The New York Times CROSSWORD ANSWER BOOK

Formerly titled *The Crossword Answer Book*

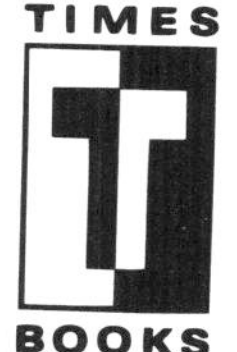

COMPILED BY
STANLEY NEWMAN
AND
DANIEL STARK

 Published in the United States by Times Books, a division of Random House, Inc., New York, and simultaneously in Canada by Random House of Canada Limited, Toronto.

This work was originally published in different form and in hardcover by Times Books, a division of Random House, Inc., in 1996 as *The Crossword Answer Book*.

ISBN 0-8129-2972-1

Random House Puzzle Website Address:
www.puzzlesatrandom.com

Text design and typography by Daniel Stark
Manufactured in the United States of America
2 4 6 8 9 7 5 3
First Paperback Edition

INTRODUCTION

Welcome to *The New York Times Crossword Answer Book.* Our objective in compiling it has been to fill what we know is an important need for crossword fans – a comprehensive one-volume source for finding troublesome puzzle answers.

If you've used crossword dictionaries, like we have, you've probably discovered that, while these books pack a lot of information, all too often the answer you're looking for just isn't there. The reason why: These books, as good as they are, have been compiled from standard reference sources (dictionaries, thesauruses, and atlases) and bear no direct relationship to the words that actually appear in crosswords.

This gap – between the true "crossword lexicon" and the information available in crossword dictionaries – has been apparent to us for a long time. So, we decided to do something about it. This is the first in what we hope will be a series of "populist" crossword references, designed to be more useful to puzzlers than the books that are currently available.

The first thing you'll notice when you open this book is that it's not organized like crossword dictionaries, where the answers are alphabetized by keywords in the clue. *The New York Times Crossword Answer Book* has no clues, only *answers*. It is this emphasis on answers and, more importantly, how we've compiled these answers, that makes this book unique.

So you can see what we mean, let's describe the process by which we selected the words for this book. First, the many thousands of crosswords we've created or edited were examined and their answers compiled. Thus, the majority of the words and phrases included here come from *actual* crosswords. This initial word list was supplemented by the latest editions of standard reference sources, *plus* "popular culture" reference books – covering such things as television, movies, literature, music and the business world. This use of "non-traditional" reference books is crucial in the quest for comprehensiveness. Today's crosswords, as exemplified by the *New York Times*, are filled with contemporary phrases, names and titles that can't be found in dictionaries and atlases.

Once all of these words were compiled, our next job was to decide which words to keep. Space considerations led us to include words up to seven letters long (adding even eight-letter words would have doubled the size of this book). This is not as limiting as you might think, because over 90% of the answers appearing in crosswords are seven letters long or less. Next, we deleted those words that, due to propriety or obscurity, are unlikely to appear in crosswords. Other categories of words that were excluded were: plurals of personal names (like HARRYS or DAVISES), multi-word partial phrases (like A HAT and IS MY), and uncommon forms of common words (such as HELIUMS and BEWARED).

Once we were finished deleting, we started adding again. In addition to ourselves, three other puzzle professionals examined our word list for completeness and consistency, and suggested words to be added. (Special thanks to Henry Hook, Trip Payne, and Rebecca Kornbluh.) Finally, we added words that are too new to be in any book, such as AMISTAD, a recent Steven Spielberg film. As a result of this word-selection process, we can say with complete confidence that no other reference of *any* kind contains all the words found here.

For this paperback edition, we have added nearly 4,000 words not in the earlier hardcover version – incorporating the very latest in contemporary American English and popular culture, as well as more comprehensive coverage of British and Canadian English. A special thank you to the people who suggested new words that we added to this edition: Diane Baldwin, Ramsey Chaffey, Philip Cohen, Chuck Deodene, Harvey Estes, Ray Hamel, Francis Heaney, Henry Hook, Phyllis Jackson, Maura Jacobson, Matt Jones, Rich Norris, Trip Payne, Mel Rosen, Robert A. Shaw, and Richard Silvestri.

For their help in the preparation of this edition, we'd like to thank the following Times Books folks: Eli Hausknecht, Lisa Arrington, Heidi North and Alejandro Moya.

Your comments on any aspect of this book are most welcome. In particular, we'd like to know how useful you find this book, as well as your suggestions for words to include in future editions. You may write to us at: Times Books Puzzles and Games, 201 East 50th Street, New York, New York 10022. We will thank the first sender of any new word we include in future editions by including his or her name in the introduction.

May all your puzzles be completely solved – with or without our help.

Stanley Newman
Daniel Stark

HOW TO USE THIS BOOK

The New York Times Crossword Answer Book is arranged first by word length, then alphabetically by the position of two given letters. So, once you have two letters of an answer filled in, you can quickly find a list of words and phrases that have those two letters in those two positions.

For example, on page 284 (right-hand column) you will find six-letter answers whose third letter is S and sixth letter is A, including: BOSNIA, CESSNA, DESICA, RUSSIA and URSULA. The context of the clue, as well as any additional letters you fill in, will help you determine which of the listed choices is the correct one.

We recognize that, unlike traditional crossword dictionaries, this book does not give additional information about words you're not familiar with. For this reason, we recommend that you do what many crossword fans do: use new words as a "springboard" to learn more about a particular subject.

AA•
AAA
AAH
AAR
AAS
AAU

A•A
AAA
ABA
ACA
ADA
AEA
AGA
AHA
AIA
AKA
ALA
AMA
ANA
APA
ARA
ASA
ATA
AVA

•AA
AAA
BAA
CAA
FAA
MAA

AB•
ABA
ABB
ABC
ABD
ABE
ABM
ABN
ABO
ABP
ABR
ABS
ABT
ABU
ABY

A•B
ABB
AFB
ALB
AMB
APB
ARB

•AB
BAB
CAB
DAB
FAB
GAB
HAB
JAB
KAB
LAB
MAB
NAB
RAB
SAB
TAB
WAB

AC•
ACA
ACC
ACE
ACH
ACK
ACP
ACR
ACS
ACT
ACU
ACV
ACY

A•C
ABC
ACC
ADC
AEC
AFC
AKC
ALC
AMC
ANC
APC
ARC
ASC
AUC
AVC

•AC
BAC
FAC
LAC
MAC
PAC
SAC
TAC
VAC
WAC

AD•
ADA
ADC
ADD
ADE
ADJ
ADL
ADM
ADO
ADP
ADS
ADV
ADZ

A•D
ABD
ADD
AID
ALD
AND
ARD
AUD

•AD
BAD
CAD
DAD
EAD
FAD
GAD
HAD
LAD
MAD
NAD
PAD
RAD
SAD
TAD
WAD
YAD

AE•
AEA
AEC
AEE
AEF
AER
AES
AET

A•E
ABE
ACE
ADE
AEE
AGE
ALE
AME
ANE
APE
ARE
ASE
ATE
AVE
AWE
AXE
AYE

•AE
BAE
HAE
LAE
MAE
NAE
RAE
SAE
TAE
UAE
VAE

AF•
AFB
AFC
AFF
AFG
AFL
AFM
AFR
AFS
AFT

A•F
AEF
AFF
ALF
AMF
ARF
ATF
AUF

•AF
KAF
OAF
QAF
RAF
WAF

AG•
AGA
AGE
AGO
AGR
AGS
AGT

A•G
AFG
ALG
ANG
ARG
AUG
AVG

•AG
BAG
DAG
GAG
HAG
JAG
LAG
MAG
NAG
PAG
RAG
SAG
TAG
WAG
YAG
ZAG

AH•
AHA
AHS
AHU

A•H
AAH
ACH
AOH
ASH
AYH

•AH
AAH
BAH
DAH
HAH
LAH
MAH
NAH
PAH
RAH
WAH
YAH

AI•
AIA
AID
AIL
AIM
AIN
AIR
AIS
AIT
AIX

A•I
ALI
AMI
ANI
API
ARI
ASI
AVI

•AI
CAI
DAI
GAI
HAI
JAI
KAI
LAI
MAI
RAI
TAI

A•J
ADJ

•AJ
HAJ
MAJ
RAJ
TAJ

AK•
AKA
AKC
AKU

A•K
ACK
ALK
AOK
ARK
ASK
AUK
AWK

•AK
DAK
OAK
PAK
YAK

AL•
ALA
ALB
ALC
ALD
ALE
ALF
ALG
ALI
ALK
ALL
ALP
ALS
ALT
ALY

A•L
ADL
AFL
AIL
ALL
AOL
APL
ASL
ATL
AWL
AXL

•AL
BAL
CAL
DAL
GAL
HAL
IAL
JAL
MAL
PAL
SAL
TAL
UAL
VAL
WAL
ZAL

AM•
AMA
AMB
AMC
AME
AMF
AMI
AMN
AMO
AMP
AMR
AMS
AMT
AMU
AMY

A•M
ABM
ADM
AFM
AIM
ARM
ATM
AUM

•AM
BAM
CAM
DAM
EAM
FAM
GAM
HAM
IAM
JAM
KAM
LAM
NAM
PAM
RAM
SAM
TAM
YAM

AN•
ANA
ANC
AND
ANE
ANG
ANI
ANN
ANO
ANS
ANT
ANU
ANY

A•N
ABN
AIN
AMN
ANN
ARN
ASN
AVN
AWN
AYN

•AN
BAN
CAN
DAN
FAN
HAN
IAN
JAN
KAN
LAN
MAN
NAN
PAN
RAN
SAN
TAN
VAN
WAN

AO•
AOH
AOK
AOL
AOR

A•O
ABO
ADO
AGO
AMO
ANO
APO
ARO
ASO
AVO
AZO

•AO
BAO
FAO
GAO
HAO
LAO
MAO
PAO
SAO
TAO
YAO

AP•
APA
APB
APC
APE
API
APL
APO
APP
APR
APS
APT
APU

A•P
ABP
ACP
ADP
ALP
AMP
APP
ARP
ASP
ATP

•AP
BAP
CAP
DAP
EAP
GAP
HAP
LAP
MAP
NAP
OAP
PAP
RAP
SAP
TAP
YAP
ZAP

•AQ
FAQ

AR•
ARA
ARB
ARC
ARD
ARE
ARF
ARG
ARI
ARK
ARM
ARN
ARO
ARP
ARR
ARS
ART
ARU
ARY

A•R
AAR
ABR
ACR
AER
AFR
AGR
AIR
AMR
AOR
APR
ARR
ASR
AYR

•AR
AAR
BAR
CAR
DAR
EAR
FAR
GAR
HAR
JAR
LAR
MAR
OAR
PAR
SAR
TAR
UAR
VAR
WAR
YAR

AS•
ASA
ASC
ASE
ASH
ASI
ASK
ASL
ASN
ASO
ASP
ASR
ASS
AST
ASU
ASV

A•S
AAS
ABS
ACS
ADS
AES
AFS
AGS
AHS
AIS
ALS
AMS
ANS
APS
ARS
ASS
AUS
AVS

•AS
AAS
BAS
CAS
DAS
FAS
GAS
HAS
JAS
KAS
LAS
MAS
NAS
OAS
PAS
RAS
SAS
TAS
VAS
WAS
YAS
ZAS

AT•
ATA
ATE
ATF
ATL
ATM
ATP
ATT
ATV

A•T
ABT
ACT
AET
AFT
AGT
AIT
ALT
AMT
ANT
APT
ART
AST
ATT
AUT

•AT
BAT
CAT
DAT
EAT
FAT
GAT
HAT
JAT
KAT
LAT
MAT
NAT
OAT
PAT
QAT
RAT
SAT
TAT
VAT
WAT
XAT
YAT

AU•
AUC
AUD
AUF
AUG
AUK
AUM
AUS
AUT
AUX

A•U
AAU
ABU
ACU
AHU
AKU
AMU
ANU
APU
ARU
ASU

•AU
AAU
DAU
EAU
PAU
RAU
SAU
TAU

AV•
AVA
AVC
AVE
AVG
AVI
AVN
AVO
AVS

A•V
ACV
ADV
ASV
ATV

•AV
CAV
DAV
JAV
LAV
MAV
NAV
TAV
VAV

AW•
AWE
AWK
AWL
AWN

•AW
CAW
DAW
GAW
HAW
JAW
KAW
LAW
MAW
NAW
PAW
RAW
SAW
TAW
UAW
WAW
YAW

AX•
AXE
AXL

A•X
AIX
AUX

•AX
BAX
DAX
FAX
LAX
MAX
PAX
RAX
SAX
TAX
WAX
ZAX

AY•
AYE
AYH
AYN
AYR

A•Y
ABY
ACY
ALY
AMY
ANY
ARY

•AY
BAY
CAY
DAY
FAY
GAY
HAY
JAY
KAY
LAY
MAY
NAY
PAY
RAY
SAY
TAY
VAY
WAY
YAY

AZ•
AZO

A•Z
ADZ

•AZ
GAZ
PAZ
YAZ

BA•
BAA
BAB
BAC
BAD
BAE
BAG
BAH
BAL
BAM
BAN
BAO
BAP
BAR
BAS
BAT
BAX
BAY

B•A
BAA
BBA
BEA
BFA
BHA
BIA
BLA
BOA
BRA
BSA

•BA
ABA
BBA
CBA
DBA
MBA
NBA
OBA
PBA
SBA
TBA
WBA

BB•
BBA
BBB
BBC
BBL
BBQ
BBS

B•B
BAB
BBB
BIB
BOB
BUB

•BB
ABB
BBB
EBB

BC•
BCE
BCG

B•C
BAC
BBC
BHC
BIC
BSC
BUC

•BC
ABC
BBC
CBC
NBC
RBC
WBC

BD•
BDL
BDS

B•D
BAD
BED
BHD
BID
BOD
BPD
BUD
BVD

•BD
ABD

MBD

BE• BEA BED BEE BEF BEG BEI BEL BEM BEN BES BET BEV BEY

B•E BAE BCE BEE BLE BME BPE BRE BYE

•BE ABE CBE DBE GBE MBE NBE OBE SBE UBE

BF• BFA

B•F BEF

BG• BGH BGS

B•G BAG BCG BEG BIG BKG BOG BUG

BH• BHA BHC BHD BHP BHT

B•H BAH BGH BPH BSH BTH

BI• BIA BIB BIC BID BIG BIL BIN BIO BIP BIS BIT BIV BIX BIZ

B•I BEI BMI BPI BWI

•BI FBI OBI RBI UBI

•BJ LBJ OBJ PBJ

BK• BKG BKS BKT

B•K BLK BOK

BL• BLA BLE BLK BLS BLT BLU BLY

B•L BAL BBL BDL BEL BIL BOL BPL BTL BUL

•BL BBL DBL OBL

BM• BME BMI BMR BMS BMW BMX

B•M BAM BEM BUM BVM

•BM ABM IBM

B•N BAN BEN BIN BON BUN

•BN ABN EBN IBN WBN

BO• BOA BOB BOD BOG BOK BOL BON BOO BOP BOR BOS BOT BOW BOX BOY BOZ

B•O BAO BIO BOO BRO BYO

•BO ABO EBO HBO IBO LBO

BP• BPD BPE BPH BPI BPL BPS

B•P BAP BHP BIP BOP

•BP ABP QBP

B•Q BBQ BXQ

•BQ BBQ

BR• BRA BRE BRO BRR BRS BRV

B•R BAR BMR BOR BRR BUR

•BR ABR

BS• BSA BSC BSH

B•S BAS BBS BDS BES BGS BIS BKS BLS BMS BOS BPS BRS BTS BUS

•BS ABS BBS CBS DBS EBS FBS GBS LBS NBS OBS PBS QBS TBS VBS WBS YBS

BT• BTH BTL BTS BTU BTW

B•T BAT BET BHT BIT BKT BLT BOT BUT BVT

•BT ABT

BU• BUB BUC BUD BUG BUL BUM BUN BUR BUS BUT BUY

B•U BLU BTU BYU

•BU ABU

BV• BVD BVM BVT

B•V BEV BIV BRV

•BV OBV

BW• BWI

B•W BMW BOW BTW

•BW NBW SBW

BX• BXQ

B•X BAX BIX BMX BOX

•BX PBX

BY• BYE BYO BYU BYZ

B•Y BAY BEY BLY BOY BUY

•BY ABY

B•Z BIZ BOZ BYZ

CA• CAA CAB CAD CAI CAL CAM CAN CAP CAR CAS CAT CAV CAW CAY

C•A CAA CBA CEA CFA CHA CIA CMA COA CPA CSA

•CA ACA FCA GCA ICA MCA OCA RCA

CB• CBA CBC CBE CBS

C•B CAB COB CPB CUB

•CB PCB

CC• CCC CCD CCI CCL CCS CCU CCV CCW CCX

C•C CBC CCC CDC CIC CSC CXC

•CC ACC CCC DCC FCC ICC JCC MCC NCC

CD• CDC CDE CDI CDL CDR CDS CDT CDV CDX

C•D CAD CCD CID CLD CMD COD CPD CUD CYD

•CD CCD GCD JCD LCD MCD RCD SCD

CE• CEA CEE CEL CEN CEO CEP CES CET CEY

C•E CBE CDE CEE CHE CIE CLE COE CUE

•CE ACE BCE GCE ICE

CF• CFA CFI CFL CFO CFS

C•F CIF CTF

•CF GCF HCF MCF

CG• CGM CGS

C•G CHG COG

•CG BCG ECG MCG

CH• CHA CHE CHG CHI CHM

•CH ACH HCH ICH OCH SCH

CI• CIA CIC CID CIE CIF CII CIM CIO CIP CIR CIS CIT CIV CIX

C•I CAI CCI CDI CFI CHI CII CLI CMI CPI CRI CUI CVI CXI

•CI CCI DCI ICI MCI SCI XCI

CK• CKW

C•K CLK CSK

•CK ACK ECK ICK OCK

CL• CLD CLE CLI CLK CLR CLS CLU CLV CLX

C•L CAL CCL CDL CEL CFL CML COL CPL CUL CXL CYL

•CL CCL DCL JCL KCL MCL

CM• CMA CMD CMI CML CMS CMV CMX

C•M CAM CGM CHM CIM COM CPM CUM CWM

•CM DCM ECM LCM MCM SCM

CN• CNN CNO CNS

C•N CAN CEN CNN CON CTN

•CN RCN

CO• COA COB COD COE COG COL COM CON COO COP COQ COR COS COT COW COX COY COZ

C•O CEO CFO CIO CNO COO CPO CRO CTO CWO CYO

•CO ECO NCO

CP• CPA CPB CPD CPI CPL CPM CPO CPR CPS CPT CPU

C•P CAP CEP CIP COP CUP CWP

•CP ACP FCP MCP RCP

C•Q COQ

•CQ MCQ

CR• CRI CRO CRS CRT CRU CRY

C•R CAR CDR CIR CLR COR CPR CTR CUR CYR

•CR ACR NCR OCR VCR

CS• CSA CSC CSK CST CSX

C•S CAS CBS CCS CDS CES CFS CGS CIS CLS CMS CNS COS CPS CRS CTS CVS

•CS ACS CCS FCS ICS JCS LCS MCS OCS PCS RCS WCS

CT• CTF CTN CTO CTR CTS

C•T CAT CDT CET CIT COT CPT CRT CST CUT CWT

•CT ACT ECT JCT LCT OCT PCT RCT

CU• CUB CUD CUE CUI CUL CUM CUP CUR CUT

C•U CCU CLU CPU CRU

•CU ACU CCU ECU ICU TCU

CV• CVI CVS

C•V CAV CCV CDV CIV CLV CMV CXV

•CV ACV CCV DCV MCV PCV XCV

CW• CWM CWO CWP CWT

C•W CAW CCW CKW COW

•CW CCW

CX• CXC CXI CXL CXV CXX

C•X CCX CDX CIX CLX CMX COX CSX CXX

•CX CCX DCX MCX

CY• CYD CYL CYO CYR

C•Y CAY CEY COY CRY

•CY ACY FCY ICY

C•Z COZ

DA• DAB DAD DAG DAH DAI DAK DAL DAM DAN DAP DAR DAS DAT DAU DAV DAW DAX DAY

D•A DBA DEA DFA DHA DIA DMA DNA DOA

•DA ADA EDA FDA IDA ODA RDA

DB• DBA DBE DBL DBS

D•B DAB DEB DIB DOB DUB

•DB EDB PDB

DC• DCC DCI DCL DCM DCV DCX

D•C DCC DEC DFC DOC DSC DUC DXC

•DC ADC CDC LDC MDC UDC

DD• DDE DDR DDS DDT

D•D DAD DED DID DMD DOD DUD DVD

•DD ADD EDD ODD PDD RDD TDD

DE• DEA DEB DEC DED DEE DEF DEG DEI DEK DEL DEM DEN DEO DEP DER DES DET DEV DEW DEX DEY

D•E DBE DDE DEE DIE DOE DRE DUE DYE

•DE ADE CDE DDE EDE IDE ODE RDE

DF• DFA DFC DFM

D•F DEF DIF

•DF RDF

D•G DAG DEG DIG DKG DOG DUG

•DG LDG

DH• DHA DHL DHS DHU

D•H DAH DOH DPH DUH

•DH EDH

DI• DIA DIB DID DIE DIF DIG DII DIK DIL DIM DIN DIO DIP DIR DIS DIT DIU DIV DIX DIY

D•I DAI DCI DEI DII DLI DOI DPI DVI DXI

•DI CDI IDI MDI SDI

DJ• DJS

D•J DOJ DRJ

•DJ ADJ

DK• DKG DKL DKM

D•K DAK DEK DIK DRK

DL• DLI DLO DLR DLS DLV DLX

D•L DAL DBL DCL DEL DHL DIL DKL DML DOL DPL DXL

•DL ADL BDL CDL HDL LDL MDL

DM• DMA DMD DML DMS DMV DMZ

D•M DAM DCM DEM DFM DIM DKM DOM DSM DUM DVM

•DM ADM EDM PDM

DN• DNA DNR

D•N DAN DEN DIN DON DUN DYN

DO• DOA DOB DOC DOD DOE DOG DOH DOI DOJ DOL DOM DON DOO DOP DOR DOS DOT DOU DOW DOZ

D•O DEO DIO DLO DOO DSO DUO

•DO ADO EDO IDO ODO UDO

DP• DPH DPI DPL DPS DPT DPW

D•P DAP DEP DIP DOP DTP DUP

•DP ADP EDP IDP

•DQ PDQ

DR• DRE DRJ DRK DRS DRU DRY

D•R DAR DDR DER DIR DLR DNR DOR

•DR CDR DDR FDR GDR LDR MDR

DS• DSC DSM DSO DST

D•S DAS DBS DDS DES DHS DIS DJS DLS DMS DOS DPS DRS DTS DYS

•DS ADS BDS CDS DDS EDS FDS GDS HDS IDS LDS MDS ODS RDS SDS TDS WDS YDS

DT• DTP DTS

D•T DAT DDT DET DIT DOT DPT DST DWT

•DT CDT DDT EDT MDT PDT VDT

DU• DUB DUC DUD DUE DUG DUH DUM DUN DUO DUP DUX DUZ

D•U DAU DHU DIU DOU DRU

•DU EDU VDU

DV• DVD DVI DVM

D•V DAV DCV DEV DIV DLV DMV DXV

•DV ADV CDV MDV

DW• DWT

D•W DAW DEW DOW DPW

•DW HDW

DX• DXC DXI DXL DXV DXX

D•X DAX DCX DEX DIX DLX DUX DXX

•DX CDX

MDX

DY• DYE DYN DYS

D•Y DAY DEY DIY DRY

D•Z DMZ DOZ DUZ

•DZ ADZ

EA• EAD EAM EAP EAR EAT EAU

E•A EDA EKA ELA ENA EPA ERA ESA ETA EVA

•EA AEA BEA CEA DEA KEA LEA MEA NEA PEA REA SEA TEA YEA ZEA

EB• EBB EBN EBO EBS

E•B EBB EDB EMB

•EB DEB FEB HEB JEB LEB NEB REB WEB

EC• ECG ECK ECM ECO ECT ECU

E•C EEC ENC ESC ETC EXC

•EC AEC DEC EEC FEC JEC NEC PEC REC SEC TEC

ED• EDA EDB EDD EDE EDH EDM EDO EDP EDS EDT EDU

E•D EAD EDD ELD END ESD ETD

•ED BED DED FED GED HED JED KED LED MED NED OED PED QED RED TED WED XED ZED

EE• EEC EEE EEG EEK EEL EEN EEO EER EES

E•E EDE EEE EKE EME ENE EOE ERE ESE ETE EVE EWE EXE EYE

•EE AEE BEE CEE DEE EEE FEE GEE HEE LEE NEE REE SEE TEE VEE WEE ZEE

EF• EFF EFG EFS EFT

E•F EFF EHF ELF EMF EOF

•EF AEF BEF DEF HEF KEF NEF QEF REF

EG• EGG EGO EGR

E•G ECG EEG EFG EGG EKG EMG ENG ERG EVG

•EG BEG DEG EEG KEG LEG MEG NEG PEG REG TEG VEG ZEG

EH• EHF EHV

E•H EDH EPH ETH

•EH HEH NEH PEH TEH VEH

EI• EIN EIS

E•I ELI EMI EPI ERI

•EI BEI DEI LEI PEI REI SEI WEI

EK• EKA EKE EKG

E•K ECK EEK ELK ERK ESK

•EK DEK EEK LEK

EL• ELA ELD ELF ELI ELK ELL ELM ELO ELS ELY

E•L EEL ELL ENL ESL

•EL BEL CEL DEL EEL GEL HEL KEL MEL REL SEL TEL VEL

EM• EMB EME EMF EMG EMI EMO EMP EMS EMT EMU

E•M EAM ECM EDM ELM EOM

•EM BEM DEM FEM GEM HEM LEM MEM OEM REM SEM TEM

EN• ENA ENC END ENE ENG ENL ENO ENS ENT ENV

E•N EBN EEN EIN EON ERN

•EN BEN CEN DEN EEN FEN GEN HEN KEN LEN MEN OEN PEN REN SEN TEN VEN WEN XEN YEN ZEN

EO• EOE EOF EOM EON EOS

E•O EBO ECO EDO EEO EGO ELO EMO ENO ESO ETO EXO

•EO CEO DEO EEO GEO LEO MEO NEO OEO REO YEO

EP• EPA EPH EPI EPS

E•P EAP EDP EMP ESP EXP

•EP CEP DEP HEP NEP PEP REP SEP YEP

E•Q ESQ

•EQ REQ SEQ

ER• ERA ERE ERG ERI ERK ERN ERR ERS ERY ERZ

E•R EAR EER EGR ERR EUR EXR EZR

•ER AER DER EER FER GER HER IER JER KER LER MER NER OER PER SER TER VER XER YER

ES• ESA ESC ESD ESE ESK ESL ESO ESP ESQ ESS EST ESU

E•S EBS EDS EES EFS EIS ELS EMS ENS EOS EPS ERS ESS ETS EVS

•ES AES BES CES DES EES HES LES MES NES PES RES SES TES WES XES YES

ET• ETA ETC ETD ETE ETH ETO ETS ETV

E•T EAT ECT EDT EFT EMT ENT EST EXT

•ET AET BET CET DET FET GET HET JET KET LET MET NET PET RET SET TET VET WET YET

EU• EUR

E•U EAU ECU EDU EMU ESU

•EU FEU JEU LEU NEU PEU

EV• EVA EVE EVG EVS

E•V EHV ENV ETV

•EV BEV DEV GEV KEV LEV MEV NEV REV ZEV

EW• EWE

•EW DEW FEW HEW JEW KEW LEW MEW NEW PEW SEW YEW

EX• EXC EXE EXO EXP EXR EXT

•EX DEX HEX LEX MEX REX SEX TEX VEX

EY• EYE

E•Y ELY ERY

•EY BEY CEY DEY FEY GEY HEY KEY LEY NEY REY TEY UEY

EZ• EZR

E•Z ERZ

•EZ FEZ NEZ PEZ SEZ

FA• FAA FAB FAC FAD FAM FAN FAO FAQ FAR FAS FAT FAX FAY

F•A FAA FCA FDA FFA FHA FLA FPA FRA

•FA BFA CFA DFA FFA MFA UFA

FB• FBI FBS

F•B FAB FEB FIB FMB FOB FRB FUB

•FB AFB LFB RFB

FC• FCA FCC FCP FCS FCY

F•C FAC FCC FEC FIC FMC FPC FTC

•FC AFC DFC KFC NFC PFC SFC

FD• FDA FDR FDS

F•D FAD FED FID FLD FTD FWD

•FD MFD NFD PFD RFD VFD

FE• FEB FEC FED FEE FEM FEN FER FET FEU FEW FEY FEZ

F•E FEE FIE FOE

•FE IFE RFE

FF• FFA FFF FFV

F•F FFF

•FF AFF EFF FFF IFF OFF

F•G FIG FOG FRG FUG

•FG AFG EFG MFG PFG

FH• FHA

F•H FTH

•FH MFH

FI• FIB FIC FID FIE FIG FIL FIN FIR FIS FIT FIX

F•I FBI FRI FYI

•FI CFI RFI

•FK JFK RFK

FL• FLA FLD FLO FLU FLY

F•L FIL FOL FPL FRL FUL

•FL AFL CFL NFL

FM• FMB FMC FMS

F•M FAM FEM FPM FUM

•FM AFM DFM

FN• FNS

F•N FAN FEN FIN FON FUN FYN

FO• FOB FOE FOG FOL FON FOO FOP FOR FOU FOX FOY

F•O FAO FLO FOO FPO FRO

•FO CFO SFO UFO

FP• FPA FPC FPL FPM FPO FPS

F•P FCP FOP

F•Q FAQ

•FQ RFQ

FR• FRA FRB FRG FRI FRL FRO FRS FRT FRY

F•R FAR FDR FER FIR FOR FUR

•FR AFR MFR TFR

FS• FSU

F•S FAS FBS FCS FDS FIS FMS FNS FPS FRS

•FS AFS CFS EFS IFS LFS

FT• FTC FTD FTH

F•T FAT FET FIT FRT FUT

•FT AFT EFT OFT UFT

FU• FUB FUG FUL FUM FUN FUR FUT

F•U FEU FLU FOU FSU

F•V FFV

•FV FFV

FW• FWD

F•W FEW

•FW UFW VFW

F•X FAX FIX FOX

FY• FYI FYN

F•Y FAY FCY FEY FLY FOY FRY

•FY IFY

F•Z FEZ

•FZ SFZ

GA• GAB GAD GAG GAI GAL GAM GAO GAP GAR GAS GAT GAW GAY GAZ

G•A GCA GIA GMA GOA GPA GSA

•GA AGA IGA PGA VGA

GB• GBE GBS

G•B GAB GIB GOB

•GB KGB RGB

GC• GCA GCD GCE GCF

G•C GMC GTC

•GC NGC

GD• GDR GDS

G•D GAD GCD GED GLD GOD GPD GTD

•GD MGD SGD

GE• GED GEE GEL GEM GEN GEO GER GET GEV GEY

G•E GBE GCE GEE GIE GRE GTE

•GE AGE LGE

G•F GCF GRF

•GF KGF NGF

G•G GAG GIG GOG

•GG EGG IGG

GH• GHI GHQ GHZ

•GH BGH HGH UGH

GI• GIA GIB GIE GIG GIL GIN GIP GIS GIT

G•I GAI GHI GUI

GL• GLD GLO

G•L GAL GEL GIL

GM• GMA GMC GMS GMT GMW

G•M GAM GEM GPM GUM GYM

•GM CGM KGM MGM

GN• GNP GNU

G•N GEN GIN GON GUN GYN

•GN IGN

GO• GOA GOB GOD GOG GON GOO GOP GOR GOT GOV

G•O GAO GEO GLO GOO GPO GRO GTO

•GO AGO EGO IGO UGO

GP• GPA GPD GPM GPO GPS

G•P GAP GIP GNP GOP GTP GYP

G•Q GHQ

GR• GRE GRF GRO GRR

G•R GAR GDR GER GOR GRR GUR

•GR AGR EGR MGR

GS• GSA GST

G•S GAS GBS GDS GIS GMS GPS GUS

•GS AGS BGS CGS JGS LGS MGS PGS RGS

GT• GTC GTD GTE GTO GTP GTT

G•T GAT GET GIT GMT GOT GST GTT GUT

•GT AGT HGT MGT RGT SGT

GU• GUI GUM GUN GUR GUS GUT GUV GUY

G•U GNU

GV• GVW

G•V GEV GOV GUV

•GV TGV

G•W GAW GMW GVW

•GW HGW

GY• GYM GYN GYP

G•Y GAY GEY GUY

•GY IGY

G•Z GAZ GHZ

HA• HAB HAD HAE HAG HAH HAI HAJ HAL HAM HAN HAO HAP HAR HAS HAT HAW HAY

H•A HUA

•HA AHA BHA CHA DHA FHA KHA SHA THA WHA

HB• HBO

H•B HAB HEB HOB HUB

•HB LHB PHB RHB THB

HC• HCF HCH

H•C HIC HOC
•HC BHC MHC OHC
HD• HDL HDS HDW
H•D HAD HED HHD HID HOD HUD HYD
•HD BHD HHD LHD PHD THD
HE• HEB HED HEE HEF HEH HEL HEM HEN HEP HER HES HET HEW HEX HEY
H•E HAE HEE HIE HOE HRE HUE
•HE CHE RHE SHE THE
H•F HCF HEF HMF HOF
•HF EHF SHF UHF VHF WHF
HG• HGH HGT HGW
H•G HAG HOG HUG
•HG CHG
HH• HHD HHH HHS
H•H HAH HCH HEH HGH HHH HIH HRH HSH HUH
•HH HHH SHH WHH
HI• HIC HID HIE HIH HIM HIN HIP HIS HIT
H•I HAI HOI HSI HUI
•HI CHI GHI NHI PHI THI
H•J HAJ
H•L HAL HDL HEL HOL
•HL DHL NHL
HM• HMF HMM HMO HMS
H•M HAM HEM HIM HMM HOM HUM HWM
•HM CHM OHM PHM THM
H•N HAN HEN HIN HON HUN
HO• HOB HOC HOD HOE HOF HOG HOI HOL HOM HON HOO HOP HOR HOS HOT HOV HOW HOY
H•O HAO HBO HMO HOO
•HO MHO OHO RHO SHO THO WHO
H•P HAP HEP HIP HOP HUP HYP
•HP BHP
HQ• HQS
•HQ GHQ
HR• HRE HRH HRS
H•R HAR HER HOR HUR
•HR IHR PHR SHR WHR
HS• HSH HSI HST
H•S HAS HDS HES HHS HIS HMS HOS HQS HRS HTS HUS
•HS AHS DHS HHS IHS JHS LHS NHS OHS VHS WHS
HT• HTS
H•T HAT HET HGT HIT HOT HST HUT
•HT BHT SHT
HU• HUA HUB HUD HUE HUG HUH HUI HUM HUN HUP HUR HUS HUT
•HU AHU DHU JHU PHU SHU THU
HV• HVY
H•V HOV
•HV EHV
HW• HWM HWY
H•W HAW HDW HEW HGW HOW
•HW MHW
H•X HEX
•HX THX
HY• HYD HYP
H•Y HAY HEY HOY HVY HWY
•HY SHY THY WHY
•HZ GHZ KHZ MHZ
IA• IAL IAM IAN
I•A ICA IDA IGA ILA INA IPA IRA ISA IVA
•IA AIA BIA CIA DIA GIA LIA MIA NIA PIA RIA TIA VIA XIA ZIA
IB• IBM IBN IBO
•IB BIB DIB FIB GIB JIB LIB MIB NIB RIB SIB
IC• ICA ICC ICE ICH ICI ICK ICS ICU ICY
I•C ICC INC IOC
•IC BIC CIC FIC HIC LIC MIC PIC RIC SIC TIC VIC
ID• IDA IDE IDI IDO IDP IDS
I•D IND IOD ITD
•ID AID BID CID DID FID HID KID LID MID OID QID RID SID TID
IE• IER
I•E ICE IDE IFE IKE ILE INE IRE ISE ITE IVE IZE
•IE CIE DIE FIE GIE HIE LIE NIE PIE SIE TIE VIE WIE
IF• IFE IFF IFS IFY
I•F IFF IMF INF
•IF CIF DIF JIF KIF RIF ZIF
IG• IGA IGG IGN IGO IGY
I•G IGG ING
•IG BIG DIG FIG GIG JIG MIG NIG PIG RIG SIG WIG ZIG
IH• IHR IHS
I•H ICH ISH
•IH HIH NIH
II• III
I•I ICI IDI III
•II CII DII III LII MII VII XII
IK• IKE
I•K ICK ILK INK IRK
•IK DIK NIK OIK PIK
IL• ILA ILE ILK ILL ILO ILS
I•L IAL ILL ISL
•IL AIL BIL DIL FIL GIL KIL LIL MIL NIL OIL SIL TIL VIL WIL
IM• IMF IMP
I•M IAM IBM IPM ISM IUM
•IM AIM CIM DIM HIM JIM KIM LIM MIM NIM PIM RIM SIM TIM VIM WIM
IN• INA INC IND INE INF ING INK INN INO INQ INS INT INV
I•N IAN IBN IGN INN ION
•IN AIN BIN DIN EIN FIN GIN HIN JIN KIN LIN MIN NIN PIN QIN RIN SIN TIN VIN WIN XIN YIN
IO• IOC IOD ION IOR IOS IOU
I•O IBO IDO IGO ILO INO IPO IRO ISO ITO IVO IWO
•IO BIO CIO DIO MIO RIO TIO
IP• IPA IPM IPO IPS
I•P IDP IMP
•IP BIP CIP DIP GIP HIP KIP LIP MIP NIP PIP RIP SIP TIP VIP WIP YIP ZIP
IQ• IQS
I•Q INQ
•IQ LIQ
IR• IRA IRE IRK IRO IRR IRS IRT IRV
I•R IER IHR IOR IRR ISR
•IR AIR CIR DIR FIR KIR MIR PIR SIR VIR
IS• ISA ISE ISH ISL ISM ISO ISR ISS IST
I•S ICS IDS IFS IHS ILS INS IOS IPS IQS IRS ISS ITS IVS
•IS AIS BIS CIS DIS EIS FIS GIS HIS LIS MIS NIS PIS SIS TIS VIS WIS XIS
IT• ITD ITE ITO ITS ITT ITV ITY
I•T INT IRT IST ITT
•IT AIT BIT CIT DIT FIT GIT HIT KIT LIT MIT NIT PIT RIT SIT UIT WIT ZIT
IU• IUM
I•U ICU IOU
•IU DIU LIU NIU PIU TIU
IV• IVA IVE IVO IVS IVY
I•V INV IRV ITV
•IV BIV CIV DIV LIV MIV RIV TIV VIV XIV ZIV
IW• IWO IWW
I•W IWW
•IX AIX BIX CIX DIX FIX KIX LIX MIX NIX PIX SIX XIX
I•Y ICY IFY IGY ITY IVY
•IY DIY
IZ• IZE
•IZ BIZ LIZ VIZ WIZ
JA• JAB JAG JAI JAL JAM JAN JAR JAS JAT JAV JAW JAY
J•B JAB JEB JIB JOB
JC• JCC JCD JCL JCS JCT
J•C JCC JEC JRC JSC JVC
J•D JCD JED JSD JUD
•JD SJD
JE• JEB JEC JED JER JET JEU JEW
J•E JOE
JF• JFK
J•F JIF
JG• JGS
J•G JAG JIG JOG JUG
JH• JHS JHU
JI• JIB JIF JIG JIM JIN
J•I JAI JOI
JK• JKP
J•K JFK
J•L JAL JCL JUL
J•M JAM JIM
•JM WJM
JN• JNT
J•N JAN JIN JON JPN JUN
JO• JOB JOE JOG JOI JON JOS JOT JOY
•JO OJO
JP• JPN JPS
J•P JKP
JR• JRC JRS
J•R JAR JER
•JR RJR
JS• JSC JSD
J•S JAS JCS JGS JHS JOS JPS JRS JUS
•JS DJS PJS VJS
J•T JAT JCT JET JNT JOT JUT
•JT OJT
JU• JUD JUG JUL JUN JUS JUT JUV
J•U JEU JHU
JV• JVC
J•V JAV JUV
•JV KJV
J•W JAW JEW
J•Y JAY JOY
KA• KAB KAF KAI KAM KAN KAS KAT KAW KAY
K•A KEA KHA KOA KRA KWA
•KA AKA EKA OKA SKA
K•B KAB KGB KOB
KC• KCL
K•C KFC
•KC AKC
K•D KED KID KOD KYD
•KD OKD
KE• KEA KED KEF KEG KEL KEN KER KET KEV KEW KEY
K•E KUE KYE
•KE EKE IKE OKE UKE XKE
KF• KFC
K•F KAF KEF KGF KIF
KG• KGB KGF KGM
K•G KEG
•KG BKG DKG EKG PKG
KH• KHA KHZ
K•H KPH KWH
KI• KID KIF KIL KIM KIN KIP KIR KIT KIX
K•I KAI KOI
•KI OKI SKI
KJ• KJV
KK• KKT
KL• KLM
K•L KCL KEL KIL KOL KUL
•KL DKL
K•M KAM KGM KIM KLM KUM
•KM DKM
KN• KNP KNT
K•N KAN KEN KIN KON KUN
KO• KOA KOB KOD KOI KOL KON KOO KOP KOR KOS
K•O KOO
•KO RKO TKO
KP• KPH KPS
K•P KIP KNP KOP KRP
•KP JKP
KR• KRA KRP
K•R KER KIR KOR KUR
K•S KAS KOS KPS KTS
•KS BKS MKS OKS PKS WKS
KT• KTS
K•T KAT KET KIT KKT KNT
•KT BKT KKT MKT PKT QKT SKT TKT
KU• KUE KUL KUM KUN KUR
•KU AKU PKU SKU
K•V KEV KJV
KW• KWA KWH
K•W KAW KEW
•KW CKW
K•X KIX
KY• KYD KYE
K•Y KAY KEY
•KY SKY
K•Z KHZ
LA• LAB LAC LAD LAE LAG LAH LAI LAM LAN LAO LAP LAR LAS LAT LAV LAW LAX LAY
L•A LEA LIA LOA
•LA ALA BLA ELA FLA ILA MLA OLA SLA
LB• LBJ LBO LBS
L•B LAB LEB LFB LHB LIB LLB LOB LUB
•LB ALB LLB
LC• LCD LCM

LCS LCT

L•C LAC LDC LIC LOC LSC LTC LUC

•LC ALC PLC TLC

LD• LDC LDG LDL LDR LDS

L•D LAD LCD LED LHD LID LLD LSD LTD

•LD ALD CLD ELD FLD GLD LLD OLD SLD YLD

LE• LEA LEB LED LEE LEG LEI LEK LEM LEN LEO LER LES LET LEU LEV LEW LEX LEY

L•E LAE LEE LGE LIE LYE

•LE ALE BLE CLE ILE OLE ULE

LF• LFB LFS

•LF ALF ELF NLF PLF ULF VLF

LG• LGE LGS

L•G LAG LDG LEG LNG LOG LPG LUG

•LG ALG

LH• LHB LHD LHS

L•H LAH

LI• LIA LIB LIC LID LIE LII LIL LIM LIN LIP LIQ LIS LIT LIU LIV LIX LIZ

L•I LAI LEI LII LOI LSI LUI LVI LXI

•LI ALI CLI DLI ELI MLI XLI

L•J LBJ

L•K LEK

•LK ALK BLK CLK ELK ILK MLK

LL• LLB LLD LLM

L•L LDL LIL

•LL ALL ELL ILL

L•M LAM LCM LEM LIM LLM LOM LPM LUM

•LM ELM KLM LLM ULM

LN• LNG

L•N LAN LEN LIN LON LPN LYN

LO• LOA LOB LOC LOG LOI LOM LON LOO LOP LOQ LOS LOT LOU LOW LOX LOY

L•O LAO LBO LEO LOO LUO LYO

•LO DLO ELO FLO GLO ILO PLO SLO

LP• LPG LPM LPN LPS

L•P LAP LIP LOP

•LP ALP

L•Q LIQ LOQ

LR• LRS LRT

L•R LAR LDR LER LTR

•LR CLR DLR SLR

LS• LSC LSD LSI LST LSU

L•S LAS LBS LCS LDS LES LFS LGS LHS LIS LOS LPS LRS LTS LYS

•LS ALS BLS CLS DLS ELS ILS MLS PLS RLS WLS XLS

LT• LTC LTD LTR LTS

L•T LAT LCT LET LIT LOT LRT LST

•LT ALT BLT ULT

LU• LUB LUC LUG LUI LUM LUO LUV LUX LUZ

L•U LEU LIU LOU LSU

•LU BLU CLU FLU PLU ULU

LV• LVI

L•V LAV LEV LIV LUV LWV LXV

•LV CLV DLV MLV XLV

LW• LWV

L•W LAW LEW LOW

•LW MLW

LX• LXI LXV LXX

L•X LAX LEX LIX LOX LUX LXX

•LX CLX DLX MLX

LY• LYE LYN LYO LYS

L•Y LAY LEY LOY

•LY ALY BLY ELY FLY PLY SLY

L•Z LIZ LUZ

MA• MAA MAB MAC MAD MAE MAG MAH MAI MAJ MAL MAN MAO MAP MAR MAS MAT MAV MAW MAX MAY

M•A MAA MBA MCA MEA MFA MIA MLA MOA MPA MTA

•MA AMA CMA DMA GMA SMA UMA YMA

MB• MBA MBD MBE

M•B MAB MIB MOB

•MB AMB EMB FMB OMB

MC• MCA MCC MCD MCF MCG MCI MCL MCM MCP MCQ MCS MCV MCX

M•C MAC MCC MDC MHC MIC MMC MOC MSC MVC MXC MYC

•MC AMC FMC GMC MMC QMC

MD• MDC MDI MDL MDR MDS MDT MDV MDX

M•D MAD MBD MCD MED MFD MGD MID MMD MOD MUD MXD

•MD CMD DMD MMD VMD

ME• MEA MED MEG MEL MEM MEN MEO MER MES MET MEV MEW MEX

M•E MAE MBE MME MOE MPE MRE

•ME AME BME EME MME UME

MF• MFA MFD MFG MFH MFR

M•F MCF MMF

•MF AMF EMF HMF IMF MMF

MG• MGD MGM MGR MGS MGT

M•G MAG MCG MEG MFG MIG MPG MSG MTG MUG

•MG EMG PMG QMG

MH• MHC MHO MHW MHZ

M•H MAH MFH MPH

MI• MIA MIB MIC MID MIG MII MIL MIM MIN MIO MIP MIR MIS MIT MIV MIX

M•I MAI MCI MDI MII MLI MMI MOI MRI MVI MXI

•MI AMI BMI CMI EMI MMI NMI OMI TMI VMI

M•J MAJ

•MJ TMJ

MK• MKS MKT

M•K MLK

•MK PMK WMK

ML• MLA MLI MLK MLS MLV MLW MLX

M•L MAL MCL MDL MEL MIL MML MOL MSL MXL

•ML CML DML MML SML

MM• MMC MMD MME MMF MMI MML MMM MMV MMX

M•M MCM MEM MGM MIM MMM MOM MTM MUM

•MM HMM MMM

MN• MNO

M•N MAN MEN MIN MON MSN MTN MUN

•MN AMN RMN

MO• MOA MOB MOC MOD MOE MOI MOL MOM MON MOO MOP MOR MOS MOT MOW

M•O MAO MEO MHO MIO MNO MOO MYO

•MO AMO EMO HMO

MP• MPA MPE MPG MPH MPS

M•P MAP MCP MIP MOP MVP

•MP AMP EMP IMP UMP

M•Q MCQ

MR• MRE MRI MRS MRT MRX

M•R MAR MDR MER MFR MGR MIR MOR

•MR AMR BMR NMR

MS• MSC MSG MSL MSN MSS MST MSU MSW

M•S MAS MCS MDS MES MGS MIS MKS MLS MOS MPS MRS MSS MTS MUS

•MS AMS BMS CMS DMS EMS FMS GMS HMS OMS RMS SMS TMS

MT• MTA MTG MTM MTN MTS MTV

M•T MAT MDT MET MGT MIT MKT MOT MRT MST MUT

•MT AMT EMT GMT PMT

MU• MUD MUG MUM MUN MUS MUT MUX MUY

M•U MSU

•MU AMU EMU NMU SMU

MV• MVC MVI MVP

M•V MAV MCV MDV MEV MIV MLV MMV MTV MXV

•MV CMV DMV MMV

M•W MAW MEW MHW MLW MOW MSW

•MW BMW GMW UMW

MX• MXC MXD MXI MXL MXV MXX

M•X MAX MCX MDX MEX MIX MLX MMX MRX MUX MXX MYX

•MX BMX CMX MMX

MY• MYC MYO MYX

M•Y MAY MUY

•MY AMY

M•Z MHZ

•MZ DMZ

NA• NAB NAD NAE NAG NAH NAM NAN NAP NAS NAT NAV NAW NAY

N•A NBA NEA NIA NRA NSA

•NA ANA DNA ENA INA ONA RNA UNA

NB• NBA NBC NBE NBS NBW

N•B NAB NEB NIB NOB NUB

NC• NCC NCO NCR

N•C NBC NCC NEC NFC NGC NRC NSC NYC

•NC ANC ENC INC UNC

N•D NAD NED NFD NOD

•ND AND END IND RND UND

NE• NEA NEB NEC NED NEE NEF NEG NEH NEO NEP NER NES NET NEU NEV NEW NEY NEZ

N•E NAE NBE NEE NIE NNE NOE NYE

•NE ANE ENE INE NNE ONE UNE

NF• NFC NFD NFL

N•F NEF NGF NLF NSF

•NF INF

NG• NGC NGF

N•G NAG NEG NIG NOG

•NG ANG ENG ING LNG SNG UNG

NH• NHI NHL NHS

N•H NAH NEH NIH NOH NTH

•NH UNH

NI• NIA NIB NIE NIG NIH NIK NIL NIM NIN NIP NIS NIT NIU NIX

N•I NHI NMI NUI

•NI ANI ONI UNI

N•K NIK NPK

•NK INK

NL• NLF

N•L NFL NHL NIL NOL NUL

•NL ENL SNL

NM• NMI NMR NMU

N•M NAM NIM NOM NUM

NN• NNE NNW

N•N NAN NIN NON NUN

•NN ANN CNN INN TNN

NO• NOB NOD NOE NOG NOH NOL NOM NON NOP NOR NOS NOT NOV NOW NOX

N•O NCO NEO

•NO ANO CNO ENO INO MNO ONO SNO UNO

NP• NPK NPR NPS

N•P NAP NEP NIP NOP

•NP GNP KNP QNP RNP UNP

•NQ INQ UNQ

NR• NRA NRC

N•R NCR NER NMR NOR NPR

•NR DNR

NS• NSA NSC NSF NSW

N•S NAS NBS NES NHS NIS NOS NPS NUS

•NS ANS CNS ENS FNS INS ONS PNS RNS TNS UNS

NT• NTH

N•T NAT NET NIT NOT NUT NWT

•NT ANT ENT INT JNT KNT ONT TNT

NU• NUB NUI NUL NUM NUN NUS NUT

N•U NEU NIU NMU NWU NYU

•NU ANU GNU UNU

N•V NAV NEV NOV

•NV ENV INV

NW• NWT NWU

N•W NAW NBW NEW NNW NOW NSW

•NW NNW WNW

N•X NIX NOX NYX

NY• NYC NYE NYU NYX

N•Y NAY NEY

•NY ANY SNY

N•Z NEZ

OA• OAF OAK OAP OAR OAS OAT

O•A OBA OCA ODA OKA OLA ONA OPA ORA OSA OTA OVA

•OA BOA COA DOA GOA KOA LOA MOA VOA ZOA

OB• OBA OBE OBI OBJ OBL OBS OBV

O•B OMB ORB OSB OTB

•OB BOB COB DOB FOB GOB HOB JOB KOB LOB MOB NOB POB ROB SOB TOB YOB

OC• OCA OCH OCK OCR OCS

OCT

O•C
OHC ORC OTC

•OC
DOC HOC IOC LOC MOC POC ROC SOC VOC

OD•
ODA ODD ODE ODO ODS

O•D
ODD OED OID OKD OLD OOD ORD OUD

•OD
BOD COD DOD GOD HOD IOD KOD MOD NOD OOD POD ROD SOD TOD YOD ZOD

OE•
OED OEM OEN OEO OER

O•E
OBE ODE OKE OLE ONE OPE ORE OSE OTE OWE

•OE
COE DOE EOE FOE HOE JOE MOE NOE POE ROE TOE WOE ZOE

OF•
OFF OFT

O•F
OAF OFF OOF OSF

•OF
EOF HOF OOF SOF

O•G
ORG

•OG
BOG COG DOG FOG GOG HOG JOG LOG NOG POG SOG TOG ZOG

OH•
OHC OHM OHO OHS

O•H
OCH OOH OSH

•OH
AOH DOH NOH OOH

OI•
OID OIK OIL

O•I
OBI OKI OMI ONI OUI OVI OWI

•OI
DOI HOI JOI KOI LOI MOI POI ROI SOI TOI

OJ•
OJO OJT

O•J
OBJ

•OJ
DOJ

OK•
OKA OKD OKE OKI OKS

O•K
OAK OCK OIK ORK

•OK
AOK BOK ROK WOK

OL•
OLA OLD OLE

O•L
OBL OIL OWL OYL

•OL
AOL BOL COL DOL FOL HOL KOL MOL NOL POL SOL VOL

OM•
OMB OMI OMS

O•M
OEM OHM OPM

•OM
COM DOM EOM HOM LOM MOM NOM POM QOM ROM TOM YOM

ON•
ONA ONE ONI ONO ONS ONT

O•N
OEN OON OWN

•ON
BON CON DON EON FON GON HON ION JON KON LON MON NON OON RON SON TON VON WON YON

OO•
OOD OOF OOH OON OOO OOP OOX

O•O
ODO OEO OHO OJO ONO OOO ORO OSO OTO OVO OXO OYO OZO

•OO
BOO COO DOO FOO GOO HOO KOO LOO MOO OOO ROO SOO TOO WOO XOO YOO ZOO

OP•
OPA OPE OPM OPP OPR OPS OPT

O•P
OAP OOP OPP

•OP
BOP COP DOP FOP GOP HOP KOP LOP MOP NOP OOP POP SOP TOP

•OQ
COQ LOQ

OR•
ORA ORB ORC ORD ORE ORG ORK ORO ORR ORS ORT ORV ORY

O•R
OAR OCR OER OPR ORR OUR

•OR
AOR BOR COR DOR FOR GOR HOR IOR KOR MOR NOR POR SOR TOR XOR

OS•
OSA OSB OSE OSF OSH OSO OSS OST OSU

O•S
OAS OBS OCS ODS OHS OKS OMS ONS OPS ORS OSS OTS OUS OZS

•OS
BOS COS DOS EOS HOS IOS JOS KOS LOS MOS NOS POS SOS VOS

OT•
OTA OTB OTC OTE OTO OTS OTT

O•T
OAT OCT OFT OJT ONT OPT ORT OST OTT OUT OZT

•OT
BOT COT DOT GOT HOT JOT LOT MOT NOT POT ROT SOT TOT WOT

OU•
OUD OUI OUR OUS OUT

O•U
OSU

•OU
DOU FOU IOU LOU SOU VOU YOU

OV•
OVA OVI OVO

O•V
OBV ORV

•OV
GOV HOV NOV POV SOV TOV

OW•
OWE OWI OWL OWN

•OW
BOW COW DOW HOW LOW MOW NOW POW ROW SOW TOW VOW WOW YOW

OX•
OXO OXX OXY

O•X
OOX OXX

•OX
BOX COX FOX LOX NOX OOX POX SOX TOX VOX XOX

OY•
OYL OYO

O•Y
ORY OXY

•OY
BOY COY FOY HOY JOY LOY ROY SOY TOY

OZ•
OZO OZS OZT

•OZ
BOZ COZ DOZ ROZ

PA•
PAC PAD PAG PAH PAK PAL PAM PAN PAO PAP PAR PAS PAT PAU PAW PAX PAY PAZ

P•A
PBA PEA PGA PIA PSA PTA PWA PYA

•PA
APA CPA EPA FPA GPA IPA MPA OPA SPA TPA WPA

PB•
PBA PBJ PBS PBX

P•B
PCB PDB PHB POB PPB PUB

•PB
APB CPB PPB

PC•
PCB PCS PCT PCV

P•C
PAC PEC PFC PIC PLC POC PRC PSC PTC PUC PVC

•PC
APC FPC UPC

PD•
PDB PDD PDM PDQ PDT

P•D
PAD PDD PED PFD PHD POD PPD

•PD
BPD CPD GPD PPD

PE•
PEA PEC PED PEG PEH PEI PEN PEP PER PES PET PEU PEW PEZ

P•E
PIE POE PRE PYE

•PE
APE BPE MPE OPE

PF•
PFC PFD PFG

P•F
PLF PRF PSF

•PF
SPF

PG•
PGA PGS

P•G
PAG PEG PFG PIG PKG PMG POG PPG PTG PUG

•PG
LPG MPG PPG RPG ZPG

PH•
PHB PHD PHI PHM PHR PHU

P•H
PAH PEH PPH PTH

•PH
BPH DPH EPH KPH MPH PPH

PI•
PIA PIC PIE PIG PIK PIM PIN PIP PIR PIS PIT PIU PIX

P•I
PEI PHI POI PSI

•PI
API BPI CPI DPI EPI RPI UPI

PJ•
PJS

P•J
PBJ

PK•
PKG PKS PKT PKU

P•K
PAK PIK PMK

•PK
NPK TPK

PL•
PLC PLF PLO PLS PLU PLY

P•L
PAL POL PTL PUL

•PL
APL BPL CPL DPL FPL

PM•
PMG PMK PMT

P•M
PAM PDM PHM PIM POM PPM PYM

•PM
CPM FPM GPM IPM LPM OPM PPM RPM WPM

PN•
PNS

P•N
PAN PEN PIN PRN PUN

•PN
JPN LPN UPN WPN

PO•
POB POC POD POE POG POI POL POM POP POR POS POT POV POW POX

P•O
PAO PLO PPO PRO PTO

•PO
APO CPO FPO GPO IPO PPO

PP•
PPB PPD PPG PPH PPM PPO PPP PPS PPT PPV

P•P
PAP PEP PIP POP PPP PRP PUP

•PP
APP OPP PPP SPP

P•Q
PDQ

•PQ
RPQ

PR•
PRC PRE PRF PRN PRO PRP PRS PRY

P•R
PAR PER PHR PIR POR PUR PWR PYR

•PR
APR CPR NPR OPR SPR TPR

PS•
PSA PSC PSF PSI PSS PST

P•S
PAS PBS PCS PES PGS PIS PJS PKS PLS PNS POS PPS PRS PSS PTS PXS

•PS
APS BPS CPS DPS EPS FPS GPS IPS JPS KPS LPS MPS NPS OPS PPS QPS RPS SPS TPS UPS VPS

PT•
PTA PTC PTG PTH PTL PTO PTS PTT PTV

P•T
PAT PCT PDT PET PIT PKT PMT POT PPT PST PTT PUT PVT PWT PXT

•PT
APT CPT DPT OPT PPT RPT SPT

PU•
PUB PUC PUG PUL PUN PUP PUR PUT

P•U
PAU PEU PHU PIU PKU PLU

•PU
APU CPU

PV•
PVC PVT

P•V
PCV POV PPV PTV

•PV
PPV

PW•
PWA PWR PWT

P•W
PAW PEW POW

•PW
DPW

PX•
PXS PXT

P•X
PAX PBX PIX POX PYX

PY•
PYA PYE PYM PYR PYX

P•Y
PAY PLY PRY

•PY
SPY

P•Z
PAZ PEZ

QA•
QAF QAT

Q•A
QUA

QB•
QBP QBS

Q•C
QMC QVC

Q•D
QED QID

QE•
QED QEF

Q•E
QUE

Q•F
QAF QEF

Q•G
QMG

QI•
QID QIN

Q•I
QUI

QK•
QKT

QM•
QMC QMG

Q•M
QOM QUM

QN•
QNP

Q•N
QIN

QO•
QOM

Q•O
QSO QTO QUO

QP•
QPS

Q•P
QBP QNP QRP

QQ•
QQV

•QQ
SQQ

QR•
QRP QRS

Q•R
QTR

QS•
QSO

Q•S
QBS QPS QRS QTS

•QS
HQS IQS

QT•
QTO QTR QTS QTY

Q•T
QAT QKT

QU•
QUA QUE QUI QUM QUO

QV•
QVC

Q•V
QQV

•QV
QQV

Q•Y
QTY

RA•
RAB RAD RAE RAF RAG RAH RAI RAJ RAM RAN RAP RAS RAT RAU RAW RAX RAY

R•A
RCA RDA REA RIA RNA RSA RYA

•RA
ARA BRA ERA FRA IRA KRA NRA ORA SRA TRA

RB•
RBC RBI

R•B
RAB REB RFB RGB RHB RIB ROB RUB

•RB
ARB FRB ORB URB

RC•
RCA RCD RCN RCP RCS RCT

R•C
RBC REC RIC ROC

•RC
ARC JRC NRC ORC PRC

RD•
RDA RDD RDE RDF RDS

R•D
RAD RCD RDD RED RFD RID RND ROD RUD

•RD
ARD ORD URD

RE•
REA REB REC RED REE REF REG REI REL REM REN REO REP REQ RES RET REV REX REY

R•E
RAE RDE REE RFE RHE ROE RTE RUE RYE

•RE
ARE BRE DRE ERE GRE HRE IRE MRE ORE PRE TRE URE

RF•
RFB RFD RFE RFI RFK RFQ

R•F
RAF RDF REF RIF

•RF
ARF GRF PRF

RG•
RGB RGS RGT

R•G
RAG REG RIG RPG RUG

•RG
ARG ERG FRG ORG

RH•
RHB RHE RHO

R•H
RAH

•RH
HRH

RI•
RIA RIB RIC RID RIF RIG

RIM RIN RIO RIP RIT RIV

R•I RAI RBI REI RFI ROI RPI

•RI ARI CRI ERI FRI MRI SRI TRI URI

RJ• RJR

R•J RAJ

•RJ DRJ

RK• RKO

R•K RFK ROK

•RK ARK DRK ERK IRK ORK

RL• RLS

R•L REL

•RL FRL URL

RM• RMN RMS

R•M RAM REM RIM ROM RPM RUM

•RM ARM VRM

RN• RNA RND RNP RNS

R•N RAN RCN REN RIN RMN RON RUN

•RN ARN ERN PRN URN

RO• ROB ROC ROD ROE ROI ROK ROM RON ROO ROT ROW ROY ROZ

R•O REO RHO RIO RKO ROO

•RO ARO BRO CRO FRO GRO IRO ORO PRO SRO URO

RP• RPG RPI RPM RPQ RPS RPT

R•P RAP RCP REP RIP RNP

•RP ARP KRP PRP QRP TRP

R•Q REQ RFQ RPQ

RR• RRR RRS

R•R RJR RRR RUR

•RR ARR BRR ERR GRR IRR ORR RRR

RS• RSA RST RSV

R•S RAS RCS RDS RES RGS RLS RMS RNS RPS RRS RTS RUS RVS

•RS ARS BRS CRS DRS ERS FRS HRS IRS JRS LRS MRS ORS PRS QRS RRS SRS TRS YRS

RT• RTE RTS RTW

R•T RAT RCT RET RGT RIT ROT RPT RST RUT

•RT ART CRT FRT IRT LRT MRT ORT

RU• RUB RUD RUE RUG RUM RUN RUR RUS RUT

R•U RAU

•RU ARU CRU DRU TRU URU

RV• RVS

R•V REV RIV RSV

•RV BRV IRV ORV

RW• RWY

R•W RAW ROW RTW

•RW TRW

R•X RAX REX

•RX MRX

RY• RYA RYE

R•Y RAY REY ROY RWY

•RY ARY CRY DRY ERY FRY ORY PRY TRY WRY

R•Z ROZ

•RZ ERZ

SA• SAB SAC SAD SAE SAG SAL SAM SAN SAO SAP SAR SAS SAT SAU SAW SAX SAY

S•A SBA SEA SHA SKA SLA SMA SPA SRA SSA STA SUA SWA

•SA ASA BSA CSA ESA GSA ISA NSA OSA PSA RSA SSA USA

SB• SBA SBE SBW

S•B SAB SIB SOB STB SUB

•SB OSB

SC• SCD SCH SCI SCM

S•C SAC SEC SFC SIC SOC SVC

•SC ASC BSC CSC DSC ESC JSC LSC MSC NSC PSC USC

SD• SDI SDS

S•D SAD SCD SGD SID SJD SLD SOD STD SUD SYD

•SD ESD JSD LSD

SE• SEA SEC SEE SEI SEL SEM SEN SEP SEQ SER SES SET SEW SEX SEZ

S•E SAE SBE SEE SHE SIE SSE STE SUE

•SE ASE ESE ISE OSE SSE TSE USE

SF• SFC SFO SFZ

S•F SHF SOF SPF SUF

•SF NSF OSF PSF

SG• SGD SGT

S•G SAG SIG SNG SOG STG SUG

•SG MSG

SH• SHA SHE SHF SHH SHO SHR SHT SHU SHY

S•H SCH SHH

•SH ASH BSH HSH ISH OSH USH

SI• SIB SIC SID SIE SIG SIL SIM SIN SIP SIR SIS SIT SIX

S•I SCI SDI SEI SKI SOI SRI SSI SUI

•SI ASI HSI LSI PSI SSI

SJ• SJD

SK• SKA SKI SKT SKU SKY

S•K STK SUK

•SK ASK CSK ESK TSK

SL• SLA SLD SLO SLR SLY

S•L SAL SEL SIL SML SNL SOL STL SYL

•SL ASL ESL ISL MSL YSL

SM• SMA SML SMS SMU

S•M SAM SCM SEM SIM STM SUM SYM

•SM DSM ISM USM

SN• SNG SNL SNO SNY

S•N SAN SEN SIN SON SSN STN SUN SYN

•SN ASN MSN SSN USN

SO• SOB SOC SOD SOF SOG SOI SOL SON SOO SOP SOR SOS SOT SOU SOV SOW SOX SOY

S•O SAO SFO SHO SLO SNO SOO SRO SUO

•SO ASO DSO ESO ISO OSO QSO USO

SP• SPA SPF SPP SPR SPS SPT SPY

S•P SAP SEP SIP SOP SPP STP SUP

•SP ASP ESP TSP USP

SQ• SQQ

S•Q SEQ SQQ SUQ

•SQ ESQ

SR• SRA SRI SRO SRS

S•R SAR SER SHR SIR SLR SOR SPR SSR STR SUR SVR SYR

•SR ASR ISR SSR TSR

SS• SSA SSE SSI SSN SSR SSS SST SSW

S•S SAS SDS SES SIS SMS SOS SPS SRS SSS STS SUS SYS

•SS ASS ESS ISS MSS OSS PSS SSS USS VSS

ST• STA STB STD STE STG STK STL STM STN STP STR STS STU STY

S•T SAT SET SGT SHT SIT SKT SOT SPT SST

•ST AST CST DST EST GST HST IST LST MST OST PST RST SST

SU• SUA SUB SUD SUE SUF SUG SUI SUK SUM SUN SUO SUP SUQ SUR SUS SUV

S•U SAU SHU SKU SMU SOU STU

•SU ASU ESU FSU LSU MSU OSU TSU USU

SV• SVC SVR

S•V SOV SUV

•SV ASV RSV

SW• SWA SWY

S•W SAW SBW SEW SOW SSW

•SW MSW NSW SSW USW WSW

S•X SAX SEX SIX SOX

•SX CSX USX

SY• SYD SYL SYM SYN SYR SYS

S•Y SAY SHY SKY SLY SNY SOY SPY STY SWY

S•Z SEZ SFZ

TA• TAB TAC TAD TAE TAG TAI TAJ TAL TAM TAN TAO TAP TAR TAS TAT TAU TAV TAW TAX TAY

T•A TBA TEA THA TIA TPA TRA TVA TWA

•TA ATA ETA MTA OTA PTA STA UTA

TB• TBA TBS

T•B TAB THB TOB TUB

•TB OTB STB

TC• TCU

T•C TAC TEC TIC TLC

•TC ETC FTC GTC LTC OTC PTC

TD• TDD TDS

T•D TAD TDD TED THD TID TOD

•TD ETD FTD GTD ITD LTD STD YTD

TE• TEA TEC TED TEE TEG TEH TEL TEM TEN TER TES TET TEX TEY

T•E TAE TEE THE TIE TOE TRE TSE TUE TYE

•TE ATE ETE GTE ITE OTE RTE STE UTE

TF• TFR

•TF ATF CTF

TG• TGV

T•G TAG TEG TOG TUG TVG

•TG MTG PTG STG

TH• THA THB THD THE THI THM THO THU THX THY

T•H TEH

•TH BTH ETH FTH NTH PTH

TI• TIA TIC TID TIE TIL TIM TIN TIO TIP TIS TIU TIV

T•I TAI THI TMI TOI TRI TUI TWI

T•J TAJ TMJ

TK• TKO TKT

T•K TPK TSK

•TK STK

TL• TLC

T•L TAL TEL TIL

•TL ATL BTL PTL STL

TM• TMI TMJ TMS

T•M TAM TEM THM TIM TOM TUM TVM

•TM ATM MTM STM

TN• TNN TNS TNT

T•N TAN TEN TIN TNN TON TUN

•TN CTN MTN STN

TO• TOB TOD TOE TOG TOI TOM TON TOO TOP TOR TOT TOV TOW TOX TOY

T•O TAO THO TIO TKO TOO TWO

•TO CTO ETO GTO ITO OTO PTO QTO UTO

TP• TPA TPK TPR TPS

T•P TAP TIP TOP TRP TSP TUP TVP TWP TYP

•TP ATP DTP GTP STP

TR• TRA TRE TRI TRP TRS TRU TRW TRY

T•R TAR TER TFR TOR TPR TSR TYR

•TR CTR LTR QTR STR VTR

TS• TSE TSK TSP TSR TSU

T•S TAS TBS TDS TES TIS TMS TNS TPS TRS TVS

•TS BTS CTS DTS ETS HTS ITS KTS LTS MTS OTS PTS QTS RTS STS UTS WTS

TT• TTY

T•T TAT TET TKT TNT TOT TUT

•TT ATT GTT ITT OTT PTT

TU• TUB TUE TUG TUI TUM TUN TUP TUT TUX TUZ

T•U TAU TCU THU TIU TRU TSU TZU

•TU BTU STU UTU

TV• TVA TVG TVM TVP TVS TVY

T•V TAV TGV TIV TOV

•TV ATV ETV ITV MTV PTV

TW• TWA TWI TWO TWP TWX

T•W TAW TOW TRW

•TW BTW RTW

T•X TAX TEX THX TOX TUX TWX

TY• TYE TYP TYR

T•Y TAY TEY THY TOY TRY TTY TVY

•TY ITY QTY STY TTY

TZ• TZU

T•Z TUZ

UA• UAE UAL UAR UAW

U•A UFA UMA UNA USA UTA UVA

•UA HUA QUA SUA

UB• UBE UBI

U•B URB

•UB BUB CUB DUB FUB HUB LUB NUB PUB RUB SUB TUB

U•C UDC UNC UPC USC

•UC AUC BUC DUC LUC PUC

UD• UDC UDO

U•D UND URD

•UD AUD BUD CUD DUD HUD JUD MUD

OUD RUD SUD WUD

UE• UEY

U•E UAE UBE UKE ULE UME UNE URE USE UTE

•UE CUE DUE HUE KUE QUE RUE SUE TUE YUE

UF• UFA UFO UFT UFW

U•F UHF ULF

•UF AUF SUF

UG• UGH UGO

U•G UNG

•UG AUG BUG DUG FUG HUG JUG LUG MUG PUG RUG SUG TUG VUG ZUG

UH• UHF

U•H UGH UNH USH

•UH DUH HUH

UI• UIT

U•I UBI UNI UPI URI UZI

•UI CUI GUI HUI LUI NUI OUI QUI SUI TUI

UK• UKE

•UK AUK SUK YUK

UL• ULE ULF ULM ULT ULU

U•L UAL URL

•UL BUL CUL FUL JUL KUL NUL PUL VUL YUL

UM• UMA UME UMP UMW

U•M ULM USM

•UM AUM BUM CUM DUM FUM GUM HUM IUM KUM LUM MUM NUM QUM RUM SUM TUM YUM

UN• UNA UNC UND UNE UNG UNH UNI UNO UNP UNQ UNS UNU

U•N UPN URN USN

•UN BUN DUN FUN GUN HUN JUN KUN MUN NUN PUN RUN SUN TUN

U•O UDO UFO UGO UNO URO USO UTO

•UO DUO LUO QUO SUO

UP• UPC UPI UPN UPS

U•P UMP UNP USP

•UP CUP DUP HUP PUP SUP TUP YUP

U•Q UNQ

•UQ SUQ

UR• URB URD URE URI URL URN URO URU

U•R UAR

•UR BUR CUR EUR FUR GUR HUR KUR OUR PUR RUR SUR

US• USA USC USE USH USM USN USO USP USS USU USW USX

U•S UNS UPS USS UTS

•US AUS BUS GUS HUS JUS MUS NUS OUS RUS SUS

UT• UTA UTE UTO UTS UTU

U•T UFT UIT ULT

•UT AUT BUT CUT FUT GUT HUT JUT MUT NUT OUT PUT RUT TUT

U•U ULU UNU URU USU UTU

UV• UVA

•UV GUV JUV LUV SUV

U•W UAW UFW UMW USW

U•X USX

•UX AUX DUX LUX MUX TUX

U•Y UEY

•UY BUY GUY MUY

UZ• UZI

•UZ DUZ LUZ TUZ

VA• VAC VAE VAL VAN VAR VAS VAT VAV VAY

V•A VGA VIA VOA

•VA AVA EVA IVA OVA TVA UVA WVA

VB• VBS

VC• VCR

V•C VAC VIC VOC

•VC AVC JVC MVC PVC QVC SVC

VD• VDT VDU

V•D VFD VMD

•VD BVD DVD

VE• VEE VEG VEH VEL VEN VER VET VEX

V•E VAE VEE VIE

•VE AVE EVE IVE

VF• VFD VFW

V•F VHF VLF

VG• VGA

V•G VEG VUG

•VG AVG EVG TVG

VH• VHF VHS

V•H VEH

VI• VIA VIC VIE VII VIL VIM VIN VIP VIR VIS VIV VIZ

V•I VII VMI

•VI AVI CVI DVI LVI MVI OVI XVI

VJ• VJS

VL• VLF

V•L VAL VEL VIL VOL VUL

VM• VMD VMI

V•M VIM VRM

•VM BVM DVM TVM

V•N VAN VEN VIN VON

•VN AVN

VO• VOA VOC VOL VON VOS VOU VOW VOX

•VO AVO IVO OVO

VP• VPS

V•P VIP

•VP MVP TVP

VR• VRM

V•R VAR VCR VER VIR VTR

•VR SVR

VS• VSS

V•S VAS VBS VHS VIS VJS VOS VPS VSS VWS

•VS AVS CVS EVS IVS RVS TVS

VT• VTR

V•T VAT VDT VET

•VT BVT PVT

VU• VUG VUL

V•U VDU VOU

V•V VAV VIV

VW• VWS

V•W VFW VOW

•VW GVW

V•X VEX VOX

V•Y VAY

•VY HVY IVY TVY

V•Z VIZ

WA• WAB WAC WAD WAF WAG WAH WAL WAN WAR WAS WAT WAW WAX WAY

W•A WBA WHA WPA WVA

•WA KWA PWA SWA TWA

WB• WBA WBC WBN WBS

W•B WAB WEB

WC• WCS

W•C WAC WBC

WD• WDS

W•D WAD WED WUD

•WD FWD

WE• WEB WED WEE WEI WEN WES WET

W•E WEE WIE WOE WYE

•WE AWE EWE OWE

W•F WAF WHF WWF

•WF WWF

W•G WAG WIG

WH• WHA WHF WHH WHO WHR WHS WHY

W•H WAH WHH

•WH KWH

WI• WIE WIG WIL WIM WIN WIP WIS WIT WIZ

W•I WEI WWI

•WI BWI OWI TWI WWI

WJ• WJM

WK• WKS

W•K WMK WOK

•WK AWK

WL• WLS

W•L WAL WIL

•WL AWL OWL

WM• WMK

W•M WIM WJM WPM

•WM CWM HWM

WN• WNW

W•N WAN WBN WEN WIN WON WPN

•WN AWN OWN

WO• WOE WOK WON WOO WOT WOW

W•O WHO WOO WYO

•WO CWO IWO TWO

WP• WPA WPM WPN

W•P WIP

•WP CWP TWP

WR• WRY

W•R WAR WHR

•WR PWR

WS• WSW

W•S WAS WBS WCS WDS WES WHS WIS WKS WLS WTS

•WS VWS

WT• WTS

W•T WAT WET WIT WOT

•WT CWT DWT NWT PWT

WU• WUD

•WU NWU

WV• WVA

•WV LWV

WW• WWF WWI WWW

W•W WAW WNW WOW WSW WWW

•WW IWW WWW

W•X WAX

•WX TWX

WY• WYE WYO

W•Y WAY WHY WRY

•WY HWY RWY SWY

W•Z WIZ

XA• XAT

X•A XIA

XC• XCI XCV

•XC CXC DXC EXC MXC

X•D XED

•XD MXD

XE• XED XEN XER XES

X•E XKE

•XE AXE EXE

XI• XIA XII XIN XIS XIV XIX

X•I XCI XII XLI XVI XXI

•XI CXI DXI LXI MXI XXI

XK• XKE

XL• XLI XLS XLV

X•L XYL

•XL AXL CXL DXL MXL

X•N XEN XIN

XO• XOO XOR XOX

X•O XOO XXO

•XO EXO OXO XXO

•XP EXP

•XQ BXQ

X•R XER XOR

•XR EXR

X•S XES XIS XLS

•XS PXS

X•T XAT

•XT EXT PXT

XV• XVI

X•V XCV XIV XLV XXV

•XV CXV DXV LXV MXV XXV

XX• XXI XXO XXV XXX

X•X XIX XOX XXX

•XX CXX DXX LXX MXX OXX XXX

XY• XYL

•XY OXY

YA• YAD YAG YAH YAK YAM YAO YAP YAR YAS YAT YAW YAY YAZ

Y•A YEA YMA

•YA PYA RYA

YB• YBS

Y•B YOB

•YC MYC NYC

YD• YDS

Y•D YAD YLD YOD YTD

•YD CYD HYD KYD SYD

YE• YEA YEN YEO YEP YER YES YET YEW

Y•E YUE

•YE AYE BYE DYE EYE KYE LYE NYE PYE RYE TYE WYE

Y•G YAG

•YG ZYG

Y•H YAH

•YH AYH

YI• YIN YIP

•YI FYI

Y•K YAK YUK

YL• YLD

Y•L YSL YUL

•YL CYL OYL SYL XYL

YM• YMA

Y•M YAM YOM YUM

•YM GYM PYM SYM ZYM

Y•N YEN YIN YON

•YN AYN DYN FYN GYN LYN SYN

YO• YOB YOD YOM YON YOO YOU YOW

Y•O YAO YEO YOO

•YO BYO CYO LYO MYO OYO WYO

Y•P YAP YEP YIP YUP

•YP GYP HYP TYP

YR• YRS

Y•R YAR YER

•YR AYR CYR PYR SYR TYR

YS• YSL

Y•S YAS YBS YDS YES YRS

•YS DYS LYS SYS

YT• YTD

Y•T YAT YET

YU• YUE YUK YUL YUM YUP

Y•U YOU

•YU BYU NYU

Y•W YAW YEW YOW

•YX MYX NYX PYX

Y•Y YAY

Y•Z YAZ

•YZ BYZ

ZA• ZAG ZAL ZAP ZAS ZAX

Z•A ZEA ZIA ZOA

Z•D ZED ZOD

ZE• ZEA ZED ZEE ZEG ZEN ZEV

Z•E ZEE ZOE

•ZE IZE

Z•F ZIF

Z•G ZAG ZEG ZIG ZOG ZPG ZUG ZYG

ZI• ZIA ZIF ZIG ZIP ZIT ZIV

•ZI UZI

Z•L ZAL

Z•M ZYM

Z•N ZEN

ZO• ZOA ZOD ZOE ZOG ZOO

Z•O ZOO

•ZO AZO OZO

ZP• ZPG

Z•P ZAP ZIP

•ZR EZR

Z•S ZAS

•ZS OZS

Z•T ZIT

•ZT OZT

ZU• ZUG

•ZU TZU

Z•V ZEV ZIV

Z•X ZAX

ZY• ZYG ZYM

ZZ• ZZZ

Z•Z ZZZ

•ZZ ZZZ

AA••
AAHS AARE AARP

A•A•
ABAS ACAD ADAH ADAK ADAM ADAR AFAR AGAR AGAS AHAB AHAZ AJAR AJAX AKAN ALAE ALAI ALAN ALAR ALAS AMAH AMAS AMAT ANAS ANAT ARAB ARAD ARAK ARAL ARAM ARAN ARAS ASAP AVAL AVAR AWAY AYAH AZAN

A••A
ABBA ACEA ACTA AFTA AGFA AGHA AGRA AGUA AIDA AIEA AIWA ALBA ALDA ALEA ALFA ALGA ALIA ALKA ALLA ALMA ALTA ALVA AMIA ANKA ANNA ANOA ANSA ANTA ANYA ANZA APIA AQUA ARCA AREA ARIA ARMA ARPA ARRA ASEA ASIA ASTA ATKA ATRA ATTA AULA AURA AVIA AYLA

•AA•
BAAL BAAS CAAN HAAG MAAM MAAR MAAS MAAT PAAR SAAB SAAR TAAL VAAL WAAC WAAF WAAL

•A•A
BABA BAJA BAMA BARA BAYA CAMA CANA CAPA CARA CASA CATA CAVA DADA DAMA DANA DATA FALA FATA FAVA GABA GAEA GAGA GAIA GALA GAMA GAPA GAYA GAZA HAHA HAMA HANA IANA JADA JAVA KAKA KAMA KANA KARA KAVA LALA LAMA LANA LARA LAVA MAIA MAJA MALA MAMA MANA MARA MATA MAYA NADA NAHA NANA NAPA NARA NASA PABA PACA PAPA PARA PASA RAGA RAJA RAMA RANA RAPA RARA RASA RATA SABA SADA SAGA SALA SANA SARA SAVA TADA TAKA TALA TAMA TANA TAPA TARA TATA TAXA VACA VARA VAYA WAKA WAWA YADA YAMA YANA ZAMA

••AA
MPAA NCAA NOAA

AB••
ABAS ABBA ABBE ABBR ABBS ABBY ABCS ABED ABEL ABER ABET ABIB ABIE ABLE ABLY ABMS ABOU ABRI ABUT ABYE ABYS

A•B•
ABBA ABBE ABBR ABBS ABBY ALBA ALBI ALBS AMBI AMBO AMBS APBS ARBS AUBE

A••B
ABIB AHAB ARAB

•AB•
BABA BABE BABI BABS BABU BABY CABS DABO DABS GABA GABE GABO GABS GABY HABE JABS KABS LABS NABE NABS PABA RABE RABI RABS SABA SABE SABU TABI TABS TABU WABS

•A•B
BARB CARB DAUB GARB IAMB JAMB KALB LAMB SAAB

••AB
AHAB ARAB BLAB CRAB DRAB FLAB GRAB JOAB MOAB SAAB SCAB SLAB STAB SWAB

AC••
ACAD ACCS ACCT ACDC ACEA ACED ACER ACES ACET ACEY ACHE ACHT ACHY ACID ACIS ACLU ACME ACNE ACRE ACRO ACTA ACTE ACTG ACTH ACTI ACTS ACTV ACYL

A•C•
ABCS ACCS ACCT ADCS AGCY ANCE ANCY ARCA ARCH ARCO ARCS ASCH ASCI ASCO

A••C
ACDC ALEC AMIC APOC AVEC

•AC•
BACH BACK BACS BACT CACO DACE EACH FACE FACP FACS FACT HACK JACK LACE LACK LACS LACT LACY MACC MACE MACH MACK MACS MACY NACL PACA PACE PACK PACS PACT RACE RACK RACY SACK SACS TACH TACK TACO TACT VACA VACS WACE WACK WACO WACS YACK ZACK

•A•C
BANC BASC CALC CANC DARC LAIC MACC MARC MASC NARC PARC TALC WAAC

••AC
BOAC BRAC GMAC HUAC WAAC WRAC

AD••
ADAH ADAK ADAM ADAR ADCS ADDN ADDS ADDY ADEN ADES ADIN ADIT ADJS ADJT ADMS ADOS ADUE ADVT ADZE

A•D•
ACDC ADDN ADDS ADDY AIDA AIDE AIDS ALDA ALDO ANDS ANDY AUDE AUDI AVDP

A••D
ABED ACAD ACED ACID AGED AMID APED ARAD ARID AULD AVID AWED AXED

•AD•
BADE CADE CADI CADS DADA DADE DADO DADS EADS FADE FADO FADS GADS HADE HADJ JADA JADE LADD LADE LADS LADY MADD MADE NADA NADH NADP PADS QADI RADM RADS SADA SADD SADE SADI SADR TADA TADS VADE VADM WADE WADI WADS YADA

•A•D
BALD BAND BARD BAUD CARD DARD DASD FAHD GAUD HAND HARD LADD LAID LAND LAPD LARD LAUD MADD MAID MAUD NARD NASD PAID PARD PATD QAID RAID RAND SADD SAID SAND SARD SAUD VAUD WALD WAND WARD YARD YAZD

••AD
ACAD ARAD BEAD BRAD CHAD CLAD DEAD DUAD DYAD EGAD FUAD GLAD GOAD GRAD HEAD HOAD JOAD LEAD LOAD MEAD OBAD ORAD QUAD READ ROAD SCAD SHAD SPAD TOAD WOAD

AE••
AEON AERO AERY

A•E•
ABED ABEL ABER ABET ACEA ACED ACER ACES ACET ACEY ADEN ADES AGED AGEE AGER AGES AHEM AIEA AKEE ALEA ALEC ALEE ALEF ALEP ALES ALEX AMEN AMER AMES AMEX ANEW APED APER APES APEX AREA AREO ARES ASEA ATEN ATES AUEL AUER AVEC AVER AVES AWED AWES AXED AXEL AXER AXES AYER AYES

A••E
AARE ABBE ABIE ABLE ABYE ACHE ACME ACNE ACRE ACTE ADUE ADZE AGEE AGUE AIDE AIME AIRE AKEE ALAE ALEE ALLE ALOE ALTE AMIE ANCE ANGE ANNE ANTE AONE APSE ARME ARNE ARTE ASHE AUBE AUDE AUGE AUNE AXLE AYME

•AE•
BAER BAEZ CAEN GAEA GAEL JAEL JAEN KAEL NAES TAEL

•A•E
AARE BABE BADE BAKE BALE BANE BARE BASE BATE CADE CAFE CAGE CAKE CALE CAME CANE CAPE CARE CASE CATE CAVE DACE DADE DALE DAME DANE DARE DATE DAVE DAZE EASE EAVE FACE FADE FAKE FAME FANE FARE FATE FAVE FAYE FAZE GABE GAGE GALE GAME GAPE GARE GATE GAVE GAYE GAZE HABE HADE HAKE HALE HAME HARE HATE HAVE HAZE JADE JAKE JANE JAPE JAYE KALE KAME KANE KATE KAYE LACE LADE LAKE LAME LANE LASE LATE LAUE LAVE LAZE MACE MADE MAGE MAKE MALE MAME MANE MARE MATE MAZE NABE NAME NAPE NATE NAVE PACE PAGE PALE PANE PARE PASE PATE PAVE RABE RACE RAGE RAKE RARE RASE RATE RAVE RAYE RAZE SABE SADE SAFE SAGE SAKE SALE SAME SANE SASE SATE SAVE SAXE TAKE TALE TAME TANE TAPE TARE TATE VADE VALE VANE VASE WACE WADE WAGE WAKE WALE WANE WARE WAVE YALE YARE ZANE

••AE
ALAE BLAE BRAE FRAE IDAE IRAE

AF••
AFAR AFGH AFRO AFTA AFTS

A•F•
AGFA ALFA AMFM

A••F
ALEF ALIF ASIF ASOF

•AF•
BAFF CAFE DAFF DAFT GAFF HAFT KAFS

OAFS QAFS RAFF RAFT SAFE SAFR TAFT WAFS WAFT

•A•F
BAFF CALF CANF DAFF GAFF HALF NAIF RAFF TAIF WAAF WAIF ZARF

••AF
DEAF GRAF LEAF LOAF OLAF PIAF RCAF USAF WAAF WRAF

AG••
AGAR AGAS AGCY AGED AGEE AGER AGES AGFA AGHA AGIN AGIO AGLY AGNI AGOG AGON AGRA AGRI AGRO AGTS AGUA AGUE

A•G•
AFGH ALGA ALGO ALGY ANGE ANGL ARGO ARGY AUGE AVGS

A••G
ACTG AGOG

•AG•
BAGS CAGE CAGY DAGS GAGA GAGE GAGS HAGI HAGS IAGO JAGR JAGS LAGO LAGS MAGE MAGI MAGS NAGS NAGY PAGE PAGO RAGA RAGE RAGG RAGS RAGU SAGA SAGE SAGO SAGS TAGS WAGE WAGS YAGI ZAGS

•A•G
BANG DANG DAWG FANG GANG HAAG HAIG HANG HAWG LANG MARG NANG PANG RAGG RANG SANG TANG VANG WANG YANG

••AG
BRAG CRAG DIAG DRAG FLAG HAAG PEAG QUAG SHAG SLAG SNAG STAG SWAG

AH••
AHAB AHAZ AHEM AHOY AHSO

A•H•
AAHS ACHE ACHT ACHY AGHA ASHE ASHY

A••H
ACTH ADAH AFGH ALPH AMAH ANKH ANTH ARCH ASCH AUTH AYAH

•AH•
AAHS BAHN BAHR BAHS BAHT CAHN DAHL DAHS FAHD FAHR HAHA HAHN HAHS JAHR KAHN LAHR MAHI NAHA OAHU PAHO PAHS SAHL TAHR WAHL ZAHN

•A•H
BACH BASH BATH CASH CATH DASH EACH FATH GASH GATH HASH HATH KAPH LAKH LASH LATH MACH MASH MATH NADH NAOH NASH OATH PASH PATH RASH RATH SASH TACH TANH WASH

••AH
ADAH AMAH AYAH BLAH ETAH EVAH LEAH NOAH OPAH PTAH SHAH UTAH YEAH

AI••
AIDA AIDE AIDS AIEA AILS AIME AIMS AINS AINT AINU AIRE AIRS AIRT AIRY AITS AIWA

A•I•
ABIB ABIE ACID ACIS ADIN ADIT AGIN AGIO AKIM AKIN ALIA ALIF ALII ALIS ALIT AMIA AMIC AMID AMIE AMIN AMIR AMIS ANIL ANIM ANIS APIA APIS ARIA ARID ARIL ARIZ ASIA ASIF ASIR ASIS ATIT AVIA AVID AVIS AVIV AXIL AXIS AYIN AZIZ

A••I
ABRI ACTI AGNI AGRI ALAI ALBI ALII ALTI ALUI AMBI AMOI ANSI ANTI AOKI AQUI ASCI ASTI ATLI ATOI ATRI AUDI AURI

•AI•
BAIL BAIN BAIO BAIT CAIN DAIN DAIS FAIL FAIN FAIR FAIT GAIA GAIL GAIN GAIT HAIG HAIK HAIL HAIM HAIR JAIL JAIN KAIN LAIC LAID LAIN LAIR LAIT MAIA MAID MAIL MAIN MAIS NAIF NAIL PAID PAIL PAIN PAIR PAIX QAID RAID RAIL RAIN SAID SAIL SAIS TAIF TAIL TAIN TAIT TAIZ VAIL VAIN VAIR WAIF WAIL WAIN WAIT

•A•I
BABI BALI BANI BARI CADI CALI CAMI DALI DARI HAGI HAJI HAPI HARI IASI KAKI KALI KAMI LARI MAGI MAHI MALI MARI MAUI MAXI MAYI NAOI PALI PARI QADI RABI RAKI RAMI RANI RAVI SADI SAKI SARI TABI TALI TATI TAVI TAXI WADI YAGI

••AI
ALAI BNAI ESAI KWAI OJAI QUAI THAI VRAI

AJ••
AJAR AJAX

A•J•
ADJS ADJT

•AJ•
BAJA HAJI HAJJ MAJA RAJA TAJS

•A•J
HADJ HAJJ

AK••
AKAN AKEE AKIM AKIN

A•K•
ALKA ANKA ANKH AOKI ARKS ASKS ATKA AUKS

A••K
ADAK AMOK ARAK

•AK•
BAKE BAKR BAKU CAKE CAKY FAKE HAKE JAKE KAKA KAKI LAKE LAKH LAKY MAKE MAKO OAKS RAKE RAKI RAKU SAKE SAKI SAKS TAKA TAKE WAKA WAKE YAKS

•A•K
BACK BALK BANK BARK BASK CALK CARK CASK DANK DARK FALK GAWK HACK HAIK HANK HARK HAWK JACK LACK LANK LARK MACK MARK MASK NARK PACK PARK RACK RANK RASK SACK SALK SANK SARK SASK SAUK TACK TALK TANK TASK WACK WALK YACK YANK ZACK

••AK
ADAK ARAK BEAK BIAK DOAK DYAK FLAK ISAK LEAK NDAK PEAK SDAK SOAK SWAK TEAK WEAK

AL••
ALAE ALAI ALAN ALAR ALAS ALBA ALBI ALBS ALDA ALDO ALEA ALEC ALEE ALEF ALEP ALES ALEX ALFA ALGA ALGO ALGY ALIA ALIF ALII ALIS ALIT ALKA ALLA ALLE ALLO ALLS ALLY ALMA ALMS ALOE ALOU ALOW ALPH ALPO ALPS ALSO ALTA ALTE ALTI ALTO ALTS ALUI ALUM ALVA

A•L•
ABLE ABLY ACLU AGLY AILS ALLA ALLE ALLO ALLS ALLY ARLO ATLI AULA AULD AWLS AXLE AYLA

A••L
ABEL ACYL AMYL ANGL ANIL APPL ARAL ARIL ARYL AUEL AVAL AWOL AXEL AXIL AZUL

•AL•
BALD BALE BALI BALK BALL BALM BALT CALC CALE CALF CALI CALK CALL CALM CALS CALX DALE DALI DALS DALY FALA FALK FALL FALX GALA GALE GALL GALS GALV HALE HALF HALL HALM HALO HALS HALT KALB KALE KALI KALT LALA LALO MALA MALE MALI MALL MALM MALO MALT PALE PALI PALL PALM PALO PALP PALS PALY RALL SALA SALE SALK SALP SALS SALT TALA TALC TALE TALI TALK TALL VALE WALD WALE WALK WALL WALT YALE YALL YALU ZALS

•A•L
BAAL BAIL BALL BAWL CALL CARL CAUL DAHL DANL EARL FAIL FALL GAEL GAIL GALL GAOL GAUL HAIL HALL HAUL JAEL JAIL JARL KAEL KARL MAIL MALL MARL MAUL NACL NAIL NASL NATL PAIL PALL PARL PAUL PAWL RAIL RALL RAUL SAHL SAIL SAML SAUL TAAL TAEL TAIL TALL VAAL VAIL WAAL WAHL WAIL WALL YALL YAWL

••AL
ARAL AVAL BAAL BEAL COAL DEAL DHAL DIAL DUAL EGAL ELAL ETAL FOAL GOAL HEAL ICAL ITAL KCAL LEAL MEAL NEAL OPAL ORAL OVAL PEAL REAL RIAL RYAL SEAL SIAL TAAL TEAL URAL VAAL VEAL VIAL WAAL WEAL ZEAL

AM••
AMAH AMAS AMAT AMBI AMBO AMBS AMEN AMER AMES AMEX AMFM AMIA AMIC AMID AMIE AMIN AMIR AMIS AMMO AMNT AMOI AMOK AMON AMOR AMOS AMOY AMPS AMTS AMUR AMYL

A•M•
ABMS ACME ADMS AIME AIMS ALMA ALMS AMMO ARMA ARME ARMS ARMY ATMO ATMS AYME

A••M
ADAM AHEM AKIM ALUM AMFM ANIM ARAM ARUM ATOM ATUM AXUM

•AM•
BAMA BAMS CAMA CAME CAMI CAMO CAMP CAMS DAMA DAME DAMN DAMP DAMS FAME GAMA GAME GAMO GAMP GAMS GAMY HAMA HAME HAMM HAMS IAMB JAMB JAMS KAMA KAME KAMI LAMA LAMB LAME LAMP LAMS LAMY MAMA MAME NAME RAMA RAMI RAMP RAMS SAME SAML SAMO SAMP TAMA TAME TAMM TAMO TAMP TAMS VAMP YAMA YAMS ZAMA

•A•M
BALM BARM BAUM CALM FARM GAUM HAIM HALM HAMM HARM MAAM MALM PALM RADM TAMM VADM WARM

••AM
ADAM ARAM BEAM BRAM CHAM CLAM CRAM DIAM DRAM EDAM ELAM EXAM FLAM FOAM FRAM GLAM GRAM GUAM IMAM LIAM LOAM MAAM NOAM PRAM QUAM REAM ROAM SCAM SEAM SHAM SIAM SLAM SPAM SWAM TEAM TRAM WHAM

AN••
ANAS ANAT ANCE ANCY ANDS ANDY ANEW ANGE ANGL ANIL ANIM ANIS ANKA ANKH ANNA ANNE ANNO ANOA ANON ANSA ANSI ANTA ANTE ANTH ANTI ANTS ANYA ANZA

A•N•
ACNE AGNI AINS AINT AINU AMNT ANNA ANNE ANNO AONE ARNE ARNO ATNO AUNE AUNT AWNS

A••N
ADDN ADEN ADIN AEON AGIN AGON AKAN AKIN ALAN AMEN AMIN AMON ANON ARAN ARON ASSN ATEN ATON ATTN AVON AXON AYIN AZAN

•AN•
BANC BAND BANE BANG BANI BANK BANS CANA CANC CANE CANF CANS CANT CANY DANA DANE DANG DANK DANL DANO DANU FANE FANG FANS GANG GANN HANA HAND HANG HANK HANS IANA JANE KANA KANE KANO KANS KANT LANA LAND LANE LANG LANK MANA MANE MANN MANO MANS MANU MANX MANY NANA NANG NANO NANU PANE PANG PANS PANT RANA RAND RANG RANI RANK RANT SANA SAND SANE SANG SANK SANO SANS SANT TANA TANE TANG TANH TANK TANS VANE VANG VANS WAND WANE WANG WANT WANY YANA YANG YANK ZANE ZANY

•A•N
BAHN BAIN BARN CAAN CAEN CAHN CAIN CAPN DAIN DAMN DARN DAWN EARN FAIN FAUN FAWN GAIN GANN GARN HAHN HAWN JAEN JAIN KAHN KAIN KAON LAIN LAWN MAIN MANN PAIN PAWN RAIN SAWN TAIN TARN VAIN WAIN WARN YARN YAWN ZAHN

••AN
AKAN ALAN ARAN AZAN BEAN BRAN CAAN CHAN CLAN CYAN DEAN DIAN DWAN DYAN EBAN EGAN ELAN EVAN FLAN FRAN GIAN GMAN GRAN GUAN IBAN IMAN IRAN IVAN JEAN JOAN JUAN KEAN KHAN KOAN KWAN LEAN LOAN MEAN MOAN OLAN OMAN ORAN PLAN ROAN RYAN SCAN SEAN SHAN SPAN STAN SWAN THAN TMAN TUAN ULAN WEAN XIAN YEAN YUAN

AO••
AOKI AONE AOUT

A•O•
ABOU ADOS AEON AGOG AGON AHOY ALOE ALOU ALOW AMOI AMOK AMON AMOR AMOS AMOY ANOA ANON APOC APOS ARON AROO ASOF ASOR ATOI ATOM ATON ATOP ATOR AVON AVOS AVOW AWOL AXON AZOV

A••O
ACRO AERO AFRO AGIO AGRO AHSO ALDO ALGO ALLO ALPO ALSO ALTO AMBO AMMO ANNO APSO AQUO ARCO AREO ARGO ARLO ARNO AROO ASCO ASTO ATMO ATNO ATTO AUTO

•AO•
GAOL HAOS KAON LAOS NAOH NAOI NAOS TAOS YAOS

•A•O
BAIO BARO CACO CAMO CAPO CARO CATO DABO DADO DANO

DAYO FADO FARO FASO GABO GAMO GATO HALO IAGO JATO KANO KARO KATO KAYO LAGO LALO MAKO MALO MANO MAYO MAZO NANO NASO NATO PAGO PAHO PALO PASO PAVO SAGO SAMO SANO SATO TACO TAMO TARO TAXO WACO

••AO
BIAO CIAO ISAO JIAO LIAO PIAO

AP••
APBS APED APER APES APEX APIA APIS APOC APOS APPL APPS APPT APRS APSE APSO APTS

A•P•
ALPH ALPO ALPS AMPS APPL APPS APPT ARPA ASPS

A••P
AARP ALEP ASAP ATOP AVDP

•AP•
BAPS BAPT CAPA CAPE CAPN CAPO CAPP CAPS CAPT DAPS GAPA GAPE GAPS HAPI HAPS JAPE KAPH LAPD LAPP LAPS MAPS NAPA NAPE NAPS PAPA PAPP RAPA RAPP RAPS RAPT SAPS TAPA TAPE TAPS YAPP YAPS ZAPS

•A•P
AARP CAMP CAPP CARP DAMP EARP FACP GAMP GARP GASP GAWP HARP HASP LAMP LAPP NADP PALP PAPP RAMP RAPP RASP SALP SAMP TAMP TARP VAMP WARP WASP YAPP YAWP

••AP
ASAP CHAP CLAP EVAP FLAP FRAP HEAP KNAP LEAP NEAP REAP SLAP SNAP SOAP SWAP TRAP WRAP

AQ••
AQUA AQUI AQUO

•AQ•
FAQS

••AQ
IRAQ SHAQ

AR••
ARAB ARAD ARAK ARAL ARAM ARAN ARAS ARBS ARCA ARCH ARCO ARCS AREA AREO ARES ARGO ARGY ARIA ARID ARIL ARIZ ARKS ARLO ARMA ARME ARMS ARMY ARNE ARNO ARON AROO ARPA ARRA ARRS ARTE ARTS ARTY ARUM ARYL

A•R•
AARE AARP ABRI ACRE ACRO AERO AERY AFRO AGRA AGRI AGRO AIRE AIRS AIRT AIRY APRS ARRA ARRS ATRA ATRI AURA AURI AWRY

A••R
ABBR ABER ACER ADAR AFAR AGAR AGER AJAR ALAR AMER AMIR AMOR AMUR APER ASIR ASOR ASTR ATOR AUER AVAR AVER AXER AYER AZUR

•AR•
AARE AARP BARA BARB BARD BARE BARI BARK BARM BARN BARO BARR BARS BART CARA CARB CARD CARE CARK CARL CARO CARP CARR CARS CART CARY DARC DARD DARE DARI DARK DARN DART EARL EARN EARP EARS FARE FARM FARO FARR FARS GARB GARE GARN GARP GARR GARS GARY HARD HARE HARI HARK HARM HARP HART HARZ JARL JARS KARA KARL KARO KART LARA LARD LARI LARK LARS MARA MARC MARE MARG MARI MARK MARL MARS MART MARU MARV MARX MARY NARA NARC NARD NARK NARY NARZ OARS PARA PARC PARD PARE PARI PARK PARL PARR PARS PART RARA RARE SARA SARD SARI SARK TARA TARE TARN TARO TARP TARS TART VARA VARY WARD WARE WARM WARN WARP WARS WART WARY YARD YARE YARN ZARF

•A•R
BAER BAHR BAKR BARR CARR FAHR FAIR FARR GARR GAUR HAIR JAGR JAHR LAHR LAIR MAAR MAWR PAAR PAIR PARR SAAR SADR SAFR SAUR TAHR VAIR

••AR
ADAR AFAR AGAR AJAR ALAR AVAR BEAR BOAR CHAR CLAR CZAR DEAR FEAR GEAR GNAR GUAR HEAR HOAR IBAR ISAR ITAR IYAR IZAR JBAR KNAR LBAR LEAR LIAR MAAR NEAR OMAR OSAR PAAR PEAR PHAR QUAR REAR ROAR SAAR SCAR SEAR SOAR SPAR STAR TBAR TEAR THAR TSAR TZAR USAR WEAR YEAR ZBAR ZOAR

AS••
ASAP ASCH ASCI ASCO ASEA ASHE ASHY ASIA ASIF ASIR ASIS ASKS ASOF ASOR ASPS ASSN ASST ASTA ASTI ASTO ASTR

A•S•
AHSO ALSO ANSA ANSI APSE APSO ASSN ASST AUST

A••S
AAHS ABAS ABBS ABCS ABMS ABYS ACCS ACES ACIS ACTS ADCS ADDS ADES ADJS ADMS ADOS AFTS AGAS AGES AGTS AIDS AILS AIMS AINS AIRS AITS ALAS ALBS ALES ALIS ALLS ALMS ALPS ALTS AMAS AMBS AMES AMIS AMOS AMPS AMTS ANAS ANDS ANIS ANTS APBS APES APIS APOS APPS APRS APTS ARAS ARBS ARCS ARES ARKS ARMS ARRS ARTS ASIS ASKS ASPS ATES ATMS ATTS ATVS AUKS AVES AVGS AVIS AVOS AWES AWLS AWNS AXES AXIS AYES

•AS•
BASC BASE BASH BASK BASS BAST CASA CASE CASH CASK CASS CAST DASD DASH EASE EAST EASY FASO FAST GASH GASP GAST HASH HASP HAST IASI LASE LASH LASS LAST MASC MASH MASK MASS MAST NASA NASD NASH NASL NASO NAST OAST PASA PASE PASH PASO PASS PAST RASA RASE RASH RASK RASP SASE SASH SASK SASS TASK TASS VASE VAST WASH WASP WAST ZASU

•A•S
AAHS BAAS BABS BACS BAGS BAHS BAMS BANS BAPS BARS BASS BATS BAYS CABS CADS CALS CAMS CANS CAPS CARS CASS CATS CAUS CAVS CAWS CAYS DABS DADS DAGS DAHS DAIS DALS DAMS DAPS DATS DAWS DAYS EADS EARS EATS FACS FADS FANS FAQS FARS FATS FAYS GABS GADS GAGS GALS GAMS GAPS GARS GATS HAGS HAHS HALS HAMS HANS HAOS HAPS HATS HAUS HAWS HAYS JABS JAGS JAMS JARS JAWS JAYS KABS KAFS KANS LABS LACS LADS LAGS LAMS LAOS LAPS LARS LASS LATS LAVS LAWS LAYS MAAS MACS MAGS MAIS MANS MAPS MARS MASS MATS MAVS MAWS MAYS NABS NAES NAGS NAOS NAPS NAYS OAFS OAKS OARS OATS PACS PADS PAHS PALS PANS PARS PASS PATS PAWS PAYS QAFS QATS RABS RADS RAGS RAMS RAPS RATS RAYS SACS SAGS SAIS SAKS SALS SANS SAPS SASS SATS SAWS SAYS TABS TADS TAGS TAJS TAMS TANS TAOS TAPS TARS TASS TATS TAUS TAWS VACS VANS VATS VAVS WABS WACS WADS WAFS WAGS WARS WATS WAWS WAYS XATS YAKS YAMS YAOS YAPS YAWS ZAGS ZALS ZAPS

••AS
ABAS AGAS ALAS AMAS ANAS ARAS BAAS BEAS BIAS BLAS BOAS BRAS CHAS CPAS DIAS ERAS ESAS ETAS EYAS FRAS GRAS IRAS KEAS KHAS LEAS MAAS MBAS MEAS MFAS MOAS OCAS ODAS PEAS PTAS RDAS RIAS RYAS SEAS SPAS SRAS STAS TEAS THAS TIAS TWAS UPAS XMAS YEAS

AT••
ATEN ATES ATIT ATKA ATLI ATMO ATMS ATNO ATOI ATOM ATON ATOP ATOR ATRA ATRI ATTA ATTN ATTO ATTS ATTU ATTY ATUM ATVS ATWT

A•T•
ACTA ACTE ACTG ACTH ACTI ACTS ACTV AFTA AFTS AGTS AITS ALTA ALTE ALTI ALTO ALTS AMTS ANTA ANTE ANTH ANTI ANTS APTS ARTE ARTS ARTY ASTA ASTI ASTO ASTR ATTA ATTN ATTO ATTS ATTU ATTY AUTH AUTO

A••T
ABET ABUT ACCT ACET ACHT ADIT ADJT ADVT AINT AIRT ALIT AMAT AMNT ANAT AOUT APPT ASST ATIT ATWT AUNT AUST

•AT•
BATE BATH BATS BATT CATA CATE CATH CATO CATS CATT CATV DATA DATE DATS EATS FATA FATE FATH FATS GATE GATH GATO GATS GATT HATE HATH HATS JATO KATE KATO KATY KATZ LATE LATH LATS MATA MATE MATH MATS MATT MATU NATE NATL NATO OATH OATS OATY PATD PATE PATH PATS QATS RATA RATE RATH RATS RATT SATE SATO SATS TATA TATE TATI TATS VATS VATU WATS WATT XATS

•A•T
BACT BAHT BAIT BALT BAPT BART BAST BATT CANT CAPT CART CAST CATT DAFT DART EAST FACT FAIT FAST FAUT GAIT GAST GATT HAFT HALT HART HAST HAUT KALT KANT KART LACT LAIT LAST MAAT MALT MART MAST MATT NAST NAUT OAST PACT PANT PART PAST PAYT RAFT RANT RAPT RATT SALT SANT TACT TAFT TAIT TART TAUT VAST WAFT WAIT WALT WANT WART WAST WATT

••AT
AMAT ANAT BEAT BLAT BOAT BRAT CHAT COAT CRAT DRAT ERAT ETAT FEAT FIAT FLAT FRAT GHAT GMAT GNAT GOAT HEAT KHAT KYAT LIAT LSAT MAAT MCAT MEAT MOAT NEAT NLAT PEAT PHAT PLAT PSAT SCAT SEAT SKAT SLAT SPAT STAT SWAT THAT TOAT WHAT

AU••
AUBE AUDE AUDI AUEL AUER AUGE AUKS AULA AULD AUNE AUNT AURA AURI AUST AUTH AUTO

A•U•
ABUT ADUE AGUA AGUE ALUI ALUM AMUR AOUT AQUA AQUI AQUO ARUM ATUM AXUM AZUL AZUR

A••U
ABOU ACLU AINU ALOU ATTU

•AU•
BAUD BAUM CAUL CAUS DAUB EAUX FAUN FAUT FAUX GAUD GAUL GAUM GAUR HAUL HAUS HAUT LAUD LAUE MAUD MAUI MAUL NAUT PAUL RAUL SAUD SAUK SAUL SAUR TAUS TAUT VAUD VAUX

•A•U
BABU BAKU DANU MANU MARU MATU NANU OAHU RAGU RAKU SABU TABU VATU YALU ZASU

••AU
BEAU BLAU ESAU FRAU GRAU LUAU PEAU UNAU VEAU

AV••
AVAL AVAR AVDP AVEC AVER AVES AVGS AVIA AVID AVIS AVIV AVON AVOS AVOW

A•V•
ADVT ALVA ATVS

A••V
ACTV AVIV AZOV

•AV•
CAVA CAVE CAVS CAVY DAVE DAVY EAVE FAVA FAVE GAVE HAVE JAVA KAVA LAVA LAVE LAVS MAVS NAVE NAVY PAVE PAVO RAVE RAVI SAVA SAVE TAVI VAVS WAVE WAVY

•A•V
CATV GALV MARV

••AV
FLAV OLAV OZAV SLAV

AW••
AWAY AWED AWES AWLS AWNS AWOL AWRY

A•W•
AIWA ATWT

A••W
ALOW ANEW AVOW

•AW•
BAWL CAWS DAWG DAWN DAWS FAWN GAWK GAWP HAWG HAWK HAWN HAWS JAWS LAWN LAWS MAWR MAWS PAWL PAWN PAWS SAWN SAWS TAWS WAWA WAWS YAWL YAWN YAWP YAWS

••AW
BRAW CHAW CLAW CRAW DRAW FLAW GNAW SHAW SKAW SLAW THAW

AX•• AXED AXEL AXER AXES AXIL AXIS AXLE AXON AXUM

A••X AJAX ALEX AMEX APEX

•AX• MAXI SAXE TAXA TAXI TAXO WAXY

•A•X CALX EAUX FALX FAUX MANX MARX PAIX VAUX

••AX AJAX COAX EDAX FLAX HOAX PLAX SFAX TRAX

AY•• AYAH AYER AYES AYIN AYLA AYME

A•Y• ABYE ABYS ACYL AMYL ANYA ARYL

A••Y ABBY ABLY ACEY ACHY ADDY AERY AGCY AGLY AHOY AIRY ALGY ALLY AMOY ANCY ANDY ARGY ARMY ARTY ASHY ATTY AWAY AWRY

•AY• BAYA BAYS CAYS DAYO DAYS FAYE FAYS GAYA GAYE HAYS JAYE JAYS KAYE KAYO LAYS MAYA MAYI MAYO MAYS NAYS PAYS PAYT RAYE RAYS SAYS VAYA WAYS

•A•Y BABY CAGY CAKY CANY CARY CAVY DALY DAVY EASY GABY GAMY GARY HAZY KATY LACY LADY LAKY LAMY LAZY MACY MANY MARY MAZY NAGY NARY NAVY OATY PALY RACY VARY WANY WARY WAVY WAXY ZANY

••AY AWAY BRAY CLAY CRAY DDAY DRAY FLAY FRAY GDAY GRAY ISAY ODAY OKAY OLAY PLAY PRAY QUAY SHAY SLAY SPAY STAY SWAY TRAY VDAY WRAY XRAY

AZ•• AZAN AZIZ AZOV AZUL AZUR

A•Z• ADZE ANZA

A••Z AHAZ ARIZ AZIZ

•AZ• DAZE FAZE GAZA GAZE HAZE HAZY JAZZ LAZE LAZY MAZE MAZO MAZY RAZE RAZZ YAZD

•A•Z BAEZ HARZ JAZZ KATZ NARZ RAZZ TAIZ

••AZ AHAZ BOAZ BRAZ CHAZ DIAZ GRAZ

BA•• BAAL BAAS BABA BABE BABI BABS BABU BABY BACH BACK BACS BACT BADE BAER BAEZ BAFF BAGS BAHN BAHR BAHS BAHT BAIL BAIN BAIO BAIT BAJA BAKE BAKR BAKU BALD BALE BALI BALK BALL BALM BALT BAMA BAMS BANC BAND BANE BANG BANI BANK BANS BAPS BAPT BARA BARB BARD BARE BARI BARK BARM BARN BARO BARR BARS BART BASC BASE BASH BASK BASS BAST BATE BATH BATS BATT BAUD BAUM BAWL BAYA BAYS

B•A• BAAL BAAS BEAD BEAK BEAL BEAM BEAN BEAR BEAS BEAT BEAU BIAK BIAO BIAS BLAB BLAE BLAH BLAS BLAT BLAU BNAI BOAC BOAR BOAS BOAT BOAZ BRAC BRAD BRAE BRAG BRAM BRAN BRAS BRAT BRAW BRAY BRAZ

B••A BABA BAJA BAMA BARA BAYA BELA BEMA BETA BIWA BOCA BOLA BOMA BONA BORA BOTA BOVA BREA BUNA

•BA• ABAS EBAN IBAN IBAR JBAR LBAR MBAS OBAD TBAR ZBAR

•B•A ABBA EBLA

••BA ABBA ALBA BABA CUBA ELBA GABA ISBA IZBA JUBA LUBA PABA REBA SABA TUBA YUBA

BB•• BBLS BBOY BBQS

B•B• BABA BABE BABI BABS BABU BABY BEBE BIBB BIBI BIBL BIBS BOBS BUBU

B••B BARB BEEB BIBB BLAB BLEB BLOB BOMB BOOB BULB BURB BYOB

•BB• ABBA ABBE ABBR ABBS ABBY EBBS

•B•B ABIB DBIB

••BB BIBB COBB GIBB ROBB TUBB WEBB

B•C• BACH BACK BACS BACT BECK BICE BICS BOCA BOCK BUCK BUCO BUCS

B••C BANC BASC BLOC BMOC BOAC BOSC BRAC BRIC BSEC

•BC• ABCS

BD•• BDRM

B•D• BADE BEDE BEDS BIDE BIDS BLDG BLDR BODE BODO BODS BODY BUDD BUDS BVDS

B••D BALD BAND BARD BAUD BEAD BEND BIGD BIND BIRD BLED BLVD BOLD BOND BOYD BRAD BRED BSED BUDD BUND BYRD

•B•D ABED IBID OBAD

••BD STBD

BE•• BEAD BEAK BEAL BEAM BEAN BEAR BEAS BEAT BEAU BEBE BECK BEDE BEDS BEEB BEEF BEEN BEEP BEER BEES BEET BEGS BEIN BELA BELG BELL BELO BELS BELT BELY BEMA BEMS BEND BENE BENG BENI BENT BENU BENZ BERG BERM BERN BERT BESO BESS BEST BETA BETE BETH BETS BETZ BEVY BEYS

B•E• BAER BAEZ BEEB BEEF BEEN BEEP BEER BEES BEET BIEL BIEN BLEB BLED BLEU BLEW BOER BREA BRED BREE BREL BREN BRER BRET BREV BREW BSEC BSED BYES

B••E BABE BADE BAKE BALE BANE BARE BASE BATE BEBE BEDE BENE BETE BICE BIDE BIKE BILE BINE BISE BITE BLAE BLUE BODE BOLE BONE BORE BOSE BOWE BPOE BRAE BREE BRIE BUTE BYME BYRE BYTE

•BE• ABED ABEL ABER ABET CBER EBEN IBET IBEX MBES OBEY UBER

•B•E ABBE ABIE ABLE ABYE IBLE OBIE OBOE

••BE ABBE AUBE BABE BEBE CUBE ELBE GABE GIBE GYBE HABE HEBE JIBE KOBE LOBE LUBE NABE NEBE RABE ROBE RUBE SABE SEBE TOBE TUBE URBE VIBE

B•F• BAFF BIFF BOFF BUFF

B••F BAFF BEEF BIFF BOFF BUFF BUMF

B•G• BAGS BEGS BIGD BOGS BOGY BUGS

B••G BANG BELG BENG BERG BING BIOG BKPG BLDG BONG BORG BRAG BRIG BULG BUNG BURG BYNG

B•H• BAHN BAHR BAHS BAHT BOHM BOHR BUHL BUHR

B••H BACH BASH BATH BETH BLAH BOSH BOTH BUSH

••BH COBH

BI•• BIAK BIAO BIAS BIBB BIBI BIBL BIBS BICE BICS BIDE BIDS BIEL BIEN BIFF BIGD BIKE BIKO BILE BILK BILL BIND BINE BING BINS BIOG BIOL BION BIOS BIRD BIRK BIRL BIRR BISE BISK BITE BITS BITT BIWA

B•I• BAIL BAIN BAIO BAIT BEIN BLIN BLIP BLIT BOIL BOIS BRIC BRIE BRIG BRIM BRIO BRIT BRIX

B••I BABI BALI BANI BARI BENI BIBI BNAI BONI BURI

•BI• ABIB ABIE DBIB IBID IBIS OBIE OBIS OBIT RBIS

•B•I ABRI

••BI ALBI AMBI BABI BIBI DEBI GOBI ORBI RABI TABI URBI

B•J• BAJA

••BJ SUBJ

BK•• BKPG BKPR

B•K• BAKE BAKR BAKU BIKE BIKO

B••K BACK BALK BANK BARK BASK BEAK BECK BIAK BILK BIRK BISK BOCK BONK BOOK BORK BOSK BUCK BULK BUNK BUSK

••BK HDBK

BL•• BLAB BLAE BLAH BLAS BLAT BLAU BLDG BLDR BLEB BLED BLEU BLEW BLIN BLIP BLIT BLOB BLOC BLOT BLOW BLTS BLUE BLUM BLUR BLVD

B•L• BALD BALE BALI BALK BALL BALM BALT BBLS BELA BELG BELL BELO BELS BELT BELY BILE BILK BILL BOLA BOLD BOLE BOLL BOLO BOLT BULB BULG BULK BULL

B••L BAAL BAIL BALL BAWL BEAL BELL BIBL BIEL BILL BIOL BIRL BOIL BOLL BOWL BREL BUHL BULL BURL

•BL• ABLE ABLY BBLS EBLA IBLE

•B•L ABEL OBOL

••BL BIBL PUBL

BM•• BMOC BMUS BMWS

B•M• BAMA BAMS BEMA BEMS BOMA BOMB BOMP BOMU BSMT BUMF BUMP BUMS BYME

B••M BALM BARM BAUM BDRM BEAM BERM BLUM BOHM BOOM BRAM BRIM BROM

•BM• ABMS

••BM ICBM IRBM SLBM

BN•• BNAI

B•N• BANC BAND BANE BANG BANI BANK BANS BEND BENE BENG BENI BENT BENU BENZ BIND BINE BING BINS BONA BOND BONE BONG BONI BONK BONN BONO BONY BRNO BUNA BUND BUNG BUNK BUNS BUNT BYNG

B••N BAHN BAIN BARN BEAN BEEN BEIN BERN BIEN BION BLIN BONN BOON BORN BOSN BRAN BREN BRYN BUON BURN

•B•N EBAN EBEN EBON IBAN

••BN ISBN NEBN NWBN

BO•• BOAC BOAR BOAS BOAT BOAZ BOBS BOCA BOCK BODE BODO BODS BODY BOER BOFF BOGS BOGY BOHM BOHR BOIL BOIS BOLA BOLD BOLE BOLL BOLO BOLT BOMA BOMB BOMP BOMU BONA BOND BONE BONG BONI BONK BONN BONO BONY BOOB BOOK BOOM BOON BOOP BOOR BOOS BOOT BOPP BOPS BORA BORE BORG BORK BORN BORO BORS BORT BOSC BOSE BOSH BOSK BOSN BOSS BOTA BOTH BOTS BOTT BOUT BOVA BOWE BOWL BOWS BOXY BOYD BOYO BOYS BOYZ BOZO

B•O• BBOY BIOG BIOL BION BIOS BLOB BLOC BLOT BLOW BMOC BOOB BOOK BOOM BOON BOOP BOOR BOOS BOOT BPOE BROM BROS BROW BROZ BUON BUOY BYOB

B••O BAIO BARO BELO BESO BIAO BIKO BODO BOLO BONO BORO BOYO BOZO BRIO BRNO BRYO BUCO

•BO• ABOU BBOY EBON IBOS LBOS MBOY OBOE OBOL

•B•O EBRO

••BO AMBO DABO GABO GOBO HOBO IGBO KOBO LOBO NEBO ROBO UMBO ZIBO

BP•• BPOE

B•P• BAPS BAPT BKPG BKPR BOPP BOPS

B••P BEEP BLIP BOMP BOOP BOPP BUMP BURP

•B•P TBSP

B•Q• BBQS

•BQ• BBQS

BR•• BRAC BRAD BRAE BRAG BRAM BRAN BRAS BRAT BRAW BRAY BRAZ BREA BRED BREE BREL BREN BRER BRET BREV BREW BRIC BRIE BRIG BRIM BRIO BRIT BRIX BRNO BROM BROS BROW BROZ BRUT BRUX BRYN BRYO

B•R• BARA BARB BARD BARE BARI BARK BARM BARN BARO BARR BARS BART BDRM BERG BERM BERN BERT BIRD BIRK BIRL BIRR BORA BORE BORG BORK BORN BORO BORS BORT BURB BURG BURI BURL BURN BURP BURR BURS BURT BURY BYRD BYRE

B••R BAER BAHR BAKR BARR BEAR BEER BIRR BKPR BLDR BLUR BOAR BOER BOHR BOOR BRER BUHR BURR

•BR• ABRI EBRO

•B•R ABBR ABER CBER IBAR JBAR LBAR TBAR UBER ZBAR

••BR ABBR GRBR GTBR

HEBR
NEBR

BS••
BSEC
BSED
BSMT

B•S•
BASC
BASE
BASH
BASK
BASS
BAST
BESO
BESS
BEST
BISE
BISK
BOSC
BOSE
BOSH
BOSK
BOSN
BOSS
BUSH
BUSK
BUSS
BUST
BUSY

B••S
BAAS
BABS
BACS
BAGS
BAHS
BAMS
BANS
BAPS
BARS
BASS
BATS
BAYS
BBLS
BBQS
BEAS
BEDS
BEES
BEGS
BELS
BEMS
BESS
BETS
BEYS
BIAS
BIBS
BICS
BIDS
BINS
BIOS
BITS
BLAS
BLTS
BMUS
BMWS
BOAS
BOBS
BODS
BOGS
BOIS
BOOS
BOPS
BORS
BOSS
BOTS
BOWS
BOYS
BRAS
BROS
BTUS
BUCS
BUDS
BUGS
BUMS
BUNS
BURS
BUSS
BUTS
BUYS
BVDS
BYES

•BS•
TBSP

•B•S
ABAS
ABBS
ABCS
ABMS
ABYS
BBLS
BBQS
EBBS
IBIS
IBOS
LBOS
MBAS
MBES
OBIS
RBIS

••BS
ABBS
ALBS
AMBS
APBS
ARBS
BABS
BIBS
BOBS
CABS
COBS
CUBS
DABS
DEBS
DIBS
DUBS
EBBS
FIBS
FOBS
FUBS
GABS
GIBS
GOBS
HOBS
HUBS
JABS
JIBS
JOBS
KABS
KOBS
LABS
LHBS
LIBS
LLBS
LOBS
MIBS
MOBS
NABS
NEBS
NIBS
NOBS
NUBS
ORBS
PCBS
PUBS
RABS
REBS
RHBS
RIBS
ROBS
RUBS
SEBS
SIBS
SOBS
SUBS
SWBS
TABS
TUBS
URBS
WABS
WEBS
YOBS

BT••
BTUS

B•T•
BATE
BATH
BATS
BATT
BETA
BETE
BETH
BETS
BETZ
BITE
BITS
BITT
BLTS
BOTA
BOTH
BOTS
BOTT
BUTE
BUTS
BUTT
BYTE

B••T
BACT
BAHT
BAIT
BALT
BAPT
BART
BAST
BATT
BEAT
BEET
BELT
BENT
BERT
BEST
BITT
BLAT
BLIT
BLOT
BOAT
BOLT
BOOT
BORT
BOTT
BOUT
BRAT
BRET
BRIT
BRUT
BSMT
BUNT
BURT
BUST
BUTT

•B•T
ABET
ABUT
IBET
OBIT

••BT
DEBT

BU••
BUBU
BUCK
BUCO
BUCS
BUDD
BUDS
BUFF
BUGS
BUHL
BUHR
BULB
BULG
BULK
BULL
BUMF
BUMP
BUMS
BUNA
BUND
BUNG
BUNK
BUNS
BUNT
BUON
BUOY
BURB
BURG
BURI
BURL
BURN
BURP
BURR
BURS
BURT
BURY
BUSH
BUSK
BUSS
BUST
BUSY
BUTE
BUTS
BUTT
BUYS
BUZZ

B•U•
BAUD
BAUM
BLUE
BLUM
BLUR
BMUS
BOUT
BRUT
BRUX
BTUS

B••U
BABU
BAKU
BEAU
BENU
BLAU
BLEU
BOMU
BUBU

•BU•
ABUT

•B•U
ABOU

••BU
BABU
BUBU
CEBU
SABU
TABU
ZEBU

BV••
BVDS

B•V•
BEVY
BLVD
BOVA

B••V
BREV

B•W•
BAWL
BIWA
BMWS
BOWE
BOWL
BOWS

B••W
BLEW
BLOW
BRAW
BREW
BROW

••BW
NWBW
SWBW

B•X•
BOXY

B••X
BRIX
BRUX

•B•X
IBEX

BY••
BYES
BYME
BYNG
BYOB
BYRD
BYRE
BYTE

B•Y•
BAYA
BAYS
BEYS
BOYD
BOYO
BOYS
BOYZ
BRYN
BRYO
BUYS

B••Y
BABY
BBOY
BELY
BEVY
BODY
BOGY
BONY
BOXY
BRAY
BUOY
BURY
BUSY

•BY•
ABYE
ABYS

•B•Y
ABBY
ABLY
BBOY
MBOY
OBEY

••BY
ABBY
BABY
DOBY
GABY
GOBY
MOBY
RUBY
TCBY
TOBY

B•Z•
BOZO
BUZZ

B••Z
BAEZ
BENZ
BETZ
BOAZ
BOYZ
BRAZ
BROZ
BUZZ

CA••
CAAN
CABS
CACO
CADE
CADI
CADS
CAEN
CAFE
CAGE
CAGY
CAHN
CAIN
CAKE
CAKY
CALC
CALE
CALF
CALI
CALK
CALL
CALM
CALS
CALX
CAMA
CAME
CAMI
CAMO
CAMP
CAMS
CANA
CANC
CANE
CANF
CANS
CANT
CANY
CAPA
CAPE
CAPN
CAPO
CAPP
CAPS
CAPT
CARA
CARB
CARD
CARE
CARK
CARL
CARO
CARP
CARR
CARS
CART
CARY
CASA
CASE
CASH
CASK
CASS
CAST
CATA
CATE
CATH
CATO
CATS
CATT
CATV
CAUL
CAUS
CAVA
CAVE
CAVS
CAVY
CAWS
CAYS

C•A•
CAAN
CHAD
CHAM
CHAN
CHAP
CHAR
CHAS
CHAT
CHAW
CHAZ
CIAO
CLAD
CLAM
CLAN
CLAP
CLAR
CLAW
CLAY
COAL
COAT
COAX
CPAS
CRAB
CRAG
CRAM
CRAT
CRAW
CRAY
CYAN
CZAR

C••A
CAMA
CANA
CAPA
CARA
CASA
CATA
CAVA
CELA
CENA
CERA
CETA
CHIA
COCA
CODA
COLA
COMA
CORA
COSA
COXA
CUBA
CUNA
CYMA

•CA•
ACAD
ICAL
KCAL
MCAT
NCAA
OCAS
RCAF
SCAB
SCAD
SCAM
SCAN
SCAR
SCAT

•C•A
ACEA
ACTA
ECUA
NCAA
OCTA
UCLA

••CA
ARCA
BOCA
COCA
DECA
FICA
INCA
MICA
ORCA
PACA
PICA
RICA
ROCA
SOCA
SPCA
VACA
YMCA
YWCA

CB••
CBER

C•B•
CABS
CEBU
COBB
COBH
COBS
CUBA
CUBE
CUBS

C••B
CARB
CHUB
CLUB
COBB
COMB
CRAB
CRIB
CURB

•CB•
ICBM
PCBS
TCBY

•C•B
SCAB

CC••
CCCI
CCCL
CCCP
CCCV
CCCX
CCII
CCIV
CCIX
CCLI
CCLV
CCLX
CCTV
CCVI
CCXC
CCXI
CCXL
CCXV
CCXX

C•C•
CACO
CCCI
CCCL
CCCP
CCCV
CCCX
COCA
COCK
COCO
CXCI
CXCV
CYCL

C••C
CALC
CANC
CCXC
CDXC
CHIC
CHOC
CINC
CIRC
CMXC
COFC
CONC
CROC

•CC•
ACCS
ACCT
CCCI
CCCL
CCCP
CCCV
CCCX
DCCC
DCCI
DCCL
DCCV
DCCX
ECCE
ECCL
MCCC
MCCI
MCCL
MCCV
MCCX

•C•C
ACDC
CCXC
DCCC
DCXC
MCCC
MCXC
SCLC

••CC
DCCC
MACC
MCCC
MDCC
MLCC
MMCC
SNCC
SPCC

CD••
CDII
CDIV
CDIX
CDLI
CDLV
CDLX
CDRS
CDVI
CDXC
CDXI
CDXL
CDXV
CDXX

C•D•
CADE
CADI
CADS
CEDE
CEDI
CIDE
CMDG
CMDR
CODA
CODE
CODS
CODY
CUDS

C••D
CARD
CHAD
CHID
CLAD
CLOD
COED
COLD
COMD
COND
CORD
CRUD
CUED
CURD

•CD•
ACDC
LCDS
MCDI
MCDL
MCDV
MCDX

•C•D
ACAD
ACED
ACID
ICED
SCAD
SCUD

••CD
MMCD
RECD

CE••
CEBU
CEDE
CEDI
CEES
CEIL
CELA
CELL
CELS
CELT
CENA
CENE
CENO
CENS
CENT
CEOS
CEPE
CEPS
CERA
CERE
CERF
CERN
CERO
CERT
CESS
CEST
CETA
CETE

C•E•
CAEN
CBER
CEES
CHEE
CHEF
CHEM
CHEN
CHER
CHET
CHEW
CHEX
CHEZ
CIEL
CLEF
CLEM
CLEO
CLEW
COED
COEL
COEN
CREE
CREW
CUED
CUER
CUES

C••E
CADE
CAFE
CAGE
CAKE
CALE
CAME
CANE
CAPE
CARE
CASE
CATE
CAVE
CEDE
CENE
CEPE
CERE
CETE
CHEE
CIDE
CINE
CIRE
CITE
CLUE
CODE
COKE
COLE
COME
CONE
COPE
CORE
COTE
COUE
COVE
CREE
CRUE
CTGE
CUBE
CUKE
CULE
CURE
CUTE
CYME
CYTE

•CE•
ACEA
ACED
ACER
ACES
ACET
ACEY
ICED
ICEL
ICER
ICES
ICET

•C•E
ACHE
ACME
ACNE
ACRE
ACTE
ECCE

••CE
ANCE
BICE
DACE
DICE
DUCE
DYCE
ECCE
ENCE
ESCE
FACE
FICE
INCE
LACE
LICE
LUCE
MACE
MICE
NICE
ONCE
PACE
PUCE
RACE
RICE
SYCE
VICE
VOCE
WACE

C•F•
CAFE
COFC
COFS
CUFF
CUFT

C••F
CALF
CANF
CERF
CHEF
CLEF
COIF
CONF
CORF
CUFF

•C•F
RCAF

C•G•
CAGE
CAGY
CHGS
CIGS
COGS
CTGE

C••G
CHUG
CLOG
CMDG
CONG
CRAG

•C•G
ACTG

••CG
USCG

CH••
CHAD
CHAM
CHAN
CHAP
CHAR
CHAS
CHAT
CHAW
CHAZ
CHEE
CHEF
CHEM
CHEN
CHER
CHET
CHEW
CHEX
CHEZ
CHGS
CHIA
CHIC
CHID
CHIN
CHIP
CHIS
CHIT
CHMN
CHOC
CHOL
CHON
CHOP
CHOU
CHOW
CHOY
CHUB
CHUG
CHUM
CHUR

C•H•
CAHN
COHN
COHO

C••H
CASH
CATH
COBH
COSH
CUSH

•CH•
ACHE
ACHT
ACHY
ECHO
ECHT
OCHO
OCHS
TCHR

•C•H
ACTH

••CH
ARCH
ASCH
BACH
DICH
EACH
ETCH
EXCH
FOCH
HOCH
INCH
ITCH
KOCH
LECH
LOCH
MACH
MECH
MICH
MUCH
ORCH
OUCH
RICH
SECH
SUCH
TACH
TECH
WYCH
YECH
ZECH

CI••
CIAO
CIDE
CIEL
CIGS
CIII
CINC
CINE
CINQ
CION
CIRC
CIRE
CIST
CITE
CITS
CITY

C•I•
CAIN
CCII
CCIV
CCIX
CDII
CDIV
CDIX
CEIL
CHIA
CHIC
CHID
CHIN
CHIP
CHIS
CHIT
CIII
CLII
CLIN
CLIO
CLIP
CLIV
CLIX
CMII
CMIV
CMIX
COIF
COIL
COIN
COIR
CRIB
CRIM
CRIN
CRIT
CUIN
CVII
CXII
CXIV
CXIX

C••I
CADI
CALI
CAMI
CCCI
CCII
CCLI
CCVI
CCXI
CDII
CDLI
CDVI
CDXI
CEDI
CIII
CLII
CLVI
CLXI
CMII
CMLI
CMVI
CMXI
CORI
COSI
CVII
CXCI
CXII
CXLI
CXVI
CXXI

•CI•
ACID
ACIS
CCII
CCIV
CCIX
DCII
DCIV
DCIX
MCII
MCIV
MCIX
SCIL
XCII
XCIV
XCIX

•C•I
ACTI
CCCI
CCII
CCLI
CCVI
CCXI
DCCI
DCII
DCLI
DCVI
DCXI
MCCI
MCDI
MCII
MCLI
MCMI
MCVI
MCXI
SCSI
XCII
XCVI

••CI
ASCI
CCCI
CXCI
DCCI
DECI
DXCI
FOCI
LOCI
LUCI
MCCI
MDCI
MMCI
MXCI
UNCI
VICI

C•J•
CUJO

C••J
CONJ

C•K•
CAKE
CAKY
COKE
COKY
CUKE

C••K
CALK
CARK
CASK
COCK
CONK
COOK
CORK
CUSK

•CK•
ICKY

••CK
BACK
BECK
BOCK
BUCK
COCK
DECK
DICK
DOCK
DUCK
DYCK
EYCK
GUCK
HACK
HECK
HICK
HOCK
HUCK
JACK
JOCK
KICK
LACK
LICK
LOCK
LUCK
MACK
MICK
MOCK
MUCK
NECK
NICK
NOCK
PACK
PECK
PICK
PUCK
RACK
RICK
ROCK
RUCK
SACK
SICK
SOCK
SUCK
TACK
TICK
TOCK
TUCK
WACK
WICK
YACK
YUCK
ZACK

CL••
CLAD
CLAM
CLAN
CLAP
CLAR
CLAW
CLAY
CLEF
CLEM
CLEO
CLEW
CLII
CLIN
CLIO
CLIP
CLIV
CLIX
CLOD
CLOG
CLOP
CLOT
CLOY
CLUB
CLUE
CLVI
CLXI
CLXV
CLXX

C•L•
CALC
CALE
CALF
CALI
CALK
CALL
CALM
CALS
CALX
CCLI
CCLV
CCLX
CDLI
CDLV
CDLX
CELA
CELL
CELS
CELT
CMLI
CMLV
CMLX
COLA
COLD
COLE
COLL
COLO
COLS
COLT
COLY
CPLS
CULE
CULL
CULM
CULP
CULS
CULT
CXLI
CXLV

C••L
CALL
CARL
CAUL
CCCL
CCXL
CDXL
CEIL
CELL
CHOL
CIEL
CMXL
COAL
COEL
COIL
COLL
COML
COOL
COWL
CULL
CURL
CYCL

•CL• ACLU CCLI CCLV CCLX DCLI DCLV DCLX MCLI MCLV MCLX SCLC UCLA

•C•L ACYL CCCL CCXL DCCL DCXL ECCL ECOL ICAL ICEL KCAL MCCL MCDL MCML MCXL SCIL

••CL CCCL CYCL DCCL DECL ECCL ENCL EXCL INCL MCCL MDCL MMCL NACL

CM•• CMDG CMDR CMII CMIV CMIX CMLI CMLV CMLX CMON CMOS CMVI CMXC CMXI CMXL CMXV CMXX

C•M• CAMA CAME CAMI CAMO CAMP CAMS CHMN COMA COMB COMD COME COML COMM COMO COMP COMR CWMS CYMA CYME

C••M CALM CHAM CHEM CHUM CLAM CLEM COMM CORM COSM CRAM CRIM CULM

•CM• ACME MCMI MCML MCMV MCMX RCMP

•C•M ICBM SCAM SCUM

••CM MMCM

CN•• CNUT

C•N• CANA CANC CANE CANF CANS CANT CANY CENA CENE CENO CENS CENT CINC CINE CINQ CONC COND CONE CONF CONG CONJ CONK CONN CONS CONT CONV CONY CTNS CUNA CUNY

C••N CAAN CAEN CAHN CAIN CAPN CERN CHAN CHEN CHIN CHMN CHON CION CLAN CLIN CMON COEN COHN COIN CONN COON CORN CRIN CUIN CYAN

•CN• ACNE

•C•N DCON ECON ICON SCAN

CO•• COAL COAT COAX COBB COBH COBS COCA COCK COCO CODA CODE CODS CODY COED COEL COEN COFC COFS COGS COHN COHO COIF COIL COIN COIR COKE COKY COLA COLD COLE COLL COLO COLS COLT COLY COMA COMB COMD COME COML COMM COMO COMP COMR CONC COND CONE CONF CONG CONJ CONK CONN CONS CONT CONV CONY COOK COOL COON COOP COOS COOT COPE COPS COPT COPY CORA CORD CORE CORF CORI CORK CORM CORN CORO CORP CORR CORS CORY COSA COSH COSI COSM COST COSY COTE COTS COTY COUE COUP COVE COWL COWS COXA COZY

C•O• CEOS CHOC CHOL CHON CHOP CHOU CHOW CHOY CION CLOD CLOG CLOP CLOT CLOY CMON CMOS COOK COOL COON COOP COOS COOT CPOS CROC CROP CROW CWOS

C••O CACO CAMO CAPO CARO CATO CENO CERO CIAO CLEO CLIO COCO COHO COLO COMO CORO CRYO CUJO CYTO

•CO• DCON ECOL ECON ICON ICOS NCOS SCOP SCOT SCOW

•C•O ACRO ECHO ECTO OCHO OCTO

••CO ARCO ASCO BUCO CACO COCO DECO EKCO LOCO MECO MYCO PICO POCO RICO TACO TICO VICO WACO

CP•• CPAS CPLS CPOS

C•P• CAPA CAPE CAPN CAPO CAPP CAPS CAPT CEPE CEPS COPE COPS COPT COPY CUPR CUPS

C••P CAMP CAPP CARP CCCP CHAP CHIP CHOP CLAP CLIP CLOP COMP COOP CORP COUP CROP CULP CUSP

•CP• RCPT

•C•P CCCP RCMP SCOP SCUP

••CP CCCP FACP FRCP

C••Q CINQ

CR•• CRAB CRAG CRAM CRAT CRAW CRAY CREE CREW CRIB CRIM CRIN CRIT CROC CROP CROW CRTS CRUD CRUE CRUS CRUX CRUZ CRYO

C•R• CARA CARB CARD CARE CARK CARL CARO CARP CARR CARS CART CARY CDRS CERA CERE CERF CERN CERO CERT CIRC CIRE CORA CORD CORE CORF CORI CORK CORM CORN CORO CORP CORR CORS CORY CURB CURD CURE CURL CURR CURS CURT

C••R CARR CBER CHAR CHER CHUR CLAR CMDR COIR COMR CORR CUER CUPR CURR CZAR

•CR• ACRE ACRO ECRU SCRY VCRS

•C•R ACER ICER SCAR TCHR

••CR INCR MICR

C•S• CASA CASE CASH CASK CASS CAST CESS CEST CIST COSA COSH COSI COSM COST COSY CUSH CUSK CUSP CUSS

C••S CABS CADS CALS CAMS CANS CAPS CARS CASS CATS CAUS CAVS CAWS CAYS CDRS CEES CELS CENS CEOS CEPS CESS CHAS CHGS CHIS CIGS CITS CMOS COBS CODS COFS COGS COLS CONS COOS COPS CORS COTS COWS CPAS CPLS CPOS CRTS CRUS CTNS CUBS CUDS CUES CULS CUPS CURS CUSS CUTS CWMS CWOS

•CS• SCSI

•C•S ACCS ACES ACIS ACTS ECUS ICES ICOS ICUS LCDS NCOS OCAS OCHS PCBS RCTS VCRS

••CS ABCS ACCS ADCS ARCS BACS BICS BUCS DOCS DSCS ENCS FACS FRCS LACS LDCS MACS MICS MOCS ORCS PACS PECS PFCS PICS PLCS RECS ROCS SACS SECS SICS TECS TICS VACS WACS

CT•• CTGE CTNS

C•T• CATA CATE CATH CATO CATS CATT CATV CCTV CETA CETE CITE CITS CITY COTE COTS COTY CRTS CUTE CUTS CYTE CYTO

C••T CANT CAPT CART CAST CATT CELT CENT CERT CEST CHAT CHET CHIT CIST CLOT CNUT COAT COLT CONT COOT COPT COST CRAT CRIT CUFT CULT CURT

•CT• ACTA ACTE ACTG ACTH ACTI ACTS ACTV CCTV ECTO OCTA OCTO RCTS SCTV WCTU

•C•T ACCT ACET ACHT ECHT ICET MCAT RCPT SCAT SCOT SCUT

••CT ACCT BACT DICT DUCT FACT FICT HECT LACT LECT PACT PICT RECT SECT TACT

CU•• CUBA CUBE CUBS CUDS CUED CUER CUES CUFF CUFT CUIN CUJO CUKE CULE CULL CULM CULP CULS CULT CUNA CUNY CUPR CUPS CURB CURD CURE CURL CURR CURS CURT CUSH CUSK CUSP CUSS CUTE CUTS

C•U• CAUL CAUS CHUB CHUG CHUM CHUR CLUB CLUE CNUT COUE COUP CRUD CRUE CRUS CRUX CRUZ

C••U CEBU CHOU

•CU• ECUA ECUS ICUS SCUD SCUM SCUP SCUT

•C•U ACLU ECRU WCTU

CV•• CVII

C•V• CAVA CAVE CAVS CAVY CCVI CDVI CLVI CMVI COVE CXVI

C••V CATV CCCV CCIV CCLV CCTV CCXV CDIV CDLV CDXV CLIV CLXV CMIV CMLV CMXV CONV CXCV CXIV CXLV CXXV

•CV• CCVI DCVI MCVI XCVI

•C•V ACTV CCCV CCIV CCLV CCTV CCXV DCCV DCIV DCLV DCXV MCCV MCDV MCIV MCLV MCMV MCXV SCTV XCIV

••CV CCCV CXCV DCCV DXCV MCCV MDCV MMCV MXCV

CW•• CWMS CWOS

C•W• CAWS COWL COWS

C••W CHAW CHEW CHOW CLAW CLEW CRAW CREW CROW

•C•W SCOW

CX•• CXCI CXCV CXII CXIV CXIX CXLI CXLV CXVI CXXI CXXV CXXX

C•X• CCXC CCXI CCXL CCXV CCXX CDXC CDXI CDXL CDXV CDXX CLXI CLXV CLXX CMXC CMXI CMXL CMXV CMXX COXA CXXI CXXV CXXX

C••X CALX CCCX CCIX CCLX CCXX CDIX CDLX CDXX CHEX CLIX CLXX CMIX CMLX CMXX COAX CRUX CXIX CXXX

•CX• CCXC CCXI CCXL CCXV CCXX DCXC DCXI DCXL DCXV DCXX MCXC MCXI MCXL MCXV MCXX

•C•X CCCX CCIX CCLX CCXX DCCX DCIX DCLX DCXX MCCX MCDX MCIX MCLX MCMX MCXX XCIX

••CX CCCX DCCX MCCX MDCX MMCX

CY•• CYAN CYCL CYMA CYME CYTE CYTO

C•Y• CAYS CRYO

C••Y CAGY CAKY CANY CARY CAVY CHOY CITY CLAY CLOY CODY COKY COLY CONY COPY CORY COSY COTY COZY CRAY CUNY

•CY• ACYL

•C•Y ACEY ACHY ICKY SCRY TCBY

••CY AGCY ANCY ENCY LACY LUCY MACY RACY SECY

CZ•• CZAR

C•Z• COZY

C••Z CHAZ CHEZ CRUZ

DA•• DABO DABS DACE DADA DADE DADO DADS DAFF DAFT DAGS DAHL DAHS DAIN DAIS DALE DALI DALS DALY DAMA DAME DAMN DAMP DAMS DANA DANE DANG DANK DANL DANO DANU DAPS DARC DARD DARE DARI DARK DARN DART DASD DASH DATA DATE DATS DAUB DAVE DAVY DAWG DAWN DAWS DAYO DAYS DAZE

D•A• DDAY DEAD DEAF DEAL DEAN DEAR DHAL DIAG DIAL DIAM DIAN DIAS DIAZ DOAK DRAB DRAG DRAM DRAT DRAW DRAY DUAD DUAL DWAN DYAD DYAK DYAN

D••A DADA DAMA DANA DATA DECA DEJA DEKA DEVA DINA DIVA DOHA DONA DOPA DORA DUMA DUNA DURA DYNA

•DA• ADAH ADAK ADAM ADAR DDAY EDAM EDAX GDAY IDAE NDAK ODAS ODAY RDAS SDAK VDAY

•D•A EDDA EDNA EDTA IDEA KDKA ODEA

••DA AIDA ALDA CODA DADA EDDA ERDA JADA LEDA NADA PODA SADA SODA TADA USDA VEDA VIDA YADA YODA

DB•• DBIB

D•B• DABO DABS DEBI DEBS DEBT DIBS DOBY DUBS

D••B DAUB DBIB DRAB DRIB DRUB DUMB

•DB• HDBK

DC•• DCCC DCCI DCCL DCCV DCCX DCII DCIV DCIX DCLI DCLV DCLX DCON DCVI DCXC DCXI DCXL DCXV DCXX

D•C• DACE DCCC DCCI DCCL DCCV DCCX DECA DECI DECK DECL DECO DICE DICH DICK DICT DOCK DOCS DSCS DUCE DUCK DUCT DXCI DXCV DYCE DYCK

D••C DARC DCCC DCXC DESC DISC

•DC• ADCS LDCS MDCC MDCI MDCL MDCV MDCX

•D•C CDXC EDUC FDIC MDCC MDXC ODIC

••DC ACDC MMDC

DD•• DDAY

D•D• DADA DADE DADO DADS DIDO DMDS DODD DODO DUDE DUDS DVDS

D••D DARD DASD DEAD DEED DIED DODD DOOD DOWD DRED DUAD DYAD DYED

•DD• ADDN ADDS ADDY EDDA EDDO EDDS EDDY ODDS

••DD BUDD DODD FUDD JUDD KIDD LADD MADD MUDD REDD RIDD RUDD SADD SUDD TODD

DE•• DEAD DEAF DEAL DEAN DEAR DEBI DEBS DEBT DECA DECI DECK DECL DECO DEED DEEM DEEP DEER DEES DEET DEFS

DEFT DEFY DEGS DEIL DEJA DEKA DEKE DELE DELI DELL DELS DELY DEME DEMI DEMO DEMS DEMY DENE DENG DENS DENT DENY DEPP DEPT DERM DERN DESC DESI DESK DETS DEUM DEUS DEUT DEUX DEVA DEVI DEVO DEWS DEWY DEYS

D•E•
DEED DEEM DEEP DEER DEES DEET DIED DIEM DIEN DIES DIET DIEU DOER DOES DRED DREE DREG DREI DREW DUEL DUES DUET DYED DYER DYES

D••E
DACE DADE DALE DAME DANE DARE DATE DAVE DAZE DEKE DELE DEME DENE DICE DIKE DIME DINE DIRE DIVE DOGE DOLE DOME DONE DOPE DORE DOSE DOTE DOVE DOZE DREE DUCE DUDE DUKE DUNE DUPE DUSE DUVE DYCE DYNE

•DE•
ADEN ADES EDEN EDER IDEA IDEE IDEM IDEO IDES ODEA ODER ODES

•D•E
ADUE ADZE EDGE EDIE HDWE IDAE IDEE IDLE MDSE ODIE

••DE
AIDE AUDE BADE BEDE BIDE BODE CADE CEDE CIDE CODE DADE DUDE ENDE ERDE FADE FIDE GIDE HADE HIDE HYDE JADE JUDE LADE LODE MADE MEDE MODE NIDE NODE NUDE OLDE PODE REDE RIDE RODE RUDE SADE SIDE TIDE TUDE VADE VIDE WADE WIDE

D•F•
DAFF DAFT DEFS DEFT DEFY DIFF DOFF DUFF DUFY

D••F
DAFF DEAF DIFF DOFF DOLF DUFF

D•G•
DAGS DEGS DIGS DOGE DOGG DOGS DOGY

D••G
DANG DAWG DENG DIAG DING DOGG DONG DOUG DRAG DREG DRUG

•DG•
EDGE EDGY

••DG
BLDG CMDG JUDG

DH••
DHAL DHOW

D•H•
DAHL DAHS DOHA

D••H
DASH DICH DISH DOTH

•DH•
EDHS

•D•H
ADAH

••DH
NADH SIDH YODH

DI••
DIAG DIAL DIAM DIAN DIAS DIAZ DIBS DICE DICH DICK DICT DIDO DIED DIEM DIEN DIES DIET DIEU DIFF DIGS DIII DIKE DILL DIME DIMS DINA DINE DING DINK DINO DINS DINT DION DIOR DIOS DIPL DIPS DIRE DIRK DIRS DIRT DISC DISH DISK DISS DIST DITS DITZ DIVA DIVE DIVS

D•I•
DAIN DAIS DBIB DCII DCIV DCIX DEIL DIII DLII DLIT DLIV DLIX DOIL DOIN DOIT DRIB DRIN DRIP DRIQ DVII DXII DXIV DXIX

D••I
DALI DARI DCCI DCII DCLI DCVI DCXI DEBI DECI DELI DEMI DESI DEVI DIII DLII DLVI DLXI DREI DVII DXCI DXII DXLI DXVI DXXI

•DI•
ADIN ADIT CDII CDIV CDIX EDIE EDIT FDIC IDIO MDII MDIV MDIX ODIC ODIE ODIN XDIN XDIV

•D•I
CDII CDLI CDVI CDXI MDCI MDII MDLI MDVI MDXI

••DI
AUDI CADI CEDI JEDI LODI MCDI MIDI MMDI NIDI NODI NUDI PEDI QADI REDI RIDI RUDI SADI VIDI WADI

D•J•
DEJA DOJO

•DJ•
ADJS ADJT

••DJ
HADJ

DK••
DKNY

D•K•
DEKA DEKE DIKE DUKE

D••K
DANK DARK DECK DESK DICK DINK DIRK DISK DOAK DOCK DUCK DUNK DUSK DYAK DYCK

•DK•
KDKA

•D•K
ADAK HDBK NDAK SDAK

DL••
DLII DLIT DLIV DLIX DLVI DLXI DLXV DLXX

D•L•
DALE DALI DALS DALY DCLI DCLV DCLX DELE DELI DELL DELS DELY DILL DOLE DOLF DOLL DOLT DULL DULY DXLI DXLV

D••L
DAHL DANL DCCL DCXL DEAL DECL DEIL DELL DHAL DIAL DILL DIPL DOIL DOLL DUAL DUEL DULL

•DL•
CDLI CDLV CDLX IDLE IDLY MDLI MDLV MDLX

•D•L
CDXL IDOL IDYL MDCL MDXL

••DL
MCDL MMDL

DM••
DMDS DMSO

D•M•
DAMA DAME DAMN DAMP DAMS DEME DEMI DEMO DEMS DEMY DIME DIMS DOME DOMO DOMS DPMS DSMS DUMA DUMB DUMP DVMS

D••M
DEEM DERM DEUM DIAM DIEM DOOM DORM DRAM DRUM

•DM•
ADMS

•D•M
ADAM BDRM EDAM EDOM IDEM ODOM

••DM
RADM VADM

D•N•
DANA DANE DANG DANK DANL DANO DANU DENE DENG DENS DENT DENY DINA DINE DING DINK DINO DINS DINT DKNY DONA DONE DONG DONS DONT DRNO DUNA DUNE DUNK DUNN DUNS DYNA DYNE

D••N
DAIN DAMN DARN DAWN DCON DEAN DERN DIAN DIEN DION DOIN DOON DORN DOWN DRIN DUNN DURN DWAN DYAN

•DN•
EDNA

•D•N
ADDN ADEN ADIN EDEN IDUN ODIN XDIN

••DN
ADDN MIDN

DO••
DOAK DOBY DOCK DOCS DODD DODO DOER DOES DOFF DOGE DOGG DOGS DOGY DOHA DOIL DOIN DOIT DOJO DOLE DOLF DOLL DOLT DOME DOMO DOMS DONA DONE DONG DONS DONT DOOD DOOM DOON DOOR DOPA DOPE DOPY DORA DORE DORM DORN DORP DORR DORS DORT DORY DOSE DOSS DOST DOTE DOTH DOTS DOUG DOUP DOUR DOUW DOUX DOVE DOWD DOWN DOZE DOZY

D•O•
DCON DHOW DION DIOR DIOS DOOD DOOM DOON DOOR DROP DSOS DUOS

D••O
DABO DADO DANO DAYO DECO DEMO DEVO DIDO DINO DMSO DODO DOJO DOMO DRNO DURO

•DO•
ADOS EDOM IDOL IDOS ODOM ODOR UDOS

•D•O
EDDO IDEO IDIO

••DO
ALDO BODO DADO DIDO DODO EDDO ENDO FADO FIDO INDO IODO JUDO LIDO ORDO PEDO PPDO REDO TODO UNDO UPDO YEDO

DP••
DPMS

D•P•
DAPS DEPP DEPT DIPL DIPS DOPA DOPE DOPY DUPE

D••P
DAMP DEEP DEPP DORP DOUP DRIP DROP DUMP

••DP
AVDP NADP

D••Q
DRIQ

DR••
DRAB DRAG DRAM DRAT DRAW DRAY DRED DREE DREG DREI DREW DRIB DRIN DRIP DRIQ DRNO DROP DRUB DRUG DRUM DRYS

D•R•
DARC DARD DARE DARI DARK DARN DART DERM DERN DIRE DIRK DIRS DIRT DORA DORE DORM DORN DORP DORR DORS DORT DORY DURA DURN DURO

D••R
DEAR DEER DIOR DOER DOOR DORR DOUR DYER

•DR•
BDRM CDRS LDRS

•D•R
ADAR EDER ODER ODOR

••DR
BLDR CMDR FLDR HYDR RMDR SADR

DS••
DSCS DSMS DSOS

D•S•
DASD DASH DESC DESI DESK DISC DISH DISK DISS DIST DMSO DOSE DOSS DOST DUSE DUSK DUST

D••S
DABS DADS DAGS DAHS DAIS DALS DAMS DAPS DATS DAWS DAYS DEBS DEES DEFS DEGS DELS DEMS DENS DETS DEUS DEWS DEYS DIAS DIBS DIES DIGS DIMS DINS DIOS DIPS DIRS DISS DITS DIVS DMDS DOCS DOES DOGS DOMS DONS DORS DOSS DOTS DPMS DRYS DSCS DSMS DSOS DUBS DUDS DUES DUNS DUOS DVDS DVMS DYES

•DS•
MDSE

•D•S
ADCS ADDS ADES ADJS ADMS ADOS CDRS EDDS EDHS IDES IDOS LDCS LDRS ODAS ODDS ODES RDAS UDOS VDTS

••DS
ADDS AIDS ANDS BEDS BIDS BODS BUDS BVDS CADS CODS CUDS DADS DMDS DUDS DVDS EADS EDDS ENDS ETDS FADS FEDS FIDS GADS GODS HODS INDS KEDS KIDS LADS LCDS LEDS LIDS LLDS LTDS MEDS MODS MUDS NODS ODDS OLDS OUDS PADS PEDS PHDS PODS RADS REDS RFDS RIDS RNDS RODS SODS STDS SUDS TADS TEDS TODS WADS WEDS YODS ZEDS

D•T•
DATA DATE DATS DETS DITS DITZ DOTE DOTH DOTS DUTY

D••T
DAFT DART DEBT DEET DEFT DENT DEPT DEUT DICT DIET DINT DIRT DIST DLIT DOIT DOLT DONT DORT DOST DRAT DUCT DUET DUST

•DT•
EDTA HDTV VDTS

•D•T
ADIT ADJT ADVT EDIT

DU••
DUAD DUAL DUBS DUCE DUCK DUCT DUDE DUDS DUEL DUES DUET DUFF DUFY DUKE DULL DULY DUMA DUMB DUMP DUNA DUNE DUNK DUNN DUNS DUOS DUPE DURA DURN DURO DUSE DUSK DUST DUTY DUVE

D•U•
DAUB DEUM DEUS DEUT DEUX DOUG DOUP DOUR DOUW DOUX DRUB DRUG DRUM

D••U
DANU DIEU

•DU•
ADUE EDUC IDUN

••DU
KUDU PUDU URDU

DV••
DVDS DVII DVMS

D•V•
DAVE DAVY DCVI DEVA DEVI DEVO DIVA DIVE DIVS DLVI DOVE DUVE DXVI

D••V
DCCV DCIV DCLV DCXV DLIV DLXV DXCV DXIV DXLV DXXV

•DV•
ADVT CDVI MDVI

•D•V
CDIV CDLV CDXV HDTV MDCV MDIV MDLV MDXV XDIV

••DV
MCDV MMDV

DW••
DWAN

D•W•
DAWG DAWN DAWS DEWS DEWY DOWD DOWN

D••W
DHOW DOUW DRAW DREW

•DW•
HDWE

DX••
DXCI DXCV DXII DXIV DXIX DXLI DXLV DXVI DXXI DXXV DXXX

D•X•
DCXC DCXI DCXL DCXV DCXX DLXI DLXV DLXX DXXI DXXV DXXX

D••X
DCCX DCIX DCLX DCXX DEUX DLIX DLXX DOUX DXIX DXXX

•DX•
CDXC CDXI CDXL CDXV CDXX MDXC MDXI MDXL MDXV MDXX

•D•X
CDIX CDLX CDXX EDAX MDCX MDIX MDLX MDXX

••DX
MCDX MMDX

DY••
DYAD DYAK DYAN DYCE DYCK DYED DYER DYES DYNA DYNE

D•Y•
DAYO DAYS DEYS DRYS

D••Y
DALY DAVY DDAY DEFY DELY DEMY DENY DEWY DKNY DOBY DOGY DOPY DORY DOZY DRAY DUFY DULY DUTY

•DY•
IDYL

•D•Y
ADDY DDAY EDDY EDGY GDAY IDLY ODAY VDAY

••DY
ADDY ANDY BODY CODY EDDY HEDY INDY JODY JUDY LADY RUDY TIDY TODY

D•Z•
DAZE DOZE DOZY

D••Z
DIAZ DITZ

•DZ•
ADZE

••DZ
LODZ

EA••
EACH EADS EARL EARN EARP EARS

EASE EAST EASY EATS EAUX EAVE

E•A•
EBAN EDAM EDAX EGAD EGAL EGAN ELAL ELAM ELAN ERAS ERAT ESAI ESAS ESAU ETAH ETAL ETAS ETAT EVAH EVAN EVAP EXAM EYAS

E••A
EBLA ECUA EDDA EDNA EDTA ELBA ELEA ELIA ELLA ELSA EMIA EMMA ENNA ENYA EPHA ERDA ERMA ESSA ESTA ETNA ETTA EYRA EZRA

•EA•
BEAD BEAK BEAL BEAM BEAN BEAR BEAS BEAT BEAU DEAD DEAF DEAL DEAN DEAR FEAR FEAT GEAR HEAD HEAL HEAP HEAR HEAT JEAN KEAN KEAS LEAD LEAF LEAH LEAK LEAL LEAN LEAP LEAR LEAS MEAD MEAL MEAN MEAS MEAT NEAL NEAP NEAR NEAT PEAG PEAK PEAL PEAR PEAS PEAT PEAU READ REAL REAM REAP REAR SEAL SEAM SEAN SEAR SEAS SEAT TEAK TEAL TEAM TEAR TEAS VEAL VEAU WEAK WEAL WEAN WEAR YEAH YEAN YEAR YEAS ZEAL

•E•A
BELA BEMA BETA CELA CENA CERA CETA DECA DEJA DEKA DEVA FEMA FETA GENA GERA GETA HEMA HERA HEXA JENA LEDA LEIA LEMA LENA MEGA MESA META NEVA PENA PEPA PETA REBA REZA SEGA SELA SERA SETA TEMA TERA TEWA VEDA VEGA VELA VENA VERA WEKA XENA ZETA

••EA
ACEA AIEA ALEA AREA ASEA BREA ELEA FLEA GAEA IDEA ITEA ODEA ONEA PLEA RHEA SHEA THEA TOEA UMEA UVEA ZOEA

EB••
EBAN EBBS EBEN EBLA EBON EBRO

E•B•
EBBS ELBA ELBE

•EB•
BEBE CEBU DEBI DEBS DEBT HEBE HEBR NEBE NEBN NEBO NEBR NEBS REBA REBS SEBE SEBS WEBB WEBS ZEBU

•E•B
BEEB HERB KERB SERB VERB WEBB WEEB

••EB
BEEB BLEB LIEB LOEB PLEB SHEB WEEB

EC••
ECCE ECCL ECHO ECHT ECOL ECON ECRU ECTO ECUA ECUS

E•C•
EACH ECCE ECCL EKCO ENCE ENCL ENCS ENCY ESCE ETCH EXCH EXCL EYCK

E••C
EDUC EEOC ELEC EMIC EPIC ERIC ETIC EXEC

•EC•
BECK DECA DECI DECK DECL DECO HECK HECT LECH LECT MECH MECO NECK PECK PECS RECD RECS RECT SECH SECS SECT SECY TECH TECS YECH ZECH

•E•C
DESC EEOC

••EC
ALEC AVEC BSEC ELEC EXEC MSEC OPEC PREC PSEC SPEC

ED••
EDAM EDAX EDDA EDDO EDDS EDDY EDEN EDER EDGE EDGY EDHS EDIE EDIT EDNA EDOM EDTA EDUC

E•D•
EADS EDDA EDDO EDDS EDDY ENDE ENDO ENDS ERDA ERDE ETDS

E••D
EGAD EKED ENID EXOD EYED

•ED•
BEDE BEDS CEDE CEDI FEDS HEDY JEDI KEDS LEDA LEDS MEDE MEDS PEDI PEDO PEDS REDD REDE REDI REDO REDS TEDS VEDA WEDS YEDO ZEDS

•E•D
BEAD BEND DEAD DEED FEED FEND FEUD GEED HEAD HEED HELD HERD LEAD LEND LEWD MEAD MEED MELD MEND NEED NEJD NERD PEND READ RECD REDD REED REGD REID REND RETD SEED SEND TEED TEND VELD VEND VERD WEED WELD WEND ZEND

••ED
ABED ACED AGED APED AWED AXED BLED BRED BSED COED CUED DEED DIED DRED DYED EKED EYED FEED FLED FRED GEED HEED HIED HOED HUED ICED IRED LIED MEED MRED NEED OHED OKED OPED OWED PIED PLED PRED REED RUED SEED SHED SKED SLED SPED SUED SWED TEED TIED TOED USED VIED WEED

EE••
EEEE EEGS EEKS EELS EELY EENY EEOC EERO EERY

E•E•
EBEN EDEN EDER EEEE EGER EKED EKES ELEA ELEC ELEM ELEV EMES EPEE ESEL ETES EVEL EVEN EVER EVES EWEN EWER EWES EXEC EXES EYED EYER EYES EZEK

E••E
EASE EAVE ECCE EDGE EDIE EEEE EINE EIRE ELBE ELIE ELKE ELLE ELSE ENCE ENDE ENNE ENSE EPEE ERDE ERIE ERLE ERNE ERSE ERTE ESCE ESME ESNE ESSE ESTE ETRE ETTE EVOE EYRE

•EE•
BEEB BEEF BEEN BEEP BEER BEES BEET CEES DEED DEEM DEEP DEER DEES DEET EEEE FEED FEEL FEES FEET GEED GEEK GEER GEES GEEZ HEED HEEL HEEP HEER HEET JEEP JEER JEEZ KEEL KEEN KEEP KEET LEEK LEER LEES LEET MEED MEEK MEER MEET NEED NEEL NEEM NEER NEET PEEK PEEL PEEN PEEP PEER REED REEF REEK REEL REES SEED SEEK SEEL SEEM SEEN SEEP SEER SEES TEED TEEM TEEN TEES VEEP VEER VEES WEEB WEED WEEK WEEN WEEP ZEES

•E•E
BEBE BEDE BENE BETE CEDE CENE CEPE CERE CETE DEKE DELE DEME DENE EEEE FEME FERE FETE GENE GERE HEBE HEME HERE JEFE JETE LESE MEDE MEME MERE METE NEBE NENE NEVE PEKE PELE PEPE PERE PETE REDE RENE RETE REVE SEBE SEME SENE SERE SEVE TELE TENE TETE UELE VERE WERE WEVE ZEKE

••EE
AGEE AKEE ALEE BREE CHEE CREE DREE EEEE EPEE FLEE FREE GHEE GLEE GREE IDEE INEE ISEE KLEE KNEE OGEE OSEE RHEE SKEE SMEE SNEE SPEE THEE TREE TWEE ULEE USEE WHEE

EF••
EFFS EFIK EFTS

E•F•
EFFS

E••F
ENUF

•EF•
DEFS DEFT DEFY HEFT JEFE JEFF LEFT NEFF REFL REFS REFT TEFF WEFT

•E•F
BEEF CERF DEAF JEFF KERF LEAF LEIF NEFF NERF NEUF NEWF OEUF PELF PERF REEF SELF SERF TEFF

••EF
ALEF BEEF CHEF CLEF FIEF LIEF PREF REEF TREF

EG••
EGAD EGAL EGAN EGER EGGO EGGS EGGY EGIS EGON EGOS

E•G•
EDGE EDGY EEGS EGGO EGGS EGGY ENGR ENGS ERGO ERGS

•EG•
BEGS DEGS EEGS KEGS LEGO LEGS MEGA NEGS PEGS REGD REGS REGT SEGA SEGO TEGS VEGA YEGG

•E•G
BELG BENG BERG DENG GEOG PEAG WENG YEGG

••EG
DREG GLEG GREG OLEG OREG ROEG SKEG

E•H•
ECHO ECHT EDHS ELHI EPHA ETHS

E••H
EACH ESTH ETAH ETCH EVAH EXCH

•EH•
JEHU LEHR NEHI PEHS SEHR

•E•H
BETH HETH IEOH LEAH LECH MECH MESH METH NETH PENH PERH RESH SECH SETH TECH TESH TETH YEAH YECH ZECH ZEPH

EI••
EINE EINS EIRE

E•I•
EDIE EDIT EFIK EGIS ELIA ELIE ELIS ELIZ EMIA EMIC EMIL EMIR EMIT ENID EPIC EPIS ERIC ERIE ERIK ERIN ERIQ ERIS ETIC EVIL EXIT EZIO

E••I
ELHI ELOI EQUI ESAI ETUI

•EI•
BEIN CEIL DEIL FEIN GEIN HEIN HEIR LEIA LEIF LEIS MEIN MEIR NEIL NEIN OEIL QEII REID REIN REIS REIT SEIN SEIS VEII VEIL VEIN WEIL WEIR ZEIN

•E•I
BENI CEDI DEBI DECI DELI DEMI DESI DEVI HELI HEMI JEDI KEPI LENI LEOI LEVI NEHI NERI NEVI PEDI PERI QEII REDI RENI SEMI SETI TERI VEII VENI YETI

••EI
DREI FREI ZWEI

•EJ•
DEJA NEJD SEJM

EK••
EKCO EKED EKES

E•K•
EEKS ELKE ELKO ELKS ERKS

E••K
EFIK ERIK EWOK EYCK EZEK

•EK•
DEKA DEKE EEKS LEKS PEKE WEKA ZEKE

•E•K
BEAK BECK DECK DESK GEEK HECK JERK LEAK LEEK LEUK MEEK NECK PEAK PECK PEEK PERK REEK SEEK TEAK WEAK WEEK WELK YERK

••EK
EZEK GEEK LEEK MEEK PEEK PREK REEK SEEK TREK WEEK

EL••
ELAL ELAM ELAN ELBA ELBE ELEA ELEC ELEM ELEV ELHI ELIA ELIE ELIS ELIZ ELKE ELKO ELKS ELLA ELLE ELLS ELLY ELMO ELMS ELOI ELON ELSA ELSE ELUL

E•L•
EBLA EELS EELY ELLA ELLE ELLS ELLY EMLY ERLE

E••L
EARL ECCL ECOL EGAL ELAL ELUL EMIL ENCL ENOL ESEL ETAL EVEL EVIL EXCL

•EL•
BELA BELG BELL BELO BELS BELT BELY CELA CELL CELS CELT DELE DELI DELL DELS DELY EELS EELY FELL FELT GELL GELS GELT HELD HELI HELL HELM HELO HELP JELL KELP LELY MELD MELL MELT NELL PELE PELF PELL PELT RELS RELY SELA SELF SELL TELE TELL TELO UELE VELA VELD WELD WELK WELL WELT YELL YELP

•E•L
BEAL BELL CEIL CELL DEAL DECL DEIL DELL FEEL FELL GELL GENL GEOL HEAL HEEL HELL HERL JELL KEEL LEAL MEAL MELL MERL MEWL NEAL NEEL NEIL NELL OEIL PEAL PEEL PELL REAL REEL REFL REPL SEAL SEEL SELL SEUL TEAL TELL VEAL VEIL WEAL WEIL WELL YELL ZEAL

••EL
ABEL AUEL AXEL BIEL BREL CIEL COEL DUEL ESEL EVEL FEEL FUEL GAEL HEEL ICEL JAEL JOEL KAEL KEEL KIEL KTEL NEEL NOEL OPEL OREL PEEL QUEL REEL RIEL SEEL SHEL TAEL

EM••
EMES EMIA EMIC EMIL EMIR EMIT EMLY EMMA EMMY EMPS EMTS EMUS

E•M•
ELMO ELMS EMMA EMMY ERMA ESME

E••M
EDAM EDOM ELAM ELEM ETYM EXAM

•EM•
BEMA BEMS DEME DEMI DEMO DEMS DEMY FEMA FEME FEMS GEMS HEMA HEME HEMI HEMO HEMP HEMS KEMO KEMP LEMA LEMS MEME MEMO MEMS NEMO REMO REMS SEME SEMI SEMS TEMA TEMP

•E•M
BEAM BERM DEEM DERM DEUM GEOM GERM GEUM HELM HERM MEUM NEEM PERM REAM SEAM SEEM SEJM TEAM TEEM TERM

••EM
AHEM CHEM CLEM DEEM DIEM ELEM FLEM IDEM ITEM NEEM OREM POEM PREM QUEM SEEM SHEM STEM TEEM THEM YLEM

EN••
ENCE
ENCL
ENCS
ENCY
ENDE
ENDO
ENDS
ENGR
ENGS
ENID
ENNA
ENNE
ENOL
ENOS
ENOW
ENRY
ENSE
ENTO
ENTR
ENTS
ENUF
ENVS
ENVY
ENYA
ENYO
ENZO

E•N•
EDNA
EENY
EINE
EINS
ENNA
ENNE
EONS
ERNE
ERNO
ERNS
ESNE
ETNA

E••N
EARN
EBAN
EBEN
EBON
ECON
EDEN
EGAN
EGON
ELAN
ELON
ERIN
ESPN
ETON
EVAN
EVEN
EWEN
EXON

•EN•
BEND
BENE
BENG
BENI
BENT
BENU
BENZ
CENA
CENE
CENO
CENS
CENT
DENE
DENG
DENS
DENT
DENY
EENY
FEND
FENN
FENS
GENA
GENE
GENL
GENS
GENT
GENU
GENX
GENY
HENS
HENT
JENA
JENS
KENO
KENS
KENT
LENA
LEND
LENI
LENO
LENS
LENT
LENZ
MEND
MENS
MENT
MENU
NENE
OENO
PENA
PEND
PENH
PENN
PENS
PENT
REND
RENE
RENI
RENO
RENT
SEND
SENE
SENS
SENT
TEND
TENE
TENN
TENO
TENS
TENT
VENA
VEND
VENI
VENN
VENT
WEND
WENG
WENS
WENT
XENA
XENO
YENS
ZEND
ZENO

•E•N
AEON
BEAN
BEEN
BEIN
BERN
CERN
DEAN
DERN
FEIN
FENN
FERN
GEIN
HEIN
HERN
HEWN
JEAN
KEAN
KEEN
KERN
LEAN
LEON
MEAN
MEIN
NEBN
NEIN
NEON
NEUN
PEEN
PENN
PEON
REIN
SEAN
SEEN
SEIN
SEWN
TEEN
TENN
TERN
VEIN
VENN
VERN
WEAN
WEEN
YEAN
ZEIN

••EN
ADEN
AMEN
ATEN
BEEN
BIEN
BREN
CAEN
CHEN
COEN
DIEN
EBEN
EDEN
EVEN
EWEN
GLEN
GMEN
GWEN
JAEN
KEEN
LIEN
MIEN
OLEN
OMEN
OPEN
OVEN
OWEN
OXEN
PEEN
RIEN
SEEN
STEN
SVEN
TEEN
THEN
TMEN
WEEN
WHEN
WIEN
WREN
XMEN

EO••
EONS
EOUS

E•O•
EBON
ECOL
ECON
EDOM
EEOC
EGON
EGOS
ELOI
ELON
ENOL
ENOS
ENOW
EPOS
EROO
EROS
ESOP
ESOS
ETON
EVOE
EWOK
EXOD
EXON
EXOR
EYOT

E••O
EBRO
ECHO
ECTO
EDDO
EERO
EGGO
EKCO
ELKO
ELMO
ENDO
ENTO
ENYO
ENZO
ERGO
ERNO
EROO
ESPO
ESSO
ESTO
EURO
EXPO
EZIO

•EO•
AEON
CEOS
EEOC
GEOG
GEOL
GEOM
IEOH
KEOS
LEOI
LEON
LEOS
MEOW
NEON
PEON
REOS

•E•O
AERO
BELO
BESO
CENO
CERO
DECO
DEMO
DEVO
EERO
HELO
HEMO
HERO
KEMO
KENO
KETO
LEGO
LENO
LETO
LEVO
MECO
MEMO
MERO
MESO
NEBO
NEMO
NERO
OENO
PEDO
PEPO
PESO
PETO
REDO
REMO
RENO
REPO
SEGO
SERO
TELO
TENO
VERO
VETO
XENO
XERO
YEDO
ZENO
ZERO

••EO
AREO
CLEO
IDEO
OLEO
OREO
PLEO
RHEO
THEO

EP••
EPEE
EPHA
EPIC
EPIS
EPOS

E•P•
EMPS
ESPN
ESPO
ESPS
ESPY
EXPO
EXPT

E••P
EARP
ESOP
EVAP

•EP•
CEPE
CEPS
DEPP
DEPT
HEPT
KEPI
KEPT
PEPA
PEPE
PEPO
PEPS
REPL
REPO
REPP
REPS
REPT
SEPT
TEPP
WEPT
ZEPH

•E•P
BEEP
DEEP
DEPP
HEAP
HEEP
HELP
HEMP
JEEP
KEEP
KELP
KEMP
LEAP
NEAP
PEEP
PERP
REAP
REPP
RESP
REUP
SEEP
TEMP
TEPP
TERP
VEEP
WEEP
YELP

••EP
ALEP
BEEP
DEEP
HEEP
JEEP
KEEP
PEEP
PREP
SEEP
SHEP
SKEP
STEP
UTEP
VEEP
WEEP

EQ••
EQUI

E•Q•
ESQS

E••Q
ERIQ

•EQ•
SEQQ

•E•Q
SEQQ

••EQ
FREQ

ER••
ERAS
ERAT
ERDA
ERDE
ERGO
ERGS
ERIC
ERIE
ERIK
ERIN
ERIQ
ERIS
ERKS
ERLE
ERMA
ERNE
ERNO
ERNS
EROO
EROS
ERRS
ERSE
ERST
ERTE

E•R•
EARL
EARN
EARP
EARS
EBRO
ECRU
EERO
EERY
EIRE
ENRY
ERRS
ETRE
EURO
EURY
EWRY
EYRA
EYRE
EYRY
EZRA

E••R
EDER
EGER
EMIR
ENGR
ENTR
EVER
EWER
EXOR
EYER

•ER•
AERO
AERY
BERG
BERM
BERN
BERT
CERA
CERE
CERF
CERN
CERO
CERT
DERM
DERN
EERO
EERY
FERE
FERN
GERA
GERE
GERM
HERA
HERB
HERD
HERE
HERL
HERM
HERN
HERO
HERR
HERS
JERK
KERB
KERF
KERN
KERR
KERT
MERE
MERL
MERO
MERS
MERV
NERD
NERF
NERI
NERO
PERE
PERF
PERH
PERI
PERK
PERM
PERP
PERS
PERT
PERU
SERA
SERB
SERE
SERF
SERO
SERS
SERT
SERV
TERA
TERI
TERM
TERN
TERP
TERR
VERA
VERB
VERD
VERE
VERN
VERO
VERS
VERT
VERY
WERE
WERT
XERO
YERK
ZERO

•E•R
BEAR
BEER
DEAR
DEER
FEAR
GEAR
GEER
HEAR
HEBR
HEER
HEIR
HERR
JEER
KERR
LEAR
LEER
LEHR
MEER
MEIR
NEAR
NEBR
NEER
PEAR
PEER
REAR
SEAR
SEER
SEHR
TEAR
TERR
VEER
WEAR
WEIR
YEAR

••ER
ABER
ACER
AGER
AMER
APER
AUER
AVER
AXER
AYER
BAER
BEER
BOER
BRER
CBER
CHER
CUER
DEER
DOER
DYER
EDER
EGER
EVER
EWER
EYER
GEER
GOER
HEER
HIER
HOER
HYER
ICER
ITER
JEER
LEER
MEER
NEER
NLER
ODER
OMER
ONER
OPER
OVER
OWER
OYER
PEER
PIER
PUER
RUER
SEER
STER
SUER
TIER
UBER
USER
VEER
VIER
YSER

ES••
ESAI
ESAS
ESAU
ESCE
ESEL
ESME
ESNE
ESOP
ESOS
ESPN
ESPO
ESPS
ESPY
ESQS
ESSA
ESSE
ESSO
ESTA
ESTE
ESTH
ESTO
ESUS

E•S•
EASE
EAST
EASY
ELSA
ELSE
ENSE
ERSE
ERST
ESSA
ESSE
ESSO

E••S
EADS
EARS
EATS
EBBS
ECUS
EDDS
EDHS
EEGS
EEKS
EELS
EFFS
EFTS
EGGS
EGIS
EGOS
EINS
EKES
ELIS
ELKS
ELLS
ELMS
EMES
EMPS
EMTS
EMUS
ENCS
ENDS
ENGS
ENOS
ENTS
ENVS
EONS
EOUS
EPIS
EPOS
ERAS
ERGS
ERIS
ERKS
ERNS
EROS
ERRS
ESAS
ESOS
ESPS
ESQS
ESUS
ETAS
ETDS
ETES
ETHS
EVES
EWES
EXES
EXTS
EYAS
EYES

•ES•
BESO
BESS
BEST
CESS
CEST
DESC
DESI
DESK
FESS
FEST
GEST
HESS
HEST
JESS
JEST
JESU
LESE
LESS
LEST
MESA
MESH
MESO
MESS
NESS
NEST
PESO
PEST
RESH
RESP
REST
SESS
TESH
TESS
TEST
VEST
WEST
ZEST

•E•S
BEAS
BEDS
BEES
BEGS
BELS
BEMS
BESS
BETS
BEYS
CEES
CELS
CENS
CEOS
CEPS
CESS
DEBS
DEES
DEFS
DEGS
DELS
DEMS
DENS
DETS
DEUS
DEWS
DEYS
EEGS
EEKS
EELS
FEDS
FEES
FEMS
FENS
FESS
GEES
GELS
GEMS
GENS
GETS
HEMS
HENS
HERS
HESS
HEWS
JENS
JESS
JETS
JEWS
KEAS
KEDS
KEGS
KENS
KEOS
KEYS
LEAS
LEDS
LEES
LEGS
LEIS
LEKS
LEMS
LENS
LEOS
LESS
LETS
MEAS
MEDS
MEMS
MENS
MERS
MESS
METS
MEWS
NEBS
NEGS
NESS
NETS
NEWS
PEAS
PECS
PEDS
PEGS
PEHS
PENS
PEPS
PERS
PETS
PEWS
REBS
RECS
REDS
REES
REFS
REGS
REIS
RELS
REMS
REOS
REPS
RETS
REVS
REYS
SEAS
SEBS
SECS
SEES
SEIS
SEMS
SENS
SERS
SESS
SETS
SEWS
TEAS
TECS
TEDS
TEES
TEGS
TENS
TESS
TETS
UEYS
VEES
VERS
VETS
WEBS
WEDS
WENS
WETS
YEAS
YENS
YEWS
ZEDS
ZEES
ZEUS

••ES
ACES
ADES
AGES
ALES
AMES
APES
ARES
ATES
AVES
AWES
AXES
AYES
BEES
BYES
CEES
CUES
DEES
DIES
DOES
DUES
DYES
EKES
EMES
ETES
EVES
EWES
EXES
EYES
FEES
FOES
GEES
GOES
HIES
HOES
HRES
HUES
ICES
IDES
ILES
INES
IRES
ITES
IVES
JOES
KYES
LEES
LIES
LYES
MBES
MIES
MMES
NAES
NOES
ODES
OLES
ONES
OPES
ORES
OWES
PIES
PRES
QUES
REES
RHES
ROES
RTES
RUES
RYES
SEES
SHES
STES
SUES
TEES
TIES
TOES
TRES
TUES
UKES
UNES
USES
UTES
VEES
VIES
WOES
WYES
YVES
ZEES

ET••
ETAH
ETAL
ETAS
ETAT
ETCH
ETDS
ETES
ETHS
ETIC
ETNA
ETON
ETRE
ETTA
ETTE
ETUI
ETUX
ETYM

E•T•
EATS
ECTO
EDTA
EFTS
EMTS
ENTO
ENTR
ENTS
ERTE
ESTA
ESTE
ESTH
ESTO
ETTA
ETTE
EXTS

E••T
EAST
ECHT
EDIT
EMIT
ERAT
ERST
ETAT
EXIT
EXPT
EYOT

•ET•
BETA
BETE
BETH
BETS
BETZ
CETA
CETE
DETS
FETA
FETE
GETA
GETS
GETZ
HETH
JETE
JETS
JETT
KETO
KETT
LETO
LETS
LETT
META
METE
METH
METS
METZ
NETH
NETS
PETA
PETE
PETO
PETS
RETD
RETE
RETS
SETA
SETH
SETI
SETS
SETT
TETE
TETH
TETS
VETO
VETS
WETS
YETI
ZETA

•E•T
BEAT
BEET
BELT
BENT
BERT
BEST
CELT
CENT
CERT
CEST
DEBT
DEET
DEFT
DENT
DEPT
DEUT
FEAT
FEET
FELT
FEST
GELT
GENT
GEST
HEAT
HECT
HEET
HEFT
HENT
HEPT
HEST
JEST
JETT
KEET
KENT
KEPT
KERT
KETT
LECT
LEET
LEFT
LENT
LEST
LETT
MEAT
MEET
MELT
MENT
NEAT
NEET
NEST
NEUT
NEWT
NEXT
PEAT
PELT
PENT
PERT
PEST
RECT
REFT
REGT
REIT
RENT
REPT
REST
SEAT
SECT
SENT
SEPT
SERT
SETT
SEXT
TENT
TEST
TEUT
TEXT
VENT
VERT
VEST
WEFT
WELT
WENT
WEPT
WERT
WEST
ZEST

••ET
ABET
ACET
BEET
BRET
CHET
DEET
DIET
DUET
FEET
FRET
HEET
IBET
ICET
KEET
LEET
MEET
NEET
NYET
PIET
POET
PRET
RHET
SPET
STET
SUET
TRET
VIET
WHET

EU••
EURO
EURY

E•U•
EAUX
ECUA
ECUS
EDUC
ELUL
EMUS
ENUF
EOUS
EQUI
ESUS
ETUI
ETUX

E••U
ECRU
ESAU

•EU•
DEUM
DEUS
DEUT
DEUX
FEUD
GEUM
JEUX
LEUK
MEUM
NEUF
NEUN
NEUT
OEUF
REUP
SEUL
TEUT
YEUX
ZEUS

•E•U
BEAU
BENU
CEBU
GENU
JEHU
JESU
LEVU
MENU
PEAU
PERU
VEAU
ZEBU

••EU
BLEU
DIEU
LIEU

EV••
EVAH
EVAN
EVAP
EVEL
EVEN
EVER
EVES
EVIL
EVOE

E•V•
EAVE
ENVS
ENVY

E••V
ELEV

•EV•
BEVY
DEVA
DEVI
DEVO
LEVI
LEVO
LEVU
LEVY
NEVA
NEVE
NEVI
REVE
REVS
SEVE
WEVE

•E•V
MERV
SERV

••EV
BREV
ELEV
KIEV
PREV

EW••
EWEN
EWER
EWES
EWOK
EWRY

E••W
ENOW

•EW• DEWS DEWY HEWN HEWS JEWS LEWD MEWL MEWS NEWF NEWS NEWT PEWS SEWN SEWS TEWA YEWS

•E•W MEOW

••EW ANEW BLEW BREW CHEW CLEW CREW DREW FLEW GREW KNEW LOEW PHEW PLEW SKEW SLEW SMEW SPEW STEW THEW VIEW WHEW

EX•• EXAM EXCH EXCL EXEC EXES EXIT EXOD EXON EXOR EXPO EXPT EXTS

E••X EAUX EDAX ETUX

•EX• HEXA NEXT SEXT SEXY TEXT

•E•X DEUX GENX JEUX YEUX

••EX ALEX AMEX APEX CHEX FLEX GREX IBEX ILEX NMEX PLEX TREX

EY•• EYAS EYCK EYED EYER EYES EYOT EYRA EYRE EYRY

E•Y• ENYA ENYO ETYM

E••Y EASY EDDY EDGY EELY EENY EERY EGGY ELLY EMLY EMMY ENCY ENRY ENVY ESPY EURY EWRY EYRY

•EY• BEYS DEYS KEYS REYS UEYS

•E•Y AERY BELY BEVY DEFY DELY DEMY DENY DEWY EELY EENY EERY GENY HEDY LELY LEVY RELY SECY SEXY VERY

••EY ACEY FLEY FREY GLEY GREY HUEY IVEY JOEY OBEY OKEY PREY SUEY THEY TREY UREY WHEY

EZ•• EZEK EZIO EZRA

E•Z• ENZO

E••Z ELIZ

•EZ• REZA

•E•Z BENZ BETZ GEEZ GETZ JEEZ LENZ METZ

••EZ BAEZ CHEZ GEEZ INEZ JEEZ OYEZ PREZ SUEZ

FA•• FACE FACP FACS FACT FADE FADO FADS FAHD FAHR FAIL FAIN FAIR FAIT FAKE FALA FALK FALL FALX FAME FANE FANG FANS FAQS FARE FARM FARO FARR FARS FASO FAST FATA FATE FATH FATS FAUN FAUT FAUX FAVA FAVE FAWN FAYE FAYS FAZE

F•A• FEAR FEAT FIAT FLAB FLAG FLAK FLAM FLAN FLAP FLAT FLAV FLAW FLAX FLAY FOAL FOAM FRAE FRAM FRAN FRAP FRAS FRAT FRAU FRAY FUAD

F••A FALA FATA FAVA FEMA FETA FICA FILA FINA FLEA FNMA FORA FRIA FULA

•FA• AFAR MFAS SFAX

•F•A AFTA

••FA AGFA ALFA SOFA TUFA URFA

F•B• FIBS FOBS FUBS

F••B FLAB FLUB FORB FTLB

F•C• FACE FACP FACS FACT FICA FICE FICT FOCH FOCI FRCP FRCS

F••C FDIC FISC FLIC FLOC

•FC• PFCS

••FC COFC KOFC

FD•• FDIC

F•D• FADE FADO FADS FEDS FIDE FIDO FIDS FLDR FUDD

F••D FAHD FEED FEND FEUD FIND FLED FOLD FOND FOOD FORD FRED FUAD FUDD FUND

•FD• RFDS

•F•D NFLD SFPD

FE•• FEAR FEAT FEDS FEED FEEL FEES FEET FEIN FELL FELT FEMA FEME FEMS FEND FENN FENS FERE FERN FESS FEST FETA FETE FEUD

F•E• FEED FEEL FEES FEET FIEF FLEA FLED FLEE FLEM FLEW FLEX FLEY FOES FRED FREE FREI FREQ FRET FREY FUEL

F••E FACE FADE FAKE FAME FANE FARE FATE FAVE FAYE FAZE FEME FERE FETE FICE FIDE FIFE FILE FINE FIRE FIVE FIXE FLEE FLOE FLUE FOIE FORE FOXE FRAE FREE FROE FRYE FUME FUSE FUZE FYKE

••FE CAFE FIFE JEFE LIFE RIFE SAFE WIFE

F•F• FIFE FIFI FIFO

F••F FIEF FUNF

•FF• EFFS IFFY OFFS PFFT

••FF BAFF BIFF BOFF BUFF CUFF DAFF DIFF DOFF DUFF GAFF GUFF HOFF HUFF JEFF JIFF LUFF MIFF MUFF NEFF ORFF PUFF RAFF RIFF RUFF SUFF TEFF TIFF TOFF TUFF

F•G• FIGS FOGG FOGS FOGY FUGS FUGU

F••G FANG FLAG FLOG FOGG FROG FRUG

•FG• AFGH

F•H• FAHD FAHR FOHN

F••H FATH FISH FOCH

•F•H AFGH

FI•• FIAT FIBS FICA FICE FICT FIDE FIDO FIDS FIEF FIFE FIFI FIFO FIGS FIJI FILA FILE FILL FILM FILS FINA FIND FINE FINI FINK FINN FINO FINS FIRE FIRM FIRN FIRS FISC FISH FISK FIST FITS FITZ FIVE FIXE FIZZ

F•I• FAIL FAIN FAIR FAIT FDIC FEIN FLIC FLIM FLIP FLIT FLIX FOIE FOIL FOIN FOIS FRIA FRIO FRIS FRIT FRIZ FWIW

F••I FIFI FIJI FINI FOCI FREI FUJI

•FI• EFIK

•F•I IFNI PFUI

••FI FIFI HIFI KOFI SUFI

F•J• FIJI FUJI

F•K• FAKE FYKE

F••K FALK FINK FISK FLAK FOLK FORK FUNK

•F•K EFIK

FL•• FLAB FLAG FLAK FLAM FLAN FLAP FLAT FLAV FLAW FLAX FLAY FLDR FLEA FLED FLEE FLEM FLEW FLEX FLEY FLIC FLIM FLIP FLIT FLIX FLOC FLOE FLOG FLOP FLOR FLOW FLOZ FLUB FLUE FLUS FLUX

F•L• FALA FALK FALL FALX FELL FELT FILA FILE FILL FILM FILS FOLD FOLK FTLB FULA FULL

F••L FAIL FALL FEEL FELL FILL FOAL FOIL FOOL FOUL FOWL FUEL FULL FURL

•FL• NFLD

••FL INFL REFL

F•M• FAME FEMA FEME FEMS FNMA FUME FUMY

F••M FARM FILM FIRM FLAM FLEM FLIM FOAM FORM FRAM FROM

••FM AMFM

FN•• FNMA

F•N• FANE FANG FANS FEND FENN FENS FINA FIND FINE FINI FINK FINN FINO FINS FOND FONS FONT FONZ FUND FUNF FUNK FUNT

F••N FAIN FAUN FAWN FEIN FENN FERN FINN FIRN FLAN FOHN FOIN FRAN

•FN• IFNI

FO•• FOAL FOAM FOBS FOCH FOCI FOES FOGG FOGS FOGY FOHN FOIE FOIL FOIN FOIS FOLD FOLK FOND FONS FONT FONZ FOOD FOOL FOOT FOPS FORA FORB FORD FORE FORK FORM FORT FOSS FOUL FOUR FOWL FOXE FOXX FOXY FOYS FOYT

F•O• FLOC FLOE FLOG FLOP FLOR FLOW FLOZ FOOD FOOL FOOT FROE FROG FROM FROW

F••O FADO FARO FASO FIDO FIFO FINO FRIO FURO

•FO• UFOS

•F•O AFRO IFSO

••FO FIFO INFO LIFO

F•P• FOPS

F••P FACP FLAP FLIP FLOP FRAP FRCP

•FP• SFPD

••FP KOFP

F•Q• FAQS

F••Q FREQ

•FQ• RFQS

FR•• FRAE FRAM FRAN FRAP FRAS FRAT FRAU FRAY FRCP FRCS FRED FREE FREI FREQ FRET FREY FRIA FRIO FRIS FRIT FRIZ FROE FROG FROM FROW FRUG FRYE

F•R• FARE FARM FARO FARR FARS FERE FERN FIRE FIRM FIRN FIRS FORA FORB FORD FORE FORK FORM FORT FURL FURO FURS FURY

F••R FAHR FAIR FARR FEAR FLDR FLOR FOUR

•FR• AFRO MFRS

•F•R AFAR

••FR SAFR

F•S• FASO FAST FESS FEST FISC FISH FISK FIST FOSS FUSE FUSS FUST

F••S FACS FADS FANS FAQS FARS FATS FAYS FEDS FEES FEMS FENS FESS FIBS FIDS FIGS FILS FINS FIRS FITS FLUS FOBS FOES FOGS FOIS FONS FOPS FOSS FOYS FRAS FRCS FRIS FUBS FUGS FURS FUSS

•FS• IFSO

•F•S AFTS EFFS EFTS MFAS MFRS OFFS PFCS RFDS RFQS UFOS

••FS COFS DEFS EFFS INFS KAFS OAFS OFFS QAFS REFS RIFS WAFS

FT•• FTLB

F•T• FATA FATE FATH FATS FETA FETE FITS FITZ FUTZ

F••T FACT FAIT FAST FAUT FEAT FEET FELT FEST FIAT FICT FIST FLAT FLIT FONT FOOT FORT FOYT FRAT FRET FRIT FUNT FUST

•FT• AFTA AFTS EFTS

•F•T PFFT

••FT CUFT DAFT DEFT GIFT HAFT HEFT LEFT LIFT LOFT LUFT PFFT RAFT REFT RIFT SIFT SOFT SQFT TAFT TOFT TUFT WAFT WEFT

FU•• FUAD FUBS FUDD FUEL FUGS FUGU FUJI FULA FULL FUME FUMY FUND FUNF FUNK FUNT FURL FURO FURS FURY FUSE FUSS FUST FUTZ FUZE FUZZ

F•U• FAUN FAUT FAUX FEUD FLUB FLUE FLUS FLUX FOUL FOUR FRUG

F••U FRAU FUGU

•FU• PFUI

••FU GIFU TOFU TUFU

F•V• FAVA FAVE FIVE

F••V FLAV

FW•• FWIW

F•W• FAWN FOWL

F••W FLAW FLEW FLOW FROW FWIW

F•X• FIXE FOXE FOXX FOXY

F••X FALX FAUX FLAX FLEX FLIX FLUX FOXX

•F•X SFAX

FY•• FYKE

F•Y• FAYE FAYS FOYS FOYT FRYE

F••Y FLAY FLEY FOGY FOXY FRAY FREY FUMY FURY

•F•Y IFFY

••FY DEFY DUFY IFFY

F•Z• FAZE FIZZ FUZE FUZZ

F••Z FITZ FIZZ FLOZ FONZ FRIZ FUTZ FUZZ

GA•• GABA GABE GABO GABS GABY GADS GAEA GAEL GAFF GAGA GAGE GAGS GAIA GAIL GAIN GAIT GALA GALE GALL GALS GALV GAMA GAME GAMO GAMP GAMS GAMY GANG GANN GAOL GAPA GAPE GAPS GARB GARE GARN GARP GARR GARS GARY GASH GASP GAST GATE GATH GATO GATS GATT GAUD GAUL GAUM GAUR GAVE GAWK GAWP GAYA GAYE GAZA GAZE

G•A• GDAY GEAR GHAT GIAN GLAD GLAM GMAC GMAN GMAT GNAR GNAT GNAW GOAD GOAL GOAT GRAB GRAD GRAF GRAM GRAN GRAS GRAU GRAY GRAZ GUAM GUAN GUAR

G••A GABA GAEA GAGA GAIA GALA GAMA GAPA GAYA GAZA GENA GERA GETA GHIA GIGA GILA GINA GITA GIZA GLIA GNMA GOYA

•GA• AGAR AGAS EGAD EGAL EGAN

•G•A AGFA AGHA AGRA AGUA

••GA ALGA GAGA GIGA INGA JUGA LPGA MEGA OLGA RAGA RIGA RUGA SAGA SEGA TOGA URGA USGA VEGA

VIGA YOGA YUGA

G•B• GABA GABE GABO GABS GABY GIBB GIBE GIBS GOBI GOBO GOBS GOBY GRBR GTBR GYBE

G••B GARB GIBB GLIB GLOB GRAB GRUB

•GB• IGBO

G•C• GUCK

G••C GLUC GLYC GMAC

•GC• AGCY

GD•• GDAY

G•D• GADS GIDE GODS

G••D GAUD GEED GILD GIRD GLAD GOAD GOLD GOND GOOD GRAD GRID

•G•D AGED EGAD

••GD BIGD REGD

GE•• GEAR GEED GEEK GEER GEES GEEZ GEIN GELL GELS GELT GEMS GENA GENE GENL GENS GENT GENU GENX GENY GEOG GEOL GEOM GERA GERE GERM GEST GETA GETS GETZ GEUM

G•E• GAEA GAEL GEED GEEK GEER GEES GEEZ GHEE GLEE GLEG GLEN GLEY GMEN GOER GOES GREE GREG GREW GREX GREY GWEN

G••E GABE GAGE GALE GAME GAPE GARE GATE GAVE GAYE GAZE GENE GERE GHEE GIBE GIDE GIVE GLEE GLUE GONE GORE GREE GYBE GYRE GYVE

•GE• AGED AGEE AGER AGES EGER OGEE

•G•E AGEE AGUE OGEE OGLE OGRE

••GE ANGE AUGE CAGE CTGE DOGE EDGE GAGE HUGE INGE LOGE LUGE MAGE MTGE PAGE RAGE SAGE STGE TIGE URGE WAGE

G•F• GAFF GIFT GIFU GUFF

G••F GAFF GOLF GOOF GRAF GUFF GULF

•GF• AGFA

•G•F TGIF

G•G• GAGA GAGE GAGS GIGA GIGI GIGO GIGS GOGH GOGI GOGO

G••G GANG GEOG GLEG GLUG GONG GREG GRIG GROG GUNG

•GG• EGGO EGGS EGGY IGGY OGGI

•G•G AGOG

••GG DOGG FOGG HOGG RAGG RIGG YEGG

GH•• GHAT GHEE GHIA

G••H GASH GATH GISH GOGH GOSH GOTH GUSH

•GH• AGHA UGHS

•G•H LGTH

••GH AFGH GOGH HIGH HUGH NIGH PUGH SIGH YOGH

GI•• GIAN GIBB GIBE GIBS GIDE GIFT GIFU GIGA GIGI GIGO GIGS GILA GILD GILL GILT GIMP GINA GINO GINS GIPS GIRD GIRL GIRN GIRO GIRT GISH GIST GITA GITS GIVE GIZA

G•I• GAIA GAIL GAIN GAIT GEIN GHIA GLIA GLIB GLIM GOIN GRID GRIG GRIM GRIN GRIP GRIS GRIT GUIN GUIS

G••I GIGI GOBI GOGI GYRI

•GI• AGIN AGIO EGIS TGIF

•G•I AGNI AGRI OGGI UGLI

••GI GIGI GOGI HAGI MAGI OGGI RIGI YAGI YOGI ZOGI

G••K GAWK GEEK GOWK GROK GUCK GUNK

GL•• GLAD GLAM GLEE GLEG GLEN GLEY GLIA GLIB GLIM GLOB GLOM GLOP GLOT GLOW GLUC GLUE GLUG GLUM GLUT GLYC GLYN

G•L• GALA GALE GALL GALS GALV GELL GELS GELT GILA GILD GILL GILT GOLD GOLF GULF GULL GULP

G••L GAEL GAIL GALL GAOL GAUL GELL GENL GEOL GILL GIRL GOAL GULL

•GL• AGLY IGLU OGLE UGLI UGLY

•G•L EGAL

••GL ANGL

GM•• GMAC GMAN GMAT GMEN

G•M• GAMA GAME GAMO GAMP GAMS GAMY GEMS GIMP GNMA GUMM GUMP GUMS GYMS

G••M GAUM GEOM GERM GEUM GLAM GLIM GLOM GLUM GRAM GRIM GUAM GUMM

•GM• MGMT

GN•• GNAR GNAT GNAW GNMA GNUS

G•N• GANG GANN GENA GENE GENL GENS GENT GENU GENX GENY GINA GINO GINS GOND GONE GONG GONY GUNG GUNK GUNN GUNS GYNT

G••N GAIN GANN GARN GEIN GIAN GIRN GLEN GLYN GMAN GMEN GOIN GOON GOWN GRAN GRIN GUAN GUIN GUNN GWEN GWYN

•GN• AGNI

•G•N AGIN AGON EGAN EGON

••GN SIGN

GO•• GOAD GOAL GOAT GOBI GOBO GOBS GOBY GODS GOER GOES GOGH GOGI GOGO GOIN GOLD GOLF GOND GONE GONG GONY GOOD GOOF GOON GOOP GOOS GORE GORP GORY GOSH GOTH GOUP GOUT GOVT GOWK GOWN GOYA

G•O• GAOL GEOG GEOL GEOM GLOB GLOM GLOP GLOT GLOW GOOD GOOF GOON GOOP GOOS GPOS GROG GROK GROS GROT GROW GTOS GYOR

G••O GABO GAMO GATO GIGO GINO GIRO GOBO GOGO GYRO

•GO• AGOG AGON EGON EGOS IGOR

•G•O AGIO AGRO EGGO IGBO

••GO ALGO ARGO EGGO ERGO GIGO GOGO HUGO IAGO LAGO LEGO LOGO NOGO PAGO POGO SAGO SEGO TOGO VIGO YUGO ZYGO

GP•• GPOS

G•P• GAPA GAPE GAPS GIPS GYPS

G••P GAMP GARP GASP GAWP GIMP GLOP GOOP GORP GOUP GRIP GULP GUMP

GR•• GRAB GRAD GRAF GRAM GRAN GRAS GRAU GRAY GRAZ GRBR GREE GREG GREW GREX GREY GRID GRIG GRIM GRIN GRIP GRIS GRIT GROG GROK GROS GROT GROW GRUB GRUS GRWT

G•R• GARB GARE GARN GARP GARR GARS GARY GERA GERE GERM GIRD GIRL GIRN GIRO GIRT GORE GORP GORY GURU GYRE GYRI GYRO

G••R GARR GAUR GEAR GEER GNAR GOER GRBR GTBR GUAR GYOR

•GR• AGRA AGRI AGRO MGRS OGRE

•G•R AGAR AGER EGER IGOR

••GR ENGR JAGR MNGR MSGR SPGR

G•S• GASH GASP GAST GEST GISH GIST GOSH GUSH GUST

G••S GABS GADS GAGS GALS GAMS GAPS GARS GATS GEES GELS GEMS GENS GETS GIBS GIGS GINS GIPS GITS GNUS GOBS GODS GOES GOOS GPOS GRAS GRIS GROS GRUS GTOS GUIS GUMS GUNS GUTS GUVS GUYS GYMS GYPS

•G•S AGAS AGES AGTS EGGS EGIS EGOS MGRS RGTS SGTS UGHS

••GS AVGS BAGS BEGS BOGS BUGS CHGS CIGS COGS DAGS DEGS DIGS DOGS EEGS EGGS ENGS ERGS FIGS FOGS FUGS GAGS GIGS HAGS HOGS HUGS JAGS JIGS JOGS JUGS KEGS LAGS LEGS LOGS LUGS MAGS MIGS MSGS MTGS MUGS NAGS NEGS NOGS ORGS PEGS PIGS PKGS POGS PUGS RAGS REGS RIGS RUGS SAGS SVGS TAGS TEGS TOGS TUGS VUGS WAGS WIGS ZAGS ZIGS

GT•• GTBR GTOS

G•T• GATE GATH GATO GATS GATT GETA GETS GETZ GITA GITS GOTH GUTS GWTW

G••T GAIT GAST GATT GELT GENT GEST GHAT GIFT GILT GIRT GIST GLOT GLUT GMAT GNAT GOAT GOUT GOVT GRIT GROT GRWT GUST GYNT

•GT• AGTS LGTH RGTS SGTS

•G•T MGMT

••GT MSGT REGT SSGT TSGT

GU•• GUAM GUAN GUAR GUCK GUFF GUIN GUIS GULF GULL GULP GUMM GUMP GUMS GUNG GUNK GUNN GUNS GURU GUSH GUST GUTS GUVS GUYS

G•U• GAUD GAUL GAUM GAUR GEUM GLUC GLUE GLUG GLUM GLUT GNUS GOUP GOUT GRUB GRUS

G••U GENU GIFU GRAU GURU

•GU• AGUA AGUE

•G•U IGLU

••GU FUGU RAGU

G•V• GAVE GIVE GOVT GUVS GYVE

G••V GALV

GW•• GWEN GWTW GWYN

G•W• GAWK GAWP GOWK GOWN GRWT

G••W GLOW GNAW GREW GROW GWTW

•GW• HGWY

G••X GENX GREX

GY•• GYBE GYMS GYNT GYOR GYPS GYRE GYRI GYRO GYVE

G•Y• GAYA GAYE GLYC GLYN GOYA GUYS GWYN

G••Y GABY GAMY GARY GDAY GENY GLEY GOBY GONY GORY GRAY GREY

•G•Y AGCY AGLY EGGY HGWY IGGY UGLY

••GY ALGY ARGY BOGY CAGY DOGY EDGY EGGY FOGY IGGY LOGY NAGY ORGY POGY

G•Z• GAZA GAZE GIZA

G••Z GEEZ GETZ GRAZ

HA•• HAAG HABE HACK HADE HADJ HAFT HAGI HAGS HAHA HAHN HAHS HAIG HAIK HAIL HAIM HAIR HAJI HAJJ HAKE HALE HALF HALL HALM HALO HALS HALT HAMA HAME HAMM HAMS HANA HAND HANG HANK HANS HAOS HAPI HAPS HARD HARE HARI HARK HARM HARP HART HARZ HASH HASP HAST HATE HATH HATS HAUL HAUS HAUT HAVE HAWG HAWK HAWN HAWS HAYS HAZE HAZY

H•A• HAAG HEAD HEAL HEAP HEAR HEAT HOAD HOAR HOAX HUAC

H••A HAHA HAMA HANA HEMA HERA HEXA HIJA HILA HOLA HORA HOYA HSIA HULA HUPA HYLA

•HA• AHAB AHAZ CHAD CHAM CHAN CHAP CHAR CHAS CHAT CHAW CHAZ DHAL GHAT KHAN KHAS KHAT PHAR PHAT SHAD SHAG SHAH SHAM SHAN SHAQ SHAW SHAY THAI THAN THAR THAS THAT THAW WHAM WHAT

•H•A CHIA GHIA RHEA SHEA THEA WHOA

••HA AGHA DOHA EPHA HAHA NAHA OSHA

H•B• HABE HDBK HEBE HEBR HOBO HOBS HUBS

H••B HERB

•HB• LHBS RHBS

•H•B AHAB CHUB SHEB

H•C• HACK HECK HECT HICK HOCH HOCK HUCK

H••C HUAC

•H•C CHIC CHOC

HD•• HDBK HDTV HDWE

H•D• HADE HADJ HEDY HIDE HODS HYDE HYDR

H••D HAND HARD HEAD HEED HELD HERD HIED HIND HOAD HOED HOLD HOND HOOD HUED HUND

•HD• PHDS

•H•D CHAD CHID OHED SHAD SHED SHOD THUD WHOD

••HD FAHD

HE•• HEAD HEAL HEAP HEAR HEAT HEBE HEBR HECK HECT HEDY HEED HEEL HEEP HEER HEET HEFT HEIN HEIR HELD HELI HELL HELM HELO HELP HEMA HEME HEMI HEMO HEMP HEMS HENS HENT HEPT HERA HERB HERD HERE HERL HERM HERN HERO HERR HERS HESS HEST HETH HEWN HEWS HEXA

H•E• HEED HEEL HEEP HEER HEET HIED HIER HIES HOED HOER HOES HRES HUED HUES

HUEY HYER

H••E
HABE HADE HAKE HALE HAME HARE HATE HAVE HAZE HDWE HEBE HEME HERE HIDE HIKE HIRE HITE HIVE HOKE HOLE HOME HONE HOPE HOSE HOTE HOVE HOWE HUGE HUME HYDE HYPE

•HE•
AHEM CHEE CHEF CHEM CHEN CHER CHET CHEW CHEX CHEZ GHEE OHED PHEW RHEA RHEE RHEO RHES RHET SHEA SHEB SHED SHEL SHEM SHEP SHES THEA THEE THEM THEN THEO THEW THEY WHEE WHEN WHET WHEW WHEY

•H•E
CHEE GHEE IHRE OHNE RHEE RHUE SHOE SHUE THEE WHEE WHSE

••HE
ACHE ASHE ROHE

H•F•
HAFT HEFT HIFI HOFF HUFF

H••F
HALF HOFF HOOF HUFF

•H•F
CHEF

HG••
HGWY

H•G•
HAGI HAGS HIGH HOGG HOGS HUGE HUGH HUGO HUGS

H••G
HAAG HAIG HANG HAWG HOGG HONG HUNG

•HG•
CHGS

•H•G
CHUG SHAG THUG WHIG

H•H•
HAHA HAHN HAHS HOHO

H••H
HASH HATH HETH HIGH HOCH HUGH HUSH

•H•H
OHOH SHAH SHIH UHOH UHUH

HI••
HICK HIDE HIED HIER HIES HIFI HIGH HIJA HIJO HIKE HILA HILL HILO HILT HIND HINS HINT HIPS HIRE HIRT HISS HIST HITE HITS HIVE HIYO

H•I•
HAIG HAIK HAIL HAIM HAIR HEIN HEIR HSIA HUIS

H••I
HAGI HAJI HAPI HARI HELI HEMI HIFI HONI HOPI

•HI•
CHIA CHIC CHID CHIN CHIP CHIS CHIT GHIA OHIO PHIL PHIS PHIZ SHIH SHIM SHIN SHIP SHIV THIN THIO THIS WHIG WHIM WHIN WHIP WHIR WHIT WHIZ

•H•I
THAI

••HI
ELHI MAHI NEHI

H•J•
HAJI HAJJ HIJA HIJO HOJO

H••J
HADJ HAJJ

H•K•
HAKE HIKE HOKE

H••K
HACK HAIK HANK HARK HAWK HDBK HECK HICK HOCK HONK HOOK HUCK HULK HUNK HUSK

H•L•
HALE HALF HALL HALM HALO HALS HALT HELD HELI HELL HELM HELO HELP HILA HILL HILO HILT HOLA HOLD HOLE HOLM HOLO HOLP HOLS HOLT HOLY HULA HULK HULL HYLA

H••L
HAIL HALL HAUL HEAL HEEL HELL HERL HILL HOWL HULL HURL

•H•L
CHOL DHAL PHIL SHEL SHUL

••HL
BUHL DAHL KOHL POHL SAHL WAHL WOHL WUHL

HM••
HMOS

H•M•
HAMA HAME HAMM HAMS HEMA HEME HEMI HEMO HEMP HEMS HOME HOMO HOMS HOMY HUME HUMP HUMS HYMN

H••M
HAIM HALM HAMM HARM HELM HERM HOLM

•HM•
CHMN OHMS OHMY

•H•M
AHEM CHAM CHEM CHUM RHUM SHAM SHEM SHIM THEM THOM WHAM WHIM WHOM

••HM
BOHM

H•N•
HANA HAND HANG HANK HANS HENS HENT HIND HINS HINT HOND HONE HONG HONI HONK HUND HUNG HUNK HUNS HUNT

H••N
HAHN HAWN HEIN HERN HEWN HORN HUON HYMN HYPN

•HN•
OHNE OHNO

•H•N
CHAN CHEN CHIN CHMN CHON KHAN PHON SHAN SHIN SHUN THAN THEN THIN WHEN WHIN

••HN
BAHN CAHN COHN FOHN HAHN JOHN KAHN KUHN SOHN ZAHN

HO••
HOAD HOAR HOAX HOBO HOBS HOCH HOCK HODS HOED HOER HOES HOFF HOGG HOGS HOHO HOJO HOKE HOLA HOLD HOLE HOLM HOLO HOLP HOLS HOLT HOLY HOME HOMO HOMS HOMY HOND HONE HONG HONI HONK HOOD HOOF HOOK HOOP HOOT HOPE HOPI HOPS HORA HORN HORS HORT HOSE HOSP HOSS HOST HOTE HOUR HOVE HOWE HOWL HOWS HOYA HOYS HOYT

H•O•
HAOS HMOS HOOD HOOF HOOK HOOP HOOT HUON

H••O
HALO HELO HEMO HERO HIJO HILO HIYO HOBO HOHO HOJO HOLO HOMO HUGO HYPO

•HO•
AHOY CHOC CHOL CHON CHOP CHOU CHOW CHOY DHOW IHOP MHOS OHOH PHON PHOT RHOS SHOD SHOE SHOO SHOP SHOT SHOW THOM THOR THOS THOU UHOH WHOA WHOD WHOM WHOP WHOS ZHOU

•H•O
AHSO OHIO OHNO RHEO SHOO THEO THIO

••HO
COHO ECHO HOHO IMHO MOHO OCHO OTHO PAHO SOHO TOHO YOHO

H•P•
HAPI HAPS HEPT HIPS HOPE HOPI HOPS HUPA HYPE HYPN HYPO

H••P
HARP HASP HEAP HEEP HELP HEMP HOLP HOOP HOSP HTTP HUMP

•HP•
SHPT

•H•P
CHAP CHIP CHOP IHOP SHEP SHIP SHOP WHIP WHOP WHUP

•H•Q
SHAQ

HR••
HRES

H•R•
HARD HARE HARI HARK HARM HARP HART HARZ HERA HERB HERD HERE HERL HERM HERN HERO HERR HERS HIRE HIRT HORA HORN HORS HORT HURL HURT

H••R
HAIR HEAR HEBR HEER HEIR HERR HIER HOAR HOER HOUR HYDR HYER

•HR•
IHRE THRU

•H•R
CHAR CHER CHUR PHAR THAR THOR THUR WHIR

••HR
BAHR BOHR BUHR FAHR JAHR KWHR LAHR LEHR RUHR SEHR TAHR TCHR

HS••
HSIA

H•S•
HASH HASP HAST HESS HEST HISS HIST HOSE HOSP HOSS HOST HUSH HUSK HUSS

H••S
HAGS HAHS HALS HAMS HANS HAOS HAPS HATS HAUS HAWS HAYS HEMS HENS HERS HESS HEWS HIES HINS HIPS HISS HITS HMOS HOBS HODS HOES HOGS HOLS HOMS HOPS HORS HOSS HOWS HOYS HRES HUBS HUES HUGS HUIS HUMS HUNS HUSS HUTS HWYS

•HS•
AHSO WHSE

•H•S
CHAS CHGS CHIS KHAS LHBS MHOS OHMS PHDS PHIS PHYS RHBS RHES RHOS RHYS SHES THAS THIS THOS THUS WHOS WHYS

••HS
AAHS BAHS DAHS EDHS ETHS HAHS MOHS OCHS OOHS PAHS PEHS UGHS

HT••
HTTP

H•T•
HATE HATH HATS HDTV HETH HITE HITS HOTE HTTP HUTS HUTT HUTU

H••T
HAFT HALT HART HAST HAUT HEAT HECT HEET HEFT HENT HEPT HEST HILT HINT HIRT HIST HOLT HOOT HORT HOST HOYT HUNT HURT HUTT

•H•T
CHAT CHET CHIT GHAT KHAT PHAT PHOT RHET SHOT SHPT SHUT THAT WHAT WHET WHIT

••HT
ACHT BAHT ECHT SPHT

HU••
HUAC HUBS HUCK HUED HUES HUEY HUFF HUGE HUGH HUGO HUGS HUIS HULA HULK HULL HUME HUMP HUMS HUND HUNG HUNK HUNS HUNT HUON HUPA HURL HURT HUSH HUSK HUSS HUTS HUTT HUTU

H•U•
HAUL HAUS HAUT HOUR

H••U
HUTU

•HU•
CHUB CHUG CHUM CHUR RHUE RHUM SHUE SHUL SHUN SHUT THUD THUG THUR THUS UHUH WHUP

•H•U
CHOU THOU THRU ZHOU

••HU
JEHU OAHU WUHU

H•V•
HAVE HIVE HOVE

H••V
HDTV

•H•V
SHIV

HW••
HWYS

H•W•
HAWG HAWK HAWN HAWS HDWE HEWN HEWS HGWY HOWE HOWL HOWS

•H•W
CHAW CHEW CHOW DHOW PHEW SHAW SHOW THAW THEW WHEW

H•X•
HEXA

H••X
HOAX

•H•X
CHEX

HY••
HYDE HYDR HYER HYLA HYMN HYPE HYPN HYPO

H•Y•
HAYS HIYO HOYA HOYS HOYT HWYS

H••Y
HAZY HEDY HGWY HOLY HOMY HUEY

•HY•
PHYS RHYS WHYS

•H•Y
AHOY CHOY OHMY SHAY THEY WHEY

••HY
ACHY ASHY

H•Z•
HAZE HAZY

H••Z
HARZ

•H•Z
AHAZ CHAZ CHEZ PHIZ WHIZ

IA••
IAGO IAMB IANA IASI

I•A•
IBAN IBAR ICAL IDAE IMAM IMAN IRAE IRAN IRAQ IRAS ISAK ISAO ISAR ISAY ITAL ITAR IVAN IYAR IZAR

I••A
IANA IDEA ILIA ILKA ILSA INCA INGA INKA IOLA IONA IOTA IOWA IRMA ISBA ISLA ITEA ITZA IXIA IZBA

•IA•
BIAK BIAO BIAS CIAO DIAG DIAL DIAM DIAN DIAS DIAZ FIAT GIAN JIAO LIAM LIAO LIAR LIAT PIAF PIAO RIAL RIAS SIAL SIAM TIAS VIAL XIAN

•I•A
AIDA AIEA AIWA BIWA DINA DIVA FICA FILA FINA GIGA GILA GINA GITA GIZA HIJA HILA JIMA KINA KIVA LILA LIMA LINA LIPA LIRA LISA LIZA MICA MINA MIRA MITA NINA NIPA NITA OITA PICA PIKA PIMA PINA PIPA PISA PITA RICA RIGA RIMA RITA SIKA SIMA TINA TIWA VIDA VIGA VILA VINA VISA VITA VIVA YIMA

••IA
ALIA AMIA APIA ARIA ASIA AVIA CHIA ELIA EMIA FRIA GAIA GHIA GLIA HSIA ILIA IXIA LEIA MAIA OPIA USIA

IB••
IBAN IBAR IBET IBEX IBID IBIS IBLE IBOS

I•B•
ICBM IGBO IRBM ISBA ISBN IZBA

I••B
IAMB

•IB•
BIBB BIBI BIBL BIBS DIBS FIBS GIBB GIBE GIBS JIBE JIBS LIBS MIBS NIBS RIBS SIBS VIBE ZIBO

•I•B
BIBB GIBB LIEB LIMB LITB

••IB
ABIB CRIB DBIB DRIB GLIB TRIB

IC••
ICAL ICBM ICED ICEL ICER ICES ICET ICKY ICON ICOS ICUS

I•C•
INCA INCE INCH INCL INCR ITCH

•IC•
BICE BICS DICE DICH DICK DICT FICA FICE FICT HICK KICK LICE LICK MICA MICE MICH MICK MICR MICS NICE NICK PICA PICK PICO PICS PICT RICA RICE RICH RICK RICO SICK SICS TICK TICO TICS VICE VICI VICO WICK

•I•C
CINC CIRC DISC FISC MISC WISC ZINC

••IC
AMIC BRIC CHIC EMIC EPIC ERIC ETIC FDIC FLIC LAIC ODIC OTIC ZOIC

ID••
IDAE IDEA IDEE IDEM IDEO IDES IDIO IDLE IDLY IDOL IDOS IDUN IDYL

I•D•
INDO INDS INDY IODO

I••D
IBID ICED IRED IRID IZOD

•ID•
AIDA AIDE

AIDS BIDE BIDS CIDE DIDO FIDE FIDO FIDS GIDE HIDE KIDD KIDS LIDO LIDS MIDI MIDN NIDE NIDI RIDD RIDE RIDI RIDS SIDE SIDH TIDE TIDY VIDA VIDE VIDI WIDE

•I•D

BIGD BIND BIRD DIED FIND GILD GIRD HIED HIND KIDD KIND LIED LIND LITD MILD MIND PIED RIDD RIND SILD SIND TIED VIED WILD WIND

••ID

ACID AMID ARID AVID CHID ENID GRID IBID IRID LAID LOID MAID OLID OOID OVID PAID QAID QUID RAID REID SAID SKID SLID VOID

IE••

IEOH

I•E•

IBET IBEX ICED ICEL ICER ICES ICET IDEA IDEE IDEM IDEO IDES ILES ILEX INEE INES INEZ IRED IRES ISEE ITEA ITEM ITER ITES IVES IVEY

I••E

IBLE IDAE IDEE IDLE IHRE ILIE ILLE IMRE INCE INEE INGE INRE IOLE IONE IPSE IRAE ISEE ISLE

•IE•

AIEA BIEL BIEN CIEL DIED DIEM DIEN DIES DIET DIEU FIEF HIED HIER HIES KIEL KIEV LIEB LIED LIEF LIEN LIES LIEU MIEN MIES PIED PIER PIES PIET RIEL RIEN TIED TIER TIES VIED VIER VIES VIET VIEW WIEN

•I•E

AIDE AIME AIRE BICE BIDE BIKE BILE BINE BISE BITE CIDE CINE CIRE CITE DICE DIKE DIME DINE DIRE DIVE EINE EIRE FICE FIDE FIFE FILE FINE FIRE FIVE FIXE GIBE GIDE GIVE HIDE HIKE HIRE HITE HIVE JIBE JIVE KINE KITE LICE LIFE LIKE LIME LINE LIRE LISE LITE LIVE MICE MIKE MILE MIME MINE MIRE MISE MITE NICE NIDE NIKE NILE NINE NITE NIUE OISE PIKE PILE PINE PIPE PIRE RICE RIDE RIFE RILE RIME RIPE RIRE RISE RITE RIVE SIDE SINE SIRE SITE SIZE TIDE TIGE TIKE TILE TIME TINE TIRE VIBE VICE VIDE VILE VINE VISE VITE VIVE WIDE WIFE WILE WINE WIPE WIRE WISE WITE XIPE YIPE ZINE

••IE

ABIE AMIE BRIE EDIE ELIE ERIE FOIE ILIE JOIE OBIE ODIE OKIE OPIE PLIE PRIE SOIE

IF••

IFFY IFNI IFSO

I•F•

IFFY INFL INFO INFS

I••F

IMPF IOOF

•IF•

BIFF DIFF FIFE FIFI FIFO GIFT GIFU HIFI JIFF LIFE LIFO LIFT MIFF RIFE RIFF RIFS RIFT SIFT TIFF WIFE

•I•F

BIFF DIFF FIEF JIFF LIEF MIFF PIAF RIFF TIFF

••IF

ALIF ASIF COIF LEIF NAIF TAIF TGIF WAIF

IG••

IGBO IGGY IGLU IGOR

I•G•

IAGO IGGY INGA INGE

•IG•

BIGD CIGS DIGS FIGS GIGA GIGI GIGO GIGS HIGH JIGS MIGS NIGH PIGS RIGA RIGG RIGI RIGS SIGH SIGN TIGE VIGA VIGO WIGS ZIGS

•I•G

BING BIOG DIAG DING KING LING MING PING RIGG RING SING TING VING WING XING ZING

••IG

BRIG GRIG HAIG ORIG PRIG SWIG TRIG TWIG WHIG

IH••

IHOP IHRE

I•H•

IMHO

I••H

IEOH INCH IPOH ISTH ITCH

•I•H

DICH DISH FISH GISH HIGH KISH KITH LITH MICH MINH NIGH PISH PITH RICH SIDH SIGH SIKH SINH TISH WISH WITH

••IH

SHIH

II••

IIII IIWI

I•I•

IBID IBIS IDIO IIII ILIA ILIE ILIO IMIT INIT IRID IRIS ISIS ITIS IWIS IXIA

I••I

IASI IFNI IIII IIWI IMPI INRI

•II•

CIII DIII IIII LIII MIII RIIS VIII XIII

•I•I

BIBI CIII DIII FIFI FIJI FINI GIGI HIFI IIII IIWI JIMI KIKI KIRI KIWI LIII LILI MIDI MIII MIMI MINI NIDI NISI PILI RIDI RIGI SIMI SISI TIKI TITI VICI VIDI VIII VINI VITI XIII ZITI

••II

ALII CCII CDII CIII CLII CMII CVII CXII DCII DIII DLII DVII DXII IIII LIII LVII LXII MCII MDII MIII MLII MMII MVII MXII QEII VEII VIII WWII XCII XIII XLII XVII XXII

•IJ•

FIJI HIJA HIJO RIJN

I•K•

ICKY ILKA ILKS INKA INKS INKY IRKS

I••K

ISAK

•IK•

BIKE BIKO DIKE HIKE KIKI LIKE MIKE NIKE OIKS PIKA PIKE SIKA SIKH TIKE TIKI

•I•K

BIAK BILK BIRK BISK DICK DINK DIRK DISK FINK FISK HICK JINK KICK KINK KIRK LICK LINK MICK MILK MINK NICK OINK PICK PINK RICK RINK RISK SICK SILK SINK TICK WICK WINK WISK

••IK

EFIK ERIK HAIK

IL••

ILES ILEX ILIA ILIE ILIO ILKA ILKS ILLE ILLS ILLY ILSA

I•L•

IBLE IDLE IDLY IGLU ILLE ILLS ILLY INLY IOLA IOLE ISLA ISLE ISLS ITLL

I••L

ICAL ICEL IDOL IDYL INCL INFL INTL ITAL ITLL ITOL

•IL•

AILS BILE BILK BILL DILL FILA FILE FILL FILM FILS GILA GILD GILL GILT HILA HILL HILO HILT JILL JILT KILL KILN KILO KILT LILA LILI LILT LILY MILD MILE MILK MILL MILO MILS MILT NILE NILS OILS OILY PILE PILI PILL RILE RILL SILD SILK SILL SILO SILT TILE TILL TILS TILT VILA VILE WILD WILE WILL WILT WILY ZILL

•I•L

BIBL BIEL BILL BIOL BIRL CIEL DIAL DILL DIPL FILL GILL GIRL HILL JILL KIEL KILL MILL PILL RIAL RIEL RILL SIAL SILL TILL VIAL VIOL WILL ZILL

••IL

ANIL ARIL AXIL BAIL BOIL CEIL COIL DEIL DOIL EMIL EVIL FAIL FOIL GAIL HAIL JAIL MAIL MOIL NAIL NEIL NOIL OEIL PAIL PHIL POIL RAIL ROIL SAIL SCIL SKIL SOIL TAIL TOIL UTIL VAIL VEIL WAIL WEIL

IM••

IMAM IMAN IMHO IMIT IMPF IMPI IMPS IMPV IMRE IMUS

I•M•

IAMB IRMA ISMS

I••M

ICBM IDEM IMAM IRBM ITEM

•IM•

AIME AIMS DIME DIMS GIMP JIMA JIMI JIMS LIMA LIMB LIME LIMN LIMO LIMP LIMY MIME MIMI MIMS PIMA RIMA RIME RIMS RIMY SIMA SIMI SIMP SIMS TIME VIMS WIMP YIMA

•I•M

DIAM DIEM FILM FIRM LIAM SIAM

••IM

AKIM ANIM BRIM CRIM FLIM GLIM GRIM HAIM PRIM SHIM SKIM SLIM SWIM TRIM URIM WHIM

IN••

INCA INCE INCH INCL INCR INDO INDS INDY INEE INES INEZ INFL INFO INFS INGA INGE INIT INKA INKS INKY INLY INNS INON INRE INRI INRO INSP INST INTL INTO INTR INTS INXS

I•N•

IANA IFNI INNS IONA IONE IONS ISNT

I••N

IBAN ICON IDUN IMAN INON IRAN IRON ISBN ISSN IVAN

•IN•

AINS AINT AINU BIND BINE BING BINS CINC CINE CINQ DINA DINE DING DINK DINO DINS DINT EINE EINS FINA FIND FINE FINI FINK FINN FINO FINS GINA GINO GINS HIND HINS HINT JINK JINN JINX KINA KIND KINE KING KINK KINO LINA LIND LINE LING LINK LINO LINT LINY LINZ MINA MIND MINE MING MINH MINI MINK MINN MINS MINT MINX NINA NINE NINO OINK PINA PINE PING PINK PINS PINT PINX PINY RIND RING RINK SIND SINE SING SINH SINK SINO SINS TINA TINE TING TINS TINT TINY VINA VINE VING VINI VINO VINS VINY WIND WINE WING WINK WINS WINY XING ZINC ZINE ZING

•I•N

BIEN BION CION DIAN DIEN DION FINN FIRN GIAN GIRN JINN KILN LIEN LIMN LION MIDN MIEN MINN PION RIEN RIJN SIGN SION TION WIEN XIAN ZION

••IN

ADIN AGIN AKIN AMIN AYIN BAIN BEIN BLIN CAIN CHIN CLIN COIN CRIN CUIN DAIN DOIN DRIN ERIN FAIN FEIN FOIN GAIN GEIN GOIN GRIN GUIN HEIN JAIN JOIN KAIN LAIN LOIN LYIN MAIN MEIN NEIN ODIN OLIN PAIN PNIN PRIN RAIN REIN RUIN SEIN SHIN SKIN SPIN SQIN TAIN THIN TWIN VAIN VEIN WAIN WHIN XDIN ZEIN

IO••

IODO IOLA IOLE IONA IONE IONS IOOF IOTA IOUS IOWA

I•O•

IBOS ICON ICOS IDOL IDOS IEOH IGOR IHOP INON IOOF IPOH IPOS IRON ITOL IVOR IZOD

I••O

IAGO IDEO IDIO IFSO IGBO ILIO IMHO INDO INFO INRO INTO IODO IPSO ISAO

•IO•

BIOG BIOL BION BIOS CION DION DIOR DIOS LION PION RIOS RIOT SION TION TIOS VIOL ZION

•I•O

BIAO BIKO CIAO DIDO DINO FIDO FIFO FINO GIGO GINO GIRO HIJO HILO HIYO JIAO KILO KINO LIAO LIDO LIFO LIMO LINO LIPO MILO MIRO MISO NINO PIAO PICO RICO SILO SINO TICO TIRO TITO VICO VIGO VINO VITO ZIBO

••IO

AGIO BAIO BRIO CLIO EZIO FRIO IDIO ILIO KRIO OHIO OLIO THIO TRIO

IP••

IPOH IPOS IPSE IPSO

I•P•

IMPF IMPI IMPS IMPV ISPY

I••P

IHOP INSP

•IP•

DIPL DIPS GIPS HIPS KIPS LIPA LIPO LIPS MIPS NIPA NIPS PIPA PIPE PIPS PIPY RIPE RIPS SIPS TIPS VIPS WIPE XIPE YIPE YIPS ZIPS

•I•P

GIMP LIMP LISP SIMP WIMP WISP

••IP

BLIP CHIP CLIP DRIP FLIP GRIP QTIP QUIP SHIP SKIP SLIP SNIP TRIP WHIP

I••Q

IRAQ

•I•Q

CINQ

••IQ

DRIQ ERIQ

IR••

IRAE IRAN IRAQ IRAS IRBM IRED IRES IRID IRIS IRKS IRMA IRON

I•R•

IHRE IMRE INRE INRI INRO

I••R

IBAR ICER IGOR INCR INTR ISAR ITAR ITER IVOR IYAR IZAR

•IR•
AIRE AIRS AIRT AIRY BIRD BIRK BIRL BIRR CIRC CIRE DIRE DIRK DIRS DIRT EIRE FIRE FIRM FIRN FIRS GIRD GIRL GIRN GIRO GIRT HIRE HIRT KIRI KIRK KIRS LIRA LIRE MIRA MIRE MIRO MIRS MIRV MIRY PIRE PIRS RIRE SIRE SIRS TIRE TIRO WIRE WIRY

•I•R
BIRR DIOR HIER LIAR MICR PIER TIER VIER

••IR
AMIR ASIR COIR EMIR FAIR HAIR HEIR LAIR MEIR MUIR NOIR PAIR SOIR STIR VAIR VOIR WEIR WHIR YMIR

IS••
ISAK ISAO ISAR ISAY ISBA ISBN ISEE ISIS ISLA ISLE ISLS ISMS ISNT ISPY ISSN ISTH ISTS

I•S•
IASI IFSO ILSA INSP INST IPSE IPSO ISSN ITSY

I••S
IBIS IBOS ICES ICOS ICUS IDES IDOS ILES ILKS ILLS IMPS IMUS INDS INES INFS INKS INNS INTS INXS IONS IOUS IPOS IRAS IRES IRIS IRKS ISIS ISLS ISMS ISTS ITES ITIS IVES IWIS

•IS•
BISE BISK CIST DISC DISH DISK DISS DIST FISC FISH FISK FIST GISH GIST HISS HIST KISH KISS LISA LISE LISP LIST MISC MISE MISO MISS MIST NISI OISE PISA PISH RISE RISK SISI TISH VISA VISE WISC WISE WISH WISK WISP

•I•S
AIDS AILS AIMS AINS AIRS AITS BIAS BIBS BICS BIDS BINS BIOS BITS CIGS CITS DIAS DIBS DIES DIGS DIMS DINS DIOS DIPS DIRS DISS DITS DIVS EINS FIBS FIDS FIGS FILS FINS FIRS FITS GIBS GIGS GINS GIPS GITS HIES HINS HIPS HISS HITS JIBS JIGS JIMS KIDS KIPS KIRS KISS KITS LIBS LIDS LIES LIPS LITS MIBS MICS MIES MIGS MILS MIMS MINS MIPS MIRS MISS NIBS NILS NIPS NITS OIKS OILS PICS PIES PIGS PINS PIPS PIRS PITS PIUS RIAS RIBS RIDS RIFS RIGS RIIS RIMS RIOS RIPS SIBS SICS SIMS SINS SIPS SIRS SITS TIAS TICS TIES TILS TINS TIOS TIPS TIVS VIES VIMS VINS VIPS WIGS WINS WITS YIPS ZIGS ZIPS

••IS
ACIS ALIS AMIS ANIS APIS ASIS AVIS AXIS BOIS CHIS DAIS EGIS ELIS EPIS ERIS FOIS FRIS GRIS GUIS HUIS IBIS IRIS ISIS ITIS IWIS KOIS KRIS LEIS LOIS LUIS MAIS OBIS OSIS OTIS OVIS PHIS POIS PSIS RBIS REIS RIIS SAIS SEIS SKIS THIS TRIS TUIS UNIS URIS UZIS

IT••
ITAL ITAR ITCH ITEA ITEM ITER ITES ITIS ITLL ITOL ITSY ITTY ITZA

I•T•
INTL INTO INTR INTS IOTA ISTH ISTS ITTY

I••T
IBET ICET IMIT INIT INST ISNT

•IT•
AITS BITE BITS BITT CITE CITS CITY DITS DITZ FITS FITZ GITA GITS HITE HITS KITE KITH KITS KITT LITB LITD LITE LITH LITS MITA MITE MITT NITA NITE NITS OITA PITA PITH PITS PITT PITY RITA RITE RITT RITZ SITE SITS SITU TITI TITO VITA VITE VITI VITO WITE WITH WITS WITT ZITI

•I•T
AINT AIRT BITT CIST DICT DIET DINT DIRT DIST FIAT FICT FIST GIFT GILT GIRT GIST HILT HINT HIRT HIST JILT KILT KITT LIAT LIFT LILT LINT LIST MILT MINT MIST MITT MIXT PICT PIET PINT PITT RIFT RIOT RITT SIFT SILT TILT TINT VIET WILT WITT

••IT
ADIT ALIT ATIT BAIT BLIT BRIT CHIT CRIT DLIT DOIT EDIT EMIT EXIT FAIT FLIT FRIT GAIT GRIT IMIT INIT KNIT LAIT NUIT OBIT OMIT QUIT REIT SKIT SLIT SMIT SNIT SPIT SUIT SWIT TAIT TWIT UNIT WAIT WHIT WRIT

I•U•
ICUS IDUN IMUS IOUS

I••U
IGLU

•IU•
NIUE PIUS

•I•U
AINU DIEU GIFU KIVU LIEU SITU

IV••
IVAN IVES IVEY IVOR

I••V
IMPV

•IV•
DIVA DIVE DIVS FIVE GIVE HIVE JIVE JIVY KIVA KIVU LIVE LIVY RIVE TIVS VIVA VIVE

•I•V
KIEV MIRV

••IV
AVIV CCIV CDIV CLIV CMIV CXIV DCIV DLIV DXIV LXIV MCIV MDIV MLIV MMIV MXIV PRIV SHIV SPIV UNIV XCIV XDIV XLIV XXIV

IW••
IWIS

I•W•
IIWI IOWA

•IW•
AIWA BIWA IIWI KIWI TIWA

•I•W
VIEW

••IW
FWIW

IX••
IXIA

I•X•
INXS

I••X
IBEX ILEX

•IX•
FIXE MIXT PIXY

•I•X
JINX MINX PINX

••IX
BRIX CCIX CDIX CLIX CMIX CXIX DCIX DLIX DXIX FLIX LXIX MCIX MDIX MLIX MMIX MXIX PAIX PRIX TRIX TWIX UNIX VOIX VSIX XCIX XLIX XXIX

IY••
IYAR

I•Y•
IDYL

I••Y
ICKY IDLY IFFY IGGY ILLY INDY INKY INLY ISAY ISPY ITSY ITTY IVEY IZZY

•IY•
HIYO

•I•Y
AIRY CITY JIVY LILY LIMY LINY LIVY MIRY OILY PINY PIPY PITY PIXY RIMY TIDY TINY VINY WILY WINY WIRY

IZ••
IZAR IZBA IZOD IZZY

I•Z•
ITZA IZZY

I••Z
INEZ

•IZ•
FIZZ GIZA LIZA PIZZ SIZE

•I•Z
DIAZ DITZ FITZ FIZZ LINZ PIZZ RITZ

••IZ
ARIZ AZIZ ELIZ FRIZ PHIZ QUIZ TAIZ WHIZ

JA••
JABS JACK JADA JADE JAEL JAEN JAGR JAGS JAHR JAIL JAIN JAKE JAMB JAMS JANE JAPE JARL JARS JATO JAVA JAWS JAYE JAYS JAZZ

J•A•
JBAR JEAN JIAO JOAB JOAD JOAN JUAN

J••A
JADA JAVA JENA JIMA JUBA JUGA JURA

•JA•
AJAR AJAX OJAI

••JA
BAJA DEJA HIJA MAJA RAJA

JB••
JBAR

J•B•
JABS JIBE JIBS JOBS JUBA

J••B
JAMB JOAB

J•C•
JACK JOCK

J••C
JUNC

J•D•
JADA JADE JEDI JODY JUDD JUDE JUDG JUDO JUDY

J••D
JOAD JUDD

••JD
NEJD

JE••
JEAN JEDI JEEP JEER JEEZ JEFE JEFF JEHU JELL JENA JENS JERK JESS JEST JESU JETE JETS JETT JEUX JEWS

J•E•
JAEL JAEN JEEP JEER JEEZ JOEL JOES JOEY

J••E
JADE JAKE JANE JAPE JAYE JEFE JETE JIBE JIVE JOIE JOKE JOSE JOVE JUDE JUKE JULE JUNE JURE JUTE

J•F•
JEFE JEFF JIFF

J••F
JEFF JIFF

J•G•
JAGR JAGS JIGS JOGS JUGA JUGS

J••G
JONG JUDG JUNG

••JG
LTJG

J•H•
JAHR JEHU JOHN

J••H
JOSH

JI••
JIAO JIBE JIBS JIFF JIGS JILL JILT JIMA JIMI JIMS JINK JINN JINX JIVE JIVY

J•I•
JAIL JAIN JOIE JOIN

J••I
JEDI JIMI JOLI JONI

•J•I
OJAI

••JI
FIJI FUJI HAJI KOJI

J•J•
JOJO JUJU

••JJ
HAJJ

J•K•
JAKE JOKE JOKY JUKE

J••K
JACK JERK JINK JOCK JUNK

J•L•
JELL JILL JILT JOLI JOLO JOLT JULE JULY

J••L
JAEL JAIL JARL JELL JILL JOEL JOWL

J•M•
JAMB JAMS JIMA JIMI JIMS JUMP

••JM
SEJM

J•N•
JANE JENA JENS JINK JINN JINX JONG JONI JUNC JUNE JUNG JUNK JUNO

J••N
JAEN JAIN JEAN JINN JOAN JOHN JOIN JOON JUAN

••JN
RIJN

JO••
JOAB JOAD JOAN JOBS JOCK JODY JOEL JOES JOEY JOGS JOHN JOIE JOIN JOJO JOKE JOKY JOLI JOLO JOLT JONG JONI JOON JOSE JOSH JOSS JOTS JOUR JOVE JOWL JOYS

J•O•
JOON

J••O
JATO JIAO JOJO JOLO JUDO JUNO

••JO
CUJO DOJO HIJO HOJO JOJO MOJO ROJO TOJO

J•P•
JAPE

J••P
JEEP JUMP

J•R•
JARL JARS JERK JURA JURE JURY

J••R
JAGR JAHR JBAR JEER JOUR

•J•R
AJAR

J•S•
JESS JEST JESU JOSE JOSH JOSS JUST

J••S
JABS JAGS JAMS JARS JAWS JAYS JENS JESS JETS JEWS JIBS JIGS JIMS JOBS JOES JOGS JOSS JOTS JOYS JUGS JUTS

••JS
ADJS TAJS

J•T•
JATO JETE JETS JETT JOTS JUTE JUTS

J••T
JEST JETT JILT JOLT JUST

••JT
ADJT

JU••
JUAN JUBA JUDD JUDE JUDG JUDO JUDY JUGA JUGS JUJU JUKE JULE JULY JUMP JUNC JUNE JUNG JUNK JUNO JURA JURE JURY JUST JUTE JUTS

J•U•
JEUX JOUR

J••U
JEHU JESU JUJU

••JU
JUJU

J•V•
JAVA JIVE JIVY JOVE

J•W•
JAWS JEWS JOWL

J••X
JEUX JINX

•J•X
AJAX

J•Y•
JAYE JAYS JOYS

J••Y
JIVY JODY JOEY JOKY JUDY JULY JURY

J•Z•
JAZZ

J••Z
JAZZ JEEZ

KA••
KABS KAEL KAFS KAHN KAIN KAKA KAKI KALB KALE KALI KALT KAMA KAME KAMI KANA KANE KANO KANS KANT KAON KAPH KARA KARL KARO KART KATE KATO KATY KATZ KAVA KAYE KAYO

K•A•
KCAL KEAN KEAS KHAN KHAS KHAT KNAP KNAR KOAN KWAI KWAN KYAT

K••A
KAKA KAMA KANA KARA KAVA KDKA KINA KIVA KOLA KONA KYRA

•KA•
AKAN OKAY SKAT SKAW

•K•A
MKSA OKLA OKRA SKUA

••KA
ALKA ANKA ATKA DEKA ILKA INKA KAKA KDKA PIKA PUKA SIKA TAKA WAKA WEKA

K•B•
KABS KOBE KOBO KOBS

K••B
KALB KERB KNOB

KC••
KCAL

K•C•
KICK KOCH

K••C
KOFC KROC

•KC•
EKCO

KD••
KDKA

K•D•
KEDS KIDD KIDS KUDU

K••D
KIDD KIND KNUD

KURD

•K•D
EKED
NKVD
OKED
SKED
SKID

KE••
KEAN
KEAS
KEDS
KEEL
KEEN
KEEP
KEET
KEGS
KELP
KEMO
KEMP
KENO
KENS
KENT
KEOS
KEPI
KEPT
KERB
KERF
KERN
KERR
KERT
KETO
KETT
KEYS

K•E•
KAEL
KEEL
KEEN
KEEP
KEET
KIEL
KIEV
KLEE
KNEE
KNEW
KTEL
KYES

K••E
KALE
KAME
KANE
KATE
KAYE
KINE
KITE
KLEE
KNEE
KOBE
KORE
KYLE

•KE•
AKEE
EKED
EKES
OKED
OKEY
SKED
SKEE
SKEG
SKEP
SKEW
UKES

•K•E
AKEE
OKIE
SKEE
SKYE

••KE
BAKE
BIKE
CAKE
COKE
CUKE
DEKE
DIKE
DUKE
ELKE
FAKE
FYKE
HAKE
HIKE
HOKE
JAKE
JOKE
JUKE
LAKE
LIKE
LUKE
MAKE
MIKE
NIKE
NUKE
PEKE
PIKE
POKE
RAKE
SAKE
SOKE
TAKE
TIKE
TOKE
TYKE
WAKE
WOKE
YOKE
ZEKE

K•F•
KAFS
KOFC
KOFI
KOFP

K••F
KERF
KOPF

K•G•
KEGS

K••G
KING
KONG
KUNG

•KG•
PKGS

•K•G
BKPG
MKTG
SKEG

KH••
KHAN
KHAS
KHAT

K•H•
KAHN
KOHL
KUHN
KWHR

K••H
KAPH
KISH
KITH
KOCH
KOPH
KUSH

••KH
ANKH
LAKH
SIKH

KI••
KICK
KIDD
KIDS
KIEL
KIEV
KIKI
KILL
KILN
KILO
KILT
KINA
KIND
KINE
KING
KINK
KINO
KIPS
KIRI
KIRK
KIRS
KISH
KISS
KITE
KITH
KITS
KITT
KIVA
KIVU
KIWI

K•I•
KAIN
KNIT
KOIS
KRIO
KRIS

K••I
KAKI
KALI
KAMI
KEPI
KIKI
KIRI
KIWI
KOFI
KOJI
KOMI
KWAI

•KI•
AKIM
AKIN
OKIE
SKID
SKIL
SKIM
SKIN
SKIP
SKIS
SKIT

••KI
AOKI
KAKI
KIKI
LOKI
RAKI
SAKI
TIKI

K•J•
KOJI

K•K•
KAKA
KAKI
KDKA
KIKI
KOKO

K••K
KICK
KINK
KIRK
KOOK
KRUK

KL••
KLEE

K•L•
KALB
KALE
KALI
KALT
KELP
KILL
KILN
KILO
KILT
KOLA
KOLN
KOLO
KYLE

K••L
KAEL
KARL
KCAL
KEEL
KIEL
KILL
KOHL
KOOL
KTEL

•KL•
OKLA
WKLY

•K•L
SKIL
SKOL

K•M•
KAMA
KAME
KAMI
KEMO
KEMP
KOMI

•K•M
AKIM
SKIM

KN••
KNAP
KNAR
KNEE
KNEW
KNIT
KNOB
KNOP
KNOT
KNOW
KNOX
KNUD
KNUR
KNUT

K•N•
KANA
KANE
KANO
KANS
KANT
KENO
KENS
KENT
KINA
KIND
KINE
KING
KINK
KINO
KONA
KONG
KUNG

K••N
KAHN
KAIN
KAON
KEAN
KEEN
KERN
KHAN
KILN
KOAN
KOLN
KUHN
KWAN
KWON

•KN•
DKNY

•K•N
AKAN
AKIN
SKIN

KO••
KOAN
KOBE
KOBO
KOBS
KOCH
KOFC
KOFI
KOFP
KOHL
KOIS
KOJI
KOKO
KOLA
KOLN
KOLO
KOMI
KONA
KONG
KOOK
KOOL
KOOP
KOPF
KOPH
KOPS
KORE
KOTO

K•O•
KAON
KEOS
KNOB
KNOP
KNOT
KNOW
KNOX
KOOK
KOOL
KOOP
KROC
KWON

K••O
KANO
KARO
KATO
KAYO
KEMO
KENO
KETO
KILO
KINO
KOBO
KOKO
KOLO
KOTO
KRIO

•KO•
SKOL
TKOS

•K•O
EKCO

••KO
BIKO
ELKO
KOKO
MAKO
YOKO

K•P•
KAPH
KEPI
KEPT
KIPS
KOPF
KOPH
KOPS

K••P
KEEP
KELP
KEMP
KNAP
KNOP
KOFP
KOOP

•KP•
BKPG
BKPR

•K•P
SKEP
SKIP
WKRP

KR••
KRIO
KRIS
KROC
KRUK

K•R•
KARA
KARL
KARO
KART
KERB
KERF
KERN
KERR
KERT
KIRI
KIRK
KIRS
KORE
KURD
KURT
KYRA

K••R
KERR
KNAR
KNUR
KWHR

•KR•
OKRA
WKRP

•K•R
BKPR

••KR
BAKR

K•S•
KISH
KISS
KUSH

K••S
KABS
KAFS
KANS
KEAS
KEDS
KEGS
KENS
KEOS
KEYS
KHAS
KIDS
KIPS
KIRS
KISS
KITS
KOBS
KOIS
KOPS
KRIS
KYES

•KS•
MKSA

•K•S
EKES
PKGS
SKIS
SKUS
SKYS
TKOS
TKTS
UKES

••KS
ARKS
ASKS
AUKS
EEKS
ELKS
ERKS
ILKS
INKS
IRKS
LEKS
LUKS
OAKS
OIKS
SAKS
SUKS
TPKS
TSKS
WOKS
YAKS
YUKS

KT••
KTEL

K•T•
KATE
KATO
KATY
KATZ
KETO
KETT
KITE
KITH
KITS
KITT
KOTO

K••T
KALT
KANT
KART
KEET
KENT
KEPT
KERT
KETT
KHAT
KILT
KITT
KNIT
KNOT
KNUT
KURT
KYAT

•KT•
MKTG
TKTS

•K•T
SKAT
SKIT

KU••
KUDU
KUHN
KUNG
KURD
KURT
KUSH

•KU•
SKUA
SKUS

K•U•
KNUD
KNUR
KNUT
KRUK

K••U
KIVU
KUDU

••KU
BAKU
PUKU
RAKU

K•V•
KAVA
KIVA
KIVU

K••V
KIEV

•KV•
NKVD

KW••
KWAI
KWAN
KWHR
KWON

K•W•
KIWI

K••W
KNEW
KNOW

•KW•
PKWY

•K•W
SKAW
SKEW

K••X
KNOX

KY••
KYAT
KYES
KYLE
KYRA

K•Y•
KAYE
KAYO
KEYS

K••Y
KATY

•KY•
SKYE
SKYS

•K•Y
DKNY
OKAY
OKEY
PKWY
WKLY

••KY
CAKY
COKY
ICKY
INKY
JOKY
LAKY
POKY

K••Z
KATZ

LA••
LABS
LACE
LACK
LACS
LACT
LACY
LADD
LADE
LADS
LADY
LAGO
LAGS
LAHR
LAIC
LAID
LAIN
LAIR
LAIT
LAKE
LAKH
LAKY
LALA
LALO
LAMA
LAMB
LAME
LAMP
LAMS
LAMY
LANA
LAND
LANE
LANG
LANK
LAOS
LAPD
LAPP
LAPS
LARA
LARD
LARI
LARK
LARS
LASE
LASH
LASS
LAST
LATE
LATH
LATS
LAUD
LAUE
LAVA
LAVE
LAVS
LAWN
LAWS
LAYS
LAZE
LAZY

L•A•
LBAR
LEAD
LEAF
LEAH
LEAK
LEAL
LEAN
LEAP
LEAR
LEAS
LIAM
LIAO
LIAR
LIAT
LOAD
LOAF
LOAM
LOAN
LSAT
LUAU

L••A
LALA
LAMA
LANA
LARA
LAVA
LEDA
LEIA
LEMA
LENA
LILA
LIMA
LINA
LIPA
LIRA
LISA
LIZA
LOLA
LOMA
LOTA
LPGA
LUBA
LUNA
LYRA

•LA•
ALAE
ALAI
ALAN
ALAR
ALAS
BLAB
BLAE
BLAH
BLAS
BLAT
BLAU
CLAD
CLAM
CLAN
CLAP
CLAR
CLAW
CLAY
ELAL
ELAM
ELAN
FLAB
FLAG
FLAK
FLAM
FLAN
FLAP
FLAT
FLAV
FLAW
FLAX
FLAY
GLAD
GLAM
NLAT
OLAF
OLAN
OLAV
OLAY
PLAN
PLAT
PLAX
PLAY
SLAB
SLAG
SLAM
SLAP
SLAT
SLAV
SLAW
SLAY
ULAN

•L•A
ALBA
ALDA
ALEA
ALFA
ALGA
ALIA
ALKA
ALLA
ALMA
ALTA
ALVA
ELBA
ELEA
ELIA
ELLA
ELSA
FLEA
GLIA
ILIA
ILKA
ILSA
OLGA
OLLA
PLEA
ULNA

••LA
ALLA
AULA
AYLA
BELA
BOLA
CELA
COLA
EBLA
ELLA
FALA
FILA
FULA
GALA
GILA
HILA
HOLA
HULA
HYLA
IOLA
ISLA
KOLA
LALA
LILA
LOLA
MALA
MOLA
NOLA
OKLA
OLLA
POLA
PULA
SALA
SELA
SOLA
TALA
TOLA
TULA
UCLA
VELA
VILA
ZOLA

LB••
LBAR
LBOS

L•B•
LABS
LHBS
LIBS
LLBS
LOBE
LOBO
LOBS
LUBA
LUBE

L••B
LAMB
LIEB
LIMB
LITB
LOEB

•LB•
ALBA
ALBI
ALBS
ELBA
ELBE
LLBS
SLBM

•L•B
BLAB
BLEB
BLOB
CLUB
FLAB
FLUB
GLIB
GLOB
NLRB
PLEB
SLAB
SLOB
SLUB

••LB
BULB
FTLB
KALB

LC••
LCDS

L•C•
LACE
LACK
LACS
LACT
LACY
LDCS
LECH
LECT
LICE
LICK
LOCH
LOCI
LOCK
LOCO
LUCE
LUCI
LUCK
LUCY

L••C
LAIC

•LC•
MLCC
PLCS

•L•C
ALEC
BLOC
ELEC
FLIC
FLOC
GLUC
GLYC
MLCC

••LC
CALC
SCLC
TALC

LD••
LDCS
LDRS

L•D•
LADD
LADE
LADS
LADY
LCDS
LEDA
LEDS
LIDO
LIDS
LLDS
LODE
LODI
LODZ
LTDS

L••D
LADD
LAID
LAND
LAPD
LARD
LAUD
LEAD
LEND
LEWD
LIED
LIND
LITD
LOAD
LOID
LORD
LOUD

•LD•
ALDA
ALDO
BLDG
BLDR
FLDR
LLDS
OLDE
OLDS

•L•D
BLED
BLVD
CLAD
CLOD
FLED
GLAD
OLID
PLED
PLOD
SLED
SLID

••LD
AULD
BALD
BOLD
COLD
FOLD
GILD
GOLD
HELD
HOLD
MELD
MILD
MOLD
NFLD
SILD
SOLD
TOLD
VELD
WALD
WELD
WILD
WOLD

LE••
LEAD
LEAF
LEAH
LEAK
LEAL
LEAN
LEAP
LEAR
LEAS
LECH
LECT
LEDA
LEDS
LEEK
LEER
LEES
LEET
LEFT
LEGO
LEGS
LEHR
LEIA
LEIF
LEIS
LEKS
LELY
LEMA
LEMS
LENA
LEND
LENI
LENO
LENS
LENT
LENZ
LEOI
LEON
LEOS
LESE
LESS
LEST
LETO
LETS
LETT
LEUK
LEVI
LEVO
LEVU
LEVY
LEWD

L•E•
LEEK
LEER
LEES
LEET
LIEB
LIED
LIEF
LIEN
LIES
LIEU
LOEB
LOEW
LYES

L••E
LACE
LADE
LAKE
LAME
LANE
LASE
LATE
LAUE
LAVE
LAZE
LESE
LICE
LIFE
LIKE
LIME
LINE
LIRE
LISE
LITE
LIVE
LOBE
LODE
LOGE
LOME
LONE
LOPE
LORE
LOSE
LOVE
LOWE
LUBE
LUCE
LUGE
LUKE
LUNE
LUPE
LURE
LUTE
LUXE
LYLE
LYNE
LYRE

•LE•
ALEA
ALEC
ALEE
ALEF
ALEP
ALES
ALEX
BLEB
BLED
BLEU
BLEW
CLEF
CLEM
CLEO
CLEW
ELEA
ELEC
ELEM
ELEV
FLEA
FLED
FLEE
FLEM
FLEW
FLEX
FLEY
GLEE
GLEG
GLEN
GLEY
ILES
ILEX
KLEE
NLER
OLEG
OLEN
OLEO
OLES
PLEA
PLEB
PLED
PLEO
PLEW
PLEX
SLED
SLEW
ULEE
YLEM

•L•E
ALAE
ALEE
ALLE
ALOE
ALTE
BLAE
BLUE
CLUE
ELBE
ELIE
ELKE
ELLE
ELSE
FLEE
FLOE
FLUE
GLEE
GLUE
ILIE
ILLE
KLEE
MLLE
OLDE
PLIE
SLOE
SLUE
SLYE
ULEE

••LE
ABLE
ALLE
AXLE
BALE
BILE
BOLE
CALE
COLE
CULE
DALE
DELE
DOLE
ELLE
ERLE
FILE
GALE
HALE
HOLE
IBLE
IDLE
ILLE
IOLE
ISLE
JULE
KALE
KYLE
LYLE
MALE
MILE
MLLE
MOLE
MULE
NILE
OGLE
ORLE
PALE
PELE
PILE
POLE
PULE
PYLE
RILE
ROLE
RULE
RYLE
SALE
SOLE
TALE
TELE
TILE
TOLE
TULE
UELE
VALE
VILE
VOLE
WALE
WILE
WOLE
YALE
YULE

L•F•
LEFT
LIFE
LIFO
LIFT
LOFT
LUFF
LUFT

L••F
LEAF
LEIF
LIEF
LOAF
LUFF

•LF•
ALFA

•L•F
ALEF
ALIF
CLEF
OLAF

••LF
CALF
DOLF
GOLF
GULF
HALF
PELF
ROLF
SELF
SULF

WOLF

LG••
LGTH

L•G•
LAGO
LAGS
LEGO
LEGS
LOGE
LOGO
LOGS
LOGY
LPGA
LUGE
LUGS

L••G
LANG
LING
LONG
LTJG
LUNG

•LG•
ALGA
ALGO
ALGY
OLGA

•L•G
BLDG
CLOG
FLAG
FLOG
GLEG
GLUG
OLEG
PLUG
SLAG
SLOG
SLUG

••LG
BELG
BULG
VULG

LH••
LHBS

L•H•
LAHR
LEHR

L••H
LAKH
LASH
LATH
LEAH
LECH
LGTH
LITH
LOCH
LUSH
LUTH

•LH•
ELHI

•L•H
ALPH
BLAH

LI••
LIAM
LIAO
LIAR
LIAT
LIBS
LICE
LICK
LIDO
LIDS
LIEB
LIED
LIEF
LIEN
LIES
LIEU
LIFE
LIFO
LIFT
LIII
LIKE
LILA
LILI
LILT
LILY
LIMA
LIMB
LIME
LIMN
LIMO
LIMP
LIMY
LINA
LIND
LINE
LING
LINK
LINO
LINT
LINY
LINZ
LION
LIPA
LIPO
LIPS
LIRA
LIRE
LISA
LISE
LISP
LIST
LITB
LITD
LITE
LITH
LITS
LIVE
LIVY
LIZA

L•I•
LAIC
LAID
LAIN
LAIR
LAIT
LEIA
LEIF
LEIS
LIII
LOID
LOIN
LOIS
LUIS

LVII
LXII
LXIV
LXIX
LYIN

L••I
LARI
LENI
LEOI
LEVI
LIII
LILI
LOCI
LODI
LOKI
LONI
LORI
LOTI
LUCI
LVII
LXII
LXVI
LXXI

•LI•
ALIA
ALIF
ALII
ALIS
ALIT
BLIN
BLIP
BLIT
CLII
CLIN
CLIO
CLIP
CLIV
CLIX
DLII
DLIT
DLIV
DLIX
ELIA
ELIE
ELIS
ELIZ
FLIC
FLIM
FLIP
FLIT
FLIX
GLIA
GLIB
GLIM
ILIA
ILIE
ILIO
MLII
MLIV
MLIX
OLID
OLIN
OLIO
PLIE
SLID
SLIM
SLIP
SLIT
XLII
XLIV
XLIX

•L•I
ALAI
ALBI
ALII
ALTI
ALUI
CLII
CLVI
CLXI
DLII
DLVI
DLXI
ELHI
ELOI
MLII
MLVI
MLXI
XLII
XLVI

••LI
ATLI
BALI
CALI
CCLI
CDLI
CMLI
CXLI
DALI
DCLI
DELI
DXLI
HELI
JOLI
KALI
LILI
MALI
MCLI
MDLI
MMLI
MXLI
NOLI
PALI
PILI
PULI
SOLI
TALI
UGLI

L•J•
LTJG

L•K•
LAKE
LAKH
LAKY
LEKS
LIKE
LOKI
LUKE
LUKS

L••K
LACK
LANK
LARK
LEAK
LEEK
LEUK
LICK
LINK
LOCK
LOOK
LUCK
LURK

•LK•
ALKA
ELKE
ELKO
ELKS
ILKA
ILKS

•L•K
FLAK

••LK
BALK
BILK
BULK
CALK
FALK
FOLK
HULK
MILK
POLK
SALK
SILK
SULK
TALK
WALK
WELK
YOLK

LL••
LLBS
LLDS
LLMS

L•L•
LALA
LALO
LELY
LILA
LILI
LILT
LILY
LOLA
LOLL
LULL
LULU
LYLE
LYLY

L••L
LEAL
LOLL
LULL

•LL•
ALLA
ALLE
ALLO
ALLS
ALLY
ELLA
ELLE
ELLS
ELLY
ILLE
ILLS
ILLY
MLLE
OLLA

•L•L
ELAL
ELUL

••LL
BALL
BELL
BILL
BOLL
BULL
CALL
CELL
COLL
CULL
DELL
DILL
DOLL
DULL
FALL
FELL
FILL
FULL
GALL
GELL
GILL
GULL
HALL
HELL
HILL
HULL
ITLL
JELL
JILL
KILL
LOLL
LULL
MALL
MELL
MILL
MOLL
MULL
NELL
NOLL
NULL
PALL
PELL
PILL
POLL
PULL
RALL
RILL
ROLL
SELL
SILL
SYLL
TALL
TELL
TILL
TOLL
TULL
WALL
WELL
WILL
YALL
YELL
ZILL

L•M•
LAMA
LAMB
LAME
LAMP
LAMS
LAMY
LEMA
LEMS
LIMA
LIMB
LIME
LIMN
LIMO
LIMP
LIMY
LLMS
LOMA
LOME
LUMP

L••M
LIAM
LOAM
LOOM

•LM•
ALMA
ALMS
ELMO
ELMS
LLMS

•L•M
ALUM
BLUM
CLAM
CLEM
ELAM
ELEM
FLAM
FLEM
FLIM
GLAM
GLIM
GLOM
GLUM
PLUM
SLAM
SLBM
SLIM
SLUM
YLEM

••LM
BALM
CALM
CULM
FILM
HALM
HELM
HOLM
MALM
PALM

L•N•
LANA
LAND
LANE
LANG
LANK
LENA
LEND
LENI
LENO
LENS
LENT
LENZ
LINA
LIND
LINE
LING
LINK
LINO
LINT
LINY
LINZ
LONE
LONG
LONI
LUNA
LUNE
LUNG
LUNN
LUNT
LYNE
LYNN
LYNX

L••N
LAIN
LAWN
LEAN
LEON
LIEN
LIMN
LION
LOAN
LOIN
LOON
LORN
LRON
LUNN
LYIN
LYNN
LYON

•LN•
ULNA

•L•N
ALAN
BLIN
CLAN
CLIN
ELAN
ELON
FLAN
GLEN
GLYN
OLAN
OLEN
OLIN
PLAN
ULAN

••LN
KILN
KOLN
SOLN

LO••
LOAD
LOAF
LOAM
LOAN
LOBE
LOBO
LOBS
LOCH
LOCI
LOCK
LOCO
LODE
LODI
LODZ
LOEB
LOEW
LOFT
LOGE
LOGO
LOGS
LOGY
LOID
LOIN
LOIS
LOKI
LOLA
LOLL
LOMA
LOME
LONE
LONG
LONI
LOOK
LOOM
LOON
LOOP
LOOS
LOOT
LOPE
LOPS
LORD
LORE
LORI
LORN
LORY
LOSE
LOSS
LOST
LOTA
LOTI
LOTS
LOTT
LOUD
LOUP
LOUT
LOVE
LOWE
LOWS

L•O•
LAOS
LBOS
LEOI
LEON
LEOS
LION
LOOK
LOOM
LOON
LOOP
LOOS
LOOT
LRON
LVOV
LYON

L••O
LAGO
LALO
LEGO
LENO
LETO
LEVO
LIAO
LIDO
LIFO
LIMO
LINO
LIPO
LOBO
LOCO
LOGO

•LO•
ALOE
ALOU
ALOW
BLOB
BLOC
BLOT
BLOW
CLOD
CLOG
CLOP
CLOT
CLOY
ELOI
ELON
FLOC
FLOE
FLOG
FLOP
FLOR
FLOW
FLOZ
GLOB
GLOM
GLOP
GLOT
GLOW
PLOD
PLOP
PLOT
PLOW
PLOY
SLOB
SLOE
SLOG
SLOP
SLOT
SLOW

•L•O
ALDO
ALGO
ALLO
ALPO
ALSO
ALTO
CLEO
CLIO
ELKO
ELMO
ILIO
OLEO
OLIO
PLEO

••LO
ALLO
ARLO
BELO
BOLO
COLO
HALO
HELO
HILO
HOLO
JOLO
KILO
KOLO
LALO
MALO
MILO
NOLO
OSLO
PALO
POLO
SILO
SOLO
STLO
TELO
XYLO

LP••
LPGA

L•P•
LAPD
LAPP
LAPS
LIPA
LIPO
LIPS
LOPE
LOPS
LUPE

L••P
LAMP
LAPP
LEAP
LIMP
LISP
LOOP
LOUP
LUMP

•LP•
ALPH
ALPO
ALPS

•L•P
ALEP
BLIP
CLAP
CLIP
CLOP
FLAP
FLIP
FLOP
GLOP
PLOP
SLAP
SLIP
SLOP

••LP
CULP
GULP
HELP
HOLP
KELP
PALP
PULP
SALP
YELP

LR••
LRON

L•R•
LARA
LARD
LARI
LARK
LARS
LDRS
LIRA
LIRE
LORD
LORE
LORI
LORN
LORY
LURE
LURK
LYRA
LYRE

L••R
LAHR
LAIR
LBAR
LEAR
LEER
LEHR
LIAR
LTYR

•LR•
NLRB
SLRS

•L•R
ALAR
BLDR
BLUR
CLAR
FLDR
FLOR
NLER
PLUR
SLUR

LS••
LSAT
LSTS

L•S•
LASE
LASH
LASS
LAST
LESE
LESS
LEST
LISA
LISE
LISP
LIST
LOSE
LOSS
LOST
LUSH
LUST

L••S
LABS
LACS
LADS
LAGS
LAMS
LAOS
LAPS
LARS
LASS
LATS
LAVS
LAWS
LAYS
LBOS
LCDS
LDCS
LDRS
LEAS
LEDS
LEES
LEGS
LEIS
LEKS
LEMS
LENS
LEOS
LESS
LETS
LHBS
LIBS
LIDS
LIES
LIPS
LITS
LLBS
LLDS
LLMS
LOBS
LOGS
LOIS
LOOS
LOPS
LOSS
LOTS
LOWS
LSTS
LTDS
LUGS
LUIS
LUKS
LUVS
LYES

•LS•
ALSO
ELSA
ELSE
ILSA

•L•S
ALAS
ALBS
ALES
ALIS
ALLS
ALMS
ALPS
ALTS
BLAS
BLTS
ELIS
ELKS
ELLS
ELMS
FLUS
ILES
ILKS
ILLS
LLBS
LLDS
LLMS
OLDS
OLES
PLCS
PLUS
SLRS
ULUS

••LS
AILS
ALLS
AWLS
BBLS
BELS
CALS
CELS
COLS
CPLS
CULS
DALS
DELS
EELS
ELLS
FILS
GALS
GELS
HALS
HOLS
ILLS
ISLS
MILS
NILS
OILS
OWLS
PALS
POLS
RELS
SALS
SOLS
SYLS
TILS
URLS
VOLS
ZALS

LT••
LTDS
LTJG
LTYR

L•T•
LATE
LATH
LATS
LETO
LETS
LETT
LGTH
LITB
LITD
LITE
LITH
LITS
LOTA
LOTI
LOTS
LOTT
LSTS
LUTE
LUTH
LUTZ

L••T
LACT
LAIT
LAST
LECT
LEET
LEFT
LENT
LEST
LETT
LIAT
LIFT
LILT
LINT
LIST
LOFT
LOOT
LOST
LOTT
LOUT
LSAT
LUFT
LUNT
LUST

•LT•
ALTA
ALTE
ALTI
ALTO
ALTS
BLTS

•L•T
ALIT
BLAT
BLIT
BLOT
CLOT
DLIT
FLAT
FLIT
GLOT
GLUT
NLAT
PLAT
PLOT
SLAT
SLIT
SLOT

••LT
BALT
BELT
BOLT
CELT
COLT
CULT
DOLT
FELT
GELT
GILT
HALT
HILT
HOLT
JILT
JOLT
KALT
KILT
LILT
MALT
MELT
MILT
MOLT
PELT
SALT
SILT
TILT
VOLT
VULT
WALT
WELT
WILT

LU••
LUAU
LUBA
LUBE
LUCE
LUCI
LUCK
LUCY
LUFF
LUFT
LUGE
LUGS
LUIS
LUKE
LUKS
LULL
LULU
LUMP
LUNA
LUNE
LUNG
LUNN
LUNT
LUPE
LURE
LURK
LUSH
LUST
LUTE
LUTH
LUTZ
LUVS
LUXE

L•U•
LAUD
LAUE
LEUK
LOUD
LOUP
LOUT

L••U
LEVU
LIEU
LUAU
LULU

•LU•
ALUI
ALUM
BLUE
BLUM
BLUR
CLUB
CLUE
ELUL
FLUB
FLUE
FLUS
FLUX
GLUC
GLUE
GLUG
GLUM
GLUT
PLUG
PLUM
PLUR
PLUS
SLUB
SLUE
SLUG
SLUM
SLUR
ULUS

•L•U
ALOU
BLAU
BLEU

••LU
ACLU
IGLU
LULU
OULU
SULU
TOLU
YALU
ZULU

LV••
LVII
LVOV

L•V•
LAVA
LAVE
LAVS
LEVI
LEVO
LEVU
LEVY
LIVE
LIVY
LOVE
LUVS
LXVI

L••V
LVOV
LXIV
LXXV

•LV•
ALVA
BLVD
CLVI
DLVI
MLVI
XLVI

•L•V
CLIV
CLXV
DLIV
DLXV
ELEV
FLAV
MLIV
MLXV
OLAV
SLAV
XLIV

••LV
CCLV
CDLV
CMLV
CXLV
DCLV
DXLV
GALV
MCLV
MDLV
MMLV
MXLV
UNLV

L•W•
LAWN
LAWS
LEWD
LOWE
LOWS

L••W
LOEW

•L•W
ALOW
BLEW
BLOW
CLAW
CLEW
FLAW
FLEW
FLOW
GLOW
PLEW
PLOW
SLAW
SLEW
SLOW

LX••
LXII
LXIV
LXIX
LXVI
LXXI
LXXV
LXXX

L•X•
LUXE
LXXI
LXXV
LXXX

L••X
LXIX
LXXX
LYNX

•LX•
CLXI
CLXV
CLXX
DLXI
DLXV
DLXX
MLXI
MLXV
MLXX

•L•X
ALEX
CLIX
CLXX
DLIX
DLXX
FLAX
FLEX
FLIX
FLUX
ILEX
MLIX
MLXX
PLAX
PLEX
XLIX

••LX
CALX
CCLX
CDLX
CMLX
DCLX
FALX
MCLX
MDLX
MMLX

LY••
LYES
LYIN
LYLE
LYLY
LYNE
LYNN
LYNX
LYON
LYRA
LYRE

L•Y•
LAYS
LTYR

L••Y
LACY
LADY
LAKY
LAMY
LAZY
LELY
LEVY
LILY
LIMY
LINY
LIVY
LOGY
LORY
LUCY
LYLY

•LY•
GLYC
GLYN
SLYE

•L•Y
ALGY
ALLY
CLAY
CLOY
ELLY
FLAY
FLEY
GLEY
ILLY
OLAY
PLAY
PLOY
SLAY

••LY
ABLY
AGLY
ALLY
BELY
COLY

DALY DELY DULY EELY ELLY EMLY HOLY IDLY ILLY INLY JULY LELY LILY LYLY MOLY OILY ONLY ORLY PALY POLY RELY ROLY UGLY WILY WKLY

L•Z•
LAZE LAZY LIZA

L••Z
LENZ LINZ LODZ LUTZ

•L•Z
ELIZ FLOZ

MA••
MAAM MAAR MAAS MAAT MACC MACE MACH MACK MACS MACY MADD MADE MAGE MAGI MAGS MAHI MAIA MAID MAIL MAIN MAIS MAJA MAKE MAKO MALA MALE MALI MALL MALM MALO MALT MAMA

MAME MANA MANE MANN MANO MANS MANU MANX MANY MAPS MARA MARC MARE MARG MARI MARK MARL MARS MART MARU MARV MARX MARY MASC MASH MASK MASS MAST MATA MATE MATH MATS MATT MATU MAUD MAUI MAUL MAVS MAWR MAWS MAXI MAYA MAYI MAYO MAYS MAZE MAZO MAZY

M•A•
MAAM MAAR MAAS MAAT MBAS MCAT MEAD MEAL MEAN MEAS MEAT MFAS MOAB MOAN MOAS MOAT MPAA

M••A
MAIA MAJA MALA MAMA MANA

MARA MATA MAYA MEGA MESA META MICA MINA MIRA MITA MKSA MOLA MOMA MONA MORA MOTA MPAA MRNA MYNA MYRA

•MA•
AMAH AMAS AMAT GMAC GMAN GMAT IMAM IMAN OMAN OMAR TMAN XMAS

•M•A
AMIA EMIA EMMA SMSA UMEA YMCA

••MA
ALMA ARMA BAMA BEMA BOMA CAMA COMA CYMA DAMA DUMA EMMA ERMA FEMA FNMA GAMA GNMA HAMA HEMA IRMA JIMA KAMA LAMA LEMA LIMA LOMA MAMA MOMA PIMA PUMA RAMA

RIMA ROMA SIMA SOMA TAMA TEMA TOMA TVMA USMA YAMA YIMA YUMA ZAMA

MB••
MBAS MBES MBOY

M•B•
MIBS MOBS MOBY

M••B
MOAB MUSB MYOB

•MB•
AMBI AMBO AMBS UMBO

••MB
BOMB COMB DUMB IAMB JAMB LAMB LIMB NUMB TOMB

MC••
MCAT MCCC MCCI MCCL MCCV MCCX MCDI MCDL MCDV MCDX MCII MCIV MCIX MCLI MCLV MCLX MCMI MCML MCMV MCMX MCVI MCXC MCXI MCXL MCXV MCXX

M•C•
MACC MACE MACH MACK MACS MACY MCCC MCCI MCCL MCCV MCCX MDCC MDCI MDCL MDCV MDCX MECH MECO MICA MICE MICH MICK MICR MICS MLCC MMCC MMCD MMCI MMCL MMCM MMCV MMCX MOCK MOCS MUCH MUCK MXCI MXCV MYCO

M••C
MACC MARC MASC MCCC MCXC MDCC MDXC MISC MLCC MMCC MMDC MMMC MMXC MSEC

•MC•
MMCC MMCD MMCI MMCL MMCM MMCV MMCX YMCA

•M•C
AMIC BMOC CMXC EMIC GMAC MMCC

MMDC MMMC MMXC

••MC
MMMC USMC

MD••
MDCC MDCI MDCL MDCV MDCX MDII MDIV MDIX MDLI MDLV MDLX MDSE MDVI MDXC MDXI MDXL MDXV MDXX

M•D•
MADD MADE MCDI MCDL MCDV MCDX MEDE MEDS MIDI MIDN MMDC MMDI MMDL MMDV MMDX MODE MODS MUDD MUDS

M••D
MADD MAID MAUD MEAD MEED MELD MEND MILD MIND MMCD MMMD MOLD MOOD MRED MUDD MUSD

•MD•
CMDG CMDR DMDS MMDC MMDI MMDL

MMDV MMDX RMDR

•M•D
AMID MMCD MMMD

••MD
COMD MMMD

ME••
MEAD MEAL MEAN MEAS MEAT MECH MECO MEDE MEDS MEED MEEK MEER MEET MEGA MEIN MEIR MELD MELL MELT MEME MEMO MEMS MEND MENS MENT MENU MEOW MERE MERL MERO MERS MERV MESA MESH MESO MESS META METE METH METS METZ MEUM MEWL MEWS

M•E•
MBES MEED MEEK MEER MEET MIEN MIES MMES MRED MSEC

M••E
MACE MADE

MAGE MAKE MALE MAME MANE MARE MATE MAZE MDSE MEDE MEME MERE METE MICE MIKE MILE MIME MINE MIRE MISE MITE MLLE MODE MOLE MOME MOPE MORE MOSE MOTE MOUE MOVE MTGE MULE MUSE MUTE

•ME•
AMEN AMER AMES AMEX EMES GMEN MMES NMEX OMEN OMER SMEE SMEW TMEN UMEA XMEN

•M•E
AMIE IMRE SMEE

••ME
ACME AIME ARME AYME BYME CAME COME CYME DAME DEME DIME DOME ESME FAME FEME

FUME GAME HAME HEME HOME HUME KAME LAME LIME LOME MAME MEME MIME MOME NAME NOME POME RIME ROME SAME SEME SOME TAME TIME TOME

MF••
MFAS MFRS

M•F•
MIFF MUFF

M••F
MIFF MUFF

•MF•
AMFM

•M•F
IMPF

••MF
BUMF

MG••
MGMT MGRS

M•G•
MAGE MAGI MAGS MEGA MIGS MNGR MSGR MSGS MSGT MTGE MTGS MUGS

M••G
MARG MING MKTG MOOG MUNG

•M•G
CMDG

SMOG SMUG

MH••
MHOS

M•H•
MAHI MOHO MOHS

M••H
MACH MASH MATH MECH MESH METH MICH MINH MOSH MOTH MUCH MUSH MYTH

•MH•
IMHO

•M•H
AMAH UMPH

MI••
MIBS MICA MICE MICH MICK MICR MICS MIDI MIDN MIEN MIES MIFF MIGS MIII MIKE MILD MILE MILK MILL MILO MILS MILT MIME MIMI MIMS MINA MIND MINE MING MINH MINI MINK MINN MINS MINT MINX MIPS MIRA MIRE MIRO

MIRS MIRV MIRY MISC MISE MISO MISS MIST MITA MITE MITT MIXT

M•I•
MAIA MAID MAIL MAIN MAIS MCII MCIV MCIX MDII MDIV MDIX MEIN MEIR MIII MLII MLIV MLIX MMII MMIV MMIX MOIL MUIR MVII MXII MXIV MXIX

M••I
MAGI MAHI MALI MARI MAUI MAXI MAYI MCCI MCDI MCII MCLI MCMI MCVI MCXI MDCI MDII MDLI MDVI MDXI MIDI MIII MIMI MINI MLII MLVI MLXI MMCI MMDI MMII MMLI MMMI MMVI

MMXI MUNI MVII MXCI MXII MXLI MXVI MXXI

•MI•
AMIA AMIC AMID AMIE AMIN AMIR AMIS CMII CMIV CMIX EMIA EMIC EMIL EMIR EMIT IMIT MMII MMIV MMIX OMIT SMIT YMIR

•M•I
AMBI AMOI CMII CMLI CMVI CMXI IMPI MMCI MMDI MMII MMLI MMMI MMVI MMXI OMNI OMRI

••MI
CAMI DEMI HEMI JIMI KAMI KOMI MCMI MIMI MMMI RAMI SEMI SIMI SQMI

M•J•
MAJA MOJO

MK••
MKSA MKTG

M•K•
MAKE MAKO MIKE

M••K
MACK MARK MASK MEEK MICK MILK MINK MOCK MONK MORK MUCK MURK MUSK

•M•K
AMOK OMSK

ML••
MLCC MLII MLIV MLIX MLLE MLVI MLXI MLXV MLXX

M•L•
MALA MALE MALI MALL MALM MALO MALT MCLI MCLV MCLX MDLI MDLV MDLX MELD MELL MELT MILD MILE MILK MILL MILO MILS MILT MLLE MMLI MMLV MMLX MOLA MOLD MOLE MOLL MOLT MOLY MULE MULL MXLI MXLV

M••L
MAIL MALL MARL MAUL MCCL MCDL MCML MCXL MDCL MDXL MEAL MELL MERL MEWL MILL MMCL MMDL MMML MMXL MOIL MOLL MULL

•ML•
CMLI CMLV CMLX EMLY MMLI MMLV MMLX

•M•L
AMYL CMXL EMIL MMCL MMDL MMML MMXL

••ML
COML MCML MMML SAML

MM••
MMCC MMCD MMCI MMCL MMCM MMCV MMCX MMDC MMDI MMDL MMDV MMDX MMES MMII MMIV MMIX MMLI MMLV MMLX MMMC MMMD MMMI MMML MMMM MMMV

MMMX MMVI MMXC MMXI MMXL MMXV MMXX

M•M•
MAMA MAME MCMI MCML MCMV MCMX MEME MEMO MEMS MGMT MIME MIMI MIMS MMMC MMMD MMMI MMML MMMM MMMV MMMX MOMA MOME MOMS MUMP MUMS MYMY

M••M
MAAM MALM MEUM MMCM MMMM MUSM

•MM•
AMMO EMMA EMMY MMMC MMMD MMMI MMML MMMM MMMV MMMX

•M•M
AMFM IMAM MMCM MMMM

••MM
COMM GUMM HAMM MMMM TAMM

MN••
MNGR

M•N•
MANA

MANE MANN MANO MANS MANU MANX MANY MEND MENS MENT MENU MINA MIND MINE MING MINH MINI MINK MINN MINS MINT MINX MONA MONK MONO MONS MONT MONY MRNA MTNS MUNG MUNI MYNA

M••N
MAIN MANN MEAN MEIN MIDN MIEN MINN MOAN MOON MORN MOWN MUON

•MN•
AMNT OMNI

•M•N
AMEN AMIN AMON CMON GMAN GMEN IMAN OMAN OMEN TMAN TMEN XMEN

••MN
CHMN DAMN HYMN LIMN

MO••
MOAB

MOAN MOAS MOAT MOBS MOBY MOCK MOCS MODE MODS MOHO MOHS MOIL MOJO MOLA MOLD MOLE MOLL MOLT MOLY MOMA MOME MOMS MONA MONK MONO MONS MONT MONY MOOD MOOG MOON MOOR MOOS MOOT MOPE MOPS MOPY MORA MORE MORK MORN MORO MORT MOSE MOSH MOSS MOST MOTA MOTE MOTH MOTO MOTS MOTT MOUE MOVE MOWN MOWS

M•O•
MBOY MEOW MHOS MOOD MOOG MOON MOOR MOOS MOOT MUON MYOB

M••O
MAKO MALO

MANO MAYO MAZO MECO MEMO MERO MESO MILO MIRO MISO MOHO MOJO MONO MORO MOTO MYCO MYXO

•MO•
AMOI AMOK AMON AMOR AMOS AMOY BMOC CMON CMOS HMOS OMOO SMOG

•M•O
AMBO AMMO DMSO IMHO OMOO UMBO

••MO
AMMO ATMO CAMO COMO DEMO DOMO ELMO GAMO HEMO HOMO KEMO LIMO MEMO NEMO POMO REMO SAMO SUMO TAMO ZYMO

MP••
MPAA

M•P•
MAPS MIPS MOPE MOPS MOPY

M••P
MUMP

•MP•
AMPS EMPS IMPF IMPI IMPS IMPV UMPH UMPS

••MP
BOMP BUMP CAMP COMP DAMP DUMP GAMP GIMP GUMP HEMP HUMP JUMP KEMP LAMP LIMP LUMP MUMP POMP PUMP RAMP RCMP ROMP RUMP SAMP SIMP SUMP TAMP TEMP TUMP TYMP VAMP WIMP

MR••
MRED MRNA

M•R•
MARA MARC MARE MARG MARI MARK MARL MARS MART MARU MARV MARX MARY MERE MERL MERO MERS MERV MFRS MGRS MIRA MIRE MIRO MIRS MIRV

MIRY MORA MORE MORK MORN MORO MORT MURK MYRA

M••R
MAAR MAWR MEER MEIR MICR MNGR MOOR MSGR MUIR

•MR•
IMRE OMRI

•M•R
AMER AMIR AMOR AMUR CMDR EMIR OMAR OMER RMDR YMIR

••MR
COMR

MS••
MSEC MSGR MSGS MSGT

M•S•
MASC MASH MASK MASS MAST MDSE MESA MESH MESO MESS MISC MISE MISO MISS MIST MKSA MOSE MOSH MOSS MOST MUSB MUSD MUSE MUSH MUSK MUSM MUSS MUST MYST

M••S
MAAS MACS MAGS MAIS MANS MAPS MARS MASS MATS MAVS MAWS MAYS MBAS MBES MEAS MEDS MEMS MENS MERS MESS METS MEWS MFAS MFRS MGRS MHOS MIBS MICS MIES MIGS MILS MIMS MINS MIPS MIRS MISS MMES MOAS MOBS MOCS MODS MOHS MOMS MONS MOOS MOPS MOSS MOTS MOWS MSGS MTGS MTNS MUDS MUGS MUMS MUSS

•MS•
DMSO OMSK SMSA

•M•S
AMAS AMBS AMES AMIS AMOS AMPS AMTS BMUS BMWS CMOS DMDS EMES EMPS EMTS EMUS HMOS IMPS IMUS MMES PMTS UMPS XMAS

••MS
ABMS ADMS AIMS ALMS ARMS ATMS BAMS BEMS BUMS CAMS CWMS DAMS DEMS DIMS DOMS DPMS DSMS DVMS ELMS FEMS GAMS GEMS GUMS GYMS HAMS HEMS HOMS HUMS ISMS JAMS JIMS LAMS LEMS LLMS MEMS MIMS MOMS MUMS NOMS OHMS POMS RAMS REMS RIMS ROMS RPMS RUMS SEMS SIMS SUMS SYMS TAMS TOMS TUMS VIMS YAMS

MT••
MTGE MTGS MTNS

M•T•
MATA MATE MATH MATS MATT MATU META METE METH METS METZ MITA MITE MITT MKTG MOTA MOTE MOTH MOTO MOTS MOTT MUTE MUTT MYTH

M••T
MAAT MALT MART MAST MATT MCAT MEAT MEET MELT MENT MGMT MILT MINT MIST MITT MIXT MOAT MOLT MONT MOOT MORT MOST MOTT MSGT MUST MUTT MYST

•MT•
AMTS EMTS PMTS

•M•T
AMAT AMNT EMIT GMAT IMIT OMIT SMIT SMUT

••MT
BSMT MGMT STMT

MU••
MUCH MUCK MUDD MUDS MUFF MUGS MUIR MULE MULL MUMP MUMS MUNG MUNI MUON MURK MUSB MUSD MUSE MUSH MUSK MUSM MUSS MUST MUTE MUTT MUZZ

M•U•
MAUD MAUI MAUL MEUM MOUE

M••U
MANU MARU MATU MENU

•MU•
AMUR BMUS EMUS IMUS SMUG SMUT

••MU
BOMU

MV••
MVII

M•V•
MAVS MCVI MDVI MLVI MMVI MOVE MXVI

M••V
MARV MCCV MCDV MCIV MCLV MCMV MCXV MDCV MDIV MDLV MDXV MERV MIRV MLIV MLXV MMCV MMDV MMIV MMLV MMMV MMXV MXCV MXIV MXLV MXXV

•MV•
CMVI MMVI

•M•V
CMIV CMLV CMXV IMPV MMCV MMDV MMIV MMLV MMMV MMXV

••MV
MCMV MMMV

M•W•
MAWR MAWS MEWL MEWS MOWN MOWS

M••W
MEOW

•MW•
BMWS

•M•W
SMEW

MX••
MXCI MXCV MXII MXIV MXIX MXLI MXLV MXVI MXXI MXXV MXXX

M•X•
MAXI MCXC MCXI MCXL MCXV MCXX MDXC MDXI MDXL MDXV MDXX MIXT MLXI MLXV MLXX MMXC MMXI MMXL MMXV MMXX MXXI MXXV MXXX MYXO

M••X
MANX MARX MCCX MCDX MCIX MCLX MCMX MCXX MDCX MDIX MDLX MDXX MINX MLIX MLXX MMCX MMDX MMIX MMLX MMMX MMXX MXIX MXXX

•MX•
CMXC CMXI CMXL CMXV CMXX MMXC MMXI MMXL MMXV MMXX

•M•X
AMEX CMIX CMLX CMXX MMCX MMDX MMIX MMLX MMMX MMXX NMEX

••MX
MCMX MMMX

MY••
MYCO MYMY MYNA MYOB MYRA MYST MYTH MYXO

M•Y•
MAYA MAYI MAYO MAYS

M••Y
MACY MANY MARY MAZY MBOY MIRY MOBY MOLY MONY MOPY MYMY

•MY•
AMYL

•M•Y
AMOY EMLY EMMY

••MY
ARMY DEMY EMMY FUMY GAMY HOMY LAMY LIMY MYMY OHMY RIMY ROMY

M•Z•
MAZE MAZO MAZY MUZZ

M••Z
METZ MUZZ

NA••
NABE NABS NACL NADA NADH NADP NAES NAGS NAGY NAHA NAIF NAIL NAME NANA NANG NANO NANU NAOH NAOI NAOS NAPA NAPE NAPS NARA NARC NARD NARK NARY NARZ NASA NASD NASH NASL NASO NAST NATE NATL NATO NAUT NAVE NAVY NAYS

N•A•
NCAA NDAK NEAL NEAP NEAR NEAT NLAT NOAA NOAH NOAM

N••A
NADA NAHA NANA NAPA NARA NASA NCAA NEVA NINA NIPA NITA NOAA NOLA NONA NORA NOTA NOVA

•NA•
ANAS ANAT BNAI GNAR GNAT GNAW KNAP KNAR SNAG SNAP UNAU

•N•A
ANKA ANNA ANOA ANSA ANTA ANYA ANZA ENNA ENYA FNMA GNMA INCA INGA INKA ONEA

••NA
ANNA BONA BUNA CANA CENA CUNA DANA DINA DONA DUNA DYNA EDNA ENNA ETNA FINA GENA GINA HANA IANA IONA JENA KANA KINA KONA LANA LENA LINA LUNA MANA MINA MONA MRNA MYNA NANA NINA NONA OONA PENA PINA PUNA RANA RONA RRNA SANA TANA TINA TRNA TUNA ULNA USNA VENA VINA XENA YANA ZONA

N•B•
NABE NABS NEBE NEBN NEBO NEBR NEBS NIBS NOBS NUBS NWBN NWBW

N••B
NLRB NTSB NUMB

•N•B
KNOB SNOB SNUB

NC••
NCAA NCOS

N•C•
NACL NECK NICE NICK NOCK

N••C
NARC NUNC

•NC•
ANCE ANCY ENCE ENCL ENCS ENCY INCA INCE INCH INCL INCR ONCE SNCC UNCI

•N•C
SNCC

••NC
BANC CANC CINC CONC JUNC NUNC SYNC ZINC

ND••
NDAK

N•D•
NADA NADH NADP NIDE NIDI NODE NODI NODS NUDE NUDI

N••D
NARD NASD NEED NEJD NERD NFLD NKVD NORD

•ND•
ANDS ANDY ENDE ENDO ENDS INDO INDS INDY RNDS UNDO

•N•D
ENID KNUD

••ND
BAND BEND BIND BOND BUND COND FEND FIND FOND FUND GOND HAND HIND HOND HUND KIND LAND LEND LIND MEND MIND PEND POND RAND REND RIND SAND SEND SIND SYND TEND VEND WAND WEND WIND YOND ZEND

NE••
NEAL NEAP NEAR NEAT NEBE NEBN NEBO NEBR NEBS NECK NEED NEEL NEEM NEER NEET NEFF NEGS NEHI NEIL NEIN NEJD NELL NEMO NENE NEON NERD NERF NERI NERO NESS NEST NETH NETS NEUF NEUN NEUT NEVA NEVE NEVI NEWF NEWS NEWT NEXT

N•E•
NAES NEED NEEL NEEM NEER NEET NLER NMEX NOEL NOES NYET

N••E
NABE NAME NAPE NATE NAVE NEBE NENE NEVE NICE NIDE NIKE NILE NINE NITE NIUE NODE NOME NONE NOPE NOSE NOTE NUDE NUKE NYSE

•NE•
ANEW INEE INES INEZ KNEE KNEW ONEA ONER ONES SNEE UNES

•N•E
ANCE ANGE ANNE ANTE ENCE ENDE ENNE ENSE INCE INEE INGE INRE KNEE ONCE SNEE

••NE
ACNE ANNE AONE ARNE AUNE BANE BENE BINE BONE CANE CENE CINE CONE DANE DENE DINE DONE DUNE DYNE EINE ENNE ERNE ESNE FANE FINE GENE GONE HONE IONE JANE JUNE KANE KINE LANE LINE LONE LUNE LYNE MANE MINE NENE NINE NONE OHNE ORNE PANE PINE PONE RENE RUNE RYNE SANE SENE SINE SONE SYNE TANE TENE TINE TONE TUNE TYNE UTNE VANE VINE WANE WINE ZANE ZINE ZONE

NF••
NFLD

N•F•
NEFF

N••F
NAIF NEFF NERF NEUF NEWF

•NF•
INFL INFO INFS

•N•F
ENUF

••NF
CANF CONF FUNF

N•G•
NAGS NAGY NEGS NIGH NOGO NOGS

N••G
NANG

•NG•
ANGE ANGL ENGR ENGS INGA INGE MNGR

•N•G
SNAG SNOG SNUG

••NG
BANG BENG BING BONG BUNG BYNG CONG DANG DENG DING DONG FANG GANG GONG GUNG HANG HONG HUNG JONG JUNG KING KONG KUNG LANG LING LONG LUNG MING MUNG NANG PANG PING PONG PUNG RANG RING RUNG SANG SING SONG SUNG TANG TING TONG TUNG VANG VING WANG WENG WING WONG XING YANG ZING

N•H•
NAHA NEHI

N••H
NADH NAOH NASH NETH NIGH NOAH NOSH

•N•H
ANKH ANTH INCH

••NH
MINH PENH SINH TANH

NI••
NIBS NICE NICK NIDE NIDI NIGH NIKE NILE NILS NINA NINE NINO NIPA NIPS NISI NITA NITE NITS NIUE

N•I•
NAIF NAIL NEIL NEIN NOIL NOIR NUIT

N••I
NAOI NEHI NERI NEVI NIDI NISI NODI NOLI NORI NOTI NUDI

•NI•
ANIL ANIM ANIS ENID INIT KNIT PNIN SNIP SNIT UNIS UNIT UNIV UNIX

•N•I
ANSI ANTI BNAI INRI UNCI

••NI
AGNI BANI BENI BONI FINI HONI IFNI JONI LENI LONI MINI MUNI OMNI RANI RENI TONI VENI VINI ZUNI

N•J•
NEJD

••NJ
CONJ

NK••
NKVD

N•K•
NIKE NUKE

N••K
NARK NDAK NECK NICK NOCK NOOK NYUK

•NK•
ANKA ANKH INKA INKS INKY

•N•K
TNPK

••NK
BANK BONK BUNK CONK DANK DINK DUNK FINK FUNK GUNK HANK HONK HUNK JINK JUNK KINK LANK LINK MINK MONK OINK PINK PUNK RANK RINK SANK SINK SUNK TANK TONK WINK WONK YANK ZONK

NL••
NLAT NLER NLRB

N•L•
NELL NFLD NILE NILS NOLA NOLI NOLL NOLO NULL

N••L
NACL NAIL NASL NATL NEAL NEEL NEIL NELL NOEL NOIL NOLL NULL

•NL•
INLY ONLY UNLV

•N•L
ANGL ANIL ENCL ENOL INCL

INFL
INTL

••NL
DANL
GENL

NM••
NMEX

N•M•
NAME
NEMO
NOME
NOMS
NUMB

N••M
NEEM
NOAM
NORM

•NM•
FNMA
GNMA

•N•M
ANIM
ONYM
UNUM

N•N•
NANA
NANG
NANO
NANU
NENE
NINA
NINE
NINO
NONA
NONE
NONO
NUNC
NUNN
NUNS

N••N
NEBN
NEIN
NEON
NEUN
NOON
NORN
NOUN
NUNN
NWBN

•NN•
ANNA
ANNE
ANNO
ENNA
ENNE
INNS

•N•N
ANON
INON
PNIN

••NN
BONN
CONN
DUNN
FENN
FINN
GANN
GUNN
JINN
LUNN
LYNN
MANN
MINN
NUNN
PENN
SUNN
TENN
VENN
WYNN

NO••
NOAA
NOAH
NOAM
NOBS
NOCK
NODE
NODI
NODS
NOEL
NOES
NOGO
NOGS
NOIL
NOIR
NOLA
NOLI
NOLL
NOLO
NOME
NOMS
NONA
NONE
NONO
NOOK
NOON
NOOP
NOOR
NOPE
NORA
NORD
NORI
NORM
NORN
NORW
NOSE
NOSH
NOSY
NOTA
NOTE
NOTI
NOTS
NOUN
NOUS
NOVA
NOVO

N•O•
NAOH
NAOI
NAOS
NCOS
NEON
NOOK
NOON
NOOP
NOOR

N••O
NANO
NASO
NATO
NEBO
NEMO
NERO
NINO
NOGO
NOLO
NONO
NOVO
NYRO

•NO•
ANOA
ANON
ENOL
ENOS
ENOW
INON
KNOB
KNOP
KNOT
KNOW
KNOX
SNOB
SNOG
SNOW

•N•O
ANNO
ENDO
ENTO
ENYO
ENZO
INDO
INFO
INRO
INTO
ONTO
UNDO
UNTO

••NO
ANNO
ARNO
ATNO
BONO
BRNO
CENO
DANO
DINO
DRNO
ERNO
FINO
GINO
JUNO
KANO
KENO
KINO
LENO
LINO
MANO
MONO
NANO
NINO
NONO
OENO
OHNO
RENO
SANO
SINO
TENO
VINO
XENO
ZENO

N•P•
NAPA
NAPE
NAPS
NIPA
NIPS
NOPE

N••P
NADP
NEAP
NOOP

•NP•
TNPK

•N•P
INSP
KNAP
KNOP
SNAP
SNIP

••NQ
CINQ

N•R•
NARA
NARC
NARD
NARK
NARY
NARZ
NERD
NERF
NERI
NERO
NLRB
NORA
NORD
NORI
NORM
NORN
NORW
NYRO

N••R
NEAR
NEBR
NEER
NLER
NOIR
NOOR

•NR•
ENRY
INRE
INRI
INRO

•N•R
ENGR
ENTR
GNAR
INCR
INTR
KNAR
KNUR
MNGR
ONER

••NR
USNR

N•S•
NASA
NASD
NASH
NASL
NASO
NAST
NESS
NEST
NISI
NOSE
NOSH
NOSY
NTSB
NYSE

N••S
NABS
NAES
NAGS
NAOS
NAPS
NAYS
NCOS
NEBS
NEGS
NESS
NETS
NEWS
NIBS
NILS
NIPS
NITS
NOBS
NODS
NOES
NOGS
NOMS
NOTS
NOUS
NUBS
NUNS
NUTS
NUYS

•NS•
ANSA
ANSI
ENSE
INSP
INST

•N•S
ANAS
ANDS
ANIS
ANTS
ENCS
ENDS
ENGS
ENOS
ENTS
ENVS
GNUS
INDS
INES
INFS
INKS
INNS
INTS
INXS
ONES
ONUS
RNDS
UNES
UNIS

••NS
AINS
AWNS
BANS
BINS
BUNS
CANS
CENS
CONS
CTNS
DENS
DINS
DONS
DUNS
EINS
EONS
ERNS
FANS
FENS
FINS
FONS
GENS
GINS
GUNS
HANS
HENS
HINS
HUNS
INNS
IONS
JENS
KANS
KENS
LENS
MANS
MENS
MINS
MONS
MTNS
NUNS
OWNS
PANS
PENS
PINS
PONS
PUNS
RUNS
SANS
SENS
SINS
SONS
SSNS
STNS
SUNS
SYNS
TANS
TENS
TINS
TONS
TUNS
URNS
VANS
VINS
WENS
WINS
WONS
WRNS
YENS

NT••
NTSB
NTWT

N•T•
NATE
NATL
NATO
NETH
NETS
NITA
NITE
NITS
NOTA
NOTE
NOTI
NOTS
NUTS
NUTT

N••T
NAST
NAUT
NEAT
NEET
NEST
NEUT
NEWT
NEXT
NLAT
NTWT
NUIT
NUTT
NYET

•NT•
ANTA
ANTE
ANTH
ANTI
ANTS
ENTO
ENTR
ENTS
INTL
INTO
INTR
INTS
ONTO
UNTO

•N•T
ANAT
CNUT
GNAT
INIT
INST
KNIT
KNOT
KNUT
SNIT
TNUT
UNIT

••NT
AINT
AMNT
AUNT
BENT
BUNT
CANT
CENT
CONT
DENT
DINT
DONT
FONT
FUNT
GENT
GYNT
HENT
HINT
HUNT
ISNT
KANT
KENT
LENT
LINT
LUNT
MENT
MINT
MONT
PANT
PENT
PINT
PONT
PUNT
RANT
RENT
RUNT
SANT
SENT
TENT
TINT
VENT
WANT
WENT
WONT

NU••
NUBS
NUDE
NUDI
NUIT
NUKE
NULL
NUMB
NUNC
NUNN
NUNS
NUTS
NUTT
NUYS

N•U•
NAUT
NEUF
NEUN
NEUT
NIUE
NOUN
NOUS
NYUK

N••U
NANU

•NU•
CNUT
ENUF
GNUS
KNUD
KNUR
KNUT
ONUS
SNUB
SNUG
TNUT
UNUM

•N•U
UNAU

••NU
AINU
BENU
DANU
GENU
MANU
MENU
NANU

N•V•
NAVE
NAVY
NEVA
NEVE
NEVI
NKVD
NOVA
NOVO

•NV•
ENVS
ENVY

•N•V
UNIV
UNLV

••NV
CONV

NW••
NWBN
NWBW

N•W•
NEWF
NEWS
NEWT
NTWT

N••W
NORW
NWBW

•N•W
ANEW
ENOW
GNAW
KNEW
KNOW
SNOW

N•X•
NEXT

N••X
NMEX

•NX•
INXS

•N•X
KNOX
ONYX
UNIX

••NX
GENX
JINX
LYNX
MANX
MINX
PINX

NY••
NYET
NYRO
NYSE
NYUK

N•Y•
NAYS
NUYS

N••Y
NAGY
NARY
NAVY
NOSY

•NY•
ANYA
ENYA
ENYO
ONYM
ONYX

•N•Y
ANCY
ANDY
ENCY
ENRY
ENVY
INDY
INKY
INLY
ONLY

••NY
BONY
CANY
CONY
CUNY
DENY
DKNY
EENY
GENY
GONY
LINY
MANY
MONY
PINY
PONY
PUNY
SONY
SUNY
TINY
TONY
VINY
WANY
WINY
ZANY

N••Z
NARZ

•NZ•
ANZA
ENZO

•N•Z
INEZ

••NZ
BENZ
FONZ
LENZ
LINZ

OA••
OAFS
OAHU
OAKS
OARS
OAST
OATH
OATS
OATY

O•A•
OBAD
OCAS
ODAS
ODAY
OJAI
OKAY
OLAF
OLAN
OLAV
OLAY
OMAN
OMAR
OPAH
OPAL
ORAD
ORAL
ORAN
OSAR
OVAL
OZAV

O••A
OCTA
ODEA
OITA
OKLA
OKRA
OLGA
OLLA
ONEA
OONA
OPIA
ORCA
OSHA
OSSA
OTRA

•OA•
BOAC
BOAR
BOAS
BOAT
BOAZ
COAL
COAT
COAX
DOAK
FOAL
FOAM
GOAD
GOAL
GOAT
HOAD
HOAR
HOAX
JOAB
JOAD
JOAN
KOAN
LOAD
LOAF
LOAM
LOAN
MOAB
MOAN
MOAS
MOAT
NOAA
NOAH
NOAM
ROAD
ROAM
ROAN
ROAR
SOAK
SOAP
SOAR
TOAD
TOAT
WOAD
ZOAR

•O•A
BOCA
BOLA
BOMA
BONA
BORA
BOTA
BOVA
COCA
CODA
COLA
COMA
CORA
COSA
COXA
DOHA
DONA
DOPA
DORA
FORA
GOYA
HOLA
HORA
HOYA
IOLA
IONA
IOTA
IOWA
KOLA
KONA
LOLA
LOMA
LOTA
MOLA
MOMA
MONA
MORA
MOTA
NOAA
NOLA
NONA
NORA
NOTA
NOVA
OONA
PODA
POLA
ROCA
ROMA
RONA
ROSA
ROTA
SOCA
SODA
SOFA
SOLA
SOMA
SORA
SOYA
TOEA
TOGA
TOLA
TOMA
TORA
YODA
YOGA
ZOEA
ZOLA
ZONA

••OA
ANOA
PROA
STOA
WHOA

OB••
OBAD
OBEY
OBIE
OBIS
OBIT
OBOE
OBOL

O•B•
ORBI
ORBS

•OB•
BOBS
COBB
COBH
COBS
DOBY
FOBS
GOBI
GOBO
GOBS
GOBY
HOBO
HOBS
JOBS
KOBE
KOBO
KOBS
LOBE
LOBO
LOBS
MOBS
MOBY
NOBS
ROBB
ROBE
ROBO
ROBS
SOBS
TOBE
TOBY
YOBS

•O•B
BOMB
BOOB
COBB
COMB
FORB
JOAB
LOEB
MOAB
ROBB
SORB
TOMB

••OB
BLOB
BOOB
BYOB
GLOB
KNOB
MYOB
PROB
SLOB
SNOB
SWOB

OC••
OCAS
OCHO
OCHS
OCTA
OCTO

O•C•
ONCE
ORCA
ORCH
ORCS
OUCH

O••C
ODIC
OPEC
OTIC

•OC•
BOCA
BOCK
COCA
COCK
COCO
DOCK
DOCS
FOCH
FOCI
HOCH
HOCK
JOCK
KOCH
LOCH
LOCI
LOCK
LOCO
MOCK
MOCS
NOCK
POCO
ROCA
ROCK
ROCS
SOCA
SOCK
TOCK
VOCE

•O•C
BOAC
BOSC
COFC
CONC
KOFC
ROTC
ZOIC

••OC
APOC
BLOC
BMOC
CHOC
CROC
EEOC
FLOC
KROC
PROC

OD••
ODAS
ODAY
ODDS
ODEA
ODER
ODES
ODIC
ODIE
ODIN
ODOM
ODOR

O•D•
ODDS
OLDE
OLDS
ORDO
OUDS

O••D
OBAD
OHED
OKED
OLID
OOID
OPED
ORAD
OVID
OWED

•OD•
BODE
BODO
BODS
BODY
CODA
CODE
CODS
CODY
DODD
DODO
GODS
HODS
IODO
JODY
LODE
LODI
LODZ
MODE
MODS
NODE
NODI
NODS
PODA
PODE
PODS
RODE
RODS
SODA
SODS
TODD
TODO
TODS
TODY
YODA
YODH
YODS

•O•D
BOLD
BOND
BOYD
COED
COLD
COMD
COND
CORD
DODD
DOOD
DOWD
FOLD
FOND
FOOD
FORD
GOAD
GOLD
GOND
GOOD
HOAD
HOED
HOLD
HOND
HOOD
JOAD
LOAD
LOID
LORD
LOUD
MOLD
MOOD
NORD
OOID
POND
POOD
ROAD
ROOD
SOLD
TOAD
TODD
TOED
TOLD
VOID
WOAD
WOLD
WOOD
WORD
YOND
YOUD

••OD
CLOD
DOOD
EXOD
FOOD
GOOD
HOOD
IZOD
MOOD
PLOD
POOD
PROD
QUOD
ROOD
SHOD
TROD
TWOD
WHOD
WOOD

OE••
OEIL
OENO
OEUF

O•E•
OBEY
ODEA
ODER
ODES
OGEE
OHED
OKED
OKEY
OLEG
OLEN
OLEO
OLES
OMEN
OMER
ONEA
ONER
ONES
OPEC
OPED
OPEL
OPEN
OPER
OPES
OREG
OREL
OREM
OREO
ORES
OSEE
OVEN
OVER
OWED
OWEN
OWER
OWES
OXEN
OYER
OYEZ

O••E
OBIE
OBOE
ODIE
OGEE
OGLE
OGRE
OHNE
OISE
OKIE
OLDE
ONCE
OOZE
OPIE
ORLE
ORNE
OSEE
OSTE
OTOE
OUSE

•OE•
BOER
COED
COEL
COEN
DOER
DOES
FOES
GOER
GOES
HOED
HOER
HOES
JOEL
JOES
JOEY
LOEB
LOEW
NOEL
NOES
POEM
POET
ROEG
ROES
TOEA
TOED
TOES
WOES
ZOEA

•O•E
AONE
BODE
BOLE
BONE
BORE
BOSE
BOWE
CODE
COKE
COLE
COME
CONE
COPE
CORE
COTE
COUE
COVE
DOGE
DOLE
DOME
DONE
DOPE
DORE
DOSE
DOTE
DOVE
DOZE
FOIE
FORE
FOXE
GONE
GORE
HOKE
HOLE
HOME
HONE
HOPE
HOSE
HOTE
HOVE
HOWE
IOLE
IONE
JOIE
JOKE
JOSE
JOVE
KOBE
KORE
LOBE
LODE
LOGE
LOME
LONE
LOPE
LORE
LOSE
LOVE
LOWE
MODE
MOLE
MOME
MOPE
MORE
MOSE
MOTE
MOUE
MOVE
NODE
NOME
NONE
NOPE
NOSE
NOTE
OOZE
PODE
POKE
POLE
POME
PONE
POPE
PORE
POSE
ROBE
RODE
ROHE
ROLE
ROME
ROPE
ROSE
ROTE
ROUE
ROVE
ROWE
SOIE
SOKE
SOLE
SOME
SONE
SORE
TOBE
TOKE
TOLE
TOME
TONE
TOPE
TORE
TOTE
VOCE
VOLE
VOTE
WOKE
WOLE
WORE
WOVE

YOKE YORE ZONE

••OE
ALOE BPOE EVOE FLOE FROE OBOE OTOE SHOE SLOE

OF••
OFFS

O•F•
OAFS OFFS ORFF

O••F
OEUF OLAF ORFF

•OF•
BOFF COFC COFS DOFF HOFF KOFC KOFI KOFP LOFT SOFA SOFT TOFF TOFT TOFU

•O•F
BOFF COIF CONF CORF DOFF DOLF GOLF GOOF HOFF HOOF IOOF KOPF LOAF POOF POUF ROLF ROOF TOFF WOLF WOOF

••OF
ASOF GOOF HOOF IOOF POOF PROF ROOF WOOF

OG••
OGEE OGGI OGLE OGRE

O•G•
OGGI OLGA ORGS ORGY

O••G
OLEG OREG ORIG

•OG•
BOGS BOGY COGS DOGE DOGG DOGS DOGY FOGG FOGS FOGY GOGH GOGI GOGO HOGG HOGS JOGS LOGE LOGO LOGS LOGY NOGO NOGS POGO POGS POGY TOGA TOGO TOGS YOGA YOGH YOGI ZOGI

•O•G
BONG BORG CONG DOGG DONG DOUG FOGG GONG HOGG HONG JONG KONG LONG MOOG PONG ROEG SONG TONG WONG

••OG
AGOG BIOG CLOG FLOG FROG GEOG GROG MOOG PROG SLOG SMOG SNOG

OH••
OHED OHIO OHMS OHMY OHNE OHNO OHOH

O•H•
OAHU OCHO OCHS OOHS OSHA OTHO

O••H
OATH OHOH OPAH ORCH ORTH OUCH

•OH•
BOHM BOHR COHN COHO DOHA FOHN HOHO JOHN KOHL MOHO MOHS OOHS POHL ROHE SOHN SOHO TOHO WOHL YOHO

•O•H
BOSH BOTH COBH COSH DOTH FOCH GOGH GOSH GOTH HOCH JOSH KOCH KOPH LOCH MOSH MOTH NOAH NOSH POOH POSH QOPH ROSH ROTH SOPH TOSH YODH YOGH

••OH
IEOH IPOH NAOH OHOH POOH UHOH

OI••
OIKS OILS OILY OINK OISE OITA

O•I•
OBIE OBIS OBIT ODIC ODIE ODIN OEIL OHIO OKIE OLID OLIN OLIO OMIT OOID OPIA OPIE ORIG OSIS OTIC OTIS OVID OVIS

O••I
OGGI OJAI OMNI OMRI ORBI

•OI•
BOIL BOIS COIF COIL COIN COIR DOIL DOIN DOIT FOIE FOIL FOIN FOIS GOIN JOIE JOIN KOIS LOID LOIN LOIS MOIL NOIL NOIR OOID POIL POIS ROIL SOIE SOIL SOIR TOIL VOID VOIR VOIX ZOIC

•O•I
AOKI BONI CORI COSI FOCI GOBI GOGI HONI HOPI JOLI JONI KOFI KOJI KOMI LOCI LODI LOKI LONI LORI LOTI NODI NOLI NORI NOTI ROTI SOLI SORI TONI TOPI TORI YOGI ZOGI ZORI

••OI
AMOI ATOI ELOI LEOI NAOI QUOI TROI

OJ••
OJAI

•OJ•
DOJO HOJO JOJO KOJI MOJO ROJO TOJO

•O•J
CONJ

OK••
OKAY OKED OKEY OKIE OKLA OKRA

O•K•
OAKS OIKS

O••K
OINK OMSK ORSK

•OK•
AOKI COKE COKY HOKE JOKE JOKY KOKO LOKI POKE POKY SOKE TOKE WOKE WOKS YOKE YOKO

•O•K
BOCK BONK BOOK BORK BOSK COCK CONK COOK CORK DOAK DOCK FOLK FORK GOWK HOCK HONK HOOK JOCK KOOK LOCK LOOK MOCK MONK MORK NOCK NOOK POLK PORK ROCK ROOK SOAK SOCK SOUK TOCK TONK TOOK TORK WONK WORK WOUK YOLK YORK ZONK ZOUK

••OK
AMOK BOOK COOK EWOK GROK HOOK KOOK LOOK NOOK ROOK TOOK

OL••
OLAF OLAN OLAV OLAY OLDE OLDS OLEG OLEN OLEO OLES OLGA OLID OLIN OLIO OLLA

O•L•
OGLE OILS OILY OKLA OLLA ONLY ORLE ORLY OSLO OULU OWLS

O••L
OBOL OEIL OPAL OPEL ORAL OREL OVAL

•OL•
BOLA BOLD BOLE BOLL BOLO BOLT COLA COLD COLE COLL COLO COLS COLT COLY DOLE DOLF DOLL DOLT FOLD FOLK GOLD GOLF HOLA HOLD HOLE HOLM HOLO HOLP HOLS HOLT HOLY IOLA IOLE JOLI JOLO JOLT KOLA KOLN KOLO LOLA LOLL MOLA MOLD MOLE MOLL MOLT MOLY NOLA NOLI NOLL NOLO POLA POLE POLK POLL POLO POLS POLY ROLE ROLF ROLL ROLY SOLA SOLD SOLE SOLI SOLN SOLO SOLS TOLA TOLD TOLE TOLL TOLU VOLE VOLS VOLT WOLD WOLE WOLF YOLK ZOLA

•O•L
BOIL BOLL BOWL COAL COEL COIL COLL COML COOL COWL DOIL DOLL FOAL FOIL FOOL FOUL FOWL GOAL HOWL JOEL JOWL KOHL KOOL LOLL MOIL MOLL NOEL NOIL NOLL POHL POIL POLL POOL ROIL ROLL ROTL SOIL SOUL TOIL TOLL TOOL WOHL WOOL YOWL ZOOL

••OL
AWOL BIOL CHOL COOL ECOL ENOL FOOL GAOL GEOL IDOL ITOL KOOL OBOL POOL SKOL STOL TOOL VIOL VTOL WOOL ZOOL

OM••
OMAN OMAR OMEN OMER OMIT OMNI OMOO OMRI OMSK

O•M•
OHMS OHMY

O••M
ODOM ONYM OREM OVUM

•OM•
BOMA BOMB BOMP BOMU COMA COMB COMD COME COML COMM COMO COMP COMR DOME DOMO DOMS HOME HOMO HOMS HOMY KOMI LOMA LOME MOMA MOME MOMS NOME NOMS POME POMO POMP POMS ROMA ROME ROMP ROMS ROMY SOMA SOME TOMA TOMB TOME TOMS

•O•M
BOHM BOOM COMM CORM COSM DOOM DORM FOAM FORM HOLM LOAM LOOM NOAM NORM POEM ROAM ROOM VOOM WORM ZOOM

••OM
ATOM BOOM BROM DOOM EDOM FROM GEOM GLOM LOOM ODOM PROM ROOM THOM VOOM WHOM ZOOM

ON••
ONCE ONEA ONER ONES ONLY ONTO ONUS ONYM ONYX

O•N•
OENO OHNE OHNO OINK OMNI OONA ORNE OWNS

O••N
ODIN OLAN OLEN OLIN OMAN OMEN OPEN ORAN OVEN OWEN OXEN OXON

•ON•
AONE BONA BOND BONE BONG BONI BONK BONN BONO BONY CONC COND CONE CONF CONG CONJ CONK CONN CONS CONT CONV CONY DONA DONE DONG DONS DONT EONS FOND FONS FONT FONZ GOND GONE GONG GONY HOND HONE HONG HONI HONK IONA IONE IONS JONG JONI KONA KONG LONE LONG LONI MONA MONK MONO MONS MONT MONY NONA NONE NONO OONA POND PONE PONG PONS PONT PONY RONA SONE SONG SONS SONY TONE TONG TONI TONK TONS TONY WONG WONK WONS WONT YOND ZONA ZONE ZONK

•O•N
BONN BOON BORN BOSN COEN COHN COIN CONN COON CORN DOIN DOON DORN DOWN FOHN FOIN GOIN GOON GOWN HORN JOAN JOHN JOIN JOON KOAN KOLN LOAN LOIN LOON LORN MOAN MOON MORN MOWN NOON NORN NOUN POON ROAN SOHN SOLN SOON SOWN TOON TORN TOWN WORN ZOON ZORN

••ON
AEON AGON AMON ANON ARON ATON AVON AXON BION BOON BUON CHON CION CMON COON DCON DION DOON EBON ECON EGON ELON ETON EXON GOON HUON ICON INON IRON JOON KAON KWON LEON LION LOON LRON LYON MOON MUON NEON NOON OXON PEON PHON PION POON PRON SION SOON TION TOON TRON UPON ZION ZOON

OO••
OOHS OOID OONA OOPS OORT OOZE OOZY

O•O•
OBOE OBOL ODOM ODOR OHOH OMOO OROS OTOE OTOS OXON

O••O
OCHO OCTO OENO OHIO OHNO OLEO OLIO OMOO ONTO OPTO ORDO OREO ORZO OSLO OSSO OTHO OTRO OTTO OUZO

•OO•
BOOB BOOK BOOM BOON BOOP BOOR BOOS BOOT COOK COOL COON COOP COOS COOT DOOD DOOM DOON DOOR FOOD FOOL FOOT GOOD GOOF GOON GOOP GOOS HOOD HOOF HOOK HOOP HOOT IOOF JOON KOOK KOOL KOOP LOOK LOOM LOON LOOP LOOS LOOT MOOD MOOG MOON MOOR MOOS MOOT NOOK NOON NOOP NOOR POOD POOF POOH POOL POON POOP POOR ROOD ROOF ROOK ROOM ROOS ROOT SOON SOOT TOOK TOOL TOON TOOT VOOM WOOD WOOF WOOL WOOS ZOOL ZOOM ZOON ZOOS ZOOT

•O•O
BODO BOLO BONO BORO BOYO BOZO COCO COHO COLO COMO CORO DODO DOJO DOMO GOBO GOGO HOBO HOHO HOJO HOLO HOMO IODO JOJO JOLO KOBO KOKO KOLO KOTO LOBO LOCO LOGO MOHO MOJO MONO MORO MOTO NOGO NOLO NONO NOVO POCO POGO POLO POMO ROBO ROJO ROTO SOHO SOLO SOSO TODO TOGO TOHO TOJO TOPO TORO TOTO YOHO YOKO YOYO

••OO
AROO EROO OMOO SHOO

OP••
OPAH OPAL OPEC OPED OPEL OPEN OPER OPES OPIA OPIE OPRY OPTO OPTS OPUS

O•P•
OOPS

•OP•
BOPP BOPS COPE COPS COPT COPY DOPA DOPE DOPY FOPS HOPE HOPI HOPS KOPF KOPH KOPS LOPE LOPS MOPE MOPS MOPY NOPE OOPS POPE POPS QOPH ROPE ROPY SOPH SOPS TOPE TOPI TOPO TOPS

•O•P
BOMP BOOP BOPP COMP COOP CORP COUP DORP DOUP GOOP GORP GOUP HOLP HOOP HOSP KOFP KOOP LOOP LOUP NOOP POMP POOP ROMP ROUP SOAP SOUP

••OP
ATOP BOOP CHOP CLOP COOP CROP DROP ESOP FLOP GLOP GOOP HOOP IHOP KNOP KOOP LOOP NOOP PLOP POOP PROP SCOP SHOP SLOP STOP SWOP TROP VSOP WHOP

OR••
ORAD ORAL ORAN ORBI ORBS ORCA ORCH ORCS ORDO OREG OREL OREM OREO ORES ORFF ORGS ORGY ORIG ORLE ORLY ORNE OROS ORSK ORTH ORTS ORVS ORYX ORZO

O•R•
OARS OGRE OKRA OMRI OORT OPRY OTRA OTRO OURS

O••R
ODER ODOR OMAR OMER ONER OPER OSAR OVER OWER OYER

•OR•
BORA BORE BORG BORK BORN BORO BORS BORT CORA CORD CORE CORF CORI CORK CORM CORN CORO CORP CORR CORS CORY DORA DORE DORM DORN DORP DORR DORS DORT DORY FORA FORB FORD FORE FORK FORM FORT GORE GORP GORY HORA HORN HORS

HORT KORE LORD LORE LORI LORN LORY MORA MORE MORK MORN MORO MORT NORA NORD NORI NORM NORN NORW OORT PORE PORK PORT RORY SORA SORB SORE SORI SORT TORA TORE TORI TORK TORN TORO TORR TORS TORT TORY WORD WORE WORK WORM WORN WORT YORE YORK ZORI ZORN

•O•R
BOAR BOER BOHR BOOR COIR COMR CORR DOER DOOR DORR DOUR FOUR GOER HOAR HOER HOUR JOUR MOOR NOIR NOOR POOR POUR ROAR SOAR SOIR SOUR TORR TOUR VOIR YOUR ZOAR

••OR
AMOR ASOR ATOR BOOR DIOR DOOR EXOR FLOR GYOR IGOR IVOR MOOR NOOR ODOR POOR THOR UXOR

OS••
OSAR OSEE OSHA OSIS OSLO OSSA OSSO OSTE

O•S•
OAST OISE OMSK ORSK OSSA OSSO OUSE OUST

O••S
OAFS OAKS OARS OATS OBIS OCAS OCHS ODAS ODDS ODES OFFS OHMS OIKS OILS OLDS OLES ONES ONUS OOHS OOPS OPES OPTS OPUS ORBS ORCS ORES ORGS OROS ORTS ORVS OSIS OTIS OTOS OUDS OURS OUTS OVIS OWES OWLS OWNS OXUS

•OS•
BOSC BOSE BOSH BOSK BOSN BOSS COSA COSH COSI COSM COST COSY DOSE DOSS DOST FOSS GOSH HOSE HOSP HOSS HOST JOSE JOSH JOSS LOSE LOSS LOST MOSE MOSH MOSS MOST NOSE NOSH NOSY POSE POSH POSS POST POSY ROSA ROSE ROSH ROSS ROSY SOSO TOSH TOSS YOST

•O•S
BOAS BOBS BODS BOGS BOIS BOOS BOPS BORS BOSS BOTS BOWS BOYS COBS CODS COFS COGS COLS CONS COOS COPS CORS COTS COWS DOCS DOES DOGS DOMS DONS DORS DOSS DOTS EONS EOUS FOBS FOES FOGS FOIS FONS FOPS FOSS FOYS GOBS GODS GOES GOOS HOBS HODS HOES HOGS HOLS HOMS HOPS HORS HOSS HOWS HOYS IONS IOUS JOBS JOES JOGS JOSS JOTS JOYS KOBS KOIS KOPS LOBS LOGS LOIS LOOS LOPS LOSS LOTS LOWS MOAS MOBS MOCS MODS MOHS MOMS MONS MOOS MOPS MOSS MOTS MOWS NOBS NODS NOES NOGS NOMS NOTS NOUS OOHS OOPS PODS POGS POIS POLS POMS PONS POPS POSS POTS POWS ROBS ROCS RODS ROES ROMS ROOS ROSS ROTS ROUS ROWS SOBS SODS SOLS SONS SOPS SOTS SOUS SOWS SOYS TODS TOES TOGS TOMS TONS TOPS TORS TOSS TOTS TOWS TOYS VOLS VOUS VOWS WOES WOKS WONS WOOS WOWS YOBS YODS ZOOS

••OS
ADOS AMOS APOS AVOS BIOS BOOS BROS CEOS CMOS COOS CPOS CWOS DIOS DSOS DUOS EGOS ENOS EPOS EROS ESOS GOOS GPOS GROS GTOS HAOS HMOS IBOS ICOS IDOS IPOS KEOS LAOS LBOS LEOS LOOS MHOS MOOS NAOS NCOS OROS OTOS PROS REOS RHOS RIOS ROOS TAOS THOS TIOS TKOS TWOS UDOS UFOS WHOS WOOS YAOS ZOOS

OT••
OTHO OTIC OTIS OTOE OTOS OTRA OTRO OTTO

O•T•
OATH OATS OATY OCTA OCTO OITA ONTO OPTO OPTS ORTH ORTS OSTE OTTO OUTS

O••T
OAST OBIT OMIT OORT OUST

•OT•
BOTA BOTH BOTS BOTT COTE COTS COTY DOTE DOTH DOTS GOTH HOTE IOTA JOTS KOTO LOTA LOTI LOTS LOTT MOTA MOTE MOTH MOTO MOTS MOTT NOTA NOTE NOTI NOTS POTS ROTA ROTC ROTE ROTH ROTI ROTL ROTO ROTS SOTS TOTE TOTO TOTS VOTE ZOTZ

•O•T
AOUT BOAT BOLT BOOT BORT BOTT BOUT COAT COLT CONT COOT COPT COST DOIT DOLT DONT DORT DOST FONT FOOT FORT FOYT GOAT GOUT GOVT HOLT HOOT HORT HOST HOYT JOLT LOFT LOOT LOST LOTT LOUT MOAT MOLT MONT MOOT MORT MOST MOTT OORT POET PONT PORT POST POUT ROOT ROUT SOFT SOOT SORT TOAT TOFT TOOT TORT TOUT VOLT WONT WORT XOUT YOST ZOOT

••OT
BLOT BOOT CLOT COOT EYOT FOOT GLOT GROT HOOT KNOT LOOT MOOT PHOT PLOT PROT QUOT RIOT ROOT RYOT SCOT SHOT SLOT SOOT SPOT STOT TOOT TROT ZOOT

OU••
OUCH OUDS OULU OURS OUSE OUST OUTS OUZO

O•U•
OEUF ONUS OPUS OVUM OXUS

O••U
OAHU OULU

•OU•
AOUT BOUT COUE COUP DOUG DOUP DOUR DOUW DOUX EOUS FOUL FOUR GOUP GOUT HOUR IOUS JOUR LOUD LOUP LOUT MOUE NOUN NOUS POUF POUR POUT ROUE ROUP ROUS ROUT ROUX SOUK SOUL SOUP SOUR SOUS TOUR TOUT VOUS WOUK XOUT YOUD YOUR ZOUK

•O•U
BOMU TOFU TOLU

••OU
ABOU ALOU CHOU THOU ZHOU

OV••
OVAL OVEN OVER OVID OVIS OVUM

O•V•
ORVS

O••V
OLAV OZAV

•OV•
BOVA COVE DOVE GOVT HOVE JOVE LOVE MOVE NOVA NOVO ROVE WOVE

•O•V
CONV

••OV
AZOV LVOV PROV

OW••
OWED OWEN OWER OWES OWLS OWNS

•OW•
BOWE BOWL BOWS COWL COWS DOWD DOWN FOWL GOWK GOWN HOWE HOWL HOWS IOWA JOWL LOWE LOWS MOWN MOWS POWS ROWE ROWS SOWN SOWS TOWN TOWS VOWS WOWS YOWL

•O•W
DOUW LOEW NORW

••OW
ALOW AVOW BLOW BROW CHOW CROW DHOW ENOW FLOW FROW GLOW GROW KNOW MEOW PLOW PROW SCOW SHOW SLOW SNOW STOW

OX••
OXEN OXON OXUS

O••X
ONYX ORYX

•OX•
BOXY COXA FOXE FOXX FOXY

•O•X
COAX DOUX FOXX HOAX ROUX VOIX

••OX
KNOX PROX

OY••
OYER OYEZ

O•Y•
ONYM ONYX ORYX

O••Y
OATY OBEY ODAY OHMY OILY OKAY OKEY OLAY ONLY OOZY OPRY ORGY ORLY OZZY

•OY•
BOYD BOYO BOYS BOYZ FOYS FOYT GOYA HOYA HOYS HOYT JOYS SOYA SOYS TOYS YOYO

•O•Y
BODY BOGY BONY BOXY CODY COKY COLY CONY COPY CORY COSY COTY COZY DOBY DOGY DOPY DORY DOZY FOGY FOXY GOBY GONY GORY HOLY HOMY JODY JOEY JOKY LOGY LORY MOBY MOLY MONY MOPY NOSY OOZY POGY POKY POLY PONY POSY ROLY ROMY ROPY RORY ROSY SONY TOBY TODY TONY TORY

••OY
AHOY AMOY BBOY BUOY CHOY CLOY MBOY PLOY TROY

OZ••
OZAV OZZY

O•Z•
OOZE OOZY ORZO OUZO OZZY

O••Z
OYEZ

•OZ•
BOZO COZY DOZE DOZY OOZE OOZY

•O•Z
BOAZ BOYZ FONZ LODZ ZOTZ

••OZ
BROZ FLOZ

PA••
PAAR PABA PACA PACE PACK PACS PACT PADS PAGE PAGO PAHO PAHS PAID PAIL PAIN PAIR PAIX PALE PALI PALL PALM PALO PALP PALS PALY PANE PANG PANS PANT PAPA PAPP PARA PARC PARD PARE PARI PARK PARL PARR PARS PART PASA PASE PASH PASO PASS PAST PATD PATE PATH PATS PAUL PAVE PAVO PAWL PAWN PAWS PAYS PAYT

P•A•
PAAR PEAG PEAK PEAL PEAR PEAS PEAT PEAU PHAR PHAT PIAF PIAO PLAN PLAT PLAX PLAY PRAM PRAY PSAT PTAH PTAS

P••A
PABA PACA PAPA PARA PASA PENA PEPA PETA PICA PIKA PIMA PINA PIPA PISA PITA PLEA PODA POLA PROA PUKA PULA PUMA PUNA PUPA

•PA•
CPAS MPAA OPAH OPAL SPAD SPAM SPAN SPAR SPAS SPAT SPAY UPAS

•P•A
APIA EPHA LPGA MPAA OPIA SPCA

••PA
ARPA CAPA DOPA GAPA HUPA LIPA NAPA NIPA PAPA PEPA PIPA PUPA RAPA TAPA

P•B•
PABA PCBS PUBL PUBS

P••B
PLEB PROB

•PB•
APBS

PC••
PCBS

P•C•
PACA PACE PACK PACS PACT PECK PECS PFCS PICA PICK PICO PICS PICT PLCS POCO PUCE PUCK

P••C
PARC PREC PROC PSEC

•PC•
SPCA SPCC

•P•C
APOC EPIC OPEC SPCC SPEC

P•D•
PADS PEDI PEDO PEDS PHDS PODA PODE PODS PPDO PUDU

P••D
PAID PARD PATD PEND PIED PLED PLOD POND POOD PRED PROD

•PD•
PPDO UPDO

•P•D
APED OPED SPAD SPED SPUD

••PD
LAPD SFPD

PE••
PEAG PEAK PEAL PEAR PEAS PEAT PEAU PECK PECS PEDI PEDO PEDS PEEK PEEL PEEN PEEP PEER PEGS PEHS PEKE PELE PELF PELL PELT PENA PEND PENH PENN PENS PENT PEON PEPA PEPE PEPO PEPS PERE PERF PERH PERI PERK PERM PERP PERS PERT PERU PESO PEST PETA PETE PETO PETS PEWS

P•E•
PEEK PEEL PEEN PEEP PEER PHEW PIED PIER PIES PIET PLEA PLEB PLED PLEO PLEW PLEX POEM POET PREC PRED PREF PREK PREM PREP PRES PRET PREV PREY PREZ PSEC PUER

P••E
PACE PAGE PALE PANE PARE PASE PATE PAVE PEKE PELE PEPE PERE PETE PIKE PILE PINE PIPE PIRE PLIE PODE POKE POLE POME PONE POPE PORE POSE PRIE PUCE PULE PURE PYLE PYRE

•PE•
APED APER APES APEX EPEE OPEC OPED OPEL OPEN OPER OPES SPEC SPED SPEE SPET SPEW

•P•E
APSE BPOE EPEE IPSE OPIE SPEE

••PE
CAPE CEPE COPE DOPE DUPE GAPE HOPE HYPE JAPE LOPE LUPE MOPE NAPE NOPE PEPE PIPE POPE RIPE ROPE SUPE TAPE TOPE TYPE WIPE XIPE YIPE

PF••
PFCS PFFT PFUI

P•F•
PFFT PUFF

P••F
PELF PERF PIAF POOF POUF PREF PROF PUFF

••PF
IMPF KOPF

P•G•
PAGE PAGO PEGS PIGS PKGS POGO POGS POGY PUGH PUGS

P••G
PANG PEAG PING PLUG PONG PRIG

PROG PUNG

•PG•
LPGA SPGR

••PG
BKPG TVPG

PH••
PHAR PHAT PHDS PHEW PHIL PHIS PHIZ PHON PHOT PHYS

P•H•
PAHO PAHS PEHS POHL

P••H
PASH PATH PENH PERH PISH PITH POOH POSH PTAH PUGH PUSH

•PH•
EPHA SPHT

•P•H
IPOH OPAH

••PH
ALPH KAPH KOPH QOPH SOPH UMPH ZEPH

PI••
PIAF PIAO PICA PICK PICO PICS PICT PIED PIER PIES PIET PIGS PIKA PIKE PILE PILI PILL PIMA PINA PINE PING PINK PINS PINT PINX PINY PION PIPA PIPE PIPS PIPY PIRE PIRS PISA PISH PITA PITH PITS PITT PITY PIUS PIXY PIZZ

P•I•
PAID PAIL PAIN PAIR PAIX PHIL PHIS PHIZ PLIE PNIN POIL POIS PRIE PRIG PRIM PRIN PRIV PRIX PSIS

P••I
PALI PARI PEDI PERI PFUI PILI PULI PUYI

•PI•
APIA APIS EPIC EPIS OPIA OPIE SPIN SPIT SPIV

••PI
HAPI HOPI IMPI KEPI TOPI TUPI

PK••
PKGS PKWY

P•K•
PEKE PIKA PIKE POKE POKY PUKA PUKU

P••K
PACK PARK PEAK PECK PEEK PERK PICK PINK POLK PORK PREK PUCK PUNK

•PK•
TPKS

••PK
TNPK

PL••
PLAN PLAT PLAX PLAY PLCS PLEA PLEB PLED PLEO PLEW PLEX PLIE PLOD PLOP PLOT PLOW PLOY PLUG PLUM PLUR PLUS

P•L•
PALE PALI PALL PALM PALO PALP PALS PALY PELE PELF PELL PELT PILE PILI PILL POLA POLE POLK POLL POLO POLS POLY PULA PULE PULI PULL PULP PYLE

P••L
PAIL PALL PARL PAUL PAWL PEAL PEEL PELL PHIL PILL POHL POIL POLL POOL PUBL PULL PURL

•PL•
CPLS

•P•L
APPL OPAL OPEL

••PL
APPL DIPL REPL

PM••
PMTS

P•M•
PIMA POME POMO POMP POMS PUMA PUMP

P••M
PALM PERM PLUM POEM PRAM PREM PRIM PROM

•PM•
DPMS RPMS

•P•M
SPAM

PN••
PNIN

P•N•
PANE PANG PANS PANT PENA PEND PENH PENN PENS PENT PINA PINE PING PINK PINS PINT PINX PINY POND PONE PONG PONS PONT PONY PUNA PUNG PUNK PUNS PUNT PUNY

P••N
PAIN PAWN PEEN PENN PEON PHON PION PLAN PNIN POON PRIN PRON

•P•N
OPEN SPAN SPIN SPUN UPON

••PN
CAPN ESPN HYPN

PO••
POCO PODA PODE PODS POEM POET POGO POGS POGY POHL POIL POIS POKE POKY POLA POLE POLK POLL POLO POLS POLY POME POMO POMP POMS POND PONE PONG PONS PONT PONY POOD POOF POOH POOL POON POOP POOR POPE POPS PORE PORK PORT POSE POSH POSS POST POSY POTS POUF POUR POUT POWS

P•O•
PEON PHON PHOT PION PLOD PLOP PLOT PLOW PLOY POOD POOF POOH POOL POON POOP POOR PROA PROB PROC PROD PROF PROG PROM PRON PROP PROS PROT PROV PROW PROX

P••O
PAGO PAHO PALO PASO PAVO PEDO PEPO PESO PETO PIAO PICO PLEO POCO POGO POLO POMO PPDO PUZO PYRO

•PO•
APOC APOS BPOE CPOS EPOS GPOS IPOH IPOS SPOT UPON

•P•O
APSO IPSO OPTO PPDO UPDO UPTO

••PO
ALPO CAPO ESPO EXPO HYPO LIPO PEPO REPO TOPO TYPO USPO

PP••
PPDO

P•P•
PAPA PAPP PEPA PEPE PEPO PEPS PIPA PIPE PIPS PIPY POPE POPS PUPA PUPS PUPU

P••P
PALP PAPP PEEP PERP PLOP POMP POOP PREP PROP PULP PUMP

•PP•
APPL APPS APPT

••PP
BOPP CAPP DEPP LAPP PAPP RAPP REPP RUPP SUPP TEPP YAPP

•PQ•
RPQS SPQR

PR••
PRAM PRAY PREC PRED PREF PREK PREM PREP PRES PRET PREV PREY PREZ PRIE PRIG PRIM PRIN PRIV PRIX PROA PROB PROC PROD PROF PROG PROM PRON PROP PROS PROT PROV PROW PROX PRUT

P•R•
PARA PARC PARD PARE PARI PARK PARL PARR PARS PART PERE PERF PERH PERI PERK PERM PERP PERS PERT PERU PIRE PIRS PORE PORK PORT PURE PURL PURR PYRE PYRO

P••R
PAAR PAIR PARR PEAR PEER PHAR PIER PLUR POOR POUR PUER PURR

•PR•
APRS OPRY SPRY

•P•R
APER OPER SPAR SPGR SPQR SPUR

••PR
BKPR CUPR SUPR

PS••
PSAT PSEC PSIS PSST

P•S•
PASA PASE PASH PASO PASS PAST PESO PEST PISA PISH POSE POSH POSS POST POSY PSST PUSH PUSS

P••S
PACS PADS PAHS PALS PANS PARS PASS PATS PAWS PAYS PCBS PEAS PECS PEDS PEGS PEHS PENS PEPS PERS PETS PEWS PFCS PHDS PHIS PHYS PICS PIES PIGS PINS PIPS PIRS PITS PIUS PKGS PLCS PLUS PMTS PODS POGS POIS POLS POMS PONS POPS POSS POTS POWS PRES PROS PSIS PTAS PUBS PUGS PUNS PUPS PUSS PUTS PVTS

•PS•
APSE APSO IPSE IPSO

•P•S
APBS APES APIS APOS APPS APRS APTS CPAS CPLS CPOS DPMS EPIS EPOS GPOS IPOS OPES OPTS OPUS RPMS RPQS RPTS SPAS TPKS UPAS

••PS
ALPS AMPS APPS ASPS BAPS BOPS CAPS CEPS COPS CUPS DAPS DIPS EMPS ESPS FOPS GAPS GIPS GYPS HAPS HIPS HOPS IMPS KIPS KOPS LAPS LIPS LOPS MAPS MIPS MOPS NAPS NIPS OOPS PEPS PIPS POPS PUPS RAPS REPS RIPS SAPS SIPS SOPS SUPS TAPS TIPS TOPS TSPS TWPS UMPS USPS VIPS YAPS YIPS ZAPS ZIPS

PT••
PTAH PTAS

P•T•
PATD PATE PATH PATS PETA PETE PETO PETS PITA PITH PITS PITT PITY PMTS POTS PUTS PUTT PVTS

P••T
PACT PANT PART PAST PAYT PEAT PELT PENT PERT PEST PFFT PHAT PHOT PICT PIET PINT PITT PLAT PLOT POET PONT PORT POST POUT PRET PROT PRUT PSAT PSST PUNT PUTT

•PT•
APTS OPTO OPTS RPTS UPTO

•P•T
APPT SPAT SPET SPHT SPIT SPOT

••PT
APPT BAPT CAPT COPT DEPT EXPT HEPT KEPT RAPT RCPT REPT SEPT SHPT SUPT WEPT

PU••
PUBL PUBS PUCE PUCK PUDU PUER PUFF PUGH PUGS PUKA PUKU PULA PULE PULI PULL PULP PUMA PUMP PUNA PUNG PUNK PUNS PUNT PUNY PUPA PUPS PUPU PURE PURL PURR PUSH PUSS PUTS PUTT PUYI PUZO

P•U•
PAUL PFUI PIUS PLUG PLUM PLUR PLUS POUF POUR POUT PRUT

P••U
PEAU PERU PUDU PUKU PUPU

•PU•
OPUS SPUD SPUN SPUR

••PU
PUPU

PV••
PVTS

P•V•
PAVE PAVO

P••V
PREV PRIV PROV

•P•V
SPIV

••PV
IMPV

P•W•
PAWL PAWN PAWS PEWS PKWY POWS

P••W
PHEW PLEW PLOW PROW

•P•W
SPEW

P•X•
PIXY

P••X
PAIX PINX PLAX PLEX PRIX PROX

•P•X
APEX

PY••
PYLE PYRE PYRO

P•Y•
PAYS PAYT PHYS PUYI

P••Y
PALY PINY PIPY PITY PIXY PKWY PLAY PLOY POGY POKY POLY PONY POSY PRAY PREY PUNY

•P•Y
OPRY SPAY SPRY

••PY
COPY DOPY ESPY ISPY MOPY PIPY ROPY TYPY

P•Z•
PIZZ PUZO

P••Z
PHIZ PIZZ PREZ

QA••
QADI QAFS QAID QATS

Q•A•
QUAD QUAG QUAI QUAM QUAR QUAY

•Q•A
AQUA

Q•D•
QADI

Q••D
QAID QUAD QUID QUOD

•Q•D
SQYD

QE••
QEII

Q•E•
QUEL QUEM QUES

Q•F•
QAFS

•QF•
SQFT

Q••G
QUAG

Q••H
QOPH

Q•I•
QAID QEII QTIP QUID QUIP QUIT QUIZ

Q••I
QADI QEII QUAI QUOI

•QI•
SQIN

•Q•I
AQUI EQUI SQMI

Q••L
QUEL

Q••M
QUAM QUEM

•QM•
SQMI

•Q•N
SQIN

QO••
QOPH

Q•O•
QUOD QUOI QUOT

•Q•O
AQUO

Q•P•
QOPH

Q••P
QTIP QUIP

••QQ
SEQQ

Q•R•
QTRS

Q••R
QUAR

••QR
SPQR

Q••S
QAFS QATS QTRS QUES

••QS
BBQS ESQS FAQS RFQS RPQS SUQS

QT••
QTIP QTRS

Q•T•
QATS

Q••T
QUIT QUOT

•Q•T
SQFT

QU••
QUAD QUAG QUAI QUAM QUAR QUAY QUEL QUEM QUES QUID QUIP QUIT QUIZ QUOD QUOI QUOT

•QU•
AQUA AQUI AQUO EQUI

Q••Y
QUAY

•QY•
SQYD

Q••Z
QUIZ

RA••
RABE RABI RABS RACE RACK RACY RADM RADS RAFF RAFT RAGA RAGE RAGG RAGS RAGU RAID RAIL RAIN RAJA RAKE RAKI RAKU RALL RAMA RAMI RAMP RAMS RANA RAND RANG RANI RANK RANT RAPA RAPP RAPS RAPT RARA RARE RASA RASE RASH RASK RASP RATA RATE RATH RATS RATT RAUL RAVE RAVI RAYE RAYS RAZE RAZZ

R•A•
RCAF RDAS READ REAL REAM REAP REAR RIAL RIAS ROAD ROAM ROAN ROAR RYAL RYAN RYAS

R••A
RAGA RAJA RAMA RANA RAPA RARA RASA RATA REBA REZA RHEA RICA RIGA RIMA RITA ROCA ROMA RONA ROSA ROTA RRNA RUGA RUTA

•RA•
ARAB ARAD ARAK ARAL ARAM ARAN ARAS BRAC BRAD BRAE BRAG BRAM BRAN BRAS BRAT BRAW BRAY BRAZ CRAB CRAG CRAM CRAT CRAW CRAY DRAB DRAG DRAM DRAT DRAW DRAY ERAS ERAT FRAE FRAM FRAN

FRAP FRAS FRAT FRAU FRAY GRAB GRAD GRAF GRAM GRAN GRAS GRAU GRAY GRAZ IRAE IRAN IRAQ IRAS ORAD ORAL ORAN PRAM PRAY SRAS TRAM TRAP TRAX TRAY URAL VRAI WRAC WRAF WRAP WRAY XRAY

•R•A
ARCA AREA ARIA ARMA ARPA ARRA BREA ERDA ERMA FRIA IRMA MRNA ORCA PROA RRNA SRTA TRNA URFA URGA URSA

••RA
AGRA ARRA ATRA AURA BARA BORA CARA CERA CORA DORA DURA EYRA EZRA FORA GERA HERA HORA JURA KARA KYRA LARA LIRA LYRA MARA MIRA MORA MYRA NARA NORA OKRA OTRA PARA RARA SARA SERA SORA SURA TARA TERA TORA VARA VERA

RB••
RBIS

R•B•
RABE RABI RABS REBA REBS RHBS RIBS ROBB ROBE ROBO ROBS RUBE RUBS RUBY

R••B
ROBB

•RB•
ARBS GRBR IRBM ORBI ORBS URBE URBI URBS

•R•B
ARAB CRAB CRIB DRAB DRIB DRUB GRAB GRUB PROB TRIB

••RB
BARB BURB CARB CURB FORB GARB HERB KERB NLRB SERB SORB VERB

RC••
RCAF RCMP RCPT RCTS

R•C•
RACE RACK RACY RECD RECS RECT RICA RICE RICH RICK RICO ROCA ROCK ROCS RUCK

R••C
ROTC

•RC•
ARCA ARCH ARCO ARCS FRCP FRCS ORCA ORCH ORCS

•R•C
BRAC BRIC CROC ERIC KROC PREC PROC WRAC

••RC
CIRC DARC MARC NARC PARC

RD••
RDAS

R•D•
RADM RADS REDD REDE REDI REDO REDS RFDS RIDD RIDE RIDI RIDS RMDR RNDS RODE RODS RUDD RUDE RUDI RUDY

R••D
RAID RAND READ RECD REDD REED REGD REID REND RETD RIDD RIND ROAD ROOD RUDD RUED

•RD•
ERDA ERDE ORDO URDU

•R•D
ARAD ARID BRAD BRED CRUD DRED FRED GRAD GRID IRED IRID MRED ORAD PRED PROD TROD

••RD
BARD BIRD BYRD CARD CORD CURD DARD FORD GIRD HARD HERD KURD LARD LORD NARD NERD NORD PARD SARD SURD VERD WARD WORD YARD

RE••
READ REAL REAM REAP REAR REBA REBS RECD RECS RECT REDD REDE REDI REDO REDS REED REEF REEK REEL REES REFL REFS REFT REGD REGS REGT REID REIN REIS REIT RELS RELY REMO REMS REND RENE RENI RENO RENT REOS REPL REPO REPP REPS REPT RESH RESP REST RETD RETE RETS REUP REVE REVS REYS REZA

R•E•
REED REEF REEK REEL REES RHEA RHEE RHEO RHES RHET RIEL RIEN ROEG ROES RTES RUED RUER RUES RYES

R••E
RABE RACE RAGE RAKE RARE RASE RATE RAVE RAYE RAZE REDE RENE RETE REVE RHEE RHUE RICE RIDE RIFE RILE RIME RIPE RIRE RISE RITE RIVE ROBE RODE ROHE ROLE ROME ROPE ROSE ROTE ROUE ROVE ROWE RUBE RUDE RULE RUNE RUSE RYLE RYNE

•RE•
AREA AREO ARES BREA BRED BREE BREL BREN BRER BRET BREV BREW CREE CREW DRED DREE DREG DREI DREW FRED FREE FREI FREQ FRET FREY GREE GREG GREW GREX GREY HRES IRED IRES MRED OREG OREL OREM OREO ORES PREC PRED PREF PREK PREM PREP PRES PRET PREV PREY PREZ TREE TREF TREK TRES TRET TREX TREY UREY WREN

•R•E
ARME ARNE ARTE BRAE BREE BRIE CREE CRUE DREE ERDE ERIE ERLE ERNE ERSE ERTE FRAE FREE FROE FRYE GREE IRAE ORLE ORNE PRIE TREE TRUE URBE URGE

••RE
AARE ACRE AIRE BARE BORE BYRE CARE CERE CIRE CORE CURE DARE DIRE DORE EIRE ETRE EYRE FARE FERE FIRE FORE GARE GERE GORE GYRE HARE HERE HIRE IHRE IMRE INRE JURE KORE LIRE LORE LURE LYRE MARE MERE MIRE MORE OGRE PARE PERE PIRE PORE PURE PYRE RARE RIRE SERE SIRE SORE SURE TARE TIRE TORE TYRE VERE WARE WERE WIRE WORE YARE YORE

RF••
RFDS RFQS

R•F•
RAFF RAFT REFL REFS REFT RIFE RIFF RIFS RIFT RUFF

R••F
RAFF RCAF REEF RIFF ROLF ROOF RUFF

•RF•
ORFF URFA

•R•F
GRAF ORFF PREF PROF TREF WRAF

••RF
CERF CORF KERF NERF PERF SERF SURF TURF ZARF

RG••
RGTS

R•G•
RAGA RAGE RAGG RAGS RAGU REGD REGS REGT RIGA RIGG RIGI RIGS RUGA RUGS

R••G
RAGG RANG RIGG RING ROEG RUNG

•RG•
ARGO ARGY ERGO ERGS ORGS ORGY URGA URGE

•R•G
BRAG BRIG CRAG DRAG DREG DRUG FROG FRUG GREG GRIG GROG OREG ORIG PRIG PROG TRIG TRUG

••RG
BERG BORG BURG MARG SURG

RH••
RHBS RHEA RHEE RHEO RHES RHET RHOS RHUE RHUM RHYS

R•H•
ROHE RUHR

R••H
RASH RATH RESH RICH ROSH ROTH RUSH RUTH

•R•H
ARCH ORCH ORTH

••RH
PERH

RI••
RIAL RIAS RIBS RICA RICE RICH RICK RICO RIDD RIDE RIDI RIDS RIEL RIEN RIFE RIFF RIFS RIFT RIGA RIGG RIGI RIGS RIIS RIJN RILE RILL RIMA RIME RIMS RIMY RIND RING RINK RIOS RIOT RIPE RIPS RIRE RISE RISK RITA RITE RITT RITZ RIVE

R•I•
RAID RAIL RAIN RBIS REID REIN REIS REIT RIIS ROIL RUIN

R••I
RABI RAKI RAMI RANI RAVI REDI RENI RIDI RIGI ROTI RUDI

•RI•
ARIA ARID ARIL ARIZ BRIC BRIE BRIG BRIM BRIO BRIT BRIX CRIB CRIM CRIN CRIT DRIB DRIN DRIP DRIQ ERIC ERIE ERIK ERIN ERIQ ERIS FRIA FRIO FRIS FRIT FRIZ GRID GRIG GRIM GRIN GRIP GRIS GRIT IRID IRIS KRIO KRIS ORIG PRIE PRIG PRIM PRIN PRIV PRIX TRIB TRIG TRIM TRIO TRIP TRIS TRIX URIM URIS WRIT

•R•I
DREI FREI ORBI TROI URBI VRAI

••RI
ABRI AGRI ATRI AURI BARI BURI CORI DARI GYRI HARI INRI KIRI LARI LORI MARI NERI NORI OMRI PARI PERI SARI SORI TERI TORI YURI ZORI

R•J•
RAJA RIJN ROJO

R•K•
RAKE RAKI RAKU

R••K
RACK RANK RASK REEK RICK RINK RISK ROCK ROOK RUCK RUSK

•RK•
ARKS ERKS IRKS

•R•K
ARAK ERIK GROK KRUK ORSK PREK TREK TRUK URUK

••RK
BARK BIRK BORK CARK CORK DARK DIRK FORK HARK JERK KIRK LARK LURK MARK MORK MURK NARK PARK PERK PORK SARK TORK TURK WORK YERK YORK

R•L•
RALL RELS RELY RILE RILL ROLE ROLF ROLL ROLY RULE RYLE

R••L
RAIL RALL RAUL REAL REEL REFL RIAL RIEL RILL ROIL ROLL ROTL RYAL

•RL•
ARLO ERLE ORLE ORLY URLS

•R•L
ARAL ARIL ARYL BREL ORAL OREL URAL

••RL
BIRL BURL CARL CURL EARL FURL GIRL HERL HURL JARL KARL MARL MERL PARL PURL

RM••
RMDR

R•M•
RAMA RAMI RAMP RAMS RCMP REMO REMS RIMA RIME RIMS RIMY ROMA ROME ROMP ROMS ROMY RPMS RUMP RUMS

R••M
RADM REAM RHUM ROAM ROOM

•RM•
ARMA ARME ARMS ARMY ERMA IRMA

•R•M
ARAM ARUM BRAM BRIM BROM CRAM CRIM DRAM DRUM FRAM FROM GRAM GRIM IRBM OREM PRAM PREM PRIM PROM TRAM TRIM URIM

••RM
BARM BDRM BERM CORM DERM DORM FARM FIRM FORM GERM HARM HERM NORM PERM TERM WARM WORM

RN••
RNDS

R•N•
RANA RAND RANG RANI RANK RANT REND RENE RENI RENO RENT RIND RING RINK RONA RRNA RUNE RUNG RUNS RUNT RYNE

R••N
RAIN REIN RIEN RIJN ROAN RUIN RYAN RYUN

•RN•
ARNE ARNO BRNO DRNO ERNE ERNO ERNS MRNA ORNE RRNA TRNA URNS WRNS

•R•N
ARAN ARON BRAN BREN BRYN CRIN DRIN ERIN FRAN GRAN GRIN IRAN IRON LRON ORAN PRIN PRON TRON WREN

••RN
BARN BERN BORN BURN CERN CORN DARN DERN DORN DURN EARN FERN FIRN GARN GIRN HERN HORN KERN LORN MORN NORN TARN TERN TORN TURN VERN WARN WORN YARN ZORN

RO••
ROAD ROAM ROAN ROAR ROBB ROBE ROBO ROBS ROCA ROCK ROCS RODE RODS ROEG ROES ROHE ROIL ROJO ROLE ROLF ROLL ROLY ROMA ROME ROMP ROMS ROMY RONA ROOD ROOF ROOK ROOM ROOS ROOT ROPE ROPY RORY ROSA ROSE ROSH ROSS ROSY ROTA ROTC ROTE ROTH ROTI ROTL ROTO ROTS ROUE ROUP ROUS ROUT ROUX ROVE ROWE ROWS

R•O•
REOS RHOS RIOS RIOT ROOD ROOF ROOK ROOM ROOS ROOT RYOT

R••O
REDO REMO RENO REPO RHEO RICO ROBO ROJO ROTO

•RO•
ARON AROO BROM BROS BROW BROZ CROC CROP CROW DROP EROO EROS FROE FROG FROM FROW GROG GROK GROS GROT GROW IRON KROC LRON OROS PROA PROB PROC PROD PROF PROG PROM PRON PROP PROS PROT PROV PROW PROX TROD TROI TRON TROP TROT TROY

•R•O
ARCO AREO ARGO ARLO ARNO AROO BRIO BRNO BRYO CRYO DRNO ERGO ERNO EROO FRIO KRIO ORDO OREO ORZO TRIO

••RO
ACRO AERO AFRO AGRO BARO BORO CARO CERO CORO DURO EBRO EERO EURO FARO FURO GIRO GYRO HERO INRO KARO MERO MIRO MORO NERO NYRO OTRO PYRO SERO TARO TIRO TORO TYRO VERO

XERO
ZERO

RP••
RPMS
RPQS
RPTS

R•P•
RAPA
RAPP
RAPS
RAPT
RCPT
REPL
REPO
REPP
REPS
REPT
RIPE
RIPS
ROPE
ROPY
RUPP

R••P
RAMP
RAPP
RASP
RCMP
REAP
REPP
RESP
REUP
ROMP
ROUP
RSVP
RUMP
RUPP

•RP•
ARPA

•R•P
CROP
DRIP
DROP
FRAP
FRCP
GRIP
PREP
PROP
TRAP
TRIP
TROP
WRAP

••RP
AARP
BURP
CARP
CORP
DORP
EARP
GARP
GORP
HARP
PERP
TARP
TERP
WARP
WKRP

R•Q•
RFQS
RPQS

•R•Q
DRIQ
ERIQ
FREQ
IRAQ

RR••
RRNA

R•R•
RARA
RARE
RIRE
RORY

R••R
REAR
RMDR
ROAR
RUER
RUHR

•RR•
ARRA
ARRS
ERRS

•R•R
BRER
GRBR

••RR
BARR
BIRR
BURR
CARR
CORR
CURR
DORR
FARR
GARR
HERR
KERR
PARR
PURR
TERR
TORR

RS••
RSVP

R•S•
RASA
RASE
RASH
RASK
RASP
RESH
RESP
REST
RISE
RISK
ROSA
ROSE
ROSH
ROSS
ROSY
RUSE
RUSH
RUSK
RUSS
RUST

R••S
RABS
RADS
RAGS
RAMS
RAPS
RATS
RAYS
RBIS
RCTS
RDAS
REBS
RECS
REDS
REES
REFS
REGS
REIS
RELS
REMS
REOS
REPS
RETS
REVS
REYS
RFDS
RFQS
RGTS
RHBS
RHES
RHOS
RHYS
RIAS
RIBS
RIDS
RIFS
RIGS
RIIS
RIMS
RIOS
RIPS
RNDS
ROBS
ROCS
RODS
ROES
ROMS
ROOS
ROSS
ROTS
ROUS
ROWS
RPMS
RPQS
RPTS
RTES
RUBS
RUES
RUGS
RUMS
RUNS
RUSS
RUTS
RYAS
RYES

•RS•
ERSE
ERST
ORSK
URSA

•R•S
ARAS
ARBS
ARCS
ARES
ARKS
ARMS
ARRS
ARTS
BRAS
BROS
CRTS
CRUS
DRYS
ERAS
ERGS
ERIS
ERKS
ERNS
EROS
ERRS
FRAS
FRCS
FRIS
GRAS
GRIS
GROS
GRUS
HRES
IRAS
IRES
IRIS
IRKS
KRIS
ORBS
ORCS
ORES
ORGS
OROS
ORTS
ORVS
PRES
PROS
SRAS
TRES
TRIS
URBS
URIS
URLS
URNS
URUS
WRNS

••RS
AIRS
APRS
ARRS
BARS
BORS
BURS
CARS
CDRS
CORS
CURS
DIRS
DORS
EARS
ERRS
FARS
FIRS
FURS
GARS
HERS
HORS
JARS
KIRS
LARS
LDRS
MARS
MERS
MFRS
MGRS
MIRS
OARS
OURS
PARS
PERS
PIRS
QTRS
SERS
SIRS
SLRS
SSRS
STRS
TARS
TORS
TSRS
VCRS
VERS
WARS

RT••
RTES

R•T•
RATA
RATE
RATH
RATS
RATT
RCTS
RETD
RETE
RETS
RGTS
RITA
RITE
RITT
RITZ
ROTA
ROTC
ROTE
ROTH
ROTI
ROTL
ROTO
ROTS
RPTS
RUTA
RUTH
RUTS

R••T
RAFT
RANT
RAPT
RATT
RCPT
RECT
REFT
REGT
REIT
RENT
REPT
REST
RHET
RIFT
RIOT
RITT
ROOT
ROUT
RUNT
RUST
RYOT

•RT•
ARTE
ARTS
ARTY
CRTS
ERTE
ORTH
ORTS
SRTA

•R•T
BRAT
BRET
BRIT
BRUT
CRAT
CRIT
DRAT
ERAT
ERST
FRAT
FRET
FRIT
GRIT
GROT
GRWT
PRET
PROT
PRUT
TRET
TROT
WRIT

••RT
AIRT
BART
BERT
BORT
BURT
CART
CERT
CURT
DART
DIRT
DORT
FORT
GIRT
HART
HIRT
HORT
HURT
KART
KERT
KURT
MART
MORT
OORT
PART
PERT
PORT
SERT
SORT
TART
TORT
VERT
WART
WERT
WORT
YURT

RU••
RUBE
RUBS
RUBY
RUCK
RUDD
RUDE
RUDI
RUDY
RUED
RUER
RUES
RUFF
RUGA
RUGS
RUHR
RUIN
RULE
RUMP
RUMS
RUNE
RUNG
RUNS
RUNT
RUPP
RUSE
RUSH
RUSK
RUSS
RUST
RUTA
RUTH
RUTS

R•U•
RAUL
REUP
RHUE
RHUM
ROUE
ROUP
ROUS
ROUT
ROUX
RYUN

R••U
RAGU
RAKU

•RU•
ARUM
BRUT
BRUX
CRUD
CRUE
CRUS
CRUX
CRUZ
DRUB
DRUG
DRUM
FRUG
GRUB
GRUS
KRUK
PRUT
TRUE
TRUG
TRUK
URUK
URUS

•R•U
FRAU
GRAU
URDU

••RU
ECRU
GURU
MARU
PERU
THRU

R•V•
RAVE
RAVI
REVE
REVS
RIVE
ROVE
RSVP

•RV•
ORVS

•R•V
BREV
PREV
PRIV
PROV

••RV
MARV
MERV
MIRV
SERV
SURV

R•W•
ROWE
ROWS

•RW•
GRWT

•R•W
BRAW
BREW
BROW
CRAW
CREW
CROW
DRAW
DREW
FROW
GREW
GROW
PROW

••RW
NORW

R••X
ROUX

•R•X
BRIX
BRUX
CRUX
GREX
ORYX
PRIX
PROX
TRAX
TREX
TRIX

••RX
MARX

RY••
RYAL
RYAN
RYAS
RYES
RYLE
RYNE
RYOT
RYUN

R•Y•
RAYE
RAYS
REYS
RHYS

R••Y
RACY
RELY
RIMY
ROLY
ROMY
ROPY
RORY
ROSY
RUBY
RUDY

•RY•
ARYL
BRYN
BRYO
CRYO
DRYS
FRYE
ORYX

•R•Y
ARGY
ARMY
ARTY
BRAY
CRAY
DRAY
FRAY
FREY
GRAY
GREY
ORGY
ORLY
PRAY
PREY
TRAY
TREY
TROY
UREY
WRAY
XRAY

••RY
AERY
AIRY
AWRY
BURY
CARY
CORY
DORY
EERY
ENRY
EURY
EWRY
EYRY
FURY
GARY
GORY
JURY
LORY
MARY
MIRY
NARY
OPRY
RORY
SCRY
SPRY
TORY
VARY
VERY
WARY
WIRY

R•Z•
RAZE
RAZZ
REZA

R••Z
RAZZ
RITZ

•RZ•
ORZO

•R•Z
ARIZ
BRAZ
BROZ
CRUZ
FRIZ
GRAZ
PREZ

••RZ
HARZ
NARZ

SA••
SAAB
SAAR
SABA
SABE
SABU
SACK
SACS
SADA
SADD
SADE
SADI
SADR
SAFE
SAFR
SAGA
SAGE
SAGO
SAGS
SAHL
SAID
SAIL
SAIS
SAKE
SAKI
SAKS
SALA
SALE
SALK
SALP
SALS
SALT
SAME
SAML
SAMO
SAMP
SANA
SAND
SANE
SANG
SANK
SANO
SANS
SANT
SAPS
SARA
SARD
SARI
SARK
SASE
SASH
SASK
SASS
SATE
SATO
SATS
SAUD
SAUK
SAUL
SAUR
SAVA
SAVE
SAWN
SAWS
SAXE
SAYS

S•A•
SAAB
SAAR
SCAB
SCAD
SCAM
SCAN
SCAR
SCAT
SDAK
SEAL
SEAM
SEAN
SEAR
SEAS
SEAT
SFAX
SHAD
SHAG
SHAH
SHAM
SHAN
SHAQ
SHAW
SHAY
SIAL
SIAM
SKAT
SKAW
SLAB
SLAG
SLAM
SLAP
SLAT
SLAV
SLAW
SLAY
SNAG
SNAP
SOAK
SOAP
SOAR
SPAD
SPAM
SPAN
SPAR
SPAS
SPAT
SPAY
SRAS
STAB
STAG
STAN
STAR
STAS
STAT
STAY
SWAB
SWAG
SWAK
SWAM
SWAN
SWAP
SWAT
SWAY

S••A
SABA
SADA
SAGA
SALA
SANA
SARA
SAVA
SEGA
SELA
SERA
SETA
SHEA
SIKA
SIMA
SKUA
SMSA
SOCA
SODA
SOFA
SOLA
SOMA
SORA
SOYA
SPCA
SRTA
STOA
SURA
SUSA
SUVA

•SA•
ASAP
ESAI
ESAS
ESAU
ISAK
ISAO
ISAR
ISAY
LSAT
OSAR
PSAT
TSAR
USAF
USAR

•S•A
ASEA
ASIA
ASTA
ESSA
ESTA
HSIA
ISBA
ISLA
OSHA
OSSA
USDA
USGA
USIA
USMA
USNA
USTA

••SA
ANSA
CASA
COSA
ELSA
ESSA
ILSA
LISA
MESA
MKSA
NASA
OSSA
PASA
PISA
RASA
ROSA
SMSA
SUSA
URSA
VISA
WUSA

S•B•
SABA
SABE
SABU
SEBE
SEBS
SIBS
SLBM
SOBS
STBD
SUBJ
SUBS
SWBS
SWBW

S••B
SAAB
SCAB
SERB
SHEB
SLAB
SLOB
SLUB
SNOB
SNUB
SORB
STAB
STUB
SWAB
SWOB

•SB•
ISBA
ISBN

••SB
MUSB
NTSB

SC••
SCAB
SCAD
SCAM
SCAN
SCAR
SCAT
SCIL
SCLC
SCOP
SCOT
SCOW
SCRY
SCSI
SCTV
SCUD
SCUM
SCUP
SCUT

S•C•
SACK
SACS
SECH
SECS
SECT
SECY
SICK
SICS
SNCC
SOCA
SOCK
SPCA
SPCC
SUCH
SUCK
SYCE

S••C
SCLC
SNCC
SPCC
SPEC
SYNC

•SC•
ASCH
ASCI
ASCO
DSCS
ESCE
USCG

•S•C
BSEC
MSEC
PSEC
USMC

••SC
BASC
BOSC
DESC
DISC
FISC
MASC
MISC
WISC

SD••
SDAK

S•D•
SADA
SADD
SADE
SADI
SADR
SIDE
SIDH
SODA
SODS
STDS
SUDD
SUDS

S••D
SADD
SAID
SAND
SARD
SAUD
SCAD
SCUD
SEED
SEND
SFPD
SHAD
SHED
SHOD
SILD
SIND
SKED
SKID
SLED
SLID
SOLD
SPAD
SPED
SPUD
SQYD
STBD
STUD
SUDD
SUED
SURD
SWED
SYND

•SD•
USDA

•S•D
BSED
USED

••SD
DASD
MUSD
NASD

SE••
SEAL
SEAM
SEAN
SEAR
SEAS
SEAT
SEBE
SEBS
SECH
SECS
SECT
SECY
SEED
SEEK
SEEL
SEEM
SEEN
SEEP
SEER
SEES
SEGA
SEGO
SEHR
SEIN
SEIS
SEJM
SELA
SELF
SELL
SEME
SEMI
SEMS
SEND
SENE
SENS
SENT
SEPT
SEQQ
SERA
SERB
SERE
SERF
SERO
SERS
SERT
SERV
SESS
SETA
SETH
SETI
SETS
SETT
SEUL
SEVE
SEWN
SEWS
SEXT
SEXY

S•E•
SEED
SEEK
SEEL
SEEM
SEEN
SEEP
SEER
SEES
SHEA
SHEB
SHED
SHEL
SHEM
SHEP
SHES
SKED
SKEE
SKEG
SKEP
SKEW
SLED
SLEW
SMEE
SMEW
SNEE
SPEC
SPED
SPEE
SPET
SPEW
STEM
STEN
STEP
STER
STES
STET
STEW
SUED
SUER
SUES
SUET
SUEY
SUEZ
SVEN
SWED

S••E
SABE
SADE
SAFE
SAGE
SAKE
SALE
SAME
SANE
SASE
SATE
SAVE
SAXE
SEBE
SEME
SENE
SERE
SEVE
SHOE
SHUE
SIDE
SINE
SIRE
SITE
SIZE
SKEE
SKYE
SLOE
SLUE
SLYE
SMEE
SNEE
SOIE
SOKE
SOLE
SOME
SONE
SORE
SPEE
STGE
SUPE
SURE
SYCE
SYNE

•SE•
ASEA
BSEC
BSED
ESEL
ISEE
MSEC
OSEE
PSEC
USED
USEE
USER
USES
YSER

•S•E
ASHE
ESCE
ESME
ESNE
ESSE
ESTE
ISEE
ISLE
OSEE
OSTE
USEE

••SE
APSE
BASE
BISE
BOSE
CASE
DOSE
DUSE
EASE
ELSE
ENSE
ERSE
ESSE
FUSE
HOSE
IPSE
JOSE
LASE
LESE
LISE
LOSE
MDSE
MISE
MOSE
MUSE
NOSE
NYSE
OISE
OUSE
PASE
POSE
RASE
RISE
ROSE
RUSE
SASE
VASE
VISE
WHSE
WISE

SF••
SFAX
SFPD

S•F•
SAFE
SAFR
SIFT
SOFA
SOFT
SQFT
SUFF
SUFI

S••F
SELF
SERF
SUFF
SULF
SURF

•S•F
ASIF
ASOF
USAF

SG••
SGTS

S•G•
SAGA
SAGE
SAGO
SAGS
SEGA
SEGO
SIGH
SIGN
SPGR
SSGT
STGE
SVGS

S••G
SANG
SHAG
SING
SKEG
SLAG
SLOG
SLUG
SMOG
SMUG
SNAG
SNOG
SNUG
SONG
STAG
SUNG
SURG
SWAG
SWIG

•SG•
MSGR
MSGS
MSGT
SSGT
TSGT
USGA

•S•G
USCG

SH••
SHAD
SHAG
SHAH
SHAM
SHAN
SHAQ

SHAW SHAY SHEA SHEB SHED SHEL SHEM SHEP SHES SHIH SHIM SHIN SHIP SHIV SHOD SHOE SHOO SHOP SHOT SHOW SHPT SHUE SHUL SHUN SHUT

S•H•
SAHL SEHR SOHN SOHO SPHT

S••H
SASH SECH SETH SHAH SHIH SIDH SIGH SIKH SINH SOPH SUCH

•SH•
ASHE ASHY OSHA

•S•H
ASCH ESTH ISTH

••SH
BASH BOSH BUSH CASH COSH CUSH DASH DISH FISH GASH GISH GOSH GUSH HASH HUSH JOSH KISH KUSH LASH LUSH MASH MESH MOSH MUSH NASH NOSH PASH PISH POSH PUSH RASH RESH ROSH RUSH SASH TESH TISH TOSH TUSH WASH WISH

SI••
SIAL SIAM SIBS SICK SICS SIDE SIDH SIFT SIGH SIGN SIKA SIKH SILD SILK SILL SILO SILT SIMA SIMI SIMP SIMS SIND SINE SING SINH SINK SINO SINS SION SIPS SIRE SIRS SISI SITE SITS SITU SIZE

S•I•
SAID SAIL SAIS SCIL SEIN SEIS SHIH SHIM SHIN SHIP SHIV SKID SKIL SKIM SKIN SKIP SKIS SKIT SLID SLIM SLIP SLIT SMIT SNIP SNIT SOIE SOIL SOIR SPIN SPIT SPIV SQIN STIR SUIT SWIG SWIM SWIT

S••I
SADI SAKI SARI SCSI SEMI SETI SIMI SISI SOLI SORI SQMI SUFI SUZI

•SI•
ASIA ASIF ASIR ASIS HSIA ISIS OSIS PSIS USIA VSIX

•S•I
ASCI ASTI ESAI

••SI
ANSI COSI DESI IASI NISI SCSI SISI

S•J•
SEJM

S••J
SUBJ

SK••
SKAT SKAW SKED SKEE SKEG SKEP SKEW SKID SKIL SKIM SKIN SKIP SKIS SKIT SKOL SKUA SKUS SKYE SKYS

S•K•
SAKE SAKI SAKS SIKA SIKH SOKE SUKS

S••K
SACK SALK SANK SARK SASK SAUK SDAK SEEK SICK SILK SINK SOAK SOCK SOUK SUCK SULK SUNK SWAK

•SK•
ASKS TSKS

•S•K
ISAK

••SK
BASK BISK BOSK BUSK CASK CUSK DESK DISK DUSK FISK HUSK MASK MUSK OMSK ORSK RASK RISK RUSK SASK TASK TUSK WISK

SL••
SLAB SLAG SLAM SLAP SLAT SLAV SLAW SLAY SLBM SLED SLEW SLID SLIM SLIP SLIT SLOB SLOE SLOG SLOP SLOT SLOW SLRS SLUB SLUE SLUG SLUM SLUR SLYE

S•L•
SALA SALE SALK SALP SALS SALT SCLC SELA SELF SELL SILD SILK SILL SILO SILT SOLA SOLD SOLE SOLI SOLN SOLO SOLS STLO SULF SULK SULU SYLL SYLS

S••L
SAHL SAIL SAML SAUL SCIL SEAL SEEL SELL SEUL SHEL SHUL SIAL SILL SKIL SKOL SOIL SOUL STOL SYLL

•SL•
ISLA ISLE ISLS OSLO

•S•L
ESEL

••SL
NASL

SM••
SMEE SMEW SMIT SMOG SMSA SMUG SMUT

S•M•
SAME SAML SAMO SAMP SEME SEMI SEMS SIMA SIMI SIMP SIMS SOMA SOME SQMI STMT SUMO SUMP SUMS SYMS

S••M
SCAM SCUM SEAM SEEM SEJM SHAM SHEM SHIM SIAM SKIM SLAM SLBM SLIM SLUM SPAM STEM STUM SUUM SWAM SWIM SWUM

•SM•
BSMT DSMS ESME ISMS USMA USMC

••SM
COSM MUSM

SN••
SNAG SNAP SNCC SNEE SNIP SNIT SNOB SNOG SNOW SNUB SNUG

S•N•
SANA SAND SANE SANG SANK SANO SANS SANT SEND SENE SENS SENT SIND SINE SING SINH SINK SINO SINS SONE SONG SONS SONY SSNS STNS SUNG SUNK SUNN SUNS SUNY SYNC SYND SYNE SYNS

S••N
SAWN SCAN SEAN SEEN SEIN SEWN SHAN SHIN SHUN SIGN SION SKIN SOHN SOLN SOON SOWN SPAN SPIN SPUN SQIN STAN STEN STUN SUNN SVEN SWAN

•SN•
ESNE ISNT SSNS USNA USNR

•S•N
ASSN ESPN ISBN ISSN

••SN
ASSN BOSN ISSN

SO••
SOAK SOAP SOAR SOBS SOCA SOCK SODA SODS SOFA SOFT SOHN SOHO SOIE SOIL SOIR SOKE SOLA SOLD SOLE SOLI SOLN SOLO SOLS SOMA SOME SONE SONG SONS SONY SOON SOOT SOPH SOPS SORA SORB SORE SORI SORT SOSO SOTS SOUK SOUL SOUP SOUR SOUS SOWN SOWS SOYA SOYS

S•O•
SCOP SCOT SCOW SHOD SHOE SHOO SHOP SHOT SHOW SION SKOL SLOB SLOE SLOG SLOP SLOT SLOW SMOG SNOB SNOG SNOW SOON SOOT SPOT STOA STOL STOP STOT STOW SWOB SWOP

S••O
SAGO SAMO SANO SATO SEGO SERO SHOO SILO SINO SOHO SOLO SOSO STLO SUMO

•SO•
ASOF ASOR DSOS ESOP ESOS VSOP

•S•O
ASCO ASTO ESPO ESSO ESTO ISAO OSLO OSSO USPO

••SO
AHSO ALSO APSO BESO DMSO ESSO FASO IFSO IPSO MESO MISO NASO OSSO PASO PESO SOSO

SP••
SPAD SPAM SPAN SPAR SPAS SPAT SPAY SPCA SPCC SPEC SPED SPEE SPET SPEW SPGR SPHT SPIN SPIT SPIV SPOT SPQR SPRY SPUD SPUN SPUR

S•P•
SAPS SEPT SFPD SHPT SIPS SOPH SOPS SUPE SUPP SUPR SUPS SUPT

S••P
SALP SAMP SCOP SCUP SEEP SHEP SHIP SHOP SIMP SKEP SKIP SLAP SLIP SLOP SNAP SNIP SOAP SOUP STEP STOP SUMP SUPP SWAP SWOP

•SP•
ASPS ESPN ESPO ESPS ESPY ISPY TSPS USPO USPS

•S•P
ASAP ESOP RSVP VSOP

••SP
CUSP GASP HASP HOSP INSP LISP RASP RESP TBSP WASP WISP

SQ••
SQFT SQIN SQMI SQYD

S•Q•
SEQQ SPQR SUQS

S••Q
SEQQ SHAQ

•SQ•
ESQS

SR••
SRAS SRTA

S•R•
SARA SARD SARI SARK SCRY SERA SERB SERE SERF SERO SERS SERT SERV SIRE SIRS SLRS SORA SORB SORE SORI SORT SPRY SSRS STRS SURA SURD SURE SURF SURG SURV

S••R
SAAR SADR SAFR SAUR SCAR SEAR SEER SEHR SLUR SOAR SOIR SOUR SPAR SPGR SPQR SPUR STAR STER STIR SUER SUPR

•SR•
SSRS TSRS

•S•R
ASIR ASOR ASTR ISAR MSGR OSAR TSAR USAR USER USNR USSR YSER

••SR
USSR

SS••
SSGT SSNS SSRS SSTS

S•S•
SASE SASH SASK SASS SCSI SESS SISI SMSA SOSO SUSA SUSS SYST

S••S
SACS SAGS SAIS SAKS SALS SANS SAPS SASS SATS SAWS SAYS SEAS SEBS SECS SEES SEIS SEMS SENS SERS SESS SETS SEWS SGTS SHES SIBS SICS SIMS SINS SIPS SIRS SITS SKIS SKUS SKYS SLRS SOBS SODS SOLS SONS SOPS SOTS SOUS SOWS SOYS SPAS SRAS SSNS SSRS SSTS STAS STDS STES STNS STRS SUBS SUDS SUES SUKS SUMS SUNS SUPS SUQS SUSS SUVS SVGS SWBS SYLS SYMS SYNS

•SS•
ASSN ASST ESSA ESSE ESSO ISSN OSSA OSSO PSST USSR

•S•S
ASIS ASKS ASPS DSCS DSMS DSOS ESAS ESOS ESPS ESQS ESUS ISIS ISLS ISMS ISTS LSTS MSGS OSIS PSIS SSNS SSRS SSTS TSKS TSPS TSRS USES USPS

••SS
BASS BESS BOSS BUSS CASS CESS CUSS DISS DOSS FESS FOSS FUSS HESS HISS HOSS HUSS JESS JOSS KISS LASS LESS LOSS MASS MESS MISS MOSS MUSS NESS PASS POSS PUSS ROSS RUSS SASS SESS SUSS TASS TESS TOSS WUSS WYSS

ST••
STAB STAG STAN STAR STAS STAT STAY STBD STDS STEM STEN STEP STER STES STET STEW STGE STIR STLO STMT STNS STOA STOL STOP STOT STOW STRS STUB STUD STUM STUN STYX

S•T•
SATE SATO SATS SCTV SETA SETH SETI SETS SETT SGTS SITE SITS SITU SOTS SRTA SSTS

S••T
SALT SANT SCAT SCOT SCUT SEAT SECT SENT SEPT SERT SETT SEXT SHOT SHPT SHUT SIFT SILT SKAT SKIT SLAT SLIT SLOT SMIT SMUT SNIT SOFT SOOT SORT SPAT SPET SPHT SPIT SPOT SQFT SSGT STAT STET STMT STOT SUET SUIT SUPT SWAT SWIT SYST

•ST•
ASTA ASTI ASTO ASTR ESTA ESTE ESTH ESTO ISTH ISTS LSTS OSTE SSTS USTA

•S•T
ASST BSMT ISNT LSAT MSGT PSAT PSST SSGT TSGT

••ST
ASST AUST BAST BEST BUST CAST CEST CIST COST DIST DOST DUST EAST ERST FAST FEST FIST FUST GAST GEST GIST GUST HAST HEST HIST HOST INST JEST JUST LAST LEST LIST LOST LUST MAST MIST MOST MUST MYST NAST NEST OAST OUST PAST PEST POST PSST REST RUST SYST TEST VAST VEST WAST WEST YOST ZEST

SU••
SUBJ SUBS SUCH SUCK SUDD SUDS SUED SUER SUES SUET SUEY SUEZ SUFF SUFI SUIT SUKS SULF SULK SULU SUMO SUMP SUMS SUNG SUNK SUNN SUNS SUNY SUPE SUPP SUPR SUPS SUPT SUQS SURA SURD SURE SURF SURG SURV SUSA SUSS SUUM SUVA SUVS SUZI SUZY

S•U•
SAUD SAUK SAUL SAUR SCUD SCUM SCUP SCUT SEUL SHUE SHUL SHUN SHUT SKUA SKUS SLUB SLUE SLUG SLUM SLUR SMUG SMUT SNUB SNUG SOUK SOUL SOUP SOUR SOUS SPUD SPUN SPUR STUB STUD STUM STUN SUUM SWUM

S••U
SABU SITU SULU

•SU•
ESUS

•S•U
ESAU

••SU
JESU ZASU

SV••
SVEN SVGS

S•V•
SAVA SAVE SEVE SUVA SUVS

S••V
SCTV SERV SHIV SLAV SPIV SURV

•SV•
RSVP

SW••
SWAB SWAG SWAK SWAM SWAN SWAP SWAT SWAY SWBS SWBW SWED SWIG SWIM SWIT SWOB SWOP SWUM

S•W•
SAWN SAWS SEWN SEWS SOWN SOWS

S••W
SCOW SHAW

SHOW SKAW SKEW SLAW SLEW SLOW SMEW SNOW SPEW STEW STOW SWBW

S•X•
SAXE SEXT SEXY

S••X
SFAX STYX

•S•X
VSIX

SY••
SYCE SYLL SYLS SYMS SYNC SYND SYNE SYNS SYST

S•Y•
SAYS SKYE SKYS SLYE SOYA SOYS SQYD STYX

S••Y
SCRY SECY SEXY SHAY SLAY SONY SPAY SPRY STAY SUEY SUNY SUZY SWAY

•S•Y
ASHY ESPY ISAY ISPY

••SY
BUSY COSY EASY ITSY NOSY POSY ROSY

S•Z•
SIZE SUZI SUZY

S••Z
SUEZ

TA••
TAAL TABI TABS TABU TACH TACK TACO TACT TADA TADS TAEL TAFT TAGS TAHR TAIF TAIL TAIN TAIT TAIZ TAJS TAKA TAKE TALA TALC TALE TALI TALK TALL TAMA TAME TAMM TAMO TAMP TAMS TANA TANE TANG TANH TANK TANS TAOS TAPA TAPE TAPS TARA TARE TARN TARO TARP TARS TART TASK TASS TATA TATE TATI TATS TAUS TAUT TAVI TAWS TAXA TAXI TAXO

T•A•
TAAL TBAR TEAK TEAL TEAM TEAR TEAS THAI THAN THAR THAS THAT THAW TIAS TMAN TOAD TOAT TRAM TRAP TRAX TRAY TSAR TUAN TWAS TZAR

T••A
TADA TAKA TALA TAMA TANA TAPA TARA TATA TAXA TEMA TERA TEWA THEA TINA TIWA TOEA TOGA TOLA TOMA TORA TRNA TUBA TUFA TULA TUNA TVMA

•TA•
ETAH ETAL ETAS ETAT ITAL ITAR PTAH PTAS STAB STAG STAN STAR STAS STAT STAY UTAH

•T•A
ATKA ATRA ATTA ETNA ETTA ITEA ITZA OTRA STOA

••TA
ACTA AFTA ALTA ANTA ASTA ATTA BETA BOTA CATA CETA DATA EDTA ESTA ETTA FATA FETA GETA GITA IOTA LOTA MATA META MITA MOTA NITA NOTA OCTA OITA PETA PITA RATA RITA ROTA RUTA SETA SRTA TATA USTA VITA ZETA

TB••
TBAR TBSP

T•B•
TABI TABS TABU TCBY TOBE TOBY TUBA TUBB TUBE TUBS

T••B
TOMB TRIB TUBB

•TB•
GTBR STBD

•T•B
FTLB NTSB STAB STUB

••TB
LITB

TC••
TCBY TCHR

T•C•
TACH TACK TACO TACT TECH TECS TICK TICO TICS TOCK TUCK

T••C
TALC

•TC•
ETCH ITCH

•T•C
ETIC OTIC

••TC
ROTC

T•D•
TADA TADS TEDS TIDE TIDY TODD TODO TODS TODY TUDE

T••D
TEED TEND THUD TIED TOAD TODD TOED TOLD TROD TWOD

•TD•
ETDS LTDS STDS

•T•D
STBD STUD

••TD
LITD PATD RETD

TE••
TEAK TEAL TEAM TEAR TEAS TECH TECS TEDS TEED TEEM TEEN TEES TEFF TEGS TELE TELL TELO TEMA TEMP TEND TENE TENN TENO TENS TENT TEPP TERA TERI TERM TERN TERP TERR TESH TESS TEST TETE TETH TETS TEUT TEWA TEXT

T•E•
TAEL TEED TEEM TEEN TEES THEA THEE THEM THEN THEO THEW THEY TIED TIER TIES TMEN TOEA TOED TOES TREE TREF TREK TRES TRET TREX TREY TUES TWEE

T••E
TAKE TALE TAME TANE TAPE TARE TATE TELE TENE TETE THEE TIDE TIGE TIKE TILE TIME TINE TIRE TOBE TOKE TOLE TOME TONE TOPE TORE TOTE TREE TRUE TUBE TUDE TULE TUNE TWEE TYKE TYNE TYPE TYRE

•TE•
ATEN ATES ETES ITEA ITEM ITER ITES KTEL RTES STEM STEN STEP STER STES STET STEW UTEP UTES

•T•E
CTGE ETRE ETTE MTGE OTOE STGE UTNE

••TE
ACTE ALTE ANTE ARTE BATE BETE BITE BUTE BYTE CATE CETE CITE COTE CUTE CYTE DATE DOTE ERTE ESTE ETTE FATE FETE GATE HATE HITE HOTE JETE JUTE KATE KITE LATE LITE LUTE MATE METE MITE MOTE MUTE NATE NITE NOTE OSTE PATE PETE RATE RETE RITE ROTE SATE SITE TATE TETE TOTE VITE VOTE WITE

T•F•
TAFT TEFF TIFF TOFF TOFT TOFU TUFA TUFF TUFT TUFU

T••F
TAIF TEFF TGIF TIFF TOFF TREF TUFF TURF

TG••
TGIF

T•G•
TAGS TEGS TIGE TOGA TOGO TOGS TSGT TUGS

T••G
TANG THUG TING TONG TRIG TRUG TUNG TVPG TWIG

•TG•
CTGE MTGE MTGS STGE

•T•G
LTJG STAG

••TG
ACTG MKTG

TH••
THAI THAN THAR THAS THAT THAW THEA THEE THEM THEN THEO THEW THEY THIN THIO THIS THOM THOR THOS THOU THRU THUD THUG THUR THUS

T•H•
TAHR TCHR TOHO

T••H
TACH TANH TECH TESH TETH TISH TOSH TUSH

•TH•
ETHS OTHO

•T•H
ETAH ETCH ITCH PTAH UTAH

••TH
ACTH ANTH AUTH BATH BETH BOTH CATH DOTH ESTH FATH GATH GOTH HATH HETH ISTH KITH LATH LGTH LITH LUTH MATH METH MOTH MYTH NETH OATH ORTH PATH PITH RATH ROTH RUTH SETH TETH WITH

TI••
TIAS TICK TICO TICS TIDE TIDY TIED TIER TIES TIFF TIGE TIKE TIKI TILE TILL TILS TILT TIME TINA TINE TING TINS TINT TINY TION TIOS TIPS TIRE TIRO TISH TITI TITO TIVS TIWA

T•I•
TAIF TAIL TAIN TAIT TAIZ TGIF THIN THIO THIS TOIL TRIB TRIG TRIM TRIO TRIP TRIS TRIX TUIS TWIG TWIN TWIT TWIX

T••I
TABI TALI TATI TAVI TAXI TERI THAI TIKI TITI TONI TOPI TORI TROI TUPI

•TI•
ATIT ETIC ITIS OTIC OTIS QTIP STIR UTIL

•T•I
ATLI ATOI ATRI ETUI

••TI
ACTI ALTI ANTI ASTI LOTI NOTI ROTI SETI TATI TITI VITI YETI ZITI

T•J•
TAJS TOJO

•TJ•
LTJG

TK••
TKOS TKTS

T•K•
TAKA TAKE TIKE TIKI TOKE TPKS TSKS TYKE

T••K
TACK TALK TANK TASK TEAK TICK TONK TOOK TORK TREK TRUK TUCK TURK TUSK

•TK•
ATKA

T•L•
TALA TALC TALE TALI TALK TALL TELE TELL TELO TILE TILL TILS TILT TOLA TOLD TOLE TOLL TOLU TULA TULE TULL

T••L
TAAL TAEL TAIL TALL TEAL TELL TILL TOIL TOLL TOOL TULL

•TL•
ATLI FTLB ITLL STLO

•T•L
ETAL ITAL ITLL ITOL KTEL STOL UTIL VTOL

••TL
INTL NATL ROTL

TM••
TMAN TMEN

T•M•
TAMA TAME TAMM TAMO TAMP TAMS TEMA TEMP TIME TOMA TOMB TOME TOMS TUMP TUMS TVMA TYMP

T••M
TAMM TEAM TEEM TERM THEM THOM TRAM TRIM TUUM

•TM•
ATMO ATMS STMT

•T•M
ATOM ATUM ETYM ITEM STEM STUM

TN••
TNPK TNUT

T•N•
TANA TANE TANG TANH TANK TANS TEND TENE TENN TENO TENS TENT TINA TINE TING TINS TINT TINY TONE TONG TONI TONK TONS TONY TRNA TUNA TUNE TUNG TUNS TYNE

T••N
TAIN TARN TEEN TENN TERN THAN THEN THIN TION TMAN TMEN TOON TORN TOWN TRON TUAN TURN TWIN

•TN•
ATNO CTNS ETNA MTNS STNS UTNE

•T•N
ATEN ATON ATTN ETON STAN STEN STUN

••TN
ATTN

TO••
TOAD TOAT TOBE TOBY TOCK TODD TODO TODS TODY TOEA TOED TOES TOFF TOFT TOFU TOGA TOGO TOGS TOHO TOIL TOJO TOKE TOLA TOLD TOLE TOLL TOLU TOMA TOMB TOME TOMS TONE TONG TONI TONK TONS TONY TOOK TOOL TOON TOOT TOPE TOPI TOPO TOPS TORA TORE TORI TORK TORN TORO TORR TORS TORT TORY TOSH TOSS TOTE TOTO TOTS TOUR TOUT TOWN TOWS TOYS

T•O•
TAOS THOM THOR THOS THOU TION TIOS TKOS TOOK TOOL TOON TOOT TROD TROI TRON TROP TROT TROY TWOD TWOS

T••O
TACO TAMO TARO TAXO TELO TENO THEO THIO TICO TIRO TITO TODO TOGO TOHO TOJO TOPO TORO TOTO TRIO TYPO TYRO

•TO•
ATOI ATOM ATON ATOP ATOR ETON GTOS ITOL OTOE OTOS STOA STOL STOP STOT STOW VTOL

•T•O
ATMO ATNO ATTO OTHO OTRO OTTO STLO

••TO
ALTO ASTO ATTO AUTO CATO CYTO ECTO ENTO ESTO GATO INTO JATO KATO KETO KOTO LETO MOTO NATO OCTO ONTO OPTO OTTO PETO ROTO SATO TITO TOTO UNTO UPTO VETO VITO

TP••
TPKS

T•P•
TAPA TAPE TAPS TEPP TIPS TNPK TOPE TOPI TOPO TOPS TSPS TUPI TVPG TWPS TYPE TYPO TYPY

T••P
TAMP TARP TBSP TEMP TEPP TERP TRAP TRIP TROP TUMP TYMP

•T•P
ATOP HTTP QTIP STEP STOP UTEP

••TP
HTTP

TR••
TRAM TRAP TRAX TRAY TREE TREF TREK TRES TRET TREX TREY TRIB TRIG TRIM TRIO TRIP TRIS TRIX TRNA TROD TROI TRON TROP TROT TROY TRUE TRUG TRUK

T•R•
TARA TARE TARN TARO TARP TARS TART TERA TERI TERM TERN TERP TERR THRU TIRE TIRO TORA TORE TORI TORK TORN TORO TORR TORS TORT TORY TSRS TURF TURK TURN TYRE TYRO

T••R
TAHR TBAR TCHR TEAR TERR THAR THOR THUR TIER TORR TOUR TSAR TZAR

•TR•
ATRA ATRI ETRE OTRA OTRO QTRS STRS

•T•R
ATOR GTBR ITAR ITER LTYR STAR STER STIR

••TR
ASTR ENTR INTR

TS••
TSAR TSGT TSKS TSPS TSRS

T•S•
TASK TASS TBSP TESH TESS TEST TISH TOSH TOSS TUSH TUSK

T••S
TABS TADS TAGS TAJS TAMS TANS TAOS TAPS

TARS
TASS
TATS
TAUS
TAWS
TEAS
TECS
TEDS
TEES
TEGS
TENS
TESS
TETS
THAS
THIS
THOS
THUS
TIAS
TICS
TIES
TILS
TINS
TIOS
TIPS
TIVS
TKOS
TKTS
TODS
TOES
TOGS
TOMS
TONS
TOPS
TORS
TOSS
TOTS
TOWS
TOYS
TPKS
TRES
TRIS
TSKS
TSPS
TSRS
TUBS
TUES
TUGS
TUIS
TUMS
TUNS
TUTS
TWAS
TWOS
TWPS

•TS•
ITSY
NTSB

•T•S
ATES
ATMS
ATTS
ATVS
BTUS
CTNS
ETAS
ETDS
ETES
ETHS
GTOS
ITES
ITIS
LTDS
MTGS
MTNS
OTIS
OTOS
PTAS
QTRS
RTES
STAS
STDS
STES
STNS
STRS
UTES

••TS
ACTS
AFTS
AGTS
AITS
ALTS
AMTS
ANTS
APTS
ARTS
ATTS
BATS
BETS
BITS
BLTS
BOTS
BUTS
CATS
CITS
COTS
CRTS
CUTS
DATS
DETS
DITS
DOTS
EATS
EFTS
EMTS
ENTS
EXTS
FATS
FITS
GATS
GETS
GITS
GUTS
HATS
HITS
HUTS
INTS
ISTS
JETS
JOTS
JUTS
KITS
LATS
LETS
LITS
LOTS
LSTS
MATS
METS
MOTS
NETS
NITS
NOTS
NUTS
OATS
OPTS
ORTS
OUTS
PATS
PETS
PITS
PMTS
POTS
PUTS
PVTS
QATS
RATS
RCTS
RETS
RGTS
ROTS
RPTS
RUTS
SATS
SETS
SGTS
SITS
SOTS
SSTS
TATS
TETS
TKTS
TOTS
TUTS
VATS
VDTS
VETS
WATS
WETS
WITS
XATS

T•T•
TATA
TATE
TATI
TATS
TETE
TETH
TETS
TITI
TITO
TKTS
TOTE
TOTO
TOTS
TUTS
TUTU

T••T
TACT
TAFT
TAIT
TART
TAUT
TENT
TEST
TEUT
TEXT
THAT
TILT
TINT
TNUT
TOAT
TOFT
TOOT
TORT
TOUT
TRET
TROT
TSGT
TUFT
TWIT

•TT•
ATTA
ATTN
ATTO
ATTS
ATTU
ATTY
ETTA
ETTE
HTTP
ITTY
OTTO

•T•T
ATIT
ATWT
ETAT
NTWT
STAT
STET
STMT
STOT

••TT
BATT
BITT
BOTT
BUTT
CATT
GATT
HUTT
JETT
KETT
KITT
LETT
LOTT
MATT
MITT
MOTT
MUTT
NUTT
PITT
PUTT
RATT
RITT
SETT
WATT
WITT

TU••
TUAN
TUBA
TUBB
TUBE
TUBS
TUCK
TUDE
TUES
TUFA
TUFF
TUFT
TUFU
TUGS
TUIS
TULA
TULE
TULL
TUMP
TUMS
TUNA
TUNE
TUNG
TUNS
TUPI
TURF
TURK
TURN
TUSH
TUSK
TUTS
TUTU
TUUM

T•U•
TAUS
TAUT
TEUT
THUD
THUG
THUR
THUS
TNUT
TOUR
TOUT
TRUE
TRUG
TRUK
TUUM

T••U
TABU
THOU
THRU
TOFU
TOLU
TUFU
TUTU

•TU•
ATUM
BTUS
ETUI
ETUX
STUB
STUD
STUM
STUN

•T•U
ATTU

••TU
ATTU
HUTU
MATU
SITU
TUTU
VATU
WCTU

TV••
TVMA
TVPG

T•V•
TAVI
TIVS

•TV•
ATVS

••TV
ACTV
CATV
CCTV
HDTV
SCTV

TW••
TWAS
TWEE
TWIG
TWIN
TWIT
TWIX
TWOD
TWOS
TWPS

T•W•
TAWS
TEWA
TIWA
TOWN
TOWS

T••W
THAW
THEW

•TW•
ATWT
NTWT

•T•W
STEW
STOW

••TW
GWTW

T•X•
TAXA
TAXI
TAXO
TEXT

T••X
TRAX
TREX
TRIX
TWIX

•T•X
ETUX
STYX

TY••
TYKE
TYMP
TYNE
TYPE
TYPO
TYPY
TYRE
TYRO

T•Y•
TOYS

T••Y
TCBY
THEY
TIDY
TINY
TOBY
TODY
TONY
TORY
TRAY
TREY
TROY
TYPY

•TY•
ETYM
LTYR
STYX

•T•Y
ATTY
ITSY
ITTY
STAY

••TY
ARTY
ATTY
CITY
COTY
DUTY
ITTY
KATY
OATY
PITY

TZ••
TZAR

T••Z
TAIZ

•TZ•
ITZA

••TZ
BETZ
DITZ
FITZ
FUTZ
GETZ
KATZ
LUTZ
METZ
RITZ
ZOTZ

U•A•
ULAN
UNAU
UPAS
URAL
USAF
USAR
UTAH

U••A
UCLA
ULNA
UMEA
URFA
URGA
URSA
USDA
USGA
USIA
USMA
USNA
USTA
UVEA

•UA•
DUAD
DUAL
FUAD
GUAM
GUAN
GUAR
HUAC
JUAN
LUAU
QUAD
QUAG
QUAI
QUAM
QUAR
QUAY
TUAN
YUAN

•U•A
AULA
AURA
BUNA
CUBA
CUNA
DUMA
DUNA
DURA
FULA
HULA
HUPA
JUBA
JUGA
JURA
LUBA
LUNA
PUKA
PULA
PUMA
PUNA
PUPA
RUGA
RUTA
SURA
SUSA
SUVA
TUBA
TUFA
TULA
TUNA
WUSA
YUBA
YUGA
YUMA

••UA
AGUA
AQUA
ECUA
SKUA

UB••
UBER

U•B•
UMBO
URBE
URBI
URBS

•UB•
AUBE
BUBU
CUBA
CUBE
CUBS
DUBS
FUBS
HUBS
JUBA
LUBA
LUBE
NUBS
PUBL
PUBS
RUBE
RUBS
RUBY
SUBJ
SUBS
TUBA
TUBB
TUBE
TUBS
YUBA

•U•B
BULB
BURB
CURB
DUMB
MUSB
NUMB
TUBB

••UB
CHUB
CLUB
DAUB
DRUB
FLUB
GRUB
SLUB
SNUB
STUB

UC••
UCLA

U•C•
UNCI
USCG

U••C
USMC

•UC•
BUCK
BUCO
BUCS
DUCE
DUCK
DUCT
GUCK
HUCK
LUCE
LUCI
LUCK
LUCY
MUCH
MUCK
OUCH
PUCE
PUCK
RUCK
SUCH
SUCK
TUCK
YUCK

•U•C
HUAC
JUNC
NUNC

••UC
EDUC
GLUC

UD••
UDOS

U•D•
UNDO
UPDO
URDU
USDA

U••D
USED

•UD•
AUDE
AUDI
BUDD
BUDS
CUDS
DUDE
DUDS
FUDD
JUDD
JUDE
JUDG
JUDO
JUDY
KUDU
MUDD
MUDS
NUDE
NUDI
OUDS
PUDU
RUDD
RUDE
RUDI
RUDY
SUDD
SUDS
TUDE

•U•D
AULD
BUDD
BUND
CUED
CURD
DUAD
FUAD
FUDD
FUND
HUED
HUND
JUDD
KURD
MUDD
MUSD
QUAD
QUID
QUOD
RUDD
RUED
SUDD
SUED
SURD

••UD
BAUD
CRUD
FEUD
GAUD
KNUD
LAUD
LOUD
MAUD
SAUD
SCUD
SPUD
STUD
THUD
VAUD
YOUD

UE••
UELE
UEYS

U•E•
UBER
UKES
ULEE
UMEA
UNES
UREY
USED
USEE
USER
USES
UTEP
UTES
UVEA

U••E
UELE
ULEE
URBE
URGE
USEE
UTNE

•UE•
AUEL
AUER
CUED
CUER
CUES
DUEL
DUES
DUET
FUEL
HUED
HUES
HUEY
PUER
QUEL
QUEM
QUES
RUED
RUER
RUES
SUED
SUER
SUES
SUET
SUEY
SUEZ
TUES

•U•E
AUBE
AUDE
AUGE
AUNE
BUTE
CUBE
CUKE
CULE
CURE
CUTE
DUCE
DUDE
DUKE
DUNE
DUPE
DUSE
DUVE
FUME
FUSE
FUZE
HUGE
HUME
JUDE
JUKE
JULE
JUNE
JURE
JUTE
LUBE
LUCE
LUGE
LUKE
LUNE
LUPE
LURE
LUTE
LUXE
MULE
MUSE
MUTE
NUDE
NUKE
OUSE
PUCE
PULE
PURE
RUBE
RUDE
RULE
RUNE
RUSE
SUPE
SURE
TUBE
TUDE
TULE
TUNE
YULE

••UE
ADUE
AGUE
BLUE
CLUE
COUE
CRUE
FLUE
GLUE
LAUE
MOUE
NIUE
RHUE
ROUE
SHUE
SLUE
TRUE

UF••
UFOS

U•F•
URFA

U••F
USAF

•UF•
BUFF
CUFF
CUFT
DUFF
DUFY
GUFF
HUFF
LUFF
LUFT
MUFF
PUFF
RUFF
SUFF
SUFI
TUFA
TUFF
TUFT
TUFU

•U•F
BUFF
BUMF
CUFF
DUFF
FUNF
GUFF
GULF
HUFF
LUFF
MUFF
PUFF
RUFF
SUFF
SULF
SURF
TUFF
TURF

••UF
ENUF
NEUF
OEUF
POUF

UG••
UGHS
UGLI
UGLY

U•G•
URGA
URGE
USGA

U••G
USCG

•UG•
AUGE
BUGS
FUGS
FUGU
HUGE
HUGH
HUGO
HUGS
JUGA
JUGS
LUGE
LUGS
MUGS
PUGH
PUGS
RUGA
RUGS
TUGS
VUGS
YUGA
YUGO

•U•G
BULG
BUNG
BURG
GUNG
HUNG
JUDG
JUNG
KUNG
LUNG
MUNG
PUNG
QUAG
RUNG
SUNG
SURG
TUNG
VULG

••UG
CHUG
DOUG
DRUG
FRUG
GLUG
PLUG
SLUG
SMUG
SNUG
THUG
TRUG

UH••
UHOH
UHUH

U•H•
UGHS

U••H
UHOH
UHUH
UMPH
UTAH

•UH•
BUHL
BUHR
KUHN
RUHR
WUHL
WUHU

•U•H
AUTH
BUSH
CUSH
GUSH
HUGH
HUSH
KUSH
LUSH
LUTH
MUCH
MUSH
OUCH
PUGH
PUSH
RUSH
RUTH
SUCH
TUSH

••UH
UHUH

U•I•
UNIS
UNIT
UNIV
UNIX
URIM
URIS
USIA
UTIL
UZIS

U••I
UGLI
UNCI
URBI

•UI•
CUIN
GUIN
GUIS
HUIS
LUIS
MUIR
NUIT
QUID
QUIP
QUIT
QUIZ
RUIN
SUIT
TUIS

•U•I
AUDI
AURI
BURI
FUJI
LUCI
MUNI
NUDI
PULI
PUYI
QUAI
QUOI
RUDI
SUFI
SUZI
TUPI
WUXI
YURI
ZUNI

••UI
ALUI
AQUI
EQUI
ETUI
MAUI
PFUI

•UJ•
CUJO
FUJI
JUJU

•U•J
SUBJ

UK••
UKES

U••K
URUK

•UK•
AUKS
CUKE
DUKE
JUKE
LUKE
LUKS
NUKE
PUKA
PUKU
SUKS
YUKS

•U•K
BUCK
BULK
BUNK
BUSK
CUSK
DUCK
DUNK
DUSK
FUNK
GUCK
GUNK
HUCK
HULK
HUNK
HUSK
JUNK
LUCK
LURK
MUCK
MURK
MUSK
PUCK
PUNK
RUCK
RUSK
SUCK
SULK
SUNK
TUCK
TURK
TUSK
YUCK

••UK
KRUK
LEUK
NYUK
SAUK
SOUK
TRUK
URUK
WOUK
ZOUK

UL••
ULAN
ULEE
ULNA
ULUS

U•L•
UCLA
UELE
UGLI
UGLY
UNLV
URLS

U••L
URAL
UTIL

•UL•
AULA
AULD
BULB
BULG
BULK
BULL
CULE
CULL
CULM
CULP
CULS
CULT
DULL
DULY
FULA
FULL
GULF
GULL
GULP
HULA
HULK
HULL
JULE
JULY
LULL
LULU
MULE
MULL
NULL
OULU
PULA
PULE
PULI
PULL
PULP
RULE
SULF
SULK
SULU
TULA
TULE
TULL
VULG
VULT
YULE
ZULU

•U•L
AUEL
BUHL
BULL
BURL
CULL
CURL
DUAL
DUEL
DULL
FUEL
FULL
FURL
GULL
HULL
HURL
LULL
MULL
NULL
PUBL
PULL
PURL
QUEL
TULL
WUHL

••UL
AZUL
CAUL
ELUL
FOUL
GAUL
HAUL
MAUL
PAUL
RAUL
SAUL
SEUL
SHUL
SOUL

UM••
UMBO
UMEA
UMPH
UMPS

U•M•
USMA
USMC

U••M
UNUM
URIM

•UM•
BUMF
BUMP
BUMS
DUMA
DUMB
DUMP
FUME
FUMY
GUMM
GUMP
GUMS
HUME
HUMP
HUMS
JUMP
LUMP
MUMP
MUMS
NUMB
PUMA
PUMP
RUMP
RUMS
SUMO
SUMP
SUMS
TUMP
TUMS
YUMA

•U•M
CULM
GUAM
GUMM
MUSM
QUAM
QUEM
SUUM
TUUM

••UM
ALUM
ARUM
ATUM
AXUM
BAUM
BLUM
CHUM
DEUM
DRUM
GAUM
GEUM
GLUM
MEUM
OVUM
PLUM
RHUM
SCUM
SLUM
STUM
SUUM
SWUM
TUUM
UNUM

UN••
UNAU
UNCI
UNDO
UNES
UNIS
UNIT
UNIV
UNIX
UNLV
UNTO
UNUM

U•N•
ULNA
URNS
USNA
USNR
UTNE

U••N
ULAN
UPON

•UN•
AUNE
AUNT
BUNA
BUND

BUNG BUNK BUNS BUNT CUNA CUNY DUNA DUNE DUNK DUNN DUNS FUND FUNF FUNK FUNT GUNG GUNK GUNN GUNS HUND HUNG HUNK HUNS HUNT JUNC JUNE JUNG JUNK JUNO KUNG LUNA LUNE LUNG LUNN LUNT MUNG MUNI NUNC NUNN NUNS PUNA PUNG PUNK PUNS PUNT PUNY RUNE RUNG RUNS RUNT SUNG SUNK SUNN SUNS SUNY TUNA TUNE TUNG TUNS ZUNI

•U•N
BUON BURN CUIN DUNN DURN GUAN GUIN GUNN HUON JUAN KUHN LUNN MUON NUNN RUIN SUNN TUAN TURN YUAN

••UN
FAUN IDUN NEUN NOUN RYUN SHUN SPUN STUN

U•O•
UDOS UFOS UHOH UPON UXOR

U••O
UMBO UNDO UNTO UPDO UPTO USPO

•UO•
BUON BUOY DUOS HUON MUON QUOD QUOI QUOT

•U•O
AUTO BUCO CUJO DURO EURO FURO HUGO JUDO JUNO OUZO PUZO SUMO YUGO

••UO
AQUO

UP••
UPAS UPDO UPON UPTO

U•P•
UMPH UMPS USPO USPS

U••P
UTEP

•UP•
CUPR CUPS DUPE HUPA LUPE PUPA PUPS PUPU RUPP SUPE SUPP SUPR SUPS SUPT TUPI

•U•P
BUMP BURP CULP CUSP DUMP GULP GUMP HUMP JUMP LUMP MUMP PULP PUMP QUIP RUMP RUPP SUMP SUPP TUMP

••UP
COUP DOUP GOUP LOUP REUP ROUP SCUP SOUP WHUP

•UQ•
SUQS

UR••
URAL URBE URBI URBS URDU UREY URFA URGA URGE URIM URIS URLS URNS URSA URUK URUS

U••R
UBER USAR USER USNR USSR UXOR

•UR•
AURA AURI BURB BURG BURI BURL BURN BURP BURR BURS BURT BURY CURB CURD CURE CURL CURR CURS CURT DURA DURN DURO EURO EURY FURL FURO FURS FURY GURU HURL HURT JURA JURE JURY KURD KURT LURE LURK MURK OURS PURE PURL PURR SURA SURD SURE SURF SURG SURV TURF TURK TURN YURI YURT

•U•R
AUER BUHR BURR CUER CUPR CURR GUAR MUIR PUER PURR QUAR RUER RUHR SUER SUPR

••UR
AMUR AZUR BLUR CHUR DOUR FOUR GAUR HOUR JOUR KNUR PLUR POUR SAUR SLUR SOUR SPUR THUR TOUR YOUR

US••
USAF USAR USCG USDA USED USEE USER USES USGA USIA USMA USMC USNA USNR USPO USPS USSR USTA

U•S•
URSA USSR

U••S
UDOS UEYS UFOS UGHS UKES ULUS UMPS UNES UNIS UPAS URBS URIS URLS URNS URUS USES USPS UTES UZIS

•US•
AUST BUSH BUSK BUSS BUST BUSY CUSH CUSK CUSP CUSS DUSE DUSK DUST FUSE FUSS FUST GUSH GUST HUSH HUSK HUSS JUST KUSH LUSH LUST MUSB MUSD MUSE MUSH MUSK MUSM MUSS MUST OUSE OUST PUSH PUSS RUSE RUSH RUSK RUSS RUST SUSA SUSS TUSH TUSK WUSA WUSS

•U•S
AUKS BUCS BUDS BUGS BUMS BUNS BURS BUSS BUTS BUYS CUBS CUDS CUES CULS CUPS CURS CUSS CUTS DUBS DUDS DUES DUNS DUOS FUBS FUGS FURS FUSS GUIS GUMS GUNS GUTS GUVS GUYS HUBS HUES HUGS HUIS HUMS HUNS HUSS HUTS JUGS JUTS LUGS LUIS LUKS LUVS MUDS MUGS MUMS MUSS NUBS NUNS NUTS NUYS OUDS OURS OUTS PUBS PUGS PUNS PUPS PUSS PUTS QUES RUBS RUES RUGS RUMS RUNS RUSS RUTS SUBS SUDS SUES SUKS SUMS SUNS SUPS SUQS SUSS SUVS TUBS TUES TUGS TUIS TUMS TUNS TUTS VUGS WUSS YUKS

••US
BMUS BTUS CAUS CRUS DEUS ECUS EMUS EOUS ESUS FLUS GNUS GRUS HAUS ICUS IMUS IOUS NOUS ONUS OPUS OXUS PIUS PLUS ROUS SKUS SOUS TAUS THUS ULUS URUS VOUS ZEUS

UT••
UTAH UTEP UTES UTIL UTNE

U•T•
UNTO UPTO USTA

U••T
UNIT

•UT•
AUTH AUTO BUTE BUTS BUTT CUTE CUTS DUTY FUTZ GUTS HUTS HUTT HUTU JUTE JUTS LUTE LUTH LUTZ MUTE MUTT NUTS NUTT OUTS PUTS PUTT RUTA RUTH RUTS TUTS TUTU

•U•T
AUNT AUST BUNT BURT BUST BUTT CUFT CULT CURT DUCT DUET DUST FUNT FUST GUST HUNT HURT HUTT JUST KURT LUFT LUNT LUST MUST MUTT NUIT NUTT OUST PUNT PUTT QUIT QUOT RUNT RUST SUET SUIT SUPT TUFT VULT YURT

••UT
ABUT AOUT BOUT BRUT CNUT DEUT FAUT GLUT GOUT HAUT KNUT LOUT NAUT NEUT POUT PRUT ROUT SCUT SHUT SMUT TAUT TEUT TNUT TOUT XOUT

U•U•
UHUH ULUS UNUM URUK URUS

U••U
UNAU URDU

•UU•
SUUM TUUM

•U•U
BUBU FUGU GURU HUTU JUJU KUDU LUAU LULU OULU PUDU PUKU PUPU SULU TUFU TUTU WUHU ZULU

UV••
UVEA

U••V
UNIV UNLV

•UV•
DUVE GUVS LUVS SUVA SUVS

•U•V
SURV

••UW
DOUW

UX••
UXOR

U••X
UNIX

•UX•
LUXE WUXI

••UX
BRUX CRUX DEUX DOUX EAUX ETUX FAUX FLUX JEUX ROUX VAUX YEUX

U•Y•
UEYS

U••Y
UGLY UREY

•UY•
BUYS GUYS NUYS PUYI

•U•Y
BUOY BURY BUSY CUNY DUFY DULY DUTY EURY FUMY FURY HUEY JUDY JULY JURY LUCY PUNY QUAY RUBY RUDY SUEY SUNY SUZY

UZ••
UZIS

•UZ•
BUZZ FUZE FUZZ MUZZ OUZO PUZO SUZI SUZY

•U•Z
BUZZ FUTZ FUZZ LUTZ MUZZ QUIZ SUEZ

••UZ
CRUZ

VA••
VAAL VACA VACS VADE VADM VAIL VAIN VAIR VALE VAMP VANE VANG VANS VARA VARY VASE VAST VATS VATU VAUD VAUX VAVS VAYA

V•A•
VAAL VDAY VEAL VEAU VIAL VRAI

V••A
VACA VARA VAYA VEDA VEGA VELA VENA VERA VIDA VIGA VILA VINA VISA VITA VIVA

•VA•
AVAL AVAR EVAH EVAN EVAP IVAN OVAL

•V•A
AVIA TVMA UVEA

••VA
ALVA BOVA CAVA DEVA DIVA FAVA JAVA KAVA KIVA LAVA NEVA NOVA SAVA SUVA VIVA

V•B•
VIBE

V••B
VERB

VC••
VCRS

V•C•
VACA VACS VICE VICI VICO VOCE

•V•C
AVEC

VD••
VDAY VDTS

V•D•
VADE VADM VEDA VIDA VIDE VIDI

V••D
VAUD VELD VEND VERD VIED VOID

•VD•
AVDP BVDS DVDS

•V•D
AVID OVID

••VD
BLVD NKVD

VE••
VEAL VEAU VEDA VEEP VEER VEES VEGA VEII VEIL VEIN VELA VELD VENA VEND VENI VENN VENT VERA VERB VERD VERE VERN VERO VERS VERT VERY VEST VETO VETS

V•E•
VEEP VEER VEES VIED VIER VIES VIET VIEW

V••E
VADE VALE VANE VASE VERE VIBE VICE VIDE VILE VINE VISE VITE VIVE VOCE VOLE VOTE

•VE•
AVEC AVER AVES EVEL EVEN EVER EVES IVES IVEY OVEN OVER SVEN UVEA YVES

•V•E
EVOE

••VE
CAVE COVE DAVE DIVE DOVE DUVE EAVE FAVE FIVE GAVE GIVE GYVE HAVE HIVE HOVE JIVE JOVE LAVE LIVE LOVE MOVE NAVE NEVE PAVE RAVE REVE RIVE ROVE SAVE SEVE VIVE WAVE WEVE WOVE

V•G•
VEGA VIGA VIGO VUGS

V••G
VANG VING VULG

•VG•
AVGS SVGS

•V•G
TVPG

•V•H
EVAH

VI••
VIAL VIBE VICE VICI VICO VIDA VIDE VIDI VIED VIER VIES VIET VIEW VIGA VIGO VIII VILA VILE VIMS VINA VINE VING VINI VINO VINS VINY VIOL VIPS VISA VISE VITA VITE VITI VITO VIVA VIVE

V•I•
VAIL VAIN VAIR VEII VEIL VEIN VIII VOID VOIR VOIX VSIX

V••I
VEII VENI VICI VIDI VIII VINI VITI VRAI

•VI•
AVIA AVID AVIS AVIV CVII DVII EVIL LVII MVII OVID OVIS XVII

•V•I
CVII DVII LVII MVII XVII

••VI
CCVI CDVI CLVI CMVI CXVI DCVI DEVI DLVI DXVI LEVI LXVI MCVI MDVI MLVI MMVI MXVI NEVI RAVI TAVI XCVI XLVI XXVI

V•L•
VALE VELA VELD VILA VILE VOLE VOLS VOLT VULG VULT

V••L
VAAL VAIL VEAL VEIL VIAL VIOL VTOL

•V•L
AVAL EVEL EVIL OVAL

V•M•
VAMP VIMS

V••M
VADM VOOM

•VM•
DVMS TVMA

•V•M
OVUM

V•N•
VANE VANG VANS VENA VEND VENI VENN VENT VINA VINE VING VINI VINO VINS VINY

V••N
VAIN VEIN VENN VERN

•V•N
AVON EVAN EVEN IVAN OVEN SVEN

VO••
VOCE VOID VOIR VOIX VOLE VOLS VOLT VOOM VOTE VOUS VOWS

V•O•
VIOL VOOM VSOP VTOL

V••O
VERO VETO VICO VIGO VINO VITO

•VO•
AVON AVOS AVOW EVOE IVOR LVOV

••VO
DEVO LEVO NOVO PAVO

V•P•
VIPS

V••P
VAMP VEEP VSOP

•VP•
TVPG

•V•P
AVDP EVAP

••VP
RSVP

VR••
VRAI

V•R•
VARA VARY VCRS VERA VERB VERD VERE VERN VERO VERS VERT VERY

V••R
VAIR VEER VIER VOIR

•V•R
AVAR AVER EVER IVOR OVER

VS••
VSIX VSOP

V•S•
VASE VAST VEST VISA VISE

V••S
VACS VANS VATS VAVS VCRS VDTS VEES VERS VETS VIES VIMS VINS VIPS VOLS VOUS VOWS VUGS

•V•S
AVES AVGS AVIS AVOS BVDS DVDS DVMS EVES IVES OVIS PVTS SVGS YVES

••VS
ATVS CAVS DIVS ENVS GUVS LAVS LUVS MAVS ORVS REVS SUVS TIVS VAVS

VT••
VTOL

V•T•
VATS VATU VDTS

VETO VETS VITA VITE VITI VITO VOTE

V••T
VAST VENT VERT VEST VIET VOLT VULT

•VT•
PVTS

••VT
ADVT GOVT

VU••
VUGS VULG VULT

V•U•
VAUD VAUX VOUS

V••U
VATU VEAU

•VU•
OVUM

••VU
KIVU LEVU

V•V•
VAVS VIVA VIVE

•V•V
AVIV LVOV

V•W•
VOWS

V••W
VIEW

•V•W
AVOW

V••X
VAUX VOIX VSIX

V•Y•
VAYA

V••Y
VARY VDAY VERY VINY

•V•Y
IVEY

••VY
BEVY CAVY DAVY ENVY JIVY LEVY LIVY NAVY WAVY

WA••
WAAC WAAF WAAL WABS WACE WACK WACO WACS WADE WADI WADS WAFS WAFT WAGE WAGS WAHL WAIF WAIL WAIN WAIT WAKA WAKE WALD WALE WALK WALL WALT WAND WANE WANG WANT WANY WARD WARE WARM WARN WARP WARS WART WARY WASH WASP WAST WATS WATT WAVE WAVY WAWA WAWS WAXY WAYS

W•A•
WAAC WAAF WAAL WEAK WEAL WEAN WEAR WHAM WHAT WOAD WRAC WRAF WRAP WRAY

W••A
WAKA WAWA WEKA WHOA WUSA

•WA•
AWAY DWAN KWAI KWAN SWAB SWAG SWAK SWAM SWAN SWAP SWAT SWAY TWAS

•W•A
YWCA

••WA
AIWA BIWA IOWA TEWA TIWA WAWA

W•B•
WABS WEBB WEBS

W••B
WEBB WEEB

•WB•
NWBN NWBW SWBS SWBW

•W•B
SWAB SWOB

WC••
WCTU

W•C•
WACE WACK WACO WACS WICK WYCH

W••C
WAAC WISC WRAC

•WC•
YWCA

W•D•
WADE WADI WADS WEDS WIDE

W••D
WALD WAND WARD WEED WELD WEND WHOD WILD WIND WOAD WOLD WOOD WORD

•W•D
AWED OWED SWED TWOD

••WD
DOWD LEWD

WE••
WEAK WEAL WEAN WEAR WEBB WEBS WEDS WEEB WEED WEEK WEEN WEEP WEFT WEIL WEIR WEKA WELD WELK WELL WELT WEND WENG WENS WENT WEPT WERE WERT WEST WETS WEVE

W•E•
WEEB WEED WEEK WEEN WEEP WHEE WHEN WHET WHEW WHEY WIEN WOES WREN WYES

W••E
WACE WADE WAGE WAKE WALE WANE WARE WAVE WERE WEVE WHEE WHSE WIDE WIFE WILE WINE WIPE WIRE WISE WITE WOKE WOLE WORE WOVE

•WE•
AWED AWES EWEN EWER EWES GWEN OWED OWEN OWER OWES SWED TWEE ZWEI

•W•E
TWEE

••WE
BOWE HDWE HOWE LOWE ROWE

W•F•
WAFS WAFT WEFT WIFE

W••F
WAAF WAIF WOLF WOOF WRAF

••WF
NEWF

W•G•
WAGE WAGS WIGS

W••G
WANG WENG WHIG WING WONG

•W•G
SWAG SWIG TWIG

••WG
DAWG HAWG

WH••
WHAM WHAT WHEE WHEN WHET WHEW WHEY WHIG WHIM WHIN WHIP WHIR WHIT WHIZ WHOA WHOD WHOM WHOP WHOS WHSE WHUP WHYS

W•H•
WAHL WOHL WUHL WUHU

W••H
WASH WISH WITH WYCH

•WH•
KWHR

WI••
WICK WIDE WIEN WIFE WIGS WILD WILE WILL WILT WILY WIMP WIND WINE WING WINK WINS WINY WIPE WIRE WIRY WISC WISE WISH WISK WISP WITE WITH WITS WITT

W•I•
WAIF WAIL WAIN WAIT WEIL WEIR WHIG WHIM WHIN WHIP WHIR WHIT WHIZ WRIT WWII

W••I
WADI WUXI WWII

•WI•
FWIW IWIS SWIG SWIM SWIT TWIG TWIN TWIT TWIX WWII

•W•I
KWAI WWII ZWEI

••WI
IIWI KIWI

WK••
WKLY WKRP

W•K•
WAKA WAKE WEKA WOKE WOKS

W••K
WACK WALK WEAK WEEK WELK WICK WINK WISK WONK WORK WOUK

•W•K
EWOK SWAK

••WK
GAWK GOWK HAWK

W•L•
WALD WALE WALK WALL WALT WELD WELK WELL WELT WILD WILE WILL WILT WILY WKLY WOLD WOLE WOLF

W••L
WAAL WAHL WAIL WALL WEAL WEIL WELL WOHL WOOL WUHL

•WL•
AWLS OWLS

•W•L
AWOL

••WL
BAWL BOWL COWL FOWL HOWL JOWL MEWL PAWL YAWL YOWL

W•M•
WIMP

W••M
WARM WHAM WHIM WHOM WORM

•WM•
CWMS

•W•M
SWAM SWIM SWUM

W•N•
WAND WANE WANG WANT WANY WEND WENG WENS WENT WIND WINE WING WINK WINS WINY WONG WONK WONS WONT WRNS WYNN

W••N
WAIN WARN WEAN WEEN WHEN WHIN WIEN WORN WREN WYNN

•WN•
AWNS OWNS

•W•N
DWAN EWEN GWEN GWYN KWAN KWON NWBN OWEN SWAN TWIN

••WN
DAWN DOWN FAWN GOWN HAWN HEWN LAWN MOWN PAWN SAWN SEWN SOWN TOWN YAWN

WO••
WOAD WOES WOHL WOKE WOKS WOLD WOLE WOLF WONG WONK WONS WONT WOOD WOOF WOOL WOOS WORD WORE WORK WORM WORN WORT WOUK WOVE WOWS

W•O•
WHOA WHOD WHOM WHOP WHOS WOOD WOOF WOOL WOOS

W••O
WACO

•WO•
AWOL CWOS EWOK KWON SWOB SWOP TWOD TWOS

W•P•
WEPT WIPE

W••P
WARP WASP WEEP WHIP WHOP WHUP WIMP WISP WKRP WRAP

•WP•
TWPS

•W•P
SWAP SWOP

••WP
GAWP YAWP

WR••
WRAC WRAF WRAP WRAY WREN WRIT WRNS

W•R•
WARD WARE WARM WARN WARP WARS WART WARY WERE WERT WIRE WIRY WKRP WORD WORE WORK WORM WORN WORT

W••R
WEAR WEIR WHIR

•WR•
AWRY EWRY

•W•R
EWER KWHR OWER

••WR
MAWR

W•S•
WASH WASP WAST WEST WHSE WISC WISE WISH WISK WISP WUSA WUSS WYSS

W••S
WABS WACS WADS WAFS WAGS WARS WATS WAWS WAYS WEBS WEDS WENS WETS WHOS WHYS WIGS WINS WITS WOES WOKS WONS WOOS WOWS WRNS WUSS WYES WYSS

•W•S
AWES AWLS AWNS CWMS CWOS EWES HWYS IWIS OWES OWLS OWNS SWBS TWAS TWOS TWPS

••WS
BMWS BOWS CAWS COWS DAWS DEWS HAWS HEWS HOWS JAWS JEWS LAWS LOWS MAWS MEWS MOWS NEWS PAWS PEWS POWS ROWS SAWS SEWS SOWS TAWS TOWS VOWS WAWS WOWS YAWS YEWS

W•T•
WATS WATT WCTU WETS WITE WITH WITS WITT

W••T
WAFT WAIT WALT WANT WART WAST WATT WEFT WELT WENT WEPT WERT WEST WHAT WHET WHIT WILT WITT WONT WORT WRIT

•WT•
GWTW

•W•T
SWAT SWIT TWIT

••WT
ATWT GRWT NEWT NTWT

WU••
WUHL WUHU WUSA WUSS WUXI

W•U•
WHUP WOUK

W••U
WCTU WUHU

•WU•
SWUM

W•V•
WAVE WAVY WEVE WOVE

WW••
WWII

W•W•
WAWA WAWS WOWS

W••W
WHEW

•W•W
FWIW GWTW NWBW SWBW

W•X•
WAXY WUXI

•W•X
TWIX

WY••
WYCH WYES WYNN WYSS

W•Y•
WAYS WHYS

W••Y
WANY WARY WAVY WAXY WHEY WILY WINY WIRY WKLY WRAY

•WY•
GWYN HWYS

•W•Y
AWAY AWRY EWRY SWAY

••WY
DEWY HGWY PKWY

W••Z
WHIZ

XA••
XATS

X•A•
XIAN XMAS XRAY

X••A
XENA

•XA•
EXAM

•X•A
IXIA

••XA
COXA HEXA TAXA

XC••
XCII XCIV XCIX XCVI

•XC•
CXCI CXCV DXCI DXCV EXCH EXCL MXCI MXCV

•X•C
EXEC

••XC
CCXC CDXC CMXC DCXC MCXC MDXC MMXC

XD••
XDIN XDIV

•X•D
AXED EXOD

XE••
XENA XENO XERO

X•E•
XMEN

X••E
XIPE

•XE•
AXED AXEL AXER AXES EXEC EXES OXEN

•X•E
AXLE

••XE
FIXE FOXE LUXE SAXE

X••G
XING

•X•H
EXCH

XI••
XIAN XIII XING XIPE

X•I•
XCII XCIV XCIX XDIN XDIV XIII XLII XLIV XLIX XVII XXII XXIV XXIX

X••I
XCII XCVI XIII XLII XLVI XVII XXII XXVI XXXI

•XI•
AXIL AXIS CXII CXIV CXIX DXII DXIV DXIX EXIT IXIA LXII LXIV LXIX MXII MXIV MXIX XXII XXIV XXIX

•X•I
CXCI CXII CXLI CXVI CXXI DXCI DXII DXLI DXVI DXXI LXII LXVI LXXI MXCI MXII MXLI MXVI MXXI XXII XXVI XXXI

••XI
CCXI CDXI CLXI CMXI CXXI DCXI DLXI DXXI LXXI MAXI MCXI MDXI MLXI MMXI MXXI TAXI WUXI XXXI

XL••
XLII XLIV XLIX XLVI

X•L•
XYLO

•XL•
AXLE CXLI CXLV DXLI DXLV MXLI MXLV

•X•L
AXEL AXIL EXCL

••XL
CCXL CDXL CMXL DCXL MCXL MDXL MMXL

XM••
XMAS XMEN

•X•M
AXUM EXAM

X•N•
XENA XENO XING

X••N
XDIN XIAN XMEN

•X•N
AXON EXON OXEN OXON

XO••
XOUT

X••O
XENO XERO XYLO

•XO•
AXON EXOD EXON EXOR OXON UXOR

•X•O
EXPO

••XO
MYXO TAXO

X•P•
XIPE

•XP•
EXPO EXPT

XR••
XRAY

X•R•
XERO

•X•R
AXER EXOR UXOR

X••S
XATS XMAS

•X•S
AXES AXIS EXES EXTS OXUS

••XS
INXS

X•T•
XATS

X••T
XOUT

•XT•
EXTS

•X•T
EXIT EXPT

••XT
MIXT NEXT SEXT TEXT

X•U•
XOUT

•XU•
AXUM OXUS

XV••
XVII

X•V•
XCVI XLVI XXVI

X••V
XCIV XDIV XLIV XXIV XXXV

•XV•
CXVI DXVI LXVI MXVI XXVI

•X•V
CXCV CXIV CXLV CXXV DXCV DXIV DXLV DXXV LXIV LXXV MXCV MXIV MXLV MXXV XXIV XXXV

••XV
CCXV CDXV

CLXV CMXV CXXV DCXV DLXV DXXV LXXV MCXV MDXV MLXV MMXV MXXV XXXV

XX••
XXII XXIV XXIX XXVI XXXI XXXV XXXX

X•X•
XXXI XXXV XXXX

X••X
XCIX XLIX XXIX XXXX

•XX•
CXXI CXXV CXXX DXXI DXXV DXXX LXXI LXXV LXXX MXXI MXXV MXXX XXXI XXXV XXXX

•X•X
CXIX CXXX DXIX DXXX LXIX LXXX MXIX MXXX XXIX XXXX

••XX
CCXX CDXX CLXX CMXX CXXX DCXX DLXX DXXX FOXX LXXX MCXX MDXX MLXX MMXX MXXX XXXX

XY••
XYLO

X••Y
XRAY

••XY
BOXY FOXY PIXY SEXY WAXY

YA••
YACK YADA YAGI YAKS YALE YALL YALU YAMA YAMS YANA YANG YANK YAOS YAPP YAPS YARD YARE YARN YAWL YAWN YAWP YAWS YAZD

Y•A•
YEAH YEAN YEAR YEAS YUAN

Y••A
YADA YAMA YANA YIMA YMCA YODA YOGA YUBA YUGA YUMA YWCA

•YA•
AYAH CYAN DYAD DYAK DYAN EYAS IYAR KYAT RYAL RYAN RYAS

•Y•A
AYLA CYMA DYNA EYRA HYLA KYRA LYRA MYNA MYRA

••YA
ANYA BAYA ENYA GAYA GOYA HOYA MAYA SOYA VAYA

Y•B•
YOBS YUBA

•YB•
GYBE

•Y•B
BYOB MYOB

Y•C•
YACK YECH YMCA YUCK YWCA

•YC•
CYCL DYCE DYCK EYCK MYCO SYCE WYCH

•Y•C
SYNC

••YC
GLYC

Y•D•
YADA YEDO YODA YODH YODS

Y••D
YARD YAZD YOND YOUD

•YD•
HYDE HYDR

•Y•D
BYRD DYAD DYED EYED SYND

••YD
BOYD SQYD

YE••
YEAH YEAN YEAR YEAS YECH YEDO YEGG YELL YELP YENS YERK YETI YEUX YEWS

Y•E•
YLEM YSER YVES

Y••E
YALE YARE YIPE YOKE YORE YULE

•YE•
AYER AYES BYES DYED DYER DYES EYED EYER EYES HYER KYES LYES NYET OYER OYEZ RYES WYES

•Y•E
AYME BYME BYRE BYTE CYME CYTE DYCE DYNE EYRE FYKE GYBE GYRE GYVE HYDE HYPE KYLE LYLE LYNE LYRE NYSE PYLE PYRE RYLE RYNE SYCE SYNE TYKE TYNE TYPE TYRE

••YE
ABYE FAYE FRYE GAYE JAYE KAYE RAYE SKYE SLYE

Y•G•
YAGI YEGG YOGA YOGH YOGI YUGA YUGO

Y••G
YANG YEGG

•YG•
ZYGO

•Y•G
BYNG

Y•H•
YOHO

Y••H
YEAH YECH YODH YOGH

•Y•H
AYAH MYTH WYCH

YI••
YIMA YIPE YIPS

Y•I•
YMIR

Y••I
YAGI YETI YOGI YURI

•YI•
AYIN LYIN

•Y•I
GYRI

••YI
MAYI PUYI

Y•K•
YAKS YOKE YOKO YUKS

Y••K
YACK YANK YERK YOLK YORK YUCK

•YK•
FYKE TYKE

•Y•K
DYAK DYCK EYCK NYUK

YL••
YLEM

Y•L•
YALE YALL YALU YELL YELP YOLK YULE

Y••L
YALL YAWL YELL YOWL

•YL•
AYLA HYLA KYLE LYLE LYLY PYLE RYLE SYLL SYLS XYLO

•Y•L
CYCL RYAL SYLL

••YL
ACYL AMYL ARYL IDYL

YM••
YMCA YMIR

Y•M•
YAMA YAMS YIMA YUMA

Y••M
YLEM

•YM•
AYME BYME CYMA CYME GYMS HYMN MYMY SYMS TYMP ZYMO

••YM
ETYM ONYM

Y•N•
YANA YANG YANK YENS YOND

Y••N
YARN YAWN YEAN YUAN

•YN•
BYNG DYNA DYNE GYNT LYNE LYNN LYNX MYNA RYNE SYNC SYND SYNE SYNS TYNE WYNN

•Y•N
AYIN CYAN DYAN HYMN HYPN LYIN LYNN LYON RYAN RYUN WYNN

••YN
BRYN GLYN GWYN

YO••
YOBS YODA YODH YODS YOGA YOGH YOGI YOHO YOKE YOKO YOLK YOND YORE YORK YOST YOUD YOUR YOWL YOYO

Y•O•
YAOS

Y••O
YEDO YOHO YOKO YOYO YUGO

•YO•
BYOB EYOT GYOR LYON MYOB RYOT

•Y•O
CYTO GYRO HYPO MYCO MYXO NYRO PYRO TYPO TYRO XYLO ZYGO ZYMO

••YO
BOYO BRYO CRYO DAYO ENYO HIYO KAYO MAYO YOYO

Y•P•
YAPP YAPS YIPE YIPS

Y••P
YAPP YAWP YELP

•YP•
GYPS HYPE HYPN HYPO TYPE TYPO TYPY

•Y•P
TYMP

Y•R•
YARD YARE YARN YERK YORE YORK YURI YURT

Y••R
YEAR YMIR YOUR YSER

•YR•
BYRD BYRE EYRA EYRE EYRY GYRE GYRI GYRO KYRA LYRA LYRE MYRA NYRO PYRE PYRO TYRE TYRO

•Y•R
AYER DYER EYER GYOR HYDR HYER IYAR OYER

••YR
LTYR

YS••
YSER

Y•S•
YOST

Y••S
YAKS YAMS YAOS YAPS YAWS YEAS YENS YEWS YIPS YOBS YODS YUKS YVES

•YS•
MYST NYSE SYST WYSS

•Y•S
AYES BYES DYES EYAS EYES GYMS GYPS KYES LYES RYAS RYES SYLS SYMS SYNS WYES WYSS

••YS
ABYS BAYS BEYS BOYS BUYS CAYS DAYS DEYS DRYS FAYS FOYS GUYS HAYS HOYS HWYS JAYS JOYS KEYS LAYS MAYS NAYS NUYS PAYS PHYS RAYS REYS RHYS SAYS SKYS SOYS TOYS UEYS WAYS WHYS

Y•T•
YETI

Y••T
YOST YURT

•YT•
BYTE CYTE CYTO MYTH

•Y•T
EYOT GYNT KYAT MYST NYET RYOT SYST

••YT
FOYT HOYT PAYT

YU••
YUAN YUBA YUCK YUGA YUGO YUKS YULE YUMA YURI YURT

Y•U•
YEUX YOUD YOUR

Y••U
YALU

•YU•
NYUK RYUN

YV••
YVES

•YV•
GYVE

YW••
YWCA

Y•W•
YAWL YAWN YAWP YAWS YEWS YOWL

Y••X
YEUX

•YX•
MYXO

•Y•X
LYNX

••YX
ONYX ORYX STYX

Y•Y•
YOYO

•Y•Y
EYRY LYLY MYMY TYPY

Y•Z•
YAZD

•Y•Z
OYEZ

••YZ
BOYZ

ZA••
ZACK ZAGS ZAHN ZALS ZAMA ZANE ZANY ZAPS ZARF ZASU

Z•A•
ZBAR ZEAL ZOAR

Z••A
ZAMA ZETA ZOEA ZOLA ZONA

•ZA•
AZAN CZAR IZAR OZAV TZAR

•Z•A
EZRA IZBA

••ZA
ANZA GAZA GIZA ITZA LIZA REZA

ZB••
ZBAR

Z•B•
ZEBU ZIBO

•ZB•
IZBA

Z•C•
ZACK ZECH

Z••C
ZINC ZOIC

Z•D•
ZEDS

Z••D
ZEND

•Z•D
IZOD

••ZD
YAZD

ZE••
ZEAL ZEBU ZECH ZEDS ZEES ZEIN ZEKE ZEND ZENO ZEPH ZERO ZEST ZETA ZEUS

Z•E•
ZEES ZOEA ZWEI

Z••E
ZANE ZEKE ZINE ZONE

•ZE•
EZEK

••ZE
ADZE DAZE DOZE FAZE FUZE GAZE HAZE LAZE MAZE OOZE RAZE SIZE

Z••F
ZARF

Z•G•
ZAGS ZIGS ZOGI ZYGO

Z••G
ZING

ZH••
ZHOU

Z•H•
ZAHN

Z••H
ZECH ZEPH

ZI••
ZIBO ZIGS ZILL ZINC ZINE ZING ZION ZIPS ZITI

Z•I•
ZEIN ZOIC

Z••I
ZITI ZOGI ZORI ZUNI ZWEI

•ZI•
AZIZ EZIO UZIS

••ZI
SUZI

Z•K•
ZEKE

Z••K
ZACK ZONK ZOUK

•Z•K
EZEK

Z•L•
ZALS ZILL ZOLA ZULU

Z••L
ZEAL ZILL ZOOL

•Z•L
AZUL

Z•M•
ZAMA ZYMO

Z••M
ZOOM

Z•N•
ZANE ZANY ZEND ZENO ZINC ZINE ZING ZONA ZONE ZONK ZUNI

Z••N
ZAHN ZEIN ZION ZOON ZORN

•Z•N
AZAN

ZO••
ZOAR ZOEA ZOGI ZOIC ZOLA ZONA ZONE ZONK ZOOL ZOOM ZOON ZOOS ZOOT ZORI ZORN ZOTZ ZOUK

Z•O•
ZHOU ZION ZOOL ZOOM ZOON ZOOS ZOOT

Z••O
ZENO ZERO ZIBO ZYGO ZYMO

•ZO•
AZOV IZOD

•Z•O
EZIO

••ZO
BOZO ENZO MAZO ORZO OUZO PUZO

Z•P•
ZAPS ZEPH ZIPS

Z•R•
ZARF ZERO ZORI ZORN

Z••R
ZBAR ZOAR

•ZR•
EZRA

•Z•R
AZUR CZAR IZAR TZAR

Z•S•
ZASU ZEST

Z••S
ZAGS ZALS ZAPS ZEDS ZEES ZEUS ZIGS ZIPS ZOOS

•Z•S
UZIS

Z•T•
ZETA ZITI ZOTZ

Z••T
ZEST ZOOT

ZU••
ZULU ZUNI

Z•U•
ZEUS ZOUK

Z••U
ZASU ZEBU ZHOU ZULU

•ZU•
AZUL AZUR

•Z•V
AZOV OZAV

ZW••
ZWEI

ZY••
ZYGO ZYMO

Z••Y
ZANY

•Z•Y
IZZY OZZY

••ZY
COZY DOZY HAZY IZZY LAZY MAZY OOZY OZZY SUZY

Z••Z
ZOTZ

•ZZ•
IZZY OZZY

•Z•Z
AZIZ

••ZZ
BUZZ FIZZ FUZZ JAZZ MUZZ PIZZ RAZZ

AA•••
AAHED
AAIUN
AALII
AALTO
AAMES
AANDE
AANDM
AARGH
AARON

A•A••
ABABA
ABACA
ABACI
ABACK
ABACO
ABAFT
ABASE
ABASH
ABATE
ABAYA
ACADS
ACARI
ADAGE
ADAIR
ADAMA
ADAMS
ADANA
ADANO
ADAPT
AEAEA
AFAIK
AFARS
AGAIN
AGALS
AGAMA
AGANA
AGAPE
AGARN
AGARS
AGASP
AGATE
AGAVE
AGAZE
ALACK
ALAIN
ALAMO
ALANA
ALAND
ALARM
ALATE
ALAVA
AMADO
AMAHL
AMAHS
AMAIN
AMANA
AMAPA
AMARA
AMASS
AMATI
AMATO
AMAZE
ANAIS
APACE
APART
AQABA
ARABS
ARABY
ARAMA
ARAME
ASAMA
ASANA
ATALL
ATARI
AVAIL
AVANT
AVARS
AVAST
AWACS
AWAIT
AWAJI
AWAKE
AWARD
AWARE
AWASH
AYAHS
AZANS

A••A•
ABBAS
ABEAM
ABRAM
ACTAS
ADDAX
ADLAI
ADMAN
ADVAL
AETAT
AFLAT
AGHAS
AHEAD
AHMAD
AIDAN
AIMAT
AKBAR
AKKAD
ALBAN
ALCAN
ALDAN
ALFAS
ALGAE
ALGAL
ALIAS
ALLAH
ALLAN
ALLAY
ALMAY
ALTAI
ALTAR
ALVAR
AMMAN
AMPAS
AMWAY
ANEAR
ANNAL
ANNAM
ANNAN
ANOAS
ANSAE
ANTAE
ANTAL
ANTAS
ANWAR
ANZAC
AODAI
AOKAY
APEAK
APIAN
APPAL
AQUAE
AQUAS
AREAL
AREAR
AREAS
ARHAT
ARIAN
ARIAS
ARNAZ
AROAR
ARPAD
ARRAN
ARRAS
ARRAU
ARRAY
ARTAL
ARYAN
ASCAP
ASIAN
ASSAD
ASSAI
ASSAM
ASSAY
ASWAN
ATBAT
ATBAY
ATEAM
ATLAS
ATMAN
ATPAR
ATTAR
ATWAR
AURAE
AURAL
AURAR
AURAS
AVGAS
AVIAN
AXIAL

A•••A
ABABA
ABACA
ABAYA
ABUJA
ACCRA
ACOMA
ACURA
ADAMA
ADANA
ADELA
ADUWA
ADYTA
AEAEA
AECIA
AETNA
AFTRA
AGAMA
AGANA
AGENA
AGITA
AGORA
AHORA
AISHA
AKELA
AKIRA
AKITA
ALANA
ALAVA
ALCOA
ALETA
ALIDA
ALOHA
ALPHA
ALULA
AMANA
AMAPA
AMARA
AMEBA
AMIGA
AMNIA
ANIMA
ANITA
ANTRA
AORTA
APNEA
AQABA
ARAMA
ARECA
ARENA
ARICA
AROMA
ARUBA
ASAMA
ASANA
ASOKA
ASPCA
ASTRA
ASYLA
ATRIA
ATSEA
AUDRA
AVENA
AVILA
AZUSA

•AA••
BAAED
BAALS
KAABA
NAACP
PAAVO
SAABS
WAAFS
WAALS

•A•A•
BABAR
BABAS
BAHAI
BALAS
BANAL
BANAT
BARAB
BASAL
BATAK
BAYAR
CABAL
CACAO
CAMAY
CANAD
CANAL
CARAT
CASAS
CAVAE
DAKAR
DALAI
DAMAN
DAMAR
DANAE
DAVAO
DAYAK
DAYAN
EAGAN
EATAT
FARAD
FARAH
FATAL
GALAH
GALAS
GALAX
GAMAL
GAMAY
GAYAL
HADAR
HADAT
HAGAR
HAHAS
HALAS
HAMAL
HAMAN
HARAR
HASAT
HAZAN
JAMAL
JAPAN
JAVAS
KADAR
KAKAS
KARAN
KARAT
KAUAI
KAVAS
KAYAK
KAZAK
KAZAN
LABAN
LAGAN
LAHAR
LALAW
LAMAR
LAMAS
LANAI
LAPAZ
LARAM
LARAS
LAVAL
LAVAS
LAZAR
MACAO
MACAW
MADAM
MAHAL
MAHAN
MALAN
MALAR
MALAY
MAMAS
MARAS
MARAT
MASAI
MAYAN
MAYAS
NAIAD
NANAK
NANAS
NARAS
NASAL
NATAL
NAVAL
NAWAB
PACAS
PAEAN
PAGAN
PALAE
PALAU
PANAM
PANAY
PAPAL
PAPAS
PAPAW
PAWAT
QATAR
RABAT
RADAR
RAGAS
RAHAB
RAHAL
RAJAH
RAJAS
RAMAN
RAMAR
RANAT
SABAH
SADAT
SAGAL
SAGAN
SAGAS
SAJAK
SAKAI
SALAD
SALAL
SALAM
SAMAR
SANAA
SARAH
SARAN
SATAN
TAKAS
TAPAS
TATAR
VARAS

•A••A
BABKA
BAHIA
BAIZA
BALSA
BANDA
BARCA
BASRA
CALLA
CANEA
CANNA
CAPRA
CARIA
CARLA
CARTA
CASCA
CAUSA
DACCA
DACHA
DACIA
DAIWA
DANZA
DARLA
DARYA
FACIA
FALLA
FANTA
FATHA
FATWA
FAUNA
GALBA
GALEA
GAMBA
GAMMA
GARDA
HABLA
HAEMA
HAIDA
HAIFA
HANNA
HANSA
HASTA
HAUSA
JABBA
JAFFA
KAABA
KAFKA
KANGA
KANSA
KAPPA
KARLA
KARMA
KASHA
LAIKA
LAMIA
LANKA
LANZA
LARVA
LAURA
LAYLA
MAGDA
MAGMA
MAGNA
MAKUA
MALTA
MAMBA
MAMMA
MANIA
MANNA
MANTA
MARIA
MARLA
MARTA
MAUNA
MAZDA
NADIA
NADJA
NAFTA
NAHUA
NAINA
NAIRA
NAMPA
NANNA
PADUA
PAISA
PALEA
PALMA
PAMPA
PANDA
PANGA
PANZA
PAPUA
PARCA
PARKA
PARMA
PASHA
PASTA
PATNA
PAULA
PAVIA
QANDA
RAISA
RASTA
SABRA
SACHA
SACRA
SAIGA
SALPA
SALSA
SALTA
SAMBA
SAMOA
SANAA
SANKA
SANTA
SASHA
SAUNA
TABLA
TAIGA
TALIA
TAMPA
TANKA
TANYA
TATRA
TAYRA
TAZZA
VACUA
VANNA
VANYA
VARIA
VARNA
WAJDA
WALLA
WANDA
WANNA
YABBA
YALTA
YAMPA
ZAMIA
ZAPPA

••AA•
ISAAC
IZAAK
KRAAL
SPAAK

••A•A
ABABA
ABACA
ABAYA
ADAMA
ADANA
AEAEA
AGAMA
AGANA
ALANA
ALAVA
AMANA
AMAPA
AMARA
AQABA
ARAMA
ASAMA
ASANA
BRAGA
BRAVA
BWANA
CHAKA
CLARA
DHAKA
DIANA
DRAMA
DRAVA
GHANA
GRAMA
GRATA
GUAVA
IPANA
IVANA
KAABA
KOALA
KUALA
LHASA
LIANA
LLAMA
MEARA
MIATA
NYALA
NYASA
OCALA
OHARA
OMAHA
OMASA
ORAMA
OSAKA
OZAWA
PLATA
PLAYA
PLAZA
PRAIA
REATA
RIATA
RUANA
SCALA
SCAPA
SHANA
TIARA
TRALA
UZALA

•••AA
SANAA

AB•••
ABABA
ABACA
ABACI
ABACK
ABACO
ABAFT
ABASE
ABASH
ABATE
ABAYA
ABBAS
ABBES
ABBEY
ABBIE
ABBOT
ABBRS
ABCTV
ABDUL
ABEAM
ABEBE
ABELE
ABEND
ABETS
ABHOR
ABIDE
ABLER
ABNER
ABODE
ABOHM
ABOIL
ABOMB
ABORT
ABOUT
ABOVE
ABOVO
ABRAM
ABRIL
ABRIS
ABUJA
ABUSE
ABUTS
ABUZZ
ABYES
ABYSM
ABYSS
ABZUG

A•B••
ABBAS
ABBES
ABBEY
ABBIE
ABBOT
ABBRS
AKBAR
ALBAN
ALBEE
ALBEN
ALBUM
AMBER
AMBIT
AMBLE
AMBOS
AMBOY
AMBRY
ARBER
ARBOR
ARBRE
ATBAT
ATBAY
AUBER

A••B•
ABABA
ABEBE
ADOBE
ALIBI
AMEBA
AQABA
ARABS
ARABY
ARUBA
ASHBY

A•••B
ABOMB
ACERB
ADLIB

•AB••
BABAR
BABAS
BABEL
BABER
BABES
BABIS
BABKA
BABUL
BABYS
CABAL
CABBY
CABER
CABIN
CABLE
CABOT
FABER
FABIO
FABLE
GABBY
GABLE
GABON
GABOR
HABER
HABIT
HABLA
JABBA
JABOT
KABOB
KABUL
LABAN
LABEL
LABIO
LABOR
MABEL
NABES
NABOB
PABLO
PABST
RABAT
RABBI
RABID
RABIN
SABAH
SABER
SABIN
SABLE
SABOT
SABRA
SABRE
TABBY
TABIS
TABLA
TABLE
TABOO
TABOR
YABBA

•A•B•
BAMBI
BARBQ
BARBS
CABBY
CANBY
CARBO
CARBS
DARBY
DAUBS
GABBY
GALBA
GAMBA
GARBO
GARBS
IAMBI
IAMBS
JABBA
JAMBS
KAABA
LAMBS
LAYBY
MAMBA
MAMBO
MAYBE
NAMBY
NASBY
PAMBY
RABBI
RAMBO
SAABS
SAMBA
SATBY
TABBY
TAMBO
YABBA

•A••B
BANDB
BARAB
CALEB
CARIB
CAROB
JACOB
KABOB
NABOB
NAMIB
NAWAB
RAHAB
RANDB
SAHIB

••AB•
ABABA
AQABA
ARABS
ARABY
BLABS
CRABS
DHABI
DRABS
GRABS
KAABA
PEABO
SAABS
SCABS
SLABS
STABS
SWABS

••A•B
PLANB

•••AB
BARAB
DCCAB
ESTAB
KEBAB
NAWAB
RAHAB
REHAB
SQUAB

AC•••
ACADS
ACARI
ACCEL
ACCRA
ACCTS
ACERB
ACERS
ACETO
ACHED
ACHES
ACHOO
ACIDS
ACIDY
ACING
ACMES
ACOMA
ACORN
ACRED
ACRES
ACRID
ACTAS
ACTED
ACTER
ACTII

ACTIN
ACTIV
ACTON
ACTOR
ACTUP
ACUFF
ACURA
ACUTE
ACYLS

A•C••
ABCTV
ACCEL
ACCRA
ACCTS
AECIA
ALCAN
ALCOA
ALCOR
ANCON
ARCED
ARCHI
ARCHY
ASCAP
ASCII
ASCOT
ASCUS

A••C•
ABACA
ABACI
ABACK
ABACO
AITCH
ALACK
ALECK
ALICE
ALYCE
AMICE
AMOCO
AMUCK
APACE
ARECA
ARICA
ASPCA
AWACS

A•••C
ADHOC
ADLOC
AFRIC
AGRIC
ANTIC
ANZAC
ASDIC
ASPIC
ASSOC
ATTIC
AURIC
AZOIC
AZTEC

•AC••
BACHS
BACKS
BACON
CACAO
CACHE
CACTI
DACCA
DACES
DACHA
DACHE
DACIA
FACED
FACER
FACES
FACET
FACIA
FACIE
FACIT
FACTO
FACTS
HACEK
HACKS
JACET
JACKS
JACKY
JACOB
LACED
LACER
LACES
LACEY
LACKS
LACTI
LACTO
MACAO
MACAW
MACED
MACES
MACHE
MACHO
MACHU
MACHY
MACLE
MACON
MACRO
MACYS
NACHO
NACHT
NACRE
PACAS
PACED
PACER
PACES
PACKS
PACTS
RACED
RACER
RACES
RACKS
RACON
SACCO
SACHA
SACHS
SACKS
SACRA
SACRE
SACRO
TACET
TACHO
TACHY
TACIT
TACKS
TACKY
TACOS
VACUA
WACKO
WACKY
XACTO
YACHT
YACKS

•A•C•
BALCH
BANCO
BANCS
BARCA
BATCH
CALCI
CASCA
CASCO
CATCH
CAYCE
DACCA
DANCE
DANCY
FANCY
FARCE
FARCI
HATCH
LAICS
LANCE
LARCH
LATCH
MANCY
MARCH
MARCO
MARCY
MATCH
NAACP
NANCY
NARCO
NARCS
NATCH
PARCA
PARCH
PASCH
PASCO
PATCH
RANCH
RATCH
SACCO
SAUCE
SAUCY
TAXCO
VANCE
VASCO
WATCH

•A••C
BARIC
BASIC
HARDC
HAVOC
MAGIC
MALIC
MANIC
PANIC
SALIC
VATIC

••AC•
ABACA
ABACI
ABACK
ABACO
ALACK
APACE
AWACS
BEACH
BLACK
BRACE
BRACT
CHACO
CLACK
COACH
COACT
CRACK
CRACY
DRACO
ENACT
EPACT
EXACT
FLACK
GLACE
GRACE
GUACO
KEACH
KNACK
KYACK
LEACH
LOACH
NAACP
NYACK
ORACH
ORACY
PEACE
PEACH
PLACE
POACH
QUACK
REACH
REACT
ROACH
SHACK
SLACK
SMACK
SNACK
SPACE
SPACY
STACK
STACY
TEACH
TRACE
TRACK
TRACT
TRACY
WHACK
WRACK
WRACS

••A•C
BLANC
FRANC
ISAAC

•••AC
ANZAC
DIRAC
ENIAC
ILIAC
ISAAC
LILAC
SERAC
SUMAC

AD•••
ADAGE
ADAIR
ADAMA
ADAMS
ADANA
ADANO
ADAPT
ADDAX
ADDED
ADDER
ADDIE
ADDIN
ADDIS
ADDLE
ADDNL
ADDON
ADDTO
ADDUP
ADEEM
ADELA
ADELE
ADENO
ADEPT
ADEUX
ADFIN
ADHEM
ADHOC
ADIEU
ADIGE
ADINT
ADIOS
ADIPO
ADITS
ADLAI
ADLER
ADLIB
ADLOC
ADMAN
ADMEN
ADMIN
ADMIT
ADMIX
ADOBE
ADOLF
ADOPT
ADORE
ADORN
ADOUT
ADREM
ADSUM
ADULT
ADUST
ADUWA
ADVAL
ADVIL
ADYTA
ADZES

A•D••
ABDUL
ADDAX
ADDED
ADDER
ADDIE
ADDIN
ADDIS
ADDLE
ADDNL
ADDON
ADDTO
ADDUP
AEDES
AIDAN
AIDED
AIDES
ALDAN
ALDEN
ALDER
ALDOL
ALDUS
ANDES
ANDIE
ANDOR
ANDRE
ANDRO
ANDRY
ANDUP
AODAI
ARDEN
ARDOR
ASDIC
AUDEN
AUDIE
AUDIO
AUDIS
AUDIT
AUDRA

A••D•
AANDE
AANDM
ABIDE
ABODE
ACADS
ACIDS
ACIDY
ALIDA
AMADO
AMIDE
AMIDO
ANODE
ASIDE
AZIDE

A•••D
AAHED
ABEND
ACHED
ACRED
ACRID
ACTED
ADDED
AHEAD
AHMAD
AHMED
AIDED
AILED
AIMED
AIRED
AKKAD
ALAND
ALGID
ALKYD
ALOUD
AMEND
AMPED
ANTED
APHID
APPTD
APTED
ARCED
ARMED
AROID
ARPAD
ASKED
ASSAD
ASSTD
AVOID
AWARD
AWNED

•AD••
BADDY
BADEN
BADER
BADGE
BADLY
CADDO
CADDY
CADET
CADGE
CADIS
CADIZ
CADRE
DADDY
DADOS
FADED
FADES
FADOS
HADAR
HADAT
HADES
HADJI
HADNT
HADON
HADST
HADTO
JADED
JADES
KADAR
LADED
LADEN
LADER
LADES
LADLE
LADON
LADYS
MADAM
MADGE
MADLY
MADRE
NADER
NADIA
NADIR
NADJA
PADDY
PADRE
PADUA
RADAR
RADII
RADIO
RADIX
RADON
SADAT
SADHE
SADHU
SADIE
SADIS
SADLY
VADER
VADIM
VADIS
VADUZ
WADDY
WADED
WADER
WADES
WADIS
WADUP
YADIM

•A•D•
AANDE
AANDM
BADDY
BALDS
BANDA
BANDB
BANDO
BANDS
BANDW
BANDY
BARDS
BAWDY
CADDO
CADDY
CANDO
CANDW
CANDY
CARDI
CARDS
DADDY
DANDY
FALDO
GANDY
GARDA
GARDE
GAUDS
GAUDY
HAIDA
HANDS
HANDY
HARDC
HARDG
HARDY
HAYDN
KANDY
LANDI
LANDO
LANDS
LARDS
LARDY
LAUDE
LAUDS
MAGDA
MAHDI
MAIDS
MAIDU
MANDY
MARDI
MAUDE
MAZDA
NALDI
NARDS
PADDY
PANDA
PANDL
PARDI
PARDO
PARDS
QANDA
RAIDS
RANDB
RANDD
RANDI
RANDR
RANDS
RANDY
SANDE
SANDH
SANDL
SANDS
SANDY
SARDS
SAUDI
TANDE
TANDY
TARDE
TARDY
WADDY
WAJDA
WALDO
WANDA
WANDS
WARDS
YARDS

•A••D
AAHED
BAAED
BAIRD
BAKED
BALED
BARED
BASED
BATED
BAYED
CAGED
CAKED
CANAD
CANED
CANID
CAPED
CARED
CASED
CAVED
CAWED
DARED
DATED
DAVID
DAZED
EARED
EASED
EAVED
FACED
FADED
FAKED
FAMED
FARAD
FARED
FATED
FAXED
FAZED
GAGED
GAMED
GAPED
GATED
GAZED
HALED
HARED
HASID
HATED
HAWED
HAYED
HAZED
JADED
JAPED
JAWED
LACED
LADED
LAIRD
LAMED
LASED
LAVED
LAZED
MACED
MANED
MATED
MAUND
MAXED
NAIAD
NAKED
NAMED
OARED
PACED
PAGED
PALED
PANED
PARED
PATED
PAVED
PAVID
PAWED
PAYED
RABID
RACED
RAGED
RAKED
RANDD
RANID
RAPID
RASED
RATED
RAVED
RAYED
RAZED
SALAD
SALUD
SAPID
SAROD
SATED
SAVED
SAWED
TAMED
TAPED
TAXED
VALID
VAPID
WADED
WAGED
WAKED
WALED
WANED
WAVED
WAXED
YAWED

••AD•
ACADS
AMADO
BEADS
BEADY
BLADE
BRADS
BRADY
DUADS
DYADS
EGADI
EGADS
EVADE
GLADE
GLADS
GOADS
GRADE
GRADS
GRADY
HEADS
HEADY
IRADE
LEADS
LEADY
LOADS
MEADE
MEADS
PRADO
QUADR
QUADS
READE
READS
READY
ROADS
SCADS
SHADE
SHADS
SHADY
SLADE
SPADE
SPADS
STADT
TOADS
TOADY
TRADE
TSADE
WOADS

••A•D
ALAND
AWARD
BAAED
BEARD
BLAND
BOARD
BRAID
BRAND
CHARD
CHAUD
ELAND
FRAUD
GLAND
GRAND
GUARD
HEARD
HOARD
IZARD
LIARD
OLAND
PLAID
QUAID
QUAND
ROALD
SCALD
SCAND
SHARD
SKALD
STAID
STAND
SWARD
VIAND
WHATD

•••AD
AHEAD
AHMAD
AKKAD
ARPAD
ASSAD
BREAD
BROAD
CANAD
CYCAD
DREAD
DRYAD
FARAD
GOBAD
HEXAD
HODAD
ILIAD
INBAD
JIHAD
KNEAD
MONAD
NAIAD
NICAD
NOMAD
NORAD
OCTAD
OREAD
PLEAD
QUOAD
REPAD
SALAD
SNEAD
SQUAD
STEAD
STRAD
TREAD
TRIAD

AE•••
AEAEA
AECIA
AEDES
AEGIR
AEGIS
AEIOU
AEONS
AERIE
AERON
AEROS
AESIR
AESOP
AETAT
AETNA

A•E••
ABEAM
ABEBE
ABELE
ABEND
ABETS
ACERB
ACERS
ACETO
ADEEM
ADELA
ADELE
ADENO
ADEPT
ADEUX
AGENA
AGENT
AGERS
AHEAD
AKEEM
AKEES
AKELA
AKENE
ALECK
ALEFS
ALENE
ALEPH
ALERT
ALETA
ALEUT
ALEVE
AMEBA
AMEER
AMEND
AMENS
AMENT
ANEAR
ANELE
ANEMO
ANENT
ANETO
APEAK
APERS
APERY
AREAL
AREAR
AREAS
ARECA
ARENA
ARENS
ARENT
ARETE
ATEAM
ATEIN
ATEUP
AVENA
AVENS
AVERS
AVERT
AVERY
AXELS
AXERS
AYERS

A••E•
AAHED
AAMES
ABBES
ABBEY
ABLER
ABNER
ABYES
ACCEL
ACHED
ACHES
ACMES
ACRED
ACRES
ACTED
ACTER
ADDED
ADDER
ADEEM
ADHEM
ADIEU
ADLER
ADMEN
ADREM
ADZES
AEAEA
AEDES
AFTER
AGLET
AGLEY
AGNES
AGNEW
AGREE
AGUES
AHMED
AIDED
AIDES
AIKEN
AILED
AILER
AILEY
AIMED
AIMEE
AIMER
AIRED
AIRES
AJMER
AKEEM
AKEES
ALBEE
ALBEN
ALDEN
ALDER
ALGER
ALIEN
ALLEE
ALLEN
ALLER
ALLES
ALLEY
ALLEZ
ALOES
ALTER
AMBER
AMEER
AMIES
AMPED
AMVET
ANDES
ANGEL
ANGER
ANGES
ANNEE
ANNES
ANNEX
ANSEL
ANSER
ANTED
ANTES
APFEL
APLEY
APNEA
APPEL
APRES
APSES
APTED
APTER
ARBER
ARCED
ARDEN
ARIEL
ARIES
ARLEN
ARLES
ARMED
ARMEE
ARMET
ARNEL
ARPEL
ARRET
ARTEL
ARTES
ASHEN
ASHER
ASHES
ASKED
ASKER
ASKEW
ASNER
ASPEN
ASSES
ASSET
ASSEZ
ASTER
ASYET
ATSEA
AUBER
AUDEN
AUGER
AUREI
AWNED
AXLES
AYRES
AZTEC

A•••E
AANDE
ABASE
ABATE
ABBIE
ABEBE
ABELE
ABIDE
ABODE
ABOVE
ABUSE
ACUTE
ADAGE
ADDIE
ADDLE
ADELE
ADIGE
ADOBE
ADORE
AERIE
AFIRE
AFORE
AGAPE
AGATE
AGAVE
AGAZE
AGGIE
AGILE
AGREE
AIMEE
AINGE
AISLE
AISNE
AKENE
ALATE
ALBEE
ALENE
ALEVE
ALFIE
ALFRE
ALGAE
ALICE
ALIKE
ALINE
ALIVE
ALLEE
ALLIE
ALONE
ALYCE
AMAZE
AMBLE
AMICE
AMIDE
AMINE
AMOLE
AMORE
AMPLE
AMUSE
ANDIE
ANDRE
ANELE
ANGIE
ANGLE
ANIME
ANISE
ANKLE
ANNEE
ANNIE
ANODE
ANOLE
ANSAE
ANTAE
ANTRE
APACE
APPLE
APURE
AQUAE
ARAME
ARBRE
ARETE
ARGUE
ARISE
ARMEE
ARNIE
AROSE
ARTIE
ASIDE
ASONE
ASTRE
ATIVE
ATONE
ATQUE
AUDIE
AURAE
AUTRE
AWAKE
AWARE
AWOKE
AXONE
AZIDE
AZINE
AZOTE
AZURE

•AE••
CAELO
FAERY
GAELS
HAEMA
HAEMO
PAEAN
PAEON
SAENS
TAEGU
TAELS

•A•E•
AAHED
AAMES
BAAED
BABEL
BABER
BABES
BADEN
BADER
BAGEL
BAKED
BAKER
BAKES
BALED
BALER
BALES
BANES
BARED
BARER
BARES
BASED
BASEL
BASER
BASES
BATED
BATES
BAUER
BAYED
BAYER
CABER
CADET
CAFES
CAGED
CAGER
CAGES
CAGEY
CAKED
CAKES
CAKEY
CALEB
CAMEL
CAMEO
CANEA
CANED
CANEM
CANER
CANES
CAPED
CAPEK
CAPER
CAPES
CAPET
CARED
CARER
CARES
CARET
CAREW
CAREY
CASED
CASES
CASEY
CATER
CATES
CAVED
CAVER
CAVES
CAWED
DACES
DALES
DALEY
DAMES
DANES
DARED
DARER
DARES
DATED
DATER
DATES
DAWES
DAZED
DAZES
EAGER
EAMES
EARED
EASED
EASEL
EASES
EATEN
EATER
EAVED
EAVES
FABER
FACED
FACER
FACES
FACET
FADED
FADES
FAHEY
FAKED
FAKER
FAKES
FAMED
FAMES
FANES
FARED
FARER
FARES
FATED
FATES
FAVES
FAXED
FAXES
FAZED
FAZES
GAGED
GAGES
GALEA
GALEN
GALES
GAMED
GAMER
GAMES
GAMEY
GANEF
GAPED
GAPER
GAPES
GASES
GATED
GATES
GAVEL
GAYER
GAZED
GAZER
GAZES
HABER
HACEK
HADES
HAGEN
HAKES
HALED
HALER
HALES
HALEY
HAMEL
HAMES
HANES
HARED
HAREM
HARES
HATED
HATER
HATES
HAUER
HAVEL
HAVEN
HAVER
HAVES
HAWED
HAYED
HAYEK
HAYES
HAZED
HAZEL
HAZER
HAZES
JACET
JADED
JADES
JAKES
JAMES
JANET
JAPED
JAPES
JASEY
JAWED
KALEL
KALES
KAREL
KAREN
KASEM
LABEL
LACED
LACER
LACES
LACEY
LADED
LADEN
LADER
LADES
LAGER
LAKER
LAKES
LAMED

LAMER LAMES LANES LAPEL LARES LASED LASER LASES LATEN LATER LATEX LAUER LAVED LAVER LAVES LAWES LAXER LAYER LAZED LAZES MABEL MACED MACES MAGEE MAGES MAHER MAKER MAKES MALES MAMET MANED MANES MANET MARES MASER MATED MATEO MATER MATES MATEY MAVEN MAXED MAXES MAYER MAZEL MAZER MAZES NABES NADER NAGEL NAKED NAMED NAMER NAMES NAPES NARES NAREW NAVEL NAVES OAKEN OAKES OARED OASES OATEN OATER OATES PACED PACER PACES PAGED PAGER PAGES PAGET PALEA

PALED PALEO PALER PALES PALEY PANED PANEL PANES PAPER PARED PAREE PAREN PARER PARES PAREU PASEO PASES PATED PATEK PATEN PATER PATES PAVED PAVER PAVES PAWED PAWER PAYED PAYEE PAYER RACED RACER RACES RAFER RAGED RAGES RAKED RAKER RAKES RAMEE RAMEN RAMET RANEE RAPEE RAREE RARER RARES RASED RASER RASES RATED RATEL RATER RATES RAVED RAVEL RAVEN RAVER RAVES RAWER RAYED RAZED RAZES SABER SAFER SAFES SAGER SAGES SAGET SAHEL SAKER SAKES SALEM SALEP

SALES SANER SASES SATED SATES SAVED SAVER SAVES SAWED SAXES SAYER TACET TAKEI TAKEN TAKER TAKES TALER TALES TAMED TAMER TAMES TANEY TAPED TAPER TAPES TARES TASER TATER TAXED TAXER TAXES VADER VALES VALET VANES VASES VATER WADED WADER WADES WAFER WAGED WAGER WAGES WAKED WAKEN WAKES WALED WALER WALES WALEY WANED WANER WANES WANEY WARES WATER WAVED WAVER WAVES WAXED WAXEN WAXER WAXES XAXES YARER YATES YAWED YAXES ZAXES ZAZEN

•A••E

AANDE BADGE BAIZE BARGE BARRE BASIE BASTE BATHE BAUME BAYLE CABLE CACHE CADGE CADRE CAFFE CAINE CALPE CALVE CANOE CARLE CARNE CARPE CARRE CARTE CARVE CASTE CAUSE CAVAE CAYCE DACHE DAFOE DAMME DANAE DANCE DANKE DANSE DANTE DAVIE DAYNE EAGLE EAGRE EARLE FABLE FACIE FAIRE FALSE FARCE FAROE FAURE FAUVE FAVRE GABLE GAFFE GARDE GASPE GAUGE GAUZE GAYLE HAGUE HAILE HALLE HALVE HANSE HAOLE HARTE HASTE HAUTE HAVRE HAWKE HAWSE JAFFE JAHRE JAIME JAMIE JANIE

JARRE JAUNE JAYNE KAFUE KATIE LADLE LAINE LAKME LANCE LANGE LAPSE LARGE LARUE LATHE LATKE LATTE LAUDE LAYNE MACHE MACLE MADGE MADRE MAGEE MAHRE MAILE MAINE MAIZE MALLE MAMIE MANSE MAPLE MARGE MARIE MARNE MASSE MATTE MAUDE MAUVE MAXIE MAYBE NACRE NAIVE NAPPE NASHE OAKIE PADRE PAIGE PAINE PALAE PALME PANNE PAREE PARLE PARSE PARTE PASSE PASTE PATHE PAUSE PAYEE PAYNE RAISE RAMEE RAMIE RANEE RANGE RANKE RAPEE RAPHE RAREE SABLE SABRE SACRE SADHE

SADIE SALLE SALVE SANDE SANTE SAONE SARGE SATIE SAUCE SAUTE TABLE TAHOE TAINE TANDE TANTE TARDE TARGE TASSE TASTE TAUPE VAGUE VALLE VALSE VALUE VALVE VANCE WAITE WAIVE WASTE WAYNE YALIE ZAIRE ZANTE

••AE•

AEAEA BAAED BRAES SHAEF STAEL

••A•E

ABASE ABATE ADAGE AGAPE AGATE AGAVE AGAZE ALATE AMAZE APACE ARAME AWAKE AWARE BLADE BLAKE BLAME BLARE BLASE BLAZE BRACE BRAHE BRAKE BRAVE BRAZE CEASE CHAFE CHASE CLARE CLAVE CRAKE CRANE CRAPE CRATE CRAVE CRAZE DEANE DIANE DNASE DRAKE DRAPE DUANE ELATE ENATE ERASE ETAGE ETAPE EVADE FLAKE FLAME FLARE FRAME GLACE GLADE GLARE GLAZE GOAPE GRACE GRADE GRAPE GRATE GRAVE GRAZE HEAVE IMAGE INANE INAWE IRADE IRATE JEANE KEANE KNAVE LEASE LEAVE LIANE MEADE NEALE OFAGE OHARE ONATE ORALE ORATE OSAGE OVATE PEACE PEALE PEASE PHAGE PHASE PLACE PLAGE PLANE PLATE PRASE PRATE QUAKE QUALE QUARE READE RNASE SCALE SCAPE SCARE SEALE SHADE SHAKE SHALE SHAME SHANE SHAPE SHARE SHAVE SKATE SLADE SLAKE SLATE SLAVE SMAZE SNAKE SNARE SOAVE SPACE SPADE SPAKE SPARE SPATE STAGE STAKE STALE STARE STATE STAVE SUAVE SWAGE SWALE TEASE THANE TRACE TRADE TRAVE TSADE UKASE USAGE WEAVE WHALE

•••AE

ALGAE ANSAE ANTAE AQUAE AURAE CAVAE COMAE COXAE CUMAE CYMAE DANAE HORAE MCRAE MORAE NOVAE NUGAE PALAE PUPAE RUGAE SETAE STOAE TOGAE ULNAE VENAE VITAE ZOEAE

AF•••

AFAIK AFARS AFFIX AFIRE AFLAT AFOFL AFOOT AFORE AFOUL AFRIC AFRIT AFROS AFTER AFTON AFTRA

A•F••

ADFIN AFFIX ALFAS ALFIE ALFRE APFEL AWFUL

A••F•

ABAFT ACUFF AFOFL ALEFS ALIFS ALOFT

A•••F

ACUFF ADOLF ALOOF

•AF••

CAFES CAFFE DAFFS DAFFY DAFOE GAFFE GAFFS HAFIZ HAFTS HAFUN JAFFA JAFFE KAFIR KAFKA KAFUE NAFTA RAFER RAFFI RAFTS SAFER SAFES TAFFY WAFER WAFTS

•A•F•

BANFF CAFFE DAFFS DAFFY GAFFE GAFFS HAIFA HANFF JAFFA JAFFE RAFFI TAFFY WAAFS WAIFS ZARFS

•A••F

BANFF CALIF GANEF HANFF

••AF•

ABAFT CHAFE CHAFF CRAFT DRAFT GRAFT KRAFT LEAFS LEAFY LOAFS QUAFF SHAFT SNAFU STAFF WAAFS WRAFS

••A•F

CHAFF DWARF QUAFF SCARF SHAEF STAFF SWARF WHARF

•••AF

DECAF PILAF SHEAF

AG•••

AGAIN AGALS AGAMA AGANA AGAPE AGARN AGARS AGASP AGATE AGAVE AGAZE AGENA AGENT AGERS AGGIE AGGRO AGHAS AGILE AGING AGIOS AGITA AGLET AGLEY AGLOW AGNES AGNEW AGNON AGNUS AGOGO AGONY AGORA AGREE AGRIC AGRON AGUES

A•G••

AEGIR AEGIS AGGIE AGGRO ALGAE ALGAL ALGER ALGID ALGIN ALGOL ANGEL ANGER ANGES ANGIE ANGIO ANGLE ANGLO ANGRY ANGST ANGUS ARGIL ARGOL ARGON ARGOS ARGOT ARGUE ARGUS AUGER AUGHT AUGUR AVGAS

A••G•

AARGH ADAGE ADIGE AGOGO AINGE ALIGN AMIGA AMIGO

A•••G

ABZUG ACING AGING ALONG AMONG APING AWING AXING

•AG••

BAGEL BAGGY BAGIT CAGED CAGER CAGES CAGEY DAGON EAGAN EAGER EAGLE EAGRE FAGIN FAGOT GAGED GAGES HAGAR HAGEN HAGIO HAGUE JAGGY LAGAN LAGER LAGOS MAGDA MAGEE MAGES MAGIC MAGMA MAGNA MAGOG MAGOO MAGOT MAGUS NAGEL NAGGY PAGAN PAGED PAGER PAGES PAGET RAGAS RAGED RAGES SAGAL SAGAN SAGAS SAGER SAGES SAGET SAGGY SAGOS TAGUP TAGUS VAGUE VAGUS WAGED WAGER WAGES WAGON

•A•G•

AARGH BADGE BAGGY BANGS BARGE BARGY BAUGH CADGE CARGO DANGS FANGS FARGO GANGS GAUGE HANGS HAWGS JAGGY KANGA LANGE LARGE LARGO LAUGH MADGE MANGO MANGY MARGE MARGO NAGGY PAIGE PANGA PANGS RANGE RANGY SAGGY SAIGA SARGE SARGO TAEGU TAIGA TANGO TANGS TANGY TARGE WAUGH

•A••G

HARDG LAING MAGOG NAVIG VARIG

••AG•

ADAGE BRAGA BRAGG BRAGS CRAGS DRAGS ETAGE FLAGG FLAGS HOAGY IMAGE IMAGO OFAGE OSAGE PHAGE PHAGO PHAGY PLAGE QUAGS SHAGS SLAGS SNAGS STAGE STAGG STAGS STAGY SWAGE SWAGS USAGE

••A•G

BRAGG CHANG CLANG CRAIG DRANG FLAGG GRAIG KIANG LIANG ORANG PRANG SLANG SPANG STAGG STANG TWANG WHANG

•••AG

DORAG GULAG IDTAG REBAG RETAG SCRAG SPRAG

AH•••

AHEAD AHMAD AHMED AHORA AHOYS AHSIN

A•H••

AAHED ABHOR ACHED ACHES ACHOO ADHEM ADHOC AGHAS ANHUI APHID APHIS ARHAT ARHUS ASHBY ASHEN ASHER ASHES ASHUR ATHOL ATHON ATHOS

A••H•

ABOHM AISHA ALOHA ALPHA ALTHO AMAHL AMAHS AMPHI AMPHR ANKHS ANTHO ARCHI ARCHY ARTHR AUGHT AYAHS

A•••H

AARGH ABASH AITCH ALEPH ALLAH AMISH APISH ARITH AWASH AZOTH

•AH••

AAHED BAHAI BAHIA BAHTS FAHEY HAHAS JAHRE KAHLO LAHAR LAHTI MAHAL MAHAN MAHDI MAHER MAHON MAHRE NAHUA NAHUM RAHAB RAHAL SAHEL SAHIB TAHOE TAHRS WAHOO YAHOO

•A•H•

BACHS BASHO BATHE BATHO BATHS BATHY CACHE CATHY DACHA DACHE DASHI FATHA KAPHS KASHA KATHY LATHE LATHS LATHY MACHE MACHO MACHU MACHY MASHY MATHS NACHO NACHT NASHE OATHS PASHA PATHE PATHO PATHS PATHY RAPHE RASHT RATHS SACHA SACHS SADHE SADHU SASHA TACHO TACHY WASHY YACHT

•A••H

AARGH BALCH BALKH BARTH BATCH BAUGH CATCH DARTH EARTH FAITH FARAH GALAH GARTH HARSH HATCH KARSH LARCH LATCH LAUGH MARCH MARSH MATCH NAISH NATCH PARCH PASCH PATCH RAJAH RALPH RANCH RATCH SABAH SAITH SANDH SARAH WALSH WATCH WAUGH

••AH•

AMAHL AMAHS AYAHS BLAHS BRAHE ICAHN IDAHO LEAHY NOAHS OMAHA OPAHS SHAHN SHAHS SPAHI SPAHN STAHL UTAHN

••A•H

ABASH AWASH BEACH BRASH CLASH COACH CRASH ELATH FLASH GNASH GRAPH HEATH KEACH LEACH LEASH LOACH LOATH NEATH ORACH PEACH PLASH PLATH POACH QUASH REACH ROACH SLASH SMASH SNATH STASH SWASH SWATH TEACH TRASH WRATH

•••AH

ALLAH BORAH DINAH EPHAH FARAH GALAH GERAH JONAH JUDAH LOTAH MICAH MYNAH NORAH OBEAH OPRAH RAJAH SABAH SARAH SELAH SHOAH SURAH TORAH URIAH

AI•••

AIDAN AIDED AIDES AIKEN AILED AILER AILEY AIMAT AIMED AIMEE AIMER AIMTO AINGE AINUS AIOLI AIRED AIRES AISHA AISLE AISNE AITCH

A•I••

AAIUN ABIDE ACIDS ACIDY ACING ADIEU ADIGE ADINT ADIOS ADIPO ADITS AEIOU AFIRE AGILE AGING AGIOS AGITA AKINS AKIRA AKITA ALIAS ALIBI ALICE ALIDA ALIEN ALIFS ALIGN ALIKE ALINE ALIOS ALIST ALIVE AMICE AMIDE AMIDO AMIES AMIGA AMIGO AMINE AMINO AMIRS AMISH AMISS AMITY ANILS ANIMA ANIME ANION ANISE ANISO ANITA APIAN APING APISH ARIAN ARIAS ARICA ARIEL ARIES ARILS ARION ARISE ARITH ARIUM ARIUS ASIAN ASIDE ATILT ATION ATIVE AVIAN AVILA AVION AVISO AWING AXIAL AXILS AXING AXIOM AXION AYINS AZIDE

AZINE

A••I•
AALII
ABBIE
ABOIL
ABRIL
ABRIS
ACRID
ACTII
ACTIN
ACTIV
ADAIR
ADDIE
ADDIN
ADDIS
ADFIN
ADLIB
ADMIN
ADMIT
ADMIX
ADVIL
AECIA
AEGIR
AEGIS
AERIE
AESIR
AFAIK
AFFIX
AFRIC
AFRIT
AGAIN
AGGIE
AGRIC
AHSIN
ALAIN
ALFIE
ALGID
ALGIN
ALLIE
ALLIN
ALVIN
AMAIN
AMBIT
AMNIA
ANAIS
ANDIE
ANGIE
ANGIO
ANNIE
ANNIV
ANTIC
ANTIQ
ANTIS
ANVIL
ANZIO
APHID
APHIS
APRIL
APSIS
ARGIL
ARKIN
ARMIS
ARNIE
AROID
ARRIS
ARSIS
ARTIE
ARTIS
ASCII
ASDIC
ASKIN
ASPIC
ASTIN
ASTIR
ATEIN
ATRIA
ATRIP
ATTIC
AUDIE
AUDIO
AUDIS
AUDIT
AULIS
AURIC
AUXIL
AUXIN
AVAIL
AVOID
AVOIR
AVRIL
AWAIT
AZOIC

A•••I
AALII
ABACI
ACARI
ACTII
ADLAI
AIOLI
ALIBI
ALTAI
AMATI
AMPHI
ANHUI
AODAI
ARCHI
ASCII
ASSAI
ATARI
AUREI
AUSSI
AWAJI

•AI••
AAIUN
BAILS
BAIRD
BAIRN
BAITS
BAIUL
BAIZA
BAIZE
CAINE
CAIRN
CAIRO
DAILY
DAIRY
DAISY
DAIWA
FAILS
FAINT
FAIRE
FAIRS
FAIRY
FAITH
GAILY
GAINS
GAITS
GAIUS
HAIDA
HAIFA
HAIKS
HAIKU
HAILE
HAILS
HAIRS
HAIRY
HAITI
JAILS
JAIME
JAINS
LAICS
LAIKA
LAINE
LAING
LAIRD
LAIRS
LAITY
LAIUS
MAIDS
MAIDU
MAILE
MAILS
MAINE
MAINS
MAINZ
MAIZE
NAIAD
NAILS
NAINA
NAIRA
NAIRN
NAISH
NAIVE
PAIGE
PAILS
PAINE
PAINS
PAINT
PAIRS
PAISA
RAIDS
RAILS
RAINS
RAINY
RAISA
RAISE
RAITT
SAIGA
SAILS
SAINT
SAITH
TAIGA
TAILS
TAINE
TAINO
TAINT
WAIFS
WAILS
WAINS
WAIST
WAITE
WAITS
WAITZ
WAIVE
ZAIRE

•A•I•
AALII
BABIS
BAGIT
BAHIA
BALIN
BARIC
BARIT
BASIC
BASIE
BASIL
BASIN
BASIS
BATIK
CABIN
CADIS
CADIZ
CALIF
CALIX
CAMIS
CANID
CANIS
CANIT
CARIA
CARIB
CASIO
CAVIL
DACIA
DANIO
DARIN
DARIO
DAVID
DAVIE
DAVIS
DAVIT
EATIN
EATIT
FABIO
FACIA
FACIE
FACIT
FAGIN
FAKIR
GAMIN
GAVIN
HABIT
HAFIZ
HAGIO
HAJIS
HAKIM
HASID
JAMIE
JAMIN
JANIE
JANIS
KAFIR
KAKIS
KANIN
KATIE
LABIO
LAMIA
LAPIN
LAPIS
LARIS
LATIN
LAVIN
LAYIN
MAGIC
MALIC
MAMIE
MANIA
MANIC
MARIA
MARIE
MARIN
MARIO
MARIS
MATIN
MAVIS
MAXIE
MAXIM
MAXIS
NADIA
NADIR
NAMIB
NARIS
NAVIG
OAKIE
OASIS
PALIN
PAMIR
PANIC
PARIS
PATIO
PAVIA
PAVID
PAVIS
PAYIN
RABID
RABIN
RADII
RADIO
RADIX
RAJIV
RAKIS
RAMIE
RAMIS
RANID
RANIN
RANIS
RAPID
RATIO
RAVIN
SABIN
SADIE
SADIS
SAHIB
SALIC
SAPID
SAPIR
SARIS
SATIE
SATIN
SAWIN
TABIS
TACIT
TAKIN
TALIA
TAMIL
TAPIN
TAPIR
TAXIS
VADIM
VADIS
VALID
VANIR
VAPID
VARIA
VARIG
VARIX
VATIC
WADIS
XAXIS
YADIM
YALIE
YASIR
YAXIS
ZAMIA
ZAXIS
ZAYIN

•A••I
AALII
BAHAI
BAMBI
BAOJI
BASSI
CACTI
CALCI
CALLI
CAPRI
CARDI
CARPI
DALAI
DASHI
FARCI
FARSI
GALLI
GARNI
HADJI
HAITI
HAJJI
HANOI
IAMBI
KANJI
KAUAI
KAURI
LACTI
LAHTI
LANAI
LANDI
MAHDI
MAORI
MAQUI
MARDI
MARTI
MASAI
MATRI
NALDI
NAMOI
NAOMI
PALPI
PAOLI
PAPPI
PARDI
PARTI
PATRI
PATTI
RABBI
RADII
RAFFI
RANDI
SAKAI
SALMI
SAUDI
TAKEI
TARSI
VALLI
YANNI
YAQUI

••AI•
ADAIR
AFAIK
AGAIN
ALAIN
AMAIN
ANAIS
AVAIL
AWAIT
BLAIR
BRAID
BRAIL
BRAIN
CHAIM
CHAIN
CHAIR
CLAIM
CLAIR
CRAIG
CRAIN
DRAIL
DRAIN
EMAIL
FLAIL
FLAIR
FRAIL
FRAIS
GHAIN
GLAIR
GRAIG
GRAIL
GRAIN
KRAIT
NGAIO
OHAIR
ONAIR
PLAID
PLAIN
PLAIT
PRAIA
QUAID
QUAIL
REAIM
REAIR
SLAIN
SMAIL
SNAIL
SPAIN
STAID
STAIN
STAIR
SWAIN
THAIS
TRAIL
TRAIN
TRAIT
TWAIN
USAIR

••A•I
ABACI
ACARI
AMATI
ATARI
AWAJI
COATI
DHABI
EGADI
ELAZI
GHALI
GHAZI
GRANI
INARI
IRANI
IRAQI
KHAKI
MIAMI
NGAMI
OKAPI
OMANI
PIAUI
PLANI
QUASI
SHARI
SPAHI
SWAMI
SWAZI

•••AI
ADLAI
ALTAI
AODAI
ASSAI
BAHAI
BOHAI
DALAI
DOUAI
DUBAI
ENLAI
KAUAI
KENAI
LANAI
MASAI
POHAI
SAKAI
SERAI
SINAI

AJ•••
AJMER

A•J••
ANJOU
AUJUS

A••J•
ABUJA
AWAJI

•AJ••
CAJUN
HAJIS
HAJJI
MAJOR
RAJAH
RAJAS
RAJIV
SAJAK
WAJDA

•A•J•
BANJO
BAOJI
HADJI
HAJJI
KANJI
NADJA

••AJ•
AWAJI

AK•••
AKBAR
AKEEM
AKEES
AKELA
AKENE
AKINS
AKIRA
AKITA
AKKAD
AKRON
AKSUM

A•K••
AIKEN
AKKAD
ALKYD
ALKYL
ANKHS
ANKLE
AOKAY
ARKIN
ASKED
ASKER
ASKEW
ASKIN

A••K•
ALIKE
ASOKA
AWAKE
AWOKE

A•••K
ABACK
AFAIK
ALACK
ALECK
AMUCK
ANOUK
APEAK

•AK••
BAKED
BAKER
BAKES
BAKST
CAKED
CAKES
CAKEY
DAKAR
FAKED
FAKER
FAKES
FAKIR
HAKES
HAKIM
JAKES
KAKAS
KAKIS
LAKER
LAKES
LAKME
MAKER
MAKES
MAKOS
MAKUA
NAKED
OAKEN
OAKES
OAKIE
OAKUM
RAKED
RAKER
RAKES
RAKIS
SAKAI
SAKER
SAKES
TAKAS
TAKEI
TAKEN
TAKER
TAKES
TAKIN
WAKED
WAKEN
WAKES
YAKOV
YAKUT

•A•K•
BABKA
BACKS
BALKH
BALKS
BALKY
BANKS
BANKY
BARKS
BARKY
BASKS
CALKS
CARKS
CASKS
DANKE
DARKS
GAWKS
GAWKY
HACKS
HAIKS
HAIKU
HANKS
HANKY
HARKS
HAWKE
HAWKS
JACKS
JACKY
KAFKA
LACKS
LAIKA
LANKA
LANKY
LARKS
LARKY
LATKE
MARKS
MASKS
NARKS
PACKS
PANKY
PARKA
PARKS
PAWKY
RACKS
RANKE
RANKS
SACKS
SANKA
SARKY
SAUKS
TACKS
TACKY
TALKS
TALKY
TANKA
TANKS
TASKS
WACKO
WACKY
WALKS
YACKS
YANKS

•A••K
BATAK
BATIK
BAULK
CAPEK
CAULK
DAYAK
HACEK
HAYEK
KAPOK
KAYAK
KAZAK
NANAK
PATEK
SAJAK
TAROK
YAPOK

••AK•
AWAKE
BEAKS
BLAKE
BRAKE
CHAKA
CRAKE
DHAKA
DRAKE
FLAKE
FLAKY
KHAKI
LEAKS
LEAKY
OSAKA
PEAKS
QUAKE
QUAKY
SHAKE
SHAKO
SHAKY
SLAKE
SNAKE
SNAKY
SOAKS
SPAKE
STAKE
TEAKS

••A•K
ABACK
AFAIK
ALACK
BLACK
BLANK
CHALK
CLACK
CLANK
CLARK
CRACK
CRANK
DMARK
DRANK
FLACK
FLANK
FLASK
FRANK
IZAAK
KNACK
KYACK
NYACK
OZARK
PLANK
PRANK
QUACK
QUARK
RUARK
SHACK
SHANK
SHARK
SKANK
SLACK
SMACK
SNACK
SNARK
SPAAK
SPANK
SPARK
STACK
STALK
STANK
STARK
SWANK
THANK
TRACK
WHACK
WRACK

•••AK
APEAK
BATAK
BLEAK
BREAK
CLOAK
CREAK
CROAK
DAYAK
FREAK
IZAAK
KAYAK
KAZAK
KODAK
KOJAK
KULAK
MUZAK
NANAK
NOVAK
SAJAK
SNEAK
SPAAK
SPEAK
STEAK
TILAK
TWEAK
UMIAK
WREAK

AL•••
ALACK
ALAIN
ALAMO
ALANA
ALAND
ALARM
ALATE
ALAVA
ALBAN
ALBEE
ALBEN
ALBUM
ALCAN
ALCOA
ALCOR
ALDAN
ALDEN
ALDER
ALDOL
ALDUS
ALECK
ALEFS
ALENE
ALEPH
ALERT
ALETA
ALEUT
ALEVE
ALFAS
ALFIE
ALFRE
ALGAE
ALGAL
ALGER
ALGID
ALGIN
ALGOL
ALIAS
ALIBI
ALICE
ALIDA
ALIEN
ALIFS
ALIGN
ALIKE
ALINE
ALIOS
ALIST
ALIVE
ALKYD
ALKYL
ALLAH
ALLAN
ALLAY
ALLEE
ALLEN
ALLER
ALLES
ALLEY
ALLEZ
ALLIE
ALLIN
ALLOT
ALLOW
ALLOY
ALLYL
ALMAY
ALOES
ALOFT
ALOHA
ALONE
ALONG
ALOOF
ALORS
ALOUD
ALPHA
ALSOP
ALTAI
ALTAR
ALTER
ALTHO
ALTON
ALTOS
ALTUS
ALULA
ALUMS
ALVAR
ALVIN
ALYCE

A•L••
AALII
AALTO
ABLER
ADLAI
ADLER
ADLIB
ADLOC
AFLAT
AGLET
AGLEY
AGLOW
AILED
AILER
AILEY
ALLAH
ALLAN
ALLAY
ALLEE
ALLEN
ALLER
ALLES
ALLEY
ALLEZ
ALLIE
ALLIN
ALLOT
ALLOW
ALLOY
ALLYL
APLEY
APLUS
ARLEN
ARLES
ATLAS
AULIS
AXLES

A••L•
ABELE
ACYLS
ADDLE
ADELA
ADELE
ADOLF
ADULT
AGALS
AGILE
AIOLI
AISLE
AKELA
ALULA
AMBLE
AMOLE
AMPLE
AMPLY
AMYLO
AMYLS
ANELE
ANGLE
ANGLO
ANILS
ANKLE
ANOLE
APPLE
APPLY
APTLY
ARILS
ASYLA
ATALL
ATILT
ATOLL
AVILA
AWOLS
AXELS
AXILS

A•••L
ABDUL
ABOIL
ABRIL
ACCEL
ADDNL
ADVAL
ADVIL
AFOFL
AFOUL
ALDOL
ALGAL
ALGOL
ALKYL
ALLYL
AMAHL
AMPUL
ANGEL
ANNAL
ANNUL
ANSEL
ANTAL
ANVIL
APFEL
APPAL
APPEL
APRIL
AREAL
ARGIL
ARGOL
ARIEL
ARNEL
ARPEL
ARTAL
ARTEL
ATALL
ATHOL
ATOLL
AURAL
AUXIL
AVAIL
AVRIL
AWFUL
AXIAL

•AL••
AALII
AALTO
BALAS
BALCH
BALDS
BALED
BALER
BALES
BALIN
BALKH
BALKS
BALKY
BALLS
BALLY
BALMS
BALMY
BALSA
BALTO
BALTS
CALCI
CALEB
CALIF
CALIX
CALKS
CALLA
CALLI
CALLS
CALMS
CALPE
CALVE
CALYX
DALAI
DALES
DALEY
DALLY
FALDO
FALLA
FALLS
FALSE
GALAH
GALAS
GALAX
GALBA
GALEA
GALEN
GALES
GALLI
GALLO
GALLS
GALOP
HALAS
HALED
HALER
HALES
HALEY
HALLE
HALLO
HALLS
HALMS
HALON
HALOS
HALTS
HALVE
KALEL
KALES
LALAW
MALAN
MALAR
MALAY
MALES
MALIC
MALLE
MALLS
MALMO
MALTA
MALTS
MALTY
NALDI
PALAE
PALAU
PALEA
PALED
PALEO
PALER
PALES
PALEY
PALIN
PALLS
PALLY
PALMA
PALME
PALMS
PALMY
PALOS
PALPI
PALPS
PALSY
RALLY
RALPH
SALAD
SALAL
SALAM
SALEM
SALEP
SALES
SALIC
SALLE
SALLY
SALMI
SALON
SALPA
SALPS
SALSA
SALTA
SALTS
SALTY
SALUD
SALUT
SALVE
SALVO
TALER
TALES
TALIA
TALKS
TALKY
TALLY
TALON
TALOS
TALUS
VALES
VALET
VALID
VALLE
VALLI
VALOR
VALSE
VALUE
VALVE
WALDO
WALED
WALER
WALES
WALEY
WALKS
WALLA
WALLS
WALLY
WALSH
WALSY
WALTZ
YALIE
YALOW
YALTA

•A•L•
BAALS
BADLY
BAILS
BALLS
BALLY
BAULK
BAWLS
BAYLE
CABLE
CAELO
CALLA
CALLI
CALLS
CARLA
CARLE
CARLO
CARLY
CAULK
CAULS
DAILY
DALLY
DARLA
EAGLE
EARLE
EARLS
EARLY
FABLE
FAILS
FALLA
FALLS
FATLY
FAULT
GABLE
GAELS
GAILY
GALLI
GALLO
GALLS
GAOLS
GAULS
GAYLE
GAYLY
HABLA
HAILE
HAILS
HALLE
HALLO
HALLS
HAOLE
HAPLO
HAPLY
HATLO
HAULM
HAULS
JAILS
JARLS
KAHLO
KARLA
LADLE
LAXLY
LAYLA
MACLE
MADLY
MAILE
MAILS
MALLE
MALLS
MANLY
MAPLE
MARLA
MARLO
MARLS
MARLY
MAULS
NAILS
PABLO
PAILS
PALLS
PALLY
PAOLI
PAOLO
PARLE
PATLY
PAULA
PAULO
PAWLS
RAILS
RALLY
RAWLS
RAWLY
SABLE
SADLY
SAILS
SALLE
SALLY
SAULT
TABLA
TABLE
TAELS
TAILS
TALLY
VALLE
VALLI
VAULT
WAALS
WAILS
WALLA
WALLS
WALLY
WANLY
YAWLS

•A••L
BABEL
BABUL
BAGEL
BAIUL
BANAL
BASAL
BASEL
BASIL
CABAL

CAMEL CANAL CAROL CAVIL DARYL EASEL FATAL GAMAL GAVEL GAYAL HAMAL HAMEL HAVEL HAZEL JAMAL KABUL KALEL KAREL KAROL LABEL LAPEL LAVAL MABEL MAHAL MAZEL NAGEL NASAL NATAL NAVAL NAVEL PANDL PANEL PAPAL PAROL RAHAL RAOUL RATEL RAVEL SAGAL SAHEL SALAL SANDL TAMIL

••AL•

AGALS ATALL BAALS BBALL BEALL BEALS BIALY CHALK COALS DEALS DEALT DHALS DIALS EXALT FOALS GHALI GOALS HEALS HEALY INALL ITALO ITALS ITALY KOALA KUALA MEALS MEALY NEALE NYALA

OCALA OPALS ORALE ORALS OVALS PEALE PEALS PSALM QUALE QUALM REALM REALS RIALS ROALD SCALA SCALD SCALE SCALP SCALY SEALE SEALS SEALY SHALE SHALL SHALT SIALS SKALD SMALL SMALT SPALL STALE STALK STALL SWALE TBALL TEALS TRALA UDALL URALS UZALA VEALY VIALS WAALS WEALS WHALE ZEALS

••A•L

AMAHL ATALL AVAIL BBALL BEALL BRAIL BRAWL CRAWL DRAIL DRAWL EMAIL FLAIL FRAIL GNARL GRAIL INALL KRAAL PEARL QUAIL SHALL SHAWL SMAIL SMALL SNAIL SNARL SPALL

STAEL STAHL STALL TBALL TRAIL TRAWL UDALL UHAUL

•••AL

ADVAL ALGAL ANNAL ANTAL APPAL AREAL ARTAL AURAL AXIAL BANAL BASAL BINAL CABAL CANAL COPAL CORAL COXAL DECAL DORAL DOTAL DUCAL EQUAL FATAL FERAL FETAL FINAL FOCAL FUGAL GAMAL GAYAL GLIAL GORAL GYRAL HAMAL HORAL IDEAL JAMAL JOUAL JUBAL JUGAL JURAL KEMAL KRAAL LAVAL LEGAL LOCAL LOYAL MAHAL MEDAL METAL MODAL MORAL MURAL NASAL NATAL NAVAL NEPAL NIVAL NOCAL NODAL NOPAL OCTAL OFFAL ONEAL PAPAL PEDAL PENAL PETAL PHIAL PIPAL PUPAL RAHAL REGAL RENAL RIVAL RIYAL ROYAL RURAL SAGAL SALAL SEGAL SEPAL SERAL SHOAL SISAL SKOAL STEAL SURAL TEPAL TICAL TIDAL TIKAL TONAL TOTAL TRIAL URIAL USUAL UXMAL VENAL VIDAL VIRAL VITAL VOCAL WHEAL ZOEAL ZONAL

AM•••

AMADO AMAHL AMAHS AMAIN AMANA AMAPA AMARA AMASS AMATI AMATO AMAZE AMBER AMBIT AMBLE AMBOS AMBOY AMBRY AMEBA AMEER AMEND AMENS AMENT AMICE AMIDE AMIDO AMIES AMIGA AMIGO AMINE AMINO AMIRS AMISH AMISS AMITY AMMAN AMMON AMMOS AMNIA AMOCO AMOLE AMONG AMORE AMORT AMORY AMOUR AMPAS AMPED AMPHI AMPHR AMPLE AMPLY AMPUL AMUCK AMUSE AMVET AMWAY AMYLO AMYLS

A•M••

AAMES ACMES ADMAN ADMEN ADMIN ADMIT ADMIX AHMAD AHMED AIMAT AIMED AIMEE AIMER AIMTO AJMER ALMAY AMMAN AMMON AMMOS ARMED ARMEE ARMET ARMIS ARMOR ATMAN ATMOS

A••M•

ABOMB ACOMA ADAMA ADAMS AGAMA ALAMO ALUMS ANEMO ANIMA ANIME ANOMY ARAMA ARAME AROMA ARUMS ASAMA ATOMS ATOMY

A•••M

AANDM ABEAM ABOHM ABRAM ABYSM ADEEM ADHEM ADREM ADSUM AKEEM AKSUM ALARM ALBUM ANNAM ANNUM ARIUM ASSAM ATEAM AURUM AXIOM

•AM••

AAMES BAMBI CAMAY CAMEL CAMEO CAMIS CAMOS CAMPO CAMPS CAMPY CAMRY CAMUS DAMAN DAMAR DAMES DAMME DAMNS DAMON DAMPS DAMUP EAMES EAMON FAMED FAMES GAMAL GAMAY GAMBA GAMED GAMER GAMES GAMEY GAMIN GAMMA GAMMY GAMOW GAMPS GAMUT HAMAL HAMAN HAMEL HAMES HAMMY IAMBI IAMBS JAMAL JAMBS JAMES JAMIE JAMIN JAMMY JAMUP LAMAR LAMAS LAMBS LAMED LAMER LAMES LAMIA LAMPS MAMAS MAMBA MAMBO MAMET MAMIE MAMMA MAMMY NAMBY NAMED NAMER NAMES NAMIB NAMOI NAMPA NAMUR PAMBY PAMIR PAMPA RAMAN RAMAR RAMBO RAMEE RAMEN RAMET RAMIE RAMIS RAMON RAMOS RAMPS SAMAR SAMBA SAMMS SAMMY SAMOA SAMOS SAMPS TAMBO TAMED TAMER TAMES TAMIL TAMMY TAMPA TAMPS VAMOS VAMPS YAMPA ZAMIA

•A•M•

BALMS BALMY BARMS BARMY BAUME CALMS DAMME FARMS GAMMA GAMMY GAUMS HAEMA HAEMO HALMS HAMMY HARMS JAIME JAMMY KARMA LAKME MAGMA MALMO MAMMA MAMMY NAOMI PALMA PALME PALMS PALMY PARMA SALMI SAMMS SAMMY TAMMY WARMS

•A••M

AANDM CANEM CAROM DATUM HAKIM HAREM HARUM HAULM KASEM LARAM MADAM MAXIM NAHUM OAKUM PANAM SALAM SALEM TATUM VADIM YADIM

••AM•

ADAMA ADAMS AGAMA ALAMO ARAMA ARAME ASAMA BEAMS BEAMY BLAME CHAMP CLAMP CLAMS CRAMP CRAMS DRAMA DRAMS EDAMS EXAMS FLAME FLAMS FLAMY FOAMS FOAMY FRAME GRAMA GRAMM GRAMP GRAMS HYAMS IMAMS ISAMU LLAMA LOAMS LOAMY MIAMI NGAMI ORAMA PRAMS REAMS ROAMS SCAMP SCAMS SEAMS SEAMY SHAME SHAMS SHAMU SLAMS SPAMS STAMP SWAMI SWAMP TEAMS TRAMP TRAMS WHAMO WHAMS

••A•M

ALARM CHAIM CHARM CHASM CLAIM GRAMM PHARM PLASM PSALM QUALM REAIM REALM REARM SHAWM SPASM SWARM UNARM

•••AM

ABEAM ABRAM ANNAM ASSAM ATEAM BREAM CERAM CREAM DREAM GLEAM GLOAM HBEAM HIRAM IBEAM ISLAM LARAM MADAM MOHAM NIZAM OCCAM OGHAM ONEAM PANAM PRIAM PROAM SALAM SCRAM SIXAM STEAM TENAM TWOAM UNJAM

AN•••

ANAIS ANCON ANDES ANDIE ANDOR ANDRE ANDRO ANDRY ANDUP ANEAR ANELE ANEMO ANENT ANETO ANGEL ANGER ANGES ANGIE ANGIO ANGLE ANGLO ANGRY ANGST ANGUS ANHUI ANILS ANIMA ANIME ANION ANISE ANISO ANITA ANJOU ANKHS ANKLE ANNAL ANNAM ANNAN ANNEE ANNES ANNEX ANNIE ANNIV ANNOY ANNUL ANNUM ANNUS ANOAS ANODE ANOLE ANOMY ANOUK ANSAE ANSEL ANSER ANSON ANTAE ANTAL ANTAS ANTED ANTES ANTHO ANTIC ANTIQ ANTIS ANTON ANTRA ANTRE ANTSY ANVIL ANWAR ANZAC ANZIO

A•N••

AANDE AANDM ABNER AGNES AGNEW AGNON AGNUS AINGE AINUS AMNIA ANNAL ANNAM ANNAN ANNEE ANNES ANNEX ANNIE ANNIV ANNOY ANNUL ANNUM ANNUS APNEA ARNAZ ARNEL ARNIE ASNER ATNOS AUNTS AUNTY AWNED

A••N•

ABEND ACING ADANA ADANO ADDNL ADENO ADINT AEONS AETNA AGANA AGENA AGENT AGING AGONY AISNE AKENE AKINS ALANA ALAND ALENE ALINE ALONE ALONG AMANA AMEND AMENS AMENT AMINE AMINO AMONG ANENT APING ARENA ARENS ARENT ASANA ASONE ASSNS ATONE ATONY AVANT AVENA AVENS AWING AXING AXONE AXONS AYINS AZANS AZINE

A•••N

AAIUN AARON ACORN ACTIN ACTON ADDIN ADDON ADFIN ADMAN ADMEN ADMIN ADORN AERON AFTON AGAIN AGARN AGNON AGRON AHSIN AIDAN AIKEN AKRON ALAIN ALBAN ALBEN ALCAN ALDAN ALDEN ALGIN ALIEN ALIGN ALLAN ALLEN ALLIN ALTON ALVIN AMAIN AMMAN AMMON ANCON ANION ANNAN ANSON ANTON APIAN APRON ARDEN ARGON ARIAN ARION ARKIN ARLEN ARRAN ARSON ARYAN ASHEN ASIAN ASKIN ASPEN ASTIN ASTON ASWAN ATEIN ATHON ATION ATMAN AUDEN AUXIN AVIAN AVION AXION

•AN••

AANDE AANDM BANAL BANAT BANCO BANCS BANDA BANDB BANDO BANDS BANDW BANDY BANES BANFF BANGS BANJO BANKS BANKY BANNS BANTU CANAD CANAL CANBY CANDO CANDW CANDY CANEA CANED CANEM CANER CANES CANID CANIS CANIT CANNA CANNY CANOE CANON CANSO CANST CANTO CANTS CANTY DANAE DANCE DANCY DANDY DANES DANGS DANIO DANKE DANNY DANSE DANTE DANZA FANCY FANES FANGS FANNY FANON FANTA GANDY GANEF GANGS HANDS HANDY HANES HANFF HANGS HANKS HANKY HANNA HANNO HANOI HANSA HANSE HANTS JANET JANIE JANIS JANUS KANDY KANGA KANIN KANJI KANSA KANZU LANAI LANCE LANDI LANDO LANDS LANES LANGE LANKA LANKY LANTZ LANZA MANCY MANDY MANED MANES MANET MANGO MANGY MANIA MANIC MANLY MANNA MANNY MANON MANOR MANOS MANSE MANTA NANAK NANAS NANCY NANNA NANNY PANAM PANAY PANDA PANDL PANED PANEL PANES PANGA PANGS PANIC PANKY PANNE PANSY PANTO PANTS PANZA QANDA RANAT RANCH RANDB RANDD RANDI RANDR RANDS RANDY RANEE RANGE RANGY RANID RANIN RANIS RANKE RANKS RANON RANTO RANTS RANUP SANAA SANDE SANDH SANDL SANDS SANDY SANER SANKA SANTA SANTE SANTO SANYO TANDE TANDY TANEY TANGO TANGS TANGY TANKA TANKS TANSY TANTE TANTO TANYA VANCE VANES VANIR VANNA VANYA WANDA WANDS WANED WANER WANES WANEY WANLY WANNA WANTS YANKS YANNI ZANTE

•A•N•

BANNS BARNS CAINE CANNA CANNY CARNE CARNY DAMNS DANNY DARNS DAUNT DAWNS DAYNE EARNS FAINT FANNY FAUNA FAUNS FAWNS GAINS GARNI GAUNT HADNT HANNA HANNO HASNT HAUNT JAINS JAUNE JAUNT JAYNE KAONS LAINE LAING LAWNS LAWNY LAYNE MAGNA MAINE MAINS MAINZ MANNA MANNY MARNE MAUNA MAUND MAYNT NAINA NANNA NANNY PAINE PAINS PAINT PANNE PATNA PAWNS PAYNE RAINS RAINY SAENS SAINT SAONE SAUNA TAINE TAINO TAINT TARNS TAUNT TAWNY VANNA VARNA VAUNT WAINS WANNA WARNS WASNT WAYNE YANNI YARNS YAWNS

•A••N

AAIUN AARON BACON BADEN BAIRN BALIN BARON BASIN BATON CABIN CAIRN CAJUN CANON CAPON CARON DAGON DAMAN DAMON DARIN DAYAN EAGAN EAMON EATEN EATIN EATON FAGIN FANON FARON GABON GALEN GAMIN GATUN GAVIN HADON HAFUN HAGEN HALON HAMAN HASON HAVEN HAYDN HAZAN JAMIN JAPAN JASON KANIN KARAN KAREN KAZAN LABAN LADEN LADON LAGAN LAPIN LATEN LATIN LAVIN LAYIN LAYON MACON MAHAN MAHON MALAN MANON MARIN MASON MATIN MAVEN MAYAN MAYON NAIRN OAKEN OATEN PAEAN PAEON PAGAN PALIN PAREN PATEN PATON PAYIN RABIN RACON RADON RAMAN RAMEN RAMON RANIN RANON RATON RAVEN RAVIN RAYON SABIN SAGAN SALON SARAN SATAN SATIN SATON SAWIN SAXON TAKEN TAKIN TALON TAPIN TAUON TAXON WAGON WAKEN WAXEN ZAYIN ZAZEN

••AN•

ADANA ADANO AGANA ALANA ALAND AMANA ASANA AVANT AZANS BEANO BEANS BEANY BLANC BLAND BLANK BRAND BRANS BRANT BWANA CHANG CHANT CLANG CLANK CLANS

CRANE
CRANK
CYANO
DEANE
DEANS
DIANA
DIANE
DRANG
DRANK
DRANO
DUANE
ELAND
EVANS
FLANK
FLANS
FRANC
FRANK
FRANS
FRANZ
GHANA
GIANT
GLAND
GRAND
GRANI
GRANT
INANE
IPANA
IRANI
IVANA
JEANE
JEANS
KEANE
KEANU
KHANS
KIANG
KOANS
LEANS
LEANT
LIANA
LIANE
LIANG
LLANO
LOANS
MEANS
MEANT
MEANY
MOANS
OLAND
OMANI
ORANG
ORANT
PHANY
PIANO
PLANB
PLANE
PLANI
PLANK
PLANO
PLANS
PLANT
PRANG
PRANK
QUAND
QUANT
RIANT
ROANS
RUANA
SCAND
SCANS
SCANT
SHANA
SHANE
SHANK
SHANS
SHANT
SKANK
SLANG
SLANT
SPANG
SPANK
SPANS
STAND
STANG
STANK
SWANK
SWANN
SWANS
THANE
THANK
THANT
TIANT
TRANS
TWANG
VIAND
WEANS
WHANG
YEANS
YUANS

••A•N
AGAIN
AGARN
ALAIN
AMAIN
BRAIN
BRAUN
BRAWN
CHAIN
CRAIN
DRAIN
DRAWN
GHAIN
GRAIN
HEARN
ICAHN
LEARN
PLAIN
PRAWN
SHAHN
SHAUN
SHAWN
SLAIN
SPAHN
SPAIN
SPAWN
STAIN
SWAIN
SWANN
TRAIN
TWAIN
UTAHN
YEARN

•••AN
ADMAN
AIDAN
ALBAN
ALCAN
ALDAN
ALLAN
AMMAN
ANNAN
APIAN
ARIAN
ARRAN
ARYAN
ASIAN
ASWAN
ATMAN
AVIAN
BEGAN
BEHAN
BRIAN
BRYAN
CLEAN
COHAN
CONAN
COPAN
CUBAN
DAMAN
DAYAN
DEWAN
DIVAN
DORAN
DUGAN
DURAN
DYLAN
EAGAN
ELMAN
ETHAN
EVIAN
FURAN
GLEAN
GOLAN
GROAN
HAMAN
HAZAN
HEMAN
HENAN
HOBAN
HOGAN
HONAN
HUMAN
HUNAN
HYMAN
INCAN
IOWAN
JAPAN
KARAN
KAZAN
KORAN
LABAN
LAGAN
LEXAN
LOGAN
LOMAN
LORAN
LUCAN
LYMAN
MAHAN
MALAN
MAYAN
MEGAN
MELAN
MIKAN
MILAN
MORAN
NEMAN
NISAN
NOLAN
OCEAN
OLEAN
ORGAN
OSCAN
OSMAN
PAEAN
PAGAN
PECAN
PERAN
PISAN
PUSAN
RAMAN
REDAN
REGAN
REHAN
REMAN
RENAN
RERAN
RODAN
ROMAN
ROWAN
SAGAN
SARAN
SATAN
SEDAN
SHEAN
SIVAN
SKEAN
SLOAN
SOLAN
SUDAN
SUSAN
TEXAN
TIRAN
TITAN
TYNAN
UCLAN
UHLAN
UNMAN
URBAN
VEGAN
WIGAN
WOMAN
WOTAN
WUHAN
WYMAN
YUMAN

AO•••
AODAI
AOKAY
AORTA

A•O••
ABODE
ABOHM
ABOIL
ABOMB
ABORT
ABOUT
ABOVE
ABOVO
ACOMA
ACORN
ADOBE
ADOLF
ADOPT
ADORE
ADORN
ADOUT
AEONS
AFOFL
AFOOT
AFORE
AFOUL
AGOGO
AGONY
AGORA
AHORA
AHOYS
AIOLI
ALOES
ALOFT
ALOHA
ALONE
ALONG
ALOOF
ALORS
ALOUD
AMOCO
AMOLE
AMONG
AMORE
AMORT
AMORY
AMOUR
ANOAS
ANODE
ANOLE
ANOMY
ANOUK
APORT
AROAR
AROID
AROMA
AROSE
ASOKA
ASONE
ATOLL
ATOMS
ATOMY
ATONE
ATONY
AVOID
AVOIR
AVOWS
AWOKE
AWOLS
AXONE
AXONS
AZOIC
AZOTE
AZOTH

A••O•
AARON
ABBOT
ABHOR
ACHOO
ACTON
ACTOR
ADDON
ADHOC
ADIOS
ADLOC
AEIOU
AERON
AEROS
AESOP
AFOOT
AFROS
AFTON
AGIOS
AGLOW
AGNON
AGRON
AKRON
ALCOA
ALCOR
ALDOL
ALGOL
ALIOS
ALLOT
ALLOW
ALLOY
ALOOF
ALSOP
ALTON
ALTOS
AMBOS
AMBOY
AMMON
AMMOS
ANCON
ANDOR
ANION
ANJOU
ANNOY
ANSON
ANTON
APRON
APSOS
ARBOR
ARDOR
ARGOL
ARGON
ARGOS
ARGOT
ARION
ARMOR
ARROW
ARROZ
ARSON
ARTOO
ASCOT
ASSOC
ASTON
ASTOR
ATHOL
ATHON
ATHOS
ATION
ATMOS
ATNOS
AUTOS
AVION
AXIOM
AXION

A•••O
AALTO
ABACO
ABOVO
ACETO
ACHOO
ADANO
ADDTO
ADENO
ADIPO
AGGRO
AGOGO
AIMTO
ALAMO
ALTHO
AMADO
AMATO
AMIDO
AMIGO
AMINO
AMOCO
AMYLO
ANDRO
ANEMO
ANETO
ANGIO
ANGLO
ANISO
ANTHO
ANZIO
ARTOO
ASTRO
AUDIO
AVISO

•AO••
BAOJI
GAOLS
HAOLE
KAONS
MAORI
NAOMI
PAOLI
PAOLO
RAOUL
SAONE

•A•O•
AARON
BACON
BARON
BASOV
BATON
BATOR
BAYOU
CABOT
CAMOS
CANOE
CANON
CAPON
CAPOS
CAROB
CAROL
CAROM
CARON
DADOS
DAFOE
DAGON
DAMON
DAVOS
EAMON
EATON
FADOS
FAGOT
FANON
FAROE
FARON
FAROS
FAVOR
GABON
GABOR
GALOP
GAMOW
GAROU
GATOR
GATOS
GAVOT
HADON
HALON
HALOS
HANOI
HASON
HAVOC
JABOT
JACOB
JASON
JATOS
KABOB
KAPOK
KAROL
KAYOS
KAZOO
LABOR
LADON
LAGOS
LAYON
MACON
MAGOG
MAGOO
MAGOT
MAHON
MAJOR
MAKOS
MANON
MANOR
MANOS
MASON
MAYON
MAYOR
NABOB
NAMOI
NAXOS
PAEON
PALOS
PAROL
PAROS
PATON
RACON
RADON
RAMON
RAMOS
RANON
RATON
RAYON
RAZOR
SABOT
SAGOS
SALON
SAMOA
SAMOS
SAPOR
SAROD
SAROS
SATON
SAVOR
SAVOY
SAXON
TABOO
TABOR
TACOS
TAHOE
TALON
TALOS
TAROK
TAROT
TAUON
TAXON
VALOR
VAMOS
VAPOR
WAGON
WAHOO
YAHOO
YAKOV
YALOW
YAPOK
YAZOO

•A••O
AALTO
BALTO
BANCO
BANDO
BANJO
BASHO
BASSO
BATHO
CACAO
CADDO
CAELO
CAIRO
CAMEO
CAMPO
CANDO
CANSO
CANTO
CARBO
CARGO
CARLO
CARPO
CASCO
CASIO
DANIO
DARIO
DAVAO
FABIO
FACTO
FALDO
FARGO
GALLO
GARBO
HADTO
HAEMO
HAGIO
HALLO
HANNO
HAPLO
HARPO
HASSO
HASTO
HATLO
IATRO
KAHLO
KAZOO
LABIO
LACTO
LANDO
LARGO
LASSO
LAYTO
MACAO
MACHO
MACRO
MAGOO
MALMO
MAMBO
MANGO
MARCO
MARGO
MARIO
MARLO
MATEO
MATRO
MATZO
MAYPO
NACHO
NARCO
PAAVO
PABLO
PALEO
PANTO
PAOLO
PARDO
PARVO
PASCO
PASEO
PASTO
PATHO
PATIO
PAULO
RADIO
RAMBO
RANTO
RATIO
RATSO
SACCO
SACRO
SALVO
SANTO
SANYO
SARGO
SARTO
SAWTO
SAYSO
TABOO
TACHO
TAINO
TAMBO
TANGO
TANTO
TASSO
TAUPO
TAURO
TAUTO
TAXCO
VASCO
WACKO
WAHOO
WALDO
XACTO
YAHOO
YAZOO

••AO•
CHAOS
MIAOW

••A•O
ABACO
ADANO
ALAMO
AMADO
AMATO
BEANO
BRAVO
CHACO
CHARO
CLARO
CYANO
DIAZO
DRACO
DRANO
ERATO
GLAXO
GUACO
IDAHO
IMAGO
ITALO
LLANO
NEATO
NGAIO
PAAVO
PEABO
PHAGO
PIANO
PLANO
PLATO
PRADO
PRATO
SEATO
SHAKO
WHAMO

•••AO
CACAO
DAVAO
DRLAO
MACAO

AP•••
APACE
APART
APEAK
APERS
APERY
APFEL
APHID
APHIS
APIAN
APING
APISH
APLEY
APLUS
APNEA
APORT
APPAL
APPEL
APPLE
APPLY
APPTD
APPTS
APRES
APRIL
APRON
APSES
APSIS
APSOS
APTED
APTER
APTLY
APURE

A•P••
ALPHA
AMPAS
AMPED
AMPHI
AMPHR
AMPLE
AMPLY
AMPUL
APPAL
APPEL
APPLE
APPLY
APPTD
APPTS
ARPAD
ARPEL
ASPCA
ASPEN
ASPIC
ATPAR

A••P•
ADAPT
ADEPT
ADIPO
ADOPT
AGAPE
ALEPH
AMAPA

A•••P
ACTUP
ADDUP
AESOP
AGASP
ALSOP
ANDUP
ASCAP
ATEUP
ATRIP

•AP••
CAPED
CAPEK
CAPER
CAPES
CAPET
CAPON
CAPOS
CAPRA
CAPRI
CAPTS
GAPED
GAPER
GAPES
HAPLO
HAPLY
HAPPY
JAPAN
JAPED
JAPES
KAPHS
KAPOK
KAPPA
KAPUT
LAPAZ
LAPEL
LAPIN
LAPIS
LAPPS
LAPSE
LAPUP
MAPLE
NAPES
NAPPE
NAPPY
PAPAL
PAPAS
PAPAW
PAPER
PAPPI
PAPPY
PAPUA
RAPEE
RAPHE
RAPID
SAPID
SAPIR
SAPOR
SAPPY
TAPAS
TAPED
TAPER
TAPES
TAPIN
TAPIR
VAPID
VAPOR
YAPOK
ZAPPA
ZAPPY

•A•P•
CALPE
CAMPO
CAMPS
CAMPY
CARPE
CARPI
CARPO
CARPS
DAMPS
GAMPS
GASPE
GASPS
GAWPS
HAPPY
HARPO
HARPS
HARPY
HASPS
KAPPA
LAMPS
LAPPS
MAYPO
NAMPA
NAPPE
NAPPY
PALPI
PALPS
PAMPA
PAPPI
PAPPY
RALPH
RAMPS
RASPS
RASPY
SALPA
SALPS
SAMPS
SAPPY
TAMPA
TAMPS
TARPS
TAUPE
TAUPO
VAMPS
WARPS
WASPS
WASPY
YAMPA
YAWPS
ZAPPA
ZAPPY

•A••P
DAMUP
EATUP
GALOP
GASUP
JAMUP
LAPUP
LAYUP
NAACP
PAYUP
RANUP
SALEP
SATUP
TAGUP
WADUP

••AP•
ADAPT
AGAPE
AMAPA
CHAPS
CLAPS
COAPT
CRAPE
CRAPS
DRAPE
ETAPE
FLAPS
FRAPS
GOAPE
GRAPE
GRAPH
GRAPY
HEAPS
INAPT
KNAPS
LEAPS
LEAPT
NEAPS
OKAPI
REAPS
SCAPA
SCAPE
SHAPE
SLAPS
SNAPS
SOAPS
SOAPY
SWAPS
TRAPP
TRAPS
UNAPT
WRAPS
WRAPT

••A•P
AGASP
CHAMP
CLAMP
CLASP
CRAMP
GRAMP
GRASP
NAACP
SCALP
SCAMP
SCARP
SCAUP
SHARP
STAMP
SWAMP
THARP
TRAMP
TRAPP

•••AP
ASCAP
CHEAP
ONTAP
PTRAP
RECAP
REMAP
RETAP
SCRAP
STRAP
UNCAP

AQ•••
AQABA
AQUAE
AQUAS

A•Q••
ATQUE

A•••Q
ANTIQ

•AQ••
MAQUI
YAQUI

•A•Q•
BARQS

•A••Q
BARBQ

••AQ•
IRAQI

AR•••
ARABS
ARABY
ARAMA
ARAME
ARBER
ARBOR
ARBRE
ARCED
ARCHI
ARCHY
ARDEN
ARDOR
AREAL
AREAR
AREAS
ARECA
ARENA
ARENS
ARENT
ARETE
ARGIL
ARGOL
ARGON
ARGOS
ARGOT
ARGUE
ARGUS
ARHAT
ARHUS
ARIAN
ARIAS
ARICA
ARIEL
ARIES
ARILS
ARION
ARISE
ARITH
ARIUM
ARIUS
ARKIN
ARLEN
ARLES
ARMED
ARMEE
ARMET
ARMIS
ARMOR
ARNAZ
ARNEL
ARNIE
AROAR
AROID
AROMA
AROSE
ARPAD
ARPEL
ARRAN
ARRAS
ARRAU
ARRAY
ARRET
ARRIS
ARROW
ARROZ
ARSIS
ARSON
ARTAL
ARTEL
ARTES
ARTHR
ARTIE
ARTIS
ARTOO
ARTSY
ARTUR
ARUBA
ARUMS
ARYAN

A•R••
AARGH
AARON
ABRAM
ABRIL
ABRIS
ACRED
ACRES
ACRID
ADREM
AERIE
AERON
AEROS
AFRIC
AFRIT
AFROS
AGREE
AGRIC
AGRON
AIRED
AIRES
AKRON
AORTA
APRES
APRIL
APRON
ARRAN
ARRAS
ARRAU
ARRAY
ARRET
ARRIS
ARROW
ARROZ
ATRIA
ATRIP
AURAE
AURAL
AURAR
AURAS
AUREI
AURIC
AURUM
AVRIL
AYRES

A••R•
ABBRS
ABORT
ACARI
ACCRA
ACERB
ACERS
ACORN
ACURA
ADORE
ADORN
AFARS
AFIRE
AFORE
AFTRA
AGARN
AGARS
AGERS
AGGRO
AGORA
AHORA
AKIRA
ALARM
ALERT
ALFRE
ALORS
AMARA
AMBRY
AMIRS
AMORE
AMORT
AMORY
ANDRE
ANDRO
ANDRY
ANGRY
ANTRA
ANTRE
APART
APERS
APERY
APORT
APURE
ARBRE
ASTRA
ASTRE
ASTRO
ATARI
AUDRA
AUTRE
AUTRY
AVARS
AVERS
AVERT
AVERY
AWARD
AWARE
AXERS
AYERS
AZURE

A•••R
ABHOR
ABLER
ABNER
ACTER
ACTOR
ADAIR
ADDER
ADLER
AEGIR
AESIR
AFTER
AILER
AIMER
AJMER
AKBAR
ALCOR
ALDER
ALGER
ALLER
ALTAR
ALTER
ALVAR
AMBER
AMEER
AMOUR
AMPHR
ANDOR
ANEAR
ANGER
ANSER
ANWAR
APTER
ARBER
ARBOR
ARDOR
AREAR
ARMOR
AROAR
ARTHR
ARTUR
ASHER
ASHUR
ASKER
ASNER
ASSUR
ASSYR
ASTER
ASTIR
ASTOR
ATPAR
ATTAR
ATWAR
AUBER
AUGER
AUGUR
AURAR
AUSTR
AVOIR

•AR••
AARGH
AARON
BARAB
BARBQ
BARBS
BARCA
BARDS
BARED
BARER
BARES
BARGE
BARGY
BARIC
BARIT
BARKS
BARKY
BARMS
BARMY
BARNS
BARON
BARQS
BARRE
BARRY
BARTH
BARTS
BARTY
CARAT
CARBO
CARBS
CARDI
CARDS
CARED
CARER
CARES
CARET
CAREW
CAREY
CARGO
CARIA
CARIB
CARKS
CARLA
CARLE
CARLO

CARLY
CARNE
CARNY
CAROB
CAROL
CAROM
CARON
CARPE
CARPI
CARPO
CARPS
CARRE
CARRY
CARTA
CARTE
CARTS
CARVE
DARBY
DARED
DARER
DARES
DARIN
DARIO
DARKS
DARLA
DARNS
DARTH
DARTS
DARYA
DARYL
EARED
EARLE
EARLS
EARLY
EARNS
EARTH
FARAD
FARAH
FARCE
FARCI
FARED
FARER
FARES
FARGO
FARMS
FAROE
FARON
FAROS
FARSI
GARBO
GARBS
GARDA
GARDE
GARNI
GAROU
GARRY
GARTH
HARAR
HARDC
HARDG
HARDY
HARED
HAREM
HARES
HARKS
HARMS
HARPO
HARPS
HARPY
HARRY
HARSH
HARTE
HARTS
HARUM
JARLS
JARRE
KARAN
KARAT
KAREL
KAREN
KARLA
KARMA
KAROL
KARSH
LARAM
LARAS
LARCH
LARDS
LARDY
LARES
LARGE
LARGO
LARIS
LARKS
LARKY
LARRY
LARUE
LARVA
MARAS
MARAT
MARCH
MARCO
MARCY
MARDI
MARES
MARGE
MARGO
MARIA
MARIE
MARIN
MARIO
MARIS
MARKS
MARLA
MARLO
MARLS
MARLY
MARNE
MARRY
MARSH
MARTA
MARTI
MARTS
MARTY
MARVY
MARYS
NARAS
NARCO
NARCS
NARDS
NARES
NAREW
NARIS
NARKS
OARED
PARCA
PARCH
PARDI
PARDO
PARDS
PARED
PAREE
PAREN
PARER
PARES
PAREU
PARIS
PARKA
PARKS
PARLE
PARMA
PAROL
PAROS
PARRY
PARSE
PARTE
PARTI
PARTS
PARTY
PARVO
RAREE
RARER
RARES
SARAH
SARAN
SARDS
SARGE
SARGO
SARIS
SARKY
SAROD
SAROS
SARTO
TARDE
TARDY
TARES
TARGE
TARNS
TAROK
TAROT
TARPS
TARRY
TARSI
TARTS
TARTU
VARAS
VARIA
VARIG
VARIX
VARNA
WARDS
WARES
WARMS
WARNS
WARPS
WARTS
WARTY
YARDS
YARER
YARNS
ZARFS

•A•R•

BAIRD
BAIRN
BARRE
BARRY
BASRA
CADRE
CAIRN
CAIRO
CAMRY
CAPRA
CAPRI
CARRE
CARRY
DAIRY
EAGRE
FAERY
FAIRE
FAIRS
FAIRY
FAURE
FAVRE
GARRY
GAURS
HAIRS
HAIRY
HARRY
HAVRE
IATRO
IATRY
JAHRE
JARRE
KAURI
LAIRD
LAIRS
LARRY
LATRY
LAURA
MACRO
MADRE
MAHRE
MAORI
MARRY
MATRI
MATRO
MAURY
NACRE
NAIRA
NAIRN
NAURU
PADRE
PAIRS
PARRY
PATRI
SABRA
SABRE
SACRA
SACRE
SACRO
SAURY
TAHRS
TARRY
TATRA
TAURO
TAYRA
ZAIRE

•A••R

BABAR
BABER
BADER
BAKER
BALER
BARER
BASER
BATOR
BAUER
BAYAR
BAYER
CABER
CAGER
CANER
CAPER
CARER
CATER
CAVER
DAKAR
DAMAR
DARER
DATER
EAGER
EATER
FABER
FACER
FAKER
FAKIR
FARER
FAVOR
GABOR
GAMER
GAPER
GASTR
GATOR
GAYER
GAZER
HABER
HADAR
HAGAR
HALER
HARAR
HATER
HAUER
HAVER
HAZER
KADAR
KAFIR
LABOR
LACER
LADER
LAGER
LAHAR
LAKER
LAMAR
LAMER
LASER
LATER
LAUER
LAVER
LAXER
LAYER
LAZAR
MAHER
MAJOR
MAKER
MALAR
MANOR
MASER
MASUR
MATER
MAYER
MAYOR
MAZER
NADER
NADIR
NAMER
NAMUR
OATER
PACER
PAGER
PALER
PAMIR
PAPER
PARER
PATER
PAVER
PAWER
PAYER
QATAR
RACER
RADAR
RAFER
RAKER
RAMAR
RANDR
RARER
RASER
RATER
RAVER
RAWER
RAZOR
SABER
SAFER
SAGER
SAKER
SAMAR
SANER
SAPIR
SAPOR
SATYR
SAVER
SAVOR
SAYER
TABOR
TAKER
TALER
TAMER
TAPER
TAPIR
TASER
TATAR
TATER
TAXER
VADER
VALOR
VANIR
VAPOR
VATER
WADER
WAFER
WAGER
WALER
WANER
WATER
WAVER
WAXER
YARER
YASIR

••AR•

ACARI
AFARS
AGARN
AGARS
ALARM
AMARA
APART
ATARI
AVARS
AWARD
AWARE
BEARD
BEARS
BLARE
BOARD
BOARS
CHARD
CHARM
CHARO
CHARS
CHART
CHARY
CLARA
CLARE
CLARK
CLARO
CLARY
CZARS
DEARS
DEARY
DIARY
DMARK
DWARF
FEARS
FLARE
GEARS
GEARY
GLARE
GLARY
GNARL
GNARS
GUARD
GUARS
HEARD
HEARN
HEARS
HEART
HOARD
HOARS
HOARY
IBARS
INARI
IZARD
IZARS
JBARS
KMART
KNARS
LEARN
LEARS
LEARY
LIARD
LIARS
MEARA
NEARS
OHARA
OHARE
OMARR
OPART
OTARU
OTARY
OZARK
PEARL
PEARS
PEARY
PHARM
QUARE
QUARK
QUART
REARM
REARS
ROARS
RUARK
SCARE
SCARF
SCARP
SCARS
SCARY
SEARS
SHARD
SHARE
SHARI
SHARK
SHARP
SMART
SNARE
SNARK
SNARL
SOARS
SPARE
SPARK
SPARS
STARE
STARK
STARR
STARS
START
STARZ
SWARD
SWARF
SWARM
SWART
TBARS
TEARS
TEARY
THARP
TIARA
TSARS
TZARS
UNARM
WEARS
WEARY
WHARF
YEARN
YEARS
ZBARS

••A•R

ADAIR
BLAIR
CHAIR
CLAIR
FLAIR
GLAIR
OHAIR
OMARR
ONAIR
QUADR
REAIR
STAIR
STARR
USAIR

•••AR

AKBAR
ALTAR
ALVAR
ANEAR
ANWAR
AREAR
AROAR
ATPAR
ATTAR
ATWAR
AURAR
BABAR
BAYAR
BIHAR
BLEAR
BOYAR
BRIAR
BYFAR
CEDAR
CESAR
CIGAR
CLEAR
DAKAR
DAMAR
DEBAR
DEWAR
DINAR
DREAR
EDGAR
EGGAR
ELGAR
EMBAR
FILAR
FRIAR
GOFAR
GULAR
HADAR
HAGAR
HARAR
HOWAR
KADAR
LAHAR
LAMAR
LAZAR
LEHAR
LEVAR
LUNAR
MALAR
MIZAR
MOLAR
MYLAR
NOPAR
OSCAR
OSKAR
PILAR
POLAR
QATAR
RADAR
RAMAR
REBAR
RETAR
SAMAR
SEGAR
SHEAR
SITAR
SMEAR
SOFAR
SOLAR
SONAR
SPEAR
SUGAR
SWEAR
TATAR
UNBAR
VELAR
VICAR
VOLAR
ZOHAR

AS•••

ASAMA
ASANA
ASCAP
ASCII
ASCOT
ASCUS
ASDIC
ASHBY
ASHEN
ASHER
ASHES
ASHUR
ASIAN
ASIDE
ASKED
ASKER
ASKEW
ASKIN
ASNER
ASOKA
ASONE
ASPCA
ASPEN
ASPIC
ASSAD
ASSAI
ASSAM
ASSAY
ASSES
ASSET
ASSEZ
ASSNS
ASSOC
ASSTD
ASSTS
ASSUR
ASSYR
ASTER
ASTIN
ASTIR
ASTON
ASTOR
ASTRA
ASTRE
ASTRO
ASWAN
ASYET
ASYLA
ASYUT

A•S••

ADSUM
AESIR
AESOP
AHSIN
AISHA
AISLE
AISNE
AKSUM
ALSOP
ANSAE
ANSEL
ANSER
ANSON
APSES
APSIS
APSOS
ARSIS
ARSON
ASSAD
ASSAI
ASSAM
ASSAY
ASSES
ASSET
ASSEZ
ASSNS
ASSOC
ASSTD
ASSTS
ASSUR
ASSYR
ATSEA
AUSSI
AUSTR

A••S•

ABASE
ABASH
ABUSE
ABYSM
ABYSS
ADUST
AGASP
ALIST
AMASS
AMISH
AMISS
AMUSE
ANGST
ANISE
ANISO
ANTSY
APISH
ARISE
AROSE
ARTSY
AUSSI
AVAST
AVISO
AWASH
AZUSA

A•••S

AAMES
ABBAS
ABBES
ABBRS
ABETS
ABRIS
ABUTS
ABYES
ABYSS
ACADS
ACCTS
ACERS
ACHES
ACIDS
ACMES
ACRES
ACTAS
ACYLS
ADAMS
ADDIS
ADIOS
ADITS
ADZES
AEDES
AEGIS
AEONS
AEROS
AFARS
AFROS
AGALS
AGARS
AGERS
AGHAS
AGIOS
AGNES
AGNUS
AGUES
AHOYS
AIDES
AINUS
AIRES
AKEES
AKINS
ALDUS
ALEFS
ALFAS
ALIAS
ALIFS
ALIOS
ALLES
ALOES
ALORS
ALTOS
ALTUS
ALUMS
AMAHS
AMASS
AMBOS
AMENS
AMIES
AMIRS
AMISS
AMMOS
AMPAS
AMYLS
ANAIS
ANDES
ANGES
ANGUS
ANILS
ANKHS
ANNES
ANNUS
ANOAS
ANTAS
ANTES
ANTIS
APERS
APHIS
APLUS
APPTS
APRES
APSES
APSIS
APSOS
AQUAS
ARABS
AREAS
ARENS
ARGOS
ARGUS
ARHUS
ARIAS
ARIES
ARILS
ARIUS
ARLES
ARMIS
ARRAS
ARRIS
ARSIS
ARTES
ARTIS
ARUMS
ASCUS
ASHES
ASSES
ASSNS
ASSTS
ATHOS
ATLAS
ATMOS
ATNOS
ATOMS
ATTYS
AUDIS
AUJUS
AULIS
AUNTS
AURAS
AUTOS
AVARS
AVENS
AVERS
AVGAS
AVOWS
AWACS
AWOLS
AXELS
AXERS
AXILS
AXLES
AXONS
AYAHS
AYERS
AYINS
AYRES
AZANS

•AS••

BASAL
BASED
BASEL
BASER
BASES
BASHO
BASIC
BASIE
BASIL
BASIN
BASIS
BASKS
BASOV
BASRA
BASSI
BASSO
BASTE
CASAS
CASCA
CASCO
CASED
CASES
CASEY
CASIO
CASKS
CASTE
CASTS
CASUS
DASHI
EASED
EASEL
EASES
EASTS
FASTS
GASES
GASPE
GASPS
GASSY
GASTR
GASUP
HASAT
HASID
HASNT
HASON
HASPS
HASSO
HASTA
HASTE
HASTO
HASTY
JASEY
JASON
JASSY
KASEM
KASHA
LASED
LASER
LASES
LASSO
LASTS
MASAI
MASER
MASHY
MASKS
MASON
MASSE
MASSY
MASTS
MASUR
NASAL
NASBY
NASHE
NASTY
OASES
OASIS
OASTS
PASCH
PASCO
PASEO
PASES
PASHA
PASSE
PASSU
PASSY
PASTA
PASTE
PASTO
PASTS
PASTY
RASED
RASER
RASES
RASHT
RASPS
RASPY
RASTA
SASES
SASHA
SASSY
TASER
TASKS
TASSE
TASSO
TASTE
TASTY
VASCO
VASES
VASTY
WASHY
WASNT
WASPS
WASPY
WASTE
YASIR

•A•S•

BAKST
BALSA
BASSI
BASSO
CANSO
CANST
CAUSA
CAUSE
DAISY
DANSE
FALSE
FARSI
FAUST
GASSY
GAUSS
HADST
HANSA
HANSE
HARSH
HASSO
HAUSA
HAWSE
JASSY
KANSA
KARSH
LAPSE
LASSO
MANSE
MARSH
MASSE
MASSY
MATSU
MAYST
NAISH
PABST
PAISA
PALSY
PANSY
PARSE
PASSE
PASSU
PASSY
PATSY
PAUSE
RAISA
RAISE
RATSO
SALSA
SASSY
SAYSO
TANSY
TARSI
TASSE
TASSO
VALSE
WAIST
WALSH
WALSY

•A••S

AAMES
BAALS
BABAS
BABES
BABIS
BABYS
BACHS
BACKS
BAHTS
BAILS
BAITS
BAKES
BALAS
BALDS
BALES
BALKS
BALLS
BALMS
BALTS
BANCS
BANDS
BANES
BANGS
BANKS
BANNS
BARBS
BARDS
BARES
BARKS
BARMS
BARNS
BARQS
BARTS
BASES
BASIS
BASKS
BATES
BATHS
BATTS
BAWLS
CADIS
CAFES
CAGES
CAKES
CALKS
CALLS
CALMS
CAMIS
CAMOS
CAMPS
CAMUS
CANES
CANIS
CANTS
CAPES
CAPOS
CAPTS
CARBS
CARDS
CARES
CARKS
CARPS
CARTS
CASAS
CASES
CASKS
CASTS
CASUS
CATES
CAULS
CAVES
DACES
DADOS
DAFFS
DALES
DAMES
DAMNS
DAMPS
DANES
DANGS
DARES
DARKS
DARNS
DARTS
DATES
DAUBS
DAVIS
DAVOS
DAVYS
DAWES
DAWNS
DAZES
EAMES
EARLS
EARNS
EASES
EASTS
EAVES
FACES
FACTS
FADES
FADOS
FAILS
FAIRS
FAKES
FALLS
FAMES
FANES
FANGS
FARES
FARMS
FAROS
FASTS
FATES
FAUNS
FAVES
FAWNS
FAXES
FAZES
GAELS
GAFFS
GAGES
GAINS
GAITS
GAIUS
GALAS
GALES
GALLS
GAMES
GAMPS
GANGS
GAOLS
GAPES
GARBS
GASES
GASPS
GATES
GATOS
GAUDS
GAULS
GAUMS
GAURS
GAUSS
GAWKS
GAWPS
GAZES
HACKS
HADES
HAFTS
HAHAS
HAIKS
HAILS
HAIRS
HAJIS
HAKES
HALAS
HALES
HALLS
HALMS
HALOS
HALTS
HAMES
HANDS
HANES
HANGS
HANKS
HANTS
HARES
HARKS
HARMS
HARPS
HARTS
HASPS
HATES
HAULS
HAVES
HAWGS
HAWKS
HAYES
HAZES
IAMBS
JACKS
JADES
JAILS
JAINS
JAKES
JAMBS
JAMES
JANIS
JANUS
JAPES
JARLS
JATOS
JAVAS
KAKAS
KAKIS
KALES
KAONS
KAPHS
KAVAS
KAYOS
LACES
LACKS
LADES
LADYS
LAGOS
LAICS
LAIRS
LAIUS
LAKES
LAMAS
LAMBS
LAMES
LAMPS
LANDS
LANES
LAPIS
LAPPS
LARAS
LARDS
LARES
LARIS
LARKS
LASES
LASTS
LATHS
LAUDS
LAVAS
LAVES
LAWES
LAWNS
LAZES
MACES
MACYS
MAGES
MAGUS
MAIDS
MAILS
MAINS
MAKES
MAKOS
MALES
MALLS
MALTS
MAMAS
MANES
MANOS
MARAS
MARES
MARIS
MARKS
MARLS
MARTS
MARYS
MASKS
MASTS
MATES
MATHS
MAULS
MAVIS
MAXES
MAXIS
MAYAS
MAZES
NABES
NAILS
NAMES

NANAS
NAPES
NARAS
NARCS
NARDS
NARES
NARIS
NARKS
NAVES
NAXOS
OAKES
OASES
OASIS
OASTS
OATES
OATHS
PACAS
PACES
PACKS
PACTS
PAGES
PAILS
PAINS
PAIRS
PALES
PALLS
PALMS
PALOS
PALPS
PANES
PANGS
PANTS
PAPAS
PARDS
PARES
PARIS
PARKS
PAROS
PARTS
PASES
PASTS
PATES
PATHS
PAVES
PAVIS
PAWLS
PAWNS
RACES
RACKS
RAFTS
RAGAS
RAGES
RAIDS
RAILS
RAINS
RAJAS
RAKES
RAKIS
RAMIS
RAMOS
RAMPS
RANDS
RANIS
RANKS
RANTS
RARES
RASES
RASPS
RATES
RATHS
RAVES
RAWLS
RAZES
SAABS
SACHS
SACKS
SADIS
SAENS
SAFES
SAGAS
SAGES
SAGOS
SAILS
SAKES
SALES
SALPS
SALTS
SAMMS
SAMOS
SAMPS
SANDS
SARDS
SARIS
SAROS
SASES
SATES
SAUKS
SAVES
SAXES
TABIS
TACKS
TACOS
TAELS
TAGUS
TAHRS
TAILS
TAKAS
TAKES
TALES
TALKS
TALOS
TALUS
TAMES
TAMPS
TANGS
TANKS
TAPAS
TAPES
TARES
TARNS
TARPS
TARTS
TASKS
TAXES
TAXIS
VADIS
VAGUS
VALES
VAMOS
VAMPS
VANES
VARAS
VASES
WAAFS
WAALS
WADES
WADIS
WAFTS
WAGES
WAIFS
WAILS
WAINS
WAITS
WAKES
WALES
WALKS
WALLS
WANDS
WANES
WANTS
WARDS
WARES
WARMS
WARNS
WARPS
WARTS
WASPS
WATTS
WAVES
WAXES
XAXES
XAXIS
YACKS
YANKS
YARDS
YARNS
YATES
YAWLS
YAWNS
YAWPS
YAXES
YAXIS
ZARFS
ZAXES
ZAXIS

••AS•

ABASE
ABASH
AGASP
AMASS
AVAST
AWASH
BEAST
BLASE
BLASS
BLAST
BOAST
BRASH
BRASS
CEASE
CHASE
CHASM
CLASH
CLASP
CLASS
COAST
CRASH
CRASS
DNASE
ERASE
FEAST
FLASH
FLASK
GLASS
GNASH
GRASP
GRASS
IPASS
KVASS
LEASE
LEASH
LEAST
LHASA
NYASA
OMASA
PEASE
PHASE
PLASH
PLASM
PRASE
QUASH
QUASI
RNASE
ROAST
SLASH
SMASH
SPASM
STASH
SWASH
TEASE
TOAST
TRASH
UKASE
YEAST

••A•S

ACADS
ADAMS
AFARS
AGALS
AGARS
AMAHS
AMASS
ANAIS
ARABS
AVARS
AWACS
AYAHS
AZANS
BAALS
BEADS
BEAKS
BEALS
BEAMS
BEANS
BEARS
BEATS
BEAUS
BLABS
BLAHS
BLASS
BLATS
BOARS
BOATS
BRADS
BRAES
BRAGS
BRANS
BRASS
BRATS
BRAYS
CHAOS
CHAPS
CHARS
CHATS
CHAWS
CLAMS
CLANS
CLAPS
CLASS
CLAUS
CLAWS
CLAYS
COALS
COATS
CRABS
CRAGS
CRAMS
CRAPS
CRASS
CRAWS
CZARS
DEALS
DEANS
DEARS
DHALS
DIALS
DRABS
DRAGS
DRAMS
DRATS
DRAWS
DRAYS
DUADS
DYADS
EDAMS
EGADS
ETATS
EVANS
EXAMS
FEARS
FEATS
FIATS
FLAGS
FLAMS
FLANS
FLAPS
FLATS
FLAWS
FLAYS
FOALS
FOAMS
FRAIS
FRANS
FRAPS
FRATS
FRAYS
GEARS
GHATS
GLADS
GLASS
GMATS
GNARS
GNATS
GNAWS
GOADS
GOALS
GOATS
GRABS
GRADS
GRAMS
GRASS
GRAYS
GUARS
HEADS
HEALS
HEAPS
HEARS
HEATS
HOARS
HYAMS
IBARS
IMAMS
IPASS
ITALS
IZARS
JBARS
JEANS
KEATS
KHANS
KLAUS
KNAPS
KNARS
KOANS
KRAUS
KVASS
KYATS
LEADS
LEAFS
LEAKS
LEANS
LEAPS
LEARS
LIARS
LOADS
LOAFS
LOAMS
LOANS
LSATS
LUAUS
MEADS
MEALS
MEANS
MEATS
MOANS
MOATS
NEAPS
NEARS
NEATS
NOAHS
OKAYS
OPAHS
OPALS
ORALS
OVALS
PEAKS
PEALS
PEARS
PEATS
PLANS
PLATS
PLAYS
PRAMS
PRAUS
PRAYS
PSATS
QUADS
QUAGS
QUAYS
READS
REALS
REAMS
REAPS
REARS
RIALS
ROADS
ROAMS
ROANS
ROARS
SAABS
SCABS
SCADS
SCAMS
SCANS
SCARS
SCATS
SEALS
SEAMS
SEARS
SEATS
SHADS
SHAGS
SHAHS
SHAMS
SHANS
SHAYS
SIALS
SLABS
SLAGS
SLAMS
SLAPS
SLATS
SLAVS
SLAWS
SLAYS
SNAGS
SNAPS
SOAKS
SOAPS
SOARS
SPADS
SPAMS
SPANS
SPARS
SPATS
SPAYS
STABS
STAGS
STARS
STATS
STAYS
SWABS
SWAGS
SWANS
SWAPS
SWATS
SWAYS
TBARS
TEAKS
TEALS
TEAMS
TEARS
THAIS
THATS
THAWS
TOADS
TRAMS
TRANS
TRAPS
TRAYS
TSARS
TZARS
UNAUS
URALS
VIALS
WAAFS
WAALS
WEALS
WEANS
WEARS
WHAMS
WHATS
WOADS
WRACS
WRAFS
WRAPS
XRAYS
YEANS
YEARS
YEATS
YUANS
ZBARS
ZEALS

•••AS

ABBAS
ACTAS
AGHAS
ALFAS
ALIAS
AMPAS
ANOAS
ANTAS
AQUAS
AREAS
ARIAS
ARRAS
ATLAS
AURAS
AVGAS
BABAS
BALAS
BEMAS
BETAS
BOLAS
BORAS
CASAS
CHIAS
CODAS
COLAS
COMAS
CUNAS
CYMAS
DEGAS
DIVAS
DONAS
DUKAS
DUMAS
EDDAS
ELIAS
EPHAS
ESTAS
ETNAS
EYRAS
FETAS
FLEAS
FULAS
GALAS
GETAS
HAHAS
HALAS
HORAS
HOYAS
HULAS
HYLAS
IDEAS
INCAS
IOTAS
ISLAS
IZBAS
JAVAS
JONAS
JOTAS
JUDAS
KAKAS
KAVAS
KINAS
KIVAS
KOLAS
LAMAS
LARAS
LAVAS
LIMAS
LIRAS
LOTAS
LUBAS
LUCAS
LUKAS
MAMAS
MARAS
MAYAS
MESAS
MICAS
MIDAS
MIMAS
MINAS
MOLAS
MORAS
MYNAS
NANAS
NARAS
NINAS
NIPAS
NOVAS
OCCAS
OKRAS
OLLAS
ORCAS
PACAS
PAPAS
PICAS
PIKAS
PIMAS
PITAS
PLEAS
PROAS
PSOAS
PULAS
PUMAS
PUNAS
PUPAS
RAGAS
RAJAS
RHEAS
ROTAS
SAGAS
SIKAS
SILAS
SKUAS
SODAS
SOFAS
SOMAS
SORAS
SOYAS
SRTAS
STOAS
SURAS
TAKAS
TAPAS
TEXAS
TOGAS
TUBAS
TUNAS
ULNAS
UNCAS
VARAS
VEDAS
VEGAS
VILAS
VINAS
VISAS
VITAS
WEKAS
YMCAS
YOGAS
YUGAS
YUMAS
YWCAS
ZETAS
ZOEAS

AT•••

ATALL
ATARI
ATBAT
ATBAY
ATEAM
ATEIN
ATEUP
ATHOL
ATHON
ATHOS
ATILT
ATION
ATIVE
ATLAS
ATMAN
ATMOS
ATNOS
ATOLL
ATOMS
ATOMY
ATONE
ATONY
ATPAR
ATQUE
ATRIA
ATRIP
ATSEA
ATTAR
ATTIC
ATTYS
ATWAR

A•T••

ACTAS
ACTED
ACTER
ACTII
ACTIN
ACTIV
ACTON
ACTOR
ACTUP
AETAT
AETNA
AFTER
AFTON
AFTRA
AITCH
ALTAI
ALTAR
ALTER
ALTHO
ALTON
ALTOS
ALTUS
ANTAE
ANTAL
ANTAS
ANTED
ANTES
ANTHO
ANTIC
ANTIQ
ANTIS
ANTON
ANTRA
ANTRE
ANTSY
APTED
APTER
APTLY
ARTAL
ARTEL
ARTES
ARTHR
ARTIE
ARTIS
ARTOO
ARTSY
ARTUR
ASTER
ASTIN
ASTIR
ASTON
ASTOR
ASTRA
ASTRE
ASTRO
ATTAR
ATTIC
ATTYS
AUTOS
AUTRE
AUTRY
AZTEC

A••T•

AALTO
ABATE
ABCTV
ABETS
ABUTS
ACCTS
ACETO
ACUTE
ADDTO
ADITS
ADYTA
AGATE
AGITA
AIMTO
AKITA
ALATE
ALETA
AMATI
AMATO
AMITY
ANETO
ANITA
AORTA
APPTD
APPTS
ARETE
ARITH
ASSTD
ASSTS
AUNTS
AUNTY
AUSTR
AZOTE
AZOTH

A•••T

ABAFT
ABBOT
ABORT
ABOUT
ADAPT
ADEPT
ADINT
ADMIT
ADOPT
ADOUT
ADULT
ADUST
AETAT
AFLAT
AFOOT
AFRIT
AGENT
AGLET
AIMAT
ALERT
ALEUT
ALIST
ALLOT
ALOFT
AMBIT
AMENT
AMORT
AMVET
ANENT
ANGST
APART
APORT
ARENT
ARGOT
ARHAT
ARMET
ARRET
ASCOT
ASSET
ASYET
ASYUT
ATBAT
ATILT
AUDIT
AUGHT
AVANT
AVAST
AVERT
AWAIT

•AT••

BATAK
BATCH
BATED
BATES
BATHE
BATHO
BATHS
BATHY
BATIK
BATON
BATOR
BATTS
BATTY
CATCH
CATER
CATES
CATHY
CATTY
DATED
DATER
DATES
DATUM
EATAT
EATEN
EATER
EATIN
EATIT
EATON
EATUP
FATAL
FATED
FATES
FATHA
FATLY
FATTY
FATWA
GATED
GATES
GATOR
GATOS
GATUN
HATCH
HATED
HATER
HATES
HATLO
IATRO
IATRY
JATOS
KATHY
KATIE
LATCH
LATEN
LATER
LATEX
LATHE
LATHS
LATHY
LATIN
LATKE
LATRY
LATTE
MATCH
MATED
MATEO
MATER
MATES
MATEY
MATHS
MATIN
MATRI
MATRO
MATSU
MATTE
MATZO
NATAL
NATCH
NATTY
OATEN
OATER
OATES
OATHS
PATCH
PATED
PATEK
PATEN
PATER
PATES
PATHE
PATHO
PATHS
PATHY
PATIO
PATLY
PATNA
PATON
PATRI
PATSY
PATTI
PATTY
QATAR
RATCH
RATED
RATEL
RATER
RATES
RATHS
RATIO
RATON
RATSO
RATTY
SATAN
SATBY
SATED
SATES
SATIE
SATIN
SATON
SATUP
SATYR
TATAR
TATER
TATRA
TATTY
TATUM
VATER
VATIC
WATCH
WATER
WATTS
YATES

•A•T•

AALTO
BAHTS
BAITS
BALTO
BALTS
BANTU
BARTH
BARTS
BARTY
BASTE
BATTS
BATTY
CACTI
CANTO
CANTS
CANTY
CAPTS
CARTA
CARTE
CARTS
CASTE
CASTS
CATTY
DANTE
DARTH
DARTS
EARTH
EASTS
FACTO
FACTS
FAITH
FANTA
FASTS
FATTY
GAITS
GARTH
GASTR
HADTO
HAFTS
HAITI
HALTS
HANTS
HARTE
HARTS
HASTA
HASTE
HASTO
HASTY
HAUTE
LACTI
LACTO
LAHTI
LAITY
LANTZ
LASTS
LATTE
LAYTO
MALTA
MALTS
MALTY
MANTA
MARTA
MARTI
MARTS
MARTY
MASTS
MATTE
NAFTA
NASTY
NATTY
OASTS
PACTS
PANTO
PANTS
PARTE
PARTI
PARTS
PARTY
PASTA
PASTE
PASTO
PASTS
PASTY
PATTI
PATTY
PAYTV
RAFTS
RAITT
RANTO
RANTS
RASTA
RATTY
SAITH
SALTA
SALTS
SALTY
SANTA
SANTE
SANTO
SARTO
SAUTE
SAWTO
TANTE
TANTO
TARTS
TARTU
TASTE
TASTY
TATTY
TAUTO
VASTY
WAFTS
WAITE
WAITS
WAITZ
WALTZ
WANTS
WARTS
WARTY
WASTE
WATTS
XACTO
YALTA
ZANTE

•A••T

BAGIT
BAKST
BANAT
BARIT
CABOT
CADET
CANIT
CANST
CAPET
CARAT
CARET
DAUNT
DAVIT
EATAT
EATIT
FACET
FACIT
FAGOT
FAINT
FAULT
FAUST
GAMUT
GAUNT
GAVOT
HABIT
HADAT
HADNT
HADST
HASAT
HASNT
HAUNT
JABOT
JACET
JANET
JAUNT
KAPUT
KARAT
MAGOT
MAMET
MANET
MARAT
MAYNT
MAYST
NACHT
PABST
PAGET
PAINT
PAWAT
RABAT
RAITT
RAMET
RANAT
RASHT
SABOT
SADAT
SAGET
SAINT
SALUT
SAULT
TACET
TACIT
TAINT
TAROT
TAUNT
VALET
VAULT
VAUNT
WAIST
WASNT
YACHT
YAKUT

••AT•

ABATE
AGATE
ALATE
AMATI
AMATO
BEATS
BLATS
BOATS
BRATS
CHATS
COATI
COATS
CRATE
DRATS
ELATE
ELATH
ENATE
ERATO
ETATS
FEATS
FIATS
FLATS
FLATT
FRATS
GHATS
GMATS
GNATS
GOATS
GRATA
GRATE
HEATH
HEATS
HYATT
IRATE
KEATS
KYATS
LOATH
LSATS
MEATS
MEATY
MIATA
MOATS
NEATH
NEATO
NEATS
ONATE
ORATE
OVATE
PEATS
PEATY
PLATA
PLATE
PLATH
PLATO
PLATS
PLATT
PLATY
PRATE
PRATO
PRATT
PSATS
REATA
RIATA
SCATS
SEATO
SEATS
SHATT
SKATE
SLATE
SLATS
SLATY
SNATH
SPATE
SPATS
STATE
STATS
SWATH
SWATS
THATS
WHATD
WHATS
WRATH
WYATT
YEATS

••A•T

ABAFT
ADAPT
APART
AVANT
AVAST
AWAIT
BEAST
BEAUT
BLAST
BOAST
BRACT
BRANT
CHANT
CHART
COACT
COAPT
COAST
CRAFT
DEALT
DRAFT
ENACT
EPACT
EXACT
EXALT
FEAST
FLATT
GIANT
GRAFT
GRANT
HEART
HYATT
INAPT
KMART
KRAFT
KRAIT
KRAUT
LEANT
LEAPT
LEAST
MEANT
OPART
ORANT
PLAIT
PLANT
PLATT
PRATT
QUANT
QUART
REACT
RIANT
ROAST
SCANT
SHAFT
SHALT
SHANT
SHATT
SLANT
SMALT
SMART
STADT
START
SWART
THANT
TIANT
TOAST
TRACT
TRAIT
UNAPT
WRAPT
WYATT
YEAST

•••AT

AETAT
AFLAT
AIMAT
ARHAT

ATBAT BANAT BEGAT BFLAT BLEAT BLOAT CARAT CERAT CFLAT CHEAT CLEAT CROAT CUGAT DEFAT DERAT DETAT DFLAT DITAT DONAT DUCAT EATAT EBOAT ECLAT EFLAT EILAT ESBAT FFLAT FLOAT FLYAT GETAT GFLAT GLOAT GOTAT GREAT GROAT HADAT HASAT HERAT JURAT KARAT KERAT LEMAT LETAT LOFAT LOPAT MARAT MURAT NEMAT NIPAT NOFAT PAWAT PLEAT RABAT RANAT RUNAT SADAT SENAT SETAT SHOAT SKEAT SPLAT SPRAT SQUAT STOAT STPAT SURAT SWEAT TREAT UBOAT VOLAT WHEAT

AU•••

AUBER AUDEN AUDIE AUDIO AUDIS AUDIT AUDRA AUGER AUGHT AUGUR AUJUS AULIS AUNTS AUNTY AURAE AURAL AURAR AURAS AUREI AURIC AURUM AUSSI AUSTR AUTOS AUTRE AUTRY AUXIL AUXIN

A•U••

ABUJA ABUSE ABUTS ABUZZ ACUFF ACURA ACUTE ADULT ADUST ADUWA AGUES ALULA ALUMS AMUCK AMUSE APURE AQUAE AQUAS ARUBA ARUMS AZURE AZUSA

A••U•

AAIUN ABDUL ABOUT ABZUG ACTUP ADDUP ADEUX ADOUT ADSUM AFOUL AGNUS AINUS AKSUM ALBUM ALDUS ALEUT ALOUD ALTUS AMOUR AMPUL ANDUP ANGUS ANHUI ANNUL ANNUM ANNUS ANOUK APLUS ARGUE ARGUS ARHUS ARIUM ARIUS ARTUR ASCUS ASHUR ASSUR ASYUT ATEUP ATQUE AUGUR AUJUS AURUM AWFUL

A•••U

ADIEU AEIOU ANJOU ARRAU

•AU••

BAUER BAUGH BAULK BAUME CAULK CAULS CAUSA CAUSE DAUBS DAUNT FAULT FAUNA FAUNS FAURE FAUST FAUVE GAUDS GAUDY GAUGE GAULS GAUMS GAUNT GAURS GAUSS GAUZE GAUZY HAUER HAULM HAULS HAUNT HAUSA HAUTE JAUNE JAUNT KAUAI KAURI LAUDE LAUDS LAUER LAUGH LAURA MAUDE MAULS MAUNA MAUND MAURY MAUVE NAURU PAULA PAULO PAUSE SAUCE SAUCY SAUDI SAUKS SAULT SAUNA SAURY SAUTE TAUNT TAUON TAUPE TAUPO TAURO TAUTO VAULT VAUNT WAUGH

•A•U•

AAIUN BABUL BAIUL CAJUN CAMUS CASUS DAMUP DATUM EATUP GAIUS GAMUT GASUP GATUN HAFUN HAGUE HARUM JAMUP JANUS KABUL KAFUE KAPUT LAIUS LAPUP LARUE LAYUP MAGUS MAKUA MAQUI MASUR NAHUA NAHUM NAMUR OAKUM PADUA PAPUA PAYUP RANUP RAOUL SALUD SALUT SATUP TAGUP TAGUS TALUS TATUM VACUA VADUZ VAGUE VAGUS VALUE WADUP YAKUT YAQUI

•A••U

BANTU BAYOU GAROU HAIKU KANZU MACHU MAIDU MATSU NAURU PALAU PAREU PASSU SADHU TAEGU TARTU

••AU•

BEAUS BEAUT BEAUX BRAUN CHAUD CLAUS FRAUD KLAUS KRAUS KRAUT LUAUS PIAUI PRAUS SCAUP SHAUN UHAUL UNAUS

••A•U

ISAMU KEANU OTARU SHAMU SNAFU

•••AU

ARRAU DONAU PALAU

AV•••

AVAIL AVANT AVARS AVAST AVENA AVENS AVERS AVERT AVERY AVGAS AVIAN AVILA AVION AVISO AVOID AVOIR AVOWS AVRIL

A•V••

ADVAL ADVIL ALVAR ALVIN AMVET ANVIL

A••V•

ABOVE ABOVO AGAVE ALAVA ALEVE ALIVE ATIVE

A•••V

ABCTV ACTIV ANNIV

•AV••

CAVAE CAVED CAVER CAVES CAVIL DAVAO DAVID DAVIE DAVIS DAVIT DAVOS DAVYS EAVED EAVES FAVES FAVOR FAVRE GAVEL GAVIN GAVOT HAVEL HAVEN HAVER HAVES HAVOC HAVRE JAVAS KAVAS LAVAL LAVAS LAVED LAVER LAVES LAVIN MAVEN MAVIS NAVAL NAVEL NAVES NAVIG NAVVY PAVED PAVER PAVES PAVIA PAVID PAVIS RAVED RAVEL RAVEN RAVER RAVES RAVIN SAVED SAVER SAVES SAVOR SAVOY SAVVY WAVED WAVER WAVES

•A•V•

CALVE CARVE FAUVE HALVE LARVA MARVY MAUVE NAIVE NAVVY PAAVO PARVO SALVE SALVO SAVVY VALVE WAIVE

•A••V

BASOV PAYTV RAJIV YAKOV

••AV•

AGAVE ALAVA BRAVA BRAVE BRAVO CLAVE CRAVE DRAVA GRAVE GRAVY GUAVA HEAVE HEAVY KNAVE LEAVE PAAVO PEAVY SHAVE SLAVE SLAVS SOAVE STAVE SUAVE TRAVE WEAVE

•••AV

SCHAV

AW•••

AWACS AWAIT AWAJI AWAKE AWARD AWARE AWASH AWFUL AWING AWNED AWOKE AWOLS

A•W••

AMWAY ANWAR ASWAN ATWAR

A••W•

ADUWA AVOWS

A•••W

AGLOW AGNEW ALLOW ARROW ASKEW

•AW••

BAWDY BAWLS CAWED DAWES DAWNS FAWNS GAWKS GAWKY GAWPS HAWED HAWGS HAWKE HAWKS HAWSE JAWED LAWES LAWNS LAWNY NAWAB PAWAT PAWED PAWER PAWKY PAWLS PAWNS RAWER RAWLS RAWLY SAWED SAWIN SAWTO TAWNY YAWED YAWLS YAWNS YAWPS

•A•W•

DAIWA FATWA

•A••W

BANDW CANDW CAREW GAMOW LALAW MACAW NAREW PAPAW YALOW

••AW•

BRAWL BRAWN CHAWS CLAWS CRAWL CRAWS DRAWL DRAWN DRAWS FLAWS FLAWY GNAWS INAWE OZAWA PRAWN SHAWL SHAWM SHAWN SLAWS SPAWN THAWS TRAWL

••A•W

MIAOW

•••AW

BYLAW INLAW LALAW MACAW PAPAW PSHAW RESAW STRAW

AX•••

AXELS AXERS AXIAL AXILS AXING AXIOM AXION AXLES AXONE AXONS

A•X••

AUXIL AUXIN

A•••X

ADDAX ADEUX ADMIX AFFIX ANNEX

•AX••

FAXED FAXES LAXER LAXLY MAXED MAXES MAXIE MAXIM MAXIS NAXOS SAXES SAXON TAXCO TAXED TAXER TAXES TAXIS TAXON WAXED WAXEN WAXER WAXES XAXES XAXIS YAXES YAXIS ZAXES ZAXIS

•A••X

CALIX CALYX GALAX LATEX RADIX VARIX

••AX•

FLAXY GLAXO

••A•X

BEAUX

•••AX

ADDAX BORAX GALAX HYRAX ICEAX LOMAX LORAX RELAX RETAX REWAX

AY•••

AYAHS AYERS AYINS AYRES

A•Y••

ABYES ABYSM ABYSS ACYLS ADYTA ALYCE AMYLO AMYLS ARYAN ASYET ASYLA ASYUT

A••Y•

ABAYA AHOYS ALKYD ALKYL ALLYL ASSYR ATTYS

A•••Y

ABBEY ACIDY AGLEY AGONY AILEY ALLAY ALLEY ALLOY ALMAY AMBOY AMBRY AMITY AMORY AMPLY AMWAY ANDRY ANGRY ANNOY ANOMY ANTSY AOKAY APERY APLEY APPLY APTLY ARABY ARCHY ARRAY ARTSY ASHBY ASSAY ATBAY ATOMY ATONY AUNTY AUTRY AVERY

•AY••

BAYAR BAYED BAYER BAYLE BAYOU CAYCE DAYAK DAYAN DAYNE GAYAL GAYER GAYLE GAYLY HAYDN HAYED HAYEK HAYES JAYNE KAYAK KAYOS LAYBY LAYER LAYIN LAYLA LAYNE LAYON LAYTO LAYUP MAYAN MAYAS MAYBE MAYER MAYNT MAYON MAYOR MAYPO MAYST PAYED PAYEE PAYER PAYIN PAYNE PAYTV PAYUP RAYED RAYON SAYER SAYSO TAYRA WAYNE ZAYIN

•A•Y•

BABYS CALYX DARYA DARYL DAVYS LADYS MACYS MARYS SANYO SATYR TANYA VANYA

•A••Y

BADDY BADLY BAGGY BALKY BALLY BALMY BANDY BANKY BARGY BARKY BARMY BARRY BARTY BATHY BATTY BAWDY CABBY CADDY CAGEY CAKEY CAMAY CAMPY CAMRY CANBY CANDY CANNY CANTY CAREY CARLY CARNY CARRY CASEY CATHY CATTY DADDY DAFFY DAILY DAIRY DAISY DALEY DALLY DANCY DANDY DANNY DARBY EARLY FAERY FAHEY FAIRY FANCY FANNY FATLY FATTY GABBY GAILY GAMAY GAMEY GAMMY GANDY GARRY GASSY GAUDY GAUZY GAWKY GAYLY HAIRY HALEY HAMMY HANDY HANKY HAPLY HAPPY HARDY HARPY HARRY HASTY IATRY JACKY JAGGY JAMMY JASEY JASSY JAZZY KANDY KATHY LACEY LAITY LANKY LARDY LARKY LARRY LATHY LATRY LAWNY LAXLY LAYBY MACHY MADLY MALAY MALTY MAMMY MANCY MANDY MANGY MANLY MANNY MARCY MARLY MARRY MARTY MARVY MASHY MASSY MATEY MAURY NAGGY NAMBY NANCY NANNY NAPPY NASBY NASTY NATTY NAVVY PADDY PALEY PALLY PALMY PALSY PAMBY PANAY PANKY PANSY PAPPY PARRY PARTY PASSY PASTY PATHY PATLY PATSY PATTY PAWKY RAINY RALLY RANDY RANGY RASPY RATTY RAWLY SADLY SAGGY SALLY SALTY SAMMY SANDY SAPPY SARKY SASSY SATBY SAUCY SAURY SAVOY SAVVY TABBY TACHY TACKY TAFFY TALKY TALLY TAMMY TANDY TANEY TANGY TANSY TARDY TARRY TASTY TATTY TAWNY VASTY WACKY WADDY WALEY WALLY WALSY WANEY WANLY WARTY WASHY WASPY ZAPPY

••AY•

ABAYA BRAYS CLAYS DRAYS FLAYS FRAYS GRAYS OKAYS PLAYA PLAYS PRAYS QUAYS SHAYS SLAYS SPAYS STAYS SWAYS TRAYS XRAYS

••A•Y

ARABY BEADY BEAMY BEANY BIALY BRADY CHARY CLARY CRACY CRAZY DEARY DIARY FLAKY FLAMY FLAWY FLAXY FOAMY GEARY GLARY GRADY GRAPY GRAVY HEADY HEALY HEAVY HOAGY HOARY ITALY KRAZY LEADY LEAFY LEAHY LEAKY LEARY LOAMY MEALY MEANY MEATY ORACY OTARY PEARY PEATY PEAVY PHAGY PHANY PLATY QUAKY READY SCALY SCARY SEALY SEAMY SHADY SHAKY SLATY SNAKY SOAPY SPACY STACY STAGY TEARY TOADY TRACY VEALY WEARY

•••AY

ALLAY ALMAY AMWAY AOKAY ARRAY ASSAY ATBAY BELAY BYWAY CAMAY COPAY DECAY DELAY DOUAY DUFAY ELWAY EMBAY ESSAY FORAY GAMAY INLAY IXNAY LEFAY LEMAY LURAY MALAY MCKAY MORAY MYWAY NOWAY OHKAY ONLAY OTWAY OYVAY PANAY POWAY RELAY REPAY SPLAY SPRAY STRAY TODAY TOKAY UNLAY UNSAY VEDAY VJDAY

AZ•••

AZANS AZIDE AZINE AZOIC AZOTE AZOTH AZTEC AZURE AZUSA

A•Z••

ABZUG ADZES ANZAC ANZIO

A••Z•

ABUZZ AGAZE AMAZE

A•••Z

ABUZZ ALLEZ ARNAZ ARROZ ASSEZ

•AZ••

DAZED DAZES FAZED FAZES GAZED GAZER GAZES HAZAN HAZED HAZEL HAZER HAZES JAZZY KAZAK KAZAN KAZOO LAZAR LAZED LAZES MAZDA MAZEL MAZER MAZES RAZED RAZES RAZOR TAZZA YAZOO ZAZEN

•A•Z•

BAIZA BAIZE DANZA GAUZE GAUZY JAZZY KANZU LANZA MAIZE MATZO PANZA TAZZA

•A••Z

CADIZ HAFIZ LANTZ LAPAZ MAINZ VADUZ WAITZ WALTZ

••AZ•

AGAZE AMAZE BLAZE BRAZE CHAZZ CRAZE CRAZY DIAZO ELAZI GHAZI GLAZE GRAZE KRAZY PLAZA SMAZE SWAZI

••A•Z

CHAZZ FRANZ STARZ

•••AZ

ARNAZ HEJAZ HIJAZ LAPAZ TOPAZ

BA•••

BAAED BAALS BABAR BABAS BABEL BABER BABES BABIS BABKA BABUL BABYS BACHS BACKS BACON BADDY BADEN BADER BADGE BADLY BAGEL BAGGY BAGIT BAHAI BAHIA BAHTS BAILS BAIRD BAIRN BAITS BAIUL BAIZA BAIZE BAKED BAKER BAKES BAKST BALAS BALCH BALDS BALED

BALER
BALES
BALIN
BALKH
BALKS
BALKY
BALLS
BALLY
BALMS
BALMY
BALSA
BALTO
BALTS
BAMBI
BANAL
BANAT
BANCO
BANCS
BANDA
BANDB
BANDO
BANDS
BANDW
BANDY
BANES
BANFF
BANGS
BANJO
BANKS
BANKY
BANNS
BANTU
BAOJI
BARAB
BARBQ
BARBS
BARCA
BARDS
BARED
BARER
BARES
BARGE
BARGY
BARIC
BARIT
BARKS
BARKY
BARMS
BARMY
BARNS
BARON
BARQS
BARRE
BARRY
BARTH
BARTS
BARTY
BASAL
BASED
BASEL
BASER
BASES
BASHO
BASIC
BASIE
BASIL
BASIN
BASIS
BASKS
BASOV
BASRA
BASSI
BASSO
BASTE
BATAK
BATCH
BATED
BATES
BATHE
BATHO
BATHS
BATHY
BATIK
BATON
BATOR
BATTS
BATTY
BAUER
BAUGH
BAULK
BAUME
BAWDY
BAWLS
BAYAR
BAYED
BAYER
BAYLE
BAYOU

B•A••

BAAED
BAALS
BBALL
BEACH
BEADS
BEADY
BEAKS
BEALL
BEALS
BEAMS
BEAMY
BEANO
BEANS
BEANY
BEARD
BEARS
BEAST
BEATS
BEAUS
BEAUT
BEAUX
BIALY
BLABS
BLACK
BLADE
BLAHS
BLAIR
BLAKE
BLAME
BLANC
BLAND
BLANK
BLARE
BLASE
BLASS
BLAST
BLATS
BLAZE
BOARD
BOARS
BOAST
BOATS
BRACE
BRACT
BRADS
BRADY
BRAES
BRAGA
BRAGG
BRAGS
BRAHE
BRAID
BRAIL
BRAIN
BRAKE
BRAND
BRANS
BRANT
BRASH
BRASS
BRATS
BRAUN
BRAVA
BRAVE
BRAVO
BRAWL
BRAWN
BRAYS
BRAZE
BWANA

B••A•

BABAR
BABAS
BAHAI
BALAS
BANAL
BANAT
BARAB
BASAL
BATAK
BAYAR
BEGAN
BEGAT
BEHAN
BELAY
BEMAS
BETAS
BFLAT
BIHAR
BINAL
BLEAK
BLEAR
BLEAT
BLOAT
BOHAI
BOLAS
BORAH
BORAS
BORAX
BOYAR
BREAD
BREAK
BREAM
BRIAN
BRIAR
BROAD
BRYAN
BYFAR
BYLAW
BYWAY

B•••A

BABKA
BAHIA
BAIZA
BALSA
BANDA
BARCA
BASRA
BELLA
BELVA
BEREA
BERRA
BETTA
BIOTA
BOHEA
BOOLA
BOSSA
BOTHA
BRAGA
BRAVA
BREDA
BROCA
BUBBA
BUENA
BUFFA
BULBA
BULLA
BURMA
BURSA
BWANA

•BA••

ABABA
ABACA
ABACI
ABACK
ABACO
ABAFT
ABASE
ABASH
ABATE
ABAYA
BBALL
IBARS
JBARS
TBALL
TBARS
ZBARS

•B•A•

ABBAS
ABEAM
ABRAM
EBOAT
HBEAM
IBEAM
OBEAH
UBOAT

•B••A

ABABA
ABACA
ABAYA
ABUJA
IBIZA
MBIRA

••BA•

ABBAS
AKBAR
ALBAN
ATBAT
ATBAY
BABAR
BABAS
CABAL
CUBAN
DEBAR
DUBAI
EMBAR
EMBAY
ESBAT
GOBAD
HOBAN
INBAD
IZBAS
JUBAL
KEBAB
LABAN
LUBAS
RABAT
REBAG
REBAR
SABAH
TUBAS
UNBAR
URBAN

••B•A

BABKA
BUBBA
COBIA
COBRA
DEBRA
DOBLA
DOBRA
HABLA
HUBBA
JABBA
LIBRA
LIBYA
NUBIA
SABRA
TABLA
TIBIA
UMBRA
YABBA
ZEBRA

•••BA

ABABA
AMEBA
AQABA
ARUBA
BUBBA
BULBA
CEIBA
CHIBA
GALBA
GAMBA
HUBBA
JABBA
KAABA
MAMBA
MELBA
PEMBA
RUMBA
SAMBA
SCUBA
SHEBA
SIMBA
SUMBA
VERBA
YABBA
YERBA
YORBA
ZORBA

BB•••

BBALL
BBGUN
BBOYS

B•B••

BABAR
BABAS
BABEL
BABER
BABES
BABIS
BABKA
BABUL
BABYS
BEBOP
BIBBS
BIBLE
BOBBY
BOBUP
BUBBA
BUBER
BUBUS

B••B•

BAMBI
BARBQ
BARBS
BEEBE
BIBBS
BILBO
BILBY
BIXBY
BLABS
BLEBS
BLOBS
BOBBY
BOMBE
BOMBS
BOOBS
BOOBY
BRIBE
BUBBA
BULBA
BULBS
BURBS
BUSBY

B•••B

BANDB
BARAB
BLURB

•BB••

ABBAS
ABBES
ABBEY
ABBIE
ABBOT
ABBRS
EBBED

•B•B•

ABABA
ABEBE

•B••B

ABOMB
HBOMB

••BB•

BIBBS
BOBBY
BUBBA
CABBY
CUBBY
DEBBY
DOBBY
GABBY
GIBBS
HOBBS
HOBBY
HUBBA
HUBBY
JABBA
LIBBY
LOBBY
NOBBY
NUBBY
RABBI
REBBE
RIBBY
ROBBY
TABBY
TIBBS
TUBBY
WEBBY
YABBA
YOBBO

••B•B

CUBEB
KABOB
KEBAB
KEBOB
NABOB

BC•••

BCELL

B•C••

BACHS
BACKS
BACON
BECHE
BECKS
BECKY
BOCCE
BOCCI
BUCKO
BUCKS
BUCKY

B••C•

BALCH
BANCO
BANCS
BARCA
BATCH
BEACH
BEECH
BELCH
BENCH
BIRCH
BLACK
BLOCH
BLOCK
BLOCS
BOCCE
BOCCI
BONCE
BOSCH
BOSCO
BOSCS
BOTCH
BRACE
BRACT
BRECK
BRICE
BRICK
BROCA
BROCK
BRUCE
BRUCH
BRYCE
BUICK
BUNCH
BUSCH
BUTCH

B•••C

BARIC
BASIC
BLANC
BORIC
BRONC

•BC••

ABCTV
NBCTV

•B•C•

ABACA
ABACI
ABACK
ABACO

••B•C

CUBIC
REBEC
SUBIC
XEBEC

•••BC

MSNBC

B•D••

BADDY
BADEN
BADER
BADGE
BADLY
BEDEW
BEDIM
BIDDY
BIDED
BIDEN
BIDES
BIDIN
BIDON
BIDUP
BLDGS
BODED
BODES
BUDDY
BUDGE

B••D•

BADDY
BALDS
BANDA
BANDB
BANDO
BANDS
BANDW
BANDY
BARDS
BAWDY
BEADS
BEADY
BENDS
BENDY
BIDDY
BINDS
BIRDS
BIRDY
BLADE
BLVDS
BONDI
BONDS
BRADS
BRADY
BREDA
BRIDE
BRODY
BSIDE
BUDDY
BUNDS
BUNDT
BUNDY
BYRDS

B•••D

BAAED
BAIRD
BAKED
BALED
BARED
BASED
BATED
BAYED
BEARD
BIDED
BIFID
BIKED
BIPED
BIPOD
BLAND
BLEED
BLEND
BLIND
BLOND
BLOOD
BLUED
BOARD
BODED
BONED
BOOED
BORED
BOUND
BOVID
BOWED
BOXED
BRAID
BRAND
BREAD
BREED
BROAD
BROOD
BUILD
BUSED

•BD••

ABDUL

•B•D•

ABIDE
ABODE

•B••D

ABEND
EBBED
EBOND
TBIRD
TBOND

••B•D

CUBED
EBBED
EMBED
GIBED
GOBAD
GYBED
INBAD
INBED
JIBED
LOBED
LUBED
NOBID
RABID
REBID
ROBED
TUBED
UNBID

BE•••

BEACH
BEADS
BEADY
BEAKS
BEALL
BEALS
BEAMS
BEAMY
BEANO
BEANS
BEANY
BEARD
BEARS
BEAST
BEATS
BEAUS
BEAUT
BEAUX
BEBOP
BECHE
BECKS
BECKY
BEDEW
BEDIM
BEEBE
BEECH
BEEFS
BEEFY
BEENE
BEEPS
BEERS
BEERY
BEETS
BEFIT
BEFOG
BEGAN
BEGAT
BEGET
BEGIN
BEGOT
BEGUM
BEGUN
BEHAN
BEIGE
BEING
BEINS
BELAY
BELCH
BELEM
BELIE
BELLA
BELLE
BELLI
BELLS
BELLY
BELOW
BELTS
BELVA
BEMAS
BENCH
BENDS
BENDY
BENES
BENET
BENIN
BENJI
BENNY
BENTS
BENUE
BENXI
BENZO
BEREA
BERET
BERGH
BERGS
BERLE
BERME
BERMS
BERNE
BERRA
BERRY
BERTH
BERYL
BESET
BESOM
BESOT
BESTS
BETAS
BETEL
BETHS
BETON
BETSY
BETTA
BETTE
BETTY
BEVEL
BEVIN
BEYLE
BEZEL

B•E••

BCELL
BEEBE
BEECH
BEEFS
BEEFY
BEENE
BEEPS
BEERS
BEERY
BEETS
BLEAK
BLEAR
BLEAT
BLEBS
BLEED
BLEEP
BLEND
BLENT
BLESS
BLEST
BOEHM
BOERS
BOEUF
BREAD
BREAK
BREAM
BRECK
BREDA
BREED
BREEN
BRENT
BRERS
BREST
BRETT
BREVE
BREWS
BUELL
BUENA
BUENO

B••E•

BAAED
BABEL
BABER
BABES
BADEN
BADER
BAGEL
BAKED
BAKER
BAKES
BALED
BALER
BALES
BANES
BARED
BARER
BARES
BASED
BASEL
BASER
BASES
BATED
BATES
BAUER
BAYED
BAYER
BEDEW
BEGET
BELEM
BENES
BENET
BEREA
BERET
BESET
BETEL
BEVEL
BEZEL
BIDED
BIDEN
BIDES
BIKED
BIKEL
BIKER
BIKES
BINES
BINET
BIPED
BISES
BITER
BITES
BIZET
BLEED
BLEEP
BLUED
BLUER
BLUES
BLUET
BLUEY
BODED
BODES
BOGEY
BOHEA
BOLES
BONED
BONER
BONES
BONET
BOOED
BOOER
BORED
BORER
BORES
BOTEL
BOWED
BOWEN
BOWER
BOWES
BOXED
BOXER
BOXES
BOYER
BRAES
BREED
BREEN
BRIEF
BRIER
BRIES
BUBER
BUSED
BUSES
BUSEY
BUTEO
BUYER
BYNER
BYRES
BYTES

B•••E

BADGE
BAIZE
BARGE
BARRE
BASIE
BASTE
BATHE
BAUME
BAYLE
BECHE
BEEBE
BEENE
BEIGE
BELIE
BELLE
BENUE
BERLE
BERME
BERNE
BETTE
BEYLE
BIBLE
BILGE
BINGE
BIOME
BIRSE
BITTE
BLADE
BLAKE
BLAME
BLARE
BLASE
BLAZE
BLIGE
BLOKE
BLUME
BOCCE
BOGIE
BOGLE
BOHME
BOISE
BOITE
BOMBE
BONCE
BONNE
BONZE
BOOLE
BOONE
BOOZE
BORGE
BORNE
BOTHE
BOULE
BOUSE
BOWIE
BOYLE
BOYNE
BRACE
BRAHE
BRAKE
BRAVE
BRAZE
BREVE
BRIBE
BRICE
BRIDE
BRINE
BRITE
BROKE
BROME
BRUCE
BRULE
BRUME
BRUTE
BRYCE
BSIDE
BUDGE
BUGLE
BULGE
BURKE
BURSE
BUTTE
BYRNE

•BE••

ABEAM
ABEBE
ABELE
ABEND
ABETS
CBERS
EBERT
HBEAM
IBEAM
IBERT
OBEAH
OBELI
OBESE
OBEYS

•B•E•

ABBES
ABBEY
ABLER
ABNER
ABYES
EBBED
EBSEN
IBSEN
OBIES
OBJET
OBOES

•B••E

ABASE
ABATE
ABBIE
ABEBE
ABELE
ABIDE
ABODE
ABOVE
ABUSE
OBESE
TBONE

••BE•

ABBES
ABBEY
ALBEE
ALBEN
AMBER
ARBER
AUBER
BABEL
BABER
BABES
BUBER
CABER
CUBEB
CUBED
CUBES
CYBER
EBBED
EMBED
EMBER
FABER
FIBER
GIBED
GIBER
GIBES
GOBEL
GYBED
GYBES
HABER
INBED
JIBED
JIBES
KIBEI
LABEL
LIBEL
LOBED
LOBES
LUBED
LUBES
MABEL
NABES
NOBEL
OMBER
REBEC
REBEL
ROBED
ROBES
RUBEN
RUBES
SABER
SOBER
TIBER
TIBET
TOBES
TOBEY
TUBED
TUBER
TUBES
UMBEL
UMBER
UZBEK
VIBES
WEBER
XEBEC
ZIBET

••B•E

ABBIE
ALBEE
AMBLE
ARBRE
BIBLE
CABLE
DOBIE
DOBLE
EUBIE
FABLE
FIBRE
GABLE
IMBUE
LIBRE
NOBLE
OMBRE
REBBE
ROBLE
RUBLE
SABLE
SABRE
TABLE

•••BE

ABEBE
ADOBE
BEEBE
BOMBE
BRIBE
COMBE
FROBE
GLEBE
GLOBE
GREBE
LETBE
MAYBE
NIOBE
PHOBE
PLEBE
PROBE
REBBE
THEBE
TRIBE

BF•••

BFLAT

B•F••

BEFIT
BEFOG
BIFFS
BIFFY
BIFID
BOFFO
BOFFS
BUFFA
BUFFI
BUFFO
BUFFS
BUFFY
BYFAR

B••F•

BANFF
BEEFS
BEEFY
BIFFS
BIFFY
BLUFF
BOFFO
BOFFS
BUFFA
BUFFI
BUFFO
BUFFS
BUFFY

B•••F

BANFF
BLUFF
BOEUF
BRIEF

•B•F•

ABAFT

BG•••

BGIRL

B•G••

BAGEL
BAGGY
BAGIT
BBGUN
BEGAN
BEGAT
BEGET
BEGIN
BEGOT
BEGUM
BEGUN
BIGGY
BIGHT
BIGLY
BIGON
BIGOS
BIGOT
BOGEY
BOGGS
BOGGY
BOGIE
BOGLE
BOGOR
BOGUS
BUGGY
BUGLE
BUGSY
BYGUM

B••G•

BADGE
BAGGY
BANGS
BARGE
BARGY
BAUGH
BEIGE
BERGH
BERGS
BIGGY
BILGE
BILGY
BINGE
BINGO
BINGS
BIOGS
BLDGS
BLIGE
BLIGH
BOGGS
BOGGY
BONGO
BONGS
BORGE
BOUGH
BRAGA
BRAGG
BRAGS
BRIGS
BUDGE
BUGGY
BULGE
BULGY
BUNGS
BURGS

B•••G

BEFOG
BEING
BOING
BOURG
BRAGG
BRING
BRUNG

•BG••

BBGUN
OBGYN

•B••G

ABZUG

••B•G

DEBUG
INBIG
MRBIG
REBAG
SOBIG

B•H••

BAHAI
BAHIA
BAHTS
BEHAN
BIHAR
BOHAI
BOHEA
BOHME
BUHLS

B••H•

BACHS
BASHO
BATHE
BATHO
BATHS
BATHY
BECHE
BETHS
BIGHT
BISHO
BLAHS
BOEHM
BOTHA
BOTHE
BRAHE
BRUHN
BUSHY

B•••H

BALCH
BALKH
BARTH
BATCH
BAUGH
BEACH
BEECH
BELCH
BENCH
BERGH
BERTH
BIRCH
BIRTH

BLIGH BLOCH BLUSH BLUTH BLYTH BOOTH BORAH BOSCH BOTCH BOUGH BRASH BRITH BROTH BRUCH BRUSH BUNCH BUSCH BUTCH

•BH••
ABHOR

•B•H•
ABOHM

•B••H
ABASH OBEAH

••B•H
SABAH

BI•••
BIALY BIBBS BIBLE BIDDY BIDED BIDEN BIDES BIDIN BIDON BIDUP BIFFS BIFFY BIFID BIGGY BIGHT BIGLY BIGON BIGOS BIGOT BIHAR BIJOU BIKED BIKEL BIKER BIKES BILBO BILBY BILGE BILGY BILKO BILKS BILLS BILLY BINAL BINDS BINES BINET BINGE BINGO BINGS BIOGS BIOKO BIOME BIONT BIOTA BIPED BIPOD BIRCH BIRDS BIRDY BIRLS BIRRS BIRSE BIRTH BISES BISHO BISON BITER BITES BITSY BITTE BITTS BITTY BIXBY BIZET

B•I••
BAILS BAIRD BAIRN BAITS BAIUL BAIZA BAIZE BEIGE BEING BEINS BGIRL BLIGE BLIGH BLIMP BLIND BLINI BLINK BLIPS BLISS BLITT BLITZ BOILS BOING BOISE BOITE BOITO BRIAN BRIAR BRIBE BRICE BRICK BRIDE BRIEF BRIER BRIES BRIGS BRILL BRIMS BRINE BRING BRINK BRINY BRISK BRITE BRITH BRITS BRITT BSIDE BUICK BUILD BUILT

B••I•
BABIS BAGIT BAHIA BALIN BARIC BARIT BASIC BASIE BASIL BASIN BASIS BATIK BEDIM BEFIT BEGIN BELIE BENIN BEVIN BIDIN BIFID BLAIR BLOIS BOGIE BORIC BORIS BOVID BOWIE BOXIN BRAID BRAIL BRAIN BROIL BRUIN BRUIT BUNIN BURIN

B•••I
BAHAI BAMBI BAOJI BASSI BELLI BENJI BENXI BLINI BOCCI BOHAI BONDI BUFFI BUZZI

•BI••
ABIDE IBIZA MBIRA OBIES TBILL TBIRD

•B•I•
ABBIE ABOIL ABRIL ABRIS QBVII

•B••I
ABACI EBOLI OBELI OBOLI QBVII

••BI•
ABBIE AMBIT BABIS CABIN COBIA CUBIC CUBIT DEBIT DOBIE DUBIN ERBIL EUBIE FABIO HABIT INBIG LABIO MOBIL MRBIG NOBID NOBIS NUBIA ORBIT RABID RABIN REBID ROBIN RUBIK RUBIN SABIN SOBIG SUBIC SYBIL TABIS TIBIA TOBIT UNBID URBIS ZUBIN

••B•I
DUBAI KIBEI RABBI

•••BI
ALIBI BAMBI DHABI IAMBI LIMBI NIMBI ORIBI RABBI

BJ•••
BJORN

B•J••
BIJOU

B••J•
BANJO BAOJI BENJI

•BJ••
OBJET

•B•J•
ABUJA

B•K••
BAKED BAKER BAKES BAKST BIKED BIKEL BIKER BIKES

B••K•
BABKA BACKS BALKH BALKS BALKY BANKS BANKY BARKS BARKY BASKS BEAKS BECKS BECKY BILKO BILKS BIOKO BLAKE BLOKE BONKS BOOKS BOSKS BOSKY BRAKE BROKE BUCKO BUCKS BUCKY BULKS BULKY BUNKO BUNKS BURKE BUSKS

B•••K
BATAK BATIK BAULK BLACK BLANK BLEAK BLINK BLOCK BREAK BRECK BRICK BRINK BRISK BROCK BROOK BUICK

•B••K
ABACK

••BK•
BABKA

••B•K
RUBIK UZBEK

BL•••
BLABS BLACK BLADE BLAHS BLAIR BLAKE BLAME BLANC BLAND BLANK BLARE BLASE BLASS BLAST BLATS BLAZE BLDGS BLEAK BLEAR BLEAT BLEBS BLEED BLEEP BLEND BLENT BLESS BLEST BLIGE BLIGH BLIMP BLIND BLINI BLINK BLIPS BLISS BLITT BLITZ BLOAT BLOBS BLOCH BLOCK BLOCS BLOIS BLOKE BLOND BLOOD BLOOM BLOOP BLOTS BLOWN BLOWS BLOWY BLUED BLUER BLUES BLUET BLUEY BLUFF BLUME BLUNT BLURB BLURS BLURT BLUSH BLUTH BLUTO BLVDS BLYTH

B•L••
BALAS BALCH BALDS BALED BALER BALES BALIN BALKH BALKS BALKY BALLS BALLY BALMS BALMY BALSA BALTO BALTS BELAY BELCH BELEM BELIE BELLA BELLE BELLI BELLS BELLY BELOW BELTS BELVA BFLAT BILBO BILBY BILGE BILGY BILKO BILKS BILLS BILLY BOLAS BOLES BOLLS BOLOS BOLTS BOLUS BPLUS BULBA BULBS BULGE BULGY BULKS BULKY BULLA BULLS BULLY BULOW BYLAW

B••L•
BAALS BADLY BAILS BALLS BALLY BAULK BAWLS BAYLE BBALL BCELL BEALL BEALS BELLA BELLE BELLI BELLS BELLY BERLE BEYLE BIALY BIBLE BIGLY BILLS BILLY BIRLS BOGLE BOILS BOLLS BOOLA BOOLE BOULE BOULT BOWLS BOYLE BRILL BRULE BUELL BUGLE BUHLS BUILD BUILT BULLA BULLS BULLY BURLS BURLY

B•••L
BABEL BABUL BAGEL BAIUL BANAL BASAL BASEL BASIL BBALL BCELL BEALL BERYL BETEL BEVEL BEZEL BGIRL BIKEL BINAL BOTEL BRAIL BRAWL BRILL BROIL BUELL BUTYL

•BL••
ABLER

•B•L•
ABELE BBALL EBOLI OBELI OBOLI OBOLS TBALL TBILL UBOLT

•B••L
ABDUL ABOIL ABRIL BBALL TBALL TBILL

••BL•
AMBLE BIBLE CABLE DOBLA DOBLE FABLE GABLE HABLA NOBLE NOBLY PABLO ROBLE RUBLE SABLE TABLA TABLE

••B•L
BABEL BABUL CABAL COBOL ERBIL GOBEL JUBAL KABUL LABEL LIBEL MABEL MOBIL NOBEL REBEL SIBYL SYBIL TOBOL UMBEL

B•M••
BAMBI BEMAS BOMBE BOMBS BUMPS BUMPY

B••M•
BALMS BALMY BARMS BARMY BAUME BEAMS BEAMY BERME BERMS BIOME BLAME BLIMP BLUME BOHME BOOMS BOOMY BRIMS BROME BROMO BRUME BURMA

B•••M
BEDIM BEGUM BELEM BESOM BLOOM BOEHM BOSOM BREAM BROOM BYGUM

•B•M•
ABOMB HBOMB MBOMU

•B••M
ABEAM ABOHM ABRAM ABYSM HBEAM IBEAM

••BM•
ICBMS

••B•M
ALBUM SEBUM

B•N••
BANAL BANAT BANCO BANCS BANDA BANDB BANDO BANDS BANDW BANDY BANES BANFF BANGS BANJO BANKS BANKY BANNS BANTU BENCH BENDS BENDY BENES BENET BENIN BENJI BENNY BENTS BENUE BENXI BENZO BINAL BINDS BINES BINET BINGE BINGO BINGS BONCE BONDI BONDS BONED BONER BONES BONET BONGO BONGS BONKS BONNE BONNY BONUS BONZE BONZO BUNCH BUNDS BUNDT BUNDY BUNGS BUNIN BUNKO BUNKS BUNNY BUNTS BYNER BYNOW

B••N•
BANNS BARNS BEANO BEANS BEANY BEENE BEING BEINS BENNY BERNE BIONT BLANC BLAND BLANK BLEND BLENT BLIND BLINI BLINK BLOND BLUNT BOING BONNE BONNY BOONE BOONS BORNE BOSNS BOUND BOYNE BRAND BRANS BRANT BRENT BRINE BRING BRINK BRINY BRONC BRONX BRUNG BRUNO BRUNT BUENA BUENO BUNNY BUONO BURNS BURNT BWANA BYRNE

B•••N
BACON BADEN BAIRN BALIN BARON BASIN BATON BBGUN BEGAN BEGIN BEGUN BEHAN BENIN BETON BEVIN BIDEN BIDIN BIDON BIGON BISON BJORN BLOWN BORON BOSON BOURN BOWEN BOXIN BRAIN BRAUN BRAWN BREEN BRIAN BROUN BROWN BRUHN BRUIN BRYAN BUNIN BURIN BYRON

•BN••
ABNER

•B•N•
ABEND EBOND EBONS EBONY TBOND TBONE

•B••N
BBGUN EBSEN IBSEN OBGYN

••B•N
ALBAN ALBEN CABIN CUBAN DUBIN GABON HOBAN LABAN RABIN ROBIN RUBEN RUBIN SABIN URBAN ZUBIN

BO•••
BOARD BOARS BOAST BOATS BOBBY BOBUP BOCCE BOCCI BODED BODES BOEHM BOERS BOEUF BOFFO BOFFS BOGEY BOGGS BOGGY BOGIE BOGLE BOGOR BOGUS BOHAI BOHEA BOHME BOILS BOING BOISE BOITE BOITO BOLAS BOLES BOLLS BOLOS BOLTS BOLUS BOMBE BOMBS BONCE BONDI BONDS BONED BONER BONES BONET BONGO BONGS BONKS BONNE BONNY BONUS BONZE BONZO BOOBS BOOBY BOOED BOOER BOOKS BOOLA BOOLE BOOMS BOOMY BOONE BOONS BOORS BOOST BOOTH BOOTS BOOTY BOOZE BORAH BORAS BORAX BORED BORER BORES BORGE BORIC BORIS BORNE BORON BOSCH BOSCO BOSCS BOSKS BOSKY BOSNS BOSOM BOSON BOSOX BOSSA BOSSY BOTCH BOTEL BOTHA BOTHE BOUGH BOULE BOULT BOUND BOURG BOURN BOUSE BOUTS BOVID BOWED BOWEN BOWER BOWES BOWIE BOWLS BOXED BOXER BOXES BOXIN BOXUP BOYAR BOYER BOYLE BOYNE BOYOS BOZOS

B•O••
BAOJI BBOYS BIOGS BIOKO BIOME BIONT BIOTA BJORN BLOAT BLOBS BLOCH BLOCK BLOCS BLOIS BLOKE BLOND BLOOD BLOOM BLOOP BLOTS BLOWN BLOWS BLOWY BOOBS BOOBY BOOED BOOER BOOKS BOOLA BOOLE BOOMS BOOMY BOONE BOONS BOORS BOOST BOOTH BOOTS BOOTY BOOZE BROAD BROCA BROCK BRODY BROIL BROKE BROME BROMO BRONC BRONX BROOD BROOK BROOM BROTH BROUN BROWN BROWS BUONO BUOYS

B••O•
BACON BARON BASOV BATON BATOR BAYOU BEBOP BEFOG BEGOT BELOW BESOM BESOT BETON BIDON BIGON BIGOS BIGOT BIJOU BIPOD BISON BLOOD BLOOM BLOOP BOGOR BOLOS BORON BOSOM BOSON BOSOX BOYOS BOZOS BROOD BROOK BROOM BULOW BYNOW BYRON

B•••O
BALTO BANCO BANDO BANJO BASHO BASSO BATHO BEANO BENZO BILBO BILKO BINGO BIOKO BISHO BLUTO BOFFO BOITO BONGO BONZO BOSCO BRAVO BROMO BRUNO BUCKO BUENO BUFFO BUNKO BUONO BURRO BUTEO

•BO••
ABODE ABOHM ABOIL ABOMB ABORT ABOUT ABOVE ABOVO BBOYS EBOAT EBOLI EBOND EBONS EBONY HBOMB MBOMU OBOES OBOLI OBOLS TBOND TBONE UBOAT UBOLT

•B•O•
ABBOT ABHOR

•B••O
ABACO ABOVO

••BO•
ABBOT AMBOS AMBOY ARBOR BEBOP CABOT COBOL DUBOS ELBOW GABON GABOR HOBOS INBOX JABOT KABOB KEBOB KOBOS LABOR LOBOS NABOB OHBOY OXBOW POBOX POBOY ROBOT SABOT TABOO TABOR TOBOL UMBOS UNBOX UPBOW

••B•O
DOBRO FABIO FIBRO LABIO PABLO TABOO YOBBO

•••BO
BILBO CARBO COMBO DUMBO GARBO GUMBO JUMBO LIMBO MAMBO MUMBO PEABO RAMBO TAMBO TURBO YOBBO

BP•••
BPLUS

B•P••
BIPED BIPOD

B••P•
BEEPS BLIPS BUMPS BUMPY BURPS

B•••P
BEBOP BIDUP BLEEP BLIMP BLOOP BOBUP BOXUP BUYUP

•B•P•
TBSPS

••B•P
BEBOP BOBUP

B••Q•
BARQS

B•••Q
BARBQ

•••BQ
BARBQ

BR•••
BRACE BRACT BRADS BRADY BRAES BRAGA BRAGG BRAGS BRAHE BRAID BRAIL BRAIN BRAKE BRAND BRANS BRANT BRASH BRASS BRATS BRAUN BRAVA BRAVE BRAVO BRAWL BRAWN BRAYS BRAZE BREAD BREAK BREAM BRECK BREDA BREED BREEN BRENT BRERS BREST BRETT BREVE BREWS BRIAN BRIAR BRIBE BRICE BRICK BRIDE BRIEF BRIER BRIES

BRIGS BRILL BRIMS BRINE BRING BRINK BRINY BRISK BRITE BRITH BRITS BRITT BROAD BROCA BROCK BRODY BROIL BROKE BROME BROMO BRONC BRONX BROOD BROOK BROOM BROTH BROUN BROWN BROWS BRUCE BRUCH BRUHN BRUIN BRUIT BRULE BRUME BRUNG BRUNO BRUNT BRUSH BRUTE BRUTS BRYAN BRYCE

B•R••
BARAB BARBQ BARBS BARCA BARDS BARED BARER BARES BARGE BARGY BARIC BARIT BARKS BARKY BARMS BARMY BARNS BARON BARQS BARRE BARRY BARTH BARTS BARTY BEREA BERET BERGH BERGS BERLE BERME BERMS BERNE BERRA BERRY BERTH BERYL BIRCH BIRDS BIRDY BIRLS BIRRS BIRSE BIRTH BORAH BORAS BORAX BORED BORER BORES BORGE BORIC BORIS BORNE BORON BURBS BURGS BURIN BURKE BURLS BURLY BURMA BURNS BURNT BURPS BURRO BURRS BURRY BURSA BURSE BURST BYRDS BYRES BYRNE BYRON

B••R•
BAIRD BAIRN BARRE BARRY BASRA BEARD BEARS BEERS BEERY BERRA BERRY BGIRL BIRRS BJORN BLARE BLURB BLURS BLURT BOARD BOARS BOERS BOORS BOURG BOURN BRERS BURRO BURRS BURRY

B•••R
BABAR BABER BADER BAKER BALER BARER BASER BATOR BAUER BAYAR BAYER BIHAR BIKER BITER BLAIR BLEAR BLUER BOGOR BONER BOOER BORER BOWER BOXER BOYAR BOYER BRIAR BRIER BUBER BUYER BYFAR BYNER

•BR••
ABRAM ABRIL ABRIS

•B•R•
ABBRS ABORT CBERS EBERT IBARS IBERT JBARS MBIRA TBARS TBIRD ZBARS

•B••R
ABHOR ABLER ABNER

••BR•
ABBRS AMBRY ARBRE COBRA DEBRA DOBRA DOBRO FIBRE FIBRO LIBRA LIBRE OMBRE SABRA SABRE UMBRA ZEBRA

••B•R
AKBAR AMBER ARBER ARBOR AUBER BABAR BABER BUBER CABER CYBER DEBAR EMBAR EMBER FABER FIBER GABOR GIBER HABER LABOR OMBER REBAR SABER SOBER TABOR TIBER TUBER UMBER UNBAR WEBER

BS•••
BSIDE

B•S••
BASAL BASED BASEL BASER BASES BASHO BASIC BASIE BASIL BASIN BASIS BASKS BASOV BASRA BASSI BASSO BASTE BESET BESOM BESOT BESTS BISES BISHO BISON BOSCH BOSCO BOSCS BOSKS BOSKY BOSNS BOSOM BOSON BOSOX BOSSA BOSSY BUSBY BUSCH BUSED BUSES BUSEY BUSHY BUSKS BUSTS

B••S•
BAKST BALSA BASSI BASSO BEAST BETSY BIRSE BITSY BLASE BLASS BLAST BLESS BLEST BLISS BLUSH BOAST BOISE BOOST BOSSA BOSSY BOUSE BRASH BRASS BREST BRISK BRUSH BUGSY BURSA BURSE BURST

B•••S
BAALS BABAS BABES BABIS BABYS BACHS BACKS BAHTS BAILS BAITS BAKES BALAS BALDS BALES BALKS BALLS BALMS BALTS BANCS BANDS BANES BANGS BANKS BANNS BARBS BARDS BARES BARKS BARMS BARNS BARQS BARTS BASES BASIS BASKS BATES BATHS BATTS BAWLS BBOYS BEADS BEAKS BEALS BEAMS BEANS BEARS BEATS BEAUS BECKS BEEFS BEEPS BEERS BEETS BEINS BELLS BELTS BEMAS BENDS BENES BENTS BERGS BERMS BESTS BETAS BETHS BIBBS BIDES BIFFS BIGOS BIKES BILKS BILLS BINDS BINES BINGS BIOGS BIRDS BIRLS BIRRS BISES BITES BITTS BLABS BLAHS BLASS BLATS BLDGS BLEBS BLESS BLIPS BLISS BLOBS BLOCS BLOIS BLOTS BLOWS BLUES BLURS BLVDS BOARS BOATS BODES BOERS BOFFS BOGGS BOGUS BOILS BOLAS BOLES BOLLS BOLOS BOLTS BOLUS BOMBS BONDS BONES BONGS BONKS BONUS BOOBS BOOKS BOOMS BOONS BOORS BOOTS BORAS BORES BORIS BOSCS BOSKS BOSNS BOUTS BOWES BOWLS BOXES BOYOS BOZOS BPLUS BRADS BRAES BRAGS BRANS BRASS BRATS BRAYS BRERS BREWS BRIES BRIGS BRIMS BRITS BROWS BRUTS BUBUS BUCKS BUFFS BUHLS BULBS BULKS BULLS BUMPS BUNDS BUNGS BUNKS BUNTS BUOYS BURBS BURGS BURLS BURNS BURPS BURRS BUSES BUSKS BUSTS BUTTS BYRDS BYRES BYTES

•BS••
CBSTV EBSEN IBSEN TBSPS

•B•S•
ABASE ABASH ABUSE ABYSM ABYSS OBESE

•B••S
ABBAS ABBES ABBRS ABETS ABRIS ABUTS ABYES ABYSS BBOYS CBERS EBONS IBARS JBARS OBEYS OBIES OBOES OBOLS TBARS TBSPS ZBARS

••BS•
FUBSY PABST

••B•S
ABBAS ABBES ABBRS AMBOS BABAS BABES BABIS BABYS BIBBS BUBUS CUBES DEBTS DUBOS GIBBS GIBES GYBES HOBBS HOBOS ICBMS IZBAS JIBES KOBOS LOBES LOBOS LUBAS LUBES NABES NOBIS REBUS ROBES RUBES TABIS TIBBS TOBES TUBAS TUBES UMBOS URBIS VIBES ZEBUS

•••BS
ARABS BARBS BIBBS BLABS BLEBS BLOBS BOMBS BOOBS BULBS BURBS CARBS CHUBS CLUBS COMBS CRABS CRIBS CURBS DAUBS DRABS DRIBS DRUBS DUMBS FLUBS FORBS FTLBS GARBS GIBBS GLOBS GRABS GRUBS HERBS HOBBS IAMBS JAMBS KERBS KNOBS KREBS LAMBS LIMBS NUMBS PLEBS PROBS SAABS SCABS SERBS SLABS SLOBS SNOBS SNUBS SORBS STABS STUBS SWABS SWOBS TIBBS VERBS

B•T••
BATAK BATCH BATED BATES BATHE BATHO BATHS BATHY BATIK BATON BATOR BATTS BATTY BETAS BETEL BETHS BETON BETSY BETTA BETTE BETTY BITER BITES BITSY BITTE BITTS BITTY BOTCH BOTEL BOTHA BOTHE BUTCH BUTEO BUTTE BUTTS BUTTY BUTUT BUTYL BYTES

B••T•
BAHTS BAITS BALTO BALTS BANTU BARTH BARTS BARTY BASTE BATTS BATTY BEATS BEETS BELTS BENTS BERTH BESTS BETTA BETTE BETTY BIOTA BIRTH BITTE BITTS BITTY BLATS BLITT BLITZ BLOTS BLUTH BLUTO BLYTH BOATS BOITE BOITO BOLTS BOOTH BOOTS BOOTY BOUTS BRATS BRETT BRITE BRITH BRITS BRITT BROTH BRUTE BRUTS BUNTS BUSTS BUTTE BUTTS BUTTY

B•••T
BAGIT BAKST BANAT BARIT BEAST BEAUT BEFIT BEGAT BEGET BEGOT BENET BERET BESET BESOT BFLAT BIGHT BIGOT BINET BIONT BIZET BLAST BLEAT BLENT BLEST BLITT BLOAT BLUET BLUNT BLURT BOAST BONET BOOST BOULT BRACT BRANT BRENT BREST BRETT BRITT BRUIT BRUNT BUILT BUNDT BURNT BURST BUTUT

•B•T•
ABATE ABCTV ABETS ABUTS CBSTV NBCTV

•B••T
ABAFT ABBOT ABORT ABOUT EBERT EBOAT IBERT OBJET UBOAT UBOLT

••BT•
DEBTS

••B•T
ABBOT AMBIT ATBAT CABOT CUBIT DEBIT DEBUT ESBAT HABIT JABOT ORBIT PABST RABAT REBUT ROBOT SABOT TIBET TOBIT ZIBET

•••BT
DOUBT

BU•••
BUBBA BUBER BUBUS BUCKO BUCKS BUCKY BUDDY BUDGE BUELL BUENA BUENO BUFFA BUFFI BUFFO BUFFS BUFFY BUGGY BUGLE BUGSY BUHLS BUICK BUILD BUILT BULBA BULBS BULGE BULGY BULKS BULKY BULLA BULLS BULLY BULOW BUMPS BUMPY BUNCH BUNDS BUNDT BUNDY BUNGS BUNIN BUNKO BUNKS BUNNY BUNTS BUONO BUOYS BURBS BURGS BURIN BURKE BURLS BURLY BURMA BURNS BURNT BURPS BURRO BURRS BURRY BURSA BURSE BURST BUSBY BUSCH BUSED BUSES BUSEY BUSHY BUSKS BUSTS BUTCH BUTEO BUTTE BUTTS BUTTY BUTUT BUTYL BUYER BUYUP BUZZI

B•U••
BAUER BAUGH BAULK BAUME BLUED BLUER BLUES BLUET BLUEY BLUFF BLUME BLUNT BLURB BLURS BLURT BLUSH BLUTH BLUTO BOUGH BOULE BOULT BOUND BOURG BOURN BOUSE BOUTS BRUCE BRUCH BRUHN BRUIN BRUIT BRULE BRUME BRUNG BRUNO BRUNT BRUSH BRUTE BRUTS

B••U•
BABUL BAIUL BBGUN BEAUS BEAUT BEAUX BEGUM BEGUN BENUE BIDUP BOBUP BOEUF BOGUS BOLUS BONUS BOXUP BPLUS BRAUN BROUN BUBUS BUTUT BUYUP BYGUM

B•••U
BANTU BAYOU BIJOU

•BU••
ABUJA ABUSE ABUTS ABUZZ

•B•U•
ABDUL ABOUT ABZUG BBGUN

•B••U
MBOMU

••BU•
ALBUM BABUL BOBUP BUBUS DEBUG DEBUT IMBUE KABUL REBUS REBUT SEBUM ZEBUS

B•V••
BEVEL BEVIN BLVDS BOVID

B••V•
BELVA BRAVA BRAVE BRAVO BREVE

B•••V
BASOV

•BV••
QBVII

•B•V•
ABOVE ABOVO

•B••V
ABCTV CBSTV NBCTV

BW•••
BWANA

B•W••
BAWDY BAWLS BOWED BOWEN BOWER BOWES BOWIE BOWLS BYWAY

B••W•
BLOWN BLOWS BLOWY BRAWL BRAWN BREWS BROWN BROWS

B•••W
BANDW BEDEW BELOW BULOW BYLAW BYNOW

••B•W
ELBOW OXBOW UPBOW

B•X••
BIXBY BOXED BOXER BOXES BOXIN BOXUP

B••X•
BENXI

B•••X
BEAUX BORAX BOSOX BRONX

••B•X
INBOX POBOX UNBOX

BY•••
BYFAR BYGUM BYLAW BYNER BYNOW BYRDS BYRES BYRNE BYRON BYTES BYWAY

B•Y••
BAYAR BAYED BAYER BAYLE BAYOU BEYLE BLYTH BOYAR BOYER BOYLE BOYNE BOYOS BRYAN BRYCE BUYER BUYUP

B••Y•
BABYS BBOYS BERYL BRAYS BUOYS BUTYL

B•••Y
BADDY BADLY BAGGY BALKY BALLY BALMY BANDY BANKY BARGY BARKY BARMY BARRY BARTY BATHY BATTY BAWDY BEADY BEAMY BEANY BECKY BEEFY BEERY BELAY BELLY BENDY BENNY BERRY BETSY BETTY BIALY BIDDY BIFFY BIGGY BIGLY BILBY BILGY BILLY BIRDY BITSY BITTY BIXBY BLOWY BLUEY BOBBY BOGEY BOGGY BONNY BOOBY BOOMY BOOTY BOSKY BOSSY BRADY BRINY BRODY BUCKY BUDDY BUFFY BUGGY BUGSY BULGY BULKY BULLY BUMPY BUNDY BUNNY BURLY BURRY BUSBY BUSEY BUSHY BUTTY BYWAY

•BY••
ABYES ABYSM ABYSS

•B•Y•
ABAYA BBOYS OBEYS OBGYN

•B••Y
ABBEY EBONY

••BY•
BABYS LIBYA SIBYL

••B•Y
ABBEY AMBOY AMBRY ATBAY BOBBY CABBY CUBBY DEBBY DOBBY EMBAY FUBSY GABBY HOBBY HUBBY LIBBY LOBBY NOBBY NOBLY NUBBY OHBOY POBOY RIBBY ROBBY TABBY TOBEY TUBBY WEBBY

•••BY
ARABY ASHBY BILBY BiXBY BOBBY BOOBY BUSBY CABBY CANBY COLBY CORBY COSBY CUBBY DARBY DEBBY DERBY DIDBY DIGBY DOBBY DOLBY FLYBY GABBY GETBY GOTBY GUMBY HERBY HOBBY HUBBY KIRBY LAYBY LIBBY LIEBY LOBBY LOOBY MOSBY NAMBY NASBY NIMBY NOBBY NUBBY PAMBY PUTBY RIBBY RIGBY ROBBY RUGBY SATBY

SETBY
SITBY
TABBY
TUBBY
VISBY
WEBBY
WELBY

B•Z••
BEZEL
BIZET
BOZOS
BUZZI

B••Z•
BAIZA
BAIZE
BENZO
BLAZE
BONZE
BONZO
BOOZE
BRAZE
BUZZI

B•••Z
BLITZ

•BZ••
ABZUG

•B•Z•
ABUZZ
IBIZA

•B••Z
ABUZZ

CA•••
CABAL
CABBY
CABER
CABIN
CABLE
CABOT
CACAO
CACHE
CACTI
CADDO
CADDY
CADET
CADGE
CADIS
CADIZ
CADRE
CAELO
CAFES
CAFFE
CAGED
CAGER
CAGES
CAGEY
CAINE
CAIRN
CAIRO
CAJUN
CAKED
CAKES
CAKEY
CALCI
CALEB
CALIF
CALIX
CALKS
CALLA
CALLI
CALLS
CALMS
CALPE
CALVE
CALYX
CAMAY
CAMEL
CAMEO
CAMIS
CAMOS
CAMPO
CAMPS
CAMPY
CAMRY
CAMUS
CANAD
CANAL
CANBY
CANDO
CANDW
CANDY
CANEA
CANED
CANEM
CANER
CANES
CANID
CANIS
CANIT
CANNA
CANNY
CANOE
CANON
CANSO
CANST
CANTO
CANTS
CANTY
CAPED
CAPEK
CAPER
CAPES
CAPET
CAPON
CAPOS
CAPRA
CAPRI
CAPTS
CARAT
CARBO
CARBS
CARDI
CARDS
CARED
CARER
CARES
CARET
CAREW
CAREY
CARGO
CARIA
CARIB
CARKS
CARLA
CARLE
CARLO
CARLY
CARNE
CARNY
CAROB
CAROL
CAROM
CARON
CARPE
CARPI
CARPO
CARPS
CARRE
CARRY
CARTA
CARTE
CARTS
CARVE
CASAS
CASCA
CASCO
CASED
CASES
CASEY
CASIO
CASKS
CASTE
CASTS
CASUS
CATCH
CATER
CATES
CATHY
CATTY
CAULK
CAULS
CAUSA
CAUSE
CAVAE
CAVED
CAVER
CAVES
CAVIL
CAWED
CAYCE

C•A••
CEASE
CHACO
CHAFE
CHAFF
CHAIM
CHAIN
CHAIR
CHAKA
CHALK
CHAMP
CHANG
CHANT
CHAOS
CHAPS
CHARD
CHARM
CHARO
CHARS
CHART
CHARY
CHASE
CHASM
CHATS
CHAUD
CHAWS
CHAZZ
CLACK
CLAIM
CLAIR
CLAMP
CLAMS
CLANG
CLANK
CLANS
CLAPS
CLARA
CLARE
CLARK
CLARO
CLARY
CLASH
CLASP
CLASS
CLAUS
CLAVE
CLAWS
CLAYS
COACH
COACT
COALS
COAPT
COAST
COATI
COATS
CRABS
CRACK
CRACY
CRAFT
CRAGS
CRAIG
CRAIN
CRAKE
CRAMP
CRAMS
CRANE
CRANK
CRAPE
CRAPS
CRASH
CRASS
CRATE
CRAVE
CRAWL
CRAWS
CRAZE
CRAZY
CYANO
CZARS

C••A•
CABAL
CACAO
CAMAY
CANAD
CANAL
CARAT
CASAS
CAVAE
CEDAR
CERAM
CERAT
CESAR
CFLAT
CHEAP
CHEAT
CHIAS
CIGAR
CLEAN
CLEAR
CLEAT
CLOAK
CODAS
COHAN
COLAS
COMAE
COMAS
CONAN
COPAL
COPAN
COPAY
CORAL
COXAE
COXAL
CREAK
CREAM
CROAK
CROAT
CUBAN
CUGAT
CUMAE
CUNAS
CYCAD
CYMAE
CYMAS

C•••A
CALLA
CANEA
CANNA
CAPRA
CARIA
CARLA
CARTA
CASCA
CAUSA
CEIBA
CELIA
CELLA
CERIA
CESTA
CEUTA
CHAKA
CHEKA
CHELA
CHIBA
CHINA
CHITA
CHULA
CIERA
CILIA
CILLA
CIRCA
CLARA
CNIDA
COBIA
COBRA
COCOA
COMMA
CONGA
COOSA
COPRA
COREA
CORIA
COSTA
COTTA
CRURA
CULPA
CUPPA
CURIA

•CA••
ACADS
ACARI
ICAHN
OCALA
SCABS
SCADS
SCALA
SCALD
SCALE
SCALP
SCALY
SCAMP
SCAMS
SCAND
SCANS
SCANT
SCAPA
SCAPE
SCARE
SCARF
SCARP
SCARS
SCARY
SCATS
SCAUP

•C•A•
ACTAS
DCCAB
ECLAT
ICEAX
MCKAY
MCRAE
OCCAM
OCCAS
OCEAN
OCTAD
OCTAL
SCHAV
SCRAG
SCRAM
SCRAP
UCLAN

•C••A
ACCRA
ACOMA
ACURA
ICOSA
OCALA
OCHOA
OCREA
SCALA
SCAPA
SCENA
SCHWA
SCUBA
SCUTA

••CA•
ALCAN
ASCAP
CACAO
CYCAD
DCCAB
DECAF
DECAL
DECAY
DUCAL
DUCAT
FOCAL
INCAN
INCAS
LOCAL
LUCAN
LUCAS
MACAO
MACAW
MICAH
MICAS
NICAD
NOCAL
OCCAM
OCCAS
ORCAS
OSCAN
OSCAR
PACAS
PECAN
PICAS
RECAP
TICAL
UNCAP
UNCAS
VICAR
VOCAL
YMCAS
YWCAS

••C•A
ACCRA
AECIA
ALCOA
COCOA
DACCA
DACHA
DACIA
DECCA
DICTA
FACIA
LICIA
LUCCA
LUCIA
LYCRA
MECCA
MICRA
MOCHA
NUCHA
SACHA
SACRA
SUCKA
USCGA
VACUA
WICCA
YUCCA

•••CA
ABACA
ARECA
ARICA
ASPCA
BARCA
BROCA
CASCA
CIRCA
DACCA
DECCA
ERICA
FINCA
LEICA
LORCA
LUCCA
MECCA
MUSCA
PARCA
PLICA
PONCA
SPICA
THECA
TOSCA
UTICA
WICCA
YUCCA

CB•••
CBERS
CBSTV

C•B••
CABAL
CABBY
CABER
CABIN
CABLE
CABOT
COBIA
COBOL
COBRA
CUBAN
CUBBY
CUBEB
CUBED
CUBES
CUBIC
CUBIT
CYBER

C••B•
CABBY
CANBY
CARBO
CARBS
CEIBA
CHIBA
CHUBS
CLUBS
COLBY
COMBE
COMBO
COMBS
CORBY
COSBY
CRABS
CRIBS
CUBBY
CURBS

C•••B
CALEB
CARIB
CAROB
CELEB
CLIMB
CRUMB
CUBEB

•CB••
ICBMS

•C•B•
SCABS
SCUBA

•C••B
ACERB
DCCAB
MCJOB
SCRUB

••C•B
DCCAB
JACOB

CC•••
CCCII
CCCIV
CCCIX
CCCLI
CCCLV
CCCLX
CCCVI
CCCXC
CCCXI
CCCXL
CCCXV
CCCXX
CCIII
CCLEF
CCLII
CCLIV
CCLIX
CCLVI
CCLXI
CCLXV
CCLXX
CCVII
CCXCI
CCXCV
CCXII
CCXIV
CCXIX
CCXLI
CCXLV
CCXVI
CCXXI
CCXXV
CCXXX

C•C••
CACAO
CACHE
CACTI
CCCII
CCCIV
CCCIX
CCCLI
CCCLV
CCCLX
CCCVI
CCCXC
CCCXI
CCCXL
CCCXV
CCCXX
CECHY
CECIL
COCKS
COCKY
COCOA
COCOS
CXCII
CXCIV
CXCIX
CXCVI
CYCAD
CYCLE
CYCLO

C••C•
CALCI
CASCA
CASCO
CATCH
CAYCE
CCXCI
CCXCV
CDXCI
CDXCV
CENCI
CHACO
CHECK
CHICK
CHICO
CHOCK
CHUCK
CINCH
CINCO
CIRCA
CIRCE
CIRCS
CISCO
CLACK
CLICK
CLOCK
CLUCK
CMXCI
CMXCV
COACH
COACT
CONCH
COUCH
CRACK
CRACY
CRECY
CRICK
CROCE
CROCI
CROCK
CROCS
CULCH
CURCI
CUZCO
CZECH

C•••C
CCCXC
CIVIC
COMIC
CONIC
COSEC
CRESC
CUBIC
CYNIC

•CC••
ACCEL
ACCRA
ACCTS
CCCII
CCCIV
CCCIX
CCCLI
CCCLV
CCCLX
CCCVI
CCCXC
CCCXI
CCCXL
CCCXV
CCCXX
DCCAB
DCCCI
DCCCL
DCCCV
DCCCX
DCCII
DCCIV
DCCIX
DCCLI
DCCLV
DCCLX
DCCVI
DCCXC
DCCXI
DCCXL
DCCXV
DCCXX
MCCCI
MCCCL
MCCCV
MCCCX
MCCII
MCCIV
MCCIX
MCCLI
MCCLV
MCCLX
MCCOO
MCCOY
MCCVI
MCCXC
MCCXI
MCCXL
MCCXV
MCCXX
OCCAM
OCCAS
OCCUR

•C•C•
CCXCI
CCXCV
DCCCI
DCCCL
DCCCV
DCCCX
DCXCI
DCXCV
MCCCI
MCCCL
MCCCV
MCCCX
MCXCI
MCXCV

•C••C
CCCXC
DCCXC
MCCXC
MCDXC
MCMXC

••CC•
BOCCE
BOCCI
DACCA
DCCCI
DCCCL
DCCCV
DCCCX
DECCA
GUCCI
LUCCA
LUCCI
MCCCI
MCCCL
MCCCV
MCCCX
MDCCC
MDCCI
MDCCL
MDCCV
MDCCX
MECCA
MMCCC
MMCCI
MMCCL
MMCCV
MMCCX
PUCCI
RECCE
RICCI
ROCCO
SACCO
SECCO
WICCA
YECCH
YUCCA

••C•C
CCCXC
DCCXC
ENCYC
MCCXC
MDCCC
MDCXC
MMCCC
MMCXC

•••CC
MDCCC
MMCCC
MMDCC
MMMCC

CD•••
CDIII
CDLII
CDLIV
CDLIX
CDLVI
CDLXI
CDLXV
CDLXX
CDROM
CDVII
CDXCI
CDXCV
CDXII
CDXIV
CDXIX
CDXLI
CDXLV
CDXVI
CDXXI
CDXXV
CDXXX

C•D••
CADDO
CADDY
CADET
CADGE
CADIS
CADIZ
CADRE
CEDAR
CEDED
CEDES
CEDIS
CIDER
CMDRS
CODAS
CODED
CODER
CODES
CODEX
CUDDY
CYDER

C••D•
CADDO
CADDY
CANDO
CANDW
CANDY
CARDI
CARDS
CHIDE
CINDY
CLODS
CLYDE
CNIDA
COEDS
COLDS
CONDE
CONDO
CORDS
CREDO
CRUDE
CUDDY
CURDS
CURDY
CYNDI

C•••D
CAGED
CAKED
CANAD
CANED
CANID
CAPED
CARED
CASED
CAVED
CAWED
CEDED
CERED
CHARD
CHAUD
CHILD
CHORD
CITED
CLOUD
CLUED
CLWYD
CODED
COKED
CONTD
COOED
COPED
CORED
COULD
COWED
COXED
CREED
CRIED
CROWD
CUBED
CUPID
CURED
CYCAD

•CD••
MCDII
MCDIV
MCDIX
MCDLI
MCDLV
MCDLX
MCDVI
MCDXC
MCDXI
MCDXL
MCDXV
MCDXX

•C•D•
ACADS
ACIDS
ACIDY
SCADS
SCUDI
SCUDO
SCUDS

•C••D
ACHED
ACRED
ACRID
ACTED
OCTAD
SCALD
SCAND
SCEND
SCHED
SCOLD
SCROD

••CD•
MMCDI
MMCDL
MMCDV
MMCDX

••C•D
ARCED
CYCAD
DICED
ELCID
FACED
LACED
LUCID
MACED
NICAD
PACED
RACED
RICED

•••CD
MMMCD
SPECD

CE•••
CEASE
CECHY
CECIL
CEDAR
CEDED
CEDES
CEDIS
CEIBA
CEILS
CELEB
CELIA
CELIE
CELLA
CELLI
CELLO
CELLS
CELTS
CENCI
CENSE
CENTI
CENTO
CENTS
CEORL
CEPES
CERAM
CERAT
CERED
CERES
CERIA
CEROS
CERRO
CERTS
CESAR
CESTA
CESTI
CETUS
CEUTA

C•E••
CAELO
CBERS
CHEAP
CHEAT
CHECK
CHEEK
CHEEP
CHEER
CHEFS
CHEJU
CHEKA
CHELA
CHERE
CHERI
CHERT
CHESS
CHEST
CHETH
CHEVY
CHEWS
CHEWY
CIERA
CLEAN
CLEAR
CLEAT
CLEEK
CLEFS
CLEFT
CLEON
CLERK
CLEWS
COEDS
COEUR
CREAK
CREAM
CRECY
CREDO
CREED
CREEK
CREEL
CREEP
CREES
CREME
CREON
CREPE
CREPT
CRESC
CRESS
CREST
CRETE
CREWS
CUEIN
CZECH

C••E•
CABER
CADET
CAFES
CAGED
CAGER
CAGES
CAGEY
CAKED
CAKES
CAKEY
CALEB
CAMEL
CAMEO
CANEA
CANED
CANEM
CANER
CANES
CAPED
CAPEK
CAPER
CAPES
CAPET
CARED
CARER
CARES
CARET
CAREW
CAREY
CASED
CASES
CASEY
CATER
CATES
CAVED
CAVER
CAVES
CAWED
CCLEF
CEDED
CEDES
CELEB
CEPES
CERED
CERES
CHEEK
CHEEP
CHEER
CHIEF
CHIEN
CIDER
CINES
CIRES
CITED
CITER
CITES
CIVET
CLEEK
CLUED
CLUES
CODED
CODER
CODES
CODEX
COHEN
COKED
COKES
COLES
COLET
COMER
COMES
COMET
COMEX
CONES
CONEY
COOED
COOEE
COOER
COPED
COPES
COREA
CORED
CORER
CORES
COREY
COSEC
COTES
COVEN
COVER
COVES
COVET
COVEY
COWED
COWER
COWES
COXED
COXES
COXEY
COYER
COZEN
COZES
CREED
CREEK
CREEL
CREEP
CREES
CRIED
CRIER
CRIES
CRUEL
CRUET
CRYER
CUBEB
CUBED
CUBES
CUKES
CULET
CULEX
CUNEO
CUPEL
CURED
CURER
CURES
CUTER
CUTEX
CUTEY
CUVEE
CYBER
CYDER
CYMES

C•••E
CABLE
CACHE
CADGE
CADRE
CAFFE
CAINE
CALPE
CALVE
CANOE
CARLE
CARNE
CARPE
CARRE
CARTE
CARVE
CASTE
CAUSE
CAVAE
CAYCE
CEASE
CELIE
CENSE
CHAFE
CHASE
CHERE
CHIDE
CHILE
CHIME
CHINE
CHIVE
CHLOE
CHOKE
CHORE
CHOSE
CHUTE
CIRCE
CLARE
CLAVE
CLIME
CLINE
CLIVE
CLONE
CLOSE
CLOVE
CLYDE
CNOTE
COMAE
COMBE
COMME
COMTE
CONDE
CONGE
CONTE
COOEE
COOKE
COPSE
COUPE
COXAE
CRAKE
CRANE
CRAPE
CRATE
CRAVE
CRAZE
CREME
CREPE
CRETE
CRIME
CROCE
CRONE
CROZE
CRUDE
CRUSE
CUMAE
CURIE
CURSE
CURVE
CUTIE
CUVEE
CYCLE
CYMAE

•CE••
ACERB
ACERS
ACETO
BCELL
ICEAX
ICEIN
ICENI
ICERS
ICEUP
OCEAN
SCENA
SCEND
SCENE
SCENT

•C•E•
ACCEL
ACHED
ACHES

ACMES
ACRED
ACRES
ACTED
ACTER
CCLEF
FCLEF
GCLEF
ICIER
ICKES
MCGEE
OCHER
OCREA
OCTET
SCHED
SCREE
SCREW
TACET
ULCER
VICES

•C••E

ACUTE
ECOLE
MCGEE
MCRAE
MCVIE
OCHRE
SCALE
SCAPE
SCARE
SCENE
SCONE
SCOPE
SCORE
SCREE
SCUTE

••C•E

BECHE
BOCCE
CACHE
CYCLE
DACHE
EMCEE
FACIE
FICHE
HECHE
LOCKE
LUCIE
LUCRE
LYCEE
MACHE
MACLE
NACRE
NICHE
ONCLE
ONCUE
RECCE
RICHE
ROCHE
RUCHE
SACRE
SOCLE
SUCRE
SYCEE
TYCHE
UNCLE

••CE•

ACCEL
ARCED
DACES
DECEM
DICED
DICER
DICES
DICEY
DUCES
EMCEE
EXCEL
FACED
FACER
FACES
FACET
FICES
HACEK
JACET
LACED
LACER
LACES
LACEY
LICET
LYCEE
MACED
MACES
NICER
PACED
PACER
PACES
RACED
RACER
RACES
RICED
RICER
RICES
SYCEE
SYCES

•••CE

ALICE
ALYCE
AMICE
APACE
BOCCE
BONCE
BRACE
BRICE
BRUCE
BRYCE
CAYCE
CIRCE
CROCE
DANCE
DEICE
DEUCE
DOLCE
DUNCE
EDUCE
FARCE
FENCE
FORCE
GLACE
GRACE
HENCE
HULCE
JOYCE
JUICE
LANCE
MERCE
MINCE
NIECE
NONCE
NOSCE
ONICE
OUNCE
PEACE
PENCE
PERCE
PIECE
PINCE
PLACE
PONCE
PRICE
PRYCE
RECCE
ROYCE
SAUCE
SINCE
SLICE
SPACE
SPICE
TRACE
TRICE
TRUCE
TWICE
VANCE
VINCE
VOICE
WINCE

CF•••

CFLAT

C•F••

CAFES
CAFFE
CUFFS

C••F•

CAFFE
CHAFE
CHAFF
CHEFS
CHUFF
CLEFS
CLEFT
CLIFF
CLIFT
COIFS
COMFY
CORFU
CRAFT
CROFT
CUFFS

C•••F

CALIF
CCLEF
CHAFF
CHIEF
CHUFF
CLIFF

•CF••

MCFLY

•C•F•

ACUFF
SCIFI
SCOFF
SCUFF

•C••F

ACUFF
CCLEF
FCLEF
GCLEF
SCARF
SCOFF
SCUFF
SCURF

••C•F

DECAF

C•G••

CAGED
CAGER
CAGES
CAGEY
CIGAR
CUGAT

C••G•

CADGE
CARGO
CHUGS
CLOGS
COIGN
CONGA
CONGE
CONGO
CORGI
COUGH
CRAGS

C•••G

CHANG
CHING
CHONG
CHUNG
CLANG
CLING
CLUNG
CRAIG
CUING

•CG••

MCGEE

•C••G

ACING
ICING
SCRAG

••CG•

USCGA

••C•G

INCOG

CH•••

CHACO
CHAFE
CHAFF
CHAIM
CHAIN
CHAIR
CHAKA
CHALK
CHAMP
CHANG
CHANT
CHAOS
CHAPS
CHARD
CHARM
CHARO
CHARS
CHART
CHARY
CHASE
CHASM
CHATS
CHAUD
CHAWS
CHAZZ
CHEAP
CHEAT
CHECK
CHEEK
CHEEP
CHEER
CHEFS
CHEJU
CHEKA
CHELA
CHERE
CHERI
CHERT
CHESS
CHEST
CHETH
CHEVY
CHEWS
CHEWY
CHIAS
CHIBA
CHICK
CHICO
CHIDE
CHIEF
CHIEN
CHILD
CHILE
CHILI
CHILL
CHILO
CHIME
CHIMP
CHINA
CHINE
CHING
CHINK
CHINO
CHINS
CHIOS
CHIPS
CHIRO
CHIRP
CHIRR
CHITA
CHITS
CHIVE
CHIVY
CHLOE
CHLOR
CHOCK
CHOIR
CHOKE
CHOKY
CHOLO
CHOMP
CHONG
CHOPS
CHORD
CHORE
CHOSE
CHOWS
CHRIS
CHROM
CHRON
CHRYS
CHUBS
CHUCK
CHUFF
CHUGS
CHULA
CHUMP
CHUMS
CHUNG
CHUNK
CHURL
CHURN
CHUTE

C•H••

COHAN
COHEN
COHOS

C••H•

CACHE
CATHY
CECHY
CUSHY

C•••H

CATCH
CHETH
CINCH
CLASH
CLOTH
COACH
CONCH
COUCH
COUGH
COUTH
CRASH
CRUSH
CULCH
CZECH

•CH••

ACHED
ACHES
ACHOO
ECHIN
ICHOR
ICHTH
OCHER
OCHOA
OCHRE
SCHAV
SCHED
SCHMO
SCHON
SCHWA
VCHIP

•C•H•

ICAHN

•C••H

ICHTH

••CH•

ARCHI
ARCHY
BACHS
BECHE
CACHE
CECHY
DACHA
DACHE
DICHO
DUCHY
FICHE
FICHU
FUCHS
HECHE
HECHT
ITCHY
KOCHI
LOCHS
MACHE
MACHO
MACHU
MACHY
MOCHA
NACHO
NACHT
NICHE
NUCHA
ORCHS
RICHE
ROCHE
RUCHE
SACHA
SACHS
SOCHI
TACHO
TACHY
TECHS
TECHY
TYCHE
TYCHO
VICHY
YACHT

••C•H

MICAH
RICOH
YECCH

•••CH

AITCH
BALCH
BATCH
BEACH
BEECH
BELCH
BENCH
BIRCH
BLOCH
BOSCH
BOTCH
BRUCH
BUNCH
BUSCH
BUTCH
CATCH
CINCH
COACH
CONCH
COUCH
CULCH
CZECH
DITCH
DUTCH
ENOCH
EPOCH
ERICH
FETCH
FILCH
FINCH
FITCH
GULCH
HATCH
HENCH
HITCH
HOOCH
HUNCH
HUTCH
ILICH
KEACH
KENCH
KETCH
KOTCH
LARCH
LATCH
LEACH
LEECH
LOACH
LUNCH
LURCH
LYNCH
MARCH
MATCH
MILCH
MITCH
MOOCH
MULCH
MUNCH
NATCH
NOTCH
ORACH
PARCH
PASCH
PATCH
PEACH
PERCH
PINCH
PITCH
POACH
PONCH
POOCH
PORCH
POUCH
PSYCH
PUNCH
RANCH
RATCH
REACH
REICH
ROACH
STICH
TEACH
TENCH
TORCH
TOUCH
URICH
VETCH
VOUCH
WATCH
WELCH
WENCH
WHICH
WINCH
WITCH
YECCH
ZILCH

CI•••

CIDER
CIERA
CIGAR
CILIA
CILLA
CINCH
CINCO
CINDY
CINES
CIRCA
CIRCE
CIRCS
CIRES
CIRRI
CIRRO
CISCO
CISSY
CITED
CITER
CITES
CIVET
CIVIC
CIVIL

C•I••

CAINE
CAIRN
CAIRO
CCIII
CDIII
CEIBA
CEILS
CHIAS
CHIBA
CHICK
CHICO
CHIDE
CHIEF
CHIEN
CHILD
CHILE
CHILI
CHILL
CHILO
CHIME
CHIMP
CHINA
CHINE
CHING
CHINK
CHINO
CHINS
CHIOS
CHIPS
CHIRO
CHIRP
CHIRR
CHITA
CHITS
CHIVE
CHIVY
CLICK
CLIFF
CLIFT
CLIII
CLIMB
CLIME
CLINE
CLING
CLINK
CLINT
CLIOS
CLIPS
CLIPT
CLIVE
CMIII
CNIDA
COIFS
COIGN
COILS
COINS
COIRS
CRIBS
CRICK
CRIED
CRIER
CRIES
CRIME
CRIMP
CRISP
CRISS
CRIST
CUING
CVIII
CXIII

C••I•

CABIN
CADIS
CADIZ
CALIF
CALIX
CAMIS
CANID
CANIS
CANIT
CARIA
CARIB
CASIO
CAVIL
CCCII
CCCIV
CCCIX
CCIII
CCLII
CCLIV
CCLIX
CCVII
CCXII
CCXIV
CCXIX
CDIII
CDLII
CDLIV
CDLIX
CDVII
CDXII
CDXIV
CDXIX
CECIL
CEDIS
CELIA
CELIE
CERIA
CHAIM
CHAIN
CHAIR
CHOIR
CHRIS
CILIA
CIVIC
CIVIL
CLAIM
CLAIR
CLIII
CLVII
CLXII
CLXIV
CLXIX
CMIII
CMLII
CMLIV
CMLIX
CMVII
CMXII
CMXIV
CMXIX
COBIA
COLIN
COMIC
COMIX
CONIC
CORIA
CRAIG
CRAIN
CROIX
CUBIC
CUBIT
CUEIN
CUMIN
CUPID
CURIA
CURIE
CURIO
CUTIE
CUTIN
CUTIS
CVIII
CXCII
CXCIV
CXCIX
CXIII
CXLII
CXLIV
CXLIX
CXVII
CXXII
CXXIV
CXXIX
CYNIC
CYRIL

C•••I

CACTI
CALCI
CALLI
CAPRI
CARDI
CARPI
CCCII
CCCLI
CCCVI
CCCXI
CCIII
CCLII
CCLVI
CCLXI
CCVII
CCXCI
CCXII
CCXLI
CCXVI
CCXXI
CDIII
CDLII
CDLVI
CDLXI
CDVII
CDXCI
CDXII
CDXLI
CDXVI
CDXXI
CELLI
CENCI
CENTI
CESTI
CHERI
CHILI
CIRRI
CLIII
CLVII
CLXII
CLXVI
CLXXI
CMIII
CMLII
CMLVI
CMLXI
CMVII
CMXCI
CMXII
CMXLI
CMXVI
CMXXI
COATI
CONTI
CORGI
CROCI
CUPRI
CURCI
CVIII
CXCII
CXCVI
CXIII
CXLII
CXLVI
CXVII
CXXII
CXXVI
CXXXI
CYNDI

•CI••

ACIDS
ACIDY
ACING
CCIII
DCIII
ICIER
ICILY
ICING
MCIII
SCIFI
SCION
XCIII

•C•I•

ACRID
ACTII
ACTIN
ACTIV
CCCII
CCCIV
CCCIX
CCIII
CCLII
CCLIV
CCLIX
CCVII
CCXII
CCXIV
CCXIX
DCCII
DCCIV
DCCIX
DCIII
DCLII
DCLIV
DCLIX
DCVII
DCXII
DCXIV
DCXIX
ECHIN
ICEIN
MCCII
MCCIV
MCCIX
MCDII
MCDIV
MCDIX
MCIII
MCLII
MCLIV
MCLIX
MCMII
MCMIV
MCMIX
MCVIE
MCVII
MCXII
MCXIV
MCXIX
SCRIM
SCRIP
VCHIP
XCIII
XCVII

•C••I

ACARI
ACTII
CCCII
CCCLI
CCCVI
CCCXI
CCIII
CCLII
CCLVI
CCLXI
CCVII
CCXCI
CCXII
CCXLI
CCXVI
CCXXI
DCCCI
DCCII
DCCLI
DCCVI
DCCXI
DCIII
DCLII
DCLVI
DCLXI
DCVII
DCXCI
DCXII
DCXLI
DCXVI
DCXXI
ECOLI
ICENI
ICOSI
MCCCI
MCCII
MCCLI
MCCVI
MCCXI
MCDII
MCDLI
MCDVI
MCDXI
MCIII
MCLII
MCLVI
MCLXI
MCMII
MCMLI
MCMVI
MCMXI
MCVII
MCXCI
MCXII
MCXLI
MCXVI
MCXXI
SCIFI
SCUDI
XCIII
XCVII

••CI•

AECIA
ASCII
CCCII
CCCIV
CCCIX
CECIL
CXCII
CXCIV
CXCIX
DACIA
DCCII
DCCIV
DCCIX
DXCII
DXCIV
DXCIX
ELCID
FACIA
FACIE
FACIT
LICIA
LICIT
LUCIA
LUCID
LUCIE
MCCII
MCCIV
MCCIX
MDCII
MDCIV
MDCIX
MMCII
MMCIV
MMCIX
MUCIN
MXCII
MXCIV
MXCIX
MYCIN
OPCIT
RECIP
SOCIO
TACIT

••C•I

ARCHI
ASCII
BOCCI
CACTI
CCCII
CCCLI
CCCVI
CCCXI
CXCII
CXCVI
DCCCI
DCCII
DCCLI
DCCVI
DCCXI
DXCII
DXCVI
GUCCI
KOCHI
LACTI
LUCCI
MCCCI
MCCII
MCCLI
MCCVI
MCCXI
MDCCI
MDCII
MDCLI
MDCVI
MDCXI
MMCCI
MMCDI
MMCII
MMCLI
MMCMI
MMCVI
MMCXI
MXCII
MXCVI
NOCTI
PUCCI
RECTI
RICCI
RICKI
SOCHI
VICKI

•••CI

ABACI
BOCCI
CALCI
CCXCI
CDXCI
CENCI
CMXCI
CROCI
CURCI
DCCCI
DCXCI
FARCI
GUCCI
LUCCI
MCCCI
MCXCI
MDCCI
MDXCI
MERCI
MMCCI
MMDCI
MMMCI
MMXCI
PESCI
PISCI
PUCCI
RICCI
SULCI
VINCI
VOICI

C•J••

CAJUN

C••J•

CHEJU

•CJ••

MCJOB

C•K••

CAKED
CAKES
CAKEY
COKED
COKES
CUKES
CUKOR

C••K•

CALKS
CARKS
CASKS
CHAKA
CHEKA
CHOKE
CHOKY
COCKS
COCKY
CONKS
COOKE
COOKS
COOKY
CORKS
CORKY
CRAKE
CUSKS

C•••K

CAPEK
CAULK
CHALK
CHECK
CHEEK
CHICK
CHINK
CHOCK
CHUCK
CHUNK
CLACK
CLANK
CLARK
CLEEK
CLERK
CLICK
CLINK
CLOAK
CLOCK
CLONK
CLUCK
CLUNK
CRACK
CRANK
CREAK
CREEK
CRICK
CROAK
CROCK
CROOK

•CK••

ICKES
MCKAY

••CK•

BACKS
BECKS
BECKY
BUCKO
BUCKS
BUCKY
COCKS
COCKY
DECKS
DICKS
DICKY
DOCKS
DUCKS
DUCKY
GECKO
HACKS
HECKS
HICKS
HOCKS
JACKS
JACKY
JOCKO
JOCKS
KICKS
KICKY
LACKS
LECKY
LICKS
LOCKE
LOCKS
LUCKS
LUCKY
MOCKS
MUCKS
MUCKY
NECKS
NICKS
NOCKS
OICKS
PACKS
PECKS
PECKY
PICKS
PICKY
PUCKS
RACKS
RICKI
RICKS
RICKY
ROCKS
ROCKY
RUCKS
SACKS
SOCKO
SOCKS
SUCKA
SUCKS
TACKS
TACKY
TICKS
TICKY
TUCKS
VICKI
VICKS
WACKO
WACKY
WICKS
YACKS
YUCKY

••C•K

HACEK

•••CK

ABACK
ALACK
ALECK
AMUCK
BLACK
BLOCK
BRECK
BRICK
BROCK
BUICK
CHECK
CHICK
CHOCK
CHUCK
CLACK
CLICK
CLOCK
CLUCK
CRACK
CRICK
CROCK
FLACK
FLECK
FLICK
FLOCK
FRICK
FROCK
GLICK
GLUCK
KNACK
KNICK
KNOCK
KYACK
MERCK
MONCK
NYACK
PLUCK
PRICK
QUACK
QUICK
SHACK
SHOCK
SHUCK
SLACK
SLICK
SMACK
SMOCK
SNACK
SNICK
SNUCK
SPECK
SPOCK
STACK
STICK
STOCK
STUCK
THICK
TRACK
TRICK
TRUCK
VNECK
WHACK
WRACK
WRECK

CL•••

CLACK
CLAIM
CLAIR
CLAMP
CLAMS
CLANG
CLANK
CLANS
CLAPS
CLARA
CLARE
CLARK
CLARO
CLARY
CLASH
CLASP
CLASS
CLAUS
CLAVE
CLAWS
CLAYS
CLEAN
CLEAR
CLEAT
CLEEK
CLEFS

CLEFT CLEON CLERK CLEWS CLICK CLIFF CLIFT CLIII CLIMB CLIME CLINE CLING CLINK CLINT CLIOS CLIPS CLIPT CLIVE CLOAK CLOCK CLODS CLOGS CLOMP CLONE CLONK CLOPS CLOSE CLOTH CLOTS CLOUD CLOUT CLOVE CLOWN CLOYS CLUBS CLUCK CLUED CLUES CLUMP CLUNG CLUNK CLUNY CLVII CLWYD CLXII CLXIV CLXIX CLXVI CLXXI CLXXV CLXXX CLYDE

C•L••

CALCI CALEB CALIF CALIX CALKS CALLA CALLI CALLS CALMS CALPE CALVE CALYX CCLEF CCLII CCLIV CCLIX CCLVI CCLXI CCLXV CCLXX CDLII CDLIV CDLIX CDLVI CDLXI CDLXV CDLXX CELEB CELIA CELIE CELLA CELLI CELLO CELLS CELTS CFLAT CHLOE CHLOR CILIA CILLA CMLII CMLIV CMLIX CMLVI CMLXI CMLXV CMLXX COLAS COLBY COLDS COLES COLET COLIN COLON COLOR COLTS COLUM CPLUS CULCH CULET CULEX CULLS CULLY CULMS CULPA CULTS CXLII CXLIV CXLIX CXLVI

C••L•

CABLE CAELO CALLA CALLI CALLS CARLA CARLE CARLO CARLY CAULK CAULS CCCLI CCCLV CCCLX CCXLI CCXLV CDXLI CDXLV CEILS CELLA CELLI CELLO CELLS CHALK CHELA CHILD CHILE CHILI CHILL CHILO CHOLO CHULA CILLA CMXLI CMXLV COALS COILS COOLS COULD COWLS COYLY CROLY CULLS CULLY CURLS CURLY CYCLE CYCLO

C•••L

CABAL CAMEL CANAL CAROL CAVIL CCCXL CECIL CEORL CHILL CHURL CIVIL COBOL COPAL CORAL COXAL CRAWL CREEL CRUEL CUMUL CUPEL CYRIL

•CL••

CCLEF CCLII CCLIV CCLIX CCLVI CCLXI CCLXV CCLXX DCLII DCLIV DCLIX DCLVI DCLXI DCLXV DCLXX ECLAT FCLEF GCLEF MCLII MCLIV MCLIX MCLVI MCLXI MCLXV MCLXX UCLAN

•C•L•

ACYLS BCELL CCCLI CCCLV CCCLX CCXLI CCXLV DCCLI DCCLV DCCLX DCXLI DCXLV ECOLE ECOLI ICILY MCCLI MCCLV MCCLX MCDLI MCDLV MCDLX MCFLY MCMLI MCMLV MCMLX MCXLI MCXLV OCALA OCULO SCALA SCALD SCALE SCALP SCALY SCOLD SCULL

•C••L

ACCEL BCELL CCCXL DCCCL DCCXL MCCCL MCCXL MCDXL MCMXL OCTAL SCOWL SCULL

••CL•

CCCLI CCCLV CCCLX CYCLE CYCLO DCCLI DCCLV DCCLX MACLE MCCLI MCCLV MCCLX MDCLI MDCLV MDCLX MMCLI MMCLV MMCLX ONCLE SOCLE UNCLE

••C•L

ACCEL CCCXL CECIL DCCCL DCCXL DECAL DUCAL EXCEL FOCAL LOCAL LTCOL MCCCL MCCXL MDCCL MDCXL MMCCL MMCDL MMCML MMCXL NICOL NOCAL PICUL TICAL VOCAL

•••CL

DCCCL MCCCL MDCCL MMCCL MMDCL MMMCL

CM•••

CMDRS CMIII CMLII CMLIV CMLIX CMLVI CMLXI CMLXV CMLXX CMVII CMXCI CMXCV CMXII CMXIV CMXIX CMXLI CMXLV CMXVI CMXXI CMXXV CMXXX

C•M••

CAMAY CAMEL CAMEO CAMIS CAMOS CAMPO CAMPS CAMPY CAMRY CAMUS COMAE COMAS COMBE COMBO COMBS COMER COMES COMET COMEX COMFY COMIC COMIX COMMA COMME COMPO COMPS COMTE COMUS CUMAE CUMIN CUMUL CYMAE CYMAS CYMES CYMRY

C••M•

CALMS CHAMP CHIME CHIMP CHOMP CHUMP CHUMS CLAMP CLAMS CLIMB CLIME CLOMP CLUMP COMMA COMME CORMS COSMO CRAMP CRAMS CREME CRIME CRIMP CRUMB CRUMP CULMS CUOMO

C•••M

CANEM CAROM CDROM CERAM CHAIM CHARM CHASM CHROM CLAIM COLUM CREAM

•CM••

ACMES MCMII MCMIV MCMIX MCMLI MCMLV MCMLX MCMVI MCMXC MCMXI MCMXL MCMXV MCMXX

•C•M•

ACOMA ICBMS SCAMP SCAMS SCHMO SCUMS

•C••M

OCCAM SCRAM SCRIM SCRUM

••CM•

MMCMI MMCML MMCMV MMCMX

••C•M

DECEM LOCUM MECUM OCCAM

CN•••

CNIDA CNOTE

C•N••

CANAD CANAL CANBY CANDO CANDW CANDY CANEA CANED CANEM CANER CANES CANID CANIS CANIT CANNA CANNY CANOE CANON CANSO CANST CANTO CANTS CANTY CENCI CENSE CENTI CENTO CENTS CINCH CINCO CINDY CINES CONAN CONCH CONDE CONDO CONES CONEY CONGA CONGE CONGO CONIC CONKS CONTD CONTE CONTI CONTR CONUS CUNAS CUNEO CYNDI CYNIC

C••N•

CAINE CANNA CANNY CARNE CARNY CHANG CHANT CHINA CHINE CHING CHINK CHINO CHINS CHONG CHUNG CHUNK CLANG CLANK CLANS CLINE CLING CLINK CLINT CLONE CLONK CLUNG CLUNK CLUNY COINS COONS CORNO CORNS CORNU CORNY COUNT CRANE CRANK CRONE CRONY CUING CYANO

C•••N

CABIN CAIRN CAJUN CANON CAPON CARON CHAIN CHIEN CHRON CHURN CLEAN CLEON CLOWN COHAN COHEN COIGN COLIN COLON CONAN COPAN COVEN COZEN CRAIN CREON CROON CROWN CUBAN CUEIN CUMIN CUTIN

•C•N•

ACING ICENI ICING ICONO ICONS SCAND SCANS SCANT SCENA SCEND SCENE SCENT SCONE

•C••N

ACORN ACTIN ACTON ECHIN ICAHN ICEIN OCEAN SCHON SCION SCORN UCLAN

••C•N

ALCAN ANCON BACON INCAN LUCAN MACON MUCIN MYCIN OSCAN PECAN RACON RECON

CO•••

COACH COACT COALS COAPT COAST COATI COATS COBIA COBOL COBRA COCKS COCKY COCOA COCOS CODAS CODED CODER CODES CODEX COEDS COEUR COHAN COHEN COHOS COIFS COIGN COILS COINS COIRS COKED COKES COLAS COLBY COLDS COLES COLET COLIN COLON COLOR COLTS COLUM COMAE COMAS COMBE COMBO COMBS COMER COMES COMET COMEX COMFY COMIC COMIX COMMA COMME COMPO COMPS COMTE COMUS CONAN CONCH CONDE CONDO CONES CONEY CONGA CONGE CONGO CONIC CONKS CONTD CONTE CONTI CONTR CONUS COOED COOEE COOER COOKE COOKS COOKY COOLS COONS COOPS COOPT COORS COOSA COOTS COPAL COPAN COPAY COPED COPES COPRA COPSE COPTS CORAL CORBY CORDS COREA CORED CORER CORES COREY CORFU CORGI CORIA CORKS CORKY CORMS CORNO CORNS CORNU CORNY COROT CORPS COSBY COSEC COSMO COSTA COSTS COTES COTTA COUCH COUGH COULD COUNT COUPE COUPS COURT COUSY COUTH COVEN COVER COVES COVET COVEY COWED COWER COWES COWLS COWRY COXAE COXAL COXED COXES COXEY COYER COYLY COYPU COZEN COZES

C•O••

CEORL CHOCK CHOIR CHOKE CHOKY CHOLO CHOMP CHONG CHOPS CHORD CHORE CHOSE CHOWS CLOAK CLOCK CLODS CLOGS CLOMP CLONE CLONK CLOPS CLOSE CLOTH CLOTS CLOUD CLOUT CLOVE CLOWN CLOYS CNOTE COOED COOEE COOER COOKE COOKS COOKY COOLS COONS COOPS COOPT COORS COOSA COOTS CROAK CROAT CROCE CROCI CROCK CROCS CROFT CROIX CROLY CRONE CRONY CROOK CROON CROPS CROSS CROUP CROWD CROWN CROWS CROZE CUOMO

C••O•

CABOT CAMOS CANOE CANON CAPON CAPOS CAROB CAROL CAROM CARON CDROM CEROS CHAOS CHIOS CHLOE CHLOR CHROM CHRON CLEON CLIOS COBOL COCOA COCOS COHOS COLON COLOR COROT CREON CROOK CROON CSPOT CUKOR

C•••O

CACAO CADDO CAELO CAIRO CAMEO CAMPO CANDO CANSO CANTO CARBO CARGO CARLO CARPO CASCO CASIO CELLO CENTO CERRO CHACO CHARO CHICO CHILO CHINO CHIRO CHOLO CINCO CIRRO CISCO CLARO COMBO COMPO CONDO CONGO CORNO COSMO CREDO CUNEO CUOMO CUPRO CURIO CUZCO CYANO CYCLO

•CO••

ACOMA ACORN ECOLE ECOLI ICONO ICONS ICOSA ICOSI SCOFF SCOLD SCONE SCOOP SCOOT SCOPE SCOPS SCOPY SCORE SCORN SCOTS SCOTT SCOUR SCOUT SCOWL SCOWS

•C•O•

ACHOO ACTON ACTOR ICHOR MCCOO MCCOY MCJOB OCHOA SCHON SCION SCOOP SCOOT SCROD

•C••O

ACETO ACHOO ICONO MCCOO OCULO SCHMO SCUDO

••CO•

ALCOA ALCOR ANCON ASCOT BACON COCOA COCOS DECOR DECOY DICOT EPCOT INCOG JACOB LOCOS LTCOL MACON MCCOO MCCOY NICOL PECOS PICOT RACON RECON RICOH TACOS

••C•O

BUCKO CACAO CYCLO DICHO FACTO GECKO HECTO JOCKO LACTO MACAO MACHO MACRO MCCOO MICRO MUCRO NACHO PICRO RECTO ROCCO SACCO SACRO SECCO SOCIO SOCKO TACHO TYCHO WACKO XACTO

•••CO

ABACO AMOCO BANCO BOSCO CASCO CHACO CHICO CINCO CISCO CUZCO DELCO DISCO DRACO GLUCO GLYCO GRECO GUACO JUNCO MARCO NARCO PASCO PHYCO PISCO ROCCO SACCO SECCO TAXCO VASCO WILCO

CP•••

CPLUS

C•P••

CAPED CAPEK CAPER CAPES CAPET CAPON CAPOS CAPRA CAPRI CAPTS CEPES COPAL COPAN COPAY COPED COPES COPRA COPSE COPTS CSPOT CUPEL CUPID CUPPA CUPRI CUPRO

C••P•

CALPE CAMPO CAMPS CAMPY CARPE CARPI CARPO CARPS CHAPS CHIPS CHOPS CLAPS CLIPS CLIPT CLOPS COAPT COMPO COMPS COOPS COOPT CORPS COUPE COUPS COYPU CRAPE CRAPS CREPE CREPT CROPS CRYPT CULPA CUPPA CUSPS

C•••P

CHAMP CHEAP CHEEP CHIMP CHIRP CHOMP CHUMP CLAMP CLASP CLOMP CLUMP CRAMP CREEP CRIMP CRISP CROUP CRUMP CUTUP

•C•P•

SCAPA SCAPE SCOPE SCOPS SCOPY SCUPS

•C••P

ACTUP ICEUP SCALP SCAMP SCARP SCAUP SCOOP SCRAP SCRIP VCHIP

••C•P

ASCAP RECAP RECIP UNCAP

•••CP

NAACP

CR•••

CRABS CRACK CRACY CRAFT CRAGS CRAIG CRAIN CRAKE CRAMP CRAMS CRANE CRANK CRAPE CRAPS CRASH CRASS CRATE CRAVE CRAWL CRAWS CRAZE CRAZY CREAK CREAM CRECY CREDO CREED CREEK CREEL CREEP CREES CREME CREON CREPE CREPT CRESC CRESS CREST CRETE CREWS CRIBS CRICK CRIED CRIER CRIES CRIME CRIMP CRISP CRISS CRIST CROAK CROAT CROCE CROCI CROCK CROCS CROFT CROIX CROLY CRONE CRONY CROOK CROON CROPS CROSS CROUP CROWD CROWN CROWS CROZE CRUDE CRUEL CRUET CRUMB CRUMP CRURA CRUSE CRUSH CRUST CRYER CRYPT

C•R••

CARAT CARBO CARBS CARDI CARDS CARED CARER CARES CARET CAREW CAREY CARGO CARIA CARIB CARKS CARLA CARLE CARLO CARLY CARNE CARNY CAROB CAROL CAROM CARON CARPE CARPI CARPO CARPS CARRE CARRY CARTA CARTE CARTS CARVE CDROM CERAM CERAT CERED CERES CERIA CEROS CERRO CERTS CHRIS

CHROM CHRON CHRYS CIRCA CIRCE CIRCS CIRES CIRRI CIRRO CORAL CORBY CORDS COREA CORED CORER CORES COREY CORFU CORGI CORIA CORKS CORKY CORMS CORNO CORNS CORNU CORNY COROT CORPS CURBS CURCI CURDS CURDY CURED CURER CURES CURIA CURIE CURIO CURLS CURLY CURRY CURSE CURST CURVE CURVY CYRIL CYRUS

C••R•

CADRE CAIRN CAIRO CAMRY CAPRA CAPRI CARRE CARRY CBERS CEORL CERRO CHARD CHARM CHARO CHARS CHART CHARY CHERE CHERI CHERT CHIRO CHIRP CHIRR CHORD CHORE CHURL CHURN CIERA CIRRI CIRRO CLARA CLARE CLARK CLARO CLARY CLERK CMDRS COBRA COIRS COORS COPRA COURT COWRY CRURA CUPRI CUPRO CURRY CYMRY CZARS

C•••R

CABER CAGER CANER CAPER CARER CATER CAVER CEDAR CESAR CHAIR CHEER CHIRR CHLOR CHOIR CIDER CIGAR CITER CLAIR CLEAR CODER COEUR COLOR COMER CONTR COOER CORER COVER COWER COYER CRIER CRYER CUKOR CURER CUTER CYBER CYDER

•CR••

ACRED ACRES ACRID ECRUS MCRAE OCREA SCRAG SCRAM SCRAP SCREE SCREW SCRIM SCRIP SCROD SCRUB SCRUM

•C•R•

ACARI ACCRA ACERB ACERS ACORN ACURA ICERS OCHRE SCARE SCARF SCARP SCARS SCARY SCORE SCORN SCURF

•C••R

ACTER ACTOR ICHOR ICIER OCCUR OCHER SCOUR

••CR•

ACCRA DECRY LUCRE LYCRA MACRO MICRA MICRO MUCRO NACRE PICRO SACRA SACRE SACRO SUCRE

••C•R

ALCOR DECOR DICER FACER INCUR LACER NICER OCCUR OSCAR PACER RACER RECUR RICER ULCER VICAR

CS•••

CSPOT

C•S••

CASAS CASCA CASCO CASED CASES CASEY CASIO CASKS CASTE CASTS CASUS CBSTV CESAR CESTA CESTI CISCO CISSY COSBY COSEC COSMO COSTA COSTS CUSHY CUSKS CUSPS

C••S•

CANSO CANST CAUSA CAUSE CEASE CENSE CHASE CHASM CHESS CHEST CHOSE CISSY CLASH CLASP CLASS CLOSE COAST COOSA COPSE COUSY CRASH CRASS CRESC CRESS CREST CRISP CRISS CRIST CROSS CRUSE CRUSH CRUST CURSE CURST

C•••S

CADIS CAFES CAGES CAKES CALKS CALLS CALMS CAMIS CAMOS CAMPS CAMUS CANES CANIS CANTS CAPES CAPOS CAPTS CARBS CARDS CARES CARKS CARPS CARTS CASAS CASES CASKS CASTS CATES CAULS CAVES CBERS CEDES CEDIS CEILS CELLS CELTS CENTS CEPES CERES CEROS CERTS CETUS CHAOS CHAPS CHARS CHATS CHAWS CHEFS CHESS CHEWS CHIAS CHINS CHIOS CHIPS CHITS CHOPS CHOWS CHRIS CHRYS CHUBS CHUGS CHUMS CINES CIRCS CIRES CITES CLAMS CLANS CLAPS CLASS CLAUS CLAWS CLAYS CLEFS CLEWS CLIOS CLIPS CLODS CLOGS CLOPS CLOTS CLOYS CLUBS CLUES CMDRS COALS COATS COCKS COCOS CODAS CODES COEDS COHOS COIFS COILS COINS COIRS COKES COLAS COLDS COLES COLTS COMAS COMBS COMES COMPS COMUS CONES CONKS CONUS COOKS COOLS COONS COOPS COORS COOTS COPES COPTS CORDS CORES CORKS CORMS CORNS CORPS COSTS COTES COUPS COVES COWES COWLS COXES COZES CPLUS CRABS CRAGS CRAMS CRAPS CRASS CRAWS CREES CRESS CREWS CRIBS CRIES CRISS CROCS CROPS CROSS CROWS CUBES CUFFS CUKES CULLS CULMS CULTS CUNAS CURBS CURDS CURES CURLS CUSKS CUSPS CUTIS CYMAS CYMES CYRUS CZARS

•C•S•

ICOSA ICOSI

•C••S

ACADS ACCTS ACERS ACHES ACIDS ACMES ACRES ACTAS ACYLS ECRUS ICBMS ICERS ICKES ICONS ICTUS OCCAS SCABS SCADS SCAMS SCANS SCARS SCATS SCOPS SCOTS SCOWS SCUDS SCUMS SCUPS SCUTS

••C•S

ACCTS ASCUS BACHS BACKS BECKS BUCKS COCKS COCOS DACES DECKS DICES DICKS DICTS DOCKS DUCES DUCKS DUCTS FACES FACTS FICES FICUS FOCUS FUCHS HACKS HECKS HICKS HOCKS HOCUS INCAS INCUS JACKS JOCKS KICKS LACES LACKS LICKS LOCHS LOCKS LOCOS LOCUS LUCAS LUCKS MACES MACYS MICAS MOCKS MUCKS NECKS NICKS NOCKS OCCAS OICKS ORCAS ORCHS ORCUS PACAS PACES PACKS PACTS PECKS PECOS PICAS PICKS PICTS POCUS PUCKS RACES RACKS RICES RICKS ROCKS RUCKS SACHS SACKS SECTS SOCKS SUCKS SYCES TACKS TACOS TECHS TICKS TUCKS UNCAS VICES VICKS WICKS YACKS YMCAS YWCAS

•••CS

AWACS BANCS BLOCS BOSCS CIRCS CROCS DISCS EPICS EXECS FISCS FLICS LAICS NARCS SPECS SYNCS WRACS ZINCS

C•T••

CATCH CATER CATES CATHY CATTY CETUS CITED CITER CITES COTES COTTA CUTER CUTEX CUTEY CUTIE CUTIN CUTIS CUTUP

C••T•

CACTI CANTO CANTS CANTY CAPTS CARTA CARTE CARTS CASTE CASTS CATTY CBSTV CELTS CENTI CENTO CENTS CERTS CESTA CESTI CEUTA CHATS CHETH CHITA CHITS CHUTE CLOTH CLOTS CNOTE COATI COATS COLTS COMTE CONTD CONTE CONTI CONTR COOTS COPTS COSTA COSTS COTTA COUTH CRATE CRETE CULTS

C•••T

CABOT CADET CANIT CANST CAPET CARAT CARET CERAT CFLAT CHANT CHART CHEAT CHERT CHEST CIVET CLEAT CLEFT CLIFT CLINT CLIPT CLOUT COACT COAPT COAST COLET COMET COOPT COROT COUNT COURT COVET CRAFT CREPT CREST CRIST CROAT CROFT CRUET CRUST CRYPT CSPOT CUBIT CUGAT CULET CURST

•CT••

ACTAS ACTED ACTER ACTII ACTIN ACTIV ACTON ACTOR ACTUP ICTUS OCTAD OCTAL OCTET

•C•T•

ACCTS ACETO ACUTE ICHTH SCATS SCOTS SCOTT SCUTA SCUTE SCUTS

•C••T

ECLAT OCTET SCANT SCENT SCOOT SCOTT SCOUT

••CT•

ABCTV ACCTS CACTI DICTA DICTS DICTU DUCTS FACTO FACTS HECTO LACTI LACTO NBCTV NOCTI PACTS PICTS RECTI RECTO SECTS XACTO

••C•T

ASCOT DICOT DUCAT EPCOT FACET FACIT HECHT JACET LICET LICIT NACHT OPCIT PICOT TACET TACIT UNCUT YACHT

•••CT

BRACT COACT EDICT EDUCT EJECT ELECT ENACT EPACT ERECT ERUCT EVICT EXACT MULCT REACT TINCT TRACT

CU•••

CUBAN CUBBY CUBEB CUBED CUBES CUBIC CUBIT CUDDY CUEIN CUFFS CUGAT CUING CUKES CUKOR CULCH CULET CULEX CULLS CULLY CULMS CULPA CULTS CUMAE CUMIN CUMUL CUNAS CUNEO CUOMO CUPEL CUPID CUPPA CUPRI CUPRO CURBS CURCI CURDS CURDY CURED CURER CURES CURIA CURIE CURIO CURLS CURLY CURRY CURSE CURST CURVE CURVY CUSHY CUSKS CUSPS CUTER CUTEX CUTEY CUTIE CUTIN CUTIS CUTUP CUVEE CUZCO

C•U••

CAULK CAULS CAUSA CAUSE CEUTA CHUBS CHUCK CHUFF CHUGS CHULA CHUMP CHUMS CHUNG CHUNK CHURL CHURN CHUTE CLUBS CLUCK CLUED CLUES CLUMP CLUNG CLUNK CLUNY COUCH COUGH COULD COUNT COUPE COUPS COURT COUSY COUTH CRUDE CRUEL CRUET CRUMB CRUMP CRURA CRUSE CRUSH CRUST

C••U•

CAJUN CAMUS CASUS CETUS CHAUD CLAUS CLOUD CLOUT COEUR COLUM COMUS CONUS CPLUS CROUP CUMUL CUTUP CYRUS

C•••U

CHEJU CORFU CORNU COYPU

•CU••

ACUFF ACURA ACUTE OCULO SCUBA SCUDI SCUDO SCUDS SCUFF SCULL SCUMS SCUPS SCURF SCUTA SCUTE SCUTS SCUZZ

•C•U•

ACTUP ECRUS ICEUP ICTUS OCCUR SCAUP SCOUR SCOUT SCRUB SCRUM

••CU•

ASCUS FICUS FOCUS HOCUS INCUR INCUS LOCUM LOCUS MECUM OCCUR ONCUE ORCUS PICUL POCUS RECUR UNCUT VACUA

••C•U

DICTU FICHU MACHU

CV•••

CVIII

C•V••

CAVAE CAVED CAVER CAVES CAVIL CCVII CDVII CIVET CIVIC CIVIL CLVII CMVII COVEN COVER COVES COVET COVEY CUVEE CXVII

C••V•

CALVE CARVE CCCVI CCLVI CCXVI CDLVI CDXVI CHEVY CHIVE CHIVY CLAVE CLIVE CLOVE CLXVI CMLVI CMXVI CRAVE CURVE CURVY CXCVI CXLVI CXXVI

C•••V

CBSTV CCCIV CCCLV CCCXV CCLIV CCLXV CCXCV CCXIV CCXLV CCXXV CDLIV CDLXV CDXCV CDXIV CDXLV CDXXV CLXIV CLXXV CMLIV CMLXV CMXCV CMXIV CMXLV CMXXV CXCIV CXLIV CXXIV CXXXV

•CV••

CCVII DCVII MCVIE MCVII XCVII

•C•V•

CCCVI CCLVI CCXVI DCCVI DCLVI DCXVI MCCVI MCDVI MCLVI MCMVI MCXVI

•C••V

ACTIV CCCIV CCCLV CCCXV CCLIV CCLXV CCXCV CCXIV CCXLV CCXXV DCCCV DCCIV DCCLV DCCXV DCLIV DCLXV DCXCV DCXIV DCXLV DCXXV MCCCV MCCIV MCCLV MCCXV MCDIV MCDLV MCDXV MCLIV MCLXV MCMIV MCMLV MCMXV MCXCV MCXIV MCXLV MCXXV SCHAV

••CV•

CCCVI CXCVI DCCVI DXCVI MCCVI MDCVI MMCVI MXCVI

••C•V

ABCTV CCCIV CCCLV CCCXV CXCIV DCCCV DCCIV DCCLV DCCXV DXCIV MCCCV MCCIV MCCLV MCCXV MDCCV MDCIV MDCLV MDCXV MMCCV MMCDV MMCIV MMCLV MMCMV MMCXV MXCIV NBCTV

•••CV

CCXCV CDXCV CMXCV DCCCV DCXCV MCCCV MCXCV MDCCV MDXCV MMCCV MMDCV MMMCV MMXCV

C•W••

CAWED CLWYD COWED COWER COWES COWLS COWRY

C••W•

CHAWS CHEWS CHEWY CHOWS CLAWS CLEWS CLOWN CRAWL CRAWS CREWS CROWD CROWN CROWS

C•••W

CANDW CAREW

•C•W•

SCHWA SCOWL SCOWS

•C••W

SCREW

••C•W

MACAW

CX•••

CXCII CXCIV CXCIX CXCVI CXIII CXLII CXLIV CXLIX CXLVI CXVII CXXII CXXIV CXXIX CXXVI CXXXI CXXXV

C•X••

CCXCI CCXCV CCXII CCXIV CCXIX CCXLI CCXLV CCXVI CCXXI CCXXV CCXXX CDXCI CDXCV CDXII CDXIV CDXIX CDXLI CDXLV CDXVI CDXXI CDXXV CDXXX CLXII CLXIV CLXIX CLXVI CLXXI CLXXV CLXXX CMXCI CMXCV CMXII CMXIV CMXIX CMXLI CMXLV CMXVI CMXXI CMXXV CMXXX COXAE COXAL COXED COXES COXEY CXXII CXXIV CXXIX CXXVI CXXXI CXXXV

C••X•

CCCXC CCCXI CCCXL CCCXV CCCXX CCLXI CCLXV CCLXX CCXXI CCXXV CCXXX CDLXI CDLXV CDLXX CDXXI CDXXV CDXXX CLXXI CLXXV CLXXX CMLXI CMLXV CMLXX CMXXI CMXXV CMXXX CXXXI CXXXV

C•••X

CALIX CALYX CCCIX

CCCLX
CCCXX
CCLIX
CCLXX
CCXIX
CCXXX
CDLIX
CDLXX
CDXIX
CDXXX
CLXIX
CLXXX
CMLIX
CMLXX
CMXIX
CMXXX
CODEX
COMEX
COMIX
CROIX
CULEX
CUTEX
CXCIX
CXLIX
CXXIX

•CX••
CCXCI
CCXCV
CCXII
CCXIV
CCXIX
CCXLI
CCXLV
CCXVI
CCXXI
CCXXV
CCXXX
DCXCI
DCXCV
DCXII
DCXIV
DCXIX
DCXLI
DCXLV
DCXVI
DCXXI
DCXXV
DCXXX
MCXCI
MCXCV
MCXII
MCXIV
MCXIX
MCXLI
MCXLV
MCXVI
MCXXI
MCXXV
MCXXX

•C•X•
CCCXC
CCCXI
CCCXL
CCCXV
CCCXX
CCLXI
CCLXV
CCLXX
CCXXI
CCXXV
CCXXX
DCCXC
DCCXI
DCCXL
DCCXV
DCCXX
DCLXI
DCLXV
DCLXX
DCXXI
DCXXV
DCXXX
MCCXC
MCCXI
MCCXL
MCCXV
MCCXX
MCDXC
MCDXI
MCDXL
MCDXV
MCDXX
MCLXI
MCLXV
MCLXX
MCMXC
MCMXI
MCMXL
MCMXV
MCMXX
MCXXI
MCXXV
MCXXX

•C••X
CCCIX
CCCLX
CCCXX
CCLIX
CCLXX
CCXIX
CCXXX
DCCCX
DCCIX
DCCLX
DCCXX
DCLIX
DCLXX
DCXIX
DCXXX
ICEAX
MCCCX
MCCIX
MCCLX
MCCXX
MCDIX
MCDLX
MCDXX
MCLIX
MCLXX
MCMIX
MCMLX
MCMXX
MCXIX
MCXXX

••CX•
CCCXC
CCCXI
CCCXL
CCCXV
CCCXX
DCCXC
DCCXI
DCCXL
DCCXV
DCCXX
MCCXC
MCCXI
MCCXL
MCCXV
MCCXX
MDCXC
MDCXI
MDCXL
MDCXV
MDCXX
MMCXC
MMCXI
MMCXL
MMCXV
MMCXX

••C•X
CCCIX
CCCLX
CCCXX
CXCIX
DCCCX
DCCIX
DCCLX
DCCXX
DXCIX
MCCCX
MCCIX
MCCLX
MCCXX
MDCCX
MDCIX
MDCLX
MDCXX
MMCCX
MMCDX
MMCIX
MMCLX
MMCMX
MMCXX
MXCIX

•••CX
DCCCX
MCCCX
MDCCX
MMCCX
MMDCX
MMMCX

CY•••
CYANO
CYBER
CYCAD
CYCLE
CYCLO
CYDER
CYMAE
CYMAS
CYMES
CYMRY
CYNDI
CYNIC
CYRIL
CYRUS

C•Y••
CAYCE
CLYDE
COYER
COYLY
COYPU
CRYER
CRYPT

C••Y•
CALYX
CHRYS
CLAYS
CLOYS
CLWYD

C•••Y
CABBY
CADDY
CAGEY
CAKEY
CAMAY
CAMPY
CAMRY
CANBY
CANDY
CANNY
CANTY
CAREY
CARLY
CARNY
CARRY
CASEY
CATHY
CATTY
CECHY
CHARY
CHEVY
CHEWY
CHIVY
CHOKY
CINDY
CISSY
CLARY
CLUNY
COCKY
COLBY
COMFY
CONEY
COOKY
COPAY
CORBY
COREY
CORKY
CORNY
COSBY
COUSY
COVEY
COWRY
COXEY
COYLY
CRACY
CRAZY
CRECY
CROLY
CRONY
CUBBY
CUDDY
CULLY
CURDY
CURLY
CURRY
CURVY
CUSHY
CUTEY
CYMRY

•CY••
ACYLS

•C••Y
ACIDY
ICILY
MCCOY
MCFLY
MCKAY
SCALY
SCARY
SCOPY

••CY•
ENCYC
MACYS

••C•Y
ARCHY
BECKY
BUCKY
CECHY
COCKY
DECAY
DECOY
DECRY
DICEY
DICKY
DUCHY
DUCKY
ITCHY
JACKY
KICKY
LACEY
LECKY
LUCKY
MACHY
MCCOY
MUCKY
ORCZY
PECKY
PICKY
RICKY
ROCKY
TACHY
TACKY
TECHY
TICKY
VICHY
WACKY
YUCKY

•••CY
CRACY
CRECY
DANCY
DEUCY
FANCY
JUICY
MANCY
MARCY
MERCY
NANCY
ORACY
PERCY
PRICY
SAUCY
SPACY
SPICY
STACY
TRACY
ZINCY

CZ•••
CZARS
CZECH

C•Z••
COZEN
COZES
CUZCO

C••Z•
CHAZZ
CRAZE
CRAZY
CROZE

C•••Z
CADIZ
CHAZZ

•C•Z•
SCUZZ

•C••Z
SCUZZ

••CZ•
ORCZY

DA•••
DACCA
DACES
DACHA
DACHE
DACIA
DADDY
DADOS
DAFFS
DAFFY
DAFOE
DAGON
DAILY
DAIRY
DAISY
DAIWA
DAKAR
DALAI
DALES
DALEY
DALLY
DAMAN
DAMAR
DAMES
DAMME
DAMNS
DAMON
DAMPS
DAMUP
DANAE
DANCE
DANCY
DANDY
DANES
DANGS
DANIO
DANKE
DANNY
DANSE
DANTE
DANZA
DARBY
DARED
DARER
DARES
DARIN
DARIO
DARKS
DARLA
DARNS
DARTH
DARTS
DARYA
DARYL
DASHI
DATED
DATER
DATES
DATUM
DAUBS
DAUNT
DAVAO
DAVID
DAVIE
DAVIS
DAVIT
DAVOS
DAVYS
DAWES
DAWNS
DAYAK
DAYAN
DAYNE
DAZED
DAZES

D•A••
DEALS
DEALT
DEANE
DEANS
DEARS
DEARY
DHABI
DHAKA
DHALS
DIALS
DIANA
DIANE
DIARY
DIAZO
DMARK
DNASE
DRABS
DRACO
DRAFT
DRAGS
DRAIL
DRAIN
DRAKE
DRAMA
DRAMS
DRANG
DRANK
DRANO
DRAPE
DRATS
DRAVA
DRAWL
DRAWN
DRAWS
DRAYS
DUADS
DUANE
DWARF
DYADS

D••A•
DAKAR
DALAI
DAMAN
DAMAR
DANAE
DAVAO
DAYAK
DAYAN
DCCAB
DEBAR
DECAF
DECAL
DECAY
DEFAT
DEGAS
DELAY
DERAT
DETAT
DEWAN
DEWAR
DFLAT
DINAH
DINAR
DIRAC
DITAT
DIVAN
DIVAS
DONAS
DONAT
DONAU
DORAG
DORAL
DORAN
DOTAL
DOUAI
DOUAY
DREAD
DREAM
DREAR
DRLAO
DRYAD
DUBAI
DUCAL
DUCAT
DUFAY
DUGAN
DUKAS
DUMAS
DURAN
DYLAN

D•••A
DACCA
DACHA
DACIA
DAIWA
DANZA
DARLA
DARYA
DEBRA
DECCA
DELLA
DELTA
DERMA
DESNA
DHAKA
DIANA
DICTA
DITKA
DOBLA
DOBRA
DOGMA
DOLMA
DONNA
DORSA
DRAMA
DRAVA
DRINA
DURRA
DVINA

•DA••
ADAGE
ADAIR
ADAMA
ADAMS
ADANA
ADANO
ADAPT
EDAMS
IDAHO
UDALL

•D•A•
ADDAX
ADLAI
ADMAN
ADVAL
EDDAS
EDGAR
IDEAL
IDEAS
IDTAG

•D••A
ADAMA
ADANA
ADELA
ADUWA
ADYTA
EDEMA
EDINA
NDOLA

••DA•
ADDAX
AIDAN
ALDAN
AODAI
CEDAR
CODAS
EDDAS
HADAR
HADAT
HODAD
JUDAH
JUDAS
KADAR
KODAK
MADAM
MEDAL
MIDAS
MODAL
NODAL
PEDAL
RADAR
REDAN
RODAN
SADAT
SEDAN
SODAS
SUDAN
TIDAL
TODAY
VEDAS
VEDAY
VIDAL
VJDAY

••D•A
AUDRA
HEDDA
HYDRA
INDIA
INDRA
JIDDA
JUDEA
LYDIA
MEDEA
MEDIA
MUDRA
NADIA
NADJA
PADUA
PODIA
SIDEA
SIDRA
SUDRA
VEDDA
VODKA

•••DA
ALIDA
BANDA
BREDA
CNIDA
FONDA
FREDA
FULDA
GARDA
GILDA
GOLDA
GOUDA
HAIDA
HEDDA
HILDA
HONDA
JIDDA
KINDA
KORDA
LINDA
LYNDA
MAGDA
MAZDA
OUIDA
PANDA
QANDA
RHODA
SKODA
SUNDA
THEDA
VEDDA
VENDA
WAJDA
WANDA
ZELDA
ZENDA

D•B••
DEBAR
DEBBY
DEBIT
DEBRA
DEBTS
DEBUG
DEBUT
DOBBY
DOBIE
DOBLA
DOBLE
DOBRA
DOBRO
DUBAI
DUBIN
DUBOS

D••B•
DARBY
DAUBS
DEBBY
DERBY
DHABI
DIDBY
DIGBY
DOBBY
DOLBY
DOUBT
DRABS
DRIBS
DRUBS
DUMBO
DUMBS

D•••B
DCCAB
DEMOB
DENEB
DWEEB

•D•B•
ADOBE

•D••B
ADLIB

••DB•
DIDBY

••D•B
REDUB
SIDEB

•••DB
BANDB
RANDB

DC•••
DCCAB
DCCCI
DCCCL
DCCCV
DCCCX
DCCII
DCCIV
DCCIX
DCCLI
DCCLV
DCCLX
DCCVI
DCCXC
DCCXI
DCCXL
DCCXV
DCCXX
DCIII
DCLII
DCLIV
DCLIX
DCLVI
DCLXI
DCLXV
DCLXX
DCVII
DCXCI
DCXCV
DCXII
DCXIV
DCXIX
DCXLI
DCXLV
DCXVI
DCXXI
DCXXV
DCXXX

D•C••
DACCA
DACES
DACHA
DACHE
DACIA
DCCAB
DCCCI
DCCCL
DCCCV
DCCCX
DCCII
DCCIV
DCCIX
DCCLI
DCCLV
DCCLX
DCCVI
DCCXC
DCCXI
DCCXL
DCCXV
DCCXX
DECAF
DECAL
DECAY
DECCA
DECEM
DECKS
DECOR
DECOY
DECRY
DICED
DICER
DICES
DICEY
DICHO
DICKS
DICKY
DICOT
DICTA
DICTS
DICTU
DOCKS
DUCAL
DUCAT
DUCES
DUCHY
DUCKS
DUCKY
DUCTS
DXCII
DXCIV
DXCIX
DXCVI

D••C•
DACCA
DANCE
DANCY
DCCCI
DCCCL
DCCCV
DCCCX
DCXCI
DCXCV
DECCA
DEICE
DELCO
DEUCE
DEUCY
DISCO
DISCS
DITCH
DOLCE
DRACO
DUNCE
DUTCH

D•••C
DCCXC
DIRAC
DORIC
DUROC

•DC••
MDCCC
MDCCI
MDCCL
MDCCV
MDCCX
MDCII
MDCIV
MDCIX
MDCLI
MDCLV
MDCLX
MDCVI
MDCXC
MDCXI
MDCXL
MDCXV
MDCXX

•D•C•
CDXCI
CDXCV
EDICT
EDUCE
EDUCT
MDCCC
MDCCI
MDCCL
MDCCV
MDCCX
MDXCI
MDXCV

•D••C
ADHOC
ADLOC
EDDIC
MDCCC
MDCXC

••DC•
MMDCC
MMDCI
MMDCL
MMDCV
MMDCX

••D•C
ASDIC
EDDIC
INDIC
IODIC
LUDIC
MCDXC
MEDIC
MEDOC
MMDCC
MMDXC
MODOC
VEDIC

•••DC
HARDC
MMMDC

D•D••
DADDY
DADOS
DIDBY
DIDIN
DIDNT
DIDOS
DIDST
DIDUP
DODGE
DODGY
DODOS
DRDRE
DUDDY
DUDES

D••D•
DADDY
DANDY
DEEDS
DENDR
DINDY
DIODE
DONDI
DOODY
DOWDY
DREDD
DUADS
DUDDY
DYADS

D•••D
DARED
DATED
DAVID
DAZED
DEKED
DELED
DEWED
DICED
DIKED
DIMED
DINED
DIVED
DOLED
DOMED
DOPED
DOSED
DOTED
DOZED
DREAD
DREDD
DRIED
DROID
DROOD
DRUID
DRYAD
DUKED
DUPED
DYFED

•DD••
ADDAX
ADDED
ADDER
ADDIE
ADDIN
ADDIS
ADDLE
ADDNL
ADDON
ADDTO
ADDUP
EDDAS
EDDIC
EDDIE
ODDER
ODDLY
UDDER

•D••D
ADDED
EDGED
IDLED

••DD•
BADDY
BIDDY
BUDDY
CADDO
CADDY
CUDDY
DADDY
DUDDY
FUDDY
GIDDY
HEDDA
JIDDA
KIDDO
KIDDY
LIDDY
MIDDY
MUDDY
NEDDY
NODDY
PADDY
REDDY
RODDY
RUDDS
RUDDY
SODDY
SUDDS
TEDDY
TODDY
VEDDA
WADDY

••D•D
ADDED
AIDED
BIDED
BODED
CEDED
CODED
ENDED
FADED
HODAD
JADED
LADED
REDED
REDID
SIDED
TIDED
UNDID
WADED

•••DD
DREDD
RANDD

DE•••
DEALS
DEALT
DEANE
DEANS
DEARS
DEARY
DEBAR
DEBBY
DEBIT
DEBRA
DEBTS
DEBUG
DEBUT
DECAF
DECAL
DECAY
DECCA
DECEM
DECKS
DECOR
DECOY
DECRY
DEEDS
DEEMS
DEEPS
DEERE
DEERS
DEFAT
DEFER
DEFOE
DEFOG
DEGAS
DEICE
DEIFY
DEIGN
DEILS
DEION
DEISM
DEIST
DEITY
DEKED
DEKES
DEKKO
DELAY
DELCO
DELED
DELES
DELFT
DELHI
DELIS
DELLA
DELLS
DELON
DELOS
DELTA
DELTS
DELVE
DEMES
DEMIT
DEMME
DEMOB
DEMON
DEMOS
DEMUR
DENDR
DENEB
DENES
DENIM
DENIS
DENNY
DENOM
DENSE
DENTE
DENTI
DENTS
DENYS
DEOXY
DEPEW
DEPOT
DEPTH
DEPTS
DERAT
DERBY
DEREK
DERIV
DERMA
DERMO
DERRY
DERSU
DESKS
DESNA
DESTE
DETAT
DETER
DETOO
DETRE
DEUCE
DEUCY
DEUTO
DEVIL
DEVON
DEVRY
DEWAN
DEWAR
DEWED
DEWEY
DEXTR

D•E••
DEEDS
DEEMS
DEEPS
DEERE
DEERS
DIEGO
DIEMS
DIENE
DIETS
DOERS
DOEST
DOETH
DREAD
DREAM
DREAR
DREDD
DREGS
DRESS
DUELS
DUETO
DUETS
DWEEB
DWELL
DWELT
DYERS

D••E•
DACES
DALES
DALEY
DAMES
DANES
DARED
DARER
DARES
DATED
DATER
DATES
DAWES
DAZED
DAZES
DECEM
DEFER
DEKED
DEKES
DELED
DELES
DEMES
DENEB
DENES
DEPEW
DEREK
DETER
DEWED
DEWEY
DICED
DICER
DICES
DICEY
DIKED
DIKES
DIMED
DIMES
DINED
DINER
DINES
DIRER
DIVED
DIVER
DIVES
DIYER
DIZEN
DOGES
DOGEY
DOLED
DOLES
DOMED
DOMES
DONEE
DONEN
DOPED
DOPES
DOPEY
DOREN
DOSED
DOSER
DOSES
DOTED
DOTER
DOTES
DOVER
DOVES
DOVEY
DOWEL
DOWER
DOYEN
DOZED
DOZEN
DOZER
DOZES
DRIED
DRIER
DRIES
DRYER
DUCES
DUDES
DUKED
DUKES
DUNES
DUPED
DUPES
DURER
DUVET
DUXES
DWEEB
DYFED

DYNEL
DYNES

D•••E
DACHE
DAFOE
DAMME
DANAE
DANCE
DANKE
DANSE
DANTE
DAVIE
DAYNE
DEANE
DEERE
DEFOE
DEICE
DELVE
DEMME
DENSE
DENTE
DESTE
DETRE
DEUCE
DHOLE
DHOTE
DIANE
DIENE
DINGE
DIODE
DIONE
DIRGE
DISME
DIXIE
DNASE
DOBIE
DOBLE
DODGE
DOGIE
DOLCE
DONEE
DONNE
DOONE
DOUSE
DOWSE
DOYLE
DRAKE
DRAPE
DRDRE
DRIVE
DROME
DRONE
DROVE
DRUPE
DRUSE
DRUZE
DUANE
DULSE
DUNCE
DUNNE
DUPLE
DUPRE

•DE••
ADEEM
ADELA
ADELE
ADENO
ADEPT
ADEUX
EDEMA
EDENS
IDEAL
IDEAS
IDEST
ODELL
ODETS
ODEUM

•D•E•
ADDED
ADDER
ADEEM
ADHEM
ADIEU
ADLER
ADMEN
ADREM
ADZES
EDGED
EDGER
EDGES
EDSEL
IDLED
IDLER
IDLES
ODDER
UDDER

•D••E
ADAGE
ADDIE
ADDLE
ADELE
ADIGE
ADOBE
ADORE
EDDIE
EDILE
EDUCE
IDINE
ODILE
UDINE

••DE•
ADDED
ADDER
AEDES
AIDED
AIDES
ALDEN
ALDER
ANDES
ARDEN
AUDEN
BADEN
BADER
BEDEW
BIDED
BIDEN
BIDES
BODED
BODES
CADET
CEDED
CEDES
CIDER
CODED
CODER
CODES
CODEX
CYDER
DUDES
EIDER
ELDER
EMDEN
ENDED
ENDER
FADED
FADES
FEDEX
FIDEI
FIDEL
FIDES
GODEL
GODET
GODEY
HADES
HIDER
HIDES
INDEF
INDEX
JADED
JADES
JUDEA
JUDEO
LADED
LADEN
LADER
LADES
LODEN
LODES
MEDEA
MEDES
MODEL
MODEM
MODES
NADER
NIDES
NODES
NUDER
NUDES
ODDER
OGDEN
OLDEN
OLDER
ORDER
REDED
REDES
RIDER
RIDES
RODEO
RUDER
RYDER
SEDER
SIDEA
SIDEB
SIDED
SIDER
SIDES
TIDED
TIDES
UDDER
UNDER
VADER
VIDEO
WADED
WADER
WADES
WEDEL
WIDEN
WIDER
WODEN
YODEL

••D•E
ADDIE
ADDLE
ANDIE
ANDRE
AUDIE
BADGE
BUDGE
CADGE
CADRE
DODGE
DRDRE
EDDIE
ENDUE
EYDIE
FUDGE
HEDGE
INDIE
JODIE
JUDGE
KEDGE
LADLE
LEDGE
LODGE
MADGE
MADRE
MIDGE
NIDRE
NUDGE
OLDIE
PADRE
REDYE
RIDGE
RUDGE
SADHE
SADIE
SEDGE
SIDHE
SIDLE
UNDUE
WEDGE
WODGE

•••DE
AANDE
ABIDE
ABODE
AMIDE
ANODE
ASIDE
AZIDE
BLADE
BRIDE
BSIDE
CHIDE
CLYDE
CONDE
CRUDE
DIODE
ELIDE
ELUDE
EPODE
ERODE
ETUDE
EVADE
EXUDE
FERDE
GARDE
GEODE
GLADE
GLEDE
GLIDE
GOLDE
GRADE
GUIDE
HORDE
IMIDE
IRADE
LAUDE
LYNDE
MAUDE
MEADE
MONDE
OXIDE
PRIDE
PRUDE
READE
RHODE
SANDE
SHADE
SLADE
SLIDE
SNIDE
SONDE
SPADE
SPODE
SUEDE
SWEDE
TANDE
TARDE
TEIDE
TILDE
TRADE
TSADE
VERDE
WILDE

DF•••
DFLAT

D•F••
DAFFS
DAFFY
DAFOE
DEFAT
DEFER
DEFOE
DEFOG
DOFFS
DUFAY
DUFFS
DUFFY
DYFED

D••F•
DAFFS
DAFFY
DEIFY
DELFT
DOFFS
DRAFT
DRIFT
DUFFS
DUFFY

D•••F
DECAF
DWARF

•DF••
ADFIN

•D•F•
EDIFY

•D••F
ADOLF

••D•F
INDEF
RIDOF

D•G••
DAGON
DEGAS
DIGBY
DIGIN
DIGIT
DIGUP
DOGES
DOGEY
DOGGO
DOGGY
DOGIE
DOGIT
DOGMA
DOGON
DUGAN
DUGIN
DUGUP

D••G•
DANGS
DEIGN
DIEGO
DINGE
DINGO
DINGS
DINGY
DIRGE
DODGE
DODGY
DOGGO
DOGGY
DONGS
DOUGH
DRAGS
DREGS
DRUGS

D•••G
DEBUG
DEFOG
DOING
DORAG
DRANG
DYING

•DG••
EDGAR
EDGED
EDGER
EDGES

•D•G•
ADAGE
ADIGE

•D••G
IDTAG

••DG•
BADGE
BLDGS
BUDGE
CADGE
DODGE
DODGY
FUDGE
HEDGE
HEDGY
JUDGE
KEDGE
LEDGE
LEDGY
LODGE
MADGE
MIDGE
NUDGE
PODGY
PUDGY
RIDGE
RIDGY
RUDGE
SEDGE
SEDGY
WEDGE
WEDGY
WODGE

•••DG
HARDG

DH•••
DHABI
DHAKA
DHALS
DHOLE
DHOTE
DHOTI
DHOWS

D••H•
DACHA
DACHE
DASHI
DELHI
DICHO
DISHY
DONHO
DUCHY

D•••H
DARTH
DEPTH
DINAH
DITCH
DOETH
DOLPH
DOUGH
DUTCH

•DH••
ADHEM
ADHOC

•D•H•
IDAHO

•D••H
EDITH

••DH•
SADHE
SADHU
SIDHE
YODHS

••D•H
JUDAH
WIDTH

•••DH
SANDH

DI•••
DIALS
DIANA
DIANE
DIARY
DIAZO
DICED
DICER
DICES
DICEY
DICHO
DICKS
DICKY
DICOT
DICTA
DICTS
DICTU
DIDBY
DIDIN
DIDNT
DIDOS
DIDST
DIDUP
DIEGO
DIEMS
DIENE
DIETS
DIGBY
DIGIN
DIGIT
DIGUP
DIJON
DIKED
DIKES
DILLS
DILLY
DIMED
DIMES
DIMLY
DINAH
DINAR
DINDY
DINED
DINER
DINES
DINGE
DINGO
DINGS
DINGY
DINKS
DINKY
DINTS
DINTY
DIODE
DIONE
DIPLO
DIPPY
DIRAC
DIRER
DIRGE
DIRKS
DIRTY
DISCO
DISCS
DISHY
DISKS
DISME
DISTR
DITAT
DITCH
DITKA
DITSY
DITTO
DITTY
DITZY
DIVAN
DIVAS
DIVED
DIVER
DIVES
DIVOT
DIVVY
DIXIE
DIXIT
DIXON
DIYER
DIZEN
DIZZY

D•I••
DAILY
DAIRY
DAISY
DAIWA
DCIII
DEICE
DEIFY
DEIGN
DEILS
DEION
DEISM
DEIST
DEITY
DJINN
DLIII
DOILY
DOING
DOITS
DRIBS
DRIED
DRIER
DRIES
DRIFT
DRILL
DRILY
DRINA
DRINK
DRIPS
DRIVE
DVIII
DVINA
DXIII
DYING

D••I•
DACIA
DANIO
DARIN
DARIO
DAVID
DAVIE
DAVIS
DAVIT
DCCII
DCCIV
DCCIX
DCIII
DCLII
DCLIV
DCLIX
DCVII
DCXII
DCXIV
DCXIX
DEBIT
DELIS
DEMIT
DENIM
DENIS
DERIV
DEVIL
DIDIN
DIGIN
DIGIT
DIXIE
DIXIT
DLIII
DLVII
DLXII
DLXIV
DLXIX
DOBIE
DOGIE
DOGIT
DORIC
DORIS
DRAIL
DRAIN
DROID
DROIT
DRUID
DUBIN
DUGIN
DVIII
DXCII
DXCIV
DXCIX
DXIII
DXLII
DXLIV
DXLIX
DXVII
DXXII
DXXIV
DXXIX

D•••I
DALAI
DASHI
DCCCI
DCCII
DCCLI
DCCVI
DCCXI
DCIII
DCLII
DCLVI
DCLXI
DCVII
DCXCI
DCXII
DCXLI
DCXVI
DCXXI
DELHI
DENTI
DHABI
DHOTI
DLIII
DLVII
DLXII
DLXVI
DLXXI
DONDI
DORSI
DOUAI
DUBAI
DVIII
DXCII
DXCVI
DXIII
DXLII
DXLVI
DXVII
DXXII
DXXVI
DXXXI

•DI••
ADIEU
ADIGE
ADINT
ADIOS
ADIPO
ADITS
CDIII
EDICT
EDIFY
EDILE
EDINA
EDITH
EDITS
IDINE
IDIOM
IDIOT
MDIII
ODILE
ODIST
ODIUM
UDINE

•D•I•
ADAIR
ADDIE
ADDIN
ADDIS
ADFIN
ADLIB
ADMIN
ADMIT
ADMIX
ADVIL
CDIII
CDLII
CDLIV
CDLIX
CDVII
CDXII
CDXIV
CDXIX
EDDIC
EDDIE
EDWIN
MDCII
MDCIV
MDCIX
MDIII
MDLII
MDLIV
MDLIX
MDVII
MDXII
MDXIV
MDXIX

•D••I
ADLAI
CDIII
CDLII
CDLVI
CDLXI
CDVII
CDXCI
CDXII
CDXLI
CDXVI
CDXXI
MDCCI
MDCII
MDCLI
MDCVI
MDCXI
MDIII
MDLII
MDLVI
MDLXI
MDVII
MDXCI
MDXII
MDXLI
MDXVI
MDXXI

••DI•
ADDIE
ADDIN
ADDIS
ANDIE
ASDIC
AUDIE
AUDIO
AUDIS
AUDIT
BEDIM
BIDIN
CADIS
CADIZ
CEDIS
DIDIN
EDDIC
EDDIE
EYDIE
HEDIN
INDIA
INDIC
INDIE
INDIO
INDIV
IODIC
JODIE
LEDIN
LUDIC
LYDIA
MCDII
MCDIV
MCDIX
MEDIA
MEDIC
MEDIT
MIDIS
MMDII
MMDIV
MMDIX
NADIA
NADIR
OLDIE
ONDIT
PODIA
RADII
RADIO
RADIX
REDID
RODIN
SADIE
SADIS
UNDID
VADIM
VADIS
VEDIC
WADIS
XEDIN
YADIM

••D•I
AODAI
FIDEI
HADJI
INDRI
MCDII
MCDLI
MCDVI
MCDXI
MMDCI
MMDII
MMDLI
MMDVI
MMDXI
RADII

•••DI
BONDI
CARDI
CYNDI
DONDI
EGADI
GONDI
HEIDI
HINDI
JEUDI
LANDI
LUNDI
MAHDI
MARDI
MMCDI
MMMDI
MUNDI
NALDI
PARDI
RANDI
SAUDI
SCUDI
SOLDI
TONDI
VERDI

DJ•••
DJINN

D•J••
DIJON
DOJOS

••DJ•
HADJI
NADJA

D•K••
DAKAR
DEKED
DEKES
DEKKO
DIKED
DIKES
DUKAS
DUKED
DUKES

D••K•
DANKE
DARKS
DECKS
DEKKO
DESKS
DHAKA
DICKS
DICKY
DINKS
DINKY
DIRKS
DISKS
DITKA
DOCKS
DRAKE
DUCKS
DUCKY
DUNKS
DUSKS
DUSKY

D•••K
DAYAK
DEREK
DMARK
DRANK
DRINK
DRUNK

••DK•
VODKA

••D•K
KODAK

DL•••
DLIII
DLVII
DLXII
DLXIV
DLXIX
DLXVI
DLXXI
DLXXV
DLXXX

D•L••
DALAI
DALES
DALEY
DALLY
DCLII
DCLIV
DCLIX
DCLVI
DCLXI
DCLXV
DCLXX
DELAY
DELCO
DELED
DELES
DELFT
DELHI
DELIS
DELLA
DELLS
DELON
DELOS
DELTA
DELTS
DELVE
DFLAT
DILLS
DILLY
DOLBY
DOLCE
DOLED
DOLES
DOLLS
DOLLY
DOLMA
DOLOR
DOLPH
DOLTS
DPLUS
DRLAO
DULLS
DULLY
DULSE
DXLII
DXLIV
DXLIX
DXLVI
DYLAN

D••L•
DAILY
DALLY
DARLA
DCCLI
DCCLV
DCCLX
DCXLI
DCXLV
DEALS
DEALT
DEILS
DELLA
DELLS
DHALS
DHOLE
DIALS
DILLS
DILLY
DIMLY
DIPLO
DOBLA
DOBLE
DOILY
DOLLS
DOLLY
DOYLE
DOYLY
DRILL
DRILY
DROLL
DRYLY
DUELS
DULLS
DULLY
DUPLE
DWELL
DWELT

D•••L
DARYL
DCCCL
DCCXL
DECAL
DEVIL
DORAL
DOTAL
DOWEL
DRAIL
DRAWL
DRILL
DROLL
DROOL
DUCAL
DWELL
DYNEL

•DL••
ADLAI
ADLER
ADLIB
ADLOC
CDLII
CDLIV
CDLIX
CDLVI
CDLXI
CDLXV
CDLXX
IDLED
IDLER
IDLES
MDLII
MDLIV
MDLIX
MDLVI
MDLXI
MDLXV
MDLXX

•D•L•
ADDLE
ADELA
ADELE
ADOLF
ADULT
CDXLI
CDXLV
EDILE
IDOLS
IDYLL
IDYLS
MDCLI
MDCLV
MDCLX
MDXLI
MDXLV
NDOLA
ODDLY
ODELL
ODILE
UDALL

•D••L
ADDNL
ADVAL
ADVIL
EDSEL
IDEAL
IDYLL
MDCCL
MDCXL
ODELL
UDALL

••DL•
ADDLE
BADLY
GODLY
LADLE
MADLY
MCDLI
MCDLV
MCDLX
MMDLI
MMDLV
MMDLX
ODDLY
REDLY
SADLY
SIDLE

••D•L
ABDUL
ADDNL
ALDOL
FIDEL
GODEL
MCDXL
MEDAL
MMDCL
MMDXL
MODAL
MODEL
NODAL
PEDAL
TIDAL
VIDAL
WEDEL
YODEL

•••DL
LENDL
MMCDL
MMMDL
PANDL
SANDL

DM•••
DMARK

D•M••
DAMAN
DAMAR
DAMES
DAMME
DAMNS
DAMON
DAMPS
DAMUP
DEMES
DEMIT
DEMME
DEMOB
DEMON
DEMOS
DEMUR
DIMED
DIMES
DIMLY
DOMED
DOMES
DUMAS
DUMBO
DUMBS
DUMMY
DUMPS
DUMPY

D••M•
DAMME
DEEMS
DEMME
DERMA
DERMO
DIEMS
DISME
DOGMA
DOLMA
DOOMS
DORMS
DRAMA
DRAMS
DROME
DRUMS
DUMMY
DUOMO

D•••M
DATUM
DECEM
DEISM
DENIM
DENOM
DREAM
DURUM

•DM••
ADMAN
ADMEN
ADMIN
ADMIT
ADMIX

•D•M•
ADAMA
ADAMS
EDAMS
EDEMA

•D••M
ADEEM
ADHEM
ADREM
ADSUM
CDROM
IDIOM
ODEUM
ODIUM

••D•M
BEDIM
MADAM
MODEM
SEDUM
SODOM
VADIM
YADIM

•••DM
AANDM

DN•••
DNASE

D•N••
DANAE
DANCE
DANCY
DANDY
DANES
DANGS
DANIO
DANKE
DANNY
DANSE
DANTE
DANZA
DENDR
DENEB
DENES
DENIM
DENIS
DENNY
DENOM
DENSE
DENTE
DENTI
DENTS
DENYS
DINAH
DINAR
DINDY
DINED
DINER
DINES

DINGE DINGO DINGS DINGY DINKS DINKY DINTS DINTY DONAS DONAT DONAU DONDI DONEE DONEN DONGS DONHO DONNA DONNE DONNY DONOR DONUT DUNCE DUNES DUNKS DUNNE DUNNO DYNEL DYNES

D••N•

DAMNS DANNY DARNS DAUNT DAWNS DAYNE DEANE DEANS DENNY DESNA DIANA DIANE DIDNT DIENE DIONE DJINN DOING DONNA DONNE DONNY DOONE DOWNS DOWNY DRANG DRANK DRANO DRINA DRINK DRONE DRUNK DUANE DUNNE DUNNO DURNS DVINA DYING

D•••N

DAGON DAMAN DAMON DARIN DAYAN DEIGN DEION DELON DEMON DEVON DEWAN DIDIN DIGIN DIJON DIVAN DIXON DIZEN DJINN DOGON DONEN DORAN DOREN DOYEN DOZEN DRAIN DRAWN DROWN DUBIN DUGAN DUGIN DURAN DYLAN

•D•N•

ADANA ADANO ADDNL ADENO ADINT EDENS EDINA IDINE ODONT UDINE

•D••N

ADDIN ADDON ADFIN ADMAN ADMEN ADMIN ADORN EDWIN

••DN•

ADDNL DIDNT HADNT

••D•N

ADDIN ADDON AIDAN ALDAN ALDEN ARDEN AUDEN BADEN BIDEN BIDIN BIDON DIDIN EMDEN ENDON FEDON HADON HEDIN LADEN LADON LEDIN LEDON LODEN OGDEN OLDEN RADON REDAN REDON RODAN RODIN SEDAN SIDON SUDAN WIDEN WODEN XEDIN

•••DN

HAYDN

DO•••

DOBBY DOBIE DOBLA DOBLE DOBRA DOBRO DOCKS DODGE DODGY DODOS DOERS DOEST DOETH DOFFS DOGES DOGEY DOGGO DOGGY DOGIE DOGIT DOGMA DOGON DOILY DOING DOITS DOJOS DOLBY DOLCE DOLED DOLES DOLLS DOLLY DOLMA DOLOR DOLPH DOLTS DOMED DOMES DONAS DONAT DONAU DONDI DONEE DONEN DONGS DONHO DONNA DONNE DONNY DONOR DONUT DOODY DOOMS DOONE DOORS DOOZY DOPED DOPES DOPEY DORAG DORAL DORAN DOREN DORIC DORIS DORMS DORPS DORSA DORSI DORSO DOSED DOSER DOSES DOTAL DOTED DOTER DOTES DOTTO DOTTY DOUAI DOUAY DOUBT DOUGH DOURO DOUSE DOVER DOVES DOVEY DOWDY DOWEL DOWER DOWNS DOWNY DOWRY DOWSE DOYEN DOYLE DOYLY DOZED DOZEN DOZER DOZES

D•O••

DEOXY DHOLE DHOTE DHOTI DHOWS DIODE DIONE DOODY DOOMS DOONE DOORS DOOZY DROID DROIT DROLL DROME DRONE DROOD DROOL DROOP DROPS DROSS DROVE DROWN DUOMO

D••O•

DADOS DAFOE DAGON DAMON DAVOS DECOR DECOY DEFOE DEFOG DEION DELON DELOS DEMOB DEMON DEMOS DENOM DEPOT DETOO DEVON DICOT DIDOS DIJON DIVOT DIXON DODOS DOGON DOJOS DOLOR DONOR DROOD DROOL DROOP DUBOS DUROC DUROS

D•••O

DANIO DARIO DAVAO DEKKO DELCO DERMO DETOO DEUTO DIAZO DICHO DIEGO DINGO DIPLO DISCO DITTO DOBRO DOGGO DONHO DORSO DOTTO DOURO DRACO DRANO DRLAO DUETO DUMBO DUNNO DUOMO

•DO••

ADOBE ADOLF ADOPT ADORE ADORN ADOUT IDOLS NDOLA ODONT ODORS ODOUR XDOUT

•D•O•

ADDON ADHOC ADIOS ADLOC CDROM IDIOM IDIOT

•D••O

ADANO ADDTO ADENO ADIPO IDAHO

••DO•

ADDON ALDOL ANDOR ARDOR BIDON DADOS DIDOS DODOS ENDON ENDOR ENDOW FADOS FEDON FODOR GODOT HADON KUDOS LADON LEDON LIDOS MEDOC MODOC MSDOS NODOZ ORDOS RADON REDON REDOX RIDOF SIDON SODOM SYDOW TODOS TUDOR UPDOS VIDOR WIDOW

••D•O

ADDTO ANDRO AUDIO CADDO HADTO HYDRO INDIO JUDEO KIDDO LEDTO PEDRO RADIO RODEO VIDEO

•••DO

AMADO AMIDO BANDO CADDO CANDO CONDO CREDO EJIDO FALDO FORDO FRODO GORDO GUIDO HONDO IMIDO IRIDO KENDO KIDDO LANDO LINDO MISDO MONDO OUTDO PARDO PRADO RHODO RONDO SCUDO SOLDO TONDO WALDO ZENDO

DP•••

DPLUS

D•P••

DEPEW DEPOT DEPTH DEPTS DIPLO DIPPY DOPED DOPES DOPEY DUPED DUPES DUPLE DUPRE

D••P•

DAMPS DEEPS DIPPY DOLPH DORPS DRAPE DRIPS DROPS DRUPE DUMPS DUMPY

D•••P

DAMUP DIDUP DIGUP DROOP DRYUP DUGUP

•D•P•

ADAPT ADEPT ADIPO ADOPT

•D••P

ADDUP

••D•P

ADDUP ANDUP BIDUP DIDUP ENDUP FEDUP WADUP

DR•••

DRABS DRACO DRAFT DRAGS DRAIL DRAIN DRAKE DRAMA DRAMS DRANG DRANK DRANO DRAPE DRATS DRAVA DRAWL DRAWN DRAWS DRAYS DRDRE DREAD DREAM DREAR DREDD DREGS DRESS DRIBS DRIED DRIER DRIES DRIFT DRILL DRILY DRINA DRINK DRIPS DRIVE DRLAO DROID DROIT DROLL DROME DRONE DROOD DROOL DROOP DROPS DROSS DROVE DROWN DRUBS DRUGS DRUID DRUMS DRUNK DRUPE DRURY DRUSE DRUZE DRYAD DRYER DRYLY DRYUP

D•R••

DARBY DARED DARER DARES DARIN DARIO DARKS DARLA DARNS DARTH DARTS DARYA DARYL DERAT DERBY DEREK DERIV DERMA DERMO DERRY DERSU DIRAC DIRER DIRGE DIRKS DIRTY DORAG DORAL DORAN DOREN DORIC DORIS DORMS DORPS DORSA DORSI DORSO DURAN DURER DURNS DUROC DUROS DURRA DURST DURUM

D••R•

DAIRY DEARS DEARY DEBRA DECRY DEERE DEERS DERRY DETRE DEVRY DIARY DMARK DOBRA DOBRO DOERS DOORS DOURO DOWRY DRDRE DRURY DUPRE DURRA DWARF DYERS

D•••R

DAKAR DAMAR DARER DATER DEBAR DECOR DEFER DEMUR DENDR DETER DEWAR DEXTR DICER DINAR DINER DIRER DISTR DIVER DIYER DOLOR DONOR DOSER DOTER DOVER DOWER DOZER DREAR DRIER DRYER DURER

•DR••

ADREM CDROM

•D•R•

ADORE ADORN ODORS

•D••R

ADAIR ADDER ADLER EDGAR EDGER IDLER ODDER ODOUR UDDER

••DR•

ANDRE ANDRO ANDRY AUDRA CADRE CMDRS DRDRE HYDRA HYDRO INDRA INDRI MADRE MUDRA NIDRE PADRE PEDRO SIDRA SUDRA

••D•R

ADDER ALDER ANDOR ARDOR BADER CEDAR CIDER CODER CYDER EIDER ELDER ENDER ENDOR FODOR HADAR HIDER KADAR LADER NADER NADIR NUDER ODDER OLDER ORDER RADAR RIDER RUDER RYDER SEDER SIDER TUDOR UDDER UNDER VADER VIDOR WADER WIDER

•••DR

DENDR QUADR RANDR

D•S••

DASHI DESKS DESNA DESTE DISCO DISCS DISHY DISKS DISME DISTR DOSED DOSER DOSES DUSKS DUSKY DUSTS DUSTY

D••S•

DAISY DANSE DEISM DEIST DENSE DERSU DIDST DITSY DNASE DOEST DORSA DORSI DORSO DOUSE DOWSE DRESS DROSS DRUSE DULSE DURST

D•••S

DACES DADOS DAFFS DALES DAMES DAMNS DAMPS DANES DANGS DARES DARKS DARNS DARTS DATES DAUBS DAVIS DAVOS DAVYS DAWES DAWNS DAZES DEALS DEANS DEARS DEBTS DECKS DEEDS DEEMS DEEPS DEERS DEGAS DEILS DEKES DELES DELIS DELLS DELOS DELTS DEMES DEMOS DENES DENIS DENTS DENYS DEPTS DESKS DHALS DHOWS DIALS DICES DICKS DICTS DIDOS DIEMS DIETS DIKES DILLS DIMES DINES DINGS DINKS DINTS DIRKS DISCS DISKS DIVAS DIVES DOCKS DODOS DOERS DOFFS DOGES DOITS DOJOS DOLES DOLLS DOLTS DOMES DONAS DONGS DOOMS DOORS DOPES DORIS DORMS DORPS DOSES DOTES DOVES DOWNS DOZES DPLUS DRABS DRAGS DRAMS DRATS DRAWS DRAYS DREGS DRESS DRIBS DRIES DRIPS DROPS DROSS DRUBS DRUGS DRUMS DUADS DUBOS DUCES DUCKS DUCTS DUDES DUELS DUETS DUFFS DUKAS DUKES DULLS DUMAS DUMBS DUMPS DUNES DUNKS DUPES DURNS DUROS DUSKS DUSTS DUXES DYADS DYERS DYNES

•DS••

ADSUM EDSEL

•D•S•

ADUST IDEST ODIST

•D••S

ADAMS ADDIS ADIOS ADITS ADZES EDAMS EDDAS EDENS EDGES EDITS IDEAS IDLES IDOLS IDYLS ODETS ODORS

••DS•

DIDST HADST MIDST SUDSY

••D•S

ADDIS AEDES AIDES ALDUS ANDES AUDIS BIDES BLDGS BODES CADIS CEDES CEDIS CMDRS CODAS CODES DADOS DIDOS DODOS DUDES EDDAS FADES FADOS FIDES HADES HIDES INDUS JADES JUDAS KUDOS KUDUS LADES LADYS LIDOS LODES MEDES MIDAS MIDIS MODES MODUS MSDOS NIDES NIDUS NODES NODUS NUDES ORDOS PUDUS REDES RIDES RUDDS SADIS SIDES SODAS SUDDS TIDES TODOS UPDOS VADIS VEDAS WADES WADIS YODHS

•••DS

ACADS ACIDS BALDS BANDS BARDS BEADS BENDS BINDS BIRDS BLVDS BONDS BRADS BUNDS BYRDS CARDS CLODS COEDS COLDS CORDS CURDS DEEDS DUADS DYADS EGADS FEEDS FENDS FEUDS FINDS FOLDS FONDS FOODS FORDS FUNDS GAUDS GILDS GIRDS GLADS GOADS GOLDS GONDS GOODS GRADS GRIDS HANDS HEADS HEEDS HERDS HINDS HOLDS HOODS KINDS KURDS LANDS LARDS LAUDS LEADS LEEDS LENDS LOADS LORDS MAIDS MEADS MEEDS MELDS MENDS MINDS MOLDS MOODS NARDS NEEDS NERDS OPEDS PARDS PENDS PIEDS PLODS PONDS POODS PRODS QUADS QUIDS QUODS RAIDS RANDS READS REEDS RENDS RINDS ROADS ROODS RUDDS SANDS SARDS SCADS SCUDS SEEDS SENDS SHADS SHEDS SKIDS SLEDS SPADS SPUDS STUDS SUDDS SURDS TENDS THUDS TOADS VELDS VENDS VOIDS WANDS WARDS WEEDS WELDS WENDS WILDS WINDS WOADS WOLDS WOODS WORDS YARDS ZENDS

D•T••

DATED DATER DATES DATUM DETAT DETER DETOO DETRE DITAT DITCH DITKA DITSY DITTO DITTY DITZY DOTAL DOTED DOTER DOTES DOTTO DOTTY DUTCH

D••T•

DANTE DARTH DARTS DEBTS DEITY DELTA DELTS DENTE DENTI DENTS DEPTH DEPTS DESTE DEUTO DEXTR DHOTE DHOTI DICTA DICTS DICTU DIETS DINTS DINTY DIRTY DISTR DITTO DITTY DOETH DOITS DOLTS DOTTO DOTTY DRATS DUCTS DUETO DUETS DUSTS DUSTY

D•••T

DAUNT DAVIT DEALT DEBIT DEBUT DEFAT DEIST DELFT DEMIT DEPOT DERAT DETAT DFLAT DICOT DIDNT DIDST DIGIT DITAT DIVOT DIXIT DOEST DOGIT DONAT DONUT DOUBT DRAFT DRIFT DROIT DUCAT DURST DUVET DWELT

•DT••

IDTAG

•D•T•

ADDTO ADITS ADYTA EDITH EDITS ODETS

•D••T

ADAPT ADEPT ADINT ADMIT ADOPT ADOUT ADULT ADUST EDICT EDUCT IDEST IDIOT ODIST ODONT XDOUT

••DT•

ADDTO HADTO LEDTO WIDTH

••D•T

AUDIT CADET DIDNT

DIDST GODET GODOT HADAT HADNT HADST MEDIT MIDST ONDIT SADAT

•••DT
BUNDT HEIDT STADT VEIDT VELDT WENDT

DU•••
DUADS DUANE DUBAI DUBIN DUBOS DUCAL DUCAT DUCES DUCHY DUCKS DUCKY DUCTS DUDDY DUDES DUELS DUETO DUETS DUFAY DUFFS DUFFY DUGAN DUGIN DUGUP DUKAS DUKED DUKES DULLS DULLY DULSE DUMAS DUMBO DUMBS DUMMY DUMPS DUMPY DUNCE DUNES DUNKS DUNNE DUNNO DUOMO DUPED DUPES DUPLE DUPRE DURAN DURER DURNS DUROC DUROS DURRA DURST DURUM DUSKS DUSKY DUSTS DUSTY DUTCH DUVET DUXES

D•U••
DAUBS DAUNT DEUCE DEUCY DEUTO DOUAI DOUAY DOUBT DOUGH DOURO DOUSE DRUBS DRUGS DRUID DRUMS DRUNK DRUPE DRURY DRUSE DRUZE

D••U•
DAMUP DATUM DEBUG DEBUT DEMUR DIDUP DIGUP DONUT DPLUS DRYUP DUGUP DURUM

D•••U
DERSU DICTU DONAU

•DU••
ADULT ADUST ADUWA EDUCE EDUCT

•D•U•
ADDUP ADEUX ADOUT ADSUM ODEUM ODIUM ODOUR XDOUT

•D••U
ADIEU

••DU•
ABDUL ADDUP ALDUS ANDUP BIDUP DIDUP ENDUE ENDUP FEDUP INDUS KUDUS MODUS NIDUS NODUS PADUA PUDUS REDUB REDUX SEDUM UNDUE VADUZ WADUP

••D•U
KUDZU SADHU

•••DU
FONDU HINDU MAIDU PERDU

DV•••
DVIII DVINA

D•V••
DAVAO DAVID DAVIE DAVIS DAVIT DAVOS DAVYS DCVII DEVIL DEVON DEVRY DIVAN DIVAS DIVED DIVER DIVES DIVOT DIVVY DLVII DOVER DOVES DOVEY DUVET DXVII

D••V•
DCCVI DCLVI DCXVI DELVE DIVVY DLXVI DRAVA DRIVE DROVE DXCVI DXLVI DXXVI

D•••V
DCCCV DCCIV DCCLV DCCXV DCLIV DCLXV DCXCV DCXIV DCXLV DCXXV DERIV DLXIV DLXXV DXCIV DXLIV DXXIV DXXXV

•DV••
ADVAL ADVIL CDVII MDVII

•D•V•
CDLVI CDXVI MDCVI MDLVI MDXVI

•D••V
CDLIV CDLXV CDXCV CDXIV CDXLV CDXXV MDCCV MDCIV MDCLV MDCXV MDLIV MDLXV MDXCV MDXIV MDXLV MDXXV

••DV•
MCDVI MMDVI

••D•V
INDIV MCDIV MCDLV MCDXV MMDCV MMDIV MMDLV MMDXV

•••DV
MMCDV MMMDV

DW•••
DWARF DWEEB DWELL DWELT

D•W••
DAWES DAWNS DEWAN DEWAR DEWED DEWEY DOWDY DOWEL DOWER DOWNS DOWNY DOWRY DOWSE

D••W•
DAIWA DHOWS DRAWL DRAWN DRAWS DROWN

D•••W
DEPEW

•DW••
EDWIN

•D•W•
ADUWA

••D•W
BEDEW ENDOW SYDOW WIDOW

•••DW
BANDW CANDW

DX•••
DXCII DXCIV DXCIX DXCVI DXIII DXLII DXLIV DXLIX DXLVI DXVII DXXII DXXIV DXXIX DXXVI DXXXI DXXXV

D•X••
DCXCI DCXCV DCXII DCXIV DCXIX DCXLI DCXLV DCXVI DCXXI DCXXV DCXXX DEXTR DIXIE DIXIT DIXON DLXII DLXIV DLXIX DLXVI DLXXI DLXXV DLXXX DUXES DXXII DXXIV DXXIX DXXVI DXXXI DXXXV

D••X•
DCCXC DCCXI DCCXL DCCXV DCCXX DCLXI DCLXV DCLXX DCXXI DCXXV DCXXX DEOXY DLXXI DLXXV DLXXX DXXXI DXXXV

D•••X
DCCCX DCCIX DCCLX DCCXX DCLIX DCLXX DCXIX DCXXX DLXIX DLXXX DXCIX DXLIX DXXIX

•DX••
CDXCI CDXCV CDXII CDXIV CDXIX CDXLI CDXLV CDXVI CDXXI CDXXV CDXXX MDXCI MDXCV MDXII MDXIV MDXIX MDXLI MDXLV MDXVI MDXXI MDXXV MDXXX

•D•X•
CDLXI CDLXV CDLXX CDXXI CDXXV CDXXX MDCXC MDCXI MDCXL MDCXV MDCXX MDLXI MDLXV MDLXX MDXXI MDXXV MDXXX

•D••X
ADDAX ADEUX ADMIX CDLIX CDLXX CDXIX CDXXX MDCCX MDCIX MDCLX MDCXX MDLIX MDLXX MDXIX MDXXX

••DX•
MCDXC MCDXI MCDXL MCDXV MCDXX MMDXC MMDXI MMDXL MMDXV MMDXX

••D•X
ADDAX CODEX FEDEX INDEX MCDIX MCDLX MCDXX MMDCX MMDIX MMDLX MMDXX RADIX REDOX REDUX

•••DX
MMCDX MMMDX

DY•••
DYADS DYERS DYFED DYING DYLAN DYNEL DYNES

D•Y••
DAYAK DAYAN DAYNE DIYER DOYEN DOYLE DOYLY DRYAD DRYER DRYLY DRYUP

D••Y•
DARYA DARYL DAVYS DENYS DRAYS

D•••Y
DADDY DAFFY DAILY DAIRY DAISY DALEY DALLY DANCY DANDY DANNY DARBY DEARY DEBBY DECAY DECOY DECRY DEIFY DEITY DELAY DENNY DEOXY DERBY DERRY DEUCY DEVRY DEWEY DIARY DICEY DICKY DIDBY DIGBY DILLY DIMLY DINDY DINGY DINKY DINTY DIPPY DIRTY DISHY DITSY DITTY DITZY DIVVY DIZZY DOBBY DODGY DOGEY DOGGY DOILY DOLBY DOLLY DONNY DOODY DOOZY DOPEY DOTTY DOUAY DOVEY DOWDY DOWNY DOWRY DOYLY DRILY DRURY DRYLY DUCHY DUCKY DUDDY DUFAY DUFFY DULLY DUMMY DUMPY DUSKY DUSTY

•DY••
ADYTA IDYLL IDYLS

•D••Y
EDIFY ODDLY

••DY•
LADYS REDYE

••D•Y
ANDRY BADDY BADLY BIDDY BUDDY CADDY CUDDY DADDY DIDBY DODGY DUDDY FUDDY GIDDY GODEY GODLY HEDGY KIDDY LEDGY LIDDY MADLY MIDDY MUDDY NEDDY NODDY ODDLY PADDY PODGY PUDGY REDDY REDLY RIDGY RODDY RUDDY SADLY SEDGY SODDY SUDSY TEDDY TODAY TODDY VEDAY VJDAY WADDY WEDGY

•••DY
ACIDY BADDY BANDY BAWDY BEADY BENDY BIDDY BIRDY BRADY BRODY BUDDY BUNDY CADDY CANDY CINDY CUDDY CURDY DADDY DANDY DINDY DOODY DOWDY DUDDY FUDDY FUNDY GANDY GAUDY GIDDY GOODY GORDY GOUDY GOWDY GRADY GRODY GURDY HANDY HARDY HEADY HOWDY HURDY KANDY KIDDY LARDY LEADY LIDDY LINDY LUNDY MANDY MIDDY MINDY MOLDY MOODY MUDDY NEDDY NEEDY NERDY NODDY PADDY RANDY READY REDDY REEDY RINDY RODDY ROWDY RUDDY SANDY SEEDY SHADY SODDY STUDY TANDY TARDY TEDDY TOADY TODDY WADDY WEEDY WENDY WINDY WOODY WORDY

D•Z••
DAZED DAZES DIZEN DIZZY DOZED DOZEN DOZER DOZES

D••Z•
DANZA DIAZO DITZY DIZZY DOOZY DRUZE

•DZ••
ADZES

••DZ•
KUDZU

••D•Z
CADIZ NODOZ VADUZ

EA•••
EAGAN EAGER EAGLE EAGRE EAMES EAMON EARED EARLE EARLS EARLY EARNS EARTH EASED EASEL EASES EASTS EATAT EATEN EATER EATIN EATIT EATON EATUP EAVED EAVES

E•A••
EDAMS EGADI EGADS ELAND ELATE ELATH ELAZI EMAIL ENACT ENATE EPACT ERASE ERATO ETAGE ETAPE ETATS EVADE EVANS EXACT EXALT EXAMS

E••A•
EAGAN EATAT EBOAT ECLAT EDDAS EDGAR EFLAT EGGAR EILAT ELGAR ELIAS ELMAN ELWAY EMBAR EMBAY ENIAC ENLAI EPHAH EPHAS EQUAL ESBAT ESSAY ESTAB ESTAS ETHAN ETNAS EVIAN EYRAS

E•••A
EDEMA EDINA ELENA ELIZA ENNEA ENOLA ENTIA ERICA ERIKA ERISA ETYMA EVITA EVORA EXTRA

•EA••
AEAEA BEACH BEADS BEADY BEAKS BEALL BEALS BEAMS BEAMY BEANO BEANS BEANY BEARD BEARS BEAST BEATS BEAUS BEAUT BEAUX CEASE DEALS DEALT DEANE DEANS DEARS DEARY FEARS FEAST FEATS GEARS GEARY HEADS HEADY HEALS HEALY HEAPS HEARD HEARN HEARS HEART HEATH HEATS HEAVE HEAVY JEANE JEANS KEACH KEANE KEANU KEATS LEACH LEADS LEADY LEAFS LEAFY LEAHY LEAKS LEAKY LEANS LEANT LEAPS LEAPT LEARN LEARS LEARY LEASE LEASH LEAST LEAVE MEADE MEADS MEALS MEALY MEANS MEANT MEANY MEARA MEATS MEATY NEALE NEAPS NEARS NEATH NEATO NEATS PEABO PEACE PEACH PEAKS PEALE PEALS PEARL PEARS PEARY PEASE PEATS PEATY PEAVY REACH REACT READE READS READY REAIM REAIR REALM REALS REAMS REAPS REARM REARS REATA SEALE SEALS SEALY SEAMS SEAMY SEARS SEATO SEATS TEACH TEAKS TEALS TEAMS TEARS TEARY TEASE VEALY WEALS WEANS WEARS WEARY WEAVE YEANS YEARN YEARS YEAST YEATS ZEALS

•E•A•
AETAT BEGAN BEGAT BEHAN BELAY BEMAS BETAS CEDAR CERAM CERAT CESAR DEBAR DECAF DECAL DECAY DEFAT DEGAS DELAY DERAT DETAT DEWAN DEWAR FERAL FETAL FETAS GERAH GETAS GETAT HEJAZ HEMAN HENAN HERAT HEXAD KEBAB KEMAL KENAI KERAT LEFAY LEGAL LEHAR LEMAT LEMAY LETAT LEVAR LEXAN MEDAL MEGAN MELAN MESAS METAL NEMAN NEMAT NEPAL PECAN PEDAL PENAL PERAN PETAL REBAG REBAR RECAP REDAN REGAL REGAN REHAB REHAN RELAX RELAY REMAN REMAP RENAL RENAN REPAD REPAY RERAN RESAW RETAG RETAP RETAR RETAX REWAX SEDAN SEGAL SEGAR SELAH SENAT SEPAL SERAC SERAI SERAL SETAE SETAT TENAM TEPAL TEXAN TEXAS VEDAS VEDAY VEGAN VEGAS VELAR VENAE VENAL WEKAS ZETAS

•E••A
AEAEA AECIA AETNA BELLA BELVA BEREA BERRA BETTA CEIBA CELIA CELLA CERIA CESTA CEUTA DEBRA DECCA DELLA DELTA DERMA DESNA FELLA FERIA FESTA GEENA GEMMA GENOA GENUA HEDDA HEKLA HELGA HENNA HEPTA KENYA LEEZA LEHUA LEICA LEILA LEMMA LENYA LEONA LEORA LEPTA MEARA MECCA MEDEA MEDIA MEHTA MELBA MENSA MESTA NEMEA PELLA PEMBA PENNA PENTA PENZA PEPLA PETRA REATA REGIA REINA RENTA RETIA SEEYA SEHNA SELMA SELVA SENNA SEPIA SEPTA SERRA SERTA TEENA TERRA TERZA TESLA TESTA TETRA VEDDA VENDA VERBA VERSA VESTA XENIA YENTA YERBA ZEBRA ZELDA ZENDA

••EA•
ABEAM AHEAD ANEAR APEAK AREAL AREAR AREAS ATEAM BLEAK BLEAR BLEAT BREAD BREAK BREAM CHEAP CHEAT CLEAN CLEAR CLEAT CREAK CREAM DREAD DREAM DREAR FLEAS FREAK GLEAM GLEAN GREAT HBEAM IBEAM ICEAX IDEAL IDEAS KNEAD OBEAH OCEAN OLEAN ONEAL ONEAM OREAD PAEAN PLEAD PLEAS PLEAT RHEAS SHEAF SHEAN SHEAR SKEAN SKEAT SMEAR SNEAD SNEAK SPEAK SPEAR STEAD STEAK STEAL STEAM SWEAR SWEAT TREAD TREAT TWEAK WHEAL WHEAT WREAK ZOEAE ZOEAL ZOEAS

••E•A
ADELA AGENA AKELA ALETA AMEBA ARECA ARENA AVENA BREDA BUENA CHEKA CHELA CIERA EDEMA ELENA FREDA FRENA FREYA GEENA GRETA HAEMA HIERA HYENA LEEZA OMEGA ONEGA OPERA OVETA PIETA PLENA SCENA

SEEYA SHEBA SHEMA SIENA SNEVA STELA TEENA THECA THEDA THEMA THERA THETA

•••EA
AEAEA APNEA ATSEA BEREA BOHEA CANEA COREA ENNEA FOVEA GALEA HOSEA JUDEA KOREA LULEA MEDEA NEMEA OCREA OSHEA PALEA PILEA SIDEA TYPEA

EB•••
EBBED EBERT EBOAT EBOLI EBOND EBONS EBONY EBSEN

E•B••
EBBED ELBOW EMBAR EMBAY EMBED EMBER ERBIL ESBAT EUBIE

E•••B
ESTAB EXURB

•EB••
BEBOP DEBAR DEBBY DEBIT DEBRA DEBTS DEBUG DEBUT KEBAB KEBOB REBAG REBAR REBBE REBEC REBEL REBID REBUS REBUT SEBUM WEBBY WEBER XEBEC ZEBRA ZEBUS

•E•B•
BEEBE CEIBA DEBBY DERBY GETBY HERBS HERBY KERBS LETBE MELBA PEABO PEMBA REBBE SERBS SETBY VERBA VERBS WEBBY WELBY YERBA

•E••B
CELEB DEMOB DENEB KEBAB KEBOB REDUB REHAB

••EB•
ABEBE AMEBA BEEBE BLEBS GLEBE GREBE KREBS LIEBY PLEBE PLEBS SHEBA THEBE

••E•B
ACERB DWEEB

•••EB
CALEB CELEB CUBEB DENEB DWEEB HOREB SIDEB STIEB TYPEB

EC•••
ECHIN ECLAT ECOLE ECOLI ECRUS

E•C••
ELCID EMCEE ENCYC EPCOT EXCEL

E••C•
EDICT EDUCE EDUCT EJECT ELECT ENACT ENOCH EPACT EPICS EPOCH ERECT ERICA ERICH ERUCT EVICT EXACT EXECS

E•••C
EDDIC ENCYC ENIAC EPISC ETHIC

•EC••
AECIA BECHE BECKS BECKY CECHY CECIL DECAF DECAL DECAY DECCA DECEM DECKS DECOR DECOY DECRY GECKO HECHE HECHT HECKS HECTO LECKY MECCA MECUM NECKS PECAN PECKS PECKY PECOS RECAP RECCE RECIP RECON RECTI RECTO RECUR SECCO SECTS TECHS TECHY YECCH

•E•C•
BEACH BEECH BELCH BENCH CENCI DECCA DEICE DELCO DEUCE DEUCY FENCE FETCH HENCE HENCH KEACH KENCH KETCH LEACH LEECH LEICA MECCA MERCE MERCI MERCK MERCY PEACE PEACH PENCE PERCE PERCH PERCY PESCI REACH REACT RECCE REICH SECCO TEACH TENCH VETCH WELCH WENCH YECCH

•E••C
GENIC HELIC MEDIC MEDOC MELIC MESIC REBEC RELIC SERAC TELIC VEDIC XEBEC XERIC ZENIC

••EC•
ALECK ARECA BEECH BRECK CHECK CRECY CZECH EJECT ELECT ERECT EXECS FLECK GRECO LEECH NIECE PIECE SPECD SPECK SPECS THECA VNECK WRECK

••E•C
CRESC OLEIC

•••EC
AZTEC COSEC OLMEC REBEC XEBEC

ED•••
EDAMS EDDAS EDDIC EDDIE EDEMA EDENS EDGAR EDGED EDGER EDGES EDICT EDIFY EDILE EDINA EDITH EDITS EDSEL EDUCE EDUCT EDWIN

E•D••
EDDAS EDDIC EDDIE EIDER ELDER EMDEN ENDED ENDER ENDON ENDOR ENDOW ENDUE ENDUP EYDIE

E••D•
EGADI EGADS EJIDO ELIDE ELUDE EPODE ERODE ETUDE EVADE EXUDE

E•••D
EARED EASED EAVED EBBED EBOND EDGED EELED EGGED ELAND ELCID EMBED EMEND ENDED EPHOD ERRED

•ED••
AEDES BEDEW BEDIM CEDAR CEDED CEDES CEDIS FEDEX FEDON FEDUP HEDDA HEDGE HEDGY HEDIN KEDGE LEDGE LEDGY LEDIN LEDON LEDTO MEDAL MEDEA MEDES MEDIA MEDIC MEDIT MEDOC NEDDY PEDAL PEDRO REDAN REDDY REDED REDES REDID REDLY REDON REDOX REDUB REDUX REDYE SEDAN SEDER SEDGE SEDGY SEDUM TEDDY VEDAS VEDAY VEDDA VEDIC WEDEL WEDGE WEDGY XEDIN

•E•D•
BEADS BEADY BENDS BENDY DEEDS DENDR FEEDS FENDS FERDE FEUDS GEODE HEADS HEADY HEDDA HEEDS HEIDI HEIDT HERDS JEUDI KENDO LEADS LEADY LEEDS LENDL LENDS MEADE MEADS MEEDS MELDS MENDS NEDDY NEEDS NEEDY NERDS NERDY PENDS PERDU READE READS READY REDDY REEDS REEDY RENDS SEEDS SEEDY SENDS TEDDY TEIDE TENDS VEDDA VEIDT VELDS VELDT VENDA VENDS VERDE VERDI WEEDS WEEDY WELDS WENDS WENDT WENDY ZELDA ZENDA ZENDO ZENDS

•E••D
BEARD CEDED CERED DEKED DELED DEWED EELED FELID FETED FETID GELID GEOID HEARD HEROD HEWED HEXAD HEXED KEYED METED MEWED NEFUD REBID REDED REDID REPAD RESOD REWED SEWED TEPID VEXED WEIRD

••ED•
BREDA COEDS CREDO DEEDS DREDD FEEDS FREDA GLEDE HEEDS LEEDS MEEDS NEEDS NEEDY OPEDS PIEDS REEDS REEDY SEEDS SEEDY SHEDS SLEDS SUEDE SWEDE THEDA WEEDS WEEDY

••E•D
ABEND AHEAD AMEND BLEED BLEND BREAD BREED CREED DREAD DREDD EMEND FIELD FIEND FJELD FREED FREUD GREED KNEAD KNEED NOEND ONEND OREAD PLEAD PSEUD SCEND SHEED SNEAD SNEED SNERD SPECD SPEED SPEND STEAD STEED THEYD TREAD TREED TREND TWEED UPEND WIELD YIELD

•••ED
AAHED ACHED ACRED ACTED ADDED AHMED AIDED AILED AIMED AIRED AMPED ANTED APTED ARCED ARMED ASKED AWNED BAAED BAKED BALED BARED BASED BATED BAYED BIDED BIKED BIPED BLEED BLUED BODED BONED BOOED BORED BOWED BOXED BREED BUSED CAGED CAKED CANED CAPED CARED CASED CAVED CAWED CEDED CERED CITED CLUED CODED COKED COOED COPED CORED COWED COXED CREED CRIED CUBED CURED DARED DATED DAZED DEKED DELED DEWED DICED DIKED DIMED DINED DIVED DOLED DOMED DOPED DOSED DOTED DOZED DRIED DUKED DUPED DYFED EARED EASED EAVED EBBED EDGED EELED EGGED EMBED ENDED ERRED FACED FADED FAKED FAMED FARED FATED FAXED FAZED FETED FIFED FILED FINED FIRED FIXED FLIED FOXED FREED FRIED FUMED FUSED FUZED GAGED GAMED GAPED GATED GAZED GIBED GLUED GORED GREED GUYED GYBED GYVED HALED HARED HATED HAWED HAYED HAZED HEWED HEXED HIKED HIRED HIVED HOKED HOLED HOMED HONED HOPED HOSED HYPED IDLED IMPED INBED INKED IRKED IVIED JADED JAPED JAWED JIBED JIVED JOKED JUKED KEYED KITED KNEED LACED LADED LAMED LASED LAVED LAZED LIKED LIMED LINED LIVED LOBED LOPED LOVED LOWED LUBED LURED MACED MANED MATED MAXED METED MEWED MIKED MIMED MINED MIRED MIXED MOOED MOPED MOVED MOWED MUSED MUTED NAKED NAMED NIXED NOSED NOTED NUKED OARED OGLED OILED OOHED OOZED OPTED OUTED OWNED PACED PAGED PALED PANED PARED PATED PAVED PAWED PAYED PIKED PILED PINED PIPED PLIED POKED POLED PORED POSED PRIED PULED RACED RAGED RAKED RASED RATED RAVED RAYED RAZED REDED REWED RICED RILED RIMED RIVED ROBED ROPED ROVED ROWED RULED SATED SAVED SAWED SCHED SEWED SHEED SHIED SHOED SHRED SIDED SIRED SITED SIXED SIZED SKIED SLUED SNEED SOLED SOWED SPEED SPIED STEED TAMED TAPED TAXED TIDED TILED TIMED TINED TIRED TONED TOPED TOTED TOWED TOYED TREED TRIED TRUED TUBED TUNED TWEED TYPED UMPED UNFED UNLED UNWED UPPED URGED USHED USTED VEXED VINED VOTED VOWED WADED WAGED WAKED WALED WANED WAVED WAXED WILED WINED WIPED WIRED WIVED WOOED WOWED YAWED YOKED ZONED

EE•••
EELED EELER EERIE

E•E••
EBERT EDEMA EDENS EGEST EIEIO EJECT ELECT ELEGY ELEMI ELENA ELENI ELEVE EMEER EMEND EMERY ENEMY ENERO EPEES ERECT EVENS EVENT EVERS EVERT EVERY EWELL EWERS EXECS EXERT EYERS EWERY

E••E•
EAGER EAMES EARED EASED EASEL EASES EATEN EATER EAVED EAVES EBBED EBSEN EDGED EDGER EDGES EDSEL EELED EELER EFREM EGGED EGRET EIDER EIGEN ELDER ELIEL ELLEN ELLER ELLES ELMER ELVER ELVES ELWES EMBED EMBER EMCEE EMDEN EMEER EMMER EMMET ENDED ENDER ENGEL ENNEA ENTER EPEES ERIES ERNES ERRED ESKER ESNES ESSEN ESSES ESSEX ESTEE ESTER ESTES ETHEL ETHER ETSEQ ETZEL EULER EXCEL EXPEL EYRES

E•••E
EAGLE EAGRE EARLE ECOLE EDDIE EDILE EDUCE EERIE EFFIE ELATE ELEVE ELIDE ELISE ELITE ELLIE ELOPE ELSIE ELUDE ELUTE ELYSE EMCEE EMILE EMOTE ENATE ENDUE ENSUE ENTRE ENURE EPODE ERASE ERNIE ERODE EROSE ESQUE ESTEE ETAGE ETAPE ETUDE EUBIE EVADE EVOKE EXILE EXUDE EYDIE EYRIE

•EE••
BEEBE BEECH BEEFS BEEFY BEENE BEEPS BEERS BEERY BEETS DEEDS DEEMS DEEPS DEERE DEERS FEEDS FEELS FEELY FEETS GEEKS GEEKY GEENA GEESE HEEDS HEELS JEEPS JEERS KEELS KEENE KEENS KEEPS KEETS LEECH LEEDS LEEKS LEERS LEERY LEETS LEEZA MEEDS MEESE MEETS NEEDS NEEDY PEEKS PEELE PEELS PEENS PEEPS PEERS PEETE PEEVE REEDS REEDY REEFS REEKS REEKY REELS REESE REEVE SEEDS SEEDY SEEIN SEEKS SEELS SEELY SEEMS SEEPS SEEPY SEERS SEETO SEEYA TEEMS TEENA TEENS TEENY TEETH TEEUP VEEPS VEERS VEERY WEEDS WEEDY WEEKS WEEMS WEENY WEEPS WEEPY WEEST

•E•E•
AEAEA AEDES BEDEW BEGET BELEM BENES BENET BEREA BERET BESET BETEL BEVEL BEZEL CEDED CEDES CELEB CEPES CERED CERES DECEM DEFER DEKED DEKES DELED DELES DEMES DENEB DENES DEPEW DEREK DETER DEWED DEWEY EELED EELER FEDEX FETED FETES FEVER FEWER FEYER GELEE GENES GENET HEFEI HEGEL HELEN HEMEN HEMET HERES HEWED HEWER HEXED HEXER HEXES JEREZ JETER JETES JEWEL KESEY KEVEL KEYED KEYES LEGER LEVEE LEVEL LEVER LEWES MEDEA MEDES MELEE MEMEL MENES MERES METED METER METES MEWED MEYER NEGEV NEMEA NENES NEVER NEVES NEWEL NEWER PEKES PELEE PELEG PERES PEREZ PETER PETES PEWEE REBEC REBEL REDED REDES REFER REHEM REKEY RELEE RELET REMET REMEX RENEE RENEW REPEG REPEL RESEE RESET RESEW REUEL REVEL REVET REWED REXES REYES SEDER SEGER SELES SERES SEVEN SEVER SEWED SEWER SEXES TEHEE TELEO TELES TELEX TENET TEPEE TETES TEVET VELEZ VENEZ VESEY VEXED VEXER VEXES WEBER WEDEL WESER XEBEC YEMEN YESES

•E••E
AERIE

BECHE BEEBE BEENE BEIGE BELIE BELLE BENUE BERLE BERME BERNE BETTE BEYLE CEASE CELIE CENSE DEANE DEERE DEFOE DEICE DELVE DEMME DENSE DENTE DESTE DETRE DEUCE EERIE FEMME FENCE FERDE GEESE GELEE GENIE GENRE GEODE GESTE GETME HEAVE HECHE HEDGE HEINE HELVE HENCE HENGE HENIE HERNE HERVE HESSE HEURE HEUTE HEYSE JEANE JESSE JEUNE KEANE KEDGE KEENE LEASE LEAVE LEDGE LEMME LEONE LETBE LETHE LEVEE LEYTE MEADE MEESE MELEE MERCE MERGE MERLE MEROE MESNE METRE MEUSE NEALE NEIGE NERVE NEUME PEACE PEALE PEASE PEELE PEETE PEEVE PEKOE PELEE PELLE PENCE PENNE PENTE PERCE PERLE PERSE PEWEE READE REBBE RECCE REDYE REESE REEVE RELEE RENEE RESEE RETIE REUNE REUSE REVUE SEALE SEDGE SEGUE SEINE SEIZE SENSE SENTE SERGE SERVE SETAE SETTE SEULE TEASE TEHEE TEIDE TEMPE TENSE TEPEE TERNE TERRE TERSE TEVYE VENAE VENUE VERDE VERGE VERNE VERRE VERSE VERTE VERVE WEAVE WEDGE YENTE

••EE•
ADEEM AKEEM AKEES AMEER BLEED BLEEP BREED BREEN CHEEK CHEEP CHEER CLEEK CREED CREEK CREEL CREEP CREES DWEEB EMEER EPEES FLEER FLEES FLEET FREED FREER FREES GHEES GLEES GREED GREEK GREEN GREER GREES GREET KNEED KNEEL KNEES OGEES PREEN QUEEG QUEEN QUEER SHEED SHEEN SHEEP SHEER SHEET SKEET SLEEK SLEEP SLEET SNEED SNEER SPEED STEED STEEL STEEN STEEP STEER SWEEP SWEET TREED TREEN TREES TWEED TWEEN TWEER TWEET WHEEL WHEEN

••E•E
ABEBE ABELE ADELE AKENE ALENE ALEVE ANELE ARETE BEEBE BEENE BREVE CHERE CREME CREPE CRETE DEERE DIENE ELEVE FRERE GEESE GLEBE GLEDE GREBE GRETE ILENE IRENE ISERE KEENE LIEGE LOEWE MEESE MNEME MYEYE NIECE OBESE OPERE OXEYE PEELE PEETE PEEVE PIECE PLEBE POEME POETE QUEUE REESE REEVE SCENE SHERE SIEGE SIETE SIEVE SKETE SPEKE STELE STERE STEVE SUEDE SUEME SWEDE THEBE THEME THERE THESE TWERE WHERE ZOEAE

•••EE
AGREE AIMEE ALBEE ALLEE ANNEE ARMEE COOEE CUVEE DONEE EMCEE ESTEE FUSEE FUZEE GELEE GOSEE LEVEE LYCEE MAGEE MCGEE MELEE NGWEE PAREE PAYEE PELEE PEWEE PUREE RAMEE RANEE RAPEE RAREE RELEE RENEE RESEE RONEE RUPEE SCREE SPREE SYCEE TEHEE TEPEE THREE TUTEE TYPEE

EF•••
EFFIE EFIKS EFLAT EFREM

E•F••
EFFIE ELFIN ENFIN

E••F•
EDIFY

•EF••
BEFIT BEFOG DEFAT DEFER DEFOE DEFOG HEFEI HEFTS HEFTY KEFIR LEFAY LEFTS LEFTY NEFUD REFER REFIT REFRY WEFTS

•E•F•
BEEFS BEEFY DEIFY DELFT FEOFF LEAFS LEAFY REEFS REIFY SERFS

•E••F
DECAF FEOFF SERIF

••EF•
ALEFS BEEFS BEEFY CHEFS CLEFS CLEFT FIEFS REEFS THEFT

••E•F
BOEUF SHEAF SHELF

•••EF
BRIEF CCLEF CHIEF FCLEF GANEF GCLEF GRIEF INDEF JOSEF SHAEF THIEF

EG•••
EGADI EGADS EGEST EGGAR EGGED EGGON EGRET EGYPT

E•G••
EAGAN EAGER EAGLE EAGRE EDGAR EDGED EDGER EDGES EGGAR EGGED EGGON EIGEN EIGHT ELGAR ELGIN ENGEL ENGRS ERGOT

E••G•
ELEGY ENUGU ETAGE

E•••G
EKING EWING

•EG••
AEGIR AEGIS BEGAN BEGAT BEGET BEGIN BEGOT BEGUM BEGUN DEGAS HEGEL LEGAL LEGER LEGGS LEGGY LEGIS LEGIT LEGOS LEGUP MEGAN NEGEV NEGRI NEGUS PEGGY REGAL REGAN REGIA REGIS REGNI REGUM SEGAL SEGAR SEGER SEGNI SEGNO SEGOS SEGUE VEGAN VEGAS YEGGS

•E•G•
BEIGE BERGH BERGS DEIGN FEIGN GETGO HEDGE HEDGY HEIGH HELGA HENGE KEDGE KEOGH LEDGE LEDGY LEGGS LEGGY LEIGH LETGO MERGE NEIGE NEIGH PEGGY PENGO REIGN SEDGE SEDGY SENGI SERGE VERGE WEDGE WEDGY WEIGH YEGGS

•E••G
BEFOG BEING DEBUG DEFOG GEORG PELEG REBAG RELIG REPEG RERIG RETAG SELIG ZELIG

••EG•
DIEGO DREGS ELEGY FUEGO GREGG LIEGE LUEGO OMEGA ONEGA PREGO SIEGE SKEGS TAEGU TIEGS

••E•G
GREGG QUEEG ZWEIG

•••EG
GRIEG IRREG KLIEG PELEG QUEEG REPEG UNPEG

E•H••
ECHIN EPHAH EPHAS EPHOD EPHOR ETHAN ETHEL ETHER ETHIC ETHNO ETHOS ETHYL

E••H•
EIGHT ELIHU

E•••H
EARTH EDITH ELATH ENOCH EPHAH EPOCH ERICH

•EH••
BEHAN LEHAR LEHUA MEHTA NEHIS NEHRU REHAB REHAN REHEM SEHNA TEHEE

•E•H•
BECHE BETHS CECHY DELHI HECHE HECHT HETHS LEAHY LETHE MESHY TECHS TECHY TETHS

•E••H
BEACH BEECH BELCH BENCH BERGH BERTH DEPTH FETCH GERAH HEATH HEIGH HENCH KEACH KEITH KENCH KEOGH KETCH LEACH LEASH LEECH LEIGH LEITH NEATH NEIGH PEACH PERCH PERTH REACH REICH SELAH TEACH TEETH TENCH TENTH VETCH WEIGH WELCH WELSH WENCH YECCH

••EH•
BOEHM FOEHN RUEHL

••E•H
ALEPH BEECH CHETH CZECH DOETH FLESH FRESH LEECH OBEAH TEETH WYETH

EI•••
EIDER EIEIO EIGEN EIGHT EILAT

E•I••
EDICT EDIFY EDILE EDINA EDITH EDITS EFIKS EJIDO EKING ELIAS ELIDE ELIEL ELIHU ELION ELIOT ELISE ELITE ELIZA EMILE EMILY EMIRS EMITS ENIAC EPICS EPISC ERICA ERICH ERIES ERIKA ERISA EVIAN EVICT EVILS EVITA EWING EXILE EXIST EXITS

E••I•
EATIN EATIT ECHIN EDDIC EDDIE EDWIN EERIE EFFIE EIEIO ELCID ELFIN ELGIN ELLIE ELLIS ELSIE ELVIN ELVIS EMAIL ENFIN ENNIO ENNIS ENTIA EOSIN EQUIP EQUIV ERBIL ERNIE ERVIL ERVIN ERWIN ETHIC ETUIS ETVIR EUBIE EYDIE EYRIE EYRIR

E•••I
EBOLI ECOLI EGADI ELAZI ELEMI ELENI ENLAI ENNUI ENVOI

•EI••
AEIOU BEIGE BEING BEINS CEIBA CEILS DEICE DEIFY DEIGN DEILS DEION DEISM DEIST DEITY FEIGN FEINT FEIST HEIDI HEIDT HEIGH HEINE HEINZ HEIRS HEISS HEIST KEITH LEICA LEIGH LEILA LEITH MEIJI MEINY NEIGE NEIGH NEILL REICH REIFY REIGN REIMS REINA REINK REINS SEIJI SEIKO SEINE SEISM SEIZE TEIDE VEIDT VEILS VEINS VEINY WEIGH WEILL WEIRD WEIRS WEISS ZEINS ZEISS ZEIST

•E•I•
AECIA AEGIR AEGIS AERIE AESIR BEDIM BEFIT BEGIN BELIE BENIN BEVIN CECIL CEDIS CELIA CELIE CERIA DEBIT DELIS DEMIT DENIM DENIS DERIV DEVIL EERIE FELID FELIS FELIX FELIZ FERIA FETID GELID GENIC GENIE GENII GEOID GETIN GETIT HEDIN HELIC HELIO HELIX HEMIN HENIE KEFIR KEPIS KEVIN KEYIN LEDIN LEGIS LEGIT LENIN LENIS LETIN LEVIN LEVIS LEWIS LEXIS MEDIA MEDIC MEDIT MELIC MERIT MESIC METIS NEHIS NEVIL NEVIN NEVIS NEXIS PEKIN PEPIN PERIL PERIS PETIT PEWIT REAIM REAIR REBID RECIP REDID REFIT REGIA REGIS RELIC RELIG RELIT REMIT REMIX RENIN REOIL REPIN RERIG RESIN RETIA RETIE REWIN SEEIN SELIG SEMIS SEPIA SERIF SERIN SETIN TELIC TEPID VEDIC VENIN XEDIN XENIA XERIC YETIS ZELIG ZENIC

•E••I
BELLI BENJI BENXI CELLI CENCI CENTI CESTI DELHI DENTI FERMI FERRI GENII HEFEI HEIDI HENRI JEUDI KENAI KERRI LEONI LEROI MEIJI MERCI NEGRI PENNI PEPSI PESCI PETRI PETTI RECTI REGNI SEGNI SEIJI SENGI SERAI TEMPI TERRI VERDI VERMI

••EI•
ATEIN CUEIN EIEIO ICEIN KLEIN LIEIN OLEIC OLEIN ONEIL PLEIO SEEIN SHEIK SKEIN STEIN THEIR TIEIN TOEIN ZWEIG

••E•I
CHERI ELEMI ELENI FLEXI ICENI OBELI SIEPI TREVI UMEKI

•••EI
AUREI FIDEI HEFEI IMPEI ISSEI KIBEI NISEI PILEI TAKEI TOMEI

EJ•••
EJECT EJIDO

E•J••
ENJOY

•EJ••
HEJAZ

•E•J•
BENJI MEIJI SEIJI

••EJ•
CHEJU VIEJO

EK•••
EKING

E•K••
ESKER

E••K•
EFIKS ENSKY ERIKA EVOKE EWOKS

•EK••
DEKED DEKES DEKKO HEKLA PEKES PEKIN PEKOE REKEY WEKAS

•E•K•
BEAKS BECKS BECKY DECKS DEKKO DESKS GECKO GEEKS GEEKY HECKS HERKY JERKS JERKY LEAKS LEAKY LECKY LEEKS NECKS PEAKS PECKS PECKY PEEKS PERKS PERKY PESKY REEKS REEKY SEEKS SEIKO TEAKS WEEKS YERKS

•E••K
DEREK MERCK REINK

••EK•
CHEKA GEEKS GEEKY LEEKS PEEKS REEKS REEKY SEEKS SPEKE TREKS UMEKI WEEKS

••E•K
ALECK APEAK BLEAK BREAK BRECK CHECK CHEEK CLEEK CLERK CREAK CREEK FLECK FREAK GREEK SHEIK SLEEK SNEAK SPEAK SPECK STEAK TWEAK VNECK WHELK WREAK WRECK

•••EK
CAPEK CHEEK CLEEK CREEK DEREK GREEK HACEK HAYEK KOPEK PATEK SLEEK UZBEK

EL•••
ELAND ELATE ELATH ELAZI ELBOW ELCID ELDER ELECT ELEGY ELEMI ELENA ELENI ELEVE ELFIN ELGAR ELGIN ELIAS ELIDE ELIEL ELIHU ELION ELIOT ELISE ELITE ELIZA ELLEN ELLER ELLES ELLIE ELLIS ELMAN ELMER ELMOS ELOPE ELROY ELSIE ELTON ELUDE ELUTE ELVER ELVES ELVIN ELVIS ELWAY ELWES ELYSE

E•L••
ECLAT EELED EELER EFLAT EILAT ELLEN ELLER ELLES ELLIE ELLIS EMLYN ENLAI EOLUS EULER

E••L•
EAGLE EARLE EARLS EARLY EBOLI ECOLE ECOLI EDILE EMILE EMILY ENOLA ENOLS EVILS EWELL EXALT EXILE EXULT

E•••L
EASEL EDSEL ELIEL EMAIL ENGEL ENROL EQUAL ERBIL ERROL ERVIL ETHEL ETHYL ETZEL EWELL EXCEL EXPEL EXTOL

•EL••
BELAY BELCH BELEM BELIE BELLA BELLE BELLI BELLS BELLY BELOW BELTS BELVA CELEB CELIA CELIE CELLA CELLI CELLO CELLS CELTS DELAY DELCO DELED DELES DELFT DELHI DELIS DELLA DELLS DELON DELOS DELTA DELTS DELVE EELED EELER FELID FELIS FELIX FELIZ FELLA FELLS FELLY FELON FELTS GELEE GELID HELEN HELGA

HELIC
HELIO
HELIX
HELLO
HELLS
HELMS
HELOS
HELOT
HELPS
HELVE
JELLO
JELLS
JELLY
KELLY
KELPS
KELPY
KELSO
MELAN
MELBA
MELDS
MELEE
MELIC
MELON
MELOS
MELTS
MELTY
NELLY
PELEE
PELEG
PELLA
PELLE
PELTS
RELAX
RELAY
RELEE
RELET
RELIC
RELIG
RELIT
SELAH
SELES
SELIG
SELLS
SELMA
SELVA
TELEO
TELES
TELEX
TELIC
TELLS
TELLY
TELOS
VELAR
VELDS
VELDT
VELEZ
VELUM
WELBY
WELCH
WELDS
WELLS
WELSH
WELTS
WELTY
YELLS
YELPS
ZELDA
ZELIG

•E•L•

BEALL
BEALS
BELLA
BELLE
BELLI
BELLS
BELLY
BERLE
BEYLE
CEILS
CELLA
CELLI
CELLO
CELLS
DEALS
DEALT
DEILS
DELLA
DELLS
FEELS
FEELY
FELLA
FELLS
FELLY
FEYLY
HEALS
HEALY
HEELS
HEKLA
HELLO
HELLS
HERLS
JELLO
JELLS
JELLY
KEELS
KELLY
LEILA
MEALS
MEALY
MENLO
MERLE
MERLS
MEWLS
NEALE
NEILL
NELLY
NEWLY
PEALE
PEALS
PEELE
PEELS
PELLA
PELLE
PEPLA
PERLE
REALM
REALS
REDLY
REELS
REPLY
SEALE
SEALS
SEALY
SEELS
SEELY
SELLS
SEULE
TEALS
TELLS
TELLY
TESLA
VEALY
VEILS
WEALS
WEILL
WELLS
WETLY
YELLS
ZEALS

•E••L

BEALL
BERYL
BETEL
BEVEL
BEZEL
CECIL
CEORL
DECAL
DEVIL
FERAL
FETAL
HEGEL
HERZL
HEXYL
JEWEL
KEMAL
KEVEL
LEGAL
LENDL
LEVEL
MEDAL
MEMEL
MERYL
METAL
NEILL
NEPAL
NEROL
NEVIL
NEWEL
PEARL
PEDAL
PENAL
PERIL
PETAL
REBEL
REGAL
RENAL
REOIL
REPEL
REUEL
REVEL
SEGAL
SEOUL
SEPAL
SERAL
TEPAL
VENAL
WEDEL
WEILL
YENTL

••EL•

ABELE
ADELA
ADELE
AKELA
ANELE
AXELS
BCELL
BUELL
CAELO
CHELA
DUELS
DWELL
DWELT
EWELL
FEELS
FEELY
FIELD
FJELD
FUELS
GAELS
HEELS
KEELS
KNELL
KNELT
KVELL
LYELL
MYELO
NIELS
NOELS
OBELI
ODELL
OPELS
PEELE
PEELS
PRELL
QUELL
REELS
RIELS
SEELS
SEELY
SHELF
SHELL
SMELL
SMELT
SNELL
SPELL
SPELT
STELA
STELE
SWELL
SZELL
TAELS
WHELK
WHELM
WHELP
WIELD
YIELD

••E•L

AREAL
BCELL
BUELL
CREEL
DWELL
EWELL
IDEAL
KNEEL
KNELL
KVELL
LYELL
ODELL
ONEAL
ONEIL
PRELL
QUELL
RUEHL
SHELL
SMELL
SNELL
SPELL
STEAL
STEEL
SWELL
SZELL
THEOL
WHEAL
WHEEL
ZOEAL

•••EL

ACCEL
ANGEL
ANSEL
APFEL
APPEL
ARIEL
ARNEL
ARPEL
ARTEL
BABEL
BAGEL
BASEL
BETEL
BEVEL
BEZEL
BIKEL
BOTEL
CAMEL
CREEL
CRUEL
CUPEL
DOWEL
DYNEL
EASEL
EDSEL
ELIEL
ENGEL
ETHEL
ETZEL
EXCEL
EXPEL
FIDEL
GAVEL
GIMEL
GOBEL
GODEL
GOMEL
GRUEL
HAMEL
HAVEL
HAZEL
HEGEL
HOSEL
HOTEL
HOVEL
IMPEL
INTEL
JEWEL
JOREL
KALEL
KAREL
KEVEL
KNEEL
KUGEL
LABEL
LAPEL
LEVEL
LIBEL
MABEL
MAZEL
MEMEL
MODEL
MONEL
MOREL
MOTEL
NAGEL
NAVEL
NEWEL
NIGEL
NOBEL
NOVEL
ORIEL
OUSEL
OUZEL
PANEL
PIXEL
RATEL
RAVEL
REBEL
REPEL
REUEL
REVEL
RIGEL
ROWEL
SAHEL
SOREL
SPIEL
STAEL
STEEL
TOWEL
UMBEL
URIEL
URKEL
VOWEL
WEDEL
WHEEL
YODEL
YOKEL

EM•••

EMAIL
EMBAR
EMBAY
EMBED
EMBER
EMCEE
EMDEN
EMEER
EMEND
EMERY
EMILE
EMILY
EMIRS
EMITS
EMLYN
EMMER
EMMET
EMMYS
EMORY
EMOTE
EMPTY

E•M••

EAMES
EAMON
ELMAN
ELMER
ELMOS
EMMER
EMMET
EMMYS

E••M•

EDAMS
EDEMA
ELEMI
ENEMY
ETYMA
EXAMS

E•••M

EFREM
ENORM
ENTOM
EPROM
EPSOM

•EM••

BEMAS
DEMES
DEMIT
DEMME
DEMOB
DEMON
DEMOS
DEMUR
FEMME
FEMTO
FEMUR
GEMMA
GEMMY
GEMOT
HEMAN
HEMEN
HEMET
HEMIN
HEMPS
JEMMY
KEMAL
KEMPS
KEMPT
LEMAT
LEMAY
LEMMA
LEMME
LEMON
LEMUR
MEMEL
MEMOS
NEMAN
NEMAT
NEMEA
PEMBA
REMAN
REMAP
REMET
REMEX
REMIT
REMIX
REMOP
REMOW
REMUS
SEMIS
TEMPE
TEMPI
TEMPO
TEMPS
TEMPT
YEMEN

•E•M•

BEAMS
BEAMY
BERME
BERMS
DEEMS
DEMME
DERMA
DERMO
FEMME
FERMI
GEMMA
GEMMY
GERMS
GERMY
GETME
GEUMS
HELMS
HERMS
JEMMY
LEMMA
LEMME
NEUME
PERMS
REAMS
REIMS
SEAMS
SEAMY
SEEMS
SELMA
TEAMS
TEEMS
TERMS
VERMI
WEEMS

•E••M

BEDIM
BEGUM
BELEM
BESOM
CERAM
DECEM
DEISM
DENIM
DENOM
MECUM
REAIM
REALM
REARM
REGUM
REHEM
RERUM
SEBUM
SEDUM
SEISM
SERUM
TENAM
TENPM
VELUM
VENOM

••EM•

ANEMO
CREME
DEEMS
DIEMS
EDEMA
ELEMI
ENEMY
HAEMA
HAEMO
ITEMS
MNEME
POEME
POEMS
SEEMS
SHEMA
SHEMP
STEMS
SUEME
TEEMS
THEMA
THEME
THEMS
WEEMS

••E•M

ABEAM
ADEEM
AKEEM
ATEAM
BOEHM
BREAM
CREAM
DREAM
GLEAM
HBEAM
IBEAM
ODEUM
OLEUM
ONEAM
ONEPM
RHEUM
STEAM
THERM
WHELM

•••EM

ADEEM
ADHEM
ADREM
AKEEM
BELEM
CANEM
DECEM
EFREM
GOLEM
HAREM
INREM
KASEM
MODEM
PROEM
REHEM
ROREM
SALEM
TOTEM
XYLEM

EN•••

ENACT
ENATE
ENCYC
ENDED
ENDER
ENDON
ENDOR
ENDOW
ENDUE
ENDUP
ENEMY
ENERO
ENFIN
ENGEL
ENGRS
ENIAC
ENJOY
ENLAI
ENNEA
ENNIO
ENNIS
ENNUI
ENOCH
ENOLA
ENOLS
ENORM
ENROL
ENSKY
ENSOR
ENSUE
ENTER
ENTIA
ENTOM
ENTRE
ENTRY
ENUGU
ENURE
ENVOI
ENVOY

E•N••

ENNEA
ENNIO
ENNIS
ENNUI
ERNES
ERNIE
ERNST
ESNES
ETNAS

E••N•

EARNS
EBOND
EBONS
EBONY
EDENS
EDINA
EKING
ELAND
ELENA
ELENI
EMEND
ETHNO
ETONS
EVANS
EVENS
EVENT
EWING
EXONS

E•••N

EAGAN
EAMON
EATEN
EATIN
EATON
EBSEN
ECHIN
EDWIN
EGGON
EIGEN
ELFIN
ELGIN
ELION
ELLEN
ELMAN
ELTON
ELVIN
EMDEN
EMLYN
ENDON
ENFIN
EOSIN
EPSON
ERVIN
ERWIN
ESSEN
ETHAN
EVIAN
EXXON

•EN••

BENCH
BENDS
BENDY
BENES
BENET
BENIN
BENJI
BENNY
BENTS
BENUE
BENXI
BENZO
CENCI
CENSE
CENTI
CENTO
CENTS
DENDR
DENEB
DENES
DENIM
DENIS
DENNY
DENOM
DENSE
DENTE
DENTI
DENTS
DENYS
FENCE
FENDS
FENNY
GENES
GENET
GENIC
GENIE
GENII
GENOA
GENRE
GENRO
GENTS
GENUA
GENUS
HENAN
HENCE
HENCH
HENGE
HENIE
HENNA
HENNY
HENRI
HENRY
HENTS
JENNY
KENAI
KENCH
KENDO
KENNY
KENOS
KENYA
LENDL
LENDS
LENIN
LENIS
LENNY
LENOS
LENOX
LENTO
LENTS
LENYA
MENDS
MENES
MENLO
MENSA
MENUS
NENES
PENAL
PENCE
PENDS
PENGO
PENNA
PENNE
PENNI
PENNY
PENTA
PENTE
PENZA
RENAL
RENAN
RENDS
RENEE
RENEW
RENIN
RENTA
RENTS
SENAT
SENDS
SENGI
SENNA
SENOR
SENSE
SENTE
TENAM
TENCH
TENDS
TENET
TENON
TENOR
TENPM
TENSE
TENTH
TENTS
VENAE
VENAL
VENDA
VENDS
VENEZ
VENIN
VENOM
VENTS
VENUE
VENUS
WENCH
WENDS
WENDT
WENDY
XENIA
XENON
YENTA
YENTE
YENTL
ZENDA
ZENDO
ZENDS
ZENIC

•E•N•

AEONS
AETNA
BEANO
BEANS
BEANY
BEENE
BEING
BEINS
BENNY
BERNE
DEANE
DEANS
DENNY
DESNA
FEINT
FENNY
FERNS
FERNY
GEENA
HEINE
HEINZ
HENNA
HENNY
HERNE
HERNS
JEANE
JEANS
JENNY
JEUNE
KEANE
KEANU
KEENE
KEENS
KENNY
KERNS
LEANS
LEANT
LENNY
LEONA
LEONE
LEONI
MEANS
MEANT
MEANY
MEINY
MESNE
NEONS
PEENS
PENNA
PENNE
PENNI
PENNY
PEONS
PEONY
REGNI
REINA
REINK
REINS
REUNE
SEGNI
SEGNO
SEHNA
SEINE
SENNA
TEENA
TEENS
TEENY
TERNE
TERNS
VEINS
VEINY
VERNE
WEANS
WEENY
YEANS
YESNO
ZEINS

•E••N

AERON
BEGAN
BEGIN
BEGUN
BEHAN
BENIN
BETON
BEVIN
DEIGN
DEION
DELON
DEMON
DEVON
DEWAN
FEDON
FEIGN
FELON
GETIN
GETON
HEARN
HEDIN
HELEN
HEMAN
HEMEN
HEMIN
HENAN
HERON
KEVIN
KEYIN
LEARN
LEDIN
LEDON
LEMON
LENIN
LETIN
LETON
LEVIN
LEVON
LEXAN
MEGAN
MELAN
MELON
MESON
NEMAN
NEVIN
PECAN
PEKIN
PEPIN
PERAN
PERON
RECON
REDAN
REDON
REGAN
REHAN
REIGN
REMAN
RENAN
RENIN
REPIN
RERAN
RERUN
RESIN
REWIN
REWON
SEDAN
SEEIN
SERIN
SETIN
SETON
SEVEN
SEWON
TENON
TETON
TEXAN
VEGAN
VENIN
XEDIN
XENON
YEARN
YEMEN
ZEVON

••EN•

ABEND
ADENO
AGENA
AGENT
AKENE
ALENE
AMEND
AMENS
AMENT
ANENT
ARENA
ARENS
ARENT
AVENA
AVENS
BEENE
BLEND
BLENT
BRENT
BUENA
BUENO
DIENE
EDENS
ELENA
ELENI
EMEND
EVENS
EVENT
FIEND
FRENA
GEENA
GHENT
GLENN
GLENS
GWENN
GWENT
HYENA
ICENI
ILENE
IRENE
KEENE
KEENS
LIENS
MIENS
NOEND
OMENS
ONEND
OPENS
OVENS
OWENS
PEENS
PHENO
PLENA
SAENS
SCENA
SCEND
SCENE
SCENT
SIENA
SPEND
SPENT
STENO
STENS
TEENA
TEENS
TEENY
TREND
TRENT
UPEND
WEENY
WRENS

••E•N

ATEIN
BREEN
CLEAN
CLEON
CREON
CUEIN
FOEHN
FREON
GLEAN
GLENN
GREEN
GWENN
ICEIN
KLEIN
LIEIN
OCEAN
OLEAN
OLEIN
PAEAN
PAEON
PLEON
PREEN
QUEEN
QUERN
SEEIN
SHEAN
SHEEN
SKEAN
SKEIN
STEEN
STEIN
STERN
TIEIN
TOEIN
TREEN
TWEEN
WHEEN

•••EN

ADMEN
AIKEN
ALBEN
ALDEN
ALIEN
ALLEN
ARDEN
ARLEN
ASHEN
ASPEN
AUDEN
BADEN
BIDEN
BOWEN
BREEN
CHIEN
COHEN
COVEN
COZEN
DIZEN
DONEN
DOREN
DOYEN
DOZEN
EATEN
EBSEN
EIGEN
ELLEN
EMDEN
ESSEN
GALEN
GIVEN
GOREN
GREEN
GUTEN
HAGEN
HAVEN
HELEN
HEMEN
IBSEN
KAREN
LADEN
LATEN
LIKEN
LIMEN
LINEN
LIVEN
LODEN
LOREN
LTGEN
LUMEN
MAVEN
NIVEN
NOMEN
NUMEN
NUYEN
OAKEN
OATEN
OFTEN
OGDEN
OLDEN
OLSEN
PAREN
PATEN
PHREN
PREEN
QUEEN
QUIEN
RAMEN
RAVEN
RIPEN
RISEN
RIVEN
ROSEN
ROUEN
ROWEN
RUBEN
RUMEN
SEVEN
SHEEN
SIREN
SOREN
STEEN
TAKEN
TOKEN
TREEN
TWEEN
UNPEN
VIXEN
WAKEN
WAXEN
WHEEN
WIDEN
WIZEN
WODEN
WOKEN
WOMEN
WOVEN
YEMEN
ZAZEN

EO•••

EOLUS
EOSIN

E•O••

EBOAT
EBOLI
EBOND
EBONS
EBONY
ECOLE
ECOLI
ELOPE
EMORY
EMOTE
ENOCH
ENOLA
ENOLS
ENORM
EPOCH
EPODE
EPOXY
ERODE
EROSE
ETONS
EVOKE
EVORA
EWOKS
EXONS
EYOTS

E••O•

EAMON
EATON
EGGON
ELBOW
ELION
ELIOT
ELMOS
ELROY
ELTON
ENDON
ENDOR
ENDOW
ENJOY
ENROL
ENSOR
ENTOM
ENVOI
ENVOY
EPCOT
EPHOD
EPHOR
EPROM
EPSOM
EPSON
ERGOT
ERROL
ERROR
ESPOO
ESTOP
ETHOS
EUROS
EXPOS
EXTOL
EXXON

E•••O

EIEIO
EJIDO
ENERO
ENNIO
ERATO
ESPOO
ETHNO
EXTRO

•EO••

AEONS
CEORL
DEOXY
FEOFF
GEODE
GEOID
GEORG
KEOGH
LEONA
LEONE
LEONI
LEORA
MEOWS
NEONS

PEONS PEONY REOIL SEOUL

•E•O•

AEIOU AERON AEROS AESOP BEBOP BEFOG BEGOT BELOW BESOM BESOT BETON CEROS DECOR DECOY DEFOE DEFOG DEION DELON DELOS DEMOB DEMON DEMOS DENOM DEPOT DETOO DEVON FEDON FELON FETOR GEMOT GENOA GETON HELOS HELOT HEROD HERON HEROS KEBOB KENOS LEDON LEGOS LEMON LENOS LENOX LEROI LEROY LETON LEVON MEDOC MELON MELOS MEMOS MEROE MESON METOO NEPOS NEROL PECOS PEKOE PEPOS PERON PEROT PESOS RECON REDON REDOX REMOP REMOW REPOS REPOT RESOD RETOP RETOW REWON SEGOS SENOR SEPOY SEROW SETON SEWON TELOS TENON TENOR TETON VENOM XENON XEROX ZEROS ZEVON

•E••O

BEANO BENZO CELLO CENTO CERRO DEKKO DELCO DERMO DETOO DEUTO FEMTO FERRO GECKO GENRO GESSO GETGO GETTO HECTO HELIO HELLO JELLO KELSO KENDO LEDTO LENTO LEPTO LETGO MENLO METOO METRO MEZZO NEATO NEURO PEABO PEDRO PENGO PESTO PETRO RECTO REPRO RETRO SEATO SECCO SEETO SEGNO SEIKO SERVO SETTO TELEO TEMPO VERSO YESNO ZENDO ZEPPO

••EO•

CLEON CREON FREON OLEOS OREOS PAEON PLEON THEOL

••E•O

ACETO ADENO ANEMO ANETO BUENO CAELO CREDO DIEGO DUETO EIEIO ENERO FIERO FUEGO GRECO HAEMO HIERO HUEVO LIETO LUEGO MYELO PHENO PLEIO PREGO PTERO SEETO SPERO STENO TIETO VIEJO

•••EO

BUTEO CAMEO CUNEO HOMEO JUDEO MATEO MIMEO MINEO ORFEO OSSEO OSTEO PALEO PASEO RODEO ROLEO ROMEO TELEO VIDEO VIREO

EP•••

EPACT EPCOT EPEES EPHAH EPHAS EPHOD EPHOR EPICS EPISC EPOCH EPODE EPOXY EPROM EPSOM EPSON

E•P••

EMPTY ESPOO EXPEL EXPOS

E••P•

EGYPT ELOPE ERUPT ETAPE

E•••P

EATUP ENDUP EQUIP ESTOP

•EP••

CEPES DEPEW DEPOT DEPTH DEPTS HEPTA KEPIS LEPPY LEPTA LEPTO LEPUS NEPAL NEPOS PEPIN PEPLA PEPOS PEPPY PEPSI PEPUP PEPYS REPAD REPAY REPEG REPEL REPIN REPLY REPOS REPOT REPPS REPRO SEPAL SEPIA SEPOY SEPTA TEPAL TEPEE TEPID ZEPPO

•E•P•

BEEPS DEEPS HEAPS HELPS HEMPS JEEPS KEEPS KELPS KELPY KEMPS KEMPT LEAPS LEAPT LEPPY NEAPS PEEPS PEPPY PERPS REAPS REPPS REUPS SEEPS SEEPY TEMPE TEMPI TEMPO TEMPS TEMPT TENPM TERPS VEEPS WEEPS WEEPY YELPS ZEPPO

•E••P

AESOP BEBOP FEDUP GETUP HETUP KEYUP LEGUP LETUP PEPUP RECAP RECIP REMAP REMOP RETAP RETOP REVUP SETUP SEWUP TEEUP

••EP•

ADEPT ALEPH BEEPS CREPE CREPT DEEPS INEPT JEEPS KEEPS ONEPM PEEPS PREPS SEEPS SEEPY SIEPI SKEPS SLEPT STEPS SWEPT VEEPS WEEPS WEEPY

••E•P

ATEUP BLEEP CHEAP CHEEP CREEP ICEUP ONEUP SHEEP SHEMP SLEEP STEEP SWEEP TEEUP TIEUP TWERP USEUP WHELP

•••EP

BLEEP CHEEP CREEP JULEP SALEP SHEEP SLEEP STEEP STREP SWEEP

EQ•••

EQUAL EQUIP EQUIV EQUUS

E•Q••

ESQUE

E••Q•

ETSQQ

E•••Q

ETSEQ ETSQQ

•••EQ

ETSEQ

ER•••

ERASE ERATO ERBIL ERECT ERGOT ERICA ERICH ERIES ERIKA ERISA ERNES ERNIE ERNST ERODE EROSE ERRED ERROL ERROR ERUCT ERUPT ERVIL ERVIN ERWIN

E•R••

EARED EARLE EARLS EARLY EARNS EARTH ECRUS EERIE EFREM EGRET ELROY ENROL EPROM ERRED ERROL ERROR EUROS EURUS EYRAS EYRES EYRIE EYRIR

E••R•

EAGRE EBERT EMERY EMIRS EMORY ENERO ENGRS ENORM ENTRE ENTRY ENURE EVERS EVERT EVERY EVORA EWERS EXERT EXTRA EXTRO EXURB EYERS

E•••R

EAGER EATER EDGAR EDGER EELER EGGAR EIDER ELDER ELGAR ELLER ELMER ELVER EMBAR EMBER EMEER EMMER ENDER ENDOR ENSOR ENTER EPHOR ERROR ESKER ESTER ETHER ETVIR EULER EYRIR

•ER••

AERIE AERON AEROS BEREA BERET BERGH BERGS BERLE BERME BERMS BERNE BERRA BERRY BERTH BERYL CERAM CERAT CERED CERES CERIA CEROS CERRO CERTS DERAT DERBY DEREK DERIV DERMA DERMO DERRY DERSU EERIE FERAL FERDE FERIA FERMI FERNS FERNY FERRI FERRO FERRY GERAH GERMS GERMY GERRY HERAT HERBS HERBY HERDS HERES HERKY HERLS HERMS HERNE HERNS HEROD HERON HEROS HERTZ HERVE HERZL JEREZ JERKS JERKY JERRY JERZY KERAT KERBS KERNS KERRI KERRY LEROI LEROY MERCE MERCI MERCK MERCY MERES MERGE MERIT MERLE MERLS MEROE MERRY MERTZ MERYL NERDS NERDY NEROL NERTS NERTZ NERVE NERVY PERAN PERCE PERCH PERCY PERDU PERES PEREZ PERIL PERIS PERKS PERKY PERLE PERMS PERON PEROT PERPS PERRY PERSE PERTH RERAN RERIG RERUM RERUN SERAC SERAI SERAL SERBS SERES SERFS SERGE SERIF SERIN SEROW SERRA SERRY SERTA SERUM SERVE SERVO TERMS TERNE TERNS TERPS TERRA TERRE TERRI TERRY TERSE TERZA VERBA VERBS VERDE VERDI VERGE VERMI VERNE VERRE VERSA VERSE VERSO VERST VERTE VERTS VERVE XERIC XEROX XERUS YERBA YERKS ZEROS

•E•R•

BEARD BEARS BEERS BEERY BERRA BERRY CEORL CERRO DEARS DEARY DEBRA DECRY DEERE DEERS DERRY DETRE DEVRY FEARS FERRI FERRO FERRY GEARS GEARY GENRE GENRO GEORG GERRY HEARD HEARN HEARS HEART HEIRS HENRI HENRY HEURE JEERS JERRY KERRI KERRY LEARN LEARS LEARY LEERS LEERY LEORA MEARA MERRY METRE METRO METRY NEARS NEGRI NEHRU NEURO PEARL PEARS PEARY PEDRO PEERS PERRY PETRA PETRI PETRO REARM REARS REFRY REPRO RETRO RETRY SEARS SEERS SERRA SERRY TEARS TEARY TERRA TERRE TERRI TERRY TETRA VEERS VEERY VERRE WEARS WEARY WEIRD WEIRS YEARN YEARS ZEBRA

•E••R

AEGIR AESIR CEDAR CESAR DEBAR DECOR DEFER DEMUR DENDR DETER DEWAR DEXTR EELER FEMUR FETOR FEVER FEWER FEYER HEWER HEXER JETER KEFIR LEGER LEHAR LEMUR LEVAR LEVER METER MEYER NEVER NEWER PETER REAIR REBAR RECUR REFER RETAR SEDER SEGAR SEGER SENOR SEVER SEWER TENOR VELAR VEXER WEBER WESER

••ER•

ACERB ACERS AGERS ALERT APERS APERY AVERS AVERT AVERY AXERS AYERS BEERS BEERY BOERS BRERS CBERS CHERE CHERI CHERT CIERA CLERK DEERE DEERS DOERS DYERS EBERT EMERY ENERO EVERS EVERT EVERY EWERS EXERT EYERS FAERY FIERO FIERY FRERE GOERS HIERA HIERO HOERS IBERT ICERS INERT ISERE ITERS JEERS LEERS LEERY MYERS NLERS OMERS ONERS OPERA OPERE OVERS OVERT OWERS PEERS PIERS PTERO QUERN QUERY RUERS SEERS SHERE SNERD SNERT SPERO STERE STERN SUERS THERA THERE THERM TIERS TWERE TWERP USERS VEERS VEERY VIERS WHERE

••E•R

AMEER ANEAR AREAR BLEAR CHEER CLEAR COEUR DREAR EMEER FLEER FLEUR FREER GREER QUEER SHEAR SHEER SIEUR SMEAR SNEER SOEUR SPEAR STEER SWEAR THEIR TWEER

•••ER

ABLER ABNER ACTER ADDER ADLER AFTER AILER AIMER AJMER ALDER ALGER ALLER ALTER AMBER AMEER ANGER ANSER APTER ARBER ASHER ASKER ASNER ASTER AUBER AUGER BABER BADER BAKER BALER BARER BASER BAUER BAYER BIKER BITER BLUER BONER BOOER BORER BOWER BOXER BOYER BRIER BUBER BUYER BYNER CABER CAGER CANER CAPER CARER CATER CAVER CHEER CIDER CITER CODER COMER COOER CORER COVER COWER COYER CRIER CRYER CURER CUTER CYBER CYDER DARER DATER DEFER DETER DICER DINER DIRER DIVER DIYER DOSER DOTER DOVER DOWER DOZER DRIER DRYER DURER EAGER EATER EDGER EELER EIDER ELDER ELLER ELMER ELVER EMBER EMEER EMMER ENDER ENTER ESKER ESTER ETHER EULER FABER FACER FAKER FARER FEVER FEWER FEYER FIBER FIFER FILER FINER FIRER FIVER FIXER FLEER FLIER FLYER FOYER FREER FRIER FRYER GAMER GAPER GAYER GAZER GIBER GIVER GLUER GOFER GOMER GONER GOWER GREER GRIER HABER HALER HATER HAUER HAVER HAZER HEWER HEXER HIDER HIKER HIRER HOMER HOPER HOVER HUGER HYPER ICIER IDLER ILLER INFER INGER INKER INNER INTER JETER JIVER JOKER KHMER KINER KITER KYSER LACER LADER LAGER LAKER LAMER LASER LATER LAUER LAVER LAXER LAYER LEGER LEVER LIGER LINER LITER LIVER LONER LOPER LOSER LOVER LOWER LUGER MAHER MAKER MASER MATER MAYER MAZER METER MEYER MILER MIMER MINER MISER MITER MIXER MOPER MOVER MOWER MUSER MUTER NADER NAMER NEVER NEWER NFLER NHLER NICER NIGER NINER NITER NIZER NOTER NUDER OATER OCHER ODDER OFFER OGLER OILER OLDER OMBER ORDER ORSER OSIER OSLER OTHER OTTER OUTER OWNER PACER PAGER PALER PAPER PARER PATER PAVER PAWER PAYER PETER PIKER PIPER POKER POLER POSER POWER PRIER PURER QUEER RACER RAFER RAKER RARER RASER RATER RAVER RAWER REFER RICER RIDER RIFER RIKER RIPER RISER RIVER ROGER ROMER ROPER ROVER ROWER RUDER RULER RYDER SABER SAFER SAGER SAKER SANER SAVER SAYER SEDER SEGER SEVER SEWER SHEER SHIER SHOER SHYER SIDER SIXER SIZER SKIER SLIER SLYER SNEER SOBER SOLER SORER SOWER SOXER STEER SUMER SUPER SURER TAKER TALER TAMER TAPER TASER TATER TAXER TIBER TIGER TILER TIMER TITER TOLER TONER TOPER TOTER TOWER TRIER TRUER TUBER TUNER TWEER TYLER TYPER UDDER ULCER UMBER UNDER UNGER UNSER UNTER UPPER URGER USHER UTHER UTTER VADER VATER VEXER VILER VIPER VOTER VOWER WADER WAFER WAGER WALER WANER WATER WAVER WAXER WEBER WESER WIDER WIPER WIRER WISER WOOER WRIER WRYER WYLER YARER

ES•••

ESBAT ESKER ESNES ESPOO ESQUE ESSAY ESSEN ESSES ESSEX ESTAB ESTAS ESTEE

ESTER ESTES ESTOP

E•S••

EASED EASEL EASES EASTS EBSEN EDSEL ELSIE ENSKY ENSOR ENSUE EOSIN EPSOM EPSON ESSAY ESSEN ESSES ESSEX ETSEQ ETSQQ

E••S•

EGEST ELISE ELYSE EPISC ERASE ERISA ERNST EROSE EXIST

E•••S

EAMES EARLS EARNS EASES EASTS EAVES EBONS ECRUS EDAMS EDDAS EDENS EDGES EDITS EFIKS EGADS ELIAS ELLES ELLIS ELMOS ELVES ELVIS ELWES EMIRS EMITS EMMYS ENGRS ENNIS ENOLS EOLUS EPEES EPHAS EPICS EQUUS ERIES ERNES ESNES ESSES

ESTAS ESTES ETATS ETHOS ETNAS ETONS ETUIS EUROS EURUS EVANS EVENS EVERS EVILS EWERS EWOKS EXAMS EXECS EXITS EXONS EXPOS EYERS EYOTS EYRAS EYRES

•ES••

AESIR AESOP BESET BESOM BESOT BESTS CESAR CESTA CESTI DESKS DESNA DESTE FESTA FESTS GESSO GESTE GESTS HESSE HESTS JESSE JESTS KESEY MESAS MESHY MESIC MESNE MESON MESSY MESTA NESTS PESCI PESKY PESOS PESTO PESTS RESAW RESEE RESET RESEW RESIN RESOD RESTS TESLA TESTA TESTS TESTY VESEY VESTA VESTS WESER WESTS YESES YESNO ZESTS ZESTY

•E•S•

BEAST BETSY CEASE CENSE DEISM DEIST DENSE DERSU FEAST FEIST GEESE GESSO HEISS HEIST HESSE HEYSE JESSE KELSO LEASE LEASH LEAST MEESE MENSA MESSY MEUSE NEWSY PEASE PEPSI PERSE REESE REUSE SEISM SENSE SEUSS TEASE TENSE TERSE VERSA VERSE VERSO VERST WEEST WEISS WELSH YEAST ZEISS ZEIST

•E••S

AEDES AEGIS AEONS AEROS BEADS BEAKS BEALS BEAMS BEANS BEARS BEATS BEAUS BECKS BEEFS BEEPS BEERS

BEETS BEINS BELLS BELTS BEMAS BENDS BENES BENTS BERGS BERMS BESTS BETAS BETHS CEDES CEDIS CEILS CELLS CELTS CENTS CEPES CERES CEROS CERTS CETUS DEALS DEANS DEARS DEBTS DECKS DEEDS DEEMS DEEPS DEERS DEGAS DEILS DEKES DELES DELIS DELLS DELOS DELTS DEMES DEMOS DENES DENIS DENTS DENYS DEPTS DESKS FEARS FEATS FEEDS FEELS FEETS FELIS FELLS FELTS FENDS FERNS FESTS FETAS FETES FEUDS GEARS GEEKS GENES GENTS GENUS GERMS GESTS GETAS GEUMS HEADS HEALS

HEAPS HEARS HEATS HECKS HEEDS HEELS HEFTS HEIRS HEISS HELLS HELMS HELOS HELPS HEMPS HENTS HERBS HERDS HERES HERLS HERMS HERNS HEROS HESTS HETHS HEXES JEANS JEEPS JEERS JELLS JERKS JESTS JETES KEATS KEELS KEENS KEEPS KEETS KELPS KEMPS KENOS KEPIS KERBS KERNS KEYES LEADS LEAFS LEAKS LEANS LEAPS LEARS LEEDS LEEKS LEERS LEETS LEFTS LEGGS LEGIS LEGOS LENDS LENIS LENOS LENTS LEPUS LETTS LEVIS LEWES LEWIS LEXIS LEXUS MEADS MEALS MEANS MEATS MEDES

MEEDS MEETS MELDS MELOS MELTS MEMOS MENDS MENES MENUS MEOWS MERES MERLS MESAS METES METIS MEWLS NEAPS NEARS NEATS NECKS NEEDS NEGUS NEHIS NENES NEONS NEPOS NERDS NERTS NESTS NEVES NEVIS NEVUS NEWTS NEXIS NEXUS PEAKS PEALS PEARS PEATS PECKS PECOS PEEKS PEELS PEENS PEEPS PEERS PEKES PELTS PENDS PEONS PEPOS PEPYS PERES PERIS PERKS PERMS PERPS PESOS PESTS PETES READS REALS REAMS REAPS REARS REBUS REDES REEDS REEFS REEKS REELS REGIS REIMS REINS

REMUS RENDS RENTS REPOS REPPS RESTS REUPS REXES REYES SEALS SEAMS SEARS SEATS SECTS SEEDS SEEKS SEELS SEEMS SEEPS SEERS SEGOS SELES SELLS SEMIS SENDS SERBS SERES SERFS SEUSS SEXES SEXTS TEAKS TEALS TEAMS TEARS TECHS TEEMS TEENS TELES TELLS TELOS TEMPS TENDS TENTS TERMS TERNS TERPS TESTS TETES TETHS TEXAS TEXTS VEDAS VEEPS VEERS VEGAS VEILS VEINS VELDS VENDS VENTS VENUS VERBS VERTS VESTS VEXES WEALS WEANS WEARS WEEDS WEEKS WEEMS WEEPS WEFTS

WEIRS WEISS WEKAS WELDS WELLS WELTS WENDS WESTS XERUS YEANS YEARS YEATS YEGGS YELLS YELPS YERKS YESES YETIS ZEALS ZEBUS ZEINS ZEISS ZENDS ZEROS ZESTS ZETAS

••ES•

BLESS BLEST BREST CHESS CHEST CRESC CRESS CREST DOEST DRESS EGEST FLESH FRESH GEESE GLESS GOEST GUESS GUEST IDEST LOESS MEESE OBESE POESY PRESS PREST QUEST REESE THESE TRESS WEEST WIEST WREST

••E•S

ABETS ACERS AGERS AKEES ALEFS AMENS APERS AREAS ARENS AVENS AVERS AXELS

AXERS AYERS BEEFS BEEPS BEERS BEETS BLEBS BLESS BOERS BRERS BREWS CBERS CHEFS CHESS CHEWS CLEFS CLEWS COEDS CREES CRESS CREWS DEEDS DEEMS DEEPS DEERS DIEMS DIETS DOERS DREGS DRESS DUELS DUETS DYERS EDENS EPEES EVENS EVERS EWERS EXECS EYERS FEEDS FEELS FEETS FIEFS FLEAS FLEES FLEWS FLEYS FREES FRETS FUELS GAELS GEEKS GHEES GLEES GLENS GLESS GLEYS GOERS GREES GREYS GUESS HEEDS HEELS HOERS ICERS IDEAS ITEMS ITERS JEEPS JEERS JOEYS KEELS KEENS

KEEPS KEETS KNEES KREBS LEEDS LEEKS LEERS LEETS LIENS LIEUS LOESS MEEDS MEETS MIENS MYERS NEEDS NIELS NLERS NOELS NYETS OBEYS ODETS OGEES OLEOS OMENS OMERS ONERS OPEDS OPELS OPENS OREOS OVENS OVERS OWENS OWERS PEEKS PEELS PEENS PEEPS PEERS PIEDS PIERS PLEAS PLEBS PLEWS POEMS POETS PREPS PRESS PREYS REEDS REEFS REEKS REELS RHEAS RIELS RUERS SAENS SEEDS SEEKS SEELS SEEMS SEEPS SEERS SHEDS SKEGS SKEPS SKEWS SLEDS SLEWS SMEWS SPECS SPETS SPEWS

STEMS STENS STEPS STETS STEWS SUERS SUETS TAELS TEEMS TEENS THEMS THEWS TIEGS TIERS TREES TREKS TRESS TREWS TREYS USERS VEEPS VEERS VIERS VIEWS WEEDS WEEKS WEEMS WEEPS WHETS WHEYS WRENS ZOEAS

•••ES

AAMES ABBES ABYES ACHES ACMES ACRES ADZES AEDES AGNES AGUES AIDES AIRES AKEES ALLES ALOES AMIES ANDES ANGES ANNES ANTES APRES APSES ARIES ARLES ARTES ASHES ASSES AXLES AYRES BABES BAKES BALES BANES BARES BASES BATES BENES BIDES BIKES BINES

BISES BITES BLUES BODES BOLES BONES BORES BOWES BOXES BRAES BRIES BUSES BYRES BYTES CAFES CAGES CAKES CANES CAPES CARES CASES CATES CAVES CEDES CEPES CERES CINES CIRES CITES CLUES CODES COKES COLES COMES CONES COPES CORES COTES COVES COWES COXES COZES CREES CRIES CUBES CUKES CURES CYMES DACES DALES DAMES DANES DARES DATES DAWES DAZES DEKES DELES DEMES DENES DICES DIKES DIMES DINES DIVES DOGES DOLES DOMES DOPES DOSES DOTES DOVES DOZES DRIES

DUCES DUDES DUKES DUNES DUPES DUXES DYNES EAMES EASES EAVES EDGES ELLES ELVES ELWES EPEES ERIES ERNES ESNES ESSES ESTES EYRES FACES FADES FAKES FAMES FANES FARES FATES FAVES FAXES FAZES FETES FICES FIDES FIFES FILES FINES FIRES FIVES FIXES FLEES FLIES FLOES FLUES FORES FOXES FREES FRIES FROES FUMES FUSES FYKES GAGES GALES GAMES GAPES GASES GATES GAZES GENES GHEES GIBES GILES GIVES GLEES GLUES GORES GREES GULES GYBES GYRES GYVES HADES HAKES

HALES HAMES HANES HARES HATES HAVES HAYES HAZES HERES HEXES HIDES HIKES HINES HIRES HIVES HOKES HOLES HOMES HONES HOPES HOSES HYPES ICKES IDLES IGNES ISLES IVIES JADES JAKES JAMES JAPES JETES JIBES JIVES JOKES JONES JUKES JULES JUTES KALES KEYES KITES KNEES LACES LADES LAKES LAMES LANES LARES LASES LAVES LAWES LAZES LEWES LIKES LIMES LINES LITES LIVES LOBES LODES LOGES LOPES LORES LOSES LOVES LOWES LOXES LUBES LUGES LUNES LURES LUTES LYRES

MACES MAGES MAKES MALES MANES MARES MATES MAXES MAZES MEDES MENES MERES METES MIKES MILES MIMES MINES MIRES MITES MIXES MLLES MODES MOLES MOPES MORES MOSES MOTES MOUES MOVES MULES MUSES MUTES MYLES NABES NAMES NAPES NARES NAVES NENES NEVES NIDES NIKES NILES NIMES NINES NITES NIXES NODES NONES NOSES NOTES NOYES NUDES NUKES OAKES OASES OATES OBIES OBOES OGEES OGLES OGRES OKIES OOZES ORLES OTOES PACES PAGES PALES PANES PARES PASES PATES PAVES

PEKES PERES PETES PIKES PILES PINES PIPES PLIES POKES POLES POMES PONES POPES PORES POSES PRIES PULES PYRES RACES RAGES RAKES RARES RASES RATES RAVES RAZES REDES REXES REYES RICES RIDES RILES RIMES RISES RITES RIVES ROBES ROLES ROPES ROSES ROTES ROUES ROVES RUBES RULES RUNES RUSES SAFES SAGES SAKES SALES SASES SATES SAVES SAXES SELES SERES SEXES SHIES SHOES SIDES SIKES SINES SIRES SITES SIXES SIZES SKIES SLOES SLUES SOKES SOLES SONES SORES

SPIES STIES SUPES SYCES TAKES TALES TAMES TAPES TARES TAXES TELES TETES TIDES TIKES TILES TIMES TINES TIRES TOBES TOMES TONES TOPES TOTES TOVES TREES TRIES TRUES TUBES TULES TUNES TUXES TYKES TYNES TYPES TYRES URGES VALES VANES VASES VEXES VIBES VICES VINES VISES VOLES VOTES WADES WAGES WAKES WALES WANES WARES WAVES WAXES WILES WINES WIPES WIRES WIVES XAXES YATES YAXES YESES YIKES YIPES YOKES YPRES ZAXES ZINES ZONES

ET•••

ETAGE ETAPE ETATS ETHAN ETHEL ETHER ETHIC ETHNO ETHOS ETHYL ETNAS ETONS ETSEQ ETSQQ ETUDE ETUIS ETVIR ETYMA ETZEL

E•T••

EATAT EATEN EATER EATIN EATIT EATON EATUP ELTON ENTER ENTIA ENTOM ENTRE ENTRY ESTAB ESTAS ESTEE ESTER ESTES ESTOP EXTOL EXTRA EXTRO

E••T•

EARTH EASTS EDITH EDITS ELATE ELATH ELITE ELUTE EMITS EMOTE EMPTY ENATE ERATO ETATS EVITA EXITS EYOTS

E•••T

EATAT EATIT EBERT EBOAT ECLAT EDICT EDUCT EFLAT EGEST EGRET EGYPT EIGHT

EILAT
EJECT
ELECT
ELIOT
EMMET
ENACT
EPACT
EPCOT
ERECT
ERGOT
ERNST
ERUCT
ERUPT
ESBAT
EVENT
EVERT
EVICT
EXACT
EXALT
EXERT
EXIST
EXULT

•ET••

AETAT
AETNA
BETAS
BETEL
BETHS
BETON
BETSY
BETTA
BETTE
BETTY
CETUS
DETAT
DETER
DETOO
DETRE
FETAL
FETAS
FETCH
FETED
FETES
FETID
FETOR
GETAS
GETAT
GETBY
GETGO
GETIN
GETIT
GETME
GETON
GETTO
GETTY
GETUP
HETHS
HETTY
HETUP
JETER
JETES
JETTY
KETCH
LETAT
LETBE
LETGO
LETHE
LETIN
LETON
LETTS
LETUP
METAL
METED
METER
METES
METIS
METOO
METRE
METRO
METRY
PETAL
PETER
PETES
PETIT
PETRA
PETRI
PETRO
PETTI
PETTY
RETAG
RETAP
RETAR
RETAX
RETIA
RETIE
RETOP
RETOW
RETRO
RETRY
SETAE
SETAT
SETBY
SETIN
SETON
SETTE
SETTO
SETUP
TETES
TETHS
TETON
TETRA
VETCH
WETLY
YETIS
ZETAS

•E•T•

BEATS
BEETS
BELTS
BENTS
BERTH
BESTS
BETTA
BETTE
BETTY
CELTS
CENTI
CENTO
CENTS
CERTS
CESTA
CESTI
CEUTA
DEBTS
DEITY
DELTA
DELTS
DENTE
DENTI
DENTS
DEPTH
DEPTS
DESTE
DEUTO
DEXTR
FEATS
FEETS
FELTS
FEMTO
FESTA
FESTS
GENTS
GESTE
GESTS
GETTO
GETTY
HEATH
HEATS
HECTO
HEFTS
HEFTY
HENTS
HEPTA
HERTZ
HESTS
HETTY
HEUTE
JESTS
JETTY
KEATS
KEETS
KEITH
LEDTO
LEETS
LEFTS
LEFTY
LEITH
LENTO
LENTS
LEPTA
LEPTO
LETTS
LEYTE
MEATS
MEATY
MEETS
MEHTA
MELTS
MELTY
MERTZ
MESTA
NEATH
NEATO
NEATS
NERTS
NERTZ
NESTS
NEWTS
PEATS
PEATY
PEETE
PELTS
PENTA
PENTE
PERTH
PESTO
PESTS
PETTI
PETTY
REATA
RECTI
RECTO
RENTA
RENTS
RESTS
SEATO
SEATS
SECTS
SEETO
SENTE
SEPTA
SERTA
SETTE
SETTO
SEXTS
TEETH
TENTH
TENTS
TESTA
TESTS
TESTY
TEXTS
VENTS
VERTE
VERTS
VESTA
VESTS
WEFTS
WELTS
WELTY
WESTS
YEATS
YENTA
YENTE
YENTL
ZESTS
ZESTY

•E••T

AETAT
BEAST
BEAUT
BEFIT
BEGAT
BEGET
BEGOT
BENET
BERET
BESET
BESOT
CERAT
DEALT
DEBIT
DEBUT
DEFAT
DEIST
DELFT
DEMIT
DEPOT
DERAT
DETAT
FEAST
FEINT
FEIST
GEMOT
GENET
GETAT
GETIT
HEART
HECHT
HEIDT
HEIST
HELOT
HEMET
HERAT
KEMPT
KERAT
LEANT
LEAPT
LEAST
LEGIT
LEMAT
LETAT
MEANT
MEDIT
MERIT
NEMAT
PEROT
PETIT
PEWIT
REACT
REBUT
REFIT
RELET
RELIT
REMET
REMIT
REPOT
RESET
REVET
SENAT
SETAT
TEMPT
TENET
TEVET
VEIDT
VELDT
VERST
WEEST
WENDT
YEAST
ZEIST

••ET•

ABETS
ACETO
ALETA
ANETO
ARETE
BEETS
BRETT
CHETH
CRETE
DIETS
DOETH
DUETO
DUETS
FEETS
FRETS
GRETA
GRETE
KEETS
LEETS
LIETO
MEETS
NYETS
ODETS
OVETA
OVETT
PEETE
PIETA
PIETY
POETE
POETS
RHETT
SEETO
SIETE
SKETE
SPETS
STETS
SUETS
SUETY
TEETH
THETA
TIETO
WHETS
WYETH

••E•T

ADEPT
AGENT
ALERT
ALEUT
AMENT
ANENT
ARENT
AVERT
BLEAT
BLENT
BLEST
BRENT
BREST
BRETT
CHEAT
CHERT
CHEST
CLEAT
CLEFT
CREPT
CREST
DOEST
DWELT
EBERT
EGEST
EJECT
ELECT
ERECT
EVENT
EVERT
EXERT
FLEET
GHENT
GOEST
GREAT
GREET
GUEST
GWENT
IBERT
IDEST
INEPT
INERT
KNELT
LIEUT
OVERT
OVETT
PLEAT
PREST
QUEST
RHETT
SCENT
SHEET
SKEAT
SKEET
SLEET
SLEPT
SMELT
SNERT
SPELT
SPENT
SWEAT
SWEET
SWEPT
THEFT
TREAT
TRENT
TWEET
WEEST
WHEAT
WIEST
WREST

•••ET

AGLET
AMVET
ARMET
ARRET
ASSET
ASYET
BEGET
BENET
BERET
BESET
BINET
BIZET
BLUET
BONET
CADET
CAPET
CARET
CIVET
COLET
COMET
COVET
CRUET
CULET
DUVET
EGRET
EMMET
FACET
FILET
FLEET
GENET
GODET
GREET
HEMET
INLET
INSET
ISLET
JACET
JANET
LICET
LUMET
MAMET
MANET
MONET
MOTET
NONET
NYMET
OBJET
OCTET
ONSET
OWLET
PAGET
PUGET
QUIET
RAMET
RELET
REMET
RESET
REVET
RIVET
ROGET
SAGET
SHEET
SKEET
SLEET
SWEET
TACET
TENET
TEVET
TIBET
TOLET
TVSET
TWEET
UNMET
UNSET
UPSET
VALET
ZIBET

EU•••

EUBIE
EULER
EUROS
EURUS

E•U••

EDUCE
EDUCT
ELUDE
ELUTE
ENUGU
ENURE
EQUAL
EQUIP
EQUIV
EQUUS
ERUCT
ERUPT
ETUDE
ETUIS
EXUDE
EXULT
EXURB

E••U•

EATUP
ECRUS
ENDUE
ENDUP
ENNUI
ENSUE
EOLUS
EQUUS
ESQUE
EURUS

E•••U

ELIHU
ENUGU

•EU••

CEUTA
DEUCE
DEUCY
DEUTO
FEUDS
GEUMS
HEURE
HEUTE
JEUDI
JEUNE
MEUSE
NEUME
NEURO
REUEL
REUNE
REUPS
REUSE
SEULE
SEUSS

•E•U•

BEAUS
BEAUT
BEAUX
BEGUM
BEGUN
BENUE
CETUS
DEBUG
DEBUT
DEMUR
FEDUP
FEMUR
GENUA
GENUS
GETUP
HETUP
KEYUP
LEGUP
LEHUA
LEMUR
LEPUS
LETUP
LEXUS
MECUM
MENUS
NEFUD
NEGUS
NEVUS
NEXUS
PEPUP
REBUS
REBUT
RECUR
REDUB
REDUX
REGUM
REMUS
RERUM
RERUN
REVUE
REVUP
SEBUM
SEDUM
SEGUE
SEOUL
SERUM
SETUP
SEWUP
TEEUP
VELUM
VENUE
VENUS
XERUS
ZEBUS

•E••U

AEIOU
DERSU
KEANU
NEHRU
PERDU

••EU•

ADEUX
ALEUT
ATEUP
BOEUF
COEUR
FLEUR
FREUD
ICEUP
LIEUS
LIEUT
ODEUM
OLEUM
ONEUP
PSEUD
QUEUE
RHEUM
SIEUR
SOEUR
TEEUP
TIEUP
USEUP

••E•U

CHEJU
TAEGU

•••EU

ADIEU
PAREU

EV•••

EVADE
EVANS
EVENS
EVENT
EVERS
EVERT
EVERY
EVIAN
EVICT
EVILS
EVITA
EVOKE
EVORA

E•V••

EAVED
EAVES
ELVER
ELVES
ELVIN
ELVIS
ENVOI
ENVOY
ERVIL
ERVIN
ETVIR

E••V•

ELEVE

E•••V

EQUIV

•EV••

BEVEL
BEVIN
DEVIL
DEVON
DEVRY
FEVER
KEVEL
KEVIN
LEVAR
LEVEE
LEVEL
LEVER
LEVIN
LEVIS
LEVON
NEVER
NEVES
NEVIL
NEVIN
NEVIS
NEVUS
REVEL
REVET
REVUE
REVUP
SEVEN
SEVER
TEVET
TEVYE
ZEVON

•E•V•

BELVA
DELVE
HEAVE
HEAVY
HELVE
HERVE
LEAVE
NERVE
NERVY
PEAVY
PEEVE
REEVE
SELVA
SERVE
SERVO
VERVE
WEAVE

•E••V

DERIV
NEGEV

••EV•

ALEVE
BREVE
CHEVY
ELEVE
HUEVO
PEEVE
REEVE
SIEVE
SNEVA
STEVE
TREVI

•••EV

NEGEV

EW•••

EWELL
EWERS
EWING
EWOKS

E•W••

EDWIN
ELWAY
ELWES
ERWIN

E•••W

ELBOW
ENDOW

•EW••

DEWAN
DEWAR
DEWED
DEWEY
FEWER
HEWED
HEWER
JEWEL
LEWES
LEWIS
MEWED
MEWLS
NEWEL
NEWER
NEWLY
NEWSY
NEWTS
PEWEE
PEWIT
REWAX
REWED
REWIN
REWON
SEWED
SEWER
SEWON
SEWUP

•E•W•

MEOWS

•E••W

BEDEW
BELOW
DEPEW
REMOW
RENEW
RESAW
RESEW
RETOW
SEROW

••EW•

BREWS
CHEWS
CHEWY
CLEWS
CREWS
FLEWS
LOEWE
LOEWY
PLEWS
SKEWS
SLEWS
SMEWS
SPEWS
STEWS
THEWS
THEWY
TREWS
VIEWS
VIEWY

•••EW

AGNEW
ASKEW
BEDEW
CAREW
DEPEW
NAREW
RENEW
RESEW
SCREW
SHREW
SINEW
STREW
THREW

EX•••

EXACT
EXALT
EXAMS
EXCEL
EXECS
EXERT
EXILE
EXIST
EXITS
EXONS
EXPEL
EXPOS
EXTOL
EXTRA
EXTRO
EXUDE
EXULT
EXURB
EXXON

E•X••

EXXON

E••X•

EPOXY

E•••X

ESSEX

•EX••

DEXTR
HEXAD
HEXED
HEXER
HEXES
HEXYL
LEXAN
LEXIS
LEXUS
NEXIS
NEXUS
REXES
SEXES
SEXTS
TEXAN
TEXAS
TEXTS
VEXED
VEXER
VEXES

•E•X•

BENXI
DEOXY

•E••X

BEAUX
FEDEX
FELIX
HELIX
LENOX
REDOX
REDUX
RELAX
REMEX
REMIX
RETAX
REWAX
TELEX
XEROX

••EX•

FLEXI
PREXY

••E•X

ADEUX
ICEAX

•••EX

ANNEX
CODEX
COMEX
CULEX
CUTEX
ESSEX
FEDEX
INDEX
LATEX
LUREX
MUREX
NYNEX
PUREX
PYREX
REMEX
ROLEX
SILEX
TELEX
TIMEX
TRUEX

EY•••

EYDIE
EYERS
EYOTS
EYRAS
EYRES
EYRIE
EYRIR

E•Y••

EGYPT
ELYSE
ETYMA

E••Y•

EMLYN
EMMYS
ENCYC
ETHYL

E•••Y

EARLY
EBONY
EDIFY
ELEGY
ELROY
ELWAY
EMBAY
EMERY
EMILY
EMORY
EMPTY
ENEMY
ENJOY
ENSKY
ENTRY
ENVOY
EPOXY
ESSAY
EVERY

•EY••

BEYLE
FEYER
FEYLY
HEYSE
KEYED
KEYES
KEYIN
KEYUP
LEYTE
MEYER
REYES

•E•Y•

BERYL
DENYS
HEXYL
KENYA
LENYA
MERYL
PEPYS
REDYE
SEEYA
TEVYE

•E••Y

BEADY
BEAMY
BEANY
BECKY
BEEFY
BEERY
BELAY
BELLY
BENDY
BENNY
BERRY
BETSY
BETTY
CECHY
DEARY
DEBBY
DECAY
DECOY
DECRY
DEIFY
DEITY
DELAY
DENNY
DEOXY
DERBY
DERRY
DEUCY
DEVRY
DEWEY
FEELY
FELLY
FENNY
FERNY
FERRY
FEYLY
GEARY
GEEKY
GEMMY
GERMY
GERRY
GETBY
GETTY
HEADY
HEALY
HEAVY
HEDGY
HEFTY
HENNY
HENRY
HERBY
HERKY
HETTY
JELLY
JEMMY
JENNY
JERKY
JERRY
JERZY
JETTY
KELLY
KELPY
KENNY
KERRY
KESEY
LEADY
LEAFY
LEAHY
LEAKY
LEARY
LECKY
LEDGY
LEERY
LEFAY
LEFTY
LEGGY
LEMAY
LENNY
LEPPY
LEROY
MEALY
MEANY
MEATY
MEINY
MELTY
MERCY
MERRY
MESHY
MESSY
METRY
NEDDY
NEEDY
NELLY
NERDY
NERVY
NEWLY
NEWSY
PEARY
PEATY
PEAVY
PECKY
PEGGY
PENNY
PEONY
PEPPY
PERCY
PERKY
PERRY
PESKY
PETTY
READY
REDDY
REDLY
REEDY
REEKY
REFRY
REIFY
REKEY
RELAY
REPAY
REPLY
RETRY
SEALY
SEAMY
SEDGY
SEEDY
SEELY
SEEPY
SEPOY
SERRY
SETBY
TEARY
TECHY
TEDDY
TEENY
TELLY
TERRY
TESTY
VEALY
VEDAY
VEERY
VEINY
VESEY
WEARY
WEBBY
WEDGY
WEEDY
WEENY
WEEPY
WELBY
WELTY
WENDY
WETLY
ZESTY

••EY•

FLEYS
FREYA
GLEYS
GREYS
JOEYS
MYEYE
OBEYS
OXEYE
PREYS
SEEYA
THEYD
TREYS
WHEYS

••E•Y

APERY
AVERY
BEEFY
BEERY
CHEVY
CHEWY
CRECY
ELEGY
EMERY
ENEMY
EVERY
FAERY
FEELY
FIERY
GEEKY
LEERY
LIEBY
LOEWY
NEEDY
PIETY
POESY
PREXY
QUERY
REEDY
REEKY
SEEDY
SEELY
SEEPY
SUETY
TEENY
THEWY
VEERY
VIEWY
WEEDY
WEENY
WEEPY

•••EY

ABBEY
AGLEY
AILEY
ALLEY
APLEY
BLUEY
BOGEY
BUSEY
CAGEY
CAKEY
CAREY
CASEY
CONEY
COREY
COVEY
COXEY
CUTEY
DALEY
DEWEY
DICEY
DOGEY
DOPEY
DOVEY
FAHEY
FOGEY
FOLEY
GAMEY
GLUEY
GODEY
GOOEY
HALEY
HOKEY
HOLEY
HOMEY
HONEY
HOOEY
HOVEY
ISLEY
JASEY
JIVEY
JOKEY
KESEY
KILEY
LACEY
LIMEY
LINEY
LOVEY
MATEY
MIKEY
MONEY
MOPEY
MOREY
MOSEY
MULEY
NOSEY
ONKEY
PALEY
PINEY
POKEY
PUSEY
REKEY
RILEY
ROPEY
ROSEY
SKYEY
SOOEY
TANEY
TOBEY
TONEY
TYPEY
UTLEY
VESEY
WALEY
WANEY
WILEY

WINEY
ZOOEY

E•Z••
ETZEL

E••Z•
ELAZI
ELIZA

•EZ••
BEZEL
MEZZO

•E•Z•
BENZO
HERZL
JERZY
LEEZA
MEZZO
PENZA
SEIZE
TERZA

•E••Z
FELIZ
HEINZ
HEJAZ
HERTZ
JEREZ
MERTZ
NERTZ
PEREZ
VELEZ
VENEZ

••EZ•
LEEZA

•••EZ
ALLEZ
ASSEZ
GOMEZ
JEREZ
LOPEZ
PEREZ
VELEZ
VENEZ

FA•••
FABER
FABIO
FABLE
FACED
FACER
FACES
FACET
FACIA
FACIE
FACIT
FACTO
FACTS
FADED
FADES
FADOS
FAERY
FAGIN
FAGOT
FAHEY
FAILS
FAINT
FAIRE
FAIRS
FAIRY
FAITH
FAKED
FAKER
FAKES
FAKIR
FALDO
FALLA
FALLS
FALSE
FAMED
FAMES
FANCY
FANES
FANGS
FANNY
FANON
FANTA
FARAD
FARAH
FARCE
FARCI
FARED
FARER
FARES
FARGO
FARMS
FAROE
FARON
FAROS
FARSI
FASTS
FATAL
FATED
FATES
FATHA
FATLY
FATTY
FATWA
FAULT
FAUNA
FAUNS
FAURE
FAUST
FAUVE
FAVES
FAVOR
FAVRE
FAWNS
FAXED
FAXES
FAZED
FAZES

F•A••
FEARS
FEAST
FEATS
FIATS
FLACK
FLAGG
FLAGS
FLAIL
FLAIR
FLAKE
FLAKY
FLAME
FLAMS
FLAMY
FLANK
FLANS
FLAPS
FLARE
FLASH
FLASK
FLATS
FLATT
FLAWS
FLAWY
FLAXY
FLAYS
FOALS
FOAMS
FOAMY
FRAIL
FRAIS
FRAME
FRANC
FRANK
FRANS
FRANZ
FRAPS
FRATS
FRAUD
FRAYS

F••A•
FARAD
FARAH
FATAL
FERAL
FETAL
FETAS
FFLAT
FILAR
FINAL
FLEAS
FLOAT
FLYAT
FOCAL
FORAY
FREAK
FRIAR
FUGAL
FULAS
FURAN

F•••A
FACIA
FALLA
FANTA
FATHA
FATWA
FAUNA
FELLA
FERIA
FESTA
FINCA
FIONA
FIRMA
FLORA
FOLIA
FONDA
FORMA
FOSSA
FOVEA
FREDA
FRENA
FREYA
FULDA

•FA••
AFAIK
AFARS
OFAGE

•F•A•
AFLAT
BFLAT
CFLAT
DFLAT
EFLAT
FFLAT
GFLAT
OFFAL

•F••A
AFTRA

••FA•
ALFAS
BYFAR
DEFAT
DUFAY
GOFAR
LEFAY
LOFAT
NOFAT
OFFAL
SOFAR
SOFAS

••F•A
BUFFA
HOFFA
INFRA
JAFFA
KAFKA
NAFTA
SOFIA

•••FA
BUFFA
HAIFA
HOFFA
JAFFA
LOOFA
SOLFA
SULFA
USOFA

F•B••
FABER
FABIO
FABLE
FIBER
FIBRE
FIBRO
FUBSY

F••B•
FLUBS
FLYBY
FORBS
FROBE
FTLBS

FC•••
FCLEF

F•C••
FACED
FACER
FACES
FACET
FACIA
FACIE
FACIT
FACTO
FACTS
FICES
FICHE
FICHU
FICUS
FOCAL
FOCUS
FUCHS

F••C•
FANCY
FARCE
FARCI
FENCE
FETCH
FILCH
FINCA
FINCH
FISCS
FITCH
FLACK
FLECK
FLICK
FLICS
FLOCK
FORCE
FRICK
FROCK

F•••C
FOLIC
FRANC
FSLIC

•F••C
AFRIC

••F•C
SOFTC

F•D••
FADED
FADES
FADOS
FEDEX
FEDON
FEDUP
FIDEI
FIDEL
FIDES
FODOR
FUDDY
FUDGE

F••D•
FALDO
FEEDS
FENDS
FERDE
FEUDS
FINDS
FOLDS
FONDA
FONDS
FONDU
FOODS
FORDO
FORDS
FREDA
FRODO
FUDDY
FULDA
FUNDS
FUNDY

F•••D
FACED
FADED
FAKED
FAMED
FARAD
FARED
FATED
FAXED
FAZED
FELID
FETED
FETID
FIELD
FIEND
FIFED
FILED
FINED
FIORD
FIRED
FIXED
FJELD
FJORD
FLIED
FLOOD
FLOYD
FLUID
FOUND
FOXED
FRAUD
FREED
FREUD
FRIED
FROID
FROND
FUMED
FUSED
FUZED

••F•D
BIFID
DYFED
FIFED
NEFUD
UNFED

FE•••
FEARS
FEAST
FEATS
FEDEX
FEDON
FEDUP
FEEDS
FEELS
FEELY
FEETS
FEIGN
FEINT
FEIST
FELID
FELIS
FELIX
FELIZ
FELLA
FELLS
FELLY
FELON
FELTS
FEMME
FEMTO
FEMUR
FENCE
FENDS
FENNY
FEOFF
FERAL
FERDE
FERIA
FERMI
FERNS
FERNY
FERRI
FERRO
FERRY
FESTA
FESTS
FETAL
FETAS
FETCH
FETED
FETES
FETID
FETOR
FEUDS
FEVER
FEWER
FEYER
FEYLY

F•E••
FAERY
FEEDS
FEELS
FEELY
FEETS
FIEFS
FIELD
FIEND
FIERO
FIERY
FJELD
FLEAS
FLECK
FLEER
FLEES
FLEET
FLESH
FLEUR
FLEWS
FLEXI
FLEYS
FOEHN
FREAK
FREDA
FREED
FREER
FREES
FRENA
FREON
FRERE
FRESH
FRETS
FREUD
FREYA
FUEGO
FUELS

F••E•
FABER
FACED
FACER
FACES
FACET
FADED
FADES
FAHEY
FAKED
FAKER
FAKES
FAMED
FAMES
FANES
FARED
FARER
FARES
FATED
FATES
FAVES
FAXED
FAXES
FAZED
FAZES
FCLEF
FEDEX
FETED
FETES
FEVER
FEWER
FEYER
FIBER
FICES
FIDEI
FIDEL
FIDES
FIFED
FIFER
FIFES
FILED
FILER
FILES
FILET
FINED
FINER
FINES
FIRED
FIRER
FIRES
FIVER
FIVES
FIXED
FIXER
FIXES
FLEER
FLEES
FLEET
FLIED
FLIER
FLIES
FLOES
FLUES
FLYER
FOGEY
FOLEY
FORES
FOVEA
FOXED
FOXES
FOYER
FREED
FREER
FREES
FRIED
FRIER
FRIES
FROES
FRYER
FUMED
FUMES
FUSED
FUSEE
FUSES
FUZED
FUZEE
FYKES

F•••E
FABLE
FACIE
FAIRE
FALSE
FARCE
FAROE
FAURE
FAUVE
FAVRE
FEMME
FENCE
FERDE
FIBRE
FICHE
FILLE
FISKE
FLAKE
FLAME
FLARE
FLUKE
FLUME
FLUTE
FOOTE
FORCE
FORGE
FORTE
FOSSE
FOYLE
FRAME
FRERE
FRISE
FROBE
FROME
FROZE
FUDGE
FUGUE
FURZE
FUSEE
FUZEE

•F•E•
AFTER
EFREM
NFLER
OFFER
OFTEN

•F••E
AFIRE
AFORE
EFFIE
MFUME
OFAGE
OFUSE

••FE•
APFEL
CAFES
DEFER
DYFED
FIFED
FIFER
FIFES
GOFER
HEFEI
INFER
OFFER
ORFEO
RAFER
REFER
RIFER
SAFER
SAFES
UNFED
WAFER

••F•E
ALFIE
ALFRE
CAFFE
DAFOE
DEFOE
EFFIE
GAFFE
JAFFE
KAFUE
RIFLE

•••FE
CAFFE
CHAFE
GAFFE
GROFE
JAFFE
KNIFE
PHYFE
ROLFE
WOLFE

FF•••
FFLAT

F•F••
FIFED
FIFER
FIFES
FIFTH
FIFTY

F••F•
FEOFF
FIEFS
FLUFF

F•••F
FCLEF
FEOFF
FLUFF

•FF••
AFFIX
EFFIE
OFFAL
OFFER

•F•F•
AFOFL

••FF•
BIFFS
BIFFY
BOFFO
BOFFS
BUFFA
BUFFI
BUFFO
BUFFS
BUFFY
CAFFE
CUFFS
DAFFS
DAFFY
DOFFS
DUFFS
DUFFY
GAFFE
GAFFS
HOFFA
HUFFS
HUFFY
JAFFA
JAFFE
JIFFY
LUFFS
MIFFS
MIFFY
MOFFO
MUFFS
PUFFS
PUFFY
RAFFI
RIFFI
RIFFS
RUFFS
TAFFY
TIFFS
TOFFS
TOFFY

•••FF
ACUFF
BANFF
BLUFF
CHAFF
CHUFF
CLIFF
FEOFF
FLUFF
GOOFF
GRUFF
HANFF
ONOFF
QUAFF
SCOFF
SCUFF
SKIFF
SNIFF
SNUFF
SPIFF
STAFF
STIFF
STUFF
WHIFF
WOLFF

F•G••
FAGIN
FAGOT
FIGHT
FOGEY
FOGGY
FOGIN
FOGUP
FUGAL
FUGGY
FUGIT
FUGUE
FUGUS

F••G•
FANGS
FARGO
FEIGN
FLAGG
FLAGS
FLOGS
FOGGY
FORGE
FORGO
FRIGG
FROGS
FUDGE
FUEGO
FUGGY
FUNGI
FUNGO

F•••G
FLAGG
FLING
FLUNG
FRIGG

•F•G•
OFAGE

••F•G
BEFOG
DEFOG
SOFTG

F•H••
FAHEY
FOHNS

F••H•
FATHA
FICHE
FICHU
FIGHT
FISHY
FOEHN
FUCHS

F•••H
FAITH
FARAH
FETCH
FIFTH
FILCH
FILTH
FINCH
FIRTH
FITCH
FLASH
FLESH
FLUSH
FORTH
FOURH
FRESH
FROSH
FROTH
FURTH

••F•H
FIFTH

FI•••
FIATS
FIBER
FIBRE
FIBRO
FICES
FICHE
FICHU
FICUS
FIDEI
FIDEL
FIDES
FIEFS
FIELD
FIEND
FIERO
FIERY
FIFED
FIFER
FIFES
FIFTH
FIFTY
FIGHT
FILAR
FILCH
FILED
FILER
FILES
FILET
FILLE
FILLS
FILLY
FILMS
FILMY
FILTH
FILUM
FINAL
FINCA
FINCH
FINDS
FINED
FINER
FINES
FINIS
FINKS
FINNO
FINNS
FINNY
FIONA
FIORD
FIRED
FIRER
FIRES
FIRMA
FIRMS
FIRNS
FIRPO
FIRRY
FIRST
FIRTH
FISCS
FISHY
FISKE
FISTS
FITCH
FITIN
FITLY
FIVER
FIVES
FIXED
FIXER
FIXES
FIXIT
FIXUP
FIZZY

F•I••
FAILS
FAINT
FAIRE
FAIRS
FAIRY
FAITH
FEIGN
FEINT
FEIST
FLICK
FLICS
FLIED
FLIER
FLIES
FLING
FLINT
FLIPS
FLIRT
FLITS
FOILS
FOINS
FOIST
FRIAR
FRICK
FRIED
FRIER
FRIES
FRIGG
FRILL
FRIML
FRISE
FRISK
FRITO
FRITS
FRITZ
FRIZZ

F••I•
FABIO
FACIA
FACIE
FACIT
FAGIN
FAKIR
FELID
FELIS
FELIX
FELIZ
FERIA
FETID
FINIS
FITIN
FIXIT
FLAIL
FLAIR
FLUID
FLYIN
FOGIN
FOLIA
FOLIC
FOLIO
FRAIL
FRAIS
FROID
FRUIT
FSLIC
FUGIT
FUSIL

F•••I
FARCI
FARSI
FERMI
FERRI
FIDEI
FLEXI
FORLI
FUNGI

•FI••
AFIRE
EFIKS

•F•I•
AFAIK
AFFIX
AFRIC
AFRIT
EFFIE

••FI•
ADFIN
AFFIX
ALFIE
BEFIT
BIFID
EFFIE
ELFIN
ENFIN
HAFIZ
HIFIS
INFIN
INFIX
KAFIR
KEFIR
REFIT
SOFIA
SUFIS
UNFIT
UNFIX

••F•I
BUFFI
HEFEI
MUFTI
RAFFI
RIFFI

•••FI
BUFFI
RAFFI
RIFFI
SCIFI

FJ•••
FJELD
FJORD

•F•J•
JFKJR

F•K••
FAKED
FAKER
FAKES
FAKIR
FYKES

F••K•
FINKS
FISKE
FLAKE
FLAKY
FLUKE
FLUKY
FOLKS
FOLKY
FORKS
FORKY
FUNKS
FUNKY

F•••K
FLACK
FLANK
FLASK
FLECK
FLICK
FLOCK
FLUNK
FRANK
FREAK
FRICK
FRISK
FROCK

•FK••
JFKJR

•F•K•
EFIKS

•F••K
AFAIK

••FK•
KAFKA

FL•••
FLACK
FLAGG
FLAGS
FLAIL
FLAIR
FLAKE
FLAKY
FLAME
FLAMS
FLAMY
FLANK
FLANS
FLAPS
FLARE
FLASH
FLASK
FLATS
FLATT
FLAWS
FLAWY
FLAXY
FLAYS
FLEAS
FLECK
FLEER
FLEES
FLEET
FLESH
FLEUR
FLEWS
FLEXI
FLEYS
FLICK
FLICS
FLIED
FLIER
FLIES
FLING
FLINT
FLIPS
FLIRT
FLITS
FLOAT
FLOCK
FLOES
FLOGS
FLOOD
FLOOR
FLOPS
FLORA
FLORY
FLOSS
FLOUR
FLOUT
FLOWN
FLOWS
FLOYD
FLUBS
FLUES
FLUFF
FLUID
FLUKE
FLUKY
FLUME
FLUNG
FLUNK
FLUOR
FLUSH
FLUTE
FLUTY
FLYAT
FLYBY
FLYER
FLYIN
FLYNN

F•L••
FALDO
FALLA
FALLS
FALSE
FCLEF
FELID
FELIS
FELIX
FELIZ
FELLA
FELLS
FELLY
FELON
FELTS
FFLAT
FILAR
FILCH
FILED
FILER
FILES
FILET
FILLE
FILLS
FILLY
FILMS
FILMY
FILTH
FILUM
FOLDS
FOLEY
FOLIA
FOLIC
FOLIO
FOLKS
FOLKY
FOLLY
FSLIC
FTLBS
FULAS
FULDA
FULLY

F••L•
FABLE
FAILS
FALLA
FALLS
FATLY
FAULT
FEELS
FEELY
FELLA
FELLS
FELLY
FEYLY
FIELD
FILLE
FILLS
FILLY
FITLY
FJELD
FOALS
FOILS
FOLLY
FOOLS
FORLI
FOULS
FOWLS
FOYLE
FRILL
FUELS
FULLY
FURLS

F•••L
FATAL
FERAL
FETAL
FIDEL
FINAL
FLAIL
FOCAL
FRAIL
FRILL
FRIML
FUGAL
FUSIL

•FL••
AFLAT
BFLAT
CFLAT
DFLAT
EFLAT
FFLAT
GFLAT
NFLER

•F••L
AFOFL
AFOUL
OFFAL

••FL•
MCFLY
NOFLY
RIFLE

••F•L
APFEL
AWFUL
OFFAL

•••FL
AFOFL

F•M••
FAMED
FAMES
FEMME
FEMTO
FEMUR
FUMED
FUMES

F••M•
FARMS
FEMME
FERMI
FILMS

FILMY FIRMA FIRMS FLAME FLAMS FLAMY FLUME FOAMS FOAMY FORMA FORMS FRAME FRIML FROME FROMM FRUMP

F•••M
FILUM FORUM FROMM

•F•M•
MFUME

•F••M
EFREM

F•N••
FANCY FANES FANGS FANNY FANON FANTA FENCE FENDS FENNY FINAL FINCA FINCH FINDS FINED FINER FINES FINIS FINKS FINNO FINNS FINNY FONDA FONDS FONDU FONTS FUNDS FUNDY FUNGI FUNGO FUNKS FUNKY FUNNY

F••N•
FAINT FANNY FAUNA FAUNS FAWNS FEINT FENNY FERNS FERNY FIEND FINNO FINNS FINNY FIONA FIRNS FLANK FLANS FLING FLINT FLUNG FLUNK FLYNN FOHNS FOINS FOUND FOUNT FRANC FRANK FRANS FRANZ FRENA FROND FRONT FUNNY

F•••N
FAGIN FANON FARON FEDON FEIGN FELON FITIN FLOWN FLYIN FLYNN FOEHN FOGIN FREON FROWN FURAN FUTON

•FN••
IFNOT

•F••N
AFTON OFTEN

••F•N
ADFIN ELFIN ENFIN HAFUN INFIN INFUN

FO•••
FOALS FOAMS FOAMY FOCAL FOCUS FODOR FOEHN FOGEY FOGGY FOGIN FOGUP FOHNS FOILS FOINS FOIST FOLDS FOLEY FOLIA FOLIC FOLIO FOLKS FOLKY FOLLY FONDA FONDS FONDU FONTS FOODS FOOLS FOOTE FOOTS FORAY FORBS FORCE FORDO FORDS FORES FORGE FORGO FORKS FORKY FORLI FORMA FORMS FORTE FORTH FORTS FORTY FORUM FOSSA FOSSE FOULS FOUND FOUNT FOURH FOURS FOUTS FOVEA FOWLS FOXED FOXES FOXTV FOYER FOYLE

F•O••
FEOFF FIONA FIORD FJORD FLOAT FLOCK FLOES FLOGS FLOOD FLOOR FLOPS FLORA FLORY FLOSS FLOUR FLOUT FLOWN FLOWS FLOYD FOODS FOOLS FOOTE FOOTS FROBE FROCK FRODO FROES FROGS FROID FROME FROMM FROND FRONT FROSH FROST FROTH FROWN FROWS FROZE

F••O•
FADOS FAGOT FANON FAROE FARON FAROS FAVOR FEDON FELON FETOR FLOOD FLOOR FLUOR FODOR FREON FSTOP FUROR FUROS FUTON

F•••O
FABIO FACTO FALDO FARGO FEMTO FERRO FIBRO FIERO FINNO FIRPO FOLIO FORDO FORGO FRITO FRODO FUEGO FUNGO

•FO••
AFOFL AFOOT AFORE AFOUL

•F•O•
AFOOT AFROS AFTON IFNOT

••FO•
BEFOG DAFOE DEFOE DEFOG GOFOR

••F•O
BOFFO BUFFO MOFFO ORFEO

•••FO
BOFFO BUFFO MOFFO

F••P•
FIRPO FLAPS FLIPS FLOPS FRAPS

F•••P
FEDUP FIXUP FOGUP FRUMP FSTOP

FR•••
FRAIL FRAIS FRAME FRANC FRANK FRANS FRANZ FRAPS FRATS FRAUD FRAYS FREAK FREDA FREED FREER FREES FRENA FREON FRERE FRESH FRETS FREUD FREYA FRIAR FRICK FRIED FRIER FRIES FRIGG FRILL FRIML FRISE FRISK FRITO FRITS FRITZ FRIZZ FROBE FROCK FRODO FROES FROGS FROID FROME FROMM FROND FRONT FROSH FROST FROTH FROWN FROWS FROZE FRUIT FRUMP FRYER

F•R••
FARAD FARAH FARCE FARCI FARED FARER FARES FARGO FARMS FAROE FARON FAROS FARSI FERAL FERDE FERIA FERMI FERNS FERNY FERRI FERRO FERRY FIRED FIRER FIRES FIRMA FIRMS FIRNS FIRPO FIRRY FIRST FIRTH FORAY FORBS FORCE FORDO FORDS FORES FORGE FORGO FORKS FORKY FORLI FORMA FORMS FORTE FORTH FORTS FORTY FORUM FURAN FURLS FUROR FUROS FURRY FURTH FURZE

F••R•
FAERY FAIRE FAIRS FAIRY FAURE FAVRE FEARS FERRI FERRO FERRY FIBRE FIBRO FIERO FIERY FIORD FIRRY FJORD FLARE FLIRT FLORA FLORY FOURH FOURS FRERE FURRY

F•••R
FABER FACER FAKER FAKIR FARER FAVOR FEMUR FETOR FEVER FEWER FEYER FIBER FIFER FILAR FILER FINER FIRER FIVER FIXER FLAIR FLEER FLEUR FLIER FLOOR FLOUR FLUOR FLYER FODOR FOYER FREER FRIAR FRIER FRYER FUROR

•FR••
AFRIC AFRIT AFROS EFREM

•F•R•
AFARS AFIRE AFORE AFTRA

•F••R
AFTER JFKJR NFLER OFFER

••FR•
ALFRE INFRA REFRY

••F•R
BYFAR DEFER FIFER GOFAR GOFER GOFOR INFER KAFIR KEFIR OFFER RAFER REFER RIFER RSFSR SAFER SOFAR WAFER

FS•••
FSLIC FSTOP

F•S••
FASTS FESTA FESTS FISCS FISHY FISKE FISTS FOSSA FOSSE FUSED FUSEE FUSES FUSIL FUSSY FUSTY

F••S•
FALSE FARSI FAUST FEAST FEIST FIRST FLASH FLASK FLESH FLOSS FLUSH FOIST FOSSA FOSSE FRESH FRISE FRISK FROSH FROST FUBSY FUSSY

F•••S
FACES FACTS FADES FADOS FAILS FAIRS FAKES FALLS FAMES FANES FANGS FARES FARMS FAROS FASTS FATES FAUNS FAVES FAWNS FAXES FAZES FEARS FEATS FEEDS FEELS FEETS FELIS FELLS FELTS FENDS FERNS FESTS FETAS FETES FEUDS FIATS FICES FICUS FIDES FIEFS FIFES FILES FILLS FILMS FINDS FINES FINIS FINKS FINNS FIRES FIRMS FIRNS FISCS FISTS FIVES FIXES FLAGS FLAMS FLANS FLAPS FLATS FLAWS FLAYS FLEAS FLEES FLEWS FLEYS FLICS FLIES FLIPS FLITS FLOES FLOGS FLOPS FLOSS FLOWS FLUBS FLUES FOALS FOAMS FOCUS FOHNS FOILS FOINS FOLDS FOLKS FONDS FONTS FOODS FOOLS FOOTS FORBS FORDS FORES FORKS FORMS FORTS FOULS FOURS FOUTS FOWLS FOXES FRAIS FRANS FRAPS FRATS FRAYS FREES FRETS FRIES FRITS FROES FROGS FROWS FTLBS FUCHS FUELS FUGUS FULAS FUMES FUNDS FUNKS FURLS FUROS FUSES FYKES

•F•S•
OFUSE

•F••S
AFARS AFROS EFIKS

••FS•
RSFSR

••F•S
ALFAS BIFFS BOFFS BUFFS CAFES CUFFS DAFFS DOFFS FIFES GAFFS GIFTS HAFTS HEFTS HIFIS HUFFS LEFTS LIFTS LOFTS LUFFS MIFFS MUFFS PUFFS RAFTS RIFFS RIFTS RUFFS RUFUS SAFES SIFTS SOFAS SUFIS TIFFS TOFFS TOFTS TUFTS WAFTS WEFTS

•••FS
ALEFS ALIFS BEEFS BIFFS BOFFS BUFFS CHEFS CLEFS COIFS CUFFS DAFFS DOFFS DUFFS FIEFS GAFFS GOLFS GOOFS GULFS HOOFS HUFFS LEAFS LOAFS LUFFS MIFFS MUFFS POUFS PROFS PUFFS REEFS RIFFS ROOFS RUFFS SERFS SURFS TIFFS TOFFS TURFS WAAFS WAIFS WOOFS WRAFS ZARFS

FT•••
FTLBS

F•T••
FATAL FATED FATES FATHA FATLY FATTY FATWA FETAL FETAS FETCH FETED FETES FETID FETOR FITCH FITIN FITLY FSTOP FUTON

F••T•
FACTO FACTS FAITH FANTA FASTS FATTY FEATS FEETS FELTS FEMTO FESTA FESTS FIATS FIFTH FIFTY FILTH FIRTH FISTS FLATS FLATT FLITS FLUTE FLUTY FONTS FOOTE FOOTS FORTE FORTH FORTS FORTY FOUTS FOXTV FRATS FRETS FRITO FRITS FRITZ FROTH FURTH FUSTY

F•••T
FACET FACIT FAGOT FAINT FAULT FAUST FEAST FEINT FEIST FFLAT FIGHT FILET FIRST FIXIT FLATT FLEET FLINT FLIRT FLOAT FLOUT FLYAT FOIST FOUNT FRONT FROST FRUIT FUGIT

•FT••
AFTER AFTON AFTRA OFTEN

•F••T
AFLAT AFOOT AFRIT BFLAT CFLAT DFLAT EFLAT FFLAT GFLAT IFNOT

••FT•
FIFTH FIFTY GIFTS HAFTS HEFTS HEFTY LEFTS LEFTY LIFTS LOFTS LOFTY MUFTI NAFTA NIFTY RAFTS RIFTS SIFTS SOFTC SOFTG SOFTY TOFTS TUFTS TUFTY WAFTS WEFTS

••F•T
BEFIT DEFAT LOFAT NOFAT REFIT UNFIT

•••FT
ABAFT ALOFT CLEFT CLIFT CRAFT CROFT DELFT DRAFT DRIFT GRAFT GRIFT KRAFT SHAFT SHIFT SWIFT THEFT

FU•••
FUBSY FUCHS FUDDY FUDGE FUEGO FUELS FUGAL FUGGY FUGIT FUGUE FUGUS FULAS FULDA FULLY FUMED FUMES FUNDS FUNDY FUNGI FUNGO FUNKS FUNKY FUNNY FURAN FURLS FUROR FUROS FURRY FURTH FURZE FUSED FUSEE FUSES FUSIL FUSSY FUSTY FUTON FUZED FUZEE FUZZY

F•U••
FAULT FAUNA FAUNS FAURE FAUST FAUVE FEUDS FLUBS FLUES FLUFF FLUID FLUKE FLUKY FLUME FLUNG FLUNK FLUOR FLUSH FLUTE FLUTY FOULS FOUND FOUNT FOURH FOURS FOUTS FRUIT FRUMP

F••U•
FEDUP FEMUR FICUS FILUM FIXUP FLEUR FLOUR FLOUT FOCUS FOGUP FORUM FRAUD FREUD FUGUE FUGUS

F•••U
FICHU FONDU

•FU••
MFUME OFUSE

•F•U•
AFOUL

••FU•
AWFUL HAFUN INFUN KAFUE NEFUD RUFUS

•••FU
CORFU KHUFU SNAFU

F•V••
FAVES FAVOR FAVRE FEVER FIVER FIVES FOVEA

F••V•
FAUVE

F•••V
FOXTV

F•W••
FAWNS FEWER FOWLS

F••W•
FATWA FLAWS FLAWY FLEWS FLOWN FLOWS FROWN FROWS

F•X••
FAXED FAXES FIXED FIXER FIXES FIXIT FIXUP FOXED FOXES FOXTV

F••X•
FLAXY FLEXI

F•••X
FEDEX FELIX

•F••X
AFFIX

••F•X
AFFIX INFIX UNFIX

FY•••
FYKES

F•Y••
FEYER FEYLY FLYAT FLYBY FLYER FLYIN FLYNN FOYER FOYLE FRYER

F••Y•
FLAYS FLEYS FLOYD FRAYS FREYA

F•••Y
FAERY FAHEY FAIRY FANCY FANNY FATLY FATTY FEELY FELLY FENNY FERNY FERRY FEYLY FIERY FIFTY FILLY FILMY FINNY FIRRY FISHY FITLY FIZZY FLAKY FLAMY FLAWY FLAXY FLORY FLUKY FLUTY FLYBY FOAMY FOGEY FOGGY FOLEY FOLKY FOLLY FORAY FORKY FORTY FUBSY FUDDY FUGGY FULLY FUNDY FUNKY FUNNY FURRY FUSSY FUSTY FUZZY

••F•Y
BIFFY BUFFY DAFFY DUFAY DUFFY FIFTY HEFTY HUFFY JIFFY LEFAY LEFTY LOFTY MCFLY MIFFY NIFTY NOFLY PUFFY REFRY SOFTY TAFFY TOFFY TUFTY

•••FY
BEEFY BIFFY BUFFY COMFY DAFFY DEIFY DUFFY EDIFY GOOFY HUFFY JIFFY LEAFY MIFFY PUFFY REIFY SURFY TAFFY TOFFY TURFY UNIFY

F•Z••
FAZED FAZES FIZZY FUZED FUZEE FUZZY

F••Z•
FIZZY FRIZZ FROZE FURZE FUZZY

F•••Z
FELIZ FRANZ FRITZ FRIZZ

••F•Z
HAFIZ

GA•••
GABBY GABLE GABON GABOR GAELS GAFFE GAFFS GAGED GAGES GAILY GAINS GAITS GAIUS GALAH GALAS GALAX GALBA GALEA GALEN GALES GALLI GALLO GALLS GALOP GAMAL GAMAY GAMBA GAMED GAMER GAMES GAMEY GAMIN GAMMA GAMMY GAMOW GAMPS GAMUT GANDY GANEF GANGS GAOLS

GAPED
GAPER
GAPES
GARBO
GARBS
GARDA
GARDE
GARNI
GAROU
GARRY
GARTH
GASES
GASPE
GASPS
GASSY
GASTR
GASUP
GATED
GATES
GATOR
GATOS
GATUN
GAUDS
GAUDY
GAUGE
GAULS
GAUMS
GAUNT
GAURS
GAUSS
GAUZE
GAUZY
GAVEL
GAVIN
GAVOT
GAWKS
GAWKY
GAWPS
GAYAL
GAYER
GAYLE
GAYLY
GAZED
GAZER
GAZES

G•A••

GEARS
GEARY
GHAIN
GHALI
GHANA
GHATS
GHAZI
GIANT
GLACE
GLADE
GLADS
GLAIR
GLAND
GLARE
GLARY
GLASS
GLAXO
GLAZE
GMATS
GNARL
GNARS
GNASH
GNATS
GNAWS
GOADS
GOALS
GOAPE
GOATS
GRABS
GRACE
GRADE
GRADS
GRADY
GRAFT
GRAIG
GRAIL
GRAIN
GRAMA
GRAMM
GRAMP
GRAMS
GRAND
GRANI
GRANT
GRAPE
GRAPH
GRAPY
GRASP
GRASS
GRATA
GRATE
GRAVE
GRAVY
GRAYS
GRAZE
GUACO
GUARD
GUARS
GUAVA

G••A•

GALAH
GALAS
GALAX
GAMAL
GAMAY
GAYAL
GERAH
GETAS
GETAT
GFLAT
GLEAM
GLEAN
GLIAL
GLOAM
GLOAT
GOBAD
GOFAR
GOLAN
GORAL
GOTAT
GREAT
GROAN
GROAT
GULAG
GULAR
GYRAL

G•••A

GALBA
GALEA
GAMBA
GAMMA
GARDA
GEENA
GEMMA
GENOA
GENUA
GHANA
GILDA
GINZA
GOLDA
GONNA
GOTHA
GOTTA
GOUDA
GRAMA
GRATA
GRETA
GROZA
GUAVA
GUNGA
GUTTA

•GA••

AGAIN
AGALS
AGAMA
AGANA
AGAPE
AGARN
AGARS
AGASP
AGATE
AGAVE
AGAZE
EGADI
EGADS
NGAIO
NGAMI

•G•A•

AGHAS
EGGAR
OGHAM

•G••A

AGAMA
AGANA
AGENA
AGITA
AGORA

••GA•

ALGAE
ALGAL
AVGAS
BEGAN
BEGAT
CIGAR
CUGAT
DEGAS
DUGAN
EAGAN
EDGAR
EGGAR
ELGAR
FUGAL
HAGAR
HOGAN
JUGAL
LAGAN
LEGAL
LOGAN
MEGAN
NUGAE
ORGAN
PAGAN
RAGAS
REGAL
REGAN
RUGAE
SAGAL
SAGAN
SAGAS
SEGAL
SEGAR
SUGAR
TOGAE
TOGAS
VEGAN
VEGAS
WIGAN
YOGAS
YUGAS

••G•A

DOGMA
LOGIA
MAGDA
MAGMA
MAGNA
REGIA
SIGMA

•••GA

AMIGA
BRAGA
CONGA
GUNGA
HELGA
KANGA
KIOGA
KYOGA
LONGA
OMEGA
ONEGA
PANGA
SAIGA
TAIGA
TONGA
USCGA
VIRGA
VOLGA

G•B••

GABBY
GABLE
GABON
GABOR
GIBBS
GIBED
GIBER
GIBES
GOBAD
GOBEL
GYBED
GYBES

G••B•

GABBY
GALBA
GAMBA
GARBO
GARBS
GETBY
GIBBS
GLEBE
GLOBE
GLOBS
GOTBY
GRABS
GREBE
GRUBS
GUMBO
GUMBY

••GB•

DIGBY
RIGBY
RUGBY

GC•••

GCLEF

G•C••

GECKO
GUCCI

G••C•

GLACE
GLICK
GLUCK
GLUCO
GLYCO
GRACE
GRECO
GUACO
GUCCI
GULCH

G•••C

GENIC

•G••C

AGRIC
UGRIC

••G•C

HIGHC
LOGIC
MAGIC
YOGIC

G•D••

GIDDY
GODEL
GODET
GODEY
GODLY
GODOT

G••D•

GANDY
GARDA
GARDE
GAUDS
GAUDY
GEODE
GIDDY
GILDA
GILDS
GIRDS
GLADE
GLADS
GLEDE
GLIDE
GOADS
GOLDA
GOLDE
GOLDS
GONDI
GONDS
GOODS
GOODY
GORDO
GORDY
GOUDA
GOUDY
GOWDY
GRADE
GRADS
GRADY
GRIDS
GRODY
GUIDE
GUIDO
GURDY

G•••D

GAGED
GAMED
GAPED
GATED
GAZED
GELID
GEOID
GIBED
GLAND
GLUED
GOBAD
GORED
GOULD
GOURD
GRAND
GREED
GRIND
GUARD
GUILD
GUYED
GYBED
GYVED

•GD••

OGDEN

•G•D•

EGADI
EGADS

•G••D

EGGED
OGLED

••GD•

MAGDA

••G•D

ALGID
CAGED
EDGED
EGGED
GAGED
OHGOD
PAGED
RAGED
RIGID
URGED
WAGED

GE•••

GEARS
GEARY
GECKO
GEEKS
GEEKY
GEENA
GEESE
GELEE
GELID
GEMMA
GEMMY
GEMOT
GENES
GENET
GENIC
GENIE
GENII
GENOA
GENRE
GENRO
GENTS
GENUA
GENUS
GEODE
GEOID
GEORG
GERAH
GERMS
GERMY
GERRY
GESSO
GESTE
GESTS
GETAS
GETAT
GETBY
GETGO
GETIN
GETIT
GETME
GETON
GETTO
GETTY
GETUP
GEUMS

G•E••

GAELS
GEEKS
GEEKY
GEENA
GEESE
GHEES
GHENT
GLEAM
GLEAN
GLEBE
GLEDE
GLEES
GLENN
GLENS
GLESS
GLEYS
GOERS
GOEST
GREAT
GREBE
GRECO
GREED
GREEK
GREEN
GREER
GREES
GREET
GREGG
GRETA
GRETE
GREYS
GUESS
GUEST
GWENN
GWENT

G••E•

GAGED
GAGES
GALEA
GALEN
GALES
GAMED
GAMER
GAMES
GAMEY
GANEF
GAPED
GAPER
GAPES
GASES
GATED
GATES
GAVEL
GAYER
GAZED
GAZER
GAZES
GCLEF
GELEE
GENES
GENET
GHEES
GIBED
GIBER
GIBES
GILES
GIMEL
GIVEN
GIVER
GIVES
GLEES
GLUED
GLUER
GLUES
GLUEY
GOBEL
GODEL
GODET
GODEY
GOFER
GOLEM
GOMEL
GOMER
GOMEZ
GONER
GOOEY
GORED
GOREN
GORES
GOSEE
GOWER
GREED
GREEK
GREEN
GREER
GREES
GREET
GRIEF
GRIEG
GRIER
GRUEL
GULES
GUTEN
GUYED
GYBED
GYBES
GYRES
GYVED
GYVES

G•••E

GABLE
GAFFE
GARDE
GASPE
GAUGE
GAUZE
GAYLE
GEESE
GELEE
GENIE
GENRE
GEODE
GESTE
GETME
GIGUE
GIJOE
GIMME
GLACE
GLADE
GLARE
GLAZE
GLEBE
GLEDE
GLIDE
GLOBE
GLOVE
GLOZE
GNOME
GOAPE
GOLDE
GOOSE
GORGE
GORME
GORSE
GOSEE
GOSSE
GOUGE
GRACE
GRADE
GRAPE
GRATE
GRAVE
GRAZE
GREBE
GRETE
GRIME
GRIPE
GROFE
GROPE
GROVE
GUIDE
GUILE
GUISE

•GE••

AGENA
AGENT
AGERS
EGEST
OGEES

•G•E•

AGLET
AGLEY
AGNES
AGNEW
AGREE
AGUES
EGGED
EGRET
IGNES
NGWEE
OGDEN
OGEES
OGLED
OGLER
OGLES
OGRES

•G••E

AGAPE
AGATE
AGAVE
AGAZE
AGGIE
AGILE
AGREE
NGWEE
OGIVE

••GE•

ALGER
ANGEL
ANGER
ANGES
AUGER
BAGEL
BEGET
BOGEY
CAGED
CAGER
CAGES
CAGEY
DOGES
DOGEY
EAGER
EDGED
EDGER
EDGES
EGGED
EIGEN
ENGEL
FOGEY
GAGED
GAGES
HAGEN
HEGEL
HUGER
INGER
KUGEL
LAGER
LEGER
LIGER
LOGES
LTGEN
LUGER
LUGES
MAGEE
MAGES
MCGEE
NAGEL
NEGEV
NIGEL
NIGER
PAGED
PAGER
PAGES
PAGET
PUGET
RAGED
RAGES
RIGEL
ROGER
ROGET
SAGER
SAGES
SAGET
SEGER
TIGER
UNGER
URGED
URGER
URGES
WAGED
WAGER
WAGES

••G•E

AGGIE
ALGAE
ANGIE
ANGLE
ARGUE
BOGIE
BOGLE
BUGLE
DOGIE
EAGLE
EAGRE
FUGUE
GIGUE
HAGUE
INGLE
LOGUE
MAGEE
MCGEE
NUGAE
ROGUE
RUGAE
SEGUE
SIGNE
TOGAE
VAGUE
VOGUE

•••GE

ADAGE
ADIGE
AINGE
BADGE
BARGE
BEIGE
BILGE
BINGE
BLIGE
BORGE
BUDGE
BULGE
CADGE
CONGE
DINGE
DIRGE
DODGE
ETAGE
FORGE
FUDGE
GAUGE
GORGE
GOUGE
HEDGE
HENGE
HINGE
IMAGE
JORGE
JUDGE
KEDGE
KLUGE
LANGE
LARGE
LEDGE
LIEGE
LODGE
LONGE
LUNGE
MADGE
MARGE
MERGE
MIDGE
NEIGE
NORGE
NUDGE
OFAGE
OSAGE
PAIGE
PHAGE
PLAGE
PURGE
RANGE
RIDGE
ROUGE
RUDGE
SARGE
SEDGE
SERGE
SIEGE
SINGE
STAGE
SURGE
SWAGE
SYNGE
TARGE
TINGE
USAGE
VERGE
WEDGE
WODGE

GF•••

GFLAT

G•F••

GAFFE
GAFFS
GIFTS
GOFAR
GOFER
GOFOR

G••F•

GAFFE
GAFFS
GOLFS
GOOFF
GOOFS
GOOFY
GRAFT
GRIFT
GROFE
GRUFF
GULFS

G•••F

GANEF
GCLEF
GOOFF
GRIEF
GRUFF

G•G••

GAGED
GAGES
GIGOT
GIGUE
GOGOL
GOGOS

G••G•

GANGS
GAUGE
GETGO
GITGO
GLOGG
GLUGS
GOLGI
GONGS
GORGE
GOUGE
GREGG
GRIGS
GROGS
GUNGA

G•••G

GEORG
GLOGG
GOING
GRAIG
GREGG
GRIEG
GULAG

•GG••

AGGIE
AGGRO
EGGAR
EGGED
EGGON

•G•G•

AGOGO

•G••G

AGING

••GG•

BAGGY
BIGGY
BOGGS
BOGGY
BUGGY
DOGGO
DOGGY
FOGGY
FUGGY
HOGGS
JAGGY
LEGGS
LEGGY
MOGGY
MUGGS
MUGGY
NAGGY
PEGGY
PIGGY
PUGGY
RIGGS
SAGGY
SOGGY
VUGGY
WIGGY
YEGGS
ZIGGY

••G•G

MAGOG

•••GG

BRAGG
FLAGG
FRIGG
GLOGG
GREGG
STAGG

GH•••

GHAIN
GHALI
GHANA
GHATS
GHAZI
GHEES
GHENT
GHOST
GHOUL

G••H•

GOTHA
GOTHS
GUSHY

G•••H

GALAH
GARTH
GERAH
GIRTH
GLYPH
GNASH
GRAPH
GULCH

•GH••

AGHAS
OGHAM

••GH•

AUGHT
BIGHT
EIGHT
FIGHT
HIGHC
HIGHS
LIGHT
MIGHT
MUGHO
NIGHT
OUGHT
RIGHT
SIGHS
SIGHT
TIGHT
WIGHT
YOGHS

•••GH

AARGH
BAUGH
BERGH
BLIGH
BOUGH
COUGH
DOUGH
HEIGH
HOUGH
KEOGH
KROGH
LAUGH
LEIGH
LOUGH
NEIGH
ROUGH
SOUGH
THIGH
TOUGH
WAUGH
WEIGH

GI•••

GIANT
GIBBS
GIBED
GIBER
GIBES
GIDDY
GIFTS
GIGOT
GIGUE
GIJOE
GIJON
GILDA
GILDS
GILES
GILLS
GILLY
GILTS
GIMEL
GIMME
GIMPS
GIMPY
GINNY
GINZA
GIPSY
GIRDS
GIRLS
GIRNS
GIROS
GIRTH
GIRTS
GISTS
GITGO
GIVEN
GIVER
GIVES
GIZMO

G•I••

GAILY
GAINS
GAITS
GAIUS
GLIAL
GLICK
GLIDE
GLIMS
GLINT
GLITZ
GOING
GRIDS
GRIEF
GRIEG
GRIER
GRIFT
GRIGS
GRILL
GRIME
GRIMM
GRIMY
GRIND
GRINS
GRIOT
GRIPE
GRIPS
GRIST
GRITS
GUIDE
GUIDO
GUILD
GUILE
GUILT
GUIRO
GUISE

G••I•

GAMIN
GAVIN
GELID
GENIC
GENIE
GENII
GEOID
GETIN
GETIT
GHAIN
GLAIR
GOTIN
GOTIT
GRAIG
GRAIL
GRAIN
GROIN
GSUIT

G•••I

GALLI
GARNI
GENII
GHALI
GHAZI
GOLGI
GONDI
GORKI
GRANI
GUCCI

•GI••

AGILE
AGING
AGIOS
AGITA
BGIRL
OGIVE

•G•I•

AGAIN
AGGIE
AGRIC
NGAIO
UGRIC

•G••I

EGADI
NGAMI

••GI•

AEGIR
AEGIS
AGGIE
ALGID
ALGIN
ANGIE
ANGIO
ARGIL
BAGIT
BEGIN
BOGIE
DIGIN
DIGIT
DOGIE
DOGIT
DUGIN
ELGIN
FAGIN
FOGIN
FUGIT
HAGIO
LEGIS
LEGIT
LOGIA
LOGIC
LOGIN
MAGIC
REGIA
REGIS
RIGID
SIGIL
VIGIL
YOGIC
YOGIS

••G•I

LIGNI
NEGRI
REGNI
SEGNI

•••GI

CORGI
FUNGI
GOLGI
LONGI
LUIGI
SENGI
SHOGI

G•J••

GIJOE
GIJON

G••K•

GAWKS
GAWKY
GECKO
GEEKS
GEEKY
GORKI
GORKY
GOWKS
GROKS
GUNKY

G•••K

GLICK
GLUCK
GREEK

GL•••

GLACE
GLADE
GLADS
GLAIR
GLAND
GLARE
GLARY
GLASS
GLAXO
GLAZE
GLEAM
GLEAN
GLEBE
GLEDE
GLEES
GLENN
GLENS
GLESS
GLEYS
GLIAL
GLICK
GLIDE
GLIMS
GLINT
GLITZ
GLOAM
GLOAT
GLOBE
GLOBS
GLOGG
GLOMS
GLOOM
GLOPS
GLORY
GLOSS
GLOVE
GLOWS
GLOZE
GLUCK
GLUCO
GLUED
GLUER
GLUES
GLUEY
GLUGS
GLUON
GLUTS
GLYCO
GLYPH

G•L••

GALAH
GALAS
GALAX
GALBA
GALEA
GALEN
GALES
GALLI
GALLO
GALLS
GALOP
GCLEF
GELEE
GELID
GFLAT
GILDA
GILDS
GILES
GILLS
GILLY
GILTS
GOLAN
GOLDA
GOLDE
GOLDS
GOLEM
GOLFS
GOLGI
GOLLY
GULAG
GULAR
GULCH
GULES
GULFS
GULLS
GULLY
GULPS
GULPY

G••L•

GABLE
GAELS
GAILY
GALLI
GALLO
GALLS
GAOLS

GAULS GAYLE GAYLY GHALI GILLS GILLY GIRLS GOALS GODLY GOLLY GOULD GRILL GUILD GUILE GUILT GULLS GULLY

G•••L
GAMAL GAVEL GAYAL GHOUL GIMEL GLIAL GNARL GOBEL GODEL GOGOL GOMEL GORAL GRAIL GRILL GROWL GRUEL GYRAL

•GL••
AGLET AGLEY AGLOW IGLOO IGLUS OGLED OGLER OGLES

•G•L•
AGALS AGILE

•G••L
BGIRL

••GL•
ANGLE ANGLO BIGLY BOGLE BUGLE EAGLE INGLE

••G•L
ALGAL ALGOL ANGEL ARGIL ARGOL BAGEL ENGEL FUGAL GOGOL HEGEL JUGAL KUGEL LEGAL MOGUL NAGEL NIGEL REGAL RIGEL SAGAL SEGAL SIGIL VIGIL

GM•••
GMATS

G•M••
GAMAL GAMAY GAMBA GAMED GAMER GAMES GAMEY GAMIN GAMMA GAMMY GAMOW GAMPS GAMUT GEMMA GEMMY GEMOT GIMEL GIMME GIMPS GIMPY GOMEL GOMER GOMEZ GUMBO GUMBY GUMMO GUMMY GUMUP GYMNO

G••M•
GAMMA GAMMY GAUMS GEMMA GEMMY GERMS GERMY GETME GEUMS GIMME GIZMO GLIMS GLOMS GNOME GORME GRAMA GRAMM GRAMP GRAMS GRIME GRIMM GRIMY GRUMP GUMMO GUMMY

G•••M
GLEAM GLOAM GLOOM GOLEM GRAMM GRIMM GROOM

•G•M•
AGAMA NGAMI

•G••M
OGHAM

••GM•
DOGMA MAGMA PYGMY SIGMA

••G•M
BEGUM BYGUM JUGUM REGUM

GN•••
GNARL GNARS GNASH GNATS GNAWS GNOME

G•N••
GANDY GANEF GANGS GENES GENET GENIC GENIE GENII GENOA GENRE GENRO GENTS GENUA GENUS GINNY GINZA GONDI GONDS GONER GONGS GONNA GONZO GUNGA GUNKY GUNNY

G••N•
GAINS GARNI GAUNT GEENA GHANA GHENT GIANT GINNY GIRNS GLAND GLENN GLENS GLINT GOING GONNA GOONS GOONY GOWNS GRAND GRANI GRANT GRIND GRINS GRUNT GUNNY GWENN GWENT GWYNN GYMNO

G•••N
GABON GALEN GAMIN GATUN GAVIN GETIN GETON GHAIN GIJON GIVEN GLEAN GLENN GLUON GOLAN GOREN GOTIN GOTON GRAIN GREEN GROAN GROIN GROWN GUTEN GWENN GWYNN GYRON

•GN••
AGNES AGNEW AGNON AGNUS IGNES

•G•N•
AGANA AGENA AGENT AGING AGONY

•G••N
AGAIN AGARN AGNON AGRON EGGON OGDEN

••GN•
LIGNI LIGNO MAGNA REGNI SEGNI SEGNO SIGNE SIGNO SIGNS VIGNY

••G•N
ALGIN ARGON BBGUN BEGAN BEGIN BEGUN BIGON DAGON DIGIN DOGON DUGAN DUGIN EAGAN EGGON EIGEN ELGIN FAGIN FOGIN HAGEN HOGAN LAGAN LOGAN LOGIN LOGON LTGEN MEGAN OBGYN ORGAN PAGAN REGAN SAGAN VEGAN WAGON WIGAN

•••GN
ALIGN COIGN DEIGN FEIGN REIGN VSIGN

GO•••
GOADS GOALS GOAPE GOATS GOBAD GOBEL GODEL GODET GODEY GODLY GODOT GOERS GOEST GOFAR GOFER GOFOR GOGOL GOGOS GOING GOLAN GOLDA GOLDE GOLDS GOLEM GOLFS GOLGI GOLLY GOMEL GOMER GOMEZ GONDI GONDS GONER GONGS GONNA GONZO GOODS GOODY GOOEY GOOFF GOOFS GOOFY GOONS GOONY GOOPS GOOPY GOOSE GOOSY GOOUT GORAL GORDO GORDY GORED GOREN GORES GORGE GORKI GORKY GORME GORPS GORSE GORSY GOSEE GOSSE GOTAT GOTBY GOTHA GOTHS GOTIN GOTIT GOTON GOTTA GOTTO GOTUP GOUDA GOUDY GOUGE GOULD GOURD GOUTY GOWDY GOWER GOWKS GOWNS

G•O••
GEODE GEOID GEORG GHOST GHOUL GLOAM GLOAT GLOBE GLOBS GLOGG GLOMS GLOOM GLOPS GLORY GLOSS GLOVE GLOWS GLOZE GNOME GOODS GOODY GOOEY GOOFF GOOFS GOOFY GOONS GOONY GOOPS GOOPY GOOSE GOOSY GOOUT GROAN GROAT GRODY GROFE GROGS GROIN GROKS GROOM GROPE GROSS GROSZ GROTS GROUP GROUT GROVE GROWL GROWN GROWS GROZA

G••O•
GABON GABOR GALOP GAMOW GAROU GATOR GATOS GAVOT GEMOT GENOA GETON GIGOT GIJOE GIJON GIROS GLOOM GLUON GODOT GOFOR GOGOL GOGOS GOTON GRIOT GROOM GUYOT GYRON GYROS

G•••O
GALLO GARBO GECKO GENRO GESSO GETGO GETTO GITGO GIZMO GLAXO GLUCO GLYCO GONZO GORDO GOTTO GRECO GUACO GUIDO GUIRO GUMBO GUMMO GUSTO GYMNO

•GO••
AGOGO AGONY AGORA

•G•O•
AGIOS AGLOW AGNON AGRON EGGON IGLOO

•G••O
AGGRO AGOGO IGLOO NGAIO

••GO•
ALGOL ARGOL ARGON ARGOS ARGOT BEGOT BIGON BIGOS BIGOT BOGOR DAGON DOGON EGGON ERGOT FAGOT GIGOT GOGOL GOGOS HUGOS INGOT LAGOS LEGOS LOGON LOGOS LTGOV MAGOG MAGOO MAGOT NOGOS OHGOD RIGOR SAGOS SEGOS VIGOR WAGON YUGOS

••G•O
AGGRO ANGIO ANGLO DOGGO HAGIO HYGRO LIGNO MAGOO MUGHO SEGNO SIGNO

•••GO
AGOGO AMIGO BINGO BONGO CARGO CONGO DIEGO DINGO DOGGO FARGO FORGO FUEGO FUNGO GETGO GITGO IMAGO INIGO JINGO LARGO LETGO LINGO LONGO LUEGO MANGO MARGO MONGO MUNGO OINGO OLIGO OUTGO PENGO PHAGO PINGO PREGO RINGO SARGO SLIGO SORGO TANGO VIRGO

G•P••
GAPED GAPER GAPES GIPSY GUPPY GYPSY

G••P•
GAMPS GASPE GASPS GAWPS GIMPS GIMPY GLOPS GLYPH GOAPE GOOPS GOOPY GORPS GRAPE GRAPH GRAPY GRIPE GRIPS GROPE GULPS GULPY GUPPY

G•••P
GALOP GASUP GETUP GOTUP GRAMP GRASP GROUP GRUMP GUMUP

•G•P•
AGAPE EGYPT

•G••P
AGASP

••G•P
DIGUP DUGUP FOGUP LEGUP RIGUP TAGUP

GR•••
GRABS GRACE GRADE GRADS GRADY GRAFT GRAIG GRAIL GRAIN GRAMA GRAMM GRAMP GRAMS GRAND GRANI GRANT GRAPE GRAPH GRAPY GRASP GRASS GRATA GRATE GRAVE GRAVY GRAYS GRAZE GREAT GREBE GRECO GREED GREEK GREEN GREER GREES GREET GREGG GRETA GRETE GREYS GRIDS GRIEF GRIEG GRIER GRIFT GRIGS GRILL GRIME GRIMM GRIMY GRIND GRINS GRIOT GRIPE GRIPS GRIST GRITS GROAN GROAT GRODY GROFE GROGS GROIN GROKS GROOM GROPE GROSS GROSZ GROTS GROUP GROUT GROVE GROWL GROWN GROWS GROZA GRUBS GRUEL GRUFF GRUMP GRUNT

G•R••
GARBO GARBS GARDA GARDE GARNI GAROU GARRY GARTH GERAH GERMS GERMY GERRY GIRDS GIRLS GIRNS GIROS GIRTH GIRTS GORAL GORDO GORDY GORED GOREN GORES GORGE GORKI GORKY GORME GORPS GORSE GORSY GURDY GURUS GYRAL GYRES GYRON GYROS GYRUS

G••R•
GARRY GAURS GEARS GEARY GENRE GENRO GEORG GERRY GLARE GLARY GLORY GNARL GNARS GOERS GOURD GUARD GUARS GUIRO

G•••R
GABOR GAMER GAPER GASTR GATOR GAYER GAZER GIBER GIVER GLAIR GLUER GOFAR GOFER GOFOR GOMER GONER GOWER GREER GRIER GULAR

•GR••
AGREE AGRIC AGRON EGRET OGRES UGRIC

•G•R•
AGARN AGARS AGERS AGGRO AGORA BGIRL

•G••R
EGGAR OGLER

••GR•
AGGRO ANGRY EAGRE ENGRS HYGRO NEGRI

••G•R
AEGIR ALGER ANGER AUGER AUGUR BOGOR CAGER CIGAR EAGER EDGAR EDGER EGGAR ELGAR HAGAR HUGER INGER LAGER LEGER LIGER LUGER NIGER PAGER RIGOR ROGER SAGER SEGAR SEGER SUGAR TIGER UIGUR UNGER URGER VIGOR WAGER

GS•••
GSUIT

G•S••
GASES GASPE GASPS GASSY GASTR GASUP GESSO GESTE GESTS GISTS GOSEE GOSSE GUSHY GUSSY GUSTO GUSTS GUSTY

G••S•
GASSY GAUSS GEESE GESSO GHOST GIPSY GLASS GLESS GLOSS GNASH GOEST GOOSE GOOSY GORSE GORSY GOSSE GRASP GRASS GRIST GROSS GROSZ GUESS GUEST GUISE GUSSY GUTSY GYPSY

G•••S
GAELS GAFFS GAGES GAINS GAITS GAIUS GALAS GALES GALLS GAMES GAMPS GANGS GAOLS GAPES GARBS GASES GASPS GATES GATOS GAUDS GAULS GAUMS GAURS GAUSS GAWKS GAWPS GAZES GEARS GEEKS GENES GENTS GENUS GERMS GESTS GETAS GEUMS GHATS GHEES GIBBS GIBES GIFTS GILDS GILES GILLS GILTS GIMPS GIRDS GIRLS GIRNS GIROS GIRTS GISTS GIVES GLADS GLASS GLEES GLENS GLESS GLEYS GLIMS GLOBS GLOMS GLOPS GLOSS GLOWS GLUES GLUGS GLUTS GMATS GNARS GNATS GNAWS GOADS GOALS GOATS GOERS GOGOS GOLDS GOLFS GONDS GONGS GOODS GOOFS GOONS GOOPS GORES GORPS GOTHS GOWKS GOWNS GRABS GRADS GRAMS GRASS GRAYS GREES GREYS GRIDS GRIGS GRINS GRIPS GRITS GROGS GROKS GROSS GROTS GROWS GRUBS GUARS GUESS GULES GULFS GULLS GULPS GURUS GUSTS GYBES GYRES GYROS GYRUS GYVES

•G•S•
AGASP EGEST

•G••S
AGALS AGARS AGERS AGHAS AGIOS AGNES AGNUS AGUES EGADS IGLUS IGNES OGEES OGLES OGRES

••GS•
ANGST BUGSY

••G•S
AEGIS ANGES ANGUS ARGOS ARGUS AVGAS BIGOS BOGGS BOGUS CAGES DEGAS DOGES EDGES ENGRS FUGUS GAGES GOGOS HIGHS HOGGS HUGOS LAGOS LEGGS LEGIS LEGOS LOGES LOGOS LUGES MAGES MAGUS MSGTS MUGGS NEGUS NOGOS PAGES RAGAS RAGES REGIS RIGGS SAGAS SAGES SAGOS SEGOS SIGHS SIGNS SSGTS TAGUS TOGAS TSGTS URGES VAGUS VEGAS WAGES YEGGS YOGAS YOGHS YOGIS YUGAS YUGOS

•••GS
BANGS BERGS BINGS BIOGS BLDGS BOGGS BONGS BRAGS BRIGS BUNGS BURGS CHUGS CLOGS CRAGS DANGS DINGS DONGS DRAGS DREGS DRUGS FANGS FLAGS FLOGS FROGS GANGS GLUGS GONGS GRIGS GROGS HANGS HAWGS HOGGS HONGS KINGS LEGGS LONGS LUNGS MINGS MOOGS MUGGS PANGS PINGS PLUGS PONGS PRIGS PROGS PUNGS QUAGS RIGGS RINGS RUNGS SHAGS SINGS SKEGS SLAGS SLOGS SLUGS SMOGS SNAGS SNOGS SNUGS SONGS STAGS SWAGS SWIGS TANGS THUGS TIEGS TINGS TONGS TRIGS TRUGS TWIGS WHIGS WINGS YEGGS ZINGS

G•T••
GATED GATES GATOR GATOS GATUN GETAS GETAT GETBY GETGO GETIN GETIT GETME GETON GETTO GETTY GETUP GITGO GOTAT GOTBY GOTHA GOTHS GOTIN GOTIT GOTON GOTTA GOTTO GOTUP GUTEN GUTSY GUTTA GUTTY

G••T•
GAITS GARTH GASTR GENTS GESTE GESTS GETTO GETTY GHATS GIFTS GILTS GIRTH GIRTS GISTS GLITZ GLUTS GMATS GNATS GOATS GOTTA GOTTO

GOUTY
GRATA
GRATE
GRETA
GRETE
GRITS
GROTS
GUSTO
GUSTS
GUSTY
GUTTA
GUTTY

G•••T
GAMUT
GAUNT
GAVOT
GEMOT
GENET
GETAT
GETIT
GFLAT
GHENT
GHOST
GIANT
GIGOT
GLINT
GLOAT
GODET
GODOT
GOEST
GOOUT
GOTAT
GOTIT
GRAFT
GRANT
GREAT
GREET
GRIFT
GRIOT
GRIST
GROAT
GROUT
GRUNT
GSUIT
GUEST
GUILT
GUYOT
GWENT

•G•T•
AGATE
AGITA

•G••T
AGENT
AGLET
EGEST
EGRET
EGYPT

••GT•
MSGTS
SSGTS
TSGTS

••G•T
ANGST
ARGOT
AUGHT
BAGIT
BEGAT
BEGET
BEGOT
BIGHT
BIGOT
CUGAT
DIGIT
DOGIT
EIGHT
ERGOT
FAGOT
FIGHT
FUGIT
GIGOT
INGOT
LEGIT
LIGHT
MAGOT
MIGHT
NIGHT
OUGHT
PAGET
PUGET
RIGHT
ROGET
SAGET
SIGHT
TIGHT
WIGHT

•••GT
VINGT

GU•••
GUACO
GUARD
GUARS
GUAVA
GUCCI
GUESS
GUEST
GUIDE
GUIDO
GUILD
GUILE
GUILT
GUIRO
GUISE
GULAG
GULAR
GULCH
GULES
GULFS
GULLS
GULLY
GULPS
GULPY
GUMBO
GUMBY
GUMMO
GUMMY
GUMUP
GUNGA
GUNKY
GUNNY
GUPPY
GURDY
GURUS
GUSHY
GUSSY
GUSTO
GUSTS
GUSTY
GUTEN
GUTSY
GUTTA
GUTTY
GUYED
GUYOT

G•U••
GAUDS
GAUDY
GAUGE
GAULS
GAUMS
GAUNT
GAURS
GAUSS
GAUZE
GAUZY
GEUMS
GLUCK
GLUCO
GLUED
GLUER
GLUES
GLUEY
GLUGS
GLUON
GLUTS
GOUDA
GOUDY
GOUGE
GOULD
GOURD
GOUTY
GRUBS
GRUEL
GRUFF
GRUMP
GRUNT
GSUIT

G••U•
GAIUS
GAMUT
GASUP
GATUN
GENUA
GENUS
GETUP
GHOUL
GIGUE
GOOUT
GOTUP
GROUP
GROUT
GUMUP
GURUS
GYRUS

G•••U
GAROU

•GU••
AGUES

•G•U•
AGNUS
IGLUS

••GU•
ANGUS
ARGUE
ARGUS
AUGUR
BBGUN
BEGUM
BEGUN
BOGUS
BYGUM
DIGUP
DUGUP
FOGUP
FUGUE
FUGUS
GIGUE
HAGUE
JUGUM
LEGUP
LOGUE
MAGUS
MOGUL
MYGUY
NEGUS
REGUM
RIGUP
ROGUE
SEGUE
TAGUP
TAGUS
UIGUR
VAGUE
VAGUS
VOGUE

••G•U
ILGWU

•••GU
ENUGU
LONGU
TAEGU
XINGU

G•V••
GAVEL
GAVIN
GAVOT
GIVEN
GIVER
GIVES
GYVED
GYVES

G••V•
GLOVE
GRAVE
GRAVY
GROVE
GUAVA

•G•V•
AGAVE
OGIVE

••G•V
LTGOV
NEGEV

GW•••
GWENN
GWENT
GWYNN

G•W••
GAWKS
GAWKY
GAWPS
GOWDY
GOWER
GOWKS
GOWNS

G••W•
GLOWS
GNAWS
GROWL
GROWN
GROWS

G•••W
GAMOW

•GW••
NGWEE

•G••W
AGLOW
AGNEW

••GW•
ILGWU

G••X•
GLAXO

G•••X
GALAX

GY•••
GYBED
GYBES
GYMNO
GYPSY
GYRAL
GYRES
GYRON
GYROS
GYRUS
GYVED
GYVES

G•Y••
GAYAL
GAYER
GAYLE
GAYLY
GLYCO
GLYPH
GUYED
GUYOT
GWYNN

G••Y•
GLEYS
GRAYS
GREYS

G•••Y
GABBY
GAILY
GAMAY
GAMEY
GAMMY
GANDY
GARRY
GASSY
GAUDY
GAUZY
GAWKY
GAYLY
GEARY
GEEKY
GEMMY
GERMY
GERRY
GETBY
GETTY
GIDDY
GILLY
GIMPY
GINNY
GIPSY
GLARY
GLORY
GLUEY
GODEY
GODLY
GOLLY
GOODY
GOOEY
GOOFY
GOONY
GOOPY
GOOSY
GORDY
GORKY
GORSY
GOTBY
GOUDY
GOUTY
GOWDY
GRADY
GRAPY
GRAVY
GRIMY
GRODY
GULLY
GULPY
GUMBY
GUMMY
GUNKY
GUNNY
GUPPY
GURDY
GUSHY
GUSSY
GUSTY
GUTSY
GUTTY
GYPSY

•GY••
EGYPT

•G••Y
AGLEY
AGONY

••GY•
OBGYN

••G•Y
ANGRY
BAGGY
BIGGY
BIGLY
BOGEY
BOGGY
BUGGY
BUGSY
CAGEY
DIGBY
DOGEY
DOGGY
FOGEY
FOGGY
FUGGY
JAGGY
LEGGY
MOGGY
MUGGY
MYGUY
NAGGY
PEGGY
PIGGY
PUGGY
PYGMY
RIGBY
RUGBY
SAGGY
SOGGY
VIGNY
VUGGY
WIGGY
ZIGGY

•••GY
BAGGY
BARGY
BIGGY
BILGY
BOGGY
BUGGY
BULGY
DINGY
DODGY
DOGGY
ELEGY
FOGGY
FUGGY
HEDGY
HOAGY
JAGGY
LEDGY
LEGGY
MANGY
MINGY
MOGGY
MUGGY
NAGGY
OLOGY
PEGGY
PHAGY
PIGGY
PODGY
PORGY
PUDGY
PUGGY
RANGY
RIDGY
SAGGY
SEDGY
SOGGY
STAGY
STOGY
TANGY
VUGGY
WEDGY
WIGGY
ZIGGY
ZINGY

G•Z••
GAZED
GAZER
GAZES
GIZMO

G••Z•
GAUZE
GAUZY
GHAZI
GINZA
GLAZE
GLOZE
GONZO
GRAZE
GROZA

G•••Z
GLITZ
GOMEZ
GROSZ

•G•Z•
AGAZE

HA•••
HABER
HABIT
HABLA
HACEK
HACKS
HADAR
HADAT
HADES
HADJI
HADNT
HADON
HADST
HADTO
HAEMA
HAEMO
HAFIZ
HAFTS
HAFUN
HAGAR
HAGEN
HAGIO
HAGUE
HAHAS
HAIDA
HAIFA
HAIKS
HAIKU
HAILE
HAILS
HAIRS
HAIRY
HAITI
HAJIS
HAJJI
HAKES
HAKIM
HALAS
HALED
HALER
HALES
HALEY
HALLE
HALLO
HALLS
HALMS
HALON
HALOS
HALTS
HALVE
HAMAL
HAMAN
HAMEL
HAMES
HAMMY
HANDS
HANDY
HANES
HANFF
HANGS
HANKS
HANKY
HANNA
HANNO
HANOI
HANSA
HANSE
HANTS
HAOLE
HAPLO
HAPLY
HAPPY
HARAR
HARDC
HARDG
HARDY
HARED
HAREM
HARES
HARKS
HARMS
HARPO
HARPS
HARPY
HARRY
HARSH
HARTE
HARTS
HARUM
HASAT
HASID
HASNT
HASON
HASPS
HASSO
HASTA
HASTE
HASTO
HASTY
HATCH
HATED
HATER
HATES
HATLO
HAUER
HAULM
HAULS
HAUNT
HAUSA
HAUTE
HAVEL
HAVEN
HAVER
HAVES
HAVOC
HAVRE
HAWED
HAWGS
HAWKE
HAWKS
HAWSE
HAYDN
HAYED
HAYEK
HAYES
HAZAN
HAZED
HAZEL
HAZER
HAZES

H•A••
HEADS
HEADY
HEALS
HEALY
HEAPS
HEARD
HEARN
HEARS
HEART
HEATH
HEATS
HEAVE
HEAVY
HOAGY
HOARD
HOARS
HOARY
HYAMS
HYATT

H••A•
HADAR
HADAT
HAGAR
HAHAS
HALAS
HAMAL
HAMAN
HARAR
HASAT
HAZAN
HBEAM
HEJAZ
HEMAN
HENAN
HERAT
HEXAD
HIJAZ
HIRAM
HOBAN
HODAD
HOGAN
HONAN
HORAE
HORAL
HORAS
HOWAR
HOYAS
HULAS
HUMAN
HUNAN
HYLAS
HYMAN
HYRAX

H•••A
HABLA
HAEMA
HAIDA
HAIFA
HANNA
HANSA
HASTA
HAUSA
HEDDA
HEKLA
HELGA
HENNA
HEPTA
HIERA
HIJRA
HILDA
HOFFA
HONDA
HOOHA
HOSEA
HOSTA
HOUMA
HUBBA
HUZZA
HYDRA
HYENA
HYPHA

•HA••
CHACO
CHAFE
CHAFF
CHAIM
CHAIN
CHAIR
CHAKA
CHALK
CHAMP
CHANG
CHANT
CHAOS
CHAPS
CHARD
CHARM
CHARO
CHARS
CHART
CHARY
CHASE
CHASM
CHATS
CHAUD
CHAWS
CHAZZ
DHABI
DHAKA
DHALS
GHAIN
GHALI
GHANA
GHATS
GHAZI
KHAKI
KHANS
LHASA
OHAIR
OHARA
OHARE
PHAGE
PHAGO
PHAGY
PHANY
PHARM
PHASE
SHACK
SHADE
SHADS
SHADY
SHAEF
SHAFT
SHAGS
SHAHN
SHAHS
SHAKE
SHAKO
SHAKY
SHALE
SHALL
SHALT
SHAME
SHAMS
SHAMU
SHANA
SHANE
SHANK
SHANS
SHANT
SHAPE
SHARD
SHARE
SHARI
SHARK
SHARP
SHATT
SHAUN
SHAVE
SHAWL
SHAWM
SHAWN
SHAYS
THAIS
THANE
THANK
THANT
THARP
THATS
THAWS
UHAUL
WHACK
WHALE
WHAMO
WHAMS
WHANG
WHARF
WHATD
WHATS

•H•A•
AHEAD
AHMAD
CHEAP
CHEAT
CHIAS
OHKAY
PHIAL
RHEAS
SHEAF
SHEAN
SHEAR
SHOAH
SHOAL
SHOAT
UHLAN
WHEAL
WHEAT

•H••A
AHORA
CHAKA
CHEKA
CHELA
CHIBA
CHINA
CHITA
CHULA
DHAKA
GHANA
LHASA
OHARA
PHYLA
RHODA
RHYTA
SHANA
SHEBA
SHEMA
SHIVA
SHULA
THECA
THEDA
THEMA
THERA
THETA
THUJA
UHURA
XHOSA

••HA•
AGHAS
ARHAT
BAHAI
BEHAN
BIHAR
BOHAI
COHAN
EPHAH
EPHAS
ETHAN
HAHAS
JIHAD
LAHAR
LEHAR
MAHAL
MAHAN
MOHAM
OGHAM
POHAI
PSHAW
RAHAB
RAHAL
REHAB
REHAN
SCHAV
WUHAN
ZOHAR

••H•A
BAHIA
BOHEA
LEHUA
MEHTA
NAHUA
OCHOA
OSHEA
SCHWA
SEHNA

•••HA
AISHA
ALOHA
ALPHA
BOTHA
DACHA
FATHA
GOTHA
HOOHA
HYPHA
KASHA
MISHA
MOCHA
NUCHA
OMAHA
PASHA
SACHA
SASHA

HB•••
HBEAM
HBOMB

H•B••
HABER
HABIT
HABLA
HOBAN
HOBBS
HOBBY
HOBOS
HUBBA
HUBBY

H••B•
HERBS
HERBY
HOBBS
HOBBY
HUBBA
HUBBY

H•••B
HBOMB
HOREB

•HB••
OHBOY

•H•B•
CHIBA
CHUBS
DHABI
PHOBE
SHEBA
THEBE

•H••B
RHOMB
RHUMB
SHRUB
THROB
THUMB

••HB•
ASHBY

••H•B
RAHAB
REHAB
SAHIB

H•C••
HACEK
HACKS
HECHE
HECHT
HECKS
HECTO
HICKS
HOCKS
HOCUS

H••C•
HATCH
HENCE
HENCH
HITCH
HOOCH
HULCE
HUNCH
HUTCH

H•••C
HARDC
HAVOC
HELIC
HIGHC

•H•C•
CHACO
CHECK
CHICK
CHICO
CHOCK
CHUCK
PHYCO
SHACK
SHOCK
SHUCK
THECA
THICK
WHACK
WHICH

••H•C
ADHOC
ETHIC

•••HC
HIGHC

H•D••
HADAR
HADAT
HADES
HADJI
HADNT
HADON
HADST
HADTO
HEDDA
HEDGE
HEDGY
HEDIN
HIDER
HIDES
HODAD
HYDRA
HYDRO

H••D•
HAIDA
HANDS
HANDY
HARDC
HARDG
HARDY
HAYDN
HEADS
HEADY
HEDDA
HEEDS
HEIDI
HEIDT
HERDS
HILDA
HINDI
HINDS
HINDU
HOLDS
HONDA
HONDO
HOODS
HORDE
HOWDY
HURDY

H•••D
HALED
HARED
HASID
HATED
HAWED
HAYED
HAZED
HEARD
HEROD
HEWED
HEXAD
HEXED
HIKED
HIRED
HIVED
HOARD
HODAD
HOKED
HOLED
HOMED
HONED
HOPED
HOSED
HOUND
HUMID
HYOID
HYPED

•H•D•
CHIDE
RHODA
RHODE
RHODO
SHADE
SHADS
SHADY
SHEDS
THEDA
THUDS

•H••D
AHEAD
AHMAD
AHMED
CHARD
CHAUD
CHILD
CHORD
OHGOD
SHARD
SHEED
SHIED
SHOED
SHRED
THEYD
THIRD
WHATD

••HD•
MAHDI

••H•D
AAHED
ACHED
APHID
EPHOD
JIHAD
OOHED
SCHED
USHED

HE•••
HEADS
HEADY
HEALS
HEALY
HEAPS
HEARD
HEARN
HEARS
HEART
HEATH
HEATS
HEAVE
HEAVY
HECHE
HECHT
HECKS
HECTO
HEDDA
HEDGE
HEDGY
HEDIN
HEEDS
HEELS
HEFEI
HEFTS
HEFTY
HEGEL
HEIDI
HEIDT
HEIGH
HEINE
HEINZ
HEIRS
HEISS
HEIST
HEJAZ
HEKLA
HELEN
HELGA
HELIC
HELIO
HELIX
HELLO
HELLS
HELMS
HELOS
HELOT
HELPS
HELVE
HEMAN
HEMEN
HEMET
HEMIN
HEMPS
HENAN
HENCE
HENCH
HENGE
HENIE
HENNA
HENNY
HENRI
HENRY
HENTS
HEPTA
HERAT
HERBS
HERBY
HERDS
HERES
HERKY
HERLS
HERMS
HERNE
HERNS
HEROD
HERON
HEROS
HERTZ
HERVE
HERZL
HESSE
HESTS
HETHS
HETTY
HETUP
HEURE
HEUTE
HEWED
HEWER
HEXAD
HEXED
HEXER
HEXES
HEXYL
HEYSE

H•E••
HAEMA
HAEMO
HBEAM
HEEDS
HEELS
HIERA
HIERO
HOERS
HUEVO
HYENA

H••E•
HABER
HACEK
HADES
HAGEN
HAKES
HALED
HALER
HALES
HALEY
HAMEL
HAMES
HANES
HARED
HAREM
HARES
HATED
HATER
HATES
HAUER
HAVEL
HAVEN
HAVER
HAVES
HAWED
HAYED
HAYEK
HAYES
HAZED
HAZEL
HAZER
HAZES
HEFEI
HEGEL
HELEN
HEMEN
HEMET
HERES
HEWED
HEWER
HEXED
HEXER
HEXES
HIDER
HIDES
HIKED
HIKER

HIKES HINES HIRED HIRER HIRES HIVED HIVES HOKED HOKES HOKEY HOLED HOLES HOLEY HOMED HOMEO HOMER HOMES HOMEY HONED HONES HONEY HOOEY HOPED HOPER HOPES HOREB HOSEA HOSED HOSEL HOSES HOTEL HOVEL HOVER HOVEY HUGER HYPED HYPER HYPES

H•••E
HAGUE HAILE HALLE HALVE HANSE HAOLE HARTE HASTE HAUTE HAVRE HAWKE HAWSE HEAVE HECHE HEDGE HEINE HELVE HENCE HENGE HENIE HERNE HERVE HESSE HEURE HEUTE HEYSE HINGE HITME HOMME HOOKE HOPPE HORAE HORDE HORNE HORSE HOUSE HOWIE HOXIE HOYLE HULCE

•HE••
AHEAD CHEAP CHEAT CHECK CHEEK CHEEP CHEER CHEFS CHEJU CHEKA CHELA CHERE CHERI CHERT CHESS CHEST CHETH CHEVY CHEWS CHEWY GHEES GHENT PHENO RHEAS RHETT RHEUM SHEAF SHEAN SHEAR SHEBA SHEDS SHEED SHEEN SHEEP SHEER SHEET SHEIK SHELF SHELL SHEMA SHEMP SHERE THEBE THECA THEDA THEFT THEIR THEMA THEME THEMS THEOL THERA THERE THERM THESE THETA THEWS THEWY THEYD WHEAL WHEAT WHEEL WHEEN WHELK WHELM WHELP WHERE WHETS WHEYS

•H•E•
AHMED CHEEK CHEEP CHEER CHIEF CHIEN GHEES KHMER NHLER PHREN SHAEF SHEED SHEEN SHEEP SHEER SHEET SHIED SHIER SHIES SHOED SHOER SHOES SHRED SHREW SHYER THIEF THREE THREW WHEEL WHEEN

•H••E
CHAFE CHASE CHERE CHIDE CHILE CHIME CHINE CHIVE CHLOE CHOKE CHORE CHOSE CHUTE DHOLE DHOTE OHARE PHAGE PHASE PHILE PHOBE PHONE PHYFE PHYLE RHINE RHODE RHONE RHYME SHADE SHAKE SHALE SHAME SHANE SHAPE SHARE SHAVE SHERE SHINE SHIRE SHONE SHORE SHOVE SHUTE THANE THEBE THEME THERE THESE THINE THOLE THOSE THREE THROE THULE THYME WHALE WHERE WHILE WHINE WHITE WHOLE WHOSE WHYME WHYRE

••HE•
AAHED ACHED ACHES ADHEM ASHEN ASHER ASHES BOHEA COHEN ETHEL ETHER FAHEY MAHER OCHER OOHED OSHEA OTHER REHEM SAHEL SCHED TEHEE USHED USHER UTHER

••H•E
BOHME JAHRE MAHRE OCHRE TAHOE TEHEE

•••HE
BATHE BECHE BOTHE BRAHE CACHE DACHE FICHE HECHE LATHE LETHE LITHE MACHE MOSHE NASHE NICHE PATHE RAPHE RICHE ROCHE RUCHE SADHE SIDHE TITHE TYCHE WITHE WYTHE

H•F••
HAFIZ HAFTS HAFUN HEFEI HEFTS HEFTY HIFIS HOFFA HUFFS HUFFY

H••F•
HAIFA HANFF HOFFA HOOFS HUFFS HUFFY

H•••F
HANFF

•H•F•
CHAFE CHAFF CHEFS CHUFF KHUFU PHYFE SHAFT SHIFT THEFT WHIFF

•H••F
CHAFF CHIEF CHUFF SHAEF SHEAF SHELF THIEF WHARF WHIFF WHOOF

H•G••
HAGAR HAGEN HAGIO HAGUE HEGEL HIGHC HIGHS HOGAN HOGGS HUGER HUGOS HYGRO

H••G•
HANGS HAWGS HEDGE HEDGY HEIGH HELGA HENGE HINGE HOAGY HOGGS HONGS HOUGH

H•••G
HARDG HMONG HYING

•HG••
OHGOD

•H•G•
CHUGS PHAGE PHAGO PHAGY SHAGS SHOGI THIGH THUGS WHIGS

•H••G
CHANG CHING CHONG CHUNG SHRUG THING THONG WHANG

HH•••
HHOUR

H•H••
HAHAS HOHOS HOHUM

H••H•
HECHE HECHT HETHS HIGHC HIGHS HOOHA HYPHA

H•••H
HARSH HATCH HEATH HEIGH HENCH HITCH HOOCH HOUGH HUMPH HUNCH HUTCH

•HH••
UHHUH

•H•H•
SHAHN SHAHS

•H••H
CHETH SHISH SHOAH SHUSH THIGH THOTH UHHUH WHICH WHISH

••H•H
EPHAH ICHTH UHHUH

HI•••
HICKS HIDER HIDES HIERA HIERO HIFIS HIGHC HIGHS HIJAZ HIJRA HIKED HIKER HIKES HILDA HILLS HILLY HILTS HILUM HINDI HINDS HINDU HINES HINGE HINNY HINTS HIPLY HIPPO HIPPY HIPTO HIRAM HIRED HIRER HIRES HISSY HITCH HITIT HITME HITON HITUP HIVED HIVES

H•I••
HAIDA HAIFA HAIKS HAIKU HAILE HAILS HAIRS HAIRY HAITI HEIDI HEIDT HEIGH HEINE HEINZ HEIRS HEISS HEIST HOIST HOITY HYING

H••I•
HABIT HAFIZ HAGIO HAJIS HAKIM HASID HEDIN HELIC HELIO HELIX HEMIN HENIE HIFIS HITIT HOPIN HOPIS HOWIE HOXIE HUMID HYOID

H•••I
HADJI HAITI HAJJI HANOI HEFEI HEIDI HENRI HINDI HOSNI HOURI

•HI••
CHIAS CHIBA CHICK CHICO CHIDE CHIEF CHIEN CHILD CHILE CHILI CHILL CHILO CHIME CHIMP CHINA CHINE CHING CHINK CHINO CHINS CHIOS CHIPS CHIRO CHIRP CHIRR CHITA CHITS CHIVE CHIVY PHIAL PHILE PHILO PHILY RHINE RHINO RHIZO SHIED SHIER SHIES SHIFT SHILL SHIMS SHINE SHINS SHINY SHIPS SHIRE SHIRK SHIRR SHIRT SHISH SHIVA SHIVS THICK THIEF THIGH THILL THINE THING THINK THINS THIRD WHICH WHIFF WHIGS WHILE WHIMS WHINE WHINS WHINY WHIPS WHIRL WHIRR WHIRS WHISH WHISK WHIST WHITE WHITS WHITY

•H•I•
AHSIN CHAIM CHAIN CHAIR CHOIR CHRIS GHAIN OHAIR SHEIK THAIS THEIR

•H••I
CHERI CHILI DHABI DHOTI GHALI GHAZI KHAKI PHYSI SHARI SHOGI SHOJI

••HI•
APHID APHIS BAHIA ECHIN ETHIC NEHIS NIHIL NOHIT OPHIR SAHIB SOHIO UNHIP VCHIP

••H•I
ANHUI BAHAI BOHAI LAHTI MAHDI POHAI

•••HI
AMPHI ARCHI DASHI DELHI KOCHI RISHI SOCHI SPAHI SUSHI

H•J••
HAJIS HAJJI HEJAZ HIJAZ HIJRA

H••J•
HADJI HAJJI

•H•J•
CHEJU SHOJI THUJA

H•K••
HAKES HAKIM HEKLA HIKED HIKER HIKES HOKED HOKES HOKEY HOKUM

H••K•
HACKS HAIKS HAIKU HANKS HANKY HARKS HAWKE HAWKS HECKS HERKY HICKS HOCKS HONKS HOOKE HOOKS HOOKY HULKS HUNKS HUSKS HUSKY

H•••K
HACEK HAYEK HUROK

•HK••
OHKAY

•H•K•
CHAKA CHEKA CHOKE CHOKY DHAKA KHAKI SHAKE SHAKO SHAKY

•H••K
CHALK CHECK CHEEK CHICK CHINK CHOCK CHUCK CHUNK SHACK SHANK SHARK SHEIK SHIRK SHOCK SHOOK SHUCK THANK THICK THINK THUNK WHACK WHELK WHISK

H•L••
HALAS HALED HALER HALES HALEY HALLE HALLO HALLS HALMS HALON HALOS HALTS HALVE HELEN HELGA HELIC HELIO HELIX HELLO HELLS HELMS HELOS HELOT HELPS HELVE HILDA HILLS HILLY HILTS HILUM HOLDS HOLED HOLES HOLEY HOLLY HOLMS HOLST HOLTZ HULAS HULCE HULKS HULLO HULLS HYLAS

H••L•
HABLA HAILE HAILS HALLE HALLO HALLS HAOLE HAPLO HAPLY HATLO HAULM HAULS HEALS HEALY HEELS HEKLA HELLO HELLS HERLS HILLS HILLY HIPLY HOLLY HOTLY HOWLS HOYLE HULLO HULLS HURLS HURLY

H•••L
HAMAL HAMEL HAVEL HAZEL HEGEL HERZL HEXYL HORAL HOROL HOSEL HOTEL HOVEL

•HL••
CHLOE CHLOR NHLER PHLOX UHLAN

•H•L•
CHALK CHELA CHILD CHILE CHILI CHILL CHILO CHOLO CHULA DHALS DHOLE GHALI PHILE PHILO PHILY PHYLA PHYLE PHYLL SHALE SHALL SHALT SHELF SHELL SHILL SHULA SHULS SHYLY THILL THOLE THULE WHALE WHELK WHELM WHELP WHILE WHOLE WHOLL WHYLL

•H••L
CHILL CHURL GHOUL PHIAL PHYLL SHALL SHAWL SHELL SHILL SHOAL THEOL THILL UHAUL WHEAL WHEEL WHIRL WHOLL WHORL WHYLL

••HL•
BUHLS KAHLO

••H•L
ATHOL ETHEL ETHYL MAHAL NIHIL RAHAL SAHEL

•••HL
AMAHL RUEHL STAHL

HM•••
HMONG

H•M••
HAMAL HAMAN HAMEL HAMES HAMMY HEMAN HEMEN HEMET HEMIN HEMPS HOMED HOMEO HOMER HOMES HOMEY HOMME HUMAN HUMID HUMOR HUMPH HUMPS HUMPY HUMUS HYMAN HYMNS

H••M•
HAEMA HAEMO HALMS HAMMY HARMS HBOMB HELMS HERMS HITME HOLMS HOMME HOUMA HYAMS

H•••M
HAKIM HAREM HARUM HAULM HBEAM HILUM HIRAM HOHUM HOKUM

•HM••
AHMAD AHMED KHMER

•H•M•
CHAMP CHIME CHIMP CHOMP CHUMP CHUMS RHOMB RHUMB RHYME SHAME SHAMS SHAMU SHEMA SHEMP SHIMS THEMA THEME THEMS THUMB THUMP THYME THYMY WHAMO WHAMS WHIMS WHOMP WHYME

•H••M
CHAIM CHARM CHASM CHROM PHARM PHNOM RHEUM SHAWM THERM THRUM WHELM

••HM•
BOHME SCHMO

••H•M
ADHEM HOHUM MOHAM NAHUM OGHAM REHEM

•••HM
ABOHM BOEHM

H•N••
HANDS HANDY HANES HANFF HANGS HANKS HANKY HANNA HANNO HANOI HANSA HANSE HANTS HENAN HENCE HENCH HENGE HENIE HENNA HENNY HENRI HENRY HENTS HINDI HINDS HINDU HINES HINGE HINNY HINTS HONAN HONDA HONDO HONED HONES HONEY HONGS HONKS HONOR HONUS HUNAN HUNCH HUNKS HUNTS HUNTZ

H••N•
HADNT HANNA HANNO HASNT HAUNT HEINE HEINZ HENNA HENNY HERNE HERNS HINNY HMONG HORNE HORNS HOSNI HOUND HYENA HYING HYMNS HYPNO

H•••N
HADON HAFUN HAGEN HALON HAMAN HASON HAVEN HAYDN HAZAN HEARN HEDIN HELEN HEMAN HEMEN HEMIN HENAN HERON HITON HOBAN HOGAN HONAN HOPIN HUMAN HUNAN HURON HYMAN HYSON

•HN••
PHNOM

•H•N•
CHANG CHANT CHINA CHINE CHING CHINK CHINO CHINS CHONG CHUNG CHUNK GHANA GHENT KHANS PHANY PHENO PHONE PHONO PHONS PHONY RHINE RHINO RHONE SHANA SHANE SHANK SHANS SHANT SHINE SHINS SHINY SHONE SHUNS SHUNT THANE THANK THANT THINE THING THINK THINS THONG THUNK WHANG WHINE WHINS WHINY

•H••N
AHSIN CHAIN CHIEN CHRON CHURN GHAIN PHREN SHAHN SHAUN SHAWN SHEAN SHEEN SHORN SHOWN THORN UHLAN WHEEN

••HN•
ETHNO FOHNS JOHNS SEHNA

••H•N
ASHEN ATHON BEHAN COHAN COHEN ECHIN ETHAN MAHAN MAHON REHAN SCHON WUHAN

•••HN
BRUHN FOEHN ICAHN SHAHN SPAHN UTAHN

HO•••
HOAGY HOARD HOARS HOARY HOBAN HOBBS HOBBY HOBOS HOCKS HOCUS HODAD HOERS HOFFA HOGAN HOGGS HOHOS HOHUM HOIST HOITY HOKED HOKES HOKEY HOKUM HOLDS HOLED HOLES HOLEY HOLLY HOLMS HOLST HOLTZ HOMED HOMEO HOMER

HOMES HOMEY HOMME HONAN HONDA HONDO HONED HONES HONEY HONGS HONKS HONOR HONUS HOOCH HOODS HOOEY HOOFS HOOHA HOOKE HOOKS HOOKY HOOPS HOOTS HOPED HOPER HOPES HOPIN HOPIS HOPPE HOPUP HORAE HORAL HORAS HORDE HOREB HORNE HORNS HOROL HORSE HORST HORSY HORUS HOSEA HOSED HOSEL HOSES HOSNI HOSTA HOSTS HOTEL HOTLY HOUGH HOUMA HOUND HOURI HOURS HOUSE HOVEL HOVER HOVEY HOWAR HOWDY HOWIE HOWLS HOWSO HOWTO HOXIE HOYAS HOYLE

H•O••

HAOLE HBOMB HHOUR HMONG HOOCH HOODS HOOEY HOOFS HOOHA HOOKE HOOKS HOOKY HOOPS HOOTS HYOID

H••O•

HADON HALON HALOS HANOI HASON HAVOC HELOS HELOT HEROD HERON HEROS HITON HOBOS HOHOS HONOR HOROL HUGOS HUMOR HUROK HURON HYPOS HYSON

H•••O

HADTO HAEMO HAGIO HALLO HANNO HAPLO HARPO HASSO HASTO HATLO HECTO HELIO HELLO HIERO HIPPO HIPTO HOMEO HONDO HOWSO HOWTO HUEVO HULLO HYDRO HYGRO HYPNO HYPSO

•HO••

AHORA AHOYS CHOCK CHOIR CHOKE CHOKY CHOLO CHOMP CHONG CHOPS CHORD CHORE CHOSE CHOWS DHOLE DHOTE DHOTI DHOWS GHOST GHOUL HHOUR PHOBE PHONE PHONO PHONS PHONY PHOTO PHOTS RHODA RHODE RHODO RHOMB RHONE SHOAH SHOAL SHOAT SHOCK SHOED SHOER SHOES SHOGI SHOJI SHONE SHOOK SHOOS SHOOT SHOPS SHORE SHORN SHORT SHOTS SHOUT SHOVE SHOWN SHOWS SHOWY SHOYU THOLE THONG THORN THORO THORP THOSE THOTH THOUS WHOLE WHOLL WHOMP WHOOF WHOOP WHOPS WHORL WHOSE WHOSO XHOSA

•H•O•

CHAOS CHIOS CHLOE CHLOR CHROM CHRON OHBOY OHGOD OHWOW PHLOX PHNOM SHOOK SHOOS SHOOT THEOL THROB THROE THROW WHOOF WHOOP

•H••O

CHACO CHARO CHICO CHILO CHINO CHIRO CHOLO PHAGO PHENO PHILO PHONO PHOTO PHYCO PHYTO RHINO RHIZO RHODO SHAKO THORO WHAMO WHOSO

••HO•

ABHOR ACHOO ADHOC ATHOL ATHON ATHOS COHOS EPHOD EPHOR ETHOS HOHOS ICHOR MAHON NOHOW OCHOA SCHON TAHOE WAHOO YAHOO

••H•O

ACHOO ETHNO KAHLO SCHMO SOHIO WAHOO YAHOO

•••HO

ALTHO ANTHO BASHO BATHO BISHO DICHO DONHO IDAHO LITHO MACHO MINHO MUGHO NACHO ORTHO PATHO SOTHO TACHO TYCHO

H•P••

HAPLO HAPLY HAPPY HEPTA HIPLY HIPPO HIPPY HIPTO HOPED HOPER HOPES HOPIN HOPIS HOPPE HOPUP HYPED HYPER HYPES HYPHA HYPNO HYPOS HYPSO

H••P•

HAPPY HARPO HARPS HARPY HASPS HEAPS HELPS HEMPS HIPPO HIPPY HOOPS HOPPE HUMPH HUMPS HUMPY

H•••P

HETUP HITUP HOPUP

•H•P•

CHAPS CHIPS CHOPS SHAPE SHIPS SHOPS WHIPS WHOPS WHUPS

•H••P

CHAMP CHEAP CHEEP CHIMP CHIRP CHOMP CHUMP SHARP SHEEP SHEMP THARP THORP THUMP WHELP WHOMP WHOOP

••H•P

UNHIP VCHIP

H•R••

HARAR HARDC HARDG HARDY HARED HAREM HARES HARKS HARMS HARPO HARPS HARPY HARRY HARSH HARTE HARTS HARUM HERAT HERBS HERBY HERDS HERES HERKY HERLS HERMS HERNE HERNS HEROD HERON HEROS HERTZ HERVE HERZL HIRAM HIRED HIRER HIRES HORAE HORAL HORAS HORDE HOREB HORNE HORNS HOROL HORSE HORST HORSY HORUS HURDY HURLS HURLY HUROK HURON HURRY HURST HURTS HYRAX

H••R•

HAIRS HAIRY HARRY HAVRE HEARD HEARN HEARS HEART HEIRS HENRI HENRY HEURE HIERA HIERO HIJRA HOARD HOARS HOARY HOERS HOURI HOURS HURRY HYDRA HYDRO HYGRO

H•••R

HABER HADAR HAGAR HALER HARAR HATER HAUER HAVER HAZER HEWER HEXER HHOUR HIDER HIKER HIRER HOMER HONOR HOPER HOVER HOWAR HUGER HUMOR HYPER

•HR••

CHRIS CHROM CHRON CHRYS PHREN SHRED SHREW SHRUB SHRUG THREE THREW THROB THROE THROW THRUM

•H•R•

AHORA CHARD CHARM CHARO CHARS CHART CHARY CHERE CHERI CHERT CHIRO CHIRP CHIRR CHORD CHORE CHURL CHURN OHARA OHARE PHARM SHARD SHARE SHARI SHARK SHARP SHERE SHIRE SHIRK SHIRR SHIRT SHORE SHORN SHORT THARP THERA THERE THERM THIRD THORN THORO THORP THURS UHURA UHURU WHARF WHERE WHIRL WHIRR WHIRS WHORL WHYRE

•H••R

CHAIR CHEER CHIRR CHLOR CHOIR HHOUR KHMER NHLER OHAIR SHEAR SHEER SHIER SHIRR SHOER SHYER THEIR WHIRR

••HR•

JAHRE MAHRE NEHRU OCHRE TAHRS

••H•R

ABHOR ASHER ASHUR BIHAR EPHOR ETHER ICHOR LAHAR LEHAR MAHER MOHUR OCHER OPHIR OTHER USHER UTHER ZOHAR

•••HR

AMPHR ARTHR

H•S••

HASAT HASID HASNT HASON HASPS HASSO HASTA HASTE HASTO HASTY HESSE HESTS HISSY HOSEA HOSED HOSEL HOSES HOSNI HOSTA HOSTS HUSKS HUSKY HUSSY HYSON

H••S•

HADST HANSA HANSE HARSH HASSO HAUSA HAWSE HEISS HEIST HESSE HEYSE HISSY HOIST HOLST HORSE HORST HORSY HOUSE HOWSO HURST HUSSY HYPSO

H•••S

HACKS HADES HAFTS HAHAS HAIKS HAILS HAIRS HAJIS HAKES HALAS HALES HALLS HALMS HALOS HALTS HAMES HANDS HANES HANGS HANKS HANTS HARES HARKS HARMS HARPS HARTS HASPS HATES HAULS HAVES HAWGS HAWKS HAYES HAZES HEADS HEALS HEAPS HEARS HEATS HECKS HEEDS HEELS HEFTS HEIRS HEISS HELLS HELMS HELOS HELPS HEMPS HENTS HERBS HERDS HERES HERLS HERMS HERNS HEROS HESTS HETHS HEXES HICKS HIDES HIFIS HIGHS HIKES HILLS HILTS HINDS HINES HINTS HIRES HIVES HOARS HOBBS HOBOS HOCKS HOCUS HOERS HOGGS HOHOS HOKES HOLDS HOLES HOLMS HOMES HONES HONGS HONKS HONUS HOODS HOOFS HOOKS HOOPS HOOTS HOPES HOPIS HORAS HORNS HORUS HOSES HOSTS HOURS HOWLS HOYAS HUFFS HUGOS HULAS HULKS HULLS HUMPS HUMUS HUNKS HUNTS HURLS HURTS HUSKS HUTUS HYAMS HYLAS HYMNS HYPES HYPOS

•HS••

AHSIN

•H•S•

CHASE CHASM CHESS CHEST CHOSE GHOST LHASA PHASE PHYSI SHISH SHUSH THESE THOSE WHISH WHISK WHIST WHOSE WHOSO XHOSA

•H••S

AHOYS CHAOS CHAPS CHARS CHATS CHAWS CHEFS CHESS CHEWS CHIAS CHINS CHIOS CHIPS CHITS CHOPS CHOWS CHRIS CHRYS CHUBS CHUGS CHUMS DHALS DHOWS GHATS GHEES KHANS PHONS PHOTS RHEAS SHADS SHAGS SHAHS SHAMS SHANS SHAYS SHEDS SHIES SHIMS SHINS SHIPS SHIVS SHOES SHOOS SHOPS SHOTS SHOWS SHULS SHUNS SHUTS THAIS THATS THAWS THEMS THEWS THINS THOUS THUDS THUGS THURS WHAMS WHATS WHETS WHEYS WHIGS WHIMS WHINS WHIPS WHIRS WHITS WHOPS WHUPS

••H•S

ACHES AGHAS APHIS ARHUS ASHES ATHOS BAHTS BUHLS COHOS EPHAS ETHOS FOHNS HAHAS HOHOS JOHNS NEHIS TAHRS

•••HS

AMAHS ANKHS AYAHS BACHS BATHS BETHS BLAHS FUCHS GOTHS HETHS HIGHS KAPHS KOPHS LATHS LITHS LOCHS MATHS MOTHS MYTHS NOAHS OATHS OPAHS ORCHS PATHS PITHS POOHS QOPHS RATHS SACHS SHAHS SIGHS SIKHS SOPHS TECHS TETHS YODHS YOGHS

H•T••

HATCH HATED HATER HATES HATLO HETHS HETTY HETUP HITCH HITIT HITME HITON HITUP HOTEL HOTLY HUTCH HUTUS

H••T•

HADTO HAFTS HAITI HALTS HANTS HARTE HARTS HASTA HASTE HASTO HASTY HAUTE HEATH HEATS HECTO HEFTS HEFTY HENTS HEPTA HERTZ HESTS HETTY HEUTE HILTS HINTS HIPTO HOITY HOLTZ HOOTS HOSTA HOSTS HOWTO HUNTS HUNTZ HURTS HYATT

H•••T

HABIT HADAT HADNT HADST HASAT HASNT HAUNT HEART HECHT HEIDT HEIST HELOT HEMET HERAT HITIT HOIST HOLST HORST HURST HYATT

•H•T•

CHATS CHETH CHITA CHITS CHUTE DHOTE DHOTI GHATS PHOTO PHOTS PHYTO RHETT RHYTA SHATT SHOTS SHUTE SHUTS THATS THETA THOTH WHATD WHATS WHETS WHITE WHITS WHITY

•H••T

CHANT CHART CHEAT CHERT CHEST GHENT GHOST RHETT SHAFT SHALT SHANT SHATT SHEET SHIFT SHIRT SHOAT SHOOT SHORT SHOUT SHUNT THANT THEFT WHEAT WHIST

••HT•

BAHTS ICHTH LAHTI MEHTA

••H•T

ARHAT NOHIT

•••HT

AUGHT BIGHT EIGHT FIGHT HECHT LIGHT MIGHT NACHT NIGHT OUGHT RASHT RIGHT SIGHT TIGHT WIGHT YACHT

HU•••

HUBBA HUBBY HUEVO HUFFS HUFFY HUGER HUGOS HULAS HULCE HULKS HULLO HULLS HUMAN HUMID HUMOR HUMPH HUMPS HUMPY HUMUS HUNAN HUNCH HUNKS HUNTS HUNTZ HURDY HURLS HURLY HUROK HURON HURRY HURST HURTS HUSKS HUSKY HUSSY HUTCH HUTUS HUZZA

H•U••

HAUER HAULM HAULS HAUNT HAUSA HAUTE HEURE HEUTE HOUGH HOUMA HOUND HOURI HOURS HOUSE

H••U•

HAFUN HAGUE HARUM HETUP HHOUR HILUM HITUP HOCUS HOHUM HOKUM HONUS HOPUP HORUS HUMUS HUTUS

H•••U

HAIKU HINDU

•HU••

CHUBS CHUCK CHUFF CHUGS CHULA CHUMP CHUMS CHUNG CHUNK CHURL CHURN CHUTE KHUFU RHUMB SHUCK SHULA SHULS SHUNS SHUNT SHUSH SHUTE SHUTS THUDS THUGS THUJA THULE THUMB THUMP THUNK THURS UHURA UHURU WHUPS

•H•U•

CHAUD GHOUL HHOUR RHEUM SHAUN SHOUT SHRUB SHRUG THOUS THRUM UHAUL UHHUH

•H••U

CHEJU KHUFU SHAMU SHOYU UHURU

••HU•

ANHUI ARHUS ASHUR HOHUM LEHUA MOHUR NAHUA NAHUM UHHUH

••H•U

NEHRU

•••HU

ELIHU FICHU MACHU SADHU WUSHU

H•V••

HAVEL HAVEN HAVER HAVES HAVOC HAVRE HIVED HIVES HOVEL HOVER HOVEY

H••V•

HALVE HEAVE HEAVY HELVE HERVE HUEVO

•H•V•

CHEVY CHIVE CHIVY SHAVE SHIVA SHIVS SHOVE

••H•V

SCHAV

H•W••

HAWED HAWGS HAWKE HAWKS HAWSE HEWED HEWER HOWAR HOWDY HOWIE HOWLS HOWSO HOWTO

•HW••

OHWOW

•H•W•

CHAWS CHEWS CHEWY CHOWS DHOWS SHAWL SHAWM SHAWN SHOWN SHOWS SHOWY THAWS THEWS THEWY

•H••W
OHWOW
SHREW
THREW
THROW

••HW•
SCHWA

••H•W
NOHOW
PSHAW

H•X••
HEXAD
HEXED
HEXER
HEXES
HEXYL
HOXIE

H•••X
HELIX
HYRAX

•H••X
PHLOX

HY•••
HYAMS
HYATT
HYDRA
HYDRO
HYENA
HYGRO
HYING
HYLAS
HYMAN
HYMNS
HYOID
HYPED
HYPER
HYPES
HYPHA
HYPNO
HYPOS
HYPSO
HYRAX
HYSON

H•Y••
HAYDN
HAYED
HAYEK
HAYES
HEYSE
HOYAS
HOYLE

H••Y•
HEXYL

H•••Y
HAIRY
HALEY
HAMMY
HANDY
HANKY
HAPLY
HAPPY
HARDY
HARPY
HARRY
HASTY
HEADY
HEALY
HEAVY
HEDGY
HEFTY
HENNY
HENRY
HERBY
HERKY
HETTY
HILLY
HINNY
HIPLY
HIPPY
HISSY
HOAGY
HOARY
HOBBY
HOITY
HOKEY
HOLEY
HOLLY
HOMEY
HONEY
HOOEY
HOOKY
HORSY
HOTLY
HOVEY
HOWDY
HUBBY
HUFFY
HUMPY
HURDY
HURLY
HURRY
HUSKY
HUSSY

•HY••
PHYCO
PHYFE
PHYLA
PHYLE
PHYLL
PHYSI
PHYTO
RHYME
RHYTA
SHYER
SHYLY
THYME
THYMY
WHYLL
WHYME
WHYRE

•H•Y•
AHOYS
CHRYS
SHAYS
SHOYU
THEYD
WHEYS

•H••Y
CHARY
CHEVY
CHEWY
CHIVY
CHOKY
OHBOY
OHKAY
PHAGY
PHANY
PHILY
PHONY
SHADY
SHAKY
SHINY
SHOWY
SHYLY
THEWY
THYMY
WHINY
WHITY

••HY•
ETHYL

••H•Y
ASHBY
FAHEY

•••HY
ARCHY
BATHY
BUSHY
CATHY
CECHY
CUSHY
DISHY
DUCHY
FISHY
GUSHY
ITCHY
KATHY
LATHY
LEAHY
MACHY
MASHY
MESHY
MOTHY
MUSHY
PATHY
PITHY
PUSHY
RUSHY
SOPHY
TACHY
TECHY
VICHY
WASHY
WISHY
WITHY

H•Z••
HAZAN
HAZED
HAZEL
HAZER
HAZES
HUZZA

H••Z•
HERZL
HUZZA

H•••Z
HAFIZ
HEINZ
HEJAZ
HERTZ
HIJAZ
HOLTZ
HUNTZ

•H•Z•
CHAZZ
GHAZI
RHIZO

•H••Z
CHAZZ

IA•••
IAMBI
IAMBS
IATRO
IATRY

I•A••
IBARS
ICAHN
IDAHO
IMAGE
IMAGO
IMAMS
INALL
INANE
INAPT
INARI
INAWE
IPANA
IPASS
IRADE
IRANI
IRAQI
IRATE
ISAAC
ISAMU
ITALO
ITALS
ITALY
IVANA
IZAAK
IZARD
IZARS

I••A•
IBEAM
ICEAX
IDEAL
IDEAS
IDTAG
ILIAC
ILIAD
INBAD
INCAN
INCAS
INLAW
INLAY
IOTAS
IOWAN
ISAAC
ISLAM
ISLAS
IXNAY
IZAAK
IZBAS

I•••A
IBIZA
ICOSA
ILONA
INDIA
INDRA
INFRA
INTRA
IONIA
IPANA
IRINA
IVANA

•IA••
BIALY
DIALS
DIANA
DIANE
DIARY
DIAZO
FIATS
GIANT
KIANG
LIANA
LIANE
LIANG
LIARD
LIARS
MIAMI
MIAOW
MIATA
PIANO
PIAUI
RIALS
RIANT
RIATA
SIALS
TIANT
TIARA
VIALS
VIAND

•I•A•
AIDAN
AIMAT
BIHAR
BINAL
CIGAR
DINAH
DINAR
DIRAC
DITAT
DIVAN
DIVAS
EILAT
FILAR
FINAL
HIJAZ
HIRAM
JIHAD
KINAS
KIVAS
LILAC
LIMAS
LIRAS
MICAH
MICAS
MIDAS
MIKAN
MILAN
MIMAS
MINAS
MIZAR
NICAD
NINAS
NIPAS
NIPAT
NISAN
NIVAL
NIZAM
PICAS
PIKAS
PILAF
PILAR
PIMAS
PIPAL
PISAN
PITAS
RIVAL
RIYAL
SIKAS
SILAS
SINAI
SISAL
SITAR
SIVAN
SIXAM
TICAL
TIDAL
TIKAL
TILAK
TIRAN
TITAN
VICAR
VIDAL
VILAS
VINAS
VIRAL
VISAS
VITAE
VITAL
VITAS
WIGAN

•I••A
AISHA
BIOTA
CIERA
CILIA
CILLA
CIRCA
DIANA
DICTA
DITKA
FINCA
FIONA
FIRMA
GILDA
GINZA
HIERA
HIJRA
HILDA
JIDDA
KINDA
KIOGA
KIOWA
KISKA
LIANA
LIBRA
LIBYA
LICIA
LINDA
LIVIA
MIATA
MICRA
MILPA
MISHA
MISSA
NINJA
PIETA
PILEA
PINNA
PINTA
PINZA
PIPPA
PITTA
PIURA
PIZZA
RIATA
RIOJA
SIDEA
SIDRA
SIENA
SIGMA
SILVA
SIMBA
SITKA
TIARA
TIBIA
TISZA
UINTA
VILLA
VILMA
VIOLA
VIRGA
VIRNA
VISTA
WICCA
WILLA
WILMA
WIRRA
ZIZKA

••IA•
ALIAS
APIAN
ARIAN
ARIAS
ASIAN
AVIAN
AXIAL
BRIAN
BRIAR
CHIAS
ELIAS
ENIAC
EVIAN
FRIAR
GLIAL
ILIAC
ILIAD
NAIAD
PHIAL
PRIAM
TRIAD
TRIAL
UMIAK
URIAH
URIAL

••I•A
AGITA
AKIRA
AKITA
ALIDA
AMIGA
ANIMA
ANITA
ARICA
AVILA
BAIZA
CEIBA
CHIBA
CHINA
CHITA
CNIDA
DAIWA
DRINA
DVINA
EDINA
ELIZA
ERICA
ERIKA
ERISA
EVITA
HAIDA
HAIFA
IBIZA
IRINA
LAIKA
LEICA
LEILA
LUISA
MBIRA
MOIRA
NAINA
NAIRA
ORIYA
OUIDA
OUIJA
PAISA
PLICA
PRIMA
RAISA
REINA
SAIGA
SHIVA
SLIWA
SPICA
SUITA
TAIGA
UTICA
VOILA

•••IA
AECIA
AMNIA
ATRIA
BAHIA
CARIA
CELIA
CERIA
CILIA
COBIA
CORIA
CURIA
DACIA
ENTIA
FACIA
FERIA
FOLIA
INDIA
IONIA
JULIA
LAMIA
LICIA
LIVIA
LOGIA
LUCIA
LURIA
LYDIA
MANIA
MARIA
MEDIA
NADIA
NORIA
NUBIA
OMNIA
OSSIA
OSTIA
PAVIA
PODIA
PRAIA
REGIA
RETIA
SEPIA
SOFIA
SONIA
STRIA
SYRIA
TALIA
TIBIA
VARIA
XENIA
ZAMIA

IB•••
IBARS
IBEAM
IBERT
IBIZA
IBSEN

I•B••
ICBMS
IMBUE
INBAD
INBED
INBIG
INBOX
IZBAS

I••B•
IAMBI
IAMBS

•IB••
BIBBS
BIBLE
FIBER
FIBRE
FIBRO
GIBBS
GIBED
GIBER
GIBES
JIBED
JIBES
KIBEI
LIBBY
LIBEL
LIBRA
LIBRE
LIBYA
RIBBY
SIBYL
TIBBS
TIBER
TIBET
TIBIA
VIBES
ZIBET

•I•B•
BIBBS
BILBO
BILBY
BIXBY
DIDBY
DIGBY
GIBBS
KIRBY
LIBBY
LIEBY
LIMBI
LIMBO
LIMBS
NIMBI
NIMBY
NIOBE
RIBBY
RIGBY
SIMBA
SITBY
TIBBS
VISBY

•I••B
SIDEB

••IB•
ALIBI
BRIBE
CEIBA
CHIBA
CRIBS
DRIBS
ORIBI
TRIBE

••I•B
CLIMB
STIEB

•••IB
ADLIB
CARIB
NAMIB
SAHIB
SQUIB

IC•••
ICAHN
ICBMS
ICEAX
ICEIN
ICENI
ICERS
ICEUP
ICHOR
ICHTH
ICIER
ICILY
ICING
ICKES
ICONO
ICONS
ICOSA
ICOSI
ICTUS

I•C••
INCAN
INCAS
INCOG
INCUR
INCUS
ITCHY

I••C•
ILICH

I•••C
ILIAC
INDIC
IODIC
IONIC
ISAAC
ISTIC

•IC••
DICED
DICER
DICES
DICEY
DICHO
DICKS
DICKY
DICOT
DICTA
DICTS
DICTU
FICES
FICHE
FICHU
FICUS
HICKS
KICKS
KICKY
LICET
LICIA
LICIT
LICKS
MICAH
MICAS
MICRA
MICRO
NICAD
NICER
NICHE
NICKS
NICOL
OICKS
PICAS
PICKS
PICKY
PICOT
PICRO
PICTS
PICUL
RICCI
RICED
RICER
RICES
RICHE
RICKI
RICKS
RICKY
RICOH
TICAL
TICKS
TICKY
VICAR
VICES
VICHY
VICKI
VICKS
WICCA
WICKS

•I•C•
AITCH
BIRCH
CINCH
CINCO
CIRCA
CIRCE
CIRCS
CISCO
DISCO
DISCS
DITCH
FILCH
FINCA
FINCH
FISCS
FITCH
HITCH
MILCH
MINCE
MITCH
NIECE
PIECE
PINCE
PINCH
PISCI
PISCO
PITCH
RICCI
SINCE
TINCT
VINCE
VINCI
WICCA
WILCO
WINCE
WINCH
WITCH
ZILCH
ZINCS
ZINCY

•I••C
CIVIC
DIRAC
HIGHC
LILAC
MIMIC

••IC•
ALICE
AMICE
ARICA
BRICE
BRICK
BUICK
CHICK
CHICO
CLICK
CRICK
DEICE
EDICT
EPICS
ERICA
ERICH
EVICT
FLICK
FLICS
FRICK
GLICK
ILICH
JUICE
JUICY
KNICK
LAICS
LEICA
ONICE
PLICA
PRICE
PRICK
PRICY
QUICK
REICH
SLICE
SLICK
SNICK
SPICA
SPICE
SPICY
STICH
STICK
THICK
TRICE
TRICK
TWICE
URICH
UTICA
VOICE
VOICI
WHICH

••I•C
ENIAC
EPISC
ILIAC

•••IC
AFRIC
AGRIC
ANTIC
ASDIC
ASPIC
ATTIC
AURIC
AZOIC
BARIC
BASIC
BORIC
CIVIC
COMIC
CONIC
CUBIC
CYNIC
DORIC
EDDIC
ETHIC
FOLIC
FSLIC
GENIC
HELIC
INDIC
IODIC
IONIC
ISTIC
LOGIC
LUDIC
LYRIC
MAGIC
MALIC
MANIC
MEDIC
MELIC
MESIC
MIMIC
MUSIC
OLEIC
OPTIC
OSMIC
OSRIC
PANIC
PUNIC
PYRIC
RELIC
RUNIC
SALIC
SONIC
STOIC
SUBIC
TELIC
TONIC
TOPIC
TORIC
TOXIC
TUNIC
UGRIC
VATIC
VEDIC
XERIC
YOGIC
ZENIC

ID•••
IDAHO
IDEAL
IDEAS
IDEST
IDINE
IDIOM
IDIOT
IDLED
IDLER
IDLES
IDOLS
IDTAG
IDYLL
IDYLS

I•D••
INDEF
INDEX
INDIA
INDIC
INDIE
INDIO
INDIV
INDRA
INDRI
INDUS
IODIC

I••D•
IMIDE
IMIDO
IRADE
IRIDO

I•••D
IDLED
ILIAD
IMPED
INBAD
INBED
INKED
IRKED
IVIED
IZARD

•ID••
AIDAN
AIDED
AIDES
BIDDY
BIDED
BIDEN
BIDES
BIDIN
BIDON
BIDUP
CIDER
DIDBY
DIDIN
DIDNT
DIDOS
DIDST
DIDUP
EIDER
FIDEI
FIDEL
FIDES
GIDDY
HIDER
HIDES
JIDDA
KIDDO
KIDDY
LIDDY
LIDOS
MIDAS
MIDDY
MIDGE
MIDIS
MIDST
NIDES
NIDRE
NIDUS
RIDER
RIDES
RIDGE
RIDGY
RIDOF
SIDEA
SIDEB
SIDED
SIDER
SIDES
SIDHE
SIDLE
SIDON
SIDRA
TIDAL
TIDED
TIDES
VIDAL
VIDEO
VIDOR
WIDEN
WIDER
WIDOW
WIDTH

•I•D•
BIDDY
BINDS
BIRDS
BIRDY
CINDY
DINDY
DIODE
FINDS
GIDDY
GILDA
GILDS
GIRDS
HILDA
HINDI
HINDS
HINDU
JIDDA
KIDDO
KIDDY
KINDA
KINDS
LIDDY
LINDA
LINDO
LINDY
MIDDY
MINDS
MINDY
MISDO
PIEDS
RINDS
RINDY
TILDE
WILDE
WILDS
WINDS
WINDY

•I••D
AIDED
AILED
AIMED
AIRED
BIDED
BIFID
BIKED
BIPED
BIPOD
CITED
DICED
DIKED
DIMED
DINED
DIVED
FIELD
FIEND
FIFED
FILED
FINED
FIORD
FIRED
FIXED
GIBED
HIKED
HIRED
HIVED
JIBED
JIHAD
JIVED
KITED
LIARD
LIKED
LIKUD
LIMED
LINED
LIPID
LIVED
LIVID
MIKED
MIMED
MINED
MIRED
MIXED
NICAD
NIXED
OILED
PIKED
PILED
PINED
PIPED
RICED
RIGID
RILED
RIMED
RIVED
SIDED
SIRED
SITED
SIXED
SIZED
TIDED
TILED
TIMED
TIMID
TINED
TIRED
VIAND
VINED
VIRID
VIVID
WIELD
WILED
WINED
WIPED
WIRED
WIVED
YIELD

••ID•
ABIDE
ACIDS
ACIDY
ALIDA
AMIDE
AMIDO
ASIDE
AZIDE
BRIDE
BSIDE
CHIDE
CNIDA
EJIDO
ELIDE
GLIDE
GRIDS
GUIDE
GUIDO
HAIDA
HEIDI
HEIDT
IMIDE
IMIDO
IRIDO
MAIDS
MAIDU
OUIDA
OXIDE
PRIDE
QUIDS
RAIDS
SKIDS
SLIDE
SNIDE
TEIDE
VEIDT
VOIDS

••I•D
BAIRD
BLIND
BUILD
CHILD
CRIED
DRIED
FLIED
FRIED
GRIND
GUILD
ILIAD
IVIED
LAIRD
NAIAD
PLIED
PRIED
SHIED
SKIED
SPIED
TBIRD
THIRD
TRIAD
TRIED
WEIRD

•••ID
ACRID
ALGID
APHID
AROID
AVOID
BIFID
BOVID
BRAID
CANID
CUPID
DAVID
DROID
DRUID
ELCID
FELID
FETID
FLUID
FROID
GELID
GEOID
HASID
HUMID
HYOID
LIPID
LIVID
LUCID
LURID
NOBID
OOTID
OVOID
PAVID
PLAID
QUAID
RABID
RANID
RAPID
REBID
REDID
RIGID
SAPID
SOLID
SQUID
STAID
TEPID
TIMID
TUMID
UNBID
UNDID
URSID
VALID
VAPID
VIRID
VIVID
ZOOID

I•E••
IBEAM
IBERT
ICEAX
ICEIN
ICENI
ICERS
ICEUP
IDEAL
IDEAS
IDEST
ILENE
INEPT
INERT
IRENE
ISERE

ITEMS
ITERS

I••E•
IBSEN
ICIER
ICKES
IDLED
IDLER
IDLES
IGNES
ILLER
IMPED
IMPEI
IMPEL
INBED
INDEF
INDEX
INFER
INGER
INKED
INKER
INLET
INNER
INREM
INSET
INTEL
INTER
IRKED
IRREG
ISLES
ISLET
ISLEY
ISSEI
IVIED
IVIES

I•••E
IDINE
ILENE
IMAGE
IMBUE
IMIDE
IMINE
INANE
INAWE
INDIE
INGLE
INKLE
INURE
INUSE
IRADE
IRATE
IRENE
ISERE
ISSUE
ISTLE
ITSME

•IE••
CIERA
DIEGO
DIEMS
DIENE
DIETS
EIEIO
FIEFS
FIELD
FIEND
FIERO
FIERY
HIERA
HIERO
LIEBY
LIEGE
LIEIN
LIENS
LIETO
LIEUS
LIEUT
MIENS
NIECE
NIELS
PIECE
PIEDS
PIERS
PIETA
PIETY
RIELS
SIEGE
SIENA
SIEPI
SIETE
SIEUR
SIEVE
TIEGS
TIEIN
TIERS
TIETO
TIEUP
VIEJO
VIERS
VIEWS
VIEWY
WIELD
WIEST
YIELD

•I•E•
AIDED
AIDES
AIKEN
AILED
AILER
AILEY
AIMED
AIMEE
AIMER
AIRED
AIRES
BIDED
BIDEN
BIDES
BIKED
BIKEL
BIKER
BIKES
BINES
BINET
BIPED
BISES
BITER
BITES
BIZET
CIDER
CINES
CIRES
CITED
CITER
CITES
CIVET
DICED
DICER
DICES
DICEY
DIKED
DIKES
DIMED
DIMES
DINED
DINER
DINES
DIRER
DIVED
DIVER
DIVES
DIYER
DIZEN
EIDER
EIGEN
FIBER
FICES
FIDEI
FIDEL
FIDES
FIFED
FIFER
FIFES
FILED
FILER
FILES
FILET
FINED
FINER
FINES
FIRED
FIRER
FIRES
FIVER
FIVES
FIXED
FIXER
FIXES
GIBED
GIBER
GIBES
GILES
GIMEL
GIVEN
GIVER
GIVES
HIDER
HIDES
HIKED
HIKER
HIKES
HINES
HIRED
HIRER
HIRES
HIVED
HIVES
JIBED
JIBES
JIVED
JIVER
JIVES
JIVEY
KIBEI
KILEY
KINER
KITED
KITER
KITES
LIBEL
LICET
LIGER
LIKED
LIKEN
LIKES
LIMED
LIMEN
LIMES
LIMEY
LINED
LINEN
LINER
LINES
LINEY
LITER
LITES
LIVED
LIVEN
LIVER
LIVES
MIKED
MIKES
MIKEY
MILER
MILES
MIMED
MIMEO
MIMER
MIMES
MINED
MINEO
MINER
MINES
MIRED
MIRES
MISER
MITER
MITES
MIXED
MIXER
MIXES
NICER
NIDES
NIGEL
NIGER
NIKES
NILES
NIMES
NINER
NINES
NISEI
NITER
NITES
NIVEN
NIXED
NIXES
NIZER
OILED
OILER
PIKED
PIKER
PIKES
PILEA
PILED
PILEI
PILES
PINED
PINES
PINEY
PIPED
PIPER
PIPES
PIXEL
RICED
RICER
RICES
RIDER
RIDES
RIFER
RIGEL
RIKER
RILED
RILES
RILEY
RIMED
RIMES
RIPEN
RIPER
RISEN
RISER
RISES
RITES
RIVED
RIVEN
RIVER
RIVES
RIVET
SIDEA
SIDEB
SIDED
SIDER
SIDES
SIKES
SILEX
SINES
SINEW
SIRED
SIREN
SIRES
SITED
SITES
SIXED
SIXER
SIXES
SIZED
SIZER
SIZES
TIBER
TIBET
TIDED
TIDES
TIGER
TIKES
TILED
TILER
TILES
TIMED
TIMER
TIMES
TIMEX
TINED
TINES
TIRED
TIRES
TITER
VIBES
VICES
VIDEO
VILER
VINED
VINES
VIPER
VIREO
VISES
VIXEN
WIDEN
WIDER
WILED
WILES
WILEY
WINED
WINES
WINEY
WIPED
WIPER
WIPES
WIRED
WIRER
WIRES
WISER
WIVED
WIVES
WIZEN
YIKES
YIPES
ZIBET
ZINES

•I••E
AIMEE
AINGE
AISLE
AISNE
BIBLE
BILGE
BINGE
BIOME
BIRSE
BITTE
CIRCE
DIANE
DIENE
DINGE
DIODE
DIONE
DIRGE
DISME
DIXIE
FIBRE
FICHE
FILLE
FISKE
GIGUE
GIJOE
GIMME
HINGE
HITME
KINTE
KITWE
LIANE
LIBRE
LIEGE
LILLE
LISLE
LISSE
LITHE
LITRE
LIVRE
MIDGE
MILLE
MILNE
MINCE
MINIE
MINKE
MITRE
NICHE
NIDRE
NIECE
NIOBE
NITRE
NIXIE
PIECE
PINCE
PIQUE
PISTE
PIXIE
RICHE
RIDGE
RIFLE
RILKE
RILLE
RINSE
SIDHE
SIDLE
SIEGE
SIETE
SIEVE
SIGNE
SINCE
SINGE
TILDE
TINGE
TITHE
TITLE
TITRE
VILLE
VINCE
VITAE
VIVRE
WILDE
WINCE
WINZE
WITHE
WITTE

••IE•
ADIEU
ALIEN
AMIES
ARIEL
ARIES
BRIEF
BRIER
BRIES
CHIEF
CHIEN
CRIED
CRIER
CRIES
DRIED
DRIER
DRIES
ELIEL
ERIES
FLIED
FLIER
FLIES
FRIED
FRIER
FRIES
GRIEF
GRIEG
GRIER
ICIER
IVIED
IVIES
KLIEG
OBIES
OKIES
ORIEL
OSIER
PLIED
PLIES
PRIED
PRIER
PRIES
QUIEN
QUIET
SHIED
SHIER
SHIES
SKIED
SKIER
SKIES
SLIER
SPIED
SPIEL
SPIES
STIEB
STIES
THIEF
TRIED
TRIER
TRIES
URIEL
WRIER

••I•E
ABIDE
ADIGE
AFIRE
AGILE
ALICE
ALIKE
ALINE
ALIVE
AMICE
AMIDE
AMINE
ANIME
ANISE
ARISE
ASIDE
ATIVE
AZIDE
AZINE
BAIZE
BEIGE
BLIGE
BOISE
BOITE
BRIBE
BRICE
BRIDE
BRINE
BRITE
BSIDE
CAINE
CHIDE
CHILE
CHIME
CHINE
CHIVE
CLIME
CLINE
CLIVE
CRIME
DEICE
DRIVE
EDILE
ELIDE
ELISE
ELITE
EMILE
EXILE
FAIRE
FRISE
GLIDE
GRIME
GRIPE
GUIDE
GUILE
GUISE
HAILE
HEINE
IDINE
IMIDE
IMINE
JAIME
JUICE
KLINE
KNIFE
KOINE
LAINE
LOIRE
LUISE
MAILE
MAINE
MAIZE
MOIRE
NAIVE
NEIGE
NOIRE
NOISE
ODILE
OGIVE
OLIVE
ONICE
OPINE
OVINE
OXIDE
PAIGE
PAINE
PHILE
POISE
PRICE
PRIDE
PRIME
PRIZE
QUIRE
QUITE
RAISE
RHINE
SEINE
SEIZE
SHINE
SHIRE
SKIVE
SLICE
SLIDE
SLIME
SMILE
SMITE
SNIDE
SNIPE
SPICE
SPIKE
SPILE
SPINE
SPIRE
SPITE
STILE
STIPE
SUITE
SWINE
SWIPE
TAINE
TEIDE
THINE
TOILE
TRIBE
TRICE
TRIKE
TRINE
TRIPE
TRITE
TWICE
TWINE
UDINE
UNITE
UTILE
VOICE
VOILE
WAITE
WAIVE
WHILE
WHINE
WHITE
WRITE
ZAIRE

•••IE
ABBIE
ADDIE
AERIE
AGGIE
ALFIE
ALLIE
ANDIE
ANGIE
ANNIE
ARNIE
ARTIE
AUDIE
BASIE
BELIE
BOGIE
BOWIE
CELIE
CURIE
CUTIE
DAVIE
DIXIE
DOBIE
DOGIE
EDDIE
EERIE
EFFIE
ELLIE
ELSIE
ERNIE
EUBIE
EYDIE
EYRIE
FACIE
GENIE
HENIE
HOWIE
HOXIE
INDIE
JAMIE
JANIE
JODIE
JOLIE
JULIE
KATIE
KYRIE
LOUIE
LUCIE
LURIE
MAMIE
MARIE
MAXIE
MCVIE
MINIE
MOVIE
MOXIE
NIXIE
OAKIE
OLDIE
OLLIE
OSSIE
OZZIE
PIXIE
PYXIE
RAMIE
RETIE
ROSIE
ROXIE
SADIE
SATIE
SUSIE
TOTIE
UNTIE
WYLIE
YALIE
ZOWIE

IF•••
IFNOT

I•F••
INFER
INFIN
INFIX
INFRA
INFUN

I•••F
INDEF

•IF••
BIFFS
BIFFY
BIFID
FIFED
FIFER
FIFES
FIFTH
FIFTY
GIFTS
HIFIS
JIFFY
LIFTS
MIFFS
MIFFY
NIFTY
RIFER
RIFFI
RIFFS
RIFLE
RIFTS
SIFTS
TIFFS

•I•F•
BIFFS
BIFFY
FIEFS
JIFFY
MIFFS
MIFFY
RIFFI
RIFFS
TIFFS

•I••F
PILAF
RIDOF

••IF•
ALIFS
CLIFF
CLIFT
COIFS
DEIFY
DRIFT
EDIFY
GRIFT
HAIFA
KNIFE
REIFY
SCIFI
SHIFT
SKIFF
SNIFF
SPIFF
STIFF
SWIFT
UNIFY
WAIFS
WHIFF

••I•F
BRIEF
CHIEF
CLIFF
GRIEF
SKIFF
SNIFF
SPIFF
STIFF
THIEF
WHIFF

•••IF
CALIF
MOTIF
SERIF

IG•••
IGLOO
IGLUS
IGNES

I•G••
ILGWU
INGER
INGLE
INGOT

I••G•
IMAGE
IMAGO
INIGO

I•••G
ICING
IDTAG
INBIG
INCOG
INORG
IRREG

•IG••
BIGGY
BIGHT
BIGLY
BIGON
BIGOS
BIGOT
CIGAR
DIGBY
DIGIN
DIGIT
DIGUP
EIGEN
EIGHT
FIGHT
GIGOT
GIGUE
HIGHC
HIGHS
LIGER
LIGHT
LIGNI
LIGNO
MIGHT
NIGEL
NIGER
NIGHT
PIGGY
RIGBY
RIGEL
RIGGS
RIGHT
RIGID
RIGOR
RIGUP
SIGHS
SIGHT
SIGIL
SIGMA
SIGNE
SIGNO
SIGNS
TIGER
TIGHT
UIGUR
VIGIL
VIGNY
VIGOR
WIGAN
WIGGY
WIGHT
ZIGGY

•I•G•
AINGE
BIGGY
BILGE
BILGY
BINGE
BINGO
BINGS
BIOGS
DIEGO
DINGE
DINGO
DINGS
DINGY
DIRGE
GITGO
HINGE
JINGO
KINGS
KIOGA
LIEGE
LINGO
MIDGE
MINGS
MINGY
OINGO
PIGGY
PINGO
PINGS
RIDGE
RIDGY
RIGGS
RINGO
RINGS
SIEGE
SINGE
SINGS
TIEGS
TINGE
TINGS
VINGT
VIRGA
VIRGO
WIGGY
WINGS
XINGU
ZIGGY
ZINGS
ZINGY

•I••G
KIANG
LIANG

••IG•
ADIGE
ALIGN
AMIGA
AMIGO
BEIGE
BLIGE
BLIGH
BRIGS
COIGN
DEIGN
FEIGN
FRIGG
GRIGS
HEIGH
INIGO
LEIGH
LUIGI
NEIGE
NEIGH
OLIGO
PAIGE
PRIGS
REIGN
SAIGA
SLIGO
SWIGS
TAIGA
THIGH
TRIGS
TWIGS
VSIGN
WEIGH
WHIGS

••I•G
ACING
AGING
APING
AWING
AXING
BEING
BOING
BRING
CHING
CLING
CUING
DOING
DYING
EKING
EWING
FLING
FRIGG
GOING
GRIEG
HYING
ICING
KLIEG
KOING
LAING
LYING
OKING
ORING
OWING
RUING
SLING
STING
SUING
SWING
THING
TYING
USING
VYING
WRING

•••IG
CRAIG
GRAIG
INBIG
MRBIG
NAVIG
RELIG
RERIG
SELIG
SOBIG
SPRIG
UNRIG
VARIG
ZELIG
ZWEIG

I•H••
ICHOR
ICHTH

I••H•
ICAHN
IDAHO
ITCHY

I•••H
ICHTH
ILICH
INISH
IRISH

•IH••
BIHAR
JIHAD
NIHIL

•I•H•
AISHA
BIGHT
BISHO
DICHO
DISHY
EIGHT
FICHE
FICHU
FIGHT
FISHY
HIGHC
HIGHS
LIGHT
LITHE
LITHO
LITHS
MIGHT
MINHO
MISHA
NICHE
NIGHT
PITHS
PITHY
RICHE
RIGHT
RISHI
SIDHE
SIGHS
SIGHT
SIKHS
TIGHT
TITHE
VICHY
WIGHT
WISHY
WITHE
WITHY

•I••H
AITCH
BIRCH
BIRTH
CINCH
DINAH
DITCH
FIFTH
FILCH
FILTH
FINCH
FIRTH
FITCH
GIRTH
HITCH
MICAH
MILCH
MIRTH
MITCH
NINTH
PINCH
PITCH
RICOH
SIXTH
TILTH
WIDTH
WINCH
WITCH
ZILCH

••IH•
ELIHU

••I•H
AMISH
APISH
ARITH
BLIGH
BRITH
EDITH
ERICH
FAITH
HEIGH
ILICH
INISH
IRISH
KEITH
KNISH
LEIGH
LEITH
NAISH
NEIGH
REICH
SAITH
SHISH
SMITH
STICH
SWISH
SWITH
THIGH
TRISH
URIAH
URICH
WEIGH
WHICH
WHISH

I•I••
IBIZA
ICIER
ICILY
ICING
IDINE
IDIOM
IDIOT
ILIAC
ILIAD
ILICH
ILION
ILIUM
IMIDE
IMIDO
IMINE
IMINO
INIGO
INION
INISH
INITS
IRIDO
IRINA
IRISH
IVIED
IVIES
IVINS
IXION

I••I•
ICEIN
ILLIN
IMMIX
INBIG
INDIA
INDIC
INDIE
INDIO
INDIV
INFIN
INFIX
INUIT
IODIC
IONIA
IONIC
IQUIT
IRVIN
IRWIN
ISLIP
ISTIC
IZMIR
IZMIT

I•••I
IAMBI
ICENI
ICOSI
IMPEI
INARI
INDRI
IRANI
IRAQI
ISSEI

•I•I•
BIDIN
BIFID
CILIA
CIVIC
CIVIL
DIDIN
DIGIN
DIGIT
DIXIE
DIXIT
EIEIO
FINIS
FITIN
FIXIT
HIFIS
HITIT
KILIM
KIRIN
KIWIS
LICIA
LICIT
LIEIN
LIMIT
LIPID
LIVIA
LIVID
MIDIS
MIMIC
MINIE
MINIM
MINIS
MIXIN
NIHIL
NIXIE
PIPIT
PIXIE
RIGID
SIGIL
SITIN
TIBIA
TIEIN
TIKIS
TIMID
TIPIN
TITIS
VIGIL
VIRID
VISIT
VIVID
ZITIS

•I••I
AIOLI
CIRRI
FIDEI
HINDI
JINNI
KIBEI
LIGNI
LIMBI
LIPPI
MIAMI
MILLI
MISTI
MITZI
NIKKI
NIMBI
NISEI
NITTI
PIAUI
PILEI
PIPPI
PISCI

RICCI RICKI RIFFI RIKKI RISHI SIEPI SINAI TIKKI TIPPI VICKI VIKKI VILLI VINCI

••II•

CCIII CDIII CLIII CMIII CVIII CXIII DCIII DLIII DVIII DXIII LVIII LXIII MCIII MDIII MLIII MMIII MVIII MXIII XCIII XLIII XVIII XXIII

••I•I

ALIBI BLINI CCIII CDIII CHILI CLIII CMIII CVIII CXIII DCIII DLIII DVIII DXIII HAITI HEIDI LUIGI LVIII LXIII MCIII MDIII MEIJI MLIII MMIII MVIII MXIII ORIBI PRIMI SCIFI SEIJI TRINI VOICI XCIII XLIII XVIII XXIII

•••II

AALII ACTII ASCII CCCII CCIII CCLII CCVII CCXII CDIII CDLII CDVII CDXII CLIII CLVII CLXII CMIII CMLII CMVII CMXII CVIII CXCII CXIII CXLII CXVII CXXII DCCII DCIII DCLII DCVII DCXII DLIII DLVII DLXII DVIII DXCII DXIII DXLII DXVII DXXII GENII LVIII LXIII LXVII LXXII MCCII MCDII MCIII MCLII MCMII MCVII MCXII MDCII MDIII MDLII MDVII MDXII MLIII MLVII MLXII MMCII MMDII MMIII MMLII MMMII MMVII MMXII MVIII MXCII MXIII MXLII MXMII MXVII MXXII QBVII RADII TORII XCIII XCVII XLIII XLVII XVIII XXIII XXVII XXXII

•IJ••

BIJOU DIJON GIJOE GIJON HIJAZ HIJRA

•I•J•

NINJA RIOJA VIEJO

••IJ•

MEIJI OUIJA SEIJI

IK•••

ICKES INKED INKER INKLE IRKED

I•••K

IZAAK

•IK••

AIKEN BIKED BIKEL BIKER BIKES DIKED DIKES HIKED HIKER HIKES LIKED LIKEN LIKES LIKUD MIKAN MIKED MIKES MIKEY NIKES NIKKI NIKKO NIKON PIKAS PIKED PIKER PIKES RIKER RIKKI SIKAS SIKES SIKHS TIKAL TIKES TIKIS TIKKI VIKKI YIKES

•I•K•

BILKO BILKS BIOKO DICKS DICKY DINKS DINKY DIRKS DISKS DITKA FINKS FISKE HICKS JINKS KICKS KICKY KINKS KINKY KIRKS KISKA LICKS LINKS MILKS MILKY MINKE MINKS MIRKY NICKS NIKKI NIKKO OICKS OINKS PICKS PICKY PINKS PINKY RICKI RICKS RICKY RIKKI RILKE RINKS RINKY RISKS RISKY SILKS SILKY SINKS SITKA TICKS TICKY TIKKI VICKI VICKS VIKKI WICKS WINKS ZIZKA

•I••K

KIOSK MINSK MIWOK PINSK TILAK

••IK•

ALIKE EFIKS ERIKA HAIKS HAIKU LAIKA SEIKO SPIKE SPIKY TRIKE

••I•K

BLINK BRICK BRINK BRISK BUICK CHICK CHINK CLICK CLINK CRICK DRINK FLICK FRICK FRISK GLICK KNICK PLINK PRICK PRINK QUICK QUIRK REINK SHIRK SKINK SLICK SLINK SMIRK SNICK STICK STINK STIRK SWINK THICK THINK TRICK UMIAK WHISK

•••IK

AFAIK BATIK LUNIK RUBIK RURIK SHEIK YUPIK

IL•••

ILENE ILGWU ILIAC ILIAD ILICH ILION ILIUM ILLER ILLIN ILLUS ILONA

I•L••

IDLED IDLER IDLES IGLOO IGLUS ILLER ILLIN ILLUS INLAW INLAY INLET ISLAM ISLAS ISLES ISLET ISLEY ISLIP

I••L•

ICILY IDOLS IDYLL IDYLS IMPLY INALL INGLE INKLE ISTLE ITALO ITALS ITALY

I•••L

IDEAL IDYLL IMPEL INALL INTEL

•IL••

AILED AILER AILEY BILBO BILBY BILGE BILGY BILKO BILKS BILLS BILLY CILIA CILLA DILLS DILLY EILAT FILAR FILCH FILED FILER FILES FILET FILLE FILLS FILLY FILMS FILMY FILTH FILUM GILDA GILDS GILES GILLS GILLY GILTS HILDA HILLS HILLY HILTS HILUM JILTS KILEY KILIM KILLS KILLY KILNS KILOS KILTS LILAC LILLE LILLY LILTS MILAN MILCH MILER MILES MILKS MILKY MILLE MILLI MILLS MILNE MILOS MILPA MILTS MILTY NILES NILLY NILOT OILED OILER PILAF PILAR PILEA PILED PILEI PILES PILLS PILOT PILUM PILUS RILED RILES RILEY RILKE RILLE RILLS SILAS SILEX SILKS SILKY SILLS SILLY SILOS SILTS SILTY SILVA TILAK TILDE TILED TILER TILES TILLS TILLY TILTH TILTS VILAS VILER VILLA VILLE VILLI VILMA WILCO WILDE WILDS WILED WILES WILEY WILLA WILLS WILLY WILMA WILTS ZILCH ZILLS

•I•L•

AIOLI AISLE BIALY BIBLE BIGLY BILLS BILLY BIRLS CILLA DIALS DILLS DILLY DIMLY DIPLO FIELD FILLE FILLS FILLY FITLY GILLS GILLY GIRLS HILLS HILLY HIPLY KILLS KILLY LILLE LILLY LISLE MILLE MILLI MILLS NIELS NILLY PILLS RIALS RIELS RIFLE RILLE RILLS SIALS SIDLE SILLS SILLY TILLS TILLY TITLE VIALS VILLA VILLE VILLI VIOLA VIOLS WIELD WILLA WILLS WILLY YIELD ZILLS

•I••L

BIKEL BINAL CIVIL FIDEL FINAL GIMEL LIBEL NICOL NIGEL NIHIL NIVAL PICUL PIPAL PIXEL RIGEL RIVAL RIYAL SIBYL SIGIL SISAL TICAL TIDAL TIKAL VIDAL VIGIL VINYL VIRAL VITAL

••IL•

AGILE ANILS ARILS ATILT AVILA AXILS BAILS BOILS BRILL BUILD BUILT CEILS CHILD CHILE CHILI CHILL CHILO COILS DAILY DEILS DOILY DRILL DRILY EDILE EMILE EMILY EVILS EXILE FAILS FOILS FRILL GAILY GRILL GUILD GUILE GUILT HAILE HAILS ICILY JAILS KRILL LEILA MAILE MAILS MOILS NAILS NEILL NOILS NOILY ODILE PAILS PHILE PHILO PHILY POILS POILU QUILL QUILP QUILT RAILS ROILS ROILY SAILS SHILL SKILL SLILY SMILE SOILS SPILE SPILL SPILT STILE STILL STILT SWILL TAILS TBILL THILL TOILE TOILS TRILL TWILL UTILE VEILS VOILA VOILE WAILS WEILL WHILE

••I•L

ARIEL AXIAL BAIUL BGIRL BRILL CHILL DRILL ELIEL FRILL FRIML GLIAL GRILL KRILL NEILL ORIEL PHIAL QUILL SHILL SKILL SKIRL SPIEL SPILL STILL SWILL SWIRL TBILL THILL TRIAL TRILL TWILL TWIRL URIAL URIEL WEILL WHIRL

•••IL

ABOIL ABRIL ADVIL ANVIL APRIL ARGIL AUXIL AVAIL AVRIL BASIL BRAIL BROIL CAVIL CECIL CIVIL CYRIL DEVIL DRAIL EMAIL ERBIL ERVIL FLAIL FRAIL FUSIL GRAIL MOBIL NEVIL NIHIL ONEIL PERIL PUPIL QUAIL REOIL SIGIL SMAIL SNAIL SPOIL SYBIL TAMIL TRAIL UNTIL VIGIL ZORIL

IM•••

IMAGE IMAGO IMAMS IMBUE IMIDE IMIDO IMINE IMINO IMMIX IMPED IMPEI IMPEL IMPLY

I•M••

IAMBI IAMBS IMMIX IZMIR IZMIT

I••M•

ICBMS IMAMS ISAMU ITEMS ITSME

I•••M

IBEAM IDIOM ILIUM INREM IPSUM ISLAM

•IM••

AIMAT AIMED AIMEE AIMER AIMTO DIMED DIMES DIMLY GIMEL GIMME GIMPS GIMPY JIMMY KIMPO LIMAS LIMBI LIMBO LIMBS LIMED LIMEN LIMES LIMEY LIMIT LIMNS LIMON LIMOS LIMPS MIMAS MIMED MIMEO MIMER MIMES MIMIC MIMSY NIMBI NIMBY NIMES NIMOY PIMAS RIMED RIMES SIMBA SIMMS SIMON SIMPS TIMED TIMER TIMES TIMEX TIMID TIMMY TIMON TIMOR WIMPS WIMPY

•I•M•

BIOME DIEMS DISME FILMS FILMY FIRMA FIRMS GIMME GIZMO HITME JIMMY MIAMI PISMO SIGMA SIMMS SIXMO TIMMY VILMA WILMA

•I••M

FILUM HILUM HIRAM KILIM MINIM NIZAM PILUM SIXAM SIXPM VISUM

••IM•

ANIMA ANIME BLIMP BRIMS CHIME CHIMP CLIMB CLIME CRIME CRIMP FRIML GLIMS GRIME GRIMM GRIMY JAIME KLIMT PRIMA PRIME PRIMI PRIMO PRIMP PRIMS REIMS SHIMS SKIMP SKIMS SLIME SLIMS SLIMY SWIMS TRIMS WHIMS

••I•M

ARIUM AXIOM DEISM GRIMM IDIOM ILIUM ODIUM OPIUM PRIAM PRISM PRIZM SEISM

•••IM

BEDIM CHAIM CLAIM DENIM HAKIM KILIM MAXIM MINIM PURIM REAIM SCRIM VADIM YADIM

IN•••

INALL INANE INAPT INARI INAWE INBAD INBED INBIG INBOX INCAN INCAS INCOG INCUR INCUS INDEF INDEX INDIA INDIC INDIE INDIO INDIV INDRA INDRI INDUS INEPT INERT INFER INFIN INFIX INFRA INFUN INGER INGLE INGOT INIGO INION INISH INITS INKED INKER INKLE INLAW INLAY INLET INNER INONU INORG INPUT INREM INSET INSTR INSTS INTEL INTER INTOW INTRA INTRO INTWO INUIT INURE INUSE

I•N••

IFNOT IGNES INNER IONIA IONIC IXNAY

I••N•

ICENI ICING ICONO ICONS IDINE ILENE ILONA IMINE IMINO INANE INONU IPANA IRANI IRENE IRINA IRONS IRONY IVANA IVINS

I•••N

IBSEN ICAHN ICEIN ILION ILLIN INCAN INFIN INFUN INION IOWAN IRVIN IRWIN IXION

•IN••

AINGE AINUS BINAL BINDS BINES BINET BINGE BINGO BINGS CINCH CINCO CINDY CINES DINAH DINAR DINDY DINED DINER DINES DINGE DINGO DINGS DINGY DINKS DINKY DINTS DINTY FINAL FINCA FINCH FINDS FINED FINER FINES FINIS FINKS FINNO FINNS FINNY GINNY GINZA HINDI HINDS HINDU HINES HINGE HINNY HINTS JINGO JINKS JINNI JINNS KINAS KINDA KINDS KINER KINGS KINKS KINKY KINTE LINDA LINDO LINDY LINED LINEN LINER LINES LINEY LINGO LINKS LINOS LINTS LINTY LINUS MINAS MINCE MINDS MINDY MINED MINEO MINER MINES MINGS MINGY MINHO MINIE MINIM MINIS MINKE MINKS MINOR MINOS MINOT MINSK MINTO MINTS MINTY MINUS NINAS NINER NINES NINJA NINNY NINON NINOS NINTH OINGO OINKS PINCE PINCH PINED PINES PINEY PINGO PINGS PINKS PINKY PINNA PINON PINOT PINSK PINTA PINTO PINTS PINUP PINZA RINDS RINDY RINGO RINGS RINKS RINKY RINSE RINSO SINAI SINCE SINES SINEW SINGE SINGS SINKS SINUS TINCT TINED TINES TINGE TINGS TINNY TINTS UINTA VINAS VINCE VINCI VINED VINES VINGT VINNY VINOS VINYL WINCE WINCH WINDS WINDY WINED WINES WINEY WINGS WINKS WINZE XINGU ZINCS ZINCY ZINES ZINGS ZINGY

•I•N•

AISNE BIONT DIANA DIANE DIDNT DIENE DIONE FIEND FINNO FINNS FINNY FIONA FIRNS GIANT GINNY GIRNS HINNY JINNI JINNS KIANG KILNS LIANA LIANE LIANG LIENS LIGNI LIGNO LIMNS LIONS MIENS MILNE NINNY PIANO PINNA PIONS RIANT SIENA SIGNE SIGNO SIGNS TIANT TINNY VIAND VIGNY VINNY VIRNA

•I••N

AIDAN AIKEN BIDEN BIDIN BIDON BIGON BISON DIDIN

DIGIN DIJON DIVAN DIXON DIZEN EIGEN FITIN GIJON GIVEN HITON KIRIN LIEIN LIKEN LIMEN LIMON LINEN LITON LIVEN MIKAN MILAN MIXIN NIKON NINON NISAN NIVEN NIXON PINON PISAN PITON RIPEN RIPON RISEN RIVEN SIDON SIMON SIREN SITIN SITON SIVAN TIEIN TIMON TIPIN TIRAN TITAN VIXEN WIDEN WIGAN WIZEN

••IN•

ACING ADINT AGING AKINS ALINE AMINE AMINO APING AWING AXING AYINS AZINE BEING BEINS BLIND BLINI BLINK BOING BRINE BRING BRINK BRINY CAINE CHINA CHINE CHING CHINK CHINO CHINS CLINE CLING CLINK CLINT COINS CUING DJINN DOING DRINA DRINK DVINA DYING EDINA EKING EWING FAINT FEINT FLING FLINT FOINS GAINS GLINT GOING GRIND GRINS HEINE HEINZ HYING ICING IDINE IMINE IMINO IRINA IVINS JAINS JOINS JOINT KLINE KOINE KOING LAINE LAING LOINS LYING MAINE MAINS MAINZ MEINY NAINA OKING OPINE ORING OVINE OWING PAINE PAINS PAINT PLINK PLINY POINT PRINK PRINT QUINN QUINO QUINT RAINS RAINY REINA REINK REINS RHINE RHINO RUING RUINS SAINT SEINE SHINE SHINS SHINY SKINK SKINS SKINT SLING SLINK SPINE SPINS SPINY STING STINK STINT SUING SUINT SWINE SWING SWINK TAINE TAINO TAINT THINE THING THINK THINS TRINE TRINI TWINE TWINS TYING UDINE USING VEINS VEINY VYING WAINS WHINE WHINS WHINY WRING ZEINS

••I•N

AAIUN ALIEN ALIGN ANION APIAN ARIAN ARION ASIAN ATION AVIAN AVION AXION BAIRN BRIAN CAIRN CHIEN COIGN DEIGN DEION DJINN ELION EVIAN FEIGN ILION INION IXION NAIRN ONION ORION PRION QUIEN QUINN REIGN SCION UNION VSIGN

•••IN

ACTIN ADDIN ADFIN ADMIN AGAIN AHSIN ALAIN ALGIN ALLIN ALVIN AMAIN ARKIN ASKIN ASTIN ATEIN AUXIN BALIN BASIN BEGIN BENIN BEVIN BIDIN BOXIN BRAIN BRUIN BUNIN BURIN CABIN CHAIN COLIN CRAIN CUEIN CUMIN CUTIN DARIN DIDIN DIGIN DRAIN DUBIN DUGIN EATIN ECHIN EDWIN ELFIN ELGIN ELVIN ENFIN EOSIN ERVIN ERWIN FAGIN FITIN FLYIN FOGIN GAMIN GAVIN GETIN GHAIN GOTIN GRAIN GROIN HEDIN HEMIN HOPIN ICEIN ILLIN INFIN IRVIN IRWIN JAMIN KANIN KEVIN KEYIN KIRIN KLEIN LAPIN LATIN LAVIN LAYIN LEDIN LENIN LETIN LEVIN LIEIN LOGIN LUPIN LYSIN MARIN MATIN MIXIN MUCIN MYCIN MYSIN NEVIN NOTIN NOWIN OLEIN OPSIN ORRIN OSLIN PALIN PAYIN PEKIN PEPIN PLAIN POPIN PUPIN PUTIN QUOIN RABIN RANIN RAVIN RENIN REPIN RESIN REWIN ROBIN RODIN ROSIN RUBIN RUNIN RUTIN SABIN SATIN SAWIN SEEIN SERIN SETIN SITIN SKEIN SLAIN SPAIN STAIN STEIN SWAIN TAKIN TAPIN TIEIN TIPIN TOEIN TOXIN TRAIN TURIN TWAIN UNPIN VENIN XEDIN ZAYIN ZUBIN

IO•••

IODIC IONIA IONIC IOTAS IOWAN

I•O••

ICONO ICONS ICOSA ICOSI IDOLS ILONA INONU INORG IRONS IRONY IVORY

I••O•

ICHOR IDIOM IDIOT IFNOT IGLOO ILION INBOX INCOG INGOT INION INTOW IXION

I•••O

IATRO ICONO IDAHO IGLOO IMAGO IMIDO IMINO INDIO INIGO INTRO INTWO IRIDO ITALO

•IO••

AIOLI BIOGS BIOKO BIOME BIONT BIOTA DIODE DIONE FIONA FIORD KIOGA KIOSK KIOWA LIONS NIOBE PIONS PIOUS RIOJA RIOTS SIOUX VIOLA VIOLS

•I•O•

BIDON BIGON BIGOS BIGOT BIJOU BIPOD BISON DICOT DIDOS DIJON DIVOT DIXON GIGOT GIJOE GIJON GIROS HITON KILOS KIROV LIDOS LIMON LIMOS LINOS LITON MIAOW MILOS MINOR MINOS MINOT MISOS MIWOK NICOL NIKON NILOT NIMOY NINON NINOS NIXON PICOT PILOT PINON PINOT PITON PITOT PIVOT RICOH RIDOF RIGOR RIPON SIDON SILOS SIMON SITON TIMON TIMOR TIROS VIDOR VIGOR VINOS VISOR WIDOW

•I••O

AIMTO BILBO BILKO BINGO BIOKO BISHO CINCO CIRRO CISCO DIAZO DICHO DIEGO DINGO DIPLO DISCO DITTO EIEIO FIBRO FIERO FINNO FIRPO GITGO GIZMO HIERO HIPPO HIPTO JINGO KIDDO KIMPO LIETO LIGNO LIMBO LINDO LINGO LIPPO LITHO MICRO MIMEO MINEO MINHO MINTO MIRRO MISDO NIKKO NITRO OINGO PIANO PICRO PINGO PINTO PISCO PISMO RINGO RINSO RIZZO SIGNO SIXMO TIETO VIDEO VIEJO VIREO VIRGO WILCO

••IO•

ADIOS AEIOU AGIOS ALIOS ANION ARION ATION AVION AXIOM AXION CHIOS CLIOS DEION ELION ELIOT GRIOT IDIOM IDIOT ILION INION IXION OLIOS ONION ORION PRION PRIOR SCION TRIOS UNION

••I•O

ADIPO AMIDO AMIGO AMINO ANISO AVISO BOITO CAIRO CHICO CHILO CHINO CHIRO EJIDO FRITO GUIDO GUIRO IMIDO IMINO INIGO IRIDO OLIGO PHILO PRIMO QUINO QUITO RHINO RHIZO SEIKO SLIGO SPIRO TAINO

•••IO

ANGIO ANZIO AUDIO CASIO CURIO DANIO DARIO EIEIO ENNIO FABIO FOLIO HAGIO HELIO INDIO JULIO LABIO MARIO NGAIO PATIO PLEIO RADIO RATIO SOCIO SOHIO TONIO

IP•••

IPANA IPASS IPSUM

I•P••

IMPED IMPEI IMPEL IMPLY INPUT

I••P•

INAPT INEPT

I•••P

ICEUP ISLIP

•IP••

BIPED BIPOD DIPLO DIPPY GIPSY HIPLY HIPPO HIPPY HIPTO LIPID LIPPI LIPPO LIPPY NIPAS NIPAT NIPPY NIPUP PIPAL PIPED PIPER PIPES PIPIT PIPPA PIPPI RIPEN RIPER RIPON RIPUP TIPIN TIPPI TIPPY TIPSY TIPUP VIPER WIPED WIPER WIPES YIPES ZIPPY ZIPUP

•I•P•

DIPPY FIRPO GIMPS GIMPY HIPPO HIPPY KIMPO LIMPS LIPPI LIPPO LIPPY LISPS MILPA NIPPY PIPPA PIPPI SIEPI SIMPS SIXPM TIPPI TIPPY WIMPS WIMPY WISPS WISPY ZIPPY

•I••P

BIDUP DIDUP DIGUP FIXUP HITUP LITUP MIXUP NIPUP PINUP RIGUP RIPUP SITUP TIEUP TIPUP ZIPUP

••IP•

ADIPO BLIPS CHIPS CLIPS CLIPT DRIPS FLIPS GRIPE GRIPS QTIPS QUIPS QUIPU SHIPS SKIPS SLIPS SLIPT SNIPE SNIPS STIPE SWIPE TRIPE TRIPS WHIPS

••I•P

BLIMP CHIMP CHIRP CRIMP CRISP PRIMP QUILP SKIMP

•••IP

ATRIP EQUIP ISLIP JOSIP OXLIP RECIP SCRIP STRIP TULIP UNHIP UNZIP VCHIP

IQ•••

IQUIT

I••Q•

IRAQI

•IQ••

PIQUE

•••IQ

ANTIQ

IR•••

IRADE IRANI IRAQI IRATE IRENE IRIDO IRINA IRISH IRKED IRONS IRONY IRREG IRVIN IRWIN

I•R••

INREM IRREG

I••R•

IATRO IATRY IBARS IBERT ICERS INARI INDRA INDRI INERT INFRA INORG INTRA INTRO INURE ISERE ITERS IVORY IZARD IZARS

I•••R

ICHOR ICIER IDLER ILLER INCUR INFER INGER INKER INNER INSTR INTER IZMIR

•IR••

AIRED AIRES BIRCH BIRDS BIRDY BIRLS BIRRS BIRSE BIRTH CIRCA CIRCE CIRCS CIRES CIRRI CIRRO DIRAC DIRER DIRGE DIRKS DIRTY FIRED FIRER FIRES FIRMA FIRMS FIRNS FIRPO FIRRY FIRST FIRTH GIRDS GIRLS GIRNS GIROS GIRTH GIRTS HIRAM HIRED HIRER HIRES KIRBY KIRIN KIRKS KIROV LIRAS MIRED MIRES MIRKY MIRRO MIRTH MIRVS SIRED SIREN SIRES TIRAN TIRED TIRES TIROS VIRAL VIREO VIRGA VIRGO VIRID VIRNA VIRTU VIRUS WIRED WIRER WIRES WIRRA

•I•R•

BIRRS CIERA CIRRI CIRRO DIARY FIBRE FIBRO FIERO FIERY FIORD FIRRY HIERA HIERO HIJRA LIARD LIARS LIBRA LIBRE LITRE LIVRE MICRA MICRO MIRRO MITRE NIDRE NITRE NITRO PICRO PIERS PIURA SIDRA TIARA TIERS TITRE VIERS VIVRE WIRRA

•I••R

AILER AIMER BIHAR BIKER BITER CIDER CIGAR CITER DICER DINAR DINER DIRER DISTR DIVER DIYER EIDER FIBER FIFER FILAR FILER FINER FIRER FIVER FIXER GIBER GIVER HIDER HIKER HIRER JIVER KINER KITER LIGER LINER LITER LIVER MILER MIMER MINER MINOR MISER MITER MIXER MIZAR NICER NIGER NINER NITER NIZER OILER PIKER PILAR PIPER RICER RIDER RIFER RIGOR RIKER RIPER RISER RIVER SIDER SIEUR SITAR SIXER SIZER TIBER TIGER TILER TIMER TIMOR TITER UIGUR VICAR VIDOR VIGOR VILER VIPER VISOR WIDER WIPER WIRER WISER

••IR•

AFIRE AKIRA AMIRS BAIRD BAIRN BGIRL CAIRN CAIRO CHIRO CHIRP CHIRR COIRS DAIRY EMIRS FAIRE FAIRS FAIRY FLIRT GUIRO HAIRS HAIRY HEIRS LAIRD LAIRS LOIRE MBIRA MOIRA MOIRE NAIRA NAIRN NOIRE PAIRS QUIRE QUIRK QUIRT SHIRE SHIRK SHIRR SHIRT SKIRL SKIRR SKIRT SMIRK SPIRE SPIRO SPIRY STIRK STIRS SWIRL TBIRD THIRD TWIRL WEIRD WEIRS WHIRL WHIRR WHIRS ZAIRE

••I•R

BRIAR BRIER CHIRR CRIER DRIER FLIER FRIAR FRIER GRIER ICIER OSIER PRIER PRIOR SHIER SHIRR SKIER SKIRR SLIER TRIER WHIRR WRIER

•••IR

ADAIR AEGIR AESIR ASTIR AVOIR BLAIR CHAIR CHOIR CLAIR ETVIR EYRIR FAKIR FLAIR GLAIR IZMIR KAFIR KEFIR NADIR NOSIR OHAIR ONAIR OPHIR PAMIR REAIR SAPIR STAIR TAPIR THEIR USAIR VANIR YASIR

IS•••

ISAAC ISAMU ISERE ISLAM ISLAS ISLES ISLET ISLEY ISLIP ISSEI ISSUE ISSUS ISTIC ISTLE ISUZU

I•S••

IBSEN INSET INSTR INSTS IPSUM ISSEI ISSUE ISSUS ITSME

I••S•

ICOSA ICOSI IDEST INISH INUSE IPASS IRISH

I•••S

IAMBS IBARS ICBMS ICERS ICKES ICONS ICTUS IDEAS IDLES IDOLS IDYLS IGLUS IGNES ILLUS IMAMS INCAS INCUS INDUS INITS INSTS IOTAS IPASS IRONS ISLAS ISLES ISSUS ITALS ITEMS ITERS IVIES IVINS IZARS IZBAS

•IS••

AISHA AISLE AISNE BISES BISHO BISON CISCO CISSY DISCO DISCS DISHY DISKS DISME DISTR FISCS FISHY FISKE FISTS GISTS HISSY KISKA LISLE LISPS LISSE LISTS LISZT MISDO MISER MISHA MISOS MISSA MISSY MISTI MISTS MISTY NISAN NISEI NISUS PISAN PISCI PISCO PISMO PISTE RISEN RISER

RISES RISHI RISKS RISKY SISAL SISSY TISZA VISAS VISBY VISES VISIT VISOR VISTA VISUM WISER WISHY WISPS WISPY

•I•S•

BIRSE BITSY CISSY DIDST DITSY FIRST GIPSY HISSY KIOSK LISSE MIDST MIMSY MINSK MISSA MISSY PINSK RINSE RINSO SISSY TIPSY WIEST

•I••S

AIDES AINUS AIRES BIBBS BIDES BIFFS BIGOS BIKES BILKS BILLS BINDS BINES BINGS BIOGS BIRDS BIRLS BIRRS BISES BITES BITTS CINES CIRCS CIRES CITES DIALS DICES DICKS DICTS DIDOS DIEMS DIETS

DIKES DILLS DIMES DINES DINGS DINKS DINTS DIRKS DISCS DISKS DIVAS DIVES FIATS FICES FICUS FIDES FIEFS FIFES FILES FILLS FILMS FINDS FINES FINIS FINKS FINNS FIRES FIRMS FIRNS FISCS FISTS FIVES FIXES GIBBS GIBES GIFTS GILDS GILES GILLS GILTS GIMPS GIRDS GIRLS GIRNS GIROS GIRTS GISTS GIVES HICKS HIDES HIFIS HIGHS HIKES HILLS HILTS HINDS HINES HINTS HIRES HIVES JIBES JILTS JINKS JINNS JIVES KICKS KILLS KILNS KILOS KILTS KINAS KINDS KINGS KINKS

KIRKS KITES KITTS KIVAS KIWIS LIARS LICKS LIDOS LIENS LIEUS LIFTS LIKES LILTS LIMAS LIMBS LIMES LIMNS LIMOS LIMPS LINES LINKS LINOS LINTS LINUS LIONS LIRAS LISPS LISTS LITES LITHS LIVES MICAS MIDAS MIDIS MIENS MIFFS MIKES MILES MILKS MILLS MILOS MILTS MIMAS MIMES MINAS MINDS MINES MINGS MINIS MINKS MINOS MINTS MINUS MIRES MIRVS MISOS MISTS MITES MITTS MIXES NICKS NIDES NIDUS NIELS NIKES NILES NIMES NINAS NINES NINOS NIPAS NISUS NITES NIXES

OICKS OINKS PICAS PICKS PICTS PIEDS PIERS PIKAS PIKES PILES PILLS PILUS PIMAS PINES PINGS PINKS PINTS PIONS PIOUS PIPES PITAS PITHS PITTS RIALS RICES RICKS RIDES RIELS RIFFS RIFTS RIGGS RILES RILLS RIMES RINDS RINGS RINKS RIOTS RISES RISKS RITES RIVES SIALS SIDES SIFTS SIGHS SIGNS SIKAS SIKES SIKHS SILAS SILKS SILLS SILOS SILTS SIMMS SIMPS SINES SINGS SINKS SINUS SIRES SITES SITUS SIXES SIZES TIBBS TICKS TIDES TIEGS TIERS TIFFS TIKES TIKIS

TILES TILLS TILTS TIMES TINES TINGS TINTS TIRES TIROS TITIS TITUS VIALS VIBES VICES VICKS VIERS VIEWS VILAS VINAS VINES VINOS VIOLS VIRUS VISAS VISES VITAS VITUS WICKS WILDS WILES WILLS WILTS WIMPS WINDS WINES WINGS WINKS WIPES WIRES WISPS WIVES YIKES YIPES ZILLS ZINCS ZINES ZINGS ZITIS

••IS•

ALIST AMISH AMISS ANISE ANISO APISH ARISE AVISO BLISS BOISE BRISK CRISP CRISS CRIST DAISY DEISM DEIST ELISE EPISC ERISA EXIST FEIST FOIST FRISE

FRISK GRIST GUISE HEISS HEIST HOIST INISH IRISH JOIST KNISH KRISS LUISA LUISE MOIST NAISH NOISE NOISY ODIST PAISA POISE PRISM RAISA RAISE SEISM SHISH SWISH SWISS TRISH TWIST WAIST WEISS WHISH WHISK WHIST WRIST ZEISS ZEIST

••I•S

ACIDS ADIOS ADITS AGIOS AKINS ALIAS ALIFS ALIOS AMIES AMIRS AMISS ANILS ARIAS ARIES ARILS ARIUS AXILS AYINS BAILS BAITS BEINS BLIPS BLISS BOILS BRIES BRIGS BRIMS BRITS CEILS CHIAS CHINS CHIOS CHIPS CHITS CLIOS

CLIPS COIFS COILS COINS COIRS CRIBS CRIES CRISS DEILS DOITS DRIBS DRIES DRIPS EDITS EFIKS ELIAS EMIRS EMITS EPICS ERIES EVILS EXITS FAILS FAIRS FLICS FLIES FLIPS FLITS FOILS FOINS FRIES FRITS GAINS GAITS GAIUS GLIMS GRIDS GRIGS GRINS GRIPS GRITS HAIKS HAILS HAIRS HEIRS HEISS INITS IVIES IVINS JAILS JAINS JOINS KNITS KRISS LAICS LAIRS LAIUS LOINS MAIDS MAILS MAINS MOILS NAILS NOILS OBIES OKIES OLIOS OMITS PAILS PAINS PAIRS PLIES POILS PRIES

PRIGS PRIMS QTIPS QUIDS QUIPS QUITS RAIDS RAILS RAINS REIMS REINS ROILS RUINS SAILS SHIES SHIMS SHINS SHIPS SHIVS SKIDS SKIES SKIMS SKINS SKIPS SKITS SLIMS SLIPS SLITS SMITS SNIPS SNITS SOILS SPIES SPINS SPITS SPIVS STIES STIRS SUITS SWIGS SWIMS SWISS TAILS THINS TOILS TRIES TRIGS TRIMS TRIOS TRIPS TWIGS TWINS TWITS UNITS UNIVS VEILS VEINS VOIDS WAIFS WAILS WAINS WAITS WEIRS WEISS WHIGS WHIMS WHINS WHIPS WHIRS WHITS WRITS ZEINS ZEISS

•••IS

ABRIS ADDIS AEGIS ANAIS ANTIS APHIS APSIS ARMIS ARRIS ARSIS ARTIS AUDIS AULIS BABIS BASIS BLOIS BORIS CADIS CAMIS CANIS CEDIS CHRIS CUTIS DAVIS DELIS DENIS DORIS ELLIS ELVIS ENNIS ETUIS FELIS FINIS FRAIS HAJIS HIFIS HOPIS JANIS KAKIS KEPIS KIWIS LAPIS LARIS LEGIS LENIS LEVIS LEWIS LEXIS LORIS LOUIS MARIS MAVIS MAXIS METIS MIDIS MINIS MUNIS NARIS NEHIS NEVIS NEXIS NOBIS NUMIS OASIS OPSIS ORNIS ORRIS PARIS PAVIS PERIS POLIS PULIS PYXIS

RAKIS RAMIS RANIS REGIS SADIS SARIS SEMIS SUFIS TABIS TAXIS THAIS TIKIS TITIS TOPIS TOTIS TROIS TUNIS URBIS VADIS WADIS XAXIS YAXIS YETIS YOGIS ZAXIS ZITIS ZORIS ZUNIS

IT•••

ITALO ITALS ITALY ITCHY ITEMS ITERS ITSME

I•T••

IATRO IATRY ICTUS IDTAG INTEL INTER INTOW INTRA INTRO INTWO IOTAS ISTIC ISTLE

I••T•

ICHTH INITS INSTR INSTS IRATE

I•••T

IBERT IDEST IDIOT IFNOT INAPT INEPT INERT INGOT INLET INPUT INSET INUIT IQUIT

ISLET IZMIT

•IT••

AITCH BITER BITES BITSY BITTE BITTS BITTY CITED CITER CITES DITAT DITCH DITKA DITSY DITTO DITTY DITZY FITCH FITIN FITLY GITGO HITCH HITIT HITME HITON HITUP KITED KITER KITES KITTS KITTY KITWE LITER LITES LITHE LITHO LITHS LITON LITRE LITUP MITCH MITER MITES MITRE MITTS MITTY MITZI NITER NITES NITRE NITRO NITTI NITTY PITAS PITCH PITHS PITHY PITON PITOT PITTA PITTS RITES RITZY SITAR SITBY SITED SITES SITIN SITKA SITON

SITUP SITUS TITAN TITER TITHE TITIS TITLE TITRE TITUS VITAE VITAL VITAS VITUS WITCH WITHE WITHY WITTE WITTY ZITIS

•I•T•

AIMTO BIOTA BIRTH BITTE BITTS BITTY DICTA DICTS DICTU DIETS DINTS DINTY DIRTY DISTR DITTO DITTY FIATS FIFTH FIFTY FILTH FIRTH FISTS GIFTS GILTS GIRTH GIRTS GISTS HILTS HINTS HIPTO JILTS KILTS KINTE KITTS KITTY LIETO LIFTS LILTS LINTS LINTY LISTS MIATA MILTS MILTY MINTO MINTS MINTY MIRTH MISTI MISTS MISTY MITTS MITTY

NIFTY NINTH NITTI NITTY PICTS PIETA PIETY PINTA PINTO PINTS PISTE PITTA PITTS RIATA RIFTS RIOTS SIETE SIFTS SILTS SILTY SIXTH SIXTY TIETO TILTH TILTS TINTS UINTA VIRTU VISTA WIDTH WILTS WITTE WITTY

•I••T

AIMAT BIGHT BIGOT BINET BIONT BIZET CIVET DICOT DIDNT DIDST DIGIT DITAT DIVOT DIXIT EIGHT EILAT FIGHT FILET FIRST FIXIT GIANT GIGOT HITIT LICET LICIT LIEUT LIGHT LIMIT LISZT MIDST MIGHT MINOT NIGHT NILOT NIPAT PICOT PILOT PINOT PIPIT

PITOT PIVOT RIANT RIGHT RIVET SIGHT TIANT TIBET TIGHT TINCT VINGT VISIT WIEST WIGHT ZIBET

••IT•

ADITS AGITA AKITA AMITY ANITA ARITH BAITS BLITT BLITZ BOITE BOITO BRITE BRITH BRITS BRITT CHITA CHITS DEITY DOITS EDITH EDITS ELITE EMITS EVITA EXITS FAITH FLITS FRITO FRITS FRITZ GAITS GLITZ GRITS HAITI HOITY INITS KEITH KNITS LAITY LEITH OMITS QUITE QUITO QUITS RAITT SAITH SKITS SLITS SMITE SMITH SMITS SNITS SPITE SPITS SPITZ SUITA SUITE

SUITS SWITH SWITZ TOITY TRITE TRITT TWITS UNITE UNITS UNITY WAITE WAITS WAITZ WHITE WHITS WHITY WRITE WRITS

••I•T

ADINT ALIST ATILT BLITT BRITT BUILT CLIFT CLINT CLIPT CRIST DEIST DRIFT EDICT ELIOT EVICT EXIST FAINT FEINT FEIST FLINT FLIRT FOIST GLINT GRIFT GRIOT GRIST GUILT HEIDT HEIST HOIST IDIOT JOINT JOIST KLIMT MOIST ODIST PAINT POINT PRINT QUIET QUILT QUINT QUIRT RAITT SAINT SHIFT SHIRT SKINT SKIRT SLIPT SPILT STILT STINT SUINT

SWIFT TAINT TRITT TWIST TWIXT VEIDT WAIST WHIST WRIST ZEIST

•••IT

ADMIT AFRIT AMBIT AUDIT AWAIT BAGIT BARIT BEFIT BRUIT CANIT CUBIT DAVIT DEBIT DEMIT DIGIT DIXIT DOGIT DROIT EATIT FACIT FIXIT FRUIT FUGIT GETIT GOTIT GSUIT HABIT HITIT INUIT IQUIT IZMIT KRAIT LEGIT LICIT LIMIT MEDIT MERIT NOHIT NOTIT ONDIT OPCIT ORBIT PETIT PEWIT PIPIT PLAIT POLIT POSIT QUOIT REFIT RELIT REMIT SPLIT SPRIT TACIT TOBIT TOWIT TRAIT UNFIT UNLIT VISIT

I•U••

INUIT INURE INUSE IQUIT ISUZU

I••U•

ICEUP ICTUS IGLUS ILIUM ILLUS IMBUE INCUR INCUS INDUS INFUN INPUT IPSUM ISSUE ISSUS

I•••U

ILGWU INONU ISAMU ISUZU

•IU••

PIURA

•I•U•

AINUS BIDUP DIDUP DIGUP FICUS FILUM FIXUP GIGUE HILUM HITUP LIEUS LIEUT LIKUD LINUS LITUP MINUS MIXUP NIDUS NIPUP NISUS PIAUI PICUL PILUM PILUS PINUP PIOUS PIQUE RIGUP RIPUP SIEUR SINUS SIOUX SITUP SITUS TIEUP TIPUP TITUS UIGUR VIRUS VISUM VITUS

ZIPUP

•I••U

BIJOU DICTU FICHU HINDU VIRTU XINGU

••IU•

AAIUN ARIUM ARIUS BAIUL GAIUS ILIUM LAIUS ODIUM OPIUM

••I•U

ADIEU AEIOU ELIHU HAIKU MAIDU POILU QUIPU

IV•••

IVANA IVIED IVIES IVINS IVORY

I•V••

IRVIN

I•••V

INDIV

•IV••

CIVET CIVIC CIVIL DIVAN DIVAS DIVED DIVER DIVES DIVOT DIVVY FIVER FIVES GIVEN GIVER GIVES HIVED HIVES JIVED JIVER JIVES JIVEY KIVAS LIVED LIVEN LIVER LIVES LIVIA LIVID LIVRE NIVAL

NIVEN PIVOT RIVAL RIVED RIVEN RIVER RIVES RIVET SIVAN VIVID VIVRE WIVED WIVES

•I•V•
DIVVY MIRVS SIEVE SILVA

•I••V
KIROV

••IV•
ALIVE ATIVE CHIVE CHIVY CLIVE DRIVE NAIVE OGIVE OLIVE PRIVY SHIVA SHIVS SKIVE SPIVS UNIVS WAIVE

•••IV
ACTIV ANNIV CCCIV CCLIV CCXIV CDLIV CDXIV CLXIV CMLIV CMXIV CXCIV CXLIV CXXIV DCCIV DCLIV DCXIV DERIV DLXIV DXCIV DXLIV DXXIV EQUIV INDIV LXXIV MCCIV MCDIV MCLIV MCMIV MCXIV MDCIV MDLIV MDXIV MLXIV MMCIV MMDIV MMLIV MMMIV MMXIV MXCIV MXLIV MXMIV MXXIV RAJIV XXXIV

I•W••
IOWAN IRWIN

I••W•
ILGWU INAWE INTWO

I•••W
INLAW INTOW

•IW••
KIWIS MIWOK

•I•W•
KIOWA KITWE VIEWS VIEWY

•I••W
MIAOW SINEW WIDOW

••IW•
DAIWA SLIWA

IX•••
IXION IXNAY

I•••X
ICEAX IMMIX INBOX INDEX INFIX

•IX••
BIXBY DIXIE DIXIT DIXON FIXED FIXER FIXES FIXIT FIXUP MIXED MIXER MIXES MIXIN MIXUP NIXED NIXES NIXIE NIXON PIXEL PIXIE SIXAM SIXED SIXER SIXES SIXMO SIXPM SIXTH SIXTY VIXEN

•I••X
SILEX SIOUX TIMEX

••IX•
TWIXT

•••IX
ADMIX AFFIX CALIX CCCIX CCLIX CCXIX CDLIX CDXIX CLXIX CMLIX CMXIX COMIX CROIX CXCIX CXLIX CXXIX DCCIX DCLIX DCXIX DLXIX DXCIX DXLIX DXXIX FELIX HELIX IMMIX INFIX KYLIX LXXIX MCCIX MCDIX MCLIX MCMIX MCXIX MDCIX MDLIX MDXIX MLXIX MMCIX MMDIX MMLIX MMMIX MMXIX MXCIX MXLIX MXXIX RADIX REMIX UNFIX VARIX XXXIX

I•Y••
IDYLL IDYLS

I•••Y
IATRY ICILY IMPLY INLAY IRONY ISLEY ITALY ITCHY IVORY IXNAY

•IY••
DIYER RIYAL

•I•Y•
LIBYA SIBYL VINYL

•I••Y
AILEY BIALY BIDDY BIFFY BIGGY BIGLY BILBY BILGY BILLY BIRDY BITSY BITTY BIXBY CINDY CISSY DIARY DICEY DICKY DIDBY DIGBY DILLY DIMLY DINDY DINGY DINKY DINTY DIPPY DIRTY DISHY DITSY DITTY DITZY DIVVY DIZZY FIERY FIFTY FILLY FILMY FINNY FIRRY FISHY FITLY FIZZY GIDDY GILLY GIMPY GINNY GIPSY HILLY HINNY HIPLY HIPPY HISSY JIFFY JIMMY JIVEY KICKY KIDDY KILEY KILLY KINKY KIRBY KITTY LIBBY LIDDY LIEBY LILLY LIMEY LINDY LINEY LINTY LIPPY MIDDY MIFFY MIKEY MILKY MILTY MIMSY MINDY MINGY MINTY MIRKY MISSY MISTY MITTY NIFTY NILLY NIMBY NIMOY NINNY NIPPY NITTY PICKY PIETY PIGGY PINEY PINKY PITHY RIBBY RICKY RIDGY RIGBY RILEY RINDY RINKY RISKY RITZY SILKY SILLY SILTY SISSY SITBY SIXTY TICKY TILLY TIMMY TINNY TIPPY TIPSY TIZZY VICHY VIEWY VIGNY VINNY VISBY WIGGY WILEY WILLY WIMPY WINDY WINEY WISHY WISPY WITHY WITTY ZIGGY ZINCY ZINGY ZIPPY

••IY•
ORIYA

••I•Y
ACIDY AMITY BRINY CHIVY DAILY DAIRY DAISY DEIFY DEITY DOILY DRILY EDIFY EMILY FAIRY GAILY GRIMY HAIRY HOITY ICILY JUICY LAITY MEINY NOILY NOISY PHILY PLINY PRICY PRIVY RAINY REIFY ROILY SHINY SLILY SLIMY SPICY SPIKY SPINY SPIRY TOITY UNIFY UNITY VEINY WHINY WHITY

IZ•••
IZAAK IZARD IZARS IZBAS IZMIR IZMIT

I••Z•
IBIZA ISUZU

•IZ••
BIZET DIZEN DIZZY FIZZY GIZMO MIZAR NIZAM NIZER PIZZA RIZZO SIZED SIZER SIZES TIZZY WIZEN ZIZKA

•I•Z•
DIAZO DITZY DIZZY FIZZY GINZA LISZT MITZI PINZA PIZZA RITZY RIZZO TISZA TIZZY WINZE

•I••Z
HIJAZ

••IZ•
BAIZA BAIZE ELIZA FRIZZ IBIZA MAIZE PRIZE PRIZM RHIZO SEIZE

••I•Z
BLITZ FRITZ FRIZZ GLITZ HEINZ MAINZ SPITZ SWITZ WAITZ

•••IZ
CADIZ FELIZ HAFIZ

JA•••
JABBA JABOT JACET JACKS JACKY JACOB JADED JADES JAFFA JAFFE JAGGY JAHRE JAILS JAIME JAINS JAKES JAMAL JAMBS JAMES JAMIE JAMIN JAMMY JAMUP JANET JANIE JANIS JANUS JAPAN JAPED JAPES JARLS JARRE JASEY JASON JASSY JATOS JAUNE JAUNT JAVAS JAWED JAYNE JAZZY

J•A••
JBARS JEANE JEANS

J••A•
JAMAL JAPAN JAVAS JIHAD JONAH JONAS JOTAS JOUAL JUBAL JUDAH JUDAS JUGAL JURAL JURAT

J•••A
JABBA JAFFA JIDDA JOLLA JUDEA JULIA JUMNA JUNTA

•J•A•
VJDAY

••JA•
HEJAZ HIJAZ KOJAK RAJAH RAJAS SAJAK UNJAM

••J•A
HIJRA WAJDA

•••JA
ABUJA NADJA NINJA OUIJA RIOJA SONJA THUJA

JB•••
JBARS

J•B••
JABBA JABOT JIBED JIBES JUBAL

J••B•
JABBA JAMBS JUMBO

J•••B
JACOB

••J•B
MCJOB

J•C••
JACET JACKS JACKY JACOB JOCKO JOCKS

J••C•
JOYCE JUICE JUICY JUNCO

•J•C•
EJECT

J•D••
JADED JADES JIDDA JODIE JUDAH JUDAS JUDEA JUDEO JUDGE

J••D•
JEUDI JIDDA

J•••D
JADED JAPED JAWED JIBED JIHAD JIVED JOKED JUKED

•JD••
VJDAY

•J•D•
EJIDO

•J••D
FJELD FJORD

••JD•
WAJDA

JE•••
JEANE JEANS JEEPS JEERS JELLO JELLS JELLY JEMMY JENNY JEREZ JERKS JERKY JERRY JERZY JESSE JESTS JETER JETES JETTY JEUDI JEUNE JEWEL

J•E••
JEEPS JEERS JOEYS

J••E•
JACET JADED JADES JAKES JAMES JANET JAPED JAPES JASEY JAWED JEREZ JETER JETES JEWEL JIBED JIBES JIVED JIVER JIVES JIVEY JOKED JOKER JOKES JOKEY JONES JOREL JOSEF JUDEA JUDEO JUKED JUKES JULEP JULES JUTES

J•••E
JAFFE JAHRE JAIME JAMIE JANIE JARRE JAUNE JAYNE JEANE JESSE JEUNE JODIE JOLIE JORGE JOULE JOYCE JUDGE JUICE JULIE JUSTE

•JE••
EJECT FJELD

•J•E•
AJMER

••JE•
OBJET

••J•E
GIJOE

•••JE
KOPJE

JF•••
JFKJR

J•F••
JAFFA JAFFE JIFFY

J••F•
JAFFA JAFFE JIFFY

J•••F
JOSEF

J•G••
JAGGY JUGAL JUGUM

J••G•
JAGGY JINGO JORGE JUDGE

J•H••
JAHRE JIHAD JOHNS

J•••H
JONAH JUDAH

••J•H
RAJAH

JI•••
JIBED JIBES JIDDA JIFFY JIHAD JILTS JIMMY JINGO JINKS JINNI JINNS JIVED JIVER JIVES JIVEY

J•I••
JAILS JAIME JAINS JOINS JOINT JOIST JUICE JUICY

J••I•
JAMIE JAMIN JANIE JANIS JODIE JOLIE JOSIP JULIA JULIE JULIO

J•••I
JEUDI JINNI

•JI••
DJINN EJIDO

••JI•
HAJIS RAJIV

••J•I
HAJJI

•••JI
AWAJI BAOJI BENJI HADJI HAJJI KANJI MEIJI SEIJI SHOJI

J•J••
JUJUS

J••J•
JFKJR

••JJ•
HAJJI

J•K••
JAKES JFKJR JOKED JOKER JOKES JOKEY JUKED JUKES

J••K•
JACKS JACKY JERKS JERKY JINKS JOCKO JOCKS JUNKS JUNKY

••J•K
KOJAK SAJAK

J•L••
JELLO JELLS JELLY JILTS JOLIE JOLLA JOLLY JOLTS JOLTY JULEP JULES JULIA JULIE JULIO

J••L•
JAILS JARLS JELLO JELLS JELLY JOLLA JOLLY JOULE JOWLS JOWLY

J•••L
JAMAL JEWEL JOREL JOUAL JUBAL JUGAL JURAL

•J•L•
FJELD

J•M••
JAMAL JAMBS JAMES JAMIE JAMIN JAMMY JAMUP JEMMY JIMMY JUMBO JUMNA JUMPS JUMPY

J••M•
JAIME JAMMY JEMMY JIMMY

J•••M
JORUM JUGUM

•JM••
AJMER

••J•M
UNJAM

J•N••
JANET JANIE JANIS JANUS JENNY JINGO JINKS JINNI JINNS JONAH JONAS JONES JUNCO JUNKS JUNKY JUNTA JUNTO

J••N•
JAINS JAUNE JAUNT JAYNE JEANE JEANS JENNY JEUNE JINNI JINNS JOHNS JOINS JOINT JUMNA

J•••N
JAMIN JAPAN JASON

•J•N•
DJINN

•J••N
BJORN DJINN

••J•N
CAJUN DIJON GIJON

JO•••
JOCKO JOCKS JODIE JOEYS JOHNS JOINS JOINT JOIST JOKED JOKER JOKES JOKEY JOLIE JOLLA JOLLY JOLTS JOLTY JONAH JONAS JONES JOREL JORGE JORUM JOSEF JOSIP JOTAS JOUAL JOULE JOUST JOWLS JOWLY JOYCE

J••O•
JABOT JACOB JASON JATOS JUROR

J•••O
JELLO JINGO JOCKO JUDEO JULIO JUMBO JUNCO JUNTO

•JO••
BJORN FJORD

•J••O
EJIDO

••JO•
ANJOU BIJOU DIJON DOJOS ENJOY GIJOE GIJON MAJOR MCJOB MOJOS

•••JO
BANJO VIEJO

J•P••
JAPAN JAPED JAPES

J••P•
JEEPS JUMPS JUMPY

J•••P
JAMUP JOSIP JULEP

J•R••
JARLS JARRE JEREZ JERKS JERKY JERRY JERZY JOREL JORGE JORUM JURAL JURAT JUROR

J••R•
JAHRE JARRE JBARS JEERS JERRY

J•••R
JETER JFKJR JIVER JOKER JUROR

•J•R•
BJORN FJORD

•J••R
AJMER

••JR•
HIJRA

••J•R
MAJOR

•••JR
JFKJR

J•S••
JASEY JASON JASSY JESSE JESTS JOSEF JOSIP JUSTE

J••S•
JASSY JESSE JOIST JOUST

J•••S
JACKS JADES JAILS JAINS JAKES JAMBS JAMES JANIS JANUS JAPES JARLS JATOS JAVAS JBARS JEANS JEEPS JEERS JELLS JERKS JESTS JETES JIBES JILTS JINKS JINNS JIVES JOCKS JOEYS JOHNS JOINS JOKES JOLTS JONAS JONES JOTAS JOWLS JUDAS JUJUS JUKES JULES JUMPS JUNKS JUTES

••J•S
AUJUS DOJOS HAJIS JUJUS MOJOS RAJAS

J•T••
JATOS JETER JETES JETTY JOTAS JUTES JUTTY

J••T•
JESTS JETTY JILTS JOLTS JOLTY JUNTA JUNTO JUSTE JUTTY

J•••T
JABOT JACET JANET JAUNT JOINT JOIST JOUST JURAT

•J••T
EJECT

••J•T
OBJET

JU•••
JUBAL JUDAH JUDAS JUDEA JUDEO JUDGE JUGAL JUGUM JUICE JUICY JUJUS JUKED JUKES JULEP JULES JULIA JULIE JULIO JUMBO JUMNA JUMPS JUMPY JUNCO JUNKS JUNKY JUNTA JUNTO JURAL JURAT JUROR JUSTE JUTES JUTTY

J•U••
JAUNE JAUNT JEUDI JEUNE

JOUAL JOULE JOUST

J••U•
JAMUP JANUS JORUM JUGUM JUJUS

••JU•
AUJUS CAJUN JUJUS

••J•U
ANJOU BIJOU

•••JU
CHEJU

J•V••
JAVAS JIVED JIVER JIVES JIVEY

••J•V
RAJIV

J•W••
JAWED JEWEL JOWLS JOWLY

J•Y••
JAYNE JOYCE

J••Y•
JOEYS

J•••Y
JACKY JAGGY JAMMY JASEY JASSY JAZZY JELLY JEMMY JENNY JERKY JERRY JERZY JETTY JIFFY JIMMY JIVEY JOKEY JOLLY JOLTY JOWLY JUICY JUMPY JUNKY JUTTY

•J••Y
VJDAY

••J•Y
ENJOY

J•Z••
JAZZY

J••Z•
JAZZY JERZY

J•••Z
JEREZ

••J•Z
HEJAZ HIJAZ

KA•••
KAABA KABOB KABUL KADAR KAFIR KAFKA KAFUE KAHLO KAKAS KAKIS KALEL KALES KANDY KANGA KANIN KANJI KANSA KANZU KAONS KAPHS KAPOK KAPPA KAPUT KARAN KARAT KAREL KAREN KARLA KARMA KAROL KARSH KASEM KASHA KATHY KATIE KAUAI KAURI KAVAS KAYAK KAYOS KAZAK KAZAN KAZOO

K•A••
KAABA KEACH KEANE KEANU KEATS KHAKI KHANS KIANG KLAUS KMART KNACK KNAPS KNARS KNAVE KOALA KOANS KRAAL KRAFT KRAIT KRAUS KRAUT KRAZY KUALA KVASS KYACK KYATS

K••A•
KADAR KAKAS KARAN KARAT KAUAI KAVAS KAYAK KAZAK KAZAN KEBAB KEMAL KENAI KERAT KINAS KIVAS KNEAD KODAK KOJAK KOLAS KORAN KRAAL KULAK

K•••A
KAABA KAFKA KANGA KANSA KAPPA KARLA KARMA KASHA KENYA KINDA KIOGA KIOWA KISKA KOALA KORDA KOREA KRONA KRUPA KUALA KUKLA KYOGA

•KA••
OKAPI OKAYS SKALD SKANK SKATE UKASE

•K•A•
AKBAR AKKAD OKRAS SKEAN SKEAT SKOAL SKUAS

•K••A
AKELA AKIRA AKITA SKODA

••KA•
AKKAD AOKAY DAKAR DUKAS KAKAS LUKAS MCKAY MIKAN OHKAY OSKAR PIKAS SAKAI SIKAS TAKAS TIKAL TOKAY WEKAS

••K•A
HEKLA KUKLA MAKUA PUKKA

•••KA
ASOKA BABKA CHAKA CHEKA DHAKA DITKA ERIKA KAFKA KISKA LAIKA LANKA OSAKA PARKA POLKA PUKKA SANKA SITKA STUKA SUCKA TANKA TONKA VODKA ZIZKA

K•B••
KABOB KABUL KEBAB KEBOB KIBEI KOBOS

K••B•
KAABA KERBS KIRBY KNOBS KREBS

K•••B
KABOB KEBAB KEBOB

•KB••
AKBAR

K•C••
KICKS KICKY KOCHI

K••C•
KEACH KENCH KETCH KNACK KNICK KNOCK KOTCH KYACK

K•D••
KADAR KEDGE KIDDO KIDDY KODAK KUDOS KUDUS KUDZU

K••D•
KANDY KENDO KIDDO KIDDY KINDA KINDS KORDA KURDS

K•••D
KEYED KITED KNEAD KNEED

•K•D•
SKIDS SKODA

•K••D
AKKAD SKALD SKIED

••K•D
AKKAD ALKYD ASKED BAKED BIKED CAKED COKED DEKED DIKED DUKED FAKED HIKED HOKED INKED IRKED JOKED JUKED LIKED LIKUD MIKED NAKED NUKED PIKED POKED RAKED WAKED YOKED

KE•••
KEACH KEANE KEANU KEATS KEBAB KEBOB KEDGE KEELS KEENE KEENS KEEPS KEETS KEFIR KEITH KELLY KELPS KELPY KELSO KEMAL KEMPS KEMPT KENAI KENCH KENDO KENNY KENOS KENYA KEOGH KEPIS KERAT KERBS KERNS KERRI KERRY KESEY KETCH KEVEL KEVIN KEYED KEYES KEYIN KEYUP

K•E••
KEELS KEENE KEENS KEEPS KEETS KLEIN KNEAD KNEED KNEEL KNEES KNELL KNELT KREBS KVELL

K••E•
KALEL KALES KAREL KAREN KASEM KESEY KEVEL KEYED KEYES KHMER KIBEI KILEY KINER KITED KITER KITES KLIEG KNEED KNEEL KNEES KOPEK KOREA KUGEL KYSER

K•••E
KAFUE KATIE KEANE KEDGE KEENE KINTE KITWE KLINE KLUGE KLUTE KNAVE KNIFE KNUTE KOINE KOPJE KRONE KYRIE

•KE••
AKEEM AKEES AKELA AKENE SKEAN SKEAT SKEET SKEGS SKEIN SKEPS SKETE SKEWS

•K•E•
AKEEM AKEES OKIES SKEET SKIED SKIER SKIES SKYEY

•K••E
AKENE SKATE SKETE SKIVE UKASE

••KE•
AIKEN ASKED ASKER ASKEW BAKED BAKER BAKES BIKED BIKEL BIKER BIKES CAKED CAKES CAKEY COKED COKES CUKES DEKED DEKES DIKED DIKES DUKED DUKES ESKER FAKED FAKER FAKES FYKES HAKES HIKED HIKER HIKES HOKED HOKES HOKEY ICKES INKED INKER IRKED JAKES JOKED JOKER JOKES JOKEY JUKED JUKES LAKER LAKES LIKED LIKEN LIKES MAKER MAKES MIKED MIKES MIKEY NAKED NIKES NUKED NUKES OAKEN OAKES ONKEY PEKES PIKED PIKER PIKES POKED POKER POKES POKEY RAKED RAKER RAKES REKEY RIKER SAKER SAKES SIKES SOKES TAKEI TAKEN TAKER TAKES TIKES TOKEN TYKES URKEL WAKED WAKEN WAKES WOKEN YIKES YOKED YOKEL YOKES

••K•E
ANKLE INKLE LAKME OAKIE PEKOE

•••KE
ALIKE AWAKE AWOKE BLAKE BLOKE BRAKE BROKE BURKE CHOKE COOKE CRAKE DANKE DRAKE EVOKE FISKE FLAKE FLUKE HAWKE HOOKE LATKE LOCKE MINKE QUAKE RANKE RILKE SHAKE SLAKE SMOKE SNAKE SPAKE SPEKE SPIKE SPOKE STAKE STOKE TRIKE

K•F••
KAFIR KAFKA KAFUE KEFIR

K••F•
KHUFU KNIFE KRAFT

K•••F
KNOPF

•K•F•
SKIFF

•K••F
SKIFF

K•G••
KUGEL

K••G•
KANGA KEDGE KEOGH KINGS KIOGA KLUGE KROGH KYOGA

K•••G
KIANG KLIEG KOING

•K•G•
SKEGS

•K••G
EKING OKING

KH•••
KHAKI KHANS KHMER KHUFU

K•H••
KAHLO

K••H•
KAPHS KASHA KATHY KOCHI KOPHS

K•••H
KARSH KEACH KEITH KENCH KEOGH KETCH KNISH KOTCH KROGH

•K••H
SKOSH

••KH•
ANKHS SIKHS

•••KH
BALKH

KI•••
KIANG KIBEI KICKS KICKY KIDDO KIDDY KILEY KILIM KILLS KILLY KILNS KILOS KILTS KIMPO KINAS KINDA KINDS KINER KINGS KINKS KINKY KINTE KIOGA KIOSK KIOWA KIRBY KIRIN KIRKS KIROV KISKA KITED KITER KITES KITTS KITTY KITWE KIVAS KIWIS

K•I••
KEITH KLIEG KLIMT KLINE KNICK KNIFE KNISH KNITS KOINE KOING KRILL KRISS

K••I•
KAFIR KAKIS KANIN KATIE KEFIR KEPIS KEVIN KEYIN KILIM KIRIN KIWIS KLEIN KRAIT KYLIX KYRIE

K•••I
KANJI KAUAI KAURI KENAI KERRI KHAKI KIBEI KOCHI

•KI••
AKINS AKIRA AKITA EKING OKIES OKING SKIDS SKIED SKIER SKIES SKIFF SKILL SKIMP SKIMS SKINK SKINS SKINT SKIPS SKIRL SKIRR SKIRT SKITS SKIVE

•K•I•
SKEIN

•K••I
OKAPI

••KI•
ARKIN ASKIN FAKIR HAKIM KAKIS OAKIE PEKIN RAKIS TAKIN TIKIS

••K•I
NIKKI RIKKI SAKAI TAKEI TIKKI VIKKI YOKOI

•••KI
GORKI KHAKI NIKKI RICKI RIKKI TIKKI UMEKI VICKI VIKKI

K•J••
KOJAK

K••J•
KANJI KOPJE

••KJ•
JFKJR

K•K••
KAKAS KAKIS KUKLA

K••K•
KAFKA KHAKI KICKS KICKY KINKS KINKY KIRKS KISKA KOOKS KOOKY

K•••K
KAPOK KAYAK KAZAK KIOSK KNACK KNICK KNOCK KODAK KOJAK KOPEK KULAK KURSK KYACK

•KK••
AKKAD

•K••K
SKANK SKINK SKULK SKUNK

••KK•
DEKKO NIKKI NIKKO PUKKA RIKKI TIKKI VIKKI

KL•••
KLAUS KLEIN KLIEG KLIMT KLINE KLUGE KLUTE KLUTZ

K•L••
KALEL KALES KELLY KELPS KELPY KELSO KILEY KILIM KILLS KILLY KILNS KILOS KILTS KOLAS KULAK KYLIX

K••L•
KAHLO KARLA KEELS KELLY KILLS KILLY KNELL KNELT KNOLL KOALA KRILL KRULL KUALA KUKLA KVELL

K•••L
KABUL KALEL KAREL KAROL KEMAL KEVEL KNEEL KNELL KNOLL KNURL KRAAL KRILL KRULL KUGEL KVELL KYZYL

•K•L•
AKELA SKALD SKILL SKULK SKULL

•K••L
SKILL SKIRL SKOAL SKULL

••KL•
ANKLE HEKLA INKLE KUKLA

••K•L
ALKYL BIKEL TIKAL URKEL YOKEL

KM•••
KMART

K•M••
KEMAL KEMPS KEMPT KHMER KIMPO

K••M•
KARMA KLIMT

K•••M
KASEM KILIM

•K•M•
SKIMP SKIMS

•K••M
AKEEM AKSUM

••KM•
LAKME

••K•M
HAKIM HOKUM OAKUM YOKUM

KN•••
KNACK KNAPS KNARS KNAVE KNEAD KNEED KNEEL KNEES KNELL KNELT KNICK KNIFE KNISH KNITS KNOBS KNOCK KNOLL KNOPF KNOPS KNORR KNOTS KNOUT KNOWN KNOWS KNURL KNURS KNUTE

K•N••
KANDY KANGA KANIN KANJI KANSA KANZU KENAI KENCH KENDO KENNY KENOS KENYA KINAS KINDA KINDS KINER KINGS KINKS KINKY KINTE

K••N•
KAONS KEANE KEANU KEENE KEENS KENNY KERNS KHANS KIANG KILNS KLINE KOANS KOINE KOING KRONA KRONE

K•••N
KANIN KARAN KAREN KAZAN KEVIN KEYIN KIRIN KLEIN KNOWN KORAN

•KN••
SKNXX

•K•N•
AKENE AKINS EKING OKING SKANK SKINK SKINS SKINT SKUNK

•K••N
AKRON SKEAN SKEIN

••K•N
AIKEN ARKIN ASKIN LIKEN MIKAN NIKON OAKEN PEKIN TAKEN TAKIN TOKEN WAKEN WOKEN YUKON

KO•••
KOALA KOANS KOBOS KOCHI KODAK KOINE KOING KOJAK KOLAS KOOKS KOOKY KOPEK KOPHS KOPJE KORAN KORDA KOREA KOTCH KOTOS KOVNO

K•O••
KAONS KEOGH KIOGA KIOSK KIOWA KNOBS KNOCK KNOLL KNOPF KNOPS KNORR KNOTS KNOUT KNOWN KNOWS KOOKS KOOKY KROGH KRONA KRONE KYOGA KYOTO

K••O•
KABOB KAPOK KAROL KAYOS KAZOO KEBOB KENOS KILOS KIROV KOBOS KOTOS KUDOS

K•••O
KAHLO KAZOO KELSO KENDO KIDDO KIMPO KOVNO KYOTO

•KO••
SKOAL SKODA SKORT SKOSH

•K•O•
AKRON

••KO•
CUKOR MAKOS NIKON PEKOE YAKOV YOKOI YUKON ZUKOR

••K•O
DEKKO MOKPO NIKKO TOKYO

•••KO
BILKO BIOKO BUCKO BUNKO DEKKO GECKO JOCKO NIKKO ROYKO SEIKO SHAKO SOCKO WACKO

K•P••
KAPHS KAPOK KAPPA KAPUT KEPIS KOPEK KOPHS KOPJE

K••P•
KAPPA KEEPS KELPS KELPY KEMPS KEMPT KIMPO KNAPS KNOPF KNOPS KRUPA KRUPP

K•••P
KEYUP KRUPP

•K•P•
OKAPI
SKEPS
SKIPS

••K•P
SKIMP

••KP•
MOKPO

KR•••
KRAAL
KRAFT
KRAIT
KRAUS
KRAUT
KRAZY
KREBS
KRILL
KRISS
KROGH
KRONA
KRONE
KRULL
KRUPA
KRUPP

K•R••
KARAN
KARAT
KAREL
KAREN
KARLA
KARMA
KAROL
KARSH
KERAT
KERBS
KERNS
KERRI
KERRY
KIRBY
KIRIN
KIRKS
KIROV
KORAN
KORDA
KOREA
KURDS
KURSK
KURTZ
KYRIE

K••R•
KAURI
KERRI
KERRY
KMART
KNARS
KNORR
KNURL
KNURS

K•••R
KADAR
KAFIR
KEFIR
KHMER
KINER
KITER
KNORR
KYSER

•KR••
AKRON
OKRAS

•K•R•
AKIRA
SKIRL
SKIRR
SKIRT
SKORT

•K••R
AKBAR
SKIER
SKIRR

••K•R
ASKER
BAKER
BIKER
CUKOR
DAKAR
ESKER
FAKER
FAKIR
HIKER
INKER
JFKJR
JOKER
LAKER
MAKER
OSKAR
PIKER
POKER
RAKER
RIKER
SAKER
TAKER
ZUKOR

K•S••
KASEM
KASHA
KESEY
KISKA
KYSER

K••S•
KANSA
KARSH
KELSO
KIOSK
KNISH
KRISS
KURSK
KVASS

K•••S
KAKAS
KAKIS
KALES
KAONS
KAPHS
KAVAS
KAYOS
KEATS
KEELS
KEENS
KEEPS
KEETS
KELPS
KEMPS
KENOS
KEPIS
KERBS
KERNS
KEYES
KHANS
KICKS
KILLS
KILNS
KILOS
KILTS
KINAS
KINDS
KINGS
KINKS
KIRKS
KITES
KITTS
KIVAS
KIWIS
KLAUS
KNAPS
KNARS
KNEES
KNITS
KNOBS
KNOPS
KNOTS
KNOWS
KNURS
KOANS
KOBOS
KOLAS
KOOKS
KOPHS
KOTOS
KRAUS
KREBS
KRISS
KUDOS
KUDUS
KURDS
KVASS
KYATS

•KS••
AKSUM

•K•S•
SKOSH
UKASE

•K••S
AKEES
AKINS
OKAYS
OKIES
OKRAS
SKEGS
SKEPS
SKEWS
SKIDS
SKIES
SKIMS
SKINS
SKIPS
SKITS
SKUAS

••KS•
BAKST

••K•S
ANKHS
BAKES
BIKES
CAKES
COKES
CUKES
DEKES
DIKES
DUKAS
DUKES
FAKES
FYKES
HAKES
HIKES
HOKES
ICKES
JAKES
JOKES
JUKES
KAKAS
KAKIS
LAKES
LIKES
LUKAS
MAKES
MAKOS
MIKES
NIKES
NUKES
OAKES
PEKES
PIKAS
PIKES
POKES
RAKES
RAKIS
SAKES
SIKAS
SIKES
SIKHS
SOKES
TAKAS
TAKES
TIKES
TIKIS
TYKES
WAKES
WEKAS
YIKES
YOKES

•••KS
BACKS
BALKS
BANKS
BARKS
BASKS
BEAKS
BECKS
BILKS
BONKS
BOOKS
BOSKS
BUCKS
BULKS
BUNKS
BUSKS
CALKS
CARKS
CASKS
COCKS
CONKS
COOKS
CORKS
CUSKS
DARKS
DECKS
DESKS
DICKS
DINKS
DIRKS
DISKS
DOCKS
DUCKS
DUNKS
DUSKS
EFIKS
EWOKS
FINKS
FOLKS
FORKS
FUNKS
GAWKS
GEEKS
GOWKS
GROKS
HACKS
HAIKS
HANKS
HARKS
HAWKS
HECKS
HICKS
HOCKS
HONKS
HOOKS
HULKS
HUNKS
HUSKS
JACKS
JERKS
JINKS
JOCKS
JUNKS
KICKS
KINKS
KIRKS
KOOKS
LACKS
LARKS
LEAKS
LEEKS
LICKS
LINKS
LOCKS
LOOKS
LUCKS
LURKS
MARKS
MASKS
MILKS
MINKS
MOCKS
MONKS
MUCKS
MUSKS
NARKS
NECKS
NICKS
NOCKS
NOOKS
OICKS
OINKS
PACKS
PARKS
PEAKS
PECKS
PEEKS
PERKS
PICKS
PINKS
PORKS
PUCKS
PUNKS
RACKS
RANKS
REEKS
RICKS
RINKS
RISKS
ROCKS
ROOKS
RUCKS
RUSKS
SACKS
SAUKS
SEEKS
SILKS
SINKS
SOAKS
SOCKS
SOUKS
SUCKS
SULKS
TACKS
TALKS
TANKS
TASKS
TEAKS
TICKS
TREKS
TUCKS
TURKS
TUSKS
VICKS
WALKS
WEEKS
WICKS
WINKS
WONKS
WORKS
YACKS
YANKS
YERKS
YOLKS
ZONKS
ZOUKS

K•T••
KATHY
KATIE
KETCH
KITED
KITER
KITES
KITTS
KITTY
KITWE
KOTCH
KOTOS

K••T•
KEATS
KEETS
KEITH
KILTS
KINTE
KITTS
KITTY
KLUTE
KLUTZ
KNITS
KNOTS
KNUTE
KURTZ
KYATS
KYOTO

K•••T
KAPUT
KARAT
KEMPT
KERAT
KLIMT
KMART
KNELT
KNOUT
KRAFT
KRAIT
KRAUT

•K•T•
AKITA
SKATE
SKETE
SKITS

•K••T
SKEAT
SKEET
SKINT
SKIRT
SKORT

••K•T
BAKST
YAKUT

KU•••
KUALA
KUDOS
KUDUS
KUDZU
KUGEL
KUKLA
KULAK
KURDS
KURSK
KURTZ

K•U••
KAUAI
KAURI
KHUFU
KLUGE
KLUTE
KLUTZ
KNURL
KNURS
KNUTE
KRULL
KRUPA
KRUPP

K••U•
KABUL
KAFUE
KAPUT
KEYUP
KLAUS
KNOUT
KRAUS
KRAUT
KUDUS

K•••U
KANZU
KEANU
KHUFU
KUDZU

•KU••
SKUAS
SKULK
SKULL
SKUNK

•K•U•
AKSUM

••KU•
HOKUM
LIKUD
MAKUA
OAKUM
YAKUT
YOKUM

•••KU
HAIKU
TURKU

KV•••
KVASS
KVELL

K•V••
KAVAS
KEVEL
KEVIN
KIVAS
KOVNO

K••V•
KNAVE

K•••V
KIROV

•K•V•
SKIVE

••K•V
YAKOV

K•W••
KIWIS

K••W•
KIOWA
KITWE
KNOWN
KNOWS

•K•W•
SKEWS

••K•W
ASKEW

K•••X
KYLIX

•K•X•
SKNXX

•K••X
SKNXX

KY•••
KYACK
KYATS
KYLIX
KYOGA
KYOTO
KYRIE
KYSER
KYZYL

K•Y••
KAYAK
KAYOS
KEYED
KEYES
KEYIN
KEYUP

K••Y•
KENYA
KYZYL

K•••Y
KANDY
KATHY
KELLY
KELPY
KENNY
KERRY
KESEY
KICKY
KIDDY
KILEY
KILLY
KINKY
KIRBY
KITTY
KOOKY
KRAZY

•KY••
SKYEY

•K•Y•
OKAYS

•K••Y
SKYEY

••KY•
ALKYD
ALKYL
TOKYO

••K•Y
AOKAY
CAKEY
HOKEY
JOKEY
MCKAY
MIKEY
OHKAY
ONKEY
POKEY
REKEY
TOKAY

•••KY
BALKY
BANKY
BARKY
BECKY
BOSKY
BUCKY
BULKY
CHOKY
COCKY
COOKY
CORKY
DICKY
DINKY
DUCKY
DUSKY
ENSKY
FLAKY
FLUKY
FOLKY
FORKY
FUNKY
GAWKY
GEEKY
GORKY
GUNKY
HANKY
HERKY
HOOKY
HUSKY
JACKY
JERKY
JUNKY
KICKY
KINKY
KOOKY
LANKY
LARKY
LEAKY
LECKY
LUCKY
MILKY
MIRKY
MUCKY
MURKY
MUSKY
PANKY
PAWKY
PECKY
PERKY
PESKY
PICKY
PINKY
PORKY
PUNKY
QUAKY
REEKY
RICKY
RINKY
RISKY
ROCKY
ROOKY
SARKY
SHAKY
SILKY
SMOKY
SNAKY
SPIKY
SULKY
TACKY
TALKY
TICKY
WACKY
WONKY
YOLKY
YUCKY

K•Z••
KAZAK
KAZAN
KAZOO
KYZYL

K••Z•
KANZU
KRAZY
KUDZU

K•••Z
KLUTZ
KURTZ

LA•••
LABAN
LABEL
LABIO
LABOR
LACED
LACER
LACES
LACEY
LACKS
LACTI
LACTO
LADED
LADEN
LADER
LADES
LADLE
LADON
LADYS
LAGAN
LAGER
LAGOS
LAHAR
LAHTI
LAICS
LAIKA
LAINE
LAING
LAIRD
LAIRS
LAITY
LAIUS
LAKER
LAKES
LAKME
LALAW
LAMAR
LAMAS
LAMBS
LAMED
LAMER
LAMES
LAMIA
LAMPS
LANAI
LANCE
LANDI
LANDO
LANDS
LANES
LANGE
LANKA
LANKY
LANTZ
LANZA
LAPAZ
LAPEL
LAPIN
LAPIS
LAPPS
LAPSE
LAPUP
LARAM
LARAS
LARCH
LARDS
LARDY
LARES
LARGE
LARGO
LARIS
LARKS
LARKY
LARRY
LARUE
LARVA
LASED
LASER
LASES
LASSO
LASTS
LATCH
LATEN
LATER
LATEX
LATHE
LATHS
LATHY
LATIN
LATKE
LATRY
LATTE
LAUDE
LAUDS
LAUER
LAUGH
LAURA
LAVAL
LAVAS
LAVED
LAVER
LAVES
LAVIN
LAWES
LAWNS
LAWNY
LAXER
LAXLY
LAYBY
LAYER
LAYIN
LAYLA
LAYNE
LAYON
LAYTO
LAYUP
LAZAR
LAZED
LAZES

L•A••
LEACH
LEADS
LEADY
LEAFS
LEAFY
LEAHY
LEAKS
LEAKY
LEANS
LEANT
LEAPS
LEAPT
LEARN
LEARS
LEARY
LEASE
LEASH
LEAST
LEAVE
LHASA
LIANA
LIANE
LIANG
LIARD
LIARS
LLAMA
LLANO
LOACH
LOADS
LOAFS
LOAMS
LOAMY
LOANS
LOATH
LSATS
LUAUS

L••A•
LABAN
LAGAN
LAHAR
LALAW
LAMAR
LAMAS
LANAI
LAPAZ
LARAM
LARAS
LAVAL
LAVAS
LAZAR
LEFAY
LEGAL
LEHAR
LEMAT
LEMAY
LETAT
LEVAR
LEXAN
LILAC
LIMAS
LIRAS
LOCAL
LOFAT
LOGAN
LOMAN
LOMAX
LOPAT
LORAN
LORAX
LOTAH
LOTAS
LOYAL
LUBAS
LUCAN
LUCAS
LUKAS
LUNAR
LURAY
LYMAN

L•••A
LAIKA
LAMIA
LANKA
LANZA
LARVA
LAURA
LAYLA
LEEZA
LEHUA
LEICA
LEILA
LEMMA
LENYA
LEONA
LEORA
LEPTA
LHASA
LIANA
LIBRA
LIBYA
LICIA
LINDA
LIVIA
LLAMA
LOGIA
LONGA
LOOFA
LORCA
LORNA
LOTTA
LUCCA
LUCIA
LUISA
LULEA
LURIA
LYCRA
LYDIA
LYNDA
LYTTA

•LA••
ALACK
ALAIN
ALAMO
ALANA
ALAND
ALARM
ALATE
ALAVA
BLABS
BLACK
BLADE
BLAHS
BLAIR
BLAKE
BLAME
BLANC
BLAND
BLANK
BLARE
BLASE
BLASS
BLAST
BLATS
BLAZE
CLACK
CLAIM
CLAIR
CLAMP
CLAMS
CLANG
CLANK
CLANS
CLAPS
CLARA
CLARE
CLARK
CLARO
CLARY
CLASH
CLASP
CLASS
CLAUS
CLAVE
CLAWS
CLAYS
ELAND
ELATE
ELATH
ELAZI
FLACK
FLAGG
FLAGS
FLAIL
FLAIR
FLAKE
FLAKY
FLAME
FLAMS
FLAMY
FLANK
FLANS
FLAPS
FLARE
FLASH
FLASK
FLATS
FLATT
FLAWS
FLAWY
FLAXY
FLAYS
GLACE
GLADE
GLADS
GLAIR
GLAND
GLARE
GLARY
GLASS
GLAXO
GLAZE
KLAUS
LLAMA
LLANO
OLAND
PLACE
PLAGE
PLAID
PLAIN
PLAIT
PLANB
PLANE
PLANI
PLANK
PLANO
PLANS
PLANT
PLASH
PLASM
PLATA
PLATE
PLATH
PLATO
PLATS
PLATT
PLATY
PLAYA
PLAYS
PLAZA
SLABS
SLACK
SLADE
SLAGS
SLAIN
SLAKE
SLAMS
SLANG
SLANT
SLAPS
SLASH
SLATE
SLATS
SLATY
SLAVE
SLAVS
SLAWS
SLAYS

•L•A•
ALBAN
ALCAN
ALDAN
ALFAS
ALGAE
ALGAL
ALIAS
ALLAH
ALLAN
ALLAY
ALMAY
ALTAI
ALTAR
ALVAR
BLEAK
BLEAR
BLEAT
BLOAT
CLEAN
CLEAR
CLEAT
CLOAK
ELGAR
ELIAS
ELMAN
ELWAY
FLEAS
FLOAT
FLYAT
GLEAM
GLEAN
GLIAL
GLOAM
GLOAT
ILIAC
ILIAD
OLEAN
OLLAS
PLEAD
PLEAS
PLEAT
SLOAN
ULNAE
ULNAS

•L••A
ALANA
ALAVA
ALCOA
ALETA
ALIDA
ALOHA
ALPHA
ALULA
CLARA
ELENA
ELIZA
FLORA
ILONA
LLAMA
PLATA
PLAYA
PLAZA
PLENA
PLICA
SLIWA
ULTRA

••LA•
ADLAI
AFLAT
ALLAH
ALLAN
ALLAY
ATLAS
BALAS
BELAY
BFLAT
BOLAS
BYLAW
CFLAT
COLAS
DALAI
DELAY
DFLAT
DRLAO
DYLAN
ECLAT
EFLAT
EILAT
ENLAI
FFLAT
FILAR
FULAS
GALAH
GALAS
GALAX
GFLAT
GOLAN
GULAG
GULAR
HALAS
HULAS
HYLAS
INLAW
INLAY
ISLAM
ISLAS
KOLAS
KULAK
LALAW
LILAC
MALAN
MALAR
MALAY
MELAN
MILAN
MOLAR
MOLAS
MYLAR
NOLAN
OLLAS
ONLAY
PALAE
PALAU
PILAF
PILAR
POLAR
PULAS
RELAX
RELAY
SALAD
SALAL
SALAM
SELAH
SILAS
SOLAN
SOLAR
SPLAT
SPLAY
TILAK
UCLAN
UHLAN
UNLAY
VELAR
VILAS
VOLAR
VOLAT

••L•A
BALSA
BELLA
BELVA
BULBA
BULLA
CALLA
CELIA
CELLA
CILIA
CILLA
CULPA
DELLA
DELTA
DOLMA
FALLA
FELLA
FOLIA
FULDA
GALBA
GALEA
GILDA
GOLDA
HELGA
HILDA
JOLLA
JULIA
LULEA
MALTA
MELBA
MILPA
PALEA
PALMA
PELLA
PILEA
POLKA
SALPA
SALSA
SALTA
SELMA
SELVA
SILVA
SOLFA
SULFA
SULLA
TALIA
TULSA
USLTA
VILLA
VILMA
VOLGA
VOLTA
VOLVA
WALLA
WILLA
WILMA
YALTA
ZELDA

•••LA
ADELA
AKELA
ALULA

ASYLA AVILA BELLA BOOLA BULLA CALLA CARLA CELLA CHELA CHULA CILLA DARLA DELLA DOBLA ENOLA FALLA FELLA HABLA HEKLA JOLLA KARLA KOALA KUALA KUKLA LAYLA LEILA MARLA MOOLA NDOLA NYALA OCALA OOOLA PAULA PELLA PEPLA PHYLA SCALA SHULA STELA STOLA SULLA TABLA TESLA TRALA TWYLA UVULA UZALA VILLA VIOLA VOILA WALLA WILLA

L•B••

LABAN LABEL LABIO LABOR LIBBY LIBEL LIBRA LIBRE LIBYA LOBBY LOBED LOBES LOBOS LUBAS LUBED LUBES

L••B•

LAMBS LAYBY LETBE LIBBY LIEBY LIMBI LIMBO LIMBS LOBBY LOOBY

•LB••

ALBAN ALBEE ALBEN ALBUM ELBOW

•L•B•

ALIBI BLABS BLEBS BLOBS CLUBS FLUBS FLYBY GLEBE GLOBE GLOBS PLEBE PLEBS SLABS SLOBS

•L••B

BLURB CLIMB PLANB PLUMB

••LB•

BILBO BILBY BULBA BULBS COLBY DOLBY FTLBS GALBA MELBA WELBY

••L•B

ADLIB CALEB CELEB

L•C••

LACED LACER LACES LACEY LACKS LACTI LACTO LECKY LICET LICIA LICIT LICKS LOCAL LOCHS LOCKE LOCKS LOCOS LOCUM LOCUS LTCOL LUCAN LUCAS LUCCA LUCCI LUCIA LUCID LUCIE LUCKS LUCKY LUCRE LYCEE LYCRA

L••C•

LAICS LANCE LARCH LATCH LEACH LEECH LEICA LOACH LORCA LUCCA LUCCI LUNCH LURCH LYNCH

L•••C

LILAC LOGIC LUDIC LYRIC

•LC••

ALCAN ALCOA ALCOR ELCID ULCER

•L•C•

ALACK ALECK ALICE ALYCE BLACK BLOCH BLOCK BLOCS CLACK CLICK CLOCK CLUCK ELECT FLACK FLECK FLICK FLICS FLOCK GLACE GLICK GLUCK GLUCO GLYCO ILICH PLACE PLICA PLUCK SLACK SLICE SLICK

•L••C

BLANC ILIAC OLEIC OLMEC

••LC•

BALCH BELCH CALCI CULCH DELCO DOLCE FILCH GULCH HULCE MILCH MULCH MULCT SULCI WELCH WILCO ZILCH

••L•C

ADLOC FOLIC FSLIC HELIC LILAC MALIC MELIC RELIC SALIC TELIC

L•D••

LADED LADEN LADER LADES LADLE LADON LADYS LEDGE LEDGY LEDIN LEDON LEDTO LIDDY LIDOS LODEN LODES LODGE LUDIC LYDIA

L••D•

LANDI LANDO LANDS LARDS LARDY LAUDE LAUDS LEADS LEADY LEEDS LENDL LENDS LIDDY LINDA LINDO LINDY LOADS LORDS LUNDI LUNDY LYNDA LYNDE

L•••D

LACED LADED LAIRD LAMED LASED LAVED LAZED LIARD LIKED LIKUD LIMED LINED LIPID LIVED LIVID LLOYD LOBED LOPED LOVED LOWED LUBED LUCID LURED LURID

•LD••

ALDAN ALDEN ALDER ALDOL ALDUS BLDGS ELDER OLDEN OLDER OLDIE

•L•D•

ALIDA BLADE BLVDS CLODS CLYDE ELIDE ELUDE GLADE GLADS GLEDE GLIDE PLODS SLADE SLEDS SLIDE

•L••D

ALAND ALGID ALKYD ALOUD BLAND BLEED BLEND BLIND BLOND BLOOD BLUED CLOUD CLUED CLWYD ELAND ELCID FLIED FLOOD FLOYD FLUID GLAND GLUED ILIAD LLOYD OLAND PLAID PLEAD PLIED SLOYD SLUED

••LD•

BALDS COLDS FALDO FOLDS FULDA GILDA GILDS GOLDA GOLDE GOLDS HILDA HOLDS MELDS MOLDS MOLDY NALDI SOLDI SOLDO TILDE VELDS VELDT WALDO WELDS WILDE WILDS WOLDS ZELDA

••L•D

AILED BALED DELED DOLED EELED FELID FILED GELID HALED HOLED IDLED OGLED OILED PALED PILED POLED PULED RILED RULED SALAD SALUD SOLED SOLID TILED UNLED VALID WALED WILED

•••LD

BUILD CHILD COULD FIELD FJELD GOULD GUILD MOULD ROALD SCALD SCOLD SKALD SZOLD WIELD WORLD WOULD YIELD

LE•••

LEACH LEADS LEADY LEAFS LEAFY LEAHY LEAKS LEAKY LEANS LEANT LEAPS LEAPT LEARN LEARS LEARY LEASE LEASH LEAST LEAVE LECKY LEDGE LEDGY LEDIN LEDON LEDTO LEECH LEEDS LEEKS LEERS LEERY LEETS LEEZA LEFAY LEFTS LEFTY LEGAL LEGER LEGGS LEGGY LEGIS LEGIT LEGOS LEGUP LEHAR LEHUA LEICA LEIGH LEILA LEITH LEMAT LEMAY LEMMA LEMME LEMON LEMUR LENDL LENDS LENIN LENIS LENNY LENOS LENOX LENTO LENTS LENYA LEONA LEONE LEONI LEORA LEPPY LEPTA LEPTO LEPUS LEROI LEROY LETAT LETBE LETGO LETHE LETIN LETON LETTS LETUP LEVAR LEVEE LEVEL LEVER LEVIN LEVIS LEVON LEWES LEWIS LEXAN LEXIS LEXUS LEYTE

L•E••

LEECH LEEDS LEEKS LEERS LEERY LEETS LEEZA LIEBY LIEGE LIEIN LIENS LIETO LIEUS LIEUT LOESS LOEWE LOEWY LUEGO LYELL

L••E•

LABEL LACED LACER LACES LACEY LADED LADEN LADER LADES LAGER LAKER LAKES LAMED LAMER LAMES LANES LAPEL LARES LASED LASER LASES LATEN LATER LATEX LAUER LAVED LAVER LAVES LAWES LAXER LAYER LAZED LAZES LEGER LEVEE LEVEL LEVER LEWES LIBEL LICET LIGER LIKED LIKEN LIKES LIMED LIMEN LIMES LIMEY LINED LINEN LINER LINES LINEY LITER LITES LIVED LIVEN LIVER LIVES LOBED LOBES LODEN LODES LOGES LONER LOPED LOPER LOPES LOPEZ LOREN LORES LOSER LOSES LOVED LOVER LOVES LOVEY LOWED LOWER LOWES LOXES LTGEN LUBED LUBES LUGER LUGES LULEA LUMEN LUMET LUNES LURED LURES LUREX LUTES LYCEE LYRES

L•••E

LADLE LAINE LAKME LANCE LANGE LAPSE LARGE LARUE LATHE LATKE LATTE LAUDE LAYNE LEASE LEAVE LEDGE LEMME LEONE LETBE LETHE LEVEE LEYTE LIANE LIBRE LIEGE LILLE LISLE LISSE LITHE LITRE LIVRE LOCKE LODGE LOEWE LOGUE LOIRE LONGE LOOSE LORNE LORRE LOTTE LOUIE LOUPE LOUSE LUCIE LUCRE LUISE LUNGE LURIE LYCEE LYNDE LYNNE

•LE••

ALECK ALEFS ALENE ALEPH ALERT ALETA ALEUT ALEVE BLEAK BLEAR BLEAT BLEBS BLEED BLEEP BLEND BLENT BLESS BLEST CLEAN CLEAR CLEAT CLEEK CLEFS CLEFT CLEON CLERK CLEWS ELECT ELEGY ELEMI ELENA ELENI ELEVE FLEAS FLECK FLEER FLEES FLEET FLESH FLEUR FLEWS FLEXI FLEYS GLEAM GLEAN GLEBE GLEDE GLEES GLENN GLENS GLESS GLEYS ILENE KLEIN NLERS OLEAN OLEIC OLEIN OLEOS OLEUM PLEAD PLEAS PLEAT PLEBE PLEBS PLEIO PLENA PLEON PLEWS SLEDS SLEEK SLEEP SLEET SLEPT SLEWS

•L•E•

ALBEE ALBEN ALDEN ALDER ALGER ALIEN ALLEE ALLEN ALLER ALLES ALLEY ALLEZ ALOES ALTER BLEED BLEEP BLUED BLUER BLUES BLUET BLUEY CLEEK CLUED CLUES ELDER ELIEL ELLEN ELLER ELLES ELMER ELVER ELVES ELWES FLEER FLEES FLEET FLIED FLIER FLIES FLOES FLUES FLYER GLEES GLUED GLUER GLUES GLUEY ILLER KLIEG MLLES OLDEN OLDER OLMEC OLSEN PLIED PLIES SLEEK SLEEP SLEET SLIER SLOES SLUED SLUES SLYER ULCER

•L••E

ALATE ALBEE ALENE ALEVE ALFIE ALFRE ALGAE ALICE ALIKE ALINE ALIVE ALLEE ALLIE ALONE ALYCE BLADE BLAKE BLAME BLARE BLASE BLAZE BLIGE BLOKE BLUME CLARE CLAVE CLIME CLINE CLIVE CLONE CLOSE CLOVE CLYDE ELATE ELEVE ELIDE ELISE ELITE ELLIE ELOPE ELSIE ELUDE ELUTE ELYSE FLAKE FLAME FLARE FLUKE FLUME FLUTE GLACE GLADE GLARE GLAZE GLEBE GLEDE GLIDE GLOBE GLOVE GLOZE ILENE KLINE KLUGE KLUTE OLDIE OLIVE OLLIE PLACE PLAGE PLANE PLATE PLEBE PLUME SLADE SLAKE SLATE SLAVE SLICE SLIDE SLIME SLOPE SLYPE ULNAE

••LE•

ABLER ADLER AGLET AGLEY AILED AILER AILEY ALLEE ALLEN ALLER ALLES ALLEY ALLEZ APLEY ARLEN ARLES AXLES BALED BALER BALES BELEM BOLES CALEB CCLEF CELEB COLES COLET CULET CULEX DALES DALEY DELED DELES DOLED DOLES EELED EELER ELLEN ELLER ELLES EULER FCLEF FILED FILER FILES FILET FOLEY GALEA GALEN GALES GCLEF GELEE GILES GOLEM GULES HALED HALER HALES HALEY HELEN HOLED HOLES HOLEY IDLED IDLER IDLES ILLER INLET ISLES ISLET ISLEY JULEP JULES KALEL KALES KILEY LULEA MALES MELEE MILER MILES MLLES MOLES MULES MULEY MYLES NFLER NHLER NILES OGLED OGLER OGLES OILED OILER ORLES OSLER OWLET PALEA PALED PALEO PALER PALES PALEY PELEE PELEG PILEA PILED PILEI PILES POLED POLER POLES PULED PULES RELEE RELET RILED RILES RILEY ROLEO ROLES ROLEX RULED RULER RULES SALEM SALEP SALES SELES SILEX SOLED SOLER SOLES TALER TALES TELEO TELES TELEX TILED TILER TILES TOLER TOLET TULES TYLER UNLED UTLEY VALES VALET VELEZ VILER VOLES WALED WALER WALES WALEY WILED WILES WILEY WYLER XYLEM

••L•E

ALLEE ALLIE BELIE BELLE BILGE BULGE CALPE CALVE CELIE CHLOE DELVE DOLCE DULSE ELLIE FALSE FILLE GELEE GOLDE HALLE HALVE HELVE HULCE JOLIE JULIE LILLE MALLE MELEE MILLE MILNE NOLLE NOLTE OLLIE PALAE PALME PELEE PELLE PULSE RELEE RILKE RILLE ROLFE ROLLE SALLE SALVE SOLVE TILDE TULLE VALLE VALSE VALUE VALVE VILLE VOLTE WILDE WOLFE WYLIE YALIE

•••LE

ABELE ADDLE ADELE AGILE AISLE AMBLE AMOLE AMPLE ANELE ANGLE ANKLE ANOLE APPLE BAYLE BELLE BERLE BEYLE BIBLE BOGLE BOOLE BOULE BOYLE BRULE BUGLE CABLE CARLE CHILE CYCLE DHOLE DOBLE DOYLE DUPLE EAGLE EARLE ECOLE EDILE EMILE EXILE FABLE FILLE FOYLE GABLE GAYLE GUILE HAILE HALLE HAOLE HOYLE INGLE INKLE ISTLE JOULE LADLE LILLE LISLE MACLE MAILE MALLE MAPLE MERLE MILLE NEALE NOBLE NOLLE ODILE ONCLE ORALE OVULE PARLE PEALE PEELE PELLE PERLE PHILE PHYLE POOLE PROLE QUALE RIFLE RILLE ROBLE ROLLE RUBLE SABLE SALLE SCALE SEALE SEULE SHALE SIDLE SMILE SOCLE SPILE STALE STELE STILE STOLE STYLE SWALE TABLE THOLE THULE TITLE TOILE TULLE UNCLE UTILE VALLE VILLE VOILE WHALE WHILE WHOLE

L•F••

LEFAY LEFTS LEFTY LIFTS LOFAT LOFTS LOFTY LUFFS

L••F•

LEAFS LEAFY LOAFS LOOFA LUFFS

•LF••

ALFAS ALFIE ALFRE ELFIN

•L•F•

ALEFS ALIFS

ALOFT
BLUFF
CLEFS
CLEFT
CLIFF
CLIFT
FLUFF

•L••F
ALOOF
BLUFF
CLIFF
FLUFF

••LF•
DELFT
GOLFS
GULFS
ROLFE
SOLFA
SULFA
WOLFE
WOLFF

••L•F
CALIF
CCLEF
FCLEF
GCLEF
PILAF
WOLFF

•••LF
ADOLF
SHELF
WOOLF

L•G••
LAGAN
LAGER
LAGOS
LEGAL
LEGER
LEGGS
LEGGY
LEGIS
LEGIT
LEGOS
LEGUP
LIGER
LIGHT
LIGNI
LIGNO
LOGAN
LOGES
LOGIA
LOGIC
LOGIN
LOGON
LOGOS
LOGUE
LTGEN
LTGOV
LUGER
LUGES

L••G•
LANGE
LARGE
LARGO
LAUGH
LEDGE
LEDGY
LEGGS
LEGGY
LEIGH
LETGO
LIEGE
LINGO
LODGE
LONGA
LONGE
LONGI
LONGO
LONGS
LONGU
LOUGH
LUEGO
LUIGI
LUNGE
LUNGS

L•••G
LAING
LIANG
LYING

•LG••
ALGAE
ALGAL
ALGER
ALGID
ALGIN
ALGOL
ELGAR
ELGIN
ILGWU

•L•G•
ALIGN
BLDGS
BLIGE
BLIGH
CLOGS
ELEGY
FLAGG
FLAGS
FLOGS
GLOGG
GLUGS
KLUGE
OLIGO
OLOGY
PLAGE
PLUGS
SLAGS
SLIGO
SLOGS
SLUGS

•L••G
ALONG
CLANG
CLING
CLUNG
FLAGG
FLING
FLUNG
GLOGG
KLIEG
SLANG
SLING
SLUNG

••LG•
BILGE
BILGY
BULGE
BULGY
GOLGI
HELGA
VOLGA

••L•G
GULAG
PELEG
RELIG
SELIG
ZELIG

LH•••
LHASA

L•H••
LAHAR
LAHTI
LEHAR
LEHUA

L••H•
LATHE
LATHS
LATHY
LEAHY
LETHE
LIGHT
LITHE
LITHO
LITHS
LOCHS

L•••H
LARCH
LATCH
LAUGH
LEACH
LEASH
LEECH
LEIGH
LEITH
LOACH
LOATH
LOTAH
LOUGH
LUNCH
LURCH
LYMPH
LYNCH

•L•H•
ALOHA
ALPHA
ALTHO
BLAHS
ELIHU

•L••H
ALEPH
ALLAH
BLIGH
BLOCH
BLUSH
BLUTH
BLYTH
CLASH
CLOTH
ELATH
FLASH
FLESH
FLUSH
GLYPH
ILICH
PLASH
PLATH
PLUSH
SLASH
SLOSH
SLOTH
SLUSH

••LH•
DELHI

••L•H
ALLAH
BALCH
BALKH
BELCH
CULCH
DOLPH
FILCH
FILTH
GALAH
GULCH
MILCH
MULCH
RALPH
SELAH
SYLPH
TILTH
WALSH
WELCH
WELSH
ZILCH

LI•••
LIANA
LIANE
LIANG
LIARD
LIARS
LIBBY
LIBEL
LIBRA
LIBRE
LIBYA
LICET
LICIA
LICIT
LICKS
LIDDY
LIDOS
LIEBY
LIEGE
LIEIN
LIENS
LIETO
LIEUS
LIEUT
LIFTS
LIGER
LIGHT
LIGNI
LIGNO
LIKED
LIKEN
LIKES
LIKUD
LILAC
LILLE
LILLY
LILTS
LIMAS
LIMBI
LIMBO
LIMBS
LIMED
LIMEN
LIMES
LIMEY
LIMIT
LIMNS
LIMON
LIMOS
LIMPS
LINDA
LINDO
LINDY
LINED
LINEN
LINER
LINES
LINEY
LINGO
LINKS
LINOS
LINTS
LINTY
LINUS
LIONS
LIPID
LIPPI
LIPPO
LIPPY
LIRAS
LISLE
LISPS
LISSE
LISTS
LISZT
LITER
LITES
LITHE
LITHO
LITHS
LITON
LITRE
LITUP
LIVED
LIVEN
LIVER
LIVES
LIVIA
LIVID
LIVRE

L•I••
LAICS
LAIKA
LAINE
LAING
LAIRD
LAIRS
LAITY
LAIUS
LEICA
LEIGH
LEILA
LEITH
LOINS
LOIRE
LUIGI
LUISA
LUISE
LVIII
LXIII
LYING

L••I•
LABIO
LAMIA
LAPIN
LAPIS
LARIS
LATIN
LAVIN
LAYIN
LEDIN
LEGIS
LEGIT
LENIN
LENIS
LETIN
LEVIN
LEVIS
LEWIS
LEXIS
LICIA
LICIT
LIEIN
LIMIT
LIPID
LIVIA
LIVID
LOGIA
LOGIC
LOGIN
LORIS
LOUIE
LOUIS
LUCIA
LUCID
LUCIE
LUDIC
LUNIK
LUPIN
LURIA
LURID
LURIE
LVIII
LXIII
LXVII
LXXII
LXXIV
LXXIX
LYDIA
LYRIC
LYSIN

L•••I
LACTI
LAHTI
LANAI
LANDI
LEONI
LEROI
LIGNI
LIMBI
LIPPI
LONGI
LUCCI
LUIGI
LUNDI
LVIII
LXIII
LXVII
LXXII
LXXVI
LXXXI

•LI••
ALIAS
ALIBI
ALICE
ALIDA
ALIEN
ALIFS
ALIGN
ALIKE
ALINE
ALIOS
ALIST
ALIVE
BLIGE
BLIGH
BLIMP
BLIND
BLINI
BLINK
BLIPS
BLISS
BLITT
BLITZ
CLICK
CLIFF
CLIFT
CLIII
CLIMB
CLIME
CLINE
CLING
CLINK
CLINT
CLIOS
CLIPS
CLIPT
CLIVE
DLIII
ELIAS
ELIDE
ELIEL
ELIHU
ELION
ELIOT
ELISE
ELITE
ELIZA
FLICK
FLICS
FLIED
FLIER
FLIES
FLING
FLINT
FLIPS
FLIRT
FLITS
GLIAL
GLICK
GLIDE
GLIMS
GLINT
GLITZ
ILIAC
ILIAD
ILICH
ILION
ILIUM
KLIEG
KLIMT
KLINE
MLIII
OLIGO
OLIOS
OLIVE
PLICA
PLIED
PLIES
PLINK
PLINY
SLICE
SLICK
SLIDE
SLIER
SLIGO
SLILY
SLIME
SLIMS
SLIMY
SLING
SLINK
SLIPS
SLIPT
SLITS
SLIWA
XLIII

•L•I•
ALAIN
ALFIE
ALGID
ALGIN
ALLIE
ALLIN
ALVIN
BLAIR
BLOIS
CLAIM
CLAIR
CLIII
CLVII
CLXII
CLXIV
CLXIX
DLIII
DLVII
DLXII
DLXIV
DLXIX
ELCID
ELFIN
ELGIN
ELLIE
ELLIS
ELSIE
ELVIN
ELVIS
FLAIL
FLAIR
FLUID
FLYIN
GLAIR
ILLIN
KLEIN
MLIII
MLVII
MLXII
MLXIV
MLXIX
OLDIE
OLEIC
OLEIN
OLLIE
PLAID
PLAIN
PLAIT
PLEIO
SLAIN
XLIII
XLVII

•L••I
ALIBI
ALTAI
BLINI
CLIII
CLVII
CLXII
CLXVI
CLXXI
DLIII
DLVII
DLXII
DLXVI
DLXXI
ELAZI
ELEMI
ELENI
FLEXI
MLIII
MLVII
MLXII
MLXVI
MLXXI
PLANI
XLIII
XLVII

••LI•
AALII
ADLIB
ALLIE
ALLIN
AULIS
BALIN
BELIE
CALIF
CALIX
CCLII
CCLIV
CCLIX
CDLII
CDLIV
CDLIX
CELIA
CELIE
CILIA
CMLII
CMLIV
CMLIX
COLIN
CXLII
CXLIV
CXLIX
DCLII
DCLIV
DCLIX
DELIS
DXLII
DXLIV
DXLIX
ELLIE
ELLIS
FELID
FELIS
FELIX
FELIZ
FOLIA
FOLIC
FOLIO
FSLIC
GELID
HELIC
HELIO
HELIX
ILLIN
ISLIP
JOLIE
JULIA
JULIE
JULIO
KILIM
KYLIX
MALIC
MCLII
MCLIV
MCLIX
MDLII
MDLIV
MDLIX
MELIC
MMLII
MMLIV
MMLIX
MXLII
MXLIV
MXLIX
OLLIE
OSLIN
OXLIP
PALIN
POLIS
POLIT
PULIS
RELIC
RELIG
RELIT
SALIC
SELIG
SOLID
SPLIT
TALIA
TELIC
TULIP
UNLIT
VALID
WYLIE
YALIE
ZELIG

••L•I
AALII
ADLAI
BELLI
CALCI
CALLI
CCLII
CCLVI
CCLXI
CDLII
CDLVI
CDLXI
CELLI
CMLII
CMLVI
CMLXI
CXLII
CXLVI
DALAI
DCLII
DCLVI
DCLXI
DELHI
DXLII
DXLVI
ENLAI
GALLI
GOLGI
MCLII
MCLVI
MCLXI
MDLII
MDLVI
MDLXI
MILLI
MMLII
MMLVI
MMLXI
MULTI
MXLII
MXLVI
NALDI
PALPI
PILEI
SALMI
SOLDI
SOLTI
SULCI
VALLI
VILLI

•••LI
AIOLI
BELLI
CALLI
CCCLI
CCXLI
CDXLI
CELLI
CHILI
CMXLI
DCCLI
DCXLI
EBOLI
ECOLI
FORLI
GALLI
GHALI
MCCLI
MCDLI
MCMLI
MCXLI
MDCLI
MDXLI
MILLI
MMCLI
MMDLI
MMMLI
MMXLI
OBELI
OBOLI
OVOLI
PAOLI
STYLI
VALLI
VILLI

L•K••
LAKER
LAKES
LAKME
LIKED
LIKEN
LIKES
LIKUD
LUKAS

L••K•
LACKS
LAIKA
LANKA
LANKY
LARKS
LARKY
LATKE
LEAKS
LEAKY
LECKY
LEEKS
LICKS
LINKS
LOCKE
LOCKS
LOOKS
LUCKS
LUCKY
LURKS

L•••K
LUNIK

•LK••
ALKYD
ALKYL

•L•K•
ALIKE
BLAKE
BLOKE
FLAKE
FLAKY
FLUKE
FLUKY
SLAKE

•L••K
ALACK
ALECK
BLACK
BLANK
BLEAK
BLINK
BLOCK
CLACK
CLANK
CLARK
CLEEK
CLERK
CLICK
CLINK
CLOAK
CLOCK
CLONK
CLUCK
CLUNK
FLACK
FLANK
FLASK
FLECK
FLICK
FLOCK
FLUNK
GLICK
GLUCK
PLANK
PLINK
PLONK
PLUCK
PLUNK
SLACK
SLEEK
SLICK
SLINK
SLUNK

••LK•
BALKH
BALKS
BALKY
BILKO
BILKS
BULKS
BULKY
CALKS
FOLKS
FOLKY
HULKS
MILKS
MILKY
POLKA
RILKE
SILKS
SILKY
SULKS
SULKY
TALKS
TALKY
WALKS
YOLKS
YOLKY

••L•K
KULAK
TILAK

•••LK
BAULK
CAULK
CHALK
SKULK
STALK
WHELK

LL•••
LLAMA
LLANO
LLOYD

L•L••
LALAW
LILAC
LILLE
LILLY
LILTS
LOLLS
LOLLY
LULEA
LULLS
LULLY
LULUS

L••L•
LADLE
LAXLY
LAYLA
LEILA
LILLE
LILLY
LISLE
LOLLS
LOLLY
LOWLY
LULLS
LULLY
LYELL

L•••L
LABEL
LAPEL
LAVAL
LEGAL
LENDL
LEVEL
LIBEL
LOCAL
LOYAL
LTCOL
LYELL
LYSOL

•LL••
ALLAH
ALLAN
ALLAY
ALLEE
ALLEN
ALLER
ALLES
ALLEY
ALLEZ
ALLIE
ALLIN
ALLOT
ALLOW
ALLOY
ALLYL
ELLEN
ELLER
ELLES
ELLIE
ELLIS
ILLER
ILLIN
ILLUS
MLLES
OLLAS
OLLIE

•L•L•
ALULA
SLILY
SLYLY

•L••L
ALDOL
ALGAL
ALGOL
ALKYL
ALLYL
ELIEL
FLAIL
GLIAL

••LL•
BALLS
BALLY
BELLA
BELLE
BELLI
BELLS
BELLY
BILLS
BILLY
BOLLS
BULLA
BULLS
BULLY
CALLA
CALLI
CALLS
CELLA
CELLI
CELLO
CELLS
CILLA
CULLS
CULLY
DALLY
DELLA
DELLS
DILLS
DILLY
DOLLS
DOLLY
DULLS
DULLY
FALLA
FALLS
FELLA
FELLS
FELLY
FILLE
FILLS
FILLY
FOLLY
FULLY
GALLI
GALLO
GALLS
GILLS
GILLY
GOLLY
GULLS
GULLY
HALLE
HALLO
HALLS
HELLO
HELLS
HILLS
HILLY
HOLLY
HULLO
HULLS
JELLO
JELLS
JELLY
JOLLA
JOLLY
KELLY
KILLS
KILLY
LILLE
LILLY
LOLLS
LOLLY
LULLS
LULLY
MALLE
MALLS
MILLE
MILLI
MILLS
MOLLS
MOLLY
MULLS
NELLY
NILLY
NOLLE
NULLS
PALLS
PALLY
PELLA
PELLE
PILLS
POLLO
POLLS
POLLY
PULLS
RALLY
RILLE
RILLS
ROLLE
ROLLO
ROLLS
SALLE
SALLY
SELLS
SILLS
SILLY
SULLA
SULLY
TALLY
TELLS
TELLY
TILLS
TILLY
TOLLS
TOLLY
TULLE
TULLY
VALLE
VALLI
VILLA
VILLE
VILLI
WALLA
WALLS
WALLY
WELLS
WILLA
WILLS
WILLY
YELLS
ZILLS

••L•L
ALLYL
KALEL
SALAL

•••LL
ATALL
ATOLL
BBALL
BCELL
BEALL
BRILL
BUELL
CHILL
DRILL
DROLL
DWELL
EWELL
FRILL
GRILL
IDYLL
INALL
KNELL
KNOLL
KRILL
KRULL
KVELL
LYELL
NEILL
ODELL
PHYLL
PRELL
QUELL
QUILL
SCULL
SHALL
SHELL
SHILL
SKILL
SKULL
SMALL
SMELL
SNELL
SPALL
SPELL
SPILL
STALL
STILL
STULL
SWELL
SWILL
SZELL
TBALL
TBILL
THILL
TRILL
TROLL
TWILL
UDALL
WEILL
WHOLL
WHYLL
YOULL

L•M••
LAMAR
LAMAS
LAMBS
LAMED
LAMER
LAMES
LAMIA
LAMPS
LEMAT
LEMAY
LEMMA
LEMME
LEMON
LEMUR
LIMAS
LIMBI
LIMBO
LIMBS
LIMED
LIMEN
LIMES
LIMEY
LIMIT
LIMNS
LIMON
LIMOS
LIMPS
LOMAN
LOMAX
LUMEN
LUMET
LUMPS
LUMPY
LYMAN
LYMON
LYMPH

L••M•
LAKME
LEMMA
LEMME
LLAMA
LOAMS
LOAMY
LOOMS

L•••M
LARAM
LOCUM

•LM••
ALMAY
ELMAN
ELMER
ELMOS
OLMEC
OLMOS

•L•M•
ALAMO
ALUMS
BLAME
BLIMP
BLUME
CLAMP
CLAMS
CLIMB
CLIME
CLOMP
CLUMP
ELEMI
FLAME
FLAMS
FLAMY
FLUME
GLIMS
GLOMS
KLIMT
LLAMA
PLUMB
PLUME
PLUMP
PLUMS
PLUMY
SLAMS
SLIME
SLIMS
SLIMY
SLOMO
SLUMP
SLUMS

•L••M
ALARM
ALBUM
BLOOM
CLAIM
GLEAM
GLOAM
GLOOM
ILIUM
OLEUM
PLASM

••LM•
BALMS
BALMY
CALMS
CULMS
DOLMA
FILMS
FILMY
HALMS
HELMS
HOLMS
MALMO
PALMA
PALME
PALMS
PALMY

SALMI
SELMA
VILMA
WILMA

••L•M
BELEM
COLUM
FILUM
GOLEM
HILUM
ISLAM
KILIM
PILUM
SALAM
SALEM
SOLUM
VELUM
XYLEM

•••LM
HAULM
PSALM
QUALM
REALM
WHELM

L•N••
LANAI
LANCE
LANDI
LANDO
LANDS
LANES
LANGE
LANKA
LANKY
LANTZ
LANZA
LENDL
LENDS
LENIN
LENIS
LENNY
LENOS
LENOX
LENTO
LENTS
LENYA
LINDA
LINDO
LINDY
LINED
LINEN
LINER
LINES
LINEY
LINGO
LINKS
LINOS
LINTS
LINTY
LINUS
LONER
LONGA
LONGE
LONGI
LONGO
LONGS
LONGU
LUNAR
LUNCH
LUNDI
LUNDY
LUNES
LUNGE
LUNGS
LUNIK
LYNCH
LYNDA
LYNDE
LYNNE

L••N•
LAINE
LAING
LAWNS
LAWNY
LAYNE
LEANS
LEANT
LENNY
LEONA
LEONE
LEONI
LIANA
LIANE
LIANG
LIENS
LIGNI
LIGNO
LIMNS
LIONS
LLANO
LOANS
LOINS
LOONS
LOONY
LORNA
LORNE
LYING
LYNNE
LYONS

L•••N
LABAN
LADEN
LADON
LAGAN
LAPIN
LATEN
LATIN
LAVIN
LAYIN
LAYON
LEARN
LEDIN
LEDON
LEMON
LENIN
LETIN
LETON
LEVIN
LEVON
LEXAN
LIEIN
LIKEN
LIMEN
LIMON
LINEN
LITON
LIVEN
LODEN
LOGAN
LOGIN
LOGON
LOMAN
LORAN
LOREN
LTGEN
LUCAN
LUMEN
LUPIN
LUZON
LYMAN
LYMON
LYSIN

•LN••
ULNAE
ULNAS

•L•N•
ALANA
ALAND
ALENE
ALINE
ALONE
ALONG
BLANC
BLAND
BLANK
BLEND
BLENT
BLIND
BLINI
BLINK
BLOND
BLUNT
CLANG
CLANK
CLANS
CLINE
CLING
CLINK
CLINT
CLONE
CLONK
CLUNG
CLUNK
CLUNY
ELAND
ELENA
ELENI
FLANK
FLANS
FLING
FLINT
FLUNG
FLUNK
FLYNN
GLAND
GLENN
GLENS
GLINT
ILENE
ILONA
KLINE
LLANO
OLAND
PLANB
PLANE
PLANI
PLANK
PLANO
PLANS
PLANT
PLENA
PLINK
PLINY
PLONK
PLUNK
SLANG
SLANT
SLING
SLINK
SLUNG
SLUNK

•L••N
ALAIN
ALBAN
ALBEN
ALCAN
ALDAN
ALDEN
ALGIN
ALIEN
ALIGN
ALLAN
ALLEN
ALLIN
ALTON
ALVIN
BLOWN
CLEAN
CLEON
CLOWN
ELFIN
ELGIN
ELION
ELLEN
ELMAN
ELTON
ELVIN
FLOWN
FLYIN
FLYNN
GLEAN
GLENN
GLUON
ILION
ILLIN
KLEIN
OLDEN
OLEAN
OLEIN
OLSEN
OLSON
PLAIN
PLEON
SLAIN
SLOAN

••LN•
KILNS
MILNE

••L•N
ALLAN
ALLEN
ALLIN
ARLEN
BALIN
COLIN
COLON
DELON
DYLAN
ELLEN
EMLYN
FELON
GALEN
GOLAN
HALON
HELEN
ILLIN
MALAN
MELAN
MELON
MILAN
NOLAN
NYLON
ORLON
OSLIN
PALIN
PYLON
SALON
SOLAN
SOLON
TALON
UCLAN
UHLAN

LO•••
LOACH
LOADS
LOAFS
LOAMS
LOAMY
LOANS
LOATH
LOBBY
LOBED
LOBES
LOBOS
LOCAL
LOCHS
LOCKE
LOCKS
LOCOS
LOCUM
LOCUS
LODEN
LODES
LODGE
LOESS
LOEWE
LOEWY
LOFAT
LOFTS
LOFTY
LOGAN
LOGES
LOGIA
LOGIC
LOGIN
LOGON
LOGOS
LOGUE
LOINS
LOIRE
LOLLS
LOLLY
LOMAN
LOMAX
LONER
LONGA
LONGE
LONGI
LONGO
LONGS
LONGU
LOOBY
LOOFA
LOOKS
LOOMS
LOONS
LOONY
LOOPS
LOOPY
LOOSE
LOOTS
LOPAT
LOPED
LOPER
LOPES
LOPEZ
LOPPY
LORAN
LORAX
LORCA
LORDS
LOREN
LORES
LORIS
LORNA
LORNE
LORRE
LORRY
LOSER
LOSES
LOSSY
LOTAH
LOTAS
LOTTA
LOTTE
LOTTO
LOTUS
LOUGH
LOUIE
LOUIS
LOUPE
LOUSE
LOUSY
LOUTS
LOVED
LOVER
LOVES
LOVEY
LOWED
LOWER
LOWES
LOWLY
LOWRY
LOXES
LOYAL

L•O••
LEONA
LEONE
LEONI
LEORA
LIONS
LLOYD
LOOBY
LOOFA
LOOKS
LOOMS
LOONS
LOONY
LOOPS
LOOPY
LOOSE
LOOTS
LYONS

L••O•
LABOR
LADON
LAGOS
LAYON
LEDON
LEGOS
LEMON
LENOS
LENOX
LEROI
LEROY
LETON
LEVON
LIDOS
LIMON
LIMOS
LINOS
LITON
LOBOS
LOCOS
LOGON
LOGOS
LTCOL
LTGOV
LUXOR
LUZON
LYMON
LYSOL

L•••O
LABIO
LACTO
LANDO
LARGO
LASSO
LAYTO
LEDTO
LENTO
LEPTO
LETGO
LIETO
LIGNO
LIMBO
LINDO
LINGO
LIPPO
LITHO
LLANO
LONGO
LOTTO
LUEGO

•LO••
ALOES
ALOFT
ALOHA
ALONE
ALONG
ALOOF
ALORS
ALOUD
BLOAT
BLOBS
BLOCH
BLOCK
BLOCS
BLOIS
BLOKE
BLOND
BLOOD
BLOOM
BLOOP
BLOTS
BLOWN
BLOWS
BLOWY
CLOAK
CLOCK
CLODS
CLOGS
CLOMP
CLONE
CLONK
CLOPS
CLOSE
CLOTH
CLOTS
CLOUD
CLOUT
CLOVE
CLOWN
CLOYS
ELOPE
FLOAT
FLOCK
FLOES
FLOGS
FLOOD
FLOOR
FLOPS
FLORA
FLORY
FLOSS
FLOUR
FLOUT
FLOWN
FLOWS
FLOYD
GLOAM
GLOAT
GLOBE
GLOBS
GLOGG
GLOMS
GLOOM
GLOPS
GLORY
GLOSS
GLOVE
GLOWS
GLOZE
ILONA
LLOYD
OLOGY
PLODS
PLONK
PLOPS
PLOTS
PLOWS
PLOYS
SLOAN
SLOBS
SLOES
SLOGS
SLOMO
SLOOP
SLOPE
SLOPS
SLOSH
SLOTH
SLOTS
SLOWS
SLOYD
ZLOTY

•L•O•
ALCOA
ALCOR
ALDOL
ALGOL
ALIOS
ALLOT
ALLOW
ALLOY
ALOOF
ALSOP
ALTON
ALTOS
BLOOD
BLOOM
BLOOP
CLEON
CLIOS
ELBOW
ELION
ELIOT
ELMOS
ELROY
ELTON
FLOOD
FLOOR
FLUOR
GLOOM
GLUON
ILION
OLEOS
OLIOS
OLMOS
OLSON
PLEON
SLOOP

•L••O
ALAMO
ALTHO
BLUTO
CLARO
GLAXO
GLUCO
GLYCO
LLANO
OLIGO
PLANO
PLATO
PLEIO
PLUTO
SLIGO
SLOMO

••LO•
ADLOC
AGLOW
ALLOT
ALLOW
ALLOY
BELOW
BOLOS
BULOW
CHLOE
CHLOR
COLON
COLOR
DELON
DELOS
DOLOR
FELON
GALOP
HALON
HALOS
HELOS
HELOT
IGLOO
KILOS
MELON
MELOS
MILOS
NILOT
NYLON
ONLOW
ORLON
ORLOP
PALOS
PHLOX
PILOT
POLOS
PYLON
SALON
SILOS
SOLON
SOLOS
TALON
TALOS
TELOS
VALOR
YALOW

••L•O
AALTO
BALTO
BILBO
BILKO
CELLO
DELCO
DRLAO
FALDO
FOLIO
GALLO
HALLO
HELIO
HELLO
HULLO
IGLOO
JELLO
JULIO
KELSO
MALMO
MOLTO
PALEO
POLLO
ROLEO
ROLLO
SALVO
SOLDO
TELEO
VOLVO
WALDO
WILCO

•••LO
AMYLO
ANGLO
CAELO
CARLO
CELLO
CHILO
CHOLO
CYCLO
DIPLO
GALLO
HALLO
HAPLO
HATLO
HELLO
HULLO
ITALO
JELLO
KAHLO
MARLO
MENLO
MYELO
OCULO
OVOLO
PABLO
PAOLO
PAULO
PHILO
POLLO
ROLLO
STYLO

L•P••
LAPAZ
LAPEL
LAPIN
LAPIS
LAPPS
LAPSE
LAPUP
LEPPY
LEPTA
LEPTO
LEPUS
LIPID
LIPPI
LIPPO
LIPPY
LOPAT
LOPED
LOPER
LOPES
LOPEZ
LOPPY
LUPIN

L••P•
LAMPS
LAPPS
LEAPS
LEAPT
LEPPY
LIMPS
LIPPI
LIPPO
LIPPY
LISPS
LOOPS
LOOPY
LOPPY
LOUPE
LUMPS
LUMPY
LYMPH

L•••P
LAPUP
LAYUP
LEGUP
LETUP
LITUP

•LP••
ALPHA

•L•P•
ALEPH
BLIPS
CLAPS
CLIPS
CLIPT
CLOPS
ELOPE
FLAPS
FLIPS
FLOPS
GLOPS
GLYPH
PLOPS
SLAPS
SLEPT
SLIPS
SLIPT
SLOPE
SLOPS
SLYPE

•L••P
ALSOP
BLEEP
BLIMP
BLOOP
CLAMP
CLASP
CLOMP
CLUMP
PLUMP
SLEEP
SLOOP
SLUMP
SLURP

••LP•
CALPE
CULPA
DOLPH
GULPS
GULPY
HELPS
KELPS
KELPY
MILPA
PALPI
PALPS
PULPS
PULPY
RALPH
SALPA
SALPS
SYLPH
YELPS

••L•P
GALOP
ISLIP
JULEP
ORLOP
OXLIP
POLYP
SALEP
TULIP

•••LP
QUILP
SCALP
WHELP

L•R••
LARAM
LARAS
LARCH
LARDS
LARDY
LARES
LARGE
LARGO
LARIS
LARKS
LARKY
LARRY
LARUE
LARVA
LEROI
LEROY
LIRAS
LORAN
LORAX
LORCA
LORDS
LOREN
LORES
LORIS
LORNA
LORNE
LORRE
LORRY
LURAY
LURCH
LURED
LURES
LUREX
LURIA
LURID
LURIE
LURKS
LYRES
LYRIC

L••R•
LAIRD
LAIRS
LARRY
LATRY
LAURA
LEARN
LEARS
LEARY
LEERS
LEERY
LEORA
LIARD
LIARS
LIBRA
LIBRE
LITRE
LIVRE
LOIRE
LORRE
LORRY
LOWRY
LUCRE
LYCRA

L•••R
LABOR
LACER
LADER
LAGER
LAHAR
LAKER
LAMAR
LAMER
LASER
LATER
LAUER
LAVER
LAXER
LAYER
LAZAR
LEGER
LEHAR
LEMUR
LEVAR
LEVER
LIGER
LINER
LITER
LIVER
LONER
LOPER
LOSER
LOVER
LOWER
LUGER
LUNAR
LUXOR

•LR••
ELROY

•L•R•
ALARM
ALERT
ALFRE
ALORS
BLARE
BLURB
BLURS
BLURT
CLARA
CLARE
CLARK
CLARO
CLARY
CLERK
FLARE
FLIRT
FLORA
FLORY
GLARE
GLARY
GLORY
NLERS
SLURP
SLURS
ULTRA

•L••R
ALCOR
ALDER
ALGER
ALLER
ALTAR
ALTER
ALVAR
BLAIR
BLEAR
BLUER
CLAIR
CLEAR
ELDER
ELGAR
ELLER
ELMER
ELVER
FLAIR
FLEER
FLEUR
FLIER
FLOOR
FLOUR
FLUOR
FLYER
GLAIR
GLUER
ILLER
OLDER
SLIER
SLYER
ULCER

••L•R
ABLER
ADLER
AILER
ALLER
BALER
CHLOR
COLOR
DOLOR
EELER
ELLER
EULER
FILAR
FILER
GULAR
HALER
IDLER
ILLER
MALAR
MILER
MOLAR
MYLAR
NFLER
NHLER
OGLER
OILER
OSLER
PALER
PILAR
POLAR
POLER
RULER
SOLAR
SOLER
TALER
TILER
TOLER
TYLER
VALOR
VELAR
VILER
VOLAR
WALER
WYLER

LS•••
LSATS

L•S••
LASED
LASER
LASES
LASSO
LASTS
LISLE
LISPS
LISSE
LISTS
LISZT
LOSER
LOSES
LOSSY
LUSTS
LUSTY
LYSIN
LYSOL

L••S•
LAPSE
LASSO
LEASE
LEASH
LEAST
LHASA
LISSE
LOESS
LOOSE
LOSSY
LOUSE
LOUSY
LUISA
LUISE

L•••S
LACES
LACKS
LADES
LADYS
LAGOS
LAICS
LAIRS
LAIUS
LAKES
LAMAS
LAMBS
LAMES
LAMPS
LANDS
LANES
LAPIS
LAPPS
LARAS
LARDS
LARES
LARIS
LARKS
LASES
LASTS
LATHS
LAUDS
LAVAS
LAVES
LAWES
LAWNS
LAZES
LEADS
LEAFS
LEAKS
LEANS
LEAPS
LEARS
LEEDS
LEEKS
LEERS
LEETS
LEFTS
LEGGS
LEGIS
LEGOS
LENDS
LENIS
LENOS
LENTS
LEPUS
LETTS
LEVIS
LEWES
LEWIS
LEXIS
LEXUS
LIARS
LICKS
LIDOS
LIENS
LIEUS
LIFTS
LIKES
LILTS
LIMAS
LIMBS
LIMES
LIMNS
LIMOS
LIMPS
LINES
LINKS
LINOS
LINTS
LINUS
LIONS
LIRAS
LISPS
LISTS
LITES
LITHS
LIVES
LOADS
LOAFS
LOAMS
LOANS
LOBES
LOBOS
LOCHS
LOCKS
LOCOS
LOCUS
LODES
LOESS
LOFTS
LOGES
LOGOS
LOINS
LOLLS
LONGS
LOOKS
LOOMS
LOONS
LOOPS
LOOTS
LOPES
LORDS
LORES
LORIS
LOSES
LOTAS
LOTUS
LOUIS
LOUTS
LOVES
LOWES
LOXES
LSATS
LUAUS
LUBAS
LUBES
LUCAS
LUCKS
LUFFS
LUGES
LUKAS
LULLS
LULUS
LUMPS
LUNES
LUNGS
LURES
LURKS
LUSTS
LUTES
LYONS
LYRES

•LS••
ALSOP
ELSIE
OLSEN
OLSON

•L•S•
ALIST
BLASE
BLASS
BLAST
BLESS
BLEST
BLISS
BLUSH
CLASH
CLASP
CLASS
CLOSE
ELISE
ELYSE
FLASH
FLASK
FLESH
FLOSS
FLUSH
GLASS
GLESS
GLOSS
PLASH
PLASM
PLUSH
SLASH
SLOSH
SLUSH

•L••S
ALDUS
ALEFS
ALFAS
ALIAS
ALIFS
ALIOS
ALLES
ALOES
ALORS
ALTOS
ALTUS
ALUMS
BLABS
BLAHS
BLASS
BLATS
BLDGS
BLEBS
BLESS
BLIPS
BLISS
BLOBS
BLOCS
BLOIS
BLOTS
BLOWS
BLUES
BLURS
BLVDS
CLAMS
CLANS
CLAPS
CLASS
CLAUS
CLAWS
CLAYS
CLEFS

CLEWS
CLIOS
CLIPS
CLODS
CLOGS
CLOPS
CLOTS
CLOYS
CLUBS
CLUES
ELIAS
ELLES
ELLIS
ELMOS
ELVES
ELVIS
ELWES
FLAGS
FLAMS
FLANS
FLAPS
FLATS
FLAWS
FLAYS
FLEAS
FLEES
FLEWS
FLEYS
FLICS
FLIES
FLIPS
FLITS
FLOES
FLOGS
FLOPS
FLOSS
FLOWS
FLUBS
FLUES
GLADS
GLASS
GLEES
GLENS
GLESS
GLEYS
GLIMS
GLOBS
GLOMS
GLOPS
GLOSS
GLOWS
GLUES
GLUGS
GLUTS
ILLUS
KLAUS
MLLES
NLERS
OLEOS
OLIOS
OLLAS
OLMOS
PLANS
PLATS
PLAYS
PLEAS
PLEBS
PLEWS
PLIES
PLODS
PLOPS
PLOTS
PLOWS
PLOYS
PLUGS
PLUMS
SLABS
SLAGS
SLAMS
SLAPS
SLATS
SLAVS
SLAWS
SLAYS
SLEDS
SLEWS
SLIMS
SLIPS
SLITS
SLOBS
SLOES
SLOGS
SLOPS
SLOTS
SLOWS
SLUES
SLUGS
SLUMS
SLURS
ULNAS

••LS•
BALSA
DULSE
FALSE
HOLST
KELSO
PALSY
PULSE
SALSA
TULSA
VALSE
WALSH
WALSY
WELSH

••L•S
ALLES
APLUS
ARLES
ATLAS
AULIS
AXLES
BALAS
BALDS
BALES
BALKS
BALLS
BALMS
BALTS
BELLS
BELTS
BILKS
BILLS
BOLAS
BOLES
BOLLS
BOLOS
BOLTS
BOLUS
BPLUS
BULBS
BULKS
BULLS
CALKS
CALLS
CALMS
CELLS
CELTS
COLAS
COLDS
COLES
COLTS
CPLUS
CULLS
CULMS
CULTS
DALES
DELES
DELIS
DELLS
DELOS
DELTS
DILLS
DOLES
DOLLS
DOLTS
DPLUS
DULLS
ELLES
ELLIS
EOLUS
FALLS
FELIS
FELLS
FELTS
FILES
FILLS
FILMS
FOLDS
FOLKS
FTLBS
FULAS
GALAS
GALES
GALLS
GILDS
GILES
GILLS
GILTS
GOLDS
GOLFS
GULES
GULFS
GULLS
GULPS
HALAS
HALES
HALLS
HALMS
HALOS
HALTS
HELLS
HELMS
HELOS
HELPS
HILLS
HILTS
HOLDS
HOLES
HOLMS
HULAS
HULKS
HULLS
HYLAS
IDLES
IGLUS
ILLUS
ISLAS
ISLES
JELLS
JILTS
JOLTS
JULES
KALES
KELPS
KILLS
KILNS
KILOS
KILTS
KOLAS
LILTS
LOLLS
LULLS
LULUS
MALES
MALLS
MALTS
MELDS
MELOS
MELTS
MILES
MILKS
MILLS
MILOS
MILTS
MLLES
MOLAS
MOLDS
MOLES
MOLLS
MOLTS
MULES
MULLS
MYLES
NILES
NULLS
OGLES
OLLAS
ORLES
PALES
PALLS
PALMS
PALOS
PALPS
PELTS
PILES
PILLS
PILUS
POLES
POLIS
POLLS
POLOS
PULAS
PULES
PULIS
PULLS
PULPS
RILES
RILLS
ROLES
ROLLS
RULES
SALES
SALPS
SALTS
SELES
SELLS
SILAS
SILKS
SILLS
SILOS
SILTS
SOLES
SOLOS
SOLUS
SULKS
TALES
TALKS
TALOS
TALUS
TELES
TELLS
TELOS
TILES
TILLS
TILTS
TOLLS
TULES
VALES
VELDS
VILAS
VOLES
VOLTS
WALES
WALKS
WALLS
WELDS
WELLS
WELTS
WILDS
WILES
WILLS
WILTS
WOLDS
YELLS
YELPS
YOLKS
ZILLS
ZULUS

•••LS
ACYLS
AGALS
AMYLS
ANILS
ARILS
AWOLS
AXELS
AXILS
BAALS
BAILS
BALLS
BAWLS
BEALS
BELLS
BILLS
BIRLS
BOILS
BOLLS
BOWLS
BUHLS
BULLS
BURLS
CALLS
CAULS
CEILS
CELLS
COALS
COILS
COOLS
COWLS
CULLS
CURLS
DEALS
DEILS
DELLS
DHALS
DIALS
DILLS
DOLLS
DUELS
DULLS
EARLS
ENOLS
EVILS
FAILS
FALLS
FEELS
FELLS
FILLS
FOALS
FOILS
FOOLS
FOULS
FOWLS
FUELS
FURLS
GAELS
GALLS
GAOLS
GAULS
GILLS
GIRLS
GOALS
GULLS
HAILS
HALLS
HAULS
HEALS
HEELS
HELLS
HERLS
HILLS
HOWLS
HULLS
HURLS
IDOLS
IDYLS
ITALS
JAILS
JARLS
JELLS
JOWLS
KEELS
KILLS
LOLLS
LULLS
MAILS
MALLS
MARLS
MAULS
MEALS
MERLS
MEWLS
MILLS
MOILS
MOLLS
MULLS
NAILS
NIELS
NOELS
NOILS
NULLS
OBOLS
OPALS
OPELS
ORALS
OVALS
PAILS
PALLS
PAWLS
PEALS
PEELS
PILLS
POILS
POLLS
POOLS
PULLS
PURLS
RAILS
RAWLS
REALS
REELS
RIALS
RIELS
RILLS
ROILS
ROLLS
ROTLS
SAILS
SEALS
SEELS
SELLS
SHULS
SIALS
SILLS
SOILS
SOULS
STOLS
TAELS
TAILS
TEALS
TELLS
TILLS
TOILS
TOLLS
TOOLS
URALS
VEILS
VIALS
VIOLS
VTOLS
WAALS
WAILS
WALLS
WEALS
WELLS
WILLS
WOOLS
YAWLS
YELLS
YOWLS
ZEALS
ZILLS

LT•••
LTCOL
LTGEN
LTGOV

L•T••
LATCH
LATEN
LATER
LATEX
LATHE
LATHS
LATHY
LATIN
LATKE
LATRY
LATTE
LETAT
LETBE
LETGO
LETHE
LETIN
LETON
LETTS
LETUP
LITER
LITES
LITHE
LITHO
LITHS
LITON
LITRE
LITUP
LOTAH
LOTAS
LOTTA
LOTTE
LOTTO
LOTUS
LUTES
LYTTA

L••T•
LACTI
LACTO
LAHTI
LAITY
LANTZ
LASTS
LATTE
LAYTO
LEDTO
LEETS
LEFTS
LEFTY
LEITH
LENTO
LENTS
LEPTA
LEPTO
LETTS
LEYTE
LIETO
LIFTS
LILTS
LINTS
LINTY
LISTS
LOATH
LOFTS
LOFTY
LOOTS
LOTTA
LOTTE
LOTTO
LOUTS
LSATS
LUSTS
LUSTY
LYTTA

L•••T
LEANT
LEAPT
LEAST
LEGIT
LEMAT
LETAT
LICET
LICIT
LIEUT
LIGHT
LIMIT
LISZT
LOFAT
LOPAT
LUMET

•LT••
ALTAI
ALTAR
ALTER
ALTHO
ALTON
ALTOS
ALTUS
ELTON
ULTRA

•L•T•
ALATE
ALETA
BLATS
BLITT
BLITZ
BLOTS
BLUTH
BLUTO
BLYTH
CLOTH
CLOTS
ELATE
ELATH
ELITE
ELUTE
FLATS
FLATT
FLITS
FLUTE
FLUTY
GLITZ
GLUTS
KLUTE
KLUTZ
PLATA
PLATE
PLATH
PLATO
PLATS
PLATT
PLATY
PLOTS
PLUTO
SLATE
SLATS
SLATY
SLITS
SLOTH
SLOTS
ZLOTY

•L••T
ALERT
ALEUT
ALIST
ALLOT
ALOFT
BLAST
BLEAT
BLENT
BLEST
BLITT
BLOAT
BLUET
BLUNT
BLURT
CLEAT
CLEFT
CLIFT
CLINT
CLIPT
CLOUT
ELECT
ELIOT
FLATT
FLEET
FLINT
FLIRT
FLOAT
FLOUT
FLYAT
GLINT
GLOAT
KLIMT
PLAIT
PLANT
PLATT
PLEAT
SLANT
SLEET
SLEPT
SLIPT

••LT•
AALTO
BALTO
BALTS
BELTS
BOLTS
CELTS
COLTS
CULTS
DELTA
DELTS
DOLTS
FELTS
FILTH
GILTS
HALTS
HILTS
HOLTZ
JILTS
JOLTS
JOLTY
KILTS
LILTS
MALTA
MALTS
MALTY
MELTS
MELTY
MILTS
MILTY
MOLTO
MOLTS
MULTI
NOLTE
PELTS
SALTA
SALTS
SALTY
SILTS
SILTY
SOLTI
TILTH
TILTS
USLTA
VOLTA
VOLTE
VOLTS
WALTZ
WELTS
WELTY
WILTS
YALTA

••L•T
AFLAT
AGLET
ALLOT
BFLAT
CFLAT
COLET
CULET
DELFT
DFLAT
ECLAT
EFLAT
EILAT
FFLAT
FILET
GFLAT
HELOT
HOLST
INLET
ISLET
MULCT
NILOT
OWLET
PILOT
POLIT
RELET
RELIT
SALUT
SPLAT
SPLIT
TOLET
UNLIT
VALET
VELDT
VOLAT

•••LT
ADULT
ATILT
BOULT
BUILT
DEALT
DWELT
EXALT
EXULT
FAULT
GUILT
KNELT
MOULT
POULT
QUILT
SAULT
SHALT
SMALT
SMELT
SMOLT
SOULT
SPELT
SPILT
STILT
UBOLT
VAULT

LU•••
LUAUS
LUBAS
LUBED
LUBES
LUCAN
LUCAS
LUCCA
LUCCI
LUCIA
LUCID
LUCIE
LUCKS
LUCKY
LUCRE
LUDIC
LUEGO
LUFFS
LUGER
LUGES
LUIGI
LUISA
LUISE
LUKAS
LULEA
LULLS
LULLY
LULUS
LUMEN
LUMET
LUMPS
LUMPY
LUNAR
LUNCH
LUNDI
LUNDY
LUNES
LUNGE
LUNGS
LUNIK
LUPIN
LURAY
LURCH
LURED
LURES
LUREX
LURIA
LURID
LURIE
LURKS
LUSTS
LUSTY
LUTES
LUXOR
LUZON

L•U••
LAUDE
LAUDS
LAUER
LAUGH
LAURA
LOUGH
LOUIE
LOUIS
LOUPE
LOUSE
LOUSY
LOUTS

L••U•
LAIUS
LAPUP
LARUE
LAYUP
LEGUP
LEHUA
LEMUR
LEPUS
LETUP
LEXUS
LIEUS
LIEUT
LIKUD
LINUS
LITUP
LOCUM
LOCUS
LOGUE
LOTUS
LUAUS
LULUS

L•••U
LONGU

•LU••
ALULA
ALUMS
BLUED
BLUER
BLUES
BLUET
BLUEY
BLUFF
BLUME
BLUNT
BLURB
BLURS
BLURT
BLUSH
BLUTH
BLUTO
CLUBS
CLUCK
CLUED
CLUES
CLUMP
CLUNG
CLUNK
CLUNY
ELUDE
ELUTE
FLUBS
FLUES
FLUFF
FLUID
FLUKE
FLUKY
FLUME
FLUNG
FLUNK
FLUOR
FLUSH
FLUTE
FLUTY
GLUCK
GLUCO
GLUED
GLUER
GLUES
GLUEY
GLUGS
GLUON
GLUTS
KLUGE
KLUTE
KLUTZ
PLUCK
PLUGS
PLUMB
PLUME
PLUMP
PLUMS
PLUMY
PLUNK
PLUSH
PLUTO
SLUED
SLUES
SLUGS
SLUMP
SLUMS
SLUNG
SLUNK
SLURP
SLURS
SLUSH

•L•U•
ALBUM
ALDUS
ALEUT
ALOUD
ALTUS
CLAUS
CLOUD
CLOUT
FLEUR
FLOUR
FLOUT
ILIUM
ILLUS
KLAUS
OLEUM

•L••U
ELIHU
ILGWU

••LU•
APLUS
BOLUS
BPLUS
COLUM
CPLUS
DPLUS
EOLUS
FILUM
HILUM
IGLUS
ILLUS
LULUS
PILUM
PILUS
SALUD
SALUT
SOLUM
SOLUS
TALUS
VALUE
VELUM
ZULUS

••L•U
PALAU

•••LU
POILU
UPOLU

LV•••
LVIII

L•V••
LAVAL
LAVAS
LAVED
LAVER
LAVES
LAVIN
LEVAR
LEVEE
LEVEL
LEVER
LEVIN
LEVIS
LEVON
LIVED
LIVEN
LIVER
LIVES
LIVIA
LIVID
LIVRE
LOVED
LOVER
LOVES
LOVEY
LXVII

L••V•
LARVA
LEAVE
LXXVI

L•••V
LTGOV
LXXIV
LXXXV

•LV••
ALVAR
ALVIN
BLVDS
CLVII
DLVII
ELVER
ELVES
ELVIN
ELVIS
MLVII
XLVII

•L•V•
ALAVA
ALEVE
ALIVE
CLAVE
CLIVE
CLOVE
CLXVI
DLXVI
ELEVE
GLOVE
MLXVI
OLIVE
SLAVE
SLAVS

•L••V
CLXIV
CLXXV
DLXIV
DLXXV
MLXIV
MLXXV

••LV•
BELVA
CALVE
CCLVI
CDLVI
CMLVI
CXLVI
DCLVI
DELVE
DXLVI
HALVE
HELVE
MCLVI
MDLVI
MMLVI
MXLVI
SALVE
SALVO
SELVA
SILVA
SOLVE
VALVE
VOLVA
VOLVO

••L•V
CCLIV
CCLXV
CDLIV
CDLXV
CMLIV
CMLXV
CXLIV
DCLIV
DCLXV
DXLIV
MCLIV
MCLXV
MDLIV
MDLXV
MMLIV
MMLXV
MXLIV

•••LV
CCCLV
CCXLV
CDXLV
CMXLV
DCCLV
DCXLV
MCCLV
MCDLV
MCMLV
MCXLV
MDCLV
MDXLV
MMCLV
MMDLV
MMMLV
MMXLV

L•W••
LAWES
LAWNS
LAWNY
LEWES
LEWIS
LOWED
LOWER
LOWES
LOWLY
LOWRY

L••W•
LOEWE
LOEWY

L•••W
LALAW

•LW••
CLWYD
ELWAY
ELWES

•L•W•
BLOWN
BLOWS
BLOWY
CLAWS
CLEWS
CLOWN
FLAWS
FLAWY
FLEWS
FLOWN
FLOWS
GLOWS
ILGWU
PLEWS
PLOWS
SLAWS
SLEWS
SLIWA
SLOWS

•L••W
ALLOW
ELBOW

••L•W
AGLOW
ALLOW
BELOW
BULOW
BYLAW
INLAW
LALAW
ONLOW
YALOW

LX•••
LXIII
LXVII
LXXII
LXXIV
LXXIX
LXXVI
LXXXI
LXXXV

L•X••
LAXER
LAXLY
LEXAN
LEXIS
LEXUS
LOXES
LUXOR
LXXII
LXXIV
LXXIX
LXXVI
LXXXI
LXXXV

L••X•
LXXXI
LXXXV

L•••X
LATEX
LENOX
LOMAX
LORAX
LUREX
LXXIX

•LX••
CLXII
CLXIV
CLXIX
CLXVI
CLXXI
CLXXV
CLXXX
DLXII
DLXIV
DLXIX
DLXVI
DLXXI
DLXXV
DLXXX
MLXII
MLXIV
MLXIX
MLXVI
MLXXI
MLXXV
MLXXX

•L•X•
CLXXI
CLXXV
CLXXX
DLXXI
DLXXV
DLXXX
FLAXY
FLEXI
GLAXO
MLXXI
MLXXV
MLXXX

•L••X
CLXIX
CLXXX
DLXIX
DLXXX
MLXIX
MLXXX

••LX•
CCLXI
CCLXV
CCLXX
CDLXI
CDLXV
CDLXX
CMLXI
CMLXV
CMLXX
DCLXI
DCLXV
DCLXX
MCLXI
MCLXV
MCLXX
MDLXI
MDLXV
MDLXX
MMLXI
MMLXV
MMLXX

••L•X
CALIX

CALYX
CCLIX
CCLXX
CDLIX
CDLXX
CMLIX
CMLXX
CULEX
CXLIX
DCLIX
DCLXX
DXLIX
FELIX
GALAX
HELIX
KYLIX
MCLIX
MCLXX
MDLIX
MDLXX
MMLIX
MMLXX
MXLIX
PHLOX
RELAX
ROLEX
SILEX
TELEX

•••LX
CCCLX
DCCLX
MCCLX
MCDLX
MCMLX
MDCLX
MMCLX
MMDLX
MMMLX

LY•••
LYCEE
LYCRA
LYDIA
LYELL
LYING
LYMAN
LYMON
LYMPH
LYNCH
LYNDA
LYNDE
LYNNE
LYONS
LYRES
LYRIC
LYSIN
LYSOL
LYTTA

L•Y••
LAYBY
LAYER
LAYIN
LAYLA
LAYNE
LAYON
LAYTO
LAYUP
LEYTE
LOYAL

L••Y•
LADYS
LENYA
LIBYA
LLOYD

L•••Y
LACEY
LAITY
LANKY
LARDY
LARKY
LARRY
LATHY
LATRY
LAWNY
LAXLY
LAYBY
LEADY
LEAFY
LEAHY
LEAKY
LEARY
LECKY
LEDGY
LEERY
LEFAY
LEFTY
LEGGY
LEMAY
LENNY
LEPPY
LEROY
LIBBY
LIDDY
LIEBY
LILLY
LIMEY
LINDY
LINEY
LINTY
LIPPY
LOAMY
LOBBY
LOEWY
LOFTY
LOLLY
LOOBY
LOONY
LOOPY
LOPPY
LORRY
LOSSY
LOUSY
LOVEY
LOWLY
LOWRY
LUCKY
LULLY
LUMPY
LUNDY
LURAY
LUSTY

•LY••
ALYCE
BLYTH
CLYDE
ELYSE
FLYAT
FLYBY
FLYER
FLYIN
FLYNN
GLYCO
GLYPH
SLYER
SLYLY
SLYPE

•L•Y•
ALKYD
ALKYL
ALLYL
CLAYS
CLOYS
CLWYD
FLAYS
FLEYS
FLOYD
GLEYS
LLOYD
PLAYA
PLAYS
PLOYS
SLAYS
SLOYD

•L••Y
ALLAY
ALLEY
ALLOY
ALMAY
BLOWY
BLUEY
CLARY
CLUNY
ELEGY
ELROY
ELWAY
FLAKY
FLAMY
FLAWY
FLAXY
FLORY
FLUKY
FLUTY
FLYBY
GLARY
GLORY
GLUEY
OLOGY
PLATY
PLINY
PLUMY
SLATY
SLILY
SLIMY
SLYLY
ZLOTY

••LY•
ALLYL
CALYX
EMLYN
POLYP

••L•Y
AGLEY
AILEY
ALLAY
ALLEY
ALLOY
APLEY
BALKY
BALLY
BALMY
BELAY
BELLY
BILBY
BILGY
BILLY
BULGY
BULKY
BULLY
COLBY
CULLY
DALEY
DALLY
DELAY
DILLY
DOLBY
DOLLY
DULLY
FELLY
FILLY
FILMY
FOLEY
FOLKY
FOLLY
FULLY
GILLY
GOLLY
GULLY
GULPY
HALEY
HILLY
HOLEY
HOLLY
INLAY
ISLEY
JELLY
JOLLY
JOLTY
KELLY
KELPY
KILEY
KILLY
LILLY
LOLLY
LULLY
MALAY
MALTY
MELTY
MILKY
MILTY
MOLDY
MOLLY
MULEY
NELLY
NILLY
ONLAY
PALEY
PALLY
PALMY
PALSY
POLLY
PULPY
RALLY
RELAY
RILEY
SALLY
SALTY
SILKY
SILLY
SILTY
SPLAY
SULKY
SULLY
TALKY
TALLY
TELLY
TILLY
TOLLY
TULLY
UNLAY
UTLEY
WALEY
WALLY
WALSY
WELBY
WELTY
WILEY
WILLY
YOLKY

•••LY
AMPLY
APPLY
APTLY
BADLY
BALLY
BELLY
BIALY
BIGLY
BILLY
BULLY
BURLY
CARLY
COYLY
CROLY
CULLY
CURLY
DAILY
DALLY
DILLY
DIMLY
DOILY
DOLLY
DOYLY
DRILY
DRYLY
DULLY
EARLY
EMILY
FATLY
FEELY
FELLY
FEYLY
FILLY
FITLY
FOLLY
FULLY
GAILY
GAYLY
GILLY
GODLY
GOLLY
GULLY
HAPLY
HEALY
HILLY
HIPLY
HOLLY
HOTLY
HURLY
ICILY
IMPLY
ITALY
JELLY
JOLLY
JOWLY
KELLY
KILLY
LAXLY
LILLY
LOLLY
LOWLY
LULLY
MADLY
MANLY
MARLY
MCFLY
MEALY
MOLLY
NELLY
NEWLY
NILLY
NOBLY
NOFLY
NOILY
ODDLY
PALLY
PATLY
PHILY
POLLY
RALLY
RAWLY
REDLY
REPLY
ROILY
SADLY
SALLY
SCALY
SEALY
SEELY
SHYLY
SILLY
SLILY
SLYLY
SULLY
SURLY
TALLY
TELLY
TILLY
TOLLY
TRULY
TULLY
VEALY
WALLY
WANLY
WETLY
WILLY
WOOLY
WRYLY

L•Z••
LAZAR
LAZED
LAZES
LUZON

L••Z•
LANZA
LEEZA
LISZT

L•••Z
LANTZ
LAPAZ
LOPEZ

•L•Z•
BLAZE
ELAZI
ELIZA
GLAZE
GLOZE
PLAZA

•L••Z
ALLEZ
BLITZ
GLITZ
KLUTZ

••L•Z
ALLEZ
FELIZ
HOLTZ
VELEZ
WALTZ

MA•••
MABEL
MACAO
MACAW
MACED
MACES
MACHE
MACHO
MACHU
MACHY
MACLE
MACON
MACRO
MACYS
MADAM
MADGE
MADLY
MADRE
MAGDA
MAGEE
MAGES
MAGIC
MAGMA
MAGNA
MAGOG
MAGOO
MAGOT
MAGUS
MAHAL
MAHAN
MAHDI
MAHER
MAHON
MAHRE
MAIDS
MAIDU
MAILE
MAILS
MAINE
MAINS
MAINZ
MAIZE
MAJOR
MAKER
MAKES
MAKOS
MAKUA
MALAN
MALAR
MALAY
MALES
MALIC
MALLE
MALLS
MALMO
MALTA
MALTS
MALTY
MAMAS
MAMBA
MAMBO
MAMET
MAMIE
MAMMA
MAMMY
MANCY
MANDY
MANED
MANES
MANET
MANGO
MANGY
MANIA
MANIC
MANLY
MANNA
MANNY
MANON
MANOR
MANOS
MANSE
MANTA
MAORI
MAPLE
MAQUI
MARAS
MARAT
MARCH
MARCO
MARCY
MARDI
MARES
MARGE
MARGO
MARIA
MARIE
MARIN
MARIO
MARIS
MARKS
MARLA
MARLO
MARLS
MARLY
MARNE
MARRY
MARSH
MARTA
MARTI
MARTS
MARTY
MARVY
MARYS
MASAI
MASER
MASHY
MASKS
MASON
MASSE
MASSY
MASTS
MASUR
MATCH
MATED
MATEO
MATER
MATES
MATEY
MATHS
MATIN
MATRI
MATRO
MATSU
MATTE
MATZO
MAUDE
MAULS
MAUNA
MAUND
MAURY
MAUVE
MAVEN
MAVIS
MAXED
MAXES
MAXIE
MAXIM
MAXIS
MAYAN
MAYAS
MAYBE
MAYER
MAYNT
MAYON
MAYOR
MAYPO
MAYST
MAZDA
MAZEL
MAZER
MAZES

M•A••
MEADE
MEADS
MEALS
MEALY
MEANS
MEANT
MEANY
MEARA
MEATS
MEATY
MIAMI
MIAOW
MIATA
MOANS
MOATS

M••A•
MACAO
MACAW
MADAM
MAHAL
MAHAN
MALAN
MALAR
MALAY
MAMAS
MARAS
MARAT
MASAI
MAYAN
MAYAS
MCKAY
MCRAE
MEDAL
MEGAN
MELAN
MESAS
METAL
MICAH
MICAS
MIDAS
MIKAN
MILAN
MIMAS
MINAS
MIZAR
MODAL
MOHAM
MOLAR
MOLAS
MONAD
MORAE
MORAL
MORAN
MORAS
MORAY
MURAL
MURAT
MUZAK
MYLAR
MYNAH
MYNAS
MYWAY

M•••A
MAGDA
MAGMA
MAGNA
MAKUA
MALTA
MAMBA
MAMMA
MANIA
MANNA
MANTA
MARIA
MARLA
MARTA
MAUNA
MAZDA
MBIRA
MEARA
MECCA
MEDEA
MEDIA
MEHTA
MELBA
MENSA
MESTA
MIATA
MICRA
MILPA
MISHA
MISSA
MOCHA
MOIRA
MOMMA
MONZA
MOOLA
MOTTA
MUDRA
MURRA
MUSCA
MYRNA

•MA••
AMADO
AMAHL
AMAHS
AMAIN
AMANA
AMAPA
AMARA
AMASS
AMATI
AMATO
AMAZE
DMARK
EMAIL
GMATS
IMAGE
IMAGO
IMAMS
KMART
OMAHA
OMANI
OMARR
OMASA
SMACK
SMAIL
SMALL
SMALT
SMART
SMASH
SMAZE

•M•A•
AMMAN
AMPAS
AMWAY
EMBAR
EMBAY
SMEAR
UMIAK
YMCAS

•M••A
AMANA
AMAPA
AMARA
AMEBA
AMIGA
AMNIA
OMAHA
OMASA
OMEGA
OMNIA
UMBRA

••MA•
ADMAN
AHMAD
AIMAT
ALMAY
AMMAN
ATMAN
BEMAS
CAMAY
COMAE
COMAS
CUMAE
CYMAE
CYMAS
DAMAN
DAMAR
DUMAS
ELMAN
GAMAL
GAMAY
HAMAL
HAMAN
HEMAN
HUMAN
HYMAN
JAMAL
KEMAL
LAMAR
LAMAS
LEMAT
LEMAY
LIMAS
LOMAN
LOMAX
LYMAN
MAMAS
MIMAS
NEMAN
NEMAT
NOMAD
OSMAN
PIMAS
PUMAS
RAMAN
RAMAR
REMAN
REMAP
ROMAN
SAMAR
SOMAS
SUMAC
UNMAN
UXMAL
WOMAN
WYMAN
YUMAN
YUMAS

••M•A
COMMA
GAMBA
GAMMA
GEMMA
JUMNA
LAMIA
LEMMA
MAMBA
MAMMA
MOMMA
NAMPA
NEMEA
PAMPA
PEMBA
RUMBA
SAMBA
SAMOA
SIMBA
SUMBA
SUMMA
TAMPA
YAMPA
ZAMIA

•••MA
ACOMA
ADAMA
AGAMA
ANIMA
ARAMA
AROMA
ASAMA
BURMA
COMMA
DERMA
DOGMA
DOLMA
DRAMA
EDEMA
ETYMA
FIRMA
FORMA
GAMMA
GEMMA
GRAMA
HAEMA
HOUMA
KARMA
LEMMA
LLAMA
MAGMA
MAMMA
MOMMA
NORMA
ORAMA
PALMA
PARMA
PRIMA
SELMA
SHEMA
SIGMA
STOMA
SUMMA
THEMA
VILMA
WILMA

MB•••
MBIRA
MBOMU

M•B••
MABEL
MOBIL
MRBIG

M••B•
MAMBA
MAMBO
MAYBE
MELBA
MOSBY
MSNBC
MUMBO

M•••B
MCJOB

•MB••
AMBER
AMBIT
AMBLE
AMBOS
AMBOY
AMBRY
EMBAR
EMBAY
EMBED
EMBER
IMBUE
OMBER
OMBRE
UMBEL
UMBER
UMBOS
UMBRA

•M•B•
AMEBA

••MB•
BAMBI
BOMBE
BOMBS
COMBE
COMBO
COMBS
DUMBO
DUMBS
GAMBA
GUMBO
GUMBY
IAMBI
IAMBS
JAMBS
JUMBO
LAMBS
LIMBI
LIMBO
LIMBS
MAMBA
MAMBO
MUMBO
NAMBY
NIMBI
NIMBY
NUMBS
PAMBY
PEMBA
RAMBO
RUMBA
SAMBA
SIMBA
SUMBA
TAMBO

••M•B
DEMOB
NAMIB

•••MB
ABOMB
CLIMB
CRUMB
HBOMB
PLUMB
RHOMB
RHUMB
THUMB

MC•••
MCCCI
MCCCL
MCCCV
MCCCX
MCCII
MCCIV
MCCIX
MCCLI
MCCLV
MCCLX
MCCOO
MCCOY
MCCVI
MCCXC
MCCXI
MCCXL
MCCXV
MCCXX
MCDII
MCDIV
MCDIX
MCDLI
MCDLV
MCDLX
MCDVI
MCDXC
MCDXI
MCDXL
MCDXV
MCDXX
MCFLY
MCGEE
MCIII
MCJOB
MCKAY
MCLII
MCLIV
MCLIX
MCLVI
MCLXI
MCLXV
MCLXX
MCMII
MCMIV
MCMIX
MCMLI
MCMLV
MCMLX
MCMVI
MCMXC
MCMXI
MCMXL
MCMXV
MCMXX
MCRAE
MCVIE
MCVII
MCXCI
MCXCV
MCXII
MCXIV
MCXIX
MCXLI
MCXLV
MCXVI
MCXXI
MCXXV
MCXXX

M•C••
MACAO
MACAW
MACED
MACES
MACHE
MACHO
MACHU
MACHY
MACLE
MACON
MACRO
MACYS
MCCCI
MCCCL
MCCCV
MCCCX
MCCII
MCCIV
MCCIX
MCCLI
MCCLV
MCCLX
MCCOO
MCCOY
MCCVI
MCCXC
MCCXI
MCCXL
MCCXV
MCCXX
MDCCC
MDCCI
MDCCL
MDCCV
MDCCX
MDCII
MDCIV
MDCIX
MDCLI
MDCLV
MDCLX
MDCVI
MDCXC
MDCXI
MDCXL
MDCXV
MDCXX
MECCA
MECUM
MICAH
MICAS
MICRA
MICRO
MMCCC
MMCCI
MMCCL
MMCCV
MMCCX
MMCDI
MMCDL
MMCDV
MMCDX
MMCII
MMCIV
MMCIX
MMCLI
MMCLV
MMCLX
MMCMI
MMCML
MMCMV
MMCMX
MMCVI
MMCXC
MMCXI
MMCXL
MMCXV
MMCXX
MOCHA
MOCKS
MUCIN
MUCKS
MUCKY
MUCRO
MXCII
MXCIV
MXCIX
MXCVI
MYCIN

M••C•
MANCY
MARCH
MARCO
MARCY
MATCH
MCCCI
MCCCL
MCCCV
MCCCX
MCXCI
MCXCV
MDCCC
MDCCI
MDCCL
MDCCV
MDCCX
MDXCI
MDXCV
MECCA
MERCE
MERCI
MERCK
MERCY
MILCH
MINCE
MITCH
MMCCC
MMCCI
MMCCL
MMCCV
MMCCX
MMDCC
MMDCI
MMDCL
MMDCV
MMDCX
MMMCC
MMMCD
MMMCI
MMMCL
MMMCV
MMMCX
MMXCI
MMXCV
MONCK
MOOCH
MULCH
MULCT
MUNCH
MUSCA

M•••C
MAGIC
MALIC
MANIC
MCCXC
MCDXC
MCMXC
MDCCC
MDCXC
MEDIC
MEDOC
MELIC
MESIC
MIMIC
MMCCC
MMCXC
MMDCC
MMDXC
MMMCC
MMMDC
MMMXC
MODOC
MSNBC
MUSIC

•MC••
EMCEE
MMCCC
MMCCI
MMCCL
MMCCV
MMCCX
MMCDI
MMCDL
MMCDV
MMCDX
MMCII
MMCIV
MMCIX
MMCLI
MMCLV
MMCLX
MMCMI
MMCML
MMCMV
MMCMX
MMCVI
MMCXC
MMCXI
MMCXL
MMCXV
MMCXX
YMCAS

•M•C•
AMICE
AMOCO
AMUCK
CMXCI
CMXCV
MMCCC
MMCCI
MMCCL
MMCCV
MMCCX
MMDCC
MMDCI
MMDCL
MMDCV
MMDCX
MMMCC
MMMCD
MMMCI
MMMCL
MMMCV
MMMCX
MMXCI
MMXCV
SMACK
SMOCK

•M••C
MMCCC
MMCXC
MMDCC
MMDXC
MMMCC
MMMDC
MMMXC

••MC•
MMMCC
MMMCD
MMMCI
MMMCL
MMMCV
MMMCX

••M•C
COMIC
MCMXC
MIMIC
MMMCC
MMMDC
MMMXC
OLMEC
OSMIC
SUMAC

MD•••
MDCCC
MDCCI
MDCCL
MDCCV
MDCII
MDCIV
MDCIX
MDCLI
MDCLV
MDCLX
MDCVI
MDCXC

MDCXI
MDCXL
MDCXV
MDCXX
MDIII
MDLII
MDLIV
MDLIX
MDLVI
MDLXI
MDLXV
MDLXX
MDVII
MDXCI
MDXCV
MDXII
MDXIV
MDXIX
MDXLI
MDXLV
MDXVI
MDXXI
MDXXV
MDXXX

M•D••
MADAM
MADGE
MADLY
MADRE
MCDII
MCDIV
MCDIX
MCDLI
MCDLV
MCDLX
MCDVI
MCDXC
MCDXI
MCDXL
MCDXV
MCDXX
MEDAL
MEDEA
MEDES
MEDIA
MEDIC
MEDIT
MEDOC
MIDAS
MIDDY
MIDGE
MIDIS
MIDST
MMDCC
MMDCI
MMDCL
MMDCV
MMDCX
MMDII
MMDIV
MMDIX
MMDLI
MMDLV
MMDLX
MMDVI
MMDXC
MMDXI
MMDXL
MMDXV
MMDXX
MODAL
MODEL
MODEM
MODES
MODOC
MODUS
MSDOS
MUDDY
MUDRA

M••D•
MAGDA
MAHDI
MAIDS
MAIDU
MANDY
MARDI
MAUDE
MAZDA
MEADE
MEADS
MEEDS
MELDS
MENDS
MIDDY
MINDS
MINDY
MISDO
MMCDI
MMCDL
MMCDV
MMCDX
MMMDC
MMMDI
MMMDL
MMMDV
MMMDX
MOLDS
MOLDY
MONDE
MONDO
MOODS
MOODY
MUDDY
MUNDI

M•••D
MACED
MANED
MATED
MAUND
MAXED
METED
MEWED
MIKED
MIMED
MINED
MIRED
MIXED
MMMCD
MONAD
MONOD
MOOED
MOPED
MOULD
MOUND
MOVED
MOWED
MUSED
MUTED

•MD••
CMDRS
EMDEN
MMDCC
MMDCI
MMDCL
MMDCV
MMDCX
MMDII
MMDIV
MMDIX
MMDLI
MMDLV
MMDLX
MMDVI
MMDXC
MMDXI
MMDXL
MMDXV
MMDXX

•M•D•
AMADO
AMIDE
AMIDO
IMIDE
IMIDO
MMCDI
MMCDL
MMCDV
MMCDX
MMMDC
MMMDI
MMMDL
MMMDV
MMMDX

•M••D
AMEND
AMPED
EMBED
EMEND
IMPED
MMMCD
UMPED

••MD•
MMMDC
MMMDI
MMMDL
MMMDV
MMMDX

••M•D
AHMAD
AHMED
AIMED
ARMED
DIMED
DOMED
FAMED
FUMED
GAMED
HOMED
HUMID
LAMED
LIMED
MIMED
MMMCD
NAMED
NOMAD
RIMED
TAMED
TIMED
TIMID
TUMID

ME•••
MEADE
MEADS
MEALS
MEALY
MEANS
MEANT
MEANY
MEARA
MEATS
MEATY
MECCA
MECUM
MEDAL
MEDEA
MEDES
MEDIA
MEDIC
MEDIT
MEDOC
MEEDS
MEESE
MEETS
MEGAN
MEHTA
MEIJI
MEINY
MELAN
MELBA
MELDS
MELEE
MELIC
MELON
MELOS
MELTS
MELTY
MEMEL
MEMOS
MENDS
MENES
MENLO
MENSA
MENUS
MEOWS
MERCE
MERCI
MERCK
MERCY
MERES
MERGE
MERIT
MERLE
MERLS
MEROE
MERRY
MERTZ
MERYL
MESAS
MESHY
MESIC
MESNE
MESON
MESSY
MESTA
METAL
METED
METER
METES
METIS
METOO
METRE
METRO
METRY
MEUSE
MEWED
MEWLS
MEYER
MEZZO

M•E••
MEEDS
MEESE
MEETS
MIENS
MNEME
MYELO
MYERS
MYEYE

M••E•
MABEL
MACED
MACES
MAGEE
MAGES
MAHER
MAKER
MAKES
MALES
MAMET
MANED
MANES
MANET
MARES
MASER
MATED
MATEO
MATER
MATES
MATEY
MAVEN
MAXED
MAXES
MAYER
MAZEL
MAZER
MAZES
MCGEE
MEDEA
MEDES
MELEE
MEMEL
MENES
MERES
METED
METER
METES
MEWED
MEYER
MIKED
MIKES
MIKEY
MILER
MILES
MIMED
MIMEO
MIMER
MIMES
MINED
MINEO
MINER
MINES
MIRED
MIRES
MISER
MITER
MITES
MIXED
MIXER
MIXES
MLLES
MODEL
MODEM
MODES
MOLES
MONEL
MONET
MONEY
MOOED
MOPED
MOPER
MOPES
MOPEY
MOREL
MORES
MOREY
MOSES
MOSEY
MOTEL
MOTES
MOTET
MOUES
MOVED
MOVER
MOVES
MOWED
MOWER
MULES
MULEY
MUREX
MUSED
MUSER
MUSES
MUTED
MUTER
MUTES
MYLES

M•••E
MACHE
MACLE
MADGE
MADRE
MAGEE
MAHRE
MAILE
MAINE
MAIZE
MALLE
MAMIE
MANSE
MAPLE
MARGE
MARIE
MARNE
MASSE
MATTE
MAUDE
MAUVE
MAXIE
MAYBE
MCGEE
MCRAE
MCVIE
MEADE
MEESE
MELEE
MERCE
MERGE
MERLE
MEROE
MESNE
METRE
MEUSE
MFUME
MIDGE
MILLE
MILNE
MINCE
MINIE
MINKE
MITRE
MNEME
MOIRE
MONDE
MONTE
MOORE
MOOSE
MORAE
MORSE
MOSHE
MOUSE
MOVIE
MOXIE
MURRE
MYEYE
MYOPE

•ME••
AMEBA
AMEER
AMEND
AMENS
AMENT
EMEER
EMEND
EMERY
OMEGA
OMENS
OMERS
SMEAR
SMELL
SMELT
SMEWS
UMEKI

•M•E•
AMBER
AMEER
AMIES
AMPED
AMVET
EMBED
EMBER
EMCEE
EMDEN
EMEER
EMMER
EMMET
IMPED
IMPEI
IMPEL
OMBER
UMBEL
UMBER
UMPED

•M••E
AMAZE
AMBLE
AMICE
AMIDE
AMINE
AMOLE
AMORE
AMPLE
AMUSE
EMCEE
EMILE
EMOTE
IMAGE
IMBUE
IMIDE
IMINE
OMBRE
SMAZE
SMILE
SMITE
SMOKE
SMOTE

••ME•
AAMES
ACMES
ADMEN
AHMED
AIMED
AIMEE
AIMER
AJMER
ARMED
ARMEE
ARMET
CAMEL
CAMEO
COMER
COMES
COMET
COMEX
CYMES
DAMES
DEMES
DIMED
DIMES
DOMED
DOMES
EAMES
ELMER
EMMER
EMMET
FAMED
FAMES
FUMED
FUMES
GAMED
GAMER
GAMES
GAMEY
GIMEL
GOMEL
GOMER
GOMEZ
HAMEL
HAMES
HEMEN
HEMET
HOMED
HOMEO
HOMER
HOMES
HOMEY
JAMES
KHMER
LAMED
LAMER
LAMES
LIMED
LIMEN
LIMES
LIMEY
LUMEN
LUMET
MAMET
MEMEL
MIMED
MIMEO
MIMER
MIMES
NAMED
NAMER
NAMES
NEMEA
NIMES
NOMEN
NUMEN
NYMET
OLMEC
POMES
RAMEE
RAMEN
RAMET
REMET
REMEX
RIMED
RIMES
ROMEO
ROMER
RUMEN
SUMER
TAMED
TAMER
TAMES
TIMED
TIMER
TIMES
TIMEX
TOMEI
TOMES
UNMET
WOMEN
YEMEN

••M•E
AIMEE
ARMEE
BOMBE
COMAE
COMBE
COMME
COMTE
CUMAE
CYMAE
DAMME
DEMME
FEMME
GIMME
HOMME
JAMIE
LEMME
MAMIE
POMME
RAMEE
RAMIE
SOMME
TEMPE

•••ME
ANIME
ARAME
BAUME
BERME
BIOME
BLAME
BLUME
BOHME
BROME
BRUME
CHIME
CLIME
COMME
CREME
CRIME
DAMME
DEMME
DISME
DROME
FEMME
FLAME
FLUME
FRAME
FROME
GETME
GIMME
GNOME
GORME
GRIME
HITME
HOMME
ITSME
JAIME
LAKME
LEMME
MFUME
MNEME
NEUME
NOTME
PALME
PLUME
POEME
POMME
PRIME
RHYME
SHAME
SLIME
SOMME
SPUME
SUEME
THEME
THYME
TORME
TRYME
WHYME

MF•••
MFUME

M•F••
MCFLY
MIFFS
MIFFY
MOFFO
MUFFS
MUFTI

M••F•
MIFFS
MIFFY
MOFFO
MUFFS

M•••F
MOTIF

•M••F
SMURF

••MF•
COMFY

M•G••
MAGDA
MAGEE
MAGES
MAGIC
MAGMA
MAGNA
MAGOG
MAGOO
MAGOT
MAGUS
MCGEE
MEGAN
MIGHT
MOGGY
MOGUL
MSGTS
MUGGS
MUGGY
MUGHO
MYGUY

M••G•
MADGE
MANGO
MANGY
MARGE
MARGO
MERGE
MIDGE
MINGS
MINGY
MOGGY
MONGO
MOOGS
MUGGS
MUGGY
MUNGO

M•••G
MAGOG
MRBIG

•M•G•
AMIGA
AMIGO
IMAGE
IMAGO
OMEGA
SMOGS

•M••G
AMONG
HMONG

M•H••
MAHAL
MAHAN
MAHDI
MAHER
MAHON
MAHRE
MEHTA
MOHAM
MOHUR

M••H•
MACHE
MACHO
MACHU
MACHY
MASHY
MATHS
MESHY
MIGHT
MINHO
MISHA
MOCHA
MOSHE
MOTHS
MOTHY
MUGHO
MUSHY
MYTHS

M•••H
MARCH
MARSH
MATCH
MICAH
MILCH
MIRTH
MITCH
MONTH
MOOCH
MORPH
MOUTH
MULCH
MUNCH
MYNAH
MYRRH

•M•H•
AMAHL
AMAHS
AMPHI
AMPHR
OMAHA

•M••H
AMISH
SMASH
SMITH
SMYTH

••M•H
HUMPH
LYMPH
NYMPH
OOMPH

MI•••
MIAMI
MIAOW
MIATA
MICAH
MICAS
MICRA
MICRO
MIDAS
MIDDY
MIDGE
MIDIS
MIDST
MIENS
MIFFS
MIFFY
MIGHT
MIKAN
MIKED
MIKES
MIKEY
MILAN
MILCH
MILER
MILES
MILKS
MILKY
MILLE
MILLI
MILLS
MILNE
MILOS
MILPA
MILTS
MILTY
MIMAS
MIMED
MIMEO
MIMER
MIMES
MIMIC
MIMSY
MINAS
MINCE
MINDS
MINDY
MINED
MINEO
MINER
MINES
MINGS
MINGY
MINHO
MINIE
MINIM
MINIS
MINKE
MINKS
MINOR
MINOS
MINOT
MINSK
MINTO
MINTS
MINTY
MINUS
MIRED
MIRES
MIRKY
MIRRO
MIRTH
MIRVS
MISDO
MISER
MISHA
MISOS
MISSA
MISSY
MISTI
MISTS
MISTY
MITCH
MITER
MITES
MITRE
MITTS
MITTY
MITZI
MIWOK
MIXED
MIXER
MIXES
MIXIN
MIXUP
MIZAR

M•I••
MAIDS
MAIDU
MAILE
MAILS
MAINE
MAINS
MAINZ
MAIZE
MBIRA
MCIII
MDIII
MEIJI
MEINY
MLIII
MMIII
MOILS
MOIRA
MOIRE
MOIST
MVIII
MXIII

M••I•
MAGIC
MALIC
MAMIE
MANIA
MANIC
MARIA
MARIE
MARIN
MARIO
MARIS
MATIN
MAVIS
MAXIE
MAXIM
MAXIS
MCCII
MCCIV
MCCIX
MCDII
MCDIV
MCDIX
MCIII
MCLII
MCLIV
MCLIX
MCMII
MCMIV
MCMIX
MCVIE
MCVII
MCXII
MCXIV
MCXIX
MDCII
MDCIV
MDCIX
MDIII
MDLII
MDLIV
MDLIX
MDVII
MDXII
MDXIV
MDXIX
MEDIA
MEDIC
MEDIT
MELIC
MERIT
MESIC
METIS
MIDIS
MIMIC
MINIE
MINIM
MINIS
MIXIN
MLIII
MLVII
MLXII
MLXIV
MLXIX
MMCII
MMCIV
MMCIX
MMDII
MMDIV
MMDIX
MMIII
MMLII
MMLIV
MMLIX
MMMII
MMMIV
MMMIX
MMVII
MMXII
MMXIV
MMXIX
MOBIL
MOTIF
MOVIE
MOXIE
MRBIG
MUCIN
MUNIS
MUSIC
MVIII
MXCII
MXCIV
MXCIX
MXIII
MXLII
MXLIV
MXLIX
MXMII
MXMIV
MXVII
MXXII
MXXIV
MXXIX
MYCIN
MYSIN

M•••I
MAHDI
MAORI
MAQUI
MARDI
MARTI
MASAI
MATRI
MCCCI
MCCII
MCCLI
MCCVI
MCCXI
MCDII
MCDLI
MCDVI
MCDXI
MCIII
MCLII
MCLVI
MCLXI
MCMII
MCMLI
MCMVI
MCMXI
MCVII
MCXCI
MCXII
MCXLI
MCXVI
MCXXI
MDCCI
MDCII
MDCLI
MDCVI
MDCXI
MDIII
MDLII
MDLVI
MDLXI
MDVII
MDXCI
MDXII
MDXLI
MDXVI
MDXXI
MEIJI
MERCI
MIAMI
MILLI
MISTI
MITZI
MLIII
MLVII
MLXII
MLXVI
MLXXI
MMCCI
MMCDI
MMCII
MMCLI
MMCMI
MMCVI
MMCXI
MMDCI
MMDII
MMDLI
MMDVI
MMDXI
MMIII
MMLII
MMLVI
MMLXI
MMMCI
MMMDI
MMMII
MMMLI
MMMVI
MMMXI
MMVII
MMXCI
MMXII
MMXLI
MMXVI
MMXXI
MUFTI
MULTI
MUNDI
MVIII
MXCII
MXCVI
MXIII
MXLII
MXLVI
MXMII
MXVII
MXXII
MXXVI
MXXXI

•MI••
AMICE
AMIDE
AMIDO
AMIES
AMIGA
AMIGO
AMINE
AMINO
AMIRS
AMISH
AMISS
AMITY
CMIII
EMILE
EMILY
EMIRS
EMITS
IMIDE
IMIDO
IMINE
IMINO
MMIII
OMITS
SMILE
SMIRK
SMITE
SMITH
SMITS
UMIAK

•M•I•
AMAIN
AMBIT
AMNIA
CMIII
CMLII
CMLIV
CMLIX
CMVII
CMXII
CMXIV
CMXIX
EMAIL
IMMIX
MMCII
MMCIV
MMCIX
MMDII
MMDIV
MMDIX
MMIII
MMLII
MMLIV
MMLIX
MMMII
MMMIV
MMMIX
MMVII
MMXII
MMXIV
MMXIX
OMNIA
SMAIL

•M••I
AMATI
AMPHI
CMIII
CMLII
CMLVI
CMLXI
CMVII
CMXCI
CMXII
CMXLI
CMXVI
CMXXI
IMPEI
MMCCI
MMCDI
MMCII
MMCLI
MMCMI
MMCVI
MMCXI
MMDCI
MMDII
MMDLI
MMDVI
MMDXI
MMIII
MMLII
MMLVI
MMLXI
MMMCI
MMMDI
MMMII
MMMLI
MMMVI
MMMXI
MMVII
MMXCI
MMXII
MMXLI
MMXVI
MMXXI
OMANI
UMEKI

••MI•
ADMIN
ADMIT
ADMIX
ARMIS
CAMIS
COMIC
COMIX
CUMIN
DEMIT
GAMIN
HEMIN
HUMID
IMMIX
IZMIR
IZMIT
JAMIE
JAMIN
LAMIA
LIMIT
MAMIE
MCMII
MCMIV
MCMIX
MIMIC
MMMII
MMMIV
MMMIX
MXMII
MXMIV
NAMIB
NUMIS
OSMIC
PAMIR
RAMIE
RAMIS
REMIT
REMIX

SEMIS
TAMIL
TIMID
TUMID
ZAMIA

••M•I
BAMBI
IAMBI
LIMBI
MCMII
MCMLI
MCMVI
MCMXI
MMMCI
MMMDI
MMMII
MMMLI
MMMVI
MMMXI
MXMII
NAMOI
NIMBI
SOMNI
TEMPI
TOMEI

•••MI
ELEMI
FERMI
MIAMI
MMCMI
NAOMI
NGAMI
NURMI
OTOMI
PRIMI
SALMI
SUOMI
SWAMI
VERMI

M•J••
MAJOR
MCJOB
MOJOS

M••J•
MEIJI

M•K••
MAKER
MAKES
MAKOS
MAKUA
MCKAY
MIKAN
MIKED
MIKES
MIKEY
MOKPO

M••K•
MARKS
MASKS
MILKS
MILKY
MINKE
MINKS
MIRKY
MOCKS
MONKS
MUCKS
MUCKY
MURKY
MUSKS
MUSKY

M•••K
MERCK
MINSK
MIWOK
MONCK
MUZAK

•M•K•
SMOKE
SMOKY
UMEKI

•M••K
AMUCK
DMARK
SMACK
SMIRK
SMOCK
UMIAK

ML•••
MLIII
MLLES
MLVII
MLXII
MLXIV
MLXIX
MLXVI
MLXXI
MLXXV
MLXXX

M•L••
MALAN
MALAR
MALAY
MALES
MALIC
MALLE
MALLS
MALMO
MALTA
MALTS
MALTY
MCLII
MCLIV
MCLIX
MCLVI
MCLXI
MCLXV
MCLXX
MDLII
MDLIV
MDLIX
MDLVI
MDLXI
MDLXV
MDLXX
MELAN
MELBA
MELDS
MELEE
MELIC
MELON
MELOS
MELTS
MELTY
MILAN
MILCH
MILER
MILES
MILKS
MILKY
MILLE
MILLI
MILLS
MILNE
MILOS
MILPA
MILTS
MILTY
MLLES
MMLII
MMLIV
MMLIX
MMLVI
MMLXI
MMLXV
MMLXX
MOLAR
MOLAS
MOLDS
MOLDY
MOLES
MOLLS
MOLLY
MOLTO
MOLTS
MULCH
MULCT
MULES
MULEY
MULLS
MULTI
MXLII
MXLIV
MXLIX
MXLVI
MYLAR
MYLES

M••L•
MACLE
MADLY
MAILE
MAILS
MALLE
MALLS
MANLY
MAPLE
MARLA
MARLO
MARLS
MARLY
MAULS
MCCLI
MCCLV
MCCLX
MCDLI
MCDLV
MCDLX
MCFLY
MCMLI
MCMLV
MCMLX
MCXLI
MCXLV
MDCLI
MDCLV
MDCLX
MDXLI
MDXLV
MEALS
MEALY
MENLO
MERLE
MERLS
MEWLS
MILLE
MILLI
MILLS
MMCLI
MMCLV
MMCLX
MMDLI
MMDLV
MMDLX
MMMLI
MMMLV
MMMLX
MMXLI
MMXLV
MOILS
MOLLS
MOLLY
MOOLA
MOULD
MOULT
MULLS
MYELO

M•••L
MABEL
MAHAL
MAZEL
MCCCL
MCCXL
MCDXL
MCMXL
MDCCL
MDCXL
MEDAL
MEMEL
MERYL
METAL
MMCCL
MMCDL
MMCML
MMCXL
MMDCL
MMDXL
MMMCL
MMMDL
MMMXL
MOBIL
MODAL
MODEL
MOGUL
MONEL
MORAL
MOREL
MOSUL
MOTEL
MURAL

•ML••
CMLII
CMLIV
CMLIX
CMLVI
CMLXI
CMLXV
CMLXX
EMLYN
MMLII
MMLIV
MMLIX
MMLVI
MMLXI
MMLXV
MMLXX

•M•L•
AMBLE
AMOLE
AMPLE
AMPLY
AMYLO
AMYLS
CMXLI
CMXLV
EMILE
EMILY
IMPLY
MMCLI
MMCLV
MMCLX
MMDLI
MMDLV
MMDLX
MMMLI
MMMLV
MMMLX
MMXLI
MMXLV
SMALL
SMALT
SMELL
SMELT
SMILE
SMOLT

•M••L
AMAHL
AMPUL
EMAIL
IMPEL
MMCCL
MMCDL
MMCML
MMCXL
MMDCL
MMDXL
MMMCL
MMMDL
MMMXL
SMAIL
SMALL
SMELL
UMBEL

••ML•
DIMLY
MCMLI
MCMLV
MCMLX
MMMLI
MMMLV
MMMLX

••M•L
CAMEL
CUMUL
GAMAL
GIMEL
GOMEL
HAMAL
HAMEL
JAMAL
KEMAL
MCMXL
MEMEL
MMMCL
MMMDL
MMMXL
TAMIL
UXMAL

•••ML
FRIML
MMCML

MM•••
MMCCC
MMCCI
MMCCL
MMCCV
MMCCX
MMCDI
MMCDL
MMCDV
MMCDX
MMCII
MMCIV
MMCIX
MMCLI
MMCLV
MMCLX
MMCMI
MMCML
MMCMV
MMCMX
MMCVI
MMCXC
MMCXI
MMCXL
MMCXV
MMCXX
MMDCC
MMDCI
MMDCL
MMDCV
MMDCX
MMDII
MMDIV
MMDIX
MMDLI
MMDLV
MMDLX
MMDVI
MMDXC
MMDXI
MMDXL
MMDXV
MMDXX
MMIII
MMLII
MMLIV
MMLIX
MMLVI
MMLXI
MMLXV
MMLXX
MMMCC
MMMCD
MMMCI
MMMCL
MMMCV
MMMCX
MMMDC
MMMDI
MMMDL
MMMDV
MMMDX
MMMII
MMMIV
MMMIX
MMMLI
MMMLV
MMMLX
MMMVI
MMMXC
MMMXI
MMMXL
MMMXV
MMMXX
MMVII
MMXCI
MMXCV
MMXII
MMXIV
MMXIX
MMXLI
MMXLV
MMXVI
MMXXI
MMXXV
MMXXX

M•M••
MAMAS
MAMBA
MAMBO
MAMET
MAMIE
MAMMA
MAMMY
MCMII
MCMIV
MCMIX
MCMLI
MCMLV
MCMLX
MCMVI
MCMXC
MCMXI
MCMXL
MCMXV
MCMXX
MEMEL
MEMOS
MIMAS
MIMED
MIMEO
MIMER
MIMES
MIMIC
MIMSY
MMMCC
MMMCD
MMMCI
MMMCL
MMMCV
MMMCX
MMMDC
MMMDI
MMMDL
MMMDV
MMMDX
MMMII
MMMIV
MMMIX
MMMLI
MMMLV
MMMLX
MMMVI
MMMXC
MMMXI
MMMXL
MMMXV
MMMXX
MOMMA
MOMMY
MOMUS
MRMOM
MUMBO
MUMMY
MUMPS
MXMII
MXMIV

M••M•
MAGMA
MALMO
MAMMA
MAMMY
MBOMU
MFUME
MIAMI
MMCMI
MMCML
MMCMV
MMCMX
MNEME
MOMMA
MOMMY
MUMMY

M•••M
MADAM
MAXIM
MECUM
MINIM
MODEM
MOHAM
MORUM
MRMOM

•MM••
AMMAN
AMMON
AMMOS
EMMER
EMMET
EMMYS
IMMIX
MMMCC
MMMCD
MMMCI
MMMCL
MMMCV
MMMCX
MMMDC
MMMDI
MMMDL
MMMDV
MMMDX
MMMII
MMMIV
MMMIX
MMMLI
MMMLV
MMMLX
MMMVI
MMMXC
MMMXI
MMMXL
MMMXV
MMMXX

•M•M•
IMAMS
MMCMI
MMCML
MMCMV
MMCMX

••MM•
COMMA
COMME
DAMME
DEMME
DUMMY
FEMME
GAMMA
GAMMY
GEMMA
GEMMY
GIMME
GUMMO
GUMMY
HAMMY
HOMME
JAMMY
JEMMY
JIMMY
LEMMA
LEMME
MAMMA
MAMMY
MOMMA
MOMMY
MUMMY
POMME
RUMMY
SAMMS
SAMMY
SIMMS
SOMME
SUMMA
TAMMY
TIMMY
TOMMY
TUMMY
YUMMY

••M•M
MRMOM

•••MM
FROMM
GRAMM
GRIMM

MN•••
MNEME

M•N••
MANCY
MANDY
MANED
MANES
MANET
MANGO
MANGY
MANIA
MANIC
MANLY
MANNA
MANNY
MANON
MANOR
MANOS
MANSE
MANTA
MENDS
MENES
MENLO
MENSA
MENUS
MINAS
MINCE
MINDS
MINDY
MINED
MINEO
MINER
MINES
MINGS
MINGY
MINHO
MINIE
MINIM
MINIS
MINKE
MINKS
MINOR
MINOS
MINOT
MINSK
MINTO
MINTS
MINTY
MINUS
MONAD
MONCK
MONDE
MONDO
MONEL
MONET
MONEY
MONGO
MONKS
MONOD
MONTE
MONTH
MONTY
MONZA
MSNBC
MUNCH
MUNDI
MUNGO
MUNIS
MUNRO
MYNAH
MYNAS

M••N•
MAGNA
MAINE
MAINS
MAINZ
MANNA
MANNY
MARNE
MAUNA
MAUND
MAYNT
MEANS
MEANT
MEANY
MEINY
MESNE
MIENS
MILNE
MOANS
MOONS
MOONY
MORNS
MOUND
MOUNT
MUONS
MYRNA

M•••N
MACON
MAHAN
MAHON
MALAN
MANON
MARIN
MASON
MATIN
MAVEN
MAYAN
MAYON
MEGAN
MELAN
MELON
MESON
MIKAN
MILAN
MIXIN
MORAN
MORON
MOURN
MUCIN
MYCIN
MYRON
MYSIN

•MN••
AMNIA
OMNIA

•M•N•
AMANA
AMEND
AMENS
AMENT
AMINE
AMINO
AMONG
EMEND
HMONG
IMINE
IMINO
OMANI
OMENS

•M••N
AMAIN
AMMAN
AMMON
EMDEN
EMLYN

••MN•
DAMNS
GYMNO
HYMNS
JUMNA
LIMNS
SOMNI

••M•N
ADMAN
ADMEN
ADMIN
AMMAN
AMMON
ATMAN
CUMIN
DAMAN
DAMON
DEMON
EAMON
ELMAN
GAMIN
HAMAN
HEMAN
HEMEN
HEMIN
HUMAN
HYMAN
JAMIN
LEMON
LIMEN
LIMON
LOMAN
LUMEN
LYMAN
LYMON
NEMAN
NOMEN
NUMEN
OSMAN
RAMAN
RAMEN
RAMON
REMAN
ROMAN
RUMEN
SIMON
TIMON
UNMAN
WOMAN
WOMEN
WOMYN
WYMAN
YEMEN
YUMAN

MO•••
MOANS
MOATS
MOBIL
MOCHA
MOCKS
MODAL
MODEL
MODEM
MODES
MODOC
MODUS
MOFFO
MOGGY
MOGUL
MOHAM
MOHUR
MOILS
MOIRA
MOIRE
MOIST
MOJOS
MOKPO
MOLAR
MOLAS
MOLDS
MOLDY
MOLES
MOLLS
MOLLY
MOLTO
MOLTS
MOMMA
MOMMY
MOMUS
MONAD
MONCK
MONDE
MONDO
MONEL
MONET
MONEY
MONGO
MONKS
MONOD
MONTE
MONTH
MONTY
MONZA
MOOCH
MOODS
MOODY
MOOED
MOOGS
MOOLA
MOONS
MOONY
MOORE
MOORS
MOORY
MOOSE
MOOTS
MOPED
MOPER
MOPES
MOPEY
MOPSY
MOPUP
MORAE
MORAL
MORAN
MORAS
MORAY
MOREL
MORES
MOREY
MORNS
MORON
MOROS
MORPH
MORRO
MORSE
MORTS
MORUM
MOSBY
MOSES
MOSEY
MOSHE
MOSSO
MOSSY
MOSUL
MOTEL
MOTES
MOTET
MOTHS
MOTHY
MOTIF
MOTOR
MOTTA
MOTTO
MOTTS
MOUES
MOULD
MOULT
MOUND
MOUNT
MOURN
MOUSE
MOUSY
MOUTH
MOVED
MOVER
MOVES
MOVIE
MOWED
MOWER
MOXIE

M•O••
MAORI
MBOMU
MEOWS
MOOCH
MOODS
MOODY
MOOED
MOOGS
MOOLA
MOONS
MOONY
MOORE
MOORS
MOORY
MOOSE
MOOTS
MUONS
MYOPE

M••O•
MACON
MAGOG
MAGOO
MAGOT
MAHON
MAJOR
MAKOS
MANON
MANOR
MANOS
MASON
MAYON
MAYOR
MCCOO
MCCOY
MCJOB
MEDOC
MELON
MELOS
MEMOS
MEROE
MESON
METOO
MIAOW
MILOS
MINOR
MINOS
MINOT
MISOS
MIWOK
MODOC
MOJOS
MONOD
MORON
MOROS
MOTOR
MRMOM
MSDOS
MYRON

M•••O
MACAO
MACHO
MACRO
MAGOO
MALMO
MAMBO
MANGO
MARCO
MARGO
MARIO
MARLO
MATEO
MATRO
MATZO
MAYPO
MCCOO
MENLO
METOO
METRO
MEZZO
MICRO
MIMEO
MINEO
MINHO
MINTO
MIRRO
MISDO
MOFFO
MOKPO
MOLTO
MONDO
MONGO
MORRO
MOSSO
MOTTO
MUCRO
MUGHO
MUMBO
MUNGO
MUNRO
MYELO

•MO••
AMOCO
AMOLE
AMONG
AMORE
AMORT
AMORY
AMOUR
EMORY
EMOTE
HMONG
SMOCK
SMOGS
SMOKE
SMOKY
SMOLT
SMOOT
SMOTE

•M•O•
AMBOS
AMBOY
AMMON
AMMOS
SMOOT
UMBOS

•M••O
AMADO
AMATO
AMIDO
AMIGO
AMINO
AMOCO
AMYLO
IMAGO
IMIDO
IMINO

••MO•
AMMON
AMMOS
ARMOR
ATMOS
CAMOS
DAMON
DEMOB
DEMON
DEMOS
EAMON
ELMOS
GAMOW
GEMOT
HUMOR
LEMON
LIMON
LIMOS
LYMON
MEMOS
MRMOM
NAMOI
NIMOY
OLMOS
POMOS
RAMON
RAMOS
REMOP
REMOW
RUMOR
SAMOA
SAMOS
SIMON
TIMON
TIMOR
VAMOS

••M•O
AIMTO
CAMEO
CAMPO
COMBO
COMPO
DUMBO
FEMTO
GUMBO
GUMMO
GYMNO
HOMEO
JUMBO
KIMPO
LIMBO
MAMBO
MIMEO
MUMBO
RAMBO
ROMEO
TAMBO
TEMPO

•••MO
ALAMO
ANEMO
BROMO
COSMO
CUOMO
DERMO
DUOMO
GIZMO
GUMMO
HAEMO
MALMO
OROMO
PISMO
PRIMO
PROMO
SCHMO
SIXMO
SLOMO
WHAMO

M•P••
MAPLE
MOPED
MOPER
MOPES
MOPEY
MOPSY
MOPUP

M••P•
MAYPO
MILPA
MOKPO
MORPH
MUMPS
MYOPE

M•••P
MIXUP
MOPUP

•MP••
AMPAS
AMPED
AMPHI
AMPHR
AMPLE
AMPLY
AMPUL
EMPTY
IMPED
IMPEI
IMPEL
IMPLY
UMPED

•M•P•
AMAPA

••MP•
BUMPS
BUMPY
CAMPO
CAMPS
CAMPY
COMPO
COMPS
DAMPS
DUMPS
DUMPY
GAMPS
GIMPS
GIMPY
HEMPS
HUMPH
HUMPS
HUMPY
JUMPS
JUMPY
KEMPS
KEMPT
KIMPO
LAMPS
LIMPS
LUMPS
LUMPY
LYMPH
MUMPS
NAMPA
NYMPH
OOMPH
PAMPA
PUMPS
RAMPS
ROMPS
RUMPS
SAMPS
SIMPS
SUMPS
TAMPA
TAMPS
TEMPE
TEMPI
TEMPO
TEMPS
TEMPT
TUMPS
VAMPS
WIMPS
WIMPY
YAMPA

••M•P
DAMUP
GUMUP
JAMUP
REMAP
REMOP
SUMUP

•••MP
BLIMP
CHAMP
CHIMP
CHOMP
CHUMP
CLAMP
CLOMP
CLUMP
CRAMP
CRIMP
CRUMP
FRUMP
GRAMP
GRUMP
PLUMP
PRIMP
SCAMP
SHEMP
SKIMP
SLUMP
STAMP
STOMP
STUMP
SWAMP
THUMP
TRAMP
TROMP
TRUMP
WHOMP

M•Q••
MAQUI

MR•••
MRBIG
MRMOM

M•R••
MARAS
MARAT
MARCH
MARCO
MARCY
MARDI
MARES
MARGE
MARGO
MARIA
MARIE
MARIN
MARIO
MARIS
MARKS
MARLA
MARLO
MARLS
MARLY
MARNE
MARRY
MARSH
MARTA
MARTI
MARTS
MARTY
MARVY
MARYS
MCRAE
MERCE
MERCI
MERCK
MERCY
MERES
MERGE
MERIT
MERLE
MERLS
MEROE
MERRY
MERTZ
MERYL
MIRED
MIRES
MIRKY
MIRRO
MIRTH
MIRVS
MORAE
MORAL
MORAN
MORAS
MORAY
MOREL
MORES
MOREY
MORNS
MORON
MOROS
MORPH
MORRO
MORSE
MORTS
MORUM
MURAL
MURAT
MUREX
MURKY
MURRA
MURRE
MYRNA
MYRON
MYRRH

M••R•
MACRO
MADRE
MAHRE
MAORI
MARRY
MATRI
MATRO
MAURY
MBIRA
MEARA
MERRY
METRE
METRO
METRY
MICRA
MICRO
MIRRO
MITRE
MOIRA
MOIRE
MOORE
MOORS
MOORY
MORRO
MOURN
MUCRO
MUDRA
MUNRO
MURRA
MURRE
MYERS
MYRRH

M•••R
MAHER
MAJOR
MAKER
MALAR
MANOR
MASER
MASUR
MATER
MAYER
MAYOR
MAZER
METER
MEYER
MILER
MIMER
MINER
MINOR
MISER
MITER
MIXER
MIZAR
MOHUR
MOLAR
MOPER
MOTOR
MOVER
MOWER
MUSER
MUTER
MYLAR

•M•R•
AMARA
AMBRY
AMIRS
AMORE
AMORT
AMORY
CMDRS
DMARK
EMERY
EMIRS
EMORY
KMART
OMARR
OMBRE
OMERS
SMART
SMIRK
SMURF
UMBRA

•M••R
AMBER
AMEER
AMOUR
AMPHR
EMBAR
EMBER
EMEER
EMMER
OMARR
OMBER
SMEAR
UMBER

••MR•
CAMRY
CYMRY

••M•R
AIMER
AJMER
ARMOR
COMER
DAMAR
DEMUR
ELMER
EMMER
FEMUR
GAMER
GOMER
HOMER
HUMOR
IZMIR
KHMER
LAMAR
LAMER
LEMUR
MIMER
NAMER
NAMUR
PAMIR
RAMAR
ROMER
RUMOR
SAMAR
SUMER
TAMER
TIMER
TIMOR

MS•••
MSDOS
MSGTS
MSNBC

M•S••
MASAI
MASER
MASHY
MASKS
MASON
MASSE
MASSY
MASTS
MASUR
MESAS
MESHY
MESIC
MESNE
MESON
MESSY
MESTA
MISDO
MISER
MISHA
MISOS
MISSA
MISSY
MISTI
MISTS
MISTY
MOSBY
MOSES
MOSEY
MOSHE
MOSSO
MOSSY
MOSUL
MUSCA
MUSED
MUSER
MUSES
MUSHY
MUSIC
MUSKS
MUSKY
MUSSY
MUSTS
MUSTY
MYSIN

M••S•
MANSE
MARSH
MASSE
MASSY
MATSU
MAYST
MEESE
MENSA
MESSY
MEUSE
MIDST
MIMSY
MINSK
MISSA
MISSY
MOIST
MOOSE
MOPSY
MORSE
MOSSO
MOSSY
MOUSE
MOUSY
MUSSY

M•••S
MACES
MACYS
MAGES
MAGUS
MAIDS
MAILS
MAINS
MAKES
MAKOS
MALES
MALLS
MALTS
MAMAS
MANES
MANOS
MARAS
MARES
MARIS
MARKS
MARLS
MARTS
MARYS
MASKS
MASTS
MATES
MATHS
MAULS
MAVIS
MAXES
MAXIS
MAYAS
MAZES
MEADS
MEALS
MEANS
MEATS
MEDES
MEEDS
MEETS
MELDS
MELOS
MELTS
MEMOS
MENDS
MENES
MENUS
MEOWS
MERES
MERLS
MESAS
METES
METIS
MEWLS
MICAS
MIDAS
MIDIS
MIENS
MIFFS
MIKES
MILES
MILKS
MILLS
MILOS
MILTS
MIMAS
MIMES
MINAS
MINDS
MINES
MINGS
MINIS
MINKS
MINOS
MINTS
MINUS
MIRES
MIRVS
MISOS
MISTS
MITES
MITTS
MIXES
MLLES
MOANS
MOATS
MOCKS
MODES
MODUS
MOILS
MOJOS
MOLAS
MOLDS
MOLES
MOLLS
MOLTS
MOMUS
MONKS
MOODS
MOOGS
MOONS
MOORS
MOOTS
MOPES
MORAS
MORES
MORNS
MOROS
MORTS
MOSES
MOTES
MOTHS
MOTTS
MOUES
MOVES
MSDOS
MSGTS
MUCKS
MUFFS
MUGGS
MULES
MULLS
MUMPS
MUNIS
MUONS
MUSES
MUSKS
MUSTS
MUTES
MUTTS
MYERS
MYLES
MYNAS
MYTHS

•M•S•
AMASS
AMISH
AMISS
AMUSE
OMASA
SMASH

•M••S
AMAHS
AMASS
AMBOS
AMENS
AMIES
AMIRS
AMISS
AMMOS
AMPAS
AMYLS
CMDRS
EMIRS
EMITS
EMMYS
GMATS
IMAMS
OMENS
OMERS
OMITS
SMEWS
SMITS
SMOGS
SMUTS
UMBOS
YMCAS

••MS•
MIMSY

••M•S
AAMES
ACMES
AMMOS
ARMIS
ATMOS
BEMAS
BOMBS
BUMPS
CAMIS
CAMOS
CAMPS
CAMUS
COMAS
COMBS
COMES
COMPS
COMUS
CYMAS
CYMES
DAMES
DAMNS
DAMPS
DEMES
DEMOS
DIMES
DOMES
DUMAS
DUMBS
DUMPS
EAMES
ELMOS
EMMYS
FAMES
FUMES
GAMES
GAMPS
GIMPS
HAMES
HEMPS
HOMES
HUMPS
HUMUS
HYMNS
IAMBS
JAMBS
JAMES
JUMPS
KEMPS
LAMAS
LAMBS
LAMES
LAMPS
LIMAS
LIMBS
LIMES
LIMNS
LIMOS
LIMPS
LUMPS
MAMAS
MEMOS
MIMAS
MIMES
MOMUS
MUMPS
NAMES
NIMES
NUMBS
NUMIS
OLMOS
PIMAS
POMES
POMOS
PUMAS
PUMPS
RAMIS
RAMOS
RAMPS
REMUS
RIMES
ROMPS
RUMPS
SAMMS
SAMOS
SAMPS
SEMIS
SIMMS
SIMPS
SOMAS
SUMPS
TAMES
TAMPS
TEMPS
TIMES
TOMES
TUMPS
VAMOS
VAMPS
WIMPS
YUMAS

•••MS
ADAMS
ALUMS
ARUMS
ATOMS
BALMS
BARMS
BEAMS
BERMS
BOOMS
BRIMS
CALMS
CHUMS
CLAMS
CORMS
CRAMS
CULMS
DEEMS
DIEMS
DOOMS
DORMS
DRAMS
DRUMS
EDAMS
EXAMS
FARMS
FILMS
FIRMS
FLAMS
FOAMS
FORMS
GAUMS
GERMS
GEUMS
GLIMS
GLOMS
GRAMS
HALMS
HARMS
HELMS
HERMS
HOLMS
HYAMS
ICBMS
IMAMS
ITEMS
LOAMS
LOOMS
NORMS
PALMS
PERMS
PLUMS
POEMS
PRAMS
PRIMS
PROMS
REAMS
REIMS
ROAMS
ROOMS
SAMMS
SCAMS
SCUMS
SEAMS
SEEMS
SHAMS
SHIMS
SIMMS
SKIMS
SLAMS
SLIMS
SLUMS
SPAMS
STEMS
STUMS
SWIMS
TEAMS
TEEMS
TERMS
THEMS
TRAMS
TRIMS
WARMS
WEEMS
WHAMS
WHIMS
WORMS
ZOOMS

M•T••
MATCH
MATED
MATEO
MATER
MATES
MATEY
MATHS
MATIN
MATRI
MATRO
MATSU
MATTE
MATZO
METAL
METED
METER
METES
METIS
METOO
METRE
METRO
METRY
MITCH
MITER
MITES
MITRE
MITTS
MITTY
MITZI
MOTEL
MOTES
MOTET
MOTHS
MOTHY
MOTIF
MOTOR
MOTTA
MOTTO
MOTTS
MUTED
MUTER
MUTES
MUTTS
MYTHS

M••T•
MALTA
MALTS
MALTY
MANTA
MARTA
MARTI
MARTS
MARTY
MASTS
MATTE
MEATS
MEATY
MEETS
MEHTA
MELTS
MELTY
MERTZ
MESTA
MIATA
MILTS
MILTY
MINTO
MINTS
MINTY
MIRTH
MISTI
MISTS
MISTY
MITTS
MITTY
MOATS
MOLTO
MOLTS
MONTE
MONTH
MONTY
MOOTS
MORTS
MOTTA
MOTTO
MOTTS
MOUTH
MSGTS
MUFTI
MULTI
MUSTS
MUSTY
MUTTS

M•••T
MAGOT
MAMET
MANET
MARAT
MAYNT
MAYST
MEANT
MEDIT
MERIT
MIDST
MIGHT
MINOT
MOIST
MONET
MOTET
MOULT
MOUNT
MULCT
MURAT

•M•T•
AMATI
AMATO
AMITY
EMITS
EMOTE
EMPTY
GMATS
OMITS
SMITE
SMITH
SMITS
SMOTE
SMUTS
SMYTH

•M••T
AMBIT
AMENT
AMORT
AMVET
EMMET
KMART
SMALT
SMART
SMELT
SMOLT
SMOOT

••MT•
AIMTO
COMTE
FEMTO

••M•T
ADMIT
AIMAT
ARMET
COMET
DEMIT
EMMET
GAMUT
GEMOT
HEMET
IZMIT
KEMPT
LEMAT
LIMIT
LUMET
MAMET
NEMAT
NYMET
RAMET
REMET
REMIT
TEMPT
UNMET

•••MT
KLIMT

MU•••
MUCIN
MUCKS
MUCKY
MUCRO
MUDDY
MUDRA
MUFFS
MUFTI
MUGGS
MUGGY
MUGHO
MULCH
MULCT
MULES
MULEY
MULLS
MULTI
MUMBO
MUMMY
MUMPS
MUNCH
MUNDI
MUNGO
MUNIS
MUNRO
MUONS
MURAL
MURAT
MUREX
MURKY
MURRA
MURRE
MUSCA
MUSED
MUSER
MUSES
MUSHY
MUSIC
MUSKS
MUSKY
MUSSY
MUSTS
MUSTY
MUTED
MUTER
MUTES
MUTTS
MUZAK
MUZZY

M•U••
MAUDE
MAULS
MAUNA
MAUND
MAURY
MAUVE
MEUSE
MFUME
MOUES
MOULD
MOULT
MOUND
MOUNT
MOURN
MOUSE
MOUSY
MOUTH

M••U•
MAGUS
MAKUA
MAQUI
MASUR
MECUM
MENUS
MINUS
MIXUP
MODUS
MOGUL
MOHUR
MOMUS
MOPUP
MORUM
MOSUL
MYGUY

M•••U
MACHU
MAIDU
MATSU
MBOMU

•MU••
AMUCK
AMUSE
SMURF
SMUTS

•M•U•
AMOUR
AMPUL
IMBUE

••MU•
CAMUS
COMUS
CUMUL
DAMUP
DEMUR
FEMUR
GAMUT
GUMUP
HUMUS
JAMUP
LEMUR
MOMUS
NAMUR
REMUS
SUMUP

•••MU
ISAMU
MBOMU
SHAMU

MV•••
MVIII

M•V••
MAVEN
MAVIS
MCVIE
MCVII
MDVII
MLVII
MMVII
MOVED
MOVER
MOVES
MOVIE
MXVII

M••V•
MARVY
MAUVE
MCCVI
MCDVI
MCLVI
MCMVI
MCXVI
MDCVI
MDLVI
MDXVI
MIRVS
MLXVI
MMCVI
MMDVI
MMLVI
MMMVI
MMXVI
MXCVI
MXLVI
MXXVI

M•••V
MCCCV
MCCIV
MCCLV
MCCXV
MCDIV
MCDLV
MCDXV
MCLIV
MCLXV
MCMIV
MCMLV
MCMXV
MCXCV
MCXIV
MCXLV
MCXXV
MDCCV
MDCIV
MDCLV
MDCXV
MDLIV
MDLXV
MDXCV
MDXIV
MDXLV
MDXXV
MLXIV
MLXXV
MMCCV
MMCDV
MMCIV
MMCLV
MMCMV
MMCXV
MMDCV
MMDIV
MMDLV
MMDXV
MMLIV
MMLXV
MMMCV
MMMDV
MMMIV
MMMLV
MMMXV
MMXCV
MMXIV
MMXLV
MMXXV
MXCIV
MXLIV
MXMIV
MXXIV
MXXXV

•MV••
AMVET
CMVII
MMVII

•M•V•
CMLVI
CMXVI
MMCVI
MMDVI
MMLVI
MMMVI
MMXVI

•M••V
CMLIV
CMLXV
CMXCV
CMXIV
CMXLV
CMXXV
MMCCV
MMCDV
MMCIV
MMCLV
MMCMV
MMCXV
MMDCV
MMDIV
MMDLV
MMDXV
MMLIV
MMLXV
MMMCV
MMMDV
MMMIV
MMMLV
MMMXV
MMXCV
MMXIV
MMXLV
MMXXV

••MV•
MCMVI
MMMVI

••M•V
MCMIV
MCMLV
MCMXV
MMMCV
MMMDV
MMMIV
MMMLV
MMMXV
MXMIV

•••MV
MMCMV

M•W••
MEWED
MEWLS
MIWOK
MOWED
MOWER
MYWAY

M••W•
MEOWS

M•••W
MACAW
MIAOW

•MW••
AMWAY

•M•W•
SMEWS

••M•W
GAMOW
REMOW

MX•••
MXCII
MXCIV
MXCIX
MXCVI
MXIII
MXLII
MXLIV
MXLIX
MXLVI
MXMII
MXMIV
MXVII
MXXII
MXXIV
MXXIX
MXXVI
MXXXI
MXXXV

M•X••
MAXED
MAXES
MAXIE
MAXIM
MAXIS
MCXCI
MCXCV
MCXII
MCXIV
MCXIX
MCXLI
MCXLV
MCXVI
MCXXI
MCXXV
MCXXX
MDXCI
MDXCV
MDXII
MDXIV
MDXIX
MDXLI
MDXLV
MDXVI
MDXXI
MDXXV
MDXXX
MIXED
MIXER
MIXES
MIXIN
MIXUP
MLXII
MLXIV
MLXIX
MLXVI
MLXXI
MLXXV
MLXXX
MMXCI
MMXCV
MMXII
MMXIV
MMXIX
MMXLI
MMXLV
MMXVI
MMXXI
MMXXV
MMXXX
MOXIE
MXXII
MXXIV
MXXIX
MXXVI
MXXXI
MXXXV

M••X•
MCCXC
MCCXI
MCCXL
MCCXV
MCCXX
MCDXC
MCDXI
MCDXL
MCDXV
MCDXX
MCLXI
MCLXV
MCLXX
MCMXC
MCMXI
MCMXL
MCMXV
MCMXX
MCXXI
MCXXV
MCXXX
MDCXC
MDCXI
MDCXL
MDCXV
MDCXX
MDLXI
MDLXV
MDLXX
MDXXI
MDXXV
MDXXX
MLXXI
MLXXV
MLXXX
MMCXC
MMCXI
MMCXL
MMCXV
MMCXX
MMDXC
MMDXI
MMDXL
MMDXV
MMDXX
MMLXI
MMLXV
MMLXX
MMMXC
MMMXI
MMMXL
MMMXV
MMMXX
MMXXI
MMXXV
MMXXX
MXXXI
MXXXV

M•••X
MCCCX
MCCIX
MCCLX
MCCXX
MCDIX
MCDLX
MCDXX
MCLIX
MCLXX
MCMIX
MCMLX
MCMXX
MCXIX
MCXXX
MDCCX
MDCIX
MDCLX
MDCXX
MDLIX
MDLXX
MDXIX
MDXXX
MLXIX
MLXXX
MMCCX
MMCDX
MMCIX
MMCLX
MMCMX
MMCXX
MMDCX
MMDIX
MMDLX
MMDXX
MMLIX
MMLXX
MMMCX
MMMDX
MMMIX
MMMLX
MMMXX
MMXIX
MMXXX
MUREX
MXCIX
MXLIX
MXXIX

•MX••
CMXCI
CMXCV
CMXII
CMXIV
CMXIX

CMXLI
CMXLV
CMXVI
CMXXI
CMXXV
CMXXX
MMXCI
MMXCV
MMXII
MMXIV
MMXIX
MMXLI
MMXLV
MMXVI
MMXXI
MMXXV
MMXXX

•M•X•
CMLXI
CMLXV
CMLXX
CMXXI
CMXXV
CMXXX
MMCXC
MMCXI
MMCXL
MMCXV
MMCXX
MMDXC
MMDXI
MMDXL
MMDXV
MMDXX
MMLXI
MMLXV
MMLXX
MMMXC
MMMXI
MMMXL
MMMXV
MMMXX
MMXXI
MMXXV
MMXXX

•M••X
CMLIX
CMLXX
CMXIX
CMXXX
IMMIX
MMCCX
MMCDX
MMCIX
MMCLX
MMCMX
MMCXX
MMDCX
MMDIX
MMDLX
MMDXX
MMLIX
MMLXX
MMMCX
MMMDX
MMMIX
MMMLX
MMMXX
MMXIX
MMXXX

••MX•
MCMXC
MCMXI
MCMXL
MCMXV
MCMXX
MMMXC
MMMXI
MMMXL
MMMXV
MMMXX

••M•X
ADMIX
COMEX
COMIX
IMMIX
LOMAX
MCMIX
MCMLX
MCMXX
MMMCX
MMMDX
MMMIX
MMMLX
MMMXX
REMEX
REMIX
TIMEX

•••MX
MMCMX

MY•••
MYCIN
MYELO
MYERS
MYEYE
MYGUY
MYLAR
MYLES
MYNAH
MYNAS
MYOPE
MYRNA
MYRON
MYRRH
MYSIN
MYTHS
MYWAY

M•Y••
MAYAN
MAYAS
MAYBE
MAYER
MAYNT
MAYON
MAYOR
MAYPO
MAYST
MEYER

M••Y•
MACYS
MARYS
MERYL
MYEYE

M•••Y
MACHY
MADLY
MALAY
MALTY
MAMMY
MANCY
MANDY
MANGY
MANLY
MANNY
MARCY
MARLY
MARRY
MARTY
MARVY
MASHY
MASSY
MATEY
MAURY
MCCOY
MCFLY
MCKAY
MEALY
MEANY
MEATY
MEINY
MELTY
MERCY
MERRY
MESHY
MESSY
METRY
MIDDY
MIFFY
MIKEY
MILKY
MILTY
MIMSY
MINDY
MINGY
MINTY
MIRKY
MISSY
MISTY
MITTY
MOGGY
MOLDY
MOLLY
MOMMY
MONEY
MONTY
MOODY
MOONY
MOORY
MOPEY
MOPSY
MORAY
MOREY
MOSBY
MOSEY
MOSSY
MOTHY
MOUSY
MUCKY
MUDDY
MUGGY
MULEY
MUMMY
MURKY
MUSHY
MUSKY
MUSSY
MUSTY
MUZZY
MYGUY
MYWAY

•MY••
AMYLO
AMYLS
SMYTH

•M•Y•
EMLYN
EMMYS

•M••Y
AMBOY
AMBRY
AMITY
AMORY
AMPLY
AMWAY
EMBAY
EMERY
EMILY
EMORY
EMPTY
IMPLY
SMOKY

••MY•
EMMYS
WOMYN

••M•Y
ALMAY
BUMPY
CAMAY
CAMPY
CAMRY
COMFY
CYMRY
DIMLY
DUMMY
DUMPY
GAMAY
GAMEY
GAMMY
GEMMY
GIMPY
GUMBY
GUMMY
HAMMY
HOMEY
HUMPY
JAMMY
JEMMY
JIMMY
JUMPY
LEMAY
LIMEY
LUMPY
MAMMY
MIMSY
MOMMY
MUMMY
NAMBY
NIMBY
NIMOY
PAMBY
RUMMY
SAMMY
TAMMY
TIMMY
TOMMY
TUMMY
WIMPY
YUMMY

•••MY
ANOMY
ATOMY
BALMY
BARMY
BEAMY
BOOMY
DUMMY
ENEMY
FILMY
FLAMY
FOAMY
GAMMY
GEMMY
GERMY
GRIMY
GUMMY
HAMMY
JAMMY
JEMMY
JIMMY
LOAMY
MAMMY
MOMMY
MUMMY
PALMY
PLUMY
PYGMY
ROOMY
RUMMY
SAMMY
SEAMY
SLIMY
SPUMY
STYMY
TAMMY
THYMY
TIMMY
TOMMY
TUMMY
WORMY
YUMMY

M•Z••
MAZDA
MAZEL
MAZER
MAZES
MEZZO
MIZAR
MUZAK
MUZZY

M••Z•
MAIZE
MATZO
MEZZO
MITZI
MONZA
MUZZY

M•••Z
MAINZ
MERTZ

•M•Z•
AMAZE
SMAZE

••M•Z
GOMEZ

NA•••
NAACP
NABES
NABOB
NACHO
NACHT
NACRE
NADER
NADIA
NADIR
NADJA
NAFTA
NAGEL
NAGGY
NAHUA
NAHUM
NAIAD
NAILS
NAINA
NAIRA
NAIRN
NAISH
NAIVE
NAKED
NALDI
NAMBY
NAMED
NAMER
NAMES
NAMIB
NAMOI
NAMPA
NAMUR
NANAK
NANAS
NANCY
NANNA
NANNY
NAOMI
NAPES
NAPPE
NAPPY
NARAS
NARCO
NARCS
NARDS
NARES
NAREW
NARIS
NARKS
NASAL
NASBY
NASHE
NASTY
NATAL
NATCH
NATTY
NAURU
NAVAL
NAVEL
NAVES
NAVIG
NAVVY
NAWAB
NAXOS

N•A••
NAACP
NEALE
NEAPS
NEARS
NEATH
NEATO
NEATS
NGAIO
NGAMI
NOAHS
NYACK
NYALA
NYASA

N••A•
NAIAD
NANAK
NANAS
NARAS
NASAL
NATAL
NAVAL
NAWAB
NEMAN
NEMAT
NEPAL
NICAD
NINAS
NIPAS
NIPAT
NISAN
NIVAL
NIZAM
NOCAL
NODAL
NOFAT
NOLAN
NOMAD
NOPAL
NOPAR
NORAD
NORAH
NOVAE
NOVAK
NOVAS
NOWAY
NUGAE

N•••A
NADIA
NADJA
NAFTA
NAHUA
NAINA
NAIRA
NAMPA
NANNA
NDOLA
NEMEA
NINJA
NORIA
NORMA
NUBIA
NUCHA
NYALA
NYASA

•NA••
ANAIS
DNASE
ENACT
ENATE
GNARL
GNARS
GNASH
GNATS
GNAWS
INALL
INANE
INAPT
INARI
INAWE
KNACK
KNAPS
KNARS
KNAVE
ONAIR
ONATE
RNASE
SNACK
SNAFU
SNAGS
SNAIL
SNAKE
SNAKY
SNAPS
SNARE
SNARK
SNARL
SNATH
UNAPT
UNARM
UNAUS

•N•A•
ANEAR
ANNAL
ANNAM
ANNAN
ANOAS
ANSAE
ANTAE
ANTAL
ANTAS
ANWAR
ANZAC
ENIAC
ENLAI
INBAD
INCAN
INCAS
INLAW
INLAY
KNEAD
ONEAL
ONEAM
ONLAY
ONTAP
SNEAD
SNEAK
UNBAR
UNCAP
UNCAS
UNJAM
UNLAY
UNMAN
UNSAY

•N••A
ANIMA
ANITA
ANTRA
CNIDA
ENNEA
ENOLA
ENTIA
INDIA
INDRA
INFRA
INTRA
ONEGA
SNEVA
UNRRA

••NA•
ANNAL
ANNAM
ANNAN
ARNAZ
BANAL
BANAT
BINAL
CANAD
CANAL
CONAN
CUNAS
DANAE
DINAH
DINAR
DONAS
DONAT
DONAU
ETNAS
FINAL
HENAN
HONAN
HUNAN
IXNAY
JONAH
JONAS
KENAI
KINAS
LANAI
LUNAR
MINAS
MONAD
MYNAH
MYNAS
NANAK
NANAS
NINAS
PANAM
PANAY
PENAL
PUNAS
RANAT
RENAL
RENAN
RUNAT
SANAA
SENAT
SINAI
SONAR
TENAM
TONAL
TUNAS
TYNAN
ULNAE
ULNAS
VENAE
VENAL
VINAS
ZONAL

••N•A
AMNIA
APNEA
BANDA
CANEA
CANNA
CONGA
DANZA
DONNA
ENNEA
FANTA
FINCA
FONDA
GENOA
GENUA
GINZA
GONNA
GUNGA
HANNA
HANSA
HENNA
HONDA
IONIA
JUNTA
KANGA
KANSA
KENYA
KINDA
LANKA
LANZA
LENYA
LINDA
LONGA
LYNDA
MANIA
MANNA
MANTA
MENSA
MONZA
NANNA
NINJA
OMNIA
PANDA
PANGA
PANZA
PENNA
PENTA
PENZA
PINNA
PINTA
PINZA
PONCA
PUNTA
QANDA
RENTA
SANAA
SANKA
SANTA
SENNA
SONIA
SONJA
SONYA
SUNDA
SUNNA
TANKA
TANYA
TONGA
TONKA
TONYA
UINTA
VANNA
VANYA
VENDA
WANDA
WANNA
XENIA
YENTA
ZENDA

•••NA
ADANA
AETNA
AGANA
AGENA
ALANA
AMANA
ARENA
ASANA
AVENA
BUENA
BWANA
CANNA
CHINA
DESNA
DIANA
DONNA
DRINA
DVINA
EDINA
ELENA
FAUNA
FIONA
FRENA
GEENA
GHANA
GONNA
HANNA
HENNA
HYENA
ILONA
IPANA
IRINA
IVANA
JUMNA
KRONA
LEONA
LIANA
LORNA
MAGNA
MANNA
MAUNA
MYRNA
NAINA
NANNA
PATNA
PENNA
PINNA
PLENA
POONA
REINA
RUANA
SAUNA
SCENA
SEHNA
SENNA
SHANA
SIENA
SUNNA
TEENA
VANNA
VARNA
VIRNA
WANNA

NB•••
NBCTV

N•B••
NABES
NABOB
NOBBY
NOBEL
NOBID
NOBIS
NOBLE
NOBLY
NUBBY
NUBIA

N••B•
NAMBY
NASBY
NIMBI
NIMBY
NIOBE
NOBBY
NUBBY
NUMBS

N•••B
NABOB
NAMIB
NAWAB

•NB••
INBAD
INBED
INBIG
INBOX
UNBAR
UNBID
UNBOX

•N•B•
KNOBS
SNOBS
SNUBS

••NB•
CANBY
MSNBC

••N•B
BANDB
DENEB
RANDB

•••NB
PLANB

N•C••
NACHO
NACHT
NACRE
NBCTV
NECKS
NICAD
NICER
NICHE
NICKS
NICOL
NOCAL
NOCKS
NOCTI
NUCHA

N••C•
NAACP
NANCY
NARCO
NARCS
NATCH
NIECE
NONCE
NOSCE
NOTCH
NYACK

•NC••
ANCON
ENCYC
INCAN
INCAS
INCOG
INCUR
INCUS
ONCLE
ONCUE
UNCAP
UNCAS
UNCLE
UNCUT

•N•C•
ENACT
ENOCH
KNACK
KNICK
KNOCK
ONICE
SNACK
SNICK
SNUCK
VNECK

•N••C
ANTIC
ANZAC
ENCYC
ENIAC
INDIC

••NC•
BANCO
BANCS
BENCH
BONCE
BUNCH
CENCI
CINCH
CINCO
CONCH
DANCE
DANCY
DUNCE
FANCY
FENCE
FINCA
FINCH
HENCE
HENCH
HUNCH
JUNCO
KENCH
LANCE
LUNCH
LYNCH
MANCY
MINCE
MONCK
MUNCH
NANCY
NONCE
OUNCE
PENCE
PINCE
PINCH
PONCA
PONCE
PONCH
PUNCH
RANCH
SINCE
SYNCS
TENCH
TINCT
VANCE
VINCE
VINCI
WENCH
WINCE
WINCH
ZINCS
ZINCY

••N•C
CONIC
CYNIC
GENIC
IONIC
MANIC
MSNBC
PANIC
PUNIC
RUNIC
SONIC
TONIC
TUNIC
ZENIC

•••NC
BLANC
BRONC
FRANC

ND•••
NDOLA

N•D••
NADER
NADIA
NADIR
NADJA
NEDDY
NIDES
NIDRE
NIDUS
NODAL
NODDY
NODES
NODOZ
NODUS
NUDER
NUDES
NUDGE

N••D•
NALDI
NARDS
NEDDY
NEEDS
NEEDY
NERDS
NERDY
NODDY

N•••D
NAIAD
NAKED
NAMED
NEFUD
NICAD
NIXED
NOBID
NOEND
NOMAD
NORAD
NOSED
NOTED
NUKED

•ND••
ANDES
ANDIE
ANDOR
ANDRE
ANDRO
ANDRY
ANDUP
ENDED
ENDER
ENDON
ENDOR
ENDOW
ENDUE
ENDUP
INDEF
INDEX
INDIA
INDIC
INDIE
INDIO
INDIV
INDRA
INDRI
INDUS
ONDIT
UNDER
UNDID
UNDUE

•N•D•
ANODE
CNIDA
SNIDE

•N••D
ANTED
ENDED
INBAD
INBED
INKED
KNEAD
KNEED
ONEND
SNEAD
SNEED
SNERD
SNOOD
UNBID
UNDID
UNFED
UNLED
UNWED

••ND•
AANDE
AANDM
BANDA
BANDB
BANDO
BANDS
BANDW
BANDY
BENDS
BENDY
BINDS
BONDI
BONDS
BUNDS
BUNDT
BUNDY
CANDO
CANDW
CANDY
CINDY
CONDE
CONDO
CYNDI
DANDY
DENDR
DINDY
DONDI
FENDS
FINDS
FONDA
FONDS
FONDU
FUNDS
FUNDY
GANDY
GONDI
GONDS
HANDS
HANDY
HINDI
HINDS
HINDU
HONDA
HONDO
KANDY
KENDO
KINDA
KINDS
LANDI
LANDO
LANDS
LENDL
LENDS
LINDA
LINDO
LINDY
LUNDI
LUNDY
LYNDA
LYNDE
MANDY
MENDS
MINDS
MINDY
MONDE
MONDO
MUNDI
PANDA
PANDL
PENDS
PONDS
QANDA
RANDB
RANDD
RANDI
RANDR
RANDS
RANDY
RENDS
RINDS
RINDY
RONDO
SANDE
SANDH
SANDL
SANDS
SANDY
SENDS
SONDE
SUNDA
TANDE
TANDY
TENDS
TONDI
TONDO
VENDA
VENDS
WANDA
WANDS
WENDS
WENDT
WENDY
WINDS
WINDY
ZENDA
ZENDO
ZENDS

••N•D
AWNED
BONED
CANAD
CANED
CANID
CONTD
DINED
FINED
HONED
LINED
MANED
MINED
MONAD
MONOD
OWNED
PANED
PINED
RANDD
RANID
SYNOD
TINED
TONED
TUNED
VINED
WANED
WINED
ZONED

•••ND
ABEND
ALAND
AMEND
BLAND
BLEND
BLIND
BLOND
BOUND
BRAND
EBOND
ELAND
EMEND
FIEND
FOUND
FROND
GLAND
GRAND
GRIND
HOUND
MAUND
MOUND
NOEND
OLAND
ONEND
POUND
QUAND
ROUND
SCAND
SCEND
SOUND
SPEND
STAND
TBOND
TREND
UPEND
VIAND
WOUND

NE•••
NEALE
NEAPS
NEARS
NEATH
NEATO
NEATS
NECKS
NEDDY
NEEDS
NEEDY
NEFUD
NEGEV
NEGRI
NEGUS
NEHIS
NEHRU
NEIGE
NEIGH
NEILL
NELLY
NEMAN
NEMAT
NEMEA
NENES
NEONS
NEPAL
NEPOS
NERDS
NERDY
NEROL
NERTS
NERTZ
NERVE
NERVY
NESTS
NEUME
NEURO
NEVER
NEVES
NEVIL
NEVIN
NEVIS
NEVUS
NEWEL
NEWER
NEWLY
NEWSY
NEWTS
NEXIS
NEXUS

N•E••
NEEDS
NEEDY
NIECE
NIELS
NLERS
NOELS
NOEND
NYETS

N••E•
NABES
NADER
NAGEL
NAKED
NAMED
NAMER
NAMES
NAPES

NARES
NAREW
NAVEL
NAVES
NEGEV
NEMEA
NENES
NEVER
NEVES
NEWEL
NEWER
NFLER
NGWEE
NHLER
NICER
NIDES
NIGEL
NIGER
NIKES
NILES
NIMES
NINER
NINES
NISEI
NITER
NITES
NIVEN
NIXED
NIXES
NIZER
NOBEL
NODES
NOMEN
NONES
NONET
NOSED
NOSES
NOSEY
NOTED
NOTER
NOTES
NOVEL
NOYES
NUDER
NUDES
NUKED
NUKES
NUMEN
NUYEN
NYMET
NYNEX

N•••E

NACRE
NAIVE
NAPPE
NASHE
NEALE
NEIGE
NERVE
NEUME
NGWEE
NICHE
NIDRE
NIECE
NIOBE
NITRE
NIXIE
NOBLE
NOIRE
NOISE
NOLLE
NOLTE
NONCE
NOONE
NOOSE
NORGE
NORSE
NORTE
NOSCE
NOTME
NOTRE
NOVAE
NUDGE
NUGAE
NURSE

•NE••

ANEAR
ANELE
ANEMO
ANENT
ANETO
ENEMY
ENERO
INEPT
INERT
KNEAD
KNEED
KNEEL
KNEES
KNELL
KNELT
MNEME
ONEAL
ONEAM
ONEGA
ONEIL
ONEND
ONEPM
ONERS
ONEUP
SNEAD
SNEAK
SNEED
SNEER
SNELL
SNERD
SNERT
SNEVA
VNECK

•N•E•

ANDES
ANGEL
ANGER
ANGES
ANNEE
ANNES
ANNEX
ANSEL
ANSER
ANTED
ANTES
ENDED
ENDER
ENGEL
ENNEA
ENTER
INBED
INDEF
INDEX
INFER
INGER
INKED
INKER
INLET
INNER
INREM
INSET
INTEL
INTER
KNEED
KNEEL
KNEES
ONKEY
ONSET
SNEED
SNEER
UNDER
UNFED
UNGER
UNLED
UNMET
UNPEG
UNPEN
UNSER
UNSET
UNTER
UNWED

•N••E

ANDIE
ANDRE
ANELE
ANGIE
ANGLE
ANIME
ANISE
ANKLE
ANNEE
ANNIE
ANODE
ANOLE
ANSAE
ANTAE
ANTRE
CNOTE
DNASE
ENATE
ENDUE
ENSUE
ENTRE
ENURE
GNOME
INANE
INAWE
INDIE
INGLE
INKLE
INURE
INUSE
KNAVE
KNIFE
KNUTE
MNEME
ONATE
ONCLE
ONCUE
ONICE
RNASE
SNAKE
SNARE
SNIDE
SNIPE
SNORE
TNOTE
UNCLE
UNDUE
UNITE
UNTIE

••NE•

ABNER
AGNES
AGNEW
ANNEE
ANNES
ANNEX
APNEA
ARNEL
ASNER
AWNED
BANES
BENES
BENET
BINES
BINET
BONED
BONER
BONES
BONET
BYNER
CANEA
CANED
CANEM
CANER
CANES
CINES
CONES
CONEY
CUNEO
DANES
DENEB
DENES
DINED
DINER
DINES
DONEE
DONEN
DUNES
DYNEL
DYNES
ENNEA
ERNES
ESNES
FANES
FINED
FINER
FINES
GANEF
GENES
GENET
GONER
HANES
HINES
HONED
HONES
HONEY
IGNES
INNER
JANET
JONES
KINER
LANES
LINED
LINEN
LINER
LINES
LINEY
LONER
LUNES
MANED
MANES
MANET
MENES
MINED
MINEO
MINER
MINES
MONEL
MONET
MONEY
NENES
NINER
NINES
NONES
NONET
NYNEX
OWNED
OWNER
PANED
PANEL
PANES
PINED
PINES
PINEY
PONES
RANEE
RENEE
RENEW
RONEE
RUNES
SANER
SINES
SINEW
SONES
TANEY
TENET
TINED
TINES
TONED
TONER
TONES
TONEY
TUNED
TUNER
TUNES
TYNES
VANES
VENEZ
VINED
VINES
WANED
WANER
WANES
WANEY
WINED
WINES
WINEY
ZINES
ZONED
ZONES

••N•E

AANDE
AINGE
ANNEE
ANNIE
ARNIE
BENUE
BINGE
BONCE
BONNE
BONZE
CANOE
CENSE
CONDE
CONGE
CONTE
DANAE
DANCE
DANKE
DANSE
DANTE
DENSE
DENTE
DINGE
DONEE
DONNE
DUNCE
DUNNE
ERNIE
FENCE
GENIE
GENRE
HANSE
HENCE
HENGE
HENIE
HINGE
JANIE
KINTE
LANCE
LANGE
LONGE
LUNGE
LYNDE
LYNNE
MANSE
MINCE
MINIE
MINKE
MONDE
MONTE
NONCE
OUNCE
PANNE
PENCE
PENNE
PENTE
PINCE
PONCE
PONTE
RANEE
RANGE
RANKE
RENEE
RINSE
RONEE
SANDE
SANTE
SENSE
SENTE
SINCE
SINGE
SONDE
SYNGE
TANDE
TANTE
TENSE
TINGE
TONNE
ULNAE
VANCE
VENAE
VENUE
VINCE
WINCE
WINZE
YENTE
ZANTE

•••NE

AISNE
AKENE
ALENE
ALINE
ALONE
AMINE
ASONE
ATONE
AXONE
AZINE
BEENE
BERNE
BONNE
BOONE
BORNE
BOYNE
BRINE
BYRNE
CAINE
CARNE
CHINE
CLINE
CLONE
CRANE
CRONE
DAYNE
DEANE
DIANE
DIENE
DIONE
DONNE
DOONE
DRONE
DUANE
DUNNE
HEINE
HERNE
HORNE
IDINE
ILENE
IMINE
INANE
IRENE
JAUNE
JAYNE
JEANE
JEUNE
KEANE
KEENE
KLINE
KOINE
KRONE
LAINE
LAYNE
LEONE
LIANE
LORNE
LYNNE
MAINE
MARNE
MESNE
MILNE
NOONE
OPINE
OVINE
OZONE
PAINE
PANNE
PAYNE
PENNE
PHONE
PLANE
PRONE
PRUNE
REUNE
RHINE
RHONE
ROONE
SAONE
SCENE
SCONE
SEINE
SHANE
SHINE
SHONE
SIGNE
SPINE
STONE
STYNE
SWINE
TAINE
TBONE
TERNE
THANE
THINE
TONNE
TOWNE
TRINE
TWINE
UDINE
VERNE
WAYNE
WHINE

NF•••

NFLER

N•F••

NAFTA
NEFUD
NIFTY
NOFAT
NOFLY

•NF••

ENFIN
INFER
INFIN
INFIX
INFRA
INFUN
UNFED
UNFIT
UNFIX

•N•F•

KNIFE
ONOFF
SNAFU
SNIFF
SNUFF
UNIFY

•N••F

INDEF
KNOPF
ONOFF
SNIFF
SNUFF

••NF•

BANFF
HANFF

••N•F

BANFF
GANEF
HANFF

NG•••

NGAIO
NGAMI
NGWEE

N•G••

NAGEL
NAGGY
NEGEV
NEGRI
NEGUS
NIGEL
NIGER
NIGHT
NOGOS
NUGAE

N••G•

NAGGY
NEIGE
NEIGH
NORGE
NUDGE

N•••G

NAVIG

•NG••

ANGEL
ANGER
ANGES
ANGIE
ANGIO
ANGLE
ANGLO
ANGRY
ANGST
ANGUS
ENGEL
ENGRS
INGER
INGLE
INGOT
UNGER

•N•G•

ENUGU
INIGO
ONEGA
SNAGS
SNOGS
SNUGS

•N••G

INBIG
INCOG
INORG
UNPEG
UNRIG

••NG•

AINGE
BANGS
BINGE
BINGO
BINGS
BONGO
BONGS
BUNGS
CONGA
CONGE
CONGO
DANGS
DINGE
DINGO
DINGS
DINGY
DONGS
FANGS
FUNGI
FUNGO
GANGS
GONGS
GUNGA
HANGS
HENGE
HINGE
HONGS
JINGO
KANGA
KINGS
LANGE
LINGO
LONGA
LONGE
LONGI
LONGO
LONGS
LONGU
LUNGE
LUNGS
MANGO
MANGY
MINGS
MINGY
MONGO
MUNGO
OINGO
PANGA
PANGS
PENGO
PINGO
PINGS
PONGS
PUNGS
RANGE
RANGY
RINGO
RINGS
RUNGS
SENGI
SINGE
SINGS
SONGS
SYNGE
TANGO
TANGS
TANGY
TINGE
TINGS
TONGA
TONGS
VINGT
WINGS
XINGU
ZINGS
ZINGY

•••NG

ACING
AGING
ALONG
AMONG
APING
AWING
AXING
BEING
BOING
BRING
BRUNG
CHANG
CHING
CHONG
CHUNG
CLANG
CLING
CLUNG
CUING
DOING
DRANG
DYING
EKING
EWING
FLING
FLUNG
GOING
HMONG
HYING
ICING
KIANG
KOING
LAING
LIANG
LYING
OKING
ORANG
ORING
OWING
PRANG
PRONG
RUING
SLANG
SLING
SLUNG
SOONG
SPANG
STANG
STING
STUNG
SUING
SWING
SWUNG
THING
THONG
TWANG
TYING
USING
VYING
WHANG
WRING
WRONG
WRUNG
YOUNG

NH•••

NHLER

N•H••

NAHUA
NAHUM
NEHIS
NEHRU
NIHIL
NOHIT
NOHOW

N••H•

NACHO
NACHT
NASHE
NICHE
NIGHT
NOAHS
NUCHA

N•••H

NAISH
NATCH
NEATH
NEIGH
NINTH
NORAH
NORTH
NOTCH
NYMPH

•NH••

ANHUI
UNHIP

•N•H•

ANKHS
ANTHO

•N••H

ENOCH
GNASH
INISH
KNISH
SNATH
UNRUH

••NH•

DONHO
MINHO

••N•H

BENCH
BUNCH
CINCH
CONCH
DINAH
FINCH
HENCH
HUNCH
JONAH
KENCH
LUNCH
LYNCH
MONTH
MUNCH
MYNAH
NINTH
PINCH
PONCH
PUNCH
RANCH
SANDH
TENCH
TENTH
WENCH
WINCH

NI•••

NICAD
NICER
NICHE
NICKS
NICOL
NIDES
NIDRE
NIDUS
NIECE
NIELS
NIFTY
NIGEL
NIGER
NIGHT
NIHIL
NIKES
NIKKI
NIKKO
NIKON
NILES
NILLY
NILOT
NIMBI
NIMBY
NIMES
NIMOY
NINAS
NINER
NINES
NINJA
NINNY
NINON
NINOS
NINTH
NIOBE
NIPAS
NIPAT
NIPPY
NIPUP
NISAN
NISEI
NISUS
NITER
NITES
NITRE
NITRO
NITTI
NITTY
NIVAL
NIVEN
NIXED
NIXES
NIXIE
NIXON
NIZAM
NIZER

N•I••

NAIAD
NAILS
NAINA
NAIRA
NAIRN
NAISH
NAIVE
NEIGE
NEIGH
NEILL
NOILS
NOILY
NOIRE
NOISE
NOISY

N••I•

NADIA
NADIR
NAMIB
NARIS
NAVIG
NEHIS
NEVIL
NEVIN
NEVIS
NEXIS
NGAIO
NIHIL
NIXIE
NOBID
NOBIS
NOHIT
NORIA
NOSIR
NOTIN
NOTIT
NOWIN
NUBIA
NUMIS

N•••I

NALDI
NAMOI
NAOMI
NEGRI
NGAMI
NIKKI
NIMBI
NISEI
NITTI
NOCTI
NURMI

•NI••

ANILS
ANIMA
ANIME
ANION
ANISE
ANISO
ANITA
CNIDA
ENIAC
INIGO
INION
INISH
INITS
KNICK
KNIFE
KNISH
KNITS
ONICE
ONION
SNICK
SNIDE
SNIFF
SNIPE
SNIPS
SNITS
UNIFY
UNION
UNITE
UNITS
UNITY
UNIVS

•N•I•

ANAIS
ANDIE
ANGIE
ANGIO
ANNIE
ANNIV
ANTIC
ANTIQ
ANTIS
ANVIL
ANZIO
ENFIN
ENNIO
ENNIS
ENTIA
INBIG
INDIA
INDIC
INDIE
INDIO
INDIV
INFIN
INFIX
INUIT
ONAIR
ONDIT
ONEIL
SNAIL
UNBID
UNDID
UNFIT
UNFIX
UNHIP
UNLIT
UNPIN
UNRIG
UNTIE
UNTIL
UNZIP

•N••I

ANHUI
ENLAI
ENNUI
ENVOI
INARI
INDRI

••NI•

AMNIA
ANNIE
ANNIV
ARNIE
BENIN
BUNIN
CANID
CANIS
CANIT
CONIC
CYNIC
DANIO
DENIM
DENIS
ENNIO
ENNIS
ERNIE
FINIS
GENIC
GENIE
GENII
HENIE
IONIA
IONIC
JANIE
JANIS
KANIN
LENIN
LENIS
LUNIK
MANIA
MANIC
MINIE
MINIM
MINIS
MUNIS
OMNIA
ORNIS
PANIC
PUNIC
RANID
RANIN
RANIS
RENIN
RUNIC
RUNIN
SONIA
SONIC
TONIC
TONIO
TUNIC
TUNIS
VANIR
VENIN
XENIA
ZENIC
ZUNIS

••N•I

BENJI
BENXI
BONDI
CENCI
CENTI
CONTI
CYNDI
DENTI
DONDI
ENNUI
FUNGI
GENII
GONDI
HANOI
HENRI
HINDI
JINNI
KANJI
KENAI
LANAI
LANDI
LONGI
LUNDI
MUNDI
PENNI
PONTI
PONZI
RANDI
SENGI
SINAI
SUNNI
TONDI
VINCI
YANNI

•••NI

BLINI
ELENI
GARNI
GRANI
HOSNI
ICENI
IRANI
JINNI
LEONI
LIGNI
OMANI
PENNI
PLANI
REGNI
SEGNI
SOMNI
SUNNI
TRINI
YANNI

N••J•

NADJA
NINJA

•NJ••

ANJOU
ENJOY
UNJAM

••NJ•

BANJO
BENJI
KANJI
NINJA
SONJA

N•K••

NAKED
NIKES
NIKKI
NIKKO
NIKON
NUKED
NUKES

N••K•

NARKS
NECKS
NICKS
NIKKI
NIKKO
NOCKS
NOOKS

N•••K

NANAK
NOVAK
NYACK

•NK••

ANKHS
ANKLE
INKED
INKER
INKLE
ONKEY

•N•K•

ENSKY
SNAKE
SNAKY

•N••K

ANOUK
KNACK
KNICK
KNOCK
SNACK
SNARK
SNEAK
SNICK
SNOOK
SNUCK
VNECK

••NK•

BANKS
BANKY
BONKS
BUNKO
BUNKS
CONKS
DANKE
DINKS
DINKY
DUNKS
FINKS
FUNKS
FUNKY
GUNKY
HANKS
HANKY
HONKS
HUNKS
JINKS
JUNKS
JUNKY
KINKS
KINKY
LANKA
LANKY
LINKS
MINKE
MINKS
MONKS
OINKS
PANKY
PINKS
PINKY
PUNKS
PUNKY
RANKE
RANKS
RINKS
RINKY
SANKA
SINKS
TANKA
TANKS
TONKA
WINKS
WONKS
WONKY
YANKS
ZONKS

••N•K

LUNIK
MINSK
MONCK
NANAK
PINSK

•••NK

BLANK
BLINK
BRINK
CHINK
CHUNK
CLANK
CLINK
CLONK
CLUNK
CRANK
DRANK
DRINK
DRUNK
FLANK
FLUNK
FRANK
PLANK
PLINK
PLONK
PLUNK

PRANK PRINK REINK SHANK SKANK SKINK SKUNK SLINK SLUNK SPANK SPUNK STANK STINK STUNK SWANK SWINK SWONK THANK THINK THUNK TRUNK

NL•••
NLERS

N•L••
NALDI NELLY NFLER NHLER NILES NILLY NILOT NOLAN NOLLE NOLTE NULLS NYLON

N••L•
NAILS NDOLA NEALE NEILL NELLY NEWLY NIELS NILLY NOBLE NOBLY NOELS NOFLY NOILS NOILY NOLLE NULLS NYALA

N•••L
NAGEL NASAL NATAL NAVAL NAVEL NEILL NEPAL NEROL NEVIL NEWEL NICOL NIGEL NIHIL NIVAL NOBEL NOCAL NODAL NOPAL NOVEL

•NL••
ENLAI INLAW INLAY INLET ONLAY ONLOW UNLAY UNLED UNLIT

•N•L•
ANELE ANGLE ANGLO ANILS ANKLE ANOLE ENOLA ENOLS INALL INGLE INKLE KNELL KNELT KNOLL ONCLE SNELL UNCLE

•N••L
ANGEL ANNAL ANNUL ANSEL ANTAL ANVIL ENGEL ENROL GNARL INALL INTEL KNEEL KNELL KNOLL KNURL ONEAL ONEIL SNAIL SNARL SNELL UNTIL

••NL•
MANLY MENLO WANLY

••N•L
ANNAL ANNUL ARNEL BANAL BINAL CANAL DYNEL FINAL LENDL MONEL PANDL PANEL PENAL RENAL SANDL TONAL VENAL VINYL YENTL ZONAL

•••NL
ADDNL

N•M••
NAMBY NAMED NAMER NAMES NAMIB NAMOI NAMPA NAMUR NEMAN NEMAT NEMEA NIMBI NIMBY NIMES NIMOY NOMAD NOMEN NUMBS NUMEN NUMIS NYMET NYMPH

N••M•
NAOMI NEUME NGAMI NORMA NORMS NOTME NURMI

N•••M
NAHUM NIZAM

•NM••
UNMAN UNMET

•N•M•
ANEMO ANIMA ANIME ANOMY ENEMY GNOME MNEME

•N••M
ANNAM ANNUM ENORM ENTOM INREM ONEAM ONEPM UNARM UNJAM

••N•M
AANDM ANNAM ANNUM CANEM DENIM DENOM MINIM PANAM PHNOM TENAM TENPM VENOM

N•N••
NANAK NANAS NANCY NANNA NANNY NENES NINAS NINER NINES NINJA NINNY NINON NINOS NINTH NIMOY NONCE NONES NONET NONOS NYNEX

N••N•
NAINA NANNA NANNY NEONS NINNY NOEND NOONE NOONS NORNS NOUNS

N•••N
NAIRN NEMAN NEVIN NIKON NINON NISAN NIVEN NIXON NOLAN NOMEN NOTIN NOWIN NUMEN NUYEN NYLON

•NN••
ANNAL ANNAM ANNAN ANNEE ANNES ANNEX ANNIE ANNIV ANNOY ANNUL ANNUM ANNUS ENNEA ENNIO ENNIS ENNUI INNER

•N•N•
ANENT INANE INONU ONEND

•N••N
ANCON ANION ANNAN ANSON ANTON ENDON ENFIN INCAN INFIN INFUN INION KNOWN ONION UNION UNMAN UNPEN UNPIN

••NN•
BANNS BENNY BONNE BONNY BUNNY CANNA CANNY DANNY DENNY DONNA DONNE DONNY DUNNE DUNNO FANNY FENNY FINNO FINNS FINNY FUNNY GINNY GONNA GUNNY HANNA HANNO HENNA HENNY HINNY JENNY JINNI JINNS KENNY LENNY LYNNE MANNA MANNY NANNA NANNY NINNY PANNE PENNA PENNE PENNI PENNY PINNA PUNNY RONNY RUNNY SENNA SONNY SUNNA SUNNI SUNNY TINNY TONNE TUNNY VANNA VINNY WANNA YANNI

••N•N
AGNON ANNAN BENIN BUNIN CANON CONAN DONEN FANON HENAN HONAN HUNAN KANIN LENIN LINEN MANON NINON PINON RANIN RANON RENAN RENIN RUNIN RUNON TENON TYNAN VENIN XENON

•••NN
DJINN FLYNN GLENN GWENN GWYNN QUINN SWANN

NO•••
NOAHS NOBBY NOBEL NOBID NOBIS NOBLE NOBLY NOCAL NOCKS NOCTI NODAL NODDY NODES NODOZ NODUS NOELS NOEND NOFAT NOFLY NOGOS NOHIT NOHOW NOILS NOILY NOIRE NOISE NOISY NOLAN NOLLE NOLTE NOMAD NOMEN NONCE NONES NONET NONOS NOOKS NOONE NOONS NOOSE NOPAL NOPAR NORAD NORAH NORGE NORIA NORMA NORMS NORNS NORSE NORTE NORTH NORVO NOSCE NOSED NOSES NOSEY NOSIR NOTCH NOTED NOTER NOTES NOTIN NOTIT NOTME NOTRE NOTSO NOTUP NOUNS NOVAE NOVAK NOVAS NOVEL NOWAY NOWIN NOYES

N•O••
NAOMI NDOLA NEONS NIOBE NOOKS NOONE NOONS NOOSE

N••O•
NABOB NAMOI NAXOS NEPOS NEROL NICOL NIKON NILOT NIMOY NINON NINOS NIXON NODOZ NOGOS NOHOW NONOS NYLON

N•••O
NACHO NARCO NEATO NEURO NGAIO NIKKO NITRO NORVO NOTSO

•NO••
ANOAS ANODE ANOLE ANOMY ANOUK CNOTE ENOCH ENOLA ENOLS ENORM GNOME INONU INORG KNOBS KNOCK KNOLL KNOPF KNOPS KNORR KNOTS KNOUT KNOWN KNOWS ONOFF SNOBS SNOGS SNOOD SNOOK SNOOP SNOOT SNORE SNORT SNOUT SNOWS SNOWY TNOTE

•N•O•
ANCON ANDOR ANION ANJOU ANNOY ANSON ANTON ENDON ENDOR ENDOW ENJOY ENROL ENSOR ENTOM ENVOI ENVOY INBOX INCOG INGOT INION INTOW ONION ONLOW ONTOP SNOOD SNOOK SNOOP SNOOT UNBOX UNION

•N••O
ANDRO ANEMO ANETO ANGIO ANGLO ANISO ANTHO ANZIO ENERO ENNIO INDIO INIGO INTRO INTWO

••NO•
AGNON ANNOY ATNOS BYNOW CANOE CANON DENOM DONOR FANON GENOA HANOI HONOR IFNOT KENOS LENOS LENOX LINOS MANON MANOR MANOS MINOR MINOS MINOT MONOD NINON NINOS NONOS PHNOM PINON PINOT RANON RUNON SENOR SYNOD TENON TENOR VENOM VINOS XENON

••N•O
BANCO BANDO BANJO BENZO BINGO BONGO BONZO BUNKO CANDO CANSO CANTO CENTO CINCO CONDO CONGO CUNEO DANIO DINGO DONHO DUNNO ENNIO FINNO FUNGO GENRO GONZO HANNO HONDO JINGO JUNCO JUNTO KENDO LANDO LENTO LINDO LINGO LONGO MANGO MENLO MINEO MINHO MINTO MONDO MONGO MUNGO MUNRO OINGO PANTO PENGO PINGO PINTO RANTO RINGO RINSO RONDO RUNTO SANTO SANYO TANGO TANTO TONDO TONIO TONTO ZENDO

•••NO
ADANO ADENO AMINO BEANO BRUNO BUENO BUONO CHINO CORNO CYANO DRANO DUNNO ETHNO FINNO GYMNO HANNO HYPNO ICONO IMINO KOVNO LIGNO LLANO ORONO PHENO PHONO PIANO PLANO QUINO RHINO ROVNO SEGNO SIGNO STENO TAINO YESNO

N•P••
NAPES NAPPE NAPPY NEPAL NEPOS NIPAS NIPAT NIPPY NIPUP NOPAL NOPAR

N••P•
NAMPA NAPPE NAPPY NEAPS NIPPY NYMPH

N•••P
NAACP NIPUP NOTUP

•NP••
INPUT UNPEG UNPEN UNPIN

•N•P•
INAPT INEPT KNAPS KNOPF KNOPS ONEPM SNAPS SNIPE SNIPS UNAPT

•N••P
ANDUP ENDUP ONEUP ONTAP ONTOP SNOOP UNCAP UNHIP UNZIP

••NP•
TENPM

••N•P
OWNUP PINUP RANUP RUNUP SUNUP

•N••Q
ANTIQ

N•R••
NARAS NARCO NARCS NARDS NARES NAREW NARIS NARKS NERDS NERDY NEROL NERTS NERTZ NERVE NERVY NORAD NORAH NORGE NORIA NORMA NORMS NORNS NORSE NORTE NORTH NORVO NURMI NURSE

N••R•
NACRE NAIRA NAIRN NAURU NEARS NEGRI NEHRU NEURO NIDRE NITRE NITRO NLERS NOIRE NOTRE

N•••R
NADER NADIR NAMER NAMUR NEVER NEWER NFLER NHLER NICER NIGER NINER NITER NIZER NOPAR NOSIR NOTER NUDER

•NR••
ENROL INREM UNRIG UNRRA UNRUH

•N•R•
ANDRE ANDRO ANDRY ANGRY ANTRA ANTRE ENERO ENGRS ENORM ENTRE ENTRY ENURE GNARL GNARS INARI INDRA INDRI INERT INFRA INORG INTRA INTRO INURE KNARS KNORR KNURL KNURS ONERS SNARE SNARK SNARL SNERD SNERT SNORE SNORT UNARM UNRRA

•N••R
ANDOR ANEAR ANGER ANSER ANWAR ENDER ENDOR ENSOR ENTER INCUR INFER INGER INKER INNER INSTR INTER KNORR ONAIR SNEER UNBAR UNDER UNGER UNSER UNTER

••NR•
GENRE GENRO HENRI HENRY MUNRO

••N•R
ABNER ASNER BONER BYNER CANER CONTR DENDR DINAR DINER DONOR FINER GONER HONOR INNER KINER LINER LONER LUNAR MANOR MINER MINOR NINER OWNER RANDR SANER SENOR SONAR TENOR TONER TUNER VANIR WANER

N•S••
NASAL NASBY NASHE NASTY NESTS NISAN NISEI NISUS NOSCE NOSED NOSES NOSEY NOSIR

N••S•
NAISH NEWSY NOISE NOISY NOOSE NORSE NOTSO NURSE NUTSY NYASA

N•••S
NABES NAILS NAMES NANAS NAPES NARAS NARCS NARDS NARES NARIS NARKS NAVES NAXOS NEAPS NEARS NEATS NECKS NEEDS NEGUS NEHIS NENES NEONS NEPOS NERDS NERTS NESTS NEVES NEVIS NEVUS NEWTS NEXIS NEXUS NICKS NIDES NIDUS NIELS NIKES NILES NIMES NINAS NINES NINOS NIPAS NISUS NITES NIXES NLERS NOAHS NOBIS NOCKS NODES NODUS NOELS NOGOS NOILS NONES NONOS NOOKS NOONS NORMS NORNS NOSES NOTES NOUNS NOVAS NOYES NUDES NUKES NULLS NUMBS NUMIS NYETS

•NS••
ANSAE ANSEL ANSER ANSON ENSKY ENSOR ENSUE INSET INSTR INSTS ONSET UNSAY UNSER UNSET

•N•S•
ANGST ANISE ANISO ANTSY DNASE GNASH INISH INUSE KNISH RNASE

•N••S
ANAIS ANDES ANGES ANGUS ANILS ANKHS ANNES ANNUS ANOAS ANTAS ANTES ANTIS ENGRS ENNIS ENOLS GNARS GNATS GNAWS INCAS INCUS INDUS INITS INSTS KNAPS KNARS KNEES KNITS KNOBS KNOPS KNOTS KNOWS KNURS ONERS SNAGS SNAPS SNIPS SNITS SNOBS SNOGS SNOWS SNUBS SNUGS TNUTS UNAUS UNCAS UNITS UNIVS

••NS•
CANSO CANST CENSE DANSE DENSE ERNST HANSA HANSE KANSA MANSE MENSA MINSK PANSY PINSK RINSE RINSO SENSE TANSY TENSE

••N•S
AGNES AGNUS AINUS ANNES ANNUS ATNOS AUNTS BANCS BANDS BANES BANGS BANKS BANNS BENDS BENES BENTS BINDS BINES BINGS BONDS BONES BONGS BONKS BONUS BUNDS BUNGS BUNKS BUNTS CANES CANIS CANTS CENTS CINES CONES CONKS CONUS CUNAS DANES DANGS DENES DENIS DENTS DENYS DINES DINGS DINKS DINTS DONAS DONGS DUNES DUNKS DYNES ENNIS ERNES ESNES ETNAS FANES FANGS FENDS FINDS FINES FINIS FINKS FINNS FONDS FONTS FUNDS FUNKS GANGS GENES GENTS GENUS GONDS GONGS HANDS HANES HANGS HANKS HANTS HENTS HINDS HINES HINTS HONES HONGS HONKS HONUS HUNKS HUNTS IGNES JANIS JANUS JINKS JINNS JONAS JONES JUNKS KENOS KINAS KINDS KINGS KINKS LANDS LANES LENDS LENIS LENOS LENTS LINES

LINKS
LINOS
LINTS
LINUS
LONGS
LUNES
LUNGS
MANES
MANOS
MENDS
MENES
MENUS
MINAS
MINDS
MINES
MINGS
MINIS
MINKS
MINOS
MINTS
MINUS
MONKS
MUNIS
MYNAS
NANAS
NENES
NINAS
NINES
NINOS
NONES
NONOS
OINKS
ORNIS
PANES
PANGS
PANTS
PENDS
PINES
PINGS
PINKS
PINTS
PONDS
PONES
PONGS
PONTS
PUNAS
PUNGS
PUNKS
PUNTS
RANDS
RANIS
RANKS
RANTS
RENDS
RENTS
RINDS
RINGS
RINKS
RUNES
RUNGS
RUNTS
SANDS
SENDS
SINES
SINGS
SINKS
SINUS
SONES
SONGS
SYNCS
TANGS
TANKS
TENDS
TENTS
TINES
TINGS
TINTS
TONES
TONGS
TONUS
TONYS
TUNAS
TUNES
TUNIS
TYNES
ULNAS
VANES
VENDS
VENTS
VENUS
VINAS
VINES
VINOS
WANDS
WANES
WANTS
WENDS
WINDS
WINES
WINGS
WINKS
WONKS
WONTS
YANKS
ZENDS
ZINCS
ZINES
ZINGS
ZONES
ZONKS
ZUNIS

•••NS
AEONS
AKINS
AMENS
ARENS
ASSNS
AVENS
AXONS
AYINS
AZANS
BANNS
BARNS
BEANS
BEINS
BOONS
BOSNS
BRANS
BURNS
CHINS
CLANS
COINS
COONS
CORNS
DAMNS
DARNS
DAWNS
DEANS
DOWNS
DURNS
EARNS
EBONS
EDENS
ETONS
EVANS
EVENS
EXONS
FAUNS
FAWNS
FERNS
FINNS
FIRNS
FLANS
FOHNS
FOINS
FRANS
GAINS
GIRNS
GLENS
GOONS
GOWNS
GRINS
HERNS
HORNS
HYMNS
ICONS
IRONS
IVINS
JAINS
JEANS
JINNS
JOHNS
JOINS
KAONS
KEENS
KERNS
KHANS
KILNS
KOANS
LAWNS
LEANS
LIENS
LIMNS
LIONS
LOANS
LOINS
LOONS
LYONS
MAINS
MEANS
MIENS
MOANS
MOONS
MORNS
MUONS
NEONS
NOONS
NORNS
NOUNS
OMENS
OPENS
OVENS
OWENS
PAINS
PAWNS
PEENS
PEONS
PHONS
PIONS
PLANS
POONS
RAINS
REINS
ROANS
RUINS
SAENS
SCANS
SHANS
SHINS
SHUNS
SIGNS
SKINS
SPANS
SPINS
STENS
STUNS
SWANS
TARNS
TEENS
TERNS
THINS
TOONS
TOWNS
TRANS
TURNS
TWINS
VEINS
WAINS
WARNS
WEANS
WHINS
WRENS
YARNS
YAWNS
YEANS
YUANS
ZEINS
ZOONS

N•T••
NATAL
NATCH
NATTY
NITER
NITES
NITRE
NITRO
NITTI
NITTY
NOTCH
NOTED
NOTER
NOTES
NOTIN
NOTIT
NOTME
NOTRE
NOTSO
NOTUP
NUTSY
NUTTY

N••T•
NAFTA
NASTY
NATTY
NBCTV
NEATH
NEATO
NEATS
NERTS
NERTZ
NESTS
NEWTS
NIFTY
NINTH
NITTI
NITTY
NOCTI
NOLTE
NORTE
NORTH
NUTTY
NYETS

N•••T
NACHT
NEMAT
NIGHT
NILOT
NIPAT
NOFAT
NOHIT
NONET
NOTIT
NYMET

•NT••
ANTAE
ANTAL
ANTAS
ANTED
ANTES
ANTHO
ANTIC
ANTIQ
ANTIS
ANTON
ANTRA
ANTRE
ANTSY
ENTER
ENTIA
ENTOM
ENTRE
ENTRY
INTEL
INTER
INTOW
INTRA
INTRO
INTWO
ONTAP
ONTOP
UNTER
UNTIE
UNTIL

•N•T•
ANETO
ANITA
CNOTE
ENATE
GNATS
INITS
INSTR
INSTS
KNITS
KNOTS
KNUTE
ONATE
SNATH
SNITS
TNOTE
TNUTS
UNITE
UNITS
UNITY

•N••T
ANENT
ANGST
ENACT
INAPT
INEPT
INERT
INGOT
INLET
INPUT
INSET
INUIT
KNELT
KNOUT
ONDIT
ONSET
SNERT
SNOOT
SNORT
SNOUT
UNAPT
UNCUT
UNFIT
UNLIT
UNMET
UNSET

••NT•
AUNTS
AUNTY
BANTU
BENTS
BUNTS
CANTO
CANTS
CANTY
CENTI
CENTO
CENTS
CONTD
CONTE
CONTI
CONTR
DANTE
DENTE
DENTI
DENTS
DINTS
DINTY
FANTA
FONTS
GENTS
HANTS
HENTS
HINTS
HUNTS
HUNTZ
JUNTA
JUNTO
KINTE
LANTZ
LENTO
LENTS
LINTS
LINTY
MANTA
MINTO
MINTS
MINTY
MONTE
MONTH
MONTY
NINTH
PANTO
PANTS
PENTA
PENTE
PINTA
PINTO
PINTS
PONTE
PONTI
PONTS
PUNTA
PUNTS
PUNTY
RANTO
RANTS
RENTA
RENTS
RUNTO
RUNTS
RUNTY
SANTA
SANTE
SANTO
SENTE
TANTE
TANTO
TENTH
TENTS
TINTS
TONTO
UINTA
VENTS
WANTS
WONTS
YENTA
YENTE
YENTL
ZANTE

••N•T
BANAT
BENET
BINET
BONET
BUNDT
CANIT
CANST
DONAT
DONUT
ERNST
GENET
IFNOT
JANET
MANET
MINOT
MONET
NONET
PINOT
RANAT
RUNAT
SENAT
TENET
TINCT
VINGT
WENDT

•••NT
ADINT
AGENT
AMENT
ANENT
ARENT
AVANT
BIONT
BLENT
BLUNT
BRANT
BRENT
BRUNT
BURNT
CHANT
CLINT
COUNT
DAUNT
DIDNT
EVENT
FAINT
FEINT
FLINT
FOUNT
FRONT
GAUNT
GHENT
GIANT
GLINT
GRANT
GRUNT
GWENT
HADNT
HASNT
HAUNT
JAUNT
JOINT
LEANT
MAYNT
MEANT
MOUNT
ODONT
ORANT
PAINT
PLANT
POINT
PRINT
QUANT
QUINT
RIANT
SAINT
SCANT
SCENT
SHANT
SHUNT
SKINT
SLANT
SPENT
STINT
STUNT
SUINT
TAINT
TAUNT
THANT
TIANT
TRENT
VAUNT
WASNT
YOUNT

NU•••
NUBBY
NUBIA
NUCHA
NUDER
NUDES
NUDGE
NUGAE
NUKED
NUKES
NULLS
NUMBS
NUMEN
NUMIS
NURMI
NURSE
NUTSY
NUTTY
NUYEN

N•U••
NAURU
NEUME
NEURO
NOUNS

N••U•
NAHUA
NAHUM
NAMUR
NEFUD
NEGUS
NEVUS
NEXUS
NIDUS
NIPUP
NISUS
NODUS
NOTUP

N•••U
NAURU
NEHRU

•NU••
ENUGU
ENURE
INUIT
INURE
INUSE
KNURL
KNURS
KNUTE
SNUBS
SNUCK
SNUFF
SNUGS
TNUTS

•N•U•
ANDUP
ANGUS
ANHUI
ANNUL
ANNUM
ANNUS
ANOUK
ENDUE
ENDUP
ENNUI
ENSUE
INCUR
INCUS
INDUS
INFUN
INPUT
KNOUT
ONCUE
ONEUP
SNOUT
UNAUS
UNCUT
UNDUE
UNRUH

•N••U
ANJOU
ENUGU
INONU
SNAFU

••NU•
AGNUS
AINUS
ANNUL
ANNUM
ANNUS
BENUE
BONUS
CONUS
DONUT
ENNUI
GENUA
GENUS
HONUS
JANUS
LINUS
MENUS
MINUS
OWNUP
PINUP
RANUP
RUNUP
SINUS
SUNUP
TONUS
VENUE
VENUS

••N•U
BANTU
DONAU
FONDU
HINDU
KANZU
LONGU
XINGU

•••NU
CORNU
INONU
KEANU

N•V••
NAVAL
NAVEL
NAVES
NAVIG
NAVVY
NEVER
NEVES
NEVIL
NEVIN
NEVIS
NEVUS
NIVAL
NIVEN
NOVAE
NOVAK
NOVAS
NOVEL

N••V•
NAIVE
NAVVY
NERVE
NERVY
NORVO

N•••V
NBCTV
NEGEV

•NV••
ANVIL
ENVOI
ENVOY

•N•V•
KNAVE
SNEVA
UNIVS

•N••V
ANNIV
INDIV

••N•V
ANNIV

N•W••
NAWAB
NEWEL
NEWER
NEWLY
NEWSY
NEWTS
NGWEE
NOWAY
NOWIN

N•••W
NAREW
NOHOW

•NW••
ANWAR
UNWED

•N•W•
GNAWS
INAWE
INTWO
KNOWN
KNOWS
SNOWS
SNOWY

•N••W
ENDOW
INLAW
INTOW
ONLOW

••N•W
AGNEW
BANDW
BYNOW
CANDW
RENEW
SINEW

N•X••
NAXOS
NEXIS
NEXUS
NIXED
NIXES
NIXIE
NIXON

N•••X
NYNEX

•N••X
ANNEX
INBOX
INDEX
INFIX
UNBOX
UNFIX

••NX•
BENXI
SKNXX

••N•X
ANNEX
LENOX
NYNEX
SKNXX

•••NX
BRONX

NY•••
NYACK
NYALA
NYASA
NYETS
NYLON
NYMET
NYMPH
NYNEX

N•Y••
NOYES
NUYEN

N•••Y
NAGGY
NAMBY
NANCY
NANNY
NAPPY
NASBY
NASTY
NATTY
NAVVY
NEDDY
NEEDY
NELLY
NERDY
NERVY
NEWLY
NEWSY
NIFTY
NILLY
NIMBY
NIMOY
NINNY
NIPPY
NITTY
NOBBY
NOBLY
NODDY
NOFLY
NOILY
NOISY
NOSEY
NOWAY
NUBBY
NUTSY
NUTTY

•N•Y•
ENCYC

•N••Y
ANDRY
ANGRY
ANNOY
ANOMY
ANTSY
ENEMY
ENJOY
ENSKY
ENTRY
ENVOY
INLAY
ONKEY
ONLAY
SNAKY
SNOWY
UNIFY
UNITY
UNLAY
UNSAY

••NY•
DENYS
KENYA
LENYA
SANYO
SONYA
TANYA
TONYA
TONYS
VANYA
VINYL

••N•Y
ANNOY
AUNTY
BANDY
BANKY
BENDY
BENNY
BONNY
BUNDY
BUNNY
CANBY
CANDY
CANNY
CANTY
CINDY
CONEY
DANCY
DANDY
DANNY
DENNY
DINDY
DINGY
DINKY
DINTY
DONNY
FANCY
FANNY
FENNY
FINNY
FUNDY
FUNKY
FUNNY
GANDY
GINNY
GUNKY
GUNNY
HANDY
HANKY
HENNY
HENRY
HINNY
HONEY
IXNAY
JENNY
JUNKY
KANDY
KENNY
KINKY
LANKY
LENNY
LINDY
LINEY
LINTY
LUNDY
MANCY
MANDY
MANGY
MANLY
MANNY
MINDY
MINGY
MINTY
MONEY
MONTY
NANCY
NANNY
NINNY
PANAY
PANKY
PANSY
PENNY
PINEY
PINKY
PUNKY
PUNNY
PUNTY
RANDY
RANGY
RINDY
RINKY
RONNY
RUNNY
RUNTY
SANDY
SONNY
SUNNY
TANDY
TANEY
TANGY
TANSY
TINNY
TONEY
TUNNY
VINNY
WANEY
WANLY
WENDY
WINDY
WINEY
WONKY
ZINCY
ZINGY

•••NY
AGONY
ATONY
BEANY
BENNY
BONNY
BRINY
BUNNY
CANNY
CARNY
CLUNY
CORNY
CRONY
DANNY
DENNY
DONNY
DOWNY
EBONY
FANNY
FENNY
FERNY
FINNY
FUNNY
GINNY
GOONY
GUNNY
HENNY
HINNY
IRONY
JENNY
KENNY
LAWNY
LENNY
LOONY
MANNY
MEANY
MEINY
MOONY
NANNY
NINNY
PENNY
PEONY
PHANY
PHONY
PLINY
PUNNY
RAINY
RONNY
RUNNY
SHINY
SONNY
SPINY
STONY
SUNNY
TAWNY
TEENY
TINNY
TOWNY
TUNNY
VEINY
VIGNY
VINNY
WEENY
WHINY

N•Z••
NIZAM
NIZER

N•••Z
NERTZ
NODOZ

•NZ••
ANZAC
ANZIO
UNZIP

••NZ•
BENZO
BONZE
BONZO
DANZA
GINZA
GONZO
KANZU
LANZA
MONZA
PANZA
PENZA
PINZA
PONZI
WINZE

••N•Z
ARNAZ
HUNTZ
LANTZ
VENEZ

•••NZ
FRANZ
HEINZ
MAINZ

OA•••
OAKEN
OAKES
OAKIE
OAKUM
OARED
OASES
OASIS
OASTS
OATEN
OATER
OATES
OATHS

O•A••
OCALA
OFAGE
OHAIR
OHARA
OHARE
OKAPI
OKAYS
OLAND
OMAHA
OMANI
OMARR
OMASA
ONAIR
ONATE
OPAHS
OPALS
OPART
ORACH
ORACY
ORALE
ORALS
ORAMA
ORANG
ORANT
ORATE
OSAGE
OSAKA
OTARU
OTARY
OVALS
OVATE
OZARK
OZAWA

O••A•
OBEAH
OCCAM
OCCAS
OCEAN
OCTAD
OCTAL
OFFAL
OGHAM
OHKAY
OKRAS
OLEAN
OLLAS
ONEAL
ONEAM
ONLAY
ONTAP
OPRAH
ORCAS
OREAD
ORGAN
OSCAN
OSCAR
OSKAR
OSMAN
OTWAY
OYVAY

O•••A
OCALA
OCHOA
OCREA
OHARA
OMAHA
OMASA
OMEGA
OMNIA
ONEGA
OOOLA
OPERA
ORAMA
ORIYA
OSAKA
OSHEA
OSSIA
OSTIA
OUIDA
OUIJA
OVETA
OZAWA

•OA••
BOARD
BOARS
BOAST
BOATS
COACH
COACT
COALS
COAPT
COAST
COATI
COATS
FOALS
FOAMS
FOAMY
GOADS
GOALS
GOAPE
GOATS
HOAGY
HOARD
HOARS
HOARY
KOALA
KOANS
LOACH
LOADS
LOAFS
LOAMS
LOAMY
LOANS
LOATH
MOANS
MOATS
NOAHS
POACH
ROACH
ROADS
ROALD
ROAMS
ROANS
ROARS
ROAST
SOAKS
SOAPS
SOAPY
SOARS
SOAVE
TOADS
TOADY
TOAST
WOADS

•O•A•
AODAI
AOKAY
BOHAI
BOLAS
BORAH
BORAS
BORAX
BOYAR
CODAS
COHAN
COLAS
COMAE
COMAS
CONAN
COPAL
COPAN
COPAY
CORAL
COXAE
COXAL
DONAS
DONAT
DONAU
DORAG
DORAL
DORAN
DOTAL
DOUAI
DOUAY
FOCAL
FORAY
GOBAD
GOFAR
GOLAN
GORAL
GOTAT
HOBAN
HODAD
HOGAN
HONAN
HORAE
HORAL
HORAS
HOWAR
HOYAS
IOTAS
IOWAN
JONAH
JONAS
JOTAS
JOUAL
KODAK
KOJAK
KOLAS
KORAN
LOCAL
LOFAT
LOGAN
LOMAN
LOMAX
LOPAT

LORAN
LORAX
LOTAH
LOTAS
LOYAL
MODAL
MOHAM
MOLAR
MOLAS
MONAD
MORAE
MORAL
MORAN
MORAS
MORAY
NOCAL
NODAL
NOFAT
NOLAN
NOMAD
NOPAL
NOPAR
NORAD
NORAH
NOVAE
NOVAK
NOVAS
NOWAY
POHAI
POLAR
POWAY
RODAN
ROMAN
ROTAS
ROWAN
ROYAL
SODAS
SOFAR
SOFAS
SOLAN
SOLAR
SOMAS
SONAR
SORAS
SOYAS
TODAY
TOGAE
TOGAS
TOKAY
TONAL
TOPAZ
TORAH
TOTAL
VOCAL
VOLAR
VOLAT
WOMAN
WOTAN
YOGAS
ZOEAE
ZOEAL
ZOEAS
ZOHAR
ZONAL

•O••A

AORTA
BOHEA
BOOLA
BOSSA
BOTHA
COBIA
COBRA
COCOA
COMMA
CONGA
COOSA
COPRA
COREA
CORIA
COSTA
COTTA
DOBLA
DOBRA
DOGMA
DOLMA
DONNA
DORSA
FOLIA
FONDA
FORMA
FOSSA
FOVEA
GOLDA
GONNA
GOTHA
GOTTA
GOUDA
HOFFA
HONDA
HOOHA
HOSEA
HOSTA
HOUMA
IONIA
JOLLA
KOALA
KORDA
KOREA
LOGIA
LONGA
LOOFA
LORCA
LORNA
LOTTA
MOCHA
MOIRA
MOMMA
MONZA
MOOLA
MOTTA
NORIA
NORMA
OOOLA
PODIA
POLKA
PONCA
POONA
POPPA
SOFIA
SOLFA
SONIA
SONJA
SONYA
SORTA
SOUSA
TONGA
TONKA
TONYA
TOSCA
VODKA
VOILA
VOLGA
VOLTA
VOLVA
YORBA
ZORBA

••OA•

ANOAS
AROAR
BLOAT
BROAD
CLOAK
CROAK
CROAT
EBOAT
FLOAT
GLOAM
GLOAT
GROAN
GROAT
PROAM
PROAS
PSOAS
QUOAD
SHOAH
SHOAL
SHOAT
SKOAL
SLOAN
STOAE
STOAS
STOAT
TWOAM
UBOAT

••O•A

ACOMA
AGORA
AHORA
ALOHA
AROMA
ASOKA
BIOTA
BOOLA
BROCA
COOSA
ENOLA
EVORA
FIONA
FLORA
GROZA
HOOHA
ICOSA
ILONA
KIOGA
KIOWA
KRONA
KYOGA
LEONA
LEORA
LOOFA
MOOLA
NDOLA
OOOLA
POONA
QUOTA
RHODA
RIOJA
SKODA
SPOSA
STOLA
STOMA
USOFA
VIOLA
XHOSA

•••OA

ALCOA
COCOA
GENOA
OCHOA
SAMOA

OB•••

OBEAH
OBELI
OBESE
OBEYS
OBGYN
OBIES
OBJET
OBOES
OBOLI
OBOLS

O•B••

OHBOY
OMBER
OMBRE
ORBIT
OXBOW

O••B•

ORIBI

•OB••

BOBBY
BOBUP
COBIA
COBOL
COBRA
DOBBY
DOBIE
DOBLA
DOBLE
DOBRA
DOBRO
GOBAD
GOBEL
HOBAN
HOBBS
HOBBY
HOBOS
KOBOS
LOBBY
LOBED
LOBES
LOBOS
MOBIL
NOBBY
NOBEL
NOBID
NOBIS
NOBLE
NOBLY
POBOX
POBOY
ROBBY
ROBED
ROBES
ROBIN
ROBLE
ROBOT
SOBER
SOBIG
TOBES
TOBEY
TOBIT
TOBOL
YOBBO

•O•B•

BOBBY
BOMBE
BOMBS
BOOBS
BOOBY
COLBY
COMBE
COMBO
COMBS
CORBY
COSBY
DOBBY
DOLBY
DOUBT
FORBS
GOTBY
HOBBS
HOBBY
LOBBY
LOOBY
MOSBY
NOBBY
ROBBY
SORBS
YOBBO
YORBA
ZORBA

•O••B

HOREB

••OB•

ADOBE
BLOBS
BOOBS
BOOBY
FROBE
GLOBE
GLOBS
KNOBS
LOOBY
NIOBE
PHOBE
PROBE
PROBS
SLOBS
SNOBS
SWOBS

••O•B

ABOMB
HBOMB
RHOMB

•••OB

CAROB
DEMOB
JACOB
KABOB
KEBOB
MCJOB
NABOB
THROB

OC•••

OCALA
OCCAM
OCCAS
OCCUR
OCEAN
OCHER
OCHOA
OCHRE
OCREA
OCTAD
OCTAL
OCTET
OCULO

O•C••

OCCAM
OCCAS
OCCUR
OICKS
ONCLE
ONCUE
OPCIT
ORCAS
ORCHS
ORCUS
ORCZY
OSCAN
OSCAR

O••C•

ONICE
ORACH
ORACY
OUNCE

O•••C

OLEIC
OLMEC
OPTIC
OSMIC
OSRIC

•OC••

BOCCE
BOCCI
COCKS
COCKY
COCOA
COCOS
DOCKS
FOCAL
FOCUS
HOCKS
HOCUS
JOCKO
JOCKS
KOCHI
LOCAL
LOCHS
LOCKE
LOCKS
LOCOS
LOCUM
LOCUS
MOCHA
MOCKS
NOCAL
NOCKS
NOCTI
POCUS
ROCCO
ROCHE
ROCKS
ROCKY
SOCHI
SOCIO
SOCKO
SOCKS
SOCLE
VOCAL

•O•C•

BOCCE
BOCCI
BONCE
BOSCH
BOSCO
BOSCS
BOTCH
COACH
COACT
CONCH
COUCH
DOLCE
FORCE
HOOCH
JOYCE
KOTCH
LOACH
LORCA
MONCK
MOOCH
NONCE
NOSCE
NOTCH
POACH
PONCA
PONCE
PONCH
POOCH
PORCH
POUCH
ROACH
ROCCO
ROYCE
TORCH
TOSCA
TOUCH
VOICE
VOICI
VOUCH

•O••C

BORIC
COMIC
CONIC
COSEC
DORIC
FOLIC
IODIC
IONIC
LOGIC
MODOC
SOFTC
SONIC
TONIC
TOPIC
TORIC
TOXIC
YOGIC

••OC•

AMOCO
BLOCH
BLOCK
BLOCS
BROCA
BROCK
CHOCK
CLOCK
CROCE
CROCI
CROCK
CROCS
ENOCH
EPOCH
FLOCK
FROCK
HOOCH
KNOCK
MOOCH
POOCH
SHOCK
SMOCK
SPOCK
STOCK

••O•C

AZOIC
BRONC
STOIC

•••OC

ADHOC
ADLOC
ASSOC
DUROC
HAVOC
MEDOC
MODOC

OD•••

ODDER
ODDLY
ODELL
ODETS
ODEUM
ODILE
ODIST
ODIUM
ODONT
ODORS
ODOUR

O•D••

ODDER
ODDLY
OGDEN
OLDEN
OLDER
OLDIE
ONDIT
ORDER
ORDOS

O••D•

OPEDS
OUIDA
OUTDO
OXIDE

O•••D

OARED
OCTAD
OGLED
OHGOD
OILED
OLAND
ONEND
OOHED
OOTID
OOZED
OPTED
OREAD
OUTED
OVOID
OWNED

•OD••

AODAI
BODED
BODES
CODAS
CODED
CODER
CODES
CODEX
DODGE
DODGY
DODOS
FODOR
GODEL
GODET
GODEY
GODLY
GODOT
HODAD
IODIC
JODIE
KODAK
LODEN
LODES
LODGE
MODAL
MODEL
MODEM
MODES
MODOC
MODUS
NODAL
NODDY
NODES
NODOZ
NODUS
PODGY
PODIA
RODAN
RODDY
RODEO
RODIN
SODAS
SODDY
SODOM
TODAY
TODDY
TODOS
VODKA
WODEN
WODGE
YODEL
YODHS

•O•D•

BONDI
BONDS
COEDS
COLDS
CONDE
CONDO
CORDS
DONDI
DOODY
DOWDY
FOLDS
FONDA
FONDS
FONDU
FOODS
FORDO
FORDS
GOADS
GOLDA
GOLDE
GOLDS
GONDI
GONDS
GOODS
GOODY
GORDO
GORDY
GOUDA
GOUDY
GOWDY
HOLDS
HONDA
HONDO
HOODS
HORDE
HOWDY
KORDA
LOADS
LORDS
MOLDS
MOLDY
MONDE
MONDO
MOODS
MOODY
NODDY
PONDS
POODS
ROADS
RODDY
RONDO
ROODS
ROWDY
SODDY
SOLDI
SOLDO
SONDE
TOADS
TOADY
TODDY
TONDI
TONDO
VOIDS
WOADS
WOLDS
WOODS
WOODY
WORDS
WORDY

•O••D

BOARD
BODED
BONED
BOOED
BORED
BOUND
BOVID
BOWED
BOXED
CODED
COKED
CONTD
COOED
COPED
CORED
COULD
COWED
COXED
DOLED
DOMED
DOPED
DOSED
DOTED
DOZED
FOUND
FOXED
GOBAD
GORED
GOULD
GOURD
HOARD
HODAD
HOKED
HOLED
HOMED
HONED
HOPED
HOSED
HOUND
JOKED
LOBED
LOPED
LOVED
LOWED
MONAD
MONOD
MOOED
MOPED
MOULD
MOUND
MOVED
MOWED
NOBID
NOEND
NOMAD
NORAD
NOSED
NOTED
OOHED
OOTID
OOZED
POKED
POLED
PORED
POSED
POUND
ROALD
ROBED
ROPED
ROUND
ROVED
ROWED
SOLED
SOLID
SOUND
SOWED
TONED
TOPED
TOTED
TOWED
TOYED
VOTED
VOWED
WOOED
WORLD
WOULD
WOUND
WOWED
YOKED
ZONED
ZOOID

••OD•

ABODE
ANODE
BRODY
CLODS
DIODE
DOODY
EPODE
ERODE
FOODS
FRODO
GEODE
GOODS
GOODY
GRODY
HOODS
MOODS
MOODY
PLODS
POODS
PRODS
QUODS
RHODA
RHODE
RHODO
ROODS
SKODA
SPODE
WOODS
WOODY

••O•D

ALOUD
AROID
AVOID
BLOND
BLOOD
BOOED
BROAD
BROOD
CHORD
CLOUD
COOED
CROWD
DROID
DROOD
EBOND
FIORD
FJORD
FLOOD
FLOYD
FROID
FROND
GEOID
HYOID
LLOYD
MOOED
OVOID
PROUD
QUOAD
SCOLD
SHOED
SLOYD
SNOOD
STOOD
SWORD
SZOLD
TBOND
WOOED
ZOOID

•••OD

BIPOD
BLOOD
BROOD
DROOD
EPHOD
FLOOD
HEROD
MONOD
OHGOD
RESOD
SAROD
SCROD
SNOOD
STOOD
SYNOD

O•E••

OBEAH
OBELI
OBESE
OBEYS
OCEAN
ODELL
ODETS
ODEUM
OGEES
OLEAN
OLEIC
OLEIN
OLEOS
OLEUM
OMEGA
OMENS
OMERS
ONEAL
ONEAM
ONEGA
ONEIL
ONEND
ONEPM
ONERS
ONEUP
OPEDS
OPELS
OPENS
OPERA
OPERE
OREAD
OREOS
OVENS
OVERS
OVERT
OVETA
OVETT
OWENS
OWERS
OXEYE

O••E•

OAKEN
OAKES
OARED
OASES
OATEN
OATER
OATES
OBIES
OBJET
OBOES
OCHER
OCREA
OCTET
ODDER
OFFER
OFTEN
OGDEN
OGEES
OGLED
OGLER
OGLES
OGRES
OILED
OILER
OKIES
OLDEN
OLDER
OLMEC
OLSEN
OMBER
ONKEY
ONSET
OOHED
OOZED
OOZES
OPTED
ORDER
ORFEO
ORIEL
ORLES
ORSER
OSHEA
OSIER
OSLER
OSSEO
OSTEO
OTHER
OTOES
OTTER
OUSEL
OUTED
OUTER
OUZEL
OWLET
OWNED
OWNER

O•••E

OAKIE
OBESE
OCHRE
ODILE
OFAGE
OFUSE
OGIVE
OHARE
OLDIE
OLIVE
OLLIE
OMBRE
ONATE
ONCLE
ONCUE
ONICE
OPERE
OPINE
ORALE
ORATE
OSAGE
OSSIE
OUNCE
OUTRE
OVATE
OVINE
OVULE
OXEYE
OXIDE
OZONE
OZZIE

•OE••

BOEHM
BOERS
BOEUF
COEDS
COEUR
DOERS
DOEST
DOETH
FOEHN
GOERS
GOEST
HOERS
JOEYS
LOESS
LOEWE
LOEWY
NOELS
NOEND
POEME
POEMS
POESY
POETE
POETS
SOEUR
TOEIN
ZOEAE
ZOEAL
ZOEAS

•O•E•

BODED
BODES
BOGEY
BOHEA
BOLES
BONED
BONER
BONES
BONET
BOOED
BOOER
BORED
BORER
BORES
BOTEL
BOWED
BOWEN
BOWER
BOWES
BOXED
BOXER
BOXES
BOYER
CODED
CODER
CODES
CODEX
COHEN
COKED
COKES
COLES
COLET
COMER
COMES
COMET
COMEX
CONES
CONEY
COOED
COOEE
COOER
COPED
COPES
COREA
CORED
CORER
CORES
COREY
COSEC
COTES
COVEN
COVER
COVES
COVET
COVEY
COWED
COWER
COWES
COXED
COXES
COXEY
COYER
COZEN
COZES
DOGES
DOGEY
DOLED
DOLES
DOMED
DOMES
DONEE
DONEN
DOPED
DOPES
DOPEY
DOREN
DOSED
DOSER
DOSES
DOTED
DOTER
DOTES
DOVER
DOVES
DOVEY
DOWEL
DOWER
DOYEN
DOZED
DOZEN
DOZER
DOZES
FOGEY
FOLEY
FORES
FOVEA
FOXED
FOXES
FOYER
GOBEL
GODEL
GODET
GODEY
GOFER
GOLEM
GOMEL
GOMER
GOMEZ
GONER
GOOEY
GORED
GOREN
GORES
GOSEE
GOWER
HOKED
HOKES
HOKEY
HOLED
HOLES
HOLEY
HOMED
HOMEO
HOMER
HOMES
HOMEY
HONED
HONES
HONEY
HOOEY
HOPED
HOPER
HOPES
HOREB
HOSEA
HOSED
HOSEL
HOSES
HOTEL
HOVEL
HOVER
HOVEY
JOKED
JOKER
JOKES
JOKEY
JONES
JOREL
JOSEF
KOPEK
KOREA
LOBED
LOBES
LODEN
LODES
LOGES
LONER
LOPED
LOPER
LOPES
LOPEZ
LOREN
LORES
LOSER
LOSES
LOVED
LOVER
LOVES
LOVEY
LOWED
LOWER
LOWES
LOXES
MODEL
MODEM
MODES
MOLES
MONEL
MONET
MONEY
MOOED
MOPED
MOPER
MOPES
MOPEY
MOREL
MORES
MOREY
MOSES
MOSEY
MOTEL
MOTES
MOTET
MOUES
MOVED
MOVER
MOVES
MOWED
MOWER
NOBEL
NODES
NOMEN
NONES
NONET
NOSED
NOSES
NOSEY
NOTED
NOTER
NOTES
NOVEL
NOYES
OOHED
OOZED
OOZES
POKED
POKER
POKES
POKEY
POLED
POLER
POLES
POMES
PONES
POPES
PORED
PORES
POSED
POSER
POSES
POWER
ROBED
ROBES
RODEO
ROGER
ROGET
ROLEO
ROLES
ROLEX
ROMEO
ROMER
RONEE
ROPED
ROPER
ROPES
ROPEY
ROREM
ROSEN
ROSES
ROSEY
ROTES
ROUEN
ROUES
ROVED
ROVER
ROVES
ROWED
ROWEL
ROWEN
ROWER
SOBER
SOKES
SOLED
SOLER
SOLES
SONES
SOOEY
SOREL
SOREN
SORER
SORES
SOWED
SOWER
SOXER
TOBES

TOBEY TOKEN TOLER TOLET TOMEI TOMES TONED TONER TONES TONEY TOPED TOPER TOPES TOTED TOTEM TOTER TOTES TOVES TOWED TOWEL TOWER TOYED VOLES VOTED VOTER VOTES VOWED VOWEL VOWER WODEN WOKEN WOMEN WOOED WOOER WOVEN WOWED YODEL YOKED YOKEL YOKES ZONED ZONES ZOOEY

•O••E

BOCCE BOGIE BOGLE BOHME BOISE BOITE BOMBE BONCE BONNE BONZE BOOLE BOONE BOOZE BORGE BORNE BOTHE BOULE BOUSE BOWIE BOYLE BOYNE COMAE COMBE COMME COMTE CONDE CONGE CONTE COOEE COOKE COPSE COUPE COXAE DOBIE DOBLE DODGE DOGIE DOLCE DONEE DONNE DOONE DOUSE DOWSE DOYLE FOOTE FORCE FORGE FORTE FOSSE FOYLE GOAPE GOLDE GOOSE GORGE GORME GORSE GOSEE GOSSE GOUGE HOMME HOOKE HOPPE HORAE HORDE HORNE HORSE HOUSE HOWIE HOXIE HOYLE JODIE JOLIE JORGE JOULE JOYCE KOINE KOPJE LOCKE LODGE LOEWE LOGUE LOIRE LONGE LOOSE LORNE LORRE LOTTE LOUIE LOUPE LOUSE MOIRE MONDE MONTE MOORE MOOSE MORAE MORSE MOSHE MOUSE MOVIE MOXIE NOBLE NOIRE NOISE NOLLE NOLTE NONCE NOONE NOOSE NORGE NORSE NORTE NOSCE NOTME NOTRE NOVAE POEME POETE POISE POMME PONCE PONTE POOLE PORTE POSSE POSTE ROBLE ROCHE ROGUE ROLFE ROLLE RONEE ROONE ROQUE ROSIE ROUGE ROUSE ROUTE ROXIE ROYCE SOAVE SOCLE SOLVE SOMME SONDE SOUSE TOGAE TOILE TONNE TOQUE TORME TORRE TORTE TOTIE TOUTE TOWNE VOGUE VOICE VOILE VOLTE VOTRE WODGE WOLFE WORSE YOURE YOUSE YOUVE ZOEAE ZOWIE

••OE•

ALOES BOOED BOOER COOED COOEE COOER FLOES FROES GOOEY HOOEY MOOED OBOES OTOES PROEM SHOED SHOER SHOES SLOES SOOEY WOOED WOOER ZOOEY

••O•E

ABODE ABOVE ADOBE ADORE AFORE ALONE AMOLE AMORE ANODE ANOLE AROSE ASONE ATONE AWOKE AXONE AZOTE BIOME BLOKE BOOLE BOONE BOOZE BROKE BROME CHOKE CHORE CHOSE CLONE CLOSE CLOVE CNOTE COOEE COOKE CROCE CRONE CROZE DHOLE DHOTE DIODE DIONE DOONE DROME DRONE DROVE ECOLE ELOPE EMOTE EPODE ERODE EROSE EVOKE FOOTE FROBE FROME FROZE GEODE GLOBE GLOVE GLOZE GNOME GOOSE GROFE GROPE GROVE HAOLE HOOKE KRONE LEONE LOOSE MOORE MOOSE MYOPE NIOBE NOONE NOOSE OZONE PHOBE PHONE POOLE PROBE PROLE PRONE PROSE PROVE QUOTE RHODE RHONE ROONE SAONE SCONE SCOPE SCORE SHONE SHORE SHOVE SLOPE SMOKE SMOTE SNORE SPODE SPOKE SPORE STOAE STOKE STOLE STONE STOPE STORE STOVE STOWE SWOPE SWORE TBONE THOLE THOSE TNOTE TROPE TROVE WHOLE WHOSE WROTE

•••OE

CANOE CHLOE DAFOE DEFOE FAROE GIJOE MEROE PEKOE TAHOE THROE

OF•••

OFAGE OFFAL OFFER OFTEN OFUSE

O•F••

OFFAL OFFER ORFEO

O••F•

ONOFF

O•••F

ONOFF

•OF••

BOFFO BOFFS DOFFS GOFAR GOFER GOFOR HOFFA LOFAT LOFTS LOFTY MOFFO NOFAT NOFLY SOFAR SOFAS SOFIA SOFTC SOFTG SOFTY TOFFS TOFFY TOFTS

•O•F•

BOFFO BOFFS COIFS COMFY CORFU DOFFS GOLFS GOOFF GOOFS GOOFY HOFFA HOOFS LOAFS LOOFA MOFFO POUFS ROLFE ROOFS SOLFA TOFFS TOFFY WOLFE WOLFF WOOFS

•O••F

BOEUF GOOFF JOSEF MOTIF WOLFF WOOLF

••OF•

AFOFL ALOFT CROFT FEOFF GOOFF GOOFS GOOFY GROFE HOOFS LOOFA ONOFF PROFS ROOFS SCOFF USOFA WOOFS

••O•F

ADOLF ALOOF FEOFF GOOFF KNOPF ONOFF PROOF SCOFF SPOOF WHOOF WOOLF

•••OF

ALOOF PROOF RIDOF SPOOF WHOOF

OG•••

OGDEN OGEES OGHAM OGIVE OGLED OGLER OGLES OGRES

O•G••

OBGYN OHGOD ORGAN OUGHT

O••G•

OFAGE OINGO OLIGO OLOGY OMEGA ONEGA OSAGE OUTGO

O•••G

OKING ORANG ORING OWING

•OG••

BOGEY BOGGS BOGGY BOGIE BOGLE BOGOR BOGUS DOGES DOGEY DOGGO DOGGY DOGIE DOGIT DOGMA DOGON FOGEY FOGGY FOGIN FOGUP GOGOL GOGOS HOGAN HOGGS LOGAN LOGES LOGIA LOGIC LOGIN LOGON LOGOS LOGUE MOGGY MOGUL NOGOS ROGER ROGET ROGUE SOGGY TOGAE TOGAS VOGUE YOGAS YOGHS YOGIC YOGIS

•O•G•

BOGGS BOGGY BONGO BONGS BORGE BOUGH COIGN CONGA CONGE CONGO CORGI COUGH DODGE DODGY DOGGO DOGGY DONGS DOUGH FOGGY FORGE FORGO GOLGI GONGS GORGE GOUGE HOAGY HOGGS HONGS HOUGH JORGE LODGE LONGA LONGE LONGI LONGO LONGS LONGU LOUGH MOGGY MONGO MOOGS NORGE PODGY PONGS PORGY ROUGE ROUGH SOGGY SONGS SORGO SOUGH TONGA TONGS TOUGH VOLGA WODGE

•O••G

BOING BOURG DOING DORAG GOING KOING SOBIG SOFTG SOONG TOPOG YOUNG

••OG•

AGOGO BIOGS CLOGS FLOGS FROGS GLOGG GROGS KEOGH KIOGA KROGH KYOGA MOOGS OLOGY PROGS SHOGI SLOGS SMOGS SNOGS STOGY

••O•G

ALONG AMONG CHONG GEORG GLOGG HMONG INORG PRONG SOONG THONG WRONG

•••OG

BEFOG DEFOG INCOG MAGOG TOPOG

OH•••

OHAIR OHARA OHARE OHBOY OHGOD OHKAY OHWOW

O•H••

OCHER OCHOA OCHRE OGHAM OOHED OPHIR OSHEA OTHER

O••H•

OATHS OMAHA OPAHS ORCHS ORTHO OUGHT

O•••H

OBEAH OOMPH OPRAH ORACH

•OH••

BOHAI BOHEA BOHME COHAN COHEN COHOS FOHNS HOHOS HOHUM JOHNS MOHAM MOHUR NOHIT NOHOW OOHED POHAI SOHIO ZOHAR

•O•H•

BOEHM BOTHA BOTHE DONHO FOEHN GOTHA GOTHS HOOHA HOOHA KOCHI KOPHS LOCHS MOCHA MOSHE MOTHS MOTHY NOAHS POOHS QOPHS ROCHE SOCHI SOPHS SOPHY SOTHO YODHS YOGHS

•O••H

BOOTH BORAH BOSCH BOTCH BOUGH COACH CONCH COUCH COUGH COUTH DOETH DOLPH DOUGH FORTH FOURH HOOCH HOUGH JONAH KOTCH LOACH LOATH LOTAH LOUGH MONTH MOOCH MORPH MOUTH NORAH NORTH NOTCH OOMPH POACH PONCH POOCH PORCH POUCH ROACH ROUGH SOOTH SOUGH SOUTH TOOTH TORAH TORCH TOUCH TOUGH VOUCH WORTH YOUTH

••OH•

ABOHM ALOHA HOOHA POOHS

••O•H

AZOTH BLOCH BOOTH BROTH CLOTH ENOCH EPOCH FROSH FROTH HOOCH KEOGH KROGH MOOCH POOCH QUOTH SHOAH SKOSH SLOSH SLOTH SOOTH THOTH TOOTH TROTH WROTH

•••OH

RICOH

OI•••

OICKS OILED OILER OINGO OINKS

O•I••

OBIES ODILE ODIST ODIUM OGIVE OKIES OKING OLIGO OLIOS OLIVE OMITS ONICE ONION OPINE OPIUM ORIBI ORIEL ORING ORION ORIYA OSIER OUIDA OUIJA OVINE OWING OXIDE

O••I•

OAKIE OASIS OHAIR OLDIE OLEIC OLEIN OLLIE OMNIA ONAIR ONDIT ONEIL OOTID OPCIT OPHIR OPSIN OPSIS OPTIC ORBIT ORNIS ORRIN ORRIS OSLIN OSMIC OSRIC OSSIA OSSIE OSTIA OVOID OXLIP OZZIE

O•••I

OBELI OBOLI OKAPI OMANI ORIBI OTOMI OVOLI

•OI••

BOILS BOING BOISE BOITE BOITO COIFS COIGN COILS COINS COIRS DOILY DOING DOITS FOILS FOINS FOIST GOING HOIST HOITY JOINS JOINT JOIST KOINE KOING LOINS LOIRE MOILS MOIRA MOIRE MOIST NOILS NOILY NOIRE NOISE NOISY POILS POILU POINT POISE ROILS ROILY SOILS TOILE TOILS TOITY VOICE VOICI VOIDS VOILA VOILE

•O•I•

BOGIE BORIC BORIS BOVID BOWIE BOXIN COBIA COLIN COMIC COMIX CONIC CORIA DOBIE DOGIE DOGIT DORIC DORIS EOSIN FOGIN FOLIA FOLIC FOLIO GOTIN GOTIT HOPIN HOPIS HOWIE HOXIE IODIC IONIA IONIC JODIE JOLIE JOSIP LOGIA LOGIC LOGIN LORIS LOUIE LOUIS MOBIL MOTIF MOVIE MOXIE NOBID NOBIS NOHIT NORIA NOSIR NOTIN NOTIT NOWIN OOTID PODIA POLIS POLIT POPIN POSIT ROBIN RODIN ROSIE ROSIN ROXIE SOBIG SOCIO SOFIA SOHIO SOLID SONIA SONIC TOBIT TOEIN TONIC TONIO TOPIC TOPIS TORIC TORII TOTIE TOTIS TOWIT TOXIC TOXIN YOGIC YOGIS ZOOID ZORIL ZORIS ZOWIE

•O••I

AODAI BOCCI BOHAI BONDI COATI CONTI CORGI DONDI DORSI DOUAI FORLI GOLGI GONDI GORKI HOSNI HOURI KOCHI LONGI NOCTI POHAI PONTI PONZI ROSSI SOCHI SOLDI SOLTI SOMNI TOMEI TONDI TOPOI TORII TORSI VOICI YOKOI

••OI•

ABOIL AROID AVOID AVOIR AZOIC BLOIS BROIL CHOIR CROIX DROID DROIT FROID GEOID GROIN HYOID OVOID QUOIN QUOIT REOIL SPOIL STOIC TROIS ZOOID

••O•I

AIOLI BAOJI CROCI DHOTI EBOLI ECOLI ICOSI LEONI MAORI NAOMI OBOLI OTOMI OVOLI PAOLI SHOGI SHOJI SUOMI

•••OI

ENVOI HANOI LEROI NAMOI TOPOI YOKOI

O•J••

OBJET

O••J•

OUIJA

•OJ••

DOJOS KOJAK MOJOS

•O•J•

KOPJE SONJA

••OJ•

BAOJI RIOJA SHOJI

OK•••

OKAPI OKAYS OKIES OKING OKRAS

O•K••

OAKEN OAKES OAKIE OAKUM OHKAY ONKEY OSKAR

O••K•

OICKS OINKS OSAKA

O•••K

OZARK

•OK••

AOKAY COKED COKES HOKED HOKES HOKEY HOKUM JOKED JOKER JOKES JOKEY MOKPO POKED POKER POKES POKEY SOKES TOKAY TOKEN TOKYO WOKEN YOKED YOKEL YOKES YOKOI YOKUM

•O•K•

BONKS BOOKS BOSKS BOSKY COCKS COCKY CONKS COOKE COOKS COOKY CORKS CORKY DOCKS FOLKS FOLKY FORKS FORKY GORKI GORKY GOWKS HOCKS HONKS HOOKE HOOKS HOOKY JOCKO JOCKS KOOKS KOOKY LOCKE LOCKS LOOKS MOCKS MONKS NOCKS NOOKS POLKA PORKS PORKY ROCKS ROCKY ROOKS ROOKY ROYKO SOAKS SOCKO SOCKS SOUKS TONKA VODKA WONKS WONKY WORKS YOLKS YOLKY ZONKS ZOUKS

•O••K

KODAK KOJAK KOPEK MONCK NOVAK POTOK

••OK•

ASOKA AWOKE BIOKO BLOKE BOOKS BROKE CHOKE CHOKY COOKE COOKS COOKY EVOKE EWOKS GROKS HOOKE HOOKS HOOKY KOOKS KOOKY LOOKS NOOKS ROOKS ROOKY SMOKE SMOKY SPOKE STOKE

••O•K

ANOUK BLOCK BROCK BROOK CHOCK CLOAK CLOCK CLONK CROAK CROCK CROOK FLOCK FROCK

KIOSK
KNOCK
PLONK
SHOCK
SHOOK
SMOCK
SNOOK
SPOCK
SPOOK
SPORK
STOCK
STOOK
STORK
SWONK

•••OK

BROOK
CROOK
HUROK
KAPOK
MIWOK
POTOK
SHOOK
SNOOK
SPOOK
STOOK
TAROK
YAPOK
YUROK

OL•••

OLAND
OLDEN
OLDER
OLDIE
OLEAN
OLEIC
OLEIN
OLEOS
OLEUM
OLIGO
OLIOS
OLIVE
OLLAS
OLLIE
OLMEC
OLMOS
OLOGY
OLSEN
OLSON

O•L••

OGLED
OGLER
OGLES
OILED
OILER
OLLAS
OLLIE
ONLAY
ONLOW
ORLES
ORLON
ORLOP
OSLER
OSLIN
OWLET
OXLIP

O••L•

OBELI
OBOLI
OBOLS
OCALA
OCULO
ODDLY
ODELL
ODILE
ONCLE
OOOLA
OPALS
OPELS
ORALE
ORALS
OVALS
OVOLI
OVOLO
OVULE

O•••L

OCTAL
ODELL
OFFAL
ONEAL
ONEIL
ORIEL
OUSEL
OUZEL

•OL••

BOLAS
BOLES
BOLLS
BOLOS
BOLTS
BOLUS
COLAS
COLBY
COLDS
COLES
COLET
COLIN
COLON
COLOR
COLTS
COLUM
DOLBY
DOLCE
DOLED
DOLES
DOLLS
DOLLY
DOLMA
DOLOR
DOLPH
DOLTS
EOLUS
FOLDS
FOLEY
FOLIA
FOLIC
FOLIO
FOLKS
FOLKY
FOLLY
GOLAN
GOLDA
GOLDE
GOLDS
GOLEM
GOLFS
GOLGI
GOLLY
HOLDS
HOLED
HOLES
HOLEY
HOLLY
HOLMS
HOLST
HOLTZ
JOLIE
JOLLA
JOLLY
JOLTS
JOLTY
KOLAS
LOLLS
LOLLY
MOLAR
MOLAS
MOLDS
MOLDY
MOLES
MOLLS
MOLLY
MOLTO
MOLTS
NOLAN
NOLLE
NOLTE
POLAR
POLED
POLER
POLES
POLIS
POLIT
POLKA
POLLO
POLLS
POLLY
POLOS
POLYP
ROLEO
ROLES
ROLEX
ROLFE
ROLLE
ROLLO
ROLLS
SOLAN
SOLAR
SOLDI
SOLDO
SOLED
SOLER
SOLES
SOLFA
SOLID
SOLON
SOLOS
SOLTI
SOLUM
SOLUS
SOLVE
TOLER
TOLET
TOLLS
TOLLY
VOLAR
VOLAT
VOLES
VOLGA
VOLTA
VOLTE
VOLTS
VOLVA
VOLVO
WOLDS
WOLFE
WOLFF
YOLKS
YOLKY

•O•L•

BOGLE
BOILS
BOLLS
BOOLA
BOOLE
BOULE
BOULT
BOWLS
BOYLE
COALS
COILS
COOLS
COULD
COWLS
COYLY
DOBLA
DOBLE
DOILY
DOLLS
DOLLY
DOYLE
DOYLY
FOALS
FOILS
FOLLY
FOOLS
FORLI
FOULS
FOWLS
FOYLE
GOALS
GODLY
GOLLY
GOULD
HOLLY
HOTLY
HOWLS
HOYLE
JOLLA
JOLLY
JOULE
JOWLS
JOWLY
KOALA
LOLLS
LOLLY
LOWLY
MOILS
MOLLS
MOLLY
MOOLA
MOULD
MOULT
NOBLE
NOBLY
NOELS
NOFLY
NOILS
NOILY
NOLLE
OOOLA
POILS
POILU
POLLO
POLLS
POLLY
POOLE
POOLS
POULT
ROALD
ROBLE
ROILS
ROILY
ROLLE
ROLLO
ROLLS
ROTLS
SOCLE
SOILS
SOULS
SOULT
TOILE
TOILS
TOLLS
TOLLY
TOOLS
VOILA
VOILE
WOOLF
WOOLS
WOOLY
WORLD
WOULD
YOULL
YOWLS

•O••L

BOTEL
COBOL
COPAL
CORAL
COXAL
DORAL
DOTAL
DOWEL
FOCAL
GOBEL
GODEL
GOGOL
GOMEL
GORAL
HORAL
HOROL
HOSEL
HOTEL
HOVEL
JOREL
JOUAL
LOCAL
LOYAL
MOBIL
MODAL
MODEL
MOGUL
MONEL
MORAL
MOREL
MOSUL
MOTEL
NOBEL
NOCAL
NODAL
NOPAL
NOVEL
ROWEL
ROYAL
SOREL
SOTOL
TOBOL
TONAL
TOPOL
TOTAL
TOWEL
VOCAL
VOWEL
YODEL
YOKEL
YOULL
ZOEAL
ZONAL
ZORIL

••OL•

ADOLF
AIOLI
AMOLE
ANOLE
ATOLL
AWOLS
BOOLA
BOOLE
CHOLO
COOLS
CROLY
DHOLE
DROLL
EBOLI
ECOLE
ECOLI
ENOLA
ENOLS
FOOLS
GAOLS
HAOLE
IDOLS
KNOLL
MOOLA
NDOLA
OBOLI
OBOLS
OOOLA
OVOLI
OVOLO
PAOLI
PAOLO
POOLE
POOLS
PROLE
SCOLD
SMOLT
STOLA
STOLE
STOLS
SZOLD
THOLE
TOOLS
TROLL
UBOLT
UPOLU
VIOLA
VIOLS
VTOLS
WHOLE
WHOLL
WOOLF
WOOLS
WOOLY

••O•L

ABOIL
AFOFL
AFOUL
ATOLL
BROIL
CEORL
DROLL
DROOL
GHOUL
GROWL
KNOLL
PROWL
RAOUL
REOIL
SCOWL
SEOUL
SHOAL
SKOAL
SPOIL
SPOOL
STOOL
TROLL
WHOLL
WHORL

•••OL

ALDOL
ALGOL
ARGOL
ATHOL
CAROL
COBOL
DROOL
ENROL
ERROL
EXTOL
GOGOL
HOROL
KAROL
LTCOL
LYSOL
NEROL
NICOL
PAROL
SOTOL
SPOOL
STOOL
THEOL
TOBOL
TOPOL
TYROL

OM•••

OMAHA
OMANI
OMARR
OMASA
OMBER
OMBRE
OMEGA
OMENS
OMERS
OMITS
OMNIA

O•M••

OLMEC
OLMOS
OOMPH
OSMAN
OSMIC

O••M•

ORAMA
OROMO
OTOMI

O•••M

OAKUM
OCCAM
ODEUM
ODIUM
OGHAM
OLEUM
ONEAM
ONEPM
OPIUM

•OM••

BOMBE
BOMBS
COMAE
COMAS
COMBE
COMBO
COMBS
COMER
COMES
COMET
COMEX
COMFY
COMIC
COMIX
COMMA
COMME
COMPO
COMPS
COMTE
COMUS
DOMED
DOMES
GOMEL
GOMER
GOMEZ
HOMED
HOMEO
HOMER
HOMES
HOMEY
HOMME
LOMAN
LOMAX
MOMMA
MOMMY
MOMUS
NOMAD
NOMEN
OOMPH
POMES
POMME
POMOS
ROMAN
ROMEO
ROMER
ROMPS
SOMAS
SOMME
SOMNI
TOMEI
TOMES
TOMMY
WOMAN
WOMEN
WOMYN

•O•M•

BOHME
BOOMS
BOOMY
COMMA
COMME
CORMS
COSMO
DOGMA
DOLMA
DOOMS
DORMS
FOAMS
FOAMY
FORMA
FORMS
GORME
HOLMS
HOMME
HOUMA
LOAMS
LOAMY
LOOMS
MOMMA
MOMMY
NORMA
NORMS
NOTME
POEME
POEMS
POMME
ROAMS
ROOMS
ROOMY
SOMME
TOMMY
TORME
WORMS
WORMY
ZOOMS

•O••M

BOEHM
BOSOM
COLUM
FORUM
GOLEM
HOHUM
HOKUM
JORUM
LOCUM
MODEM
MOHAM
MORUM
ROREM
SODOM
SOLUM
TOTEM
YOKUM

••OM•

ABOMB
ACOMA
ANOMY
AROMA
ATOMS
ATOMY
BIOME
BOOMS
BOOMY
BROME
BROMO
CHOMP
CLOMP
CUOMO
DOOMS
DROME
DUOMO
FROME
FROMM
GLOMS
GNOME
HBOMB
LOOMS
MBOMU
NAOMI
OROMO
OTOMI
PROMO
PROMS
RHOMB
ROOMS
ROOMY
SLOMO
STOMA
STOMP
SUOMI
TROMP
WHOMP
ZOOMS

••O•M

ABOHM
BLOOM
BROOM
ENORM
FROMM
GLOAM
GLOOM
GROOM
PROAM
PROEM
STORM
TWOAM
TWOPM
VROOM

•••OM

AXIOM
BESOM
BLOOM
BOSOM
BROOM
CAROM
CDROM
CHROM
DENOM
ENTOM
EPROM
EPSOM
GLOOM
GROOM
IDIOM
MRMOM
PHNOM
SODOM
STROM
VENOM
VROOM

ON•••

ONAIR
ONATE
ONCLE
ONCUE
ONDIT
ONEAL
ONEAM
ONEGA
ONEIL
ONEND
ONEPM
ONERS
ONEUP
ONICE
ONION
ONKEY
ONLAY
ONLOW
ONOFF
ONSET
ONTAP
ONTOP

O•N••

OINGO
OINKS
OMNIA
ORNIS
OUNCE
OWNED
OWNER
OWNUP

O••N•

ODONT
OKING
OLAND
OMANI
OMENS
ONEND
OPENS
OPINE
ORANG
ORANT
ORING
ORONO
OVENS
OVINE
OWENS
OWING
OZONE

O•••N

OAKEN
OATEN
OBGYN
OCEAN
OFTEN
OGDEN
OLDEN
OLEAN
OLEIN
OLSEN
OLSON
ONION
OPSIN
ORGAN
ORION
ORLON
ORRIN
ORSON
ORTON
OSCAN
OSLIN
OSMAN

•ON••

BONCE
BONDI
BONDS
BONED
BONER
BONES
BONET
BONGO
BONGS
BONKS
BONNE
BONNY
BONUS
BONZE
BONZO
CONAN
CONCH
CONDE
CONDO
CONES
CONEY
CONGA
CONGE
CONGO
CONIC
CONKS
CONTD
CONTE
CONTI
CONTR
CONUS
DONAS
DONAT
DONAU
DONDI
DONEE
DONEN
DONGS
DONHO
DONNA
DONNE
DONNY
DONOR
DONUT
FONDA
FONDS
FONDU
FONTS
GONDI
GONDS
GONER
GONGS
GONNA
GONZO
HONAN
HONDA
HONDO
HONED
HONES
HONEY
HONGS
HONKS
HONOR
HONUS
IONIA
IONIC
JONAH
JONAS
JONES
LONER
LONGA
LONGE
LONGI
LONGO
LONGS
LONGU
MONAD
MONCK
MONDE
MONDO
MONEL
MONET
MONEY
MONGO
MONKS
MONOD
MONTE
MONTH
MONTY
MONZA
NONCE
NONES
NONET
NONOS
PONCA
PONCE
PONCH
PONDS
PONES
PONGS
PONTE
PONTI
PONTS
PONZI
RONDO
RONEE
RONNY
SONAR
SONDE
SONES
SONGS
SONIA
SONIC
SONJA
SONNY
SONYA
TONAL
TONDI
TONDO
TONED
TONER
TONES
TONEY
TONGA
TONGS
TONIC
TONIO
TONKA
TONNE
TONTO
TONUS
TONYA
TONYS
WONKS
WONKY
WONTS
ZONAL
ZONED
ZONES
ZONKS

•O•N•

BOING
BONNE
BONNY
BOONE
BOONS
BORNE
BOSNS
BOUND
BOYNE
COINS
COONS
CORNO
CORNS
CORNU
CORNY
COUNT
DOING
DONNA
DONNE
DONNY
DOONE
DOWNS
DOWNY
FOHNS
FOINS
FOUND
FOUNT
GOING
GONNA
GOONS
GOONY
GOWNS
HORNE
HORNS
HOSNI
HOUND
JOHNS
JOINS
JOINT
KOANS
KOINE
KOING
KOVNO
LOANS
LOINS
LOONS
LOONY
LORNA
LORNE
MOANS
MOONS
MOONY
MORNS
MOUND
MOUNT
NOEND
NOONE
NOONS
NORNS
NOUNS
POINT
POONA
POONS
POUND
ROANS
RONNY
ROONE
ROUND
ROVNO
SOMNI
SONNY
SOONG
SOUND
TONNE
TOONS
TOWNE
TOWNS
TOWNY
WOUND
YOUNG
YOUNT
ZOONS

•O••N

BORON
BOSON
BOURN
BOWEN
BOXIN
COHAN
COHEN
COIGN
COLIN
COLON
CONAN
COPAN
COVEN
COZEN
DOGON
DONEN
DORAN
DOREN
DOYEN
DOZEN
EOSIN
FOEHN
FOGIN
GOLAN
GOREN
GOTIN
GOTON
HOBAN
HOGAN
HONAN
HOPIN
IOWAN
KORAN
LODEN
LOGAN
LOGIN
LOGON
LOMAN
LORAN
LOREN
MORAN
MORON
MOURN
NOLAN
NOMEN
NOTIN
NOWIN
POPIN
ROBIN
RODAN
RODIN
ROMAN
ROSEN
ROSIN
ROUEN
ROWAN
ROWEN
SOLAN
SOLON
SOREN
TOEIN
TOKEN
TOXIN
TOYON
WODEN
WOKEN
WOMAN
WOMEN
WOMYN
WOTAN
WOVEN

••ON•

AEONS
AGONY
ALONE
ALONG
AMONG
ASONE
ATONE
ATONY
AXONE
AXONS
BIONT
BLOND
BOONE
BOONS
BRONC
BRONX
BUONO
CHONG
CLONE
CLONK
COONS
CRONE
CRONY
DIONE
DOONE
DRONE
EBOND
EBONS
EBONY
ETONS
EXONS
FIONA
FROND
FRONT
GOONS
GOONY
HMONG
ICONO
ICONS
ILONA
INONU
IRONS
IRONY
KAONS
KRONA
KRONE
LEONA
LEONE
LEONI
LIONS
LOONS
LOONY
LYONS
MOONS
MOONY
MUONS
NEONS
NOONE
NOONS
ODONT
ORONO
OZONE
PEONS
PEONY
PHONE
PHONO
PHONS
PHONY
PIONS
PLONK
POONA
POONS
PRONE
PRONG
RHONE
ROONE
SAONE
SCONE
SHONE
SOONG
STONE
STONY
SWONK
TBOND
TBONE
THONG
TOONS
WRONG
ZOONS

••O•N

ACORN
ADORN
BJORN
BLOWN
BROUN
BROWN
CLOWN
CROON
CROWN
DROWN
FLOWN
FROWN
GROAN
GROIN
GROWN
KNOWN
QUOIN
SCORN
SHORN
SHOWN
SLOAN
SPOON
SWOON
SWORN
THORN

•••ON

AARON
ACTON
ADDON
AERON
AFTON
AGNON
AGRON
AKRON
ALTON
AMMON
ANCON
ANION
ANSON
ANTON
APRON
ARGON
ARION
ARSON
ASTON
ATHON
ATION
AVION
AXION
BACON
BARON
BATON
BETON
BIDON
BIGON
BISON
BORON
BOSON
BYRON
CANON
CAPON
CARON
CHRON
CLEON
COLON
CREON
CROON
DAGON
DAMON
DEION
DELON
DEMON
DEVON
DIJON
DIXON
DOGON
EAMON
EATON
EGGON
ELION
ELTON
ENDON
EPSON
EXXON
FANON
FARON
FEDON
FELON
FREON
FUTON
GABON
GETON
GIJON
GLUON
GOTON
GYRON
HADON
HALON
HASON
HERON
HITON
HURON
HYSON
ILION
INION
IXION
JASON
LADON
LAYON
LEDON
LEMON
LETON
LEVON
LIMON
LITON
LOGON
LUZON
LYMON
MACON
MAHON
MANON
MASON
MAYON
MELON
MESON
MORON
MYRON
NIKON
NINON
NIXON
NYLON
OLSON
ONION
ORION
ORLON
ORSON
ORTON
PAEON
PATON
PERON
PINON
PITON
PLEON
PRION

PUTON PYLON RACON RADON RAMON RANON RATON RAYON RECON REDON REWON RIPON RUNON SALON SATON SAXON SCHON SCION SETON SEWON SIDON SIMON SITON SOLON SPOON SPYON SWOON TALON TAUON TAXON TENON TETON TIMON TOYON TRYON TYSON UNION UPTON WAGON XENON YUKON ZEVON

OO•••

OOHED OOMPH OOOLA OOTID OOZED OOZES

O•O••

OBOES OBOLI OBOLS ODONT ODORS ODOUR OLOGY ONOFF OOOLA OROMO ORONO OTOES OTOMI OVOID OVOLI OVOLO OZONE

O••O•

OCHOA OHBOY OHGOD OHWOW OLEOS OLIOS OLMOS OLSON ONION ONLOW ONTOP ORDOS OREOS ORION ORLON ORLOP ORSON ORTON ORZOS OUZOS OXBOW

O•••O

OCULO OINGO OLIGO ORFEO OROMO ORONO ORTHO ORURO OSSEO OSTEO OUTDO OUTGO OVOLO

•OO••

BOOBS BOOBY BOOED BOOER BOOKS BOOLA BOOLE BOOMS BOOMY BOONE BOONS BOORS BOOST BOOTH BOOTS BOOTY BOOZE COOED COOEE COOER COOKE COOKS COOKY COOLS COONS COOPS COOPT COORS COOSA COOTS DOODY DOOMS DOONE DOORS DOOZY FOODS FOOLS FOOTE FOOTS GOODS GOODY GOOEY GOOFF GOOFS GOOFY GOONS GOONY GOOPS GOOPY GOOSE GOOSY GOOUT HOOCH HOODS HOOEY HOOFS HOOHA HOOKE HOOKS HOOKY HOOPS HOOTS KOOKS KOOKY LOOBY LOOFA LOOKS LOOMS LOONS LOONY LOOPS LOOPY LOOSE LOOTS MOOCH MOODS MOODY MOOED MOOGS MOOLA MOONS MOONY MOORE MOORS MOORY MOOSE MOOTS NOOKS NOONE NOONS NOOSE OOOLA POOCH POODS POOHS POOLE POOLS POONA POONS POOPS ROODS ROOFS ROOKS ROOKY ROOMS ROOMY ROONE ROOST ROOTS ROOTY SOOEY SOONG SOOTH SOOTS SOOTY TOOLS TOONS TOOTH TOOTS WOODS WOODY WOOED WOOER WOOFS WOOLF WOOLS WOOLY WOOZY ZOOEY ZOOID ZOOMS ZOONS

•O•O•

BOGOR BOLOS BORON BOSOM BOSON BOSOX BOYOS BOZOS COBOL COCOA COCOS COHOS COLON COLOR COROT DODOS DOGON DOJOS DOLOR DONOR FODOR GODOT GOFOR GOGOL GOGOS GOTON HOBOS HOHOS HONOR HOROL KOBOS KOTOS LOBOS LOCOS LOGON LOGOS MODOC MOJOS MONOD MORON MOROS MOTOR NODOZ NOGOS NOHOW NONOS POBOX POBOY POLOS POMOS POPOV POTOK ROBOT ROTOR ROTOS SODOM SOLON SOLOS SOPOR SOTOL TOBOL TODOS TOPOG TOPOI TOPOL TOPOS TOROS TOYON YOKOI YOYOS

•O••O

BOFFO BOITO BONGO BONZO BOSCO COMBO COMPO CONDO CONGO CORNO COSMO DOBRO DOGGO DONHO DORSO DOTTO DOURO FOLIO FORDO FORGO GONZO GORDO GOTTO HOMEO HONDO HOWSO HOWTO JOCKO KOVNO LONGO LOTTO MOFFO MOKPO MOLTO MONDO MONGO MORRO MOSSO MOTTO NORVO NOTSO POLLO PORTO POTTO ROCCO RODEO ROLEO ROLLO ROMEO RONDO ROVNO ROYKO SOCIO SOCKO SOHIO SOLDO SORGO SOTHO SOTTO TOKYO TONDO TONIO TONTO TORSO VOLVO YOBBO ZORRO

••OO•

AFOOT ALOOF BLOOD BLOOM BLOOP BROOD BROOK BROOM CROOK CROON DROOD DROOL DROOP FLOOD FLOOR GLOOM GROOM PROOF SCOOP SCOOT SHOOK SHOOS SHOOT SLOOP SMOOT SNOOD SNOOK SNOOP SNOOT SPOOF SPOOK SPOOL SPOON SPOOR STOOD STOOK STOOL STOOP SWOON SWOOP TROOP VROOM WHOOF WHOOP

••O•O

ABOVO AGOGO AMOCO BIOKO BROMO BUONO CHOLO CUOMO DUOMO FRODO ICONO KYOTO OROMO ORONO OVOLO PAOLO PHONO PHOTO PROMO PROTO PROVO RHODO SLOMO THORO TROPO WHOSO

•••OO

ACHOO ARTOO DETOO ESPOO IGLOO KAZOO MAGOO MCCOO METOO TABOO WAHOO YAHOO YAZOO

OP•••

OPAHS OPALS OPART OPCIT OPEDS OPELS OPENS OPERA OPERE OPHIR OPINE OPIUM OPRAH OPSIN OPSIS OPTED OPTIC

O••P•

OKAPI ONEPM OOMPH

O•••P

ONEUP ONTAP ONTOP ORLOP OWNUP OXLIP

•OP••

COPAL COPAN COPAY COPED COPES COPRA COPSE COPTS DOPED DOPES DOPEY HOPED HOPER HOPES HOPIN HOPIS HOPPE HOPUP KOPEK KOPHS KOPJE LOPAT LOPED LOPER LOPES LOPEZ LOPPY MOPED MOPER MOPES MOPEY MOPSY MOPUP NOPAL NOPAR POPES POPIN POPOV POPPA POPPY POPUP QOPHS ROPED ROPER ROPES ROPEY SOPHS SOPHY SOPOR SOPPY SOPUP TOPAZ TOPED TOPER TOPES TOPIC TOPIS TOPOG TOPOI TOPOL TOPOS TOPPS TOPSY

•O•P•

COAPT COMPO COMPS COOPS COOPT CORPS COUPE COUPS COYPU DOLPH DORPS GOAPE GOOPS GOOPY GORPS HOOPS HOPPE LOOPS LOOPY LOPPY LOUPE MOKPO MORPH OOMPH POOPS POPPA POPPY ROMPS SOAPS SOAPY SOPPY SOUPS SOUPY TOPPS

•O••P

BOBUP BOXUP FOGUP GOTUP HOPUP JOSIP MOPUP NOTUP POLYP POPUP SOPUP TOTUP

••OP•

ADOPT CHOPS CLOPS COOPS COOPT CROPS DROPS ELOPE FLOPS GLOPS GOOPS GOOPY GROPE HOOPS KNOPF KNOPS LOOPS LOOPY MYOPE PLOPS POOPS PROPS SCOPE SCOPS SCOPY SHOPS SLOPE SLOPS STOPE STOPS SWOPE SWOPS TROPE TROPO TWOPM WHOPS

••O•P

BLOOP CHOMP CLOMP CROUP DROOP GROUP SCOOP SLOOP SNOOP STOMP STOOP STOUP SWOOP THORP TROMP TROOP WHOMP WHOOP

•••OP

AESOP ALSOP BEBOP BLOOP DROOP ESTOP FSTOP GALOP ONTOP ORLOP REMOP RETOP SCOOP SLOOP SNOOP STOOP STROP SWOOP SYSOP TROOP WHOOP ZZTOP

•OQ••

ROQUE TOQUE

OR•••

ORACH ORACY ORALE ORALS ORAMA ORANG ORANT ORATE ORBIT ORCAS ORCHS ORCUS ORCZY ORDER ORDOS OREAD OREOS ORFEO ORGAN ORIBI ORIEL ORING ORION ORIYA ORLES ORLON ORLOP ORNIS OROMO ORONO ORRIN ORRIS ORSER ORSON ORTHO ORTON ORURO ORZOS

O•R••

OARED OCREA OGRES OKRAS OPRAH ORRIN ORRIS OSRIC

O••R•

OCHRE ODORS OHARA OHARE OMARR OMBRE OMERS ONERS OPART OPERA OPERE ORURO OTARU OTARY OUTRE OVERS OVERT OWERS OZARK

O•••R

OATER OCCUR OCHER ODDER ODOUR OFFER OGLER OHAIR OILER OLDER OMARR OMBER ONAIR OPHIR ORDER ORSER OSCAR OSIER OSKAR OSLER OTHER OTTER OUTER OWNER

•OR••

AORTA BORAH BORAS BORAX BORED BORER BORES BORGE BORIC BORIS BORNE BORON CORAL CORBY CORDS COREA CORED CORER CORES COREY CORFU CORGI CORIA CORKS CORKY CORMS CORNO CORNS CORNU CORNY COROT CORPS DORAG DORAL DORAN DOREN DORIC DORIS DORMS DORPS DORSA DORSI DORSO FORAY FORBS FORCE FORDO FORDS FORES FORGE FORGO FORKS FORKY FORLI FORMA FORMS FORTE FORTH FORTS FORTY FORUM GORAL GORDO GORDY GORED GOREN GORES GORGE GORKI GORKY GORME GORPS GORSE GORSY HORAE HORAL HORAS HORDE HOREB HORNE HORNS HOROL HORSE HORST HORSY HORUS JOREL JORGE JORUM KORAN KORDA KOREA LORAN LORAX LORCA LORDS LOREN LORES LORIS LORNA LORNE LORRE LORRY MORAE MORAL MORAN MORAS MORAY MOREL MORES MOREY MORNS MORON MOROS MORPH MORRO MORSE MORTS MORUM NORAD NORAH NORGE NORIA NORMA NORMS NORNS NORSE NORTE NORTH NORVO PORCH PORED PORES PORGY PORKS PORKY PORTE PORTO PORTS ROREM SORAS SORBS SOREL SOREN SORER SORES SORGO SORRY SORTA SORTS SORUS TORAH TORCH TORIC TORII TORME TOROS TORRE TORRS TORSI TORSO TORTE TORTS TORUS WORDS WORDY WORKS WORLD WORMS WORMY WORRY WORSE WORST WORTH WORTS YORBA ZORBA ZORIL ZORIS ZORRO

•O•R•

BOARD BOARS BOERS BOORS BOURG BOURN COBRA COIRS COORS COPRA COURT COWRY DOBRA DOBRO DOERS DOORS DOURO DOWRY FOURH FOURS GOERS GOURD HOARD HOARS HOARY HOERS HOURI HOURS LOIRE LORRE LORRY LOWRY MOIRA MOIRE MOORE MOORS MOORY MORRO MOURN NOIRE NOTRE POURS ROARS SOARS SORRY SOURS TORRE TORRS TOURS VOTRE WORRY YOURE YOURS ZORRO

•O••R

BOGOR BONER BOOER BORER BOWER BOXER BOYAR BOYER CODER COEUR COLOR COMER CONTR COOER CORER COVER COWER COYER DOLOR DONOR DOSER DOTER DOVER DOWER DOZER FODOR FOYER GOFAR GOFER GOFOR GOMER GONER GOWER HOMER HONOR HOPER HOVER HOWAR JOKER LONER LOPER LOSER LOVER LOWER MOHUR MOLAR MOPER MOTOR MOVER MOWER NOPAR NOSIR NOTER POKER POLAR POLER POSER POWER ROGER ROMER ROPER ROTOR ROVER ROWER SOBER SOEUR SOFAR SOLAR SOLER SONAR SOPOR SORER SOWER SOXER TOLER TONER TOPER TOTER TOWER VOLAR VOTER VOWER WOOER ZOHAR

••OR•

ABORT ACORN ADORE ADORN AFORE AGORA AHORA ALORS AMORE AMORT AMORY APORT BJORN BOORS CEORL CHORD CHORE COORS DOORS EMORY ENORM EVORA FIORD FJORD FLORA FLORY GEORG GLORY INORG IVORY KNORR LEORA MAORI MOORE MOORS MOORY ODORS SCORE SCORN SHORE SHORN SHORT SKORT SNORE SNORT SPORE SPORK SPORT STORE STORK STORM STORY SWORD SWORE SWORN THORN THORO THORP WHORL

••O•R

AMOUR AROAR AVOIR BOOER CHOIR COOER FLOOR FLOUR HHOUR KNORR ODOUR SCOUR SHOER SPOOR WOOER

•••OR

ABHOR ACTOR ALCOR ANDOR ARBOR ARDOR ARMOR ASTOR BATOR BOGOR CHLOR COLOR CUKOR DECOR DOLOR DONOR ENDOR ENSOR EPHOR ERROR FAVOR FETOR FLOOR FLUOR FODOR FUROR GABOR GATOR GOFOR HONOR HUMOR ICHOR JUROR LABOR LUXOR MAJOR MANOR MAYOR MINOR MOTOR PRIOR PRYOR RAZOR RIGOR ROTOR RUMOR SAPOR SAVOR SENOR SOPOR SPOOR TABOR TENOR TIMOR TUDOR TUTOR VALOR VAPOR VIDOR VIGOR VISOR ZUKOR

OS•••

OSAGE OSAKA OSCAN OSCAR OSHEA OSIER OSKAR OSLER OSLIN OSMAN OSMIC OSRIC OSSEO OSSIA OSSIE OSTEO OSTIA

O•S••

OASES OASIS OASTS OLSEN OLSON ONSET OPSIN OPSIS ORSER ORSON OSSEO OSSIA OSSIE OUSEL OUSTS

O••S•

OBESE ODIST OFUSE OMASA

O•••S

OAKES OASES OASIS OASTS OATES OATHS OBEYS OBIES OBOES OBOLS OCCAS ODETS ODORS OGEES OGLES OGRES OICKS OINKS OKAYS OKIES OKRAS

OLEOS OLIOS OLLAS OLMOS OMENS OMERS OMITS ONERS OOZES OPAHS OPALS OPEDS OPELS OPENS OPSIS ORALS ORCAS ORCHS ORCUS ORDOS OREOS ORLES ORNIS ORRIS ORZOS OTOES OUSTS OUZOS OVALS OVENS OVERS OWENS OWERS

•OS••

BOSCH BOSCO BOSCS BOSKS BOSKY BOSNS BOSOM BOSON BOSOX BOSSA BOSSY COSBY COSEC COSMO COSTA COSTS DOSED DOSER DOSES EOSIN FOSSA FOSSE GOSEE GOSSE HOSEA HOSED HOSEL HOSES HOSNI HOSTA HOSTS JOSEF JOSIP LOSER LOSES LOSSY MOSBY MOSES MOSEY MOSHE MOSSO MOSSY MOSUL NOSCE NOSED NOSES NOSEY NOSIR POSED POSER POSES POSIT POSSE POSTE POSTS ROSEN ROSES ROSEY ROSIE ROSIN ROSSI TOSCA

•O•S•

BOAST BOISE BOOST BOSSA BOSSY BOUSE COAST COOSA COPSE COUSY DOEST DORSA DORSI DORSO DOUSE DOWSE FOIST FOSSA FOSSE GOEST GOOSE GOOSY GORSE GORSY GOSSE HOIST HOLST HORSE HORST HORSY HOUSE HOWSO JOIST JOUST LOESS LOOSE LOSSY LOUSE LOUSY MOIST MOOSE MOPSY MORSE MOSSO MOSSY MOUSE MOUSY NOISE NOISY NOOSE NORSE NOTSO POESY POISE POSSE POTSY ROAST ROOST ROSSI ROUSE ROUST SOUSA SOUSE TOAST TOPSY TORSI TORSO WORSE WORST YOUSE

•O••S

BOARS BOATS BODES BOERS BOFFS BOGGS BOGUS BOILS BOLAS BOLES BOLLS BOLOS BOLTS BOLUS BOMBS BONDS BONES BONGS BONKS BONUS BOOBS BOOKS BOOMS BOONS BOORS BOOTS BORAS BORES BORIS BOSCS BOSKS BOSNS BOUTS BOWES BOWLS BOXES BOYOS BOZOS COALS COATS COCKS COCOS CODAS CODES COEDS COHOS COIFS COILS COINS COIRS COKES COLAS COLDS COLES COLTS COMAS COMBS COMES COMPS COMUS CONES CONKS CONUS COOKS COOLS COONS COOPS COORS COOTS COPES COPTS CORDS CORES CORKS CORMS CORNS CORPS COSTS COTES COUPS COVES COWES COWLS COXES COZES DOCKS DODOS DOERS DOFFS DOGES DOITS DOJOS DOLES DOLLS DOLTS DOMES DONAS DONGS DOOMS DOORS DOPES DORIS DORMS DORPS DOSES DOTES DOVES DOWNS DOZES EOLUS FOALS FOAMS FOCUS FOHNS FOILS FOINS FOLDS FOLKS FONDS FONTS FOODS FOOLS FOOTS FORBS FORDS FORES FORKS FORMS FORTS FOULS FOURS FOUTS FOWLS FOXES GOADS GOALS GOATS GOERS GOGOS GOLDS GOLFS GONDS GONGS GOODS GOOFS GOONS GOOPS GORES GORPS GOTHS GOWKS GOWNS HOARS HOBBS HOBOS HOCKS HOCUS HOERS HOGGS HOHOS HOKES HOLDS HOLES HOLMS HOMES HONES HONGS HONKS HONUS HOODS HOOFS HOOKS HOOPS HOOTS HOPES HOPIS HORAS HORNS HORUS HOSES HOSTS HOURS HOWLS HOYAS IOTAS JOCKS JOEYS JOHNS JOINS JOKES JOLTS JONAS JONES JOTAS JOWLS KOANS KOBOS KOLAS KOOKS KOPHS KOTOS LOADS LOAFS LOAMS LOANS LOBES LOBOS LOCHS LOCKS LOCOS LOCUS LODES LOESS LOFTS LOGES LOGOS LOINS LOLLS LONGS LOOKS LOOMS LOONS LOOPS LOOTS LOPES LORDS LORES LORIS LOSES LOTAS LOTUS LOUIS LOUTS LOVES LOWES LOXES MOANS MOATS MOCKS MODES MODUS MOILS MOJOS MOLAS MOLDS MOLES MOLLS MOLTS MOMUS MONKS MOODS MOOGS MOONS MOORS MOOTS MOPES MORAS MORES MORNS MOROS MORTS MOSES MOTES MOTHS MOTTS MOUES MOVES NOAHS NOBIS NOCKS NODES NODUS NOELS NOGOS NOILS NONES NONOS NOOKS NOONS NORMS NORNS NOSES NOTES NOUNS NOVAS NOYES OOZES POCUS POEMS POETS POILS POKES POLES POLIS POLLS POLOS POMES POMOS PONDS PONES PONGS PONTS POODS POOHS POOLS POONS POOPS POPES PORES PORKS PORTS POSES POSTS POTTS POUFS POURS POUTS POWYS QOPHS ROADS ROAMS ROANS ROARS ROBES ROCKS ROILS ROLES ROLLS ROMPS ROODS ROOFS ROOKS ROOMS ROOTS ROPES ROSES ROTAS ROTES ROTLS ROTOS ROUES ROUTS ROVES SOAKS SOAPS SOARS SOCKS SODAS SOFAS SOILS SOKES SOLES SOLOS SOLUS SOMAS SONES SONGS SOOTS SOPHS SORAS SORBS SORES SORTS SORUS SOUKS SOULS SOUPS SOURS SOYAS TOADS TOBES TODOS TOFFS TOFTS TOGAS TOILS TOLLS TOMES TONES TONGS TONUS TONYS TOOLS TOONS TOOTS TOPES TOPIS TOPOS TOPPS TOROS TORRS TORTS TORUS TOTES TOTIS TOURS TOUTS TOVES TOWNS VOIDS VOLES VOLTS VOTES WOADS WOLDS WONKS WONTS WOODS WOOFS WOOLS WORDS WORKS WORMS WORTS YODHS YOGAS YOGHS YOGIS YOKES YOLKS YOURS YOWLS YOYOS ZOEAS ZONES ZONKS ZOOMS ZOONS ZORIS ZOUKS

••OS•

AROSE BOOST CHOSE CLOSE COOSA CROSS DROSS EROSE FLOSS FROSH FROST GHOST GLOSS GOOSE GOOSY GROSS GROSZ ICOSA ICOSI KIOSK LOOSE MOOSE NOOSE PROSE PROST PROSY ROOST SKOSH SLOSH SPOSA STOSS THOSE WHOSE WHOSO XHOSA

••O•S

AEONS AHOYS ALOES ALORS ANOAS ATOMS AVOWS AWOLS AXONS BBOYS BIOGS BLOBS BLOCS BLOIS BLOTS BLOWS BOOBS BOOKS BOOMS BOONS BOORS BOOTS BROWS BUOYS CHOPS CHOWS CLODS CLOGS CLOPS CLOTS CLOYS COOKS COOLS COONS COOPS COORS COOTS CROCS CROPS CROSS CROWS DHOWS DOOMS DOORS DROPS DROSS EBONS ENOLS ETONS EWOKS EXONS EYOTS FLOES FLOGS FLOPS FLOSS FLOWS FOODS FOOLS FOOTS FROES FROGS FROWS GAOLS GLOBS GLOMS GLOPS GLOSS GLOWS GOODS GOOFS GOONS GOOPS GROGS GROKS GROSS GROTS GROWS HOODS HOOFS HOOKS HOOPS HOOTS ICONS IDOLS IRONS KAONS KNOBS KNOPS KNOTS KNOWS KOOKS LIONS LOOKS LOOMS LOONS LOOPS LOOTS LYONS MEOWS MOODS MOOGS MOONS MOORS MOOTS MUONS NEONS NOOKS NOONS OBOES OBOLS ODORS OTOES PEONS PHONS PHOTS PIONS PIOUS PLODS PLOPS PLOTS PLOWS PLOYS POODS POOHS POOLS POONS POOPS PROAS PROBS PRODS PROFS PROGS PROMS PROPS PROTS PROWS PSOAS QUODS RIOTS ROODS ROOFS ROOKS ROOMS ROOTS RYOTS SCOPS SCOTS SCOWS SHOES SHOOS SHOPS SHOTS SHOWS SLOBS SLOES SLOGS SLOPS SLOTS SLOWS SMOGS SNOBS SNOGS SNOWS SOOTS SPOTS STOAS STOLS STOPS STOSS STOTS STOWS SWOBS SWOPS THOUS TOOLS TOONS TOOTS TROIS TROTS VIOLS VTOLS WHOPS WOODS WOOFS WOOLS ZOOMS ZOONS

•••OS

ADIOS AEROS AFROS AGIOS ALIOS ALTOS AMBOS AMMOS APSOS ARGOS ATHOS ATMOS ATNOS AUTOS BIGOS BOLOS BOYOS BOZOS CAMOS CAPOS CEROS CHAOS CHIOS CLIOS COCOS COHOS DADOS DAVOS DELOS DEMOS DIDOS DODOS DOJOS DUBOS DUROS ELMOS ETHOS EUROS EXPOS FADOS FAROS FUROS GATOS GIROS GOGOS GYROS HALOS HELOS HEROS HOBOS HOHOS HUGOS HYPOS JATOS KAYOS KENOS KILOS KOBOS KOTOS KUDOS LAGOS LEGOS LENOS LIDOS LIMOS LINOS LOBOS LOCOS LOGOS MAKOS MANOS MELOS MEMOS MILOS MINOS MISOS MOJOS MOROS MSDOS NAXOS NEPOS NINOS NOGOS NONOS OLEOS OLIOS OLMOS ORDOS OREOS ORZOS OUZOS PALOS PAROS PECOS PEPOS PESOS POLOS POMOS RAMOS REPOS ROTOS SAGOS SAMOS SAROS SEGOS SHOOS SILOS SOLOS TACOS TALOS TELOS TIROS TODOS TOPOS TOROS TRIOS TYPOS TYROS UMBOS UPDOS VAMOS VINOS YOYOS YUGOS ZEROS

OT•••

OTARU OTARY OTHER OTOES OTOMI OTTER OTWAY

O•T••

OATEN OATER OATES OATHS OCTAD OCTAL OCTET OFTEN ONTAP ONTOP OOTID OPTED OPTIC ORTHO ORTON OSTEO OSTIA OTTER OUTDO OUTED OUTER OUTGO OUTRE

O••T•

OASTS ODETS OMITS ONATE ORATE OUSTS OVATE OVETA OVETT

O•••T

OBJET OCTET ODIST ODONT ONDIT ONSET OPART OPCIT ORANT ORBIT OUGHT OVERT OVETT OWLET

•OT••

BOTCH BOTEL BOTHA BOTHE COTES COTTA DOTAL DOTED DOTER DOTES DOTTO DOTTY GOTAT GOTBY GOTHA GOTHS GOTIN GOTIT GOTON GOTTA GOTTO GOTUP HOTEL HOTLY IOTAS JOTAS KOTCH KOTOS LOTAH LOTAS LOTTA LOTTE LOTTO LOTUS MOTEL MOTES MOTET MOTHS MOTHY MOTIF MOTOR MOTTA MOTTO MOTTS NOTCH NOTED NOTER NOTES NOTIN NOTIT NOTME NOTRE NOTSO NOTUP OOTID POTOK POTSY POTTO POTTS POTTY ROTAS ROTES ROTLS ROTOR ROTOS SOTHO SOTOL SOTTO TOTAL TOTED TOTEM TOTER TOTES TOTIE TOTIS TOTUP VOTED VOTER VOTES VOTRE WOTAN

•O•T•

AORTA BOATS BOITE BOITO BOLTS BOOTH BOOTS BOOTY BOUTS COATI COATS COLTS COMTE CONTD CONTE CONTI CONTR COOTS COPTS COSTA COSTS COTTA COUTH DOETH DOITS DOLTS DOTTO DOTTY FONTS FOOTE FOOTS FORTE FORTH FORTS FORTY FOUTS FOXTV GOATS GOTTA GOTTO GOUTY HOITY HOLTZ HOOTS HOSTA HOSTS HOWTO JOLTS JOLTY LOATH LOFTS LOFTY LOOTS LOTTA LOTTE LOTTO LOUTS MOATS MOLTO MOLTS MONTE MONTH MONTY MOOTS MORTS MOTTA MOTTO MOTTS MOUTH NOCTI NOLTE NORTE NORTH POETE POETS PONTE PONTI PONTS PORTE PORTO PORTS POSTE POSTS POTTO POTTS POTTY POUTS POUTY ROOTS ROOTY ROUTE ROUTS SOFTC SOFTG SOFTY SOLTI SOOTH SOOTS SOOTY SORTA SORTS SOTTO SOUTH TOFTS TOITY TONTO TOOTH TOOTS TORTE TORTS TOUTE TOUTS VOLTA VOLTE VOLTS WONTS WORTH WORTS YOUTH

•O••T

BOAST BONET BOOST BOULT COACT COAPT COAST COLET COMET COOPT COROT COUNT COURT COVET DOEST DOGIT DONAT DONUT DOUBT FOIST FOUNT GODET GODOT GOEST GOOUT GOTAT GOTIT HOIST HOLST HORST JOINT JOIST JOUST LOFAT LOPAT MOIST MONET MOTET MOULT MOUNT NOFAT NOHIT NONET NOTIT POINT POLIT POSIT POULT ROAST ROBOT ROGET ROOST ROUST SOULT TOAST TOBIT TOLET TOWIT VOLAT WORST YOUNT

••OT•

AZOTE AZOTH BIOTA BLOTS BOOTH BOOTS BOOTY BROTH CLOTH CLOTS CNOTE COOTS DHOTE DHOTI EMOTE EYOTS FOOTE FOOTS FROTH GROTS HOOTS KNOTS KYOTO LOOTS MOOTS PHOTO PHOTS PLOTS PROTO PROTS QUOTA QUOTE QUOTH RIOTS ROOTS ROOTY RYOTS SCOTS SCOTT SHOTS SLOTH SLOTS SMOTE SOOTH SOOTS SOOTY SPOTS

STOTS
THOTH
TNOTE
TOOTH
TOOTS
TROTH
TROTS
WROTE
WROTH
ZLOTY

••O•T
ABORT
ABOUT
ADOPT
ADOUT
AFOOT
ALOFT
AMORT
APORT
BIONT
BLOAT
BOOST
CLOUT
COOPT
CROAT
CROFT
DROIT
EBOAT
FLOAT
FLOUT
FRONT
FROST
GHOST
GLOAT
GOOUT
GROAT
GROUT
KNOUT
ODONT
PROST
QUOIT
ROOST
SCOOT
SCOTT
SCOUT
SHOAT
SHOOT
SHORT
SHOUT
SKORT
SMOLT
SMOOT
SNOOT
SNORT
SNOUT
SPORT
SPOUT
STOAT
STOUT
TROUT
UBOAT
UBOLT
XDOUT
XSOUT

•••OT
ABBOT
AFOOT
ALLOT
ARGOT
ASCOT
BEGOT
BESOT
BIGOT
CABOT
COROT
CSPOT
DEPOT
DICOT
DIVOT
ELIOT
EPCOT
ERGOT
FAGOT
GAVOT
GEMOT
GIGOT
GODOT
GRIOT
GUYOT
HELOT
IDIOT
IFNOT
INGOT
JABOT
MAGOT
MINOT
NILOT
PEROT
PICOT
PILOT
PINOT
PITOT
PIVOT
REPOT
ROBOT
SABOT
SCOOT
SHOOT
SMOOT
SNOOT
TAROT

OU•••
OUGHT
OUIDA
OUIJA
OUNCE
OUSEL
OUSTS
OUTDO
OUTED
OUTER
OUTGO
OUTRE
OUZEL
OUZOS

O•U••
OCULO
OFUSE
ORURO
OVULE

O••U•
OAKUM
OCCUR
ODEUM
ODIUM
ODOUR
OLEUM
ONCUE
ONEUP
OPIUM
ORCUS
OWNUP

O•••U
OTARU

•OU••
BOUGH
BOULE
BOULT
BOUND
BOURG
BOURN
BOUSE
BOUTS
COUCH
COUGH
COULD
COUNT
COUPE
COUPS
COURT
COUSY
COUTH
DOUAI
DOUAY
DOUBT
DOUGH
DOURO
DOUSE
FOULS
FOUND
FOUNT
FOURH
FOURS
FOUTS
GOUDA
GOUDY
GOUGE
GOULD
GOURD
GOUTY
HOUGH
HOUMA
HOUND
HOURI
HOURS
HOUSE
JOUAL
JOULE
JOUST
LOUGH
LOUIE
LOUIS
LOUPE
LOUSE
LOUSY
LOUTS
MOUES
MOULD
MOULT
MOUND
MOUNT
MOURN
MOUSE
MOUSY
MOUTH
NOUNS
POUCH
POUFS
POULT
POUND
POURS
POUTS
POUTY
ROUEN
ROUES
ROUGE
ROUGH
ROUND
ROUSE
ROUST
ROUTE
ROUTS
SOUGH
SOUKS
SOULS
SOULT
SOUND
SOUPS
SOUPY
SOURS
SOUSA
SOUSE
SOUTH
TOUCH
TOUGH
TOURS
TOUTE
TOUTS
VOUCH
WOULD
WOUND
YOULL
YOUNG
YOUNT
YOURE
YOURS
YOUSE
YOUTH
YOUVE
ZOUKS

•O•U•
BOBUP
BOEUF
BOGUS
BOLUS
BONUS
BOXUP
COEUR
COLUM
COMUS
CONUS
DONUT
EOLUS
FOCUS
FOGUP
FORUM
GOOUT
GOTUP
HOCUS
HOHUM
HOKUM
HONUS
HOPUP
HORUS
JORUM
LOCUM
LOCUS
LOGUE
LOTUS
MODUS
MOGUL
MOHUR
MOMUS
MOPUP
MORUM
MOSUL
NODUS
NOTUP
POCUS
POPUP
ROGUE
ROQUE
SOEUR
SOLUM
SOLUS
SOPUP
SORUS
SOYUZ
TONUS
TOQUE
TORUS
TOTUP
VOGUE
YOKUM

•O••U
CORFU
CORNU
COYPU
DONAU
FONDU
LONGU
POILU

••OU•
ABOUT
ADOUT
AFOUL
ALOUD
AMOUR
ANOUK
BROUN
CLOUD
CLOUT
CROUP
FLOUR
FLOUT
GHOUL
GOOUT
GROUP
GROUT
HHOUR
KNOUT
ODOUR
PIOUS
PROUD
RAOUL
SCOUR
SCOUT
SEOUL
SHOUT
SIOUX
SNOUT
SPOUT
STOUP
STOUT
THOUS
TROUT
XDOUT
XSOUT

••O•U
INONU
MBOMU
SHOYU
UPOLU

•••OU
AEIOU
ANJOU
BAYOU
BIJOU
GAROU

OV•••
OVALS
OVATE
OVENS
OVERS
OVERT
OVETA
OVETT
OVINE
OVOID
OVOLI
OVOLO
OVULE

O•V••
OYVAY

O••V•
OGIVE
OLIVE

•OV••
BOVID
COVEN
COVER
COVES
COVET
COVEY
DOVER
DOVES
DOVEY
FOVEA
HOVEL
HOVER
HOVEY
KOVNO
LOVED
LOVER
LOVES
LOVEY
MOVED
MOVER
MOVES
MOVIE
NOVAE
NOVAK
NOVAS
NOVEL
ROVED
ROVER
ROVES
ROVNO
TOVES
WOVEN

•O•V•
NORVO
SOAVE
SOLVE
VOLVA
VOLVO
YOUVE

•O••V
FOXTV
POPOV

••OV•
ABOVE
ABOVO
CLOVE
DROVE
GLOVE
GROVE
PROVE
PROVO
SHOVE
STOVE
TROVE

•••OV
BASOV
KIROV
LTGOV
POPOV
YAKOV

OW•••
OWENS
OWERS
OWING
OWLET
OWNED
OWNER
OWNUP

O•W••
OHWOW
OTWAY

O••W•
OZAWA

O•••W
OHWOW
ONLOW
OXBOW

•OW••
BOWED
BOWEN
BOWER
BOWES
BOWIE
BOWLS
COWED
COWER
COWES
COWLS
COWRY
DOWDY
DOWEL
DOWER
DOWNS
DOWNY
DOWRY
DOWSE
FOWLS
GOWDY
GOWER
GOWKS
GOWNS
HOWAR
HOWDY
HOWIE
HOWLS
HOWSO
HOWTO
IOWAN
JOWLS
JOWLY
LOWED
LOWER
LOWES
LOWLY
LOWRY
MOWED
MOWER
NOWAY
NOWIN
POWAY
POWER
POWYS
ROWAN
ROWDY
ROWED
ROWEL
ROWEN
ROWER
SOWED
SOWER
TOWED
TOWEL
TOWER
TOWIT
TOWNE
TOWNS
TOWNY
VOWED
VOWEL
VOWER
WOWED
YOWLS
ZOWIE

•O•W•
LOEWE
LOEWY

•O••W
NOHOW

••OW•
AVOWS
BLOWN
BLOWS
BLOWY
BROWN
BROWS
CHOWS
CLOWN
CROWD
CROWN
CROWS
DHOWS
DROWN
FLOWN
FLOWS
FROWN
FROWS
GLOWS
GROWL
GROWN
GROWS
KIOWA
KNOWN
KNOWS
MEOWS
PLOWS
PROWL
PROWS
SCOWL
SCOWS
SHOWN
SHOWS
SHOWY
SLOWS
SNOWS
SNOWY
STOWE
STOWS

•••OW
AGLOW
ALLOW
ARROW
BELOW
BULOW
BYNOW
ELBOW
ENDOW
GAMOW
INTOW
MIAOW
NOHOW
OHWOW
ONLOW
OXBOW
REMOW
RETOW
SEROW
SYDOW
THROW
TUROW
UPBOW
WIDOW
YALOW

OX•••
OXBOW
OXEYE
OXIDE
OXLIP

•OX••
BOXED
BOXER
BOXES
BOXIN
BOXUP
COXAE
COXAL
COXED
COXES
COXEY
FOXED
FOXES
FOXTV
HOXIE
LOXES
MOXIE
ROXIE
SOXER
TOXIC
TOXIN

•O••X
BORAX
BOSOX
CODEX
COMEX
COMIX
LOMAX
LORAX
POBOX
ROLEX

••OX•
DEOXY
EPOXY
PROXY

••O•X
BRONX
CROIX
SIOUX

•••OX
BOSOX
INBOX
LENOX
PHLOX
POBOX
REDOX
UNBOX
XEROX

OY•••
OYVAY

O••Y•
OBEYS
OBGYN
OKAYS
ORIYA
OXEYE

O•••Y
ODDLY
OHBOY
OHKAY
OLOGY
ONKEY
ONLAY
ORACY
ORCZY
OTARY
OTWAY
OYVAY

•OY••
BOYAR
BOYER
BOYLE
BOYNE
BOYOS
COYER
COYLY
COYPU
DOYEN
DOYLE
DOYLY
FOYER
FOYLE
HOYAS
HOYLE
JOYCE
LOYAL
NOYES
ROYAL
ROYCE
ROYKO
SOYAS
SOYUZ
TOYED
TOYON
YOYOS

•O•Y•
JOEYS
POLYP
POWYS
SONYA
TOKYO
TONYA
TONYS
WOMYN

•O••Y
AOKAY
BOBBY
BOGEY
BOGGY
BONNY
BOOBY
BOOMY
BOOTY
BOSKY
BOSSY
COCKY
COLBY
COMFY
CONEY
COOKY
COPAY
CORBY
COREY
CORKY
CORNY
COSBY
COUSY
COVEY
COWRY
COXEY
COYLY
DOBBY
DODGY
DOGEY
DOGGY
DOILY
DOLBY
DOLLY
DONNY
DOODY
DOOZY
DOPEY
DOTTY
DOUAY
DOVEY
DOWDY
DOWNY
DOWRY
DOYLY
FOAMY
FOGEY
FOGGY
FOLEY
FOLKY
FOLLY
FORAY
FORKY
FORTY
GODEY
GODLY
GOLLY
GOODY
GOOEY
GOOFY
GOONY
GOOPY
GOOSY
GORDY
GORKY
GORSY
GOTBY
GOUDY
GOUTY
GOWDY
HOAGY
HOARY
HOBBY
HOITY
HOKEY
HOLEY
HOLLY
HOMEY
HONEY
HOOEY
HOOKY
HORSY
HOTLY
HOVEY
HOWDY
JOKEY
JOLLY
JOLTY
JOWLY
KOOKY
LOAMY
LOBBY
LOEWY
LOFTY
LOLLY
LOOBY
LOONY
LOOPY
LOPPY
LORRY
LOSSY
LOUSY
LOVEY
LOWLY
LOWRY
MOGGY
MOLDY
MOLLY
MOMMY
MONEY
MONTY
MOODY
MOONY
MOORY
MOPEY
MOPSY
MORAY
MOREY
MOSBY
MOSEY
MOSSY
MOTHY
MOUSY
NOBBY
NOBLY
NODDY
NOFLY
NOILY
NOISY
NOSEY
NOWAY
POBOY
PODGY
POESY
POKEY
POLLY
POPPY
PORGY
PORKY
POTSY
POTTY
POUTY
POWAY
ROBBY
ROCKY
RODDY
ROILY
RONNY
ROOKY
ROOMY
ROOTY
ROPEY
ROSEY
ROWDY
SOAPY
SODDY
SOFTY
SOGGY
SONNY
SOOEY
SOOTY
SOPHY
SOPPY
SORRY
SOUPY
TOADY
TOBEY
TODAY
TODDY
TOFFY
TOITY
TOKAY
TOLLY
TOMMY
TONEY
TOPSY
TOWNY
WONKY
WOODY
WOOLY
WOOZY
WORDY
WORMY
WORRY
YOLKY
ZOOEY

••OY•
AHOYS
BBOYS
BUOYS
CLOYS
FLOYD
LLOYD
PLOYS
SHOYU
SLOYD

••O•Y
AGONY
AMORY
ANOMY
ATOMY
ATONY
BLOWY
BOOBY
BOOMY
BOOTY
BRODY
CHOKY
COOKY
CROLY
CRONY
DEOXY
DOODY
DOOZY
EBONY
EMORY
EPOXY
FLORY
GLORY
GOODY
GOOEY
GOOFY
GOONY
GOOPY
GOOSY
GRODY
HOOEY
HOOKY
IRONY
IVORY
KOOKY
LOOBY
LOONY
LOOPY
MOODY
MOONY
MOORY
OLOGY
PEONY
PHONY
PROSY
PROXY
ROOKY
ROOMY
ROOTY
SCOPY
SHOWY
SMOKY
SNOWY
SOOEY
SOOTY
STOGY
STONY
STORY
WOODY
WOOLY
WOOZY
ZLOTY
ZOOEY

•••OY
ALLOY
AMBOY
ANNOY
DECOY
ELROY
ENJOY
ENVOY
LEROY
MCCOY
NIMOY
OHBOY
POBOY
SAVOY
SEPOY

OZ•••
OZARK
OZAWA
OZONE
OZZIE

O•Z••
OOZED
OOZES
ORZOS
OUZEL
OUZOS
OZZIE

O••Z•
ORCZY

•OZ••
BOZOS
COZEN
COZES
DOZED
DOZEN
DOZER
DOZES
OOZED
OOZES

•O•Z•
BONZE
BONZO
BOOZE
DOOZY
GONZO
MONZA
PONZI
WOOZY

•O••Z
GOMEZ
HOLTZ
LOPEZ
NODOZ
SOYUZ
TOPAZ

••OZ•
BOOZE
CROZE
DOOZY
FROZE
GLOZE
GROZA
WOOZY

••O•Z
GROSZ

•••OZ
ARROZ
NODOZ

PA•••
PAAVO
PABLO
PABST
PACAS
PACED
PACER
PACES
PACKS
PACTS
PADDY
PADRE
PADUA
PAEAN
PAEON
PAGAN
PAGED
PAGER
PAGES
PAGET
PAIGE
PAILS
PAINE
PAINS
PAINT
PAIRS
PAISA
PALAE
PALAU
PALEA
PALED
PALEO
PALER
PALES
PALEY
PALIN
PALLS
PALLY
PALMA
PALME
PALMS
PALMY
PALOS
PALPI
PALPS
PALSY
PAMBY
PAMIR
PAMPA
PANAM
PANAY
PANDA
PANDL
PANED
PANEL
PANES
PANGA
PANGS
PANIC
PANKY
PANNE
PANSY
PANTO
PANTS
PANZA
PAOLI
PAOLO
PAPAL
PAPAS
PAPAW
PAPER
PAPPI
PAPPY
PAPUA
PARCA
PARCH
PARDI
PARDO
PARDS
PARED
PAREE
PAREN
PARER
PARES
PAREU
PARIS
PARKA
PARKS
PARLE
PARMA
PAROL
PAROS
PARRY
PARSE
PARTE
PARTI
PARTS
PARTY
PARVO
PASCH
PASCO
PASEO
PASES
PASHA
PASSE
PASSU
PASSY
PASTA
PASTE
PASTO
PASTS
PASTY
PATCH
PATED
PATEK
PATEN
PATER
PATES
PATHE
PATHO
PATHS
PATHY
PATIO
PATLY
PATNA
PATON
PATRI
PATSY
PATTI
PATTY
PAULA
PAULO
PAUSE
PAVED
PAVER
PAVES
PAVIA
PAVID
PAVIS
PAWAT
PAWED
PAWER
PAWKY
PAWLS
PAWNS
PAYED
PAYEE
PAYER
PAYIN
PAYNE
PAYTV
PAYUP

P•A••
PAAVO
PEABO
PEACE
PEACH
PEAKS
PEALE
PEALS
PEARL
PEARS
PEARY
PEASE
PEATS
PEATY
PEAVY
PHAGE
PHAGO
PHAGY
PHANY
PHARM
PHASE
PIANO
PIAUI
PLACE
PLAGE
PLAID
PLAIN
PLAIT
PLANB
PLANE
PLANI
PLANK
PLANO
PLANS
PLANT
PLASH
PLASM
PLATA
PLATE
PLATH
PLATO
PLATS
PLATT
PLATY
PLAYA
PLAYS
PLAZA
POACH
PRADO
PRAIA
PRAMS
PRANG
PRANK
PRASE
PRATE
PRATO
PRATT
PRAUS
PRAWN
PRAYS
PSALM
PSATS

P••A•
PACAS
PAEAN
PAGAN
PALAE
PALAU
PANAM
PANAY
PAPAL
PAPAS
PAPAW
PAWAT
PECAN
PEDAL
PENAL
PERAN
PETAL
PHIAL
PICAS
PIKAS
PILAF
PILAR
PIMAS
PIPAL
PISAN
PITAS
PLEAD
PLEAS
PLEAT
POHAI
POLAR
POWAY
PRIAM
PROAM
PROAS

PSHAW
PSOAS
PTRAP
PULAS
PUMAS
PUNAS
PUPAE
PUPAL
PUPAS
PUSAN

P•••A
PADUA
PAISA
PALEA
PALMA
PAMPA
PANDA
PANGA
PANZA
PAPUA
PARCA
PARKA
PARMA
PASHA
PASTA
PATNA
PAULA
PAVIA
PELLA
PEMBA
PENNA
PENTA
PENZA
PEPLA
PETRA
PHYLA
PIETA
PILEA
PINNA
PINTA
PINZA
PIPPA
PITTA
PIURA
PIZZA
PLATA
PLAYA
PLAZA
PLENA
PLICA
PODIA
POLKA
PONCA
POONA
POPPA
PRAIA
PRIMA
PUKKA
PUNTA

•PA••
APACE
APART
EPACT
IPANA
IPASS
OPAHS
OPALS
OPART
SPAAK
SPACE
SPACY
SPADE
SPADS
SPAHI
SPAHN
SPAIN
SPAKE
SPALL
SPAMS
SPANG
SPANK
SPANS
SPARE
SPARK
SPARS
SPASM
SPATE
SPATS
SPAWN
SPAYS

•P•A•
APEAK
APIAN
APPAL
EPHAH
EPHAS
OPRAH
SPAAK
SPEAK
SPEAR
SPLAT
SPLAY
SPRAG
SPRAT
SPRAY

•P••A
APNEA
IPANA
OPERA
SPICA
SPOSA

••PA•
AMPAS
APPAL
ARPAD
ATPAR
COPAL
COPAN
COPAY
JAPAN
LAPAZ
LOPAT
NEPAL
NIPAS
NIPAT
NOPAL
NOPAR
PAPAL
PAPAS
PAPAW
PIPAL
PUPAE
PUPAL
PUPAS
REPAD
REPAY
SEPAL
STPAT
TAPAS
TEPAL
TOPAZ

••P•A
ALPHA
ASPCA
CAPRA
COPRA
CUPPA
HEPTA
HYPHA
KAPPA
LEPTA
PAPUA
PEPLA
PIPPA
POPPA
SEPIA
SEPTA
SUPRA
TYPEA
ZAPPA

•••PA
AMAPA
CULPA
CUPPA
KAPPA
KRUPA
MILPA
NAMPA
PAMPA
PIPPA
POPPA
SALPA
SCAPA
STUPA
TAMPA
YAMPA
ZAPPA

P•B••
PABLO
PABST
POBOX
POBOY

P••B•
PAMBY
PEABO
PEMBA
PHOBE
PLEBE
PLEBS
PROBE
PROBS
PUTBY

P•••B
PLANB
PLUMB

•PB••
UPBOW

••P•B
TYPEB

P•C••
PACAS
PACED
PACER
PACES
PACKS
PACTS
PECAN
PECKS
PECKY
PECOS
PICAS
PICKS
PICKY
PICOT
PICRO
PICTS
PICUL
POCUS
PUCCI
PUCKS

P••C•
PARCA
PARCH
PASCH
PASCO
PATCH
PEACE
PEACH
PENCE
PERCE
PERCH
PERCY
PESCI
PHYCO
PIECE
PINCE
PINCH
PISCI
PISCO
PITCH
PLACE
PLICA
PLUCK
POACH
PONCA
PONCE
PONCH
POOCH
PORCH
POUCH
PRICE
PRICK
PRICY
PRYCE
PSYCH
PUCCI
PUNCH

P•••C
PANIC
PUNIC
PYRIC

•PC••
EPCOT
OPCIT

•P•C•
APACE
EPACT
EPICS
EPOCH
SPACE
SPACY
SPECD
SPECK
SPECS
SPICA
SPICE
SPICY
SPOCK

•P••C
EPISC
OPTIC

••PC•
ASPCA

••P•C
ASPIC
TOPIC

P•D••
PADDY
PADRE
PADUA
PEDAL
PEDRO
PODGY
PODIA
PUDGY
PUDUS

P••D•
PADDY
PANDA
PANDL
PARDI
PARDO
PARDS
PENDS
PERDU
PIEDS
PLODS
PONDS
POODS
PRADO
PRIDE
PRODS
PRUDE

P•••D
PACED
PAGED
PALED
PANED
PARED
PATED
PAVED
PAVID
PAWED
PAYED
PIKED
PILED
PINED
PIPED
PLAID
PLEAD
PLIED
POKED
POLED
PORED
POSED
POUND
PRIED
PROUD
PSEUD
PULED

•PD••
UPDOS

•P•D•
EPODE
OPEDS
SPADE
SPADS
SPODE
SPUDS

•P••D
APHID
APPTD
APTED
EPHOD
OPTED
SPECD
SPEED
SPEND
SPIED
UPEND
UPPED

••P•D
AMPED
APPTD
ARPAD
BIPED
BIPOD
CAPED
COPED
CUPID
DOPED
DUPED
GAPED
HOPED
HYPED
IMPED
JAPED
LIPID
LOPED
MOPED
PIPED
RAPID
REPAD
ROPED
SAPID
TAPED
TEPID
TOPED
TYPED
UMPED
UPPED
VAPID
WIPED

•••PD
RSVPD

PE•••
PEABO
PEACE
PEACH
PEAKS
PEALE
PEALS
PEARL
PEARS
PEARY
PEASE
PEATS
PEATY
PEAVY
PECAN
PECKS
PECKY
PECOS
PEDAL
PEDRO
PEEKS
PEELE
PEELS
PEENS
PEEPS
PEERS
PEETE
PEEVE
PEGGY
PEKES
PEKIN
PEKOE
PELEE
PELEG
PELLA
PELLE
PELTS
PEMBA
PENAL
PENCE
PENDS
PENGO
PENNA
PENNE
PENNI
PENNY
PENTA
PENTE
PENZA
PEONS
PEONY
PEPIN
PEPLA
PEPOS
PEPPY
PEPSI
PEPUP
PEPYS
PERAN
PERCE
PERCH
PERCY
PERDU
PERES
PEREZ
PERIL
PERIS
PERKS
PERKY
PERLE
PERMS
PERON
PEROT
PERPS
PERRY
PERSE
PERTH
PESCI
PESKY
PESOS
PESTO
PESTS
PETAL
PETER
PETES
PETIT
PETRA
PETRI
PETRO
PETTI
PETTY
PEWEE
PEWIT

P•E••
PAEAN
PAEON
PEEKS
PEELE
PEELS
PEENS
PEEPS
PEERS
PEETE
PEEVE
PHENO
PIECE
PIEDS
PIERS
PIETA
PIETY
PLEAD
PLEAS
PLEAT
PLEBE
PLEBS
PLEIO
PLENA
PLEON
PLEWS
POEME
POEMS
POESY
POETE
POETS
PREEN
PREGO
PRELL
PREPS
PRESS
PREST
PREXY
PREYS
PSEUD
PTERO

P••E•
PACED
PACER
PACES
PAGED
PAGER
PAGES
PAGET
PALEA
PALED
PALEO
PALER
PALES
PALEY
PANED
PANEL
PANES
PAPER
PARED
PAREE
PAREN
PARER
PARES
PAREU
PASEO
PASES
PATED
PATEK
PATEN
PATER
PATES
PAVED
PAVER
PAVES
PAWED
PAWER
PAYED
PAYEE
PAYER
PEKES
PELEE
PELEG
PERES
PEREZ
PETER
PETES
PEWEE
PHREN
PIKED
PIKER
PIKES
PILEA
PILED
PILEI
PILES
PINED
PINES
PINEY
PIPED
PIPER
PIPES
PIXEL
PLIED
PLIES
POKED
POKER
POKES
POKEY
POLED
POLER
POLES
POMES
PONES
POPES
PORED
PORES
POSED
POSER
POSES
POWER
PREEN
PRIED
PRIER
PRIES
PROEM
PUGET
PULED
PULES
PUREE
PURER
PUREX
PUSEY
PYRES
PYREX

P•••E
PADRE
PAIGE
PAINE
PALAE
PALME
PANNE
PAREE
PARLE
PARSE
PARTE
PASSE
PASTE
PATHE
PAUSE
PAYEE
PAYNE
PEACE
PEALE
PEASE
PEELE
PEETE
PEEVE
PEKOE
PELEE
PELLE
PENCE
PENNE
PENTE
PERCE
PERLE
PERSE
PEWEE
PHAGE
PHASE
PHILE
PHOBE
PHONE
PHYFE
PHYLE
PIECE
PINCE
PIQUE
PISTE
PIXIE
PLACE
PLAGE
PLANE
PLATE
PLEBE
PLUME
POEME
POETE
POISE
POMME
PONCE
PONTE
POOLE
PORTE
POSSE
POSTE
PRASE
PRATE
PRICE
PRIDE
PRIME
PRIZE
PROBE
PROLE
PRONE
PROSE
PROVE
PRUDE
PRUNE
PRYCE
PULSE
PUPAE
PUREE
PURGE
PURSE
PYXIE

•PE••
APEAK
APERS
APERY
EPEES
OPEDS
OPELS
OPENS
OPERA
OPERE
SPEAK
SPEAR
SPECD
SPECK
SPECS
SPEED
SPEKE
SPELL
SPELT
SPEND
SPENT
SPERO
SPETS
SPEWS
UPEND

•P•E•
APFEL
APLEY
APNEA
APPEL
APRES
APSES
APTED
APTER
EPEES
OPTED
SPEED
SPIED
SPIEL
SPIES
SPREE
UPPED
UPPER
UPSET
YPRES

•P••E
APACE
APPLE
APURE
EPODE
OPERE
OPINE
SPACE
SPADE
SPAKE
SPARE
SPATE
SPEKE
SPICE
SPIKE
SPILE
SPINE
SPIRE
SPITE
SPODE
SPOKE
SPORE
SPREE
SPRUE
SPUME

••PE•
AMPED
APPEL
ARPEL
ASPEN
BIPED
CAPED
CAPEK
CAPER
CAPES
CAPET
CEPES
COPED
COPES
CUPEL
DEPEW
DOPED
DOPES
DOPEY
DUPED
DUPES
EXPEL
GAPED
GAPER
GAPES
HOPED
HOPER
HOPES
HYPED
HYPER
HYPES
IMPED
IMPEI
IMPEL
JAPED
JAPES
KOPEK
LAPEL
LOPED
LOPER
LOPES
LOPEZ
MOPED
MOPER
MOPES
MOPEY
NAPES
PAPER
PIPED
PIPER
PIPES
POPES
RAPEE
REPEG
REPEL
RIPEN
RIPER
ROPED
ROPER
ROPES
ROPEY
RUPEE
SUPER
SUPES
TAPED
TAPER
TAPES
TEPEE
TOPED
TOPER
TOPES
TYPEA
TYPEB
TYPED
TYPEE
TYPER
TYPES
TYPEY
UMPED
UNPEG
UNPEN
UPPED
UPPER
VIPER
WIPED
WIPER
WIPES
YIPES

••P•E
AMPLE
APPLE
COPSE
DUPLE
DUPRE
HOPPE
KOPJE
LAPSE
MAPLE
NAPPE
PUPAE
RAPEE
RAPHE
RUPEE
TEPEE
TYPEE

•••PE
AGAPE
CALPE
CARPE
COUPE
CRAPE
CREPE
DRAPE
DRUPE
ELOPE
ETAPE
GASPE
GOAPE
GRAPE
GRIPE
GROPE
HOPPE
LOUPE
MYOPE
NAPPE
SCAPE
SCOPE
SHAPE
SLOPE
SLYPE
SNIPE
STIPE
STOPE
STUPE
SWIPE
SWOPE
TAUPE
TEMPE
TRIPE
TROPE

P•F••
PUFFS
PUFFY

P••F•
PHYFE
POUFS
PROFS
PUFFS
PUFFY

P•••F
PILAF
PROOF

•PF••
APFEL

•P•F•
SPIFF

•P••F
SPIFF
SPOOF

•••PF
KNOPF

P•G••
PAGAN
PAGED
PAGER
PAGES
PAGET
PEGGY
PIGGY
PUGET
PUGGY
PYGMY

P••G•
PAIGE
PANGA
PANGS
PEGGY
PENGO
PHAGE
PHAGO
PHAGY
PIGGY
PINGO
PINGS
PLAGE
PLUGS
PODGY
PONGS
PORGY
PREGO
PRIGS
PROGS
PUDGY
PUGGY
PUNGS
PURGE

P•••G
PELEG
PRANG
PRONG

•P••G
APING
SPANG
SPRAG
SPRIG

••P•G
REPEG
TOPOG
UNPEG

PH•••
PHAGE
PHAGO
PHAGY
PHANY
PHARM
PHASE
PHENO
PHIAL
PHILE
PHILO
PHILY
PHLOX
PHNOM
PHOBE
PHONE
PHONO
PHONS
PHONY
PHOTO
PHOTS
PHREN
PHYCO
PHYFE
PHYLA
PHYLE
PHYLL
PHYSI
PHYTO

P•H••
POHAI
PSHAW

P••H•
PASHA
PATHE
PATHO
PATHS
PATHY
PITHS
PITHY
POOHS
PUSHY

P•••H
PARCH
PASCH
PATCH
PEACH
PERCH
PERTH
PINCH
PITCH
PLASH
PLATH
PLUSH
POACH
PONCH
POOCH
PORCH
POUCH
PSYCH
PUNCH

•PH••
APHID
APHIS
EPHAH
EPHAS
EPHOD
EPHOR
OPHIR

•P•H•
OPAHS
SPAHI
SPAHN

•P••H
APISH
EPHAH
EPOCH
OPRAH

••PH•
ALPHA
AMPHI
AMPHR
HYPHA
KAPHS
KOPHS
QOPHS
RAPHE
SOPHS
SOPHY

••P•H
DEPTH

•••PH
ALEPH
DOLPH
GLYPH
GRAPH
HUMPH
LYMPH
MORPH
NYMPH
OOMPH
RALPH
SYLPH

PI•••
PIANO
PIAUI
PICAS
PICKS
PICKY
PICOT
PICRO
PICTS
PICUL
PIECE
PIEDS
PIERS
PIETA
PIETY
PIGGY
PIKAS
PIKED
PIKER
PIKES
PILAF
PILAR
PILEA
PILED
PILEI
PILES
PILLS
PILOT
PILUM
PILUS
PIMAS
PINCE
PINCH
PINED
PINES
PINEY
PINGO
PINGS
PINKS
PINKY
PINNA
PINON
PINOT
PINSK
PINTA
PINTO
PINTS
PINUP
PINZA
PIONS
PIOUS
PIPAL
PIPED
PIPER
PIPES
PIPIT
PIPPA
PIPPI
PIQUE
PISAN
PISCI
PISCO
PISMO
PISTE
PITAS
PITCH
PITHS
PITHY
PITON
PITOT
PITTA
PITTS
PIURA
PIVOT
PIXEL
PIXIE
PIZZA

P•I••
PAIGE
PAILS
PAINE
PAINS
PAINT
PAIRS
PAISA
PHIAL
PHILE
PHILO
PHILY
PLICA
PLIED
PLIES
PLINK
PLINY
POILS
POILU
POINT
POISE
PRIAM
PRICE
PRICK
PRICY
PRIDE
PRIED
PRIER
PRIES
PRIGS
PRIMA
PRIME
PRIMI
PRIMO
PRIMP
PRIMS
PRINK
PRINT
PRION
PRIOR
PRISM
PRIVY
PRIZE
PRIZM

P••I•
PALIN
PAMIR
PANIC
PARIS
PATIO
PAVIA
PAVID
PAVIS
PAYIN
PEKIN
PEPIN
PERIL
PERIS
PETIT
PEWIT
PIPIT
PIXIE
PLAID
PLAIN
PLAIT
PLEIO
PODIA
POLIS
POLIT
POPIN
POSIT
PRAIA
PULIS
PUNIC
PUPIL
PUPIN
PURIM
PUTIN
PYRIC
PYXIE
PYXIS

P•••I
PALPI
PAOLI
PAPPI
PARDI
PARTI
PATRI
PATTI
PENNI
PEPSI
PESCI
PETRI
PETTI
PHYSI
PIAUI
PILEI
PIPPI
PISCI
PLANI
POHAI
PONTI
PONZI
PRIMI
PUCCI

PUTTI

•PI••
APIAN APING APISH EPICS EPISC OPINE OPIUM SPICA SPICE SPICY SPIED SPIEL SPIES SPIFF SPIKE SPIKY SPILE SPILL SPILT SPINE SPINS SPINY SPIRE SPIRO SPIRY SPITE SPITS SPITZ SPIVS

•P•I•
APHID APHIS APRIL APSIS OPCIT OPHIR OPSIN OPSIS OPTIC SPAIN SPLIT SPOIL SPRIG SPRIT

•P••I
SPAHI SPYRI

••PI•
ASPIC CUPID HOPIN HOPIS KEPIS LAPIN LAPIS LIPID LUPIN PEPIN PIPIT POPIN PUPIL PUPIN RAPID REPIN SAPID SAPIR SEPIA TAPIN TAPIR TEPID TIPIN TOPIC TOPIS UNPIN VAPID YUPIK

••P•I
AMPHI CAPRI CUPRI IMPEI LIPPI PAPPI PEPSI PIPPI TIPPI TOPOI

•••PI
CARPI LIPPI OKAPI PALPI PAPPI PIPPI SIEPI TEMPI TIPPI

••PJ•
KOPJE

P•K••
PEKES PEKIN PEKOE PIKAS PIKED PIKER PIKES POKED POKER POKES POKEY PUKKA

P••K•
PACKS PANKY PARKA PARKS PAWKY PEAKS PECKS PECKY PEEKS PERKS PERKY PESKY PICKS PICKY PINKS PINKY POLKA PORKS PORKY PUCKS PUKKA PUNKS PUNKY

P•••K
PATEK PINSK PLANK PLINK PLONK PLUCK PLUNK POTOK PRANK PRICK PRINK

•P•K•
SPAKE SPEKE SPIKE SPIKY SPOKE

•P••K
APEAK SPAAK SPANK SPARK SPEAK SPECK SPOCK SPOOK SPORK SPUNK

••P•K
CAPEK KAPOK KOPEK YAPOK YUPIK

PL•••
PLACE PLAGE PLAID PLAIN PLAIT PLANB PLANE PLANI PLANK PLANO PLANS PLANT PLASH PLASM PLATA PLATE PLATH PLATO PLATS PLATT PLATY PLAYA PLAYS PLAZA PLEAD PLEAS PLEAT PLEBE PLEBS PLEIO PLENA PLEON PLEWS PLICA PLIED PLIES PLINK PLINY PLODS PLONK PLOPS PLOTS PLOWS PLOYS PLUCK PLUGS PLUMB PLUME PLUMP PLUMS PLUMY PLUNK PLUSH PLUTO

P•L••
PALAE PALAU PALEA PALED PALEO PALER PALES PALEY PALIN PALLS PALLY PALMA PALME PALMS PALMY PALOS PALPI PALPS PALSY PELEE PELEG PELLA PELLE PELTS PHLOX PILAF PILAR PILEA PILED PILEI PILES PILLS PILOT PILUM PILUS POLAR POLED POLER POLES POLIS POLIT POLKA POLLO POLLS POLLY POLOS POLYP PULAS PULED PULES PULIS PULLS PULPS PULPY PULSE PYLON

P••L•
PABLO PAILS PALLS PALLY PAOLI PAOLO PARLE PATLY PAULA PAULO PAWLS PEALE PEALS PEELE PEELS PELLA PELLE PEPLA PERLE PHILE PHILO PHILY PHYLA PHYLE PHYLL PILLS POILS POILU POLLO POLLS POLLY POOLE POOLS POULT PRELL PROLE PSALM PULLS PURLS

P•••L
PANDL PANEL PAPAL PAROL PEARL PEDAL PENAL PERIL PETAL PHIAL PHYLL PICUL PIPAL PIXEL PRELL PROWL PUPAL PUPIL

•PL••
APLEY APLUS BPLUS CPLUS DPLUS SPLAT SPLAY SPLIT

•P•L•
APPLE APPLY APTLY OPALS OPELS SPALL SPELL SPELT SPILE SPILL SPILT UPOLU

•P••L
APFEL APPAL APPEL APRIL SPALL SPELL SPIEL SPILL SPOIL SPOOL

••PL•
AMPLE AMPLY APPLE APPLY DIPLO DUPLE HAPLO HAPLY HIPLY IMPLY MAPLE PEPLA REPLY

••P•L
AMPUL APPAL APPEL ARPEL COPAL CUPEL EXPEL IMPEL LAPEL NEPAL NOPAL PAPAL PIPAL PUPAL PUPIL REPEL SEPAL TEPAL TOPOL

P•M••
PAMBY PAMIR PAMPA PEMBA PIMAS POMES POMME POMOS PUMAS PUMPS

P••M•
PALMA PALME PALMS PALMY PARMA PERMS PISMO PLUMB PLUME PLUMP PLUMS PLUMY POEME POEMS POMME PRAMS PRIMA PRIME PRIMI PRIMO PRIMP PRIMS PROMO PROMS PYGMY

P•••M
PANAM PHARM PHNOM PILUM PLASM PRIAM PRISM PRIZM PROAM PROEM PSALM PURIM

•P•M•
SPAMS SPUME SPUMY

•P••M
EPROM EPSOM IPSUM OPIUM SPASM

•••PM
ONEPM SIXPM TENPM TWOPM

P•N••
PANAM PANAY PANDA PANDL PANED PANEL PANES PANGA PANGS PANIC PANKY PANNE PANSY PANTO PANTS PANZA PENAL PENCE PENDS PENGO PENNA PENNE PENNI PENNY PENTA PENTE PENZA PHNOM PINCE PINCH PINED PINES PINEY PINGO PINGS PINKS PINKY PINNA PINON PINOT PINSK PINTA PINTO PINTS PINUP PINZA PONCA PONCE PONCH PONDS PONES PONGS PONTE PONTI PONTS PONZI PUNAS PUNCH PUNGS PUNIC PUNKS PUNKY PUNNY PUNTA PUNTS PUNTY

P••N•
PAINE PAINS PAINT PANNE PATNA PAWNS PAYNE PEENS PENNA PENNE PENNI PENNY PEONS PEONY PHANY PHENO PHONE PHONO PHONS PHONY PIANO PINNA PIONS PLANB PLANE PLANI PLANK PLANO PLANS PLANT PLENA PLINK PLINY PLONK PLUNK POINT POONA POONS POUND PRANG PRANK PRINK PRINT PRONE PRONG PRUNE PUNNY

P•••N
PAEAN PAEON PAGAN PALIN PAREN PATEN PATON PAYIN PECAN PEKIN PEPIN PERAN PERON PHREN PINON PISAN PITON PLAIN PLEON POPIN PRAWN PREEN PRION PUPIN PUSAN PUTIN PUTON PYLON

•PN••
APNEA

•P•N•
APING IPANA OPENS OPINE SPANG SPANK SPANS SPEND SPENT SPINE SPINS SPINY SPUNK UPEND

•P••N
APIAN APRON EPSON OPSIN SPAHN SPAIN SPAWN SPOON SPURN SPYON UPTON

••PN•
HYPNO

••P•N
ASPEN CAPON COPAN HOPIN JAPAN LAPIN LUPIN PEPIN POPIN PUPIN REPIN RIPEN RIPON TAPIN TIPIN UNPEN UNPIN

PO•••
POACH POBOX POBOY POCUS PODGY PODIA POEME POEMS POESY POETE POETS POHAI POILS POILU POINT POISE POKED POKER POKES POKEY POLAR POLED POLER POLES POLIS POLIT POLKA POLLO POLLS POLLY POLOS POLYP POMES POMME POMOS PONCA PONCE PONCH PONDS PONES PONGS PONTE PONTI PONTS PONZI POOCH POODS POOHS POOLE POOLS POONA POONS POOPS POPES POPIN POPOV POPPA POPPY POPUP PORCH PORED PORES PORGY PORKS PORKY PORTE PORTO PORTS POSED POSER POSES POSIT POSSE POSTE POSTS POTOK POTSY POTTO POTTS POTTY POUCH POUFS POULT POUND POURS POUTS POUTY POWAY POWER POWYS

P•O••
PAOLI PAOLO PEONS PEONY PHOBE PHONE PHONO PHONS PHONY PHOTO PHOTS PIONS PIOUS PLODS PLONK PLOPS PLOTS PLOWS PLOYS POOCH POODS POOHS POOLE POOLS POONA POONS POOPS PROAM PROAS PROBE PROBS PRODS PROEM PROFS PROGS PROLE PROMO PROMS PRONE PRONG PROOF PROPS PROSE PROST PROSY PROTO PROTS PROUD PROVE PROVO PROWL PROWS PROXY PSOAS

P••O•
PAEON PALOS PAROL PAROS PATON PECOS PEKOE PEPOS PERON PEROT PESOS PHLOX PHNOM PICOT PILOT PINON PINOT PITON PITOT PIVOT PLEON POBOX POBOY POLOS POMOS POPOV POTOK PRION PRIOR PROOF PRYOR PUTON PYLON

P•••O
PAAVO PABLO PALEO PANTO PAOLO PARDO PARVO PASCO PASEO PASTO PATHO PATIO PAULO PEABO PEDRO PENGO PESTO PETRO PHAGO PHENO PHILO PHONO PHOTO PHYCO PHYTO PIANO PICRO PINGO PINTO PISCO PISMO PLANO PLATO PLEIO PLUTO POLLO PORTO POTTO PRADO PRATO PREGO PRIMO PROMO PROTO PROVO PTERO PUTTO

•PO••
APORT EPOCH EPODE EPOXY SPOCK SPODE SPOIL SPOKE SPOOF SPOOK SPOOL SPOON SPOOR SPORE SPORK SPORT SPOSA SPOTS SPOUT UPOLU

•P•O•
APRON APSOS EPCOT EPHOD EPHOR EPROM EPSOM EPSON SPOOF SPOOK SPOOL SPOON SPOOR SPYON UPBOW UPDOS UPTON

•P••O
SPERO SPIRO

••PO•
BIPOD CAPON CAPOS CSPOT DEPOT ESPOO EXPOS HYPOS KAPOK NEPOS PEPOS POPOV REPOS REPOT RIPON SAPOR SEPOY SOPOR TOPOG TOPOI TOPOL TOPOS TYPOS VAPOR YAPOK

••P•O
CUPRO DIPLO ESPOO HAPLO HIPPO HIPTO HYPNO HYPSO LEPTO LIPPO REPRO ZEPPO

•••PO
ADIPO CAMPO CARPO COMPO FIRPO HARPO HIPPO KIMPO LIPPO MAYPO MOKPO TAUPO TEMPO TROPO ZEPPO

P•P••
PAPAL PAPAS PAPAW PAPER PAPPI PAPPY PAPUA PEPIN PEPLA PEPOS PEPPY PEPSI PEPUP PEPYS PIPAL PIPED PIPER PIPES PIPIT PIPPA PIPPI POPES POPIN POPOV POPPA POPPY POPUP PUPAE PUPAL PUPAS PUPIL PUPIN PUPPY PUPUS

P••P•
PALPI PALPS PAMPA PAPPI PAPPY PEEPS PEPPY PERPS PIPPA PIPPI PLOPS POOPS POPPA POPPY PREPS PROPS PULPS PULPY PUMPS PUPPY

P•••P
PAYUP PEPUP PINUP PLUMP POLYP POPUP PRIMP PTRAP PUTUP

•PP••
APPAL APPEL APPLE APPLY APPTD APPTS UPPED UPPER

••PP•
CUPPA DIPPY GUPPY HAPPY HIPPO HIPPY HOPPE KAPPA LAPPS LEPPY LIPPI LIPPO LIPPY LOPPY NAPPE NAPPY NIPPY PAPPI PAPPY PEPPY PIPPA PIPPI POPPA POPPY PUPPY REPPS SAPPY SOPPY TIPPI TIPPY TOPPS ZAPPA ZAPPY ZEPPO ZIPPY

••P•P
HOPUP LAPUP MOPUP NIPUP PEPUP POPUP RIPUP SOPUP TIPUP ZIPUP

•••PP
KRUPP TRAPP

P•Q••
PIQUE

PR•••
PRADO PRAIA PRAMS PRANG PRANK PRASE PRATE PRATO PRATT PRAUS PRAWN PRAYS PREEN PREGO PRELL PREPS PRESS PREST PREXY PREYS PRIAM PRICE PRICK PRICY PRIDE PRIED PRIER PRIES PRIGS PRIMA PRIME PRIMI PRIMO PRIMP PRIMS PRINK PRINT PRION PRIOR PRISM PRIVY PRIZE PRIZM PROAM PROAS PROBE PROBS PRODS PROEM PROFS PROGS PROLE PROMO PROMS PRONE PRONG PROOF PROPS PROSE PROST PROSY PROTO PROTS PROUD PROVE PROVO PROWL PROWS PROXY PRUDE PRUNE PRYCE PRYOR

P•R••
PARCA PARCH PARDI PARDO PARDS PARED PAREE PAREN PARER PARES PAREU PARIS PARKA PARKS PARLE PARMA PAROL PAROS PARRY PARSE PARTE PARTI PARTS PARTY PARVO PERAN PERCE PERCH PERCY PERDU PERES PEREZ PERIL PERIS PERKS PERKY PERLE PERMS PERON PEROT PERPS PERRY PERSE PERTH PHREN PORCH PORED PORES PORGY PORKS PORKY PORTE PORTO PORTS PTRAP PUREE PURER PUREX PURGE PURIM PURLS PURRS PURSE PURSY PURUS PYRES PYREX PYRIC

P••R•
PADRE PAIRS PARRY PATRI PEARL PEARS PEARY PEDRO PEERS PERRY

PETRA
PETRI
PETRO
PHARM
PICRO
PIERS
PIURA
POURS
PTERO
PURRS

P•••R
PACER
PAGER
PALER
PAMIR
PAPER
PARER
PATER
PAVER
PAWER
PAYER
PETER
PIKER
PILAR
PIPER
POKER
POLAR
POLER
POSER
POWER
PRIER
PRIOR
PRYOR
PURER

•PR••
APRES
APRIL
APRON
EPROM
OPRAH
SPRAG
SPRAT
SPRAY
SPREE
SPRIG
SPRIT
SPRUE
YPRES

•P•R•
APART
APERS
APERY
APORT
APURE
OPART
OPERA
OPERE
SPARE
SPARK
SPARS
SPERO
SPIRE
SPIRO
SPIRY
SPORE
SPORK
SPORT
SPURN
SPURS
SPURT
SPYRI

•P••R
APTER
EPHOR
OPHIR
SPEAR
SPOOR
UPPER

••PR•
CAPRA
CAPRI
COPRA
CUPRI
CUPRO
DUPRE
REPRO
SUPRA

••P•R
AMPHR
ATPAR
CAPER
GAPER
HOPER
HYPER
LOPER
MOPER
NOPAR
PAPER
PIPER
RIPER
ROPER
SAPIR
SAPOR
SOPOR
SUPER
SUPVR
TAPER
TAPIR
TOPER
TYPER
UPPER
VAPOR
VIPER
WIPER

PS•••
PSALM
PSATS
PSEUD
PSHAW
PSOAS
PSYCH

P•S••
PASCH
PASCO
PASEO
PASES
PASHA
PASSE
PASSU
PASSY
PASTA
PASTE
PASTO
PASTS
PASTY
PESCI
PESKY
PESOS
PESTO
PESTS
PISAN
PISCI
PISCO
PISMO
PISTE
POSED
POSER
POSES
POSIT
POSSE
POSTE
POSTS
PUSAN
PUSEY
PUSHY

P••S•
PABST
PAISA
PALSY
PANSY
PARSE
PASSE
PASSU
PASSY
PATSY
PAUSE
PEASE
PEPSI
PERSE
PHASE
PHYSI
PINSK
PLASH
PLASM
PLUSH
POESY
POISE
POSSE
POTSY
PRASE
PRESS
PREST
PRISM
PROSE
PROST
PROSY
PULSE
PURSE
PURSY

P•••S
PACAS
PACES
PACKS
PACTS
PAGES
PAILS
PAINS
PAIRS
PALES
PALLS
PALMS
PALOS
PALPS
PANES
PANGS
PANTS
PAPAS
PARDS
PARES
PARIS
PARKS
PAROS
PARTS
PASES
PASTS
PATES
PATHS
PAVES
PAVIS
PAWLS
PAWNS
PEAKS
PEALS
PEARS
PEATS
PECKS
PECOS
PEEKS
PEELS
PEENS
PEEPS
PEERS
PEKES
PELTS
PENDS
PEONS
PEPOS
PEPYS
PERES
PERIS
PERKS
PERMS
PERPS
PESOS
PESTS
PETES
PHONS
PHOTS
PICAS
PICKS
PICTS
PIEDS
PIERS
PIKAS
PIKES
PILES
PILLS
PILUS
PIMAS
PINES
PINGS
PINKS
PINTS
PIONS
PIOUS
PIPES
PITAS
PITHS
PITTS
PLANS
PLATS
PLAYS
PLEAS
PLEBS
PLEWS
PLIES
PLODS
PLOPS
PLOTS
PLOWS
PLOYS
PLUGS
PLUMS
POCUS
POEMS
POETS
POILS
POKES
POLES
POLIS
POLLS
POLOS
POMES
POMOS
PONDS
PONES
PONGS
PONTS
POODS
POOHS
POOLS
POONS
POOPS
POPES
PORES
PORKS
PORTS
POSES
POSTS
POTTS
POUFS
POURS
POUTS
POWYS
PRAMS
PRAUS
PRAYS
PREPS
PRESS
PREYS
PRIES
PRIGS
PRIMS
PROAS
PROBS
PRODS
PROFS
PROGS
PROMS
PROPS
PROTS
PROWS
PSATS
PSOAS
PUCKS
PUDUS
PUFFS
PULAS
PULES
PULIS
PULLS
PULPS
PUMAS
PUMPS
PUNAS
PUNGS
PUNKS
PUNTS
PUPAS
PUPUS
PURLS
PURRS
PURUS
PUTTS
PYRES
PYXIS

•PS••
APSES
APSIS
APSOS
EPSOM
EPSON
IPSUM
OPSIN
OPSIS
UPSET

•P•S•
APISH
EPISC
IPASS
SPASM
SPOSA

•P••S
APERS
APHIS
APLUS
APPTS
APRES
APSES
APSIS
APSOS
BPLUS
CPLUS
DPLUS
EPEES
EPHAS
EPICS
IPASS
OPAHS
OPALS
OPEDS
OPELS
OPENS
OPSIS
SPADS
SPAMS
SPANS
SPARS
SPATS
SPAYS
SPECS
SPETS
SPEWS
SPIES
SPINS
SPITS
SPIVS
SPOTS
SPUDS
SPURS
UPDOS
YPRES

••PS•
COPSE
GIPSY
GYPSY
HYPSO
LAPSE
MOPSY
PEPSI
TIPSY
TOPSY

••P•S
AMPAS
APPTS
CAPES
CAPOS
CAPTS
CEPES
COPES
COPTS
DEPTS
DOPES
DUPES
EXPOS
GAPES
HOPES
HOPIS
HYPES
HYPOS
JAPES
KAPHS
KEPIS
KOPHS
LAPIS
LAPPS
LEPUS
LOPES
MOPES
NAPES
NEPOS
NIPAS
PAPAS
PEPOS
PEPYS
PIPES
POPES
PUPAS
PUPUS
QOPHS
REPOS
REPPS
ROPES
SOPHS
SUPES
SUPTS
TAPAS
TAPES
TOPES
TOPIS
TOPOS
TOPPS
TYPES
TYPOS
WIPES
YIPES

•••PS
BEEPS
BLIPS
BUMPS
BURPS
CAMPS
CARPS
CHAPS
CHIPS
CHOPS
CLAPS
CLIPS
CLOPS
COMPS
COOPS
CORPS
COUPS
CRAPS
CROPS
CUSPS
DAMPS
DEEPS
DORPS
DRIPS
DROPS
DUMPS
FLAPS
FLIPS
FLOPS
FRAPS
GAMPS
GASPS
GAWPS
GIMPS
GLOPS
GOOPS
GORPS
GRIPS
GULPS
HARPS
HASPS
HEAPS
HELPS
HEMPS
HOOPS
HUMPS
JEEPS
JUMPS
KEEPS
KELPS
KEMPS
KNAPS
KNOPS
LAMPS
LAPPS
LEAPS
LIMPS
LISPS
LOOPS
LUMPS
MUMPS
NEAPS
PALPS
PEEPS
PERPS
PLOPS
POOPS
PREPS
PROPS
PULPS
PUMPS
QTIPS
QUIPS
RAMPS
RASPS
REAPS
REPPS
REUPS
ROMPS
RSVPS
RUMPS
SALPS
SAMPS
SCOPS
SCUPS
SEEPS
SHIPS
SHOPS
SIMPS
SKEPS
SKIPS
SLAPS
SLIPS
SLOPS
SNAPS
SNIPS
SOAPS
SOUPS
STEPS
STOPS
SUMPS
SWAPS
SWOPS
TAMPS
TARPS
TBSPS
TEMPS
TERPS
TOPPS
TRAPS
TRIPS
TUMPS
VAMPS
VEEPS
WARPS
WASPS
WEEPS
WHIPS
WHOPS
WHUPS
WIMPS
WISPS
WRAPS
YAWPS
YELPS

PT•••
PTERO
PTRAP

P•T••
PATCH
PATED
PATEK
PATEN
PATER
PATES
PATHE
PATHO
PATHS
PATHY
PATIO
PATLY
PATNA
PATON
PATRI
PATSY
PATTI
PATTY
PETAL
PETER
PETES
PETIT
PETRA
PETRI
PETRO
PETTI
PETTY
PITAS
PITCH
PITHS
PITHY
PITON
PITOT
PITTA
PITTS
POTOK
POTSY
POTTO
POTTS
POTTY
PUTBY
PUTIN
PUTON
PUTTI
PUTTO
PUTTS
PUTTY
PUTUP

P••T•
PACTS
PANTO
PANTS
PARTE
PARTI
PARTS
PARTY
PASTA
PASTE
PASTO
PASTS
PASTY
PATTI
PATTY
PAYTV
PEATS
PEATY
PEETE
PELTS
PENTA
PENTE
PERTH
PESTO
PESTS
PETTI
PETTY
PHOTO
PHOTS
PHYTO
PICTS
PIETA
PIETY
PINTA
PINTO
PINTS
PISTE
PITTA
PITTS
PLATA
PLATE
PLATH
PLATO
PLATS
PLATT
PLATY
PLOTS
PLUTO
POETE
POETS
PONTE
PONTI
PONTS
PORTE
PORTO
PORTS
POSTE
POSTS
POTTO
POTTS
POTTY
POUTS
POUTY
PRATE
PRATO
PRATT
PROTO
PROTS
PSATS
PUNTA
PUNTS
PUNTY
PUTTI
PUTTO
PUTTS
PUTTY

P•••T
PABST
PAGET
PAINT
PAWAT
PEROT
PETIT
PEWIT
PICOT
PILOT
PINOT
PIPIT
PITOT
PIVOT
PLAIT
PLANT
PLATT
PLEAT
POINT
POLIT
POSIT
POULT
PRATT
PREST
PRINT
PROST
PUGET

•PT••
APTED
APTER
APTLY
OPTED
OPTIC
UPTON

•P•T•
APPTD
APPTS
SPATE
SPATS
SPETS
SPITE
SPITS
SPITZ
SPOTS

•P••T
APART
APORT
EPACT
EPCOT
OPART
OPCIT
SPELT
SPENT
SPILT
SPLAT
SPLIT
SPORT
SPOUT
SPRAT
SPRIT
SPURT
UPSET

••PT•
APPTD
APPTS
CAPTS
COPTS
DEPTH
DEPTS
EMPTY
HEPTA
HIPTO
LEPTA
LEPTO
SEPTA
SUPTS

••P•T
CAPET
CSPOT
DEPOT
INPUT
KAPUT
LOPAT
NIPAT
PIPIT
REPOT
STPAT

•••PT
ADAPT
ADEPT
ADOPT
CLIPT
COAPT
COOPT
CREPT
CRYPT
EGYPT
ERUPT
INAPT
INEPT
KEMPT
LEAPT
SLEPT
SLIPT
SWEPT
TEMPT
UNAPT
WRAPT

PU•••
PUCCI
PUCKS
PUDGY
PUDUS
PUFFS
PUFFY
PUGET
PUGGY
PUKKA
PULAS
PULED
PULES
PULIS
PULLS
PULPS
PULPY
PULSE
PUMAS
PUMPS
PUNAS
PUNCH
PUNGS
PUNIC
PUNKS
PUNKY
PUNNY
PUNTA
PUNTS
PUNTY
PUPAE
PUPAL
PUPAS
PUPIL
PUPIN
PUPPY
PUPUS
PUREE
PURER
PUREX
PURGE
PURIM
PURLS
PURRS
PURSE
PURSY
PURUS
PUSAN
PUSEY
PUSHY
PUTBY
PUTIN
PUTON
PUTTI
PUTTO
PUTTS
PUTTY
PUTUP

P•U••
PAULA
PAULO
PAUSE
PIURA
PLUCK
PLUGS
PLUMB
PLUME
PLUMP
PLUMS
PLUMY
PLUNK
PLUSH
PLUTO
POUCH
POUFS
POULT
POUND
POURS
POUTS
POUTY
PRUDE
PRUNE

P••U•
PADUA
PAPUA
PAYUP
PEPUP
PIAUI
PICUL
PILUM
PILUS
PINUP
PIOUS
PIQUE
POCUS
POPUP
PRAUS
PROUD
PSEUD
PUDUS
PUPUS
PURUS
PUTUP

P•••U
PALAU
PAREU
PASSU
PERDU
POILU

•PU••
APURE
SPUDS
SPUME
SPUMY
SPUNK
SPURN
SPURS
SPURT

•P•U•
APLUS
BPLUS
CPLUS
DPLUS
IPSUM
OPIUM
SPOUT
SPRUE

•P••U
UPOLU

••PU•
AMPUL
HOPUP
INPUT
KAPUT
LAPUP
LEPUS
MOPUP
NIPUP
PAPUA
PEPUP
POPUP
PUPUS
RIPUP
SOPUP
TIPUP
ZIPUP

•••PU
COYPU
QUIPU

P•V••
PAVED
PAVER
PAVES
PAVIA
PAVID
PAVIS
PIVOT

P••V•
PAAVO
PARVO
PEAVY
PEEVE
PRIVY
PROVE
PROVO

P•••V
PAYTV
POPOV

•P•V•
SPIVS

••PV•
SUPVR

••P•V
POPOV

P•W••
PAWAT
PAWED
PAWER
PAWKY
PAWLS
PAWNS
PEWEE
PEWIT
POWAY
POWER
POWYS

P••W•
PLEWS
PLOWS
PRAWN
PROWL
PROWS

P•••W
PAPAW
PSHAW

•P•W•
SPAWN
SPEWS

•P••W
UPBOW

••P•W
DEPEW
PAPAW

P•X••
PIXEL
PIXIE
PYXIE
PYXIS

P••X•
PREXY
PROXY

P•••X
PHLOX
POBOX
PUREX
PYREX

•P•X•
EPOXY

PY•••
PYGMY
PYLON
PYRES
PYREX
PYRIC
PYXIE
PYXIS

P•Y••
PAYED
PAYEE
PAYER
PAYIN
PAYNE
PAYTV
PAYUP
PHYCO
PHYFE
PHYLA
PHYLE
PHYLL
PHYSI
PHYTO
PRYCE
PRYOR
PSYCH

P••Y•
PEPYS
PLAYA
PLAYS
PLOYS
POLYP
POWYS
PRAYS
PREYS

P•••Y
PADDY
PALEY
PALLY
PALMY
PALSY
PAMBY
PANAY
PANKY
PANSY
PAPPY
PARRY
PARTY
PASSY
PASTY
PATHY
PATLY
PATSY
PATTY
PAWKY
PEARY
PEATY
PEAVY
PECKY
PEGGY
PENNY
PEONY
PEPPY
PERCY
PERKY
PERRY
PESKY
PETTY
PHAGY
PHANY
PHILY
PHONY
PICKY
PIETY
PIGGY
PINEY
PINKY
PITHY
PLATY
PLINY
PLUMY
POBOY
PODGY
POESY
POKEY
POLLY
POPPY
PORGY
PORKY
POTSY
POTTY
POUTY
POWAY
PREXY
PRICY
PRIVY
PROSY
PROXY
PUDGY
PUFFY
PUGGY
PULPY
PUNKY
PUNNY
PUNTY
PUPPY
PURSY
PUSEY
PUSHY
PUTBY
PUTTY
PYGMY

•PY••
SPYON
SPYRI

•P•Y•
SPAYS

•P••Y
APERY
APLEY
APPLY
APTLY
EPOXY
SPACY
SPICY
SPIKY
SPINY
SPIRY
SPLAY
SPRAY
SPUMY

••PY•
PEPYS

••P•Y
AMPLY
APPLY
COPAY
DIPPY
DOPEY
EMPTY
GIPSY
GUPPY
GYPSY
HAPLY
HAPPY
HIPLY
HIPPY
IMPLY
LEPPY
LIPPY
LOPPY
MOPEY
MOPSY
NAPPY
NIPPY
PAPPY
PEPPY
POPPY
PUPPY
REPAY
REPLY
ROPEY
SAPPY
SEPOY
SOPHY
SOPPY
TIPPY
TIPSY
TOPSY
TYPEY
ZAPPY
ZIPPY

•••PY
BUMPY
CAMPY
DIPPY
DUMPY
GIMPY
GOOPY
GRAPY
GULPY
GUPPY
HAPPY
HARPY
HIPPY
HUMPY
JUMPY
KELPY
LEPPY
LIPPY
LOOPY
LOPPY
LUMPY
NAPPY
NIPPY
PAPPY
PEPPY
POPPY
PULPY
PUPPY
RASPY
SAPPY
SCOPY
SEEPY
SOAPY
SOPPY
SOUPY
TIPPY
WASPY
WEEPY
WIMPY
WISPY
ZAPPY
ZIPPY

P•Z••
PIZZA

P••Z•
PANZA PENZA PINZA PIZZA PLAZA PONZI PRIZE PRIZM

P•••Z
PEREZ

•P••Z
SPITZ

••P•Z
LAPAZ LOPEZ TOPAZ

QA•••
QANDA QATAR

Q•A••
QUACK QUADR QUADS QUAFF QUAGS QUAID QUAIL QUAKE QUAKY QUALE QUALM QUAND QUANT QUARE QUARK QUART QUASH QUASI QUAYS

Q••A•
QATAR QUOAD

Q•••A
QANDA QUOTA

•QA••
AQABA

•Q•A•
AQUAE AQUAS EQUAL SQUAB SQUAD SQUAT

•Q••A
AQABA

QB•••
QBVII

•Q•B•
AQABA

•Q••B
SQUAB SQUIB

Q••C•
QUACK QUICK

Q••D•
QANDA QUADR QUADS QUIDS QUODS

Q•••D
QUAID QUAND QUOAD

•Q••D
SQUAD SQUID

Q•E••
QUEEG QUEEN QUEER QUELL QUERN QUERY QUEST QUEUE

Q••E•
QUEEG QUEEN QUEER QUIEN QUIET

Q•••E
QUAKE QUALE QUARE QUEUE QUIRE QUITE QUOTE

•Q••E
AQUAE

••Q•E
ATQUE ESQUE PIQUE ROQUE TOQUE TUQUE USQUE

Q••F•
QUAFF

Q•••F
QUAFF

Q••G•
QUAGS

Q•••G
QUEEG

Q••H•
QOPHS

Q•••H
QUASH QUOTH

Q•I••
QTIPS QUICK QUIDS QUIEN QUIET QUILL QUILP QUILT QUINN QUINO QUINT QUIPS QUIPU QUIRE QUIRK QUIRT QUITE QUITO QUITS

Q••I•
QBVII QUAID QUAIL QUOIN QUOIT

Q•••I
QBVII QUASI

•Q•I•
EQUIP EQUIV IQUIT SQUIB SQUID

••Q•I
MAQUI YAQUI

•••QI
IRAQI

Q••K•
QUAKE QUAKY

Q•••K
QUACK QUARK QUICK QUIRK

Q••L•
QUALE QUALM QUELL QUILL QUILP QUILT

Q•••L
QUAIL QUELL QUILL

•Q••L
EQUAL

Q•••M
QUALM

Q•N••
QANDA

Q••N•
QUAND QUANT QUINN QUINO QUINT

Q•••N
QUEEN QUERN QUIEN QUINN QUOIN

QO•••
QOPHS

Q•O••
QUOAD QUODS QUOIN QUOIT QUOTA QUOTE QUOTH

Q•••O
QUINO QUITO

Q•P••
QOPHS

Q••P•
QTIPS QUIPS QUIPU

Q•••P
QUILP

•Q••P
EQUIP

•••QQ
ETSQQ

Q••R•
QUARE QUARK QUART QUERN QUERY QUIRE QUIRK QUIRT

Q•••R
QATAR QUADR QUEER

Q••S•
QUASH QUASI QUEST

Q•••S
QOPHS QTIPS QUADS QUAGS QUAYS QUIDS QUIPS QUITS QUODS

•Q••S
AQUAS EQUUS

•••QS
BARQS

QT•••
QTIPS

Q•T••
QATAR

Q••T•
QUITE QUITO QUITS QUOTA QUOTE QUOTH

Q•••T
QUANT QUART QUEST QUIET QUILT QUINT QUIRT QUOIT

•Q••T
IQUIT SQUAT

QU•••
QUACK QUADR QUADS QUAFF QUAGS QUAID QUAIL QUAKE QUAKY QUALE QUALM QUAND QUANT QUARE QUARK QUART QUASH QUASI QUAYS QUEEG QUEEN QUEER QUELL QUERN QUERY QUEST QUEUE QUICK QUIDS QUIEN QUIET QUILL QUILP QUILT QUINN QUINO QUINT QUIPS QUIPU QUIRE QUIRK QUIRT QUITE QUITO QUITS QUOAD QUODS QUOIN QUOIT QUOTA QUOTE QUOTH

Q••U•
QUEUE

Q•••U
QUIPU

•QU••
AQUAE AQUAS EQUAL EQUIP EQUIV EQUUS IQUIT SQUAB SQUAD SQUAT SQUIB SQUID

•Q•U•
EQUUS

••QU•
ATQUE ESQUE MAQUI PIQUE ROQUE TOQUE TUQUE USQUE YAQUI

Q•V••
QBVII

•Q••V
EQUIV

Q••Y•
QUAYS

Q•••Y
QUAKY QUERY

RA•••
RABAT RABBI RABID RABIN RACED RACER RACES RACKS RACON RADAR RADII RADIO RADIX RADON RAFER RAFFI RAFTS RAGAS RAGED RAGES RAHAB RAHAL RAIDS RAILS RAINS RAINY RAISA RAISE RAITT RAJAH RAJAS RAJIV RAKED RAKER RAKES RAKIS RALLY RALPH RAMAN RAMAR RAMBO RAMEE RAMEN RAMET RAMIE RAMIS RAMON RAMOS RAMPS RANAT RANCH RANDB RANDD RANDI RANDR RANDS RANDY RANEE RANGE RANGY RANID RANIN RANIS RANKE RANKS RANON RANTO RANTS RANUP RAOUL RAPEE RAPHE RAPID RAREE RARER RARES RASED RASER RASES RASHT RASPS RASPY RASTA RATCH RATED RATEL RATER RATES RATHS RATIO RATON RATSO RATTY RAVED RAVEL RAVEN RAVER RAVES RAVIN RAWER RAWLS RAWLY RAYED RAYON RAZED RAZES RAZOR

R•A••
REACH REACT READE READS READY REAIM REAIR REALM REALS REAMS REAPS REARM REARS REATA RIALS RIANT RIATA RNASE ROACH ROADS ROALD ROAMS ROANS ROARS ROAST RUANA RUARK

R••A•
RABAT RADAR RAGAS RAHAB RAHAL RAJAH RAJAS RAMAN RAMAR RANAT REBAG REBAR RECAP REDAN REGAL REGAN REHAB REHAN RELAX RELAY REMAN REMAP RENAL RENAN REPAD REPAY RERAN RESAW RETAG RETAP RETAR RETAX REWAX RHEAS RIVAL RIYAL RODAN ROMAN ROTAS ROWAN ROYAL RUGAE RUNAT RURAL

R•••A
RAISA RASTA REATA REGIA REINA RENTA RETIA RHODA RHYTA RIATA RIOJA RUANA RUMBA

•RA••
ARABS ARABY ARAMA ARAME BRACE BRACT BRADS BRADY BRAES BRAGA BRAGG BRAGS BRAHE BRAID BRAIL BRAIN BRAKE BRAND BRANS BRANT BRASH BRASS BRATS BRAUN BRAVA BRAVE BRAVO BRAWL BRAWN BRAYS BRAZE CRABS CRACK CRACY CRAFT CRAGS CRAIG CRAIN CRAKE CRAMP CRAMS CRANE CRANK CRAPE CRAPS CRASH CRASS CRATE CRAVE CRAWL CRAWS CRAZE CRAZY DRABS DRACO DRAFT DRAGS DRAIL DRAIN DRAKE DRAMA DRAMS DRANG DRANK DRANO DRAPE DRATS DRAVA DRAWL DRAWN DRAWS DRAYS ERASE ERATO FRAIL FRAIS FRAME FRANC FRANK FRANS FRANZ FRAPS FRATS FRAUD FRAYS GRABS GRACE GRADE GRADS GRADY GRAFT GRAIG GRAIL GRAIN GRAMA GRAMM GRAMP GRAMS GRAND GRANI GRANT GRAPE GRAPH GRAPY GRASP GRASS GRATA GRATE GRAVE GRAVY GRAYS GRAZE IRADE IRANI IRAQI IRATE KRAAL KRAFT KRAIT KRAUS KRAUT KRAZY ORACH ORACY ORALE ORALS ORAMA ORANG ORANT ORATE PRADO PRAIA PRAMS PRANG PRANK PRASE PRATE PRATO PRATT PRAUS PRAWN PRAYS TRACE TRACK TRACT TRACY TRADE TRAIL TRAIN TRAIT TRALA TRAMP TRAMS TRANS TRAPP TRAPS TRASH TRAVE TRAWL TRAYS URALS WRACK WRACS WRAFS WRAPS WRAPT WRATH XRAYS

•R•A•
AREAL AREAR AREAS ARHAT ARIAN ARIAS ARNAZ AROAR ARPAD ARRAN ARRAS ARRAU ARRAY ARTAL ARYAN BREAD BREAK BREAM BRIAN BRIAR BROAD BRYAN CREAK CREAM CROAK CROAT DREAD DREAM DREAR DRLAO DRYAD FREAK FRIAR GREAT GROAN GROAT KRAAL ORCAS OREAD ORGAN PRIAM PROAM PROAS SRTAS TREAD TREAT TRIAD TRIAL URBAN URIAH URIAL WREAK

•R••A
ARAMA ARECA ARENA ARICA AROMA ARUBA BRAGA BRAVA BREDA BROCA CRURA DRAMA DRAVA DRINA ERICA ERIKA ERISA FREDA FRENA FREYA GRAMA GRATA GRETA GROZA IRINA KRONA KRUPA ORAMA ORIYA PRAIA PRIMA TRALA

••RA•
ABRAM ARRAN ARRAS ARRAU ARRAY AURAE AURAL AURAR AURAS BARAB BORAH BORAS BORAX CARAT CERAM CERAT CORAL DERAT DIRAC DORAG DORAL DORAN DURAN EYRAS FARAD FARAH FERAL FORAY FURAN GERAH GORAL GYRAL HARAR HERAT HIRAM HORAE HORAL HORAS HYRAX JURAL JURAT KARAN KARAT KERAT KORAN LARAM LARAS LIRAS LORAN LORAX LURAY MARAS MARAT MCRAE MORAE MORAL MORAN MORAS MORAY MURAL MURAT NARAS NORAD NORAH OKRAS OPRAH PERAN PTRAP RERAN RURAL SARAH SARAN SCRAG SCRAM SCRAP SERAC SERAI SERAL SORAS SPRAG SPRAT SPRAY STRAD STRAP STRAW STRAY SURAH SURAL SURAS SURAT TIRAN TORAH VARAS VIRAL

••R•A
AORTA ATRIA BARCA BEREA BERRA BURMA BURSA CARIA CARLA CARTA CERIA CIRCA COREA CORIA CURIA DARLA DARYA DERMA DORSA DURRA FERIA FIRMA FORMA GARDA KARLA KARMA KORDA KOREA LARVA LORCA LORNA LURIA MARIA MARLA MARTA MURRA MYRNA NORIA NORMA OCREA PARCA PARKA PARMA SERRA SERTA SORTA STRIA SYRIA TERRA TERZA UNRRA VARIA VARNA VERBA VERSA VIRGA VIRNA WIRRA YERBA YORBA ZORBA

•••RA
ACCRA ACURA AFTRA AGORA AHORA AKIRA AMARA ANTRA ASTRA AUDRA BASRA BERRA CAPRA CIERA CLARA COBRA COPRA CRURA DEBRA DOBRA DURRA EVORA EXTRA FLORA HIERA HIJRA HYDRA INDRA INFRA INTRA LAURA LEORA LIBRA LYCRA MBIRA MEARA MICRA MOIRA MUDRA MURRA NAIRA OHARA OPERA PETRA PIURA SABRA SACRA SERRA SIDRA SUDRA SUPRA SUTRA TATRA TAYRA TERRA TETRA THERA TIARA UHURA ULTRA UMBRA UNRRA WIRRA ZEBRA

R•B••
RABAT RABBI RABID RABIN REBAG REBAR REBBE REBEC REBEL REBID REBUS REBUT RIBBY ROBBY ROBED ROBES ROBIN ROBLE ROBOT RUBEN RUBES RUBIK RUBIN RUBLE

R••B•
RABBI RAMBO REBBE RIBBY RIGBY ROBBY RUGBY RUMBA

R•••B
RAHAB RANDB REDUB REHAB RHOMB RHUMB

•RB••
ARBER ARBOR ARBRE ERBIL MRBIG ORBIT URBAN URBIS

•R•B•
ARABS ARABY ARUBA BRIBE CRABS CRIBS DRABS DRIBS DRUBS FROBE GRABS GREBE GRUBS KREBS ORIBI PROBE PROBS TRIBE

•R••B
CRUMB

••RB•
BARBQ BARBS BURBS CARBO CARBS CORBY CURBS DARBY DERBY FORBS GARBO GARBS HERBS HERBY KERBS KIRBY SERBS SORBS TURBO VERBA VERBS YERBA YORBA ZORBA

••R•B
BARAB CARIB CAROB HOREB SCRUB SHRUB THROB

•••RB
ACERB BLURB EXURB

R•C••
RACED RACER RACES RACKS RACON RECAP RECCE RECIP RECON RECTI RECTO RECUR RICCI RICED RICER RICES RICHE RICKI RICKS RICKY RICOH ROCCO ROCHE ROCKS ROCKY RUCHE RUCKS

R••C•
RANCH RATCH REACH REACT RECCE REICH RICCI ROACH ROCCO ROYCE

R•••C
REBEC RELIC RUNIC

•RC••
ARCED ARCHI ARCHY ORCAS ORCHS ORCUS ORCZY

•R•C•
ARECA ARICA BRACE BRACT BRECK BRICE BRICK BROCA BROCK BRUCE BRUCH BRYCE CRACK CRACY CRECY CRICK CROCE CROCI CROCK CROCS DRACO ERECT ERICA ERICH ERUCT FRICK FROCK GRACE GRECO

ORACH ORACY PRICE PRICK PRICY PRYCE TRACE TRACK TRACT TRACY TRICE TRICK TRUCE TRUCK URICH WRACK WRACS WRECK

•R••C

BRONC CRESC FRANC

••RC•

BARCA BIRCH CIRCA CIRCE CIRCS CURCI FARCE FARCI FORCE LARCH LORCA LURCH MARCH MARCO MARCY MERCE MERCI MERCK MERCY NARCO NARCS PARCA PARCH PERCE PERCH PERCY PORCH TORCH

••R•C

AFRIC AGRIC AURIC BARIC BORIC DIRAC DORIC DUROC HARDC LYRIC OSRIC PYRIC SERAC TORIC UGRIC XERIC

R•D••

RADAR RADII RADIO RADIX RADON REDAN REDDY REDED REDES REDID REDLY REDON REDOX REDUB REDUX REDYE RIDER RIDES RIDGE RIDGY RIDOF RODAN RODDY RODEO RODIN RUDDS RUDDY RUDER RUDGE RYDER

R••D•

RAIDS RANDB RANDD RANDI RANDR RANDS RANDY READE READS READY REDDY REEDS REEDY RENDS RHODA RHODE RHODO RINDS RINDY ROADS RODDY RONDO ROODS ROWDY RUDDS RUDDY

R•••D

RABID RACED RAGED RAKED RANDD RANID RAPID RASED RATED RAVED RAYED RAZED REBID REDED REDID REPAD RESOD REWED RICED RIGID RILED RIMED RIVED ROALD ROBED ROPED ROUND ROVED ROWED RSVPD RULED

•RD••

ARDEN ARDOR DRDRE ORDER ORDOS

•R•D•

BRADS BRADY BREDA BRIDE BRODY CREDO CRUDE DREDD ERODE FREDA FRODO GRADE GRADS GRADY GRIDS GRODY IRADE IRIDO PRADO PRIDE PRODS PRUDE TRADE

•R••D

ARCED ARMED AROID ARPAD BRAID BRAND BREAD BREED BROAD BROOD CREED CRIED CROWD DREAD DREDD DRIED DROID DROOD DRUID DRYAD ERRED FRAUD FREED FREUD FRIED FROID FROND GRAND GREED GRIND IRKED OREAD PRIED PROUD TREAD TREED TREND TRIAD TRIED TRUED URGED URSID

••RD•

BARDS BIRDS BIRDY BYRDS CARDI CARDS CORDS CURDS CURDY FERDE FORDO FORDS GARDA GARDE GIRDS GORDO GORDY GURDY HARDC HARDG HARDY HERDS HORDE HURDY KORDA KURDS LARDS LARDY LORDS MARDI NARDS NERDS NERDY PARDI PARDO PARDS PERDU SARDS SURDS TARDE TARDY VERDE VERDI WARDS WORDS WORDY YARDS

••R•D

ACRED ACRID AIRED BARED BORED CARED CERED CORED CURED DARED EARED ERRED FARAD FARED FIRED GORED HARED HEROD HIRED LURED LURID MIRED NORAD OARED PARED PORED SAROD SCROD SHRED SIRED STRAD TIRED VIRID WIRED WORLD

•••RD

AWARD BAIRD BEARD BOARD CHARD CHORD FIORD FJORD GOURD GUARD HEARD HOARD IZARD LAIRD LIARD SHARD SNERD SWARD SWORD TBIRD THIRD WEIRD

RE•••

REACH REACT READE READS READY REAIM REAIR REALM REALS REAMS REAPS REARM REARS REATA REBAG REBAR REBBE REBEC REBEL REBID REBUS REBUT RECAP RECCE RECIP RECON RECTI RECTO RECUR REDAN REDDY REDED REDES REDID REDLY REDON REDOX REDUB REDUX REDYE REEDS REEDY REEFS REEKS REEKY REELS REESE REEVE REFER REFIT REFRY REGAL REGAN REGIA REGIS REGNI REGUM REHAB REHAN REHEM REICH REIFY REIGN REIMS REINA REINK REINS REKEY RELAX RELAY RELEE RELET RELIC RELIG RELIT REMAN REMAP REMET REMEX REMIT REMIX REMOP REMOW REMUS RENAL RENAN RENDS RENEE RENEW RENIN RENTA RENTS REOIL REPAD REPAY REPEG REPEL REPIN REPLY REPOS REPOT REPPS REPRO RERAN RERIG RERUM RERUN RESAW RESEE RESET RESEW RESIN RESOD RESTS RETAG RETAP RETAR RETAX RETIA RETIE RETOP RETOW RETRO RETRY REUEL REUNE REUPS REUSE REVEL REVET REVUE REVUP REWAX REWED REWIN REWON REXES REYES

R•E••

REEDS REEDY REEFS REEKS REEKY REELS REESE REEVE RHEAS RHETT RHEUM RIELS RUEHL RUERS

R••E•

RACED RACER RACES RAFER RAGED RAGES RAKED RAKER RAKES RAMEE RAMEN RAMET RANEE RAPEE RAREE RARER RARES RASED RASER RASES RATED RATEL RATER RATES RAVED RAVEL RAVEN RAVER RAVES RAWER RAYED RAZED RAZES REBEC REBEL REDED REDES REFER REHEM REKEY RELEE RELET REMET REMEX RENEE RENEW REPEG REPEL RESEE RESET RESEW REUEL REVEL REVET REWED REXES REYES RICED RICER RICES RIDER RIDES RIFER RIGEL RIKER RILED RILES RILEY RIMED RIMES RIPEN RIPER RISEN RISER RISES RITES RIVED RIVEN RIVER RIVES RIVET ROBED ROBES RODEO ROGER ROGET ROLEO ROLES ROLEX ROMEO ROMER RONEE ROPED ROPER ROPES ROPEY ROREM ROSEN ROSES ROSEY ROTES ROUEN ROUES ROVED ROVER ROVES ROWED ROWEL ROWEN ROWER RUBEN RUBES RUDER RULED RULER RULES RUMEN RUNES RUPEE RUSES RYDER

R•••E

RAISE RAMEE RAMIE RANEE RANGE RANKE RAPEE RAPHE RAREE READE REBBE RECCE REDYE REESE REEVE RELEE RENEE RESEE RETIE REUNE REUSE REVUE RHINE RHODE RHONE RHYME RICHE RIDGE RIFLE RILKE RILLE RINSE RNASE ROBLE ROCHE ROGUE ROLFE ROLLE RONEE ROONE ROQUE ROSIE ROUGE ROUSE ROUTE ROXIE ROYCE RUBLE RUCHE RUDGE RUGAE RUPEE RUSSE

•RE••

AREAL AREAR AREAS ARECA ARENA ARENS ARENT ARETE BREAD BREAK BREAM BRECK BREDA BREED BREEN BRENT BRERS BREST BRETT BREVE BREWS CREAK CREAM CRECY CREDO CREED CREEK CREEL CREEP CREES CREME CREON CREPE CREPT CRESC CRESS CREST CRETE CREWS DREAD DREAM DREAR DREDD DREGS DRESS ERECT FREAK FREDA FREED FREER FREES FRENA FREON FRERE FRESH FRETS FREUD FREYA GREAT GREBE GRECO GREED GREEK GREEN GREER GREES GREET GREGG GRETA GRETE GREYS IRENE KREBS OREAD OREOS PREEN PREGO PRELL PREPS PRESS PREST PREXY PREYS TREAD TREAT TREED TREEN TREES TREKS TREND TRENT TRESS TREVI TREWS TREYS WREAK WRECK WRENS WREST

•R•E•

ARBER ARCED ARDEN ARIEL ARIES ARLEN ARLES ARMED ARMEE ARMET ARNEL ARPEL ARRET ARTEL ARTES BRAES BREED BREEN BRIEF BRIER BRIES CREED CREEK CREEL CREEP CREES CRIED CRIER CRIES CRUEL CRUET CRYER DRIED DRIER DRIES DRYER ERIES ERNES ERRED FREED FREER FREES FRIED FRIER FRIES FROES FRYER GREED GREEK GREEN GREER GREES GREET GRIEF GRIEG GRIER GRUEL IRKED IRREG ORDER ORFEO ORIEL ORLES ORSER PREEN PRIED PRIER PRIES PROEM TREED TREEN TREES TRIED TRIER TRIES TRUED TRUER TRUES TRUEX URGED URGER URGES URIEL URKEL WRIER WRYER

•R••E

ARAME ARBRE ARETE ARGUE ARISE ARMEE ARNIE AROSE ARTIE BRACE BRAHE BRAKE BRAVE BRAZE BREVE BRIBE BRICE BRIDE BRINE BRITE BROKE BROME BRUCE BRULE BRUME BRUTE BRYCE CRAKE CRANE CRAPE CRATE CRAVE CRAZE CREME CREPE CRETE CRIME CROCE CRONE CROZE CRUDE CRUSE DRAKE DRAPE DRDRE DRIVE DROME DRONE DROVE DRUPE DRUSE DRUZE ERASE ERNIE ERODE EROSE FRAME FRERE FRISE FROBE FROME FROZE GRACE GRADE GRAPE GRATE GRAVE GRAZE GREBE GRETE GRIME GRIPE GROFE GROPE GROVE IRADE IRATE IRENE KRONE ORALE ORATE PRASE PRATE PRICE PRIDE PRIME PRIZE PROBE PROLE PRONE PROSE PROVE PRUDE PRUNE PRYCE TRACE TRADE TRAVE TRIBE TRICE TRIKE TRINE TRIPE TRITE TROPE TROVE TRUCE TRYME WRITE WROTE

••RE•

ACRED ACRES ADREM AGREE AIRED AIRES APRES ARRET AUREI AYRES BARED BARER BARES BEREA BERET BORED BORER BORES BYRES CARED CARER CARES CARET CAREW CAREY CERED CERES CIRES COREA CORED CORER CORES COREY CURED CURER CURES DARED DARER DARES DEREK DIRER DOREN DURER EARED EFREM EGRET ERRED EYRES FARED FARER FARES FIRED FIRER FIRES FORES GORED GOREN GORES GYRES HARED HAREM HARES HERES HIRED HIRER HIRES HOREB INREM IRREG JEREZ JOREL KAREL KAREN KOREA LARES LOREN LORES LURED LURES LUREX LYRES MARES MERES MIRED MIRES MOREL MORES MOREY MUREX NARES NAREW OARED OCREA OGRES PARED PAREE PAREN PARER PARES PAREU PERES PEREZ PHREN PORED PORES PUREE PURER PUREX PYRES PYREX RAREE RARER RARES ROREM SCREE SCREW SERES SHRED SHREW SIRED SIREN SIRES SOREL SOREN SORER SORES SPREE STREP STREW SURER TARES THREE THREW TIRED TIRES TYRES VIREO WARES WIRED WIRER WIRES YARER YPRES

••R•E

AERIE AGREE AURAE BARGE BARRE BERLE BERME BERNE BIRSE BORGE BORNE BURKE BURSE BYRNE CARLE CARNE CARPE CARRE CARTE CARVE CIRCE CURIE CURSE CURVE DIRGE EARLE EERIE EYRIE FARCE FAROE FERDE FORCE FORGE FORTE FURZE GARDE GORGE GORME GORSE HARTE HERNE HERVE HORAE HORDE HORNE HORSE JARRE JORGE KYRIE LARGE LARUE LORNE LORRE LURIE MARGE MARIE MARNE MCRAE MERCE MERGE MERLE MEROE MORAE MORSE MURRE NERVE NORGE NORSE NORTE NURSE PAREE PARLE PARSE PARTE PERCE PERLE PERSE PORTE PUREE PURGE PURSE RAREE SARGE SCREE SERGE SERVE SPREE SPRUE SURGE TARDE TARGE TERNE TERRE TERSE THREE THROE TORME TORRE TORTE VERDE VERGE VERNE VERRE VERSE VERTE VERVE WORSE

•••RE

ADORE AFIRE AFORE ALFRE AMORE ANDRE ANTRE APURE ARBRE ASTRE AUTRE AWARE AZURE BARRE BLARE CADRE CARRE CHERE CHORE CLARE DEERE DETRE DRDRE DUPRE EAGRE ENTRE ENURE FAIRE FAURE FAVRE FIBRE FLARE FRERE GENRE GLARE HAVRE HEURE INURE ISERE JAHRE JARRE LIBRE LITRE LIVRE LOIRE LORRE LUCRE MADRE MAHRE METRE MITRE MOIRE MOORE MURRE NACRE NIDRE NITRE NOIRE NOTRE OCHRE OHARE OMBRE OPERE OUTRE PADRE QUARE QUIRE SABRE SACRE SCARE SCORE SHARE SHERE SHIRE SHORE SNARE SNORE SPARE SPIRE SPORE STARE STERE STORE SUCRE SWORE TERRE THERE TITRE TORRE TWERE VERRE

VIVRE VOTRE WHERE WHYRE YOURE ZAIRE

R•F••
RAFER RAFFI RAFTS REFER REFIT REFRY RIFER RIFFI RIFFS RIFLE RIFTS RSFSR RUFFS RUFUS

R••F•
RAFFI REEFS REIFY RIFFI RIFFS ROLFE ROOFS RUFFS

R•••F
RIDOF

•RF••
ORFEO

•R•F•
CRAFT CROFT DRAFT DRIFT GRAFT GRIFT GROFE GRUFF KRAFT PROFS WRAFS

•R••F
BRIEF GRIEF GRUFF PROOF

••RF•
CORFU SERFS SURFS SURFY TURFS TURFY ZARFS

••R•F
SERIF

•••RF
DWARF SCARF SCURF SMURF SWARF WHARF

R•G••
RAGAS RAGED RAGES REGAL REGAN REGIA REGIS REGNI REGUM RIGBY RIGEL RIGGS RIGHT RIGID RIGOR RIGUP ROGER ROGET ROGUE RUGAE RUGBY

R••G•
RANGE RANGY REIGN RIDGE RIDGY RIGGS RINGO RINGS ROUGE ROUGH RUDGE RUNGS

R•••G
REBAG RELIG REPEG RERIG RETAG RUING

•RG••
ARGIL ARGOL ARGON ARGOS ARGOT ARGUE ARGUS ERGOT ORGAN URGED URGER URGES

•R•G•
BRAGA BRAGG BRAGS BRIGS CRAGS DRAGS DREGS DRUGS FRIGG FROGS GREGG GRIGS GROGS KROGH PREGO PRIGS PROGS TRIGS TRUGS

•R••G
BRAGG BRING BRUNG CRAIG DRANG FRIGG GRAIG GREGG GRIEG IRREG MRBIG ORANG ORING PRANG PRONG WRING WRONG WRUNG

••RG•
AARGH BARGE BARGY BERGH BERGS BORGE BURGS CARGO CORGI DIRGE FARGO FORGE FORGO GORGE JORGE LARGE LARGO MARGE MARGO MERGE NORGE PORGY PURGE SARGE SARGO SERGE SORGO SURGE TARGE VERGE VIRGA VIRGO

••R•G
DORAG HARDG IRREG RERIG SCRAG SHRUG SPRAG SPRIG STRUG UNRIG VARIG

•••RG
BOURG GEORG INORG

RH•••
RHEAS RHETT RHEUM RHINE RHINO RHIZO RHODA RHODE RHODO RHOMB RHONE RHUMB RHYME RHYTA

R•H••
RAHAB RAHAL REHAB REHAN REHEM

R••H•
RAPHE RASHT RATHS RICHE RIGHT RISHI ROCHE RUCHE RUEHL RUSHY

R•••H
RAJAH RALPH RANCH RATCH REACH REICH RICOH ROACH ROUGH

•RH••
ARHAT ARHUS

•R•H•
ARCHI ARCHY ARTHR BRAHE BRUHN ORCHS ORTHO

•R••H
ARITH BRASH BRITH BROTH BRUCH BRUSH CRASH CRUSH ERICH FRESH FROSH FROTH GRAPH IRISH KROGH ORACH TRASH TRISH TROTH TRUTH URIAH URICH WRATH WROTH

••R•H
AARGH BARTH BERGH BERTH BIRCH BIRTH BORAH DARTH EARTH FARAH FIRTH FORTH FURTH GARTH GERAH GIRTH HARSH KARSH LARCH LURCH MARCH MARSH MIRTH MORPH MYRRH NORAH NORTH OPRAH PARCH PERCH PERTH PORCH SARAH SURAH TORAH TORCH UNRUH WORTH

•••RH
FOURH MYRRH

RI•••
RIALS RIANT RIATA RIBBY RICCI RICED RICER RICES RICHE RICKI RICKS RICKY RICOH RIDER RIDES RIDGE RIDGY RIDOF RIELS RIFER RIFFI RIFFS RIFLE RIFTS RIGBY RIGEL RIGGS RIGHT RIGID RIGOR RIGUP RIKER RIKKI RILED RILES RILEY RILKE RILLE RILLS RIMED RIMES RINDS RINDY RINGO RINGS RINKS RINKY RINSE RINSO RIOJA RIOTS RIPEN RIPER RIPON RIPUP RISEN RISER RISES RISHI RISKS RISKY RITES RITZY RIVAL RIVED RIVEN RIVER RIVES RIVET RIYAL RIZZO

R•I••
RAIDS RAILS RAINS RAINY RAISA RAISE RAITT REICH REIFY REIGN REIMS REINA REINK REINS RHINE RHINO RHIZO ROILS ROILY RUING RUINS

R••I•
RABID RABIN RADII RADIO RADIX RAJIV RAKIS RAMIE RAMIS RANID RANIN RANIS RAPID RATIO RAVIN REAIM REAIR REBID RECIP REDID REFIT REGIA REGIS RELIC RELIG RELIT REMIT REMIX RENIN REOIL REPIN RERIG RESIN RETIA RETIE REWIN RIGID ROBIN RODIN ROSIE ROSIN ROXIE RUBIK RUBIN RUNIC RUNIN RURIK RUTIN

R•••I
RABBI RADII RAFFI RANDI RECTI REGNI RICCI RICKI RIFFI RIKKI RISHI ROSSI

•RI••
ARIAN ARIAS ARICA ARIEL ARIES ARILS ARION ARISE ARITH ARIUM ARIUS BRIAN BRIAR BRIBE BRICE BRICK BRIDE BRIEF BRIER BRIES BRIGS BRILL BRIMS BRINE BRING BRINK BRINY BRISK BRITE BRITH BRITS BRITT CRIBS CRICK CRIED CRIER CRIES CRIME CRIMP CRISP CRISS CRIST DRIBS DRIED DRIER DRIES DRIFT DRILL DRILY DRINA DRINK DRIPS DRIVE ERICA ERICH ERIES ERIKA ERISA FRIAR FRICK FRIED FRIER FRIES FRIGG FRILL FRIML FRISE FRISK FRITO FRITS FRITZ FRIZZ GRIDS GRIEF GRIEG GRIER GRIFT GRIGS GRILL GRIME GRIMM GRIMY GRIND GRINS GRIOT GRIPE GRIPS GRIST GRITS IRIDO IRINA IRISH KRILL KRISS ORIBI ORIEL ORING ORION ORIYA PRIAM PRICE PRICK PRICY PRIDE PRIED PRIER PRIES PRIGS PRIMA PRIME PRIMI PRIMO PRIMP PRIMS PRINK PRINT PRION PRIOR PRISM PRIVY PRIZE PRIZM TRIAD TRIAL TRIBE TRICE TRICK TRIED TRIER TRIES TRIGS TRIKE TRILL TRIMS TRINE TRINI TRIOS TRIPE TRIPS TRISH TRITE TRITT URIAH URIAL URICH URIEL WRIER WRING WRIST WRITE WRITS

•R•I•
ARGIL ARKIN ARMIS ARNIE AROID ARRIS ARSIS ARTIE ARTIS BRAID BRAIL BRAIN BROIL BRUIN BRUIT CRAIG CRAIN CROIX DRAIL DRAIN DROID DROIT DRUID ERBIL ERNIE ERVIL ERVIN ERWIN FRAIL FRAIS FROID FRUIT GRAIG GRAIL GRAIN GROIN IRVIN IRWIN KRAIT MRBIG ORBIT ORNIS ORRIN ORRIS PRAIA TRAIL TRAIN TRAIT TROIS URBIS URSID

•R••I
ARCHI CROCI GRANI IRANI IRAQI ORIBI PRIMI TREVI TRINI

••RI•
ABRIL ABRIS ACRID AERIE AFRIC AFRIT AGRIC APRIL ARRIS ATRIA ATRIP AURIC AVRIL BARIC BARIT BORIC BORIS BURIN CARIA CARIB CERIA CHRIS CORIA CURIA CURIE CURIO CYRIL DARIN DARIO DERIV DORIC DORIS EERIE EYRIE EYRIR FERIA KIRIN KYRIE LARIS LORIS LURIA LURID LURIE LYRIC MARIA MARIE MARIN MARIO MARIS MERIT NARIS NORIA ORRIN ORRIS OSRIC PARIS PERIL PERIS PURIM PYRIC RERIG RURIK SARIS SCRIM SCRIP SERIF SERIN SPRIG SPRIT STRIA STRIP SYRIA TORIC TORII TURIN UGRIC UNRIG VARIA VARIG VARIX VIRID XERIC ZORIL ZORIS

••R•I
AUREI CARDI CARPI CIRRI CORGI CURCI DORSI FARCI FARSI FERMI FERRI FORLI GARNI GORKI KERRI LEROI MARDI MARTI MERCI NURMI PARDI PARTI SERAI TARSI TERRI TORII TORSI VERDI VERMI

•••RI
ACARI ATARI CAPRI CHERI CIRRI CUPRI FERRI HENRI HOURI INARI INDRI KAURI KERRI MAORI MATRI NEGRI PATRI PETRI SHARI SPYRI TERRI

R•J••
RAJAH RAJAS RAJIV

R••J•
RIOJA

R•K••
RAKED RAKER RAKES RAKIS REKEY RIKER RIKKI

R••K•
RACKS RANKE RANKS REEKS REEKY RICKI RICKS RICKY RIKKI RILKE RINKS RINKY RISKS RISKY ROCKS ROCKY ROOKS ROOKY ROYKO RUCKS RUSKS

R•••K
REINK RUARK RUBIK RURIK

•RK••
ARKIN IRKED URKEL

•R•K•
BRAKE BROKE CRAKE DRAKE ERIKA GROKS TREKS TRIKE

•R••K
BREAK BRECK BRICK BRINK BRISK BROCK BROOK CRACK CRANK CREAK CREEK CRICK CROAK CROCK CROOK DRANK DRINK DRUNK FRANK FREAK FRICK FRISK FROCK GREEK PRANK PRICK PRINK TRACK TRICK TRUCK TRUNK WRACK WREAK WRECK

••RK•
BARKS BARKY BURKE CARKS CORKS CORKY DARKS DIRKS FORKS FORKY GORKI GORKY HARKS HERKY JERKS JERKY KIRKS LARKS LARKY LURKS MARKS MIRKY MURKY NARKS PARKA PARKS PERKS PERKY PORKS PORKY SARKY TURKS TURKU WORKS YERKS

••R•K
DEREK HUROK KURSK MERCK RURIK TAROK YUROK

•••RK
CLARK CLERK DMARK OZARK QUARK QUIRK RUARK SHARK SHIRK SMIRK SNARK SPARK SPORK STARK STIRK STORK

R•L••
RALLY RALPH RELAX RELAY RELEE RELET RELIC RELIG RELIT RILED RILES RILEY RILKE RILLE RILLS ROLEO ROLES ROLEX ROLFE ROLLE ROLLO ROLLS RULED RULER RULES

R••L•
RAILS RALLY RAWLS RAWLY REALM REALS REDLY REELS REPLY RIALS RIELS RIFLE RILLE RILLS ROALD ROBLE ROILS ROILY ROLLE ROLLO ROLLS ROTLS RUBLE

R•••L
RAHAL RAOUL RATEL RAVEL REBEL REGAL RENAL REOIL REPEL REUEL REVEL RIGEL RIVAL RIYAL ROWEL ROYAL RUEHL RURAL

•RL••
ARLEN ARLES DRLAO ORLES ORLON ORLOP

•R•L•
ARILS BRILL BRULE CROLY DRILL DRILY DROLL DRYLY FRILL GRILL KRILL KRULL ORALE ORALS PRELL PROLE TRALA TRILL TROLL TRULY URALS WRYLY

•R••L
AREAL ARGIL ARGOL ARIEL ARNEL ARPEL ARTAL ARTEL BRAIL BRAWL BRILL BROIL CRAWL CREEL CRUEL DRAIL DRAWL DRILL DROLL DROOL ERBIL ERROL ERVIL FRAIL FRILL FRIML GRAIL GRILL GROWL GRUEL KRAAL KRILL KRULL ORIEL PRELL PROWL TRAIL TRAWL TRIAL TRILL TROLL URIAL URIEL URKEL

••RL•
BERLE BIRLS BURLS BURLY CARLA CARLE CARLO CARLY CURLS CURLY DARLA EARLE EARLS EARLY FORLI FURLS GIRLS HERLS HURLS HURLY JARLS KARLA MARLA MARLO MARLS MARLY MERLE MERLS PARLE PERLE PURLS SURLY WORLD

••R•L
ABRIL APRIL AURAL AVRIL BERYL CAROL CORAL CYRIL DARYL DORAL ENROL ERROL FERAL GORAL GYRAL HERZL HORAL HOROL JOREL JURAL KAREL KAROL MERYL MORAL MOREL MURAL NEROL PAROL PERIL RURAL SERAL SOREL SURAL TYROL VIRAL ZORIL

•••RL
BGIRL CEORL CHURL GNARL KNURL PEARL SKIRL SNARL SWIRL TWIRL WHIRL WHORL

R•M••
RAMAN RAMAR RAMBO RAMEE RAMEN RAMET RAMIE RAMIS RAMON RAMOS RAMPS REMAN REMAP REMET REMEX REMIT REMIX REMOP REMOW REMUS RIMED RIMES ROMAN ROMEO ROMER ROMPS RUMBA RUMEN RUMMY RUMOR RUMPS

R••M•
REAMS REIMS RHOMB RHUMB RHYME ROAMS ROOMS ROOMY RUMMY

R•••M
REAIM REALM REARM REGUM REHEM RERUM RHEUM ROREM

•RM••
ARMED ARMEE ARMET ARMIS ARMOR

MRMOM

•R•M•
ARAMA ARAME AROMA ARUMS BRIMS BROME BROMO BRUME CRAMP CRAMS CREME CRIME CRIMP CRUMB CRUMP DRAMA DRAMS DROME DRUMS FRAME FRIML FROME FROMM FRUMP GRAMA GRAMM GRAMP GRAMS GRIME GRIMM GRIMY GRUMP ORAMA OROMO PRAMS PRIMA PRIME PRIMI PRIMO PRIMP PRIMS PROMO PROMS TRAMP TRAMS TRIMS TROMP TRUMP TRYME

•R••M
ARIUM BREAM BROOM CREAM DREAM FROMM GRAMM GRIMM GROOM MRMOM PRIAM PRISM PRIZM PROAM PROEM VROOM

••RM•
BARMS BARMY BERME BERMS BURMA CORMS DERMA DERMO DORMS FARMS FERMI FIRMA FIRMS FORMA FORMS GERMS GERMY GORME HARMS HERMS KARMA NORMA NORMS NURMI PARMA PERMS TERMS TORME VERMI WARMS WORMS WORMY

••R•M
ABRAM ADREM AURUM CAROM CDROM CERAM CHROM DURUM EFREM EPROM FORUM HAREM HARUM HIRAM INREM JORUM LARAM MORUM PURIM RERUM ROREM SCRAM SCRIM SCRUM SERUM STROM STRUM THRUM

•••RM
ALARM CHARM ENORM PHARM REARM STORM STURM SWARM THERM UNARM

RN•••
RNASE

R•N••
RANAT RANCH RANDB RANDD RANDI RANDR RANDS RANDY RANEE RANGE RANGY RANID RANIN RANIS RANKE RANKS RANON RANTO RANTS RANUP RENAL RENAN RENDS RENEE RENEW RENIN RENTA RENTS RINDS RINDY RINGO RINGS RINKS RINKY RINSE RINSO RONDO RONEE RONNY RUNAT RUNES RUNGS RUNIC RUNIN RUNNY RUNON RUNTO RUNTS RUNTY RUNUP

R••N•
RAINS RAINY REGNI REINA REINK REINS REUNE RHINE RHINO RHONE RIANT ROANS RONNY ROONE ROUND ROVNO RUANA RUING RUINS RUNNY

R•••N
RABIN RACON RADON RAMAN RAMEN RAMON RANIN RANON RATON RAVEN RAVIN RAYON RECON REDAN REDON REGAN REHAN REIGN REMAN RENAN RENIN REPIN RERAN RERUN RESIN REWIN REWON RIPEN RIPON RISEN RIVEN ROBIN RODAN RODIN ROMAN ROSEN ROSIN ROUEN ROWAN ROWEN RUBEN RUBIN RUMEN RUNIN RUNON RUTIN

•RN••
ARNAZ ARNEL ARNIE ERNES ERNIE ERNST ORNIS

•R•N•
ARENA ARENS ARENT BRAND BRANS BRANT BRENT BRINE BRING BRINK BRINY BRONC BRONX BRUNG BRUNO BRUNT CRANE CRANK CRONE CRONY DRANG DRANK DRANO DRINA DRINK DRONE DRUNK FRANC FRANK FRANS FRANZ FRENA FROND FRONT GRAND GRANI GRANT GRIND GRINS GRUNT IRANI IRENE IRINA IRONS IRONY KRONA KRONE ORANG ORANT ORING ORONO PRANG PRANK PRINK PRINT PRONE PRONG PRUNE TRANS TREND TRENT TRINE TRINI TRUNK WRENS WRING WRONG WRUNG

•R••N
ARDEN ARGON ARIAN ARION ARKIN ARLEN ARRAN ARSON ARYAN BRAIN BRAUN BRAWN BREEN BRIAN BROUN BROWN BRUHN BRUIN BRYAN CRAIN CREON CROON CROWN DRAIN DRAWN DROWN ERVIN ERWIN FREON FROWN GRAIN GREEN GROAN GROIN GROWN IRVIN IRWIN ORGAN ORION ORLON ORRIN ORSON ORTON PRAWN PREEN PRION TRAIN TREEN TRYON URBAN

••RN•
BARNS BERNE BORNE BURNS BURNT BYRNE CARNE CARNY CORNO CORNS CORNU CORNY DARNS DURNS EARNS FERNS FERNY FIRNS GARNI GIRNS HERNE HERNS HORNE HORNS KERNS LORNA LORNE MARNE MORNS MYRNA NORNS TARNS TERNE TERNS TURNS VARNA VERNE VIRNA WARNS YARNS

••R•N
AARON AERON AGRON AKRON APRON ARRAN BARON BORON BURIN BYRON CARON CHRON DARIN DORAN DOREN DURAN FARON FURAN GOREN GYRON HERON HURON KARAN KAREN KIRIN KORAN LORAN LOREN MARIN MORAN MORON MYRON ORRIN PAREN PERAN PERON PHREN RERAN RERUN SARAN SERIN SIREN SOREN TIRAN TURIN

•••RN
ACORN ADORN AGARN BAIRN BJORN BOURN CAIRN CHURN HEARN LEARN MOURN NAIRN QUERN SCORN SHORN SPURN STERN SWORN THORN UTURN YEARN

RO•••
ROACH ROADS ROALD ROAMS ROANS ROARS ROAST ROBBY ROBED ROBES ROBIN ROBLE ROBOT ROCCO ROCHE ROCKS ROCKY RODAN RODDY RODEO RODIN ROGER ROGET ROGUE ROILS ROILY ROLEO ROLES ROLEX ROLFE ROLLE ROLLO ROLLS ROMAN ROMEO ROMER ROMPS RONDO RONEE RONNY ROODS ROOFS ROOKS ROOKY ROOMS ROOMY ROONE ROOST ROOTS ROOTY ROPED ROPER ROPES ROPEY ROQUE ROREM ROSEN ROSES ROSEY ROSIE ROSIN ROSSI ROTAS ROTES ROTLS ROTOR ROTOS ROUEN ROUES ROUGE ROUGH ROUND ROUSE ROUST ROUTE ROUTS ROVED ROVER ROVES ROVNO ROWAN ROWDY ROWED ROWEL ROWEN ROWER ROXIE ROYAL ROYCE ROYKO

R•O••
RAOUL REOIL RHODA RHODE RHODO RHOMB RHONE RIOJA RIOTS ROODS ROOFS ROOKS ROOKY ROOMS ROOMY ROONE ROOST ROOTS ROOTY RYOTS

R••O•
RACON RADON RAMON RAMOS RANON RATON RAYON RAZOR RECON REDON REDOX REMOP REMOW REPOS REPOT RESOD RETOP RETOW REWON RICOH RIDOF RIGOR RIPON ROBOT ROTOR ROTOS RUMOR RUNON

R•••O
RADIO RAMBO RANTO RATIO RATSO RECTO REPRO RETRO RHINO RHIZO RHODO RINGO RINSO RIZZO ROCCO RODEO ROLEO ROLLO ROMEO RONDO ROVNO ROYKO RUNTO RUSSO

•RO••
AROAR AROID AROMA AROSE BROAD BROCA BROCK BRODY BROIL BROKE BROME BROMO BRONC BRONX BROOD BROOK BROOM BROTH BROUN BROWN BROWS CROAK CROAT CROCE CROCI CROCK CROCS CROFT CROIX CROLY CRONE CRONY CROOK CROON CROPS CROSS CROUP CROWD CROWN CROWS CROZE DROID DROIT DROLL DROME DRONE DROOD DROOL DROOP DROPS DROSS DROVE DROWN ERODE EROSE FROBE FROCK FRODO FROES FROGS FROID FROME FROMM FROND FRONT FROSH FROST FROTH FROWN FROWS FROZE GROAN GROAT GRODY GROFE GROGS GROIN GROKS GROOM GROPE GROSS GROSZ GROTS GROUP GROUT GROVE GROWL GROWN GROWS GROZA IRONS IRONY KROGH KRONA KRONE OROMO ORONO PROAM PROAS PROBE PROBS PRODS PROEM PROFS PROGS PROLE PROMO PROMS PRONE PRONG PROOF PROPS PROSE PROST PROSY PROTO PROTS PROUD PROVE PROVO PROWL PROWS PROXY TROIS TROLL TROMP TROOP TROPE TROPO TROTH TROTS TROUT TROVE VROOM WRONG WROTE WROTH

•R•O•
ARBOR ARDOR ARGOL ARGON ARGOS ARGOT ARION ARMOR ARROW ARROZ ARSON ARTOO BROOD BROOK BROOM CREON CROOK CROON DROOD DROOL DROOP ERGOT ERROL ERROR FREON GRIOT GROOM MRMOM ORDOS OREOS ORION ORLON ORLOP ORSON ORTON ORZOS PRION PRIOR PROOF PRYOR TRIOS TROOP TRYON VROOM

•R••O
ARTOO BRAVO BROMO BRUNO CREDO DRACO DRANO DRLAO ERATO FRITO FRODO GRECO IRIDO ORFEO OROMO ORONO ORTHO ORURO PRADO PRATO PREGO PRIMO PROMO PROTO PROVO TROPO TRURO

••RO•
AARON AERON AEROS AFROS AGRON AKRON APRON ARROW ARROZ BARON BORON BYRON CAROB CAROL CAROM CARON CDROM CEROS CHROM CHRON COROT DUROC DUROS ELROY ENROL EPROM ERROL ERROR EUROS FAROE FARON FAROS FUROR FUROS GAROU GIROS GYRON GYROS HEROD HERON HEROS HOROL HUROK HURON JUROR KAROL KIROV LEROI LEROY MEROE MORON MOROS MYRON NEROL PAROL PAROS PERON PEROT SAROD SAROS SCROD SEROW STROM STROP TAROK TAROT THROB THROE THROW TIROS TOROS TUROW TYROL TYROS XEROX YUROK ZEROS

••R•O
BURRO CARBO CARGO CARLO CARPO CERRO CIRRO CORNO CURIO DARIO DERMO DORSO FARGO FERRO FIRPO FORDO FORGO GARBO GORDO HARPO LARGO MARCO MARGO MARIO MARLO MIRRO MORRO NARCO NORVO PARDO PARVO PORTO SARGO SARTO SERVO SORGO TORSO TURBO VERSO VIREO VIRGO ZORRO

•••RO
AGGRO ANDRO ASTRO BURRO CAIRO CERRO CHARO CHIRO CIRRO CLARO CUPRO DOBRO DOURO ENERO EXTRO FERRO FIBRO FIERO GENRO GUIRO HIERO HYDRO HYGRO IATRO INTRO MACRO MATRO METRO MICRO MIRRO MORRO MUCRO MUNRO NEURO NITRO ORURO PEDRO PETRO PICRO PTERO REPRO RETRO SACRO SPERO SPIRO TAURO THORO TRURO ZORRO

R•P••
RAPEE RAPHE RAPID REPAD REPAY REPEG REPEL REPIN REPLY REPOS REPOT REPPS REPRO RIPEN RIPER RIPON RIPUP ROPED ROPER ROPES ROPEY RUPEE

R••P•
RALPH RAMPS RASPS RASPY REAPS REPPS REUPS ROMPS RSVPD RSVPS RUMPS

R•••P
RANUP RECAP RECIP REMAP REMOP RETAP RETOP REVUP RIGUP RIPUP RUNUP

•RP••
ARPAD ARPEL

•R•P•
CRAPE CRAPS CREPE CREPT CROPS CRYPT DRAPE DRIPS DROPS DRUPE ERUPT FRAPS GRAPE GRAPH GRAPY GRIPE GRIPS GROPE KRUPA KRUPP PREPS PROPS TRAPP TRAPS TRIPE TRIPS TROPE TROPO WRAPS WRAPT

•R••P
CRAMP CREEP CRIMP CRISP CROUP CRUMP DROOP DRYUP FRUMP GRAMP GRASP GROUP GRUMP KRUPP ORLOP PRIMP TRAMP TRAPP TROMP TROOP TRUMP

••RP•
BURPS CARPE CARPI CARPO CARPS CORPS DORPS FIRPO GORPS HARPO HARPS HARPY MORPH PERPS TARPS TERPS WARPS

••R•P
ATRIP PTRAP SCRAP SCRIP STRAP STREP STRIP STROP SYRUP

•••RP
CHIRP SCARP SHARP SLURP THARP THORP TWERP USURP

R•Q••
ROQUE

•R•Q•
IRAQI

••RQ•
BARQS

••R•Q
BARBQ

R•R••
RAREE RARER RARES RERAN RERIG RERUM RERUN ROREM RURAL RURIK

R••R•
REARM REARS REFRY REPRO RETRO RETRY ROARS RUARK RUERS

R•••R
RACER RADAR RAFER RAKER RAMAR RANDR RARER RASER RATER RAVER RAWER RAZOR REAIR REBAR RECUR REFER RETAR RICER RIDER RIFER RIGOR RIKER RIPER RISER RIVER ROGER ROMER ROPER ROTOR ROVER ROWER RSFSR RUDER RULER RUMOR RYDER

•RR••
ARRAN ARRAS ARRAU ARRAY ARRET ARRIS ARROW ARROZ ERRED ERROL ERROR IRREG ORRIN ORRIS

•R•R•
ARBRE BRERS CRURA DRDRE DRURY FRERE ORURO TRURO

•R••R
ARBER ARBOR ARDOR AREAR ARMOR AROAR ARTHR ARTUR BRIAR

BRIER CRIER CRYER DREAR DRIER DRYER ERROR FREER FRIAR FRIER FRYER GREER GRIER ORDER ORSER PRIER PRIOR PRYOR TRIER TRUER URGER WRIER WRYER

••RR•

BARRE BARRY BERRA BERRY BIRRS BURRO BURRS BURRY CARRE CARRY CERRO CIRRI CIRRO CURRY DERRY DURRA FERRI FERRO FERRY FIRRY FURRY GARRY GERRY HARRY HURRY JARRE JERRY KERRI KERRY LARRY LORRE LORRY MARRY MERRY MIRRO MORRO MURRA MURRE MYRRH PARRY PERRY PURRS SERRA SERRY SORRY TARRY TERRA TERRE TERRI TERRY TORRE TORRS UNRRA VERRE WIRRA WORRY ZORRO

••R•R

AURAR BARER BORER CARER CORER CURER DARER DIRER DURER ERROR EYRIR FARER FIRER FUROR HARAR HIRER JUROR PARER PURER RARER SORER SURER WIRER YARER

•••RR

CHIRR KNORR OMARR SHIRR SKIRR STARR WHIRR

RS•••

RSFSR RSVPD RSVPS

R•S••

RASED RASER RASES RASHT RASPS RASPY RASTA RESAW RESEE RESET RESEW RESIN RESOD RESTS RISEN RISER RISES RISHI RISKS RISKY ROSEN ROSES ROSEY ROSIE ROSIN ROSSI RUSES RUSHY RUSKS RUSSE RUSSO RUSTS RUSTY

R••S•

RAISA RAISE RATSO REESE REUSE RINSE RINSO RNASE ROAST ROOST ROSSI ROUSE ROUST RSFSR RUSSE RUSSO

R•••S

RACES RACKS RAFTS RAGAS RAGES RAIDS RAILS RAINS RAJAS RAKES RAKIS RAMIS RAMOS RAMPS RANDS RANIS RANKS RANTS RARES RASES RASPS RATES RATHS RAVES RAWLS RAZES READS REALS REAMS REAPS REARS REBUS REDES REEDS REEFS REEKS REELS REGIS REIMS REINS REMUS RENDS RENTS REPOS REPPS RESTS REUPS REXES REYES RHEAS RIALS RICES RICKS RIDES RIELS RIFFS RIFTS RIGGS RILES RILLS RIMES RINDS RINGS RINKS RIOTS RISES RISKS RITES RIVES ROADS ROAMS ROANS ROARS ROBES ROCKS ROILS ROLES ROLLS ROMPS ROODS ROOFS ROOKS ROOMS ROOTS ROPES ROSES ROTAS ROTES ROTLS ROTOS ROUES ROUTS ROVES RSVPS RUBES RUCKS RUDDS RUERS RUFFS RUFUS RUINS RULES RUMPS RUNES RUNGS RUNTS RUSES RUSKS RUSTS RYOTS

•RS••

ARSIS ARSON ORSER ORSON URSID

•R•S•

ARISE AROSE ARTSY BRASH BRASS BREST BRISK BRUSH CRASH CRASS CRESC CRESS CREST CRISP CRISS CRIST CROSS CRUSE CRUSH CRUST DRESS DROSS DRUSE ERASE ERISA ERNST EROSE FRESH FRISE FRISK FROSH FROST GRASP GRASS GRIST GROSS GROSZ IRISH KRISS PRASE PRESS PREST PRISM PROSE PROST PROSY TRASH TRESS TRISH TRUSS TRUST TRYST WREST WRIST

•R••S

ARABS AREAS ARENS ARGOS ARGUS ARHUS ARIAS ARIES ARILS ARIUS ARLES ARMIS ARRAS ARRIS ARSIS ARTES ARTIS ARUMS BRADS BRAES BRAGS BRANS BRASS BRATS BRAYS BRERS BREWS BRIES BRIGS BRIMS BRITS BROWS BRUTS CRABS CRAGS CRAMS CRAPS CRASS CRAWS CREES CRESS CREWS CRIBS CRIES CRISS CROCS CROPS CROSS CROWS DRABS DRAGS DRAMS DRATS DRAWS DRAYS DREGS DRESS DRIBS DRIES DRIPS DROPS DROSS DRUBS DRUGS DRUMS ERIES ERNES FRAIS FRANS FRAPS FRATS FRAYS FREES FRETS FRIES FRITS FROES FROGS FROWS GRABS GRADS GRAMS GRASS GRAYS GREES GREYS GRIDS GRIGS GRINS GRIPS GRITS GROGS GROKS GROSS GROTS GROWS GRUBS IRONS KRAUS KREBS KRISS ORALS ORCAS ORCHS ORCUS ORDOS OREOS ORLES ORNIS ORRIS ORZOS PRAMS PRAUS PRAYS PREPS PRESS PREYS PRIES PRIGS PRIMS PROAS PROBS PRODS PROFS PROGS PROMS PROPS PROTS PROWS SRTAS TRAMS TRANS TRAPS TRAYS TREES TREKS TRESS TREWS TREYS TRIES TRIGS TRIMS TRIOS TRIPS TROIS TROTS TRUES TRUGS TRUSS URALS URBIS URGES WRACS WRAFS WRAPS WRENS WRITS XRAYS

••RS•

BIRSE BURSA BURSE BURST CURSE CURST DERSU DORSA DORSI DORSO DURST FARSI FIRST GORSE GORSY HARSH HORSE HORST HORSY HURST KARSH KURSK MARSH MORSE NORSE NURSE PARSE PERSE PURSE PURSY TARSI TERSE TORSI TORSO VERSA VERSE VERSO VERST WORSE WORST WURST

••R•S

ABRIS ACRES AEROS AFROS AIRES APRES ARRAS ARRIS AURAS AYRES BARBS BARDS BARES BARKS BARMS BARNS BARQS BARTS BERGS BERMS BIRDS BIRLS BIRRS BORAS BORES BORIS BURBS BURGS BURLS BURNS BURPS BURRS BYRDS BYRES CARBS CARDS CARES CARKS CARPS CARTS CERES CEROS CERTS CHRIS CHRYS CIRCS CIRES CORDS CORES CORKS CORMS CORNS CORPS CURBS CURDS CURES CURLS CYRUS DARES DARKS DARNS DARTS DIRKS DORIS DORMS DORPS DURNS DUROS EARLS EARNS ECRUS EUROS EURUS EYRAS EYRES FARES FARMS FAROS FERNS FIRES FIRMS FIRNS FORBS FORDS FORES FORKS FORMS FORTS FURLS FUROS GARBS GERMS GIRDS GIRLS GIRNS GIROS GIRTS GORES GORPS GURUS GYRES GYROS GYRUS HARES HARKS HARMS HARPS HARTS HERBS HERDS HERES HERLS HERMS HERNS HEROS HIRES HORAS HORNS HORUS HURLS HURTS JARLS JERKS KERBS KERNS KIRKS KURDS LARAS LARDS LARES LARIS LARKS LIRAS LORDS LORES LORIS LURES LURKS LYRES MARAS MARES MARIS MARKS MARLS MARTS MARYS MERES MERLS MIRES MIRVS MORAS MORES MORNS MOROS MORTS NARAS NARCS NARDS NARES NARIS NARKS NERDS NERTS NORMS NORNS OGRES OKRAS ORRIS PARDS PARES PARIS PARKS PAROS PARTS PERES PERIS PERKS PERMS PERPS PORES PORKS PORTS PURLS PURRS PURUS PYRES RARES SARDS SARIS SAROS SERBS SERES SERFS SIRES SORAS SORBS SORES SORTS SORUS SURAS SURDS SURFS TARES TARNS TARPS TARTS TERMS TERNS TERPS TIRES TIROS TOROS TORRS TORTS TORUS TURFS TURKS TURNS TYRES TYROS VARAS VERBS VERTS VIRUS WARDS WARES WARMS WARNS WARPS WARTS WIRES WORDS WORKS WORMS WORTS XERUS YARDS YARNS YERKS YPRES YURTS ZARFS ZEROS ZORIS

•••RS

ABBRS ACERS AFARS AGARS AGERS ALORS AMIRS APERS AVARS AVERS AXERS AYERS BEARS BEERS BIRRS BLURS BOARS BOERS BOORS BRERS BURRS CBERS CHARS CMDRS COIRS COORS CZARS DEARS DEERS DOERS DOORS DYERS EMIRS ENGRS EVERS EWERS EYERS FAIRS FEARS FOURS GAURS GEARS GNARS GOERS GUARS HAIRS HEARS HEIRS HOARS HOERS HOURS IBARS ICERS ITERS IZARS JBARS JEERS KNARS KNURS LAIRS LEARS LEERS LIARS MOORS MYERS NEARS NLERS ODORS OMERS ONERS OVERS OWERS PAIRS PEARS PEERS PIERS POURS PURRS REARS ROARS RUERS SCARS SEARS SEERS SLURS SOARS SOURS SPARS SPURS STARS STIRS SUERS TAHRS TBARS TEARS THURS TIERS TORRS TOURS TSARS TZARS USERS VEERS VIERS WEARS WEIRS WHIRS YEARS YOURS ZBARS

R•T••

RATCH RATED RATEL RATER RATES RATHS RATIO RATON RATSO RATTY RETAG RETAP RETAR RETAX RETIA RETIE RETOP RETOW RETRO RETRY RITES RITZY ROTAS ROTES ROTLS ROTOR ROTOS RUTIN RUTTY

R••T•

RAFTS RAITT RANTO RANTS RASTA RATTY REATA RECTI RECTO RENTA RENTS RESTS RHETT RHYTA RIATA RIFTS RIOTS ROOTS ROOTY ROUTE ROUTS RUNTO RUNTS RUNTY RUSTS RUSTY RUTTY RYOTS

R•••T

RABAT RAITT RAMET RANAT RASHT REACT REBUT REFIT RELET RELIT REMET REMIT REPOT RESET REVET RHETT RIANT RIGHT RIVET ROAST ROBOT ROGET ROOST ROUST RUNAT

•RT••

ARTAL ARTEL ARTES ARTHR ARTIE ARTIS ARTOO ARTSY ARTUR ORTHO ORTON SRTAS

•R•T•

ARETE ARITH BRATS BRETT BRITE BRITH BRITS BRITT BROTH BRUTE BRUTS CRATE CRETE DRATS ERATO FRATS FRETS FRITO FRITS FRITZ FROTH GRATA GRATE GRETA GRETE GRITS GROTS IRATE ORATE PRATE PRATO PRATT PROTO PROTS TRITE TRITT TROTH TROTS TRUTH WRATH WRITE WRITS WROTE WROTH

•R••T

ARENT ARGOT ARHAT ARMET ARRET BRACT BRANT BRENT BREST BRETT BRITT BRUIT BRUNT CRAFT CREPT CREST CRIST CROAT CROFT CRUET CRUST CRYPT DRAFT DRIFT DROIT ERECT ERGOT ERNST ERUCT ERUPT FRONT FROST FRUIT GRAFT GRANT GREAT GREET GRIFT GRIOT GRIST GROAT GROUT GRUNT KRAFT KRAIT KRAUT ORANT ORBIT PRATT PREST PRINT PROST TRACT TRAIT TREAT TRENT TRITT TROUT TRUST TRYST WRAPT WREST WRIST

••RT•

AORTA BARTH BARTS BARTY BERTH BIRTH CARTA CARTE CARTS CERTS DARTH DARTS DIRTY EARTH FIRTH FORTE FORTH FORTS FORTY FURTH GARTH GIRTH GIRTS HARTE HARTS HERTZ HURTS KURTZ MARTA MARTI MARTS MARTY MERTZ MIRTH MORTS NERTS NERTZ NORTE NORTH PARTE PARTI PARTS PARTY PERTH PORTE PORTO PORTS SARTO SERTA SORTA SORTS TARTS TARTU TORTE TORTS VERTE VERTS VIRTU WARTS WARTY WORTH WORTS YURTS

••R•T

AFRIT ARRET BARIT BERET BURNT BURST CARAT CARET CERAT COROT CURST DERAT DURST EGRET FIRST HERAT HORST HURST JURAT KARAT KERAT MARAT MERIT MURAT PEROT SPRAT SPRIT STRUT SURAT TAROT VERST WORST WURST

•••RT

ABORT ALERT AMORT APART APORT AVERT BLURT CHART CHERT COURT EBERT EVERT EXERT FLIRT HEART IBERT INERT KMART OPART OVERT QUART QUIRT SHIRT SHORT SKIRT SKORT SMART SNERT SNORT SPORT SPURT START SWART

RU•••

RUANA RUARK RUBEN RUBES RUBIK RUBIN RUBLE RUCHE RUCKS RUDDS RUDDY RUDER RUDGE RUEHL RUERS RUFFS RUFUS RUGAE RUGBY RUING RUINS RULED RULER RULES RUMBA RUMEN RUMMY RUMOR RUMPS RUNAT RUNES RUNGS RUNIC RUNIN RUNNY RUNON RUNTO RUNTS RUNTY RUNUP RUPEE RURAL RURIK RUSES RUSHY RUSKS RUSSE RUSSO RUSTS RUSTY RUTIN RUTTY

R•U••

REUEL REUNE REUPS REUSE RHUMB ROUEN ROUES ROUGE ROUGH ROUND ROUSE ROUST ROUTE ROUTS

R••U•

RANUP RAOUL REBUS REBUT RECUR REDUB REDUX REGUM REMUS RERUM RERUN REVUE REVUP RHEUM RIGUP RIPUP ROGUE ROQUE RUFUS RUNUP

•RU••

ARUBA ARUMS BRUCE BRUCH BRUHN BRUIN BRUIT BRULE BRUME BRUNG BRUNO BRUNT BRUSH BRUTE BRUTS CRUDE CRUEL CRUET CRUMB CRUMP CRURA CRUSE CRUSH CRUST DRUBS DRUGS DRUID DRUMS DRUNK DRUPE DRURY DRUSE DRUZE ERUCT ERUPT FRUIT FRUMP GRUBS GRUEL GRUFF GRUMP GRUNT KRULL KRUPA KRUPP ORURO PRUDE PRUNE TRUCE TRUCK TRUED TRUER TRUES TRUEX TRUGS TRULY TRUMP TRUNK TRURO TRUSS TRUST TRUTH WRUNG

•R•U•

ARGUE ARGUS ARHUS ARIUM ARIUS ARTUR BRAUN BROUN CROUP DRYUP FRAUD FREUD GROUP GROUT KRAUS KRAUT ORCUS PRAUS PROUD TROUT

•R••U

ARRAU

••RU•

AURUM CYRUS DURUM ECRUS EURUS FORUM GURUS GYRUS HARUM HORUS JORUM LARUE MORUM PURUS RERUM RERUN SCRUB SCRUM SERUM SHRUB SHRUG SORUS SPRUE STRUG STRUM STRUT SYRUP THRUM TORUS UNRUH VIRUS XERUS

••R•U

ARRAU CORFU CORNU DERSU GAROU PAREU PERDU TARTU TURKU VIRTU

•••RU

NAURU NEHRU OTARU UHURU

R•V••

RAVED RAVEL RAVEN RAVER RAVES RAVIN REVEL REVET REVUE REVUP RIVAL RIVED RIVEN RIVER RIVES RIVET ROVED ROVER ROVES ROVNO RSVPD RSVPS

R••V•

REEVE

R•••V

RAJIV

•RV••

ERVIL ERVIN IRVIN

•R•V•

BRAVA BRAVE BRAVO BREVE CRAVE DRAVA DRIVE DROVE GRAVE GRAVY GROVE PRIVY PROVE PROVO TRAVE TREVI TROVE

••RV•

CARVE CURVE CURVY HERVE LARVA MARVY MIRVS NERVE NERVY NORVO PARVO SERVE SERVO TURVY VERVE

••R•V

DERIV KIROV

R•W••

RAWER RAWLS RAWLY REWAX REWED REWIN REWON ROWAN ROWDY ROWED ROWEL ROWEN ROWER

R•••W

REMOW RENEW RESAW RESEW RETOW

•RW••

ERWIN IRWIN

•R•W•

BRAWL BRAWN BREWS BROWN BROWS CRAWL CRAWS CREWS CROWD CROWN CROWS DRAWL DRAWN DRAWS DROWN FROWN FROWS GROWL GROWN GROWS PRAWN PROWL PROWS TRAWL TREWS

•R••W

ARROW

••R•W

ARROW CAREW NAREW SCREW SEROW SHREW STRAW STREW THREW THROW TUROW

R•X••

REXES ROXIE

R•••X

RADIX REDOX REDUX RELAX REMEX REMIX RETAX REWAX ROLEX

•R•X•

PREXY PROXY

•R••X

BRONX CROIX TRUEX

••R•X

BORAX HYRAX LORAX LUREX MUREX PUREX PYREX VARIX XEROX

RY•••

RYDER RYOTS

R•Y••

RAYED RAYON REYES RHYME RHYTA RIYAL ROYAL ROYCE ROYKO

R••Y•

REDYE

R•••Y

RAINY RALLY RANDY RANGY RASPY RATTY RAWLY READY REDDY REDLY REEDY REEKY REFRY REIFY REKEY RELAY REPAY REPLY RETRY RIBBY RICKY RIDGY RIGBY RILEY RINDY RINKY RISKY RITZY ROBBY ROCKY RODDY ROILY RONNY ROOKY ROOMY ROOTY ROPEY ROSEY ROWDY RUDDY RUGBY RUMMY RUNNY RUNTY RUSHY RUSTY RUTTY

•RY••

ARYAN BRYAN BRYCE CRYER CRYPT DRYAD DRYER DRYLY DRYUP FRYER PRYCE PRYOR TRYME TRYON TRYST WRYER WRYLY

•R•Y•

BRAYS DRAYS FRAYS FREYA GRAYS GREYS ORIYA PRAYS PREYS TRAYS TREYS XRAYS

•R••Y

ARABY ARCHY ARRAY ARTSY BRADY BRINY BRODY CRACY CRAZY CRECY CROLY CRONY DRILY DRURY DRYLY GRADY GRAPY GRAVY GRIMY GRODY IRONY KRAZY ORACY ORCZY PREXY PRICY PRIVY PROSY PROXY TRACY TRULY WRYLY

••RY•

BERYL CHRYS DARYA DARYL MARYS MERYL

••R•Y

ARRAY BARGY BARKY BARMY BARRY BARTY BERRY BIRDY BURLY BURRY CAREY CARLY CARNY CARRY CORBY COREY CORKY CORNY CURDY CURLY CURRY CURVY DARBY DERBY DERRY DIRTY EARLY ELROY FERNY FERRY FIRRY FORAY FORKY FORTY FURRY GARRY GERMY GERRY GORDY GORKY GORSY GURDY HARDY HARPY HARRY HERBY HERKY HORSY HURDY HURLY HURRY JERKY JERRY JERZY KERRY KIRBY LARDY LARKY LARRY LEROY LORRY LURAY MARCY MARLY MARRY MARTY MARVY MERCY MERRY MIRKY MORAY MOREY MURKY NERDY NERVY PARRY PARTY PERCY PERKY PERRY PORGY PORKY PURSY SARKY SERRY SORRY SPRAY STRAY SURFY SURLY TARDY TARRY TERRY TURFY TURVY WARTY WORDY WORMY WORRY

•••RY

AMBRY AMORY ANDRY ANGRY APERY AUTRY AVERY BARRY BEERY BERRY BURRY CAMRY CARRY CHARY CLARY COWRY CURRY CYMRY DAIRY DEARY DECRY DERRY DEVRY DIARY DOWRY DRURY EMERY EMORY ENTRY EVERY FAERY FAIRY FERRY FIERY FIRRY FLORY FURRY GARRY GEARY GERRY GLARY GLORY HAIRY HARRY HENRY HOARY HURRY IATRY IVORY JERRY KERRY LARRY LATRY LEARY LEERY LORRY LOWRY MARRY MAURY MERRY METRY MOORY OTARY PARRY PEARY PERRY QUERY REFRY RETRY SAURY SCARY SERRY SORRY SPIRY STORY TARRY TEARY TERRY USURY VEERY WEARY WORRY

R•Z••

RAZED RAZES RAZOR RIZZO

R••Z•

RHIZO RITZY RIZZO

•RZ••

ORZOS

•R•Z•

BRAZE CRAZE CRAZY CROZE DRUZE FRIZZ FROZE GRAZE GROZA KRAZY ORCZY PRIZE PRIZM

•R••Z

ARNAZ ARROZ FRANZ FRITZ FRIZZ GROSZ

••RZ•

FURZE HERZL JERZY TERZA

••R•Z

ARROZ HERTZ JEREZ KURTZ MERTZ NERTZ PEREZ

•••RZ

STARZ

SA•••

SAABS SABAH SABER SABIN SABLE SABOT SABRA SABRE SACCO SACHA SACHS SACKS SACRA SACRE SACRO SADAT SADHE SADHU SADIE SADIS SADLY SAENS SAFER SAFES SAGAL SAGAN SAGAS SAGER SAGES SAGET SAGGY SAGOS SAHEL SAHIB SAIGA SAILS SAINT SAITH SAJAK SAKAI SAKER SAKES SALAD SALAL SALAM SALEM SALEP SALES SALIC SALLE SALLY SALMI SALON SALPA SALPS SALSA SALTA SALTS SALTY SALUD SALUT SALVE SALVO SAMAR SAMBA SAMMS SAMMY SAMOA SAMOS SAMPS SANAA SANDE SANDH SANDL SANDS SANDY SANER SANKA SANTA SANTE SANTO SANYO SAONE SAPID SAPIR SAPOR SAPPY SARAH SARAN SARDS SARGE SARGO SARIS SARKY SAROD SAROS SARTO SASES SASHA SASSY SATAN SATBY SATED SATES SATIE SATIN SATON SATUP SATYR SAUCE SAUCY SAUDI SAUKS SAULT SAUNA SAURY SAUTE SAVED SAVER SAVES SAVOR SAVOY SAVVY SAWED SAWIN SAWTO SAXES SAXON SAYER SAYSO

S•A••

SAABS SCABS SCADS SCALA SCALD SCALE SCALP SCALY SCAMP SCAMS SCAND SCANS SCANT SCAPA SCAPE SCARE SCARF SCARP SCARS SCARY SCATS SCAUP SEALE SEALS SEALY SEAMS SEAMY SEARS SEATO SEATS SHACK SHADE SHADS SHADY SHAEF SHAFT SHAGS SHAHN SHAHS SHAKE SHAKO SHAKY SHALE SHALL SHALT SHAME SHAMS SHAMU SHANA SHANE SHANK SHANS SHANT SHAPE SHARD SHARE SHARI SHARK SHARP SHATT SHAUN SHAVE SHAWL SHAWM SHAWN SHAYS SIALS SKALD SKANK SKATE SLABS SLACK SLADE SLAGS SLAIN SLAKE SLAMS SLANG SLANT SLAPS SLASH SLATE SLATS SLATY SLAVE SLAVS SLAWS SLAYS SMACK SMAIL SMALL SMALT SMART SMASH SMAZE SNACK SNAFU SNAGS SNAIL SNAKE SNAKY SNAPS SNARE SNARK SNARL SNATH SOAKS SOAPS SOAPY SOARS SOAVE SPAAK SPACE SPACY SPADE SPADS SPAHI SPAHN SPAIN SPAKE SPALL SPAMS SPANG SPANK SPANS SPARE SPARK SPARS SPASM SPATE SPATS SPAWN SPAYS STABS STACK STACY STADT STAEL STAFF STAGE STAGG STAGS STAGY STAHL STAID STAIN STAIR STAKE STALE STALK STALL STAMP STAND STANG STANK STARE STARK STARR STARS START STARZ STASH STATE STATS STAVE STAYS SUAVE SWABS SWAGE SWAGS SWAIN SWALE SWAMI SWAMP SWANK SWANN SWANS SWAPS SWARD SWARF SWARM SWART SWASH SWATH SWATS SWAYS SWAZI

S••A•

SABAH SADAT SAGAL SAGAN SAGAS SAJAK SAKAI SALAD SALAL SALAM SAMAR SANAA SARAH SARAN SATAN SCHAV SCRAG SCRAM SCRAP SEDAN SEGAL SEGAR SELAH SENAT SEPAL SERAC SERAI SERAL SETAE SETAT SHEAF SHEAN SHEAR SHOAH SHOAL SHOAT SIKAS SILAS SINAI SISAL SITAR SIVAN SIXAM SKEAN SKEAT SKOAL SKUAS SLOAN SMEAR SNEAD SNEAK SODAS SOFAR SOFAS SOLAN SOLAR SOMAS SONAR SORAS SOYAS SPAAK SPEAK SPEAR SPLAT SPLAY SPRAG SPRAT SPRAY SQUAB SQUAD SQUAT SRTAS STEAD STEAK STEAL STEAM STOAE STOAS STOAT STPAT STRAD STRAP STRAW STRAY SUDAN SUGAR SUMAC SURAH SURAL SURAS SURAT SUSAN SWEAR SWEAT

S•••A

SABRA SACHA SACRA SAIGA SALPA SALSA SALTA SAMBA SAMOA SANAA SANKA SANTA SASHA SAUNA SCALA SCAPA SCENA SCHWA SCUBA SCUTA SEEYA SEHNA SELMA SELVA SENNA SEPIA SEPTA SERRA SERTA SHANA SHEBA SHEMA SHIVA SHULA SIDEA SIDRA SIENA SIGMA SILVA SIMBA SITKA SKODA SLIWA SNEVA SOFIA SOLFA SONIA SONJA SONYA SORTA SOUSA SPICA SPOSA STELA STOLA STOMA STRIA STUKA STUPA SUCKA SUDRA SUITA SULFA SULLA SUMBA SUMMA SUNDA SUNNA SUPRA SUTRA SYRIA

•SA••

ASAMA ASANA ISAAC ISAMU LSATS OSAGE OSAKA PSALM PSATS TSADE TSARS USAGE USAIR

•S•A•

ASCAP ASIAN ASSAD ASSAI ASSAM ASSAY ASWAN ESBAT ESSAY ESTAB ESTAS ISAAC ISLAM ISLAS OSCAN OSCAR OSKAR OSMAN PSHAW PSOAS USUAL

•S••A

ASAMA ASANA ASOKA ASPCA ASTRA ASYLA OSAKA OSHEA OSSIA OSTIA USCGA USLTA USOFA

••SA•

ANSAE ASSAD ASSAI ASSAM ASSAY BASAL CASAS CESAR ESSAY HASAT MASAI MESAS NASAL NISAN PISAN PUSAN RESAW SISAL SUSAN UNSAY VISAS

••S•A

AISHA ATSEA BASRA BOSSA CASCA CESTA COSTA DESNA FESTA FOSSA HASTA HOSEA HOSTA KASHA KISKA MESTA MISHA MISSA MUSCA OSSIA PASHA PASTA RASTA SASHA TESLA TESTA TISZA TOSCA VESTA VISTA

•••SA

AZUSA BALSA BOSSA BURSA CAUSA COOSA DORSA

ERISA FOSSA HANSA HAUSA ICOSA KANSA LHASA LUISA MENSA MISSA NYASA OMASA PAISA RAISA SALSA SOUSA SPOSA TULSA VERSA XHOSA

S•B••
SABAH SABER SABIN SABLE SABOT SABRA SABRE SEBUM SIBYL SOBER SOBIG SUBIC SYBIL

S••B•
SAABS SAMBA SATBY SCABS SCUBA SERBS SETBY SHEBA SIMBA SITBY SLABS SLOBS SNOBS SNUBS SORBS STABS STUBS SUMBA SWABS SWOBS

S•••B
SAHIB SCRUB SHRUB SIDEB SQUAB SQUIB STIEB

•SB••
ESBAT

•S•B•
ASHBY MSNBC

•S••B
ESTAB

••SB•
BUSBY COSBY MOSBY NASBY VISBY

SC•••
SCABS SCADS SCALA SCALD SCALE SCALP SCALY SCAMP SCAMS SCAND SCANS SCANT SCAPA SCAPE SCARE SCARF SCARP SCARS SCARY SCATS SCAUP SCENA SCEND SCENE SCENT SCHAV SCHED SCHMO SCHON SCHWA SCIFI SCION SCOFF SCOLD SCONE SCOOP SCOOT SCOPE SCOPS SCOPY SCORE SCORN SCOTS SCOTT SCOUR SCOUT SCOWL SCOWS SCRAG SCRAM SCRAP SCREE SCREW SCRIM SCRIP SCROD SCRUB SCRUM SCUBA SCUDI SCUDO SCUDS SCUFF SCULL SCUMS SCUPS SCURF SCUTA SCUTE SCUTS SCUZZ

S•C••
SACCO SACHA SACHS SACKS SACRA SACRE SACRO SECCO SECTS SOCHI SOCIO SOCKO SOCKS SOCLE SUCKA SUCKS SUCRE SYCEE SYCES

S••C•
SACCO SAUCE SAUCY SECCO SHACK SHOCK SHUCK SINCE SLACK SLICE SLICK SMACK SMOCK SNACK SNICK SNUCK SPACE SPACY SPECD SPECK SPECS SPICA SPICE SPICY SPOCK STACK STACY STICH STICK STOCK STUCK SULCI SYNCS

S•••C
SALIC SERAC SOFTC SONIC STOIC SUBIC SUMAC

•SC••
ASCAP ASCII ASCOT ASCUS OSCAN OSCAR USCGA

•S•C•
ASPCA PSYCH

•S••C
ASDIC ASPIC ASSOC FSLIC ISAAC ISTIC MSNBC OSMIC OSRIC

••SC•
BOSCH BOSCO BOSCS BUSCH CASCA CASCO CISCO DISCO DISCS FISCS MUSCA NOSCE PASCH PASCO PESCI PISCI PISCO TOSCA VASCO

••S•C
ASSOC BASIC COSEC MESIC MUSIC

•••SC
CRESC EPISC

S•D••
SADAT SADHE SADHU SADIE SADIS SADLY SEDAN SEDER SEDGE SEDGY SEDUM SIDEA SIDEB SIDED SIDER SIDES SIDHE SIDLE SIDON SIDRA SODAS SODDY SODOM SUDAN SUDDS SUDRA SUDSY SYDOW

S••D•
SANDE SANDH SANDL SANDS SANDY SARDS SAUDI SCADS SCUDI SCUDO SCUDS SEEDS SEEDY SENDS SHADE SHADS SHADY SHEDS SKIDS SKODA SLADE SLEDS SLIDE SNIDE SODDY SOLDI SOLDO SONDE SPADE SPADS SPODE SPUDS STADT STUDS STUDY SUDDS SUEDE SUNDA SURDS SWEDE

S•••D
SALAD SALUD SAPID SAROD SATED SAVED SAWED SCALD SCAND SCEND SCHED SCOLD SCROD SEWED SHARD SHEED SHIED SHOED SHRED SIDED SIRED SITED SIXED SIZED SKALD SKIED SLOYD SLUED SNEAD SNEED SNERD SNOOD SOLED SOLID SOUND SOWED SPECD SPEED SPEND SPIED SQUAD SQUID STAID STAND STEAD STEED STOOD STRAD SWARD SWORD SYNOD SZOLD

•SD••
ASDIC MSDOS

•S•D•
ASIDE BSIDE TSADE

•S••D
ASKED ASSAD ASSTD PSEUD RSVPD USHED USTED

••SD•
MISDO

••S•D
ASSAD ASSTD BASED BUSED CASED DOSED EASED FUSED HASID HOSED LASED MUSED NOSED POSED RASED RESOD URSID

SE•••
SEALE SEALS SEALY SEAMS SEAMY SEARS SEATO SEATS SEBUM SECCO SECTS SEDAN SEDER SEDGE SEDGY SEDUM SEEDS SEEDY SEEIN SEEKS SEELS SEELY SEEMS SEEPS SEEPY SEERS SEETO SEEYA SEGAL SEGAR SEGER SEGNI SEGNO SEGOS SEGUE SEHNA SEIJI SEIKO SEINE SEISM SEIZE SELAH SELES SELIG SELLS SELMA SELVA SEMIS SENAT SENDS SENGI SENNA SENOR SENSE SENTE SEOUL SEPAL SEPIA SEPOY SEPTA SERAC SERAI SERAL SERBS SERES SERFS SERGE SERIF SERIN SEROW SERRA SERRY SERTA SERUM SERVE SERVO SETAE SETAT SETBY SETIN SETON SETTE SETTO SETUP SEULE SEUSS SEVEN SEVER SEWED SEWER SEWON SEWUP SEXES SEXTS

S•E••
SAENS SCENA SCEND SCENE SCENT SEEDS SEEDY SEEIN SEEKS SEELS SEELY SEEMS SEEPS SEEPY SEERS SEETO SEEYA SHEAF SHEAN SHEAR SHEBA SHEDS SHEED SHEEN SHEEP SHEER SHEET SHEIK SHELF SHELL SHEMA SHEMP SHERE SIEGE SIENA SIEPI SIETE SIEUR SIEVE SKEAN SKEAT SKEET SKEGS SKEIN SKEPS SKETE SKEWS SLEDS SLEEK SLEEP SLEET SLEPT SLEWS SMEAR SMELL SMELT SMEWS SNEAD SNEAK SNEED SNEER SNELL SNERD SNERT SNEVA SOEUR SPEAK SPEAR SPECD SPECK SPECS SPEED SPEKE SPELL SPELT SPEND SPENT SPERO SPETS SPEWS STEAD STEAK STEAL STEAM STEED STEEL STEEN STEEP STEER STEIN STELA STELE STEMS STENO STENS STEPS STERE STERN STETS STEVE STEWS SUEDE SUEME SUERS SUETS SUETY SWEAR SWEAT SWEDE SWEEP SWEET SWELL SWEPT SZELL

S••E•
SABER SAFER SAFES SAGER SAGES SAGET SAHEL SAKER SAKES SALEM SALEP SALES SANER SASES SATED SATES SAVED SAVER SAVES SAWED SAXES SAYER SCHED SCREE SCREW SEDER SEGER SELES SERES SEVEN SEVER SEWED SEWER SEXES SHAEF SHEED SHEEN SHEEP SHEER SHEET SHIED SHIER SHIES SHOED SHOER SHOES SHRED SHREW SHYER SIDEA SIDEB SIDED SIDER SIDES SIKES SILEX SINES SINEW SIRED SIREN SIRES SITED SITES SIXED SIXER SIXES SIZED SIZER SIZES SKEET SKIED SKIER SKIES SKYEY SLEEK SLEEP SLEET SLIER SLOES SLUED SLUES SLYER SNEED SNEER SOBER SOKES SOLED SOLER SOLES SONES SOOEY SOREL SOREN SORER SORES SOWED SOWER SOXER SPEED SPIED SPIEL SPIES SPREE STAEL STEED STEEL STEEN STEEP STEER STIEB STIES STREP STREW SUMER SUPER SUPES SURER SWEEP SWEET SYCEE SYCES

S•••E
SABLE SABRE SACRE SADHE SADIE SALLE SALVE SANDE SANTE SAONE SARGE SATIE SAUCE SAUTE SCALE SCAPE SCARE SCENE SCONE SCOPE SCORE SCREE SCUTE SEALE SEDGE SEGUE SEINE SEIZE SENSE SENTE SERGE SERVE SETAE SETTE SEULE SHADE SHAKE SHALE SHAME SHANE SHAPE SHARE SHAVE SHERE SHINE SHIRE SHONE SHORE SHOVE SHUTE SIDHE SIDLE SIEGE SIETE SIEVE SIGNE SINCE SINGE SKATE SKETE SKIVE SLADE SLAKE SLATE SLAVE SLICE SLIDE SLIME SLOPE SLYPE SMAZE SMILE SMITE SMOKE SMOTE SNAKE SNARE SNIDE SNIPE SNORE SOAVE SOCLE SOLVE SOMME SONDE SOUSE SPACE SPADE SPAKE SPARE SPATE SPEKE SPICE SPIKE SPILE SPINE SPIRE SPITE SPODE SPOKE SPORE SPREE SPRUE SPUME STAGE STAKE STALE STARE STATE STAVE STELE STERE STEVE STILE STIPE STOAE STOKE STOLE STONE STOPE STORE STOVE STOWE STUPE STYLE STYNE SUAVE SUCRE SUEDE SUEME SUITE SURGE SUSIE SWAGE SWALE SWEDE SWINE SWIPE SWOPE SWORE SYCEE SYNGE

•SE••
ISERE PSEUD USERS USEUP

•S•E•
ASHEN ASHER ASHES ASKED ASKER ASKEW ASNER ASPEN ASSES ASSET ASSEZ ASTER ASYET ESKER ESNES ESSEN ESSES ESSEX ESTEE ESTER ESTES ISLES ISLET ISLEY ISSEI OSHEA OSIER OSLER OSSEO OSTEO USHED USHER USTED

•S••E
ASIDE ASONE ASTRE BSIDE ESQUE ESTEE ISERE ISSUE ISTLE OSAGE OSSIE TSADE USAGE USQUE

••SE•
ANSEL ANSER APSES ASSES ASSET ASSEZ ATSEA BASED BASEL BASER BASES BESET BISES BUSED BUSES BUSEY CASED CASES CASEY COSEC DOSED DOSER DOSES EASED EASEL EASES EBSEN EDSEL ESSEN ESSES ESSEX ETSEQ FUSED FUSEE FUSES GASES GOSEE HOSEA HOSED HOSEL HOSES IBSEN INSET ISSEI JASEY JOSEF KASEM KESEY KYSER LASED LASER LASES LOSER LOSES MASER MISER MOSES MOSEY MUSED MUSER MUSES NISEI NOSED NOSES NOSEY OASES OLSEN ONSET ORSER OSSEO OUSEL PASEO PASES POSED POSER POSES PUSEY RASED RASER RASES RESEE RESET RESEW RISEN RISER RISES ROSEN ROSES ROSEY RUSES SASES TASER TVSET UNSER UNSET UPSET VASES VESEY VISES WESER WISER YESES

••S•E
AISLE AISNE ANSAE BASIE BASTE CASTE DESTE DISME ELSIE ENSUE FISKE FOSSE FUSEE GASPE GESTE GOSEE GOSSE HASTE HESSE ISSUE ITSME JESSE JUSTE LISLE LISSE MASSE MESNE MOSHE NASHE NOSCE OSSIE PASSE PASTE PISTE POSSE POSTE RESEE ROSIE RUSSE SUSIE TASSE TASTE WASTE

•••SE
ABASE ABUSE AMUSE ANISE ARISE AROSE BIRSE BLASE BOISE BOUSE BURSE CAUSE CEASE CENSE CHASE CHOSE CLOSE COPSE CRUSE CURSE DANSE DENSE DNASE DOUSE DOWSE DRUSE DULSE ELISE ELYSE ERASE EROSE FALSE FOSSE FRISE GEESE GOOSE GORSE GOSSE GUISE HANSE HAWSE HESSE HEYSE HORSE HOUSE INUSE JESSE LAPSE LEASE LISSE LOOSE LOUSE LUISE MANSE MASSE MEESE MEUSE MOOSE MORSE MOUSE NOISE NOOSE NORSE NURSE OBESE OFUSE PARSE PASSE PAUSE PEASE PERSE PHASE POISE POSSE PRASE PROSE PULSE PURSE RAISE REESE REUSE RINSE RNASE ROUSE RUSSE SENSE SOUSE TASSE TEASE TENSE TERSE THESE THOSE UKASE VALSE VERSE WHOSE WORSE YOUSE

S•F••
SAFER SAFES SIFTS SOFAR SOFAS SOFIA SOFTC SOFTG SOFTY SUFIS

S••F•
SCIFI SCOFF SCUFF SERFS SHAFT SHIFT SKIFF SNAFU SNIFF SNUFF SOLFA SPIFF STAFF STIFF STUFF SULFA SURFS SURFY SWIFT

S•••F
SCARF SCOFF SCUFF SCURF SERIF SHAEF SHEAF SHELF SKIFF SMURF SNIFF SNUFF SPIFF SPOOF STAFF STIFF STUFF SWARF

•SF••
RSFSR

•S•F•
USOFA

••S•F
JOSEF

S•G••
SAGAL SAGAN SAGAS SAGER SAGES SAGET SAGGY SAGOS SEGAL SEGAR SEGER SEGNI SEGNO SEGOS SEGUE SIGHS SIGHT SIGIL SIGMA SIGNE SIGNO SIGNS SOGGY SSGTS SUGAR

S••G•
SAGGY SAIGA SARGE SARGO SEDGE SEDGY SENGI SERGE SHAGS SHOGI SIEGE SINGE

SINGS SKEGS SLAGS SLIGO SLOGS SLUGS SMOGS SNAGS SNOGS SNUGS SOGGY SONGS SORGO SOUGH STAGE STAGG STAGS STAGY STOGY SURGE SWAGE SWAGS SWIGS SYNGE

S•••G

SCRAG SELIG SHRUG SLANG SLING SLUNG SOBIG SOFTG SOONG SPANG SPRAG SPRIG STAGG STANG STING STRUG STUNG SUING SWING SWUNG

•SG••

MSGTS SSGTS TSGTS

•S•G•

OSAGE USAGE USCGA VSIGN

•S••G

USING

SH•••

SHACK SHADE SHADS SHADY SHAEF SHAFT SHAGS SHAHN SHAHS SHAKE SHAKO SHAKY SHALE SHALL SHALT SHAME SHAMS SHAMU SHANA SHANE SHANK SHANS SHANT SHAPE SHARD SHARE SHARI SHARK SHARP SHATT SHAUN SHAVE SHAWL SHAWM SHAWN SHAYS SHEAF SHEAN SHEAR SHEBA SHEDS SHEED SHEEN SHEEP SHEER SHEET SHEIK SHELF SHELL SHEMA SHEMP SHERE SHIED SHIER SHIES SHIFT SHILL SHIMS SHINE SHINS SHINY SHIPS SHIRE SHIRK SHIRR SHIRT SHISH SHIVA SHIVS SHOAH SHOAL SHOAT SHOCK SHOED SHOER SHOES SHOGI SHOJI SHONE SHOOK SHOOS SHOOT SHOPS SHORE SHORN SHORT SHOTS SHOUT SHOVE SHOWN SHOWS SHOWY SHOYU SHRED SHREW SHRUB SHRUG SHUCK SHULA SHULS SHUNS SHUNT SHUSH SHUTE SHUTS SHYER SHYLY

S•H••

SAHEL SAHIB SCHAV SCHED SCHMO SCHON SCHWA SEHNA SOHIO

S••H•

SACHA SACHS SADHE SADHU SASHA SHAHN SHAHS SIDHE SIGHS SIGHT SIKHS SOCHI SOPHS SOPHY SOTHO SPAHI SPAHN STAHL SUSHI

S•••H

SABAH SAITH SANDH SARAH SELAH SHISH SHOAH SHUSH SIXTH SKOSH SLASH SLOSH SLOTH SLUSH SMASH SMITH SMYTH SNATH SOOTH SOUGH SOUTH STASH STICH SURAH SWASH SWATH SWISH SWITH SYLPH

•SH••

ASHBY ASHEN ASHER ASHES ASHUR OSHEA PSHAW USHED USHER

•S••H

PSYCH

••SH•

AISHA BASHO BISHO BUSHY CUSHY DASHI DISHY FISHY GUSHY KASHA MASHY MESHY MISHA MOSHE MUSHY NASHE PASHA PUSHY RASHT RISHI RUSHY SASHA SUSHI WASHY WISHY WUSHU

••S•H

BOSCH BUSCH PASCH

•••SH

ABASH AMISH APISH AWASH BLUSH BRASH BRUSH CLASH CRASH CRUSH FLASH FLESH FLUSH FRESH FROSH GNASH HARSH INISH IRISH KARSH KNISH LEASH MARSH NAISH PLASH PLUSH QUASH SHISH SHUSH SKOSH SLASH SLOSH SLUSH SMASH STASH SWASH SWISH TRASH TRISH WALSH WELSH WHISH

SI•••

SIALS SIBYL SIDEA SIDEB SIDED SIDER SIDES SIDHE SIDLE SIDON SIDRA SIEGE SIENA SIEPI SIETE SIEUR SIEVE SIFTS SIGHS SIGHT SIGIL SIGMA SIGNE SIGNO SIGNS SIKAS SIKES SIKHS SILAS SILEX SILKS SILKY SILLS SILLY SILOS SILTS SILTY SILVA SIMBA SIMMS SIMON SIMPS SINAI SINCE SINES SINEW SINGE SINGS SINKS SINUS SIOUX SIRED SIREN SIRES SISAL SISSY SITAR SITBY SITED SITES SITIN SITKA SITON SITUP SITUS SIVAN SIXAM SIXED SIXER SIXES SIXMO SIXPM SIXTH SIXTY SIZED SIZER SIZES

S•I••

SAIGA SAILS SAINT SAITH SCIFI SCION SEIJI SEIKO SEINE SEISM SEIZE SHIED SHIER SHIES SHIFT SHILL SHIMS SHINE SHINS SHINY SHIPS SHIRE SHIRK SHIRR SHIRT SHISH SHIVA SHIVS SKIDS SKIED SKIER SKIES SKIFF SKILL SKIMP SKIMS SKINK SKINS SKINT SKIPS SKIRL SKIRR SKIRT SKITS SKIVE SLICE SLICK SLIDE SLIER SLIGO SLILY SLIME SLIMS SLIMY SLING SLINK SLIPS SLIPT SLITS SLIWA SMILE SMIRK SMITE SMITH SMITS SNICK SNIDE SNIFF SNIPE SNIPS SNITS SOILS SPICA SPICE SPICY SPIED SPIEL SPIES SPIFF SPIKE SPIKY SPILE SPILT SPINE SPINS SPINY SPIRE SPIRO SPIRY SPITE SPITS SPITZ SPIVS STICH STICK STIEB STIES STIFF STILE STILL STILT STING STINK STINT STIPE STIRK STIRS SUING SUINT SUITA SUITE SUITS SWIFT SWIGS SWILL SWIMS SWINE SWING SWINK SWIPE SWIRL SWISH SWISS SWITH SWITZ

S••I•

SABIN SADIE SADIS SAHIB SALIC SAPID SAPIR SARIS SATIE SATIN SAWIN SCRIM SCRIP SEEIN SELIG SEMIS SEPIA SERIF SERIN SETIN SHEIK SIGIL SITIN SKEIN SLAIN SMAIL SNAIL SOBIG SOCIO SOFIA SOHIO SOLID SONIA SONIC SPAIN SPLIT SPOIL SPRIG SPRIT SQUIB SQUID STAID STAIN STAIR STEIN STOIC STRIA STRIP SUBIC SUFIS SUSIE SWAIN SYBIL SYRIA

S•••I

SAKAI SALMI SAUDI SCIFI SCUDI SEGNI SEIJI SENGI SERAI SHARI SHOGI SHOJI SIEPI SINAI SOCHI SOLDI SOLTI SOMNI SPAHI SPYRI STYLI SULCI SUNNI SUOMI SUSHI SWAMI SWAZI

•SI••

ASIAN ASIDE BSIDE OSIER USING VSIGN

•S•I•

ASCII ASDIC ASKIN ASPIC ASTIN ASTIR FSLIC GSUIT ISLIP ISTIC OSLIN OSMIC OSRIC OSSIA OSSIE OSTIA USAIR

•S••I

ASCII ASSAI ISSEI

••SI•

AESIR AHSIN APSIS ARSIS BASIC BASIE BASIL BASIN BASIS CASIO ELSIE EOSIN FUSIL HASID JOSIP LYSIN MESIC MUSIC MYSIN NOSIR OASIS OPSIN OPSIS OSSIA OSSIE POSIT RESIN ROSIE ROSIN SUSIE URSID VISIT YASIR

••S•I

ASSAI AUSSI BASSI CESTI DASHI HOSNI ISSEI MASAI MISTI NISEI PESCI PISCI RISHI ROSSI SUSHI

•••SI

AUSSI BASSI DORSI FARSI ICOSI PEPSI PHYSI QUASI ROSSI TARSI TORSI

S•J••

SAJAK

S••J•

SEIJI SHOJI SONJA

SK•••

SKALD SKANK SKATE SKEAN SKEAT SKEET SKEGS SKEIN SKEPS SKETE SKEWS SKIDS SKIED SKIER SKIES SKIFF SKILL SKIMP SKIMS SKINK SKINS SKINT SKIPS SKIRL SKIRR SKIRT SKITS SKIVE SKNXX SKOAL SKODA SKORT SKOSH SKUAS SKULK SKULL SKUNK SKYEY

S•K••

SAKAI SAKER SAKES SIKAS SIKES SIKHS SOKES

S••K•

SACKS SANKA SARKY SAUKS SEEKS SEIKO SHAKE SHAKO SHAKY SILKS SILKY SINKS SITKA SLAKE SMOKE SMOKY SNAKE SNAKY SOAKS SOCKO SOCKS SOUKS SPAKE SPEKE SPIKE SPIKY SPOKE STAKE STOKE STUKA SUCKA SUCKS SULKS SULKY

S•••K

SAJAK SHACK SHANK SHARK SHEIK SHIRK SHOCK SHOOK SHUCK SKANK SKINK SKULK SKUNK SLACK SLEEK SLICK SLINK SLUNK SMACK SMIRK SMOCK SNACK SNARK SNEAK SNICK SNOOK SNUCK SPAAK SPANK SPARK SPEAK SPECK SPOCK SPOOK SPORK SPUNK STACK STALK STANK STARK STEAK STICK STINK STIRK STOCK STOOK STORK STUCK STUNK SWANK SWINK SWONK

•SK••

ASKED ASKER ASKEW ASKIN ESKER OSKAR

•S•K•

ASOKA OSAKA

••SK•

BASKS BOSKS BOSKY BUSKS CASKS CUSKS DESKS DISKS DUSKS DUSKY ENSKY FISKE HUSKS HUSKY KISKA MASKS MUSKS MUSKY PESKY RISKS RISKY RUSKS TASKS TUSKS

•••SK

BRISK FLASK FRISK KIOSK KURSK MINSK PINSK WHISK

SL•••

SLABS SLACK SLADE SLAGS SLAIN SLAKE SLAMS SLANG SLANT SLAPS SLASH SLATE SLATS SLATY SLAVE SLAVS SLAWS SLAYS SLEDS SLEEK SLEEP SLEET SLEPT SLEWS SLICE SLICK SLIDE SLIER SLIGO SLILY SLIME SLIMS SLIMY SLING SLINK SLIPS SLIPT SLITS SLIWA SLOAN SLOBS SLOES SLOGS SLOMO SLOOP SLOPE SLOPS SLOSH SLOTH SLOTS SLOWS SLOYD SLUED SLUES SLUGS SLUMP SLUMS SLUNG SLUNK SLURP SLURS SLUSH SLYER SLYLY SLYPE

S•L••

SALAD SALAL SALAM SALEM SALEP SALES SALIC SALLE SALLY SALMI SALON SALPA SALPS SALSA SALTA SALTS SALTY SALUD SALUT SALVE SALVO SELAH SELES SELIG SELLS SELMA SELVA SILAS SILEX SILKS SILKY SILLS SILLY SILOS SILTS SILTY SILVA SOLAN SOLAR SOLDI SOLDO SOLED SOLER SOLES SOLFA SOLID SOLON SOLOS SOLTI SOLUM SOLUS SOLVE SPLAT SPLAY SPLIT SULCI SULFA SULKS SULKY SULLA SULLY SYLPH

S••L•

SABLE SADLY SAILS SALLE SALLY SAULT SCALA SCALD SCALE SCALP SCALY SCOLD SCULL SEALE SEALS SEALY SEELS SEELY SELLS SEULE SHALE SHALL SHALT SHELF SHELL SHILL SHULA SHULS SHYLY SIALS SIDLE SILLS SILLY SKALD SKILL SKULK SKULL SLILY SLYLY SMALL SMALT SMELL SMELT SMILE SMOLT SNELL SOCLE SOILS SOULS SOULT SPALL SPELL SPELT SPILE SPILL SPILT STALE STALK STALL STELA STELE STILE STILL STILT STOLA STOLE STOLS STULL STYLE STYLI STYLO SULLA SULLY SURLY SWALE SWELL SWILL SZELL SZOLD

S•••L

SAGAL SAHEL SALAL SANDL SCOWL SCULL SEGAL SEOUL SEPAL SERAL SHALL SHAWL SHELL SHILL SHOAL SIBYL SIGIL SISAL SKILL SKIRL SKOAL SKULL SMAIL SMALL SMELL SNAIL SNARL SNELL SOREL SOTOL SPALL SPELL SPIEL SPILL SPOIL SPOOL STAEL STAHL STALL STEAL STEEL STILL STOOL STULL SURAL SWELL SWILL SWIRL SYBIL SZELL

•SL••

FSLIC ISLAM ISLAS ISLES ISLET ISLEY ISLIP OSLER OSLIN USLTA

•S•L•

ASYLA ISTLE PSALM

•S••L

USUAL

••SL•

AISLE LISLE TESLA

••S•L

ANSEL BASAL BASEL BASIL EASEL EDSEL FUSIL HOSEL LYSOL MOSUL NASAL OUSEL SISAL

SM•••

SMACK SMAIL SMALL SMALT SMART SMASH SMAZE SMEAR SMELL SMELT SMEWS SMILE SMIRK SMITE SMITH SMITS SMOCK SMOGS SMOKE SMOKY SMOLT SMOOT SMOTE SMURF SMUTS SMYTH

S•M••

SAMAR SAMBA SAMMS SAMMY SAMOA SAMOS SAMPS SEMIS SIMBA SIMMS SIMON SIMPS SOMAS SOMME SOMNI SUMAC SUMBA SUMER SUMMA SUMPS SUMUP

S••M•

SALMI SAMMS SAMMY SCAMP SCAMS SCHMO SCUMS SEAMS SEAMY SEEMS SELMA SHAME SHAMS SHAMU SHEMA SHEMP SHIMS SIGMA SIMMS SIXMO SKIMP SKIMS SLAMS SLIME SLIMS SLIMY SLOMO SLUMP SLUMS SOMME SPAMS SPUME SPUMY STAMP STEMS STOMA STOMP STUMP STUMS STYMY SUEME SUMMA SUOMI SWAMI SWAMP SWIMS

S•••M

SALAM SALEM SCRAM SCRIM SCRUM SEBUM SEDUM SEISM SERUM SHAWM SIXAM SIXPM SODOM SOLUM SPASM STEAM STORM STROM STRUM STURM

SWARM

•SM••
OSMAN
OSMIC

•S•M•
ASAMA
ISAMU

•S••M
ASSAM
ISLAM
PSALM

••SM•
COSMO
DISME
ITSME
PISMO

••S•M
ADSUM
AKSUM
ASSAM
BESOM
BOSOM
EPSOM
IPSUM
KASEM
VISUM

•••SM
ABYSM
CHASM
DEISM
PLASM
PRISM
SEISM
SPASM

SN•••
SNACK
SNAFU
SNAGS
SNAIL
SNAKE
SNAKY
SNAPS
SNARE
SNARK
SNARL
SNATH
SNEAD
SNEAK
SNEED
SNEER
SNELL
SNERD
SNERT
SNEVA
SNICK
SNIDE
SNIFF
SNIPE
SNIPS
SNITS
SNOBS
SNOGS
SNOOD
SNOOK
SNOOP
SNOOT
SNORE
SNORT
SNOUT
SNOWS
SNOWY
SNUBS
SNUCK
SNUFF
SNUGS

S•N••
SANAA
SANDE
SANDH
SANDL
SANDS
SANDY
SANER
SANKA
SANTA
SANTE
SANTO
SANYO
SENAT
SENDS
SENGI
SENNA
SENOR
SENSE
SENTE
SINAI
SINCE
SINES
SINEW
SINGE
SINGS
SINKS
SINUS
SKNXX
SONAR
SONDE
SONES
SONGS
SONIA
SONIC
SONJA
SONNY
SONYA
SUNDA
SUNNA
SUNNI
SUNNY
SUNUP
SYNCS
SYNGE
SYNOD

S••N•
SAENS
SAINT
SAONE
SAUNA
SCAND
SCANS
SCANT
SCENA
SCEND
SCENE
SCENT
SCONE
SEGNI
SEGNO
SEHNA
SEINE
SENNA
SHANA
SHANE
SHANK
SHANS
SHANT
SHINE
SHINS
SHINY
SHONE
SHUNS
SHUNT
SIENA
SIGNE
SIGNO
SIGNS
SKANK
SKINK
SKINS
SKINT
SKUNK
SLANG
SLANT
SLING
SLINK
SLUNG
SLUNK
SOMNI
SONNY
SOONG
SOUND
SPANG
SPANK
SPANS
SPEND
SPENT
SPINE
SPINS
SPINY
SPUNK
STAND
STANG
STANK
STENO
STENS
STING
STINK
STINT
STONE
STONY
STUNG
STUNK
STUNS
STUNT
STYNE
SUING
SUINT
SUNNA
SUNNI
SUNNY
SWANK
SWANN
SWANS
SWINE
SWING
SWINK
SWONK
SWUNG

S•••N
SABIN
SAGAN
SALON
SARAN
SATAN
SATIN
SATON
SAWIN
SAXON
SCHON
SCION
SCORN
SEDAN
SEEIN
SERIN
SETIN
SETON
SEVEN
SEWON
SHAHN
SHAUN
SHAWN
SHEAN
SHEEN
SHORN
SHOWN
SIDON
SIMON
SIREN
SITIN
SITON
SIVAN
SKEAN
SKEIN
SLAIN
SLOAN
SOLAN
SOLON
SOREN
SPAHN
SPAIN
SPAWN
SPOON
SPURN
SPYON
STAIN
STEEN
STEIN
STERN
SUDAN
SUSAN
SWAIN
SWANN
SWOON
SWORN

•SN••
ASNER
ESNES
MSNBC

•S•N•
ASANA
ASONE
ASSNS
USING

•S••N
ASHEN
ASIAN
ASKIN
ASPEN
ASTIN
ASTON
ASWAN
ESSEN
OSCAN
OSLIN
OSMAN
VSIGN

••SN•
AISNE
ASSNS
BOSNS
DESNA
HASNT
HOSNI
MESNE
WASNT
YESNO

••S•N
AHSIN
ANSON
ARSON
BASIN
BISON
BOSON
EBSEN
EOSIN
EPSON
ESSEN
HASON
HYSON
IBSEN
JASON
LYSIN
MASON
MESON
MYSIN
NISAN
OLSEN
OLSON
OPSIN
ORSON
PISAN
PUSAN
RESIN
RISEN
ROSEN
ROSIN
SUSAN
TYSON

SO•••
SOAKS
SOAPS
SOAPY
SOARS
SOAVE
SOBER
SOBIG
SOCHI
SOCIO
SOCKO
SOCKS
SOCLE
SODAS
SODDY
SODOM
SOEUR
SOFAR
SOFAS
SOFIA
SOFTC
SOFTG
SOFTY
SOGGY
SOHIO
SOILS
SOKES
SOLAN
SOLAR
SOLDI
SOLDO
SOLED
SOLER
SOLES
SOLFA
SOLID
SOLON
SOLOS
SOLTI
SOLUM
SOLUS
SOLVE
SOMAS
SOMME
SOMNI
SONAR
SONDE
SONES
SONGS
SONIA
SONIC
SONJA
SONNY
SONYA
SOOEY
SOONG
SOOTH
SOOTS
SOOTY
SOPHS
SOPHY
SOPOR
SOPPY
SOPUP
SORAS
SORBS
SOREL
SOREN
SORER
SORES
SORGO
SORRY
SORTA
SORTS
SORUS
SOTHO
SOTOL
SOTTO
SOUGH
SOUKS
SOULS
SOULT
SOUND
SOUPS
SOUPY
SOURS
SOUSA
SOUSE
SOUTH
SOWED
SOWER
SOXER
SOYAS
SOYUZ

S•O••
SAONE
SCOFF
SCOLD
SCONE
SCOOP
SCOOT
SCOPE
SCOPS
SCOPY
SCORE
SCORN
SCOTS
SCOTT
SCOUR
SCOUT
SCOWL
SCOWS
SEOUL
SHOAH
SHOAL
SHOAT
SHOCK
SHOED
SHOER
SHOES
SHOGI
SHOJI
SHONE
SHOOK
SHOOS
SHOOT
SHOPS
SHORE
SHORN
SHORT
SHOTS
SHOUT
SHOVE
SHOWN
SHOWS
SHOWY
SHOYU
SIOUX
SKOAL
SKODA
SKORT
SKOSH
SLOAN
SLOBS
SLOES
SLOGS
SLOMO
SLOOP
SLOPE
SLOPS
SLOSH
SLOTH
SLOTS
SLOWS
SLOYD
SMOCK
SMOGS
SMOKE
SMOKY
SMOLT
SMOOT
SMOTE
SNOBS
SNOGS
SNOOD
SNOOK
SNOOP
SNOOT
SNORE
SNORT
SNOUT
SNOWS
SNOWY
SOOEY
SOONG
SOOTH
SOOTS
SOOTY
SPOCK
SPODE
SPOIL
SPOKE
SPOOF
SPOOK
SPOOL
SPOON
SPOOR
SPORE
SPORK
SPORT
SPOSA
SPOTS
SPOUT
STOAE
STOAS
STOAT
STOCK
STOGY
STOIC
STOKE
STOLA
STOLE
STOLS
STOMA
STOMP
STONE
STONY
STOOD
STOOK
STOOL
STOOP
STOPE
STOPS
STORE
STORK
STORM
STORY
STOSS
STOTS
STOUP
STOUT
STOVE
STOWE
STOWS
SUOMI
SWOBS
SWONK
SWOON
SWOOP
SWOPE
SWOPS
SWORD
SWORE
SWORN
SZOLD

S••O•
SABOT
SAGOS
SALON
SAMOA
SAMOS
SAPOR
SAROD
SAROS
SATON
SAVOR
SAVOY
SAXON
SCHON
SCION
SCOOP
SCOOT
SCROD
SEGOS
SENOR
SEPOY
SEROW
SETON
SEWON
SHOOK
SHOOS
SHOOT
SIDON
SILOS
SIMON
SITON
SLOOP
SMOOT
SNOOD
SNOOK
SNOOP
SNOOT
SODOM
SOLON
SOLOS
SOPOR
SOTOL
SPOOF
SPOOK
SPOOL
SPOON
SPOOR
SPYON
STOOD
STOOK
STOOL
STOOP
STROM
STROP
SWOON
SWOOP
SYDOW
SYNOD
SYSOP

S•••O
SACCO
SACRO
SALVO
SANTO
SANYO
SARGO
SARTO
SAWTO
SAYSO
SCHMO
SCUDO
SEATO
SECCO
SEETO
SEGNO
SEIKO
SERVO
SETTO
SHAKO
SIGNO
SIXMO
SLIGO
SLOMO
SOCIO
SOCKO
SOHIO
SOLDO
SORGO
SOTHO
SOTTO
SPERO
SPIRO
STENO
STYLO

•SO••
ASOKA
ASONE
PSOAS
USOFA
XSOUT

•S•O•
ASCOT
ASSOC
ASTON
ASTOR
CSPOT
ESPOO
ESTOP
FSTOP
MSDOS

•S••O
ASTRO
ESPOO
OSSEO
OSTEO

••SO•
AESOP
ALSOP
ANSON
APSOS
ARSON
ASSOC
BASOV
BESOM
BESOT
BISON
BOSOM
BOSON
BOSOX
ENSOR
EPSOM
EPSON
HASON
HYSON
JASON
LYSOL
MASON
MESON
MISOS
OLSON
ORSON
PESOS
RESOD
SYSOP
TYSON
VISOR

••S•O
BASHO
BASSO
BISHO
BOSCO
CASCO
CASIO
CISCO
COSMO
DISCO
GESSO
GUSTO
HASSO
HASTO
LASSO
MISDO
MOSSO
OSSEO
PASCO
PASEO
PASTO
PESTO
PISCO
PISMO
RUSSO
TASSO
VASCO
YESNO

•••SO
ANISO
AVISO
BASSO
CANSO
DORSO
GESSO
HASSO
HOWSO
HYPSO
KELSO
LASSO
MOSSO
NOTSO
RATSO
RINSO
RUSSO
SAYSO
TASSO
TORSO
VERSO
WHOSO

SP•••
SPAAK
SPACE
SPACY
SPADE
SPADS
SPAHI
SPAHN
SPAIN
SPAKE
SPALL
SPAMS
SPANG
SPANK
SPANS
SPARE
SPARK
SPARS
SPASM
SPATE
SPATS
SPAWN
SPAYS
SPEAK
SPEAR
SPECD
SPECK
SPECS
SPEED
SPEKE
SPELL
SPELT
SPEND
SPENT
SPERO
SPETS
SPEWS
SPICA
SPICE
SPICY
SPIED
SPIEL
SPIES
SPIFF
SPIKE
SPIKY
SPILE
SPILL
SPILT
SPINE
SPINS
SPINY
SPIRE
SPIRO
SPIRY
SPITE
SPITS
SPITZ
SPIVS
SPLAT
SPLAY
SPLIT
SPOCK
SPODE
SPOIL
SPOKE
SPOOF
SPOOK
SPOOL
SPOON
SPOOR
SPORE
SPORK
SPORT
SPOSA
SPOTS
SPOUT
SPRAG
SPRAT
SPRAY
SPREE
SPRIG
SPRIT
SPRUE
SPUDS
SPUME
SPUMY
SPUNK
SPURN
SPURS
SPURT
SPYON
SPYRI

S•P••
SAPID
SAPIR
SAPOR
SAPPY
SEPAL
SEPIA
SEPOY
SEPTA
SOPHS
SOPHY
SOPOR
SOPPY
SOPUP
STPAT
SUPER
SUPES
SUPRA
SUPTS
SUPVR

S••P•
SALPA
SALPS
SAMPS
SAPPY
SCAPA
SCAPE
SCOPE
SCOPS
SCOPY
SCUPS
SEEPS
SEEPY
SHAPE
SHIPS
SHOPS
SIEPI
SIMPS
SIXPM
SKEPS
SKIPS
SLAPS
SLEPT
SLIPS
SLIPT
SLOPE
SLOPS
SLYPE
SNAPS
SNIPE
SNIPS
SOAPS
SOAPY
SOPPY
SOUPS
SOUPY
STEPS
STIPE
STOPE
STOPS
STUPA
STUPE
SUMPS
SWAPS
SWEPT
SWIPE
SWOPE
SWOPS
SYLPH

S•••P
SALEP
SATUP
SCALP
SCAMP
SCARP
SCAUP
SCOOP
SCRAP
SCRIP
SETUP
SEWUP
SHARP
SHEEP
SHEMP
SITUP
SKIMP
SLEEP
SLOOP
SLUMP
SLURP
SNOOP
SOPUP
STAMP
STEEP
STOMP
STOOP
STOUP
STRAP
STREP
STRIP
STROP
STUMP
SUMUP
SUNUP
SWAMP
SWEEP
SWOOP
SYRUP
SYSOP

•SP••
ASPCA
ASPEN
ASPIC
CSPOT
ESPOO

•S•P•
RSVPD
RSVPS

•S••P
ASCAP
ESTOP
FSTOP
ISLIP
USEUP
USURP

••SP•
CUSPS
GASPE
GASPS
HASPS
LISPS
RASPS
RASPY
TBSPS
WASPS
WASPY
WISPS
WISPY

••S•P
AESOP
ALSOP
GASUP
JOSIP
SYSOP

•••SP
AGASP
CLASP
CRISP
GRASP

SQ•••
SQUAB
SQUAD
SQUAT
SQUIB
SQUID

•SQ••
ESQUE
USQUE

••SQ•
ETSQQ

••S•Q
ETSEQ
ETSQQ

SR•••
SRTAS

S•R••
SARAH
SARAN
SARDS
SARGE
SARGO
SARIS
SARKY
SAROD
SAROS
SARTO
SCRAG
SCRAM
SCRAP
SCREE
SCREW
SCRIM
SCRIP
SCROD
SCRUB
SCRUM
SERAC
SERAI
SERAL
SERBS
SERES
SERFS
SERGE
SERIF
SERIN
SEROW
SERRA
SERRY
SERTA
SERUM
SERVE
SERVO
SHRED
SHREW
SHRUB
SHRUG
SIRED
SIREN
SIRES
SORAS
SORBS
SOREL
SOREN
SORER
SORES
SORGO
SORRY
SORTA
SORTS
SORUS
SPRAG
SPRAT
SPRAY
SPREE
SPRIG
SPRIT
SPRUE
STRAD
STRAP
STRAW
STRAY
STREP
STREW
STRIA
STRIP
STROM
STROP
STRUG
STRUM
STRUT
SURAH
SURAL
SURAS
SURAT
SURDS
SURER
SURFS
SURFY
SURGE
SURLY
SYRIA
SYRUP

S••R•
SABRA
SABRE
SACRA
SACRE
SACRO
SAURY
SCARE
SCARF
SCARP
SCARS
SCARY
SCORE
SCORN
SCURF
SEARS
SEERS
SERRA
SERRY
SHARD
SHARE
SHARI
SHARK
SHARP
SHERE
SHIRE
SHIRK
SHIRR
SHIRT
SHORE
SHORN
SHORT
SIDRA
SKIRL
SKIRR
SKIRT
SKORT
SLURP
SLURS
SMART
SMIRK
SMURF
SNARE
SNARK
SNARL
SNERD
SNERT
SNORE
SNORT
SOARS
SORRY
SOURS
SPARE
SPARK
SPARS
SPERO
SPIRE
SPIRO
SPIRY
SPORE
SPORK
SPORT
SPURN
SPURS
SPURT
SPYRI
STARE
STARK
STARR
STARS
START
STARZ
STERE
STERN
STIRK
STIRS
STORE
STORK
STORM
STORY
STURM
SUCRE
SUDRA
SUERS
SUPRA
SUTRA
SWARD
SWARF
SWARM
SWART
SWIRL
SWORD
SWORE
SWORN

S•••R
SABER
SAFER
SAGER
SAKER
SAMAR
SANER
SAPIR
SAPOR
SATYR
SAVER
SAVOR
SAYER
SCOUR
SEDER
SEGAR
SEGER
SENOR
SEVER
SEWER
SHEAR
SHEER
SHIER
SHIRR
SHOER
SHYER
SIDER
SIEUR
SITAR
SIXER
SIZER
SKIER
SKIRR
SLIER
SLYER
SMEAR
SNEER
SOBER
SOEUR
SOFAR
SOLAR
SOLER
SONAR
SOPOR
SORER
SOWER
SOXER
SPEAR
SPOOR
STAIR
STARR
STEER
SUGAR
SUMER
SUPER
SUPVR
SURER
SWEAR

•SR••
OSRIC

•S•R•
ASTRA
ASTRE
ASTRO
ISERE
TSARS
USERS
USURP
USURY

•S••R
ASHER
ASHUR
ASKER
ASNER
ASSUR
ASSYR
ASTER
ASTIR
ASTOR
ESKER
ESTER
OSCAR
OSIER
OSKAR
OSLER
RSFSR
USAIR
USHER

••SR•
BASRA

••S•R
AESIR ANSER ASSUR ASSYR AUSTR BASER CESAR DISTR DOSER ENSOR GASTR INSTR KYSER LASER LOSER MASER MASUR MISER MUSER NOSIR ORSER POSER RASER RISER TASER UNSER VISOR WESER WISER YASIR

•••SR
RSFSR

SS•••
SSGTS

S•S••
SASES SASHA SASSY SISAL SISSY SUSAN SUSHI SUSIE SYSOP

S••S•
SALSA SASSY SAYSO SEISM SENSE SEUSS SHISH SHUSH SISSY SKOSH SLASH SLOSH SLUSH SMASH SOUSA SOUSE SPASM SPOSA STASH STOSS SUDSY SWASH SWISH SWISS

S•••S
SAABS SACHS SACKS SADIS SAENS SAFES SAGAS SAGES SAGOS SAILS SAKES SALES SALPS SALTS SAMMS SAMOS SAMPS SANDS SARDS SARIS SAROS SASES SATES SAUKS SAVES SAXES SCABS SCADS SCAMS SCANS SCARS SCATS SCOPS SCOTS SCOWS SCUDS SCUMS SCUPS SCUTS SEALS SEAMS SEARS SEATS SECTS SEEDS SEEKS SEELS SEEMS SEEPS SEERS SEGOS SELES SELLS SEMIS SENDS SERBS SERES SERFS SEUSS SEXES SEXTS SHADS SHAGS SHAHS SHAMS SHANS SHAYS SHEDS SHIES SHIMS SHINS SHIPS SHIVS SHOES SHOOS SHOPS SHOTS SHOWS SHULS SHUNS SHUTS SIALS SIDES SIFTS SIGHS SIGNS SIKAS SIKES SIKHS SILAS SILKS SILLS SILOS SILTS SIMMS SIMPS SINES SINGS SINKS SINUS SIRES SITES SITUS SIXES SIZES SKEGS SKEPS SKEWS SKIDS SKIES SKIMS SKINS SKIPS SKITS SKUAS SLABS SLAGS SLAMS SLAPS SLATS SLAVS SLAWS SLAYS SLEDS SLEWS SLIMS SLIPS SLITS SLOBS SLOES SLOGS SLOPS SLOTS SLOWS SLUES SLUGS SLUMS SLURS SMEWS SMITS SMOGS SMUTS SNAGS SNAPS SNIPS SNITS SNOBS SNOGS SNOWS SNUBS SNUGS SOAKS SOAPS SOARS SOCKS SODAS SOFAS SOILS SOKES SOLES SOLOS SOLUS SOMAS SONES SONGS SOOTS SOPHS SORAS SORBS SORES SORTS SORUS SOUKS SOULS SOUPS SOURS SOYAS SPADS SPAMS SPANS SPARS SPATS SPAYS SPECS SPETS SPEWS SPIES SPINS SPITS SPIVS SPOTS SPUDS SPURS SRTAS SSGTS STABS STAGS STARS STATS STAYS STEMS STENS STEPS STETS STEWS STIES STIRS STOAS STOLS STOPS STOSS STOTS STOWS STUBS STUDS STUMS STUNS SUCKS SUDDS SUERS SUETS SUFIS SUITS SULKS SUMPS SUPES SUPTS SURAS SURDS SURFS SWABS SWAGS SWANS SWAPS SWATS SWAYS SWIGS SWIMS SWISS SWOBS SWOPS SYCES SYNCS

•SS••
ASSAD ASSAI ASSAM ASSAY ASSES ASSET ASSEZ ASSNS ASSOC ASSTD ASSTS ASSUR ASSYR ESSAY ESSEN ESSES ESSEX ISSEI ISSUE ISSUS OSSEO OSSIA OSSIE

•S•S•
RSFSR

•S••S
ASCUS ASHES ASSES ASSNS ASSTS ESNES ESSES ESTAS ESTES ISLAS ISLES ISSUS LSATS MSDOS MSGTS PSATS PSOAS RSVPS SSGTS TSARS TSGTS USERS

••SS•
AUSSI BASSI BASSO BOSSA BOSSY CISSY FOSSA FOSSE FUSSY GASSY GESSO GOSSE GUSSY HASSO HESSE HISSY HUSSY JASSY JESSE LASSO LISSE LOSSY MASSE MASSY MESSY MISSA MISSY MOSSO MOSSY MUSSY PASSE PASSU PASSY POSSE ROSSI RUSSE RUSSO SASSY SISSY TASSE TASSO

••S•S
APSES APSIS APSOS ARSIS ASSES ASSNS ASSTS BASES BASIS BASKS BESTS BISES BOSCS BOSKS BOSNS BUSES BUSKS BUSTS CASAS CASES CASKS CASTS CASUS COSTS CUSKS CUSPS DESKS DISCS DISKS DOSES DUSKS DUSTS EASES EASTS ESSES FASTS FESTS FISCS FISTS FUSES GASES GASPS GESTS GISTS GUSTS HASPS HESTS HOSES HOSTS HUSKS INSTS ISSUS JESTS LASES LASTS LISPS LISTS LOSES LUSTS MASKS MASTS MESAS MISOS MISTS MOSES MUSES MUSKS MUSTS NESTS NISUS NOSES OASES OASIS OASTS OPSIS OUSTS PASES PASTS PESOS PESTS POSES POSTS RASES RASPS RESTS RISES RISKS ROSES RUSES RUSKS RUSTS SASES TASKS TBSPS TESTS TUSKS VASES VESTS VISAS VISES WASPS WESTS WISPS YESES ZESTS

•••SS
ABYSS AMASS AMISS BLASS BLESS BLISS BRASS CHESS CLASS CRASS CRESS CRISS CROSS DRESS DROSS FLOSS GAUSS GLASS GLESS GLOSS GRASS GROSS GUESS HEISS IPASS KRISS KVASS LOESS PRESS SEUSS STOSS SWISS TRESS TRUSS WEISS ZEISS

ST•••
STABS STACK STACY STADT STAEL STAFF STAGE STAGG STAGS STAGY STAHL STAID STAIN STAIR STAKE STALE STALK STALL STAMP STAND STANG STANK STARE STARK STARR STARS START STARZ STASH STATE STATS STAVE STAYS STEAD STEAK STEAL STEAM STEED STEEL STEEN STEEP STEER STEIN STELA STELE STEMS STENO STENS STEPS STERE STERN STETS STEVE STEWS STICH STICK STIEB STIES STIFF STILE STILL STILT STING STINK STINT STIPE STIRK STIRS STOAE STOAS STOAT STOCK STOGY STOIC STOKE STOLA STOLE STOLS STOMA STOMP STONE STONY STOOD STOOK STOOL STOOP STOPE STOPS STORE STORK STORM STORY STOSS STOTS STOUP STOUT STOVE STOWE STOWS STPAT STRAD STRAP STRAW STRAY STREP STREW STRIA STRIP STROM STROP STRUG STRUM STRUT STUBS STUCK STUDS STUDY STUFF STUKA STULL STUMP STUMS STUNG STUNK STUNS STUNT STUPA STUPE STURM STUTZ STYLE STYLI STYLO STYMY STYNE

S•T••
SATAN SATBY SATED SATES SATIE SATIN SATON SATUP SATYR SETAE SETAT SETBY SETIN SETON SETTE SETTO SETUP SITAR SITBY SITED SITES SITIN SITKA SITON SITUP SITUS SOTHO SOTOL SOTTO SRTAS SUTRA

S••T•
SAITH SALTA SALTS SALTY SANTA SANTE SANTO SARTO SAUTE SAWTO SCATS SCOTS SCOTT SCUTA SCUTE SCUTS SEATO SEATS SECTS SEETO SENTE SEPTA SERTA SETTE SETTO SEXTS SHATT SHOTS SHUTE SHUTS SIETE SIFTS SILTS SILTY SIXTH SIXTY SKATE SKETE SKITS SLATE SLATS SLATY SLITS SLOTH SLOTS SMITE SMITH SMITS SMOTE SMUTS SMYTH SNATH SNITS SOFTC SOFTG SOFTY SOLTI SOOTH SOOTS SOOTY SORTA SORTS SOTTO SOUTH SPATE SPATS SPETS SPITE SPITS SPITZ SPOTS SSGTS STATE STATS STETS STOTS STUTZ SUETS SUETY SUITA SUITE SUITS SUPTS SWATH SWATS SWITH SWITZ

S•••T
SABOT SADAT SAGET SAINT SALUT SAULT SCANT SCENT SCOOT SCOTT SCOUT SENAT SETAT SHAFT SHALT SHANT SHATT SHEET SHIFT SHIRT SHOAT SHOOT SHORT SHOUT SHUNT SIGHT SKEAT SKEET SKINT SKIRT SKORT SLANT SLEET SLEPT SLIPT SMALT SMART SMELT SMOLT SMOOT SNERT SNOOT SNORT SNOUT SOULT SPELT SPENT SPILT SPLAT SPLIT SPORT SPOUT SPRAT SPRIT SPURT SQUAT STADT START STILT STINT STOAT STOUT STPAT STRUT STUNT SUINT SURAT SWART SWEAT SWEET SWEPT SWIFT

•ST••
ASTER ASTIN ASTIR ASTON ASTOR ASTRA ASTRE ASTRO ESTAB ESTAS ESTEE ESTER ESTES ESTOP FSTOP ISTIC ISTLE OSTEO OSTIA USTED

•S•T•
ASSTD ASSTS LSATS MSGTS PSATS SSGTS TSGTS USLTA

•S••T
ASCOT ASSET ASYET ASYUT CSPOT ESBAT GSUIT ISLET XSOUT

••ST•
ASSTD ASSTS AUSTR BASTE BESTS BUSTS CASTE CASTS CBSTV CESTA CESTI COSTA COSTS DESTE DISTR DUSTS DUSTY EASTS FASTS FESTA FESTS FISTS FUSTY GASTR GESTE GESTS GISTS GUSTO GUSTS GUSTY HASTA HASTE HASTO HASTY HESTS HOSTA HOSTS INSTR INSTS JESTS JUSTE LASTS LISTS LUSTS LUSTY MASTS MESTA MISTI MISTS MISTY MUSTS MUSTY NASTY NESTS OASTS OUSTS PASTA PASTE PASTO PASTS PASTY PESTO PESTS PISTE POSTE POSTS RASTA RESTS RUSTS RUSTY TASTE TASTY TESTA TESTS TESTY VASTY VESTA VESTS VISTA WASTE WESTS ZESTS ZESTY

••S•T
ASSET BESET BESOT HASAT HASNT INSET LISZT ONSET POSIT RASHT RESET TVSET UNSET UPSET VISIT WASNT

•••ST
ADUST ALIST ANGST AVAST BAKST BEAST BLAST BLEST BOAST BOOST BREST BURST CANST CHEST COAST CREST CRIST CRUST CURST DEIST DIDST DOEST DURST EGEST ERNST EXIST FAUST FEAST FEIST FIRST FOIST FROST GHOST GOEST GRIST GUEST HADST HEIST HOIST HOLST HORST HURST IDEST JOIST JOUST LEAST MAYST MIDST MOIST ODIST PABST PREST PROST QUEST ROAST ROOST ROUST TOAST TRUST TRYST TWIST VERST WAIST WEEST WHIST WIEST WORST WREST WRIST WURST YEAST ZEIST

SU•••
SUAVE SUBIC SUCKA SUCKS SUCRE SUDAN SUDDS SUDRA SUDSY SUEDE SUEME SUERS SUETS SUETY SUFIS SUGAR SUING SUINT SUITA SUITE SUITS SULCI SULFA SULKS SULKY SULLA SULLY SUMAC SUMBA SUMER SUMMA SUMPS SUMUP SUNDA SUNNA SUNNI SUNNY SUNUP SUOMI SUPER SUPES SUPRA SUPTS SUPVR SURAH SURAL SURAS SURAT SURDS SURER SURFS SURFY SURGE SURLY SUSAN SUSHI SUSIE SUTRA

S•U••
SAUCE SAUCY SAUDI SAUKS SAULT SAUNA SAURY SAUTE SCUBA SCUDI SCUDO SCUDS SCUFF SCULL SCUMS SCUPS SCURF SCUTA SCUTE SCUTS SCUZZ SEULE SEUSS SHUCK SHULA SHULS SHUNS SHUNT SHUSH SHUTE SHUTS SKUAS SKULK SKULL SKUNK SLUED SLUES SLUGS SLUMP SLUMS SLUNG SLUNK SLURP SLURS SLUSH SMURF SMUTS SNUBS SNUCK SNUFF SNUGS SOUGH SOUKS SOULS SOULT SOUND SOUPS SOUPY SOURS SOUSA SOUSE SOUTH SPUDS SPUME SPUMY SPUNK SPURN SPURS SPURT SQUAB SQUAD SQUAT SQUIB SQUID STUBS STUCK STUDS STUDY STUFF STUKA STULL STUMP STUMS STUNG STUNK STUNS STUNT STUPA STUPE STURM STUTZ SWUNG

S••U•
SALUD SALUT SATUP SCAUP SCOUR SCOUT SCRUB SCRUM SEBUM SEDUM SEGUE SEOUL SERUM SETUP SEWUP SHAUN SHOUT SHRUB SHRUG SIEUR SINUS SIOUX SITUP SITUS SNOUT SOEUR SOLUM SOLUS SOPUP SORUS SOYUZ SPOUT SPRUE STOUP STOUT STRUG STRUM STRUT SUMUP SUNUP SYRUP

S•••U
SADHU SHAMU SHOYU SNAFU

•SU••
GSUIT ISUZU USUAL USURP USURY

•S•U•
ASCUS ASHUR ASSUR ASYUT ESQUE

ISSUE
ISSUS
PSEUD
USEUP
USQUE
XSOUT

•S••U
ISAMU
ISUZU

••SU•
ADSUM
AKSUM
ASSUR
CASUS
ENSUE
GASUP
IPSUM
ISSUE
ISSUS
MASUR
MOSUL
NISUS
VISUM

••S•U
PASSU
WUSHU

•••SU
DERSU
MATSU
PASSU

S•V••
SAVED
SAVER
SAVES
SAVOR
SAVOY
SAVVY
SEVEN
SEVER
SIVAN

S••V•
SALVE
SALVO
SAVVY
SELVA
SERVE
SERVO
SHAVE
SHIVA
SHIVS
SHOVE
SIEVE
SILVA
SKIVE
SLAVE
SLAVS
SNEVA
SOAVE
SOLVE
SPIVS
STAVE
STEVE
STOVE
SUAVE
SUPVR

S•••V
SCHAV

•SV••
RSVPD
RSVPS

••S•V
BASOV
CBSTV

SW•••
SWABS
SWAGE
SWAGS
SWAIN
SWALE
SWAMI
SWAMP
SWANK
SWANN
SWANS
SWAPS
SWARD
SWARF
SWARM
SWART
SWASH
SWATH
SWATS
SWAYS
SWAZI
SWEAR
SWEAT
SWEDE
SWEEP
SWEET
SWELL
SWEPT
SWIFT
SWIGS
SWILL
SWIMS
SWINE
SWING
SWINK
SWIPE
SWIRL
SWISH
SWISS
SWITH
SWITZ
SWOBS
SWONK
SWOON
SWOOP
SWOPE
SWOPS
SWORD
SWORE
SWORN
SWUNG

S•W••
SAWED
SAWIN
SAWTO
SEWED
SEWER
SEWON
SEWUP
SOWED
SOWER

S••W•
SCHWA
SCOWL
SCOWS
SHAWL
SHAWM
SHAWN
SHOWN
SHOWS
SHOWY
SKEWS
SLAWS
SLEWS
SLIWA
SLOWS
SMEWS
SNOWS
SNOWY
SPAWN
SPEWS
STEWS
STOWE
STOWS

S•••W
SCREW
SEROW
SHREW
SINEW
STRAW
STREW
SYDOW

•SW••
ASWAN

•S••W
ASKEW
PSHAW

••S•W
RESAW
RESEW

S•X••
SAXES
SAXON
SEXES
SEXTS
SIXAM
SIXED
SIXER
SIXES
SIXMO
SIXPM
SIXTH
SIXTY
SOXER

S••X•
SKNXX

S•••X
SILEX
SIOUX
SKNXX

•S••X
ESSEX

••S•X
BOSOX
ESSEX

SY•••
SYBIL
SYCEE
SYCES
SYDOW
SYLPH
SYNCS
SYNGE
SYNOD
SYRIA
SYRUP
SYSOP

S•Y••
SAYER
SAYSO
SHYER
SHYLY
SKYEY
SLYER
SLYLY
SLYPE
SMYTH
SOYAS
SOYUZ
SPYON
SPYRI
STYLE
STYLI
STYLO
STYMY
STYNE

S••Y•
SANYO
SATYR
SEEYA
SHAYS
SHOYU
SIBYL
SLAYS
SLOYD
SONYA
SPAYS
STAYS
SWAYS

S•••Y
SADLY
SAGGY
SALLY
SALTY
SAMMY
SANDY
SAPPY
SARKY
SASSY
SATBY
SAUCY
SAURY
SAVOY
SAVVY
SCALY
SCARY
SCOPY
SEALY
SEAMY
SEDGY
SEEDY
SEELY
SEEPY
SEPOY
SERRY
SETBY
SHADY
SHAKY
SHINY
SHOWY
SHYLY
SILKY
SILLY
SILTY
SISSY
SITBY
SIXTY
SKYEY
SLATY
SLILY
SLIMY
SLYLY
SMOKY
SNAKY
SNOWY
SOAPY
SODDY
SOFTY
SOGGY
SONNY
SOOEY
SOOTY
SOPHY
SOPPY
SORRY
SOUPY
SPACY
SPICY
SPIKY
SPINY
SPIRY
SPLAY
SPRAY
SPUMY
STACY
STAGY
STOGY
STONY
STORY
STRAY
STUDY
STYMY
SUDSY
SUETY
SULKY
SULLY
SUNNY
SURFY
SURLY

•SY••
ASYET
ASYLA
ASYUT
PSYCH

•S•Y•
ASSYR

•S••Y
ASHBY
ASSAY
ESSAY
ISLEY
USURY

••SY•
ASSYR

••S•Y
ASSAY
BOSKY
BOSSY
BUSBY
BUSEY
BUSHY
CASEY
CISSY
COSBY
CUSHY
DISHY
DUSKY
DUSTY
ENSKY
ESSAY
FISHY
FUSSY
FUSTY
GASSY
GUSHY
GUSSY
GUSTY
HASTY
HISSY
HUSKY
HUSSY
JASEY
JASSY
KESEY
LOSSY
LUSTY
MASHY
MASSY
MESHY
MESSY
MISSY
MISTY
MOSBY
MOSEY
MOSSY
MUSHY
MUSKY
MUSSY
MUSTY
NASBY
NASTY
NOSEY
PASSY
PASTY
PESKY
PUSEY
PUSHY
RASPY
RISKY
ROSEY
RUSHY
RUSTY
SASSY
SISSY
TASTY
TESTY
UNSAY
VASTY
VESEY
VISBY
WASHY
WASPY
WISHY
WISPY
ZESTY

•••SY
ANTSY
ARTSY
BETSY
BITSY
BOSSY
BUGSY
CISSY
COUSY
DAISY
DITSY
FUBSY
FUSSY
GASSY
GIPSY
GOOSY
GORSY
GUSSY
GUTSY
GYPSY
HISSY
HORSY
HUSSY
JASSY
LOSSY
LOUSY
MASSY
MESSY
MIMSY
MISSY
MOPSY
MOSSY
MOUSY
MUSSY
NEWSY
NOISY
NUTSY
PALSY
PANSY
PASSY
PATSY
POESY
POTSY
PROSY
PURSY
SASSY
SISSY
SUDSY
TANSY
TIPSY
TOPSY
WALSY

SZ•••
SZELL
SZOLD

S•Z••
SIZED
SIZER
SIZES

S••Z•
SCUZZ
SEIZE
SMAZE
SWAZI

S•••Z
SCUZZ
SOYUZ
SPITZ
STARZ
STUTZ
SWITZ

•S•Z•
ISUZU

•S••Z
ASSEZ

••SZ•
LISZT
TISZA

••S•Z
ASSEZ

•••SZ
GROSZ

TA•••
TABBY
TABIS
TABLA
TABLE
TABOO
TABOR
TACET
TACHO
TACHY
TACIT
TACKS
TACKY
TACOS
TAEGU
TAELS
TAFFY
TAGUP
TAGUS
TAHOE
TAHRS
TAIGA
TAILS
TAINE
TAINO
TAINT
TAKAS
TAKEI
TAKEN
TAKER
TAKES
TAKIN
TALER
TALES
TALIA
TALKS
TALKY
TALLY
TALON
TALOS
TALUS
TAMBO
TAMED
TAMER
TAMES
TAMIL
TAMMY
TAMPA
TAMPS
TANDE
TANDY
TANEY
TANGO
TANGS
TANGY
TANKA
TANKS
TANSY
TANTE
TANTO
TANYA
TAPAS
TAPED
TAPER
TAPES
TAPIN
TAPIR
TARDE
TARDY
TARES
TARGE
TARNS
TAROK
TAROT
TARPS
TARRY
TARSI
TARTS
TARTU
TASER
TASKS
TASSE
TASSO
TASTE
TASTY
TATAR
TATER
TATRA
TATTY
TATUM
TAUNT
TAUON
TAUPE
TAUPO
TAURO
TAUTO
TAWNY
TAXCO
TAXED
TAXER
TAXES
TAXIS
TAXON
TAYRA
TAZZA

T•A••
TBALL
TBARS
TEACH
TEAKS
TEALS
TEAMS
TEARS
TEARY
TEASE
THAIS
THANE
THANK
THANT
THARP
THATS
THAWS
TIANT
TIARA
TOADS
TOADY
TOAST
TRACE
TRACK
TRACT
TRACY
TRADE
TRAIL
TRAIN
TRAIT
TRALA
TRAMP
TRAMS
TRANS
TRAPP
TRAPS
TRASH
TRAVE
TRAWL
TRAYS
TSADE
TSARS
TWAIN
TWANG
TZARS

T••A•
TAKAS
TAPAS
TATAR
TENAM
TEPAL
TEXAN
TEXAS
TICAL
TIDAL
TIKAL
TILAK
TIRAN
TITAN
TODAY
TOGAE
TOGAS
TOKAY
TONAL
TOPAZ
TORAH
TOTAL
TREAD
TREAT
TRIAD
TRIAL
TUBAS
TUNAS
TWEAK
TWOAM
TYNAN

T•••A
TABLA
TAIGA
TALIA
TAMPA
TANKA
TANYA
TATRA
TAYRA
TAZZA
TEENA
TERRA
TERZA
TESLA
TESTA
TETRA
THECA
THEDA
THEMA
THERA
THETA
THUJA
TIARA
TIBIA
TISZA
TONGA
TONKA
TONYA
TOSCA
TRALA
TULSA
TWYLA
TYPEA

•TA••
ATALL
ATARI
ETAGE
ETAPE
ETATS
ITALO
ITALS
ITALY
OTARU
OTARY
STABS
STACK
STACY
STADT
STAEL
STAFF
STAGE
STAGG
STAGS
STAGY
STAHL
STAID
STAIN
STAIR
STAKE
STALE
STALK
STALL
STAMP
STAND
STANG
STANK
STARE
STARK
STARR
STARS
START
STARZ
STASH
STATE
STATS
STAVE
STAYS
UTAHN

•T•A•
ATBAT
ATBAY
ATEAM
ATLAS
ATMAN
ATPAR
ATTAR
ATWAR
ETHAN
ETNAS
OTWAY
PTRAP
STEAD
STEAK
STEAL
STEAM
STOAE
STOAS
STOAT
STPAT
STRAD
STRAP
STRAW
STRAY

•T••A
ATRIA
ATSEA
ETYMA
STELA
STOLA
STOMA
STRIA
STUKA
STUPA
UTICA

••TA•
ACTAS
AETAT
ALTAI
ALTAR
ANTAE
ANTAL
ANTAS
ARTAL
ATTAR
BATAK
BETAS
DETAT
DITAT
DOTAL
EATAT
ESTAB
ESTAS
FATAL
FETAL
FETAS
GETAS
GETAT
GOTAT
IDTAG
IOTAS
JOTAS
LETAT
LOTAH
LOTAS
METAL
NATAL
OCTAD
OCTAL
ONTAP
PETAL
PITAS
QATAR
RETAG
RETAP
RETAR
RETAX
ROTAS
SATAN
SETAE
SETAT
SITAR
SRTAS
TATAR
TITAN
TOTAL
VITAE
VITAL
VITAS
WOTAN
ZETAS

••T•A
AETNA
AFTRA
ANTRA
ASTRA
BETTA
BOTHA
COTTA
DITKA
ENTIA
EXTRA
FATHA
FATWA
GOTHA
GOTTA
GUTTA
INTRA
LOTTA
LYTTA
MOTTA
OSTIA
PATNA
PETRA
PITTA
RETIA
SITKA
SUTRA
TATRA
TETRA
ULTRA

•••TA
ADYTA
AGITA
AKITA
ALETA
ANITA
AORTA
BETTA
BIOTA
CARTA
CESTA
CEUTA
CHITA
COSTA
COTTA
DELTA
DICTA
EVITA
FANTA
FESTA
GOTTA
GRATA
GRETA
GUTTA
HASTA
HEPTA
HOSTA
JUNTA
LEPTA
LOTTA
LYTTA
MALTA
MANTA
MARTA
MEHTA
MESTA
MIATA
MOTTA
NAFTA
OVETA
PASTA
PENTA
PIETA
PINTA
PITTA
PLATA
PUNTA
QUOTA
RASTA
REATA
RENTA
RHYTA
RIATA
SALTA
SANTA
SCUTA
SEPTA
SERTA
SORTA
SUITA
TESTA
THETA
UINTA
USLTA
VESTA
VISTA
VOLTA
YALTA
YENTA

TB•••
TBALL
TBARS
TBILL
TBIRD
TBOND
TBONE
TBSPS

T•B••
TABBY
TABIS
TABLA
TABLE
TABOO
TABOR
TIBBS
TIBER
TIBET
TIBIA
TOBES
TOBEY
TOBIT
TOBOL
TUBAS
TUBBY
TUBED
TUBER
TUBES

T••B•
TABBY
TAMBO
THEBE
TIBBS
TRIBE
TUBBY
TURBO

T•••B
THROB
THUMB
TYPEB

•TB••
ATBAT
ATBAY

•T•B•
FTLBS
STABS
STUBS

•T••B
STIEB

••TB•
GETBY
GOTBY
LETBE
PUTBY
SATBY
SETBY
SITBY

••T•B
ESTAB

T•C••
TACET
TACHO
TACHY
TACIT
TACKS
TACKY
TACOS
TECHS
TECHY
TICAL
TICKS
TICKY
TUCKS
TYCHE
TYCHO

T••C•
TAXCO
TEACH
TENCH
THECA
THICK
TINCT
TORCH
TOSCA
TOUCH
TRACE
TRACK
TRACT
TRACY
TRICE
TRICK
TRUCE
TRUCK
TWICE

T•••C
TELIC
TONIC
TOPIC
TORIC
TOXIC
TUNIC

•TC••
ITCHY
LTCOL

•T•C•
STACK
STACY
STICH
STICK
STOCK
STUCK
UTICA

•T••C
ATTIC
ETHIC
STOIC

••TC•
AITCH
BATCH
BOTCH
BUTCH
CATCH
DITCH
DUTCH
FETCH
FITCH
HATCH
HITCH
HUTCH
KETCH
KOTCH
LATCH
MATCH
MITCH
NATCH
NOTCH
PATCH
PITCH
RATCH
VETCH
WATCH
WITCH

••T•C
ANTIC
ATTIC
AZTEC
ISTIC
OPTIC
VATIC

•••TC
SOFTC

T•D••
TEDDY
TIDAL
TIDED
TIDES
TODAY
TODDY
TODOS
TUDOR

T••D•
TANDE
TANDY
TARDE
TARDY
TEDDY
TEIDE
TENDS
THEDA
THUDS
TILDE
TOADS
TOADY
TODDY
TONDI
TONDO
TRADE
TSADE

T•••D
TAMED
TAPED
TAXED
TBIRD
TBOND
TEPID
THEYD
THIRD
TIDED
TILED
TIMED
TIMID
TINED
TIRED
TONED
TOPED
TOTED
TOWED
TOYED
TREAD
TREED
TREND
TRIAD
TRIED
TRUED
TUBED
TUMID
TUNED
TWEED
TYPED

•T•D•
ETUDE
STADT
STUDS
STUDY

•T••D
STAID
STAND
STEAD
STEED
STOOD
STRAD

••TD•
OUTDO

••T•D
ACTED
ANTED
APTED
BATED
CITED
DATED
DOTED
FATED
FETED
FETID
GATED
HATED
KITED
MATED
METED
MUTED
NOTED
OCTAD
OOTID
OPTED
OUTED
PATED
RATED
SATED
SITED
TOTED
USTED
VOTED

•••TD
APPTD
ASSTD
CONTD
WHATD

TE•••
TEACH
TEAKS
TEALS
TEAMS
TEARS
TEARY
TEASE
TECHS
TECHY
TEDDY
TEEMS
TEENA
TEENS
TEENY
TEETH
TEEUP
TEHEE
TEIDE
TELEO
TELES
TELEX
TELIC
TELLS
TELLY
TELOS
TEMPE
TEMPI
TEMPO
TEMPS
TEMPT
TENAM
TENCH
TENDS
TENET
TENON
TENOR
TENPM
TENSE
TENTH
TENTS
TEPAL
TEPEE
TEPID
TERMS
TERNE
TERNS
TERPS
TERRA
TERRE
TERRI
TERRY
TERSE
TERZA
TESLA
TESTA

TESTS TESTY TETES TETHS TETON TETRA TEVET TEVYE TEXAN TEXAS TEXTS

T•E••

TAEGU TAELS TEEMS TEENA TEENS TEENY TEETH TEEUP THEBE THECA THEDA THEFT THEIR THEMA THEME THEMS THEOL THERA THERE THERM THESE THETA THEWS THEWY THEYD TIEGS TIEIN TIERS TIETO TIEUP TOEIN TREAD TREAT TREED TREEN TREES TREKS TREND TRENT TRESS TREVI TREWS TREYS TWEAK TWEED TWEEN TWEER TWEET TWERE TWERP

T••E•

TACET TAKEI TAKEN TAKER TAKES TALER TALES TAMED TAMER TAMES TANEY TAPED TAPER TAPES TARES TASER TATER TAXED TAXER TAXES TEHEE TELEO TELES TELEX TENET TEPEE TETES TEVET THIEF THREE THREW TIBER TIBET TIDED TIDES TIGER TIKES TILED TILER TILES TIMED TIMER TIMES TIMEX TINED TINES TIRED TIRES TITER TOBES TOBEY TOKEN TOLER TOLET TOMEI TOMES TONED TONER TONES TONEY TOPED TOPER TOPES TOTED TOTEM TOTER TOTES TOVES TOWED TOWEL TOWER TOYED TREED TREEN TREES TRIED TRIER TRIES TRUED TRUER TRUES TRUEX TUBED TUBER TUBES TULES TUNED TUNER TUNES TUTEE TUXES TVSET TWEED TWEEN TWEER TWEET TYKES TYLER TYNES TYPEA TYPEB TYPED TYPEE TYPER TYPES TYPEY TYRES

T•••E

TABLE TAHOE TAINE TANDE TANTE TARDE TARGE TASSE TASTE TAUPE TBONE TEASE TEHEE TEIDE TEMPE TENSE TEPEE TERNE TERRE TERSE TEVYE THANE THEBE THEME THERE THESE THINE THOLE THOSE THREE THROE THULE THYME TILDE TINGE TITHE TITLE TITRE TNOTE TOGAE TOILE TONNE TOQUE TORME TORRE TORTE TOTIE TOUTE TOWNE TRACE TRADE TRAVE TRIBE TRICE TRIKE TRINE TRIPE TRITE TROPE TROVE TRUCE TRYME TSADE TULLE TUQUE TUTEE TWERE TWICE TWINE TYCHE TYPEE

•TE••

ATEAM ATEIN ATEUP ITEMS ITERS PTERO STEAD STEAK STEAL STEAM STEED STEEL STEEN STEEP STEER STEIN STELA STELE STEMS STENO STENS STEPS STERE STERN STETS STEVE STEWS

•T•E•

ATSEA ETHEL ETHER ETSEQ ETZEL LTGEN OTHER OTOES OTTER STAEL STEED STEEL STEEN STEEP STEER STIEB STIES STREP STREW UTHER UTLEY UTTER

•T••E

ATIVE ATONE ATQUE ETAGE ETAPE ETUDE ITSME STAGE STAKE STALE STARE STATE STAVE STELE STERE STEVE STILE STIPE STOAE STOKE STOLE STONE STOPE STORE STOVE STOWE STUPE STYLE STYNE UTILE

••TE•

ACTED ACTER AFTER ALTER ANTED ANTES APTED APTER ARTEL ARTES ASTER AZTEC BATED BATES BETEL BITER BITES BOTEL BUTEO BYTES CATER CATES CITED CITER CITES COTES CUTER CUTEX CUTEY DATED DATER DATES DETER DOTED DOTER DOTES EATEN EATER ENTER ESTEE ESTER ESTES FATED FATES FETED FETES GATED GATES GUTEN HATED HATER HATES HOTEL INTEL INTER JETER JETES JUTES KITED KITER KITES LATEN LATER LATEX LITER LITES LUTES MATED MATEO MATER MATES MATEY METED METER METES MITER MITES MOTEL MOTES MOTET MUTED MUTER MUTES NITER NITES NOTED NOTER NOTES OATEN OATER OATES OCTET OFTEN OPTED OSTEO OTTER OUTED OUTER PATED PATEK PATEN PATER PATES PETER PETES RATED RATEL RATER RATES RITES ROTES SATED SATES SITED SITES TATER TETES TITER TOTED TOTEM TOTER TOTES TUTEE UNTER USTED UTTER VATER VOTED VOTER VOTES WATER YATES

••T•E

ANTAE ANTRE ARTIE ASTRE AUTRE BATHE BETTE BITTE BOTHE BUTTE CUTIE DETRE ENTRE ESTEE GETME HITME ISTLE KATIE KITWE LATHE LATKE LATTE LETBE LETHE LITHE LITRE LOTTE MATTE METRE MITRE NITRE NOTME NOTRE OUTRE PATHE RETIE SATIE SETAE SETTE TITHE TITLE TITRE TOTIE TUTEE UNTIE VITAE VOTRE WITHE WITTE WYTHE

•••TE

ABATE ACUTE AGATE ALATE ARETE AZOTE BASTE BETTE BITTE BOITE BRITE BRUTE BUTTE CARTE CASTE CHUTE CNOTE COMTE CONTE CRATE CRETE DANTE DENTE DESTE DHOTE ELATE ELITE ELUTE EMOTE ENATE FLUTE FOOTE FORTE GESTE GRATE GRETE HARTE HASTE HAUTE HEUTE IRATE JUSTE KINTE KLUTE KNUTE LATTE LEYTE LOTTE MATTE MONTE NOLTE NORTE ONATE ORATE OVATE PARTE PASTE PEETE PENTE PISTE PLATE POETE PONTE PORTE POSTE PRATE QUITE QUOTE ROUTE SANTE SAUTE SCUTE SENTE SETTE SHUTE SIETE SKATE SKETE SLATE SMITE SMOTE SPATE SPITE STATE SUITE TANTE TASTE TNOTE TORTE TOUTE TRITE UNITE VERTE VOLTE WAITE WASTE WHITE WITTE WRITE WROTE YENTE ZANTE

T•F••

TAFFY TIFFS TOFFS TOFFY TOFTS TUFTS TUFTY

T••F•

TAFFY THEFT TIFFS TOFFS TOFFY TURFS TURFY

T•••F

THIEF

•T•F•

STAFF STIFF STUFF

•T••F

STAFF STIFF STUFF

••T•F

MOTIF

T•G••

TAGUP TAGUS TIGER TIGHT TOGAE TOGAS TSGTS

T••G•

TAEGU TAIGA TANGO TANGS TANGY TARGE THIGH THUGS TIEGS TINGE TINGS TONGA TONGS TOUGH TRIGS TRUGS TWIGS

T•••G

THING THONG TOPOG TWANG TYING

•TG••

LTGEN LTGOV

•T•G•

ETAGE STAGE STAGG STAGS STAGY STOGY

•T••G

STAGG STANG STING STRUG STUNG

••TG•

GETGO GITGO LETGO OUTGO

••T•G

IDTAG RETAG

•••TG

SOFTG

TH•••

THAIS THANE THANK THANT THARP THATS THAWS THEBE THECA THEDA THEFT THEIR THEMA THEME THEMS THEOL THERA THERE THERM THESE THETA THEWS THEWY THEYD THICK THIEF THIGH THILL THINE THING THINK THINS THIRD THOLE THONG THORN THORO THORP THOSE THOTH THOUS THREE THREW THROB THROE THROW THRUM THUDS THUGS THUJA THULE THUMB THUMP THUNK THURS THYME THYMY

T•H••

TAHOE TAHRS TEHEE

T••H•

TACHO TACHY TECHS TECHY TETHS TIGHT TITHE TYCHE TYCHO

T•••H

TEACH TEETH TENCH TENTH THIGH THOTH TILTH TOOTH TORAH TORCH TOUCH TOUGH TRASH TRISH TROTH TRUTH

•TH••

ATHOL ATHON ATHOS ETHAN ETHEL ETHER ETHIC ETHNO ETHOS ETHYL OTHER UTHER

•T•H•

ITCHY STAHL UTAHN

•T••H

STASH STICH

••TH•

ALTHO ANTHO ARTHR BATHE BATHO BATHS BATHY BETHS BOTHA BOTHE CATHY FATHA GOTHA GOTHS HETHS KATHY LATHE LATHS LATHY LETHE LITHE LITHO LITHS MATHS MOTHS MOTHY MYTHS OATHS ORTHO PATHE PATHO PATHS PATHY PITHS PITHY RATHS SOTHO TETHS TITHE WITHE WITHY WYTHE

••T•H

AITCH BATCH BOTCH BUTCH CATCH DITCH DUTCH FETCH FITCH HATCH HITCH HUTCH KETCH KOTCH LATCH LOTAH MATCH MITCH NATCH NOTCH PATCH PITCH RATCH VETCH WATCH WITCH

•••TH

ARITH AZOTH BARTH BERTH BIRTH BLUTH BLYTH BOOTH BRITH BROTH CHETH CLOTH COUTH DARTH DEPTH DOETH EARTH EDITH ELATH FAITH FIFTH FILTH FIRTH FORTH FROTH FURTH GARTH GIRTH HEATH ICHTH KEITH LEITH LOATH MIRTH MONTH MOUTH NEATH NINTH NORTH PERTH PLATH QUOTH SAITH SIXTH SLOTH SMITH SMYTH SNATH SOOTH SOUTH SWATH SWITH TEETH TENTH THOTH TILTH TOOTH TROTH TRUTH WIDTH WORTH WRATH WROTH WYETH YOUTH

TI•••

TIANT TIARA TIBBS TIBER TIBET TIBIA TICAL TICKS TICKY TIDAL TIDED TIDES TIEGS TIEIN TIERS TIETO TIEUP TIFFS TIGER TIGHT TIKAL TIKES TIKIS TIKKI TILAK TILDE TILED TILER TILES TILLS TILLY TILTH TILTS TIMED TIMER TIMES TIMEX TIMID TIMMY TIMON TIMOR TINCT TINED TINES TINGE TINGS TINNY TINTS TIPIN TIPPI TIPPY TIPSY TIPUP TIRAN TIRED TIRES TIROS TISZA TITAN TITER TITHE TITIS TITLE TITRE TITUS TIZZY

T•I••

TAIGA TAILS TAINE TAINO TAINT TBILL TBIRD TEIDE THICK THIEF THIGH THILL THINE THING THINK THINS THIRD TOILE TOILS TOITY TRIAD TRIAL TRIBE TRICE TRICK TRIED TRIER TRIES TRIGS TRIKE TRILL TRIMS TRINE TRINI TRIOS TRIPE TRIPS TRISH TRITE TRITT TWICE TWIGS TWILL TWINE TWINS TWIRL TWIST TWITS TWIXT TYING

T••I•

TABIS TACIT TAKIN TALIA TAMIL TAPIN TAPIR TAXIS TELIC TEPID THAIS THEIR TIBIA TIEIN TIKIS TIMID TIPIN TITIS TOBIT TOEIN TONIC TONIO TOPIC TOPIS TORIC TORII TOTIE TOTIS TOWIT TOXIC TOXIN TRAIL TRAIN TRAIT TROIS TULIP TUMID TUNIC TUNIS TURIN TWAIN

T•••I

TAKEI TARSI TEMPI TERRI TIKKI TIPPI TOMEI TONDI TOPOI TORII TORSI TREVI TRINI TUTTI

•TI••

ATILT ATION ATIVE QTIPS STICH STICK STIEB STIES STIFF STILE STILL STILT STING STINK STINT STIPE STIRK STIRS UTICA UTILE

•T•I•

ATEIN ATRIA ATRIP ATTIC ETHIC ETUIS ETVIR STAID STAIN STAIR STEIN STOIC STRIA STRIP

•T••I

ATARI OTOMI STYLI

••TI•

ACTII ACTIN ACTIV ANTIC ANTIQ ANTIS ARTIE ARTIS ASTIN ASTIR ATTIC BATIK CUTIE CUTIN CUTIS EATIN EATIT ENTIA FETID FITIN GETIN GETIT GOTIN GOTIT HITIT ISTIC KATIE LATIN LETIN MATIN METIS MOTIF NOTIN NOTIT OOTID OPTIC OSTIA PATIO PETIT PUTIN RATIO RETIA RETIE RUTIN SATIE SATIN SETIN SITIN TITIS TOTIE TOTIS UNTIE UNTIL VATIC YETIS ZITIS

••T•I

ACTII ALTAI MATRI MITZI NITTI PATRI PATTI PETRI PETTI PUTTI TUTTI

•••TI

AMATI CACTI CENTI CESTI COATI CONTI DENTI DHOTI HAITI LACTI LAHTI MARTI MISTI MUFTI MULTI NITTI NOCTI PARTI PATTI PETTI PONTI PUTTI RECTI SOLTI TUTTI

T••J•

THUJA

T•K••

TAKAS TAKEI TAKEN TAKER TAKES TAKIN TIKAL TIKES TIKIS TIKKI TOKAY TOKEN TOKYO TYKES

T••K•

TACKS TACKY TALKS TALKY TANKA TANKS TASKS TEAKS TICKS TICKY TIKKI TONKA TREKS TRIKE

TUCKS TURKS TURKU TUSKS

T•••K
TAROK THANK THICK THINK THUNK TILAK TRACK TRICK TRUCK TRUNK TWEAK

•T•K•
STAKE STOKE STUKA

•T••K
STACK STALK STANK STARK STEAK STICK STINK STIRK STOCK STOOK STORK STUCK STUNK

••TK•
DITKA LATKE SITKA

••T•K
BATAK BATIK PATEK POTOK

T•L••
TALER TALES TALIA TALKS TALKY TALLY TALON TALOS TALUS TELEO TELES TELEX TELIC TELLS TELLY TELOS TILAK TILDE TILED TILER TILES TILLS TILLY TILTH TILTS TOLER TOLET TOLLS TOLLY TULES TULIP TULLE TULLY TULSA TYLER

T••L•
TABLA TABLE TAELS TAILS TALLY TBALL TBILL TEALS TELLS TELLY TESLA THILL THOLE THULE TILLS TILLY TITLE TOILE TOILS TOLLS TOLLY TOOLS TRALA TRILL TROLL TRULY TULLE TULLY TWILL TWYLA

T•••L
TAMIL TBALL TBILL TEPAL THEOL THILL TICAL TIDAL TIKAL TOBOL TONAL TOPOL TOTAL TOWEL TRAIL TRAWL TRIAL TRILL TROLL TWILL TWIRL TYROL

•TL••
ATLAS FTLBS UTLEY

•T•L•
ATALL ATILT ATOLL ITALO ITALS ITALY STALE STALK STALL STELA STELE STILE STILL STILT STOLA STOLE STOLS STULL STYLE STYLI STYLO UTILE VTOLS

•T••L
ATALL ATHOL ATOLL ETHEL ETHYL ETZEL LTCOL STAEL STAHL STALL STEAL STEEL STILL STOOL STULL

••TL•
APTLY FATLY FITLY HATLO HOTLY ISTLE PATLY ROTLS TITLE WETLY

••T•L
ANTAL ARTAL ARTEL BETEL BOTEL BUTYL DOTAL EXTOL FATAL FETAL HOTEL INTEL METAL MOTEL NATAL OCTAL PETAL RATEL SOTOL TOTAL UNTIL VITAL

•••TL
YENTL

T•M••
TAMBO TAMED TAMER TAMES TAMIL TAMMY TAMPA TAMPS TEMPE TEMPI TEMPO TEMPS TEMPT TIMED TIMER TIMES TIMEX TIMID TIMMY TIMON TIMOR TOMEI TOMES TOMMY TUMID TUMMY TUMPS

T••M•
TAMMY TEAMS TEEMS TERMS THEMA THEME THEMS THUMB THUMP THYME THYMY TIMMY TOMMY TORME TRAMP TRAMS TRIMS TROMP TRUMP TRYME TUMMY

T•••M
TATUM TENAM TENPM THERM THRUM TOTEM TWOAM TWOPM

•TM••
ATMAN ATMOS

•T•M•
ATOMS ATOMY ETYMA ITEMS ITSME OTOMI STAMP STEMS STOMA STOMP STUMP STUMS STYMY

•T••M
ATEAM STEAM STORM STROM STRUM STURM

••TM•
GETME HITME NOTME

••T•M
DATUM ENTOM TATUM TOTEM

TN•••
TNOTE TNUTS

T•N••
TANDE TANDY TANEY TANGO TANGS TANGY TANKA TANKS TANSY TANTE TANTO TANYA TENAM TENCH TENDS TENET TENON TENOR TENPM TENSE TENTH TENTS TINCT TINED TINES TINGE TINGS TINNY TINTS TONAL TONDI TONDO TONED TONER TONES TONEY TONGA TONGS TONIC TONIO TONKA TONNE TONTO TONUS TONYA TONYS TUNAS TUNED TUNER TUNES TUNIC TUNIS TUNNY TYNAN TYNES

T••N•
TAINE TAINO TAINT TARNS TAUNT TAWNY TBOND TBONE TEENA TEENS TEENY TERNE TERNS THANE THANK THANT THINE THING THINK THINS THONG THUNK TIANT TINNY TONNE TOONS TOWNE TOWNS TOWNY TRANS TREND TRENT TRINE TRINI TRUNK TUNNY TURNS TWANG TWINE TWINS TYING

T•••N
TAKEN TAKIN TALON TAPIN TAUON TAXON TENON TETON TEXAN THORN TIEIN TIMON TIPIN TIRAN TITAN TOEIN TOKEN TOXIN TOYON TRAIN TREEN TRYON TURIN TWAIN TWEEN TYNAN TYSON

•TN••
ATNOS ETNAS

•T•N•
ATONE ATONY ETHNO ETONS STAND STANG STANK STENO STENS STING STINK STINT STONE STONY STUNG STUNK STUNS STUNT STYNE

•T••N
ATEIN ATHON ATION ATMAN ETHAN LTGEN STAIN STEEN STEIN STERN UTAHN UTURN

••TN•
AETNA PATNA

••T•N
ACTIN ACTON AFTON ALTON ANTON ASTIN ASTON BATON BETON CUTIN EATEN EATIN EATON ELTON FITIN FUTON GATUN GETIN GETON GOTIN GOTON GUTEN HITON LATEN LATIN LETIN LETON LITON MATIN NOTIN OATEN OFTEN ORTON PATEN PATON PITON PUTIN PUTON RATON RUTIN SATAN SATIN SATON SETIN SETON SITIN SITON TETON TITAN UPTON WOTAN

TO•••
TOADS TOADY TOAST TOBES TOBEY TOBIT TOBOL TODAY TODDY TODOS TOEIN TOFFS TOFFY TOFTS TOGAE TOGAS TOILE TOILS TOITY TOKAY TOKEN TOKYO TOLER TOLET TOLLS TOLLY TOMEI TOMES TOMMY TONAL TONDI TONDO TONED TONER TONES TONEY TONGA TONGS TONIC TONIO TONKA TONNE TONTO TONUS TONYA TONYS TOOLS TOONS TOOTH TOOTS TOPAZ TOPED TOPER TOPES TOPIC TOPIS TOPOG TOPOI TOPOL TOPOS TOPPS TOPSY TOQUE TORAH TORCH TORIC TORII TORME TOROS TORRE TORRS TORSI TORSO TORTE TORTS TORUS TOSCA TOTAL TOTED TOTEM TOTER TOTES TOTIE TOTIS TOTUP TOUCH TOUGH TOURS TOUTE TOUTS TOVES TOWED TOWEL TOWER TOWIT TOWNE TOWNS TOWNY TOXIC TOXIN TOYED TOYON

T•O••
TBOND TBONE THOLE THONG THORN THORO THORP THOSE THOTH THOUS TNOTE TOOLS TOONS TOOTH TOOTS TROIS TROLL TROMP TROOP TROPE TROPO TROTH TROTS TROUT TROVE TWOAM TWOPM

T••O•
TABOO TABOR TACOS TAHOE TALON TALOS TAROK TAROT TAUON TAXON TELOS TENON TENOR TETON THEOL THROB THROE THROW TIMON TIMOR TIROS TOBOL TODOS TOPOG TOPOI TOPOL TOPOS TOROS TOYON TRIOS TROOP TRYON TUDOR TUROW TUTOR TYPOS TYROL TYROS TYSON

T•••O
TABOO TACHO TAINO TAMBO TANGO TANTO TASSO TAUPO TAURO TAUTO TAXCO TELEO TEMPO THORO TIETO TOKYO TONDO TONIO TONTO TORSO TROPO TRURO TURBO TYCHO

•TO••
ATOLL ATOMS ATOMY ATONE ATONY ETONS OTOES OTOMI STOAE STOAS STOAT STOCK STOGY STOIC STOKE STOLA STOLE STOLS STOMA STOMP STONE STONY STOOD STOOK STOOL STOOP STOPE STOPS STORE STORK STORM STORY STOSS STOTS STOUP STOUT STOVE STOWE STOWS VTOLS

•T•O•
ATHOL ATHON ATHOS ATION ATMOS ATNOS ETHOS LTCOL LTGOV STOOD STOOK STOOL STOOP STROM STROP

•T••O
ETHNO ITALO PTERO STENO STYLO

••TO•
ACTON ACTOR AFTON ALTON ALTOS ANTON ARTOO ASTON ASTOR AUTOS BATON BATOR BETON DETOO EATON ELTON ENTOM ESTOP EXTOL FETOR FSTOP FUTON GATOR GATOS GETON GOTON HITON INTOW JATOS KOTOS LETON LITON METOO MOTOR ONTOP ORTON PATON PITON PITOT POTOK PUTON RATON RETOP RETOW ROTOR ROTOS SATON SETON SITON SOTOL TETON TUTOR UPTON ZZTOP

••T•O
ALTHO ANTHO ARTOO ASTRO BATHO BUTEO DETOO DITTO DOTTO EXTRO GETGO GETTO GITGO GOTTO HATLO IATRO INTRO INTWO LETGO LITHO LOTTO MATEO MATRO MATZO METOO METRO MOTTO NITRO NOTSO ORTHO OSTEO OUTDO OUTGO PATHO PATIO PETRO POTTO PUTTO RATIO RATSO RETRO SETTO SOTHO SOTTO

•••TO
AALTO ACETO ADDTO AIMTO AMATO ANETO BALTO BLUTO BOITO CANTO CENTO DEUTO DITTO DOTTO DUETO ERATO FACTO FEMTO FRITO GETTO GOTTO GUSTO HADTO HASTO HECTO HIPTO HOWTO JUNTO KYOTO LACTO LAYTO LEDTO LENTO LEPTO LIETO LOTTO MINTO MOLTO MOTTO NEATO PANTO PASTO PESTO PHOTO PHYTO PINTO PLATO PLUTO PORTO POTTO PRATO PROTO PUTTO QUITO RANTO RECTO RUNTO SANTO SARTO SAWTO SEATO SEETO SETTO SOTTO TANTO TAUTO TIETO TONTO XACTO

T•P••
TAPAS TAPED TAPER TAPES TAPIN TAPIR TEPAL TEPEE TEPID TIPIN TIPPI TIPPY TIPSY TIPUP TOPAZ TOPED TOPER TOPES TOPIC TOPIS TOPOG TOPOI TOPOL TOPOS TOPPS TOPSY TYPEA TYPEB TYPED TYPEE TYPER TYPES TYPEY TYPOS

T••P•
TAMPA TAMPS TARPS TAUPE TAUPO TBSPS TEMPE TEMPI TEMPO TEMPS TEMPT TENPM TERPS TIPPI TIPPY TOPPS TRAPP TRAPS TRIPE TRIPS TROPE TROPO TUMPS TWOPM

T•••P
TAGUP TEEUP THARP THORP THUMP TIEUP TIPUP TOTUP TRAMP TRAPP TROMP TROOP TRUMP TULIP TWERP

•TP••
ATPAR STPAT

•T•P•
ETAPE QTIPS STEPS STIPE STOPE STOPS STUPA STUPE

•T••P
ATEUP ATRIP PTRAP STAMP STEEP STOMP STOOP STOUP STRAP STREP STRIP STROP STUMP

••T•P
ACTUP CUTUP EATUP ESTOP FSTOP GETUP GOTUP HETUP HITUP LETUP LITUP NOTUP ONTAP ONTOP PUTUP RETAP RETOP SATUP SETUP SITUP TOTUP ZZTOP

T•Q••
TOQUE TUQUE

•TQ••
ATQUE

•T•Q•
ETSQQ

•T••Q
ETSEQ ETSQQ

••T•Q
ANTIQ

TR•••
TRACE TRACK TRACT TRACY TRADE TRAIL TRAIN TRAIT TRALA TRAMP TRAMS TRANS TRAPP TRAPS TRASH TRAVE TRAWL TRAYS TREAD TREAT TREED TREEN TREES TREKS TREND TRENT TRESS TREVI TREWS TREYS TRIAD TRIAL TRIBE TRICE TRICK TRIED TRIER TRIES TRIGS TRIKE TRILL TRIMS TRINE TRINI TRIOS TRIPE TRIPS TRISH TRITE TRITT TROIS TROLL TROMP TROOP TROPE TROPO TROTH TROTS TROUT TROVE TRUCE TRUCK TRUED TRUER TRUES TRUEX TRUGS TRULY TRUMP TRUNK TRURO TRUSS TRUST TRUTH TRYME TRYON TRYST

T•R••
TARDE TARDY TARES TARGE TARNS TAROK TAROT TARPS TARRY TARSI TARTS TARTU TERMS TERNE TERNS TERPS TERRA TERRE TERRI TERRY TERSE TERZA THREE THREW THROB THROE THROW THRUM TIRAN TIRED TIRES TIROS TORAH TORCH TORIC TORII TORME TOROS TORRE TORRS TORSI TORSO TORTE TORTS TORUS TURBO TURFS TURFY TURIN TURKS TURKU TURNS TUROW TURVY TYRES TYROL TYROS

T••R•
TAHRS TARRY TATRA TAURO TAYRA TBARS TBIRD TEARS TEARY TERRA TERRE TERRI TERRY TETRA THARP THERA THERE THERM THIRD THORN THORO THORP THURS TIARA TIERS TITRE TORRE TORRS TOURS TRURO TSARS TWERE TWERP TWIRL TZARS

T•••R
TABOR TAKER TALER TAMER TAPER TAPIR TASER TATAR TATER

TAXER TENOR THEIR TIBER TIGER TILER TIMER TIMOR TITER TOLER TONER TOPER TOTER TOWER TRIER TRUER TUBER TUDOR TUNER TUTOR TWEER TYLER TYPER

•TR••
ATRIA ATRIP PTRAP STRAD STRAP STRAW STRAY STREP STREW STRIA STRIP STROM STROP STRUG STRUM STRUT

•T•R•
ATARI ITERS OTARU OTARY PTERO STARE STARK STARR STARS START STARZ STERE STERN STIRK STIRS STORE STORK STORM STORY STURM UTURN

•T••R
ATPAR ATTAR ATWAR ETHER ETVIR OTHER OTTER STAIR STARR STEER UTHER UTTER

••TR•
AFTRA ANTRA ANTRE ASTRA ASTRE ASTRO AUTRE AUTRY DETRE ENTRE ENTRY EXTRA EXTRO IATRO IATRY INTRA INTRO LATRY LITRE MATRI MATRO METRE METRO METRY MITRE NITRE NITRO NOTRE OUTRE PATRI PETRA PETRI PETRO RETRO RETRY SUTRA TATRA TETRA TITRE ULTRA VOTRE

••T•R
ACTER ACTOR AFTER ALTAR ALTER APTER ARTHR ARTUR ASTER ASTIR ASTOR ATTAR BATOR BITER CATER CITER CUTER DATER DETER DOTER EATER ENTER ESTER FETOR GATOR HATER INTER JETER KITER LATER LITER MATER METER MITER MOTOR MUTER NITER NOTER OATER OTTER OUTER PATER PETER QATAR RATER RETAR ROTOR SATYR SITAR TATAR TATER TITER TOTER TUTOR UNTER UTTER VATER VOTER WATER

•••TR
AUSTR CONTR DEXTR DISTR GASTR INSTR

TS•••
TSADE TSARS TSGTS

T•S••
TASER TASKS TASSE TASSO TASTE TASTY TBSPS TESLA TESTA TESTS TESTY TISZA TOSCA TUSKS TVSET TYSON

T••S•
TANSY TARSI TASSE TASSO TEASE TENSE TERSE THESE THOSE TIPSY TOAST TOPSY TORSI TORSO TRASH TRESS TRISH TRUSS TRUST TRYST TULSA TWIST

T•••S
TABIS TACKS TACOS TAELS TAGUS TAHRS TAILS TAKAS TAKES TALES TALKS TALOS TALUS TAMES TAMPS TANGS TANKS TAPAS TAPES TARES TARNS TARPS TARTS TASKS TAXES TAXIS TBARS TBSPS TEAKS TEALS TEAMS TEARS TECHS TEEMS TEENS TELES TELLS TELOS TEMPS TENDS TENTS TERMS TERNS TERPS TESTS TETES TETHS TEXAS TEXTS THAIS THATS THAWS THEMS THEWS THINS THOUS THUDS THUGS THURS TIBBS TICKS TIDES TIEGS TIERS TIFFS TIKES TIKIS TILES TILLS TILTS TIMES TINES TINGS TINTS TIRES TIROS TITIS TITUS TNUTS TOADS TOBES TODOS TOFFS TOFTS TOGAS TOILS TOLLS TOMES TONES TONGS TONUS TONYS TOOLS TOONS TOOTS TOPES TOPIS TOPOS TOPPS TOROS TORRS TORTS TORUS TOTES TOTIS TOURS TOUTS TOVES TOWNS TRAMS TRANS TRAPS TRAYS TREES TREKS TRESS TREWS TREYS TRIES TRIGS TRIMS TRIOS TRIPS TROIS TROTS TRUES TRUGS TRUSS TSARS TSGTS TUBAS TUBES TUCKS TUFTS TULES TUMPS TUNAS TUNES TUNIS TURFS TURKS TURNS TUSKS TUTUS TUXES TWIGS TWINS TWITS TYKES TYNES TYPES TYPOS TYRES TYROS TZARS

•TS••
ATSEA ETSEQ ETSQQ ITSME

•T•S•
STASH STOSS

•T••S
ATHOS ATLAS ATMOS ATNOS ATOMS ATTYS ETATS ETHOS ETNAS ETONS ETUIS FTLBS ITALS ITEMS ITERS OTOES QTIPS STABS STAGS STARS STATS STAYS STEMS STENS STEPS STETS STEWS STIES STIRS STOAS STOLS STOPS STOSS STOTS STOWS STUBS STUDS STUMS STUNS VTOLS

••TS•
ANTSY ARTSY BETSY BITSY DITSY GUTSY MATSU NOTSO NUTSY PATSY POTSY RATSO

••T•S
ACTAS ALTOS ALTUS ANTAS ANTES ANTIS ARTES ARTIS ATTYS AUTOS BATES BATHS BATTS BETAS BETHS BITES BITTS BUTTS BYTES CATES CETUS CITES COTES CUTIS DATES DOTES ESTAS ESTES FATES FETAS FETES GATES GATOS GETAS GOTHS HATES HETHS HUTUS ICTUS IOTAS JATOS JETES JOTAS JUTES KITES KITTS KOTOS LATHS LETTS LITES LITHS LOTAS LOTUS LUTES MATES MATHS METES METIS MITES MITTS MOTES MOTHS MOTTS MUTES MUTTS MYTHS NITES NOTES OATES OATHS PATES PATHS PETES PITAS PITHS PITTS POTTS PUTTS RATES RATHS RITES ROTAS ROTES ROTLS ROTOS SATES SITES SITUS SRTAS TETES TETHS TITIS TITUS TOTES TOTIS TUTUS VITAS VITUS VOTES WATTS YATES YETIS ZETAS ZITIS

•••TS
ABETS ABUTS ACCTS ADITS APPTS ASSTS AUNTS BAHTS BAITS BALTS BARTS BATTS BEATS BEETS BELTS BENTS BESTS BITTS BLATS BLOTS BOATS BOLTS BOOTS BOUTS BRATS BRITS BRUTS BUNTS BUSTS BUTTS CANTS CAPTS CARTS CASTS CELTS CENTS CERTS CHATS CHITS CLOTS COATS COLTS COOTS COPTS COSTS CULTS DARTS DEBTS DELTS DENTS DEPTS DICTS DIETS DINTS DOITS DOLTS DRATS DUCTS DUETS DUSTS EASTS EDITS EMITS ETATS EXITS EYOTS FACTS FASTS FEATS FEETS FELTS FESTS FIATS FISTS FLATS FLITS FONTS FOOTS FORTS FOUTS FRATS FRETS FRITS GAITS GENTS GESTS GHATS GIFTS GILTS GIRTS GISTS GLUTS GMATS GNATS GOATS GRITS GROTS GUSTS HAFTS HALTS HANTS HARTS HEATS HEFTS HENTS HESTS HILTS HINTS HOOTS HOSTS HUNTS HURTS INITS INSTS JESTS JILTS JOLTS KEATS KEETS KILTS KITTS KNITS KNOTS KYATS LASTS LEETS LEFTS LENTS LETTS LIFTS LILTS LINTS LISTS LOFTS LOOTS LOUTS LSATS LUSTS MALTS MARTS MASTS MEATS MEETS MELTS MILTS MINTS MISTS MITTS MOATS MOLTS MOOTS MORTS MOTTS MSGTS MUSTS MUTTS NEATS NERTS NESTS NEWTS NYETS OASTS ODETS OMITS OUSTS PACTS PANTS PARTS PASTS PEATS PELTS PESTS PHOTS PICTS PINTS PITTS PLATS PLOTS POETS PONTS PORTS POSTS POTTS POUTS PROTS PSATS PUNTS PUTTS QUITS RAFTS RANTS RENTS RESTS RIFTS RIOTS ROOTS ROUTS RUNTS RUSTS RYOTS SALTS SCATS SCOTS SCUTS SEATS SECTS SEXTS SHOTS SHUTS SIFTS SILTS SKITS SLATS SLITS SLOTS SMITS SMUTS SNITS SOOTS SORTS SPATS SPETS SPITS SPOTS SSGTS STATS STETS STOTS SUETS SUITS SUPTS SWATS TARTS TENTS TESTS TEXTS THATS TILTS TINTS TNUTS TOFTS TOOTS TORTS TOUTS TROTS TSGTS TUFTS TWITS UNITS VENTS VERTS VESTS VOLTS WAFTS WAITS WANTS WARTS WATTS WEFTS WELTS WESTS WHATS WHETS WHITS WILTS WONTS WORTS WRITS YEATS YURTS ZESTS

T•T••
TATAR TATER TATRA TATTY TATUM TETES TETHS TETON TETRA TITAN TITER TITHE TITIS TITLE TITRE TITUS TOTAL TOTED TOTEM TOTER TOTES TOTIE TOTIS TOTUP TUTEE TUTOR TUTTI TUTUS

T••T•
TANTE TANTO TARTS TARTU TASTE TASTY TATTY TAUTO TEETH TENTH TENTS TESTA TESTS TESTY TEXTS THATS THETA THOTH TIETO TILTH TILTS TINTS TNOTE TNUTS TOFTS TOITY TONTO TOOTH TOOTS TORTE TORTS TOUTE TOUTS TRITE TRITT TROTH TROTS TRUTH TSGTS TUFTS TUFTY TUTTI TWITS

T•••T
TACET TACIT TAINT TAROT TAUNT TEMPT TENET TEVET THANT THEFT TIANT TIBET TIGHT TINCT TOAST TOBIT TOLET TOWIT TRACT TRAIT TREAT TRENT TRITT TROUT TRUST TRYST TVSET TWEET TWIST TWIXT

•TT••
ATTAR ATTIC ATTYS OTTER UTTER

•T•T•
ETATS STATE STATS STETS STOTS STUTZ

•T••T
ATBAT ATILT STADT START STILT STINT STOAT STOUT STPAT STRUT STUNT

••TT•
BATTS BATTY BETTA BETTE BETTY BITTE BITTS BITTY BUTTE BUTTS BUTTY CATTY COTTA DITTO DITTY DOTTO DOTTY FATTY GETTO GETTY GOTTA GOTTO GUTTA GUTTY HETTY JETTY JUTTY KITTS KITTY LATTE LETTS LOTTA LOTTE LOTTO LYTTA MATTE MITTS MITTY MOTTA MOTTO MOTTS MUTTS NATTY NITTI NITTY NUTTY PATTI PATTY PETTI PETTY PITTA PITTS POTTO POTTS POTTY PUTTI PUTTO PUTTS PUTTY RATTY RUTTY SETTE SETTO SOTTO TATTY TUTTI WATTS WITTE WITTY

••T•T
AETAT BUTUT DETAT DITAT EATAT EATIT GETAT GETIT GOTAT GOTIT HITIT LETAT MOTET NOTIT OCTET PETIT PITOT SETAT

•••TT
BLITT BRETT BRITT FLATT HYATT OVETT PLATT PRATT RAITT RHETT SCOTT SHATT TRITT WYATT

TU•••
TUBAS TUBBY TUBED TUBER TUBES TUCKS TUDOR TUFTS TUFTY TULES TULIP TULLE TULLY TULSA TUMID TUMMY TUMPS TUNAS TUNED TUNER TUNES TUNIC TUNIS TUNNY TUQUE TURBO TURFS TURFY TURIN TURKS TURKU TURNS TUROW TURVY TUSKS TUTEE TUTOR TUTTI TUTUS TUXES

T•U••
TAUNT TAUON TAUPE TAUPO TAURO TAUTO THUDS THUGS THUJA THULE THUMB THUMP THUNK THURS TNUTS TOUCH TOUGH TOURS TOUTE TOUTS TRUCE TRUCK TRUED TRUER TRUES TRUEX TRUGS TRULY TRUMP TRUNK TRURO TRUSS TRUST TRUTH

T••U•
TAGUP TAGUS TALUS TATUM TEEUP THOUS THRUM TIEUP TIPUP TITUS TONUS TOQUE TORUS TOTUP TROUT TUQUE TUTUS

T•••U
TAEGU TARTU TURKU

•TU••
ETUDE ETUIS STUBS STUCK STUDS STUDY STUFF STUKA STULL STUMP STUMS STUNG STUNK STUNS STUNT STUPA STUPE STURM STUTZ UTURN

•T•U•
ATEUP ATQUE STOUP STOUT STRUG STRUM STRUT

•T••U
OTARU

••TU•
ACTUP ALTUS ARTUR BUTUT CETUS CUTUP DATUM EATUP GATUN GETUP GOTUP HETUP HITUP HUTUS ICTUS LETUP LITUP LOTUS NOTUP PUTUP SATUP SETUP SITUP SITUS TATUM TITUS TOTUP TUTUS VITUS

••T•U
MATSU

•••TU
BANTU DICTU TARTU VIRTU

TV•••
TVSET

T•V••
TEVET TEVYE TOVES

T••V•
TRAVE TREVI TROVE TURVY

•TV••
ETVIR

•T•V•
ATIVE STAVE STEVE STOVE

•T••V
LTGOV

••T•V
ACTIV

•••TV
ABCTV CBSTV FOXTV NBCTV PAYTV

TW•••
TWAIN TWANG TWEAK TWEED TWEEN TWEER TWEET TWERE TWERP TWICE TWIGS TWILL TWINE TWINS TWIRL TWIST TWITS TWIXT TWOAM TWOPM TWYLA

T•W••
TAWNY TOWED TOWEL TOWER TOWIT TOWNE TOWNS TOWNY

T••W•
THAWS THEWS THEWY TRAWL

TREWS

T•••W
THREW THROW TUROW

•TW••
ATWAR OTWAY

•T•W•
STEWS STOWE STOWS

•T••W
STRAW STREW

••TW•
FATWA INTWO KITWE

••T•W
INTOW RETOW

T•X••
TAXCO TAXED TAXER TAXES TAXIS TAXON TEXAN TEXAS TEXTS TOXIC TOXIN TUXES

T••X•
TWIXT

T•••X
TELEX TIMEX TRUEX

••T•X
CUTEX LATEX RETAX

TY•••
TYCHE TYCHO TYING TYKES TYLER TYNAN TYNES TYPEA TYPEB TYPED TYPEE TYPER TYPES TYPEY TYPOS TYRES TYROL TYROS TYSON

T•Y••
TAYRA THYME THYMY TOYED TOYON TRYME TRYON TRYST TWYLA

T••Y•
TANYA TEVYE THEYD TOKYO TONYA TONYS TRAYS TREYS

T•••Y
TABBY TACHY TACKY TAFFY TALKY TALLY TAMMY TANDY TANEY TANGY TANSY TARDY TARRY TASTY TATTY TAWNY TEARY TECHY TEDDY TEENY TELLY TERRY TESTY THEWY THYMY TICKY TILLY TIMMY TINNY TIPPY TIPSY TIZZY TOADY TOBEY TODAY TODDY TOFFY TOITY TOKAY TOLLY TOMMY TONEY TOPSY TOWNY TRACY TRULY TUBBY TUFTY TULLY TUMMY TUNNY TURFY TURVY TYPEY

•TY••
ETYMA STYLE STYLI STYLO STYMY STYNE

•T•Y•
ATTYS ETHYL STAYS

•T••Y
ATBAY ATOMY ATONY ITALY ITCHY OTARY OTWAY STACY STAGY STOGY STONY STORY STRAY STUDY STYMY UTLEY

••TY•
ATTYS BUTYL SATYR

••T•Y
ANTSY APTLY ARTSY AUTRY BATHY BATTY BETSY BETTY BITSY BITTY BUTTY CATHY CATTY CUTEY DITSY DITTY DITZY DOTTY ENTRY FATLY FATTY FITLY GETBY GETTY GOTBY GUTSY GUTTY HETTY HOTLY IATRY JETTY JUTTY KATHY KITTY LATHY LATRY MATEY METRY MITTY MOTHY NATTY NITTY NUTSY NUTTY PATHY PATLY PATSY PATTY PETTY PITHY POTSY POTTY PUTBY PUTTY RATTY RETRY RITZY RUTTY SATBY SETBY SITBY TATTY WETLY WITHY WITTY

•••TY
AMITY AUNTY BARTY BATTY BETTY BITTY BOOTY BUTTY CANTY CATTY DEITY DINTY DIRTY DITTY DOTTY DUSTY EMPTY FATTY FIFTY FLUTY FORTY FUSTY GETTY GOUTY GUSTY GUTTY HASTY HEFTY HETTY HOITY JETTY JOLTY JUTTY KITTY LAITY LEFTY LINTY LOFTY LUSTY MALTY MARTY MEATY MELTY MILTY MINTY MISTY MITTY MONTY MUSTY NASTY NATTY NIFTY NITTY NUTTY PARTY PASTY PATTY PEATY PETTY PIETY PLATY POTTY POUTY PUNTY PUTTY RATTY ROOTY RUNTY RUSTY RUTTY SALTY SILTY SIXTY SLATY SOFTY SOOTY SUETY TASTY TATTY TESTY TOITY TUFTY UNITY VASTY WARTY WELTY WHITY WITTY ZESTY ZLOTY

TZ•••
TZARS

T•Z••
TAZZA TIZZY

T••Z•
TAZZA TERZA TISZA TIZZY

T•••Z
TOPAZ

•TZ••
ETZEL

•T••Z
STARZ STUTZ

••TZ•
DITZY MATZO MITZI RITZY

•••TZ
BLITZ FRITZ GLITZ HERTZ HOLTZ HUNTZ KLUTZ KURTZ LANTZ MERTZ NERTZ SPITZ STUTZ SWITZ WAITZ WALTZ

U•A••
UDALL UHAUL UKASE UNAPT UNARM UNAUS URALS USAGE USAIR UTAHN UZALA

U••A•
UBOAT UCLAN UHLAN ULNAE ULNAS UMIAK UNBAR UNCAP UNCAS UNJAM UNLAY UNMAN UNSAY URBAN URIAH URIAL USUAL UXMAL

U•••A
UHURA UINTA ULTRA UMBRA UNRRA USCGA USLTA USOFA UTICA UVULA UZALA

•UA••
DUADS DUANE GUACO GUARD GUARS GUAVA KUALA LUAUS QUACK QUADR QUADS QUAFF QUAGS QUAID QUAIL QUAKE QUAKY QUALE QUALM QUAND QUANT QUARE QUARK QUART QUASH QUASI QUAYS RUANA RUARK SUAVE YUANS

•U•A•
AURAE AURAL AURAR AURAS CUBAN CUGAT CUMAE CUNAS DUBAI DUCAL DUCAT DUFAY DUGAN DUKAS DUMAS DURAN FUGAL FULAS FURAN GULAG GULAR HULAS HUMAN HUNAN JUBAL JUDAH JUDAS JUGAL JURAL JURAT KULAK LUBAS LUCAN LUCAS LUKAS LUNAR LURAY MURAL MURAT MUZAK NUGAE PULAS PUMAS PUNAS PUPAE PUPAL PUPAS PUSAN QUOAD RUGAE RUNAT RURAL SUDAN SUGAR SUMAC SURAH SURAL SURAS SURAT SUSAN TUBAS TUNAS WUHAN YUGAS YUMAN YUMAS

•U••A
AUDRA BUBBA BUENA BUFFA BULBA BULLA BURMA BURSA CULPA CUPPA CURIA DURRA FULDA GUAVA GUNGA GUTTA HUBBA HUZZA JUDEA JULIA JUMNA JUNTA KUALA KUKLA LUCCA LUCIA LUISA LULEA LURIA MUDRA MURRA MUSCA NUBIA NUCHA OUIDA OUIJA PUKKA PUNTA QUOTA RUANA RUMBA SUCKA SUDRA SUITA SULFA SULLA SUMBA SUMMA SUNDA SUNNA SUPRA SUTRA TULSA YUCCA

••UA•
AQUAE AQUAS DOUAI DOUAY EQUAL JOUAL KAUAI SKUAS SQUAB SQUAD SQUAT USUAL

••U•A
ABUJA ACURA ADUWA ALULA ARUBA AZUSA CAUSA CEUTA CHULA CRURA FAUNA GOUDA HAUSA HOUMA KRUPA LAURA MAUNA PAULA PIURA SAUNA SCUBA SCUTA SHULA SOUSA STUKA STUPA THUJA UHURA UVULA

•••UA
GENUA LEHUA MAKUA NAHUA PADUA PAPUA VACUA

UB•••
UBOAT UBOLT

U•B••
UMBEL UMBER UMBOS UMBRA UNBAR UNBID UNBOX UPBOW URBAN URBIS UZBEK

•UB••
AUBER BUBBA BUBER BUBUS CUBAN CUBBY CUBEB CUBED CUBES CUBIC CUBIT DUBAI DUBIN DUBOS EUBIE FUBSY HUBBA HUBBY JUBAL LUBAS LUBED LUBES NUBBY NUBIA RUBEN RUBES RUBIK RUBIN RUBLE SUBIC TUBAS TUBBY TUBED TUBER TUBES ZUBIN

•U•B•
BUBBA BULBA BULBS BURBS BUSBY CUBBY CURBS DUMBO DUMBS GUMBO GUMBY HUBBA HUBBY JUMBO MUMBO NUBBY NUMBS PUTBY RUGBY RUMBA SUMBA TUBBY TURBO

•U••B
CUBEB

••UB•
ARUBA CHUBS CLUBS DAUBS DOUBT DRUBS FLUBS GRUBS SCUBA SNUBS STUBS

••U•B
BLURB CRUMB EXURB PLUMB RHUMB SQUAB SQUIB THUMB

•••UB
REDUB SCRUB SHRUB

UC•••
UCLAN

U•C••
ULCER UNCAP UNCAS UNCLE UNCUT USCGA

U••C•
URICH UTICA

U•••C
UGRIC

•UC••
BUCKO BUCKS BUCKY DUCAL DUCAT DUCES DUCHY DUCKS DUCKY DUCTS FUCHS GUCCI LUCAN LUCAS LUCCA LUCCI LUCIA LUCID LUCIE LUCKS LUCKY LUCRE MUCIN MUCKS MUCKY MUCRO NUCHA PUCCI PUCKS RUCHE RUCKS SUCKA SUCKS SUCRE TUCKS YUCCA YUCKY

•U•C•
BUICK BUNCH BUSCH BUTCH CULCH CURCI CUZCO DUNCE DUTCH GUACO GUCCI GULCH HULCE HUNCH HUTCH JUICE JUICY JUNCO LUCCA LUCCI LUNCH LURCH MULCH MULCT MUNCH MUSCA OUNCE PUCCI PUNCH QUACK QUICK SULCI YUCCA

•U••C
AURIC CUBIC DUROC LUDIC MUSIC PUNIC RUNIC SUBIC SUMAC TUNIC

••UC•
AMUCK BRUCE BRUCH CHUCK CLUCK COUCH DEUCE DEUCY EDUCE EDUCT ERUCT GLUCK GLUCO PLUCK POUCH SAUCE SAUCY SHUCK SNUCK STUCK TOUCH TRUCE TRUCK VOUCH

UD•••
UDALL UDDER UDINE

U•D••
UDDER UNDER UNDID UNDUE UPDOS

U•••D
UMPED UNBID UNDID UNFED UNLED UNWED UPEND UPPED URGED URSID USHED USTED

•UD••
AUDEN AUDIE AUDIO AUDIS AUDIT AUDRA BUDDY BUDGE CUDDY DUDDY DUDES FUDDY FUDGE JUDAH JUDAS JUDEA JUDEO JUDGE KUDOS KUDUS KUDZU LUDIC MUDDY MUDRA NUDER NUDES NUDGE PUDGY PUDUS RUDDS RUDDY RUDER RUDGE SUDAN SUDDS SUDRA SUDSY TUDOR

•U•D•
BUDDY BUNDS BUNDT BUNDY CUDDY CURDS CURDY DUADS DUDDY FUDDY FULDA FUNDS FUNDY GUIDE GUIDO GURDY HURDY KURDS LUNDI LUNDY MUDDY MUNDI OUIDA OUTDO QUADR QUADS QUIDS QUODS RUDDS RUDDY SUDDS SUEDE SUNDA SURDS

•U••D
BUILD BUSED CUBED CUPID CURED DUKED DUPED FUMED FUSED FUZED GUARD GUILD GUYED HUMID JUKED LUBED LUCID LURED LURID MUSED MUTED NUKED OUTED PULED QUAID QUAND QUOAD RULED TUBED TUMID TUNED

••UD•
CRUDE ELUDE ETUDE EXUDE FEUDS GAUDS GAUDY GOUDA GOUDY JEUDI LAUDE LAUDS MAUDE PRUDE SAUDI SCUDI SCUDO SCUDS SPUDS STUDS STUDY THUDS

••U•D
BLUED BOUND CLUED COULD DRUID FLUID FOUND GLUED GOULD GOURD HOUND MAUND MOULD MOUND POUND ROUND SLUED SOUND SQUAD SQUID TRUED WOULD WOUND

•••UD
ALOUD CHAUD CLOUD FRAUD FREUD LIKUD NEFUD PROUD PSEUD SALUD

U•E••
UMEKI UPEND USERS USEUP

U••E•
UDDER ULCER UMBEL UMBER UMPED UNDER UNFED UNGER UNLED UNMET UNPEG UNPEN UNSER UNSET UNTER UNWED UPPED UPPER UPSET URGED URGER URGES URIEL URKEL USHED USHER USTED UTHER UTLEY UTTER UZBEK

U•••E
UDINE UKASE ULNAE UNCLE UNDUE UNITE UNTIE USAGE USQUE UTILE

•UE••
BUELL BUENA BUENO CUEIN DUELS DUETO DUETS FUEGO FUELS GUESS GUEST HUEVO LUEGO QUEEG QUEEN QUEER QUELL QUERN QUERY QUEST QUEUE RUEHL RUERS SUEDE SUEME SUERS SUETS SUETY

•U•E•
AUBER AUDEN AUGER AUREI BUBER BUSED BUSES BUSEY BUTEO BUYER CUBEB CUBED CUBES CUKES CULET CULEX CUNEO CUPEL CURED CURER CURES CUTER CUTEX CUTEY CUVEE DUCES DUDES DUKED DUKES DUNES DUPED DUPES DURER DUVET DUXES EULER FUMED FUMES FUSED FUSEE FUSES FUZED FUZEE GULES GUTEN GUYED HUGER JUDEA JUDEO JUKED JUKES JULEP JULES JUTES KUGEL LUBED LUBES LUGER LUGES LULEA LUMEN LUMET LUNES LURED LURES LUREX LUTES MULES MULEY MUREX MUSED MUSER MUSES MUTED MUTER MUTES NUDER NUDES NUKED NUKES NUMEN NUYEN OUSEL OUTED OUTER OUZEL PUGET PULED PULES PUREE PURER PUREX PUSEY QUEEG QUEEN QUEER QUIEN QUIET RUBEN RUBES RUDER RULED RULER RULES RUMEN RUNES RUPEE RUSES SUMER SUPER SUPES SURER TUBED TUBER TUBES TULES TUNED TUNER TUNES TUTEE TUXES

•U••E
AUDIE AURAE AUTRE BUDGE BUGLE BULGE BURKE BURSE BUTTE CUMAE CURIE CURSE CURVE CUTIE CUVEE DUANE DULSE DUNCE DUNNE DUPLE DUPRE EUBIE FUDGE FUGUE FURZE FUSEE FUZEE GUIDE GUILE GUISE HULCE JUDGE JUICE JULIE JUSTE LUCIE LUCRE

LUISE LUNGE LURIE MURRE NUDGE NUGAE NURSE OUNCE OUTRE PULSE PUPAE PUREE PURGE PURSE QUAKE QUALE QUARE QUEUE QUIRE QUITE QUOTE RUBLE RUCHE RUDGE RUGAE RUPEE RUSSE SUAVE SUCRE SUEDE SUEME SUITE SURGE SUSIE TULLE TUQUE TUTEE

••UE•

AGUES BAUER BLUED BLUER BLUES BLUET BLUEY CLUED CLUES CRUEL CRUET FLUES GLUED GLUER GLUES GLUEY GRUEL HAUER LAUER MOUES REUEL ROUEN ROUES SLUED SLUES TRUED TRUER TRUES TRUEX

••U•E

ABUSE ACUTE AMUSE APURE AQUAE AZURE BAUME BLUME BOULE BOUSE BRUCE BRULE BRUME BRUTE CAUSE CHUTE COUPE CRUDE CRUSE DEUCE DOUSE DRUPE DRUSE DRUZE EDUCE ELUDE ELUTE ENURE ETUDE EXUDE FAURE FAUVE FLUKE FLUME FLUTE GAUGE GAUZE GOUGE HAUTE HEURE HEUTE HOUSE INURE INUSE JAUNE JEUNE JOULE KLUGE KLUTE KNUTE LAUDE LOUIE LOUPE LOUSE MAUDE MAUVE MEUSE MFUME MOUSE NEUME OFUSE OVULE PAUSE PLUME PRUDE PRUNE REUNE REUSE ROUGE ROUSE ROUTE SAUCE SAUTE SCUTE SEULE SHUTE SOUSE SPUME STUPE TAUPE THULE TOUTE TRUCE YOURE YOUSE YOUVE

•••UE

ARGUE ATQUE BENUE ENDUE ENSUE ESQUE FUGUE GIGUE HAGUE IMBUE ISSUE KAFUE LARUE LOGUE ONCUE PIQUE QUEUE REVUE ROGUE ROQUE SEGUE SPRUE TOQUE TUQUE UNDUE USQUE VAGUE VALUE VENUE VOGUE

U•F••

UNFED UNFIT UNFIX

U••F•

UNIFY USOFA

•UF••

BUFFA BUFFI BUFFO BUFFS BUFFY CUFFS DUFAY DUFFS DUFFY HUFFS HUFFY LUFFS MUFFS MUFTI PUFFS PUFFY RUFFS RUFUS SUFIS TUFTS TUFTY

•U•F•

BUFFA BUFFI BUFFO BUFFS BUFFY CUFFS DUFFS DUFFY GULFS HUFFS HUFFY LUFFS MUFFS PUFFS PUFFY QUAFF RUFFS SULFA SURFS SURFY TURFS TURFY

•U••F

QUAFF

••UF•

ACUFF BLUFF CHUFF FLUFF GRUFF KHUFU POUFS SCUFF SNUFF STUFF

••U•F

ACUFF BLUFF CHUFF FLUFF GRUFF SCUFF SCURF SMURF SNUFF STUFF

•••UF

BOEUF

UG•••

UGRIC

U•G••

UIGUR UNGER URGED URGER URGES

U••G•

USAGE USCGA

U•••G

UNPEG UNRIG USING

•UG••

AUGER AUGHT AUGUR BUGGY BUGLE BUGSY CUGAT DUGAN DUGIN DUGUP FUGAL FUGGY FUGIT FUGUE FUGUS HUGER HUGOS JUGAL JUGUM KUGEL LUGER LUGES MUGGS MUGGY MUGHO NUGAE OUGHT PUGET PUGGY RUGAE RUGBY SUGAR VUGGY YUGAS YUGOS

•U•G•

BUDGE BUGGY BULGE BULGY BUNGS BURGS FUDGE FUEGO FUGGY FUNGI FUNGO GUNGA JUDGE LUEGO LUIGI LUNGE LUNGS MUGGS MUGGY MUNGO NUDGE OUTGO PUDGY PUGGY PUNGS PURGE QUAGS RUDGE RUNGS SURGE VUGGY

•U••G

CUING GULAG QUEEG RUING SUING

••UG•

BAUGH BOUGH CHUGS COUGH DOUGH DRUGS ENUGU GAUGE GLUGS GOUGE HOUGH KLUGE LAUGH LOUGH PLUGS ROUGE ROUGH SLUGS SNUGS SOUGH THUGS TOUGH TRUGS WAUGH

••U•G

BOURG BRUNG CHUNG CLUNG FLUNG SLUNG STUNG SWUNG WRUNG YOUNG

•••UG

ABZUG DEBUG SHRUG STRUG

UH•••

UHAUL UHHUH UHLAN UHURA UHURU

U•H••

UHHUH UNHIP USHED USHER UTHER

U••H•

UTAHN

U•••H

UHHUH UNRUH URIAH URICH

•UH••

BUHLS WUHAN

•U•H•

AUGHT BUSHY CUSHY DUCHY FUCHS GUSHY MUGHO MUSHY NUCHA OUGHT PUSHY RUCHE RUEHL RUSHY SUSHI WUSHU

•U••H

BUNCH BUSCH BUTCH CULCH DUTCH FURTH GULCH HUMPH HUNCH HUTCH JUDAH LUNCH LURCH MULCH MUNCH PUNCH QUASH QUOTH SURAH

••UH•

BRUHN

••U•H

BAUGH BLUSH BLUTH BOUGH BRUCH BRUSH COUCH COUGH COUTH CRUSH DOUGH FLUSH FOURH HOUGH LAUGH LOUGH MOUTH PLUSH POUCH ROUGH SHUSH SLUSH SOUGH SOUTH TOUCH TOUGH TRUTH VOUCH WAUGH YOUTH

•••UH

UHHUH UNRUH

UI•••

UIGUR UINTA

U•I••

UDINE UMIAK UNIFY UNION UNITE UNITS UNITY UNIVS URIAH URIAL URICH URIEL USING UTICA UTILE

U••I•

UGRIC UNBID UNDID UNFIT UNFIX UNHIP UNLIT UNPIN UNRIG UNTIE UNTIL UNZIP URBIS URSID USAIR

U•••I

UMEKI

•UI••

BUICK BUILD BUILT CUING GUIDE GUIDO GUILD GUILE GUILT GUIRO GUISE JUICE JUICY LUIGI LUISA LUISE OUIDA OUIJA QUICK QUIDS QUIEN QUIET QUILL QUILP QUILT QUINN QUINO QUINT QUIPS QUIPU QUIRE QUIRK QUIRT QUITE QUITO QUITS RUING RUINS SUING SUINT SUITA SUITE SUITS

•U•I•

AUDIE AUDIO AUDIS AUDIT AULIS AURIC AUXIL AUXIN BUNIN BURIN CUBIC CUBIT CUEIN CUMIN CUPID CURIA CURIE CURIO CUTIE CUTIN CUTIS DUBIN DUGIN EUBIE FUGIT FUSIL HUMID JULIA JULIE JULIO LUCIA LUCID LUCIE LUDIC LUNIK LUPIN LURIA LURID LURIE MUCIN MUNIS MUSIC NUBIA NUMIS PULIS PUNIC PUPIL PUPIN PURIM PUTIN QUAID QUAIL QUOIN QUOIT RUBIK RUBIN RUNIC RUNIN RURIK RUTIN SUBIC SUFIS SUSIE TULIP TUMID TUNIC TUNIS TURIN YUPIK ZUBIN ZUNIS

•U••I

AUREI AUSSI BUFFI BUZZI CUPRI CURCI DUBAI FUNGI GUCCI LUCCI LUIGI LUNDI MUFTI MULTI MUNDI NURMI PUCCI PUTTI QUASI SULCI SUNNI SUOMI SUSHI TUTTI

••UI•

BRUIN BRUIT DRUID EQUIP EQUIV ETUIS FLUID FRUIT GSUIT INUIT IQUIT LOUIE LOUIS SQUIB SQUID

••U•I

DOUAI HOURI JEUDI KAUAI KAURI SAUDI SCUDI

•••UI

ANHUI ENNUI MAQUI PIAUI YAQUI

U•J••

UNJAM

•UJ••

AUJUS JUJUS

•U•J•

OUIJA

••UJ•

ABUJA THUJA

UK•••

UKASE

U•K••

URKEL

U••K•

UMEKI

U•••K

UMIAK UZBEK

•UK••

CUKES CUKOR DUKAS DUKED DUKES JUKED JUKES KUKLA LUKAS NUKED NUKES PUKKA YUKON ZUKOR

•U•K•

BUCKO BUCKS BUCKY BULKS BULKY BUNKO BUNKS BURKE BUSKS CUSKS DUCKS DUCKY DUNKS DUSKS DUSKY FUNKS FUNKY GUNKY HULKS HUNKS HUSKS HUSKY JUNKS JUNKY LUCKS LUCKY LURKS MUCKS MUCKY MURKY MUSKS MUSKY PUCKS PUKKA PUNKS PUNKY QUAKE QUAKY RUCKS RUSKS SUCKA SUCKS SULKS SULKY TUCKS TURKS TURKU TUSKS YUCKY

•U••K

BUICK HUROK KULAK KURSK LUNIK MUZAK QUACK QUARK QUICK QUIRK RUARK RUBIK RURIK YUPIK YUROK

••UK•

FLUKE FLUKY SAUKS SOUKS STUKA ZOUKS

••U•K

AMUCK BAULK CAULK CHUCK CHUNK CLUCK CLUNK DRUNK FLUNK GLUCK PLUCK PLUNK SHUCK SKULK SKUNK SLUNK SNUCK SPUNK STUCK STUNK THUNK TRUCK TRUNK

•••UK

ANOUK

UL•••

ULCER ULNAE ULNAS ULTRA

U•L••

UCLAN UHLAN UNLAY UNLED UNLIT USLTA UTLEY

U••L•

UBOLT UDALL UNCLE UPOLU URALS UTILE UVULA UZALA

U•••L

UDALL UHAUL UMBEL UNTIL URIAL URIEL URKEL USUAL UXMAL

•UL••

AULIS BULBA BULBS BULGE BULGY BULKS BULKY BULLA BULLS BULLY BULOW CULCH CULET CULEX CULLS CULLY CULMS CULPA CULTS DULLS DULLY DULSE EULER FULAS FULDA FULLY GULAG GULAR GULCH GULES GULFS GULLS GULLY GULPS GULPY HULAS HULCE HULKS HULLO HULLS JULEP JULES JULIA JULIE JULIO KULAK LULEA LULLS LULLY LULUS MULCH MULCT MULES MULEY MULLS MULTI NULLS PULAS PULED PULES PULIS PULLS PULPS PULPY PULSE RULED RULER RULES SULCI SULFA SULKS SULKY SULLA SULLY TULES TULIP TULLE TULLY TULSA ZULUS

•U•L•

BUELL BUGLE BUHLS BUILD BUILT BULLA BULLS BULLY BURLS BURLY CULLS CULLY CURLS CURLY DUELS DULLS DULLY DUPLE FUELS FULLY FURLS GUILD GUILE GUILT GULLS GULLY HULLO HULLS HURLS HURLY KUALA KUKLA LULLS LULLY MULLS NULLS PULLS PURLS QUALE QUALM QUELL QUILL QUILP QUILT RUBLE SULLA SULLY SURLY TULLE TULLY

•U••L

AURAL AUXIL BUELL BUTYL CUMUL CUPEL DUCAL FUGAL FUSIL JUBAL JUGAL JURAL KUGEL MURAL OUSEL OUZEL PUPAL PUPIL QUAIL QUELL QUILL RUEHL RURAL SURAL

••UL•

ADULT ALULA BAULK BOULE BOULT BRULE CAULK CAULS CHULA COULD EXULT FAULT FOULS GAULS GOULD HAULM HAULS JOULE KRULL MAULS MOULD MOULT OCULO OVULE PAULA PAULO POULT SAULT SCULL SEULE SHULA SHULS SKULK SKULL SOULS SOULT STULL THULE TRULY UVULA VAULT WOULD YOULL

••U•L

CHURL CRUEL EQUAL GRUEL JOUAL KNURL KRULL REUEL SCULL SKULL STULL USUAL YOULL

•••UL

ABDUL AFOUL AMPUL ANNUL AWFUL BABUL BAIUL CUMUL GHOUL KABUL MOGUL MOSUL PICUL RAOUL SEOUL UHAUL

UM•••

UMBEL UMBER UMBOS UMBRA UMEKI UMIAK UMPED

U•M••

UNMAN UNMET UXMAL

U•••M

UNARM UNJAM

•UM••

BUMPS BUMPY CUMAE CUMIN CUMUL DUMAS DUMBO DUMBS DUMMY DUMPS DUMPY FUMED FUMES GUMBO GUMBY GUMMO GUMMY GUMUP HUMAN HUMID HUMOR HUMPH HUMPS HUMPY HUMUS JUMBO JUMNA JUMPS JUMPY LUMEN LUMET LUMPS LUMPY MUMBO MUMMY MUMPS NUMBS NUMEN NUMIS PUMAS PUMPS RUMBA RUMEN RUMMY RUMOR RUMPS SUMAC SUMBA SUMER SUMMA SUMPS SUMUP TUMID TUMMY TUMPS YUMAN YUMAS YUMMY

•U•M•

BURMA CULMS CUOMO DUMMY DUOMO GUMMO GUMMY MUMMY NURMI RUMMY SUEME SUMMA SUOMI TUMMY YUMMY

•U••M

AURUM DURUM JUGUM PURIM QUALM

••UM•

ALUMS ARUMS BAUME BLUME BRUME CHUMP CHUMS CLUMP CRUMB CRUMP DRUMS FLUME FRUMP GAUMS GEUMS GRUMP HOUMA MFUME NEUME PLUMB PLUME PLUMP PLUMS PLUMY RHUMB SCUMS SLUMP SLUMS SPUME SPUMY STUMP STUMS THUMB THUMP TRUMP

••U•M

HAULM STURM

•••UM

ADSUM AKSUM ALBUM ANNUM ARIUM AURUM BEGUM BYGUM COLUM DATUM DURUM FILUM FORUM HARUM HILUM HOHUM HOKUM ILIUM IPSUM JORUM JUGUM LOCUM MECUM MORUM NAHUM

OAKUM ODEUM ODIUM OLEUM OPIUM PILUM REGUM RERUM RHEUM SCRUM SEBUM SEDUM SERUM SOLUM STRUM TATUM THRUM VELUM VISUM YOKUM

UN•••

UNAPT UNARM UNAUS UNBAR UNBID UNBOX UNCAP UNCAS UNCLE UNCUT UNDER UNDID UNDUE UNFED UNFIT UNFIX UNGER UNHIP UNIFY UNION UNITE UNITS UNITY UNIVS UNJAM UNLAY UNLED UNLIT UNMAN UNMET UNPEG UNPEN UNPIN UNRIG UNRRA UNRUH UNSAY UNSER UNSET UNTER UNTIE UNTIL UNWED UNZIP

U•N••

UINTA ULNAE ULNAS

U••N•

UDINE UPEND USING

U•••N

UCLAN UHLAN UNION UNMAN UNPEN UNPIN UPTON URBAN UTAHN UTURN

•UN••

AUNTS AUNTY BUNCH BUNDS BUNDT BUNDY BUNGS BUNIN BUNKO BUNKS BUNNY BUNTS CUNAS CUNEO DUNCE DUNES DUNKS DUNNE DUNNO FUNDS FUNDY FUNGI FUNGO FUNKS FUNKY FUNNY GUNGA GUNKY GUNNY HUNAN HUNCH HUNKS HUNTS HUNTZ JUNCO JUNKS JUNKY JUNTA JUNTO LUNAR LUNCH LUNDI LUNDY LUNES LUNGE LUNGS LUNIK MUNCH MUNDI MUNGO MUNIS MUNRO OUNCE PUNAS PUNCH PUNGS PUNIC PUNKS PUNKY PUNNY PUNTA PUNTS PUNTY RUNAT RUNES RUNGS RUNIC RUNIN RUNNY RUNON RUNTO RUNTS RUNTY RUNUP SUNDA SUNNA SUNNI SUNNY SUNUP TUNAS TUNED TUNER TUNES TUNIC TUNIS TUNNY ZUNIS

•U•N•

BUENA BUENO BUNNY BUONO BURNS BURNT CUING DUANE DUNNE DUNNO DURNS FUNNY GUNNY JUMNA MUONS PUNNY QUAND QUANT QUINN QUINO QUINT RUANA RUING RUINS RUNNY SUING SUINT SUNNA SUNNI SUNNY TUNNY TURNS YUANS

•U••N

AUDEN AUXIN BUNIN BURIN CUBAN CUEIN CUMIN CUTIN DUBIN DUGAN DUGIN DURAN FURAN FUTON GUTEN HUMAN HUNAN HURON LUCAN LUMEN LUPIN LUZON MUCIN NUMEN NUYEN PUPIN PUSAN PUTIN PUTON QUEEN QUERN QUIEN QUINN QUOIN RUBEN RUBIN RUMEN RUNIN RUNON RUTIN SUDAN SUSAN TURIN WUHAN YUKON YUMAN ZUBIN

••UN•

BLUNT BOUND BRUNG BRUNO BRUNT CHUNG CHUNK CLUNG CLUNK CLUNY COUNT DAUNT DRUNK FAUNA FAUNS FLUNG FLUNK FOUND FOUNT GAUNT GRUNT HAUNT HOUND JAUNE JAUNT JEUNE MAUNA MAUND MOUND MOUNT NOUNS PLUNK POUND PRUNE REUNE ROUND SAUNA SHUNS SHUNT SKUNK SLUNG SLUNK SOUND SPUNK STUNG STUNK STUNS STUNT SWUNG TAUNT THUNK TRUNK VAUNT WOUND WRUNG YOUNG YOUNT

••U•N

BOURN BRUHN BRUIN CHURN GLUON MOURN ROUEN SPURN TAUON UTURN

•••UN

AAIUN BBGUN BEGUN BRAUN BROUN CAJUN GATUN HAFUN INFUN RERUN SHAUN

U•O••

UBOAT UBOLT UPOLU USOFA

U••O•

UMBOS UNBOX UNION UPBOW UPDOS UPTON

•UO••

BUONO BUOYS CUOMO DUOMO MUONS QUOAD QUODS QUOIN QUOIT QUOTA QUOTE QUOTH SUOMI

•U•O•

AUTOS BULOW CUKOR DUBOS DUROC DUROS EUROS FUROR FUROS FUTON GUYOT HUGOS HUMOR HUROK HURON JUROR KUDOS LUXOR LUZON OUZOS PUTON RUMOR RUNON TUDOR TUROW TUTOR YUGOS YUKON YUROK ZUKOR

•U••O

AUDIO BUCKO BUENO BUFFO BUNKO BUONO BURRO BUTEO CUNEO CUOMO CUPRO CURIO CUZCO DUETO DUMBO DUNNO DUOMO FUEGO FUNGO GUACO GUIDO GUIRO GUMBO GUMMO GUSTO HUEVO HULLO JUDEO JULIO JUMBO JUNCO JUNTO LUEGO MUCRO MUGHO MUMBO MUNGO MUNRO OUTDO OUTGO PUTTO QUINO QUITO RUNTO RUSSO TURBO

••UO•

FLUOR GLUON TAUON

••U•O

BLUTO BRUNO DEUTO DOURO GLUCO NEURO OCULO ORURO PAULO PLUTO SCUDO TAUPO TAURO TAUTO TRURO

UP•••

UPBOW UPDOS UPEND UPOLU UPPED UPPER UPSET UPTON

U•P••

UMPED UNPEG UNPEN UNPIN UPPED UPPER

U••P•

UNAPT

U•••P

UNCAP UNHIP UNZIP USEUP USURP

•UP••

CUPEL CUPID CUPPA CUPRI CUPRO DUPED DUPES DUPLE DUPRE GUPPY LUPIN PUPAE PUPAL PUPAS PUPIL PUPIN PUPPY PUPUS RUPEE SUPER SUPES SUPRA SUPTS SUPVR YUPIK

•U•P•

BUMPS BUMPY BURPS CULPA CUPPA CUSPS DUMPS DUMPY GULPS GULPY GUPPY HUMPH HUMPS HUMPY JUMPS JUMPY LUMPS LUMPY MUMPS PULPS PULPY PUMPS PUPPY QUIPS QUIPU RUMPS SUMPS TUMPS

•U••P

BUYUP CUTUP DUGUP GUMUP JULEP PUTUP QUILP RUNUP SUMUP SUNUP TULIP

••UP•

COUPE COUPS DRUPE ERUPT KRUPA KRUPP LOUPE REUPS SCUPS SOUPS SOUPY STUPA STUPE TAUPE TAUPO WHUPS

••U•P

CHUMP CLUMP CRUMP EQUIP FRUMP GRUMP KRUPP PLUMP SLUMP SLURP STUMP THUMP TRUMP USURP

•••UP

ACTUP ADDUP ANDUP ATEUP BIDUP BOBUP BOXUP BUYUP CROUP CUTUP DAMUP DIDUP DIGUP DRYUP DUGUP EATUP ENDUP FEDUP FIXUP FOGUP GASUP GETUP GOTUP GROUP GUMUP HETUP HITUP HOPUP ICEUP JAMUP KEYUP LAPUP LAYUP LEGUP LETUP LITUP MIXUP MOPUP NIPUP NOTUP ONEUP OWNUP PAYUP PEPUP PINUP POPUP PUTUP RANUP REVUP RIGUP RIPUP RUNUP SATUP SCAUP SETUP SEWUP SITUP SOPUP STOUP SUMUP SUNUP SYRUP TAGUP TEEUP TIEUP TIPUP TOTUP USEUP WADUP ZIPUP

U•Q••

USQUE

•UQ••

TUQUE

UR•••

URALS URBAN URBIS URGED URGER URGES URIAH URIAL URICH URIEL URKEL URSID

U•R••

UGRIC UNRIG UNRRA UNRUH

U••R•

UHURA UHURU ULTRA UMBRA UNARM UNRRA USERS USURP USURY UTURN

U•••R

UDDER UIGUR ULCER UMBER UNBAR UNDER UNGER UNSER UNTER UPPER URGER USAIR USHER UTHER UTTER

•UR••

AURAE AURAL AURAR AURAS AUREI AURIC AURUM BURBS BURGS BURIN BURKE BURLS BURLY BURMA BURNS BURNT BURPS BURRO BURRS BURRY BURSA BURSE BURST CURBS CURCI CURDS CURDY CURED CURER CURES CURIA CURIE CURIO CURLS CURLY CURRY CURSE CURST CURVE CURVY DURAN DURER DURNS DUROC DUROS DURRA DURST DURUM EUROS EURUS FURAN FURLS FUROR FUROS FURRY FURTH FURZE GURDY GURUS HURDY HURLS HURLY HUROK HURON HURRY HURST HURTS JURAL JURAT JUROR KURDS KURSK KURTZ LURAY LURCH LURED LURES LUREX LURIA LURID LURIE LURKS MURAL MURAT MUREX MURKY MURRA MURRE NURMI NURSE PUREE PURER PUREX PURGE PURIM PURLS PURRS PURSE PURSY PURUS RURAL RURIK SURAH SURAL SURAS SURAT SURDS SURER SURFS SURFY SURGE SURLY TURBO TURFS TURFY TURIN TURKS TURKU TURNS TUROW TURVY WURST YUROK YURTS

•U•R•

AUDRA AUTRE AUTRY BURRO BURRS BURRY CUPRI CUPRO CURRY DUPRE DURRA FURRY GUARD GUARS GUIRO HURRY LUCRE MUCRO MUDRA MUNRO MURRA MURRE OUTRE PURRS QUARE QUARK QUART QUERN QUERY QUIRE QUIRK QUIRT RUARK RUERS SUCRE SUDRA SUERS SUPRA SUTRA

•U••R

AUBER AUGER AUGUR AURAR AUSTR BUBER BUYER CUKOR CURER CUTER DURER EULER FUROR GULAR HUGER HUMOR JUROR LUGER LUNAR LUXOR MUSER MUTER NUDER OUTER PURER QUADR QUEER RUDER RULER RUMOR SUGAR SUMER SUPER SUPVR SURER TUBER TUDOR TUNER TUTOR ZUKOR

••UR•

ACURA APURE AZURE BLURB BLURS BLURT BOURG BOURN CHURL CHURN COURT CRURA DOURO DRURY ENURE EXURB FAURE FOURH FOURS GAURS GOURD HEURE HOURI HOURS INURE KAURI KNURL KNURS LAURA MAURY MOURN NAURU NEURO ORURO PIURA POURS SAURY SCURF SLURP SLURS SMURF SOURS SPURN SPURS SPURT STURM TAURO THURS TOURS TRURO UHURA UHURU USURP USURY UTURN YOURE YOURS

••U•R

BAUER BLUER FLUOR GLUER HAUER LAUER TRUER

•••UR

AMOUR ARTUR ASHUR ASSUR AUGUR COEUR DEMUR FEMUR FLEUR FLOUR HHOUR INCUR LEMUR MASUR MOHUR NAMUR OCCUR ODOUR RECUR SCOUR SIEUR SOEUR UIGUR

US•••

USAGE USAIR USCGA USERS USEUP USHED USHER USING USLTA USOFA USQUE USTED USUAL USURP USURY

U•S••

UNSAY UNSER UNSET UPSET URSID

U••S•

UKASE

U•••S

ULNAS UMBOS UNAUS UNCAS UNITS UNIVS UPDOS URALS URBIS URGES USERS

•US••

AUSSI AUSTR BUSBY BUSCH BUSED BUSES BUSEY BUSHY BUSKS BUSTS CUSHY CUSKS CUSPS DUSKS DUSKY DUSTS DUSTY FUSED FUSEE FUSES FUSIL FUSSY FUSTY GUSHY GUSSY GUSTO GUSTS GUSTY HUSKS HUSKY HUSSY JUSTE LUSTS LUSTY MUSCA MUSED MUSER MUSES MUSHY MUSIC MUSKS MUSKY MUSSY MUSTS MUSTY OUSEL OUSTS PUSAN PUSEY PUSHY RUSES RUSHY RUSKS RUSSE RUSSO RUSTS RUSTY SUSAN SUSHI SUSIE TUSKS WUSHU

•U•S•

AUSSI BUGSY BURSA BURSE BURST CURSE CURST DULSE DURST FUBSY FUSSY GUESS GUEST GUISE GUSSY GUTSY HURST HUSSY KURSK LUISA LUISE MUSSY NURSE NUTSY PULSE PURSE PURSY QUASH QUASI QUEST RUSSE RUSSO SUDSY TULSA WURST

•U••S

AUDIS AUJUS AULIS AUNTS AURAS AUTOS BUBUS BUCKS BUFFS BUHLS BULBS BULKS BULLS BUMPS BUNDS BUNGS BUNKS BUNTS BUOYS BURBS BURGS BURLS BURNS BURPS BURRS BUSES BUSKS BUSTS BUTTS CUBES CUFFS CUKES CULLS CULMS CULTS CUNAS CURBS CURDS CURES CURLS CUSKS CUSPS CUTIS DUADS DUBOS DUCES DUCKS DUCTS DUDES DUELS DUETS DUFFS DUKAS DUKES DULLS DUMAS DUMBS DUMPS DUNES DUNKS DUPES DURNS DUROS DUSKS DUSTS DUXES EUROS EURUS FUCHS FUELS FUGUS FULAS FUMES FUNDS FUNKS FURLS FUROS FUSES GUARS GUESS GULES GULFS GULLS GULPS GURUS GUSTS HUFFS HUGOS HULAS HULKS HULLS HUMPS HUMUS HUNKS HUNTS HURLS HURTS HUSKS HUTUS JUDAS JUJUS JUKES JULES JUMPS JUNKS JUTES KUDOS KUDUS KURDS LUAUS LUBAS LUBES LUCAS LUCKS LUFFS LUGES LUKAS LULLS LULUS LUMPS LUNES LUNGS LURES LURKS LUSTS LUTES MUCKS MUFFS MUGGS MULES MULLS MUMPS MUNIS MUONS MUSES MUSKS MUSTS MUTES MUTTS NUDES NUKES NULLS NUMBS NUMIS OUSTS OUZOS PUCKS PUDUS PUFFS PULAS PULES PULIS PULLS PULPS

PUMAS
PUMPS
PUNAS
PUNGS
PUNKS
PUNTS
PUPAS
PUPUS
PURLS
PURRS
PURUS
PUTTS
QUADS
QUAGS
QUAYS
QUIDS
QUIPS
QUITS
QUODS
RUBES
RUCKS
RUDDS
RUERS
RUFFS
RUFUS
RUINS
RULES
RUMPS
RUNES
RUNGS
RUNTS
RUSES
RUSKS
RUSTS
SUCKS
SUDDS
SUERS
SUETS
SUFIS
SUITS
SULKS
SUMPS
SUPES
SUPTS
SURAS
SURDS
SURFS
TUBAS
TUBES
TUCKS
TUFTS
TULES
TUMPS
TUNAS
TUNES
TUNIS
TURFS
TURKS
TURNS
TUSKS
TUTUS
TUXES
YUANS
YUGAS
YUGOS
YUMAS
YURTS
ZULUS
ZUNIS

••US•
ABUSE
ADUST
AMUSE
AZUSA
BLUSH
BOUSE
BRUSH
CAUSA
CAUSE
COUSY
CRUSE
CRUSH
CRUST
DOUSE
DRUSE
FAUST
FLUSH
GAUSS
HAUSA
HOUSE
INUSE
JOUST
LOUSE
LOUSY
MEUSE
MOUSE
MOUSY
OFUSE
PAUSE
PLUSH
REUSE
ROUSE
ROUST
SEUSS
SHUSH
SLUSH
SOUSA
SOUSE
TRUSS
TRUST
YOUSE

••U•S
ABUTS
AGUES
ALUMS
AQUAS
ARUMS
BLUES
BLURS
BOUTS
BRUTS
CAULS
CHUBS
CHUGS
CHUMS
CLUBS
CLUES
COUPS
DAUBS
DRUBS
DRUGS
DRUMS
EQUUS
ETUIS
FAUNS
FEUDS
FLUBS
FLUES
FOULS
FOURS
FOUTS
GAUDS
GAULS
GAUMS
GAURS
GAUSS
GEUMS
GLUES
GLUGS
GLUTS
GRUBS
HAULS
HOURS
KNURS
LAUDS
LOUIS
LOUTS
MAULS
MOUES
NOUNS
PLUGS
PLUMS
POUFS
POURS
POUTS
REUPS
ROUES
ROUTS
SAUKS
SCUDS
SCUMS
SCUPS
SCUTS
SEUSS
SHULS
SHUNS
SHUTS
SKUAS
SLUES
SLUGS
SLUMS
SLURS
SMUTS
SNUBS
SNUGS
SOUKS
SOULS
SOUPS
SOURS
SPUDS
SPURS
STUBS
STUDS
STUMS
STUNS
THUDS
THUGS
THURS
TNUTS
TOURS
TOUTS
TRUES
TRUGS
TRUSS
WHUPS
YOURS
ZOUKS

•••US
AGNUS
AINUS
ALDUS
ALTUS
ANGUS
ANNUS
APLUS
ARGUS
ARHUS
ARIUS
ASCUS
AUJUS
BEAUS
BOGUS
BOLUS
BONUS
BPLUS
BUBUS
CAMUS
CASUS
CETUS
CLAUS
COMUS
CONUS
CPLUS
CYRUS
DPLUS
ECRUS
EOLUS
EQUUS
EURUS
FICUS
FOCUS
FUGUS
GAIUS
GENUS
GURUS
GYRUS
HOCUS
HONUS
HORUS
HUMUS
HUTUS
ICTUS
IGLUS
ILLUS
INCUS
INDUS
ISSUS
JANUS
JUJUS
KLAUS
KRAUS
KUDUS
LAIUS
LEPUS
LEXUS
LIEUS
LINUS
LOCUS
LOTUS
LUAUS
LULUS
MAGUS
MENUS
MINUS
MODUS
MOMUS
NEGUS
NEVUS
NEXUS
NIDUS
NISUS
NODUS
ORCUS
PILUS
PIOUS
POCUS
PRAUS
PUDUS
PUPUS
PURUS
REBUS
REMUS
RUFUS
SINUS
SITUS
SOLUS
SORUS
TAGUS
TALUS
THOUS
TITUS
TONUS
TORUS
TUTUS
UNAUS
VAGUS
VENUS
VIRUS
VITUS
XERUS
ZEBUS
ZULUS

UT•••
UTAHN
UTHER
UTICA
UTILE
UTLEY
UTTER
UTURN

U•T••
ULTRA
UNTER
UNTIE
UNTIL
UPTON
USTED
UTTER

U••T•
UINTA
UNITE
UNITS
UNITY
USLTA

U•••T
UBOAT
UBOLT
UNAPT
UNCUT
UNFIT
UNLIT
UNMET
UNSET
UPSET

•UT••
AUTOS
AUTRE
AUTRY
BUTCH
BUTEO
BUTTE
BUTTS
BUTTY
BUTUT
BUTYL
CUTER
CUTEX
CUTEY
CUTIE
CUTIN
CUTIS
CUTUP
DUTCH
FUTON
GUTEN
GUTSY
GUTTA
GUTTY
HUTCH
HUTUS
JUTES
JUTTY
LUTES
MUTED
MUTER
MUTES
MUTTS
NUTSY
NUTTY
OUTDO
OUTED
OUTER
OUTGO
OUTRE
PUTBY
PUTIN
PUTON
PUTTI
PUTTO
PUTTS
PUTTY
PUTUP
RUTIN
RUTTY
SUTRA
TUTEE
TUTOR
TUTTI
TUTUS

•U•T•
AUNTS
AUNTY
AUSTR
BUNTS
BUSTS
BUTTE
BUTTS
BUTTY
CULTS
DUCTS
DUETO
DUETS
DUSTS
DUSTY
FURTH
FUSTY
GUSTO
GUSTS
GUSTY
GUTTA
GUTTY
HUNTS
HUNTZ
HURTS
JUNTA
JUNTO
JUSTE
JUTTY
KURTZ
LUSTS
LUSTY
MUFTI
MULTI
MUSTS
MUSTY
MUTTS
NUTTY
OUSTS
PUNTA
PUNTS
PUNTY
PUTTI
PUTTO
PUTTS
PUTTY
QUITE
QUITO
QUITS
QUOTA
QUOTE
QUOTH
RUNTO
RUNTS
RUNTY
RUSTS
RUSTY
RUTTY
SUETS
SUETY
SUITA
SUITE
SUITS
SUPTS
TUFTS
TUFTY
TUTTI
YURTS

•U••T
AUDIT
AUGHT
BUILT
BUNDT
BURNT
BURST
BUTUT
CUBIT
CUGAT
CULET
CURST
DUCAT
DURST
DUVET
FUGIT
GUEST
GUILT
GUYOT
HURST
JURAT
LUMET
MULCT
MURAT
OUGHT
PUGET
QUANT
QUART
QUEST
QUIET
QUILT
QUINT
QUIRT
QUOIT
RUNAT
SUINT
SURAT
WURST

••UT•
ABUTS
ACUTE
BLUTH
BLUTO
BOUTS
BRUTE
BRUTS
CEUTA
CHUTE
COUTH
DEUTO
ELUTE
FLUTE
FLUTY
FOUTS
GLUTS
GOUTY
HAUTE
HEUTE
KLUTE
KLUTZ
KNUTE
LOUTS
MOUTH
PLUTO
POUTS
POUTY
ROUTE
ROUTS
SAUTE
SCUTA
SCUTE
SCUTS
SHUTE
SHUTS
SMUTS
SOUTH
STUTZ
TAUTO
TNUTS
TOUTE
TOUTS
TRUTH
YOUTH

••U•T
ADULT
ADUST
BLUET
BLUNT
BLURT
BOULT
BRUIT
BRUNT
COUNT
COURT
CRUET
CRUST
DAUNT
DOUBT
EDUCT
ERUCT
ERUPT
EXULT
FAULT
FAUST
FOUNT
FRUIT
GAUNT
GRUNT
GSUIT
HAUNT
INUIT
IQUIT
JAUNT
JOUST
MOULT
MOUNT
POULT
ROUST
SAULT
SHUNT
SOULT
SPURT
SQUAT
STUNT
TAUNT
TRUST
VAULT
VAUNT
YOUNT

•••UT
ABOUT
ADOUT
ALEUT
ASYUT
BEAUT
BUTUT
CLOUT
DEBUT
DONUT
FLOUT
GAMUT
GOOUT
GROUT
INPUT
KAPUT
KNOUT
KRAUT
LIEUT
REBUT
SALUT
SCOUT
SHOUT
SNOUT
SPOUT
STOUT
STRUT
TROUT
UNCUT
XDOUT
XSOUT
YAKUT

U•U••
UHURA
UHURU
USUAL
USURP
USURY
UTURN
UVULA

U••U•
UHAUL
UHHUH
UIGUR
UNAUS
UNCUT
UNDUE
UNRUH
USEUP
USQUE

U•••U
UHURU
UPOLU

•U•U•
AUGUR
AUJUS
AURUM
BUBUS
BUTUT
BUYUP
CUMUL
CUTUP
DUGUP
DURUM
EURUS
FUGUE
FUGUS
GUMUP
GURUS
HUMUS
HUTUS
JUGUM
JUJUS
KUDUS
LUAUS
LULUS
PUDUS
PUPUS
PURUS
PUTUP
QUEUE
RUFUS
RUNUP
SUMUP
SUNUP
TUQUE
TUTUS
ZULUS

•U••U
KUDZU
QUIPU
TURKU
WUSHU

••UU•
EQUUS

••U•U
ENUGU
ISUZU
KHUFU
NAURU
UHURU

UV•••
UVULA

U••V•
UNIVS

•UV••
CUVEE
DUVET

•U•V•
CURVE
CURVY
GUAVA
HUEVO
SUAVE
SUPVR
TURVY

••UV•
FAUVE
MAUVE
YOUVE

••U•V
EQUIV

U•W••
UNWED

U•••W
UPBOW

•U••W
BULOW
TUROW

••UW•
ADUWA

UX•••
UXMAL

U•••X
UNBOX
UNFIX

•UX••
AUXIL
AUXIN
DUXES
LUXOR
TUXES

•U••X
CULEX
CUTEX
LUREX
MUREX
PUREX

••U•X
TRUEX

•••UX
ADEUX
BEAUX
REDUX
SIOUX

U•••Y
UNIFY
UNITY
UNLAY
UNSAY
USURY
UTLEY

•UY••
BUYER
BUYUP
GUYED
GUYOT
NUYEN

•U•Y•
BUOYS
BUTYL
QUAYS

•U••Y
AUNTY
AUTRY
BUCKY
BUDDY
BUFFY
BUGGY
BUGSY
BULGY
BULKY
BULLY
BUMPY
BUNDY
BUNNY
BURLY
BURRY
BUSBY
BUSEY
BUSHY
BUTTY
CUBBY
CUDDY
CULLY
CURDY
CURLY
CURRY
CURVY
CUSHY
CUTEY
DUCHY
DUCKY
DUDDY
DUFAY
DUFFY
DULLY
DUMMY
DUMPY
DUSKY
DUSTY
FUBSY
FUDDY
FUGGY
FULLY
FUNDY
FUNKY
FUNNY
FURRY
FUSSY
FUSTY
FUZZY
GULLY
GULPY
GUMBY
GUMMY
GUNKY
GUNNY
GUPPY
GURDY
GUSHY
GUSSY
GUSTY
GUTSY
GUTTY
HUBBY
HUFFY
HUMPY
HURDY
HURLY
HURRY
HUSKY
HUSSY
JUICY
JUMPY
JUNKY
JUTTY
LUCKY
LULLY
LUMPY
LUNDY
LURAY
LUSTY
MUCKY
MUDDY
MUGGY
MULEY
MUMMY
MURKY
MUSHY
MUSKY
MUSSY
MUSTY
MUZZY
NUBBY
NUTSY
NUTTY
PUDGY
PUFFY
PUGGY
PULPY
PUNKY
PUNNY
PUNTY
PUPPY
PURSY
PUSEY
PUSHY
PUTBY
PUTTY
QUAKY
QUERY
RUDDY
RUGBY
RUMMY
RUNNY
RUNTY
RUSHY
RUSTY
RUTTY
SUDSY
SUETY
SULKY
SULLY
SUNNY
SURFY
SURLY
TUBBY
TUFTY
TULLY
TUMMY
TUNNY
TURFY
TURVY
VUGGY
YUCKY
YUMMY

••U•Y
BLUEY
CLUNY
COUSY
DEUCY
DOUAY
DRURY
FLUKY
FLUTY
GAUDY
GAUZY
GLUEY
GOUDY
GOUTY
LOUSY
MAURY
MOUSY
PLUMY
POUTY
SAUCY
SAURY
SOUPY
SPUMY
STUDY
TRULY
USURY

•••UY
MYGUY

UZ•••
UZALA
UZBEK

U•Z••
UNZIP

•UZ••
BUZZI
CUZCO
FUZED
FUZEE
FUZZY
HUZZA
LUZON
MUZAK
MUZZY
OUZEL
OUZOS

•U•Z•
BUZZI
FURZE
FUZZY
HUZZA
KUDZU
MUZZY

•U••Z
HUNTZ
KURTZ

••UZ•
ABUZZ
DRUZE
GAUZE
GAUZY
ISUZU
SCUZZ

••U•Z
ABUZZ
KLUTZ
SCUZZ
STUTZ

•••UZ
SOYUZ
VADUZ

VA•••
VACUA
VADER
VADIM
VADIS
VADUZ
VAGUE
VAGUS
VALES
VALET
VALID
VALLE
VALLI
VALOR
VALSE
VALUE
VALVE
VAMOS
VAMPS
VANCE
VANES
VANIR
VANNA
VANYA
VAPID
VAPOR
VARAS
VARIA
VARIG
VARIX
VARNA
VASCO
VASES
VASTY
VATER
VATIC
VAULT
VAUNT

V•A••
VEALY
VIALS
VIAND

V••A•
VARAS
VEDAS
VEDAY
VEGAN
VEGAS
VELAR
VENAE
VENAL
VICAR
VIDAL
VILAS
VINAS
VIRAL
VISAS
VITAE
VITAL
VITAS
VJDAY
VOCAL
VOLAR
VOLAT

V•••A
VACUA
VANNA
VANYA
VARIA
VARNA
VEDDA
VENDA
VERBA
VERSA
VESTA
VILLA
VILMA
VIOLA
VIRGA
VIRNA
VISTA
VODKA
VOILA
VOLGA
VOLTA
VOLVA

•VA••
AVAIL
AVANT
AVARS
AVAST
EVADE
EVANS
IVANA
KVASS
OVALS
OVATE

•V•A•
AVGAS
AVIAN
EVIAN

•V••A
AVENA
AVILA
DVINA
EVITA
EVORA
IVANA
OVETA
UVULA

••VA•
ADVAL
ALVAR
CAVAE
DAVAO
DIVAN
DIVAS
JAVAS
KAVAS
KIVAS
LAVAL
LAVAS
LEVAR
NAVAL
NIVAL
NOVAE
NOVAK
NOVAS
OYVAY
RIVAL
SIVAN

••V•A
FOVEA
LIVIA
PAVIA

•••VA
ALAVA
BELVA
BRAVA
DRAVA
GUAVA
LARVA
SELVA
SHIVA
SILVA
SNEVA
VOLVA

V•B••
VIBES

V••B•
VERBA
VERBS
VISBY

VC•••
VCHIP

V•C••
VACUA
VICAR
VICES
VICHY
VICKI
VICKS
VOCAL

V••C•
VANCE
VASCO
VETCH
VINCE
VINCI
VNECK
VOICE
VOICI
VOUCH

V•••C
VATIC
VEDIC

•V•C•
EVICT

••V•C
CIVIC
HAVOC

V•D••
VADER
VADIM
VADIS
VADUZ
VEDAS
VEDAY
VEDDA
VEDIC
VIDAL
VIDEO
VIDOR
VJDAY
VODKA

V••D•
VEDDA
VEIDT
VELDS
VELDT
VENDA
VENDS
VERDE
VERDI
VOIDS

V•••D
VALID
VAPID
VEXED
VIAND
VINED
VIRID
VIVID
VOTED
VOWED

•V•D•
EVADE

•V••D
AVOID
IVIED
OVOID

••VD•
BLVDS

••V•D
BOVID
CAVED
DAVID
DIVED
EAVED
GYVED
HIVED
JIVED
LAVED
LIVED
LIVID
LOVED
MOVED
PAVED
PAVID
RAVED
RIVED
ROVED
RSVPD
SAVED
VIVID
WAVED
WIVED

VE•••
VEALY
VEDAS
VEDAY
VEDDA
VEDIC
VEEPS
VEERS
VEERY
VEGAN
VEGAS
VEIDT
VEILS
VEINS
VEINY
VELAR
VELDS
VELDT
VELEZ
VELUM
VENAE
VENAL
VENDA
VENDS
VENEZ
VENIN
VENOM
VENTS
VENUE
VENUS
VERBA
VERBS
VERDE
VERDI
VERGE
VERMI

VERNE VERRE VERSA VERSE VERSO VERST VERTE VERTS VERVE VESEY VESTA VESTS VETCH VEXED VEXER VEXES

V•E••
VEEPS VEERS VEERY VIEJO VIERS VIEWS VIEWY VNECK

V••E•
VADER VALES VALET VANES VASES VATER VELEZ VENEZ VESEY VEXED VEXER VEXES VIBES VICES VIDEO VILER VINED VINES VIPER VIREO VISES VIXEN VOLES VOTED VOTER VOTES VOWED VOWEL VOWER

V•••E
VAGUE VALLE VALSE VALUE VALVE VANCE VENAE VENUE VERDE VERGE VERNE VERRE VERSE VERTE VERVE VILLE VINCE VITAE VIVRE VOGUE VOICE VOILE VOLTE VOTRE

•VE••
AVENA AVENS AVERS AVERT AVERY EVENS EVENT EVERS EVERT EVERY KVELL OVENS OVERS OVERT OVETA OVETT

•V•E•
IVIED IVIES TVSET

•V••E
EVADE EVOKE OVATE OVINE OVULE

••VE•
AMVET BEVEL CAVED CAVER CAVES CIVET COVEN COVER COVES COVET COVEY CUVEE DIVED DIVER DIVES DOVER DOVES DOVEY DUVET EAVED EAVES ELVER ELVES FAVES FEVER FIVER FIVES FOVEA GAVEL GIVEN GIVER GIVES GYVED GYVES HAVEL HAVEN HAVER HAVES HIVED HIVES HOVEL HOVER HOVEY JIVED JIVER JIVES JIVEY KEVEL LAVED LAVER LAVES LEVEE LEVEL LEVER LIVED LIVEN LIVER LIVES LOVED LOVER LOVES LOVEY MAVEN MOVED MOVER MOVES NAVEL NAVES NEVER NEVES NIVEN NOVEL PAVED PAVER PAVES RAVED RAVEL RAVEN RAVER RAVES REVEL REVET RIVED RIVEN RIVER RIVES RIVET ROVED ROVER ROVES SAVED SAVER SAVES SEVEN SEVER TEVET TOVES WAVED WAVER WAVES WIVED WIVES WOVEN

••V•E
CAVAE CUVEE DAVIE FAVRE HAVRE LEVEE LIVRE MCVIE MOVIE NOVAE REVUE TEVYE VIVRE

•••VE
ABOVE AGAVE ALEVE ALIVE ATIVE BRAVE BREVE CALVE CARVE CHIVE CLAVE CLIVE CLOVE CRAVE CURVE DELVE DRIVE DROVE ELEVE FAUVE GLOVE GRAVE GROVE HALVE HEAVE HELVE HERVE KNAVE LEAVE MAUVE NAIVE NERVE OGIVE OLIVE PEEVE PROVE REEVE SALVE SERVE SHAVE SHOVE SIEVE SKIVE SLAVE SOAVE SOLVE STAVE STEVE STOVE SUAVE TRAVE TROVE VALVE VERVE WAIVE WEAVE YOUVE

V•G••
VAGUE VAGUS VEGAN VEGAS VIGIL VIGNY VIGOR VOGUE VUGGY

V••G•
VERGE VINGT VIRGA VIRGO VOLGA VSIGN VUGGY

V•••G
VARIG VYING

•VG••
AVGAS

••V•G
NAVIG

V•H••
VCHIP

V••H•
VICHY

V•••H
VETCH VOUCH

VI•••
VIALS VIAND VIBES VICAR VICES VICHY VICKI VICKS VIDAL VIDEO VIDOR VIEJO VIERS VIEWS VIEWY VIGIL VIGNY VIGOR VIKKI VILAS VILER VILLA VILLE VILLI VILMA VINAS VINCE VINCI VINED VINES VINGT VINNY VINOS VINYL VIOLA VIOLS VIPER VIRAL VIREO VIRGA VIRGO VIRID VIRNA VIRTU VIRUS VISAS VISBY VISES VISIT VISOR VISTA VISUM VITAE VITAL VITAS VITUS VIVID VIVRE VIXEN

V•I••
VEIDT VEILS VEINS VEINY VOICE VOICI VOIDS VOILA VOILE VSIGN VYING

V••I•
VADIM VADIS VALID VANIR VAPID VARIA VARIG VARIX VATIC VCHIP VEDIC VENIN VIGIL VIRID VISIT VIVID

V•••I
VALLI VERDI VERMI VICKI VIKKI VILLI VINCI VOICI

•VI••
AVIAN AVILA AVION AVISO CVIII DVIII DVINA EVIAN EVICT EVILS EVITA IVIED IVIES IVINS LVIII MVIII OVINE XVIII

•V•I•
AVAIL AVOID AVOIR AVRIL CVIII DVIII LVIII MVIII OVOID XVIII

•V••I
CVIII DVIII LVIII MVIII OVOLI XVIII

••VI•
ADVIL ALVIN ANVIL BEVIN BOVID CAVIL CCVII CDVII CIVIC CIVIL CLVII CMVII CXVII DAVID DAVIE DAVIS DAVIT DCVII DEVIL DLVII DXVII ELVIN ELVIS ERVIL ERVIN ETVIR GAVIN IRVIN KEVIN LAVIN LEVIN LEVIS LIVIA LIVID LXVII MAVIS MCVIE MCVII MDVII MLVII MMVII MOVIE MXVII NAVIG NEVIL NEVIN NEVIS PAVIA PAVID PAVIS QBVII RAVIN VIVID XCVII XLVII XXVII

••V•I
CCVII CDVII CLVII CMVII CXVII DCVII DLVII DXVII ENVOI LXVII MCVII MDVII MLVII MMVII MXVII QBVII XCVII XLVII XXVII

•••VI
CCCVI CCLVI CCXVI CDLVI CDXVI CLXVI CMLVI CMXVI CXCVI CXLVI CXXVI DCCVI DCLVI DCXVI DLXVI DXCVI DXLVI DXXVI LXXVI MCCVI MCDVI MCLVI MCMVI MCXVI MDCVI MDLVI MDXVI MLXVI MMCVI MMDVI MMLVI MMMVI MMXVI MXCVI MXLVI MXXVI TREVI XXXVI

VJ•••
VJDAY

V••J•
VIEJO

V•K••
VIKKI

V••K•
VICKI VICKS VIKKI VODKA

V•••K
VNECK

•V•K•
EVOKE

••V•K
NOVAK

V•L••
VALES VALET VALID VALLE VALLI VALOR VALSE VALUE VALVE VELAR VELDS VELDT VELEZ VELUM VILAS VILER VILLA VILLE VILLI VILMA VOLAR VOLAT VOLES VOLGA VOLTA VOLTE VOLTS VOLVA VOLVO

V••L•
VALLE VALLI VAULT VEALY VEILS VIALS VILLA VILLE VILLI VIOLA VIOLS VOILA VOILE VTOLS

V•••L
VENAL VIDAL VIGIL VINYL VIRAL VITAL VOCAL VOWEL

•V•L•
AVILA EVILS KVELL OVALS OVOLI OVOLO OVULE UVULA

•V••L
AVAIL AVRIL KVELL

••V•L
ADVAL ADVIL ANVIL BEVEL CAVIL CIVIL DEVIL ERVIL GAVEL HAVEL HOVEL KEVEL LAVAL LEVEL NAVAL NAVEL NEVIL NIVAL NOVEL RAVEL REVEL RIVAL

V•M••
VAMOS VAMPS

V••M•
VERMI VILMA

V•••M
VADIM VELUM VENOM VISUM VROOM

VN•••
VNECK

V•N••
VANCE VANES VANIR VANNA VANYA VENAE VENAL VENDA VENDS VENEZ VENIN VENOM VENTS VENUE VENUS VINAS VINCE VINCI VINED VINES VINGT VINNY VINOS VINYL

V••N•
VANNA VARNA VAUNT VEINS VEINY VERNE VIAND VIGNY VINNY VIRNA VYING

V•••N
VEGAN VENIN VIXEN VSIGN

•V•N•
AVANT AVENA AVENS DVINA EVANS EVENS EVENT IVANA IVINS OVENS OVINE

•V••N
AVIAN AVION EVIAN

••VN•
KOVNO ROVNO

••V•N
ALVIN BEVIN COVEN DEVON DIVAN ELVIN ERVIN GAVIN GIVEN HAVEN IRVIN KEVIN LAVIN LEVIN LEVON LIVEN MAVEN NEVIN NIVEN RAVEN RAVIN RIVEN SEVEN SIVAN WOVEN ZEVON

VO•••
VOCAL VODKA VOGUE VOICE VOICI VOIDS VOILA VOILE VOLAR VOLAT VOLES VOLGA VOLTA VOLTE VOLTS VOLVA VOLVO VOTED VOTER VOTES VOTRE VOUCH VOWED VOWEL VOWER

V•O••
VIOLA VIOLS VROOM VTOLS

V••O•
VALOR VAMOS VAPOR VENOM VIDOR VIGOR VINOS VISOR VROOM

V•••O
VASCO VERSO VIDEO VIEJO VIREO VIRGO VOLVO

•VO••
AVOID AVOIR AVOWS EVOKE EVORA IVORY OVOID OVOLI OVOLO

•V•O•
AVION

•V••O
AVISO OVOLO

••VO•
DAVOS DEVON DIVOT ENVOI ENVOY FAVOR GAVOT HAVOC LEVON PIVOT SAVOR SAVOY ZEVON

••V•O
DAVAO KOVNO ROVNO

•••VO
ABOVO BRAVO HUEVO NORVO PAAVO PARVO PROVO SALVO SERVO VOLVO

V•P••
VAPID VAPOR VIPER

V••P•
VAMPS VEEPS

V•••P
VCHIP

••VP•
RSVPD RSVPS

••V•P
REVUP

VR•••
VROOM

V•R••
VARAS VARIA VARIG VARIX VARNA VERBA VERBS VERDE VERDI VERGE VERMI VERNE VERRE VERSA VERSE VERSO VERST VERTE VERTS VERVE VIRAL VIREO VIRGA VIRGO VIRID VIRNA VIRTU VIRUS

V••R•
VEERS VEERY VERRE VIERS VIVRE VOTRE

V•••R
VADER VALOR VANIR VAPOR VATER VELAR VEXER VICAR VIDOR VIGOR VILER VIPER VISOR VOLAR VOTER VOWER

•VR••
AVRIL

•V•R•
AVARS AVERS AVERT AVERY EVERS EVERT EVERY EVORA IVORY OVERS OVERT

•V••R
AVOIR

••VR•
DEVRY FAVRE HAVRE LIVRE VIVRE

••V•R
ALVAR CAVER COVER DIVER DOVER ELVER ETVIR FAVOR FEVER FIVER GIVER HAVER HOVER JIVER LAVER LEVAR LEVER LIVER LOVER MOVER NEVER PAVER RAVER RIVER ROVER SAVER SAVOR SEVER WAVER

•••VR
SUPVR

VS•••
VSIGN

V•S••
VASCO VASES VASTY VESEY VESTA VESTS VISAS VISBY VISES VISIT VISOR VISTA VISUM

V••S•
VALSE VERSA VERSE VERSO VERST

V•••S
VADIS VAGUS VALES VAMOS VAMPS VANES VARAS VASES VEDAS VEEPS VEERS VEGAS VEILS VEINS VELDS VENDS VENTS VENUS VERBS VERTS VESTS VEXES VIALS VIBES VICES VICKS VIERS VIEWS VILAS VINAS VINES VINOS VIOLS VIRUS VISAS VISES VITAS VITUS VOIDS VOLES VOLTS VOTES VTOLS

•VS••
TVSET

•V•S•
AVAST AVISO KVASS

•V••S
AVARS AVENS AVERS AVGAS AVOWS EVANS EVENS EVERS EVILS IVIES IVINS KVASS OVALS OVENS OVERS

••V•S
BLVDS CAVES COVES DAVIS DAVOS DAVYS DIVAS DIVES DOVES EAVES ELVES ELVIS FAVES FIVES GIVES GYVES HAVES HIVES JAVAS JIVES KAVAS KIVAS LAVAS LAVES LEVIS LIVES LOVES MAVIS MOVES NAVES NEVES NEVIS NEVUS NOVAS PAVES PAVIS RAVES RIVES ROVES RSVPS SAVES TOVES WAVES WIVES

•••VS
MIRVS SHIVS SLAVS SPIVS UNIVS

VT•••
VTOLS

V•T••
VATER VATIC VETCH VITAE VITAL VITAS VITUS VOTED VOTER VOTES VOTRE

V••T•
VASTY VENTS VERTE VERTS VESTA VESTS VIRTU VISTA VOLTA VOLTE VOLTS

V•••T
VALET VAULT VAUNT VEIDT VELDT VERST VINGT VISIT VOLAT

•V•T•
EVITA OVATE OVETA OVETT

•V••T
AVANT AVAST AVERT EVENT EVERT EVICT OVERT OVETT TVSET

••V•T
AMVET CIVET COVET DAVIT DIVOT DUVET GAVOT PIVOT REVET RIVET TEVET

VU•••
VUGGY

V•U••
VAULT VAUNT VOUCH

V••U•
VACUA VADUZ VAGUE VAGUS VALUE VELUM VENUE VENUS VIRUS VISUM VITUS VOGUE

V•••U
VIRTU

•VU••
OVULE UVULA

••VU•
NEVUS REVUE REVUP

V•V••
VIVID VIVRE

V••V•
VALVE VERVE VOLVA VOLVO

••VV•
DIVVY
NAVVY
SAVVY

V•W••
VOWED
VOWEL
VOWER

V••W•
VIEWS
VIEWY

•V•W•
AVOWS

V•X••
VEXED
VEXER
VEXES
VIXEN

V•••X
VARIX

VY•••
VYING

V••Y•
VANYA
VINYL

V•••Y
VASTY
VEALY
VEDAY
VEERY
VEINY
VESEY
VICHY
VIEWY
VIGNY
VINNY
VISBY
VJDAY
VUGGY

•V••Y
AVERY
EVERY
IVORY

••VY•
DAVYS
TEVYE

••V•Y
COVEY
DEVRY
DIVVY
DOVEY
ENVOY
HOVEY
JIVEY
LOVEY
NAVVY
OYVAY
SAVOY
SAVVY

•••VY
CHEVY
CHIVY
CURVY
DIVVY
GRAVY
HEAVY
MARVY
NAVVY
NERVY
PEAVY
PRIVY
SAVVY
TURVY

V•••Z
VADUZ
VELEZ
VENEZ

WA•••
WAAFS
WAALS
WACKO
WACKY
WADDY
WADED
WADER
WADES
WADIS
WADUP
WAFER
WAFTS
WAGED
WAGER
WAGES
WAGON
WAHOO
WAIFS
WAILS
WAINS
WAIST
WAITE
WAITS
WAITZ
WAIVE
WAJDA
WAKED
WAKEN
WAKES
WALDO
WALED
WALER
WALES
WALEY
WALKS
WALLA
WALLS
WALLY
WALSH
WALSY
WALTZ
WANDA
WANDS
WANED
WANER
WANES
WANEY
WANLY
WANNA
WANTS
WARDS
WARES
WARMS
WARNS
WARPS
WARTS
WARTY
WASHY
WASNT
WASPS
WASPY
WASTE
WATCH
WATER
WATTS
WAUGH
WAVED
WAVER
WAVES
WAXED
WAXEN
WAXER
WAXES
WAYNE

W•A••
WAAFS
WAALS
WEALS
WEANS
WEARS
WEARY
WEAVE
WHACK
WHALE
WHAMO
WHAMS
WHANG
WHARF
WHATD
WHATS
WOADS
WRACK
WRACS
WRAFS
WRAPS
WRAPT
WRATH
WYATT

W••A•
WEKAS
WHEAL
WHEAT
WIGAN
WOMAN
WOTAN
WREAK
WUHAN
WYMAN

W•••A
WAJDA
WALLA
WANDA
WANNA
WICCA
WILLA
WILMA
WIRRA

•WA••
AWACS
AWAIT
AWAJI
AWAKE
AWARD
AWARE
AWASH
BWANA
DWARF
SWABS
SWAGE
SWAGS
SWAIN
SWALE
SWAMI
SWAMP
SWANK
SWANN
SWANS
SWAPS
SWARD
SWARF
SWARM
SWART
SWASH
SWATH
SWATS
SWAYS
SWAZI
TWAIN
TWANG

•W•A•
SWEAR
SWEAT
TWEAK
TWOAM
YWCAS

•W••A
BWANA
TWYLA

••WA•
AMWAY
ANWAR
ASWAN
ATWAR
BYWAY
DEWAN
DEWAR
ELWAY
HOWAR
IOWAN
MYWAY
NAWAB
NOWAY
OTWAY
PAWAT
POWAY
REWAX
ROWAN

•••WA
ADUWA
DAIWA
FATWA
KIOWA
OZAWA
SCHWA
SLIWA

W•B••
WEBBY
WEBER

W••B•
WEBBY
WELBY

•W•B•
SWABS
SWOBS

•W••B
DWEEB

••W•B
NAWAB

W•C••
WACKO
WACKY
WICCA
WICKS

W••C•
WATCH
WELCH
WENCH
WHACK
WHICH
WICCA
WILCO
WINCE
WINCH
WITCH
WRACK
WRACS
WRECK

•WC••
YWCAS

•W•C•
AWACS
TWICE

W•D••
WADDY
WADED
WADER
WADES
WADIS
WADUP
WEDEL
WEDGE
WEDGY
WIDEN
WIDER
WIDOW
WIDTH
WODEN
WODGE

W••D•
WADDY
WAJDA
WALDO
WANDA
WANDS
WARDS
WEEDS
WEEDY
WELDS
WENDS
WENDT
WENDY
WILDE
WILDS
WINDS
WINDY
WOADS
WOLDS
WOODS
WOODY
WORDS
WORDY

W•••D
WADED
WAGED
WAKED
WALED
WANED
WAVED
WAXED
WEIRD
WHATD
WIELD
WILED
WINED
WIPED
WIRED
WIVED
WOOED
WORLD
WOULD
WOUND
WOWED

•W•D•
SWEDE

•W••D
AWARD
AWNED
OWNED
SWARD
SWORD
TWEED

••WD•
BAWDY
DOWDY
GOWDY
HOWDY
ROWDY

••W•D
BOWED
CAWED
CLWYD
COWED
DEWED
HAWED
HEWED
JAWED
LOWED
MEWED
MOWED
PAWED
REWED
ROWED
SAWED
SEWED
SOWED
TOWED
UNWED
VOWED
WOWED
YAWED

•••WD
CROWD

WE•••
WEALS
WEANS
WEARS
WEARY
WEAVE
WEBBY
WEBER
WEDEL
WEDGE
WEDGY
WEEDS
WEEDY
WEEKS
WEEMS
WEENY
WEEPS
WEEPY
WEEST
WEFTS
WEIGH
WEILL
WEIRD
WEIRS
WEISS
WEKAS
WELBY
WELCH
WELDS
WELLS
WELSH
WELTS
WELTY
WENCH
WENDS
WENDT
WENDY
WESER
WESTS
WETLY

W•E••
WEEDS
WEEDY
WEEKS
WEEMS
WEENY
WEEPS
WEEPY
WEEST
WHEAL
WHEAT
WHEEL
WHEEN
WHELK
WHELM
WHELP
WHERE
WHETS
WHEYS
WIELD
WIEST
WREAK
WRECK
WRENS
WREST
WYETH

W••E•
WADED
WADER
WADES
WAFER
WAGED
WAGER
WAGES
WAKED
WAKEN
WAKES
WALED
WALER
WALES
WALEY
WANED
WANER
WANES
WANEY
WARES
WATER
WAVED
WAVER
WAVES
WAXED
WAXEN
WAXER
WAXES
WEBER
WEDEL
WESER
WHEEL
WHEEN
WIDEN
WIDER
WILED
WILES
WILEY
WINED
WINES
WINEY
WIPED
WIPER
WIPES
WIRED
WIRER
WIRES
WISER
WIVED
WIVES
WIZEN
WODEN
WOKEN
WOMEN
WOOED
WOOER
WOVEN
WOWED
WRIER
WRYER
WYLER

W•••E
WAITE
WAIVE
WASTE
WAYNE
WEAVE
WEDGE
WHALE
WHERE
WHILE
WHINE
WHITE
WHOLE
WHOSE
WHYME
WHYRE
WILDE
WINCE
WINZE
WITHE
WITTE
WODGE
WOLFE
WORSE
WRITE
WROTE
WYLIE
WYTHE

•WE••
DWEEB
DWELL
DWELT
EWELL
EWERS
GWENN
GWENT
OWENS
OWERS
SWEAR
SWEAT
SWEDE
SWEEP
SWEET
SWELL
SWEPT
TWEAK
TWEED
TWEEN
TWEER
TWEET
TWERE
TWERP
ZWEIG

•W•E•
AWNED
DWEEB
OWLET
OWNED
OWNER
SWEEP
SWEET
TWEED
TWEEN
TWEER
TWEET

•W••E
AWAKE
AWARE
AWOKE
SWAGE
SWALE
SWEDE
SWINE
SWIPE
SWOPE
SWORE
TWERE
TWICE
TWINE

••WE•
BOWED
BOWEN
BOWER
BOWES
CAWED
COWED
COWER
COWES
DAWES
DEWED
DEWEY
DOWEL
DOWER
ELWES
FEWER
GOWER
HAWED
HEWED
HEWER
JAWED
JEWEL
LAWES
LEWES
LOWED
LOWER
LOWES
MEWED
MOWED
MOWER
NEWEL
NEWER
NGWEE
PAWED
PAWER
PEWEE
POWER
RAWER
REWED
ROWED
ROWEL
ROWEN
ROWER
SAWED
SEWED
SEWER
SOWED
SOWER
TOWED
TOWEL
TOWER
UNWED
VOWED
VOWEL
VOWER
WOWED
YAWED

••W•E
BOWIE
DOWSE
HAWKE
HAWSE
HOWIE
NGWEE
PEWEE
TOWNE
ZOWIE

•••WE
INAWE
KITWE
LOEWE
STOWE

W•F••
WAFER
WAFTS
WEFTS

W••F•
WAAFS
WAIFS
WHIFF
WOLFE
WOLFF
WOOFS
WRAFS

W•••F
WHARF
WHIFF
WHOOF
WOLFF
WOOLF

•WF••
AWFUL

•W•F•
SWIFT

•W••F
DWARF
SWARF

W•G••
WAGED
WAGER
WAGES
WAGON
WIGAN
WIGGY
WIGHT

W••G•
WAUGH
WEDGE
WEDGY
WEIGH
WHIGS
WIGGY
WINGS
WODGE

W•••G
WHANG
WRING
WRONG
WRUNG

•W•G•
SWAGE
SWAGS
SWIGS
TWIGS

•W••G
AWING
EWING
OWING
SWING
SWUNG
TWANG
ZWEIG

••WG•
HAWGS

WH•••
WHACK
WHALE
WHAMO
WHAMS
WHANG
WHARF
WHATD
WHATS
WHEAL
WHEAT
WHEEL
WHEEN
WHELK
WHELM
WHELP
WHERE
WHETS
WHEYS
WHICH
WHIFF
WHIGS
WHILE
WHIMS
WHINE
WHINS
WHINY
WHIPS
WHIRL
WHIRR
WHIRS
WHISH
WHISK
WHIST
WHITE
WHITS
WHITY
WHOLE
WHOLL
WHOMP
WHOOF
WHOOP
WHOPS
WHORL
WHOSE
WHOSO
WHUPS
WHYLL
WHYME
WHYRE

W•H••
WAHOO
WUHAN

W••H•
WASHY
WIGHT
WISHY
WITHE
WITHY
WUSHU
WYTHE

W•••H
WALSH
WATCH
WAUGH
WEIGH
WELCH
WELSH
WENCH
WHICH
WHISH
WIDTH
WINCH
WITCH
WORTH
WRATH
WROTH
WYETH

•W••H
AWASH
SWASH
SWATH
SWISH
SWITH

WI•••
WICCA
WICKS
WIDEN
WIDER
WIDOW
WIDTH
WIELD
WIEST
WIGAN
WIGGY
WIGHT
WILCO
WILDE
WILDS
WILED
WILES
WILEY
WILLA
WILLS
WILLY
WILMA
WILTS
WIMPS
WIMPY
WINCE
WINCH
WINDS
WINDY
WINED
WINES
WINEY
WINGS
WINKS
WINZE
WIPED
WIPER
WIPES
WIRED
WIRER
WIRES
WIRRA
WISER
WISHY
WISPS
WISPY
WITCH
WITHE
WITHY
WITTE
WITTY
WIVED
WIVES
WIZEN

W•I••
WAIFS
WAILS
WAINS
WAIST
WAITE
WAITS
WAITZ
WAIVE
WEIGH
WEILL
WEIRD
WEIRS
WEISS
WHICH
WHIFF
WHIGS
WHILE
WHIMS
WHINE
WHINS
WHINY
WHIPS
WHIRL
WHIRR
WHIRS
WHISH
WHISK
WHIST
WHITE
WHITS
WHITY
WRIER
WRING
WRIST
WRITE
WRITS

W••I•
WADIS
WYLIE

•WI••
AWING
EWING
OWING
SWIFT
SWIGS
SWILL
SWIMS
SWINE
SWING
SWINK
SWIPE
SWIRL
SWISH
SWISS
SWITH
SWITZ
TWICE
TWIGS
TWILL
TWINE
TWINS
TWIRL
TWIST
TWITS
TWIXT

•W•I•
AWAIT
SWAIN
TWAIN
ZWEIG

•W••I
AWAJI
SWAMI
SWAZI

••WI•
BOWIE
EDWIN
ERWIN
HOWIE
IRWIN
KIWIS
LEWIS
NOWIN
PEWIT
REWIN
SAWIN
TOWIT
ZOWIE

W•J••
WAJDA

•W•J•
AWAJI

W•K••
WAKED
WAKEN
WAKES
WEKAS
WOKEN

W••K•
WACKO
WACKY
WALKS
WEEKS
WICKS
WINKS
WONKS
WONKY
WORKS

W•••K
WHACK
WHELK
WHISK
WRACK
WREAK
WRECK

•W•K•
AWAKE
AWOKE
EWOKS

•W••K
SWANK
SWINK
SWONK
TWEAK

••WK•
GAWKS
GAWKY
GOWKS
HAWKE
HAWKS
PAWKY

••W•K
MIWOK

W•L••
WALDO
WALED
WALER
WALES
WALEY
WALKS
WALLA
WALLS
WALLY
WALSH
WALSY
WALTZ
WELBY
WELCH
WELDS
WELLS
WELSH
WELTS
WELTY
WILCO
WILDE
WILDS
WILED
WILES
WILEY
WILLA
WILLS
WILLY
WILMA
WILTS
WOLDS
WOLFE
WOLFF
WYLER
WYLIE

W••L•
WAALS
WAILS
WALLA
WALLS
WALLY
WANLY
WEALS
WEILL
WELLS
WETLY
WHALE
WHELK
WHELM
WHELP
WHILE
WHOLE
WHOLL
WHYLL
WIELD
WILLA
WILLS
WILLY
WOOLF
WOOLS
WOOLY
WORLD
WOULD
WRYLY

W•••L
WEDEL
WEILL
WHEAL
WHEEL
WHIRL
WHOLL
WHORL
WHYLL

•WL••
OWLET

•W•L•
AWOLS
DWELL
DWELT
EWELL
SWALE
SWELL
SWILL
TWILL
TWYLA

•W••L
AWFUL
DWELL
EWELL
SWELL
SWILL
SWIRL
TWILL
TWIRL

••WL•
BAWLS
BOWLS
COWLS
FOWLS
HOWLS
JOWLS
JOWLY
LOWLY
MEWLS
NEWLY
PAWLS
RAWLS
RAWLY
YAWLS
YOWLS

••W•L
DOWEL
JEWEL
NEWEL
ROWEL
TOWEL
VOWEL

•••WL
BRAWL
CRAWL
DRAWL
GROWL
PROWL
SCOWL
SHAWL
TRAWL

W•M••
WIMPS
WIMPY
WOMAN
WOMEN
WOMYN
WYMAN

W••M•
WARMS
WEEMS
WHAMO
WHAMS
WHIMS
WHOMP
WHYME
WILMA
WORMS
WORMY

W•••M
WHELM

•W•M•
SWAMI
SWAMP
SWIMS

•W••M
SWARM
TWOAM
TWOPM

•••WM
SHAWM

W•N••
WANDA
WANDS
WANED
WANER
WANES
WANEY
WANLY
WANNA
WANTS
WENCH
WENDS
WENDT
WENDY
WINCE
WINCH
WINDS
WINDY
WINED
WINES
WINEY
WINGS
WINKS
WINZE
WONKS
WONKY
WONTS

W••N•
WAINS
WANNA
WARNS
WASNT
WAYNE
WEANS
WEENY
WHANG
WHINE
WHINS
WHINY
WOUND
WRENS
WRING
WRONG
WRUNG

W•••N
WAGON
WAKEN
WAXEN
WHEEN
WIDEN
WIGAN
WIZEN
WODEN
WOKEN
WOMAN
WOMEN
WOMYN
WOTAN
WOVEN
WUHAN
WYMAN

•WN••
AWNED

OWNED OWNER OWNUP

•W•N•
AWING BWANA EWING GWENN GWENT GWYNN OWENS OWING SWANK SWANN SWANS SWINE SWING SWINK SWONK SWUNG TWANG TWINE TWINS

•W••N
GWENN GWYNN SWAIN SWANN SWOON SWORN TWAIN TWEEN

••WN•
DAWNS DOWNS DOWNY FAWNS GOWNS LAWNS LAWNY PAWNS TAWNY TOWNE TOWNS TOWNY YAWNS

••W•N
ASWAN BOWEN DEWAN EDWIN ERWIN IOWAN IRWIN NOWIN REWIN REWON ROWAN ROWEN SAWIN SEWON

•••WN
BLOWN BRAWN BROWN CLOWN CROWN DRAWN DROWN FLOWN FROWN GROWN KNOWN PRAWN SHAWN SHOWN SPAWN

WO•••
WOADS WODEN WODGE WOKEN WOLDS WOLFE WOLFF WOMAN WOMEN WOMYN WONKS WONKY WONTS WOODS WOODY WOOED WOOER WOOFS WOOLF WOOLS WOOLY WOOZY WORDS WORDY WORKS WORLD WORMS WORMY WORRY WORSE WORST WORTH WORTS WOTAN WOULD WOUND WOVEN WOWED

W•O••
WHOLE WHOLL WHOMP WHOOF WHOOP WHOPS WHORL WHOSE WHOSO WOODS WOODY WOOED WOOER WOOFS WOOLF WOOLS WOOLY WOOZY WRONG WROTE WROTH

W••O•
WAGON WAHOO WHOOF WHOOP WIDOW

W•••O
WACKO WAHOO WALDO WHAMO WHOSO WILCO

•WO••
AWOKE AWOLS EWOKS SWOBS SWONK SWOON SWOOP SWOPE SWOPS SWORD SWORE SWORN TWOAM TWOPM

•W•O•
SWOON SWOOP

••WO•
MIWOK OHWOW REWON SEWON

••W•O
HOWSO HOWTO SAWTO

•••WO
INTWO

W•P••
WIPED WIPER WIPES

W••P•
WARPS WASPS WASPY WEEPS WEEPY WHIPS WHOPS WHUPS WIMPS WIMPY WISPS WISPY WRAPS WRAPT

W•••P
WADUP WHELP WHOMP WHOOP

•W•P•
SWAPS SWEPT SWIPE SWOPE SWOPS TWOPM

•W••P
OWNUP SWAMP SWEEP SWOOP TWERP

••WP•
GAWPS YAWPS

••W•P
SEWUP

WR•••
WRACK WRACS WRAFS WRAPS WRAPT WRATH WREAK WRECK WRENS WREST WRIER WRING WRIST WRITE WRITS WRONG WROTE WROTH WRUNG WRYER WRYLY

W•R••
WARDS WARES WARMS WARNS WARPS WARTS WARTY WIRED WIRER WIRES WIRRA WORDS WORDY WORKS WORLD WORMS WORMY WORRY WORSE WORST WORTH WORTS WURST

W••R•
WEARS WEARY WEIRD WEIRS WHARF WHERE WHIRL WHIRR WHIRS WHORL WHYRE WIRRA WORRY

W•••R
WADER WAFER WAGER WALER WANER WATER WAVER WAXER WEBER WESER WHIRR WIDER WIPER WIRER WISER WOOER WRIER WRYER WYLER

•W•R•
AWARD AWARE DWARF EWERS OWERS SWARD SWARF SWARM SWART SWIRL SWORD SWORE SWORN TWERE TWERP TWIRL

•W••R
OWNER SWEAR TWEER

••WR•
COWRY DOWRY LOWRY

••W•R
ANWAR ATWAR BOWER COWER DEWAR DOWER FEWER GOWER HEWER HOWAR LOWER MOWER NEWER PAWER POWER RAWER ROWER SEWER SOWER TOWER VOWER

W•S••
WASHY WASNT WASPS WASPY WASTE WESER WESTS WISER WISHY WISPS WISPY WUSHU

W••S•
WAIST WALSH WALSY WEEST WEISS WELSH WHISH WHISK WHIST WHOSE WHOSO WIEST WORSE WORST WREST WRIST WURST

W•••S
WAAFS WAALS WADES WADIS WAFTS WAGES WAIFS WAILS WAINS WAITS WAKES WALES WALKS WALLS WANDS WANES WANTS WARDS WARES WARMS WARNS WARPS WARTS WASPS WATTS WAVES WAXES WEALS WEANS WEARS WEEDS WEEKS WEEMS WEEPS WEFTS WEIRS WEISS WEKAS WELDS WELLS WELTS WENDS WESTS WHAMS WHATS WHETS WHEYS WHIGS WHIMS WHINS WHIPS WHIRS WHITS WHOPS WHUPS WICKS WILDS WILES WILLS WILTS WIMPS WINDS WINES WINGS WINKS WIPES WIRES WISPS WIVES WOADS WOLDS WONKS WONTS WOODS WOOFS WOOLS WORDS WORKS WORMS WORTS WRACS WRAFS WRAPS WRENS WRITS

•W•S•
AWASH SWASH SWISH SWISS TWIST

•W••S
AWACS AWOLS EWERS EWOKS OWENS OWERS SWABS SWAGS SWANS SWAPS SWATS SWAYS SWIGS SWIMS SWISS SWOBS SWOPS TWIGS TWINS TWITS YWCAS

••WS•
DOWSE HAWSE HOWSO NEWSY

••W•S
BAWLS BOWES BOWLS COWES COWLS DAWES DAWNS DOWNS ELWES FAWNS FOWLS GAWKS GAWPS GOWKS GOWNS HAWGS HAWKS HOWLS JOWLS KIWIS LAWES LAWNS LEWES LEWIS LOWES MEWLS NEWTS PAWLS PAWNS POWYS RAWLS TOWNS YAWLS YAWNS YAWPS YOWLS

•••WS
AVOWS BLOWS BREWS BROWS CHAWS CHEWS CHOWS CLAWS CLEWS CRAWS CREWS CROWS DHOWS DRAWS FLAWS FLEWS FLOWS FROWS GLOWS GNAWS GROWS KNOWS MEOWS PLEWS PLOWS PROWS SCOWS SHOWS SKEWS SLAWS SLEWS SLOWS SMEWS SNOWS SPEWS STEWS STOWS THAWS THEWS TREWS VIEWS

W•T••
WATCH WATER WATTS WETLY WITCH WITHE WITHY WITTE WITTY WOTAN WYTHE

W••T•
WAFTS WAITE WAITS WAITZ WALTZ WANTS WARTS WARTY WASTE WATTS WEFTS WELTS WELTY WESTS WHATD WHATS WHETS WHITE WHITS WHITY WIDTH WILTS WITTE WITTY WONTS WORTH WORTS WRATH WRITE WRITS WROTE WROTH WYATT WYETH

W•••T
WAIST WASNT WEEST WENDT WHEAT WHIST WIEST WIGHT WORST WRAPT WREST WRIST WURST WYATT

•W•T•
SWATH SWATS SWITH SWITZ TWITS

•W••T
AWAIT DWELT GWENT OWLET SWART SWEAT SWEET SWEPT SWIFT TWEET TWIST TWIXT

••WT•
HOWTO NEWTS SAWTO

••W•T
PAWAT PEWIT TOWIT

WU•••
WUHAN WURST WUSHU

W•U••
WAUGH WHUPS WOULD WOUND WRUNG

W••U•
WADUP

W•••U
WUSHU

•WU••
SWUNG

•W•U•
AWFUL OWNUP

••WU•
SEWUP

•••WU
ILGWU

W•V••
WAVED WAVER WAVES WIVED WIVES WOVEN

W••V•
WAIVE WEAVE

W•W••
WOWED

W•••W
WIDOW

••W•W
OHWOW

W•X••
WAXED WAXEN WAXER WAXES

•W•X•
TWIXT

••W•X
REWAX

WY•••
WYATT WYETH WYLER WYLIE WYMAN WYTHE

W•Y••
WAYNE WHYLL WHYME WHYRE WRYER WRYLY

W••Y•
WHEYS WOMYN

W•••Y
WACKY WADDY WALEY WALLY WALSY WANEY WANLY WARTY WASHY WASPY WEARY WEBBY WEDGY WEEDY WEENY WEEPY WELBY WELTY WENDY WETLY WHINY WHITY WIGGY WILEY WILLY WIMPY WINDY WINEY WISHY WISPY WITHY WITTY WONKY WOODY WOOLY WOOZY WORDY WORMY WORRY WRYLY

•WY••
GWYNN TWYLA

•W•Y•
SWAYS

••WY•
CLWYD POWYS

••W•Y
AMWAY BAWDY BYWAY COWRY DEWEY DOWDY DOWNY DOWRY ELWAY GAWKY GOWDY HOWDY JOWLY LAWNY LOWLY LOWRY MYWAY NEWLY NEWSY NOWAY OTWAY PAWKY POWAY RAWLY ROWDY TAWNY TOWNY

•••WY
BLOWY CHEWY FLAWY LOEWY SHOWY SNOWY THEWY VIEWY

W•Z••
WIZEN

W••Z•
WINZE WOOZY

W•••Z
WAITZ WALTZ

•W•Z•
SWAZI

•W••Z
SWITZ

XA•••
XACTO XAXES XAXIS

X•A••
XRAYS

X•••A
XENIA XHOSA

•XA••
EXACT EXALT EXAMS

•X•A•
AXIAL IXNAY UXMAL

•X••A
EXTRA

••XA•
COXAE COXAL HEXAD LEXAN SIXAM TEXAN TEXAS

X•B••
XEBEC

•XB••
OXBOW

•X••B
EXURB

••XB•
BIXBY

XC•••
XCIII XCVII

X•C••
XACTO

X•••C
XEBEC XERIC

•XC••
CXCII CXCIV CXCIX CXCVI DXCII DXCIV DXCIX DXCVI EXCEL MXCII MXCIV MXCIX MXCVI

•X•C•
EXACT EXECS

••XC•
CCXCI CCXCV CDXCI CDXCV CMXCI CMXCV DCXCI DCXCV MCXCI MCXCV MDXCI MDXCV MMXCI MMXCV TAXCO

••X•C
TOXIC

•••XC
CCCXC DCCXC MCCXC MCDXC MCMXC MDCXC MMCXC MMDXC MMMXC

XD•••
XDOUT

X•D••
XEDIN

•X•D•
EXUDE OXIDE

••X•D
BOXED COXED FAXED FIXED FOXED HEXAD HEXED MAXED MIXED NIXED SIXED TAXED VEXED WAXED

XE•••
XEBEC XEDIN XENIA XENON XERIC XEROX XERUS

X••E•
XAXES XEBEC XYLEM

•XE••
AXELS AXERS EXECS EXERT OXEYE

•X•E•
AXLES EXCEL EXPEL

•X••E
AXONE EXILE EXUDE OXEYE OXIDE

••XE•
BOXED BOXER BOXES COXED COXES COXEY DUXES FAXED FAXES FIXED FIXER FIXES FOXED FOXES HEXED HEXER HEXES LAXER LOXES MAXED MAXES MIXED MIXER MIXES NIXED NIXES PIXEL REXES SAXES SEXES SIXED SIXER SIXES SOXER TAXED TAXER TAXES TUXES VEXED VEXER VEXES VIXEN WAXED WAXEN WAXER WAXES XAXES YAXES ZAXES

••X•E
COXAE DIXIE HOXIE MAXIE MOXIE NIXIE PIXIE PYXIE ROXIE

X••G•
XINGU

•X••G
AXING

XH•••
XHOSA

••X•H
SIXTH

XI•••
XINGU

X•I••
XCIII XLIII XVIII XXIII

X••I•
XAXIS XCIII XCVII XEDIN XENIA XERIC XLIII XLVII XVIII XXIII XXVII XXXII XXXIV XXXIX

X•••I
XCIII XCVII XLIII XLVII XVIII XXIII XXVII XXXII XXXVI

•XI••
AXIAL AXILS AXING AXIOM AXION CXIII DXIII EXILE EXIST EXITS IXION LXIII MXIII OXIDE XXIII

•X•I•
CXCII CXCIV CXCIX CXIII CXLII CXLIV CXLIX CXVII CXXII CXXIV CXXIX DXCII DXCIV DXCIX DXIII DXLII DXLIV DXLIX DXVII DXXII DXXIV DXXIX LXIII LXVII LXXII LXXIV LXXIX MXCII MXCIV MXCIX MXIII MXLII MXLIV MXLIX MXMII MXMIV MXVII MXXII MXXIV MXXIX OXLIP XXIII XXVII XXXII XXXIV XXXIX

•X••I
CXCII CXCVI CXIII CXLII CXLVI CXVII CXXII CXXVI CXXXI DXCII DXCVI DXIII DXLII DXLVI DXVII DXXII DXXVI DXXXI LXIII LXVII LXXII LXXVI LXXXI MXCII MXCVI MXIII MXLII MXLVI MXMII MXVII MXXII MXXVI MXXXI XXIII XXVII XXXII XXXVI

••XI•
AUXIL AUXIN BOXIN CCXII CCXIV CCXIX CDXII CDXIV CDXIX CLXII CLXIV CLXIX CMXII CMXIV CMXIX CXXII CXXIV CXXIX DCXII DCXIV DCXIX DIXIE DIXIT DLXII DLXIV DLXIX DXXII DXXIV DXXIX FIXIT HOXIE LEXIS LXXII LXXIV LXXIX MAXIE MAXIM MAXIS MCXII MCXIV MCXIX MDXII MDXIV MDXIX MIXIN MLXII

MLXIV MLXIX MMXII MMXIV MMXIX MOXIE MXXII MXXIV MXXIX NEXIS NIXIE PIXIE PYXIE PYXIS ROXIE TAXIS TOXIC TOXIN XAXIS XXXII XXXIV XXXIX YAXIS ZAXIS

••X•I
CCXCI CCXII CCXLI CCXVI CCXXI CDXCI CDXII CDXLI CDXVI CDXXI CLXII CLXVI CLXXI CMXCI CMXII CMXLI CMXVI CMXXI CXXII CXXVI CXXXI DCXCI DCXII DCXLI DCXVI DCXXI DLXII DLXVI DLXXI DXXII DXXVI DXXXI LXXII LXXVI LXXXI MCXCI MCXII MCXLI MCXVI MCXXI MDXCI MDXII MDXLI MDXVI MDXXI MLXII MLXVI MLXXI MMXCI MMXII MMXLI MMXVI MMXXI MXXII MXXVI MXXXI XXXII XXXVI

•••XI
BENXI CCCXI CCLXI CCXXI CDLXI CDXXI CLXXI CMLXI CMXXI CXXXI DCCXI DCLXI DCXXI DLXXI DXXXI FLEXI LXXXI MCCXI MCDXI MCLXI MCMXI MCXXI MDCXI MDLXI MDXXI MLXXI MMCXI MMDXI MMLXI MMMXI MMXXI MXXXI

XL•••
XLIII XLVII

X•L••
XYLEM

•XL••
AXLES CXLII CXLIV CXLIX CXLVI DXLII DXLIV DXLIX DXLVI MXLII MXLIV MXLIX MXLVI OXLIP

•X•L•
AXELS AXILS EXALT EXILE EXULT

•X••L
AXIAL EXCEL EXPEL EXTOL UXMAL

••XL•
CCXLI CCXLV CDXLI CDXLV CMXLI CMXLV DCXLI DCXLV LAXLY MCXLI MCXLV MDXLI MDXLV MMXLI MMXLV

••X•L
AUXIL COXAL HEXYL PIXEL

•••XL
CCCXL DCCXL MCCXL MCDXL MCMXL MDCXL MMCXL MMDXL MMMXL

X•••M
XYLEM

•XM••
MXMII MXMIV UXMAL

•X•M•
EXAMS

•X••M
AXIOM

••XM•
SIXMO

••X•M
MAXIM SIXAM SIXPM

X•N••
XENIA XENON XINGU

X•••N
XEDIN XENON

•XN••
IXNAY

•X•N•
AXING AXONE AXONS EXONS

•X••N
AXION EXXON IXION

••X•N
AUXIN BOXIN DIXON EXXON LEXAN MIXIN NIXON SAXON TAXON TEXAN TOXIN VIXEN WAXEN

X•O••
XDOUT XHOSA XSOUT

X••O•
XENON XEROX

X•••O
XACTO

•XO••
AXONE AXONS EXONS

•X•O•
AXIOM AXION EXPOS EXTOL EXXON IXION OXBOW

•X••O
EXTRO

••XO•
DIXON EXXON LUXOR NAXOS NIXON SAXON TAXON

••X•O
SIXMO TAXCO

•••XO
GLAXO

•XP••
EXPEL EXPOS

•X••P
OXLIP

••XP•
SIXPM

••X•P
BOXUP FIXUP MIXUP

XR•••
XRAYS

X•R••
XERIC XEROX XERUS

•X•R•
AXERS EXERT EXTRA EXTRO EXURB

••X•R
BOXER DEXTR FIXER HEXER LAXER LUXOR MIXER SIXER SOXER TAXER VEXER WAXER

XS•••
XSOUT

X••S•
XHOSA

X•••S
XAXES XAXIS XERUS XRAYS

•X•S•
EXIST

•X••S
AXELS AXERS AXILS AXLES AXONS EXAMS EXECS EXITS EXONS EXPOS

••X•S
BOXES COXES DUXES FAXES FIXES FOXES HEXES LEXIS LEXUS LOXES MAXES MAXIS MIXES NAXOS NEXIS NEXUS NIXES PYXIS REXES SAXES SEXES SEXTS SIXES TAXES TAXIS TEXAS TEXTS TUXES VEXES WAXES XAXES XAXIS YAXES YAXIS ZAXES ZAXIS

X••T•
XACTO

X•••T
XDOUT XSOUT

•XT••
EXTOL EXTRA EXTRO

•X•T•
EXITS

•X••T
EXACT EXALT EXERT EXIST EXULT

••XT•
DEXTR FOXTV SEXTS SIXTH SIXTY TEXTS

••X•T
DIXIT FIXIT

•••XT
TWIXT

X••U•
XDOUT XERUS XSOUT

X•••U
XINGU

•XU••
EXUDE EXULT EXURB

••XU•
BOXUP FIXUP LEXUS MIXUP NEXUS

XV•••
XVIII

X•V••
XCVII XLVII XXVII

X••V•
XXXVI

X•••V
XXXIV

•XV••
CXVII DXVII LXVII MXVII XXVII

•X•V•
CXCVI CXLVI CXXVI DXCVI DXLVI DXXVI LXXVI MXCVI MXLVI MXXVI XXXVI

•X••V
CXCIV CXLIV CXXIV CXXXV DXCIV DXLIV DXXIV DXXXV LXXIV LXXXV MXCIV MXLIV MXMIV MXXIV MXXXV XXXIV

••XV•
CCXVI CDXVI CLXVI CMXVI CXXVI DCXVI DLXVI DXXVI LXXVI MCXVI MDXVI MLXVI MMXVI MXXVI XXXVI

••X•V
CCXCV CCXIV CCXLV CCXXV CDXCV CDXIV CDXLV CDXXV CLXIV CLXXV CMXCV CMXIV CMXLV CMXXV CXXIV CXXXV DCXCV DCXIV DCXLV DCXXV DLXIV DLXXV DXXIV DXXXV FOXTV LXXIV LXXXV MCXCV MCXIV MCXLV MCXXV MDXCV MDXIV MDXLV MDXXV MLXIV MLXXV MMXCV MMXIV MMXLV MMXXV MXXIV MXXXV XXXIV

•••XV
CCCXV CCLXV CCXXV CDLXV CDXXV CLXXV CMLXV CMXXV CXXXV DCCXV DCLXV DCXXV DLXXV DXXXV LXXXV MCCXV MCDXV MCLXV MCMXV MCXXV MDCXV MDLXV MDXXV MLXXV MMCXV MMDXV MMLXV MMMXV MMXXV MXXXV

•X••W
OXBOW

XX•••
XXIII XXVII XXXII XXXIV XXXIX XXXVI

X•X••
XAXES XAXIS XXXII XXXIV XXXIX XXXVI

X•••X
XEROX XXXIX

•XX••
CXXII CXXIV CXXIX CXXVI CXXXI CXXXV DXXII DXXIV DXXIX DXXVI DXXXI DXXXV EXXON LXXII LXXIV LXXIX LXXVI LXXXI LXXXV MXXII MXXIV MXXIX MXXVI MXXXI MXXXV XXXII XXXIV XXXIX XXXVI

•X•X•
CXXXI CXXXV DXXXI DXXXV LXXXI LXXXV MXXXI MXXXV XXXII XXXIV XXXIX XXXVI LXXXV MXXXI MXXXV

•X••X
CXCIX CXLIX CXXIX DXCIX DXLIX DXXIX LXXIX MXCIX MXLIX MXXIX XXXIX

••XX•
CCXXI CCXXV CCXXX CDXXI CDXXV CDXXX CLXXI CLXXV CLXXX CMXXI CMXXV CMXXX CXXXI CXXXV DCXXI DCXXV DCXXX DLXXI DLXXV DLXXX DXXXI DXXXV LXXXI LXXXV MCXXI MCXXV MCXXX MDXXI MDXXV MDXXX MLXXI MLXXV MLXXX MMXXI MMXXV MMXXX MXXXI MXXXV

••X•X
CCXIX CCXXX CDXIX CDXXX CLXIX CLXXX CMXIX CMXXX CXXIX DCXIX DCXXX DLXIX DLXXX DXXIX LXXIX MCXIX MCXXX MDXIX MDXXX MLXIX MLXXX MMXIX MMXXX MXXIX XXXIX

•••XX
CCCXX CCLXX CCXXX CDLXX CDXXX CLXXX CMLXX CMXXX DCCXX DCLXX DCXXX DLXXX MCCXX MCDXX MCLXX MCMXX MCXXX MDCXX MDLXX MDXXX MLXXX MMCXX MMDXX MMLXX MMMXX MMXXX SKNXX

XY•••
XYLEM

X••Y•
XRAYS

•X•Y•
OXEYE

•X••Y
IXNAY

••XY•
HEXYL

••X•Y
BIXBY COXEY LAXLY SIXTY

•••XY
DEOXY EPOXY FLAXY PREXY PROXY

YA•••
YABBA YACHT YACKS YADIM YAHOO YAKOV YAKUT YALIE YALOW YALTA YAMPA YANKS YANNI YAPOK YAQUI YARDS YARER YARNS YASIR YATES YAWED YAWLS YAWNS YAWPS YAXES YAXIS YAZOO

Y•A••
YEANS YEARN YEARS YEAST YEATS YUANS

Y••A•
YMCAS YOGAS YUGAS YUMAN YUMAS YWCAS

Y•••A
YABBA YALTA YAMPA YENTA YERBA YORBA YUCCA

•YA••
AYAHS CYANO DYADS HYAMS HYATT KYACK KYATS NYACK NYALA NYASA WYATT

•Y•A•
BYFAR BYLAW BYWAY CYCAD CYMAE CYMAS DYLAN EYRAS GYRAL HYLAS HYMAN HYRAX LYMAN MYLAR MYNAH MYNAS MYWAY OYVAY TYNAN WYMAN

•Y••A
HYDRA HYENA HYPHA KYOGA LYCRA LYDIA LYNDA LYTTA MYRNA NYALA NYASA SYRIA TYPEA

••YA•
ARYAN BAYAR BOYAR BRYAN DAYAK DAYAN DRYAD FLYAT GAYAL HOYAS KAYAK LOYAL MAYAN MAYAS RIYAL ROYAL SOYAS

••Y•A
ADYTA ASYLA ETYMA LAYLA PHYLA RHYTA TAYRA TWYLA

•••YA
ABAYA DARYA FREYA KENYA LENYA LIBYA ORIYA PLAYA SEEYA SONYA TANYA TONYA VANYA

Y•B••
YABBA YOBBO

Y••B•
YABBA YERBA YOBBO YORBA

•YB••
CYBER GYBED GYBES SYBIL

•Y••B
TYPEB

••YB•
FLYBY LAYBY MAYBE

Y•C••
YACHT YACKS YECCH YMCAS YUCCA YUCKY YWCAS

Y••C•
YECCH YUCCA

Y•••C
YOGIC

•YC••
CYCAD CYCLE CYCLO LYCEE LYCRA MYCIN SYCEE SYCES TYCHE TYCHO

•Y•C•
KYACK LYNCH NYACK SYNCS

•Y••C
CYNIC LYRIC PYRIC

••YC•
ALYCE BRYCE CAYCE GLYCO JOYCE PHYCO PRYCE PSYCH ROYCE

•••YC
ENCYC

Y•D••
YADIM YODEL YODHS

Y••D•
YARDS

Y•••D
YAWED YIELD YOKED

•YD••
CYDER EYDIE HYDRA HYDRO LYDIA RYDER SYDOW

•Y•D•
BYRDS CYNDI DYADS LYNDA LYNDE

•Y••D
CYCAD DYFED GYBED GYVED HYOID HYPED SYNOD TYPED

••YD•
CLYDE HAYDN

••Y•D
BAYED DRYAD GUYED HAYED KEYED PAYED RAYED TOYED

•••YD
ALKYD CLWYD FLOYD LLOYD SLOYD THEYD

YE•••
YEANS YEARN YEARS YEAST YEATS YECCH YEGGS YELLS YELPS YEMEN YENTA YENTE YENTL YERBA YERKS YESES YESNO YETIS

Y•E••
YIELD

Y••E•
YARER YATES YAWED YAXES YEMEN YESES YIKES YIPES YODEL YOKED YOKEL YOKES YPRES

Y•••E
YALIE YENTE YOURE YOUSE YOUVE

•YE••
AYERS DYERS EYERS HYENA LYELL MYELO MYERS MYEYE NYETS WYETH

•Y•E•
AYRES BYNER BYRES BYTES CYBER CYDER CYMES DYFED DYNEL DYNES EYRES FYKES GYBED GYBES GYRES GYVED GYVES HYPED HYPER HYPES KYSER LYCEE LYRES MYLES NYMET NYNEX PYRES PYREX RYDER SYCEE SYCES TYKES TYLER TYNES TYPEA TYPEB TYPED TYPEE TYPER TYPES TYPEY TYRES WYLER XYLEM

•Y••E
BYRNE CYCLE CYMAE EYDIE EYRIE KYRIE LYCEE LYNDE LYNNE MYEYE MYOPE PYXIE SYCEE SYNGE TYCHE TYPEE WYLIE WYTHE

••YE•
ABYES ASYET BAYED BAYER BOYER BUYER COYER CRYER DIYER DOYEN DRYER FEYER FLYER FOYER FRYER GAYER GUYED HAYED HAYEK HAYES KEYED KEYES LAYER MAYER MEYER NOYES NUYEN PAYED PAYEE PAYER RAYED REYES SAYER SHYER SKYEY SLYER TOYED WRYER

••Y•E
ALYCE BAYLE BEYLE BOYLE BOYNE BRYCE CAYCE CLYDE DAYNE DOYLE ELYSE FOYLE GAYLE HEYSE HOYLE JAYNE JOYCE LAYNE LEYTE MAYBE PAYEE PAYNE PHYFE PHYLE PRYCE RHYME ROYCE SLYPE STYLE STYNE THYME TRYME WAYNE WHYME WHYRE

•••YE
MYEYE OXEYE REDYE TEVYE

•YF••
BYFAR DYFED

••YF•
PHYFE

Y•G••
YEGGS YOGAS YOGHS YOGIC YOGIS YUGAS YUGOS

Y••G•
YEGGS

Y•••G
YOUNG

•YG••
BYGUM HYGRO MYGUY PYGMY

•Y•G•
KYOGA SYNGE

•Y••G
DYING

HYING LYING TYING VYING

Y•H••
YAHOO

Y••H•
YACHT YODHS YOGHS

Y•••H
YECCH YOUTH

•Y•H•
AYAHS HYPHA MYTHS TYCHE TYCHO WYTHE

•Y••H
LYMPH LYNCH MYNAH MYRRH NYMPH SYLPH WYETH

••Y•H
BLYTH GLYPH PSYCH SMYTH

YI•••
YIELD YIKES YIPES

Y••I•
YADIM YALIE YASIR YAXIS YETIS YOGIC YOGIS YUPIK

Y•••I
YANNI YAQUI YOKOI

•YI••
AYINS DYING HYING LYING TYING VYING

•Y•I•
CYNIC CYRIL EYDIE EYRIE EYRIR HYOID KYLIX KYRIE LYDIA LYRIC LYSIN MYCIN MYSIN PYRIC PYXIE PYXIS SYBIL SYRIA WYLIE

•Y••I
CYNDI

••YI•
FLYIN KEYIN LAYIN PAYIN ZAYIN

••Y•I
PHYSI SPYRI STYLI

Y•K••
YAKOV YAKUT YIKES YOKED YOKEL YOKES YOKOI YOKUM YUKON

Y••K•
YACKS YANKS YERKS YOLKS YOLKY YUCKY

Y•••K
YAPOK YUPIK YUROK

•YK••
FYKES TYKES

•Y••K
KYACK NYACK

••YK•
ROYKO

••Y•K
DAYAK HAYEK KAYAK

Y•L••
YALIE YALOW YALTA YELLS YELPS YOLKS YOLKY

Y••L•
YAWLS YELLS YIELD YOULL YOWLS

Y•••L
YENTL YODEL YOKEL YOULL

•YL••
BYLAW DYLAN HYLAS KYLIX MYLAR MYLES NYLON PYLON SYLPH TYLER WYLER WYLIE XYLEM

•Y•L•
CYCLE CYCLO LYELL MYELO NYALA

•Y••L
CYRIL DYNEL GYRAL KYZYL LYELL LYSOL SYBIL TYROL

••YL•
ACYLS AMYLO AMYLS ASYLA BAYLE BEYLE BOYLE COYLY DOYLE DOYLY DRYLY FEYLY FOYLE GAYLE GAYLY HOYLE IDYLL IDYLS LAYLA PHYLA PHYLE PHYLL SHYLY SLYLY STYLE STYLI STYLO TWYLA WHYLL WRYLY

••Y•L
GAYAL IDYLL LOYAL PHYLL RIYAL ROYAL WHYLL

•••YL
ALKYL ALLYL BERYL BUTYL DARYL ETHYL HEXYL KYZYL MERYL SIBYL VINYL

YM•••
YMCAS

Y•M••
YAMPA YEMEN YUMAN YUMAS YUMMY

Y••M•
YUMMY

Y•••M
YADIM YOKUM

•YM••
CYMAE CYMAS CYMES CYMRY GYMNO HYMAN HYMNS LYMAN LYMON LYMPH NYMET NYMPH WYMAN

•Y•M•
HYAMS PYGMY

•Y••M
BYGUM XYLEM

••YM•
ETYMA RHYME STYMY THYME THYMY TRYME WHYME

••Y•M
ABYSM

Y•N••
YANKS YANNI YENTA YENTE YENTL

Y••N•
YANNI YARNS YAWNS YEANS YESNO YOUNG YOUNT YUANS

Y•••N
YEARN YEMEN YUKON YUMAN

•YN••
BYNER BYNOW CYNDI CYNIC DYNEL DYNES LYNCH LYNDA LYNDE LYNNE MYNAH MYNAS NYNEX SYNCS SYNGE SYNOD TYNAN TYNES

•Y•N•
AYINS BYRNE CYANO DYING GYMNO HYENA HYING HYMNS HYPNO LYING LYNNE LYONS MYRNA TYING VYING

•Y••N
BYRON DYLAN GYRON HYMAN HYSON LYMAN LYMON LYSIN MYCIN MYRON MYSIN NYLON PYLON TYNAN TYSON WYMAN

••YN•
BOYNE DAYNE FLYNN GWYNN JAYNE LAYNE MAYNT PAYNE STYNE WAYNE

••Y•N
ARYAN BRYAN DAYAN DOYEN FLYIN FLYNN GWYNN HAYDN KEYIN LAYIN LAYON MAYAN MAYON NUYEN PAYIN RAYON SPYON TOYON TRYON ZAYIN

•••YN
EMLYN OBGYN WOMYN

YO•••
YOBBO YODEL YODHS YOGAS YOGHS YOGIC YOGIS YOKED YOKEL YOKES YOKOI YOKUM YOLKS YOLKY YORBA YOULL YOUNG YOUNT YOURE YOURS YOUSE YOUTH YOUVE YOWLS YOYOS

Y••O•
YAHOO YAKOV YALOW YAPOK YAZOO YOKOI YOYOS YUGOS YUKON YUROK

Y•••O
YAHOO YAZOO YESNO YOBBO

•YO••
EYOTS HYOID KYOGA KYOTO LYONS MYOPE RYOTS

•Y•O•
BYNOW BYRON GYRON GYROS HYPOS HYSON LYMON LYSOL MYRON NYLON PYLON SYDOW SYNOD SYSOP TYPOS TYROL TYROS TYSON

•Y••O
CYANO CYCLO GYMNO HYDRO HYGRO HYPNO HYPSO KYOTO MYELO TYCHO

••YO•
BAYOU BOYOS GUYOT KAYOS LAYON MAYON MAYOR PRYOR RAYON SPYON TOYON TRYON YOYOS

••Y•O
AMYLO GLYCO LAYTO MAYPO PHYCO PHYTO ROYKO SAYSO STYLO

•••YO
SANYO TOKYO

YP•••
YPRES

Y•P••
YAPOK YIPES YUPIK

Y••P•
YAMPA YAWPS YELPS

•YP••
GYPSY HYPED HYPER HYPES HYPHA HYPNO HYPOS HYPSO TYPEA TYPEB TYPED TYPEE TYPER TYPES TYPEY TYPOS

•Y•P•
LYMPH MYOPE NYMPH SYLPH

•Y••P
SYRUP SYSOP

••YP•
COYPU CRYPT EGYPT GLYPH MAYPO SLYPE

••Y•P
BUYUP DRYUP KEYUP LAYUP PAYUP

•••YP
POLYP

Y•Q••
YAQUI

Y•R••
YARDS YARER YARNS YERBA YERKS YORBA YPRES YUROK YURTS

Y••R•
YEARN YEARS YOURE YOURS

Y•••R
YARER YASIR

•YR••
AYRES BYRDS BYRES BYRNE BYRON CYRIL CYRUS EYRAS EYRES EYRIE EYRIR GYRAL GYRES GYRON GYROS GYRUS HYRAX KYRIE LYRES LYRIC MYRNA MYRON MYRRH PYRES PYREX PYRIC SYRIA SYRUP TYRES TYROL TYROS

•Y•R•
AYERS CYMRY DYERS EYERS HYDRA HYDRO HYGRO LYCRA MYERS MYRRH

•Y••R
BYFAR BYNER CYBER CYDER EYRIR HYPER KYSER MYLAR RYDER TYLER TYPER WYLER

••YR•
SPYRI TAYRA WHYRE

••Y•R
BAYAR BAYER BOYAR BOYER BUYER COYER CRYER DIYER DRYER FEYER FLYER FOYER FRYER GAYER LAYER MAYER MAYOR MEYER PAYER PRYOR SAYER SHYER SLYER WRYER

•••YR
ASSYR SATYR

Y•S••
YASIR YESES YESNO

Y••S•
YEAST YOUSE

Y•••S
YACKS YANKS YARDS YARNS YATES YAWLS YAWNS YAWPS YAXES YAXIS YEANS YEARS YEATS YEGGS YELLS YELPS YERKS YESES YETIS YIKES YIPES YMCAS YODHS YOGAS YOGHS YOGIS YOKES YOLKS YOURS YOWLS YOYOS YPRES YUANS YUGAS YUGOS YUMAS YURTS YWCAS

•YS••
HYSON KYSER LYSIN LYSOL MYSIN SYSOP TYSON

•Y•S•
GYPSY HYPSO NYASA

•Y••S
AYAHS AYERS AYINS AYRES BYRDS BYRES BYTES CYMAS CYMES CYRUS DYADS DYERS DYNES EYERS EYOTS EYRAS EYRES FYKES GYBES GYRES GYROS GYRUS GYVES HYAMS HYLAS HYMNS HYPES HYPOS KYATS LYONS LYRES MYERS MYLES MYNAS MYTHS NYETS PYRES PYXIS RYOTS SYCES SYNCS TYKES TYNES TYPES TYPOS TYRES TYROS

••YS•
ABYSM ABYSS ELYSE HEYSE MAYST PHYSI SAYSO TRYST

••Y•S
ABYES ABYSS ACYLS AMYLS BOYOS HAYES HOYAS IDYLS KAYOS KEYES MAYAS NOYES REYES SOYAS YOYOS

•••YS
AHOYS ATTYS BABYS BBOYS BRAYS BUOYS CHRYS CLAYS CLOYS DAVYS DENYS DRAYS EMMYS FLAYS FLEYS FRAYS GLEYS GRAYS GREYS JOEYS LADYS MACYS MARYS OBEYS OKAYS PEPYS PLAYS PLOYS POWYS PRAYS PREYS QUAYS SHAYS SLAYS SPAYS STAYS SWAYS TONYS TRAYS TREYS WHEYS XRAYS

Y•T••
YATES YETIS

Y••T•
YALTA YEATS YENTA YENTE YENTL YOUTH YURTS

Y•••T
YACHT YAKUT YEAST YOUNT

•YT••
BYTES LYTTA MYTHS WYTHE

•Y•T•
EYOTS HYATT KYATS KYOTO LYTTA NYETS RYOTS WYATT WYETH

•Y••T
HYATT NYMET WYATT

••YT•
ADYTA BLYTH LAYTO LEYTE PAYTV PHYTO RHYTA SMYTH

••Y•T
ASYET ASYUT CRYPT EGYPT FLYAT GUYOT MAYNT MAYST TRYST

YU•••
YUANS YUCCA YUCKY YUGAS YUGOS YUKON YUMAN YUMAS YUMMY YUPIK YUROK YURTS

Y•U••
YOULL YOUNG YOUNT YOURE YOURS YOUSE YOUTH YOUVE

Y••U•
YAKUT YAQUI YOKUM

•Y•U•
BYGUM CYRUS GYRUS MYGUY SYRUP

••YU•
ASYUT BUYUP DRYUP KEYUP LAYUP PAYUP SOYUZ

••Y•U
BAYOU COYPU

•••YU
SHOYU

Y••V•
YOUVE

Y•••V
YAKOV

•YV••
GYVED GYVES OYVAY

••Y•V
PAYTV

YW•••
YWCAS

Y•W••
YAWED YAWLS YAWNS YAWPS YOWLS

Y•••W
YALOW

•YW••
BYWAY MYWAY

•Y••W
BYLAW BYNOW SYDOW

Y•X••
YAXES YAXIS

•YX••
PYXIE PYXIS

•Y••X
HYRAX KYLIX NYNEX PYREX

•••YX
CALYX

Y•Y••
YOYOS

Y•••Y
YOLKY YUCKY YUMMY

•Y•Y•
KYZYL MYEYE

•Y••Y
BYWAY CYMRY GYPSY MYGUY MYWAY OYVAY PYGMY TYPEY

••Y•Y
COYLY DOYLY DRYLY FEYLY FLYBY GAYLY LAYBY SHYLY SKYEY SLYLY STYMY THYMY WRYLY

Y•Z••
YAZOO

•YZ••
KYZYL

••Y•Z
SOYUZ

ZA•••
ZAIRE ZAMIA ZANTE ZAPPA ZAPPY ZARFS ZAXES ZAXIS ZAYIN ZAZEN

Z•A••
ZBARS ZEALS

Z••A•
ZETAS ZOEAE ZOEAL ZOEAS ZOHAR ZONAL

Z•••A
ZAMIA ZAPPA ZEBRA ZELDA ZENDA ZIZKA ZORBA

•ZA••
AZANS CZARS IZAAK IZARD IZARS OZARK OZAWA TZARS UZALA

•Z•A•
IZAAK IZBAS

•Z••A
AZUSA OZAWA UZALA

••ZA•
ANZAC HAZAN KAZAK KAZAN LAZAR MIZAR MUZAK NIZAM

••Z•A
HUZZA MAZDA PIZZA TAZZA ZIZKA

•••ZA
BAIZA DANZA ELIZA GINZA GROZA HUZZA IBIZA LANZA LEEZA MONZA PANZA PENZA PINZA PIZZA PLAZA TAZZA TERZA TISZA

ZB•••
ZBARS

Z•B••
ZEBRA ZEBUS ZIBET ZUBIN

Z••B•
ZORBA

•ZB••
IZBAS UZBEK

Z••C•
ZILCH ZINCS ZINCY

Z•••C
ZENIC

•Z•C•
CZECH

•Z••C
AZOIC AZTEC

••ZC•
CUZCO

••Z•C
ANZAC

Z••D•
ZELDA ZENDA ZENDO ZENDS

Z•••D
ZONED ZOOID

•Z•D•
AZIDE

•Z••D
IZARD SZOLD

••ZD•
MAZDA

••Z•D
DAZED DOZED FAZED FUZED GAZED HAZED LAZED OOZED RAZED SIZED

ZE•••
ZEALS ZEBRA ZEBUS ZEINS ZEISS ZEIST ZELDA ZELIG ZENDA ZENDO ZENDS ZENIC ZEPPO ZEROS ZESTS ZESTY ZETAS ZEVON

Z•E••
ZOEAE ZOEAL ZOEAS ZWEIG

Z••E•
ZAXES ZAZEN ZIBET ZINES ZONED ZONES ZOOEY

Z•••E
ZAIRE ZANTE ZOEAE ZOWIE

•ZE••
CZECH SZELL

•Z•E•
AZTEC UZBEK

•Z••E
AZIDE AZINE AZOTE AZURE OZONE OZZIE

••ZE•
ADZES BEZEL BIZET COZEN COZES DAZED DAZES

DIZEN
DOZED
DOZEN
DOZER
DOZES
ETZEL
FAZED
FAZES
FUZED
FUZEE
GAZED
GAZER
GAZES
HAZED
HAZEL
HAZER
HAZES
LAZED
LAZES
MAZEL
MAZER
MAZES
NIZER
OOZED
OOZES
OUZEL
RAZED
RAZES
SIZED
SIZER
SIZES
WIZEN
ZAZEN

••Z•E
FUZEE
OZZIE

•••ZE
AGAZE
AMAZE
BAIZE
BLAZE
BONZE
BOOZE
BRAZE
CRAZE
CROZE
DRUZE
FROZE
FURZE
GAUZE
GLAZE
GLOZE
GRAZE
MAIZE
PRIZE
SEIZE
SMAZE
WINZE

Z••F•
ZARFS

Z•G••
ZIGGY

Z••G•
ZIGGY
ZINGS
ZINGY

Z•••G
ZELIG
ZWEIG

••Z•G
ABZUG

Z•H••
ZOHAR

Z•••H
ZILCH

•Z••H
AZOTH
CZECH

ZI•••
ZIBET
ZIGGY
ZILCH
ZILLS
ZINCS
ZINCY
ZINES
ZINGS
ZINGY
ZIPPY
ZIPUP
ZITIS
ZIZKA

Z•I••
ZAIRE
ZEINS
ZEISS
ZEIST

Z••I•
ZAMIA
ZAXIS
ZAYIN
ZELIG
ZENIC
ZITIS
ZOOID
ZORIL
ZORIS
ZOWIE
ZUBIN
ZUNIS
ZWEIG

•ZI••
AZIDE
AZINE

•Z•I•
AZOIC
IZMIR
IZMIT
OZZIE

••ZI•
ANZIO
OZZIE
UNZIP

••Z•I
BUZZI

•••ZI
BUZZI
ELAZI
GHAZI
MITZI
PONZI
SWAZI

Z•K••
ZUKOR

Z••K•
ZIZKA
ZONKS
ZOUKS

•Z••K
IZAAK
OZARK
UZBEK

••ZK•
ZIZKA

••Z•K
KAZAK
MUZAK

ZL•••
ZLOTY

Z•L••
ZELDA
ZELIG
ZILCH
ZILLS
ZULUS

Z••L•
ZEALS
ZILLS

Z•••L
ZOEAL
ZONAL
ZORIL

•Z•L•
SZELL
SZOLD
UZALA

•Z••L
SZELL

••Z•L
BEZEL
ETZEL
HAZEL
KYZYL
MAZEL
OUZEL

•••ZL
HERZL

Z•M••
ZAMIA

Z••M•
ZOOMS

•ZM••
IZMIR
IZMIT

••ZM•
GIZMO

••Z•M
NIZAM

•••ZM
PRIZM

Z•N••
ZANTE
ZENDA
ZENDO
ZENDS
ZENIC
ZINCS
ZINCY
ZINES
ZINGS
ZINGY
ZONAL
ZONED
ZONES
ZONKS
ZUNIS

Z••N•
ZEINS
ZOONS

Z•••N
ZAYIN
ZAZEN
ZEVON
ZUBIN

•Z•N•
AZANS
AZINE
OZONE

••Z•N
COZEN
DIZEN
DOZEN
HAZAN
KAZAN
LUZON
WIZEN
ZAZEN

ZO•••
ZOEAE
ZOEAL
ZOEAS
ZOHAR
ZONAL
ZONED
ZONES
ZONKS
ZOOEY
ZOOID
ZOOMS
ZOONS
ZORBA
ZORIL
ZORIS
ZORRO
ZOUKS
ZOWIE

Z•O••
ZLOTY
ZOOEY
ZOOID
ZOOMS
ZOONS

Z••O•
ZEROS
ZEVON
ZUKOR
ZZTOP

Z•••O
ZENDO
ZEPPO
ZORRO

•ZO••
AZOIC
AZOTE
AZOTH
OZONE
SZOLD

•Z•O•
ZZTOP

••ZO•
BOZOS
KAZOO
LUZON
ORZOS
OUZOS
RAZOR
YAZOO

••Z•O
ANZIO
CUZCO
GIZMO
KAZOO
MEZZO
RIZZO
YAZOO

•••ZO
BENZO
BONZO
DIAZO
GONZO
MATZO
MEZZO
RHIZO
RIZZO

Z•P••
ZAPPA
ZAPPY
ZEPPO
ZIPPY
ZIPUP

Z••P•
ZAPPA
ZAPPY
ZEPPO
ZIPPY

Z•••P
ZIPUP
ZZTOP

•Z••P
ZZTOP

••Z•P
UNZIP

Z•R••
ZARFS
ZEROS
ZORBA
ZORIL
ZORIS
ZORRO

Z••R•
ZAIRE
ZBARS
ZEBRA
ZORRO

Z•••R
ZOHAR
ZUKOR

•Z•R•
AZURE
CZARS
IZARD
IZARS
OZARK
TZARS

•Z••R
IZMIR

••Z•R
DOZER
GAZER
HAZER
LAZAR
MAZER
MIZAR
NIZER
RAZOR
SIZER

Z•S••
ZESTS
ZESTY

Z••S•
ZEISS
ZEIST

Z•••S
ZARFS
ZAXES
ZAXIS
ZBARS
ZEALS
ZEBUS
ZEINS
ZEISS
ZENDS
ZEROS
ZESTS
ZETAS
ZILLS
ZINCS
ZINES
ZINGS
ZITIS
ZOEAS
ZONES
ZONKS
ZOOMS
ZOONS
ZORIS
ZOUKS
ZULUS
ZUNIS

•Z•S•
AZUSA

•Z••S
AZANS
CZARS
IZARS
IZBAS
TZARS

••Z•S
ADZES
BOZOS
COZES
DAZES
DOZES
FAZES
GAZES
HAZES
LAZES
MAZES
OOZES
ORZOS
OUZOS
RAZES
SIZES

Z•T••
ZETAS
ZITIS
ZZTOP

Z••T•
ZANTE
ZESTS
ZESTY
ZLOTY

Z•••T
ZEIST
ZIBET

•ZT••
AZTEC
ZZTOP

•Z•T•
AZOTE
AZOTH

•Z••T
IZMIT

••Z•T
BIZET

•••ZT
LISZT

ZU•••
ZUBIN
ZUKOR
ZULUS
ZUNIS

Z•U••
ZOUKS

Z••U•
ZEBUS
ZIPUP
ZULUS

•ZU••
AZURE
AZUSA

••ZU•
ABZUG

•••ZU
ISUZU
KANZU
KUDZU

Z•V••
ZEVON

ZW•••
ZWEIG

Z•W••
ZOWIE

•Z•W•
OZAWA

Z•X••
ZAXES
ZAXIS

Z•Y••
ZAYIN

Z•••Y
ZAPPY
ZESTY
ZIGGY
ZINCY
ZINGY
ZIPPY
ZLOTY
ZOOEY

••ZY•
KYZYL

••Z•Y
DIZZY
FIZZY
FUZZY
JAZZY
MUZZY
TIZZY

•••ZY
CRAZY
DITZY
DIZZY
DOOZY
FIZZY
FUZZY
GAUZY
JAZZY
JERZY
KRAZY
MUZZY
ORCZY
RITZY
TIZZY
WOOZY

ZZ•••
ZZTOP

Z•Z••
ZAZEN
ZIZKA

•ZZ••
OZZIE

••ZZ•
BUZZI
DIZZY
FIZZY
FUZZY
HUZZA
JAZZY
MEZZO
MUZZY
PIZZA
RIZZO
TAZZA
TIZZY

•••ZZ
ABUZZ
CHAZZ
FRIZZ
SCUZZ

AA••••
AACHEN
AAFAIR
AAHING

A•A•••
ABACAS
ABACUS
ABASED
ABASES
ABATED
ABATES
ABATIS
ACACIA
ACADIA
ACAJOU
ACARID
ACARUS
ADAGES
ADAGIO
ADAPTS
AGADIR
AGAMAS
AGARIC
AGASSI
AGATES
AGATHA
AGAVES
AJANTA
ALAMOS
ALANIS
ALANON
ALARIC
ALARMS
ALARUM
ALASKA
ALATAU
ALATED
AMADIS
AMADOU
AMAJOR
AMALFI
AMALIE
AMANDA
AMATIS
AMATOL
AMAZED
AMAZES
AMAZON
ANACIN
ANADEM
ANALOG
ANANDA
ANATTO
APACHE
APATHY
ARABIA
ARABIC
ARABLE
ARAFAT
ARAGON
ARALIA
ARALLU
ARAMIS
ARARAT
ARAWAK
ASANAS
ATAMAN
AVAILS
AVALON
AVANTI
AVATAR
AVAUNT
AWAITS
AWAKED
AWAKEN
AWAKES
AWARDS
AZALEA

A••A••
AAFAIR
ABBACY
ABLATE
ABLAUT
ABLAZE
ABOARD
ABRADE
ABRAMS
ACHAEA
ACKACK
ACUATE
ADDAMS
ADJANI
ADMASS
ADNATE
AERATE
AFEARD
AFFAIR
AFLAME
AFLATS
AFRAID
AFRAME
AGHAST
AGLAIA
AGLARE
AGNATE
AIRARM
AKUAKU
ALBANO
ALBANY
ALCAPP
ALEAST
ALKALI
ALLAYS
ALMATY
ALPACA
ALSACE
ALTAIC
ALTAIR
ALTARS
ALWAYS
AMBATO
AMHARA
ANKARA
ANNABA
ANNALS
ANSARA
ANSATE
ANWANG
ANYANG
AODAIS
APIARY
APPALL
APPALS
AQUATE
ARCADE
ARCANA
ARCANE
ARCARO
ARGALI
ARMADA
ARMAGH
ARMAND
ARMANI
ARRACK
ARRANT
ARRAYS
ARVADA
ARYANS
ASGARD
ASHARP
ASIANS
ASKARI
ASLANT
ASMARA
ASSAIL
ASSAYS
ATBATS
ATEAMS
ATEASE
ATHAND
ATLAST
ATLATL
ATTACH
ATTACK
ATTAIN
ATTARS
AUBADE
AUFAIT
AULAIT
AUPAIR
AVIANS
AVIARY
AVIATE
AWEARY
AYEAYE
AYMARA

A•••A•
ABACAS
ABORAL
ABROAD
ABSCAM
ACETAL
ACTSAS
ACTUAL
ADIDAS
ADONAI
ADRIAN
AEGEAN
AENEAS
AERIAL
AFFRAY
AFGHAN
AFLOAT
AGAMAS
AGENAS
AGLEAM
AGORAE
AGORAS
AIMSAT
AIRBAG
AIRDAM
AIRMAN
AIRSAC
AIRWAY
AKELAS
AKITAS
ALATAU
ALEGAR
ALEMAN
ALLDAY
ALLMAN
ALOHAS
ALOMAR
ALPHAS
ALTMAN
ALULAE
ALULAR
AMEBAE
AMEBAS
AMIGAS
AMORAL
AMTRAC
AMTRAK
AMYTAN
ANDEAN
ANIMAL
ANIMAS
ANNEAL
ANNUAL
ANORAK
ANSGAR
ANURAN
ANYDAY
ANYWAY
AORTAE
AORTAL
AORTAS
AOUDAD
APEMAN
APICAL
APODAL
APPEAL
APPEAR
APPIAN
ARAFAT
ARARAT
ARAWAK
ARCTAN
ARECAS
ARENAS
AROMAS
ARREAR
ARUBAN
ASANAS
ASCHAM
ASHCAN
ASHLAR
ASHRAM
ASOSAN
ASTRAL
ASTRAY
ATAMAN
ATONAL
ATRIAL
ATTHAT
AUDIAL
AUGEAN
AVATAR
AVOWAL
AXONAL

A••••A
ABOLLA
ACACIA
ACADIA
ACEDIA
ACHAEA
ADNEXA
AEOLIA
AFRICA
AGATHA
AGENDA
AGLAIA
AHIMSA
AJANTA
ALASKA
ALEXIA
ALICIA
ALPACA
ALTHEA
ALTIMA
ALUMNA
ALYSSA
AMANDA
AMELIA
AMENRA
AMHARA
AMOEBA
ANANDA
ANCONA
ANDREA
ANEMIA
ANGELA
ANGLIA
ANGOLA
ANGORA
ANITRA
ANKARA
ANNABA
ANNIKA
ANSARA
APULIA
AQUILA
ARABIA
ARALIA
ARBELA
ARCANA
AREOLA
ARETHA
ARISTA
ARJUNA
ARMADA
ARNICA
ARRIBA
ARROBA
ARVADA
ASMARA
ASPERA
ATHENA
ATTICA
ATTILA
AURIGA
AURORA
AVESTA
AXILLA
AYESHA
AYMARA
AZALEA

•AA•••
BAAING
LAAGER
PAANGA

•A•A••
AAFAIR
BABALU
BACALL
BAHAMA
BALAAM
BALATA
BAMAKO
BANANA
BASALT
BATAAN
BAYARD
BAZAAR
CABALA
CABALS
CABANA
CACAOS
CALAIS
CALASH
CAMARO
CANAAN
CANADA
CANALS
CANAPE
CANARD
CANARY
CARAFE
CARATS
CASABA
CASALS
CASAVA
DACAPO
DAGAMA
DALASI
DAMAGE
DAMASK
DAMATO
DANANG
DANAUS
DATARY
FACADE
FALANA
FARADS
FATALE
GALAGO
GALAHS
GALATA
GALAXY
GAMAYS
GARAGE
GAWAIN
GAYALS
HABANA
HAMALS
HARALD
HARARE
HARASS
HATARI
HAVANA
HAVASU
HAWAII
HAZANS
HAZARD
JACALS
JACANA
JALAPA
JAMAAL
JAPANS
JAVARI
KAKAPO
KALAKH
KAMALA
KANAKA
KARATE
KARATS
KAYAKS
KAZAKH
KAZAKS
LAGASH
LALALA
LAMARR
LAMAZE
LANAIS
LANARK
LANATE
LARAMS
LAVABO
LAVAGE
MACACO
MACAWS
MADAME
MADAMS
MAKALU
MALABO
MALADY
MALAGA
MALATE
MALAWI
MALAYA
MALAYS
MANAGE
MANAMA
MANANA
MANAUS
MARACA
MARAUD
MASADA
MASAIS
MAYANS
NAGANO
NAIADS
NAMATH
NASALS
NATANT
NAVAHO
NAVAJO
NAWABS
OAXACA
PADANG
PAEANS
PAGANS
PAHANG
PAHARI
PAJAMA
PALACE
PALAEO
PALATE
PANADA
PANAMA
PAPACY
PAPAGO
PAPAIN
PAPAWS
PAPAYA
PARADE
PARANA
PARANG
PARAPH
PATACA
PAVANE
QATARI
RABATO
RAFAEL
RAJAHS
RAMADA
RAMATE
RAVAGE
SABATO
SAFARI
SAHARA
SALAAM
SALADO
SALADS
SALALS
SALAMI
SALARY
SAMARA
SARANS
SATANG
SAVAGE
SAVAII
SAVANT
SAVATE
TABARD
TAMALE
TAMARA
TAMAYO
TANAKA
TANANA
TARAWA
TATAMI
TATARS
UAKARI
VACANT
VACATE
VAGARY
WABASH
WASABI
WAYANS
XANADU
YAMAHA
ZAPATA

•A••A•
BABKAS
BADHAM
BADMAN
BAGDAD
BAHIAN
BAIKAL
BAIZAS
BALAAM
BALKAN
BALLAD
BALSAM
BALZAC
BANTAM
BANYAN
BANZAI
BAOBAB
BARCAR
BARKAT
BARMAN
BARTAB
BATAAN
BATEAU
BATMAN
BATYAM
BAZAAR
CAESAR
CAFTAN
CAGUAS
CAIMAN
CALLAO
CALLAS
CALPAC
CAMEAT
CANAAN
CANCAN
CANNAE
CANTAB
CANVAS
CAPIAS
CAPTAN
CARMAN
CARNAL
CARPAL
CASBAH
CASPAR
CASUAL
CATHAY
CATNAP
CAUDAL
CAUSAL
CAVEAT
CAVIAR
CAYMAN
DACHAS
DAEDAL
DAGMAR
DALLAS
DAMMAR
DANNAY
DARNAY
EARLAP
EARWAX
EATSAT
FABIAN
FABRAY
FACIAL
FACIAS
FAISAL
FANTAN
FARRAH
FARRAR
FATCAT
FATWAS
FAUNAE
FAUNAL
FAUNAS
GAGLAW
GAGMAN
GALEAE
GALPAL
GALWAY
GALYAK
GAMMAS
GASBAG
GASCAP
GASMAN
GASPAR
GATEAU
GAVIAL
HABEAS
HAEMAT
HAGMAN
HAIDAS
HAINAN
HALVAH
HANGAR
HANNAH
HARLAN
HASSAM
HASSAN
HAUSAS
HAVEAT
HAWHAW
JABBAR
JACKAL
JAGUAR
JAMAAL
JARRAH
KALKAN
KALMAR
KANSAN
KANSAS
KAPLAN
KAPPAS
KARNAK
KARRAS
KASBAH
KASDAN
KATMAI
KAUNAS
LABIAL
LAMIAS
LAMMAS
LANDAU
LAPHAM
LARIAT
LARVAE
LARVAL
LARVAS
LASCAR
LAWMAN
LAYMAN
MACRAE
MADCAP
MADMAN
MADMAX
MADRAS
MAENAD
MAGMAS
MAGYAR
MAITAI
MAMBAS
MAMMAL
MAMMAS
MANDAN
MANDAY
MANIAC
MANIAS
MANRAY
MANTAS
MANUAL
MAOTAI
MARGAY
MARIAH
MARIAN
MAUMAU
MAYDAY
MAYHAP
MAYTAG
NAIRAS
NARIAL
NARWAL
NASCAR
NASDAQ
NASSAU
NATHAN
NAYSAY
PACMAN
PADUAN
PAISAS
PALEAE
PALLAS
PALMAS
PAMPAS
PANDAS
PAPPAS
PAPUAN
PARCAE
PARIAH
PARKAS
PARKAY
PARLAY
PASCAL
PASHAS
PASTAS
PATHAN
PAWPAW
PAWSAT
PAYDAY
QANTAS
RACIAL
RADIAL
RADIAN
RAGBAG
RAGLAN
RAGMAN
RAGTAG
RAHRAH
RAILAT
RAMEAU
RAMSAY
RASCAL
RASHAD
RATTAN
SABRAS
SACRAL
SADDAM
SAIGAS
SAIPAN
SALAAM
SALMAN
SALSAS
SAMBAL
SAMBAR
SAMBAS
SAMIAM
SAMOAN
SAMPAN
SANDAL
SASHAY
SATRAP
SAUNAS
TABLAS
TAGDAY
TAIGAS
TAINAN
TAIPAN
TAIWAN
TALKAT
TAMTAM
TANKAS
TANOAK
TANOAN
TAPPAN
TARMAC
TARPAN
TARSAL

TARTAN
TARTAR
TARZAN
TASMAN
TAXMAN
TAYRAS
TAZZAS
VACLAV
VANDAL
VARNAS
VASLAV
VASSAL
VASSAR
WAHWAH
WANTAD
WARSAW
WAUSAU
WAYLAY
ZAMIAS

•A•••A

BAHAMA
BAKULA
BALATA
BALBOA
BANANA
BANGKA
BARBRA
BAROJA
CABALA
CABANA
CAMERA
CANADA
CANOLA
CANOVA
CAPITA
CARINA
CASABA
CASAVA
CASSIA
CATENA
CAYUGA
DAGAMA
DAHLIA
DAKOTA
DAMITA
DATURA
EARTHA
FACULA
FAENZA
FAJITA
FALANA
FARINA
FASCIA
FATIMA
GALATA
GALENA
GALLIA
GAMBIA
GARCIA
HABANA
HAVANA
JACANA
JALAPA
JASCHA
KAGERA
KAHLUA
KAHUNA
KAILUA
KAMALA
KANAKA
KARIBA
KAUNDA
LABREA
LACUNA
LADIDA
LADOGA
LAGUNA
LAKOTA
LALALA
LAMBDA
LAMESA
LAMINA
LAPUTA
LAROSA
LATINA
LATONA
LATOYA
LATVIA
MACULA
MADURA
MAKEBA
MAKUTA
MALAGA
MALAYA
MANAMA
MANANA
MANCHA
MANILA
MANTRA
MANTUA
MARACA
MARCIA
MARINA
MARISA
MARKKA
MARSHA
MARTHA
MASADA
MATTEA
MAURYA
MAXIMA
MAZOLA
MAZUMA
NAGOYA
NARNIA
NASHUA
NATURA
NAUSEA
OAXACA
PAANGA
PAELLA
PAGODA
PAJAMA
PAKULA
PALLIA
PALOMA
PAMELA
PANADA
PANAMA
PAPAYA
PARANA
PARULA
PATACA
PATINA
PAYOLA
RADULA
RAFFIA
RAMADA
RAMBLA
RAMONA
SABENA
SAHARA
SALINA
SALIVA
SALVIA
SAMARA
SAMOSA
SANCTA
SANDIA
SANDRA
SARNIA
TABULA
TACOMA
TAMARA
TANAKA
TANANA
TANTRA
TARAWA
VAISYA
VARUNA
WALESA
YAKIMA
YAKUZA
YAMAHA
ZADORA
ZAMBIA
ZAPATA
ZAREBA

••AA••

KRAALS

••A•A•

ABACAS
AGAMAS
ALATAU
ARAFAT
ARARAT
ARAWAK
ASANAS
ATAMAN
AVATAR
BRAVAS
BWANAS
CRAVAT
DRAMAS
FRACAS
GOAWAY
GRABAT
GRAHAM
GRAMAS
GUAVAS
HIATAL
IBADAN
IMAMAN
INAJAM
INAWAY
ISAIAH
IZABAL
KOALAS
LIANAS
LLAMAS
MCADAM
NYALAS
OMAHAN
OMAHAS
PLAGAL
PLANAR
PLAYAS
PLAYAT
PLAZAS
QUASAR
REAGAN
REATAS
RIATAS
RUANAS
RYAZAN
SCALAR
SCARAB
SEABAG
SEAFAN
SEAGAL
SEALAB
SEAMAN
SEAWAY
SHABAN
SHAMAN
SHAZAM
SNAPAT
SRANAN
STABAT
STALAG
SWARAJ
TEABAG
TEARAT
TIARAS
TOAMAN
TRAJAN
UTAHAN

••A••A

ACACIA
ACADIA
AGATHA
AJANTA
ALASKA
AMANDA
ANANDA
ARABIA
ARALIA
AZALEA
BIAFRA
BIANCA
BLANCA
BLANDA
BRAHMA
BRAILA
BRAZZA
CHACHA
CHACMA
CRANIA
DEANNA
DHARMA
ETALIA
EXACTA
FLAVIA
FRANCA
GOANNA
GRADEA
GRAMPA
GRAPPA
GRATIA
ICARIA
ITALIA
ITASCA
JOANNA
KWACHA
KWANZA
LUANDA
MIAMIA
MIASMA
NYASSA
PAANGA
PIAZZA
PLASMA
PRAJNA
PRAVDA
QUAGGA
QUANTA
REALIA
RUANDA
RWANDA
SCALIA
SHANIA
SHARIA
SHASTA
SPARTA
STADIA
STANZA
THALIA
TRAUMA
UGANDA
URANIA
ZSAZSA

•••AA•

BALAAM
BATAAN
BAZAAR
CANAAN
GSTAAD
JAMAAL
SALAAM

•••A•A

ACHAEA
AGLAIA
ALPACA
AMHARA
ANKARA
ANNABA
ANSARA
ARCANA
ARMADA
ARVADA
ASMARA
AYMARA
BAHAMA
BALATA
BANANA
BEMATA
CABALA
CABANA
CANADA
CASABA
CASAVA
CICADA
CLOACA
COLADA
CUIABA
CUNAXA
DAGAMA
DOUALA
ERRATA
ESPANA
FALANA
GALATA
GELADA
GEMARA
GUIANA
GUYANA
HABANA
HAVANA
HIVAOA
IGUANA
ILEANA
IMPALA
INDABA
ITHACA
JACANA
JALAPA
JICAMA
JUDAEA
JUMADA
KAMALA
KANAKA
KERALA
LALALA
LUSAKA
MALAGA
MALAYA
MANAMA
MANANA
MARACA
MASADA
MEDAKA
MEGARA
MORAVA
MUFASA
NEVADA
NICAEA
OAXACA
OGLALA
OKSANA
OOLALA
ORGANA
ORIANA
OSHAWA
OTTAVA
OTTAWA
PAJAMA
PANADA
PANAMA
PAPAYA
PARANA
PATACA
PESAWA
PICARA
PINATA
PIRANA
POSADA
PYJAMA
RAMADA
RENATA
ROXANA
SAHARA
SAMARA
SEDAKA
SOMATA
SONATA
STRATA
TAMARA
TANAKA
TANANA
TARAWA
TIRANA
TUCANA
UMTATA
URBANA
YAMAHA
YUKATA
YUKAWA
ZAPATA
ZENANA

AB••••

ABACAS
ABACUS
ABASED
ABASES
ABATED
ABATES
ABATIS
ABBACY
ABBESS
ABBEYS
ABBOTS
ABBOTT
ABDUCT
ABELES
ABESSE
ABHORS
ABIDED
ABIDES
ABJECT
ABJURE
ABLATE
ABLAUT
ABLAZE
ABLEST
ABLOOM
ABLUSH
ABOARD
ABODES
ABOHMS
ABOLLA
ABOMBS
ABORAL
ABORTS
ABOUND
ABRADE
ABRAMS
ABROAD
ABRUPT
ABSCAM
ABSENT
ABSORB
ABSURD
ABUKIR
ABUSED
ABUSER
ABUSES
ABYDOS
ABYING
ABYSMS

A•B•••

ABBACY
ABBESS
ABBEYS
ABBOTS
ABBOTT
ALBANO
ALBANY
ALBEDO
ALBEIT
ALBERT
ALBINO
ALBION
ALBOIN
ALBORG
ALBUMS
AMBATO
AMBERS
AMBERY
AMBITS
AMBLED
AMBLER
AMBLES
AMBLIN
AMBUSH
ARBELA
ARBORS
ARBOUR
ASBURY
ATBATS
ATBEST
AUBADE
AUBREY
AUBURN

A••B••

ADOBES
AIRBAG
AIRBUS
ALIBIS
ALIBLE
ALLBUT
AMEBAE
AMEBAS
AMEBIC
ANUBIS
ARABIA
ARABIC
ARABLE
ARUBAN

A•••B•

ABOMBS
ACHEBE
ADLIBS
AEROBE
AKIMBO
AMOEBA
ANNABA
ARDEBS
ARRIBA
ARROBA

A••••B

ABSORB
ADSORB
ADVERB
APLOMB

•AB•••

BABALU
BABBLE
BABELS
BABIED
BABIES
BABKAS
BABOON
BABSON
BABULS
CABALA
CABALS
CABANA
CABBED
CABBIE
CABERS
CABINS
CABLED
CABLER
CABLES
DABBED
DABBLE
DABNEY
FABIAN
FABLED
FABLER
FABLES
FABRAY
FABRIC
GABBED
GABBER
GABBLE
GABBRO
GABIES
GABION
GABLED
GABLER
GABLES
HABANA
HABEAS
HABILE
HABITS
JABBAR
JABBED
JABBER
JABIRU
JABOTS
KABOBS
KABOOM
KABUKI
LABELS
LABIAL
LABILE
LABORS
LABOUR
LABREA
LABRET
LABRUM
MABELL
NABBED
NABBER
NABOBS
NABORS
PABLUM
RABATO
RABBET
RABBIS
RABBIT
RABBLE
RABIES
SABATO
SABENA
SABERS
SABINE
SABINS
SABLES
SABOTS
SABRAS
SABRES
TABARD
TABBED
TABLAS
TABLED
TABLES
TABLET
TABOOS
TABORS
TABRIZ
TABULA
WABASH
YABBER

•A•B••

BABBLE
BADBOY
BALBOA
BAMBOO
BAOBAB
BARBED
BARBEL
BARBER
BARBET
BARBIE
BARBRA
BATBOY
BAUBLE
CABBED
CABBIE
CAMBER
CARBON
CARBOS
CARBOY
CASBAH
DABBED
DABBLE
DAUBED
DAUBER
DAUBES
DAYBED
DAYBOY
GABBED
GABBER
GABBLE
GABBRO
GAMBIA
GAMBIT
GAMBLE
GAMBOL
GARBED
GARBLE
GASBAG
HARBIN
HARBOR
HASBRO
HATBOX
IAMBIC
JABBAR
JABBED
JABBER
KASBAH
LAMBDA
LAMBED
LAYBYS
LAZBOY
MAMBAS
MAMBOS
MARBLE
MARBLY
MAYBES
NABBED
NABBER
PAYBOX
RABBET
RABBIS
RABBIT
RABBLE
RAGBAG
RAMBLA
RAMBLE
SAMBAL
SAMBAR
SAMBAS
TABBED
TALBOT
WAMBLE
WAMBLY
WARBLE
YABBER
ZAMBIA

•A••B•

CAMEBY
CARIBE
CARIBS
CAROBS
CASABA
DANUBE
GATSBY
GAZEBO
HARDBY
JACOBI
KABOBS
KARIBA
LAIDBY
LAVABO
LAYSBY
MAKEBA
MALABO
MALIBU
NABOBS
NASEBY
NAWABS
PASSBY
SAHIBS
SASEBO
WASABI
ZAREBA

•A•••B

BAOBAB
BARTAB
CANTAB
DAYJOB
ZAGREB

••AB••

ARABIA
ARABIC
ARABLE
BLABBY
CRABBE
CRABBY
DIABLO
DOABLE
DRABLY
ENABLE
FLABBY
GRABAT
GRABBY
GRABEN
GRABLE
ISABEL
IZABAL
LIABLE
RHABDO
SCABBY
SEABAG
SEABED
SEABEE
SHABAN
SHABBY
STABAT
STABLE
STABLY
SWABBY
TEABAG
UNABLE
USABLE
USABLY
VIABLE
VIABLY

••A•B•

BLABBY
CRABBE
CRABBY
CRAMBO
FLABBY
FLAMBE
GRABBY
NEARBY
SCABBY
SHABBY
SWABBY

••A••B

SCARAB
SEALAB

•••AB•

ANNABA
CASABA
CUIABA
INDABA
KEBABS
LAVABO
MALABO
MCCABE
MESABI
MUGABE
NAWABS
PICABO
REHABS
SQUABS
STRABO
WASABI

•••A•B

BEDAUB
BICARB
DEKALB
STRAUB

••••AB

BAOBAB
BARTAB
CANTAB
CONFAB
MIHRAB
PREFAB
PUNJAB
SCARAB
SCHWAB
SEALAB
SKYLAB

AC••••

ACACIA
ACADIA
ACAJOU
ACARID
ACARUS
ACCEDE
ACCENT
ACCEPT
ACCESS
ACCORD
ACCOST
ACCRUE
ACCUSE
ACEDIA
ACEOUS
ACEOUT
ACESUP
ACETAL
ACETIC
ACETYL
ACHAEA
ACHEBE
ACHENE
ACHIER
ACHING
ACIDIC
ACIDLY
ACINUS
ACKACK
ACORNS
ACQUIT
ACROSS
ACTIII
ACTING
ACTINO
ACTION
ACTIUM
ACTIVE
ACTONE
ACTORS
ACTOUT
ACTSAS
ACTSON
ACTSUP
ACTTWO
ACTUAL
ACUATE
ACUITY
ACUMEN

A•C•••

AACHEN
ACCEDE
ACCENT
ACCEPT
ACCESS
ACCORD
ACCOST
ACCRUE
ACCUSE
AHCHOO
ALCAPP
ALCOTT
ALCOVE
ALCUIN
ANCHOR
ANCIEN
ANCONA
ARCADE
ARCANA
ARCANE
ARCARO
ARCCOS
ARCHED
ARCHER
ARCHES
ARCHIE
ARCHLY
ARCHON
ARCING
ARCTAN
ARCTIC
ASCEND
ASCENT
ASCHAM
ASCOTS
ATCOST

A••C••

ABACAS
ABACUS
ABSCAM
ACACIA
AFLCIO
ALECKY
ALECTO
ALICIA
AMECHE
AMICES
AMICUS
ANACIN
ANTCOW
APACHE
APICAL
APICES
ARCCOS
ARECAS
ASHCAN
AVOCET

A•••C•

ABBACY
ABDUCT
ABJECT
ACKACK
ADDUCE
ADDUCT
ADVICE
AFFECT
AFRICA
AGENCY
ALNICO
ALPACA
ALSACE
AMERCE
ANTICS
APERCU
APIECE
ARNICA
ARRACK
ASDICS
ASPECT
ASPICS
ATONCE
ATTACH
ATTACK
ATTICA
ATTICS
AVOUCH
AZTECS

A••••C

ACETIC
ACIDIC
AEOLIC
AGARIC
AIRSAC
ALARIC
ALTAIC
AMEBIC
AMTRAC
ANEMIC
ANGLIC
ANODIC
ANOMIC
AORTIC
ARABIC
ARCTIC
ATOMIC
ATONIC

•AC•••

AACHEN
BACALL
BACHED
BACKED
BACKER
BACKIN
BACKUP
BACKUS
CACAOS
CACHED
CACHES
CACHET
CACHOU
CACKLE
CACTUS
DACAPO
DACHAS
DACOIT
DACRON
DACTYL
FACADE
FACETS
FACEUP
FACIAL
FACIAS
FACIES
FACILE
FACING
FACTOR
FACULA
HACEKS
HACKED
HACKER
HACKIE
HACKLE
HACKLY
JACALS
JACANA
JACKAL
JACKED
JACKET
JACKEY
JACKIE
JACKUP
JACLYN
JACOBI
LACERS
LACEUP
LACHES
LACIER
LACILY
LACING
LACKED
LACKEY
LACTIC
LACUNA
MACACO
MACAWS
MACEIO
MACHES
MACHOS
MACOUN
MACRAE
MACRON
MACROS
MACULA
NACHOS
NACRES
PACERS
PACIFY
PACING
PACINO
PACKED
PACKER
PACKET
PACKUP
PACMAN
RACEME
RACERS
RACHEL
RACHIS
RACIAL
RACIER
RACILY
RACINE
RACING
RACKED
RACKET
RACKUP
RACONS
SACHEM
SACHET
SACKED
SACKER
SACQUE
SACRAL
SACRED
SACRUM
TACKED
TACKER
TACKLE
TACKON
TACOMA
TACTIC
VACANT
VACATE
VACHEL
VACLAV
VACUUM
WACKOS
YACHTS
YACKED

•A•C••

BARCAR
BAUCIS
CAICOS
CALCES
CANCAN
CANCEL
CANCUN
CATCHY
CAUCHO
CAUCHY
CAUCUS
DANCED
DANCER
DANCES
FALCES
FALCON
FARCED
FARCES
FARCRY
FASCES
FASCIA
FATCAT
FAUCES
FAUCET
GARCIA
GARCON
GASCAP
GASCON
GAUCHE
GAUCHO
JASCHA
JAYCEE
LANCED
LANCER
LANCES
LANCET
LASCAR
MADCAP
MANCHA
MANCHU
MARCEL
MARCHE
MARCIA
MARCIE
MARCOS
MARCUS
MASCOT
NASCAR
PANCHO
PARCAE
PARCEL
PASCAL
PATCHY
PAUCIS
RANCHO
RANCID
RANCOR
RASCAL
SANCHO
SANCTA
SAUCED
SAUCER
SAUCES
TAICHI
TALCED

TALCUM
WARCRY

•A••C•
BARUCH
BASICS
CALICO
HAUNCH
HAVOCS
JANICE
LAMECH
LAUNCH
MACACO
MALICE
MARACA
NATICK
NAUTCH
OAXACA
PALACE
PANICS
PAPACY
PATACA
PAUNCH
SAMECH
ZANUCK

•A•••C
BALTIC
BALZAC
BARDIC
CADMIC
CALPAC
FABRIC
GAELIC
GALLIC
GARLIC
IAMBIC
IATRIC
KARMIC
LACTIC
MANIAC
MANIOC
MANTIC
MASTIC
PARSEC
TACTIC
TANNIC
TARMAC

••AC••
ABACAS
ABACUS
ACACIA
ANACIN
APACHE
BEACHY
BEACON
BLACKS
BRACED
BRACER
BRACES
BRACHY
BRACTS
CHACHA
CHACMA
CLACKS
CRACKS
CRACKY
DEACON
DRACHM
ENACTS
EXACTA
EXACTO
EXACTS
FIACRE
FLACKS
FLACON
FRACAS
GLACES
GLACIS
GRACED
GRACES
GRACIE
GUACOS
KNACKS
KWACHA
KYACKS
LEACHY
NIACIN
ORACHS
ORACLE
PEACHY
PLACED
PLACER
PLACES
PLACET
PLACID
POACHY
QUACKS
REACTS
SEACOW
SHACKS
SLACKS
SMACKS
SNACKS
SPACED
SPACEK
SPACER
SPACES
SPACEY
STACEY
STACKS
STACTE
TEACUP
TRACED
TRACER
TRACES
TRACEY
TRACHY
TRACKS
TRACTS
URACIL
VIACOM
WHACKS
WHACKY
WRACKS

••A•C•
BIANCA
BLANCA
BLANCH
BRANCH
CHALCO
CHANCE
CHANCY
CLANCY
EPARCH
EXARCH
FIANCE
FIASCO
FRANCA
FRANCE
FRANCK
FRANCO
FRANCS
GLANCE
GRAECO
INARCH
ITASCA
KLATCH
NUANCE
PLAICE
PLANCK
PRANCE
SCARCE
SEANCE
SEARCH
SNATCH
STANCE
STANCH
STARCH
SWATCH
THATCH
TRANCE
USANCE

••A••C
AGARIC
ALARIC
ARABIC
CYANIC
DYADIC
ITALIC
PHATIC
SLAVIC
STATIC
TLALOC
TRAGIC
URALIC
URANIC

•••AC•
ABBACY
ACKACK
ALPACA
ALSACE
ARRACK
ATTACH
ATTACK
BLEACH
BREACH
BROACH
CLOACA
CURACY
CUSACK
DEFACE
DETACH
DIDACT
EFFACE
ENLACE
GOBACK
HIJACK
HORACE
IGNACE
IGUACU
IMPACT
INFACT
INTACT
ITHACA
KOVACS
LEGACY
LILACS
LUNACY
MACACO
MARACA
MENACE
MONACO
OAXACA
ONEACT
ORBACH
OUTACT
PALACE
PAPACY
PATACA
PESACH
PIRACY
PLEACH
POMACE
PREACH
PURACE
REDACT
REFACE
RELACE
SERACS
SOLACE
SUMACS
TENACE
TEXACO
THRACE
THWACK
UNLACE
UNPACK
UNTACK
VIVACE

•••A•C
ALTAIC
JUDAIC
MOSAIC
ROMAIC

••••AC
AIRSAC
AMTRAC
BALZAC
BIGMAC
CALPAC
CHIRAC
COGNAC
CONTAC
IPECAC
MANIAC
MELMAC
MICMAC
OVISAC
PROZAC
SENLAC
TARMAC
TICTAC
TOMBAC
UNIVAC
ZODIAC

AD••••
ADAGES
ADAGIO
ADAPTS
ADDAMS
ADDEND
ADDERS
ADDING
ADDLED
ADDLES
ADDONS
ADDSIN
ADDSON
ADDSTO
ADDSUP
ADDUCE
ADDUCT
ADEEMS
ADELIE
ADELLE
ADEPTS
ADESTE
ADHERE
ADIDAS
ADIEUS
ADIEUX
ADJANI
ADJOIN
ADJURE
ADJUST
ADLIBS
ADMASS
ADMIRE
ADMITS
ADNATE
ADNEXA
ADOBES
ADOLPH
ADONAI
ADONIS
ADOPTS
ADORED
ADOREE
ADORER
ADORES
ADORNS
ADRENO
ADRIAN
ADRIEN
ADRIFT
ADROIT
ADSORB
ADULTS
ADVENT
ADVERB
ADVERT
ADVICE
ADVISE
ADWEEK
ADYTUM
ADZUKI

A•D•••
ABDUCT
ADDAMS
ADDEND
ADDERS
ADDING
ADDLED
ADDLES
ADDONS
ADDSIN
ADDSON
ADDSTO
ADDSUP
ADDUCE
ADDUCT
AEDILE
AIDERS
AIDFUL
AIDING
ALDERS
ALDINE
ALDOSE
ALDOUS
ALDRIN
ANDEAN
ANDHOW
ANDREA
ANDREI
ANDRES
ANDREW
ANDREY
ANDROS
AODAIS
ARDEBS
ARDENT
ARDORS
ARDOUR
ASDICS
AUDENS
AUDIAL
AUDILE
AUDIOS
AUDITS
AUDREY

A••D••
ABIDED
ABIDES
ABODES
ABYDOS
ACADIA
ACEDIA
ACIDIC
ACIDLY
ADIDAS
AGADIR
AIRDAM
AIRDRY
ALLDAY
AMADIS
AMADOU
AMEDEO
AMIDES
AMIDOL
AMIDST
ANADEM
ANODES
ANODIC
ANYDAY
AOUDAD
APODAL
ARIDLY
ASIDES
ATODDS
AVEDON
AVIDLY
AWEDLY
AZIDES
AZODYE

A•••D•
ABRADE
ACCEDE
AGENDA
AIKIDO
ALBEDO
ALKYDS
ALLUDE
AMANDA
AMENDS
ANANDA
ANHYDR
APHIDS
ARCADE
ARENDT
ARMADA
AROIDS
ARVADA
ATODDS
AUBADE
AVOIDS
AWARDS

A••••D
ABASED
ABATED
ABIDED
ABOARD
ABOUND
ABROAD
ABSURD
ABUSED
ACARID
ACCORD
ADDEND
ADDLED
ADORED
AENEID
AFEARD
AFFORD
AFIELD
AFRAID
AGEOLD
AGREED
ALATED
ALFRED
ALLIED
ALMOND
AMAZED
AMBLED
AMPHID
AMUSED
ANELED
ANGLED
ANKLED
ANTEED
AOUDAD
APPEND
ARCHED
ARGUED
ARMAND
ARNOLD
AROUND
ASCEND
ASGARD
ASTRID
ATHAND
ATONED
ATSTUD
ATTEND
ATWOOD
AUFOND
AUGEND
AVOWED
AWAKED
AXSEED

•AD•••
BADBOY
BADDER
BADDIE
BADEGG
BADGER
BADGES
BADGUY
BADHAM
BADLOT
BADMAN
BADMEN
CADDIE
CADDIS
CADENT
CADETS
CADGED
CADGER
CADGES
CADMIC
CADMUS
CADRES
DADDYO
DADOED
DADOES
FADEIN
FADING
GADDED
GADDER
GADFLY
GADGET
HADDIE
HADJES
HADJIS
HADRON
JADING
JADISH
LADDER
LADDIE
LADERS
LADIDA
LADIES
LADING
LADINO
LADLED
LADLER
LADLES
LADOGA
MADAME
MADAMS
MADCAP
MADDEN
MADDER
MADDIE
MADEDO
MADEIT
MADERO
MADEUP
MADMAN
MADMAX
MADMEN
MADRAS
MADRES
MADRID
MADSEN
MADTOM
MADURA
MADURO
NADINE
NADIRS
PADANG
PADDED
PADDER
PADDLE
PADRES
PADUAN
RADDLE
RADIAL
RADIAN
RADIOS
RADISH
RADIUM
RADIUS
RADNER
RADOME
RADULA
SADDAM
SADDEN
SADDER
SADDLE
SADHES
SADHUS
VADOSE
WADDED
WADDLE
WADDLY
WADEIN
WADERS
WADING
WADSUP
ZADDIK
ZADORA

•A•D••
BADDER
BADDIE
BAGDAD
BALDER
BALDLY
BANDED
BANDIT
BANDOG
BARDIC
BARDOT
CADDIE
CADDIS
CALDER
CAMDEN
CANDID
CANDLE
CANDOR
CARDED
CARDER
CARDIN
CARDIO
CAUDAL
CAUDEX
CAUDLE
CAWDOR
DADDYO
DAEDAL
DANDER
DANDIE
DANDLE
DAWDLE
FANDOM
GADDED
GADDER
GANDER
GANDHI
GARDEN
HADDIE
HAGDON
HAIDAS
HANDED
HANDEL
HANDIN
HANDLE
HANDON
HANDUP
HARDBY
HARDEN
HARDER
HARDLY
HARDUP
HAYDEN
KANDER
KASDAN
LADDER
LADDIE
LAIDBY
LAIDIN
LAIDON
LAIDTO
LAIDUP
LANDAU
LANDED
LANDER
LANDHO
LANDIS
LANDON
LANDRY
LAPDOG
LARDED
LARDER
LARDON
LAUDED
LAUDER
MADDEN
MADDER
MADDIE
MAHDIS
MAIDEN
MAIDUS
MALDEN
MANDAN
MANDAY
MARDUK
MAYDAY
NASDAQ
PADDED
PADDER
PADDLE
PAIDIN
PAIDUP
PANDAS
PANDER
PANDIT
PARDON
PAYDAY
RADDLE
RAIDED
RAIDER
RANDOM
RANDRY
SADDAM
SADDEN
SADDER
SADDLE
SANDAL
SANDED
SANDER
SANDIA
SANDRA
SARDIS
SAUDIS
TAGDAY
TANDEM
TAWDRY
VALDEZ
VANDAL
VARDEN
WADDED
WADDLE
WADDLY
WALDEN
WANDER
WARDED
WARDEN
WARDER
YARDED
ZADDIK
ZANDER

•A••D•
CANADA
CANIDS
FACADE
FARADS
HAIRDO
HALIDE
KAUNDA
LADIDA
LAIRDS
LAMBDA
LAMEDH
LAMEDS
LAREDO
MADEDO
MAKEDO
MALADY
MASADA
MAUNDY
NAIADS
PAGODA
PANADA
PARADE
PARODY
RAMADA
RANIDS
RAPIDS
RATEDG
RATEDR
RATEDX
SALADO
SALADS
SARODS
XANADU

•A•••D
BABIED
BACHED
BACKED
BAGDAD
BAGGED
BAILED
BAITED
BALKED
BALLAD
BANDED
BANGED
BANKED
BANNED
BARBED
BARGED
BARKED
BARRED
BASHED
BASKED
BASTED
BATHED
BATTED
BAWLED
BAYARD
CABBED
CABLED
CACHED
CADGED
CALKED
CALLED
CALMED
CALVED
CAMPED
CANARD
CANDID
CANNED
CANOED
CANTED
CAPPED
CAPSID
CARDED
CARKED
CARPED
CARTED
CARVED
CASHED
CATTED
CAUSED
DABBED
DADOED
DAFFED
DAMMED
DAMNED
DAMPED
DANCED
DAPPED
DARNED
DARTED
DASHED
DAUBED
DAWNED
DAYBED
EAGLED
EARNED
FABLED
FAGEND
FAGGED
FAILED
FAIRED
FANGED
FANNED
FARCED
FARMED
FASTED
FATTED
FAWNED
GABBED
GABLED
GADDED
GAFFED
GAGGED
GAINED
GAITED
GALLED
GAMMED
GANGED
GAOLED
GAPPED
GARBED
GASHED
GASPED
GASSED
GAUGED
GAUMED
GAWKED
GAWPED
HACKED
HAFTED
HAILED
HAIRED
HALOED
HALOID
HALTED
HALVED
HAMMED
HANDED
HANGED
HAPPED
HARALD
HARKED
HARMED
HAROLD
HARPED
HASHED
HASPED
HATRED
HATTED
HAULED
HAWKED
HAZARD
JABBED
JACKED
JAGGED
JAILED
JAMMED
JARRED
JAZZED
KAYOED
LACKED
LADLED
LAGGED
LAMBED
LAMMED
LANCED
LANDED
LAPPED
LAPSED
LARDED
LARKED
LASHED
LASTED
LATHED
LAUDED
MADRID
MAENAD
MAILED
MALTED
MANNED
MAPPED
MARAUD
MARKED
MARLED
MARRED
MASHED
MASKED
MASSED
MATTED
MAULED
NABBED
NAGGED
NAILED
NAPPED
PACKED
PADDED
PAINED
PAIRED
PALLED
PALLID
PALMED
PANNED
PANTED
PARKED
PARRED
PARSED
PARTED
PASSED
PASTED
PATTED
PAUSED
PAWNED
RACKED
RAFTED
RAGGED
RAIDED
RAILED
RAINED
RAISED
RAMMED
RAMPED
RAMROD
RANCID
RANGED
RANKED
RANTED
RAPPED
RASHAD
RASHID
RASPED
RATTED
RAZZED
SACKED
SACRED
SAGGED
SAILED
SALTED
SALVED
SANDED
SAPPED
SASHED
SASSED
SAUCED
SAWRED
SAYYID
TABARD
TABBED
TABLED
TACKED
TAGEND
TAGGED
TAILED
TALCED
TALKED
TALMUD
TAMPED
TANGED
TANKED
TANNED
TAPPED
TARRED
TASKED
TASTED
TATTED
TAXIED
VALUED
VALVED
VAMPED
VANNED
VARIED
VATTED
WADDED
WAFTED
WAGGED
WAILED
WAITED
WAIVED
WALKED
WALLED
WANNED
WANTAD
WANTED
WARDED
WARGOD
WARMED
WARNED
WARPED
WARRED
WASHED
WASTED
YACKED
YAKKED
YANKED
YAPPED
YARDED
YARNED
YAWNED
YAWPED
ZAGGED
ZAPPED

••AD••
ACADIA
AGADIR
AMADIS
AMADOU
ANADEM
BEADED
BEADLE
BEADUP
BLADED
BLADER
BLADES
CHADOR
CRADLE
DEADEN
DEADER
DEADLY
DEADON
DIADEM
DYADIC
EVADED
EVADER
EVADES
GLADES
GLADLY
GLADYS
GOADED
GRADEA
GRADED
GRADER
GRADES
GRADIN
GRADUS
HEADED
HEADER
HEADIN
HEADON
HEADUP
HYADES
IBADAN
ISADOR
LEADED
LEADEN
LEADER
LEADIN
LEADON
LEADTO
LEADUP
LOADED
LOADER
MCADAM
MCADOO
MEADOW
QUADRI
READER
READIN
ROADIE
SEADOG
SHADED
SHADES
SHADOW
SPADED
SPADER
SPADES
SPADIX
STADIA
TRADED
TRADER
TRADES

••A•D•
AMANDA
ANANDA
AWARDS
BEARDS
BLANDA
BOARDS
BRAIDS
BRANDO
BRANDS
BRANDT
BRANDX
BRANDY
CIARDI
CLAUDE
ELANDS
FRAIDY
FRAUDS
GLANDS
GRANDE
GRANDS
GUARDS
HOARDS
LUANDA
PLAIDS
PRAVDA
RHABDO
RUANDA
RWANDA
SCALDS
SHANDY
SHARDS
SKALDS
STANDS
SWARDS
UGANDA
VIANDS

••A••D
ABASED
ABATED
ACARID
ALATED
AMAZED
AWAKED
BEADED
BEAKED
BEAMED
BEANED
BIASED
BLADED
BLAMED
BLARED
BLAZED
BOATED
BRACED
BRAKED
BRAVED
BRAYED
BRAZED
CEASED
CHAFED
CHASED
CLAWED
COATED
COAXED
CRANED
CRATED
CRAVED
CRAZED
DIALED
DRAPED
DRAYED
ELAPID
ELATED
ERASED
EVADED
FEARED
FLAKED
FLAMED
FLARED
FLAWED
FLAYED

FOALED
FOAMED
FRAMED
FRAYED
GEARED
GLARED
GLAZED
GNAWED
GOADED
GRACED
GRADED
GRATED
GRAVED
GRAVID
GRAYED
GRAZED
HEADED
HEALED
HEAPED
HEATED
HEAVED
HOAXED
IMAGED
KHALID
LEADED
LEAFED
LEAKED
LEANED
LEAPED
LEASED
LEAVED
LOADED
LOAFED
LOAMED
LOANED
MOANED
MOATED
NEARED
OKAYED
ORATED
PEAKED
PEALED
PEAPOD
PHASED
PLACED
PLACID
PLANED
PLATED
PLAYED
PRATED
PRAYED
QUAKED
REAMED
REAPED
REARED
ROAMED
ROARED
RRATED
SCALED
SCAPED
SCARED
SEABED
SEALED
SEAMED
SEARED
SEATED
SHADED
SHAMED
SHAPED
SHARED
SHAVED
SKATED
SLAKED
SLATED
SLAVED
SLAYED
SNAKED
SNARED
SOAKED
SOAPED
SOARED
SPACED
SPADED
SPARED
SPAYED
STAGED
STAKED
STALED
STARED
STATED
STAVED
STAYED
SWAGED
SWAYED
TEAMED
TEARED
TEASED
THAWED
TRACED
TRADED
UNAGED
UNAWED
WEANED
WEAVED
XRATED
XRAYED
YEANED

•••AD•

ABRADE
ARCADE
ARMADA
ARVADA
AUBADE
BREADS
BROADS
CANADA
CICADA
COLADA
CYCADS
DECADE
DORADO
DREADS
DRYADS
FACADE
FARADS
GELADA
HEXADS
HODADS
INVADE
JIHADS
JUMADA
JURADO
KNEADS
MALADY
MASADA
MENADO
MIKADO
MILADY
MONADS
NAIADS
NEVADA
NOMADS
OCTADS
OREADS
PANADA
PARADE
PLEADS
POMADE
POSADA
RAMADA
REMADE
REPADS
RIYADH
SALADO
SALADS
SQUADS
STEADS
STEADY
STRADS
TIRADE
TREADS
TRIADS
UNLADE
UNMADE
XANADU

•••A•D

ABOARD
AFEARD
AFRAID
ARMAND
ASGARD
ATHAND
BAYARD
BRIAND
BRIARD
BYHAND
CANARD
COWARD
CUNARD
DEMAND
DONALD
DOTARD
EDGARD
EDUARD
EDVARD
EDWARD
ERHARD
ERRAND
EXPAND
EZZARD
FUGARD
GERALD
GERARD
GIRARD
GODARD
GSTAAD
HARALD
HAZARD
HERALD
HOWARD
IDCARD
INHAND
INLAID
INLAND
INWARD
ISLAND
IZZARD
LELAND
LIGAND
LIZARD
MARAUD
ONHAND
ONLAND
ONWARD
OSWALD
OXNARD
PETARD
PICARD
POLAND
REGARD
RELAID
REMAND
REPAID
REPAND
RESAND
RETARD
REWARD
RIBALD
RIBAND
RITARD
ROLAND
RONALD
SEWARD
STRAND
TABARD
TOGAED
TOWARD
UNHAND
UNLAID
UNPAID
UNSAID
UPLAND
UPWARD
VISAED
WIZARD

••••AD

ABROAD
AOUDAD
BAGDAD
BALLAD
BEHEAD
BYROAD
CIUDAD
CONRAD
DOODAD
EMQUAD
ENNEAD
ENQUAD
FORBAD
GETMAD
GILEAD
GOTMAD
GSTAAD
HEPTAD
INROAD
KEYPAD
KONRAD
MAENAD
MSQUAD
MYRIAD
NOLEAD
NOLOAD
NOTBAD
OGDOAD
PENTAD
PLEIAD
RASHAD
RELOAD
REREAD
SINBAD
SINEAD
SPREAD
TETRAD
THREAD
TOOBAD
UNCLAD
UNLEAD
UNLOAD
UNREAD
UPLOAD
WANTAD

AE••••

AEDILE
AEETES
AEGEAN
AENEAS
AENEID
AEOLIA
AEOLIC
AEOLUS
AERATE
AERIAL
AERIES
AERIFY
AERILY
AEROBE
AETHER

A•E•••

ABELES
ABESSE
ACEDIA
ACEOUS
ACEOUT
ACESUP
ACETAL
ACETIC
ACETYL
ADEEMS
ADELIE
ADELLE
ADEPTS
ADESTE
AEETES
AFEARD
AGEING
AGEISM
AGEIST
AGENAS
AGENCY
AGENDA
AGENTS
AGEOLD
AHERNE
AIELLO
AKELAS
AKENES
ALEAST
ALECKY
ALECTO
ALEGAR
ALEGRE
ALEMAN
ALEPHS
ALEPPO
ALERTS
ALEUTS
ALEVEL
ALEXEI
ALEXIA
ALEXIS
AMEBAE
AMEBAS
AMEBIC
AMECHE
AMEDEO
AMEERS
AMELIA
AMENDS
AMENRA
AMENTS
AMERCE
AMERSP
ANELED
ANELES
ANEMIA
ANEMIC
ANERGY
APEMAN
APEMEN
APERCU
APEXES
ARECAS
ARENAS
ARENDT
AREOLA
ARETES
ARETHA
AREZZO
ASEITY
ASEVER
ATEAMS
ATEASE
ATEMPO
ATEOUT
ATERGO
ATESTS
AVEDON
AVENGE
AVENUE
AVERNO
AVERSE
AVERTS
AVESTA
AWEARY
AWEDLY
AWEIGH
AYEAYE
AYESHA

A••E••

ABBESS
ABBEYS
ABJECT
ABLEST
ABSENT
ACCEDE
ACCENT
ACCEPT
ACCESS
ACHEBE
ACHENE
ADDEND
ADDERS
ADEEMS
ADHERE
ADIEUS
ADIEUX
ADNEXA
ADRENO
ADVENT
ADVERB
ADVERT
ADWEEK
AEGEAN
AENEAS
AENEID
AFFECT
AFIELD
AFREET
AFRESH
AGLEAM
AGLETS
AGREED
AGREES
AIDERS
AILEEN
AILERS
ALBEDO
ALBEIT
ALBERT
ALDERS
ALIENS
ALKENE
ALLEES
ALLEGE
ALLELE
ALLEYS
ALPERT
ALTERS
ALWEST
AMBERS
AMBERY
AMEERS
AMIENS
AMOEBA
AMPERE
AMVETS
ANDEAN
ANGELA
ANGELI
ANGELL
ANGELO
ANGELS
ANGERS
ANNEAL
ANNEXE
ANSELM
ANTEED
ANTERO
ANTEUP
APIECE
APPEAL
APPEAR
APPEND
APTEST
ARBELA
ARDEBS
ARDENT
ARGENT
ARLEEN
ARLENE
ARMETS
ARNESS
ARNETT
ARPENT
ARREAR
ARREST
ARSENE
ARTELS
ARTERY
ASCEND
ASCENT
ASKERS
ASLEEP
ASPECT
ASPENS
ASPERA
ASSENT
ASSERT
ASSESS
ASSETS
ASTERN
ASTERS
ASWELL
ATBEST
ATHENA
ATHENE
ATHENS
ATREST
ATREUS
ATTEND
ATTEST
AUDENS
AUGEAN
AUGEND
AUGERS
AUREUS
AUTEUR
AXSEED
AZTECS

A•••E•

AACHEN
ABASED
ABASES
ABATED
ABATES
ABELES
ABIDED
ABIDES
ABODES
ABUSED
ABUSER
ABUSES
ACHAEA
ACHIER
ACUMEN
ADAGES
ADDLED
ADDLES
ADOBES
ADORED
ADOREE
ADORER
ADORES
ADRIEN
ADWEEK
AEETES
AERIES
AETHER
AFREET
AGATES
AGAVES
AGGIES
AGREED
AGREES
AIGRET
AILEEN
AIRIER
AIRMEN
AISLES
AKENES
ALATED
ALEVEL
ALEXEI
ALFRED
ALFVEN
ALINES
ALITER
ALLEES
ALLIED
ALLIES
ALLSET
ALLWET
ALTHEA
AMAZED
AMAZES
AMBLED
AMBLER
AMBLES
AMEDEO
AMICES
AMIDES
AMINES
AMOLES
AMPLER
AMSTEL
AMULET
AMUSED
AMUSES
ANADEM
ANCIEN
ANDREA
ANDREI
ANDRES
ANDREW
ANDREY
ANELED
ANELES
ANGLED
ANGLER
ANGLES
ANIMES
ANKLED
ANKLES
ANKLET
ANNLEE
ANODES
ANOLES
ANSWER
ANTEED
ANTHEM
ANTHER
ANTLER
ANTRES
APEMEN
APEXES
APICES
APOGEE
APPLES
APPLET
ARCHED
ARCHER
ARCHES
ARETES
ARGUED
ARGUER
ARGUES
ARISEN
ARISES
ARLEEN
ARMIES
ARMLET
ARNHEM
ARTIER
ASEVER
ASHIER
ASHLEY
ASIDES
ASLEEP
ATONED
ATONES
ATTLEE
AUBREY
AUDREY
AUKLET
AUSPEX
AUSTEN
AVOCET
AVOWED
AVOWER
AWAKED
AWAKEN
AWAKES
AWOKEN
AXSEED
AZALEA
AZIDES
AZINES
AZORES

A••••E

ABESSE
ABJURE
ABLATE
ABLAZE
ABRADE
ACCEDE
ACCRUE
ACCUSE
ACHEBE
ACHENE
ACTIVE
ACTONE
ACUATE
ADDUCE
ADELIE
ADELLE
ADESTE
ADHERE
ADJURE
ADMIRE
ADNATE
ADOREE
ADVICE
ADVISE
AEDILE
AERATE
AEROBE
AFFINE
AFLAME
AFRAME
AGLARE
AGNATE
AGORAE
AHERNE
ALCOVE
ALDINE
ALDOSE
ALEGRE
ALFINE
ALGORE
ALIBLE
ALKENE
ALLEGE
ALLELE
ALLUDE
ALLURE
ALPINE
ALSACE
ALULAE
AMALIE
AMEBAE
AMECHE
AMERCE
AMPERE
AMPULE
ANNEXE
ANNLEE
ANOMIE
ANSATE
ANYONE
AORTAE
APACHE
APIECE
APLITE
APOGEE
APPOSE
AQUATE
ARABLE
ARCADE
ARCANE
ARCHIE
ARGIVE
ARGYLE
ARIOSE
ARLENE
ARMURE
AROUSE
ARRIVE
ARSENE
ASHORE
ASLOPE
ASPIRE
ASSIZE
ASSUME
ASSURE
ASTUTE
ATEASE
ATHENE
ATHOME
ATONCE
ATTIRE
ATTLEE
ATTUNE
AUBADE
AUDILE
AUNTIE
AUSSIE
AVENGE
AVENUE
AVERSE
AVIATE
AVULSE
AWHILE
AXLIKE
AYEAYE
AZODYE

•AE•••

CAESAR
DAEDAL
FAENZA
FAERIE
FAEROE
GAELIC
HAEMAT
HAEMON
JAEGER
MAENAD
PAEANS
PAELLA
PAEONS

•A•E••

BABELS
BADEGG
BAGELS
BAKERS
BAKERY
BALEEN
BALERS
BAREGE
BARELY
BAREST
BASELY
BASEST
BATEAU
BAYEUX
CABERS
CADENT
CADETS
CAGERS
CAMEAT
CAMEBY
CAMEIN
CAMELS
CAMEON
CAMEOS
CAMERA
CAMETO
CAMEUP
CANERS
CAPERS
CAREEN
CAREER
CARESS
CARETO
CARETS
CASEFY
CASERN
CATENA
CATERS
CAVEAT
CAVEIN
CAVELL
CAVERN
CAVERS
CAVETT
DALETH
DARENT
DARETO
DATERS
EASEIN
EASELS
EASEUP
EATERS
EATERY
FACETS
FACEUP
FADEIN
FAGEND
FAKERS
FAKERY
FARERS
GAIETY
GALEAE
GALENA
GAMELY
GAMEST
GAMETE
GAPERS
GARETH
GATEAU
GATERS
GAVEIN
GAVELS
GAVEUP
GAYEST
GAZEBO
HABEAS
HACEKS
HALERS
HALERU
HALEST
HALEVY
HAMELN
HAREMS
HATERS
HAVEAT
HAVENS
HAVENT
HAVEON
HAVERS
HAZELS
HAZERS
JAPERS
JAPERY
JASEYS
KAGERA
KAREEM
LABELS
LACERS
LACEUP
LADERS
LAGERS
LAKERS
LAMECH
LAMEDH
LAMEDS
LAMELY
LAMENT
LAMESA
LAMEST
LAPELS
LAREDO
LASERS
LATEEN
LATELY
LATENE
LATENS
LATENT
LATEST
LAVERS
LAXEST
LAYERS
MABELL
MACEIO
MADEDO
MADEIT
MADERO
MADEUP
MAKEBA
MAKEDO
MAKEIT
MAKERS
MAKEUP
MANEGE
MASERS
MASERU
MATERS
MATEYS
MAVENS
MAXENE
MAZERS
NAMELY
NAMERS
NAPERY
NASEBY
NAVELS
OATERS
PACERS
PAGERS
PALEAE
PALELY
PALEST
PAMELA
PANELS
PAPERS
PAPERY
PARENS
PARENT
PARERS
PARETO
PAREVE
PASEOS
PATENS
PATENT
PATERS
PAVERS
PAWERS
PAYEES
PAYERS
RACEME
RACERS
RAKEIN
RAKERS
RAKEUP
RAMEAU
RAMETS
RANEES
RAREFY
RARELY
RAREST
RASERS
RATEDG
RATEDR
RATEDX
RATELS
RATERS
RAVELS
RAVENS
RAVERS
RAVEUP
RAWEGG
RAWEST
SABENA
SABERS
SAFELY
SAFEST
SAFETY
SAGELY
SAGEST
SAKERS
SAMECH
SAMEKH
SANELY
SANEST
SASEBO
SATEEN
SAVERS
SAVEUP
SAYERS
TAGEND
TAKEIN
TAKEON
TAKERS
TAKETH
TAKETO
TAKEUP
TALENT
TALERS
TALESE
TAMELY
TAMERS
TAMEST
TAPERS
TASERS
TATERS
TAVERN
TAXERS
VALENS
VALENT
VALERY
VALETS
VARESE
WADEIN
WADERS
WAFERS
WAFERY
WAGERS
WAKENS
WAKEUP
WALERS
WALESA
WANERS
WATERS
WATERY
WAVEIN
WAVERS
WAVERY
WAXERS
YARELY
YAREST
ZAREBA
ZAZENS

•A••E•

AACHEN
BABIED
BABIES
BACHED
BACKED
BACKER
BADDER
BADGER
BADGES
BADMEN
BAGGED
BAGGER
BAILED
BAILEE
BAILER
BAILEY
BAINES
BAITED
BALDER
BALEEN
BALKED
BALLET
BANDED
BANGED
BANGER
BANKED
BANKER
BANNED
BANNER
BANTER
BARBED
BARBEL
BARBER
BARBET
BARGED
BARGES
BARKED
BARKER
BARLEY
BARMEN
BARNES
BARNEY
BARRED
BARREL
BARREN
BARRES
BARTER
BASHED
BASHES
BASKED
BASKET
BASSES
BASSET
BASTED
BASTER
BASTES
BATHED
BATHER
BATHES
BATMEN
BATTED
BATTEL
BATTEN
BATTER
BAWLED
BAWLER
BAXTER
CABBED
CABLED
CABLER
CABLES
CACHED
CACHES
CACHET
CADGED
CADGER
CADGES
CADRES
CAGIER
CAGNEY
CAHIER
CAKIER
CALCES
CALDER
CALKED
CALLED
CALLER
CALLES
CALMED
CALMER
CALVED
CALVES
CALXES
CAMBER
CAMDEN
CAMLET
CAMPED
CAMPER
CANCEL
CANIER
CANKER
CANNED
CANNEL
CANNER
CANNES
CANOED
CANOES
CANTED
CANTER
CAPLET
CAPPED
CAPPER
CARDED
CARDER
CAREEN
CAREER
CARIES
CARKED
CARMEL
CARMEN
CARNES
CARNET
CARNEY
CARPED
CARPEL
CARPER
CARPET
CARREL
CARREY
CARTED
CARTEL
CARTER
CARTES
CARVED
CARVER
CARVES
CARVEY
CASHED
CASHES
CASHEW
CASPER

CASTER
CASTES
CATHER
CATTED
CAUDEX
CAUSED
CAUSES
DABBED
DABNEY
DADOED
DADOES
DAFFED
DAFTER
DAGGER
DAILEY
DAIREN
DAISES
DALLES
DAMIEN
DAMMED
DAMNED
DAMPED
DAMPEN
DAMPER
DAMSEL
DANCED
DANCER
DANCES
DANDER
DANGER
DANIEL
DANKER
DANNER
DANTES
DAPPED
DAPPER
DARIEN
DARKEN
DARKER
DARNED
DARNEL
DARNER
DARREN
DARTED
DARTER
DASHED
DASHER
DASHES
DAUBED
DAUBER
DAUBES
DAVIES
DAWNED
DAYBED
EAGLED
EAGLES
EAGLET
EAGRES
EARNED
EARNER
EASIER
EASTER
FABLED
FABLER
FABLES
FACIES
FAGGED
FAILED
FAIRED
FAIRER
FALCES
FALLEN
FALSER
FALTER

FANGED
FANJET
FANNED
FARCED
FARCES
FARLEY
FARMED
FARMER
FASCES
FASTED
FASTEN
FASTER
FATHER
FATTED
FATTEN
FATTER
FAUCES
FAUCET
FAWKES
FAWNED
FAWNER
GABBED
GABBER
GABIES
GABLED
GABLER
GABLES
GADDED
GADDER
GADGET
GAFFED
GAFFER
GAFFES
GAGGED
GAGMEN
GAINED
GAINER
GAITED
GAITER
GALLED
GALLEY
GAMIER
GAMMED
GAMMER
GANDER
GANGED
GANGER
GANGES
GANNET
GAOLED
GAOLER
GAPPED
GARBED
GARDEN
GARNER
GARNET
GARRET
GARTER
GARVEY
GASHED
GASHES
GASJET
GASKET
GASMEN
GASPED
GASPER
GASSED
GASSER
GASSES
GATHER
GAUGED
GAUGER
GAUGES
GAUMED

GAUZES
GAWKED
GAWKER
GAWPED
HACKED
HACKER
HADJES
HAFTED
HAILED
HAILEY
HAINES
HAIRED
HAJJES
HALLEL
HALLEY
HALOED
HALOES
HALSEY
HALTED
HALTER
HALVED
HALVES
HAMLET
HAMMED
HAMMER
HAMPER
HANDED
HANDEL
HANGED
HANGER
HANKER
HANLEY
HANSEL
HAOLES
HAPPED
HAPPEN
HARDEN
HARDER
HARKED
HARKEN
HARKER
HARLEM
HARLEY
HARMED
HARPED
HARPER
HARVEY
HASHED
HASHES
HASPED
HASTEN
HASTES
HATRED
HATTED
HATTER
HAULED
HAULER
HAWKED
HAWKER
HAWSER
HAWSES
HAYDEN
HAYLEY
HAZIER
JABBED
JABBER
JACKED
JACKET
JACKEY
JAEGER
JAGGED
JAGGER
JAILED
JAILER

JAMMED
JAMMER
JANSEN
JARRED
JASPER
JAURES
JAVIER
JAYCEE
JAYVEE
JAZZED
JAZZES
KAISER
KANDER
KAREEM
KAVNER
KAYOED
LAAGER
LABREA
LABRET
LACHES
LACIER
LACKED
LACKEY
LADDER
LADIES
LADLED
LADLER
LADLES
LAFFER
LAGGED
LAGGER
LAKIER
LAMBED
LAMMED
LANCED
LANCER
LANCES
LANCET
LANDED
LANDER
LANIER
LANKER
LAPPED
LAPPET
LAPSED
LAPSES
LAPTEV
LARDED
LARDER
LARGER
LARGES
LARKED
LARSEN
LASHED
LASHER
LASHES
LASSEN
LASSER
LASSES
LASTED
LASTEX
LATEEN
LATHED
LATHER
LATHES
LATKES
LATTEN
LATTER
LAUDED
LAUDER
LAUPER
LAUREL
LAUREN
LAWMEN

LAWYER
LAYMEN
LAZIER
MACHES
MADDEN
MADDER
MADMEN
MADRES
MADSEN
MAGNET
MAGUEY
MAHLER
MAIDEN
MAILED
MAILER
MAILES
MAIZES
MAJGEN
MALDEN
MALLEE
MALLEI
MALLET
MALTED
MANGER
MANNED
MANNER
MANSES
MANTEL
MANUEL
MAPLES
MAPPED
MAPPER
MARCEL
MARGES
MARIEL
MARKED
MARKER
MARKET
MARLED
MARLEE
MARLEY
MARMEE
MARNER
MARRED
MARTEL
MARTEN
MARVEL
MASHED
MASHER
MASHES
MASKED
MASKER
MASSED
MASSES
MASSEY
MASTER
MATHER
MATTEA
MATTED
MATTEL
MATTER
MATTES
MAULED
MAULER
MAUMEE
MAUSER
MAUVES
MAYBES
MAYHEM
MAZIER
NABBED
NABBER
NACRES
NAGGED

NAGGER
NAILED
NAILER
NANSEN
NANTES
NAPIER
NAPLES
NAPPED
NAPPER
NAPPES
NASSER
NATTER
NAUSEA
NAVIES
OAKLEY
OATIER
PACKED
PACKER
PACKET
PADDED
PADDER
PADRES
PAINED
PAIRED
PALAEO
PALIER
PALLED
PALLET
PALMED
PALMER
PALTER
PAMPER
PANDER
PANNED
PANNER
PANNES
PANTED
PANZER
PAPIER
PARCEL
PARGET
PARKED
PARKER
PARLEY
PARRED
PARREL
PARSEC
PARSED
PARSEE
PARSER
PARSES
PARTED
PASSED
PASSEL
PASSER
PASSES
PASTED
PASTEL
PASTES
PATTED
PATTEN
PATTER
PAULEY
PAUPER
PAUSED
PAUSES
PAWNED
PAWNEE
PAWNER
PAYEES
RABBET
RABIES
RACHEL
RACIER

RACKED
RACKET
RADNER
RAFAEL
RAFTED
RAFTER
RAGGED
RAGMEN
RAIDED
RAIDER
RAILED
RAILER
RAINED
RAINER
RAINES
RAINEY
RAISED
RAISER
RAISES
RAMIES
RAMJET
RAMMED
RAMPED
RAMSES
RAMSEY
RANEES
RANGED
RANGER
RANGES
RANKED
RANKER
RANTED
RANTER
RAPIER
RAPPED
RAPPEE
RAPPEL
RAPPER
RAQUEL
RASHER
RASHES
RASPED
RASPER
RASTER
RATHER
RATTED
RATTER
RAZZED
RAZZES
SABLES
SABRES
SACHEM
SACHET
SACKED
SACKER
SACRED
SADDEN
SADDER
SADHES
SAGGED
SAILED
SALLET
SALTED
SALTEN
SALTER
SALVED
SALVER
SALVES
SAMLET
SAMUEL
SANDED
SANDER
SANGER
SANSEI

SANTEE
SAPPED
SAPPER
SARGES
SASHED
SASHES
SASSED
SASSER
SASSES
SATEEN
SAUCED
SAUCER
SAUCES
SAUGER
SAUREL
SAUTES
SAWRED
SAWYER
SAYLES
SAYYES
TABBED
TABLED
TABLES
TABLET
TACKED
TACKER
TAGGED
TAILED
TAIPEI
TALCED
TALKED
TALKER
TALLER
TAMPED
TAMPER
TANDEM
TANGED
TANKED
TANKER
TANNED
TANNER
TANTES
TAPPED
TAPPER
TAPPET
TARGES
TARGET
TARRED
TARTER
TASKED
TASSEL
TASSES
TASTED
TASTER
TASTES
TATTED
TATTER
TAUPES
TAUTEN
TAUTER
TAXIED
TAXIES
TAXMEN
VACHEL
VAGUER
VAINER
VALDEZ
VALLEE
VALLEY
VALUED
VALUES
VALVED
VALVES
VAMPED

VAMPER
VANIER
VANNED
VARDEN
VARIED
VARIES
VARLET
VARNEY
VASTER
VATTED
WADDED
WAFTED
WAGGED
WAGNER
WAILED
WAILER
WAITED
WAITER
WAIVED
WAIVER
WAIVES
WALDEN
WALKED
WALKEN
WALKER
WALLED
WALLER
WALLET
WALTER
WANDER
WANIER
WANNED
WANNER
WANTED
WAPNER
WARDED
WARDEN
WARDER
WARIER
WARMED
WARMER
WARNED
WARNER
WARPED
WARRED
WARREN
WASHED
WASHER
WASHES
WASTED
WASTER
WASTES
WATNEY
WAVIER
WAXIER
XAVIER
YABBER
YACKED
YAHWEH
YAKKED
YAKKER
YALIES
YAMMER
YANKED
YANKEE
YAPPED
YARDED
YARNED
YASSER
YAWNED
YAWNER
YAWPED
YAWPER
ZAFFER

ZAGGED
ZAGREB
ZAIRES
ZANDER
ZANIER
ZANIES
ZAPPED
ZAPPER

•A•••E

BABBLE
BADDIE
BAFFLE
BAGGIE
BAILEE
BANGLE
BARBIE
BAREGE
BARITE
BARQUE
BARRIE
BASQUE
BATTLE
BATTUE
BAUBLE
CABBIE
CACKLE
CADDIE
CAIQUE
CAJOLE
CALQUE
CAMISE
CANAPE
CANDLE
CANINE
CANNAE
CANTLE
CANUTE
CAPONE
CAPOTE
CARAFE
CARIBE
CAROLE
CARRIE
CASQUE
CASTLE
CATTLE
CAUDLE
CAYUSE
DABBLE
DAMAGE
DAMONE
DAMORE
DANDIE
DANDLE
DANGLE
DANGME
DANUBE
DAPHNE
DAPPLE
DARKLE
DATIVE
DAWDLE
DAYONE
DAZZLE
FACADE
FACILE
FAERIE
FAEROE
FAILLE
FALINE
FAMINE
FANNIE
FATALE

FAUNAE
GABBLE
GAGGLE
GALEAE
GALORE
GAMBLE
GAMETE
GAMINE
GANGLE
GANGUE
GARAGE
GARBLE
GARGLE
GAUCHE
HABILE
HACKIE
HACKLE
HADDIE
HAGGLE
HALIDE
HALITE
HAMITE
HANDLE
HANKIE
HARARE
HASSLE
HATTIE
JACKIE
JAMOKE
JANGLE
JANICE
JANINE
JAYCEE
JAYVEE
KALINE
KARATE
KATHIE
LABILE
LADDIE
LAHORE
LAINIE
LAMAZE
LANATE
LANOSE
LAOTSE
LARVAE
LASSIE
LATENE
LAURIE
LAVAGE
MACRAE
MADAME
MADDIE
MAGGIE
MAGPIE
MAISIE
MAITRE
MALATE
MALICE
MALLEE
MALONE
MANAGE
MANEGE
MANGLE
MANQUE
MANTLE
MARBLE
MARCHE
MARCIE
MARGIE
MARINE
MARLEE
MARMEE
MARNIE

MARPLE
MARQUE
MASHIE
MASQUE
MATTIE
MATURE
MAUMEE
MAXENE
MAXINE
MAXIXE
NADINE
NANNIE
NAPPIE
NATIVE
NATURE
PADDLE
PAIUTE
PALACE
PALATE
PALEAE
PARADE
PARCAE
PAREVE
PAROLE
PARSEE
PARURE
PATINE
PAVANE
PAWNEE
RABBLE
RACEME
RACINE
RADDLE
RADOME
RAFFLE
RAMATE
RAMBLE
RAMONE
RAMOSE
RANKLE
RAPINE
RAPPEE
RASSLE
RATINE
RATITE
RATTLE
RAVAGE
RAVINE
RAZZLE
SABINE
SACQUE
SADDLE
SAFIRE
SAINTE
SALINE
SALOME
SALUTE
SAMITE
SAMMIE
SAMPLE
SANTEE
SARTRE
SATIRE
SAVAGE
SAVATE
SAVOIE
TACKLE
TAGORE
TAILLE
TALESE
TALKIE
TAMALE
TANGLE
TATTLE

VACATE
VADOSE
VALISE
VALLEE
VARESE
WADDLE
WAFFLE
WAGGLE
WAHINE
WALKIE
WAMBLE
WANGLE
WARBLE
WASHOE
WATTLE
YANKEE

••AE••

GRAECO
URAEUS

••A•E•

ABASED
ABASES
ABATED
ABATES
ADAGES
AGATES
AGAVES
ALATED
AMAZED
AMAZES
ANADEM
AWAKED
AWAKEN
AWAKES
AZALEA
BEADED
BEAKED
BEAKER
BEAMED
BEANED
BEARER
BEATEN
BEATER
BEAVER
BIASED
BIASES
BLADED
BLADER
BLADES
BLAMED
BLAMES
BLARED
BLARES
BLAZED
BLAZER
BLAZES
BOATED
BOATEL
BOATER
BRACED
BRACER
BRACES
BRAKED
BRAKES
BRAVED
BRAVER
BRAVES
BRAYED
BRAYER
BRAZED
BRAZEN
BRAZER

BRAZES
CEASED
CEASES
CHAFED
CHAFES
CHALET
CHANEL
CHANEY
CHAPEL
CHASED
CHASER
CHASES
CHAVEZ
CLARET
CLAVES
CLAWED
CLAWER
CLAYEY
COALER
COATED
COAXED
COAXER
COAXES
CRAKES
CRANED
CRANES
CRAPES
CRATED
CRATER
CRATES
CRAVED
CRAVEN
CRAVER
CRAVES
CRAZED
CRAZES
DEADEN
DEADER
DEAFEN
DEAFER
DEALER
DEARER
DIADEM
DIALED
DIALER
DIAPER
DLAYER
DRAGEE
DRAKES
DRAPED
DRAPER
DRAPES
DRAWER
DRAYED
EDAMES
ELATED
ELATER
ELATES
ELAYER
ENAMEL
ENATES
ERASED
ERASER
ERASES
ETAPES
EVADED
EVADER
EVADES
FEARED
FEARER
FLAKED
FLAKER
FLAKES
FLAKEY

FLAMED
FLAMES
FLARED
FLARES
FLAWED
FLAXEN
FLAXES
FLAYED
FLAYER
FOALED
FOAMED
FRAMED
FRAMES
FRASER
FRAUEN
FRAYED
FRAZER
GEARED
GLACES
GLADES
GLARED
GLARES
GLASER
GLAZED
GLAZER
GLAZES
GNAWED
GNAWER
GOADED
GOATEE
GRABEN
GRACED
GRACES
GRADEA
GRADED
GRADER
GRADES
GRAPES
GRAPEY
GRATED
GRATER
GRATES
GRAVED
GRAVEL
GRAVEN
GRAVER
GRAVES
GRAYED
GRAYER
GRAZED
GRAZER
GRAZES
HEADED
HEADER
HEALED
HEALER
HEANEY
HEAPED
HEARER
HEATED
HEATER
HEAVED
HEAVEN
HEAVER
HEAVES
HOAXED
HOAXER
HOAXES
HYADES
IMAGED
IMAGER
IMAGES
IMARET
INANER

INAPET
IRATER
ISABEL
JUAREZ
KNAVES
KRAKEN
KRAMER
KRATER
LAAGER
LEADED
LEADEN
LEADER
LEAFED
LEAKED
LEAKER
LEAKEY
LEANED
LEANER
LEAPED
LEAPER
LEASED
LEASER
LEASES
LEAVED
LEAVEN
LEAVES
LIANES
LOADED
LOADER
LOAFED
LOAFER
LOAMED
LOANED
LOANER
LOAVES
MEAGER
MEANER
MOANED
MOANER
MOATED
NEARED
NEARER
NEATEN
NEATER
NIAMEY
OCASEK
OCASEY
OKAYED
ONAGER
ORALES
ORATED
ORATES
OSAGES
PEAHEN
PEAKED
PEALED
PEAVEY
PHAGES
PHASED
PHASER
PHASES
PIAGET
PLACED
PLACER
PLACES
PLACET
PLAGES
PLANED
PLANER
PLANES
PLANET
PLATED
PLATEN
PLATER

PLATES PLAYED PLAYER PRASES PRATED PRATER PRATES PRAXES PRAYED PRAYER QUAKED QUAKER QUAKES QUAVER READER REALER REALES REAMED REAMER REAPED REAPER REARED REARER RHAMES ROAMED ROAMER ROARED ROARER RRATED SCALED SCALER SCALES SCAPED SCAPES SCARED SCARER SCARES SEABED SEABEE SEALED SEALER SEAMED SEAMEN SEARED SEATED SEATER SHADED SHADES SHAKEN SHAKER SHAKES SHALES SHALEY SHAMED SHAMES SHAPED SHAPER SHAPES SHARED SHARER SHARES SHAVED SHAVEN SHAVER SHAVES SKATED SKATER SKATES SLAKED SLAKES SLATED SLATER SLATES SLAVED SLAVER SLAVES SLAVEY SLAYED SLAYER SNAKED SNAKES SNARED SNARES SOAKED SOAKER SOAPED SOAPER SOARED SOARER SOARES SOAVES SPACED SPACEK SPACER SPACES SPACEY SPADED SPADER SPADES SPARED SPARER SPARES SPATES SPAYED STACEY STAGED STAGER STAGES STAKED STAKES STALED STALER STALES STAMEN STAPES STARED STARER STARES STASES STATED STATEN STATER STATES STAVED STAVES STAYED SUAVER SWAGED SWAGES SWALES SWANEE SWAYED SWAYER TEAMED TEARED TEASED TEASEL TEASER TEASES TEASET THALER THALES THAMES THANES THAWED THAYER TOATEE TRACED TRACER TRACES TRACEY TRADED TRADER TRADES TRALEE TRAVEL TRAVES TUAREG UKASES UNAGED UNAWED UPASES USAGES WEAKEN WEAKER WEANED WEARER WEASEL WEAVED WEAVER WEAVES WHALER WHALES XIAMEN XRATED XRAYED YEAGER YEANED

••A••E

AMALIE APACHE ARABLE BEADLE BEAGLE BEANIE BEATLE BLAINE BLAISE BRAISE BRAQUE CHAINE CHAISE CHANCE CHANGE CHARGE CHASSE CHASTE CLAIRE CLAQUE CLARKE CLAUDE CLAUSE COARSE CRABBE CRADLE DEARIE DEARME DIANNE DOABLE DRAGEE DUARTE DWAYNE ECARTE ELAINE ELAPSE ELAYNE ENABLE FIACRE FIANCE FLAMBE FLANGE FRAISE FRANCE FRAPPE GLANCE GOALIE GOATEE GRABLE GRACIE GRAMME GRANDE GRANGE HEARYE HOAGIE HOARSE JEANNE JOANIE JOANNE KHAFRE LEAGUE LIABLE LIAISE LOATHE MEAGRE MEALIE MEANIE NUANCE OPAQUE ORACLE ORANGE PIAFFE PLAGUE PLAICE PLANTE PLAQUE PLATTE PRAGUE PRAISE PRANCE QUAYLE ROADIE RVALUE SCARCE SCARNE SCATHE SEABEE SEANCE SEARLE SHAYNE SNATHE SPARGE SPARSE SPATHE STABLE STACTE STANCE STAPLE STARVE STATUE SWANEE SWATHE SWAYZE TOATEE TRALEE TRANCE UNABLE USABLE USANCE UVALUE VIABLE WHATVE WRASSE

•••AE•

ACHAEA ISRAEL JUDAEA NICAEA PALAEO RAFAEL TOGAED VISAED

•••A•E

ABLATE ABLAZE ABRADE ACUATE ADNATE AERATE AFLAME AFRAME AGLARE AGNATE ALSACE ANSATE AQUATE ARCADE ARCANE ATEASE AUBADE AVIATE AYEAYE BECAME BEDAZE BEHAVE BERATE BETAKE BEWARE BINATE BORAGE BORATE BUTANE BYNAME CANAPE CARAFE CERATE CESARE CETANE CHOATE CLEAVE COMATE CREASE CREATE CUBAGE CURARE CURATE DAMAGE DEBASE DEBATE DECADE DEFACE DEFAME DEGAGE DELATE DILATE DONATE DOSAGE DOTAGE EFFACE ENCAGE ENCASE ENGAGE ENLACE ENRAGE EQUATE ERGATE ERRARE ESCAPE ESTATE ETHANE EXHALE FACADE FATALE FEMALE FINALE FIXATE FORAGE GARAGE GREASE GREAVE GYRATE HARARE HECATE HOMAGE HORACE HUMANE ICEAGE IDEATE IGNACE IMPALE INCASE INHALE INMATE INNAGE INNATE INSANE INTAKE INVADE IODATE KARATE LAMAZE LANATE LAVAGE LEGATE LENAPE LESAGE LIGATE LINAGE LIPASE LOBATE LOCALE LOCATE LOVAGE LUNATE LUXATE MADAME MALATE MANAGE MCCABE MCHALE MENACE MENAGE METATE MIRAGE MOHAVE MOJAVE MORALE MUGABE MUTATE NEGATE NEWAGE NONAGE NONAME NOSALE NOTATE NUTATE OBLATE OCTANE OCTAVE OFLATE OLDAGE OLEATE ONSALE ONTAPE OPIATE ORGATE ORNATE OUTAGE OUTATE PALACE PALATE PARADE PAVANE PEDATE PELAGE PHRASE PIKAKE PILATE PIRATE PLEASE POMACE POMADE POTAGE PURACE RAMATE RAVAGE REBATE RECANE REDATE REFACE REGALE RELACE RELATE REMADE REMAKE RENAME REPAVE RERATE RESALE RETAKE RETAPE ROTATE ROXANE ROYALE RUGATE SAVAGE SAVATE SCRAPE SEDATE SENATE SERAPE SESAME SEWAGE SHEAVE SILAGE SLEAVE SLEAZE SLOANE SOCAGE SOLACE SQUARE STRAFE STRAKE TAMALE TENACE THRACE THRALE TIRADE TIRANE TISANE TODATE TOWAGE TRIAGE TUBATE TULANE TULARE ULLAGE UNCAGE UNCASE UNEASE UNIATE UNLACE UNLADE UNMADE UNMAKE UNSAFE UPDATE UPTAKE URBANE VACATE VISAGE VITALE VIVACE VOLARE VOYAGE ZONATE ZOUAVE ZYMASE

••••AE

AGORAE ALULAE AMEBAE AORTAE BULLAE BURSAE CANNAE CELLAE CHELAE CNIDAE COSTAE CURIAE FAUNAE FLORAE FOSSAE FOVEAE GALEAE GEMMAE GUTTAE HYDRAE LARVAE MACRAE MENSAE NUCHAE OCREAE PALEAE PARCAE PENNAE PHILAE PHYLAE PINNAE PLICAE REGGAE STELAE STRIAE SUMMAE SUNDAE TESTAE THECAE TIBIAE UMBRAE UVULAE

AF••••

AFEARD AFFAIR AFFECT AFFINE AFFIRM AFFORD AFFRAY AFGHAN AFIELD AFLAME AFLATS AFLCIO AFLOAT AFRAID AFRAME AFREET AFRESH AFRICA AFRITS

A•F•••

AAFAIR AFFAIR AFFECT AFFINE AFFIRM AFFORD AFFRAY AJFOYT ALFINE ALFRED ALFVEN AUFAIT AUFOND

A••F••

AIDFUL AIMFOR AIMFUL ALLFOR ARAFAT ARMFUL ARTFUL ASKFOR

A•••F•

ADRIFT AERIFY AMALFI ARGUFY AURIFY

•AF•••

AAFAIR BAFFIN BAFFLE CAFTAN DAFFED DAFTER DAFTLY FAFNIR GAFFED GAFFER GAFFES HAFTED KAFFIR KAFIRS LAFFER OAFISH RAFAEL RAFFIA RAFFLE RAFTED RAFTER SAFARI SAFELY SAFEST SAFETY SAFIRE WAFERS WAFERY WAFFLE WAFFLY WAFTED ZAFFER ZAFTIG

•A•F••

BAFFIN BAFFLE BAGFUL BARFLY CANFUL CAPFUL CARFUL DAFFED EARFUL GADFLY GAFFED GAFFER GAFFES HATFUL JARFUL KAFFIR LAFFER LAPFUL LAWFUL LAYFOR MANFUL MAYFLY PANFRY PANFUL PAYFOR RAFFIA RAFFLE RANFOR SAWFIT VATFUL WAFFLE WAFFLY ZAFFER

•A••F•

BASIFY CANIFF CARAFE CASEFY FAROFF GASIFY LAYOFF PACIFY PAYOFF RAMIFY RANOFF RAREFY RARIFY RATIFY SALIFY SAWOFF TAPOFF TARIFF

•A•••F

CANIFF FAROFF LAYOFF MASSIF PAYOFF RANOFF SAWOFF TAPOFF TARIFF

••AF••

ARAFAT BIAFRA CHAFED CHAFES CHAFFS CHAFFY CRAFTS CRAFTY DEAFEN DEAFER DEAFLY DRAFTS DRAFTY GRAFTS INAFIX INAFOG KHAFRE LEAFED LOAFED LOAFER PIAFFE QUAFFS SEAFAN SEAFOX SHAFTS SNAFUS STAFFS

••A•F•

AMALFI CHAFFS CHAFFY DWARFS PIAFFE QUAFFS SCARFS STAFFS WHARFS

••A••F

HEAROF SHARIF STAPUF WHATIF

•••AF•

CARAFE DECAFS PILAFS SCLAFF SHEAFS STRAFE UNSAFE

•••A•F

BEHALF INHALF SCLAFF

AG••••

AGADIR AGAMAS AGARIC AGASSI AGATES AGATHA AGAVES AGEING AGEISM AGEIST AGENAS AGENCY AGENDA AGENTS AGEOLD AGGIES AGGROS AGHAST AGLAIA AGLARE AGLEAM AGLETS AGLINT AGNATE AGORAE AGORAS AGOROT AGOUTI AGREED AGREES AGUISH

A•G•••

AEGEAN AFGHAN AGGIES AGGROS AIGRET ALGORE ANGELA ANGELI ANGELL ANGELO ANGELS ANGERS ANGKOR ANGLED ANGLER ANGLES ANGLIA ANGLIC ANGLOS ANGOLA ANGORA ARGALI ARGENT ARGIVE ARGOSY ARGOTS ARGUED ARGUER ARGUES ARGUFY ARGYLE ARGYLL ASGARD AUGEAN AUGEND AUGERS AUGHTS AUGURS AUGURY AUGUST

A••G••

ADAGES ADAGIO AIRGUN ALEGAR ALEGRE ALIGHT ALIGNS AMIGAS AMIGOS ANSGAR APOGEE ARAGON ARIGHT ARTGUM

A•••G•

ALLEGE ANERGY ARMAGH ASSIGN ATERGO AURIGA AVENGE AWEIGH

A••••G

AAHING ABYING ACHING ACTING ADDING AGEING AIDING AILING AIMING AIRBAG AIRING ALBORG ANALOG ANWANG ANYANG ARCING ARMING ASKING AWNING

•AG•••

BAGDAD BAGELS BAGFUL BAGGED BAGGER BAGGIE BAGSIT BAGUIO CAGERS CAGIER CAGILY CAGING CAGNEY CAGUAS DAGAMA DAGGER DAGMAR EAGLED EAGLES EAGLET EAGRES FAGEND FAGGED FAGOTS GAGGED GAGGLE GAGING GAGLAW GAGMAN GAGMEN HAGDON HAGGIS HAGGLE HAGMAN JAGGED JAGGER JAGUAR KAGERA LAGASH LAGERS LAGGED LAGGER LAGOON LAGUNA MAGGIE MAGGIO MAGMAS MAGNET MAGNON MAGNUM MAGNUS MAGPIE MAGUEY MAGYAR NAGANO NAGGED NAGGER NAGOYA PAGANS PAGERS PAGING PAGODA RAGBAG RAGGED RAGING RAGLAN RAGMAN RAGMEN RAGMOP RAGOUT RAGRUG RAGTAG RAGTOP SAGELY SAGEST SAGGED TAGDAY TAGEND TAGGED TAGORE TAGOUT TAGSUP VAGARY VAGUER WAGERS WAGGED WAGGLE WAGGLY WAGGON WAGING WAGNER WAGONS ZAGGED ZAGREB

•A•G••

BADGER BADGES BADGUY BAGGED BAGGER BAGGIE BANGED BANGER BANGKA BANGLE BANGOR BANGUI BANGUP BARGED BARGES CADGED CADGER CADGES CAPGUN CARGOS CATGUT CAUGHT DAGGER DANGER DANGLE DANGLY DANGME DAYGLO FAGGED FANGED GADGET GAGGED GAGGLE GANGED GANGER GANGES GANGLE GANGLY GANGUE GANGUP GARGLE GAUGED GAUGER GAUGES HAGGIS HAGGLE HAIGHT HANGAR HANGED HANGER HANGIN HANGON HANGUL HANGUP JAEGER JAGGED JAGGER JANGLE JANGLY JARGON LAAGER LAGGED LAGGER LANGUR LARGER LARGES LARGOS LAUGHS MAGGIE MAGGIO MAJGEN MANGER MANGLE MANGOS MARGAY MARGES MARGIE MARGIN MARGOT NAGGED NAGGER NAUGHT PARGET RAGGED RANGED RANGER RANGES RANGUP RAYGUN SAGGED SAIGAS SAIGON SANGER SANGTO SARGES SARGON SARGOS SAUGER TAGGED TAIGAS TANGED TANGLE TANGLY TANGOS TANGUY TARGES TARGET TAUGHT VAUGHN WAGGED WAGGLE WAGGLY WAGGON WANGLE WARGOD YANGON ZAGGED

•A••G•

BADEGG BAREGE CAYUGA DAMAGE GALAGO GARAGE LADOGA LATIGO LAVAGE MALAGA MALIGN MANAGE MANEGE PAANGA PAPAGO RAVAGE RAWEGG SAVAGE

•A•••G

AAHING BAAING BADEGG BAKING BALING BANDOG BARING BARONG BASING BATING BAYING CAGING CAKING CANING CARING CASING CATRIG CAVING CAWING DANANG DANZIG DARING DATING DATONG DAZING EALING

EARING
EARWIG
EASING
EATING
FACING
FADING
FAKING
FARING
FAXING
FAZING
GAGING
GAMING
GAPING
GASBAG
GASLOG
GATING
GAZING
HALING
HARING
HATING
HAVING
HAWING
HAYING
HAZING
JADING
JAPING
JAWING
LACING
LADING
LAMING
LAPDOG
LAVING
LAWING
LAYING
LAZING
MAKING
MATING
MAYTAG
NAMING
OARING
PACING
PADANG
PAGING
PAHANG
PALING
PARANG
PARING
PAVING
PAWING
PAYING
RACING
RAGBAG
RAGING
RAGRUG
RAGTAG
RAKING
RARING
RASING
RATEDG
RATING
RAVING
RAWEGG
RAZING
SARONG
SATANG
SATING
SAVING
SAWING
SAWLOG
SAYING
TAKING
TAMING
TAPING
TARING
TAUTOG
TAWING
TAXING
WADING
WAGING
WAKING
WANING
WARING
WAVING
WAXING
YAWING
ZAFTIG

••AG••

ADAGES
ADAGIO
ARAGON
BEAGLE
CRAGGY
DRAGEE
DRAGGY
DRAGIN
DRAGON
FLAGGY
FLAGON
HOAGIE
IMAGED
IMAGER
IMAGES
KNAGGY
LAAGER
LEAGUE
MEAGER
MEAGRE
ONAGER
OSAGES
PHAGES
PIAGET
PLAGAL
PLAGES
PLAGIO
PLAGUE
PRAGUE
QUAGGA
QUAGGY
REAGAN
SEAGAL
SHAGGY
SLAGGY
SNAGGY
STAGED
STAGER
STAGES
SWAGED
SWAGES
TRAGIC
UNAGED
USAGES
YEAGER

••A•G•

CHANGE
CHARGE
CLANGS
CRAGGY
DRAGGY
FLAGGY
FLANGE
GRANGE
KIANGS
KNAGGY
LIANGS
ORANGE
ORANGS
ORANGY
PAANGA
PRANGS
QUAGGA
QUAGGY
QUANGO
SHAGGY
SLAGGY
SLANGS
SLANGY
SNAGGY
SPARGE
TWANGS
TWANGY
UBANGI
WHANGS

••A••G

ANALOG
BAAING
DIALOG
INAFOG
QUAHOG
SEABAG
SEADOG
STALAG
TEABAG
TUAREG

•••AG•

ARMAGH
BORAGE
CUBAGE
DAMAGE
DEGAGE
DORAGS
DOSAGE
DOTAGE
ENCAGE
ENGAGE
ENRAGE
FORAGE
GALAGO
GARAGE
GULAGS
HOMAGE
ICEAGE
IDTAGS
INNAGE
LAVAGE
LESAGE
LINAGE
LOVAGE
MALAGA
MANAGE
MENAGE
MIRAGE
NEWAGE
NONAGE
OLDAGE
OUTAGE
PAPAGO
PELAGE
POTAGE
RAVAGE
REBAGS
RETAGS
SAVAGE
SCRAGS
SEWAGE
SILAGE
SOCAGE
SPRAGS
TOBAGO
TOWAGE
TRIAGE
ULLAGE
UNCAGE
VIRAGO
VISAGE
VOYAGE

•••A•G

ANWANG
ANYANG
CHIANG
DANANG
KDLANG
PADANG
PAHANG
PARANG
PENANG
REHANG
SATANG
SPRANG

••••AG

AIRBAG
DOGTAG
GASBAG
GOSTAG
GYMBAG
ICEBAG
JETLAG
KITBAG
MAYTAG
RAGBAG
RAGTAG
REDTAG
REFLAG
SEABAG
SONTAG
STALAG
TEABAG
UNSNAG
WIGWAG
ZIGZAG

AH••••

AHCHOO
AHERNE
AHIMSA

A•H•••

AAHING
ABHORS
ACHAEA
ACHEBE
ACHENE
ACHIER
ACHING
ADHERE
AGHAST
ALHIRT
AMHARA
ANHYDR
APHIDS
ASHARP
ASHCAN
ASHIER
ASHLAR
ASHLEY
ASHORE
ASHRAM
ATHAND
ATHENA
ATHENE
ATHENS
ATHOME
AWHILE
AWHIRL

A••H••

AACHEN
ABOHMS
AETHER
AFGHAN
AHCHOO
ALOHAS
ALPHAS
ALTHEA
AMPHID
ANCHOR
ANDHOW
ANNHON
ANTHEM
ANTHER
ANYHOW
ARCHED
ARCHER
ARCHES
ARCHIE
ARCHLY
ARCHON
ARNHEM
ARTHRO
ARTHUR
ASCHAM
ATTHAT
AUGHTS
AUTHOR

A•••H•

AGATHA
ALEPHS
ALIGHT
AMECHE
APACHE
APATHY
ARETHA
ARIGHT
AYESHA

A••••H

ABLUSH
ADOLPH
AFRESH
AGUISH
AMBUSH
ARMAGH
ASPISH
ATTACH
AVOUCH
AWEIGH

•AH•••

AAHING
BAHAMA
BAHIAN
CAHIER
CAHOWS
DAHLIA
KAHLIL
KAHLUA
KAHUNA
LAHORE
MAHDIS
MAHLER
MAHOUT
MAHZOR
PAHANG
PAHARI
RAHRAH
SAHARA
SAHIBS
TAHINI
TAHITI
WAHINE
WAHOOS
WAHWAH
YAHOOS
YAHWEH

•A•H••

AACHEN
BACHED
BADHAM
BARHOP
BASHED
BASHES
BATHED
BATHER
BATHES
BATHOS
CACHED
CACHES
CACHET
CACHOU
CARHOP
CASHED
CASHES
CASHEW
CASHIN
CATHAY
CATHER
DACHAS
DAPHNE
DASHED
DASHER
DASHES
DASHIS
FATHER
FATHOM
GASHED
GASHES
GATHER
HASHED
HASHES
HATHOR
HAWHAW
JANHUS
KATHIE
LACHES
LAPHAM
LASHED
LASHER
LASHES
LASHIO
LASHUP
LATHED
LATHER
LATHES
MACHES
MACHOS
MASHED
MASHER
MASHES
MASHIE
MATHER
MATHIS
MAYHAP
MAYHEM
NACHOS
NASHUA
NATHAN
PASHAS
PASHTO
PATHAN
PATHOL
PATHOS
RACHEL
RACHIS
RASHAD
RASHER
RASHES
RASHID
RASHLY
RATHER
SACHEM
SACHET
SADHES
SADHUS
SASHAY
SASHED
SASHES
VACHEL
VASHTI
WARHOL
WASHED
WASHER
WASHES
WASHOE
WASHUP
YACHTS

•A••H•

CANTHI
CATCHY
CAUCHO
CAUCHY
CAUGHT
EARTHA
EARTHY
FAITHS
GALAHS
GANDHI
GARTHS
GAUCHE
GAUCHO
HAIGHT
JASCHA
JAWOHL
LANDHO
LAUGHS
MANCHA
MANCHU
MARCHE
MARSHA
MARSHY
MARTHA
NAUGHT
NAVAHO
PANCHO
PATCHY
RAJAHS
RANCHO
SANCHO
SAPPHO
TAICHI
TAUGHT
VAUGHN
XANTHO
YAMAHA

•A•••H

BANISH
BARISH
BARUCH
CALASH
CALIPH
CASBAH
DALETH
DANISH
FAMISH
FARRAH
GALOSH
GARETH
GARISH
HALVAH
HANNAH
HAUNCH
JADISH
JARRAH
KALAKH
KASBAH
KAZAKH
LAGASH
LAMECH
LAMEDH
LATISH
LAUNCH
LAVISH
MARIAH
MARISH
MATZOH
NAMATH
NAUTCH
OAFISH
PALISH
PARAPH
PARIAH
PARISH
PAUNCH
RADISH
RAHRAH
RAKISH
RAVISH
RAWISH
SALISH
SAMECH
SAMEKH
TAKETH
VANISH
WABASH
WAHWAH
WARMTH
YAHWEH

••AH••

BRAHMA
BRAHMS
GRAHAM
OMAHAN
OMAHAS
PEAHEN
QUAHOG
SPAHIS
UTAHAN

••A•H•

AGATHA
APACHE
APATHY
BEACHY
BRACHY
BRASHY
CHACHA
DRACHM
FLASHY
GRAPHS
GRAPHY
HEATHS
HEATHY
KWACHA
LEACHY
LOATHE
ORACHS
PEACHY
PLASHY
POACHY
SCATHE
SNATHE
SNATHS
SPATHE
SWATHE
SWATHS
TRACHY
TRASHY
WRATHS
WRATHY

••A••H

BLANCH
BRANCH
DEARTH
EPARCH
EXARCH
HEALTH
HEARTH
INARCH
ISAIAH
KLATCH
SEARCH
SNATCH
STANCH
STARCH
SWARTH
SWATCH
THATCH
WEALTH
WRAITH

•••AH•

EPHAHS
GALAHS
GERAHS
JONAHS
LOTAHS
MYNAHS
NAVAHO
OBEAHS
RAJAHS
SURAHS
TORAHS
YAMAHA

•••A•H

ARMAGH
ATTACH
BLEACH
BREACH
BREATH
BROACH
BYPATH
CALASH
DETACH
EMDASH
ENDASH
INCASH
KALAKH
KAZAKH
LAGASH
NAMATH
ORBACH
PARAPH
PESACH
PLEACH
POTASH
PREACH
REHASH
REWASH
RIYADH
SERAPH
SHEATH
SIWASH
SPLASH
SQUASH
TERAPH
THRASH
UNLASH
WABASH
WREATH

••••AH

BEULAH
CASBAH
DOODAH
ELIJAH
FARRAH
FELLAH
GULLAH
HALVAH
HANNAH
HIJRAH
HOOHAH
HOOKAH
HOORAH
HOWDAH
HURRAH
HUZZAH
ISAIAH
JARRAH
JINNAH
JOSIAH
JUBBAH
KASBAH
LOOFAH
MARIAH
MOOLAH
MULLAH
NULLAH
OHYEAH
OOMPAH
PARIAH
PISGAH
PUNKAH
PURDAH
RAHRAH
RUPIAH
SIRRAH
SUKKAH
TUSSAH
UZZIAH
WAHWAH
WHYDAH
ZILPAH

AI••••

AIDERS
AIDFUL
AIDING
AIELLO
AIGRET
AIKIDO
AILEEN
AILERS
AILING
AIMFOR
AIMFUL
AIMING
AIMSAT
AIMSTO
AIRARM
AIRBAG
AIRBUS
AIRDAM
AIRDRY
AIRGUN
AIRIER
AIRILY
AIRING
AIRMAN
AIRMEN
AIROUT
AIRSAC
AIRWAY
AISLES

A•I•••

ABIDED
ABIDES
ACIDIC
ACIDLY
ACINUS
ADIDAS
ADIEUS
ADIEUX
AFIELD
AHIMSA
AKIMBO
AKITAS
ALIBIS
ALIBLE
ALICIA
ALIENS
ALIGHT
ALIGNS
ALINES
ALIOTO
ALISON
ALITER
AMICES
AMICUS
AMIDES
AMIDOL
AMIDST
AMIENS
AMIGAS
AMIGOS
AMINES
AMINOR
AMINUS
ANIMAL
ANIMAS
ANIMES
ANIMUS
ANIONS
ANITRA
APIARY
APICAL
APICES
APIECE
ARIDLY
ARIGHT
ARIOSE
ARIOSO
ARISEN
ARISES
ARISTA
ARISTO
ASIANS
ASIDES
ASIMOV
AVIANS
AVIARY
AVIATE
AVIDLY
AVISOS
AXILLA
AXIOMS
AXIONS
AZIDES
AZINES

A••I••

AAHING
ABYING
ACHIER
ACHING
ACTIII
ACTING
ACTINO
ACTION
ACTIUM
ACTIVE
ACUITY
ADDING
ADLIBS
ADMIRE
ADMITS
ADRIAN
ADRIEN
ADRIFT
ADVICE
ADVISE
AEDILE
AERIAL
AERIES
AERIFY
AERILY
AFFINE
AFFIRM
AFRICA
AFRITS
AGEING
AGEISM
AGEIST
AGGIES
AGLINT
AGUISH
AIDING
AIKIDO
AILING
AIMING
AIRIER
AIRILY
AIRING
ALBINO
ALBION
ALDINE
ALFINE
ALHIRT
ALLIED
ALLIES
ALLIUM
ALNICO
ALOINS
ALPINE
ALTIMA
ALTIUS
AMBITS
AMNION
ANCIEN
ANNIKA
ANOINT
ANTICS
ANVILS
AORIST
APHIDS
APLITE
APPIAN
AQUILA
AQUINO
ARCING
ARGIVE
ARLISS
ARMIES
ARMING
ARNICA
AROIDS
ARRIBA
ARRIVE
ARTIER
ARTILY
ARTIST
ASDICS
ASEITY
ASHIER
ASKING
ASPICS
ASPIRE
ASPISH
ASSIGN
ASSISI
ASSIST
ASSIZE
ASWIRL
ATKINS
ATRIAL
ATRISK
ATRIUM
ATTICA
ATTICS
ATTILA
ATTIRE
ATWILL
AUDIAL
AUDILE
AUDIOS
AUDITS
AURIFY
AURIGA
AUXINS
AVAILS
AVOIDS
AWAITS
AWEIGH
AWHILE
AWHIRL
AWNING
AXLIKE

A•••I•

AAFAIR
ABATIS
ABUKIR
ACACIA
ACADIA
ACARID
ACEDIA
ACETIC
ACIDIC
ACQUIT
ACTIII
ADAGIO
ADDSIN
ADELIE
ADJOIN
ADONIS
ADROIT
AENEID
AEOLIA
AEOLIC
AFFAIR
AFLCIO
AFRAID
AGADIR
AGARIC
AGLAIA
ALANIS
ALARIC
ALBEIT
ALBOIN
ALCUIN
ALDRIN
ALEXIA
ALEXIS
ALIBIS
ALICIA
ALTAIC
ALTAIR
AMADIS
AMALIE
AMATIS
AMBLIN
AMEBIC
AMELIA
AMPHID
ANACIN
ANEMIA
ANEMIC
ANGLIA
ANGLIC
ANNUIT
ANODIC
ANOMIC
ANOMIE
ANTRIM
ANUBIS
AODAIS
AORTIC
APULIA
ARABIA
ARABIC
ARALIA
ARAMIS
ARCHIE
ARCTIC
ARMPIT
ARTOIS
ASKSIN
ASSAIL
ASTRID
ATOMIC
ATONIC
ATTAIN
ATTRIT
AUFAIT
AULAIT
AUNTIE
AUPAIR
AUSSIE
AUSTIN
AZORIN

A••••I

ACTIII
ADJANI
ADONAI
ADZUKI
AGASSI
AGOUTI
ALEXEI
ALKALI
ALUMNI
AMALFI
ANDREI
ANGELI
ANNULI
ARGALI
ARMANI
ASKARI
ASSISI
AVANTI

•AI•••

BAIKAL
BAILED
BAILEE
BAILER
BAILEY
BAILOR
BAINES
BAIRNS
BAITED
BAIZAS
CAICOS
CAIMAN
CAIQUE
CAIRNS
DAIKON
DAILEY
DAIMON
DAIMYO
DAINTY
DAIREN
DAISES
FAILED
FAILLE
FAINTS
FAIRED
FAIRER
FAIRLY
FAIRUP
FAISAL
FAITHS
FAIYUM
GAIETY
GAIJIN
GAINED
GAINER
GAINLY
GAINON
GAINST
GAITED
GAITER
HAIDAS
HAIGHT
HAIKUS
HAILED
HAILEY
HAINAN
HAINES
HAIRDO
HAIRED
JAILED
JAILER
JAIPUR
KAILUA
KAISER
LAIDBY
LAIDIN
LAIDON
LAIDTO
LAIDUP
LAINIE
LAIRDS
MAIDEN
MAIDUS
MAILED
MAILER
MAILES
MAILIN
MAINLY
MAISIE
MAITAI
MAITRE
MAIZES
NAIADS
NAILED
NAILER
NAILIN
NAIRAS
PAIDIN
PAIDUP
PAILOU
PAINED
PAINTS
PAINTY
PAIRED
PAIRUP
PAISAS
PAIUTE
RAIDED
RAIDER
RAILAT
RAILED
RAILER
RAINED
RAINER
RAINES
RAINEY
RAIPUR
RAISED
RAISER
RAISES
RAISIN
SAIGAS
SAIGON
SAILED
SAILOR
SAINTE
SAINTS
SAIPAN
TAICHI
TAIGAS
TAILED
TAILLE
TAILOR
TAINAN
TAINOS
TAINTS
TAIPAN
TAIPEI
TAIWAN
VAINER
VAINLY
VAISYA
WAILED
WAILER
WAISTS
WAITED
WAITER
WAITON
WAITUP
WAIVED
WAIVER
WAIVES
ZAIRES

•A•I••

AAHING
BAAING
BABIED
BABIES
BAHIAN

BAKING
BALING
BANISH
BARING
BARISH
BARITE
BARIUM
BASICS
BASIFY
BASING
BASINS
BATIKS
BATING
BAYING
CABINS
CAGIER
CAGILY
CAGING
CAHIER
CAKIER
CAKING
CALICO
CALIPH
CAMINO
CAMION
CAMISE
CANIDS
CANIER
CANIFF
CANINE
CANING
CAPIAS
CAPITA
CARIBE
CARIBS
CARIES
CARINA
CARING
CASING
CASINO
CATION
CAVIAR
CAVILS
CAVING
CAVITY
CAWING
DAMIEN
DAMITA
DANIEL
DANISH
DARIEN
DARING
DARIUS
DATING
DATIVE
DAVIES
DAVITS
DAZING
EALING
EARING
EASIER
EASILY
EASING
EATING
FABIAN
FACIAL
FACIAS
FACIES
FACILE
FACING
FADING
FAJITA
FAKING
FAKIRS
FALINE
FAMILY
FAMINE
FAMISH
FANION
FARINA
FARING
FATIMA
FAXING
FAZING
GABIES
GABION
GAGING
GAMIER
GAMILY
GAMINE
GAMING
GAMINS
GAPING
GARISH
GASIFY
GATING
GAVIAL
GAZING
HABILE
HABITS
HAKIMS
HALIDE
HALING
HALITE
HAMILL
HAMITE
HARING
HATING
HAVING
HAWING
HAYING
HAZIER
HAZILY
HAZING
JABIRU
JADING
JADISH
JANICE
JANINE
JAPING
JAVIER
JAWING
KAFIRS
KALINE
KARIBA
LABIAL
LABILE
LACIER
LACILY
LACING
LADIDA
LADIES
LADING
LADINO
LAKIER
LAMIAS
LAMINA
LAMING
LANIER
LAPINS
LARIAT
LATIGO
LATINA
LATINI
LATINO
LATINS
LATISH
LATIUM
LAVING
LAVISH
LAWING
LAXITY
LAYING
LAZIER
LAZILY
LAZING
MAKING
MALIBU
MALICE
MALIGN
MANIAC
MANIAS
MANILA
MANIOC
MAOISM
MAOIST
MARIAH
MARIAN
MARIEL
MARIKO
MARILU
MARINA
MARINE
MARINO
MARION
MARISA
MARISH
MARIST
MARIUS
MATING
MATINS
MAXIMA
MAXIMS
MAXINE
MAXIXE
MAZIER
MAZILY
NADINE
NADIRS
NAMING
NAPIER
NARIAL
NATICK
NATION
NATIVE
NAVIES
OAFISH
OARING
OATIER
PACIFY
PACING
PACINO
PAGING
PALIER
PALING
PALISH
PAMIRS
PANICS
PAPIER
PARIAH
PARING
PARISH
PARITY
PATINA
PATINE
PATIOS
PAVING
PAWING
PAYING
RABIES
RACIAL
RACIER
RACILY
RACINE
RACING
RADIAL
RADIAN
RADIOS
RADISH
RADIUM
RADIUS
RAGING
RAKING
RAKISH
RAMIES
RAMIFY
RANIDS
RAPIDS
RAPIER
RAPINE
RAPINI
RARIFY
RARING
RARITY
RASING
RATIFY
RATINE
RATING
RATION
RATIOS
RATITE
RAVINE
RAVING
RAVISH
RAWISH
RAZING
SABINE
SABINS
SAFIRE
SAHIBS
SALIFY
SALINA
SALINE
SALISH
SALIVA
SAMIAM
SAMITE
SANITY
SATING
SATINS
SATINY
SATIRE
SAVING
SAVIOR
SAWING
SAYING
TAHINI
TAHITI
TAKING
TAKINS
TALION
TAMILS
TAMING
TANIST
TAOISM
TAOIST
TAPING
TAPINS
TAPIRS
TARIFF
TARING
TAWING
TAXIED
TAXIES
TAXING
VALISE
VALIUM
VANIER
VANISH
VANITY
VARIED
VARIES
WADING
WAGING
WAHINE
WAKING
WANIER
WANING
WAPITI
WARIER
WARILY
WARING
WAVIER
WAVILY
WAVING
WAXIER
WAXILY
WAXING
XAVIER
YAKIMA
YALIES
YAWING
ZAMIAS
ZANIER
ZANIES
ZANILY
ZAYINS

•A••I•

AAFAIR
BACKIN
BADDIE
BAFFIN
BAGGIE
BAGSIT
BAGUIO
BALTIC
BANDIT
BARBIE
BARDIC
BARKIN
BARRIE
BARRIO
BARRIS
BAUCIS
CABBIE
CADDIE
CADDIS
CADMIC
CALAIS
CALLIN
CALVIN
CAMEIN
CANDID
CANLIT
CAPRIS
CAPSID
CARDIN
CARDIO
CARLIN
CARRIE
CASHIN
CASSIA
CASSIO
CASSIS
CATKIN
CATNIP
CATRIG
CAVEIN
DACOIT
DAHLIA
DANDIE
DANZIG
DARNIT
DARWIN
DASHIS
DASSIN
DAYLIT
EARWIG
EASEIN
EATSIN
FABRIC
FADEIN
FAERIE
FAFNIR
FALLIN
FANNIE
FASCIA
GAELIC
GAIJIN
GALLIA
GALLIC
GALOIS
GAMBIA
GAMBIT
GARCIA
GARLIC
GASKIN
GASLIT
GATLIN
GAVEIN
GAWAIN
HACKIE
HADDIE
HADJIS
HAGGIS
HAJJIS
HALOID
HAMLIN
HANDIN
HANGIN
HANKIE
HARBIN
HARLIN
HARRIS
HATPIN
HATTIE
HAWAII
IAMBIC
IATRIC
JACKIE
JAMSIN
KAFFIR
KAHLIL
KAOLIN
KARMIC
KATHIE
KAURIS
LACTIC
LADDIE
LAIDIN
LAINIE
LANAIS
LANDIS
LANVIN
LASHIO
LASSIE
LATVIA
LAURIE
LAYSIN
MACEIO
MADDIE
MADEIT
MADRID
MAGGIE
MAGGIO
MAGPIE
MAHDIS
MAILIN
MAISIE
MAJLIS
MAKEIT
MALKIN
MALTIN
MANNIX
MANTIC
MANTIS
MAORIS
MAQUIS
MARCIA
MARCIE
MARGIE
MARGIN
MARLIN
MARNIE
MARTIN
MARVIN
MASAIS
MASHIE
MASSIF
MASTIC
MATHIS
MATLIN
MATRIX
MATTIE
NAILIN
NANNIE
NAPKIN
NAPPIE
NARNIA
NARVIK
PAIDIN
PALLIA
PALLID
PANDIT
PAPAIN
PAQUIN
PARNIS
PARRIS
PARVIS
PASSIM
PASTIS
PATOIS
PAUCIS
PAYSIN
RABBIS
RABBIT
RACHIS
RAFFIA
RAISIN
RAKEIN
RANCID
RANKIN
RASHID
RATLIN
SALVIA
SAMMIE
SANDIA
SANTIR
SARDIS
SARNIA
SAUDIS
SAVAII
SAVOIE
SAVOIR
SAWFIT
SAYYID
TABRIZ
TACTIC
TAKEIN
TALKIE
TANNIC
TANNIN
TARPIT
VALOIS
WADEIN
WALKIE
WALKIN
WALLIS
WANTIN
WAVEIN
YAQUIS
ZADDIK
ZAFTIG
ZAMBIA

•A•••I

BANGUI
BANZAI
BATUMI
CANTHI
CARONI
DALASI
GANDHI
HATARI
HAWAII
JACOBI
JAVARI
KABUKI
KATMAI
LATINI
LAZULI
MAITAI
MALAWI
MALLEI
MALOTI
MAOTAI
NAPOLI
PAHARI
PAPYRI
QATARI
RAPINI
SAFARI
SALAMI
SALUKI
SANSEI
SATORI
SAVAII
TAHINI
TAHITI
TAICHI
TAIPEI
TATAMI
UAKARI
VASHTI
WAPITI
WASABI
WATUSI
YANQUI

••AI••

AVAILS
AWAITS
BAAING
BLAINE
BLAISE
BRAIDS
BRAILA
BRAILS
BRAINS
BRAINY
BRAISE
CHAINE
CHAINS
CHAIRS
CHAISE
CLAIMS
CLAIRE
DRAILS
DRAINS
ELAINE
EMAILS
FLAILS
FLAIRS
FRAIDY
FRAISE
GHAINS
GLAIRS
GLAIRY
GRAILS
GRAINS
GRAINY
ISAIAH
KRAITS
LIAISE
PLAICE
PLAIDS
PLAINS
PLAINT
PLAITS
PRAISE
QUAILS
QUAINT
REAIMS
REAIRS
SNAILS
STAINS
STAIRS
SWAINS
TRAILS
TRAINS
TRAITS
WRAITH

••A•I•

ABATIS
ACACIA
ACADIA
ACARID
ADAGIO
AGADIR
AGARIC
ALANIS
ALARIC
AMADIS
AMALIE
AMATIS
ANACIN
ARABIA
ARABIC
ARALIA
ARAMIS
BEANIE
BEATIT
BEAVIS
BRAZIL
CHAPIN
CLAVIN
COATIS
CRANIA
CRANIO
CYANIC
DEALIN
DEARIE
DEASIL
DRAGIN
DRAWIN
DYADIC
ELAPID
ETALIA
ETALII
FLAVIA
GHAZIS
GLACIS
GOALIE
GRACIE
GRADIN
GRATIA
GRATIN
GRATIS
GRAVID
HEADIN
HOAGIE
ICARIA
INAFIX
IRANIS
IRAQIS
ITALIA
ITALIC
JOANIE
KHAKIS
KHALID
LEADIN
MEALIE
MEANIE
MIAMIA
NIACIN
OKAPIS
OMANIS
OXALIS
PHATIC
PLACID
PLAGIO
PRAXIS
READIN
REALIA
ROADIE
SCALIA
SHAMIR
SHANIA
SHARIA
SHARIF
SLAVIC
SPADIX
SPAHIS
SPAVIN
STADIA
STALIN
STASIS
STATIC
SWAMIS
SWAZIS
THALIA
THATIS
TRAGIC
TRAVIS
URACIL
URALIC
URANIA
URANIC
WHATIF

••A••I

AGASSI
AMALFI
AVANTI
BHAKTI
BRAZZI
CIARDI
ETALII
QUADRI
SCAMPI
SHAKTI
SMALTI
UBANGI

•••AI•

AAFAIR
AFFAIR
AFRAID
AGLAIA
ALTAIC
ALTAIR
AODAIS
ASSAIL
ATTAIN
AUFAIT
AULAIT
AUPAIR
BELAIR
BEWAIL
CALAIS
DERAIL
DETAIL
DETAIN
DOMAIN
ECLAIR
ENTAIL
EURAIL
GAWAIN
HAWAII
HOTAIR
IMPAIR
INLAID
INVAIN
JUDAIC
KUWAIT
LANAIS
LCHAIM
LORAIN
MASAIS
MCBAIN
MCLAIN
MCNAIR
MIDAIR
MOHAIR
MOSAIC
OBTAIN
ORDAIN
OXTAIL
PAPAIN
PETAIN
REGAIN
RELAID
REMAIL
REMAIN
RENAIL
REPAID
REPAIR
RETAIL
RETAIN
ROMAIC
SAVAII
SERAIS
SPRAIN
STRAIN
STRAIT
UJJAIN
UNFAIR
UNLAID
UNPAID
UNSAID
USMAIL

•••A•I

ADJANI
ALKALI
ARGALI
ARMANI
ASKARI
BIHARI
BONAMI
DALASI
DENALI
DOMANI
DORATI
ERNANI
FULANI
GELATI
HATARI
HAWAII
HEGARI
ITHAKI
JAVARI
KIGALI
MALAWI
MESABI
NEPALI
PAHARI
QATARI
ROMAJI
RUBATI
SAFARI
SALAMI
SAVAII
SOMALI
SOUARI
STRATI
TATAMI
UAKARI
WASABI

••••AI

ADONAI
BANZAI
BONSAI
KATMAI
KUBLAI
MAITAI
MAOTAI
NILGAI

AJ••••

AJANTA
AJFOYT

A•J•••

ABJECT
ABJURE
ADJANI
ADJOIN
ADJURE
ADJUST
ANJOUS
ARJUNA

A••J••

ACAJOU
AMAJOR

•AJ•••

CAJOLE
CAJUNS
FAJITA
HAJJES
HAJJIS
MAJGEN
MAJLIS
MAJORS
PAJAMA
RAJAHS
RAJPUT

•A•J••

BANJOS
BANJUL
DAYJOB
FANJET
GAIJIN
GASJET
HADJES
HADJIS
HAJJES
HAJJIS
RAMJET

•A••J•

BAROJA
NAVAJO

••AJ••

ACAJOU
AMAJOR
BMAJOR
CMAJOR
DMAJOR
EMAJOR
FMAJOR
GMAJOR
INAJAM
PRAJNA
TRAJAN

••A••J

SWARAJ

•••AJ•

NAVAJO
ROMAJI

••••AJ

SGTMAJ
SWARAJ
THEHAJ

AK••••

AKELAS
AKENES
AKIMBO
AKITAS
AKUAKU

A•K•••

ACKACK
AIKIDO
ALKALI
ALKENE
ALKYDS
ALKYLS
ANKARA
ANKLED
ANKLES
ANKLET
ASKARI
ASKERS
ASKFOR
ASKING
ASKOUT
ASKSIN
ATKINS
AUKLET

A••K••

ABUKIR
ANGKOR
AWAKED
AWAKEN
AWAKES
AWOKEN

A•••K•

ADZUKI
AKUAKU
ALASKA
ALECKY
ANNIKA
AXLIKE

A••••K

ACKACK
ADWEEK
AMTRAK
ANORAK
ARAWAK
ARRACK
ATRISK
ATTACK
ATWORK

•AK•••

BAKERS
BAKERY
BAKING
BAKULA
CAKIER
CAKING
DAKOTA
FAKERS
FAKERY
FAKING
FAKIRS
HAKIMS
KAKAPO
LAKERS
LAKIER
LAKOTA
MAKALU
MAKEBA
MAKEDO
MAKEIT
MAKERS
MAKEUP
MAKING
MAKUTA
OAKLEY
PAKULA
RAKEIN
RAKERS
RAKEUP
RAKING
RAKISH
SAKERS
TAKEIN
TAKEON
TAKERS
TAKETH
TAKETO
TAKEUP
TAKING
TAKINS
UAKARI
WAKENS
WAKEUP
WAKING
YAKIMA
YAKKED
YAKKER
YAKUTS
YAKUZA

•A•K••

BABKAS
BACKED
BACKER
BACKIN
BACKUP
BACKUS
BAIKAL
BALKAN
BALKED
BANKED
BANKER
BANKON
BARKAT
BARKED
BARKER
BARKIN
BASKED
BASKET
CACKLE
CALKED
CANKER
CARKED
CATKIN
DAIKON
DANKER
DANKLY
DARKEN
DARKER
DARKLE
DARKLY
FAWKES
GASKET
GASKIN
GAWKED
GAWKER
HACKED
HACKER
HACKIE
HACKLE
HACKLY
HAIKUS
HANKER
HANKIE
HARKED
HARKEN
HARKER
HAWKED
HAWKER
JACKAL
JACKED
JACKET
JACKEY
JACKIE
JACKUP
KALKAN
LACKED
LACKEY
LANKER
LANKLY
LARKED
LATKES
MALKIN
MARKED
MARKER
MARKET
MARKKA
MARKUP
MASKED
MASKER
NAPKIN
PACKED
PACKER
PACKET
PACKUP
PARKAS
PARKAY
PARKED
PARKER
RACKED
RACKET
RACKUP
RANKED
RANKER
RANKIN
RANKLE
RANKLY
SACKED
SACKER
TACKED
TACKER
TACKLE
TACKON
TALKAT
TALKED
TALKER
TALKIE
TALKTO
TALKUP
TANKAS
TANKED
TANKER
TANKUP
TASKED
WACKOS
WALKED
WALKEN
WALKER
WALKIE
WALKIN
WALKON
WALKUP
YACKED
YAKKED
YAKKER
YANKED
YANKEE

•A••K•

BAMAKO
BANGKA
BATIKS
BAULKS
CAULKS
HACEKS
JAMOKE
JANSKY
KABUKI
KALAKH
KANAKA
KAYAKS
KAZAKH
KAZAKS
MARIKO
MARKKA
SALUKI
SAMEKH
TANAKA
YAPOKS

•A•••K

BARTOK
DAMASK
FAROUK

GALYAK
KARNAK
LANARK
MARDUK
NANOOK
NARVIK
NATICK
TANOAK
ZADDIK
ZANUCK

••AK••

AWAKED
AWAKEN
AWAKES
BEAKED
BEAKER
BHAKTI
BRAKED
BRAKES
CRAKES
DRAKES
FLAKED
FLAKER
FLAKES
FLAKEY
KHAKIS
KRAKEN
KRAKOW
LEAKED
LEAKER
LEAKEY
PEAKED
QUAKED
QUAKER
QUAKES
SHAKEN
SHAKER
SHAKES
SHAKOS
SHAKTI
SLAKED
SLAKES
SNAKED
SNAKES
SOAKED
SOAKER
SOAKUP
STAKED
STAKES
WEAKEN
WEAKER
WEAKLY

••A•K•

ALASKA
BLACKS
BLANKS
CHALKS
CHALKY
CLACKS
CLANKS
CLANKY
CLARKE
CRACKS
CRACKY
CRANKS
CRANKY
DMARKS
FLACKS
FLANKS
FLASKS
FRANKS
KNACKS
KYACKS
OZARKS
PLANKS
PRANKS
QUACKS
QUARKS
SHACKS
SHANKS
SHARKS
SKANKS
SLACKS
SMACKS
SNACKS
SPANKS
SPANKY
SPARKS
SPARKY
STACKS
STALKS
STALKY
STANKY
SWANKS
SWANKY
THANKS
TRACKS
WHACKS
WHACKY
WRACKS

••A••K

ARAWAK
BRATSK
FRANCK
GDANSK
OCASEK
PLANCK
SPACEK
URALSK

•••AK•

AKUAKU
BAMAKO
BETAKE
BREAKS
CLOAKS
CREAKS
CREAKY
CROAKS
CROAKY
FREAKS
FREAKY
INTAKE
ITHAKI
KALAKH
KANAKA
KAYAKS
KAZAKH
KAZAKS
KULAKS
LUSAKA
MEDAKA
PIKAKE
REMAKE
RETAKE
SEDAKA
SNEAKS
SNEAKY
SPEAKS
STEAKS
STRAKE
TANAKA
TILAKS
TWEAKS
UMIAKS
UNMAKE
UPTAKE
WREAKS

•••A•K

ACKACK
ARRACK
ATTACK
BYTALK
CUSACK
DAMASK
DEBARK
EMBANK
EMBARK
GOBACK
HIJACK
LANARK
MOHAWK
NEWARK
REMARK
SHRANK
SQUAWK
STMARK
THWACK
UNMASK
UNPACK
UNTACK
UPTALK

••••AK

AMTRAK
ANORAK
ARAWAK
BUROAK
DEEPAK
DVORAK
GALYAK
ITZHAK
KARNAK
KODIAK
PINOAK
REDOAK
SCREAK
SENDAK
SLEZAK
SLOVAK
SPIVAK
SQUEAK
STREAK
TANOAK

AL••••

ALAMOS
ALANIS
ALANON
ALARIC
ALARMS
ALARUM
ALASKA
ALATAU
ALATED
ALBANO
ALBANY
ALBEDO
ALBEIT
ALBERT
ALBINO
ALBION
ALBOIN
ALBORG
ALBUMS
ALCAPP
ALCOTT
ALCOVE
ALCUIN
ALDERS
ALDINE
ALDOSE
ALDOUS
ALDRIN
ALEAST
ALECKY
ALECTO
ALEGAR
ALEGRE
ALEMAN
ALEPHS
ALEPPO
ALERTS
ALEUTS
ALEVEL
ALEXEI
ALEXIA
ALEXIS
ALFINE
ALFRED
ALFVEN
ALGORE
ALHIRT
ALIBIS
ALIBLE
ALICIA
ALIENS
ALIGHT
ALIGNS
ALINES
ALIOTO
ALISON
ALITER
ALKALI
ALKENE
ALKYDS
ALKYLS
ALLAYS
ALLBUT
ALLDAY
ALLEES
ALLEGE
ALLELE
ALLEYS
ALLFOR
ALLIED
ALLIES
ALLIUM
ALLMAN
ALLOTS
ALLOUT
ALLOWS
ALLOYS
ALLPRO
ALLSET
ALLUDE
ALLURE
ALLWET
ALMATY
ALMOND
ALMOST
ALNICO
ALOHAS
ALOINS
ALOMAR
ALONSO
ALONZO
ALPACA
ALPERT
ALPHAS
ALPINE
ALSACE
ALTAIC
ALTAIR
ALTARS
ALTERS
ALTHEA
ALTIMA
ALTIUS
ALTMAN
ALULAE
ALULAR
ALUMNA
ALUMNI
ALWAYS
ALWEST
ALYSSA

A•L•••

ABLATE
ABLAUT
ABLAZE
ABLEST
ABLOOM
ABLUSH
ADLIBS
AFLAME
AFLATS
AFLCIO
AFLOAT
AGLAIA
AGLARE
AGLEAM
AGLETS
AGLINT
AILEEN
AILERS
AILING
ALLAYS
ALLBUT
ALLDAY
ALLEES
ALLEGE
ALLELE
ALLEYS
ALLFOR
ALLIED
ALLIES
ALLIUM
ALLMAN
ALLOTS
ALLOUT
ALLOWS
ALLOYS
ALLPRO
ALLSET
ALLUDE
ALLURE
ALLWET
APLITE
APLOMB
ARLEEN
ARLENE
ARLISS
ASLANT
ASLEEP
ASLOPE
ATLAST
ATLATL
AULAIT
AXLIKE

A••L••

ABELES
ABOLLA
ADDLED
ADDLES
ADELIE
ADELLE
ADOLPH
ADULTS
AEOLIA
AEOLIC
AEOLUS
AIELLO
AISLES
AKELAS
ALULAE
ALULAR
AMALFI
AMALIE
AMBLED
AMBLER
AMBLES
AMBLIN
AMELIA
AMOLES
AMPLER
AMULET
ANALOG
ANELED
ANELES
ANGLED
ANGLER
ANGLES
ANGLIA
ANGLIC
ANGLOS
ANKLED
ANKLES
ANKLET
ANNLEE
ANOLES
ANTLER
APOLLO
APPLES
APPLET
APULIA
ARALIA
ARALLU
ARMLET
ASHLAR
ASHLEY
ASYLUM
ATOLLS
ATTLEE
AUKLET
AVALON
AVULSE
AXILLA
AZALEA

A•••L•

ABOLLA
ACIDLY
ADELLE
AEDILE
AERILY
AFIELD
AGEOLD
AIELLO
AIRILY
ALIBLE
ALKALI
ALKYLS
ALLELE
AMPULE
AMPULS
ANGELA
ANGELI
ANGELL
ANGELO
ANGELS
ANGOLA
ANNALS
ANNULI
ANNULS
ANSELM
ANVILS
APOLLO
APPALL
APPALS
AQUILA
ARABLE
ARALLU
ARBELA
ARCHLY
AREOLA
ARGALI
ARGYLE
ARGYLL
ARIDLY
ARNOLD
ARTELS
ARTILY
ASWELL
ATOLLS
ATTILA
ATWILL
AUDILE
AVAILS
AVIDLY
AWEDLY
AWHILE
AXILLA

A••••L

ABORAL
ACETAL
ACETYL
ACTUAL
AERIAL
AIDFUL
AIMFUL
ALEVEL
AMATOL
AMIDOL
AMORAL
AMSTEL
ANGELL
ANIMAL
ANNEAL
ANNUAL
AORTAL
APICAL
APODAL
APPALL
APPEAL
ARGYLL
ARMFUL
ARTFUL
ASSAIL
ASTRAL
ASWELL
ASWIRL
ATLATL
ATONAL
ATRIAL
ATWILL
AUDIAL
AVOWAL
AWHIRL
AXONAL

•AL•••

BALAAM
BALATA
BALBOA
BALDER
BALDLY
BALEEN
BALERS
BALING
BALKAN
BALKED
BALLAD
BALLET
BALLON
BALLOT
BALLOU
BALLUP
BALSAM
BALTIC
BALZAC
CALAIS
CALASH
CALCES
CALDER
CALICO
CALIPH
CALKED
CALLAO
CALLAS
CALLED
CALLER
CALLES
CALLIN
CALLON
CALLOW
CALLUP
CALLUS
CALMED
CALMER
CALMLY
CALPAC
CALQUE
CALVED
CALVES
CALVIN
CALXES
DALASI
DALETH
DALLAS
DALLES
DALTON
EALING
FALANA
FALCES
FALCON
FALINE
FALLEN
FALLIN
FALLON
FALLOW
FALLTO
FALSER
FALTER
GALAGO
GALAHS
GALATA
GALAXY
GALEAE
GALENA
GALLED
GALLEY
GALLIA
GALLIC
GALLON
GALLOP
GALLUP
GALOIS
GALOOT
GALOPS
GALORE
GALOSH
GALPAL
GALWAY
GALYAK
HALERS
HALERU
HALEST
HALEVY
HALIDE
HALING
HALITE
HALLEL
HALLEY
HALLOO
HALLOS
HALLOW
HALLUX
HALOED
HALOES
HALOID
HALSEY
HALTED
HALTER
HALVAH
HALVED
HALVES
JALAPA
JALOPY
KALAKH
KALINE
KALKAN
KALMAR
LALALA
MALABO
MALADY
MALAGA
MALATE
MALAWI
MALAYA
MALAYS
MALDEN
MALIBU
MALICE
MALIGN
MALKIN
MALLEE
MALLEI
MALLET
MALLOW
MALONE
MALORY
MALOTI
MALTED
MALTIN
PALACE
PALAEO
PALATE
PALEAE
PALELY
PALEST
PALIER
PALING
PALISH
PALLAS
PALLED
PALLET
PALLIA
PALLID
PALLOR
PALMAS
PALMED
PALMER
PALOMA
PALPUS
PALTER
PALTRY
SALAAM
SALADO
SALADS
SALALS
SALAMI
SALARY
SALIFY
SALINA
SALINE
SALISH
SALIVA
SALLET
SALLOW
SALMAN
SALMON
SALOME
SALONS
SALOON
SALSAS
SALTED
SALTEN
SALTER
SALTON
SALTUM
SALUKI
SALUTE
SALVED
SALVER
SALVES
SALVIA
SALVOR
SALVOS
SALYUT
TALBOT
TALCED
TALCUM
TALENT
TALERS
TALESE
TALION
TALKAT
TALKED
TALKER
TALKIE
TALKTO
TALKUP
TALLER
TALLOW
TALMUD
TALONS
VALDEZ
VALENS
VALENT
VALERY
VALETS
VALISE
VALIUM
VALLEE
VALLEY
VALOIS
VALOUR
VALUED
VALUES
VALVED
VALVES
WALDEN
WALERS
WALESA
WALKED
WALKEN
WALKER
WALKIE
WALKIN
WALKON
WALKUP
WALLED
WALLER
WALLET
WALLIS
WALLOP
WALLOW
WALLUP
WALNUT
WALRUS
WALTER
WALTON
YALIES

•A•L••

BADLOT
BAILED
BAILEE
BAILER
BAILEY
BAILOR
BALLAD
BALLET
BALLON
BALLOT
BALLOU
BALLUP
BANLON
BARLEY
BAULKS
BAWLED
BAWLER
BAYLOR
CABLED
CABLER
CABLES
CALLAO
CALLAS
CALLED
CALLER
CALLES
CALLIN
CALLON
CALLOW
CALLUP
CALLUS
CAMLET
CANLIT
CAPLET
CARLIN
CARLOS
CARLOT
CAULKS
DAHLIA
DAILEY
DALLAS
DALLES
DAYLIT
EAGLED
EAGLES
EAGLET
EARLAP
FABLED
FABLER
FABLES
FAILED
FAILLE
FALLEN
FALLIN
FALLON
FALLOW
FALLTO
FARLEY
FARLOW
FAULTS
FAULTY
FAWLTY
GABLED
GABLER
GABLES
GAELIC
GAGLAW
GALLED
GALLEY
GALLIA
GALLIC
GALLON
GALLOP
GALLUP
GAOLED
GAOLER
GARLIC
GASLIT
GASLOG
GATLIN
HAILED
HAILEY
HALLEL
HALLEY
HALLOO
HALLOS
HALLOW
HALLUX
HAMLET
HAMLIN
HANLEY
HAOLES
HARLAN
HARLEM
HARLEY
HARLIN
HARLOW
HAULED
HAULER
HAULMS
HAULUP
HAYLEY
JACLYN
JAILED
JAILER
KAHLIL
KAHLUA
KAILUA
KAOLIN
KAPLAN
LADLED
LADLER
LADLES
LAYLOW
MAHLER
MAILED
MAILER
MAILES
MAILIN
MAJLIS
MALLEE
MALLEI
MALLET
MALLOW
MAPLES
MARLED
MARLEE
MARLEY
MARLIN
MARLON
MATLIN
MAULED
MAULER
NAILED
NAILER
NAILIN
NAPLES
OAKLEY
PABLUM
PAELLA
PAILOU
PALLAS
PALLED
PALLET
PALLIA
PALLID
PALLOR
PARLAY
PARLEY
PARLOR
PAULEY
PAVLOV
RAGLAN
RAILAT
RAILED
RAILER
RATLIN
SABLES
SAILED
SAILOR
SALLET
SALLOW
SAMLET
SAULTS
SAWLOG
SAYLES
TABLAS
TABLED
TABLES
TABLET
TAILED
TAILLE
TAILOR
TALLER
TALLOW
TAYLOR
VACLAV
VALLEE
VALLEY
VARLET
VASLAV
VAULTS
VAULTY
WAILED
WAILER
WALLED
WALLER
WALLET
WALLIS
WALLOP
WALLOW
WALLUP
WAYLAY
WAYLON

•A••L•

BABALU
BABBLE
BABELS
BABULS
BACALL
BAFFLE
BAGELS
BAKULA
BALDLY
BANGLE
BARELY
BARFLY
BAROLO
BASALT
BASELY
BASSLY
BATTLE
BAUBLE
CABALA
CABALS
CACKLE
CAGILY
CAJOLE
CALMLY
CAMELS
CANALS
CANDLE
CANOLA
CANTLE
CAROLE
CAROLS
CASALS
CASTLE
CATTLE
CAUDLE
CAVELL
CAVILS
DABBLE
DAFTLY
DAMPLY
DANDLE
DANGLE
DANGLY
DANKLY
DAPPLE
DARKLE
DARKLY
DAWDLE
DAYGLO
DAZZLE
EASELS
EASILY
FACILE
FACULA
FAILLE
FAIRLY
FAMILY
FATALE
GABBLE
GADFLY
GAGGLE
GAINLY
GAMBLE
GAMELY
GAMILY
GANGLE
GANGLY
GARBLE
GARGLE
GAVELS
GAYALS
HABILE
HACKLE
HACKLY
HAGGLE
HAMALS
HAMELN
HAMILL
HANDLE
HARALD
HARDLY
HAROLD
HASSLE
HAZELS
HAZILY
JACALS
JANGLE
JANGLY
KAMALA
LABELS
LABILE
LACILY
LALALA
LAMELY
LANKLY
LAPELS
LASTLY
LATELY
LAZILY
LAZULI
MABELL
MACULA
MAINLY
MAKALU
MANGLE
MANILA
MANTLE
MARBLE
MARBLY
MARILU
MARPLE
MAYFLY
MAZILY
MAZOLA
NAMELY
NAPOLI
NASALS
NAVELS
PADDLE
PAELLA
PAKULA
PALELY
PAMELA
PANELS
PAROLE
PARTLY
PARULA
PAYOLA
RABBLE
RACILY
RADDLE
RADULA
RAFFLE
RAMBLA
RAMBLE
RANKLE
RANKLY
RAPTLY
RARELY
RASHLY
RASSLE
RATELS
RATTLE
RATTLY
RAVELS
RAZZLE
SADDLE
SAFELY
SAGELY
SALALS
SAMPLE
SANELY
TABULA
TACKLE
TAILLE
TAMALE
TAMELY
TAMILS
TANGLE
TANGLY
TARTLY
TATTLE
TAUTLY
VAINLY
VASTLY
WADDLE
WADDLY
WAFFLE
WAFFLY
WAGGLE
WAGGLY
WAMBLE
WAMBLY
WANGLE
WARBLE
WARILY
WARMLY
WATTLE
WAVILY
WAXILY
YARELY
ZANILY

•A•••L

BACALL
BAGFUL
BAIKAL
BANJUL
BARBEL
BARREL
BATTEL
CANCEL
CANFUL
CANNEL
CAPFUL
CARFUL
CARMEL
CARNAL
CARPAL
CARPEL
CARREL
CARROL
CARTEL
CASUAL
CAUDAL
CAUSAL
CAVELL
DACTYL
DAEDAL
DAMSEL
DANIEL
DARNEL
DARRYL
EARFUL
FACIAL
FAISAL
FAUNAL
FAZOOL
GALPAL
GAMBOL
GAVIAL
HALLEL
HAMILL
HANDEL
HANGUL

HANSEL
HATFUL
JACKAL
JAMAAL
JARFUL
JAWOHL
KAHLIL
LABIAL
LAPFUL
LARVAL
LAUREL
LAWFUL
MABELL
MAMMAL
MANFUL
MANTEL
MANUAL
MANUEL
MARCEL
MARIEL
MARTEL
MARVEL
MATTEL
NARIAL
NARWAL
PANFUL
PARCEL
PARREL
PASCAL
PASSEL
PASTEL
PATHOL
PATROL
RACHEL
RACIAL
RADIAL
RAFAEL
RAPPEL
RAQUEL
RASCAL
SACRAL
SAMBAL
SAMUEL
SANDAL
SAUREL
TARSAL
TASSEL
VACHEL
VANDAL
VASSAL
VATFUL
WARHOL

••AL••
AMALFI
AMALIE
ANALOG
ARALIA
ARALLU
AVALON
AZALEA
CHALCO
CHALET
CHALKS
CHALKY
COALER
DEALER
DEALIN
DIALED
DIALER
DIALOG
DIALUP
DUALLY
ETALIA

ETALII
EXALTS
FEALTY
FOALED
GOALIE
HEALED
HEALER
HEALTH
ITALIA
ITALIC
KHALID
KOALAS
LEALTY
MEALIE
NYALAS
ORALES
ORALLY
OVALLY
OXALIS
PEALED
PSALMS
QUALMS
REALER
REALES
REALIA
REALLY
REALMS
REALTY
RIALTO
RVALUE
SCALAR
SCALDS
SCALED
SCALER
SCALES
SCALIA
SCALPS
SEALAB
SEALED
SEALER
SEALUP
SHALES
SHALEY
SHALLY
SHALOM
SKALDS
SLALOM
SMALLS
SMALTI
SMALTO
SPALLS
STALAG
STALED
STALER
STALES
STALIN
STALKS
STALKY
STALLS
SWALES
THALER
THALES
THALIA
TLALOC
TRALEE
URALIC
URALSK
UVALUE
WEALTH
WHALER
WHALES
ZEALOT

••A•L•
ARABLE
ARALLU
AVAILS
BEADLE
BEAGLE
BEATLE
BRAILA
BRAILS
BRAWLS
CHARLY
CRADLE
CRAWLS
CRAWLY
DEADLY
DEAFLY
DEARLY
DIABLO
DOABLE
DRABLY
DRAILS
DRAWLS
DRAWLY
DUALLY
EMAILS
ENABLE
FEATLY
FLAILS
FLATLY
GLADLY
GNARLS
GNARLY
GRABLE
GRAILS
GRAYLY
KRAALS
LEANLY
LIABLE
MEANLY
MEASLY
NEARLY
NEATLY
ORACLE
ORALLY
OVALLY
PEARLS
PEARLY
QUAILS
QUAYLE
REALLY
SEARLE
SHALLY
SHAWLS
SMALLS
SNAILS
SNARLS
SNARLY
SPALLS
STABLE
STABLY
STALLS
STAPLE
THATLL
TRAILS
TRAWLS
UNABLE
USABLE
USABLY
VIABLE
VIABLY
WEAKLY
WHATLL
YEARLY

••A••L
AMATOL
BOATEL
BRAZIL
CHANEL
CHAPEL
DEASIL
ENAMEL
GRAVEL
HIATAL
ISABEL
IZABAL
PLAGAL
SEAGAL
TEASEL
THATLL
TRAVEL
URACIL
WEASEL
WHATLL

•••AL•
ALKALI
ANNALS
APPALL
APPALS
ARGALI
BABALU
BACALL
BASALT
BECALM
BEFALL
BEHALF
BYTALK
CABALA
CABALS
CANALS
CASALS
COBALT
CORALS
DECALS
DEKALB
DENALI
DESALT
DONALD
DOUALA
DUVALL
ENDALL
ENHALO
EQUALS
EXHALE
FATALE
FEMALE
FINALE
FINALS
GAYALS
GERALD
GORALS
HAMALS
HARALD
HERALD
IDEALS
IMPALA
IMPALE
INHALE
INHALF
JACALS
KAMALA
KERALA
KIGALI
KODALY
KRAALS
KURALT
LALALA

LEGALS
LOCALE
LOCALS
MAKALU
MCHALE
MEDALS
MEGALO
METALS
MORALE
MORALS
MURALS
NASALS
NEPALI
NOSALE
OGLALA
ONCALL
ONSALE
OOLALA
OSWALD
PEDALS
PETALS
PHIALS
PIPALS
RECALL
REGALE
RESALE
RESALT
RIBALD
RIVALS
RIYALS
ROBALO
RONALD
ROYALE
ROYALS
SALALS
SEPALS
SHOALS
SHOALY
SISALS
SKOALS
SOMALI
SQUALL
STEALS
STMALO
TAMALE
TEPALS
THRALE
THRALL
TICALS
TOTALS
TRIALS
TUVALU
TYBALT
UPTALK
URIALS
USUALS
VITALE
VITALS
VOCALS
WHEALS
YOUALL

•••A•L
APPALL
ASSAIL
ATLATL
BACALL
BEFALL
BEWAIL
DEPAUL
DERAIL
DETAIL
DUVALL
ENDALL

ENTAIL
EURAIL
INHAUL
ISRAEL
JAMAAL
ONCALL
OXTAIL
RAFAEL
RECALL
REMAIL
RENAIL
RETAIL
RUPAUL
SCRAWL
SPRAWL
SQUALL
STPAUL
THRALL
USMAIL
YOUALL

••••AL
ABORAL
ACETAL
ACTUAL
AERIAL
AMORAL
ANIMAL
ANNEAL
ANNUAL
AORTAL
APICAL
APODAL
APPEAL
ASTRAL
ATONAL
ATRIAL
AUDIAL
AVOWAL
AXONAL
BAIKAL
BELIAL
BENGAL
BHOPAL
BOREAL
BRIDAL
BRUMAL
BRUTAL
BUCCAL
BURSAL
CARNAL
CARPAL
CASUAL
CAUDAL
CAUSAL
CEREAL
CHEVAL
CHORAL
COEVAL
CORRAL
COSTAL
CRURAL
CUNEAL
CURIAL
CYMBAL
DAEDAL
DENIAL
DENTAL
DERMAL
DISMAL
DISTAL
DORSAL
DOSSAL
DUCTAL

EPICAL
EPINAL
ESPIAL
FACIAL
FAISAL
FAUNAL
FERIAL
FESTAL
FEUDAL
FILIAL
FINIAL
FISCAL
FLORAL
FOETAL
FONTAL
FORMAL
FRUGAL
GALPAL
GAVIAL
GENIAL
GENUAL
GIMBAL
GLOBAL
HERBAL
HIATAL
HIEMAL
HYETAL
HYMNAL
INSTAL
IRREAL
IZABAL
JACKAL
JAMAAL
JOVIAL
LABIAL
LARVAL
LETHAL
LINEAL
LOREAL
LOWCAL
MAMMAL
MANUAL
MEDIAL
MENIAL
MENSAL
MENTAL
MESCAL
MISSAL
MITRAL
MORTAL
MUSIAL
MUTUAL
MYRDAL
NARIAL
NARWAL
NEURAL
NORMAL
NUCHAL
ORDEAL
OSTEAL
PASCAL
PENPAL
PINEAL
PLAGAL
PLEXAL
PLURAL
PORTAL
POSTAL
PRIMAL
RACIAL
RADIAL
RASCAL
REDEAL
REDIAL

REGNAL
REHEAL
RENTAL
REPEAL
RESEAL
RETIAL
RETRAL
REVEAL
RHINAL
RITUAL
SACRAL
SAMBAL
SANDAL
SEAGAL
SEPTAL
SERIAL
SERVAL
SIGNAL
SOCIAL
SPINAL
SPIRAL
SQUEAL
TARSAL
THECAL
TIBIAL
TIMBAL
TINCAL
TRIBAL
TRINAL
UMBRAL
UNCIAL
UNGUAL
UNITAL
UNOCAL
UNREAL
UNSEAL
VANDAL
VASSAL
VEINAL
VENIAL
VERBAL
VERNAL
VESTAL
VISUAL
WITHAL

AM••••
AMADIS
AMADOU
AMAJOR
AMALFI
AMALIE
AMANDA
AMATIS
AMATOL
AMAZED
AMAZES
AMAZON
AMBATO
AMBERS
AMBERY
AMBITS
AMBLED
AMBLER
AMBLES
AMBLIN
AMBUSH
AMEBAE
AMEBAS
AMEBIC
AMECHE
AMEDEO
AMEERS
AMELIA

AMENDS
AMENRA
AMENTS
AMERCE
AMERSP
AMHARA
AMICES
AMICUS
AMIDES
AMIDOL
AMIDST
AMIENS
AMIGAS
AMIGOS
AMINES
AMINOR
AMINUS
AMNION
AMOEBA
AMOLES
AMORAL
AMOSOZ
AMOUNT
AMOURS
AMPERE
AMPHID
AMPLER
AMPULE
AMPULS
AMSTEL
AMTRAC
AMTRAK
AMULET
AMUSED
AMUSES
AMVETS
AMYTAN

A•M•••
ADMASS
ADMIRE
ADMITS
AIMFOR
AIMFUL
AIMING
AIMSAT
AIMSTO
ALMATY
ALMOND
ALMOST
ARMADA
ARMAGH
ARMAND
ARMANI
ARMETS
ARMFUL
ARMIES
ARMING
ARMLET
ARMORS
ARMORY
ARMOUR
ARMPIT
ARMURE
ASMARA
ATMOST
AUMONT
AYMARA

A••M••
ABOMBS
ACUMEN
AGAMAS
AHIMSA

AIRMAN
AIRMEN
AKIMBO
ALAMOS
ALEMAN
ALLMAN
ALOMAR
ALTMAN
ALUMNA
ALUMNI
ANEMIA
ANEMIC
ANIMAL
ANIMAS
ANIMES
ANIMUS
ANOMIC
ANOMIE
APEMAN
APEMEN
ARAMIS
AROMAS
ASIMOV
ATAMAN
ATEMPO
ATOMIC

A•••M•
ABOHMS
ABRAMS
ABYSMS
ADDAMS
ADEEMS
AFLAME
AFRAME
ALARMS
ALBUMS
ALTIMA
APLOMB
ASSUME
ATEAMS
ATHOME
AUTUMN
AXIOMS

A••••M
ABLOOM
ABSCAM
ACTIUM
ADYTUM
AFFIRM
AGEISM
AGLEAM
AIRARM
AIRDAM
ALARUM
ALLIUM
ANADEM
ANONYM
ANSELM
ANTHEM
ANTRIM
ANTRUM
ARNHEM
ARTGUM
ASCHAM
ASHRAM
ASYLUM
ATRIUM

•AM•••
BAMAKO
BAMBOO
CAMARO

CAMBER
CAMDEN
CAMEAT
CAMEBY
CAMEIN
CAMELS
CAMEON
CAMEOS
CAMERA
CAMETO
CAMEUP
CAMINO
CAMION
CAMISE
CAMLET
CAMPED
CAMPER
CAMPOS
CAMPUS
DAMAGE
DAMASK
DAMATO
DAMIEN
DAMITA
DAMMAR
DAMMED
DAMNED
DAMONE
DAMORE
DAMOUR
DAMPED
DAMPEN
DAMPER
DAMPLY
DAMSEL
DAMSON
DAMSUP
FAMILY
FAMINE
FAMISH
FAMOUS
GAMAYS
GAMBIA
GAMBIT
GAMBLE
GAMBOL
GAMELY
GAMEST
GAMETE
GAMIER
GAMILY
GAMINE
GAMING
GAMINS
GAMMAS
GAMMED
GAMMER
GAMMON
GAMUTS
HAMALS
HAMELN
HAMILL
HAMITE
HAMLET
HAMLIN
HAMMED
HAMMER
HAMPER
IAMBIC
JAMAAL
JAMMED
JAMMER
JAMOKE
JAMSIN

JAMSUP
JAMUPS
KAMALA
LAMARR
LAMAZE
LAMBDA
LAMBED
LAMECH
LAMEDH
LAMEDS
LAMELY
LAMENT
LAMESA
LAMEST
LAMIAS
LAMINA
LAMING
LAMMAS
LAMMED
LAMONT
LAMOUR
MAMBAS
MAMBOS
MAMMAL
MAMMAS
MAMMON
NAMATH
NAMELY
NAMERS
NAMING
PAMELA
PAMIRS
PAMPAS
PAMPER
RAMADA
RAMATE
RAMBLA
RAMBLE
RAMEAU
RAMETS
RAMIES
RAMIFY
RAMJET
RAMMED
RAMONA
RAMONE
RAMOSE
RAMOUS
RAMPED
RAMROD
RAMSAY
RAMSES
RAMSEY
RAMSON
SAMARA
SAMBAL
SAMBAR
SAMBAS
SAMECH
SAMEKH
SAMIAM
SAMITE
SAMLET
SAMMIE
SAMOAN
SAMOSA
SAMPAN
SAMPLE
SAMSON
SAMUEL
TAMALE
TAMARA
TAMAYO
TAMELY

TAMERS
TAMEST
TAMILS
TAMING
TAMMUZ
TAMPED
TAMPER
TAMTAM
VAMPED
VAMPER
WAMBLE
WAMBLY
WAMPUM
YAMAHA
YAMMER
ZAMBIA
ZAMIAS

•A•M••
BADMAN
BADMEN
BARMAN
BARMEN
BATMAN
BATMEN
CADMIC
CADMUS
CAIMAN
CALMED
CALMER
CALMLY
CARMAN
CARMEL
CARMEN
CAYMAN
DAGMAR
DAIMON
DAIMYO
DAMMAR
DAMMED
FARMED
FARMER
GAGMAN
GAGMEN
GAMMAS
GAMMED
GAMMER
GAMMON
GASMAN
GASMEN
GAUMED
HAEMAT
HAEMON
HAGMAN
HAMMED
HAMMER
HARMED
HARMON
HAYMOW
JAMMED
JAMMER
KALMAR
KARMIC
KATMAI
LAMMAS
LAMMED
LAWMAN
LAWMEN
LAYMAN
LAYMEN
MADMAN
MADMAX
MADMEN
MAGMAS

MAMMAL
MAMMAS
MAMMON
MARMEE
MARMOT
MAUMAU
MAUMEE
PACMAN
PALMAS
PALMED
PALMER
PATMOS
RAGMAN
RAGMEN
RAGMOP
RAMMED
SALMAN
SALMON
SAMMIE
TALMUD
TAMMUZ
TARMAC
TASMAN
TAXMAN
TAXMEN
WARMED
WARMER
WARMLY
WARMTH
WARMUP
YAMMER

•A••M•
BAHAMA
BATUMI
CAROMS
DAGAMA
DANGME
FATIMA
GAZUMP
HAKIMS
HAREMS
HAULMS
LARAMS
MADAME
MADAMS
MANAMA
MAXIMA
MAXIMS
MAZUMA
PAJAMA
PALOMA
PANAMA
RACEME
RADOME
SALAMI
SALOME
TACOMA
TATAMI
YAKIMA

•A•••M
BADHAM
BALAAM
BALSAM
BANTAM
BARIUM
BARNUM
BATYAM
BAYRUM
FAIYUM
FANDOM
FATHOM
HANSOM

HARLEM
HASSAM
KABOOM
KAREEM
LABRUM
LAPHAM
LATIUM
MADTOM
MAGNUM
MAOISM
MAYHEM
PABLUM
PASSIM
RADIUM
RANDOM
RANSOM
SACHEM
SACRUM
SADDAM
SALAAM
SALTUM
SAMIAM
TALCUM
TAMTAM
TANDEM
TAOISM
VACUUM
VALIUM
WAMPUM

••AM••
AGAMAS
ALAMOS
ARAMIS
ATAMAN
BEAMED
BEAMON
BEAMUP
BLAMED
BLAMES
CHAMMY
CHAMPS
CLAMMY
CLAMOR
CLAMPS
CLAMUP
CRAMBO
CRAMPS
DRAMAS
EDAMES
ENAMEL
ENAMOR
FLAMBE
FLAMED
FLAMES
FOAMED
FRAMED
FRAMES
GLAMOR
GRAMAS
GRAMME
GRAMMY
GRAMPA
GRAMPS
IMAMAN
KRAMER
LLAMAS
LOAMED
MIAMIA
NIAMEY
REAMED
REAMER
RHAMES
ROAMED

ROAMER
SCAMPI
SCAMPS
SEAMAN
SEAMED
SEAMEN
SEAMUS
SHAMAN
SHAMED
SHAMES
SHAMIR
SHAMUS
STAMEN
STAMPS
SWAMIS
SWAMPS
SWAMPY
TEAMED
TEAMUP
THAMES
TOAMAN
TRAMPS
WHAMMO
WHAMMY
XIAMEN

••A•M•
ALARMS
BRAHMA
BRAHMS
CHACMA
CHAMMY
CHARMS
CHASMS
CLAIMS
CLAMMY
DEARME
DHARMA
GRAMME
GRAMMY
MIASMA
PLASMA
PLASMO
PSALMS
QUALMS
REAIMS
REALMS
REARMS
SHAWMS
SMARMY
SPASMS
SWARMS
TRAUMA
UNARMS
WHAMMO
WHAMMY

••A••M
ALARUM
ANADEM
DIADEM
DIATOM
DRACHM
GRAHAM
INAJAM
MCADAM
OMASUM
SCARUM
SHALOM
SHAZAM
SLALOM
VIACOM

•••AM•

ABRAMS ADDAMS AFLAME AFRAME ATEAMS BAHAMA BECAME BIGAMY BONAMI BREAMS BYNAME CCLAMP CREAMS CREAMY DAGAMA DECAMP DEFAME DREAMS DREAMT DREAMY DYNAMO ENCAMP GLEAMS GLEAMY HBEAMS IBEAMS INFAMY JICAMA LARAMS MADAME MADAMS MANAMA NONAME OGHAMS PAJAMA PANAMA PREAMP PROAMS PYJAMA RENAME REVAMP SALAMI SCRAMS SESAME STEAMS STEAMY TATAMI UGGAMS UNJAMS

•••A•M

AIRARM BALAAM BECALM DISARM LCHAIM REWARM SALAAM

••••AM

ABSCAM AGLEAM AIRDAM ASCHAM ASHRAM BADHAM BALAAM BALSAM BANTAM BATYAM BEDLAM BELDAM COBHAM DIGRAM DIRHAM DUNHAM DURHAM ENGRAM FIVEAM FOURAM GOTHAM GRAHAM HASSAM INAJAM INGRAM INSEAM JETSAM LAPHAM LOGJAM MCADAM MIRIAM NINEAM OLDHAM PUTNAM RODHAM SADDAM SALAAM SAMIAM SCREAM SHAZAM SILOAM STREAM TAMTAM WIGWAM

AN••••

ANACIN ANADEM ANALOG ANANDA ANATTO ANCHOR ANCIEN ANCONA ANDEAN ANDHOW ANDREA ANDREI ANDRES ANDREW ANDREY ANDROS ANELED ANELES ANEMIA ANEMIC ANERGY ANGELA ANGELI ANGELL ANGELO ANGELS ANGERS ANGKOR ANGLED ANGLER ANGLES ANGLIA ANGLIC ANGLOS ANGOLA ANGORA ANHYDR ANIMAL ANIMAS ANIMES ANIMUS ANIONS ANITRA ANJOUS ANKARA ANKLED ANKLES ANKLET ANNABA ANNALS ANNEAL ANNEXE ANNHON ANNIKA ANNLEE ANNOYS ANNUAL ANNUIT ANNULI ANNULS ANODES ANODIC ANOINT ANOLES ANOMIC ANOMIE ANONYM ANORAK ANSARA ANSATE ANSELM ANSGAR ANSWER ANTCOW ANTEED ANTERO ANTEUP ANTHEM ANTHER ANTICS ANTLER ANTONY ANTRES ANTRIM ANTRON ANTRUM ANUBIS ANURAN ANVILS ANWANG ANYANG ANYDAY ANYHOW ANYONE ANYWAY

A•N•••

ADNATE ADNEXA AENEAS AENEID AGNATE ALNICO AMNION ANNABA ANNALS ANNEAL ANNEXE ANNHON ANNIKA ANNLEE ANNOYS ANNUAL ANNUIT ANNULI ANNULS ARNESS ARNETT ARNHEM ARNICA ARNOLD AUNTIE AWNING

A••N••

ACINUS ADONAI ADONIS AGENAS AGENCY AGENDA AGENTS AJANTA AKENES ALANIS ALANON ALINES ALONSO ALONZO AMANDA AMENDS AMENRA AMENTS AMINES AMINOR AMINUS ANANDA ANONYM ARENAS ARENDT ASANAS ATONAL ATONCE ATONED ATONES ATONIC AVANTI AVENGE AVENUE AXONAL AZINES

A•••N•

AAHING ABOUND ABSENT ABYING ACCENT ACHENE ACHING ACORNS ACTING ACTINO ACTONE ADDEND ADDING ADDONS ADJANI ADORNS ADRENO ADVENT AFFINE AGEING AGLINT AHERNE AIDING AILING AIMING AIRING ALBANO ALBANY ALBINO ALDINE ALFINE ALIENS ALIGNS ALKENE ALMOND ALOINS ALPINE ALUMNA ALUMNI AMIENS AMOUNT ANCONA ANIONS ANOINT ANTONY ANWANG ANYANG ANYONE APPEND APRONS AQUINO ARCANA ARCANE ARCING ARDENT ARGENT ARJUNA ARLENE ARMAND ARMANI ARMING AROUND ARPENT ARRANT ARSENE ARSONS ARYANS ASCEND ASCENT ASIANS ASKING ASLANT ASPENS ASSENT ATHAND ATHENA ATHENE ATHENS ATKINS ATTEND ATTUNE AUDENS AUFOND AUGEND AUMONT AUXINS AVAUNT AVERNO AVIANS AWNING AXIONS

A••••N

AACHEN ACTION ACTSON ACUMEN ADDSIN ADDSON ADJOIN ADRIAN ADRIEN AEGEAN AFGHAN AILEEN AIRGUN AIRMAN AIRMEN ALANON ALBION ALBOIN ALCUIN ALDRIN ALEMAN ALFVEN ALISON ALLMAN ALTMAN AMAZON AMBLIN AMNION AMYTAN ANACIN ANCIEN ANDEAN ANNHON ANTRON ANURAN APEMAN APEMEN APPIAN ARAGON ARCHON ARCTAN ARISEN ARLEEN ARUBAN ASHCAN ASKSIN ASOSAN ASSIGN ASTERN ASWOON ATAMAN ATTAIN AUBURN AUGEAN AUSTEN AUSTIN AUTUMN AVALON AVEDON AWAKEN AWOKEN AZORIN

•AN•••

BANANA BANDED BANDIT BANDOG BANGED BANGER BANGKA BANGLE BANGOR BANGUI BANGUP BANISH BANJOS BANJUL BANKED BANKER BANKON BANLON BANNED BANNER BANQUO BANTAM BANTER BANTUS BANYAN BANZAI CANAAN CANADA CANALS CANAPE CANARD CANARY CANCAN CANCEL CANCUN CANDID CANDLE CANDOR CANERS CANFUL CANIDS CANIER CANIFF CANINE CANING CANKER CANLIT CANNAE CANNED CANNEL CANNER CANNES CANNON CANNOT CANOED CANOES CANOLA CANONS CANOPY CANOVA CANTAB CANTED CANTER CANTHI CANTLE CANTON CANTOR CANTOS CANUTE CANVAS CANYON DANANG DANAUS DANCED DANCER DANCES DANDER DANDIE DANDLE DANGER DANGLE DANGLY DANGME DANIEL DANISH DANKER DANKLY DANNAY DANNER DANSON DANTES DANTON DANUBE DANZIG FANDOM FANGED FANION FANJET FANNED FANNIE FANONS FANOUT FANTAN GANDER GANDHI GANGED GANGER GANGES GANGLE GANGLY GANGUE GANGUP GANNET GANTRY HANDED HANDEL HANDIN HANDLE HANDON HANDUP HANGAR HANGED HANGER HANGIN HANGON HANGUL HANGUP HANKER HANKIE HANLEY HANNAH HANSEL HANSOM HANSON JANGLE JANGLY JANHUS JANICE JANINE JANSEN JANSKY KANAKA KANDER KANSAN KANSAS KANTOR LANAIS LANARK LANATE LANCED LANCER LANCES LANCET LANDAU LANDED LANDER LANDHO LANDIS LANDON LANDRY LANGUR LANIER LANKER LANKLY LANOSE LANSON LANVIN MANAGE MANAMA MANANA MANAUS MANCHA MANCHU MANDAN MANDAY MANEGE MANFUL MANGER MANGLE MANGOS MANIAC MANIAS MANILA MANIOC MANNED MANNER MANNIX MANORS MANQUE MANRAY MANSES MANTAS MANTEL MANTIC MANTIS MANTLE MANTRA MANTUA MANUAL MANUEL NANNIE NANOOK NANSEN NANTES PANADA PANAMA PANCHO PANDAS PANDER PANDIT PANELS PANFRY PANFUL PANICS PANNED PANNER PANNES PANOUT PANTED PANTOS PANTRY PANZER QANTAS RANCHO RANCID RANCOR RANDOM RANDRY RANEES RANFOR RANGED RANGER RANGES RANGUP RANIDS RANKED RANKER RANKIN RANKLE RANKLY RANOFF RANOUT RANSOM RANTED RANTER SANCHO SANCTA SANDAL SANDED SANDER SANDIA SANDRA SANELY SANEST SANGER SANGTO SANITY SANNUP SANSEI SANTEE SANTIR SANTOS TANAKA TANANA TANDEM TANGED TANGLE TANGLY TANGOS TANGUY TANIST TANKAS TANKED TANKER TANKUP TANNED TANNER TANNIC TANNIN TANOAK TANOAN TANTES TANTRA VANDAL VANIER VANISH VANITY VANNED VANRYN WANDER WANERS WANGLE WANIER WANING WANNED WANNER WANTAD WANTED WANTIN WANTON WANTTO XANADU XANTHO YANGON YANKED YANKEE YANQUI ZANDER ZANIER ZANIES ZANILY ZANUCK

•A•N••

BAINES BANNED BANNER BARNES BARNEY BARNUM CAGNEY CANNAE CANNED CANNEL CANNER CANNES CANNON CANNOT CAPNUT CARNAL CARNES CARNET CARNEY CARNOT CATNAP CATNIP DABNEY DAINTY DAMNED DANNAY DANNER DARNAY DARNED DARNEL DARNER DARNIT DAUNTS DAWNED DAWNON EARNED EARNER FAENZA FAFNIR FAINTS FANNED FANNIE FAUNAE FAUNAL FAUNAS FAUNUS FAWNED FAWNER GAINED GAINER GAINLY GAINON GAINST GANNET GARNER GARNET GAYNOR HAINAN HAINES HANNAH HAUNCH HAUNTS JAUNTS JAUNTY KARNAK KAUNAS KAUNDA KAVNER LAINIE LAUNCH MAENAD MAGNET MAGNON MAGNUM MAGNUS MAINLY MANNED MANNER MANNIX MARNER MARNIE MAUNDY NANNIE NARNIA PAANGA PAINED PAINTS PAINTY PANNED PANNER PANNES PARNIS PAUNCH PAWNED PAWNEE PAWNER RADNER RAINED RAINER RAINES RAINEY SAINTE SAINTS SANNUP SARNIA SAUNAS TAINAN TAINOS TAINTS TANNED TANNER TANNIC TANNIN TAUNTS VAINER VAINLY VANNED VARNAS VARNEY VAUNTS WAGNER WALNUT WANNED WANNER WAPNER WARNED WARNER WATNEY YARNED YAWNED YAWNER

•A••N•

AAHING BAAING BAIRNS BAKING BALING BANANA BARING BARONG BARONS BARONY BASING BASINS BATING BATONS BAYING CABANA CABINS CADENT CAGING CAIRNS CAJUNS CAKING CAMINO CANINE CANING CANONS CAPONE CAPONS CARINA CARING CARONI CASING CASINO CATENA CAVING CAWING DAMONE DANANG DAPHNE DARENT DARING DATING DATONG DAYONE DAZING EALING EARING EASING EATING FACING FADING FAGEND FAKING FALANA FALINE FAMINE FANONS FARINA FARING FAXING FAZING GAGING GALENA GAMINE GAMING GAMINS GAPING GATING GAZING HABANA HALING HARING HATING HAVANA HAVENS HAVENT HAVING HAWING HAYING HAZANS HAZING JACANA JADING JANINE JAPANS JAPING JAWING KAHUNA KALINE LACING LACUNA LADING LADINO LAGUNA LAMENT LAMINA LAMING LAMONT LAPINS LARYNX LATENE LATENS LATENT LATINA LATINI LATINO LATINS LATONA LAVING LAWING LAYING LAZING MAKING MALONE MANANA MARINA MARINE MARINO MASONS MATING MATINS MAVENS MAXENE MAXINE MAYANS NADINE NAGANO NAMING NATANT OARING PACING PACINO PADANG PAEANS PAEONS PAGANS PAGING PAHANG PALING PARANA PARANG PARENS PARENT PARING PATENS PATENT PATINA PATINE PAVANE PAVING PAWING PAYING RACINE RACING RACONS RAGING RAKING RAMONA RAMONE RAPINE RAPINI RARING RASING RATINE RATING RAVENS RAVINE RAVING RAYONS RAZING SABENA SABINE SABINS SALINA SALINE SALONS SARANS SARONG SATANG SATING SATINS SATINY SAVANT SAVING SAWING SAXONS SAXONY SAYING TAGEND TAHINI TAKING TAKINS TALENT TALONS TAMING TANANA TAPING TAPINS TARING TAUONS TAWING TAXING VACANT VALENS VALENT VARUNA WADING WAGING WAGONS WAHINE WAKENS WAKING WANING WARING WAVING WAXING WAYANS YAWING ZAYINS ZAZENS

•A•••N

AACHEN BABOON BABSON BACKIN BADMAN BADMEN BAFFIN BAHIAN BALEEN BALKAN BALLON BANKON BANLON BANYAN BARKIN BARMAN BARMEN BARREN BARRON BARTON BARYON BARZUN BATAAN BATMAN BATMEN BATTEN CAFTAN CAIMAN CALLIN CALLON CALVIN CAMDEN CAMEIN CAMEON CAMION CANAAN CANCAN CANCUN CANNON CANTON CANYON CAPGUN CAPTAN CARBON CARDIN CAREEN CARLIN CARMAN CARMEN CARSON CARTON CASERN CASHIN CASTON CATION CATKIN CATTON CAVEIN CAVERN CAXTON CAYMAN DACRON DAIKON DAIMON DAIREN DALTON DAMIEN DAMPEN DAMSON DANSON DANTON DARIEN DARKEN DARREN DARWIN DASSIN DATSUN DAWNON DAWSON DAYTON EASEIN EASTON EATSIN FABIAN FADEIN FALCON FALLEN FALLIN

FALLON FANION FANTAN FASTEN FATTEN GABION GAGMAN GAGMEN GAIJIN GAINON GALLON GAMMON GARCON GARDEN GARSON GASCON GASKIN GASMAN GASMEN GASTON GATLIN GAVEIN GAWAIN HADRON HAEMON HAGDON HAGMAN HAINAN HAMELN HAMLIN HANDIN HANDON HANGIN HANGON HANSON HAPPEN HARBIN HARDEN HARKEN HARLAN HARLIN HARMON HARPON HASSAN HASTEN HATPIN HAVEON HAYDEN JACLYN JAMSIN JANSEN JARGON KALKAN KANSAN KAOLIN KAPLAN KASDAN LAGOON LAIDIN LAIDON LANDON LANSON LANVIN LARDON LARSEN LARSON LASSEN LATEEN LATTEN LAUREN LAWMAN LAWMEN LAWSON LAWTON

LAYMAN LAYMEN LAYSIN LAYSON MACOUN MACRON MADDEN MADMAN MADMEN MADSEN MAGNON MAIDEN MAILIN MAJGEN MALDEN MALIGN MALKIN MALTIN MAMMON MANDAN MARGIN MARIAN MARION MARLIN MARLON MAROON MARRON MARTEN MARTIN MARVIN MATLIN MATRON NAILIN NANSEN NAPKIN NATHAN NATION NATRON PACMAN PADUAN PAIDIN PAPAIN PAPUAN PAQUIN PARDON PARSON PARTON PASSON PATHAN PATRON PATTEN PATTON PAXTON PAYSIN PAYSON RADIAN RAGLAN RAGMAN RAGMEN RAISIN RAKEIN RAMSON RANKIN RATION RATLIN RATSON RATTAN RAYGUN SADDEN SAIGON SAIPAN SALMAN SALMON SALOON

SALTEN SALTON SAMOAN SAMPAN SAMSON SARGON SARTON SATEEN SATURN TACKON TAINAN TAIPAN TAIWAN TAKEIN TAKEON TALION TANNIN TANOAN TAPPAN TARPAN TARPON TARTAN TARZAN TASMAN TAUTEN TAVERN TAXMAN TAXMEN VANRYN VARDEN VAUGHN WADEIN WAGGON WAITON WALDEN WALKEN WALKIN WALKON WALTON WANTIN WANTON WARDEN WARREN WATSON WAVEIN WAYLON YANGON YAUPON

••AN••

AJANTA ALANIS ALANON AMANDA ANANDA ASANAS AVANTI BEANED BEANIE BEANOS BIANCA BLANCA BLANCH BLANDA BLANKS BRANCH BRANDO BRANDS BRANDT BRANDX BRANDY BRANNY BRANTS BWANAS

CHANCE CHANCY CHANEL CHANEY CHANGE CHANTS CLANCY CLANGS CLANKS CLANKY CRANED CRANES CRANIA CRANIO CRANKS CRANKY CRANNY CYANIC DEANNA DIANNE ELANDS FIANCE FLANGE FLANKS FRANCA FRANCE FRANCK FRANCO FRANCS FRANKS FRANNY GDANSK GIANTS GLANCE GLANDS GOANNA GRANDE GRANDS GRANGE GRANNY GRANTS HEANEY INANER IRANIS JEANNE JOANIE JOANNA JOANNE KIANGS KRANTZ KWANZA LEANED LEANER LEANLY LEANON LEANTO LIANAS LIANES LIANGS LLANOS LOANED LOANER LUANDA MEANER MEANIE MEANLY MOANED MOANER NUANCE OMANIS ORANGE ORANGS ORANGY ORANTS

PAANGA PEANUT PIANOS PLANAR PLANCK PLANED PLANER PLANES PLANET PLANKS PLANON PLANTE PLANTS PRANCE PRANGS PRANKS QUANGO QUANTA RUANAS RUANDA RWANDA SCANTS SCANTY SEANCE SHANDY SHANIA SHANKS SHANNY SHANTY SKANKS SLANGS SLANGY SLANTS SPANKS SPANKY SRANAN STANCE STANCH STANDS STANKY STANZA SWANEE SWANKS SWANKY THANES THANKS TRANCE TWANGS TWANGY UBANGI UGANDA URANIA URANIC URANUS USANCE VIANDS WEANED WHANGS YEANED

••A•N•

AVAUNT BAAING BLAINE BRAINS BRAINY BRANNY BRAWNY CHAINE CHAINS CRANNY DEANNA DIANNE DRAINS

DWAYNE ELAINE ELAYNE FLAUNT FRANNY GHAINS GOANNA GRAINS GRAINY GRANNY JEANNE JOANNA JOANNE KEARNY KRASNY LEARNS LEARNT PLAINS PLAINT PRAJNA PRAWNS QUAINT SCARNE SHANNY SHAYNE SPAWNS STAINS SWAINS TRAINS YEARNS

••A••N

ALANON AMAZON ANACIN ARAGON ATAMAN AVALON AWAKEN BEACON BEAMON BEARON BEATEN BEATON BLAZON BRAZEN CHAPIN CHARON CLAVIN CRAVEN CRAYON DEACON DEADEN DEADON DEAFEN DEALIN DRAGIN DRAGON DRAWIN DRAWON FLACON FLAGON FLAXEN FRAUEN GRABEN GRADIN GRATIN GRAVEN HEADIN HEADON HEAVEN IBADAN IMAMAN KEATON

KLAXON KRAKEN LEADEN LEADIN LEADON LEANON LEAVEN NEATEN NIACIN OMAHAN PEAHEN PLANON PLATEN PLAYON READIN REAGAN REASON RYAZAN SEAFAN SEAMAN SEAMEN SEASON SEATON SHABAN SHAKEN SHAMAN SHARON SHAVEN SPAVIN SRANAN STALIN STAMEN STATEN STAYON TOAMAN TRAJAN UTAHAN WEAKEN WEAPON XIAMEN

•••AN•

ADJANI ALBANO ALBANY ANWANG ANYANG ARCANA ARCANE ARMAND ARMANI ARRANT ARYANS ASIANS ASLANT ATHAND AVIANS BANANA BESANT BEZANT BOTANY BRIAND BRIANS BRYANT BUTANE BYHAND CABANA CEDANT CETANE CHIANG CLEANS CONANT CYRANO DANANG

DECANT DELANO DELANY DEMAND DISANT DIVANS DOMANI DOPANT DUNANT DURANT EMBANK ENFANT ERNANI ERRAND ERRANT ESPANA ETHANE EXPAND EXTANT FALANA FULANI GITANO GLEANS GROANS GUIANA GUYANA HABANA HAVANA HAZANS HOGANS HUMANE HUMANS IGUANA ILEANA INCANS INFANT INHAND INLAND INSANE IOWANS ISLAND JACANA JAPANS JOHANN KDLANG LELAND LEMANS LEVANT LIGAND LITANY MANANA MAYANS MCCANN MELANO MILANO MORANT MURANO MUTANT NAGANO NATANT OCEANS OCTANE OCTANT OKSANA ONHAND ONLAND ORGANA ORGANS ORIANA PADANG PAEANS PAGANS PAHANG PARANA

PARANG PAVANE PECANS PEDANT PENANG PIRANA PISANO PISANS PLIANT POLAND RECANE RECANT REDANT REHANG REMAND REMANS REPAND RESAND RIBAND ROLAND ROMANO ROMANS ROMANY ROXANA ROXANE SARANS SATANG SAVANT SECANT SEDANS SEJANT SHRANK SKEANS SLOANE SOLANS SOMANY SONANT SPRANG STRAND SUSANN TANANA TEJANO TENANT TEXANS TIRANA TIRANE TISANE TITANS TRUANT TUCANA TULANE TYRANT UCLANS UHLANS UNHAND UNMANS UPLAND URBANA URBANE UTHANT VACANT VEGANS VIVANT VOLANS VOLANT WAYANS ZENANA

•••A•N

ATTAIN BATAAN CANAAN DETAIN DOMAIN

GAWAIN INVAIN JOHANN LORAIN MCBAIN MCCANN MCLAIN OBTAIN ORDAIN PAPAIN PETAIN REGAIN REMAIN RESAWN RETAIN SPRAIN STRAIN SUSANN UJJAIN

••••AN

ADRIAN AEGEAN AFGHAN AIRMAN ALEMAN ALLMAN ALTMAN AMYTAN ANDEAN ANURAN APEMAN APPIAN ARCTAN ARUBAN ASHCAN ASOSAN ATAMAN AUGEAN BADMAN BAHIAN BALKAN BANYAN BARMAN BATAAN BATMAN BEMOAN BHUTAN BORMAN BOWMAN BROGAN BUCHAN BUNYAN BURMAN BUSMAN CAFTAN CAIMAN CANAAN CANCAN CAPTAN CARMAN CAYMAN COLMAN CONMAN COOGAN CORBAN CORMAN COWMAN CRETAN DEMEAN DESMAN DOLMAN DORIAN DOTHAN

DUNCAN DURBAN DURIAN ELFMAN ENDMAN EOLIAN EONIAN FABIAN FANTAN FBIMAN FENIAN FENMAN FEZZAN FIJIAN FINNAN FIRMAN FLYMAN FORMAN FRYPAN FUJIAN GAGMAN GASMAN GENOAN GERMAN GIBRAN GUNMAN HAGMAN HAINAN HARLAN HASSAN HERMAN HETMAN HITMAN IBADAN ICEMAN IMAMAN INDIAN INSPAN IONIAN JORDAN JOVIAN JULIAN KALKAN KANSAN KAPLAN KASDAN KEENAN KENYAN KERMAN KIDMAN KIRMAN KLIBAN KOREAN KORMAN KURGAN LAWMAN LAYMAN LEGMAN LIBYAN LLBEAN LONGAN LUCIAN MADMAN MANDAN MARIAN MCLEAN MEDIAN MERMAN MIDIAN MINOAN MINYAN MORGAN NATHAN NETMAN

NEUMAN NEWMAN NICEAN NISSAN NOONAN NORMAN NUBIAN OBIWAN OBRIAN OHIOAN OILCAN OILMAN OILPAN OLDMAN OMAHAN ONEMAN ONLOAN ORPHAN OSSIAN OUTRAN PACMAN PADUAN PAPUAN PATHAN PENMAN PIEMAN PIEPAN PITMAN QUMRAN RADIAN RAGLAN RAGMAN RATTAN REAGAN REPLAN RODMAN RUDMAN RUTTAN RYAZAN RYOKAN SAIPAN SALMAN SAMOAN SAMPAN SEAFAN SEAMAN SHABAN SHAMAN SHORAN SIMIAN SIOUAN SLOGAN SOLDAN SRANAN STEFAN STJOAN SULTAN SUNTAN SYLVAN SYRIAN TAINAN TAIPAN TAIWAN TANOAN TAPPAN TARPAN TARTAN TARZAN TASMAN TAXMAN TERRAN TINCAN TINMAN TINPAN

TITIAN TOAMAN TODMAN TONGAN TOUCAN TRAJAN TREPAN TROJAN TRUMAN TUBMAN TULSAN TUPIAN TURBAN TUSCAN TYRIAN UGRIAN ULLMAN UTAHAN VIVIAN VULCAN WICCAN WYSTAN YEOMAN YESMAN YUNNAN ZEEMAN

AO••••

AODAIS AORIST AORTAE AORTAL AORTAS AORTIC AOUDAD

A•O•••

ABOARD ABODES ABOHMS ABOLLA ABOMBS ABORAL ABORTS ABOUND ACORNS ADOBES ADOLPH ADONAI ADONIS ADOPTS ADORED ADOREE ADORER ADORES ADORNS AEOLIA AEOLIC AEOLUS AGORAE AGORAS AGOROT AGOUTI ALOHAS ALOINS ALOMAR ALONSO ALONZO AMOEBA AMOLES AMORAL AMOSOZ AMOUNT AMOURS

ANODES ANODIC ANOINT ANOLES ANOMIC ANOMIE ANONYM ANORAK APODAL APOGEE APOLLO AROIDS AROMAS AROUND AROUSE ASOSAN ATODDS ATOLLS ATOMIC ATONAL ATONCE ATONED ATONES ATONIC AVOCET AVOIDS AVOUCH AVOWAL AVOWED AVOWER AWOKEN AXONAL AZODYE AZORES AZORIN

A••O••

ABBOTS ABBOTT ABHORS ABLOOM ABROAD ABSORB ACCORD ACCOST ACEOUS ACEOUT ACROSS ACTONE ACTORS ACTOUT ADDONS ADJOIN ADROIT ADSORB AEROBE AFFORD AFLOAT AGEOLD AIROUT AJFOYT ALBOIN ALBORG ALCOTT ALCOVE ALDOSE ALDOUS ALGORE ALIOTO ALLOTS ALLOUT ALLOWS ALLOYS ALMOND

ALMOST ANCONA ANGOLA ANGORA ANIONS ANJOUS ANNOYS ANTONY ANYONE APLOMB APPOSE APRONS ARBORS ARBOUR ARDORS ARDOUR AREOLA ARGOSY ARGOTS ARIOSE ARIOSO ARMORS ARMORY ARMOUR ARNOLD ARROBA ARROWS ARROYO ARSONS ARTOIS ASCOTS ASHORE ASKOUT ASLOPE ASSORT ASWOON ATCOST ATEOUT ATHOME ATMOST ATWOOD ATWORK AUFOND AUMONT AURORA AUROUS AXIOMS AXIONS

A•••O•

ABLOOM ABYDOS ACAJOU ACTION ACTSON ADDSON AGGROS AGOROT AHCHOO AIMFOR ALAMOS ALANON ALBION ALISON ALLFOR AMADOU AMAJOR AMATOL AMAZON AMIDOL AMIGOS AMINOR AMNION AMOSOZ

ANALOG ANCHOR ANDHOW ANDROS ANGKOR ANGLOS ANNHON ANTCOW ANTRON ANYHOW ARAGON ARCCOS ARCHON ASIMOV ASKFOR ASTROS ASWOON ATWOOD AUDIOS AUTHOR AVALON AVEDON AVISOS

A••••O

ACTINO ACTTWO ADAGIO ADDSTO ADRENO AFLCIO AHCHOO AIELLO AIKIDO AIMSTO AKIMBO ALBANO ALBEDO ALBINO ALECTO ALEPPO ALIOTO ALLPRO ALNICO ALONSO ALONZO AMBATO AMEDEO ANATTO ANGELO ANTERO APOLLO AQUINO ARCARO AREZZO ARIOSO ARISTO ARROYO ARTHRO ARTURO ATEMPO ATERGO AUSTRO AVERNO

•AO•••

BAOBAB GAOLED GAOLER HAOLES KAOLIN LAOTSE LAOTZU MAOISM

MAOIST
MAORIS
MAOTAI
TAOISM
TAOIST

•A•O••
BABOON
BAROJA
BAROLO
BARONG
BARONS
BARONY
BATONS
BAYOUS
CAHOWS
CAJOLE
CANOED
CANOES
CANOLA
CANONS
CANOPY
CANOVA
CAPONE
CAPONS
CAPOTE
CAROBS
CAROLE
CAROLS
CAROMS
CARONI
CAVORT
DACOIT
DADOED
DADOES
DAKOTA
DAMONE
DAMORE
DAMOUR
DATONG
DAYONE
EATOUT
FAGOTS
FAMOUS
FANONS
FANOUT
FAROFF
FAROUK
FAROUT
FAVORS
FAVOUR
FAZOOL
GALOIS
GALOOT
GALOPS
GALORE
GALOSH
GATORS
HALOED
HALOES
HALOID
HAROLD
HAVOCS
JABOTS
JACOBI
JALOPY
JAMOKE
JAWOHL
KABOBS
KABOOM
KAROSS
KAYOED
KAZOOS
LABORS
LABOUR
LADOGA
LAGOON
LAHORE
LAKOTA
LAMONT
LAMOUR
LANOSE
LAROSA
LATONA
LATOUR
LATOYA
LAYOFF
LAYOUT
MACOUN
MAHOUT
MAJORS
MALONE
MALORY
MALOTI
MANORS
MAROON
MASONS
MAXOUT
MAYORS
MAZOLA
NABOBS
NABORS
NAGOYA
NANOOK
NAPOLI
PAEONS
PAGODA
PALOMA
PANOUT
PARODY
PAROLE
PATOIS
PAYOFF
PAYOLA
PAYOUT
RACONS
RADOME
RAGOUT
RAMONA
RAMONE
RAMOSE
RAMOUS
RANOFF
RANOUT
RAYONS
RAZORS
SABOTS
SALOME
SALONS
SALOON
SAMOAN
SAMOSA
SAPORS
SARODS
SARONG
SATORI
SATOUT
SAVOIE
SAVOIR
SAVORS
SAVORY
SAVOUR
SAWOFF
SAWOUT
SAXONS
SAXONY
TABOOS
TABORS
TACOMA
TAGORE
TAGOUT
TALONS
TANOAK
TANOAN
TAPOFF
TAPOUT
TAROTS
TAUONS
VADOSE
VALOIS
VALOUR
VAPORS
VAPORY
VAPOUR
WAGONS
WAHOOS
WAYOUT
YAHOOS
YAPOKS
ZADORA

•A••O•
BABOON
BABSON
BADBOY
BADLOT
BAILOR
BALBOA
BALLON
BALLOT
BALLOU
BAMBOO
BANDOG
BANGOR
BANJOS
BANKON
BANLON
BARDOT
BARHOP
BARRON
BARROW
BARTOK
BARTON
BARYON
BASSOS
BATBOY
BATHOS
BAYLOR
CACAOS
CACHOU
CAICOS
CALLON
CALLOW
CAMEON
CAMEOS
CAMION
CAMPOS
CANDOR
CANNON
CANNOT
CANTON
CANTOR
CANTOS
CANYON
CAPTOR
CARBON
CARBOS
CARBOY
CARGOS
CARHOP
CARLOS
CARLOT
CARNOT
CARROL
CARROT
CARSON
CARTON
CASTON
CASTOR
CATION
CATTON
CAWDOR
CAXTON
DACRON
DAIKON
DAIMON
DALTON
DAMSON
DANSON
DANTON
DARROW
DAWNON
DAWSON
DAYBOY
DAYJOB
DAYTON
EASTON
FACTOR
FAEROE
FALCON
FALLON
FALLOW
FANDOM
FANION
FARLOW
FARROW
FATHOM
FAZOOL
GABION
GAINON
GALLON
GALLOP
GALOOT
GAMBOL
GAMMON
GARCON
GARSON
GASCON
GASLOG
GASTON
GAYNOR
HADRON
HAEMON
HAGDON
HALLOO
HALLOS
HALLOW
HANDON
HANGON
HANSOM
HARBOR
HARLOW
HARMON
HARPON
HARROW
HATBOX
HATHOR
HAVEON
HAYMOW
JARGON
KABOOM
KANTOR
KARPOV
KARROO
KAZOOS
LAGOON
LAIDON
LANDON
LANSON
LAPDOG
LAPTOP
LARDON
LARGOS
LARSON
LASSOS
LAWSON
LAWTON
LAYFOR
LAYLOW
LAYSON
LAZBOY
MACHOS
MACRON
MACROS
MADTOM
MAGNON
MAHZOR
MALLOW
MAMBOS
MAMMON
MANGOS
MANIOC
MARCOS
MARGOT
MARION
MARLON
MARMOT
MAROON
MARRON
MARROW
MASCOT
MATRON
MATZOH
MATZOS
MAYPOP
NACHOS
NANOOK
NARROW
NATION
NATRON
PAILOU
PALLOR
PANTOS
PARDON
PARLOR
PARROT
PARSON
PARTON
PASEOS
PASSON
PASTOR
PATHOL
PATHOS
PATIOS
PATMOS
PATROL
PATRON
PATTON
PAVLOV
PAXTON
PAYBOX
PAYFOR
PAYSON
RADIOS
RAGMOP
RAGTOP
RAMROD
RAMSON
RANCOR
RANDOM
RANFOR
RANSOM
RAPTOR
RATION
RATIOS
RATSON
SAIGON
SAILOR
SALLOW
SALMON
SALOON
SALTON
SALVOR
SALVOS
SAMSON
SANTOS
SARGON
SARGOS
SARTON
SAVIOR
SAWLOG
SAYSOS
TABOOS
TACKON
TAILOR
TAINOS
TAKEON
TALBOT
TALION
TALLOW
TANGOS
TARPON
TATTOO
TAUTOG
TAYLOR
WACKOS
WAGGON
WAHOOS
WAITON
WALKON
WALLOP
WALLOW
WALTON
WANTON
WARGOD
WARHOL
WASHOE
WATSON
WAYLON
YAHOOS
YANGON
YARROW
YAUPON

•A•••O
BAGUIO
BAMAKO
BAMBOO
BANQUO
BAROLO
BARRIO
CALICO
CALLAO
CAMARO
CAMETO
CAMINO
CARDIO
CARETO
CARUSO
CASINO
CASSIO
CASTRO
CAUCHO
DACAPO
DADDYO
DAIMYO
DAMATO
DARETO
DAYGLO
FALLTO
GABBRO
GALAGO
GASTRO
GAUCHO
GAZEBO
HAIRDO
HALLOO
HASBRO
KAKAPO
KARROO
LADINO
LAIDTO
LANDHO
LAREDO
LASHIO
LATIGO
LATINO
LAVABO
LAYSTO
MACACO
MACEIO
MADEDO
MADERO
MADURO
MAGGIO
MAKEDO
MALABO
MAPUTO
MARIKO
MARINO
NAGANO
NAVAHO
NAVAJO
PACINO
PALAEO
PANCHO
PAPAGO
PARETO
PASHTO
RABATO
RANCHO
SABATO
SALADO
SANCHO
SANGTO
SAPPHO
SASEBO
TAKETO
TALKTO
TAMAYO
TATTOO
WANTTO
XANTHO

••A•O•
ACAJOU
ALAMOS
ALANON
AMADOU
AMAJOR
AMATOL
AMAZON
ANALOG
ARAGON
AVALON
BEACON
BEAMON
BEANOS
BEARON
BEATON
BLAZON
BMAJOR
BRASOV
BRAVOS
BRAZOS
CHADOR
CHARON
CLAMOR
CLAROS
CMAJOR
CRAYON
DEACON
DEADON
DIALOG
DIATOM
DMAJOR
DRAGON
DRAWON
EMAJOR
ENAMOR
FLACON
FLAGON
FLAVOR
FMAJOR
GLAMOR
GMAJOR
GUACOS
HEADON
HEAROF
INAFOG
INAROW
ISADOR
KEATON
KLAXON
KRAKOW
LEADON
LEANON
LLANOS
MCADOO
MEADOW
ORATOR
PEAPOD
PHAROS
PIANOS
PLANON
PLAYON
QUAHOG
REASON
SEACOW
SEADOG
SEAFOX
SEASON
SEATON
SHADOW
SHAKOS
SHALOM
SHARON
SLALOM
STATOR
STAYON
TEAPOT
TEAPOY
TLALOC
VIACOM
WEAPON
ZEALOT

••A••O
ADAGIO
ANATTO
BRANDO
CHALCO
CHARRO
CRAMBO
CRANIO
DIABLO
EXACTO
FIASCO
FRANCO
GEARTO
GRAECO
GRASSO
LEADTO
LEANTO
MCADOO
NEARTO
PLAGIO
PLASMO
QUANGO
QUARTO
RHABDO
RIALTO
SMALTO
SNAPTO
SOASTO
WHAMMO

•••AO•
CACAOS
HIVAOA

•••A•O
ALBANO
AMBATO
ARCARO
BAMAKO
BORAXO
CAMARO
CHEAPO
CITATO
CYRANO
DACAPO
DAMATO
DELANO
DORADO
DYNAMO
ELPASO
ENHALO
FIGARO
GALAGO
GELATO
GITANO
HEMATO
JURADO
KAKAPO
LAVABO
LEGATO
MACACO
MALABO
MEGALO
MELANO
MENADO
MIKADO
MILANO
MONACO
MURANO
MUTATO
NAGANO
NAVAHO
NAVAJO
NEMATO
NOVATO
OCTAVO
PALAEO
PAPAGO
PICABO
PICARO
PISANO
POTATO
RABATO
ROBALO
ROMANO
RUBATO
SABATO
SALADO
SOMATO
STMALO
STRABO
STRATO
TAMAYO
TEJANO
TERATO
TEXACO
TOBAGO
TOMATO
VIRAGO

••••AO
BILBAO
CALLAO
TODDAO

AP••••
APACHE
APATHY
APEMAN
APEMEN
APERCU
APEXES
APHIDS
APIARY
APICAL
APICES
APIECE
APLITE
APLOMB
APODAL
APOGEE
APOLLO
APPALL
APPALS
APPEAL
APPEAR
APPEND
APPIAN
APPLES
APPLET
APPOSE
APRONS
APTEST
APULIA

A•P•••
ALPACA
ALPERT
ALPHAS
ALPINE
AMPERE
AMPHID
AMPLER
AMPULE
AMPULS
APPALL
APPALS
APPEAL
APPEAR
APPEND
APPIAN
APPLES
APPLET
APPOSE
ARPENT
ASPECT
ASPENS
ASPERA
ASPICS
ASPIRE
ASPISH
AUPAIR

A••P••
ADAPTS
ADEPTS
ADOPTS
ALEPHS
ALEPPO
ALLPRO
ARMPIT
AUSPEX

A•••P•
ABRUPT
ACCEPT
ADOLPH
ALCAPP
ALEPPO
ASLOPE
ATEMPO

A••••P
ACESUP
ACTSUP
ADDSUP
ALCAPP
AMERSP
ANTEUP
ASHARP
ASLEEP

•AP•••
CAPERS
CAPFUL
CAPGUN
CAPIAS
CAPITA
CAPLET
CAPNUT
CAPONE
CAPONS
CAPOTE
CAPPED
CAPPER
CAPRIS
CAPSID
CAPTAN
CAPTOR
DAPHNE
DAPPED
DAPPER
DAPPLE
GAPERS
GAPING
GAPPED
HAPPED
HAPPEN
JAPANS
JAPERS
JAPERY
JAPING
KAPLAN
KAPPAS
LAPDOG
LAPELS
LAPFUL
LAPHAM
LAPINS
LAPPED
LAPPET
LAPSED
LAPSES
LAPSUP
LAPTEV
LAPTOP
LAPUTA
MAPLES
MAPPED
MAPPER
MAPUTO
NAPERY
NAPIER
NAPKIN
NAPLES
NAPOLI
NAPPED
NAPPER
NAPPES
NAPPIE
PAPACY
PAPAGO
PAPAIN
PAPAWS
PAPAYA
PAPERS
PAPERY
PAPIER
PAPPAS
PAPPUS
PAPUAN
PAPYRI
RAPIDS
RAPIER
RAPINE
RAPINI
RAPPED
RAPPEE
RAPPEL
RAPPER
RAPTLY
RAPTOR
SAPORS
SAPPED
SAPPER
SAPPHO
TAPERS
TAPING
TAPINS
TAPIRS
TAPOFF
TAPOUT
TAPPAN
TAPPED
TAPPER
TAPPET
VAPORS
VAPORY
VAPOUR
WAPITI
WAPNER
YAPOKS
YAPPED
ZAPATA
ZAPPED
ZAPPER

•A•P••
CALPAC
CAMPED
CAMPER
CAMPOS
CAMPUS
CAPPED
CAPPER
CARPAL
CARPED
CARPEL
CARPER
CARPET
CARPUS
CASPAR
CASPER
DAMPED
DAMPEN
DAMPER
DAMPLY
DAPPED
DAPPER
DAPPLE
GALPAL
GAPPED
GASPAR
GASPED
GASPER
GAWPED
HAMPER
HAPPED
HAPPEN
HARPED
HARPER
HARPON
HASPED
HATPIN
JAIPUR
JASPER
KAPPAS
KARPOV
LAPPED
LAPPET
LAUPER
MAGPIE
MAPPED
MAPPER
MARPLE
MAYPOP
NAPPED
NAPPER
NAPPES
NAPPIE
PALPUS
PAMPAS
PAMPER
PAPPAS
PAPPUS
PAUPER
PAWPAW
RAIPUR
RAJPUT
RAMPED
RAPPED
RAPPEE
RAPPEL
RAPPER
RASPED
RASPER
SAIPAN
SAMPAN
SAMPLE
SAPPED
SAPPER
SAPPHO
TAIPAN
TAIPEI
TAMPED
TAMPER
TAPPAN
TAPPED
TAPPER
TAPPET
TARPAN
TARPIT
TARPON
TAUPES
VAMPED
VAMPER
WAMPUM
WARPED
YAPPED
YAUPON
YAWPED
YAWPER
ZAPPED
ZAPPER

•A••P•
CALIPH
CANAPE
CANOPY
DACAPO
GALOPS
JALAPA
JALOPY
JAMUPS
KAKAPO
LAYUPS
PARAPH

•A•••P
BACKUP
BALLUP
BANGUP
BARHOP
CALLUP
CAMEUP
CARHOP
CATNAP
CATNIP
CATSUP
DAMSUP
EARLAP
EASEUP
EATSUP
FACEUP
FAIRUP
GALLOP
GALLUP
GANGUP
GASCAP
GAVEUP
GAZUMP
HANDUP
HANGUP
HARDUP
HAULUP
JACKUP
JAMSUP
JAZZUP
LACEUP
LAIDUP
LAPSUP
LAPTOP
LARRUP
LASHUP
LAYSUP
MADCAP
MADEUP
MAKEUP
MARKUP
MAYHAP
MAYPOP
PACKUP
PAIDUP
PAIRUP
PASSUP
PAYSUP
RACKUP
RAGMOP
RAGTOP
RAKEUP
RANGUP
RAVEUP
SANNUP
SATRAP
SAVEUP
TAGSUP
TAKEUP
TALKUP
TANKUP
WADSUP
WAITUP
WAKEUP
WALKUP
WALLOP
WALLUP
WARMUP
WASHUP

••AP••
ADAPTS
CHAPEL
CHAPIN
COAPTS
CRAPES
DIAPER
DRAPED
DRAPER
DRAPES
ELAPID
ELAPSE
ETAPES
FLAPPY
FRAPPE
GRAPES
GRAPEY
GRAPHS
GRAPHY
GRAPPA
HEAPED
INAPET
LEAPED
LEAPER
OKAPIS
PEAPOD
REAPED
REAPER
SCAPED
SCAPES
SHAPED
SHAPER
SHAPES
SLAPPY
SLAPUP
SNAPAT
SNAPPY
SNAPTO
SNAPUP
SOAPED
SOAPER
STAPES
STAPLE
STAPUF
TEAPOT
TEAPOY
TRAPPY
WEAPON
WRAPUP

••A•P•
CHAMPS
CLAMPS
CLASPS
CRAMPS
FLAPPY
FRAPPE
GRAMPA
GRAMPS
GRAPPA
GRASPS
SCALPS
SCAMPI
SCAMPS
SCARPS
SCAUPS
SHARPS
SLAPPY
SNAPPY
STAMPS
SWAMPS
SWAMPY
TRAMPS
TRAPPY

••A••P
BEADUP
BEAMUP
BEARUP
BEATUP
CHATUP
CLAMUP
DIALUP
DRAWUP
GEARUP
HEADUP
HEATUP
LEADUP
PLAYUP
REARUP
SEALUP
SLAPUP
SNAPUP
SOAKUP
STAYUP
TEACUP
TEAMUP
TEARUP
WRAPUP

•••AP•
ALCAPP
CANAPE
CHEAPO
DACAPO
ENRAPT
ESCAPE
JALAPA
KAKAPO
LENAPE
ONTAPE
PARAPH
PTRAPS
RECAPS
REMAPS
RETAPE
RETAPS
SCRAPE

SCRAPS SERAPE SERAPH STRAPS TERAPH UNCAPS

•••A•P

ALCAPP ASHARP BSHARP CCLAMP CSHARP DECAMP DSHARP ENCAMP ESCARP ESHARP FSHARP GSHARP PREAMP REVAMP

••••AP

BITMAP BUMRAP BURLAP CATNAP DEWLAP EARLAP ENTRAP ENWRAP GASCAP HOTCAP HUBCAP ICECAP KIDNAP MADCAP MAYHAP MILSAP MISHAP MOBCAP NOSOAP REDCAP REWRAP RIPRAP SATRAP SKYCAP TOECAP TOETAP UNSNAP UNTRAP UNWRAP

AQ••••

AQUATE AQUILA AQUINO

A•Q•••

ACQUIT

•AQ•••

MAQUIS PAQUIN RAQUEL YAQUIS

•A•Q••

BANQUO BARQUE BASQUE CAIQUE CALQUE CASQUE MANQUE MARQUE MASQUE SACQUE YANQUI

•A•••Q

NASDAQ

••AQ••

BRAQUE CLAQUE IRAQIS OPAQUE PLAQUE

••••AQ

COMPAQ NASDAQ

AR••••

ARABIA ARABIC ARABLE ARAFAT ARAGON ARALIA ARALLU ARAMIS ARARAT ARAWAK ARBELA ARBORS ARBOUR ARCADE ARCANA ARCANE ARCARO ARCCOS ARCHED ARCHER ARCHES ARCHIE ARCHLY ARCHON ARCING ARCTAN ARCTIC ARDEBS ARDENT ARDORS ARDOUR ARECAS ARENAS ARENDT AREOLA ARETES ARETHA AREZZO ARGALI ARGENT ARGIVE ARGOSY ARGOTS ARGUED ARGUER ARGUES ARGUFY ARGYLE ARGYLL ARIDLY ARIGHT ARIOSE ARIOSO ARISEN ARISES ARISTA ARISTO ARJUNA ARLEEN ARLENE ARLISS ARMADA ARMAGH ARMAND ARMANI ARMETS ARMFUL ARMIES ARMING ARMLET ARMORS ARMORY ARMOUR ARMPIT ARMURE ARNESS ARNETT ARNHEM ARNICA ARNOLD AROIDS AROMAS AROUND AROUSE ARPENT ARRACK ARRANT ARRAYS ARREAR ARREST ARRIBA ARRIVE ARROBA ARROWS ARROYO ARSENE ARSONS ARTELS ARTERY ARTFUL ARTGUM ARTHRO ARTHUR ARTIER ARTILY ARTIST ARTOIS ARTURO ARUBAN ARVADA ARYANS

A•R•••

ABRADE ABRAMS ABROAD ABRUPT ACROSS ADRENO ADRIAN ADRIEN ADRIFT ADROIT AERATE AERIAL AERIES AERIFY AERILY AEROBE AFRAID AFRAME AFREET AFRESH AFRICA AFRITS AGREED AGREES AIRARM AIRBAG AIRBUS AIRDAM AIRDRY AIRGUN AIRIER AIRILY AIRING AIRMAN AIRMEN AIROUT AIRSAC AIRWAY AORIST AORTAE AORTAL AORTAS AORTIC APRONS ARRACK ARRANT ARRAYS ARREAR ARREST ARRIBA ARRIVE ARROBA ARROWS ARROYO ATREST ATREUS ATRIAL ATRISK ATRIUM AUREUS AURIFY AURIGA AURORA AUROUS

A••R••

ABORAL ABORTS ACARID ACARUS ACCRUE ACORNS ADORED ADOREE ADORER ADORES ADORNS AFFRAY AGARIC AGGROS AGORAE AGORAS AGOROT AHERNE AIGRET ALARIC ALARMS ALARUM ALDRIN ALERTS ALFRED AMERCE AMERSP AMORAL AMTRAC AMTRAK ANDREA ANDREI ANDRES ANDREW ANDREY ANDROS ANERGY ANORAK ANTRES ANTRIM ANTRON ANTRUM ANURAN APERCU ARARAT ASHRAM ASTRAL ASTRAY ASTRID ASTROS ATERGO ATTRIT AUBREY AUDREY AVERNO AVERSE AVERTS AWARDS AZORES AZORIN

A•••R•

ABHORS ABJURE ABOARD ABSORB ABSURD ACCORD ACTORS ADDERS ADHERE ADJURE ADMIRE ADSORB ADVERB ADVERT AFEARD AFFIRM AFFORD AGLARE AIDERS AILERS AIRARM AIRDRY ALBERT ALBORG ALDERS ALEGRE ALGORE ALHIRT ALLPRO ALLURE ALPERT ALTARS ALTERS AMBERS AMBERY AMEERS AMENRA AMHARA AMOURS AMPERE ANGERS ANGORA ANITRA ANKARA ANSARA ANTERO APIARY ARBORS ARCARO ARDORS ARMORS ARMORY ARMURE ARTERY ARTHRO ARTURO ASBURY ASGARD ASHARP ASHORE ASKARI ASKERS ASMARA ASPERA ASPIRE ASSERT ASSORT ASSURE ASTERN ASTERS ASWIRL ATTARS ATTIRE ATWORK AUBURN AUGERS AUGURS AUGURY AURORA AUSTRO AVIARY AWEARY AWHIRL AYMARA

A••••R

AAFAIR ABUKIR ABUSER ACHIER ADORER AETHER AFFAIR AGADIR AIMFOR AIRIER ALEGAR ALITER ALLFOR ALOMAR ALTAIR ALULAR AMAJOR AMBLER AMINOR AMPLER ANCHOR ANGKOR ANGLER ANHYDR ANSGAR ANSWER ANTHER ANTLER APPEAR ARBOUR ARCHER ARDOUR ARGUER ARMOUR ARREAR ARTHUR ARTIER ASEVER ASHIER ASHLAR ASKFOR AUPAIR AUTEUR AUTHOR AVATAR AVOWER

•AR•••

BARBED BARBEL BARBER BARBET BARBIE BARBRA BARCAR BARDIC BARDOT BAREGE BARELY BAREST BARFLY BARGED BARGES BARHOP BARING BARISH BARITE BARIUM BARKAT BARKED BARKER BARKIN BARLEY BARMAN BARMEN BARNES BARNEY BARNUM BAROJA BAROLO BARONG BARONS BARONY BARQUE BARRED BARREL BARREN BARRES BARRIE BARRIO BARRIS BARRON BARROW BARTAB BARTER BARTOK BARTON BARUCH BARYON BARZUN CARAFE CARATS CARBON CARBOS CARBOY CARDED CARDER CARDIN CARDIO CAREEN CAREER CARESS CARETO CARETS CARFUL CARGOS CARHOP CARIBE CARIBS CARIES CARINA CARING CARKED CARLIN CARLOS CARLOT CARMAN CARMEL CARMEN CARNAL CARNES CARNET CARNEY CARNOT CAROBS CAROLE CAROLS CAROMS CARONI CARPAL CARPED CARPEL CARPER CARPET CARPUS CARREL CARREY CARRIE CARROL CARROT CARSON CARTED CARTEL CARTER CARTES CARTON CARUSO CARVED CARVER CARVES CARVEY DARENT DARETO DARIEN DARING DARIUS DARKEN DARKER DARKLE DARKLY DARNAY DARNED DARNEL DARNER DARNIT DARREN DARROW DARRYL DARTED DARTER DARWIN EARFUL EARING EARLAP EARNED EARNER EARTHA EARTHY EARWAX EARWIG FARADS FARCED FARCES FARCRY FARERS FARINA FARING FARLEY FARLOW FARMED FARMER FAROFF FAROUK FAROUT FARRAH FARRAR FARROW GARAGE GARBED GARBLE GARCIA GARCON GARDEN GARETH GARGLE GARISH GARLIC GARNER GARNET GARRET GARSON GARTER GARTHS GARVEY HARALD HARARE HARASS HARBIN HARBOR HARDBY HARDEN HARDER HARDLY HARDUP HAREMS HARING HARKED HARKEN HARKER HARLAN HARLEM HARLEY HARLIN HARLOW HARMED HARMON HAROLD HARPED HARPER HARPON HARRIS HARROW HARVEY JARFUL JARGON JARRAH JARRED KARATE KARATS KAREEM KARIBA KARMIC KARNAK KAROSS KARPOV KARRAS KARROO KARSTS LARAMS LARDED LARDER LARDON LAREDO LARGER LARGES LARGOS LARIAT LARKED LAROSA LARRUP LARSEN LARSON LARVAE LARVAL LARVAS LARYNX MARACA MARAUD MARBLE MARBLY MARCEL MARCHE MARCIA MARCIE MARCOS MARCUS MARDUK MARGAY MARGES MARGIE MARGIN MARGOT MARIAH MARIAN MARIEL MARIKO MARILU MARINA MARINE MARINO MARION MARISA MARISH MARIST MARIUS MARKED MARKER MARKET MARKKA MARKUP MARLED MARLEE MARLEY MARLIN MARLON MARMEE MARMOT MARNER MARNIE MAROON MARPLE MARQUE MARRED MARRON MARROW MARSHA MARSHY MARTEL MARTEN MARTHA MARTIN MARTYR MARVEL MARVIN NARIAL NARNIA NARROW NARVIK NARWAL OARING PARADE PARANA PARANG PARAPH PARCAE PARCEL PARDON PARENS PARENT PARERS PARETO PAREVE PARGET PARIAH PARING PARISH PARITY PARKAS PARKAY PARKED PARKER PARLAY PARLEY PARLOR PARNIS PARODY PAROLE PARRED PARREL PARRIS PARROT PARSEC PARSED PARSEE PARSER PARSES PARSON PARTED PARTLY PARTON PARULA PARURE PARVIS RAREFY RARELY RAREST RARIFY RARING RARITY SARANS SARDIS SARGES SARGON SARGOS SARNIA SARODS SARONG SARTON SARTRE TARAWA TARGES TARGET TARIFF TARING TARMAC TAROTS TARPAN TARPIT TARPON TARRED TARSAL TARSUS TARTAN TARTAR TARTER TARTLY TARZAN VARDEN VARESE VARIED VARIES VARLET VARNAS VARNEY VARUNA WARBLE WARCRY WARDED WARDEN WARDER WARGOD WARHOL WARIER WARILY WARING WARMED WARMER WARMLY WARMTH WARMUP WARNED WARNER WARPED WARRED WARREN WARSAW YARDED YARELY YAREST YARNED YARROW ZAREBA

•A•R••

BAIRNS BARRED BARREL BARREN BARRES BARRIE BARRIO BARRIS BARRON BARROW BAYRUM CADRES CAIRNS CAPRIS CARREL CARREY CARRIE CARROL CARROT CATRIG DACRON DAIREN DARREN DARROW DARRYL EAGRES FABRAY FABRIC FAERIE FAEROE FAIRED FAIRER FAIRLY FAIRUP FARRAH FARRAR FARROW GARRET HADRON HAIRDO HAIRED HARRIS HARROW HATRED IATRIC JARRAH JARRED JAURES KARRAS KARROO KAURIS LABREA LABRET LABRUM LAIRDS LARRUP LAUREL LAUREN LAURIE MACRAE MACRON MACROS MADRAS MADRES MADRID MANRAY MAORIS MARRED MARRON MARROW MATRIX MATRON MAURYA NACRES NAIRAS NARROW NATRON PADRES PAIRED PAIRUP PARRED PARREL PARRIS PARROT PATROL PATRON RAGRUG RAHRAH RAMROD SABRAS SABRES SACRAL SACRED SACRUM SATRAP SAUREL SAWRED TABRIZ TARRED TAURUS TAYRAS VANRYN WALRUS WARRED WARREN YARROW ZAGREB ZAIRES

•A••R•

BAKERS BAKERY BALERS BARBRA BAYARD CABERS CAGERS CAMARO CAMERA CANARD CANARY CANERS CAPERS CASERN CASTRO CATERS CAVERN CAVERS CAVORT DAMORE DATARY DATERS DATURA EATERS EATERY FAKERS FAKERY FAKIRS FARCRY FARERS FAVORS GABBRO GALORE GANTRY GAPERS GASTRO GATERS GATORS HALERS HALERU HARARE HASBRO HATARI HATERS HAVERS HAZARD HAZERS JABIRU JAPERS JAPERY JAVARI KAFIRS KAGERA LABORS LACERS LADERS LAGERS LAHORE LAKERS LAMARR LANARK LANDRY LASERS LAVERS LAYERS MADERO MADURA MADURO MAITRE MAJORS MAKERS MALORY MANORS MANTRA MASERS MASERU MATERS MATURE MAYORS MAZERS NABORS NADIRS NAMERS NAPERY NATURA NATURE OATERS PACERS PAGERS PAHARI PALTRY PAMIRS PANFRY PANTRY PAPERS PAPERY PAPYRI PARERS PARURE PASTRY PATERS PAVERS PAWERS PAYERS QATARI RACERS RAKERS RANDRY RASERS RATERS RAVERS RAZORS SABERS SAFARI SAFIRE SAHARA SAKERS SALARY SAMARA SANDRA SAPORS SARTRE SATIRE SATORI SATURN SATYRS SAVERS SAVORS SAVORY SAYERS TABARD TABORS TAGORE TAKERS TALERS TAMARA TAMERS TANTRA TAPERS TAPIRS TASERS TATARS TATERS TAVERN TAWDRY TAXERS UAKARI VAGARY VALERY VAPORS VAPORY WADERS WAFERS WAFERY WAGERS WALERS WANERS WARCRY WATERS WATERY WAVERS WAVERY WAXERS ZADORA

•A•••R

AAFAIR BACKER BADDER BADGER BAGGER BAILER BAILOR BALDER BANGER BANGOR BANKER BANNER BANTER BARBER BARCAR BARKER BARTER BASTER BATHER BATTER BAWLER

BAXTER
BAYLOR
BAZAAR
CABLER
CADGER
CAESAR
CAGIER
CAHIER
CAKIER
CALDER
CALLER
CALMER
CAMBER
CAMPER
CANDOR
CANIER
CANKER
CANNER
CANTER
CANTOR
CAPPER
CAPTOR
CARDER
CAREER
CARPER
CARTER
CARVER
CASPAR
CASPER
CASTER
CASTOR
CATHER
CAVIAR
CAWDOR
DAFTER
DAGGER
DAGMAR
DAMMAR
DAMOUR
DAMPER
DANCER
DANDER
DANGER
DANKER
DANNER
DAPPER
DARKER
DARNER
DARTER
DASHER
DAUBER
EARNER
EASIER
EASTER
FABLER
FACTOR
FAFNIR
FAIRER
FALSER
FALTER
FARMER
FARRAR
FASTER
FATHER
FATTER
FAVOUR
FAWNER
GABBER
GABLER
GADDER
GAFFER
GAINER
GAITER
GAMIER
GAMMER
GANDER
GANGER
GAOLER
GARNER
GARTER
GASPAR
GASPER
GASSER
GATHER
GAUGER
GAWKER
GAYNOR
HACKER
HALTER
HAMMER
HAMPER
HANGAR
HANGER
HANKER
HARBOR
HARDER
HARKER
HARPER
HATHOR
HATTER
HAULER
HAWKER
HAWSER
HAZIER
JABBAR
JABBER
JAEGER
JAGGER
JAGUAR
JAILER
JAIPUR
JAMMER
JASPER
JAVIER
KAFFIR
KAISER
KALMAR
KANDER
KANTOR
KAVNER
LAAGER
LABOUR
LACIER
LADDER
LADLER
LAFFER
LAGGER
LAKIER
LAMARR
LAMOUR
LANCER
LANDER
LANGUR
LANIER
LANKER
LARDER
LARGER
LASCAR
LASHER
LASSER
LATHER
LATOUR
LATTER
LAUDER
LAUPER
LAWYER
LAYFOR
LAZIER
MADDER
MAGYAR
MAHLER
MAHZOR
MAILER
MANGER
MANNER
MAPPER
MARKER
MARNER
MARTYR
MASHER
MASKER
MASTER
MATHER
MATTER
MAULER
MAUSER
MAZIER
NABBER
NAGGER
NAILER
NAPIER
NAPPER
NASCAR
NASSER
NATTER
OATIER
PACKER
PADDER
PALIER
PALLOR
PALMER
PALTER
PAMPER
PANDER
PANNER
PANZER
PAPIER
PARKER
PARLOR
PARSER
PASSER
PASTOR
PATTER
PAUPER
PAWNER
PAYFOR
RACIER
RADNER
RAFTER
RAIDER
RAILER
RAINER
RAIPUR
RAISER
RANCOR
RANFOR
RANGER
RANKER
RANTER
RAPIER
RAPPER
RAPTOR
RASHER
RASPER
RASTER
RATEDR
RATHER
RATTER
SACKER
SADDER
SAILOR
SALTER
SALVER
SALVOR
SAMBAR
SANDER
SANGER
SANTIR
SAPPER
SASSER
SAUCER
SAUGER
SAVIOR
SAVOIR
SAVOUR
SAWYER
TACKER
TAILOR
TALKER
TALLER
TAMPER
TANKER
TANNER
TAPPER
TARTAR
TARTER
TASTER
TATTER
TAUTER
TAYLOR
VAGUER
VAINER
VALOUR
VAMPER
VANIER
VAPOUR
VASSAR
VASTER
WAGNER
WAILER
WAITER
WAIVER
WALKER
WALLER
WALTER
WANDER
WANIER
WANNER
WAPNER
WARDER
WARIER
WARMER
WARNER
WASHER
WASTER
WAVIER
WAXIER
XAVIER
YABBER
YAKKER
YAMMER
YASSER
YAWNER
YAWPER
ZAFFER
ZANDER
ZANIER
ZAPPER

••AR••

ACARID
ACARUS
AGARIC
ALARIC
ALARMS
ALARUM
ARARAT
AWARDS
BEARDS
BEARER
BEARON
BEARUP
BLARED
BLARES
BOARDS
CHARGE
CHARLY
CHARMS
CHARON
CHARRO
CHARTS
CIARDI
CLARET
CLARKE
CLAROS
COARSE
DEARER
DEARIE
DEARLY
DEARME
DEARTH
DHARMA
DMARKS
DUARTE
DWARFS
ECARTE
EPARCH
EXARCH
FEARED
FEARER
FLARED
FLARES
GEARED
GEARTO
GEARUP
GHARRY
GLARED
GLARES
GNARLS
GNARLY
GUARDS
HEARER
HEAROF
HEARST
HEARTH
HEARTS
HEARTY
HEARYE
HOARDS
HOARSE
ICARIA
ICARUS
IMARET
INARCH
INAROW
INARUT
JUAREZ
KEARNY
KNARRY
LEARNS
LEARNT
NEARBY
NEARED
NEARER
NEARLY
NEARTO
OZARKS
PEARLS
PEARLY
PHAROS
QUARKS
QUARRY
QUARTO
QUARTS
QUARTZ
REARED
REARER
REARMS
REARUP
ROARED
ROARER
SCARAB
SCARCE
SCARED
SCARER
SCARES
SCARFS
SCARNE
SCARPS
SCARRY
SCARUM
SEARCH
SEARED
SEARLE
SHARDS
SHARED
SHARER
SHARES
SHARIA
SHARIF
SHARKS
SHARON
SHARPS
SMARMY
SMARTS
SMARTY
SNARED
SNARES
SNARLS
SNARLY
SOARED
SOARER
SOARES
SPARED
SPARER
SPARES
SPARGE
SPARKS
SPARKY
SPARSE
SPARTA
STARCH
STARED
STARER
STARES
STARRY
STARTS
STARVE
SWARAJ
SWARDS
SWARMS
SWARTH
TEARAT
TEARED
TEARUP
TIARAS
TUAREG
UNARMS
WEARER
WHARFS
YEARLY
YEARNS

••A•R•

BIAFRA
CHAIRS
CHARRO
CLAIRE
FIACRE
FLAIRS
GHARRY
GLAIRS
GLAIRY
GOAWRY
KHAFRE
KNARRY
MEAGRE
QUADRI
QUARRY
REAIRS
SCARRY
STAIRS
STARRY

••A••R

AGADIR
AMAJOR
AVATAR
BEAKER
BEARER
BEATER
BEAVER
BLADER
BLAZER
BMAJOR
BOATER
BRACER
BRAVER
BRAYER
BRAZER
CHADOR
CHASER
CLAMOR
CLAWER
CMAJOR
COALER
COAXER
CRATER
CRAVER
DEADER
DEAFER
DEALER
DEARER
DIALER
DIAPER
DLAYER
DMAJOR
DRAPER
DRAWER
ELATER
ELAYER
EMAJOR
ENAMOR
ERASER
EVADER
FEARER
FLAKER
FLAVOR
FLAYER
FMAJOR
FRASER
FRAZER
GLAMOR
GLASER
GLAZER
GMAJOR
GNAWER
GRADER
GRATER
GRAVER
GRAYER
GRAZER
HEADER
HEALER
HEARER
HEATER
HEAVER
HOAXER
IMAGER
INANER
IRATER
ISADOR
KRAMER
KRATER
LAAGER
LEADER
LEAKER
LEANER
LEAPER
LEASER
LOADER
LOAFER
LOANER
MEAGER
MEANER
MOANER
NEARER
NEATER
ONAGER
ORATOR
PHASER
PLACER
PLANAR
PLANER
PLATER
PLAYER
PRATER
PRAYER
QUAKER
QUASAR
QUAVER
READER
REALER
REAMER
REAPER
REARER
ROAMER
ROARER
SCALAR
SCALER
SCARER
SEALER
SEATER
SHAKER
SHAMIR
SHAPER
SHARER
SHAVER
SKATER
SLATER
SLAVER
SLAYER
SOAKER
SOAPER
SOARER
SPACER
SPADER
SPARER
STAGER
STALER
STARER
STATER
STATOR
SUAVER
SWAYER
TEASER
THALER
THAYER
TRACER
TRADER
WEAKER
WEARER
WEAVER
WHALER
YEAGER

•••AR•

ABOARD
AFEARD
AGLARE
AIRARM
ALTARS
AMHARA
ANKARA
ANSARA
APIARY
ARCARO
ASGARD
ASHARP
ASKARI
ASMARA
ATTARS
AVIARY
AWEARY
AYMARA
BAYARD
BEWARE
BICARB
BIHARI
BINARY
BLEARS
BLEARY
BOGART
BOVARY
BOYARS
BRIARD
BRIARS
BSHARP
CAMARO
CANARD
CANARY
CEDARS
CESARE
CIGARS
CLEARS
COWARD
CSHARP
CUNARD
CURARE
DATARY
DEBARK
DEBARS
DENARY
DEPART
DINARS
DISARM
DOTARD
DREARY
DSHARP
EDGARD
EDGARS
EDUARD
EDVARD
EDWARD
EMBARK
ERHARD
ERRARE
ESCARP
ESHARP
EZZARD
FIGARO
FRIARS
FRIARY
FSHARP
FUGARD
GEMARA
GERARD
GIRARD
GOCART
GODARD
GOKART
GSHARP
HARARE
HATARI
HAZARD
HEGARI
HILARY
HOBART
HOWARD
IDCARD
IMPART
INPART
INWARD
IZZARD
JAVARI
LAMARR
LANARK
LIZARD
MEGARA
MOLARS
MOZART
NEWARK
NONARY
NOTARY
OLEARY
ONWARD
OSCARS
OXCART
OXNARD
PAHARI
PETARD
PICARA
PICARD
PICARO
POPART
QATARI
REBARS
REGARD
REMARK
RETARD
RETARS
REWARD
REWARM
RITARD
ROSARY
ROTARY
SAFARI
SAHARA
SALARY
SAMARA
SENARY
SEWARD
SHEARS
SITARS
SMEARS
SMEARY
SOLARS
SOUARI
SPEARS
SQUARE
STMARK
STUART
SUBARU
SUGARS
SUGARY
SWEARS
TABARD
TAMARA
TATARS
THWART
TOWARD
TULARE
UAKARI
UNBARS
UNWARY
UPWARD
VAGARY
VICARS
VOLARE
VOTARY
WIZARD

•••A•R

AAFAIR
AFFAIR
ALTAIR
AUPAIR
BAZAAR
BELAIR
ECLAIR
HOTAIR
IMPAIR
LAMARR
MCNAIR
MIDAIR
MOHAIR
REPAIR
UNFAIR

••••AR

ALEGAR
ALOMAR
ALULAR
ANSGAR
APPEAR
ARREAR
ASHLAR
AVATAR
BARCAR
BAZAAR
BEGGAR
BOWOAR
BOXCAR
BULGAR
BURSAR
BUSBAR
CAESAR
CASPAR
CAVIAR
CELLAR
CHUKAR
COLLAR
COSTAR
COUGAR
DAGMAR
DAMMAR
DELMAR
DEODAR
DISBAR
DOGEAR
DOLLAR
DUNBAR
DURBAR
ENDEAR
FARRAR
FOLIAR
FULMAR
GASPAR
GUITAR
GUNNAR
HANGAR
HOTCAR
HOTWAR
HUSSAR
INGEAR
INGMAR
INSTAR
ISHTAR
ISOBAR
JABBAR
JAGUAR
KALMAR
KEVLAR
LASCAR
LEKVAR
LINEAR
LOTHAR
LUMBAR
MAGYAR
MEDGAR
MEDLAR
MOLNAR
MORTAR
NASCAR
NECTAR
NEWMAR
OCULAR
OVULAR
PEDLAR
PILLAR
PINDAR
PLANAR
POPLAR
PREWAR
PSYWAR
PULSAR
QINTAR
QUASAR
REHEAR
RETEAR
SAMBAR
SCALAR
SHIKAR
SHOFAR
SIRDAR
STELAR
SUBPAR
TARTAR
THENAR
TINEAR
TOWCAR
TROCAR
UPROAR
UVULAR
VASSAR
VULGAR
WEIMAR
WETBAR
ZEDBAR

AS••••

ASANAS
ASBURY
ASCEND
ASCENT
ASCHAM
ASCOTS
ASDICS
ASEITY
ASEVER
ASGARD
ASHARP
ASHCAN
ASHIER
ASHLAR
ASHLEY
ASHORE
ASHRAM
ASIANS
ASIDES
ASIMOV
ASKARI
ASKERS
ASKFOR
ASKING
ASKOUT
ASKSIN
ASLANT
ASLEEP
ASLOPE
ASMARA
ASOSAN
ASPECT
ASPENS
ASPERA
ASPICS
ASPIRE
ASPISH
ASSAIL
ASSAYS
ASSENT
ASSERT
ASSESS
ASSETS
ASSIGN
ASSISI
ASSIST
ASSIZE
ASSORT
ASSUME
ASSURE
ASTERN
ASTERS
ASTRAL
ASTRAY
ASTRID
ASTROS
ASTUTE
ASWELL
ASWIRL
ASWOON
ASYLUM

A•S•••

ABSCAM
ABSENT
ABSORB
ABSURD
ADSORB
AISLES
ALSACE
AMSTEL
ANSARA
ANSATE
ANSELM
ANSGAR
ANSWER
ARSENE
ARSONS
ASSAIL
ASSAYS
ASSENT
ASSERT
ASSESS
ASSETS
ASSIGN
ASSISI
ASSIST
ASSIZE
ASSORT
ASSUME
ASSURE
ATSTUD
AUSPEX
AUSSIE
AUSTEN
AUSTIN
AUSTRO
AXSEED

A••S••

ABASED
ABASES
ABESSE
ABUSED
ABUSER
ABUSES
ABYSMS
ACESUP
ACTSAS
ACTSON
ACTSUP
ADDSIN
ADDSON
ADDSTO
ADDSUP
ADESTE
AGASSI
AIMSAT
AIMSTO
AIRSAC
ALASKA
ALISON
ALLSET
ALYSSA
AMOSOZ
AMUSED
AMUSES
ARISEN
ARISES
ARISTA
ARISTO
ASKSIN
ASOSAN
ATESTS
AUSSIE
AVESTA
AVISOS
AYESHA

A•••S•

ABBESS
ABESSE
ABLEST
ABLUSH
ACCESS
ACCOST
ACCUSE
ACROSS
ADJUST
ADMASS
ADVISE
AFRESH
AGASSI
AGEISM
AGEIST
AGHAST
AGUISH
AHIMSA
ALDOSE
ALEAST
ALMOST
ALONSO
ALWEST
ALYSSA
AMBUSH
AMERSP
AMIDST
AORIST
APPOSE
APTEST
ARGOSY
ARIOSE
ARIOSO
ARLISS
ARNESS
AROUSE
ARREST
ARTIST
ASPISH
ASSESS
ASSISI
ASSIST
ATBEST
ATCOST
ATEASE
ATLAST
ATMOST
ATREST
ATRISK
ATTEST
AUGUST
AVERSE
AVULSE

A••••S

ABACAS
ABACUS
ABASES
ABATES
ABATIS
ABBESS
ABBEYS
ABBOTS
ABELES
ABHORS
ABIDES
ABODES
ABOHMS
ABOMBS
ABORTS
ABRAMS
ABUSES
ABYDOS
ABYSMS
ACARUS
ACCESS
ACEOUS
ACINUS
ACORNS
ACROSS
ACTORS
ACTSAS
ADAGES
ADAPTS
ADDAMS
ADDERS
ADDLES
ADDONS
ADEEMS
ADEPTS
ADIDAS
ADIEUS
ADLIBS
ADMASS
ADMITS
ADOBES
ADONIS
ADOPTS
ADORES
ADORNS
ADULTS
AEETES
AENEAS
AEOLUS
AERIES
AFLATS
AFRITS
AGAMAS
AGATES
AGAVES
AGENAS
AGENTS
AGGIES
AGGROS
AGLETS
AGORAS
AGREES
AIDERS
AILERS
AIRBUS
AISLES
AKELAS
AKENES
AKITAS
ALAMOS
ALANIS
ALARMS
ALBUMS
ALDERS
ALDOUS
ALEPHS
ALERTS
ALEUTS
ALEXIS
ALIBIS
ALIENS
ALIGNS
ALINES
ALKYDS
ALKYLS
ALLAYS
ALLEES
ALLEYS
ALLIES
ALLOTS
ALLOWS
ALLOYS
ALOHAS
ALOINS
ALPHAS
ALTARS
ALTERS
ALTIUS
ALWAYS
AMADIS
AMATIS
AMAZES
AMBERS
AMBITS
AMBLES
AMEBAS
AMEERS

AMENDS
AMENTS
AMICES
AMICUS
AMIDES
AMIENS
AMIGAS
AMIGOS
AMINES
AMINUS
AMOLES
AMOURS
AMPULS
AMUSES
AMVETS
ANDRES
ANDROS
ANELES
ANGELS
ANGERS
ANGLES
ANGLOS
ANIMAS
ANIMES
ANIMUS
ANIONS
ANJOUS
ANKLES
ANNALS
ANNOYS
ANNULS
ANODES
ANOLES
ANTICS
ANTRES
ANUBIS
ANVILS
AODAIS
AORTAS
APEXES
APHIDS
APICES
APPALS
APPLES
APRONS
ARAMIS
ARBORS
ARCCOS
ARCHES
ARDEBS
ARDORS
ARECAS
ARENAS
ARETES
ARGOTS
ARGUES
ARISES
ARLISS
ARMETS
ARMIES
ARMORS
ARNESS
AROIDS
AROMAS
ARRAYS
ARROWS
ARSONS
ARTELS
ARTOIS
ARYANS
ASANAS
ASCOTS
ASDICS
ASIANS
ASIDES
ASKERS
ASPENS
ASPICS
ASSAYS
ASSESS
ASSETS
ASTERS
ASTROS
ATBATS
ATEAMS
ATESTS
ATHENS
ATKINS
ATODDS
ATOLLS
ATONES
ATREUS
ATTARS
ATTICS
AUDENS
AUDIOS
AUDITS
AUGERS
AUGHTS
AUGURS
AUREUS
AUROUS
AUXINS
AVAILS
AVERTS
AVIANS
AVISOS
AVOIDS
AWAITS
AWAKES
AWARDS
AXIOMS
AXIONS
AZIDES
AZINES
AZORES
AZTECS

•AS•••

BASALT
BASELY
BASEST
BASHED
BASHES
BASICS
BASIFY
BASING
BASINS
BASKED
BASKET
BASQUE
BASSES
BASSET
BASSLY
BASSOS
BASTED
BASTER
BASTES
CASABA
CASALS
CASAVA
CASBAH
CASEFY
CASERN
CASHED
CASHES
CASHEW
CASHIN
CASING
CASINO
CASPAR
CASPER
CASQUE
CASSIA
CASSIO
CASSIS
CASTER
CASTES
CASTLE
CASTON
CASTOR
CASTRO
CASUAL
DASHED
DASHER
DASHES
DASHIS
DASSIN
EASEIN
EASELS
EASEUP
EASIER
EASILY
EASING
EASTER
EASTON
FASCES
FASCIA
FASTED
FASTEN
FASTER
GASBAG
GASCAP
GASCON
GASHED
GASHES
GASIFY
GASJET
GASKET
GASKIN
GASLIT
GASLOG
GASMAN
GASMEN
GASPAR
GASPED
GASPER
GASSED
GASSER
GASSES
GASTON
GASTRO
HASBRO
HASHED
HASHES
HASPED
HASSAM
HASSAN
HASSLE
HASTEN
HASTES
JASCHA
JASEYS
JASPER
KASBAH
KASDAN
LASCAR
LASERS
LASHED
LASHER
LASHES
LASHIO
LASHUP
LASSEN
LASSER
LASSES
LASSIE
LASSOS
LASTED
LASTEX
LASTLY
MASADA
MASAIS
MASCOT
MASERS
MASERU
MASHED
MASHER
MASHES
MASHIE
MASKED
MASKER
MASONS
MASQUE
MASSED
MASSES
MASSEY
MASSIF
MASTER
MASTIC
NASALS
NASCAR
NASDAQ
NASEBY
NASHUA
NASSAU
NASSER
PASCAL
PASEOS
PASHAS
PASHTO
PASSBY
PASSED
PASSEL
PASSER
PASSES
PASSIM
PASSON
PASSUP
PASTAS
PASTED
PASTEL
PASTES
PASTIS
PASTOR
PASTRY
RASCAL
RASERS
RASHAD
RASHER
RASHES
RASHID
RASHLY
RASING
RASPED
RASPER
RASSLE
RASTER
SASEBO
SASHAY
SASHED
SASHES
SASSED
SASSER
SASSES
TASERS
TASKED
TASMAN
TASSEL
TASSES
TASTED
TASTER
TASTES
VASHTI
VASLAV
VASSAL
VASSAR
VASTER
VASTLY
WASABI
WASHED
WASHER
WASHES
WASHOE
WASHUP
WASTED
WASTER
WASTES
YASSER

•A•S••

BABSON
BAGSIT
BALSAM
BASSES
BASSET
BASSLY
BASSOS
CAESAR
CAPSID
CARSON
CASSIA
CASSIO
CASSIS
CATSUP
CAUSAL
CAUSED
CAUSES
DAISES
DAMSEL
DAMSON
DAMSUP
DANSON
DASSIN
DATSUN
DAWSON
EATSAT
EATSIN
EATSUP
FAISAL
FALSER
GARSON
GASSED
GASSER
GASSES
GATSBY
HALSEY
HANSEL
HANSOM
HANSON
HASSAM
HASSAN
HASSLE
HAUSAS
HAWSER
HAWSES
JAMSIN
JAMSUP
JANSEN
JANSKY
KAISER
KANSAN
KANSAS
KARSTS
LANSON
LAPSED
LAPSES
LAPSUP
LARSEN
LARSON
LASSEN
LASSER
LASSES
LASSIE
LASSOS
LAWSON
LAYSBY
LAYSIN
LAYSON
LAYSTO
LAYSUP
MADSEN
MAISIE
MANSES
MARSHA
MARSHY
MASSED
MASSES
MASSEY
MASSIF
MAUSER
NANSEN
NASSAU
NASSER
NAUSEA
NAYSAY
PAISAS
PARSEC
PARSED
PARSEE
PARSER
PARSES
PARSON
PASSBY
PASSED
PASSEL
PASSER
PASSES
PASSIM
PASSON
PASSUP
PAUSED
PAUSES
PAWSAT
PAYSIN
PAYSON
PAYSUP
RAISED
RAISER
RAISES
RAISIN
RAMSAY
RAMSES
RAMSEY
RAMSON
RANSOM
RASSLE
RATSON
SALSAS
SAMSON
SANSEI
SASSED
SASSER
SASSES
SAYSOS
TAGSUP
TARSAL
TARSUS
TASSEL
TASSES
VAISYA
VASSAL
VASSAR
WADSUP
WAISTS
WARSAW
WATSON
WAUSAU
YASSER

•A••S•

BANISH
BAREST
BARISH
BASEST
CALASH
CAMISE
CARESS
CARUSO
CAYUSE
DALASI
DAMASK
DANISH
FAMISH
GAINST
GALOSH
GAMEST
GARISH
GAYEST
HALEST
HARASS
HAVASU
JADISH
KAROSS
LAGASH
LAMESA
LAMEST
LANOSE
LAOTSE
LAROSA
LATEST
LATISH
LAVISH
LAXEST
MAOISM
MAOIST
MARISA
MARISH
MARIST
OAFISH
PALEST
PALISH
PARISH
RADISH
RAKISH
RAMOSE
RAREST
RAVISH
RAWEST
RAWISH
SAFEST
SAGEST
SALISH
SAMOSA
SANEST
TALESE
TAMEST
TANIST
TAOISM
TAOIST
VADOSE
VALISE
VANISH
VARESE
WABASH
WALESA
WATUSI
YAREST

•A•••S

BABELS
BABIES
BABKAS
BABULS
BACKUS
BADGES
BAGELS
BAINES
BAIRNS
BAIZAS
BAKERS
BALERS
BANJOS
BANTUS
BARGES
BARNES
BARONS
BARRES
BARRIS
BASHES
BASICS
BASINS
BASSES
BASSOS
BASTES
BATHES
BATHOS
BATIKS
BATONS
BAUCIS
BAULKS
BAYOUS
CABALS
CABERS
CABINS
CABLES
CACAOS
CACHES
CACTUS
CADDIS
CADETS
CADGES
CADMUS
CADRES
CAGERS
CAGUAS
CAHOWS
CAICOS
CAIRNS
CAJUNS
CALAIS
CALCES
CALLAS
CALLES
CALLUS
CALVES
CALXES
CAMELS
CAMEOS
CAMPOS
CAMPUS
CANALS
CANERS
CANIDS
CANNES
CANOES
CANONS
CANTOS
CANVAS
CAPERS
CAPIAS
CAPONS
CAPRIS
CARATS
CARBOS
CARESS
CARETS
CARGOS
CARIBS
CARIES
CARLOS
CARNES
CAROBS
CAROLS
CAROMS
CARPUS
CARTES
CARVES
CASALS
CASHES
CASSIS
CASTES
CATERS
CAUCUS
CAULKS
CAUSES
CAVERS
CAVILS
DACHAS
DADOES
DAISES
DALLAS
DALLES
DANAUS
DANCES
DANTES
DARIUS
DASHES
DASHIS
DATERS
DAUBES
DAUNTS
DAVIES
DAVITS
EAGLES
EAGRES
EASELS
EATERS
FABLES
FACETS
FACIAS
FACIES
FAGOTS
FAINTS
FAITHS
FAKERS
FAKIRS
FALCES
FAMOUS
FANONS
FARADS
FARCES
FARERS
FASCES
FATWAS
FAUCES
FAULTS
FAUNAS
FAUNUS
FAVORS
FAWKES
GABIES
GABLES
GAFFES
GALAHS
GALOIS
GALOPS
GAMAYS
GAMINS
GAMMAS
GAMUTS
GANGES
GAPERS
GARTHS
GASHES
GASSES
GATERS
GATORS
GAUGES
GAUZES
GAVELS
GAYALS
HABEAS
HABITS
HACEKS
HADJES
HADJIS
HAGGIS
HAIDAS
HAIKUS
HAINES
HAJJES
HAJJIS
HAKIMS
HALERS
HALLOS
HALOES
HALVES
HAMALS
HAOLES
HARASS
HAREMS
HARRIS
HASHES
HASTES
HATERS
HAULMS
HAUNTS
HAUSAS
HAVENS
HAVERS
HAVOCS
HAWSES
HAZANS
HAZELS
HAZERS
JABOTS
JACALS
JAMUPS
JANHUS
JAPANS
JAPERS
JASEYS
JAUNTS
JAURES
JAZZES
KABOBS
KAFIRS
KANSAS
KAPPAS
KARATS
KAROSS
KARRAS
KARSTS
KAUNAS
KAURIS
KAYAKS
KAZAKS
KAZOOS
LABELS
LABORS
LACERS
LACHES
LADERS
LADIES
LADLES
LAGERS
LAIRDS
LAKERS
LAMEDS
LAMIAS
LAMMAS
LANAIS
LANCES
LANDIS
LAPELS
LAPINS
LAPSES
LARAMS
LARGES
LARGOS
LARVAS
LASERS
LASHES
LASSES
LASSOS
LATENS
LATHES
LATINS
LATKES
LAUGHS
LAVERS
LAYBYS
LAYERS
LAYUPS
MACAWS
MACHES
MACHOS
MACROS
MADAMS
MADRAS
MADRES
MAGMAS
MAGNUS
MAHDIS
MAIDUS
MAILES
MAIZES
MAJLIS
MAJORS
MAKERS
MALAYS
MAMBAS
MAMBOS
MAMMAS
MANAUS
MANGOS
MANIAS
MANORS
MANSES
MANTAS
MANTIS
MAORIS
MAPLES
MAQUIS
MARCOS
MARCUS
MARGES
MARIUS
MASAIS
MASERS
MASHES
MASONS
MASSES
MATERS
MATEYS
MATHIS
MATINS
MATTES
MATZOS
MAUVES
MAVENS
MAXIMS
MAYANS
MAYBES
MAYORS
MAZERS
NABOBS
NABORS
NACHOS
NACRES
NADIRS
NAIADS
NAIRAS
NAMERS
NANTES
NAPLES
NAPPES
NASALS
NAVELS
NAVIES
NAWABS
OATERS
PACERS
PADRES
PAEANS
PAEONS
PAGANS
PAGERS
PAINTS
PAISAS
PALLAS
PALMAS
PALPUS
PAMIRS
PAMPAS
PANDAS
PANELS
PANICS
PANNES
PANTOS
PAPAWS
PAPERS
PAPPAS
PAPPUS
PARENS
PARERS
PARKAS
PARNIS
PARRIS
PARSES
PARVIS
PASEOS
PASHAS
PASSES
PASTAS
PASTES
PASTIS
PATENS
PATERS
PATHOS
PATIOS
PATMOS
PATOIS
PAUCIS
PAUSES
PAVERS
PAWERS
PAYEES
PAYERS
QANTAS
RABBIS
RABIES
RACERS
RACHIS
RACONS
RADIOS
RADIUS
RAINES
RAISES
RAJAHS
RAKERS
RAMETS
RAMIES
RAMOUS
RAMSES
RANEES
RANGES
RANIDS
RAPIDS
RASERS
RASHES
RATELS
RATERS
RATIOS
RAVELS
RAVENS
RAVERS
RAYONS
RAZORS
RAZZES
SABERS
SABINS
SABLES
SABOTS
SABRAS
SABRES
SADHES
SADHUS
SAHIBS
SAIGAS
SAINTS
SAKERS
SALADS
SALALS
SALONS
SALSAS
SALVES
SALVOS
SAMBAS
SANTOS
SAPORS
SARANS
SARDIS
SARGES
SARGOS
SARODS
SASHES
SASSES
SATINS
SATYRS
SAUCES
SAUDIS
SAULTS
SAUNAS
SAUTES
SAVERS
SAVORS
SAXONS
SAYERS
SAYLES
SAYSOS
SAYYES
TABLAS
TABLES
TABOOS
TABORS
TAIGAS
TAINOS
TAINTS
TAKERS
TAKINS
TALERS
TALONS
TAMERS
TAMILS
TANGOS
TANKAS
TANTES
TAPERS
TAPINS
TAPIRS
TARGES
TAROTS
TARSUS
TASERS
TASSES
TASTES
TATARS
TATERS
TAUNTS
TAUONS
TAUPES
TAURUS
TAXERS
TAXIES
TAYRAS
TAZZAS
VALENS
VALETS
VALOIS
VALUES
VALVES
VAPORS
VARIES
VARNAS
VAULTS
VAUNTS
WACKOS
WADERS
WAFERS
WAGERS
WAGONS
WAHOOS
WAISTS
WAIVES
WAKENS
WALERS
WALLIS
WALRUS
WANERS
WASHES
WASTES
WATERS
WAVERS
WAXERS
WAYANS
YACHTS
YAHOOS
YAKUTS
YALIES
YAPOKS
YAQUIS
ZAIRES
ZAMIAS
ZANIES
ZAYINS
ZAZENS

••AS••

ABASED
ABASES
AGASSI
ALASKA
BEASTS
BIASED
BIASES
BLASTS
BOASTS
BRASHY
BRASOV
BRASSY
CEASED
CEASES
CHASED
CHASER
CHASES
CHASMS
CHASSE
CHASTE
CLASPS
CLASSY
COASTS
DEASIL
ERASED
ERASER
ERASES
FEASTS
FIASCO
FLASHY
FLASKS
FRASER
GLASER
GLASSY
GRASPS
GRASSO
GRASSY
ITASCA
KRASNY
LEASED
LEASER
LEASES
MEASLY
MIASMA
NYASSA
OCASEK
OCASEY
OMASUM
PHASED
PHASER
PHASES
PLASHY
PLASMA
PLASMO
PLASTY
PRASES
QUASAR
REASON
ROASTS
SEASON
SHASTA
SOASTO
SPASMS
STASES
STASIS
TEASED
TEASEL
TEASER
TEASES
TEASET
TOASTS
TOASTY
TRASHY
UKASES
UPASES
WEASEL
WRASSE
YEASTS
YEASTY

••A•S•

AGASSI
BLAISE
BRAISE
BRASSY
BRATSK
CHAISE
CHASSE
CLASSY
CLAUSE
COARSE
ELAPSE
FRAISE
GDANSK
GLASSY
GRASSO
GRASSY
HEARST
HOARSE
LIAISE
NYASSA
PRAISE
SPARSE
URALSK
WRASSE
ZSAZSA

••A••S

ABACAS
ABACUS
ABASES
ABATES
ABATIS
ACARUS
ADAGES
ADAPTS
AGAMAS
AGATES
AGAVES
ALAMOS
ALANIS
ALARMS
AMADIS
AMATIS
AMAZES
ARAMIS
ASANAS
AVAILS
AWAITS
AWAKES
AWARDS
BEANOS
BEARDS
BEASTS

BEAUTS
BEAVIS
BIASES
BLACKS
BLADES
BLAMES
BLANKS
BLARES
BLASTS
BLAZES
BOARDS
BOASTS
BRACES
BRACTS
BRAHMS
BRAIDS
BRAILS
BRAINS
BRAKES
BRANDS
BRANTS
BRAVAS
BRAVES
BRAVOS
BRAWLS
BRAZES
BRAZOS
BWANAS
CEASES
CHAFES
CHAFFS
CHAINS
CHAIRS
CHALKS
CHAMPS
CHANTS
CHARMS
CHARTS
CHASES
CHASMS
CLACKS
CLAIMS
CLAMPS
CLANGS
CLANKS
CLAROS
CLASPS
CLAVES
COAPTS
COASTS
COATIS
COAXES
CRACKS
CRAFTS
CRAKES
CRAMPS
CRANES
CRANKS
CRAPES
CRATES
CRAVES
CRAWLS
CRAZES
DMARKS
DRAFTS
DRAILS
DRAINS
DRAKES
DRAMAS
DRAPES
DRAWLS
DWARFS
EDAMES
ELANDS
ELATES
EMAILS
ENACTS
ENATES
ERASES
ETAPES
EVADES
EXACTS
EXALTS
FEASTS
FLACKS
FLAILS
FLAIRS
FLAKES
FLAMES
FLANKS
FLARES
FLASKS
FLAXES
FRACAS
FRAMES
FRANCS
FRANKS
FRAUDS
GHAINS
GHAZIS
GIANTS
GLACES
GLACIS
GLADES
GLADYS
GLAIRS
GLANDS
GLARES
GLAZES
GNARLS
GRACES
GRADES
GRADUS
GRAFTS
GRAILS
GRAINS
GRAMAS
GRAMPS
GRANDS
GRANTS
GRAPES
GRAPHS
GRASPS
GRATES
GRATIS
GRAVES
GRAZES
GUACOS
GUARDS
GUAVAS
HEARTS
HEATHS
HEAVES
HIATUS
HOARDS
HOAXES
HYADES
ICARUS
IMAGES
IRANIS
IRAQIS
KHAKIS
KIANGS
KNACKS
KNAVES
KOALAS
KRAALS
KRAITS
KYACKS
LEARNS
LEASES
LEAVES
LIANAS
LIANES
LIANGS
LLAMAS
LLANOS
LOAVES
NYALAS
OKAPIS
OMAHAS
OMANIS
ORACHS
ORALES
ORANGS
ORANTS
ORATES
OSAGES
OXALIS
OZARKS
PEARLS
PHAGES
PHAROS
PHASES
PIANOS
PLACES
PLAGES
PLAIDS
PLAINS
PLAITS
PLANES
PLANKS
PLANTS
PLATES
PLAYAS
PLAZAS
PRANGS
PRANKS
PRASES
PRATES
PRAWNS
PRAXES
PRAXIS
PSALMS
QUACKS
QUAFFS
QUAILS
QUAKES
QUALMS
QUARKS
QUARTS
REACTS
REAIMS
REAIRS
REALES
REALMS
REARMS
REATAS
RHAMES
RIATAS
ROASTS
RUANAS
SCALDS
SCALES
SCALPS
SCAMPS
SCANTS
SCAPES
SCARES
SCARFS
SCARPS
SCAUPS
SEAMUS
SHACKS
SHADES
SHAFTS
SHAKES
SHAKOS
SHALES
SHAMES
SHAMUS
SHANKS
SHAPES
SHARDS
SHARES
SHARKS
SHARPS
SHAVES
SHAWLS
SHAWMS
SKALDS
SKANKS
SKATES
SLACKS
SLAKES
SLANGS
SLANTS
SLATES
SLAVES
SMACKS
SMALLS
SMARTS
SNACKS
SNAFUS
SNAILS
SNAKES
SNARES
SNARLS
SNATHS
SOARES
SOAVES
SPACES
SPADES
SPAHIS
SPALLS
SPANKS
SPARES
SPARKS
SPASMS
SPATES
SPAWNS
STACKS
STAFFS
STAGES
STAINS
STAIRS
STAKES
STALES
STALKS
STALLS
STAMPS
STANDS
STAPES
STARES
STARTS
STASES
STASIS
STATES
STATUS
STAVES
SWAGES
SWAINS
SWALES
SWAMIS
SWAMPS
SWANKS
SWARDS
SWARMS
SWATHS
SWAZIS
TEASES
THALES
THAMES
THANES
THANKS
THATIS
TIARAS
TOASTS
TRACES
TRACKS
TRACTS
TRADES
TRAILS
TRAINS
TRAITS
TRAMPS
TRAVES
TRAVIS
TRAWLS
TWANGS
UKASES
UNARMS
UPASES
URAEUS
URANUS
USAGES
VIANDS
WEAVES
WHACKS
WHALES
WHANGS
WHARFS
WRACKS
WRATHS
YEARNS
YEASTS

•••AS•

ADMASS
AGHAST
ALEAST
ATEASE
ATLAST
BREAST
BYPASS
BYPAST
CALASH
CREASE
CREASY
DALASI
DAMASK
DEBASE
DYNAST
ELPASO
EMDASH
ENCASE
ENDASH
GOEASY
GREASE
GREASY
HARASS
HAVASU
INCASE
INCASH
KUVASZ
LAGASH
LIPASE
MORASS
MUFASA
NLEAST
OBLAST
PHRASE
PLEASE
POTASH
QUEASY
RECAST
REHASH
REPAST
REWASH
SIWASH
SPLASH
SQUASH
STRASS
THRASH
UNCASE
UNEASE
UNEASY
UNLASH
UNMASK
UPCAST
WABASH
ZYMASE

•••A•S

ABRAMS
ADDAMS
ADMASS
AFLATS
ALLAYS
ALTARS
ALWAYS
ANNALS
AODAIS
APPALS
ARRAYS
ARYANS
ASIANS
ASSAYS
ATBATS
ATEAMS
ATTARS
AVIANS
BELAYS
BLEARS
BLEATS
BLOATS
BOYARS
BREADS
BREAKS
BREAMS
BRIANS
BRIARS
BROADS
BYLAWS
BYPASS
BYWAYS
CABALS
CACAOS
CALAIS
CANALS
CARATS
CASALS
CEDARS
CHEATS
CHIAUS
CIGARS
CLEANS
CLEARS
CLEATS
CLOAKS
COPAYS
CORALS
CREAKS
CREAMS
CROAKS
CROATS
CYCADS
DANAUS
DEBARS
DECAFS
DECALS
DECAYS
DEFATS
DELAYS
DINARS
DIVANS
DORAGS
DREADS
DREAMS
DRYADS
DUCATS
EBOATS
ECLATS
EDGARS
EFLATS
EMBAYS
EPHAHS
EQUALS
ESSAYS
FARADS
FINALS
FLOATS
FORAYS
FREAKS
FRIARS
GALAHS
GAMAYS
GAYALS
GERAHS
GLEAMS
GLEANS
GLOATS
GORALS
GREATS
GROANS
GROATS
GULAGS
HAMALS
HARASS
HAZANS
HBEAMS
HEXADS
HODADS
HOGANS
HUMANS
IBEAMS
IDEALS
IDTAGS
INCANS
INLAWS
INLAYS
IOWANS
JACALS
JAPANS
JIHADS
JONAHS
JURATS
KARATS
KAYAKS
KAZAKS
KEBABS
KNEADS
KORATS
KOVACS
KRAALS
KULAKS
LANAIS
LARAMS
LEGALS
LEMANS
LILACS
LOCALS
LOTAHS
MACAWS
MADAMS
MALAYS
MANAUS
MASAIS
MAYANS
MEDALS
METALS
MOLARS
MONADS
MORALS
MORASS
MORAYS
MURALS
MYNAHS
NAIADS
NASALS
NAWABS
NOMADS
OBEAHS
OCEANS
OCTADS
OGHAMS
OREADS
ORGANS
OSCARS
PAEANS
PAGANS
PAPAWS
PECANS
PEDALS
PETALS
PHIALS
PILAFS
PIPALS
PISANS
PLEADS
PLEATS
PROAMS
PTRAPS
RAJAHS
REBAGS
REBARS
RECAPS
REHABS
RELAYS
REMANS
REMAPS
REPADS
REPAYS
RESAWS
RETAGS
RETAPS
RETARS
RIVALS
RIYALS
ROMANS
ROYALS
SALADS
SALALS
SARANS
SCRAGS
SCRAMS
SCRAPS
SEDANS
SEPALS
SERACS
SERAIS
SHEAFS
SHEARS
SHOALS
SHOATS
SISALS
SITARS
SKEANS
SKOALS
SMEARS
SNEAKS
SOLANS
SOLARS
SPEAKS
SPEARS
SPLATS
SPLAYS
SPRAGS
SPRATS
SPRAYS
SQUABS
SQUADS
SQUATS
STEADS
STEAKS
STEALS
STEAMS
STOATS
STRADS
STRAPS
STRASS
STRAUS
STRAWS
STRAYS
SUGARS
SUMACS
SURAHS
SWEARS
SWEATS
TATARS
TEPALS
TEXANS
TICALS
TILAKS
TITANS
TOKAYS
TORAHS
TOTALS
TREADS
TREATS
TRIADS
TRIALS
TWEAKS
UBOATS
UCLANS
UGGAMS
UHLANS
UMIAKS
UNBARS
UNCAPS
UNIATS
UNJAMS
UNMANS
UNSAYS
URIALS
USUALS
VEGANS
VICARS
VITALS
VOCALS
VOLANS
WAYANS
WHEALS
WHEATS
WREAKS

••••AS

ABACAS
ACTSAS
ADIDAS
AENEAS
AGAMAS
AGENAS
AGORAS
AKELAS
AKITAS
ALOHAS
ALPHAS
AMEBAS
AMIGAS
ANIMAS
AORTAS
ARECAS
ARENAS
AROMAS
ASANAS
BABKAS
BAIZAS
BETTAS
BIOGAS
BIOTAS
BOREAS
BRAVAS
BURGAS
BURSAS
BWANAS
CAGUAS
CALLAS
CANVAS
CAPIAS
CEIBAS
CESTAS
CHELAS
COBIAS
COBRAS
COCOAS
COMMAS
CONGAS
COSTAS
COTTAS
CUPPAS
CYCLAS
DACHAS
DALLAS
DEBRAS
DELTAS
DOBLAS
DOBRAS
DOGMAS
DOLMAS
DONNAS
DORCAS
DRAMAS
ESDRAS
EXTRAS
FACIAS
FATWAS
FAUNAS
FELLAS
FERIAS
FESTAS
FLORAS
FORTAS
FOSSAS
FRACAS
GAMMAS
GRAMAS
GUAVAS
HABEAS
HAIDAS
HAUSAS
HELLAS
HENNAS
HOOHAS
HOSTAS
HUZZAS
HYDRAS
HYENAS
JUNTAS
KANSAS
KAPPAS
KARRAS
KAUNAS
KIOWAS
KOALAS
LAMIAS
LAMMAS
LARVAS
LEHUAS
LEMMAS
LIANAS
LLAMAS
LOOFAS
MADRAS
MAGMAS
MAMBAS
MAMMAS
MANIAS
MANTAS
MECCAS
MEDIAS
MENSAS
MILPAS
MOCHAS
MOMMAS
MUDRAS
MULLAS
NAIRAS
NINJAS
NORIAS
NYALAS
OMAHAS
OMEGAS
OPERAS
PAISAS
PALLAS
PALMAS
PAMPAS
PANDAS
PAPPAS
PARKAS
PASHAS
PASTAS
PIETAS
PINNAS
PIZZAS
PLAYAS
PLAZAS
POLKAS
POPPAS
QANTAS
QUOTAS
REATAS
REINAS
RIATAS
RIOJAS
RUANAS
RUMBAS
SABRAS
SAIGAS
SALSAS
SAMBAS
SAUNAS
SCENAS
SCHWAS
SCUBAS
SENNAS
SEPIAS
SIGMAS
SILVAS
SOLFAS
SPICAS
STOMAS
STUPAS
SUCHAS
SUCKAS
SUDRAS
SUMMAS
SUTRAS
TABLAS
TAIGAS
TANKAS
TAYRAS
TAZZAS
TESLAS
TETRAS
THETAS
THOMAS
THUJAS
TIARAS
TIBIAS
TOBIAS
TOKLAS
UINTAS
ULTRAS
UMBRAS
UNITAS
UVULAS
VARNAS
VESTAS
VILLAS
VIOLAS
VISTAS
VODKAS
VOLVAS
XHOSAS
YENTAS
YUCCAS
ZAMIAS
ZEBRAS

AT••••

ATAMAN
ATBATS
ATBEST
ATCOST
ATEAMS
ATEASE
ATEMPO
ATEOUT
ATERGO
ATESTS
ATHAND
ATHENA
ATHENE
ATHENS
ATHOME
ATKINS
ATLAST
ATLATL
ATMOST
ATODDS
ATOLLS
ATOMIC
ATONAL
ATONCE
ATONED
ATONES
ATONIC
ATREST
ATREUS
ATRIAL
ATRISK
ATRIUM
ATSTUD
ATTACH
ATTACK
ATTAIN
ATTARS
ATTEND
ATTEST
ATTHAT
ATTICA
ATTICS
ATTILA
ATTIRE
ATTLEE
ATTRIT
ATTUNE
ATWILL
ATWOOD
ATWORK

A•T•••

ACTIII
ACTING
ACTINO
ACTION
ACTIUM
ACTIVE
ACTONE
ACTORS
ACTOUT
ACTSAS
ACTSON
ACTSUP
ACTTWO
ACTUAL
AETHER
ALTAIC
ALTAIR
ALTARS
ALTERS
ALTHEA
ALTIMA
ALTIUS
ALTMAN
AMTRAC
AMTRAK
ANTCOW
ANTEED
ANTERO
ANTEUP
ANTHEM
ANTHER
ANTICS
ANTLER
ANTONY
ANTRES
ANTRIM
ANTRON
ANTRUM
APTEST
ARTELS
ARTERY
ARTFUL
ARTGUM
ARTHRO
ARTHUR
ARTIER
ARTILY
ARTIST
ARTOIS
ARTURO
ASTERN
ASTERS
ASTRAL
ASTRAY
ASTRID
ASTROS
ASTUTE
ATTACH
ATTACK
ATTAIN
ATTARS
ATTEND
ATTEST
ATTHAT
ATTICA
ATTICS
ATTILA
ATTIRE
ATTLEE
ATTRIT
ATTUNE
AUTEUR
AUTHOR
AUTUMN
AZTECS

A••T••

ABATED
ABATES
ABATIS
ACETAL
ACETIC
ACETYL
ACTTWO
ADYTUM
AEETES
AGATES
AGATHA
AKITAS
ALATAU
ALATED
ALITER
AMATIS
AMATOL
AMSTEL
AMYTAN
ANATTO
ANITRA
AORTAE
AORTAL
AORTAS
AORTIC
APATHY
ARCTAN
ARCTIC
ARETES
ARETHA
ATSTUD
AUNTIE
AUSTEN
AUSTIN
AUSTRO
AVATAR

A•••T•

ABBOTS
ABBOTT
ABLATE
ABORTS
ACUATE
ACUITY
ADAPTS
ADDSTO
ADEPTS
ADESTE
ADMITS
ADNATE
ADOPTS
ADULTS
AERATE
AFLATS
AFRITS
AGENTS
AGLETS
AGNATE
AGOUTI
AIMSTO
AJANTA
ALCOTT
ALECTO
ALERTS
ALEUTS
ALIOTO
ALLOTS
ALMATY
AMBATO
AMBITS
AMENTS
AMVETS
ANATTO
ANSATE
APLITE
AQUATE
ARGOTS
ARISTA
ARISTO
ARMETS
ARNETT
ASCOTS
ASEITY
ASSETS
ASTUTE
ATBATS
ATESTS
ATLATL
AUDITS
AUGHTS
AVANTI
AVERTS
AVESTA
AVIATE
AWAITS

A••••T

ABBOTT
ABDUCT
ABJECT
ABLAUT
ABLEST
ABRUPT
ABSENT
ACCENT
ACCEPT
ACCOST
ACEOUT
ACQUIT
ACTOUT
ADDUCT
ADJUST
ADRIFT
ADROIT
ADVENT
ADVERT
AFFECT
AFLOAT
AFREET
AGEIST
AGHAST
AGLINT
AGOROT
AIGRET
AIMSAT
AIROUT
AJFOYT
ALBEIT
ALBERT
ALCOTT
ALEAST
ALHIRT
ALIGHT
ALLBUT
ALLOUT
ALLSET
ALLWET
ALMOST
ALPERT
ALWEST
AMIDST
AMOUNT
AMULET
ANKLET
ANNUIT
ANOINT
AORIST
APPLET
APTEST
ARAFAT
ARARAT
ARDENT
ARENDT
ARGENT
ARIGHT
ARMLET
ARMPIT
ARNETT
ARPENT
ARRANT
ARREST
ARTIST
ASCENT
ASKOUT
ASLANT
ASPECT
ASSENT
ASSERT
ASSIST
ASSORT
ATBEST
ATCOST
ATEOUT
ATLAST
ATMOST
ATREST
ATTEST
ATTHAT
ATTRIT
AUFAIT
AUGUST
AUKLET
AULAIT
AUMONT
AVAUNT
AVOCET

•AT•••

BATAAN
BATBOY
BATEAU
BATHED
BATHER

BATHES
BATHOS
BATIKS
BATING
BATMAN
BATMEN
BATONS
BATTED
BATTEL
BATTEN
BATTER
BATTLE
BATTUE
BATUMI
BATYAM
CATCHY
CATENA
CATERS
CATGUT
CATHAY
CATHER
CATION
CATKIN
CATNAP
CATNIP
CATRIG
CATSUP
CATTED
CATTLE
CATTON
DATARY
DATERS
DATING
DATIVE
DATONG
DATSUN
DATURA
EATERS
EATERY
EATING
EATOUT
EATSAT
EATSIN
EATSUP
FATALE
FATCAT
FATHER
FATHOM
FATIMA
FATTED
FATTEN
FATTER
FATWAS
GATEAU
GATERS
GATHER
GATING
GATLIN
GATORS
GATSBY
HATARI
HATBOX
HATERS
HATFUL
HATHOR
HATING
HATPIN
HATRED
HATTED
HATTER
HATTIE
IATRIC
KATHIE
KATMAI
LATEEN
LATELY
LATENE
LATENS
LATENT
LATEST
LATHED
LATHER
LATHES
LATIGO
LATINA
LATINI
LATINO
LATINS
LATISH
LATIUM
LATKES
LATONA
LATOUR
LATOYA
LATTEN
LATTER
LATVIA
MATERS
MATEYS
MATHER
MATHIS
MATING
MATINS
MATLIN
MATRIX
MATRON
MATTEA
MATTED
MATTEL
MATTER
MATTES
MATTIE
MATURE
MATZOH
MATZOS
NATANT
NATHAN
NATICK
NATION
NATIVE
NATRON
NATTER
NATURA
NATURE
OATERS
OATIER
PATACA
PATCHY
PATENS
PATENT
PATERS
PATHAN
PATHOL
PATHOS
PATINA
PATINE
PATIOS
PATMOS
PATOIS
PATROL
PATRON
PATTED
PATTEN
PATTER
PATTON
QATARI
RATEDG
RATEDR
RATEDX
RATELS
RATERS
RATHER
RATIFY
RATINE
RATING
RATION
RATIOS
RATITE
RATLIN
RATSON
RATTAN
RATTED
RATTER
RATTLE
RATTLY
SATANG
SATEEN
SATING
SATINS
SATINY
SATIRE
SATORI
SATOUT
SATRAP
SATURN
SATYRS
TATAMI
TATARS
TATERS
TATTED
TATTER
TATTLE
TATTOO
VATFUL
VATTED
WATERS
WATERY
WATNEY
WATSON
WATTLE
WATUSI

•A•T••

BAITED
BALTIC
BANTAM
BANTER
BANTUS
BARTAB
BARTER
BARTOK
BARTON
BASTED
BASTER
BASTES
BATTED
BATTEL
BATTEN
BATTER
BATTLE
BATTUE
BAXTER
CACTUS
CAFTAN
CANTAB
CANTED
CANTER
CANTHI
CANTLE
CANTON
CANTOR
CANTOS
CAPTAN
CAPTOR
CARTED
CARTEL
CARTER
CARTES
CARTON
CASTER
CASTES
CASTLE
CASTON
CASTOR
CASTRO
CATTED
CATTLE
CATTON
CAXTON
DACTYL
DAFTER
DAFTLY
DALTON
DANTES
DANTON
DARTED
DARTER
DAYTON
EARTHA
EARTHY
EASTER
EASTON
FACTOR
FAITHS
FALTER
FANTAN
FASTED
FASTEN
FASTER
FATTED
FATTEN
FATTER
GAITED
GAITER
GANTRY
GARTER
GARTHS
GASTON
GASTRO
HAFTED
HALTED
HALTER
HASTEN
HASTES
HATTED
HATTER
HATTIE
KANTOR
LACTIC
LAOTSE
LAOTZU
LAPTEV
LAPTOP
LASTED
LASTEX
LASTLY
LATTEN
LATTER
LAWTON
MADTOM
MAITAI
MAITRE
MALTED
MALTIN
MANTAS
MANTEL
MANTIC
MANTIS
MANTLE
MANTRA
MANTUA
MAOTAI
MARTEL
MARTEN
MARTHA
MARTIN
MARTYR
MASTER
MASTIC
MATTEA
MATTED
MATTEL
MATTER
MATTES
MATTIE
MAYTAG
NANTES
NATTER
NAUTCH
PALTER
PALTRY
PANTED
PANTOS
PANTRY
PARTED
PARTLY
PARTON
PASTAS
PASTED
PASTEL
PASTES
PASTIS
PASTOR
PASTRY
PATTED
PATTEN
PATTER
PATTON
PAXTON
QANTAS
RAFTED
RAFTER
RAGTAG
RAGTOP
RANTED
RANTER
RAPTLY
RAPTOR
RASTER
RATTAN
RATTED
RATTER
RATTLE
RATTLY
SALTED
SALTEN
SALTER
SALTON
SALTUM
SANTEE
SANTIR
SANTOS
SARTON
SARTRE
SAUTES
TACTIC
TAMTAM
TANTES
TANTRA
TARTAN
TARTAR
TARTER
TARTLY
TASTED
TASTER
TASTES
TATTED
TATTER
TATTLE
TATTOO
TAUTEN
TAUTER
TAUTLY
TAUTOG
VASTER
VASTLY
VATTED
WAFTED
WAITED
WAITER
WAITON
WAITUP
WALTER
WALTON
WANTAD
WANTED
WANTIN
WANTON
WANTTO
WASTED
WASTER
WASTES
WATTLE
XANTHO
ZAFTIG

•A••T•

BALATA
BARITE
CADETS
CAMETO
CANUTE
CAPITA
CAPOTE
CARATS
CARETO
CARETS
CAVETT
CAVITY
DAINTY
DAKOTA
DALETH
DAMATO
DAMITA
DARETO
DAUNTS
DAVITS
FACETS
FAGOTS
FAINTS
FAJITA
FALLTO
FAULTS
FAULTY
FAWLTY
GAIETY
GALATA
GAMETE
GAMUTS
GARETH
HABITS
HALITE
HAMITE
HAUNTS
JABOTS
JAUNTS
JAUNTY
KARATE
KARATS
KARSTS
LAIDTO
LAKOTA
LANATE
LAPUTA
LAXITY
LAYSTO
MAKUTA
MALATE
MALOTI
MAPUTO
NAMATH
PAINTS
PAINTY
PAIUTE
PALATE
PARETO
PARITY
PASHTO
RABATO
RAMATE
RAMETS
RARITY
RATITE
SABATO
SABOTS
SAFETY
SAINTE
SAINTS
SALUTE
SAMITE
SANCTA
SANGTO
SANITY
SAULTS
SAVATE
TAHITI
TAINTS
TAKETH
TAKETO
TALKTO
TAROTS
TAUNTS
VACATE
VALETS
VANITY
VASHTI
VAULTS
VAULTY
VAUNTS
WAISTS
WANTTO
WAPITI
WARMTH
YACHTS
YAKUTS
ZAPATA

•A•••T

BADLOT
BAGSIT
BALLET
BALLOT
BANDIT
BARBET
BARDOT
BAREST
BARKAT
BASALT
BASEST
BASKET
BASSET
CACHET
CADENT
CAMEAT
CAMLET
CANLIT
CANNOT
CAPLET
CAPNUT
CARLOT
CARNET
CARNOT
CARPET
CARROT
CATGUT
CAUGHT
CAVEAT
CAVETT
CAVORT
DACOIT
DARENT
DARNIT
DAYLIT
EAGLET
EATOUT
EATSAT
FANJET
FANOUT
FAROUT
FATCAT
FAUCET
GADGET
GAINST
GALOOT
GAMBIT
GAMEST
GANNET
GARNET
GARRET
GASJET
GASKET
GASLIT
GAYEST
HAEMAT
HAIGHT
HALEST
HAMLET
HAVEAT
HAVENT
JACKET
LABRET
LAMENT
LAMEST
LAMONT
LANCET
LAPPET
LARIAT
LATENT
LATEST
LAXEST
LAYOUT
MADEIT
MAGNET
MAHOUT
MAKEIT
MALLET
MAOIST
MARGOT
MARIST
MARKET
MARMOT
MASCOT
MAXOUT
NATANT
NAUGHT
PACKET
PALEST
PALLET
PANDIT
PANOUT
PARENT
PARGET
PARROT
PATENT
PAWSAT
PAYOUT
RABBET
RABBIT
RACKET
RAGOUT
RAILAT
RAJPUT
RAMJET
RANOUT
RAREST
RAWEST
SACHET
SAFEST
SAGEST
SALLET
SALYUT
SAMLET
SANEST
SATOUT
SAVANT
SAWFIT
SAWOUT
TABLET
TAGOUT
TALBOT
TALENT
TALKAT
TAMEST
TANIST
TAOIST
TAPOUT
TAPPET
TARGET
TARPIT
TAUGHT
VACANT
VALENT
VARLET
WALLET
WALNUT
WAYOUT
YAREST

••AT••

ABATED
ABATES
ABATIS
AGATES
AGATHA
ALATAU
ALATED
AMATIS
AMATOL
ANATTO
APATHY
AVATAR
BEATEN
BEATER
BEATIT
BEATLE
BEATON
BEATTY
BEATUP
BLATTY
BOATED
BOATEL
BOATER
BRATSK
BRATTY
CHATTY
CHATUP
COATED
COATIS
CRATED
CRATER
CRATES
DIATOM
ELATED
ELATER
ELATES
ENATES
FEATLY
FLATLY
GNATTY
GOATEE
GRATED
GRATER
GRATES
GRATIA
GRATIN
GRATIS
HEATED
HEATER
HEATHS
HEATHY
HEATUP
HIATAL
HIATUS
IRATER
KEATON
KLATCH
KRATER
LOATHE
MOATED
NEATEN
NEATER
NEATLY
ORATED
ORATES
ORATOR
PHATIC
PLATED
PLATEN
PLATER
PLATES
PLATTE
PRATED
PRATER
PRATES
REATAS
RIATAS
RRATED
SCATHE
SCATTY
SEATED
SEATER
SEATON
SKATED
SKATER
SKATES
SLATED
SLATER
SLATES
SNATCH
SNATHE
SNATHS
SPATES
SPATHE
STATED
STATEN
STATER
STATES
STATIC
STATOR
STATUE
STATUS
SWATCH
SWATHE
SWATHS
THATCH
THATIS
THATLL
TOATEE
WHATIF
WHATLL
WHATVE
WRATHS
WRATHY
XRATED

••A•T•

ADAPTS
AJANTA
ANATTO
AVANTI
AWAITS
BEASTS
BEATTY
BEAUTS
BEAUTY
BHAKTI
BLASTS
BLATTY
BOASTS
BRACTS
BRANTS
BRATTY
CHANTS
CHARTS
CHASTE
CHATTY
COAPTS
COASTS
CRAFTS
CRAFTY
DEARTH
DRAFTS
DRAFTY
DUARTE
ECARTE
ENACTS
EXACTA
EXACTO
EXACTS
EXALTS
FEALTY
FEASTS
GEARTO
GIANTS
GNATTY
GRAFTS
GRANTS
HEALTH
HEARTH
HEARTS
HEARTY
KRAITS
KRANTZ
LEADTO
LEALTY
LEANTO
NEARTO
ORANTS
PLAITS
PLANTE
PLANTS
PLASTY
PLATTE
QUANTA
QUARTO
QUARTS
QUARTZ
REACTS
REALTY
RIALTO
ROASTS
SCANTS
SCANTY
SCATTY
SHAFTS
SHAKTI
SHANTY
SHASTA
SLANTS
SMALTI
SMALTO
SMARTS
SMARTY
SNAPTO
SOASTO
SPARTA
STACTE
STARTS
SWARTH
TOASTS
TOASTY
TRACTS
TRAITS
WEALTH
WRAITH
YEASTS
YEASTY

••A••T

ARAFAT
ARARAT
AVAUNT
BEATIT
BRANDT
CHALET
CLARET
CRAVAT
FLAUNT
GRABAT
HEARST
IMARET
INAPET
INARUT
LEARNT
PEANUT
PIAGET
PLACET
PLAINT
PLANET
PLAYAT
QUAINT
SNAPAT
STABAT
TEAPOT
TEARAT
TEASET
ZEALOT

•••AT•

ABLATE
ACUATE
ADNATE
AERATE
AFLATS
AGNATE
ALMATY
AMBATO
ANSATE
AQUATE
ATBATS
ATLATL
AVIATE
BALATA
BEMATA
BERATE
BINATE
BLEATS
BLOATS
BORATE
BREATH
BYPATH
CARATS
CERATE
CHEATS
CHOATE
CITATO
CLEATS
COMATE
CREATE
CROATS
CURATE
DAMATO
DEBATE
DEFATS
DELATE
DILATE
DONATE
DORATI
DUCATS
EBOATS
ECLATS
EFLATS
EQUATE
ERGATE
ERRATA
ERSATZ
ESTATE
FIXATE
FLOATS
FLOATY
GALATA
GELATI
GELATO
GLOATS
GREATS
GROATS
GYRATE
HECATE
HEMATO
IDEATE
IGNATZ
INMATE
INNATE
IODATE
JURATS
KARATE
KARATS
KORATS
LANATE
LEGATE
LEGATO
LIGATE
LOBATE
LOCATE
LUNATE
LUXATE
MALATE
METATE
MUTATE
MUTATO
NAMATH
NEGATE
NEMATO
NOTATE
NOVATO
NUTATE
OBLATE
OFLATE
OLEATE
OPIATE
ORGATE
ORNATE
OUTATE
PALATE
PEDATE
PILATE
PINATA
PIRATE
PLEATS
POTATO
RABATO
RAMATE
REBATE
REDATE
RELATE
RENATA
RERATE
ROTATE
RUBATI
RUBATO
RUGATE
SABATO
SAVATE
SEDATE
SENATE
SHEATH
SHOATS
SOMATA
SOMATO
SONATA
SPLATS
SPRATS
SQUATS
STOATS
STRATA
STRATI
STRATO
SWEATS
SWEATY
TERATO
TODATE
TOMATO
TREATS
TREATY
TUBATE
UBOATS
UMTATA
UNIATE
UNIATS
UPDATE
VACATE
WHEATS
WREATH
YUKATA
ZAPATA
ZONATE

•••A•T

ABLAUT
AGHAST
ALEAST
ARRANT
ASLANT
ATLAST
AUFAIT
AULAIT
BASALT
BESANT
BEZANT
BOGART
BREAST
BRYANT
BYPAST
CEDANT
COBALT
CONANT
DECANT
DEPART
DESALT
DIDACT
DISANT
DOPANT
DREAMT
DUNANT
DURANT
DYNAST
ENFANT
ENRAPT
ERRANT
EXTANT
GOCART
GOKART
HOBART
IMPACT
IMPART
INFACT
INFANT
INPART
INTACT
KURALT
KUWAIT
LEVANT
MORANT
MOZART
MUTANT
NATANT
NLEAST
OBLAST
OCTANT
ONEACT
OUTACT
OXCART
PEDANT
PLIANT
POPART
RECANT
RECAST
REDACT
REDANT
REPAST
RESALT
SAVANT
SECANT
SEJANT
SONANT
STRAIT
STUART
TENANT
THWART
TRUANT
TYBALT
TYRANT
UMLAUT
UPCAST
UTHANT
VACANT
VIVANT
VOLANT

••••AT

AFLOAT
AIMSAT
ARAFAT
ARARAT
ATTHAT
BARKAT
BOBCAT
CAMEAT
CAVEAT
COMBAT
COMEAT
COMSAT
CRAVAT
DEFEAT
DIKTAT
DOGSAT
EATSAT
FATCAT
FERMAT
FLEWAT
FOGHAT
FORMAT
GETSAT
GOESAT
GRABAT
HAEMAT
HAVEAT
HEPCAT
HEREAT
HINTAT
HISSAT
HOOTAT
JEERAT
JUMPAT
KEEPAT
KEPTAT
KITKAT
KOMBAT
LARIAT
LEERAT
LESTAT
LETSAT
LOOKAT
LOQUAT
LOWFAT
MEDLAT
MUDCAT
MUSCAT
NIPSAT
NONFAT
NOUGAT
NUMBAT
OLDHAT
ORGEAT
OUTEAT
PAWSAT
PECKAT
PEEKAT
PEERAT
PICKAT
PLAYAT
POKEAT
PTBOAT
RAILAT
RECOAT

REDHAT REGNAT REHEAT REPEAT RESEAT REXCAT RUNSAT SETSAT SEURAT SHEVAT SHOTAT SNAPAT SNOCAT SOTHAT SOWHAT STABAT STOMAT TALKAT TEARAT THREAT THROAT TINHAT TOMCAT TOPCAT TOPHAT TOREAT UNSEAT UPBEAT WENTAT WINKAT WOMBAT

AU••••

AUBADE AUBREY AUBURN AUDENS AUDIAL AUDILE AUDIOS AUDITS AUDREY AUFAIT AUFOND AUGEAN AUGEND AUGERS AUGHTS AUGURS AUGURY AUGUST AUKLET AULAIT AUMONT AUNTIE AUPAIR AUREUS AURIFY AURIGA AURORA AUROUS AUSPEX AUSSIE AUSTEN AUSTIN AUSTRO AUTEUR AUTHOR AUTUMN AUXINS

A•U•••

ABUKIR ABUSED ABUSER ABUSES ACUATE ACUITY ACUMEN ADULTS AGUISH AKUAKU ALULAE ALULAR ALUMNA ALUMNI AMULET AMUSED AMUSES ANUBIS ANURAN AOUDAD APULIA AQUATE AQUILA AQUINO ARUBAN AVULSE

A••U••

ABDUCT ABJURE ABLUSH ABOUND ABRUPT ABSURD ACCUSE ACQUIT ACTUAL ADDUCE ADDUCT ADJURE ADJUST ADZUKI AGOUTI ALBUMS ALCUIN ALEUTS ALLUDE ALLURE AMBUSH AMOUNT AMOURS AMPULE AMPULS ANNUAL ANNUIT ANNULI ANNULS ARGUED ARGUER ARGUES ARGUFY ARJUNA ARMURE AROUND AROUSE ARTURO ASBURY ASSUME ASSURE ASTUTE ATTUNE AUBURN AUGURS AUGURY AUGUST AUTUMN AVAUNT AVOUCH

A•••U•

ABACUS ABLAUT ACARUS ACCRUE ACEOUS ACEOUT ACESUP ACINUS ACTIUM ACTOUT ACTSUP ADDSUP ADIEUS ADIEUX ADYTUM AEOLUS AIDFUL AIMFUL AIRBUS AIRGUN AIROUT ALARUM ALDOUS ALLBUT ALLIUM ALLOUT ALTIUS AMICUS AMINUS ANIMUS ANJOUS ANTEUP ANTRUM ARBOUR ARDOUR ARMFUL ARMOUR ARTFUL ARTGUM ARTHUR ASKOUT ASYLUM ATEOUT ATREUS ATRIUM ATSTUD AUREUS AUROUS AUTEUR AVENUE

A••••U

ACAJOU AKUAKU ALATAU AMADOU APERCU ARALLU

•AU•••

BAUBLE BAUCIS BAULKS CAUCHO CAUCHY CAUCUS CAUDAL CAUDEX CAUDLE CAUGHT CAULKS CAUSAL CAUSED CAUSES DAUBED DAUBER DAUBES DAUNTS FAUCES FAUCET FAULTS FAULTY FAUNAE FAUNAL FAUNAS FAUNUS GAUCHE GAUCHO GAUGED GAUGER GAUGES GAUMED GAUZES HAULED HAULER HAULMS HAULUP HAUNCH HAUNTS HAUSAS JAUNTS JAUNTY JAURES KAUNAS KAUNDA KAURIS LAUDED LAUDER LAUGHS LAUNCH LAUPER LAUREL LAUREN LAURIE MAULED MAULER MAUMAU MAUMEE MAUNDY MAURYA MAUSER MAUVES NAUGHT NAUSEA NAUTCH PAUCIS PAULEY PAUNCH PAUPER PAUSED PAUSES SAUCED SAUCER SAUCES SAUDIS SAUGER SAULTS SAUNAS SAUREL SAUTES TAUGHT TAUNTS TAUONS TAUPES TAURUS TAUTEN TAUTER TAUTLY TAUTOG VAUGHN VAULTS VAULTY VAUNTS WAUSAU YAUPON

•A•U••

BABULS BAGUIO BAKULA BARUCH BATUMI CAGUAS CAJUNS CANUTE CARUSO CASUAL CAYUGA CAYUSE DANUBE DATURA FACULA GAMUTS GAZUMP JAGUAR JAMUPS KABUKI KAHUNA LACUNA LAGUNA LAPUTA LAYUPS LAZULI MACULA MADURA MADURO MAGUEY MAKUTA MANUAL MANUEL MAPUTO MAQUIS MATURE MAZUMA NATURA NATURE PADUAN PAIUTE PAKULA PAPUAN PAQUIN PARULA PARURE RADULA RAQUEL SALUKI SALUTE SAMUEL SATURN TABULA VACUUM VAGUER VALUED VALUES VARUNA WATUSI YAKUTS YAKUZA YAQUIS ZANUCK

•A••U•

BACKUP BACKUS BADGUY BAGFUL BALLUP BANGUI BANGUP BANJUL BANQUO BANTUS BARIUM BARNUM BARQUE BARZUN BASQUE BATTUE BAYEUX BAYOUS BAYRUM CACTUS CADMUS CAIQUE CALLUP CALLUS CALQUE CAMEUP CAMPUS CANCUN CANFUL CAPFUL CAPGUN CAPNUT CARFUL CARPUS CASQUE CATGUT CATSUP CAUCUS DAMOUR DAMSUP DANAUS DARIUS DATSUN EARFUL EASEUP EATOUT EATSUP FACEUP FAIRUP FAIYUM FAMOUS FANOUT FAROUK FAROUT FAUNUS FAVOUR GALLUP GANGUE GANGUP GAVEUP HAIKUS HALLUX HANDUP HANGUL HANGUP HARDUP HATFUL HAULUP JACKUP JAIPUR JAMSUP JANHUS JARFUL JAZZUP KAHLUA KAILUA LABOUR LABRUM LACEUP LAIDUP LAMOUR LANGUR LAPFUL LAPSUP LARRUP LASHUP LATIUM LATOUR LAWFUL LAYOUT LAYSUP MACOUN MADEUP MAGNUM MAGNUS MAHOUT MAIDUS MAKEUP MANAUS MANFUL MANQUE MANTUA MARAUD MARCUS MARDUK MARIUS MARKUP MARQUE MASQUE MAXOUT NASHUA PABLUM PACKUP PAIDUP PAIRUP PALPUS PANFUL PANOUT PAPPUS PASSUP PAYOUT PAYSUP RACKUP RADIUM RADIUS RAGOUT RAGRUG RAIPUR RAJPUT RAKEUP RAMOUS RANGUP RANOUT RAVEUP RAYGUN SACQUE SACRUM SADHUS SALTUM SALYUT SANNUP SATOUT SAVEUP SAVOUR SAWOUT TAGOUT TAGSUP TAKEUP TALCUM TALKUP TALMUD TAMMUZ TANGUY TANKUP TAPOUT TARSUS TAURUS VACUUM VALIUM VALOUR VAPOUR VATFUL WADSUP WAITUP WAKEUP WALKUP WALLUP WALNUT WALRUS WAMPUM WARMUP WASHUP WAYOUT YANQUI

•A•••U

BABALU BALLOU BATEAU CACHOU GATEAU HALERU HAVASU JABIRU LANDAU LAOTZU MAKALU MALIBU MANCHU MARILU MASERU MAUMAU NASSAU PAILOU RAMEAU WAUSAU XANADU

••AU••

AVAUNT BEAUTS BEAUTY CLAUDE CLAUSE FLAUNT FRAUDS FRAUEN SCAUPS TRAUMA

••A•U•

ABACUS ACARUS ALARUM BEADUP BEAMUP BEARUP BEATUP BRAQUE CHATUP CLAMUP CLAQUE DIALUP DRAWUP GEARUP GRADUS HEADUP HEATUP HIATUS ICARUS INARUT LEADUP LEAGUE OMASUM OPAQUE PEANUT PLAGUE PLAQUE PLAYUP PRAGUE REARUP RVALUE SCARUM SEALUP SEAMUS SHAMUS SLAPUP SNAFUS SNAPUP SOAKUP STAPUF STATUE STATUS STAYUP TEACUP TEAMUP TEARUP URAEUS URANUS UVALUE WRAPUP

••A••U

ACAJOU ALATAU AMADOU ARALLU

•••AU•

ABLAUT BEDAUB CHIAUS DANAUS DEPAUL DEPAUW INHAUL MANAUS MARAUD RUPAUL STPAUL STRAUB STRAUS UMLAUT

•••A•U

AKUAKU BABALU DEJAVU HAVASU IGUACU MAKALU SUBARU TUVALU XANADU

••••AU

ALATAU BATEAU BISSAU BUREAU GATEAU JUNEAU LANDAU MAUMAU MOLDAU MOREAU NASSAU NIIHAU RAMEAU RESEAU ROSEAU WAUSAU

AV••••

AVAILS AVALON AVANTI AVATAR AVAUNT AVEDON AVENGE AVENUE AVERNO AVERSE AVERTS AVESTA AVIANS AVIARY AVIATE AVIDLY AVISOS AVOCET AVOIDS AVOUCH AVOWAL AVOWED AVOWER AVULSE

A•V•••

ADVENT ADVERB ADVERT ADVICE ADVISE AMVETS ANVILS ARVADA

A••V••

AGAVES ALEVEL ALFVEN ASEVER

A•••V•

ACTIVE ALCOVE ARGIVE ARRIVE

A••••V

ASIMOV

•AV•••

CAVEAT CAVEIN CAVELL CAVERN CAVERS CAVETT CAVIAR CAVILS CAVING CAVITY CAVORT DAVIES DAVITS FAVORS FAVOUR GAVEIN GAVELS GAVEUP GAVIAL HAVANA HAVASU HAVEAT HAVENS HAVENT HAVEON HAVERS HAVING HAVOCS JAVARI JAVIER KAVNER LAVABO LAVAGE LAVERS LAVING LAVISH MAVENS NAVAHO NAVAJO NAVELS NAVIES PAVANE PAVERS PAVING PAVLOV RAVAGE RAVELS RAVENS RAVERS RAVEUP RAVINE RAVING RAVISH SAVAGE SAVAII SAVANT SAVATE SAVERS SAVEUP SAVING SAVIOR SAVOIE SAVOIR SAVORS SAVORY SAVOUR TAVERN WAVEIN WAVERS WAVERY WAVIER WAVILY WAVING XAVIER

•A•V••

CALVED CALVES CALVIN CANVAS CARVED CARVER CARVES CARVEY GARVEY HALVAH HALVED HALVES HARVEY JAYVEE LANVIN LARVAE LARVAL LARVAS LATVIA MARVEL MARVIN MAUVES NARVIK PARVIS SALVED SALVER SALVES SALVIA SALVOR SALVOS VALVED VALVES WAIVED WAIVER WAIVES

•A••V•

CANOVA CASAVA DATIVE HALEVY NATIVE PAREVE SALIVA

•A•••V

KARPOV LAPTEV PAVLOV VACLAV VASLAV

••AV••

AGAVES BEAVER BEAVIS BRAVAS BRAVED BRAVER BRAVES BRAVOS CHAVEZ CLAVES CLAVIN CRAVAT CRAVED CRAVEN CRAVER CRAVES FLAVIA FLAVOR GRAVED GRAVEL GRAVEN GRAVER GRAVES GRAVID GUAVAS HEAVED HEAVEN HEAVER HEAVES KNAVES LEAVED LEAVEN LEAVES LOAVES PEAVEY PRAVDA QUAVER SHAVED SHAVEN SHAVER SHAVES SLAVED SLAVER SLAVES SLAVEY SLAVIC SOAVES SPAVIN STAVED STAVES SUAVER TRAVEL TRAVES TRAVIS WEAVED WEAVER WEAVES

••A•V•

STARVE WHATVE

••A••V

BRASOV

•••AV•

BEHAVE CASAVA CLEAVE DEJAVU GREAVE MOHAVE MOJAVE MORAVA OCTAVE OCTAVO OTTAVA REPAVE SHEAVE SLEAVE ZOUAVE

••••AV

GUSTAV MOSHAV VACLAV VASLAV

AW••••

AWAITS AWAKED AWAKEN AWAKES AWARDS AWEARY AWEDLY AWEIGH AWHILE AWHIRL AWNING AWOKEN

A•W•••

ADWEEK ALWAYS ALWEST ANWANG ASWELL ASWIRL ASWOON ATWILL ATWOOD ATWORK

A••W••

AIRWAY ALLWET ANSWER ANYWAY ARAWAK AVOWAL AVOWED AVOWER

A•••W•

ACTTWO ALLOWS ARROWS

A••••W

ANDHOW ANDREW ANTCOW ANYHOW

•AW•••

BAWLED BAWLER CAWDOR CAWING DAWDLE DAWNED DAWNON DAWSON FAWKES FAWLTY FAWNED FAWNER GAWAIN GAWKED GAWKER GAWPED HAWAII HAWHAW HAWING HAWKED HAWKER HAWSER HAWSES JAWING JAWOHL LAWFUL LAWING LAWMAN LAWMEN LAWSON LAWTON LAWYER NAWABS PAWERS PAWING PAWNED PAWNEE PAWNER PAWPAW PAWSAT RAWEGG RAWEST RAWISH SAWFIT SAWING SAWLOG SAWOFF SAWOUT SAWRED SAWYER TAWDRY TAWING YAWING YAWNED YAWNER YAWPED YAWPER

•A•W••

DARWIN EARWAX EARWIG FATWAS GALWAY NARWAL TAIWAN WAHWAH YAHWEH

•A••W•

CAHOWS MACAWS MALAWI PAPAWS TARAWA

•A•••W

BARROW CALLOW CASHEW DARROW FALLOW FARLOW FARROW GAGLAW HALLOW HARLOW HARROW HAWHAW HAYMOW LAYLOW MALLOW MARROW NARROW PAWPAW SALLOW TALLOW WALLOW WARSAW YARROW

••AW••

ARAWAK BRAWLS BRAWNY CLAWED CLAWER CRAWLS CRAWLY DRAWER DRAWIN DRAWLS DRAWLY DRAWON DRAWUP FLAWED GNAWED GNAWER GOAWAY GOAWRY INAWAY PRAWNS SEAWAY SHAWLS SHAWMS SPAWNS THAWED TRAWLS UNAWED

••A••W

INAROW KRAKOW MEADOW SEACOW SHADOW

•••AW•

BYLAWS INLAWS MACAWS MALAWI MOHAWK OSHAWA OTTAWA PAPAWS PESAWA RESAWN RESAWS SCRAWL SPRAWL SQUAWK STRAWS STRAWY TARAWA YUKAWA

•••A•W

DEPAUW

••••AW

BOWSAW BROKAW CUSHAW GAGLAW GEEGAW GEWGAW GUFFAW HAWHAW HEEHAW JIGSAW MCGRAW OLDSAW OUTLAW PAWPAW PITSAW PRELAW REDRAW RIPSAW SEESAW

UNDRAW
WARSAW

AX••••
AXILLA
AXIOMS
AXIONS
AXLIKE
AXONAL
AXSEED

A•X•••
AUXINS

A••X••
ALEXEI
ALEXIA
ALEXIS
APEXES

A•••X•
ADNEXA
ANNEXE

A••••X
ADIEUX
AUSPEX

•AX•••
BAXTER
CAXTON
FAXING
LAXEST
LAXITY
MAXENE
MAXIMA
MAXIMS
MAXINE
MAXIXE
MAXOUT
OAXACA
PAXTON
SAXONS
SAXONY
TAXERS
TAXIED
TAXIES
TAXING
TAXMAN
TAXMEN
WAXERS
WAXIER
WAXILY
WAXING

•A•X••
CALXES

•A••X•
GALAXY
MAXIXE

•A•••X
BAYEUX
CAUDEX
EARWAX
HALLUX
HATBOX
LARYNX
LASTEX
MADMAX
MANNIX
MATRIX
PAYBOX
RATEDX

••AX••
COAXED
COAXER
COAXES
FLAXEN
FLAXES
HOAXED
HOAXER
HOAXES
KLAXON
PRAXES
PRAXIS

••A••X
BRANDX
INAFIX
SEAFOX
SPADIX

•••AX•
BORAXO
CUNAXA
EUTAXY
GALAXY

••••AX
CLIMAX
COLFAX
EARWAX
KOUFAX
MADMAX
PICKAX
POLEAX
PRETAX
PROTAX
SINTAX
SMILAX
SURTAX
SYNTAX
THORAX

AY••••
AYEAYE
AYESHA
AYMARA

A•Y•••
ABYDOS
ABYING
ABYSMS
ADYTUM
ALYSSA
AMYTAN
ANYANG
ANYDAY
ANYHOW
ANYONE
ANYWAY
ARYANS
ASYLUM

A••Y••
ALKYDS
ALKYLS
ANHYDR
ARGYLE
ARGYLL

A•••Y•
ABBEYS
ACETYL
AJFOYT
ALLAYS
ALLEYS
ALLOYS
ALWAYS
ANNOYS
ANONYM
ARRAYS
ARROYO
ASSAYS
AYEAYE
AZODYE

A••••Y
ABBACY
ACIDLY
ACUITY
AERIFY
AERILY
AFFRAY
AGENCY
AIRDRY
AIRILY
AIRWAY
ALBANY
ALECKY
ALLDAY
ALMATY
AMBERY
ANDREY
ANERGY
ANTONY
ANYDAY
ANYWAY
APATHY
APIARY
ARCHLY
ARGOSY
ARGUFY
ARIDLY
ARMORY
ARTERY
ARTILY
ASBURY
ASEITY
ASHLEY
ASTRAY
AUBREY
AUDREY
AUGURY
AURIFY
AVIARY
AVIDLY
AWEARY
AWEDLY

•AY•••
BAYARD
BAYEUX
BAYING
BAYLOR
BAYOUS
BAYRUM
CAYMAN
CAYUGA
CAYUSE
DAYBED
DAYBOY
DAYGLO
DAYJOB
DAYLIT
DAYONE
DAYTON
GAYALS
GAYEST
GAYNOR
HAYDEN
HAYING
HAYLEY
HAYMOW
JAYCEE
JAYVEE
KAYAKS
KAYOED
LAYBYS
LAYERS
LAYFOR
LAYING
LAYLOW
LAYMAN
LAYMEN
LAYOFF
LAYOUT
LAYSBY
LAYSIN
LAYSON
LAYSTO
LAYSUP
LAYUPS
MAYANS
MAYBES
MAYDAY
MAYFLY
MAYHAP
MAYHEM
MAYORS
MAYPOP
MAYTAG
NAYSAY
PAYBOX
PAYDAY
PAYEES
PAYERS
PAYFOR
PAYING
PAYOFF
PAYOLA
PAYOUT
PAYSIN
PAYSON
PAYSUP
RAYGUN
RAYONS
SAYERS
SAYING
SAYLES
SAYSOS
SAYYES
SAYYID
TAYLOR
TAYRAS
WAYANS
WAYLAY
WAYLON
WAYOUT
ZAYINS

•A•Y••
BANYAN
BARYON
BATYAM
CANYON
FAIYUM
GALYAK
LARYNX
LAWYER
MAGYAR
PAPYRI
SALYUT
SATYRS
SAWYER
SAYYES
SAYYID

•A••Y•
DACTYL
DADDYO
DAIMYO
DARRYL
GAMAYS
JACLYN
JASEYS
LATOYA
LAYBYS
MALAYA
MALAYS
MARTYR
MATEYS
MAURYA
NAGOYA
PAPAYA
TAMAYO
VAISYA
VANRYN

•A•••Y
BADBOY
BADGUY
BAILEY
BAKERY
BALDLY
BARELY
BARFLY
BARLEY
BARNEY
BARONY
BASELY
BASIFY
BASSLY
BATBOY
CAGILY
CAGNEY
CALMLY
CAMEBY
CANARY
CANOPY
CARBOY
CARNEY
CARREY
CARVEY
CASEFY
CATCHY
CATHAY
CAUCHY
CAVITY
DABNEY
DAFTLY
DAILEY
DAINTY
DAMPLY
DANGLY
DANKLY
DANNAY
DARKLY
DARNAY
DATARY
DAYBOY
EARTHY
EASILY
EATERY
FABRAY
FAIRLY
FAKERY
FAMILY
FARCRY
FARLEY
FAULTY
FAWLTY
GADFLY
GAIETY
GAINLY
GALAXY
GALLEY
GALWAY
GAMELY
GAMILY
GANGLY
GANTRY
GARVEY
GASIFY
GATSBY
HACKLY
HAILEY
HALEVY
HALLEY
HALSEY
HANLEY
HARDBY
HARDLY
HARLEY
HARVEY
HAYLEY
HAZILY
JACKEY
JALOPY
JANGLY
JANSKY
JAPERY
JAUNTY
LACILY
LACKEY
LAIDBY
LAMELY
LANDRY
LANKLY
LASTLY
LATELY
LAXITY
LAYSBY
LAZBOY
LAZILY
MAGUEY
MAINLY
MALADY
MALORY
MANDAY
MANRAY
MARBLY
MARGAY
MARLEY
MARSHY
MASSEY
MAUNDY
MAYDAY
MAYFLY
MAZILY
NAMELY
NAPERY
NASEBY
NAYSAY
OAKLEY
PACIFY
PAINTY
PALELY
PALTRY
PANFRY
PANTRY
PAPACY
PAPERY
PARITY
PARKAY
PARLAY
PARLEY
PARODY
PARTLY
PASSBY
PASTRY
PATCHY
PAULEY
PAYDAY
RACILY
RAINEY
RAMIFY
RAMSAY
RAMSEY
RANDRY
RANKLY
RAPTLY
RAREFY
RARELY
RARIFY
RARITY
RASHLY
RATIFY
RATTLY
SAFELY
SAFETY
SAGELY
SALARY
SALIFY
SANELY
SANITY
SASHAY
SATINY
SAVORY
SAXONY
TAGDAY
TAMELY
TANGLY
TANGUY
TARTLY
TAUTLY
TAWDRY
VAGARY
VAINLY
VALERY
VALLEY
VANITY
VAPORY
VARNEY
VASTLY
VAULTY
WADDLY
WAFERY
WAFFLY
WAGGLY
WAMBLY
WARCRY
WARILY
WARMLY
WATERY
WATNEY
WAVERY
WAVILY
WAXILY
WAYLAY
YARELY
ZANILY

••AY••
BRAYED
BRAYER
CLAYEY
CRAYON
DLAYER
DRAYED
DWAYNE
ELAYER
ELAYNE
FLAYED
FLAYER
FRAYED
GRAYED
GRAYER
GRAYLY
OKAYED
PLAYAS
PLAYAT
PLAYED
PLAYER
PLAYON
PLAYUP
PRAYED
PRAYER
QUAYLE
SHAYNE
SLAYED
SLAYER
SPAYED
STAYED
STAYON
STAYUP
SWAYED
SWAYER
SWAYZE
THAYER
XRAYED

••A•Y•
GLADYS
HEARYE

••A••Y
APATHY
BEACHY
BEATTY
BEAUTY
BLABBY
BLATTY
BRACHY
BRAINY
BRANDY
BRANNY
BRASHY
BRASSY
BRATTY
BRAWNY
CHAFFY
CHALKY
CHAMMY
CHANCY
CHANEY
CHARLY
CHATTY
CLAMMY
CLANCY
CLANKY
CLASSY
CLAYEY
CRABBY
CRACKY
CRAFTY
CRAGGY
CRANKY
CRANNY
CRAWLY
DEADLY
DEAFLY
DEARLY
DRABLY
DRAFTY
DRAGGY
DRAWLY
DUALLY
FEALTY
FEATLY
FLABBY
FLAGGY
FLAKEY
FLAPPY
FLASHY
FLATLY
FRAIDY
FRANNY
GHARRY
GLADLY
GLAIRY
GLASSY
GNARLY
GNATTY
GOAWAY
GOAWRY
GRABBY
GRAINY
GRAMMY
GRANNY
GRAPEY
GRAPHY
GRASSY
GRAYLY
HEANEY
HEARTY
HEATHY
INAWAY
KEARNY
KNAGGY
KNARRY
KRASNY
LEACHY
LEAKEY
LEALTY
LEANLY
MEANLY
MEASLY
NEARBY
NEARLY
NEATLY
NIAMEY
OCASEY
ORALLY
ORANGY
OVALLY
PEACHY
PEARLY
PEAVEY
PLASHY
PLASTY
POACHY
QUAGGY
QUARRY
REALLY
REALTY
SCABBY
SCANTY
SCARRY
SCATTY
SEAWAY
SHABBY
SHAGGY
SHALEY
SHALLY
SHANDY
SHANNY
SHANTY
SLAGGY
SLANGY
SLAPPY
SLAVEY
SMARMY
SMARTY
SNAGGY
SNAPPY
SNARLY
SNAZZY
SPACEY
SPANKY
SPARKY
STABLY
STACEY
STALKY
STANKY
STARRY
SWABBY
SWAMPY
SWANKY
TEAPOY
TOASTY
TRACEY
TRACHY
TRAPPY
TRASHY
TWANGY
USABLY
VIABLY
WEAKLY
WHACKY
WHAMMY
WRATHY
YEARLY
YEASTY

•••AY•
ALLAYS
ALWAYS
ARRAYS
ASSAYS
AYEAYE
BELAYS
BYWAYS
COPAYS
DECAYS
DELAYS
EMBAYS
ESSAYS
FORAYS
GAMAYS
INLAYS
MALAYA
MALAYS
MORAYS
PAPAYA
RELAYS
REPAYS
SPLAYS
SPRAYS
STRAYS
TAMAYO
TOKAYS
UNSAYS

•••A•Y
ABBACY
ALBANY
ALMATY
APIARY
AVIARY
AWEARY
BIGAMY
BINARY
BLEARY
BOTANY
BOVARY
CANARY
CREAKY
CREAMY
CREASY
CROAKY
CURACY
DATARY
DELANY
DENARY
DREAMY
DREARY
EUTAXY
FLOATY
FREAKY
FRIARY
GALAXY
GLEAMY
GOEASY
GREASY
HILARY
INFAMY
KODALY
LEGACY
LITANY
LUNACY
MALADY
MILADY
NONARY
NOTARY
OLEARY
PAPACY
PIRACY
QUEASY
ROMANY
ROSARY
ROTARY
SALARY
SENARY
SHOALY
SLEAZY
SMEARY
SNEAKY
SOMANY
STEADY
STEAMY
STRAWY
SUGARY
SWEATY
TREATY
UNEASY
UNWARY
VAGARY
VOTARY

••••AY
AFFRAY
AIRWAY
ALLDAY
ANYDAY
ANYWAY
ASTRAY
BELLAY
BENDAY
BENGAY
BETRAY
BEWRAY
BISCAY
BOMBAY
BYPLAY
CATHAY
CONWAY
CORDAY
DANNAY
DARNAY
DEEJAY
DEFRAY
DELRAY
DISMAY
DOGDAY
ESTRAY
FABRAY
FENWAY
FLYWAY
FRIDAY
GALWAY
GOAWAY
HEYDAY
HOORAY
HURRAY
ILLSAY
INAWAY
INPLAY
JETWAY
KEYWAY
LEEWAY
MANDAY
MANRAY
MARGAY
MAYDAY
MIDDAY
MIDWAY
MILLAY
MISLAY
MISSAY
MONDAY
MORNAY
MURRAY
NAYSAY
NETPAY
NORGAY
NORWAY
OFFDAY
ONEDAY
ONEWAY
OUTLAY
PARKAY
PARLAY
PAYDAY
PEDWAY
PREPAY
RAMSAY
REDBAY
REPLAY
RUNWAY
SASHAY
SEAWAY
SKYWAY
SUBWAY
SUNDAY
SUNRAY
TAGDAY
TWOWAY
VEEJAY
WAYLAY

AZ••••
AZALEA
AZIDES
AZINES
AZODYE
AZORES
AZORIN
AZTECS

A•Z•••
ADZUKI

A••Z••
AMAZED
AMAZES
AMAZON
AREZZO

A•••Z•
ABLAZE
ALONZO
AREZZO
ASSIZE

A••••Z
AMOSOZ

•AZ•••
BAZAAR
DAZING
DAZZLE
FAZING
FAZOOL
GAZEBO
GAZING
GAZUMP
HAZANS
HAZARD
HAZELS
HAZERS
HAZIER
HAZILY
HAZING
JAZZED
JAZZES
JAZZUP
KAZAKH
KAZAKS
KAZOOS
LAZBOY
LAZIER
LAZILY
LAZING
LAZULI
MAZERS
MAZIER
MAZILY
MAZOLA
MAZUMA
RAZING
RAZORS
RAZZED
RAZZES
RAZZLE
TAZZAS
ZAZENS

•A•Z••
BAIZAS
BALZAC
BANZAI
BARZUN
DANZIG
DAZZLE
GAUZES
JAZZED
JAZZES
JAZZUP
MAHZOR
MAIZES
MATZOH
MATZOS
PANZER
RAZZED
RAZZES
RAZZLE
TARZAN
TAZZAS

•A••Z•
FAENZA
LAMAZE
LAOTZU
YAKUZA

•A•••Z
TABRIZ
TAMMUZ
VALDEZ

••AZ••
AMAZED
AMAZES
AMAZON
BLAZED
BLAZER
BLAZES
BLAZON
BRAZED
BRAZEN
BRAZER
BRAZES
BRAZIL
BRAZOS
BRAZZA
BRAZZI
CRAZED
CRAZES
FRAZER
GHAZIS
GLAZED
GLAZER
GLAZES
GRAZED
GRAZER
GRAZES
PIAZZA
PLAZAS
RYAZAN
SHAZAM
SNAZZY
SWAZIS
ZSAZSA

••A•Z•
BRAZZA
BRAZZI
KWANZA
PIAZZA
SNAZZY
STANZA
SWAYZE

••A••Z
CHAVEZ
JUAREZ
KRANTZ
QUARTZ

•••AZ•
ABLAZE
BEDAZE
LAMAZE
PIZAZZ
SLEAZE
SLEAZY

•••A•Z
ERSATZ
IGNATZ
KUVASZ
PIZAZZ

••••AZ
SHIRAZ

BA••••
BAAING
BABALU
BABBLE
BABELS
BABIED
BABIES
BABKAS
BABOON
BABSON
BABULS
BACALL
BACHED
BACKED
BACKER
BACKIN
BACKUP
BACKUS
BADBOY
BADDER
BADDIE
BADEGG
BADGER
BADGES
BADGUY
BADHAM
BADLOT
BADMAN
BADMEN
BAFFIN
BAFFLE
BAGDAD
BAGELS
BAGFUL
BAGGED
BAGGER
BAGGIE
BAGSIT
BAGUIO
BAHAMA
BAHIAN
BAIKAL
BAILED
BAILEE
BAILER
BAILEY
BAILOR
BAINES
BAIRNS
BAITED
BAIZAS
BAKERS
BAKERY
BAKING
BAKULA
BALAAM
BALATA
BALBOA
BALDER
BALDLY
BALEEN
BALERS
BALING
BALKAN
BALKED
BALLAD
BALLET
BALLON
BALLOT
BALLOU
BALLUP
BALSAM
BALTIC
BALZAC
BAMAKO
BAMBOO
BANANA
BANDED
BANDIT
BANDOG
BANGED
BANGER
BANGKA
BANGLE
BANGOR
BANGUI
BANGUP
BANISH
BANJOS
BANJUL
BANKED
BANKER
BANKON
BANLON
BANNED
BANNER
BANQUO
BANTAM
BANTER
BANTUS
BANYAN
BANZAI
BAOBAB
BARBED
BARBEL
BARBER
BARBET
BARBIE
BARBRA
BARCAR
BARDIC
BARDOT
BAREGE
BARELY
BAREST
BARFLY
BARGED
BARGES
BARHOP
BARING
BARISH
BARITE
BARIUM
BARKAT
BARKED
BARKER
BARKIN
BARLEY
BARMAN
BARMEN
BARNES
BARNEY
BARNUM
BAROJA

BAROLO
BARONG
BARONS
BARONY
BARQUE
BARRED
BARREL
BARREN
BARRES
BARRIE
BARRIO
BARRIS
BARRON
BARROW
BARTAB
BARTER
BARTOK
BARTON
BARUCH
BARYON
BARZUN
BASALT
BASELY
BASEST
BASHED
BASHES
BASICS
BASIFY
BASING
BASINS
BASKED
BASKET
BASQUE
BASSES
BASSET
BASSLY
BASSOS
BASTED
BASTER
BASTES
BATAAN
BATBOY
BATEAU
BATHED
BATHER
BATHES
BATHOS
BATIKS
BATING
BATMAN
BATMEN
BATONS
BATTED
BATTEL
BATTEN
BATTER
BATTLE
BATTUE
BATUMI
BATYAM
BAUBLE
BAUCIS
BAULKS
BAWLED
BAWLER
BAXTER
BAYARD
BAYEUX
BAYING
BAYLOR
BAYOUS
BAYRUM
BAZAAR

B•A•••

BAAING
BEACHY
BEACON
BEADED
BEADLE
BEADUP
BEAGLE
BEAKED
BEAKER
BEAMED
BEAMON
BEAMUP
BEANED
BEANIE
BEANOS
BEARDS
BEARER
BEARON
BEARUP
BEASTS
BEATEN
BEATER
BEATIT
BEATLE
BEATON
BEATTY
BEATUP
BEAUTS
BEAUTY
BEAVER
BEAVIS
BHAKTI
BIAFRA
BIANCA
BIASED
BIASES
BLABBY
BLACKS
BLADED
BLADER
BLADES
BLAINE
BLAISE
BLAMED
BLAMES
BLANCA
BLANCH
BLANDA
BLANKS
BLARED
BLARES
BLASTS
BLATTY
BLAZED
BLAZER
BLAZES
BLAZON
BMAJOR
BOARDS
BOASTS
BOATED
BOATEL
BOATER
BRACED
BRACER
BRACES
BRACHY
BRACTS
BRAHMA
BRAHMS
BRAIDS
BRAILA
BRAILS
BRAINS
BRAINY
BRAISE
BRAKED
BRAKES
BRANCH
BRANDO
BRANDS
BRANDT
BRANDX
BRANDY
BRANNY
BRANTS
BRAQUE
BRASHY
BRASOV
BRASSY
BRATSK
BRATTY
BRAVAS
BRAVED
BRAVER
BRAVES
BRAVOS
BRAWLS
BRAWNY
BRAYED
BRAYER
BRAZED
BRAZEN
BRAZER
BRAZES
BRAZIL
BRAZOS
BRAZZA
BRAZZI
BWANAS

B••A••

BABALU
BACALL
BAHAMA
BALAAM
BALATA
BAMAKO
BANANA
BASALT
BATAAN
BAYARD
BAZAAR
BECALM
BECAME
BEDAUB
BEDAZE
BEFALL
BEHALF
BEHAVE
BELAIR
BELAYS
BEMATA
BERATE
BESANT
BETAKE
BEWAIL
BEWARE
BEZANT
BICARB
BIGAMY
BIHARI
BINARY
BINATE
BLEACH
BLEARS
BLEARY
BLEATS
BLOATS
BOGART
BONAMI
BORAGE
BORATE
BORAXO
BOTANY
BOVARY
BOYARS
BREACH
BREADS
BREAKS
BREAMS
BREAST
BREATH
BRIAND
BRIANS
BRIARD
BRIARS
BROACH
BROADS
BRYANT
BSHARP
BUTANE
BYHAND
BYLAWS
BYNAME
BYPASS
BYPAST
BYPATH
BYTALK
BYWAYS

B•••A•

BABKAS
BADHAM
BADMAN
BAGDAD
BAHIAN
BAIKAL
BAIZAS
BALAAM
BALKAN
BALLAD
BALSAM
BALZAC
BANTAM
BANYAN
BANZAI
BAOBAB
BARCAR
BARKAT
BARMAN
BARTAB
BATAAN
BATEAU
BATMAN
BATYAM
BAZAAR
BEDLAM
BEGGAR
BEHEAD
BELDAM
BELIAL
BELLAY
BEMOAN
BENDAY
BENGAL
BENGAY
BETRAY
BETTAS
BEULAH
BEWRAY
BHOPAL
BHUTAN
BIGMAC
BILBAO
BIOGAS
BIOTAS
BISCAY
BISSAU
BITMAP
BOBCAT
BOMBAY
BONSAI
BOREAL
BOREAS
BORMAN
BOWMAN
BOWOAR
BOWSAW
BOXCAR
BRAVAS
BRIDAL
BROGAN
BROKAW
BRUMAL
BRUTAL
BUCCAL
BUCHAN
BULGAR
BULLAE
BUMRAP
BUNYAN
BUREAU
BURGAS
BURLAP
BURMAN
BUROAK
BURSAE
BURSAL
BURSAR
BURSAS
BUSBAR
BUSMAN
BWANAS
BYPLAY
BYROAD

B••••A

BAHAMA
BAKULA
BALATA
BALBOA
BANANA
BANGKA
BARBRA
BAROJA
BELUGA
BEMATA
BERTHA
BETCHA
BIAFRA
BIANCA
BIKILA
BITOLA
BLANCA
BLANDA
BODEGA
BOGOTA
BORGIA
BOSNIA
BRAHMA
BRAILA
BRAZZA
BRENDA
BUDDHA
BULOVA
BUQSHA
BUSHWA

•BA•••

ABACAS
ABACUS
ABASED
ABASES
ABATED
ABATES
ABATIS
IBADAN
UBANGI

•B•A••

ABBACY
ABLATE
ABLAUT
ABLAZE
ABOARD
ABRADE
ABRAMS
EBOATS
HBEAMS
IBEAMS
OBEAHS
OBLAST
OBLATE
OBTAIN
UBOATS

•B••A•

ABACAS
ABORAL
ABROAD
ABSCAM
FBIMAN
IBADAN
OBIWAN
OBRIAN

•B•••A

ABOLLA
IBERIA
OBELIA

••BA••

ABBACY
ALBANO
ALBANY
AMBATO
ATBATS
AUBADE
BABALU
CABALA
CABALS
CABANA
COBALT
CUBAGE
DEBARK
DEBARS
DEBASE
DEBATE
EMBANK
EMBARK
EMBAYS
GOBACK
HABANA
HOBART
KEBABS
LOBATE
MCBAIN
ORBACH
RABATO
REBAGS
REBARS
REBATE
RIBALD
RIBAND
ROBALO
RUBATI
RUBATO
SABATO
SUBARU
TABARD
TOBAGO
TUBATE
TYBALT
UNBARS
URBANA
URBANE
WABASH

••B•A•

BABKAS
BOBCAT
COBHAM
COBIAS
COBRAS
DEBRAS
DOBLAS
DOBRAS
FABIAN
FABRAY
GIBRAN
HABEAS
HUBCAP
JABBAR
JUBBAH
KUBLAI
LABIAL
LIBYAN
LLBEAN
MOBCAP
NUBIAN
PTBOAT
SABRAS
SUBPAR
SUBWAY
TABLAS
TIBIAE
TIBIAL
TIBIAS
TOBIAS
TUBMAN
UMBRAE
UMBRAL
UMBRAS
UPBEAT
ZEBRAS

••B••A

ARBELA
CABALA
CABANA
CIBOLA
EUBOEA
FIBULA
HABANA
LABREA
NEBULA
ROBBIA
SABENA
TABULA
UMBRIA
URBANA

•••BA•

AIRBAG
AMEBAE
AMEBAS
ARUBAN
BAOBAB
BILBAO
BOMBAY
BUSBAR
CASBAH
CEIBAS
COMBAT
CORBAN
CYMBAL
DISBAR
DUNBAR
DURBAN
DURBAR
FORBAD
GASBAG
GIMBAL
GLOBAL
GRABAT
GYMBAG
HERBAL
ICEBAG
ISOBAR
IZABAL
JABBAR
JUBBAH
KASBAH
KITBAG
KLIBAN
KOMBAT
LUMBAR
MAMBAS
NOTBAD
NUMBAT
RAGBAG
REDBAY
RUMBAS
SAMBAL
SAMBAR
SAMBAS
SCUBAS
SEABAG
SHABAN
SINBAD
STABAT
TEABAG
TIMBAL
TOMBAC
TOOBAD
TRIBAL
TURBAN
VERBAL
WETBAR
WOMBAT
ZEDBAR

•••B•A

ARABIA
BALBOA
BARBRA
GAMBIA
JERBOA
LAMBDA
LISBOA
OJIBWA
PHOBIA
PUEBLA
RAMBLA
ROBBIA
SERBIA
ZAMBIA

••••BA

AMOEBA
ANNABA
ARRIBA
ARROBA
CASABA
CUIABA
DJERBA
HECUBA
INDABA
JOJOBA
KARIBA
MAKEBA
RHUMBA
YORUBA
ZAREBA

BB••••

BBKING

B•B•••

BABALU
BABBLE
BABELS
BABIED
BABIES
BABKAS
BABOON
BABSON
BABULS
BEBOPS
BIBBED
BIBLES
BIBLIO
BOBBED
BOBBER
BOBBIE
BOBBIN
BOBBLE
BOBCAT
BOBSUP
BUBBLE
BUBBLY

B••B••

BABBLE
BADBOY
BALBOA
BAMBOO
BAOBAB
BARBED
BARBEL
BARBER
BARBET
BARBIE
BARBRA
BATBOY
BAUBLE
BEDBUG
BERBER
BIBBED
BIGBEN
BIGBOY
BILBAO
BIOBIO
BLABBY
BOBBED
BOBBER
BOBBIE
BOBBIN
BOBBLE
BOMBAY
BOMBED
BOMBER
BOMBES
BONBON
BOOBOO
BOUBOU
BOXBOY
BRIBED
BRIBES
BUBBLE
BUBBLY
BULBIL
BULBUL
BUMBLE
BUMBRY
BURBLE
BURBLY
BURBOT
BUSBAR
BUSBOY
BYEBYE

B•••B•

BLABBY
BLURBS
BRUMBY

B••••B

BAOBAB
BARTAB
BEDAUB
BENUMB
BICARB

•BB•••

ABBACY
ABBESS
ABBEYS
ABBOTS
ABBOTT
EBBING

•B•B••

IBIBIO

•B••B•

ABOMBS
HBOMBS

•B•••B

ABSORB

••BB••

BABBLE
BIBBED
BOBBED
BOBBER
BOBBIE
BOBBIN
BOBBLE
BUBBLE
BUBBLY
CABBED
CABBIE
COBBLE
DABBED
DABBLE
DEBBIE
DIBBLE
DOBBER
DOBBIN
DUBBED
DUBBIN
DYBBUK
FIBBED
FIBBER
FOBBED
FUBBED
GABBED
GABBER
GABBLE
GABBRO
GIBBED
GIBBER
GIBBET
GIBBON
GOBBLE
HOBBES
HOBBIT
HOBBLE
HUBBLE
HUBBLY
HUBBUB
JABBAR
JABBED
JABBER
JIBBED
JOBBED
JOBBER
JUBBAH
KIBBLE
LIBBED
LIBBER
LOBBED
LOBBER
LUBBER
MOBBED
NABBED
NABBER
NIBBLE
NOBBLE
NUBBED
NUBBIN
NUBBLE
NUBBLY
PEBBLE
PEBBLY
RABBET
RABBIS
RABBIT
RABBLE
REBBES
RIBBED
RIBBON
ROBBED
ROBBER
ROBBIA
ROBBIE
RUBBED
RUBBER
RUBBLE
RUBBLY
SOBBED
SOBBER
SUBBED
TABBED
TUBBED
WEBBED
WEBBER
WOBBLE
WOBBLY
YABBER
YOBBOS

••B•B•

CUBEBS
IMBIBE
KABOBS
KEBABS
KEBOBS
NABOBS

••B••B

COBWEB
HOBNOB
HUBBUB
SUBDEB
SUBURB

•••BB•

BLABBY
CHUBBY
CLUBBY
CRABBE
CRABBY
FLABBY
GRABBY
GRUBBY
KNOBBY
SCABBY
SHABBY
SLOBBY
SNOBBY
SNUBBY
STUBBY
SWABBY

•••B•B

BAOBAB
HUBBUB
SKIBOB

••••BB

SQUIBB
TYCOBB

BC••••

BCELLS

B•C•••

BACALL
BACHED
BACKED
BACKER
BACKIN
BACKUP
BACKUS
BECALM
BECAME
BECKER
BECKET
BECKON
BECOME
BICARB
BICEPS
BICKER
BICORN
BOCCIE
BOCHCO
BUCCAL
BUCHAN
BUCKED
BUCKET
BUCKLE
BUCKUP

B••C••

BARCAR
BAUCIS
BEACHY
BEACON
BETCHA
BISCAY
BLACKS
BLOCKS
BLOCKY
BOBCAT
BOCCIE
BONCES
BOTCHY
BOUCLE
BOXCAR
BRACED
BRACER
BRACES
BRACHY
BRACTS
BRECHT
BRICKS
BRICKY
BUCCAL
BUNCHE
BUNCHY
BUNCOS

B•••C•

BARUCH
BASICS
BEDECK
BIANCA
BIERCE
BISECT
BLANCA
BLANCH
BLEACH
BLENCH
BLOTCH
BOCHCO
BODICE
BORSCH
BOUNCE
BOUNCY
BRANCH
BREACH
BREECH
BROACH
BRONCO
BRONCS
BROOCH
BRUNCH

B••••C

BALTIC
BALZAC
BARDIC
BELLOC
BIGMAC
BIONIC
BIOTIC

•B•C••

ABACAS
ABACUS
ABSCAM

•B••C•

ABBACY
ABDUCT
ABJECT
OBJECT

••BC••

BOBCAT
DUBCEK
HUBCAP
MOBCAP

••B•C•

ABBACY
CUBICS
GOBACK
LUBECK
ORBACH
REBECS
XEBECS

••B••C

ENBLOC
FABRIC
PUBLIC
RUBRIC

•••B•C

AMEBIC
ARABIC
IAMBIC
PHOBIC
QUEBEC
SORBIC
TOMBAC

B•D•••

BADBOY
BADDER
BADDIE
BADEGG
BADGER
BADGES
BADGUY
BADHAM
BADLOT
BADMAN
BADMEN
BEDAUB
BEDAZE
BEDBUG
BEDECK
BEDEWS
BEDIMS
BEDLAM
BIDDEN
BIDDER
BIDDLE
BIDING
BIDSIN
BIDSON
BIDSUP
BODEGA
BODICE
BODIED
BODIES
BODILY
BODING
BODKIN
BODONI
BUDDED
BUDDHA
BUDGED
BUDGES
BUDGET
BUDGIE

B••D••

BADDER
BADDIE
BAGDAD
BALDER
BALDLY
BANDED
BANDIT
BANDOG
BARDIC
BARDOT
BEADED
BEADLE
BEADUP
BELDAM
BENDAY
BENDED
BENDER
BENDIX
BIDDEN
BIDDER
BIDDLE
BINDER
BINDUP
BIRDED
BIRDER
BIRDIE
BLADED
BLADER
BLADES
BOLDER
BOLDLY
BONDED
BOODLE
BORDEN
BORDER
BOUDIN
BRIDAL
BRIDES
BRIDGE
BRIDLE
BRODIE
BRUDER
BSIDES
BUDDED
BUDDHA
BUNDLE
BURDEN

B•••D•

BEARDS
BESIDE
BETIDE
BIONDI
BIPEDS
BIPODS
BLANDA
BLEEDS
BLENDE
BLENDS
BLINDS
BLONDE
BLONDS
BLOODY
BOARDS
BOLIDE
BORIDE
BOUNDS
BOVIDS
BRAIDS
BRANDO
BRANDS
BRANDT
BRANDX
BRANDY
BREADS
BREEDS
BRENDA
BROADS
BROODS
BROODY
BUILDS

B••••D

BABIED
BACHED
BACKED
BAGDAD
BAGGED
BAILED
BAITED
BALKED
BALLAD
BANDED
BANGED
BANKED
BANNED
BARBED
BARGED
BARKED
BARRED
BASHED
BASKED
BASTED
BATHED
BATTED
BAWLED
BAYARD
BEADED
BEAKED
BEAMED
BEANED
BEEFED
BEEPED
BEGGED
BEHEAD
BEHELD
BEHIND
BEHOLD
BELIED
BELLED
BELTED
BENDED
BESTED
BEYOND
BIASED
BIBBED
BIFFED
BIFOLD
BIGRED
BILKED
BILLED
BINGED
BINNED
BIRDED
BIRLED
BITTED
BLADED
BLAMED
BLARED
BLAZED
BOATED
BOBBED
BODIED
BOFFED
BOGGED
BOILED
BOLTED
BOMBED
BONDED
BONGED
BOOKED
BOOMED
BOOTED
BOPPED
BOSSED
BOUSED

BOWLED
BRACED
BRAKED
BRAVED
BRAYED
BRAZED
BREWED
BRIAND
BRIARD
BRIBED
BRIGID
BRINED
BRUXED
BUCKED
BUDDED
BUDGED
BUFFED
BUGGED
BUGLED
BUJOLD
BULGED
BULKED
BULLED
BUMMED
BUMPED
BUNGED
BUNKED
BUNTED
BUOYED
BURIED
BURLED
BURNED
BURPED
BURRED
BUSHED
BUSIED
BUSKED
BUSSED
BUSTED
BUTTED
BUZZED
BYHAND
BYROAD
BYWORD

•BD•••
ABDUCT

•B•D••
ABIDED
ABIDES
ABODES
ABYDOS
IBADAN
IBIDEM

•B••D•
ABRADE
EBONDS
MBUNDU
TBIRDS
TBONDS

•B•••D
ABASED
ABATED
ABIDED
ABOARD
ABOUND
ABROAD
ABSURD
ABUSED
OBEYED
OBTUND

••BD••
EMBDEN
SUBDEB
SUBDUE

••B•D•
ALBEDO
AUBADE
EMBEDS
EMBODY
LIBIDO
NOBODY
REBIDS

••B••D
AMBLED
BABIED
BIBBED
BOBBED
CABBED
CABLED
CUBOID
DABBED
DUBBED
FABLED
FIBBED
FOBBED
FUBBED
GABBED
GABLED
GIBBED
HYBRID
IMBUED
INBRED
JABBED
JIBBED
JOBBED
KOBOLD
LIBBED
LOBBED
MOBBED
NABBED
NUBBED
REBEND
REBIND
RIBALD
RIBAND
RIBBED
ROBBED
RUBBED
RUBIED
SOBBED
SUBBED
TABARD
TABBED
TABLED
TUBBED
UNBEND
UNBIND
WEBBED

•••BD•
LAMBDA
RHABDO

•••B•D
BARBED
BIBBED
BOBBED
BOMBED
BRIBED
CABBED
COMBED
CURBED
DABBED
DAUBED
DAYBED
DUBBED
FIBBED
FOBBED
FORBAD
FORBID
FUBBED
GABBED
GARBED
GIBBED
GLOBED
HOTBED
JABBED
JIBBED
JOBBED
LAMBED
LIBBED
LIMBED
LOBBED
MOBBED
MORBID
NABBED
NOTBAD
NUBBED
NUMBED
OUTBID
PROBED
REDBUD
RIBBED
ROBBED
RUBBED
SEABED
SINBAD
SOBBED
SUBBED
TABBED
TOOBAD
TUBBED
TURBID
WEBBED

BE••••
BEACHY
BEACON
BEADED
BEADLE
BEADUP
BEAGLE
BEAKED
BEAKER
BEAMED
BEAMON
BEAMUP
BEANED
BEANIE
BEANOS
BEARDS
BEARER
BEARON
BEARUP
BEASTS
BEATEN
BEATER
BEATIT
BEATLE
BEATON
BEATTY
BEATUP
BEAUTS
BEAUTY
BEAVER
BEAVIS
BEBOPS
BECALM
BECAME
BECKER
BECKET
BECKON
BECOME
BEDAUB
BEDAZE
BEDBUG
BEDECK
BEDEWS
BEDIMS
BEDLAM
BEEFED
BEEFUP
BEEGUM
BEEPED
BEEPER
BEETLE
BEEVES
BEFALL
BEFELL
BEFITS
BEFOGS
BEFORE
BEFOUL
BEGETS
BEGGAR
BEGGED
BEGINS
BEGLEY
BEGOFF
BEGONE
BEGUMS
BEHALF
BEHAVE
BEHEAD
BEHELD
BEHEST
BEHIND
BEHOLD
BEHOOF
BEHOVE
BEIGES
BEINGS
BEIRUT
BEKESY
BELAIR
BELAYS
BELDAM
BELFRY
BELIAL
BELIED
BELIEF
BELIES
BELIKE
BELIZE
BELLAY
BELLED
BELLES
BELLOC
BELLOW
BELOIT
BELONG
BELTED
BELUGA
BEMATA
BEMINE
BEMIRE
BEMOAN
BEMUSE
BENDAY
BENDED
BENDER
BENDIX
BENGAL
BENGAY
BENHUR
BENIGN
BENING
BENITO
BENOIT
BENONI
BENSON
BENTON
BENUMB
BENZOL
BERATE
BERBER
BEREFT
BERETS
BERGEN
BERING
BERLIN
BERNIE
BERTHA
BERTHS
BERTIE
BESANT
BESETS
BESIDE
BESOMS
BESOTS
BESSER
BESSIE
BESTED
BESTIR
BESTOW
BETAKE
BETCHA
BETELS
BETHEL
BETIDE
BETISE
BETONY
BETOOK
BETRAY
BETSEY
BETSON
BETTAS
BETTER
BETTOR
BEULAH
BEURRE
BEVELS
BEVIES
BEWAIL
BEWARE
BEWRAY
BEYOND
BEZANT
BEZELS

B•E•••
BCELLS
BEEFED
BEEFUP
BEEGUM
BEEPED
BEEPER
BEETLE
BEEVES
BIERCE
BLEACH
BLEARS
BLEARY
BLEATS
BLEEDS
BLEEPS
BLENCH
BLENDE
BLENDS
BLENNY
BLEWIT
BLEWUP
BOEING
BREACH
BREADS
BREAKS
BREAMS
BREAST
BREATH
BRECHT
BREECH
BREEDS
BREEZE
BREEZY
BREMEN
BRENDA
BRENTS
BRETON
BREUER
BREVES
BREVET
BREVIS
BREWED
BREWER
BREYER
BUENOS
BYEBYE

B••E••
BABELS
BADEGG
BAGELS
BAKERS
BAKERY
BALEEN
BALERS
BAREGE
BARELY
BAREST
BASELY
BASEST
BATEAU
BAYEUX
BEDECK
BEDEWS
BEFELL
BEGETS
BEHEAD
BEHELD
BEHEST
BEKESY
BEREFT
BERETS
BESETS
BETELS
BEVELS
BEZELS
BICEPS
BIKERS
BIPEDS
BIREME
BISECT
BITERS
BLEEDS
BLEEPS
BLUELY
BLUEOX
BLUEST
BLUESY
BLUETS
BLUEYS
BODEGA
BOGEYS
BOLERO
BOLEYN
BONERS
BONEUP
BOPEEP
BOREAL
BOREAS
BOREON
BORERS
BOREUP
BOTELS
BOWERS
BOWERY
BOXERS
BREECH
BREEDS
BREEZE
BREEZY
BRIEFS
BRIENZ
BRIERS
BRIERY
BUREAU
BUTENE
BUTEOS
BUYERS

B•••E•
BABIED
BABIES
BACHED
BACKED
BACKER
BADDER
BADGER
BADGES
BADMEN
BAGGED
BAGGER
BAILED
BAILEE
BAILER
BAILEY
BAINES
BAITED
BALDER
BALEEN
BALKED
BALLET
BANDED
BANGED
BANGER
BANKED
BANKER
BANNED
BANNER
BANTER
BARBED
BARBEL
BARBER
BARBET
BARGED
BARGES
BARKED
BARKER
BARLEY
BARMEN
BARNES
BARNEY
BARRED
BARREL
BARREN
BARRES
BARTER
BASHED
BASHES
BASKED
BASKET
BASSES
BASSET
BASTED
BASTER
BASTES
BATHED
BATHER
BATHES
BATMEN
BATTED
BATTEL
BATTEN
BATTER
BAWLED
BAWLER
BAXTER
BEADED
BEAKED
BEAKER
BEAMED
BEANED
BEARER
BEATEN
BEATER
BEAVER
BECKER
BECKET
BEEFED
BEEPED
BEEPER
BEEVES
BEGGED
BEGLEY
BEIGES
BELIED
BELIEF
BELIES
BELLED
BELLES
BELTED
BENDED
BENDER
BERBER
BERGEN
BESSER
BESTED
BETHEL
BETSEY
BETTER
BEVIES
BIASED
BIASES
BIBBED
BIBLES
BICKER
BIDDEN
BIDDER
BIFFED
BIGBEN
BIGGER
BIGRED
BIGTEN
BILGES
BILKED
BILLED
BILLET
BINDER
BINGED
BINGES
BINNED
BIOMES
BIRDED
BIRDER
BIRLED
BIRNEY
BISSET
BITTED
BITTEN
BITTER
BLADED
BLADER
BLADES
BLAMED
BLAMES
BLARED
BLARES
BLAZED
BLAZER
BLAZES
BLIMEY
BLIXEN
BLOKES
BLOOEY
BLOWER
BOATED
BOATEL
BOATER
BOBBED
BOBBER
BODIED
BODIES
BOFFED
BOGGED
BOGIES
BOGLES
BOILED
BOILER
BOITES
BOLDER
BOLGER
BOLTED
BOMBED
BOMBER
BOMBES
BONCES
BONDED
BONGED
BONIER
BONNES
BONNET
BONZES
BOOKED
BOOKER
BOOMED
BOOMER
BOOTED
BOOTEE
BOOTES
BOPEEP
BOPPED
BOPPER
BORDEN
BORDER
BORNEO
BOSKET
BOSLEY
BOSSED
BOSSES
BOTHER
BOTREE
BOULES
BOULEZ
BOUSED
BOUSES
BOVVER
BOWLED
BOWLER
BOWLES
BOWMEN
BOWNET
BOWSER
BOWYER
BOXIER
BOXSET
BRACED
BRACER
BRACES
BRAKED
BRAKES
BRAVED
BRAVER
BRAVES
BRAYED
BRAYER
BRAZED
BRAZEN
BRAZER
BRAZES
BREMEN
BREUER
BREVES
BREVET
BREWED
BREWER
BREYER
BRIBED
BRIBES
BRIDES
BRINED
BRINES
BROKEN
BROKER
BRUDER
BRUGES
BRULES
BRUMES
BRUNEI
BRUNET
BRUTES
BRUXED
BRUXES
BSIDES
BUCKED
BUCKET
BUDDED
BUDGED
BUDGES
BUDGET
BUFFED
BUFFER
BUFFET
BUGGED
BUGLED
BUGLER
BUGLES
BULGED
BULGES
BULKED
BULLED
BULLET
BULWER
BUMMED
BUMMER
BUMPED
BUMPER
BUNGED
BUNGEE
BUNKED
BUNKER
BUNSEN
BUNTED
BUNTER
BUNUEL
BUOYED
BURDEN
BURGEE
BURGER
BURIED
BURIES
BURLED
BURLEY
BURNED
BURNER
BURNET
BURNEY
BURPED
BURRED
BURSES
BUSHED
BUSHEL
BUSHES
BUSIED
BUSIER
BUSIES
BUSKED
BUSMEN
BUSSED
BUSSES
BUSTED
BUSTER
BUTLER
BUTTED
BUTTER
BUTTES
BUZZED
BUZZER
BUZZES
BYRNES

B••••E
BABBLE
BADDIE
BAFFLE
BAGGIE
BAILEE
BANGLE
BARBIE
BAREGE
BARITE
BARQUE
BARRIE
BASQUE
BATTLE
BATTUE
BAUBLE
BEADLE
BEAGLE
BEANIE
BEATLE
BECAME
BECOME
BEDAZE
BEETLE
BEFORE
BEGONE
BEHAVE
BEHOVE
BELIKE
BELIZE
BEMINE
BEMIRE
BEMUSE
BERATE
BERNIE
BERTIE
BESIDE
BESSIE
BETAKE
BETIDE
BETISE
BEURRE
BEWARE
BIDDLE
BIERCE
BIGGIE
BIGLIE
BIGTOE
BILLIE
BINATE
BIRDIE
BIREME
BISQUE
BLAINE
BLAISE
BLENDE
BLITHE
BLONDE
BLOUSE
BLYTHE
BMOVIE
BOBBIE
BOBBLE
BOCCIE
BODICE
BOGGLE
BOLIDE
BONNIE
BOODLE
BOOGIE
BOOKIE
BOOTEE
BOOTHE
BOOTIE
BORAGE
BORATE
BORIDE
BOTREE
BOTTLE
BOUCLE
BOUFFE
BOULLE
BOUNCE
BOURKE
BOURNE
BOURSE
BOVINE
BOWTIE
BRAISE
BRAQUE
BREEZE
BRIDGE
BRIDLE
BRODIE
BROGUE
BRONTE
BRONZE
BROOKE
BROWNE
BROWSE
BRUISE
BUBBLE
BUCKLE
BUDGIE
BULLAE
BUMBLE
BUNCHE
BUNDLE
BUNGEE
BUNGLE
BURBLE
BURGEE
BURGLE
BURSAE
BUSTLE
BUTANE
BUTENE
BYEBYE
BYGONE
BYJOVE
BYLINE
BYNAME
BYROTE
BYSSHE

•BE•••
ABELES
ABESSE
EBERLY
HBEAMS
IBEAMS
IBERIA
IBEXES
OBEAHS
OBELIA
OBELUS
OBERON
OBEYED

•B•E••
ABBESS
ABBEYS
ABJECT
ABLEST
ABSENT
OBJECT
OBSESS
OBTEST
OBVERT
UBIETY

•B••E•
ABASED
ABASES
ABATED
ABATES
ABELES
ABIDED
ABIDES
ABODES
ABUSED
ABUSER
ABUSES
FBIMEN
IBEXES
IBIDEM
IBISES
OBEYED
OBITER
OBRIEN
OBSTET
TBONES

•B•••E
ABESSE
ABJURE
ABLATE
ABLAZE
ABRADE
OBLATE
OBLIGE
OBTUSE
UBIQUE

••BE••
ABBESS
ABBEYS
ALBEDO
ALBEIT
ALBERT
AMBERS
AMBERY
ARBELA
ATBEST
BABELS
CABERS
CUBEBS
CYBELE
EDBERG
EGBERT
EKBERG
ELBERT
EMBEDS
EMBERS
FIBERS
GIBERS
HABEAS
HUBERT
JOBETH
LABELS
LIBELS
LIBERI
LLBEAN
LUBECK
MABELL
REBECS
REBELS
REBEND
REBENT
RIBEYE
ROBERT
RUBENS
SABENA
SABERS
SEBERG
SOBEIT
SOBERS
TUBERS
UMBELS
UMBERS
UNBELT
UNBEND
UNBENT
UPBEAT
UZBEKS
WEBERN
XEBECS
ZIBETS

••B•E•
AMBLED
AMBLER
AMBLES
AUBREY
BABIED
BABIES
BIBBED
BIBLES
BOBBED
BOBBER
CABBED
CABLED
CABLER
CABLES
COBWEB
DABBED
DABNEY
DOBBER
DUBBED
DUBCEK
EMBDEN
EMBLEM
EUBOEA
FABLED
FABLER
FABLES
FIBBED
FIBBER
FIBRES
FOBBED
FUBBED
GABBED
GABBER
GABIES
GABLED
GABLER
GABLES
GIBBED
GIBBER
GIBBET
GIBLET
GOBIES
GOBLET
HEBREW
HOBBES
HOBOES
IMBUED
IMBUES
INBRED
JABBED
JABBER
JIBBED
JOBBED
JOBBER
LABREA
LABRET
LIBBED
LIBBER
LOBBED
LOBBER
LUBBER
MOBBED
MOBLEY
NABBED
NABBER
NOBLER
NOBLES
NUBBED
RABBET
RABIES
REBBES
RIBBED
ROBBED
ROBBER
ROBLES
RUBBED
RUBBER
RUBIED
RUBIES
RUBLES
RUBLEV
SABLES
SABRES
SOBBED
SOBBER
SUBBED
SUBDEB
SUBLET
SUBSET
TABBED
TABLED
TABLES
TABLET
TOBIES
TUBBED
VEBLEN
WEBBED
WEBBER
YABBER

••B••E
AUBADE
BABBLE
BOBBIE
BOBBLE
BUBBLE
CABBIE
COBBLE
CUBAGE
CYBELE
DABBLE
DEBASE
DEBATE
DEBBIE
DEBONE
DIBBLE
GABBLE
GOBBLE
HABILE
HOBBLE
HUBBLE
IMBIBE
IMBRUE
KIBBLE
LABILE
LOBATE
LOBULE
MOBILE
MRBLUE
NIBBLE
NOBBLE
NUBBLE
NUBILE
PEBBLE
RABBLE
REBATE
REBUKE
RIBEYE
RIBOSE
ROBBIE
RUBBLE
SABINE
SUBDUE
SUBTLE
TIBIAE
TUBATE
UMBRAE
URBANE
WOBBLE

•••BE•
ADOBES
BARBED
BARBEL
BARBER
BARBET
BERBER
BIBBED

BIGBEN
BOBBED
BOBBER
BOMBED
BOMBER
BOMBES
BRIBED
BRIBES
CABBED
CAMBER
COMBED
COMBER
COMBES
CORBEL
CUMBER
CURBED
DABBED
DAUBED
DAUBER
DAUBES
DAYBED
DOBBER
DUBBED
DUMBER
FERBER
FIBBED
FIBBER
FOBBED
FORBES
FUBBED
GABBED
GABBER
GARBED
GERBER
GIBBED
GIBBER
GIBBET
GIMBEL
GLEBES
GLOBED
GLOBES
GOOBER
GRABEN
GREBES
GUMBEL
HOBBES
HOTBED
ISABEL
JABBED
JABBER
JIBBED
JOBBED
JOBBER
KHYBER
LAMBED
LIBBED
LIBBER
LIMBED
LIMBER
LOBBED
LOBBER
LUBBER
LUMBER
MAYBES
MEMBER
MOBBED
NABBED
NABBER
NUBBED
NUMBED
NUMBER
PLEBES
PROBED
PROBER

PROBES
QUEBEC
RABBET
REBBES
REUBEN
RIBBED
ROBBED
ROBBER
RUBBED
RUBBER
SEABED
SEABEE
SIMBEL
SOBBED
SOBBER
SOMBER
SORBET
SUBBED
TABBED
THEBES
TIMBER
TREBEK
TRIBES
TUBBED
WEBBED
WEBBER
YABBER
YOUBET

•••B•E
ALIBLE
AMEBAE
ARABLE
BABBLE
BARBIE
BAUBLE
BOBBIE
BOBBLE
BUBBLE
BUMBLE
BURBLE
BYEBYE
CABBIE
COBBLE
CRABBE
DABBLE
DEBBIE
DIBBLE
DOABLE
DOOBIE
DOUBLE
EDIBLE
ENABLE
FEEBLE
FOIBLE
FUMBLE
GABBLE
GAMBLE
GARBLE
GOBBLE
GRABLE
HEEBIE
HERBIE
HOBBLE
HOMBRE
HUBBLE
HUMBLE
JUMBLE
KIBBLE
LIABLE
MARBLE
MUMBLE
NIBBLE
NIMBLE

NOBBLE
NUBBLE
PEBBLE
RABBLE
RAMBLE
ROBBIE
ROUBLE
RUBBLE
RUMBLE
SEABEE
SOMBRE
STABLE
TIMBRE
TREBLE
TUMBLE
UNABLE
USABLE
VIABLE
WAMBLE
WARBLE
WIMBLE
WOBBLE
ZOMBIE

••••BE
ACHEBE
AEROBE
CARIBE
CRABBE
DANUBE
ENROBE
EPHEBE
FLAMBE
IMBIBE
JUJUBE
LETSBE
MCCABE
MUGABE
PHOEBE
SCRIBE
STROBE
THISBE
UNROBE

B•F•••
BAFFIN
BAFFLE
BEFALL
BEFELL
BEFITS
BEFOGS
BEFORE
BEFOUL
BIFFED
BIFOLD
BOFFED
BOFFIN
BOFFOS
BUFFED
BUFFER
BUFFET
BUFFON
BUFFOS

B••F••
BAFFIN
BAFFLE
BAGFUL
BARFLY
BEEFED
BEEFUP
BELFRY
BIAFRA
BIFFED

BLUFFS
BOFFED
BOFFIN
BOFFOS
BOTFLY
BOUFFE
BOWFIN
BOXFUL
BUFFED
BUFFER
BUFFET
BUFFON
BUFFOS

B•••F•
BASIFY
BEGOFF
BEREFT
BITOFF
BLUFFS
BOUFFE
BRIEFS
BUGOFF
BUYOFF

B••••F
BEGOFF
BEHALF
BEHOOF
BELIEF
BITOFF
BUGOFF
BUYOFF

••BF••
SOBFUL

••B•F•
FOBOFF
REBUFF
RUBIFY
RUBOFF

••B••F
FOBOFF
REBUFF
RUBOFF

BG••••
BGIRLS

B•G•••
BAGDAD
BAGELS
BAGFUL
BAGGED
BAGGER
BAGGIE
BAGSIT
BAGUIO
BEGETS
BEGGAR
BEGGED
BEGINS
BEGLEY
BEGOFF
BEGONE
BEGUMS
BIGAMY
BIGBEN
BIGBOY
BIGGER
BIGGIE
BIGGUN

BIGHTS
BIGLIE
BIGMAC
BIGOTS
BIGRED
BIGSUR
BIGTEN
BIGTOE
BIGTOP
BIGWIG
BOGART
BOGEYS
BOGGED
BOGGLE
BOGIES
BOGLES
BOGONG
BOGOTA
BUGGED
BUGLED
BUGLER
BUGLES
BUGOFF
BUGOUT
BYGONE
BYGOSH

B••G••
BADGER
BADGES
BADGUY
BAGGED
BAGGER
BAGGIE
BANGED
BANGER
BANGKA
BANGLE
BANGOR
BANGUI
BANGUP
BARGED
BARGES
BEAGLE
BEEGUM
BEGGAR
BEGGED
BEIGES
BENGAL
BENGAY
BERGEN
BIGGER
BIGGIE
BIGGUN
BILGES
BINGED
BINGES
BIOGAS
BIRGIT
BLIGHT
BOGGED
BOGGLE
BOIGNY
BOLGER
BONGED
BONGOS
BOOGIE
BORGIA
BOUGHS
BOUGHT
BRIGGS
BRIGHT
BRIGID
BROGAN

BROGUE
BRUGES
BUDGED
BUDGES
BUDGET
BUDGIE
BUGGED
BULGAR
BULGED
BULGES
BULGUR
BUNGED
BUNGEE
BUNGLE
BURGAS
BURGEE
BURGER
BURGHS
BURGLE
BURGOO
BURGOS

B•••G•
BADEGG
BAREGE
BEFOGS
BEINGS
BELUGA
BENIGN
BODEGA
BOINGO
BORAGE
BRIDGE
BRIGGS
BRINGS

B••••G
BAAING
BADEGG
BAKING
BALING
BANDOG
BARING
BARONG
BASING
BATING
BAYING
BBKING
BEDBUG
BELONG
BENING
BERING
BIDING
BIGWIG
BIKING
BITING
BLUING
BODING
BOEING
BOGONG
BONING
BOOING
BORING
BOWING
BOXING
BUSING
BUTUNG
BUYING

•B••G•
OBLIGE
UBANGI

•B•••G
ABYING
BBKING
EBBING
OBLONG

••BG••
SUBGUM

••B•G•
CUBAGE
DEBUGS
REBAGS
TOBAGO

••B••G
ALBORG
COBURG
CUBING
CYBORG
EBBING
EDBERG
EKBERG
GIBING
GYBING
JIBING
LUBING
ORBING
ROBING
SEBERG
TUBING
VYBORG

•••B•G
AIRBAG
BEDBUG
GASBAG
GYMBAG
HUMBUG
ICEBAG
KITBAG
LIEBIG
RAGBAG
SEABAG
SOWBUG
TEABAG

BH••••
BHAKTI
BHOPAL
BHUTAN
BHUTTO

B•H•••
BAHAMA
BAHIAN
BEHALF
BEHAVE
BEHEAD
BEHELD
BEHEST
BEHIND
BEHOLD
BEHOOF
BEHOVE
BIHARI
BSHARP
BYHAND

B••H••
BACHED
BADHAM
BARHOP
BASHED

BASHES
BATHED
BATHER
BATHES
BATHOS
BENHUR
BETHEL
BIGHTS
BISHOP
BOCHCO
BOOHOO
BOTHER
BRAHMA
BRAHMS
BUCHAN
BUSHED
BUSHEL
BUSHES
BUSHWA

B•••H•
BEACHY
BERTHA
BERTHS
BETCHA
BIRTHS
BLIGHT
BLITHE
BLYTHE
BOLSHY
BOOTHE
BOOTHS
BOTCHY
BOUGHS
BOUGHT
BRACHY
BRASHY
BRECHT
BRIGHT
BROTHS
BRUSHY
BUDDHA
BUNCHE
BUNCHY
BUQSHA
BURGHS
BYSSHE

B••••H
BANISH
BARISH
BARUCH
BEULAH
BLANCH
BLEACH
BLENCH
BLOTCH
BLUISH
BORSCH
BOYISH
BRANCH
BREACH
BREATH
BREECH
BROACH
BROOCH
BRUNCH
BYGOSH
BYPATH

•BH•••
ABHORS

•B•H••
ABOHMS

•B••H•
OBEAHS

•B•••H
ABLUSH

••BH••
COBHAM
JOBHOP

••B••H
AMBUSH
JOBETH
JUBBAH
KIBOSH
ORBACH
WABASH

•••B•H
CASBAH
JUBBAH
KASBAH

BI••••
BIAFRA
BIANCA
BIASED
BIASES
BIBBED
BIBLES
BIBLIO
BICARB
BICEPS
BICKER
BICORN
BIDDEN
BIDDER
BIDDLE
BIDING
BIDSIN
BIDSON
BIDSUP
BIERCE
BIFFED
BIFOLD
BIGAMY
BIGBEN
BIGBOY
BIGGER
BIGGIE
BIGGUN
BIGHTS
BIGLIE
BIGMAC
BIGOTS
BIGRED
BIGSUR
BIGTEN
BIGTOE
BIGTOP
BIGWIG
BIHARI
BIJOUX
BIKERS
BIKILA
BIKING
BIKINI
BILBAO
BILGES
BILKED
BILLED

BILLET
BILLIE
BILLON
BILLOW
BILOXI
BIMINI
BINARY
BINATE
BINDER
BINDUP
BINGED
BINGES
BINNED
BIOBIO
BIOGAS
BIOMES
BIONDI
BIONIC
BIOTAS
BIOTIC
BIOTIN
BIPEDS
BIPODS
BIRDED
BIRDER
BIRDIE
BIREME
BIRGIT
BIRLED
BIRNEY
BIRTHS
BISCAY
BISECT
BISHOP
BISONS
BISQUE
BISSAU
BISSET
BISTRO
BITERS
BITING
BITMAP
BITOFF
BITOLA
BITTED
BITTEN
BITTER

B•I•••
BAIKAL
BAILED
BAILEE
BAILER
BAILEY
BAILOR
BAINES
BAIRNS
BAITED
BAIZAS
BEIGES
BEINGS
BEIRUT
BGIRLS
BLIGHT
BLIMEY
BLIMPS
BLINDS
BLINIS
BLINKS
BLINTZ
BLITHE
BLIXEN
BMINOR
BMINUS

BOIGNY
BOILED
BOILER
BOINGO
BOITES
BRIAND
BRIANS
BRIARD
BRIARS
BRIBED
BRIBES
BRICKS
BRICKY
BRIDAL
BRIDES
BRIDGE
BRIDLE
BRIEFS
BRIENZ
BRIERS
BRIERY
BRIGGS
BRIGHT
BRIGID
BRILLO
BRILLS
BRINED
BRINES
BRINGS
BRINKS
BRITON
BSIDES
BUILDS

B••I••
BAAING
BABIED
BABIES
BAHIAN
BAKING
BALING
BANISH
BARING
BARISH
BARITE
BARIUM
BASICS
BASIFY
BASING
BASINS
BATIKS
BATING
BAYING
BBKING
BEDIMS
BEFITS
BEGINS
BEHIND
BELIAL
BELIED
BELIEF
BELIES
BELIKE
BELIZE
BEMINE
BEMIRE
BENIGN
BENING
BENITO
BERING
BESIDE
BETIDE
BETISE
BEVIES

BIDING
BIKILA
BIKING
BIKINI
BIMINI
BITING
BLAINE
BLAISE
BLUING
BLUISH
BODICE
BODIED
BODIES
BODILY
BODING
BOEING
BOGIES
BOLIDE
BONIER
BONING
BONITO
BOOING
BORIDE
BORING
BOVIDS
BOVINE
BOWING
BOXIER
BOXING
BOYISH
BRAIDS
BRAILA
BRAILS
BRAINS
BRAINY
BRAISE
BROILS
BRUINS
BRUISE
BRUITS
BUNION
BURIED
BURIES
BURINS
BUSIED
BUSIER
BUSIES
BUSILY
BUSING
BUYING
BYLINE

B•••I•
BACKIN
BADDIE
BAFFIN
BAGGIE
BAGSIT
BAGUIO
BALTIC
BANDIT
BARBIE
BARDIC
BARKIN
BARRIE
BARRIO
BARRIS
BAUCIS
BEANIE
BEATIT
BEAVIS
BELAIR
BELOIT
BENDIX

BENOIT
BERLIN
BERNIE
BERTIE
BESSIE
BESTIR
BEWAIL
BIBLIO
BIDSIN
BIGGIE
BIGLIE
BIGWIG
BILLIE
BIOBIO
BIONIC
BIOTIC
BIOTIN
BIRDIE
BIRGIT
BLEWIT
BLINIS
BLOWIN
BLOWIT
BMOVIE
BOBBIE
BOBBIN
BOCCIE
BODKIN
BOFFIN
BOLLIX
BONNIE
BOOGIE
BOOKIE
BOOTIE
BORGIA
BOSNIA
BOUDIN
BOWFIN
BOWTIE
BRAZIL
BREVIS
BRIGID
BRODIE
BROLIN
BUDGIE
BULBIL
BUNYIP
BUSKIN
BUSTIN
BUTTIN

B••••I
BANGUI
BANZAI
BATUMI
BENONI
BHAKTI
BIHARI
BIKINI
BILOXI
BIMINI
BIONDI
BODONI
BONAMI
BONSAI
BORZOI
BRAZZI
BRUNEI
BUSONI

•BI•••
ABIDED
ABIDES
FBIMAN

FBIMEN
IBIBIO
IBIDEM
IBISES
OBISPO
OBITER
OBIWAN
TBILLS
TBIRDS
UBIETY
UBIQUE

•B•I••
ABYING
BBKING
EBBING
OBLIGE
OBOIST
OBRIAN
OBRIEN

•B••I•
ABATIS
ABUKIR
IBERIA
IBIBIO
OBELIA
OBTAIN

•B•••I
UBANGI

••BI••
ALBINO
ALBION
AMBITS
BABIED
BABIES
CABINS
COBIAS
CUBICS
CUBING
CUBISM
CUBIST
CUBITS
CYBILL
DEBITS
EBBING
ERBIUM
FABIAN
GABIES
GABION
GIBILL
GIBING
GOBIES
GYBING
HABILE
HABITS
IMBIBE
JABIRU
JIBING
KIBITZ
LABIAL
LABILE
LIBIDO
LUBING
MOBILE
MOBIUS
NUBIAN
NUBILE
ORBING
ORBITS
RABIES
REBIDS

REBIND
ROBING
ROBINS
RUBIED
RUBIES
RUBIFY
SABINE
SABINS
SUBITO
TIBIAE
TIBIAL
TIBIAS
TOBIAS
TOBIES
TUBING
TUBIST
UNBIND

••B•I•
ALBEIT
ALBOIN
AMBLIN
BIBLIO
BOBBIE
BOBBIN
CABBIE
CUBOID
DEBBIE
DEBRIS
DOBBIN
DOBLIN
DUBBIN
DUBLIN
DUBOIS
FABRIC
FIBRIL
FIBRIN
GOBLIN
HOBBIT
HUBRIS
HYBRID
LIBRIS
LUBLIN
MCBAIN
NUBBIN
PUBLIC
RABBIS
RABBIT
REBOIL
ROBBIA
ROBBIE
RUBRIC
RUBSIN
SOBEIT
SUBMIT
TABRIZ
UMBRIA

••B••I
KABUKI
KUBLAI
LIBERI
RUBATI

•••BI•
ALIBIS
AMEBIC
ANUBIS
ARABIA
ARABIC
BARBIE
BIOBIO
BOBBIE
BOBBIN

BULBIL
CABBIE
CORBIN
DEBBIE
DOBBIN
DOOBIE
DUBBIN
DURBIN
FORBID
GAMBIA
GAMBIT
GERBIL
GLOBIN
HARBIN
HEEBIE
HENBIT
HERBIE
HOBBIT
IAMBIC
IBIBIO
LIEBIG
MORBID
NUBBIN
ORIBIS
OUTBID
PHOBIA
PHOBIC
RABBIS
RABBIT
ROBBIA
ROBBIE
SERBIA
SORBIC
TIDBIT
TITBIT
TURBID
TURBIT
TWOBIT
VERBIS
ZAMBIA
ZOMBIE

••••BI
ITURBI
JACOBI
MESABI
RHOMBI
WASABI

B•J•••
BIJOUX
BUJOLD
BYJOVE

B••J••
BANJOS
BANJUL
BMAJOR
BOOJUM

B•••J•
BAROJA

•BJ•••
ABJECT
ABJURE
OBJECT

B•K•••
BAKERS
BAKERY
BAKING
BAKULA
BBKING

BEKESY BIKERS BIKILA BIKING BIKINI

B••K••

BABKAS BACKED BACKER BACKIN BACKUP BACKUS BAIKAL BALKAN BALKED BANKED BANKER BANKON BARKAT BARKED BARKER BARKIN BASKED BASKET BEAKED BEAKER BECKER BECKET BECKON BHAKTI BICKER BILKED BLOKES BODKIN BOOKED BOOKER BOOKIE BOSKET BRAKED BRAKES BROKAW BROKEN BROKER BUCKED BUCKET BUCKLE BUCKUP BULKED BUNKED BUNKER BUNKOS BUNKUM BUSKED BUSKIN

B•••K•

BAMAKO BANGKA BATIKS BAULKS BELIKE BETAKE BLACKS BLANKS BLINKS BLOCKS BLOCKY BOURKE BREAKS BRICKS BRICKY BRINKS BROOKE BROOKS BROOKY

B••••K

BARTOK BEDECK BETOOK BRATSK BUROAK BYTALK

•BK•••

BBKING

•B•K••

ABUKIR

••BK••

BABKAS

••B•K•

KABUKI REBUKE UZBEKS

••B••K

DEBARK DEBUNK DUBCEK DYBBUK EMBANK EMBARK GOBACK INBULK LUBECK TOBRUK

•••B•K

DYBBUK LOMBOK REEBOK RHEBOK TREBEK

BL••••

BLABBY BLACKS BLADED BLADER BLADES BLAINE BLAISE BLAMED BLAMES BLANCA BLANCH BLANDA BLANKS BLARED BLARES BLASTS BLATTY BLAZED BLAZER BLAZES BLAZON BLEACH BLEARS BLEARY BLEATS BLEEDS BLEEPS BLENCH BLENDE BLENDS BLENNY BLEWIT BLEWUP BLIGHT BLIMEY BLIMPS BLINDS BLINIS BLINKS BLINTZ BLITHE BLIXEN BLOATS BLOCKS BLOCKY BLOKES BLONDE BLONDS BLOODY BLOOEY BLOOMS BLOOMY BLOOPS BLOTCH BLOTTO BLOTTY BLOUSE BLOWER BLOWIN BLOWIT BLOWSY BLOWUP BLOWZY BLUELY BLUEOX BLUEST BLUESY BLUETS BLUEYS BLUFFS BLUING BLUISH BLUNTS BLURBS BLURRY BLURTS BLYTHE

B•L•••

BALAAM BALATA BALBOA BALDER BALDLY BALEEN BALERS BALING BALKAN BALKED BALLAD BALLET BALLON BALLOT BALLOU BALLUP BALSAM BALTIC BALZAC BELAIR BELAYS BELDAM BELFRY BELIAL BELIED BELIEF BELIES BELIKE BELIZE BELLAY BELLED BELLES BELLOC BELLOW BELOIT BELONG BELTED BELUGA BILBAO BILGES BILKED BILLED BILLET BILLIE BILLON BILLOW BILOXI BOLDER BOLDLY BOLERO BOLEYN BOLGER BOLIDE BOLLIX BOLSHY BOLTED BOLTON BULBIL BULBUL BULGAR BULGED BULGES BULGUR BULKED BULLAE BULLED BULLET BULOVA BULWER BYLAWS BYLINE

B••L••

BADLOT BAILED BAILEE BAILER BAILEY BAILOR BALLAD BALLET BALLON BALLOT BALLOU BALLUP BANLON BARLEY BAULKS BAWLED BAWLER BAYLOR BCELLS BEDLAM BEGLEY BELLAY BELLED BELLES BELLOC BELLOW BERLIN BEULAH BIBLES BIBLIO BIGLIE BILLED BILLET BILLIE BILLON BILLOW BIRLED BOGLES BOILED BOILER BOLLIX BOSLEY BOULES BOULEZ BOULLE BOWLED BOWLER BOWLES BRILLO BRILLS BROLIN BROLLY BRULES BUGLED BUGLER BUGLES BUILDS BULLAE BULLED BULLET BURLAP BURLED BURLEY BUTLER BYPLAY

B•••L•

BABALU BABBLE BABELS BABULS BACALL BAFFLE BAGELS BAKULA BALDLY BANGLE BARELY BARFLY BAROLO BASALT BASELY BASSLY BATTLE BAUBLE BCELLS BEADLE BEAGLE BEATLE BECALM BEETLE BEFALL BEFELL BEHALF BEHELD BEHOLD BETELS BEVELS BEZELS BGIRLS BIDDLE BIFOLD BIKILA BITOLA BLUELY BOBBLE BODILY BOGGLE BOLDLY BOODLE BOTELS BOTFLY BOTTLE BOUCLE BOULLE BRAILA BRAILS BRAWLS BRIDLE BRILLO BRILLS BROILS BROLLY BUBBLE BUBBLY BUCKLE BUJOLD BUMBLE BUNDLE BUNGLE BURBLE BURBLY BURGLE BUSILY BUSTLE BYTALK

B••••L

BACALL BAGFUL BAIKAL BANJUL BARBEL BARREL BATTEL BEFALL BEFELL BEFOUL BELIAL BENGAL BENZOL BETHEL BEWAIL BHOPAL BOATEL BOREAL BOXFUL BRAZIL BRIDAL BRUMAL BRUTAL BUCCAL BULBIL BULBUL BUNUEL BURSAL BUSHEL

•BL•••

ABLATE ABLAUT ABLAZE ABLEST ABLOOM ABLUSH OBLAST OBLATE OBLIGE OBLONG

•B•L••

ABELES ABOLLA OBELIA OBELUS TBILLS UBOLTS

•B••L•

ABOLLA EBERLY TBILLS

•B•••L

ABORAL

••BL••

AMBLED AMBLER AMBLES AMBLIN BIBLES BIBLIO CABLED CABLER CABLES DOBLAS DOBLIN DUBLIN EMBLEM ENBLOC FABLED FABLER FABLES GABLED GABLER GABLES GIBLET GOBLET GOBLIN JOBLOT KUBLAI LUBLIN MOBLEY MRBLUE NOBLER NOBLES PABLUM PUBLIC ROBLES RUBLES RUBLEV SABLES SUBLET TABLAS TABLED TABLES TABLET VEBLEN

••B•L•

ARBELA BABALU BABBLE BABELS BABULS BOBBLE BUBBLE BUBBLY CABALA CABALS CIBOLA COBALT COBBLE CYBELE CYBILL DABBLE DIBBLE FIBULA GABBLE GIBILL GOBBLE HABILE HOBBLE HUBBLE HUBBLY INBULK KIBBLE KOBOLD LABELS LABILE LIBELS LOBULE MABELL MOBILE NEBULA NIBBLE NOBBLE NUBBLE NUBBLY NUBILE PEBBLE PEBBLY RABBLE REBELS REBOLT RIBALD ROBALO RUBBLE RUBBLY SIBYLS SUBTLE SUBTLY TABULA TYBALT UMBELS UNBELT UNBOLT WOBBLE WOBBLY

••B••L

CYBILL FIBRIL GIBILL LABIAL MABELL REBOIL SOBFUL TIBIAL UMBRAL

•••BL•

ALIBLE ARABLE BABBLE BAUBLE BOBBLE BUBBLE BUBBLY BUMBLE BURBLE BURBLY COBBLE DABBLE DIABLO DIBBLE DOABLE DOUBLE DOUBLY DRABLY DUMBLY EDIBLE ENABLE FEEBLE FEEBLY FOIBLE FUMBLE GABBLE GAMBLE GARBLE GLIBLY GOBBLE GRABLE HOBBLE HUBBLE HUBBLY HUMBLE HUMBLY JUMBLE KIBBLE LIABLE MARBLE MARBLY MUMBLE MUMBLY NIBBLE NIMBLE NIMBLY NOBBLE NUBBLE NUBBLY NUMBLY PEBBLE PEBBLY PUEBLA PUEBLO RABBLE RAMBLA RAMBLE ROUBLE RUBBLE RUBBLY RUMBLE RUMBLY STABLE STABLY TREBLE TREBLY TUMBLE UNABLE USABLE USABLY VIABLE VIABLY WAMBLE WAMBLY WARBLE WIMBLE WOBBLE WOBBLY

•••B•L

BARBEL BULBIL BULBUL CORBEL CYMBAL GAMBOL GERBIL GIMBAL GIMBEL GLOBAL GUMBEL HERBAL ISABEL IZABAL SAMBAL SIMBEL SYMBOL TIMBAL TRIBAL TYDBOL VERBAL

BM••••

BMAJOR BMINOR BMINUS BMOVIE

B•M•••

BAMAKO BAMBOO BEMATA BEMINE BEMIRE BEMOAN BEMUSE BIMINI BOMBAY BOMBED BOMBER BOMBES BUMBLE BUMBRY BUMMED BUMMER BUMOUT BUMPED BUMPER BUMPPO BUMPUP BUMRAP

B••M••

BADMAN BADMEN BARMAN BARMEN BATMAN BATMEN BEAMED BEAMON BEAMUP BIGMAC BIOMES BITMAP BLAMED BLAMES BLIMEY BLIMPS BONMOT BOOMED BOOMER BORMAN BOWMAN BOWMEN BREMEN BRUMAL BRUMBY BRUMES BUMMED BUMMER BURMAN BUSMAN BUSMEN

B•••M•

BAHAMA BATUMI BECAME BECOME BEDIMS BEGUMS BENUMB BESOMS BIGAMY BIREME BLOOMS BLOOMY BONAMI BRAHMA BRAHMS BREAMS BROOMS BROOMY BYNAME

B••••M

BADHAM BALAAM BALSAM BANTAM BARIUM BARNUM BATYAM BAYRUM BECALM BEDLAM BEEGUM BELDAM BOOJUM BOTTOM BUNKUM

•B•M••

ABOMBS FBIMAN FBIMEN HBOMBS

•B••M•

ABOHMS ABRAMS ABYSMS HBEAMS IBEAMS

•B•••M

ABLOOM ABSCAM IBIDEM

••BM••

SUBMIT TUBMAN

••B•M•

ALBUMS

••B••M

COBHAM CUBISM EMBLEM ERBIUM KABOOM LABRUM PABLUM SHBOOM SUBGUM

B•N•••

BANANA BANDED BANDIT BANDOG BANGED BANGER BANGKA BANGLE BANGOR BANGUI BANGUP BANISH BANJOS BANJUL BANKED BANKER BANKON BANLON BANNED BANNER BANQUO BANTAM BANTER BANTUS BANYAN BANZAI BENDAY BENDED BENDER BENDIX BENGAL BENGAY BENHUR BENIGN BENING BENITO BENOIT BENONI BENSON BENTON BENUMB BENZOL BINARY BINATE BINDER BINDUP BINGED BINGES BINNED BONAMI BONBON BONCES BONDED BONERS BONEUP BONGED BONGOS BONIER BONING BONITO BONMOT BONNES BONNET BONNIE BONSAI BONTON BONZES BUNCHE BUNCHY BUNCOS BUNDLE BUNGED BUNGEE BUNGLE BUNION BUNKED BUNKER BUNKOS BUNKUM BUNSEN BUNTED BUNTER BUNUEL BUNYAN BUNYIP BYNAME

B••N••

BAINES BANNED BANNER BARNES BARNEY BARNUM BEANED BEANIE BEANOS BEINGS BERNIE BIANCA BINNED BIONDI BIONIC BIRNEY BLANCA BLANCH BLANDA BLANKS BLENCH BLENDE BLENDS BLENNY BLINDS BLINIS BLINKS BLINTZ BLONDE BLONDS BLUNTS BMINOR BMINUS BOINGO BONNES BONNET BONNIE BORNEO BOSNIA BOUNCE BOUNCY BOUNDS BOUNTY BOWNET BRANCH BRANDO BRANDS BRANDT BRANDX BRANDY BRANNY BRANTS BRENDA BRENTS BRINED BRINES BRINGS BRINKS BRONCO BRONCS BRONTE BRONZE BRONZY BRUNCH BRUNEI BRUNET BRUNTS BUENOS BURNED BURNER BURNET BURNEY BURNUP BWANAS BYRNES

B•••N•

BAAING BAIRNS BAKING BALING BANANA BARING BARONG BARONS BARONY BASING BASINS BATING BATONS BAYING BBKING BEGINS BEGONE BEHIND BELONG BEMINE BENING BENONI BERING BESANT BETONY BEYOND BEZANT BIDING BIKING BIKINI BIMINI BISONS BITING BLAINE BLENNY BLUING BODING BODONI BOEING BOGONG BOIGNY BONING BOOING BORING BOSONS BOSUNS BOTANY BOURNE BOVINE BOWING BOXING BRAINS BRAINY BRANNY BRAWNY BRIAND BRIANS BRIENZ BROWNE BROWNS BROWNY BRUINS BRYANT BRYONY BURINS BUSING BUSONI BUTANE BUTENE BUTUNG BUYING BYGONE BYHAND BYLINE

B••••N

BABOON BABSON BACKIN BADMAN BADMEN BAFFIN BAHIAN BALEEN BALKAN BALLON BANKON BANLON BANYAN BARKIN BARMAN BARMEN BARREN BARRON BARTON BARYON BARZUN BATAAN BATMAN BATMEN BATTEN BEACON BEAMON BEARON BEATEN BEATON BECKON BEMOAN BENIGN BENSON BENTON BERGEN BERLIN BETSON BHUTAN BICORN BIDDEN BIDSIN BIDSON BIGBEN BIGGUN BIGTEN BILLON BIOTIN BITTEN BLAZON BLIXEN BLOWIN BOBBIN BODKIN BOFFIN BOLEYN BOLTON BONBON BONTON BORDEN BOREON BORMAN BOSTON BOUDIN BOWFIN BOWMAN BOWMEN BRAZEN BREMEN BRETON BRITON BROGAN BROKEN BROLIN BRYSON BUCHAN BUFFON BUNION BUNSEN BUNYAN BURDEN BURMAN BURTON BUSKIN BUSMAN BUSMEN BUSTIN BUTTIN BUTTON

•B•N••

EBONDS MBUNDU TBONDS TBONES UBANGI

•B••N•

ABOUND ABSENT ABYING BBKING EBBING OBLONG OBTUND

•B•••N

FBIMAN FBIMEN IBADAN OBERON OBIWAN OBRIAN OBRIEN OBTAIN

••BN••

DABNEY HOBNOB

••B•N•
ALBANO
ALBANY
ALBINO
CABANA
CABINS
CUBING
DEBONE
DEBUNK
EBBING
EMBANK
GIBING
GYBING
HABANA
JIBING
LUBING
ORBING
REBEND
REBENT
REBIND
RIBAND
ROBING
ROBINS
RUBENS
SABENA
SABINE
SABINS
TUBING
UNBEND
UNBENT
UNBIND
URBANA
URBANE

••B••N
ALBION
ALBOIN
AMBLIN
AUBURN
BABOON
BABSON
BOBBIN
COBURN
DOBBIN
DOBLIN
DOBSON
DUBBIN
DUBLIN
EMBDEN
FABIAN
FIBRIN
GABION
GIBBON
GIBRAN
GIBSON
GOBLIN
HEBRON
HOBSON
INBORN
LEBRUN
LIBYAN
LLBEAN
LUBLIN
MCBAIN
NUBBIN
NUBIAN
OSBORN
REBORN
RIBBON
ROBSON
RUBSIN
SUBORN
TUBMAN
UNBORN
VEBLEN
WEBERN

•••B•N
ARUBAN
BIGBEN
BOBBIN
BONBON
CARBON
CORBAN
CORBIN
DOBBIN
DUBBIN
DURBAN
DURBIN
GIBBON
GLOBIN
GRABEN
HARBIN
KLIBAN
LISBON
NUBBIN
REUBEN
RIBBON
SHABAN
TURBAN

BO••••
BOARDS
BOASTS
BOATED
BOATEL
BOATER
BOBBED
BOBBER
BOBBIE
BOBBIN
BOBBLE
BOBCAT
BOBSUP
BOCCIE
BOCHCO
BODEGA
BODICE
BODIED
BODIES
BODILY
BODING
BODKIN
BODONI
BOEING
BOFFED
BOFFIN
BOFFOS
BOGART
BOGEYS
BOGGED
BOGGLE
BOGIES
BOGLES
BOGONG
BOGOTA
BOIGNY
BOILED
BOILER
BOINGO
BOITES
BOLDER
BOLDLY
BOLERO
BOLEYN
BOLGER
BOLIDE
BOLLIX
BOLSHY
BOLTED
BOLTON
BOMBAY
BOMBED
BOMBER
BOMBES
BONAMI
BONBON
BONCES
BONDED
BONERS
BONEUP
BONGED
BONGOS
BONIER
BONING
BONITO
BONMOT
BONNES
BONNET
BONNIE
BONSAI
BONTON
BONZES
BOOBOO
BOODLE
BOOGIE
BOOHOO
BOOING
BOOJUM
BOOKED
BOOKER
BOOKIE
BOOMED
BOOMER
BOOSTS
BOOTED
BOOTEE
BOOTES
BOOTHE
BOOTHS
BOOTIE
BOOTSY
BOOTUP
BOPEEP
BOPPED
BOPPER
BORAGE
BORATE
BORAXO
BORDEN
BORDER
BOREAL
BOREAS
BOREON
BORERS
BOREUP
BORGIA
BORIDE
BORING
BORMAN
BORNEO
BORROW
BORSCH
BORZOI
BOSKET
BOSLEY
BOSNIA
BOSONS
BOSSED
BOSSES
BOSTON
BOSUNS
BOTANY
BOTCHY
BOTELS
BOTFLY
BOTHER
BOTREE
BOTTLE
BOTTOM
BOUBOU
BOUCLE
BOUDIN
BOUFFE
BOUGHS
BOUGHT
BOULES
BOULEZ
BOULLE
BOUNCE
BOUNCY
BOUNDS
BOUNTY
BOURKE
BOURNE
BOURSE
BOUSED
BOUSES
BOVARY
BOVIDS
BOVINE
BOVVER
BOWERS
BOWERY
BOWFIN
BOWING
BOWLED
BOWLER
BOWLES
BOWMAN
BOWMEN
BOWNET
BOWOAR
BOWOUT
BOWSAW
BOWSER
BOWTIE
BOWWOW
BOWYER
BOXBOY
BOXCAR
BOXERS
BOXFUL
BOXIER
BOXING
BOXSET
BOXTOP
BOYARS
BOYISH

B•O•••
BAOBAB
BHOPAL
BIOBIO
BIOGAS
BIOMES
BIONDI
BIONIC
BIOTAS
BIOTIC
BIOTIN
BLOATS
BLOCKS
BLOCKY
BLOKES
BLONDE
BLONDS
BLOODY
BLOOEY
BLOOMS
BLOOMY
BLOOPS
BLOTCH
BLOTTO
BLOTTY
BLOUSE
BLOWER
BLOWIN
BLOWIT
BLOWSY
BLOWUP
BLOWZY
BMOVIE
BOOBOO
BOODLE
BOOGIE
BOOHOO
BOOING
BOOJUM
BOOKED
BOOKER
BOOKIE
BOOMED
BOOMER
BOOSTS
BOOTED
BOOTEE
BOOTES
BOOTHE
BOOTHS
BOOTIE
BOOTSY
BOOTUP
BROACH
BROADS
BRODIE
BROGAN
BROGUE
BROILS
BROKAW
BROKEN
BROKER
BROLIN
BROLLY
BRONCO
BRONCS
BRONTE
BRONZE
BRONZY
BROOCH
BROODS
BROODY
BROOKE
BROOKS
BROOKY
BROOMS
BROOMY
BROTHS
BROWNE
BROWNS
BROWNY
BROWSE
BUOYED
BUOYUP

B••O••
BABOON
BAROJA
BAROLO
BARONG
BARONS
BARONY
BATONS
BAYOUS
BEBOPS
BECOME
BEFOGS
BEFORE
BEFOUL
BEGOFF
BEGONE
BEHOLD
BEHOOF
BEHOVE
BELOIT
BELONG
BEMOAN
BENOIT
BENONI
BESOMS
BESOTS
BETONY
BETOOK
BEYOND
BICORN
BIFOLD
BIGOTS
BIJOUX
BILOXI
BIPODS
BISONS
BITOFF
BITOLA
BLOODY
BLOOEY
BLOOMS
BLOOMY
BLOOPS
BODONI
BOGONG
BOGOTA
BOSONS
BOWOAR
BOWOUT
BROOCH
BROODS
BROODY
BROOKE
BROOKS
BROOKY
BROOMS
BROOMY
BRYONY
BUGOFF
BUGOUT
BUJOLD
BULOVA
BUMOUT
BUROAK
BUSONI
BUYOFF
BUYOUT
BYGONE
BYGOSH
BYJOVE
BYROAD
BYROTE
BYWORD

B•••O•
BABOON
BABSON
BADBOY
BADLOT
BAILOR
BALBOA
BALLON
BALLOT
BALLOU
BAMBOO
BANDOG
BANGOR
BANJOS
BANKON
BANLON
BARDOT
BARHOP
BARRON
BARROW
BARTOK
BARTON
BARYON
BASSOS
BATBOY
BATHOS
BAYLOR
BEACON
BEAMON
BEANOS
BEARON
BEATON
BECKON
BEHOOF
BELLOC
BELLOW
BENSON
BENTON
BENZOL
BESTOW
BETOOK
BETSON
BETTOR
BIDSON
BIGBOY
BIGTOE
BIGTOP
BILLON
BILLOW
BISHOP
BLAZON
BLUEOX
BMAJOR
BMINOR
BOFFOS
BOLTON
BONBON
BONGOS
BONMOT
BONTON
BOOBOO
BOOHOO
BOREON
BORROW
BORZOI
BOSTON
BOTTOM
BOUBOU
BOWWOW
BOXBOY
BOXTOP
BRASOV
BRAVOS
BRAZOS
BRETON
BRITON
BRYSON
BUENOS
BUFFON
BUFFOS
BUNCOS
BUNION
BUNKOS
BURBOT
BURGOO
BURGOS
BURROS
BURROW
BURTON
BUSBOY
BUTEOS
BUTTON

B••••O
BAGUIO
BAMAKO
BAMBOO
BANQUO
BAROLO
BARRIO
BENITO
BHUTTO
BIBLIO
BILBAO
BIOBIO
BISTRO
BLOTTO
BOCHCO
BOINGO
BOLERO
BONITO
BOOBOO
BOOHOO
BORAXO
BORNEO
BRANDO
BRILLO
BRONCO
BUMPPO
BURGOO

•BO•••
ABOARD
ABODES
ABOHMS
ABOLLA
ABOMBS
ABORAL
ABORTS
ABOUND
EBOATS
EBONDS
HBOMBS
OBOIST
TBONDS
TBONES
UBOATS
UBOLTS

•B•O••
ABBOTS
ABBOTT
ABHORS
ABLOOM
ABROAD
ABSORB
OBLONG

•B••O•
ABLOOM
ABYDOS
OBERON

•B•••O
IBIBIO
OBISPO

••BO••
ABBOTS
ABBOTT
ALBOIN
ALBORG
ARBORS
ARBOUR
BABOON
BEBOPS
CIBOLA
CUBOID
CYBORG
DEBONE
DUBOIS
ELBOWS
EMBODY
EMBOSS
EUBOEA
FOBOFF
HOBOES
INBORN
JABOTS
KABOBS
KABOOM
KEBOBS
KIBOSH
KOBOLD
LABORS
LABOUR
NABOBS
NABORS
NOBODY
OSBORN
OXBOWS
POBOYS
PTBOAT
REBOIL
REBOLT
REBOOT
REBORN
REBOZO
RIBOSE
ROBOTS
RUBOFF
RUBOUT
SABOTS
SHBOOM
SUBORN
TABOOS
TABORS
TOBOOT
UNBOLT
UNBORN
UPBOWS
VYBORG

••B•O•
ALBION
BABOON
BABSON
DEBTOR
DOBROS
DOBSON
ENBLOC
GABION
GIBBON
GIBSON
HEBRON
HOBNOB
HOBSON
JOBHOP
JOBLOT
KABOOM
REBOOT
RIBBON
ROBROY
ROBSON
SHBOOM
TABOOS
TOBOOT
YOBBOS

••B••O
ALBANO
ALBEDO
ALBINO
AMBATO
BIBLIO
EMBRYO
GABBRO
LIBIDO
RABATO
REBOZO
ROBALO
RUBATO
SABATO
SUBITO
TOBAGO

•••BO•
BADBOY
BALBOA
BAMBOO
BATBOY
BIGBOY
BONBON
BOOBOO
BOUBOU
BOXBOY
BURBOT
BUSBOY
CARBON
CARBOS
CARBOY
COMBOS
COWBOY
DAYBOY
FLYBOY
FOGBOW
GAMBOL
GIBBON
GUMBOS
HARBOR
HATBOX
HOTBOX
ICEBOX
IROBOT
JERBOA
JUMBOS
LAZBOY
LESBOS
LIMBOS
LISBOA
LISBON
LOMBOK
LOWBOY
MAMBOS
OLDBOY
OUTBOX
PAYBOX
PHOBOS
REEBOK
RHEBOK
RIBBON
SKIBOB
SKYBOX
SYMBOL
TALBOT
TOMBOY
TURBOS
TURBOT
TYDBOL
YOBBOS

•••B•O
BAMBOO
BILBAO
BIOBIO
BOOBOO
DIABLO
GABBRO
HASBRO
IBIBIO
PUEBLO
RHABDO

••••BO
AKIMBO
CRAMBO
GAZEBO
LAVABO
MALABO
NINGBO
PHLEBO
PICABO
SASEBO
STRABO

B•P•••
BIPEDS
BIPODS
BOPEEP
BOPPED
BOPPER
BYPASS
BYPAST
BYPATH
BYPLAY

B••P••
BEEPED
BEEPER
BHOPAL
BOPPED
BOPPER
BUMPED
BUMPER
BUMPPO
BUMPUP
BURPED

B•••P•
BEBOPS
BICEPS
BLEEPS
BLIMPS
BLOOPS
BUMPPO

B••••P
BACKUP
BALLUP
BANGUP
BARHOP
BEADUP
BEAMUP
BEARUP
BEATUP
BEEFUP
BIDSUP
BIGTOP
BINDUP
BISHOP
BITMAP
BLEWUP
BLOWUP
BOBSUP
BONEUP
BOOTUP
BOPEEP
BOREUP
BOXTOP
BSHARP
BUCKUP
BUMPUP
BUMRAP
BUNYIP
BUOYUP
BURLAP
BURNUP
BUYSUP

•B••P•
ABRUPT
OBISPO

••BP••
SUBPAR

••B•P•
BEBOPS

••B••P
BOBSUP
HUBCAP
JOBHOP
MOBCAP

B•Q•••
BUQSHA

B••Q••
BANQUO
BARQUE
BASQUE
BISQUE
BRAQUE

•B•Q••
UBIQUE

BR••••
BRACED
BRACER
BRACES
BRACHY
BRACTS
BRAHMA
BRAHMS
BRAIDS
BRAILA
BRAILS
BRAINS
BRAINY
BRAISE
BRAKED
BRAKES
BRANCH
BRANDO
BRANDS
BRANDT
BRANDX
BRANDY
BRANNY
BRANTS
BRAQUE
BRASHY
BRASOV
BRASSY
BRATSK
BRATTY
BRAVAS
BRAVED
BRAVER
BRAVES
BRAVOS
BRAWLS
BRAWNY
BRAYED
BRAYER
BRAZED
BRAZEN
BRAZER
BRAZES
BRAZIL
BRAZOS
BRAZZA
BRAZZI
BREACH
BREADS
BREAKS
BREAMS
BREAST
BREATH
BRECHT
BREECH
BREEDS
BREEZE
BREEZY
BREMEN
BRENDA
BRENTS
BRETON
BREUER
BREVES
BREVET
BREVIS
BREWED
BREWER
BREYER
BRIAND
BRIANS
BRIARD
BRIARS
BRIBED
BRIBES
BRICKS
BRICKY
BRIDAL
BRIDES
BRIDGE
BRIDLE
BRIEFS
BRIENZ
BRIERS
BRIERY
BRIGGS
BRIGHT
BRIGID
BRILLO
BRILLS
BRINED
BRINES
BRINGS
BRINKS
BRITON
BROACH
BROADS
BRODIE
BROGAN
BROGUE
BROILS
BROKAW
BROKEN
BROKER
BROLIN
BROLLY
BRONCO
BRONCS
BRONTE
BRONZE
BRONZY
BROOCH
BROODS
BROODY
BROOKE
BROOKS
BROOKY
BROOMS
BROOMY
BROTHS
BROWNE
BROWNS
BROWNY
BROWSE
BRUDER
BRUGES
BRUINS
BRUISE
BRUITS
BRULES
BRUMAL
BRUMBY
BRUMES
BRUNCH
BRUNEI
BRUNET
BRUNTS
BRUSHY
BRUTAL
BRUTES
BRUTUS
BRUXED
BRUXES
BRYANT
BRYONY
BRYSON

B•R•••
BARBED
BARBEL
BARBER
BARBET
BARBIE
BARBRA
BARCAR
BARDIC
BARDOT
BAREGE
BARELY
BAREST
BARFLY
BARGED
BARGES
BARHOP
BARING
BARISH
BARITE
BARIUM
BARKAT
BARKED
BARKER
BARKIN
BARLEY
BARMAN
BARMEN
BARNES
BARNEY
BARNUM
BAROJA
BAROLO
BARONG
BARONS
BARONY
BARQUE
BARRED
BARREL
BARREN
BARRES
BARRIE
BARRIO
BARRIS
BARRON
BARROW
BARTAB
BARTER
BARTOK
BARTON
BARUCH
BARYON
BARZUN
BERATE
BERBER
BEREFT
BERETS
BERGEN
BERING
BERLIN
BERNIE
BERTHA
BERTHS
BERTIE
BIRDED
BIRDER
BIRDIE
BIREME
BIRGIT
BIRLED
BIRNEY
BIRTHS
BORAGE
BORATE
BORAXO
BORDEN
BORDER
BOREAL
BOREAS
BOREON
BORERS
BOREUP
BORGIA
BORIDE
BORING
BORMAN
BORNEO
BORROW
BORSCH
BORZOI
BURBLE
BURBLY
BURBOT
BURDEN
BUREAU
BURGAS
BURGEE
BURGER
BURGHS
BURGLE
BURGOO
BURGOS
BURIED
BURIES
BURINS
BURLAP
BURLED
BURLEY
BURMAN
BURNED
BURNER
BURNET
BURNEY
BURNUP
BUROAK
BURPED
BURRED
BURROS
BURROW
BURSAE
BURSAL
BURSAR
BURSAS
BURSES
BURSTS
BURTON
BYRNES
BYROAD
BYROTE

B••R••
BAIRNS
BARRED
BARREL
BARREN
BARRES
BARRIE
BARRIO
BARRIS
BARRON
BARROW
BAYRUM
BEARDS
BEARER
BEARON
BEARUP
BEIRUT
BETRAY
BEURRE
BEWRAY
BGIRLS
BIERCE
BIGRED
BLARED
BLARES
BLURBS
BLURRY
BLURTS
BOARDS
BORROW
BOTREE
BOURKE
BOURNE
BOURSE
BUMRAP
BURRED
BURROS
BURROW

B•••R•
BAKERS BAKERY BALERS BARBRA BAYARD BEFORE BELFRY BEMIRE BEURRE BEWARE BIAFRA BICARB BICORN BIHARI BIKERS BINARY BISTRO BITERS BLEARS BLEARY BLURRY BOGART BOLERO BONERS BORERS BOVARY BOWERS BOWERY BOXERS BOYARS BRIARD BRIARS BRIERS BRIERY BSHARP BUMBRY BUYERS BYWORD

B••••R
BACKER BADDER BADGER BAGGER BAILER BAILOR BALDER BANGER BANGOR BANKER BANNER BANTER BARBER BARCAR BARKER BARTER BASTER BATHER BATTER BAWLER BAXTER BAYLOR BAZAAR BEAKER BEARER BEATER BEAVER BECKER BEEPER BEGGAR BELAIR BENDER BENHUR BERBER BESSER BESTIR BETTER BETTOR BICKER BIDDER BIGGER BIGSUR BINDER BIRDER BITTER BLADER BLAZER BLOWER BMAJOR BMINOR BOATER BOBBER BOILER BOLDER BOLGER BOMBER BONIER BOOKER BOOMER BOPPER BORDER BOTHER BOVVER BOWLER BOWOAR BOWSER BOWYER BOXCAR BOXIER BRACER BRAVER BRAYER BRAZER BREUER BREWER BREYER BROKER BRUDER BUFFER BUGLER BULGAR BULGUR BULWER BUMMER BUMPER BUNKER BUNTER BURGER BURNER BURSAR BUSBAR BUSIER BUSTER BUTLER BUTTER BUZZER

•BR•••
ABRADE ABRAMS ABROAD ABRUPT OBRIAN OBRIEN

•B•R••
ABORAL ABORTS EBERLY IBERIA OBERON TBIRDS

•B••R•
ABHORS ABJURE ABOARD ABSORB ABSURD OBVERT

•B•••R
ABUKIR ABUSER OBITER

••BR••
AUBREY COBRAS DEBRAS DEBRIS DOBRAS DOBROS ELBRUS EMBRYO FABRAY FABRIC FIBRES FIBRIL FIBRIN GIBRAN HEBREW HEBRON HUBRIS HYBRID IMBRUE INBRED LABREA LABRET LABRUM LEBRUN LIBRIS ROBROY RUBRIC SABRAS SABRES TABRIZ TOBRUK UMBRAE UMBRAL UMBRAS UMBRIA ZEBRAS

••B•R•
ALBERT ALBORG AMBERS AMBERY ARBORS ASBURY AUBURN CABERS COBURG COBURN CYBORG DEBARK DEBARS EDBERG EGBERT EKBERG ELBERT EMBARK EMBERS FIBERS GABBRO GIBERS HOBART HUBERT INBORN JABIRU LABORS LIBERI NABORS OSBORN REBARS REBORN REBURY ROBERT SABERS SEBERG SOBERS SUBARU SUBORN SUBURB TABARD TABORS TUBERS UMBERS UNBARS UNBORN VYBORG WEBERN

••B••R
AMBLER ARBOUR BOBBER CABLER DEBTOR DOBBER FABLER FIBBER GABBER GABLER GIBBER JABBAR JABBER JOBBER LABOUR LIBBER LOBBER LUBBER NABBER NOBLER ROBBER RUBBER SOBBER SUBPAR WEBBER YABBER

•••BR•
BARBRA BUMBRY GABBRO HASBRO HOMBRE SOMBRE TIMBRE

•••B•R
BARBER BERBER BOBBER BOMBER BUSBAR CAMBER COMBER CUMBER DAUBER DISBAR DOBBER DUMBER DUNBAR DURBAR FERBER FIBBER GABBER GERBER GIBBER GOOBER HARBOR ISOBAR JABBAR JABBER JOBBER KHYBER LIBBER LIMBER LOBBER LUBBER LUMBAR LUMBER MEMBER NABBER NUMBER PROBER ROBBER RUBBER SAMBAR SOBBER SOMBER TIMBER WEBBER WETBAR WILBUR YABBER ZEDBAR

BS••••
BSHARP BSIDES

B•S•••
BASALT BASELY BASEST BASHED BASHES BASICS BASIFY BASING BASINS BASKED BASKET BASQUE BASSES BASSET BASSLY BASSOS BASTED BASTER BASTES BESANT BESETS BESIDE BESOMS BESOTS BESSER BESSIE BESTED BESTIR BESTOW BISCAY BISECT BISHOP BISONS BISQUE BISSAU BISSET BISTRO BOSKET BOSLEY BOSNIA BOSONS BOSSED BOSSES BOSTON BOSUNS BUSBAR BUSBOY BUSHED BUSHEL BUSHES BUSHWA BUSIED BUSIER BUSIES BUSILY BUSING BUSKED BUSKIN BUSMAN BUSMEN BUSONI BUSSED BUSSES BUSTED BUSTER BUSTIN BUSTLE BYSSHE BYSSUS

B••S••
BABSON BAGSIT BALSAM BASSES BASSET BASSLY BASSOS BEASTS BENSON BESSER BESSIE BETSEY BETSON BIASED BIASES BIDSIN BIDSON BIDSUP BIGSUR BISSAU BISSET BLASTS BOASTS BOBSUP BOLSHY BONSAI BOOSTS BORSCH BOSSED BOSSES BOUSED BOUSES BOWSAW BOWSER BOXSET BRASHY BRASOV BRASSY BRUSHY BRYSON BUNSEN BUQSHA BURSAE BURSAL BURSAR BURSAS BURSES BURSTS BUSSED BUSSES BUYSUP BYSSHE BYSSUS

B•••S•
BANISH BAREST BARISH BASEST BEHEST BEKESY BEMUSE BETISE BLAISE BLOUSE BLOWSY BLUEST BLUESY BLUISH BOOTSY BOURSE BOYISH BRAISE BRASSY BRATSK BREAST BROWSE BRUISE BYGOSH BYPASS BYPAST

B••••S
BABELS BABIES BABKAS BABULS BACKUS BADGES BAGELS BAINES BAIRNS BAIZAS BAKERS BALERS BANJOS BANTUS BARGES BARNES BARONS BARRES BARRIS BASHES BASICS BASINS BASSES BASSOS BASTES BATHES BATHOS BATIKS BATONS BAUCIS BAULKS BAYOUS BCELLS BEANOS BEARDS BEASTS BEAUTS BEAVIS BEBOPS BEDEWS BEDIMS BEEVES BEFITS BEFOGS BEGETS BEGINS BEGUMS BEIGES BEINGS BELAYS BELIES BELLES BERETS BERTHS BESETS BESOMS BESOTS BETELS BETTAS BEVELS BEVIES BEZELS BGIRLS BIASES BIBLES BICEPS BIGHTS BIGOTS BIKERS BILGES BINGES BIOGAS BIOMES BIOTAS BIPEDS BIPODS BIRTHS BISONS BITERS BLACKS BLADES BLAMES BLANKS BLARES BLASTS BLAZES BLEARS BLEATS BLEEDS BLEEPS BLENDS BLIMPS BLINDS BLINIS BLINKS BLOATS BLOCKS BLOKES BLONDS BLOOMS BLOOPS BLUETS BLUEYS BLUFFS BLUNTS BLURBS BLURTS BMINUS BOARDS BOASTS BODIES BOFFOS BOGEYS BOGIES BOGLES BOITES BOMBES BONCES BONERS BONGOS BONNES BONZES BOOSTS BOOTES BOOTHS BOREAS BORERS BOSONS BOSSES BOSUNS BOTELS BOUGHS BOULES BOUNDS BOUSES BOVIDS BOWERS BOWLES BOXERS BOYARS BRACES BRACTS BRAHMS BRAIDS BRAILS BRAINS BRAKES BRANDS BRANTS BRAVAS BRAVES BRAVOS BRAWLS BRAZES BRAZOS BREADS BREAKS BREAMS BREEDS BRENTS BREVES BREVIS BRIANS BRIARS BRIBES BRICKS BRIDES BRIEFS BRIERS BRIGGS BRILLS BRINES BRINGS BRINKS BROADS BROILS BRONCS BROODS BROOKS BROOMS BROTHS BROWNS BRUGES BRUINS BRUITS BRULES BRUMES BRUNTS BRUTES BRUTUS BRUXES BSIDES BUDGES BUENOS BUFFOS BUGLES BUILDS BULGES BUNCOS BUNKOS BURGAS BURGHS BURGOS BURIES BURINS BURROS BURSAS BURSES BURSTS BUSHES BUSIES BUSSES BUTEOS BUTTES BUTUTS BUYERS BUZZES BWANAS BYLAWS BYPASS BYRNES BYSSUS BYWAYS

•BS•••
ABSCAM ABSENT ABSORB ABSURD OBSESS OBSTET

•B•S••
ABASED ABASES ABESSE ABUSED ABUSER ABUSES ABYSMS IBISES OBISPO

•B••S•
ABBESS ABESSE ABLEST ABLUSH OBLAST OBOIST OBSESS OBTEST OBTUSE

•B•••S
ABACAS ABACUS ABASES ABATES ABATIS ABBESS ABBEYS ABBOTS ABELES ABHORS ABIDES ABODES ABOHMS ABOMBS ABORTS ABRAMS ABUSES ABYDOS ABYSMS EBOATS EBONDS HBEAMS HBOMBS IBEAMS IBEXES IBISES OBEAHS OBELUS OBSESS TBILLS TBIRDS TBONDS TBONES UBOATS UBOLTS

••BS••
BABSON BOBSUP DOBSON GIBSON HOBSON ROBSON RUBSIN SUBSET

••B•S•
ABBESS AMBUSH ATBEST CUBISM CUBIST DEBASE EMBOSS GOBUST KIBOSH RIBOSE ROBUST TUBIST UNBUSY WABASH

••B••S
ABBESS ABBEYS ABBOTS ALBUMS AMBERS AMBITS AMBLES ARBORS ATBATS BABELS BABIES BABKAS BABULS BEBOPS BIBLES CABALS CABERS CABINS CABLES COBIAS COBRAS CUBEBS CUBICS CUBITS DEBARS DEBITS DEBRAS DEBRIS DEBUGS DEBUTS DOBLAS DOBRAS DOBROS DUBOIS ELBOWS ELBRUS EMBAYS EMBEDS EMBERS EMBOSS FABLES FIBERS FIBRES GABIES GABLES GIBERS GOBIES HABEAS HABITS HOBBES HOBOES HUBRIS IMBUES JABOTS KABOBS KEBABS KEBOBS LABELS LABORS LIBELS LIBRIS MOBIUS NABOBS NABORS NOBLES ORBITS OXBOWS POBOYS RABBIS RABIES REBAGS REBARS REBBES REBECS REBELS REBIDS REBUTS ROBINS ROBLES ROBOTS RUBENS RUBIES RUBLES SABERS SABINS SABLES SABOTS SABRAS SABRES SIBYLS SOBERS TABLAS TABLES TABOOS TABORS TIBIAS TOBIAS TOBIES TUBERS UMBELS UMBERS UMBRAS UNBARS UPBOWS UZBEKS XEBECS YOBBOS ZEBRAS ZIBETS

•••B•S
ADOBES AIRBUS ALIBIS AMEBAS ANUBIS BOMBES BRIBES CARBOS CEIBAS COMBES COMBOS DAUBES DOUBTS EREBUS FLYBYS FORBES GLEBES GLOBES GREBES GUMBOS HOBBES JUMBOS LAYBYS LESBOS LIEBYS LIMBOS LIMBUS MAMBAS MAMBOS MAYBES NIMBUS ORIBIS PHOBOS PLEBES PROBES RABBIS REBBES RUMBAS SAMBAS SCUBAS THEBES TRIBES TURBOS VERBIS YOBBOS

••••BS
ABOMBS ADLIBS ARDEBS BLURBS CARIBS CAROBS CELEBS CLIMBS CRUMBS CUBEBS DEMOBS DWEEBS EXURBS HBOMBS KABOBS KEBABS KEBOBS MCJOBS NABOBS NAWABS PLUMBS REDUBS REHABS RHOMBS RHUMBS SAHIBS SCRUBS SHRUBS SQUABS SQUIBS THROBS THUMBS

B•T•••
BATAAN BATBOY BATEAU BATHED BATHER BATHES BATHOS BATIKS BATING BATMAN BATMEN BATONS BATTED BATTEL BATTEN BATTER BATTLE BATTUE BATUMI BATYAM BETAKE BETCHA BETELS BETHEL BETIDE BETISE BETONY BETOOK BETRAY BETSEY BETSON BETTAS BETTER BETTOR BITERS BITING BITMAP BITOFF BITOLA BITTED BITTEN BITTER BOTANY BOTCHY BOTELS BOTFLY BOTHER BOTREE BOTTLE BOTTOM BUTANE BUTENE BUTEOS BUTLER BUTTED BUTTER BUTTES BUTTIN BUTTON BUTUNG BUTUTS BYTALK

B••T••
BAITED BALTIC BANTAM BANTER BANTUS BARTAB BARTER BARTOK BARTON BASTED BASTER BASTES BATTED BATTEL BATTEN BATTER BATTLE BATTUE BAXTER BEATEN BEATER BEATIT BEATLE BEATON BEATTY BEATUP BEETLE BELTED BENTON BERTHA BERTHS BERTIE BESTED BESTIR BESTOW BETTAS BETTER BETTOR BHUTAN BHUTTO BIGTEN BIGTOE BIGTOP BIOTAS BIOTIC BIOTIN BIRTHS BISTRO BITTED BITTEN BITTER BLATTY BLITHE BLOTCH BLOTTO BLOTTY BLYTHE BOATED BOATEL BOATER BOITES BOLTED BOLTON BONTON BOOTED BOOTEE BOOTES BOOTHE BOOTHS BOOTIE BOOTSY BOOTUP BOSTON BOTTLE BOTTOM BOWTIE BOXTOP BRATSK BRATTY BRETON BRITON BROTHS BRUTAL BRUTES BRUTUS BUNTED BUNTER BURTON BUSTED BUSTER BUSTIN BUSTLE BUTTED BUTTER BUTTES BUTTIN BUTTON

B•••T•
BALATA BARITE BEASTS BEATTY BEAUTS BEAUTY BEFITS BEGETS BEMATA BENITO BERATE

BERETS
BESETS
BESOTS
BHAKTI
BHUTTO
BIGHTS
BIGOTS
BINATE
BLASTS
BLATTY
BLEATS
BLINTZ
BLOATS
BLOTTO
BLOTTY
BLUETS
BLUNTS
BLURTS
BOASTS
BOGOTA
BONITO
BOOSTS
BORATE
BOUNTY
BRACTS
BRANTS
BRATTY
BREATH
BRENTS
BRONTE
BRUITS
BRUNTS
BURSTS
BUTUTS
BYPATH
BYROTE

B••••T
BADLOT
BAGSIT
BALLET
BALLOT
BANDIT
BARBET
BARDOT
BAREST
BARKAT
BASALT
BASEST
BASKET
BASSET
BEATIT
BECKET
BEHEST
BEIRUT
BELOIT
BENOIT
BEREFT
BESANT
BEZANT
BILLET
BIRGIT
BISECT
BISSET
BLEWIT
BLIGHT
BLOWIT
BLUEST
BOBCAT
BOGART
BONMOT
BONNET
BOSKET
BOUGHT
BOWNET
BOWOUT
BOXSET
BRANDT
BREAST
BRECHT
BREVET
BRIGHT
BRUNET
BRYANT
BUCKET
BUDGET
BUFFET
BUGOUT
BULLET
BUMOUT
BURBOT
BURNET
BUYOUT
BYPAST

•BT•••
OBTAIN
OBTEST
OBTUND
OBTUSE

•B•T••
ABATED
ABATES
ABATIS
OBITER
OBSTET

•B••T•
ABBOTS
ABBOTT
ABLATE
ABORTS
EBOATS
OBLATE
UBIETY
UBOATS
UBOLTS

•B•••T
ABBOTT
ABDUCT
ABJECT
ABLAUT
ABLEST
ABRUPT
ABSENT
OBJECT
OBLAST
OBOIST
OBSTET
OBTEST
OBVERT

••BT••
DEBTOR
SUBTLE
SUBTLY

••B•T•
ABBOTS
ABBOTT
AMBATO
AMBITS
ATBATS
CUBITS
DEBATE
DEBITS
DEBUTS
HABITS
JABOTS
JOBETH
KIBITZ
LOBATE
ORBITS
RABATO
REBATE
REBUTS
ROBOTS
RUBATI
RUBATO
SABATO
SABOTS
SUBITO
TUBATE
ZIBETS

••B••T
ABBOTT
ALBEIT
ALBERT
ATBEST
BOBCAT
COBALT
CUBIST
EGBERT
ELBERT
GIBBET
GIBLET
GOBLET
GOBUST
HOBART
HOBBIT
HUBERT
JOBLOT
LABRET
PTBOAT
RABBET
RABBIT
REBENT
REBOLT
REBOOT
ROBERT
ROBUST
RUBOUT
SOBEIT
SUBLET
SUBMIT
SUBSET
TABLET
TOBOOT
TUBIST
TYBALT
UNBELT
UNBENT
UNBOLT
UPBEAT

•••BT•
DOUBTS

•••B•T
ALLBUT
BARBET
BURBOT
COMBAT
GAMBIT
GIBBET
GRABAT
HENBIT
HOBBIT
IROBOT
KOMBAT
KORBUT
NUMBAT
RABBET
RABBIT
SORBET
STABAT
TALBOT
TIDBIT
TITBIT
TURBIT
TURBOT
TWOBIT
WOMBAT
YOUBET

••••BT
INDEBT

BU••••
BUBBLE
BUBBLY
BUCCAL
BUCHAN
BUCKED
BUCKET
BUCKLE
BUCKUP
BUDDED
BUDDHA
BUDGED
BUDGES
BUDGET
BUDGIE
BUENOS
BUFFED
BUFFER
BUFFET
BUFFON
BUFFOS
BUGGED
BUGLED
BUGLER
BUGLES
BUGOFF
BUGOUT
BUILDS
BUJOLD
BULBIL
BULBUL
BULGAR
BULGED
BULGES
BULGUR
BULKED
BULLAE
BULLED
BULLET
BULOVA
BULWER
BUMBLE
BUMBRY
BUMMED
BUMMER
BUMOUT
BUMPED
BUMPER
BUMPPO
BUMPUP
BUMRAP
BUNCHE
BUNCHY
BUNCOS
BUNDLE
BUNGED
BUNGEE
BUNGLE
BUNION
BUNKED
BUNKER
BUNKOS
BUNKUM
BUNSEN
BUNTED
BUNTER
BUNUEL
BUNYAN
BUNYIP
BUOYED
BUOYUP
BUQSHA
BURBLE
BURBLY
BURBOT
BURDEN
BUREAU
BURGAS
BURGEE
BURGER
BURGHS
BURGLE
BURGOO
BURGOS
BURIED
BURIES
BURINS
BURLAP
BURLED
BURLEY
BURMAN
BURNED
BURNER
BURNET
BURNEY
BURNUP
BUROAK
BURPED
BURRED
BURROS
BURROW
BURSAE
BURSAL
BURSAR
BURSAS
BURSES
BURSTS
BURTON
BUSBAR
BUSBOY
BUSHED
BUSHEL
BUSHES
BUSHWA
BUSIED
BUSIER
BUSIES
BUSILY
BUSING
BUSKED
BUSKIN
BUSMAN
BUSMEN
BUSONI
BUSSED
BUSSES
BUSTED
BUSTER
BUSTIN
BUSTLE
BUTANE
BUTENE
BUTEOS
BUTLER
BUTTED
BUTTER
BUTTES
BUTTIN
BUTTON
BUTUNG
BUTUTS
BUYERS
BUYING
BUYOFF
BUYOUT
BUYSUP
BUZZED
BUZZER
BUZZES

B•U•••
BAUBLE
BAUCIS
BAULKS
BEULAH
BEURRE
BHUTAN
BHUTTO
BLUELY
BLUEOX
BLUEST
BLUESY
BLUETS
BLUEYS
BLUFFS
BLUING
BLUISH
BLUNTS
BLURBS
BLURRY
BLURTS
BOUBOU
BOUCLE
BOUDIN
BOUFFE
BOUGHS
BOUGHT
BOULES
BOULEZ
BOULLE
BOUNCE
BOUNCY
BOUNDS
BOUNTY
BOURKE
BOURNE
BOURSE
BOUSED
BOUSES
BRUDER
BRUGES
BRUINS
BRUISE
BRUITS
BRULES
BRUMAL
BRUMBY
BRUMES
BRUNCH
BRUNEI
BRUNET
BRUNTS
BRUSHY
BRUTAL
BRUTES
BRUTUS
BRUXED
BRUXES

B••U••
BABULS
BAGUIO
BAKULA
BARUCH
BATUMI
BEAUTS
BEAUTY
BEGUMS
BELUGA
BEMUSE
BENUMB
BLOUSE
BOSUNS
BREUER
BUNUEL
BUTUNG
BUTUTS

B•••U•
BACKUP
BACKUS
BADGUY
BAGFUL
BALLUP
BANGUI
BANGUP
BANJUL
BANQUO
BANTUS
BARIUM
BARNUM
BARQUE
BARZUN
BASQUE
BATTUE
BAYEUX
BAYOUS
BAYRUM
BEADUP
BEAMUP
BEARUP
BEATUP
BEDAUB
BEDBUG
BEEFUP
BEEGUM
BEFOUL
BEIRUT
BENHUR
BIDSUP
BIGGUN
BIGSUR
BIJOUX
BINDUP
BISQUE
BLEWUP
BLOWUP
BMINUS
BOBSUP
BONEUP
BOOJUM
BOOTUP
BOREUP
BOWOUT
BOXFUL
BRAQUE
BROGUE
BRUTUS
BUCKUP
BUGOUT
BULBUL
BULGUR
BUMOUT
BUMPUP
BUNKUM
BUOYUP
BURNUP
BUYOUT
BUYSUP
BYSSUS

B••••U
BABALU
BALLOU
BATEAU
BISSAU
BOUBOU
BUREAU

•BU•••
ABUKIR
ABUSED
ABUSER
ABUSES
MBUNDU

•B•U••
ABDUCT
ABJURE
ABLUSH
ABOUND
ABRUPT
ABSURD
OBTUND
OBTUSE

•B••U•
ABACUS
ABLAUT
OBELUS
UBIQUE

•B•••U
MBUNDU

••BU••
ALBUMS
AMBUSH
ASBURY
AUBURN
BABULS
COBURG
COBURN
DEBUGS
DEBUNK
DEBUTS
FIBULA
GOBUST
IMBUED
IMBUES
INBULK
KABUKI
LOBULE
NEBULA
REBUFF
REBUKE
REBURY
REBUTS
ROBUST
SUBURB
TABULA
UNBUSY

••B•U•
ARBOUR
BOBSUP
DYBBUK
ELBRUS
ERBIUM
HUBBUB
IMBRUE
LABOUR
LABRUM
LEBRUN
MOBIUS
MRBLUE
PABLUM
RUBOUT
SOBFUL
SUBDUE
SUBGUM
TOBRUK

••B••U
BABALU
JABIRU
SUBARU

•••BU•
AIRBUS
ALLBUT
BEDBUG
BULBUL
DYBBUK
EREBUS
HUBBUB
HUMBUG
KORBUT
LIMBUS
NIMBUS
REDBUD
SOWBUG
WILBUR

•••B•U
BOUBOU

••••BU
MALIBU

B•V•••
BEVELS
BEVIES
BOVARY
BOVIDS
BOVINE
BOVVER

B••V••
BEAVER
BEAVIS
BEEVES
BMOVIE
BOVVER
BRAVAS
BRAVED
BRAVER
BRAVES
BRAVOS
BREVES
BREVET
BREVIS

B•••V•
BEHAVE
BEHOVE
BULOVA
BYJOVE

B••••V
BRASOV

•BV•••
OBVERT

••B••V
RUBLEV

BW••••
BWANAS

B•W•••
BAWLED
BAWLER
BEWAIL
BEWARE
BEWRAY
BOWERS
BOWERY
BOWFIN
BOWING
BOWLED
BOWLER
BOWLES
BOWMAN
BOWMEN
BOWNET
BOWOAR
BOWOUT
BOWSAW
BOWSER
BOWTIE
BOWWOW
BOWYER
BYWAYS
BYWORD

B••W••
BIGWIG
BLEWIT
BLEWUP
BLOWER
BLOWIN
BLOWIT
BLOWSY
BLOWUP
BLOWZY
BOWWOW
BRAWLS
BRAWNY
BREWED
BREWER
BROWNE
BROWNS
BROWNY
BROWSE
BULWER

B•••W•
BEDEWS
BUSHWA
BYLAWS

B••••W
BARROW
BELLOW
BESTOW
BILLOW
BORROW
BOWSAW
BOWWOW
BROKAW
BURROW

•B•W••
OBIWAN

••BW••
COBWEB
SUBWAY

••B•W•
ELBOWS
OXBOWS
UPBOWS

••B••W
HEBREW

•••BW•
OJIBWA

•••B•W
FOGBOW

B•X•••
BAXTER
BOXBOY
BOXCAR
BOXERS
BOXFUL
BOXIER
BOXING
BOXSET
BOXTOP

B••X••
BLIXEN
BRUXED
BRUXES

B•••X•
BILOXI
BORAXO

B••••X
BAYEUX
BENDIX
BIJOUX
BLUEOX
BOLLIX
BRANDX

•B•X••
IBEXES

•••B•X
HATBOX
HOTBOX
ICEBOX
OUTBOX
PAYBOX
SKYBOX

BY••••
BYEBYE
BYGONE
BYGOSH
BYHAND
BYJOVE
BYLAWS
BYLINE
BYNAME
BYPASS
BYPAST
BYPATH
BYPLAY
BYRNES
BYROAD
BYROTE
BYSSHE
BYSSUS
BYTALK
BYWAYS
BYWORD

B•Y•••
BAYARD
BAYEUX
BAYING
BAYLOR
BAYOUS
BAYRUM
BEYOND
BLYTHE
BOYARS
BOYISH
BRYANT
BRYONY
BRYSON
BUYERS
BUYING
BUYOFF
BUYOUT
BUYSUP

B••Y••
BANYAN
BARYON
BATYAM
BOWYER
BRAYED
BRAYER
BREYER
BUNYAN
BUNYIP
BUOYED
BUOYUP

B•••Y•
BELAYS
BLUEYS
BOGEYS
BOLEYN
BYEBYE
BYWAYS

B••••Y
BADBOY
BADGUY
BAILEY
BAKERY
BALDLY
BARELY
BARFLY
BARLEY
BARNEY
BARONY
BASELY
BASIFY
BASSLY
BATBOY
BEACHY
BEATTY
BEAUTY
BEGLEY
BEKESY
BELFRY
BELLAY
BENDAY
BENGAY
BETONY
BETRAY
BETSEY
BEWRAY
BIGAMY
BIGBOY
BINARY
BIRNEY
BISCAY
BLABBY
BLATTY
BLEARY
BLENNY
BLIMEY
BLOCKY
BLOODY
BLOOEY
BLOOMY
BLOTTY
BLOWSY
BLOWZY
BLUELY
BLUESY
BLURRY
BODILY
BOIGNY
BOLDLY
BOLSHY
BOMBAY
BOOTSY
BOSLEY
BOTANY
BOTCHY
BOTFLY
BOUNCY
BOUNTY
BOVARY
BOWERY
BOXBOY
BRACHY
BRAINY
BRANDY
BRANNY
BRASHY
BRASSY
BRATTY
BRAWNY
BREEZY
BRICKY
BRIERY
BROLLY
BRONZY
BROODY
BROOKY
BROOMY
BROWNY
BRUMBY
BRUSHY
BRYONY
BUBBLY
BUMBRY
BUNCHY
BURBLY
BURLEY
BURNEY
BUSBOY
BUSILY
BYPLAY

•BY•••
ABYDOS
ABYING
ABYSMS

•B•Y••
OBEYED

•B••Y•
ABBEYS

•B•••Y
ABBACY
EBERLY
UBIETY

••BY••
LIBYAN
SIBYLS

••B•Y•
ABBEYS
EMBAYS
EMBRYO
POBOYS
RIBEYE

••B••Y
ABBACY
ALBANY
AMBERY
ASBURY
AUBREY
BUBBLY
DABNEY
EMBODY
FABRAY
HUBBLY
MOBLEY
NOBODY
NUBBLY
PEBBLY
REBURY
ROBROY
RUBBLY
RUBIFY
SUBTLY
SUBWAY
UNBUSY
WOBBLY

•••BY•
BYEBYE
FLYBYS
LAYBYS
LIEBYS

•••B•Y
BADBOY
BATBOY
BIGBOY
BLABBY
BOMBAY
BOXBOY
BUBBLY
BUMBRY
BURBLY
BUSBOY
CARBOY
CHUBBY
CLUBBY
COWBOY
CRABBY
DAYBOY
DOUBLY
DRABLY
DUMBLY
FEEBLY
FLABBY
FLYBOY
GLIBLY
GRABBY
GRUBBY
HUBBLY
HUMBLY
KNOBBY
LAZBOY
LOWBOY
MARBLY
MUMBLY
NIMBLY
NUBBLY
NUMBLY
OLDBOY
PEBBLY
REDBAY
RUBBLY
RUMBLY
SCABBY
SHABBY
SLOBBY
SNOBBY
SNUBBY
STABLY
STUBBY
SWABBY
TOMBOY
TREBLY
USABLY
VIABLY
WAMBLY
WOBBLY

••••BY
BLABBY
BRUMBY
CAMEBY
CHUBBY
CLUBBY
COMEBY
CRABBY
CROSBY
CRUMBY
DOESBY
DROPBY
FLABBY
GATSBY
GETSBY
GOESBY
GONEBY
GOODBY
GRABBY
GRUBBY
HARDBY
HEREBY
KNOBBY
LAIDBY
LAYSBY
NASEBY
NEARBY
PASSBY
PHILBY
PUTSBY
SCABBY
SETSBY
SHABBY
SITSBY
SLOBBY
SNOBBY
SNUBBY
STUBBY
SWABBY
TRILBY
WENTBY

B•Z•••
BAZAAR
BEZANT
BEZELS
BUZZED
BUZZER
BUZZES

B••Z••
BAIZAS
BALZAC
BANZAI
BARZUN
BENZOL
BLAZED
BLAZER
BLAZES
BLAZON
BONZES
BORZOI
BRAZED
BRAZEN
BRAZER
BRAZES
BRAZIL
BRAZOS
BRAZZA
BRAZZI
BUZZED
BUZZER
BUZZES

B•••Z•
BEDAZE
BELIZE
BLOWZY
BRAZZA
BRAZZI
BREEZE
BREEZY
BRONZE
BRONZY

B••••Z
BLINTZ
BOULEZ
BRIENZ

•B••Z•
ABLAZE

••B•Z•
REBOZO

••B••Z
KIBITZ
TABRIZ

CA••••
CABALA
CABALS
CABANA
CABBED
CABBIE
CABERS
CABINS
CABLED

CABLER
CABLES
CACAOS
CACHED
CACHES
CACHET
CACHOU
CACKLE
CACTUS
CADDIE
CADDIS
CADENT
CADETS
CADGED
CADGER
CADGES
CADMIC
CADMUS
CADRES
CAESAR
CAFTAN
CAGERS
CAGIER
CAGILY
CAGING
CAGNEY
CAGUAS
CAHIER
CAHOWS
CAICOS
CAIMAN
CAIQUE
CAIRNS
CAJOLE
CAJUNS
CAKIER
CAKING
CALAIS
CALASH
CALCES
CALDER
CALICO
CALIPH
CALKED
CALLAO
CALLAS
CALLED
CALLER
CALLES
CALLIN
CALLON
CALLOW
CALLUP
CALLUS
CALMED
CALMER
CALMLY
CALPAC
CALQUE
CALVED
CALVES
CALVIN
CALXES
CAMARO
CAMBER
CAMDEN
CAMEAT
CAMEBY
CAMEIN
CAMELS
CAMEON
CAMEOS
CAMERA
CAMETO
CAMEUP
CAMINO
CAMION
CAMISE
CAMLET
CAMPED
CAMPER
CAMPOS
CAMPUS
CANAAN
CANADA
CANALS
CANAPE
CANARD
CANARY
CANCAN
CANCEL
CANCUN
CANDID
CANDLE
CANDOR
CANERS
CANFUL
CANIDS
CANIER
CANIFF
CANINE
CANING
CANKER
CANLIT
CANNAE
CANNED
CANNEL
CANNER
CANNES
CANNON
CANNOT
CANOED
CANOES
CANOLA
CANONS
CANOPY
CANOVA
CANTAB
CANTED
CANTER
CANTHI
CANTLE
CANTON
CANTOR
CANTOS
CANUTE
CANVAS
CANYON
CAPERS
CAPFUL
CAPGUN
CAPIAS
CAPITA
CAPLET
CAPNUT
CAPONE
CAPONS
CAPOTE
CAPPED
CAPPER
CAPRIS
CAPSID
CAPTAN
CAPTOR
CARAFE
CARATS
CARBON
CARBOS
CARBOY
CARDED
CARDER
CARDIN
CARDIO
CAREEN
CAREER
CARESS
CARETO
CARETS
CARFUL
CARGOS
CARHOP
CARIBE
CARIBS
CARIES
CARINA
CARING
CARKED
CARLIN
CARLOS
CARLOT
CARMAN
CARMEL
CARMEN
CARNAL
CARNES
CARNET
CARNEY
CARNOT
CAROBS
CAROLE
CAROLS
CAROMS
CARONI
CARPAL
CARPED
CARPEL
CARPER
CARPET
CARPUS
CARREL
CARREY
CARRIE
CARROL
CARROT
CARSON
CARTED
CARTEL
CARTER
CARTES
CARTON
CARUSO
CARVED
CARVER
CARVES
CARVEY
CASABA
CASALS
CASAVA
CASBAH
CASEFY
CASERN
CASHED
CASHES
CASHEW
CASHIN
CASING
CASINO
CASPAR
CASPER
CASQUE
CASSIA
CASSIO
CASSIS
CASTER
CASTES
CASTLE
CASTON
CASTOR
CASTRO
CASUAL
CATCHY
CATENA
CATERS
CATGUT
CATHAY
CATHER
CATION
CATKIN
CATNAP
CATNIP
CATRIG
CATSUP
CATTED
CATTLE
CATTON
CAUCHO
CAUCHY
CAUCUS
CAUDAL
CAUDEX
CAUDLE
CAUGHT
CAULKS
CAUSAL
CAUSED
CAUSES
CAVEAT
CAVEIN
CAVELL
CAVERN
CAVERS
CAVETT
CAVIAR
CAVILS
CAVING
CAVITY
CAVORT
CAWDOR
CAWING
CAXTON
CAYMAN
CAYUGA
CAYUSE

C•A•••

CEASED
CEASES
CHACHA
CHACMA
CHADOR
CHAFED
CHAFES
CHAFFS
CHAFFY
CHAINE
CHAINS
CHAIRS
CHAISE
CHALCO
CHALET
CHALKS
CHALKY
CHAMMY
CHAMPS
CHANCE
CHANCY
CHANEL
CHANEY
CHANGE
CHANTS
CHAPEL
CHAPIN
CHARGE
CHARLY
CHARMS
CHARON
CHARRO
CHARTS
CHASED
CHASER
CHASES
CHASMS
CHASSE
CHASTE
CHATTY
CHATUP
CHAVEZ
CIARDI
CLACKS
CLAIMS
CLAIRE
CLAMMY
CLAMOR
CLAMPS
CLAMUP
CLANCY
CLANGS
CLANKS
CLANKY
CLAQUE
CLARET
CLARKE
CLAROS
CLASPS
CLASSY
CLAUDE
CLAUSE
CLAVES
CLAVIN
CLAWED
CLAWER
CLAYEY
CMAJOR
COALER
COAPTS
COARSE
COASTS
COATED
COATIS
COAXED
COAXER
COAXES
CRABBE
CRABBY
CRACKS
CRACKY
CRADLE
CRAFTS
CRAFTY
CRAGGY
CRAKES
CRAMBO
CRAMPS
CRANED
CRANES
CRANIA
CRANIO
CRANKS
CRANKY
CRANNY
CRAPES
CRATED
CRATER
CRATES
CRAVAT
CRAVED
CRAVEN
CRAVER
CRAVES
CRAWLS
CRAWLY
CRAYON
CRAZED
CRAZES
CYANIC

C••A••

CABALA
CABALS
CABANA
CACAOS
CALAIS
CALASH
CAMARO
CANAAN
CANADA
CANALS
CANAPE
CANARD
CANARY
CARAFE
CARATS
CASABA
CASALS
CASAVA
CCLAMP
CEDANT
CEDARS
CERATE
CESARE
CETANE
CHEAPO
CHEATS
CHIANG
CHIAUS
CHOATE
CICADA
CIGARS
CITATO
CLEANS
CLEARS
CLEATS
CLEAVE
CLOACA
CLOAKS
COBALT
COLADA
COMATE
CONANT
COPAYS
CORALS
COWARD
CREAKS
CREAKY
CREAMS
CREAMY
CREASE
CREASY
CREATE
CROAKS
CROAKY
CROATS
CSHARP
CUBAGE
CUIABA
CUNARD
CUNAXA
CURACY
CURARE
CURATE
CUSACK
CYCADS
CYRANO

C•••A•

CAESAR
CAFTAN
CAGUAS
CAIMAN
CALLAO
CALLAS
CALPAC
CAMEAT
CANAAN
CANCAN
CANNAE
CANTAB
CANVAS
CAPIAS
CAPTAN
CARMAN
CARNAL
CARPAL
CASBAH
CASPAR
CASUAL
CATHAY
CATNAP
CAUDAL
CAUSAL
CAVEAT
CAVIAR
CAYMAN
CEIBAS
CELLAE
CELLAR
CEREAL
CESTAS
CHELAE
CHELAS
CHEVAL
CHIRAC
CHORAL
CHUKAR
CIUDAD
CLIMAX
CNIDAE
COBHAM
COBIAS
COBRAS
COCOAS
COEVAL
COGNAC
COLFAX
COLLAR
COLMAN
COMBAT
COMEAT
COMMAS
COMPAQ
COMSAT
CONFAB
CONGAS
CONMAN
CONRAD
CONTAC
CONWAY
COOGAN
CORBAN
CORDAY
CORMAN
CORRAL
COSTAE
COSTAL
COSTAR
COSTAS
COTTAS
COUGAR
COWMAN
CRAVAT
CRETAN
CRURAL
CUNEAL
CUPPAS
CURIAE
CURIAL
CUSHAW
CYCLAS
CYMBAL

C••••A

CABALA
CABANA
CAMERA
CANADA
CANOLA
CANOVA
CAPITA
CARINA
CASABA
CASAVA
CASSIA
CATENA
CAYUGA
CESSNA
CETERA
CHACHA
CHACMA
CHICHA
CHOLLA
CHOPRA
CHROMA
CHUKKA
CIBOLA
CICADA
CINEMA
CLOACA
COLADA
COLIMA
CONCHA
CONTRA
COPULA
CORNEA
CORONA
CORYZA
COULDA
COVINA
COWPEA
CRANIA
CRENNA
CREUSA
CRIMEA
CUESTA
CUIABA
CUNAXA
CUPOLA

•CA•••

ACACIA
ACADIA
ACAJOU
ACARID
ACARUS
ECARTE
ICARIA
ICARUS
MCADAM
MCADOO
OCASEK
OCASEY
SCABBY
SCALAR
SCALDS
SCALED
SCALER
SCALES
SCALIA
SCALPS
SCAMPI
SCAMPS
SCANTS
SCANTY
SCAPED
SCAPES
SCARAB
SCARCE
SCARED
SCARER
SCARES
SCARFS
SCARNE
SCARPS
SCARRY
SCARUM
SCATHE
SCATTY
SCAUPS

•C•A••

ACHAEA
ACKACK
ACUATE
CCLAMP
ECLAIR
ECLATS
ICEAGE
LCHAIM
MCBAIN
MCCABE
MCCANN
MCHALE
MCLAIN
MCNAIR
OCEANS
OCTADS
OCTANE
OCTANT
OCTAVE
OCTAVO
SCLAFF
SCRAGS
SCRAMS
SCRAPE
SCRAPS
SCRAWL
UCLANS

•C••A•

ACETAL
ACTSAS
ACTUAL
ICEBAG
ICECAP
ICEMAN
MCADAM
MCGRAW
MCLEAN
OCREAE
OCULAR
SCALAR
SCARAB
SCENAS
SCHWAB
SCHWAS
SCREAK
SCREAM
SCUBAS

•C•••A

ACACIA
ACADIA
ACEDIA
ACHAEA
ICARIA
MCCREA
RCCOLA
SCALIA
SCHEMA
SCLERA
SCORIA
SCOTIA
SCYLLA

••CA••

ALCAPP
ARCADE
ARCANA
ARCANE
ARCARO
BACALL
BECALM
BECAME
BICARB
CACAOS
CICADA
CYCADS
DACAPO
DECADE
DECAFS
DECALS
DECAMP
DECANT
DECAYS
DUCATS
ENCAGE
ENCAMP
ENCASE
ESCAPE
ESCARP
FACADE
GOCART
HECATE
IDCARD
INCANS
INCASE
INCASH
JACALS
JACANA
JICAMA
LOCALE
LOCALS
LOCATE
MACACO
MACAWS
MCCABE
MCCANN
NICAEA
ONCALL
OSCARS
OXCART
PECANS
PICABO
PICARA
PICARD
PICARO
RECALL
RECANE
RECANT
RECAPS
RECAST
SECANT
SOCAGE
TICALS
TUCANA
UNCAGE
UNCAPS
UNCASE
UPCAST
VACANT
VACATE
VICARS
VOCALS

••C•A•

ARCTAN
ASCHAM
BUCCAL
BUCHAN
COCOAS
CYCLAS
DACHAS
DUCTAL
FACIAL
FACIAS
JACKAL
LUCIAN
MACRAE
MECCAS
MICMAC
MOCHAS
NECTAR
NICEAN
NUCHAE
NUCHAL
PACMAN
PECKAT
PICKAT
PICKAX
RACIAL
RECOAT
SACRAL
SOCIAL
SUCHAS
SUCKAS
TICTAC
UNCIAL
UNCLAD
VACLAV
WICCAN
YUCCAS

••C••A

ANCONA
ARCANA
CICADA
ENCINA
FACULA
HECUBA
ISCHIA
JACANA
JICAMA
LACUNA
MACULA
MCCREA
MUCOSA
NICAEA
NICOLA
OSCULA
PICARA
RCCOLA
TACOMA
TUCANA
VICUNA

•••CA•

ABACAS
ABSCAM
APICAL
ARECAS
ASHCAN
BARCAR
BISCAY
BOBCAT
BOXCAR
BUCCAL
CANCAN
DORCAS
DUNCAN
EPICAL
FATCAT
FISCAL
FRACAS
GASCAP
HEPCAT
HOTCAP
HOTCAR
HUBCAP
ICECAP
IPECAC
LASCAR
LOWCAL
MADCAP
MECCAS
MESCAL
MOBCAP
MUDCAT
MUSCAT
NASCAR
OILCAN
PARCAE
PASCAL
PLICAE
RASCAL
REDCAP
REXCAT
SKYCAP
SNOCAT
SPICAS
THECAE
THECAL
TINCAL
TINCAN
TOECAP
TOMCAT
TOPCAT
TOUCAN
TOWCAR
TROCAR
TUSCAN
UNOCAL
VULCAN
WICCAN
YUCCAS

•••C•A

ACACIA
ALICIA
BETCHA
CHACHA
CHACMA
CHICHA
CONCHA
EJECTA
EXACTA
FASCIA
FLICKA
FULCRA
GARCIA
GOTCHA
JASCHA
KWACHA
MANCHA
MARCIA
MISCHA
MURCIA
PERCHA
SANCTA
TRICIA

••••CA

AFRICA
ALPACA
ARNICA
ATTICA
BIANCA
BLANCA
CLOACA
DESICA
DODECA
EROICA
FRANCA
FRESCA
ITASCA
ITHACA
KONICA
LEXICA
LORICA
MARACA
MONICA
OAXACA
PATACA
SENECA
SILICA
SIRICA
TOLUCA
TUNICA

C•B•••

CABALA
CABALS
CABANA
CABBED
CABBIE
CABERS
CABINS
CABLED
CABLER
CABLES
CIBOLA
COBALT
COBBLE
COBHAM
COBIAS
COBRAS
COBURG
COBURN
COBWEB
CUBAGE
CUBEBS
CUBICS
CUBING
CUBISM
CUBIST
CUBITS
CUBOID
CYBELE
CYBILL
CYBORG

C••B••

CABBED
CABBIE
CAMBER
CARBON
CARBOS
CARBOY
CASBAH
CEIBAS
CHUBBY
CLUBBY
COBBLE
COMBAT
COMBED
COMBER
COMBES
COMBOS
CORBAN
CORBEL
CORBIN
COWBOY
CRABBE
CRABBY
CUMBER
CURBED
CYMBAL

C•••B•

CAMEBY
CARIBE
CARIBS
CAROBS
CASABA
CELEBS
CHUBBY
CLIMBS
CLUBBY
COMEBY
CRABBE
CRABBY
CRAMBO
CROSBY
CRUMBS
CRUMBY
CUBEBS
CUIABA

C••••B

CANTAB
CHERUB
COBWEB
CONFAB
CONJOB

•CB•••

MCBAIN

•C•B••

ICEBAG
ICEBOX
SCABBY
SCUBAS

•C••B•

ACHEBE
MCCABE
MCJOBS
SCABBY
SCRIBE
SCRUBS

•C•••B

SCARAB
SCHWAB

••C•B•

HECUBA
JACOBI
MCCABE
PICABO
TYCOBB

••C••B

BICARB
TYCOBB

CC••••

CCLAMP

C•C•••

CACAOS
CACHED
CACHES
CACHET
CACHOU
CACKLE
CACTUS
CECILE
CECILY
CICADA
CICELY
CICERO
COCCID
COCCUS
COCCYX
COCHIN
COCKED
COCKER
COCKLE
COCOAS
COCOON
CUCKOO
CYCADS
CYCLAS
CYCLED
CYCLER
CYCLES
CYCLIC
CYCLOS

C••C••

CAICOS
CALCES
CANCAN
CANCEL
CANCUN
CATCHY
CAUCHO
CAUCHY
CAUCUS
CHACHA
CHACMA
CHECKS
CHICHA
CHICHI
CHICKS
CHICLE
CHICLY
CHOCKS
CHUCKS
CIRCLE
CIRCUM
CIRCUS
CISCOS
CLACKS
CLICHE
CLICKS
CLOCHE
CLOCKS
CLUCKS
COCCID
COCCUS
COCCYX
CONCHA
CONCHS
CONCUR
CRACKS
CRACKY
CRECHE
CRICKS
CROCKS
CROCUS
CRUCES
CZECHS

C•••C•

CALICO
CHALCO
CHANCE
CHANCY
CHEECH
CHINCH
CHOICE
CHURCH
CIVICS
CLANCY
CLENCH
CLINCH
CLOACA
CLUTCH
COERCE
COMICS
CONICS
CONOCO
CRISCO
CROUCH
CRUNCH
CRUTCH
CUBICS
CURACY
CUSACK
CYNICS

C••••C

CADMIC
CALPAC
CEDRIC
CELTIC
CHIRAC
CITRIC
CLERIC
CLINIC
COGNAC
CONTAC
COPTIC
COSMIC
COURIC
CRITIC
CULTIC
CUPRIC
CYANIC
CYCLIC
CYMRIC

•CC•••
ACCEDE ACCENT ACCEPT ACCESS ACCORD ACCOST ACCRUE ACCUSE ECCLES MCCABE MCCANN MCCREA OCCULT OCCUPY OCCURS RCCOLA

•C•C••
ACACIA ICECAP ICICLE

•C••C•
ACKACK OCLOCK SCARCE SCHICK SCONCE SCORCH SCOTCH SCUTCH

•C•••C
ACETIC ACIDIC ECESIC ECHOIC ICONIC SCENIC

••CC••
ARCCOS BOCCIE BUCCAL COCCID COCCUS COCCYX HICCUP MECCAS PICCHU SICCED SOCCER SUCCES SUCCOR WICCAN YUCCAS

••C•C•
BOCHCO DECOCT MACACO ROCOCO

••C••C
ARCTIC CYCLIC HECTIC LACTIC MICMAC PECTIC PICNIC TACTIC TICTAC UNCHIC

•••CC•
STUCCO

•••C•C
IPECAC

CD••••
CDROMS

C•D•••
CADDIE CADDIS CADENT CADETS CADGED CADGER CADGES CADMIC CADMUS CADRES CEDANT CEDARS CEDING CEDRIC CIDERS CODDLE CODERS CODGER CODIFY CODING CODONS CUDDLE CUDDLY CUDGEL CYDERS

C••D••
CADDIE CADDIS CALDER CAMDEN CANDID CANDLE CANDOR CARDED CARDER CARDIN CARDIO CAUDAL CAUDEX CAUDLE CAWDOR CHADOR CHIDED CHIDER CHIDES CINDER CIUDAD CLODDY CNIDAE CNIDUS CODDLE COEDIT COLDER COLDLY CONDOR CONDOS COODER CORDAY CORDED CORDON CRADLE CREDIT CREDOS CRUDDY CRUDER CUDDLE CUDDLY CURDED CURDLE

C•••D•
CANADA CANIDS CHILDE CHILDS CHORDS CIARDI CICADA CLAUDE CLODDY CLOUDS CLOUDY COLADA COMEDY COULDA CREEDS CROWDS CRUDDY CUPIDS CYCADS

C••••D
CABBED CABLED CACHED CADGED CALKED CALLED CALMED CALVED CAMPED CANARD CANDID CANNED CANOED CANTED CAPPED CAPSID CARDED CARKED CARPED CARTED CARVED CASHED CATTED CAUSED CEASED CEILED CELLED CENSED CERVID CESSED CHAFED CHASED CHEWED CHIDED CHIMED CHOKED CHOWED CHUTED CIUDAD CLAWED CLEPED CLEWED CLONED CLOSED CLOYED COATED COAXED COCCID COCKED COGGED COIFED COILED COINED COMBED CONFED CONKED CONNED CONOID CONRAD COOKED COOLED COOPED COPIED COPPED CORDED CORKED CORNED COSHED COSIED COWARD COWLED COZIED CRANED CRATED CRAVED CRAZED CREWED CROWED CUBOID CUFFED CULLED CUNARD CUPPED CURBED CURDED CURLED CURRED CURSED CURVED CUSPED CUSPID CUSSED CYCLED

•C•D••
ACADIA ACEDIA ACIDIC ACIDLY ICEDIN ICEDUP MCADAM MCADOO

•C••D•
ACCEDE OCTADS SCALDS SCENDS SCOLDS SCRODS

•C•••D
ACARID ACCORD ECHOED SCALED SCAPED SCARED SCOPED SCORED SCREED

••C•D•
ACCEDE ARCADE CICADA CYCADS DECADE DECIDE DECODE ENCODE ESCUDO FACADE RECEDE RECODE SECEDE

••C••D
ACCORD ARCHED ASCEND BACHED BACKED BUCKED CACHED COCCID COCKED CYCLED DECKED DOCKED DUCKED EMCEED ETCHED EUCLID EXCEED FECUND HACKED HOCKED IDCARD INCHED ITCHED JACKED JOCUND KICKED LACKED LICKED LOCKED LUCKED MOCKED MUCKED NECKED NICKED ORCHID PACKED PECKED PICARD PICKED RACKED RECORD RICKED ROCKED RUCKED SACKED SACRED SECOND SICCED SOCKED SUCKED TACKED TICKED TUCKED UNCLAD WICKED YACKED

•••C•D
BRACED COCCID DANCED DEICED DEUCED EDUCED FARCED FENCED FORCED GRACED JUICED LANCED MERCED MINCED PIECED PLACED PLACID PRICED RANCID SAUCED SICCED SLICED SPACED SPICED SYNCED TALCED TRACED TRICED VISCID VOICED WINCED

CE••••
CEASED CEASES CECILE CECILY CEDANT CEDARS CEDING CEDRIC CEIBAS CEILED CELEBS CELERY CELINE CELLAE CELLAR CELLED CELLOS CELTIC CEMENT CENOTE CENSED CENSER CENSES CENSOR CENSUS CENTER CENTOS CENTRE CENTRI CENTRO CEORLS CERATE CEREAL CEREUS CERIPH CERISE CERIUM CERMET CERROS CERTIF CERUSE CERVID CESARE CESIUM CESSED CESSES CESSNA CESTAS CESTOS CESTUS CETANE CETERA CEYLON

C•E•••
CAESAR CHEAPO CHEATS CHECKS CHEECH CHEEKS CHEEKY CHEEPS CHEERS CHEERY CHEESE CHEESY CHEKOV CHELAE CHELAS CHEMIN CHENIN CHEOPS CHEQUE CHERIE CHERRY CHERTY CHERUB CHERYL CHESTS CHESTY CHETHS CHEVAL CHEVET CHEVRE CHEWED CHEWER CHEWUP CLEANS CLEARS CLEATS CLEAVE CLEEKS CLEESE CLEFTS CLENCH CLEPED CLERGY CLERIC CLERKS CLEVER CLEVES CLEVIS CLEWED COEDIT COELOM COERCE COEVAL CREAKS CREAKY CREAMS CREAMY CREASE CREASY CREATE CRECHE CREDIT CREDOS CREEDS CREEKS CREELS CREEPS CREEPY CREMES CRENEL CRENNA CREOLE CREPES CRESOL CRESTS CRETAN CRETIN CREUSA CREWED CREWEL CUESTA CZECHS CZERNY

C••E••
CABERS CADENT CADETS CAGERS CAMEAT CAMEBY CAMEIN CAMELS CAMEON CAMEOS CAMERA CAMETO CAMEUP CANERS CAPERS CAREEN CAREER CARESS CARETO CARETS CASEFY CASERN CATENA CATERS CAVEAT CAVEIN CAVELL CAVERN CAVERS CAVETT CELEBS CELERY CEMENT CEREAL CEREUS CETERA CHEECH CHEEKS CHEEKY CHEEPS CHEERS CHEERY CHEESE CHEESY CHIEFS CICELY CICERO CIDERS CINEMA CITERS CIVETS CLEEKS CLEESE CLIENT CLUEIN CODERS COGENT COHEIR COHERE COLEUS COMEAT COMEBY COMEDY COMEIN COMELY COMEON COMERS COMETH COMETO COMETS COMEUP CONEYS COOERS CORERS COSELL COVENS COVENT COVERS COVERT COVETS COVEYS COWENS COWERS COYEST COZENS CREEDS CREEKS CREELS CREEPS CREEPY CRIERS CRUETS CRYERS CUBEBS CULETS CUNEAL CUPELS CURERS CUTELY CUTEST CUTESY CUVEES CYBELE CYDERS

C•••E•
CABBED CABLED CABLER CABLES CACHED CACHES CACHET CADGED CADGER CADGES CADRES CAGIER CAGNEY CAHIER CAKIER CALCES CALDER CALKED CALLED CALLER CALLES CALMED CALMER CALVED CALVES CALXES CAMBER CAMDEN CAMLET CAMPED CAMPER CANCEL CANIER CANKER CANNED CANNEL CANNER CANNES CANOED CANOES CANTED CANTER CAPLET CAPPED CAPPER CARDED CARDER CAREEN CAREER CARIES CARKED CARMEL CARMEN CARNES CARNET CARNEY CARPED CARPEL CARPER CARPET CARREL CARREY CARTED CARTEL CARTER CARTES CARVED CARVER CARVES CARVEY CASHED CASHES CASHEW CASPER CASTER CASTES CATHER CATTED CAUDEX CAUSED CAUSES CEASED CEASES CEILED CELLED CENSED CENSER CENSES CENTER CERMET CESSED CESSES CHAFED CHAFES CHALET CHANEL CHANEY CHAPEL CHASED CHASER CHASES CHAVEZ CHEVET CHEWED CHEWER CHIDED CHIDER CHIDES CHIMED CHIMES CHINES CHISEL CHIVES CHOKED CHOKER CHOKES CHOLER CHORES CHOSEN CHOWED CHUTED CHUTES CINDER CIPHER CISKEI CITIES CLARET CLAVES CLAWED CLAWER CLAYEY CLEPED CLEVER CLEVES CLEWED CLIMES CLINES CLONED CLONES CLOSED CLOSER CLOSES CLOSET CLOVEN CLOVER CLOVES CLOYED CNOTES COALER COATED COAXED COAXER COAXES COBWEB COCKED COCKER CODGER COFFEE COFFER COGGED COIFED COILED COINED COINER COKIER COLDER COLIES COLLET COLTER COMBED COMBER COMBES COMPEL COMTES CONFED CONFER CONGER CONIES CONKED CONKER CONMEN CONNED CONNER CONTES CONVEX CONVEY COODER COOKED COOKER COOLED COOLER COONEY COOPED COOPER COOTER COPIED COPIER COPIES COPLEY COPPED COPPER COPSES COPTER COQUET CORBEL CORDED CORKED CORKER CORNEA CORNED CORNEL CORNER CORNET CORREL CORSET CORTES CORTEX CORTEZ CORVEE CORVES COSHED COSHES COSIED COSIER COSIES COSSET COTTEN COTTER COULEE COUPES COUTER COWLED COWLEY COWMEN COWPEA COWPER COZIED COZIER COZIES CRAKES CRANED CRANES CRAPES CRATED CRATER CRATES CRAVED CRAVEN CRAVER CRAVES CRAZED CRAZES CREMES CRENEL CREPES CREWED CREWEL CRIKEY CRIMEA CRIMES CRIPES CRISES CRONES CROWED CROWER CROZES CRUCES CRUDER CRUSES CRUXES CUDGEL CUFFED CULLED CULLEN CULLER CULLET CULVER CUMBER CUPPED CURBED CURDED CURFEW CURLED CURLER CURLEW CURLEY CURRED CURSED CURSES CURTER CURVED CURVES CURVET CUSPED CUSSED CUSSES CUSTER CUTIES CUTLER CUTLET CUTTER CUVEES CYCLED CYCLER CYCLES CYGNET CYPHER

C••••E
CABBIE CACKLE CADDIE CAIQUE CAJOLE CALQUE CAMISE CANAPE CANDLE CANINE CANNAE CANTLE CANUTE CAPONE CAPOTE CARAFE CARIBE CAROLE CARRIE CASQUE CASTLE CATTLE CAUDLE CAYUSE CECILE CELINE CELLAE CENOTE CENTRE CERATE CERISE CERUSE CESARE CETANE CHAINE CHAISE CHANCE CHANGE CHARGE CHASSE CHASTE CHEESE CHELAE CHEQUE CHERIE CHEVRE CHICLE CHIGOE CHILDE CHILOE CHOATE CHOICE CHOOSE CHROME CINQUE CIRCLE CIRQUE CLAIRE CLAQUE CLARKE CLAUDE CLAUSE CLEAVE CLEESE CLICHE CLIQUE CLOCHE CLOQUE CLOTHE CNIDAE COARSE COBBLE COCKLE CODDLE COERCE COFFEE COHERE COHUNE COLLIE COMATE CONNIE CONTRE CONURE COOKIE COOTIE CORVEE COSINE COSTAE COULEE COUPLE COURSE COWRIE COYOTE CRABBE CRADLE CREASE CREATE CRECHE CREOLE CRINGE CROSSE CROUSE CROUTE CRUISE CRUSOE CUBAGE CUDDLE CUIQUE CUISSE CURARE CURATE CURDLE CURIAE CURULE CYBELE

•CE•••
ACEDIA ACEOUS ACEOUT ACESUP ACETAL ACETIC ACETYL BCELLS ECESIC ECESIS ICEAGE ICEBAG ICEBOX ICECAP ICEDIN ICEDUP ICEFOG ICEMAN ICEMEN ICEOUT ICESIN ICESUP OCEANS OCELLI OCELOT SCENAS SCENDS SCENES SCENIC SCENTS

•C•E••
ACCEDE ACCENT ACCEPT ACCESS ACHEBE ACHENE ICIEST MCLEAN OCHERS OCHERY OCREAE OCTETS SCHELL SCHEMA SCHEME SCLERA SCLERO SCREAK SCREAM SCREED SCREEN SCREES SCREWS SCREWY

•C••E•
ACHAEA ACHIER ACUMEN ECCLES ECHOED ECHOES ECOLES ICEMEN ICKIER MCCREA MCGREW MCKUEN OCASEK OCASEY OCHRES SCALED SCALER SCALES SCAPED SCAPES SCARED SCARER SCARES SCENES SCHLEP SCONES SCOPED SCOPES SCORED SCORER SCORES SCOTER SCREED SCREEN SCREES SCUTES

•C•••E
ACCEDE ACCRUE ACCUSE ACHEBE ACHENE ACTIVE ACTONE ACUATE ECARTE

ECTYPE ICEAGE ICICLE MCCABE MCHALE OCREAE OCTANE OCTAVE SCARCE SCARNE SCATHE SCHEME SCONCE SCOUSE SCRAPE SCRIBE SCURVE SCYTHE

••CE••

ACCEDE ACCENT ACCEPT ACCESS ASCEND ASCENT BICEPS CICELY CICERO DECEIT DECENT DICERS DOCENT EMCEED EMCEES EOCENE ESCENT EXCEED EXCELS EXCEPT EXCESS FACETS FACEUP HACEKS INCEPT LACERS LACEUP LUCENT LYCEES LYCEUM MACEIO NICEAN NICELY NICENE NICEST NICETY NOCENT PACERS RACEME RACERS RECEDE RECENT RECESS RICERS SECEDE SECERN ULCERS

••C•E•

AACHEN ANCIEN ARCHED ARCHER ARCHES BACHED BACKED BACKER BECKER BECKET BICKER BUCKED BUCKET CACHED CACHES CACHET COCKED COCKER CYCLED CYCLER CYCLES DECKED DECKER DECREE DICIER DICKER DICKEY DOCKED DOCKER DOCKET DUCKED ECCLES EMCEED EMCEES ESCHER ESCHEW ETCHED ETCHER ETCHES EXCEED FACIES FICHES HACKED HACKER HICKEY HOCKED HOCKEY INCHED INCHES ITCHED ITCHES JACKED JACKET JACKEY JOCKEY KICKED KICKER KUCHEN LACHES LACIER LACKED LACKEY LECTER LICHEN LICKED LOCKED LOCKER LOCKET LUCKED LYCEES MACHES MCCREA MICHEL MICKEY MOCKED MOCKER MUCKED NACRES NECKED NICAEA NICHES NICKED NICKEL NICKER NUCLEI NUCLEO PACKED PACKER PACKET PECKED PICKED PICKER PICKET POCKET PUCKER RACHEL RACIER RACKED RACKET RICHEN RICHER RICHES RICKED RICKEY ROCHET ROCKED ROCKER ROCKET RUCHES RUCKED SACHEM SACHET SACKED SACKER SACRED SECKEL SECRET SICCED SICKEN SICKER SOCCER SOCKED SOCKET SOCLES SUCCES SUCKED SUCKER TACKED TACKER TICKED TICKER TICKET TUCKED TUCKER TUCKET UNCLES VACHEL WICKED WICKER WICKET YACKED

••C••E

ACCEDE ACCRUE ACCUSE ALCOVE ARCADE ARCANE ARCHIE BECAME BECOME BOCCIE BUCKLE CACKLE CECILE COCKLE DECADE DECIDE DECKLE DECODE DECREE DOCILE ENCAGE ENCASE ENCODE ENCORE EOCENE ESCAPE EUCHRE EXCISE EXCITE EXCUSE FACADE FACILE FICHTE FICKLE FOCSLE HACKIE HACKLE HECATE HECKLE INCASE INCISE INCITE INCOME INCUSE JACKIE JECKLE JOCOSE LOCALE LOCATE LUCITE MACRAE MCCABE NICENE NICOLE NUCHAE OOCYTE OSCINE PICKLE RACEME RACINE RECANE RECEDE RECIFE RECIPE RECITE RECODE RECUSE RICHIE ROCKNE SACQUE SECEDE SECURE SICKLE SOCAGE TACKLE TECHIE TICKLE UNCAGE UNCASE VACATE

•••CE•

AMICES APICES AVOCET BONCES BRACED BRACER BRACES CALCES CANCEL CRUCES DANCED DANCER DANCES DEICED DEICER DEICES DEUCED DEUCES DUBCEK DULCET DUNCES EDUCED EDUCES FALCES FARCED FARCES FASCES FAUCES FAUCET FENCED FENCER FENCES FORCED FORCER FORCES GLACES GRACED GRACES GROCER JAYCEE JUICED JUICER JUICES LANCED LANCER LANCES LANCET MARCEL MERCED MERCER MINCED MINCER MINCES NIECES NUECES OUNCES PARCEL PENCEL PIECED PIECER PIECES PINCER PISCES PLACED PLACER PLACES PLACET PONCES PRICED PRICER PRICES PRICEY SAUCED SAUCER SAUCES SICCED SLICED SLICER SLICES SOCCER SPACED SPACEK SPACER SPACES SPACEY SPICED SPICES STACEY SUCCES SYNCED TALCED TERCEL TERCET TRACED TRACER TRACES TRACEY TRICED TRICEP TRICES TRUCES UNICEF VINCES VOICED VOICES WENCES WINCED WINCER WINCES

•••C•E

AMECHE APACHE BOCCIE BOUCLE BUNCHE CHICLE CIRCLE CLICHE CLOCHE CRECHE FESCUE FIACRE FLECHE GAUCHE GRACIE ICICLE JAYCEE LOUCHE MARCHE MARCIE MISCUE MUNCIE MUSCLE ORACLE PARCAE PLICAE PROCNE PSYCHE QUICHE RESCUE ROSCOE RUNCIE SEICHE SIECLE SPECIE STACTE THECAE THICKE TOUCHE TROCHE

••••CE

ADDUCE ADVICE ALSACE AMERCE APIECE ATONCE BIERCE BODICE BOUNCE CHANCE CHOICE COERCE DEDUCE DEFACE DEVICE DRYICE EFFACE ELLICE ENLACE ENTICE EUNICE EVINCE FIANCE FIERCE FLEECE FRANCE GLANCE GREECE HORACE IGNACE INDUCE JANICE JOUNCE MALICE MENACE NODICE NOTICE NOVICE NUANCE OFFICE PALACE PEERCE PIERCE PLAICE POLICE POMACE POUNCE PRANCE PRINCE PUMICE PURACE QUINCE REDUCE REFACE RELACE SCARCE SCONCE SEANCE SEDUCE SLUICE SOLACE SOURCE SPLICE SPRUCE STANCE TENACE THENCE THRACE THRICE TIERCE TRANCE UNLACE USANCE VELOCE VENICE VIVACE WHENCE

C•F•••

CAFTAN COFFEE COFFER CUFFED

C••F••

CANFUL CAPFUL CARFUL CHAFED CHAFES CHAFFS CHAFFY CHUFFY CLEFTS CLIFFS CLIFFY COFFEE COFFER COIFED COLFAX COMFIT CONFAB CONFED CONFER CRAFTS CRAFTY CROFTS CUFFED CUPFUL CURFEW

C•••F•

CANIFF CARAFE CASEFY CHAFFS CHAFFY CHIEFS CHUFFY CITIFY CLIFFS CLIFFY CODIFY CRYOFF CUTOFF

C••••F

CANIFF CERTIF CRYOFF CUTOFF

•C•F••

ICEFOG SCIFIS SCOFFS SCUFFS

•C••F•

SCARFS SCHIFF SCLAFF SCOFFS SCRUFF SCUFFS SCURFY

•C•••F

SCHIFF SCLAFF SCRUFF

••C•F•

DECAFS PACIFY RECIFE

•••C•F

UNICEF

C•G•••

CAGERS CAGIER CAGILY CAGING CAGNEY CAGUAS CIGARS COGENT COGGED COGITO COGNAC CYGNET CYGNUS

C••G••

CADGED CADGER CADGES CAPGUN CARGOS CATGUT CAUGHT CHIGOE CLOGGY CLOGUP CODGER COGGED COIGNS CONGAS CONGER CONGOU COOGAN CORGIS COUGAR COUGHS CRAGGY CUDGEL

C•••G•

CAYUGA CHANGE CHARGE CHOUGH CLANGS CLERGY CLINGS CLINGY CLOGGY COLUGO COSIGN CRAGGY CRINGE CUBAGE

C••••G

CAGING CAKING CANING CARING CASING CATRIG CAVING CAWING CEDING CHIANG CITING CLUING COBURG CODING COMING COOING COPING CORING COWING CRYING CUBING CURING CYBORG

•CG•••

MCGRAW MCGREW

•C••G•

ICEAGE ICINGS MCHUGH SCRAGS

•C•••G

ACHING ACTING ICEBAG ICEFOG ICHING

••C•G•

ENCAGE SOCAGE UNCAGE

••C••G

ARCING DICING FACING LACING PACING RACING RICING UNCLOG

CH••••

CHACHA CHACMA CHADOR CHAFED CHAFES CHAFFS CHAFFY CHAINE CHAINS CHAIRS CHAISE CHALCO CHALET CHALKS CHALKY CHAMMY CHAMPS CHANCE CHANCY CHANEL CHANEY CHANGE CHANTS CHAPEL CHAPIN CHARGE CHARLY CHARMS CHARON CHARRO CHARTS CHASED CHASER CHASES CHASMS CHASSE CHASTE CHATTY CHATUP CHAVEZ CHEAPO CHEATS CHECKS CHEECH CHEEKS CHEEKY CHEEPS CHEERS CHEERY CHEESE CHEESY CHEKOV CHELAE CHELAS CHEMIN CHENIN CHEOPS CHEQUE CHERIE CHERRY CHERTY CHERUB CHERYL CHESTS CHESTY CHETHS CHEVAL CHEVET CHEVRE CHEWED CHEWER CHEWUP CHIANG CHIAUS CHICHA CHICHI CHICKS CHICLE CHICLY CHIDED CHIDER CHIDES CHIEFS CHIGOE CHILDE CHILDS CHILLI CHILLS CHILLY CHILOE CHIMED CHIMES CHIMPS CHINCH CHINES CHINKS CHINKY CHINOS CHINTZ CHINUP CHIPIN CHIRAC CHIRON CHIRPS CHIRPY CHIRRS CHISEL CHISOX CHITIN CHITON CHIVES CHLORO CHOATE CHOCKS CHOICE CHOIRS CHOKED CHOKER CHOKES CHOLER CHOLLA CHOLOS CHOMPS CHONJU CHOOSE CHOOSY CHOOYU CHOPIN CHOPPY CHOPRA CHORAL CHORDS CHORES CHORUS CHOSEN CHOUGH CHOWED CHRISM CHROMA CHROME CHROMO CHROMY CHRONO CHUBBY CHUCKS CHUFFY CHUHSI CHUKAR CHUKKA CHUMMY CHUMPS CHUNKS CHUNKY CHURCH CHURLS CHURNS CHURRO CHURRS CHUTED CHUTES CHYRON

C•H•••

CAHIER CAHOWS COHEIR COHERE COHORT COHOST COHUNE CSHARP

C••H••

CACHED CACHES CACHET CACHOU CARHOP CASHED CASHES CASHEW CASHIN CATHAY CATHER CHUHSI CIPHER COBHAM COCHIN COSHED COSHES CUSHAW CYPHER

C•••H•

CANTHI CATCHY CAUCHO CAUCHY CAUGHT CHACHA CHETHS CHICHA CHICHI CLICHE CLOCHE CLOTHE CLOTHO CLOTHS CONCHA CONCHS COUGHS CRECHE CZECHS

C••••H

CALASH CALIPH CASBAH CERIPH CHEECH CHINCH CHOUGH CHURCH CLENCH CLINCH CLUTCH COMETH COYISH CROUCH CRUNCH CRUTCH

•CH•••

ACHAEA ACHEBE ACHENE ACHIER ACHING ECHINO ECHOED ECHOES ECHOIC ICHING ICHTHY LCHAIM MCHALE MCHUGH OCHERS OCHERY OCHRES SCHELL SCHEMA SCHEME SCHICK SCHIFF SCHISM SCHIST SCHIZY SCHLEP SCHMOO SCHMOS SCHNOZ SCHOOL SCHORL SCHULZ SCHUSS SCHWAB SCHWAS VCHIPS

•C••H•

ICHTHY SCATHE SCYTHE

•C•••H

MCHUGH SCORCH SCOTCH SCUTCH

••CH••

AACHEN AHCHOO ANCHOR ARCHED ARCHER ARCHES ARCHIE ARCHLY ARCHON ASCHAM BACHED BOCHCO BUCHAN CACHED CACHES CACHET CACHOU COCHIN DACHAS DUCHIN ESCHER ESCHEW ETCHED ETCHER ETCHES EUCHRE FICHES FICHTE FICHUS INCHED INCHES INCHON ISCHIA ITCHED ITCHES KUCHEN LACHES LICHEN MACHES MACHOS MICHEL MOCHAS NACHOS NICHES NUCHAE NUCHAL ORCHID ORCHIL RACHEL RACHIS RICHEN RICHER RICHES RICHIE RICHLY ROCHET RUCHES SACHEM SACHET SUCHAS TECHIE TECHNO TUCHUN UNCHIC URCHIN VACHEL YACHTS

••C•H•

PICCHU

••C••H

INCASH

•••CH•

AMECHE APACHE BEACHY BETCHA BOTCHY BRACHY BRECHT BUNCHE BUNCHY CATCHY CAUCHO CAUCHY CHACHA CHICHA CHICHI CLICHE CLOCHE CONCHA CONCHS CRECHE CZECHS DRACHM EPOCHS FLECHE GAUCHE GAUCHO GOTCHA HONCHO JASCHA KIMCHI KWACHA LEACHY LITCHI LOUCHE LUNCHY MANCHA MANCHU MARCHE MISCHA MUNCHY NOTCHY ORACHS PANCHO PATCHY PEACHY PERCHA PICCHU PITCHY POACHY PONCHO POUCHY PSYCHE PSYCHO PSYCHS PUNCHY QUICHE RANCHO REECHO SANCHO SEICHE TAICHI TETCHY TORCHY TOUCHE TOUCHY TRACHY TRICHO TROCHE WITCHY

••••CH

ATTACH AVOUCH BARUCH BLANCH BLEACH BLENCH BLOTCH BORSCH BRANCH BREACH BREECH BROACH BROOCH BRUNCH CHEECH CHINCH CHURCH CLENCH CLINCH CLUTCH CROUCH CRUNCH CRUTCH DETACH DRACHM DRENCH EDKOCH ENRICH EPARCH EXARCH FLETCH FLINCH FLITCH FRENCH GLITCH GRINCH GROUCH

HAUNCH
HIRSCH
HITECH
HOOTCH
INARCH
KIRSCH
KITSCH
KLATCH
KVETCH
LAMECH
LAUNCH
MENSCH
MOLOCH
MUNICH
NAUTCH
ORBACH
PAUNCH
PESACH
PLEACH
PREACH
PUTSCH
QUENCH
SAMECH
SCORCH
SCOTCH
SCUTCH
SEARCH
SKETCH
SKITCH
SLOUCH
SMIRCH
SMOOCH
SMUTCH
SNATCH
SNITCH
SPEECH
STANCH
STARCH
STENCH
STITCH
STORCH
SWATCH
SWITCH
THATCH
TRENCH
TWITCH
VOTECH
WRENCH
WRETCH
ZURICH

CI••••
CIARDI
CIBOLA
CICADA
CICELY
CICERO
CIDERS
CIGARS
CILIUM
CINDER
CINEMA
CINQUE
CIPHER
CIRCLE
CIRCUM
CIRCUS
CIRQUE
CIRRUS
CISCOS
CISKEI
CITATO
CITERS
CITIES
CITIFY
CITING
CITIUS
CITRIC
CITRON
CITRUS
CIUDAD
CIVETS
CIVICS

C•I•••
CAICOS
CAIMAN
CAIQUE
CAIRNS
CEIBAS
CEILED
CHIANG
CHIAUS
CHICHA
CHICHI
CHICKS
CHICLE
CHICLY
CHIDED
CHIDER
CHIDES
CHIEFS
CHIGOE
CHILDE
CHILDS
CHILLI
CHILLS
CHILLY
CHILOE
CHIMED
CHIMES
CHIMPS
CHINCH
CHINES
CHINKS
CHINKY
CHINOS
CHINTZ
CHINUP
CHIPIN
CHIRAC
CHIRON
CHIRPS
CHIRPY
CHIRRS
CHISEL
CHISOX
CHITIN
CHITON
CHIVES
CLICHE
CLICKS
CLIENT
CLIFFS
CLIFFY
CLIMAX
CLIMBS
CLIMES
CLINCH
CLINES
CLINGS
CLINGY
CLINIC
CLINKS
CLIPON
CLIQUE
CLIQUY
CMINOR
CMINUS
CNIDAE
CNIDUS
COIFED
COIGNS
COILED
COILUP
COINED
COINER
CRICKS
CRIERS
CRIKEY
CRIMEA
CRIMES
CRIMPS
CRIMPY
CRINGE
CRIPES
CRISCO
CRISES
CRISIS
CRISPS
CRISPY
CRISTO
CRITIC
CUIABA
CUIQUE
CUISSE

C••I••
CABINS
CAGIER
CAGILY
CAGING
CAHIER
CAKIER
CAKING
CALICO
CALIPH
CAMINO
CAMION
CAMISE
CANIDS
CANIER
CANIFF
CANINE
CANING
CAPIAS
CAPITA
CARIBE
CARIBS
CARIES
CARINA
CARING
CASING
CASINO
CATION
CAVIAR
CAVILS
CAVING
CAVITY
CAWING
CECILE
CECILY
CEDING
CELINE
CERIPH
CERISE
CERIUM
CESIUM
CHAINE
CHAINS
CHAIRS
CHAISE
CHOICE
CHOIRS
CHRISM
CILIUM
CITIES
CITIFY
CITING
CITIUS
CIVICS
CLAIMS
CLAIRE
CLUING
COBIAS
CODIFY
CODING
COGITO
COKIER
COLIES
COLIMA
COMICS
COMING
COMITY
CONICS
CONIES
CONIUM
COOING
COPIED
COPIER
COPIES
COPING
CORING
CORIUM
COSIED
COSIER
COSIES
COSIGN
COSILY
COSINE
COVINA
COWING
COYISH
COZIED
COZIER
COZIES
COZILY
CRUISE
CRYING
CUBICS
CUBING
CUBISM
CUBIST
CUBITS
CUPIDS
CURIAE
CURIAL
CURING
CURIOS
CURIUM
CUTIES
CUTINS
CYBILL
CYNICS

C•••I•
CABBIE
CADDIE
CADDIS
CADMIC
CALAIS
CALLIN
CALVIN
CAMEIN
CANDID
CANLIT
CAPRIS
CAPSID
CARDIN
CARDIO
CARLIN
CARRIE
CASHIN
CASSIA
CASSIO
CASSIS
CATKIN
CATNIP
CATRIG
CAVEIN
CEDRIC
CELTIC
CERTIF
CERVID
CHAPIN
CHEMIN
CHENIN
CHERIE
CHIPIN
CHITIN
CHOPIN
CITRIC
CLAVIN
CLERIC
CLEVIS
CLINIC
CLORIS
CLOVIS
CLUEIN
COATIS
COCCID
COCHIN
COEDIT
COHEIR
COLLIE
COMEIN
COMFIT
COMMIT
COMMIX
CONNIE
CONOID
COOKIE
COOLIT
COOTIE
COPTIC
CORBIN
CORGIS
COSMIC
COURIC
COUSIN
COWRIE
CRANIA
CRANIO
CREDIT
CRETIN
CRISIS
CRITIC
CRONIN
CUBOID
CULKIN
CULLIS
CULTIC
CUPRIC
CURTIN
CURTIS
CURTIZ
CUSPID
CUSTIS
CUTSIN
CYANIC
CYCLIC
CYMRIC

C••••I
CANTHI
CARONI
CENTRI
CHICHI
CHILLI
CHUHSI
CIARDI
CISKEI
CUMULI

•CI•••
ACIDIC
ACIDLY
ACINUS
ICICLE
ICIEST
ICINGS
SCIFIS
SCIONS
SCIPIO

•C•I••
ACHIER
ACHING
ACTIII
ACTING
ACTINO
ACTION
ACTIUM
ACTIVE
ACUITY
ECHINO
ICHING
ICKIER
SCHICK
SCHIFF
SCHISM
SCHIST
SCHIZY
SCRIBE
SCRIMP
SCRIMS
SCRIPS
SCRIPT
VCHIPS

•C••I•
ACACIA
ACADIA
ACARID
ACEDIA
ACETIC
ACIDIC
ACQUIT
ACTIII
ECESIC
ECESIS
ECHOIC
ECLAIR
ICARIA
ICEDIN
ICESIN
ICONIC
LCHAIM
MCBAIN
MCLAIN
MCNAIR
SCALIA
SCENIC
SCIFIS
SCIPIO
SCORIA
SCOTIA

•C•••I
ACTIII
OCELLI
OCTOPI
OCTROI
SCAMPI

••CI••
ANCIEN
ARCING
CECILE
CECILY
DECIDE
DICIER
DICING
DOCILE
ENCINA
ENCINO
EXCISE
EXCITE
FACIAL
FACIAS
FACIES
FACILE
FACING
INCISE
INCITE
LACIER
LACILY
LACING
LUCIAN
LUCITE
LUCIUS
MUCINS
OSCINE
PACIFY
PACING
PACINO
RACIAL
RACIER
RACILY
RACINE
RACING
RECIFE
RECIPE
RECITE
RICING
SICILY
SOCIAL
UNCIAL

••C•I•
ALCUIN
ARCHIE
ARCTIC
BACKIN
BOCCIE
COCCID
COCHIN
CYCLIC
DACOIT
DECEIT
DUCHIN
EUCLID
HACKIE
HECTIC
ISCHIA
JACKIE
KICKIN
LACTIC
LOCKIN
MACEIO
ORCHID
ORCHIL
PECTIC
PECTIN
PICNIC
RACHIS
RECOIL
RICHIE
SOCKIN
SUCKIN
TACTIC
TECHIE
TOCSIN
TUCKIN
UNCHIC
UNCOIL
URCHIN
VICTIM
VICTIS

••C••I
JACOBI
NUCLEI

•••CI•
ACACIA
AFLCIO
ALICIA
ANACIN
BAUCIS
BOCCIE
COCCID
ELICIT
FASCIA
GARCIA
GLACIS
GRACIE
MARCIA
MARCIE
MUNCIE
MURCIA
NIACIN
NUNCIO
PAUCIS
PENCIL
PHOCIS
PLACID
PRECIS
RANCID
RUNCIE
SPECIE
TRICIA
URACIL
VINCIT
VISCID

•••C•I
CHICHI
KIMCHI
LITCHI
TAICHI

••••CI
MEDICI

C•J•••
CAJOLE
CAJUNS

C••J••
CMAJOR
CONJOB

C•••J•
CHONJU

•CJ•••
MCJOBS

•C•J••
ACAJOU

C•K•••
CAKIER
CAKING
COKIER

C••K••
CACKLE
CALKED
CANKER
CARKED
CATKIN
CHEKOV
CHOKED
CHOKER
CHOKES
CHUKAR
CHUKKA
CISKEI
COCKED
COCKER
COCKLE
CONKED
CONKER
COOKED
COOKER
COOKIE
COOKUP
CORKED
CORKER
CRAKES
CRIKEY
CUCKOO
CULKIN

C•••K•
CAULKS
CHALKS
CHALKY
CHECKS
CHEEKS
CHEEKY
CHICKS
CHINKS
CHINKY
CHOCKS
CHUCKS
CHUKKA
CHUNKS
CHUNKY
CLACKS
CLANKS
CLANKY
CLARKE
CLEEKS
CLERKS
CLICKS
CLINKS
CLOAKS
CLOCKS
CLONKS
CLUCKS
CLUNKS
CLUNKY
CRACKS
CRACKY
CRANKS
CRANKY
CREAKS
CREAKY
CREEKS
CRICKS
CROAKS
CROAKY
CROCKS
CROOKS

C••••K
CUSACK

•CK•••
ACKACK
ICKIER
MCKUEN

•C•••K
ACKACK
OCASEK
OCLOCK
SCHICK
SCREAK

••CK••
BACKED
BACKER
BACKIN
BACKUP
BACKUS
BECKER
BECKET
BECKON
BICKER
BUCKED
BUCKET
BUCKLE
BUCKUP
CACKLE
COCKED
COCKER
COCKLE
CUCKOO
DECKED
DECKER
DECKLE
DICKER
DICKEY
DOCKED
DOCKER
DOCKET
DUCKED
FICKLE
GECKOS
HACKED
HACKER
HACKIE
HACKLE
HACKLY
HECKLE
HICKEY
HICKOK
HOCKED
HOCKEY
JACKAL
JACKED
JACKET
JACKEY
JACKIE
JACKUP
JECKLE
JOCKEY
KICKED
KICKER
KICKIN
KICKUP
LACKED
LACKEY
LICKED
LOCKED
LOCKER
LOCKET
LOCKIN
LOCKON
LOCKUP
LUCKED
MICKEY
MOCKED
MOCKER
MOCKUP
MUCKED
MUCKUP
NECKED
NICKED
NICKEL
NICKER
PACKED
PACKER
PACKET
PACKUP
PECKAT
PECKED
PICKAT
PICKAX
PICKED
PICKER
PICKET
PICKLE
PICKON
PICKUP
POCKET
PUCKER
RACKED
RACKET
RACKUP
RECKON
RICKED
RICKEY
ROCKED
ROCKER
ROCKET
ROCKNE
ROCKYV
RUCKED
RUCKUS
SACKED
SACKER
SECKEL
SICKEN
SICKER
SICKLE
SICKLY
SOCKED
SOCKET
SOCKIN
SUCKAS
SUCKED
SUCKER
SUCKIN
TACKED
TACKER
TACKLE
TACKON
TICKED
TICKER
TICKET
TICKLE
TICKLY
TUCKED
TUCKER
TUCKET
TUCKIN
WACKOS
WICKED
WICKER
WICKET
YACKED

••C•K•
HACEKS

••C••K
HICKOK
RECORK
UNCORK

•••CK•
ALECKY
BLACKS
BLOCKS
BLOCKY
BRICKS
BRICKY
CHECKS
CHICKS
CHOCKS
CHUCKS
CLACKS
CLICKS
CLOCKS
CLUCKS
CRACKS
CRACKY
CRICKS
CROCKS
FLACKS
FLECKS
FLECKY
FLICKA
FLICKS
FLOCKS
FLOCKY
FROCKS
KNACKS
KNICKS
KNOCKS
KYACKS
PLUCKS
PLUCKY
PRICKS
QUACKS
SHACKS
SHOCKS
SHUCKS
SLACKS
SLICKS
SMACKS
SMOCKS
SNACKS
SNICKS
SPECKS
STACKS
STICKS
STICKY
STOCKS
STOCKY
THICKE
TRACKS
TRICKS
TRICKY
TRUCKS
VNECKS
WHACKS
WHACKY
WRACKS
WRECKS
YOICKS

•••C•K
DUBCEK
SPACEK

••••CK
ACKACK
ARRACK
ATTACK
BEDECK
CUSACK
FRANCK
GOBACK
HIJACK
INLUCK
KOPECK
LUBECK
MOHOCK
NATICK
OCLOCK
ONDECK
PLANCK
RELOCK
REMICK
SCHICK
SHTICK
STRICK
STRUCK
THWACK
UNLOCK
UNPACK
UNTACK
UPTICK
YORICK
ZANUCK

CL••••
CLACKS
CLAIMS
CLAIRE
CLAMMY
CLAMOR
CLAMPS
CLAMUP
CLANCY
CLANGS
CLANKS
CLANKY
CLAQUE
CLARET
CLARKE
CLAROS
CLASPS
CLASSY
CLAUDE
CLAUSE
CLAVES
CLAVIN
CLAWED
CLAWER
CLAYEY
CLEANS
CLEARS
CLEATS
CLEAVE
CLEEKS
CLEESE
CLEFTS
CLENCH
CLEPED
CLERGY
CLERIC
CLERKS
CLEVER
CLEVES
CLEVIS
CLEWED
CLICHE
CLICKS
CLIENT
CLIFFS
CLIFFY
CLIMAX
CLIMBS
CLIMES
CLINCH
CLINES
CLINGS
CLINGY
CLINIC
CLINKS
CLIPON
CLIQUE
CLIQUY
CLOACA
CLOAKS
CLOCHE
CLOCKS
CLODDY
CLOGGY
CLOGUP
CLOMPS
CLONED
CLONES
CLONKS
CLONUS
CLOQUE
CLORIS
CLOROX
CLOSED
CLOSER
CLOSES
CLOSET
CLOTHE
CLOTHO
CLOTHS
CLOTTY
CLOUDS
CLOUDY
CLOUTS
CLOVEN
CLOVER
CLOVES
CLOVIS
CLOWNS
CLOYED
CLUBBY
CLUCKS
CLUEIN
CLUING
CLUMPS
CLUMPY
CLUMSY
CLUNKS
CLUNKY
CLUTCH

C•L•••
CALAIS
CALASH
CALCES
CALDER
CALICO
CALIPH
CALKED
CALLAO
CALLAS
CALLED
CALLER
CALLES
CALLIN
CALLON
CALLOW
CALLUP
CALLUS
CALMED
CALMER
CALMLY
CALPAC
CALQUE
CALVED
CALVES
CALVIN
CALXES
CCLAMP
CELEBS
CELERY
CELINE
CELLAE
CELLAR
CELLED
CELLOS
CELTIC
CHLORO
CILIUM
COLADA
COLDER
COLDLY
COLEUS
COLFAX
COLIES
COLIMA
COLLAR
COLLET
COLLIE
COLLOP
COLLOQ
COLMAN
COLONS
COLONY
COLORS
COLOUR
COLTER
COLUGO
COLUMN
CULETS
CULKIN
CULLED
CULLEN
CULLER
CULLET
CULLIS
CULTIC
CULVER

C••L••
CABLED
CABLER
CABLES
CALLAO
CALLAS
CALLED
CALLER
CALLES
CALLIN
CALLON
CALLOW
CALLUP
CALLUS
CAMLET
CANLIT
CAPLET
CARLIN
CARLOS
CARLOT
CAULKS
CEILED
CELLAE
CELLAR
CELLED
CELLOS
CEYLON
CHALCO
CHALET
CHALKS
CHALKY
CHELAE
CHELAS
CHILDE
CHILDS
CHILLI
CHILLS
CHILLY
CHILOE
CHOLER
CHOLLA
CHOLOS
COALER
COELOM
COILED
COILUP
COLLAR
COLLET
COLLIE
COLLOP
COLLOQ
COOLED
COOLER
COOLIT
COOLLY
COPLEY
COULDA
COULEE
COWLED
COWLEY
CULLED
CULLEN
CULLER
CULLET
CULLIS
CURLED
CURLER
CURLEW
CURLEY
CURLUP
CUTLER
CUTLET
CYCLAS
CYCLED
CYCLER
CYCLES
CYCLIC
CYCLOS

C•••L•
CABALA
CABALS
CACKLE
CAGILY

CAJOLE
CALMLY
CAMELS
CANALS
CANDLE
CANOLA
CANTLE
CAROLE
CAROLS
CASALS
CASTLE
CATTLE
CAUDLE
CAVELL
CAVILS
CECILE
CECILY
CEORLS
CHARLY
CHICLE
CHICLY
CHILLI
CHILLS
CHILLY
CHOLLA
CHURLS
CIBOLA
CICELY
CIRCLE
COBALT
COBBLE
COCKLE
CODDLE
COLDLY
COMELY
COMPLY
COOLLY
COPULA
CORALS
COSELL
COSILY
COSTLY
COUPLE
COZILY
CRADLE
CRAWLS
CRAWLY
CREELS
CREOLE
CUDDLE
CUDDLY
CUMULI
CUMULO
CUPELS
CUPOLA
CURDLE
CURTLY
CURULE
CUTELY
CYBELE
CYBILL

C••••L
CANCEL
CANFUL
CANNEL
CAPFUL
CARFUL
CARMEL
CARNAL
CARPAL
CARPEL
CARREL
CARROL
CARTEL
CASUAL
CAUDAL
CAUSAL
CAVELL
CEREAL
CHANEL
CHAPEL
CHERYL
CHEVAL
CHISEL
CHORAL
COEVAL
COMPEL
CONSUL
CORBEL
CORNEL
CORRAL
CORREL
COSELL
COSTAL
CRENEL
CRESOL
CREWEL
CRURAL
CUDGEL
CUNEAL
CUPFUL
CURIAL
CYBILL
CYMBAL

•CL•••
CCLAMP
ECLAIR
ECLATS
MCLAIN
MCLEAN
OCLOCK
SCLAFF
SCLERA
SCLERO
UCLANS

•C•L••
BCELLS
ECCLES
ECOLES
OCELLI
OCELOT
OCULAR
SCALAR
SCALDS
SCALED
SCALER
SCALES
SCALIA
SCALPS
SCHLEP
SCOLDS
SCULLS
SCULLY
SCULPT
SCYLLA

•C••L•
ACIDLY
BCELLS
ICICLE
MCHALE
OCCULT
OCELLI
RCCOLA
SCHELL
SCHULZ
SCOWLS
SCROLL
SCULLS
SCULLY
SCYLLA

•C•••L
ACETAL
ACETYL
ACTUAL
SCHELL
SCHOOL
SCHORL
SCRAWL
SCROLL

••CL••
CYCLAS
CYCLED
CYCLER
CYCLES
CYCLIC
CYCLOS
ECCLES
EUCLID
JACLYN
NUCLEI
NUCLEO
SOCLES
UNCLAD
UNCLES
UNCLOG
VACLAV

••C•L•
ARCHLY
BACALL
BECALM
BUCKLE
CACKLE
CECILE
CECILY
CICELY
COCKLE
DECALS
DECKLE
DOCILE
EXCELS
FACILE
FACULA
FICKLE
FOCSLE
HACKLE
HACKLY
HECKLE
INCULT
JACALS
JECKLE
LACILY
LOCALE
LOCALS
MACULA
NICELY
NICOLA
NICOLE
NICOLO
OCCULT
ONCALL
OSCULA
PICKLE
PICULS
RACILY
RCCOLA
RECALL
RICHLY
SICILY
SICKLE
SICKLY
TACKLE
TICALS
TICKLE
TICKLY
VOCALS

••C••L
BACALL
BUCCAL
DACTYL
DUCTAL
FACIAL
JACKAL
MICHEL
MRCOOL
NICKEL
NUCHAL
ONCALL
ORCHIL
RACHEL
RACIAL
RECALL
RECOIL
SACRAL
SECKEL
SOCIAL
UNCIAL
UNCOIL
UNCOOL
UNCURL
VACHEL

•••CL•
BOUCLE
CHICLE
CHICLY
CIRCLE
ICICLE
MUSCLE
MUSCLY
ORACLE
SIECLE

•••C•L
APICAL
BUCCAL
CANCEL
EPICAL
FISCAL
GLYCOL
LOWCAL
MARCEL
MESCAL
PARCEL
PASCAL
PENCEL
PENCIL
RASCAL
TERCEL
THECAL
TINCAL
UNOCAL
URACIL

CM••••
CMAJOR
CMINOR
CMINUS

C•M•••
CAMARO
CAMBER
CAMDEN
CAMEAT
CAMEBY
CAMEIN
CAMELS
CAMEON
CAMEOS
CAMERA
CAMETO
CAMEUP
CAMINO
CAMION
CAMISE
CAMLET
CAMPED
CAMPER
CAMPOS
CAMPUS
CEMENT
COMATE
COMBAT
COMBED
COMBER
COMBES
COMBOS
COMEAT
COMEBY
COMEDY
COMEIN
COMELY
COMEON
COMERS
COMETH
COMETO
COMETS
COMEUP
COMFIT
COMICS
COMING
COMITY
COMMAS
COMMIT
COMMIX
COMMON
COMPAQ
COMPEL
COMPLY
COMPOS
COMSAT
COMTES
CUMBER
CUMULI
CUMULO
CYMBAL
CYMRIC

C••M••
CADMIC
CADMUS
CAIMAN
CALMED
CALMER
CALMLY
CARMAN
CARMEL
CARMEN
CAYMAN
CERMET
CHAMMY
CHAMPS
CHEMIN
CHIMED
CHIMES
CHIMPS
CHOMPS
CHUMMY
CHUMPS
CLAMMY
CLAMOR
CLAMPS
CLAMUP
CLIMAX
CLIMBS
CLIMES
CLOMPS
CLUMPS
CLUMPY
CLUMSY
COLMAN
COMMAS
COMMIT
COMMIX
COMMON
CONMAN
CONMEN
CORMAN
COSMIC
COSMOS
COWMAN
COWMEN
CRAMBO
CRAMPS
CREMES
CRIMEA
CRIMES
CRIMPS
CRIMPY
CRUMBS
CRUMBY
CRUMMY

C•••M•
CAROMS
CCLAMP
CDROMS
CHACMA
CHAMMY
CHARMS
CHASMS
CHROMA
CHROME
CHROMO
CHROMY
CHUMMY
CINEMA
CLAIMS
CLAMMY
COLIMA
COLUMN
CREAMS
CREAMY
CRUMMY

C••••M
CERIUM
CESIUM
CHRISM
CILIUM
CIRCUM
COBHAM
COELOM
CONIUM
CORIUM
CUBISM
CURIUM
CUSTOM

•C•M••
ACUMEN
ICEMAN
ICEMEN
SCAMPI
SCAMPS
SCHMOO
SCHMOS
SCUMMY

•C••M•
CCLAMP
SCHEMA
SCHEME
SCRAMS
SCRIMP
SCRIMS
SCRUMS
SCUMMY

•C•••M
ACTIUM
LCHAIM
MCADAM
SCARUM
SCHISM
SCREAM

••CM••
MICMAC
PACMAN

••C•M•
BECAME
BECOME
DECAMP
ENCAMP
INCOME
JICAMA
RACEME
TACOMA

••C••M
ASCHAM
BECALM
DICTUM
LYCEUM
SACHEM
SACRUM
VACUUM
VICTIM

•••CM•
CHACMA

•••C•M
ABSCAM
CIRCUM
DRACHM
NONCOM
SITCOM
TALCUM
VIACOM

CN••••
CNIDAE
CNIDUS
CNOTES

C•N•••
CANAAN
CANADA
CANALS
CANAPE
CANARD
CANARY
CANCAN
CANCEL
CANCUN
CANDID
CANDLE
CANDOR
CANERS
CANFUL
CANIDS
CANIER
CANIFF
CANINE
CANING
CANKER
CANLIT
CANNAE
CANNED
CANNEL
CANNER
CANNES
CANNON
CANNOT
CANOED
CANOES
CANOLA
CANONS
CANOPY
CANOVA
CANTAB
CANTED
CANTER
CANTHI
CANTLE
CANTON
CANTOR
CANTOS
CANUTE
CANVAS
CANYON
CENOTE
CENSED
CENSER
CENSES
CENSOR
CENSUS
CENTER
CENTOS
CENTRE
CENTRI
CENTRO
CINDER
CINEMA
CINQUE
CONANT
CONCHA
CONCHS
CONCUR
CONDOR
CONDOS
CONEYS
CONFAB
CONFED
CONFER
CONGAS
CONGER
CONGOU
CONICS
CONIES
CONIUM
CONJOB
CONKED
CONKER
CONMAN
CONMEN
CONNED
CONNER
CONNIE
CONNOR
CONOCO
CONOID
CONRAD
CONROY
CONSUL
CONTAC
CONTES
CONTRA
CONTRE
CONURE
CONVEX
CONVEY
CONVOY
CONWAY
CUNARD
CUNAXA
CUNEAL
CYNICS

C••N••
CAGNEY
CANNAE
CANNED
CANNEL
CANNER
CANNES
CANNON
CANNOT
CAPNUT
CARNAL
CARNES
CARNET
CARNEY
CARNOT
CATNAP
CATNIP
CHANCE
CHANCY
CHANEL
CHANEY
CHANGE
CHANTS
CHENIN
CHINCH
CHINES
CHINKS
CHINKY
CHINOS
CHINTZ
CHINUP
CHONJU
CHUNKS
CHUNKY
CLANCY
CLANGS
CLANKS
CLANKY
CLENCH
CLINCH
CLINES
CLINGS
CLINGY
CLINIC
CLINKS
CLONED
CLONES
CLONKS
CLONUS
CLUNKS
CLUNKY
CMINOR
CMINUS
COGNAC
COINED
COINER
CONNED
CONNER
CONNIE
CONNOR
COONEY
CORNEA
CORNED
CORNEL
CORNER
CORNET
COUNTS
COUNTY
CPSNOW
CRANED
CRANES
CRANIA
CRANIO
CRANKS
CRANKY
CRANNY
CRENEL
CRENNA
CRINGE
CRONES
CRONIN
CRONUS
CRONYN
CRUNCH
CYANIC
CYGNET
CYGNUS

C•••N•
CABANA
CABINS
CADENT
CAGING
CAIRNS
CAJUNS
CAKING
CAMINO
CANINE
CANING
CANONS
CAPONE
CAPONS
CARINA
CARING
CARONI
CASING
CASINO
CATENA
CAVING
CAWING
CEDANT
CEDING
CELINE
CEMENT
CESSNA
CETANE
CHAINE
CHAINS
CHIANG
CHRONO
CHURNS
CITING
CLEANS
CLIENT
CLOWNS
CLUING
CODING
CODONS
COGENT
COHUNE
COIGNS
COLONS
COLONY
COMING
CONANT
COOING
COPING
CORING
CORONA
COSINE
COVENS
COVENT
COVINA
COWENS
COWING
COZENS
CRANNY
CRENNA
CROONS
CROWNS
CRYING
CUBING
CURING
CUTINS
CYRANO
CZERNY

C••••N
CAFTAN
CAIMAN
CALLIN
CALLON
CALVIN
CAMDEN
CAMEIN
CAMEON
CAMION
CANAAN
CANCAN
CANCUN
CANNON
CANTON
CANYON
CAPGUN
CAPTAN
CARBON
CARDIN
CAREEN
CARLIN
CARMAN
CARMEN
CARSON
CARTON
CASERN
CASHIN
CASTON
CATION
CATKIN
CATTON
CAVEIN
CAVERN
CAXTON
CAYMAN
CEYLON
CHAPIN
CHARON
CHEMIN
CHENIN
CHIPIN
CHIRON
CHITIN
CHITON
CHOPIN
CHOSEN
CHYRON
CITRON
CLAVIN
CLIPON
CLOVEN
CLUEIN
COBURN
COCHIN
COCOON
COLMAN
COLUMN
COMEIN
COMEON
COMMON
CONMAN
CONMEN
COOGAN
CORBAN
CORBIN
CORDON
CORMAN
COSIGN
COTTEN
COTTON
COUPON
COUSIN
COWMAN
COWMEN
CRAVEN
CRAYON
CRETAN
CRETIN
CRONIN
CRONYN
CROTON
CULKIN
CULLEN
CURTIN
CURZON
CUTSIN

•CN•••
MCNAIR

•C•N••
ACINUS
ICINGS
ICONIC
SCANTS
SCANTY
SCENAS
SCENDS
SCENES
SCENIC
SCENTS
SCHNOZ
SCONCE
SCONES

•C••N•
ACCENT
ACHENE
ACHING
ACORNS
ACTING
ACTINO
ACTONE
ECHINO
ICHING
MCCANN
OCEANS
OCTANE
OCTANT
SCARNE
SCIONS
SCORNS
UCLANS

•C•••N
ACTION
ACTSON
ACUMEN
ICEDIN
ICEMAN
ICEMEN
ICESIN
MCBAIN
MCCANN
MCKUEN
MCLAIN
MCLEAN
SCREEN

••CN••
PICNIC

••C•N•
ACCENT
ANCONA
ARCANA
ARCANE
ARCING
ASCEND
ASCENT
DECANT
DECENT
DICING
DOCENT
ENCINA
ENCINO
EOCENE
ESCENT
FACING
FECUND
INCANS
JACANA
JOCUND
LACING
LACUNA
LUCENT
MCCANN
MUCINS
NICENE
NOCENT
OSCINE
PACING
PACINO
PECANS
POCONO
RACINE
RACING
RACONS
RECANE
RECANT
RECENT
RECONS
RICING
ROCKNE
SECANT
SECOND
TECHNO
TUCANA
VACANT
VICUNA

••C••N
AACHEN
ALCUIN
ANCIEN
ARCHON
ARCTAN
BACKIN
BECKON
BICORN
BUCHAN
COCHIN
COCOON
DACRON
DUCHIN
INCHON
JACLYN
KICKIN
KUCHEN
LICHEN
LOCKIN
LOCKON
LUCIAN
MACOUN
MACRON
MCCANN
MICRON
NICEAN
PACMAN
PECTIN
PICKON
RECKON
RICHEN
SECERN
SICKEN
SOCKIN
SUCKIN
TACKON
TOCSIN
TUCHUN
TUCKIN
TUCSON
TYCOON
URCHIN
WICCAN

•••CN•
PROCNE

•••C•N
ANACIN
ASHCAN
BEACON
CANCAN
CANCUN
DEACON
DUNCAN
FALCON
FLACON
GARCON
GASCON
NIACIN
OILCAN
TINCAN
TOUCAN
TUSCAN
VULCAN
WICCAN
ZIRCON

CO••••
COALER
COAPTS
COARSE
COASTS
COATED
COATIS
COAXED
COAXER
COAXES
COBALT
COBBLE
COBHAM
COBIAS
COBRAS
COBURG
COBURN
COBWEB
COCCID
COCCUS
COCCYX
COCHIN
COCKED
COCKER
COCKLE
COCOAS
COCOON
CODDLE
CODERS
CODGER
CODIFY
CODING
CODONS
COEDIT
COELOM
COERCE
COEVAL
COFFEE
COFFER
COGENT
COGGED
COGITO
COGNAC
COHEIR
COHERE
COHORT
COHOST
COHUNE
COIFED
COIGNS
COILED
COILUP
COINED
COINER
COKIER
COLADA
COLDER
COLDLY
COLEUS
COLFAX
COLIES
COLIMA
COLLAR
COLLET
COLLIE
COLLOP
COLLOQ
COLMAN
COLONS
COLONY
COLORS
COLOUR
COLTER
COLUGO
COLUMN
COMATE
COMBAT
COMBED
COMBER
COMBES
COMBOS
COMEAT
COMEBY
COMEDY
COMEIN
COMELY
COMEON
COMERS
COMETH
COMETO
COMETS
COMEUP
COMFIT
COMICS
COMING
COMITY
COMMAS
COMMIT
COMMIX
COMMON
COMPAQ
COMPEL
COMPLY
COMPOS
COMSAT
COMTES
CONANT
CONCHA
CONCHS
CONCUR
CONDOR
CONDOS
CONEYS
CONFAB
CONFED
CONFER
CONGAS
CONGER
CONGOU
CONICS
CONIES
CONIUM
CONJOB
CONKED
CONKER
CONMAN
CONMEN
CONNED
CONNER
CONNIE
CONNOR
CONOCO
CONOID
CONRAD
CONROY
CONSUL
CONTAC
CONTES
CONTRA
CONTRE
CONURE
CONVEX
CONVEY
CONVOY
CONWAY
COODER
COOERS
COOGAN

COOING
COOKED
COOKER
COOKIE
COOKUP
COOLED
COOLER
COOLIT
COOLLY
COONEY
COOPED
COOPER
COOPTS
COOPUP
COOTER
COOTIE
COPAYS
COPIED
COPIER
COPIES
COPING
COPLEY
COPOUT
COPPED
COPPER
COPSES
COPTER
COPTIC
COPULA
COQUET
CORALS
CORBAN
CORBEL
CORBIN
CORDAY
CORDED
CORDON
CORERS
CORGIS
CORING
CORIUM
CORKED
CORKER
CORMAN
CORNEA
CORNED
CORNEL
CORNER
CORNET
CORONA
CORPUS
CORRAL
CORREL
CORSET
CORTES
CORTEX
CORTEZ
CORVEE
CORVES
CORYZA
COSELL
COSHED
COSHES
COSIED
COSIER
COSIES
COSIGN
COSILY
COSINE
COSMIC
COSMOS
COSSET
COSTAE
COSTAL
COSTAR
COSTAS
COSTLY
COTTAS
COTTEN
COTTER
COTTON
COUGAR
COUGHS
COULDA
COULEE
COUNTS
COUNTY
COUPES
COUPLE
COUPON
COURIC
COURSE
COURTS
COUSIN
COUTER
COVENS
COVENT
COVERS
COVERT
COVETS
COVEYS
COVINA
COWARD
COWBOY
COWENS
COWERS
COWING
COWLED
COWLEY
COWMAN
COWMEN
COWPEA
COWPER
COWPOX
COWRIE
COYEST
COYISH
COYOTE
COYPUS
COZENS
COZIED
COZIER
COZIES
COZILY

C•O•••

CEORLS
CHOATE
CHOCKS
CHOICE
CHOIRS
CHOKED
CHOKER
CHOKES
CHOLER
CHOLLA
CHOLOS
CHOMPS
CHONJU
CHOOSE
CHOOSY
CHOOYU
CHOPIN
CHOPPY
CHOPRA
CHORAL
CHORDS
CHORES
CHORUS
CHOSEN
CHOUGH
CHOWED
CLOACA
CLOAKS
CLOCHE
CLOCKS
CLODDY
CLOGGY
CLOGUP
CLOMPS
CLONED
CLONES
CLONKS
CLONUS
CLOQUE
CLORIS
CLOROX
CLOSED
CLOSER
CLOSES
CLOSET
CLOTHE
CLOTHO
CLOTHS
CLOTTY
CLOUDS
CLOUDY
CLOUTS
CLOVEN
CLOVER
CLOVES
CLOVIS
CLOWNS
CLOYED
CNOTES
COODER
COOERS
COOGAN
COOING
COOKED
COOKER
COOKIE
COOKUP
COOLED
COOLER
COOLIT
COOLLY
COONEY
COOPED
COOPER
COOPTS
COOPUP
COOTER
COOTIE
CROAKS
CROAKY
CROATS
CROCKS
CROCUS
CROFTS
CRONES
CRONIN
CRONUS
CRONYN
CROOKS
CROONS
CROPUP
CROSBY
CROSSE
CROTON
CROUCH
CROUPY
CROUSE
CROUTE
CROWDS
CROWED
CROWER
CROWNS
CROZES

C••O••

CAHOWS
CAJOLE
CANOED
CANOES
CANOLA
CANONS
CANOPY
CANOVA
CAPONE
CAPONS
CAPOTE
CAROBS
CAROLE
CAROLS
CAROMS
CARONI
CAVORT
CDROMS
CENOTE
CHEOPS
CHLORO
CHOOSE
CHOOSY
CHOOYU
CHROMA
CHROME
CHROMO
CHROMY
CHRONO
CIBOLA
COCOAS
COCOON
CODONS
COHORT
COHOST
COLONS
COLONY
COLORS
COLOUR
CONOCO
CONOID
COPOUT
CORONA
COYOTE
CREOLE
CROOKS
CROONS
CRYOFF
CSPOTS
CUBOID
CUPOLA
CUTOFF
CUTOUT
CYBORG

C•••O•

CACAOS
CACHOU
CAICOS
CALLON
CALLOW
CAMEON
CAMEOS
CAMION
CAMPOS
CANDOR
CANNON
CANNOT
CANTON
CANTOR
CANTOS
CANYON
CAPTOR
CARBON
CARBOS
CARBOY
CARGOS
CARHOP
CARLOS
CARLOT
CARNOT
CARROL
CARROT
CARSON
CARTON
CASTON
CASTOR
CATION
CATTON
CAWDOR
CAXTON
CELLOS
CENSOR
CENTOS
CERROS
CESTOS
CEYLON
CHADOR
CHARON
CHEKOV
CHIGOE
CHILOE
CHINOS
CHIRON
CHISOX
CHITON
CHOLOS
CHYRON
CISCOS
CITRON
CLAMOR
CLAROS
CLIPON
CLOROX
CMAJOR
CMINOR
COCOON
COELOM
COLLOP
COLLOQ
COMBOS
COMEON
COMMON
COMPOS
CONDOR
CONDOS
CONGOU
CONJOB
CONNOR
CONROY
CONVOY
CORDON
COSMOS
COTTON
COUPON
COWBOY
COWPOX
CPSNOW
CRAYON
CREDOS
CRESOL
CROTON
CRUSOE
CUCKOO
CURIOS
CURSOR
CURZON
CUSTOM
CUSTOS
CYCLOS

C••••O

CALICO
CALLAO
CAMARO
CAMETO
CAMINO
CARDIO
CARETO
CARUSO
CASINO
CASSIO
CASTRO
CAUCHO
CENTRO
CHALCO
CHARRO
CHEAPO
CHLORO
CHROMO
CHRONO
CHURRO
CICERO
CITATO
CLOTHO
COGITO
COLUGO
COMETO
CONOCO
CRAMBO
CRANIO
CRISCO
CRISTO
CRYPTO
CUCKOO
CUMULO
CYRANO

•CO•••

ACORNS
ECOLES
ICONIC
SCOFFS
SCOLDS
SCONCE
SCONES
SCOOPS
SCOOTS
SCOPED
SCOPES
SCORCH
SCORED
SCORER
SCORES
SCORIA
SCORNS
SCOTCH
SCOTER
SCOTIA
SCOTTO
SCOTTY
SCOURS
SCOUSE
SCOUTS
SCOWLS

•C•O••

ACCORD
ACCOST
ACEOUS
ACEOUT
ACROSS
ACTONE
ACTORS
ACTOUT
ECHOED
ECHOES
ECHOIC
ICEOUT
MCJOBS
OCLOCK
OCTOPI
RCCOLA
SCHOOL
SCHORL
SCIONS
SCOOPS
SCOOTS
SCRODS
SCROLL
SCROOP

•C••O•

ACAJOU
ACTION
ACTSON
ICEBOX
ICEFOG
MCADOO
OCELOT
OCTROI
SCHMOO
SCHMOS
SCHNOZ
SCHOOL
SCROOP

•C•••O

ACTINO
ACTTWO
ECHINO
MCADOO
OCTAVO
SCHMOO
SCIPIO
SCLERO
SCOTTO

••CO••

ACCORD
ACCOST
ALCOTT
ALCOVE
ANCONA
ASCOTS
ATCOST
BECOME
BICORN
COCOAS
COCOON
DACOIT
DECOCT
DECODE
DECORS
DECOYS
DICOTS
ENCODE
ENCORE
ESCORT
INCOME
JACOBI
JOCOSE
MACOUN
MRCOOL
MUCOSA
MUCOUS
NICOLA
NICOLE
NICOLO
PICOTS
POCONO
RACONS
RCCOLA
RECOAT
RECODE
RECOIL
RECONS
RECOPY
RECORD
RECORK
RECOUP
ROCOCO
SECOND
TACOMA
TYCOBB
TYCOON
UNCOIL
UNCOOL
UNCORK
WICOPY

••C•O•

AHCHOO
ANCHOR
ARCCOS
ARCHON
BECKON
CACAOS
CACHOU
COCOON
CUCKOO
CYCLOS
DACRON
DOCTOR
ESCROW
FACTOR
GECKOS
HECTOR
HICKOK
INCHON
LECTOR
LICTOR
LOCKON
MACHOS
MACRON
MACROS
MICRON
MICROS
MRCOOL
NACHOS
PICKON
RECKON
RECTOR
RECTOS
SECTOR
SUCCOR
TACKON
TUCSON
TYCOON
UNCLOG
UNCOOL
VECTOR
VICTOR
WACKOS

••C••O

AHCHOO
ARCARO
BOCHCO
CICERO
CUCKOO
DACAPO
ENCINO
ESCUDO
MACACO
MACEIO
NICOLO
NUCLEO
PACINO
PICABO
PICARO
POCONO
ROCOCO
TECHNO

•••CO•

ANTCOW
ARCCOS
BEACON
BUNCOS
CAICOS
CISCOS
DEACON
DISCOS
FALCON
FLACON
GARCON
GASCON
GLYCOL
GUACOS
JUNCOS
MARCOS
MASCOT
MOSCOW
NONCOM
PESCOW
RANCOR
ROSCOE
SEACOW
SITCOM
SUCCOR
TRICOT
VIACOM
WILCOX
ZIRCON

•••C•O

AFLCIO
ALECTO
CAUCHO
EXACTO
GAUCHO
HONCHO
NUNCIO
PANCHO
PONCHO
PSYCHO
RANCHO
REECHO
SANCHO
STUCCO
TRICHO
VELCRO

••••CO

ALNICO
BOCHCO
BRONCO
CALICO
CHALCO
CONOCO
CRISCO
ENESCO
ENRICO
FIASCO
FRANCO
FRESCO
FRISCO
GRAECO
MACACO
MEDICO
MEJICO
MEXICO
MONACO
OROZCO
ROCOCO
STUCCO
SUNOCO
TEXACO
UNESCO
ZYDECO

CP••••

CPSNOW

C•P•••

CAPERS
CAPFUL
CAPGUN
CAPIAS
CAPITA
CAPLET
CAPNUT
CAPONE
CAPONS
CAPOTE
CAPPED
CAPPER
CAPRIS
CAPSID
CAPTAN
CAPTOR
CIPHER
COPAYS
COPIED
COPIER
COPIES
COPING
COPLEY
COPOUT
COPPED
COPPER
COPSES
COPTER
COPTIC
COPULA
CSPOTS
CUPELS
CUPFUL
CUPIDS
CUPOLA
CUPPAS
CUPPED
CUPRIC
CYPHER
CYPRUS

C••P••

CALPAC
CAMPED
CAMPER
CAMPOS
CAMPUS
CAPPED
CAPPER
CARPAL
CARPED
CARPEL
CARPER
CARPET
CARPUS
CASPAR
CASPER
CHAPEL
CHAPIN
CHIPIN
CHOPIN
CHOPPY
CHOPRA
CLEPED
CLIPON
COAPTS
COMPAQ
COMPEL
COMPLY
COMPOS
COOPED
COOPER
COOPTS
COOPUP
COPPED
COPPER
CORPUS
COUPES
COUPLE
COUPON
COWPEA
COWPER
COWPOX
COYPUS
CRAPES
CREPES
CRIPES
CROPUP
CRYPTO
CRYPTS
CUPPAS
CUPPED
CUSPED
CUSPID

C•••P•

CALIPH
CANAPE
CANOPY
CERIPH
CHAMPS
CHEAPO
CHEEPS
CHEOPS
CHIMPS
CHIRPS
CHIRPY
CHOMPS
CHOPPY
CHUMPS
CLAMPS
CLASPS
CLOMPS
CLUMPS
CLUMPY
CRAMPS
CREEPS
CREEPY
CRIMPS
CRIMPY
CRISPS
CRISPY
CROUPY
CUTUPS

C••••P

CALLUP
CAMEUP
CARHOP
CATNAP
CATNIP
CATSUP
CCLAMP
CHATUP
CHEWUP
CHINUP
CLAMUP
CLOGUP
COILUP
COLLOP
COMEUP
COOKUP
COOPUP
CROPUP
CSHARP
CURLUP
CUTSUP

•C•P••

SCAPED
SCAPES
SCIPIO
SCOPED
SCOPES

•C••P•

ACCEPT
ECTYPE
OCCUPY
OCTOPI
SCALPS
SCAMPI
SCAMPS
SCARPS
SCAUPS
SCOOPS
SCRAPE
SCRAPS
SCRIPS
SCRIPT
SCULPT
VCHIPS

•C•••P

ACESUP
ACTSUP
CCLAMP
ICECAP
ICEDUP
ICESUP
SCHLEP
SCRIMP
SCROOP

••C•P•

ACCEPT
ALCAPP
BICEPS
DACAPO
ESCAPE
EXCEPT
INCEPT
OCCUPY
RECAPS
RECIPE
RECOPY
UNCAPS
WICOPY

••C••P

ALCAPP
BACKUP
BUCKUP
DECAMP
ENCAMP
ESCARP
FACEUP
HICCUP
JACKUP
KICKUP
LACEUP
LOCKUP
MOCKUP
MUCKUP
PACKUP
PICKUP
RACKUP
RECOUP

•••C•P

EGGCUP
EYECUP
GASCAP
HICCUP
HOTCAP
HUBCAP
ICECAP
MADCAP
MOBCAP
REDCAP
SKYCAP
TEACUP
TOECAP
TRICEP

C•Q•••

COQUET

C••Q••

CAIQUE
CALQUE
CASQUE
CHEQUE
CINQUE
CIRQUE
CLAQUE
CLIQUE
CLIQUY
CLOQUE
CUIQUE

C••••Q

COLLOQ
COMPAQ

•CQ•••

ACQUIT

••CQ••

SACQUE

CR••••

CRABBE
CRABBY
CRACKS
CRACKY
CRADLE
CRAFTS
CRAFTY
CRAGGY
CRAKES
CRAMBO
CRAMPS
CRANED
CRANES
CRANIA
CRANIO
CRANKS
CRANKY
CRANNY
CRAPES
CRATED
CRATER
CRATES
CRAVAT
CRAVED
CRAVEN
CRAVER
CRAVES
CRAWLS
CRAWLY
CRAYON
CRAZED
CRAZES
CREAKS
CREAKY
CREAMS
CREAMY
CREASE
CREASY
CREATE
CRECHE
CREDIT
CREDOS
CREEDS
CREEKS
CREELS
CREEPS
CREEPY
CREMES
CRENEL
CRENNA
CREOLE
CREPES
CRESOL
CRESTS
CRETAN
CRETIN
CREUSA
CREWED
CREWEL
CRICKS
CRIERS
CRIKEY
CRIMEA
CRIMES
CRIMPS
CRIMPY
CRINGE
CRIPES
CRISCO
CRISES
CRISIS
CRISPS
CRISPY
CRISTO
CRITIC
CROAKS
CROAKY
CROATS
CROCKS
CROCUS
CROFTS
CRONES
CRONIN
CRONUS
CRONYN
CROOKS
CROONS
CROPUP
CROSBY
CROSSE
CROTON
CROUCH
CROUPY
CROUSE
CROUTE
CROWDS
CROWED
CROWER
CROWNS
CROZES
CRUCES
CRUDDY
CRUDER
CRUETS
CRUISE
CRUMBS
CRUMBY
CRUMMY
CRUNCH
CRURAL
CRUSES
CRUSOE
CRUSTS
CRUSTY
CRUTCH
CRUXES
CRYERS
CRYING
CRYOFF
CRYPTO
CRYPTS

C•R•••

CARAFE
CARATS
CARBON
CARBOS
CARBOY
CARDED
CARDER
CARDIN
CARDIO
CAREEN
CAREER
CARESS
CARETO
CARETS
CARFUL
CARGOS
CARHOP
CARIBE
CARIBS
CARIES
CARINA
CARING
CARKED
CARLIN
CARLOS
CARLOT
CARMAN
CARMEL
CARMEN
CARNAL
CARNES
CARNET
CARNEY
CARNOT
CAROBS
CAROLE
CAROLS
CAROMS
CARONI
CARPAL
CARPED
CARPEL
CARPER
CARPET
CARPUS
CARREL
CARREY
CARRIE
CARROL
CARROT
CARSON
CARTED
CARTEL
CARTER
CARTES
CARTON
CARUSO
CARVED
CARVER
CARVES
CARVEY
CDROMS
CERATE
CEREAL
CEREUS
CERIPH
CERISE
CERIUM
CERMET
CERROS
CERTIF
CERUSE
CERVID
CHRISM
CHROMA
CHROME
CHROMO
CHROMY
CHRONO
CIRCLE
CIRCUM
CIRCUS
CIRQUE
CIRRUS
CORALS
CORBAN
CORBEL
CORBIN
CORDAY
CORDED
CORDON
CORERS
CORGIS
CORING
CORIUM
CORKED
CORKER
CORMAN
CORNEA
CORNED

CORNEL
CORNER
CORNET
CORONA
CORPUS
CORRAL
CORREL
CORSET
CORTES
CORTEX
CORTEZ
CORVEE
CORVES
CORYZA
CURACY
CURARE
CURATE
CURBED
CURDED
CURDLE
CURERS
CURFEW
CURIAE
CURIAL
CURING
CURIOS
CURIUM
CURLED
CURLER
CURLEW
CURLEY
CURLUP
CURRED
CURSED
CURSES
CURSOR
CURTER
CURTIN
CURTIS
CURTIZ
CURTLY
CURTSY
CURULE
CURVED
CURVES
CURVET
CURZON
CYRANO

C••R••

CADRES
CAIRNS
CAPRIS
CARREL
CARREY
CARRIE
CARROL
CARROT
CATRIG
CEDRIC
CEORLS
CERROS
CHARGE
CHARLY
CHARMS
CHARON
CHARRO
CHARTS
CHERIE
CHERRY
CHERTY
CHERUB
CHERYL
CHIRAC
CHIRON
CHIRPS
CHIRPY
CHIRRS
CHORAL
CHORDS
CHORES
CHORUS
CHURCH
CHURLS
CHURNS
CHURRO
CHURRS
CHYRON
CIARDI
CIRRUS
CITRIC
CITRON
CITRUS
CLARET
CLARKE
CLAROS
CLERGY
CLERIC
CLERKS
CLORIS
CLOROX
COARSE
COBRAS
COERCE
CONRAD
CONROY
CORRAL
CORREL
COURIC
COURSE
COURTS
COWRIE
CRURAL
CUPRIC
CURRED
CYMRIC
CYPRUS
CZERNY

C•••R•

CABERS
CAGERS
CAMARO
CAMERA
CANARD
CANARY
CANERS
CAPERS
CASERN
CASTRO
CATERS
CAVERN
CAVERS
CAVORT
CEDARS
CELERY
CENTRE
CENTRI
CENTRO
CESARE
CETERA
CHAIRS
CHARRO
CHEERS
CHEERY
CHERRY
CHEVRE
CHIRRS
CHLORO
CHOIRS
CHOPRA
CHURRO
CHURRS
CICERO
CIDERS
CIGARS
CITERS
CLAIRE
CLEARS
COBURG
COBURN
CODERS
COHERE
COHORT
COLORS
COMERS
CONTRA
CONTRE
CONURE
COOERS
CORERS
COVERS
COVERT
COWARD
COWERS
CRIERS
CRYERS
CSHARP
CUNARD
CURARE
CURERS
CYBORG
CYDERS

C••••R

CABLER
CADGER
CAESAR
CAGIER
CAHIER
CAKIER
CALDER
CALLER
CALMER
CAMBER
CAMPER
CANDOR
CANIER
CANKER
CANNER
CANTER
CANTOR
CAPPER
CAPTOR
CARDER
CAREER
CARPER
CARTER
CARVER
CASPAR
CASPER
CASTER
CASTOR
CATHER
CAVIAR
CAWDOR
CELLAR
CENSER
CENSOR
CENTER
CHADOR
CHASER
CHEWER
CHIDER
CHOKER
CHOLER
CHUKAR
CINDER
CIPHER
CLAMOR
CLAWER
CLEVER
CLOSER
CLOVER
CMAJOR
CMINOR
COALER
COAXER
COCKER
CODGER
COFFER
COHEIR
COINER
COKIER
COLDER
COLLAR
COLOUR
COLTER
COMBER
CONCUR
CONDOR
CONFER
CONGER
CONKER
CONNER
CONNOR
COODER
COOKER
COOLER
COOPER
COOTER
COPIER
COPPER
COPTER
CORKER
CORNER
COSIER
COSTAR
COTTER
COUGAR
COUTER
COWPER
COZIER
CRATER
CRAVER
CROWER
CRUDER
CULLER
CULVER
CUMBER
CURLER
CURSOR
CURTER
CUSTER
CUTLER
CUTTER
CYCLER
CYPHER

•CR•••

ACROSS
OCREAE
SCRAGS
SCRAMS
SCRAPE
SCRAPS
SCRAWL
SCREAK
SCREAM
SCREED
SCREEN
SCREES
SCREWS
SCREWY
SCRIBE
SCRIMP
SCRIMS
SCRIPS
SCRIPT
SCRODS
SCROLL
SCROOP
SCRUBS
SCRUFF
SCRUMS

•C•R••

ACARID
ACARUS
ACCRUE
ACORNS
ECARTE
ICARIA
ICARUS
MCCREA
MCGRAW
MCGREW
OCHRES
OCTROI
SCARAB
SCARCE
SCARED
SCARER
SCARES
SCARFS
SCARNE
SCARPS
SCARRY
SCARUM
SCORCH
SCORED
SCORER
SCORES
SCORIA
SCORNS
SCURFY
SCURRY
SCURVE
SCURVY

•C••R•

ACCORD
ACTORS
OCCURS
OCHERS
OCHERY
SCARRY
SCHORL
SCLERA
SCLERO
SCOURS
SCURRY

•C•••R

ACHIER
ECLAIR
ICKIER
MCNAIR
OCULAR
SCALAR
SCALER
SCARER
SCORER
SCOTER

••CR••

ACCRUE
DACRON
DECREE
ESCROW
MACRAE
MACRON
MACROS
MCCREA
MICRON
MICROS
NACRES
SACRAL
SACRED
SACRUM
SECRET

••C•R•

ACCORD
ARCARO
BICARB
BICORN
CICERO
DECORS
DICERS
ENCORE
ESCARP
ESCORT
EUCHRE
GOCART
IDCARD
INCURS
LACERS
OCCURS
OSCARS
OXCART
PACERS
PICARA
PICARD
PICARO
RACERS
RECORD
RECORK
RECURS
RICERS
SECERN
SECURE
ULCERS
UNCORK
UNCURL
VICARS

••C••R

ANCHOR
ARCHER
BACKER
BECKER
BICKER
COCKER
CYCLER
DECKER
DICIER
DICKER
DOCKER
DOCTOR
ESCHER
ETCHER
FACTOR
HACKER
HECTOR
KICKER
LACIER
LECTER
LECTOR
LICTOR
LOCKER
MOCKER
NECTAR
NICKER
PACKER
PICKER
PUCKER
RACIER
RECTOR
RICHER
ROCKER
SACKER
SECTOR
SICKER
SOCCER
SUCCOR
SUCKER
TACKER
TICKER
TUCKER
VECTOR
VICTOR
WICKER

•••CR•

DESCRY
FARCRY
FIACRE
FULCRA
OUTCRY
VELCRO
WARCRY

•••C•R

BARCAR
BOXCAR
BRACER
CONCUR
DANCER
DEICER
FENCER
FORCER
GROCER
HOTCAR
JUICER
LANCER
LASCAR
MERCER
MINCER
NASCAR
PIECER
PINCER
PLACER
PRICER
RANCOR
SAUCER
SLICER
SOCCER
SPACER
SUCCOR
TOWCAR
TRACER
TROCAR
WINCER

CS••••

CSHARP
CSPOTS

C•S•••

CASABA
CASALS
CASAVA
CASBAH
CASEFY
CASERN
CASHED
CASHES
CASHEW
CASHIN
CASING
CASINO
CASPAR
CASPER
CASQUE
CASSIA
CASSIO
CASSIS
CASTER
CASTES
CASTLE
CASTON
CASTOR
CASTRO
CASUAL
CESARE
CESIUM
CESSED
CESSES
CESSNA
CESTAS
CESTOS
CESTUS
CISCOS
CISKEI
COSELL
COSHED
COSHES
COSIED
COSIER
COSIES
COSIGN
COSILY
COSINE
COSMIC
COSMOS
COSSET
COSTAE
COSTAL
COSTAR
COSTAS
COSTLY
CPSNOW
CUSACK
CUSHAW
CUSPED
CUSPID
CUSSED
CUSSES
CUSTER
CUSTIS
CUSTOM
CUSTOS

C••S••

CAESAR
CAPSID
CARSON
CASSIA
CASSIO
CASSIS
CATSUP
CAUSAL
CAUSED
CAUSES
CEASED
CEASES
CENSED
CENSER
CENSES
CENSOR
CENSUS
CESSED
CESSES
CESSNA
CHASED
CHASER
CHASES
CHASMS
CHASSE
CHASTE
CHESTS
CHESTY
CHISEL
CHISOX
CHOSEN
CLASPS
CLASSY
CLOSED
CLOSER
CLOSES
CLOSET
COASTS
COMSAT
CONSUL
COPSES
CORSET
COSSET
COUSIN
CRESOL
CRESTS
CRISCO
CRISES
CRISIS
CRISPS
CRISPY
CRISTO
CROSBY
CROSSE
CRUSES
CRUSOE
CRUSTS
CRUSTY
CUESTA
CUISSE
CURSED
CURSES
CURSOR
CUSSED
CUSSES
CUTSIN
CUTSUP

C•••S•

CALASH
CAMISE
CARESS
CARUSO
CAYUSE
CERISE
CERUSE
CHAISE
CHASSE
CHEESE
CHEESY
CHOOSE
CHOOSY
CHRISM
CHUHSI
CLASSY
CLAUSE
CLEESE
CLUMSY
COARSE
COHOST
COURSE
COYEST
COYISH
CREASE
CREASY
CREUSA
CROSSE
CROUSE
CRUISE
CUBISM
CUBIST
CUISSE
CURTSY
CUTEST
CUTESY

C••••S

CABALS
CABERS
CABINS
CABLES
CACAOS
CACHES
CACTUS
CADDIS
CADETS
CADGES
CADMUS
CADRES
CAGERS
CAGUAS
CAHOWS
CAICOS
CAIRNS
CAJUNS
CALAIS
CALCES
CALLAS
CALLES
CALLUS
CALVES
CALXES
CAMELS
CAMEOS
CAMPOS
CAMPUS
CANALS
CANERS
CANIDS
CANNES
CANOES
CANONS
CANTOS
CANVAS
CAPERS
CAPIAS
CAPONS
CAPRIS
CARATS
CARBOS
CARESS
CARETS
CARGOS
CARIBS
CARIES
CARLOS
CARNES
CAROBS
CAROLS
CAROMS
CARPUS
CARTES
CARVES
CASALS
CASHES
CASSIS
CASTES
CATERS
CAUCUS
CAULKS
CAUSES
CAVERS
CAVILS
CDROMS
CEASES
CEDARS
CEIBAS
CELEBS
CELLOS
CENSES
CENSUS
CENTOS
CEORLS
CEREUS
CERROS
CESSES
CESTAS
CESTOS
CESTUS
CHAFES
CHAFFS
CHAINS
CHAIRS
CHALKS
CHAMPS
CHANTS
CHARMS
CHARTS
CHASES
CHASMS
CHEATS
CHECKS
CHEEKS
CHEEPS
CHEERS
CHELAS
CHEOPS
CHESTS
CHETHS
CHIAUS
CHICKS
CHIDES
CHIEFS
CHILDS
CHILLS
CHIMES
CHIMPS
CHINES
CHINKS
CHINOS
CHIRPS
CHIRRS
CHIVES
CHOCKS
CHOIRS
CHOKES
CHOLOS
CHOMPS
CHORDS
CHORES
CHORUS
CHUCKS
CHUMPS
CHUNKS
CHURLS
CHURNS
CHURRS
CHUTES
CIDERS
CIGARS
CIRCUS
CIRRUS
CISCOS
CITERS
CITIES
CITIUS
CITRUS
CIVETS
CIVICS
CLACKS
CLAIMS
CLAMPS
CLANGS
CLANKS
CLAROS
CLASPS
CLAVES
CLEANS
CLEARS
CLEATS
CLEEKS
CLEFTS
CLERKS
CLEVES
CLEVIS
CLICKS
CLIFFS
CLIMBS
CLIMES
CLINES
CLINGS
CLINKS
CLOAKS
CLOCKS
CLOMPS
CLONES
CLONKS
CLONUS
CLORIS
CLOSES
CLOTHS
CLOUDS
CLOUTS
CLOVES
CLOVIS
CLOWNS
CLUCKS
CLUMPS
CLUNKS
CMINUS
CNIDUS
CNOTES
COAPTS
COASTS
COATIS
COAXES
COBIAS
COBRAS
COCCUS
COCOAS
CODERS
CODONS
COIGNS
COLEUS
COLIES
COLONS
COLORS
COMBES
COMBOS
COMERS
COMETS
COMICS
COMMAS
COMPOS
COMTES
CONCHS
CONDOS
CONEYS
CONGAS
CONICS
CONIES
CONTES
COOERS
COOPTS
COPAYS
COPIES
COPSES
CORALS
CORERS
CORGIS
CORPUS
CORTES
CORVES
COSHES
COSIES
COSMOS
COSTAS
COTTAS
COUGHS
COUNTS
COUPES
COURTS
COVENS
COVERS
COVETS
COVEYS
COWENS
COWERS
COYPUS
COZENS
COZIES
CRACKS
CRAFTS
CRAKES
CRAMPS
CRANES
CRANKS
CRAPES
CRATES
CRAVES
CRAWLS
CRAZES
CREAKS
CREAMS
CREDOS
CREEDS
CREEKS
CREELS
CREEPS
CREMES
CREPES
CRESTS
CRICKS
CRIERS
CRIMES
CRIMPS
CRIPES
CRISES
CRISIS
CRISPS
CROAKS
CROATS
CROCKS
CROCUS
CROFTS
CRONES
CRONUS
CROOKS
CROONS
CROWDS
CROWNS
CROZES
CRUCES
CRUETS
CRUMBS
CRUSES
CRUSTS
CRUXES
CRYERS
CRYPTS
CSPOTS
CUBEBS
CUBICS
CUBITS
CULETS
CULLIS
CUPELS
CUPIDS
CUPPAS
CURERS
CURIOS
CURSES
CURTIS
CURVES
CUSSES
CUSTIS
CUSTOS
CUTIES
CUTINS
CUTUPS
CUVEES
CYCADS
CYCLAS
CYCLES
CYCLOS
CYDERS
CYGNUS
CYNICS
CYPRUS
CZECHS

•C•S••

ACESUP
ACTSAS
ACTSON
ACTSUP
ECESIC
ECESIS
ICESIN
ICESUP
OCASEK
OCASEY

•C••S•

ACCESS
ACCOST
ACCUSE
ACROSS
ICIEST
SCHISM
SCHIST
SCHUSS
SCOUSE

•C•••S

ACARUS
ACCESS
ACEOUS
ACINUS
ACORNS
ACROSS
ACTORS
ACTSAS
BCELLS
ECCLES
ECESIS
ECHOES
ECLATS
ECOLES
ICARUS
ICINGS
MCJOBS
OCCURS
OCEANS
OCHERS
OCHRES
OCTADS
OCTETS
SCALDS
SCALES
SCALPS
SCAMPS
SCANTS
SCAPES
SCARES
SCARFS
SCARPS
SCAUPS
SCENAS
SCENDS
SCENES
SCENTS
SCHMOS
SCHUSS
SCHWAS
SCIFIS
SCIONS
SCOFFS
SCOLDS
SCONES
SCOOPS
SCOOTS
SCOPES
SCORES
SCORNS
SCOURS
SCOUTS
SCOWLS
SCRAGS
SCRAMS
SCRAPS
SCREES
SCREWS
SCRIMS
SCRIPS
SCRODS
SCRUBS
SCRUMS
SCUBAS
SCUFFS
SCULLS
SCUTES
UCLANS
VCHIPS

••CS••

FOCSLE
TOCSIN
TUCSON

••C•S•

ACCESS
ACCOST
ACCUSE
ATCOST
ENCASE
EXCESS
EXCISE
EXCUSE
INCASE
INCASH
INCISE
INCUSE
JOCOSE
LOCUST
MUCOSA
NICEST
RECAST
RECESS
RECUSE
UNCASE
UPCAST

••C••S

ACCESS
ARCCOS
ARCHES
ASCOTS
BACKUS
BICEPS
CACAOS
CACHES
CACTUS
COCCUS
COCOAS
CYCADS
CYCLAS
CYCLES
CYCLOS
DACHAS
DECAFS
DECALS
DECAYS
DECORS
DECOYS
DICERS
DICOTS
DICTUS
DUCATS
ECCLES
EMCEES
ETCHES
EXCELS
EXCESS
FACETS
FACIAS
FACIES
FICHES
FICHUS
GECKOS
HACEKS
INCANS
INCHES
INCURS
ITCHES
JACALS
LACERS
LACHES
LOCALS

LUCIUS
LYCEES
MACAWS
MACHES
MACHOS
MACROS
MECCAS
MICROS
MOCHAS
MUCINS
MUCOUS
NACHOS
NACRES
NICHES
OCCURS
OSCARS
PACERS
PECANS
PICOTS
PICULS
RACERS
RACHIS
RACONS
RECAPS
RECESS
RECONS
RECTOS
RECTUS
RECURS
RICERS
RICHES
RUCHES
RUCKUS
SOCLES
SUCCES
SUCHAS
SUCKAS
TICALS
ULCERS
UNCAPS
UNCLES
VICARS
VICTIS
VOCALS
WACKOS
YACHTS
YUCCAS

•••C•S

ABACAS
ABACUS
AMICES
AMICUS
APICES
ARCCOS
ARECAS
BAUCIS
BLACKS
BLOCKS
BONCES
BRACES
BRACTS
BRICKS
BUNCOS
CAICOS
CALCES
CAUCUS
CHECKS
CHICKS
CHOCKS
CHUCKS
CIRCUS
CISCOS
CLACKS
CLICKS
CLOCKS
CLUCKS
COCCUS
CONCHS
CRACKS
CRICKS
CROCKS
CROCUS
CRUCES
CZECHS
DANCES
DEICES
DEUCES
DISCOS
DISCUS
DORCAS
DUNCES
EDICTS
EDUCES
EJECTS
ELECTS
ENACTS
EPOCHS
ERECTS
ERUCTS
EVICTS
EXACTS
FALCES
FARCES
FASCES
FAUCES
FENCES
FLACKS
FLECKS
FLICKS
FLOCKS
FORCES
FRACAS
FROCKS
GLACES
GLACIS
GRACES
GUACOS
JUICES
JUNCOS
KNACKS
KNICKS
KNOCKS
KYACKS
LANCES
MARCOS
MARCUS
MECCAS
MINCES
MULCTS
NIECES
NUECES
ORACHS
OUNCES
PAUCIS
PHOCIS
PIECES
PISCES
PLACES
PLUCKS
PONCES
PRECIS
PRICES
PRICKS
PSYCHS
QUACKS
REACTS
SAUCES
SHACKS
SHOCKS
SHUCKS
SLACKS
SLICES
SLICKS
SMACKS
SMOCKS
SNACKS
SNICKS
SPACES
SPECKS
SPICAS
SPICES
STACKS
STICKS
STOCKS
SUCCES
SULCUS
TINCTS
TRACES
TRACKS
TRACTS
TRICES
TRICKS
TRUCES
TRUCKS
VINCES
VNECKS
VOICES
WENCES
WHACKS
WINCES
WRACKS
WRECKS
YOICKS
YUCCAS

••••CS

ANTICS
ASDICS
ASPICS
ATTICS
AZTECS
BASICS
BRONCS
CIVICS
COMICS
CONICS
CUBICS
CYNICS
DUROCS
ETHICS
FRANCS
HAVOCS
IONICS
KOVACS
LILACS
LYRICS
MEDICS
MIMICS
MODOCS
OLMECS
OPTICS
OSMICS
PANICS
REBECS
RELICS
SERACS
SONICS
STOICS
SUMACS
TONICS
TOPICS
TOXICS
TUNICS
XEBECS

C•T•••

CATCHY
CATENA
CATERS
CATGUT
CATHAY
CATHER
CATION
CATKIN
CATNAP
CATNIP
CATRIG
CATSUP
CATTED
CATTLE
CATTON
CETANE
CETERA
CITATO
CITERS
CITIES
CITIFY
CITING
CITIUS
CITRIC
CITRON
CITRUS
COTTAS
COTTEN
COTTER
COTTON
CUTELY
CUTEST
CUTESY
CUTIES
CUTINS
CUTLER
CUTLET
CUTOFF
CUTOUT
CUTSIN
CUTSUP
CUTTER
CUTUPS

C••T••

CACTUS
CAFTAN
CANTAB
CANTED
CANTER
CANTHI
CANTLE
CANTON
CANTOR
CANTOS
CAPTAN
CAPTOR
CARTED
CARTEL
CARTER
CARTES
CARTON
CASTER
CASTES
CASTLE
CASTON
CASTOR
CASTRO
CATTED
CATTLE
CATTON
CAXTON
CELTIC
CENTER
CENTOS
CENTRE
CENTRI
CENTRO
CERTIF
CESTAS
CESTOS
CESTUS
CHATTY
CHATUP
CHETHS
CHITIN
CHITON
CHUTED
CHUTES
CLOTHE
CLOTHO
CLOTHS
CLOTTY
CLUTCH
CNOTES
COATED
COATIS
COLTER
COMTES
CONTAC
CONTES
CONTRA
CONTRE
COOTER
COOTIE
COPTER
COPTIC
CORTES
CORTEX
CORTEZ
COSTAE
COSTAL
COSTAR
COSTAS
COSTLY
COTTAS
COTTEN
COTTER
COTTON
COUTER
CRATED
CRATER
CRATES
CRETAN
CRETIN
CRITIC
CROTON
CRUTCH
CULTIC
CURTER
CURTIN
CURTIS
CURTIZ
CURTLY
CURTSY
CUSTER
CUSTIS
CUSTOM
CUSTOS
CUTTER

C•••T•

CADETS
CAMETO
CANUTE
CAPITA
CAPOTE
CARATS
CARETO
CARETS
CAVETT
CAVITY
CENOTE
CERATE
CHANTS
CHARTS
CHASTE
CHATTY
CHEATS
CHERTY
CHESTS
CHESTY
CHINTZ
CHOATE
CITATO
CIVETS
CLEATS
CLEFTS
CLOTTY
CLOUTS
COAPTS
COASTS
COGITO
COMATE
COMETH
COMETO
COMETS
COMITY
COOPTS
COUNTS
COUNTY
COURTS
COVETS
COYOTE
CRAFTS
CRAFTY
CREATE
CRESTS
CRISTO
CROATS
CROFTS
CROUTE
CRUETS
CRUSTS
CRUSTY
CRYPTO
CRYPTS
CSPOTS
CUBITS
CUESTA
CULETS
CURATE

C••••T

CACHET
CADENT
CAMEAT
CAMLET
CANLIT
CANNOT
CAPLET
CAPNUT
CARLOT
CARNET
CARNOT
CARPET
CARROT
CATGUT
CAUGHT
CAVEAT
CAVETT
CAVORT
CEDANT
CEMENT
CERMET
CHALET
CHEVET
CLARET
CLIENT
CLOSET
COBALT
COEDIT
COGENT
COHORT
COHOST
COLLET
COMBAT
COMEAT
COMFIT
COMMIT
COMSAT
CONANT
COOLIT
COPOUT
COQUET
CORNET
CORSET
COSSET
COVENT
COVERT
COYEST
CRAVAT
CREDIT
CUBIST
CULLET
CURVET
CUTEST
CUTLET
CUTOUT
CYGNET

•CT•••

ACTIII
ACTING
ACTINO
ACTION
ACTIUM
ACTIVE
ACTONE
ACTORS
ACTOUT
ACTSAS
ACTSON
ACTSUP
ACTTWO
ACTUAL
ECTYPE
OCTADS
OCTANE
OCTANT
OCTAVE
OCTAVO
OCTETS
OCTOPI
OCTROI

•C•T••

ACETAL
ACETIC
ACETYL
ACTTWO
ICHTHY
SCATHE
SCATTY
SCOTCH
SCOTER
SCOTIA
SCOTTO
SCOTTY
SCUTCH
SCUTES
SCYTHE

•C••T•

ACUATE
ACUITY
ECARTE
ECLATS
OCTETS
SCANTS
SCANTY
SCATTY
SCENTS
SCOOTS
SCOTTO
SCOTTY
SCOUTS

•C•••T

ACCENT
ACCEPT
ACCOST
ACEOUT
ACQUIT
ACTOUT
ICEOUT
ICIEST
OCCULT
OCELOT
OCTANT
SCHIST
SCRIPT
SCULPT

••CT••

ARCTAN
ARCTIC
CACTUS
DACTYL
DICTUM
DICTUS
DOCTOR
DUCTAL
FACTOR
HECTIC
HECTOR
LACTIC
LECTER
LECTOR
LICTOR
NECTAR
PECTIC
PECTIN
RECTOR
RECTOS
RECTUS
SECTOR
TACTIC
TICTAC
VECTOR
VICTIM
VICTIS
VICTOR

••C•T•

ALCOTT
ASCOTS
DICOTS
DUCATS
EXCITE
FACETS
FICHTE
HECATE
INCITE
LOCATE
LUCITE
NICETY
OOCYTE
PICOTS
RECITE
VACATE
YACHTS

••C••T

ACCENT
ACCEPT
ACCOST
ALCOTT
ASCENT
ATCOST
BECKET
BUCKET
CACHET
DACOIT
DECANT
DECEIT
DECENT
DECOCT
DOCENT
DOCKET
ESCENT
ESCORT
EXCEPT
GOCART
INCEPT
INCULT
JACKET
LOCKET
LOCUST
LUCENT
NICEST
NOCENT
OCCULT
OXCART
PACKET
PECKAT
PICKAT
PICKET
POCKET
RACKET
RECANT
RECAST
RECENT
RECOAT
ROCHET
ROCKET
SACHET
SECANT
SECRET
SOCKET
TICKET
TUCKET
UPCAST
VACANT
WICKET

•••CT•

ALECTO
BRACTS
EDICTS
EJECTA
EJECTS
ELECTS
ENACTS
ERECTS
ERUCTS
EVICTS
EXACTA
EXACTO
EXACTS
HINCTY
MULCTS
REACTS
SANCTA
STACTE
TINCTS
TRACTS

•••C•T

AVOCET
BOBCAT
BRECHT
DULCET
ELICIT
FATCAT
FAUCET
HEPCAT
LANCET
MASCOT
MUDCAT
MUSCAT
PLACET
REXCAT
SNOCAT
TERCET
TOMCAT
TOPCAT
TRICOT
VINCIT

••••CT

ABDUCT
ABJECT
ADDUCT
AFFECT
ASPECT
BISECT
DECOCT
DEDUCT
DEFECT
DEJECT
DELICT
DEPICT
DETECT
DIDACT
DIRECT
EFFECT
EXPECT
IMPACT
INDICT
INDUCT
INFACT
INFECT
INJECT
INSECT
INTACT
OBJECT
ONEACT
OUTACT
REDACT
REJECT
RELICT
RELUCT
RESECT
SELECT
STRICT

CU••••

CUBAGE
CUBEBS
CUBICS
CUBING
CUBISM
CUBIST
CUBITS
CUBOID
CUCKOO
CUDDLE
CUDDLY
CUDGEL
CUESTA
CUFFED
CUIABA
CUIQUE
CUISSE
CULETS
CULKIN
CULLED
CULLEN
CULLER
CULLET
CULLIS
CULTIC
CULVER
CUMBER
CUMULI
CUMULO
CUNARD
CUNAXA
CUNEAL
CUPELS
CUPFUL
CUPIDS
CUPOLA
CUPPAS
CUPPED
CUPRIC
CURACY
CURARE
CURATE
CURBED
CURDED
CURDLE
CURERS
CURFEW
CURIAE
CURIAL
CURING
CURIOS
CURIUM
CURLED
CURLER
CURLEW
CURLEY
CURLUP
CURRED
CURSED
CURSES
CURSOR
CURTER
CURTIN
CURTIS
CURTIZ
CURTLY
CURTSY
CURULE
CURVED
CURVES
CURVET
CURZON
CUSACK
CUSHAW
CUSPED
CUSPID
CUSSED
CUSSES
CUSTER
CUSTIS
CUSTOM
CUSTOS
CUTELY
CUTEST
CUTESY
CUTIES
CUTINS
CUTLER
CUTLET
CUTOFF
CUTOUT
CUTSIN
CUTSUP
CUTTER
CUTUPS
CUVEES

C•U•••

CAUCHO
CAUCHY
CAUCUS
CAUDAL
CAUDEX
CAUDLE
CAUGHT
CAULKS
CAUSAL
CAUSED
CAUSES
CHUBBY
CHUCKS
CHUFFY
CHUHSI
CHUKAR
CHUKKA
CHUMMY
CHUMPS
CHUNKS
CHUNKY
CHURCH
CHURLS
CHURNS
CHURRO
CHURRS
CHUTED
CHUTES
CIUDAD
CLUBBY
CLUCKS
CLUEIN
CLUING
CLUMPS
CLUMPY
CLUMSY
CLUNKS
CLUNKY
CLUTCH
COUGAR
COUGHS
COULDA
COULEE
COUNTS
COUNTY
COUPES
COUPLE
COUPON
COURIC
COURSE
COURTS
COUSIN
COUTER
CRUCES
CRUDDY
CRUDER
CRUETS
CRUISE
CRUMBS
CRUMBY
CRUMMY
CRUNCH
CRURAL
CRUSES
CRUSOE
CRUSTS
CRUSTY
CRUTCH
CRUXES

C••U••

CAGUAS
CAJUNS
CANUTE
CARUSO
CASUAL
CAYUGA
CAYUSE
CERUSE
CHOUGH
CLAUDE
CLAUSE
CLOUDS
CLOUDY
CLOUTS
COBURG
COBURN
COHUNE
COLUGO
COLUMN
CONURE
COPULA
COQUET
CREUSA
CROUCH
CROUPY
CROUSE
CROUTE
CUMULI
CUMULO
CURULE
CUTUPS

C•••U•

CACTUS
CADMUS
CAIQUE
CALLUP
CALLUS
CALQUE
CAMEUP
CAMPUS
CANCUN
CANFUL
CAPFUL
CAPGUN
CAPNUT
CARFUL
CARPUS
CASQUE
CATGUT
CATSUP
CAUCUS
CENSUS
CEREUS
CERIUM
CESIUM
CESTUS
CHATUP
CHEQUE
CHERUB
CHEWUP
CHIAUS
CHINUP
CHORUS
CILIUM
CINQUE
CIRCUM
CIRCUS
CIRQUE
CIRRUS
CITIUS
CITRUS
CLAMUP
CLAQUE
CLIQUE
CLIQUY
CLOGUP
CLONUS
CLOQUE
CMINUS
CNIDUS
COCCUS
COILUP
COLEUS
COLOUR
COMEUP
CONCUR
CONIUM
CONSUL
COOKUP
COOPUP
COPOUT
CORIUM
CORPUS
COYPUS
CROCUS
CRONUS
CROPUP
CUIQUE
CUPFUL
CURIUM
CURLUP
CUTOUT
CUTSUP
CYGNUS
CYPRUS

C••••U

CACHOU
CHONJU
CHOOYU
CONGOU

•CU•••

ACUATE
ACUITY
ACUMEN
OCULAR
SCUBAS
SCUFFS
SCULLS
SCULLY
SCULPT
SCUMMY
SCURFY
SCURRY
SCURVE
SCURVY
SCUTCH
SCUTES
SCUZZY

•C•U••

ACCUSE
ACQUIT
ACTUAL
MCHUGH
MCKUEN
OCCULT
OCCUPY
OCCURS
SCAUPS
SCHULZ
SCHUSS
SCOURS
SCOUSE
SCOUTS
SCRUBS
SCRUFF
SCRUMS

•C••U•

ACARUS
ACCRUE
ACEOUS
ACEOUT
ACESUP
ACINUS
ACTIUM
ACTOUT
ACTSUP
ICARUS
ICEDUP
ICEOUT
ICESUP
SCARUM

•C•••U

ACAJOU

••CU••

ACCUSE
ALCUIN
ESCUDO
EXCUSE
FACULA
FECUND
HECUBA
INCULT
INCURS
INCUSE
JOCUND
LACUNA
LOCUST
MACULA
OCCULT
OCCUPY
OCCURS
OSCULA
PICULS
RECURS
RECUSE
SECURE
UNCURL
VACUUM
VICUNA

••C•U•

ACCRUE
BACKUP
BACKUS
BUCKUP
CACTUS
COCCUS
DICTUM
DICTUS
FACEUP
FICHUS
HICCUP
JACKUP
KICKUP
LACEUP
LOCKUP
LUCIUS
LYCEUM
MACOUN
MOCKUP
MUCKUP
MUCOUS
PACKUP
PICKUP
RACKUP
RECOUP
RECTUS
RUCKUS
SACQUE
SACRUM
TUCHUN
VACUUM

••C••U

CACHOU
PICCHU

•••CU•

ABACUS
AMICUS
CANCUN
CAUCUS
CIRCUM
CIRCUS
COCCUS
CONCUR
CROCUS
DISCUS
EGGCUP
EYECUP
FESCUE
HICCUP
MARCUS
MISCUE
RESCUE
SULCUS
TALCUM
TEACUP

•••C•U

MANCHU
PICCHU

••••CU

APERCU
IGUACU

C•V•••

CAVEAT
CAVEIN
CAVELL
CAVERN

CAVERS
CAVETT
CAVIAR
CAVILS
CAVING
CAVITY
CAVORT
CIVETS
CIVICS
COVENS
COVENT
COVERS
COVERT
COVETS
COVEYS
COVINA
CUVEES

C••V••
CALVED
CALVES
CALVIN
CANVAS
CARVED
CARVER
CARVES
CARVEY
CERVID
CHAVEZ
CHEVAL
CHEVET
CHEVRE
CHIVES
CLAVES
CLAVIN
CLEVER
CLEVES
CLEVIS
CLOVEN
CLOVER
CLOVES
CLOVIS
COEVAL
CONVEX
CONVEY
CONVOY
CORVEE
CORVES
CRAVAT
CRAVED
CRAVEN
CRAVER
CRAVES
CULVER
CURVED
CURVES
CURVET

C•••V•
CANOVA
CASAVA
CLEAVE

C••••V
CHEKOV

•C••V•
ACTIVE
OCTAVE
OCTAVO
SCURVE
SCURVY

••C•V•
ALCOVE

••C••V
ROCKYV
VACLAV

C•W•••
CAWDOR
CAWING
COWARD
COWBOY
COWENS
COWERS
COWING
COWLED
COWLEY
COWMAN
COWMEN
COWPEA
COWPER
COWPOX
COWRIE

C••W••
CHEWED
CHEWER
CHEWUP
CHOWED
CLAWED
CLAWER
CLEWED
CLOWNS
COBWEB
CONWAY
CRAWLS
CRAWLY
CREWED
CREWEL
CROWDS
CROWED
CROWER
CROWNS

C•••W•
CAHOWS

C••••W
CALLOW
CASHEW
CPSNOW
CURFEW
CURLEW
CUSHAW

•C•W••
SCHWAB
SCHWAS
SCOWLS

•C••W•
ACTTWO
SCRAWL
SCREWS
SCREWY

•C•••W
MCGRAW
MCGREW

••C•W•
MACAWS

••C••W
ESCHEW
ESCROW

•••C•W
ANTCOW
MOSCOW
PESCOW
SEACOW

C•X•••
CAXTON

C••X••
CALXES
COAXED
COAXER
COAXES
CRUXES

C•••X•
CUNAXA

C••••X
CAUDEX
CHISOX
CLIMAX
CLOROX
COCCYX
COLFAX
COMMIX
CONVEX
CORTEX
COWPOX

•C•••X
ICEBOX

••C••X
COCCYX
PICKAX

•••C•X
COCCYX
WILCOX

CY••••
CYANIC
CYBELE
CYBILL
CYBORG
CYCADS
CYCLAS
CYCLED
CYCLER
CYCLES
CYCLIC
CYCLOS
CYDERS
CYGNET
CYGNUS
CYMBAL
CYMRIC
CYNICS
CYPHER
CYPRUS
CYRANO

C•Y•••
CAYMAN
CAYUGA
CAYUSE
CEYLON
CHYRON
COYEST
COYISH
COYOTE
COYPUS
CRYERS
CRYING
CRYOFF
CRYPTO
CRYPTS

C••Y••
CANYON
CLAYEY
CLOYED
CORYZA
CRAYON

C•••Y•
CHERYL
CHOOYU
COCCYX
CONEYS
COPAYS
COVEYS
CRONYN

C••••Y
CAGILY
CAGNEY
CALMLY
CAMEBY
CANARY
CANOPY
CARBOY
CARNEY
CARREY
CARVEY
CASEFY
CATCHY
CATHAY
CAUCHY
CAVITY
CECILY
CELERY
CHAFFY
CHALKY
CHAMMY
CHANCY
CHANEY
CHARLY
CHATTY
CHEEKY
CHEERY
CHEESY
CHERRY
CHERTY
CHESTY
CHICLY
CHILLY
CHINKY
CHIRPY
CHOOSY
CHOPPY
CHROMY
CHUBBY
CHUFFY
CHUMMY
CHUNKY
CICELY
CITIFY
CLAMMY
CLANCY
CLANKY
CLASSY
CLAYEY
CLERGY
CLIFFY
CLINGY
CLIQUY
CLODDY
CLOGGY
CLOTTY
CLOUDY
CLUBBY
CLUMPY
CLUMSY
CLUNKY
CODIFY
COLDLY
COLONY
COMEBY
COMEDY
COMELY
COMITY
COMPLY
CONROY
CONVEY
CONVOY
CONWAY
COOLLY
COONEY
COPLEY
CORDAY
COSILY
COSTLY
COUNTY
COWBOY
COWLEY
COZILY
CRABBY
CRACKY
CRAFTY
CRAGGY
CRANKY
CRANNY
CRAWLY
CREAKY
CREAMY
CREASY
CREEPY
CRIKEY
CRIMPY
CRISPY
CROAKY
CROSBY
CROUPY
CRUDDY
CRUMBY
CRUMMY
CRUSTY
CUDDLY
CURACY
CURLEY
CURTLY
CURTSY
CUTELY
CUTESY
CZERNY

•CY•••
SCYLLA
SCYTHE

•C•Y••
ECTYPE

•C••Y•
ACETYL

•C•••Y
ACIDLY
ACUITY
ICHTHY
OCASEY
OCCUPY
OCHERY
SCABBY
SCANTY
SCARRY
SCATTY
SCHIZY
SCOTTY
SCREWY
SCULLY
SCUMMY
SCURFY
SCURRY
SCURVY
SCUZZY

••CY••
OOCYTE

••C•Y•
COCCYX
DACTYL
DECAYS
DECOYS
JACLYN
ROCKYV

••C••Y
ARCHLY
CECILY
CICELY
DICKEY
HACKLY
HICKEY
HOCKEY
JACKEY
JOCKEY
LACILY
LACKEY
MICKEY
NICELY
NICETY
OCCUPY
PACIFY
RACILY
RECOPY
RICHLY
RICKEY
SICILY
SICKLY
TICKLY
WICOPY

•••CY•
COCCYX

•••C•Y
ALECKY
BEACHY
BISCAY
BLOCKY
BOTCHY
BRACHY
BRICKY
BUNCHY
CATCHY
CAUCHY
CHICLY
CRACKY
DESCRY
FARCRY
FLECKY
FLOCKY
HINCTY
LEACHY
LUNCHY
MUNCHY
MUSCLY
NOTCHY
OUTCRY
PATCHY
PEACHY
PITCHY
PLUCKY
POACHY
POUCHY
PRICEY
PUNCHY
SPACEY
STACEY
STICKY
STOCKY
TETCHY
TORCHY
TOUCHY
TRACEY
TRACHY
TRICKY
WARCRY
WHACKY
WITCHY

••••CY
ABBACY
AGENCY
BOUNCY
CHANCY
CLANCY
CURACY
FLEECY
IDIOCY
JOUNCY
LEGACY
LUNACY
PAPACY
PIRACY
POLICY
QUINCY

CZ••••
CZECHS
CZERNY

C•Z•••
COZENS
COZIED
COZIER
COZIES
COZILY

C••Z••
CRAZED
CRAZES
CROZES
CURZON

C•••Z•
CORYZA

C••••Z
CHAVEZ
CHINTZ
CORTEZ
CURTIZ

•C•Z••
SCUZZY

•C••Z•
SCHIZY
SCUZZY

•C•••Z
SCHNOZ
SCHULZ

DA••••
DABBED
DABBLE
DABNEY
DACAPO
DACHAS
DACOIT
DACRON
DACTYL
DADDYO
DADOED
DADOES
DAEDAL
DAFFED
DAFTER
DAFTLY
DAGAMA
DAGGER
DAGMAR
DAHLIA
DAIKON
DAILEY
DAIMON
DAIMYO
DAINTY
DAIREN
DAISES
DAKOTA
DALASI
DALETH
DALLAS
DALLES
DALTON
DAMAGE
DAMASK
DAMATO
DAMIEN
DAMITA
DAMMAR
DAMMED
DAMNED
DAMONE
DAMORE
DAMOUR
DAMPED
DAMPEN
DAMPER
DAMPLY
DAMSEL
DAMSON
DAMSUP
DANANG
DANAUS
DANCED
DANCER
DANCES
DANDER
DANDIE
DANDLE
DANGER
DANGLE
DANGLY
DANGME
DANIEL
DANISH
DANKER
DANKLY
DANNAY
DANNER
DANSON
DANTES
DANTON
DANUBE
DANZIG
DAPHNE
DAPPED
DAPPER
DAPPLE
DARENT
DARETO
DARIEN
DARING
DARIUS
DARKEN
DARKER
DARKLE
DARKLY
DARNAY
DARNED
DARNEL
DARNER
DARNIT
DARREN
DARROW
DARRYL
DARTED
DARTER
DARWIN
DASHED
DASHER
DASHES
DASHIS
DASSIN
DATARY
DATERS
DATING
DATIVE
DATONG
DATSUN
DATURA
DAUBED
DAUBER
DAUBES
DAUNTS
DAVIES
DAVITS
DAWDLE
DAWNED
DAWNON
DAWSON
DAYBED
DAYBOY
DAYGLO
DAYJOB
DAYLIT
DAYONE
DAYTON
DAZING
DAZZLE

D•A•••
DEACON
DEADEN
DEADER
DEADLY
DEADON
DEAFEN
DEAFER
DEAFLY
DEALER
DEALIN
DEANNA
DEARER
DEARIE
DEARLY
DEARME
DEARTH
DEASIL
DHARMA
DIABLO
DIADEM
DIALED
DIALER
DIALOG
DIALUP
DIANNE
DIAPER
DIATOM
DLAYER
DMAJOR
DMARKS
DOABLE
DRABLY
DRACHM
DRAFTS
DRAFTY
DRAGEE
DRAGGY
DRAGIN
DRAGON
DRAILS
DRAINS
DRAKES
DRAMAS
DRAPED
DRAPER
DRAPES
DRAWER
DRAWIN
DRAWLS
DRAWLY
DRAWON
DRAWUP
DRAYED
DUALLY
DUARTE
DWARFS
DWAYNE
DYADIC

D••A••
DACAPO
DAGAMA
DALASI
DAMAGE
DAMASK
DAMATO
DANANG
DANAUS
DATARY
DEBARK
DEBARS
DEBASE
DEBATE
DECADE
DECAFS
DECALS
DECAMP
DECANT
DECAYS
DEFACE
DEFAME
DEFATS
DEGAGE
DEJAVU
DEKALB
DELANO
DELANY
DELATE
DELAYS
DEMAND
DENALI
DENARY
DEPART
DEPAUL
DEPAUW
DERAIL
DESALT
DETACH
DETAIL
DETAIN
DIDACT
DILATE
DINARS
DISANT
DISARM
DIVANS
DOMAIN
DOMANI
DONALD
DONATE
DOPANT
DORADO
DORAGS
DORATI
DOSAGE
DOTAGE
DOTARD
DOUALA
DREADS
DREAMS
DREAMT
DREAMY
DREARY
DRYADS
DSHARP
DUCATS
DUNANT
DURANT
DUVALL
DYNAMO
DYNAST

D•••A•
DACHAS
DAEDAL
DAGMAR
DALLAS
DAMMAR
DANNAY
DARNAY
DEBRAS
DEEJAY
DEEPAK
DEFEAT
DEFRAY
DELMAR
DELRAY
DELTAS
DEMEAN
DENIAL
DENTAL
DEODAR
DERMAL
DESMAN
DEWLAP
DIGRAM
DIKTAT
DIRHAM
DISBAR
DISMAL
DISMAY
DISTAL
DOBLAS
DOBRAS
DOGDAY
DOGEAR
DOGMAS
DOGSAT
DOGTAG
DOLLAR
DOLMAN
DOLMAS
DONNAS
DOODAD
DOODAH
DORCAS
DORIAN
DORSAL
DOSSAL
DOTHAN
DRAMAS
DUCTAL
DUNBAR
DUNCAN
DUNHAM
DURBAN
DURBAR
DURHAM
DURIAN
DVORAK

D••••A
DAGAMA
DAHLIA
DAKOTA
DAMITA
DATURA
DEANNA
DEFLEA
DESICA
DHARMA
DJERBA
DODECA
DODOMA
DOUALA
DUENNA
DULLEA
DUNERA
DURYEA

•DA•••
ADAGES
ADAGIO
ADAPTS
EDAMES
GDANSK

•D•A••
ADDAMS
ADJANI
ADMASS
ADNATE
EDGARD
EDGARS
EDUARD
EDVARD
EDWARD
IDCARD
IDEALS
IDEATE
IDTAGS
KDLANG

•D••A•
ADIDAS
ADONAI
ADRIAN

•D•••A
ADNEXA
EDESSA
ODESSA
ODETTA

••DA••
ADDAMS
AODAIS
BEDAUB
BEDAZE
CEDANT
CEDARS
DIDACT
EMDASH
ENDALL
ENDASH
GODARD
HODADS
INDABA
IODATE
JUDAEA
JUDAIC
KODALY
MADAME
MADAMS
MEDAKA
MEDALS
MIDAIR
OLDAGE
ORDAIN
PADANG
PEDALS
PEDANT
PEDATE
REDACT
REDANT
REDATE
SEDAKA
SEDANS
SEDATE
TODATE
UPDATE

••D•A•
ANDEAN
AUDIAL
BADHAM
BADMAN
BEDLAM
ENDEAR
ENDMAN
ESDRAS
HYDRAE
HYDRAS
INDIAN
KIDMAN
KIDNAP
KODIAK
MADCAP
MADMAN
MADMAX
MADRAS
MEDGAR
MEDIAL
MEDIAN
MEDIAS
MEDLAR
MEDLAT
MIDDAY
MIDIAN
MIDWAY
MUDCAT
MUDRAS
OGDOAD
OLDHAM
OLDHAT
OLDMAN
OLDSAW
ORDEAL
PADUAN
PEDLAR
PEDWAY
RADIAL
RADIAN
REDBAY
REDCAP
REDEAL
REDHAT
REDIAL
REDOAK
REDRAW
REDTAG
RODHAM
RODMAN
RUDMAN
SADDAM
SUDRAS
TODDAO
TODMAN
UNDRAW
VODKAS
ZEDBAR
ZODIAC

••D••A
ANDREA
BODEGA
BUDDHA
DODECA
DODOMA
EIDOLA
ENDORA
EUDORA
FEDORA
GODIVA
INDABA
INDIRA
JUDAEA
JUDOKA
LADIDA
LADOGA
MADURA
MEDAKA
MEDINA
MEDUSA
MODELA
MODENA
OEDEMA
RADULA
REDSEA
SEDAKA
ZADORA

•••DA•
ADIDAS
AIRDAM
ALLDAY
ANYDAY
AOUDAD
APODAL
BAGDAD
BELDAM
BENDAY
BRIDAL
CAUDAL
CIUDAD
CNIDAE
CORDAY
DAEDAL
DEODAR
DOGDAY
DOODAD
DOODAH
FEUDAL
FRIDAY
HAIDAS
HEYDAY
HOWDAH
IBADAN
JORDAN
KASDAN
LANDAU
MANDAN
MANDAY
MAYDAY
MCADAM
MIDDAY
MOLDAU
MONDAY
MYRDAL
NASDAQ
OFFDAY
ONEDAY
PANDAS
PAYDAY
PINDAR
PURDAH
SADDAM
SANDAL
SENDAK
SIRDAR
SOLDAN
SUNDAE
SUNDAY
TAGDAY
TODDAO
VANDAL
WHYDAH

•••D•A
ACADIA
ACEDIA
BUDDHA
EXEDRA
GRADEA
SANDIA
SANDRA
STADIA
TREDIA
TUNDRA

••••DA
AGENDA
AMANDA
ANANDA
ARMADA
ARVADA
BLANDA
BRENDA
CANADA
CICADA
COLADA
COULDA
GELADA
GLENDA
IMELDA
JUMADA
KAUNDA
LADIDA
LAMBDA
LERIDA
LUANDA
MASADA
MERIDA
NERUDA
NEVADA
OLINDA
ONEIDA
OREIDA
PAGODA
PANADA
POSADA
PRAVDA
RAMADA
REMUDA
RESEDA
RHONDA
RUANDA
RWANDA
UGANDA
VIGODA

D•B•••
DABBED
DABBLE
DABNEY
DEBARK
DEBARS
DEBASE
DEBATE
DEBBIE
DEBITS
DEBONE
DEBRAS
DEBRIS
DEBTOR
DEBUGS
DEBUNK
DEBUTS
DIBBLE
DOBBER
DOBBIN
DOBLAS
DOBLIN
DOBRAS
DOBROS
DOBSON
DUBBED
DUBBIN
DUBCEK
DUBLIN
DUBOIS
DYBBUK

D••B••
DABBED
DABBLE
DAUBED
DAUBER
DAUBES
DAYBED
DAYBOY
DEBBIE

DIABLO DIBBLE DISBAR DOABLE DOBBER DOBBIN DOOBIE DOUBLE DOUBLY DOUBTS DRABLY DUBBED DUBBIN DUMBER DUMBLY DUNBAR DURBAN DURBAR DURBIN DYBBUK

D•••B•
DANUBE DEMOBS DJERBA DOESBY DROPBY DWEEBS

D••••B
DAYJOB DEKALB DIONEB

•DB•••
EDBERG

•D•B••
ADOBES EDIBLE

•D••B•
ADLIBS

•D•••B
ADSORB ADVERB ODDJOB

••DB••
BADBOY BEDBUG OLDBOY REDBAY REDBUD TIDBIT TYDBOL ZEDBAR

••D•B•
ARDEBS INDABA INDEBT REDUBS

••D••B
BEDAUB MIDRIB ODDJOB

•••DB•
GOODBY HARDBY LAIDBY

•••D•B
SUBDEB

D•C•••
DACAPO DACHAS DACOIT DACRON DACTYL DECADE DECAFS DECALS DECAMP DECANT DECAYS DECEIT DECENT DECIDE DECKED DECKER DECKLE DECOCT DECODE DECORS DECOYS DECREE DICERS DICIER DICING DICKER DICKEY DICOTS DICTUM DICTUS DOCENT DOCILE DOCKED DOCKER DOCKET DOCTOR DUCATS DUCHIN DUCKED DUCTAL

D••C••
DANCED DANCER DANCES DEACON DEICED DEICER DEICES DESCRY DEUCED DEUCES DISCOS DISCUS DORCAS DRACHM DUBCEK DULCET DUNCAN DUNCES

D•••C•
DECOCT DEDUCE DEDUCT DEFACE DEFECT DEJECT DELICT DEPICT DESICA DETACH DETECT DEVICE DIDACT DIRECT DODECA DRENCH DRYICE DUROCS

D••••C
DELTIC DYADIC

•DC•••
IDCARD

•D•C••
EDICTS EDUCED EDUCES

•D••C•
ADDUCE ADDUCT ADVICE EDKOCH IDIOCY

•D•••C
EDENIC

••DC••
MADCAP MUDCAT REDCAP

••D•C•
ABDUCT ADDUCE ADDUCT ASDICS BEDECK BODICE DEDUCE DEDUCT DIDACT DODECA INDICT INDUCE INDUCT MEDICI MEDICO MEDICS MODOCS NODICE ONDECK REDACT REDUCE SEDUCE ZYDECO

••D••C
CADMIC CEDRIC JUDAIC OLDVIC ZODIAC

•••D•C
ACIDIC ANODIC BARDIC DYADIC IRIDIC NORDIC OXIDIC RUNDMC SYNDIC ZENDIC

D•D•••
DADDYO DADOED DADOES DEDUCE DEDUCT DIDACT DIDDLE DIDDLY DIDIES DIDION DODDER DODECA DODGED DODGER DODGES DODODO DODOES DODOMA DUDEEN DUDISH DUDLEY

D••D••
DADDYO DAEDAL DANDER DANDIE DANDLE DAWDLE DEADEN DEADER DEADLY DEADON DEEDED DEEDEE DEIDRE DENDRI DENDRO DEODAR DIADEM DIDDLE DIDDLY DIKDIK DIODES DODDER DOGDAY DOGDOM DONDER DOODAD DOODAH DOODLE DREDGE DRUDGE DRYDEN DUMDUM DUNDEE DYADIC

D•••D•
DECADE DECIDE DECODE DELUDE DEMODE DENUDE DERIDE DIPODY DIRNDL DIVIDE DODODO DORADO DOSIDO DREADS DROIDS DRUIDS DRYADS

D••••D
DABBED DADOED DAFFED DAMMED DAMNED DAMPED DANCED DAPPED DARNED DARTED DASHED DAUBED DAWNED DAYBED DECKED DEEDED DEEMED DEFEND DEFIED DEICED DELVED DEMAND DEMOND DENIED DENNED DENTED DEPEND DEUCED DEVOID DIALED DIETED DIMMED DINGED DINNED DINTED DIPPED DISHED DISKED DISSED DOCKED DODGED DOFFED DOGGED DOGOOD DOLLED DONALD DONNED DOODAD DOOMED DOSSED DOTARD DOTTED DOUSED DOWNED DOWSED DRAPED DRAYED DRONED DUBBED DUCKED DUELED DULLED DUMPED DUNKED DUNNED DURNED DUSTED

•DD•••
ADDAMS ADDEND ADDERS ADDING ADDLED ADDLES ADDONS ADDSIN ADDSON ADDSTO ADDSUP ADDUCE ADDUCT EDDIED EDDIES EDDOES ODDEST ODDITY ODDJOB ODDLOT ODDSON UDDERS

•D•D••
ADIDAS

•D••D•
IDOIDO

•D•••D
ADDEND ADDLED ADORED EDDIED EDGARD EDITED EDMOND EDMUND EDUARD EDUCED EDVARD EDWARD EDWOOD IDCARD

••DD••
BADDER BADDIE BIDDEN BIDDER BIDDLE BUDDED BUDDHA CADDIE CADDIS CODDLE CUDDLE CUDDLY DADDYO DIDDLE DIDDLY DODDER FIDDLE FODDER FUDDLE GADDED GADDER HADDIE HEDDLE HIDDEN HUDDLE JUDDER KIDDED KIDDER KIDDIE LADDER LADDIE LIDDED LUDDEN MADDEN MADDER MADDIE MEDDLE MIDDAY MIDDEN MIDDLE MUDDED MUDDER MUDDLE NODDED NODDLE PADDED PADDER PADDLE PEDDLE PODDED PUDDLE PUDDLY RADDLE REDDEN REDDER REDDOG RIDDED RIDDEN RIDDLE RODDED RUDDER RUDDLE SADDAM SADDEN SADDER SADDLE SIDDUR SODDED SODDEN SUDDEN TEDDED TEDDER TIDDLY TODDAO TODDLE VEDDER WADDED WADDLE WADDLY WEDDED ZADDIK

••D•D•
DODODO HODADS IODIDE LADIDA MADEDO

••D••D
ADDEND ADDLED BODIED BUDDED BUDGED CADGED DADOED DODGED EDDIED ENDUED FUDGED GADDED GODARD HEDGED INDEED JUDGED KEDGED KIDDED KIDVID LADLED LIDDED LODGED MADRID MUDDED NODDED NUDGED OGDOAD PADDED PODDED REDBUD REDYED RIDDED RIDGED RODDED SIDLED SODDED SUDSED TEDDED TIDIED UNDYED WADDED WEDDED WEDGED

•••DD•
ATODDS CLODDY CRUDDY FREDDY QUIDDE SHODDY SKIDDY

•••D•D
ABIDED AOUDAD BAGDAD BANDED BEADED BENDED BIRDED BLADED BONDED BUDDED CANDID CARDED CHIDED CIUDAD CORDED CURDED DEEDED DOODAD ELIDED ELUDED ERODED EVADED EXUDED FENDED FEUDED FOLDED FORDED FUNDED GADDED GILDED GIRDED GLIDED GOADED GRADED GUIDED HANDED HEADED HEEDED HERDED HOODED KIDDED LANDED LARDED LAUDED LEADED LIDDED LOADED LORDED MELDED MENDED MINDED MISDID MOLDED MUDDED NEEDED NODDED OUTDID PADDED PENDED PODDED PRIDED RAIDED RIDDED RODDED SANDED SEEDED SHADED SODDED SORDID SPADED TEDDED TENDED TRADED VENDED VOIDED WADDED WARDED WEDDED WEEDED WELDED WENDED WINDED WOODED WORDED YARDED

DE••••
DEACON DEADEN DEADER DEADLY DEADON DEAFEN DEAFER DEAFLY DEALER DEALIN DEANNA DEARER DEARIE DEARLY DEARME DEARTH DEASIL DEBARK DEBARS DEBASE DEBATE DEBBIE DEBITS DEBONE DEBRAS DEBRIS DEBTOR DEBUGS DEBUNK DEBUTS DECADE DECAFS DECALS DECAMP DECANT DECAYS DECEIT DECENT DECIDE DECKED DECKER DECKLE DECOCT DECODE DECORS DECOYS DECREE DEDUCE DEDUCT DEEDED DEEDEE DEEJAY DEEMED DEEPAK DEEPEN DEEPER DEEPLY DEFACE DEFAME DEFATS DEFEAT DEFECT DEFEND DEFERS DEFIED DEFIES DEFILE DEFINE DEFLEA DEFOGS DEFORM DEFRAY DEFTER DEFTLY DEFUSE DEGAGE DEGREE DEGUST DEHORN DEICED DEICER DEICES DEIDRE DEIGNS DEIMOS DEISTS DEJAVU DEJECT DEJURE DEKALB DEKING DEKKOS DELANO DELANY DELATE DELAYS DELEON DELETE DELFTS DELICT DELIST DELIUS DELMAR DELONG DELPHI DELRAY DELRIO DELROY DELTAS DELTIC DELUDE DELUGE DELUXE DELVED DELVER DELVES DEMAND DEMEAN DEMIES DEMISE DEMITS DEMOBS DEMODE DEMOND DEMONS DEMOTE DEMURE DEMURS DENALI DENARY DENDRI DENDRO DENGUE DENIAL DENIED DENIER DENIES DENIMS DENIRO DENISE DENNED DENNIS DENOTE DENOVO DENSER DENTAL DENTED DENTIL DENTIN DENTON DENUDE DENVER DENZEL DEODAR DEPART DEPAUL DEPAUW DEPEND DEPICT DEPLOY DEPONE DEPORT DEPOSE DEPOTS DEPTHS DEPUTE DEPUTY DERAIL DERIDE DERIVE DERMAL DERMIS DERRIS DESALT DESCRY DESERT DESICA DESIGN DESILU DESIRE DESIST DESMAN DESOTO DESPOT DESTRY DETACH DETAIL DETAIN DETECT DETENT DETERS DETEST DETOUR DETROP DEUCED DEUCES DEVEIN DEVEST DEVICE DEVILS DEVINE DEVISE DEVITO DEVOID DEVOIR DEVOTE DEVOTO DEVOUR DEVOUT DEWIER DEWILY DEWING DEWITT DEWLAP DEXTER DEXTRO

D•E•••
DAEDAL DEEDED DEEDEE DEEJAY DEEMED DEEPAK DEEPEN DEEPER DEEPLY DIEOFF DIEOUT DIEPPE DIESEL DIESES DIESIS DIETED DIETER DJERBA DOESBY DOESIN DOESNT DOESUP DREADS DREAMS DREAMT DREAMY DREARY DREDGE DRENCH DRESSY DREWIN DREWON DREWUP DREXEL DUELED DUELER DUELLO DUENNA DWEEBS DWELLS DYEING DYELOT

D••E••
DALETH DARENT DARETO DATERS DECEIT DECENT DEFEAT DEFECT DEFEND DEFERS DEJECT DELEON DELETE DEMEAN DEPEND DESERT DETECT DETENT DETERS DETEST DEVEIN DEVEST DICERS DIGEST DINEIN DINEON DINERO DINERS DIRECT DIRELY DIREST DIVEIN DIVERS DIVERT DIVEST DIYERS DIZENS DOCENT DODECA DOGEAR DOGEYS DOLENZ DONEES DONEIN DONETS DONEUP DOREMI DOSERS DOTELL DOTEON DOVEIN DOWELS DOWERS DOWERY DOYENS DOZENS DOZERS DRIERS DRIEST DRYERS DRYEST DUDEEN DUNERA DUPERY DURESS DUVETS DWEEBS

D•••E•
DABBED DABNEY DADOED DADOES DAFFED DAFTER DAGGER DAILEY DAIREN DAISES DALLES DAMIEN DAMMED DAMNED DAMPED DAMPEN DAMPER DAMSEL DANCED DANCER DANCES DANDER DANGER DANIEL DANKER DANNER DANTES DAPPED DAPPER DARIEN DARKEN DARKER DARNED DARNEL DARNER DARREN DARTED DARTER DASHED DASHER DASHES DAUBED DAUBER DAUBES DAVIES DAWNED DAYBED DEADEN DEADER DEAFEN DEAFER DEALER DEARER DECKED DECKER DECREE DEEDED DEEDEE DEEMED DEEPEN DEEPER DEFIED DEFIES DEFLEA DEFTER DEGREE DEICED DEICER DEICES DELVED DELVER DELVES DEMIES DENIED DENIER DENIES DENNED DENSER DENTED DENVER DENZEL DEUCED DEUCES DEWIER DEXTER DHOLES DHOTEL DIADEM DIALED DIALER DIAPER DICIER DICKER DICKEY DIDIES DIESEL DIESES DIETED DIETER DIFFER DIGGER DILLER DILSEY DIMMED DIMMER DINGED DINKEY DINNED DINNER DINTED DIODES DIONEB DIPPED DIPPER DIRGES DISHED DISHES DISKED DISMES DISNEY DISPEL DISSED DITHER DITZES DLAYER DOBBER DOCKED DOCKER DOCKET DODDER DODGED DODGER DODGES DODOES DOFFED DOGGED DOGGER DOGIES DOGLEG DOLLED DOLMEN DOMREP DONDER DONEES DONKEY DONNED DONNEE DONNER DOOLEY DOOMED DOPIER DORIES DORMER DORSET DORSEY DOSSED DOSSEL DOSSER DOSSES DOTTED DOURER DOUSED DOUSES DOWNED DOWNER DOWNEY DOWSED DOWSER DOWSES DOZIER DRAGEE DRAKES DRAPED DRAPER DRAPES DRAWER DRAYED DREXEL DRIVEL DRIVEN DRIVER DRIVES DRONED DRONER DRONES DROVER DROVES DRUPES DRUZES DRYDEN DUBBED DUBCEK DUCKED DUDEEN DUDLEY DUELED DUELER DUFFEL

DUFFER DUIKER DULCET DULLEA DULLED DULLER DULLES DUMBER DUMPED DUMPER DUNCES DUNDEE DUNKED DUNKER DUNNED DUPLEX DURFEY DURNED DURYEA DUSTED DUSTER DUTIES

D••••E

DABBLE DAMAGE DAMONE DAMORE DANDIE DANDLE DANGLE DANGME DANUBE DAPHNE DAPPLE DARKLE DATIVE DAWDLE DAYONE DAZZLE DEARIE DEARME DEBASE DEBATE DEBBIE DEBONE DECADE DECIDE DECKLE DECODE DECREE DEDUCE DEEDEE DEFACE DEFAME DEFILE DEFINE DEFUSE DEGAGE DEGREE DEIDRE DEJURE DELATE DELETE DELUDE DELUGE DELUXE DEMISE DEMODE DEMOTE DEMURE DENGUE DENISE DENOTE DENUDE DEPONE DEPOSE DEPUTE DERIDE DERIVE DESIRE DEVICE DEVINE DEVISE DEVOTE DIANNE DIBBLE DIDDLE DIEPPE DILATE DILUTE DIMPLE DINGLE DIONNE DIPOLE DIRIGE DISUSE DIVIDE DIVINE DOABLE DOCILE DOGGIE DOMINE DONATE DONGLE DONNEE DOOBIE DOODLE DOOGIE DOOZIE DOSAGE DOTAGE DOTTIE DOTTLE DOUBLE DRAGEE DREDGE DROGUE DROWSE DRUDGE DRYICE DUARTE DUNDEE DWAYNE

•DE•••

ADEEMS ADELIE ADELLE ADEPTS ADESTE EDENIC EDERLE EDESSA IDEALS IDEATE ODENSE ODESSA ODETTA ODETTE

•D•E••

ADDEND ADDERS ADEEMS ADHERE ADIEUS ADIEUX ADNEXA ADRENO ADVENT ADVERB ADVERT ADWEEK EDBERG EDGEIN EDGERS EDSELS IDLERS IDLEST ODDEST UDDERS

•D••E•

ADAGES ADDLED ADDLES ADOBES ADORED ADOREE ADORER ADORES ADRIEN ADWEEK EDAMES EDDIED EDDIES EDDOES EDGIER EDILES EDITED EDUCED EDUCES

•D•••E

ADDUCE ADELIE ADELLE ADESTE ADHERE ADJURE ADMIRE ADNATE ADOREE ADVICE ADVISE EDERLE EDIBLE IDEATE ODENSE ODETTE

••DE••

ADDEND ADDERS AIDERS ALDERS ANDEAN ARDEBS ARDENT AUDENS BADEGG BEDECK BEDEWS BODEGA CADENT CADETS CIDERS CODERS CYDERS DODECA DUDEEN EIDERS ELDERS ELDEST ENDEAR ENDERS FADEIN GIDEON GODETS HIDEHO HIDEKI HIDERS INDEBT INDEED INDENE INDENT LADERS LODENS LUDENS MADEDO MADEIT MADERO MADEUP MODELA MODELS MODELT MODEMS MODENA MODERN MODEST MUDEEL NUDELY NUDEST ODDEST OEDEMA OLDEST ONDECK ORDEAL ORDERS REDEAL REDEEM REDENY REDEYE RIDENT RIDERS RODENT RODEOS RUDELY RUDEST RYDELL SEDERS SIDERO SIDERS TEDEUM UDDERS VIDEOS VIDERI WADEIN WADERS WEDELN WIDELY WIDENS WIDEST YODELS ZYDECO

••D•E•

ADDLED ADDLES ANDREA ANDREI ANDRES ANDREW ANDREY AUDREY BADDER BADGER BADGES BADMEN BIDDEN BIDDER BODIED BODIES BUDDED BUDGED BUDGES BUDGET CADGED CADGER CADGES CADRES CODGER CUDGEL DADOED DADOES DIDIES DODDER DODGED DODGER DODGES DODOES DUDEEN DUDLEY EDDIED EDDIES EDDOES ENDMEN ENDUED ENDUES FIDGET FODDER FUDGED FUDGES GADDED GADDER GADGET GIDGET HADJES HEDGED HEDGER HEDGES HEDREN HIDDEN HODGES INDEED INDIES JUDAEA JUDDER JUDGED JUDGES KEDGED KEDGES KIDDED KIDDER KIDNEY LADDER LADIES LADLED LADLER LADLES LEDGER LEDGES LIDDED LODGED LODGER LODGES LUDDEN MADDEN MADDER MADMEN MADRES MADSEN MEDLEY MIDDEN MIDGES MIDGET MIDLER MUDDED MUDDER MUDEEL MUDHEN NODDED NUDGED NUDGER NUDGES OLDIES OLDMEN OODLES PADDED PADDER PADRES PODDED RADNER REDDEN REDDER REDEEM REDOES REDREW REDSEA REDYED REDYES RIDDED RIDDEN RIDGED RIDGES RIDLEY RODDED RODNEY RUDDER SADDEN SADDER SADHES SEDGES SIDLED SIDLES SIDNEY SODDED SODDEN SUDDEN SUDSED SUDSES SYDNEY TEDDED TEDDER TEDKEY TIDIED TIDIER TIDIES UNDIES UNDOER UNDOES UNDYED VEDDER WADDED WEDDED WEDGED WEDGES WIDGET WODGES

••D••E

ADDUCE AEDILE ALDINE ALDOSE AUDILE BADDIE BEDAZE BIDDLE BODICE BUDGIE CADDIE CODDLE CUDDLE DEDUCE DIDDLE ENDIVE ENDURE ENDUSE FIDDLE FUDDLE HADDIE HEDDLE HUDDLE HYDRAE INDENE INDITE INDORE INDUCE IODATE IODIDE IODINE IODISE IODIZE KIDDIE LADDIE MADAME MADDIE MEDDLE MIDDLE MODINE MODULE MUDDLE MUDPIE NADINE NODDLE NODICE NODOSE NODULE OLDAGE ONDINE ORDURE PADDLE PEDATE PEDDLE PUDDLE RADDLE RADOME REDATE REDEYE REDONE REDUCE RIDDLE RUDDLE SADDLE SEDATE SEDILE SEDUCE TODATE TODDLE UNDINE UNDONE UPDATE UPDIKE VADOSE WADDLE WEDGIE

•••DE•

ABIDED ABIDES ABODES AMEDEO AMIDES ANADEM ANODES ASIDES AZIDES BADDER BALDER BANDED BEADED BENDED BENDER BIDDEN BIDDER BINDER BIRDED BIRDER BLADED BLADER BLADES BOLDER BONDED BORDEN BORDER BRIDES BRUDER BSIDES BUDDED BURDEN CALDER CAMDEN CARDED CARDER CAUDEX CHIDED CHIDER CHIDES CINDER COLDER COODER CORDED CRUDER CURDED DANDER DEADEN DEADER DEEDED DEEDEE DIADEM DIODES DODDER DONDER DRYDEN DUNDEE ELIDED ELIDES ELUDED ELUDER ELUDES EMBDEN EPODES ERODED ERODES ETUDES EVADED EVADER EVADES EXUDED EXUDES FEEDER FENDED FENDER FEUDED FINDER FODDER FOLDED FOLDER FONDER FORDED FUNDED GADDED GADDER GANDER GARDEN GENDER GEODES GILDED GILDER GIRDED GIRDER GLADES GLIDED GLIDER GLIDES GOADED GOLDEN GOODEN GRADEA GRADED GRADER GRADES GUIDED GUIDES HANDED HANDEL HARDEN HARDER HAYDEN HEADED HEADER HEEDED HEEDER HEIDEN HERDED HERDER HIDDEN HINDER HOLDEN HOLDER HOODED HORDES HOYDEN HYADES IBIDEM IRIDES JUDDER KANDER KIDDED KIDDER KINDER LADDER LANDED LANDER LARDED LARDER LAUDED LAUDER LEADED LEADEN LEADER LEIDEN LENDER LEWDER LEYDEN LIDDED LIEDER LINDEN LOADED LOADER LORDED LOUDEN LOUDER LUDDEN LUNDEN MADDEN MADDER MAIDEN MALDEN MELDED MENDED MENDEL MENDER MENDES MIDDEN MILDER MILDEW MINDED MINDER MOLDED MOLDER MUDDED MUDDER MURDER NEEDED NODDED OXIDES PADDED PADDER PANDER PEEDEE PENDED PODDED POLDER PONDER POWDER PRIDED PRIDES PRUDES RAIDED RAIDER READER REDDEN REDDER RENDER RHODES RIDDED RIDDEN RODDED RONDEL RUDDER SADDEN SADDER SANDED SANDER SEEDED SEEDER SEIDEL SENDER SHADED SHADES SLIDER SLIDES SNIDER SNYDER SODDED SODDEN SOLDER SONDES SPADED SPADER SPADES SPIDER SUBDEB SUDDEN SUEDES SUNDER SUNDEW SWEDEN SWEDES TANDEM TEDDED TEDDER TENDED TENDER TILDEN TILDES TINDER TRADED TRADER TRADES VALDEZ VARDEN VEDDER VENDED VENDEE VOIDED WADDED WALDEN WANDER WARDED WARDEN WARDER WEDDED WEEDED WEEDER WELDED WELDER WENDED WILDER WINDED WINDER WINDEX WONDER WOODED WOODEN WORDED YARDED YONDER ZANDER ZUIDER

•••D•E

AZODYE BADDIE BEADLE BIDDLE BIRDIE BOODLE BRIDGE BRIDLE BRODIE BUNDLE CADDIE CANDLE CAUDLE CNIDAE CODDLE CRADLE CUDDLE CURDLE DANDIE DANDLE DAWDLE DEEDEE DEIDRE DIDDLE DOODLE DREDGE DRUDGE DUNDEE FIDDLE FLEDGE FONDLE FONDUE FOODIE FRIDGE FUDDLE GIRDLE GOLDIE GOODIE GORDIE GRUDGE HADDIE HANDLE HEDDLE HUDDLE HURDLE KIDDIE KINDLE KLUDGE LADDIE MADDIE MEDDLE MIDDLE MUDDLE NEEDLE NODDLE NOODLE ONEDGE PADDLE PEDDLE PEEDEE PERDUE PHEDRE PLEDGE POODLE PUDDLE PURDUE QUIDDE RADDLE RIDDLE ROADIE RUDDLE RUNDLE SADDLE SLEDGE SLUDGE SMUDGE STODGE SUBDUE SUNDAE TIEDYE TODDLE TRUDGE VENDEE WADDLE

••••DE

ABRADE ACCEDE ALLUDE ARCADE AUBADE BESIDE BETIDE BLENDE BLONDE BOLIDE BORIDE CHILDE CLAUDE DECADE DECIDE DECODE DELUDE DEMODE DENUDE DERIDE DIVIDE ENCODE FACADE GOURDE GRANDE HALIDE IMPEDE INSIDE INVADE IODIDE ISOLDE LIPIDE MRHYDE ONSIDE OROIDE PARADE POMADE QUIDDE RECEDE RECODE REMADE RESIDE SECEDE STRIDE STRODE TIRADE TRIODE UNLADE UNMADE UPSIDE

D•F•••

DAFFED DAFTER DAFTLY DEFACE DEFAME DEFATS DEFEAT DEFECT DEFEND DEFERS DEFIED DEFIES DEFILE DEFINE DEFLEA DEFOGS DEFORM DEFRAY DEFTER DEFTLY DEFUSE DIFFER DOFFED DUFFEL DUFFER

D••F••

DAFFED DEAFEN DEAFER DEAFLY DELFTS DIFFER DOFFED DOOFUS DRAFTS DRAFTY DRIFTS DRIFTY DRYFLY DUFFEL DUFFER DURFEY

D•••F•

DECAFS DIEOFF DRYOFF DWARFS

D••••F

DIEOFF DRYOFF

•D••F•

ADRIFT

••DF••

AIDFUL GADFLY MEDFLY REDFIN REDFIR REDFOX

••D•F•

CODIFY LEDOFF MODIFY NIDIFY NODOFF

••D••F

LEDOFF NODOFF RIDSOF RUDOLF

•••D•F

KINDOF TOLDOF

D•G•••

DAGAMA DAGGER DAGMAR DEGAGE DEGREE DEGUST DIGEST DIGGER DIGITS DIGLOT DIGOUT DIGRAM DIGSIN DIGSUP DOGDAY DOGDOM DOGEAR DOGEYS DOGGED DOGGER DOGGIE DOGIES DOGLEG DOGMAS DOGONS DOGOOD DOGSAT DOGSIT DOGTAG DUGONG DUGOUT

D••G••

DAGGER DANGER DANGLE DANGLY DANGME DAYGLO DEIGNS DENGUE DIGGER DINGED DINGHY DINGLE DINGUS DIRGES DODGED DODGER DODGES DOGGED DOGGER DOGGIE DONGLE DOOGIE DOUGHS DOUGHY DRAGEE DRAGGY DRAGIN DRAGON DROGUE DWIGHT

D•••G•

DAMAGE DEBUGS DEFOGS DEGAGE DELUGE DESIGN DIRIGE DIRIGO DOINGS DORAGS DOSAGE DOTAGE DRAGGY DREDGE DRINGS DRUDGE

D••••G

DANANG DANZIG DARING DATING DATONG DAZING DEKING DELONG DEWING DIALOG DICING DIKING DINING DIVING DOGLEG DOGTAG DOLING DOMING DOPING DOSING DOTING DOZING DRYING DUGONG DUKING DUPING DURING DYEING

•DG•••

EDGARD EDGARS EDGEIN EDGERS EDGIER EDGILY EDGING

•D•G••

ADAGES ADAGIO

•D••G•

IDTAGS

•D•••G

ADDING EDBERG EDGING IDLING KDLANG

••DG••

BADGER BADGES BADGUY BUDGED BUDGES BUDGET BUDGIE CADGED CADGER CADGES CODGER CUDGEL DODGED DODGER DODGES FIDGET FUDGED FUDGES GADGET GIDGET HEDGED HEDGER HEDGES HODGES JUDGED JUDGES KEDGED KEDGES LEDGER LEDGES LODGED LODGER LODGES

MEDGAR MIDGES MIDGET NUDGED NUDGER NUDGES PIDGIN REDGUM RIDGED RIDGES SEDGES WEDGED WEDGES WEDGIE WIDGET WODGES

••D•G•

BADEGG BODEGA INDIGO LADOGA OLDAGE

••D••G

ADDING AIDING BADEGG BEDBUG BIDING BODING CEDING CODING ENDING FADING HIDING JADING LADING LUDWIG PADANG REDDOG REDING REDTAG RIDING SIDING TIDING WADING

•••DG•

BRIDGE DREDGE DRUDGE FLEDGE FLEDGY FRIDGE GRUDGE KLUDGE ONEDGE PLEDGE SLEDGE SLUDGE SLUDGY SMUDGE SMUDGY STODGE STODGY TRUDGE

•••D•G

BANDOG GUNDOG HOTDOG LAPDOG PYEDOG REDDOG SEADOG SUNDOG TOPDOG TOYDOG

••••DG

RATEDG

DH••••

DHARMA DHOLES DHOTEL DHOTIS

D•H•••

DAHLIA DEHORN DRHOOK DSHARP

D••H••

DACHAS DAPHNE DASHED DASHER DASHES DASHIS DIRHAM DISHED DISHES DITHER DOTHAN DUCHIN DUNHAM DURHAM

D•••H•

DELPHI DEPTHS DINGHY DOUGHS DOUGHY DRACHM DWIGHT

D••••H

DALETH DANISH DEARTH DETACH DOODAH DOVISH DRENCH DUDISH DULUTH

•DH•••

ADHERE

•D•••H

ADOLPH EDKOCH

••DH••

ANDHOW BADHAM MUDHEN OLDHAM OLDHAT REDHAT REDHOT RODHAM SADHES SADHUS

••D•H•

BUDDHA HIDEHO WIDTHS

••D••H

DUDISH EMDASH ENDASH JADISH JUDITH MODISH OLDISH RADISH WIDISH

•••DH•

BUDDHA GANDHI LANDHO

•••D•H

DOODAH GOODOH HOWDAH PURDAH WHYDAH

••••DH

LAMEDH RIYADH

DI••••

DIABLO DIADEM DIALED DIALER DIALOG DIALUP DIANNE DIAPER DIATOM DIBBLE DICERS DICIER DICING DICKER DICKEY DICOTS DICTUM DICTUS DIDACT DIDDLE DIDDLY DIDIES DIDION DIEOFF DIEOUT DIEPPE DIESEL DIESES DIESIS DIETED DIETER DIFFER DIGEST DIGGER DIGITS DIGLOT DIGOUT DIGRAM DIGSIN DIGSUP DIKDIK DIKING DIKTAT DILATE DILLER DILLON DILSEY DILUTE DIMITY DIMMED DIMMER DIMOUT DIMPLE DIMPLY DIMSUM DIMWIT DINARS DINEIN DINEON DINERO DINERS DINGED DINGHY DINGLE DINGUS DINING DINKEY DINNED DINNER DINTED DIODES DIONEB DIONNE DIOXIN DIPODY DIPOLE DIPPED DIPPER DIRECT DIRELY DIREST DIRGES DIRHAM DIRIGE DIRIGO DIRNDL DISANT DISARM DISBAR DISCOS DISCUS DISHED DISHES DISKED DISMAL DISMAY DISMES DISNEY DISOWN DISPEL DISSED DISTAL DISTIL DISUSE DITHER DITTOS DITZES DIVANS DIVEIN DIVERS DIVERT DIVEST DIVIDE DIVINE DIVING DIVINO DIVOTS DIXITS DIYERS DIZENS

D•I•••

DAIKON DAILEY DAIMON DAIMYO DAINTY DAIREN DAISES DEICED DEICER DEICES DEIDRE DEIGNS DEIMOS DEISTS DMINOR DMINUS DMITRI DOINGS DRIERS DRIEST DRIFTS DRIFTY DRILLS DRINGS DRINKS DRIPPY DRIVEL DRIVEN DRIVER DRIVES DUIKER DWIGHT

D••I••

DAMIEN DAMITA DANIEL DANISH DARIEN DARING DARIUS DATING DATIVE DAVIES DAVITS DAZING DEBITS DECIDE DEFIED DEFIES DEFILE DEFINE DEKING DELICT DELIST DELIUS DEMIES DEMISE DEMITS DENIAL DENIED DENIER DENIES DENIMS DENIRO DENISE DEPICT DERIDE DERIVE DESICA DESIGN DESILU DESIRE DESIST DEVICE DEVILS DEVINE DEVISE DEVITO DEWIER DEWILY DEWING DEWITT DICIER DICING DIDIES DIDION DIGITS DIKING DIMITY DINING DIRIGE DIRIGO DIVIDE DIVINE DIVING DIVINO DIXITS DOCILE DOGIES DOLING DOMINE DOMING DOMINI DOMINO DONITZ DOPIER DOPING DORIAN DORIES DOSIDO DOSING DOTING DOVISH DOZIER DOZILY DOZING DRAILS DRAINS DROIDS DROITS DRUIDS DRYICE DRYING DRYINK DUDISH DUKING DUPING DURIAN DURING DUTIES DYEING

D•••I•

DACOIT DAHLIA DANDIE DANZIG DARNIT DARWIN DASHIS DASSIN DAYLIT DEALIN DEARIE DEASIL DEBBIE DEBRIS DECEIT DELRIO DELTIC DENNIS DENTIL DENTIN DERAIL DERMIS DERRIS DETAIL DETAIN DEVEIN DEVOID DEVOIR DHOTIS DIESIS DIGSIN DIKDIK DIMWIT DINEIN DIOXIN DISTIL DIVEIN DOBBIN DOBLIN DOESIN DOGGIE DOGSIT DOMAIN DONEIN DOOBIE DOOGIE DOOZIE DORRIT DOTTIE DOVEIN DRAGIN DRAWIN DREWIN DROPIN DROPIT DUBBIN DUBLIN DUBOIS DUCHIN DUNLIN DURBIN DUSTIN DYADIC

D••••I

DALASI DELPHI DENALI DENDRI DMITRI DOMANI DOMINI DORATI DOREMI DROMOI

•DI•••

ADIDAS ADIEUS ADIEUX EDIBLE EDICTS EDILES EDISON EDITED EDITIO EDITOR IDIOCY IDIOMS IDIOTS ODIOUS ODISTS ODIUMS

•D•I••

ADDING ADLIBS ADMIRE ADMITS ADRIAN ADRIEN ADRIFT ADVICE ADVISE EDDIED EDDIES EDGIER EDGILY EDGING IDLING IDOIDO ODDITY

•D••I•

ADAGIO ADDSIN ADELIE ADJOIN ADONIS ADROIT EDENIC EDGEIN EDITIO

•D•••I

ADJANI ADONAI ADZUKI

••DI••

ADDING AEDILE AIDING ALDINE ASDICS AUDIAL AUDILE AUDIOS AUDITS BEDIMS BIDING BODICE BODIED BODIES BODILY BODING CEDING CODIFY CODING DIDIES DIDION DUDISH EDDIED EDDIES ENDING ENDIVE FADING GODIVA HIDING INDIAN INDICT INDIES INDIGO INDIRA INDITE INDIUM IODIDE IODINE IODISE IODIZE JADING JADISH JUDITH KODIAK LADIDA LADIES LADING LADINO MEDIAL MEDIAN MEDIAS MEDICI MEDICO MEDICS MEDINA MEDIUM MIDIAN MODIFY MODINE MODISH NADINE NADIRS NIDIFY NODICE NUDIST NUDITY ODDITY OLDIES OLDISH ONDINE PODIUM RADIAL RADIAN RADIOS RADISH RADIUM RADIUS REDIAL REDING REDINK RIDING SEDILE SIDING SODIUM TEDIUM TIDIED TIDIER TIDIES TIDILY TIDING UNDIES UNDINE UPDIKE WADING WIDISH ZODIAC

••D•I•

ADDSIN ALDRIN AODAIS BADDIE BIDSIN BODKIN BUDGIE CADDIE CADDIS CADMIC CEDRIC FADEIN GODWIN GODWIT HADDIE HADJIS JUDAIC KIDDIE KIDVID LADDIE LUDWIG MADDIE MADEIT MADRID MIDAIR MIDRIB MUDPIE NUDNIK OLDVIC ORDAIN PIDGIN REDFIN REDFIR TIDBIT WADEIN WEDGIE ZADDIK

••D••I

ANDREI BODONI HIDEKI MEDICI MIDORI VIDERI

•••DI•

ACADIA ACEDIA ACIDIC AGADIR AMADIS ANODIC BADDIE BANDIT BARDIC BENDIX BIRDIE BOUDIN BRODIE CADDIE CADDIS CANDID CARDIN CARDIO COEDIT CREDIT DANDIE DIKDIK DYADIC FOODIE GOLDIE GOODIE GORDIE GRADIN GRODIN HADDIE HANDIN HEADIN HELDIN HOLDIN HOLDIT ICEDIN IRIDIC KIDDIE LADDIE LAIDIN LANDIS LEADIN MADDIE MAHDIS MISDID NORDIC OUTDID OXIDIC PAIDIN PANDIT PUNDIT READIN REEDIT ROADIE SANDIA SARDIS SAUDIS SENDIN SLIDIN SORDID SPADIX STADIA STUDIO SYNDIC TIEDIN TOEDIN TREDIA VERDIN ZADDIK ZENDIC

•••D•I

DENDRI GANDHI QUADRI

••••DI

BIONDI CIARDI SOLIDI YEHUDI

DJ••••

DJERBA

D•J•••

DEJAVU DEJECT DEJURE

D••J••

DAYJOB DEEJAY DMAJOR DONJON

•DJ•••

ADJANI ADJOIN ADJURE ADJUST

•D•J••

ODDJOB

••DJ••

HADJES HADJIS ODDJOB

D•K•••

DAKOTA DEKALB DEKING DEKKOS DIKDIK DIKING DIKTAT DUKING

D••K••

DAIKON DANKER DANKLY DARKEN DARKER DARKLE DARKLY DECKED DECKER DECKLE DEKKOS DICKER DICKEY DINKEY DISKED DOCKED DOCKER DOCKET DONKEY DRAKES DUCKED DUIKER DUNKED DUNKER

D•••K•

DMARKS DRINKS

D••••K

DAMASK DEBARK DEBUNK DEEPAK DIKDIK DRHOOK DRYINK DUBCEK DVORAK DYBBUK

•DK•••

EDKOCH

•D••K•

ADZUKI

•D•••K

ADWEEK GDANSK

••DK••

BODKIN TEDKEY VODKAS

••D•K•

HIDEKI JUDOKA MEDAKA SEDAKA UPDIKE

••D••K

BEDECK KODIAK NUDNIK ONDECK PODUNK REDINK REDOAK ZADDIK

•••D•K

DIKDIK MARDUK SENDAK ZADDIK

DL••••

DLAYER

D•L•••

DALASI DALETH DALLAS DALLES DALTON DELANO DELANY DELATE DELAYS DELEON DELETE DELFTS DELICT DELIST DELIUS DELMAR DELONG DELPHI DELRAY DELRIO DELROY DELTAS DELTIC DELUDE DELUGE DELUXE DELVED DELVER DELVES DILATE DILLER DILLON DILSEY DILUTE DOLENZ DOLING DOLLAR DOLLED DOLLOP DOLLUP DOLMAN DOLMAS DOLMEN DOLORS DOLOUR DULCET DULLEA DULLED DULLER DULLES DULUTH

D••L••

DAHLIA DAILEY DALLAS DALLES DAYLIT DEALER DEALIN DEFLEA DEPLOY DEWLAP DHOLES DIALED DIALER DIALOG DIALUP DIGLOT DILLER DILLON DOBLAS DOBLIN DOGLEG DOLLAR DOLLED DOLLOP DOLLUP DOOLEY DRILLS DROLLS DROLLY DUALLY DUBLIN DUDLEY DUELED DUELER DUELLO DULLEA DULLED DULLER DULLES DUNLIN DUNLOP DUPLEX DWELLS DYELOT

D•••L•

DABBLE DAFTLY DAMPLY DANDLE DANGLE DANGLY DANKLY DAPPLE DARKLE DARKLY DAWDLE DAYGLO DAZZLE DEADLY DEAFLY DEARLY DECALS DECKLE DEEPLY DEFILE DEFTLY DEKALB DENALI DESALT DESILU DEVILS DEWILY DIABLO DIBBLE DIDDLE DIDDLY DIMPLE DIMPLY DINGLE DIPOLE DIRELY DOABLE DOCILE DONALD DONGLE DOODLE DOTELL DOTTLE DOUALA DOUBLE DOUBLY DOURLY DOWELS DOZILY DRABLY DRAILS DRAWLS DRAWLY DRILLS DROLLS DROLLY DROOLS DROOLY DRYFLY DUALLY DUELLO DUMBLY DUVALL DWELLS

D••••L

DACTYL DAEDAL DAMSEL DANIEL DARNEL DARRYL DEASIL DENIAL DENTAL DENTIL DENZEL DEPAUL DERAIL DERMAL DETAIL DHOTEL DIESEL DIRNDL DISMAL DISPEL DISTAL DISTIL DORSAL DOSSAL DOSSEL DOTELL DREXEL DRIVEL DUCTAL DUFFEL DUVALL

•DL•••

ADLIBS IDLERS IDLEST IDLING KDLANG

•D•L••

ADDLED ADDLES ADELIE ADELLE ADOLPH ADULTS EDILES IDYLLS ODDLOT

•D••L•

ADELLE EDERLE EDGILY EDIBLE EDSELS IDEALS IDYLLS

••DL••

ADDLED ADDLES BADLOT BEDLAM DUDLEY LADLED LADLER LADLES LUDLUM MEDLAR MEDLAT MEDLEY MIDLER ODDLOT OODLES PEDLAR RIDLEY SIDLED SIDLES

••D•L•

AEDILE AUDILE BIDDLE BODILY CODDLE CUDDLE CUDDLY DIDDLE DIDDLY EIDOLA ENDALL FIDDLE FUDDLE GADFLY HEDDLE HUDDLE KODALY MEDALS

MEDDLE
MEDFLY
MIDDLE
MODELA
MODELS
MODELT
MODULE
MODULO
MUDDLE
NODDLE
NODULE
NUDELY
PADDLE
PEDALS
PEDDLE
PUDDLE
PUDDLY
RADDLE
RADULA
RIDDLE
RUDDLE
RUDELY
RUDOLF
RYDELL
SADDLE
SEDILE
TIDDLY
TIDILY
TODDLE
UNDULY
WADDLE
WADDLY
WEDELN
WIDELY
YODELS

••D••L

AIDFUL
AUDIAL
CUDGEL
ENDALL
MEDIAL
MUDEEL
ORDEAL
RADIAL
REDEAL
REDIAL
RYDELL
TYDBOL

•••DL•

ACIDLY
ARIDLY
AVIDLY
AWEDLY
BALDLY
BEADLE
BIDDLE
BOLDLY
BOODLE
BRIDLE
BUNDLE
CANDLE
CAUDLE
CODDLE
COLDLY
CRADLE
CUDDLE
CUDDLY
CURDLE
DANDLE
DAWDLE
DEADLY
DIDDLE
DIDDLY
DOODLE
FIDDLE
FONDLE
FONDLY
FUDDLE
GIRDLE
GLADLY
GOODLY
HANDLE
HARDLY
HEDDLE
HUDDLE
HURDLE
KINDLE
KINDLY
LEWDLY
LORDLY
LOUDLY
MEDDLE
MIDDLE
MILDLY
MUDDLE
NEEDLE
NODDLE
NOODLE
PADDLE
PEDDLE
POODLE
PUDDLE
PUDDLY
RADDLE
RIDDLE
RUDDLE
RUNDLE
SADDLE
TIDDLY
TODDLE
WADDLE
WADDLY
WILDLY

•••D•L

AMIDOL
APODAL
BRIDAL
CAUDAL
DAEDAL
FEUDAL
HANDEL
MENDEL
MYRDAL
OXYDOL
RONDEL
SANDAL
SEIDEL
VANDAL

••••DL

DIRNDL

DM••••

DMAJOR
DMARKS
DMINOR
DMINUS
DMITRI

D•M•••

DAMAGE
DAMASK
DAMATO
DAMIEN
DAMITA
DAMMAR
DAMMED
DAMNED
DAMONE
DAMORE
DAMOUR
DAMPED
DAMPEN
DAMPER
DAMPLY
DAMSEL
DAMSON
DAMSUP
DEMAND
DEMEAN
DEMIES
DEMISE
DEMITS
DEMOBS
DEMODE
DEMOND
DEMONS
DEMOTE
DEMURE
DEMURS
DIMITY
DIMMED
DIMMER
DIMOUT
DIMPLE
DIMPLY
DIMSUM
DIMWIT
DOMAIN
DOMANI
DOMINE
DOMING
DOMINI
DOMINO
DOMREP
DUMBER
DUMBLY
DUMDUM
DUMONT
DUMPED
DUMPER

D••M••

DAGMAR
DAIMON
DAIMYO
DAMMAR
DAMMED
DEEMED
DEIMOS
DELMAR
DERMAL
DERMIS
DESMAN
DIMMED
DIMMER
DISMAL
DISMAY
DISMES
DOGMAS
DOLMAN
DOLMAS
DOLMEN
DOOMED
DORMER
DRAMAS
DROMOI
DROMOS
DRUMUP
DUOMOS

D•••M•

DAGAMA
DANGME
DEARME
DECAMP
DEFAME
DENIMS
DHARMA
DODOMA
DOREMI
DREAMS
DREAMT
DREAMY
DYNAMO

D••••M

DEFORM
DIADEM
DIATOM
DICTUM
DIGRAM
DIMSUM
DIRHAM
DISARM
DOGDOM
DORSUM
DRACHM
DUMDUM
DUNHAM
DURHAM

•DM•••

ADMASS
ADMIRE
ADMITS
EDMOND
EDMUND

•D•M••

EDAMES

•D••M•

ADDAMS
ADEEMS
CDROMS
IDIOMS
ODIUMS

•D•••M

ADYTUM

••DM••

BADMAN
BADMEN
CADMIC
CADMUS
ENDMAN
ENDMEN
KIDMAN
MADMAN
MADMAX
MADMEN
OLDMAN
OLDMEN
RODMAN
RUDMAN
TODMAN

••D•M•

ADDAMS
BEDIMS
DODOMA
MADAME
MADAMS
MODEMS
OEDEMA
RADOME
SEDUMS

••D••M

BADHAM
BEDLAM
INDIUM
LUDLUM
MADTOM
MEDIUM
OLDHAM
PODIUM
RADIUM
REDEEM
REDGUM
RODHAM
SADDAM
SODIUM
TEDEUM
TEDIUM

•••DM•

RUNDMC

•••D•M

AIRDAM
ANADEM
BELDAM
DIADEM
DOGDOM
DUMDUM
FANDOM
IBIDEM
MCADAM
RANDOM
SADDAM
SELDOM
TANDEM
WINDOM
WISDOM

D•N•••

DANANG
DANAUS
DANCED
DANCER
DANCES
DANDER
DANDIE
DANDLE
DANGER
DANGLE
DANGLY
DANGME
DANIEL
DANISH
DANKER
DANKLY
DANNAY
DANNER
DANSON
DANTES
DANTON
DANUBE
DANZIG
DENALI
DENARY
DENDRI
DENDRO
DENGUE
DENIAL
DENIED
DENIER
DENIES
DENIMS
DENIRO
DENISE
DENNED
DENNIS
DENOTE
DENOVO
DENSER
DENTAL
DENTED
DENTIL
DENTIN
DENTON
DENUDE
DENVER
DENZEL
DINARS
DINEIN
DINEON
DINERO
DINERS
DINGED
DINGHY
DINGLE
DINGUS
DINING
DINKEY
DINNED
DINNER
DINTED
DONALD
DONATE
DONDER
DONEES
DONEIN
DONETS
DONEUP
DONGLE
DONITZ
DONJON
DONKEY
DONNAS
DONNED
DONNEE
DONNER
DONORS
DONUTS
DUNANT
DUNBAR
DUNCAN
DUNCES
DUNDEE
DUNERA
DUNHAM
DUNKED
DUNKER
DUNLIN
DUNLOP
DUNNED
DYNAMO
DYNAST

D••N••

DABNEY
DAINTY
DAMNED
DANNAY
DANNER
DARNAY
DARNED
DARNEL
DARNER
DARNIT
DAUNTS
DAWNED
DAWNON
DEANNA
DENNED
DENNIS
DIANNE
DINNED
DINNER
DIONEB
DIONNE
DIRNDL
DISNEY
DMINOR
DMINUS
DOINGS
DONNAS
DONNED
DONNEE
DONNER
DOWNED
DOWNER
DOWNEY
DOWNON
DRENCH
DRINGS
DRINKS
DRONED
DRONER
DRONES
DUENNA
DUNNED
DURNED

D•••N•

DAMONE
DANANG
DAPHNE
DARENT
DARING
DATING
DATONG
DAYONE
DAZING
DEANNA
DEBONE
DEBUNK
DECANT
DECENT
DEFEND
DEFINE
DEIGNS
DEKING
DELANO
DELANY
DELONG
DEMAND
DEMOND
DEMONS
DEPEND
DEPONE
DETENT
DEVINE
DEWING
DIANNE
DICING
DIKING
DINING
DIONNE
DISANT
DIVANS
DIVINE
DIVING
DIVINO
DIZENS
DOCENT
DOESNT
DOGONS
DOLENZ
DOLING
DOMANI
DOMINE
DOMING
DOMINI
DOMINO
DOPANT
DOPING
DOSING
DOTING
DOYENS
DOZENS
DOZING
DRAINS
DROWNS
DRYING
DRYINK
DUENNA
DUGONG
DUKING
DUMONT
DUNANT
DUPING
DUPONT
DURANT
DURING
DWAYNE
DYEING

D••••N

DACRON
DAIKON
DAIMON
DAIREN
DALTON
DAMIEN
DAMPEN
DAMSON
DANSON
DANTON
DARIEN
DARKEN
DARREN
DARWIN
DASSIN
DATSUN
DAWNON
DAWSON
DAYTON
DEACON
DEADEN
DEADON
DEAFEN
DEALIN
DEEPEN
DEHORN
DELEON
DEMEAN
DENTIN
DENTON
DESIGN
DESMAN
DETAIN
DEVEIN
DIDION
DIGSIN
DILLON
DINEIN
DINEON
DIOXIN
DISOWN
DIVEIN
DOBBIN
DOBLIN
DOBSON
DOESIN
DOLMAN
DOLMEN
DOMAIN
DONEIN
DONJON
DORIAN
DOTEON
DOTHAN
DOVEIN
DOWNON
DRAGIN
DRAGON
DRAWIN
DRAWON
DREWIN
DREWON
DRIVEN
DROPIN
DRYDEN
DRYRUN
DUBBIN
DUBLIN
DUCHIN
DUDEEN
DUNCAN
DUNLIN
DURBAN
DURBIN
DURIAN
DUSTIN

•DN•••

ADNATE
ADNEXA

•D•N••

ADONAI
ADONIS
EDENIC
GDANSK
ODENSE
ODONTO

•D••N•

ADDEND
ADDING
ADDONS
ADJANI
ADORNS
ADRENO
ADVENT
EDGING
EDMOND
EDMUND
EDWYNN
IDLING
KDLANG

•D•••N

ADDSIN
ADDSON
ADJOIN
ADRIAN
ADRIEN
EDGEIN
EDISON
EDWYNN
ODDSON

••DN••

KIDNAP
KIDNEY
NUDNIK
RADNER
RODNEY
SIDNEY
SYDNEY

••D•N•

ADDEND
ADDING
ADDONS
AIDING
ALDINE
ARDENT
AUDENS
BIDING
BODING
BODONI
CADENT
CEDANT
CEDING
CODING
CODONS
ENDING
FADING
HIDING
INDENE
INDENT
IODINE
JADING
LADING
LADINO
LODENS
LUDENS
MEDINA
MODENA
MODINE
NADINE
ONDINE
PADANG
PEDANT
PODUNK
REDANT
REDENY
REDING
REDINK
REDONE
RIDENT
RIDING
RODENT
SEDANS
SIDING
TIDING
UNDINE
UNDONE
WADING
WIDENS

••D••N

ADDSIN
ADDSON
ALDRIN
ANDEAN
BADMAN
BADMEN
BIDDEN
BIDSIN
BIDSON
BODKIN
DIDION
DUDEEN
ENDMAN
ENDMEN
ENDRUN
FADEIN
GIDEON
GODOWN
GODSON
GODWIN
GUDRUN
HADRON
HEDREN
HEDRON
HIDDEN
HUDSON
INDIAN
KIDMAN
LUDDEN
MADDEN
MADMAN
MADMEN
MADSEN
MEDIAN
MIDDEN
MIDIAN
MODERN
MUDHEN
ODDSON
OLDMAN
OLDMEN
ORDAIN
PADUAN
PIDGIN
RADIAN
REDDEN
REDFIN
RIDDEN
RODMAN
RUDMAN
SADDEN
SODDEN
SUDDEN
TODMAN
WADEIN
WEDELN

•••DN•

GRODNO
NEEDNT

•••D•N

AVEDON
BIDDEN
BORDEN
BOUDIN
BURDEN
CAMDEN
CARDIN
CORDON
DEADEN
DEADON
DRYDEN
EMBDEN
FEEDON
FELDON
GARDEN
GOLDEN
GOODEN
GORDON
GRADIN
GRODIN
GUIDON
HAGDON
HANDIN
HANDON
HARDEN
HAYDEN
HEADIN
HEADON
HEIDEN
HELDIN
HELDON
HIDDEN
HOLDEN
HOLDIN
HOLDON
HOYDEN
IBADAN
ICEDIN
JORDAN
KASDAN
LAIDIN
LAIDON
LANDON
LARDON
LEADEN
LEADIN
LEADON
LEIDEN
LEYDEN
LINDEN
LONDON
LOUDEN
LUDDEN
LUNDEN
LYNDON
MADDEN
MAIDEN
MALDEN
MANDAN
MIDDEN
PAIDIN
PARDON
READIN
REDDEN
RIDDEN
SADDEN
SENDIN
SLIDIN
SODDEN
SOLDAN
SOLDON
SUDDEN
SWEDEN
TENDON
TIEDIN
TILDEN
TOEDIN
TOLDON
VARDEN
VERDIN
VERDON
VERDUN
WALDEN
WARDEN
WOODEN

DO••••

DOABLE
DOBBER
DOBBIN
DOBLAS
DOBLIN
DOBRAS
DOBROS
DOBSON
DOCENT
DOCILE
DOCKED
DOCKER
DOCKET
DOCTOR
DODDER
DODECA
DODGED
DODGER
DODGES
DODODO
DODOES
DODOMA
DOESBY
DOESIN
DOESNT
DOESUP
DOFFED
DOGDAY
DOGDOM
DOGEAR
DOGEYS
DOGGED
DOGGER
DOGGIE
DOGIES
DOGLEG
DOGMAS
DOGONS
DOGOOD
DOGSAT
DOGSIT
DOGTAG
DOINGS
DOLENZ
DOLING
DOLLAR
DOLLED
DOLLOP
DOLLUP
DOLMAN
DOLMAS
DOLMEN
DOLORS
DOLOUR
DOMAIN
DOMANI
DOMINE
DOMING
DOMINI
DOMINO
DOMREP
DONALD
DONATE
DONDER
DONEES
DONEIN
DONETS
DONEUP
DONGLE
DONITZ
DONJON
DONKEY
DONNAS
DONNED
DONNEE
DONNER
DONORS
DONUTS
DOOBIE
DOODAD
DOODAH
DOODLE
DOOFUS
DOOGIE
DOOLEY
DOOMED
DOOWOP
DOOZIE
DOPANT
DOPIER
DOPING
DORADO
DORAGS
DORATI
DORCAS
DOREMI
DORIAN
DORIES
DORMER
DORRIT
DORSAL
DORSET
DORSEY
DORSUM
DOSAGE
DOSERS
DOSIDO
DOSING
DOSSAL
DOSSED
DOSSEL
DOSSER
DOSSES
DOTAGE
DOTARD
DOTELL
DOTEON
DOTHAN
DOTING
DOTTED
DOTTIE
DOTTLE
DOUALA
DOUBLE
DOUBLY
DOUBTS
DOUGHS
DOUGHY
DOURER
DOURLY
DOUSED
DOUSES
DOVEIN
DOVISH
DOWELS
DOWERS
DOWERY
DOWNED
DOWNER
DOWNEY
DOWNON
DOWSED
DOWSER
DOWSES
DOYENS
DOZENS
DOZERS
DOZIER
DOZILY
DOZING

D•O•••

DEODAR
DHOLES
DHOTEL
DHOTIS
DIODES
DIONEB
DIONNE
DIOXIN
DOOBIE
DOODAD
DOODAH
DOODLE
DOOFUS
DOOGIE
DOOLEY
DOOMED
DOOWOP
DOOZIE
DROGUE
DROIDS
DROITS
DROLLS
DROLLY
DROMOI
DROMOS
DRONED
DRONER
DRONES
DROOLS
DROOLY
DROOPS
DROOPY
DROPBY
DROPIN
DROPIT
DROVER
DROVES
DROWNS
DROWSE
DROWSY
DUOMOS
DVORAK

D••O••

DACOIT
DADOED
DADOES
DAKOTA
DAMONE
DAMORE
DAMOUR
DATONG
DAYONE
DEBONE
DECOCT
DECODE
DECORS
DECOYS
DEFOGS
DEFORM
DEHORN
DELONG
DEMOBS
DEMODE
DEMOND
DEMONS
DEMOTE
DENOTE
DENOVO
DEPONE
DEPORT
DEPOSE
DEPOTS
DESOTO
DETOUR
DEVOID
DEVOIR
DEVOTE
DEVOTO
DEVOUR
DEVOUT
DICOTS
DIEOFF
DIEOUT
DIGOUT
DIMOUT
DIPODY
DIPOLE
DISOWN
DIVOTS
DODODO
DODOES
DODOMA
DOGONS
DOGOOD
DOLORS
DOLOUR
DONORS
DRHOOK
DROOLS
DROOLY
DROOPS
DROOPY
DRYOFF
DRYOUT
DUBOIS
DUGONG
DUGOUT
DUMONT
DUPONT
DUROCS

D•••O•

DACRON
DAIKON
DAIMON
DALTON
DAMSON
DANSON
DANTON
DARROW
DAWNON
DAWSON
DAYBOY
DAYJOB
DAYTON
DEACON
DEADON
DEBTOR
DEIMOS
DEKKOS
DELEON
DELROY
DENTON
DEPLOY
DESPOT
DETROP
DIALOG
DIATOM
DIDION
DIGLOT
DILLON
DINEON
DISCOS
DITTOS
DMAJOR
DMINOR
DOBROS
DOBSON
DOCTOR
DOGDOM

DOGOOD
DOLLOP
DONJON
DOOWOP
DOTEON
DOWNON
DRAGON
DRAWON
DREWON
DRHOOK
DROMOI
DROMOS
DRYROT
DUNLOP
DUOMOS
DYELOT

D••••O

DACAPO
DADDYO
DAIMYO
DAMATO
DARETO
DAYGLO
DELANO
DELRIO
DENDRO
DENIRO
DENOVO
DESOTO
DEVITO
DEVOTO
DEXTRO
DIABLO
DINERO
DIRIGO
DIVINO
DODODO
DOMINO
DORADO
DOSIDO
DUELLO
DYNAMO

•DO•••

ADOBES
ADOLPH
ADONAI
ADONIS
ADOPTS
ADORED
ADOREE
ADORER
ADORES
ADORNS
IDOIDO
ODONTO
ODOURS

•D•O••

ADDONS
ADJOIN
ADROIT
ADSORB
CDROMS
EDDOES
EDKOCH
EDMOND
EDWOOD
IDIOCY
IDIOMS
IDIOTS
ODIOUS

•D••O•

ADDSON
EDISON
EDITOR
EDWOOD
ODDJOB
ODDLOT
ODDSON

•D•••O

ADAGIO
ADDSTO
ADRENO
EDITIO
IDOIDO
ODONTO

••DO••

ADDONS
ALDOSE
ALDOUS
ARDORS
ARDOUR
BODONI
CODONS
DADOED
DADOES
DODODO
DODOES
DODOMA
EDDOES
EIDOLA
ENDORA
ENDOWS
EUDORA
FEDORA
GODOWN
HIDOUT
INDOOR
INDORE
JUDOKA
KIDORY
LADOGA
LEDOFF
LEDOUT
MIDORI
MODOCS
NODOFF
NODOSE
OGDOAD
RADOME
REDOAK
REDOES
REDONE
RUDOLF
TUDORS
UNDOER
UNDOES
UNDONE
VADOSE
WIDOWS
XEDOUT
ZADORA

••D•O•

ADDSON
ANDHOW
ANDROS
AUDIOS
BADBOY
BADLOT
BIDSON
DIDION
GIDEON
GODSON
HADRON
HEDRON
HUDSON
HYDROS
INDOOR
KUDROW
MADTOM
ODDJOB
ODDLOT
ODDSON
OLDBOY
RADIOS
REDDOG
REDFOX
REDHOT
REDSOX
REDTOP
RIDSOF
RODEOS
TYDBOL
VIDEOS

••D••O

ADDSTO
DADDYO
DODODO
ENDURO
HIDEHO
INDIGO
LADINO
MADEDO
MADERO
MADURO
MEDICO
MODULO
OLDPRO
SIDERO
TODDAO
ZYDECO

•••DO•

ABYDOS
AMADOU
AMIDOL
AVEDON
BANDOG
BARDOT
CANDOR
CAWDOR
CHADOR
CONDOR
CONDOS
CORDON
CREDOS
DEADON
DOGDOM
EJIDOS
FANDOM
FEEDON
FELDON
FYODOR
GOODOH
GORDON
GUIDON
GUNDOG
HAGDON
HANDON
HEADON
HELDON
HOLDON
HOODOO
HOTDOG
ISADOR
KINDOF
LAIDON
LANDON
LAPDOG
LARDON
LEADON
LONDON
LYNDON
MCADOO
MEADOW
OXYDOL
PARDON
PYEDOG
RANDOM
REDDOG
RONDOS
SEADOG
SELDOM
SHADOW
SOLDON
SUNDOG
TENDON
TOLDOF
TOLDON
TONDOS
TOPDOG
TOYDOG
VENDOR
VERDON
VOODOO
WINDOM
WINDOW
WISDOM
ZENDOS

•••D•O

AMEDEO
CARDIO
DADDYO
DENDRO
GRODNO
HELDTO
HOLDTO
HOODOO
LAIDTO
LANDHO
LEADTO
MCADOO
STUDIO
TENDTO
TIEDTO
TODDAO
USEDTO
VOODOO

••••DO

AIKIDO
ALBEDO
BRANDO
DODODO
DORADO
DOSIDO
ESCUDO
HAIRDO
IDOIDO
JURADO
KOMODO
LAREDO
LIBIDO
MADEDO
MAKEDO
MENADO
MIKADO
OVERDO
OVIEDO
PSEUDO
RHABDO
SALADO
SPEEDO
TEREDO
TOLEDO
TUXEDO
WEIRDO

D•P•••

DAPHNE
DAPPED
DAPPER
DAPPLE
DEPART
DEPAUL
DEPAUW
DEPEND
DEPICT
DEPLOY
DEPONE
DEPORT
DEPOSE
DEPOTS
DEPTHS
DEPUTE
DEPUTY
DIPODY
DIPOLE
DIPPED
DIPPER
DOPANT
DOPIER
DOPING
DUPERY
DUPING
DUPLEX
DUPONT

D••P••

DAMPED
DAMPEN
DAMPER
DAMPLY
DAPPED
DAPPER
DAPPLE
DEEPAK
DEEPEN
DEEPER
DEEPLY
DELPHI
DESPOT
DIAPER
DIEPPE
DIMPLE
DIMPLY
DIPPED
DIPPER
DISPEL
DRAPED
DRAPER
DRAPES
DRIPPY
DROPBY
DROPIN
DROPIT
DRUPES
DUMPED
DUMPER

D•••P•

DACAPO
DIEPPE
DRIPPY
DROOPS
DROOPY

D••••P

DAMSUP
DECAMP
DETROP
DEWLAP
DIALUP
DIGSUP
DOESUP
DOLLOP
DOLLUP
DOMREP
DONEUP
DOOWOP
DRAWUP
DREWUP
DRUMUP
DSHARP
DUNLOP
DUSTUP

•D•P••

ADAPTS
ADEPTS
ADOPTS

•D••P•

ADOLPH

•D•••P

ADDSUP

••DP••

MUDPIE
OLDPRO

••D••P

ADDSUP
BIDSUP
ENDSUP
KIDNAP
MADCAP
MADEUP
REDCAP
REDTOP
TIDYUP
WADSUP

•••D•P

BEADUP
BINDUP
FOLDUP
HANDUP
HARDUP
HEADUP
HELDUP
HOLDUP
ICEDUP
LAIDUP
LEADUP
PAIDUP
SENDUP
SPEDUP
TEEDUP
TIEDUP
USEDUP
WINDUP

•••D•Q

NASDAQ

DR••••

DRABLY
DRACHM
DRAFTS
DRAFTY
DRAGEE
DRAGGY
DRAGIN
DRAGON
DRAILS
DRAINS
DRAKES
DRAMAS
DRAPED
DRAPER
DRAPES
DRAWER
DRAWIN
DRAWLS
DRAWLY
DRAWON
DRAWUP
DRAYED
DREADS
DREAMS
DREAMT
DREAMY
DREARY
DREDGE
DRENCH
DRESSY
DREWIN
DREWON
DREWUP
DREXEL
DRHOOK
DRIERS
DRIEST
DRIFTS
DRIFTY
DRILLS
DRINGS
DRINKS
DRIPPY
DRIVEL
DRIVEN
DRIVER
DRIVES
DROGUE
DROIDS
DROITS
DROLLS
DROLLY
DROMOI
DROMOS
DRONED
DRONER
DRONES
DROOLS
DROOLY
DROOPS
DROOPY
DROPBY
DROPIN
DROPIT
DROVER
DROVES
DROWNS
DROWSE
DROWSY
DRUDGE
DRUIDS
DRUMUP
DRUPES
DRUZES
DRYADS
DRYDEN
DRYERS
DRYEST
DRYFLY
DRYICE
DRYING
DRYINK
DRYOFF
DRYOUT
DRYROT
DRYRUN

D•R•••

DARENT
DARETO
DARIEN
DARING
DARIUS
DARKEN
DARKER
DARKLE
DARKLY
DARNAY
DARNED
DARNEL
DARNER
DARNIT
DARREN
DARROW
DARRYL
DARTED
DARTER
DARWIN
DERAIL
DERIDE
DERIVE
DERMAL
DERMIS
DERRIS
DIRECT
DIRELY
DIREST
DIRGES
DIRHAM
DIRIGE
DIRIGO
DIRNDL
DORADO
DORAGS
DORATI
DORCAS
DOREMI
DORIAN
DORIES
DORMER
DORRIT
DORSAL
DORSET
DORSEY
DORSUM
DURANT
DURBAN
DURBAR
DURBIN
DURESS
DURFEY
DURHAM
DURIAN
DURING
DURNED
DUROCS
DURYEA

D••R••

DACRON
DAIREN
DARREN
DARROW
DARRYL
DEARER
DEARIE
DEARLY
DEARME
DEARTH
DEBRAS
DEBRIS
DECREE
DEFRAY
DEGREE
DELRAY
DELRIO
DELROY
DERRIS
DETROP
DHARMA
DIGRAM
DJERBA
DMARKS
DOBRAS
DOBROS
DOMREP
DORRIT
DOURER
DOURLY
DRYROT
DRYRUN
DUARTE
DVORAK
DWARFS

D•••R•

DAMORE
DATARY
DATERS
DATURA
DEBARK
DEBARS
DECORS
DEFERS
DEFORM
DEHORN
DEIDRE
DEJURE
DEMURE
DEMURS
DENARY
DENDRI
DENDRO
DENIRO
DEPART
DEPORT
DESCRY
DESERT
DESIRE
DESTRY
DETERS
DEXTRO
DICERS
DINARS
DINERO
DINERS
DISARM
DIVERS
DIVERT
DIYERS
DMITRI
DOLORS
DONORS
DOSERS
DOTARD
DOWERS
DOWERY
DOZERS
DREARY
DRIERS
DRYERS
DSHARP
DUNERA
DUPERY

D••••R

DAFTER
DAGGER
DAGMAR
DAMMAR
DAMOUR
DAMPER
DANCER
DANDER
DANGER
DANKER
DANNER
DAPPER
DARKER
DARNER
DARTER
DASHER
DAUBER
DEADER
DEAFER
DEALER
DEARER
DEBTOR
DECKER
DEEPER
DEFTER
DEICER
DELMAR
DELVER
DENIER
DENSER
DENVER
DEODAR
DETOUR
DEVOIR
DEVOUR
DEWIER
DEXTER
DIALER
DIAPER
DICIER
DICKER
DIETER
DIFFER
DIGGER
DILLER
DIMMER
DINNER
DIPPER
DISBAR
DITHER
DLAYER
DMAJOR
DMINOR
DOBBER
DOCKER
DOCTOR
DODDER
DODGER
DOGEAR
DOGGER
DOLLAR
DOLOUR
DONDER
DONNER
DOPIER
DORMER
DOSSER
DOURER
DOWNER
DOWSER
DOZIER
DRAPER
DRAWER
DRIVER
DRONER
DROVER
DUELER
DUFFER
DUIKER
DULLER
DUMBER
DUMPER
DUNBAR
DUNKER
DURBAR
DUSTER

•DR•••

ADRENO
ADRIAN
ADRIEN
ADRIFT
ADROIT
CDROMS

•D•R••

ADORED
ADOREE
ADORER
ADORES
ADORNS
EDERLE

•D••R•

ADDERS
ADHERE
ADJURE
ADMIRE
ADSORB
ADVERB
ADVERT
EDBERG
EDGARD
EDGARS
EDGERS
EDUARD
EDVARD
EDWARD
IDCARD
IDLERS
ODOURS
UDDERS

•D•••R

ADORER
EDGIER
EDITOR

••DR••

ALDRIN
ANDREA
ANDREI
ANDRES
ANDREW
ANDREY
ANDROS
AUDREY
CADRES
CEDRIC
ENDRUN
ESDRAS
GUDRUN
HADRON
HEDREN
HEDRON
HYDRAE
HYDRAS
HYDROS
INDRIS
KUDROW
MADRAS
MADRES
MADRID
MIDRIB
MUDRAS
PADRES
REDRAW
REDREW
SUDRAS
UNDRAW

••D•R•

ADDERS
AIDERS
ALDERS
ARDORS
CEDARS
CIDERS
CODERS
CYDERS
EIDERS
ELDERS
ENDERS
ENDORA
ENDURE
ENDURO
EUDORA
FEDORA
GODARD
HIDERS
INDIRA
INDORE
KIDORY
LADERS
MADERO
MADURA
MADURO
MIDORI
MODERN
NADIRS
OLDPRO
ORDERS
ORDURE
RIDERS
SEDERS
SIDERO
SIDERS
TUDORS
UDDERS
VIDERI
WADERS
ZADORA

••D••R

ARDOUR
BADDER
BADGER
BIDDER
CADGER
CODGER
DODDER
DODGER
ENDEAR
FODDER
GADDER
HEDGER
INDOOR
JUDDER
KIDDER
LADDER
LADLER
LEDGER
LODGER
MADDER
MEDGAR
MEDLAR
MIDAIR
MIDLER
MUDDER
NUDGER
PADDER
PEDLAR
RADNER
REDDER
REDFIR
RUDDER
SADDER
SIDDUR
TEDDER
TIDIER
UNDOER
VEDDER
ZEDBAR

•••DR•

AIRDRY
DEIDRE
DENDRI
DENDRO
EXEDRA
LANDRY
PHEDRE
QUADRI
RANDRY
RUNDRY
SANDRA
SUNDRY
TAWDRY
TUNDRA

•••D•R

AGADIR
BADDER
BALDER
BENDER
BIDDER
BINDER
BIRDER
BLADER
BOLDER
BORDER
BRUDER
CALDER
CANDOR
CARDER
CAWDOR
CHADOR
CHIDER
CINDER
COLDER
CONDOR
COODER
CRUDER
DANDER
DEADER
DEODAR
DODDER
DONDER
ELUDER
EVADER
FEEDER
FENDER
FINDER
FODDER
FOLDER
FONDER
FYODOR
GADDER
GANDER
GENDER
GILDER
GIRDER
GLIDER
GRADER
HARDER
HEADER
HEEDER
HERDER
HINDER
HOLDER
ISADOR
JUDDER
KANDER
KIDDER
KINDER
LADDER
LANDER
LARDER
LAUDER
LEADER
LENDER
LEWDER
LIEDER
LOADER
LOUDER
MADDER
MENDER
MILDER
MINDER
MOLDER
MUDDER
MURDER
PADDER
PANDER
PINDAR
POLDER
PONDER
POWDER
RAIDER
READER
REDDER
RENDER
RUDDER
SADDER
SANDER
SEEDER
SENDER
SIDDUR
SIRDAR
SLIDER
SNIDER
SNYDER
SOLDER
SPADER
SPIDER
SUNDER
TEDDER
TENDER
TINDER
TRADER
VEDDER
VENDOR
WANDER
WARDER
WEEDER
WELDER
WILDER
WINDER
WONDER
YONDER
ZANDER
ZUIDER

••••DR

ANHYDR
RATEDR

DS••••

DSHARP

D•S•••

DASHED
DASHER
DASHES
DASHIS
DASSIN
DESALT
DESCRY
DESERT
DESICA
DESIGN
DESILU
DESIRE
DESIST
DESMAN
DESOTO
DESPOT
DESTRY
DISANT
DISARM
DISBAR
DISCOS
DISCUS
DISHED
DISHES
DISKED
DISMAL
DISMAY
DISMES
DISNEY
DISOWN
DISPEL
DISSED
DISTAL
DISTIL
DISUSE
DOSAGE
DOSERS
DOSIDO
DOSING
DOSSAL
DOSSED
DOSSEL
DOSSER
DOSSES
DUSTED
DUSTER
DUSTIN
DUSTUP

D••S••

DAISES
DAMSEL
DAMSON
DAMSUP
DANSON
DASSIN
DATSUN
DAWSON
DEASIL
DEISTS
DENSER
DIESEL
DIESES
DIESIS
DIGSIN
DIGSUP
DILSEY
DIMSUM
DISSED
DOBSON
DOESBY
DOESIN
DOESNT
DOESUP
DOGSAT
DOGSIT
DORSAL
DORSET
DORSEY
DORSUM
DOSSAL
DOSSED
DOSSEL
DOSSER
DOSSES
DOUSED
DOUSES
DOWSED
DOWSER
DOWSES
DRESSY

D•••S•

DALASI
DAMASK
DANISH
DEBASE
DEFUSE
DEGUST
DELIST
DEMISE
DENISE
DEPOSE
DESIST
DETEST
DEVEST
DEVISE
DIGEST
DIREST
DISUSE
DIVEST
DOVISH
DRESSY
DRIEST
DROWSE
DROWSY
DRYEST
DUDISH
DURESS
DYNAST

D••••S

DACHAS

DADOES
DAISES
DALLAS
DALLES
DANAUS
DANCES
DANTES
DARIUS
DASHES
DASHIS
DATERS
DAUBES
DAUNTS
DAVIES
DAVITS
DEBARS
DEBITS
DEBRAS
DEBRIS
DEBUGS
DEBUTS
DECAFS
DECALS
DECAYS
DECORS
DECOYS
DEFATS
DEFERS
DEFIES
DEFOGS
DEICES
DEIGNS
DEIMOS
DEISTS
DEKKOS
DELAYS
DELFTS
DELIUS
DELTAS
DELVES
DEMIES
DEMITS
DEMOBS
DEMONS
DEMURS
DENIES
DENIMS
DENNIS
DEPOTS
DEPTHS
DERMIS
DERRIS
DETERS
DEUCES
DEVILS
DHOLES
DHOTIS
DICERS
DICOTS
DICTUS
DIDIES
DIESES
DIESIS
DIGITS
DINARS
DINERS
DINGUS
DIODES
DIRGES
DISCOS
DISCUS
DISHES
DISMES
DITTOS
DITZES
DIVANS
DIVERS
DIVOTS
DIXITS
DIYERS
DIZENS
DMARKS
DMINUS
DOBLAS
DOBRAS
DOBROS
DODGES
DODOES
DOGEYS
DOGIES
DOGMAS
DOGONS
DOINGS
DOLMAS
DOLORS
DONEES
DONETS
DONNAS
DONORS
DONUTS
DOOFUS
DORAGS
DORCAS
DORIES
DOSERS
DOSSES
DOUBTS
DOUGHS
DOUSES
DOWELS
DOWERS
DOWSES
DOYENS
DOZENS
DOZERS
DRAFTS
DRAILS
DRAINS
DRAKES
DRAMAS
DRAPES
DRAWLS
DREADS
DREAMS
DRIERS
DRIFTS
DRILLS
DRINGS
DRINKS
DRIVES
DROIDS
DROITS
DROLLS
DROMOS
DRONES
DROOLS
DROOPS
DROVES
DROWNS
DRUIDS
DRUPES
DRUZES
DRYADS
DRYERS
DUBOIS
DUCATS
DULLES
DUNCES
DUOMOS
DURESS
DUROCS
DUTIES
DUVETS
DWARFS
DWEEBS
DWELLS

•DS•••
ADSORB
EDSELS

•D•S••
ADDSIN
ADDSON
ADDSTO
ADDSUP
ADESTE
EDESSA
EDISON
ODDSON
ODESSA
ODISTS

•D••S•
ADJUST
ADMASS
ADVISE
EDESSA
GDANSK
IDLEST
ODDEST
ODENSE
ODESSA

•D•••S
ADAGES
ADAPTS
ADDAMS
ADDERS
ADDLES
ADDONS
ADEEMS
ADEPTS
ADIDAS
ADIEUS
ADLIBS
ADMASS
ADMITS
ADOBES
ADONIS
ADOPTS
ADORES
ADORNS
ADULTS
CDROMS
EDAMES
EDDIES
EDDOES
EDGARS
EDGERS
EDICTS
EDILES
EDSELS
EDUCES
IDEALS
IDIOMS
IDIOTS
IDLERS
IDTAGS
IDYLLS
ODIOUS
ODISTS
ODIUMS
ODOURS
UDDERS

••DS••
ADDSIN
ADDSON
ADDSTO
ADDSUP
BIDSIN
BIDSON
BIDSUP
ENDSUP
GODSON
HUDSON
MADSEN
ODDSON
OLDSAW
REDSEA
REDSOX
RIDSOF
SUDSED
SUDSES
WADSUP

••D•S•
ALDOSE
DUDISH
ELDEST
EMDASH
ENDASH
ENDUSE
IODISE
JADISH
MEDUSA
MODEST
MODISH
NODOSE
NUDEST
NUDIST
ODDEST
OLDEST
OLDISH
RADISH
RUDEST
VADOSE
WIDEST
WIDISH

••D••S
ADDAMS
ADDERS
ADDLES
ADDONS
AIDERS
ALDERS
ALDOUS
ANDRES
ANDROS
AODAIS
ARDEBS
ARDORS
ASDICS
AUDENS
AUDIOS
AUDITS
BADGES
BEDEWS
BEDIMS
BODIES
BUDGES
CADDIS
CADETS
CADGES
CADMUS
CADRES
CEDARS
CIDERS
CODERS
CODONS
CYDERS
DADOES
DIDIES
DODGES
DODOES
EDDIES
EDDOES
EIDERS
ELDERS
ENDERS
ENDOWS
ENDUES
ESDRAS
FUDGES
GODETS
HADJES
HADJIS
HEDGES
HIDERS
HODADS
HODGES
HYDRAS
HYDROS
INDIES
INDRIS
JUDGES
KEDGES
KUDZUS
LADERS
LADIES
LADLES
LEDGES
LODENS
LODGES
LUDENS
MADAMS
MADRAS
MADRES
MEDALS
MEDIAS
MEDICS
MIDGES
MODELS
MODEMS
MODOCS
MUDRAS
NADIRS
NUDGES
OLDIES
OODLES
ORDERS
PADRES
PEDALS
RADIOS
RADIUS
REDOES
REDUBS
REDYES
RIDERS
RIDGES
RODEOS
SADHES
SADHUS
SEDANS
SEDERS
SEDGES
SEDUMS
SIDERS
SIDLES
SUDRAS
SUDSES
TIDIES
TUDORS
UDDERS
UNDIES
UNDOES
VIDEOS
VODKAS
WADERS
WEDGES
WIDENS
WIDOWS
WIDTHS
WODGES
YODELS

•••DS•
AMIDST
WOODSY

•••D•S
ABIDES
ABODES
ABYDOS
ADIDAS
AMADIS
AMIDES
ANODES
ASIDES
ATODDS
AZIDES
BLADES
BRIDES
BSIDES
CADDIS
CHIDES
CNIDUS
CONDOS
CREDOS
DIODES
EJIDOS
ELIDES
ELUDES
EPODES
ERODES
ETUDES
EVADES
EXODUS
EXUDES
GEODES
GLADES
GLADYS
GLIDES
GRADES
GRADUS
GUIDES
HAIDAS
HINDUS
HORDES
HYADES
IRIDES
LANDIS
MAHDIS
MAIDUS
MENDES
OXIDES
PANDAS
PINDUS
PRIDES
PRUDES
RHODES
RONDOS
SARDIS
SAUDIS
SHADES
SLIDES
SONDES
SPADES
SUEDES
SWEDES
TILDES
TONDOS
TRADES
VELDTS
ZENDOS

••••DS
ALKYDS
AMENDS
APHIDS
AROIDS
ATODDS
AVOIDS
AWARDS
BEARDS
BIPEDS
BIPODS
BLEEDS
BLENDS
BLINDS
BLONDS
BOARDS
BOUNDS
BOVIDS
BRAIDS
BRANDS
BREADS
BREEDS
BROADS
BROODS
BUILDS
CANIDS
CHILDS
CHORDS
CLOUDS
CREEDS
CROWDS
CUPIDS
CYCADS
DREADS
DROIDS
DRUIDS
DRYADS
EBONDS
ELANDS
EMBEDS
EMENDS
EPHODS
FARADS
FIELDS
FIENDS
FIORDS
FJELDS
FJORDS
FLOODS
FLUIDS
FOUNDS
FRAUDS
FRONDS
GLANDS
GOURDS
GRANDS
GRINDS
GUARDS
GUILDS
HEXADS
HOARDS
HODADS
HOUNDS
JIHADS
KNEADS
LAIRDS
LAMEDS
LIPIDS
LLOYDS
MONADS
MOPEDS
MOULDS
MOUNDS
NAIADS
NOMADS
OCTADS
OREADS
OVOIDS
PLAIDS
PLEADS
POUNDS
PSEUDS
RANIDS
RAPIDS
REBIDS
REPADS
RESODS
REWEDS
ROUNDS
SALADS
SARODS
SCALDS
SCENDS
SCOLDS
SCRODS
SHARDS
SHREDS
SKALDS
SNOODS
SOLIDS
SOUNDS
SPEEDS
SPENDS
SQUADS
SQUIDS
STANDS
STEADS
STEEDS
STRADS
SWARDS
SWORDS
SYNODS
TBIRDS
TBONDS
THIRDS
TREADS
TRENDS
TRIADS
TWEEDS
UPENDS
URSIDS
VIANDS
WIELDS
WORLDS
WOUNDS
YIELDS
ZOOIDS
ZOUNDS
DATONG
DATSUN
DATURA
DETACH
DETAIL
DETAIN
DETECT
DETENT
DETERS
DETEST
DETOUR
DETROP
DITHER
DITTOS
DITZES
DOTAGE
DOTARD
DOTELL
DOTEON
DOTHAN
DOTING
DOTTED
DOTTIE
DOTTLE
DUTIES

D••T••
DACTYL
DAFTER
DAFTLY
DALTON
DANTES
DANTON
DARTED
DARTER
DAYTON
DEBTOR
DEFTER
DEFTLY
DELTAS
DELTIC
DENTAL
DENTED
DENTIL
DENTIN
DENTON
DEPTHS
DESTRY
DEXTER
DEXTRO
DHOTEL
DHOTIS
DIATOM
DICTUM
DICTUS
DIETED
DIETER
DIKTAT
DINTED
DISTAL
DISTIL
DITTOS
DMITRI
DOCTOR
DOGTAG
DOTTED
DOTTIE
DOTTLE
DUCTAL
DUSTED
DUSTER
DUSTIN
DUSTUP

D•T•••
DATARY
DATERS
DATING
DATIVE

D•••T•
DAINTY
DAKOTA
DALETH
DAMATO
DAMITA
DARETO
DAUNTS
DAVITS
DEARTH
DEBATE
DEBITS
DEBUTS
DEFATS
DEISTS
DELATE
DELETE
DELFTS
DEMITS
DEMOTE
DENOTE
DEPOTS
DEPUTE
DEPUTY
DESOTO
DEVITO
DEVOTE
DEVOTO
DEWITT
DICOTS
DIGITS
DILATE
DILUTE
DIMITY
DIVOTS
DIXITS
DONATE
DONETS
DONITZ
DONUTS
DORATI
DOUBTS
DRAFTS
DRAFTY
DRIFTS
DRIFTY
DROITS
DUARTE
DUCATS
DULUTH
DUVETS

D••••T
DACOIT
DARENT
DARNIT
DAYLIT
DECANT
DECEIT
DECENT
DECOCT
DEDUCT
DEFEAT
DEFECT
DEGUST
DEJECT
DELICT
DELIST
DEPART
DEPICT
DEPORT
DESALT
DESERT
DESIST
DESPOT
DETECT
DETENT
DETEST
DEVEST
DEVOUT
DEWITT
DIDACT
DIEOUT
DIGEST
DIGLOT
DIGOUT
DIKTAT
DIMOUT
DIMWIT
DIRECT
DIREST
DISANT
DIVERT
DIVEST
DOCENT
DOCKET
DOESNT
DOGSAT
DOGSIT
DOPANT
DORRIT
DORSET
DREAMT
DRIEST
DROPIT
DRYEST
DRYOUT
DRYROT
DUGOUT
DULCET
DUMONT
DUNANT
DUPONT
DURANT
DWIGHT
DYELOT
DYNAST

•DT•••
IDTAGS

•D•T••
ADYTUM
EDITED
EDITIO
EDITOR
ODETTA
ODETTE

•D••T•
ADAPTS
ADDSTO
ADEPTS
ADESTE
ADMITS
ADNATE
ADOPTS
ADULTS
EDICTS
IDEATE
IDIOTS
ODDITY
ODETTA
ODETTE
ODISTS
ODONTO

•D•••T
ADDUCT
ADJUST
ADRIFT
ADROIT
ADVENT
ADVERT
IDLEST
ODDEST
ODDLOT

••DT••
MADTOM
REDTAG
REDTOP
WIDTHS

••D•T•
ADDSTO
AUDITS
CADETS
GODETS
INDITE
IODATE
JUDITH
NUDITY
ODDITY
PEDATE
REDATE
SEDATE
TODATE
UPDATE

••D••T
ABDUCT
ADDUCT
ARDENT
BADLOT
BUDGET
CADENT
CEDANT
DEDUCT
DIDACT
ELDEST
FIDGET
GADGET
GIDGET
GODWIT
HIDOUT
INDEBT
INDENT
INDICT
INDUCT
LEDOUT
MADEIT
MEDLAT
MIDGET
MODELT
MODEST
MUDCAT
NUDEST
NUDIST
ODDEST
ODDLOT
OLDEST
OLDHAT
PEDANT
REDACT
REDANT
REDHAT
REDHOT
RIDENT
RODENT
RUDEST
TIDBIT
WIDEST
WIDGET
XEDOUT

•••DT•
HELDTO
HOLDTO
LAIDTO
LEADTO
TENDTO
TIEDTO
USEDTO
VELDTS

•••D•T
AMIDST
BANDIT
BARDOT
COEDIT
CREDIT
HOLDIT
NEEDNT
PANDIT
PUNDIT
REEDIT

••••DT
ARENDT
BRANDT

DU••••
DUALLY
DUARTE
DUBBED
DUBBIN
DUBCEK
DUBLIN
DUBOIS
DUCATS
DUCHIN
DUCKED
DUCTAL
DUDEEN
DUDISH
DUDLEY
DUELED
DUELER
DUELLO
DUENNA
DUFFEL
DUFFER
DUGONG
DUGOUT
DUIKER
DUKING
DULCET
DULLEA
DULLED
DULLER
DULLES
DULUTH
DUMBER
DUMBLY
DUMDUM
DUMONT
DUMPED
DUMPER
DUNANT
DUNBAR
DUNCAN
DUNCES
DUNDEE
DUNERA
DUNHAM
DUNKED
DUNKER
DUNLIN
DUNLOP
DUNNED
DUOMOS
DUPERY
DUPING
DUPLEX
DUPONT
DURANT
DURBAN
DURBAR
DURBIN
DURESS
DURFEY
DURHAM
DURIAN
DURING
DURNED
DUROCS
DURYEA
DUSTED
DUSTER
DUSTIN
DUSTUP
DUTIES
DUVALL
DUVETS

D•U•••
DAUBED
DAUBER
DAUBES
DAUNTS
DEUCED
DEUCES
DOUALA
DOUBLE
DOUBLY
DOUBTS
DOUGHS
DOUGHY
DOURER
DOURLY
DOUSED
DOUSES
DRUDGE
DRUIDS
DRUMUP
DRUPES
DRUZES

D••U••
DANUBE
DATURA
DEBUGS
DEBUNK
DEBUTS
DEDUCE
DEDUCT
DEFUSE
DEGUST
DEJURE
DELUDE
DELUGE
DELUXE
DEMURE
DEMURS
DENUDE
DEPUTE
DEPUTY
DILUTE
DISUSE
DONUTS
DULUTH

D•••U•
DAMOUR
DAMSUP
DANAUS
DARIUS
DATSUN
DELIUS
DENGUE
DEPAUL
DEPAUW
DETOUR
DEVOUR
DEVOUT
DIALUP
DICTUM
DICTUS
DIEOUT
DIGOUT
DIGSUP
DIMOUT
DIMSUM
DINGUS
DISCUS
DMINUS
DOESUP
DOLLUP
DOLOUR
DONEUP
DOOFUS
DORSUM
DRAWUP
DREWUP
DROGUE
DRUMUP
DRYOUT
DRYRUN
DUGOUT
DUMDUM
DUSTUP
DYBBUK

D••••U
DEJAVU
DESILU

•DU•••
ADULTS
EDUARD
EDUCED
EDUCES

•D•U••
ADDUCE
ADDUCT
ADJURE
ADJUST
ADZUKI
EDMUND
ODIUMS
ODOURS

•D••U•
ADDSUP
ADIEUS
ADIEUX
ADYTUM
ODIOUS

••DU••
ABDUCT
ADDUCE
ADDUCT
DEDUCE
DEDUCT
ENDUED
ENDUES
ENDURE
ENDURO
ENDUSE
INDUCE
INDUCT
MADURA
MADURO
MEDUSA
MODULE
MODULO
NODULE
ORDURE
PADUAN
PODUNK
RADULA
REDUBS
REDUCE
SEDUCE
SEDUMS
UNDULY

••D•U•
ADDSUP
AIDFUL
ALDOUS
ARDOUR
BADGUY
BEDAUB
BEDBUG
BIDSUP
CADMUS
ENDRUN
ENDSUP
GUDRUN
HIDOUT
INDIUM
KUDZUS
LEDOUT
LUDLUM
MADEUP
MEDIUM
PODIUM
RADIUM
RADIUS
REDBUD
REDGUM
SADHUS
SIDDUR
SODIUM
TEDEUM
TEDIUM
TIDYUP
WADSUP
XEDOUT

•••DU•
BEADUP
BINDUP
CNIDUS
DUMDUM
EXODUS
FOLDUP
FONDUE
GRADUS
HANDUP
HARDUP
HEADUP
HELDUP

HINDUS HOLDUP ICEDUP LAIDUP LEADUP MAIDUS MARDUK PAIDUP PERDUE PINDUS PURDUE SENDUP SIDDUR SPEDUP SUBDUE TEEDUP TIEDUP USEDUP VERDUN WINDUP

•••D•U
AMADOU LANDAU MOLDAU

••••DU
MBUNDU TELEDU XANADU

DV••••
DVORAK

D•V•••
DAVIES DAVITS DEVEIN DEVEST DEVICE DEVILS DEVINE DEVISE DEVITO DEVOID DEVOIR DEVOTE DEVOTO DEVOUR DEVOUT DIVANS DIVEIN DIVERS DIVERT DIVEST DIVIDE DIVINE DIVING DIVINO DIVOTS DOVEIN DOVISH DUVALL DUVETS

D••V••
DELVED DELVER DELVES DENVER DRIVEL DRIVEN DRIVER DRIVES DROVER DROVES

D•••V•
DATIVE DEJAVU DENOVO DERIVE

•DV•••
ADVENT ADVERB ADVERT ADVICE ADVISE EDVARD

••DV••
KIDVID OLDVIC

••D•V•
ENDIVE GODIVA

DW••••
DWARFS DWAYNE DWEEBS DWELLS DWIGHT

D•W•••
DAWDLE DAWNED DAWNON DAWSON DEWIER DEWILY DEWING DEWITT DEWLAP DOWELS DOWERS DOWERY DOWNED DOWNER DOWNEY DOWNON DOWSED DOWSER DOWSES

D••W••
DARWIN DIMWIT DOOWOP DRAWER DRAWIN DRAWLS DRAWLY DRAWON DRAWUP DREWIN DREWON DREWUP DROWNS DROWSE DROWSY

D•••W•
DISOWN

D••••W
DARROW DEPAUW

•DW•••
ADWEEK EDWARD EDWOOD EDWYNN

••DW••
GODWIN GODWIT LUDWIG MIDWAY PEDWAY

••D•W•
BEDEWS ENDOWS GODOWN WIDOWS

••D••W
ANDHOW ANDREW KUDROW OLDSAW REDRAW REDREW UNDRAW

•••D•W
MEADOW MILDEW SHADOW SUNDEW WINDOW

D•X•••
DEXTER DEXTRO DIXITS

D••X••
DIOXIN DREXEL

D•••X•
DELUXE

D••••X
DUPLEX

•D••X•
ADNEXA

•D•••X
ADIEUX

••D••X
MADMAX REDFOX REDSOX

•••D•X
BENDIX CAUDEX SPADIX WINDEX

••••DX
BRANDX RATEDX

DY••••
DYADIC DYBBUK DYEING DYELOT DYNAMO DYNAST

D•Y•••
DAYBED DAYBOY DAYGLO DAYJOB DAYLIT DAYONE DAYTON DIYERS DOYENS DRYADS DRYDEN DRYERS DRYEST DRYFLY DRYICE DRYING DRYINK DRYOFF DRYOUT DRYROT DRYRUN

D••Y••
DLAYER DRAYED DURYEA DWAYNE

D•••Y•
DACTYL DADDYO DAIMYO DARRYL DECAYS DECOYS DELAYS DOGEYS

D••••Y
DABNEY DAFTLY DAILEY DAINTY DAMPLY DANGLY DANKLY DANNAY DARKLY DARNAY DATARY DAYBOY DEADLY DEAFLY DEARLY DEEJAY DEEPLY DEFRAY DEFTLY DELANY DELRAY DELROY DENARY DEPLOY DEPUTY DESCRY DESTRY DEWILY DICKEY DIDDLY DILSEY DIMITY DIMPLY DINGHY DINKEY DIPODY DIRELY DISMAY DISNEY DOESBY DOGDAY DONKEY DOOLEY DORSEY DOUBLY DOUGHY DOURLY DOWERY DOWNEY DOZILY DRABLY DRAFTY DRAGGY DRAWLY DREAMY DREARY DRESSY DRIFTY DRIPPY DROLLY DROOLY DROOPY DROPBY DROWSY DRYFLY DUALLY DUDLEY DUMBLY DUPERY DURFEY

•DY•••
ADYTUM IDYLLS

•D•Y••
EDWYNN

•D•••Y
EDGILY IDIOCY ODDITY

••DY••
REDYED REDYES TIDYUP UNDYED

••D•Y•
DADDYO REDEYE

••D••Y
ANDREY AUDREY BADBOY BADGUY BODILY CODIFY CUDDLY DIDDLY DUDLEY GADFLY KIDNEY KIDORY KODALY MEDFLY MEDLEY MIDDAY MIDWAY MODIFY NIDIFY NUDELY NUDITY ODDITY OLDBOY PEDWAY PUDDLY REDBAY REDENY RIDLEY RODNEY RUDELY SIDNEY SYDNEY TEDKEY TIDDLY TIDILY UNDULY WADDLY WIDELY

•••DY•
AZODYE DADDYO GLADYS TIEDYE

•••D•Y
ACIDLY AIRDRY ALLDAY ANYDAY ARIDLY AVIDLY AWEDLY BALDLY BENDAY BOLDLY CLODDY COLDLY CORDAY CRUDDY CUDDLY DEADLY DIDDLY DOGDAY FLEDGY FONDLY FREDDY FRIDAY GLADLY GOODBY GOODLY HARDBY HARDLY HEYDAY KINDLY LAIDBY LANDRY LEWDLY LORDLY LOUDLY MANDAY MAYDAY MIDDAY MILDLY MONDAY OFFDAY ONEDAY PAYDAY PUDDLY RANDRY RUNDRY SHODDY SKIDDY SLUDGY SMUDGY STODGY SUNDAY SUNDRY TAGDAY TAWDRY TIDDLY WADDLY WILDLY WOODSY

••••DY
BLOODY BRANDY BROODY CLODDY CLOUDY COMEDY CRUDDY DIPODY EMBODY FRAIDY FREDDY GREEDY GRUNDY HOUNDY MALADY MAUNDY MELODY MILADY MONODY MOULDY NOBODY PARODY REMEDY SHANDY SHEEDY SHINDY SHODDY SKIDDY SPEEDY STEADY STURDY TRENDY TWEEDY UNTIDY WEIRDY

D•Z•••
DAZING DAZZLE DIZENS DOZENS DOZERS DOZIER DOZILY DOZING

D••Z••
DANZIG DAZZLE DENZEL DITZES DOOZIE DRUZES

D••••Z
DOLENZ DONITZ

•DZ•••
ADZUKI

••DZ••
KUDZUS

••D•Z•
BEDAZE IODIZE

•••D•Z
VALDEZ

EA••••
EAGLED EAGLES EAGLET EAGRES EALING EARFUL EARING EARLAP EARNED EARNER EARTHA EARTHY EARWAX EARWIG EASEIN EASELS EASEUP EASIER EASILY EASING EASTER EASTON EATERS EATERY EATING EATOUT EATSAT EATSIN EATSUP

E•A•••
ECARTE EDAMES ELAINE ELANDS ELAPID ELAPSE ELATED ELATER ELATES ELAYER ELAYNE EMAILS EMAJOR ENABLE ENACTS ENAMEL ENAMOR ENATES EPARCH ERASED ERASER ERASES ETALIA ETALII ETAPES EVADED EVADER EVADES EXACTA EXACTO EXACTS EXALTS EXARCH

E••A••
EBOATS ECLAIR ECLATS EDGARD EDGARS EDUARD EDVARD EDWARD EFFACE EFLATS ELPASO EMBANK EMBARK EMBAYS EMDASH ENCAGE ENCAMP ENCASE ENDALL ENDASH ENFANT ENGAGE ENHALO ENLACE ENRAGE ENRAPT ENTAIL EPHAHS EQUALS EQUATE ERGATE ERHARD ERNANI ERRAND ERRANT ERRARE ERRATA ERSATZ ESCAPE ESCARP ESHARP ESPANA ESSAYS ESTATE ETHANE EURAIL EUTAXY EXHALE EXPAND EXTANT EZZARD

E•••A•
EARLAP EARWAX EATSAT ELFMAN ELIJAH EMQUAD ENDEAR ENDMAN ENGRAM ENNEAD ENQUAD ENTRAP ENWRAP EOLIAN EONIAN EPICAL EPINAL ESDRAS ESPIAL ESTRAY EXTRAS

E••••A
EARTHA EDESSA EGERIA EGESTA EIDOLA EJECTA ELISHA ELISSA ELMIRA ELVIRA EMILIA ENCINA ENDORA ENIGMA EROICA ERRATA ESPANA ESPOSA ETALIA EUBOEA EUDORA EUPNEA EUREKA EUROPA EXACTA EXEDRA

•EA•••
BEACHY BEACON BEADED BEADLE BEADUP BEAGLE BEAKED BEAKER BEAMED BEAMON BEAMUP BEANED BEANIE BEANOS BEARDS BEARER BEARON BEARUP BEASTS BEATEN BEATER BEATIT BEATLE BEATON BEATTY BEATUP BEAUTS BEAUTY BEAVER BEAVIS CEASED CEASES DEACON DEADEN DEADER DEADLY DEADON DEAFEN DEAFER DEAFLY DEALER DEALIN DEANNA DEARER DEARIE DEARLY DEARME DEARTH DEASIL FEALTY FEARED FEARER FEASTS FEATLY GEARED GEARTO GEARUP HEADED HEADER HEADIN HEADON HEADUP HEALED HEALER HEALTH HEANEY HEAPED HEARER HEAROF HEARST HEARTH HEARTS HEARTY HEARYE HEATED HEATER HEATHS HEATHY HEATUP HEAVED HEAVEN HEAVER HEAVES JEANNE KEARNY KEATON LEACHY LEADED LEADEN LEADER LEADIN LEADON LEADTO LEADUP LEAFED LEAGUE LEAKED LEAKER LEAKEY LEALTY LEANED LEANER LEANLY LEANON LEANTO LEAPED LEAPER LEARNS LEARNT LEASED LEASER LEASES LEAVED LEAVEN LEAVES MEADOW MEAGER MEAGRE MEALIE MEANER MEANIE MEANLY MEASLY NEARBY NEARED NEARER NEARLY NEARTO NEATEN NEATER NEATLY PEACHY PEAHEN PEAKED PEALED PEANUT PEAPOD PEARLS PEARLY PEAVEY REACTS READER READIN REAGAN REAIMS REAIRS REALER REALES REALIA REALLY REALMS REALTY REAMED REAMER REAPED REAPER REARED REARER REARMS REARUP REASON REATAS SEABAG SEABED SEABEE SEACOW SEADOG SEAFAN SEAFOX SEAGAL SEALAB SEALED SEALER SEALUP SEAMAN SEAMED SEAMEN SEAMUS SEANCE SEARCH SEARED SEARLE SEASON SEATED SEATER SEATON SEAWAY TEABAG TEACUP TEAMED TEAMUP TEAPOT TEAPOY TEARAT TEARED TEARUP TEASED TEASEL TEASER TEASES TEASET WEAKEN WEAKER WEAKLY WEALTH WEANED WEAPON WEARER WEASEL WEAVED WEAVER WEAVES YEAGER YEANED YEARLY YEARNS YEASTS YEASTY ZEALOT

•E•A••
AERATE BECALM BECAME BEDAUB BEDAZE BEFALL BEHALF BEHAVE BELAIR BELAYS BEMATA BERATE BESANT BETAKE BEWAIL BEWARE BEZANT CEDANT CEDARS CERATE CESARE CETANE DEBARK DEBARS DEBASE DEBATE DECADE DECAFS DECALS DECAMP DECANT DECAYS DEFACE DEFAME DEFATS DEGAGE DEJAVU DEKALB DELANO DELANY DELATE DELAYS DEMAND DENALI DENARY DEPART DEPAUL DEPAUW DERAIL DESALT DETACH DETAIL DETAIN FEMALE GELADA GELATI GELATO GEMARA GERAHS GERALD GERARD HECATE HEGARI HEMATO HERALD HEXADS KEBABS KERALA LEGACY LEGALS LEGATE LEGATO LELAND LEMANS LENAPE LESAGE LEVANT MEDAKA MEDALS MEGALO MEGARA MELANO MENACE MENADO MENAGE MESABI METALS METATE NEGATE NEMATO NEPALI NEVADA NEWAGE NEWARK PECANS PEDALS PEDANT PEDATE PELAGE PENANG PESACH PESAWA PETAIN PETALS PETARD REBAGS REBARS REBATE RECALL RECANE RECANT RECAPS RECAST REDACT REDANT REDATE REFACE REGAIN REGALE REGARD REHABS REHANG REHASH RELACE RELAID RELATE RELAYS REMADE REMAIL REMAIN REMAKE REMAND REMANS REMAPS REMARK RENAIL RENAME RENATA REPADS REPAID REPAIR REPAND REPAST REPAVE REPAYS RERATE RESALE RESALT RESAND RESAWN RESAWS RETAGS RETAIL RETAIN RETAKE RETAPE RETAPS RETARD RETARS REVAMP REWARD REWARM REWASH SECANT SEDAKA SEDANS SEDATE SEJANT SENARY SENATE SEPALS SERACS SERAIS SERAPE SERAPH SESAME SEWAGE SEWARD TEJANO TENACE TENANT TEPALS TERAPH TERATO TEXACO TEXANS VEGANS ZENANA

•E••A•
AEGEAN AENEAS AERIAL BEDLAM BEGGAR BEHEAD BELDAM BELIAL BELLAY BEMOAN BENDAY BENGAL BENGAY BETRAY BETTAS BEULAH BEWRAY CEIBAS CELLAE CELLAR CEREAL CESTAS DEBRAS DEEJAY DEEPAK DEFEAT DEFRAY DELMAR DELRAY DELTAS DEMEAN DENIAL DENTAL DEODAR DERMAL DESMAN DEWLAP FELLAH FELLAS FENIAN FENMAN FENWAY FERIAL FERIAS FERMAT FESTAL FESTAS FEUDAL FEZZAN GEEGAW GEMMAE GENIAL GENOAN GENUAL GERMAN GETMAD GETSAT GEWGAW HEEHAW HELLAS HENNAS

HEPCAT
HEPTAD
HERBAL
HEREAT
HERMAN
HETMAN
HEYDAY
JEERAT
JETLAG
JETSAM
JETWAY
KEENAN
KEEPAT
KENYAN
KEPTAT
KERMAN
KEVLAR
KEYPAD
KEYWAY
LEERAT
LEEWAY
LEGMAN
LEHUAS
LEKVAR
LEMMAS
LESTAT
LETHAL
LETSAT
MECCAS
MEDGAR
MEDIAL
MEDIAN
MEDIAS
MEDLAR
MEDLAT
MELMAC
MENIAL
MENSAE
MENSAL
MENSAS
MENTAL
MERMAN
MESCAL
NECTAR
NETMAN
NETPAY
NEUMAN
NEURAL
NEWMAN
NEWMAR
PECKAT
PEDLAR
PEDWAY
PEEKAT
PEERAT
PENMAN
PENNAE
PENPAL
PENTAD
REAGAN
REATAS
RECOAT
REDBAY
REDCAP
REDEAL
REDHAT
REDIAL
REDOAK
REDRAW
REDTAG
REFLAG
REGGAE
REGNAL
REGNAT
REHEAL
REHEAR
REHEAT
REINAS
RELOAD
RENTAL
REPEAL
REPEAT
REPLAN
REPLAY
REREAD
RESEAL
RESEAT
RESEAU
RETEAR
RETIAL
RETRAL
REVEAL
REWRAP
REXCAT
SEABAG
SEAFAN
SEAGAL
SEALAB
SEAMAN
SEAWAY
SEESAW
SENDAK
SENLAC
SENNAS
SEPIAS
SEPTAL
SERIAL
SERVAL
SETSAT
SEURAT
TEABAG
TEARAT
TERRAN
TESLAS
TESTAE
TETRAD
TETRAS
VEEJAY
VEINAL
VENIAL
VERBAL
VERNAL
VESTAL
VESTAS
WEIMAR
WENTAT
WETBAR
YENTAS
YEOMAN
YESMAN
ZEBRAS
ZEDBAR
ZEEMAN

•E•••A

AEOLIA
BELUGA
BEMATA
BERTHA
BETCHA
CESSNA
CETERA
DEANNA
DEFLEA
DESICA
FEDORA
FEMORA
GEISHA
GELADA
GEMARA
GENERA
GENEVA
GEZIRA
HECUBA
HEGIRA
HELENA
HESTIA
JERBOA
KERALA
KESHIA
LERIDA
LEXICA
MEDAKA
MEDINA
MEDUSA
MEGARA
MELINA
MERIDA
NEBULA
NERUDA
NESTEA
NEVADA
OEDEMA
PELOTA
PENNIA
PEORIA
PEPITA
PERCHA
PERSIA
PERUGA
PESAWA
PESETA
PETULA
REALIA
REDSEA
REGINA
REMORA
REMUDA
RENATA
RESEDA
RETINA
SEDAKA
SEGURA
SELENA
SENECA
SENEGA
SENORA
SENTRA
SERBIA
SERENA
SEROSA
TEPHRA
TERESA
VERONA
ZENANA
ZEUGMA

••EA••

AFEARD
ALEAST
ATEAMS
ATEASE
AWEARY
AYEAYE
BLEACH
BLEARS
BLEARY
BLEATS
BREACH
BREADS
BREAKS
BREAMS
BREAST
BREATH
CHEAPO
CHEATS
CLEANS
CLEARS
CLEATS
CLEAVE
CREAKS
CREAKY
CREAMS
CREAMY
CREASE
CREASY
CREATE
DREADS
DREAMS
DREAMT
DREAMY
DREARY
FREAKS
FREAKY
GLEAMS
GLEAMY
GLEANS
GOEASY
GREASE
GREASY
GREATS
GREAVE
HBEAMS
IBEAMS
ICEAGE
IDEALS
IDEATE
ILEANA
KNEADS
NLEAST
OBEAHS
OCEANS
OLEARY
OLEATE
ONEACT
OREADS
PAEANS
PLEACH
PLEADS
PLEASE
PLEATS
PREACH
PREAMP
QUEASY
SHEAFS
SHEARS
SHEATH
SHEAVE
SKEANS
SLEAVE
SLEAZE
SLEAZY
SMEARS
SMEARY
SNEAKS
SNEAKY
SPEAKS
SPEARS
STEADS
STEADY
STEAKS
STEALS
STEAMS
STEAMY
SWEARS
SWEATS
SWEATY
TREADS
TREATS
TREATY
TWEAKS
UNEASE
UNEASY
WHEALS
WHEATS
WREAKS
WREATH

••E•A•

ACETAL
AGENAS
AKELAS
ALEGAR
ALEMAN
AMEBAE
AMEBAS
APEMAN
ARECAS
ARENAS
CAESAR
CHELAE
CHELAS
CHEVAL
COEVAL
CRETAN
DAEDAL
DEEJAY
DEEPAK
FLEWAT
FOETAL
GEEGAW
GOESAT
HAEMAT
HEEHAW
HIEMAL
HYENAS
HYETAL
ICEBAG
ICECAP
ICEMAN
IPECAC
JEERAT
KEENAN
KEEPAT
LEERAT
LEEWAY
MAENAD
OMEGAS
ONEDAY
ONEMAN
ONEWAY
OPERAS
PEEKAT
PEERAT
PIEMAN
PIEPAN
PIETAS
PLEIAD
PLEXAL
PREFAB
PRELAW
PREPAY
PRETAX
PREWAR
SCENAS
SEESAW
SHEVAT
SLEZAK
STEFAN
STELAE
STELAR
THECAE
THECAL
THEHAJ
THENAR
THETAS
TOECAP
TOETAP
TREPAN
VEEJAY
ZEEMAN

••E••A

ACEDIA
AGENDA
ALEXIA
AMELIA
AMENRA
ANEMIA
AREOLA
ARETHA
AVESTA
AYESHA
BRENDA
CRENNA
CREUSA
CUESTA
DJERBA
DUENNA
EDESSA
EGERIA
EGESTA
EJECTA
EXEDRA
FAENZA
FIESTA
FRESCA
GLENDA
GRETNA
IBERIA
ILEANA
ILESHA
IMELDA
OBELIA
ODESSA
ODETTA
OMERTA
ONEIDA
OREIDA
PAELLA
PLEURA
PNEUMA
PUEBLA
QUETTA
SHEENA
SHEILA
SHERPA
SIENNA
SIERRA
SIESTA
STELLA
STERNA
THELMA
THESEA
TIERRA
TREDIA
VIENNA

•••EA•

AEGEAN
AENEAS
AGLEAM
ANDEAN
ANNEAL
APPEAL
APPEAR
ARREAR
AUGEAN
BATEAU
BEHEAD
BOREAL
BOREAS
BUREAU
CAMEAT
CAVEAT
CEREAL
COMEAT
CUNEAL
DEFEAT
DEMEAN
DOGEAR
ENDEAR
ENNEAD
FIVEAM
FOVEAE
GALEAE
GATEAU
GILEAD
HABEAS
HAVEAT
HEREAT
INGEAR
INSEAM
IRREAL
JUNEAU
KOREAN
LINEAL
LINEAR
LLBEAN
LOREAL
MCLEAN
MOREAU
NICEAN
NINEAM
NOLEAD
OCREAE
OHYEAH
ORDEAL
ORGEAT
OSTEAL
OUTEAT
PALEAE
PINEAL
POKEAT
POLEAX
RAMEAU
REDEAL
REHEAL
REHEAR
REHEAT
REPEAL
REPEAT
REREAD
RESEAL
RESEAT
RESEAU
RETEAR
REVEAL
ROSEAU
SCREAK
SCREAM
SINEAD
SPREAD
SQUEAK
SQUEAL
STREAK
STREAM
THREAD
THREAT
TINEAR
TOREAT
UNLEAD
UNREAD
UNREAL
UNSEAL
UNSEAT
UPBEAT

•••E•A

ADNEXA
AMOEBA
ANGELA
ARBELA
ASPERA
ATHENA
BODEGA
CAMERA
CATENA
CETERA
CINEMA
DODECA
DUNERA
EUREKA
GALENA
GENERA
GENEVA
HELENA
KAGERA
KINEMA
LAMESA
MAKEBA
MODELA
MODENA
MONERA
MONETA
MULETA
NOVENA
OEDEMA
ORTEGA
PAMELA
PESETA
RESEDA
RIVERA
ROWENA
SABENA
SCHEMA
SCLERA
SELENA
SENECA
SENEGA
SERENA
SHEENA
SISERA
TERESA
TOPEKA
WALESA
XIMENA
ZAREBA

••••EA

ACHAEA
ALTHEA
ANDREA
AZALEA
CORNEA
COWPEA
CRIMEA
DEFLEA
DULLEA
DURYEA
EUBOEA
EUPNEA
GRADEA
GUINEA
HOTTEA
JUDAEA
LABREA
MATTEA
MCCREA
NAUSEA
NESTEA
NICAEA
NOUMEA
REDSEA
SPIREA
THESEA

EB••••

EBBING
EBERLY
EBOATS
EBONDS

E•B•••

EBBING
EDBERG
EGBERT
EKBERG
ELBERT
ELBOWS
ELBRUS
EMBANK
EMBARK
EMBAYS
EMBDEN
EMBEDS
EMBERS
EMBLEM
EMBODY
EMBOSS
EMBRYO
ENBLOC
ERBIUM
EUBOEA

E••B••

EDIBLE
ENABLE
EREBUS

E•••B•

ENROBE
EPHEBE
EXURBS

•EB•••

BEBOPS
DEBARK
DEBARS
DEBASE
DEBATE
DEBBIE
DEBITS
DEBONE
DEBRAS
DEBRIS
DEBTOR
DEBUGS
DEBUNK
DEBUTS
HEBREW
HEBRON
KEBABS
KEBOBS
LEBRUN
NEBULA
PEBBLE
PEBBLY
REBAGS
REBARS
REBATE
REBBES
REBECS
REBELS
REBEND
REBENT
REBIDS
REBIND
REBOIL
REBOLT
REBOOT
REBORN
REBOZO
REBUFF
REBUKE
REBURY
REBUTS
SEBERG
VEBLEN
WEBBED
WEBBER
WEBERN
XEBECS
ZEBRAS

•E•B••

BEDBUG
BERBER
CEIBAS
DEBBIE
FEEBLE
FEEBLY
FERBER
GERBER
GERBIL
HEEBIE
HENBIT
HERBAL
HERBIE
JERBOA
LESBOS
MEMBER
PEBBLE
PEBBLY
REBBES
REDBAY
REDBUD
REEBOK
REUBEN
SEABAG
SEABED
SEABEE
SERBIA
TEABAG
VERBAL
VERBIS
WEBBED
WEBBER
WETBAR
ZEDBAR

•E••B•

AEROBE
CELEBS
DEMOBS
GETSBY
HECUBA
HEREBY
KEBABS
KEBOBS
LETSBE
MESABI
NEARBY
REDUBS
REHABS
SETSBY
WENTBY

•E•••B

BEDAUB
BENUMB
DEKALB
RESORB
REVERB
SEALAB

••EB••

AMEBAE
AMEBAS
AMEBIC
BYEBYE
EREBUS
FEEBLE
FEEBLY
GLEBES
GREBES
HEEBIE
ICEBAG
ICEBOX
LIEBIG
LIEBYS
PLEBES
PUEBLA
PUEBLO
QUEBEC
REEBOK
RHEBOK
THEBES
TREBEK
TREBLE
TREBLY

••E•B•

DJERBA
DOESBY
DWEEBS
GOESBY

••E••B

CHERUB
PREFAB
THEWEB

•••EB•

ACHEBE
AMOEBA
ARDEBS
CAMEBY
CELEBS
COMEBY
CUBEBS
DWEEBS
EPHEBE
GAZEBO
GONEBY
HEREBY
INDEBT
MAKEBA
NASEBY
PHLEBO
PHOEBE
SASEBO
ZAREBA

•••E•B

ADVERB
REVERB
SUPERB

••••EB

COBWEB
DIONEB
SUBDEB
THEWEB
ZAGREB

EC••••

ECARTE
ECCLES
ECESIC
ECESIS
ECHINO
ECHOED
ECHOES
ECHOIC
ECLAIR
ECLATS
ECOLES
ECTYPE

E•C•••

ECCLES
EMCEED
EMCEES
ENCAGE
ENCAMP
ENCASE
ENCINA
ENCINO
ENCODE
ENCORE
EOCENE
ESCAPE
ESCARP
ESCENT
ESCHER
ESCHEW
ESCORT
ESCROW
ESCUDO
ETCHED
ETCHER
ETCHES
EUCHRE
EUCLID
EXCEED
EXCELS
EXCEPT
EXCESS
EXCISE
EXCITE
EXCUSE

E••C••

EDICTS
EDUCED
EDUCES
EGGCUP
EJECTA
EJECTS
ELECTS
ELICIT
ENACTS
EPICAL
EPOCHS
ERECTS
ERUCTS
EVICTS
EXACTA
EXACTO
EXACTS
EYECUP

E•••C•

EDKOCH
EFFACE
EFFECT
ELLICE
ENESCO
ENLACE
ENRICH
ENRICO
ENTICE
EPARCH
EROICA
ETHICS
EUNICE
EVINCE
EXARCH
EXPECT

E••••C

ECESIC
ECHOIC
EDENIC
ENBLOC
EROTIC
ETHNIC
ETONIC
EXILIC
EXOTIC

•EC•••

BECALM
BECAME
BECKER
BECKET
BECKON
BECOME
CECILE
CECILY
DECADE
DECAFS
DECALS
DECAMP
DECANT
DECAYS
DECEIT
DECENT
DECIDE
DECKED
DECKER
DECKLE
DECOCT
DECODE
DECORS
DECOYS
DECREE
FECUND
GECKOS
HECATE
HECKLE
HECTIC
HECTOR
HECUBA
JECKLE
LECTER
LECTOR
MECCAS
NECKED
NECTAR
PECANS
PECKAT
PECKED
PECTIC
PECTIN
RECALL
RECANE
RECANT
RECAPS
RECAST
RECEDE
RECENT
RECESS
RECIFE
RECIPE
RECITE
RECKON
RECOAT
RECODE
RECOIL
RECONS
RECOPY
RECORD
RECORK
RECOUP
RECTOR
RECTOS
RECTUS
RECURS
RECUSE
SECANT
SECEDE
SECERN
SECKEL
SECOND
SECRET
SECTOR
SECURE
TECHIE
TECHNO
VECTOR

•E•C••

BEACHY
BEACON
BETCHA
DEACON
DEICED
DEICER
DEICES
DESCRY
DEUCED
DEUCES
FENCED
FENCER
FENCES
FESCUE
HEPCAT
LEACHY
MECCAS
MERCED
MERCER
MESCAL
PEACHY
PENCEL
PENCIL
PERCHA
PESCOW
REACTS
REDCAP
REECHO
RESCUE
REXCAT
SEACOW
SEICHE
TEACUP
TERCEL
TERCET
TETCHY
VELCRO
WENCES

•E••C•

BEDECK
DECOCT
DEDUCE
DEDUCT
DEFACE
DEFECT
DEJECT
DELICT
DEPICT
DESICA
DETACH
DETECT
DEVICE
LEGACY
LEXICA
MEDICI
MEDICO
MEDICS
MEJICO
MENACE
MENSCH
MEXICO
PEERCE
PESACH
REBECS
REDACT
REDUCE
REFACE
REJECT
RELACE
RELICS
RELICT
RELOCK
RELUCT
REMICK
RESECT
SEANCE
SEARCH
SEDUCE
SELECT
SENECA
SERACS
TENACE
TEXACO
VELOCE
VENICE
XEBECS

•E•••C

AEOLIC
BELLOC
CEDRIC
CELTIC
DELTIC
FENNEC
FERENC
FERRIC
GESTIC
HECTIC
HEROIC
MELMAC
METRIC
PECTIC
PELVIC
PEPTIC
SENLAC
SEPTIC
TENREC
ZENDIC

••EC••

ALECKY
ALECTO
AMECHE
ARECAS
BRECHT
CHECKS
CRECHE
CZECHS
EJECTA
EJECTS
ELECTS
ERECTS
EYECUP
FLECHE
FLECKS
FLECKY
ICECAP
IPECAC
NIECES
NUECES
PIECED
PIECER
PIECES
PRECIS
REECHO
SIECLE
SPECIE
SPECKS
THECAE
THECAL
TOECAP
VNECKS
WRECKS

••E•C•

AGENCY
AMERCE
APERCU
BIERCE
BLEACH
BLENCH
BREACH
BREECH
CHEECH
CLENCH
COERCE
DRENCH
ENESCO
FIERCE
FLEECE
FLEECY
FLETCH
FRENCH
FRESCA
FRESCO
GREECE
KVETCH
ONEACT
PEERCE
PIERCE
PLEACH
PREACH
QUENCH
SKETCH
SPEECH
STENCH
THENCE
TIERCE
TRENCH

UNESCO
WHENCE
WRENCH
WRETCH

••E••C
ACETIC
AMEBIC
ANEMIC
CLERIC
ECESIC
EDENIC
GAELIC
IPECAC
IRENIC
NOETIC
POETIC
QUEBEC
SCENIC
THETIC

•••EC•
ABJECT
AFFECT
APIECE
ASPECT
AZTECS
BEDECK
BISECT
BREECH
CHEECH
DEFECT
DEJECT
DETECT
DIRECT
DODECA
EFFECT
EXPECT
FLEECE
FLEECY
GRAECO
GREECE
HITECH
INFECT
INJECT
INSECT
KOPECK
LAMECH
LUBECK
OBJECT
OLMECS
ONDECK
REBECS
REJECT
RESECT
SAMECH
SELECT
SENECA
SPEECH
VOTECH
XEBECS
ZYDECO

•••E•C
FERENC
HOMEEC

••••EC
FENNEC
HOMEEC
MIXTEC
ONSPEC
PARSEC
QUEBEC
TENREC
TOLTEC

ED••••
EDAMES
EDBERG
EDDIED
EDDIES
EDDOES
EDENIC
EDERLE
EDESSA
EDGARD
EDGARS
EDGEIN
EDGERS
EDGIER
EDGILY
EDGING
EDIBLE
EDICTS
EDILES
EDISON
EDITED
EDITIO
EDITOR
EDKOCH
EDMOND
EDMUND
EDSELS
EDUARD
EDUCED
EDUCES
EDVARD
EDWARD
EDWOOD
EDWYNN

E•D•••
EDDIED
EDDIES
EDDOES
EIDERS
EIDOLA
ELDERS
ELDEST
EMDASH
ENDALL
ENDASH
ENDEAR
ENDERS
ENDING
ENDIVE
ENDMAN
ENDMEN
ENDORA
ENDOWS
ENDRUN
ENDSUP
ENDUED
ENDUES
ENDURE
ENDURO
ENDUSE
ESDRAS
EUDORA

E••D••
EJIDOS
ELIDED
ELIDES
ELUDED
ELUDER
ELUDES
EMBDEN
EPODES
ERODED
ERODES
ETUDES
EVADED
EVADER
EVADES
EXEDRA
EXODUS
EXUDED
EXUDES

E•••D•
EBONDS
ELANDS
EMBEDS
EMBODY
EMENDS
ENCODE
EPHODS
ESCUDO

E••••D
EAGLED
EARNED
ECHOED
EDDIED
EDGARD
EDITED
EDMOND
EDMUND
EDUARD
EDUCED
EDVARD
EDWARD
EDWOOD
ELAPID
ELATED
ELIDED
ELOPED
ELUDED
ELUTED
ELWOOD
EMCEED
EMOTED
EMQUAD
ENDUED
ENFOLD
ENGIRD
ENNEAD
ENQUAD
ENSUED
ENURED
ENVIED
ERASED
ERHARD
ERODED
ERRAND
ESPIED
ETCHED
EUCLID
EVADED
EVENED
EVOKED
EXCEED
EXILED
EXITED
EXPAND
EXPEND
EXTEND
EXUDED
EYELID
EZZARD

•ED•••
AEDILE
BEDAUB
BEDAZE
BEDBUG
BEDECK
BEDEWS
BEDIMS
BEDLAM
CEDANT
CEDARS
CEDING
CEDRIC
DEDUCE
DEDUCT
FEDORA
HEDDLE
HEDGED
HEDGER
HEDGES
HEDREN
HEDRON
KEDGED
KEDGES
LEDGER
LEDGES
LEDOFF
LEDOUT
MEDAKA
MEDALS
MEDDLE
MEDFLY
MEDGAR
MEDIAL
MEDIAN
MEDIAS
MEDICI
MEDICO
MEDICS
MEDINA
MEDIUM
MEDLAR
MEDLAT
MEDLEY
MEDUSA
OEDEMA
PEDALS
PEDANT
PEDATE
PEDDLE
PEDLAR
PEDWAY
REDACT
REDANT
REDATE
REDBAY
REDBUD
REDCAP
REDDEN
REDDER
REDDOG
REDEAL
REDEEM
REDENY
REDEYE
REDFIN
REDFIR
REDFOX
REDGUM
REDHAT
REDHOT
REDIAL
REDING
REDINK
REDOAK
REDOES
REDONE
REDRAW
REDREW
REDSEA
REDSOX
REDTAG
REDTOP
REDUBS
REDUCE
REDYED
REDYES
SEDAKA
SEDANS
SEDATE
SEDERS
SEDGES
SEDILE
SEDUCE
SEDUMS
TEDDED
TEDDER
TEDEUM
TEDIUM
TEDKEY
VEDDER
WEDDED
WEDELN
WEDGED
WEDGES
WEDGIE
XEDOUT
ZEDBAR

•E•D••
BEADED
BEADLE
BEADUP
BELDAM
BENDAY
BENDED
BENDER
BENDIX
DEADEN
DEADER
DEADLY
DEADON
DEEDED
DEEDEE
DEIDRE
DENDRI
DENDRO
DEODAR
FEEDER
FEEDON
FELDON
FENDED
FENDER
FEUDAL
FEUDED
GENDER
GEODES
HEADED
HEADER
HEADIN
HEADON
HEADUP
HEDDLE
HEEDED
HEEDER
HEIDEN
HELDIN
HELDON
HELDTO
HELDUP
HERDED
HERDER
HEYDAY
LEADED
LEADEN
LEADER
LEADIN
LEADON
LEADTO
LEADUP
LEIDEN
LENDER
LEWDER
LEWDLY
LEYDEN
MEADOW
MEDDLE
MELDED
MENDED
MENDEL
MENDER
MENDES
NEEDED
NEEDLE
NEEDNT
PEDDLE
PEEDEE
PENDED
PERDUE
READER
READIN
REDDEN
REDDER
REDDOG
REEDIT
RENDER
SEADOG
SEEDED
SEEDER
SEIDEL
SELDOM
SENDAK
SENDER
SENDIN
SENDUP
TEDDED
TEDDER
TEEDUP
TENDED
TENDER
TENDON
TENDTO
VEDDER
VELDTS
VENDED
VENDEE
VENDOR
VERDIN
VERDON
VERDUN
WEDDED
WEEDED
WEEDER
WELDED
WELDER
WENDED
ZENDIC
ZENDOS

•E••D•
BEARDS
BESIDE
BETIDE
DECADE
DECIDE
DECODE
DELUDE
DEMODE
DENUDE
DERIDE
GELADA
HEXADS
LERIDA
MELODY
MENADO
MERIDA
NERUDA
NEVADA
REBIDS
RECEDE
RECODE
REMADE
REMEDY
REMUDA
REPADS
RESEDA
RESIDE
RESODS
REWEDS
SECEDE
TELEDU
TEREDO
WEIRDO
WEIRDY
YEHUDI

•E•••D
AENEID
BEADED
BEAKED
BEAMED
BEANED
BEEFED
BEEPED
BEGGED
BEHEAD
BEHELD
BEHIND
BEHOLD
BELIED
BELLED
BELTED
BENDED
BESTED
BEYOND
CEASED
CEILED
CELLED
CENSED
CERVID
CESSED
DECKED
DEEDED
DEEMED
DEFEND
DEFIED
DEICED
DELVED
DEMAND
DEMOND
DENIED
DENNED
DENTED
DEPEND
DEUCED
DEVOID
FEARED
FECUND
FELLED
FELTED
FENCED
FENDED
FERVID
FESSED
FEUDED
GEARED
GELLED
GEMMED
GERALD
GERARD
GERUND
GETMAD
HEADED
HEALED
HEAPED
HEATED
HEAVED
HEDGED
HEEDED
HEELED
HEFTED
HELMED
HELPED
HEMMED
HENTED
HEPTAD
HERALD
HERDED
HESIOD
JEERED
JELLED
JERKED
JESTED
JETTED
KEDGED
KEELED
KEENED
KEGGED
KENNED
KERNED
KEYPAD
LEADED
LEAFED
LEAKED
LEANED
LEAPED
LEASED
LEAVED
LEERED
LEGEND
LEGGED
LELAND
LEMOND
LENSED
LEONID
LETTED
LEVEED
LEVIED
MELDED
MELTED
MENDED
MEOWED
MERCED
MERGED
MESHED
MESSED
METHOD
MEWLED
NEARED
NECKED
NEEDED
NEREID
NESTED
NETTED
PEAKED
PEALED
PEAPOD
PECKED
PEEKED
PEELED
PEENED
PEEPED
PEERED
PEEVED
PEGGED
PELTED
PENDED
PENNED
PENROD
PENTAD
PEPPED
PEQUOD
PERIOD
PERKED
PERMED
PERNOD
PETARD
PETTED
REAMED
REAPED
REARED
REBEND
REBIND
RECORD
REDBUD
REDYED
REEFED
REEKED
REELED
REEVED
REFFED
REFUND
REGARD
REHELD
REINED
RELAID
RELIED
RELOAD
REMAND
REMEND
REMIND
REMOLD
RENTED
REPAID
REPAND
REREAD
RESAND
RESEED
RESEND
RESHOD
RESOLD
RESTED
RETARD
RETIED
RETOLD
REUSED
REVVED
REWARD
REWELD
REWIND
REWORD
SEABED
SEALED
SEAMED
SEARED
SEATED
SECOND
SEEDED
SEEMED
SEEPED
SEERED
SEGUED
SEINED
SEIZED
SENSED
SERVED
SEWARD
TEAMED
TEARED
TEASED
TEDDED
TEEMED
TEHEED
TEMPED
TENDED
TENSED
TENTED
TERMED
TESTED
TETRAD
VEERED
VEGGED
VEILED
VEINED
VENDED
VENTED
VERGED
VERSED
VESPID
VESTED
VETOED
VETTED
WEANED
WEAVED
WEBBED
WEDDED
WEDGED
WEEDED
WELDED
WELLED
WELTED
WENDED
WETTED
YEANED
YELLED
YELPED
YENNED
YERKED
YESSED
ZEROED
ZESTED

••ED••
ACEDIA
AMEDEO
AVEDON
AWEDLY
COEDIT
CREDIT
CREDOS
DAEDAL
DEEDED
DEEDEE
DREDGE
EXEDRA
FEEDER
FEEDON
FLEDGE
FLEDGY
FREDDY
HEEDED
HEEDER
ICEDIN
ICEDUP
LIEDER
NEEDED
NEEDLE
NEEDNT
ONEDAY
ONEDGE
PEEDEE
PHEDRE
PLEDGE
PYEDOG
REEDIT
SEEDED
SEEDER
SLEDGE
SPEDUP
SUEDES
SWEDEN
SWEDES
TEEDUP
TIEDIN
TIEDTO
TIEDUP
TIEDYE
TOEDIN
TREDIA
USEDTO
USEDUP
WEEDED
WEEDER

••E•D•
AGENDA
AMENDS
ARENDT
BLEEDS
BLENDE
BLENDS
BREADS
BREEDS
BRENDA
CREEDS
DREADS
EMENDS
FIELDS
FIENDS
FJELDS
FREDDY
GLENDA
GREEDY
IMELDA
KNEADS
ONEIDA
OREADS
OREIDA
OVERDO
PLEADS
PSEUDO
PSEUDS
SCENDS
SHEEDY
SPEEDO
SPEEDS
SPEEDY
SPENDS
STEADS
STEADY
STEEDS
TREADS
TRENDS
TRENDY
TWEEDS
TWEEDY
UPENDS
WIELDS
YIELDS

••E••D
AFEARD
AGEOLD
ANELED
BEEFED
BEEPED
BREWED
CHEWED
CLEPED
CLEWED
CREWED
DEEDED
DEEMED
DIETED
DUELED
EVENED
EYELID
FLEXED
FLEYED
FOETID
FUELED
GREYED
HEEDED
HEELED
JEERED
KEELED
KEENED
LEERED
MAENAD
NEEDED
OBEYED
OPENED
PEEKED
PEELED
PEENED
PEEPED
PEERED
PEEVED
PIECED
PLEIAD
PREMED
PREYED
QUEUED
REEFED
REEKED
REELED
REEVED
SEEDED
SEEMED
SEEPED
SEERED
SIEGED
SIEVED
SKEWED
SLEWED
SPEWED
STEWED
TEEMED
THEEND
THEFED
THEKID
THEMED
TIERED
TIEROD
TREPID
USERID
VEERED
VIEWED
WEEDED
WHERED

•••ED•
ACCEDE
ALBEDO
BIPEDS
BLEEDS
BREEDS
COMEDY
CREEDS
EMBEDS
GREEDY
IMPEDE
LAMEDH
LAMEDS
LAREDO
MADEDO
MAKEDO
MOPEDS
OVIEDO
RATEDG
RATEDR
RATEDX
RECEDE
REMEDY
RESEDA
REWEDS
SECEDE
SHEEDY
SHREDS
SPEEDO
SPEEDS
SPEEDY
STEEDS
TELEDU
TEREDO
TOLEDO
TUXEDO
TWEEDS
TWEEDY

•••E•D
ADDEND
AENEID
AFIELD
AGREED
ANTEED
APPEND
ASCEND
ATTEND
AUGEND
AXSEED
BEHEAD
BEHELD
DEFEND
DEPEND
EMCEED
ENNEAD
EXCEED
EXPEND
EXTEND
FAGEND
FRIEND
GILEAD
IMPEND
INDEED
INNEED
INTEND
LEGEND
LEVEED
LOWEND
NEREID
NOLEAD
OFFEND
OSTEND
PUREED
REBEND
REHELD
REMEND
REREAD
RESEED
RESEND
REWELD
SCREED
SHIELD
SHREWD
SINEAD
SPREAD
TAGEND
TEHEED
THEEND
THREAD
THREED
UNBEND
UNHEED
UNLEAD
UNREAD
UPHELD

••••ED
ABASED
ABATED
ABIDED
ABUSED
ADDLED
ADORED
AGREED
ALATED
ALFRED
ALLIED
AMAZED
AMBLED
AMUSED
ANELED
ANGLED
ANKLED
ANTEED
ARCHED
ARGUED
ATONED
AVOWED
AWAKED
AXSEED
BABIED
BACHED
BACKED
BAGGED
BAILED
BAITED
BALKED
BANDED
BANGED
BANKED
BANNED
BARBED
BARGED
BARKED
BARRED
BASHED
BASKED
BASTED
BATHED
BATTED
BAWLED
BEADED
BEAKED
BEAMED
BEANED
BEEFED
BEEPED
BEGGED
BELIED
BELLED
BELTED
BENDED
BESTED
BIASED
BIBBED
BIFFED
BIGRED
BILKED
BILLED
BINGED
BINNED
BIRDED
BIRLED
BITTED
BLADED
BLAMED
BLARED
BLAZED
BOATED
BOBBED
BODIED
BOFFED
BOGGED
BOILED
BOLTED
BOMBED
BONDED
BONGED
BOOKED
BOOMED
BOOTED
BOPPED
BOSSED
BOUSED
BOWLED
BRACED
BRAKED
BRAVED
BRAYED
BRAZED
BREWED
BRIBED
BRINED
BRUXED
BUCKED
BUDDED
BUDGED
BUFFED
BUGGED
BUGLED
BULGED
BULKED
BULLED
BUMMED
BUMPED
BUNGED
BUNKED
BUNTED
BUOYED
BURIED
BURLED
BURNED
BURPED
BURRED
BUSHED
BUSIED
BUSKED
BUSSED
BUSTED
BUTTED
BUZZED
CABBED
CABLED
CACHED
CADGED
CALKED
CALLED
CALMED
CALVED
CAMPED
CANNED
CANOED
CANTED
CAPPED
CARDED
CARKED
CARPED
CARTED
CARVED
CASHED
CATTED
CAUSED
CEASED
CEILED
CELLED
CENSED
CESSED
CHAFED
CHASED
CHEWED
CHIDED
CHIMED
CHOKED
CHOWED
CHUTED
CLAWED
CLEPED
CLEWED
CLONED
CLOSED
CLOYED
COATED
COAXED
COCKED
COGGED
COIFED
COILED
COINED
COMBED
CONFED
CONKED
CONNED
COOKED
COOLED
COOPED
COPIED
COPPED
CORDED
CORKED
CORNED
COSHED
COSIED
COWLED
COZIED
CRANED
CRATED
CRAVED
CRAZED
CREWED
CROWED

CUFFED
CULLED
CUPPED
CURBED
CURDED
CURLED
CURRED
CURSED
CURVED
CUSPED
CUSSED
CYCLED
DABBED
DADOED
DAFFED
DAMMED
DAMNED
DAMPED
DANCED
DAPPED
DARNED
DARTED
DASHED
DAUBED
DAWNED
DAYBED
DECKED
DEEDED
DEEMED
DEFIED
DEICED
DELVED
DENIED
DENNED
DENTED
DEUCED
DIALED
DIETED
DIMMED
DINGED
DINNED
DINTED
DIPPED
DISHED
DISKED
DISSED
DOCKED
DODGED
DOFFED
DOGGED
DOLLED
DONNED
DOOMED
DOSSED
DOTTED
DOUSED
DOWNED
DOWSED
DRAPED
DRAYED
DRONED
DUBBED
DUCKED
DUELED
DULLED
DUMPED
DUNKED
DUNNED
DURNED
DUSTED
EAGLED
EARNED
ECHOED
EDDIED

EDITED
EDUCED
ELATED
ELIDED
ELOPED
ELUDED
ELUTED
EMCEED
EMOTED
ENDUED
ENSUED
ENURED
ENVIED
ERASED
ERODED
ESPIED
ETCHED
EVADED
EVENED
EVOKED
EXCEED
EXILED
EXITED
EXUDED
FABLED
FAGGED
FAILED
FAIRED
FANGED
FANNED
FARCED
FARMED
FASTED
FATTED
FAWNED
FEARED
FELLED
FELTED
FENCED
FENDED
FESSED
FEUDED
FIBBED
FILLED
FILMED
FINKED
FINNED
FIRMED
FISHED
FISTED
FITTED
FIZZED
FLAKED
FLAMED
FLARED
FLAWED
FLAYED
FLEXED
FLEYED
FLOWED
FLUTED
FLUXED
FOALED
FOAMED
FOBBED
FOGGED
FOILED
FOINED
FOLDED
FOOLED
FOOTED
FORCED
FORDED
FORGED

FORKED
FORMED
FOULED
FOWLED
FRAMED
FRAYED
FUBBED
FUDGED
FUELED
FUNDED
FUNKED
FUNNED
FURLED
FURRED
FUSSED
FUTZED
FUZZED
GABBED
GABLED
GADDED
GAFFED
GAGGED
GAINED
GAITED
GALLED
GAMMED
GANGED
GAOLED
GAPPED
GARBED
GASHED
GASPED
GASSED
GAUGED
GAUMED
GAWKED
GAWPED
GEARED
GELLED
GEMMED
GIBBED
GIFTED
GIGGED
GILDED
GILLED
GINNED
GIPPED
GIRDED
GIRNED
GIRTED
GLARED
GLAZED
GLIDED
GLOBED
GLOVED
GLOWED
GLOZED
GNAWED
GOADED
GOLFED
GONGED
GOOFED
GOOSED
GORGED
GOUGED
GOWNED
GRACED
GRADED
GRATED
GRAVED
GRAYED
GRAZED
GREYED
GRIMED

GRIPED
GROPED
GUIDED
GULFED
GULLED
GULPED
GUMMED
GUNNED
GUSHED
GUSTED
GUTTED
GYPPED
HACKED
HAFTED
HAILED
HAIRED
HALOED
HALTED
HALVED
HAMMED
HANDED
HANGED
HAPPED
HARKED
HARMED
HARPED
HASHED
HASPED
HATRED
HATTED
HAULED
HAWKED
HEADED
HEALED
HEAPED
HEATED
HEAVED
HEDGED
HEEDED
HEELED
HEFTED
HELMED
HELPED
HEMMED
HENTED
HERDED
HILLED
HINGED
HINTED
HIPPED
HISSED
HOAXED
HOCKED
HOGGED
HONIED
HONKED
HOODED
HOOFED
HOOKED
HOOPED
HOOTED
HOPPED
HORNED
HORSED
HOSTED
HOTBED
HOUSED
HOWLED
HUFFED
HUGGED
HULKED
HULLED
HUMMED
HUMPED

HUNTED
HURLED
HUSHED
HUSKED
HUTTED
HYMNED
HYPOED
ILLFED
IMAGED
IMBUED
INBRED
INCHED
INDEED
INNEED
INURED
IRONED
ISSUED
ITCHED
JABBED
JACKED
JAGGED
JAILED
JAMMED
JARRED
JAZZED
JEERED
JELLED
JERKED
JESTED
JETTED
JIBBED
JIGGED
JILTED
JINKED
JINXED
JOBBED
JOGGED
JOINED
JOLTED
JOSHED
JOTTED
JUDGED
JUGGED
JUICED
JUMPED
JUNKED
JUTTED
KAYOED
KEDGED
KEELED
KEENED
KEGGED
KENNED
KERNED
KICKED
KIDDED
KILLED
KILNED
KILTED
KINGED
KINKED
KISSED
KNIFED
LACKED
LADLED
LAGGED
LAMBED
LAMMED
LANCED
LANDED
LAPPED
LAPSED
LARDED
LARKED

LASHED
LASTED
LATHED
LAUDED
LEADED
LEAFED
LEAKED
LEANED
LEAPED
LEASED
LEAVED
LEERED
LEGGED
LENSED
LETTED
LEVEED
LEVIED
LIBBED
LICKED
LIDDED
LIFTED
LILTED
LIMBED
LIMNED
LIMPED
LINKED
LIPPED
LISPED
LISTED
LOADED
LOAFED
LOAMED
LOANED
LOBBED
LOCKED
LODGED
LOFTED
LOGGED
LOLLED
LONGED
LOOKED
LOOMED
LOOPED
LOOSED
LOOTED
LOPPED
LORDED
LOTTED
LOUSED
LUCKED
LUFFED
LUGGED
LULLED
LUMPED
LUNGED
LURKED
LUSTED
MAILED
MALTED
MANNED
MAPPED
MARKED
MARLED
MARRED
MASHED
MASKED
MASSED
MATTED
MAULED
MELDED
MELTED
MENDED
MEOWED
MERCED

MERGED
MESHED
MESSED
MEWLED
MIFFED
MILKED
MILLED
MINCED
MINDED
MINTED
MISLED
MISSED
MISTED
MITRED
MOANED
MOATED
MOBBED
MOCKED
MOILED
MOLDED
MOLTED
MONIED
MOONED
MOORED
MOOTED
MOPPED
MOSHED
MOSSED
MOUSED
MUCKED
MUDDED
MUFFED
MUGGED
MULLED
MUMMED
MUMPED
MUSHED
MUSSED
MUZZED
NABBED
NAGGED
NAILED
NAPPED
NEARED
NECKED
NEEDED
NESTED
NETTED
NICKED
NIPPED
NODDED
NOISED
NOOSED
NOSHED
NUBBED
NUDGED
NULLED
NUMBED
NURSED
NUTTED
OBEYED
OINKED
OKAYED
OPENED
OPINED
ORATED
OUSTED
PACKED
PADDED
PAINED
PAIRED
PALLED
PALMED
PANNED

PANTED
PARKED
PARRED
PARSED
PARTED
PASSED
PASTED
PATTED
PAUSED
PAWNED
PEAKED
PEALED
PECKED
PEEKED
PEELED
PEENED
PEEPED
PEERED
PEEVED
PEGGED
PELTED
PENDED
PENNED
PEPPED
PERKED
PERMED
PETTED
PHASED
PHONED
PHYSED
PICKED
PIECED
PIGGED
PILLED
PINGED
PINKED
PINNED
PIPPED
PIQUED
PITHED
PITIED
PITTED
PLACED
PLANED
PLATED
PLAYED
PLOWED
PLUMED
PODDED
POISED
POLLED
PONGED
PONIED
POOHED
POOLED
POOPED
POPPED
PORTED
POSTED
POTTED
POURED
POUTED
PRATED
PRAYED
PREMED
PREYED
PRICED
PRIDED
PRIMED
PRIZED
PROBED
PROSED
PROVED
PRUNED

PUFFED
PUGGED
PULLED
PULPED
PULSED
PUMPED
PUNNED
PUNTED
PUREED
PURGED
PURLED
PURRED
PURSED
PUSHED
PUTTED
QUAKED
QUEUED
QUOTED
RACKED
RAFTED
RAGGED
RAIDED
RAILED
RAINED
RAISED
RAMMED
RAMPED
RANGED
RANKED
RANTED
RAPPED
RASPED
RATTED
RAZZED
REAMED
REAPED
REARED
REDYED
REEFED
REEKED
REELED
REEVED
REFFED
REINED
RELIED
RENTED
RESEED
RESTED
RETIED
REUSED
REVVED
RHYMED
RIBBED
RICKED
RIDDED
RIDGED
RIFFED
RIFLED
RIFTED
RIGGED
RIMMED
RINGED
RINSED
RIOTED
RIPPED
RISKED
ROAMED
ROARED
ROBBED
ROCKED
RODDED
ROILED
ROLLED
ROMPED

ROOFED
ROOKED
ROOMED
ROOTED
ROTTED
ROUGED
ROUSED
ROUTED
RRATED
RSVPED
RUBBED
RUBIED
RUCKED
RUFFED
RUGGED
RUINED
RUSHED
RUSTED
RUTTED
SACKED
SACRED
SAGGED
SAILED
SALTED
SALVED
SANDED
SAPPED
SASHED
SASSED
SAUCED
SAWRED
SCALED
SCAPED
SCARED
SCOPED
SCORED
SCREED
SEABED
SEALED
SEAMED
SEARED
SEATED
SEEDED
SEEMED
SEEPED
SEERED
SEGUED
SEINED
SEIZED
SENSED
SERVED
SHADED
SHAMED
SHAPED
SHARED
SHAVED
SHINED
SHOOED
SHORED
SHOVED
SHOWED
SICCED
SIDLED
SIEGED
SIEVED
SIFTED
SIGHED
SIGNED
SILKED
SILOED
SILTED
SINGED
SINNED
SIPPED

SKATED
SKEWED
SKIVED
SLAKED
SLATED
SLAVED
SLAYED
SLEWED
SLICED
SLIMED
SLOPED
SLOWED
SMILED
SMOKED
SNAKED
SNARED
SNIPED
SNORED
SNOWED
SOAKED
SOAPED
SOARED
SOBBED
SOCKED
SODDED
SOILED
SOLOED
SOLVED
SOPPED
SORTED
SOTTED
SOURED
SOUSED
SPACED
SPADED
SPARED
SPAYED
SPEWED
SPICED
SPIKED
SPINED
SPIRED
SPITED
SPOKED
SPUMED
STAGED
STAKED
STALED
STARED
STATED
STAVED
STAYED
STEWED
STOKED
STONED
STORED
STOWED
STYLED
SUBBED
SUCKED
SUDSED
SUITED
SULKED
SUMMED
SUNNED
SUPPED
SURFED
SURGED
SUSSED
SWAGED
SWAYED
SWIPED
SYNCED
TABBED

TABLED
TACKED
TAGGED
TAILED
TALCED
TALKED
TAMPED
TANGED
TANKED
TANNED
TAPPED
TARRED
TASKED
TASTED
TATTED
TAXIED
TEAMED
TEARED
TEASED
TEDDED
TEEMED
TEHEED
TEMPED
TENDED
TENSED
TENTED
TERMED
TESTED
THAWED
THEFED
THEMED
THREED
TICKED
TIDIED
TIERED
TIFFED
TILLED
TILTED
TINGED
TINNED
TINTED
TIPPED
TITHED
TITLED
TITRED
TOGAED
TOGGED
TOILED
TOLLED
TOOLED
TOOTED
TOPPED
TOSSED
TOTTED
TOURED
TOUTED
TRACED
TRADED
TRICED
TROWED
TUBBED
TUCKED
TUFTED
TUGGED
TUMMED
TURFED
TURNED
TUSKED
TUTUED
TWINED
UNAGED
UNAWED
UNDYED
UNHEED

UNITED
UNSHED
UNTIED
UNUSED
VALUED
VALVED
VAMPED
VANNED
VARIED
VATTED
VEERED
VEGGED
VEILED
VEINED
VENDED
VENTED
VERGED
VERSED
VESTED
VETOED
VETTED
VIEWED
VISAED
VOICED
VOIDED
WADDED
WAFTED
WAGGED
WAILED
WAITED
WAIVED
WALKED
WALLED
WANNED
WANTED
WARDED
WARMED
WARNED
WARPED
WARRED
WASHED
WASTED
WEANED
WEAVED
WEBBED
WEDDED
WEDGED
WEEDED
WELDED
WELLED
WELTED
WENDED
WETTED
WHERED
WHILED
WHINED
WICKED
WIGGED
WILLED
WILTED
WINCED
WINDED
WINGED
WINKED
WISHED
WISPED
WITHED
WITTED
WOLFED
WONNED
WONTED
WOODED
WOOFED
WORDED

WORKED
WORMED
XRATED
XRAYED
YACKED
YAKKED
YANKED
YAPPED
YARDED
YARNED
YAWNED
YAWPED
YEANED
YELLED
YELPED
YENNED
YERKED
YESSED
YIPPED
YOLKED
YOWLED
YOYOED
YUKKED
ZAGGED
ZAPPED
ZEROED
ZESTED
ZIGGED
ZINGED
ZIPPED
ZONKED
ZOOMED

EE••••

EELERS
EELIER
EERIER
EERILY
EEYORE

E•E•••

EBERLY
ECESIC
ECESIS
EDENIC
EDERLE
EDESSA
EGERIA
EGESTA
EGESTS
EJECTA
EJECTS
EKEOUT
ELECTS
ELEGIT
ELEMIS
ELEVEN
ELEVES
EMEERS
EMENDS
EMERGE
EMEUTE
ENERGY
ENESCO
EREBUS
ERECTS
ERENOW
ERESTU
ETERNE
EVELYN
EVENED
EVENER
EVENKI
EVENLY
EVENSO
EVENTS
EVENUP
EVERLY
EVERSO
EVERTS
EXEDRA
EXEMPT
EXERTS
EXETER
EXEUNT
EYECUP
EYEFUL
EYEING
EYELET
EYELID

E••E••

EASEIN
EASELS
EASEUP
EATERS
EATERY
EDBERG
EDGEIN
EDGERS
EDSELS
EELERS
EFFECT
EFFETE
EGBERT
EGRESS
EGRETS
EIDERS
EILEEN
EKBERG
ELBERT
ELDERS
ELDEST
ELLERY
ELVERS
EMBEDS
EMBERS
EMCEED
EMCEES
EMEERS
EMMETS
EMMETT
EMPERY
ENDEAR
ENDERS
ENGELS
ENMESH
ENNEAD
ENTERO
ENTERS
EOCENE
EPHEBE
ERNEST
ESCENT
ESKERS
ESSENE
ESTEEM
ESTERS
ETHENE
ETHERS
ETSEQQ
EUGENE
EUREKA
EXCEED
EXCELS
EXCEPT
EXCESS
EXLEGE
EXPECT
EXPELS
EXPEND
EXPERT
EXSERT
EXTEND
EXTENT
EXTERN

E•••E•

EAGLED
EAGLES
EAGLET
EAGRES
EARNED
EARNER
EASIER
EASTER
ECCLES
ECHOED
ECHOES
ECOLES
EDAMES
EDDIED
EDDIES
EDDOES
EDGIER
EDILES
EDITED
EDUCED
EDUCES
EELIER
EERIER
EGGIER
EIFFEL
EILEEN
EISNER
EITHER
ELATED
ELATER
ELATES
ELAYER
ELEVEN
ELEVES
ELIDED
ELIDES
ELITES
ELOPED
ELOPER
ELOPES
ELUDED
ELUDER
ELUDES
ELUTED
ELUTES
ELYSEE
EMBDEN
EMBLEM
EMCEED
EMCEES
EMOTED
EMOTER
EMOTES
ENAMEL
ENATES
ENDMEN
ENDUED
ENDUES
ENSUED
ENSUES
ENTREE
ENURED
ENURES
ENVIED

ENVIER
ENVIES
EPODES
EPOPEE
ERASED
ERASER
ERASES
ERODED
ERODES
ESCHER
ESCHEW
ESPIED
ESPIES
ESTEEM
ESTHER
ETAPES
ETCHED
ETCHER
ETCHES
ETUDES
EUBOEA
EUPNEA
EVADED
EVADER
EVADES
EVENED
EVENER
EVILER
EVOKED
EVOKER
EVOKES
EXCEED
EXETER
EXILED
EXILES
EXITED
EXUDED
EXUDES
EYELET
EYRIES

E••••E

ECARTE
ECTYPE
EDERLE
EDIBLE
EEYORE
EFFACE
EFFETE
EFFUSE
ELAINE
ELAPSE
ELAYNE
ELLICE
ELMORE
ELOISE
ELYSEE
EMERGE
EMEUTE
EMIGRE
EMPIRE
ENABLE
ENCAGE
ENCASE
ENCODE
ENCORE
ENDIVE
ENDURE
ENDUSE
ENGAGE
ENGINE
ENISLE
ENLACE
ENRAGE

ENROBE
ENSILE
ENSURE
ENTICE
ENTIRE
ENTREE
ENZYME
EOCENE
EPHEBE
EPOPEE
EQUATE
EQUINE
ERGATE
ERMINE
ERRARE
ESCAPE
ESSENE
ESTATE
ETERNE
ETHANE
ETHENE
ETOILE
EUCHRE
EUGENE
EUNICE
EUROPE
EVINCE
EVOLVE
EVONNE
EVULSE
EVZONE
EXCISE
EXCITE
EXCUSE
EXHALE
EXLEGE
EXMORE
EXPIRE
EXPOSE
EXWIFE

•EE•••

AEETES
BEEFED
BEEFUP
BEEGUM
BEEPED
BEEPER
BEETLE
BEEVES
DEEDED
DEEDEE
DEEJAY
DEEMED
DEEPAK
DEEPEN
DEEPER
DEEPLY
FEEBLE
FEEBLY
FEEDER
FEEDON
FEEING
FEELER
GEEGAW
GEEGEE
GEEING
GEEZER
HEEBIE
HEEDED
HEEDER
HEEHAW
HEELED
HEELER

JEERAT
JEERED
JEERER
JEETER
JEEVES
KEELED
KEELER
KEENAN
KEENED
KEENEN
KEENER
KEENLY
KEEPAT
KEEPER
KEEPIN
KEEPON
KEEPTO
KEEPUP
LEERAT
LEERED
LEERER
LEEWAY
MEEKER
MEEKLY
MEERUT
MEETER
MEETLY
NEEDED
NEEDLE
NEEDNT
NEESON
PEEDEE
PEEKAT
PEEKED
PEELED
PEELER
PEENED
PEEPED
PEEPER
PEERAT
PEERCE
PEERED
PEERIN
PEEVED
PEEVES
PEEWEE
REEBOK
REECHO
REEDIT
REEFED
REEFER
REEKED
REELED
REELIN
REESES
REEVED
REEVES
SEEDED
SEEDER
SEEFIT
SEEGER
SEEING
SEEKER
SEELEY
SEEMED
SEEMLY
SEENIN
SEENTO
SEEOFF
SEEOUT
SEEPED
SEEPIN
SEERED
SEESAW

SEESIN
SEESTO
SEETHE
TEEDUP
TEEHEE
TEEING
TEEMED
TEENER
TEENSY
TEEOFF
TEESUP
TEETER
TEETHE
TEEVEE
VEEJAY
VEERED
WEEDED
WEEDER
WEEKLY
WEENIE
WEENSY
WEEPER
WEEPIE
WEEVIL
ZEEMAN

•E•E••

AEGEAN
AENEAS
AENEID
BEDECK
BEDEWS
BEFELL
BEGETS
BEHEAD
BEHELD
BEHEST
BEKESY
BEREFT
BERETS
BESETS
BETELS
BEVELS
BEZELS
CELEBS
CELERY
CEMENT
CEREAL
CEREUS
CETERA
DECEIT
DECENT
DEFEAT
DEFECT
DEFEND
DEFERS
DEJECT
DELEON
DELETE
DEMEAN
DEPEND
DESERT
DETECT
DETENT
DETERS
DETEST
DEVEIN
DEVEST
EELERS
FERENC
FEVERS
FEWEST
FEYEST
GELEES

GENERA
GENETS
GENEVA
GENEVE
GERENT
HELENA
HELENE
HELENS
HEREAT
HEREBY
HEREIN
HEREOF
HEREON
HERESY
HERETO
HETERO
HEWERS
HEXERS
JEREMY
JEWELS
JEWETT
KEVELS
LEGEND
LEVEED
LEVEES
LEVELS
LEVENE
LEVERS
LEXEME
MELEES
MERELY
MEREST
METEOR
METERS
NENETS
NEREID
NEREIS
NEREUS
NEVERS
NEWELS
NEWEST
OEDEMA
PELEUS
PESETA
PETERS
PEWEES
REBECS
REBELS
REBEND
REBENT
RECEDE
RECENT
RECESS
REDEAL
REDEEM
REDENY
REDEYE
REFERS
REGENT
REHEAL
REHEAR
REHEAT
REHEEL
REHELD
REHEMS
REJECT
REKEYS
RELENT
RELETS
RELEVY
REMEDY
REMELT
REMEND
RENEGE

RENEWS
REPEAL
REPEAT
REPEGS
REPELS
REPENT
REREAD
RERENT
RESEAL
RESEAT
RESEAU
RESECT
RESEDA
RESEED
RESEEN
RESEES
RESELL
RESEND
RESENT
RESETS
RESEWN
RESEWS
RETEAR
RETELL
RETENE
RETEST
REVEAL
REVELS
REVERB
REVERE
REVERS
REVERT
REVETS
REWEDS
REWELD
SEBERG
SECEDE
SECERN
SEDERS
SELECT
SELENA
SELENE
SELENO
SEMELE
SENECA
SENEGA
SERENA
SERENE
SEVENS
SEVERE
SEVERN
SEVERS
SEVERY
SEWELL
SEWERS
TEDEUM
TEHEED
TEHEES
TELEDU
TENENS
TENETS
TEPEES
TEREDO
TERESA
TERETE
TEREUS
VENEER
VENETO
VEREEN
VEXERS
WEBERN
WEDELN
WERENT
XEBECS

YEMENI

•E••E•

AEETES
AERIES
AETHER
BEADED
BEAKED
BEAKER
BEAMED
BEANED
BEARER
BEATEN
BEATER
BEAVER
BECKER
BECKET
BEEFED
BEEPED
BEEPER
BEEVES
BEGGED
BEGLEY
BEIGES
BELIED
BELIEF
BELIES
BELLED
BELLES
BELTED
BENDED
BENDER
BERBER
BERGEN
BESSER
BESTED
BETHEL
BETSEY
BETTER
BEVIES
CEASED
CEASES
CEILED
CELLED
CENSED
CENSER
CENSES
CENTER
CERMET
CESSED
CESSES
DEADEN
DEADER
DEAFEN
DEAFER
DEALER
DEARER
DECKED
DECKER
DECREE
DEEDED
DEEDEE
DEEMED
DEEPEN
DEEPER
DEFIED
DEFIES
DEFLEA
DEFTER
DEGREE
DEICED
DEICER
DEICES
DELVED

DELVER
DELVES
DEMIES
DENIED
DENIER
DENIES
DENNED
DENSER
DENTED
DENVER
DENZEL
DEUCED
DEUCES
DEWIER
DEXTER
EELIER
EERIER
FEARED
FEARER
FEEDER
FEELER
FELLED
FELLER
FELTED
FEMMES
FENCED
FENCER
FENCES
FENDED
FENDER
FENMEN
FENNEC
FENNEL
FERBER
FERRER
FERRET
FESSED
FESSES
FESTER
FETTER
FEUDED
FEZZES
GEARED
GEEGEE
GEEZER
GEIGER
GEISEL
GELEES
GELLED
GELSEY
GEMMED
GENDER
GENIES
GENRES
GEODES
GERBER
GESTES
GETSET
GETTER
GEYSER
HEADED
HEADER
HEALED
HEALER
HEANEY
HEAPED
HEARER
HEATED
HEATER
HEAVED
HEAVEN
HEAVER
HEAVES
HEBREW

HEDGED
HEDGER
HEDGES
HEDREN
HEEDED
HEEDER
HEELED
HEELER
HEFNER
HEFTED
HEIDEN
HEIFER
HELLER
HELMED
HELMET
HELPED
HELPER
HELTER
HELVES
HEMMED
HEMMER
HENLEY
HENNER
HENTED
HEPPER
HERDED
HERDER
HERMES
HEROES
HERSEY
HESTER
JEERED
JEERER
JEETER
JEEVES
JELLED
JENNER
JENNET
JENNEY
JENSEN
JERKED
JERSEY
JESSEL
JESTED
JESTER
JETSET
JETTED
KEDGED
KEDGES
KEELED
KEELER
KEENED
KEENEN
KEENER
KEEPER
KEGGED
KEGLER
KEITEL
KELLER
KELLEY
KELSEY
KENNED
KENNEL
KENNER
KEPLER
KERMES
KERNED
KERNEL
KERSEE
KERSEY
KEYNES
LEADED
LEADEN
LEADER

LEAFED
LEAKED
LEAKER
LEAKEY
LEANED
LEANER
LEAPED
LEAPER
LEASED
LEASER
LEASES
LEAVED
LEAVEN
LEAVES
LECTER
LEDGER
LEDGES
LEERED
LEERER
LEGGED
LEGMEN
LEGREE
LEHRER
LEIDEN
LEMUEL
LENDER
LENSED
LENSES
LENTEN
LEONES
LERNER
LESLEY
LESSEE
LESSEN
LESSER
LESTER
LETTED
LETTER
LEVEED
LEVEES
LEVIED
LEVIER
LEVIES
LEWDER
LEYDEN
MEAGER
MEANER
MEDLEY
MEEKER
MEETER
MELDED
MELEES
MELTED
MEMBER
MENDED
MENDEL
MENDER
MENDES
MENKEN
MENNEN
MEOWED
MERCED
MERCER
MERGED
MERGER
MERGES
MERKEL
MERMEN
MERSEY
MESHED
MESHES
MESMER
MESSED
MESSES

METIER
METRES
MEWLED
MEWLER
NEARED
NEARER
NEATEN
NEATER
NECKED
NEEDED
NEPHEW
NERVES
NESSES
NESTEA
NESTED
NESTER
NETHER
NETMEN
NETTED
NEUMES
NEUTER
NEWLEY
OERTER
PEAHEN
PEAKED
PEALED
PEAVEY
PECKED
PEEDEE
PEEKED
PEELED
PEELER
PEENED
PEEPED
PEEPER
PEERED
PEEVED
PEEVES
PEEWEE
PEGGED
PEGLER
PEKOES
PELLET
PELMET
PELTED
PELTER
PENCEL
PENDED
PENMEN
PENNED
PENNER
PENNEY
PENSEE
PEPPED
PEPPER
PERKED
PERMED
PERTER
PESTER
PETREL
PETTED
PETTER
PEWEES
PEWTER
READER
REALER
REALES
REAMED
REAMER
REAPED
REAPER
REARED
REARER
REBBES

REDDEN
REDDER
REDEEM
REDOES
REDREW
REDSEA
REDYED
REDYES
REEFED
REEFER
REEKED
REELED
REESES
REEVED
REEVES
REFFED
REFLEX
REFUEL
REGLET
REGRET
REHEEL
REINED
REINER
RELIED
RELIEF
RELIES
RENDER
RENNES
RENNET
RENTED
RENTER
REOPEN
RESEED
RESEEN
RESEES
RESHES
RESTED
RESTER
RETIED
RETIES
REUBEN
REUNES
REUSED
REUSES
REUTER
REVIEW
REVUES
REVVED
SEABED
SEABEE
SEALED
SEALER
SEAMED
SEAMEN
SEARED
SEATED
SEATER
SECKEL
SECRET
SEDGES
SEEDED
SEEDER
SEEGER
SEEKER
SEELEY
SEEMED
SEEPED
SEERED
SEGUED
SEGUES
SEIDEL
SEINED
SEINER
SEINES

SEIZED
SEIZER
SEIZES
SELLER
SELVES
SEMPER
SENDER
SENNET
SENSED
SENSEI
SENSES
SEPTET
SEQUEL
SERGEI
SERGES
SERIES
SERVED
SERVER
SERVES
SESTET
SETTEE
SETTER
SEVRES
SEXIER
SEXTET
TEAMED
TEARED
TEASED
TEASEL
TEASER
TEASES
TEASET
TEDDED
TEDDER
TEDKEY
TEEHEE
TEEMED
TEENER
TEETER
TEEVEE
TEHEED
TEHEES
TELLER
TEMPED
TEMPEH
TEMPER
TENDED
TENDER
TENREC
TENSED
TENSER
TENSES
TENTED
TENTER
TEPEES
TERCEL
TERCET
TERKEL
TERMED
TERNES
TERRET
TERSER
TESTED
TESTEE
TESTER
TETHER
TETZEL
TEXMEX
VEBLEN
VEDDER
VEERED
VEGGED
VEILED
VEINED

VELVET
VENDED
VENDEE
VENEER
VENTED
VENTER
VENUES
VEREEN
VERGED
VERGER
VERGES
VERSED
VERSES
VERTEX
VERVES
VERVET
VESPER
VESSEL
VESTED
VESTEE
VETOED
VETOER
VETOES
VETTED
WEAKEN
WEAKER
WEANED
WEARER
WEASEL
WEAVED
WEAVER
WEAVES
WEBBED
WEBBER
WEDDED
WEDGED
WEDGES
WEEDED
WEEDER
WEEPER
WELDED
WELDER
WELLED
WELLER
WELLES
WELTED
WELTER
WENCES
WENDED
WERFEL
WERNER
WESLEY
WESSEX
WETHER
WETTED
WETTER
XERXES
YEAGER
YEANED
YELLED
YELLER
YELPED
YELPER
YENNED
YEOMEN
YERKED
YERKES
YESMEN
YESSED
YESSES
YESTER
ZENGER
ZEROED
ZEROES

ZESTED

•E•••E

AEDILE
AERATE
AEROBE
BEADLE
BEAGLE
BEANIE
BEATLE
BECAME
BECOME
BEDAZE
BEETLE
BEFORE
BEGONE
BEHAVE
BEHOVE
BELIKE
BELIZE
BEMINE
BEMIRE
BEMUSE
BERATE
BERNIE
BERTIE
BESIDE
BESSIE
BETAKE
BETIDE
BETISE
BEURRE
BEWARE
CECILE
CELINE
CELLAE
CENOTE
CENTRE
CERATE
CERISE
CERUSE
CESARE
CETANE
DEARIE
DEARME
DEBASE
DEBATE
DEBBIE
DEBONE
DECADE
DECIDE
DECKLE
DECODE
DECREE
DEDUCE
DEEDEE
DEFACE
DEFAME
DEFILE
DEFINE
DEFUSE
DEGAGE
DEGREE
DEIDRE
DEJURE
DELATE
DELETE
DELUDE
DELUGE
DELUXE
DEMISE
DEMODE
DEMOTE
DEMURE

DENGUE
DENISE
DENOTE
DENUDE
DEPONE
DEPOSE
DEPUTE
DERIDE
DERIVE
DESIRE
DEVICE
DEVINE
DEVISE
DEVOTE
EEYORE
FEEBLE
FELINE
FELIPE
FELLOE
FEMALE
FERGIE
FERULE
FESCUE
FETTLE
GEEGEE
GEMMAE
GEMOTE
GENEVE
GENOME
GENTLE
GEORGE
GERTIE
HEARYE
HECATE
HECKLE
HEDDLE
HEEBIE
HELENE
HERBIE
HETTIE
JEANNE
JECKLE
JEJUNE
JENNIE
JEROME
JESSIE
KELPIE
KERSEE
KETONE
KETTLE
KEWPIE
LEAGUE
LEFTIE
LEGATE
LEGREE
LEGUME
LENAPE
LENNIE
LENORE
LEONIE
LESAGE
LESLIE
LESSEE
LETSBE
LEVENE
LEVINE
LEVITE
LEXEME
MEAGRE
MEALIE
MEANIE
MEDDLE
MENACE
MENAGE

MENSAE
MEROPE
METATE
METOPE
METTLE
NEEDLE
NEGATE
NEISSE
NELLIE
NESSIE
NESTLE
NETTLE
NEWAGE
OENONE
OEUVRE
PEBBLE
PEDATE
PEDDLE
PEEDEE
PEERCE
PEEWEE
PELAGE
PELIKE
PENNAE
PENSEE
PEOPLE
PERDUE
PERUKE
PERUSE
PESTLE
PETITE
PETRIE
PEYOTE
REBATE
REBUKE
RECANE
RECEDE
RECIFE
RECIPE
RECITE
RECODE
RECUSE
REDATE
REDEYE
REDONE
REDUCE
REFACE
REFILE
REFINE
REFUGE
REFUSE
REFUTE
REGALE
REGGAE
REGGIE
REGIME
REGLUE
REHIRE
RELACE
RELATE
RELINE
RELIVE
RELUME
REMADE
REMAKE
REMISE
REMOTE
REMOVE
RENAME
RENEGE
RENNIE
RENOTE
REPAVE
REPINE
REPOSE
REPUTE
RERATE
RESALE
RESCUE
RESHOE
RESIDE
RESILE
RESOLE
RESUME
RETAKE
RETAPE
RETENE
RETILE
RETIME
RETIRE
RETUNE
RETYPE
REVERE
REVILE
REVISE
REVIVE
REVOKE
REWIRE
REWOVE
REZONE
SEABEE
SEANCE
SEARLE
SECEDE
SECURE
SEDATE
SEDILE
SEDUCE
SEETHE
SEICHE
SELENE
SEMELE
SEMITE
SEMPRE
SENATE
SERAPE
SERENE
SERINE
SESAME
SETOSE
SETTEE
SETTLE
SEVERE
SEWAGE
TECHIE
TEEHEE
TEETHE
TEEVEE
TEMPLE
TENACE
TENURE
TERETE
TESSIE
TESTAE
TESTEE
VEGGIE
VELOCE
VENDEE
VENICE
VENIRE
VENITE
VERITE
VESTEE
WEDGIE
WEENIE
WEEPIE

••EE••

ADEEMS
AMEERS
BLEEDS
BLEEPS
BREECH
BREEDS
BREEZE
BREEZY
CHEECH
CHEEKS
CHEEKY
CHEEPS
CHEERS
CHEERY
CHEESE
CHEESY
CLEEKS
CLEESE
CREEDS
CREEKS
CREELS
CREEPS
CREEPY
DWEEBS
EMEERS
FLEECE
FLEECY
FLEERS
FLEETS
FREELY
FREEST
FREEZE
GREECE
GREEDY
GREEKS
GREENE
GREENS
GREENY
GREETS
KNEELS
OKEEFE
PREENS
QUEENS
SHEEDY
SHEEHY
SHEENA
SHEENS
SHEEPS
SHEERS
SHEETS
SLEEKS
SLEEKY
SLEEPS
SLEEPY
SLEETS
SLEETY
SLEEVE
SNEERS
SNEERY
SNEEZE
SNEEZY
SPEECH
SPEEDO
SPEEDS
SPEEDY
STEEDS
STEELE
STEELS
STEELY
STEEPS
STEERS
STEEVE
SWEEPS
SWEETS
THEEND
TWEEDS
TWEEDY
TWEENS
TWEENY
TWEEST
TWEETS
TWEETY
TWEEZE
WHEELS
WHEEZE
WHEEZY

••E•E•

ABELES
AEETES
AKENES
ALEVEL
ALEXEI
AMEDEO
ANELED
ANELES
APEMEN
APEXES
ARETES
ASEVER
BEEFED
BEEPED
BEEPER
BEEVES
BREMEN
BREUER
BREVES
BREVET
BREWED
BREWER
BREYER
CHEVET
CHEWED
CHEWER
CLEPED
CLEVER
CLEVES
CLEWED
CREMES
CRENEL
CREPES
CREWED
CREWEL
DEEDED
DEEDEE
DEEMED
DEEPEN
DEEPER
DIESEL
DIESES
DIETED
DIETER
DREXEL
DUELED
DUELER
ELEVEN
ELEVES
EVENED
EVENER
EXETER
EYELET
FEEDER
FEELER
FLEXED
FLEXES
FLEYED
FUELED
FUELER
GEEGEE
GEEZER
GLEBES
GREBES
GRETEL
GREYED
GREYER
HEEDED
HEEDER
HEELED
HEELER
IBEXES
ICEMEN
ILEXES
IRENES
JAEGER
JEERED
JEERER
JEETER
JEEVES
JOETEX
KEELED
KEELER
KEENED
KEENEN
KEENER
KEEPER
KIEFER
LEERED
LEERER
LIEDER
LIEFER
LIEGES
LIENEE
MEEKER
MEETER
NEEDED
NIECES
NUECES
OBEYED
OLEVEL
OMELET
OPENED
OPENER
OXEYES
PEEDEE
PEEKED
PEELED
PEELER
PEENED
PEEPED
PEEPER
PEERED
PEEVED
PEEVES
PEEWEE
PIECED
PIECER
PIECES
PIEMEN
PIETER
PLEBES
PREFER
PREMED
PRESET
PRETER
PREYED
QUEBEC
QUEUED
QUEUER
QUEUES
REEFED
REEFER
REEKED
REELED
REESES
REEVED
REEVES
SCENES
SEEDED
SEEDER
SEEGER
SEEKER
SEELEY
SEEMED
SEEPED
SEERED
SHEKEL
SHEREE
SIEGED
SIEGEL
SIEGES
SIEVED
SIEVES
SKEWED
SKEWER
SLEWED
SPEWED
STELES
STEREO
STERES
STEVEN
STEWED
STEWER
SUEDES
SWEDEN
SWEDES
TEEHEE
TEEMED
TEENER
TEETER
TEEVEE
THEBES
THEFED
THEMED
THEMES
THERES
THESEA
THESES
THEWEB
TIERED
TREBEK
UNEVEN
USENET
VEERED
VIEWED
VIEWER
WEEDED
WEEDER
WEEPER
WHERED
WHERES
WIENER
WIESEL

••E••E

ABESSE
ADELIE
ADELLE
ADESTE
AHERNE
ALEGRE
AMEBAE
AMECHE
AMERCE
ATEASE
AVENGE
AVENUE
AVERSE
AYEAYE
BEETLE
BIERCE
BLENDE
BREEZE
BYEBYE
CHEESE
CHELAE
CHEQUE
CHERIE
CHEVRE
CLEAVE
CLEESE
COERCE
CREASE
CREATE
CRECHE
CREOLE
DEEDEE
DIEPPE
DREDGE
EDERLE
EMERGE
EMEUTE
ETERNE
FAERIE
FAEROE
FEEBLE
FIERCE
FLECHE
FLEDGE
FLEECE
FLENSE
FREEZE
GEEGEE
GLENNE
GOETHE
GREASE
GREAVE
GREECE
GREENE
GREIGE
GUERRE
HEEBIE
ICEAGE
IDEATE
INESSE
KPELLE
KRESGE
LIENEE
LIERNE
NEEDLE
ODENSE
ODETTE
OKEEFE
OLEATE
ONEDGE
ORELSE
PEEDEE
PEERCE
PEEWEE
PHEDRE
PIERCE
PIERRE
PLEASE
PLEDGE
PREMIE
PUENTE
SEETHE
SHEAVE
SHELVE
SHEREE
SIECLE
SLEAVE
SLEAZE
SLEDGE
SLEEVE
SNEEZE
SPECIE
STEELE
STEEVE
STELAE
STEPPE
STERNE
STEVIE
SVELTE
SWERVE
TEEHEE
TEETHE
TEEVEE
THECAE
THENCE
THEYRE
THEYVE
TIEDYE
TIERCE
TREBLE
TSETSE
TWEEZE
TWELVE
UNEASE
VIENNE
WEENIE
WEEPIE
WHEEZE
WHENCE
YVETTE

•••EE•

ADWEEK
AFREET
AGREED
AGREES
AILEEN
ALLEES
ANTEED
ARLEEN
ASLEEP
AXSEED
BALEEN
BOPEEP
CAREEN
CAREER
CUVEES
DONEES
DUDEEN
EILEEN
EMCEED
EMCEES
ESTEEM
EXCEED
FUSEES
FUZEES
GELEES
HOMEEC
INDEED
INNEED
KAREEM
LATEEN
LEVEED
LEVEES
LYCEES
MELEES
MOREEN
MUDEEL
PAYEES
PEWEES
POTEEN
PUREED
PUREES
RANEES
REDEEM
REHEEL
RESEED
RESEEN
RESEES
RUPEES
SATEEN
SCREED
SCREEN
SCREES
SPLEEN
SPREES
STREEP
STREET
TEHEED
TEHEES
TEPEES
THREED
THREES
TUREEN
UNHEED
UNMEET
UNREEL
UNSEEN
UPKEEP
VENEER
VEREEN

•••E•E

ACCEDE
ACHEBE
ACHENE
ADHERE
ALKENE
ALLEGE
ALLELE
AMPERE
ANNEXE
APIECE
ARLENE
ARSENE
ATHENE
BAREGE
BIREME
BREEZE
BUTENE
CHEESE
CLEESE
COHERE
CYBELE
DELETE
EFFETE
EOCENE
EPHEBE
ESSENE
ETHENE
EUGENE
EXLEGE
FILENE
FLEECE
FOVEAE
FREEZE
FRIEZE
GALEAE
GAMETE
GENEVE
GREECE
GREENE
GRIEVE
GYRENE
HELENE
IMPEDE
INDENE
INHERE
IRLENE
ISMENE
JOLENE
LATENE
LEVENE
LEXEME
MANEGE
MAXENE
NICENE
OCREAE
OKEEFE
OSSETE
PALEAE
PAREVE
PHOEBE
POPEYE
RACEME
RECEDE
REDEYE
RENEGE
RETENE
REVERE
RIBEYE
SCHEME
SECEDE
SELENE
SEMELE
SERENE
SEVERE
SLEEVE
SNEEZE
SPHERE
STEELE
STEEVE
STPETE
SURETE
TALESE
TERETE
THIEVE
TUYERE
TWEEZE
VARESE
WHEEZE
XYLENE

••••EE

ADOREE
ANNLEE
APOGEE
ATTLEE
BAILEE
BOOTEE
BOTREE
BUNGEE
BURGEE
COFFEE
CORVEE
COULEE
DECREE
DEEDEE
DEGREE
DONNEE
DRAGEE
DUNDEE
ELYSEE
ENTREE
EPOPEE
FRISEE
GEEGEE
GOATEE
HUMVEE
JAYCEE
JAYVEE
KERSEE
LEGREE
LESSEE
LIENEE
LISTEE
MALLEE
MARLEE
MARMEE
MAUMEE
PARSEE
PAWNEE
PEEDEE
PEEWEE
PENSEE
POMMEE
PONGEE
PUGREE
PUTTEE
RAPPEE
RUSHEE
SANTEE
SEABEE
SETTEE
SHEREE
SIGNEE
SIRREE
SOIREE
SWANEE
TEEHEE
TEEVEE
TESTEE
TOATEE
TOFFEE
TOUPEE
TOWHEE
TRALEE
UNFREE
VALLEE
VENDEE
VESTEE
YANKEE
YIPPEE

EF••••

EFFACE
EFFECT
EFFETE
EFFIGY
EFFLUX
EFFORT
EFFUSE
EFLATS

E•F•••

EFFACE
EFFECT
EFFETE
EFFIGY
EFFLUX
EFFORT
EFFUSE
EIFFEL
ELFISH
ELFMAN
ENFANT
ENFOLD
ERFURT

E••F••

EARFUL
EIFFEL
EYEFUL

E•••F•

EXWIFE

E••••F

ENGULF

•EF•••

BEFALL
BEFELL
BEFITS
BEFOGS
BEFORE
BEFOUL
DEFACE
DEFAME
DEFATS
DEFEAT
DEFECT
DEFEND
DEFERS
DEFIED
DEFIES
DEFILE
DEFINE
DEFLEA
DEFOGS
DEFORM
DEFRAY
DEFTER
DEFTLY
DEFUSE
HEFLIN
HEFNER
HEFTED
KEFIRS
LEFTIE
LEFTIN
REFACE
REFERS
REFFED
REFILE
REFILL
REFINE
REFITS
REFLAG
REFLEX
REFLUX
REFORM
REFUEL
REFUGE
REFUND
REFUSE
REFUTE
TEFLON

•E•F••

BEEFED
BEEFUP
BELFRY
DEAFEN
DEAFER
DEAFLY
DELFTS
HEIFER
LEAFED
LETFLY
MEDFLY
PEPFUL
REDFIN
REDFIR
REDFOX
REEFED
REEFER
REFFED
SEAFAN
SEAFOX
SEEFIT
WERFEL
WETFLY

•E••F•

AERIFY
BEGOFF
BEREFT
DECAFS
GETOFF
LEDOFF
LETOFF
REBUFF
RECIFE
SEEOFF
SENUFO
SERIFS
SETOFF
TEEOFF
VERIFY

•E•••F

BEGOFF
BEHALF
BEHOOF
BELIEF
CERTIF
GETOFF
HEAROF
HEREOF
LEDOFF
LETOFF
REBUFF
RELIEF
SEEOFF
SETOFF
TEEOFF
TELLOF

••EF••

BEEFED
BEEFUP
CLEFTS
EYEFUL
ICEFOG
IREFUL
KIEFER
LIEFER
LIEFLY
OLEFIN
PREFAB
PREFER
PREFIX
REEFED
REEFER
RUEFUL
SEEFIT
STEFAN
STEFFI
STEFOY
THEFED
THEFLY
THEFTS
USEFUL
WOEFUL

••E•F•

DIEOFF
OKEEFE
SEEOFF
SHEAFS
STEFFI
TEEOFF

••E••F

DIEOFF
SEEOFF
SHERIF
TEEOFF

•••EF•

BEREFT
BRIEFS
CASEFY
CHIEFS
GRIEFS
OKEEFE
RAREFY
TUMEFY

•••E•F

HEREOF
IMPERF
ITSELF
MYSELF

••••EF

BELIEF
RELIEF
UNICEF

EG••••

EGBERT
EGERIA
EGESTA
EGESTS
EGGCUP
EGGIER
EGGING
EGGNOG
EGGSON
EGMONT
EGOISM
EGOIST
EGRESS
EGRETS

E•G•••

EAGLED
EAGLES
EAGLET
EAGRES
EDGARD
EDGARS
EDGEIN
EDGERS
EDGIER
EDGILY
EDGING
EGGCUP
EGGIER
EGGING
EGGNOG
EGGSON
EIGHTH
EIGHTS
EIGHTY
ENGAGE
ENGELS
ENGINE
ENGIRD
ENGIRT
ENGLUT
ENGRAM
ENGULF
ERGATE
ERGOTS
EUGENE

E••G••

ELEGIT
EMIGRE
ENIGMA

E•••G•

EFFIGY
ELOIGN
EMERGE
ENCAGE
ENERGY
ENGAGE
ENOUGH
ENRAGE
ENSIGN
ERYNGO
EULOGY
EXLEGE

E••••G

EALING
EARING
EARWIG
EASING
EATING
EBBING
EDBERG
EDGING
EGGING
EGGNOG
EKBERG
ENDING
EPILOG
EPPING
ERRING
ERVING
EYEING

•EG•••

AEGEAN
BEGETS
BEGGAR
BEGGED
BEGINS
BEGLEY
BEGOFF
BEGONE
BEGUMS
DEGAGE
DEGREE
DEGUST
HEGARI
HEGIRA
KEGGED
KEGLER
LEGACY
LEGALS
LEGATE
LEGATO
LEGEND
LEGGED
LEGION
LEGIST
LEGMAN
LEGMEN
LEGREE
LEGUIN
LEGUME
MEGALO
MEGARA
MEGILP
MEGOHM
NEGATE
PEGGED
PEGLER
PEGTOP
REGAIN
REGALE
REGARD
REGENT
REGGAE
REGGIE
REGIME
REGINA
REGION
REGIUS
REGLET
REGLUE
REGNAL
REGNAT
REGRET
SEGUED
SEGUES
SEGURA
VEGANS
VEGGED
VEGGIE

•E•G••

BEAGLE
BEEGUM
BEGGAR
BEGGED
BEIGES
BENGAL
BENGAY
BERGEN
DEIGNS
DENGUE
FEIGNS
FERGIE
FERGUS
GEEGAW
GEEGEE
GEIGER
GEWGAW
HEDGED
HEDGER
HEDGES
HEIGHT
JETGUN
KEDGED
KEDGES
KEGGED
LEAGUE
LEDGER
LEDGES
LEGGED
LENGTH
MEAGER
MEAGRE
MEDGAR
MERGED
MERGER
MERGES
NEIGHS
PEGGED
PENGHU
REAGAN
REDGUM
REGGAE
REGGIE

REIGNS
SEAGAL
SEDGES
SEEGER
SERGEI
SERGES
SERGIO
VEGGED
VEGGIE
VEIGHT
VERGED
VERGER
VERGES
WEDGED
WEDGES
WEDGIE
WEIGHS
WEIGHT
YEAGER
ZENGER
ZEUGMA

•E••G•

BEFOGS
BEINGS
BELUGA
BENIGN
DEBUGS
DEFOGS
DEGAGE
DELUGE
DESIGN
GEORGE
GEORGY
LEHIGH
LESAGE
LETSGO
MENAGE
NEWAGE
PELAGE
PERUGA
REBAGS
REFUGE
RENEGE
REPEGS
REPUGN
RESIGN
RETAGS
SENEGA
SEWAGE
TELUGU

•E•••G

BEDBUG
BELONG
BENING
BERING
CEDING
DEKING
DELONG
DEWING
FEEING
FETING
GEEING
GEHRIG
HERZOG
HEWING
HEXING
JETLAG
KENNYG
KEYING
MEKONG
METING
MEWING
PEKING
PENANG
PETROG
REDDOG
REDING
REDTAG
REFLAG
REHANG
REHUNG
RESING
SEABAG
SEADOG
SEBERG
SEEING
SEWING
TEABAG
TEEING
VEXING
WETTIG

••EG••

ALEGAR
ALEGRE
BEEGUM
ELEGIT
GEEGAW
GEEGEE
GREGOR
JAEGER
LIEGES
OMEGAS
OREGON
SEEGER
SIEGED
SIEGEL
SIEGES

••E•G•

ANERGY
ATERGO
AVENGE
AWEIGH
CLERGY
DREDGE
EMERGE
ENERGY
FLEDGE
FLEDGY
GREIGE
ICEAGE
KRESGE
ONEDGE
PLEDGE
SLEDGE
SLEIGH

••E••G

AGEING
BOEING
DYEING
EYEING
FEEING
GEEING
HIEING
HOEING
ICEBAG
ICEFOG
KOENIG
LIEBIG
PYEDOG
SEEING
STENOG
TEEING
TIEING
TOEING

•••EG•

ALLEGE
BADEGG
BAREGE
BODEGA
EXLEGE
FOREGO
MANEGE
NONEGO
ORTEGA
OSWEGO
PHLEGM
RAWEGG
RENEGE
REPEGS
SENEGA
UNPEGS

•••E•G

BADEGG
EDBERG
EKBERG
LIPENG
RATEDG
RAWEGG
SEBERG

••••EG

DOGLEG
MUSKEG
NUTMEG
TUAREG

E•H•••

ECHINO
ECHOED
ECHOES
ECHOIC
ENHALO
EPHAHS
EPHEBE
EPHODS
EPHORI
EPHORS
EPHRON
ERHARD
ESHARP
ETHANE
ETHENE
ETHERS
ETHICS
ETHNIC
ETHNOS
EXHALE
EXHORT

E••H••

EIGHTH
EIGHTS
EIGHTY
EITHER
ELOHIM
ESCHER
ESCHEW
ESTHER
ETCHED
ETCHER
ETCHES
EUCHRE

E•••H•

EARTHA
EARTHY
ELISHA
EPHAHS
EPOCHS

E••••H

EDKOCH
EIGHTH
ELFISH
ELIJAH
ELVISH
EMDASH
ENDASH
ENMESH
ENOUGH
ENRICH
EOLITH
EPARCH
EXARCH

•EH•••

BEHALF
BEHAVE
BEHEAD
BEHELD
BEHEST
BEHIND
BEHOLD
BEHOOF
BEHOVE
DEHORN
GEHRIG
LEHIGH
LEHRER
LEHUAS
REHABS
REHANG
REHASH
REHEAL
REHEAR
REHEAT
REHEEL
REHELD
REHEMS
REHIRE
REHOOK
REHUNG
TEHEED
TEHEES
YEHUDI

•E•H••

AETHER
BENHUR
BETHEL
HEEHAW
JETHRO
KESHIA
LETHAL
MENHIR
MESHED
MESHES
METHOD
METHYL
NEPHEW
NEPHRO
NETHER
PEAHEN
REDHAT
REDHOT
RESHES
RESHIP
RESHOD
RESHOE
RESHOT
SENHOR
TECHIE
TECHNO
TEEHEE
TEPHRA
TETHER
TETHYS
WETHER
ZEPHYR

•E••H•

BEACHY
BERTHA
BERTHS
BETCHA
DELPHI
DEPTHS
GEISHA
GERAHS
HEATHS
HEATHY
HEIGHT
LEACHY
MEGOHM
NEIGHS
PEACHY
PENGHU
PERCHA
REECHO
SEETHE
SEICHE
TEETHE
TENTHS
TETCHY
VEIGHT
WEIGHS
WEIGHT

•E•••H

BEULAH
CERIPH
DEARTH
DETACH
FELLAH
FETISH
HEALTH
HEARTH
JEWISH
LEHIGH
LENGTH
MENSCH
NEWISH
PERISH
PESACH
REHASH
RELISH
REWASH
SEARCH
SERAPH
TEMPEH
TERAPH
WEALTH
ZENITH
ZEROTH

••EH••

FOEHNS
HEEHAW
TEEHEE
THEHAJ

••E•H•

ALEPHS
AMECHE
ARETHA
AYESHA
BRECHT
CHETHS
CRECHE
CZECHS
FLECHE
FLESHY
GOETHE
ILESHA
OBEAHS
REECHO
SEETHE
SHEEHY
TEETHE

••E••H

AWEIGH
BLEACH
BLENCH
BREACH
BREATH
BREECH
CHEECH
CLENCH
DRENCH
FLETCH
FRENCH
GUELPH
KVETCH
PLEACH
PREACH
QUENCH
SHEATH
SKETCH
SLEIGH
SLEUTH
SMERSH
SPEECH
STENCH
TRENCH
WREATH
WRENCH
WRETCH

•••EH•

HIDEHO
SHEEHY

•••E•H

AFRESH
BREECH
CHEECH
COMETH
DALETH
ENMESH
GARETH
HITECH
JOBETH
JOSEPH
LAMECH
LAMEDH
OHYEAH
SAMECH
SAMEKH
SPEECH
TAKETH
THRESH
UNMESH
VOTECH

••••EH

TEMPEH
YAHWEH

EI••••

EIDERS
EIDOLA
EIFFEL
EIGHTH
EIGHTS
EIGHTY
EILEEN
EISNER
EITHER

E•I•••

EDIBLE
EDICTS
EDILES
EDISON
EDITED
EDITIO
EDITOR
EJIDOS
ELICIT
ELIDED
ELIDES
ELIJAH
ELINOR
ELISHA
ELISSA
ELITES
ELIXIR
EMIGRE
EMILIA
EMILIO
EMINOR
ENIGMA
ENISLE
EOIPSO
EPICAL
EPILOG
EPINAL
EPIRUS
ERINYS
EVICTS
EVILER
EVILLY
EVINCE
EXILED
EXILES
EXILIC
EXISTS
EXITED

E••I••

EALING
EARING
EASIER
EASILY
EASING
EATING
EBBING
ECHINO
EDDIED
EDDIES
EDGIER
EDGILY
EDGING
EELIER
EERIER
EERILY
EFFIGY
EGGIER
EGGING
EGOISM
EGOIST
ELAINE
ELFISH
ELLICE
ELLIOT
ELMIRA
ELNINO
ELOIGN
ELOISE
ELVIRA
ELVISH
EMAILS
EMPIRE
ENCINA
ENCINO
ENDING
ENDIVE
ENGINE
ENGIRD
ENGIRT
ENLIST
ENMITY
ENNIUS
ENRICH
ENRICO
ENSIGN
ENSILE
ENTICE
ENTIRE
ENTITY
ENVIED
ENVIER
ENVIES
EOLIAN
EOLITH
EONIAN
EOSINS
EPPING
EQUINE
EQUIPS
EQUITY
ERBIUM
ERMINE
EROICA
ERRING
ERVING
ESKIMO
ESPIAL
ESPIED
ESPIES
ETHICS
ETOILE
EUNICE
EXCISE
EXCITE
EXPIRE
EXPIRY
EXWIFE
EYEING
EYRIES

E•••I•

EARWIG
EASEIN
EATSIN
ECESIC
ECESIS
ECHOIC
ECLAIR
EDENIC
EDGEIN
EDITIO
EGERIA
ELAPID
ELEGIT
ELEMIS
ELICIT
ELIXIR
ELOHIM
EMILIA
EMILIO
ENJOIN
ENOKIS
ENOSIS
ENTAIL
ENVOIS
EROTIC
ESPRIT
ETALIA
ETALII
ETHNIC
ETONIC
EUCLID
EURAIL
EXILIC
EXOTIC
EYELID

E••••I

EPHORI
ERNANI
ETALII
EVENKI

•EI•••

BEIGES
BEINGS
BEIRUT
CEIBAS
CEILED
DEICED
DEICER
DEICES
DEIDRE
DEIGNS
DEIMOS
DEISTS
FEIGNS
FEINTS
FEISTY
GEIGER
GEISEL
GEISHA
HEIDEN
HEIFER
HEIGHT
HEISTS
KEITEL
LEIDEN
NEIGHS
NEISSE
REIGNS
REILLY
REINAS
REINED
REINER
REININ
REINKS
SEICHE
SEIDEL
SEINED
SEINER
SEINES
SEISMO
SEISMS
SEIZED
SEIZER
SEIZES
VEIGHT
VEILED
VEINAL
VEINED
WEIGHS
WEIGHT
WEIMAR
WEIRDO
WEIRDY

•E•I••

AEDILE
AERIAL
AERIES
AERIFY
AERILY
BEDIMS
BEFITS
BEGINS
BEHIND
BELIAL
BELIED
BELIEF
BELIES
BELIKE
BELIZE
BEMINE
BEMIRE
BENIGN
BENING
BENITO
BERING
BESIDE
BETIDE
BETISE
BEVIES
CECILE
CECILY
CEDING
CELINE
CERIPH
CERISE
CERIUM
CESIUM
DEBITS
DECIDE
DEFIED
DEFIES
DEFILE
DEFINE
DEKING
DELICT
DELIST
DELIUS
DEMIES
DEMISE
DEMITS
DENIAL
DENIED
DENIER
DENIES
DENIMS
DENIRO
DENISE
DEPICT
DERIDE
DERIVE
DESICA
DESIGN
DESILU
DESIRE
DESIST
DEVICE
DEVILS
DEVINE
DEVISE
DEVITO
DEWIER
DEWILY
DEWING
DEWITT
EELIER
EERIER
EERILY
FEEING
FELINE
FELIPE
FENIAN
FERIAL
FERIAS
FERITY
FETING
FETISH
GEEING
GEMINI
GENIAL
GENIES
GENIUS
GEZIRA
HEGIRA
HELIOS
HELIUM
HERIOT
HESIOD
HEWING
HEXING
JEWISH
KEFIRS
KEYING
LEGION
LEGIST
LEHIGH
LENITY
LERIDA
LEVIED
LEVIER
LEVIES
LEVINE
LEVITE
LEVITY
LEXICA
MEDIAL
MEDIAN
MEDIAS
MEDICI
MEDICO
MEDICS
MEDINA
MEDIUM
MEGILP
MEJICO
MELINA
MENIAL
MENINX
MERIDA
MERINO
MERITS
METIER
METING
MEWING
MEXICO
NEVINS
NEWISH
PEKING
PEKINS
PELIKE
PELION
PEPINO
PEPITA
PERILS
PERIOD
PERISH
PETITE
PEWITS
REAIMS
REAIRS
REBIDS
REBIND
RECIFE
RECIPE
RECITE
REDIAL
REDING
REDINK
REFILE
REFILL
REFINE
REFITS
REGIME
REGINA
REGION
REGIUS
REHIRE
RELICS
RELICT
RELIED
RELIEF
RELIES
RELINE
RELISH
RELIST
RELIVE
REMICK
REMIND
REMISE
REMISS
REMITS
REOILS
REPINE
REPINS
RESIDE
RESIGN
RESILE
RESING
RESINS
RESINY
RESIST
RETIAL
RETIED
RETIES
RETILE
RETIME
RETINA
RETIRE
REVIEW
REVILE
REVISE
REVIVE
REWIND
REWINS
REWIRE
SEDILE
SEEING
SEMITE
SENIOR
SENITI
SEPIAS
SERIAL
SERIES
SERIFS
SERINE
SERINS
SETINS
SEWING
SEXIER
SEXILY
SEXIST
TEDIUM
TEEING
VENIAL
VENICE
VENIRE
VENITE
VERIFY
VERILY
VERISM
VERITE
VERITY
VEXING
ZENITH

•E••I•

AENEID
AEOLIA
AEOLIC
BEANIE
BEATIT
BEAVIS
BELAIR
BELOIT
BENDIX
BENOIT
BERLIN
BERNIE
BERTIE
BESSIE
BESTIR
BEWAIL
CEDRIC
CELTIC
CERTIF
CERVID
DEALIN
DEARIE
DEASIL
DEBBIE
DEBRIS
DECEIT
DELRIO
DELTIC
DENNIS
DENTIL
DENTIN
DERAIL
DERMIS
DERRIS
DETAIL
DETAIN
DEVEIN
DEVOID
DEVOIR
FELLIN
FERGIE
FERRIC
FERRIS
FERVID
GEHRIG
GERBIL
GERTIE
GESTIC
GETSIN
GETSIT
HEADIN
HECTIC
HEEBIE
HEFLIN
HELDIN
HEMSIN
HENBIT
HENNIN
HENRIK
HERBIE
HEREIN
HERMIT
HEROIC
HESTIA
HETTIE
JENNIE
JERKIN
JESSIE
JESUIT
KEEPIN
KELPIE
KELVIN
KEMPIS
KERMIS
KERMIT
KESHIA
KEWPIE
KEYSIN
LEADIN
LEFTIE
LEFTIN
LEGUIN
LENNIE
LENTIL
LEONID
LEONIE
LESLIE
LETSIN
MEALIE
MEANIE
MELVIL
MELVIN
MEMOIR
MENHIR
MENTIS
MERLIN
METRIC
NELLIE
NEREID
NEREIS
NESSIE
PECTIC
PECTIN
PEERIN
PELVIC
PELVIS
PENCIL
PENNIA
PENNIS
PEORIA
PEPSIN
PEPTIC
PERMIT
PERNIO
PERSIA
PETAIN
PETRIE
PETTIT
READIN
REALIA
REBOIL
RECOIL
REDFIN
REDFIR
REEDIT
REELIN
REGAIN
REGGIE
REININ
REJOIN
RELAID
REMAIL
REMAIN
RENAIL
RENNIE
RENNIN
RENOIR
REPAID
REPAIR
RESHIP
RESNIK
RESPIN
RETAIL
RETAIN
RETRIM
REVOIR
SEEFIT
SEENIN
SEEPIN
SEESIN
SENDIN
SENNIT
SENTIN
SEPTIC
SEQUIN
SERAIS
SERBIA
SERGIO
SERKIN
SETSIN
TECHIE
TENNIS
TENPIN
TESSIE
TETRIS
VEGGIE
VERBIS
VERDIN
VERMIN
VESPID
WEDGIE
WEENIE
WEEPIE
WEEVIL
WELKIN
WENTIN
WESKIT
WETTIG
YESSIR
ZENDIC
ZEROIN
ZEUXIS

•E•••I

BENONI
CENTRI
DELPHI
DENALI
DENDRI
GELATI
GEMINI
HEGARI
JETSKI
KERNOI
MEDICI
MESABI
NEPALI
NEROLI
SENITI
SENSEI
SERGEI
SESQUI
YEHUDI
YEMENI

••EI••

AGEING
AGEISM
AGEIST
ASEITY
AWEIGH
BOEING
DYEING
EYEING
FEEING
GEEING
GNEISS
GREIGE
HIEING
HOEING
KLEIST
KWEISI
ONEIDA
ONEILL
OREIDA
PLEIAD
SEEING
SHEIKS
SHEILA
SKEINS
SLEIGH
STEINS
TEEING
THEIRS
THEISM
THEIST
TIEING
TIEINS
TOEING
TOEINS

••E•I•

ACEDIA
ACETIC
ADELIE
ALEXIA
ALEXIS
AMEBIC
AMELIA
ANEMIA
ANEMIC
BLEWIT
BREVIS
CHEMIN
CHENIN
CHERIE
CLERIC
CLEVIS
COEDIT
CREDIT
CRETIN
DIESIS
DOESIN
DREWIN
ECESIC
ECESIS
EDENIC
EGERIA
ELEGIT
ELEMIS
EYELID
FAERIE
FLEWIN
FOETID
GAELIC
GOESIN

HEEBIE
IBERIA
ICEDIN
ICESIN
IGETIT
IRENIC
ISELIN
KEEPIN
KOENIG
LIEBIG
LIESIN
MYELIN
NOESIS
NOETIC
NOEXIT
OBELIA
OLEFIN
PEERIN
PIETIN
POETIC
PRECIS
PREFIX
PRELIM
PREMIE
PREVIN
REEDIT
REELIN
SCENIC
SEEFIT
SEENIN
SEEPIN
SEESIN
SHERIF
SPECIE
STEPIN
STEVIE
THEKID
THELIP
THESIS
THESIX
THETIC
THETIS
THEWIZ
TIEDIN
TIEPIN
TIESIN
TMESIS
TOEDIN
TOESIN
TREDIA
TREPID
USERID
WEENIE
WEEPIE
WEEVIL

••E••I

ALEXEI
EVENKI
KWEISI
NIELLI
OCELLI
RIENZI
STEFFI

•••EI•

AENEID
ALBEIT
CAMEIN
CAVEIN
CLUEIN
COHEIR
COMEIN
DECEIT
DEVEIN
DINEIN
DIVEIN
DONEIN
DOVEIN
EASEIN
EDGEIN
FADEIN
GAVEIN
GIVEIN
HEREIN
LIVEIN
LOMEIN
LOSEIT
LOVEIN
MACEIO
MADEIT
MAKEIT
MOVEIN
NEREID
NEREIS
OSSEIN
PILEIN
RAKEIN
ROPEIN
SOBEIT
SOLEIL
TAKEIN
TUNEIN
UNVEIL
VOTEIN
WADEIN
WAVEIN

•••E•I

ANGELI
DOREMI
HIDEKI
HUMERI
LIBERI
SILENI
VIDERI
YEMENI

••••EI

ALEXEI
ANDREI
BRUNEI
CISKEI
GLUTEI
MALLEI
NIKKEI
NUCLEI
PROTEI
SANSEI
SENSEI
SERGEI
TAIPEI

EJ••••

EJECTA
EJECTS
EJIDOS

E•J•••

ENJOIN
ENJOYS

E••J••

ELIJAH
EMAJOR

•EJ•••

DEJAVU
DEJECT
DEJURE
JEJUNE
MEJICO
REJECT
REJOIN
SEJANT
TEJANO

•E•J••

DEEJAY
MENJOU
SELJUK
VEEJAY

••EJ••

DEEJAY
VEEJAY

••E••J

THEHAJ

•••E•J

INTERJ

EK••••

EKBERG
EKEOUT

E•K•••

EDKOCH
ESKERS
ESKIMO

E••K••

ENOKIS
EVOKED
EVOKER
EVOKES

E•••K•

EUREKA
EVENKI

E••••K

EMBANK
EMBARK

•EK•••

BEKESY
DEKALB
DEKING
DEKKOS
JEKYLL
LEKVAR
MEKONG
NEKTON
PEKING
PEKINS
PEKOES
REKEYS

•E•K••

BEAKED
BEAKER
BECKER
BECKET
BECKON
DECKED
DECKER
DECKLE
DEKKOS
GECKOS
HECKLE
JECKLE
JERKED
JERKIN
LEAKED
LEAKER
LEAKEY
MEEKER
MEEKLY
MENKEN
MERKEL
NECKED
PEAKED
PECKAT
PECKED
PEEKAT
PEEKED
PERKED
PERKUP
RECKON
REEKED
SECKEL
SEEKER
SERKIN
TEDKEY
TERKEL
WEAKEN
WEAKER
WEAKLY
WEEKLY
WELKIN
WESKIT
YERKED
YERKES

•E••K•

BELIKE
BETAKE
JETSKI
MEDAKA
NEVSKY
PELIKE
PERUKE
REBUKE
REINKS
REMAKE
RETAKE
REVOKE
SEDAKA

•E•••K

BEDECK
BETOOK
DEBARK
DEBUNK
DEEPAK
HENRIK
NEWARK
RECORK
REDINK
REDOAK
REEBOK
REHOOK
RELOCK
REMARK
REMICK
RESNIK
RETOOK
REWORK
SELJUK
SENDAK

••EK••

CHEKOV
MEEKER
MEEKLY
PEEKAT
PEEKED
REEKED
SEEKER
SHEKEL
THEKID
WEEKLY

••E•K•

ALECKY
BREAKS
CHECKS
CHEEKS
CHEEKY
CLEEKS
CLERKS
CREAKS
CREAKY
CREEKS
EVENKI
FLECKS
FLECKY
FREAKS
FREAKY
GREEKS
SHEIKS
SLEEKS
SLEEKY
SNEAKS
SNEAKY
SPEAKS
SPECKS
STEAKS
TWEAKS
VNECKS
WHELKS
WREAKS
WRECKS

••E••K

DEEPAK
REEBOK
RHEBOK
SLEZAK
TREBEK

•••EK•

CHEEKS
CHEEKY
CLEEKS
CREEKS
EUREKA
GREEKS
HACEKS
HIDEKI
KOPEKS
SAMEKH
SLEEKS
SLEEKY
TOPEKA
UZBEKS

•••E•K

ADWEEK
BEDECK
KOPECK
LUBECK
ONDECK
SCREAK
SQUEAK
STREAK

••••EK

ADWEEK
DUBCEK
OCASEK
SHRIEK
SPACEK
TREBEK

EL••••

ELAINE
ELANDS
ELAPID
ELAPSE
ELATED
ELATER
ELATES
ELAYER
ELAYNE
ELBERT
ELBOWS
ELBRUS
ELDERS
ELDEST
ELECTS
ELEGIT
ELEMIS
ELEVEN
ELEVES
ELFISH
ELFMAN
ELICIT
ELIDED
ELIDES
ELIJAH
ELINOR
ELISHA
ELISSA
ELITES
ELIXIR
ELLERY
ELLICE
ELLIOT
ELMIRA
ELMORE
ELNINO
ELOHIM
ELOIGN
ELOISE
ELOPED
ELOPER
ELOPES
ELPASO
ELUDED
ELUDER
ELUDES
ELUTED
ELUTES
ELVERS
ELVIRA
ELVISH
ELWOOD
ELYSEE

E•L•••

EALING
ECLAIR
ECLATS
EELERS
EELIER
EFLATS
EILEEN
ELLERY
ELLICE
ELLIOT
ENLACE
ENLIST
EOLIAN
EOLITH
EULOGY
EXLEGE

E••L••

EAGLED
EAGLES
EAGLET
EARLAP
ECCLES
ECOLES
EDILES
EFFLUX
EMBLEM
EMILIA
EMILIO
EMPLOY
ENBLOC
ENGLUT
EPILOG
ETALIA
ETALII
EUCLID
EVELYN
EVILER
EVILLY
EVOLVE
EVULSE
EXALTS
EXILED
EXILES
EXILIC
EXULTS
EYELET
EYELID

E•••L•

EASELS
EASILY
EBERLY
EDERLE
EDGILY
EDIBLE
EDSELS
EERILY
EIDOLA
EMAILS
ENABLE
ENDALL
ENFOLD
ENGELS
ENGULF
ENHALO
ENISLE
ENROLL
ENROLS
ENSILE
EQUALS
ERROLL
ETOILE
EVENLY
EVERLY
EVILLY
EXCELS
EXHALE
EXPELS
EXTOLS

E••••L

EARFUL
EIFFEL
ENAMEL
ENDALL
ENROLL
ENSOUL
ENTAIL
EPICAL
EPINAL
ERROLL
ESPIAL
ETYMOL
EURAIL
EYEFUL

•EL•••

BELAIR
BELAYS
BELDAM
BELFRY
BELIAL
BELIED
BELIEF
BELIES
BELIKE
BELIZE
BELLAY
BELLED
BELLES
BELLOC
BELLOW
BELOIT
BELONG
BELTED
BELUGA
CELEBS
CELERY
CELINE
CELLAE
CELLAR
CELLED
CELLOS
CELTIC
DELANO
DELANY
DELATE
DELAYS
DELEON
DELETE
DELFTS
DELICT
DELIST
DELIUS
DELMAR
DELONG
DELPHI
DELRAY
DELRIO
DELROY
DELTAS
DELTIC
DELUDE
DELUGE
DELUXE
DELVED
DELVER
DELVES
EELERS
EELIER
FELDON
FELINE
FELIPE
FELLAH
FELLAS
FELLED
FELLER
FELLIN
FELLOE
FELLON
FELLOW
FELLTO
FELONS
FELONY
FELTED
GELADA
GELATI
GELATO
GELEES
GELLED
GELSEY
HELDIN
HELDON
HELDTO
HELDUP
HELENA
HELENE
HELENS
HELIOS
HELIUM
HELLAS
HELLER
HELLOS
HELMED
HELMET
HELMUT
HELOTS
HELPED
HELPER
HELTER
HELVES
JELLED
KELLER
KELLEY
KELPIE
KELSEY
KELVIN
LELAND
MELANO
MELDED
MELEES
MELINA
MELLON
MELLOW
MELMAC
MELODY
MELONS
MELOTT
MELTED
MELTON
MELVIL
MELVIN
MELVYN
NELLIE
NELSON
PELAGE
PELEUS
PELIKE
PELION
PELLET
PELMET
PELOPS
PELOTA
PELTED
PELTER
PELTRY
PELVIC
PELVIS
RELACE
RELAID
RELATE
RELAYS
RELENT
RELETS
RELEVY
RELICS
RELICT
RELIED
RELIEF
RELIES
RELINE
RELISH
RELIST
RELIVE
RELOAD
RELOCK
RELUCT
RELUME
SELDOM
SELECT
SELENA
SELENE
SELENO
SELJUK
SELLER
SELVES
TELEDU
TELLER
TELLOF
TELLON
TELUGU
VELCRO
VELDTS
VELLUM
VELOCE
VELOUR
VELVET
WELDED
WELDER
WELKIN
WELLED
WELLER
WELLES
WELLUP
WELTED
WELTER
YELLED
YELLER
YELLOW
YELPED
YELPER

•E•L••

AEOLIA
AEOLIC
AEOLUS
BEDLAM
BEGLEY
BELLAY
BELLED
BELLES
BELLOC
BELLOW
BERLIN
BEULAH
CEILED
CELLAE
CELLAR
CELLED
CELLOS
CEYLON
DEALER
DEALIN
DEFLEA
DEPLOY
DEWLAP
FEALTY
FEELER
FELLAH
FELLAS
FELLED
FELLER
FELLIN
FELLOE
FELLON
FELLOW
FELLTO
GELLED
HEALED
HEALER
HEALTH
HEELED
HEELER
HEFLIN
HELLAS
HELLER
HELLOS
HENLEY
JELLED
JETLAG
KEELED
KEELER
KEGLER
KELLER
KELLEY
KEPLER
KEVLAR
LEALTY
LESLEY
LESLIE
MEALIE
MEDLAR
MEDLAT
MEDLEY
MELLON
MELLOW
MERLIN
MERLON
MERLOT
MEWLED
MEWLER
NELLIE
NEWLEY
PEALED
PEDLAR
PEELED
PEELER
PEGLER
PELLET
PEPLOS
PEPLUM
REALER
REALES
REALIA
REALLY
REALMS
REALTY
REELED
REELIN
REFLAG
REFLEX
REFLUX
REGLET
REGLUE
REILLY
REPLAN
REPLAY
REPLOW
REVLON
SEALAB
SEALED
SEALER
SEALUP
SEELEY
SELLER
SENLAC
TEFLON
TELLER
TELLOF
TELLON
TESLAS
VEBLEN
VEILED
VELLUM
WEALTH
WELLED
WELLER
WELLES
WELLUP
WESLEY
YELLED
YELLER
YELLOW
ZEALOT

•E••L•

AEDILE
AERILY
BEADLE
BEAGLE
BEATLE
BECALM
BEETLE
BEFALL
BEFELL
BEHALF
BEHELD
BEHOLD
BETELS
BEVELS
BEZELS
CECILE
CECILY
CEORLS
DEADLY
DEAFLY
DEARLY
DECALS
DECKLE
DEEPLY
DEFILE
DEFTLY
DEKALB
DENALI
DESALT
DESILU
DEVILS
DEWILY
EERILY
FEATLY
FEEBLE
FEEBLY
FEMALE
FERULE
FETTLE
GENTLE
GENTLY
GERALD
HECKLE
HEDDLE
HERALD
JECKLE
JEKYLL
JEWELS
KEENLY
KERALA
KETTLE
KEVELS
LEANLY
LEGALS
LETFLY
LEVELS
LEWDLY
MEANLY
MEASLY
MEDALS
MEDDLE
MEDFLY
MEEKLY
MEETLY
MEGALO
MEGILP
MERELY
METALS
METTLE
NEARLY
NEATLY
NEBULA
NEEDLE
NEPALI
NEROLI
NESTLE
NETTLE
NETTLY
NEWELS
PEARLS
PEARLY
PEBBLE
PEBBLY
PEDALS
PEDDLE
PENULT
PEOPLE
PERILS
PERTLY
PESTLE
PETALS
PETULA
REALLY
REBELS
REBOLT
RECALL
REFILE
REFILL
REGALE
REHELD
REILLY
REMELT
REMOLD
REOILS
REPELS
REPOLL
RESALE
RESALT
RESELL
RESILE
RESOLD
RESOLE
RESULT
RETELL
RETILE
RETOLD
REVELS
REVILE
REVOLT
REWELD
SEARLE
SEDILE
SEEMLY
SEMELE
SEPALS
SETTLE
SEWELL
SEXILY
TEMPLE
TEPALS
VERILY
WEAKLY
WEDELN
WEEKLY
WETFLY
YEARLY

•E•••L

AERIAL
BEFALL
BEFELL
BEFOUL
BELIAL
BENGAL
BENZOL
BETHEL
BEWAIL
CEREAL
DEASIL
DENIAL
DENTAL
DENTIL
DENZEL
DEPAUL
DERAIL
DERMAL
DETAIL
FENNEL
FERIAL
FESTAL
FEUDAL
GEISEL
GENIAL
GENUAL
GERBIL
HERBAL
JEKYLL
JESSEL
KEITEL
KENNEL
KERNEL
LEMUEL
LENTIL
LETHAL
MEDIAL
MELVIL
MENDEL
MENIAL
MENSAL
MENTAL
MERKEL
MESCAL
METHYL
NEURAL
NEUROL
PENCEL
PENCIL
PENPAL
PEPFUL
PETREL
PETROL
REBOIL
RECALL
RECOIL
REDEAL
REDIAL
REFILL
REFUEL
REGNAL
REHEAL
REHEEL
REMAIL
RENAIL
RENTAL
REPEAL
REPOLL
RESEAL
RESELL
RETAIL
RETELL
RETIAL
RETOOL
RETRAL
REVEAL
SEAGAL
SECKEL
SEIDEL
SEPTAL
SEQUEL
SERIAL
SERVAL
SEWELL
TEASEL
TERCEL
TERKEL
TETZEL
VEINAL
VENIAL
VERBAL
VERNAL
VESSEL
VESTAL
WEASEL
WEEVIL
WERFEL

••EL••

ABELES
ADELIE
ADELLE
AIELLO
AKELAS
AMELIA
ANELED
ANELES
BCELLS
CHELAE
CHELAS
COELOM
DUELED
DUELER
DUELLO
DWELLS
DYELOT
EVELYN
EYELET
EYELID
FEELER
FIELDS
FJELDS
FUELED
FUELER
GAELIC
GUELPH
HEELED
HEELER
IMELDA
ISELIN
KEELED
KEELER
KNELLS
KPELLE
KVELLS
LIELOW
MYELIN
NIELLI
NIELLO
OBELIA
OBELUS
OCELLI
OCELOT
OKELLY
OMELET
ORELSE
OTELLO
PAELLA
PEELED
PEELER
PRELAW
PRELIM
QUELLS
REELED
REELIN
SEELEY
SHELLS
SHELLY
SHELTY
SHELVE
SMELLS
SMELLY
SMELTS
SNELLS
SPELLS
STELAE
STELAR
STELES
STELLA
STELMO
SVELTE
SWELLS
THELIP
THELMA
TWELVE
WHELKS
WHELMS
WHELPS
WIELDS
YIELDS

••E•L•

ADELLE
AGEOLD
AIELLO
AREOLA
AWEDLY
BCELLS
BEETLE
CREELS
CREOLE
DEEPLY
DUELLO
DWELLS
EBERLY
EDERLE
EVENLY
EVERLY
FEEBLE
FEEBLY
FREELY
GREYLY
IDEALS
ISEULT
KEENLY

KNEELS
KNELLS
KPELLE
KVELLS
LIEFLY
MEEKLY
MEETLY
NEEDLE
NIELLI
NIELLO
OCELLI
OKELLY
ONEILL
OPENLY
OTELLO
OVERLY
PAELLA
PUEBLA
PUEBLO
QUELLS
SEEMLY
SHEILA
SHELLS
SHELLY
SIECLE
SMELLS
SMELLY
SNELLS
SPELLS
STEALS
STEELE
STEELS
STEELY
STELLA
SWELLS
THEFLY
THEYLL
TREBLE
TREBLY
WEEKLY
WHEALS
WHEELS

••E••L
ACETAL
ACETYL
ALEVEL
CHERYL
CHEVAL
COEVAL
CRENEL
CRESOL
CREWEL
DAEDAL
DIESEL
DREXEL
EYEFUL
FOETAL
GRETEL
HIEMAL
HYETAL
IREFUL
OLEVEL
ONEILL
PHENOL
PHENYL
PLEXAL
RUEFUL
SHEKEL
SHERYL
SIEGEL
STEROL
THECAL
THEYLL
USEFUL
WEEVIL
WIESEL
WOEFUL

•••EL•
AFIELD
ALLELE
ANGELA
ANGELI
ANGELL
ANGELO
ANGELS
ANSELM
ARBELA
ARTELS
ASWELL
BABELS
BAGELS
BARELY
BASELY
BEFELL
BEHELD
BETELS
BEVELS
BEZELS
BLUELY
BOTELS
CAMELS
CAVELL
CICELY
COMELY
COSELL
CREELS
CUPELS
CUTELY
CYBELE
DIRELY
DOTELL
DOWELS
EASELS
EDSELS
ENGELS
EXCELS
EXPELS
FINELY
FREELY
GAMELY
GAVELS
GIMELS
GRUELS
HAMELN
HAZELS
HOMELY
HOSELS
HOTELS
HOVELS
HOWELL
HUGELY
IMPELS
ITSELF
JEWELS
KEVELS
KNEELS
LABELS
LAMELY
LAPELS
LATELY
LEVELS
LIBELS
LIKELY
LIVELY
LONELY
LOVELL
LOVELY
LOWELL
MABELL
MERELY
MODELA
MODELS
MODELT
MORELS
MOTELS
MUTELY
MYSELF
NAMELY
NAVELS
NEWELS
NICELY
NOVELS
NUDELY
OHWELL
ORIELS
ORWELL
OUSELS
OUZELS
PALELY
PAMELA
PANELS
PIXELS
POMELO
POWELL
PURELY
RARELY
RATELS
RAVELS
REBELS
REHELD
REMELT
REPELS
RESELL
RETELL
REVELS
REWELD
RIFELY
RIPELY
RONELY
ROWELS
RUDELY
RYDELL
SAFELY
SAGELY
SANELY
SCHELL
SEMELE
SEWELL
SHIELD
SOLELY
SORELY
SPIELS
STEELE
STEELS
STEELY
SURELY
TAMELY
TIMELY
TOWELS
TUPELO
UMBELS
UNBELT
UNWELL
UPHELD
UPWELL
VILELY
VOWELS
VOWELY
WEDELN
WHEELS
WIDELY
WIFELY
WISELY
YARELY
YODELS
YOKELS

•••E•L
ANGELL
ANNEAL
APPEAL
ASWELL
BEFELL
BOREAL
CAVELL
CEREAL
COSELL
CUNEAL
DOTELL
HOWELL
IRREAL
LINEAL
LOREAL
LOVELL
LOWELL
MABELL
MUDEEL
OHWELL
ORDEAL
ORWELL
OSTEAL
PINEAL
POWELL
REDEAL
REHEAL
REHEEL
REPEAL
RESEAL
RESELL
RETELL
REVEAL
RYDELL
SCHELL
SEWELL
SHTETL
SOLEIL
SQUEAL
UNREAL
UNREEL
UNSEAL
UNVEIL
UNWELL
UPWELL

••••EL
ALEVEL
AMSTEL
BARBEL
BARREL
BATTEL
BETHEL
BOATEL
BUNUEL
BUSHEL
CANCEL
CANNEL
CARMEL
CARPEL
CARREL
CARTEL
CHANEL
CHAPEL
CHISEL
COMPEL
CORBEL
CORNEL
CORREL
CRENEL
CREWEL
CUDGEL
DAMSEL
DANIEL
DARNEL
DENZEL
DHOTEL
DIESEL
DISPEL
DOSSEL
DREXEL
DRIVEL
DUFFEL
EIFFEL
ENAMEL
FENNEL
FUNNEL
GEISEL
GIMBEL
GOSPEL
GRAVEL
GRETEL
GROVEL
GUMBEL
GUNNEL
HALLEL
HANDEL
HANSEL
HILLEL
HORMEL
HOSTEL
IJSSEL
ISABEL
ISOHEL
ISRAEL
JESSEL
KEITEL
KENNEL
KERNEL
KOPPEL
KUMMEL
LAUREL
LEMUEL
LINTEL
LIONEL
LISTEL
MANTEL
MANUEL
MARCEL
MARIEL
MARTEL
MARVEL
MATTEL
MENDEL
MERKEL
MICHEL
MIGUEL
MONTEL
MORSEL
MOSTEL
MUDEEL
MURIEL
MUSSEL
NICKEL
OLEVEL
PARCEL
PARREL
PASSEL
PASTEL
PENCEL
PETREL
POMMEL
PROPEL
PUMMEL
RACHEL
RAFAEL
RAPPEL
RAQUEL
REFUEL
REHEEL
ROMMEL
RONDEL
RUNNEL
SAMUEL
SAUREL
SECKEL
SEIDEL
SEQUEL
SHEKEL
SHOVEL
SIEGEL
SIMBEL
SIMNEL
SISKEL
SNIVEL
SORREL
SPINEL
STIPEL
SWIVEL
TASSEL
TEASEL
TERCEL
TERKEL
TETZEL
TINSEL
TRAVEL
TROWEL
TUNNEL
UNREEL
VACHEL
VESSEL
WEASEL
WERFEL
WIESEL

EM••••
EMAILS
EMAJOR
EMBANK
EMBARK
EMBAYS
EMBDEN
EMBEDS
EMBERS
EMBLEM
EMBODY
EMBOSS
EMBRYO
EMCEED
EMCEES
EMDASH
EMEERS
EMENDS
EMERGE
EMEUTE
EMIGRE
EMILIA
EMILIO
EMINOR
EMMETS
EMMETT
EMOTED
EMOTER
EMOTES
EMPERY
EMPIRE
EMPLOY
EMPTOR
EMQUAD

E•M•••
EDMOND
EDMUND
EGMONT
ELMIRA
ELMORE
EMMETS
EMMETT
ENMESH
ENMITY
ERMINE
EXMOOR
EXMORE

E••M••
EDAMES
ELEMIS
ELFMAN
ENAMEL
ENAMOR
ENDMAN
ENDMEN
ETYMOL
ETYMON
EXEMPT

E•••M•
ENCAMP
ENIGMA
ENTOMO
ENZYME
EPROMS
ESKIMO

E••••M
EGOISM
ELOHIM
EMBLEM
ENGRAM
EPONYM
ERBIUM
ESTEEM

•EM•••
BEMATA
BEMINE
BEMIRE
BEMOAN
BEMUSE
CEMENT
DEMAND
DEMEAN
DEMIES
DEMISE
DEMITS
DEMOBS
DEMODE
DEMOND
DEMONS
DEMOTE
DEMURE
DEMURS
FEMALE
FEMMES
FEMORA
FEMURS
GEMARA
GEMINI
GEMMAE
GEMMED
GEMOTE
GEMOTS
HEMATO
HEMMED
HEMMER
HEMSIN
KEMPIS
LEMANS
LEMMAS
LEMMON
LEMNOS
LEMOND
LEMONS
LEMONY
LEMUEL
LEMURS
MEMBER
MEMNON
MEMOIR
MEMORY
NEMATO
REMADE
REMAIL
REMAIN
REMAKE
REMAND
REMANS
REMAPS
REMARK
REMEDY
REMELT
REMEND
REMICK
REMIND
REMISE
REMISS
REMITS
REMOLD
REMOPS
REMORA
REMOTE
REMOVE
REMOWN
REMOWS
REMUDA
SEMELE
SEMITE
SEMPER
SEMPRE
TEMPED
TEMPEH
TEMPER
TEMPLE
TEMPOS
TEMPTS
TEMPUS
YEMENI

•E•M••
BEAMED
BEAMON
BEAMUP
CERMET
DEEMED
DEIMOS
DELMAR
DERMAL
DERMIS
DESMAN
FEMMES
FENMAN
FENMEN
FERMAT
GEMMAE
GEMMED
GERMAN
GETMAD
HELMED
HELMET
HELMUT
HEMMED
HEMMER
HERMAN
HERMES
HERMIT
HERMON
HETMAN
KERMAN
KERMES
KERMIS
KERMIT
LEGMAN
LEGMEN
LEMMAS
LEMMON
MELMAC
MERMAN
MERMEN
MESMER
NETMAN
NETMEN
NEUMAN
NEUMES
NEWMAN
NEWMAR
PELMET
PENMAN
PENMEN
PERMED
PERMIT
REAMED
REAMER
SEAMAN
SEAMED
SEAMEN
SEAMUS
SEEMED
SEEMLY
SERMON
TEAMED
TEAMUP
TEEMED
TERMED
TEXMEX
VERMIN
WEIMAR
WETMOP
YEOMAN
YEOMEN
YESMAN
YESMEN
ZEEMAN

•E••M•
BECAME
BECOME
BEDIMS
BEGUMS
BENUMB
BESOMS
DEARME
DECAMP
DEFAME
DENIMS
GENOME
JEREMY
JEROME
LEGUME
LEXEME
OEDEMA
REAIMS
REALMS
REARMS
REGIME
REHEMS
RELUME
RENAME
RESUME
RETIME
REVAMP
SEDUMS
SEISMO
SEISMS
SERUMS
SESAME
VENOMS
ZEUGMA

•E•••M
BECALM
BEDLAM
BEEGUM
BELDAM
CERIUM
CESIUM
DEFORM
HELIUM
JETSAM
MEDIUM
MEGOHM
PEPLUM
REDEEM
REDGUM
REFORM
RETRIM
REWARM
SELDOM
SEPTUM
TEDEUM
TEDIUM
VELLUM
VERISM

••EM••
ALEMAN
ANEMIA
ANEMIC
APEMAN
APEMEN
ATEMPO
BREMEN
CHEMIN
CREMES
DEEMED
ELEMIS
EXEMPT
HAEMAT
HAEMON
HIEMAL
ICEMAN
ICEMEN
ONEMAN
PIEMAN
PIEMEN
PREMED
PREMIE
QUEMOY
SEEMED
SEEMLY
TEEMED
THEMED
THEMES
TREMOR
ZEEMAN

••E•M•
ADEEMS
ATEAMS
BREAMS
CREAMS
CREAMY
DREAMS
DREAMT
DREAMY
GLEAMS
GLEAMY
HBEAMS
IBEAMS
PNEUMA
PREAMP
RHEUMS
RHEUMY
STEAMS
STEAMY
STELMO
THELMA
THERMO
THERMS
WHELMS

••E••M
AGEISM
BEEGUM
COELOM
FRENUM
PHENOM
PLENUM
PRELIM
THEISM

•••EM•
ADEEMS
BIREME
CINEMA
DOREMI
GOLEMS
HAREMS
JEREMY
KINEMA
LEXEME
MODEMS
OEDEMA
PROEMS
RACEME
REHEMS
SCHEMA
SCHEME
SOLEMN
TOTEMS

•••E•M
AGLEAM
ANSELM
ESTEEM
FIVEAM
FIVEPM
INSEAM
KAREEM
LYCEUM
MUSEUM
NINEAM
NINEPM
PHLEGM
PILEUM
REDEEM
SCREAM
STREAM
TEDEUM

••••EM
ANADEM
ANTHEM
ARNHEM
DIADEM
EMBLEM
ESTEEM
HARLEM
IBIDEM
KAREEM
MAYHEM
MOSLEM
PHLOEM
PROTEM
REDEEM
SACHEM
SHOLEM
SYSTEM
TANDEM
WILLEM

EN••••
ENABLE
ENACTS
ENAMEL
ENAMOR
ENATES
ENBLOC
ENCAGE
ENCAMP
ENCASE
ENCINA
ENCINO
ENCODE
ENCORE
ENDALL
ENDASH
ENDEAR
ENDERS
ENDING
ENDIVE
ENDMAN
ENDMEN
ENDORA
ENDOWS
ENDRUN
ENDSUP
ENDUED
ENDUES
ENDURE
ENDURO
ENDUSE
ENERGY
ENESCO
ENFANT
ENFOLD
ENGAGE
ENGELS
ENGINE
ENGIRD
ENGIRT
ENGLUT
ENGRAM
ENGULF
ENHALO
ENIGMA
ENISLE
ENJOIN
ENJOYS
ENLACE
ENLIST
ENMESH
ENMITY
ENNEAD
ENNIUS
ENOKIS
ENOSIS
ENOUGH
ENQUAD
ENRAGE
ENRAPT
ENRICH
ENRICO
ENROBE
ENROLL
ENROLS
ENROOT
ENSIGN
ENSILE
ENSOUL
ENSUED
ENSUES
ENSURE
ENTAIL
ENTERO
ENTERS
ENTICE
ENTIRE
ENTITY
ENTOMO
ENTRAP
ENTREE
ENURED
ENURES
ENVIED
ENVIER
ENVIES
ENVOIS
ENVOYS
ENWRAP
ENZYME

E•N•••
ELNINO
ENNEAD
ENNIUS
EONIAN
ERNANI
ERNEST
EUNICE

E••N••
EARNED
EARNER
EBONDS
EDENIC
EGGNOG
EISNER
ELANDS
ELINOR
EMENDS
EMINOR
EPINAL
EPONYM
ERENOW
ERINYS
ERYNGO
ETHNIC
ETHNOS
ETONIC
EUPNEA
EVENED
EVENER
EVENKI
EVENLY
EVENSO
EVENTS
EVENUP
EVINCE
EVONNE

E•••N•
EALING
EARING
EASING
EATING
EBBING
ECHINO
EDGING
EDMOND
EDMUND
EDWYNN
EGGING
EGMONT
ELAINE
ELAYNE
ELNINO
EMBANK
ENCINA
ENCINO
ENDING
ENFANT
ENGINE
EOCENE
EOSINS
EPPING
EQUINE
ERMINE
ERNANI
ERRAND
ERRANT
ERRING
ERVING
ESCENT
ESPANA
ESSENE
ETERNE
ETHANE
ETHENE
EUGENE
EVONNE
EVZONE
EXEUNT
EXPAND
EXPEND
EXTANT
EXTEND
EXTENT
EYEING

E••••N
EASEIN
EASTON
EATSIN
EDGEIN
EDISON
EDWYNN
EGGSON
EILEEN
ELEVEN
ELFMAN
ELOIGN
EMBDEN
ENDMAN
ENDMEN
ENDRUN
ENJOIN
ENSIGN
EOLIAN
EONIAN
EPHRON
ETYMON
EVELYN
EXTERN

•EN•••
AENEAS
AENEID
BENDAY
BENDED
BENDER
BENDIX
BENGAL
BENGAY
BENHUR
BENIGN
BENING
BENITO
BENOIT
BENONI
BENSON
BENTON
BENUMB
BENZOL
CENOTE
CENSED
CENSER
CENSES
CENSOR
CENSUS
CENTER
CENTOS
CENTRE
CENTRI
CENTRO
DENALI
DENARY
DENDRI
DENDRO
DENGUE
DENIAL
DENIED
DENIER
DENIES
DENIMS
DENIRO
DENISE
DENNED
DENNIS
DENOTE
DENOVO
DENSER
DENTAL
DENTED
DENTIL
DENTIN
DENTON
DENUDE
DENVER
DENZEL
FENCED
FENCER
FENCES
FENDED
FENDER
FENIAN
FENMAN
FENMEN
FENNEC
FENNEL
FENWAY
GENDER
GENERA
GENETS
GENEVA
GENEVE
GENIAL
GENIES
GENIUS
GENOAN
GENOME
GENRES
GENTLE
GENTLY
GENTRY
GENUAL
HENBIT
HENLEY
HENNAS
HENNER
HENNIN
HENRIK
HENRYV
HENSON
HENTED
JENNER
JENNET
JENNEY
JENNIE
JENSEN
KENNED
KENNEL
KENNER
KENNYG
KENTON
KENYAN
LENAPE
LENDER
LENGTH
LENITY
LENNIE
LENNON
LENNOX
LENORE
LENSED
LENSES
LENTEN
LENTIL
MENACE
MENADO
MENAGE
MENDED
MENDEL
MENDER
MENDES
MENHIR
MENIAL
MENINX
MENJOU
MENKEN
MENNEN
MENSAE
MENSAL
MENSAS
MENSCH
MENTAL
MENTIS
MENTOR
NENETS
OENONE
PENANG
PENCEL
PENCIL
PENDED
PENGHU

PENMAN
PENMEN
PENNAE
PENNED
PENNER
PENNEY
PENNIA
PENNIS
PENNON
PENPAL
PENROD
PENSEE
PENTAD
PENTUP
PENULT
PENURY
RENAIL
RENAME
RENATA
RENDER
RENEGE
RENEWS
RENNES
RENNET
RENNIE
RENNIN
RENOIR
RENOTE
RENOWN
RENTAL
RENTED
RENTER
SENARY
SENATE
SENDAK
SENDER
SENDIN
SENDUP
SENECA
SENEGA
SENHOR
SENIOR
SENITI
SENLAC
SENNAS
SENNET
SENNIT
SENORA
SENORS
SENSED
SENSEI
SENSES
SENSOR
SENTIN
SENTRA
SENTRY
SENTUP
SENUFO
TENACE
TENANT
TENDED
TENDER
TENDON
TENDTO
TENENS
TENETS
TENNIS
TENONS
TENORS
TENPIN
TENREC
TENSED
TENSER
TENSES

TENSOR
TENTED
TENTER
TENTHS
TENURE
TENUTO
VENDED
VENDEE
VENDOR
VENEER
VENETO
VENIAL
VENICE
VENIRE
VENITE
VENOMS
VENOUS
VENTED
VENTER
VENUES
WENCES
WENDED
WENTAT
WENTBY
WENTIN
WENTON
WENTUP
YENNED
YENTAS
ZENANA
ZENDIC
ZENDOS
ZENGER
ZENITH

•E•N••

BEANED
BEANIE
BEANOS
BEINGS
BERNIE
DEANNA
DENNED
DENNIS
FEINTS
FENNEC
FENNEL
HEANEY
HEFNER
HENNAS
HENNER
HENNIN
HEXNUT
JEANNE
JENNER
JENNET
JENNEY
JENNIE
KEENAN
KEENED
KEENEN
KEENER
KEENLY
KENNED
KENNEL
KENNER
KENNYG
KERNED
KERNEL
KERNOI
KERNOS
KEYNES
LEANED
LEANER

LEANLY
LEANON
LEANTO
LEMNOS
LENNIE
LENNON
LENNOX
LEONES
LEONID
LEONIE
LERNER
MEANER
MEANIE
MEANLY
MEMNON
MENNEN
PEANUT
PEENED
PENNAE
PENNED
PENNER
PENNEY
PENNIA
PENNIS
PENNON
PERNIO
PERNOD
REGNAL
REGNAT
REINAS
REINED
REINER
REININ
REINKS
RENNES
RENNET
RENNIE
RENNIN
RESNIK
REUNES
SEANCE
SEENIN
SEENTO
SEINED
SEINER
SEINES
SENNAS
SENNET
SENNIT
SEWNON
SEWNUP
TEENER
TEENSY
TENNIS
TERNES
VEINAL
VEINED
VERNAL
VERNON
WEANED
WEENIE
WEENSY
WERNER
YEANED
YENNED

•E••N•

BEGINS
BEGONE
BEHIND
BELONG
BEMINE
BENING
BENONI

BERING
BESANT
BETONY
BEYOND
BEZANT
CEDANT
CEDING
CELINE
CEMENT
CESSNA
CETANE
DEANNA
DEBONE
DEBUNK
DECANT
DECENT
DEFEND
DEFINE
DEIGNS
DEKING
DELANO
DELANY
DELONG
DEMAND
DEMOND
DEMONS
DEPEND
DEPONE
DETENT
DEVINE
DEWING
FECUND
FEEING
FEIGNS
FELINE
FELONS
FELONY
FERENC
FETING
GEEING
GEMINI
GERENT
GERONT
GERUND
HELENA
HELENE
HELENS
HERONS
HEWING
HEXING
JEANNE
JEJUNE
KEARNY
KETONE
KEYING
LEARNS
LEARNT
LEGEND
LELAND
LEMANS
LEMOND
LEMONS
LEMONY
LEVANT
LEVENE
LEVINE
MEDINA
MEKONG
MELANO
MELINA
MELONS
MENINX
MERINO
MESONS

METING
MEWING
NEEDNT
NEVINS
OENONE
PECANS
PEDANT
PEKING
PEKINS
PENANG
PEPINO
REBEND
REBENT
REBIND
RECANE
RECANT
RECENT
RECONS
REDANT
REDENY
REDING
REDINK
REDONE
REFINE
REFUND
REGENT
REGINA
REHANG
REHUNG
REIGNS
RELENT
RELINE
REMAND
REMANS
REMEND
REMIND
REPAND
REPENT
REPINE
REPINS
RERENT
RERUNS
RESAND
RESEND
RESENT
RESING
RESINS
RESINY
RETENE
RETINA
RETUNE
REWIND
REWINS
REZONE
SECANT
SECOND
SEDANS
SEEING
SEJANT
SELENA
SELENE
SELENO
SERENA
SERENE
SERINE
SERINS
SETINS
SEVENS
SEWING
TECHNO
TEEING
TEJANO
TENANT
TENENS

TENONS
TETONS
TEXANS
VEGANS
VERONA
VEXING
WERENT
YEARNS
YEMENI
ZENANA

•E•••N

AEGEAN
BEACON
BEAMON
BEARON
BEATEN
BEATON
BECKON
BEMOAN
BENIGN
BENSON
BENTON
BERGEN
BERLIN
BETSON
CEYLON
DEACON
DEADEN
DEADON
DEAFEN
DEALIN
DEEPEN
DEHORN
DELEON
DEMEAN
DENTIN
DENTON
DESIGN
DESMAN
DETAIN
DEVEIN
FEEDON
FELDON
FELLIN
FELLON
FENIAN
FENMAN
FENMEN
FEZZAN
GENOAN
GERMAN
GETSIN
GETSON
HEADIN
HEADON
HEAVEN
HEBRON
HEDREN
HEDRON
HEFLIN
HEIDEN
HELDIN
HELDON
HEMSIN
HENNIN
HENSON
HEREIN
HEREON
HERMAN
HERMON
HESTON
HETMAN
JENSEN

JERKIN
JETGUN
JETSON
KEATON
KEENAN
KEENEN
KEEPIN
KEEPON
KELVIN
KENTON
KENYAN
KEPTON
KERMAN
KEYSIN
LEADEN
LEADIN
LEADON
LEANON
LEAVEN
LEBRUN
LEFTIN
LEGION
LEGMAN
LEGMEN
LEGUIN
LEIDEN
LEMMON
LENNON
LENTEN
LEPTON
LESSEN
LESSON
LETSIN
LETSON
LEYDEN
MEDIAN
MELLON
MELTON
MELVIN
MELVYN
MEMNON
MENKEN
MENNEN
MERLIN
MERLON
MERMAN
MERMEN
MERTON
MERVYN
NEATEN
NEESON
NEKTON
NELSON
NETMAN
NETMEN
NETTON
NEUMAN
NEURON
NEWMAN
NEWTON
PEAHEN
PECTIN
PEERIN
PELION
PENMAN
PENMEN
PENNON
PEPSIN
PERSON
PETAIN
PEYTON
READIN
REAGAN
REASON

REBORN
RECKON
REDDEN
REDFIN
REELIN
REGAIN
REGION
REININ
REJOIN
REMAIN
REMOWN
RENNIN
RENOWN
REOPEN
REPLAN
REPUGN
RESAWN
RESEEN
RESEWN
RESIGN
RESPIN
RESTON
RETAIN
RETTON
RETURN
REUBEN
REVLON
REVSON
SEAFAN
SEAMAN
SEAMEN
SEASON
SEATON
SECERN
SEENIN
SEEPIN
SEESIN
SENDIN
SENTIN
SEQUIN
SERKIN
SERMON
SETSIN
SETSON
SEVERN
SEWNON
SEWSON
SEXTON
TEFLON
TELLON
TENDON
TENPIN
TERRAN
TEUTON
VEBLEN
VERDIN
VERDON
VERDUN
VEREEN
VERMIN
VERNON
WEAKEN
WEAPON
WEBERN
WEDELN
WELKIN
WENTIN
WENTON
WESSON
YEOMAN
YEOMEN
YESMAN
YESMEN
ZEEMAN

ZEROIN

••EN••

AGENAS
AGENCY
AGENDA
AGENTS
AKENES
AMENDS
AMENRA
AMENTS
ARENAS
ARENDT
AVENGE
AVENUE
BLENCH
BLENDE
BLENDS
BLENNY
BRENDA
BRENTS
BUENOS
CHENIN
CLENCH
CRENEL
CRENNA
DRENCH
DUENNA
EDENIC
EMENDS
ERENOW
EVENED
EVENER
EVENKI
EVENLY
EVENSO
EVENTS
EVENUP
FAENZA
FIENDS
FLENSE
FRENCH
FRENUM
FRENZY
GLENDA
GLENNE
GUENON
HYENAS
IRENES
IRENIC
KEENAN
KEENED
KEENEN
KEENER
KEENLY
KOENIG
LIENEE
MAENAD
ODENSE
OHENRY
OPENED
OPENER
OPENLY
OPENTO
OPENUP
PEENED
PHENOL
PHENOM
PHENYL
PLENTY
PLENUM
PRENUP
PUENTE
QUENCH

RIENZI
SCENAS
SCENDS
SCENES
SCENIC
SCENTS
SEENIN
SEENTO
SIENNA
SPENDS
STENCH
STENOG
STENOS
TEENER
TEENSY
THENAR
THENCE
TRENCH
TRENDS
TRENDY
TWENTY
UPENDS
USENET
VIENNA
VIENNE
WEENIE
WEENSY
WHENCE
WIENER
WRENCH

••E•N•

AGEING
AHERNE
AVERNO
BLENNY
BOEING
CLEANS
CRENNA
CZERNY
DOESNT
DUENNA
DYEING
ETERNE
EXEUNT
EYEING
FEEING
FOEHNS
FRESNO
GEEING
GLEANS
GLENNE
GREENE
GREENS
GREENY
GRETNA
HIEING
HOEING
ILEANA
LIERNE
NEEDNT
OCEANS
PAEANS
PAEONS
PREENS
QUEENS
QUERNS
SEEING
SHEENA
SHEENS
SIENNA
SKEANS
SKEINS
STEINS

STERNA
STERNE
STERNO
STERNS
TEEING
THEEND
TIEING
TIEINS
TOEING
TOEINS
TWEENS
TWEENY
VIENNA
VIENNE

••E••N

ALEMAN
APEMAN
APEMEN
AVEDON
BREMEN
BRETON
CHEMIN
CHENIN
CRETAN
CRETIN
DEEPEN
DOESIN
DREWIN
DREWON
ELEVEN
EVELYN
FEEDON
FLEWIN
GOESIN
GOESON
GREWON
GUENON
HAEMON
HIERON
ICEDIN
ICEMAN
ICEMEN
ICESIN
ISELIN
KEENAN
KEENEN
KEEPIN
KEEPON
KMESON
LIESIN
MYELIN
NEESON
OBERON
OLEFIN
OLESON
ONEMAN
OREGON
PEERIN
PIEMAN
PIEMEN
PIEPAN
PIETIN
PREVIN
PREYON
QUEZON
REELIN
SEENIN
SEEPIN
SEESIN
STEFAN
STEPIN
STEPON
STEVEN

SWEDEN
TIEDIN
TIEPIN
TIESIN
TOEDIN
TOESIN
TREPAN
UNEVEN
ZEEMAN

•••EN•

ABSENT
ACCENT
ACHENE
ADDEND
ADRENO
ADVENT
ALIENS
ALKENE
AMIENS
APPEND
ARDENT
ARGENT
ARLENE
ARPENT
ARSENE
ASCEND
ASCENT
ASPENS
ASSENT
ATHENA
ATHENE
ATHENS
ATTEND
AUDENS
AUGEND
BRIENZ
BUTENE
CADENT
CATENA
CEMENT
CLIENT
COGENT
COVENS
COVENT
COWENS
COZENS
DARENT
DECENT
DEFEND
DEPEND
DETENT
DIZENS
DOCENT
DOLENZ
DOYENS
DOZENS
EOCENE
ESCENT
ESSENE
ETHENE
EUGENE
EXPEND
EXTEND
EXTENT
FAGEND
FERENC
FILENE
FLUENT
FOMENT
FRIEND
GALENA
GERENT
GIVENS

GREENE
GREENS
GREENY
GYRENE
HAVENS
HAVENT
HELENA
HELENE
HELENS
IMPEND
INDENE
INDENT
INTEND
INTENS
INTENT
INVENT
IRLENE
ISMENE
JOLENE
LAMENT
LATENE
LATENS
LATENT
LEGEND
LEVENE
LIKENS
LIMENS
LINENS
LINENY
LIPENG
LIVENS
LODENS
LORENZ
LOWEND
LUCENT
LUDENS
LUMENS
MAVENS
MAXENE
MIZENS
MODENA
MOMENT
MORENO
NICENE
NOCENT
NOLENS
NOVENA
NUGENT
OFFEND
ORIENT
OSTEND
PARENS
PARENT
PATENS
PATENT
POTENT
PREENS
QUEENS
RAVENS
REBEND
REBENT
RECENT
REDENY
REGENT
RELENT
REMEND
REPENT
RERENT
RESEND
RESENT
RETENE
RIDENT
RIPENS
RODENT

ROWENA
ROWENS
RUBENS
RUMENS
SABENA
SELENA
SELENE
SELENO
SERENA
SERENE
SEVENS
SHEENA
SHEENS
SILENI
SILENT
SIRENS
SOLENT
STHENO
TAGEND
TALENT
TENENS
THEEND
TOKENS
TWEENS
TWEENY
UNBEND
UNBENT
UNPENS
URGENT
VALENS
VALENT
VIXENS
VOLENS
WAKENS
WERENT
WIDENS
WISENT
WIZENS
WOMENS
XIMENA
XYLENE
YEMENI
ZAZENS

•••E•N

AEGEAN
AILEEN
ANDEAN
ARLEEN
ASTERN
AUGEAN
BALEEN
BOLEYN
BOREON
CAMEIN
CAMEON
CAREEN
CASERN
CAVEIN
CAVERN
CLUEIN
COMEIN
COMEON
DELEON
DEMEAN
DEVEIN
DINEIN
DINEON
DIVEIN
DONEIN
DOTEON
DOVEIN
DUDEEN
EASEIN

EDGEIN
EILEEN
EXTERN
FADEIN
GAVEIN
GIDEON
GIVEIN
GOVERN
HAMELN
HAVEON
HEREIN
HEREON
HIREON
INTERN
KOREAN
LATEEN
LIVEIN
LIVEON
LLBEAN
LOMEIN
LOVEIN
MCLEAN
MODERN
MOREEN
MOVEIN
MOVEON
NICEAN
OSSEIN
PIGEON
PILEIN
PILEON
POLEYN
POTEEN
RAKEIN
RESEEN
RESEWN
ROPEIN
RULEON
SATEEN
SCREEN
SECERN
SEVERN
SIMEON
SOLEMN
SPLEEN
STREWN
TAKEIN
TAKEON
TAVERN
TUNEIN
TUREEN
UNSEEN
UNSEWN
VEREEN
VOTEIN
WADEIN
WAVEIN
WEBERN
WEDELN
WOREON
WYVERN

••••EN

AACHEN
ACUMEN
ADRIEN
AILEEN
AIRMEN
ALFVEN
ANCIEN
APEMEN
ARISEN
ARLEEN
AUSTEN

AWAKEN
AWOKEN
BADMEN
BALEEN
BARMEN
BARREN
BATMEN
BATTEN
BEATEN
BERGEN
BIDDEN
BIGBEN
BIGTEN
BITTEN
BLIXEN
BORDEN
BOWMEN
BRAZEN
BREMEN
BROKEN
BUNSEN
BURDEN
BUSMEN
CAMDEN
CAREEN
CARMEN
CHOSEN
CLOVEN
CONMEN
COTTEN
COWMEN
CRAVEN
CULLEN
DAIREN
DAMIEN
DAMPEN
DARIEN
DARKEN
DARREN
DEADEN
DEAFEN
DEEPEN
DOLMEN
DRIVEN
DRYDEN
DUDEEN
EILEEN
ELEVEN
EMBDEN
ENDMEN
FALLEN
FASTEN
FATTEN
FBIMEN
FENMEN
FLAXEN
FLYMEN
FRAUEN
FROZEN
GAGMEN
GARDEN
GASMEN
GLUTEN
GOLDEN
GOODEN
GOSHEN
GOTTEN
GRABEN
GRAVEN
GUNMEN
HAPPEN
HARDEN
HARKEN
HASTEN

HAYDEN
HEAVEN
HEDREN
HEIDEN
HIDDEN
HITMEN
HOLDEN
HOYDEN
HYPHEN
ICEMEN
IMOGEN
JANSEN
JENSEN
KEENEN
KITTEN
KJOLEN
KRAKEN
KUCHEN
LARSEN
LASSEN
LATEEN
LATTEN
LAUREN
LAWMEN
LAYMEN
LEADEN
LEAVEN
LEGMEN
LEIDEN
LENTEN
LESSEN
LEYDEN
LICHEN
LINDEN
LISTEN
LOOSEN
LOUDEN
LUDDEN
LUMPEN
LUNDEN
MADDEN
MADMEN
MADSEN
MAIDEN
MAJGEN
MALDEN
MARTEN
MCKUEN
MENKEN
MENNEN
MERMEN
MIDDEN
MIRREN
MITTEN
MIZZEN
MOLTEN
MOREEN
MORGEN
MUDHEN
NANSEN
NEATEN
NETMEN
NGUYEN
NISSEN
OBRIEN
OILMEN
OLDMEN
ORIGEN
OXYGEN
PATTEN
PEAHEN
PENMEN
PIEMEN
PIGPEN
PINKEN
PITMEN
PLATEN
POLLEN
POTEEN
PROVEN
RAGMEN
REDDEN
REOPEN
RESEEN
REUBEN
RICHEN
RIDDEN
RIPKEN
ROTTEN
SADDEN
SALTEN
SATEEN
SCREEN
SEAMEN
SHAKEN
SHAVEN
SICKEN
SILKEN
SLOVEN
SODDEN
SOFTEN
SPLEEN
SPOKEN
STAMEN
STATEN
STEVEN
STOLEN
SUDDEN
SULLEN
SUNKEN
SWEDEN
TAUTEN
TAXMEN
TILDEN
TINMEN
TOPTEN
TUREEN
UNEVEN
UNOPEN
UNSEEN
USOPEN
VARDEN
VEBLEN
VEREEN
VIVIEN
WALDEN
WALKEN
WARDEN
WARREN
WEAKEN
WHITEN
WOODEN
WOOLEN
WORSEN
XIAMEN
YEOMEN
YESMEN

EO••••
EOCENE
EOIPSO
EOLIAN
EOLITH
EONIAN
EOSINS

E•O•••
EBOATS
EBONDS
ECOLES
EGOISM
EGOIST
ELOHIM
ELOIGN
ELOISE
ELOPED
ELOPER
ELOPES
EMOTED
EMOTER
EMOTES
ENOKIS
ENOSIS
ENOUGH
EPOCHS
EPODES
EPONYM
EPOPEE
ERODED
ERODES
EROICA
EROTIC
ETOILE
ETONIC
EVOKED
EVOKER
EVOKES
EVOLVE
EVONNE
EXODUS
EXOTIC

E••O••
EATOUT
ECHOED
ECHOES
ECHOIC
EDDOES
EDKOCH
EDMOND
EDWOOD
EEYORE
EFFORT
EGMONT
EIDOLA
EKEOUT
ELBOWS
ELMORE
ELWOOD
EMBODY
EMBOSS
ENCODE
ENCORE
ENDORA
ENDOWS
ENFOLD
ENJOIN
ENJOYS
ENROBE
ENROLL
ENROLS
ENROOT
ENSOUL
ENTOMO
ENVOIS
ENVOYS
EPHODS
EPHORI
EPHORS
EPROMS
ERGOTS
ERROLL
ERRORS
ESCORT
ESPOSA
ESPOSO
ESTOPS
EUBOEA
EUDORA
EULOGY
EUROPA
EUROPE
EVZONE
EXHORT
EXMOOR
EXMORE
EXPORT
EXPOSE
EXPOST
EXTOLS
EXTORT
EXVOTO

E•••O•
EASTON
EDISON
EDITOR
EDWOOD
EGGNOG
EGGSON
EJIDOS
ELINOR
ELLIOT
ELWOOD
EMAJOR
EMINOR
EMPLOY
EMPTOR
ENAMOR
ENBLOC
ENROOT
EPHRON
EPILOG
ERENOW
ESCROW
ETHNOS
ETUXOR
ETYMOL
ETYMON
EXMOOR

E••••O
ECHINO
EDITIO
ELNINO
ELPASO
EMBRYO
EMILIO
ENCINO
ENDURO
ENESCO
ENHALO
ENRICO
ENTERO
ENTOMO
EOIPSO
ERYNGO
ESCUDO
ESKIMO
ESPOSO
EVENSO
EVERSO
EXACTO
EXVOTO

•EO•••
AEOLIA
AEOLIC
AEOLUS
CEORLS
DEODAR
GEODES
GEORGE
GEORGY
LEONES
LEONID
LEONIE
MEOWED
PEOPLE
PEORIA
REOILS
REOPEN
YEOMAN
YEOMEN

•E•O••
AEROBE
BEBOPS
BECOME
BEFOGS
BEFORE
BEFOUL
BEGOFF
BEGONE
BEHOLD
BEHOOF
BEHOVE
BELOIT
BELONG
BEMOAN
BENOIT
BENONI
BESOMS
BESOTS
BETONY
BETOOK
BEYOND
CENOTE
DEBONE
DECOCT
DECODE
DECORS
DECOYS
DEFOGS
DEFORM
DEHORN
DELONG
DEMOBS
DEMODE
DEMOND
DEMONS
DEMOTE
DENOTE
DENOVO
DEPONE
DEPORT
DEPOSE
DEPOTS
DESOTO
DETOUR
DEVOID
DEVOIR
DEVOTE
DEVOTO
DEVOUR
DEVOUT
EEYORE
FEDORA
FELONS
FELONY
FEMORA
GEMOTE
GEMOTS
GENOAN
GENOME
GERONT
GETOFF
GETOUT
HELOTS
HEROES
HEROIC
HERONS
JEROME
KEBOBS
KETONE
LEDOFF
LEDOUT
LEMOND
LEMONS
LEMONY
LENORE
LETOFF
LETOUT
MEGOHM
MEKONG
MELODY
MELONS
MELOTT
MEMOIR
MEMORY
MEROPE
MESONS
METOPE
NEROLI
OENONE
PEKOES
PELOPS
PELOTA
PEYOTE
REBOIL
REBOLT
REBOOT
REBORN
REBOZO
RECOAT
RECODE
RECOIL
RECONS
RECOPY
RECORD
RECORK
RECOUP
REDOAK
REDOES
REDONE
REFORM
REHOOK
REJOIN
RELOAD
RELOCK
REMOLD
REMOPS
REMORA
REMOTE
REMOVE
REMOWN
REMOWS
RENOIR
RENOTE
RENOWN
REPOLL
REPORT
REPOSE
REPOST
REPOTS
RESODS
RESOLD
RESOLE
RESORB
RESORT
RETOLD
RETOOK
RETOOL
RETOPS
RETORT
RETOUR
RETOWS
REVOIR
REVOKE
REVOLT
REWORD
REWORK
REWOVE
REZONE
SECOND
SEEOFF
SEEOUT
SENORA
SENORS
SEPOYS
SEROSA
SEROUS
SEROWS
SETOFF
SETOSE
SETOUT
TEEOFF
TENONS
TENORS
TETONS
VELOCE
VELOUR
VENOMS
VENOUS
VERONA
VETOED
VETOER
VETOES
XEDOUT
ZEROED
ZEROES
ZEROIN
ZEROTH

•E••O•
BEACON
BEAMON
BEANOS
BEARON
BEATON
BECKON
BEHOOF
BELLOC
BELLOW
BENSON
BENTON
BENZOL
BESTOW
BETOOK
BETSON
BETTOR
CELLOS
CENSOR
CENTOS
CERROS
CESTOS
CEYLON
DEACON
DEADON
DEBTOR
DEIMOS
DEKKOS
DELEON
DELROY
DENTON
DEPLOY
DESPOT
DETROP
FEEDON
FELDON
FELLOE
FELLON
FELLOW
FERVOR
GECKOS
GETSON
HEADON
HEAROF
HEBRON
HECTOR
HEDRON
HELDON
HELIOS
HELLOS
HENSON
HEREOF
HEREON
HERIOT
HERMON
HERZOG
HESIOD
HESTON
HEYYOU
JERBOA
JETSON
KEATON
KEEPON
KENTON
KEPTON
KERNOI
KERNOS
LEADON
LEANON
LECTOR
LEGION
LEMMON
LEMNOS
LENNON
LENNOX
LEPTON
LESBOS
LESSON
LESSOR
LETSON
MEADOW
MELLON
MELLOW
MELTON
MEMNON
MENJOU
MENTOR
MERLON
MERLOT
MERTON
METEOR
METHOD
METROS
MEZZOS
NEESON
NEKTON
NELSON
NESTOR
NETTON
NEUROL
NEURON
NEWTON
PEAPOD
PEGTOP
PELION
PENNON
PENROD
PEPLOS
PEQUOD
PEQUOT
PERIOD
PERNOD
PERROT
PERSON
PESCOW
PESTOS
PETROG
PETROL
PEYTON
REASON
REBOOT
RECKON
RECTOR
RECTOS
REDDOG
REDFOX
REDHOT
REDSOX
REDTOP
REEBOK
REGION
REHOOK
REPLOW
REPROS
RESHOD
RESHOE
RESHOT
RESTON
RETOOK
RETOOL
RETROS
RETTON
REVLON
REVSON
SEACOW
SEADOG
SEAFOX
SEASON
SEATON
SECTOR
SELDOM
SENHOR
SENIOR
SENSOR
SERMON
SERVOS
SESTOS
SETSON
SETTOS
SEWNON
SEWSON
SEXTON
TEAPOT
TEAPOY
TEFLON
TELLOF
TELLON
TEMPOS
TENDON
TENSOR
TERROR
TEUTON
VECTOR
VENDOR
VERDON
VERNON
VERSOS
WEAPON
WENTON
WESSON
WETMOP
YELLOW
ZEALOT
ZENDOS

•E•••O
BENITO
CENTRO
DELANO
DELRIO
DENDRO
DENIRO
DENOVO
DESOTO
DEVITO
DEVOTO
DEXTRO
FELLTO
GEARTO
GELATO
GETSTO
HELDTO
HEMATO
HERETO
HETERO
JETHRO
KEEPTO
LEADTO
LEANTO
LEGATO
LETSGO
MEDICO
MEGALO
MEJICO
MELANO
MENADO
MERINO
MEXICO
NEARTO
NEMATO
NEPHRO
NEXTTO
PEPINO
PERNIO
REBOZO
REECHO
SEENTO
SEESTO
SEISMO
SELENO
SENUFO
SERGIO
TECHNO
TEJANO
TENDTO
TENUTO
TERATO
TEREDO
TEXACO
VELCRO
VENETO
WEIRDO

••EO••
ACEOUS
ACEOUT
AGEOLD
AREOLA
ATEOUT
CHEOPS
CREOLE
DIEOFF
DIEOUT
EKEOUT
ICEOUT
PAEONS
SEEOFF
SEEOUT
TEEOFF
THEORY

••E•O•
AVEDON
BRETON
BUENOS
CHEKOV
COELOM
CREDOS
CRESOL
DREWON
DYELOT
ERENOW
FAEROE
FEEDON
FLEXOR
FOETOR
GOESON
GREGOR
GREWON
GUENON
HAEMON
HIERON
HUEVOS
ICEBOX
ICEFOG
KEEPON
KMESON
LIELOW
NEESON
OBERON
OCELOT
OLESON
OREGON
PHENOL
PHENOM
PLEXOR
PREYON
PYEDOG
QUEMOY
QUEZON
REEBOK
RHEBOK
RHETOR
STEFOY
STENOG
STENOS
STEPON
STEROL
THETOY
TIEROD
TREMOR
TREVOR

••E••O
AIELLO
ALECTO
ALEPPO
AMEDEO
AREZZO
ATEMPO
ATERGO
AVERNO
CHEAPO
DUELLO
ENESCO
EVENSO
EVERSO
FRESCO
FRESNO
GHETTO
KEEPTO
LIESTO
NIELLO
ONETWO
OPENTO
OTELLO
OVERDO
PIETRO
PRESTO
PSEUDO
PUEBLO
PUERTO
REECHO
SEENTO
SEESTO
SPEEDO
STELMO
STEREO
STERNO
THERMO
TIEDTO
TIESTO
UNESCO
USEDTO

•••EO•
BLUEOX
BOREON
BUTEOS
CAMEON
CAMEOS
COMEON
DELEON
DINEON
DOTEON
GIDEON
HAVEON
HEREOF
HEREON
HIREON
LIVEON
METEOR
MIMEOS
MOVEON
PASEOS
PIGEON
PILEON
RODEOS
ROLEOS
ROMEOS
RULEON
SIMEON
TAKEON
VIDEOS
VIREOS
WOREON

•••E•O
ADRENO
ALBEDO
ANGELO
ANTERO
BOLERO
CAMETO
CARETO
CICERO
COMETO
DARETO
DINERO
ENTERO
FOREGO
GAZEBO
GIVETO
GRAECO
HERETO
HETERO
HIDEHO
HOVETO
LAREDO
MACEIO
MADEDO
MADERO
MAKEDO
MORENO
NONEGO
NUMERO
OSWEGO
OVIEDO
PARETO
PHLEBO
PINERO
POMELO
ROMERO
SASEBO
SCLERO
SELENO
SIDERO
SOWETO
SPEEDO
STHENO
TAKETO
TEREDO
TOLEDO
TORERO
TUPELO
TUXEDO
VENETO
WISETO
ZYDECO

••••EO
AMEDEO
BORNEO
NUCLEO
PALAEO
STEREO

EP••••
EPARCH
EPHAHS
EPHEBE
EPHODS
EPHORI
EPHORS
EPHRON
EPICAL
EPILOG
EPINAL
EPIRUS
EPOCHS
EPODES
EPONYM
EPOPEE
EPPING
EPROMS

E•P•••
ELPASO
EMPERY
EMPIRE
EMPLOY
EMPTOR
EPPING
ESPANA
ESPIAL
ESPIED
ESPIES
ESPOSA
ESPOSO
ESPRIT
EUPNEA
EXPAND
EXPECT
EXPELS
EXPEND
EXPERT
EXPIRE
EXPIRY
EXPORT
EXPOSE
EXPOST

E••P••
ELAPID
ELAPSE
ELOPED
ELOPER
ELOPES
EOIPSO
EPOPEE
ERUPTS
ETAPES

E•••P•
ECTYPE
ENRAPT
EQUIPS
ESCAPE
ESTOPS
EUROPA
EUROPE
EXCEPT
EXEMPT

E••••P
EARLAP
EASEUP
EATSUP
EGGCUP
ENCAMP
ENDSUP
ENTRAP
ENWRAP
ESCARP
ESHARP
EVENUP
EYECUP

•EP•••
DEPART
DEPAUL
DEPAUW
DEPEND
DEPICT
DEPLOY
DEPONE
DEPORT
DEPOSE
DEPOTS
DEPTHS
DEPUTE
DEPUTY
HEPCAT
HEPPER
HEPTAD
KEPLER
KEPTAT
KEPTON
KEPTUP
LEPTON
NEPALI
NEPHEW
NEPHRO
PEPFUL
PEPINO
PEPITA
PEPLOS
PEPLUM
PEPPED
PEPPER
PEPSIN
PEPSUP
PEPTIC
REPADS
REPAID
REPAIR
REPAND
REPAST
REPAVE
REPAYS
REPEAL
REPEAT
REPEGS
REPELS
REPENT
REPINE
REPINS
REPLAN
REPLAY
REPLOW
REPOLL
REPORT
REPOSE
REPOST
REPOTS
REPROS
REPUGN
REPUTE
SEPALS
SEPIAS
SEPOYS
SEPTAL
SEPTET
SEPTIC
SEPTUM
TEPALS
TEPEES
TEPHRA
ZEPHYR

•E•P••
BEEPED
BEEPER
DEEPAK
DEEPEN
DEEPER
DEEPLY
DELPHI
DESPOT
HEAPED
HELPED
HELPER
HEPPER
KEEPAT
KEEPER
KEEPIN
KEEPON
KEEPTO
KEEPUP
KELPIE
KEMPIS
KEWPIE
KEYPAD
LEAPED
LEAPER
NETPAY
PEAPOD
PEEPED
PEEPER
PENPAL
PEOPLE
PEPPED
PEPPER
REAPED
REAPER
REOPEN
RESPIN
SEEPED
SEEPIN
SEMPER
SEMPRE
TEAPOT
TEAPOY
TEMPED
TEMPEH
TEMPER
TEMPLE
TEMPOS
TEMPTS
TEMPUS
TENPIN
VESPER
VESPID
WEAPON
WEEPER
WEEPIE
YELPED
YELPER

•E••P•
BEBOPS
CERIPH
FELIPE
GETUPS
LENAPE
LETUPS
MEROPE
METOPE
PELOPS
RECAPS
RECIPE
RECOPY
REMAPS
REMOPS
RETAPE
RETAPS
RETOPS
RETYPE
SERAPE
SERAPH
SETUPS
TERAPH

•E•••P
BEADUP
BEAMUP
BEARUP
BEATUP

BEEFUP DECAMP DETROP DEWLAP FESSUP GEARUP GETSUP HEADUP HEATUP HELDUP KEEPUP KEPTUP KEYSUP LEADUP LETSUP MEGILP MESSUP PEGTOP PENTUP PEPSUP PERKUP REARUP RECOUP REDCAP REDTOP RESHIP RESTUP REVAMP REVSUP REWRAP SEALUP SENDUP SENTUP SETSUP SEWNUP SEWSUP TEACUP TEAMUP TEARUP TEEDUP TEESUP WELLUP WENTUP WETMOP

••EP••

ADEPTS ALEPHS ALEPPO BEEPED BEEPER CLEPED CREPES DEEPAK DEEPEN DEEPER DEEPLY DIEPPE KEEPAT KEEPER KEEPIN KEEPON KEEPTO KEEPUP PEEPED PEEPER PIEPAN PREPAY PREPPY SEEPED SEEPIN STEPIN STEPON STEPPE STEPUP TIEPIN TREPAN TREPID WEEPER WEEPIE

••E•P•

ALEPPO ATEMPO BLEEPS CHEAPO CHEEPS CHEOPS CREEPS CREEPY DIEPPE EXEMPT GUELPH ONEUPS PREPPY SHEEPS SHERPA SLEEPS SLEEPY STEEPS STEPPE SWEEPS TIEUPS TWERPS WHELPS

••E••P

ACESUP AMERSP BEEFUP BLEWUP CHEWUP DOESUP DREWUP EVENUP EYECUP GOESUP GREWUP ICECAP ICEDUP ICESUP KEEPUP OPENUP PREAMP PRENUP SPEDUP STEPUP TEEDUP TEESUP THELIP TIEDUP TIESUP TOECAP TOETAP USEDUP USESUP

•••EP•

ACCEPT BICEPS BLEEPS CHEEPS CREEPS CREEPY EXCEPT FIVEPM INCEPT JOSEPH JULEPS NINEPM SHEEPS SLEEPS SLEEPY STEEPS SWEEPS

•••E•P

ANTEUP ASLEEP BONEUP BOPEEP BOREUP CAMEUP COMEUP DONEUP EASEUP FACEUP FIREUP GAVEUP GIVEUP HIKEUP HOLEUP HYPEUP LACEUP LINEUP MADEUP MAKEUP MOVEUP PILEUP PIPEUP RAKEUP RAVEUP RILEUP SAVEUP SIZEUP STREEP TAKEUP TONEUP TOREUP TUNEUP TYPEUP UPKEEP WAKEUP WIPEUP WISEUP WOKEUP

••••EP

ASLEEP BOPEEP DOMREP INSTEP SCHLEP STREEP TRICEP UPKEEP

EQ••••

EQUALS EQUATE EQUINE EQUIPS EQUITY

E•Q•••

EMQUAD ENQUAD

E•••Q•

ETSEQQ

E••••Q

ETSEQQ

•EQ•••

PEQUOD PEQUOT SEQUEL SEQUIN

•E•Q••

SESQUI

••EQ••

CHEQUE

•••EQ•

ETSEQQ

•••E•Q

ETSEQQ

••••EQ

SUSIEQ

ER••••

ERASED ERASER ERASES ERBIUM EREBUS ERECTS ERENOW ERESTU ERFURT ERGATE ERGOTS ERHARD ERINYS ERMINE ERNANI ERNEST ERODED ERODES EROICA EROTIC ERRAND ERRANT ERRARE ERRATA ERRING ERROLL ERRORS ERSATZ ERUCTS ERUPTS ERVING ERYNGO

E•R•••

EARFUL EARING EARLAP EARNED EARNER EARTHA EARTHY EARWAX EARWIG EERIER EERILY EGRESS EGRETS ENRAGE ENRAPT ENRICH ENRICO ENROBE ENROLL ENROLS ENROOT EPROMS ERRAND ERRANT ERRARE ERRATA ERRING ERROLL ERRORS EURAIL EUREKA EUROPA EUROPE EYRIES

E••R••

EAGRES EBERLY ECARTE EDERLE EGERIA ELBRUS EMBRYO EMERGE ENDRUN ENERGY ENGRAM ENTRAP ENTREE ENURED ENURES ENWRAP EPARCH EPHRON EPIRUS ESCROW ESDRAS ESPRIT ESTRAY ETERNE EVERLY EVERSO EVERTS EXARCH EXERTS EXTRAS EXURBS

E•••R•

EATERS EATERY EDBERG EDGARD EDGARS EDGERS EDUARD EDVARD EDWARD EELERS EEYORE EFFORT EGBERT EIDERS EKBERG ELBERT ELDERS ELLERY ELMIRA ELMORE ELVERS ELVIRA EMBARK EMBERS EMEERS EMIGRE EMPERY EMPIRE ENCORE ENDERS ENDORA ENDURE ENDURO ENGIRD ENGIRT ENSURE ENTERO ENTERS ENTIRE EPHORI EPHORS ERFURT ERHARD ERRARE ERRORS ESCARP ESCORT ESHARP ESKERS ESTERS ETHERS EUCHRE EUDORA EXEDRA EXHORT EXMORE EXPERT EXPIRE EXPIRY EXPORT EXSERT EXTERN EXTORT EZZARD

E••••R

EARNER EASIER EASTER ECLAIR EDGIER EDITOR EELIER EERIER EGGIER EISNER EITHER ELATER ELAYER ELINOR ELIXIR ELOPER ELUDER EMAJOR EMINOR EMOTER EMPTOR ENAMOR ENDEAR ENVIER ERASER ESCHER ESTHER ETCHER ETUXOR EVADER EVENER EVILER EVOKER EXETER EXMOOR

•ER•••

AERATE AERIAL AERIES AERIFY AERILY AEROBE BERATE BERBER BEREFT BERETS BERGEN BERING BERLIN BERNIE BERTHA BERTHS BERTIE CERATE CEREAL CEREUS CERIPH CERISE CERIUM CERMET CERROS CERTIF CERUSE CERVID DERAIL DERIDE DERIVE DERMAL DERMIS DERRIS EERIER EERILY FERBER FERENC FERGIE FERGUS FERIAL FERIAS FERITY FERMAT FERRER FERRET FERRIC FERRIS FERULE FERVID FERVOR GERAHS GERALD GERARD GERBER GERBIL GERENT GERMAN GERONT GERTIE GERUND HERALD HERBAL HERBIE HERDED HERDER HEREAT HEREBY HEREIN HEREOF HEREON HERESY HERETO HERIOT HERMAN HERMES HERMIT HERMON HEROES HEROIC HERONS HERSEY HERZOG JERBOA JEREMY JERKED JERKIN JEROME JERSEY KERALA KERMAN KERMES KERMIS KERMIT KERNED KERNEL KERNOI KERNOS KERSEE KERSEY LERIDA LERNER MERCED MERCER MERELY MEREST MERGED MERGER MERGES MERIDA MERINO MERITS MERKEL MERLIN MERLON MERLOT MERMAN MERMEN MEROPE MERSEY MERTON MERVYN NEREID NEREIS NEREUS NEROLI NERUDA NERVES OERTER PERCHA PERDUE PERILS PERIOD PERISH PERKED PERKUP PERMED PERMIT PERNIO PERNOD PERROT PERSIA PERSON PERTER PERTLY PERUGA PERUKE PERUSE RERATE REREAD RERENT RERUNS SERACS SERAIS SERAPE SERAPH SERBIA SERENA SERENE SERGEI SERGES SERGIO SERIAL SERIES SERIFS SERINE SERINS SERKIN SERMON SEROSA SEROUS SEROWS SERUMS SERVAL SERVED SERVER SERVES SERVOS TERAPH TERATO TERCEL TERCET TEREDO TERESA TERETE TEREUS TERKEL TERMED TERNES TERRAN TERRET TERROR TERSER VERBAL VERBIS VERDIN VERDON VERDUN VEREEN VERGED VERGER VERGES VERIFY VERILY VERISM VERITE VERITY VERMIN VERNAL VERNON VERONA VERSED VERSES VERSOS VERSTS VERSUS VERTEX VERVES VERVET WERENT WERFEL WERNER XERXES YERKED YERKES ZEROED ZEROES ZEROIN ZEROTH

•E•R••

BEARDS BEARER BEARON BEARUP BEIRUT BETRAY BEURRE BEWRAY CEDRIC CEORLS CERROS DEARER DEARIE DEARLY DEARME DEARTH DEBRAS DEBRIS DECREE DEFRAY DEGREE DELRAY DELRIO DELROY DERRIS DETROP FEARED FEARER FERRER FERRET FERRIC FERRIS GEARED GEARTO GEARUP GEHRIG GENRES GEORGE GEORGY HEARER HEAROF HEARST HEARTH HEARTS HEARTY HEARYE HEBREW HEBRON HEDREN HEDRON HENRIK HENRYV JEERAT JEERED JEERER KEARNY LEARNS LEARNT LEBRUN LEERAT LEERED LEERER LEGREE LEHRER MEERUT METRES METRIC METROS NEARBY NEARED NEARER NEARLY NEARTO NEURAL NEUROL NEURON PEARLS PEARLY PEERAT PEERCE PEERED PEERIN PENROD PEORIA PERROT PETREL PETRIE PETROG PETROL REARED REARER REARMS REARUP REDRAW REDREW REGRET REPROS RETRAL RETRIM RETROS REWRAP SEARCH SEARED SEARLE SECRET SEERED SEURAT SEVRES TEARAT TEARED TEARUP TENREC TERRAN TERRET TERROR TETRAD TETRAS TETRIS VEERED WEARER WEIRDO WEIRDY YEARLY YEARNS ZEBRAS

•E••R•

BEFORE BELFRY BEMIRE BEURRE BEWARE CEDARS CELERY CENTRE CENTRI CENTRO CESARE CETERA DEBARK DEBARS DECORS DEFERS DEFORM DEHORN DEIDRE DEJURE DEMURE DEMURS DENARY DENDRI DENDRO DENIRO DEPART DEPORT DESCRY DESERT DESIRE DESTRY DETERS DEXTRO EELERS EEYORE FEDORA FEMORA FEMURS FEVERS GEMARA GENERA GENTRY GERARD GEZIRA HEGARI HEGIRA HETERO HEWERS HEXERS JETHRO KEFIRS LEMURS LENORE LEVERS MEAGRE MEGARA MEMORY MESSRS METERS NEPHRO NEVERS NEWARK OEUVRE PELTRY PENURY PETARD PETERS REAIRS REBARS REBORN REBURY RECORD RECORK RECURS REFERS REFORM REGARD REHIRE REMARK REMORA REPORT RESORB RESORT RETARD RETARS RETIRE RETORT RETURN REVERB REVERE REVERS REVERT REWARD REWARM REWIRE REWORD REWORK SEBERG SECERN SECURE SEDERS SEGURA SEMPRE SENARY SENORA SENORS SENTRA SENTRY SEVERE SEVERN SEVERS SEVERY SEWARD SEWERS TENORS TENURE TEPHRA VELCRO VENIRE VESTRY VEXERS WEBERN

•E•••R

AETHER BEAKER BEARER BEATER BEAVER BECKER BEEPER BEGGAR BELAIR BENDER BENHUR BERBER BESSER BESTIR BETTER BETTOR CELLAR CENSER CENSOR CENTER DEADER DEAFER DEALER DEARER DEBTOR DECKER DEEPER DEFTER DEICER DELMAR DELVER DENIER DENSER DENVER DEODAR DETOUR DEVOIR DEVOUR DEWIER DEXTER EELIER EERIER FEARER FEEDER FEELER FELLER FENCER FENDER FERBER FERRER FERVOR FESTER FETTER GEEZER GEIGER GENDER GERBER GETTER GEYSER HEADER HEALER HEARER HEATER HEAVER HECTOR HEDGER HEEDER HEELER HEFNER HEIFER HELLER HELPER HELTER HEMMER HENNER HEPPER HERDER HESTER JEERER JEETER JENNER JESTER KEELER KEENER KEEPER KEGLER KELLER KENNER KEPLER KEVLAR LEADER LEAKER LEANER LEAPER LEASER LECTER LECTOR LEDGER LEERER LEHRER LEKVAR LENDER LERNER LESSER LESSOR LESTER LETTER LEVIER LEWDER MEAGER MEANER MEDGAR MEDLAR MEEKER MEETER MEMBER MEMOIR MENDER MENHIR MENTOR MERCER MERGER MESMER METEOR METIER MEWLER NEARER NEATER NECTAR NESTER NESTOR NETHER NEUTER NEWMAR OERTER PEDLAR PEELER PEEPER PEGLER PELTER PENNER PEPPER PERTER PESTER PETTER PEWTER READER REALER REAMER REAPER REARER RECTOR REDDER REDFIR REEFER REHEAR REINER RENDER RENOIR RENTER REPAIR RESTER RETEAR RETOUR REUTER REVOIR SEALER SEATER SECTOR SEEDER SEEGER SEEKER SEINER SEIZER SELLER SEMPER SENDER SENHOR SENIOR SENSOR SERVER SETTER SEXIER TEASER TEDDER TEENER TEETER TELLER TEMPER TENDER TENSER TENSOR TENTER TERROR TERSER TESTER TETHER VECTOR VEDDER VELOUR VENDOR VENEER VENTER VERGER VESPER VETOER WEAKER WEARER WEAVER WEBBER WEEDER WEEPER WEIMAR WELDER WELLER WELTER WERNER WETBAR WETHER WETTER YEAGER YELLER YELPER YESSIR YESTER ZEDBAR ZENGER ZEPHYR

••ER••

AHERNE ALERTS AMERCE AMERSP ANERGY APERCU ATERGO AVERNO AVERSE AVERTS BIERCE CHERIE CHERRY CHERTY CHERUB CHERYL CLERGY CLERIC

CLERKS
COERCE
CZERNY
DJERBA
EBERLY
EDERLE
EGERIA
EMERGE
ENERGY
ETERNE
EVERLY
EVERSO
EVERTS
EXERTS
FAERIE
FAEROE
FIERCE
GUERRE
HIERON
IBERIA
JEERAT
JEERED
JEERER
LEERAT
LEERED
LEERER
LIERNE
MEERUT
OBERON
OMERTA
OPERAS
OVERDO
OVERLY
PEERAT
PEERCE
PEERED
PEERIN
PIERCE
PIERRE
PUERTO
QUERNS
QWERTY
SEERED
SHEREE
SHERIF
SHERPA
SHERRY
SHERYL
SIERRA
SKERRY
SMERSH
SPERRY
STEREO
STERES
STERNA
STERNE
STERNO
STERNS
STEROL
SWERVE
THERES
THERMO
THERMS
TIERCE
TIERED
TIEROD
TIERRA
TWERPS
USERID
VEERED
WHERED
WHERES
WHERRY

••E•R•

AFEARD
ALEGRE
AMEERS
AMENRA
AWEARY
BLEARS
BLEARY
CHEERS
CHEERY
CHERRY
CHEVRE
CLEARS
DREARY
EMEERS
EXEDRA
FLEERS
FLEURY
GUERRE
OHENRY
OLEARY
PHEDRE
PIERRE
PIETRO
PLEURA
POETRY
SHEARS
SHEERS
SHERRY
SIERRA
SKERRY
SMEARS
SMEARY
SNEERS
SNEERY
SOEURS
SPEARS
SPERRY
STEERS
SWEARS
THEIRS
THEORY
THEYRE
TIERRA
WHERRY

••E••R

ALEGAR
ASEVER
BEEPER
BREUER
BREWER
BREYER
CAESAR
CHEWER
CLEVER
DEEPER
DIETER
DUELER
EVENER
EXETER
FEEDER
FEELER
FLEXOR
FOETOR
FUELER
GEEZER
GREGOR
GREYER
HEEDER
HEELER
JAEGER
JEERER
JEETER
KEELER
KEENER
KEEPER
KIEFER
LEERER
LIEDER
LIEFER
MEEKER
MEETER
OPENER
PEELER
PEEPER
PIECER
PIETER
PLEXOR
PREFER
PRETER
PREWAR
QUEUER
REEFER
RHETOR
SEEDER
SEEGER
SEEKER
SKEWER
STELAR
STEWER
TEENER
TEETER
THENAR
TREMOR
TREVOR
VIEWER
WEEDER
WEEPER
WIENER

•••ER•

ADDERS
ADHERE
ADVERB
ADVERT
AIDERS
AILERS
ALBERT
ALDERS
ALPERT
ALTERS
AMBERS
AMBERY
AMEERS
AMPERE
ANGERS
ANTERO
ARTERY
ASKERS
ASPERA
ASSERT
ASTERN
ASTERS
AUGERS
BAKERS
BAKERY
BALERS
BIKERS
BITERS
BOLERO
BONERS
BORERS
BOWERS
BOWERY
BOXERS
BRIERS
BRIERY
BUYERS
CABERS
CAGERS
CAMERA
CANERS
CAPERS
CASERN
CATERS
CAVERN
CAVERS
CELERY
CETERA
CHEERS
CHEERY
CICERO
CIDERS
CITERS
CODERS
COHERE
COMERS
COOERS
CORERS
COVERS
COVERT
COWERS
CRIERS
CRYERS
CURERS
CYDERS
DATERS
DEFERS
DESERT
DETERS
DICERS
DINERO
DINERS
DIVERS
DIVERT
DIYERS
DOSERS
DOWERS
DOWERY
DOZERS
DRIERS
DRYERS
DUNERA
DUPERY
EATERS
EATERY
EDBERG
EDGERS
EELERS
EGBERT
EIDERS
EKBERG
ELBERT
ELDERS
ELLERY
ELVERS
EMBERS
EMEERS
EMPERY
ENDERS
ENTERO
ENTERS
ESKERS
ESTERS
ETHERS
EXPERT
EXSERT
EXTERN
FAKERS
FAKERY
FARERS
FEVERS
FIBERS
FIFERS
FILERS
FINERY
FIRERS
FIVERS
FIXERS
FLEERS
FLIERS
FLYERS
FOYERS
FRIERS
FRYERS
GAPERS
GATERS
GENERA
GIBERS
GIVERS
GLUERS
GOFERS
GONERS
GOVERN
HALERS
HALERU
HATERS
HAVERS
HAZERS
HETERO
HEWERS
HEXERS
HIDERS
HIKERS
HIRERS
HOMERS
HOPERS
HOVERS
HUBERT
HUMERI
IDLERS
IMPERF
INFERS
INHERE
INKERS
INSERT
INTERJ
INTERN
INVERT
JAPERS
JAPERY
JIVERS
JOKERS
KAGERA
KHMERS
KITERS
LACERS
LADERS
LAGERS
LAKERS
LASERS
LAVERS
LAYERS
LEVERS
LIBERI
LIFERS
LIGERS
LINERS
LITERS
LIVERS
LIVERY
LONERS
LOPERS
LOSERS
LOVERS
LOWERS
LOWERY
LUGERS
MADERO
MAKERS
MASERS
MASERU
MATERS
MAZERS
METERS
MILERS
MIMERS
MINERS
MISERS
MISERY
MITERS
MIXERS
MODERN
MONERA
MOPERS
MOPERY
MOVERS
MOWERS
MOYERS
MUSERS
NAMERS
NAPERY
NEVERS
NFLERS
NHLERS
NINERS
NITERS
NITERY
NOTERS
NUMERO
OATERS
OBVERT
OCHERS
OCHERY
OFFERS
OGLERS
OILERS
ORDERS
ORNERY
ORRERY
OSIERS
OTHERS
OTTERS
OWNERS
PACERS
PAGERS
PAPERS
PAPERY
PARERS
PATERS
PAVERS
PAWERS
PAYERS
PETERS
PIKERS
PINERO
PINERY
PIPERS
PLIERS
POKERS
POKERY
POLERS
POSERS
POWERS
PRIERS
RACERS
RAKERS
RASERS
RATERS
RAVERS
REFERS
REVERB
REVERE
REVERS
REVERT
RICERS
RIDERS
RISERS
RIVERA
RIVERS
ROBERT
ROGERS
ROMERO
ROPERS
ROVERS
ROWERS
RULERS
RUPERT
SABERS
SAKERS
SAVERS
SAYERS
SCLERA
SCLERO
SEBERG
SECERN
SEDERS
SEVERE
SEVERN
SEVERS
SEVERY
SEWERS
SHEERS
SHOERS
SIDERO
SIDERS
SISERA
SIXERS
SIZERS
SKIERS
SNEERS
SNEERY
SOBERS
SOLERS
SOMERS
SOWERS
SOXERS
SPHERE
SPHERY
SPIERS
STEERS
SUPERB
SUPERS
TAKERS
TALERS
TAMERS
TAPERS
TASERS
TATERS
TAVERN
TAXERS
TIGERS
TILERS
TIMERS
TITERS
TONERS
TOPERS
TORERO
TOTERS
TOWERS
TOWERY
TRIERS
TUBERS
TUNERS
TUYERE
TYPERS
UDDERS
ULCERS
UMBERS
UPPERS
URGERS
USHERS
UTTERS
VALERY
VEXERS
VIDERI
VINERY
VIPERS
VOTERS
VOWERS
WADERS
WAFERS
WAFERY
WAGERS
WALERS
WANERS
WATERS
WATERY
WAVERS
WAVERY
WAXERS
WEBERN
WINERY
WIPERS
WIRERS
WOOERS
WYVERN

•••E•R

APPEAR
ARREAR
AUTEUR
CAREER
COHEIR
DOGEAR
ENDEAR
INGEAR
LINEAR
METEOR
POSEUR
RATEDR
REHEAR
RETEAR
TINEAR
VENEER

••••ER

ABUSER
ACHIER
ADORER
AETHER
AIRIER
ALITER
AMBLER
AMPLER
ANGLER
ANSWER
ANTHER
ANTLER
ARCHER
ARGUER
ARTIER
ASEVER
ASHIER
AVOWER
BACKER
BADDER
BADGER
BAGGER
BAILER
BALDER
BANGER
BANKER
BANNER
BANTER
BARBER
BARKER
BARTER
BASTER
BATHER
BATTER
BAWLER
BAXTER
BEAKER
BEARER
BEATER
BEAVER
BECKER
BEEPER
BENDER
BERBER
BESSER
BETTER
BICKER
BIDDER
BIGGER
BINDER
BIRDER
BITTER
BLADER
BLAZER
BLOWER
BOATER
BOBBER
BOILER
BOLDER
BOLGER
BOMBER
BONIER
BOOKER
BOOMER
BOPPER
BORDER
BOTHER
BOVVER
BOWLER
BOWSER
BOWYER
BOXIER
BRACER
BRAVER
BRAYER
BRAZER
BREUER
BREWER
BREYER
BROKER
BRUDER
BUFFER
BUGLER
BULWER
BUMMER
BUMPER
BUNKER
BUNTER
BURGER
BURNER
BUSIER
BUSTER
BUTLER
BUTTER
BUZZER
CABLER
CADGER
CAGIER
CAHIER
CAKIER
CALDER
CALLER
CALMER
CAMBER
CAMPER
CANIER
CANKER
CANNER
CANTER
CAPPER
CARDER
CAREER
CARPER
CARTER
CARVER
CASPER
CASTER
CATHER
CENSER
CENTER
CHASER
CHEWER
CHIDER
CHOKER
CHOLER
CINDER
CIPHER
CLAWER
CLEVER
CLOSER
CLOVER
COALER
COAXER
COCKER
CODGER
COFFER
COINER
COKIER
COLDER
COLTER
COMBER
CONFER
CONGER
CONKER
CONNER
COODER
COOKER
COOLER
COOPER
COOTER
COPIER
COPPER
COPTER
CORKER
CORNER
COSIER
COTTER
COUTER
COWPER
COZIER
CRATER
CRAVER
CROWER
CRUDER
CULLER
CULVER
CUMBER
CURLER
CURTER
CUSTER
CUTLER
CUTTER
CYCLER
CYPHER
DAFTER
DAGGER
DAMPER
DANCER
DANDER
DANGER
DANKER
DANNER
DAPPER
DARKER
DARNER
DARTER
DASHER
DAUBER
DEADER
DEAFER
DEALER
DEARER
DECKER
DEEPER
DEFTER
DEICER
DELVER
DENIER
DENSER
DENVER
DEWIER
DEXTER
DIALER
DIAPER
DICIER
DICKER
DIETER
DIFFER
DIGGER
DILLER
DIMMER
DINNER
DIPPER
DITHER
DLAYER
DOBBER
DOCKER
DODDER
DODGER
DOGGER
DONDER
DONNER
DOPIER
DORMER
DOSSER
DOURER
DOWNER
DOWSER
DOZIER
DRAPER
DRAWER
DRIVER
DRONER
DROVER
DUELER
DUFFER
DUIKER
DULLER
DUMBER
DUMPER
DUNKER
DUSTER
EARNER
EASIER
EASTER
EDGIER
EELIER
EERIER
EGGIER
EISNER
EITHER
ELATER
ELAYER
ELOPER
ELUDER
EMOTER
ENVIER
ERASER
ESCHER
ESTHER
ETCHER
EVADER
EVENER
EVILER
EVOKER
EXETER
FABLER
FAIRER
FALSER
FALTER
FARMER
FASTER
FATHER
FATTER
FAWNER
FEARER
FEEDER
FEELER
FELLER
FENCER
FENDER
FERBER
FERRER
FESTER
FETTER
FIBBER
FILLER
FILTER
FINDER
FINGER
FIRMER
FISHER
FITTER
FLAKER
FLAYER
FLOWER
FODDER
FOGGER
FOKKER
FOLDER
FONDER
FOOLER
FOOTER
FORCER
FORGER
FORKER
FORMER
FOSTER
FOULER
FOWLER
FOXIER
FRASER
FRAZER
FUELER
FULLER
FUMIER
GABBER
GABLER
GADDER
GAFFER
GAINER
GAITER
GAMIER
GAMMER
GANDER
GANGER
GAOLER
GARNER
GARTER
GASPER
GASSER
GATHER
GAUGER
GAWKER
GEEZER
GEIGER
GENDER
GERBER
GETTER
GEYSER
GIBBER
GILDER
GINGER
GIPPER
GIRDER
GLASER
GLAZER
GLIDER
GLOVER
GLOWER
GLUIER
GNAWER
GOLFER
GOOBER
GOOIER
GOOVER
GOPHER
GORIER
GOUGER
GRADER
GRATER
GRAVER
GRAYER
GRAZER
GREYER
GRIPER
GROCER
GROVER
GROWER
GULPER
GUNNER
GUNTER
GUSHER
GUTTER
GYPPER
HACKER
HALTER
HAMMER
HAMPER
HANGER
HANKER
HARDER
HARKER
HARPER
HATTER
HAULER
HAWKER
HAWSER
HAZIER
HEADER
HEALER
HEARER
HEATER
HEAVER
HEDGER
HEEDER
HEELER
HEFNER
HEIFER
HELLER
HELPER
HELTER
HEMMER
HENNER
HEPPER
HERDER
HESTER
HIGHER
HILLER
HINDER
HINTER
HIPPER
HISSER
HITHER
HITTER
HOAXER
HOKIER
HOLDER
HOLIER
HOLLER
HOMIER
HONKER
HOOFER
HOOPER
HOOTER
HOOVER
HOPPER
HORNER
HOSIER
HOTTER
HOWLER
HUGGER
HULLER
HUMMER
HUNGER
HUNKER
HUNTER
HURLER
HUSKER
ICKIER
IFFIER
IMAGER
INANER
INKIER
IRATER
IRONER
ISOMER
ISSUER
JABBER
JAEGER
JAGGER
JAILER
JAMMER
JASPER
JAVIER
JEERER
JEETER
JENNER
JESTER
JIGGER
JITTER
JIVIER
JOBBER
JOGGER
JOINER
JOKIER
JOSSER
JOYNER
JUDDER
JUICER
JUMPER
JUNKER
JUSTER
KAISER
KANDER
KAVNER
KEELER
KEENER
KEEPER
KEGLER
KELLER
KENNER
KEPLER
KHYBER
KICKER
KIDDER
KIEFER
KILLER
KILMER
KILTER
KINDER
KIPPER
KISSER
KNOWER
KOHLER
KOSHER
KOTTER
KRAMER
KRATER
KRONER
KRUGER
LAAGER
LACIER
LADDER
LADLER
LAFFER
LAGGER
LAKIER
LANCER
LANDER
LANIER
LANKER
LARDER
LARGER
LASHER
LASSER
LATHER
LATTER
LAUDER
LAUPER
LAWYER
LAZIER
LEADER
LEAKER
LEANER
LEAPER
LEASER
LECTER
LEDGER
LEERER
LEHRER
LENDER
LERNER
LESSER
LESTER
LETTER
LEVIER
LEWDER
LIBBER
LIEDER
LIEFER
LIFTER
LIMBER
LIMIER
LIMNER
LIMPER
LINGER
LINIER
LINKER
LINTER
LISTER
LITTER
LOADER
LOAFER
LOANER
LOBBER
LOCKER
LODGER
LOGGER
LOGIER
LOITER
LONGER
LOOKER
LOOPER
LOOSER
LOOTER
LOPPER
LOUDER
LOUVER
LUBBER
LUGGER
LUMBER
LUMPER
LUNKER
LUSHER
LUSTER
LUTHER
MADDER
MAHLER
MAILER
MANGER
MANNER
MAPPER
MARKER
MARNER
MASHER
MASKER
MASTER
MATHER
MATTER
MAULER
MAUSER
MAZIER
MEAGER
MEANER
MEEKER
MEETER
MEMBER
MENDER
MERCER
MERGER
MESMER
METIER
MEWLER
MIDLER
MILDER
MILKER
MILLER
MILNER
MINCER
MINDER
MINTER

MIRIER
MISTER
MOANER
MOCKER
MOILER
MOLDER
MOLTER
MONGER
MOPIER
MOPPER
MOSHER
MOTHER
MOUSER
MUDDER
MUGGER
MULLER
MUMMER
MURDER
MUSHER
MUSTER
MUTTER
NABBER
NAGGER
NAILER
NAPIER
NAPPER
NASSER
NATTER
NEARER
NEATER
NESTER
NETHER
NEUTER
NICKER
NIGHER
NIPPER
NOBLER
NOSHER
NOSIER
NUDGER
NUMBER
NURSER
NUTTER
OATIER
OBITER
OERTER
OILIER
OLIVER
ONAGER
OOZIER
OPENER
OPINER
OSTLER
OUSTER
OYSTER
PACKER
PADDER
PALIER
PALMER
PALTER
PAMPER
PANDER
PANNER
PANZER
PAPIER
PARKER
PARSER
PASSER
PATTER
PAUPER
PAWNER
PEELER
PEEPER
PEGLER

PELTER
PENNER
PEPPER
PERTER
PESTER
PETTER
PEWTER
PFIZER
PHASER
PICKER
PIECER
PIETER
PILFER
PINCER
PINIER
PINKER
PINNER
PINTER
PIPIER
PITIER
PITTER
PLACER
PLANER
PLATER
PLAYER
PLOVER
PLOWER
POKIER
POLDER
POLLER
PONDER
POORER
POPPER
PORKER
PORTER
POSHER
POSTER
POTHER
POTTER
POURER
POUTER
POWDER
PRATER
PRAYER
PREFER
PRETER
PRICER
PRIMER
PROBER
PROPER
PROSER
PROVER
PRUNER
PUCKER
PUFFER
PUMPER
PUNIER
PUNKER
PUNTER
PURRER
PURSER
PUTTER
QUAKER
QUAVER
QUEUER
QUIVER
QUOTER
RACIER
RADNER
RAFTER
RAIDER
RAILER
RAINER
RAISER

RANGER
RANKER
RANTER
RAPIER
RAPPER
RASHER
RASPER
RASTER
RATHER
RATTER
READER
REALER
REAMER
REAPER
REARER
REDDER
REEFER
REINER
RENDER
RENTER
RESTER
REUTER
RHYMER
RICHER
RIFLER
RIGGER
RIMIER
RINGER
RIOTER
RIPPER
RISKER
RITTER
ROAMER
ROARER
ROBBER
ROCKER
ROHMER
ROLLER
ROMPER
ROOFER
ROOMER
ROOTER
ROPIER
ROSIER
ROSTER
ROTTER
ROUSER
ROUTER
ROZZER
RUBBER
RUDDER
RUINER
RUMMER
RUNNER
RUTGER
SACKER
SADDER
SALTER
SALVER
SANDER
SANGER
SAPPER
SASSER
SAUCER
SAUGER
SAWYER
SCALER
SCARER
SCORER
SCOTER
SEALER
SEATER
SEEDER
SEEGER

SEEKER
SEINER
SEIZER
SELLER
SEMPER
SENDER
SERVER
SETTER
SEXIER
SHAKER
SHAPER
SHARER
SHAVER
SHINER
SHIRER
SHIVER
SHOVER
SHOWER
SICKER
SIFTER
SIGHER
SIGNER
SILVER
SIMMER
SIMPER
SINGER
SINKER
SINNER
SINTER
SIPPER
SISLER
SISTER
SITTER
SKATER
SKEWER
SKIVER
SLATER
SLAVER
SLAYER
SLICER
SLIDER
SLIVER
SLOWER
SMILER
SMOKER
SNIDER
SNIPER
SNORER
SNYDER
SOAKER
SOAPER
SOARER
SOBBER
SOCCER
SOFTER
SOLDER
SOLVER
SOMBER
SOMMER
SOONER
SORTER
SOURER
SOUTER
SPACER
SPADER
SPARER
SPIDER
SPIKER
SPRIER
SPRYER
STAGER
STALER
STARER
STATER

STEWER
STIVER
STOKER
STONER
STORER
STOVER
STUMER
STYLER
SUAVER
SUCKER
SUFFER
SULKER
SUMMER
SUMNER
SUMTER
SUNDER
SUPPER
SURFER
SUTLER
SUTTER
SWAYER
SWIPER
TACKER
TALKER
TALLER
TAMPER
TANKER
TANNER
TAPPER
TARTER
TASTER
TATTER
TAUTER
TEASER
TEDDER
TEENER
TEETER
TELLER
TEMPER
TENDER
TENSER
TENTER
TERSER
TESTER
TETHER
THALER
THAYER
TICKER
TIDIER
TIGGER
TILLER
TILTER
TIMBER
TINDER
TINIER
TINKER
TINNER
TINTER
TIPPER
TITFER
TITHER
TITTER
TOILER
TONIER
TOOTER
TOPPER
TOSSER
TOTHER
TOTTER
TOURER
TOUTER
TOWNER
TRACER
TRADER

TRITER
TUCKER
TUGGER
TURNER
TUSKER
TWOFER
TYPIER
UGLIER
ULSTER
UNDOER
UNITER
USURER
VAGUER
VAINER
VAMPER
VANIER
VASTER
VEDDER
VENEER
VENTER
VERGER
VESPER
VETOER
VIEWER
VINIER
VIZIER
WAGNER
WAILER
WAITER
WAIVER
WALKER
WALLER
WALTER
WANDER
WANIER
WANNER
WAPNER
WARDER
WARIER
WARMER
WARNER
WASHER
WASTER
WAVIER
WAXIER
WEAKER
WEARER
WEAVER
WEBBER
WEEDER
WEEPER
WELDER
WELLER
WELTER
WERNER
WETHER
WETTER
WHALER
WHINER
WHITER
WICKER
WIENER
WILDER
WILIER
WINCER
WINDER
WINGER
WINIER
WINKER
WINNER
WINTER
WIRIER
WISHER
WISTER

WITHER
WOHLER
WOLPER
WONDER
WOOFER
WORKER
WOWSER
WRITER
WYNTER
XAVIER
XYSTER
YABBER
YAKKER
YAMMER
YASSER
YAWNER
YAWPER
YEAGER
YELLER
YELPER
YESTER
YONDER
YORKER
ZAFFER
ZANDER
ZANIER
ZAPPER
ZENGER
ZIMMER
ZINGER
ZIPPER
ZITHER
ZONKER
ZUIDER

ES••••

ESCAPE
ESCARP
ESCENT
ESCHER
ESCHEW
ESCORT
ESCROW
ESCUDO
ESDRAS
ESHARP
ESKERS
ESKIMO
ESPANA
ESPIAL
ESPIED
ESPIES
ESPOSA
ESPOSO
ESPRIT
ESSAYS
ESSENE
ESTATE
ESTEEM
ESTERS
ESTHER
ESTOPS
ESTRAY

E•S•••

EASEIN
EASELS
EASEUP
EASIER
EASILY
EASING
EASTER
EASTON
EDSELS
EISNER
ENSIGN
ENSILE
ENSOUL
ENSUED
ENSUES
ENSURE
EOSINS
ERSATZ
ESSAYS
ESSENE
ETSEQQ
EXSERT

E••S••

EATSAT
EATSIN
EATSUP
ECESIC
ECESIS
EDESSA
EDISON
EGESTA
EGESTS
EGGSON
ELISHA
ELISSA
ELYSEE
ENDSUP
ENESCO
ENISLE
ENOSIS
ERASED
ERASER
ERASES
ERESTU
EXISTS

E•••S•

EDESSA
EFFUSE
EGOISM
EGOIST
EGRESS
ELAPSE
ELDEST
ELFISH
ELISSA
ELOISE
ELPASO
ELVISH
EMBOSS
EMDASH
ENCASE
ENDASH
ENDUSE
ENLIST
ENMESH
EOIPSO
ERNEST
ESPOSA
ESPOSO
EVENSO
EVERSO
EVULSE
EXCESS
EXCISE
EXCUSE
EXPOSE
EXPOST

E••••S

EAGLES
EAGRES
EASELS
EATERS
EBOATS
EBONDS
ECCLES
ECESIS
ECHOES
ECLATS
ECOLES
EDAMES
EDDIES
EDDOES
EDGARS
EDGERS
EDICTS
EDILES
EDSELS
EDUCES
EELERS
EFLATS
EGESTS
EGRESS
EGRETS
EIDERS
EIGHTS
EJECTS
EJIDOS
ELANDS
ELATES
ELBOWS
ELBRUS
ELDERS
ELECTS
ELEMIS
ELEVES
ELIDES
ELITES
ELOPES
ELUDES
ELUTES
ELVERS
EMAILS
EMBAYS
EMBEDS
EMBERS
EMBOSS
EMCEES
EMEERS
EMENDS
EMMETS
EMOTES
ENACTS
ENATES
ENDERS
ENDOWS
ENDUES
ENGELS
ENJOYS
ENNIUS
ENOKIS
ENOSIS
ENROLS
ENSUES
ENTERS
ENURES
ENVIES
ENVOIS
ENVOYS
EOSINS
EPHAHS
EPHODS
EPHORS
EPIRUS
EPOCHS
EPODES
EPROMS
EQUALS
EQUIPS
ERASES
EREBUS
ERECTS
ERGOTS
ERINYS
ERODES
ERRORS
ERUCTS
ERUPTS
ESDRAS
ESKERS
ESPIES
ESSAYS
ESTERS
ESTOPS
ETAPES
ETCHES
ETHERS
ETHICS
ETHNOS
ETUDES
EVADES
EVENTS
EVERTS
EVICTS
EVOKES
EXACTS
EXALTS
EXCELS
EXCESS
EXERTS
EXILES
EXISTS
EXODUS
EXPELS
EXTOLS
EXTRAS
EXUDES
EXULTS
EXURBS
EYRIES

•ES•••

BESANT
BESETS
BESIDE
BESOMS
BESOTS
BESSER
BESSIE
BESTED
BESTIR
BESTOW
CESARE
CESIUM
CESSED
CESSES
CESSNA
CESTAS
CESTOS
CESTUS
DESALT
DESCRY
DESERT
DESICA
DESIGN
DESILU
DESIRE
DESIST
DESMAN
DESOTO
DESPOT
DESTRY
FESCUE
FESSED
FESSES
FESSUP
FESTAL
FESTAS
FESTER
FESTUS
GESTES
GESTIC
HESIOD
HESTER
HESTIA
HESTON
JESSEL
JESSIE
JESTED
JESTER
JESUIT
KESHIA
LESAGE
LESBOS
LESLEY
LESLIE
LESSEE
LESSEN
LESSER
LESSON
LESSOR
LESTAT
LESTER
MESABI
MESCAL
MESHED
MESHES
MESMER
MESONS
MESSED
MESSES
MESSRS
MESSUP
NESSES
NESSIE
NESTEA
NESTED
NESTER
NESTLE
NESTOR
PESACH
PESAWA
PESCOW
PESETA
PESTER
PESTLE
PESTOS
RESALE
RESALT
RESAND
RESAWN
RESAWS
RESCUE
RESEAL
RESEAT
RESEAU
RESECT
RESEDA
RESEED
RESEEN
RESEES
RESELL
RESEND
RESENT
RESETS
RESEWN
RESEWS
RESHES
RESHIP
RESHOD
RESHOE
RESHOT
RESIDE
RESIGN
RESILE
RESING
RESINS
RESINY
RESIST
RESNIK
RESODS
RESOLD
RESOLE
RESORB
RESORT
RESPIN
RESTED
RESTER
RESTON
RESTUP
RESULT
RESUME
SESAME
SESQUI
SESTET
SESTOS
TESLAS
TESSIE
TESTAE
TESTED
TESTEE
TESTER
VESPER
VESPID
VESSEL
VESTAL
VESTAS
VESTED
VESTEE
VESTRY
WESKIT
WESLEY
WESSEX
WESSON
YESMAN
YESMEN
YESSED
YESSES
YESSIR
YESTER
ZESTED

•E•S••

BEASTS
BENSON
BESSER
BESSIE
BETSEY
BETSON
CEASED
CEASES
CENSED
CENSER
CENSES
CENSOR
CENSUS
CESSED
CESSES
CESSNA
DEASIL
DEISTS
DENSER
FEASTS
FEISTY
FESSED
FESSES
FESSUP
GEISEL
GEISHA
GELSEY
GETSAT
GETSBY
GETSET
GETSIN
GETSIT
GETSON
GETSTO
GETSUP
GEYSER
HEISTS
HEMSIN
HENSON
HERSEY
JENSEN
JERSEY
JESSEL
JESSIE
JETSAM
JETSET
JETSKI
JETSON
KELSEY
KERSEE
KERSEY
KEYSIN
KEYSUP
LEASED
LEASER
LEASES
LENSED
LENSES
LESSEE
LESSEN
LESSER
LESSON
LESSOR
LETSAT
LETSBE
LETSGO
LETSIN
LETSON
LETSUP
MEASLY
MENSAE
MENSAL
MENSAS
MENSCH
MERSEY
MESSED
MESSES
MESSRS
MESSUP
NEESON
NEISSE
NELSON
NESSES
NESSIE
NEVSKY
PENSEE
PEPSIN
PEPSUP
PERSIA
PERSON
REASON
REDSEA
REDSOX
REESES
REUSED
REUSES
REVSON
REVSUP
SEASON
SEESAW
SEESIN
SEESTO
SEISMO
SEISMS
SENSED
SENSEI
SENSES
SENSOR
SETSAT
SETSBY
SETSIN
SETSON
SETSUP
SEWSON
SEWSUP
TEASED
TEASEL
TEASER
TEASES
TEASET
TEESUP
TENSED
TENSER
TENSES
TENSOR
TERSER
TESSIE
VERSED
VERSES
VERSOS
VERSTS
VERSUS
VESSEL
WEASEL
WESSEX
WESSON
YEASTS
YEASTY
YESSED
YESSES
YESSIR

•E••S•

BEHEST
BEKESY
BEMUSE
BETISE
CERISE
CERUSE
DEBASE
DEFUSE
DEGUST
DELIST
DEMISE
DENISE
DEPOSE
DESIST
DETEST
DEVEST
DEVISE
FETISH
FEWEST
FEYEST
HEARST
HERESY
JEWISH
LEGIST
MEDUSA
MEREST
NEISSE
NEWEST
NEWISH
PERISH
PERUSE
RECAST
RECESS
RECUSE
REFUSE
REHASH
RELISH
RELIST
REMISE
REMISS
REPAST
REPOSE
REPOST
RESIST
RETEST
REVISE
REWASH
SEROSA
SETOSE
SEXIST
TEENSY
TERESA
VERISM
WEENSY

•E•••S

AEETES
AENEAS
AEOLUS
AERIES
BEANOS
BEARDS
BEASTS
BEAUTS
BEAVIS
BEBOPS
BEDEWS
BEDIMS
BEEVES
BEFITS
BEFOGS
BEGETS
BEGINS
BEGUMS
BEIGES
BEINGS
BELAYS
BELIES
BELLES
BERETS
BERTHS
BESETS
BESOMS
BESOTS
BETELS
BETTAS
BEVELS
BEVIES
BEZELS
CEASES
CEDARS
CEIBAS
CELEBS
CELLOS
CENSES
CENSUS
CENTOS
CEORLS
CEREUS
CERROS
CESSES
CESTAS
CESTOS
CESTUS
DEBARS
DEBITS
DEBRAS
DEBRIS
DEBUGS
DEBUTS
DECAFS
DECALS
DECAYS
DECORS
DECOYS
DEFATS
DEFERS
DEFIES
DEFOGS
DEICES
DEIGNS
DEIMOS
DEISTS
DEKKOS
DELAYS
DELFTS
DELIUS
DELTAS
DELVES
DEMIES
DEMITS
DEMOBS
DEMONS
DEMURS
DENIES
DENIMS
DENNIS
DEPOTS
DEPTHS
DERMIS
DERRIS
DETERS
DEUCES
DEVILS
EELERS
FEASTS
FEIGNS
FEINTS
FELLAS
FELONS
FEMMES
FEMURS
FENCES
FERGUS
FERIAS
FERRIS
FESSES
FESTAS
FESTUS
FEVERS
FEZZES
GECKOS
GELEES
GEMOTS
GENETS
GENIES
GENIUS

GENRES GEODES GERAHS GESTES GETUPS HEARTS HEATHS HEAVES HEDGES HEISTS HELENS HELIOS HELLAS HELLOS HELOTS HELVES HENNAS HERMES HEROES HERONS HEWERS HEXADS HEXERS JEEVES JEWELS KEBABS KEBOBS KEDGES KEFIRS KEMPIS KERMES KERMIS KERNOS KEVELS KEYNES LEARNS LEASES LEAVES LEDGES LEGALS LEHUAS LEMANS LEMMAS LEMNOS LEMONS LEMURS LENSES LEONES LESBOS LETUPS LEVEES LEVELS LEVERS LEVIES MECCAS MEDALS MEDIAS MEDICS MELEES MELONS MENDES MENSAS MENTIS MERGES MERITS MESHES MESONS MESSES MESSRS METALS METERS METRES METROS MEZZOS

NEIGHS NENETS NEREIS NEREUS NERVES NESSES NEUMES NEVERS NEVINS NEWELS PEARLS PECANS PEDALS PEEVES PEKINS PEKOES PELEUS PELOPS PELVIS PENNIS PEPLOS PERILS PESTOS PETALS PETERS PEWEES PEWITS REACTS REAIMS REAIRS REALES REALMS REARMS REATAS REBAGS REBARS REBBES REBECS REBELS REBIDS REBUTS RECAPS RECESS RECONS RECTOS RECTUS RECURS REDOES REDUBS REDYES REESES REEVES REFERS REFITS REGIUS REHABS REHEMS REIGNS REINAS REINKS REKEYS RELAYS RELETS RELICS RELIES REMANS REMAPS REMISS REMITS REMOPS REMOWS RENEWS RENNES REOILS

REPADS REPAYS REPEGS REPELS REPINS REPOTS REPROS RERUNS RESAWS RESEES RESETS RESEWS RESHES RESINS RESODS RETAGS RETAPS RETARS RETIES RETOPS RETOWS RETROS REUNES REUSES REVELS REVERS REVETS REVUES REWEDS REWINS SEAMUS SEDANS SEDERS SEDGES SEDUMS SEGUES SEINES SEISMS SEIZES SELVES SENNAS SENORS SENSES SEPALS SEPIAS SEPOYS SERACS SERAIS SERGES SERIES SERIFS SERINS SEROUS SEROWS SERUMS SERVES SERVOS SESTOS SETINS SETTOS SETUPS SEVENS SEVERS SEVRES SEWERS TEASES TEHEES TEMPOS TEMPTS TEMPUS TENENS TENETS TENNIS TENONS

TENORS TENSES TENTHS TEPALS TEPEES TEREUS TERNES TESLAS TETHYS TETONS TETRAS TETRIS TEXANS VEGANS VELDTS VENOMS VENOUS VENUES VERBIS VERGES VERSES VERSOS VERSTS VERSUS VERVES VESTAS VETOES VEXERS WEAVES WEDGES WEIGHS WELLES WENCES XEBECS XERXES YEARNS YEASTS YENTAS YERKES YESSES ZEBRAS ZENDOS ZEROES ZEUXIS

••ES••

ABESSE ACESUP ADESTE ATESTS AVESTA AYESHA CAESAR CHESTS CHESTY CRESOL CRESTS CUESTA DIESEL DIESES DIESIS DOESBY DOESIN DOESNT DOESUP DRESSY ECESIC ECESIS EDESSA EGESTA EGESTS ENESCO ERESTU FIESTA FLESHY FRESCA FRESCO FRESNO GOESAT GOESBY GOESIN GOESON GOESUP GUESTS ICESIN ICESUP ILESHA INESSE KMESON KRESGE LIESIN LIESTO NEESON NOESIS ODESSA OLESON PRESET PRESTO QUESTS REESES RHESUS SEESAW SEESIN SEESTO SIESTA TEESUP THESEA THESES THESIS THESIX TIESIN TIESTO TIESUP TMESIS TOESIN UNESCO USESUP WIESEL WRESTS

••E•S•

ABESSE AGEISM AGEIST ALEAST AMERSP ATEASE AVERSE BREAST CHEESE CHEESY CLEESE CREASE CREASY CREUSA DRESSY EDESSA EVENSO EVERSO FLENSE FREEST GNEISS GOEASY GREASE GREASY INESSE KLEIST KWEISI NLEAST ODENSE ODESSA ORELSE PLEASE QUEASY SMERSH TEENSY THEISM THEIST TSETSE TWEEST UNEASE UNEASY WEENSY

••E••S

ABELES ACEOUS ADEEMS ADEPTS AEETES AGENAS AGENTS AKELAS AKENES ALEPHS ALERTS ALEUTS ALEXIS AMEBAS AMEERS AMENDS AMENTS ANELES APEXES ARECAS ARENAS ARETES ATEAMS ATESTS AVERTS BCELLS BEEVES BLEARS BLEATS BLEEDS BLEEPS BLENDS BREADS BREAKS BREAMS BREEDS BRENTS BREVES BREVIS BUENOS CHEATS CHECKS CHEEKS CHEEPS CHEERS CHELAS CHEOPS CHESTS CHETHS CLEANS CLEARS CLEATS CLEEKS CLEFTS CLERKS CLEVES CLEVIS

CREAKS CREAMS CREDOS CREEDS CREEKS CREELS CREEPS CREMES CREPES CRESTS CZECHS DIESES DIESIS DREADS DREAMS DWEEBS DWELLS ECESIS EGESTS EJECTS ELECTS ELEMIS ELEVES EMEERS EMENDS EREBUS ERECTS EVENTS EVERTS EXERTS FIELDS FIENDS FJELDS FLECKS FLEERS FLEETS FLEXES FOEHNS FOETUS FREAKS GLEAMS GLEANS GLEBES GNEISS GREATS GREBES GREEKS GREENS GREETS GUESTS HBEAMS HUEVOS HYENAS IBEAMS IBEXES IDEALS ILEXES IRENES JEEVES KNEADS KNEELS KNELLS KVELLS LIEBYS LIEGES LIEUTS NIECES NOESIS NUECES OBEAHS OBELUS OCEANS OMEGAS ONEUPS

OPERAS OREADS OXEYES PAEANS PAEONS PEEVES PIECES PIETAS PLEADS PLEATS PLEBES PLEXUS PRECIS PREENS PSEUDS QUEENS QUELLS QUERNS QUESTS QUEUES REESES REEVES RHESUS RHEUMS SCENAS SCENDS SCENES SCENTS SHEAFS SHEARS SHEENS SHEEPS SHEERS SHEETS SHEIKS SHELLS SIEGES SIEVES SKEANS SKEINS SLEEKS SLEEPS SLEETS SMEARS SMELLS SMELTS SNEAKS SNEERS SNELLS SOEURS SPEAKS SPEARS SPECKS SPEEDS SPELLS SPENDS STEADS STEAKS STEALS STEAMS STEEDS STEELS STEEPS STEERS STEINS STELES STENOS STERES STERNS SUEDES SWEARS SWEATS SWEDES SWEEPS

SWEETS SWELLS THEBES THEFTS THEIRS THEMES THERES THERMS THESES THESIS THETAS THETIS TIEINS TIEUPS TMESIS TOEINS TREADS TREATS TRENDS TWEAKS TWEEDS TWEENS TWEETS TWERPS UPENDS VNECKS WHEALS WHEATS WHEELS WHELKS WHELMS WHELPS WHERES WIELDS WREAKS WRECKS WRESTS YIELDS

•••ES•

ABBESS ABLEST ACCESS AFRESH ALWEST APTEST ARNESS ARREST ASSESS ATBEST ATREST ATTEST BAREST BASEST BEHEST BEKESY BLUEST BLUESY CARESS CHEESE CHEESY CLEESE COYEST CUTEST CUTESY DETEST DEVEST DIGEST DIREST DIVEST DRIEST DRYEST DURESS EGRESS

ELDEST ENMESH ERNEST EXCESS FEWEST FEYEST FINEST FOREST FREEST GAMEST GAYEST GOWEST HALEST HERESY HONEST HUGEST ICIEST IDLEST ILLEST INFEST INGEST INJEST INNESS INVEST IQTEST LAMESA LAMEST LATEST LAXEST LOWEST MEREST MODEST MOLEST MUTEST NEWEST NICEST NLWEST NOLESS NUDEST OBSESS OBTEST ODDEST OGRESS OLDEST PALEST PRIEST PUREST RAREST RAWEST RECESS RETEST RIFEST RIPEST RUDEST SAFEST SAGEST SANEST SHIEST SHYEST SLIEST SLYEST SOREST STRESS SUREST TALESE TAMEST TERESA THRESH TRUEST TWEEST UNLESS UNMESH UNREST VARESE

VILEST WALESA WIDEST WISEST WRIEST WRYEST YAREST

•••E•S

ABBESS ABBEYS ACCESS ADDERS ADEEMS ADIEUS AENEAS AGLETS AGREES AIDERS AILERS ALDERS ALIENS ALLEES ALLEYS ALTERS AMBERS AMEERS AMIENS AMVETS ANGELS ANGERS ARDEBS ARMETS ARNESS ARTELS ASKERS ASPENS ASSESS ASSETS ASTERS ATHENS ATREUS AUDENS AUGERS AUREUS AZTECS BABELS BAGELS BAKERS BALERS BEDEWS BEGETS BERETS BESETS BETELS BEVELS BEZELS BICEPS BIKERS BIPEDS BITERS BLEEDS BLEEPS BLUETS BLUEYS BOGEYS BONERS BOREAS BORERS BOTELS BOWERS BOXERS BREEDS BRIEFS

BRIERS BUTEOS BUYERS CABERS CADETS CAGERS CAMELS CAMEOS CANERS CAPERS CARESS CARETS CATERS CAVERS CELEBS CEREUS CHEEKS CHEEPS CHEERS CHIEFS CIDERS CITERS CIVETS CLEEKS CODERS COLEUS COMERS COMETS CONEYS COOERS CORERS COVENS COVERS COVETS COVEYS COWENS COWERS COZENS CREEDS CREEKS CREELS CREEPS CRIERS CRUETS CRYERS CUBEBS CULETS CUPELS CURERS CUVEES CYDERS DATERS DEFERS DETERS DICERS DINERS DIVERS DIYERS DIZENS DOGEYS DONEES DONETS DOSERS DOWELS DOWERS DOYENS DOZENS DOZERS DRIERS DRYERS DURESS DUVETS DWEEBS EASELS

EATERS EDGERS EDSELS EELERS EGRESS EGRETS EIDERS ELDERS ELVERS EMBEDS EMBERS EMCEES EMEERS EMMETS ENDERS ENGELS ENTERS ESKERS ESTERS ETHERS EXCELS EXCESS EXPELS FACETS FAKERS FARERS FEVERS FIBERS FIFERS FILERS FILETS FIRERS FIVERS FIVEWS FIXERS FLEERS FLEETS FLIERS FLYERS FOGEYS FOYERS FRIERS FRYERS FUSEES FUZEES GAPERS GATERS GAVELS GELEES GENETS GIBERS GIMELS GIVENS GIVERS GLUERS GODETS GOFERS GOLEMS GONERS GREEKS GREENS GREETS GRIEFS GRUELS HABEAS HACEKS HALERS HAREMS HATERS HAVENS HAVERS HAZELS HAZERS HELENS

HEWERS HEXERS HIDERS HIKERS HIRERS HOMERS HONEYS HOPERS HOSELS HOTELS HOVELS HOVERS IDLERS IMPELS INFERS INKERS INLETS INNESS INSETS INTENS ISLETS JAPERS JASEYS JEWELS JIVERS JOKERS JULEPS KEVELS KHMERS KITERS KNEELS KOPEKS LABELS LACERS LADERS LAGERS LAKERS LAMEDS LAPELS LASERS LATENS LAVERS LAYERS LEVEES LEVELS LEVERS LIBELS LIFERS LIGERS LIKENS LIMENS LIMEYS LINENS LINERS LITERS LIVENS LIVERS LODENS LONERS LOPERS LOSERS LOVERS LOWERS LUDENS LUGERS LUMENS LYCEES MAKERS MASERS MATERS MATEYS MAVENS MAZERS MELEES

METERS MILERS MIMEOS MIMERS MINERS MISERS MITERS MIXERS MIZENS MODELS MODEMS MONEYS MOPEDS MOPERS MORELS MOSEYS MOTELS MOTETS MOVERS MOWERS MOYERS MULEYS MUSERS NAMERS NAVELS NENETS NEREIS NEREUS NEVERS NEWELS NFLERS NHLERS NINERS NITERS NOLENS NOLESS NONETS NOPETS NOTERS NOVELS NYMETS OATERS OBSESS OCHERS OCTETS OFFERS OGLERS OGRESS OILERS OLMECS ONSETS ORDERS ORIELS OSIERS OTHERS OTTERS OUSELS OUZELS OWLETS OWNERS PACERS PAGERS PANELS PAPERS PARENS PARERS PASEOS PATENS PATERS PAVERS PAWERS PAYEES PAYERS PELEUS

PETERS PEWEES PIKERS PILEUS PIPERS PIXELS PLIERS POKERS POKEYS POLERS POSERS POWERS PREENS PRIERS PROEMS PUREES QUEENS QUIETS RACERS RAKERS RAMETS RANEES RASERS RATELS RATERS RAVELS RAVENS RAVERS REBECS REBELS RECESS REFERS REHEMS REKEYS RELETS RENEWS REPEGS REPELS RESEES RESETS RESEWS REVELS REVERS REVETS REWEDS RICERS RIDERS RIPENS RISERS RIVERS RIVETS RODEOS ROGERS ROLEOS ROMEOS ROPERS ROVERS ROWELS ROWENS ROWERS RUBENS RULERS RUMENS RUPEES SABERS SAKERS SAVERS SAYERS SCREES SCREWS SEDERS SEVENS SEVERS SEWERS

SHEENS
SHEEPS
SHEERS
SHEETS
SHOERS
SHREDS
SHREWS
SIDERS
SINEWS
SIRENS
SIXERS
SIZERS
SKIERS
SLEEKS
SLEEPS
SLEETS
SNEERS
SOBERS
SOLERS
SOLEUS
SOMERS
SOWERS
SOXERS
SPEEDS
SPIELS
SPIERS
SPREES
STEEDS
STEELS
STEEPS
STEERS
STRESS
STREWS
SUPERS
SWEEPS
SWEETS
TAKERS
TALERS
TAMERS
TAPERS
TASERS
TATERS
TAXERS
TEHEES
TENENS
TENETS
TEPEES
TEREUS
THREES
TIGERS
TILERS
TIMERS
TITERS
TOKENS
TONERS
TOPERS
TOTEMS
TOTERS
TOWELS
TOWERS
TRIERS
TUBERS
TUNERS
TVSETS
TWEEDS
TWEENS
TWEETS
TYPERS
UDDERS
ULCERS
UMBELS
UMBERS
UNLESS
UNPEGS
UNPENS
UNSEWS
UPPERS
UPSETS
URAEUS
URGERS
USHERS
UTTERS
UZBEKS
VALENS
VALETS
VEXERS
VIDEOS
VIPERS
VIREOS
VIXENS
VOLENS
VOTERS
VOWELS
VOWERS
WADERS
WAFERS
WAGERS
WAKENS
WALERS
WANERS
WATERS
WAVERS
WAXERS
WHEELS
WIDENS
WIPERS
WIRERS
WIZENS
WOMENS
WOOERS
XEBECS
YODELS
YOKELS
ZAZENS
ZIBETS

••••ES

ABASES
ABATES
ABELES
ABIDES
ABODES
ABUSES
ADAGES
ADDLES
ADOBES
ADORES
AEETES
AERIES
AGATES
AGAVES
AGGIES
AGREES
AISLES
AKENES
ALINES
ALLEES
ALLIES
AMAZES
AMBLES
AMICES
AMIDES
AMINES
AMOLES
AMUSES
ANDRES
ANELES
ANGLES
ANIMES
ANKLES
ANODES
ANOLES
ANTRES
APEXES
APICES
APPLES
ARCHES
ARETES
ARGUES
ARISES
ARMIES
ASIDES
ATONES
AWAKES
AZIDES
AZINES
AZORES
BABIES
BADGES
BAINES
BARGES
BARNES
BARRES
BASHES
BASSES
BASTES
BATHES
BEEVES
BEIGES
BELIES
BELLES
BEVIES
BIASES
BIBLES
BILGES
BINGES
BIOMES
BLADES
BLAMES
BLARES
BLAZES
BLOKES
BODIES
BOGIES
BOGLES
BOITES
BOMBES
BONCES
BONNES
BONZES
BOOTES
BOSSES
BOULES
BOUSES
BOWLES
BRACES
BRAKES
BRAVES
BRAZES
BREVES
BRIBES
BRIDES
BRINES
BRUGES
BRULES
BRUMES
BRUTES
BRUXES
BSIDES
BUDGES
BUGLES
BULGES
BURIES
BURSES
BUSHES
BUSIES
BUSSES
BUTTES
BUZZES
BYRNES
CABLES
CACHES
CADGES
CADRES
CALCES
CALLES
CALVES
CALXES
CANNES
CANOES
CARIES
CARNES
CARTES
CARVES
CASHES
CASTES
CAUSES
CEASES
CENSES
CESSES
CHAFES
CHASES
CHIDES
CHIMES
CHINES
CHIVES
CHOKES
CHORES
CHUTES
CITIES
CLAVES
CLEVES
CLIMES
CLINES
CLONES
CLOSES
CLOVES
CNOTES
COAXES
COLIES
COMBES
COMTES
CONIES
CONTES
COPIES
COPSES
CORTES
CORVES
COSHES
COSIES
COUPES
COZIES
CRAKES
CRANES
CRAPES
CRATES
CRAVES
CRAZES
CREMES
CREPES
CRIMES
CRIPES
CRISES
CRONES
CROZES
CRUCES
CRUSES
CRUXES
CURSES
CURVES
CUSSES
CUTIES
CUVEES
CYCLES
DADOES
DAISES
DALLES
DANCES
DANTES
DASHES
DAUBES
DAVIES
DEFIES
DEICES
DELVES
DEMIES
DENIES
DEUCES
DHOLES
DIDIES
DIESES
DIODES
DIRGES
DISHES
DISMES
DITZES
DODGES
DODOES
DOGIES
DONEES
DORIES
DOSSES
DOUSES
DOWSES
DRAKES
DRAPES
DRIVES
DRONES
DROVES
DRUPES
DRUZES
DULLES
DUNCES
DUTIES
EAGLES
EAGRES
ECCLES
ECHOES
ECOLES
EDAMES
EDDIES
EDDOES
EDILES
EDUCES
ELATES
ELEVES
ELIDES
ELITES
ELOPES
ELUDES
ELUTES
EMCEES
EMOTES
ENATES
ENDUES
ENSUES
ENURES
ENVIES
EPODES
ERASES
ERODES
ESPIES
ETAPES
ETCHES
ETUDES
EVADES
EVOKES
EXILES
EXUDES
EYRIES
FABLES
FACIES
FALCES
FARCES
FASCES
FAUCES
FAWKES
FEMMES
FENCES
FESSES
FEZZES
FIBRES
FICHES
FILLES
FISHES
FIZZES
FLAKES
FLAMES
FLARES
FLAXES
FLEXES
FLORES
FLUKES
FLUMES
FLUTES
FLUXES
FOGIES
FORBES
FORCES
FORGES
FORTES
FOSSES
FOWLES
FRAMES
FRISES
FUDGES
FUGUES
FURIES
FURZES
FUSEES
FUSSES
FUTZES
FUZEES
FUZZES
GABIES
GABLES
GAFFES
GANGES
GASHES
GASSES
GAUGES
GAUZES
GELEES
GENIES
GENRES
GEODES
GESTES
GIGUES
GIJOES
GIMMES
GLACES
GLADES
GLARES
GLAZES
GLEBES
GLIDES
GLOBES
GLOVES
GLOZES
GLUTES
GNOMES
GOBIES
GOOSES
GORGES
GORSES
GOUGES
GRACES
GRADES
GRAPES
GRATES
GRAVES
GRAZES
GREBES
GRIMES
GRIPES
GROPES
GROVES
GUIDES
GUILES
GUISES
GUSHES
HADJES
HAINES
HAJJES
HALOES
HALVES
HAOLES
HASHES
HASTES
HAWSES
HEAVES
HEDGES
HELVES
HERMES
HEROES
HINGES
HISSES
HOAXES
HOBBES
HOBOES
HODGES
HOLMES
HOOVES
HORDES
HORSES
HOUSES
HUGHES
HUSHES
HYADES
IBEXES
IBISES
ILEXES
IMAGES
IMBUES
INCHES
INDIES
INGLES
INGRES
INKLES
INURES
IRENES
IRIDES
IRISES
ISSUES
ISTLES
ITCHES
JAURES
JAZZES
JEEVES
JINXES
JOSHES
JOSSES
JOULES
JUDGES
JUICES
JURIES
KEDGES
KERMES
KEYNES
KISSES
KNAVES
KNIFES
KNIVES
KOPJES
LACHES
LADIES
LADLES
LANCES
LAPSES
LARGES
LASHES
LASSES
LATHES
LATKES
LEASES
LEAVES
LEDGES
LENSES
LEONES
LEVEES
LEVIES
LIANES
LIEGES
LILIES
LISLES
LITRES
LIVRES
LOAVES
LODGES
LONGES
LOOIES
LOOSES
LORIES
LOSSES
LOUPES
LOUSES
LUNGES
LUTZES
LYCEES
LYNXES
MACHES
MADRES
MAILES
MAIZES
MANSES
MAPLES
MARGES
MASHES
MASSES
MATTES
MAUVES
MAYBES
MELEES
MENDES
MERGES
MESHES
MESSES
METRES
MIDGES
MINCES
MINKES
MINXES
MISSES
MITRES
MOINES
MOIRES
MONIES
MONTES
MOSHES
MOSSES
MOUSES
MOVIES
MURRES
MUSHES
MUSSES
MUZZES
MYOPES
NACRES
NANTES
NAPLES
NAPPES
NAVIES
NERVES
NESSES
NEUMES
NICHES
NIECES
NITRES
NIXIES
NOBLES
NOISES
NOONES
NOOSES
NOSHES
NUDGES
NUECES
NURSES
OCHRES
OGIVES
OLDIES
OLIVES
ONUSES
ONYXES
OODLES
OPINES
OPUSES
ORALES
ORATES
ORGIES
ORTLES
ORYXES
OSAGES
OUNCES
OVULES
OXEYES
OXIDES
PADRES
PANNES
PARSES
PASSES
PASTES
PAUSES
PAYEES
PEEVES
PEKOES
PEWEES
PHAGES
PHASES
PHONES
PIECES
PIQUES
PISCES
PISTES
PITIES
PIXIES
PLACES
PLAGES
PLANES
PLATES
PLEBES
PLUMES
PLUSES
POGIES
POISES
PONCES
PONIES
PONTES
POSIES
POSSES
PRASES
PRATES
PRAXES
PRICES
PRIDES
PRIMES
PRIZES
PROBES
PROLES
PROSES
PROVES
PRUDES
PRUNES
PULSES
PUREES
PURGES
PURSES
PUSHES
PUSSES
PYXIES
QUAKES
QUEUES
QUIRES
QUOTES
RABIES
RAINES
RAISES
RAMIES
RAMSES
RANEES
RANGES
RASHES
RAZZES
REALES
REBBES
REDOES
REDYES
REESES
REEVES
RELIES
RENNES
RESEES
RESHES
RETIES
REUNES
REUSES
REVUES
RHAMES
RHODES
RHYMES
RICHES
RIDGES
RIFLES
RILLES
RINSES
ROBLES
ROGUES
ROUGES
ROUSES
ROUTES
RUBIES
RUBLES
RUCHES
RUPEES
RUSHES
SABLES
SABRES
SADHES
SALVES
SARGES
SASHES
SASSES
SAUCES
SAUTES
SAYLES
SAYYES
SCALES
SCAPES
SCARES
SCENES
SCONES
SCOPES
SCORES
SCREES
SCUTES
SEDGES
SEGUES
SEINES
SEIZES
SELVES
SENSES
SERGES
SERIES
SERVES
SEVRES
SHADES
SHAKES
SHALES
SHAMES
SHAPES
SHARES
SHAVES
SHINES
SHIRES
SHORES
SHOVES
SIDLES
SIEGES
SIEVES
SINGES
SKATES
SKIVES
SLAKES
SLATES
SLAVES
SLICES
SLIDES
SLIMES
SLOPES
SLYPES
SMILES
SMITES
SMOKES
SNAKES
SNARES
SNIPES
SNOPES
SNORES
SOARES
SOAVES
SOCLES
SOLVES
SONDES
SOUSES
SPACES
SPADES
SPARES
SPATES
SPICES
SPIKES
SPILES
SPINES
SPIRES
SPITES
SPOKES
SPORES
SPREES
SPRUES
SPUMES
STAGES
STAKES
STALES
STAPES
STARES
STASES
STATES
STAVES
STELES
STERES
STILES
STIPES
STOKES
STOLES
STONES
STOPES
STORES
STOVES
STUPES
STYLES
SUCCES
SUDSES
SUEDES
SUITES
SURGES
SUSSES
SWAGES
SWALES
SWEDES
SWIPES
TABLES
TANTES
TARGES
TASSES
TASTES
TAUPES
TAXIES
TBONES
TEASES
TEHEES
TENSES
TEPEES
TERNES
THALES
THAMES
THANES
THEBES
THEMES
THERES
THESES
THOLES
THREES
THROES
TIDIES
TILDES
TINGES
TITHES
TITLES
TITRES
TNOTES
TOBIES
TOILES
TONNES
TOQUES
TORIES
TORRES
TORTES
TOSSES
TRACES
TRADES
TRAVES
TRIBES
TRICES
TRIKES
TRINES
TROPES
TROVES
TRUCES
TULLES
TUQUES
TURVES
TWINES
UGLIES
UKASES
UNCLES
UNDIES
UNDOES
UNGUES
UNITES
UNTIES
UPASES
URUSES
USAGES
VALUES
VALVES
VARIES
VENUES
VERGES
VERSES
VERVES
VETOES
VINCES
VOGUES
VOICES
VOILES
VOSGES
VSIXES
WAIVES
WASHES
WASTES
WEAVES
WEDGES
WELLES
WENCES
WHALES
WHERES
WHILES
WHINES
WHITES
WHOLES
WILKES
WINCES
WINZES
WISHES
WITHES
WODGES
WOLVES
WRITES
WUSSES
XERXES
XFILES
YALIES
YERKES
YESSES
ZAIRES
ZANIES
ZEROES

ET••••

ETALIA
ETALII
ETAPES
ETCHED
ETCHER
ETCHES
ETERNE
ETHANE
ETHENE
ETHERS
ETHICS
ETHNIC
ETHNOS
ETOILE
ETONIC
ETSEQQ
ETUDES
ETUXOR
ETYMOL
ETYMON

E•T•••

EATERS
EATERY
EATING
EATOUT
EATSAT
EATSIN
EATSUP
ECTYPE
EITHER
ENTAIL
ENTERO
ENTERS
ENTICE
ENTIRE
ENTITY
ENTOMO
ENTRAP
ENTREE
ESTATE
ESTEEM
ESTERS
ESTHER
ESTOPS
ESTRAY
EUTAXY
EXTANT
EXTEND
EXTENT
EXTERN
EXTOLS
EXTORT
EXTRAS

E••T••

EARTHA
EARTHY
EASTER
EASTON
EDITED
EDITIO
EDITOR
ELATED
ELATER
ELATES
ELITES
ELUTED
ELUTES
EMOTED
EMOTER
EMOTES
EMPTOR
ENATES
EROTIC
EXETER
EXITED
EXOTIC

E•••T•

EBOATS
ECARTE
ECLATS
EDICTS
EFFETE
EFLATS
EGESTA
EGESTS
EGRETS
EIGHTH
EIGHTS
EIGHTY
EJECTA
EJECTS
ELECTS
EMEUTE
EMMETS
EMMETT
ENACTS
ENMITY
ENTITY
EOLITH
EQUATE
EQUITY
ERECTS
ERESTU
ERGATE
ERGOTS
ERRATA
ERSATZ
ERUCTS
ERUPTS
ESTATE
EVENTS
EVERTS
EVICTS
EXACTA
EXACTO
EXACTS
EXALTS
EXCITE
EXERTS
EXISTS
EXULTS
EXVOTO

E••••T

EAGLET
EATOUT
EATSAT
EFFECT
EFFORT
EGBERT
EGMONT
EGOIST
EKEOUT
ELBERT
ELDEST
ELEGIT
ELICIT
ELLIOT
EMMETT
ENFANT
ENGIRT
ENGLUT
ENLIST
ENRAPT
ENROOT
ERFURT
ERNEST
ERRANT
ESCENT
ESCORT
ESPRIT
EXCEPT
EXEMPT
EXEUNT
EXHORT
EXPECT
EXPERT
EXPORT
EXPOST
EXSERT
EXTANT
EXTENT
EXTORT
EYELET

•ET•••

AETHER
BETAKE
BETCHA
BETELS
BETHEL
BETIDE
BETISE
BETONY
BETOOK
BETRAY
BETSEY
BETSON
BETTAS
BETTER
BETTOR
CETANE
CETERA
DETACH
DETAIL
DETAIN
DETECT
DETENT
DETERS
DETEST
DETOUR
DETROP
FETING
FETISH
FETTER
FETTLE
GETMAD
GETOFF
GETOUT
GETSAT
GETSBY
GETSET
GETSIN
GETSIT
GETSON
GETSTO
GETSUP
GETTER
GETUPS
HETERO
HETMAN
HETTIE
JETGUN
JETHRO

JETLAG
JETSAM
JETSET
JETSKI
JETSON
JETTED
JETWAY
KETONE
KETTLE
LETFLY
LETHAL
LETOFF
LETOUT
LETSAT
LETSBE
LETSGO
LETSIN
LETSON
LETSUP
LETTED
LETTER
LETUPS
METALS
METATE
METEOR
METERS
METHOD
METHYL
METIER
METING
METOPE
METRES
METRIC
METROS
METTLE
NETHER
NETMAN
NETMEN
NETPAY
NETTED
NETTLE
NETTLY
NETTON
PETAIN
PETALS
PETARD
PETERS
PETITE
PETREL
PETRIE
PETROG
PETROL
PETTED
PETTER
PETTIT
PETULA
RETAGS
RETAIL
RETAIN
RETAKE
RETAPE
RETAPS
RETARD
RETARS
RETEAR
RETELL
RETENE
RETEST
RETIAL
RETIED
RETIES
RETILE
RETIME
RETINA
RETIRE
RETOLD
RETOOK
RETOOL
RETOPS
RETORT
RETOUR
RETOWS
RETRAL
RETRIM
RETROS
RETTON
RETUNE
RETURN
RETYPE
SETINS
SETOFF
SETOSE
SETOUT
SETSAT
SETSBY
SETSIN
SETSON
SETSUP
SETTEE
SETTER
SETTLE
SETTOS
SETUPS
TETCHY
TETHER
TETHYS
TETONS
TETRAD
TETRAS
TETRIS
TETZEL
VETOED
VETOER
VETOES
VETTED
WETBAR
WETFLY
WETHER
WETMOP
WETTED
WETTER
WETTIG

•E•T••

AEETES
BEATEN
BEATER
BEATIT
BEATLE
BEATON
BEATTY
BEATUP
BEETLE
BELTED
BENTON
BERTHA
BERTHS
BERTIE
BESTED
BESTIR
BESTOW
BETTAS
BETTER
BETTOR
CELTIC
CENTER
CENTOS
CENTRE
CENTRI
CENTRO
CERTIF
CESTAS
CESTOS
CESTUS
DEBTOR
DEFTER
DEFTLY
DELTAS
DELTIC
DENTAL
DENTED
DENTIL
DENTIN
DENTON
DEPTHS
DESTRY
DEXTER
DEXTRO
FEATLY
FELTED
FESTAL
FESTAS
FESTER
FESTUS
FETTER
FETTLE
GENTLE
GENTLY
GENTRY
GERTIE
GESTES
GESTIC
GETTER
HEATED
HEATER
HEATHS
HEATHY
HEATUP
HECTIC
HECTOR
HEFTED
HELTER
HENTED
HEPTAD
HESTER
HESTIA
HESTON
HETTIE
JEETER
JESTED
JESTER
JETTED
KEATON
KEITEL
KENTON
KEPTAT
KEPTON
KEPTUP
KETTLE
LECTER
LECTOR
LEFTIE
LEFTIN
LENTEN
LENTIL
LEPTON
LESTAT
LESTER
LETTED
LETTER
MEETER
MEETLY
MELTED
MELTON
MENTAL
MENTIS
MENTOR
MERTON
METTLE
NEATEN
NEATER
NEATLY
NECTAR
NEKTON
NESTEA
NESTED
NESTER
NESTLE
NESTOR
NETTED
NETTLE
NETTLY
NETTON
NEUTER
NEWTON
NEXTTO
OERTER
PECTIC
PECTIN
PEGTOP
PELTED
PELTER
PELTRY
PENTAD
PENTUP
PEPTIC
PERTER
PERTLY
PESTER
PESTLE
PESTOS
PETTED
PETTER
PETTIT
PEWTER
PEYTON
REATAS
RECTOR
RECTOS
RECTUS
REDTAG
REDTOP
RENTAL
RENTED
RENTER
RESTED
RESTER
RESTON
RESTUP
RETTON
REUTER
SEATED
SEATER
SEATON
SECTOR
SEETHE
SENTIN
SENTRA
SENTRY
SENTUP
SEPTAL
SEPTET
SEPTIC
SEPTUM
SESTET
SESTOS
SETTEE
SETTER
SETTLE
SETTOS
SEXTET
SEXTON
TEETER
TEETHE
TENTED
TENTER
TENTHS
TESTAE
TESTED
TESTEE
TESTER
TEUTON
VECTOR
VENTED
VENTER
VERTEX
VESTAL
VESTAS
VESTED
VESTEE
VESTRY
VETTED
WELTED
WELTER
WENTAT
WENTBY
WENTIN
WENTON
WENTUP
WETTED
WETTER
WETTIG
YENTAS
YESTER
ZESTED

•E••T•

AERATE
BEASTS
BEATTY
BEAUTS
BEAUTY
BEFITS
BEGETS
BEMATA
BENITO
BERATE
BERETS
BESETS
BESOTS
CENOTE
CERATE
DEARTH
DEBATE
DEBITS
DEBUTS
DEFATS
DEISTS
DELATE
DELETE
DELFTS
DEMITS
DEMOTE
DENOTE
DEPOTS
DEPUTE
DEPUTY
DESOTO
DEVITO
DEVOTE
DEVOTO
DEWITT
FEALTY
FEASTS
FEINTS
FEISTY
FELLTO
FERITY
GEARTO
GELATI
GELATO
GEMOTE
GEMOTS
GENETS
GETSTO
HEALTH
HEARTH
HEARTS
HEARTY
HECATE
HEISTS
HELDTO
HELOTS
HEMATO
HERETO
JEWETT
KEEPTO
LEADTO
LEALTY
LEANTO
LEGATE
LEGATO
LENGTH
LENITY
LEVITE
LEVITY
MELOTT
MERITS
METATE
NEARTO
NEGATE
NEMATO
NENETS
NEXTTO
PEDATE
PELOTA
PEPITA
PESETA
PETITE
PEWITS
PEYOTE
REACTS
REALTY
REBATE
REBUTS
RECITE
REDATE
REFITS
REFUTE
RELATE
RELETS
REMITS
REMOTE
RENATA
RENOTE
REPOTS
REPUTE
RERATE
RESETS
REVETS
SEDATE
SEENTO
SEESTO
SEMITE
SENATE
SENITI
TEMPTS
TENDTO
TENETS
TENUTO
TERATO
TERETE
VELDTS
VENETO
VENITE
VERITE
VERITY
VERSTS
WEALTH
YEASTS
YEASTY
ZENITH
ZEROTH

•E•••T

BEATIT
BECKET
BEHEST
BEIRUT
BELOIT
BENOIT
BEREFT
BESANT
BEZANT
CEDANT
CEMENT
CERMET
DECANT
DECEIT
DECENT
DECOCT
DEDUCT
DEFEAT
DEFECT
DEGUST
DEJECT
DELICT
DELIST
DEPART
DEPICT
DEPORT
DESALT
DESERT
DESIST
DESPOT
DETECT
DETENT
DETEST
DEVEST
DEVOUT
DEWITT
FERMAT
FERRET
FEWEST
FEYEST
GERENT
GERONT
GETOUT
GETSAT
GETSET
GETSIT
HEARST
HEIGHT
HELMET
HELMUT
HENBIT
HEPCAT
HEREAT
HERIOT
HERMIT
HEXNUT
JEERAT
JENNET
JESUIT
JETSET
JEWETT
KEEPAT
KEPTAT
KERMIT
LEARNT
LEDOUT
LEERAT
LEGIST
LESTAT
LETOUT
LETSAT
LEVANT
MEDLAT
MEERUT
MELOTT
MEREST
MERLOT
NEEDNT
NEWEST
PEANUT
PECKAT
PEDANT
PEEKAT
PEERAT
PELLET
PELMET
PENULT
PEQUOT
PERMIT
PERROT
PETTIT
REBENT
REBOLT
REBOOT
RECANT
RECAST
RECENT
RECOAT
REDACT
REDANT
REDHAT
REDHOT
REEDIT
REGENT
REGLET
REGNAT
REGRET
REHEAT
REJECT
RELENT
RELICT
RELIST
RELUCT
REMELT
RENNET
REPAST
REPEAT
REPENT
REPORT
REPOST
RERENT
RESALT
RESEAT
RESECT
RESENT
RESHOT
RESIST
RESORT
RESULT
RETEST
RETORT
REVERT
REVOLT
REXCAT
SECANT
SECRET
SEEFIT
SEEOUT
SEJANT
SELECT
SENNET
SENNIT
SEPTET
SESTET
SETOUT
SETSAT
SEURAT
SEXIST
SEXTET
TEAPOT
TEARAT
TEASET
TENANT
TERCET
TERRET
VEIGHT
VELVET
VERVET
WEIGHT
WENTAT
WERENT
WESKIT
XEDOUT
ZEALOT

••ET••

ACETAL
ACETIC
ACETYL
AEETES
ARETES
ARETHA
BEETLE
BRETON
CHETHS
CRETAN
CRETIN
DIETED
DIETER
EXETER
FLETCH
FOETAL
FOETID
FOETOR
FOETUS
FRETTY
GHETTO
GOETHE
GRETEL
GRETNA
HYETAL
IGETIT
JEETER
JOETEX
KVETCH
MEETER
MEETLY
NOETIC
ODETTA
ODETTE
ONETWO
PIETAS
PIETER
PIETIN
PIETRO
POETIC
POETRY
PRETAX
PRETER
PRETTY
QUETTA
RHETOR
SEETHE
SKETCH
TEETER
TEETHE
THETAS
THETIC
THETIS
THETOY
TOETAP
TSETSE
WRETCH
YVETTE

••E•T•

ADEPTS
ADESTE
AGENTS
ALECTO
ALERTS
ALEUTS
AMENTS
ASEITY
ATESTS
AVERTS
AVESTA
BLEATS
BREATH
BRENTS
CHEATS
CHERTY
CHESTS
CHESTY
CLEATS
CLEFTS
CREATE
CRESTS
CUESTA
EGESTA
EGESTS
EJECTA
EJECTS
ELECTS
EMEUTE
ERECTS
ERESTU
EVENTS
EVERTS
EXERTS
FIESTA
FLEETS
FRETTY
GHETTO
GREATS
GREETS
GUESTS
IDEATE
KEEPTO
LIESTO
LIEUTS
ODETTA
ODETTE
OLEATE
OMERTA
OPENTO
PLEATS
PLENTY
PRESTO
PRETTY
PUENTE
PUERTO
QUESTS
QUETTA
QWERTY
SCENTS
SEENTO
SEESTO
SHEATH
SHEETS
SHELTY
SIESTA
SLEETS
SLEETY
SLEUTH
SMELTS
SVELTE
SWEATS
SWEATY
SWEETS
THEFTS
TIEDTO
TIESTO
TREATS
TREATY
TWEETS
TWEETY
TWENTY
USEDTO
WHEATS
WREATH
WRESTS
YVETTE

••E••T

ACEOUT
AGEIST
ALEAST
ARENDT
ATEOUT
BLEWIT
BREAST
BRECHT
BREVET
CHEVET
COEDIT
CREDIT
DIEOUT
DOESNT
DREAMT
DYELOT
EKEOUT
ELEGIT
EXEMPT
EXEUNT
EYELET
FLEWAT
FREEST
GOESAT
HAEMAT
ICEOUT
IGETIT
ISEULT
JEERAT
KEEPAT
KLEIST
LEERAT
MEERUT
NEEDNT
NLEAST
NOEXIT
OCELOT
OMELET
ONEACT
PEEKAT
PEERAT
PRESET
REEDIT
SEEFIT
SEEOUT
SHEVAT
THEIST
TWEEST
USENET

•••ET•

AGLETS
AMVETS
ARMETS
ARNETT
ASSETS
BEGETS
BERETS
BESETS
BLUETS
CADETS
CAMETO
CARETO
CARETS
CAVETT
CIVETS
COMETH
COMETO
COMETS
COVETS
CRUETS
CULETS
DALETH
DARETO
DELETE
DONETS
DUVETS
EFFETE
EGRETS
EMMETS
EMMETT
FACETS
FILETS
FLEETS
GAIETY
GAMETE
GARETH
GENETS
GIVETO
GODETS
GREETS
HERETO
HOVETO
INLETS
INSETS
ISLETS
JEWETT
JOBETH
JOWETT
LOVETT
MOIETY
MONETA
MOTETS
MULETA
NENETS
NICETY
NINETY
NONETS
NOPETS
NYMETS
OCTETS
ONSETS
OSSETE
OWLETS
PARETO
PESETA
QUIETS
RAMETS
RELETS
RESETS
REVETS
RIVETS
SAFETY
SHEETS
SHTETL
SLEETS
SLEETY
SOWETO
STPETE
SURETE
SURETY
SWEETS
TAKETH
TAKETO
TENETS
TERETE
TVSETS
TWEETS
TWEETY
UBIETY
UPSETS
VALETS
VENETO
WISETO
ZIBETS

•••E•T

ABJECT
ABLEST
ABSENT
ACCENT
ACCEPT
ADVENT
ADVERT
AFFECT
AFREET
ALBEIT
ALBERT
ALPERT
ALWEST
APTEST
ARDENT
ARGENT
ARNETT
ARPENT
ARREST
ASCENT
ASPECT
ASSENT
ASSERT
ATBEST
ATREST
ATTEST
BAREST
BASEST
BEHEST
BEREFT
BISECT
BLUEST
CADENT
CAMEAT
CAVEAT
CAVETT
CEMENT
CLIENT
COGENT
COMEAT
COVENT
COVERT
COYEST
CUTEST
DARENT
DECEIT
DECENT
DEFEAT
DEFECT
DEJECT
DESERT
DETECT
DETENT
DETEST
DEVEST
DIGEST
DIRECT
DIREST
DIVERT
DIVEST
DOCENT
DRIEST
DRYEST
EFFECT
EGBERT
ELBERT
ELDEST
EMMETT
ERNEST
ESCENT
EXCEPT
EXPECT
EXPERT
EXSERT
EXTENT
FEWEST
FEYEST
FINEST
FLUENT
FOMENT
FOREST
FREEST
GAMEST
GAYEST
GERENT
GOWEST
HALEST
HAVEAT
HAVENT
HEREAT
HONEST
HUBERT
HUGEST
ICIEST
IDLEST
ILLEST
INCEPT
INDEBT
INDENT
INFECT
INFEST
INGEST
INJECT
INJEST
INSECT
INSERT
INTENT
INVENT
INVERT
INVEST
IQTEST
JEWETT
JOWETT
LAMENT
LAMEST
LATENT
LATEST
LAXEST
LOSEIT
LOVETT
LOWEST
LUCENT
MADEIT
MAKEIT
MEREST
MODELT
MODEST
MOLEST
MOMENT
MUTEST
NEWEST
NICEST
NLWEST
NOCENT
NUDEST
NUGENT
OBJECT
OBTEST
OBVERT
ODDEST
OLDEST
ORGEAT
ORIENT
OUTEAT
PALEST
PARENT
PATENT
POKEAT
POTENT
PRIEST
PUREST
RAREST
RAWEST
REBENT
RECENT
REGENT
REHEAT
REJECT
RELENT
REMELT
REPEAT
REPENT
RERENT
RESEAT
RESECT
RESENT
RETEST
REVERT
RIDENT
RIFEST
RIPEST
ROBERT
RODENT
RUDEST
RUPERT
SAFEST
SAGEST
SANEST
SELECT
SHIEST
SHYEST
SILENT
SLIEST
SLYEST
SOBEIT
SOLENT
SOREST
STREET
SUREST
TALENT
TAMEST
THREAT
TOREAT
TRUEST
TWEEST
UNBELT
UNBENT
UNMEET
UNREST
UNSEAT
UPBEAT
URGENT
URTEXT
VALENT
VILEST
WERENT
WIDEST
WISENT
WISEST
WRIEST
WRYEST
YAREST

••••ET

AFREET
AIGRET
ALLSET
ALLWET
AMULET
ANKLET
APPLET
ARMLET
AUKLET
AVOCET
BALLET
BARBET
BASKET
BASSET
BECKET
BILLET
BISSET
BONNET
BOSKET
BOWNET
BOXSET
BREVET
BRUNET
BUCKET
BUDGET
BUFFET
BULLET
BURNET
CACHET
CAMLET
CAPLET
CARNET
CARPET
CERMET
CHALET
CHEVET
CLARET
CLOSET
COLLET
COQUET
CORNET
CORSET
COSSET

CULLET
CURVET
CUTLET
CYGNET
DOCKET
DORSET
DULCET
EAGLET
EYELET
FANJET
FAUCET
FERRET
FIDGET
FILLET
FLORET
FLYNET
FORGET
GADGET
GANNET
GARNET
GARRET
GASJET
GASKET
GETSET
GIBBET
GIBLET
GIDGET
GIMLET
GOBLET
GORGET
GOTSET
GOULET
GRIVET
GULLET
GUSSET
HAMLET
HELMET
HOGGET
HORNET
ILLMET
IMARET
INAPET
INKJET
JACKET
JENNET
JETSET
JOLIET
JULIET
JUNKET
KISMET
LABRET
LANCET
LAPPET
LIMPET
LINNET
LIONET
LOCKET
MAGNET
MALLET
MARKET
MIDGET
MILLET
MINUET
MOPPET
MULLET
MUPPET
MUSKET
NOTYET
NUGGET
NUTLET
OBSTET
OFFSET
OMELET
OUTLET
OUTSET
PACKET
PALLET
PARGET
PELLET
PELMET
PIAGET
PICKET
PIGLET
PIOLET
PIQUET
PLACET
PLANET
POCKET
POPPET
POSSET
PRESET
PRIPET
PRIVET
PULLET
PUNNET
PUPPET
RABBET
RACKET
RAMJET
REGLET
REGRET
RENNET
RILLET
ROCHET
ROCKET
RUNLET
RUSSET
SACHET
SALLET
SAMLET
SECRET
SENNET
SEPTET
SESTET
SEXTET
SIGNET
SIPPET
SOCKET
SONNET
SORBET
SOVIET
SPINET
STREET
STYLET
SUBLET
SUBSET
SUNSET
SWIVET
TABLET
TAPPET
TARGET
TEASET
TERCET
TERRET
TICKET
TIPPET
TOILET
TRIJET
TRIVET
TUCKET
TUFFET
TURRET
UNMEET
USENET
VARLET
VELVET
VERVET
VIOLET
WALLET
WICKET
WIDGET
WIGLET
WILLET
YOUBET

EU••••
EUBOEA
EUCHRE
EUCLID
EUDORA
EUGENE
EULOGY
EUNICE
EUPNEA
EURAIL
EUREKA
EUROPA
EUROPE
EUTAXY

E•U•••
EDUARD
EDUCED
EDUCES
ELUDED
ELUDER
ELUDES
ELUTED
ELUTES
ENURED
ENURES
EQUALS
EQUATE
EQUINE
EQUIPS
EQUITY
ERUCTS
ERUPTS
ETUDES
ETUXOR
EVULSE
EXUDED
EXUDES
EXULTS
EXURBS

E••U••
EDMUND
EFFUSE
EMEUTE
EMQUAD
ENDUED
ENDUES
ENDURE
ENDURO
ENDUSE
ENGULF
ENOUGH
ENQUAD
ENSUED
ENSUES
ENSURE
ERFURT
ESCUDO
EXCUSE
EXEUNT

E•••U•
EARFUL
EASEUP
EATOUT
EATSUP
EFFLUX
EGGCUP
EKEOUT
ELBRUS
ENDRUN
ENDSUP
ENGLUT
ENNIUS
ENSOUL
EPIRUS
ERBIUM
EREBUS
EVENUP
EXODUS
EYECUP
EYEFUL

E••••U
ERESTU

•EU•••
BEULAH
BEURRE
DEUCED
DEUCES
FEUDAL
FEUDED
NEUMAN
NEUMES
NEURAL
NEUROL
NEURON
NEUTER
OEUVRE
REUBEN
REUNES
REUSED
REUSES
REUTER
SEURAT
TEUTON
ZEUGMA
ZEUXIS

•E•U••
BEAUTS
BEAUTY
BEGUMS
BELUGA
BEMUSE
BENUMB
CERUSE
DEBUGS
DEBUNK
DEBUTS
DEDUCE
DEDUCT
DEFUSE
DEGUST
DEJURE
DELUDE
DELUGE
DELUXE
DEMURE
DEMURS
DENUDE
DEPUTE
DEPUTY
FECUND
FEMURS
FERULE
GENUAL
GERUND
GETUPS
HECUBA
JEJUNE
JESUIT
LEGUIN
LEGUME
LEHUAS
LEMUEL
LEMURS
LETUPS
MEDUSA
NEBULA
NERUDA
PENULT
PENURY
PEQUOD
PEQUOT
PERUGA
PERUKE
PERUSE
PETULA
REBUFF
REBUKE
REBURY
REBUTS
RECURS
RECUSE
REDUBS
REDUCE
REFUEL
REFUGE
REFUND
REFUSE
REFUTE
REHUNG
RELUCT
RELUME
REMUDA
REPUGN
REPUTE
RERUNS
RESULT
RESUME
RETUNE
RETURN
REVUES
SECURE
SEDUCE
SEDUMS
SEGUED
SEGUES
SEGURA
SENUFO
SEQUEL
SEQUIN
SERUMS
SETUPS
TELUGU
TENURE
TENUTO
VENUES
YEHUDI

•E••U•
AEOLUS
BEADUP
BEAMUP
BEARUP
BEATUP
BEDAUB
BEDBUG
BEEFUP
BEEGUM
BEFOUL
BEIRUT
BENHUR
CENSUS
CEREUS
CERIUM
CESIUM
CESTUS
DELIUS
DENGUE
DEPAUL
DEPAUW
DETOUR
DEVOUR
DEVOUT
FERGUS
FESCUE
FESSUP
FESTUS
GEARUP
GENIUS
GETOUT
GETSUP
HEADUP
HEATUP
HELDUP
HELIUM
HELMUT
HEXNUT
JETGUN
KEEPUP
KEPTUP
KEYSUP
LEADUP
LEAGUE
LEBRUN
LEDOUT
LETOUT
LETSUP
MEDIUM
MEERUT
MESSUP
NEREUS
PEANUT
PELEUS
PENTUP
PEPFUL
PEPLUM
PEPSUP
PERDUE
PERKUP
REARUP
RECOUP
RECTUS
REDBUD
REDGUM
REFLUX
REGIUS
REGLUE
RESCUE
RESTUP
RETOUR
REVSUP
SEALUP
SEAMUS
SEEOUT
SELJUK
SENDUP
SENTUP
SEPTUM
SEROUS
SESQUI
SETOUT
SETSUP
SEWNUP
SEWSUP
TEACUP
TEAMUP
TEARUP
TEDEUM
TEDIUM
TEEDUP
TEESUP
TEMPUS
TEREUS
VELLUM
VELOUR
VENOUS
VERDUN
VERSUS
WELLUP
WENTUP
XEDOUT

•E•••U
DEJAVU
DESILU
HEYYOU
MENJOU
PENGHU
RESEAU
TELEDU
TELUGU

••EU••
ALEUTS
BREUER
CREUSA
EMEUTE
EXEUNT
FLEURY
ISEULT
LIEUTS
ONEUPS
PLEURA
PNEUMA
PSEUDO
PSEUDS
QUEUED
QUEUER
QUEUES
RHEUMS
RHEUMY
SLEUTH
SOEURS
TIEUPS

••E•U•
ACEOUS
ACEOUT
ACESUP
ATEOUT
AVENUE
BEEFUP
BEEGUM
BLEWUP
CHEQUE
CHERUB
CHEWUP
DIEOUT
DOESUP
DREWUP
EKEOUT
EREBUS
EVENUP
EYECUP
EYEFUL
FOETUS
FRENUM
GOESUP
GREWUP
ICEDUP
ICEOUT
ICESUP
IREFUL
KEEPUP
MEERUT
OBELUS
OPENUP
PLENUM
PLEXUS
PRENUP
RHESUS
RUEFUL
SEEOUT
SPEDUP
STEPUP
TEEDUP
TEESUP
TIEDUP
TIESUP
USEDUP
USEFUL
USESUP
WOEFUL

••E••U
APERCU
ERESTU

•••EU•
ADIEUS
ADIEUX
ANTEUP
ATREUS
AUREUS
AUTEUR
BAYEUX
BONEUP
BOREUP
CAMEUP
CEREUS
COLEUS
COMEUP
DONEUP
EASEUP
FACEUP
FIREUP
GAVEUP
GIVEUP
HIKEUP
HOLEUP
HYPEUP
LACEUP
LINEUP
LYCEUM
MADEUP
MAKEUP
MOVEUP
MUSEUM
NEREUS
PELEUS
PILEUM
PILEUP
PILEUS
PIPEUP
POSEUR
RAKEUP
RAVEUP
RILEUP
SAVEUP
SIZEUP
SOLEUS
TAKEUP
TEDEUM
TEREUS
TONEUP
TOREUP
TUNEUP
TYPEUP
URAEUS
WAKEUP
WIPEUP
WISEUP
WOKEUP

•••E•U
BATEAU
BUREAU
GATEAU
HALERU
JUNEAU
MASERU
MOREAU
RAMEAU
RESEAU
ROSEAU
TELEDU

••••EU
MILIEU

EV••••
EVADED
EVADER
EVADES
EVELYN
EVENED
EVENER
EVENKI
EVENLY
EVENSO
EVENTS
EVENUP
EVERLY
EVERSO
EVERTS
EVICTS
EVILER
EVILLY
EVINCE
EVOKED
EVOKER
EVOKES
EVOLVE
EVONNE
EVULSE
EVZONE

E•V•••
EDVARD
ELVERS
ELVIRA
ELVISH
ENVIED
ENVIER
ENVIES
ENVOIS
ENVOYS
ERVING
EXVOTO

E••V••
ELEVEN
ELEVES

E•••V•
ENDIVE
EVOLVE

•EV•••
BEVELS
BEVIES
DEVEIN
DEVEST
DEVICE
DEVILS
DEVINE
DEVISE
DEVITO
DEVOID
DEVOIR
DEVOTE
DEVOTO
DEVOUR
DEVOUT
FEVERS
KEVELS
KEVLAR
LEVANT
LEVEED
LEVEES
LEVELS
LEVENE
LEVERS
LEVIED
LEVIER
LEVIES
LEVINE
LEVITE
LEVITY
NEVADA
NEVERS
NEVINS
NEVSKY
REVAMP
REVEAL
REVELS
REVERB
REVERE
REVERS
REVERT
REVETS
REVIEW
REVILE
REVISE
REVIVE
REVLON
REVOIR
REVOKE
REVOLT
REVSON
REVSUP
REVUES
REVVED
SEVENS
SEVERE
SEVERN
SEVERS
SEVERY
SEVRES

•E•V••
BEAVER
BEAVIS
BEEVES
CERVID
DELVED
DELVER
DELVES
DENVER
FERVID
FERVOR
HEAVED
HEAVEN
HEAVER
HEAVES
HELVES
JEEVES
KELVIN
LEAVED
LEAVEN
LEAVES
LEKVAR
MELVIL
MELVIN
MELVYN
MERVYN
NERVES
OEUVRE
PEAVEY
PEEVED
PEEVES
PELVIC
PELVIS
REEVED
REEVES
REVVED
SELVES
SERVAL
SERVED
SERVER
SERVES
SERVOS
TEEVEE
VELVET
VERVES
VERVET
WEAVED
WEAVER
WEAVES
WEEVIL

•E••V•
BEHAVE
BEHOVE
DEJAVU
DENOVO
DERIVE
GENEVA
GENEVE
RELEVY
RELIVE
REMOVE
REPAVE
REVIVE
REWOVE

•E•••V
HENRYV

••EV••
ALEVEL
ASEVER
BEEVES
BREVES
BREVET
BREVIS
CHEVAL
CHEVET
CHEVRE
CLEVER
CLEVES
CLEVIS
COEVAL
ELEVEN
ELEVES
HUEVOS
JEEVES
OLEVEL
PEEVED
PEEVES
PREVIN
REEVED
REEVES
SHEVAT
SIEVED
SIEVES
STEVEN
STEVIE
TEEVEE
TREVOR
UNEVEN
WEEVIL

••E•V•
CLEAVE
GREAVE
SHEAVE
SHELVE
SLEAVE
SLEEVE
STEEVE
SWERVE
THEYVE
TWELVE

••E••V
CHEKOV

•••EV•
GENEVA
GENEVE
GRIEVE
HALEVY
PAREVE
RELEVY
SLEEVE
STEEVE
THIEVE

••••EV
KISLEV
LAPTEV
RUBLEV

E•W•••
EDWARD
EDWOOD
EDWYNN
ELWOOD
ENWRAP
EXWIFE

E••W••
EARWAX
EARWIG

E•••W•
ELBOWS
ENDOWS

E••••W
ERENOW
ESCHEW
ESCROW

•EW•••
BEWAIL
BEWARE
BEWRAY
DEWIER
DEWILY
DEWING
DEWITT
DEWLAP
FEWEST
GEWGAW
HEWERS
HEWING
JEWELS
JEWETT
JEWISH
KEWPIE
LEWDER
LEWDLY
MEWING
MEWLED
MEWLER
NEWAGE
NEWARK
NEWELS
NEWEST
NEWISH
NEWLEY
NEWMAN
NEWMAR
NEWTON
PEWEES
PEWITS
PEWTER
REWARD
REWARM
REWASH
REWEDS
REWELD
REWIND
REWINS
REWIRE
REWORD
REWORK
REWOVE
REWRAP
SEWAGE
SEWARD
SEWELL
SEWERS
SEWING
SEWNON
SEWNUP
SEWSON
SEWSUP

•E•W••
FENWAY
JETWAY
KEYWAY
LEEWAY
MEOWED
PEDWAY
PEEWEE
SEAWAY

•E••W•
BEDEWS
PESAWA
REMOWN
REMOWS
RENEWS
RENOWN
RESAWN
RESAWS
RESEWN
RESEWS
RETOWS
SEROWS

•E•••W
BELLOW
BESTOW
DEPAUW
FELLOW
GEEGAW
GEWGAW
HEBREW
HEEHAW
MEADOW
MELLOW
NEPHEW
PESCOW
REDRAW
REDREW
REPLOW
REVIEW
SEACOW
SEESAW
YELLOW

••EW••
BLEWIT
BLEWUP
BREWED
BREWER
CHEWED
CHEWER
CHEWUP
CLEWED
CREWED
CREWEL
DREWIN
DREWON
DREWUP
FLEWAT
FLEWIN
GREWON
GREWUP
LEEWAY
ONEWAY
PEEWEE
PREWAR
SKEWED
SKEWER
SLEWED
SPEWED
STEWED
STEWER
THEWEB
THEWIZ
VIEWED
VIEWER

••E•W•
ONETWO

••E••W
ERENOW
GEEGAW
HEEHAW
LIELOW
PRELAW
SEESAW

•••EW•
BEDEWS
FIVEWS
RENEWS
RESEWN
RESEWS
SCREWS
SCREWY
SHREWD
SHREWS
SINEWS
SINEWY
STREWN
STREWS
UNSEWN
UNSEWS

••••EW
ANDREW
CASHEW
CURFEW
CURLEW
ESCHEW
HEBREW
MCGREW
MILDEW
NEPHEW
ONVIEW
REDREW
REVIEW
SUNDEW

EX••••
EXACTA
EXACTO
EXACTS
EXALTS
EXARCH
EXCEED
EXCELS
EXCEPT
EXCESS
EXCISE
EXCITE
EXCUSE
EXEDRA
EXEMPT
EXERTS
EXETER
EXEUNT
EXHALE
EXHORT
EXILED
EXILES
EXILIC
EXISTS
EXITED
EXLEGE
EXMOOR
EXMORE
EXODUS
EXOTIC
EXPAND
EXPECT
EXPELS
EXPEND
EXPERT
EXPIRE
EXPIRY
EXPORT
EXPOSE
EXPOST
EXSERT
EXTANT
EXTEND
EXTENT
EXTERN
EXTOLS
EXTORT
EXTRAS
EXUDED
EXUDES
EXULTS
EXURBS
EXVOTO
EXWIFE

E••X••
ELIXIR
ETUXOR

E•••X•
EUTAXY

E••••X
EARWAX
EFFLUX

•EX•••
DEXTER
DEXTRO
HEXADS
HEXERS
HEXING
HEXNUT
LEXEME
LEXICA
MEXICO
NEXTTO
REXCAT
SEXIER
SEXILY
SEXIST
SEXTET
SEXTON
TEXACO
TEXANS
TEXMEX
VEXERS
VEXING

•E•X••
XERXES
ZEUXIS

•E••X•
DELUXE

•E•••X
BENDIX
LENNOX
MENINX
REDFOX
REDSOX
REFLEX
REFLUX
SEAFOX
TEXMEX
VERTEX
WESSEX

••EX••
ALEXEI
ALEXIA
ALEXIS
APEXES
DREXEL
FLEXED
FLEXES
FLEXOR
IBEXES
ILEXES
NOEXIT
PLEXAL

PLEXOR
PLEXUS

••E••X
ICEBOX
JOETEX
PREFIX
PRETAX
THESIX

•••EX•
ADNEXA
ANNEXE
URTEXT

•••E•X
ADIEUX
BAYEUX
BLUEOX
POLEAX
RATEDX

••••EX
AUSPEX
CAUDEX
CONVEX
CORTEX
DUPLEX
JOETEX
LASTEX
POLLEX
REFLEX
SUSSEX
TEXMEX
UNISEX
VERTEX
VORTEX
WESSEX
WINDEX

EY••••
EYECUP
EYEFUL
EYEING
EYELET
EYELID
EYRIES

E•Y•••
EEYORE
ELYSEE
ERYNGO
ETYMOL
ETYMON

E••Y••
ECTYPE
EDWYNN
ELAYER
ELAYNE
ENZYME

E•••Y•
EMBAYS
EMBRYO
ENJOYS
ENVOYS
EPONYM
ERINYS
ESSAYS
EVELYN

E••••Y
EARTHY
EASILY
EATERY
EBERLY
EDGILY
EERILY
EFFIGY
EIGHTY
ELLERY
EMBODY
EMPERY
EMPLOY
ENERGY
ENMITY
ENTITY
EQUITY
ESTRAY
EULOGY
EUTAXY
EVENLY
EVERLY
EVILLY
EXPIRY

•EY•••
BEYOND
CEYLON
EEYORE
FEYEST
GEYSER
HEYDAY
HEYYOU
KEYING
KEYNES
KEYPAD
KEYSIN
KEYSUP
KEYWAY
LEYDEN
PEYOTE
PEYTON

•E•Y••
HEYYOU
JEKYLL
KENYAN
REDYED
REDYES
RETYPE

•E••Y•
BELAYS
DECAYS
DECOYS
DELAYS
HEARYE
HENRYV
KENNYG
MELVYN
MERVYN
METHYL
REDEYE
REKEYS
RELAYS
REPAYS
SEPOYS
TETHYS
ZEPHYR

•E•••Y
AERIFY
AERILY
BEACHY
BEATTY
BEAUTY
BEGLEY
BEKESY
BELFRY
BELLAY
BENDAY
BENGAY
BETONY
BETRAY
BETSEY
BEWRAY
CECILY
CELERY
DEADLY
DEAFLY
DEARLY
DEEJAY
DEEPLY
DEFRAY
DEFTLY
DELANY
DELRAY
DELROY
DENARY
DEPLOY
DEPUTY
DESCRY
DESTRY
DEWILY
EERILY
FEALTY
FEATLY
FEEBLY
FEISTY
FELONY
FENWAY
FERITY
GELSEY
GENTLY
GENTRY
GEORGY
GETSBY
HEANEY
HEARTY
HEATHY
HENLEY
HEREBY
HERESY
HERSEY
HEYDAY
JENNEY
JEREMY
JERSEY
JETWAY
KEARNY
KEENLY
KELLEY
KELSEY
KERSEY
KEYWAY
LEACHY
LEAKEY
LEALTY
LEANLY
LEEWAY
LEGACY
LEMONY
LENITY
LESLEY
LETFLY
LEVITY
LEWDLY
MEANLY
MEASLY
MEDFLY
MEDLEY
MEEKLY
MEETLY
MELODY
MEMORY
MERELY
MERSEY
NEARBY
NEARLY
NEATLY
NETPAY
NETTLY
NEVSKY
NEWLEY
PEACHY
PEARLY
PEAVEY
PEBBLY
PEDWAY
PELTRY
PENNEY
PENURY
PERTLY
REALLY
REALTY
REBURY
RECOPY
REDBAY
REDENY
REILLY
RELEVY
REMEDY
REPLAY
RESINY
SEAWAY
SEELEY
SEEMLY
SENARY
SENTRY
SETSBY
SEVERY
SEXILY
TEAPOY
TEDKEY
TEENSY
TETCHY
VEEJAY
VERIFY
VERILY
VERITY
VESTRY
WEAKLY
WEEKLY
WEENSY
WEIRDY
WENTBY
WESLEY
WETFLY
YEARLY
YEASTY

••EY••
BREYER
FLEYED
GREYED
GREYER
GREYLY
OBEYED
OXEYES
PREYED
PREYON
THEYLL
THEYRE
THEYVE

••E•Y•
ACETYL
AYEAYE
BYEBYE
CHERYL
EVELYN
LIEBYS
PHENYL
SHERYL
TIEDYE

••E••Y
AGENCY
ALECKY
ANERGY
ASEITY
AWEARY
AWEDLY
BLEARY
BLENNY
BREEZY
CHEEKY
CHEERY
CHEESY
CHERRY
CHERTY
CHESTY
CLERGY
CREAKY
CREAMY
CREASY
CREEPY
CZERNY
DEEJAY
DEEPLY
DOESBY
DREAMY
DREARY
DRESSY
EBERLY
ENERGY
EVENLY
EVERLY
FEEBLY
FLECKY
FLEDGY
FLEECY
FLESHY
FLEURY
FREAKY
FREDDY
FREELY
FRENZY
FRETTY
GLEAMY
GOEASY
GOESBY
GREASY
GREEDY
GREENY
GREYLY
KEENLY
LEEWAY
LIEFLY
MEEKLY
MEETLY
OHENRY
OKELLY
OLEARY
ONEDAY
ONEWAY
OPENLY
OVERLY
PLENTY
POETRY
PREPAY
PREPPY
PRETTY
QUEASY
QUEMOY
QWERTY
RHEUMY
SEELEY
SEEMLY
SHEEDY
SHEEHY
SHELLY
SHELTY
SHERRY
SKERRY
SLEAZY
SLEEKY
SLEEPY
SLEETY
SMEARY
SMELLY
SNEAKY
SNEERY
SNEEZY
SPEEDY
SPERRY
STEADY
STEAMY
STEELY
STEFOY
SWEATY
TEENSY
THEFLY
THEORY
THETOY
TREATY
TREBLY
TRENDY
TWEEDY
TWEENY
TWEETY
TWENTY
UNEASY
VEEJAY
WEEKLY
WEENSY
WHEEZY
WHERRY

•••EY•
ABBEYS
ALLEYS
BLUEYS
BOGEYS
BOLEYN
CONEYS
COVEYS
DOGEYS
FOGEYS
HONEYS
JASEYS
LIMEYS
MATEYS
MONEYS
MOSEYS
MULEYS
POKEYS
POLEYN
POPEYE
REDEYE
REKEYS
RIBEYE

•••E•Y
AMBERY
ARTERY
BAKERY
BARELY
BASELY
BEKESY
BLUELY
BLUESY
BOWERY
BREEZY
BRIERY
CAMEBY
CASEFY
CELERY
CHEEKY
CHEERY
CHEESY
CICELY
COMEBY
COMEDY
COMELY
CREEPY
CUTELY
CUTESY
DIRELY
DOWERY
DUPERY
EATERY
ELLERY
EMPERY
FAKERY
FINELY
FINERY
FLEECY
FREELY
GAIETY
GAMELY
GONEBY
GREEDY
GREENY
HALEVY
HEREBY
HERESY
HOMELY
HUGELY
JAPERY
JEREMY
LAMELY
LATELY
LIKELY
LINENY
LIVELY
LIVERY
LONELY
LOVELY
LOWERY
MERELY
MISERY
MOIETY
MOPERY
MUTELY
NAMELY
NAPERY
NASEBY
NICELY
NICETY
NINETY
NITERY
NUDELY
OCHERY
ORNERY
ORRERY
PALELY
PAPERY
PINERY
POKERY
PURELY
RAREFY
RARELY
REDENY
RELEVY
REMEDY
RIFELY
RIPELY
RONELY
RUDELY
SAFELY
SAFETY
SAGELY
SANELY
SCREWY
SEVERY
SHEEDY
SHEEHY
SINEWY
SLEEKY
SLEEPY
SLEETY
SNEERY
SNEEZY
SOLELY
SORELY
SPEEDY
SPHERY
STEELY
SURELY
SURETY
TAMELY
TIMELY
TOWERY
TUMEFY
TWEEDY
TWEENY
TWEETY
UBIETY
VALERY
VILELY
VINERY
VOWELY
WAFERY
WATERY
WAVERY
WHEEZY
WIDELY
WIFELY
WINERY
WISELY
YARELY

••••EY
ANDREY
ASHLEY
AUBREY
AUDREY
BAILEY
BARLEY
BARNEY
BEGLEY
BETSEY
BIRNEY
BLIMEY
BLOOEY
BOSLEY
BURLEY
BURNEY
CAGNEY
CARNEY
CARREY
CARVEY
CHANEY
CLAYEY
CONVEY
COONEY
COPLEY
COWLEY
CRIKEY
CURLEY
DABNEY
DAILEY
DICKEY
DILSEY
DINKEY
DISNEY
DONKEY
DOOLEY
DORSEY
DOWNEY
DUDLEY
DURFEY
FARLEY
FINNEY
FLAKEY
FLOOEY
FLUKEY
FLUTEY
FOSSEY
GALLEY
GARVEY
GELSEY
GOOSEY
GRAPEY
GURLEY
GURNEY
HAILEY
HALLEY
HALSEY
HANLEY
HARLEY
HARVEY
HAYLEY
HEANEY
HENLEY
HERSEY
HICKEY
HOCKEY
HORNEY
HORSEY
HURLEY
HUSSEY
HUXLEY
JACKEY
JENNEY
JERSEY
JITNEY
JOCKEY
KELLEY
KELSEY
KERSEY
KIDNEY
KINSEY
LACKEY
LEAKEY
LESLEY
LINNEY
LINSEY
LOONEY
LOWKEY
LYNLEY
MAGUEY
MARLEY
MASSEY
MEDLEY
MERSEY
MICKEY
MOBLEY
MONKEY
MOONEY
MORLEY
MOTLEY
MOUSEY
MURREY
NEWLEY
NIAMEY
NIPSEY
OAKLEY
OCASEY
OFFKEY
ORKNEY
OSPREY
PARLEY
PAULEY
PEAVEY
PENNEY
PHONEY
PHOOEY
POMPEY
PRICEY
PULLEY
PURVEY
RAINEY
RAMSEY
RICKEY
RIDLEY
RIPLEY
RODNEY
ROMNEY
ROONEY
SEELEY
SHALEY
SIDNEY
SISLEY
SLAVEY
SMILEY
SMOKEY
SPACEY
STACEY
STOREY
SURREY
SURVEY
SYDNEY
TEDKEY
TORREY
TRACEY
TUNNEY
TURKEY
VALLEY
VARNEY
VOLLEY
WATNEY
WESLEY
WHINEY
WIMSEY
WOLSEY
WOOLEY
WURLEY

EZ••••
EZZARD

E•Z•••
ENZYME
EVZONE
EZZARD

E••••Z
ERSATZ

•EZ•••
BEZANT
BEZELS
FEZZAN
FEZZES
GEZIRA
MEZZOS
REZONE

•E•Z••
BENZOL
DENZEL
FEZZAN
FEZZES
GEEZER
HERZOG
MEZZOS
SEIZED
SEIZER
SEIZES
TETZEL

•E••Z•
BEDAZE
BELIZE
REBOZO

••EZ••
AREZZO
GEEZER
QUEZON
SLEZAK

••E•Z•
AREZZO
BREEZE
BREEZY
FAENZA
FREEZE
FRENZY
RIENZI
SLEAZE
SLEAZY
SNEEZE
SNEEZY
TWEEZE
WHEEZE
WHEEZY

••E••Z
THEWIZ

•••EZ•
BREEZE
BREEZY
FREEZE
FRIEZE
SNEEZE
SNEEZY
TWEEZE
WHEEZE
WHEEZY

•••E•Z
BRIENZ
DOLENZ
LORENZ

••••EZ
BOULEZ
CHAVEZ
CORTEZ
JUAREZ
MONTEZ
TROPEZ
VALDEZ

FA••••
FABIAN
FABLED
FABLER
FABLES
FABRAY
FABRIC
FACADE
FACETS
FACEUP
FACIAL
FACIAS
FACIES
FACILE
FACING
FACTOR
FACULA
FADEIN
FADING
FAENZA
FAERIE
FAEROE
FAFNIR
FAGEND
FAGGED
FAGOTS
FAILED
FAILLE
FAINTS
FAIRED
FAIRER
FAIRLY
FAIRUP
FAISAL
FAITHS
FAIYUM
FAJITA
FAKERS
FAKERY
FAKING
FAKIRS
FALANA
FALCES
FALCON
FALINE
FALLEN
FALLIN
FALLON
FALLOW
FALLTO
FALSER
FALTER
FAMILY
FAMINE
FAMISH
FAMOUS
FANDOM
FANGED
FANION
FANJET
FANNED
FANNIE
FANONS
FANOUT
FANTAN
FARADS
FARCED
FARCES
FARCRY
FARERS
FARINA
FARING
FARLEY
FARLOW
FARMED
FARMER
FAROFF
FAROUK
FAROUT
FARRAH
FARRAR
FARROW
FASCES
FASCIA
FASTED
FASTEN
FASTER
FATALE
FATCAT
FATHER
FATHOM
FATIMA
FATTED
FATTEN
FATTER
FATWAS
FAUCES
FAUCET
FAULTS
FAULTY
FAUNAE
FAUNAL
FAUNAS
FAUNUS
FAVORS
FAVOUR
FAWKES
FAWLTY
FAWNED
FAWNER
FAXING
FAZING
FAZOOL

F•A•••
FEALTY
FEARED
FEARER
FEASTS
FEATLY
FIACRE
FIANCE
FIASCO
FLABBY
FLACKS
FLACON
FLAGGY
FLAGON
FLAILS
FLAIRS
FLAKED
FLAKER
FLAKES
FLAKEY
FLAMBE
FLAMED
FLAMES
FLANGE
FLANKS
FLAPPY
FLARED
FLARES
FLASHY
FLASKS
FLATLY
FLAUNT
FLAVIA
FLAVOR
FLAWED
FLAXEN
FLAXES
FLAYED
FLAYER
FMAJOR
FOALED
FOAMED
FRACAS
FRAIDY
FRAISE
FRAMED
FRAMES
FRANCA
FRANCE
FRANCK
FRANCO
FRANCS
FRANKS
FRANNY
FRAPPE
FRASER
FRAUDS
FRAUEN
FRAYED
FRAZER

F••A••
FACADE
FALANA
FARADS
FATALE
FEMALE
FIGARO
FINALE
FINALS
FIXATE
FLOATS
FLOATY
FORAGE
FORAYS
FREAKS
FREAKY
FRIARS
FRIARY
FSHARP
FUGARD
FULANI

F•••A•
FABIAN
FABRAY
FACIAL
FACIAS
FAISAL
FANTAN
FARRAH
FARRAR
FATCAT
FATWAS
FAUNAE
FAUNAL
FAUNAS
FBIMAN
FELLAH
FELLAS
FENIAN
FENMAN
FENWAY
FERIAL
FERIAS
FERMAT
FESTAL
FESTAS
FEUDAL
FEZZAN
FIJIAN
FILIAL
FINIAL
FINNAN
FIRMAN
FISCAL
FIVEAM
FLEWAT
FLORAE
FLORAL
FLORAS
FLYMAN
FLYWAY
FOETAL
FOGHAT
FOLIAR
FONTAL
FORBAD
FORMAL
FORMAN
FORMAT
FORTAS
FOSSAE
FOSSAS
FOURAM
FOVEAE
FRACAS
FRIDAY
FRUGAL
FRYPAN
FUJIAN
FULMAR

F••••A
FACULA
FAENZA
FAJITA
FALANA
FARINA
FASCIA
FATIMA
FEDORA
FEMORA
FIBULA
FIESTA
FLAVIA
FLICKA
FRANCA
FRESCA
FULCRA

•F•A••
AFEARD
AFFAIR
AFLAME
AFLATS
AFRAID
AFRAME
EFFACE
EFLATS
OFLATE

•F••A•
AFFRAY
AFGHAN
AFLOAT
OFFDAY

•F•••A
AFRICA
SFORZA

••FA••
AAFAIR
AFFAIR
AUFAIT
BEFALL
DEFACE
DEFAME
DEFATS
EFFACE
ENFANT
INFACT
INFAMY
INFANT
MUFASA
RAFAEL
REFACE
SAFARI
UNFAIR

••F•A•
AFFRAY
CAFTAN
DEFEAT
DEFRAY
ELFMAN
GUFFAW
OFFDAY
REFLAG

••F••A
DEFLEA
MUFASA
RAFFIA

•••FA•
ARAFAT
COLFAX
CONFAB
GUFFAW
KOUFAX
LOOFAH
LOOFAS
LOWFAT
NONFAT
PREFAB
SEAFAN
SHOFAR
SOLFAS
STEFAN

•••F•A
BIAFRA
RAFFIA

FB••••
FBIMAN
FBIMEN

F•B•••
FABIAN
FABLED
FABLER
FABLES
FABRAY
FABRIC
FIBBED
FIBBER
FIBERS

FIBRES FIBRIL FIBRIN FIBULA FOBBED FOBOFF FUBBED

F••B••

FEEBLE FEEBLY FERBER FIBBED FIBBER FLABBY FLYBOY FLYBYS FOBBED FOGBOW FOIBLE FORBAD FORBES FORBID FUBBED FUMBLE

F•••B•

FLABBY FLAMBE

•••F•B

CONFAB PREFAB

F•C•••

FACADE FACETS FACEUP FACIAL FACIAS FACIES FACILE FACING FACTOR FACULA FECUND FICHES FICHTE FICHUS FICKLE FOCSLE

F••C••

FALCES FALCON FARCED FARCES FARCRY FASCES FASCIA FATCAT FAUCES FAUCET FENCED FENCER FENCES FESCUE FIACRE FISCAL FLACKS FLACON FLECHE FLECKS FLECKY FLICKA FLICKS FLOCKS FLOCKY FORCED FORCER FORCES FRACAS FROCKS FULCRA

F•••C•

FIANCE FIASCO FIERCE FLEECE FLEECY FLETCH FLINCH FLITCH FRANCA FRANCE FRANCK FRANCO FRANCS FRENCH FRESCA FRESCO FRISCO

F••••C

FABRIC FENNEC FERENC FERRIC FINNIC FISTIC FORMIC FROLIC FUSTIC

•F•C••

AFLCIO

•F••C•

AFFECT AFRICA EFFACE EFFECT OFFICE

••F•C•

AFFECT DEFACE DEFECT EFFACE EFFECT INFACT INFECT OFFICE REFACE

•••F•C

UNIFIC

F•D•••

FADEIN FADING FEDORA FIDDLE FIDGET FODDER FUDDLE FUDGED FUDGES

F••D••

FANDOM FEEDER FEEDON FELDON FENDED FENDER FEUDAL FEUDED FIDDLE FINDER FLEDGE FLEDGY FODDER FOLDED FOLDER FOLDUP FONDER FONDLE FONDLY FONDUE FOODIE FORDED FREDDY FRIDAY FRIDGE FUDDLE FUNDED FYODOR

F•••D•

FACADE FARADS FIELDS FIENDS FIORDS FJELDS FJORDS FLOODS FLUIDS FOUNDS FRAIDY FRAUDS FREDDY FRONDS

F••••D

FABLED FAGEND FAGGED FAILED FAIRED FANGED FANNED FARCED FARMED FASTED FATTED FAWNED FEARED FECUND FELLED FELTED FENCED FENDED FERVID FESSED FEUDED FIBBED FILLED FILMED FINKED FINNED FIRMED FISHED FISTED FITTED FIZZED FLAKED FLAMED FLARED FLAWED FLAYED FLEXED FLEYED FLORID FLOWED FLUTED FLUXED FLYROD FOALED FOAMED FOBBED FOETID FOGGED FOILED FOINED FOLDED FOOLED FOOTED FORBAD FORBID FORCED FORDED FORGED FORKED FORMED FOULED FOWLED FRAMED FRAYED FRIEND FRIGID FUBBED FUDGED FUELED FUGARD FUNDED FUNKED FUNNED FURLED FURRED FUSSED FUTZED FUZZED

•F•D••

OFFDAY

•F•••D

AFEARD AFFORD AFIELD AFRAID OFFEND

••FD••

OFFDAY

••F••D

AFFORD ALFRED AUFOND BIFFED BIFOLD BOFFED BUFFED CUFFED DAFFED DEFEND DEFIED DOFFED ENFOLD GAFFED GIFTED HAFTED HEFTED HUFFED INFOLD LIFTED LOFTED LUFFED MIFFED MUFFED OFFEND OXFORD PUFFED RAFTED REFFED REFUND RIFFED RIFLED RIFTED RUFFED SIFTED TIFFED TUFTED UNFOLD WAFTED

•••F•D

BEEFED BIFFED BOFFED BUFFED CHAFED COIFED CONFED CUFFED DAFFED DOFFED GAFFED GOLFED GOOFED GULFED HOOFED HUFFED ILLFED KNIFED LEAFED LOAFED LUFFED MIFFED MUFFED PUFFED REEFED REFFED RIFFED ROOFED RUFFED SURFED THEFED TIFFED TRIFID TURFED WOLFED WOOFED

FE••••

FEALTY FEARED FEARER FEASTS FEATLY FECUND FEDORA FEEBLE FEEBLY FEEDER FEEDON FEEING FEELER FEIGNS FEINTS FEISTY FELDON FELINE FELIPE FELLAH FELLAS FELLED FELLER FELLIN FELLOE FELLON FELLOW FELLTO FELONS FELONY FELTED FEMALE FEMMES FEMORA FEMURS FENCED FENCER FENCES FENDED FENDER FENIAN FENMAN FENMEN FENNEC FENNEL FENWAY FERBER FERENC FERGIE FERGUS FERIAL FERIAS FERITY FERMAT FERRER FERRET FERRIC FERRIS FERULE FERVID FERVOR FESCUE FESSED FESSES FESSUP FESTAL FESTAS FESTER FESTUS FETING FETISH FETTER FETTLE FEUDAL FEUDED FEVERS FEWEST FEYEST FEZZAN FEZZES

F•E•••

FAENZA FAERIE FAEROE FEEBLE FEEBLY FEEDER FEEDON FEEING FEELER FIELDS FIENDS FIERCE FIESTA FJELDS FLECHE FLECKS FLECKY FLEDGE FLEDGY FLEECE FLEECY FLEERS FLEETS FLENSE FLESHY FLETCH FLEURY FLEWAT FLEWIN FLEXED FLEXES FLEXOR FLEYED FOEHNS FOETAL FOETID FOETOR FOETUS FREAKS FREAKY FREDDY FREELY FREEST FREEZE FRENCH FRENUM FRENZY FRESCA FRESCO FRESNO FRETTY FUELED FUELER

F••E••

FACETS FACEUP FADEIN FAGEND FAKERS FAKERY FARERS FERENC FEVERS FEWEST FEYEST FIBERS FIFERS FILENE FILERS FILETS FINELY FINERY FINEST FIRERS FIREUP FIVEAM FIVEPM FIVERS FIVEWS FIXERS FLEECE FLEECY FLEERS FLEETS FLIERS FLUENT FLYERS FOGEYS FOMENT FOREGO FOREST FOVEAE FOYERS FREELY FREEST FREEZE FRIEND FRIERS FRIEZE FRYERS FUSEES FUZEES

F•••E•

FABLED FABLER FABLES FACIES FAGGED FAILED FAIRED FAIRER FALCES FALLEN FALSER FALTER FANGED FANJET FANNED FARCED FARCES FARLEY FARMED FARMER FASCES FASTED FASTEN FASTER FATHER FATTED FATTEN FATTER FAUCES FAUCET FAWKES FAWNED FAWNER FBIMEN FEARED FEARER FEEDER FEELER FELLED FELLER FELTED FEMMES FENCED FENCER FENCES FENDED FENDER FENMEN FENNEC FENNEL FERBER FERRER FERRET FESSED FESSES FESTER FETTER FEUDED FEZZES FIBBED FIBBER FIBRES FICHES FIDGET FILLED FILLER FILLES FILLET FILMED FILTER FINDER FINGER FINKED FINNED FINNEY FIRMED FIRMER FISHED FISHER FISHES FISTED FITTED FITTER FIZZED FIZZES FLAKED FLAKER FLAKES FLAKEY FLAMED FLAMES FLARED FLARES FLAWED FLAXEN FLAXES FLAYED FLAYER FLEXED FLEXES FLEYED FLOOEY FLORES FLORET FLOWED FLOWER FLUKES FLUKEY FLUMES FLUTED FLUTES FLUTEY FLUXED FLUXES FLYMEN FLYNET FOALED FOAMED FOBBED FODDER FOGGED FOGGER FOGIES FOILED FOINED FOKKER FOLDED FOLDER FONDER FOOLED FOOLER FOOTED FOOTER FORBES FORCED FORCER FORCES FORDED FORGED FORGER FORGES FORGET FORKED FORKER FORMED FORMER FORTES FOSSES FOSSEY FOSTER FOULED FOULER FOWLED FOWLER FOWLES FOXIER FRAMED FRAMES FRASER FRAUEN FRAYED FRAZER FRISEE FRISES FROZEN FUBBED FUDGED FUDGES FUELED FUELER FUGUES FULLER FUMIER FUNDED FUNKED FUNNED FUNNEL FURIES FURLED FURRED FURZES FUSEES FUSSED FUSSES FUTZED FUTZES FUZEES FUZZED FUZZES

F••••E

FACADE FACILE FAERIE FAEROE FAILLE FALINE FAMINE FANNIE FATALE FAUNAE FEEBLE FELINE FELIPE FELLOE FEMALE FERGIE FERULE FESCUE FETTLE FIACRE FIANCE FICHTE FICKLE FIDDLE FIERCE FIGURE FILENE FILOSE FINALE FINITE FIPPLE FIXATE FIZZLE FLAMBE FLANGE FLECHE FLEDGE FLEECE FLENSE FLORAE FOCSLE FOIBLE FOLKIE FONDLE FONDUE FOODIE FOOZLE FORAGE FOSSAE FOVEAE FOZZIE FRAISE FRANCE FRAPPE FREEZE FRIDGE FRIEZE FRINGE FRISEE FUDDLE FUMBLE FURORE FUTILE FUTURE

•FE•••

AFEARD

•F•E••

AFFECT AFIELD AFREET AFRESH EFFECT EFFETE NFLERS OFFEND OFFERS

•F••E•

AFREET IFFIER OFFKEY OFFSET PFIZER XFILES

•F•••E

AFFINE AFLAME AFRAME EFFACE EFFETE EFFUSE OFFICE OFLATE

••FE••

AFFECT BEFELL DEFEAT DEFECT DEFEND DEFERS EFFECT EFFETE FIFERS GOFERS INFECT INFERS INFEST LIFERS OFFEND OFFERS REFERS RIFELY RIFEST SAFELY SAFEST SAFETY WAFERS WAFERY WIFELY

••F•E•

ALFRED ALFVEN BIFFED BOFFED BUFFED BUFFER BUFFET COFFEE COFFER CUFFED DAFFED DAFTER DEFIED DEFIES DEFLEA DEFTER DIFFER DOFFED DUFFEL DUFFER EIFFEL GAFFED GAFFER GAFFES GIFTED HAFTED HEFNER HEFTED HUFFED IFFIER LAFFER LIFTED LIFTER LOFTED LUFFED MIFFED MUFFED OFFKEY OFFSET PUFFED PUFFER RAFAEL RAFTED RAFTER REFFED REFLEX REFUEL RIFFED RIFLED RIFLER RIFLES RIFTED RUFFED SIFTED SIFTER SOFTEN SOFTER SUFFER TIFFED TOFFEE TUFFET TUFTED UNFREE WAFTED ZAFFER

••F••E

AFFINE ALFINE BAFFLE BEFORE COFFEE DEFACE DEFAME DEFILE DEFINE DEFUSE EFFACE EFFETE EFFUSE IMFINE INFUSE LEFTIE MIFUNE MUFFLE OFFICE ONFILE ONFIRE PIFFLE RAFFLE REFACE REFILE REFINE REFUGE REFUSE REFUTE RIFFLE RUFFLE SAFIRE SOFINE SOFTIE TOFFEE UNFREE WAFFLE

•••FE•

BEEFED BIFFED BOFFED BUFFED BUFFER BUFFET CHAFED CHAFES COFFEE COFFER COIFED CONFED CONFER CUFFED CURFEW DAFFED DEAFEN DEAFER DIFFER DOFFED DUFFEL DUFFER DURFEY EIFFEL GAFFED GAFFER GAFFES GOLFED GOLFER GOOFED GULFED HEIFER HOOFED HOOFER HUFFED ILLFED KIEFER KNIFED KNIFES LAFFER LEAFED LIEFER LOAFED LOAFER LUFFED MIFFED MUFFED PILFER PREFER PUFFED PUFFER REEFED REEFER REFFED RIFFED ROOFED ROOFER RUFFED SUFFER SURFED SURFER THEFED TIFFED TITFER TOFFEE TUFFET TURFED TWOFER WERFEL WOLFED WOOFED WOOFER ZAFFER

•••F•E

BAFFLE BOUFFE COFFEE KHAFRE MUFFLE PIAFFE PIFFLE PURFLE RAFFLE RIFFLE RUFFLE STIFLE TOFFEE TRIFLE WAFFLE

••••FE

BOUFFE CARAFE EXWIFE OKEEFE PIAFFE RECIFE STRAFE STRIFE TOLIFE UNSAFE

F•F•••

FAFNIR FIFERS FIFING FIFTHS

F••F••

FITFUL FLUFFS FLUFFY FULFIL

F•••F•

FAROFF FLUFFS FLUFFY FOBOFF

F••••F

FAROFF FOBOFF

•FF•••

AFFAIR AFFECT AFFINE AFFIRM AFFORD AFFRAY EFFACE EFFECT EFFETE EFFIGY EFFLUX EFFORT EFFUSE IFFIER OFFDAY OFFEND OFFERS OFFICE OFFING OFFISH OFFKEY OFFSET

••FF••

BAFFIN BAFFLE BIFFED BOFFED BOFFIN BOFFOS BUFFED BUFFER BUFFET BUFFON BUFFOS COFFEE COFFER CUFFED DAFFED DIFFER DOFFED DUFFEL DUFFER EIFFEL GAFFED GAFFER GAFFES GUFFAW HUFFED KAFFIR LAFFER LUFFED MIFFED MUFFED MUFFIN MUFFLE PIFFLE PUFFED PUFFER PUFFIN RAFFIA RAFFLE REFFED RIFFED RIFFLE RUFFED RUFFLE RUFFLY SOFFIT SUFFER SUFFIX TIFFED TIFFIN TOFFEE TUFFET WAFFLE WAFFLY ZAFFER

••F•F•

RIFIFI

•••FF•
BLUFFS BOUFFE CHAFFS CHAFFY CHUFFY CLIFFS CLIFFY FLUFFS FLUFFY PIAFFE QUAFFS SCOFFS SCUFFS SKIFFS SNIFFS SNIFFY SNUFFS SNUFFY SPIFFS SPIFFY STAFFS STEFFI STIFFS STUFFS STUFFY WHIFFS

••••FF
BEGOFF BITOFF BUGOFF BUYOFF CANIFF CRYOFF CUTOFF DIEOFF DRYOFF FAROFF FOBOFF GETOFF GOTOFF HOPOFF LAYOFF LEDOFF LETOFF LOGOFF NODOFF PAYOFF POPOFF PUTOFF RANOFF REBUFF RIPOFF RUBOFF RUNOFF SAWOFF SCHIFF SCLAFF SCRUFF SEEOFF SETOFF TAPOFF TARIFF TEEOFF TIPOFF TOPOFF

F•G•••
FAGEND FAGGED FAGOTS FIGARO FIGHTS FIGURE FOGBOW FOGEYS FOGGED FOGGER FOGHAT FOGIES FOGSIN FOGSUP FUGARD FUGUES

F••G••
FAGGED FANGED FEIGNS FERGIE FERGUS FIDGET FINGER FIZGIG FLAGGY FLAGON FLIGHT FOGGED FOGGER FORGED FORGER FORGES FORGET FORGOT FOUGHT FRIGHT FRIGID FROGGY FRUGAL FUDGED FUDGES FUNGUS

F•••G•
FLAGGY FLANGE FLEDGE FLEDGY FLINGS FORAGE FOREGO FRIDGE FRINGE FRINGY FROGGY

F••••G
FACING FADING FAKING FARING FAXING FAZING FEEING FETING FIFING FILING FINING FIRING FIXING FIZGIG FLYING FOXING FRYING FUMING FUSING FUZING

•FG•••
AFGHAN

•F••G•
EFFIGY

•F•••G
OFFING

••F•G•
BEFOGS DEFOGS EFFIGY REFUGE

••F••G
FIFING OFFING REFLAG ZAFTIG

•••F•G
ICEFOG INAFOG

F•H•••
FSHARP

F••H••
FATHER FATHOM FICHES FICHTE FICHUS FIGHTS FISHED FISHER FISHES FOEHNS FOGHAT FUZHOU

F•••H•
FAITHS FIFTHS FILTHY FIRTHS FLASHY FLECHE FLESHY FLIGHT FOUGHT FRIGHT FROTHS FROTHY

F••••H
FAMISH FARRAH FELLAH FETISH FINISH FLETCH FLINCH FLITCH FOURTH FRENCH

•F•H••
AFGHAN

•F•••H
AFRESH OFFISH

••F•H•
FIFTHS

••F••H
ELFISH GOFISH OAFISH OFFISH

•••F•H
LOOFAH

FI••••
FIACRE FIANCE FIASCO FIBBED FIBBER FIBERS FIBRES FIBRIL FIBRIN FIBULA FICHES FICHTE FICHUS FICKLE FIDDLE FIDGET FIELDS FIENDS FIERCE FIESTA FIFERS FIFING FIFTHS FIGARO FIGHTS FIGURE FIJIAN FILENE FILERS FILETS FILIAL FILING FILIUS FILLED FILLER FILLES FILLET FILLIN FILLIP FILLUP FILMED FILOSE FILTER FILTHY FINALE FINALS FINDER FINELY FINERY FINEST FINGER FINIAL FINING FINISH FINITE FINITO FINKED FINNAN FINNED FINNEY FINNIC FIORDS FIPPLE FIRERS FIREUP FIRING FIRKIN FIRMAN FIRMED FIRMER FIRMLY FIRMUP FIRSTS FIRTHS FISCAL FISHED FISHER FISHES FISTED FISTIC FITFUL FITSIN FITTED FITTER FIVEAM FIVEPM FIVERS FIVEWS FIXATE FIXERS FIXING FIXITY FIXUPS FIZGIG FIZZED FIZZES FIZZLE

F•I•••
FAILED FAILLE FAINTS FAIRED FAIRER FAIRLY FAIRUP FAISAL FAITHS FAIYUM FBIMAN FBIMEN FEIGNS FEINTS FEISTY FLICKA FLICKS FLIERS FLIGHT FLIMSY FLINCH FLINGS FLINTS FLINTY FLIPUP FLIRTS FLIRTY FLITCH FMINOR FOIBLE FOILED FOINED FOISTS FRIARS FRIARY FRIDAY FRIDGE FRIEND FRIERS FRIEZE FRIGHT FRIGID FRIJOL FRILLS FRILLY FRINGE FRINGY FRISCO FRISEE FRISES FRISKS FRISKY FRITOS FRIZZY

F••I••
FABIAN FACIAL FACIAS FACIES FACILE FACING FADING FAJITA FAKING FAKIRS FALINE FAMILY FAMINE FAMISH FANION FARINA FARING FATIMA FAXING FAZING FEEING FELINE FELIPE FENIAN FERIAL FERIAS FERITY FETING FETISH FIFING FIJIAN FILIAL FILING FILIUS FINIAL FINING FINISH FINITE FINITO FIRING FIXING FIXITY FLAILS FLAIRS FLUIDS FLYING FLYINS FOGIES FOLIAR FOLIOS FOLIUM FORINT FOXIER FOXILY FOXING FRAIDY FRAISE FRUITS FRUITY FRYING FUJIAN FUMIER FUMING FURIES FUSILS FUSING FUSION FUTILE FUZING

F•••I•
FABRIC FADEIN FAERIE FAFNIR FALLIN FANNIE FASCIA FELLIN FERGIE FERRIC FERRIS FERVID FIBRIL FIBRIN FILLIN FILLIP FINNIC FIRKIN FISTIC FITSIN FIZGIG FLAVIA FLEWIN FLORID FLORIN FLORIO FOETID FOGSIN FOLKIE FOODIE FORBID FORMIC FOSSIL FOZZIE FRIGID FROLIC FULFIL FUSTIC

F••••I
FRUTTI FULANI

•FI•••
AFIELD PFIZER XFILES

•F•I••
AFFINE AFFIRM AFRICA AFRITS EFFIGY IFFIER OFFICE OFFING OFFISH

•F••I•
AFFAIR AFLCIO AFRAID

••FI••
AFFINE AFFIRM ALFINE BEFITS DEFIED DEFIES DEFILE DEFINE EFFIGY ELFISH FIFING GOFISH IFFIER IMFINE INFIRM KAFIRS KEFIRS OAFISH OFFICE OFFING OFFISH ONFILE ONFIRE REFILE REFILL REFINE REFITS RIFIFI SAFIRE SOFINE SUFISM UNFITS

••F•I•
AAFAIR AFFAIR AUFAIT BAFFIN BOFFIN FAFNIR HEFLIN KAFFIR LEFTIE LEFTIN MUFFIN MUFTIS PUFFIN RAFFIA SOFFIT SOFTIE SUFFIX TIFFIN UNFAIR ZAFTIG

••F••I
RIFIFI SAFARI

•••FI•
BAFFIN BOFFIN BOWFIN COMFIT FULFIL HOOFIT INAFIX KAFFIR MISFIT MUFFIN OLEFIN OUTFIT PREFIX PROFIT PUFFIN RAFFIA REDFIN REDFIR SAWFIT SCIFIS SEEFIT SOFFIT SUFFIX TIFFIN TRIFID UNIFIC

•••F•I
STEFFI

••••FI
AMALFI RIFIFI STEFFI

FJ••••
FJELDS FJORDS

F•J•••
FAJITA FIJIAN FUJIAN

F••J••
FANJET FMAJOR FRIJOL

F•K•••
FAKERS FAKERY FAKING FAKIRS FOKKER

F••K••
FAWKES FICKLE FINKED FIRKIN FLAKED FLAKER FLAKES FLAKEY FLUKES FLUKEY FOKKER FOLKIE FOLKSY FORKED FORKER FUNKED

F•••K•
FLACKS FLANKS FLASKS FLECKS FLECKY FLICKA FLICKS FLOCKS FLOCKY FLUNKS FLUNKY FRANKS FREAKS FREAKY FRISKS FRISKY FROCKS

F••••K
FAROUK FRANCK

•F•K••
OFFKEY

••FK••
OFFKEY

FL••••
FLABBY FLACKS FLACON FLAGGY FLAGON FLAILS FLAIRS FLAKED FLAKER FLAKES FLAKEY FLAMBE FLAMED FLAMES FLANGE FLANKS FLAPPY FLARED FLARES FLASHY FLASKS FLATLY FLAUNT FLAVIA FLAVOR FLAWED FLAXEN FLAXES FLAYED FLAYER FLECHE FLECKS FLECKY FLEDGE FLEDGY FLEECE FLEECY FLEERS FLEETS FLENSE FLESHY FLETCH FLEURY FLEWAT FLEWIN FLEXED FLEXES FLEXOR FLEYED FLICKA FLICKS FLIERS FLIGHT FLIMSY FLINCH FLINGS FLINTS FLINTY FLIPUP FLIRTS FLIRTY FLITCH FLOATS FLOATY FLOCKS FLOCKY FLOODS FLOOEY FLOORS FLOPPY FLOPSY FLORAE FLORAL FLORAS FLORES FLORET FLORID FLORIN FLORIO FLOSSY FLOURS FLOURY FLOUTS FLOWED FLOWER FLUENT FLUFFS FLUFFY FLUIDS FLUKES FLUKEY FLUMES FLUNKS FLUNKY FLUORO FLURRY FLUTED FLUTES FLUTEY FLUXED FLUXES FLYBOY FLYBYS FLYERS FLYING FLYINS FLYMAN FLYMEN FLYNET FLYOUT FLYROD FLYWAY

F•L•••
FALANA FALCES FALCON FALINE FALLEN FALLIN FALLON FALLOW FALLTO FALSER FALTER FELDON FELINE FELIPE FELLAH FELLAS FELLED FELLER FELLIN FELLOE FELLON FELLOW FELLTO FELONS FELONY FELTED FILENE FILERS FILETS FILIAL FILING FILIUS FILLED FILLER FILLES FILLET FILLIN FILLIP FILLUP FILMED FILOSE FILTER FILTHY FOLDED FOLDER FOLDUP FOLIAR FOLIOS FOLIUM FOLKIE FOLKSY FOLLOW FOLSOM FULANI FULCRA FULFIL FULLER FULMAR FULTON

F••L••
FABLED FABLER FABLES FAILED FAILLE FALLEN FALLIN FALLON FALLOW FALLTO FARLEY FARLOW FAULTS FAULTY FAWLTY FEALTY FEELER FELLAH FELLAS FELLED FELLER FELLIN FELLOE FELLON FELLOW FELLTO FIELDS FILLED FILLER FILLES FILLET FILLIN FILLIP FILLUP FJELDS FOALED FOILED FOLLOW FOOLED FOOLER FOULED FOULER FOULLY FOULUP FOWLED FOWLER FOWLES FRILLS FRILLY FROLIC FUELED FUELER FULLER FURLED

F•••L•
FACILE FACULA FAILLE FAIRLY FAMILY FATALE FEATLY FEEBLE FEEBLY FEMALE FERULE FETTLE FIBULA FICKLE FIDDLE FINALE FINALS FINELY FIPPLE FIRMLY FIZZLE FLAILS FLATLY FOCSLE FOIBLE FONDLE FONDLY FOOZLE FOULLY FOXILY FREELY FRILLS FRILLY FUDDLE FUMBLE FUSILS FUTILE

F••••L
FACIAL FAISAL FAUNAL FAZOOL FENNEL FERIAL FESTAL FEUDAL FIBRIL FILIAL FINIAL FISCAL FITFUL FLORAL FOETAL FONTAL FORMAL FOSSIL FRIJOL FRUGAL FULFIL FUNNEL

•FL•••
AFLAME AFLATS AFLCIO AFLOAT EFLATS NFLERS OFLATE

•F•L••
EFFLUX XFILES

•F••L•
AFIELD

••FL••
DEFLEA EFFLUX HEFLIN INFLOW INFLUX REFLAG REFLEX REFLUX RIFLED RIFLER RIFLES TEFLON

••F•L•
BAFFLE BEFALL BEFELL BIFOLD DAFTLY DEFILE DEFTLY ENFOLD INFOLD INFULL MUFFLE ONFILE PIFFLE RAFFLE REFILE REFILL RIFELY RIFFLE RUFFLE RUFFLY SAFELY SOFTLY UNFOLD WAFFLE WAFFLY WIFELY

••F••L
BEFALL BEFELL BEFOUL DUFFEL EIFFEL INFULL RAFAEL REFILL REFUEL UNFURL

•••FL•
BAFFLE BARFLY BOTFLY DEAFLY DRYFLY GADFLY LETFLY LIEFLY MAYFLY MEDFLY MUFFLE OUTFLY PIFFLE POPFLY PURFLE RAFFLE RIFFLE RUFFLE RUFFLY STIFLE THEFLY TRIFLE WAFFLE WAFFLY WETFLY

•••F•L
AIDFUL AIMFUL ARMFUL ARTFUL BAGFUL BOXFUL CANFUL CAPFUL CARFUL CUPFUL DUFFEL EARFUL EIFFEL EYEFUL FITFUL FULFIL HATFUL IREFUL JARFUL JOYFUL JUGFUL LAPFUL LAWFUL MANFUL PANFUL PEPFUL POTFUL RUEFUL SINFUL SOBFUL USEFUL VATFUL WERFEL WILFUL WOEFUL

FM••••
FMAJOR FMINOR

F•M•••
FAMILY FAMINE FAMISH FAMOUS FEMALE FEMMES FEMORA FEMURS FOMENT FUMBLE FUMIER FUMING

F••M••
FARMED FARMER FBIMAN FBIMEN FEMMES FENMAN FENMEN FERMAT FILMED FIRMAN FIRMED FIRMER FIRMLY FIRMUP FLAMBE FLAMED FLAMES FLIMSY FLUMES FLYMAN FLYMEN FOAMED FORMAL FORMAN FORMAT FORMED FORMER FORMIC FRAMED FRAMES FRUMPS FRUMPY FULMAR

F•••M•
FATIMA FORUMS

F••••M
FAIYUM FANDOM FATHOM FIVEAM FIVEPM FOLIUM FOLSOM FOURAM FOURPM

FRENUM

•F••M•
AFLAME
AFRAME

•F•••M
AFFIRM

••FM••
ELFMAN

••F•M•
DEFAME
INFAMY

••F••M
AFFIRM
DEFORM
INFIRM
INFORM
REFORM
SUFISM

F•N•••
FANDOM
FANGED
FANION
FANJET
FANNED
FANNIE
FANONS
FANOUT
FANTAN
FENCED
FENCER
FENCES
FENDED
FENDER
FENIAN
FENMAN
FENMEN
FENNEC
FENNEL
FENWAY
FINALE
FINALS
FINDER
FINELY
FINERY
FINEST
FINGER
FINIAL
FINING
FINISH
FINITE
FINITO
FINKED
FINNAN
FINNED
FINNEY
FINNIC
FONDER
FONDLE
FONDLY
FONDUE
FONTAL
FUNDED
FUNGUS
FUNKED
FUNNED
FUNNEL

F••N••
FAENZA
FAFNIR
FAINTS
FANNED
FANNIE
FAUNAE
FAUNAL
FAUNAS
FAUNUS
FAWNED
FAWNER
FEINTS
FENNEC
FENNEL
FIANCE
FIENDS
FINNAN
FINNED
FINNEY
FINNIC
FLANGE
FLANKS
FLENSE
FLINCH
FLINGS
FLINTS
FLINTY
FLUNKS
FLUNKY
FLYNET
FMINOR
FOINED
FOUNDS
FOUNTS
FRANCA
FRANCE
FRANCK
FRANCO
FRANCS
FRANKS
FRANNY
FRENCH
FRENUM
FRENZY
FRINGE
FRINGY
FRONDS
FRONTS
FUNNED
FUNNEL

F•••N•
FACING
FADING
FAGEND
FAKING
FALANA
FALINE
FAMINE
FANONS
FARINA
FARING
FAXING
FAZING
FECUND
FEEING
FEIGNS
FELINE
FELONS
FELONY
FERENC
FETING
FIFING
FILENE
FILING
FINING
FIRING
FIXING
FLAUNT
FLUENT
FLYING
FLYINS
FOEHNS
FOMENT
FORINT
FOXING
FRANNY
FRESNO
FRIEND
FROWNS
FRYING
FULANI
FUMING
FUSING
FUTONS
FUZING

F••••N
FABIAN
FADEIN
FALCON
FALLEN
FALLIN
FALLON
FANION
FANTAN
FASTEN
FATTEN
FBIMAN
FBIMEN
FEEDON
FELDON
FELLIN
FELLON
FENIAN
FENMAN
FENMEN
FEZZAN
FIBRIN
FIJIAN
FILLIN
FINNAN
FIRKIN
FIRMAN
FITSIN
FLACON
FLAGON
FLAXEN
FLEWIN
FLORIN
FLYMAN
FLYMEN
FOGSIN
FORMAN
FRAUEN
FROZEN
FRYPAN
FUJIAN
FULTON
FUSION

•F••N•
AFFINE
OFFEND
OFFING

•F•••N
AFGHAN

••FN••
FAFNIR
HEFNER

••F•N•
AFFINE
ALFINE
AUFOND
DEFEND
DEFINE
ENFANT
FIFING
IMFINE
INFANT
MIFUNE
OFFEND
OFFING
REFINE
REFUND
SOFINE

••F••N
ALFVEN
BAFFIN
BOFFIN
BUFFON
CAFTAN
ELFMAN
HEFLIN
LEFTIN
MUFFIN
PUFFIN
SOFTEN
TEFLON
TIFFIN

•••F•N
BAFFIN
BOFFIN
BOWFIN
BUFFON
DEAFEN
MUFFIN
OLEFIN
PUFFIN
REDFIN
SEAFAN
STEFAN
TIFFIN

FO••••
FOALED
FOAMED
FOBBED
FOBOFF
FOCSLE
FODDER
FOEHNS
FOETAL
FOETID
FOETOR
FOETUS
FOGBOW
FOGEYS
FOGGED
FOGGER
FOGHAT
FOGIES
FOGSIN
FOGSUP
FOIBLE
FOILED
FOINED
FOISTS
FOKKER
FOLDED
FOLDER
FOLDUP
FOLIAR
FOLIOS
FOLIUM
FOLKIE
FOLKSY
FOLLOW
FOLSOM
FOMENT
FONDER
FONDLE
FONDLY
FONDUE
FONTAL
FOODIE
FOOLED
FOOLER
FOOTED
FOOTER
FOOZLE
FORAGE
FORAYS
FORBAD
FORBES
FORBID
FORCED
FORCER
FORCES
FORDED
FOREGO
FOREST
FORGED
FORGER
FORGES
FORGET
FORGOT
FORINT
FORKED
FORKER
FORMAL
FORMAN
FORMAT
FORMED
FORMER
FORMIC
FORTAS
FORTES
FORUMS
FOSSAE
FOSSAS
FOSSES
FOSSEY
FOSSIL
FOSTER
FOUGHT
FOULED
FOULER
FOULLY
FOULUP
FOUNDS
FOUNTS
FOURAM
FOURPM
FOURTH
FOVEAE
FOWLED
FOWLER
FOWLES
FOXIER
FOXILY
FOXING
FOYERS
FOZZIE

F•O•••
FIORDS
FJORDS
FLOATS
FLOATY
FLOCKS
FLOCKY
FLOODS
FLOOEY
FLOORS
FLOPPY
FLOPSY
FLORAE
FLORAL
FLORAS
FLORES
FLORET
FLORID
FLORIN
FLORIO
FLOSSY
FLOURS
FLOURY
FLOUTS
FLOWED
FLOWER
FOODIE
FOOLED
FOOLER
FOOTED
FOOTER
FOOZLE
FROCKS
FROGGY
FROLIC
FRONDS
FRONTS
FROSTS
FROSTY
FROTHS
FROTHY
FROWNS
FROWZY
FROZEN
FYODOR

F••O••
FAGOTS
FAMOUS
FANONS
FANOUT
FAROFF
FAROUK
FAROUT
FAVORS
FAVOUR
FAZOOL
FEDORA
FELONS
FELONY
FEMORA
FILOSE
FLOODS
FLOOEY
FLOORS
FLUORO
FLYOUT
FOBOFF
FSTOPS
FTROOP
FURORE
FURORS
FUTONS

F•••O•
FACTOR
FAEROE
FALCON
FALLON
FALLOW
FANDOM
FANION
FARLOW
FARROW
FATHOM
FAZOOL
FEEDON
FELDON
FELLOE
FELLON
FELLOW
FERVOR
FLACON
FLAGON
FLAVOR
FLEXOR
FLYBOY
FLYROD
FMAJOR
FMINOR
FOETOR
FOGBOW
FOLIOS
FOLLOW
FOLSOM
FORGOT
FRIJOL
FRITOS
FTROOP
FULTON
FURROW
FUSION
FUZHOU
FYODOR

F••••O
FALLTO
FELLTO
FIASCO
FIGARO
FINITO
FLORIO
FLUORO
FOREGO
FRANCO
FRESCO
FRESNO
FRISCO

•FO•••
SFORZA

•F•O••
AFFORD
AFLOAT
EFFORT

•F•••O
AFLCIO

••FO••
AFFORD
AJFOYT
AUFOND
BEFOGS
BEFORE
BEFOUL
BIFOLD
DEFOGS
DEFORM
EFFORT
ENFOLD
INFOLD
INFORM
ONFOOT
OXFORD
REFORM
RUFOUS
UNFOLD

••F•O•
BOFFOS
BUFFON
BUFFOS
INFLOW
ONFOOT
TEFLON

•••FO•
AIMFOR
ALLFOR
ASKFOR
BOFFOS
BUFFON
BUFFOS
GUNFOR
ICEFOG
INAFOG
KITFOX
LAYFOR
OPTFOR
OUTFOX
PAYFOR
RANFOR
REDFOX
RUNFOR
SEAFOX
STEFOY
TRYFOR

••••FO
SENUFO

F•P•••
FIPPLE

F••P••
FIPPLE
FLAPPY
FLIPUP
FLOPPY
FLOPSY
FRAPPE
FRYPAN

F•••P•
FELIPE
FIVEPM
FIXUPS
FLAPPY
FLOPPY
FOURPM
FRAPPE
FRUMPS
FRUMPY
FSTOPS

F••••P
FACEUP
FAIRUP
FESSUP
FILLIP
FILLUP
FIREUP
FIRMUP
FLIPUP
FOGSUP
FOLDUP
FOULUP
FSHARP
FTROOP

••F••P
LIFTUP

•••F•P
BEEFUP
GOOFUP

FR••••
FRACAS
FRAIDY
FRAISE
FRAMED
FRAMES
FRANCA
FRANCE
FRANCK
FRANCO
FRANCS
FRANKS
FRANNY
FRAPPE
FRASER
FRAUDS
FRAUEN
FRAYED
FRAZER
FREAKS
FREAKY
FREDDY
FREELY
FREEST
FREEZE
FRENCH
FRENUM
FRENZY
FRESCA
FRESCO
FRESNO
FRETTY
FRIARS
FRIARY
FRIDAY
FRIDGE
FRIEND
FRIERS
FRIEZE
FRIGHT
FRIGID
FRIJOL
FRILLS
FRILLY
FRINGE
FRINGY
FRISCO
FRISEE
FRISES
FRISKS
FRISKY
FRITOS
FRIZZY
FROCKS
FROGGY
FROLIC
FRONDS
FRONTS
FROSTS
FROSTY
FROTHS
FROTHY
FROWNS
FROWZY
FROZEN
FRUGAL
FRUITS
FRUITY
FRUMPS
FRUMPY
FRUTTI
FRYERS
FRYING
FRYPAN

F•R•••
FARADS
FARCED
FARCES
FARCRY
FARERS
FARINA
FARING
FARLEY
FARLOW
FARMED
FARMER
FAROFF
FAROUK
FAROUT
FARRAH
FARRAR
FARROW
FERBER
FERENC
FERGIE
FERGUS
FERIAL
FERIAS
FERITY
FERMAT
FERRER
FERRET
FERRIC
FERRIS
FERULE
FERVID
FERVOR
FIRERS
FIREUP
FIRING
FIRKIN
FIRMAN
FIRMED
FIRMER
FIRMLY
FIRMUP
FIRSTS
FIRTHS
FORAGE
FORAYS
FORBAD
FORBES
FORBID
FORCED
FORCER
FORCES
FORDED
FOREGO
FOREST
FORGED
FORGER
FORGES
FORGET
FORGOT
FORINT
FORKED
FORKER
FORMAL
FORMAN
FORMAT
FORMED
FORMER
FORMIC
FORTAS
FORTES
FORUMS
FTROOP
FURIES
FURLED
FURORE
FURORS
FURRED
FURROW
FURZES

F••R••
FABRAY
FABRIC
FAERIE
FAEROE
FAIRED
FAIRER
FAIRLY
FAIRUP
FARRAH
FARRAR
FARROW
FEARED
FEARER
FERRER
FERRET
FERRIC
FERRIS
FIBRES
FIBRIL
FIBRIN
FIERCE
FIORDS
FJORDS
FLARED
FLARES
FLIRTS
FLIRTY
FLORAE
FLORAL
FLORAS
FLORES
FLORET
FLORID
FLORIN
FLORIO
FLURRY
FLYROD
FOURAM
FOURPM
FOURTH
FURRED
FURROW

F•••R•
FAKERS
FAKERY
FAKIRS
FARCRY
FARERS
FAVORS
FEDORA
FEMORA
FEMURS
FEVERS
FIACRE
FIBERS
FIFERS
FIGARO
FIGURE
FILERS
FINERY
FIRERS
FIVERS
FIXERS
FLAIRS
FLEERS
FLEURY
FLIERS
FLOORS
FLOURS
FLOURY
FLUORO
FLURRY
FLYERS
FOYERS
FRIARS
FRIARY
FRIERS
FRYERS
FSHARP
FUGARD
FULCRA
FURORE
FURORS
FUTURE

F••••R
FABLER
FACTOR
FAFNIR
FAIRER
FALSER
FALTER
FARMER
FARRAR
FASTER
FATHER
FATTER
FAVOUR
FAWNER
FEARER
FEEDER
FEELER
FELLER
FENCER
FENDER
FERBER
FERRER
FERVOR
FESTER
FETTER
FIBBER
FILLER
FILTER
FINDER
FINGER
FIRMER
FISHER
FITTER
FLAKER
FLAVOR
FLAYER
FLEXOR
FLOWER
FMAJOR
FMINOR
FODDER
FOETOR
FOGGER
FOKKER
FOLDER
FOLIAR
FONDER
FOOLER
FOOTER
FORCER
FORGER
FORKER
FORMER
FOSTER
FOULER
FOWLER
FOXIER
FRASER
FRAZER
FUELER
FULLER
FULMAR
FUMIER
FYODOR

•FR•••
AFRAID
AFRAME
AFREET
AFRESH
AFRICA
AFRITS

•F•R••
AFFRAY
SFORZA

•F••R•
AFEARD
AFFIRM
AFFORD
EFFORT
NFLERS
OFFERS

•F•••R
AFFAIR
IFFIER
PFIZER

••FR••
AFFRAY
ALFRED
DEFRAY
UNFREE

••F•R•
AFFIRM
AFFORD
BEFORE
DEFERS
DEFORM
EFFORT
ERFURT
FIFERS
GOFERS
INFERS
INFIRM
INFORM
KAFIRS
KEFIRS
LIFERS
OFFERS
ONFIRE
OXFORD
REFERS
REFORM
SAFARI
SAFIRE
UNFURL
WAFERS
WAFERY

••F••R
AAFAIR
AFFAIR
BUFFER
COFFER
DAFTER
DEFTER
DIFFER
DUFFER
FAFNIR
GAFFER
HEFNER
IFFIER
KAFFIR
LAFFER
LIFTER
PUFFER
RAFTER
RIFLER
SIFTER
SOFTER
SUFFER
UNFAIR
ZAFFER

•••FR•
BELFRY
BIAFRA
KHAFRE
PANFRY

•••F•R
AIMFOR
ALLFOR
ASKFOR
BUFFER
COFFER
CONFER
DEAFER
DIFFER
DUFFER
GAFFER
GOLFER
GUNFOR
HEIFER
HOOFER
KAFFIR
KIEFER
LAFFER
LAYFOR
LIEFER
LOAFER
OPTFOR
PAYFOR
PILFER
PREFER
PUFFER
RANFOR
REDFIR
REEFER
ROOFER
RUNFOR
SHOFAR
SUFFER
SULFUR
SURFER
TITFER
TRYFOR
TWOFER
WOOFER
ZAFFER

FS••••
FSHARP
FSTOPS

F•S•••
FASCES
FASCIA
FASTED
FASTEN
FASTER
FESCUE
FESSED
FESSES
FESSUP
FESTAL
FESTAS
FESTER
FESTUS
FISCAL
FISHED
FISHER
FISHES
FISTED
FISTIC
FOSSAE
FOSSAS
FOSSES
FOSSEY
FOSSIL
FOSTER
FUSEES
FUSILS
FUSING
FUSION
FUSSED
FUSSES
FUSTIC

F••S••
FAISAL
FALSER
FEASTS
FEISTY
FESSED
FESSES
FESSUP
FIASCO
FIESTA
FIRSTS
FITSIN
FLASHY
FLASKS
FLESHY
FLOSSY
FOCSLE
FOGSIN
FOGSUP
FOISTS
FOLSOM
FOSSAE
FOSSAS
FOSSES
FOSSEY
FOSSIL
FRASER
FRESCA
FRESCO
FRESNO
FRISCO
FRISEE
FRISES
FRISKS
FRISKY
FROSTS
FROSTY
FUSSED
FUSSES

F•••S•
FAMISH
FETISH
FEWEST
FEYEST
FILOSE
FINEST
FINISH
FLENSE
FLIMSY
FLOPSY
FLOSSY
FOLKSY
FOREST
FRAISE
FREEST

F••••S
FABLES
FACETS
FACIAS
FACIES
FAGOTS
FAINTS
FAITHS
FAKERS
FAKIRS
FALCES
FAMOUS
FANONS
FARADS
FARCES
FARERS
FASCES
FATWAS
FAUCES
FAULTS
FAUNAS
FAUNUS
FAVORS
FAWKES
FEASTS
FEIGNS
FEINTS
FELLAS
FELONS
FEMMES
FEMURS
FENCES
FERGUS
FERIAS
FERRIS
FESSES
FESTAS

FESTUS FEVERS FEZZES FIBERS FIBRES FICHES FICHUS FIELDS FIENDS FIFERS FIFTHS FIGHTS FILERS FILETS FILIUS FILLES FINALS FIORDS FIRERS FIRSTS FIRTHS FISHES FIVERS FIVEWS FIXERS FIXUPS FIZZES FJELDS FJORDS FLACKS FLAILS FLAIRS FLAKES FLAMES FLANKS FLARES FLASKS FLAXES FLECKS FLEERS FLEETS FLEXES FLICKS FLIERS FLINGS FLINTS FLIRTS FLOATS FLOCKS FLOODS FLOORS FLORAS FLORES FLOURS FLOUTS FLUFFS FLUIDS FLUKES FLUMES FLUNKS FLUTES FLUXES FLYBYS FLYERS FLYINS FOEHNS FOETUS FOGEYS FOGIES FOISTS FOLIOS FORAYS FORBES FORCES FORGES FORTAS FORTES FORUMS FOSSAS FOSSES FOUNDS FOUNTS FOWLES FOYERS FRACAS FRAMES FRANCS FRANKS FRAUDS FREAKS FRIARS FRIERS FRILLS FRISES FRISKS FRITOS FROCKS FRONDS FRONTS FROSTS FROTHS FROWNS FRUITS FRUMPS FRYERS FSTOPS FUDGES FUGUES FUNGUS FURIES FURORS FURZES FUSEES FUSILS FUSSES FUTONS FUTZES FUZEES FUZZES

•F•S••
OFFSET

•F••S•
AFRESH EFFUSE OFFISH

•F•••S
AFLATS AFRITS EFLATS NFLERS OFFERS XFILES

••FS••
OFFSET

••F•S•
DEFUSE EFFUSE ELFISH GOFISH INFEST INFUSE MUFASA OAFISH OFFISH REFUSE RIFEST SAFEST SUFISM

••F••S
BEFITS BEFOGS BOFFOS BUFFOS DEFATS DEFERS DEFIES DEFOGS FIFERS FIFTHS GAFFES GOFERS INFERS KAFIRS KEFIRS LIFERS MUFTIS OFFERS REFERS REFITS RIFLES RUFOUS UNFITS WAFERS

•••F•S
BLUFFS BOFFOS BUFFOS CHAFES CHAFFS CLEFTS CLIFFS CRAFTS CROFTS DELFTS DOOFUS DRAFTS DRIFTS FLUFFS GAFFES GRAFTS GRIFTS KNIFES LOOFAS QUAFFS SCIFIS SCOFFS SCUFFS SHAFTS SHIFTS SKIFFS SNAFUS SNIFFS SNUFFS SOLFAS SPIFFS STAFFS STIFFS STUFFS SWIFTS THEFTS WHIFFS

••••FS
BLUFFS BRIEFS CHAFFS CHIEFS CLIFFS DECAFS DWARFS FLUFFS GRIEFS KLOOFS MOTIFS PILAFS PROOFS QUAFFS SCARFS SCOFFS SCUFFS SERIFS SHEAFS SKIFFS SMURFS SNIFFS SNUFFS SPIFFS SPOOFS STAFFS STIFFS STUFFS WHARFS WHIFFS WHOOFS

FT••••
FTROOP

F•T•••
FATALE FATCAT FATHER FATHOM FATIMA FATTED FATTEN FATTER FATWAS FETING FETISH FETTER FETTLE FITFUL FITSIN FITTED FITTER FSTOPS FUTILE FUTONS FUTURE FUTZED FUTZES

F••T••
FACTOR FAITHS FALTER FANTAN FASTED FASTEN FASTER FATTED FATTEN FATTER FEATLY FELTED FESTAL FESTAS FESTER FESTUS FETTER FETTLE FIFTHS FILTER FILTHY FIRTHS FISTED FISTIC FITTED FITTER FLATLY FLETCH FLITCH FLUTED FLUTES FLUTEY FOETAL FOETID FOETOR FOETUS FONTAL FOOTED FOOTER FORTAS FORTES FOSTER FRETTY FRITOS FROTHS FROTHY FRUTTI FULTON FUSTIC

F•••T•
FACETS FAGOTS FAINTS FAJITA FALLTO FAULTS FAULTY FAWLTY FEALTY FEASTS FEINTS FEISTY FELLTO FERITY FICHTE FIESTA FIGHTS FILETS FINITE FINITO FIRSTS FIXATE FIXITY FLEETS FLINTS FLINTY FLIRTS FLIRTY FLOATS FLOATY FLOUTS FOISTS FOUNTS FOURTH FRETTY FRONTS FROSTS FROSTY FRUITS FRUITY FRUTTI

F••••T
FANJET FANOUT FAROUT FATCAT FAUCET FERMAT FERRET FEWEST FEYEST FIDGET FILLET FINEST FLAUNT FLEWAT FLIGHT FLORET FLUENT FLYNET FLYOUT FOGHAT FOMENT FOREST FORGET FORGOT FORINT FORMAT FOUGHT FREEST FRIGHT

•F••T•
AFLATS AFRITS EFFETE EFLATS OFLATE

•F•••T
AFFECT AFLOAT AFREET EFFECT EFFORT OFFSET

••FT••
CAFTAN DAFTER DAFTLY DEFTER DEFTLY FIFTHS GIFTED HAFTED HEFTED LEFTIE LEFTIN LIFTED LIFTER LIFTUP LOFTED MUFTIS RAFTED RAFTER RIFTED SIFTED SIFTER SOFTEN SOFTER SOFTIE SOFTLY TUFTED WAFTED ZAFTIG

••F•T•
BEFITS DEFATS EFFETE REFITS REFUTE SAFETY UNFITS

••F••T
AFFECT AJFOYT AUFAIT BUFFET DEFEAT DEFECT EFFECT EFFORT ENFANT ERFURT INFACT INFANT INFECT INFEST OFFSET ONFOOT RIFEST SAFEST SOFFIT TUFFET

•••FT•
CLEFTS CRAFTS CRAFTY CROFTS DELFTS DRAFTS DRAFTY DRIFTS DRIFTY GRAFTS GRIFTS SHAFTS SHIFTS SHIFTY SWIFTS THEFTS

•••F•T
ARAFAT BUFFET COMFIT HOOFIT LOWFAT MISFIT NONFAT OUTFIT PROFIT SAWFIT SEEFIT SOFFIT TUFFET

••••FT
ADRIFT BEREFT GOSOFT SHRIFT THRIFT UPLIFT

FU••••
FUBBED FUDDLE FUDGED FUDGES FUELED FUELER FUGARD FUGUES FUJIAN FULANI FULCRA FULFIL FULLER FULMAR FULTON FUMBLE FUMIER FUMING FUNDED FUNGUS FUNKED FUNNED FUNNEL FURIES FURLED FURORE FURORS FURRED FURROW FURZES FUSEES FUSILS FUSING FUSION FUSSED FUSSES FUSTIC FUTILE FUTONS FUTURE FUTZED FUTZES FUZEES FUZHOU FUZING FUZZED FUZZES

F•U•••
FAUCES FAUCET FAULTS FAULTY FAUNAE FAUNAL FAUNAS FAUNUS FEUDAL FEUDED FLUENT FLUFFS FLUFFY FLUIDS FLUKES FLUKEY FLUMES FLUNKS FLUNKY FLUORO FLURRY FLUTED FLUTES FLUTEY FLUXED FLUXES FOUGHT FOULED FOULER FOULLY FOULUP FOUNDS FOUNTS FOURAM FOURPM FOURTH FRUGAL FRUITS FRUITY FRUMPS FRUMPY FRUTTI

F••U••
FACULA FECUND FEMURS FERULE FIBULA FIGURE FIXUPS FLAUNT FLEURY FLOURS FLOURY FLOUTS FORUMS FRAUDS FRAUEN FUGUES FUTURE

F•••U•
FACEUP FAIRUP FAIYUM FAMOUS FANOUT FAROUK FAROUT FAUNUS FAVOUR FERGUS FESCUE FESSUP FESTUS FICHUS FILIUS FILLUP FIREUP FIRMUP FITFUL FLIPUP FLYOUT FOETUS FOGSUP FOLDUP FOLIUM FONDUE FOULUP FRENUM FUNGUS

F••••U
FUZHOU

•F•U••
EFFUSE

•F••U•
EFFLUX

••FU••
DEFUSE EFFUSE ERFURT INFULL INFUSE MIFUNE REFUEL REFUGE REFUND REFUSE REFUTE UNFURL

••F•U•
BEFOUL EFFLUX INFLUX LIFTUP REFLUX RUFOUS

•••FU•
AIDFUL AIMFUL ARMFUL ARTFUL BAGFUL BEEFUP BOXFUL CANFUL CAPFUL CARFUL CUPFUL DOOFUS EARFUL EYEFUL FITFUL GOOFUP HATFUL IREFUL JARFUL JOYFUL JUGFUL LAPFUL LAWFUL MANFUL PANFUL PEPFUL POTFUL RUEFUL SINFUL SNAFUS SOBFUL SULFUR USEFUL VATFUL WILFUL WOEFUL

••••FU
KUNGFU

F•V•••
FAVORS FAVOUR FEVERS FIVEAM FIVEPM FIVERS FIVEWS FOVEAE

F••V••
FERVID FERVOR FLAVIA FLAVOR

••FV••
ALFVEN

F•W•••
FAWKES FAWLTY FAWNED FAWNER FEWEST FOWLED FOWLER FOWLES

F••W••
FATWAS FENWAY FLAWED FLEWAT FLEWIN FLOWED FLOWER FLYWAY FROWNS FROWZY

F•••W•
FIVEWS

F••••W
FALLOW FARLOW FARROW FELLOW FOGBOW FOLLOW FURROW

••F••W
GUFFAW INFLOW

•••F•W
CURFEW GUFFAW

F•X•••
FAXING FIXATE FIXERS FIXING FIXITY FIXUPS FOXIER FOXILY FOXING

F••X••
FLAXEN FLAXES FLEXED FLEXES FLEXOR FLUXED FLUXES

•F•••X
EFFLUX

••F••X
EFFLUX INFLUX REFLEX REFLUX SUFFIX

•••F•X
COLFAX INAFIX KITFOX KOUFAX OUTFOX PREFIX REDFOX SEAFOX SUFFIX

FY••••
FYODOR

F•Y•••
FEYEST FLYBOY FLYBYS FLYERS FLYING FLYINS FLYMAN FLYMEN FLYNET FLYOUT FLYROD FLYWAY FOYERS FRYERS FRYING FRYPAN

F••Y••
FAIYUM FLAYED FLAYER FLEYED FRAYED

F•••Y•
FLYBYS FOGEYS FORAYS

F••••Y
FABRAY FAIRLY FAKERY FAMILY FARCRY FARLEY FAULTY FAWLTY FEALTY FEATLY FEEBLY FEISTY FELONY FENWAY FERITY FILTHY FINELY FINERY FINNEY FIRMLY FIXITY FLABBY FLAGGY FLAKEY FLAPPY FLASHY FLATLY FLECKY FLEDGY FLEECY FLESHY FLEURY FLIMSY FLINTY FLIRTY FLOATY FLOCKY FLOOEY FLOPPY FLOPSY FLOSSY FLOURY FLUFFY FLUKEY FLUNKY FLURRY FLUTEY FLYBOY FLYWAY FOLKSY FONDLY FOSSEY FOULLY FOXILY FRAIDY FRANNY FREAKY FREDDY FREELY FRENZY FRETTY FRIARY FRIDAY FRILLY FRINGY FRISKY FRIZZY FROGGY FROSTY FROTHY FROWZY FRUITY FRUMPY

•F•••Y
AFFRAY EFFIGY OFFDAY OFFKEY

••F•Y•
AJFOYT

••F••Y
AFFRAY DAFTLY DEFRAY DEFTLY EFFIGY INFAMY OFFDAY OFFKEY RIFELY RUFFLY SAFELY SAFETY SOFTLY WAFERY WAFFLY WIFELY

•••F•Y
BARFLY BELFRY BOTFLY CHAFFY CHUFFY CLIFFY CRAFTY DEAFLY DRAFTY DRIFTY DRYFLY DURFEY FLUFFY GADFLY LETFLY LIEFLY MAYFLY MEDFLY OUTFLY PANFRY POPFLY RUFFLY SHIFTY SNIFFY SNUFFY SPIFFY STEFOY STUFFY THEFLY WAFFLY WETFLY

••••FY
AERIFY ARGUFY AURIFY BASIFY CASEFY CHAFFY CHUFFY CITIFY CLIFFY CODIFY FLUFFY GASIFY MINIFY MODIFY NIDIFY NOTIFY OSSIFY PACIFY PURIFY RAMIFY RAREFY RARIFY RATIFY RUBIFY SALIFY SCURFY SNIFFY SNUFFY SPIFFY STUFFY TUMEFY TYPIFY UGLIFY VERIFY VILIFY VINIFY VIVIFY

F•Z•••
FAZING FAZOOL FEZZAN FEZZES FIZGIG FIZZED FIZZES FIZZLE FOZZIE FUZEES FUZHOU FUZING FUZZED FUZZES

F••Z••
FEZZAN FEZZES FIZZED FIZZES FIZZLE FOOZLE FOZZIE FRAZER FRIZZY FROZEN FURZES FUTZED FUTZES FUZZED FUZZES

F•••Z•
FAENZA FREEZE FRENZY FRIEZE FRIZZY FROWZY

•F•Z••
PFIZER

•F••Z•
SFORZA

GA••••
GABBED GABBER GABBLE GABBRO GABIES GABION GABLED GABLER GABLES GADDED GADDER GADFLY GADGET GAELIC GAFFED GAFFER GAFFES GAGGED GAGGLE GAGING GAGLAW GAGMAN GAGMEN GAIETY GAIJIN GAINED GAINER GAINLY GAINON GAINST GAITED GAITER GALAGO GALAHS GALATA GALAXY GALEAE GALENA GALLED GALLEY GALLIA GALLIC GALLON GALLOP GALLUP GALOIS GALOOT GALOPS GALORE GALOSH GALPAL GALWAY GALYAK GAMAYS GAMBIA GAMBIT GAMBLE GAMBOL GAMELY GAMEST GAMETE GAMIER GAMILY GAMINE GAMING GAMINS GAMMAS GAMMED GAMMER GAMMON GAMUTS GANDER GANDHI GANGED GANGER GANGES GANGLE GANGLY GANGUE GANGUP GANNET GANTRY GAOLED GAOLER GAPERS GAPING GAPPED GARAGE GARBED

GARBLE
GARCIA
GARCON
GARDEN
GARETH
GARGLE
GARISH
GARLIC
GARNER
GARNET
GARRET
GARSON
GARTER
GARTHS
GARVEY
GASBAG
GASCAP
GASCON
GASHED
GASHES
GASIFY
GASJET
GASKET
GASKIN
GASLIT
GASLOG
GASMAN
GASMEN
GASPAR
GASPED
GASPER
GASSED
GASSER
GASSES
GASTON
GASTRO
GATEAU
GATERS
GATHER
GATING
GATLIN
GATORS
GATSBY
GAUCHE
GAUCHO
GAUGED
GAUGER
GAUGES
GAUMED
GAUZES
GAVEIN
GAVELS
GAVEUP
GAVIAL
GAWAIN
GAWKED
GAWKER
GAWPED
GAYALS
GAYEST
GAYNOR
GAZEBO
GAZING
GAZUMP

G•A•••

GDANSK
GEARED
GEARTO
GEARUP
GHAINS
GHARRY
GHAZIS
GIANTS
GLACES
GLACIS
GLADES
GLADLY
GLADYS
GLAIRS
GLAIRY
GLAMOR
GLANCE
GLANDS
GLARED
GLARES
GLASER
GLASSY
GLAZED
GLAZER
GLAZES
GMAJOR
GNARLS
GNARLY
GNATTY
GNAWED
GNAWER
GOADED
GOALIE
GOANNA
GOATEE
GOAWAY
GOAWRY
GRABAT
GRABBY
GRABEN
GRABLE
GRACED
GRACES
GRACIE
GRADEA
GRADED
GRADER
GRADES
GRADIN
GRADUS
GRAECO
GRAFTS
GRAHAM
GRAILS
GRAINS
GRAINY
GRAMAS
GRAMME
GRAMMY
GRAMPA
GRAMPS
GRANDE
GRANDS
GRANGE
GRANNY
GRANTS
GRAPES
GRAPEY
GRAPHS
GRAPHY
GRAPPA
GRASPS
GRASSO
GRASSY
GRATED
GRATER
GRATES
GRATIA
GRATIN
GRATIS
GRAVED
GRAVEL
GRAVEN
GRAVER
GRAVES
GRAVID
GRAYED
GRAYER
GRAYLY
GRAZED
GRAZER
GRAZES
GUACOS
GUARDS
GUAVAS

G••A••

GALAGO
GALAHS
GALATA
GALAXY
GAMAYS
GARAGE
GAWAIN
GAYALS
GELADA
GELATI
GELATO
GEMARA
GERAHS
GERALD
GERARD
GIRARD
GITANO
GLEAMS
GLEAMY
GLEANS
GLOATS
GOBACK
GOCART
GODARD
GOEASY
GOKART
GORALS
GREASE
GREASY
GREATS
GREAVE
GROANS
GROATS
GSHARP
GSTAAD
GUIANA
GULAGS
GUYANA
GYRATE

G•••A•

GAGLAW
GAGMAN
GALEAE
GALPAL
GALWAY
GALYAK
GAMMAS
GASBAG
GASCAP
GASMAN
GASPAR
GATEAU
GAVIAL
GEEGAW
GEMMAE
GENIAL
GENOAN
GENUAL
GERMAN
GETMAD
GETSAT
GEWGAW
GIBRAN
GILEAD
GIMBAL
GLOBAL
GOAWAY
GOESAT
GOSTAG
GOTHAM
GOTMAD
GRABAT
GRAHAM
GRAMAS
GSTAAD
GUAVAS
GUFFAW
GUITAR
GULLAH
GUNMAN
GUNNAR
GUSTAV
GUTTAE
GYMBAG

G••••A

GALATA
GALENA
GALLIA
GAMBIA
GARCIA
GEISHA
GELADA
GEMARA
GENERA
GENEVA
GEZIRA
GLENDA
GLINKA
GLORIA
GLOSSA
GOANNA
GODIVA
GOTCHA
GRADEA
GRAMPA
GRAPPA
GRATIA
GRETNA
GUIANA
GUINEA
GURKHA
GUYANA

•GA•••

AGADIR
AGAMAS
AGARIC
AGASSI
AGATES
AGATHA
AGAVES
UGANDA

•G•A••

AGHAST
AGLAIA
AGLARE
AGNATE
IGNACE
IGNATZ
IGUACU
IGUANA
OGHAMS
OGLALA
UGGAMS

•G••A•

AGAMAS
AGENAS
AGLEAM
AGORAE
AGORAS
OGDOAD
SGTMAJ
UGRIAN

•G•••A

AGATHA
AGENDA
AGLAIA
EGERIA
EGESTA
IGUANA
OGLALA
UGANDA

••GA••

ARGALI
ASGARD
BIGAMY
BOGART
CIGARS
DAGAMA
DEGAGE
EDGARD
EDGARS
ENGAGE
ERGATE
FIGARO
FUGARD
HEGARI
HOGANS
KIGALI
LAGASH
LEGACY
LEGALS
LEGATE
LEGATO
LIGAND
LIGATE
MEGALO
MEGARA
MUGABE
NAGANO
NEGATE
ORGANA
ORGANS
ORGATE
PAGANS
REGAIN
REGALE
REGARD
RUGATE
SUGARS
SUGARY
TOGAED
UGGAMS
VAGARY
VEGANS

••G•A•

AEGEAN
AFGHAN
AUGEAN
BAGDAD
BEGGAR
BIGMAC
CAGUAS
COGNAC
DAGMAR
DIGRAM
DOGDAY
DOGEAR
DOGMAS
DOGSAT
DOGTAG
ENGRAM
FOGHAT
GAGLAW
GAGMAN
HAGMAN
INGEAR
INGMAR
INGRAM
JAGUAR
JIGSAW
LEGMAN
LOGJAM
MAGMAS
MAGYAR
MCGRAW
ORGEAT
RAGBAG
RAGLAN
RAGMAN
RAGTAG
REGGAE
REGNAL
REGNAT
SIGMAS
SIGNAL
TAGDAY
UNGUAL
WIGWAG
WIGWAM
ZIGZAG

••G••A

ANGELA
ANGLIA
ANGOLA
ANGORA
BOGOTA
DAGAMA
HEGIRA
KAGERA
LAGUNA
LIGULA
LOGGIA
MEGARA
NAGOYA
ORGANA
PAGODA
REGINA
SEGURA
VIGODA

•••GA•

ALEGAR
AMIGAS
ANSGAR
BEGGAR
BENGAL
BENGAY
BIOGAS
BROGAN
BULGAR
BURGAS
CONGAS
COOGAN
COUGAR
FRUGAL
GEEGAW
GEWGAW
HANGAR
KURGAN
LONGAN
MARGAY
MEDGAR
MORGAN
NILGAI
NORGAY
NOUGAT
OMEGAS
PISGAH
PLAGAL
REAGAN
REGGAE
SAIGAS
SEAGAL
SLOGAN
TAIGAS
TONGAN
VULGAR

•••G•A

BANGKA
BORGIA
ENIGMA
LINGUA
LOGGIA
QUAGGA
STIGMA
ZEUGMA

••••GA

AURIGA
BELUGA
BODEGA
CAYUGA
LADOGA
MALAGA
ORTEGA
PAANGA
PERUGA
QUAGGA
SENEGA

G•B•••

GABBED
GABBER
GABBLE
GABBRO
GABIES
GABION
GABLED
GABLER
GABLES
GIBBED
GIBBER
GIBBET
GIBBON
GIBERS
GIBILL
GIBING
GIBLET
GIBRAN
GIBSON
GOBACK
GOBBLE
GOBIES
GOBLET
GOBLIN
GOBUST
GYBING

G••B••

GABBED
GABBER
GABBLE
GABBRO
GAMBIA
GAMBIT
GAMBLE
GAMBOL
GARBED
GARBLE
GASBAG
GERBER
GERBIL
GIBBED
GIBBER
GIBBET
GIBBON
GIMBAL
GIMBEL
GLEBES
GLIBLY
GLOBAL
GLOBED
GLOBES
GLOBIN
GOBBLE
GOOBER
GRABAT
GRABBY
GRABEN
GRABLE
GREBES
GRUBBY
GUMBEL
GUMBOS
GYMBAG

G•••B•

GATSBY
GAZEBO
GETSBY
GOESBY
GONEBY
GOODBY
GRABBY
GRUBBY

•GB•••

EGBERT

••GB••

BIGBEN
BIGBOY
FOGBOW
RAGBAG

••G•B•

MUGABE

••G••B

ZAGREB

•••GB•

NINGBO

G••C••

GARCIA
GARCON
GASCAP
GASCON
GAUCHE
GAUCHO
GLACES
GLACIS
GLYCOL
GOTCHA
GRACED
GRACES
GRACIE
GROCER
GUACOS

G•••C•

GLANCE
GLITCH
GOBACK
GRAECO
GREECE
GRINCH
GROUCH

G••••C

GAELIC
GALLIC
GARLIC
GESTIC
GNOMIC
GOTHIC

•G•C••

EGGCUP

•G••C•

AGENCY
IGNACE
IGUACU

•G•••C

AGARIC

••GC••

EGGCUP

••G•C•

LEGACY

••G••C

ANGLIC
BIGMAC
COGNAC

•••G•C

TRAGIC

GD••••

GDANSK

G•D•••

GADDED
GADDER
GADFLY
GADGET
GIDEON
GIDGET
GODARD
GODETS
GODIVA
GODOWN
GODSON
GODWIN
GODWIT
GUDRUN

G••D••

GADDED
GADDER
GANDER
GANDHI
GARDEN
GENDER
GEODES
GILDED
GILDER
GIRDED
GIRDER
GIRDLE
GLADES
GLADLY
GLADYS
GLIDED
GLIDER
GLIDES
GOADED
GOLDEN
GOLDIE
GOODBY
GOODEN
GOODIE
GOODLY
GOODOH
GORDIE
GORDON
GRADEA
GRADED
GRADER
GRADES
GRADIN
GRADUS
GRODIN
GRODNO
GRUDGE
GUIDED
GUIDES
GUIDON
GUNDOG

G•••D•

GELADA
GLANDS
GLENDA
GOURDE
GOURDS
GRANDE
GRANDS
GREEDY
GRINDS
GRUNDY
GUARDS
GUILDS

G••••D

GABBED
GABLED
GADDED
GAFFED
GAGGED
GAINED
GAITED
GALLED
GAMMED
GANGED
GAOLED
GAPPED
GARBED
GASHED
GASPED
GASSED
GAUGED
GAUMED
GAWKED
GAWPED
GEARED
GELLED
GEMMED
GERALD
GERARD
GERUND
GETMAD
GIBBED
GIFTED
GIGGED
GILDED
GILEAD
GILLED
GINNED
GIPPED
GIRARD
GIRDED
GIRNED
GIRTED
GLARED
GLAZED
GLIDED
GLOBED
GLOVED
GLOWED
GLOZED
GNAWED
GOADED
GODARD
GOLFED
GONGED
GOOFED
GOOSED
GORGED
GOTMAD
GOUGED
GOUNOD
GOWILD
GOWNED
GRACED
GRADED
GRATED
GRAVED
GRAVID
GRAYED
GRAZED
GREYED
GRIMED
GRIPED
GROPED
GROUND
GSTAAD
GUIDED
GULFED
GULLED
GULPED
GUMMED
GUNNED
GUSHED
GUSTED
GUTTED
GYPPED

•GD•••

OGDOAD

•G•D••

AGADIR

•G••D•

AGENDA
UGANDA

•G•••D

AGEOLD
AGREED
OGDOAD

••GD••

BAGDAD
DOGDAY
DOGDOM
HAGDON
TAGDAY

••G•D•

PAGODA
VIGODA

••G••D

ANGLED
ARGUED
ASGARD
AUGEND
BAGDAD
BAGGED
BEGGED
BIGRED
BOGGED
BUGGED
BUGLED
COGGED
DOGGED
DOGOOD
EAGLED
EDGARD
ENGIRD
FAGEND
FAGGED
FOGGED
FUGARD
GAGGED
GIGGED
HOGGED
HUGGED
INGRID
JAGGED
JIGGED
JOGGED
JUGGED
KEGGED
LAGGED
LEGEND
LEGGED
LIGAND
LOGGED
LUGGED
MUGGED
NAGGED
NOGOOD
OSGOOD
PEGGED
PIGGED
PUGGED
RAGGED
REGARD
RIGGED
RUGGED
SAGGED
SEGUED
SIGHED
SIGNED
SIGURD
TAGEND
TAGGED
TOGAED
TOGGED
TUGGED
UNGIRD
VEGGED
WAGGED
WIGGED
ZAGGED
ZIGGED

•••G•D

BAGGED
BANGED
BARGED
BEGGED
BINGED
BOGGED
BONGED
BRIGID
BUDGED
BUGGED
BULGED
BUNGED
CADGED
COGGED
DINGED
DODGED
DOGGED
FAGGED
FANGED
FOGGED
FORGED
FRIGID
FUDGED
GAGGED
GANGED
GAUGED
GIGGED
GONGED
GORGED
GOUGED
HANGED
HEDGED
HINGED
HOGGED
HUGGED
IMAGED
JAGGED
JIGGED
JOGGED
JUDGED
JUGGED
KEDGED
KEGGED
KINGED
LAGGED
LEGGED
LODGED
LOGGED
LONGED
LUGGED
LUNGED
MERGED
MUGGED
NAGGED
NUDGED
PEGGED
PIGGED
PINGED
PONGED
PONGID
PUGGED
PURGED
RAGGED
RANGED
RIDGED
RIGGED
RINGED
ROUGED
RUGGED
SAGGED
SIEGED
SINGED
STAGED
SUNGOD
SURGED
SWAGED
TAGGED
TANGED
TINGED
TINGOD
TOGGED
TUGGED
TURGID
UNAGED
VEGGED
VERGED
WAGGED
WARGOD
WEDGED
WIGGED
WINGED
ZAGGED
ZIGGED
ZINGED

GE••••

GEARED
GEARTO
GEARUP
GECKOS
GEEGAW
GEEGEE
GEEING
GEEZER
GEHRIG
GEIGER
GEISEL
GEISHA
GELADA
GELATI
GELATO
GELEES
GELLED
GELSEY
GEMARA
GEMINI
GEMMAE
GEMMED
GEMOTE
GEMOTS
GENDER
GENERA
GENETS
GENEVA
GENEVE
GENIAL
GENIES
GENIUS
GENOAN
GENOME
GENRES
GENTLE
GENTLY
GENTRY
GENUAL
GEODES
GEORGE
GEORGY
GERAHS
GERALD
GERARD
GERBER
GERBIL
GERENT
GERMAN
GERONT
GERTIE
GERUND
GESTES
GESTIC
GETMAD
GETOFF
GETOUT
GETSAT
GETSBY
GETSET
GETSIN
GETSIT
GETSON
GETSTO
GETSUP
GETTER
GETUPS
GEWGAW
GEYSER
GEZIRA

G•E•••

GAELIC
GEEGAW
GEEGEE
GEEING
GEEZER
GHETTO
GLEAMS
GLEAMY
GLEANS
GLEBES
GLENDA
GLENNE
GNEISS
GOEASY
GOESAT
GOESBY
GOESIN
GOESON
GOESUP
GOETHE
GREASE
GREASY
GREATS
GREAVE
GREBES
GREECE
GREEDY
GREEKS
GREENE
GREENS
GREENY
GREETS
GREGOR
GREIGE
GRETEL
GRETNA
GREWON
GREWUP
GREYED
GREYER
GREYLY
GUELPH
GUENON
GUERRE
GUESTS

G••E••

GAIETY
GALEAE
GALENA
GAMELY
GAMEST
GAMETE
GAPERS
GARETH
GATEAU
GATERS
GAVEIN
GAVELS
GAVEUP
GAYEST
GAZEBO
GELEES
GENERA
GENETS
GENEVA
GENEVE
GERENT
GIBERS
GIDEON
GILEAD
GIMELS
GIVEIN
GIVENS
GIVERS
GIVETO
GIVEUP
GLUERS
GODETS
GOFERS
GOLEMS
GONEBY
GONERS
GOVERN
GOWEST
GRAECO
GREECE
GREEDY
GREEKS
GREENE
GREENS
GREENY
GREETS
GRIEFS
GRIEVE
GRUELS
GYRENE

G•••E•

GABBED
GABBER
GABIES
GABLED
GABLER
GABLES
GADDED
GADDER
GADGET
GAFFED
GAFFER
GAFFES
GAGGED

GAGMEN
GAINED
GAINER
GAITED
GAITER
GALLED
GALLEY
GAMIER
GAMMED
GAMMER
GANDER
GANGED
GANGER
GANGES
GANNET
GAOLED
GAOLER
GAPPED
GARBED
GARDEN
GARNER
GARNET
GARRET
GARTER
GARVEY
GASHED
GASHES
GASJET
GASKET
GASMEN
GASPED
GASPER
GASSED
GASSER
GASSES
GATHER
GAUGED
GAUGER
GAUGES
GAUMED
GAUZES
GAWKED
GAWKER
GAWPED
GEARED
GEEGEE
GEEZER
GEIGER
GEISEL
GELEES
GELLED
GELSEY
GEMMED
GENDER
GENIES
GENRES
GEODES
GERBER
GESTES
GETSET
GETTER
GEYSER
GIBBED
GIBBER
GIBBET
GIBLET
GIDGET
GIFTED
GIGGED
GIGUES
GIJOES
GILDED
GILDER
GILLED

GIMBEL
GIMLET
GIMMES
GINGER
GINNED
GIPPED
GIPPER
GIRDED
GIRDER
GIRNED
GIRTED
GLACES
GLADES
GLARED
GLARES
GLASER
GLAZED
GLAZER
GLAZES
GLEBES
GLIDED
GLIDER
GLIDES
GLOBED
GLOBES
GLOVED
GLOVER
GLOVES
GLOWED
GLOWER
GLOZED
GLOZES
GLUIER
GLUTEI
GLUTEN
GLUTES
GNAWED
GNAWER
GNOMES
GOADED
GOATEE
GOBIES
GOBLET
GOLDEN
GOLFED
GOLFER
GONGED
GOOBER
GOODEN
GOOFED
GOOIER
GOOSED
GOOSES
GOOSEY
GOOVER
GOPHER
GORGED
GORGES
GORGET
GORIER
GORSES
GOSHEN
GOSPEL
GOTSET
GOTTEN
GOUGED
GOUGER
GOUGES
GOULET
GOWNED
GRABEN
GRACED
GRACES
GRADEA

GRADED
GRADER
GRADES
GRAPES
GRAPEY
GRATED
GRATER
GRATES
GRAVED
GRAVEL
GRAVEN
GRAVER
GRAVES
GRAYED
GRAYER
GRAZED
GRAZER
GRAZES
GREBES
GRETEL
GREYED
GREYER
GRIMED
GRIMES
GRIPED
GRIPER
GRIPES
GRIVET
GROCER
GROPED
GROPES
GROVEL
GROVER
GROVES
GROWER
GUIDED
GUIDES
GUILES
GUINEA
GUISES
GULFED
GULLED
GULLET
GULPED
GULPER
GUMBEL
GUMMED
GUNMEN
GUNNED
GUNNEL
GUNNER
GUNTER
GURLEY
GURNEY
GUSHED
GUSHER
GUSHES
GUSSET
GUSTED
GUTTED
GUTTER
GYPPED
GYPPER

G••••E

GABBLE
GAGGLE
GALEAE
GALORE
GAMBLE
GAMETE
GAMINE
GANGLE
GANGUE
GARAGE
GARBLE
GARGLE
GAUCHE
GEEGEE
GEMMAE
GEMOTE
GENEVE
GENOME
GENTLE
GEORGE
GERTIE
GIGGLE
GILLIE
GIRDLE
GLANCE
GLENNE
GOALIE
GOATEE
GOBBLE
GOETHE
GOGGLE
GOHOME
GOLDIE
GOODIE
GOOGLE
GORDIE
GOURDE
GRABLE
GRACIE
GRAMME
GRANDE
GRANGE
GREASE
GREAVE
GREECE
GREENE
GREIGE
GRIEVE
GRILLE
GRILSE
GRIMKE
GRIPPE
GROOVE
GROSSE
GROUSE
GRUDGE
GRUNGE
GUERRE
GUIMPE
GUNITE
GURGLE
GUTTAE
GUZZLE
GWYNNE
GYRATE
GYRENE
GYROSE

•GE•••

AGEING
AGEISM
AGEIST
AGENAS
AGENCY
AGENDA
AGENTS
AGEOLD
EGERIA
EGESTA
EGESTS
IGETIT

•G•E••

AGLEAM
AGLETS
AGREED
AGREES
EGBERT
EGRESS
EGRETS
OGLERS
OGRESS

•G••E•

AGATES
AGAVES
AGGIES
AGREED
AGREES
EGGIER
NGUYEN
OGIVES
UGLIER
UGLIES

•G•••E

AGLARE
AGNATE
AGORAE
IGNACE
IGNITE
IGNORE
UGSOME

••GE••

AEGEAN
ANGELA
ANGELI
ANGELL
ANGELO
ANGELS
ANGERS
ARGENT
AUGEAN
AUGEND
AUGERS
BAGELS
BEGETS
BOGEYS
CAGERS
COGENT
DIGEST
DOGEAR
DOGEYS
EDGEIN
EDGERS
ENGELS
EUGENE
FAGEND
FOGEYS
HUGELY
HUGEST
INGEAR
INGEST
KAGERA
LAGERS
LEGEND
LIGERS
LUGERS
NUGENT
ORGEAT
PAGERS
PIGEON
REGENT
ROGERS
SAGELY
SAGEST
TAGEND
TIGERS
URGENT
URGERS
WAGERS

••G•E•

AGGIES
AIGRET
ANGLED
ANGLER
ANGLES
ARGUED
ARGUER
ARGUES
BAGGED
BAGGER
BEGGED
BEGLEY
BIGBEN
BIGGER
BIGRED
BIGTEN
BOGGED
BOGIES
BOGLES
BUGGED
BUGLED
BUGLER
BUGLES
CAGIER
CAGNEY
COGGED
CYGNET
DAGGER
DEGREE
DIGGER
DOGGED
DOGGER
DOGIES
DOGLEG
EAGLED
EAGLES
EAGLET
EAGRES
EDGIER
EGGIER
FAGGED
FOGGED
FOGGER
FOGIES
FUGUES
GAGGED
GAGMEN
GIGGED
GIGUES
HIGHER
HOGGED
HOGGET
HUGGED
HUGGER
HUGHES
INGLES
INGRES
JAGGED
JAGGER
JIGGED
JIGGER
JOGGED
JOGGER
JUGGED
KEGGED
KEGLER
LAGGED
LAGGER
LEGGED
LEGMEN
LEGREE
LOGGED
LOGGER
LOGIER
LUGGED
LUGGER
MAGNET
MAGUEY
MCGREW
MIGUEL
MUGGED
MUGGER
NAGGED
NAGGER
NIGHER
NUGGET
ORGIES
PEGGED
PEGLER
PIGGED
PIGLET
PIGPEN
POGIES
PUGGED
PUGREE
RAGGED
RAGMEN
REGLET
REGRET
RIGGED
RIGGER
ROGUES
RUGGED
SAGGED
SEGUED
SEGUES
SIGHED
SIGHER
SIGNED
SIGNEE
SIGNER
SIGNET
TAGGED
TIGGER
TOGAED
TOGGED
TUGGED
TUGGER
UNGUES
VAGUER
VEGGED
VOGUES
WAGGED
WAGNER
WIGGED
WIGLET
ZAGGED
ZAGREB
ZIGGED

••G••E

ALGORE
ARGIVE
ARGYLE
BAGGIE
BEGONE
BIGGIE
BIGLIE
BIGTOE
BOGGLE
BYGONE
DEGAGE
DEGREE
DOGGIE
ENGAGE
ENGINE
ERGATE
EUGENE
FIGURE
GAGGLE
GIGGLE
GOGGLE
HAGGLE
HIGGLE
HOGTIE
JIGGLE
JOGGLE
JUGGLE
LEGATE
LEGREE
LEGUME
LIGATE
LIGURE
MAGGIE
MAGPIE
MIGGLE
MUGABE
NEGATE
NIGGLE
ORGATE
PIGGIE
PUGREE
REGALE
REGGAE
REGGIE
REGIME
REGLUE
RUGATE
RUGOSE
SIGNEE
TAGORE
TOGGLE
UNGLUE
VEGGIE
WAGGLE
WIGGLE
ZYGOTE

•••GE•

ADAGES
APOGEE
BADGER
BADGES
BAGGED
BAGGER
BANGED
BANGER
BARGED
BARGES
BEGGED
BEIGES
BERGEN
BIGGER
BILGES
BINGED
BINGES
BOGGED
BOLGER
BONGED
BRUGES
BUDGED
BUDGES
BUDGET
BUGGED
BULGED
BULGES
BUNGED
BUNGEE
BURGEE
BURGER
CADGED
CADGER
CADGES
CODGER
COGGED
CONGER
CUDGEL
DAGGER
DANGER
DIGGER
DINGED
DIRGES
DODGED
DODGER
DODGES
DOGGED
DOGGER
DRAGEE
FAGGED
FANGED
FIDGET
FINGER
FOGGED
FOGGER
FORGED
FORGER
FORGES
FORGET
FUDGED
FUDGES
GADGET
GAGGED
GANGED
GANGER
GANGES
GAUGED
GAUGER
GAUGES
GEEGEE
GEIGER
GIDGET
GIGGED
GINGER
GONGED
GORGED
GORGES
GORGET
GOUGED
GOUGER
GOUGES
HANGED
HANGER
HEDGED
HEDGER
HEDGES
HINGED
HINGES
HODGES
HOGGED
HOGGET
HUGGED
HUGGER
HUNGER
IMAGED
IMAGER
IMAGES
IMOGEN
JAEGER
JAGGED
JAGGER
JIGGED
JIGGER
JOGGED
JOGGER
JUDGED
JUDGES
JUGGED
KEDGED
KEDGES
KEGGED
KINGED
KRUGER
LAAGER
LAGGED
LAGGER
LARGER
LARGES
LEDGER
LEDGES
LEGGED
LIEGES
LINGER
LODGED
LODGER
LODGES
LOGGED
LOGGER
LONGED
LONGER
LONGES
LUGGED
LUGGER
LUNGED
LUNGES
MAJGEN
MANGER
MARGES
MEAGER
MERGED
MERGER
MERGES
MIDGES
MIDGET
MONGER
MORGEN
MUGGED
MUGGER
NAGGED
NAGGER
NUDGED
NUDGER
NUDGES
NUGGET
ONAGER
ORIGEN
OSAGES
OXYGEN
PARGET
PEGGED
PHAGES
PIAGET
PIGGED
PINGED
PLAGES
PONGED
PONGEE
PUGGED
PURGED
PURGES
RAGGED
RANGED
RANGER
RANGES
RIDGED
RIDGES
RIGGED
RIGGER
RINGED
RINGER
ROUGED
ROUGES
RUGGED
RUTGER
SAGGED
SANGER
SARGES
SAUGER
SEDGES
SEEGER
SERGEI
SERGES
SIEGED
SIEGEL
SIEGES
SINGED
SINGER
SINGES
STAGED
STAGER
STAGES
SURGED
SURGES
SWAGED
SWAGES
TAGGED
TANGED
TARGES
TARGET
TIGGER
TINGED
TINGES
TOGGED
TUGGED
TUGGER
UNAGED
USAGES
VEGGED
VERGED
VERGER
VERGES
VOSGES
WAGGED
WEDGED
WEDGES
WIDGET
WIGGED
WINGED
WINGER
WODGES
YEAGER
ZAGGED
ZENGER
ZIGGED
ZINGED
ZINGER

•••G•E

ALEGRE
APOGEE
BAGGIE
BANGLE
BEAGLE
BIGGIE
BOGGLE
BOOGIE
BROGUE
BUDGIE
BUNGEE
BUNGLE
BURGEE
BURGLE
CHIGOE
DANGLE
DANGME
DENGUE
DINGLE
DOGGIE
DONGLE
DOOGIE
DRAGEE
DROGUE
EMIGRE
FERGIE
GAGGLE
GANGLE
GANGUE
GARGLE
GEEGEE
GIGGLE
GOGGLE
GOOGLE
GURGLE
HAGGLE
HIGGLE
HOAGIE
JANGLE
JIGGLE
JINGLE
JOGGLE
JUGGLE
JUNGLE
KINGME
LEAGUE
LONGUE
MAGGIE
MANGLE
MARGIE
MEAGRE
MIGGLE
MINGLE
NIGGLE
PIGGIE
PLAGUE
PONGEE
PRAGUE
REGGAE
REGGIE
SINGLE
SOIGNE
STOGIE
TANGLE
TINGLE
TOGGLE
TONGUE
VEGGIE
WAGGLE
WANGLE
WEDGIE
WIGGLE
WOOGIE

••••GE

ALLEGE
AVENGE
BAREGE
BORAGE
BRIDGE
CHANGE
CHARGE
CRINGE
CUBAGE
DAMAGE
DEGAGE
DELUGE
DIRIGE
DOSAGE
DOTAGE
DREDGE
DRUDGE
EMERGE
ENCAGE
ENGAGE
ENRAGE
EXLEGE
FLANGE
FLEDGE
FORAGE
FRIDGE
FRINGE
GARAGE
GEORGE
GRANGE
GREIGE
GRUDGE
GRUNGE
HOMAGE
ICEAGE
INNAGE
KLUDGE
KRESGE
LAVAGE
LESAGE
LINAGE
LOUNGE
LOVAGE
MANAGE
MANEGE
MENAGE
MIRAGE
NEWAGE
NONAGE
OBLIGE
OLDAGE
ONEDGE
ORANGE
OUTAGE
PELAGE
PLEDGE
PLUNGE
POTAGE
RAVAGE
REFUGE
RENEGE
SAVAGE
SEWAGE
SILAGE
SLEDGE
SLUDGE
SMUDGE
SOCAGE
SPARGE
SPONGE
SPURGE
STODGE
STOOGE
TOWAGE
TRIAGE
TRUDGE
TWINGE
ULLAGE
UNCAGE
VISAGE
VOYAGE

G•F•••

GAFFED
GAFFER
GAFFES
GIFTED
GOFERS
GOFISH
GUFFAW

G••F••

GADFLY
GAFFED
GAFFER
GAFFES
GOLFED
GOLFER
GOOFED
GOOFUP
GRAFTS
GRIFTS
GUFFAW
GULFED
GUNFOR

G•••F•

GASIFY
GETOFF
GOSOFT
GOTOFF
GRIEFS

G••••F

GETOFF
GOTOFF

•G••F•

UGLIFY

••GF••

BAGFUL
JUGFUL

••G•F•

ARGUFY
BEGOFF
BUGOFF
LOGOFF

••G••F

BEGOFF
BUGOFF
ENGULF
LOGOFF

•••GF•

KUNGFU

G•G•••

GAGGED
GAGGLE
GAGING
GAGLAW
GAGMAN
GAGMEN
GIGGED
GIGGLE
GIGGLY
GIGOLO
GIGOTS
GIGUES
GOGGLE
GOGGLY

G••G••

GADGET
GAGGED
GAGGLE
GANGED
GANGER
GANGES
GANGLE
GANGLY
GANGUE
GANGUP
GARGLE
GAUGED
GAUGER
GAUGES
GEEGAW
GEEGEE
GEIGER
GEWGAW
GIDGET
GIGGED
GIGGLE
GIGGLY
GILGUY
GINGER
GLOGGS
GOGGLE
GOGGLY
GONGED
GOOGLE
GOOGLY
GOOGOL
GOOGOO
GORGED
GORGES
GORGET
GORGON
GOUGED
GOUGER
GOUGES
GREGOR
GRIGRI
GROGGY
GUNGHO
GURGLE

G•••G•

GALAGO
GARAGE
GEORGE
GEORGY
GINKGO
GLOGGS
GOINGS
GONOGO
GRANGE
GREIGE
GRINGO
GROGGY
GRUDGE
GRUNGE
GRUNGY
GULAGS

G••••G

GAGING
GAMING
GAPING
GASBAG
GASLOG
GATING
GAZING
GEEING
GEHRIG
GIBING
GIVING
GLUING
GORING
GOSTAG
GUNDOG
GUYING
GYBING
GYMBAG

•GG•••

AGGIES
AGGROS
EGGCUP
EGGIER
EGGING
EGGNOG
EGGSON
UGGAMS

•G•••G

AGEING
EGGING
EGGNOG
OGLING

••GG••

BAGGED
BAGGER
BAGGIE
BEGGAR
BEGGED
BIGGER
BIGGIE
BIGGUN
BOGGED
BOGGLE
BUGGED
COGGED
DAGGER
DIGGER
DOGGED
DOGGER
DOGGIE
FAGGED
FOGGED
FOGGER
GAGGED
GAGGLE
GIGGED
GIGGLE
GIGGLY
GOGGLE
GOGGLY
HAGGIS
HAGGLE
HIGGLE
HOGGED
HOGGET
HUGGED
HUGGER
JAGGED
JAGGER
JIGGED
JIGGER
JIGGLE
JIGGLY
JOGGED
JOGGER
JOGGLE
JUGGED
JUGGLE
KEGGED
LAGGED

LAGGER
LEGGED
LOGGED
LOGGER
LOGGIA
LUGGED
LUGGER
MAGGIE
MAGGIO
MIGGLE
MUGGED
MUGGER
NAGGED
NAGGER
NIGGLE
NOGGIN
NUGGET
PEGGED
PIGGED
PIGGIE
PUGGED
RAGGED
REGGAE
REGGIE
RIGGED
RIGGER
RUGGED
SAGGED
TAGGED
TIGGER
TOGGED
TOGGLE
TUGGED
TUGGER
VEGGED
VEGGIE
WAGGED
WAGGLE
WAGGLY
WAGGON
WIGGED
WIGGLE
WIGGLY
ZAGGED
ZIGGED

••G•G•
DEGAGE
ENGAGE

••G••G
BIGWIG
BOGONG
CAGING
DOGLEG
DOGTAG
DUGONG
EDGING
EGGING
EGGNOG
GAGING
PAGING
RAGBAG
RAGING
RAGRUG
RAGTAG
URGING
WAGING
WIGWAG
ZIGZAG

•••GG•
BRIGGS
CLOGGY
CRAGGY
DRAGGY
FLAGGY
FROGGY
GLOGGS
GROGGY
KNAGGY
QUAGGA
QUAGGY
SHAGGY
SLAGGY
SLUGGO
SMOGGY
SNAGGY
TWIGGY

•••G•G
FIZGIG

••••GG
BADEGG
RAWEGG

GH••••
GHAINS
GHARRY
GHAZIS
GHETTO
GHOSTS
GHOULS

G•H•••
GEHRIG
GOHOME
GSHARP

G••H••
GASHED
GASHES
GATHER
GOPHER
GOSHEN
GOTHAM
GOTHIC
GRAHAM
GUSHED
GUSHER
GUSHES

G•••H•
GALAHS
GANDHI
GARTHS
GAUCHE
GAUCHO
GEISHA
GERAHS
GIRTHS
GLYPHS
GOETHE
GOTCHA
GRAPHS
GRAPHY
GUNGHO
GUNSHY
GURKHA

G••••H
GALOSH
GARETH
GARISH
GLITCH
GOFISH
GOODOH
GOWITH
GRINCH
GROUCH
GROWTH
GUELPH
GULLAH

•GH•••
AGHAST
OGHAMS

•G••H•
AGATHA

•G•••H
AGUISH
OGRISH

••GH••
AFGHAN
AUGHTS
BIGHTS
EIGHTH
EIGHTS
EIGHTY
FIGHTS
FOGHAT
HIGHER
HIGHIQ
HIGHLY
HIGHUP
HUGHES
LIGHTS
MIGHTY
MUGHOS
NIGHER
NIGHTS
NIGHTY
OUGHTS
RIGHTO
RIGHTS
RIGHTY
SIGHED
SIGHER
SIGHTS
TIGHTS
WIGHTS

••G•H•
MEGOHM

••G••H
BYGOSH
EIGHTH
LAGASH

•••GH•
ALIGHT
ARIGHT
BLIGHT
BOUGHS
BOUGHT
BRIGHT
BURGHS
CAUGHT
COUGHS
DINGHY
DOUGHS
DOUGHY
DWIGHT
FLIGHT
FOUGHT
FRIGHT
GUNGHO
HAIGHT
HEIGHT
HOUGHS
KNIGHT
LAUGHS
LOUGHS
NAUGHT
NEIGHS
NOUGHT
PENGHU
PLIGHT
ROUGHS
ROUGHY
SLIGHT
SOUGHS
SOUGHT
TAUGHT
THIGHS
TOUGHS
TOUGHY
VAUGHN
VEIGHT
VOIGHT
WEIGHS
WEIGHT
WRIGHT

•••G•H
LENGTH
PISGAH

••••GH
ARMAGH
AWEIGH
CHOUGH
ENOUGH
LEHIGH
MCHUGH
ONHIGH
PLOUGH
SLEIGH
SLOUGH
THOUGH
TROUGH

GI••••
GIANTS
GIBBED
GIBBER
GIBBET
GIBBON
GIBERS
GIBILL
GIBING
GIBLET
GIBRAN
GIBSON
GIDEON
GIDGET
GIFTED
GIGGED
GIGGLE
GIGGLY
GIGOLO
GIGOTS
GIGUES
GIJOES
GILDED
GILDER
GILEAD
GILGUY
GILLED
GILLIE
GILLIS
GIMBAL
GIMBEL
GIMELS
GIMLET
GIMMES
GINGER
GINKGO
GINNED
GIOTTO
GIPPED
GIPPER
GIRARD
GIRDED
GIRDER
GIRDLE
GIRNED
GIRTED
GIRTHS
GITANO
GIVEIN
GIVENS
GIVERS
GIVETO
GIVEUP
GIVING
GIZMOS

G•I•••
GAIETY
GAIJIN
GAINED
GAINER
GAINLY
GAINON
GAINST
GAITED
GAITER
GEIGER
GEISEL
GEISHA
GLIBLY
GLIDED
GLIDER
GLIDES
GLINKA
GLINTS
GLITCH
GLITZY
GMINOR
GOINGS
GOINTO
GRIEFS
GRIEVE
GRIFTS
GRIGRI
GRILLE
GRILLS
GRILSE
GRIMED
GRIMES
GRIMKE
GRIMLY
GRINCH
GRINDS
GRINGO
GRIOTS
GRIPED
GRIPER
GRIPES
GRIPPE
GRISLY
GRISON
GRISTS
GRITTY
GRIVET
GUIANA
GUIDED
GUIDES
GUIDON
GUILDS
GUILES
GUILTY
GUIMPE
GUINEA
GUIROS
GUISES
GUITAR
GUITRY

G••I••
GABIES
GABION
GAGING
GAMIER
GAMILY
GAMINE
GAMING
GAMINS
GAPING
GARISH
GASIFY
GATING
GAVIAL
GAZING
GEEING
GEMINI
GENIAL
GENIES
GENIUS
GEZIRA
GHAINS
GIBILL
GIBING
GIVING
GLAIRS
GLAIRY
GLUIER
GLUING
GNEISS
GOBIES
GODIVA
GOFISH
GOLINO
GOOIER
GORIER
GORILY
GORING
GOWILD
GOWITH
GRAILS
GRAINS
GRAINY
GREIGE
GROINS
GSUITS
GUNITE
GUYING
GYBING

G•••I•
GAELIC
GAIJIN
GALLIA
GALLIC
GALOIS
GAMBIA
GAMBIT
GARCIA
GARLIC
GASKIN
GASLIT
GATLIN
GAVEIN
GAWAIN
GEHRIG
GERBIL
GERTIE
GESTIC
GETSIN
GETSIT
GHAZIS
GILLIE
GILLIS
GIVEIN
GLACIS
GLOBIN
GLORIA
GLYNIS
GNOMIC
GNOSIS
GOALIE
GOBLIN
GODWIN
GODWIT
GOESIN
GOLDIE
GOODIE
GORDIE
GOSSIP
GOTHIC
GOTOIT
GRACIE
GRADIN
GRATIA
GRATIN
GRATIS
GRAVID
GRODIN

G••••I
GANDHI
GELATI
GEMINI
GLUTEI
GRIGRI

•GI•••
BGIRLS
OGIVES

•G•I••
AGEING
AGEISM
AGEIST
AGGIES
AGLINT
AGUISH
EGGIER
EGGING
EGOISM
EGOIST
IGNITE
OGLING
OGRISH
UGLIER
UGLIES
UGLIFY
UGLILY
UGRIAN

•G••I•
AGADIR
AGARIC
AGLAIA
EGERIA
IGETIT
IGOTIT

•G•••I
AGASSI
AGOUTI

••GI••
AGGIES
ARGIVE
BEGINS
BOGIES
CAGIER
CAGILY
CAGING
COGITO
DIGITS
DOGIES
EDGIER
EDGILY
EDGING
EGGIER
EGGING
ENGINE
ENGIRD
ENGIRT
FOGIES
GAGING
HEGIRA
LEGION
LEGIST
LOGIER
LOGILY
LOGION
MEGILP
MYGIRL
ORGIES
PAGING
POGIES
RAGING
REGIME
REGINA
REGION
REGIUS
SIGILS
UNGIRD
UNGIRT
URGING
VIGILS
WAGING
YOGINI
YOGISM

••G•I•
ANGLIA
ANGLIC
BAGGIE
BAGSIT
BAGUIO
BIGGIE
BIGLIE
BIGWIG
DIGSIN
DOGGIE
DOGSIT
EDGEIN
FOGSIN
HAGGIS
HIGHIQ
HOGTIE
INGRID
LEGUIN
LIGNIN
LOGGIA
LOGSIN
MAGGIE
MAGGIO
MAGPIE
NOGGIN
PIGGIE
REGAIN
REGGIE
SIGNIN
TIGRIS
TUGRIK
UNGUIS
VEGGIE

••G••I
ANGELI
ARGALI
HEGARI
KIGALI
LUGOSI
YOGINI

•••GI•
ADAGIO
BAGGIE
BIGGIE
BIRGIT
BOOGIE
BORGIA
BRIGID
BUDGIE
CORGIS
DOGGIE
DOOGIE
DRAGIN
ELEGIT
FERGIE
FIZGIG
FRIGID
HAGGIS
HANGIN
HINGIS
HOAGIE
HUNGIN
LOGGIA
MAGGIE
MAGGIO
MARGIE
MARGIN
NOGGIN
ORIGIN
PIDGIN
PIGGIE
PLAGIO
PLUGIN
PONGID
REGGIE
SERGIO
SINGIN
STOGIE
TRAGIC
TURGID
VEGGIE
VIRGIL
VIRGIN
WEDGIE
WINGIT
WOOGIE
XINGIN

•••G•I
BANGUI
GRIGRI
MOWGLI
NILGAI
SERGEI
SNUGLI

••••GI
UBANGI

G•J•••
GIJOES

G••J••
GAIJIN
GASJET
GMAJOR

•G•••J
SGTMAJ

••GJ••
LOGJAM

G•K•••
GOKART

G••K••
GASKET
GASKIN
GAWKED
GAWKER
GECKOS
GINKGO
GURKHA

G•••K•
GLINKA
GREEKS
GRIMKE

G••••K
GALYAK
GDANSK
GOBACK

••GK••
ANGKOR

••G••K
TUGRIK

•••GK•
BANGKA

GL••••
GLACES
GLACIS
GLADES
GLADLY
GLADYS
GLAIRS
GLAIRY
GLAMOR
GLANCE
GLANDS
GLARED
GLARES
GLASER
GLASSY
GLAZED
GLAZER
GLAZES
GLEAMS
GLEAMY
GLEANS
GLEBES
GLENDA
GLENNE
GLIBLY
GLIDED
GLIDER
GLIDES
GLINKA
GLINTS
GLITCH
GLITZY
GLOATS
GLOBAL
GLOBED
GLOBES
GLOBIN
GLOGGS
GLOOMS
GLOOMY
GLOPPY
GLORIA
GLOSSA
GLOSSO
GLOSSY
GLOVED
GLOVER
GLOVES
GLOWED
GLOWER
GLOZED
GLOZES
GLUERS
GLUIER
GLUING
GLUMLY
GLUONS
GLUTEI
GLUTEN
GLUTES
GLYCOL
GLYNIS
GLYPHS

G•L•••
GALAGO
GALAHS
GALATA
GALAXY
GALEAE
GALENA
GALLED
GALLEY
GALLIA
GALLIC
GALLON
GALLOP
GALLUP
GALOIS
GALOOT
GALOPS
GALORE
GALOSH
GALPAL
GALWAY
GALYAK
GELADA
GELATI
GELATO
GELEES
GELLED
GELSEY
GILDED
GILDER
GILEAD
GILGUY
GILLED
GILLIE
GILLIS
GOLDEN
GOLDIE
GOLEMS
GOLFED
GOLFER
GOLINO
GOLLUM
GULAGS
GULFED
GULLAH
GULLED
GULLET
GULPED
GULPER

G••L••
GABLED
GABLER
GABLES
GAELIC
GAGLAW
GALLED
GALLEY
GALLIA
GALLIC
GALLON
GALLOP
GALLUP
GAOLED
GAOLER
GARLIC
GASLIT
GASLOG
GATLIN
GELLED
GIBLET
GILLED
GILLIE
GILLIS
GIMLET
GOALIE
GOBLET
GOBLIN
GOLLUM
GOSLOW
GOULET
GRILLE
GRILLS
GRILSE
GUELPH
GUILDS
GUILES
GUILTY
GULLAH
GULLED
GULLET
GURLEY

G•••L•
GABBLE
GADFLY
GAGGLE
GAINLY
GAMBLE
GAMELY
GAMILY
GANGLE
GANGLY
GARBLE
GARGLE
GAVELS
GAYALS
GENTLE
GENTLY
GERALD
GHOULS
GIBILL
GIGGLE
GIGGLY
GIGOLO
GIMELS
GIRDLE
GLADLY
GLIBLY
GLUMLY
GNARLS
GNARLY
GOBBLE
GOGGLE
GOGGLY
GOODLY
GOOGLE
GOOGLY
GORALS
GORILY
GOWILD
GRABLE
GRAILS
GRAYLY
GREYLY
GRILLE
GRILLS
GRIMLY
GRISLY
GROWLS
GROWLY
GRUELS
GURGLE
GUZZLE

G••••L
GALPAL
GAMBOL
GAVIAL
GEISEL
GENIAL
GENUAL
GERBIL
GIBILL
GIMBAL
GIMBEL
GLOBAL
GLYCOL
GOOGOL
GOSPEL
GRAVEL
GRETEL
GROVEL
GUMBEL
GUNNEL

•GL•••
AGLAIA
AGLARE
AGLEAM
AGLETS
AGLINT
IGLOOS
OGLALA
OGLERS
OGLING
UGLIER
UGLIES
UGLIFY
UGLILY

•G••L•
AGEOLD
BGIRLS
OGLALA
UGLILY

••GL••
ANGLED
ANGLER
ANGLES
ANGLIA
ANGLIC
ANGLOS
BEGLEY
BIGLIE
BOGLES
BUGLED
BUGLER
BUGLES
DIGLOT
DOGLEG
EAGLED
EAGLES
EAGLET
ENGLUT
GAGLAW
INGLES
KEGLER
PEGLER
PIGLET
RAGLAN
REGLET
REGLUE
TIGLON
UNGLUE
WIGLET

••G•L•
ANGELA
ANGELI
ANGELL
ANGELO
ANGELS
ANGOLA
ARGALI
ARGYLE
ARGYLL
BAGELS
BOGGLE
CAGILY
EDGILY
ENGELS
ENGULF
GAGGLE
GIGGLE
GIGGLY
GIGOLO
GOGGLE
GOGGLY
HAGGLE
HIGGLE
HIGHLY
HUGELY
JIGGLE
JIGGLY
JOGGLE
JUGGLE
KIGALI
LEGALS
LIGULA
LOGILY
MEGALO
MEGILP
MIGGLE
MOGULS
NIGGLE
REGALE
SAGELY
SIGILS
TOGGLE
VIGILS
WAGGLE
WAGGLY
WIGGLE
WIGGLY

••G••L
ANGELL
ARGYLL
BAGFUL
JUGFUL
MIGUEL
MYGIRL
REGNAL
SIGNAL
UNGUAL

•••GL•
BANGLE
BEAGLE
BOGGLE
BUNGLE
BURGLE
DANGLE
DANGLY
DAYGLO
DINGLE
DONGLE
GAGGLE
GANGLE
GANGLY
GARGLE
GIGGLE
GIGGLY
GOGGLE
GOGGLY
GOOGLE
GOOGLY
GURGLE
HAGGLE
HIGGLE
JANGLE
JANGLY
JIGGLE
JIGGLY
JINGLE
JINGLY
JOGGLE
JUGGLE
JUNGLE
JUNGLY
KINGLY
LONGLY
MANGLE
MIGGLE
MINGLE
MOWGLI
NIGGLE
SINGLE
SINGLY
SMUGLY
SNUGLI
SNUGLY
TANGLE
TANGLY
TINGLE
TINGLY
TOGGLE
TRIGLY
WAGGLE
WAGGLY
WANGLE
WIGGLE
WIGGLY
YUNGLO

•••G•L
BENGAL
CUDGEL
FRUGAL
GOOGOL
HANGUL
MONGOL
PLAGAL
SEAGAL
SIEGEL
VIRGIL

GM••••
GMAJOR
GMINOR

G•M•••
GAMAYS
GAMBIA
GAMBIT
GAMBLE
GAMBOL
GAMELY
GAMEST
GAMETE
GAMIER
GAMILY
GAMINE
GAMING
GAMINS
GAMMAS
GAMMED
GAMMER
GAMMON
GAMUTS
GEMARA
GEMINI
GEMMAE
GEMMED
GEMOTE
GEMOTS
GIMBAL
GIMBEL
GIMELS
GIMLET
GIMMES
GUMBEL
GUMBOS
GUMMED
GUMSUP
GYMBAG

G••M••
GAGMAN
GAGMEN
GAMMAS
GAMMED
GAMMER
GAMMON
GASMAN
GASMEN

GAUMED GEMMAE GEMMED GERMAN GETMAD GIMMES GIZMOS GLAMOR GLUMLY GNOMES GNOMIC GNOMON GOTMAD GRAMAS GRAMME GRAMMY GRAMPA GRAMPS GRIMED GRIMES GRIMKE GRIMLY GRUMPS GRUMPY GUIMPE GUMMED GUNMAN GUNMEN

G•••M•

GAZUMP GENOME GLEAMS GLEAMY GLOOMS GLOOMY GOHOME GOLEMS GRAMME GRAMMY GROOMS

G••••M

GOLLUM GOTHAM GRAHAM GYPSUM

•GM•••

EGMONT

•G•M••

AGAMAS SGTMAJ

•G••M•

OGHAMS UGGAMS UGSOME

•G•••M

AGEISM AGLEAM EGOISM

••GM••

BIGMAC DAGMAR DOGMAS GAGMAN GAGMEN HAGMAN INGMAR LEGMAN LEGMEN MAGMAS RAGMAN RAGMEN RAGMOP SIGMAS

••G•M•

BEGUMS BIGAMY DAGAMA LEGUME REGIME UGGAMS

••G••M

DIGRAM DOGDOM ENGRAM INGRAM LOGJAM MAGNUM MEGOHM WIGWAM YOGISM

•••GM•

DANGME ENIGMA KINGME STIGMA ZEUGMA

•••G•M

ARTGUM BEEGUM REDGUM SUBGUM

••••GM

PHLEGM

GN••••

GNARLS GNARLY GNATTY GNAWED GNAWER GNEISS GNOMES GNOMIC GNOMON GNOSIS

G•N•••

GANDER GANDHI GANGED GANGER GANGES GANGLE GANGLY GANGUE GANGUP GANNET GANTRY GENDER GENERA GENETS GENEVA GENEVE GENIAL GENIES GENIUS GENOAN GENOME GENRES GENTLE GENTLY GENTRY GENUAL GINGER GINKGO GINNED GONEBY GONERS GONGED GONOGO GUNDOG GUNFOR GUNGHO GUNITE GUNMAN GUNMEN GUNNAR GUNNED GUNNEL GUNNER GUNSHY GUNTER

G••N••

GAINED GAINER GAINLY GAINON GAINST GANNET GARNER GARNET GAYNOR GDANSK GIANTS GINNED GIRNED GLANCE GLANDS GLENDA GLENNE GLINKA GLINTS GLYNIS GMINOR GOANNA GOINGS GOINTO GOUNOD GOWNED GRANDE GRANDS GRANGE GRANNY GRANTS GRINCH GRINDS GRINGO GRUNDY GRUNGE GRUNGY GRUNTS GUENON GUINEA GUNNAR GUNNED GUNNEL GUNNER GURNEY GWYNNE

G•••N•

GAGING GALENA GAMINE GAMING GAMINS GAPING GATING GAZING GEEING GEMINI GERENT GERONT GERUND GHAINS GIBING GITANO GIVENS GIVING GLEANS GLENNE GLUING GLUONS GOANNA GOLINO GORING GRAINS GRAINY GRANNY GREENE GREENS GREENY GRETNA GROANS GRODNO GROINS GROUND GROZNY GUIANA GUYANA GUYING GWYNNE GYBING GYRENE GYRONS

G••••N

GABION GAGMAN GAGMEN GAIJIN GAINON GALLON GAMMON GARCON GARDEN GARSON GASCON GASKIN GASMAN GASMEN GASTON GATLIN GAVEIN GAWAIN GENOAN GERMAN GETSIN GETSON GIBBON GIBRAN GIBSON GIDEON GIVEIN GLOBIN GLUTEN GNOMON GOBLIN GODOWN GODSON GODWIN GOESIN GOESON GOLDEN GOODEN GORDON GORGON GOSHEN GOTTEN GOVERN GRABEN GRADIN GRATIN GRAVEN GREWON GRISON GRODIN GROTON GROWON GUDRUN GUENON GUIDON GUNMAN GUNMEN

•GN•••

AGNATE IGNACE IGNATZ IGNITE IGNORE

•G•N••

AGENAS AGENCY AGENDA AGENTS EGGNOG UGANDA

•G••N•

AGEING AGLINT EGGING EGMONT IGUANA OGLING

•G•••N

EGGSON NGUYEN UGRIAN

••GN••

CAGNEY COGNAC CYGNET CYGNUS EGGNOG LIGNIN LUGNUT MAGNET MAGNON MAGNUM MAGNUS MIGNON PIGNUT REGNAL REGNAT SIGNAL SIGNED SIGNEE SIGNER SIGNET SIGNIN SIGNON SIGNOR SIGNUP WAGNER

••G•N•

ARGENT AUGEND BEGINS BEGONE BOGONG BYGONE CAGING COGENT DOGONS DUGONG EDGING EGGING ENGINE EUGENE FAGEND GAGING HOGANS LAGUNA LEGEND LIGAND NAGANO NUGENT ORGANA ORGANS PAGANS PAGING RAGING REGENT REGINA TAGEND URGENT URGING VEGANS WAGING WAGONS YOGINI

••G••N

AEGEAN AFGHAN AUGEAN BIGBEN BIGGUN BIGTEN DIGSIN EDGEIN EGGSON FOGSIN GAGMAN GAGMEN HAGDON HAGMAN LAGOON LEGION LEGMAN LEGMEN LEGUIN LIGNIN LOGION LOGSIN LOGSON MAGNON MIGNON NOGGIN PIGEON PIGPEN RAGLAN RAGMAN RAGMEN REGAIN REGION SIGNIN SIGNON TIGLON WAGGON

•••GN•

ALIGNS BOIGNY COIGNS DEIGNS FEIGNS REIGNS SOIGNE VSIGNS

•••G•N

AIRGUN ARAGON BERGEN BIGGUN BROGAN CAPGUN COOGAN DRAGIN DRAGON FLAGON GORGON HANGIN HANGON HUNGIN HUNGON IMOGEN ISOGON JARGON JETGUN KURGAN LONGAN MAJGEN MARGIN MORGAN MORGEN NOGGIN OREGON ORIGEN ORIGIN OUTGUN OXYGEN PIDGIN PLUGIN POPGUN RAYGUN REAGAN SAIGON SARGON SHOGUN SINGIN SIXGUN SLOGAN TONGAN TOPGUN TRIGON TROGON VAUGHN VIRGIN WAGGON XINGIN YANGON

••••GN

ASSIGN BENIGN COSIGN DESIGN ELOIGN ENSIGN IMPUGN MALIGN OPPUGN REPUGN RESIGN

GO••••

GOADED GOALIE GOANNA GOATEE GOAWAY GOAWRY GOBACK GOBBLE GOBIES GOBLET GOBLIN GOBUST GOCART GODARD GODETS GODIVA GODOWN GODSON GODWIN GODWIT GOEASY GOESAT GOESBY GOESIN GOESON GOESUP GOETHE GOFERS GOFISH GOGGLE GOGGLY GOHOME GOINGS GOINTO GOKART GOLDEN GOLDIE GOLEMS GOLFED GOLFER GOLINO GOLLUM GONEBY GONERS GONGED GONOGO GOOBER GOODBY GOODEN GOODIE GOODLY GOODOH GOOFED GOOFUP GOOGLE GOOGLY GOOGOL GOOGOO GOOIER GOOSED GOOSES GOOSEY GOOVER GOPHER GORALS GORDIE GORDON GORGED GORGES GORGET GORGON GORIER GORILY GORING GORSES GOSHEN GOSLOW GOSOFT GOSPEL GOSSIP GOSTAG GOTCHA GOTHAM GOTHIC GOTMAD GOTOFF GOTOIT GOTOUT GOTSET GOTTEN GOUGED GOUGER GOUGES GOULET GOUNOD GOURDE GOURDS GOVERN GOWEST GOWILD GOWITH GOWNED

G•O•••

GAOLED GAOLER GEODES GEORGE GEORGY GHOSTS GHOULS GIOTTO GLOATS GLOBAL GLOBED GLOBES GLOBIN GLOGGS GLOOMS GLOOMY GLOPPY GLORIA GLOSSA GLOSSO GLOSSY GLOVED GLOVER GLOVES GLOWED GLOWER GLOZED GLOZES GNOMES GNOMIC GNOMON GNOSIS GOOBER GOODBY GOODEN GOODIE GOODLY GOODOH GOOFED GOOFUP GOOGLE GOOGLY GOOGOL GOOGOO GOOIER GOOSED GOOSES GOOSEY GOOVER GROANS GROATS GROCER GRODIN GRODNO GROGGY GROINS GROOMS GROOVE GROOVY GROPED GROPES GROSSE GROSSO GROSZY GROTON GROTTO GROTTY GROUCH GROUND GROUPS GROUSE GROUTS GROUTY GROVEL GROVER GROVES GROWER GROWLS GROWLY GROWON GROWTH GROWUP GROZNY

G••O••

GALOIS GALOOT GALOPS GALORE GALOSH GATORS GEMOTE GEMOTS GENOAN GENOME GERONT GETOFF GETOUT GIGOLO GIGOTS GIJOES GLOOMS GLOOMY GLUONS GODOWN GOHOME GONOGO GOSOFT GOTOFF GOTOIT GOTOUT GRIOTS GROOMS GROOVE GROOVY GUYOTS GYRONS GYROSE

G•••O•

GABION GAINON GALLON GALLOP GALOOT GAMBOL GAMMON GARCON GARSON GASCON GASLOG GASTON GAYNOR GECKOS GETSON GIBBON GIBSON GIDEON GIZMOS GLAMOR GLYCOL GMAJOR GMINOR GNOMON GODSON GOESON GOODOH GOOGOL GOOGOO GORDON GORGON GOSLOW GOUNOD GREGOR GREWON GRISON GROTON GROWON GUACOS GUENON GUIDON GUIROS GUMBOS GUNDOG GUNFOR

G••••O

GABBRO GALAGO GASTRO GAUCHO GAZEBO GEARTO GELATO GETSTO GHETTO GIGOLO GINKGO GIOTTO GITANO GIVETO GLOSSO GOINTO GOLINO GONOGO GOOGOO GRAECO GRASSO GRINGO GRODNO GROSSO GROTTO GUNGHO

•GO•••

AGORAE AGORAS AGOROT AGOUTI EGOISM EGOIST IGOTIT

•G•O••

AGEOLD EGMONT IGLOOS IGNORE OGDOAD UGSOME

•G••O•

AGGROS AGOROT EGGNOG EGGSON IGLOOS

••GO••

ALGORE ANGOLA ANGORA ARGOSY ARGOTS BEGOFF BEGONE BIGOTS BOGONG BOGOTA BUGOFF BUGOUT BYGONE BYGOSH DIGOUT DOGONS DOGOOD DUGONG DUGOUT ERGOTS FAGOTS GIGOLO GIGOTS INGOTS LAGOON LOGOFF LOGOUT LUGOSI MEGOHM NAGOYA NOGOOD OSGOOD PAGODA PIGOUT RAGOUT RIGORS RIGOUR RUGOSE TAGORE TAGOUT VIGODA VIGORS VIGOUR WAGONS WIGOUT ZYGOTE

••G•O•

AGGROS ANGKOR ANGLOS BIGBOY BIGTOE BIGTOP DIGLOT DOGDOM DOGOOD EGGNOG EGGSON FOGBOW HAGDON LAGOON LEGION LOGION LOGSON MAGNON MIGNON MUGHOS NOGOOD OSGOOD PEGTOP PIGEON RAGMOP RAGTOP REGION SIGNON SIGNOR TIGLON WAGGON

••G••O

ANGELO BAGUIO COGITO FIGARO GIGOLO LEGATO MAGGIO MEGALO NAGANO RIGHTO

•••GO•

AMIGOS ARAGON BANGOR BONGOS BURGOO BURGOS CARGOS CHIGOE CONGOU DRAGON FLAGON FORGOT GOOGOL GOOGOO GORGON GREGOR HANGON HUNGON ISOGON JARGON LARGOS MANGOS MARGOT MONGOL MUNGOS OREGON SAIGON SARGON SARGOS SPIGOT SUNGOD TANGOS TINGOD TRIGON TROGON TURGOR WAGGON WARGOD YANGON

•••G•O

ADAGIO BURGOO DAYGLO GOOGOO GUNGHO MAGGIO NINGBO PLAGIO SANGTO SERGIO SINGTO SLUGGO YUNGLO

••••GO

ATERGO BOINGO COLUGO DIRIGO ERYNGO FOREGO GALAGO GINKGO GONOGO GRINGO INDIGO LATIGO LETSGO NONEGO OLINGO OSWEGO PAPAGO QUANGO SLUGGO STINGO TOBAGO VIRAGO

G•P•••

GAPERS GAPING GAPPED GIPPED GIPPER GOPHER GYPPED GYPPER GYPSUM

G••P••

GALPAL GAPPED GASPAR GASPED GASPER GAWPED GIPPED GIPPER GLOPPY GLYPHS GOSPEL GRAPES GRAPEY GRAPHS GRAPHY GRAPPA GRIPED GRIPER GRIPES GRIPPE GROPED GROPES GULPED GULPER GYPPED GYPPER

G•••P•

GALOPS GETUPS GLOPPY GRAMPA GRAMPS GRAPPA GRASPS GRIPPE GROUPS GRUMPS GRUMPY GUELPH GUIMPE

G••••P

GALLOP GALLUP GANGUP GASCAP GAVEUP GAZUMP GEARUP GETSUP GIVEUP GOESUP GOOFUP GOSSIP GREWUP GROWUP GSHARP GUMSUP

•G•••P

EGGCUP

••GP••

MAGPIE PIGPEN

••G••P

BIGTOP DIGSUP EGGCUP FOGSUP HIGHUP MEGILP PEGTOP RAGMOP RAGTOP RIGSUP SIGNUP TAGSUP

•••G•P

BANGUP CLOGUP GANGUP HANGUP HUNGUP RANGUP RINGUP RUNGUP

••G••Q

HIGHIQ

GR••••

GRABAT GRABBY GRABEN GRABLE GRACED GRACES GRACIE GRADEA GRADED GRADER GRADES GRADIN GRADUS GRAECO GRAFTS GRAHAM GRAILS GRAINS GRAINY GRAMAS GRAMME GRAMMY GRAMPA GRAMPS GRANDE GRANDS GRANGE GRANNY GRANTS GRAPES GRAPEY GRAPHS GRAPHY GRAPPA GRASPS GRASSO GRASSY GRATED GRATER GRATES GRATIA GRATIN GRATIS GRAVED GRAVEL GRAVEN

GRAVER
GRAVES
GRAVID
GRAYED
GRAYER
GRAYLY
GRAZED
GRAZER
GRAZES
GREASE
GREASY
GREATS
GREAVE
GREBES
GREECE
GREEDY
GREEKS
GREENE
GREENS
GREENY
GREETS
GREGOR
GREIGE
GRETEL
GRETNA
GREWON
GREWUP
GREYED
GREYER
GREYLY
GRIEFS
GRIEVE
GRIFTS
GRIGRI
GRILLE
GRILLS
GRILSE
GRIMED
GRIMES
GRIMKE
GRIMLY
GRINCH
GRINDS
GRINGO
GRIOTS
GRIPED
GRIPER
GRIPES
GRIPPE
GRISLY
GRISON
GRISTS
GRITTY
GRIVET
GROANS
GROATS
GROCER
GRODIN
GRODNO
GROGGY
GROINS
GROOMS
GROOVE
GROOVY
GROPED
GROPES
GROSSE
GROSSO
GROSZY
GROTON
GROTTO
GROTTY
GROUCH
GROUND
GROUPS
GROUSE
GROUTS
GROUTY
GROVEL
GROVER
GROVES
GROWER
GROWLS
GROWLY
GROWON
GROWTH
GROWUP
GROZNY
GRUBBY
GRUDGE
GRUELS
GRUMPS
GRUMPY
GRUNDY
GRUNGE
GRUNGY
GRUNTS

G•R•••
GARAGE
GARBED
GARBLE
GARCIA
GARCON
GARDEN
GARETH
GARGLE
GARISH
GARLIC
GARNER
GARNET
GARRET
GARSON
GARTER
GARTHS
GARVEY
GERAHS
GERALD
GERARD
GERBER
GERBIL
GERENT
GERMAN
GERONT
GERTIE
GERUND
GIRARD
GIRDED
GIRDER
GIRDLE
GIRNED
GIRTED
GIRTHS
GORALS
GORDIE
GORDON
GORGED
GORGES
GORGET
GORGON
GORIER
GORILY
GORING
GORSES
GURGLE
GURKHA
GURLEY
GURNEY
GYRATE
GYRENE
GYRONS
GYROSE

G••R••
GARRET
GEARED
GEARTO
GEARUP
GEHRIG
GENRES
GEORGE
GEORGY
GHARRY
GIBRAN
GLARED
GLARES
GLORIA
GNARLS
GNARLY
GOURDE
GOURDS
GUARDS
GUDRUN
GUERRE
GUIROS

G•••R•
GABBRO
GALORE
GANTRY
GAPERS
GASTRO
GATERS
GATORS
GEMARA
GENERA
GENTRY
GERARD
GEZIRA
GHARRY
GIBERS
GIRARD
GIVERS
GLAIRS
GLAIRY
GLUERS
GOAWRY
GOCART
GODARD
GOFERS
GOKART
GONERS
GOVERN
GRIGRI
GSHARP
GUERRE
GUITRY

G••••R
GABBER
GABLER
GADDER
GAFFER
GAINER
GAITER
GAMIER
GAMMER
GANDER
GANGER
GAOLER
GARNER
GARTER
GASPAR
GASPER
GASSER
GATHER
GAUGER
GAWKER
GAYNOR
GEEZER
GEIGER
GENDER
GERBER
GETTER
GEYSER
GIBBER
GILDER
GINGER
GIPPER
GIRDER
GLAMOR
GLASER
GLAZER
GLIDER
GLOVER
GLOWER
GLUIER
GMAJOR
GMINOR
GNAWER
GOLFER
GOOBER
GOOIER
GOOVER
GOPHER
GORIER
GOUGER
GRADER
GRATER
GRAVER
GRAYER
GRAZER
GREGOR
GREYER
GRIPER
GROCER
GROVER
GROWER
GUITAR
GULPER
GUNFOR
GUNNAR
GUNNER
GUNTER
GUSHER
GUTTER
GYPPER

•GR•••
AGREED
AGREES
EGRESS
EGRETS
OGRESS
OGRISH
UGRIAN

•G•R••
AGARIC
AGGROS
AGORAE
AGORAS
AGOROT
BGIRLS
EGERIA

•G••R•
AGLARE
EGBERT
IGNORE
OGLERS

•G•••R
AGADIR
EGGIER
UGLIER

••GR••
AGGROS
AIGRET
BIGRED
DEGREE
DIGRAM
EAGRES
ENGRAM
INGRAM
INGRES
INGRID
LEGREE
MCGRAW
MCGREW
PUGREE
RAGRUG
REGRET
TIGRIS
TUGRIK
ZAGREB

••G•R•
ALGORE
ANGERS
ANGORA
ASGARD
AUGERS
AUGURS
AUGURY
BOGART
CAGERS
CIGARS
EDGARD
EDGARS
EDGERS
ENGIRD
ENGIRT
FIGARO
FIGURE
FUGARD
HEGARI
HEGIRA
KAGERA
LAGERS
LIGERS
LIGURE
LUGERS
MEGARA
MYGIRL
PAGERS
REGARD
RIGORS
ROGERS
SEGURA
SIGURD
SUGARS
SUGARY
TAGORE
TIGERS
UIGURS
UNGIRD
UNGIRT
URGERS
VAGARY
VIGORS
WAGERS
YOGURT

••G••R
ANGKOR
ANGLER
ARGUER
BAGGER
BEGGAR
BIGGER
BIGSUR
BUGLER
CAGIER
DAGGER
DAGMAR
DIGGER
DOGEAR
DOGGER
EDGIER
EGGIER
FOGGER
HIGHER
HUGGER
INGEAR
INGMAR
JAGGER
JAGUAR
JIGGER
JOGGER
KEGLER
LAGGER
LOGGER
LOGIER
LUGGER
MAGYAR
MUGGER
NAGGER
NIGHER
PEGLER
RIGGER
RIGOUR
SIGHER
SIGNER
SIGNOR
TIGGER
TUGGER
VAGUER
VIGOUR
WAGNER

•••GR•
ALEGRE
EMIGRE
GRIGRI
HUNGRY
MEAGRE

•••G•R
ALEGAR
ANSGAR
BADGER
BAGGER
BANGER
BANGOR
BEGGAR
BIGGER
BOLGER
BULGAR
BULGUR
BURGER
CADGER
CODGER
CONGER
COUGAR
DAGGER
DANGER
DIGGER
DODGER
DOGGER
FINGER
FOGGER
FORGER
GANGER
GAUGER
GEIGER
GINGER
GOUGER
GREGOR
HANGAR
HANGER
HEDGER
HUGGER
HUNGER
IMAGER
JAEGER
JAGGER
JIGGER
JOGGER
KRUGER
LAAGER
LAGGER
LANGUR
LARGER
LEDGER
LINGER
LODGER
LOGGER
LONGER
LUGGER
MANGER
MEAGER
MEDGAR
MERGER
MONGER
MUGGER
NAGGER
NUDGER
ONAGER
RANGER
RIGGER
RINGER
RUTGER
SANGER
SAUGER
SEEGER
SINGER
STAGER
TIGGER
TUGGER
TURGOR
VERGER
VULGAR
WINGER
YEAGER
ZENGER
ZINGER

GS••••
GSHARP
GSTAAD
GSUITS

G•S•••
GASBAG
GASCAP
GASCON
GASHED
GASHES
GASIFY
GASJET
GASKET
GASKIN
GASLIT
GASLOG
GASMAN
GASMEN
GASPAR
GASPED
GASPER
GASSED
GASSER
GASSES
GASTON
GASTRO
GESTES
GESTIC
GOSHEN
GOSLOW
GOSOFT
GOSPEL
GOSSIP
GOSTAG
GUSHED
GUSHER
GUSHES
GUSSET
GUSTAV
GUSTED

G••S••
GARSON
GASSED
GASSER
GASSES
GATSBY
GEISEL
GEISHA
GELSEY
GETSAT
GETSBY
GETSET
GETSIN
GETSIT
GETSON
GETSTO
GETSUP
GEYSER
GHOSTS
GIBSON
GLASER
GLASSY
GLOSSA
GLOSSO
GLOSSY
GNOSIS
GODSON
GOESAT
GOESBY
GOESIN
GOESON
GOESUP
GOOSED
GOOSES
GOOSEY
GORSES
GOSSIP
GOTSET
GRASPS
GRASSO
GRASSY
GRISLY
GRISON
GRISTS
GROSSE
GROSSO
GROSZY
GUESTS
GUISES
GUMSUP
GUNSHY
GUSSET
GYPSUM

G•••S•
GAINST
GALOSH
GAMEST
GARISH
GAYEST
GDANSK
GLASSY
GLOSSA
GLOSSO
GLOSSY
GNEISS
GOBUST
GOEASY
GOFISH
GOWEST
GRASSO
GRASSY
GREASE
GREASY
GRILSE
GROSSE
GROSSO
GROUSE
GYROSE

G••••S
GABIES
GABLES
GAFFES
GALAHS
GALOIS
GALOPS
GAMAYS
GAMINS
GAMMAS
GAMUTS
GANGES
GAPERS
GARTHS
GASHES
GASSES
GATERS
GATORS
GAUGES
GAUZES
GAVELS
GAYALS
GECKOS
GELEES
GEMOTS
GENETS
GENIES
GENIUS
GENRES
GEODES
GERAHS
GESTES
GETUPS
GHAINS
GHAZIS
GHOSTS
GHOULS
GIANTS
GIBERS
GIGOTS
GIGUES
GIJOES
GILLIS
GIMELS
GIMMES
GIRTHS
GIVENS
GIVERS
GIZMOS
GLACES
GLACIS
GLADES
GLADYS
GLAIRS
GLANDS
GLARES
GLAZES
GLEAMS
GLEANS
GLEBES
GLIDES
GLINTS
GLOATS
GLOBES
GLOGGS
GLOOMS
GLOVES
GLOZES
GLUERS
GLUONS
GLUTES
GLYNIS
GLYPHS
GNARLS
GNEISS
GNOMES
GNOSIS
GOBIES
GODETS
GOFERS
GOINGS
GOLEMS
GONERS
GOOSES
GORALS
GORGES
GORSES
GOUGES
GOURDS
GRACES
GRADES
GRADUS
GRAFTS
GRAILS
GRAINS
GRAMAS
GRAMPS
GRANDS
GRANTS
GRAPES
GRAPHS
GRASPS
GRATES
GRATIS
GRAVES
GRAZES
GREATS
GREBES
GREEKS
GREENS
GREETS
GRIEFS
GRIFTS
GRILLS
GRIMES
GRINDS
GRIOTS
GRIPES
GRISTS
GROANS
GROATS
GROINS
GROOMS
GROPES
GROUPS
GROUTS
GROVES
GROWLS
GRUELS
GRUMPS
GRUNTS
GSUITS
GUACOS
GUARDS
GUAVAS
GUESTS
GUIDES
GUILDS
GUILES
GUIROS
GUISES
GULAGS
GUMBOS
GUSHES
GUYOTS
GYRONS

•GS•••
UGSOME

•G•S••
AGASSI
EGESTA
EGESTS
EGGSON

•G••S•
AGASSI
AGEISM
AGEIST
AGHAST
AGUISH
EGOISM
EGOIST
EGRESS
OGRESS
OGRISH

•G•••S
AGAMAS
AGATES
AGAVES
AGENAS
AGENTS
AGGIES
AGGROS
AGLETS
AGORAS
AGREES
BGIRLS
EGESTS
EGRESS
EGRETS
IGLOOS
OGHAMS
OGIVES
OGLERS
OGRESS
UGGAMS
UGLIES

••GS••
BAGSIT
BIGSUR
DIGSIN
DIGSUP
DOGSAT
DOGSIT
EGGSON
FOGSIN
FOGSUP
JIGSAW
LOGSIN
LOGSON
PIGSTY
RIGSUP
TAGSUP

••G•S•
ARGOSY
AUGUST
BYGOSH
DEGUST
DIGEST
HUGEST
INGEST
LAGASH
LEGIST
LUGOSI
RUGOSE
SAGEST
YOGISM

••G••S
AGGIES
AGGROS
ANGELS
ANGERS
ANGLES
ANGLOS
ARGOTS
ARGUES
AUGERS
AUGHTS
AUGURS
BAGELS
BEGETS
BEGINS
BEGUMS
BIGHTS
BIGOTS
BOGEYS
BOGIES
BOGLES
BUGLES
CAGERS
CAGUAS
CIGARS
CYGNUS
DIGITS
DOGEYS
DOGIES
DOGMAS
DOGONS
EAGLES
EAGRES
EDGARS
EDGERS
EIGHTS
ENGELS
ERGOTS
FAGOTS
FIGHTS
FOGEYS
FOGIES
FUGUES
GIGOTS
GIGUES
HAGGIS
HOGANS
HUGHES
INGLES
INGOTS
INGRES
LAGERS
LEGALS
LIGERS
LIGHTS
LUGERS
MAGMAS
MAGNUS
MOGULS
MUGHOS
NIGHTS
ORGANS
ORGIES
OUGHTS
PAGANS
PAGERS
POGIES
REGIUS
RIGHTS
RIGORS
ROGERS
ROGUES
SEGUES
SIGHTS
SIGILS
SIGMAS
SUGARS
TIGERS
TIGHTS
TIGRIS
UGGAMS
UIGURS
UNGUES
UNGUIS
URGERS
VEGANS
VIGILS
VIGORS
VOGUES
WAGERS
WAGONS
WIGHTS

•••G•S
ADAGES
ALIGNS
AMIGAS
AMIGOS
BADGES
BARGES
BEIGES
BILGES
BINGES
BIOGAS
BONGOS
BOUGHS
BRIGGS
BRUGES
BUDGES
BULGES
BURGAS
BURGHS
BURGOS
CADGES
CARGOS
COIGNS
CONGAS
CORGIS
COUGHS
DEIGNS
DINGUS
DIRGES
DODGES
DOUGHS
FEIGNS
FERGUS
FORGES
FUDGES
FUNGUS
GANGES
GAUGES
GLOGGS
GORGES
GOUGES
HAGGIS
HEDGES
HINGES
HINGIS
HODGES
HOUGHS
IMAGES
JUDGES
KEDGES
LARGES
LARGOS
LAUGHS
LEDGES
LIEGES
LODGES
LONGES
LOUGHS
LUNGES
MANGOS
MARGES
MERGES
MIDGES
MUNGOS
NEIGHS
NUDGES
OMEGAS
OSAGES
PHAGES
PLAGES
PURGES
RANGES
REIGNS
RIDGES
ROUGES
ROUGHS
SAIGAS
SARGES
SARGOS
SEDGES
SERGES
SIEGES
SINGES
SOUGHS
STAGES
SURGES
SWAGES
TAIGAS
TANGOS
TARGES
THIGHS
TINGES
TOUGHS
USAGES
VERGES
VOSGES
VSIGNS
WEDGES
WEIGHS
WODGES

••••GS
BEFOGS
BEINGS
BRIGGS
BRINGS
CLANGS
CLINGS
DEBUGS
DEFOGS
DOINGS
DORAGS
DRINGS
FLINGS
GLOGGS
GOINGS
GULAGS
HMONGS
ICINGS
IDTAGS
KIANGS
LIANGS
ORANGS
ORINGS
PRANGS
PRONGS
REBAGS
REPEGS
RETAGS
SCRAGS
SHRUGS
SLANGS
SLINGS
SPRAGS
SPRIGS
STINGS
SWINGS
THINGS
THONGS
TWANGS
UNPEGS
UNRIGS
WHANGS
WRINGS
WRONGS

G•T•••
GATEAU
GATERS
GATHER
GATING
GATLIN
GATORS
GATSBY
GETMAD
GETOFF
GETOUT
GETSAT
GETSBY
GETSET
GETSIN
GETSIT
GETSON
GETSTO
GETSUP
GETTER
GETUPS
GITANO
GOTCHA
GOTHAM
GOTHIC
GOTMAD
GOTOFF
GOTOIT
GOTOUT
GOTSET
GOTTEN
GSTAAD
GUTTAE
GUTTED
GUTTER

G••T••
GAITED
GAITER
GANTRY
GARTER
GARTHS
GASTON
GASTRO
GENTLE
GENTLY
GENTRY
GERTIE
GESTES
GESTIC
GETTER
GHETTO
GIFTED
GIOTTO
GIRTED
GIRTHS
GLITCH
GLITZY
GLUTEI
GLUTEN
GLUTES
GNATTY
GOATEE
GOETHE
GOSTAG
GOTTEN
GRATED
GRATER
GRATES
GRATIA
GRATIN
GRATIS
GRETEL
GRETNA
GRITTY
GROTON
GROTTO
GROTTY
GUITAR
GUITRY
GUNTER
GUSTAV
GUSTED
GUTTAE
GUTTED
GUTTER

G•••T•
GAIETY
GALATA
GAMETE

GAMUTS GARETH GEARTO GELATI GELATO GEMOTE GEMOTS GENETS GETSTO GHETTO GHOSTS GIANTS GIGOTS GIOTTO GIVETO GLINTS GLOATS GNATTY GODETS GOINTO GOWITH GRAFTS GRANTS GREATS GREETS GRIFTS GRIOTS GRISTS GRITTY GROATS GROTTO GROTTY GROUTS GROUTY GROWTH GRUNTS GSUITS GUESTS GUILTY GUNITE GUYOTS GYRATE

G••••T

GADGET GAINST GALOOT GAMBIT GAMEST GANNET GARNET GARRET GASJET GASKET GASLIT GAYEST GERENT GERONT GETOUT GETSAT GETSET GETSIT GIBBET GIBLET GIDGET GIMLET GOBLET GOBUST GOCART GODWIT GOESAT GOKART GORGET GOSOFT GOTOIT GOTOUT GOTSET GOULET GOWEST GRABAT GRIVET GULLET GUSSET

•GT•••

SGTMAJ

•G•T••

AGATES AGATHA IGETIT IGOTIT

•G••T•

AGENTS AGLETS AGNATE AGOUTI EGESTA EGESTS EGRETS IGNATZ IGNITE

•G•••T

AGEIST AGHAST AGLINT AGOROT EGBERT EGMONT EGOIST IGETIT IGOTIT

••GT••

BIGTEN BIGTOE BIGTOP DOGTAG HOGTIE PEGTOP RAGTAG RAGTOP

••G•T•

ARGOTS AUGHTS BEGETS BIGHTS BIGOTS BOGOTA COGITO DIGITS EIGHTH EIGHTS EIGHTY ERGATE ERGOTS FAGOTS FIGHTS GIGOTS INGOTS LEGATE LEGATO LIGATE LIGHTS MIGHTY NEGATE NIGHTS NIGHTY ORGATE OUGHTS PIGSTY RIGHTO RIGHTS RIGHTY RUGATE SIGHTS TIGHTS WIGHTS ZYGOTE

••G••T

AIGRET ARGENT AUGUST BAGSIT BOGART BUGOUT COGENT CYGNET DEGUST DIGEST DIGLOT DIGOUT DOGSAT DOGSIT DUGOUT EAGLET ENGIRT ENGLUT FOGHAT HOGGET HUGEST INGEST LEGIST LOGOUT LUGNUT MAGNET NUGENT NUGGET ORGEAT PIGLET PIGNUT PIGOUT RAGOUT REGENT REGLET REGNAT REGRET SAGEST SIGNET TAGOUT UNGIRT URGENT WIGLET WIGOUT YOGURT

•••GT•

LENGTH SANGTO SINGTO

•••G•T

ALIGHT ARIGHT BIRGIT BLIGHT BOUGHT BRIGHT BUDGET CATGUT CAUGHT DWIGHT ELEGIT FIDGET FLIGHT FORGET FORGOT FOUGHT FRIGHT GADGET GIDGET GORGET HAIGHT HEIGHT HOGGET KNIGHT MARGOT MIDGET NAUGHT NOUGAT NOUGHT NUGGET PARGET PIAGET PLIGHT ROTGUT SLIGHT SOUGHT SPIGOT TARGET TAUGHT VEIGHT VOIGHT WEIGHT WIDGET WINGIT WRIGHT

GU••••

GUACOS GUARDS GUAVAS GUDRUN GUELPH GUENON GUERRE GUESTS GUFFAW GUIANA GUIDED GUIDES GUIDON GUILDS GUILES GUILTY GUIMPE GUINEA GUIROS GUISES GUITAR GUITRY GULAGS GULFED GULLAH GULLED GULLET GULPED GULPER GUMBEL GUMBOS GUMMED GUMSUP GUNDOG GUNFOR GUNGHO GUNITE GUNMAN GUNMEN GUNNAR GUNNED GUNNEL GUNNER GUNSHY GUNTER GURGLE GURKHA GURLEY GURNEY GUSHED GUSHER GUSHES GUSSET GUSTAV GUSTED GUTTAE GUTTED GUTTER GUYANA GUYING GUYOTS GUZZLE

G•U•••

GAUCHE GAUCHO GAUGED GAUGER GAUGES GAUMED GAUZES GLUERS GLUIER GLUING GLUMLY GLUONS GLUTEI GLUTEN GLUTES GOUGED GOUGER GOUGES GOULET GOUNOD GOURDE GOURDS GRUBBY GRUDGE GRUELS GRUMPS GRUMPY GRUNDY GRUNGE GRUNGY GRUNTS GSUITS

G••U••

GAMUTS GAZUMP GENUAL GERUND GETUPS GHOULS GIGUES GOBUST GROUCH GROUND GROUPS GROUSE GROUTS GROUTY

G•••U•

GALLUP GANGUE GANGUP GAVEUP GEARUP GENIUS GETOUT GETSUP GILGUY GIVEUP GOESUP GOLLUM GOOFUP GOTOUT GRADUS GREWUP GROWUP GUDRUN GUMSUP GYPSUM

G••••U

GATEAU

•GU•••

AGUISH IGUACU IGUANA NGUYEN

•G•U••

AGOUTI

•G••U•

EGGCUP

•G•••U

IGUACU

••GU••

ARGUED ARGUER ARGUES ARGUFY AUGURS AUGURY AUGUST BAGUIO BEGUMS CAGUAS DEGUST ENGULF FIGURE FUGUES GIGUES JAGUAR LAGUNA LEGUIN LEGUME LIGULA LIGURE MAGUEY MIGUEL MOGULS ROGUES SEGUED SEGUES SEGURA SIGURD UIGURS UNGUAL UNGUES UNGUIS VAGUER VOGUES YOGURT

••G•U•

BAGFUL BIGGUN BIGSUR BUGOUT CYGNUS DIGOUT DIGSUP DUGOUT EGGCUP ENGLUT FOGSUP HIGHUP JUGFUL LOGOUT LUGNUT MAGNUM MAGNUS PIGNUT PIGOUT RAGOUT RAGRUG REGIUS REGLUE RIGOUR RIGSUP SIGNUP TAGOUT TAGSUP UNGLUE VIGOUR WIGOUT

•••GU•

AIRGUN ARTGUM BADGUY BANGUI BANGUP BEEGUM BIGGUN BROGUE BULGUR CAPGUN CATGUT CLOGUP DENGUE DINGUS DROGUE FERGUS FUNGUS GANGUE GANGUP GILGUY HANGUL HANGUP HUNGUP JETGUN LANGUR LEAGUE LINGUA LONGUE OUTGUN PLAGUE POPGUN PRAGUE RANGUP RAYGUN REDGUM RINGUP ROTGUT RUNGUP SHOGUN SIXGUN SUBGUM TANGUY TONGUE TOPGUN

•••G•U

CONGOU HUNGWU KUNGFU PENGHU

••••GU

TELUGU

G•V•••

GAVEIN GAVELS GAVEUP GAVIAL GIVEIN GIVENS GIVERS GIVETO GIVEUP GIVING GOVERN

G••V••

GARVEY GLOVED GLOVER GLOVES GOOVER GRAVED GRAVEL GRAVEN GRAVER GRAVES GRAVID GRIVET GROVEL GROVER GROVES GUAVAS

G•••V•

GENEVA GENEVE GODIVA GREAVE GRIEVE GROOVE GROOVY

G••••V

GUSTAV

•G•V••

AGAVES OGIVES

••G•V•

ARGIVE

GW••••

GWYNNE

G•W•••

GAWAIN GAWKED GAWKER GAWPED GEWGAW GOWEST GOWILD GOWITH GOWNED

G••W••

GALWAY GLOWED GLOWER GNAWED GNAWER GOAWAY GOAWRY GODWIN GODWIT GREWON GREWUP GROWER GROWLS GROWLY GROWON GROWTH GROWUP

G•••W•

GODOWN

G••••W

GAGLAW GEEGAW GEWGAW GOSLOW GUFFAW

••GW••

BIGWIG WIGWAG WIGWAM

••G••W

FOGBOW GAGLAW JIGSAW MCGRAW MCGREW

•••GW•

HUNGWU

•••G•W

GEEGAW GEWGAW

G•••X•

GALAXY

GY••••

GYBING GYMBAG GYPPED GYPPER GYPSUM GYRATE GYRENE GYRONS GYROSE

G•Y•••

GAYALS GAYEST GAYNOR GEYSER GLYCOL GLYNIS GLYPHS GUYANA GUYING GUYOTS GWYNNE

G••Y••

GALYAK GRAYED GRAYER GRAYLY GREYED GREYER GREYLY

G•••Y•

GAMAYS GLADYS

G••••Y

GADFLY GAIETY GAINLY GALAXY GALLEY GALWAY GAMELY GAMILY GANGLY GANTRY GARVEY GASIFY GATSBY GELSEY GENTLY GENTRY GEORGY GETSBY GHARRY GIGGLY GILGUY GLADLY GLAIRY GLASSY GLEAMY GLIBLY GLITZY GLOOMY GLOPPY GLOSSY GLUMLY GNARLY GNATTY GOAWAY GOAWRY GOEASY GOESBY GOGGLY GONEBY GOODBY GOODLY GOOGLY GOOSEY GORILY GRABBY GRAINY GRAMMY GRANNY GRAPEY GRAPHY GRASSY GRAYLY GREASY GREEDY GREENY GREYLY GRIMLY GRISLY GRITTY GROGGY GROOVY GROSZY GROTTY GROUTY GROWLY GROZNY GRUBBY GRUMPY GRUNDY GRUNGY GUILTY GUITRY GUNSHY GURLEY GURNEY

•G•Y••

NGUYEN

•G•••Y

AGENCY UGLIFY UGLILY

••GY••

ARGYLE ARGYLL MAGYAR

••G•Y•

BOGEYS DOGEYS FOGEYS NAGOYA

••G••Y

ARGOSY ARGUFY AUGURY BEGLEY BIGAMY BIGBOY CAGILY CAGNEY DOGDAY EDGILY EIGHTY GIGGLY GOGGLY HIGHLY HUGELY JIGGLY LEGACY LOGILY MAGUEY MIGHTY NIGHTY PIGSTY RIGHTY SAGELY SUGARY TAGDAY VAGARY WAGGLY WIGGLY

•••G•Y

BADGUY BENGAY BOIGNY CLOGGY CRAGGY DANGLY DINGHY DOUGHY DRAGGY FLAGGY FROGGY GANGLY GIGGLY GILGUY GOGGLY GOOGLY GROGGY HUNGRY JANGLY JIGGLY JINGLY JUNGLY KINGLY KNAGGY LONGLY MARGAY NORGAY QUAGGY ROUGHY SHAGGY SINGLY SLAGGY SMOGGY SMUGLY SNAGGY SNUGLY TANGLY TANGUY TINGLY TOUGHY TRIGLY TWIGGY WAGGLY WIGGLY

••••GY

ANERGY CLERGY CLINGY CLOGGY CRAGGY DRAGGY EFFIGY ENERGY EULOGY FLAGGY FLEDGY FRINGY FROGGY GEORGY GROGGY GRUNGY KNAGGY OOLOGY ORANGY QUAGGY SHAGGY SLAGGY SLANGY SLUDGY SMOGGY SMUDGY SNAGGY SPONGY STINGY STODGY SWINGY SYZYGY THINGY TWANGY TWIGGY

G•Z•••

GAZEBO GAZING GAZUMP GEZIRA GIZMOS GUZZLE

G••Z••

GAUZES GEEZER GHAZIS GLAZED GLAZER GLAZES GLOZED GLOZES GRAZED GRAZER GRAZES GROZNY GUZZLE

G•••Z•

GLITZY GROSZY

•G•••Z

IGNATZ

••GZ••

ZIGZAG

HA••••

HABANA HABEAS HABILE HABITS HACEKS HACKED HACKER HACKIE HACKLE HACKLY HADDIE HADJES HADJIS HADRON HAEMAT HAEMON HAFTED HAGDON HAGGIS HAGGLE HAGMAN HAIDAS HAIGHT HAIKUS HAILED HAILEY HAINAN HAINES HAIRDO HAIRED HAJJES HAJJIS HAKIMS HALERS HALERU HALEST HALEVY HALIDE HALING HALITE HALLEL HALLEY HALLOO HALLOS HALLOW HALLUX HALOED HALOES HALOID HALSEY HALTED HALTER HALVAH HALVED HALVES HAMALS HAMELN HAMILL HAMITE HAMLET HAMLIN HAMMED HAMMER HAMPER HANDED HANDEL HANDIN HANDLE HANDON HANDUP HANGAR HANGED HANGER HANGIN HANGON HANGUL HANGUP HANKER HANKIE HANLEY HANNAH HANSEL HANSOM HANSON HAOLES HAPPED HAPPEN HARALD HARARE HARASS HARBIN HARBOR HARDBY HARDEN HARDER HARDLY HARDUP HAREMS HARING HARKED HARKEN HARKER HARLAN HARLEM HARLEY HARLIN HARLOW HARMED HARMON HAROLD HARPED HARPER HARPON HARRIS HARROW HARVEY HASBRO HASHED HASHES HASPED HASSAM HASSAN HASSLE HASTEN HASTES HATARI HATBOX HATERS HATFUL HATHOR HATING HATPIN HATRED HATTED HATTER HATTIE HAULED HAULER HAULMS HAULUP HAUNCH HAUNTS HAUSAS HAVANA HAVASU HAVEAT HAVENS HAVENT HAVEON HAVERS HAVING HAVOCS HAWAII HAWHAW HAWING HAWKED HAWKER HAWSER HAWSES HAYDEN HAYING HAYLEY HAYMOW HAZANS HAZARD HAZELS HAZERS HAZIER HAZILY HAZING

H•A•••

HEADED HEADER HEADIN HEADON HEADUP HEALED HEALER HEALTH HEANEY HEAPED HEARER HEAROF HEARST HEARTH HEARTS HEARTY HEARYE HEATED HEATER HEATHS HEATHY HEATUP HEAVED HEAVEN HEAVER HEAVES HIATAL HIATUS HOAGIE HOARDS HOARSE HOAXED HOAXER HOAXES HYADES

H••A••

HABANA HAMALS HARALD HARARE HARASS HATARI HAVANA HAVASU HAWAII HAZANS HAZARD HBEAMS HECATE HEGARI HEMATO HERALD HEXADS HIJACK HILARY HIVAOA HOBART HODADS HOGANS HOMAGE HORACE HOTAIR HOWARD HUMANE HUMANS

H•••A•

HABEAS HAEMAT HAGMAN HAIDAS HAINAN

HALVAH HANGAR HANNAH HARLAN HASSAM HASSAN HAUSAS HAVEAT HAWHAW HEEHAW HELLAS HENNAS HEPCAT HEPTAD HERBAL HEREAT HERMAN HETMAN HEYDAY HIATAL HIEMAL HIJRAH HINTAT HISSAT HITMAN HOOHAH HOOHAS HOOKAH HOORAH HOORAY HOOTAT HOSTAS HOTCAP HOTCAR HOTWAR HOWDAH HUBCAP HURRAH HURRAY HUSSAR HUZZAH HUZZAS HYDRAE HYDRAS HYENAS HYETAL HYMNAL

H••••A
HABANA HAVANA HECUBA HEGIRA HELENA HESTIA HIVAOA HOOPLA HOTTEA HULLOA

•HA•••
BHAKTI CHACHA CHACMA CHADOR CHAFED CHAFES CHAFFS CHAFFY CHAINE CHAINS CHAIRS CHAISE CHALCO CHALET CHALKS CHALKY CHAMMY CHAMPS CHANCE CHANCY CHANEL CHANEY CHANGE CHANTS CHAPEL CHAPIN CHARGE CHARLY CHARMS CHARON CHARRO CHARTS CHASED CHASER CHASES CHASMS CHASSE CHASTE CHATTY CHATUP CHAVEZ DHARMA GHAINS GHARRY GHAZIS KHAFRE KHAKIS KHALID PHAGES PHAROS PHASED PHASER PHASES PHATIC RHABDO RHAMES SHABAN SHABBY SHACKS SHADED SHADES SHADOW SHAFTS SHAGGY SHAKEN SHAKER SHAKES SHAKOS SHAKTI SHALES SHALEY SHALLY SHALOM SHAMAN SHAMED SHAMES SHAMIR SHAMUS SHANDY SHANIA SHANKS SHANNY SHANTY SHAPED SHAPER SHAPES SHARDS SHARED SHARER SHARES SHARIA SHARIF SHARKS SHARON SHARPS SHASTA SHAVED SHAVEN SHAVER SHAVES SHAWLS SHAWMS SHAYNE SHAZAM THALER THALES THALIA THAMES THANES THANKS THATCH THATIS THATLL THAWED THAYER WHACKS WHACKY WHALER WHALES WHAMMO WHAMMY WHANGS WHARFS WHATIF WHATLL WHATVE

•H•A••
CHEAPO CHEATS CHIANG CHIAUS CHOATE PHIALS PHRASE SHEAFS SHEARS SHEATH SHEAVE SHOALS SHOALY SHOATS SHRANK THRACE THRALE THRALL THRASH THWACK THWART UHLANS WHEALS WHEATS

•H••A•
BHOPAL BHUTAN CHELAE CHELAS CHEVAL CHIRAC CHORAL CHUKAR OHIOAN OHYEAH PHILAE PHYLAE RHINAL SHABAN SHAMAN SHAZAM SHEVAT SHIKAR SHIRAZ SHOFAR SHORAN SHOTAT THECAE THECAL THEHAJ THENAR THETAS THOMAS THORAX THREAD THREAT THROAT THUJAS WHYDAH XHOSAS

•H•••A
AHIMSA CHACHA CHACMA CHICHA CHOLLA CHOPRA CHROMA CHUKKA DHARMA PHOBIA RHONDA RHUMBA SHANIA SHARIA SHASTA SHEENA SHEILA SHERPA SHORTA THALIA THELMA THESEA

••HA••
ACHAEA AGHAST AMHARA ASHARP ATHAND BAHAMA BEHALF BEHAVE BIHARI BSHARP BYHAND CSHARP DSHARP ENHALO EPHAHS ERHARD ESHARP ETHANE EXHALE FSHARP GSHARP INHALE INHALF INHAND INHAUL ITHACA ITHAKI JIHADS JOHANN LCHAIM MCHALE MOHAIR MOHAVE MOHAWK OGHAMS ONHAND OSHAWA PAHANG PAHARI REHABS REHANG REHASH SAHARA UNHAND UTHANT

••H•A•
ASHCAN ASHLAR ASHRAM BAHIAN BEHEAD ISHTAR LEHUAS MIHRAB RAHRAH REHEAL REHEAR REHEAT SCHWAB SCHWAS WAHWAH

••H••A
ACHAEA AMHARA ATHENA BAHAMA DAHLIA ITHACA KAHLUA KAHUNA OSHAWA SAHARA SCHEMA

•••HA•
AFGHAN ALOHAS ALPHAS ASCHAM ATTHAT BADHAM BUCHAN CATHAY COBHAM CUSHAW DACHAS DIRHAM DOTHAN DUNHAM DURHAM FOGHAT GOTHAM GRAHAM HAWHAW HEEHAW HOOHAH HOOHAS ITZHAK LAPHAM LETHAL LOTHAR MAYHAP MISHAP MOCHAS MOSHAV NATHAN NIIHAU NUCHAE NUCHAL OLDHAM OLDHAT OMAHAN OMAHAS ORPHAN PASHAS PATHAN RASHAD REDHAT RODHAM SASHAY SOTHAT SOWHAT SUCHAS THEHAJ TINHAT TOPHAT UTAHAN WITHAL

•••H•A
ALTHEA BRAHMA BUSHWA ISCHIA JOSHUA KESHIA MOTHRA NASHUA PYTHIA SOPHIA TEPHRA

••••HA
AGATHA ARETHA AYESHA BERTHA BETCHA BUDDHA BUQSHA CHACHA CHICHA CONCHA EARTHA ELISHA GEISHA GOTCHA GURKHA ILESHA JASCHA KWACHA MANCHA MARSHA MARTHA MISCHA PERCHA QUOTHA TRISHA YAMAHA

HB••••
HBEAMS HBOMBS

H•B•••
HABANA HABEAS HABILE HABITS HEBREW HEBRON HOBART HOBBES HOBBIT HOBBLE HOBNOB HOBOES HOBSON HUBBLE HUBBLY HUBBUB HUBCAP HUBERT HUBRIS HYBRID

H••B••
HARBIN HARBOR HASBRO HATBOX HEEBIE HENBIT HERBAL HERBIE HOBBES HOBBIT HOBBLE HOMBRE HOTBED HOTBOX HUBBLE HUBBLY HUBBUB HUMBLE HUMBLY HUMBUG

H•••B•
HARDBY HBOMBS HECUBA HEREBY

H••••B
HOBNOB HOTTUB HUBBUB

•HB•••
SHBOOM

•H•B••
CHUBBY KHYBER PHOBIA PHOBIC PHOBOS RHABDO RHEBOK SHABAN SHABBY THEBES

•H••B•
CHUBBY PHILBY PHLEBO PHOEBE RHOMBI RHOMBS RHUMBA RHUMBS SHABBY SHRUBS THISBE THROBS THUMBS

•H•••B
CHERUB THEWEB

••H•B•
ACHEBE EPHEBE REHABS SAHIBS

••H••B
MIHRAB SCHWAB

H•C•••
HACEKS HACKED HACKER HACKIE HACKLE HACKLY HECATE HECKLE HECTIC HECTOR HECUBA HICCUP HICKEY HICKOK HOCKED HOCKEY

H••C••
HEPCAT HICCUP HINCTY HONCHO HOTCAP HOTCAR HUBCAP

H•••C•
HAUNCH HAVOCS HIJACK HIRSCH HITECH HOOTCH HORACE

H••••C
HECTIC HEROIC HOMEEC

•HC•••
AHCHOO

•H•C••
CHACHA CHACMA CHECKS CHICHA CHICHI CHICKS CHICLE CHICLY CHOCKS CHUCKS PHOCIS SHACKS SHOCKS SHUCKS THECAE THECAL THICKE WHACKS WHACKY

•H••C•
CHALCO CHANCE CHANCY CHEECH CHINCH CHOICE CHURCH SHTICK THATCH THENCE THRACE THRICE THWACK WHENCE

•H•••C
CHIRAC PHATIC PHOBIC PHONIC PHOTIC THETIC

••HC••
ASHCAN

••H•C•
ETHICS ITHACA MOHOCK SCHICK

••H••C
ECHOIC ETHNIC

•••HC•
BOCHCO

•••H•C
GOTHIC LITHIC MYTHIC ORPHIC UNCHIC

H•D•••
HADDIE HADJES HADJIS HADRON HEDDLE HEDGED HEDGER HEDGES HEDREN HEDRON HIDDEN HIDEHO HIDEKI HIDERS HIDING HIDOUT HODADS HODGES HUDDLE HUDSON HYDRAE HYDRAS HYDROS

H••D••
HADDIE HAGDON HAIDAS HANDED HANDEL HANDIN HANDLE HANDON HANDUP HARDBY HARDEN HARDER HARDLY HARDUP HAYDEN HEADED HEADER HEADIN HEADON HEADUP HEDDLE HEEDED HEEDER HEIDEN HELDIN HELDON HELDTO HELDUP HERDED HERDER HEYDAY HIDDEN HINDER HINDUS HOLDEN HOLDER HOLDIN HOLDIT HOLDON HOLDTO HOLDUP HOODED HOODOO HORDES HOTDOG HOWDAH HOYDEN HUDDLE HURDLE HYADES

H•••D•
HAIRDO HALIDE HEXADS HOARDS HODADS HOUNDS HOUNDY

H••••D
HACKED HAFTED HAILED HAIRED HALOED HALOID HALTED HALVED HAMMED HANDED HANGED HAPPED HARALD HARKED HARMED HAROLD HARPED HASHED HASPED HATRED HATTED HAULED HAWKED HAZARD HEADED HEALED HEAPED HEATED HEAVED HEDGED HEEDED HEELED HEFTED HELMED HELPED HEMMED HENTED HEPTAD HERALD HERDED HESIOD HILLED HINGED HINTED HIPPED HISPID HISSED HOAXED HOCKED HOGGED HONIED HONKED HOODED HOOFED HOOKED HOOPED HOOTED HOPPED HORNED HORRID HORSED HOSTED HOTBED HOTROD HOUSED HOWARD HOWLED HUFFED HUGGED HULKED HULLED HUMMED HUMPED HUNTED HURLED HUSHED HUSKED HUTTED HYBRID HYMNED HYPOED

•H•D••
CHADOR CHIDED CHIDER CHIDES PHEDRE RHODES SHADED SHADES SHADOW SHODDY WHYDAH

•H••D•
CHILDE CHILDS CHORDS RHABDO RHONDA SHANDY SHARDS SHEEDY SHINDY SHODDY SHREDS THIRDS

•H•••D
CHAFED CHASED CHEWED CHIDED CHIMED CHOKED CHOWED CHUTED KHALID PHASED PHONED PHYSED RHYMED SHADED SHAMED SHAPED SHARED SHAVED SHIELD SHINED SHOOED SHORED SHOULD SHOVED SHOWED SHREWD SHROUD THAWED THEEND THEFED THEKID THEMED THREAD THREED WHERED WHILED WHINED

••HD••
MAHDIS

••H•D•
ANHYDR APHIDS EPHODS JIHADS MRHYDE YEHUDI

••H••D
ATHAND BEHEAD BEHELD BEHIND BEHOLD BYHAND ECHOED ERHARD INHAND ONHAND ONHOLD REHELD TEHEED UNHAND UNHEED UPHELD UPHOLD

•••H•D
AMPHID ARCHED BACHED BASHED BATHED BUSHED CACHED CASHED COSHED DASHED DISHED ETCHED FISHED GASHED GUSHED HASHED HUSHED INCHED ITCHED JOSHED LASHED LATHED MASHED MESHED METHOD MOSHED MUSHED NOSHED ORCHID PITHED POOHED PUSHED RASHAD RASHID RESHOD RUSHED SASHED SIGHED TITHED UNSHED UNSHOD WASHED WISHED WITHED

HE••••
HEADED HEADER HEADIN HEADON HEADUP HEALED HEALER HEALTH HEANEY HEAPED HEARER HEAROF HEARST HEARTH HEARTS HEARTY HEARYE HEATED HEATER HEATHS HEATHY HEATUP HEAVED HEAVEN HEAVER HEAVES HEBREW HEBRON HECATE HECKLE HECTIC HECTOR HECUBA HEDDLE HEDGED HEDGER HEDGES HEDREN HEDRON HEEBIE HEEDED HEEDER HEEHAW HEELED HEELER HEFLIN HEFNER HEFTED HEGARI HEGIRA HEIDEN HEIFER HEIGHT HEISTS HELDIN HELDON HELDTO HELDUP HELENA HELENE HELENS HELIOS HELIUM HELLAS HELLER HELLOS HELMED HELMET HELMUT HELOTS HELPED HELPER HELTER HELVES HEMATO HEMMED HEMMER HEMSIN HENBIT HENLEY HENNAS HENNER HENNIN HENRIK HENRYV HENSON HENTED HEPCAT HEPPER HEPTAD HERALD HERBAL HERBIE HERDED HERDER HEREAT HEREBY HEREIN HEREOF HEREON HERESY HERETO HERIOT HERMAN HERMES HERMIT HERMON HEROES HEROIC HERONS HERSEY HERZOG HESIOD HESTER HESTIA HESTON HETERO HETMAN HETTIE HEWERS HEWING HEXADS HEXERS HEXING HEXNUT HEYDAY HEYYOU

H•E•••
HAEMAT HAEMON HBEAMS HEEBIE HEEDED HEEDER HEEHAW HEELED HEELER HIEING HIEMAL HIERON HOEING HUEVOS HYENAS HYETAL

H••E••
HABEAS HACEKS HALERS HALERU HALEST HALEVY HAMELN HAREMS HATERS HAVEAT HAVENS HAVENT HAVEON HAVERS HAZELS HAZERS HELENA HELENE HELENS HEREAT HEREBY HEREIN HEREOF HEREON HERESY HERETO HETERO HEWERS HEXERS HIDEHO HIDEKI HIDERS HIKERS HIKEUP HIREON HIRERS HITECH HOLEUP HOMEEC HOMELY HOMERS HONEST HONEYS HOPERS HOSELS HOTELS HOVELS HOVERS HOVETO HOWELL HUBERT HUGELY HUGEST HUMERI HYPEUP

H•••E•
HACKED HACKER HADJES HAFTED HAILED

HAILEY HAINES HAIRED HAJJES HALLEL HALLEY HALOED HALOES HALSEY HALTED HALTER HALVED HALVES HAMLET HAMMED HAMMER HAMPER HANDED HANDEL HANGED HANGER HANKER HANLEY HANSEL HAOLES HAPPED HAPPEN HARDEN HARDER HARKED HARKEN HARKER HARLEM HARLEY HARMED HARPED HARPER HARVEY HASHED HASHES HASPED HASTEN HASTES HATRED HATTED HATTER HAULED HAULER HAWKED HAWKER HAWSER HAWSES HAYDEN HAYLEY HAZIER HEADED HEADER HEALED HEALER HEANEY HEAPED HEARER HEATED HEATER HEAVED HEAVEN HEAVER HEAVES HEBREW HEDGED HEDGER HEDGES HEDREN HEEDED

HEEDER HEELED HEELER HEFNER HEFTED HEIDEN HEIFER HELLER HELMED HELMET HELPED HELPER HELTER HELVES HEMMED HEMMER HENLEY HENNER HENTED HEPPER HERDED HERDER HERMES HEROES HERSEY HESTER HICKEY HIDDEN HIGHER HILLED HILLEL HILLER HINDER HINGED HINGES HINTED HINTER HIPPED HIPPER HISSED HISSER HISSES HITHER HITMEN HITTER HOAXED HOAXER HOAXES HOBBES HOBOES HOCKED HOCKEY HODGES HOGGED HOGGET HOKIER HOLDEN HOLDER HOLIER HOLLER HOLMES HOMEEC HOMIER HONIED HONKED HONKER HOODED HOOFED HOOFER HOOKED HOOPED HOOPER HOOTED HOOTER

HOOVER HOOVES HOPPED HOPPER HORDES HORMEL HORNED HORNER HORNET HORNEY HORSED HORSES HORSEY HOSIER HOSTED HOSTEL HOTBED HOTTEA HOTTER HOUSED HOUSES HOWLED HOWLER HOYDEN HUFFED HUGGED HUGGER HUGHES HULKED HULLED HULLER HUMMED HUMMER HUMPED HUMVEE HUNGER HUNKER HUNTED HUNTER HURLED HURLER HURLEY HUSHED HUSHES HUSKED HUSKER HUSSEY HUTTED HUXLEY HYADES HYMNED HYPHEN HYPOED

H••••E

HABILE HACKIE HACKLE HADDIE HAGGLE HALIDE HALITE HAMITE HANDLE HANKIE HARARE HASSLE HATTIE HEARYE HECATE HECKLE HEDDLE HEEBIE HELENE HERBIE HETTIE HIGGLE HIPPIE HOAGIE HOARSE HOBBLE HOGTIE HOMAGE HOMBRE HONORE HOOPLE HOOPOE HOOTIE HOPPLE HORACE HUBBLE HUDDLE HUMANE HUMBLE HUMVEE HURDLE HURTLE HUSTLE HYDRAE

•HE•••

AHERNE CHEAPO CHEATS CHECKS CHEECH CHEEKS CHEEKY CHEEPS CHEERS CHEERY CHEESE CHEESY CHEKOV CHELAE CHELAS CHEMIN CHENIN CHEOPS CHEQUE CHERIE CHERRY CHERTY CHERUB CHERYL CHESTS CHESTY CHETHS CHEVAL CHEVET CHEVRE CHEWED CHEWER CHEWUP GHETTO OHENRY PHEDRE PHENOL PHENOM PHENYL RHEBOK RHESUS RHETOR RHEUMS RHEUMY SHEAFS SHEARS SHEATH SHEAVE SHEEDY SHEEHY SHEENA SHEENS SHEEPS SHEERS SHEETS SHEIKS SHEILA SHEKEL SHELLS SHELLY SHELTY SHELVE SHEREE SHERIF SHERPA SHERRY SHERYL SHEVAT THEBES THECAE THECAL THEEND THEFED THEFLY THEFTS THEHAJ THEIRS THEISM THEIST THEKID THELIP THELMA THEMED THEMES THENAR THENCE THEORY THERES THERMO THERMS THESEA THESES THESIS THESIX THETAS THETIC THETIS THETOY THEWEB THEWIZ THEYLL THEYRE THEYVE WHEALS WHEATS WHEELS WHEEZE WHEEZY WHELKS WHELMS WHELPS WHENCE WHERED WHERES WHERRY

•H•E••

CHEECH CHEEKS CHEEKY CHEEPS CHEERS CHEERY CHEESE CHEESY CHIEFS KHMERS NHLERS OHWELL OHYEAH PHLEBO PHLEGM PHOEBE SHEEDY SHEEHY SHEENA SHEENS SHEEPS SHEERS SHEETS SHIELD SHIEST SHOERS SHREDS SHREWD SHREWS SHTETL SHYEST THEEND THIEVE THREAD THREAT THREED THREES THRESH WHEELS WHEEZE WHEEZY

•H••E•

CHAFED CHAFES CHALET CHANEL CHANEY CHAPEL CHASED CHASER CHASES CHAVEZ CHEVET CHEWED CHEWER CHIDED CHIDER CHIDES CHIMED CHIMES CHINES CHISEL CHIVES CHOKED CHOKER CHOKES CHOLER CHORES CHOSEN CHOWED CHUTED CHUTES DHOLES DHOTEL KHYBER PHAGES PHASED PHASER PHASES PHLOEM PHONED PHONES PHONEY PHOOEY PHYSED RHAMES RHODES RHYMED RHYMER RHYMES SHADED SHADES SHAKEN SHAKER SHAKES SHALES SHALEY SHAMED SHAMES SHAPED SHAPER SHAPES SHARED SHARER SHARES SHAVED SHAVEN SHAVER SHAVES SHEKEL SHEREE SHINED SHINER SHINES SHIRER SHIRES SHIVER SHOLEM SHOOED SHORED SHORES SHOVED SHOVEL SHOVER SHOVES SHOWED SHOWER SHRIEK THALER THALES THAMES THANES THAWED THAYER THEBES THEFED THEMED THEMES THERES THESEA THESES THEWEB THOLES THREED THREES THROES WHALER WHALES WHERED WHERES WHILED WHILES WHINED WHINER WHINES WHINEY WHITEN WHITER WHITES WHOLES

•H•••E

AHERNE CHAINE CHAISE CHANCE CHANGE CHARGE CHASSE CHASTE CHEESE CHELAE CHEQUE CHERIE CHEVRE CHICLE CHIGOE CHILDE CHILOE CHOATE CHOICE CHOOSE CHROME KHAFRE LHOTSE PHEDRE PHILAE PHOEBE PHRASE PHYLAE SHAYNE SHEAVE SHELVE SHEREE SHIITE SHOPPE SHORTE SHOWME SHRIKE SHRINE SHRIVE SHROVE THECAE THENCE THEYRE THEYVE THICKE THIEVE THISBE THORPE THRACE THRALE THRICE THRIVE THRONE THROVE WHATVE WHEEZE WHENCE

••HE••

ACHEBE ACHENE ADHERE ATHENA ATHENE ATHENS BEHEAD BEHELD BEHEST COHEIR COHERE EPHEBE ETHENE ETHERS INHERE OCHERS OCHERY OTHERS REHEAL REHEAR REHEAT REHEEL REHELD REHEMS SCHELL SCHEMA SCHEME SPHERE SPHERY STHENO TEHEED TEHEES UNHEED UPHELD USHERS

••H•E•

ACHAEA ACHIER ASHIER ASHLEY CAHIER ECHOED ECHOES KOHLER LEHRER MAHLER OCHRES REHEEL ROHMER SCHLEP TEHEED TEHEES UNHEED WOHLER YAHWEH

••H••E

ACHEBE ACHENE ADHERE ASHORE ATHENE ATHOME AWHILE BEHAVE BEHOVE COHERE COHUNE EPHEBE ETHANE ETHENE EXHALE GOHOME INHALE INHERE JOHORE LAHORE MCHALE MOHAVE MRHYDE OPHITE REHIRE SCHEME SPHERE WAHINE

•••HE•

AACHEN AETHER ALTHEA ANTHEM ANTHER ARCHED ARCHER ARCHES ARNHEM BACHED BASHED BASHES BATHED BATHER BATHES BETHEL BOTHER BUSHED BUSHEL BUSHES CACHED CACHES CACHET CASHED CASHES CASHEW CATHER CIPHER COSHED COSHES CYPHER DASHED DASHER DASHES DISHED DISHES DITHER EITHER ESCHER ESCHEW ESTHER ETCHED ETCHER ETCHES FATHER FICHES FISHED FISHER FISHES GASHED GASHES GATHER GOPHER GOSHEN GUSHED GUSHER GUSHES HASHED HASHES HIGHER HITHER HUGHES HUSHED HUSHES HYPHEN INCHED INCHES ISOHEL ITCHED ITCHES JOSHED JOSHES KOSHER KUCHEN LACHES LASHED LASHER LASHES LATHED LATHER LATHES LICHEN LUSHER LUTHER MACHES MASHED MASHER MASHES MATHER MAYHEM MESHED MESHES MICHEL MOSHED MOSHER MOSHES MOTHER MUDHEN MUSHED MUSHER MUSHES NEPHEW NETHER NICHES NIGHER NOSHED NOSHER NOSHES PEAHEN PITHED POOHED POSHER POTHER PUSHED PUSHES RACHEL RASHER RASHES RATHER RESHES RICHEN RICHER RICHES ROCHET RUCHES RUSHED RUSHEE RUSHES SACHEM SACHET SADHES SASHED SASHES SIGHED SIGHER TEEHEE TETHER TITHED TITHER TITHES TOTHER TOWHEE UNSHED VACHEL WASHED WASHER WASHES WETHER WISHED WISHER WISHES WITHED WITHER WITHES ZITHER

•••H•E

ARCHIE DAPHNE EUCHRE FICHTE KATHIE KISHKE MASHIE NUCHAE RESHOE RICHIE RUSHEE SOPHIE TECHIE TEEHEE TOWHEE WASHOE

••••HE

AMECHE APACHE BLITHE BLYTHE BOOTHE BUNCHE BYSSHE CLICHE CLOCHE CLOTHE CRECHE FLECHE GAUCHE GOETHE LOATHE LOUCHE MARCHE PSYCHE QUICHE SCATHE SCYTHE SEETHE SEICHE SNATHE SOOTHE SPATHE SWATHE TEETHE TOUCHE TROCHE WRITHE

H•F•••

HAFTED HEFLIN HEFNER HEFTED HUFFED

H••F••

HATFUL HEIFER HOOFED HOOFER HOOFIT HUFFED

H•••F•

HOPOFF

H••••F

HEAROF HEREOF HOPOFF

•H•F••

CHAFED CHAFES CHAFFS CHAFFY CHUFFY KHAFRE SHAFTS SHIFTS SHIFTY SHOFAR THEFED THEFLY THEFTS WHIFFS

•H••F•

CHAFFS CHAFFY CHIEFS CHUFFY SHEAFS SHRIFT THRIFT WHARFS WHIFFS WHOOFS

•H•••F

SHARIF SHERIF WHATIF

••H•F•

SCHIFF

••H••F

BEHALF BEHOOF INHALF SCHIFF

H•G•••

HAGDON HAGGIS HAGGLE HAGMAN HEGARI HEGIRA HIGGLE HIGHER HIGHIQ HIGHLY HIGHUP HOGANS HOGGED HOGGET HOGTIE HUGELY HUGEST HUGGED HUGGER HUGHES

H••G••

HAGGIS HAGGLE HAIGHT HANGAR HANGED HANGER HANGIN HANGON HANGUL HANGUP HEDGED HEDGER HEDGES HEIGHT HIGGLE HINGED HINGES HINGIS HOAGIE HODGES HOGGED HOGGET HOUGHS HUGGED HUGGER HUNGER HUNGIN HUNGON HUNGRY HUNGUP HUNGWU

H•••G•

HMONGS HOMAGE

H••••G

HALING HARING HATING HAVING HAWING HAYING HAZING HERZOG HEWING HEXING HIDING HIEING HIKING HIRING HIVING HOEING HOLING HOMING HONING HOPING HOSING HOTDOG HUMBUG HYPING

•H•G••

CHIGOE PHAGES SHAGGY SHOGUN THIGHS

•H••G•

CHANGE CHARGE CHOUGH PHLEGM SHAGGY SHRUGS THINGS THINGY THONGS THOUGH WHANGS

•H•••G

CHIANG PHOTOG SHYING THRONG

••H•G•

LEHIGH MCHUGH ONHIGH

••H••G

AAHING ACHING GEHRIG ICHING OOHING PAHANG REHANG REHUNG

•••H•G

LITHOG QUAHOG

H•H•••

HLHUNT HOHOHO

H••H••

HASHED HASHES HATHOR HAWHAW HEEHAW HIGHER HIGHIQ HIGHLY HIGHUP HIPHOP HITHER HOOHAH HOOHAS HUGHES HUSHED HUSHES HYPHEN

H•••H•

HAIGHT HEATHS HEATHY HEIGHT HIDEHO HOHOHO HONCHO HONSHU HOUGHS HUMPHS

H••••H

HALVAH HANNAH HAUNCH HEALTH HEARTH HIJRAH HIRSCH HITECH HOOHAH HOOKAH HOORAH HOOTCH HOWDAH HURRAH HUZZAH

•H•H••

AHCHOO CHUHSI THEHAJ

•H••H•

CHACHA CHETHS CHICHA CHICHI RHYTHM SHEEHY THIGHS

•H•••H

CHEECH CHINCH CHOUGH CHURCH OHYEAH SHEATH SHILOH THATCH THOUGH THRASH THRESH THRUSH WHOOSH WHYDAH

••H•H•

EPHAHS HOHOHO ICHTHY YOHOHO

••H••H

LEHIGH MCHUGH ONHIGH RAHRAH REHASH WAHWAH YAHWEH

•••H•H

EIGHTH HOOHAH

HI••••

HIATAL HIATUS HICCUP HICKEY

HICKOK
HIDDEN
HIDEHO
HIDEKI
HIDERS
HIDING
HIDOUT
HIEING
HIEMAL
HIERON
HIGGLE
HIGHER
HIGHIQ
HIGHLY
HIGHUP
HIJACK
HIJRAH
HIKERS
HIKEUP
HIKING
HILARY
HILLED
HILLEL
HILLER
HILTON
HINCTY
HINDER
HINDUS
HINGED
HINGES
HINGIS
HINTAT
HINTED
HINTER
HINTON
HIPHOP
HIPPED
HIPPER
HIPPIE
HIPPOS
HIREON
HIRERS
HIRING
HIRSCH
HISPID
HISSAT
HISSED
HISSER
HISSES
HITECH
HITHER
HITMAN
HITMEN
HITOUT
HITSIT
HITSON
HITSUP
HITTER
HIVAOA
HIVING

H•I•••

HAIDAS
HAIGHT
HAIKUS
HAILED
HAILEY
HAINAN
HAINES
HAIRDO
HAIRED
HEIDEN
HEIFER
HEIGHT
HEISTS
HOISTS

H••I••

HABILE
HABITS
HAKIMS
HALIDE
HALING
HALITE
HAMILL
HAMITE
HARING
HATING
HAVING
HAWING
HAYING
HAZIER
HAZILY
HAZING
HEGIRA
HELIOS
HELIUM
HERIOT
HESIOD
HEWING
HEXING
HIDING
HIEING
HIKING
HIRING
HIVING
HOEING
HOKIER
HOLIER
HOLILY
HOLING
HOLISM
HOLIST
HOMIER
HOMILY
HOMING
HOMINY
HONIED
HONING
HOPING
HOSIER
HOSING
HYPING

H•••I•

HACKIE
HADDIE
HADJIS
HAGGIS
HAJJIS
HALOID
HAMLIN
HANDIN
HANGIN
HANKIE
HARBIN
HARLIN
HARRIS
HATPIN
HATTIE
HAWAII
HEADIN
HECTIC
HEEBIE
HEFLIN
HELDIN
HEMSIN
HENBIT
HENNIN
HENRIK
HERBIE
HEREIN
HERMIT
HEROIC
HESTIA
HETTIE
HIGHIQ
HINGIS
HIPPIE
HISPID
HITSIT
HOAGIE
HOBBIT
HOGTIE
HOLDIN
HOLDIT
HOOFIT
HOOTIE
HOPSIN
HORNIN
HORRID
HOTAIR
HOTTIP
HOURIS
HOWLIN
HUBRIS
HUNGIN
HYBRID

H••••I

HATARI
HAWAII
HEGARI
HIDEKI
HUMERI

•HI•••

AHIMSA
CHIANG
CHIAUS
CHICHA
CHICHI
CHICKS
CHICLE
CHICLY
CHIDED
CHIDER
CHIDES
CHIEFS
CHIGOE
CHILDE
CHILDS
CHILLI
CHILLS
CHILLY
CHILOE
CHIMED
CHIMES
CHIMPS
CHINCH
CHINES
CHINKS
CHINKY
CHINOS
CHINTZ
CHINUP
CHIPIN
CHIRAC
CHIRON
CHIRPS
CHIRPY
CHIRRS
CHISEL
CHISOX
CHITIN
CHITON
CHIVES
OHIOAN
PHIALS
PHILAE
PHILBY
PHILIP
PHILLY
PHILOL
PHILOS
RHINAL
RHINOS
SHIELD
SHIEST
SHIFTS
SHIFTY
SHIISM
SHIITE
SHIKAR
SHILLS
SHILLY
SHILOH
SHIMMY
SHIMON
SHINDY
SHINED
SHINER
SHINES
SHINNY
SHINTO
SHIRAZ
SHIRER
SHIRES
SHIRKS
SHIRRS
SHIRTS
SHIRTY
SHIVER
THICKE
THIEVE
THIGHS
THILLS
THINGS
THINGY
THINKS
THINLY
THIRDS
THIRST
THIRTY
THISBE
WHIFFS
WHILED
WHILES
WHILOM
WHILST
WHIMSY
WHINED
WHINER
WHINES
WHINEY
WHINNY
WHIPPY
WHIPUP
WHIRLS
WHIRLY
WHIRRS
WHISKS
WHISKY
WHITEN
WHITER
WHITES
WHITTY
WHIZZO

•H•I••

CHAINE
CHAINS
CHAIRS
CHAISE
CHOICE
CHOIRS
CHRISM
GHAINS
SHEIKS
SHEILA
SHIISM
SHIITE
SHRIEK
SHRIFT
SHRIKE
SHRILL
SHRIMP
SHRINE
SHRINK
SHRIVE
SHTICK
SHYING
THEIRS
THEISM
THEIST
THRICE
THRIFT
THRILL
THRIPS
THRIVE

•H••I•

CHAPIN
CHEMIN
CHENIN
CHERIE
CHIPIN
CHITIN
CHOPIN
DHOTIS
GHAZIS
KHAKIS
KHALID
PHATIC
PHILIP
PHOBIA
PHOBIC
PHOCIS
PHONIC
PHOTIC
PHYSIO
SHAMIR
SHANIA
SHARIA
SHARIF
SHERIF
SHOJIS
SHOOIN
SHOWIN
SHUTIN
THALIA
THATIS
THEKID
THELIP
THESIS
THESIX
THETIC
THETIS
THEWIZ
WHATIF

•H•••I

BHAKTI
CHICHI
CHILLI
CHUHSI
RHOMBI
SHAKTI
SHORTI
THYRSI
WHOOPI

••HI••

AAHING
ACHIER
ACHING
ALHIRT
APHIDS
ASHIER
AWHILE
AWHIRL
BAHIAN
BEHIND
CAHIER
ECHINO
ETHICS
ICHING
LEHIGH
NIHILO
NOHITS
ONHIGH
OOHING
OPHITE
REHIRE
SAHIBS
SCHICK
SCHIFF
SCHISM
SCHIST
SCHIZY
SPHINX
TAHINI
TAHITI
TSHIRT
UPHILL
VCHIPS
WAHINE

••H•I•

COHEIR
DAHLIA
ECHOIC
ETHNIC
GEHRIG
KAHLIL
LCHAIM
MAHDIS
MOHAIR

••H••I

BIHARI
EPHORI
ITHAKI
PAHARI
TAHINI
TAHITI
YEHUDI

•••HI•

AMPHID
ARCHIE
CASHIN
COCHIN
DASHIS
DUCHIN
ELOHIM
GOTHIC
HIGHIQ
ISCHIA
KATHIE
KESHIA
LASHIO
LITHIC
MASHIE
MATHIS
MENHIR
MISHIT
MUZHIK
MYTHIC
ORCHID
ORCHIL
ORPHIC
OUTHIT
PYTHIA
RACHIS
RASHID
RESHIP
RICHIE
SOPHIA
SOPHIE
SPAHIS
TECHIE
UNCHIC
URCHIN
WITHIN
WITHIT

•••H•I

CHUHSI
ISTHMI
MYTHOI
TISHRI
TZUHSI
VASHTI

••••HI

CANTHI
CHICHI
DELPHI
GANDHI
KIMCHI
LITCHI
TAICHI

H•J•••

HAJJES
HAJJIS
HIJACK
HIJRAH

H••J••

HADJES
HADJIS
HAJJES
HAJJIS

•H•J••

SHOJIS
THUJAS

•H••J•

CHONJU

•H•••J

THEHAJ

•••H•J

THEHAJ

H•K•••

HAKIMS
HIKERS
HIKEUP
HIKING
HOKIER
HYKSOS

H••K••

HACKED
HACKER
HACKIE
HACKLE
HACKLY
HAIKUS
HANKER
HANKIE
HARKED
HARKEN
HARKER
HAWKED
HAWKER
HECKLE
HICKEY
HICKOK
HOCKED
HOCKEY
HONKED
HONKER
HOOKAH
HOOKED
HOOKUP
HULKED
HUNKER
HUSKED
HUSKER

H•••K•

HACEKS
HIDEKI

H••••K

HENRIK
HICKOK
HIJACK

•H•K••

BHAKTI
CHEKOV
CHOKED
CHOKER
CHOKES
CHUKAR
CHUKKA
KHAKIS
SHAKEN
SHAKER
SHAKES
SHAKOS
SHAKTI
SHEKEL
SHIKAR
THEKID
ZHUKOV

•H••K•

CHALKS
CHALKY
CHECKS
CHEEKS
CHEEKY
CHICKS
CHINKS
CHINKY
CHOCKS
CHUCKS
CHUKKA
CHUNKS
CHUNKY
SHACKS
SHANKS
SHARKS
SHEIKS
SHIRKS
SHOCKS
SHOOKS
SHRIKE
SHUCKS
THANKS
THICKE
THINKS
THUNKS
WHACKS
WHACKY
WHELKS
WHISKS
WHISKY

•H•••K

RHEBOK
SHRANK
SHRIEK
SHRINK
SHRUNK
SHTICK
THWACK

••H•K•

ITHAKI

••H••K

DRHOOK
MOHAWK
MOHOCK
REHOOK
SCHICK
UNHOOK

•••HK•

KISHKE
ROTHKO

•••H•K

ITZHAK
MUZHIK

HL••••

HLHUNT

H•L•••

HALERS
HALERU
HALEST
HALEVY
HALIDE
HALING
HALITE
HALLEL
HALLEY
HALLOO
HALLOS
HALLOW
HALLUX
HALOED
HALOES
HALOID
HALSEY
HALTED
HALTER
HALVAH
HALVED
HALVES
HELDIN
HELDON
HELDTO
HELDUP
HELENA
HELENE
HELENS
HELIOS
HELIUM
HELLAS
HELLER
HELLOS
HELMED
HELMET
HELMUT
HELOTS
HELPED
HELPER
HELTER
HELVES
HILARY
HILLED
HILLEL
HILLER
HILTON
HOLDEN
HOLDER
HOLDIN
HOLDIT
HOLDON
HOLDTO
HOLDUP
HOLEUP
HOLIER
HOLILY
HOLING
HOLISM
HOLIST
HOLLER
HOLLOW
HOLMES
HULKED
HULLED
HULLER
HULLOA
HULLOS

H••L••

HAILED
HAILEY
HALLEL
HALLEY
HALLOO
HALLOS
HALLOW
HALLUX
HAMLET
HAMLIN
HANLEY
HAOLES
HARLAN
HARLEM
HARLEY
HARLIN
HARLOW
HAULED
HAULER
HAULMS
HAULUP
HAYLEY
HEALED
HEALER
HEALTH
HEELED
HEELER
HEFLIN
HELLAS
HELLER
HELLOS
HENLEY
HILLED
HILLEL
HILLER
HOLLER
HOLLOW
HOWLED
HOWLER
HOWLIN
HULLED
HULLER
HULLOA
HULLOS
HURLED
HURLER
HURLEY
HUXLEY

H•••L•

HABILE
HACKLE
HACKLY
HAGGLE
HAMALS
HAMELN
HAMILL
HANDLE
HARALD
HARDLY
HAROLD
HASSLE
HAZELS
HAZILY
HECKLE
HEDDLE
HERALD
HIGGLE
HIGHLY
HOBBLE
HOLILY
HOMELY
HOMILY
HOOPLA
HOOPLE
HOPPLE
HOSELS
HOSTLY
HOTELS
HOURLY
HOVELS
HOWELL
HUBBLE
HUBBLY
HUDDLE
HUGELY
HUMBLE
HUMBLY
HURDLE
HURTLE
HUSTLE

H••••L

HALLEL
HAMILL
HANDEL
HANGUL
HANSEL
HATFUL
HERBAL
HIATAL
HIEMAL
HILLEL
HORMEL
HOSTEL
HOWELL
HYETAL
HYMNAL

•HL•••

CHLORO
NHLERS
PHLEBO
PHLEGM
PHLOEM
UHLANS

•H•L••

CHALCO
CHALET
CHALKS
CHALKY
CHELAE
CHELAS
CHILDE
CHILDS
CHILLI
CHILLS
CHILLY
CHILOE
CHOLER
CHOLLA
CHOLOS
DHOLES
KHALID
PHILAE
PHILBY
PHILIP
PHILLY
PHILOL
PHILOS
PHYLAE
PHYLLO
PHYLUM
SHALES
SHALEY
SHALLY
SHALOM
SHELLS
SHELLY
SHELTY
SHELVE
SHILLS
SHILLY
SHILOH
SHOLEM
SHOLOM
THALER
THALES
THALIA
THELIP
THELMA
THILLS
THOLES
WHALER
WHALES
WHELKS
WHELMS
WHELPS
WHILED
WHILES
WHILOM
WHILST
WHOLES
WHOLLY

•H••L•

CHARLY
CHICLE
CHICLY
CHILLI
CHILLS
CHILLY
CHOLLA
CHURLS
GHOULS
OHWELL
PHIALS
PHILLY
PHYLLO
SHALLY
SHAWLS
SHEILA
SHELLS
SHELLY
SHIELD
SHILLS
SHILLY
SHOALS
SHOALY
SHOULD
SHRILL
THATLL
THEFLY
THEYLL
THILLS
THINLY
THRALE
THRALL
THRILL
THUSLY
WHATLL
WHEALS
WHEELS
WHIRLS
WHIRLY
WHOLLY
WHORLS

•H•••L

BHOPAL
CHANEL
CHAPEL
CHERYL
CHEVAL
CHISEL
CHORAL
DHOTEL
OHWELL
PHENOL
PHENYL
PHILOL
RHINAL
SHEKEL
SHERYL
SHOVEL
SHRILL
SHTETL
THATLL
THECAL
THEYLL
THRALL
THRILL
WHATLL

••HL••

ASHLAR
ASHLEY
DAHLIA
KAHLIL
KAHLUA
KOHLER
MAHLER
SCHLEP
WOHLER

••H•L•

AWHILE
BEHALF
BEHELD
BEHOLD
ENHALO
EXHALE
INHALE
INHALF
MCHALE
NIHILO
ONHOLD
REHELD
SCHELL
SCHULZ
UNHOLY
UPHELD
UPHILL
UPHOLD

••H••L

AWHIRL
INHAUL
KAHLIL
REHEAL
REHEEL
SCHELL
SCHOOL
SCHORL
UPHILL

•••HL•

ARCHLY
HIGHLY
LUSHLY
POSHLY
RASHLY
RICHLY

•••H•L

BETHEL
BUSHEL
ISOHEL
LETHAL
METHYL
MICHEL
MYTHOL
NUCHAL
ORCHIL
PATHOL
RACHEL
VACHEL
WARHOL
WITHAL

••••HL

JAWOHL

HM••••

HMONGS

H•M•••

HAMALS
HAMELN
HAMILL
HAMITE
HAMLET
HAMLIN
HAMMED
HAMMER
HAMPER
HEMATO
HEMMED
HEMMER
HEMSIN
HOMAGE
HOMBRE
HOMEEC
HOMELY
HOMERS
HOMIER
HOMILY
HOMING
HOMINY
HUMANE
HUMANS
HUMBLE
HUMBLY
HUMBUG
HUMERI
HUMMED
HUMMER
HUMMUS
HUMORS
HUMOUR
HUMPED
HUMPHS
HUMVEE
HYMNAL
HYMNED

H••M••

HAEMAT
HAEMON
HAGMAN
HAMMED
HAMMER
HARMED
HARMON
HAYMOW
HBOMBS
HELMED
HELMET
HELMUT
HEMMED
HEMMER
HERMAN
HERMES
HERMIT
HERMON
HETMAN
HIEMAL
HITMAN
HITMEN
HOLMES
HORMEL
HORMUZ
HUMMED
HUMMER
HUMMUS

H•••M•

HAKIMS
HAREMS
HAULMS
HBEAMS

H••••M

HANSOM
HARLEM
HASSAM
HELIUM
HOLISM

•HM•••

KHMERS

•H•M••

AHIMSA
CHAMMY
CHAMPS
CHEMIN
CHIMED
CHIMES
CHIMPS
CHOMPS
CHUMMY
CHUMPS
RHAMES
RHOMBI
RHOMBS
RHUMBA
RHUMBS
RHYMED
RHYMER
RHYMES
SHAMAN
SHAMED
SHAMES
SHAMIR
SHAMUS
SHIMMY
SHIMON
THAMES
THEMED
THEMES
THOMAS
THUMBS
THUMPS
THYMUS
WHAMMO
WHAMMY
WHIMSY
WHOMPS
WHOMSO

•H••M•

CHACMA
CHAMMY
CHARMS
CHASMS
CHROMA
CHROME
CHROMO
CHROMY
CHUMMY
DHARMA
KHOUMS
RHEUMS
RHEUMY
SHAWMS
SHIMMY
SHOWME
SHRIMP
THELMA
THERMO
THERMS
THRUMS
WHAMMO
WHAMMY
WHELMS

•H••M

CHRISM PHENOM PHLEGM PHLOEM PHYLUM RHYTHM SHALOM SHAZAM SHBOOM SHIISM SHOLEM SHOLOM THEISM WHILOM

••HM••

ROHMER SCHMOO SCHMOS

••H•M•

ATHOME BAHAMA GOHOME OGHAMS REHEMS SCHEMA SCHEME

••H••M

ASHRAM LCHAIM SCHISM

•••HM•

ABOHMS BRAHMA BRAHMS ISTHMI MYOHMY

•••H•M

ANTHEM ARNHEM ASCHAM BADHAM COBHAM DIRHAM DUNHAM DURHAM ELOHIM FATHOM GOTHAM GRAHAM LAPHAM MAYHEM OLDHAM RODHAM SACHEM

••••HM

DRACHM MEGOHM RHYTHM

H•N•••

HANDED HANDEL HANDIN HANDLE HANDON HANDUP HANGAR HANGED HANGER HANGIN HANGON HANGUL HANGUP HANKER HANKIE HANLEY HANNAH HANSEL HANSOM HANSON HENBIT HENLEY HENNAS HENNER HENNIN HENRIK HENRYV HENSON HENTED HINCTY HINDER HINDUS HINGED HINGES HINGIS HINTAT HINTED HINTER HINTON HONCHO HONEST HONEYS HONIED HONING HONKED HONKER HONORE HONORS HONOUR HONSHU HUNGER HUNGIN HUNGON HUNGRY HUNGUP HUNGWU HUNKER HUNTED HUNTER

H••N••

HAINAN HAINES HANNAH HAUNCH HAUNTS HEANEY HEFNER HENNAS HENNER HENNIN HEXNUT HMONGS HOBNOB HORNED HORNER HORNET HORNEY HORNIN HOUNDS HOUNDY HOWNOW HYENAS HYMNAL HYMNED HYPNOS

H•••N•

HABANA HALING HARING HATING HAVANA HAVENS HAVENT HAVING HAWING HAYING HAZANS HAZING HELENA HELENE HELENS HERONS HEWING HEXING HIDING HIEING HIKING HIRING HIVING HLHUNT HOEING HOGANS HOLING HOMING HOMINY HONING HOPING HOSING HUMANE HUMANS HURONS HYPING

H••••N

HADRON HAEMON HAGDON HAGMAN HAINAN HAMELN HAMLIN HANDIN HANDON HANGIN HANGON HANSON HAPPEN HARBIN HARDEN HARKEN HARLAN HARLIN HARMON HARPON HASSAN HASTEN HATPIN HAVEON HAYDEN HEADIN HEADON HEAVEN HEBRON HEDREN HEDRON HEFLIN HEIDEN HELDIN HELDON HEMSIN HENNIN HENSON HEREIN HEREON HERMAN HERMON HESTON HETMAN HIDDEN HIERON HILTON HINTON HIREON HITMAN HITMEN HITSON HOBSON HOLDEN HOLDIN HOLDON HOPSIN HORNIN HORTON HOWLIN HOYDEN HUDSON HUNGIN HUNGON HUSTON HUTTON HYPHEN

•H•N••

CHANCE CHANCY CHANEL CHANEY CHANGE CHANTS CHENIN CHINCH CHINES CHINKS CHINKY CHINOS CHINTZ CHINUP CHONJU CHUNKS CHUNKY OHENRY PHENOL PHENOM PHENYL PHONED PHONES PHONEY PHONIC PHONON PHONOS RHINAL RHINOS RHONDA SHANDY SHANIA SHANKS SHANNY SHANTY SHINDY SHINED SHINER SHINES SHINNY SHINTO SHUNTS THANES THANKS THENAR THENCE THINGS THINGY THINKS THINLY THONGS THUNKS WHANGS WHENCE WHINED WHINER WHINES WHINEY WHINNY WHYNOT

•H••N•

AHERNE CHAINE CHAINS CHIANG CHRONO CHURNS GHAINS SHANNY SHAYNE SHEENA SHEENS SHINNY SHRANK SHRINE SHRINK SHRUNK SHYING THEEND THORNS THORNY THRONE THRONG UHLANS WHINNY

•H•••N

BHUTAN CHAPIN CHARON CHEMIN CHENIN CHIPIN CHIRON CHITIN CHITON CHOPIN CHOSEN CHYRON OHIOAN PHONON PHOTON RHYTON SHABAN SHAKEN SHAMAN SHARON SHAVEN SHIMON SHOGUN SHOOIN SHORAN SHOWIN SHUTIN THROWN WHITEN

••HN••

ETHNIC ETHNOS JOHNNY SCHNOZ

••H•N•

AAHING ACHENE ACHING ATHAND ATHENA ATHENE ATHENS BEHIND BYHAND COHUNE ECHINO ETHANE ETHENE ICHING INHAND JOHANN JOHNNY KAHUNA ONHAND OOHING PAHANG REHANG REHUNG SPHINX STHENO TAHINI UNHAND UTHANT WAHINE

••H••N

ASHCAN BAHIAN DEHORN EPHRON JOHANN

•••HN•

DAPHNE FOEHNS TECHNO VISHNU

•••H•N

AACHEN AFGHAN ANNHON ARCHON BUCHAN CASHIN COCHIN DOTHAN DUCHIN GOSHEN HYPHEN INCHON KUCHEN LICHEN MUDHEN NATHAN OMAHAN ORPHAN PATHAN PEAHEN PUSHON PYTHON RICHEN SIPHON SYPHON TUCHUN URCHIN UTAHAN WITHIN

••••HN

STJOHN UPJOHN VAUGHN

HO••••

HOAGIE HOARDS HOARSE HOAXED HOAXER HOAXES HOBART HOBBES HOBBIT HOBBLE HOBNOB HOBOES HOBSON HOCKED HOCKEY HODADS HODGES HOEING HOGANS HOGGED HOGGET HOGTIE HOHOHO HOISTS HOKIER HOLDEN HOLDER HOLDIN HOLDIT HOLDON HOLDTO HOLDUP HOLEUP HOLIER HOLILY HOLING HOLISM HOLIST HOLLER HOLLOW HOLMES HOMAGE HOMBRE HOMEEC HOMELY HOMERS HOMIER HOMILY HOMING HOMINY HONCHO HONEST HONEYS HONIED HONING HONKED HONKER HONORE HONORS HONOUR HONSHU HOODED HOODOO HOOFED HOOFER HOOFIT HOOHAH HOOHAS HOOKAH HOOKED HOOKUP HOOPED HOOPER HOOPLA HOOPLE HOOPOE HOORAH HOORAY HOOTAT HOOTCH HOOTED HOOTER HOOTIE HOOVER HOOVES HOPERS HOPING HOPOFF HOPPED HOPPER HOPPLE HOPSIN HOPSUP HORACE HORDES HORMEL HORMUZ HORNED HORNER HORNET HORNEY HORNIN HORRID HORROR HORSED HORSES HORSEY HORTON HOSELS HOSIER HOSING HOSTAS HOSTED HOSTEL HOSTLY HOTAIR HOTBED HOTBOX HOTCAP HOTCAR HOTDOG HOTELS HOTPOT HOTROD HOTTEA HOTTER HOTTIP HOTTUB HOTWAR HOUGHS HOUNDS HOUNDY HOURIS HOURLY HOUSED HOUSES HOVELS HOVERS HOVETO HOWARD HOWDAH HOWELL HOWLED HOWLER HOWLIN HOWNOW HOWTOS HOYDEN

H•O•••

HAOLES HBOMBS HMONGS HOODED HOODOO HOOFED HOOFER HOOFIT HOOHAH HOOHAS HOOKAH HOOKED HOOKUP HOOPED HOOPER HOOPLA HOOPLE HOOPOE HOORAH HOORAY HOOTAT HOOTCH HOOTED HOOTER HOOTIE HOOVER HOOVES

H••O••

HALOED HALOES HALOID HAROLD HAVOCS HELOTS HEROES HEROIC HERONS HIDOUT HITOUT HOBOES HOHOHO HONORE HONORS HONOUR HOPOFF HUMORS HUMOUR HURONS HYPOED

H•••O•

HADRON HAEMON HAGDON HALLOO HALLOS HALLOW HANDON HANGON HANSOM HANSON HARBOR HARLOW HARMON HARPON HARROW HATBOX HATHOR HAVEON HAYMOW HEADON HEAROF HEBRON HECTOR HEDRON HELDON HELIOS HELLOS HENSON HEREOF HEREON HERIOT HERMON HERZOG HESIOD HESTON HEYYOU HICKOK HIERON HILTON HINTON HIPHOP HIPPOS HIREON HITSON HIVAOA HOBNOB HOBSON HOLDON HOLLOW HOODOO HOOPOE HORROR HORTON HOTBOX HOTDOG HOTPOT HOTROD HOWNOW HOWTOS HUDSON HUEVOS HULLOA HULLOS HUNGON HUSTON HUTTON HYDROS HYKSOS HYPNOS HYSSOP

H••••O

HAIRDO HALLOO HASBRO HELDTO HEMATO HERETO HETERO HIDEHO HOHOHO HOLDTO HONCHO HOODOO HOVETO

•HO•••

BHOPAL CHOATE CHOCKS CHOICE CHOIRS CHOKED CHOKER CHOKES CHOLER CHOLLA CHOLOS CHOMPS CHONJU CHOOSE CHOOSY CHOOYU CHOPIN CHOPPY CHOPRA CHORAL CHORDS CHORES CHORUS CHOSEN CHOUGH CHOWED DHOLES DHOTEL DHOTIS GHOSTS GHOULS KHOUMS LHOTSE PHOBIA PHOBIC PHOBOS PHOCIS PHOEBE PHONED PHONES PHONEY PHONIC PHONON PHONOS PHOOEY PHOTIC PHOTOG PHOTON PHOTOS RHODES RHOMBI RHOMBS RHONDA SHOALS SHOALY SHOATS SHOCKS SHODDY SHOERS SHOFAR SHOGUN SHOJIS SHOLEM SHOLOM SHOOED SHOOIN SHOOKS SHOOTS SHOPPE SHORAN SHORED SHORES SHORTA SHORTE SHORTI SHORTO SHORTS SHORTU SHORTY SHOTAT SHOTUP SHOULD SHOUTS SHOVED SHOVEL SHOVER SHOVES SHOWED SHOWER SHOWIN SHOWME SHOWUP THOLES THOMAS THONGS THORAX THORNS THORNY THORPE THORPS THOUGH WHOLES WHOLLY WHOMPS WHOMSO WHOOFS WHOOPI WHOOPS WHOOSH WHORLS XHOSAS

•H•O••

CHEOPS CHLORO CHOOSE CHOOSY CHOOYU CHROMA CHROME CHROMO CHROMY CHRONO OHIOAN PHLOEM PHOOEY SHBOOM SHOOED SHOOIN SHOOKS SHOOTS SHROUD SHROVE THEORY THROAT THROBS THROES THRONE THRONG THROVE THROWN THROWS WHOOFS WHOOPI WHOOPS WHOOSH

•H••O•

AHCHOO CHADOR CHARON CHEKOV CHIGOE CHILOE CHINOS CHIRON CHISOX CHITON CHOLOS CHYRON PHAROS PHENOL PHENOM PHILOL PHILOS PHOBOS PHONON PHONOS PHOTOG PHOTON PHOTOS RHEBOK RHETOR RHINOS RHYTON SHADOW SHAKOS SHALOM SHARON SHBOOM SHILOH SHIMON SHOLOM THETOY WHILOM WHYNOT ZHUKOV

•H•••O

AHCHOO BHUTTO CHALCO CHARRO CHEAPO CHLORO CHROMO CHRONO CHURRO GHETTO PHLEBO PHYLLO PHYSIO RHABDO SHINTO SHORTO THERMO WHAMMO WHIZZO WHOMSO

••HO••

ABHORS ASHORE ATHOME BEHOLD BEHOOF BEHOVE CAHOWS COHORT COHOST DEHORN DRHOOK ECHOED ECHOES ECHOIC EPHODS EPHORI EPHORS EXHORT GOHOME HOHOHO JOHORE LAHORE MAHOUT MOHOCK ONHOLD REHOOK SCHOOL SCHORL UNHOLY UNHOOK UPHOLD WAHOOS YAHOOS YOHOHO

••H•O•

BEHOOF DRHOOK EPHRON ETHNOS MAHZOR REHOOK SCHMOO SCHMOS SCHNOZ SCHOOL UNHOOK WAHOOS YAHOOS

••H••O

ECHINO ENHALO HOHOHO NIHILO SCHMOO STHENO YOHOHO

•••HO•

AHCHOO ANCHOR ANDHOW ANNHON ANYHOW ARCHON AUTHOR BARHOP BATHOS BISHOP BOOHOO CACHOU CARHOP FATHOM FUZHOU HATHOR HIPHOP INCHON JOBHOP LITHOG LITHOS LUTHOR MACHOS METHOD MUGHOS MYTHOI MYTHOL MYTHOS NACHOS NOSHOW PATHOL PATHOS PUSHON PYTHON QUAHOG REDHOT RESHOD RESHOE RESHOT SENHOR SIPHON SYPHON TVSHOW UNSHOD UPSHOT WARHOL WASHOE YOOHOO

•••H•O

AHCHOO ARTHRO BOCHCO BOOHOO JETHRO LASHIO NEPHRO PASHTO RIGHTO ROTHKO TECHNO YOOHOO

••••HO

CAUCHO CLOTHO GAUCHO GUNGHO HIDEHO HOHOHO HONCHO LANDHO MORPHO NAVAHO PANCHO PONCHO PSYCHO RANCHO REECHO SANCHO SAPPHO TRICHO XANTHO YOHOHO

H•P•••

HAPPED HAPPEN HEPCAT HEPPER HEPTAD HIPHOP HIPPED HIPPER HIPPIE HIPPOS HOPERS HOPING HOPOFF HOPPED HOPPER HOPPLE HOPSIN HOPSUP HYPEUP HYPHEN HYPING HYPNOS HYPOED

H••P••

HAMPER HAPPED HAPPEN HARPED HARPER HARPON HASPED HATPIN HEAPED HELPED HELPER HEPPER HIPPED HIPPER HIPPIE HIPPOS HISPID HOOPED HOOPER HOOPLA HOOPLE HOOPOE HOPPED HOPPER HOPPLE HOTPOT HUMPED HUMPHS

H••••P

HANDUP HANGUP HARDUP HAULUP HEADUP HEATUP HELDUP HICCUP HIGHUP HIKEUP HIPHOP HITSUP HOLDUP HOLEUP HOOKUP HOPSUP

HOTCAP
HOTTIP
HUBCAP
HUNGUP
HYPEUP
HYSSOP

•H•P••
BHOPAL
CHAPEL
CHAPIN
CHIPIN
CHOPIN
CHOPPY
CHOPRA
SHAPED
SHAPER
SHAPES
SHOPPE
WHIPPY
WHIPUP

•H••P•
CHAMPS
CHEAPO
CHEEPS
CHEOPS
CHIMPS
CHIRPS
CHIRPY
CHOMPS
CHOPPY
CHUMPS
SHARPS
SHEEPS
SHERPA
SHOPPE
THORPE
THORPS
THRIPS
THUMPS
WHELPS
WHIPPY
WHOMPS
WHOOPI
WHOOPS

•H•••P
CHATUP
CHEWUP
CHINUP
PHILIP
SHOTUP
SHOWUP
SHRIMP
SHUTUP
THELIP
WHIPUP

••H•P•
VCHIPS

••H••P
ASHARP
BSHARP
CSHARP
DSHARP
ESHARP
FSHARP
GSHARP
SCHLEP

•••H•P
BARHOP
BISHOP
CARHOP
HIGHUP
HIPHOP
JOBHOP
LASHUP
MAYHAP
MISHAP
PUSHUP
RESHIP
WASHUP

H••••Q
HIGHIQ

•H•Q••
CHEQUE

•••H•Q
HIGHIQ

H•R•••
HARALD
HARARE
HARASS
HARBIN
HARBOR
HARDBY
HARDEN
HARDER
HARDLY
HARDUP
HAREMS
HARING
HARKED
HARKEN
HARKER
HARLAN
HARLEM
HARLEY
HARLIN
HARLOW
HARMED
HARMON
HAROLD
HARPED
HARPER
HARPON
HARRIS
HARROW
HARVEY
HERALD
HERBAL
HERBIE
HERDED
HERDER
HEREAT
HEREBY
HEREIN
HEREOF
HEREON
HERESY
HERETO
HERIOT
HERMAN
HERMES
HERMIT
HERMON
HEROES
HEROIC
HERONS
HERSEY
HERZOG
HIREON
HIRERS
HIRING
HIRSCH
HORACE
HORDES
HORMEL
HORMUZ
HORNED
HORNER
HORNET
HORNEY
HORNIN
HORRID
HORROR
HORSED
HORSES
HORSEY
HORTON
HURDLE
HURLED
HURLER
HURLEY
HURONS
HURRAH
HURRAY
HURTLE

H••R••
HADRON
HAIRDO
HAIRED
HARRIS
HARROW
HATRED
HEARER
HEAROF
HEARST
HEARTH
HEARTS
HEARTY
HEARYE
HEBREW
HEBRON
HEDREN
HEDRON
HENRIK
HENRYV
HIERON
HIJRAH
HOARDS
HOARSE
HOORAH
HOORAY
HORRID
HORROR
HOTROD
HOURIS
HOURLY
HUBRIS
HURRAH
HURRAY
HYBRID
HYDRAE
HYDRAS
HYDROS

H•••R•
HALERS
HALERU
HARARE
HASBRO
HATARI
HATERS
HAVERS
HAZARD
HAZERS
HEGARI
HEGIRA
HETERO
HEWERS
HEXERS
HIDERS
HIKERS
HILARY
HIRERS
HOBART
HOMBRE
HOMERS
HONORE
HONORS
HOPERS
HOVERS
HOWARD
HUBERT
HUMERI
HUMORS
HUNGRY

H••••R
HACKER
HALTER
HAMMER
HAMPER
HANGAR
HANGER
HANKER
HARBOR
HARDER
HARKER
HARPER
HATHOR
HATTER
HAULER
HAWKER
HAWSER
HAZIER
HEADER
HEALER
HEARER
HEATER
HEAVER
HECTOR
HEDGER
HEEDER
HEELER
HEFNER
HEIFER
HELLER
HELPER
HELTER
HEMMER
HENNER
HEPPER
HERDER
HESTER
HIGHER
HILLER
HINDER
HINTER
HIPPER
HISSER
HITHER
HITTER
HOAXER
HOKIER
HOLDER
HOLIER
HOLLER
HOMIER
HONKER
HONOUR
HOOFER
HOOPER
HOOTER
HOOVER
HOPPER
HORNER
HORROR
HOSIER
HOTAIR
HOTCAR
HOTTER
HOTWAR
HOWLER
HUGGER
HULLER
HUMMER
HUMOUR
HUNGER
HUNKER
HUNTER
HURLER
HUSKER
HUSSAR

•HR•••
CHRISM
CHROMA
CHROME
CHROMO
CHROMY
CHRONO
PHRASE
SHRANK
SHREDS
SHREWD
SHREWS
SHRIEK
SHRIFT
SHRIKE
SHRILL
SHRIMP
SHRINE
SHRINK
SHRIVE
SHROUD
SHROVE
SHRUBS
SHRUGS
SHRUNK
THRACE
THRALE
THRALL
THRASH
THREAD
THREAT
THREED
THREES
THRESH
THRICE
THRIFT
THRILL
THRIPS
THRIVE
THROAT
THROBS
THROES
THRONE
THRONG
THROVE
THROWN
THROWS
THRUMS
THRUSH
THRUST

•H•R••
AHERNE
CHARGE
CHARLY
CHARMS
CHARON
CHARRO
CHARTS
CHERIE
CHERRY
CHERTY
CHERUB
CHERYL
CHIRAC
CHIRON
CHIRPS
CHIRPY
CHIRRS
CHORAL
CHORDS
CHORES
CHORUS
CHURCH
CHURLS
CHURNS
CHURRO
CHURRS
CHYRON
DHARMA
GHARRY
PHAROS
SHARDS
SHARED
SHARER
SHARES
SHARIA
SHARIF
SHARKS
SHARON
SHARPS
SHEREE
SHERIF
SHERPA
SHERRY
SHERYL
SHIRAZ
SHIRER
SHIRES
SHIRKS
SHIRRS
SHIRTS
SHIRTY
SHORAN
SHORED
SHORES
SHORTA
SHORTE
SHORTI
SHORTO
SHORTS
SHORTU
SHORTY
THERES
THERMO
THERMS
THIRDS
THIRST
THIRTY
THORAX
THORNS
THORNY
THORPE
THORPS
THYRSI
WHARFS
WHERED
WHERES
WHERRY
WHIRLS
WHIRLY
WHIRRS
WHORLS

•H••R•
CHAIRS
CHARRO
CHEERS
CHEERY
CHERRY
CHEVRE
CHIRRS
CHIRRS
CHLORO
CHOIRS
CHOPRA
CHURRO
CHURRS
GHARRY
KHAFRE
KHMERS
NHLERS
OHENRY
PHEDRE
SHEARS
SHEERS
SHERRY
SHIRRS
SHOERS
THEIRS
THEORY
THEYRE
THWART
WHERRY
WHIRRS

•H•••R
CHADOR
CHASER
CHEWER
CHIDER
CHOKER
CHOLER
CHUKAR
KHYBER
PHASER
RHETOR
RHYMER
SHAKER
SHAMIR
SHAPER
SHARER
SHAVER
SHIKAR
SHINER
SHIRER
SHIVER
SHOFAR
SHOVER
SHOWER
THALER
THAYER
THENAR
WHALER
WHINER
WHITER

••HR••
ASHRAM
EPHRON
GEHRIG
LEHRER
MIHRAB
OCHRES
RAHRAH

••H•R•
ABHORS
ADHERE
ALHIRT
AMHARA
ASHARP
ASHORE
AWHIRL
BIHARI
BSHARP
COHERE
COHORT
CSHARP
DEHORN
DSHARP
EPHORI
EPHORS
ERHARD
ESHARP
ETHERS
EXHORT
FSHARP
GSHARP
INHERE
JOHORE
LAHORE
MOHURS
OCHERS
OCHERY
OTHERS
PAHARI
REHIRE
SAHARA
SCHORL
SPHERE
SPHERY
TSHIRT
UNHURT
USHERS

••H••R
ACHIER
ANHYDR
ASHIER
ASHLAR
CAHIER
COHEIR
ISHTAR
KOHLER
LEHRER
MAHLER
MAHZOR
MOHAIR
REHEAR
ROHMER
WOHLER

•••HR•
ARTHRO
EUCHRE
JETHRO
MOTHRA
NEPHRO
TEPHRA
TISHRI

•••H•R
AETHER
ANCHOR
ANTHER
ARCHER
ARTHUR
AUTHOR
BATHER
BENHUR
BOTHER
CATHER
CIPHER
CYPHER
DASHER
DITHER
EITHER
ESCHER
ESTHER
ETCHER
FATHER
FISHER
GATHER
GOPHER
GUSHER
HATHOR
HIGHER
HITHER
KOSHER
LASHER
LATHER
LOTHAR
LUSHER
LUTHER
LUTHOR
MASHER
MATHER
MENHIR
MOSHER
MOTHER
MUSHER
NETHER
NIGHER
NOSHER
POSHER
POTHER
RASHER
RATHER
RICHER
SENHOR
SIGHER
TETHER
TITHER
TOTHER
WASHER
WETHER
WISHER
WITHER
ZEPHYR
ZITHER

H•S•••
HASBRO
HASHED
HASHES
HASPED
HASSAM
HASSAN
HASSLE
HASTEN
HASTES
HESIOD
HESTER
HESTIA
HESTON
HISPID
HISSAT
HISSED
HISSER
HISSES
HOSELS
HOSIER
HOSING
HOSTAS
HOSTED
HOSTEL
HOSTLY
HUSHED
HUSHES
HUSKED
HUSKER
HUSSAR
HUSSEY
HUSTLE
HUSTON
HYSSOP

H••S••
HALSEY
HANSEL
HANSOM
HANSON
HASSAM
HASSAN
HASSLE
HAUSAS
HAWSER
HAWSES
HEISTS
HEMSIN
HENSON
HERSEY
HIRSCH
HISSAT
HISSED
HISSER
HISSES
HITSIT
HITSON
HITSUP
HOBSON
HOISTS
HONSHU
HOPSIN
HOPSUP
HORSED
HORSES
HORSEY
HOUSED
HOUSES
HUDSON
HUSSAR
HUSSEY
HYKSOS
HYSSOP

H•••S•
HALEST
HARASS
HAVASU
HEARST
HERESY
HOARSE
HOLISM
HOLIST
HONEST
HUGEST

H••••S
HABEAS
HABITS
HACEKS
HADJES
HADJIS
HAGGIS
HAIDAS
HAIKUS
HAINES
HAJJES
HAJJIS
HAKIMS
HALERS
HALLOS
HALOES
HALVES
HAMALS
HAOLES
HARASS
HAREMS
HARRIS
HASHES
HASTES
HATERS
HAULMS
HAUNTS
HAUSAS
HAVENS
HAVERS
HAVOCS
HAWSES
HAZANS
HAZELS
HAZERS
HBEAMS
HBOMBS
HEARTS
HEATHS
HEAVES
HEDGES
HEISTS
HELENS
HELIOS
HELLAS
HELLOS
HELOTS
HELVES
HENNAS
HERMES
HEROES
HERONS
HEWERS
HEXADS
HEXERS
HIATUS
HIDERS
HIKERS
HINDUS
HINGES
HINGIS
HIPPOS
HIRERS
HISSES
HMONGS
HOARDS
HOAXES
HOBBES
HOBOES
HODADS
HODGES
HOGANS
HOISTS
HOLMES
HOMERS
HONEYS
HONORS
HOOHAS
HOOVES
HOPERS
HORDES
HORSES
HOSELS
HOSTAS
HOTELS
HOUGHS
HOUNDS
HOURIS
HOUSES
HOVELS
HOVERS
HOWTOS
HUBRIS
HUEVOS
HUGHES
HULLOS
HUMANS
HUMMUS
HUMORS
HUMPHS
HURONS
HUSHES
HUZZAS
HYADES
HYDRAS
HYDROS
HYENAS
HYKSOS
HYPNOS

•H•S••
CHASED
CHASER
CHASES
CHASMS
CHASSE
CHASTE
CHESTS
CHESTY
CHISEL
CHISOX
CHOSEN
GHOSTS
PHASED
PHASER
PHASES
PHYSED
PHYSIO
RHESUS
SHASTA
THESEA
THESES
THESIS
THESIX
THISBE
THUSLY
WHISKS
WHISKY
XHOSAS

•H••S•
AHIMSA
CHAISE
CHASSE
CHEESE
CHEESY
CHOOSE
CHOOSY
CHRISM
CHUHSI
LHOTSE
PHRASE
SHIEST
SHIISM
SHYEST
THEISM
THEIST
THIRST
THRASH
THRESH
THRUSH
THRUST
THYRSI
WHILST
WHIMSY
WHOMSO
WHOOSH

•H•••S
CHAFES
CHAFFS
CHAINS
CHAIRS
CHALKS
CHAMPS
CHANTS
CHARMS
CHARTS
CHASES
CHASMS
CHEATS
CHECKS
CHEEKS
CHEEPS
CHEERS
CHELAS
CHEOPS
CHESTS
CHETHS
CHIAUS
CHICKS
CHIDES
CHIEFS
CHILDS
CHILLS
CHIMES
CHIMPS
CHINES
CHINKS
CHINOS
CHIRPS
CHIRRS
CHIVES
CHOCKS
CHOIRS
CHOKES
CHOLOS
CHOMPS
CHORDS
CHORES
CHORUS
CHUCKS
CHUMPS
CHUNKS
CHURLS
CHURNS
CHURRS
CHUTES
DHOLES
DHOTIS
GHAINS
GHAZIS
GHOSTS
GHOULS
KHAKIS
KHMERS
KHOUMS
NHLERS
PHAGES
PHAROS
PHASES
PHIALS
PHILOS
PHOBOS
PHOCIS
PHONES
PHONOS
PHOTOS
RHAMES
RHESUS
RHEUMS
RHINOS
RHODES
RHOMBS
RHUMBS
RHYMES
SHACKS
SHADES
SHAFTS
SHAKES
SHAKOS
SHALES
SHAMES
SHAMUS
SHANKS
SHAPES
SHARDS
SHARES
SHARKS
SHARPS
SHAVES
SHAWLS
SHAWMS
SHEAFS
SHEARS
SHEENS
SHEEPS
SHEERS
SHEETS
SHEIKS
SHELLS
SHIFTS
SHILLS
SHINES
SHIRES
SHIRKS
SHIRRS
SHIRTS
SHOALS
SHOATS
SHOCKS
SHOERS
SHOJIS
SHOOKS
SHOOTS
SHORES
SHORTS
SHOUTS
SHOVES
SHREDS
SHREWS
SHRUBS
SHRUGS
SHUCKS
SHUNTS
THALES
THAMES
THANES
THANKS
THATIS
THEBES
THEFTS
THEIRS
THEMES
THERES
THERMS
THESES
THESIS
THETAS
THETIS
THIGHS
THILLS
THINGS
THINKS
THIRDS
THOLES
THOMAS
THONGS
THORNS
THORPS
THREES
THRIPS
THROBS
THROES
THROWS
THRUMS
THUJAS
THUMBS
THUMPS
THUNKS
THYMUS
UHLANS
WHACKS
WHALES
WHANGS
WHARFS
WHEALS
WHEATS
WHEELS
WHELKS
WHELMS
WHELPS
WHERES
WHIFFS
WHILES
WHINES
WHIRLS
WHIRRS
WHISKS
WHITES
WHOLES
WHOMPS
WHOOFS
WHOOPS
WHORLS
XHOSAS

••H•S•
AGHAST
BEHEST
COHOST
REHASH
SCHISM
SCHIST
SCHUSS

••H••S
ABHORS
APHIDS
ATHENS
CAHOWS
ECHOES
EPHAHS
EPHODS
EPHORS
ETHERS
ETHICS
ETHNOS
JIHADS
LEHUAS
MAHDIS
MOHURS
NOHITS
OCHERS
OCHRES
OGHAMS
OTHERS
REHABS
REHEMS
SAHIBS
SCHMOS
SCHUSS
SCHWAS
TEHEES
USHERS
VCHIPS
WAHOOS
YAHOOS

•••HS•
CHUHSI
TZUHSI

•••H•S
ABOHMS
ALOHAS
ALPHAS
ARCHES
AUGHTS
BASHES
BATHES
BATHOS
BIGHTS
BRAHMS
BUSHES
CACHES
CASHES
COSHES
DACHAS
DASHES
DASHIS
DISHES
EIGHTS
ETCHES
FICHES
FICHUS
FIGHTS
FISHES
FOEHNS
GASHES
GUSHES
HASHES
HOOHAS
HUGHES
HUSHES
INCHES
ITCHES
JANHUS
JOSHES
LACHES
LASHES
LATHES
LIGHTS
LITHOS

MACHES MACHOS MASHES MATHIS MESHES MOCHAS MOSHES MUGHOS MUSHES MYTHOS NACHOS NICHES NIGHTS NOSHES OMAHAS OUGHTS PASHAS PATHOS PUSHES RACHIS RASHES RESHES RICHES RIGHTS RUCHES RUSHES SADHES SADHUS SASHES SIGHTS SPAHIS SUCHAS TETHYS TIGHTS TITHES TOPHUS TYPHUS WASHES WIGHTS WISHES WITHES YACHTS

••••HS

ALEPHS BERTHS BIRTHS BOOTHS BOUGHS BROTHS BURGHS CHETHS CLOTHS CONCHS COUGHS CZECHS DEPTHS DOUGHS EPHAHS EPOCHS FAITHS FIFTHS FIRTHS FROTHS GALAHS GARTHS GERAHS GIRTHS GLYPHS GRAPHS HEATHS HOUGHS HUMPHS JONAHS LAUGHS LOTAHS LOUGHS LYMPHS MONTHS MORPHS MOUTHS MYNAHS MYRRHS NEIGHS NINTHS NORTHS NYMPHS OBEAHS ORACHS PSYCHS RAJAHS ROUGHS SIXTHS SLOTHS SMITHS SNATHS SOUGHS SOUTHS SURAHS SWATHS SYLPHS TENTHS THIGHS TORAHS TOUGHS TROTHS TRUTHS WEIGHS WIDTHS WORTHS WRATHS YOUTHS

H•T•••

HATARI HATBOX HATERS HATFUL HATHOR HATING HATPIN HATRED HATTED HATTER HATTIE HETERO HETMAN HETTIE HITECH HITHER HITMAN HITMEN HITOUT HITSIT HITSON HITSUP HITTER HOTAIR HOTBED HOTBOX HOTCAP HOTCAR HOTDOG HOTELS HOTPOT HOTROD HOTTEA HOTTER HOTTIP HOTTUB HOTWAR HUTTED HUTTON

H••T••

HAFTED HALTED HALTER HASTEN HASTES HATTED HATTER HATTIE HEATED HEATER HEATHS HEATHY HEATUP HECTIC HECTOR HEFTED HELTER HENTED HEPTAD HESTER HESTIA HESTON HETTIE HIATAL HIATUS HILTON HINTAT HINTED HINTER HINTON HITTER HOGTIE HOOTAT HOOTCH HOOTED HOOTER HOOTIE HORTON HOSTAS HOSTED HOSTEL HOSTLY HOTTEA HOTTER HOTTIP HOTTUB HOWTOS HUNTED HUNTER HURTLE HUSTLE HUSTON HUTTED HUTTON HYETAL

H•••T•

HABITS HALITE HAMITE HAUNTS HEALTH HEARTH HEARTS HEARTY HECATE HEISTS HELDTO HELOTS HEMATO HERETO HINCTY HOISTS HOLDTO HOVETO

H••••T

HAEMAT HAIGHT HALEST HAMLET HAVEAT HAVENT HEARST HEIGHT HELMET HELMUT HENBIT HEPCAT HEREAT HERIOT HERMIT HEXNUT HIDOUT HINTAT HISSAT HITOUT HITSIT HLHUNT HOBART HOBBIT HOGGET HOLDIT HOLIST HONEST HOOFIT HOOTAT HORNET HOTPOT HUBERT HUGEST

•HT•••

SHTETL SHTICK

•H•T••

BHUTAN BHUTTO CHATTY CHATUP CHETHS CHITIN CHITON CHUTED CHUTES DHOTEL DHOTIS GHETTO LHOTSE PHATIC PHOTIC PHOTOG PHOTON PHOTOS RHETOR RHYTHM RHYTON SHOTAT SHOTUP SHUTIN SHUTUP THATCH THATIS THATLL THETAS THETIC THETIS THETOY WHATIF WHATLL WHATVE WHITEN WHITER WHITES WHITTY

•H••T•

BHAKTI BHUTTO CHANTS CHARTS CHASTE CHATTY CHEATS CHERTY CHESTS CHESTY CHINTZ CHOATE GHETTO GHOSTS SHAFTS SHAKTI SHANTY SHASTA SHEATH SHEETS SHELTY SHIFTS SHIFTY SHIITE SHINTO SHIRTS SHIRTY SHOATS SHOOTS SHORTA SHORTE SHORTI SHORTO SHORTS SHORTU SHORTY SHOUTS SHTETL SHUNTS THEFTS THIRTY WHEATS WHITTY

•H•••T

CHALET CHEVET SHEVAT SHIEST SHOTAT SHRIFT SHYEST THEIST THIRST THREAT THRIFT THROAT THRUST THWART WHILST WHYNOT

••HT••

ICHTHY ISHTAR

••H•T•

NOHITS OPHITE TAHITI

••H••T

AGHAST ALHIRT BEHEST COHORT COHOST EXHORT HLHUNT MAHOUT REHEAT SCHIST TSHIRT UNHURT UTHANT

•••HT•

AUGHTS BIGHTS EIGHTH EIGHTS EIGHTY FICHTE FIGHTS LIGHTS MIGHTY NIGHTS NIGHTY OUGHTS PASHTO RIGHTO RIGHTS RIGHTY SIGHTS TIGHTS VASHTI WIGHTS YACHTS

•••H•T

ATTHAT CACHET FOGHAT MISHIT OLDHAT OUTHIT REDHAT REDHOT RESHOT ROCHET SACHET SOTHAT SOWHAT TINHAT TOPHAT UPSHOT WITHIT

••••HT

ALIGHT ARIGHT BLIGHT BOUGHT BRECHT BRIGHT CAUGHT DWIGHT FLIGHT FOUGHT FRIGHT HAIGHT HEIGHT KNIGHT NAUGHT NOUGHT PLIGHT SLIGHT SOUGHT TAUGHT VEIGHT VOIGHT WEIGHT WRIGHT

HU••••

HUBBLE HUBBLY HUBBUB HUBCAP HUBERT HUBRIS HUDDLE HUDSON HUEVOS HUFFED HUGELY HUGEST HUGGED HUGGER HUGHES HULKED HULLED HULLER HULLOA HULLOS HUMANE HUMANS HUMBLE HUMBLY HUMBUG HUMERI HUMMED HUMMER HUMMUS HUMORS HUMOUR HUMPED HUMPHS HUMVEE HUNGER HUNGIN HUNGON HUNGRY HUNGUP HUNGWU HUNKER HUNTED HUNTER HURDLE HURLED HURLER HURLEY HURONS HURRAH HURRAY HURTLE HUSHED HUSHES HUSKED HUSKER HUSSAR HUSSEY HUSTLE HUSTON HUTTED HUTTON HUXLEY HUZZAH HUZZAS

H•U•••

HAULED HAULER HAULMS HAULUP HAUNCH HAUNTS HAUSAS HOUGHS HOUNDS HOUNDY HOURIS HOURLY HOUSED HOUSES

H••U••

HECUBA HLHUNT

H•••U•

HAIKUS HALLUX HANDUP HANGUL HANGUP HARDUP HATFUL HAULUP HEADUP HEATUP HELDUP HELIUM HELMUT HEXNUT HIATUS HICCUP HIDOUT HIGHUP HIKEUP HINDUS HITOUT HITSUP HOLDUP HOLEUP HONOUR HOOKUP HOPSUP HORMUZ HOTTUB HUBBUB HUMBUG HUMMUS HUMOUR HUNGUP HYPEUP

H••••U

HALERU HAVASU HEYYOU HONSHU HUNGWU

•HU•••

BHUTAN BHUTTO CHUBBY CHUCKS CHUFFY CHUHSI CHUKAR CHUKKA CHUMMY CHUMPS CHUNKS CHUNKY CHURCH CHURLS CHURNS CHURRO CHURRS CHUTED CHUTES RHUMBA RHUMBS SHUCKS SHUNTS SHUTIN SHUTUP THUJAS THUMBS THUMPS THUNKS THUSLY ZHUKOV

•H•U••

CHOUGH GHOULS KHOUMS RHEUMS RHEUMY SHOULD SHOUTS SHRUBS SHRUGS SHRUNK THOUGH THRUMS THRUSH THRUST

•H••U•

CHATUP CHEQUE CHERUB CHEWUP CHIAUS CHINUP CHORUS PHYLUM RHESUS SHAMUS SHOGUN SHOTUP SHOWUP SHROUD SHUTUP THYMUS WHIPUP

•H•••U

CHONJU CHOOYU SHORTU

••HU••

COHUNE HLHUNT KAHUNA LEHUAS MCHUGH MOHURS REHUNG SCHULZ SCHUSS UNHURT YEHUDI

••H•U•

INHAUL KAHLUA MAHOUT

•••HU•

ARTHUR BENHUR FICHUS HIGHUP JANHUS JOSHUA LASHUP NASHUA PUSHUP SADHUS TOPHUS TUCHUN TYPHUS WASHUP

•••H•U

CACHOU FUZHOU NIIHAU VISHNU

••••HU

HONSHU KYUSHU MANCHU PENGHU PICCHU

H•V•••

HAVANA HAVASU HAVEAT HAVENS HAVENT HAVEON HAVERS HAVING HAVOCS HIVAOA HIVING HOVELS HOVERS HOVETO

H••V••

HALVAH HALVED HALVES HARVEY HEAVED HEAVEN HEAVER HEAVES HELVES HOOVER HOOVES HUEVOS HUMVEE

H•••V•

HALEVY

H••••V

HENRYV

•H•V••

CHAVEZ CHEVAL CHEVET CHEVRE CHIVES SHAVED SHAVEN SHAVER SHAVES SHEVAT SHIVER SHOVED SHOVEL SHOVER SHOVES

•H••V•

SHEAVE SHELVE SHRIVE SHROVE THEYVE THIEVE THRIVE THROVE WHATVE

•H•••V

CHEKOV ZHUKOV

••H•V•

BEHAVE BEHOVE MOHAVE

•••H•V

MOSHAV

H•W•••

HAWAII HAWHAW HAWING HAWKED HAWKER HAWSER HAWSES HEWERS HEWING HOWARD HOWDAH HOWELL HOWLED HOWLER HOWLIN HOWNOW HOWTOS

H••W••

HOTWAR

H•••W•

HUNGWU

H••••W

HALLOW HARLOW HARROW HAWHAW HAYMOW HEBREW HEEHAW HOLLOW HOWNOW

•HW•••

OHWELL THWACK THWART

•H•W••

CHEWED CHEWER CHEWUP CHOWED SHAWLS SHAWMS SHOWED SHOWER SHOWIN SHOWME SHOWUP THAWED THEWEB THEWIZ

•H••W•

SHREWD SHREWS THROWN THROWS

•H•••W

SHADOW

••HW••

SCHWAB SCHWAS WAHWAH YAHWEH

••H•W•

CAHOWS MOHAWK OSHAWA

•••HW•

BUSHWA

•••H•W

ANDHOW ANYHOW CASHEW CUSHAW ESCHEW HAWHAW HEEHAW NEPHEW NOSHOW TVSHOW

H•X•••

HEXADS HEXERS HEXING HEXNUT HUXLEY

H••X••

HOAXED HOAXER HOAXES

H••••X

HALLUX HATBOX HOTBOX

•H•••X

CHISOX THESIX THORAX

••H••X

SPHINX

HY••••

HYADES HYBRID HYDRAE HYDRAS HYDROS HYENAS HYETAL HYKSOS HYMNAL HYMNED HYPEUP HYPHEN HYPING HYPNOS HYPOED HYSSOP

H•Y•••

HAYDEN HAYING HAYLEY HAYMOW HEYDAY HEYYOU HOYDEN

H••Y••

HEYYOU

H•••Y•

HEARYE HENRYV HONEYS

H••••Y

HACKLY HAILEY HALEVY HALLEY HALSEY HANLEY HARDBY HARDLY HARLEY HARVEY HAYLEY HAZILY HEANEY HEARTY HEATHY HENLEY HEREBY HERESY HERSEY HEYDAY HICKEY HIGHLY HILARY HINCTY HOCKEY HOLILY HOMELY HOMILY HOMINY HOORAY HORNEY HORSEY HOSTLY HOUNDY HOURLY HUBBLY HUGELY HUMBLY HUNGRY HURLEY HURRAY HUSSEY HUXLEY

•HY•••

CHYRON KHYBER OHYEAH PHYLAE PHYLLO PHYLUM PHYSED PHYSIO RHYMED RHYMER RHYMES RHYTHM RHYTON SHYEST SHYING THYMUS THYRSI WHYDAH WHYNOT

•H•Y••

SHAYNE THAYER THEYLL THEYRE THEYVE

•H••Y•

CHERYL CHOOYU PHENYL SHERYL

•H•••Y

CHAFFY CHALKY CHAMMY CHANCY CHANEY CHARLY CHATTY CHEEKY CHEERY CHEESY CHERRY CHERTY CHESTY CHICLY CHILLY CHINKY CHIRPY CHOOSY CHOPPY CHROMY CHUBBY CHUFFY CHUMMY CHUNKY GHARRY OHENRY PHILBY PHILLY PHONEY PHOOEY RHEUMY SHABBY SHAGGY SHALEY SHALLY SHANDY SHANNY SHANTY SHEEDY SHEEHY SHELLY SHELTY SHERRY SHIFTY SHILLY SHIMMY SHINDY SHINNY SHIRTY SHOALY SHODDY SHORTY THEFLY THEORY THETOY THINGY THINLY THIRTY THORNY THUSLY WHACKY WHAMMY WHEEZY WHERRY WHIMSY WHINEY WHINNY WHIPPY WHIRLY WHISKY WHITTY WHOLLY

••HY••

ANHYDR MRHYDE

••H••Y

ASHLEY ICHTHY JOHNNY OCHERY SCHIZY SPHERY UNHOLY

•••HY•

METHYL TETHYS ZEPHYR

•••H•Y

ARCHLY CATHAY EIGHTY HIGHLY LUSHLY MIGHTY MYOHMY NIGHTY POSHLY RASHLY RICHLY RIGHTY SASHAY

••••HY

APATHY BEACHY BOLSHY BOTCHY BRACHY BRASHY BRUSHY BUNCHY CATCHY CAUCHY DINGHY DOUGHY EARTHY FILTHY FLASHY FLESHY FROTHY GRAPHY GUNSHY HEATHY ICHTHY LEACHY LUNCHY MARSHY MORPHY MOUTHY MUNCHY MURPHY NOTCHY PATCHY PEACHY PITCHY PLASHY PLUSHY POACHY POUCHY PUNCHY ROUGHY SHEEHY SLITHY SLOSHY SLUSHY SMITHY STITHY TETCHY TOOTHY TORCHY TOUCHY TOUGHY

TRACHY
TRASHY
TROPHY
WITCHY
WORTHY
WRATHY

H•Z•••
HAZANS
HAZARD
HAZELS
HAZERS
HAZIER
HAZILY
HAZING
HUZZAH
HUZZAS

H••Z••
HERZOG
HUZZAH
HUZZAS

H••••Z
HORMUZ

•H•Z••
GHAZIS
SHAZAM
WHIZZO

•H••Z•
WHEEZE
WHEEZY
WHIZZO

•H•••Z
CHAVEZ
CHINTZ
SHIRAZ
THEWIZ

••HZ••
MAHZOR

••H•Z•
SCHIZY

••H••Z
SCHNOZ
SCHULZ

IA••••
IAMBIC
IATRIC

I•A•••
IBADAN
ICARIA
ICARUS
IMAGED
IMAGER
IMAGES
IMAMAN
IMARET
INAFIX
INAFOG
INAJAM
INANER
INAPET
INARCH
INAROW
INARUT
INAWAY
IRANIS
IRAQIS
IRATER
ISABEL
ISADOR
ISAIAH
ITALIA
ITALIC
ITASCA
IZABAL

I••A••
IBEAMS
ICEAGE
IDCARD
IDEALS
IDEATE
IDTAGS
IGNACE
IGNATZ
IGUACU
IGUANA
ILEANA
IMPACT
IMPAIR
IMPALA
IMPALE
IMPART
INCANS
INCASE
INCASH
INDABA
INFACT
INFAMY
INFANT
INHALE
INHALF
INHAND
INHAUL
INLAID
INLAND
INLAWS
INLAYS
INMATE
INNAGE
INNATE
INPART
INSANE
INTACT
INTAKE
INVADE
INVAIN
INWARD
IODATE
IOWANS
ISLAND
ISRAEL
ITHACA
ITHAKI
IZZARD

I•••A•
IBADAN
ICEBAG
ICECAP
ICEMAN
ILLSAY
IMAMAN
INAJAM
INAWAY
INDIAN
INGEAR
INGMAR
INGRAM
INPLAY
INROAD
INSEAM
INSPAN
INSTAL
INSTAR
IONIAN
IPECAC
IRREAL
ISAIAH
ISHTAR
ISOBAR
ITZHAK
IZABAL

I••••A
IBERIA
ICARIA
IGUANA
ILEANA
ILESHA
IMELDA
IMPALA
INDABA
INDIRA
INTIMA
ISCHIA
ISTRIA
ITALIA
ITASCA
ITHACA

•IA•••
BIAFRA
BIANCA
BIASED
BIASES
CIARDI
DIABLO
DIADEM
DIALED
DIALER
DIALOG
DIALUP
DIANNE
DIAPER
DIATOM
FIACRE
FIANCE
FIASCO
GIANTS
HIATAL
HIATUS
KIANGS
LIABLE
LIAISE
LIANAS
LIANES
LIANGS
MIAMIA
MIASMA
NIACIN
NIAMEY
PIAFFE
PIAGET
PIANOS
PIAZZA
RIALTO
RIATAS
TIARAS
VIABLE
VIABLY
VIACOM
VIANDS
XIAMEN

•I•A••
AIRARM
BICARB
BIGAMY
BIHARI
BINARY
BINATE
CICADA
CIGARS
CITATO
DIDACT
DILATE
DINARS
DISANT
DISARM
DIVANS
FIGARO
FINALE
FINALS
FIXATE
GIRARD
GITANO
HIJACK
HILARY
HIVAOA
JICAMA
JIHADS
KIGALI
LIGAND
LIGATE
LILACS
LINAGE
LIPASE
LITANY
LIZARD
MIDAIR
MIKADO
MILADY
MILANO
MIRAGE
NICAEA
PICABO
PICARA
PICARD
PICARO
PIKAKE
PILAFS
PILATE
PINATA
PIPALS
PIRACY
PIRANA
PIRATE
PISANO
PISANS
PIZAZZ
RIBALD
RIBAND
RITARD
RIVALS
RIYADH
RIYALS
SILAGE
SISALS
SITARS
SIWASH
TICALS
TILAKS
TIRADE
TIRANA
TIRANE
TISANE
TITANS
VICARS
VIRAGO
VISAED
VISAGE
VITALE
VITALS
VIVACE
VIVANT
WIZARD

•I••A•
AIMSAT
AIRBAG
AIRDAM
AIRMAN
AIRSAC
AIRWAY
BIGMAC
BILBAO
BIOGAS
BIOTAS
BISCAY
BISSAU
BITMAP
CIUDAD
DIGRAM
DIKTAT
DIRHAM
DISBAR
DISMAL
DISMAY
DISTAL
FIJIAN
FILIAL
FINIAL
FINNAN
FIRMAN
FISCAL
FIVEAM
GIBRAN
GILEAD
GIMBAL
HIATAL
HIEMAL
HIJRAH
HINTAT
HISSAT
HITMAN
JIGSAW
JINNAH
KIDMAN
KIDNAP
KIOWAS
KIRMAN
KITBAG
KITKAT
LIANAS
LIBYAN
LINEAL
LINEAR
MICMAC
MIDDAY
MIDIAN
MIDWAY
MIHRAB
MILLAY
MILPAS
MILSAP
MINOAN
MINYAN
MIRIAM
MISHAP
MISLAY
MISSAL
MISSAY
MITRAL
NICEAN
NIIHAU
NILGAI
NINEAM
NINJAS
NIPSAT
NISSAN
OILCAN
OILMAN
OILPAN
PICKAT
PICKAX
PIEMAN
PIEPAN
PIETAS
PILLAR
PINDAR
PINEAL
PINNAE
PINNAS
PINOAK
PISGAH
PITMAN
PITSAW
PIZZAS
QINTAR
RIATAS
RIOJAS
RIPRAP
RIPSAW
RITUAL
SIGMAS
SIGNAL
SILOAM
SILVAS
SIMIAN
SINBAD
SINEAD
SINTAX
SIOUAN
SIRDAR
SIRRAH
TIARAS
TIBIAE
TIBIAL
TIBIAS
TICTAC
TIMBAL
TINCAL
TINCAN
TINEAR
TINHAT
TINMAN
TINPAN
TITIAN
UINTAS
VILLAS
VIOLAS
VISTAS
VISUAL
VIVIAN
WICCAN
WIGWAG
WIGWAM
WINKAT
WITHAL
ZIGZAG
ZILPAH

•I•••A
BIAFRA
BIANCA
BIKILA
BITOLA
CIBOLA
CICADA
CINEMA
EIDOLA
FIBULA
FIESTA
HIVAOA
JICAMA
KINEMA
LIGULA
LINGUA
LIOTTA
LISBOA
MIAMIA
MIASMA
MIKITA
MIMOSA
MINIMA
MISCHA
NICAEA
NICOLA
NIKITA
NIKOLA
PIAZZA
PICARA
PINATA
PIRANA
RIVERA
SIENNA
SIERRA
SIESTA
SILICA
SIRICA
SISERA
SISTRA
TIERRA
TIRANA
VICUNA
VIENNA
VIGODA
VIZSLA
WINONA
XIMENA
ZINNIA

••IA••
APIARY
ASIANS
AVIANS
AVIARY
AVIATE
BRIAND
BRIANS
BRIARD
BRIARS
CHIANG
CHIAUS
CUIABA
FRIARS
FRIARY
GUIANA
NAIADS
OPIATE
ORIANA
PHIALS
PLIANT
TRIADS
TRIAGE
TRIALS
UMIAKS
UNIATE
UNIATS
URIALS

••I•A•
ADIDAS
AKITAS
AMIGAS
ANIMAL
ANIMAS
APICAL
BAIKAL
BAIZAS
BRIDAL
CAIMAN
CEIBAS
CHIRAC
CLIMAX
CNIDAE
ELIJAH
EPICAL
EPINAL
FAISAL
FBIMAN
FRIDAY
GUITAR
HAIDAS
HAINAN
KLIBAN
MAITAI
NAIRAS
NIIHAU
OBIWAN
OHIOAN
OVISAC
PAISAS
PHILAE
PLICAE
PRIMAL
RAILAT
REINAS
RHINAL
SAIGAS
SAIPAN
SHIKAR
SHIRAZ
SMILAX
SPICAS
SPINAL
SPIRAL
SPIVAK
TAIGAS
TAINAN
TAIPAN
TAIWAN
TRIBAL
TRINAL
UNITAL
UNITAS
UNIVAC
VEINAL
WEIMAR

••I••A
AHIMSA
ALICIA
ANITRA
ARISTA
AXILLA
CHICHA
CRIMEA
CUIABA
ELISHA
ELISSA
EMILIA
ENIGMA
FLICKA
GEISHA
GLINKA
GUIANA
GUINEA
KAILUA
OJIBWA
OLINDA
OLIVIA
ORIANA
ORISSA
QUINOA
SPIREA
STIGMA
TRICIA
TRISHA
TRIVIA
VAISYA

•••IA•
ADRIAN
AERIAL
APPIAN
ATRIAL
AUDIAL
BAHIAN
BELIAL
CAPIAS
CAVIAR
COBIAS
CURIAE
CURIAL
DENIAL
DORIAN
DURIAN
EOLIAN
EONIAN
ESPIAL
FABIAN
FACIAL
FACIAS
FENIAN
FERIAL
FERIAS
FIJIAN
FILIAL
FINIAL
FOLIAR
FUJIAN
GAVIAL
GENIAL
INDIAN
IONIAN
ISAIAH
JOSIAH
JOVIAL
JOVIAN
JULIAN
KODIAK
LABIAL
LAMIAS
LARIAT
LUCIAN
MANIAC
MANIAS
MARIAH
MARIAN
MEDIAL
MEDIAN
MEDIAS
MENIAL
MIDIAN
MIRIAM
MUSIAL
MYRIAD
NARIAL
NORIAS
NUBIAN
OBRIAN
OSSIAN
PARIAH
PLEIAD
RACIAL
RADIAL
RADIAN
REDIAL
RETIAL
RUPIAH
SAMIAM
SEPIAS
SERIAL
SIMIAN
SOCIAL
STRIAE
SYRIAN
TIBIAE
TIBIAL
TIBIAS
TITIAN
TOBIAS
TUPIAN
TYRIAN
UGRIAN
UNCIAL
UZZIAH
VENIAL
VIVIAN
ZAMIAS
ZODIAC

•••I•A
AFRICA
ALTIMA
ANNIKA
AQUILA
ARNICA
ATTICA
ATTILA
AURIGA
BIKILA
BRAILA
CAPITA
CARINA
COLIMA
COVINA
DAMITA
DESICA
ELMIRA
ELVIRA
ENCINA
EROICA
FAJITA
FARINA
FATIMA
GEZIRA
GODIVA
HEGIRA
INDIRA
INTIMA
KARIBA
KONICA
LADIDA
LAMINA
LATINA
LERIDA
LEXICA
LOLITA
LORICA
LOUISA
LUMINA
MANILA
MARINA
MARISA
MAXIMA
MEDINA
MELINA
MERIDA
MIKITA
MINIMA
MONICA
MORITA
NIKITA
NUMINA
ONEIDA
OPTIMA
OREIDA
PATINA
PEPITA
PURINA
REGINA
RETINA
ROSITA
RUMINA
SALINA
SALIVA
SHEILA
SILICA
SIRICA
TROIKA
TUNICA
ULTIMA
YAKIMA

••••IA
ACACIA
ACADIA
ACEDIA
AEOLIA
AGLAIA
ALEXIA
ALICIA
AMELIA
ANEMIA
ANGLIA
APULIA
ARABIA
ARALIA
BORGIA
BOSNIA
CASSIA
CRANIA
DAHLIA
EGERIA
EMILIA
ETALIA
FASCIA
FLAVIA
GALLIA
GAMBIA
GARCIA
GLORIA
GRATIA
HESTIA
IBERIA
ICARIA
ISCHIA
ISTRIA
ITALIA
KESHIA
LATVIA
LOGGIA
MARCIA
MIAMIA
MURCIA
MYOPIA
NARNIA
NUTRIA
OBELIA
OLIVIA
PALLIA
PENNIA
PEORIA
PERSIA
PHOBIA
PORTIA
PYTHIA
RAFFIA
REALIA
ROBBIA
RUSSIA
SALVIA
SANDIA
SARNIA
SCALIA
SCORIA
SCOTIA
SERBIA
SHANIA
SHARIA
SOPHIA
STADIA
STYRIA
SYLVIA
THALIA
TREDIA
TRICIA
TRIVIA
UMBRIA
URANIA
UTOPIA
ZAMBIA
ZINNIA
ZOYSIA

IB••••
IBADAN
IBEAMS
IBERIA
IBEXES
IBIBIO
IBIDEM
IBISES

I•B•••
IMBIBE
IMBRUE
IMBUED
IMBUES
INBORN
INBRED
INBULK

I••B••
IAMBIC
IBIBIO
ICEBAG
ICEBOX
IROBOT
ISABEL
ISOBAR
IZABAL

I•••B•
IMBIBE
INDABA
INDEBT
ITURBI

•IB•••
BIBBED
BIBLES
BIBLIO
CIBOLA
DIBBLE
FIBBED
FIBBER
FIBERS
FIBRES
FIBRIL
FIBRIN
FIBULA
GIBBED
GIBBER
GIBBET
GIBBON
GIBERS
GIBILL
GIBING
GIBLET
GIBRAN
GIBSON
JIBBED
JIBING
KIBBLE
KIBITZ
KIBOSH
LIBBED
LIBBER
LIBELS
LIBERI
LIBIDO
LIBRIS
LIBYAN
NIBBLE
RIBALD
RIBAND
RIBBED
RIBBON
RIBEYE
RIBOSE
SIBYLS
TIBIAE
TIBIAL
TIBIAS
ZIBETS

•I•B••
AIRBAG
AIRBUS
BIBBED
BIGBEN
BIGBOY
BILBAO
BIOBIO
DIABLO
DIBBLE
DISBAR
FIBBED
FIBBER
GIBBED
GIBBER
GIBBET
GIBBON
GIMBAL
GIMBEL
JIBBED
KIBBLE
KITBAG
LIABLE
LIBBED
LIBBER
LIEBIG
LIEBYS
LIMBED
LIMBER
LIMBOS
LIMBUS
LISBOA
LISBON
NIBBLE
NIMBLE
NIMBLY
NIMBUS
RIBBED
RIBBON
SIMBEL
SINBAD
TIDBIT
TIMBAL
TIMBER
TIMBRE
TITBIT
VIABLE
VIABLY
WILBUR
WIMBLE

•I••B•
NINGBO
PICABO
SITSBY

•I•••B
BICARB
DIONEB
MIDRIB
MIHRAB

••IB••
ALIBIS
ALIBLE
BRIBED
BRIBES
CEIBAS
EDIBLE
FOIBLE
GLIBLY
IBIBIO
KLIBAN
OJIBWA
ORIBIS
SKIBOB
TRIBAL
TRIBES

••I•B•
AKIMBO
CLIMBS
CUIABA
LAIDBY
PHILBY
THISBE
TRILBY

••I••B
SKIBOB

•••IB•
ADLIBS
ARRIBA
CARIBE
CARIBS
IMBIBE
KARIBA
MALIBU
SAHIBS
SCRIBE
SQUIBB
SQUIBS

•••I•B
SQUIBB

••••IB
MIDRIB

IC••••
ICARIA
ICARUS
ICEAGE
ICEBAG
ICEBOX
ICECAP
ICEDIN
ICEDUP
ICEFOG
ICEMAN
ICEMEN
ICEOUT
ICESIN
ICESUP
ICHING
ICHTHY
ICICLE
ICIEST
ICINGS
ICKIER
ICONIC

I•C•••
IDCARD
INCANS
INCASE
INCASH
INCEPT
INCHED
INCHES
INCHON
INCISE
INCITE
INCOME
INCULT
INCURS
INCUSE
ISCHIA
ITCHED
ITCHES

I••C••
ICECAP
ICICLE
IPECAC

I•••C•
IDIOCY
IGNACE
IGUACU
IMPACT
INARCH
INDICT
INDUCE
INDUCT
INFACT
INFECT
INJECT
INLUCK
INSECT
INTACT
IONICS
ITASCA
ITHACA

I••••C
IAMBIC
IATRIC
ICONIC
INSYNC
IPECAC
IRENIC
IRIDIC
IRONIC
ITALIC

•IC•••
BICARB
BICEPS
BICKER
BICORN
CICADA
CICELY
CICERO
DICERS
DICIER
DICING
DICKER
DICKEY
DICOTS
DICTUM
DICTUS
FICHES
FICHTE
FICHUS
FICKLE
HICCUP
HICKEY
HICKOK
JICAMA
KICKED
KICKER
KICKIN
KICKUP
LICHEN
LICKED
LICTOR
MICHEL
MICKEY
MICMAC
MICRON
MICROS
NICAEA
NICEAN
NICELY
NICENE
NICEST
NICETY
NICHES
NICKED
NICKEL
NICKER
NICOLA
NICOLE
NICOLO
PICABO
PICARA
PICARD
PICARO
PICCHU
PICKAT
PICKAX
PICKED

PICKER
PICKET
PICKLE
PICKON
PICKUP
PICNIC
PICOTS
PICULS
RICERS
RICHEN
RICHER
RICHES
RICHIE
RICHLY
RICING
RICKED
RICKEY
SICCED
SICILY
SICKEN
SICKER
SICKLE
SICKLY
TICALS
TICKED
TICKER
TICKET
TICKLE
TICKLY
TICTAC
VICARS
VICTIM
VICTIS
VICTOR
VICUNA
WICCAN
WICKED
WICKER
WICKET
WICOPY

•I•C••

BISCAY
CIRCLE
CIRCUM
CIRCUS
CISCOS
DISCOS
DISCUS
FIACRE
FISCAL
HICCUP
HINCTY
KIMCHI
LITCHI
MINCED
MINCER
MINCES
MISCHA
MISCUE
NIACIN
NIECES
OILCAN
PICCHU
PIECED
PIECER
PIECES
PINCER
PISCES
PITCHY
SICCED
SIECLE
SITCOM
TINCAL
TINCAN
TINCTS
VIACOM
VINCES
VINCIT
VISCID
WICCAN
WILCOX
WINCED
WINCER
WINCES
WITCHY
ZIRCON

•I••C•

BIANCA
BIERCE
BISECT
CIVICS
DIDACT
DIRECT
FIANCE
FIASCO
FIERCE
HIJACK
HIRSCH
HITECH
KIRSCH
KITSCH
LILACS
MIMICS
PIERCE
PIRACY
SILICA
SIRICA
TIERCE
VIVACE

•I•••C

AIRSAC
BIGMAC
BIONIC
BIOTIC
CITRIC
FINNIC
FISTIC
LITHIC
MICMAC
MIXTEC
NITRIC
PICNIC
TICTAC
VITRIC
ZIPLOC

••IC••

ALICIA
AMICES
AMICUS
APICAL
APICES
BRICKS
BRICKY
CAICOS
CHICHA
CHICHI
CHICKS
CHICLE
CHICLY
CLICHE
CLICKS
CRICKS
DEICED
DEICER
DEICES
EDICTS
ELICIT
EPICAL
EVICTS
FLICKA
FLICKS
ICICLE
JUICED
JUICER
JUICES
KNICKS
PLICAE
PRICED
PRICER
PRICES
PRICEY
PRICKS
QUICHE
SEICHE
SLICED
SLICER
SLICES
SLICKS
SNICKS
SPICAS
SPICED
SPICES
STICKS
STICKY
TAICHI
THICKE
TRICED
TRICEP
TRICES
TRICHO
TRICIA
TRICKS
TRICKY
TRICOT
UNICEF
VOICED
VOICES
YOICKS

••I•C•

APIECE
CHINCH
CLINCH
CRISCO
EVINCE
FLINCH
FLITCH
FRISCO
GLITCH
GRINCH
IDIOCY
PRINCE
QUINCE
QUINCY
SKITCH
SMIRCH
SNITCH
STITCH
SWITCH
TWITCH

••I••C

ACIDIC
CHIRAC
CLINIC
CRITIC
EXILIC
IRIDIC
OTITIC
OVISAC
OXIDIC
STIVIC
UNIFIC
UNIVAC

•••IC•

ADVICE
AFRICA
ALNICO
ANTICS
ARNICA
ASDICS
ASPICS
ATTICA
ATTICS
BASICS
BODICE
CALICO
CHOICE
CIVICS
COMICS
CONICS
CUBICS
CYNICS
DELICT
DEPICT
DESICA
DEVICE
DRYICE
ELLICE
ENRICH
ENRICO
ENTICE
EROICA
ETHICS
EUNICE
INDICT
IONICS
JANICE
KONICA
LEXICA
LORICA
LYRICS
MALICE
MEDICI
MEDICO
MEDICS
MEJICO
MEXICO
MIMICS
MONICA
MUNICH
NATICK
NODICE
NOTICE
NOVICE
OFFICE
OPTICS
OSMICS
PANICS
PLAICE
POLICE
POLICY
PUMICE
RELICS
RELICT
REMICK
SCHICK
SHTICK
SILICA
SIRICA
SLUICE
SONICS
SPLICE
STOICS
STRICK
STRICT
THRICE
TONICS
TOPICS
TOXICS
TUNICA
TUNICS
UPTICK
VENICE
YORICK
ZURICH

•••I•C

MANIAC
MANIOC
ZODIAC

••••IC

ACETIC
ACIDIC
AEOLIC
AGARIC
ALARIC
ALTAIC
AMEBIC
ANEMIC
ANGLIC
ANODIC
ANOMIC
AORTIC
ARABIC
ARCTIC
ATOMIC
ATONIC
BALTIC
BARDIC
BIONIC
BIOTIC
CADMIC
CEDRIC
CELTIC
CITRIC
CLERIC
CLINIC
COPTIC
COSMIC
COURIC
CRITIC
CULTIC
CUPRIC
CYANIC
CYCLIC
CYMRIC
DELTIC
DYADIC
ECESIC
ECHOIC
EDENIC
EROTIC
ETHNIC
ETONIC
EXILIC
EXOTIC
FABRIC
FERRIC
FINNIC
FISTIC
FORMIC
FROLIC
FUSTIC
GAELIC
GALLIC
GARLIC
GESTIC
GNOMIC
GOTHIC
HECTIC
HEROIC
IAMBIC
IATRIC
ICONIC
IRENIC
IRIDIC
IRONIC
ITALIC
JUDAIC
KARMIC
LACTIC
LITHIC
MANTIC
MASTIC
METRIC
MOSAIC
MYOPIC
MYSTIC
MYTHIC
NITRIC
NOETIC
NORDIC
OLDVIC
ORPHIC
OTITIC
OXIDIC
OZONIC
PECTIC
PELVIC
PEPTIC
PHATIC
PHOBIC
PHONIC
PHOTIC
PICNIC
POETIC
PONTIC
PUBLIC
PYKNIC
ROMAIC
RUBRIC
RUSTIC
SCENIC
SEPTIC
SLAVIC
SORBIC
STATIC
STIVIC
SYNDIC
TACTIC
TANNIC
THETIC
TRAGIC
TROPIC
TURKIC
UNCHIC
UNIFIC
URALIC
URANIC
VITRIC
ZENDIC

ID••••

IDCARD
IDEALS
IDEATE
IDIOCY
IDIOMS
IDIOTS
IDLERS
IDLEST
IDLING
IDOIDO
IDTAGS
IDYLLS

I•D•••

INDABA
INDEBT
INDEED
INDENE
INDENT
INDIAN
INDICT
INDIES
INDIGO
INDIRA
INDITE
INDIUM
INDOOR
INDORE
INDRIS
INDUCE
INDUCT
IODATE
IODIDE
IODINE
IODISE
IODIZE

I••D••

IBADAN
IBIDEM
ICEDIN
ICEDUP
IRIDES
IRIDIC
ISADOR

I•••D•

IDOIDO
IMELDA
IMPEDE
INSIDE
INVADE
IODIDE
ISOLDE

I••••D

IDCARD
ILLFED
IMAGED
IMBUED
IMPEND
INBRED
INCHED
INDEED
INFOLD
INGRID
INHAND
INKIND
INLAID
INLAND
INNEED
INROAD
INTEND
INURED
INWARD
IRONED
ISLAND
ISOPOD
ISSUED
ITCHED
IZZARD

•ID•••

AIDERS
AIDFUL
AIDING
BIDDEN
BIDDER
BIDDLE
BIDING
BIDSIN
BIDSON
BIDSUP
CIDERS
DIDACT
DIDDLE
DIDDLY
DIDIES
DIDION
EIDERS
EIDOLA
FIDDLE
FIDGET
GIDEON
GIDGET
HIDDEN
HIDEHO
HIDEKI
HIDERS
HIDING
HIDOUT
KIDDED
KIDDER
KIDDIE
KIDMAN
KIDNAP
KIDNEY
KIDORY
KIDVID
LIDDED
MIDAIR
MIDDAY
MIDDEN
MIDDLE
MIDGES
MIDGET
MIDIAN
MIDLER
MIDORI
MIDRIB
MIDWAY
NIDIFY
PIDGIN
RIDDED
RIDDEN
RIDDLE
RIDENT
RIDERS
RIDGED
RIDGES
RIDING
RIDLEY
RIDSOF
SIDDUR
SIDERO
SIDERS
SIDING
SIDLED
SIDLES
SIDNEY
TIDBIT
TIDDLY
TIDIED
TIDIER
TIDIES
TIDILY
TIDING
TIDYUP
VIDEOS
VIDERI
WIDELY
WIDENS
WIDEST
WIDGET
WIDISH
WIDOWS
WIDTHS

•I•D••

AIRDAM
AIRDRY
BIDDEN
BIDDER
BIDDLE
BINDER
BINDUP
BIRDED
BIRDER
BIRDIE
CINDER
CIUDAD
DIADEM
DIDDLE
DIDDLY
DIKDIK
DIODES
FIDDLE
FINDER
GILDED
GILDER
GIRDED
GIRDER
GIRDLE
HIDDEN
HINDER
HINDUS
KIDDED
KIDDER
KIDDIE
KINDER
KINDLE
KINDLY
KINDOF
LIDDED
LIEDER
LINDEN
MIDDAY
MIDDEN
MIDDLE
MILDER
MILDEW
MILDLY
MINDED
MINDER
MISDID
PINDAR
PINDUS
RIDDED
RIDDEN
RIDDLE
SIDDUR
SIRDAR
TIDDLY
TIEDIN
TIEDTO
TIEDUP
TIEDYE
TILDEN
TILDES
TINDER
WILDER
WILDLY
WINDED
WINDER
WINDEX
WINDOM
WINDOW
WINDUP
WISDOM

•I••D•

AIKIDO
BIONDI
BIPEDS
BIPODS
CIARDI
CICADA
DIPODY
DIRNDL
DIVIDE
FIELDS
FIENDS
FIORDS
JIHADS
LIBIDO
LIPIDE
LIPIDS
MIKADO
MILADY
RIYADH
TIRADE
VIANDS
VIGODA
WIELDS
YIELDS

•I•••D

BIASED
BIBBED
BIFFED
BIFOLD
BIGRED
BILKED
BILLED
BINGED
BINNED
BIRDED
BIRLED
BITTED
CIUDAD
DIALED
DIETED
DIMMED
DINGED
DINNED
DINTED
DIPPED
DISHED
DISKED
DISSED
FIBBED
FILLED
FILMED
FINKED
FINNED
FIRMED
FISHED
FISTED
FITTED
FIZZED
GIBBED
GIFTED
GIGGED
GILDED
GILEAD
GILLED
GINNED
GIPPED
GIRARD
GIRDED
GIRNED
GIRTED
HILLED
HINGED
HINTED
HIPPED
HISPID
HISSED
JIBBED
JIGGED
JILTED
JINKED
JINXED
KICKED
KIDDED
KIDVID
KILLED
KILNED
KILTED
KINGED
KINKED
KISSED
LIBBED
LICKED
LIDDED
LIFTED
LIGAND
LILTED
LIMBED
LIMNED
LIMPED
LIMPID
LINKED
LIPOID
LIPPED
LIQUID
LISPED
LISTED
LIZARD
MIFFED
MILKED
MILLED
MILORD
MINCED
MINDED
MINTED
MISDID
MISLED
MISSED
MISTED
MITRED
NICKED
NIMROD
NIPPED
OINKED
PICARD
PICKED
PIECED
PIGGED
PILLED
PINGED
PINKED
PINNED
PIPPED
PIQUED
PITHED
PITIED
PITTED
RIBALD
RIBAND
RIBBED
RICKED
RIDDED
RIDGED
RIFFED
RIFLED
RIFTED
RIGGED
RIMMED
RINGED
RINSED
RIOTED
RIPPED
RISKED
RITARD
SICCED
SIDLED
SIEGED
SIEVED
SIFTED
SIGHED
SIGNED
SIGURD
SILKED
SILOED
SILTED
SINBAD
SINEAD
SINGED
SINNED
SIPPED
TICKED
TIDIED
TIERED
TIEROD
TIFFED
TILLED
TILTED
TINGED
TINGOD
TINNED
TINTED
TIPPED
TITHED
TITLED
TITRED
VIEWED
VISAED
VISCID
WICKED
WIGGED
WILLED
WILTED
WINCED
WINDED
WINGED
WINKED
WISHED
WISPED
WITHED
WITTED
WIZARD
YIPPED
ZIGGED
ZINGED
ZIPPED

••ID••

ABIDED
ABIDES
ACIDIC
ACIDLY
ADIDAS
AMIDES
AMIDOL
AMIDST
ARIDLY
ASIDES
AVIDLY
AZIDES
BRIDAL
BRIDES
BRIDGE
BRIDLE
BSIDES
CHIDED
CHIDER
CHIDES
CNIDAE
CNIDUS
DEIDRE
EJIDOS
ELIDED
ELIDES
FRIDAY
FRIDGE
GLIDED
GLIDER
GLIDES
GUIDED
GUIDES
GUIDON
HAIDAS
HEIDEN
IBIDEM
IRIDES
IRIDIC
LAIDBY
LAIDIN
LAIDON
LAIDTO
LAIDUP
LEIDEN
MAIDEN
MAIDUS
OXIDES
OXIDIC
PAIDIN
PAIDUP
PRIDED
PRIDES
QUIDDE
RAIDED
RAIDER
SEIDEL
SKIDDY
SLIDER
SLIDES
SLIDIN
SNIDER
SPIDER
VOIDED
ZUIDER

••I•D•

BLINDS
BUILDS
CHILDE
CHILDS
GRINDS
GUILDS
HAIRDO
LAIRDS
NAIADS
OLINDA
OVIEDO
QUIDDE
SHINDY
SKIDDY
TBIRDS
THIRDS
TRIADS
TRIODE
WEIRDO
WEIRDY

••I••D

ABIDED
AFIELD
BAILED
BAITED
BOILED
BRIAND
BRIARD
BRIBED
BRIGID
BRINED
CEILED
CHIDED
CHIMED
COIFED
COILED
COINED
DEICED
EDITED
ELIDED
EXILED
EXITED
FAILED
FAIRED
FOILED
FOINED
FRIEND
FRIGID
GAINED
GAITED
GLIDED
GRIMED
GRIPED
GUIDED
HAILED
HAIRED
JAILED
JOINED
JUICED
KNIFED
MAILED
MOILED
NAILED
NOISED
OPINED
PAINED
PAIRED
POISED
PRICED
PRIDED
PRIMED
PRIZED
RAIDED
RAILED
RAINED
RAISED
REINED
ROILED
RUINED
SAILED
SEINED
SEIZED
SHIELD
SHINED
SKIVED
SLICED
SLIMED
SMILED
SNIPED
SOILED
SPICED
SPIKED
SPINED
SPIRED
SPITED
SUITED
SWIPED
TAILED
TOILED
TRICED
TRIFID
TRIPOD
TWINED
UNIPOD
UNITED
VEILED
VEINED
VOICED
VOIDED
WAILED
WAITED
WAIVED
WHILED
WHINED

•••ID•

AIKIDO
APHIDS
AROIDS
AVOIDS
BESIDE
BETIDE
BOLIDE
BORIDE
BOVIDS
BRAIDS
CANIDS
CUPIDS
DECIDE
DERIDE
DIVIDE
DOSIDO
DROIDS
DRUIDS
FLUIDS
FRAIDY
HALIDE
IDOIDO
INSIDE
IODIDE
LADIDA
LERIDA
LIBIDO
LIPIDE
LIPIDS
MERIDA
ONEIDA
ONSIDE
OREIDA
OROIDE
OVOIDS
PLAIDS
RANIDS
RAPIDS
REBIDS
RESIDE
SOLIDI
SOLIDS
SQUIDS
STRIDE
UNTIDY
UPSIDE
URSIDS
ZOOIDS

•••I•D

ALLIED
BABIED
BEHIND
BELIED
BODIED
BURIED
BUSIED
COPIED
COSIED
COZIED
DEFIED
DENIED
EDDIED
ENGIRD
ENVIED
ESPIED
GOWILD
HESIOD
HONIED
INKIND
LEVIED
MONIED
MYRIAD
PERIOD
PITIED
PLEIAD
PONIED
REBIND
RELIED
REMIND
RETIED
REWIND
RUBIED
TAXIED
TIDIED
UNBIND
UNGIRD
UNKIND
UNTIED
UNWIND
UPWIND
VARIED

••••ID

ACARID
AENEID
AFRAID
AMPHID
ASTRID
BRIGID
CANDID
CAPSID
CERVID
COCCID
CONOID
CUBOID
CUSPID
DEVOID
ELAPID
EUCLID
EYELID

FERVID
FLORID
FOETID
FORBID
FRIGID
GRAVID
HALOID
HISPID
HORRID
HYBRID
INGRID
INLAID
KHALID
KIDVID
LEONID
LIMPID
LIPOID
LIQUID
MADRID
MISDID
MORBID
NEREID
ORCHID
OUTBID
OUTDID
PALLID
PLACID
PONGID
PUTRID
RANCID
RASHID
RELAID
REPAID
SAYYID
SORDID
STOLID
STUPID
THEKID
TOROID
TORPID
TORRID
TREPID
TRIFID
TURBID
TURGID
UNLAID
UNPAID
UNSAID
USERID
VESPID
VISCID
XYLOID

I•E•••

IBEAMS
IBERIA
IBEXES
ICEAGE
ICEBAG
ICEBOX
ICECAP
ICEDIN
ICEDUP
ICEFOG
ICEMAN
ICEMEN
ICEOUT
ICESIN
ICESUP
IDEALS
IDEATE
IGETIT
ILEANA
ILESHA
ILEXES
IMELDA
INESSE
IPECAC
IREFUL
IRENES
IRENIC
ISELIN
ISEULT

I••E••

ICIEST
IDLERS
IDLEST
ILLEST
IMPEDE
IMPELS
IMPEND
IMPERF
INCEPT
INDEBT
INDEED
INDENE
INDENT
INFECT
INFERS
INFEST
INGEAR
INGEST
INHERE
INJECT
INJEST
INKERS
INLETS
INNEED
INNESS
INSEAM
INSECT
INSERT
INSETS
INTEND
INTENS
INTENT
INTERJ
INTERN
INVENT
INVERT
INVEST
IQTEST
IRLENE
IRREAL
ISLETS
ISMENE
ITSELF

I•••E•

IBEXES
IBIDEM
IBISES
ICEMEN
ICKIER
IFFIER
IJSSEL
ILEXES
ILLFED
ILLMET
IMAGED
IMAGER
IMAGES
IMARET
IMBUED
IMBUES
IMOGEN
INANER
INAPET
INBRED
INCHED
INCHES
INDEED
INDIES
INGLES
INGRES
INKIER
INKJET
INKLES
INNEED
INSTEP
INURED
INURES
IRATER
IRENES
IRIDES
IRISES
IRONED
IRONER
ISABEL
ISOHEL
ISOMER
ISRAEL
ISSUED
ISSUER
ISSUES
ISTLES
ITCHED
ITCHES

I••••E

ICEAGE
ICICLE
IDEATE
IGNACE
IGNITE
IGNORE
ILLUME
ILLUSE
IMBIBE
IMBRUE
IMFINE
IMMUNE
IMMURE
IMPALE
IMPEDE
IMPOSE
IMPURE
IMPUTE
INCASE
INCISE
INCITE
INCOME
INCUSE
INDENE
INDITE
INDORE
INDUCE
INESSE
INFUSE
INHALE
INHERE
INJOKE
INJURE
INLINE
INLOVE
INMATE
INNAGE
INNATE
INOUYE
INSANE
INSIDE
INSOLE
INSURE
INTAKE
INTIME
INTINE
INTONE
INTUNE
INVADE
INVITE
INVOKE
IODATE
IODIDE
IODINE
IODISE
IODIZE
IOLITE
IONISE
IONIZE
IRLENE
IRVINE
ISMENE
ISOLDE

•IE•••

AIELLO
BIERCE
DIEOFF
DIEOUT
DIEPPE
DIESEL
DIESES
DIESIS
DIETED
DIETER
FIELDS
FIENDS
FIERCE
FIESTA
HIEING
HIEMAL
HIERON
KIEFER
LIEBIG
LIEBYS
LIEDER
LIEFER
LIEFLY
LIEGES
LIELOW
LIENEE
LIERNE
LIESIN
LIESTO
LIEUTS
NIECES
NIELLI
NIELLO
PIECED
PIECER
PIECES
PIEMAN
PIEMEN
PIEPAN
PIERCE
PIERRE
PIETAS
PIETER
PIETIN
PIETRO
RIENZI
SIECLE
SIEGED
SIEGEL
SIEGES
SIENNA
SIERRA
SIESTA
SIEVED
SIEVES
TIEDIN
TIEDTO
TIEDUP
TIEDYE
TIEING
TIEINS
TIEPIN
TIERCE
TIERED
TIEROD
TIERRA
TIESIN
TIESTO
TIESUP
TIEUPS
VIENNA
VIENNE
VIEWED
VIEWER
WIELDS
WIENER
WIESEL
YIELDS

•I•E••

AIDERS
AILEEN
AILERS
BICEPS
BIKERS
BIPEDS
BIREME
BISECT
BITERS
CICELY
CICERO
CIDERS
CINEMA
CITERS
CIVETS
DICERS
DIGEST
DINEIN
DINEON
DINERO
DINERS
DIRECT
DIRELY
DIREST
DIVEIN
DIVERS
DIVERT
DIVEST
DIYERS
DIZENS
EIDERS
EILEEN
FIBERS
FIFERS
FILENE
FILERS
FILETS
FINELY
FINERY
FINEST
FIRERS
FIREUP
FIVEAM
FIVEPM
FIVERS
FIVEWS
FIXERS
GIBERS
GIDEON
GILEAD
GIMELS
GIVEIN
GIVENS
GIVERS
GIVETO
GIVEUP
HIDEHO
HIDEKI
HIDERS
HIKERS
HIKEUP
HIREON
HIRERS
HITECH
JIVERS
KINEMA
KITERS
LIBELS
LIBERI
LIFERS
LIGERS
LIKELY
LIKENS
LIMENS
LIMEYS
LINEAL
LINEAR
LINENS
LINENY
LINERS
LINEUP
LIPENG
LITERS
LIVEIN
LIVELY
LIVENS
LIVEON
LIVERS
LIVERY
MILERS
MIMEOS
MIMERS
MINERS
MISERS
MISERY
MITERS
MIXERS
MIZENS
NICEAN
NICELY
NICENE
NICEST
NICETY
NINEAM
NINEPM
NINERS
NINETY
NITERS
NITERY
OILERS
PIGEON
PIKERS
PILEIN
PILEON
PILEUM
PILEUP
PILEUS
PINEAL
PINERO
PINERY
PIPERS
PIPEUP
PIXELS
RIBEYE
RICERS
RIDENT
RIDERS
RIFELY
RIFEST
RILEUP
RIPELY
RIPENS
RIPEST
RISERS
RIVERA
RIVERS
RIVETS
SIDERO
SIDERS
SILENI
SILENT
SIMEON
SINEAD
SINEWS
SINEWY
SIRENS
SISERA
SIXERS
SIZERS
SIZEUP
TIGERS
TILERS
TIMELY
TIMERS
TINEAR
TITERS
VIDEOS
VIDERI
VILELY
VILEST
VINERY
VIPERS
VIREOS
VIXENS
WIDELY
WIDENS
WIDEST
WIFELY
WINERY
WIPERS
WIPEUP
WIRERS
WISELY
WISENT
WISEST
WISETO
WISEUP
WIZENS
XIMENA
ZIBETS

•I••E•

AIGRET
AILEEN
AIRIER
AIRMEN
AISLES
BIASED
BIASES
BIBBED
BIBLES
BICKER
BIDDEN
BIDDER
BIFFED
BIGBEN
BIGGER
BIGRED
BIGTEN
BILGES
BILKED
BILLED
BILLET
BINDER
BINGED
BINGES
BINNED
BIOMES
BIRDED
BIRDER
BIRLED
BIRNEY
BISSET
BITTED
BITTEN
BITTER
CINDER
CIPHER
CISKEI
CITIES
DIADEM
DIALED
DIALER
DIAPER
DICIER
DICKER
DICKEY
DIDIES
DIESEL
DIESES
DIETED
DIETER
DIFFER
DIGGER
DILLER
DILSEY
DIMMED
DIMMER
DINGED
DINKEY
DINNED
DINNER
DINTED
DIODES
DIONEB
DIPPED
DIPPER
DIRGES
DISHED
DISHES
DISKED
DISMES
DISNEY
DISPEL
DISSED
DITHER
DITZES
EIFFEL
EILEEN
EISNER
EITHER
FIBBED
FIBBER
FIBRES
FICHES
FIDGET
FILLED
FILLER
FILLES
FILLET
FILMED
FILTER
FINDER
FINGER
FINKED
FINNED
FINNEY
FIRMED
FIRMER
FISHED
FISHER
FISHES
FISTED
FITTED
FITTER
FIZZED
FIZZES
GIBBED
GIBBER
GIBBET
GIBLET
GIDGET
GIFTED
GIGGED
GIGUES
GIJOES
GILDED
GILDER
GILLED
GIMBEL
GIMLET
GIMMES
GINGER
GINNED
GIPPED
GIPPER
GIRDED
GIRDER
GIRNED
GIRTED
HICKEY
HIDDEN
HIGHER
HILLED
HILLEL
HILLER
HINDER
HINGED
HINGES
HINTED
HINTER
HIPPED
HIPPER
HISSED
HISSER
HISSES
HITHER
HITMEN
HITTER
JIBBED
JIGGED
JIGGER
JILTED
JINKED
JINXED
JINXES
JITNEY
JITTER
JIVIER
KICKED
KICKER
KIDDED
KIDDER
KIDNEY
KIEFER
KILLED
KILLER
KILMER
KILNED
KILTED
KILTER
KINDER
KINGED
KINKED
KINSEY
KIPPER
KISLEV
KISMET
KISSED
KISSER
KISSES
KITTEN
LIANES
LIBBED
LIBBER
LICHEN
LICKED
LIDDED
LIEDER
LIEFER
LIEGES
LIENEE
LIFTED
LIFTER
LILIES
LILTED
LIMBED
LIMBER
LIMIER
LIMNED
LIMNER
LIMPED
LIMPER
LIMPET
LINDEN
LINGER
LINIER
LINKED
LINKER
LINNET
LINNEY
LINSEY
LINTEL
LINTER
LIONEL
LIONET
LIPPED
LISLES
LISPED
LISTED
LISTEE
LISTEL
LISTEN
LISTER
LITRES
LITTER
LIVRES
MICHEL
MICKEY
MIDDEN
MIDGES
MIDGET
MIDLER
MIFFED
MIGUEL
MILDER
MILDEW
MILIEU
MILKED
MILKER
MILLED
MILLER
MILLET
MILNER
MINCED
MINCER
MINCES
MINDED
MINDER
MINKES
MINTED
MINTER
MINUET
MINXES
MIRIER
MIRREN
MISLED
MISSED
MISSES
MISTED
MISTER
MITRED
MITRES
MITTEN
MIXTEC
MIZZEN
NIAMEY
NICAEA
NICHES
NICKED
NICKEL
NICKER
NIECES
NIGHER
NIKKEI
NIPPED
NIPPER
NIPSEY
NISSEN
NITRES
NIXIES
OILIER
OILMEN
OINKED
PIAGET
PICKED
PICKER
PICKET
PIECED
PIECER
PIECES
PIEMEN
PIETER
PIGGED
PIGLET
PIGPEN
PILFER
PILLED
PINCER
PINGED
PINIER
PINKED
PINKEN
PINKER
PINNED
PINNER
PINTER
PIOLET
PIPIER
PIPPED
PIQUED
PIQUES
PIQUET
PISCES
PISTES
PITHED
PITIED
PITIER
PITIES
PITMEN
PITTED
PITTER
PIXIES
RIBBED
RICHEN
RICHER
RICHES
RICKED
RICKEY
RIDDED
RIDDEN
RIDGED
RIDGES
RIDLEY
RIFFED
RIFLED
RIFLER
RIFLES
RIFTED
RIGGED
RIGGER
RILLES
RILLET
RIMIER
RIMMED
RINGED
RINGER
RINSED
RINSES
RIOTED
RIOTER
RIPKEN
RIPLEY
RIPPED
RIPPER
RISKED
RISKER
RITTER
SICCED
SICKEN
SICKER
SIDLED
SIDLES
SIDNEY
SIEGED
SIEGEL
SIEGES
SIEVED
SIEVES
SIFTED
SIFTER
SIGHED
SIGHER
SIGNED
SIGNEE
SIGNER
SIGNET
SILKED
SILKEN
SILOED
SILTED
SILVER
SIMBEL
SIMMER
SIMNEL
SIMPER
SINGED
SINGER
SINGES
SINKER
SINNED
SINNER
SINTER
SIPPED
SIPPER
SIPPET
SIRREE
SISKEL
SISLER
SISLEY
SISTER
SITTER
TICKED
TICKER
TICKET
TIDIED
TIDIER
TIDIES
TIERED
TIFFED
TIGGER
TILDEN
TILDES
TILLED
TILLER
TILTED
TILTER
TIMBER
TINDER
TINGED
TINGES
TINIER
TINKER
TINMEN
TINNED
TINNER
TINSEL
TINTED
TINTER
TIPPED
TIPPER
TIPPET
TITFER
TITHED
TITHER
TITHES
TITLED
TITLES
TITRED
TITRES
TITTER
VIEWED
VIEWER
VINCES
VINIER
VIOLET
VISAED
VIVIEN
VIZIER
WICKED
WICKER
WICKET
WIDGET
WIENER
WIESEL
WIGGED
WIGLET
WILDER
WILIER
WILKES
WILLED
WILLEM
WILLET
WILTED
WIMSEY
WINCED
WINCER
WINCES
WINDED
WINDER
WINDEX
WINGED
WINGER
WINIER
WINKED
WINKER
WINNER
WINTER
WINZES
WIRIER
WISHED
WISHER
WISHES
WISPED
WISTER
WITHED
WITHER
WITHES
WITTED
XIAMEN
YIPPED
YIPPEE
ZIGGED
ZIMMER
ZINGED
ZINGER
ZIPPED
ZIPPER
ZITHER

•I•••E

BIDDLE
BIERCE
BIGGIE
BIGLIE
BIGTOE
BILLIE
BINATE
BIRDIE
BIREME
BISQUE
CINQUE
CIRCLE
CIRQUE
DIANNE
DIBBLE
DIDDLE
DIEPPE
DILATE
DILUTE
DIMPLE
DINGLE
DIONNE
DIPOLE
DIRIGE
DISUSE
DIVIDE
DIVINE
FIACRE
FIANCE
FICHTE
FICKLE
FIDDLE
FIERCE
FIGURE
FILENE
FILOSE
FINALE
FINITE
FIPPLE
FIXATE
FIZZLE
GIGGLE
GILLIE
GIRDLE
HIGGLE
HIPPIE
JIGGLE
JIMMIE
JINGLE
KIBBLE
KIDDIE
KILTIE
KINDLE
KINGME
KIRTLE
KISHKE
LIABLE
LIAISE
LIENEE
LIERNE
LIGATE
LIGURE
LILLIE
LINAGE
LIPASE
LIPIDE
LISTEE
LITTLE
LIZZIE
MIDDLE
MIFUNE
MIGGLE
MILLIE
MILTIE
MINGLE
MINNIE
MINUTE
MIRAGE
MISCUE
MISUSE
MIZZLE
NIBBLE
NICENE
NICOLE
NIGGLE
NIMBLE
PIAFFE
PICKLE
PIERCE
PIERRE
PIFFLE
PIGGIE
PIKAKE
PILATE
PILOSE
PINITE
PINKIE
PINNAE
PINOLE
PINTLE
PIRATE
RIBEYE
RIBOSE
RICHIE
RIDDLE
RIFFLE
RIMOSE
RIMPLE
RIPPLE
RISQUE
SICKLE
SIECLE
SIGNEE
SILAGE
SILONE
SIMILE
SIMONE
SIMPLE
SINGLE
SINISE
SIRREE
SIZZLE
TIBIAE
TICKLE
TIEDYE
TIERCE
TILLIE
TIMBRE
TINGLE
TINKLE
TIPPLE
TIPTOE
TIRADE
TIRANE
TISANE
TISSUE
TITTLE
VIABLE
VIENNE
VINNIE
VIRILE
VIRTUE
VISAGE
VISINE
VITALE
VIVACE
WIGGLE
WILLIE
WIMBLE
WIMPLE
WINKIE
WINKLE
WINNIE
YIPPEE

••IE••

ADIEUS
ADIEUX
AFIELD
ALIENS
AMIENS
APIECE
BRIEFS
BRIENZ
BRIERS
BRIERY
CHIEFS
CLIENT
CRIERS
DRIERS
DRIEST
FLIERS
FRIEND
FRIERS
FRIEZE
GAIETY
GRIEFS

GRIEVE
ICIEST
MOIETY
ORIELS
ORIENT
OSIERS
OVIEDO
PLIERS
PRIERS
PRIEST
QUIETS
SHIELD
SHIEST
SKIERS
SLIEST
SPIELS
SPIERS
THIEVE
TRIERS
UBIETY
WRIEST

••I•E•

ABIDED
ABIDES
ALINES
ALITER
AMICES
AMIDES
AMINES
ANIMES
APICES
ARISEN
ARISES
ASIDES
AZIDES
AZINES
BAILED
BAILEE
BAILER
BAILEY
BAINES
BAITED
BEIGES
BLIMEY
BLIXEN
BOILED
BOILER
BOITES
BRIBED
BRIBES
BRIDES
BRINED
BRINES
BSIDES
CEILED
CHIDED
CHIDER
CHIDES
CHIMED
CHIMES
CHINES
CHISEL
CHIVES
CLIMES
CLINES
COIFED
COILED
COINED
COINER
CRIKEY
CRIMEA
CRIMES
CRIPES
CRISES
DAILEY
DAIREN
DAISES
DEICED
DEICER
DEICES
DRIVEL
DRIVEN
DRIVER
DRIVES
DUIKER
EDILES
EDITED
ELIDED
ELIDES
ELITES
EVILER
EXILED
EXILES
EXITED
FAILED
FAIRED
FAIRER
FBIMEN
FOILED
FOINED
FRISEE
FRISES
GAINED
GAINER
GAITED
GAITER
GEIGER
GEISEL
GLIDED
GLIDER
GLIDES
GRIMED
GRIMES
GRIPED
GRIPER
GRIPES
GRIVET
GUIDED
GUIDES
GUILES
GUINEA
GUISES
HAILED
HAILEY
HAINES
HAIRED
HEIDEN
HEIFER
IBIDEM
IBISES
IRIDES
IRISES
JAILED
JAILER
JOINED
JOINER
JUICED
JUICER
JUICES
KAISER
KEITEL
KNIFED
KNIFES
KNIVES
LEIDEN
LOITER
MAIDEN
MAILED
MAILER
MAILES
MAIZES
MOILED
MOILER
MOINES
MOIRES
NAILED
NAILER
NOISED
NOISES
OBITER
OGIVES
OLIVER
OLIVES
OPINED
OPINER
OPINES
ORIGEN
OXIDES
PAINED
PAIRED
PFIZER
POISED
POISES
PRICED
PRICER
PRICES
PRICEY
PRIDED
PRIDES
PRIMED
PRIMER
PRIMES
PRIPET
PRIVET
PRIZED
PRIZES
QUIRES
QUIVER
RAIDED
RAIDER
RAILED
RAILER
RAINED
RAINER
RAINES
RAINEY
RAISED
RAISER
RAISES
REINED
REINER
ROILED
RUINED
RUINER
SAILED
SEIDEL
SEINED
SEINER
SEINES
SEIZED
SEIZER
SEIZES
SHINED
SHINER
SHINES
SHIRER
SHIRES
SHIVER
SKIVED
SKIVER
SKIVES
SLICED
SLICER
SLICES
SLIDER
SLIDES
SLIMED
SLIMES
SLIVER
SMILED
SMILER
SMILES
SMILEY
SMITES
SNIDER
SNIPED
SNIPER
SNIPES
SNIVEL
SOILED
SOIREE
SPICED
SPICES
SPIDER
SPIKED
SPIKER
SPIKES
SPILES
SPINED
SPINEL
SPINES
SPINET
SPIREA
SPIRED
SPIRES
SPITED
SPITES
STILES
STIPEL
STIPES
STIVER
SUITED
SUITES
SWIPED
SWIPER
SWIPES
SWIVEL
SWIVET
TAILED
TAIPEI
TOILED
TOILER
TOILES
TOILET
TRIBES
TRICED
TRICEP
TRICES
TRIJET
TRIKES
TRINES
TRITER
TRIVET
TWINED
TWINES
UNICEF
UNISEX
UNITED
UNITER
UNITES
VAINER
VEILED
VEINED
VOICED
VOICES
VOIDED
VOILES
VSIXES
WAILED
WAILER
WAITED
WAITER
WAIVED
WAIVER
WAIVES
WHILED
WHILES
WHINED
WHINER
WHINES
WHINEY
WHITEN
WHITER
WHITES
WRITER
WRITES
XFILES
ZAIRES
ZUIDER

••I••E

ALIBLE
APIECE
ARIOSE
AVIATE
BAILEE
BLITHE
BRIDGE
BRIDLE
CAIQUE
CHICLE
CHIGOE
CHILDE
CHILOE
CLICHE
CLIQUE
CNIDAE
CRINGE
CUIQUE
CUISSE
DEIDRE
EDIBLE
EMIGRE
ENISLE
EVINCE
FAILLE
FOIBLE
FRIDGE
FRIEZE
FRINGE
FRISEE
GRIEVE
GRILLE
GRILSE
GRIMKE
GRIPPE
GUIMPE
ICICLE
LAINIE
MAISIE
MAITRE
NEISSE
OPIATE
ORIOLE
OTIOSE
PAIUTE
PHILAE
PLICAE
PLISSE
POINTE
PRINCE
PUISNE
QUICHE
QUIDDE
QUINCE
SAINTE
SEICHE
SHIITE
SOIGNE
SOIREE
STIFLE
SUISSE
TAILLE
THICKE
THIEVE
THISBE
TRIAGE
TRIFLE
TRIODE
TRIPLE
TRISTE
TRIUNE
TRIXIE
TUILLE
TWINGE
UBIQUE
UNIATE
UNIQUE
WRITHE

•••IE•

ACHIER
ADRIEN
AERIES
AGGIES
AIRIER
ALLIED
ALLIES
ANCIEN
ARMIES
ARTIER
ASHIER
BABIED
BABIES
BELIED
BELIEF
BELIES
BEVIES
BODIED
BODIES
BOGIES
BONIER
BOXIER
BURIED
BURIES
BUSIED
BUSIER
BUSIES
CAGIER
CAHIER
CAKIER
CANIER
CARIES
CITIES
COKIER
COLIES
CONIES
COPIED
COPIER
COPIES
COSIED
COSIER
COSIES
COZIED
COZIER
COZIES
CUTIES
DAMIEN
DANIEL
DARIEN
DAVIES
DEFIED
DEFIES
DEMIES
DENIED
DENIER
DENIES
DEWIER
DICIER
DIDIES
DOGIES
DOPIER
DORIES
DOZIER
DUTIES
EASIER
EDDIED
EDDIES
EDGIER
EELIER
EERIER
EGGIER
ENVIED
ENVIER
ENVIES
ESPIED
ESPIES
EYRIES
FACIES
FOGIES
FOXIER
FUMIER
FURIES
GABIES
GAMIER
GENIES
GLUIER
GOBIES
GOOIER
GORIER
HAZIER
HOKIER
HOLIER
HOMIER
HONIED
HOSIER
ICKIER
IFFIER
INDIES
INKIER
JAVIER
JIVIER
JOKIER
JOLIET
JULIET
JURIES
LACIER
LADIES
LAKIER
LANIER
LAZIER
LEVIED
LEVIER
LEVIES
LILIES
LIMIER
LINIER
LOGIER
LOOIES
LORIES
MARIEL
MAZIER
METIER
MILIEU
MIRIER
MONIED
MONIES
MOPIER
MOVIES
MURIEL
NAPIER
NAVIES
NIXIES
NOSIER
OATIER
OBRIEN
OILIER
OLDIES
ONVIEW
OOZIER
ORGIES
PALIER
PAPIER
PINIER
PIPIER
PITIED
PITIER
PITIES
PIXIES
POGIES
POKIER
PONIED
PONIES
POSIES
PUNIER
PYXIES
RABIES
RACIER
RAMIES
RAPIER
RELIED
RELIEF
RELIES
RETIED
RETIES
REVIEW
RIMIER
ROPIER
ROSIER
RUBIED
RUBIES
SERIES
SEXIER
SHRIEK
SOVIET
SPRIER
SUSIEQ
TAXIED
TAXIES
TIDIED
TIDIER
TIDIES
TINIER
TOBIES
TONIER
TORIES
TYPIER
UGLIER
UGLIES
UNDIES
UNTIED
UNTIES
VANIER
VARIED
VARIES
VINIER
VIVIEN
VIZIER
WANIER
WARIER
WAVIER
WAXIER
WILIER
WINIER
WIRIER
XAVIER
YALIES
ZANIER
ZANIES

•••I•E

ACTIVE
ADMIRE
ADVICE
ADVISE
AEDILE
AFFINE
ALDINE
ALFINE
ALPINE
APLITE
ARGIVE
ARRIVE
ASPIRE
ASSIZE
ATTIRE
AUDILE
AWHILE
AXLIKE
BARITE
BELIKE
BELIZE
BEMINE
BEMIRE
BESIDE
BETIDE
BETISE
BLAINE
BLAISE
BODICE
BOLIDE
BORIDE
BOVINE
BRAISE
BRUISE
BYLINE
CAMISE
CANINE
CARIBE
CECILE
CELINE
CERISE
CHAINE
CHAISE
CHOICE
CLAIRE
COSINE
CRUISE
CURIAE
DATIVE
DECIDE
DEFILE
DEFINE
DEMISE
DENISE
DERIDE
DERIVE
DESIRE
DEVICE
DEVINE
DEVISE
DIRIGE
DIVIDE
DIVINE
DOCILE
DOMINE
DRYICE
ELAINE
ELLICE
ELOISE
EMPIRE
ENDIVE
ENGINE
ENSILE
ENTICE
ENTIRE
EQUINE
ERMINE
ETOILE
EUNICE
EXCISE
EXCITE
EXPIRE
EXWIFE
FACILE
FALINE
FAMINE
FELINE
FELIPE
FINITE
FRAISE
FUTILE
GAMINE
GREIGE
GUNITE
HABILE
HALIDE
HALITE
HAMITE
IGNITE
IMBIBE
IMFINE
INCISE
INCITE
INDITE
INLINE
INSIDE
INTIME
INTINE
INVITE
IODIDE
IODINE
IODISE
IODIZE
IOLITE
IONISE
IONIZE
IRVINE
JANICE
JANINE
KALINE
KURILE
LABILE
LEVINE
LEVITE
LIAISE
LIPIDE
LOUISE
LUCITE
LUPINE
LYSINE
MALICE
MARINE
MAXINE
MAXIXE
MOBILE
MODINE
MOLINE
MOTILE
MOTIVE
MURINE
NADINE
NATIVE
NODICE
NOMINE
NOTICE
NOVICE
NOWISE
NUBILE
OBLIGE
OFFICE
ONDINE
ONFILE
ONFIRE
ONLINE
ONSIDE
ONSITE
ONTIME
OOLITE
OPHITE
OROIDE
ORPINE
OSCINE
OXLIKE
PATINE
PELIKE
PETITE
PINITE
PLAICE
POLICE
POLITE
PRAISE
PUMICE
PURINE
PYRITE
RACINE
RAPINE
RATINE
RATITE
RAVINE
RECIFE
RECIPE
RECITE
REFILE
REFINE
REGIME
REHIRE
RELINE
RELIVE
REMISE
REPINE
RESIDE
RESILE
RETILE
RETIME
RETIRE
REVILE
REVISE
REVIVE
REWIRE
RUTILE
SABINE
SAFIRE
SALINE
SAMITE
SATIRE
SCRIBE
SEDILE
SEMITE
SERINE
SHIITE
SHRIKE
SHRINE
SHRIVE
SIMILE
SINISE
SLUICE
SOFINE
SPLICE
SPLINE
SPRITE
SQUIRE
STRIAE
STRIDE
STRIFE
STRIKE
STRINE
STRIPE
STRIVE
SUPINE
THRICE
THRIVE
TIBIAE
TOLIFE
TONITE
UMPIRE
UNDINE
UNLIKE
UNPILE
UNRIPE
UNWISE
UPDIKE
UPRISE
UPSIDE
UPTIME
URSINE
VALISE
VENICE
VENIRE
VENITE
VERITE
VIRILE
VISINE
VOTIVE
WAHINE

••••IE

ADELIE
AMALIE
ANOMIE
ARCHIE
AUNTIE
AUSSIE
BADDIE
BAGGIE
BARBIE
BARRIE
BEANIE
BERNIE
BERTIE
BESSIE
BIGGIE
BIGLIE
BILLIE
BIRDIE
BMOVIE
BOBBIE
BOCCIE
BONNIE
BOOGIE
BOOKIE
BOOTIE
BOWTIE
BRODIE
BUDGIE
CABBIE
CADDIE
CARRIE
CHERIE
COLLIE
CONNIE
COOKIE
COOTIE
COWRIE
DANDIE
DEARIE
DEBBIE
DOGGIE
DOOBIE
DOOGIE
DOOZIE
DOTTIE
FAERIE
FANNIE
FERGIE
FOLKIE
FOODIE
FOZZIE
GERTIE
GILLIE
GOALIE
GOLDIE
GOODIE
GORDIE
GRACIE
HACKIE
HADDIE
HANKIE
HATTIE
HEEBIE
HERBIE
HETTIE
HIPPIE
HOAGIE
HOGTIE
HOOTIE
JACKIE
JENNIE
JESSIE
JIMMIE
JOANIE
JUNKIE
KATHIE
KELPIE
KEWPIE
KIDDIE
KILTIE
KOOKIE
LADDIE
LAINIE
LASSIE
LAURIE
LEFTIE
LENNIE
LEONIE
LESLIE
LILLIE
LIZZIE
LOONIE
MADDIE
MAGGIE
MAGPIE
MAISIE
MARCIE
MARGIE
MARNIE
MASHIE
MATTIE
MEALIE
MEANIE
MILLIE
MILTIE
MINNIE
MOMMIE
MUDPIE
MUNCIE
MUSKIE
NANNIE
NAPPIE
NELLIE
NESSIE
PETRIE
PIGGIE
PINKIE
POTPIE
PREMIE
PUNKIE
REGGIE
RENNIE
RICHIE
ROADIE
ROBBIE
ROLLIE
RONNIE
ROOKIE
ROOMIE
RUNCIE
SAMMIE
SAVOIE
SKOKIE
SOFTIE
SOPHIE
SORTIE
SPECIE
STEVIE
STOGIE
STYMIE
TALKIE
TECHIE
TESSIE
TILLIE
TOONIE
TOWNIE
TRIXIE
VEGGIE
VINNIE
WALKIE
WEDGIE
WEENIE
WEEPIE
WILLIE
WINKIE
WINNIE
WOOGIE
WOOKIE
YORKIE
YUPPIE
ZOMBIE

IF••••

IFFIER

I•F•••

IFFIER
IMFINE
INFACT
INFAMY
INFANT
INFECT
INFERS
INFEST
INFIRM
INFLOW
INFLUX
INFOLD
INFORM
INFULL
INFUSE

I••F••

ICEFOG
ILLFED
INAFIX
INAFOG
IREFUL

I••••F

IMPERF
INHALF
ITSELF

•IF•••

BIFFED
BIFOLD
DIFFER
EIFFEL
FIFERS
FIFING
FIFTHS
GIFTED
LIFERS
LIFTED
LIFTER
LIFTUP
MIFFED
MIFUNE
PIFFLE
RIFELY
RIFEST
RIFFED
RIFFLE
RIFIFI
RIFLED
RIFLER
RIFLES
RIFTED
SIFTED
SIFTER
TIFFED
TIFFIN
WIFELY

•I•F••

AIDFUL
AIMFOR
AIMFUL
BIAFRA
BIFFED
DIFFER
EIFFEL
FITFUL
KIEFER
KITFOX
LIEFER
LIEFLY
MIFFED
MISFIT
PIAFFE
PIFFLE
PILFER
RIFFED
RIFFLE
SINFUL
TIFFED
TIFFIN
TITFER
WILFUL

•I••F•

BITOFF
CITIFY
DIEOFF
MINIFY
NIDIFY
PIAFFE
PILAFS
RIFIFI
RIPOFF
TIPOFF
VILIFY
VINIFY
VIVIFY

•I•••F

BITOFF
DIEOFF
KINDOF
RIDSOF
RIPOFF
TIPOFF

••IF••

CLIFFS
CLIFFY
COIFED
DRIFTS
DRIFTY
GRIFTS
HEIFER
KNIFED
KNIFES
SCIFIS
SHIFTS
SHIFTY
SKIFFS
SNIFFS
SNIFFY
SPIFFS
SPIFFY
STIFFS
STIFLE
SWIFTS
TRIFID
TRIFLE
UNIFIC
WHIFFS

••I•F•

BRIEFS
CHIEFS
CLIFFS
CLIFFY
GRIEFS
SKIFFS
SNIFFS
SNIFFY
SPIFFS
SPIFFY
STIFFS
WHIFFS

••I••F

UNICEF

•••IF•
ADRIFT
AERIFY
AURIFY
BASIFY
CANIFF
CITIFY
CODIFY
EXWIFE
GASIFY
MINIFY
MODIFY
MOTIFS
NIDIFY
NOTIFY
OSSIFY
PACIFY
PURIFY
RAMIFY
RARIFY
RATIFY
RECIFE
RIFIFI
RUBIFY
SALIFY
SCHIFF
SERIFS
SHRIFT
STRIFE
TARIFF
THRIFT
TOLIFE
TYPIFY
UGLIFY
UPLIFT
VERIFY
VILIFY
VINIFY
VIVIFY

•••I•F
BELIEF
CANIFF
RELIEF
SCHIFF
TARIFF

••••IF
CERTIF
MASSIF
SHARIF
SHERIF
WHATIF

IG••••
IGETIT
IGLOOS
IGNACE
IGNATZ
IGNITE
IGNORE
IGOTIT
IGUACU
IGUANA

I•G•••
INGEAR
INGEST
INGLES
INGMAR
INGOTS
INGRAM
INGRES
INGRID

I••G••
IMAGED
IMAGER
IMAGES
IMOGEN
ISOGON

I•••G•
ICEAGE
ICINGS
IDTAGS
IMPUGN
INDIGO
INNAGE

I••••G
ICEBAG
ICEFOG
ICHING
IDLING
IMPING
INAFOG
INKING
INNING
IRKING
IRVING

•IG•••
AIGRET
BIGAMY
BIGBEN
BIGBOY
BIGGER
BIGGIE
BIGGUN
BIGHTS
BIGLIE
BIGMAC
BIGOTS
BIGRED
BIGSUR
BIGTEN
BIGTOE
BIGTOP
BIGWIG
CIGARS
DIGEST
DIGGER
DIGITS
DIGLOT
DIGOUT
DIGRAM
DIGSIN
DIGSUP
EIGHTH
EIGHTS
EIGHTY
FIGARO
FIGHTS
FIGURE
GIGGED
GIGGLE
GIGGLY
GIGOLO
GIGOTS
GIGUES
HIGGLE
HIGHER
HIGHIQ
HIGHLY
HIGHUP
JIGGED
JIGGER
JIGGLE
JIGGLY
JIGSAW
KIGALI
LIGAND
LIGATE
LIGERS
LIGHTS
LIGNIN
LIGULA
LIGURE
MIGGLE
MIGHTY
MIGNON
MIGUEL
NIGGLE
NIGHER
NIGHTS
NIGHTY
PIGEON
PIGGED
PIGGIE
PIGLET
PIGNUT
PIGOUT
PIGPEN
PIGSTY
RIGGED
RIGGER
RIGHTO
RIGHTS
RIGHTY
RIGORS
RIGOUR
RIGSUP
SIGHED
SIGHER
SIGHTS
SIGILS
SIGMAS
SIGNAL
SIGNED
SIGNEE
SIGNER
SIGNET
SIGNIN
SIGNON
SIGNOR
SIGNUP
SIGURD
TIGERS
TIGGER
TIGHTS
TIGLON
TIGRIS
UIGURS
VIGILS
VIGODA
VIGORS
VIGOUR
WIGGED
WIGGLE
WIGGLY
WIGHTS
WIGLET
WIGOUT
WIGWAG
WIGWAM
ZIGGED
ZIGZAG

•I•G••
AIRGUN
BIGGER
BIGGIE
BIGGUN
BILGES
BINGED
BINGES
BIOGAS
BIRGIT
DIGGER
DINGED
DINGHY
DINGLE
DINGUS
DIRGES
FIDGET
FINGER
FIZGIG
GIDGET
GIGGED
GIGGLE
GIGGLY
GILGUY
GINGER
HIGGLE
HINGED
HINGES
HINGIS
JIGGED
JIGGER
JIGGLE
JIGGLY
JINGLE
JINGLY
KINGED
KINGLY
KINGME
LIEGES
LINGER
LINGUA
MIDGES
MIDGET
MIGGLE
MINGLE
NIGGLE
NILGAI
NINGBO
PIAGET
PIDGIN
PIGGED
PIGGIE
PINGED
PISGAH
RIDGED
RIDGES
RIGGED
RIGGER
RINGED
RINGER
RINGUP
SIEGED
SIEGEL
SIEGES
SINGED
SINGER
SINGES
SINGIN
SINGLE
SINGLY
SINGTO
SIXGUN
TIGGER
TINGED
TINGES
TINGLE
TINGLY
TINGOD
VIRGIL
VIRGIN
WIDGET
WIGGED
WIGGLE
WIGGLY
WINGED
WINGER
WINGIT
XINGIN
ZIGGED
ZINGED
ZINGER

•I••G•
DIRIGE
DIRIGO
GINKGO
KIANGS
LIANGS
LINAGE
MIRAGE
SILAGE
VIRAGO
VISAGE

•I•••G
AIDING
AILING
AIMING
AIRBAG
AIRING
BIDING
BIGWIG
BIKING
BITING
CITING
DIALOG
DICING
DIKING
DINING
DIVING
FIFING
FILING
FINING
FIRING
FIXING
FIZGIG
GIBING
GIVING
HIDING
HIEING
HIKING
HIRING
HIVING
JIBING
JIVING
KITBAG
KITING
LIEBIG
LIKING
LIMING
LINING
LIPENG
LITHOG
LIVING
MIKING
MIMING
MINING
MIRING
MIXING
NIXING
OILING
OILRIG
PIKING
PILING
PINING
PIPING
RICING
RIDING
RILING
RIMING
RISING
RIVING
SIDING
SIRING
SITING
SIXING
SIZING
TIDING
TIEING
TILING
TIMING
TIRING
VIKING
VINING
WIGWAG
WILING
WINING
WIPING
WIRING
ZIGZAG

••IG••
ALIGHT
ALIGNS
AMIGAS
AMIGOS
ARIGHT
BEIGES
BLIGHT
BOIGNY
BRIGGS
BRIGHT
BRIGID
CHIGOE
COIGNS
DEIGNS
DWIGHT
EMIGRE
ENIGMA
FEIGNS
FLIGHT
FRIGHT
FRIGID
GEIGER
GRIGRI
HAIGHT
HEIGHT
KNIGHT
NEIGHS
ORIGEN
ORIGIN
PLIGHT
REIGNS
SAIGAS
SAIGON
SLIGHT
SOIGNE
SPIGOT
STIGMA
TAIGAS
THIGHS
TRIGLY
TRIGON
TWIGGY
VEIGHT
VOIGHT
VSIGNS
WEIGHS
WEIGHT
WRIGHT

••I•G•
BEINGS
BOINGO
BRIDGE
BRIGGS
BRINGS
CLINGS
CLINGY
CRINGE
DOINGS
DRINGS
FLINGS
FRIDGE
FRINGE
FRINGY
GOINGS
GRINGO
ICINGS
OLINGO
ORINGS
SLINGS
STINGO
STINGS
STINGY
SWINGS
SWINGY
THINGS
THINGY
TRIAGE
TWIGGY
TWINGE
WRINGS

••I••G
CHIANG
EPILOG
SKIING

•••IG•
ASSIGN
AURIGA
AWEIGH
BENIGN
COSIGN
DESIGN
DIRIGE
DIRIGO
EFFIGY
ELOIGN
ENSIGN
GREIGE
INDIGO
LATIGO
LEHIGH
MALIGN
OBLIGE
ONHIGH
RESIGN
SLEIGH
SPRIGS
UNRIGS

•••I•G
AAHING
ABYING
ACHING
ACTING
ADDING
AGEING
AIDING
AILING
AIMING
AIRING
ARCING
ARMING
ASKING
AWNING
BAAING
BAKING
BALING
BARING
BASING
BATING
BAYING
BBKING
BENING
BERING
BIDING
BIKING
BITING
BLUING
BODING
BOEING
BONING
BOOING
BORING
BOWING
BOXING
BUSING
BUYING
CAGING
CAKING
CANING
CARING
CASING
CAVING
CAWING
CEDING
CITING
CLUING
CODING
COMING
COOING
COPING
CORING
COWING
CRYING
CUBING
CURING
DARING
DATING
DAZING
DEKING
DEWING
DICING
DIKING
DINING
DIVING
DOLING
DOMING
DOPING
DOSING
DOTING
DOZING
DRYING
DUKING
DUPING
DURING
DYEING
EALING
EARING
EASING
EATING
EBBING
EDGING
EGGING
ENDING
EPPING
ERRING
ERVING
EYEING
FACING
FADING
FAKING
FARING
FAXING
FAZING
FEEING
FETING
FIFING
FILING
FINING
FIRING
FIXING
FLYING
FOXING
FRYING
FUMING
FUSING
FUZING
GAGING
GAMING
GAPING
GATING
GAZING
GEEING
GIBING
GIVING
GLUING
GORING
GUYING
GYBING
HALING
HARING
HATING
HAVING
HAWING
HAYING
HAZING
HEWING
HEXING
HIDING
HIEING
HIKING
HIRING
HIVING
HOEING
HOLING
HOMING
HONING
HOPING
HOSING
HYPING
ICHING
IDLING
IMPING
INKING
INNING
IRKING
IRVING
JADING
JAPING
JAWING
JIBING
JIVING
JOKING
JUKING
KEYING
KITING
LACING
LADING
LAMING
LAVING
LAWING
LAYING
LAZING
LIKING
LIMING
LINING
LIVING
LOPING
LOSING
LOVING
LOWING
LUBING
LURING
LUTING
MAKING
MATING
METING
MEWING
MIKING
MIMING
MINING
MIRING
MIXING
MOOING
MOPING
MOVING
MOWING
MUSING
MUTING
NAMING
NIXING
NOSING
NOTING
NUKING
OARING
OFFING
OGLING
OILING
OOHING
OOZING
OPTING
ORBING
OUTING
OWNING
PACING
PAGING
PALING
PARING
PAVING
PAWING
PAYING
PEKING
PIKING
PILING
PINING
PIPING
PLYING
POKING
POLING
PORING
POSING
PRYING
PULING
RACING
RAGING
RAKING
RARING
RASING
RATING
RAVING
RAZING
REDING
RESING
RICING
RIDING
RILING
RIMING
RISING
RIVING
ROBING
ROPING
ROVING
ROWING
RULING
SATING
SAVING
SAWING
SAYING
SEEING
SEWING
SHYING
SIDING
SIRING
SITING
SIXING
SIZING
SKIING
SKYING
SLUING
SOLING
SOWING
SPRING
SPYING
STRING
TAKING
TAMING
TAPING
TARING
TAWING
TAXING
TEEING
TIDING
TIEING
TILING
TIMING
TIRING
TOEING
TONING
TOTING
TOWING
TOYING
TRUING
TRYING
TUBING
TUNING
TURING
TYPING
UPPING
URGING
VEXING
VIKING
VINING
VOTING
VOWING
WADING
WAGING
WAKING
WANING
WARING
WAVING
WAXING
WILING
WINING
WIPING
WIRING
WOOING
WOWING
YAWING
YOKING
ZONING

••••IG
BIGWIG
CATRIG
DANZIG
EARWIG
FIZGIG
GEHRIG
KOENIG
LIEBIG
LUDWIG
OILRIG
WETTIG
ZAFTIG

I•H•••
ICHING
ICHTHY
INHALE
INHALF
INHAND
INHAUL
INHERE
ISHTAR
ITHACA
ITHAKI

I••H••
INCHED
INCHES
INCHON
ISCHIA
ISOHEL
ISTHMI
ITCHED
ITCHES
ITZHAK

I•••H•
ICHTHY
ILESHA

I••••H
IMPISH
INARCH
INCASH
INRUSH
INWITH
IOMOTH
IRTYSH
ISAIAH

•IH•••
BIHARI
JIHADS
MIHRAB
NIHILO

•I•H••
BIGHTS
BISHOP
CIPHER
DIRHAM
DISHED
DISHES
DITHER
EIGHTH
EIGHTS
EIGHTY
EITHER
FICHES
FICHTE
FICHUS
FIGHTS
FISHED
FISHER
FISHES
HIGHER
HIGHIQ
HIGHLY
HIGHUP
HIPHOP
HITHER
KISHKE
LICHEN
LIGHTS
LITHIC
LITHOG
LITHOS
MICHEL
MIGHTY
MISHAP
MISHIT
NICHES
NIGHER
NIGHTS
NIGHTY
NIIHAU
PITHED
RICHEN
RICHER
RICHES
RICHIE
RICHLY
RIGHTO
RIGHTS
RIGHTY
SIGHED
SIGHER
SIGHTS
SIPHON
TIGHTS
TINHAT
TISHRI
TITHED
TITHER
TITHES
VISHNU
WIGHTS
WISHED
WISHER
WISHES
WITHAL
WITHED
WITHER
WITHES
WITHIN
WITHIT
ZITHER

•I••H•
BIRTHS
DINGHY
FIFTHS
FILTHY
FIRTHS
GIRTHS
HIDEHO
KIMCHI
LITCHI
MISCHA
NINTHS
PICCHU
PITCHY
SIXTHS
WIDTHS
WITCHY

•I•••H
EIGHTH
FINISH
HIJRAH
HIRSCH
HITECH
JINNAH
KIBOSH
KIRSCH
KITSCH
LILITH
PISGAH
RIYADH
SIRRAH
SIWASH
WIDISH
WINISH
ZILPAH
ZIZITH

••IH••
NIIHAU

••I•H•
ALIGHT
ARIGHT
BLIGHT
BLITHE
BRIGHT
CHICHA
CHICHI
CLICHE
DWIGHT
ELISHA
FAITHS
FLIGHT
FRIGHT
GEISHA
HAIGHT
HEIGHT
KNIGHT
NEIGHS
PLIGHT
QUICHE
SEICHE
SLIGHT
SLITHY
SMITHS
SMITHY
STITHY
TAICHI
THIGHS
TRICHO
TRISHA
VEIGHT
VOIGHT
WEIGHS
WEIGHT
WRIGHT
WRITHE

••I••H
CHINCH
CLINCH
ELIJAH
FLINCH
FLITCH
GLITCH
GRINCH
PLINTH
SHILOH
SKITCH
SMIRCH
SNITCH
SPILTH
STITCH
SWITCH
TWITCH

•••I•H
AGUISH
ASPISH
AWEIGH
BANISH
BARISH
BLUISH
BOYISH
CALIPH
CERIPH
COYISH
DANISH
DOVISH
DUDISH
ELFISH
ELVISH
ENRICH
EOLITH
FAMISH
FETISH
FINISH
GARISH
GOFISH
GOWITH
IMPISH
INWITH
ISAIAH
JADISH
JEWISH
JOSIAH
JUDITH
JUTISH
LATISH
LAVISH
LEHIGH
LILITH
LOWISH
MARIAH
MARISH
MODISH
MOPISH
MULISH
MUNICH
NEWISH
OAFISH
OFFISH
OGRISH
OLDISH
ONHIGH
OOLITH
ORNITH
OWLISH
PALISH
PARIAH
PARISH
PERISH
POLISH
PUNISH
RADISH
RAKISH
RAVISH
RAWISH
RELISH
RUPIAH
SALISH
SLEIGH
SQUISH
TONISH
UNWISH
UPPISH
UZZIAH
VANISH
WIDISH
WINISH
WRAITH
ZENITH
ZIZITH
ZURICH

I•I•••
IBIBIO
IBIDEM
IBISES
ICICLE
ICIEST
ICINGS
IDIOCY
IDIOMS
IDIOTS
INIONS
INITIO
IRIDES
IRIDIC
IRISES
IRISIN

I••I••
ICHING
ICKIER
IDLING
IDOIDO
IFFIER
IGNITE
ILLINI
ILOILO
IMBIBE
IMFINE
IMPING
IMPISH
INCISE
INCITE
INDIAN
INDICT
INDIES
INDIGO
INDIRA
INDITE
INDIUM
INFIRM
INKIER
INKIND
INKING
INLINE
INNING
INSIDE
INSIST
INSITU
INTIMA
INTIME
INTINE
INUITS
INVITE
INVIVO
INWITH
IODIDE

IODINE
IODISE
IODIZE
IOLITE
IONIAN
IONICS
IONISE
IONIUM
IONIZE
IRKING
IRVINE
IRVING
ISAIAH

I•••I•
IAMBIC
IATRIC
IBERIA
IBIBIO
ICARIA
ICEDIN
ICESIN
ICONIC
IGETIT
IGOTIT
ILORIN
IMPAIR
INAFIX
INDRIS
INGRID
INITIO
INLAID
INSTIL
INTUIT
INVAIN
IRANIS
IRAQIS
IRENIC
IRIDIC
IRISIN
IRONIC
ISCHIA
ISELIN
ISTRIA
ITALIA
ITALIC

I••••I
ILLINI
ISTHMI
ITHAKI
ITURBI

•II•••
NIIHAU

•I•I••
AIDING
AIKIDO
AILING
AIMING
AIRIER
AIRILY
AIRING
BIDING
BIKILA
BIKING
BIKINI
BIMINI
BITING
CILIUM
CITIES
CITIFY
CITING
CITIUS
CIVICS
DICIER
DICING
DIDIES
DIDION
DIGITS
DIKING
DIMITY
DINING
DIRIGE
DIRIGO
DIVIDE
DIVINE
DIVING
DIVINO
DIXITS
FIFING
FIJIAN
FILIAL
FILING
FILIUS
FINIAL
FINING
FINISH
FINITE
FINITO
FIRING
FIXING
FIXITY
GIBILL
GIBING
GIVING
HIDING
HIEING
HIKING
HIRING
HIVING
JIBING
JIMINY
JIVIER
JIVING
KIBITZ
KILIMS
KITING
LIAISE
LIBIDO
LIKING
LILIES
LILITH
LIMIER
LIMING
LIMITS
LINIER
LINING
LIPIDE
LIPIDS
LIVING
MIDIAN
MIKING
MIKITA
MILIEU
MIMICS
MIMING
MINIFY
MINIMA
MINIMS
MINING
MINION
MINIUM
MIRIAM
MIRIER
MIRING
MIXING
NIDIFY
NIHILO
NIKITA
NIMINY
NIMITZ
NIXIES
NIXING
OILIER
OILILY
OILING
PIKING
PILING
PIMINY
PINIER
PINING
PINION
PINITE
PIPIER
PIPING
PIPITS
PITIED
PITIER
PITIES
PIXIES
QIVIUT
RICING
RIDING
RIFIFI
RILING
RIMIER
RIMING
RIMINI
RISING
RIVING
SICILY
SIDING
SIGILS
SILICA
SIMIAN
SIMILE
SINISE
SIRICA
SIRING
SIRIUS
SITING
SITINS
SIXING
SIZING
TIBIAE
TIBIAL
TIBIAS
TIDIED
TIDIER
TIDIES
TIDILY
TIDING
TIEING
TIEINS
TILING
TIMING
TINIER
TINILY
TIPINS
TIRING
TITIAN
VIGILS
VIKING
VILIFY
VINIER
VINIFY
VINING
VIRILE
VISINE
VISION
VISITS
VIVIAN
VIVIEN
VIVIFY
VIZIER
WIDISH
WILIER
WILILY
WILING
WINIER
WINING
WINISH
WIPING
WIRIER
WIRILY
WIRING
ZIZITH

•I••I•
BIBLIO
BIDSIN
BIGGIE
BIGLIE
BIGWIG
BILLIE
BIOBIO
BIONIC
BIOTIC
BIOTIN
BIRDIE
BIRGIT
CITRIC
DIESIS
DIGSIN
DIKDIK
DIMWIT
DINEIN
DIOXIN
DISTIL
DIVEIN
FIBRIL
FIBRIN
FILLIN
FILLIP
FINNIC
FIRKIN
FISTIC
FITSIN
FIZGIG
GILLIE
GILLIS
GIVEIN
HIGHIQ
HINGIS
HIPPIE
HISPID
HITSIT
JIMMIE
KICKIN
KIDDIE
KIDVID
KILTIE
LIBRIS
LIEBIG
LIESIN
LIGNIN
LILLIE
LIMPID
LIPOID
LIQUID
LITHIC
LIVEIN
LIZZIE
MIAMIA
MIDAIR
MIDRIB
MILLIE
MILTIE
MINNIE
MINUIT
MIOSIS
MISDID
MISFIT
MISHIT
MISSIS
NIACIN
NITRIC
NITWIT
OILRIG
PICNIC
PIDGIN
PIETIN
PIGGIE
PILEIN
PINKIE
PINXIT
PINYIN
PIPKIN
PIPPIN
PIRRIP
PISTIL
RICHIE
RIZZIO
SIGNIN
SIKKIM
SINGIN
SINKIN
SISKIN
SITSIN
TIDBIT
TIEDIN
TIEPIN
TIESIN
TIFFIN
TIGRIS
TILLIE
TILLIS
TILSIT
TIPSIN
TITBIT
VICTIM
VICTIS
VINCIT
VINNIE
VIOLIN
VIRGIL
VIRGIN
VISCID
VITRIC
WILLIE
WILLIS
WINGIT
WINKIE
WINNIE
WINWIN
WITHIN
WITHIT
XINGIN
ZINNIA

•I•••I
BIHARI
BIKINI
BILOXI
BIMINI
BIONDI
CIARDI
CISKEI
HIDEKI
KIGALI
KIMCHI
KINSKI
LIBERI
LITCHI
MIDORI
NIELLI
NIKKEI
NILGAI
PILOTI
RIENZI
RIFIFI
RIMINI
SILENI
TISHRI
TIVOLI
VIDERI

••II••
SHIISM
SHIITE
SKIING

••I•I•
ACIDIC
ALIBIS
ALICIA
BLINIS
BRIGID
CHIPIN
CHITIN
CLINIC
CRISIS
CRITIC
EDITIO
ELICIT
ELIXIR
EMILIA
EMILIO
EXILIC
FRIGID
GAIJIN
IBIBIO
INITIO
IRIDIC
IRISIN
JOININ
LAIDIN
LAINIE
MAILIN
MAISIE
NAILIN
OLIVIA
ORIBIS
ORIGIN
OSIRIS
OTITIC
OTITIS
OXIDIC
PAIDIN
PHILIP
QUITIT
RAISIN
REININ
SCIFIS
SCIPIO
SKIPIT
SLIDIN
SLIPIN
SMILIN
SPIRIT
STIRIN
STIVIC
TRICIA
TRIFID
TRIVIA
TRIXIE
TWILIT
UNIFIC

••I••I
CHICHI
CHILLI
DMITRI
GRIGRI
MAITAI
PRIORI
TAICHI
TAIPEI

•••II•
ACTIII

•••I•I
ACTIII
ASSISI
BIKINI
BIMINI
DOMINI
GEMINI
ILLINI
KWEISI
LATINI
MEDICI
RAPINI
RIFIFI
RIMINI
ROTINI
SENITI
SOLIDI
SURIMI
TAHINI
TAHITI
WAPITI
YOGINI

••••II
ACTIII
ETALII
HAWAII
SAVAII

IJ••••
IJSSEL

I•J•••
INJECT
INJEST
INJOKE
INJURE
INJURY

I••J••
INAJAM
INKJET

I••••J
INTERJ

•IJ•••
BIJOUX
FIJIAN
GIJOES
HIJACK
HIJRAH

•I•J••
NINJAS
RIOJAS

••IJ••
ELIJAH
FRIJOL
GAIJIN
TRIJET

I•K•••
ICKIER
INKERS
INKIER
INKIND
INKING
INKJET
INKLES
IRKING

I•••K•
INJOKE
INTAKE
INVOKE
ITHAKI

I••••K
INBULK
INLUCK
ITZHAK

•IK•••
AIKIDO
BIKERS
BIKILA
BIKING
BIKINI
DIKDIK
DIKING
DIKTAT
HIKERS
HIKEUP
HIKING
KIKUYU
LIKELY
LIKENS
LIKING
MIKADO
MIKING
MIKITA
NIKITA
NIKKEI
NIKOLA
PIKAKE
PIKERS
PIKING
SIKKIM
VIKING

•I•K••
BICKER
BILKED
CISKEI
DICKER
DICKEY
DINKEY
DISKED
FICKLE
FINKED
FIRKIN
GINKGO
HICKEY
HICKOK
JINKED
KICKED
KICKER
KICKIN
KICKUP
KINKED
KITKAT
LICKED
LINKED
LINKER
LINKUP
MICKEY
MILKED
MILKER
MINKES
NICKED
NICKEL
NICKER
NIKKEI
OINKED
PICKAT
PICKAX
PICKED
PICKER
PICKET
PICKLE
PICKON
PICKUP
PINKED
PINKEN
PINKER
PINKIE
PIPKIN
RICKED
RICKEY
RIPKEN
RISKED
RISKER
SICKEN
SICKER
SICKLE
SICKLY
SIKKIM
SILKED
SILKEN
SINKER
SINKIN
SISKEL
SISKIN
TICKED
TICKER
TICKET
TICKLE
TICKLY
TINKER
TINKLE
TINKLY
WICKED
WICKER
WICKET
WILKES
WINKAT
WINKED
WINKER
WINKIE
WINKLE

•I••K•
HIDEKI
KINSKI
KIOSKS
KISHKE
MIWOKS
PIKAKE
RIMSKY
TILAKS

•I•••K
DIKDIK
HICKOK
HIJACK
PINOAK

••IK••
BAIKAL
CRIKEY
DAIKON
DUIKER
HAIKUS
SHIKAR
SPIKED
SPIKER
SPIKES
TRIKES

••I•K•
BLINKS
BRICKS
BRICKY
BRINKS
CHICKS
CHINKS
CHINKY
CLICKS
CLINKS
CRICKS
DRINKS
FLICKA
FLICKS
FRISKS
FRISKY
GLINKA
GRIMKE
KNICKS
PLINKS
PRICKS
PRINKS
QUIRKS
QUIRKY
REINKS
SHIRKS
SKINKS
SLICKS
SLINKS
SLINKY
SMIRKS
SMIRKY
SNICKS
SPINKS
STICKS
STICKY
STINKS
STINKY
STIRKS
THICKE
THINKS
TRICKS
TRICKY
UMIAKS
WHISKS
WHISKY
YOICKS

••I••K
SPIVAK

•••IK•
ANNIKA
AXLIKE
BATIKS
BELIKE
MARIKO
OXLIKE
PELIKE
SHEIKS
SHRIKE
STRIKE
TROIKA
UNLIKE
UPDIKE

•••I•K
ATRISK
DRYINK
KODIAK
NATICK
REDINK
REMICK
SCHICK
SHRIEK
SHRINK
SHTICK
STRICK
UNKINK
UNLINK
UPLINK
UPTICK
YORICK

••••IK
DIKDIK
HENRIK
MUZHIK
NARVIK
NUDNIK
RESNIK
SLOVIK
SUSLIK
TUGRIK
ZADDIK

IL••••
ILEANA
ILESHA
ILEXES
ILLEST
ILLFED
ILLINI
ILLMET
ILLSAY
ILLUME
ILLUSE
ILOILO
ILORIN

I•L•••
IDLERS
IDLEST
IDLING
IGLOOS
ILLEST
ILLFED
ILLINI
ILLMET
ILLSAY
ILLUME
ILLUSE
INLAID
INLAND
INLAWS
INLAYS
INLETS
INLINE
INLOVE
INLUCK
IOLITE
IRLENE
ISLAND
ISLETS

I••L••
IDYLLS
IMELDA
INFLOW
INFLUX
INGLES
INKLES
INPLAY
ISELIN
ISOLDE
ISTLES
ITALIA
ITALIC

I•••L•
ICICLE
IDEALS
IDYLLS
ILOILO
IMPALA
IMPALE
IMPELS
INBULK
INCULT
INFOLD
INFULL
INHALE
INHALF
INSOLE
INSULT
ISEULT
ITSELF

I••••L
IJSSEL
INFULL
INHAUL
INSTAL
INSTIL
IREFUL
IRREAL
ISABEL
ISOHEL
ISRAEL
IZABAL

•IL•••
AILEEN
AILERS
AILING
BILBAO
BILGES
BILKED
BILLED
BILLET
BILLIE
BILLON
BILLOW
BILOXI
CILIUM
DILATE
DILLER
DILLON
DILSEY
DILUTE
EILEEN
FILENE
FILERS
FILETS
FILIAL
FILING
FILIUS
FILLED
FILLER
FILLES
FILLET
FILLIN
FILLIP
FILLUP
FILMED
FILOSE
FILTER
FILTHY
GILDED
GILDER
GILEAD
GILGUY
GILLED
GILLIE
GILLIS
HILARY
HILLED
HILLEL
HILLER
HILTON
JILTED
KILIMS
KILLED
KILLER
KILMER
KILNED
KILROY
KILTED
KILTER
KILTIE
LILACS
LILIES
LILITH
LILLIE
LILTED
MILADY
MILANO
MILDER
MILDEW
MILDLY
MILERS
MILIEU
MILKED
MILKER
MILLAY
MILLED
MILLER
MILLET
MILLIE
MILNER
MILORD
MILOSZ
MILPAS
MILSAP
MILTIE
MILTON
NILGAI
OILCAN
OILERS
OILIER
OILILY
OILING
OILMAN
OILMEN
OILPAN
OILRIG
PILAFS
PILATE
PILEIN
PILEON
PILEUM
PILEUP
PILEUS
PILFER
PILING
PILLAR
PILLED
PILLOW
PILOSE
PILOTI
PILOTS
RILEUP
RILING
RILLES
RILLET
SILAGE
SILENI
SILENT
SILICA
SILKED
SILKEN
SILOAM
SILOED
SILONE
SILTED
SILVAS
SILVER
TILAKS
TILDEN
TILDES
TILERS
TILING
TILLED
TILLER
TILLIE
TILLIS
TILSIT
TILTED
TILTER
VILELY
VILEST
VILIFY
VILLAS
VILLON
VILLUS
WILBUR
WILCOX
WILDER
WILDLY
WILFUL
WILIER
WILILY
WILING
WILKES
WILLED
WILLEM
WILLET
WILLIE
WILLIS
WILLOW
WILSON
WILTED
WILTON
ZILPAH

•I•L••
AIELLO
AISLES
BIBLES
BIBLIO
BIGLIE
BILLED
BILLET
BILLIE
BILLON
BILLOW
BIRLED
DIALED
DIALER
DIALOG
DIALUP
DIGLOT
DILLER
DILLON
FIELDS
FILLED
FILLER
FILLES
FILLET
FILLIN
FILLIP
FILLUP
GIBLET
GILLED
GILLIE
GILLIS
GIMLET
HILLED
HILLEL
HILLER
KILLED
KILLER
KISLEV
LIELOW
LILLIE
LISLES
MIDLER
MILLAY
MILLED
MILLER
MILLET
MILLIE
MISLAY
MISLED
NIELLI
NIELLO
PIGLET
PILLAR
PILLED
PILLOW
PIOLET
RIALTO
RIDLEY
RIFLED
RIFLER
RIFLES
RILLES
RILLET
RIPLEY
SIDLED
SIDLES
SISLER
SISLEY
TIGLON
TILLED
TILLER
TILLIE
TILLIS
TITLED
TITLES
VILLAS
VILLON
VILLUS
VIOLAS
VIOLET
VIOLIN
WIELDS
WIGLET
WILLED
WILLEM
WILLET
WILLIE
WILLIS
WILLOW
YIELDS
ZIPLOC

•I••L•
AIELLO
AIRILY
BIDDLE
BIFOLD
BIKILA
BITOLA
CIBOLA
CICELY
CIRCLE
DIABLO
DIBBLE
DIDDLE
DIDDLY
DIMPLE
DIMPLY
DINGLE
DIPOLE
DIRELY
EIDOLA
FIBULA
FICKLE
FIDDLE
FINALE
FINALS
FINELY
FIPPLE
FIRMLY
FIZZLE
GIBILL
GIGGLE
GIGGLY
GIGOLO
GIMELS
GIRDLE
HIGGLE
HIGHLY
JIGGLE
JIGGLY
JINGLE
JINGLY
KIBBLE
KIGALI
KINDLE
KINDLY
KINGLY
KIRTLE
LIABLE
LIBELS
LIEFLY
LIGULA
LIKELY
LIMPLY
LIONLY
LITTLE
LIVELY
MIDDLE
MIGGLE
MILDLY
MINGLE
MIZZLE

NIBBLE
NICELY
NICOLA
NICOLE
NICOLO
NIELLI
NIELLO
NIGGLE
NIHILO
NIKOLA
NIMBLE
NIMBLY
OILILY
PICKLE
PICULS
PIFFLE
PINOLE
PINTLE
PIPALS
PIXELS
RIBALD
RICHLY
RIDDLE
RIFELY
RIFFLE
RIMPLE
RIPELY
RIPPLE
RIPPLY
RIVALS
RIYALS
SIBYLS
SICILY
SICKLE
SICKLY
SIECLE
SIGILS
SIMILE
SIMPLE
SIMPLY
SINGLE
SINGLY
SISALS
SIZZLE
TICALS
TICKLE
TICKLY
TIDDLY
TIDILY
TIMELY
TINGLE
TINGLY
TINILY
TINKLE
TINKLY
TIPPLE
TITTLE
TIVOLI
VIABLE
VIABLY
VIGILS
VILELY
VINYLS
VIRILE
VITALE
VITALS
VIZSLA
WIDELY
WIFELY
WIGGLE
WIGGLY
WILDLY
WILILY
WIMBLE
WIMPLE
WINKLE
WIRILY
WISELY

•I•••L

AIDFUL
AIMFUL
DIESEL
DIRNDL
DISMAL
DISPEL
DISTAL
DISTIL
EIFFEL
FIBRIL
FILIAL
FINIAL
FISCAL
FITFUL
GIBILL
GIMBAL
GIMBEL
HIATAL
HIEMAL
HILLEL
LINEAL
LINTEL
LIONEL
LISTEL
MICHEL
MIGUEL
MISSAL
MITRAL
NICKEL
PINEAL
PISTIL
PISTOL
RITUAL
SIEGEL
SIGNAL
SIMBEL
SIMNEL
SINFUL
SISKEL
TIBIAL
TIMBAL
TINCAL
TINSEL
VIRGIL
VISUAL
WIESEL
WILFUL
WITHAL

••IL••

AXILLA
BAILED
BAILEE
BAILER
BAILEY
BAILOR
BOILED
BOILER
BRILLO
BRILLS
BUILDS
CEILED
CHILDE
CHILDS
CHILLI
CHILLS
CHILLY
CHILOE
COILED
COILUP
DAILEY
DRILLS
EDILES
EMILIA
EMILIO
EPILOG
EVILER
EVILLY
EXILED
EXILES
EXILIC
FAILED
FAILLE
FOILED
FRILLS
FRILLY
GRILLE
GRILLS
GRILSE
GUILDS
GUILES
GUILTY
HAILED
HAILEY
JAILED
JAILER
KAILUA
MAILED
MAILER
MAILES
MAILIN
MOILED
MOILER
NAILED
NAILER
NAILIN
PAILOU
PHILAE
PHILBY
PHILIP
PHILLY
PHILOL
PHILOS
POILUS
QUILLS
QUILTS
RAILAT
RAILED
RAILER
REILLY
ROILED
SAILED
SAILOR
SHILLS
SHILLY
SHILOH
SKILLS
SMILAX
SMILED
SMILER
SMILES
SMILEY
SMILIN
SOILED
SPILES
SPILLS
SPILTH
STILES
STILLS
STILLY
STILTS
SWILLS
TAILED
TAILLE
TAILOR
TBILLS
THILLS
TOILED
TOILER
TOILES
TOILET
TRILBY
TRILLS
TUILLE
TWILIT
TWILLS
VEILED
VOILES
WAILED
WAILER
WHILED
WHILES
WHILOM
WHILST
XFILES

••I•L•

ACIDLY
AFIELD
ALIBLE
ARIDLY
AVIDLY
AXILLA
BGIRLS
BRIDLE
BRILLO
BRILLS
CHICLE
CHICLY
CHILLI
CHILLS
CHILLY
DRILLS
EDIBLE
ENISLE
EVILLY
FAILLE
FAIRLY
FOIBLE
FRILLS
FRILLY
GAINLY
GLIBLY
GRILLE
GRILLS
GRIMLY
GRISLY
ICICLE
MAINLY
ORIELS
ORIOLE
PHIALS
PHILLY
PRIMLY
QUILLS
REILLY
SHIELD
SHILLS
SHILLY
SKILLS
SKIRLS
SLIMLY
SPIELS
SPILLS
STIFLE
STILLS
STILLY
SWILLS
SWIRLS
SWIRLY
TAILLE
TBILLS
THILLS
THINLY
TRIALS
TRIFLE
TRIGLY
TRILLS
TRIMLY
TRIPLE
TRIPLY
TUILLE
TWILLS
TWIRLS
URIALS
VAINLY
WHIRLS
WHIRLY

••I••L

AMIDOL
ANIMAL
APICAL
BAIKAL
BRIDAL
CHISEL
DRIVEL
EPICAL
EPINAL
FAISAL
FRIJOL
GEISEL
KEITEL
PHILOL
PRIMAL
RHINAL
SEIDEL
SNIVEL
SPINAL
SPINEL
SPIRAL
STIPEL
SWIVEL
TRIBAL
TRINAL
UNITAL
VEINAL

•••IL•

AEDILE
AERILY
AIRILY
ANVILS
AQUILA
ARTILY
ATTILA
ATWILL
AUDILE
AVAILS
AWHILE
BIKILA
BODILY
BRAILA
BRAILS
BROILS
BUSILY
CAGILY
CAVILS
CECILE
CECILY
COSILY
COZILY
CYBILL
DEFILE
DESILU
DEVILS
DEWILY
DOCILE
DOZILY
DRAILS
EASILY
EDGILY
EERILY
EMAILS
ENSILE
ETOILE
FACILE
FAMILY
FLAILS
FOXILY
FUSILS
FUTILE
GAMILY
GIBILL
GORILY
GOWILD
GRAILS
HABILE
HAMILL
HAZILY
HOLILY
HOMILY
ILOILO
JOKILY
KURILE
LABILE
LACILY
LAZILY
LOGILY
MANILA
MARILU
MAZILY
MEGILP
MOBILE
MOTILE
NIHILO
NOSILY
NUBILE
OILILY
ONEILL
ONFILE
OOZILY
PERILS
POKILY
PUNILY
PUPILS
QUAILS
RACILY
REFILE
REFILL
REOILS
RESILE
RETILE
REVILE
ROSILY
RUTILE
SEDILE
SEXILY
SHEILA
SHRILL
SICILY
SIGILS
SIMILE
SNAILS
SPOILS
SPOILT
SQUILL
TAMILS
THRILL
TIDILY
TINILY
TRAILS
UGLILY
UNOILY
UNPILE
UNWILY
UPHILL
VERILY
VIGILS
VIRILE
WARILY
WAVILY
WAXILY
WILILY
WIRILY
ZANILY
ZORILS

•••I•L

AERIAL
ASWIRL
ATRIAL
ATWILL
AUDIAL
AWHIRL
BELIAL
CURIAL
CYBILL
DANIEL
DENIAL
ESPIAL
FACIAL
FERIAL
FILIAL
FINIAL
GAVIAL
GENIAL
GIBILL
HAMILL
JOVIAL
LABIAL
MARIEL
MEDIAL
MENIAL
MURIEL
MUSIAL
MYGIRL
NARIAL
ONEILL
RACIAL
RADIAL
REDIAL
REFILL
RETIAL
SERIAL
SHRILL
SOCIAL
SQUILL
THRILL
TIBIAL
UNCIAL
UPHILL
VENIAL

••••IL

ASSAIL
BEWAIL
BRAZIL
BULBIL
DEASIL
DENTIL
DERAIL
DETAIL
DISTIL
ENTAIL
EURAIL
FIBRIL
FOSSIL
FULFIL
GERBIL
INSTIL
KAHLIL
LENTIL
MELVIL
NYQUIL
ORCHIL
OXTAIL
PENCIL
PISTIL
REBOIL
RECOIL
REMAIL
RENAIL
RETAIL
SOLEIL
TONSIL
UNCOIL
UNVEIL
URACIL
USMAIL
VIRGIL
WEEVIL

IM••••

IMAGED
IMAGER
IMAGES
IMAMAN
IMARET
IMBIBE
IMBRUE
IMBUED
IMBUES
IMELDA
IMFINE
IMMUNE
IMMUNO
IMMURE
IMOGEN
IMPACT
IMPAIR
IMPALA
IMPALE
IMPART
IMPEDE
IMPELS
IMPEND
IMPERF
IMPING
IMPISH
IMPORT
IMPOSE
IMPOST
IMPROV
IMPUGN
IMPURE
IMPUTE

I•M•••

IAMBIC
IMMUNE
IMMUNO
IMMURE
INMATE
INMOST
IOMOTH
ISMENE

I••M••

ICEMAN
ICEMEN
ILLMET
IMAMAN
INGMAR
ISOMER

I•••M•

IBEAMS
IDIOMS
ILLUME
INCOME
INFAMY
INTIMA
INTIME
ISTHMI

I••••M

IBIDEM
INAJAM
INDIUM
INFIRM
INFORM
INGRAM
INSEAM
IONIUM

•IM•••

AIMFOR
AIMFUL
AIMING
AIMSAT
AIMSTO
BIMINI
DIMITY
DIMMED
DIMMER
DIMOUT
DIMPLE
DIMPLY
DIMSUM
DIMWIT
GIMBAL
GIMBEL
GIMELS
GIMLET
GIMMES
JIMINY
JIMMIE
JIMSON
KIMCHI
KIMONO
LIMBED
LIMBER
LIMBOS
LIMBUS
LIMENS
LIMEYS
LIMIER
LIMING
LIMITS
LIMNED
LIMNER
LIMPED
LIMPER
LIMPET
LIMPID
LIMPLY
MIMEOS
MIMERS
MIMICS
MIMING
MIMOSA
NIMBLE
NIMBLY
NIMBUS
NIMINY
NIMITZ
NIMROD
PIMINY
RIMIER
RIMING
RIMINI
RIMMED
RIMOSE
RIMPLE
RIMSKY
SIMBEL
SIMEON
SIMIAN
SIMILE
SIMMER
SIMNEL
SIMONE
SIMONY
SIMPER
SIMPLE
SIMPLY
TIMBAL
TIMBER
TIMBRE
TIMELY
TIMERS
TIMING
WIMBLE
WIMPLE
WIMSEY
XIMENA
ZIMMER

•I•M••

AIRMAN
AIRMEN
BIGMAC
BIOMES
BITMAP
DIMMED
DIMMER
DISMAL
DISMAY
DISMES
FILMED
FIRMAN
FIRMED
FIRMER
FIRMLY
FIRMUP
GIMMES
GIZMOS
HIEMAL
HITMAN
HITMEN
JIMMIE
KIDMAN
KILMER
KIRMAN
KISMET
LITMUS
MIAMIA
MICMAC
NIAMEY
OILMAN
OILMEN
PIEMAN
PIEMEN
PITMAN
PITMEN
RIMMED
SIGMAS
SIMMER
TINMAN
TINMEN
XIAMEN
ZIMMER

•I••M•

BIGAMY
BIREME
CINEMA
JICAMA
KILIMS
KINEMA
KINGME
MIASMA
MINIMA
MINIMS

•I•••M

AIRARM
AIRDAM
CILIUM
CIRCUM
DIADEM
DIATOM
DICTUM
DIGRAM
DIMSUM
DIRHAM
DISARM
FIVEAM
FIVEPM
MINIUM
MIRIAM
NINEAM
NINEPM
PILEUM
SIKKIM
SILOAM
SITCOM
VIACOM
VICTIM
WIGWAM
WILLEM
WINDOM
WISDOM

••IM••

AHIMSA
AKIMBO
ANIMAL
ANIMAS
ANIMES
ANIMUS
ASIMOV
BLIMEY
BLIMPS
CAIMAN
CHIMED
CHIMES
CHIMPS
CLIMAX
CLIMBS
CLIMES
CRIMEA
CRIMES
CRIMPS
CRIMPY
DAIMON
DAIMYO
DEIMOS
FBIMAN
FBIMEN
FLIMSY
GRIMED
GRIMES
GRIMKE
GRIMLY
GUIMPE
PRIMAL
PRIMED
PRIMER
PRIMES
PRIMLY
PRIMOS
PRIMPS
PRIMUM
PRIMUS
SHIMMY
SHIMON
SKIMPS
SKIMPY
SLIMED
SLIMES
SLIMLY
SLIMSY
STIMPY
TRIMLY
WEIMAR
WHIMSY

••I•M•

AXIOMS
ENIGMA
IDIOMS
ODIUMS
PRISMS
SEISMO
SEISMS
SHIMMY
STIGMA

••I••M

FAIYUM
IBIDEM
PRIMUM
SHIISM
WHILOM

•••IM•

ALTIMA
BEDIMS
CLAIMS
COLIMA
DENIMS
ESKIMO
FATIMA
HAKIMS
INTIMA
INTIME
KILIMS
MAXIMA
MAXIMS
MINIMA
MINIMS
ONTIME
OPTIMA
REAIMS
REGIME
RETIME
SCRIMP
SCRIMS
SHRIMP
SURIMI
ULTIMA
ULTIMO
UPTIME
YAKIMA

•••I•M

ACTIUM
AFFIRM
AGEISM
ALLIUM
ATRIUM
BARIUM
CERIUM
CESIUM
CHRISM
CILIUM
CONIUM
CORIUM
CUBISM
CURIUM
EGOISM
ERBIUM
FOLIUM
HELIUM
HOLISM
INDIUM
INFIRM
IONIUM
LATIUM
MAOISM
MEDIUM
MINIUM
MIRIAM
MONISM
OMNIUM
OSMIUM
OSTIUM
PODIUM
PURISM
RADIUM
SAMIAM
SCHISM
SHIISM
SODIUM
SQUIRM
SUFISM
TAOISM
TEDIUM
THEISM
TRUISM
VALIUM
VERISM
YOGISM

••••IM

ANTRIM
ELOHIM
LCHAIM
MUSLIM
PASSIM
PRELIM
RETRIM
SIKKIM
VICTIM

IN••••

INAFIX
INAFOG
INAJAM
INANER
INAPET
INARCH
INAROW
INARUT
INAWAY
INBORN
INBRED
INBULK
INCANS
INCASE
INCASH
INCEPT
INCHED
INCHES
INCHON
INCISE
INCITE
INCOME
INCULT
INCURS
INCUSE
INDABA
INDEBT
INDEED
INDENE
INDENT
INDIAN
INDICT
INDIES
INDIGO
INDIRA
INDITE
INDIUM
INDOOR
INDORE
INDRIS
INDUCE
INDUCT
INESSE
INFACT
INFAMY
INFANT
INFECT
INFERS
INFEST
INFIRM
INFLOW
INFLUX
INFOLD
INFORM
INFULL
INFUSE
INGEAR
INGEST
INGLES
INGMAR
INGOTS
INGRAM
INGRES
INGRID
INHALE
INHALF
INHAND
INHAUL
INHERE
INIONS
INITIO
INJECT
INJEST
INJOKE
INJURE
INJURY
INKERS
INKIER
INKIND
INKING
INKJET
INKLES
INLAID
INLAND
INLAWS
INLAYS
INLETS
INLINE
INLOVE
INLUCK
INMATE
INMOST
INNAGE
INNATE
INNEED
INNESS
INNING
INOUYE
INPART
INPLAY
INPORT
INPOUR
INPUTS
INROAD
INRUSH
INSANE
INSEAM
INSECT
INSERT
INSETS
INSIDE
INSIST
INSITU
INSOLE
INSPAN
INSTAL
INSTAR
INSTEP
INSTIL
INSULT
INSURE
INSYNC
INTACT
INTAKE
INTEND
INTENS
INTENT
INTERJ
INTERN
INTIMA
INTIME
INTINE
INTONE
INTOTO
INTOWN
INTROS
INTUIT
INTUNE
INTURN
INUITS
INURED
INURES
INVADE
INVAIN
INVENT
INVERT
INVEST
INVITE
INVIVO
INVOKE
INWARD
INWITH

I•N•••

IGNACE
IGNATZ
IGNITE
IGNORE
INNAGE
INNATE
INNEED
INNESS
INNING
IONIAN
IONICS
IONISE
IONIUM
IONIZE

I••N••

ICINGS
ICONIC
INANER
IRANIS
IRENES
IRENIC
IRONED
IRONER
IRONIC
IRONON

I•••N•

ICHING
IDLING
IGUANA
ILEANA
ILLINI
IMFINE
IMMUNE
IMMUNO
IMPEND
IMPING
INCANS
INDENE
INDENT
INFANT
INHAND
INIONS
INKIND
INKING
INLAND
INLINE
INNING
INSANE
INSYNC
INTEND
INTENS
INTENT
INTINE
INTONE
INTUNE
INVENT
IODINE
IOWANS
IRKING
IRLENE
IRVINE
IRVING
ISLAND
ISMENE

I••••N

IBADAN
ICEDIN
ICEMAN
ICEMEN
ICESIN

ILORIN
IMAMAN
IMOGEN
IMPUGN
INBORN
INCHON
INDIAN
INSPAN
INTERN
INTOWN
INTURN
INVAIN
IONIAN
IRISIN
IRONON
ISELIN
ISOGON

•IN•••

BINARY
BINATE
BINDER
BINDUP
BINGED
BINGES
BINNED
CINDER
CINEMA
CINQUE
DINARS
DINEIN
DINEON
DINERO
DINERS
DINGED
DINGHY
DINGLE
DINGUS
DINING
DINKEY
DINNED
DINNER
DINTED
FINALE
FINALS
FINDER
FINELY
FINERY
FINEST
FINGER
FINIAL
FINING
FINISH
FINITE
FINITO
FINKED
FINNAN
FINNED
FINNEY
FINNIC
GINGER
GINKGO
GINNED
HINCTY
HINDER
HINDUS
HINGED
HINGES
HINGIS
HINTAT
HINTED
HINTER
HINTON
JINGLE
JINGLY
JINKED
JINNAH
JINXED
JINXES
KINDER
KINDLE
KINDLY
KINDOF
KINEMA
KINGED
KINGLY
KINGME
KINKED
KINSEY
KINSKI
LINAGE
LINDEN
LINEAL
LINEAR
LINENS
LINENY
LINERS
LINEUP
LINGER
LINGUA
LINIER
LINING
LINKED
LINKER
LINKUP
LINNET
LINNEY
LINSEY
LINTEL
LINTER
MINCED
MINCER
MINCES
MINDED
MINDER
MINERS
MINGLE
MINIFY
MINIMA
MINIMS
MINING
MINION
MINIUM
MINKES
MINNIE
MINNOW
MINOAN
MINORS
MINTED
MINTER
MINUET
MINUIT
MINUTE
MINXES
MINYAN
NINEAM
NINEPM
NINERS
NINETY
NINGBO
NINJAS
NINTHS
OINKED
PINATA
PINCER
PINDAR
PINDUS
PINEAL
PINERO
PINERY
PINGED
PINIER
PINING
PINION
PINITE
PINKED
PINKEN
PINKER
PINKIE
PINNAE
PINNAS
PINNED
PINNER
PINOAK
PINOLE
PINONS
PINOTS
PINSON
PINTER
PINTLE
PINTOS
PINUPS
PINXIT
PINYIN
PINYON
PINZON
QINTAR
RINGED
RINGER
RINGUP
RINSED
RINSES
SINBAD
SINEAD
SINEWS
SINEWY
SINFUL
SINGED
SINGER
SINGES
SINGIN
SINGLE
SINGLY
SINGTO
SINISE
SINKER
SINKIN
SINNED
SINNER
SINTAX
SINTER
TINCAL
TINCAN
TINCTS
TINDER
TINEAR
TINGED
TINGES
TINGLE
TINGLY
TINGOD
TINHAT
TINIER
TINILY
TINKER
TINKLE
TINKLY
TINMAN
TINMEN
TINNED
TINNER
TINPAN
TINPOT
TINSEL
TINTED
TINTER
UINTAS
VINCES
VINCIT
VINERY
VINIER
VINIFY
VINING
VINNIE
VINOUS
VINTON
VINYLS
WINCED
WINCER
WINCES
WINDED
WINDER
WINDEX
WINDOM
WINDOW
WINDUP
WINERY
WINGED
WINGER
WINGIT
WINIER
WINING
WINISH
WINKAT
WINKED
WINKER
WINKIE
WINKLE
WINNER
WINNIE
WINNOW
WINONA
WINOUT
WINSOR
WINTER
WINTRY
WINWIN
WINZES
XINGIN
ZINGED
ZINGER
ZINNIA

•I•N••

BIANCA
BINNED
BIONDI
BIONIC
BIRNEY
DIANNE
DINNED
DINNER
DIONEB
DIONNE
DIRNDL
DISNEY
EISNER
FIANCE
FIENDS
FINNAN
FINNED
FINNEY
FINNIC
GIANTS
GINNED
GIRNED
JINNAH
JITNEY
KIANGS
KIDNAP
KIDNEY
KILNED
LIANAS
LIANES
LIANGS
LIENEE
LIGNIN
LIMNED
LIMNER
LINNET
LINNEY
LIONEL
LIONET
LIONLY
MIGNON
MILNER
MINNIE
MINNOW
PIANOS
PICNIC
PIGNUT
PINNAE
PINNAS
PINNED
PINNER
RIENZI
SIDNEY
SIENNA
SIGNAL
SIGNED
SIGNEE
SIGNER
SIGNET
SIGNIN
SIGNON
SIGNOR
SIGNUP
SIMNEL
SINNED
SINNER
TINNED
TINNER
VIANDS
VIENNA
VIENNE
VINNIE
WIENER
WINNER
WINNIE
WINNOW
ZINNIA

•I••N•

AIDING
AILING
AIMING
AIRING
BIDING
BIKING
BIKINI
BIMINI
BISONS
BITING
CITING
DIANNE
DICING
DIKING
DINING
DIONNE
DISANT
DIVANS
DIVINE
DIVING
DIVINO
DIZENS
FIFING
FILENE
FILING
FINING
FIRING
FIXING
GIBING
GITANO
GIVENS
GIVING
HIDING
HIEING
HIKING
HIRING
HIVING
JIBING
JIMINY
JIVING
KIMONO
KITING
LIERNE
LIGAND
LIKENS
LIKING
LIMENS
LIMING
LINENS
LINENY
LINING
LIPENG
LITANY
LIVENS
LIVING
MIFUNE
MIKING
MILANO
MIMING
MINING
MIRING
MIXING
MIZENS
NICENE
NIMINY
NIXING
OILING
PIKING
PILING
PIMINY
PINING
PINONS
PIPING
PIRANA
PISANO
PISANS
PITONS
RIBAND
RICING
RIDENT
RIDING
RILING
RIMING
RIMINI
RIPENS
RISING
RIVING
SIDING
SIENNA
SILENI
SILENT
SILONE
SIMONE
SIMONY
SIRENS
SIRING
SITING
SITINS
SIXING
SIZING
TIDING
TIEING
TIEINS
TILING
TIMING
TIPINS
TIRANA
TIRANE
TIRING
TISANE
TITANS
VICUNA
VIENNA
VIENNE
VIKING
VINING
VISHNU
VISINE
VIVANT
VIXENS
WIDENS
WILING
WINING
WINONA
WIPING
WIRING
WISENT
WIZENS
XIMENA

•I•••N

AILEEN
AIRGUN
AIRMAN
AIRMEN
BICORN
BIDDEN
BIDSIN
BIDSON
BIGBEN
BIGGUN
BIGTEN
BILLON
BIOTIN
BITTEN
CITRON
DIDION
DIGSIN
DILLON
DINEIN
DINEON
DIOXIN
DISOWN
DIVEIN
EILEEN
FIBRIN
FIJIAN
FILLIN
FINNAN
FIRKIN
FIRMAN
FITSIN
GIBBON
GIBRAN
GIBSON
GIDEON
GIVEIN
HIDDEN
HIERON
HILTON
HINTON
HIREON
HITMAN
HITMEN
HITSON
JIMSON
KICKIN
KIDMAN
KIRMAN
KITTEN
LIBYAN
LICHEN
LIESIN
LIGNIN
LINDEN
LIPTON
LISBON
LISTEN
LISTON
LIVEIN
LIVEON
MICRON
MIDDEN
MIDIAN
MIGNON
MILTON
MINION
MINOAN
MINYAN
MIRREN
MITTEN
MIZZEN
NIACIN
NICEAN
NIPPON
NISSAN
NISSEN
OILCAN
OILMAN
OILMEN
OILPAN
PICKON
PIDGIN
PIEMAN
PIEMEN
PIEPAN
PIETIN
PIGEON
PIGPEN
PILEIN
PILEON
PINION
PINKEN
PINSON
PINYIN
PINYON
PINZON
PIPKIN
PIPPIN
PISTON
PITMAN
PITMEN
RIBBON
RICHEN
RIDDEN
RIPKEN
SICKEN
SIGNIN
SIGNON
SILKEN
SIMEON
SIMIAN
SINGIN
SINKIN
SIOUAN
SIPHON
SISKIN
SITSIN
SITSON
SIXGUN
TIEDIN
TIEPIN
TIESIN
TIFFIN
TIGLON
TILDEN
TINCAN
TINMAN
TINMEN
TINPAN
TIPSIN
TITIAN
VILLON
VINTON
VIOLIN
VIRGIN
VISION
VIVIAN
VIVIEN
WICCAN
WILSON
WILTON
WINWIN
WITHIN
XIAMEN
XINGIN
ZIRCON

••IN••

ACINUS
ALINES
AMINES
AMINOR
AMINUS
AZINES
BAINES
BEINGS
BLINDS
BLINIS
BLINKS
BLINTZ
BMINOR
BMINUS
BOINGO
BRINED
BRINES
BRINGS
BRINKS
CHINCH
CHINES
CHINKS
CHINKY
CHINOS
CHINTZ
CHINUP
CLINCH
CLINES
CLINGS
CLINGY
CLINIC
CLINKS
CMINOR
CMINUS
COINED
COINER
CRINGE
DAINTY
DMINOR
DMINUS
DOINGS
DRINGS
DRINKS
ELINOR
EMINOR
EPINAL
ERINYS
EVINCE
FAINTS
FEINTS
FLINCH
FLINGS
FLINTS
FLINTY
FMINOR
FOINED
FRINGE
FRINGY
GAINED
GAINER
GAINLY
GAINON
GAINST
GLINKA
GLINTS
GMINOR
GOINGS
GOINTO
GRINCH
GRINDS
GRINGO
GUINEA
HAINAN
HAINES
ICINGS
JOINED
JOINER
JOININ
JOINTS
JOINUP
LAINIE
MAINLY
MOINES
OLINDA
OLINGO
OPINED
OPINER
OPINES
ORINGS
PAINED
PAINTS
PAINTY
PLINKS
PLINTH
POINTE
POINTS
POINTY
PRINCE
PRINKS
PRINTS
QUINCE
QUINCY
QUINOA
QUINTS
RAINED
RAINER
RAINES
RAINEY
REINAS
REINED
REINER
REININ
REINKS
RHINAL
RHINOS
RUINED
RUINER
SAINTE
SAINTS
SEINED
SEINER
SEINES
SHINDY
SHINED
SHINER
SHINES
SHINNY
SHINTO
SKINKS
SKINNY
SLINGS
SLINKS
SLINKY
SPINAL
SPINED
SPINEL
SPINES
SPINET
SPINKS
SPINTO
STINGO
STINGS
STINGY
STINKS
STINKY
STINTS
SWINGS
SWINGY
TAINAN
TAINOS
TAINTS
THINGS
THINGY
THINKS
THINLY
TRINAL
TRINES
TWINED
TWINES
TWINGE
VAINER
VAINLY
VEINAL
VEINED
WHINED
WHINER
WHINES
WHINEY
WHINNY
WRINGS

••I•N•

ALIENS
ALIGNS
AMIENS
ANIONS
ASIANS
AVIANS
AXIONS
BAIRNS
BOIGNY
BRIAND
BRIANS
BRIENZ
CAIRNS
CHIANG
CLIENT
COIGNS
DEIGNS
FEIGNS
FRIEND
GUIANA
INIONS
ONIONS
ONIONY
ORIANA
ORIENT
PLIANT
PRIONS
PUISNE
REIGNS
SCIONS
SHINNY
SKIING
SKINNY
SOIGNE
TRIUNE
UNIONS
VSIGNS
WHINNY

••I••N

ALISON
ARISEN
BLIXEN
BRITON
CAIMAN
CHIPIN
CHIRON
CHITIN
CHITON
CLIPON
DAIKON
DAIMON
DAIREN
DRIVEN
EDISON
FBIMAN
FBIMEN
GAIJIN
GAINON
GRISON
GUIDON
HAINAN
HEIDEN
IRISIN
JOININ
KLIBAN
LAIDIN
LAIDON
LEIDEN
MAIDEN
MAILIN
NAILIN
NOIRON
OBIWAN
OHIOAN
ORIGEN
ORIGIN
ORISON
PAIDIN
POISON
PRISON
RAISIN
REININ
SAIGON
SAIPAN
SHIMON
SKIRUN
SLIDIN
SLIPIN
SLIPON
SMILIN
STIRIN
TAINAN
TAIPAN
TAIWAN
TRIGON
TRITON
UNISON
WAITON
WHITEN

•••IN•

AAHING
ABYING
ACHING
ACTING
ACTINO
ADDING
AFFINE
AGEING
AGLINT
AIDING
AILING
AIMING
AIRING
ALBINO
ALDINE
ALFINE
ALOINS
ALPINE
ANOINT
AQUINO
ARCING
ARMING
ASKING
ATKINS
AUXINS
AWNING
BAAING
BAKING
BALING
BARING
BASING
BASINS
BATING
BAYING
BBKING
BEGINS
BEHIND
BEMINE
BENING
BERING
BIDING
BIKING
BIKINI
BIMINI
BITING
BLAINE
BLUING
BODING
BOEING
BONING
BOOING
BORING
BOVINE
BOWING
BOXING
BRAINS
BRAINY
BRUINS
BURINS
BUSING
BUYING
BYLINE
CABINS
CAGING
CAKING
CAMINO
CANINE
CANING
CARINA
CARING
CASING
CASINO
CAVING
CAWING
CEDING
CELINE
CHAINE
CHAINS
CITING
CLUING
CODING
COMING
COOING
COPING
CORING
COSINE
COVINA
COWING
CRYING
CUBING
CURING
CUTINS
DARING
DATING
DAZING
DEFINE
DEKING
DEVINE
DEWING
DICING
DIKING
DINING
DIVINE
DIVING
DIVINO
DOLING
DOMINE
DOMING
DOMINI
DOMINO
DOPING
DOSING
DOTING
DOZING
DRAINS
DRYING
DRYINK
DUKING
DUPING
DURING
DYEING
EALING
EARING
EASING
EATING
EBBING
ECHINO
EDGING
EGGING
ELAINE
ELNINO
ENCINA
ENCINO
ENDING
ENGINE
EOSINS
EPPING
EQUINE
ERMINE
ERRING
ERVING
EYEING
FACING
FADING
FAKING
FALINE
FAMINE
FARINA
FARING
FAXING
FAZING
FEEING
FELINE
FETING
FIFING
FILING
FINING
FIRING
FIXING
FLYING
FLYINS
FORINT
FOXING
FRYING
FUMING
FUSING
FUZING
GAGING
GAMINE
GAMING
GAMINS
GAPING
GATING
GAZING
GEEING
GEMINI
GHAINS
GIBING
GIVING
GLUING
GOLINO
GORING
GRAINS
GRAINY
GROINS
GUYING
GYBING
HALING
HARING
HATING
HAVING
HAWING
HAYING
HAZING
HEWING
HEXING
HIDING
HIEING
HIKING
HIRING
HIVING
HOEING
HOLING
HOMING
HOMINY
HONING
HOPING
HOSING
HYPING
ICHING
IDLING
ILLINI
IMFINE
IMPING
INKIND
INKING
INLINE
INNING
INTINE
IODINE
IRKING
IRVINE
IRVING
JADING
JANINE
JAPING
JAWING
JIBING
JIMINY
JIVING
JOKING
JUKING
KALINE
KEYING
KITING
LACING
LADING
LADINO
LAMINA
LAMING
LAPINS
LATINA
LATINI
LATINO
LATINS
LAVING
LAWING
LAYING
LAZING
LEVINE
LIKING
LIMING
LINING
LIVING
LOPING
LOSING
LOVING
LOWING
LUBING
LUMINA
LUPINE
LUPINO
LURING
LUTING
LYSINE
LYSINS
MAKING
MARINA
MARINE
MARINO
MATING
MATINS
MAXINE
MEDINA
MELINA
MENINX
MERINO
METING

MEWING
MIKING
MIMING
MINING
MIRING
MIXING
MODINE
MOLINE
MOOING
MOPING
MOVING
MOWING
MUCINS
MURINE
MUSING
MUTING
MUTINY
NADINE
NAMING
NEVINS
NIMINY
NIXING
NOMINE
NOSING
NOTING
NUKING
NUMINA
OARING
OFFING
OGLING
OILING
ONDINE
ONLINE
OOHING
OOZING
OPTING
ORBING
ORPINE
ORSINO
OSCINE
OUTING
OWNING
PACING
PACINO
PAGING
PALING
PARING
PATINA
PATINE
PAVING
PAWING
PAYING
PEKING
PEKINS
PEPINO
PIKING
PILING
PIMINY
PINING
PIPING
PLAINS
PLAINT
PLYING
POKING
POLING
PORING
POSING
PRYING
PULING
PURINA
PURINE
QUAINT
QUOINS
RACINE
RACING
RAGING
RAKING
RAPINE
RAPINI
RARING
RASING
RATINE
RATING
RAVINE
RAVING
RAZING
REBIND
REDING
REDINK
REFINE
REGINA
RELINE
REMIND
REPINE
REPINS
RESING
RESINS
RESINY
RETINA
REWIND
REWINS
RICING
RIDING
RILING
RIMING
RIMINI
RISING
RIVING
ROBING
ROBINS
ROPING
ROSINS
ROSINY
ROTINI
ROVING
ROWING
RULING
RUMINA
RUNINS
SABINE
SABINS
SALINA
SALINE
SATING
SATINS
SATINY
SAVING
SAWING
SAYING
SEEING
SERINE
SERINS
SETINS
SEWING
SHRINE
SHRINK
SHYING
SIDING
SIRING
SITING
SITINS
SIXING
SIZING
SKEINS
SKIING
SKYING
SLUING
SOFINE
SOLING
SOWING
SPHINX
SPLINE
SPLINT
SPRING
SPRINT
SPYING
SQUINT
STAINS
STEINS
STRINE
STRING
SUPINE
SWAINS
SYRINX
TAHINI
TAKING
TAKINS
TAMING
TAPING
TAPINS
TARING
TAWING
TAXING
TEEING
TIDING
TIEING
TIEINS
TILING
TIMING
TIPINS
TIRING
TOEING
TOEINS
TONING
TORINO
TOTING
TOWING
TOXINS
TOYING
TRAINS
TRUING
TRYING
TUBING
TUNING
TURING
TYPING
UNBIND
UNDINE
UNKIND
UNKINK
UNLINK
UNPINS
UNWIND
UPLINK
UPPING
UPWIND
URGING
URSINE
VEXING
VIKING
VINING
VISINE
VOTING
VOWING
WADING
WAGING
WAHINE
WAKING
WANING
WARING
WAVING
WAXING
WILING
WINING
WIPING
WIRING
WOOING
WOWING
YAWING
YOGINI
YOKING
ZAYINS
ZONING

•••I•N

ACTION
ADRIAN
ADRIEN
ALBION
AMNION
ANCIEN
APPIAN
ASSIGN
BAHIAN
BENIGN
BUNION
CAMION
CATION
COSIGN
DAMIEN
DARIEN
DESIGN
DIDION
DORIAN
DURIAN
ELOIGN
ENSIGN
EOLIAN
EONIAN
FABIAN
FANION
FENIAN
FIJIAN
FUJIAN
FUSION
GABION
INDIAN
IONIAN
JOVIAN
JULIAN
LEGION
LOGION
LOTION
LUCIAN
MALIGN
MARIAN
MARION
MEDIAN
MIDIAN
MINION
MORION
MOTION
NATION
NOTION
NUBIAN
OBRIAN
OBRIEN
OPTION
OSSIAN
PELION
PINION
POTION
RADIAN
RATION
REGION
RESIGN
SIMIAN
SYRIAN
TALION
TITIAN
TUPIAN
TYRIAN
UGRIAN
VISION
VIVIAN
VIVIEN

••••IN

ADDSIN
ADJOIN
ALBOIN
ALCUIN
ALDRIN
AMBLIN
ANACIN
ASKSIN
ATTAIN
AUSTIN
AZORIN
BACKIN
BAFFIN
BARKIN
BERLIN
BIDSIN
BIOTIN
BLOWIN
BOBBIN
BODKIN
BOFFIN
BOUDIN
BOWFIN
BROLIN
BUSKIN
BUSTIN
BUTTIN
CALLIN
CALVIN
CAMEIN
CARDIN
CARLIN
CASHIN
CATKIN
CAVEIN
CHAPIN
CHEMIN
CHENIN
CHIPIN
CHITIN
CHOPIN
CLAVIN
CLUEIN
COCHIN
COMEIN
CORBIN
COUSIN
CRETIN
CRONIN
CULKIN
CURTIN
CUTSIN
DARWIN
DASSIN
DEALIN
DENTIN
DETAIN
DEVEIN
DIGSIN
DINEIN
DIOXIN
DIVEIN
DOBBIN
DOBLIN
DOESIN
DOMAIN
DONEIN
DOVEIN
DRAGIN
DRAWIN
DREWIN
DROPIN
DUBBIN
DUBLIN
DUCHIN
DUNLIN
DURBIN
DUSTIN
EASEIN
EATSIN
EDGEIN
ENJOIN
FADEIN
FALLIN
FELLIN
FIBRIN
FILLIN
FIRKIN
FITSIN
FLEWIN
FLORIN
FOGSIN
GAIJIN
GASKIN
GATLIN
GAVEIN
GAWAIN
GETSIN
GIVEIN
GLOBIN
GOBLIN
GODWIN
GOESIN
GRADIN
GRATIN
GRODIN
HAMLIN
HANDIN
HANGIN
HARBIN
HARLIN
HATPIN
HEADIN
HEFLIN
HELDIN
HEMSIN
HENNIN
HEREIN
HOLDIN
HOPSIN
HORNIN
HOWLIN
HUNGIN
ICEDIN
ICESIN
ILORIN
INVAIN
IRISIN
ISELIN
JAMSIN
JERKIN
JOININ
JOPLIN
JOSKIN
JUMPIN
JUSTIN
KAOLIN
KEEPIN
KELVIN
KEYSIN
KICKIN
LAIDIN
LANVIN
LAYSIN
LEADIN
LEFTIN
LEGUIN
LETSIN
LIESIN
LIGNIN
LIVEIN
LOCKIN
LOGSIN
LOMEIN
LOOKIN
LORAIN
LOVEIN
LUBLIN
MAILIN
MALKIN
MALTIN
MARGIN
MARLIN
MARTIN
MARVIN
MATLIN
MCBAIN
MCLAIN
MELVIN
MERLIN
MOULIN
MOVEIN
MUFFIN
MUNTIN
MUSLIN
MYELIN
MYOSIN
NAILIN
NAPKIN
NIACIN
NOGGIN
NUBBIN
NUTKIN
OBTAIN
OLEFIN
ORDAIN
ORIGIN
OSSEIN
PAIDIN
PAPAIN
PAQUIN
PAYSIN
PECTIN
PEERIN
PEPSIN
PETAIN
PIDGIN
PIETIN
PILEIN
PINYIN
PIPKIN
PIPPIN
PLUGIN
POPLIN
POPSIN
POURIN
PREVIN
PUFFIN
PULLIN
PURLIN
PUTSIN
RAISIN
RAKEIN
RANKIN
RATLIN
READIN
REDFIN
REELIN
REGAIN
REININ
REJOIN
REMAIN
RENNIN
RESPIN
RETAIN
ROLLIN
ROPEIN
RUBSIN
RUNSIN
RUSKIN
SEENIN
SEEPIN
SEESIN
SENDIN
SENTIN
SEQUIN
SERKIN
SETSIN
SHOOIN
SHOWIN
SHUTIN
SIGNIN
SINGIN
SINKIN
SISKIN
SITSIN
SLIDIN
SLIPIN
SMILIN
SNOWIN
SOCKIN
SPAVIN
SPRAIN
STALIN
STEPIN
STIRIN
STOPIN
STOTIN
STRAIN
SUCKIN
TAKEIN
TANNIN
TENPIN
TIEDIN
TIEPIN
TIESIN
TIFFIN
TIPSIN
TOCSIN
TOEDIN
TOESIN
TOMLIN
TONKIN
TOOKIN
TUCKIN
TUNEIN
TURNIN
TURPIN
UJJAIN
URCHIN
VERDIN
VERMIN
VIOLIN
VIRGIN
VOTEIN
WADEIN
WALKIN
WANTIN
WAVEIN
WELKIN
WENTIN
WINWIN
WITHIN
WORKIN
XINGIN
ZEROIN
ZOOMIN

IO••••

IODATE
IODIDE
IODINE
IODISE
IODIZE
IOLITE
IOMOTH
IONIAN
IONICS
IONISE
IONIUM
IONIZE
IOWANS

I•O•••

ICONIC
IDOIDO
IGOTIT
ILOILO
ILORIN
IMOGEN
INOUYE
IROBOT
IRONED
IRONER
IRONIC
IRONON
ISOBAR
ISOGON
ISOHEL
ISOLDE
ISOMER
ISOPOD

I••O••

ICEOUT
IDIOCY
IDIOMS
IDIOTS
IGLOOS
IGNORE
IMPORT
IMPOSE
IMPOST
INBORN
INCOME
INDOOR
INDORE
INFOLD
INFORM
INGOTS
INIONS
INJOKE
INLOVE
INMOST
INPORT
INPOUR
INROAD
INSOLE
INTONE
INTOTO
INTOWN
INVOKE
IOMOTH

I•••O•

ICEBOX
ICEFOG
IGLOOS
IMPROV
INAFOG
INAROW
INCHON
INDOOR
INFLOW
INTROS
IROBOT
IRONON
ISADOR
ISOGON
ISOPOD

I••••O

IBIBIO
IDOIDO
ILOILO
IMMUNO
INDIGO
INITIO
INTOTO
INVIVO

•IO•••

BIOBIO
BIOGAS
BIOMES
BIONDI
BIONIC
BIOTAS
BIOTIC
BIOTIN
DIODES
DIONEB
DIONNE
DIOXIN
FIORDS
GIOTTO
KIOSKS
KIOWAS
LIONEL
LIONET
LIONLY
LIOTTA
MIOSIS
PIOLET
RIOJAS
RIOTED
RIOTER
SIOUAN
VIOLAS
VIOLET
VIOLIN

•I•O••

AIROUT
BICORN
BIFOLD
BIGOTS
BIJOUX
BILOXI
BIPODS
BISONS
BITOFF
BITOLA
CIBOLA
DICOTS
DIEOFF
DIEOUT
DIGOUT
DIMOUT
DIPODY
DIPOLE
DISOWN
DIVOTS
EIDOLA
FILOSE
GIGOLO
GIGOTS
GIJOES
HIDOUT
HITOUT
KIBOSH
KIDORY
KIMONO
LIPOID
LITOUT
MIDORI
MILORD
MILOSZ
MIMOSA
MINOAN
MINORS
MIWOKS
NICOLA
NICOLE
NICOLO
NIKOLA
PICOTS
PIGOUT
PILOSE
PILOTI
PILOTS
PINOAK
PINOLE
PINONS
PINOTS
PITONS
PIVOTS
RIBOSE
RIGORS
RIGOUR
RIMOSE
RIPOFF
RIPOUT
SILOAM
SILOED
SILONE
SIMONE
SIMONY
SITOUT
TIPOFF
TIVOLI
VIGODA
VIGORS
VIGOUR
VINOUS
VISORS
WICOPY
WIDOWS
WIGOUT
WINONA
WINOUT

•I••O•

AIMFOR
BIDSON
BIGBOY
BIGTOE
BIGTOP
BILLON
BILLOW
BISHOP
CISCOS
CITRON
DIALOG
DIATOM
DIDION
DIGLOT
DILLON
DINEON
DISCOS
DITTOS
GIBBON
GIBSON
GIDEON
GIZMOS
HICKOK
HIERON
HILTON
HINTON
HIPHOP
HIPPOS
HIREON
HITSON
HIVAOA
JIMSON
KILROY
KINDOF
KITFOX
LICTOR
LIELOW
LIMBOS
LIPTON
LIQUOR
LISBOA
LISBON
LISTON
LITHOG
LITHOS
LIVEON
MICRON
MICROS
MIGNON
MILTON
MIMEOS
MINION
MINNOW
MIRROR
NIMROD
NIPPON
PIANOS
PICKON
PIGEON
PILEON
PILLOW
PINION
PINSON
PINTOS
PINYON
PINZON
PISTOL
PISTON
RIBBON
RIDSOF
SIGNON
SIGNOR
SIMEON
SIPHON
SITCOM
SITSON
TIEROD
TIGLON
TINGOD
TINPOT
TIPTOE
TIPTOP
VIACOM
VICTOR
VIDEOS
VILLON
VINTON
VIREOS
VISION
WILCOX
WILLOW
WILSON
WILTON
WINDOM
WINDOW
WINNOW
WINSOR
WISDOM
ZIPLOC
ZIRCON

•I•••O

AIELLO
AIKIDO
AIMSTO
BIBLIO
BILBAO
BIOBIO
BISTRO
CICERO
CITATO
DIABLO
DINERO
DIRIGO
DIVINO
FIASCO
FIGARO
FINITO
GIGOLO
GINKGO
GIOTTO
GITANO
GIVETO
HIDEHO
KIMONO
LIBIDO
LIESTO
MIKADO
MILANO
NICOLO
NIELLO
NIHILO
NINGBO
PICABO
PICARO
PIETRO
PINERO
PISANO
RIALTO
RIGHTO
RIZZIO
SIDERO
SINGTO
TIEDTO
TIESTO
VIRAGO
WISETO

••IO••

ALIOTO
ANIONS
ARIOSE
ARIOSO
AXIOMS
AXIONS
GRIOTS
IDIOCY
IDIOMS
IDIOTS
INIONS
ODIOUS
OHIOAN
ONIONS
ONIONY
ORIOLE
OTIOSE
PRIONS
PRIORI
PRIORS
PRIORY
SCIONS
TRIODE
UNIONS

••I•O•

ALISON
AMIDOL
AMIGOS
AMINOR
ASIMOV
AVISOS
BAILOR
BMINOR
BRITON
CAICOS
CHIGOE
CHILOE
CHINOS
CHIRON
CHISOX
CHITON
CLIPON
CMINOR
DAIKON
DAIMON
DEIMOS
DMINOR
EDISON
EDITOR
EJIDOS
ELINOR
EMINOR
EPILOG
FMINOR
FRIJOL
FRITOS
GAINON
GMINOR
GRISON
GUIDON
GUIROS
LAIDON
NOIRON
ORISON
PAILOU
PHILOL
PHILOS
POIROT
POISON
PRIMOS
PRISON
QUINOA
RHINOS
SAIGON
SAILOR
SHILOH
SHIMON
SKIBOB
SKIROS
SKITOW
SLIPON
SPIGOT
SPIROS
SUITOR
TAILOR
TAINOS
TRICOT
TRIGON
TRIPOD
TRIPOS
TRITON
UNIPOD
UNISON
WAITON
WHILOM

••I••O

AKIMBO
ALIOTO
ARIOSO
ARISTO
BOINGO
BRILLO
CRISCO
CRISTO
DAIMYO
EDITIO
EMILIO
EOIPSO
FRISCO
GOINTO
GRINGO
HAIRDO
IBIBIO
INITIO
LAIDTO
OBISPO
OLINGO
OVIEDO
SCIPIO
SEISMO
SHINTO
SPINTO
STINGO
TRICHO
WEIRDO
WHIZZO

•••IO•

ACTION
ALBION
AMNION
AUDIOS
BUNION
CAMION
CATION
CURIOS
DIDION
ELLIOT
FANION
FOLIOS
FUSION
GABION
HELIOS
HERIOT
HESIOD
JOLIOT
JUNIOR
LEGION
LOGION
LOTION
MANIOC
MARION
MINION
MORION
MOTION
NATION
NOTION
OPTION
PATIOS
PELION
PERIOD
PINION
POTION
RADIOS
RATION
RATIOS
REGION
SAVIOR
SENIOR
TALION
VISION

•••I•O

ACTINO
AIKIDO
ALBINO
ALNICO
AQUINO
BENITO
BONITO
CALICO
CAMINO
CASINO
COGITO
DENIRO
DEVITO
DIRIGO
DIVINO
DOMINO
DOSIDO
ECHINO
ELNINO
ENCINO
ENRICO
ESKIMO
FINITO
GOLINO
IDOIDO
ILOILO
INDIGO
INVIVO
LADINO
LATIGO
LATINO
LIBIDO
LUPINO
MARIKO
MARINO
MEDICO
MEJICO
MERINO
MEXICO
NIHILO
ORSINO
PACINO
PEPINO
SUBITO
TORINO
ULTIMO

••••IO

ADAGIO

AFLCIO
BAGUIO
BARRIO
BIBLIO
BIOBIO
CARDIO
CASSIO
CRANIO
DELRIO
EDITIO
EMILIO
FLORIO
IBIBIO
INITIO
KUOPIO
LASHIO
MACEIO
MAGGIO
NUNCIO
PERNIO
PHYSIO
PLAGIO
RIZZIO
SCIPIO
SERGIO
STUDIO

IP••••

IPECAC

I•P•••

IMPACT
IMPAIR
IMPALA
IMPALE
IMPART
IMPEDE
IMPELS
IMPEND
IMPERF
IMPING
IMPISH
IMPORT
IMPOSE
IMPOST
IMPROV
IMPUGN
IMPURE
IMPUTE
INPART
INPLAY
INPORT
INPOUR
INPUTS

I••P••

INAPET
INSPAN
ISOPOD

I•••P•

INCEPT
IRRUPT

I••••P

ICECAP
ICEDUP
ICESUP
INSTEP

•IP•••

BIPEDS
BIPODS
CIPHER
DIPODY
DIPOLE
DIPPED
DIPPER
FIPPLE
GIPPED
GIPPER
HIPHOP
HIPPED
HIPPER
HIPPIE
HIPPOS
KIPPER
KIPPUR
LIPASE
LIPENG
LIPIDE
LIPIDS
LIPOID
LIPPED
LIPTON
NIPPED
NIPPER
NIPPON
NIPPUR
NIPSAT
NIPSEY
NIPUPS
PIPALS
PIPERS
PIPEUP
PIPIER
PIPING
PIPITS
PIPKIN
PIPPED
PIPPIN
RIPELY
RIPENS
RIPEST
RIPKEN
RIPLEY
RIPOFF
RIPOUT
RIPPED
RIPPER
RIPPLE
RIPPLY
RIPRAP
RIPSAW
RIPSUP
SIPHON
SIPPED
SIPPER
SIPPET
TIPINS
TIPOFF
TIPPED
TIPPER
TIPPET
TIPPLE
TIPSIN
TIPTOE
TIPTOP
TIPUPS
VIPERS
WIPERS
WIPEUP
WIPING
YIPPED
YIPPEE
ZIPLOC
ZIPPED
ZIPPER
ZIPSUP

•I•P••

DIAPER
DIEPPE
DIMPLE
DIMPLY
DIPPED
DIPPER
DISPEL
FIPPLE
GIPPED
GIPPER
HIPPED
HIPPER
HIPPIE
HIPPOS
HISPID
KIPPER
KIPPUR
LIMPED
LIMPER
LIMPET
LIMPID
LIMPLY
LIPPED
LISPED
MILPAS
NIPPED
NIPPER
NIPPON
NIPPUR
OILPAN
PIEPAN
PIGPEN
PIPPED
PIPPIN
RIMPLE
RIPPED
RIPPER
RIPPLE
RIPPLY
SIMPER
SIMPLE
SIMPLY
SIPPED
SIPPER
SIPPET
TIEPIN
TINPAN
TINPOT
TIPPED
TIPPER
TIPPET
TIPPLE
WIMPLE
WISPED
YIPPED
YIPPEE
ZILPAH
ZIPPED
ZIPPER

•I••P•

BICEPS
DIEPPE
FIVEPM
FIXUPS
MIXUPS
NINEPM
NIPUPS
PINUPS
SITUPS
TIEUPS
TIPUPS
WICOPY

•I•••P

BIDSUP
BIGTOP
BINDUP
BISHOP
BITMAP
DIALUP
DIGSUP
FILLIP
FILLUP
FIREUP
FIRMUP
GIVEUP
HICCUP
HIGHUP
HIKEUP
HIPHOP
HITSUP
KICKUP
KIDNAP
LIFTUP
LINEUP
LINKUP
MILSAP
MISHAP
PICKUP
PILEUP
PIPEUP
PIRRIP
RIGSUP
RILEUP
RINGUP
RIPRAP
RIPSUP
SIGNUP
SITSUP
SIZEUP
TIDYUP
TIEDUP
TIESUP
TIPTOP
TITTUP
WINDUP
WIPEUP
WISEUP
ZIPSUP

••IP••

CHIPIN
CLIPON
CRIPES
DRIPPY
EOIPSO
FLIPUP
GRIPED
GRIPER
GRIPES
GRIPPE
JAIPUR
PRIPET
QUIPPY
QUIPUS
RAIPUR
SAIPAN
SCIPIO
SKIPIT
SKIPPY
SLIPIN
SLIPON
SLIPPY
SLIPUP
SNIPED
SNIPER
SNIPES
SNIPPY
STIPEL
STIPES
SWIPED
SWIPER
SWIPES
TAIPAN
TAIPEI
TRIPLE
TRIPLY
TRIPOD
TRIPOS
TRIPUP
UNIPOD
WHIPPY
WHIPUP

••I•P•

BLIMPS
CHIMPS
CHIRPS
CHIRPY
CRIMPS
CRIMPY
CRISPS
CRISPY
DRIPPY
GRIPPE
GUIMPE
OBISPO
PRIMPS
QUIPPY
SKIMPS
SKIMPY
SKIPPY
SLIPPY
SNIPPY
STIMPY
WHIPPY

••I••P

CHINUP
COILUP
FAIRUP
FLIPUP
JOINUP
LAIDUP
PAIDUP
PAIRUP
PHILIP
SLIPUP
STIRUP
SUITUP
TRICEP
TRIPUP
WAITUP
WHIPUP

•••IP•

CALIPH
CERIPH
EQUIPS
FELIPE
OXLIPS
RECIPE
SCRIPS
SCRIPT
STRIPE
STRIPS
STRIPY
THRIPS
TULIPS
UNRIPE
UNZIPS
VCHIPS

•••I•P

MEGILP
SCRIMP
SHRIMP

••••IP

BUNYIP
CATNIP
FILLIP
GOSSIP
HOTTIP
PHILIP
PIRRIP
RESHIP
THELIP
TURNIP

IQ••••

IQTEST

I••Q••

IRAQIS

•IQ•••

LIQUID
LIQUOR
PIQUED
PIQUES
PIQUET

•I•Q••

BISQUE
CINQUE
CIRQUE
RISQUE

•I•••Q

HIGHIQ

••IQ••

CAIQUE
CLIQUE
CLIQUY
CUIQUE
UBIQUE
UNIQUE

•••I•Q

SUSIEQ

••••IQ

HIGHIQ

IR••••

IRANIS
IRAQIS
IRATER
IREFUL
IRENES
IRENIC
IRIDES
IRIDIC
IRISES
IRISIN
IRKING
IRLENE
IROBOT
IRONED
IRONER
IRONIC
IRONON
IRREAL
IRRUPT
IRTYSH
IRVINE
IRVING

I•R•••

INROAD
INRUSH
IRREAL
IRRUPT
ISRAEL

I••R••

IATRIC
IBERIA
ICARIA
ICARUS
ILORIN
IMARET
IMBRUE
IMPROV
INARCH
INAROW
INARUT
INBRED
INDRIS
INGRAM
INGRES
INGRID
INTROS
INURED
INURES
ISTRIA
ITURBI

I•••R•

IDCARD
IDLERS
IGNORE
IMMURE
IMPART
IMPERF
IMPORT
IMPURE
INBORN
INCURS
INDIRA
INDORE
INFERS
INFIRM
INFORM
INHERE
INJURE
INJURY
INKERS
INPART
INPORT
INSERT
INSURE
INTERJ
INTERN
INTURN
INVERT
INWARD
IZZARD

I••••R

ICKIER
IFFIER
IMAGER
IMPAIR
INANER
INDOOR
INGEAR
INGMAR
INKIER
INPOUR
INSTAR
IRATER
IRONER
ISADOR
ISHTAR
ISOBAR
ISOMER
ISSUER

•IR•••

AIRARM
AIRBAG
AIRBUS
AIRDAM
AIRDRY
AIRGUN
AIRIER
AIRILY
AIRING
AIRMAN
AIRMEN
AIROUT
AIRSAC
AIRWAY
BIRDED
BIRDER
BIRDIE
BIREME
BIRGIT
BIRLED
BIRNEY
BIRTHS
CIRCLE
CIRCUM
CIRCUS
CIRQUE
CIRRUS
DIRECT
DIRELY
DIREST
DIRGES
DIRHAM
DIRIGE
DIRIGO
DIRNDL
FIRERS
FIREUP
FIRING
FIRKIN
FIRMAN
FIRMED
FIRMER
FIRMLY
FIRMUP
FIRSTS
FIRTHS
GIRARD
GIRDED
GIRDER
GIRDLE
GIRNED
GIRTED
GIRTHS
HIREON
HIRERS
HIRING
HIRSCH
KIRMAN
KIRSCH
KIRTLE
MIRAGE
MIRIAM
MIRIER
MIRING
MIRREN
MIRROR
PIRACY
PIRANA
PIRATE
PIRRIP
SIRDAR
SIRENS
SIRICA
SIRING
SIRIUS
SIRRAH
SIRREE
TIRADE
TIRANA
TIRANE
TIRING
VIRAGO
VIREOS
VIRGIL
VIRGIN
VIRILE
VIRTUE
VIRTUS
WIRERS
WIRIER
WIRILY
WIRING
ZIRCON

•I•R••

AIGRET
BIERCE
BIGRED
CIARDI
CIRRUS
CITRIC
CITRON
CITRUS
DIGRAM
FIBRES
FIBRIL
FIBRIN
FIERCE
FIORDS
GIBRAN
HIERON
HIJRAH
KILROY
LIBRIS
LIERNE
LITRES
LIVRES
MICRON
MICROS
MIDRIB
MIHRAB
MIRREN
MIRROR
MITRAL
MITRED
MITRES
NIMROD
NITRES
NITRIC
OILRIG
PIERCE
PIERRE
PIRRIP
RIPRAP
SIERRA
SIRRAH
SIRREE
TIARAS
TIERCE
TIERED
TIEROD
TIERRA
TIGRIS
TITRED
TITRES
VITRIC

•I••R•

AIDERS
AILERS
AIRARM
AIRDRY
BIAFRA
BICARB
BICORN
BIHARI
BIKERS
BINARY
BISTRO
BITERS
CICERO
CIDERS
CIGARS
CITERS
DICERS
DINARS
DINERO
DINERS
DISARM
DIVERS
DIVERT
DIYERS
EIDERS
FIACRE
FIBERS
FIFERS
FIGARO
FIGURE
FILERS
FINERY
FIRERS
FIVERS
FIXERS
GIBERS
GIRARD
GIVERS
HIDERS
HIKERS
HILARY
HIRERS
JIVERS
KIDORY
KITERS
LIBERI
LIFERS
LIGERS
LIGURE
LINERS
LITERS
LIVERS
LIVERY
LIZARD
MIDORI
MILERS
MILORD
MIMERS
MINERS
MINORS
MISERS
MISERY
MITERS
MIXERS
NINERS
NITERS
NITERY
OILERS
PICARA
PICARD
PICARO
PIERRE
PIETRO
PIKERS
PINERO
PINERY
PIPERS
RICERS
RIDERS
RIGORS
RISERS
RITARD
RIVERA
RIVERS
SIDERO
SIDERS
SIERRA
SIGURD
SISERA
SISTRA
SITARS
SIXERS
SIZERS
TIERRA
TIGERS
TILERS
TIMBRE
TIMERS
TISHRI
TITERS
UIGURS
VICARS
VIDERI
VIGORS
VINERY
VIPERS
VISORS
WINERY
WINTRY
WIPERS
WIRERS
WIZARD

•I•••R

AIMFOR
AIRIER
BICKER
BIDDER
BIGGER
BIGSUR
BINDER
BIRDER
BITTER
CINDER
CIPHER
DIALER
DIAPER
DICIER
DICKER
DIETER
DIFFER
DIGGER
DILLER
DIMMER
DINNER
DIPPER
DISBAR
DITHER
EISNER
EITHER
FIBBER
FILLER
FILTER
FINDER
FINGER
FIRMER
FISHER
FITTER
GIBBER
GILDER
GINGER
GIPPER
GIRDER
HIGHER
HILLER
HINDER
HINTER
HIPPER
HISSER
HITHER
HITTER
JIGGER
JITTER
JIVIER
KICKER
KIDDER
KIEFER
KILLER
KILMER
KILTER
KINDER
KIPPER
KIPPUR
KISSER
LIBBER
LICTOR
LIEDER
LIEFER
LIFTER
LIMBER
LIMIER
LIMNER
LIMPER
LINEAR
LINGER
LINIER
LINKER
LINTER
LIQUOR
LISTER
LITTER
MIDAIR
MIDLER
MILDER
MILKER
MILLER
MILNER
MINCER
MINDER
MINTER
MIRIER
MIRROR
MISTER
NICKER
NIGHER
NIPPER
NIPPUR
OILIER
PICKER
PIECER
PIETER
PILFER
PILLAR
PINCER
PINDAR
PINIER
PINKER
PINNER
PINTER
PIPIER
PITIER
PITTER
QINTAR
RICHER
RIFLER
RIGGER
RIGOUR
RIMIER
RINGER
RIOTER
RIPPER
RISKER
RITTER
SICKER
SIDDUR
SIFTER
SIGHER
SIGNER
SIGNOR
SILVER
SIMMER
SIMPER
SINGER
SINKER
SINNER
SINTER
SIPPER
SIRDAR
SISLER
SISTER
SITTER
TICKER
TIDIER
TIGGER
TILLER
TILTER
TIMBER
TINDER
TINEAR
TINIER
TINKER
TINNER
TINTER
TIPPER
TITFER
TITHER
TITTER
VICTOR
VIEWER
VIGOUR
VINIER
VIZIER
WICKER
WIENER
WILBUR
WILDER
WILIER
WINCER
WINDER
WINGER
WINIER
WINKER
WINNER
WINSOR
WINTER
WIRIER
WISHER
WISTER
WITHER
ZIMMER
ZINGER
ZIPPER
ZITHER

••IR••

BAIRNS
BEIRUT
BGIRLS
CAIRNS
CHIRAC
CHIRON
CHIRPS
CHIRPY
CHIRRS
DAIREN
EPIRUS
FAIRED
FAIRER
FAIRLY
FAIRUP
FLIRTS
FLIRTY
GUIROS
HAIRDO
HAIRED
LAIRDS
MOIRES
NAIRAS
NOIRON
OSIRIS
PAIRED
PAIRUP
POIROT
QUIRES
QUIRKS
QUIRKY
QUIRTS
SHIRAZ
SHIRER
SHIRES
SHIRKS
SHIRRS
SHIRTS
SHIRTY
SKIRLS
SKIROS
SKIRRS
SKIRTS
SKIRUN
SMIRCH
SMIRKS
SMIRKY
SOIREE
SPIRAL
SPIREA
SPIRED
SPIRES
SPIRIT
SPIROS
STIRIN
STIRKS
STIRUP
SWIRLS
SWIRLY
TBIRDS
THIRDS
THIRST
THIRTY
TWIRLS
WEIRDO
WEIRDY
WHIRLS
WHIRLY
WHIRRS
ZAIRES

••I•R•

ANITRA
APIARY
AVIARY
BRIARD
BRIARS
BRIERS
BRIERY
CHIRRS
CRIERS
DEIDRE
DMITRI
DRIERS
EMIGRE
FLIERS
FRIARS
FRIARY
FRIERS
GRIGRI
GUITRY
MAITRE
OSIERS
PLIERS
PRIERS
PRIORI
PRIORS
PRIORY
SHIRRS
SKIERS
SKIRRS
SPIERS
TRIERS
WHIRRS

••I••R

ALITER
AMINOR
BAILER
BAILOR
BMINOR
BOILER
CHIDER
CMINOR
COINER
DEICER
DMINOR
DRIVER
DUIKER
EDITOR
ELINOR
ELIXIR
EMINOR
EVILER
FAIRER
FMINOR
GAINER
GAITER
GEIGER
GLIDER
GMINOR
GRIPER
GUITAR
HEIFER
JAILER
JAIPUR
JOINER
JUICER
KAISER
LOITER
MAILER
MOILER
NAILER
OBITER
OLIVER
OPINER
PFIZER
PRICER
PRIMER
QUIVER
RAIDER
RAILER
RAINER
RAIPUR
RAISER
REINER
RUINER
SAILOR
SEINER
SEIZER
SHIKAR
SHINER
SHIRER
SHIVER
SKIVER
SLICER
SLIDER
SLIVER
SMILER
SNIDER
SNIPER
SPIDER
SPIKER
STIVER
SUITOR
SWIPER
TAILOR
TOILER
TRITER
UNITER
VAINER
WAILER
WAITER
WAIVER
WEIMAR
WHINER
WHITER
WRITER
ZUIDER

•••IR•

ADMIRE
AFFIRM
ALHIRT
ASPIRE
ASWIRL
ATTIRE
AWHIRL
BEMIRE
CHAIRS
CHOIRS
CLAIRE
DENIRO
DESIRE
ELMIRA
ELVIRA
EMPIRE

ENGIRD
ENGIRT
ENTIRE
EXPIRE
EXPIRY
FAKIRS
FLAIRS
GEZIRA
GLAIRS
GLAIRY
HEGIRA
INDIRA
INFIRM
JABIRU
KAFIRS
KEFIRS
MYGIRL
NADIRS
ONFIRE
PAMIRS
REAIRS
REHIRE
RETIRE
REWIRE
SAFIRE
SATIRE
SQUIRE
SQUIRM
SQUIRT
STAIRS
TAPIRS
THEIRS
TSHIRT
UMPIRE
UNGIRD
UNGIRT
VENIRE

•••I•R

ACHIER
AIRIER
ARTIER
ASHIER
BONIER
BOXIER
BUSIER
CAGIER
CAHIER
CAKIER
CANIER
CAVIAR
COKIER
COPIER
COSIER
COZIER
DENIER
DEWIER
DICIER
DOPIER
DOZIER
EASIER
EDGIER
EELIER
EERIER
EGGIER
ENVIER
FOLIAR
FOXIER
FUMIER
GAMIER
GLUIER
GOOIER
GORIER
HAZIER
HOKIER
HOLIER
HOMIER
HOSIER
ICKIER
IFFIER
INKIER
JAVIER
JIVIER
JOKIER
JUNIOR
LACIER
LAKIER
LANIER
LAZIER
LEVIER
LIMIER
LINIER
LOGIER
MAZIER
METIER
MIRIER
MOPIER
NAPIER
NOSIER
OATIER
OILIER
OOZIER
PALIER
PAPIER
PINIER
PIPIER
PITIER
POKIER
PUNIER
RACIER
RAPIER
RIMIER
ROPIER
ROSIER
SAVIOR
SENIOR
SEXIER
SPRIER
TIDIER
TINIER
TONIER
TYPIER
UGLIER
VANIER
VINIER
VIZIER
WANIER
WARIER
WAVIER
WAXIER
WILIER
WINIER
WIRIER
XAVIER
ZANIER

••••IR

AAFAIR
ABUKIR
AFFAIR
AGADIR
ALTAIR
AUPAIR
BELAIR
BESTIR
COHEIR
DEVOIR
ECLAIR
ELIXIR
FAFNIR
HOTAIR
IMPAIR
KAFFIR
MCNAIR
MEMOIR
MENHIR
MIDAIR
MOHAIR
REDFIR
RENOIR
REPAIR
REVOIR
SANTIR
SAVOIR
SHAMIR
UNFAIR
YESSIR

IS••••

ISABEL
ISADOR
ISAIAH
ISCHIA
ISELIN
ISEULT
ISHTAR
ISLAND
ISLETS
ISMENE
ISOBAR
ISOGON
ISOHEL
ISOLDE
ISOMER
ISOPOD
ISRAEL
ISSUED
ISSUER
ISSUES
ISTHMI
ISTLES
ISTRIA

I•S•••

IJSSEL
INSANE
INSEAM
INSECT
INSERT
INSETS
INSIDE
INSIST
INSITU
INSOLE
INSPAN
INSTAL
INSTAR
INSTEP
INSTIL
INSULT
INSURE
INSYNC
ISSUED
ISSUER
ISSUES
ITSELF

I••S••

IBISES
ICESIN
ICESUP
IJSSEL
ILESHA
ILLSAY
INESSE
IRISES
IRISIN
ITASCA

I•••S•

ICIEST
IDLEST
ILLEST
ILLUSE
IMPISH
IMPOSE
IMPOST
INCASE
INCASH
INCISE
INCUSE
INESSE
INFEST
INFUSE
INGEST
INJEST
INMOST
INNESS
INRUSH
INSIST
INVEST
IODISE
IONISE
IQTEST
IRTYSH

I••••S

IBEAMS
IBEXES
IBISES
ICARUS
ICINGS
IDEALS
IDIOMS
IDIOTS
IDLERS
IDTAGS
IDYLLS
IGLOOS
ILEXES
IMAGES
IMBUES
IMPELS
INCANS
INCHES
INCURS
INDIES
INDRIS
INFERS
INGLES
INGOTS
INGRES
INIONS
INKERS
INKLES
INLAWS
INLAYS
INLETS
INNESS
INPUTS
INSETS
INTENS
INTROS
INUITS
INURES
IONICS
IOWANS
IRANIS
IRAQIS
IRENES
IRIDES
IRISES
ISLETS
ISSUES
ISTLES
ITCHES

•IS•••

AISLES
BISCAY
BISECT
BISHOP
BISONS
BISQUE
BISSAU
BISSET
BISTRO
CISCOS
CISKEI
DISANT
DISARM
DISBAR
DISCOS
DISCUS
DISHED
DISHES
DISKED
DISMAL
DISMAY
DISMES
DISNEY
DISOWN
DISPEL
DISSED
DISTAL
DISTIL
DISUSE
EISNER
FISCAL
FISHED
FISHER
FISHES
FISTED
FISTIC
HISPID
HISSAT
HISSED
HISSER
HISSES
KISHKE
KISLEV
KISMET
KISSED
KISSER
KISSES
LISBOA
LISBON
LISLES
LISPED
LISTED
LISTEE
LISTEL
LISTEN
LISTER
LISTON
MISCHA
MISCUE
MISDID
MISERS
MISERY
MISFIT
MISHAP
MISHIT
MISLAY
MISLED
MISSAL
MISSAY
MISSED
MISSES
MISSIS
MISSUS
MISTED
MISTER
MISUSE
NISSAN
NISSEN
PISANO
PISANS
PISCES
PISGAH
PISTES
PISTIL
PISTOL
PISTON
RISERS
RISING
RISKED
RISKER
RISQUE
SISALS
SISERA
SISKEL
SISKIN
SISLER
SISLEY
SISTER
SISTRA
TISANE
TISHRI
TISSUE
VISAED
VISAGE
VISCID
VISHNU
VISINE
VISION
VISITS
VISORS
VISTAS
VISUAL
WISDOM
WISELY
WISENT
WISEST
WISETO
WISEUP
WISHED
WISHER
WISHES
WISPED
WISTER

•I•S••

AIMSAT
AIMSTO
AIRSAC
BIASED
BIASES
BIDSIN
BIDSON
BIDSUP
BIGSUR
BISSAU
BISSET
DIESEL
DIESES
DIESIS
DIGSIN
DIGSUP
DILSEY
DIMSUM
DISSED
FIASCO
FIESTA
FIRSTS
FITSIN
GIBSON
HIRSCH
HISSAT
HISSED
HISSER
HISSES
HITSIT
HITSON
HITSUP
JIGSAW
JIMSON
KINSEY
KINSKI
KIOSKS
KIRSCH
KISSED
KISSER
KISSES
KITSCH
LIESIN
LIESTO
LINSEY
MIASMA
MILSAP
MIOSIS
MISSAL
MISSAY
MISSED
MISSES
MISSIS
MISSUS
NIPSAT
NIPSEY
NISSAN
NISSEN
PIGSTY
PINSON
PITSAW
RIDSOF
RIGSUP
RIMSKY
RINSED
RINSES
RIPSAW
RIPSUP
SIESTA
SITSBY
SITSIN
SITSON
SITSUP
TIESIN
TIESTO
TIESUP
TILSIT
TINSEL
TIPSIN
TISSUE
VIZSLA
WIESEL
WILSON
WIMSEY
WINSOR
ZIPSUP

•I••S•

DIGEST
DIREST
DISUSE
DIVEST
FILOSE
FINEST
FINISH
KIBOSH
LIAISE
LIPASE
MILOSZ
MIMOSA
MISUSE
NICEST
PILOSE
RIBOSE
RIFEST
RIMOSE
RIPEST
SINISE
SIWASH
VILEST
WIDEST
WIDISH
WINISH
WISEST

•I•••S

AIDERS
AILERS
AIRBUS
AISLES
BIASES
BIBLES
BICEPS
BIGHTS
BIGOTS
BIKERS
BILGES
BINGES
BIOGAS
BIOMES
BIOTAS
BIPEDS
BIPODS
BIRTHS
BISONS
BITERS
CIDERS
CIGARS
CIRCUS
CIRRUS
CISCOS
CITERS
CITIES
CITIUS
CITRUS
CIVETS
CIVICS
DICERS
DICOTS
DICTUS
DIDIES
DIESES
DIESIS
DIGITS
DINARS
DINERS
DINGUS
DIODES
DIRGES
DISCOS
DISCUS
DISHES
DISMES
DITTOS
DITZES
DIVANS
DIVERS
DIVOTS
DIXITS
DIYERS
DIZENS
EIDERS
EIGHTS
FIBERS
FIBRES
FICHES
FICHUS
FIELDS
FIENDS
FIFERS
FIFTHS
FIGHTS
FILERS
FILETS
FILIUS
FILLES
FINALS
FIORDS
FIRERS
FIRSTS
FIRTHS
FISHES
FIVERS
FIVEWS
FIXERS
FIXUPS
FIZZES
GIANTS
GIBERS
GIGOTS
GIGUES
GIJOES
GILLIS
GIMELS
GIMMES
GIRTHS
GIVENS
GIVERS
GIZMOS
HIATUS
HIDERS
HIKERS
HINDUS
HINGES
HINGIS
HIPPOS
HIRERS
HISSES
JIHADS
JINXES
JIVERS
KIANGS
KILIMS
KIOSKS
KIOWAS
KISSES
KITERS
LIANAS
LIANES
LIANGS
LIBELS
LIBRIS
LIEBYS
LIEGES
LIEUTS
LIFERS
LIGERS
LIGHTS
LIKENS
LILACS
LILIES
LIMBOS
LIMBUS
LIMENS
LIMEYS
LIMITS
LINENS
LINERS
LIPIDS
LISLES
LITERS
LITHOS
LITMUS
LITRES
LIVENS
LIVERS
LIVRES
MICROS
MIDGES
MILERS
MILPAS
MIMEOS
MIMERS
MIMICS
MINCES
MINERS
MINIMS
MINKES
MINORS
MINXES
MIOSIS
MISERS
MISSES
MISSIS
MISSUS
MITERS
MITRES
MIWOKS
MIXERS
MIXUPS
MIZENS
NICHES
NIECES
NIGHTS
NIMBUS
NINERS
NINJAS
NINTHS
NIPUPS
NITERS
NITRES
NIXIES
OILERS
PIANOS
PICOTS
PICULS
PIECES
PIETAS
PIKERS
PILAFS
PILEUS
PILOTS
PINDUS
PINNAS
PINONS
PINOTS
PINTOS
PINUPS
PIPALS
PIPERS
PIPITS
PIQUES
PISANS
PISCES
PISTES
PITIES
PITONS
PIVOTS
PIXELS
PIXIES
PIZZAS
RIATAS
RICERS
RICHES
RIDERS
RIDGES
RIFLES
RIGHTS
RIGORS
RILLES
RINSES
RIOJAS
RIPENS
RISERS
RIVALS
RIVERS
RIVETS
RIYALS
SIBYLS
SIDERS
SIDLES
SIEGES
SIEVES
SIGHTS
SIGILS
SIGMAS
SILVAS
SINEWS
SINGES
SIRENS
SIRIUS
SISALS
SITARS
SITINS
SITUPS
SIXERS
SIXTHS
SIXTUS
SIZERS
TIARAS
TIBIAS
TICALS
TIDIES
TIEINS
TIEUPS
TIGERS
TIGHTS
TIGRIS
TILAKS
TILDES
TILERS
TILLIS
TIMERS
TINCTS
TINGES
TIPINS
TIPUPS
TITANS
TITERS
TITHES
TITLES
TITRES
UIGURS
UINTAS
VIANDS
VICARS
VICTIS
VIDEOS
VIGILS
VIGORS
VILLAS
VILLUS
VINCES
VINOUS
VINYLS
VIOLAS
VIPERS
VIREOS
VIRTUS
VISITS
VISORS
VISTAS
VITALS
VIXENS
WIDENS
WIDOWS
WIDTHS
WIELDS
WIGHTS
WILKES
WILLIS
WINCES
WINZES
WIPERS
WIRERS
WISHES
WITHES
WIZENS
YIELDS
ZIBETS

••IS••

ALISON
ARISEN
ARISES
ARISTA
ARISTO
AVISOS
CHISEL
CHISOX
CRISCO
CRISES
CRISIS
CRISPS
CRISPY
CRISTO
CUISSE
DAISES
DEISTS
EDISON
ELISHA
ELISSA
ENISLE
EXISTS
FAISAL
FEISTY
FOISTS
FRISCO
FRISEE
FRISES
FRISKS
FRISKY
GEISEL
GEISHA
GRISLY
GRISON
GRISTS
GUISES
HEISTS
HOISTS
IBISES
IRISES
IRISIN
JOISTS
KAISER
MAISIE
NEISSE
NOISED
NOISES
OBISPO
ODISTS
ORISON
ORISSA
OVISAC
PAISAS
PLISSE
POISED
POISES
POISON
PRISMS
PRISON
PRISSY
PUISNE
RAISED
RAISER
RAISES
RAISIN
SEISMO
SEISMS
SUISSE
THISBE
TRISHA
TRISTE
TWISTS
TWISTY
UNISEX
UNISON
UNISYS
VAISYA
WAISTS
WHISKS
WHISKY
WRISTS

••I•S•

AHIMSA
AMIDST
ARIOSE
ARIOSO
CUISSE
DRIEST
ELISSA
EOIPSO
FLIMSY
GAINST
GRILSE
ICIEST
NEISSE
ORISSA
OTIOSE
PLISSE
PRIEST
PRISSY
SHIEST
SHIISM
SLIEST
SLIMSY
SUISSE
THIRST
WHILST
WHIMSY
WRIEST

••I••S

ABIDES
ACINUS
ADIDAS
ADIEUS
AKITAS
ALIBIS
ALIENS
ALIGNS
ALINES
AMICES
AMICUS
AMIDES
AMIENS
AMIGAS
AMIGOS
AMINES
AMINUS
ANIMAS
ANIMES
ANIMUS
ANIONS
APICES
ARISES
ASIANS
ASIDES
AVIANS
AVISOS
AXIOMS
AXIONS
AZIDES
AZINES
BAINES
BAIRNS
BAIZAS
BEIGES
BEINGS
BGIRLS
BLIMPS
BLINDS
BLINIS
BLINKS
BMINUS
BOITES
BRIANS
BRIARS
BRIBES
BRICKS
BRIDES
BRIEFS
BRIERS
BRIGGS
BRILLS
BRINES
BRINGS
BRINKS
BSIDES
BUILDS
CAICOS
CAIRNS
CEIBAS
CHIAUS
CHICKS
CHIDES
CHIEFS
CHILDS
CHILLS
CHIMES
CHIMPS
CHINES
CHINKS
CHINOS
CHIRPS
CHIRRS
CHIVES
CLICKS
CLIFFS
CLIMBS
CLIMES
CLINES
CLINGS
CLINKS
CMINUS
CNIDUS
COIGNS
CRICKS
CRIERS
CRIMES
CRIMPS
CRIPES
CRISES
CRISIS
CRISPS
DAISES
DEICES
DEIGNS
DEIMOS
DEISTS
DMINUS
DOINGS
DRIERS
DRIFTS
DRILLS
DRINGS
DRINKS
DRIVES
EDICTS
EDILES
EJIDOS
ELIDES
ELITES
EPIRUS
ERINYS
EVICTS
EXILES
EXISTS
FAINTS
FAITHS
FEIGNS
FEINTS
FLICKS
FLIERS
FLINGS
FLINTS
FLIRTS
FOISTS
FRIARS
FRIERS
FRILLS
FRISES
FRISKS
FRITOS
GLIDES
GLINTS
GOINGS
GRIEFS
GRIFTS
GRILLS
GRIMES
GRINDS
GRIOTS
GRIPES
GRISTS
GUIDES
GUILDS
GUILES
GUIROS
GUISES
HAIDAS
HAIKUS
HAINES
HEISTS
HOISTS
IBISES
ICINGS
IDIOMS
IDIOTS
INIONS
IRIDES
IRISES
JOINTS
JOISTS
JUICES
KNICKS
KNIFES
KNIVES
LAIRDS
MAIDUS
MAILES
MAIZES
MOINES
MOIRES
NAIADS
NAIRAS
NEIGHS
NOISES
ODIOUS
ODISTS
ODIUMS
OGIVES
OLIVES
ONIONS
OPINES
ORIBIS
ORIELS
ORINGS
OSIERS
OSIRIS
OTITIS
OXIDES
PAINTS
PAISAS
PHIALS
PHILOS
PLIERS
PLINKS
POILUS
POINTS
POISES
PRICES
PRICKS
PRIDES
PRIERS
PRIMES
PRIMOS
PRIMPS
PRIMUS
PRINKS
PRINTS
PRIONS
PRIORS
PRISMS
PRIZES
QUIETS
QUILLS
QUILTS
QUINTS
QUIPUS

QUIRES QUIRKS QUIRTS RAINES RAISES REIGNS REINAS REINKS RHINOS SAIGAS SAINTS SCIFIS SCIONS SEINES SEISMS SEIZES SHIFTS SHILLS SHINES SHIRES SHIRKS SHIRRS SHIRTS SKIERS SKIFFS SKILLS SKIMPS SKINKS SKIRLS SKIROS SKIRRS SKIRTS SKIVES SLICES SLICKS SLIDES SLIMES SLINGS SLINKS SMILES SMIRKS SMITES SMITHS SNICKS SNIFFS SNIPES SPICAS SPICES SPIELS SPIERS SPIFFS SPIKES SPILES SPILLS SPINES SPINKS SPIRES SPIROS SPITES STICKS STIFFS STILES STILLS STILTS STINGS STINKS STINTS STIPES STIRKS SUITES SWIFTS SWILLS SWINGS SWIPES

SWIRLS TAIGAS TAINOS TAINTS TBILLS TBIRDS THIGHS THILLS THINGS THINKS THIRDS TOILES TRIADS TRIALS TRIBES TRICES TRICKS TRIERS TRIKES TRILLS TRINES TRIPOS TWILLS TWINES TWIRLS TWISTS UMIAKS UNIATS UNIONS UNISYS UNITAS UNITES URIALS VOICES VOILES VSIGNS VSIXES WAISTS WAIVES WEIGHS WHIFFS WHILES WHINES WHIRLS WHIRRS WHISKS WHITES WRINGS WRISTS WRITES XFILES YOICKS ZAIRES

•••IS•

ADVISE AGEISM AGEIST AGUISH AORIST ARLISS ARTIST ASPISH ASSISI ASSIST ATRISK BANISH BARISH BETISE BLAISE BLUISH BOYISH BRAISE BRUISE CAMISE CERISE CHAISE CHRISM COYISH CRUISE CUBISM CUBIST DANISH DELIST DEMISE DENISE DESIST DEVISE DOVISH DUDISH EGOISM EGOIST ELFISH ELOISE ELVISH ENLIST EXCISE FAMISH FETISH FINISH FRAISE GARISH GNEISS GOFISH HOLISM HOLIST IMPISH INCISE INSIST IODISE IONISE JADISH JEWISH JURIST JUTISH KLEIST KUMISS KWEISI LATISH LAVISH LEGIST LIAISE LOUISA LOUISE LOWISH LUTIST LYRIST MAOISM MAOIST MARISA MARISH MARIST MODISH MONISM MONIST MOPISH MULISH NEWISH NOWISE NUDIST OAFISH OBOIST OFFISH OGRISH OLDISH OWLISH PALISH PARISH PERISH POLISH PRAISE PUNISH PURISM PURIST RADISH RAKISH RAVISH RAWISH RELISH RELIST REMISE REMISS RESIST REVISE SALISH SCHISM SCHIST SEXIST SHIISM SINISE SQUISH SUFISM TANIST TAOISM TAOIST THEISM THEIST TONISH TRUISM TUBIST TYPIST UNWISE UNWISH UPPISH UPRISE VALISE VANISH VERISM WIDISH WINISH YOGISM

•••I•S

ADLIBS ADMITS AERIES AFRITS AGGIES ALLIES ALOINS ALTIUS AMBITS ANTICS ANVILS APHIDS ARLISS ARMIES AROIDS ASDICS ASPICS ATKINS ATTICS AUDIOS AUDITS AUXINS AVAILS AVOIDS AWAITS BABIES BASICS BASINS BATIKS BEDIMS BEFITS BEGINS BELIES BEVIES BODIES BOGIES BOVIDS BRAIDS BRAILS BRAINS BROILS BRUINS BRUITS BURIES BURINS BUSIES CABINS CANIDS CAPIAS CARIBS CARIES CAVILS CHAINS CHAIRS CHOIRS CITIES CITIUS CIVICS CLAIMS COBIAS COLIES COMICS CONICS CONIES COPIES COSIES COZIES CUBICS CUBITS CUPIDS CURIOS CUTIES CUTINS CYNICS DARIUS DAVIES DAVITS DEBITS DEFIES DELIUS DEMIES DEMITS DENIES DENIMS DEVILS DIDIES DIGITS DIXITS DOGIES DORIES DRAILS DRAINS DROIDS DROITS DRUIDS DUTIES EDDIES EMAILS ENNIUS ENVIES EOSINS EQUIPS ESPIES ETHICS EYRIES FACIAS FACIES FAKIRS FERIAS FILIUS FLAILS FLAIRS FLUIDS FLYINS FOGIES FOLIOS FRUITS FURIES FUSILS GABIES GAMINS GENIES GENIUS GHAINS GLAIRS GNEISS GOBIES GRAILS GRAINS GROINS GSUITS HABITS HAKIMS HELIOS INDIES INUITS IONICS JULIUS JURIES KAFIRS KEFIRS KILIMS KRAITS KUMISS LADIES LAMIAS LAPINS LATINS LEVIES LILIES LIMITS LIPIDS LOOIES LORIES LUCIUS LYRICS LYSINS MANIAS MARIUS MATINS MAXIMS MEDIAS MEDICS MERITS MIMICS MINIMS MOBIUS MONIES MOTIFS MOVIES MUCINS NADIRS NAVIES NEVINS NIXIES NOHITS NORIAS OLDIES OPTICS ORBITS ORGIES OSMICS OVOIDS OXLIPS PAMIRS PANICS PATIOS PEKINS PERILS PEWITS PIPITS PITIES PIXIES PLAIDS PLAINS PLAITS POGIES PONIES POSIES POSITS PUPILS PYXIES QUAILS QUOINS QUOITS RABIES RADIOS RADIUS RAMIES RANIDS RAPIDS RATIOS REAIMS REAIRS REBIDS REFITS REGIUS RELICS RELIES REMISS REMITS REOILS REPINS RESINS RETIES REWINS ROBINS ROSINS RUBIES RUNINS SABINS SAHIBS SATINS SCRIMS SCRIPS SEPIAS SERIES SERIFS SERINS SETINS SHEIKS SIGILS SIRIUS SITINS SKEINS SNAILS SOLIDS SONICS SPLITS SPOILS SPRIGS SPRITS SQUIBS SQUIDS STAINS STAIRS STEINS STOICS STRIPS SWAINS TAKINS TAMILS TAPINS TAPIRS TAXIES THEIRS THRIPS TIBIAS TIDIES TIEINS TIPINS TOBIAS TOBIES TOEINS TONICS TOPICS TORIES TOXICS TOXINS TRAILS TRAINS TRAITS TULIPS TUNICS UGLIES UNDIES UNFITS UNPINS UNRIGS UNTIES UNZIPS URSIDS VARIES VCHIPS VIGILS VISITS YALIES ZAMIAS ZANIES ZAYINS ZOOIDS ZORILS

••••IS

ABATIS ADONIS ALANIS ALEXIS ALIBIS AMADIS AMATIS ANUBIS AODAIS ARAMIS ARTOIS BARRIS BAUCIS BEAVIS BLINIS BREVIS CADDIS CALAIS CAPRIS CASSIS CLEVIS CLORIS CLOVIS COATIS CORGIS CRISIS CULLIS CURTIS CUSTIS DASHIS DEBRIS DENNIS DERMIS DERRIS DHOTIS DIESIS DUBOIS ECESIS ELEMIS ENOKIS ENOSIS ENVOIS FERRIS GALOIS GHAZIS GILLIS GLACIS GLYNIS GNOSIS GRATIS HADJIS HAGGIS HAJJIS HARRIS HINGIS HOURIS HUBRIS INDRIS IRANIS IRAQIS KAURIS KEMPIS KERMIS KHAKIS KUKRIS LANAIS LANDIS LIBRIS MAHDIS MAJLIS MANTIS MAORIS MAQUIS MASAIS MATHIS MENTIS MIOSIS MISSIS MORRIS MUFTIS MYOSIS NEREIS NOESIS NORRIS OKAPIS OMANIS ORIBIS OSIRIS OTITIS OXALIS PARNIS PARRIS PARVIS PASTIS PATOIS PAUCIS PELVIS PENNIS PHOCIS PRAXIS PRECIS RABBIS RACHIS SARDIS SAUDIS SCIFIS SERAIS SHOJIS SPAHIS STASIS SUNNIS SWAMIS SWAZIS TENNIS TETRIS THATIS THESIS THETIS TIGRIS TILLIS TMESIS TRAVIS TSURIS UNGUIS VALOIS VERBIS VICTIS WALLIS WILLIS YAQUIS ZEUXIS

IT••••

ITALIA ITALIC ITASCA ITCHED ITCHES ITHACA ITHAKI ITSELF ITURBI ITZHAK

I•T•••

IATRIC IDTAGS INTACT INTAKE INTEND INTENS INTENT INTERJ INTERN INTIMA INTIME INTINE INTONE INTOTO INTOWN INTROS INTUIT INTUNE INTURN IQTEST IRTYSH ISTHMI ISTLES ISTRIA

I••T••

ICHTHY IGETIT IGOTIT INITIO INSTAL INSTAR INSTEP INSTIL IRATER ISHTAR

I•••T•

IDEATE IDIOTS IGNATZ IGNITE IMPUTE INCITE INDITE INGOTS INLETS INMATE INNATE INPUTS INSETS INSITU INTOTO INUITS INVITE INWITH IODATE IOLITE IOMOTH ISLETS

I••••T

ICEOUT ICIEST IDLEST IGETIT IGOTIT ILLEST ILLMET IMARET IMPACT IMPART IMPORT IMPOST INAPET INARUT INCEPT INCULT INDEBT INDENT INDICT INDUCT INFACT INFANT INFECT INFEST INGEST INJECT INJEST INKJET INMOST INPART INPORT INSECT INSERT INSIST INSULT INTACT INTENT INTUIT INVENT INVERT INVEST IQTEST IROBOT IRRUPT ISEULT

•IT•••

BITERS BITING BITMAP BITOFF BITOLA BITTED BITTEN BITTER CITATO CITERS CITIES CITIFY CITING CITIUS CITRIC CITRON CITRUS DITHER DITTOS DITZES EITHER FITFUL FITSIN FITTED FITTER GITANO HITECH HITHER HITMAN HITMEN HITOUT HITSIT HITSON HITSUP HITTER JITNEY JITTER KITBAG KITERS KITFOX KITING KITKAT KITSCH KITTEN LITANY LITCHI LITERS LITHIC LITHOG LITHOS LITMUS LITOUT LITRES LITTER LITTLE MITERS MITRAL MITRED MITRES MITTEN NITERS NITERY NITRES NITRIC NITWIT PITCHY PITHED PITIED PITIER PITIES PITMAN PITMEN PITONS PITSAW PITTED PITTER RITARD RITTER RITUAL SITARS SITCOM SITING SITINS SITOUT SITSBY SITSIN SITSON SITSUP SITTER SITUPS TITANS TITBIT TITERS TITFER TITHED TITHER TITHES TITIAN TITLED TITLES TITRED TITRES TITTER TITTLE TITTUP VITALE VITALS VITRIC WITCHY WITHAL WITHED WITHER WITHES WITHIN WITHIT WITTED ZITHER

•I•T••

BIGTEN BIGTOE BIGTOP BIOTAS BIOTIC BIOTIN BIRTHS BISTRO BITTED BITTEN BITTER DIATOM DICTUM DICTUS DIETED DIETER DIKTAT DINTED DISTAL DISTIL DITTOS FIFTHS FILTER FILTHY FIRTHS FISTED FISTIC FITTED FITTER GIFTED GIOTTO GIRTED GIRTHS HIATAL HIATUS HILTON HINTAT HINTED HINTER HINTON HITTER JILTED JITTER KILTED KILTER KILTIE KIRTLE KITTEN LICTOR LIFTED LIFTER LIFTUP LILTED LINTEL LINTER LIOTTA LIPTON LISTED LISTEE LISTEL LISTEN LISTER LISTON LITTER LITTLE MILTIE MILTON MINTED MINTER MISTED MISTER MITTEN MIXTEC NINTHS PIETAS PIETER PIETIN PIETRO PINTER PINTLE PINTOS PISTES PISTIL PISTOL PISTON PITTED PITTER QINTAR RIATAS RIFTED RIOTED RIOTER RITTER SIFTED SIFTER SILTED SINTAX SINTER SISTER SISTRA SITTER SIXTHS SIXTUS TICTAC TILTED TILTER TINTED TINTER TIPTOE TIPTOP TITTER TITTLE TITTUP UINTAS VICTIM VICTIS VICTOR VINTON VIRTUE VIRTUS VISTAS WIDTHS WILTED WILTON WINTER WINTRY WISTER WITTED

•I••T•

AIMSTO BIGHTS BIGOTS BINATE CITATO CIVETS DICOTS DIGITS DILATE DILUTE DIMITY DIVOTS DIXITS EIGHTH EIGHTS EIGHTY FICHTE FIESTA FIGHTS FILETS FINITE FINITO FIRSTS FIXATE FIXITY GIANTS GIGOTS GIOTTO GIVETO HINCTY KIBITZ LIESTO LIEUTS LIGATE LIGHTS LILITH LIMITS LIOTTA MIGHTY MIKITA MINUTE NICETY NIGHTS NIGHTY NIKITA NIMITZ NINETY PICOTS PIGSTY PILATE PILOTI PILOTS PINATA PINITE PINOTS PIPITS PIRATE PIVOTS RIALTO RIGHTO RIGHTS RIGHTY RIVETS SIESTA SIGHTS SINGTO TIEDTO TIESTO TIGHTS TINCTS VISITS WIGHTS WISETO ZIBETS ZIZITH

•I•••T

AIGRET AIMSAT AIROUT BILLET BIRGIT BISECT BISSET DIDACT DIEOUT DIGEST DIGLOT DIGOUT DIKTAT DIMOUT DIMWIT DIRECT DIREST DISANT DIVERT DIVEST FIDGET FILLET FINEST GIBBET GIBLET GIDGET GIMLET HIDOUT HINTAT HISSAT HITOUT HITSIT KISMET KITKAT

LIMPET
LINNET
LIONET
LITOUT
MIDGET
MILLET
MINUET
MINUIT
MISFIT
MISHIT
NICEST
NIPSAT
NITWIT
PIAGET
PICKAT
PICKET
PIGLET
PIGNUT
PIGOUT
PINXIT
PIOLET
PIQUET
QIVIUT
RIDENT
RIFEST
RILLET
RIPEST
RIPOUT
SIGNET
SILENT
SIPPET
SITOUT
TICKET
TIDBIT
TILSIT
TINHAT
TINPOT
TIPPET
TITBIT
VILEST
VINCIT
VIOLET
VIVANT
WICKET
WIDEST
WIDGET
WIGLET
WIGOUT
WILLET
WINGIT
WINKAT
WINOUT
WISENT
WISEST
WITHIT

••IT••
AKITAS
ALITER
ANITRA
BAITED
BLITHE
BOITES
BRITON
CHITIN
CHITON
CRITIC
DMITRI
EDITED
EDITIO
EDITOR
ELITES
EXITED
FAITHS
FLITCH
FRITOS
GAITED
GAITER
GLITCH
GLITZY
GRITTY
GUITAR
GUITRY
INITIO
KEITEL
LOITER
MAITAI
MAITRE
OBITER
OTITIC
OTITIS
QUITIT
SKITCH
SKITOW
SLITHY
SLITTY
SMITES
SMITHS
SMITHY
SNITCH
SPITED
SPITES
STITCH
STITHY
SUITED
SUITES
SUITOR
SUITUP
SWITCH
TRITER
TRITON
TWITCH
TWITTY
UNITAL
UNITAS
UNITED
UNITER
UNITES
WAITED
WAITER
WAITON
WAITUP
WHITEN
WHITER
WHITES
WHITTY
WRITER
WRITES
WRITHE

••I•T•
ALIOTO
ARISTA
ARISTO
AVIATE
BLINTZ
CHINTZ
CRISTO
DAINTY
DEISTS
DRIFTS
DRIFTY
EDICTS
EVICTS
EXISTS
FAINTS
FEINTS
FEISTY
FLINTS
FLINTY
FLIRTS
FLIRTY
FOISTS
GAIETY
GLINTS
GOINTO
GRIFTS
GRIOTS
GRISTS
GRITTY
GUILTY
HEISTS
HOISTS
IDIOTS
JOINTS
JOISTS
LAIDTO
MOIETY
ODISTS
OPIATE
PAINTS
PAINTY
PAIUTE
PLINTH
POINTE
POINTS
POINTY
PRINTS
QUIETS
QUILTS
QUINTS
QUIRTS
SAINTE
SAINTS
SHIFTS
SHIFTY
SHIITE
SHINTO
SHIRTS
SHIRTY
SKIRTS
SLITTY
SPILTH
SPINTO
STILTS
STINTS
SWIFTS
TAINTS
THIRTY
TRISTE
TWISTS
TWISTY
TWITTY
UBIETY
UNIATE
UNIATS
WAISTS
WHITTY
WRISTS

••I••T
ALIGHT
AMIDST
ARIGHT
BEIRUT
BLIGHT
BRIGHT
CLIENT
DRIEST
DWIGHT
ELICIT
FLIGHT
FRIGHT
GAINST
GRIVET
HAIGHT
HEIGHT
ICIEST
KNIGHT
ORIENT
PLIANT
PLIGHT
POIROT
PRIEST
PRIPET
PRIVET
QUITIT
RAILAT
SHIEST
SKIPIT
SLIEST
SLIGHT
SPIGOT
SPINET
SPIRIT
SWIVET
THIRST
TOILET
TRICOT
TRIJET
TRIVET
TWILIT
VEIGHT
VOIGHT
WEIGHT
WHILST
WRIEST
WRIGHT

•••IT•
ACUITY
ADMITS
AFRITS
AMBITS
APLITE
ASEITY
AUDITS
AWAITS
BARITE
BEFITS
BENITO
BONITO
BRUITS
CAPITA
CAVITY
COGITO
COMITY
CUBITS
DAMITA
DAVITS
DEBITS
DEMITS
DEVITO
DEWITT
DIGITS
DIMITY
DIXITS
DONITZ
DROITS
ENMITY
ENTITY
EOLITH
EQUITY
EXCITE
FAJITA
FERITY
FINITE
FINITO
FIXITY
FRUITS
FRUITY
GOWITH
GSUITS
GUNITE
HABITS
HALITE
HAMITE
IGNITE
INCITE
INDITE
INSITU
INUITS
INVITE
INWITH
IOLITE
JUDITH
KIBITZ
KRAITS
LAXITY
LENITY
LEVITE
LEVITY
LILITH
LIMITS
LOLITA
LUCITE
MERITS
MIKITA
MORITA
MORITZ
NIKITA
NIMITZ
NOHITS
NUDITY
ODDITY
ONSITE
OOLITE
OOLITH
OPHITE
ORBITS
ORNITH
PARITY
PEPITA
PETITE
PEWITS
PINITE
PIPITS
PLAITS
POLITE
POLITY
POSITS
PURITY
PYRITE
QUOITS
RARITY
RATITE
RECITE
REFITS
REMITS
ROSITA
SAMITE
SANITY
SEMITE
SENITI
SHIITE
SPLITS
SPRITE
SPRITS
SPRITZ
SUBITO
TAHITI
TONITE
TRAITS
UNFITS
UPPITY
VANITY
VENITE
VERITE
VERITY
VISITS
WAPITI
WRAITH
ZENITH
ZIZITH

•••I•T
ADRIFT
AGEIST
AGLINT
ALHIRT
ANOINT
AORIST
ARTIST
ASSIST
CUBIST
DELICT
DELIST
DEPICT
DESIST
DEWITT
EGOIST
ELLIOT
ENGIRT
ENLIST
FORINT
HERIOT
HOLIST
INDICT
INSIST
JOLIET
JOLIOT
JULIET
JURIST
KLEIST
LARIAT
LEGIST
LUTIST
LYRIST
MAOIST
MARIST
MONIST
NUDIST
OBOIST
PLAINT
PURIST
QIVIUT
QUAINT
RELICT
RELIST
RESIST
SCHIST
SCRIPT
SEXIST
SHRIFT
SOVIET
SPLINT
SPOILT
SPRINT
SQUINT
SQUIRT
STRICT
TANIST
TAOIST
THEIST
THRIFT
TSHIRT
TUBIST
TYPIST
UNGIRT
UPLIFT

••••IT
ACQUIT
ADROIT
ALBEIT
ANNUIT
ARMPIT
ATTRIT
AUFAIT
AULAIT
BAGSIT
BANDIT
BEATIT
BELOIT
BENOIT
BIRGIT
BLEWIT
BLOWIT
CANLIT
COEDIT
COMFIT
COMMIT
COOLIT
CREDIT
DACOIT
DARNIT
DAYLIT
DECEIT
DIMWIT
DOGSIT
DORRIT
DROPIT
ELEGIT
ELICIT
ESPRIT
GAMBIT
GASLIT
GETSIT
GODWIT
GOTOIT
HENBIT
HERMIT
HITSIT
HOBBIT
HOLDIT
HOOFIT
IGETIT
IGOTIT
INTUIT
JESUIT
KERMIT
KUWAIT
LOSEIT
LOSTIT
MADEIT
MAKEIT
MINUIT
MISFIT
MISHIT
NITWIT
NOEXIT
OUTFIT
OUTHIT
OUTWIT
PANDIT
PERMIT
PETTIT
PINXIT
POSTIT
PROFIT
PROSIT
PULPIT
PUNDIT
QUITIT
RABBIT
REEDIT
SAWFIT
SEEFIT
SENNIT
SKIPIT
SOBEIT
SOFFIT
SPIRIT
STOPIT
STRAIT
SUBMIT
SUMMIT
SUNLIT
TARPIT
TIDBIT
TILSIT
TITBIT
TOMTIT
TOOKIT
TURBIT
TWILIT
TWOBIT
UNKNIT
VINCIT
WESKIT
WINGIT
WITHIT

I•U•••
IGUACU
IGUANA
INUITS
INURED
INURES
ITURBI

I••U••
ILLUME
ILLUSE
IMBUED
IMBUES
IMMUNE
IMMUNO
IMMURE
IMPUGN
IMPURE
IMPUTE
INBULK
INCULT
INCURS
INCUSE
INDUCE
INDUCT
INFULL
INFUSE
INJURE
INJURY
INLUCK
INOUYE
INPUTS
INRUSH
INSULT
INSURE
INTUIT
INTUNE
INTURN
IRRUPT
ISEULT
ISSUED
ISSUER
ISSUES

I•••U•
ICARUS
ICEDUP
ICEOUT
ICESUP
IMBRUE
INARUT
INDIUM
INFLUX
INHAUL
INPOUR
IONIUM
IREFUL

I••••U
IGUACU
INSITU

•IU•••
CIUDAD

•I•U••
DILUTE
DISUSE
FIBULA
FIGURE
FIXUPS
GIGUES
KIKUYU
LIEUTS
LIGULA
LIGURE
LIQUID
LIQUOR
MIFUNE
MIGUEL
MINUET
MINUIT
MINUTE
MISUSE
MIXUPS
NIPUPS
PICULS
PINUPS
PIQUED
PIQUES
PIQUET
RITUAL
SIGURD
SIOUAN
SITUPS
TIEUPS
TIPUPS
UIGURS
VICUNA
VISUAL

•I••U•
AIDFUL
AIMFUL
AIRBUS
AIRGUN
AIROUT
BIDSUP
BIGGUN
BIGSUR
BIJOUX
BINDUP
BISQUE
CILIUM
CINQUE
CIRCUM
CIRCUS
CIRQUE
CIRRUS
CITIUS
CITRUS
DIALUP
DICTUM
DICTUS
DIEOUT
DIGOUT
DIGSUP
DIMOUT
DIMSUM
DINGUS
DISCUS
FICHUS
FILIUS
FILLUP
FIREUP
FIRMUP
FITFUL
GILGUY
GIVEUP
HIATUS
HICCUP
HIDOUT
HIGHUP
HIKEUP
HINDUS
HITOUT
HITSUP
KICKUP
KIPPUR
LIFTUP
LIMBUS
LINEUP
LINGUA
LINKUP
LITMUS
LITOUT
MINIUM
MISCUE
MISSUS
NIMBUS
NIPPUR
PICKUP
PIGNUT
PIGOUT
PILEUM
PILEUP
PILEUS
PINDUS
PIPEUP
QIVIUT
RIGOUR
RIGSUP
RILEUP
RINGUP
RIPOUT
RIPSUP
RISQUE
SIDDUR
SIGNUP
SINFUL
SIRIUS
SITOUT
SITSUP
SIXGUN
SIXTUS
SIZEUP
TIDYUP
TIEDUP
TIESUP
TISSUE
TITTUP
VIGOUR
VILLUS
VINOUS
VIRTUE
VIRTUS
WIGOUT
WILBUR
WILFUL
WINDUP
WINOUT
WIPEUP
WISEUP
ZIPSUP

•I•••U
BISSAU
KIKUYU
MILIEU
NIIHAU
PICCHU
VISHNU

••IU••
ODIUMS
PAIUTE
TRIUNE

••I•U•
ACINUS
ADIEUS
ADIEUX
AMICUS
AMINUS
ANIMUS
BEIRUT
BMINUS
CAIQUE
CHIAUS
CHINUP
CLIQUE
CLIQUY
CMINUS
CNIDUS
COILUP
CUIQUE
DMINUS
EPIRUS
FAIRUP
FAIYUM
FLIPUP
HAIKUS
JAIPUR
JOINUP
KAILUA
LAIDUP
MAIDUS
ODIOUS
PAIDUP
PAIRUP
POILUS
PRIMUM
PRIMUS
QUIPUS
RAIPUR
SKIRUN
SLIPUP
STIRUP
SUITUP
TRIPUP
UBIQUE
UNIQUE
WAITUP
WHIPUP

••I••U
NIIHAU
PAILOU

•••IU•
ACTIUM
ALLIUM
ALTIUS
ATRIUM
BARIUM
CERIUM
CESIUM
CILIUM
CITIUS
CONIUM
CORIUM
CURIUM
DARIUS
DELIUS
ENNIUS
ERBIUM
FILIUS
FOLIUM
GENIUS
HELIUM
INDIUM
IONIUM
JULIUS
LATIUM
LUCIUS
MARIUS
MEDIUM
MINIUM
MOBIUS
OMNIUM
OSMIUM
OSTIUM
PODIUM
QIVIUT
RADIUM
RADIUS
REGIUS
SIRIUS
SODIUM
TEDIUM
VALIUM

•••I•U
DESILU
INSITU
JABIRU
MALIBU
MARILU
MILIEU

I•V•••
INVADE
INVAIN
INVENT
INVERT
INVEST
INVITE
INVIVO
INVOKE
IRVINE
IRVING

I•••V•
INLOVE
INVIVO

I••••V
IMPROV

•IV•••
CIVETS
CIVICS
DIVANS
DIVEIN
DIVERS
DIVERT
DIVEST
DIVIDE
DIVINE
DIVING
DIVINO
DIVOTS
FIVEAM
FIVEPM
FIVERS
FIVEWS
GIVEIN
GIVENS
GIVERS
GIVETO
GIVEUP
GIVING
HIVAOA
HIVING
JIVERS
JIVIER
JIVING
LIVEIN
LIVELY
LIVENS
LIVEON
LIVERS
LIVERY
LIVING
LIVRES
PIVOTS
QIVIUT
RIVALS
RIVERA
RIVERS
RIVETS
RIVING
TIVOLI
VIVACE
VIVANT
VIVIAN
VIVIEN
VIVIFY

•I•V••
KIDVID
SIEVED
SIEVES
SILVAS
SILVER

•I•••V
KISLEV

••IV••
CHIVES
DRIVEL
DRIVEN
DRIVER
DRIVES
GRIVET
KNIVES
OGIVES
OLIVER
OLIVES
OLIVIA
PRIVET
QUIVER
SHIVER
SKIVED
SKIVER
SKIVES
SKIVVY
SLIVER
SNIVEL
SPIVAK
SPIVVY
STIVER
STIVIC
SWIVEL
SWIVET
TRIVET
TRIVIA
UNIVAC
WAIVED
WAIVER
WAIVES

••I•V•
GRIEVE
SKIVVY
SPIVVY
THIEVE

••I••V
ASIMOV

•••IV•
ACTIVE
ARGIVE
ARRIVE
DATIVE
DERIVE
ENDIVE
GODIVA
INVIVO
MOTIVE
NATIVE
RELIVE
REVIVE
SALIVA
SHRIVE
STRIVE
THRIVE
VOTIVE

I•W•••
INWARD
INWITH
IOWANS

I••W••
INAWAY

I•••W•
INLAWS
INTOWN

I••••W
INAROW
INFLOW

•IW•••
MIWOKS
SIWASH

•I•W••
AIRWAY
BIGWIG
DIMWIT
KIOWAS
MIDWAY
NITWIT
VIEWED
VIEWER
WIGWAG
WIGWAM
WINWIN

•I••W•
DISOWN
FIVEWS
SINEWS
SINEWY
WIDOWS

•I•••W
BILLOW
JIGSAW
LIELOW
MILDEW
MINNOW
PILLOW
PITSAW
RIPSAW
WILLOW
WINDOW
WINNOW

••IW••
OBIWAN
TAIWAN

••I•W•
OJIBWA

••I••W
SKITOW

•••I•W
ONVIEW
REVIEW

I••X••
IBEXES
ILEXES

I••••X
ICEBOX
INAFIX
INFLUX

•IX•••
DIXITS
FIXATE
FIXERS
FIXING
FIXITY
FIXUPS
MIXERS
MIXING
MIXTEC
MIXUPS
NIXIES
NIXING
PIXELS
PIXIES
SIXERS
SIXGUN
SIXING
SIXTHS
SIXTUS
VIXENS

•I•X••
DIOXIN
JINXED
JINXES
MINXES
PINXIT

•I••X•
BILOXI

•I•••X
BIJOUX
KITFOX
PICKAX
SINTAX
WILCOX
WINDEX

••IX••
BLIXEN
ELIXIR
TRIXIE
VSIXES

••I••X
ADIEUX
CHISOX
CLIMAX
SMILAX
UNISEX

•••IX•
MAXIXE

•••I•X
MENINX
SPHINX
SYRINX

••••IX
BENDIX
BOLLIX
COMMIX
INAFIX
MANNIX
MATRIX
PREFIX
PROLIX
SPADIX
SUFFIX
THESIX
TOMMIX

I•Y•••
IDYLLS

I••Y••
INSYNC
IRTYSH

I•••Y•
INLAYS
INOUYE

I••••Y
ICHTHY
IDIOCY
ILLSAY
INAWAY
INFAMY
INJURY
INPLAY

•IY•••
DIYERS
RIYADH
RIYALS

•I•Y••
LIBYAN
MINYAN
PINYIN
PINYON
SIBYLS
TIDYUP
VINYLS

•I••Y•
KIKUYU
LIEBYS
LIMEYS
RIBEYE
TIEDYE

•I•••Y
AIRDRY
AIRILY
AIRWAY
BIGAMY
BIGBOY
BINARY
BIRNEY
BISCAY
CICELY
CITIFY
DICKEY
DIDDLY
DILSEY
DIMITY
DIMPLY
DINGHY
DINKEY
DIPODY
DIRELY
DISMAY
DISNEY
EIGHTY
FILTHY
FINELY
FINERY
FINNEY
FIRMLY
FIXITY
GIGGLY
GILGUY
HICKEY
HIGHLY
HILARY
HINCTY
JIGGLY
JIMINY
JINGLY
JITNEY
KIDNEY
KIDORY
KILROY
KINDLY
KINGLY
KINSEY
LIEFLY
LIKELY
LIMPLY
LINENY
LINNEY
LINSEY
LIONLY
LITANY
LIVELY
LIVERY
MICKEY
MIDDAY
MIDWAY
MIGHTY
MILADY
MILDLY
MILLAY
MINIFY
MISERY
MISLAY
MISSAY
NIAMEY
NICELY
NICETY
NIDIFY
NIGHTY
NIMBLY
NIMINY
NINETY
NIPSEY
NITERY
OILILY
PIGSTY
PIMINY
PINERY
PIRACY
PITCHY
RICHLY
RICKEY
RIDLEY
RIFELY
RIGHTY
RIMSKY
RIPELY
RIPLEY
RIPPLY
SICILY
SICKLY
SIDNEY
SIMONY
SIMPLY
SINEWY
SINGLY
SISLEY
SITSBY
TICKLY
TIDDLY
TIDILY
TIMELY
TINGLY
TINILY
TINKLY
VIABLY
VILELY
VILIFY
VINERY
VINIFY
VIVIFY
WICOPY
WIDELY
WIFELY
WIGGLY
WILDLY
WILILY
WIMSEY
WINERY
WINTRY
WIRILY
WISELY
WITCHY

••IY••
FAIYUM

••I•Y•
DAIMYO
ERINYS
UNISYS
VAISYA

••I••Y
ACIDLY
APIARY
ARIDLY
AVIARY
AVIDLY
BAILEY
BLIMEY
BOIGNY
BRICKY
BRIERY
CHICLY
CHILLY
CHINKY
CHIRPY
CLIFFY
CLINGY
CLIQUY
CRIKEY
CRIMPY
CRISPY
DAILEY
DAINTY
DRIFTY
DRIPPY
EVILLY
FAIRLY
FEISTY
FLIMSY
FLINTY
FLIRTY
FRIARY
FRIDAY
FRILLY
FRINGY
FRISKY
FRIZZY
GAIETY
GAINLY
GLIBLY
GLITZY
GRIMLY
GRISLY
GRITTY
GUILTY
GUITRY
HAILEY
IDIOCY
LAIDBY
MAINLY
MOIETY
ONIONY
PAINTY
PHILBY
PHILLY
POINTY
PRICEY
PRIMLY
PRIORY
PRISSY
QUINCY
QUIPPY
QUIRKY
RAINEY
REILLY
SHIFTY
SHILLY
SHIMMY
SHINDY
SHINNY
SHIRTY
SKIDDY
SKIMPY
SKINNY
SKIPPY
SKIVVY
SLIMLY
SLIMSY
SLINKY
SLIPPY
SLITHY
SLITTY
SMILEY
SMIRKY
SMITHY
SNIFFY
SNIPPY
SPIFFY
SPIVVY
STICKY
STILLY
STIMPY
STINGY
STINKY
STITHY
SWINGY
SWIRLY
THINGY
THINLY
THIRTY
TRICKY
TRIGLY
TRILBY
TRIMLY
TRIPLY
TWIGGY
TWISTY
TWITTY
UBIETY
VAINLY
WEIRDY
WHIMSY
WHINEY
WHINNY
WHIPPY
WHIRLY
WHISKY
WHITTY

•••I•Y
ACUITY
AERIFY
AERILY
AIRILY
ARTILY
ASEITY
AURIFY
BASIFY
BODILY
BRAINY
BUSILY
CAGILY
CAVITY
CECILY
CITIFY
CODIFY
COMITY
COSILY
COZILY
DEWILY
DIMITY
DOZILY
EASILY
EDGILY
EERILY
EFFIGY
ENMITY
ENTITY
EQUITY
EXPIRY
FAMILY
FERITY
FIXITY
FOXILY
FRAIDY
FRUITY
GAMILY
GASIFY
GLAIRY
GORILY
GRAINY
HAZILY
HOLILY
HOMILY
HOMINY
JIMINY
JOKILY
LACILY
LAXITY
LAZILY
LENITY
LEVITY
LOGILY
MAZILY
MINIFY
MODIFY
MUTINY
NIDIFY
NIMINY
NOSILY
NOTIFY
NUDITY
ODDITY
OILILY
OOZILY
OSSIFY
PACIFY
PARITY
PIMINY
POKILY
POLICY
POLITY
PUNILY
PURIFY
PURITY
RACILY
RAMIFY
RARIFY
RARITY
RATIFY
RESINY
ROSILY
ROSINY
RUBIFY
SALIFY
SANITY
SATINY
SCHIZY
SEXILY
SICILY
STRIPY
TIDILY
TINILY
TYPIFY
UGLIFY
UGLILY
UNOILY
UNTIDY
UNWILY
UPPITY
VANITY
VERIFY
VERILY
VERITY
VILIFY
VINIFY
VIVIFY
WARILY
WAVILY
WAXILY
WILILY
WIRILY
ZANILY

IZ••••
IZABAL
IZZARD

I•Z•••
ITZHAK
IZZARD

I•••Z•
IODIZE
IONIZE

I••••Z
IGNATZ

•IZ•••
DIZENS
FIZGIG
FIZZED
FIZZES
FIZZLE
GIZMOS
LIZARD
LIZZIE
MIZENS
MIZZEN
MIZZLE
PIZAZZ
PIZZAS
RIZZIO
SIZERS
SIZEUP
SIZING
SIZZLE
VIZIER
VIZSLA
WIZARD
WIZENS
ZIZITH

•I•Z••
DITZES
FIZZED
FIZZES
FIZZLE
LIZZIE
MIZZEN
MIZZLE
PIAZZA
PINZON
PIZZAS
RIZZIO
SIZZLE
WINZES
ZIGZAG

•I••Z•
PIAZZA
PIZAZZ
RIENZI

•I•••Z
KIBITZ
MILOSZ
NIMITZ
PIZAZZ

••IZ••
BAIZAS
FRIZZY
MAIZES
PFIZER
PRIZED
PRIZES
SEIZED
SEIZER
SEIZES
WHIZZO

••I•Z•
FRIEZE
FRIZZY
GLITZY
WHIZZO

••I••Z
BLINTZ
BRIENZ
CHINTZ
SHIRAZ

•••IZ•
ASSIZE
BELIZE
IODIZE
IONIZE
SCHIZY

•••I•Z
DONITZ
KIBITZ
MORITZ
NIMITZ
SPRITZ

••••IZ
CURTIZ
TABRIZ
THEWIZ

JA••••
JABBAR
JABBED
JABBER
JABIRU
JABOTS
JACALS
JACANA
JACKAL
JACKED
JACKET
JACKEY
JACKIE
JACKUP
JACLYN
JACOBI
JADING
JADISH
JAEGER
JAGGED
JAGGER
JAGUAR
JAILED
JAILER
JAIPUR
JALAPA
JALOPY
JAMAAL
JAMMED
JAMMER
JAMOKE
JAMSIN
JAMSUP
JAMUPS
JANGLE
JANGLY
JANHUS
JANICE
JANINE
JANSEN
JANSKY
JAPANS
JAPERS
JAPERY
JAPING
JARFUL
JARGON
JARRAH
JARRED
JASCHA
JASEYS
JASPER
JAUNTS
JAUNTY
JAURES
JAVARI
JAVIER
JAWING
JAWOHL
JAYCEE
JAYVEE
JAZZED
JAZZES
JAZZUP

J•A•••
JEANNE
JOANIE
JOANNA
JOANNE
JUAREZ

J••A••
JACALS
JACANA
JALAPA
JAMAAL
JAPANS
JAVARI
JICAMA
JIHADS
JOHANN
JONAHS
JUDAEA
JUDAIC
JUMADA
JURADO
JURATS

J•••A•
JABBAR
JACKAL
JAGUAR
JAMAAL
JARRAH
JEERAT
JETLAG
JETSAM
JETWAY
JIGSAW
JINNAH
JORDAN
JOSIAH
JOVIAL
JOVIAN
JUBBAH
JULIAN
JUMPAT
JUNEAU
JUNTAS

J••••A
JACANA
JALAPA
JASCHA
JERBOA
JICAMA
JOANNA
JOJOBA
JOSHUA
JUDAEA
JUDOKA
JUMADA

•JA•••
AJANTA

•J•A••
UJJAIN

•J•••A
AJANTA
DJERBA
EJECTA
OJIBWA

••JA••
ADJANI
DEJAVU
HIJACK
MOJAVE
PAJAMA
PYJAMA
RAJAHS
SEJANT
TEJANO
UJJAIN
UNJAMS

••J•A•
FIJIAN
FUJIAN
HIJRAH
STJOAN

••J••A
ARJUNA
FAJITA
JOJOBA
PAJAMA
PYJAMA

•••JA•
DEEJAY
ELIJAH
INAJAM
LOGJAM
NINJAS
PUNJAB
RIOJAS
THUJAS
TRAJAN
TROJAN
VEEJAY

•••J•A
PRAJNA

••••JA
BAROJA

J•B•••
JABBAR
JABBED
JABBER
JABIRU
JABOTS
JIBBED
JIBING
JOBBED
JOBBER
JOBETH
JOBHOP
JOBLOT
JUBBAH

J••B••
JABBAR
JABBED
JABBER
JERBOA
JIBBED
JOBBED
JOBBER
JUBBAH
JUMBLE
JUMBOS

J•••B•
JACOBI
JOJOBA
JUJUBE

•J•B••
OJIBWA

•J••B•
DJERBA

••J•B•
JOJOBA
JUJUBE
MCJOBS

•••J•B
CONJOB
DAYJOB
ODDJOB
PUNJAB
TOPJOB

J•C•••
JACALS
JACANA
JACKAL
JACKED
JACKET
JACKEY
JACKIE
JACKUP
JACLYN
JACOBI
JECKLE
JICAMA
JOCKEY
JOCOSE
JOCUND

J••C••
JASCHA
JAYCEE
JUICED
JUICER
JUICES
JUNCOS

J•••C•
JANICE
JOUNCE
JOUNCY

J••••C
JUDAIC

•J•C••
EJECTA
EJECTS

••J•C•
ABJECT
DEJECT
HIJACK
INJECT
MEJICO
OBJECT
REJECT

J•D•••
JADING
JADISH
JUDAEA
JUDAIC
JUDDER
JUDGED
JUDGES
JUDITH
JUDOKA

J••D••
JORDAN
JUDDER

J•••D•
JIHADS
JUMADA
JURADO

J••••D
JABBED
JACKED
JAGGED
JAILED
JAMMED
JARRED
JAZZED
JEERED
JELLED
JERKED
JESTED
JETTED
JIBBED
JIGGED
JILTED
JINKED
JINXED
JOBBED
JOCUND
JOGGED
JOINED
JOLTED
JOSHED
JOTTED
JUDGED
JUGGED
JUICED
JUMPED
JUNKED
JUTTED

•J•D••
EJIDOS

•J••D•
FJELDS
FJORDS

••J••D
BUJOLD

JE••••
JEANNE
JECKLE
JEERAT
JEERED
JEERER
JEETER
JEEVES
JEJUNE
JEKYLL
JELLED
JENNER
JENNET
JENNEY
JENNIE
JENSEN
JERBOA
JEREMY
JERKED
JERKIN
JEROME
JERSEY
JESSEL
JESSIE
JESTED
JESTER
JESUIT
JETGUN
JETHRO
JETLAG
JETSAM
JETSET
JETSKI
JETSON
JETTED
JETWAY
JEWELS
JEWETT
JEWISH

J•E•••
JAEGER
JEERAT
JEERED
JEERER
JEETER
JEEVES
JOETEX

J••E••
JAPERS
JAPERY
JASEYS
JEREMY
JEWELS
JEWETT
JIVERS
JOBETH
JOKERS
JOLENE
JOSEPH
JOWETT
JULEPS
JUNEAU

J•••E•
JABBED
JABBER
JACKED
JACKET
JACKEY
JAEGER
JAGGED
JAGGER
JAILED
JAILER
JAMMED
JAMMER
JANSEN
JARRED
JASPER
JAURES
JAVIER
JAYCEE
JAYVEE
JAZZED
JAZZES
JEERED
JEERER
JEETER
JEEVES
JELLED
JENNER
JENNET
JENNEY
JENSEN
JERKED
JERSEY
JESSEL
JESTED
JESTER
JETSET
JETTED
JIBBED
JIGGED
JIGGER
JILTED
JINKED
JINXED
JINXES
JITNEY
JITTER
JIVIER
JOBBED
JOBBER
JOCKEY
JOETEX
JOGGED
JOGGER
JOINED
JOINER
JOKIER
JOLIET
JOLTED
JOSHED
JOSHES
JOSSER
JOSSES
JOTTED
JOULES
JOYNER
JUAREZ
JUDAEA
JUDDER
JUDGED
JUDGES
JUGGED
JUICED
JUICER
JUICES
JULIET
JUMPED
JUMPER
JUNKED
JUNKER
JUNKET
JURIES
JUSTER
JUTTED

J••••E
JACKIE
JAMOKE
JANGLE
JANICE
JANINE
JAYCEE
JAYVEE
JEANNE
JECKLE
JEJUNE
JENNIE
JEROME
JESSIE
JIGGLE
JIMMIE
JINGLE
JOANIE
JOANNE
JOCOSE
JOGGLE
JOHORE
JOLENE
JOSTLE
JOUNCE
JUGGLE
JUJUBE
JUMBLE
JUNGLE
JUNKIE

•JE•••
DJERBA
EJECTA
EJECTS
FJELDS

•J••E•
IJSSEL
KJOLEN

••JE••
ABJECT
DEJECT
INJECT
INJEST
OBJECT
REJECT

••J•E•
GIJOES
HAJJES
MAJGEN

••J••E
ABJURE
ADJURE
BYJOVE
CAJOLE
DEJURE
INJOKE
INJURE
JEJUNE
JUJUBE
MOJAVE

•••JE•
FANJET
GASJET
HADJES
HAJJES
INKJET
KOPJES
RAMJET
TRIJET

••••JE
SKOPJE

J••F••
JARFUL
JOYFUL
JUGFUL

•JF•••
AJFOYT

J•G•••
JAGGED
JAGGER
JAGUAR
JIGGED
JIGGER
JIGGLE
JIGGLY
JIGSAW
JOGGED
JOGGER
JOGGLE
JUGFUL
JUGGED
JUGGLE

J••G••
JAEGER
JAGGED
JAGGER
JANGLE
JANGLY
JARGON
JETGUN
JIGGED
JIGGER
JIGGLE
JIGGLY
JINGLE
JINGLY
JOGGED
JOGGER
JOGGLE
JUDGED
JUDGES
JUGGED
JUGGLE
JUNGLE
JUNGLY

J••••G
JADING
JAPING
JAWING
JETLAG
JIBING
JIVING
JOKING
JUKING

••JG••
MAJGEN

J•H•••
JIHADS
JOHANN
JOHNNY
JOHORE

J••H••
JANHUS
JETHRO
JOBHOP
JOSHED
JOSHES
JOSHUA

J•••H•
JASCHA
JAWOHL
JONAHS

J••••H
JADISH
JARRAH
JEWISH
JINNAH
JOBETH
JOSEPH
JOSIAH
JUBBAH
JUDITH
JUTISH

••J•H•
RAJAHS
STJOHN
UPJOHN

••J••H
HIJRAH

•••J•H
ELIJAH

JI••••
JIBBED
JIBING
JICAMA
JIGGED
JIGGER
JIGGLE
JIGGLY
JIGSAW
JIHADS
JILTED
JIMINY
JIMMIE

JIMSON
JINGLE
JINGLY
JINKED
JINNAH
JINXED
JINXES
JITNEY
JITTER
JIVERS
JIVIER
JIVING

J•I•••
JAILED
JAILER
JAIPUR
JOINED
JOINER
JOININ
JOINTS
JOINUP
JOISTS
JUICED
JUICER
JUICES

J••I••
JABIRU
JADING
JADISH
JANICE
JANINE
JAPING
JAVIER
JAWING
JEWISH
JIBING
JIMINY
JIVIER
JIVING
JOKIER
JOKILY
JOKING
JOLIET
JOLIOT
JOSIAH
JOVIAL
JOVIAN
JUDITH
JUKING
JULIAN
JULIET
JULIUS
JUNIOR
JURIES
JURIST
JUTISH

J•••I•
JACKIE
JAMSIN
JENNIE
JERKIN
JESSIE
JESUIT
JIMMIE
JOANIE
JOININ
JOPLIN
JOSKIN
JUDAIC
JUMPIN
JUNKIE
JUSTIN

J••••I
JACOBI
JAVARI
JETSKI

•JI•••
EJIDOS
OJIBWA

•J••I•
UJJAIN

••JI••
FAJITA
FIJIAN
FUJIAN
MEJICO

••J•I•
ADJOIN
ENJOIN
HAJJIS
MAJLIS
REJOIN
UJJAIN

••J••I
ADJANI

•••JI•
GAIJIN
HADJIS
HAJJIS
SHOJIS

••••JI
ROMAJI

J•J•••
JEJUNE
JOJOBA
JUJUBE

•JJ•••
UJJAIN

••JJ••
HAJJES
HAJJIS

J•K•••
JEKYLL
JOKERS
JOKIER
JOKILY
JOKING
JUKING

J••K••
JACKAL
JACKED
JACKET
JACKEY
JACKIE
JACKUP
JECKLE
JERKED
JERKIN
JINKED
JOCKEY
JOSKIN
JUNKED
JUNKER
JUNKET
JUNKIE

J•••K•
JAMOKE
JANSKY
JETSKI
JUDOKA

••J•K•
INJOKE

••J••K
HIJACK

•••JK•
STOJKO

•••J•K
SELJUK

J•L•••
JALAPA
JALOPY
JELLED
JILTED
JOLENE
JOLIET
JOLIOT
JOLSON
JOLTED
JULEPS
JULIAN
JULIET
JULIUS

J••L••
JACLYN
JAILED
JAILER
JELLED
JETLAG
JOBLOT
JOPLIN
JOULES

J•••L•
JACALS
JANGLE
JANGLY
JECKLE
JEKYLL
JEWELS
JIGGLE
JIGGLY
JINGLE
JINGLY
JOGGLE
JOKILY
JOSTLE
JUGGLE
JUMBLE
JUNGLE
JUNGLY
JUSTLY

J••••L
JACKAL
JAMAAL
JARFUL
JAWOHL
JEKYLL
JESSEL
JOVIAL
JOYFUL
JUGFUL

•J•L••
FJELDS
KJOLEN

•J•••L
IJSSEL

••JL••
MAJLIS

••J•L•
BUJOLD
CAJOLE

•••J•L
BANJUL
FRIJOL

J•M•••
JAMAAL
JAMMED
JAMMER
JAMOKE
JAMSIN
JAMSUP
JAMUPS
JIMINY
JIMMIE
JIMSON
JUMADA
JUMBLE
JUMBOS
JUMPAT
JUMPED
JUMPER
JUMPIN
JUMPON
JUMPUP

J••M••
JAMMED
JAMMER
JIMMIE

J•••M•
JEREMY
JEROME
JICAMA
JORUMS

J••••M
JETSAM

••J•M•
PAJAMA
PYJAMA
UNJAMS

•••J•M
BOOJUM
INAJAM
LOGJAM

J•N•••
JANGLE
JANGLY
JANHUS
JANICE
JANINE
JANSEN
JANSKY
JENNER
JENNET
JENNEY
JENNIE
JENSEN
JINGLE
JINGLY
JINKED
JINNAH
JINXED
JINXES
JONAHS
JONSON
JUNCOS
JUNEAU
JUNGLE
JUNGLY
JUNIOR
JUNKED
JUNKER
JUNKET
JUNKIE
JUNTAS
JUNTOS

J••N••
JAUNTS
JAUNTY
JEANNE
JENNER
JENNET
JENNEY
JENNIE
JINNAH
JITNEY
JOANIE
JOANNA
JOANNE
JOHNNY
JOINED
JOINER
JOININ
JOINTS
JOINUP
JOUNCE
JOUNCY
JOYNER

J•••N•
JACANA
JADING
JANINE
JAPANS
JAPING
JAWING
JEANNE
JEJUNE
JIBING
JIMINY
JIVING
JOANNA
JOANNE
JOCUND
JOHANN
JOHNNY
JOKING
JOLENE
JOURNO
JUKING

J••••N
JACLYN
JAMSIN
JANSEN
JARGON
JENSEN
JERKIN
JETGUN
JETSON
JIMSON
JOHANN
JOININ
JOLSON
JONSON
JOPLIN
JORDAN
JOSKIN
JOVIAN
JULIAN
JUMPIN
JUMPON
JUSTIN

•J•N••
AJANTA

•J•••N
KJOLEN
UJJAIN

••J•N•
ADJANI
ARJUNA
CAJUNS
JEJUNE
SEJANT
TEJANO

••J••N
ADJOIN
ENJOIN
FIJIAN
FUJIAN
MAJGEN
REJOIN
STJOAN
STJOHN
UJJAIN
UPJOHN

•••JN•
PRAJNA

•••J•N
DONJON
GAIJIN
TRAJAN
TROJAN

JO••••
JOANIE
JOANNA
JOANNE
JOBBED
JOBBER
JOBETH
JOBHOP
JOBLOT
JOCKEY
JOCOSE
JOCUND
JOETEX
JOGGED
JOGGER
JOGGLE
JOHANN
JOHNNY
JOHORE
JOINED
JOINER
JOININ
JOINTS
JOINUP
JOISTS
JOJOBA
JOKERS
JOKIER
JOKILY
JOKING
JOLENE
JOLIET
JOLIOT
JOLSON
JOLTED
JONAHS
JONSON
JOPLIN
JORDAN
JORUMS
JOSEPH
JOSHED
JOSHES
JOSHUA
JOSIAH
JOSKIN
JOSSER
JOSSES
JOSTLE
JOTTED
JOULES
JOUNCE
JOUNCY
JOURNO
JOUSTS
JOVIAL
JOVIAN
JOWETT
JOYFUL
JOYNER
JOYOUS

J••O••
JABOTS
JACOBI
JALOPY
JAMOKE
JAWOHL
JEROME
JOCOSE
JOHORE
JOJOBA
JUDOKA
JURORS

J•••O•
JARGON
JERBOA
JETSON
JIMSON
JOBHOP
JOBLOT
JOLIOT
JOLSON
JONSON
JUMBOS
JUMPON
JUNCOS
JUNIOR
JUNTOS

J••••O
JETHRO
JOURNO
JURADO

•JO•••
FJORDS
KJOLEN

•J•O••
AJFOYT

•J••O•
EJIDOS

••JO••
ADJOIN
ANJOUS
BIJOUX
BUJOLD
BYJOVE
CAJOLE
ENJOIN
ENJOYS
GIJOES
INJOKE
JOJOBA
MAJORS
MCJOBS
REJOIN
STJOAN
STJOHN
UPJOHN

••J••O
MEJICO
TEJANO

•••JO•
ACAJOU
AMAJOR
BANJOS
BMAJOR
CMAJOR
CONJOB
DAYJOB
DMAJOR
DONJON
EMAJOR
FMAJOR
FRIJOL
GMAJOR
MENJOU
ODDJOB
TOPJOB

•••J•O
STOJKO

••••JO
NAVAJO

J•P•••
JAPANS
JAPERS
JAPERY
JAPING
JOPLIN

J••P••
JAIPUR
JASPER
JUMPAT
JUMPED
JUMPER
JUMPIN
JUMPON
JUMPUP

J•••P•
JALAPA
JALOPY
JAMUPS
JOSEPH
JULEPS

J••••P
JACKUP
JAMSUP
JAZZUP
JOBHOP
JOINUP
JUMPUP

••JP••
RAJPUT

J•R•••
JARFUL
JARGON
JARRAH
JARRED
JERBOA
JEREMY
JERKED
JERKIN
JEROME
JERSEY
JORDAN
JORUMS
JURADO
JURATS
JURIES
JURIST
JURORS

J••R••
JARRAH
JARRED
JAURES
JEERAT
JEERED
JEERER
JOURNO
JUAREZ

J•••R•
JABIRU
JAPERS
JAPERY
JAVARI
JETHRO
JIVERS
JOHORE
JOKERS
JURORS

J••••R
JABBAR
JABBER
JAEGER
JAGGER
JAGUAR
JAILER
JAIPUR
JAMMER
JASPER
JAVIER
JEERER
JEETER
JENNER
JESTER
JIGGER
JITTER
JIVIER
JOBBER
JOGGER
JOINER
JOKIER
JOSSER
JOYNER
JUDDER
JUICER
JUMPER
JUNIOR
JUNKER
JUSTER

•J•R••
DJERBA
FJORDS

••JR••
HIJRAH

••J•R•
ABJURE
ADJURE
DEJURE
INJURE
INJURY
MAJORS

•••J•R
AMAJOR
BMAJOR
CMAJOR
DMAJOR
EMAJOR
FMAJOR
GMAJOR

J•S•••
JASCHA
JASEYS
JASPER
JESSEL
JESSIE
JESTED
JESTER
JESUIT
JOSEPH
JOSHED
JOSHES
JOSHUA
JOSIAH
JOSKIN
JOSSER
JOSSES
JOSTLE
JUSTER
JUSTIN
JUSTLY

J••S••
JAMSIN
JAMSUP
JANSEN
JANSKY
JENSEN
JERSEY
JESSEL
JESSIE
JETSAM
JETSET
JETSKI
JETSON
JIGSAW
JIMSON
JOISTS
JOLSON
JONSON
JOSSER
JOSSES
JOUSTS

J•••S•
JADISH
JEWISH
JOCOSE
JURIST
JUTISH

J••••S
JABOTS
JACALS
JAMUPS
JANHUS
JAPANS
JAPERS
JASEYS
JAUNTS
JAURES
JAZZES
JEEVES
JEWELS
JIHADS
JINXES
JIVERS
JOINTS
JOISTS
JOKERS
JONAHS
JORUMS
JOSHES
JOSSES
JOULES
JOUSTS
JOYOUS
JUDGES
JUICES
JULEPS
JULIUS
JUMBOS
JUNCOS
JUNTAS
JUNTOS
JURATS
JURIES
JURORS

•JS•••
IJSSEL

•J•S••
IJSSEL

•J•••S
EJECTS
EJIDOS
FJELDS
FJORDS

••J•S•
ADJUST
INJEST
UNJUST

••J••S
ANJOUS
CAJUNS
ENJOYS
GIJOES
HAJJES
HAJJIS
MAJLIS
MAJORS
MCJOBS
RAJAHS
UNJAMS

•••J•S
BANJOS
HADJES
HADJIS
HAJJES
HAJJIS
KOPJES
NINJAS
RIOJAS
SHOJIS
THUJAS

J•T•••
JETGUN
JETHRO
JETLAG
JETSAM
JETSET
JETSKI
JETSON
JETTED
JETWAY
JITNEY
JITTER
JOTTED
JUTISH
JUTTED

J••T••
JEETER
JESTED
JESTER
JETTED
JILTED
JITTER
JOETEX
JOLTED
JOSTLE
JOTTED
JUNTAS
JUNTOS
JUSTER
JUSTIN
JUSTLY
JUTTED

J•••T•
JABOTS
JAUNTS
JAUNTY
JEWETT
JOBETH
JOINTS
JOISTS
JOUSTS
JOWETT
JUDITH
JURATS

J••••T
JACKET
JEERAT
JENNET
JESUIT
JETSET
JEWETT
JOBLOT
JOLIET
JOLIOT
JOWETT
JULIET
JUMPAT
JUNKET
JURIST

•J••T•
AJANTA
EJECTA
EJECTS

•J•••T
AJFOYT

••J•T•
FAJITA

••J••T
ABJECT
ADJUST
DEJECT
INJECT
INJEST
OBJECT
RAJPUT
REJECT
SEJANT
UNJUST

•••J•T
FANJET
GASJET
INKJET
RAMJET
TRIJET

JU••••
JUAREZ
JUBBAH
JUDAEA
JUDAIC
JUDDER
JUDGED
JUDGES
JUDITH
JUDOKA
JUGFUL
JUGGED
JUGGLE
JUICED
JUICER
JUICES
JUJUBE
JUKING
JULEPS
JULIAN
JULIET
JULIUS
JUMADA
JUMBLE
JUMBOS
JUMPAT
JUMPED
JUMPER
JUMPIN
JUMPON
JUMPUP
JUNCOS
JUNEAU
JUNGLE
JUNGLY
JUNIOR
JUNKED
JUNKER
JUNKET
JUNKIE
JUNTAS
JUNTOS
JURADO
JURATS
JURIES
JURIST
JURORS
JUSTER
JUSTIN
JUSTLY
JUTISH
JUTTED

J•U•••
JAUNTS
JAUNTY
JAURES
JOULES
JOUNCE
JOUNCY
JOURNO
JOUSTS

J••U••
JAGUAR
JAMUPS
JEJUNE
JESUIT
JOCUND
JORUMS
JUJUBE

J•••U•
JACKUP
JAIPUR
JAMSUP
JANHUS
JARFUL
JAZZUP
JETGUN
JOINUP
JOSHUA
JOYFUL
JOYOUS
JUGFUL
JULIUS
JUMPUP

J••••U
JABIRU
JUNEAU

••JU••
ABJURE
ADJURE
ADJUST
ARJUNA
CAJUNS
DEJURE
INJURE
INJURY
JEJUNE
JUJUBE
UNJUST

••J•U•
ANJOUS
BIJOUX
RAJPUT

••J••U
DEJAVU

•••JU•
BANJUL
BOOJUM
SELJUK

•••J•U
ACAJOU
MENJOU

••••JU
CHONJU

J•V•••
JAVARI
JAVIER
JIVERS
JIVIER
JIVING
JOVIAL
JOVIAN

J••V••
JAYVEE
JEEVES

••J•V•
BYJOVE
DEJAVU
MOJAVE

J•W•••
JAWING
JAWOHL
JEWELS
JEWETT
JEWISH
JOWETT

J••W••
JETWAY

J••••W
JIGSAW

•J••W•
OJIBWA

J••X••
JINXED
JINXES

J••••X
JOETEX

••J••X
BIJOUX

J•Y•••
JAYCEE
JAYVEE
JOYFUL
JOYNER
JOYOUS

J••Y••
JEKYLL

J•••Y•
JACLYN
JASEYS

J••••Y
JACKEY
JALOPY
JANGLY
JANSKY
JAPERY
JAUNTY
JENNEY
JEREMY
JERSEY
JETWAY
JIGGLY
JIMINY
JINGLY
JITNEY
JOCKEY
JOHNNY
JOKILY
JOUNCY
JUNGLY
JUSTLY

•J••Y•
AJFOYT

••J•Y•
ENJOYS

••J••Y
INJURY

•••J•Y
DEEJAY
VEEJAY

J•Z•••
JAZZED
JAZZES
JAZZUP

J••Z••
JAZZED
JAZZES
JAZZUP

J••••Z
JUAREZ

KA••••
KABOBS
KABOOM
KABUKI
KAFFIR
KAFIRS
KAGERA
KAHLIL
KAHLUA
KAHUNA
KAILUA
KAISER
KAKAPO
KALAKH
KALINE
KALKAN
KALMAR
KAMALA
KANAKA

KANDER KANSAN KANSAS KANTOR KAOLIN KAPLAN KAPPAS KARATE KARATS KAREEM KARIBA KARMIC KARNAK KAROSS KARPOV KARRAS KARROO KARSTS KASBAH KASDAN KATHIE KATMAI KAUNAS KAUNDA KAURIS KAVNER KAYAKS KAYOED KAZAKH KAZAKS KAZOOS

K•A•••

KEARNY KEATON KHAFRE KHAKIS KHALID KIANGS KLATCH KLAXON KNACKS KNAGGY KNARRY KNAVES KOALAS KRAALS KRAITS KRAKEN KRAKOW KRAMER KRANTZ KRASNY KRATER KWACHA KWANZA KYACKS

K••A••

KAKAPO KALAKH KAMALA KANAKA KARATE KARATS KAYAKS KAZAKH KAZAKS KDLANG KEBABS KERALA KIGALI KNEADS KODALY KORATS KOVACS KRAALS KULAKS KURALT KUVASZ KUWAIT

K•••A•

KALKAN KALMAR KANSAN KANSAS KAPLAN KAPPAS KARNAK KARRAS KASBAH KASDAN KATMAI KAUNAS KEENAN KEEPAT KENYAN KEPTAT KERMAN KEVLAR KEYPAD KEYWAY KIDMAN KIDNAP KIOWAS KIRMAN KITBAG KITKAT KLIBAN KOALAS KODIAK KOMBAT KONRAD KOREAN KORMAN KOUFAX KUBLAI KURGAN

K••••A

KAGERA KAHLUA KAHUNA KAILUA KAMALA KANAKA KARIBA KAUNDA KERALA KESHIA KINEMA KONICA KORUNA KWACHA KWANZA

•KA•••

OKAPIS OKAYED SKALDS SKANKS SKATED SKATER SKATES UKASES

•K•A••

AKUAKU OKSANA SKEANS SKOALS

•K••A•

AKELAS AKITAS SKYCAP SKYLAB SKYWAY

•K•••A

OKSANA

••KA••

ACKACK ALKALI ANKARA ASKARI DEKALB GOKART KAKAPO MAKALU MIKADO PIKAKE TOKAYS UAKARI YUKATA YUKAWA

••K•A•

DIKTAT LEKVAR POKEAT SUKKAH TOKLAS

••K••A

ANKARA BAKULA BIKILA DAKOTA LAKOTA MAKEBA MAKUTA MIKITA NIKITA NIKOLA PAKULA YAKIMA YAKUZA YUKATA YUKAWA

•••KA•

BABKAS BAIKAL BALKAN BARKAT BROKAW CHUKAR HOOKAH JACKAL KALKAN KITKAT LOOKAT PARKAS PARKAY PECKAT PEEKAT PICKAT PICKAX POLKAS PUNKAH RYOKAN SHIKAR SUCKAS SUKKAH TALKAT TANKAS VODKAS WINKAT

•••K•A

CHUKKA GURKHA MARKKA MOSKVA QUOKKA

••••KA

ALASKA ANNIKA BANGKA CHUKKA EUREKA FLICKA GLINKA JUDOKA KANAKA LUSAKA MARKKA MEDAKA NOOTKA QUOKKA SEDAKA TANAKA TOPEKA TROIKA WOVOKA

K•B•••

KABOBS KABOOM KABUKI KEBABS KEBOBS KIBBLE KIBITZ KIBOSH KOBOLD KUBLAI

K••B••

KASBAH KHYBER KIBBLE KITBAG KLIBAN KNOBBY KOMBAT KORBUT

K•••B•

KABOBS KARIBA KEBABS KEBOBS KNOBBY

•KB•••

EKBERG

•K•B••

SKIBOB SKYBOX

•K••B•

AKIMBO

•K•••B

SKIBOB SKYLAB

••K•B•

MAKEBA

••K••B

DEKALB

K•C•••

KICKED KICKER KICKIN KICKUP KUCHEN

K••C••

KIMCHI KNACKS KNICKS KNOCKS KWACHA KYACKS

K•••C•

KIRSCH KITSCH KLATCH KONICA KOPECK KOVACS KVETCH

K••••C

KARMIC

•K•C••

SKYCAP

•K••C•

SKETCH SKITCH

••K•C•

ACKACK EDKOCH

••K••C

PYKNIC

•••K•C

TURKIC

KD••••

KDLANG

K•D•••

KEDGED KEDGES KIDDED KIDDER KIDDIE KIDMAN KIDNAP KIDNEY KIDORY KIDVID KODALY KODIAK KUDROW KUDZUS

K••D••

KANDER KASDAN KIDDED KIDDER KIDDIE KINDER KINDLE KINDLY KINDOF KLUDGE

K•••D•

KAUNDA KNEADS KOMODO

K••••D

KAYOED KEDGED KEELED KEENED KEGGED KENNED KERNED KEYPAD KHALID KICKED KIDDED KIDVID KILLED KILNED KILTED KINGED KINKED KISSED KNIFED KOBOLD KONRAD

•K•D••

SKIDDY

•K••D•

SKALDS SKIDDY

•K•••D

OKAYED SKATED SKEWED SKIVED

••KD••

DIKDIK

••K•D•

AIKIDO ALKYDS MAKEDO MIKADO

••K••D

ANKLED INKIND UNKIND YAKKED YUKKED

•••K•D

AWAKED BACKED BALKED BANKED BARKED BASKED BEAKED BILKED BOOKED BRAKED BUCKED BULKED BUNKED BUSKED CALKED CARKED CHOKED COCKED CONKED COOKED CORKED DECKED DISKED DOCKED DUCKED DUNKED EVOKED FINKED FLAKED FORKED FUNKED GAWKED HACKED HARKED HAWKED HOCKED HONKED HOOKED HULKED HUSKED JACKED JERKED JINKED JUNKED KICKED KINKED LACKED LARKED LEAKED LICKED LINKED LOCKED LOOKED LUCKED LURKED MARKED MASKED MILKED MOCKED MUCKED NECKED NICKED OINKED PACKED PARKED PEAKED PECKED PEEKED PERKED PICKED PINKED QUAKED RACKED RANKED REEKED RICKED RISKED ROCKED ROOKED RUCKED SACKED SILKED SLAKED SMOKED SNAKED SOAKED SOCKED SPIKED SPOKED STAKED STOKED SUCKED SULKED TACKED TALKED TANKED TASKED THEKID TICKED TUCKED TUSKED WALKED WICKED WINKED WORKED YACKED YAKKED YANKED YERKED YOLKED YUKKED ZONKED

KE••••

KEARNY KEATON KEBABS KEBOBS KEDGED KEDGES KEELED KEELER KEENAN KEENED KEENEN KEENER KEENLY KEEPAT KEEPER KEEPIN KEEPON KEEPTO KEEPUP KEFIRS KEGGED KEGLER KEITEL KELLER KELLEY KELPIE KELSEY KELVIN KEMPIS KENNED KENNEL KENNER KENNYG KENTON KENYAN KEPLER KEPTAT KEPTON KEPTUP KERALA KERMAN KERMES KERMIS KERMIT KERNED KERNEL KERNOI KERNOS KERSEE KERSEY KESHIA KETONE KETTLE KEVELS KEVLAR KEWPIE KEYING KEYNES KEYPAD KEYSIN KEYSUP KEYWAY

K•E•••

KEELED KEELER KEENAN KEENED KEENEN KEENER KEENLY KEEPAT KEEPER KEEPIN KEEPON KEEPTO KEEPUP KIEFER KLEIST KMESON KNEADS KNEELS KNELLS KOENIG KPELLE KRESGE KVELLS KVETCH KWEISI

K••E••

KAGERA KAREEM KEVELS KHMERS KINEMA KITERS KNEELS KOPECK KOPEKS KOREAN

K•••E•

KAISER KANDER KAREEM KAVNER KAYOED KEDGED KEDGES KEELED KEELER KEENED KEENEN KEENER KEEPER KEGGED KEGLER KEITEL KELLER KELLEY KELSEY KENNED KENNEL KENNER KEPLER KERMES KERNED KERNEL KERSEE KERSEY KEYNES KHYBER KICKED KICKER KIDDED KIDDER KIDNEY KIEFER KILLED KILLER KILMER KILNED KILTED KILTER KINDER KINGED KINKED KINSEY KIPPER KISLEV KISMET KISSED KISSER KISSES KITTEN KJOLEN KNAVES KNIFED KNIFES KNIVES KNOWER KOHLER KOPJES KOPPEL KOSHER KOTTER KRAKEN KRAMER KRATER KRONER KRUGER KUCHEN KUMMEL

K••••E

KALINE KARATE KATHIE KELPIE KERSEE KETONE KETTLE KEWPIE KHAFRE KIBBLE KIDDIE KILTIE KINDLE KINGME KIRTLE KISHKE KLUDGE KOOKIE KPELLE KRESGE KURILE

•KE•••

AKELAS AKENES EKEOUT OKEEFE OKELLY SKEANS SKEINS SKERRY SKETCH SKEWED SKEWER

•K•E••

EKBERG OKEEFE SKIERS

•K••E•

AKENES OKAYED SKATED SKATER SKATES SKEWED SKEWER SKIVED SKIVER SKIVES UKASES

•K•••E

OKEEFE SKOKIE SKOPJE

••KE••

ALKENE ASKERS BAKERS BAKERY BEKESY BIKERS ESKERS FAKERS FAKERY HIKERS HIKEUP INKERS JOKERS LAKERS LIKELY LIKENS MAKEBA MAKEDO MAKEIT MAKERS MAKEUP PIKERS POKEAT POKERS POKERY POKEYS RAKEIN RAKERS RAKEUP REKEYS SAKERS TAKEIN TAKEON TAKERS TAKETH TAKETO TAKEUP TOKENS UPKEEP WAKENS WAKEUP WOKEUP YOKELS

••K•E•

ANKLED ANKLES ANKLET AUKLET CAKIER COKIER FOKKER HOKIER ICKIER INKIER INKJET INKLES JOKIER LAKIER MCKUEN NIKKEI OAKLEY ORKNEY PEKOES POKIER UPKEEP YAKKED YAKKER YUKKED

••K••E

ALKENE PIKAKE

•••KE•

AWAKED AWAKEN AWAKES AWOKEN BACKED BACKER BALKED BANKED BANKER BARKED BARKER BASKED BASKET BEAKED BEAKER BECKER BECKET BICKER BILKED BLOKES BOOKED BOOKER BOSKET BRAKED BRAKES BROKEN BROKER BUCKED BUCKET BULKED BUNKED BUNKER BUSKED CALKED CANKER CARKED CHOKED CHOKER CHOKES CISKEI COCKED COCKER CONKED CONKER COOKED COOKER CORKED CORKER CRAKES CRIKEY DANKER DARKEN DARKER DECKED DECKER DICKER DICKEY DINKEY DISKED DOCKED DOCKER DOCKET DONKEY DRAKES DUCKED DUIKER DUNKED DUNKER EVOKED EVOKER EVOKES FAWKES FINKED FLAKED FLAKER FLAKES FLAKEY FLUKES FLUKEY FOKKER FORKED FORKER FUNKED GASKET GAWKED GAWKER HACKED HACKER HANKER HARKED HARKEN HARKER HAWKED HAWKER HICKEY HOCKED HOCKEY HONKED HONKER HOOKED HULKED HUNKER HUSKED HUSKER JACKED JACKET JACKEY JERKED JINKED JOCKEY JUNKED JUNKER JUNKET KICKED KICKER KINKED KRAKEN LACKED LACKEY LANKER LARKED LATKES LEAKED LEAKER LEAKEY LICKED LINKED LINKER LOCKED LOCKER LOCKET LOOKED LOOKER LOWKEY LUCKED LUNKER LURKED MARKED MARKER MARKET MASKED MASKER MEEKER MENKEN MERKEL MICKEY MILKED MILKER MINKES MOCKED MOCKER MONKEY MUCKED MUSKEG MUSKET NECKED NICKED NICKEL NICKER NIKKEI OFFKEY OINKED PACKED PACKER PACKET PARKED PARKER PEAKED PECKED PEEKED PERKED PICKED PICKER PICKET PINKED PINKEN PINKER POCKET PORKER PUCKER PUNKER QUAKED QUAKER QUAKES RACKED RACKET RANKED RANKER REEKED RICKED RICKEY RIPKEN RISKED RISKER ROCKED ROCKER ROCKET ROOKED RUCKED SACKED SACKER SECKEL SEEKER SHAKEN SHAKER SHAKES SHEKEL SICKEN SICKER SILKED SILKEN SINKER SISKEL SLAKED SLAKES SMOKED SMOKER SMOKES SMOKEY SNAKED SNAKES SOAKED SOAKER SOCKED SOCKET SPIKED SPIKER SPIKES SPOKED SPOKEN SPOKES STAKED STAKES STOKED STOKER STOKES SUCKED SUCKER SULKED SULKER SUNKEN TACKED TACKER TALKED TALKER TANKED TANKER TASKED TEDKEY TERKEL TICKED TICKER TICKET TINKER TRIKES TUCKED TUCKER TUCKET TURKEY TUSKED TUSKER WALKED WALKEN WALKER WEAKEN WEAKER WICKED WICKER WICKET WILKES WINKED WINKER WORKED WORKER YACKED YAKKED YAKKER YANKED YANKEE YERKED YERKES YOLKED YORKER YUKKED ZONKED ZONKER

•••K•E

BOOKIE BUCKLE CACKLE COCKLE COOKIE DARKLE DECKLE FICKLE FOLKIE HACKIE HACKLE HANKIE HECKLE JACKIE JECKLE JUNKIE KOOKIE MUSKIE PICKLE PINKIE PUNKIE RANKLE ROCKNE ROOKIE SICKLE SKOKIE TACKLE TALKIE TICKLE TINKLE

WALKIE
WINKIE
WINKLE
WOOKIE
YANKEE
YORKIE

••••KE
AXLIKE
BELIKE
BETAKE
BOURKE
BROOKE
CLARKE
GRIMKE
INJOKE
INTAKE
INVOKE
JAMOKE
KISHKE
MOLTKE
OXLIKE
PELIKE
PERUKE
PIKAKE
REBUKE
REMAKE
RETAKE
REVOKE
ROURKE
SHRIKE
STLUKE
STRAKE
STRIKE
STROKE
THICKE
UNLIKE
UNMAKE
UNYOKE
UPDIKE
UPTAKE

K•F•••
KAFFIR
KAFIRS
KEFIRS

K••F••
KAFFIR
KHAFRE
KIEFER
KITFOX
KNIFED
KNIFES
KOUFAX

K•••F•
KLOOFS
KUNGFU

K••••F
KINDOF

•K•F••
SKIFFS

•K••F•
OKEEFE
SKIFFS

••KF••
ASKFOR

K•G•••
KAGERA
KEGGED
KEGLER
KIGALI

K••G••
KEDGED
KEDGES
KEGGED
KINGED
KINGLY
KINGME
KNAGGY
KNIGHT
KRUGER
KUNGFU
KURGAN

K•••G•
KIANGS
KLUDGE
KNAGGY
KRESGE

K••••G
KDLANG
KENNYG
KEYING
KITBAG
KITING
KOENIG

•K•••G
EKBERG
SKIING
SKYING

••K••G
ASKING
BAKING
BBKING
BIKING
CAKING
DEKING
DIKING
DUKING
FAKING
HIKING
INKING
IRKING
JOKING
JUKING
LIKING
MAKING
MEKONG
MIKING
NUKING
PEKING
PIKING
POKING
RAKING
TAKING
VIKING
WAKING
YOKING

•••KG•
GINKGO

•••K•G
MUSKEG

KH••••
KHAFRE
KHAKIS
KHALID
KHMERS
KHOUMS
KHYBER

K•H•••
KAHLIL
KAHLUA
KAHUNA
KOHLER

K••H••
KATHIE
KESHIA
KISHKE
KOSHER
KUCHEN

K•••H•
KIMCHI
KNIGHT
KWACHA
KYUSHU

K••••H
KALAKH
KASBAH
KAZAKH
KIBOSH
KIRSCH
KITSCH
KLATCH
KVETCH

•K•••H
SKETCH
SKITCH

••K••H
EDKOCH
RAKISH
SUKKAH
TAKETH

•••KH•
GURKHA

•••K•H
HOOKAH
PUNKAH
SUKKAH

••••KH
KALAKH
KAZAKH
SAMEKH

KI••••
KIANGS
KIBBLE
KIBITZ
KIBOSH
KICKED
KICKER
KICKIN
KICKUP
KIDDED
KIDDER
KIDDIE
KIDMAN
KIDNAP
KIDNEY
KIDORY
KIDVID
KIEFER
KIGALI
KIKUYU
KILIMS
KILLED
KILLER
KILMER
KILNED
KILROY
KILTED
KILTER
KILTIE
KIMCHI
KIMONO
KINDER
KINDLE
KINDLY
KINDOF
KINEMA
KINGED
KINGLY
KINGME
KINKED
KINSEY
KINSKI
KIOSKS
KIOWAS
KIPPER
KIPPUR
KIRMAN
KIRSCH
KIRTLE
KISHKE
KISLEV
KISMET
KISSED
KISSER
KISSES
KITBAG
KITERS
KITFOX
KITING
KITKAT
KITSCH
KITTEN

K•I•••
KAILUA
KAISER
KEITEL
KLIBAN
KNICKS
KNIFED
KNIFES
KNIGHT
KNIVES

K••I••
KAFIRS
KALINE
KARIBA
KEFIRS
KEYING
KIBITZ
KILIMS
KITING
KLEIST
KODIAK
KONICA
KRAITS
KUMISS
KURILE
KWEISI

K•••I•
KAFFIR
KAHLIL
KAOLIN
KARMIC
KATHIE
KAURIS
KEEPIN
KELPIE
KELVIN
KEMPIS
KERMIS
KERMIT
KESHIA
KEWPIE
KEYSIN
KHAKIS
KHALID
KICKIN
KIDDIE
KIDVID
KILTIE
KOENIG
KOOKIE
KUKRIS
KUOPIO
KUWAIT

K••••I
KABUKI
KATMAI
KERNOI
KIGALI
KIMCHI
KINSKI
KUBLAI
KWEISI

•KI•••
AKIMBO
AKITAS
SKIBOB
SKIDDY
SKIERS
SKIFFS
SKIING
SKILLS
SKIMPS
SKIMPY
SKINKS
SKINNY
SKIPIT
SKIPPY
SKIRLS
SKIROS
SKIRRS
SKIRTS
SKIRUN
SKITCH
SKITOW
SKIVED
SKIVER
SKIVES
SKIVVY

•K•I••
SKEINS
SKIING
SKYING

•K••I•
OKAPIS
SKIPIT
SKOKIE

••KI••
AIKIDO
ASKING
ATKINS
BAKING
BBKING
BIKILA
BIKING
BIKINI
CAKIER
CAKING
COKIER
DEKING
DIKING
DUKING
ESKIMO
FAKING
FAKIRS
HAKIMS
HIKING
HOKIER
ICKIER
INKIER
INKIND
INKING
IRKING
JOKIER
JOKILY
JOKING
JUKING
LAKIER
LIKING
MAKING
MIKING
MIKITA
NIKITA
NUKING
PEKING
PEKINS
PIKING
POKIER
POKILY
POKING
RAKING
RAKISH
TAKING
TAKINS
UNKIND
UNKINK
VIKING
WAKING
YAKIMA
YOKING

••K•I•
ASKSIN
DIKDIK
KUKRIS
MAKEIT
PYKNIC
RAKEIN
SIKKIM
TAKEIN
UNKNIT

••K••I
ALKALI
ASKARI
BIKINI
NIKKEI
UAKARI

•••KI•
ABUKIR
BACKIN
BARKIN
BODKIN
BOOKIE
BUSKIN
CATKIN
COOKIE
CULKIN
ENOKIS
FIRKIN
FOLKIE
GASKIN
HACKIE
HANKIE
JACKIE
JERKIN
JOSKIN
JUNKIE
KHAKIS
KICKIN
KOOKIE
LOCKIN
LOOKIN
MALKIN
MUSKIE
NAPKIN
NUTKIN
PINKIE
PIPKIN
PUNKIE
RANKIN
ROOKIE
RUSKIN
SERKIN
SIKKIM
SINKIN
SISKIN
SKOKIE
SOCKIN
SUCKIN
TALKIE
THEKID
TONKIN
TOOKIN
TOOKIT
TUCKIN
TURKIC
WALKIE
WALKIN
WELKIN
WESKIT
WINKIE
WOOKIE
WORKIN
YORKIE

•••K•I
BHAKTI
CISKEI
NIKKEI
SHAKTI

••••KI
ADZUKI
EVENKI
HIDEKI
ITHAKI
JETSKI
KABUKI
KINSKI
SALUKI
SUZUKI

KJ••••
KJOLEN

K••J••
KOPJES

•K••J•
SKOPJE

••KJ••
INKJET

K•K•••
KAKAPO
KIKUYU
KOKOMO
KUKRIS

K••K••
KALKAN
KHAKIS
KICKED
KICKER
KICKIN
KICKUP
KINKED
KITKAT
KOOKIE
KRAKEN
KRAKOW

K•••K•
KABUKI
KALAKH
KANAKA
KAYAKS
KAZAKH
KAZAKS
KINSKI
KIOSKS
KISHKE
KNACKS
KNICKS
KNOCKS
KOPEKS
KULAKS
KYACKS

K••••K
KARNAK
KODIAK
KOPECK
KUSPUK

•K•K••
SKOKIE

•K••K•
AKUAKU
SKANKS
SKINKS
SKULKS
SKUNKS
SKUNKY

••KK••
DEKKOS
FOKKER
NIKKEI
SIKKIM
SUKKAH
YAKKED
YAKKER
YUKKED

••K•K•
PIKAKE

••K••K
ACKACK
DIKDIK
MUKLUK
UNKINK

•••KK•
CHUKKA
MARKKA
QUOKKA

•••K•K
HICKOK

KL••••
KLATCH
KLAXON
KLEIST
KLIBAN
KLOOFS
KLUDGE
KLUTZY

K•L•••
KALAKH
KALINE
KALKAN
KALMAR
KDLANG
KELLER
KELLEY
KELPIE
KELSEY
KELVIN
KILIMS
KILLED
KILLER
KILMER
KILNED
KILROY
KILTED
KILTER
KILTIE
KULAKS
KULTUR

K••L••
KAHLIL
KAHLUA
KAILUA
KAOLIN
KAPLAN
KEELED
KEELER
KEGLER
KELLER
KELLEY
KEPLER
KEVLAR
KHALID
KILLED
KILLER
KISLEV
KJOLEN
KNELLS
KNOLLS
KNOLLY
KOALAS
KOHLER
KPELLE
KUBLAI
KUNLUN
KVELLS

K•••L•
KAMALA
KEENLY
KERALA
KETTLE
KEVELS
KIBBLE
KIGALI
KINDLE
KINDLY
KINGLY
KIRTLE
KNEELS
KNELLS
KNOLLS
KNOLLY
KNURLS
KNURLY
KOBOLD
KODALY
KPELLE
KRAALS
KURALT
KURILE
KVELLS

K••••L
KAHLIL
KEITEL
KENNEL
KERNEL
KOPPEL
KUMMEL

•K•L••
AKELAS
OKELLY
SKALDS
SKILLS
SKULKS
SKULLS
SKYLAB

•K••L•
OKELLY
SKILLS
SKIRLS
SKOALS
SKULLS

••KL••
ANKLED
ANKLES
ANKLET
AUKLET
INKLES
MUKLUK
OAKLEY
TOKLAS

••K•L•
ALKALI
ALKYLS
BAKULA
BIKILA
DEKALB
JEKYLL
JOKILY
LIKELY
MAKALU
NIKOLA
PAKULA
POKILY
YOKELS

••K••L
JEKYLL

•••KL•
BUCKLE
CACKLE
COCKLE
DANKLY
DARKLE
DARKLY
DECKLE
FICKLE
HACKLE
HACKLY
HECKLE
JECKLE
LANKLY
MEEKLY
PICKLE
RANKLE
RANKLY
SICKLE
SICKLY
TACKLE
TICKLE
TICKLY
TINKLE
TINKLY
WEAKLY
WEEKLY
WINKLE

•••K•L
BAIKAL
JACKAL
MERKEL
NICKEL
SECKEL
SHEKEL
SISKEL
TERKEL

KM••••
KMESON

K•M•••
KAMALA
KEMPIS
KHMERS
KIMCHI
KIMONO
KOMBAT
KOMODO
KUMISS
KUMMEL

K••M••
KALMAR
KARMIC
KATMAI
KERMAN
KERMES
KERMIS
KERMIT
KIDMAN
KILMER
KIRMAN
KISMET
KORMAN
KRAMER
KUMMEL

K•••M•
KHOUMS
KILIMS
KINEMA
KINGME
KOKOMO

K••••M
KABOOM
KAREEM

•K•M••
AKIMBO
SKIMPS
SKIMPY

••K•M•
ESKIMO
HAKIMS
KOKOMO
YAKIMA

••K••M
SIKKIM

•••K•M
BUNKUM
SIKKIM

KN••••
KNACKS
KNAGGY
KNARRY
KNAVES
KNEADS
KNEELS
KNELLS
KNICKS
KNIFED
KNIFES
KNIGHT
KNIVES
KNOBBY
KNOCKS
KNOLLS
KNOLLY
KNOTTS
KNOTTY
KNOUTS
KNOWER
KNOWNS
KNURLS
KNURLY

K•N•••
KANAKA
KANDER
KANSAN
KANSAS
KANTOR
KENNED
KENNEL
KENNER
KENNYG
KENTON
KENYAN
KINDER
KINDLE
KINDLY
KINDOF
KINEMA
KINGED
KINGLY
KINGME
KINKED
KINSEY
KINSKI
KONICA
KONRAD
KUNGFU
KUNLUN

K••N••
KARNAK
KAUNAS
KAUNDA
KAVNER
KEENAN
KEENED
KEENEN
KEENER
KEENLY
KENNED
KENNEL
KENNER
KENNYG
KERNED
KERNEL
KERNOI
KERNOS
KEYNES
KIANGS
KIDNAP
KIDNEY
KILNED
KOENIG
KOONTZ
KRANTZ
KRONER
KRONOR
KRONUR
KWANZA

K•••N•
KAHUNA
KALINE
KDLANG
KEARNY
KETONE
KEYING
KIMONO
KITING
KNOWNS
KORUNA
KRASNY

K••••N
KALKAN
KANSAN
KAOLIN
KAPLAN
KASDAN
KEATON
KEENAN
KEENEN
KEEPIN
KEEPON
KELVIN
KENTON
KENYAN
KEPTON
KERMAN
KEYSIN
KICKIN
KIDMAN
KIRMAN
KITTEN
KJOLEN
KLAXON
KLIBAN
KMESON
KOREAN
KORMAN
KRAKEN
KUCHEN
KUNLUN
KURGAN

•KN•••
SKNXXX

•K•N••
AKENES
SKANKS
SKINKS
SKINNY
SKUNKS
SKUNKY

•K••N•
OKSANA
SKEANS
SKEINS
SKIING
SKINNY
SKYING

•K•••N
SKIRUN

••KN••
ORKNEY
PYKNIC
UNKNIT
UNKNOT

••K•N•
ALKENE
ASKING
ATKINS
BAKING
BBKING
BIKING
BIKINI
CAKING
DEKING
DIKING
DUKING
FAKING
HIKING
INKIND
INKING
IRKING
JOKING
JUKING
LIKENS
LIKING
MAKING
MEKONG
MIKING
NUKING
PEKING
PEKINS
PIKING
POKING
RAKING
TAKING
TAKINS
TOKENS
UNKIND
UNKINK
VIKING
WAKENS
WAKING
YOKING

••K••N
ASKSIN
MCKUEN
NEKTON
RAKEIN
TAKEIN
TAKEON

•••KN•
ROCKNE

•••K•N
AWAKEN
AWOKEN
BACKIN
BALKAN
BANKON
BARKIN
BECKON
BODKIN
BROKEN
BUSKIN
CATKIN
CULKIN
DAIKON
DARKEN
FIRKIN
GASKIN
HARKEN
JERKIN
JOSKIN
KALKAN
KICKIN
KRAKEN
LOCKIN
LOCKON
LOOKIN
LOOKON
MALKIN
MENKEN
NAPKIN
NUTKIN
PICKON
PINKEN
PIPKIN
RANKIN
RECKON
RIPKEN
RUSKIN
RYOKAN
SERKIN
SHAKEN
SICKEN
SILKEN
SINKIN
SISKIN
SOCKIN
SPOKEN
SUCKIN
SUNKEN
TACKON
TONKIN
TOOKIN
TOOKON
TUCKIN
WALKEN
WALKIN
WALKON
WEAKEN
WELKIN
WORKIN
WORKON

KO••••
KOALAS
KOBOLD
KODALY
KODIAK
KOENIG
KOHLER
KOKOMO
KOMBAT
KOMODO
KONICA
KONRAD
KOOKIE
KOONTZ
KOPECK
KOPEKS
KOPJES
KOPPEL
KORATS
KORBUT
KOREAN
KORMAN
KORUNA
KOSHER
KOSOVO
KOTTER
KOUFAX
KOVACS
KOWTOW

K•O•••
KAOLIN
KHOUMS
KIOSKS
KIOWAS
KJOLEN
KLOOFS
KNOBBY
KNOCKS
KNOLLS
KNOLLY
KNOTTS
KNOTTY
KNOUTS
KNOWER
KNOWNS
KOOKIE
KOONTZ
KRONER
KRONOR
KRONUR
KUOPIO

K••O••
KABOBS
KABOOM
KAROSS
KAYOED
KAZOOS
KEBOBS
KETONE
KIBOSH
KIDORY
KIMONO

KLOOFS
KOBOLD
KOKOMO
KOMODO
KOSOVO

K•••O•
KABOOM
KANTOR
KARPOV
KARROO
KAZOOS
KEATON
KEEPON
KENTON
KEPTON
KERNOI
KERNOS
KILROY
KINDOF
KITFOX
KLAXON
KMESON
KOWTOW
KRAKOW
KRONOR
KUDROW

K••••O
KAKAPO
KARROO
KEEPTO
KIMONO
KOKOMO
KOMODO
KOSOVO
KUOPIO

•KO•••
SKOALS
SKOKIE
SKOPJE
SKORTS

•K•O••
EKEOUT

•K••O•
SKIBOB
SKIROS
SKITOW
SKYBOX

•K•••O
AKIMBO

••KO••
ASKOUT
DAKOTA
EDKOCH
KOKOMO
LAKOTA
MEKONG
NIKOLA
PEKOES

••K•O•
ASKFOR
DEKKOS
HYKSOS
NEKTON
TAKEON
UNKNOT

••K••O
AIKIDO
ESKIMO
KAKAPO
KOKOMO
MAKEDO
MIKADO
TAKETO

•••KO•
ANGKOR
BANKON
BECKON
BUNKOS
CHEKOV
CUCKOO
DAIKON
DEKKOS
GECKOS
HICKOK
KRAKOW
LOCKON
LOOKON
MUSKOX
PICKON
RECKON
SHAKOS
TACKON
TOOKON
WACKOS
WALKON
WORKON
ZHUKOV

•••K•O
CUCKOO
GINKGO
LOOKTO
TALKTO
TOOKTO

••••KO
BAMAKO
MARIKO
ROTHKO
STOJKO

KP••••
KPELLE

K•P•••
KAPLAN
KAPPAS
KEPLER
KEPTAT
KEPTON
KEPTUP
KIPPER
KIPPUR
KOPECK
KOPEKS
KOPJES
KOPPEL

K••P••
KAPPAS
KARPOV
KEEPAT
KEEPER
KEEPIN
KEEPON
KEEPTO
KEEPUP
KELPIE
KEMPIS
KEWPIE
KEYPAD
KIPPER
KIPPUR
KOPPEL
KUOPIO
KUSPUK

K•••P•
KAKAPO

K••••P
KEEPUP
KEPTUP
KEYSUP
KICKUP
KIDNAP

•K•P••
OKAPIS
SKIPIT
SKIPPY
SKOPJE

•K••P•
SKIMPS
SKIMPY
SKIPPY

•K•••P
SKYCAP

••K•P•
KAKAPO

••K••P
HIKEUP
MAKEUP
RAKEUP
TAKEUP
UPKEEP
WAKEUP
WOKEUP

•••K•P
BACKUP
BUCKUP
COOKUP
HOOKUP
JACKUP
KICKUP
LINKUP
LOCKUP
LOOKUP
MARKUP
MOCKUP
MUCKUP
PACKUP
PERKUP
PICKUP
RACKUP
SOAKUP
TALKUP
TANKUP
TOOKUP
WALKUP
WORKUP

KR••••
KRAALS
KRAITS
KRAKEN
KRAKOW
KRAMER
KRANTZ
KRASNY
KRATER
KRESGE
KRONER
KRONOR
KRONUR
KRUGER

K•R•••
KARATE
KARATS
KAREEM
KARIBA
KARMIC
KARNAK
KAROSS
KARPOV
KARRAS
KARROO
KARSTS
KERALA
KERMAN
KERMES
KERMIS
KERMIT
KERNED
KERNEL
KERNOI
KERNOS
KERSEE
KERSEY
KIRMAN
KIRSCH
KIRTLE
KORATS
KORBUT
KOREAN
KORMAN
KORUNA
KURALT
KURGAN
KURILE

K••R••
KARRAS
KARROO
KAURIS
KEARNY
KILROY
KNARRY
KNURLS
KNURLY
KONRAD
KUDROW
KUKRIS

K•••R•
KAFIRS
KAGERA
KEFIRS
KHAFRE
KHMERS
KIDORY
KITERS
KNARRY

K••••R
KAFFIR
KAISER
KALMAR
KANDER
KANTOR
KAVNER
KEELER
KEENER
KEEPER
KEGLER
KELLER
KENNER
KEPLER
KEVLAR
KHYBER
KICKER
KIDDER
KIEFER
KILLER
KILMER
KILTER
KINDER
KIPPER
KIPPUR
KISSER
KNOWER
KOHLER
KOSHER
KOTTER
KRAMER
KRATER
KRONER
KRONOR
KRONUR
KRUGER
KULTUR

•K•R••
SKERRY
SKIRLS
SKIROS
SKIRRS
SKIRTS
SKIRUN
SKORTS

•K••R•
EKBERG
SKERRY
SKIERS
SKIRRS

•K•••R
SKATER
SKEWER
SKIVER

••KR••
KUKRIS

••K•R•
ANKARA
ASKARI
ASKERS
BAKERS
BAKERY
BIKERS
ESKERS
FAKERS
FAKERY
FAKIRS
GOKART
HIKERS
INKERS
JOKERS
LAKERS
MAKERS
PIKERS
POKERS
POKERY
RAKERS
SAKERS
TAKERS
UAKARI

••K••R
ASKFOR
CAKIER
COKIER
FOKKER
HOKIER
ICKIER
INKIER
JOKIER
LAKIER
LEKVAR
POKIER
YAKKER

•••K•R
ABUKIR
ANGKOR
BACKER
BANKER
BARKER
BEAKER
BECKER
BICKER
BOOKER
BROKER
BUNKER
CANKER
CHOKER
CHUKAR
COCKER
CONKER
COOKER
CORKER
DANKER
DARKER
DECKER
DICKER
DOCKER
DUIKER
DUNKER
EVOKER
FLAKER
FOKKER
FORKER
GAWKER
HACKER
HANKER
HARKER
HAWKER
HONKER
HUNKER
HUSKER
JUNKER
KICKER
LANKER
LEAKER
LINKER
LOCKER
LOOKER
LUNKER
MARKER
MASKER
MEEKER
MILKER
MOCKER
NICKER
PACKER
PARKER
PICKER
PINKER
PORKER
PUCKER
PUNKER
QUAKER
RANKER
RISKER
ROCKER
SACKER
SEEKER
SHAKER
SHIKAR
SICKER
SINKER
SMOKER
SOAKER
SPIKER
STOKER
SUCKER
SULKER
TACKER
TALKER
TANKER
TICKER
TINKER
TUCKER
TUSKER
WALKER
WEAKER
WICKER
WINKER
WORKER
YAKKER
YORKER
ZONKER

K•S•••
KASBAH
KASDAN
KESHIA
KISHKE
KISLEV
KISMET
KISSED
KISSER
KISSES
KOSHER
KOSOVO
KUSPUK

K••S••
KAISER
KANSAN
KANSAS
KARSTS
KELSEY
KERSEE
KERSEY
KEYSIN
KEYSUP
KINSEY
KINSKI
KIOSKS
KIRSCH
KISSED
KISSER
KISSES
KITSCH
KMESON
KRASNY
KRESGE
KYUSHU

K•••S•
KAROSS
KIBOSH
KLEIST
KUMISS
KUVASZ
KWEISI

K••••S
KABOBS
KAFIRS
KANSAS
KAPPAS
KARATS
KAROSS
KARRAS
KARSTS
KAUNAS
KAURIS
KAYAKS
KAZAKS
KAZOOS
KEBABS
KEBOBS
KEDGES
KEFIRS
KEMPIS
KERMES
KERMIS
KERNOS
KEVELS
KEYNES
KHAKIS
KHMERS
KHOUMS
KIANGS
KILIMS
KIOSKS
KIOWAS
KISSES
KITERS
KLOOFS
KNACKS
KNAVES
KNEADS
KNEELS
KNELLS
KNICKS
KNIFES
KNIVES
KNOCKS
KNOLLS
KNOTTS
KNOUTS
KNOWNS
KNURLS
KOALAS
KOPEKS
KOPJES
KORATS
KOVACS
KRAALS
KRAITS
KUDZUS
KUKRIS
KULAKS
KUMISS
KVELLS
KYACKS

•KS•••
OKSANA

•K•S••
UKASES

•K•••S
AKELAS
AKENES
AKITAS
OKAPIS
SKALDS
SKANKS
SKATES
SKEANS
SKEINS
SKIERS
SKIFFS
SKILLS
SKIMPS
SKINKS
SKIRLS
SKIROS
SKIRRS
SKIRTS
SKIVES
SKOALS
SKORTS
SKULKS
SKULLS
SKUNKS
UKASES

••KS••
ASKSIN
HYKSOS

••K•S•
BEKESY
RAKISH

••K••S
ALKYDS
ALKYLS
ANKLES
ASKERS
ATKINS
BAKERS
BIKERS
DEKKOS
ESKERS
FAKERS
FAKIRS
HAKIMS
HIKERS
HYKSOS
INKERS
INKLES
JOKERS
KUKRIS
LAKERS
LIKENS
MAKERS
PEKINS
PEKOES
PIKERS
POKERS
POKEYS
RAKERS
REKEYS
SAKERS
TAKERS
TAKINS
TOKAYS
TOKENS
TOKLAS
WAKENS
YAKUTS
YOKELS
YOKUTS

•••KS•
FOLKSY

•••K•S
AWAKES
BABKAS
BACKUS
BLOKES
BRAKES
BUNKOS
CHOKES
CRAKES
DEKKOS
DRAKES
ENOKIS
EVOKES
FAWKES
FLAKES
FLUKES
GECKOS
HAIKUS
KHAKIS
LATKES
MINKES
PARKAS
POLKAS
QUAKES
RUCKUS
SHAKES
SHAKOS
SLAKES
SMOKES
SNAKES
SPIKES
SPOKES
STAKES
STOKES
SUCKAS
TANKAS
TRIKES
VODKAS
WACKOS
WILKES
YERKES

••••KS
BATIKS
BAULKS
BLACKS
BLANKS
BLINKS
BLOCKS
BREAKS
BRICKS
BRINKS
BROOKS
CAULKS
CHALKS
CHECKS
CHEEKS
CHICKS
CHINKS
CHOCKS
CHUCKS
CHUNKS
CLACKS
CLANKS
CLEEKS
CLERKS
CLICKS
CLINKS
CLOAKS
CLOCKS
CLONKS
CLUCKS
CLUNKS
CRACKS
CRANKS
CREAKS
CREEKS
CRICKS
CROAKS
CROCKS
CROOKS
DMARKS
DRINKS
FLACKS
FLANKS
FLASKS
FLECKS
FLICKS
FLOCKS
FLUNKS
FRANKS
FREAKS
FRISKS
FROCKS
GREEKS
HACEKS
KAYAKS
KAZAKS
KIOSKS
KNACKS
KNICKS
KNOCKS
KOPEKS
KULAKS
KYACKS
MIWOKS
OZARKS
PLANKS
PLINKS
PLONKS
PLUCKS
PLUNKS
PRANKS
PRICKS
PRINKS
QUACKS
QUARKS
QUIRKS
REINKS
SHACKS
SHANKS
SHARKS
SHEIKS
SHIRKS
SHOCKS
SHOOKS
SHUCKS
SKANKS
SKINKS
SKULKS
SKUNKS
SLACKS
SLEEKS
SLICKS
SLINKS
SMACKS
SMIRKS
SMOCKS
SNACKS
SNEAKS
SNICKS
SNOOKS
SPANKS
SPARKS
SPEAKS
SPECKS
SPINKS
SPOOKS
STACKS
STALKS
STEAKS
STICKS
STINKS
STIRKS
STOCKS
STOOKS
STORKS
SWANKS
THANKS
THINKS
THUNKS
TILAKS
TRACKS
TRICKS
TRUCKS
TRUNKS
TWEAKS
UMIAKS
UZBEKS
VNECKS
WHACKS
WHELKS
WHISKS
WRACKS
WREAKS
WRECKS
YAPOKS
YOICKS
YUROKS

K•T•••
KATHIE
KATMAI
KETONE
KETTLE
KITBAG
KITERS
KITFOX
KITING
KITKAT
KITSCH
KITTEN
KOTTER

K••T••
KANTOR
KEATON
KEITEL
KENTON
KEPTAT
KEPTON
KEPTUP
KETTLE
KILTED
KILTER
KILTIE
KIRTLE
KITTEN
KLATCH
KLUTZY
KNOTTS
KNOTTY
KOTTER
KOWTOW
KRATER
KULTUR
KVETCH

K•••T•
KARATE
KARATS
KARSTS
KEEPTO
KIBITZ
KNOTTS
KNOTTY
KNOUTS
KOONTZ
KORATS
KRAITS
KRANTZ

K••••T
KEEPAT
KEPTAT
KERMIT
KISMET
KITKAT
KLEIST
KNIGHT
KOMBAT
KORBUT
KURALT
KUWAIT

•K•T••
AKITAS
SKATED
SKATER
SKATES
SKETCH
SKITCH
SKITOW

•K••T•
SKIRTS
SKORTS

•K•••T
EKEOUT
SKIPIT

••KT••
DIKTAT
NEKTON

••K•T•
DAKOTA
LAKOTA
MAKUTA
MIKITA
NIKITA
TAKETH
TAKETO
YAKUTS
YOKUTS
YUKATA

••K••T
ANKLET
ASKOUT
AUKLET
DIKTAT
GOKART
INKJET
MAKEIT
POKEAT
UNKNIT
UNKNOT

•••KT•
BHAKTI
LOOKTO
SHAKTI
TALKTO
TOOKTO

•••K•T
BARKAT
BASKET
BECKET
BOSKET
BUCKET
DOCKET
GASKET
JACKET
JUNKET
KITKAT
LOCKET
LOOKAT
MARKET
MUSKET
PACKET
PECKAT
PEEKAT
PICKAT
PICKET
POCKET
RACKET
ROCKET
SOCKET
TALKAT
TICKET
TOOKIT
TUCKET
WESKIT
WICKET
WINKAT

KU••••
KUBLAI
KUCHEN
KUDROW
KUDZUS
KUKRIS
KULAKS
KULTUR
KUMISS
KUMMEL
KUNGFU
KUNLUN
KUOPIO
KURALT
KURGAN
KURILE
KUSPUK
KUVASZ
KUWAIT

K•U•••
KAUNAS
KAUNDA
KAURIS
KLUDGE
KLUTZY
KNURLS
KNURLY
KOUFAX
KRUGER
KYUSHU

K••U••
KABUKI
KAHUNA
KHOUMS
KIKUYU
KNOUTS
KORUNA

K•••U•
KAHLUA
KAILUA
KEEPUP
KEPTUP
KEYSUP
KICKUP
KIPPUR
KORBUT
KRONUR
KUDZUS
KULTUR
KUNLUN
KUSPUK

K••••U
KIKUYU
KUNGFU
KYUSHU

•KU•••
AKUAKU
SKULKS
SKULLS
SKUNKS
SKUNKY

•K••U•
EKEOUT
SKIRUN

•K•••U
AKUAKU

••KU••
BAKULA
KIKUYU
MAKUTA
MCKUEN
PAKULA
YAKUTS
YAKUZA
YOKUTS

••K•U•
ASKOUT
HIKEUP
MAKEUP
MUKLUK
RAKEUP
TAKEUP
WAKEUP
WOKEUP

••K••U
KIKUYU
MAKALU

•••KU•
BACKUP
BACKUS
BUCKUP
BUNKUM
COOKUP
HAIKUS
HOOKUP
JACKUP
KICKUP
LINKUP
LOCKUP
LOOKUP
MARKUP
MOCKUP
MUCKUP
PACKUP
PERKUP
PICKUP
RACKUP
RUCKUS
SOAKUP
TALKUP
TANKUP
TOOKUP
WALKUP
WORKUP

•••K•U
RYUKYU

••••KU
AKUAKU

KV••••
KVELLS
KVETCH

K•V•••
KAVNER
KEVELS
KEVLAR
KOVACS
KUVASZ

K••V••
KELVIN
KIDVID
KNAVES
KNIVES

K•••V•
KOSOVO

K••••V
KARPOV
KISLEV

•K•V••
SKIVED
SKIVER
SKIVES
SKIVVY

•K••V•
SKIVVY

••KV••
LEKVAR

•••KV•
MOSKVA

•••K•V
CHEKOV
ROCKYV
ZHUKOV

KW••••
KWACHA
KWANZA
KWEISI

K•W•••
KEWPIE

KOWTOW
KUWAIT

K••W••
KEYWAY
KIOWAS
KNOWER
KNOWNS

K••••W
KOWTOW
KRAKOW
KUDROW

•K•W••
SKEWED
SKEWER
SKYWAY

•K•••W
SKITOW

••K•W•
YUKAWA

•••K•W
BROKAW
KRAKOW

K••X••
KLAXON

K••••X
KITFOX
KOUFAX

•K•X••
SKNXXX

•K••X•
SKNXXX

•K•••X
SKNXXX
SKYBOX

•••K•X
MUSKOX
PICKAX

KY••••
KYACKS
KYUSHU

K•Y•••
KAYAKS
KAYOED
KEYING
KEYNES
KEYPAD
KEYSIN
KEYSUP
KEYWAY
KHYBER

K••Y••
KENYAN

K•••Y•
KENNYG
KIKUYU

K••••Y
KEARNY
KEENLY
KELLEY
KELSEY
KERSEY
KEYWAY
KIDNEY
KIDORY
KILROY
KINDLY
KINGLY
KINSEY
KLUTZY
KNAGGY
KNARRY
KNOBBY
KNOLLY
KNOTTY
KNURLY
KODALY
KRASNY

•KY•••
SKYBOX
SKYCAP
SKYING
SKYLAB
SKYWAY

•K•Y••
OKAYED

•K•••Y
OKELLY
SKERRY
SKIDDY
SKIMPY
SKINNY
SKIPPY
SKIVVY
SKUNKY
SKYWAY

••KY••
ALKYDS
ALKYLS
JEKYLL

••K•Y•
KIKUYU
POKEYS
REKEYS
TOKAYS

••K••Y
BAKERY
BEKESY
FAKERY
JOKILY
LIKELY
OAKLEY
ORKNEY
POKERY
POKILY

•••KY•
ROCKYV
RYUKYU

•••K•Y
CRIKEY
DANKLY
DARKLY
DICKEY
DINKEY
DONKEY
FLAKEY
FLUKEY
FOLKSY
HACKLY
HICKEY
HOCKEY
JACKEY
JOCKEY
LACKEY
LANKLY
LEAKEY
LOWKEY
MEEKLY
MICKEY
MONKEY
OFFKEY
PARKAY
RANKLY
RICKEY
SICKLY
SMOKEY
TEDKEY
TICKLY
TINKLY
TURKEY
WEAKLY
WEEKLY

••••KY
ALECKY
BLOCKY
BRICKY
BROOKY
CHALKY
CHEEKY
CHINKY
CHUNKY
CLANKY
CLUNKY
CRACKY
CRANKY
CREAKY
CROAKY
FLECKY
FLOCKY
FLUNKY
FREAKY
FRISKY
JANSKY
NEVSKY
PLUCKY
PROSKY
QUIRKY
RIMSKY
SKUNKY
SLEEKY
SLINKY
SMIRKY
SNEAKY
SNOOKY
SPANKY
SPARKY
SPOOKY
SPUNKY
STALKY
STANKY
STICKY
STINKY
STOCKY
SWANKY
TRICKY
WHACKY
WHISKY

K•Z•••
KAZAKH
KAZAKS
KAZOOS

K••Z••
KUDZUS

K•••Z•
KLUTZY
KWANZA

K••••Z
KIBITZ
KOONTZ
KRANTZ
KUVASZ

••K•Z•
YAKUZA

LA••••
LAAGER
LABELS
LABIAL
LABILE
LABORS
LABOUR
LABREA
LABRET
LABRUM
LACERS
LACEUP
LACHES
LACIER
LACILY
LACING
LACKED
LACKEY
LACTIC
LACUNA
LADDER
LADDIE
LADERS
LADIDA
LADIES
LADING
LADINO
LADLED
LADLER
LADLES
LADOGA
LAFFER
LAGASH
LAGERS
LAGGED
LAGGER
LAGOON
LAGUNA
LAHORE
LAIDBY
LAIDIN
LAIDON
LAIDTO
LAIDUP
LAINIE
LAIRDS
LAKERS
LAKIER
LAKOTA
LALALA
LAMARR
LAMAZE
LAMBDA
LAMBED
LAMECH
LAMEDH
LAMEDS
LAMELY
LAMENT
LAMESA
LAMEST
LAMIAS
LAMINA
LAMING
LAMMAS
LAMMED
LAMONT
LAMOUR
LANAIS
LANARK
LANATE
LANCED
LANCER
LANCES
LANCET
LANDAU
LANDED
LANDER
LANDHO
LANDIS
LANDON
LANDRY
LANGUR
LANIER
LANKER
LANKLY
LANOSE
LANSON
LANVIN
LAOTSE
LAOTZU
LAPDOG
LAPELS
LAPFUL
LAPHAM
LAPINS
LAPPED
LAPPET
LAPSED
LAPSES
LAPSUP
LAPTEV
LAPTOP
LAPUTA
LARAMS
LARDED
LARDER
LARDON
LAREDO
LARGER
LARGES
LARGOS
LARIAT
LARKED
LAROSA
LARRUP
LARSEN
LARSON
LARVAE
LARVAL
LARVAS
LARYNX
LASCAR
LASERS
LASHED
LASHER
LASHES
LASHIO
LASHUP
LASSEN
LASSER
LASSES
LASSIE
LASSOS
LASTED
LASTEX
LASTLY
LATEEN
LATELY
LATENE
LATENS
LATENT
LATEST
LATHED
LATHER
LATHES
LATIGO
LATINA
LATINI
LATINO
LATINS
LATISH
LATIUM
LATKES
LATONA
LATOUR
LATOYA
LATTEN
LATTER
LATVIA
LAUDED
LAUDER
LAUGHS
LAUNCH
LAUPER
LAUREL
LAUREN
LAURIE
LAVABO
LAVAGE
LAVERS
LAVING
LAVISH
LAWFUL
LAWING
LAWMAN
LAWMEN
LAWSON
LAWTON
LAWYER
LAXEST
LAXITY
LAYBYS
LAYERS
LAYFOR
LAYING
LAYLOW
LAYMAN
LAYMEN
LAYOFF
LAYOUT
LAYSBY
LAYSIN
LAYSON
LAYSTO
LAYSUP
LAYUPS
LAZBOY
LAZIER
LAZILY
LAZING
LAZULI

L•A•••
LAAGER
LEACHY
LEADED
LEADEN
LEADER
LEADIN
LEADON
LEADTO
LEADUP
LEAFED
LEAGUE
LEAKED
LEAKER
LEAKEY
LEALTY
LEANED
LEANER
LEANLY
LEANON
LEANTO
LEAPED
LEAPER
LEARNS
LEARNT
LEASED
LEASER
LEASES
LEAVED
LEAVEN
LEAVES
LIABLE
LIAISE
LIANAS
LIANES
LIANGS
LLAMAS
LLANOS
LOADED
LOADER
LOAFED
LOAFER
LOAMED
LOANED
LOANER
LOATHE
LOAVES
LUANDA

L••A••
LAGASH
LALALA
LAMARR
LAMAZE
LANAIS
LANARK
LANATE
LARAMS
LAVABO
LAVAGE
LCHAIM
LEGACY
LEGALS
LEGATE
LEGATO
LELAND
LEMANS
LENAPE
LESAGE
LEVANT
LIGAND
LIGATE
LILACS
LINAGE
LIPASE
LITANY
LIZARD
LOBATE
LOCALE
LOCALS
LOCATE
LORAIN
LOTAHS
LOVAGE
LUNACY
LUNATE
LUSAKA
LUXATE

L•••A•
LABIAL
LAMIAS
LAMMAS
LANDAU
LAPHAM
LARIAT
LARVAE
LARVAL
LARVAS
LASCAR
LAWMAN
LAYMAN
LEERAT
LEEWAY
LEGMAN
LEHUAS
LEKVAR
LEMMAS
LESTAT
LETHAL
LETSAT
LIANAS
LIBYAN
LINEAL
LINEAR
LLAMAS
LLBEAN
LOGJAM
LONGAN
LOOFAH
LOOFAS
LOOKAT
LOQUAT
LOREAL
LOTHAR
LOWCAL
LOWFAT
LUCIAN
LUMBAR

L••••A
LABREA
LACUNA
LADIDA
LADOGA
LAGUNA
LAKOTA
LALALA
LAMBDA
LAMESA
LAMINA
LAPUTA
LAROSA
LATINA
LATONA
LATOYA
LATVIA
LERIDA
LEXICA
LIGULA
LINGUA
LIOTTA
LISBOA
LOGGIA
LOLITA
LORICA
LOUISA
LOYOLA
LUANDA
LUMINA
LUNULA
LUSAKA

•LA•••
ALAMOS
ALANIS
ALANON
ALARIC
ALARMS
ALARUM
ALASKA
ALATAU
ALATED
BLABBY
BLACKS
BLADED
BLADER
BLADES
BLAINE
BLAISE
BLAMED
BLAMES
BLANCA
BLANCH
BLANDA
BLANKS
BLARED
BLARES
BLASTS
BLATTY
BLAZED
BLAZER
BLAZES
BLAZON
CLACKS
CLAIMS
CLAIRE
CLAMMY
CLAMOR
CLAMPS
CLAMUP
CLANCY
CLANGS
CLANKS
CLANKY
CLAQUE
CLARET
CLARKE
CLAROS
CLASPS
CLASSY
CLAUDE
CLAUSE
CLAVES
CLAVIN
CLAWED
CLAWER
CLAYEY
DLAYER
ELAINE
ELANDS
ELAPID
ELAPSE
ELATED
ELATER
ELATES
ELAYER
ELAYNE
FLABBY
FLACKS
FLACON
FLAGGY
FLAGON
FLAILS
FLAIRS
FLAKED
FLAKER
FLAKES
FLAKEY
FLAMBE
FLAMED
FLAMES
FLANGE
FLANKS
FLAPPY
FLARED
FLARES
FLASHY
FLASKS
FLATLY
FLAUNT
FLAVIA
FLAVOR
FLAWED
FLAXEN
FLAXES
FLAYED
FLAYER
GLACES
GLACIS
GLADES
GLADLY
GLADYS
GLAIRS
GLAIRY
GLAMOR
GLANCE
GLANDS
GLARED
GLARES
GLASER
GLASSY
GLAZED
GLAZER
GLAZES
KLATCH
KLAXON
LLAMAS
LLANOS
PLACED
PLACER
PLACES
PLACET
PLACID
PLAGAL
PLAGES
PLAGIO
PLAGUE
PLAICE
PLAIDS
PLAINS
PLAINT
PLAITS
PLANAR
PLANCK
PLANED
PLANER
PLANES
PLANET
PLANKS
PLANON
PLANTE
PLANTS
PLAQUE
PLASHY
PLASMA
PLASMO
PLASTY
PLATED
PLATEN
PLATER
PLATES
PLATTE
PLAYAS
PLAYAT
PLAYED
PLAYER
PLAYON
PLAYUP
PLAZAS
SLACKS
SLAGGY
SLAKED
SLAKES
SLALOM
SLANGS
SLANGY
SLANTS
SLAPPY
SLAPUP
SLATED
SLATER
SLATES
SLAVED
SLAVER
SLAVES
SLAVEY
SLAVIC
SLAYED
SLAYER
TLALOC

•L•A••
ALBANO
ALBANY
ALCAPP
ALEAST
ALKALI
ALLAYS
ALMATY
ALPACA
ALSACE
ALTAIC
ALTAIR
ALTARS
ALWAYS
BLEACH
BLEARS
BLEARY
BLEATS
BLOATS
CLEANS
CLEARS
CLEATS
CLEAVE
CLOACA
CLOAKS
ELPASO
FLOATS
FLOATY
GLEAMS
GLEAMY
GLEANS
GLOATS
ILEANA
NLEAST
OLDAGE
OLEARY
OLEATE
PLEACH
PLEADS
PLEASE
PLEATS
PLIANT
SLEAVE
SLEAZE
SLEAZY
SLOANE
ULLAGE

•L••A•
ALATAU
ALEGAR
ALEMAN
ALLDAY
ALLMAN
ALOHAS
ALOMAR
ALPHAS
ALTMAN
ALULAE
ALULAR
CLIMAX
ELFMAN
ELIJAH
FLEWAT
FLORAE
FLORAL
FLORAS
FLYMAN
FLYWAY
GLOBAL
ILLSAY
KLIBAN
LLAMAS
LLBEAN
OLDHAM
OLDHAT
OLDMAN
OLDSAW
PLAGAL
PLANAR
PLAYAS
PLAYAT
PLAZAS
PLEIAD
PLEXAL
PLICAE
PLURAL
SLEZAK
SLOGAN
SLOVAK
ULLMAN
ULTRAS

•L•••A
ALASKA
ALEXIA
ALICIA
ALPACA
ALTHEA
ALTIMA
ALUMNA
ALYSSA
BLANCA
BLANDA
CLOACA
ELISHA
ELISSA
ELMIRA
ELVIRA
FLAVIA
FLICKA
GLENDA
GLINKA
GLORIA
GLOSSA
ILEANA
ILESHA
OLINDA
OLIVIA
PLASMA
PLEURA
ULTIMA

••LA••
ABLATE
ABLAUT
ABLAZE
AFLAME
AFLATS
AGLAIA
AGLARE
ALLAYS
ASLANT
ATLAST
ATLATL
AULAIT
BALAAM
BALATA
BELAIR
BELAYS
BYLAWS
CALAIS
CALASH
CCLAMP
COLADA
DALASI
DELANO
DELANY
DELATE
DELAYS
DILATE
ECLAIR
ECLATS
EFLATS
ENLACE
FALANA
FULANI
GALAGO
GALAHS
GALATA
GALAXY
GELADA
GELATI
GELATO
GULAGS
HILARY
INLAID
INLAND
INLAWS
INLAYS
ISLAND
JALAPA
KALAKH
KDLANG
KULAKS
LALALA
LELAND
LILACS
MALABO
MALADY
MALAGA
MALATE
MALAWI
MALAYA
MALAYS
MCLAIN
MELANO
MILADY
MILANO
MOLARS
OBLAST
OBLATE
OFLATE
OGLALA
ONLAND
OOLALA
PALACE
PALAEO
PALATE
PELAGE
PILAFS
PILATE
POLAND
RELACE
RELAID
RELATE
RELAYS
ROLAND
SALAAM
SALADO
SALADS
SALALS
SALAMI
SALARY
SCLAFF
SILAGE
SOLACE
SOLANS
SOLARS
SPLASH
SPLATS
SPLAYS
TILAKS
TULANE
TULARE
UCLANS
UHLANS
ULLAGE
UMLAUT
UNLACE
UNLADE
UNLAID
UNLASH
UPLAND
VOLANS
VOLANT
VOLARE

••L•A•
AFLOAT
AGLEAM
ALLDAY
ALLMAN
BALAAM
BALKAN
BALLAD
BALSAM
BALZAC
BELDAM
BELIAL
BELLAY
BILBAO
BULGAR
BULLAE
CALLAO
CALLAS
CALPAC
CELLAE
CELLAR
COLFAX
COLLAR
COLMAN
DALLAS
DELMAR
DELRAY
DELTAS
DOLLAR
DOLMAN
DOLMAS
EOLIAN
FELLAH
FELLAS
FILIAL
FOLIAR
FULMAR
GALEAE
GALPAL
GALWAY
GALYAK
GILEAD
GULLAH
HALVAH
HELLAS
ILLSAY
JULIAN
KALKAN
KALMAR
MCLEAN
MELMAC
MILLAY
MILPAS
MILSAP
MOLDAU
MOLNAR
MULLAH
MULLAS
NILGAI
NOLEAD
NOLOAD
NULLAH
OILCAN
OILMAN
OILPAN
ONLOAN
PALEAE
PALLAS
PALMAS
PILLAR
POLEAX
POLKAS
PULSAR
RELOAD
SALAAM
SALMAN
SALSAS
SILOAM
SILVAS
SOLDAN
SOLFAS
SULTAN
SYLVAN
TALKAT
TULSAN
ULLMAN
UNLEAD
UNLOAD
UPLOAD
VILLAS
VOLVAS
VULCAN
VULGAR
ZILPAH

••L••A
AGLAIA
BALATA
BALBOA
BELUGA
BULOVA
COLADA
COLIMA
DULLEA
FALANA
FULCRA
GALATA
GALENA
GALLIA
GELADA
HELENA
HULLOA
JALAPA
LALALA
LOLITA
MALAGA
MALAYA
MELINA
MULETA
OGLALA
OOLALA
PALLIA
PALOMA
PELOTA
SALINA
SALIVA
SALVIA
SCLERA
SELENA
SILICA
SYLVIA
TOLUCA
WALESA

•••LA•
AKELAS
ALULAE
ALULAR
ASHLAR
BALLAD
BEDLAM
BELLAY
BEULAH
BULLAE
BURLAP
BYPLAY
CALLAO
CALLAS
CELLAE
CELLAR
CHELAE
CHELAS
COLLAR
CYCLAS
DALLAS
DEWLAP
DOBLAS
DOLLAR

EARLAP
FELLAH
FELLAS
GAGLAW
GULLAH
HARLAN
HELLAS
INPLAY
JETLAG
KAPLAN
KEVLAR
KOALAS
KUBLAI
MEDLAR
MEDLAT
MILLAY
MISLAY
MOOLAH
MULLAH
MULLAS
NULLAH
NYALAS
OCULAR
OUTLAW
OUTLAY
OVULAR
PALLAS
PARLAY
PEDLAR
PHILAE
PHYLAE
PILLAR
POPLAR
PRELAW
RAGLAN
RAILAT
REFLAG
REPLAN
REPLAY
SCALAR
SEALAB
SENLAC
SKYLAB
SMILAX
STALAG
STELAE
STELAR
TABLAS
TESLAS
TOKLAS
UNCLAD
UVULAE
UVULAR
UVULAS
VACLAV
VASLAV
VILLAS
VIOLAS
WAYLAY

•••L•A
ABOLLA
AEOLIA
AMELIA
ANGLIA
APULIA
ARALIA
AXILLA
AZALEA
CHOLLA
COULDA
DAHLIA
DEFLEA
DULLEA
EMILIA
ETALIA
GALLIA
HULLOA
IMELDA
ITALIA
KAHLUA
KAILUA
OBELIA
PAELLA
PALLIA
PSYLLA
REALIA
SCALIA
SCYLLA
STELLA
THALIA
THELMA

••••LA
ABOLLA
ANGELA
ANGOLA
AQUILA
ARBELA
AREOLA
ATTILA
AXILLA
BAKULA
BIKILA
BITOLA
BRAILA
CABALA
CANOLA
CHOLLA
CIBOLA
COPULA
CUPOLA
DOUALA
EIDOLA
FACULA
FIBULA
HOOPLA
IMPALA
KAMALA
KERALA
LALALA
LIGULA
LOYOLA
LUNULA
MACULA
MANILA
MAZOLA
MODELA
NEBULA
NICOLA
NIKOLA
OGLALA
OOLALA
OSCULA
PAELLA
PAKULA
PAMELA
PARULA
PAYOLA
PETULA
PSYLLA
PUEBLA
RADULA
RAMBLA
RCCOLA
ROMOLA
SCYLLA
SHEILA
STELLA
TABULA
URSULA
VIZSLA

L•B•••
LABELS
LABIAL
LABILE
LABORS
LABOUR
LABREA
LABRET
LABRUM
LEBRUN
LIBBED
LIBBER
LIBELS
LIBERI
LIBIDO
LIBRIS
LIBYAN
LLBEAN
LOBATE
LOBBED
LOBBER
LOBULE
LUBBER
LUBECK
LUBING
LUBLIN

L••B••
LAMBDA
LAMBED
LAYBYS
LAZBOY
LESBOS
LIABLE
LIBBED
LIBBER
LIEBIG
LIEBYS
LIMBED
LIMBER
LIMBOS
LIMBUS
LISBOA
LISBON
LOBBED
LOBBER
LOMBOK
LOWBOY
LUBBER
LUMBAR
LUMBER

L•••B•
LAIDBY
LAVABO
LAYSBY
LETSBE

•LB•••
ALBANO
ALBANY
ALBEDO
ALBEIT
ALBERT
ALBINO
ALBION
ALBOIN
ALBORG
ALBUMS
ELBERT
ELBOWS
ELBRUS
LLBEAN

•L•B••
ALIBIS
ALIBLE
ALLBUT
BLABBY
CLUBBY
FLABBY
FLYBOY
FLYBYS
GLEBES
GLIBLY
GLOBAL
GLOBED
GLOBES
GLOBIN
KLIBAN
OLDBOY
PLEBES
SLOBBY

•L••B•
BLABBY
BLURBS
CLIMBS
CLUBBY
FLABBY
FLAMBE
PLUMBS
SLOBBY

••LB••
ALLBUT
BALBOA
BILBAO
BULBIL
BULBUL
TALBOT
WILBUR

••L•B•
ADLIBS
CELEBS
MALABO
MALIBU
PHLEBO

••L••B
APLOMB

•••LB•
PHILBY
TRILBY

•••L•B
SEALAB
SKYLAB

••••LB
DEKALB

LC••••
LCHAIM

L•C•••
LACERS
LACEUP
LACHES
LACIER
LACILY
LACING
LACKED
LACKEY
LACTIC
LACUNA
LECTER
LECTOR
LICHEN
LICKED
LICTOR
LOCALE
LOCALS
LOCATE
LOCKED
LOCKER
LOCKET
LOCKIN
LOCKON
LOCKUP
LOCUST
LUCENT
LUCIAN
LUCITE
LUCIUS
LUCKED
LYCEES
LYCEUM

L••C••
LANCED
LANCER
LANCES
LANCET
LASCAR
LEACHY
LITCHI
LOUCHE
LOWCAL
LUNCHY

L•••C•
LAMECH
LAUNCH
LEGACY
LEXICA
LILACS
LORICA
LUBECK
LUNACY
LYRICS

L••••C
LACTIC
LITHIC

•LC•••
ALCAPP
ALCOTT
ALCOVE
ALCUIN
ULCERS

•L•C••
ALECKY
ALECTO
ALICIA
BLACKS
BLOCKS
BLOCKY
CLACKS
CLICHE
CLICKS
CLOCHE
CLOCKS
CLUCKS
ELECTS
ELICIT
FLACKS
FLACON
FLECHE
FLECKS
FLECKY
FLICKA
FLICKS
FLOCKS
FLOCKY
GLACES
GLACIS
GLYCOL
PLACED
PLACER
PLACES
PLACET
PLACID
PLICAE
PLUCKS
PLUCKY
SLACKS
SLICED
SLICER
SLICES
SLICKS

•L••C•
ALNICO
ALPACA
ALSACE
BLANCA
BLANCH
BLEACH
BLENCH
BLOTCH
CLANCY
CLENCH
CLINCH
CLOACA
CLUTCH
ELLICE
FLEECE
FLEECY
FLETCH
FLINCH
FLITCH
GLANCE
GLITCH
KLATCH
OLMECS
PLAICE
PLANCK
PLEACH
SLOUCH
SLUICE

•L•••C
ALARIC
ALTAIC
CLERIC
CLINIC
OLDVIC
SLAVIC
TLALOC

••LC••
AFLCIO
CALCES
DULCET
FALCES
FALCON
FULCRA
MULCTS
OILCAN
SULCUS
TALCED
TALCUM
VELCRO
VULCAN
WILCOX

••L•C•
CALICO
DELICT
ELLICE
ENLACE
INLUCK
LILACS
MALICE
MOLOCH
OCLOCK
PALACE
POLICE
POLICY
RELACE
RELICS
RELICT
RELOCK
RELUCT
SELECT
SILICA
SOLACE
SPLICE
TOLUCA
UNLACE
UNLOCK
VELOCE

••L••C
BALTIC
BALZAC
BELLOC
CALPAC
CELTIC
CULTIC
DELTIC
GALLIC
MELMAC
PELVIC
TOLTEC

•••LC•
CHALCO

•••L•C
AEOLIC
ANGLIC
BELLOC
CYCLIC
ENBLOC
EXILIC
FROLIC
GAELIC
GALLIC
GARLIC
ITALIC
PUBLIC
SENLAC
TLALOC
URALIC
ZIPLOC

L•D•••
LADDER
LADDIE
LADERS
LADIDA
LADIES
LADING
LADINO
LADLED
LADLER
LADLES
LADOGA
LEDGER
LEDGES
LEDOFF
LEDOUT
LIDDED
LODENS
LODGED
LODGER
LODGES
LUDDEN
LUDENS
LUDLUM
LUDWIG

L••D••
LADDER
LADDIE
LAIDBY
LAIDIN
LAIDON
LAIDTO
LAIDUP
LANDAU
LANDED
LANDER
LANDHO
LANDIS
LANDON
LANDRY
LAPDOG
LARDED
LARDER
LARDON
LAUDED
LAUDER
LEADED
LEADEN
LEADER
LEADIN
LEADON
LEADTO
LEADUP
LEIDEN
LENDER
LEWDER
LEWDLY
LEYDEN
LIDDED
LIEDER
LINDEN
LOADED
LOADER
LONDON
LORDED
LORDLY
LOUDEN
LOUDER
LOUDLY
LUDDEN
LUNDEN
LYNDON

L•••D•
LADIDA
LAIRDS
LAMBDA
LAMEDH
LAMEDS
LAREDO
LERIDA
LIBIDO
LIPIDE
LIPIDS
LLOYDS
LUANDA

L••••D
LACKED
LADLED
LAGGED
LAMBED
LAMMED
LANCED
LANDED
LAPPED
LAPSED
LARDED
LARKED
LASHED
LASTED
LATHED
LAUDED
LEADED
LEAFED
LEAKED
LEANED
LEAPED
LEASED
LEAVED
LEERED
LEGEND
LEGGED
LELAND
LEMOND
LENSED
LEONID
LETTED
LEVEED
LEVIED
LIBBED
LICKED
LIDDED
LIFTED
LIGAND
LILTED
LIMBED
LIMNED
LIMPED
LIMPID
LINKED
LIPOID
LIPPED
LIQUID
LISPED
LISTED
LIZARD
LOADED
LOAFED
LOAMED
LOANED
LOBBED
LOCKED
LODGED
LOFTED
LOGGED
LOLLED
LOMOND
LONGED
LOOKED
LOOMED
LOOPED
LOOSED
LOOTED
LOPPED
LORDED
LOTTED
LOUSED
LOWEND
LUCKED
LUFFED
LUGGED
LULLED
LUMPED
LUNGED
LURKED
LUSTED
LYNYRD

•LD•••
ALDERS
ALDINE
ALDOSE
ALDOUS
ALDRIN
ELDERS
ELDEST
OLDAGE
OLDBOY
OLDEST
OLDHAM
OLDHAT
OLDIES
OLDISH
OLDMAN
OLDMEN
OLDPRO
OLDSAW
OLDVIC

•L•D••
ALLDAY
BLADED
BLADER
BLADES
CLODDY
ELIDED
ELIDES
ELUDED
ELUDER
ELUDES
FLEDGE
FLEDGY
GLADES
GLADLY
GLADYS
GLIDED
GLIDER
GLIDES
KLUDGE
PLEDGE
SLEDGE
SLIDER
SLIDES
SLIDIN
SLUDGE
SLUDGY

•L••D•
ALBEDO
ALKYDS
ALLUDE
BLANDA
BLEEDS
BLENDE
BLENDS
BLINDS
BLONDE
BLONDS
BLOODY
CLAUDE
CLODDY
CLOUDS
CLOUDY
ELANDS
FLOODS
FLUIDS
GLANDS
GLENDA
LLOYDS
OLINDA
PLAIDS
PLEADS

•L•••D
ALATED
ALFRED
ALLIED
ALMOND
BLADED
BLAMED
BLARED
BLAZED
CLAWED
CLEPED
CLEWED
CLONED
CLOSED
CLOYED
ELAPID
ELATED
ELIDED
ELOPED
ELUDED
ELUTED
ELWOOD
FLAKED
FLAMED
FLARED
FLAWED
FLAYED
FLEXED
FLEYED
FLORID
FLOWED
FLUTED
FLUXED
FLYROD
GLARED
GLAZED
GLIDED
GLOBED
GLOVED
GLOWED
GLOZED
ILLFED
PLACED
PLACID
PLANED
PLATED
PLAYED
PLEIAD
PLOWED
PLUMED
SLAKED
SLATED
SLAVED
SLAYED
SLEWED
SLICED
SLIMED
SLOPED
SLOWED

••LD••
ALLDAY
BALDER
BALDLY
BELDAM
BOLDER
BOLDLY
CALDER
COLDER
COLDLY
FELDON
FOLDED
FOLDER
FOLDUP
GILDED
GILDER
GOLDEN
GOLDIE
HELDIN
HELDON
HELDTO
HELDUP
HOLDEN
HOLDER
HOLDIN
HOLDIT
HOLDON
HOLDTO
HOLDUP
MALDEN
MELDED
MILDER
MILDEW
MILDLY
MOLDAU
MOLDED
MOLDER
POLDER
SELDOM
SOLDAN
SOLDER
SOLDON
TILDEN
TILDES
TOLDOF
TOLDON
VALDEZ
VELDTS
WALDEN
WELDED
WELDER
WILDER
WILDLY

••L•D•
ALLUDE
BOLIDE
COLADA
DELUDE
GELADA
HALIDE
MALADY
MELODY
MILADY
SALADO
SALADS
SOLIDI
SOLIDS
TELEDU
TOLEDO
UNLADE

••L••D
ALLIED
BALKED
BALLAD
BELIED
BELLED
BELTED
BILKED
BILLED
BOLTED
BULGED
BULKED
BULLED
CALKED
CALLED
CALMED
CALVED
CELLED
CULLED
DELVED
DOLLED
DULLED
FELLED
FELTED
FILLED
FILMED
FOLDED
GALLED
GELLED
GILDED
GILEAD
GILLED
GOLFED
GULFED
GULLED
GULPED
HALOED
HALOID
HALTED
HALVED
HELMED
HELPED
HILLED
HULKED
HULLED
ILLFED
INLAID
INLAND
ISLAND
JELLED
JILTED
JOLTED
KILLED
KILNED
KILTED
LELAND
LILTED
LOLLED
LULLED
MALTED
MELDED
MELTED
MILKED
MILLED
MILORD
MOLDED
MOLTED
MULLED
NOLEAD
NOLOAD
NULLED
ONLAND
PALLED
PALLID
PALMED
PELTED
PILLED
POLAND
POLLED
PULLED
PULPED
PULSED
RELAID
RELIED
RELOAD
ROLAND
ROLLED
SALTED
SALVED
SILKED
SILOED
SILTED
SOLOED
SOLVED
SULKED
TALCED
TALKED
TALMUD
TILLED
TILTED
TOLLED
UNLAID
UNLEAD
UNLOAD
UPLAND
UPLOAD
VALUED
VALVED
WALKED
WALLED
WELDED
WELLED
WELTED
WILLED
WILTED
WOLFED
XYLOID
YELLED
YELPED
YOLKED

•••LD•
BUILDS
CHILDE
CHILDS
COULDA
FIELDS
FJELDS
GUILDS
IMELDA
ISOLDE
MOULDS
MOULDY
SCALDS
SCOLDS
SKALDS
WIELDS
WORLDS
YIELDS

•••L•D
ADDLED
AMBLED
ANELED
ANGLED
ANKLED
BAILED
BALLAD
BAWLED
BELLED
BILLED
BIRLED
BOILED
BOWLED
BUGLED
BULLED
BURLED
CABLED
CALLED
CEILED
CELLED
COILED
COOLED
COWLED
CULLED
CURLED
CYCLED
DIALED
DOLLED
DUELED
DULLED
EAGLED
EUCLID
EXILED
EYELID
FABLED
FAILED
FELLED
FILLED
FOALED
FOILED
FOOLED
FOULED
FOWLED
FUELED
FURLED
GABLED
GALLED
GAOLED
GELLED
GILLED
GULLED
HAILED
HAULED
HEALED
HEELED
HILLED
HOWLED
HULLED
HURLED
JAILED
JELLED
KEELED
KHALID
KILLED
LADLED
LOLLED
LULLED
MAILED
MARLED
MAULED
MEWLED
MILLED
MISLED
MOILED
MULLED
NAILED
NULLED
PALLED
PALLID
PEALED
PEELED
PILLED
POLLED
POOLED
PULLED
PURLED
RAILED
REELED
RIFLED
ROILED
ROLLED
SAILED
SCALED
SEALED
SIDLED
SMILED
SOILED
STALED
STOLID
STYLED
TABLED
TAILED
TILLED
TITLED
TOILED
TOLLED
TOOLED
UNCLAD
VEILED
WAILED
WALLED
WELLED
WHILED
WILLED
YELLED
YOWLED

••••LD
AFIELD
AGEOLD
ARNOLD
BEHELD
BEHOLD
BIFOLD
BUJOLD
DONALD
ENFOLD
GERALD
GOWILD
HARALD
HAROLD
HERALD
INFOLD
KOBOLD
ONHOLD
OSWALD
REHELD
REMOLD
RESOLD
RETOLD
REWELD
RIBALD
RONALD
SHIELD
SHOULD
UNFOLD
UNSOLD
UNTOLD
UPHELD
UPHOLD

LE••••
LEACHY
LEADED
LEADEN
LEADER
LEADIN
LEADON
LEADTO
LEADUP
LEAFED
LEAGUE
LEAKED
LEAKER
LEAKEY
LEALTY
LEANED
LEANER
LEANLY
LEANON
LEANTO
LEAPED
LEAPER
LEARNS
LEARNT
LEASED
LEASER
LEASES
LEAVED
LEAVEN
LEAVES
LEBRUN
LECTER
LECTOR
LEDGER
LEDGES
LEDOFF
LEDOUT
LEERAT
LEERED
LEERER
LEEWAY
LEFTIE
LEFTIN
LEGACY
LEGALS
LEGATE
LEGATO
LEGEND
LEGGED
LEGION
LEGIST
LEGMAN
LEGMEN
LEGREE
LEGUIN
LEGUME
LEHIGH
LEHRER
LEHUAS
LEIDEN
LEKVAR
LELAND
LEMANS
LEMMAS
LEMMON
LEMNOS
LEMOND
LEMONS
LEMONY
LEMUEL
LEMURS
LENAPE
LENDER
LENGTH
LENITY
LENNIE
LENNON
LENNOX
LENORE
LENSED
LENSES
LENTEN
LENTIL
LEONES
LEONID
LEONIE
LEPTON
LERIDA
LERNER
LESAGE
LESBOS
LESLEY
LESLIE
LESSEE
LESSEN
LESSER
LESSON
LESSOR
LESTAT
LESTER
LETFLY
LETHAL
LETOFF
LETOUT
LETSAT
LETSBE
LETSGO
LETSIN
LETSON
LETSUP
LETTED
LETTER
LETUPS
LEVANT
LEVEED
LEVEES
LEVELS
LEVENE
LEVERS
LEVIED
LEVIER
LEVIES
LEVINE
LEVITE
LEVITY
LEWDER
LEWDLY
LEXEME
LEXICA
LEYDEN

L•E•••
LEERAT
LEERED
LEERER
LEEWAY
LIEBIG
LIEBYS
LIEDER
LIEFER
LIEFLY
LIEGES
LIELOW
LIENEE
LIERNE
LIESIN
LIESTO
LIEUTS

L••E••
LABELS
LACERS
LACEUP
LADERS
LAGERS
LAKERS
LAMECH
LAMEDH
LAMEDS
LAMELY
LAMENT
LAMESA
LAMEST
LAPELS
LAREDO
LASERS
LATEEN
LATELY
LATENE
LATENS
LATENT
LATEST
LAVERS
LAXEST
LAYERS
LEGEND
LEVEED
LEVEES
LEVELS
LEVENE
LEVERS
LEXEME
LIBELS
LIBERI
LIFERS
LIGERS
LIKELY
LIKENS
LIMENS
LIMEYS
LINEAL
LINEAR
LINENS
LINENY
LINERS
LINEUP
LIPENG
LITERS
LIVEIN
LIVELY
LIVENS
LIVEON
LIVERS
LIVERY
LLBEAN
LODENS
LOMEIN
LONELY
LONERS
LOPERS
LOREAL
LORENZ
LOSEIT
LOSERS
LOVEIN
LOVELL
LOVELY
LOVERS
LOVETT
LOWELL
LOWEND
LOWERS
LOWERY
LOWEST
LUBECK
LUCENT
LUDENS
LUGERS
LUMENS
LYCEES
LYCEUM

L•••E•
LAAGER
LABREA
LABRET
LACHES
LACIER
LACKED
LACKEY
LADDER
LADIES
LADLED
LADLER
LADLES
LAFFER
LAGGED
LAGGER
LAKIER
LAMBED
LAMMED
LANCED
LANCER
LANCES
LANCET
LANDED
LANDER
LANIER
LANKER
LAPPED
LAPPET
LAPSED
LAPSES
LAPTEV
LARDED
LARDER
LARGER
LARGES
LARKED
LARSEN
LASHED
LASHER
LASHES
LASSEN
LASSER
LASSES
LASTED
LASTEX
LATEEN
LATHED
LATHER
LATHES
LATKES
LATTEN
LATTER
LAUDED
LAUDER
LAUPER
LAUREL
LAUREN
LAWMEN
LAWYER
LAYMEN
LAZIER
LEADED
LEADEN
LEADER
LEAFED
LEAKED
LEAKER
LEAKEY
LEANED
LEANER
LEAPED
LEAPER
LEASED
LEASER
LEASES
LEAVED
LEAVEN
LEAVES
LECTER
LEDGER
LEDGES
LEERED
LEERER
LEGGED
LEGMEN
LEGREE
LEHRER
LEIDEN
LEMUEL
LENDER
LENSED
LENSES
LENTEN
LEONES
LERNER
LESLEY
LESSEE
LESSEN
LESSER
LESTER
LETTED
LETTER
LEVEED
LEVEES
LEVIED
LEVIER
LEVIES
LEWDER
LEYDEN
LIANES
LIBBED
LIBBER
LICHEN
LICKED
LIDDED
LIEDER
LIEFER
LIEGES
LIENEE
LIFTED
LIFTER
LILIES
LILTED
LIMBED
LIMBER
LIMIER
LIMNED
LIMNER
LIMPED
LIMPER
LIMPET
LINDEN
LINGER
LINIER
LINKED
LINKER
LINNET
LINNEY
LINSEY
LINTEL
LINTER
LIONEL
LIONET
LIPPED
LISLES
LISPED
LISTED
LISTEE
LISTEL
LISTEN
LISTER
LITRES
LITTER
LIVRES
LOADED
LOADER
LOAFED
LOAFER
LOAMED
LOANED
LOANER
LOAVES
LOBBED
LOBBER
LOCKED
LOCKER
LOCKET
LODGED
LODGER
LODGES
LOFTED
LOGGED
LOGGER
LOGIER
LOITER
LOLLED
LONGED
LONGER
LONGES
LOOIES
LOOKED
LOOKER
LOOMED
LOONEY
LOOPED
LOOPER
LOOSED
LOOSEN
LOOSER
LOOSES
LOOTED
LOOTER
LOPPED
LOPPER
LORDED
LORIES
LOSSES
LOTTED
LOUDEN
LOUDER
LOUPES
LOUSED
LOUSES
LOUVER
LOWKEY
LUBBER
LUCKED
LUDDEN
LUFFED
LUGGED
LUGGER
LULLED
LUMBER
LUMPED
LUMPEN
LUMPER
LUNDEN
LUNGED
LUNGES
LUNKER
LURKED
LUSHER
LUSTED
LUSTER
LUTHER
LUTZES
LYCEES
LYNLEY
LYNXES

L••••E
LABILE
LADDIE
LAHORE
LAINIE
LAMAZE
LANATE
LANOSE
LAOTSE
LARVAE
LASSIE
LATENE
LAURIE
LAVAGE
LEAGUE
LEFTIE
LEGATE
LEGREE
LEGUME
LENAPE
LENNIE
LENORE
LEONIE
LESAGE
LESLIE
LESSEE
LETSBE
LEVENE
LEVINE
LEVITE
LEXEME
LHOTSE
LIABLE
LIAISE
LIENEE
LIERNE
LIGATE
LIGURE
LILLIE
LINAGE
LIPASE
LIPIDE
LISTEE
LITTLE
LIZZIE
LOATHE
LOBATE
LOBULE
LOCALE
LOCATE
LONGUE
LOONIE
LOUCHE
LOUISE
LOUNGE
LOUVRE
LOVAGE
LUCITE
LUNATE
LUPINE
LUPONE
LUSTRE
LUXATE
LYSINE

•LE•••
ALEAST
ALECKY
ALECTO
ALEGAR
ALEGRE
ALEMAN
ALEPHS
ALEPPO
ALERTS
ALEUTS
ALEVEL
ALEXEI
ALEXIA
ALEXIS
BLEACH
BLEARS
BLEARY
BLEATS
BLEEDS
BLEEPS
BLENCH
BLENDE
BLENDS
BLENNY
BLEWIT
BLEWUP
CLEANS
CLEARS
CLEATS
CLEAVE
CLEEKS
CLEESE
CLEFTS
CLENCH
CLEPED
CLERGY
CLERIC
CLERKS
CLEVER
CLEVES
CLEVIS
CLEWED
ELECTS
ELEGIT
ELEMIS
ELEVEN
ELEVES
FLECHE
FLECKS
FLECKY
FLEDGE
FLEDGY
FLEECE
FLEECY
FLEERS
FLEETS
FLENSE
FLESHY
FLETCH
FLEURY
FLEWAT
FLEWIN
FLEXED
FLEXES
FLEXOR
FLEYED
GLEAMS
GLEAMY
GLEANS
GLEBES
GLENDA
GLENNE
ILEANA
ILESHA
ILEXES
KLEIST
NLEAST
OLEARY
OLEATE
OLEFIN
OLESON
OLEVEL
PLEACH
PLEADS
PLEASE
PLEATS
PLEBES
PLEDGE
PLEIAD
PLENTY
PLENUM
PLEURA
PLEXAL
PLEXOR
PLEXUS
SLEAVE
SLEAZE
SLEAZY
SLEDGE
SLEEKS
SLEEKY
SLEEPS
SLEEPY
SLEETS
SLEETY
SLEEVE
SLEIGH
SLEUTH
SLEWED
SLEZAK

•L•E••
ALBEDO
ALBEIT
ALBERT
ALDERS
ALIENS
ALKENE
ALLEES
ALLEGE
ALLELE
ALLEYS
ALPERT
ALTERS
ALWEST
BLEEDS
BLEEPS
BLUELY
BLUEOX
BLUEST
BLUESY
BLUETS
BLUEYS
CLEEKS
CLEESE
CLIENT
CLUEIN
ELBERT
ELDERS
ELDEST
ELLERY
ELVERS
FLEECE
FLEECY
FLEERS
FLEETS
FLIERS
FLUENT
FLYERS
GLUERS
ILLEST
LLBEAN
NLWEST
OLDEST
OLMECS
PLIERS
SLEEKS
SLEEKY
SLEEPS
SLEEPY
SLEETS
SLEETY
SLEEVE
SLIEST
SLYEST
ULCERS

•L••E•
ALATED
ALEVEL
ALEXEI
ALFRED
ALFVEN
ALINES
ALITER
ALLEES
ALLIED
ALLIES
ALLSET
ALLWET
ALTHEA
BLADED
BLADER
BLADES
BLAMED
BLAMES
BLARED
BLARES
BLAZED
BLAZER
BLAZES
BLIMEY
BLIXEN
BLOKES
BLOOEY
BLOWER
CLARET
CLAVES
CLAWED
CLAWER
CLAYEY
CLEPED
CLEVER
CLEVES
CLEWED
CLIMES
CLINES
CLONED
CLONES
CLOSED
CLOSER
CLOSES
CLOSET
CLOVEN
CLOVER
CLOVES
CLOYED
DLAYER
ELATED
ELATER
ELATES
ELAYER
ELEVEN
ELEVES
ELIDED
ELIDES
ELITES
ELOPED
ELOPER
ELOPES
ELUDED
ELUDER
ELUDES
ELUTED
ELUTES
ELYSEE
FLAKED
FLAKER
FLAKES
FLAKEY
FLAMED
FLAMES
FLARED
FLARES
FLAWED
FLAXEN
FLAXES
FLAYED
FLAYER
FLEXED
FLEXES
FLEYED
FLOOEY
FLORES
FLORET
FLOWED
FLOWER
FLUKES
FLUKEY
FLUMES
FLUTED
FLUTES
FLUTEY
FLUXED
FLUXES
FLYMEN
FLYNET
GLACES
GLADES
GLARED
GLARES
GLASER
GLAZED
GLAZER
GLAZES
GLEBES
GLIDED
GLIDER
GLIDES
GLOBED
GLOBES
GLOVED
GLOVER
GLOVES
GLOWED
GLOWER
GLOZED
GLOZES
GLUIER
GLUTEI
GLUTEN
GLUTES
ILEXES
ILLFED
ILLMET
OLDIES
OLDMEN
OLEVEL
OLIVER
OLIVES
PLACED
PLACER
PLACES
PLACET
PLAGES
PLANED
PLANER
PLANES
PLANET
PLATED
PLATEN
PLATER
PLATES
PLAYED
PLAYER
PLEBES
PLOVER
PLOWED
PLOWER
PLUMED
PLUMES
PLUSES
SLAKED
SLAKES
SLATED
SLATER
SLATES
SLAVED
SLAVER
SLAVES
SLAVEY
SLAYED
SLAYER
SLEWED
SLICED
SLICER
SLICES
SLIDER
SLIDES
SLIMED
SLIMES
SLIVER
SLOPED
SLOPES
SLOVEN
SLOWED
SLOWER
SLYPES
ULSTER

•L•••E
ALCOVE
ALDINE
ALDOSE
ALEGRE
ALFINE
ALGORE
ALIBLE
ALKENE
ALLEGE
ALLELE
ALLUDE
ALLURE
ALPINE
ALSACE
ALULAE
BLAINE
BLAISE
BLENDE
BLITHE
BLONDE
BLOUSE
BLYTHE
CLAIRE
CLAQUE
CLARKE
CLAUDE
CLAUSE
CLEAVE
CLEESE
CLICHE
CLIQUE
CLOCHE
CLOQUE
CLOTHE
ELAINE
ELAPSE
ELAYNE
ELLICE
ELMORE
ELOISE
ELYSEE
FLAMBE
FLANGE
FLECHE
FLEDGE
FLEECE
FLENSE
FLORAE
GLANCE
GLENNE
ILLUME
ILLUSE
KLUDGE
OLDAGE
OLEATE
PLAGUE
PLAICE
PLANTE
PLAQUE
PLATTE
PLEASE
PLEDGE
PLICAE
PLISSE
PLUNGE
SLEAVE
SLEAZE
SLEDGE
SLEEVE
SLOANE
SLUDGE
SLUICE
ULLAGE

••LE••
ABLEST
AGLEAM
AGLETS
AILEEN
AILERS
ALLEES
ALLEGE
ALLELE
ALLEYS
ARLEEN
ARLENE
ASLEEP
BALEEN
BALERS
BOLERO
BOLEYN
CELEBS
CELERY
COLEUS
CULETS
DALETH
DELEON
DELETE
DOLENZ
EELERS
EILEEN
ELLERY
EXLEGE
FILENE
FILERS
FILETS
GALEAE
GALENA
GELEES
GILEAD
GOLEMS
HALERS
HALERU
HALEST
HALEVY
HELENA
HELENE
HELENS
HOLEUP
IDLERS
IDLEST
ILLEST
INLETS
IRLENE
ISLETS
JOLENE
JULEPS
MCLEAN
MELEES
MILERS
MOLEST
MULETA
MULEYS
NFLERS
NHLERS
NOLEAD
NOLENS
NOLESS
OGLERS
OILERS
OWLETS
PALEAE
PALELY
PALEST
PELEUS
PHLEBO
PHLEGM
PILEIN
PILEON
PILEUM
PILEUP
PILEUS
POLEAX
POLERS
POLEYN
RELENT
RELETS
RELEVY
RILEUP
ROLEOS
RULEON
RULERS
SCLERA
SCLERO
SELECT
SELENA
SELENE
SELENO
SILENI
SILENT
SOLEIL
SOLELY
SOLEMN
SOLENT
SOLERS
SOLEUS
SPLEEN
TALENT
TALERS
TALESE
TELEDU
TILERS
TOLEDO
UNLEAD
UNLESS
VALENS
VALENT
VALERY
VALETS
VILELY
VILEST
VOLENS
WALERS
WALESA
XYLENE

••L•E•
AILEEN
ALLEES
ALLIED
ALLIES
ALLSET
ALLWET
ARLEEN
ASLEEP
BALDER
BALEEN
BALKED
BALLET
BELIED
BELIEF
BELIES
BELLED
BELLES
BELTED
BILGES
BILKED
BILLED
BILLET
BOLDER
BOLGER
BOLTED
BULGED
BULGES
BULKED
BULLED
BULLET
BULWER
CALCES
CALDER
CALKED
CALLED
CALLER
CALLES
CALMED
CALMER
CALVED
CALVES
CALXES
CELLED
COLDER
COLIES
COLLET
COLTER
CULLED
CULLEN
CULLER
CULLET
CULVER
DALLES
DELVED
DELVER
DELVES
DILLER
DILSEY
DOLLED
DOLMEN
DULCET
DULLEA
DULLED
DULLER
DULLES
EELIER
EILEEN
FALCES
FALLEN
FALSER
FALTER
FELLED
FELLER
FELTED
FILLED
FILLER
FILLES
FILLET
FILMED
FILTER
FOLDED
FOLDER
FULLER
GALLED
GALLEY
GELEES
GELLED
GELSEY
GILDED
GILDER
GILLED
GOLDEN
GOLFED
GOLFER
GULFED
GULLED
GULLET
GULPED
GULPER
HALLEL
HALLEY
HALOED
HALOES
HALSEY
HALTED
HALTER
HALVED
HALVES

HELLER
HELMED
HELMET
HELPED
HELPER
HELTER
HELVES
HILLED
HILLEL
HILLER
HOLDEN
HOLDER
HOLIER
HOLLER
HOLMES
HULKED
HULLED
HULLER
ILLFED
ILLMET
JELLED
JILTED
JOLIET
JOLTED
JULIET
KELLER
KELLEY
KELSEY
KILLED
KILLER
KILMER
KILNED
KILTED
KILTER
LILIES
LILTED
LOLLED
LULLED
MALDEN
MALLEE
MALLEI
MALLET
MALTED
MELDED
MELEES
MELTED
MILDER
MILDEW
MILIEU
MILKED
MILKER
MILLED
MILLER
MILLET
MILNER
MOLDED
MOLDER
MOLTED
MOLTEN
MOLTER
MULLED
MULLER
MULLET
NULLED
OILIER
OILMEN
PALAEO
PALIER
PALLED
PALLET
PALMED
PALMER
PALTER
PELLET
PELMET
PELTED
PELTER
PHLOEM
PILFER
PILLED
POLDER
POLLED
POLLEN
POLLER
POLLEX
PULLED
PULLET
PULLEY
PULPED
PULSED
PULSES
RELIED
RELIEF
RELIES
RILLES
RILLET
ROLLED
ROLLER
SALLET
SALTED
SALTEN
SALTER
SALVED
SALVER
SALVES
SELLER
SELVES
SILKED
SILKEN
SILOED
SILTED
SILVER
SOLDER
SOLOED
SOLVED
SOLVER
SOLVES
SPLEEN
SULKED
SULKER
SULLEN
TALCED
TALKED
TALKER
TALLER
TELLER
TILDEN
TILDES
TILLED
TILLER
TILTED
TILTER
TOLLED
TOLTEC
TULLES
UGLIER
UGLIES
VALDEZ
VALLEE
VALLEY
VALUED
VALUES
VALVED
VALVES
VELVET
VOLLEY
WALDEN
WALKED
WALKEN
WALKER
WALLED
WALLER
WALLET
WALTER
WELDED
WELDER
WELLED
WELLER
WELLES
WELTED
WELTER
WILDER
WILIER
WILKES
WILLED
WILLEM
WILLET
WILTED
WOLFED
WOLPER
WOLSEY
WOLVES
YALIES
YELLED
YELLER
YELPED
YELPER
YOLKED

••L••E

ABLATE
ABLAZE
AFLAME
AGLARE
ALLEGE
ALLELE
ALLUDE
ALLURE
APLITE
ARLENE
ASLOPE
AXLIKE
BELIKE
BELIZE
BILLIE
BOLIDE
BULLAE
BYLINE
CALQUE
CELINE
CELLAE
COLLIE
DELATE
DELETE
DELUDE
DELUGE
DELUXE
DILATE
DILUTE
ELLICE
ENLACE
EXLEGE
FALINE
FELINE
FELIPE
FELLOE
FILENE
FILOSE
FOLKIE
GALEAE
GALORE
GILLIE
GOLDIE
HALIDE
HALITE
HELENE
ILLUME
ILLUSE
INLINE
INLOVE
IOLITE
IRLENE
JOLENE
KALINE
KELPIE
KILTIE
LILLIE
MALATE
MALICE
MALLEE
MALONE
MILLIE
MILTIE
MOLINE
MOLTKE
NELLIE
NOLOSE
OBLATE
OBLIGE
OFLATE
ONLINE
OOLITE
OXLIKE
PALACE
PALATE
PALEAE
PELAGE
PELIKE
PILATE
PILOSE
POLICE
POLITE
PULQUE
RELACE
RELATE
RELINE
RELIVE
RELUME
ROLLIE
SALINE
SALOME
SALUTE
SELENE
SILAGE
SILONE
SOLACE
SOLUTE
SPLICE
SPLINE
STLUKE
TALESE
TALKIE
TILLIE
TOLIFE
TULANE
TULARE
ULLAGE
UNLACE
UNLADE
UNLIKE
VALISE
VALLEE
VELOCE
VOLARE
VOLUME
VOLUTE
WALKIE
WILLIE
XYLENE

•••LE•

ABELES
ADDLED
ADDLES
AISLES
AMBLED
AMBLER
AMBLES
AMOLES
AMPLER
AMULET
ANELED
ANELES
ANGLED
ANGLER
ANGLES
ANKLED
ANKLES
ANKLET
ANNLEE
ANOLES
ANTLER
APPLES
APPLET
ARMLET
ASHLEY
ATTLEE
AUKLET
AZALEA
BAILED
BAILEE
BAILER
BAILEY
BALLET
BARLEY
BAWLED
BAWLER
BEGLEY
BELLED
BELLES
BIBLES
BILLED
BILLET
BIRLED
BOGLES
BOILED
BOILER
BOSLEY
BOULES
BOULEZ
BOWLED
BOWLER
BOWLES
BRULES
BUGLED
BUGLER
BUGLES
BULLED
BULLET
BURLED
BURLEY
BUTLER
CABLED
CABLER
CABLES
CALLED
CALLER
CALLES
CAMLET
CAPLET
CEILED
CELLED
CHALET
CHOLER
COALER
COILED
COLLET
COOLED
COOLER
COPLEY
COULEE
COWLED
COWLEY
CULLED
CULLEN
CULLER
CULLET
CURLED
CURLER
CURLEW
CURLEY
CUTLER
CUTLET
CYCLED
CYCLER
CYCLES
DAILEY
DALLES
DEALER
DEFLEA
DHOLES
DIALED
DIALER
DILLER
DOGLEG
DOLLED
DOOLEY
DUDLEY
DUELED
DUELER
DULLEA
DULLED
DULLER
DULLES
DUPLEX
EAGLED
EAGLES
EAGLET
ECCLES
ECOLES
EDILES
EMBLEM
EVILER
EXILED
EXILES
EYELET
FABLED
FABLER
FABLES
FAILED
FALLEN
FARLEY
FEELER
FELLED
FELLER
FILLED
FILLER
FILLES
FILLET
FOALED
FOILED
FOOLED
FOOLER
FOULED
FOULER
FOWLED
FOWLER
FOWLES
FUELED
FUELER
FULLER
FURLED
GABLED
GABLER
GABLES
GALLED
GALLEY
GAOLED
GAOLER
GELLED
GIBLET
GILLED
GIMLET
GOBLET
GOULET
GUILES
GULLED
GULLET
GURLEY
HAILED
HAILEY
HALLEL
HALLEY
HAMLET
HANLEY
HAOLES
HARLEM
HARLEY
HAULED
HAULER
HAYLEY
HEALED
HEALER
HEELED
HEELER
HELLER
HENLEY
HILLED
HILLEL
HILLER
HOLLER
HOWLED
HOWLER
HULLED
HULLER
HURLED
HURLER
HURLEY
HUXLEY
INGLES
INKLES
ISTLES
JAILED
JAILER
JELLED
JOULES
KEELED
KEELER
KEGLER
KELLER
KELLEY
KEPLER
KILLED
KILLER
KISLEV
KJOLEN
KOHLER
LADLED
LADLER
LADLES
LESLEY
LISLES
LOLLED
LULLED
LYNLEY
MAHLER
MAILED
MAILER
MAILES
MALLEE
MALLEI
MALLET
MAPLES
MARLED
MARLEE
MARLEY
MAULED
MAULER
MEDLEY
MEWLED
MEWLER
MIDLER
MILLED
MILLER
MILLET
MISLED
MOBLEY
MOILED
MOILER
MORLEY
MOSLEM
MOTLEY
MULLED
MULLER
MULLET
NAILED
NAILER
NAPLES
NEWLEY
NOBLER
NOBLES
NUCLEI
NUCLEO
NULLED
NUTLET
OAKLEY
OMELET
OODLES
ORALES
ORTLES
OSTLER
OUTLET
OVULES
PALLED
PALLET
PARLEY
PAULEY
PEALED
PEELED
PEELER
PEGLER
PELLET
PIGLET
PILLED
PIOLET
POLLED
POLLEN
POLLER
POLLEX
POOLED
PROLES
PULLED
PULLET
PULLEY
PURLED
RAILED
RAILER
REALER
REALES
REELED
REFLEX
REGLET
RIDLEY
RIFLED
RIFLER
RIFLES
RILLES
RILLET
RIPLEY
ROBLES
ROILED
ROLLED
ROLLER
RUBLES
RUBLEV
RUNLET
SABLES
SAILED
SALLET
SAMLET
SAYLES
SCALED
SCALER
SCALES
SCHLEP
SEALED
SEALER
SEELEY
SELLER
SHALES
SHALEY
SHOLEM
SIDLED
SIDLES
SISLER
SISLEY
SMILED
SMILER
SMILES
SMILEY
SOCLES
SOILED
SPILES
STALED
STALER
STALES
STELES
STILES
STOLEN
STOLES
STYLED
STYLER
STYLES
STYLET
SUBLET
SULLEN
SUTLER
SWALES
TABLED
TABLES
TABLET
TAILED
TALLER
TELLER
THALER
THALES
THOLES
TILLED
TILLER
TITLED
TITLES
TOILED
TOILER
TOILES
TOILET
TOLLED
TOOLED
TRALEE
TULLES
UNCLES
VALLEE
VALLEY
VARLET
VEBLEN
VEILED
VIOLET
VOILES
VOLLEY
WAILED
WAILER
WALLED
WALLER
WALLET
WELLED
WELLER
WELLES
WESLEY
WHALER
WHALES
WHILED
WHILES
WHOLES
WIGLET
WILLED
WILLEM
WILLET
WOHLER
WOOLEN
WOOLEY
WURLEY
XFILES
YELLED
YELLER
YOWLED

•••L•E

ADELIE
ADELLE
ALULAE
AMALIE
ANNLEE
ATTLEE
AVULSE
BAILEE
BIGLIE
BILLIE
BOULLE
BULLAE
CELLAE
CHELAE
CHILDE
CHILOE
COLLIE
COULEE
EVOLVE
EVULSE
FAILLE
FELLOE
GILLIE
GOALIE
GRILLE
GRILSE
ISOLDE
KPELLE
LESLIE
LILLIE
MALLEE
MARLEE
MEALIE
MILLIE
MRBLUE
NELLIE
ORELSE
PHILAE
PHYLAE
REGLUE
ROLLIE
RVALUE
SHELVE
STELAE
STOLLE
SVELTE
TAILLE
TILLIE
TRALEE
TUILLE
TWELVE
UNGLUE
UVALUE
UVULAE
VALLEE
WILLIE

••••LE

ADELLE
AEDILE
ALIBLE
ALLELE
AMPULE
ARABLE
ARGYLE
AUDILE
AWHILE
BABBLE
BAFFLE
BANGLE
BATTLE
BAUBLE
BEADLE
BEAGLE
BEATLE
BEETLE
BIDDLE
BOBBLE
BOGGLE
BOODLE
BOTTLE
BOUCLE
BOULLE
BRIDLE
BUBBLE
BUCKLE
BUMBLE
BUNDLE
BUNGLE
BURBLE
BURGLE
BUSTLE
CACKLE
CAJOLE
CANDLE
CANTLE
CAROLE
CASTLE
CATTLE
CAUDLE
CECILE
CHICLE
CIRCLE
COBBLE
COCKLE
CODDLE
COUPLE
CRADLE
CREOLE
CUDDLE
CURDLE
CURULE
CYBELE
DABBLE
DANDLE
DANGLE
DAPPLE
DARKLE
DAWDLE
DAZZLE
DECKLE
DEFILE
DIBBLE
DIDDLE
DIMPLE
DINGLE
DIPOLE
DOABLE
DOCILE
DONGLE
DOODLE
DOTTLE
DOUBLE
EDERLE
EDIBLE
ENABLE
ENISLE
ENSILE
ETOILE
EXHALE
FACILE
FAILLE
FATALE
FEEBLE
FEMALE
FERULE
FETTLE
FICKLE
FIDDLE
FINALE
FIPPLE
FIZZLE
FOCSLE
FOIBLE
FONDLE
FOOZLE
FUDDLE
FUMBLE
FUTILE
GABBLE
GAGGLE
GAMBLE
GANGLE
GARBLE
GARGLE
GENTLE
GIGGLE
GIRDLE
GOBBLE
GOGGLE
GOOGLE
GRABLE
GRILLE
GURGLE
GUZZLE
HABILE
HACKLE
HAGGLE
HANDLE
HASSLE
HECKLE
HEDDLE
HIGGLE
HOBBLE
HOOPLE
HOPPLE
HUBBLE
HUDDLE
HUMBLE
HURDLE
HURTLE
HUSTLE
ICICLE
IMPALE
INHALE
INSOLE
JANGLE
JECKLE
JIGGLE
JINGLE
JOGGLE
JOSTLE
JUGGLE
JUMBLE
JUNGLE
KETTLE
KIBBLE
KINDLE
KIRTLE
KPELLE
KURILE
LABILE
LIABLE
LITTLE
LOBULE
LOCALE
MANGLE
MANTLE
MARBLE
MARPLE
MCHALE
MEDDLE
METTLE
MIDDLE
MIGGLE
MINGLE
MIZZLE
MOBILE
MODULE
MORALE
MOTILE
MOTTLE
MUDDLE
MUFFLE
MUMBLE
MUSCLE
MUZZLE
MYRTLE
NEEDLE
NESTLE
NETTLE
NIBBLE
NICOLE
NIGGLE
NIMBLE
NOBBLE
NODDLE
NODULE
NOODLE
NOSALE
NOZZLE
NUBBLE
NUBILE
NUZZLE
ONFILE
ONSALE
ORACLE
ORIOLE
OTOOLE
PADDLE
PAROLE
PEBBLE
PEDDLE
PEOPLE
PESTLE
PICKLE
PIFFLE
PINOLE
PINTLE
POODLE
POPPLE
POTTLE
PUDDLE
PURFLE
PURPLE
PUZZLE
QUAYLE
RABBLE
RADDLE
RAFFLE
RAMBLE
RANKLE
RASSLE
RATTLE
RAZZLE
REFILE
REGALE
RESALE
RESILE
RESOLE
RETILE
REVILE
RIDDLE
RIFFLE
RIMPLE
RIPPLE
ROUBLE
ROYALE
RUBBLE
RUDDLE
RUFFLE
RUMBLE
RUMPLE
RUNDLE
RUSTLE
RUTILE
SADDLE
SAMPLE
SEARLE
SEDILE
SEMELE
SETTLE
SICKLE
SIECLE
SIMILE
SIMPLE
SINGLE
SIZZLE
STABLE
STAPLE
STEELE
STIFLE
STOLLE
SUBTLE
SUPPLE
TACKLE
TAILLE
TAMALE
TANGLE
TATTLE
TEMPLE
THRALE
TICKLE
TINGLE
TINKLE
TIPPLE
TITTLE
TODDLE
TOGGLE
TOOTLE
TOPPLE
TOUSLE
TREBLE
TRIFLE
TRIPLE
TUILLE
TUMBLE
TURTLE
TUSSLE
UNABLE
UNPILE
USABLE
VIABLE
VIRILE
VITALE
WADDLE
WAFFLE
WAGGLE
WAMBLE
WANGLE
WARBLE
WATTLE
WIGGLE
WIMBLE
WIMPLE
WINKLE
WOBBLE

L•F•••

LAFFER
LEFTIE
LEFTIN
LIFERS
LIFTED
LIFTER
LIFTUP
LOFTED
LUFFED

L••F••

LAFFER
LAPFUL
LAWFUL
LAYFOR
LEAFED
LETFLY
LIEFER
LIEFLY
LOAFED
LOAFER
LOOFAH
LOOFAS
LOWFAT
LUFFED

L•••F•

LAYOFF
LEDOFF
LETOFF
LOGOFF

L••••F

LAYOFF
LEDOFF
LETOFF
LOGOFF

•LF•••

ALFINE
ALFRED
ALFVEN
ELFISH
ELFMAN

•L•F••

ALLFOR
BLUFFS
CLEFTS
CLIFFS
CLIFFY
FLUFFS
FLUFFY
ILLFED
OLEFIN

•L••F•

BLUFFS
CLIFFS
CLIFFY
FLUFFS
FLUFFY
KLOOFS

••LF••

ALLFOR
BELFRY
COLFAX
DELFTS
FULFIL
GOLFED
GOLFER
GULFED
ILLFED
PILFER
SOLFAS
SULFUR
WILFUL
WOLFED

••L•F•

PILAFS
SALIFY
SCLAFF
TOLIFE
UGLIFY
UPLIFT
VILIFY

••L••F

BELIEF
RELIEF
SCLAFF
TELLOF
TOLDOF

•••LF•

AMALFI

•••L•F
TELLOF

••••LF
BEHALF
ENGULF
INHALF
ITSELF
MYSELF
RUDOLF

L•G•••
LAGASH
LAGERS
LAGGED
LAGGER
LAGOON
LAGUNA
LEGACY
LEGALS
LEGATE
LEGATO
LEGEND
LEGGED
LEGION
LEGIST
LEGMAN
LEGMEN
LEGREE
LEGUIN
LEGUME
LIGAND
LIGATE
LIGERS
LIGHTS
LIGNIN
LIGULA
LIGURE
LOGGED
LOGGER
LOGGIA
LOGIER
LOGILY
LOGION
LOGJAM
LOGOFF
LOGOUT
LOGSIN
LOGSON
LUGERS
LUGGED
LUGGER
LUGNUT
LUGOSI

L••G••
LAAGER
LAGGED
LAGGER
LANGUR
LARGER
LARGES
LARGOS
LAUGHS
LEAGUE
LEDGER
LEDGES
LEGGED
LENGTH
LIEGES
LINGER
LINGUA
LODGED
LODGER
LODGES
LOGGED
LOGGER
LOGGIA
LONGAN
LONGED
LONGER
LONGES
LONGLY
LONGUE
LOUGHS
LUGGED
LUGGER
LUNGED
LUNGES

L•••G•
LADOGA
LATIGO
LAVAGE
LEHIGH
LESAGE
LETSGO
LIANGS
LINAGE
LOUNGE
LOVAGE

L••••G
LACING
LADING
LAMING
LAPDOG
LAVING
LAWING
LAYING
LAZING
LIEBIG
LIKING
LIMING
LINING
LIPENG
LITHOG
LIVING
LOPING
LOSING
LOVING
LOWING
LUBING
LUDWIG
LURING
LUTING

•LG•••
ALGORE

•L•G••
ALEGAR
ALEGRE
ALIGHT
ALIGNS
BLIGHT
CLOGGY
CLOGUP
ELEGIT
FLAGGY
FLAGON
FLIGHT
GLOGGS
PLAGAL
PLAGES
PLAGIO
PLAGUE
PLIGHT
PLUGIN
SLAGGY
SLIGHT
SLOGAN
SLUGGO

•L••G•
ALLEGE
CLANGS
CLERGY
CLINGS
CLINGY
CLOGGY
ELOIGN
FLAGGY
FLANGE
FLEDGE
FLEDGY
FLINGS
GLOGGS
KLUDGE
OLDAGE
OLINGO
PLEDGE
PLOUGH
PLUNGE
SLAGGY
SLANGS
SLANGY
SLEDGE
SLEIGH
SLINGS
SLOUGH
SLUDGE
SLUDGY
SLUGGO
ULLAGE

•L•••G
ALBORG
BLUING
CLUING
FLYING
GLUING
PLYING
SLUING

••LG••
BILGES
BOLGER
BULGAR
BULGED
BULGES
BULGUR
GILGUY
NILGAI
VULGAR

••L•G•
ALLEGE
BELUGA
COLUGO
DELUGE
EULOGY
EXLEGE
GALAGO
GULAGS
MALAGA
MALIGN
OBLIGE
OOLOGY
PELAGE
PHLEGM
SILAGE
TELUGU
ULLAGE

••L••G
AILING
BALING
BELONG
DELONG
DOLING
EALING
FILING
HALING
HOLING
IDLING
KDLANG
OBLONG
OGLING
OILING
OILRIG
OOLONG
PALING
PILING
POLING
PULING
RILING
RULING
SOLING
SOLONG
TILING
WILING

•••L•G
ANALOG
DIALOG
DOGLEG
EPILOG
GASLOG
JETLAG
PROLOG
REFLAG
SAWLOG
STALAG
UNCLOG
UNPLUG

LH••••
LHOTSE

L•H•••
LAHORE
LCHAIM
LEHIGH
LEHRER
LEHUAS

L••H••
LACHES
LAPHAM
LASHED
LASHER
LASHES
LASHIO
LASHUP
LATHED
LATHER
LATHES
LETHAL
LICHEN
LIGHTS
LITHIC
LITHOG
LITHOS
LOTHAR
LUSHER
LUSHLY
LUTHER
LUTHOR

L•••H•
LANDHO
LAUGHS
LEACHY
LITCHI
LOATHE
LOTAHS
LOUCHE
LOUGHS
LUNCHY
LYMPHS

L••••H
LAGASH
LAMECH
LAMEDH
LATISH
LAUNCH
LAVISH
LEHIGH
LENGTH
LILITH
LOOFAH
LOWISH

•LH•••
ALHIRT
HLHUNT

•L•H••
ALOHAS
ALPHAS
ALTHEA
ELOHIM
OLDHAM
OLDHAT

•L••H•
ALEPHS
ALIGHT
BLIGHT
BLITHE
BLYTHE
CLICHE
CLOCHE
CLOTHE
CLOTHO
CLOTHS
ELISHA
FLASHY
FLECHE
FLESHY
FLIGHT
GLYPHS
ILESHA
PLASHY
PLIGHT
PLUSHY
SLIGHT
SLITHY
SLOSHY
SLOTHS
SLUSHY

•L•••H
BLANCH
BLEACH
BLENCH
BLOTCH
BLUISH
CLENCH
CLINCH
CLUTCH
ELFISH
ELIJAH
ELVISH
FLETCH
FLINCH
FLITCH
GLITCH
KLATCH
OLDISH
PLEACH
PLINTH
PLOUGH
SLEIGH
SLEUTH
SLOUCH
SLOUGH

••L•H•
BOLSHY
DELPHI
FILTHY
GALAHS
SYLPHS

••L••H
ABLUSH
CALASH
CALIPH
DALETH
DULUTH
EOLITH
FELLAH
GALOSH
GULLAH
HALVAH
KALAKH
LILITH
MOLOCH
MULISH
MULLAH
NULLAH
OOLITH
OWLISH
PALISH
POLISH
RELISH
SALISH
SPLASH
SPLOSH
UNLASH
ZILPAH

•••L•H
ADOLPH
BEULAH
FELLAH
GUELPH
GULLAH
HEALTH
MOOLAH
MULLAH
NULLAH
SHILOH
SPLITH
WEALTH

LI••••
LIABLE
LIAISE
LIANAS
LIANES
LIANGS
LIBBED
LIBBER
LIBELS
LIBERI
LIBIDO
LIBRIS
LIBYAN
LICHEN
LICKED
LICTOR
LIDDED
LIEBIG
LIEBYS
LIEDER
LIEFER
LIEFLY
LIEGES
LIELOW
LIENEE
LIERNE
LIESIN
LIESTO
LIEUTS
LIFERS
LIFTED
LIFTER
LIFTUP
LIGAND
LIGATE
LIGERS
LIGHTS
LIGNIN
LIGULA
LIGURE
LIKELY
LIKENS
LIKING
LILACS
LILIES
LILITH
LILLIE
LILTED
LIMBED
LIMBER
LIMBOS
LIMBUS
LIMENS
LIMEYS
LIMIER
LIMING
LIMITS
LIMNED
LIMNER
LIMPED
LIMPER
LIMPET
LIMPID
LIMPLY
LINAGE
LINDEN
LINEAL
LINEAR
LINENS
LINENY
LINERS
LINEUP
LINGER
LINGUA
LINIER
LINING
LINKED
LINKER
LINKUP
LINNET
LINNEY
LINSEY
LINTEL
LINTER
LIONEL
LIONET
LIONLY
LIOTTA
LIPASE
LIPENG
LIPIDE
LIPIDS
LIPOID
LIPPED
LIPTON
LIQUID
LIQUOR
LISBOA
LISBON
LISLES
LISPED
LISTED
LISTEE
LISTEL
LISTEN
LISTER
LISTON
LITANY
LITCHI
LITERS
LITHIC
LITHOG
LITHOS
LITMUS
LITOUT
LITRES
LITTER
LITTLE
LIVEIN
LIVELY
LIVENS
LIVEON
LIVERS
LIVERY
LIVING
LIVRES
LIZARD
LIZZIE

L•I•••
LAIDBY
LAIDIN
LAIDON
LAIDTO
LAIDUP
LAINIE
LAIRDS
LEIDEN
LOITER

L••I••
LABIAL
LABILE
LACIER
LACILY
LACING
LADIDA
LADIES
LADING
LADINO
LAKIER
LAMIAS
LAMINA
LAMING
LANIER
LAPINS
LARIAT
LATIGO
LATINA
LATINI
LATINO
LATINS
LATISH
LATIUM
LAVING
LAVISH
LAWING
LAXITY
LAYING
LAZIER
LAZILY
LAZING
LEGION
LEGIST
LEHIGH
LENITY
LERIDA
LEVIED
LEVIER
LEVIES
LEVINE
LEVITE
LEVITY
LEXICA
LIAISE
LIBIDO
LIKING
LILIES
LILITH
LIMIER
LIMING
LIMITS
LINIER
LINING
LIPIDE
LIPIDS
LIVING
LOGIER
LOGILY
LOGION
LOLITA
LOOIES
LOPING
LORICA
LORIES
LOSING
LOTION
LOUISA
LOUISE
LOVING
LOWING
LOWISH
LUBING
LUCIAN
LUCITE
LUCIUS
LUMINA
LUPINE
LUPINO
LURING
LUTING
LUTIST
LYRICS
LYRIST
LYSINE
LYSINS

L•••I•
LACTIC
LADDIE
LAIDIN
LAINIE
LANAIS
LANDIS
LANVIN
LASHIO
LASSIE
LATVIA
LAURIE
LAYSIN
LCHAIM
LEADIN
LEFTIE
LEFTIN
LEGUIN
LENNIE
LENTIL
LEONID
LEONIE
LESLIE
LETSIN
LIBRIS
LIEBIG
LIESIN
LIGNIN
LILLIE
LIMPID
LIPOID
LIQUID
LITHIC
LIVEIN
LIZZIE
LOCKIN
LOGGIA
LOGSIN
LOMEIN
LOOKIN
LOONIE
LORAIN
LOSEIT
LOSTIT
LOVEIN
LUBLIN
LUDWIG

L••••I
LATINI
LAZULI
LIBERI
LITCHI
LUGOSI

•LI•••
ALIBIS
ALIBLE
ALICIA
ALIENS
ALIGHT
ALIGNS
ALINES
ALIOTO
ALISON
ALITER
BLIGHT
BLIMEY
BLIMPS
BLINDS
BLINIS
BLINKS
BLINTZ
BLITHE
BLIXEN
CLICHE
CLICKS
CLIENT
CLIFFS
CLIFFY
CLIMAX
CLIMBS
CLIMES
CLINCH
CLINES
CLINGS
CLINGY
CLINIC
CLINKS
CLIPON
CLIQUE
CLIQUY
ELICIT
ELIDED
ELIDES
ELIJAH
ELINOR
ELISHA
ELISSA
ELITES
ELIXIR
FLICKA
FLICKS
FLIERS
FLIGHT
FLIMSY
FLINCH
FLINGS
FLINTS
FLINTY
FLIPUP
FLIRTS
FLIRTY
FLITCH
GLIBLY
GLIDED
GLIDER
GLIDES
GLINKA
GLINTS
GLITCH
GLITZY
KLIBAN
OLINDA
OLINGO
OLIVER
OLIVES
OLIVIA
PLIANT
PLICAE
PLIERS
PLIGHT
PLINKS
PLINTH
PLISSE
SLICED
SLICER
SLICES
SLICKS
SLIDER
SLIDES
SLIDIN
SLIEST
SLIGHT
SLIMED
SLIMES
SLIMLY
SLIMSY
SLINGS
SLINKS
SLINKY
SLIPIN
SLIPON
SLIPPY
SLIPUP
SLITHY
SLITTY
SLIVER

•L•I••
ALBINO
ALBION
ALDINE
ALFINE
ALHIRT
ALLIED
ALLIES
ALLIUM
ALNICO
ALOINS
ALPINE
ALTIMA
ALTIUS
BLAINE
BLAISE
BLUING
BLUISH
CLAIMS
CLAIRE
CLUING
ELAINE
ELFISH
ELLICE
ELLIOT
ELMIRA
ELNINO
ELOIGN
ELOISE
ELVIRA
ELVISH
FLAILS
FLAIRS
FLUIDS
FLYING
FLYINS
GLAIRS
GLAIRY
GLUIER
GLUING
ILLINI
ILOILO
KLEIST
OLDIES
OLDISH
PLAICE
PLAIDS
PLAINS
PLAINT
PLAITS
PLEIAD
PLYING
SLEIGH
SLUICE
SLUING
ULTIMA
ULTIMO

•L••I•
ALANIS
ALARIC
ALBEIT
ALBOIN
ALCUIN
ALDRIN
ALEXIA
ALEXIS
ALIBIS
ALICIA
ALTAIC
ALTAIR
BLEWIT
BLINIS
BLOWIN
BLOWIT
CLAVIN
CLERIC
CLEVIS
CLINIC
CLORIS
CLOVIS
CLUEIN
ELAPID
ELEGIT
ELEMIS
ELICIT
ELIXIR
ELOHIM
FLAVIA
FLEWIN
FLORID
FLORIN
FLORIO
GLACIS
GLOBIN
GLORIA
GLYNIS
ILORIN
OLDVIC
OLEFIN
OLIVIA
PLACID
PLAGIO
PLUGIN
SLAVIC
SLIDIN
SLIPIN
SLOVIK

•L•••I
ALEXEI
ALKALI
ALUMNI
GLUTEI
ILLINI

••LI••
ADLIBS
AGLINT
AILING
ALLIED
ALLIES
ALLIUM
APLITE
ARLISS
AXLIKE
BALING
BELIAL
BELIED
BELIEF
BELIES
BELIKE
BELIZE
BOLIDE
BYLINE
CALICO
CALIPH
CELINE
CILIUM
COLIES
COLIMA
DELICT
DELIST
DELIUS
DOLING
EALING
EELIER
ELLICE
ELLIOT
ENLIST
EOLIAN
EOLITH
FALINE
FELINE
FELIPE
FILIAL
FILING
FILIUS
FOLIAR
FOLIOS
FOLIUM
GOLINO
HALIDE
HALING
HALITE
HELIOS
HELIUM
HOLIER
HOLILY
HOLING
HOLISM
HOLIST
IDLING
ILLINI
INLINE
IOLITE
JOLIET
JOLIOT
JULIAN
JULIET
JULIUS
KALINE
KILIMS
LILIES
LILITH
LOLITA
MALIBU
MALICE
MALIGN
MELINA
MILIEU
MOLINE
MULISH
OBLIGE
OGLING
OILIER
OILILY
OILING
ONLINE
OOLITE
OOLITH
OWLISH
OXLIKE
OXLIPS
PALIER
PALING
PALISH
PELIKE
PELION
PILING
POLICE
POLICY
POLING
POLISH
POLITE
POLITY
PULING
RELICS
RELICT
RELIED
RELIEF
RELIES
RELINE
RELISH
RELIST
RELIVE
RILING
RULING
SALIFY
SALINA
SALINE
SALISH
SALIVA
SILICA
SOLIDI
SOLIDS
SOLING
SPLICE
SPLINE
SPLINT
SPLITS
TALION
TILING
TOLIFE
TULIPS
UGLIER
UGLIES
UGLIFY
UGLILY
UNLIKE
UNLINK
UPLIFT
UPLINK
VALISE
VALIUM
VILIFY
WILIER
WILILY
WILING
YALIES

••L•I•
AFLCIO
AGLAIA
AULAIT
BALTIC
BELAIR
BELOIT
BILLIE
BOLLIX
BULBIL
CALAIS
CALLIN
CALVIN
CELTIC
COLLIE
CULKIN
CULLIS
CULTIC
DELRIO
DELTIC
ECLAIR
FALLIN
FELLIN
FILLIN
FILLIP
FOLKIE
FULFIL
GALLIA
GALLIC
GALOIS
GILLIE
GILLIS
GOLDIE
HALOID
HELDIN
HOLDIN
HOLDIT
INLAID
KELPIE
KELVIN
KILTIE
LILLIE
MALKIN
MALTIN
MCLAIN
MELVIL
MELVIN
MILLIE
MILTIE
NELLIE
OILRIG
PALLIA
PALLID
PELVIC
PELVIS
PILEIN
PULLIN
PULPIT
RELAID
ROLLIE
ROLLIN
SALVIA
SOLEIL
SYLVIA
TALKIE
TILLIE
TILLIS
TILSIT
UNLAID
VALOIS
WALKIE
WALKIN
WALLIS
WELKIN
WILLIE
WILLIS
XYLOID

••L••I
BILOXI
DALASI
DELPHI
FULANI
GELATI
ILLINI
MALAWI
MALLEI
MALOTI
NILGAI
PILOTI
POLLOI
SALAMI
SALUKI
SILENI
SOLIDI

•••LI•
ADELIE

AEOLIA
AEOLIC
AMALIE
AMBLIN
AMELIA
ANGLIA
ANGLIC
APULIA
ARALIA
BERLIN
BIBLIO
BIGLIE
BILLIE
BOLLIX
BROLIN
CALLIN
CANLIT
CARLIN
COLLIE
COOLIT
CULLIS
CYCLIC
DAHLIA
DAYLIT
DEALIN
DOBLIN
DUBLIN
DUNLIN
EMILIA
EMILIO
ETALIA
ETALII
EUCLID
EXILIC
EYELID
FALLIN
FELLIN
FILLIN
FILLIP
FROLIC
GAELIC
GALLIA
GALLIC
GARLIC
GASLIT
GATLIN
GILLIE
GILLIS
GOALIE
GOBLIN
HAMLIN
HARLIN
HEFLIN
HOWLIN
ISELIN
ITALIA
ITALIC
JOPLIN
KAHLIL
KAOLIN
KHALID
LESLIE
LILLIE
LUBLIN
MAILIN
MAJLIS
MARLIN
MATLIN
MEALIE
MERLIN
MILLIE
MOULIN
MUSLIM
MUSLIN
MYELIN
NAILIN
NELLIE
OBELIA
OXALIS
PALLIA
PALLID
PHILIP
POPLIN
PRELIM
PROLIX
PUBLIC
PULLIN
PURLIN
RATLIN
REALIA
REELIN
ROLLIE
ROLLIN
SCALIA
SMILIN
STALIN
STOLID
SUNLIT
SUSLIK
THALIA
THELIP
TILLIE
TILLIS
TOMLIN
TWILIT
URALIC
VIOLIN
WALLIS
WILLIE
WILLIS

•••L•I
AMALFI
CHILLI
ETALII
KUBLAI
MALLEI
NIELLI
NUCLEI
OCELLI
POLLOI
SMALTI

••••LI
ALKALI
ANGELI
ANNULI
ARGALI
CHILLI
CUMULI
DENALI
KIGALI
LAZULI
MOWGLI
NAPOLI
NEPALI
NEROLI
NIELLI
OCELLI
POPULI
SNUGLI
SOMALI
TIVOLI
TUMULI

L••J••
LOGJAM

•L•J••
ELIJAH

••LJ••
SELJUK

L•K•••
LAKERS
LAKIER
LAKOTA
LEKVAR
LIKELY
LIKENS
LIKING

L••K••
LACKED
LACKEY
LANKER
LANKLY
LARKED
LATKES
LEAKED
LEAKER
LEAKEY
LICKED
LINKED
LINKER
LINKUP
LOCKED
LOCKER
LOCKET
LOCKIN
LOCKON
LOCKUP
LOOKAT
LOOKED
LOOKER
LOOKIN
LOOKON
LOOKTO
LOOKUP
LOWKEY
LUCKED
LUNKER
LURKED

L•••K•
LUSAKA

L••••K
LANARK
LOMBOK
LUBECK

•LK•••
ALKALI
ALKENE
ALKYDS
ALKYLS

•L•K••
BLOKES
FLAKED
FLAKER
FLAKES
FLAKEY
FLUKES
FLUKEY
SLAKED
SLAKES

•L••K•
ALASKA
ALECKY
BLACKS
BLANKS
BLINKS
BLOCKS
BLOCKY
CLACKS
CLANKS
CLANKY
CLARKE
CLEEKS
CLERKS
CLICKS
CLINKS
CLOAKS
CLOCKS
CLONKS
CLUCKS
CLUNKS
CLUNKY
FLACKS
FLANKS
FLASKS
FLECKS
FLECKY
FLICKA
FLICKS
FLOCKS
FLOCKY
FLUNKS
FLUNKY
GLINKA
PLANKS
PLINKS
PLONKS
PLUCKS
PLUCKY
PLUNKS
SLACKS
SLEEKS
SLEEKY
SLICKS
SLINKS
SLINKY

•L•••K
PLANCK
SLEZAK
SLOVAK
SLOVIK

••LK••
BALKAN
BALKED
BILKED
BULKED
CALKED
CULKIN
FOLKIE
FOLKSY
HULKED
KALKAN
MALKIN
MILKED
MILKER
POLKAS
SILKED
SILKEN
SULKED
SULKER
TALKAT
TALKED
TALKER
TALKIE
TALKTO
TALKUP
WALKED
WALKEN
WALKER
WALKIE
WALKIN
WALKON
WALKUP
WELKIN
WILKES
YOLKED

••L•K•
AXLIKE
BELIKE
KALAKH
KULAKS
MOLTKE
OXLIKE
PELIKE
SALUKI
STLUKE
TILAKS
UNLIKE

••L••K
GALYAK
INLUCK
OCLOCK
RELOCK
SELJUK
UNLINK
UNLOCK
UPLINK

•••LK•
BAULKS
CAULKS
CHALKS
CHALKY
SKULKS
STALKS
STALKY
WHELKS

•••L•K
MUKLUK
SUSLIK
URALSK

••••LK
BYTALK
INBULK
UPTALK

LL••••
LLAMAS
LLANOS
LLBEAN
LLOYDS

L•L•••
LALALA
LELAND
LILACS
LILIES
LILITH
LILLIE
LILTED
LOLITA
LOLLED
LOLLOP
LULLED

L••L••
LADLED
LADLER
LADLES
LAYLOW
LEALTY
LESLEY
LESLIE
LIELOW
LILLIE
LISLES
LOLLED
LOLLOP
LUBLIN
LUDLUM
LULLED
LYNLEY

L•••L•
LABELS
LABILE
LACILY
LALALA
LAMELY
LANKLY
LAPELS
LASTLY
LATELY
LAZILY
LAZULI
LEANLY
LEGALS
LETFLY
LEVELS
LEWDLY
LIABLE
LIBELS
LIEFLY
LIGULA
LIKELY
LIMPLY
LIONLY
LITTLE
LIVELY
LOBULE
LOCALE
LOCALS
LOGILY
LONELY
LONGLY
LORDLY
LOUDLY
LOVELL
LOVELY
LOWELL
LOYOLA
LUNULA
LUSHLY

L••••L
LABIAL
LAPFUL
LARVAL
LAUREL
LAWFUL
LEMUEL
LENTIL
LETHAL
LINEAL
LINTEL
LIONEL
LISTEL
LONNOL
LOREAL
LOVELL
LOWCAL
LOWELL

•LL•••
ALLAYS
ALLBUT
ALLDAY
ALLEES
ALLEGE
ALLELE
ALLEYS
ALLFOR
ALLIED
ALLIES
ALLIUM
ALLMAN
ALLOTS
ALLOUT
ALLOWS
ALLOYS
ALLPRO
ALLSET
ALLUDE
ALLURE
ALLWET
ELLERY
ELLICE
ELLIOT
ILLEST
ILLFED
ILLINI
ILLMET
ILLSAY
ILLUME
ILLUSE
ULLAGE
ULLMAN

•L•L••
ALULAE
ALULAR
SLALOM
TLALOC

•L••L•
ALIBLE
ALKALI
ALKYLS
ALLELE
BLUELY
FLAILS
FLATLY
GLADLY
GLIBLY
GLUMLY
ILOILO
SLIMLY
SLOWLY

•L•••L
ALEVEL
FLORAL
GLOBAL
GLYCOL
OLEVEL
PLAGAL
PLEXAL
PLURAL

••LL••
BALLAD
BALLET
BALLON
BALLOT
BALLOU
BALLUP
BELLAY
BELLED
BELLES
BELLOC
BELLOW
BILLED
BILLET
BILLIE
BILLON
BILLOW
BOLLIX
BULLAE
BULLED
BULLET
CALLAO
CALLAS
CALLED
CALLER
CALLES
CALLIN
CALLON
CALLOW
CALLUP
CALLUS
CELLAE
CELLAR
CELLED
CELLOS
COLLAR
COLLET
COLLIE
COLLOP
COLLOQ
CULLED
CULLEN
CULLER
CULLET
CULLIS
DALLAS
DALLES
DILLER
DILLON
DOLLAR
DOLLED
DOLLOP
DOLLUP
DULLEA
DULLED
DULLER
DULLES
FALLEN
FALLIN
FALLON
FALLOW
FALLTO
FELLAH
FELLAS
FELLED
FELLER
FELLIN
FELLOE
FELLON
FELLOW
FELLTO
FILLED
FILLER
FILLES
FILLET
FILLIN
FILLIP
FILLUP
FOLLOW
FULLER
GALLED
GALLEY
GALLIA
GALLIC
GALLON
GALLOP
GALLUP
GELLED
GILLED
GILLIE
GILLIS
GOLLUM
GULLAH
GULLED
GULLET
HALLEL
HALLEY
HALLOO
HALLOS
HALLOW
HALLUX
HELLAS
HELLER
HELLOS
HILLED
HILLEL
HILLER
HOLLER
HOLLOW
HULLED
HULLER
HULLOA
HULLOS
JELLED
KELLER
KELLEY
KILLED
KILLER
LILLIE
LOLLED
LOLLOP
LULLED
MALLEE
MALLEI
MALLET
MALLOW
MELLON
MELLOW
MILLAY
MILLED
MILLER
MILLET
MILLIE
MULLAH
MULLAS
MULLED
MULLER
MULLET
NELLIE
NULLAH
NULLED
PALLAS
PALLED
PALLET
PALLIA
PALLID
PALLOR
PELLET
PILLAR
PILLED
PILLOW
POLLED
POLLEN
POLLER
POLLEX
POLLOI
POLLUX
PULLED
PULLET
PULLEY
PULLIN
PULLON
PULLUP
RILLES
RILLET
ROLLED
ROLLER
ROLLIE
ROLLIN
ROLLON
ROLLUP
SALLET
SALLOW
SELLER
SULLEN
TALLER
TALLOW
TELLER
TELLOF
TELLON
TILLED
TILLER
TILLIE
TILLIS
TOLLED
TULLES
VALLEE
VALLEY
VELLUM
VILLAS
VILLON
VILLUS
VOLLEY
WALLED
WALLER
WALLET
WALLIS
WALLOP
WALLOW
WALLUP
WELLED
WELLER
WELLES
WELLUP
WILLED
WILLEM
WILLET
WILLIE
WILLIS
WILLOW
YELLED
YELLER
YELLOW

••L•L•
ALLELE
BALDLY
BOLDLY
CALMLY
COLDLY
HOLILY
LALALA
MILDLY
OGLALA
OILILY
OOLALA
PALELY
SALALS
SOLELY
UGLILY
VILELY
WILDLY
WILILY

••L••L
ATLATL
BELIAL
BULBIL
BULBUL
FILIAL
FULFIL
GALPAL
HALLEL
HILLEL
MELVIL
SOLEIL
WILFUL

•••LL•
ABOLLA
ADELLE
AIELLO
APOLLO
ARALLU
ATOLLS
AXILLA
BCELLS
BOULLE
BRILLO
BRILLS
BROLLY
CHILLI
CHILLS
CHILLY
CHOLLA
COOLLY
DRILLS
DROLLS
DROLLY
DUALLY
DUELLO
DWELLS
EVILLY
FAILLE
FOULLY
FRILLS
FRILLY
GRILLE
GRILLS
IDYLLS
KNELLS
KNOLLS
KNOLLY
KPELLE
KVELLS
NIELLI
NIELLO
OCELLI
OKELLY
ORALLY
OTELLO
OVALLY
PAELLA
PHILLY
PHYLLO
PSYLLA
QUELLS
QUILLS
REALLY
REILLY
SCULLS
SCULLY
SCYLLA
SHALLY
SHELLS
SHELLY
SHILLS
SHILLY
SKILLS
SKULLS
SMALLS
SMELLS
SMELLY
SNELLS
SPALLS
SPELLS
SPILLS
STALLS
STELLA
STILLS
STILLY
STOLLE
STULLS
SWELLS
SWILLS
TAILLE
TBILLS
THILLS
TRILLS
TROLLS
TUILLE
TWILLS
WHOLLY
WOOLLY

•••L•L
HALLEL
HILLEL
KAHLIL
PHILOL

••••LL
ANGELL
APPALL
ARGYLL
ASWELL
ATWILL
BACALL
BEFALL
BEFELL
CAVELL
COSELL
CYBILL
DOTELL
DUVALL
ENDALL
ENROLL
ERROLL
GIBILL
HAMILL
HOWELL
INFULL
JEKYLL
LOVELL
LOWELL
MABELL
OHWELL
ONCALL
ONEILL
ORWELL
POWELL
RECALL
REFILL
REPOLL
RESELL
RETELL
RYDELL
SCHELL
SCROLL
SEWELL
SHRILL
SQUALL
SQUILL
STROLL
THATLL
THEYLL
THRALL
THRILL
UNROLL
UNWELL
UPHILL
UPWELL
WHATLL
YOUALL

L•M•••
LAMARR
LAMAZE
LAMBDA
LAMBED
LAMECH
LAMEDH
LAMEDS
LAMELY
LAMENT
LAMESA
LAMEST
LAMIAS
LAMINA
LAMING
LAMMAS
LAMMED
LAMONT
LAMOUR
LEMANS
LEMMAS
LEMMON
LEMNOS
LEMOND
LEMONS
LEMONY
LEMUEL
LEMURS
LIMBED
LIMBER
LIMBOS
LIMBUS
LIMENS
LIMEYS
LIMIER
LIMING
LIMITS
LIMNED
LIMNER
LIMPED
LIMPER
LIMPET
LIMPID
LIMPLY
LOMBOK
LOMEIN
LOMOND
LUMBAR
LUMBER
LUMENS
LUMINA
LUMMOX
LUMPED
LUMPEN
LUMPER
LUMPUR
LYMPHS

L••M••
LAMMAS
LAMMED
LAWMAN
LAWMEN
LAYMAN
LAYMEN
LEGMAN
LEGMEN
LEMMAS
LEMMON
LITMUS
LLAMAS
LOAMED
LOOMED
LUMMOX

L•••M•
LARAMS
LEGUME
LEXEME

L••••M
LABRUM
LAPHAM
LATIUM
LCHAIM
LOGJAM
LUDLUM
LYCEUM

•LM•••
ALMATY
ALMOND
ALMOST
ELMIRA
ELMORE
OLMECS

•L•M••
ALAMOS
ALEMAN
ALLMAN
ALOMAR
ALTMAN
ALUMNA
ALUMNI
BLAMED
BLAMES
BLIMEY
BLIMPS
CLAMMY
CLAMOR
CLAMPS
CLAMUP
CLIMAX
CLIMBS
CLIMES
CLOMPS
CLUMPS
CLUMPY
CLUMSY
ELEMIS
ELFMAN
FLAMBE
FLAMED
FLAMES
FLIMSY
FLUMES
FLYMAN
FLYMEN
GLAMOR
GLUMLY
ILLMET
LLAMAS
OLDMAN
OLDMEN
PLUMBS
PLUMED
PLUMES
PLUMMY
PLUMPS
SLIMED
SLIMES
SLIMLY
SLIMSY
SLUMMY
SLUMPS
ULLMAN

•L••M•
ALARMS
ALBUMS
ALTIMA
BLOOMS
BLOOMY
CLAIMS
CLAMMY
GLEAMS
GLEAMY
GLOOMS
GLOOMY
ILLUME
PLASMA
PLASMO
PLUMMY
SLUMMY
ULTIMA
ULTIMO

•L•••M
ALARUM
ALLIUM
ELOHIM
OLDHAM
PLENUM
SLALOM

••LM••
ALLMAN
CALMED
CALMER
CALMLY
COLMAN
DELMAR
DOLMAN
DOLMAS
DOLMEN
FILMED
FULMAR
HELMED
HELMET
HELMUT
HOLMES
ILLMET
KALMAR
KILMER
MELMAC
OILMAN
OILMEN
PALMAS
PALMED
PALMER
PELMET
SALMAN
SALMON
TALMUD
ULLMAN

••L•M•
AFLAME
APLOMB
CCLAMP
COLIMA
COLUMN
GOLEMS
ILLUME
KILIMS
PALOMA
RELUME
SALAMI
SALOME
SOLEMN
VOLUME

••L••M
ABLOOM
AGLEAM
ALLIUM
BALAAM
BALSAM
BELDAM
CILIUM
FOLIUM
FOLSOM
GOLLUM
HELIUM
HOLISM
MULTUM
PHLEGM
PHLOEM
PILEUM
SALAAM
SALTUM
SELDOM
SILOAM
TALCUM
VALIUM
VELLUM
WILLEM

•••LM•
HAULMS
PSALMS
QUALMS
REALMS
STELMO
THELMA
WHELMS

•••L•M
ASYLUM
BEDLAM
COELOM
EMBLEM
GOLLUM
HARLEM
LUDLUM
MOSLEM
MUSLIM
PABLUM
PEPLUM
PHYLUM
PRELIM
SHALOM
SHOLEM
SHOLOM

SLALOM
VELLUM
WHILOM
WILLEM

••••LM

ANSELM
BECALM

L•N•••

LANAIS
LANARK
LANATE
LANCED
LANCER
LANCES
LANCET
LANDAU
LANDED
LANDER
LANDHO
LANDIS
LANDON
LANDRY
LANGUR
LANIER
LANKER
LANKLY
LANOSE
LANSON
LANVIN
LENAPE
LENDER
LENGTH
LENITY
LENNIE
LENNON
LENNOX
LENORE
LENSED
LENSES
LENTEN
LENTIL
LINAGE
LINDEN
LINEAL
LINEAR
LINENS
LINENY
LINERS
LINEUP
LINGER
LINGUA
LINIER
LINING
LINKED
LINKER
LINKUP
LINNET
LINNEY
LINSEY
LINTEL
LINTER
LONDON
LONELY
LONERS
LONGAN
LONGED
LONGER
LONGES
LONGLY
LONGUE
LONNOL
LUNACY
LUNATE
LUNCHY
LUNDEN
LUNGED
LUNGES
LUNKER
LUNULA
LYNDON
LYNLEY
LYNXES
LYNYRD

L••N••

LAINIE
LAUNCH
LEANED
LEANER
LEANLY
LEANON
LEANTO
LEMNOS
LENNIE
LENNON
LENNOX
LEONES
LEONID
LEONIE
LERNER
LIANAS
LIANES
LIANGS
LIENEE
LIGNIN
LIMNED
LIMNER
LINNET
LINNEY
LIONEL
LIONET
LIONLY
LLANOS
LOANED
LOANER
LONNOL
LOONEY
LOONIE
LOUNGE
LUANDA
LUGNUT

L•••N•

LACING
LACUNA
LADING
LADINO
LAGUNA
LAMENT
LAMINA
LAMING
LAMONT
LAPINS
LARYNX
LATENE
LATENS
LATENT
LATINA
LATINI
LATINO
LATINS
LATONA
LAVING
LAWING
LAYING
LAZING
LEARNS
LEARNT
LEGEND
LELAND
LEMANS
LEMOND
LEMONS
LEMONY
LEVANT
LEVENE
LEVINE
LIERNE
LIGAND
LIKENS
LIKING
LIMENS
LIMING
LINENS
LINENY
LINING
LIPENG
LITANY
LIVENS
LIVING
LODENS
LOMOND
LOPING
LORENZ
LOSING
LOVING
LOWEND
LOWING
LUBING
LUCENT
LUDENS
LUMENS
LUMINA
LUPINE
LUPINO
LUPONE
LURING
LUTING
LYSINE
LYSINS

L••••N

LAGOON
LAIDIN
LAIDON
LANDON
LANSON
LANVIN
LARDON
LARSEN
LARSON
LASSEN
LATEEN
LATTEN
LAUREN
LAWMAN
LAWMEN
LAWSON
LAWTON
LAYMAN
LAYMEN
LAYSIN
LAYSON
LEADEN
LEADIN
LEADON
LEANON
LEAVEN
LEBRUN
LEFTIN
LEGION
LEGMAN
LEGMEN
LEGUIN
LEIDEN
LEMMON
LENNON
LENTEN
LEPTON
LESSEN
LESSON
LETSIN
LETSON
LEYDEN
LIBYAN
LICHEN
LIESIN
LIGNIN
LINDEN
LIPTON
LISBON
LISTEN
LISTON
LIVEIN
LIVEON
LLBEAN
LOCKIN
LOCKON
LOGION
LOGSIN
LOGSON
LOMEIN
LONDON
LONGAN
LOOKIN
LOOKON
LOOSEN
LORAIN
LOTION
LOUDEN
LOVEIN
LUBLIN
LUCIAN
LUDDEN
LUMPEN
LUNDEN
LYNDON
LYTTON

•LN•••

ALNICO
ELNINO

•L•N••

ALANIS
ALANON
ALINES
ALONSO
ALONZO
BLANCA
BLANCH
BLANDA
BLANKS
BLENCH
BLENDE
BLENDS
BLENNY
BLINDS
BLINIS
BLINKS
BLINTZ
BLONDE
BLONDS
BLUNTS
CLANCY
CLANGS
CLANKS
CLANKY
CLENCH
CLINCH
CLINES
CLINGS
CLINGY
CLINIC
CLINKS
CLONED
CLONES
CLONKS
CLONUS
CLUNKS
CLUNKY
ELANDS
ELINOR
FLANGE
FLANKS
FLENSE
FLINCH
FLINGS
FLINTS
FLINTY
FLUNKS
FLUNKY
FLYNET
GLANCE
GLANDS
GLENDA
GLENNE
GLINKA
GLINTS
GLYNIS
LLANOS
OLINDA
OLINGO
PLANAR
PLANCK
PLANED
PLANER
PLANES
PLANET
PLANKS
PLANON
PLANTE
PLANTS
PLENTY
PLENUM
PLINKS
PLINTH
PLONKS
PLUNGE
PLUNKS
SLANGS
SLANGY
SLANTS
SLINGS
SLINKS
SLINKY

•L••N•

ALBANO
ALBANY
ALBINO
ALDINE
ALFINE
ALIENS
ALIGNS
ALKENE
ALMOND
ALOINS
ALPINE
ALUMNA
ALUMNI
BLAINE
BLENNY
BLUING
CLEANS
CLIENT
CLOWNS
CLUING
ELAINE
ELAYNE
ELNINO
FLAUNT
FLUENT
FLYING
FLYINS
GLEANS
GLENNE
GLUING
GLUONS
HLHUNT
ILEANA
ILLINI
PLAINS
PLAINT
PLIANT
PLYING
SLOANE
SLUING

•L•••N

ALANON
ALBION
ALBOIN
ALCUIN
ALDRIN
ALEMAN
ALFVEN
ALISON
ALLMAN
ALTMAN
BLAZON
BLIXEN
BLOWIN
CLAVIN
CLIPON
CLOVEN
CLUEIN
ELEVEN
ELFMAN
ELOIGN
FLACON
FLAGON
FLAXEN
FLEWIN
FLORIN
FLYMAN
FLYMEN
GLOBIN
GLUTEN
ILORIN
KLAXON
KLIBAN
LLBEAN
OLDMAN
OLDMEN
OLEFIN
OLESON
PLANON
PLATEN
PLAYON
PLUGIN
SLIDIN
SLIPIN
SLIPON
SLOGAN
SLOVEN
ULLMAN

••LN••

KILNED
MILNER
MOLNAR
WALNUT

••L•N•

AGLINT
AILING
ARLENE
ASLANT
BALING
BELONG
BYLINE
CELINE
COLONS
COLONY
DELANO
DELANY
DELONG
DOLENZ
DOLING
EALING
FALANA
FALINE
FELINE
FELONS
FELONY
FILENE
FILING
FULANI
GALENA
GOLINO
HALING
HELENA
HELENE
HELENS
HOLING
IDLING
ILLINI
INLAND
INLINE
IRLENE
ISLAND
JOLENE
KALINE
KDLANG
LELAND
MALONE
MELANO
MELINA
MELONS
MILANO
MOLINE
NOLENS
NYLONS
OBLONG
OGLING
OILING
ONLAND
ONLINE
OOLONG
PALING
PILING
POLAND
POLING
PULING
PYLONS
RELENT
RELINE
RILING
ROLAND
RULING
SALINA
SALINE
SALONS
SELENA
SELENE
SELENO
SILENI
SILENT
SILONE
SOLANS
SOLENT
SOLING
SOLONG
SPLINE
SPLINT
TALENT
TALONS
TILING
TULANE
UCLANS
UHLANS
UNLINK
UPLAND
UPLINK
VALENS
VALENT
VOLANS
VOLANT
VOLENS
WILING
XYLENE

••L••N

AILEEN
ALLMAN
ARLEEN
BALEEN
BALKAN
BALLON
BILLON
BOLEYN
BOLTON
CALLIN
CALLON
CALVIN
COLMAN
COLUMN
CULKIN
CULLEN
DALTON
DELEON
DILLON
DOLMAN
DOLMEN
EILEEN
EOLIAN
FALCON
FALLEN
FALLIN
FALLON
FELDON
FELLIN
FELLON
FILLIN
FULTON
GALLON
GOLDEN
HELDIN
HELDON
HILTON
HOLDEN
HOLDIN
HOLDON
JOLSON
JULIAN
KALKAN
KELVIN
MALDEN
MALIGN
MALKIN
MALTIN
MCLAIN
MCLEAN
MELLON
MELTON
MELVIN
MELVYN
MILTON
MOLTEN
NELSON
OILCAN
OILMAN
OILMEN
OILPAN
ONLOAN
PELION
PILEIN
PILEON
POLEYN
POLLEN
PULLIN
PULLON
ROLLIN
ROLLON
RULEON
SALMAN
SALMON
SALOON
SALTEN
SALTON
SILKEN
SOLDAN
SOLDON
SOLEMN
SPLEEN
SULLEN
SULTAN
SYLVAN
TALION
TELLON
TILDEN
TOLDON
TULSAN
ULLMAN
VILLON
VULCAN
WALDEN
WALKEN
WALKIN
WALKON
WALTON
WELKIN
WILSON
WILTON

•••L•N

AMBLIN
AVALON
BALLON
BANLON
BERLIN
BILLON
BROLIN
CALLIN
CALLON
CARLIN
CEYLON
CULLEN
DEALIN
DILLON
DOBLIN
DUBLIN
DUNLIN
EVELYN
FALLEN
FALLIN
FALLON
FELLIN
FELLON
FILLIN
GALLON
GATLIN
GOBLIN
HAMLIN
HARLAN
HARLIN
HEFLIN
HOWLIN
ISELIN
JACLYN
JOPLIN
KAOLIN
KAPLAN
KJOLEN
KUNLUN
LUBLIN
MAILIN
MARLIN
MARLON
MATLIN
MELLON
MERLIN
MERLON
MOULIN
MUSLIN
MYELIN
NAILIN
POLLEN
POPLIN
PULLIN
PULLON
PURLIN
RAGLAN
RATLIN
REELIN
REPLAN
REVLON
ROLLIN
ROLLON
SMILIN
STALIN
STOLEN
STOLON
SULLEN
TEFLON
TELLON
TIGLON
TOMLIN
TOULON
TRYLON
VEBLEN
VILLON
VIOLIN
WAYLON
WOOLEN

••••LN

HAMELN
WEDELN

LO••••

LOADED
LOADER
LOAFED
LOAFER
LOAMED
LOANED
LOANER
LOATHE
LOAVES
LOBATE
LOBBED
LOBBER
LOBULE
LOCALE
LOCALS
LOCATE
LOCKED
LOCKER
LOCKET
LOCKIN
LOCKON
LOCKUP
LOCUST
LODENS
LODGED
LODGER
LODGES
LOFTED
LOGGED
LOGGER
LOGGIA
LOGIER
LOGILY
LOGION
LOGJAM
LOGOFF
LOGOUT
LOGSIN
LOGSON
LOITER
LOLITA
LOLLED
LOLLOP
LOMBOK
LOMEIN
LOMOND
LONDON
LONELY
LONERS
LONGAN
LONGED
LONGER
LONGES
LONGLY
LONGUE
LONNOL
LOOFAH
LOOFAS
LOOIES
LOOKAT
LOOKED
LOOKER
LOOKIN
LOOKON
LOOKTO
LOOKUP
LOOMED
LOONEY
LOONIE
LOOPED
LOOPER
LOOSED
LOOSEN
LOOSER
LOOSES
LOOTED
LOOTER
LOPERS
LOPING
LOPPED
LOPPER
LOQUAT
LORAIN
LORDED
LORDLY
LOREAL
LORENZ
LORICA
LORIES
LOSEIT
LOSERS
LOSING
LOSSES
LOSTIT
LOTAHS
LOTHAR
LOTION
LOTTED
LOTTOS
LOUCHE
LOUDEN
LOUDER
LOUDLY
LOUGHS
LOUISA
LOUISE
LOUNGE
LOUPES
LOUSED
LOUSES
LOUVER
LOUVRE
LOVAGE
LOVEIN
LOVELL
LOVELY
LOVERS
LOVETT
LOVING
LOWBOY
LOWCAL
LOWELL
LOWEND
LOWERS
LOWERY
LOWEST
LOWFAT
LOWING
LOWISH
LOWKEY
LOYOLA

L•O•••

LAOTSE
LAOTZU
LEONES
LEONID
LEONIE
LHOTSE
LIONEL
LIONET
LIONLY
LIOTTA
LLOYDS
LOOFAH
LOOFAS
LOOIES
LOOKAT
LOOKED
LOOKER
LOOKIN
LOOKON
LOOKTO
LOOKUP
LOOMED
LOONEY
LOONIE
LOOPED
LOOPER
LOOSED
LOOSEN
LOOSER
LOOSES
LOOTED
LOOTER

L••O••

LABORS
LABOUR
LADOGA
LAGOON
LAHORE
LAKOTA
LAMONT
LAMOUR
LANOSE
LAROSA
LATONA
LATOUR
LATOYA
LAYOFF
LAYOUT
LEDOFF
LEDOUT
LEMOND
LEMONS
LEMONY
LENORE
LETOFF
LETOUT
LIPOID
LITOUT
LOGOFF
LOGOUT
LOMOND
LOYOLA
LUGOSI
LUPONE

L•••O•

LAGOON
LAIDON
LANDON
LANSON
LAPDOG
LAPTOP
LARDON
LARGOS
LARSON
LASSOS
LAWSON
LAWTON
LAYFOR
LAYLOW
LAYSON
LAZBOY
LEADON
LEANON
LECTOR
LEGION
LEMMON
LEMNOS
LENNON
LENNOX
LEPTON
LESBOS
LESSON
LESSOR
LETSON
LICTOR
LIELOW
LIMBOS
LIPTON
LIQUOR
LISBOA
LISBON
LISTON
LITHOG
LITHOS
LIVEON
LLANOS
LOCKON
LOGION
LOGSON
LOLLOP
LOMBOK
LONDON
LONNOL
LOOKON
LOTION
LOTTOS
LOWBOY
LUMMOX
LUTHOR
LYNDON
LYTTON

L••••O

LADINO
LAIDTO
LANDHO
LAREDO
LASHIO
LATIGO
LATINO
LAVABO
LAYSTO
LEADTO
LEANTO
LEGATO
LETSGO
LIBIDO
LIESTO
LOOKTO
LUPINO

•LO•••

ALOHAS
ALOINS
ALOMAR
ALONSO
ALONZO
BLOATS
BLOCKS
BLOCKY
BLOKES
BLONDE
BLONDS
BLOODY
BLOOEY
BLOOMS
BLOOMY
BLOOPS
BLOTCH
BLOTTO
BLOTTY
BLOUSE
BLOWER
BLOWIN
BLOWIT
BLOWSY
BLOWUP
BLOWZY
CLOACA
CLOAKS
CLOCHE
CLOCKS
CLODDY
CLOGGY
CLOGUP
CLOMPS
CLONED
CLONES
CLONKS
CLONUS
CLOQUE
CLORIS
CLOROX
CLOSED
CLOSER
CLOSES
CLOSET
CLOTHE
CLOTHO
CLOTHS
CLOTTY
CLOUDS
CLOUDY
CLOUTS
CLOVEN
CLOVER
CLOVES
CLOVIS
CLOWNS
CLOYED
ELOHIM
ELOIGN
ELOISE
ELOPED
ELOPER
ELOPES
FLOATS
FLOATY
FLOCKS
FLOCKY
FLOODS
FLOOEY
FLOORS
FLOPPY
FLOPSY
FLORAE
FLORAL
FLORAS
FLORES
FLORET
FLORID
FLORIN
FLORIO
FLOSSY
FLOURS
FLOURY
FLOUTS
FLOWED
FLOWER
GLOATS
GLOBAL
GLOBED
GLOBES
GLOBIN
GLOGGS
GLOOMS
GLOOMY
GLOPPY
GLORIA
GLOSSA
GLOSSO
GLOSSY
GLOVED
GLOVER
GLOVES
GLOWED
GLOWER
GLOZED
GLOZES
ILOILO
ILORIN
KLOOFS
LLOYDS
PLONKS
PLOTTY
PLOUGH
PLOVER
PLOWED
PLOWER
SLOANE
SLOBBY
SLOGAN
SLOOPS
SLOPED
SLOPES
SLOPPY
SLOSHY
SLOTHS
SLOUCH
SLOUGH
SLOVAK
SLOVEN
SLOVIK
SLOWED
SLOWER
SLOWLY
SLOWUP
ZLOTYS

•L•O••

ALBOIN
ALBORG
ALCOTT
ALCOVE
ALDOSE
ALDOUS
ALGORE
ALIOTO
ALLOTS
ALLOUT
ALLOWS
ALLOYS
ALMOND
ALMOST
BLOODY
BLOOEY
BLOOMS
BLOOMY
BLOOPS
ELBOWS
ELMORE
ELWOOD
FLOODS
FLOOEY

FLOORS FLUORO FLYOUT GLOOMS GLOOMY GLUONS KLOOFS SLOOPS

•L••O•

ALAMOS ALANON ALBION ALISON ALLFOR BLAZON BLUEOX CLAMOR CLAROS CLIPON CLOROX ELINOR ELLIOT ELWOOD FLACON FLAGON FLAVOR FLEXOR FLYBOY FLYROD GLAMOR GLYCOL KLAXON LLANOS OLDBOY OLESON PLANON PLAYON PLEXOR SLALOM SLIPON TLALOC

•L•••O

ALBANO ALBEDO ALBINO ALECTO ALEPPO ALIOTO ALLPRO ALNICO ALONSO ALONZO BLOTTO CLOTHO ELNINO ELPASO FLORIO FLUORO GLOSSO ILOILO OLDPRO OLINGO PLAGIO PLASMO SLUGGO ULTIMO

••LO••

ABLOOM AFLOAT ALLOTS ALLOUT ALLOWS ALLOYS APLOMB ASLOPE BELOIT BELONG BILOXI BULOVA CHLORO COLONS COLONY COLORS COLOUR DELONG DOLORS DOLOUR EULOGY FELONS FELONY FILOSE GALOIS GALOOT GALOPS GALORE GALOSH HALOED HALOES HALOID HELOTS IGLOOS INLOVE JALOPY MALONE MALORY MALOTI MELODY MELONS MELOTT MILORD MILOSZ MOLOCH MOLOPO NOLOAD NOLOSE NYLONS OBLONG OCLOCK ONLOAN OOLOGY OOLONG ORLOPS PALOMA PELOPS PELOTA PHLOEM PILOSE PILOTI PILOTS PYLONS RELOAD RELOCK SALOME SALONS SALOON SILOAM SILOED SILONE SOLOED SOLONG SPLOSH TALONS UNLOAD UNLOCK UPLOAD VALOIS VALOUR VELOCE VELOUR XYLOID

••L•O•

ABLOOM ALLFOR BALBOA BALLON BALLOT BALLOU BELLOC BELLOW BILLON BILLOW BOLTON CALLON CALLOW CELLOS COLLOP COLLOQ DALTON DELEON DELROY DILLON DOLLOP ELLIOT FALCON FALLON FALLOW FELDON FELLOE FELLON FELLOW FOLIOS FOLLOW FOLSOM FULTON GALLON GALLOP GALOOT HALLOO HALLOS HALLOW HELDON HELIOS HELLOS HILTON HOLDON HOLLOW HULLOA HULLOS IGLOOS JOLIOT JOLSON KILROY LOLLOP MALLOW MELLON MELLOW MELTON MILTON NELSON PALLOR PELION PILEON PILLOW POLLOI POLPOT PULLON ROLEOS ROLLON RULEON SALLOW SALMON SALOON SALTON SALVOR SALVOS SELDOM SOLDON TALBOT TALION TALLOW TELLOF TELLON TOLDOF TOLDON VILLON VOLVOX WALKON WALLOP WALLOW WALTON WILCOX WILLOW WILSON WILTON YELLOW

••L••O

AFLCIO ALLPRO BILBAO BOLERO CALICO CALLAO CHLORO COLUGO DELANO DELRIO FALLTO FELLTO GALAGO GELATO GOLINO HALLOO HELDTO HOLDTO MALABO MELANO MILANO MOLOPO PALAEO PHLEBO SALADO SCLERO SELENO TALKTO TOLEDO VELCRO

•••LO•

ANALOG ANGLOS AVALON BADLOT BAILOR BALLON BALLOT BALLOU BANLON BAYLOR BELLOC BELLOW BILLON BILLOW CALLON CALLOW CARLOS CARLOT CELLOS CEYLON CHILOE CHOLOS COELOM COLLOP COLLOQ CYCLOS DEPLOY DIALOG DIGLOT DILLON DOLLOP DUNLOP DYELOT EMPLOY ENBLOC EPILOG FALLON FALLOW FARLOW FELLOE FELLON FELLOW FOLLOW GALLON GALLOP GASLOG GOSLOW HALLOO HALLOS HALLOW HARLOW HELLOS HOLLOW HULLOA HULLOS INFLOW JOBLOT LAYLOW LIELOW LOLLOP MALLOW MARLON MELLON MELLOW MERLON MERLOT OCELOT ODDLOT PAILOU PALLOR PARLOR PAVLOV PEPLOS PHILOL PHILOS PILLOW POLLOI PROLOG PULLON REPLOW REVLON ROLLON SAILOR SALLOW SAWLOG SHALOM SHILOH SHOLOM SLALOM STOLON TAILOR TALLOW TAYLOR TEFLON TELLOF TELLON TIGLON TLALOC TOULON TRYLON UNCLOG VILLON WALLOP WALLOW WAYLON WHILOM WILLOW YELLOW ZEALOT ZIPLOC

•••L•O

AIELLO APOLLO BIBLIO BRILLO CALLAO CHALCO DUELLO EMILIO FALLTO FELLTO HALLOO NIELLO NUCLEO OTELLO PHYLLO RIALTO SMALTO STELMO

••••LO

AIELLO ANGELO APOLLO BAROLO BRILLO CUMULO DAYGLO DIABLO DUELLO ENHALO GIGOLO ILOILO MEGALO MODULO NICOLO NIELLO NIHILO OTELLO PHYLLO POMELO PUEBLO ROBALO STMALO TUPELO YUNGLO

L•P•••

LAPDOG LAPELS LAPFUL LAPHAM LAPINS LAPPED LAPPET LAPSED LAPSES LAPSUP LAPTEV LAPTOP LAPUTA LEPTON LIPASE LIPENG LIPIDE LIPIDS LIPOID LIPPED LIPTON LOPERS LOPING LOPPED LOPPER LUPINE LUPINO LUPONE

L••P••

LAPPED LAPPET LAUPER LEAPED LEAPER LIMPED LIMPER LIMPET LIMPID LIMPLY LIPPED LISPED LOOPED LOOPER LOPPED LOPPER LOUPES LUMPED LUMPEN LUMPER LUMPUR LYMPHS

L•••P•

LAYUPS LENAPE LETUPS

L••••P

LACEUP LAIDUP LAPSUP LAPTOP LARRUP LASHUP LAYSUP LEADUP LETSUP LIFTUP LINEUP LINKUP LOCKUP LOLLOP LOOKUP

•LP•••

ALPACA ALPERT ALPHAS ALPINE ELPASO

•L•P••

ALEPHS ALEPPO ALLPRO CLEPED CLIPON ELAPID ELAPSE ELOPED ELOPER ELOPES FLAPPY FLIPUP FLOPPY FLOPSY GLOPPY GLYPHS OLDPRO SLAPPY SLAPUP SLIPIN SLIPON SLIPPY SLIPUP SLOPED SLOPES SLOPPY SLYPES

•L••P•

ALCAPP ALEPPO BLEEPS BLIMPS BLOOPS CLAMPS CLASPS CLOMPS CLUMPS CLUMPY FLAPPY FLOPPY GLOPPY PLUMPS SLAPPY SLEEPS SLEEPY SLIPPY SLOOPS SLOPPY SLUMPS SLURPS

•L•••P

ALCAPP BLEWUP BLOWUP CLAMUP CLOGUP FLIPUP PLAYUP SLAPUP SLIPUP SLOWUP

••LP••

ALLPRO CALPAC DELPHI GALPAL GULPED GULPER HELPED HELPER KELPIE MILPAS OILPAN PALPUS POLPOT PULPED PULPIT SYLPHS WOLPER YELPED YELPER ZILPAH

••L•P•

ASLOPE CALIPH FELIPE GALOPS JALAPA JALOPY JULEPS MOLOPO ORLOPS OXLIPS PELOPS POLYPS TULIPS

••L••P

ASLEEP BALLUP CALLUP CCLAMP COLLOP DOLLOP DOLLUP FILLIP FILLUP FOLDUP GALLOP GALLUP HELDUP HOLDUP HOLEUP LOLLOP MILSAP PILEUP PULLUP RILEUP ROLLUP TALKUP WALKUP WALLOP WALLUP WELLUP

•••LP•

ADOLPH GUELPH SCALPS SCULPT WHELPS

•••L•P

BALLUP BURLAP CALLUP COILUP COLLOP CURLUP DEWLAP DIALUP DOLLOP DOLLUP DUNLOP EARLAP FILLIP FILLUP FOULUP GALLOP GALLUP HAULUP LOLLOP PHILIP PULLUP ROLLUP SCHLEP SEALUP THELIP TOOLUP WALLOP WALLUP WELLUP

••••LP

MEGILP

L•Q•••

LIQUID LIQUOR LOQUAT

•L•Q••

CLAQUE CLIQUE CLIQUY CLOQUE PLAQUE

••LQ••

CALQUE PULQUE

••L••Q

COLLOQ

•••L•Q

COLLOQ

••••LQ

POSSLQ

L•R•••

LARAMS LARDED LARDER LARDON LAREDO LARGER LARGES LARGOS LARIAT LARKED LAROSA LARRUP LARSEN LARSON LARVAE LARVAL LARVAS LARYNX LERIDA LERNER LORAIN LORDED LORDLY LOREAL LORENZ LORICA LORIES LURING LURKED LYRICS LYRIST

L••R••

LABREA LABRET LABRUM LAIRDS LARRUP LAUREL LAUREN LAURIE LEARNS LEARNT LEBRUN LEERAT LEERED LEERER LEGREE LEHRER LIBRIS LIERNE LITRES LIVRES

L•••R•

LABORS LACERS LADERS LAGERS LAHORE LAKERS LAMARR LANARK LANDRY LASERS LAVERS LAYERS LEMURS LENORE LEVERS LIBERI LIFERS LIGERS LIGURE LINERS LITERS LIVERS LIVERY LIZARD LONERS LOPERS LOSERS LOUVRE LOVERS LOWERS LOWERY LUGERS LUSTRE LUXURY LYNYRD

L••••R

LAAGER LABOUR LACIER LADDER LADLER LAFFER LAGGER LAKIER LAMARR LAMOUR LANCER LANDER LANGUR LANIER LANKER LARDER LARGER LASCAR LASHER LASSER LATHER LATOUR LATTER LAUDER LAUPER LAWYER LAYFOR LAZIER LEADER LEAKER LEANER LEAPER LEASER LECTER LECTOR LEDGER LEERER LEHRER LEKVAR LENDER LERNER LESSER LESSOR LESTER LETTER LEVIER LEWDER LIBBER LICTOR LIEDER LIEFER LIFTER LIMBER LIMIER LIMNER LIMPER LINEAR LINGER LINIER LINKER LINTER LIQUOR LISTER LITTER LOADER LOAFER LOANER LOBBER LOCKER LODGER LOGGER LOGIER LOITER LONGER LOOKER LOOPER LOOSER LOOTER LOPPER LOTHAR LOUDER LOUVER LUBBER LUGGER LUMBAR LUMBER LUMPER LUMPUR LUNKER LUSHER LUSTER LUTHER LUTHOR

•L•R••

ALARIC ALARMS ALARUM ALDRIN ALERTS ALFRED BLARED BLARES BLURBS BLURRY BLURTS CLARET CLARKE CLAROS CLERGY CLERIC CLERKS CLORIS CLOROX ELBRUS FLARED FLARES FLIRTS FLIRTY FLORAE FLORAL FLORAS FLORES FLORET FLORID FLORIN FLORIO FLURRY FLYROD GLARED GLARES GLORIA ILORIN PLURAL SLURPS SLURRY ULTRAS

•L••R•

ALBERT ALBORG ALDERS ALEGRE ALGORE ALHIRT ALLPRO ALLURE ALPERT ALTARS ALTERS BLEARS BLEARY BLURRY CLAIRE CLEARS ELBERT ELDERS ELLERY ELMIRA ELMORE ELVERS ELVIRA FLAIRS FLEERS FLEURY FLIERS FLOORS FLOURS FLOURY FLUORO FLURRY FLYERS GLAIRS GLAIRY GLUERS OLDPRO OLEARY PLEURA PLIERS SLURRY ULCERS

•L•••R

ALEGAR ALITER ALLFOR ALOMAR ALTAIR ALULAR BLADER BLAZER BLOWER CLAMOR CLAWER CLEVER CLOSER CLOVER DLAYER ELATER ELAYER ELINOR ELIXIR ELOPER ELUDER FLAKER FLAVOR FLAYER FLEXOR FLOWER GLAMOR GLASER GLAZER GLIDER GLOVER GLOWER GLUIER OLIVER PLACER PLANAR PLANER PLATER PLAYER PLEXOR PLOVER PLOWER SLATER SLAVER SLAYER SLICER SLIDER SLIVER SLOWER ULSTER

••LR••

DELRAY DELRIO DELROY KILROY OILRIG WALRUS

••L•R•

AGLARE AILERS ALLPRO ALLURE BALERS BELFRY BOLERO CELERY CHLORO COLORS DOLORS EELERS ELLERY FILERS FULCRA GALORE HALERS HALERU HILARY IDLERS MALORY MILERS MILORD MOLARS NFLERS NHLERS OGLERS OILERS PALTRY PELTRY POLERS RULERS SALARY SCLERA SCLERO SOLARS SOLERS SULTRY TALERS TILERS TULARE VALERY VELCRO VOLARE WALERS

••L••R

ALLFOR BALDER BELAIR BOLDER BOLGER BULGAR BULGUR BULWER CALDER CALLER CALMER CELLAR COLDER COLLAR COLOUR COLTER CULLER CULVER DELMAR DELVER DILLER DOLLAR DOLOUR DULLER ECLAIR EELIER FALSER FALTER FELLER FILLER FILTER FOLDER FOLIAR FULLER FULMAR GILDER GOLFER GULPER HALTER HELLER HELPER HELTER HILLER HOLDER HOLIER HOLLER HULLER KALMAR KELLER KILLER KILMER KILTER KULTUR MILDER MILKER MILLER MILNER MOLDER MOLNAR MOLTER MULLER OILIER PALIER PALLOR PALMER PALTER PELTER PILFER PILLAR POLDER POLLER PULSAR ROLLER SALTER SALVER SALVOR SELLER SILVER SOLDER

SOLVER
SULFUR
SULKER
TALKER
TALLER
TELLER
TILLER
TILTER
UGLIER
VALOUR
VELOUR
VULGAR
WALKER
WALLER
WALTER
WELDER
WELLER
WELTER
WILBUR
WILDER
WILIER
WOLPER
YELLER
YELPER

•••L•R

ALULAR
AMBLER
AMPLER
ANGLER
ANTLER
ASHLAR
BAILER
BAILOR
BAWLER
BAYLOR
BOILER
BOWLER
BUGLER
BUTLER
CABLER
CALLER
CELLAR
CHOLER
COALER
COLLAR
COOLER
CULLER
CURLER
CUTLER
CYCLER
DEALER
DIALER
DILLER
DOLLAR
DUELER
DULLER
EVILER
FABLER
FEELER
FELLER
FILLER
FOOLER
FOULER
FOWLER
FUELER
FULLER
GABLER
GAOLER
HAULER
HEALER
HEELER
HELLER
HILLER
HOLLER
HOWLER
HULLER
HURLER
JAILER
KEELER
KEGLER
KELLER
KEPLER
KEVLAR
KILLER
KOHLER
LADLER
MAHLER
MAILER
MAULER
MEDLAR
MEWLER
MIDLER
MILLER
MOILER
MULLER
NAILER
NOBLER
OCULAR
OSTLER
OVULAR
PALLOR
PARLOR
PEDLAR
PEELER
PEGLER
PILLAR
POLLER
POPLAR
RAILER
REALER
RIFLER
ROLLER
SAILOR
SCALAR
SCALER
SEALER
SELLER
SISLER
SMILER
STALER
STELAR
STYLER
SUTLER
TAILOR
TALLER
TAYLOR
TELLER
THALER
TILLER
TOILER
UVULAR
WAILER
WALLER
WELLER
WHALER
WOHLER
YELLER

L•S•••

LASCAR
LASERS
LASHED
LASHER
LASHES
LASHIO
LASHUP
LASSEN
LASSER
LASSES
LASSIE
LASSOS
LASTED
LASTEX
LASTLY
LESAGE
LESBOS
LESLEY
LESLIE
LESSEE
LESSEN
LESSER
LESSON
LESSOR
LESTAT
LESTER
LISBOA
LISBON
LISLES
LISPED
LISTED
LISTEE
LISTEL
LISTEN
LISTER
LISTON
LOSEIT
LOSERS
LOSING
LOSSES
LOSTIT
LUSAKA
LUSHER
LUSHLY
LUSTED
LUSTER
LUSTRE
LYSINE
LYSINS

L••S••

LANSON
LAPSED
LAPSES
LAPSUP
LARSEN
LARSON
LASSEN
LASSER
LASSES
LASSIE
LASSOS
LAWSON
LAYSBY
LAYSIN
LAYSON
LAYSTO
LAYSUP
LEASED
LEASER
LEASES
LENSED
LENSES
LESSEE
LESSEN
LESSER
LESSON
LESSOR
LETSAT
LETSBE
LETSGO
LETSIN
LETSON
LETSUP
LIESIN
LIESTO
LINSEY
LOGSIN
LOGSON
LOOSED
LOOSEN
LOOSER
LOOSES
LOSSES
LOUSED
LOUSES

L•••S•

LAGASH
LAMESA
LAMEST
LANOSE
LAOTSE
LAROSA
LATEST
LATISH
LAVISH
LAXEST
LEGIST
LHOTSE
LIAISE
LIPASE
LOCUST
LOUISA
LOUISE
LOWEST
LOWISH
LUGOSI
LUTIST
LYRIST

L••••S

LABELS
LABORS
LACERS
LACHES
LADERS
LADIES
LADLES
LAGERS
LAIRDS
LAKERS
LAMEDS
LAMIAS
LAMMAS
LANAIS
LANCES
LANDIS
LAPELS
LAPINS
LAPSES
LARAMS
LARGES
LARGOS
LARVAS
LASERS
LASHES
LASSES
LASSOS
LATENS
LATHES
LATINS
LATKES
LAUGHS
LAVERS
LAYBYS
LAYERS
LAYUPS
LEARNS
LEASES
LEAVES
LEDGES
LEGALS
LEHUAS
LEMANS
LEMMAS
LEMNOS
LEMONS
LEMURS
LENSES
LEONES
LESBOS
LETUPS
LEVEES
LEVELS
LEVERS
LEVIES
LIANAS
LIANES
LIANGS
LIBELS
LIBRIS
LIEBYS
LIEGES
LIEUTS
LIFERS
LIGERS
LIGHTS
LIKENS
LILACS
LILIES
LIMBOS
LIMBUS
LIMENS
LIMEYS
LIMITS
LINENS
LINERS
LIPIDS
LISLES
LITERS
LITHOS
LITMUS
LITRES
LIVENS
LIVERS
LIVRES
LLAMAS
LLANOS
LLOYDS
LOAVES
LOCALS
LODENS
LODGES
LONERS
LONGES
LOOFAS
LOOIES
LOOSES
LOPERS
LORIES
LOSERS
LOSSES
LOTAHS
LOTTOS
LOUGHS
LOUPES
LOUSES
LOVERS
LOWERS
LUCIUS
LUDENS
LUGERS
LUMENS
LUNGES
LUTZES
LYCEES
LYMPHS
LYNXES
LYRICS
LYSINS

•LS•••

ALSACE
ULSTER

•L•S••

ALASKA
ALISON
ALLSET
ALYSSA
BLASTS
CLASPS
CLASSY
CLOSED
CLOSER
CLOSES
CLOSET
ELISHA
ELISSA
ELYSEE
FLASHY
FLASKS
FLESHY
FLOSSY
GLASER
GLASSY
GLOSSA
GLOSSO
GLOSSY
ILESHA
ILLSAY
OLDSAW
OLESON
PLASHY
PLASMA
PLASMO
PLASTY
PLISSE
PLUSES
PLUSHY
SLOSHY
SLUSHY

•L••S•

ALDOSE
ALEAST
ALMOST
ALONSO
ALWEST
ALYSSA
BLAISE
BLOUSE
BLOWSY
BLUEST
BLUESY
BLUISH
CLASSY
CLAUSE
CLEESE
CLUMSY
ELAPSE
ELDEST
ELFISH
ELISSA
ELOISE
ELPASO
ELVISH
FLENSE
FLIMSY
FLOPSY
FLOSSY
GLASSY
GLOSSA
GLOSSO
GLOSSY
ILLEST
ILLUSE
KLEIST
NLEAST
NLWEST
OLDEST
OLDISH
PLEASE
PLISSE
SLIEST
SLIMSY
SLYEST

•L•••S

ALAMOS
ALANIS
ALARMS
ALBUMS
ALDERS
ALDOUS
ALEPHS
ALERTS
ALEUTS
ALEXIS
ALIBIS
ALIENS
ALIGNS
ALINES
ALKYDS
ALKYLS
ALLAYS
ALLEES
ALLEYS
ALLIES
ALLOTS
ALLOWS
ALLOYS
ALOHAS
ALOINS
ALPHAS
ALTARS
ALTERS
ALTIUS
ALWAYS
BLACKS
BLADES
BLAMES
BLANKS
BLARES
BLASTS
BLAZES
BLEARS
BLEATS
BLEEDS
BLEEPS
BLENDS
BLIMPS
BLINDS
BLINIS
BLINKS
BLOATS
BLOCKS
BLOKES
BLONDS
BLOOMS
BLOOPS
BLUETS
BLUEYS
BLUFFS
BLUNTS
BLURBS
BLURTS
CLACKS
CLAIMS
CLAMPS
CLANGS
CLANKS
CLAROS
CLASPS
CLAVES
CLEANS
CLEARS
CLEATS
CLEEKS
CLEFTS
CLERKS
CLEVES
CLEVIS
CLICKS
CLIFFS
CLIMBS
CLIMES
CLINES
CLINGS
CLINKS
CLOAKS
CLOCKS
CLOMPS
CLONES
CLONKS
CLONUS
CLORIS
CLOSES
CLOTHS
CLOUDS
CLOUTS
CLOVES
CLOVIS
CLOWNS
CLUCKS
CLUMPS
CLUNKS
ELANDS
ELATES
ELBOWS
ELBRUS
ELDERS
ELECTS
ELEMIS
ELEVES
ELIDES
ELITES
ELOPES
ELUDES
ELUTES
ELVERS
FLACKS
FLAILS
FLAIRS
FLAKES
FLAMES
FLANKS
FLARES
FLASKS
FLAXES
FLECKS
FLEERS
FLEETS
FLEXES
FLICKS
FLIERS
FLINGS
FLINTS
FLIRTS
FLOATS
FLOCKS
FLOODS
FLOORS
FLORAS
FLORES
FLOURS
FLOUTS
FLUFFS
FLUIDS
FLUKES
FLUMES
FLUNKS
FLUTES
FLUXES
FLYBYS
FLYERS
FLYINS
GLACES
GLACIS
GLADES
GLADYS
GLAIRS
GLANDS
GLARES
GLAZES
GLEAMS
GLEANS
GLEBES
GLIDES
GLINTS
GLOATS
GLOBES
GLOGGS
GLOOMS
GLOVES
GLOZES
GLUERS
GLUONS
GLUTES
GLYNIS
GLYPHS
ILEXES
KLOOFS
LLAMAS
LLANOS
LLOYDS
OLDIES
OLIVES
OLMECS
PLACES
PLAGES
PLAIDS
PLAINS
PLAITS
PLANES
PLANKS
PLANTS
PLATES
PLAYAS
PLAZAS
PLEADS
PLEATS
PLEBES
PLEXUS
PLIERS
PLINKS
PLONKS
PLUCKS
PLUMBS
PLUMES
PLUMPS
PLUNKS
PLUSES
SLACKS
SLAKES
SLANGS
SLANTS
SLATES
SLAVES
SLEEKS
SLEEPS
SLEETS
SLICES
SLICKS
SLIDES
SLIMES
SLINGS
SLINKS
SLOOPS
SLOPES
SLOTHS
SLUMPS
SLURPS
SLYPES
ULCERS
ULTRAS
ZLOTYS

••LS••

ALLSET
BALSAM
BOLSHY
DILSEY
FALSER
FOLSOM
GELSEY
HALSEY
ILLSAY
JOLSON
KELSEY
MILSAP
NELSON
PULSAR
PULSED
PULSES
SALSAS
TILSIT
TULSAN
WILSON
WOLSEY

••L•S•

ABLEST
ABLUSH
ARLISS
ATLAST
CALASH
DALASI
DELIST
ENLIST
FILOSE
FOLKSY
GALOSH
HALEST
HOLISM
HOLIST
IDLEST
ILLEST
ILLUSE
MILOSZ
MOLEST
MULISH
NOLESS
NOLOSE
OBLAST
OWLISH
PALEST
PALISH
PILOSE
POLISH
RELISH
RELIST
SALISH
SPLASH
SPLOSH
TALESE
UNLASH
UNLESS
VALISE
VILEST
WALESA

••L••S

ADLIBS
AFLATS
AGLETS
AILERS
ALLAYS
ALLEES
ALLEYS
ALLIES
ALLOTS
ALLOWS
ALLOYS
ARLISS
BALERS
BELAYS
BELIES
BELLES
BILGES
BULGES
BYLAWS
CALAIS
CALCES
CALLAS
CALLES
CALLUS
CALVES
CALXES
CELEBS
CELLOS
COLEUS
COLIES
COLONS
COLORS
CULETS
CULLIS
DALLAS
DALLES
DELAYS
DELFTS
DELIUS
DELTAS
DELVES
DOLMAS
DOLORS
DULLES
ECLATS
EELERS
EFLATS
FALCES
FELLAS
FELONS
FILERS
FILETS
FILIUS
FILLES
FOLIOS
GALAHS
GALOIS
GALOPS
GELEES
GILLIS
GOLEMS
GULAGS
HALERS
HALLOS
HALOES
HALVES
HELENS
HELIOS
HELLAS
HELLOS
HELOTS
HELVES
HOLMES
HULLOS
IDLERS
IGLOOS
INLAWS
INLAYS
INLETS
ISLETS
JULEPS
JULIUS
KILIMS
KULAKS
LILACS
LILIES
MALAYS
MELEES
MELONS
MILERS
MILPAS
MOLARS
MULCTS
MULEYS
MULLAS
NFLERS
NHLERS
NOLENS
NOLESS
NYLONS
OGLERS
OILERS
ORLOPS
OWLETS
OXLIPS
PALLAS
PALMAS
PALPUS
PELEUS
PELOPS
PELVIS
PILAFS
PILEUS
PILOTS
POLERS
POLKAS
POLYPS
PULSES
PYLONS
RELAYS
RELETS
RELICS
RELIES
RILLES
ROLEOS
RULERS
SALADS
SALALS
SALONS
SALSAS
SALVES
SALVOS
SELVES
SILVAS
SOLANS
SOLARS
SOLERS
SOLEUS
SOLFAS
SOLIDS
SOLVES
SPLATS
SPLAYS
SPLITS
SULCUS
SYLPHS
TALERS
TALONS
TILAKS
TILDES
TILERS
TILLIS
TULIPS
TULLES
UCLANS
UGLIES
UHLANS
UNLESS
VALENS
VALETS
VALOIS
VALUES
VALVES
VELDTS
VILLAS
VILLUS
VOLANS
VOLENS
VOLVAS
WALERS
WALLIS
WALRUS
WELLES
WILKES
WILLIS
WOLVES
YALIES

•••LS•

AVULSE
EVULSE
GRILSE
ORELSE
URALSK
WHILST

•••L•S

ABELES
ADDLES
ADULTS
AEOLUS
AISLES
AKELAS
AMBLES
AMOLES
ANELES
ANGLES
ANGLOS
ANKLES
ANOLES
APPLES
ATOLLS
BAULKS
BCELLS
BELLES
BIBLES
BOGLES
BOULES
BOWLES
BRILLS
BRULES
BUGLES
BUILDS
CABLES
CALLAS
CALLES
CALLUS
CARLOS
CAULKS
CELLOS
CHALKS
CHELAS
CHILDS
CHILLS
CHOLOS
CULLIS
CYCLAS
CYCLES
CYCLOS
DALLAS
DALLES
DHOLES
DOBLAS
DRILLS
DROLLS
DULLES
DWELLS
EAGLES
ECCLES
ECOLES
EDILES
EXALTS
EXILES
EXULTS
FABLES
FAULTS
FELLAS
FIELDS
FILLES
FJELDS
FOWLES
FRILLS
GABLES
GILLIS
GRILLS
GUILDS
GUILES
HALLOS
HAOLES
HAULMS
HELLAS
HELLOS
HULLOS
IDYLLS
INGLES
INKLES
ISTLES
JOULES
KNELLS
KNOLLS
KOALAS
KVELLS
LADLES
LISLES
MAILES
MAJLIS
MAPLES
MOULDS
MOULTS
MULLAS
NAPLES
NOBLES
NYALAS
OBELUS
OODLES
ORALES
ORTLES
OVULES
OXALIS
PALLAS
PEPLOS
PHILOS
POILUS
POULTS
PROLES
PSALMS
QUALMS
QUELLS
QUILLS
QUILTS
REALES
REALMS
RIFLES
RILLES
ROBLES
RUBLES
SABLES
SAULTS
SAYLES
SCALDS
SCALES
SCALPS
SCOLDS
SCULLS
SHALES
SHELLS
SHILLS
SIDLES
SKALDS
SKILLS
SKULKS
SKULLS
SMALLS
SMELLS
SMELTS
SMILES
SMOLTS
SNELLS
SOCLES
SPALLS
SPELLS
SPILES
SPILLS
STALES
STALKS
STALLS
STELES
STILES
STILLS
STILTS
STOLES
STULLS
STYLES
STYLUS
SWALES
SWELLS
SWILLS
TABLAS
TABLES
TBILLS
TESLAS
THALES
THILLS
THOLES
TILLIS
TITLES
TOILES
TOKLAS
TRILLS
TROLLS
TULLES
TWILLS
UBOLTS
UNCLES
UVULAS
VAULTS
VILLAS
VILLUS
VIOLAS
VOILES
WALLIS
WELLES
WHALES
WHELKS
WHELMS
WHELPS
WHILES
WHOLES
WIELDS
WILLIS
WORLDS
XFILES
YIELDS

••••LS

ALKYLS
AMPULS
ANGELS
ANNALS
ANNULS
ANVILS
APPALS
ARTELS
ATOLLS
AVAILS
BABELS
BABULS
BAGELS
BCELLS
BETELS
BEVELS
BEZELS
BGIRLS
BOTELS
BRAILS
BRAWLS
BRILLS
BROILS
CABALS
CAMELS
CANALS
CAROLS
CASALS
CAVILS
CEORLS
CHILLS
CHURLS
CORALS
CRAWLS
CREELS

CUPELS
DECALS
DEVILS
DOWELS
DRAILS
DRAWLS
DRILLS
DROLLS
DROOLS
DWELLS
EASELS
EDSELS
EMAILS
ENGELS
ENROLS
EQUALS
EXCELS
EXPELS
EXTOLS
FINALS
FLAILS
FRILLS
FUSILS
GAVELS
GAYALS
GHOULS
GIMELS
GNARLS
GORALS
GRAILS
GRILLS
GROWLS
GRUELS
HAMALS
HAZELS
HOSELS
HOTELS
HOVELS
IDEALS
IDYLLS
IMPELS
JACALS
JEWELS
KEVELS
KNEELS
KNELLS
KNOLLS
KNURLS
KRAALS
KVELLS
LABELS
LAPELS
LEGALS
LEVELS
LIBELS
LOCALS
MEDALS
METALS
MODELS
MOGULS
MORALS
MORELS
MOTELS
MURALS
NASALS
NAVELS
NEWELS
NOVELS
ORIELS
OUSELS
OUZELS
PANELS
PEARLS
PEDALS
PERILS
PETALS
PHIALS
PICULS
PIPALS
PIXELS
PROWLS
PUPILS
QUAILS
QUELLS
QUILLS
RATELS
RAVELS
REBELS
REOILS
REPELS
REVELS
RIVALS
RIYALS
ROWELS
ROYALS
SALALS
SCOWLS
SCULLS
SEPALS
SHAWLS
SHELLS
SHILLS
SHOALS
SIBYLS
SIGILS
SISALS
SKILLS
SKIRLS
SKOALS
SKULLS
SMALLS
SMELLS
SNAILS
SNARLS
SNELLS
SOTOLS
SPALLS
SPELLS
SPIELS
SPILLS
SPOILS
SPOOLS
STALLS
STEALS
STEELS
STILLS
STOOLS
STULLS
SWELLS
SWILLS
SWIRLS
TAMILS
TBILLS
TEPALS
THILLS
TICALS
TOTALS
TOWELS
TRAILS
TRAWLS
TRIALS
TRILLS
TROLLS
TWILLS
TWIRLS
UMBELS
URIALS
USUALS
VIGILS
VINYLS
VITALS
VOCALS
VOWELS
WHEALS
WHEELS
WHIRLS
WHORLS
YODELS
YOKELS
ZORILS

L•T•••
LATEEN
LATELY
LATENE
LATENS
LATENT
LATEST
LATHED
LATHER
LATHES
LATIGO
LATINA
LATINI
LATINO
LATINS
LATISH
LATIUM
LATKES
LATONA
LATOUR
LATOYA
LATTEN
LATTER
LATVIA
LETFLY
LETHAL
LETOFF
LETOUT
LETSAT
LETSBE
LETSGO
LETSIN
LETSON
LETSUP
LETTED
LETTER
LETUPS
LITANY
LITCHI
LITERS
LITHIC
LITHOG
LITHOS
LITMUS
LITOUT
LITRES
LITTER
LITTLE
LOTAHS
LOTHAR
LOTION
LOTTED
LOTTOS
LUTHER
LUTHOR
LUTING
LUTIST
LUTZES
LYTTON

L••T••
LACTIC
LAOTSE
LAOTZU
LAPTEV
LAPTOP
LASTED
LASTEX
LASTLY
LATTEN
LATTER
LAWTON
LECTER
LECTOR
LEFTIE
LEFTIN
LENTEN
LENTIL
LEPTON
LESTAT
LESTER
LETTED
LETTER
LHOTSE
LICTOR
LIFTED
LIFTER
LIFTUP
LILTED
LINTEL
LINTER
LIOTTA
LIPTON
LISTED
LISTEE
LISTEL
LISTEN
LISTER
LISTON
LITTER
LITTLE
LOATHE
LOFTED
LOITER
LOOTED
LOOTER
LOSTIT
LOTTED
LOTTOS
LUSTED
LUSTER
LUSTRE
LYTTON

L•••T•
LAIDTO
LAKOTA
LANATE
LAPUTA
LAXITY
LAYSTO
LEADTO
LEALTY
LEANTO
LEGATE
LEGATO
LENGTH
LENITY
LEVITE
LEVITY
LIESTO
LIEUTS
LIGATE
LIGHTS
LILITH
LIMITS
LIOTTA
LOBATE
LOCATE
LOLITA
LOOKTO
LOVETT
LUCITE
LUNATE
LUXATE

L••••T
LABRET
LAMENT
LAMEST
LAMONT
LANCET
LAPPET
LARIAT
LATENT
LATEST
LAXEST
LAYOUT
LEARNT
LEDOUT
LEERAT
LEGIST
LESTAT
LETOUT
LETSAT
LEVANT
LIMPET
LINNET
LIONET
LITOUT
LOCKET
LOCUST
LOGOUT
LOOKAT
LOQUAT
LOSEIT
LOSTIT
LOVETT
LOWEST
LOWFAT
LUCENT
LUGNUT
LUTIST
LYRIST

•LT•••
ALTAIC
ALTAIR
ALTARS
ALTERS
ALTHEA
ALTIMA
ALTIUS
ALTMAN
ULTIMA
ULTIMO
ULTRAS

•L•T••
ALATAU
ALATED
ALITER
BLATTY
BLITHE
BLOTCH
BLOTTO
BLOTTY
BLYTHE
CLOTHE
CLOTHO
CLOTHS
CLOTTY
CLUTCH
ELATED
ELATER
ELATES
ELITES
ELUTED
ELUTES
FLATLY
FLETCH
FLITCH
FLUTED
FLUTES
FLUTEY
GLITCH
GLITZY
GLUTEI
GLUTEN
GLUTES
KLATCH
KLUTZY
PLATED
PLATEN
PLATER
PLATES
PLATTE
PLOTTY
SLATED
SLATER
SLATES
SLITHY
SLITTY
SLOTHS
ULSTER
ZLOTYS

•L••T•
ALCOTT
ALECTO
ALERTS
ALEUTS
ALIOTO
ALLOTS
ALMATY
BLASTS
BLATTY
BLEATS
BLINTZ
BLOATS
BLOTTO
BLOTTY
BLUETS
BLUNTS
BLURTS
CLEATS
CLEFTS
CLOTTY
CLOUTS
ELECTS
FLEETS
FLINTS
FLINTY
FLIRTS
FLIRTY
FLOATS
FLOATY
FLOUTS
GLINTS
GLOATS
OLEATE
PLAITS
PLANTE
PLANTS
PLASTY
PLATTE
PLEATS
PLENTY
PLINTH
PLOTTY
SLANTS
SLEETS
SLEETY
SLEUTH
SLITTY

•L•••T
ALBEIT
ALBERT
ALCOTT
ALEAST
ALHIRT
ALIGHT
ALLBUT
ALLOUT
ALLSET
ALLWET
ALMOST
ALPERT
ALWEST
BLEWIT
BLIGHT
BLOWIT
BLUEST
CLARET
CLIENT
CLOSET
ELBERT
ELDEST
ELEGIT
ELICIT
ELLIOT
FLAUNT
FLEWAT
FLIGHT
FLORET
FLUENT
FLYNET
FLYOUT
HLHUNT
ILLEST
ILLMET
KLEIST
NLEAST
NLWEST
OLDEST
OLDHAT
PLACET
PLAINT
PLANET
PLAYAT
PLIANT
PLIGHT
SLIEST
SLIGHT
SLYEST

••LT••
BALTIC
BELTED
BOLTED
BOLTON
CELTIC
COLTER
CULTIC
DALTON
DELTAS
DELTIC
FALTER
FELTED
FILTER
FILTHY
FULTON
HALTED
HALTER
HELTER
HILTON
JILTED
JOLTED
KILTED
KILTER
KILTIE
KULTUR
LILTED
MALTED
MALTIN
MELTED
MELTON
MILTIE
MILTON
MOLTED
MOLTEN
MOLTER
MOLTKE
MULTUM
PALTER
PALTRY
PELTED
PELTER
PELTRY
SALTED
SALTEN
SALTER
SALTON
SALTUM
SILTED
SULTAN
SULTRY
TILTED
TILTER
TOLTEC
WALTER
WALTON
WELTED
WELTER
WILTED
WILTON

••L•T•
ABLATE
AFLATS
AGLETS
ALLOTS
APLITE
ATLATL
BALATA
CULETS
DALETH
DELATE
DELETE
DELFTS
DILATE
DILUTE
DULUTH
ECLATS
EFLATS
EOLITH
FALLTO
FELLTO
FILETS
GALATA
GELATI
GELATO
HALITE
HELDTO
HELOTS
HOLDTO
INLETS
IOLITE
ISLETS
LILITH
LOLITA
MALATE
MALOTI
MELOTT
MULCTS
MULETA
OBLATE
OFLATE
OOLITE
OOLITH
OWLETS
PALATE
PELOTA
PILATE
PILOTI
PILOTS
POLITE
POLITY
RELATE
RELETS
SALUTE
SOLUTE
SPLATS
SPLITS
TALKTO
VALETS
VELDTS
VOLUTE

••L••T
ABLAUT
ABLEST
AFLOAT
AGLINT
ALLBUT
ALLOUT
ALLSET
ALLWET
ASLANT
ATLAST
AULAIT
BALLET
BALLOT
BELOIT
BILLET
BULLET
COLLET
CULLET
DELICT
DELIST
DULCET
ELLIOT
ENLIST
FILLET
GALOOT
GULLET
HALEST
HELMET
HELMUT
HOLDIT
HOLIST
IDLEST
ILLEST
ILLMET
JOLIET
JOLIOT
JULIET
MALLET
MELOTT
MILLET
MOLEST
MULLET
OBLAST
PALEST
PALLET
PELLET
PELMET
POLPOT
PULLET
PULPIT
RELENT
RELICT
RELIST
RELUCT
RILLET
SALLET
SALYUT
SELECT
SILENT
SOLENT
SPLINT
TALBOT
TALENT
TALKAT
TILSIT
UMLAUT
UPLIFT
VALENT
VELVET
VILEST
VOLANT
WALLET
WALNUT
WILLET

•••LT•
ADULTS
EXALTS
EXULTS
FALLTO
FAULTS
FAULTY
FAWLTY
FEALTY
FELLTO
GUILTY
HEALTH
LEALTY
MOULTS
POULTS
QUILTS
REALTY
RIALTO
SAULTS
SHELTY
SMALTI
SMALTO
SMELTS
SMOLTS
SPILTH
STILTS
SVELTE
UBOLTS
VAULTS
VAULTY
WEALTH

•••L•T
AMULET
ANKLET
APPLET
ARMLET
AUKLET
BADLOT
BALLET
BALLOT
BILLET
BULLET
CAMLET
CANLIT
CAPLET
CARLOT
CHALET
COLLET
COOLIT
CULLET
CUTLET
DAYLIT
DIGLOT
DYELOT
EAGLET
ENGLUT
EYELET
FILLET
GASLIT
GIBLET
GIMLET
GOBLET
GOULET
GULLET
HAMLET
JOBLOT
MALLET
MEDLAT
MERLOT
MILLET
MULLET
NUTLET
OCELOT
ODDLOT
OMELET
OUTLET
PALLET
PELLET
PIGLET
PIOLET
PULLET
RAILAT
REGLET
RILLET
RUNLET
SALLET
SAMLET
SCULPT
STYLET
SUBLET
SUNLIT
TABLET
TOILET
TWILIT
VARLET
VIOLET
WALLET
WHILST
WIGLET
WILLET
ZEALOT

••••LT
BASALT
COBALT
DESALT
INCULT
INSULT
ISEULT
KURALT
MODELT
OCCULT
PENULT
REBOLT
REMELT
RESALT
RESULT
REVOLT
SPOILT
TUMULT
TYBALT
UNBELT
UNBOLT

LU••••
LUANDA
LUBBER
LUBECK
LUBING
LUBLIN
LUCENT
LUCIAN
LUCITE
LUCIUS
LUCKED
LUDDEN
LUDENS
LUDLUM
LUDWIG
LUFFED
LUGERS
LUGGED
LUGGER
LUGNUT
LUGOSI
LULLED
LUMBAR
LUMBER
LUMENS
LUMINA
LUMMOX
LUMPED
LUMPEN
LUMPER
LUMPUR
LUNACY
LUNATE
LUNCHY
LUNDEN
LUNGED
LUNGES
LUNKER
LUNULA
LUPINE
LUPINO
LUPONE
LURING
LURKED
LUSAKA
LUSHER
LUSHLY
LUSTED
LUSTER
LUSTRE
LUTHER
LUTHOR
LUTING
LUTIST
LUTZES
LUXATE
LUXURY

L•U•••
LAUDED
LAUDER
LAUGHS
LAUNCH
LAUPER
LAUREL
LAUREN
LAURIE
LOUCHE
LOUDEN
LOUDER
LOUDLY
LOUGHS
LOUISA
LOUISE
LOUNGE
LOUPES
LOUSED
LOUSES
LOUVER
LOUVRE

L••U••
LACUNA
LAGUNA
LAPUTA
LAYUPS
LAZULI
LEGUIN
LEGUME
LEHUAS
LEMUEL
LEMURS
LETUPS
LIEUTS
LIGULA
LIGURE
LIQUID
LIQUOR
LOBULE
LOCUST
LOQUAT
LUNULA
LUXURY

L•••U•
LABOUR
LABRUM
LACEUP
LAIDUP
LAMOUR
LANGUR
LAPFUL
LAPSUP
LARRUP
LASHUP
LATIUM
LATOUR
LAWFUL
LAYOUT
LAYSUP
LEADUP
LEAGUE
LEBRUN
LEDOUT
LETOUT
LETSUP
LIFTUP
LIMBUS
LINEUP
LINGUA
LINKUP
LITMUS
LITOUT
LOCKUP
LOGOUT
LONGUE
LOOKUP
LUCIUS
LUDLUM
LUGNUT
LUMPUR
LYCEUM

L••••U
LANDAU
LAOTZU

•LU•••
ALULAE
ALULAR
ALUMNA
ALUMNI
BLUELY
BLUEOX
BLUEST
BLUESY
BLUETS
BLUEYS
BLUFFS
BLUING
BLUISH
BLUNTS
BLURBS
BLURRY
BLURTS
CLUBBY
CLUCKS
CLUEIN
CLUING
CLUMPS
CLUMPY
CLUMSY
CLUNKS
CLUNKY
CLUTCH
ELUDED
ELUDER
ELUDES
ELUTED
ELUTES
FLUENT
FLUFFS
FLUFFY
FLUIDS
FLUKES
FLUKEY
FLUMES
FLUNKS
FLUNKY
FLUORO
FLURRY
FLUTED
FLUTES
FLUTEY
FLUXED
FLUXES
GLUERS
GLUIER
GLUING
GLUMLY
GLUONS
GLUTEI
GLUTEN
GLUTES
KLUDGE
KLUTZY
PLUCKS
PLUCKY
PLUGIN
PLUMBS
PLUMED
PLUMES
PLUMMY
PLUMPS
PLUNGE
PLUNKS
PLURAL
PLUSES
PLUSHY
SLUDGE
SLUDGY
SLUGGO
SLUICE
SLUING
SLUMMY
SLUMPS
SLURPS
SLURRY
SLUSHY

•L•U••
ALBUMS
ALCUIN
ALEUTS
ALLUDE
ALLURE
BLOUSE
CLAUDE
CLAUSE
CLOUDS
CLOUDY
CLOUTS
FLAUNT
FLEURY
FLOURS
FLOURY
FLOUTS
HLHUNT
ILLUME
ILLUSE
PLEURA
PLOUGH
SLEUTH
SLOUCH
SLOUGH

•L••U•
ALARUM
ALDOUS
ALLBUT
ALLIUM
ALLOUT
ALTIUS
BLEWUP
BLOWUP
CLAMUP
CLAQUE
CLIQUE
CLIQUY
CLOGUP
CLONUS
CLOQUE
ELBRUS
FLIPUP
FLYOUT
PLAGUE
PLAQUE
PLAYUP
PLENUM
PLEXUS
SLAPUP
SLIPUP
SLOWUP

•L•••U
ALATAU

••LU••
ABLUSH
ALLUDE
ALLURE
BELUGA
COLUGO
COLUMN
DELUDE
DELUGE
DELUXE
DILUTE
DULUTH
ILLUME
ILLUSE
INLUCK
RELUCT
RELUME
SALUKI
SALUTE
SOLUTE
STLUKE
TELUGU
TOLUCA
VALUED
VALUES
VOLUME
VOLUTE

••L•U•
ABLAUT
ALLBUT
ALLIUM
ALLOUT
BALLUP
BULBUL
BULGUR
CALLUP
CALLUS
CALQUE
CILIUM
COLEUS
COLOUR
DELIUS
DOLLUP
DOLOUR
FILIUS
FILLUP
FOLDUP
FOLIUM
GALLUP
GILGUY
GOLLUM
HALLUX
HELDUP
HELIUM
HELMUT
HOLDUP
HOLEUP
JULIUS
KULTUR
MULTUM
PALPUS
PELEUS
PILEUM

PILEUP
PILEUS
POLLUX
PULLUP
PULQUE
RILEUP
ROLLUP
SALTUM
SALYUT
SELJUK
SOLEUS
SULCUS
SULFUR
TALCUM
TALKUP
TALMUD
UMLAUT
VALIUM
VALOUR
VELLUM
VELOUR
VILLUS
WALKUP
WALLUP
WALNUT
WALRUS
WELLUP
WILBUR
WILFUL

••L••U
BALLOU
HALERU
MALIBU
MILIEU
MOLDAU
TELEDU
TELUGU

•••LU•
AEOLUS
ASYLUM
BALLUP
CALLUP
CALLUS
COILUP
CURLUP
DIALUP
DOLLUP
EFFLUX
ENGLUT
FILLUP
FOULUP
GALLUP
GOLLUM
HALLUX
HAULUP
INFLUX
KAHLUA
KAILUA
KUNLUN
LUDLUM
MRBLUE
MUKLUK
OBELUS
PABLUM
PEPLUM
PHYLUM
POILUS
POLLUX
PULLUP
REFLUX
REGLUE
ROLLUP
RVALUE
SEALUP
STYLUS
TOOLUP
UNGLUE
UNPLUG
UVALUE
VELLUM
VILLUS
WALLUP
WELLUP

•••L•U
ARALLU
BALLOU
PAILOU

••••LU
ARALLU
BABALU
DESILU
MAKALU
MARILU
ORMOLU
TUVALU

L•V•••
LAVABO
LAVAGE
LAVERS
LAVING
LAVISH
LEVANT
LEVEED
LEVEES
LEVELS
LEVENE
LEVERS
LEVIED
LEVIER
LEVIES
LEVINE
LEVITE
LEVITY
LIVEIN
LIVELY
LIVENS
LIVEON
LIVERS
LIVERY
LIVING
LIVRES
LOVAGE
LOVEIN
LOVELL
LOVELY
LOVERS
LOVETT
LOVING

L••V••
LANVIN
LARVAE
LARVAL
LARVAS
LATVIA
LEAVED
LEAVEN
LEAVES
LEKVAR
LOAVES
LOUVER
LOUVRE

L••••V
LAPTEV

•LV•••
ELVERS
ELVIRA
ELVISH

•L•V••
ALEVEL
ALFVEN
CLAVES
CLAVIN
CLEVER
CLEVES
CLEVIS
CLOVEN
CLOVER
CLOVES
CLOVIS
ELEVEN
ELEVES
FLAVIA
FLAVOR
GLOVED
GLOVER
GLOVES
OLDVIC
OLEVEL
OLIVER
OLIVES
OLIVIA
PLOVER
SLAVED
SLAVER
SLAVES
SLAVEY
SLAVIC
SLIVER
SLOVAK
SLOVEN
SLOVIK

•L••V•
ALCOVE
CLEAVE
SLEAVE
SLEEVE

••LV••
CALVED
CALVES
CALVIN
CULVER
DELVED
DELVER
DELVES
HALVAH
HALVED
HALVES
HELVES
KELVIN
MELVIL
MELVIN
MELVYN
PELVIC
PELVIS
SALVED
SALVER
SALVES
SALVIA
SALVOR
SALVOS
SELVES
SILVAS
SILVER
SOLVED
SOLVER
SOLVES
SYLVAN
SYLVIA
VALVED
VALVES
VELVET
VOLVAS
VOLVOX
WOLVES

••L•V•
BULOVA
HALEVY
INLOVE
RELEVY
RELIVE
SALIVA

•••LV•
EVOLVE
SHELVE
TWELVE

•••L•V
KISLEV
PAVLOV
RUBLEV
VACLAV
VASLAV

L•W•••
LAWFUL
LAWING
LAWMAN
LAWMEN
LAWSON
LAWTON
LAWYER
LEWDER
LEWDLY
LOWBOY
LOWCAL
LOWELL
LOWEND
LOWERS
LOWERY
LOWEST
LOWFAT
LOWING
LOWISH
LOWKEY

L••W••
LEEWAY
LUDWIG

L••••W
LAYLOW
LIELOW

•LW•••
ALWAYS
ALWEST
ELWOOD
NLWEST

•L•W••
ALLWET
BLEWIT
BLEWUP
BLOWER
BLOWIN
BLOWIT
BLOWSY
BLOWUP
BLOWZY
CLAWED
CLAWER
CLEWED
CLOWNS
FLAWED
FLEWAT
FLEWIN
FLOWED
FLOWER
FLYWAY
GLOWED
GLOWER
PLOWED
PLOWER
SLEWED
SLOWED
SLOWER
SLOWLY
SLOWUP

•L••W•
ALLOWS
ELBOWS

•L•••W
OLDSAW

••LW••
ALLWET
BULWER
GALWAY

••L•W•
ALLOWS
BYLAWS
INLAWS
MALAWI

••L••W
BELLOW
BILLOW
CALLOW
FALLOW
FELLOW
FOLLOW
HALLOW
HOLLOW
MALLOW
MELLOW
MILDEW
PILLOW
SALLOW
TALLOW
WALLOW
WILLOW
YELLOW

•••L•W
BELLOW
BILLOW
CALLOW
CURLEW
FALLOW
FARLOW
FELLOW
FOLLOW
GAGLAW
GOSLOW
HALLOW
HARLOW
HOLLOW
INFLOW
LAYLOW
LIELOW
MALLOW
MELLOW
OUTLAW
PILLOW
PRELAW
REPLOW
SALLOW
TALLOW
WALLOW
WILLOW
YELLOW

L•X•••
LAXEST
LAXITY
LEXEME
LEXICA
LUXATE
LUXURY

L••X••
LYNXES

L••••X
LARYNX
LASTEX
LENNOX
LUMMOX

•L•X••
ALEXEI
ALEXIA
ALEXIS
BLIXEN
ELIXIR
FLAXEN
FLAXES
FLEXED
FLEXES
FLEXOR
FLUXED
FLUXES
ILEXES
KLAXON
PLEXAL
PLEXOR
PLEXUS

•L•••X
BLUEOX
CLIMAX
CLOROX

••LX••
CALXES

••L•X•
BILOXI
DELUXE
GALAXY

••L••X
BOLLIX
COLFAX
HALLUX
POLEAX
POLLEX
POLLUX
VOLVOX
WILCOX

•••L•X
BOLLIX
DUPLEX
EFFLUX
HALLUX
INFLUX
POLLEX
POLLUX
PROLIX
REFLEX
REFLUX
SMILAX

LY••••
LYCEES
LYCEUM
LYMPHS
LYNDON
LYNLEY
LYNXES
LYNYRD
LYRICS
LYRIST
LYSINE
LYSINS
LYTTON

L•Y•••
LAYBYS
LAYERS
LAYFOR
LAYING
LAYLOW
LAYMAN
LAYMEN
LAYOFF
LAYOUT
LAYSBY
LAYSIN
LAYSON
LAYSTO
LAYSUP
LAYUPS
LEYDEN
LOYOLA

L••Y••
LARYNX
LAWYER
LIBYAN
LLOYDS
LYNYRD

L•••Y•
LATOYA
LAYBYS
LIEBYS
LIMEYS

L••••Y
LACILY
LACKEY
LAIDBY
LAMELY
LANDRY
LANKLY
LASTLY
LATELY
LAXITY
LAYSBY
LAZBOY
LAZILY
LEACHY
LEAKEY
LEALTY
LEANLY
LEEWAY
LEGACY
LEMONY
LENITY
LESLEY
LETFLY
LEVITY
LEWDLY
LIEFLY
LIKELY
LIMPLY
LINENY
LINNEY
LINSEY
LIONLY
LITANY
LIVELY
LIVERY
LOGILY
LONELY
LONGLY
LOONEY
LORDLY
LOUDLY
LOVELY
LOWBOY
LOWERY
LOWKEY
LUNACY
LUNCHY
LUSHLY
LUXURY
LYNLEY

•LY•••
ALYSSA
BLYTHE
ELYSEE
FLYBOY
FLYBYS
FLYERS
FLYING
FLYINS
FLYMAN
FLYMEN
FLYNET
FLYOUT
FLYROD
FLYWAY
GLYCOL
GLYNIS
GLYPHS
PLYING
SLYEST
SLYPES

•L•Y••
ALKYDS
ALKYLS
CLAYEY
CLOYED
DLAYER
ELAYER
ELAYNE
FLAYED
FLAYER
FLEYED
LLOYDS
PLAYAS
PLAYAT
PLAYED
PLAYER
PLAYON
PLAYUP
SLAYED
SLAYER

•L••Y•
ALLAYS
ALLEYS
ALLOYS
ALWAYS
BLUEYS
FLYBYS
GLADYS
ZLOTYS

•L•••Y
ALBANY
ALECKY
ALLDAY
ALMATY
BLABBY
BLATTY
BLEARY
BLENNY
BLIMEY
BLOCKY
BLOODY
BLOOEY
BLOOMY
BLOTTY
BLOWSY
BLOWZY
BLUELY
BLUESY
BLURRY
CLAMMY
CLANCY
CLANKY
CLASSY
CLAYEY
CLERGY
CLIFFY
CLINGY
CLIQUY
CLODDY
CLOGGY
CLOTTY
CLOUDY
CLUBBY
CLUMPY
CLUMSY
CLUNKY
ELLERY
FLABBY
FLAGGY
FLAKEY
FLAPPY
FLASHY
FLATLY
FLECKY
FLEDGY
FLEECY
FLESHY
FLEURY
FLIMSY
FLINTY
FLIRTY
FLOATY
FLOCKY
FLOOEY
FLOPPY
FLOPSY
FLOSSY
FLOURY
FLUFFY
FLUKEY
FLUNKY
FLURRY
FLUTEY
FLYBOY
FLYWAY
GLADLY
GLAIRY
GLASSY
GLEAMY
GLIBLY
GLITZY
GLOOMY
GLOPPY
GLOSSY
GLUMLY
ILLSAY
KLUTZY
OLDBOY
OLEARY
PLASHY
PLASTY
PLENTY
PLOTTY
PLUCKY
PLUMMY
PLUSHY
SLAGGY
SLANGY
SLAPPY
SLAVEY
SLEAZY
SLEEKY
SLEEPY
SLEETY
SLIMLY
SLIMSY
SLINKY
SLIPPY
SLITHY
SLITTY
SLOBBY
SLOPPY
SLOSHY
SLOWLY
SLUDGY
SLUMMY
SLURRY
SLUSHY

••LY••
GALYAK
POLYPS
SALYUT

••L•Y•
ALLAYS
ALLEYS
ALLOYS
BELAYS
BOLEYN
DELAYS
INLAYS
MALAYA
MALAYS
MELVYN
MULEYS
POLEYN
RELAYS
SPLAYS

••L••Y
ALLDAY
BALDLY
BELFRY
BELLAY
BOLDLY
BOLSHY
CALMLY
CELERY
COLDLY
COLONY
DELANY
DELRAY
DELROY
DILSEY
ELLERY
EULOGY
FELONY
FILTHY
FOLKSY
GALAXY
GALLEY
GALWAY
GELSEY
GILGUY
HALEVY
HALLEY
HALSEY
HILARY
HOLILY
ILLSAY
JALOPY
KELLEY
KELSEY
KILROY
MALADY
MALORY
MELODY
MILADY
MILDLY
MILLAY
OILILY
OOLOGY
PALELY
PALTRY
PELTRY
POLICY
POLITY
PULLEY
RELEVY
SALARY
SALIFY
SOLELY
SULTRY
UGLIFY
UGLILY
VALERY
VALLEY
VILELY
VILIFY
VOLLEY
WILDLY
WILILY
WOLSEY

•••LY•
EVELYN
JACLYN

•••L•Y
ASHLEY
BAILEY
BARLEY
BEGLEY
BELLAY
BOSLEY
BROLLY
BURLEY
BYPLAY
CHALKY
CHILLY
COOLLY
COPLEY
COWLEY
CURLEY
DAILEY
DEPLOY
DOOLEY
DROLLY
DUALLY
DUDLEY
EMPLOY
EVILLY
FARLEY
FAULTY
FAWLTY
FEALTY
FOULLY
FRILLY
GALLEY
GUILTY
GURLEY
HAILEY
HALLEY
HANLEY
HARLEY
HAYLEY
HENLEY
HURLEY
HUXLEY
INPLAY
KELLEY
KNOLLY
LEALTY
LESLEY
LYNLEY
MARLEY
MEDLEY
MILLAY
MISLAY
MOBLEY
MORLEY
MOTLEY
MOULDY
NEWLEY
OAKLEY
OKELLY
ORALLY
OUTLAY
OVALLY
PARLAY
PARLEY
PAULEY
PHILBY
PHILLY
PULLEY
REALLY
REALTY
REILLY
REPLAY
RIDLEY
RIPLEY
SCULLY
SEELEY
SHALEY
SHALLY
SHELLY
SHELTY
SHILLY
SISLEY
SMELLY
SMILEY
STALKY
STILLY
TRILBY
VALLEY
VAULTY
VOLLEY
WAYLAY
WESLEY
WHOLLY
WOOLEY
WOOLLY
WURLEY

••••LY
ACIDLY
AERILY
AIRILY
ARCHLY
ARIDLY
ARTILY
AVIDLY
AWEDLY
BALDLY
BARELY
BARFLY
BASELY
BASSLY
BLUELY
BODILY
BOLDLY
BOTFLY
BROLLY
BUBBLY
BURBLY
BUSILY
CAGILY
CALMLY
CECILY
CHARLY
CHICLY
CHILLY
CICELY
COLDLY
COMELY
COMPLY
COOLLY
COSILY
COSTLY
COZILY
CRAWLY
CUDDLY
CURTLY
CUTELY
DAFTLY
DAMPLY
DANGLY
DANKLY
DARKLY
DEADLY
DEAFLY
DEARLY
DEEPLY
DEFTLY
DEWILY
DIDDLY
DIMPLY
DIRELY
DOUBLY
DOURLY
DOZILY
DRABLY
DRAWLY
DROLLY
DROOLY
DRYFLY
DUALLY
DUMBLY
EASILY
EBERLY
EDGILY
EERILY
EVENLY
EVERLY
EVILLY
FAIRLY
FAMILY
FEATLY
FEEBLY
FINELY
FIRMLY
FLATLY
FONDLY
FOULLY
FOXILY
FREELY
FRILLY
GADFLY
GAINLY
GAMELY
GAMILY
GANGLY
GENTLY
GIGGLY
GLADLY
GLIBLY
GLUMLY
GNARLY
GOGGLY
GOODLY
GOOGLY
GORILY
GRAYLY
GREYLY
GRIMLY
GRISLY
GROWLY
HACKLY
HARDLY
HAZILY
HIGHLY
HOLILY
HOMELY
HOMILY
HOSTLY
HOURLY
HUBBLY
HUGELY
HUMBLY
JANGLY
JIGGLY
JINGLY
JOKILY
JUNGLY
JUSTLY
KEENLY
KINDLY
KINGLY
KNOLLY
KNURLY
KODALY
LACILY
LAMELY
LANKLY
LASTLY
LATELY
LAZILY
LEANLY
LETFLY
LEWDLY
LIEFLY
LIKELY
LIMPLY
LIONLY
LIVELY
LOGILY
LONELY
LONGLY
LORDLY
LOUDLY
LOVELY
LUSHLY
MAINLY
MARBLY
MAYFLY
MAZILY
MEANLY
MEASLY
MEDFLY
MEEKLY
MEETLY
MERELY
MILDLY
MOSTLY
MUMBLY
MUSCLY
MUTELY
NAMELY
NEARLY
NEATLY
NETTLY
NICELY
NIMBLY
NOSILY
NUBBLY
NUDELY
NUMBLY
OILILY
OKELLY
OOZILY
OPENLY
ORALLY
OUTFLY
OVALLY
OVERLY
PALELY
PARTLY
PEARLY
PEBBLY
PERTLY
PHILLY
POKILY
POORLY
POPFLY
PORTLY
POSHLY
PRIMLY
PUDDLY
PUNILY
PURELY
PURPLY
RACILY
RANKLY
RAPTLY
RARELY
RASHLY
RATTLY
REALLY
REILLY
RICHLY
RIFELY
RIPELY
RIPPLY
RONELY
ROSILY
RUBBLY
RUDELY
RUFFLY
RUMBLY
RUMPLY
SAFELY
SAGELY
SANELY
SCULLY
SEEMLY
SEXILY
SHALLY
SHELLY
SHILLY
SHOALY
SICILY
SICKLY
SIMPLY
SINGLY
SLIMLY
SLOWLY
SMELLY
SMUGLY
SNARLY
SNUGLY
SOFTLY
SOLELY
SORELY
SOURLY
SPRYLY
STABLY
STEELY
STILLY
STOOLY
SUBTLY
SUPPLY
SURELY
SWIRLY
TAMELY
TANGLY
TARTLY
TAUTLY
THEFLY
THINLY
THUSLY
TICKLY
TIDDLY
TIDILY
TIMELY
TINGLY
TINILY
TINKLY
TREBLY
TRIGLY
TRIMLY
TRIPLY
TWOPLY
UGLILY
UNDULY
UNHOLY
UNOILY
UNRULY
UNWILY
USABLY
VAINLY
VASTLY
VERILY
VIABLY

VILELY
VOWELY
WADDLY
WAFFLY
WAGGLY
WAMBLY
WARILY
WARMLY
WAVILY
WAXILY
WEAKLY
WEEKLY
WETFLY
WHIRLY
WHOLLY
WIDELY
WIFELY
WIGGLY
WILDLY
WILILY
WIRILY
WISELY
WOBBLY
WOOLLY
YARELY
YEARLY
ZANILY

L•Z•••
LAZBOY
LAZIER
LAZILY
LAZING
LAZULI
LIZARD
LIZZIE

L••Z••
LIZZIE
LUTZES

L•••Z•
LAMAZE
LAOTZU

L••••Z
LORENZ

•L•Z••
BLAZED
BLAZER
BLAZES
BLAZON
GLAZED
GLAZER
GLAZES
GLOZED
GLOZES
PLAZAS
SLEZAK

•L••Z•
ALONZO
BLOWZY
GLITZY
KLUTZY
SLEAZE
SLEAZY

•L•••Z
BLINTZ

••LZ••
BALZAC

••L•Z•
ABLAZE
BELIZE

••L••Z
DOLENZ
MILOSZ
VALDEZ

•••L•Z
BOULEZ

••••LZ
SCHULZ

MA••••
MABELL
MACACO
MACAWS
MACEIO
MACHES
MACHOS
MACOUN
MACRAE
MACRON
MACROS
MACULA
MADAME
MADAMS
MADCAP
MADDEN
MADDER
MADDIE
MADEDO
MADEIT
MADERO
MADEUP
MADMAN
MADMAX
MADMEN
MADRAS
MADRES
MADRID
MADSEN
MADTOM
MADURA
MADURO
MAENAD
MAGGIE
MAGGIO
MAGMAS
MAGNET
MAGNON
MAGNUM
MAGNUS
MAGPIE
MAGUEY
MAGYAR
MAHDIS
MAHLER
MAHOUT
MAHZOR
MAIDEN
MAIDUS
MAILED
MAILER
MAILES
MAILIN
MAINLY
MAISIE
MAITAI
MAITRE
MAIZES
MAJGEN
MAJLIS
MAJORS
MAKALU
MAKEBA
MAKEDO
MAKEIT
MAKERS
MAKEUP
MAKING
MAKUTA
MALABO
MALADY
MALAGA
MALATE
MALAWI
MALAYA
MALAYS
MALDEN
MALIBU
MALICE
MALIGN
MALKIN
MALLEE
MALLEI
MALLET
MALLOW
MALONE
MALORY
MALOTI
MALTED
MALTIN
MAMBAS
MAMBOS
MAMMAL
MAMMAS
MAMMON
MANAGE
MANAMA
MANANA
MANAUS
MANCHA
MANCHU
MANDAN
MANDAY
MANEGE
MANFUL
MANGER
MANGLE
MANGOS
MANIAC
MANIAS
MANILA
MANIOC
MANNED
MANNER
MANNIX
MANORS
MANQUE
MANRAY
MANSES
MANTAS
MANTEL
MANTIC
MANTIS
MANTLE
MANTRA
MANTUA
MANUAL
MANUEL
MAOISM
MAOIST
MAORIS
MAOTAI
MAPLES
MAPPED
MAPPER
MAPUTO
MAQUIS
MARACA
MARAUD
MARBLE
MARBLY
MARCEL
MARCHE
MARCIA
MARCIE
MARCOS
MARCUS
MARDUK
MARGAY
MARGES
MARGIE
MARGIN
MARGOT
MARIAH
MARIAN
MARIEL
MARIKO
MARILU
MARINA
MARINE
MARINO
MARION
MARISA
MARISH
MARIST
MARIUS
MARKED
MARKER
MARKET
MARKKA
MARKUP
MARLED
MARLEE
MARLEY
MARLIN
MARLON
MARMEE
MARMOT
MARNER
MARNIE
MAROON
MARPLE
MARQUE
MARRED
MARRON
MARROW
MARSHA
MARSHY
MARTEL
MARTEN
MARTHA
MARTIN
MARTYR
MARVEL
MARVIN
MASADA
MASAIS
MASCOT
MASERS
MASERU
MASHED
MASHER
MASHES
MASHIE
MASKED
MASKER
MASONS
MASQUE
MASSED
MASSES
MASSEY
MASSIF
MASTER
MASTIC
MATERS
MATEYS
MATHER
MATHIS
MATING
MATINS
MATLIN
MATRIX
MATRON
MATTEA
MATTED
MATTEL
MATTER
MATTES
MATTIE
MATURE
MATZOH
MATZOS
MAULED
MAULER
MAUMAU
MAUMEE
MAUNDY
MAURYA
MAUSER
MAUVES
MAVENS
MAXENE
MAXIMA
MAXIMS
MAXINE
MAXIXE
MAXOUT
MAYANS
MAYBES
MAYDAY
MAYFLY
MAYHAP
MAYHEM
MAYORS
MAYPOP
MAYTAG
MAZERS
MAZIER
MAZILY
MAZOLA
MAZUMA

M•A•••
MCADAM
MCADOO
MEADOW
MEAGER
MEAGRE
MEALIE
MEANER
MEANIE
MEANLY
MEASLY
MIAMIA
MIASMA
MOANED
MOANER
MOATED

M••A••
MACACO
MACAWS
MADAME
MADAMS
MAKALU
MALABO
MALADY
MALAGA
MALATE
MALAWI
MALAYA
MALAYS
MANAGE
MANAMA
MANANA
MANAUS
MARACA
MARAUD
MASADA
MASAIS
MAYANS
MCBAIN
MCCABE
MCCANN
MCHALE
MCLAIN
MCNAIR
MEDAKA
MEDALS
MEGALO
MEGARA
MELANO
MENACE
MENADO
MENAGE
MESABI
METALS
METATE
MIDAIR
MIKADO
MILADY
MILANO
MIRAGE
MOHAIR
MOHAVE
MOHAWK
MOJAVE
MOLARS
MONACO
MONADS
MORALE
MORALS
MORANT
MORASS
MORAVA
MORAYS
MOSAIC
MOZART
MUFASA
MUGABE
MURALS
MURANO
MUTANT
MUTATE
MUTATO
MYNAHS

M•••A•
MACRAE
MADCAP
MADMAN
MADMAX
MADRAS
MAENAD
MAGMAS
MAGYAR
MAITAI
MAMBAS
MAMMAL
MAMMAS
MANDAN
MANDAY
MANIAC
MANIAS
MANRAY
MANTAS
MANUAL
MAOTAI
MARGAY
MARIAH
MARIAN
MAUMAU
MAYDAY
MAYHAP
MAYTAG
MCADAM
MCGRAW
MCLEAN
MECCAS
MEDGAR
MEDIAL
MEDIAN
MEDIAS
MEDLAR
MEDLAT
MELMAC
MENIAL
MENSAE
MENSAL
MENSAS
MENTAL
MERMAN
MESCAL
MICMAC
MIDDAY
MIDIAN
MIDWAY
MIHRAB
MILLAY
MILPAS
MILSAP
MINOAN
MINYAN
MIRIAM
MISHAP
MISLAY
MISSAL
MISSAY
MITRAL
MOBCAP
MOCHAS
MOLDAU
MOLNAR
MOMMAS
MONDAY
MOOLAH
MOREAU
MORGAN
MORNAY
MORTAL
MORTAR
MOSHAV
MSQUAD
MUDCAT
MUDRAS
MULLAH
MULLAS
MURRAY
MUSCAT
MUSIAL
MUTUAL
MYRDAL
MYRIAD

M••••A
MACULA
MADURA
MAKEBA
MAKUTA
MALAGA
MALAYA
MANAMA
MANANA
MANCHA
MANILA
MANTRA
MANTUA
MARACA
MARCIA
MARINA
MARISA
MARKKA
MARSHA
MARTHA
MASADA
MATTEA
MAURYA
MAXIMA
MAZOLA
MAZUMA
MCCREA
MEDAKA
MEDINA
MEDUSA
MEGARA
MELINA
MERIDA
MIAMIA
MIASMA
MIKITA
MIMOSA
MINIMA
MISCHA
MODELA
MODENA
MONERA
MONETA
MONICA
MORAVA
MORITA
MOSKVA
MOTHRA
MUCOSA
MUFASA
MULETA
MURCIA
MYOPIA

•MA•••
AMADIS
AMADOU
AMAJOR
AMALFI
AMALIE
AMANDA
AMATIS
AMATOL
AMAZED
AMAZES
AMAZON
BMAJOR
CMAJOR
DMAJOR
DMARKS
EMAILS
EMAJOR
FMAJOR
GMAJOR
IMAGED
IMAGER
IMAGES
IMAMAN
IMARET
OMAHAN
OMAHAS
OMANIS
OMASUM
SMACKS
SMALLS
SMALTI
SMALTO
SMARMY
SMARTS
SMARTY

•M•A••
AMBATO
AMHARA
EMBANK
EMBARK
EMBAYS
EMDASH
IMPACT
IMPAIR
IMPALA
IMPALE
IMPART
SMEARS
SMEARY
UMIAKS
UMLAUT
UMTATA

•M••A•
AMEBAE
AMEBAS
AMIGAS
AMORAL
AMTRAC
AMTRAK
AMYTAN
EMQUAD
IMAMAN
OMAHAN
OMAHAS
OMEGAS
SMILAX
UMBRAE
UMBRAL
UMBRAS

•M•••A
AMANDA
AMELIA
AMENRA
AMHARA
AMOEBA
EMILIA
IMELDA
IMPALA
OMERTA
SMYRNA
UMBRIA
UMTATA

••MA••
ADMASS
ALMATY
ARMADA
ARMAGH
ARMAND
ARMANI
ASMARA
AYMARA
BAMAKO
BEMATA
CAMARO
COMATE
DAMAGE
DAMASK
DAMATO
DEMAND
DOMAIN
DOMANI
FEMALE
GAMAYS
GEMARA
HAMALS
HEMATO
HOMAGE
HUMANE
HUMANS
INMATE
JAMAAL
JUMADA
KAMALA
LAMARR
LAMAZE
LEMANS
NAMATH
NEMATO
NOMADS
POMACE
POMADE
RAMADA
RAMATE
REMADE
REMAIL
REMAIN
REMAKE
REMAND
REMANS
REMAPS
REMARK
ROMAIC
ROMAJI
ROMANO
ROMANS
ROMANY
SAMARA
SOMALI
SOMANY
SOMATA
SOMATO
STMALO
STMARK
SUMACS
TAMALE
TAMARA
TAMAYO
TOMATO
UNMADE
UNMAKE
UNMANS
UNMASK
USMAIL
YAMAHA
ZYMASE

••M•A•
AIMSAT
BEMOAN
BOMBAY
BUMRAP
CAMEAT
COMBAT
COMEAT
COMMAS
COMPAQ
COMSAT
CYMBAL
DAMMAR
DEMEAN
GAMMAS
GEMMAE
GIMBAL
GYMBAG
HYMNAL
JAMAAL
JUMPAT
KOMBAT
LAMIAS
LAMMAS
LEMMAS
LUMBAR
MAMBAS
MAMMAL
MAMMAS
MOMMAS
NUMBAT
OOMPAH
PAMPAS
QUMRAN
RAMEAU
RAMSAY
RUMBAS
SAMBAL
SAMBAR
SAMBAS
SAMIAM
SAMOAN
SAMPAN
SIMIAN
SUMMAE
SUMMAS
TAMTAM
TIMBAL
TOMBAC
TOMCAT
WOMBAT
ZAMIAS

••M••A
ARMADA
ASMARA
AYMARA
BEMATA
CAMERA
DAMITA
ELMIRA
FEMORA
GAMBIA
GEMARA
JUMADA
KAMALA
LAMBDA
LAMESA
LAMINA
LUMINA
MIMOSA
NUMINA
PAMELA
POMONA
RAMADA
RAMBLA
RAMONA
REMORA
REMUDA
ROMOLA
RUMINA
SAMARA
SAMOSA
SOMATA
TAMARA
XIMENA
YAMAHA
ZAMBIA

•••MA•
AGAMAS
AIRMAN
ALEMAN
ALLMAN
ALOMAR
ALTMAN
ANIMAL
ANIMAS
APEMAN
AROMAS
ATAMAN
BADMAN
BARMAN
BATMAN
BIGMAC
BITMAP
BORMAN
BOWMAN
BRUMAL
BURMAN
BUSMAN
CAIMAN
CARMAN
CAYMAN
CLIMAX
COLMAN
COMMAS
CONMAN
CORMAN
COWMAN
DAGMAR
DAMMAR
DELMAR
DERMAL
DESMAN
DISMAL
DISMAY
DOGMAS
DOLMAN
DOLMAS
DRAMAS
ELFMAN
ENDMAN
FBIMAN
FENMAN
FERMAT
FIRMAN
FLYMAN
FORMAL
FORMAN
FORMAT
FULMAR
GAGMAN
GAMMAS
GASMAN
GEMMAE
GERMAN
GETMAD
GOTMAD
GRAMAS
GUNMAN
HAEMAT
HAGMAN
HERMAN
HETMAN
HIEMAL
HITMAN
ICEMAN
IMAMAN
INGMAR
KALMAR
KATMAI
KERMAN
KIDMAN
KIRMAN
KORMAN
LAMMAS
LAWMAN
LAYMAN
LEGMAN
LEMMAS
LLAMAS
MADMAN
MADMAX
MAGMAS
MAMMAL
MAMMAS
MAUMAU
MELMAC
MERMAN
MICMAC
MOMMAS
NETMAN
NEUMAN
NEWMAN
NEWMAR
NORMAL
NORMAN
OILMAN
OLDMAN
ONEMAN
PACMAN
PALMAS
PENMAN
PIEMAN
PITMAN
PRIMAL
RAGMAN
RODMAN
RUDMAN
SALMAN
SEAMAN
SGTMAJ
SHAMAN
SIGMAS
STOMAS
STOMAT
SUMMAE
SUMMAS
TARMAC
TASMAN
TAXMAN
THOMAS
TINMAN
TOAMAN
TODMAN
TRUMAN
TUBMAN
ULLMAN
WEIMAR
YEOMAN
YESMAN
ZEEMAN

•••M•A
AHIMSA
ALUMNA
ANEMIA
CRIMEA
GRAMPA
MIAMIA
NOUMEA
RHUMBA

••••MA
ALTIMA
BAHAMA
BRAHMA
CHACMA
CHROMA
CINEMA
COLIMA
DAGAMA
DHARMA
DODOMA
ENIGMA
FATIMA
INTIMA
JICAMA
KINEMA
MANAMA
MAXIMA
MAZUMA
MIASMA
MINIMA
OEDEMA
OPTIMA
PAJAMA
PALOMA
PANAMA
PLASMA
PNEUMA
PYJAMA
SCHEMA
SONOMA
STIGMA
TACOMA
THELMA
TRAUMA
ULTIMA
YAKIMA
YOYOMA
ZEUGMA

MB••••
MBUNDU

M•B•••
MABELL
MCBAIN
MOBBED
MOBCAP
MOBILE
MOBIUS
MOBLEY
MRBLUE

M••B••
MAMBAS
MAMBOS
MARBLE
MARBLY
MAYBES
MEMBER
MOBBED
MORBID
MUMBLE
MUMBLY

M•••B•
MAKEBA
MALABO
MALIBU
MCCABE
MCJOBS
MESABI
MUGABE

M••••B
MIDRIB
MIHRAB

•MB•••
AMBATO
AMBERS
AMBERY
AMBITS
AMBLED
AMBLER
AMBLES
AMBLIN
AMBUSH
EMBANK
EMBARK
EMBAYS
EMBDEN
EMBEDS
EMBERS
EMBLEM
EMBODY
EMBOSS
EMBRYO
IMBIBE
IMBRUE
IMBUED
IMBUES
UMBELS
UMBERS
UMBRAE
UMBRAL
UMBRAS
UMBRIA

•M•B••
AMEBAE
AMEBAS
AMEBIC

•M••B•
AMOEBA
IMBIBE

••MB••
BAMBOO
BOMBAY
BOMBED
BOMBER
BOMBES
BUMBLE
BUMBRY
CAMBER
COMBAT
COMBED
COMBER
COMBES
COMBOS
CUMBER
CYMBAL
DUMBER
DUMBLY
FUMBLE
GAMBIA
GAMBIT
GAMBLE
GAMBOL
GIMBAL
GIMBEL
GUMBEL
GUMBOS
GYMBAG
HOMBRE
HUMBLE
HUMBLY
HUMBUG
IAMBIC
JUMBLE
JUMBOS
KOMBAT
LAMBDA
LAMBED
LIMBED
LIMBER
LIMBOS
LIMBUS
LOMBOK
LUMBAR
LUMBER
MAMBAS
MAMBOS
MEMBER
MUMBLE
MUMBLY
NIMBLE
NIMBLY
NIMBUS
NUMBAT
NUMBED
NUMBER
NUMBLY
RAMBLA
RAMBLE
RUMBAS
RUMBLE
RUMBLY
SAMBAL
SAMBAR
SAMBAS
SIMBEL
SOMBER
SOMBRE
SYMBOL
TIMBAL
TIMBER
TIMBRE
TOMBAC
TOMBOY
TUMBLE
WAMBLE
WAMBLY
WIMBLE
WOMBAT
ZAMBIA
ZOMBIE

••M•B•
CAMEBY
COMEBY
DEMOBS

•••MB•
ABOMBS
AKIMBO
BRUMBY
CLIMBS
CRAMBO
CRUMBS
CRUMBY

FLAMBE
HBOMBS
PLUMBS
RHOMBI
RHOMBS
RHUMBA
RHUMBS
THUMBS

••••MB

APLOMB
BENUMB

MC••••

MCADAM
MCADOO
MCBAIN
MCCABE
MCCANN
MCCREA
MCGRAW
MCGREW
MCHALE
MCHUGH
MCJOBS
MCKUEN
MCLAIN
MCLEAN
MCNAIR

M•C•••

MACACO
MACAWS
MACEIO
MACHES
MACHOS
MACOUN
MACRAE
MACRON
MACROS
MACULA
MCCABE
MCCANN
MCCREA
MECCAS
MICHEL
MICKEY
MICMAC
MICRON
MICROS
MOCHAS
MOCKED
MOCKER
MOCKUP
MRCOOL
MUCINS
MUCKED
MUCKUP
MUCOSA
MUCOUS

M••C••

MADCAP
MANCHA
MANCHU
MARCEL
MARCHE
MARCIA
MARCIE
MARCOS
MARCUS
MASCOT
MECCAS
MERCED
MERCER
MESCAL
MINCED
MINCER
MINCES
MISCHA
MISCUE
MOBCAP
MOSCOW
MUDCAT
MULCTS
MUNCHY
MUNCIE
MURCIA
MUSCAT
MUSCLE
MUSCLY

M•••C•

MACACO
MALICE
MARACA
MEDICI
MEDICO
MEDICS
MEJICO
MENACE
MENSCH
MEXICO
MIMICS
MODOCS
MOHOCK
MOLOCH
MONACO
MONICA
MUNICH

M••••C

MANIAC
MANIOC
MANTIC
MASTIC
MELMAC
METRIC
MICMAC
MIXTEC
MOSAIC
MYOPIC
MYSTIC
MYTHIC

•MC•••

EMCEED
EMCEES

•M•C••

AMECHE
AMICES
AMICUS
SMACKS
SMOCKS

•M••C•

AMERCE
IMPACT
SMIRCH
SMOOCH
SMUTCH

•M•••C

AMEBIC
AMTRAC

••MC••

KIMCHI
TOMCAT

••M•C•

COMICS
LAMECH
MIMICS
OLMECS
OSMICS
POMACE
PUMICE
REMICK
SAMECH
SUMACS

••M••C

CYMRIC
HOMEEC
IAMBIC
ROMAIC
TOMBAC

•••M•C

ANEMIC
ANOMIC
ATOMIC
BIGMAC
CADMIC
COSMIC
FORMIC
GNOMIC
KARMIC
MELMAC
MICMAC
TARMAC

••••MC

RUNDMC

M•D•••

MADAME
MADAMS
MADCAP
MADDEN
MADDER
MADDIE
MADEDO
MADEIT
MADERO
MADEUP
MADMAN
MADMAX
MADMEN
MADRAS
MADRES
MADRID
MADSEN
MADTOM
MADURA
MADURO
MEDAKA
MEDALS
MEDDLE
MEDFLY
MEDGAR
MEDIAL
MEDIAN
MEDIAS
MEDICI
MEDICO
MEDICS
MEDINA
MEDIUM
MEDLAR
MEDLAT
MEDLEY
MEDUSA
MIDAIR
MIDDAY
MIDDEN
MIDDLE
MIDGES
MIDGET
MIDIAN
MIDLER
MIDORI
MIDRIB
MIDWAY
MODELA
MODELS
MODELT
MODEMS
MODENA
MODERN
MODEST
MODIFY
MODINE
MODISH
MODOCS
MODULE
MODULO
MUDCAT
MUDDED
MUDDER
MUDDLE
MUDEEL
MUDHEN
MUDPIE
MUDRAS

M••D••

MADDEN
MADDER
MADDIE
MAHDIS
MAIDEN
MAIDUS
MALDEN
MANDAN
MANDAY
MARDUK
MAYDAY
MCADAM
MCADOO
MEADOW
MEDDLE
MELDED
MENDED
MENDEL
MENDER
MENDES
MIDDAY
MIDDEN
MIDDLE
MILDER
MILDEW
MILDLY
MINDED
MINDER
MISDID
MOLDAU
MOLDED
MOLDER
MONDAY
MUDDED
MUDDER
MUDDLE
MURDER
MYRDAL

M•••D•

MADEDO
MAKEDO
MALADY
MASADA
MAUNDY
MBUNDU
MELODY
MENADO
MERIDA
MIKADO
MILADY
MONADS
MONODY
MOPEDS
MOULDS
MOULDY
MOUNDS
MRHYDE

M••••D

MADRID
MAENAD
MAILED
MALTED
MANNED
MAPPED
MARAUD
MARKED
MARLED
MARRED
MASHED
MASKED
MASSED
MATTED
MAULED
MELDED
MELTED
MENDED
MEOWED
MERCED
MERGED
MESHED
MESSED
METHOD
MEWLED
MIFFED
MILKED
MILLED
MILORD
MINCED
MINDED
MINTED
MISDID
MISLED
MISSED
MISTED
MITRED
MOANED
MOATED
MOBBED
MOCKED
MOILED
MOLDED
MOLTED
MONIED
MOONED
MOORED
MOOTED
MOPPED
MORBID
MOSHED
MOSSED
MOUSED
MSQUAD
MUCKED
MUDDED
MUFFED
MUGGED
MULLED
MUMMED
MUMPED
MUSHED
MUSSED
MUZZED
MYRIAD
MYWORD

•MD•••

EMDASH

•M•D••

AMADIS
AMADOU
AMEDEO
AMIDES
AMIDOL
AMIDST
EMBDEN
SMUDGE
SMUDGY

•M••D•

AMANDA
AMENDS
EMBEDS
EMBODY
EMENDS
IMELDA
IMPEDE

•M•••D

AMAZED
AMBLED
AMPHID
AMUSED
EMCEED
EMOTED
EMQUAD
IMAGED
IMBUED
IMPEND
SMILED
SMOKED

••MD••

CAMDEN
DUMDUM

••M•D•

ARMADA
COMEDY
DEMODE
JUMADA
KOMODO
LAMBDA
LAMEDH
LAMEDS
NOMADS
POMADE
RAMADA
REMADE
REMEDY
REMUDA
UNMADE

••M••D

ALMOND
ARMAND
BOMBED
BUMMED
BUMPED
CAMPED
COMBED
DAMMED
DAMNED
DAMPED
DEMAND
DEMOND
DIMMED
DUMPED
EDMOND
EDMUND
GAMMED
GEMMED
GUMMED
HAMMED
HEMMED
HUMMED
HUMPED
HYMNED
JAMMED
JUMPED
LAMBED
LAMMED
LEMOND
LIMBED
LIMNED
LIMPED
LIMPID
LOMOND
LUMPED
MUMMED
MUMPED
NIMROD
NUMBED
ORMOND
OSMOND
OSMUND
PUMPED
RAMMED
RAMPED
RAMROD
REMAND
REMEND
REMIND
REMOLD
RIMMED
ROMPED
SUMMED
TAMPED
TEMPED
TUMMED
VAMPED

•••M•D

BEAMED
BLAMED
BOOMED
BUMMED
CALMED
CHIMED
DAMMED
DEEMED
DIMMED
DOOMED
FARMED
FILMED
FIRMED
FLAMED
FOAMED
FORMED
FRAMED
GAMMED
GAUMED
GEMMED
GETMAD
GOTMAD
GRIMED
GUMMED
HAMMED
HARMED
HELMED
HEMMED
HUMMED
JAMMED
LAMMED
LOAMED
LOOMED
MUMMED
PALMED
PERMED
PLUMED
PREMED
PRIMED
RAMMED
REAMED
RHYMED
RIMMED
ROAMED
ROOMED
SEAMED
SEEMED
SHAMED
SLIMED
SPUMED
SUMMED
TALMUD
TEAMED
TEEMED
TERMED
THEMED
TUMMED
WARMED
WORMED
ZOOMED

ME••••

MEADOW
MEAGER
MEAGRE
MEALIE
MEANER
MEANIE
MEANLY
MEASLY
MECCAS
MEDAKA
MEDALS
MEDDLE
MEDFLY
MEDGAR
MEDIAL
MEDIAN
MEDIAS
MEDICI
MEDICO
MEDICS
MEDINA
MEDIUM
MEDLAR
MEDLAT
MEDLEY
MEDUSA
MEEKER
MEEKLY
MEERUT
MEETER
MEETLY
MEGALO
MEGARA
MEGILP
MEGOHM
MEJICO
MEKONG
MELANO
MELDED
MELEES
MELINA
MELLON
MELLOW
MELMAC
MELODY
MELONS
MELOTT
MELTED
MELTON
MELVIL
MELVIN
MELVYN
MEMBER
MEMNON
MEMOIR
MEMORY
MENACE
MENADO
MENAGE
MENDED
MENDEL
MENDER
MENDES
MENHIR
MENIAL
MENINX
MENJOU
MENKEN
MENNEN
MENSAE
MENSAL
MENSAS
MENSCH
MENTAL
MENTIS
MENTOR
MEOWED
MERCED
MERCER
MERELY
MEREST
MERGED
MERGER
MERGES
MERIDA
MERINO
MERITS
MERKEL
MERLIN
MERLON
MERLOT
MERMAN
MERMEN
MEROPE
MERSEY
MERTON
MERVYN
MESABI
MESCAL
MESHED
MESHES
MESMER
MESONS
MESSED
MESSES
MESSRS
MESSUP
METALS
METATE
METEOR
METERS
METHOD
METHYL
METIER
METING
METOPE
METRES
METRIC
METROS
METTLE
MEWING
MEWLED
MEWLER
MEXICO
MEZZOS

M•E•••

MAENAD
MEEKER
MEEKLY
MEERUT
MEETER
MEETLY
MYELIN

M••E••

MABELL
MACEIO
MADEDO
MADEIT
MADERO
MADEUP
MAKEBA
MAKEDO
MAKEIT
MAKERS
MAKEUP
MANEGE
MASERS
MASERU
MATERS
MATEYS
MAVENS
MAXENE
MAZERS
MCLEAN
MELEES
MERELY
MEREST
METEOR
METERS
MILERS
MIMEOS
MIMERS
MINERS
MISERS
MISERY
MITERS
MIXERS
MIZENS
MODELA
MODELS
MODELT
MODEMS
MODENA
MODERN
MODEST
MOIETY
MOLEST
MOMENT
MONERA
MONETA
MONEYS
MOPEDS
MOPERS
MOPERY
MOREAU
MOREEN
MORELS
MORENO
MOSEYS
MOTELS
MOTETS
MOVEIN
MOVEON
MOVERS
MOVEUP
MOWERS
MOYERS
MUDEEL
MULETA
MULEYS
MUSERS
MUSEUM
MUTELY
MUTEST
MYSELF

M•••E•

MACHES
MADDEN
MADDER
MADMEN
MADRES
MADSEN
MAGNET
MAGUEY
MAHLER
MAIDEN
MAILED
MAILER
MAILES
MAIZES
MAJGEN
MALDEN
MALLEE
MALLEI
MALLET
MALTED
MANGER
MANNED
MANNER
MANSES
MANTEL
MANUEL
MAPLES
MAPPED
MAPPER
MARCEL
MARGES
MARIEL
MARKED
MARKER
MARKET
MARLED
MARLEE
MARLEY
MARMEE
MARNER
MARRED
MARTEL
MARTEN
MARVEL
MASHED
MASHER
MASHES
MASKED
MASKER
MASSED
MASSES
MASSEY
MASTER
MATHER
MATTEA
MATTED
MATTEL
MATTER
MATTES
MAULED
MAULER
MAUMEE
MAUSER
MAUVES
MAYBES
MAYHEM
MAZIER
MCCREA
MCGREW
MCKUEN
MEAGER
MEANER
MEDLEY
MEEKER
MEETER
MELDED
MELEES
MELTED
MEMBER
MENDED
MENDEL
MENDER
MENDES
MENKEN
MENNEN
MEOWED
MERCED
MERCER
MERGED
MERGER
MERGES
MERKEL
MERMEN
MERSEY
MESHED
MESHES
MESMER
MESSED
MESSES
METIER
METRES
MEWLED
MEWLER
MICHEL
MICKEY
MIDDEN
MIDGES
MIDGET
MIDLER
MIFFED
MIGUEL
MILDER
MILDEW
MILIEU
MILKED
MILKER
MILLED
MILLER
MILLET
MILNER
MINCED
MINCER
MINCES
MINDED
MINDER
MINKES
MINTED
MINTER
MINUET
MINXES
MIRIER
MIRREN
MISLED
MISSED
MISSES
MISTED
MISTER
MITRED
MITRES
MITTEN
MIXTEC
MIZZEN
MOANED
MOANER
MOATED
MOBBED
MOBLEY
MOCKED
MOCKER
MOILED
MOILER
MOINES
MOIRES
MOLDED
MOLDER
MOLTED
MOLTEN
MOLTER
MONGER
MONIED
MONIES
MONKEY
MONTEL
MONTES
MONTEZ
MOONED
MOONEY
MOORED
MOOTED
MOPIER
MOPPED
MOPPER
MOPPET
MOREEN
MORGEN
MORLEY
MORSEL
MOSHED
MOSHER
MOSHES
MOSLEM
MOSSED
MOSSES
MOSTEL
MOTHER
MOTLEY
MOUSED
MOUSER
MOUSES
MOUSEY
MOVIES
MUCKED
MUDDED
MUDDER
MUDEEL
MUDHEN
MUFFED
MUGGED
MUGGER
MULLED
MULLER
MULLET
MUMMED
MUMMER
MUMPED
MUPPET
MURDER
MURIEL
MURRES
MURREY
MUSHED
MUSHER
MUSHES
MUSKEG
MUSKET
MUSSED
MUSSEL
MUSSES
MUSTER
MUTTER
MUZZED
MUZZES
MYOPES

M••••E

MACRAE
MADAME
MADDIE
MAGGIE
MAGPIE
MAISIE
MAITRE
MALATE
MALICE
MALLEE
MALONE
MANAGE
MANEGE
MANGLE
MANQUE
MANTLE
MARBLE
MARCHE
MARCIE
MARGIE
MARINE
MARLEE
MARMEE
MARNIE
MARPLE
MARQUE
MASHIE
MASQUE
MATTIE
MATURE
MAUMEE
MAXENE
MAXINE
MAXIXE
MCCABE
MCHALE
MEAGRE
MEALIE
MEANIE
MEDDLE
MENACE
MENAGE
MENSAE
MEROPE
METATE
METOPE
METTLE
MIDDLE
MIFUNE
MIGGLE
MILLIE
MILTIE
MINGLE
MINNIE
MINUTE
MIRAGE
MISCUE
MISUSE
MIZZLE
MOBILE
MODINE
MODULE
MOHAVE
MOJAVE
MOLINE
MOLTKE
MOMMIE
MONROE
MORALE
MOROSE
MOSQUE
MOTILE
MOTIVE
MOTTLE
MOUSSE
MRBLUE
MRHYDE
MUDDLE
MUDPIE
MUFFLE
MUGABE
MUMBLE
MUNCIE
MURINE
MUSCLE
MUSKIE
MUTATE
MUZZLE
MYRTLE
MYSORE

•ME•••

AMEBAE
AMEBAS
AMEBIC
AMECHE
AMEDEO
AMEERS
AMELIA
AMENDS
AMENRA
AMENTS
AMERCE
AMERSP
EMEERS
EMENDS
EMERGE
EMEUTE
IMELDA
KMESON
OMEGAS
OMELET
OMERTA
SMEARS
SMEARY
SMELLS
SMELLY
SMELTS
SMERSH
TMESIS

•M•E••

AMBERS
AMBERY
AMEERS
AMIENS
AMOEBA
AMPERE
AMVETS
EMBEDS
EMBERS
EMCEED
EMCEES
EMEERS
EMMETS
EMMETT
EMPERY
IMPEDE
IMPELS
IMPEND
IMPERF
UMBELS
UMBERS

•M••E•

AMAZED
AMAZES
AMBLED
AMBLER
AMBLES
AMEDEO
AMICES
AMIDES
AMINES
AMOLES
AMPLER
AMSTEL
AMULET
AMUSED
AMUSES
EMBDEN
EMBLEM
EMCEED
EMCEES
EMOTED
EMOTER
EMOTES
IMAGED
IMAGER
IMAGES
IMARET
IMBUED
IMBUES
IMOGEN
OMELET
SMILED
SMILER
SMILES
SMILEY
SMITES
SMOKED
SMOKER
SMOKES
SMOKEY

•M•••E
AMALIE
AMEBAE
AMECHE
AMERCE
AMPERE
AMPULE
BMOVIE
EMERGE
EMEUTE
EMIGRE
EMPIRE
IMBIBE
IMBRUE
IMFINE
IMMUNE
IMMURE
IMPALE
IMPEDE
IMPOSE
IMPURE
IMPUTE
SMUDGE
UMBRAE
UMPIRE

••ME••
ARMETS
CAMEAT
CAMEBY
CAMEIN
CAMELS
CAMEON
CAMEOS
CAMERA
CAMETO
CAMEUP
CEMENT
COMEAT
COMEBY
COMEDY
COMEIN
COMELY
COMEON
COMERS
COMETH
COMETO
COMETS
COMEUP
DEMEAN
EMMETS
EMMETT
ENMESH
FOMENT
GAMELY
GAMEST
GAMETE
GIMELS
HAMELN
HOMEEC
HOMELY
HOMERS
HUMERI
ISMENE
KHMERS
LAMECH
LAMEDH
LAMEDS
LAMELY
LAMENT
LAMESA
LAMEST
LIMENS
LIMEYS
LOMEIN
LUMENS
MIMEOS
MIMERS
MOMENT
NAMELY
NAMERS
NUMERO
NYMETS
OLMECS
PAMELA
POMELO
RAMEAU
RAMETS
REMEDY
REMELT
REMEND
ROMEOS
ROMERO
RUMENS
SAMECH
SAMEKH
SEMELE
SIMEON
SOMERS
TAMELY
TAMERS
TAMEST
TIMELY
TIMERS
TUMEFY
UNMEET
UNMESH
WOMENS
XIMENA
YEMENI

••M•E•
ARMIES
ARMLET
BOMBED
BOMBER
BOMBES
BUMMED
BUMMER
BUMPED
BUMPER
CAMBER
CAMDEN
CAMLET
CAMPED
CAMPER
COMBED
COMBER
COMBES
COMPEL
COMTES
CUMBER
DAMIEN
DAMMED
DAMNED
DAMPED
DAMPEN
DAMPER
DAMSEL
DEMIES
DIMMED
DIMMER
DOMREP
DUMBER
DUMPED
DUMPER
FEMMES
FUMIER
GAMIER
GAMMED
GAMMER
GEMMED
GIMBEL
GIMLET
GIMMES
GUMBEL
GUMMED
HAMLET
HAMMED
HAMMER
HAMPER
HEMMED
HEMMER
HOMEEC
HOMIER
HUMMED
HUMMER
HUMPED
HUMVEE
HYMNED
JAMMED
JAMMER
JUMPED
JUMPER
KUMMEL
LAMBED
LAMMED
LEMUEL
LIMBED
LIMBER
LIMIER
LIMNED
LIMNER
LIMPED
LIMPER
LIMPET
LUMBER
LUMPED
LUMPEN
LUMPER
MEMBER
MUMMED
MUMMER
MUMPED
NUMBED
NUMBER
PAMPER
POMMEE
POMMEL
POMPEY
PUMMEL
PUMPED
PUMPER
RAMIES
RAMJET
RAMMED
RAMPED
RAMSES
RAMSEY
RIMIER
RIMMED
ROMMEL
ROMNEY
ROMPED
ROMPER
RUMMER
SAMLET
SAMUEL
SEMPER
SIMBEL
SIMMER
SIMNEL
SIMPER
SOMBER
SOMMER
SUMMED
SUMMER
SUMNER
SUMTER
TAMPED
TAMPER
TEMPED
TEMPEH
TEMPER
TIMBER
TUMMED
UNMEET
VAMPED
VAMPER
WIMSEY
YAMMER
ZIMMER

••M••E
ADMIRE
ARMURE
BEMINE
BEMIRE
BEMUSE
BUMBLE
CAMISE
COMATE
DAMAGE
DAMONE
DAMORE
DEMISE
DEMODE
DEMOTE
DEMURE
DIMPLE
DOMINE
ELMORE
ERMINE
EXMORE
FAMINE
FEMALE
FUMBLE
GAMBLE
GAMETE
GAMINE
GEMMAE
GEMOTE
HAMITE
HOMAGE
HOMBRE
HUMANE
HUMBLE
HUMVEE
IMMUNE
IMMURE
INMATE
ISMENE
JAMOKE
JIMMIE
JUMBLE
LAMAZE
MOMMIE
MUMBLE
NIMBLE
NOMINE
NOMORE
OSMOSE
POMACE
POMADE
POMMEE
PUMICE
RAMATE
RAMBLE
RAMONE
RAMOSE
REMADE
REMAKE
REMISE
REMOTE
REMOVE
RIMOSE
RIMPLE
RUMBLE
RUMPLE
SAMITE
SAMMIE
SAMPLE
SEMELE
SEMITE
SEMPRE
SIMILE
SIMONE
SIMPLE
SOMBRE
SUMMAE
TAMALE
TEMPLE
TIMBRE
TUMBLE
UNMADE
UNMAKE
WAMBLE
WIMBLE
WIMPLE
ZOMBIE
ZYMASE

•••ME•
ACUMEN
AIRMEN
ANIMES
APEMEN
BADMEN
BARMEN
BATMEN
BEAMED
BIOMES
BLAMED
BLAMES
BLIMEY
BOOMED
BOOMER
BOWMEN
BREMEN
BRUMES
BUMMED
BUMMER
BUSMEN
CALMED
CALMER
CARMEL
CARMEN
CERMET
CHIMED
CHIMES
CLIMES
CONMEN
COWMEN
CREMES
CRIMEA
CRIMES
DAMMED
DEEMED
DIMMED
DIMMER
DISMES
DOLMEN
DOOMED
DORMER
EDAMES
ENAMEL
ENDMEN
FARMED
FARMER
FBIMEN
FEMMES
FENMEN
FILMED
FIRMED
FIRMER
FLAMED
FLAMES
FLUMES
FLYMEN
FOAMED
FORMED
FORMER
FRAMED
FRAMES
GAGMEN
GAMMED
GAMMER
GASMEN
GAUMED
GEMMED
GIMMES
GNOMES
GRIMED
GRIMES
GUMMED
GUNMEN
HAMMED
HAMMER
HARMED
HELMED
HELMET
HEMMED
HEMMER
HERMES
HITMEN
HOLMES
HORMEL
HUMMED
HUMMER
ICEMEN
ILLMET
ISOMER
JAMMED
JAMMER
KERMES
KILMER
KISMET
KRAMER
KUMMEL
LAMMED
LAWMEN
LAYMEN
LEGMEN
LOAMED
LOOMED
MADMEN
MARMEE
MAUMEE
MERMEN
MESMER
MUMMED
MUMMER
NETMEN
NEUMES
NIAMEY
NOUMEA
NUTMEG
OILMEN
OLDMEN
PALMED
PALMER
PELMET
PENMEN
PERMED
PIEMEN
PITMEN
PLUMED
PLUMES
POMMEE
POMMEL
PREMED
PRIMED
PRIMER
PRIMES
PUMMEL
RAGMEN
RAMMED
REAMED
REAMER
RHAMES
RHYMED
RHYMER
RHYMES
RIMMED
ROAMED
ROAMER
ROHMER
ROMMEL
ROOMED
ROOMER
RUMMER
SEAMED
SEAMEN
SEEMED
SHAMED
SHAMES
SIMMER
SLIMED
SLIMES
SOMMER
SPUMED
SPUMES
STAMEN
STUMER
SUMMED
SUMMER
TAXMEN
TEAMED
TEEMED
TERMED
TEXMEX
THAMES
THEMED
THEMES
TINMEN
TUMMED
WARMED
WARMER
WORMED
XIAMEN
YAMMER
YEOMEN
YESMEN
ZIMMER
ZOOMED

•••M•E
ANOMIE
FLAMBE
GEMMAE
GRAMME
GRIMKE
GUIMPE
JIMMIE
MARMEE
MAUMEE
MOMMIE
POMMEE
PREMIE
ROOMIE
SAMMIE
STYMIE
SUMMAE
TROMPE

••••ME
AFLAME
AFRAME
ASSUME
ATHOME
BECAME
BECOME
BIREME
BYNAME
CHROME
DANGME
DEARME
DEFAME
ENZYME
GENOME
GOHOME
GRAMME
ILLUME
INCOME
INTIME
JEROME
KINGME
LEGUME
LEXEME
MADAME
NONAME
ONTIME
RACEME
RADOME
REGIME
RELUME
RENAME
RESUME
RETIME
SALOME
SCHEME
SESAME
SHOWME
UGSOME
UPTIME
VOLUME

M•F•••
MIFFED
MIFUNE
MUFASA
MUFFED
MUFFIN
MUFFLE
MUFTIS

M••F••
MANFUL
MAYFLY
MEDFLY
MIFFED
MISFIT
MUFFED
MUFFIN
MUFFLE

M•••F•
MINIFY
MODIFY
MOTIFS

M••••F
MASSIF
MYSELF

•MF•••
IMFINE

•M••F•
AMALFI
SMURFS

•M•••F
IMPERF

••MF••
AIMFOR
AIMFUL
ARMFUL
COMFIT

••M•F•
RAMIFY
TUMEFY

M•G•••
MAGGIE
MAGGIO
MAGMAS
MAGNET
MAGNON
MAGNUM
MAGNUS
MAGPIE
MAGUEY
MAGYAR
MCGRAW
MCGREW
MEGALO
MEGARA
MEGILP
MEGOHM
MIGGLE
MIGHTY
MIGNON
MIGUEL
MOGULS
MUGABE
MUGGED
MUGGER
MUGHOS
MYGIRL

M••G••
MAGGIE
MAGGIO
MAJGEN
MANGER
MANGLE
MANGOS
MARGAY
MARGES
MARGIE
MARGIN
MARGOT
MEAGER
MEAGRE
MEDGAR
MERGED
MERGER
MERGES
MIDGES
MIDGET
MIGGLE
MINGLE
MONGER
MONGOL
MORGAN
MORGEN
MOWGLI
MUGGED
MUGGER
MUNGOS

M•••G•
MALAGA
MALIGN
MANAGE
MANEGE
MCHUGH
MENAGE
MIRAGE

M••••G
MAKING
MATING
MAYTAG
MEKONG
METING
MEWING
MIKING
MIMING
MINING
MIRING
MIXING
MOOING
MOPING
MOVING
MOWING
MUSING
MUSKEG
MUTING

•M•G••
AMIGAS
AMIGOS
EMIGRE
IMAGED
IMAGER
IMAGES
IMOGEN
OMEGAS
SMOGGY
SMUGLY

•M••G•
EMERGE
HMONGS
IMPUGN
SMOGGY
SMUDGE
SMUDGY

•M•••G
IMPING

••M•G•
ARMAGH
DAMAGE
HOMAGE

••M••G
AIMING
ARMING
COMING
DOMING
FUMING
GAMING
GYMBAG
HOMING
HUMBUG
LAMING
LIMING
MIMING
NAMING
RIMING
TAMING
TIMING

•••M•G
NUTMEG
WONMUG

M•H•••
MAHDIS
MAHLER
MAHOUT
MAHZOR
MCHALE
MCHUGH
MIHRAB
MOHAIR
MOHAVE
MOHAWK
MOHOCK
MOHURS
MRHYDE

M••H••
MACHES
MACHOS
MASHED
MASHER
MASHES
MASHIE
MATHER
MATHIS
MAYHAP
MAYHEM
MENHIR
MESHED
MESHES
METHOD
METHYL
MICHEL
MIGHTY
MISHAP
MISHIT
MOCHAS
MOSHAV
MOSHED
MOSHER
MOSHES
MOTHER
MOTHRA
MUDHEN
MUGHOS
MUSHED
MUSHER
MUSHES
MUZHIK
MYOHMY
MYTHIC
MYTHOI
MYTHOL
MYTHOS

M•••H•
MANCHA
MANCHU
MARCHE
MARSHA
MARSHY
MARTHA
MEGOHM
MISCHA
MONTHS
MORPHO
MORPHS
MORPHY
MOUTHS
MOUTHY
MUNCHY
MURPHY
MYNAHS
MYRRHS

M••••H
MARIAH
MARISH
MATZOH
MCHUGH
MENSCH
MODISH
MOLOCH
MOOLAH
MOPISH
MULISH
MULLAH
MUNICH

•MH•••
AMHARA

•M•H••
AMPHID
OMAHAN
OMAHAS

•M••H•
AMECHE
SMITHS
SMITHY

•M•••H
AMBUSH
EMDASH
IMPISH
SMERSH
SMIRCH
SMOOCH
SMOOTH
SMUTCH

••M•H•
HUMPHS
KIMCHI
LYMPHS
NYMPHS
YAMAHA

••M••H
ARMAGH
COMETH
ENMESH
FAMISH
IOMOTH
LAMECH
LAMEDH
NAMATH
OOMPAH
SAMECH
SAMEKH
TEMPEH
UNMESH

•••M•H
WARMTH

MI••••
MIAMIA
MIASMA
MICHEL
MICKEY
MICMAC
MICRON
MICROS
MIDAIR
MIDDAY
MIDDEN
MIDDLE
MIDGES
MIDGET
MIDIAN
MIDLER
MIDORI
MIDRIB
MIDWAY
MIFFED
MIFUNE
MIGGLE
MIGHTY
MIGNON
MIGUEL
MIHRAB
MIKADO
MIKING
MIKITA
MILADY
MILANO
MILDER
MILDEW
MILDLY
MILERS
MILIEU
MILKED
MILKER
MILLAY
MILLED
MILLER
MILLET
MILLIE
MILNER
MILORD
MILOSZ
MILPAS
MILSAP
MILTIE
MILTON
MIMEOS
MIMERS
MIMICS
MIMING
MIMOSA
MINCED
MINCER
MINCES
MINDED
MINDER
MINERS
MINGLE
MINIFY
MINIMA
MINIMS
MINING
MINION
MINIUM
MINKES
MINNIE
MINNOW
MINOAN
MINORS
MINTED
MINTER
MINUET
MINUIT
MINUTE
MINXES
MINYAN
MIOSIS
MIRAGE
MIRIAM
MIRIER
MIRING
MIRREN
MIRROR
MISCHA
MISCUE
MISDID
MISERS
MISERY
MISFIT
MISHAP
MISHIT
MISLAY
MISLED
MISSAL
MISSAY
MISSED
MISSES
MISSIS
MISSUS
MISTED
MISTER
MISUSE
MITERS
MITRAL
MITRED
MITRES
MITTEN
MIWOKS
MIXERS
MIXING
MIXTEC
MIXUPS
MIZENS
MIZZEN
MIZZLE

M•I•••
MAIDEN
MAIDUS
MAILED
MAILER
MAILES
MAILIN
MAINLY
MAISIE
MAITAI
MAITRE
MAIZES
MOIETY
MOILED
MOILER
MOINES
MOIRES

M••I••
MAKING
MALIBU
MALICE
MALIGN
MANIAC
MANIAS
MANILA
MANIOC
MAOISM
MAOIST
MARIAH
MARIAN
MARIEL
MARIKO
MARILU
MARINA
MARINE
MARINO
MARION
MARISA
MARISH
MARIST
MARIUS
MATING
MATINS
MAXIMA
MAXIMS
MAXINE
MAXIXE
MAZIER
MAZILY
MEDIAL
MEDIAN
MEDIAS
MEDICI
MEDICO
MEDICS
MEDINA
MEDIUM
MEGILP
MEJICO
MELINA
MENIAL
MENINX
MERIDA
MERINO
MERITS
METIER
METING
MEWING
MEXICO
MIDIAN
MIKING
MIKITA
MILIEU
MIMICS
MIMING
MINIFY
MINIMA
MINIMS
MINING
MINION
MINIUM
MIRIAM
MIRIER
MIRING
MIXING
MOBILE
MOBIUS
MODIFY
MODINE
MODISH
MOLINE
MONICA
MONIED
MONIES
MONISM
MONIST
MOOING
MOPIER
MOPING
MOPISH
MORION
MORITA
MORITZ
MOTIFS
MOTILE
MOTION
MOTIVE
MOVIES
MOVING
MOWING
MUCINS
MULISH
MUNICH
MURIEL
MURINE
MUSIAL
MUSING
MUTING
MUTINY
MYGIRL
MYRIAD

M•••I•
MACEIO
MADDIE
MADEIT
MADRID
MAGGIE
MAGGIO
MAGPIE
MAHDIS
MAILIN
MAISIE
MAJLIS
MAKEIT
MALKIN
MALTIN
MANNIX
MANTIC
MANTIS
MAORIS
MAQUIS
MARCIA
MARCIE
MARGIE
MARGIN
MARLIN
MARNIE
MARTIN
MARVIN
MASAIS
MASHIE
MASSIF
MASTIC
MATHIS
MATLIN
MATRIX
MATTIE
MCBAIN
MCLAIN
MCNAIR
MEALIE
MEANIE
MELVIL
MELVIN

MEMOIR MENHIR MENTIS MERLIN METRIC MIAMIA MIDAIR MIDRIB MILLIE MILTIE MINNIE MINUIT MIOSIS MISDID MISFIT MISHIT MISSIS MOHAIR MOMMIE MORBID MORRIS MOSAIC MOULIN MOVEIN MUDPIE MUFFIN MUFTIS MUNCIE MUNTIN MURCIA MUSKIE MUSLIM MUSLIN MUZHIK MYELIN MYOPIA MYOPIC MYOSIN MYOSIS MYSTIC MYTHIC

M••••I

MAITAI MALAWI MALLEI MALOTI MAOTAI MEDICI MESABI MIDORI MORONI MOWGLI MYTHOI

•MI•••

AMICES AMICUS AMIDES AMIDOL AMIDST AMIENS AMIGAS AMIGOS AMINES AMINOR AMINUS BMINOR BMINUS CMINOR CMINUS DMINOR DMINUS DMITRI EMIGRE EMILIA EMILIO EMINOR FMINOR GMINOR SMILAX SMILED SMILER SMILES SMILEY SMILIN SMIRCH SMIRKS SMIRKY SMITES SMITHS SMITHY UMIAKS

•M•I••

AMBITS AMNION EMAILS EMPIRE IMBIBE IMFINE IMPING IMPISH OMNIUM UMPIRE

•M••I•

AMADIS AMALIE AMATIS AMBLIN AMEBIC AMELIA AMPHID BMOVIE EMILIA EMILIO IMPAIR OMANIS SMILIN TMESIS UMBRIA

•M•••I

AMALFI DMITRI SMALTI

••MI••

ADMIRE ADMITS AIMING ARMIES ARMING BEMINE BEMIRE BIMINI CAMINO CAMION CAMISE COMICS COMING COMITY DAMIEN DAMITA DEMIES DEMISE DEMITS DIMITY DOMINE DOMING DOMINI DOMINO ELMIRA ENMITY ERMINE FAMILY FAMINE FAMISH FUMIER FUMING GAMIER GAMILY GAMINE GAMING GAMINS GEMINI HAMILL HAMITE HOMIER HOMILY HOMING HOMINY JIMINY KUMISS LAMIAS LAMINA LAMING LIMIER LIMING LIMITS LUMINA MIMICS MIMING NAMING NIMINY NIMITZ NOMINE NUMINA OSMICS OSMIUM PAMIRS PIMINY PUMICE RAMIES RAMIFY REMICK REMIND REMISE REMISS REMITS RIMIER RIMING RIMINI RUMINA SAMIAM SAMITE SEMITE SIMIAN SIMILE TAMILS TAMING TIMING ZAMIAS

••M•I•

ARMPIT CAMEIN COMEIN COMFIT COMMIT COMMIX CYMRIC DIMWIT DOMAIN GAMBIA GAMBIT HAMLIN HEMSIN IAMBIC JAMSIN JIMMIE JUMPIN KEMPIS LIMPID LOMEIN MEMOIR MOMMIE REMAIL REMAIN ROMAIC SAMMIE SUMMIT TOMLIN TOMMIX TOMTIT USMAIL ZAMBIA ZOMBIE

••M••I

ARMANI BIMINI CUMULI DOMANI DOMINI GEMINI HUMERI KIMCHI RIMINI ROMAJI SOMALI TUMULI YEMENI

•••MI•

ANEMIA ANEMIC ANOMIC ANOMIE ARAMIS ATOMIC CADMIC CHEMIN COMMIT COMMIX COSMIC DERMIS ELEMIS FORMIC GNOMIC HERMIT JIMMIE KARMIC KERMIS KERMIT MIAMIA MOMMIE PERMIT PREMIE ROOMIE SAMMIE SHAMIR STYMIE SUBMIT SUMMIT SWAMIS TOMMIX VERMIN ZOOMIN

•••M•I

ALUMNI DROMOI KATMAI RHOMBI SCAMPI

••••MI

BATUMI BONAMI DOREMI ISTHMI SALAMI SURIMI TATAMI

M•J•••

MAJGEN MAJLIS MAJORS MCJOBS MEJICO MOJAVE

M••J••

MENJOU

•M•J••

AMAJOR BMAJOR CMAJOR DMAJOR EMAJOR FMAJOR GMAJOR

••MJ••

RAMJET

••M•J•

ROMAJI

•••M•J

SGTMAJ

M•K•••

MAKALU MAKEBA MAKEDO MAKEIT MAKERS MAKEUP MAKING MAKUTA MCKUEN MEKONG MIKADO MIKING MIKITA MUKLUK

M••K••

MALKIN MARKED MARKER MARKET MARKKA MARKUP MASKED MASKER MEEKER MEEKLY MENKEN MERKEL MICKEY MILKED MILKER MINKES MOCKED MOCKER MOCKUP MONKEY MOSKVA MUCKED MUCKUP MUSKEG MUSKET MUSKIE MUSKOX

M•••K•

MARIKO MARKKA MEDAKA MIWOKS MOLTKE

M••••K

MARDUK MOHAWK MOHOCK MUKLUK MUZHIK

•M•K••

SMOKED SMOKER SMOKES SMOKEY

•M••K•

DMARKS SMACKS SMIRKS SMIRKY SMOCKS UMIAKS

•M•••K

AMTRAK EMBANK EMBARK

••M•K•

BAMAKO JAMOKE REMAKE RIMSKY SAMEKH UNMAKE

••M••K

DAMASK LOMBOK REMARK REMICK STMARK UNMASK

•••MK•

GRIMKE

M•L•••

MALABO MALADY MALAGA MALATE MALAWI MALAYA MALAYS MALDEN MALIBU MALICE MALIGN MALKIN MALLEE MALLEI MALLET MALLOW MALONE MALORY MALOTI MALTED MALTIN MCLAIN MCLEAN MELANO MELDED MELEES MELINA MELLON MELLOW MELMAC MELODY MELONS MELOTT MELTED MELTON MELVIL MELVIN MELVYN MILADY MILANO MILDER MILDEW MILDLY MILERS MILIEU MILKED MILKER MILLAY MILLED MILLER MILLET MILLIE MILNER MILORD MILOSZ MILPAS MILSAP MILTIE MILTON MOLARS MOLDAU MOLDED MOLDER MOLEST MOLINE MOLNAR MOLOCH MOLOPO MOLTED MOLTEN MOLTER MOLTKE MULCTS MULETA MULEYS MULISH MULLAH MULLAS MULLED MULLER MULLET MULTUM

M••L••

MAHLER MAILED MAILER MAILES MAILIN MAJLIS MALLEE MALLEI MALLET MALLOW MAPLES MARLED MARLEE MARLEY MARLIN MARLON MATLIN MAULED MAULER MEALIE MEDLAR MEDLAT MEDLEY MELLON MELLOW MERLIN MERLON MERLOT MEWLED MEWLER MIDLER MILLAY MILLED MILLER MILLET MILLIE MISLAY MISLED MOBLEY MOILED MOILER MOOLAH MORLEY MOSLEM MOTLEY MOULDS MOULDY MOULIN MOULTS MRBLUE MUKLUK MULLAH MULLAS MULLED MULLER MULLET MUSLIM MUSLIN MYELIN

M•••L•

MABELL MACULA MAINLY MAKALU MANGLE MANILA MANTLE MARBLE MARBLY MARILU MARPLE MAYFLY MAZILY MAZOLA MCHALE MEANLY MEASLY MEDALS MEDDLE MEDFLY MEEKLY MEETLY MEGALO MEGILP MERELY METALS METTLE MIDDLE MIGGLE MILDLY MINGLE MIZZLE MOBILE MODELA MODELS MODELT MODULE MODULO MOGULS MORALE MORALS MORELS MOSTLY MOTELS MOTILE MOTTLE MOWGLI MUDDLE MUFFLE MUMBLE MUMBLY MURALS MUSCLE MUSCLY MUTELY MUZZLE MYRTLE MYSELF

M••••L

MABELL MAMMAL MANFUL MANTEL MANUAL MANUEL MARCEL MARIEL MARTEL MARVEL MATTEL MEDIAL MELVIL MENDEL MENIAL MENSAL MENTAL MERKEL MESCAL METHYL MICHEL MIGUEL MISSAL MITRAL MONGOL MONTEL MORSEL MORTAL MOSTEL MRCOOL MUDEEL MURIEL MUSIAL MUSSEL MUTUAL MYGIRL MYRDAL MYTHOL

•ML•••

UMLAUT

•M•L••

AMALFI AMALIE AMBLED AMBLER AMBLES AMBLIN AMELIA AMOLES AMPLER AMULET EMBLEM EMILIA EMILIO EMPLOY IMELDA OMELET SMALLS SMALTI SMALTO SMELLS SMELLY SMELTS SMILAX SMILED SMILER SMILES SMILEY SMILIN SMOLTS

•M••L•

AMPULE AMPULS EMAILS IMPALA IMPALE IMPELS SMALLS SMELLS SMELLY SMUGLY UMBELS

•M•••L

AMATOL AMIDOL AMORAL AMSTEL UMBRAL

••ML••

ARMLET CAMLET GIMLET HAMLET HAMLIN SAMLET TOMLIN

••M•L•

BUMBLE CAMELS COMELY COMPLY CUMULI CUMULO DAMPLY DIMPLE DIMPLY DUMBLY FAMILY FEMALE FUMBLE GAMBLE GAMELY GAMILY GIMELS HAMALS HAMELN HAMILL HOMELY HOMILY HUMBLE HUMBLY JUMBLE KAMALA LAMELY LIMPLY MUMBLE MUMBLY NAMELY NIMBLE NIMBLY NUMBLY ORMOLU PAMELA POMELO RAMBLA RAMBLE REMELT REMOLD RIMPLE ROMOLA RUMBLE RUMBLY RUMPLE RUMPLY SAMPLE SEMELE SIMILE SIMPLE SIMPLY SOMALI STMALO TAMALE TAMELY TAMILS TEMPLE TIMELY TUMBLE TUMULI TUMULT WAMBLE WAMBLY WIMBLE WIMPLE

••M••L

AIMFUL ARMFUL COMPEL CYMBAL DAMSEL GAMBOL GIMBAL GIMBEL GUMBEL HAMILL HYMNAL JAMAAL KUMMEL LEMUEL MAMMAL POMMEL PUMMEL REMAIL ROMMEL SAMBAL SAMUEL SIMBEL SIMNEL SYMBOL TIMBAL USMAIL

•••ML•

CALMLY FIRMLY GLUMLY GRIMLY PRIMLY SEEMLY SLIMLY TRIMLY WARMLY

•••M•L

ANIMAL BRUMAL CARMEL DERMAL DISMAL ENAMEL ETYMOL FORMAL HIEMAL HORMEL KUMMEL MAMMAL NORMAL POMMEL PRIMAL PUMMEL ROMMEL

M•M•••

MAMBAS MAMBOS MAMMAL MAMMAS MAMMON MEMBER MEMNON MEMOIR MEMORY MIMEOS MIMERS MIMICS MIMING MIMOSA MOMENT MOMMAS MOMMIE MRMOTO MUMBLE MUMBLY MUMMED MUMMER MUMPED

M••M••

MADMAN MADMAX MADMEN MAGMAS MAMMAL MAMMAS MAMMON MARMEE MARMOT MAUMAU MAUMEE MELMAC MERMAN MERMEN MESMER MIAMIA MICMAC MOMMAS MOMMIE MORMON MOTMOT MUMMED MUMMER MURMUR MUUMUU

M•••M•

MADAME MADAMS MANAMA MAXIMA MAXIMS MAZUMA MIASMA MINIMA MINIMS MODEMS MYOHMY

M••••M

MADTOM MAGNUM MAOISM MAYHEM MCADAM MEDIUM MEGOHM MINIUM MIRIAM MONISM MOSLEM MULTUM MUSEUM MUSLIM

•MM•••

EMMETS EMMETT IMMUNE IMMUNO IMMURE

•M•M••

IMAMAN

•M••M•

SMARMY

•M•••M

EMBLEM OMASUM OMNIUM

••MM••

BUMMED BUMMER COMMAS COMMIT COMMIX COMMON DAMMAR DAMMED DIMMED DIMMER FEMMES GAMMAS GAMMED GAMMER GAMMON GEMMAE GEMMED GIMMES GUMMED HAMMED HAMMER HEMMED HEMMER HUMMED HUMMER HUMMUS JAMMED JAMMER JIMMIE KUMMEL LAMMAS LAMMED LEMMAS LEMMON LUMMOX MAMMAL MAMMAS MAMMON MOMMAS MOMMIE MUMMED MUMMER POMMEE POMMEL PUMMEL RAMMED RIMMED ROMMEL RUMMER SAMMIE SIMMER SOMMER SUMMAE SUMMAS SUMMED SUMMER SUMMIT SUMMON TAMMUZ TOMMIX TUMMED YAMMER ZIMMER

••M••M

DIMSUM DUMDUM OSMIUM POMPOM SAMIAM TAMTAM TOMTOM WAMPUM YUMYUM

•••MM•

CHAMMY CHUMMY CLAMMY CRUMMY GRAMME GRAMMY PLUMMY SCUMMY SHIMMY SLUMMY WHAMMO WHAMMY

•••M•M

PRIMUM

M•N•••

MANAGE MANAMA MANANA MANAUS MANCHA MANCHU MANDAN MANDAY MANEGE MANFUL MANGER MANGLE MANGOS MANIAC MANIAS MANILA MANIOC MANNED MANNER MANNIX MANORS MANQUE MANRAY MANSES MANTAS MANTEL MANTIC MANTIS MANTLE MANTRA MANTUA MANUAL MANUEL MCNAIR MENACE MENADO MENAGE MENDED MENDEL MENDER MENDES MENHIR MENIAL MENINX MENJOU MENKEN MENNEN MENSAE MENSAL MENSAS MENSCH MENTAL MENTIS MENTOR MINCED MINCER MINCES MINDED MINDER MINERS MINGLE MINIFY MINIMA MINIMS MINING MINION MINIUM MINKES MINNIE MINNOW MINOAN MINORS MINTED MINTER MINUET MINUIT MINUTE MINXES MINYAN MONACO MONADS MONDAY MONERA MONETA MONEYS MONGER MONGOL MONICA MONIED MONIES MONISM MONIST MONKEY MONODY MONROE MONTEL MONTES MONTEZ MONTHS MUNCHY MUNCIE MUNGOS MUNICH MUNTIN MYNAHS

M••N••

MAENAD MAGNET MAGNON MAGNUM MAGNUS MAINLY

MANNED
MANNER
MANNIX
MARNER
MARNIE
MAUNDY
MBUNDU
MEANER
MEANIE
MEANLY
MEMNON
MENNEN
MIGNON
MILNER
MINNIE
MINNOW
MOANED
MOANER
MOINES
MOLNAR
MOONED
MOONEY
MORNAY
MOUNDS
MOUNTS
MOUNTY

M•••N•

MAKING
MALONE
MANANA
MARINA
MARINE
MARINO
MASONS
MATING
MATINS
MAVENS
MAXENE
MAXINE
MAYANS
MCCANN
MEDINA
MEKONG
MELANO
MELINA
MELONS
MENINX
MERINO
MESONS
METING
MEWING
MIFUNE
MIKING
MILANO
MIMING
MINING
MIRING
MIXING
MIZENS
MODENA
MODINE
MOLINE
MOMENT
MOOING
MOPING
MORANT
MORENO
MORONI
MORONS
MOURNS
MOVING
MOWING
MUCINS
MURANO
MURINE
MUSING
MUSTNT
MUTANT
MUTING
MUTINY

M••••N

MACOUN
MACRON
MADDEN
MADMAN
MADMEN
MADSEN
MAGNON
MAIDEN
MAILIN
MAJGEN
MALDEN
MALIGN
MALKIN
MALTIN
MAMMON
MANDAN
MARGIN
MARIAN
MARION
MARLIN
MARLON
MAROON
MARRON
MARTEN
MARTIN
MARVIN
MATLIN
MATRON
MCBAIN
MCCANN
MCKUEN
MCLAIN
MCLEAN
MEDIAN
MELLON
MELTON
MELVIN
MELVYN
MEMNON
MENKEN
MENNEN
MERLIN
MERLON
MERMAN
MERMEN
MERTON
MERVYN
MICRON
MIDDEN
MIDIAN
MIGNON
MILTON
MINION
MINOAN
MINYAN
MIRREN
MITTEN
MIZZEN
MODERN
MOLTEN
MOREEN
MORGAN
MORGEN
MORION
MORMON
MORTON
MOTION
MOTOWN
MOULIN
MOUTON
MOVEIN
MOVEON
MUDHEN
MUFFIN
MUNTIN
MUSLIN
MUTTON
MYELIN
MYOSIN

•MN•••

AMNION
OMNIUM

•M•N••

AMANDA
AMENDS
AMENRA
AMENTS
AMINES
AMINOR
AMINUS
BMINOR
BMINUS
CMINOR
CMINUS
DMINOR
DMINUS
EMENDS
EMINOR
FMINOR
GMINOR
HMONGS
OMANIS

•M••N•

AMIENS
AMOUNT
EMBANK
IMFINE
IMMUNE
IMMUNO
IMPEND
IMPING
SMYRNA

•M•••N

AMAZON
AMBLIN
AMNION
AMYTAN
EMBDEN
IMAMAN
IMOGEN
IMPUGN
KMESON
OMAHAN
SMILIN

••MN••

DAMNED
HYMNAL
HYMNED
LEMNOS
LIMNED
LIMNER
MEMNON
ROMNEY
SIMNEL
SUMNER

••M•N•

AIMING
ALMOND
ARMAND
ARMANI
ARMING
AUMONT
BEMINE
BIMINI
CAMINO
CEMENT
COMING
DAMONE
DEMAND
DEMOND
DEMONS
DOMANI
DOMINE
DOMING
DOMINI
DOMINO
DUMONT
EDMOND
EDMUND
EGMONT
ERMINE
FAMINE
FOMENT
FUMING
GAMINE
GAMING
GAMINS
GEMINI
HOMING
HOMINY
HUMANE
HUMANS
IMMUNE
IMMUNO
ISMENE
JIMINY
KIMONO
LAMENT
LAMINA
LAMING
LAMONT
LEMANS
LEMOND
LEMONS
LEMONY
LIMENS
LIMING
LOMOND
LUMENS
LUMINA
MIMING
MOMENT
NAMING
NIMINY
NOMINE
NUMINA
ORMOND
OSMOND
OSMUND
PIMINY
POMONA
RAMONA
RAMONE
REMAND
REMANS
REMEND
REMIND
RIMING
RIMINI
ROMANO
ROMANS
ROMANY
RUMENS
RUMINA
SIMONE
SIMONY
SOMANY
TAMING
TIMING
UNMANS
WOMENS
XIMENA
YEMENI

••M••N

BEMOAN
CAMDEN
CAMEIN
CAMEON
CAMION
COMEIN
COMEON
COMMON
DAMIEN
DAMPEN
DAMSON
DEMEAN
DOMAIN
GAMMON
HAMELN
HAMLIN
HEMSIN
JAMSIN
JIMSON
JUMPIN
JUMPON
LEMMON
LOMEIN
LUMPEN
MAMMON
MEMNON
POMPON
QUMRAN
RAMSON
REMAIN
REMOWN
SAMOAN
SAMPAN
SAMSON
SIMEON
SIMIAN
SUMMON
TOMLIN

•••MN•

ALUMNA
ALUMNI

•••M•N

ACUMEN
AIRMAN
AIRMEN
ALEMAN
ALLMAN
ALTMAN
APEMAN
APEMEN
ATAMAN
BADMAN
BADMEN
BARMAN
BARMEN
BATMAN
BATMEN
BEAMON
BORMAN
BOWMAN
BOWMEN
BREMEN
BURMAN
BUSMAN
BUSMEN
CAIMAN
CARMAN
CARMEN
CAYMAN
CHEMIN
COLMAN
COMMON
CONMAN
CONMEN
CORMAN
COWMAN
COWMEN
DAIMON
DESMAN
DOLMAN
DOLMEN
ELFMAN
ENDMAN
ENDMEN
ETYMON
FBIMAN
FBIMEN
FENMAN
FENMEN
FIRMAN
FLYMAN
FLYMEN
FORMAN
GAGMAN
GAGMEN
GAMMON
GASMAN
GASMEN
GERMAN
GNOMON
GUNMAN
GUNMEN
HAEMON
HAGMAN
HARMON
HERMAN
HERMON
HETMAN
HITMAN
HITMEN
ICEMAN
ICEMEN
IMAMAN
KERMAN
KIDMAN
KIRMAN
KORMAN
LAWMAN
LAWMEN
LAYMAN
LAYMEN
LEGMAN
LEGMEN
LEMMON
MADMAN
MADMEN
MAMMON
MERMAN
MERMEN
MORMON
NETMAN
NETMEN
NEUMAN
NEWMAN
NORMAN
OILMAN
OILMEN
OLDMAN
OLDMEN
ONEMAN
PACMAN
PENMAN
PENMEN
PIEMAN
PIEMEN
PITMAN
PITMEN
RAGMAN
RAGMEN
RODMAN
RUDMAN
SALMAN
SALMON
SEAMAN
SEAMEN
SERMON
SHAMAN
SHIMON
STAMEN
SUMMON
TASMAN
TAXMAN
TAXMEN
TINMAN
TINMEN
TOAMAN
TODMAN
TRUMAN
TUBMAN
ULLMAN
VERMIN
XIAMEN
YEOMAN
YEOMEN
YESMAN
YESMEN
ZEEMAN
ZOOMIN

••••MN

AUTUMN
COLUMN
SOLEMN

MO••••

MOANED
MOANER
MOATED
MOBBED
MOBCAP
MOBILE
MOBIUS
MOBLEY
MOCHAS
MOCKED
MOCKER
MOCKUP
MODELA
MODELS
MODELT
MODEMS
MODENA
MODERN
MODEST
MODIFY
MODINE
MODISH
MODOCS
MODULE
MODULO
MOGULS
MOHAIR
MOHAVE
MOHAWK
MOHOCK
MOHURS
MOIETY
MOILED
MOILER
MOINES
MOIRES
MOJAVE
MOLARS
MOLDAU
MOLDED
MOLDER
MOLEST
MOLINE
MOLNAR
MOLOCH
MOLOPO
MOLTED
MOLTEN
MOLTER
MOLTKE
MOMENT
MOMMAS
MOMMIE
MONACO
MONADS
MONDAY
MONERA
MONETA
MONEYS
MONGER
MONGOL
MONICA
MONIED
MONIES
MONISM
MONIST
MONKEY
MONODY
MONROE
MONTEL
MONTES
MONTEZ
MONTHS
MOOING
MOOLAH
MOONED
MOONEY
MOORED
MOOTED
MOPEDS
MOPERS
MOPERY
MOPIER
MOPING
MOPISH
MOPPED
MOPPER
MOPPET
MOPSUP
MOPTOP
MOPUPS
MORALE
MORALS
MORANT
MORASS
MORAVA
MORAYS
MORBID
MOREAU
MOREEN
MORELS
MORENO
MORGAN
MORGEN
MORION
MORITA
MORITZ
MORLEY
MORMON
MORNAY
MORONI
MORONS
MOROSE
MORPHO
MORPHS
MORPHY
MORRIS
MORROW
MORSEL
MORTAL
MORTAR
MORTON
MOSAIC
MOSCOW
MOSEYS
MOSHAV
MOSHED
MOSHER
MOSHES
MOSKVA
MOSLEM
MOSQUE
MOSSED
MOSSES
MOSTEL
MOSTLY
MOTELS
MOTETS
MOTHER
MOTHRA
MOTIFS
MOTILE
MOTION
MOTIVE
MOTLEY
MOTMOT
MOTORS
MOTOWN
MOTTLE
MOTTOS
MOULDS
MOULDY
MOULIN
MOULTS
MOUNDS
MOUNTS
MOUNTY
MOURNS
MOUSED
MOUSER
MOUSES
MOUSEY
MOUSSE
MOUTHS
MOUTHY
MOUTON
MOVEIN
MOVEON
MOVERS
MOVEUP
MOVIES
MOVING
MOWERS
MOWGLI
MOWING
MOYERS
MOZART

M•O•••

MAOISM
MAOIST
MAORIS
MAOTAI
MEOWED
MIOSIS
MOOING
MOOLAH
MOONED
MOONEY
MOORED
MOOTED
MYOHMY
MYOPES
MYOPIA
MYOPIC
MYOSIN
MYOSIS

M••O••

MACOUN
MAHOUT
MAJORS
MALONE
MALORY
MALOTI
MANORS
MAROON
MASONS
MAXOUT
MAYORS
MAZOLA
MCJOBS
MEGOHM
MEKONG
MELODY
MELONS
MELOTT
MEMOIR
MEMORY
MEROPE
MESONS
METOPE
MIDORI
MILORD
MILOSZ
MIMOSA
MINOAN
MINORS
MIWOKS
MODOCS
MOHOCK
MOLOCH
MOLOPO
MONODY
MORONI
MORONS
MOROSE
MOTORS
MOTOWN
MRCOOL
MRMOTO
MUCOSA
MUCOUS
MYSORE
MYWORD

M•••O•

MACHOS
MACRON
MACROS
MADTOM
MAGNON
MAHZOR
MALLOW
MAMBOS
MAMMON
MANGOS
MANIOC
MARCOS
MARGOT
MARION
MARLON
MARMOT
MAROON
MARRON
MARROW
MASCOT
MATRON
MATZOH
MATZOS
MAYPOP
MCADOO
MEADOW
MELLON
MELLOW
MELTON
MEMNON
MENJOU
MENTOR
MERLON
MERLOT
MERTON
METEOR
METHOD
METROS
MEZZOS
MICRON
MICROS
MIGNON
MILTON
MIMEOS
MINION
MINNOW
MIRROR
MONGOL
MONROE
MOPTOP
MORION
MORMON
MORROW
MORTON
MOSCOW
MOTION
MOTMOT
MOTTOS
MOUTON
MOVEON
MRCOOL
MUGHOS
MUNGOS
MURROW
MUSKOX
MUTTON
MYTHOI
MYTHOL
MYTHOS

M••••O

MACACO
MACEIO
MADEDO
MADERO
MADURO
MAGGIO
MAKEDO
MALABO
MAPUTO
MARIKO
MARINO
MCADOO
MEDICO
MEGALO
MEJICO
MELANO
MENADO
MERINO
MEXICO
MIKADO
MILANO
MODULO
MOLOPO
MONACO
MORENO
MORPHO
MRMOTO
MURANO
MUTATO

•MO•••

AMOEBA
AMOLES
AMORAL
AMOSOZ
AMOUNT
AMOURS
BMOVIE
EMOTED
EMOTER
EMOTES
HMONGS
IMOGEN
SMOCKS
SMOGGY
SMOKED
SMOKER
SMOKES
SMOKEY
SMOLTS
SMOOCH
SMOOTH

•M•O••

EMBODY
EMBOSS
IMPORT
IMPOSE
IMPOST
SMOOCH
SMOOTH

•M••O•

AMADOU
AMAJOR
AMATOL
AMAZON
AMIDOL
AMIGOS
AMINOR
AMNION
AMOSOZ
BMAJOR
BMINOR
CMAJOR
CMINOR
DMAJOR
DMINOR
EMAJOR
EMINOR
EMPLOY
EMPTOR
FMAJOR
FMINOR
GMAJOR
GMINOR
IMPROV
KMESON

•M•••O

AMBATO
AMEDEO
EMBRYO
EMILIO
IMMUNO
SMALTO

••MO••

ALMOND
ALMOST
ARMORS
ARMORY
ARMOUR
ATMOST
AUMONT
BEMOAN
BUMOUT
DAMONE
DAMORE
DAMOUR
DEMOBS
DEMODE
DEMOND
DEMONS
DEMOTE
DIMOUT
DUMONT
EDMOND
EGMONT
ELMORE
EXMOOR
EXMORE
FAMOUS
FEMORA
GEMOTE
GEMOTS
HUMORS
HUMOUR
INMOST
IOMOTH
JAMOKE
KIMONO
KOMODO
LAMONT
LAMOUR
LEMOND
LEMONS
LEMONY
LOMOND
MEMOIR
MEMORY
MIMOSA
MRMOTO
NOMORE
ORMOLU
ORMOND
OSMOND
OSMOSE
POMONA
RAMONA
RAMONE
RAMOSE
RAMOUS
REMOLD
REMOPS
REMORA
REMOTE
REMOVE
REMOWN
REMOWS
RIMOSE
ROMOLA
RUMORS
RUMOUR
SAMOAN
SAMOSA
SIMONE
SIMONY
UNMOOR
UPMOST
UTMOST

••M•O•

AIMFOR
BAMBOO
CAMEON
CAMEOS
CAMION
CAMPOS
COMBOS
COMEON
COMMON
COMPOS
DAMSON
EXMOOR
GAMBOL
GAMMON
GUMBOS
JIMSON
JUMBOS
JUMPON
LEMMON
LEMNOS
LIMBOS
LOMBOK
LUMMOX
MAMBOS
MAMMON
MEMNON
MIMEOS
NIMROD
POMPOM
POMPON
RAMROD
RAMSON
ROMEOS
SAMSON
SIMEON
SUMMON
SYMBOL
TEMPOS
TOMBOY
TOMTOM
UNMOOR
YOMTOV

••M••O

AIMSTO
BAMAKO
BAMBOO
BUMPPO
CAMARO
CAMETO
CAMINO
COMETO
CUMULO
DAMATO
DOMINO
HEMATO
IMMUNO
KIMONO
KOMODO
MRMOTO
NEMATO
NUMERO
POMELO
ROMANO
ROMERO
SOMATO
STMALO
TAMAYO
TOMATO

•••MO•

ALAMOS
ASIMOV
BEAMON
BONMOT
CLAMOR
COMMON
COSMOS
DAIMON
DEIMOS
DROMOI
DROMOS
DUOMOS
ENAMOR
ETYMOL
ETYMON
GAMMON
GIZMOS
GLAMOR
GNOMON
HAEMON
HARMON
HAYMOW
HERMON
LEMMON
LUMMOX
MAMMON
MARMOT
MORMON
MOTMOT
OROMOS
PATMOS
PRIMOS
PROMOS
QUEMOY
RAGMOP
SALMON
SCHMOO
SCHMOS
SERMON
SHIMON
SUMMON
TREMOR
WETMOP

•••M•O

AKIMBO
ATEMPO
CRAMBO
DAIMYO
SCHMOO
WHAMMO
WHOMSO

••••MO

CHROMO
DYNAMO
ENTOMO
ESKIMO
KOKOMO
PLASMO
SEISMO
STELMO
THERMO
ULTIMO
WHAMMO

M•P•••

MAPLES
MAPPED
MAPPER
MAPUTO
MOPEDS
MOPERS
MOPERY
MOPIER
MOPING
MOPISH
MOPPED
MOPPER
MOPPET
MOPSUP
MOPTOP
MOPUPS
MUPPET

M••P••

MAGPIE
MAPPED
MAPPER
MARPLE
MAYPOP
MILPAS
MOPPED
MOPPER
MOPPET
MORPHO
MORPHS
MORPHY
MUDPIE
MUMPED
MUPPET
MURPHY
MYOPES
MYOPIA
MYOPIC

M•••P•

MEROPE
METOPE
MIXUPS
MOLOPO
MOPUPS

M••••P

MADCAP
MADEUP
MAKEUP
MARKUP
MAYHAP
MAYPOP

MEGILP
MESSUP
MILSAP
MISHAP
MOBCAP
MOCKUP
MOPSUP
MOPTOP
MOVEUP
MUCKUP
MUSSUP

•MP•••

AMPERE
AMPHID
AMPLER
AMPULE
AMPULS
EMPERY
EMPIRE
EMPLOY
EMPTOR
IMPACT
IMPAIR
IMPALA
IMPALE
IMPART
IMPEDE
IMPELS
IMPEND
IMPERF
IMPING
IMPISH
IMPORT
IMPOSE
IMPOST
IMPROV
IMPUGN
IMPURE
IMPUTE
UMPIRE

•M•••P

AMERSP

••MP••

ARMPIT
BUMPED
BUMPER
BUMPPO
BUMPUP
CAMPED
CAMPER
CAMPOS
CAMPUS
COMPAQ
COMPEL
COMPLY
COMPOS
DAMPED
DAMPEN
DAMPER
DAMPLY
DIMPLE
DIMPLY
DUMPED
DUMPER
HAMPER
HUMPED
HUMPHS
JUMPAT
JUMPED
JUMPER
JUMPIN
JUMPON
JUMPUP
KEMPIS
LIMPED
LIMPER
LIMPET
LIMPID
LIMPLY
LUMPED
LUMPEN
LUMPER
LUMPUR
LYMPHS
MUMPED
NYMPHS
OOMPAH
PAMPAS
PAMPER
POMPEY
POMPOM
POMPON
PUMPED
PUMPER
PUMPUP
RAMPED
RIMPLE
ROMPED
ROMPER
RUMPLE
RUMPLY
RUMPUS
SAMPAN
SAMPLE
SEMPER
SEMPRE
SIMPER
SIMPLE
SIMPLY
TAMPED
TAMPER
TEMPED
TEMPEH
TEMPER
TEMPLE
TEMPOS
TEMPTS
TEMPUS
VAMPED
VAMPER
WAMPUM
WIMPLE

••M•P•

BUMPPO
JAMUPS
REMAPS
REMOPS
SUMUPS

••M••P

BUMPUP
BUMRAP
CAMEUP
COMEUP
DAMSUP
DOMREP
GUMSUP
JAMSUP
JUMPUP
PUMPUP
SUMSUP

•••MP•

ATEMPO
BLIMPS
CHAMPS
CHIMPS
CHOMPS
CHUMPS
CLAMPS
CLOMPS
CLUMPS
CLUMPY
CRAMPS
CRIMPS
CRIMPY
EXEMPT
FRUMPS
FRUMPY
GRAMPA
GRAMPS
GRUMPS
GRUMPY
GUIMPE
PLUMPS
PRIMPS
PROMPT
SCAMPI
SCAMPS
SKIMPS
SKIMPY
SLUMPS
STAMPS
STIMPY
STOMPS
STUMPS
STUMPY
SWAMPS
SWAMPY
THUMPS
TRAMPS
TROMPE
TROMPS
TRUMPS
WHOMPS

•••M•P

BEAMUP
BITMAP
CLAMUP
DRUMUP
FIRMUP
RAGMOP
TEAMUP
WARMUP
WETMOP

••••MP

CCLAMP
DECAMP
ENCAMP
GAZUMP
PREAMP
REVAMP
SCRIMP
SHRIMP

M•Q•••

MAQUIS
MSQUAD

M••Q••

MANQUE
MARQUE
MASQUE
MOSQUE

•MQ•••

EMQUAD

••M••Q

COMPAQ

MR••••

MRBLUE
MRCOOL
MRHYDE
MRMOTO

M•R•••

MARACA
MARAUD
MARBLE
MARBLY
MARCEL
MARCHE
MARCIA
MARCIE
MARCOS
MARCUS
MARDUK
MARGAY
MARGES
MARGIE
MARGIN
MARGOT
MARIAH
MARIAN
MARIEL
MARIKO
MARILU
MARINA
MARINE
MARINO
MARION
MARISA
MARISH
MARIST
MARIUS
MARKED
MARKER
MARKET
MARKKA
MARKUP
MARLED
MARLEE
MARLEY
MARLIN
MARLON
MARMEE
MARMOT
MARNER
MARNIE
MAROON
MARPLE
MARQUE
MARRED
MARRON
MARROW
MARSHA
MARSHY
MARTEL
MARTEN
MARTHA
MARTIN
MARTYR
MARVEL
MARVIN
MERCED
MERCER
MERELY
MEREST
MERGED
MERGER
MERGES
MERIDA
MERINO
MERITS
MERKEL
MERLIN
MERLON
MERLOT
MERMAN
MERMEN
MEROPE
MERSEY
MERTON
MERVYN
MIRAGE
MIRIAM
MIRIER
MIRING
MIRREN
MIRROR
MORALE
MORALS
MORANT
MORASS
MORAVA
MORAYS
MORBID
MOREAU
MOREEN
MORELS
MORENO
MORGAN
MORGEN
MORION
MORITA
MORITZ
MORLEY
MORMON
MORNAY
MORONI
MORONS
MOROSE
MORPHO
MORPHS
MORPHY
MORRIS
MORROW
MORSEL
MORTAL
MORTAR
MORTON
MURALS
MURANO
MURCIA
MURDER
MURIEL
MURINE
MURMUR
MURPHY
MURRAY
MURRES
MURREY
MURROW
MYRDAL
MYRIAD
MYRRHS
MYRTLE

M••R••

MACRAE
MACRON
MACROS
MADRAS
MADRES
MADRID
MANRAY
MAORIS
MARRED
MARRON
MARROW
MATRIX
MATRON
MAURYA
MCCREA
MCGRAW
MCGREW
MEERUT
METRES
METRIC
METROS
MICRON
MICROS
MIDRIB
MIHRAB
MIRREN
MIRROR
MITRAL
MITRED
MITRES
MOIRES
MONROE
MOORED
MORRIS
MORROW
MOURNS
MUDRAS
MURRAY
MURRES
MURREY
MURROW
MYRRHS

M•••R•

MADERO
MADURA
MADURO
MAITRE
MAJORS
MAKERS
MALORY
MANORS
MANTRA
MASERS
MASERU
MATERS
MATURE
MAYORS
MAZERS
MEAGRE
MEGARA
MEMORY
MESSRS
METERS
MIDORI
MILERS
MILORD
MIMERS
MINERS
MINORS
MISERS
MISERY
MITERS
MIXERS
MODERN
MOHURS
MOLARS
MONERA
MOPERS
MOPERY
MOTHRA
MOTORS
MOVERS
MOWERS
MOYERS
MOZART
MUSERS
MYGIRL
MYSORE
MYWORD

M••••R

MADDER
MAGYAR
MAHLER
MAHZOR
MAILER
MANGER
MANNER
MAPPER
MARKER
MARNER
MARTYR
MASHER
MASKER
MASTER
MATHER
MATTER
MAULER
MAUSER
MAZIER
MCNAIR
MEAGER
MEANER
MEDGAR
MEDLAR
MEEKER
MEETER
MEMBER
MEMOIR
MENDER
MENHIR
MENTOR
MERCER
MERGER
MESMER
METEOR
METIER
MEWLER
MIDAIR
MIDLER
MILDER
MILKER
MILLER
MILNER
MINCER
MINDER
MINTER
MIRIER
MIRROR
MISTER
MOANER
MOCKER
MOHAIR
MOILER
MOLDER
MOLNAR
MOLTER
MONGER
MOPIER
MOPPER
MORTAR
MOSHER
MOTHER
MOUSER
MUDDER
MUGGER
MULLER
MUMMER
MURDER
MURMUR
MUSHER
MUSTER
MUTTER

•M•R••

AMERCE
AMERSP
AMORAL
AMTRAC
AMTRAK
DMARKS
EMBRYO
EMERGE
IMARET
IMBRUE
IMPROV
OMERTA
SMARMY
SMARTS
SMARTY
SMERSH
SMIRCH
SMIRKS
SMIRKY
SMURFS
SMYRNA
UMBRAE
UMBRAL
UMBRAS
UMBRIA

•M••R•

AMBERS
AMBERY
AMEERS
AMENRA
AMHARA
AMOURS
AMPERE
DMITRI
EMBARK
EMBERS
EMEERS
EMIGRE
EMPERY
EMPIRE
IMMURE
IMPART
IMPERF
IMPORT
IMPURE
SMEARS
SMEARY
UMBERS
UMPIRE

•M•••R

AMAJOR
AMBLER
AMINOR
AMPLER
BMAJOR
BMINOR
CMAJOR
CMINOR
DMAJOR
DMINOR
EMAJOR
EMINOR
EMOTER
EMPTOR
FMAJOR
FMINOR
GMAJOR
GMINOR
IMAGER
IMPAIR
SMILER
SMOKER

••MR••

BUMRAP
CYMRIC
DOMREP
NIMROD
QUMRAN
RAMROD

••M•R•

ADMIRE
ARMORS
ARMORY
ARMURE
ASMARA
AYMARA
BEMIRE
BUMBRY
CAMARO
CAMERA
COMERS
DAMORE
DEMURE
DEMURS
ELMIRA
ELMORE
EXMORE
FEMORA
FEMURS
GEMARA
HOMBRE
HOMERS
HUMERI
HUMORS
IMMURE
KHMERS
LAMARR
LEMURS
MEMORY
MIMERS
NAMERS
NOMORE
NUMERO
PAMIRS
REMARK
REMORA
ROMERO
RUMORS
SAMARA
SEMPRE
SOMBRE
SOMERS
STMARK
TAMARA
TAMERS
TIMBRE
TIMERS

••M••R

AIMFOR
ARMOUR
BOMBER
BUMMER
BUMPER
CAMBER
CAMPER
COMBER
CUMBER
DAMMAR
DAMOUR
DAMPER
DIMMER
DUMBER
DUMPER
EXMOOR
FUMIER
GAMIER
GAMMER
HAMMER
HAMPER
HEMMER
HOMIER
HUMMER
HUMOUR
JAMMER
JUMPER
LAMARR
LAMOUR
LIMBER
LIMIER
LIMNER
LIMPER
LUMBAR
LUMBER
LUMPER
LUMPUR
MEMBER
MEMOIR
MUMMER
NUMBER
PAMPER
PUMPER
RIMIER
ROMPER
RUMMER
RUMOUR
SAMBAR
SEMPER
SIMMER
SIMPER
SOMBER
SOMMER
SUMMER
SUMNER
SUMTER
TAMPER
TEMPER
TIMBER
UNMOOR
VAMPER
YAMMER
ZIMMER

•••M•R

ALOMAR
BOOMER
BUMMER
CALMER
CLAMOR
DAGMAR
DAMMAR
DELMAR
DIMMER
DORMER
ENAMOR
FARMER
FIRMER
FORMER
FULMAR
GAMMER
GLAMOR
HAMMER
HEMMER
HUMMER
INGMAR
ISOMER
JAMMER
KALMAR
KILMER
KRAMER
MESMER
MUMMER
MURMUR
NEWMAR
PALMER
PRIMER
REAMER
RHYMER
ROAMER
ROHMER
ROOMER
RUMMER
SHAMIR
SIMMER
SOMMER
STUMER
SUMMER
TREMOR
WARMER
WEIMAR
YAMMER
ZIMMER

MS••••

MSQUAD

M•S•••

MASADA
MASAIS
MASCOT
MASERS
MASERU
MASHED
MASHER
MASHES
MASHIE
MASKED
MASKER
MASONS
MASQUE
MASSED
MASSES
MASSEY
MASSIF
MASTER
MASTIC
MESABI
MESCAL
MESHED
MESHES
MESMER
MESONS
MESSED
MESSES
MESSRS
MESSUP
MISCHA
MISCUE
MISDID
MISERS
MISERY
MISFIT
MISHAP
MISHIT
MISLAY
MISLED
MISSAL
MISSAY
MISSED
MISSES
MISSIS
MISSUS
MISTED
MISTER
MISUSE
MOSAIC
MOSCOW
MOSEYS
MOSHAV
MOSHED
MOSHER
MOSHES
MOSKVA
MOSLEM
MOSQUE
MOSSED
MOSSES
MOSTEL
MOSTLY
MUSCAT
MUSCLE
MUSCLY
MUSERS
MUSEUM
MUSHED
MUSHER
MUSHES
MUSIAL
MUSING
MUSKEG
MUSKET
MUSKIE
MUSKOX
MUSLIM
MUSLIN
MUSSED
MUSSEL
MUSSES
MUSSUP
MUSTER
MUSTNT
MYSELF
MYSORE
MYSTIC

M••S••

MADSEN
MAISIE
MANSES
MARSHA
MARSHY
MASSED
MASSES
MASSEY
MASSIF
MAUSER
MEASLY
MENSAE
MENSAL
MENSAS
MENSCH
MERSEY
MESSED
MESSES
MESSRS
MESSUP
MIASMA
MILSAP
MIOSIS
MISSAL
MISSAY
MISSED
MISSES
MISSIS
MISSUS
MOPSUP
MORSEL
MOSSED
MOSSES
MOUSED
MOUSER
MOUSES
MOUSEY
MOUSSE
MUSSED
MUSSEL
MUSSES
MUSSUP
MYOSIN
MYOSIS

M•••S•

MAOISM
MAOIST
MARISA
MARISH
MARIST
MEDUSA
MEREST
MILOSZ
MIMOSA
MISUSE
MODEST
MODISH
MOLEST
MONISM
MONIST
MOPISH
MORASS
MOROSE
MOUSSE
MUCOSA
MUFASA
MULISH
MUTEST

M••••S

MACAWS
MACHES
MACHOS
MACROS
MADAMS
MADRAS
MADRES
MAGMAS
MAGNUS
MAHDIS
MAIDUS
MAILES
MAIZES
MAJLIS
MAJORS
MAKERS
MALAYS
MAMBAS
MAMBOS
MAMMAS
MANAUS
MANGOS
MANIAS
MANORS
MANSES
MANTAS
MANTIS
MAORIS
MAPLES
MAQUIS
MARCOS
MARCUS
MARGES
MARIUS
MASAIS
MASERS
MASHES
MASONS
MASSES
MATERS
MATEYS
MATHIS
MATINS
MATTES
MATZOS
MAUVES
MAVENS
MAXIMS
MAYANS
MAYBES
MAYORS
MAZERS
MCJOBS
MECCAS
MEDALS
MEDIAS
MEDICS
MELEES
MELONS
MENDES
MENSAS
MENTIS
MERGES
MERITS
MESHES
MESONS
MESSES
MESSRS
METALS
METERS
METRES
METROS
MEZZOS
MICROS
MIDGES
MILERS
MILPAS
MIMEOS
MIMERS
MIMICS
MINCES
MINERS
MINIMS
MINKES
MINORS
MINXES
MIOSIS
MISERS
MISSES
MISSIS
MISSUS
MITERS
MITRES
MIWOKS
MIXERS
MIXUPS
MIZENS
MOBIUS
MOCHAS
MODELS
MODEMS
MODOCS
MOGULS
MOHURS
MOINES
MOIRES
MOLARS
MOMMAS
MONADS
MONEYS
MONIES
MONTES
MONTHS
MOPEDS
MOPERS
MOPUPS
MORALS
MORASS
MORAYS
MORELS
MORONS
MORPHS
MORRIS
MOSEYS
MOSHES
MOSSES
MOTELS
MOTETS
MOTIFS
MOTORS
MOTTOS
MOULDS
MOULTS
MOUNDS
MOUNTS
MOURNS
MOUSES
MOUTHS
MOVERS
MOVIES
MOWERS
MOYERS
MUCINS
MUCOUS
MUDRAS
MUFTIS
MUGHOS
MULCTS
MULEYS
MULLAS
MUNGOS
MURALS
MURRES
MUSERS
MUSHES
MUSSES
MUZZES
MYNAHS
MYOPES
MYOSIS
MYRRHS
MYTHOS

•MS•••

AMSTEL

•M•S••

AMOSOZ
AMUSED
AMUSES
KMESON
OMASUM
TMESIS

•M••S•

AMBUSH
AMERSP
AMIDST
EMBOSS
EMDASH
IMPISH
IMPOSE
IMPOST
SMERSH

•M•••S

AMADIS
AMATIS
AMAZES
AMBERS
AMBITS
AMBLES
AMEBAS
AMEERS
AMENDS
AMENTS
AMICES
AMICUS
AMIDES
AMIENS
AMIGAS
AMIGOS
AMINES
AMINUS
AMOLES
AMOURS
AMPULS
AMUSES
AMVETS
BMINUS
CMINUS
DMARKS
DMINUS
EMAILS
EMBAYS
EMBEDS
EMBERS
EMBOSS
EMCEES
EMEERS
EMENDS
EMMETS
EMOTES
HMONGS
IMAGES
IMBUES
IMPELS
OMAHAS
OMANIS
OMEGAS
SMACKS
SMALLS
SMARTS
SMEARS
SMELLS
SMELTS
SMILES
SMIRKS
SMITES
SMITHS

SMOCKS
SMOKES
SMOLTS
SMURFS
TMESIS
UMBELS
UMBERS
UMBRAS
UMIAKS

••MS••

AIMSAT
AIMSTO
COMSAT
DAMSEL
DAMSON
DAMSUP
DIMSUM
GUMSUP
HEMSIN
JAMSIN
JAMSUP
JIMSON
RAMSAY
RAMSES
RAMSEY
RAMSON
RIMSKY
SAMSON
SUMSUP
WIMSEY

••M•S•

ADMASS
ALMOST
ATMOST
BEMUSE
CAMISE
DAMASK
DEMISE
ENMESH
FAMISH
GAMEST
INMOST
KUMISS
LAMESA
LAMEST
MIMOSA
OSMOSE
RAMOSE
REMISE
REMISS
RIMOSE
SAMOSA
TAMEST
UNMASK
UNMESH
UPMOST
UTMOST
ZYMASE

••M••S

ADMASS
ADMITS
ARMETS
ARMIES
ARMORS
BOMBES
CAMELS
CAMEOS
CAMPOS
CAMPUS
COMBES
COMBOS
COMERS
COMETS
COMICS
COMMAS
COMPOS
COMTES
DEMIES
DEMITS
DEMOBS
DEMONS
DEMURS
EMMETS
FAMOUS
FEMMES
FEMURS
GAMAYS
GAMINS
GAMMAS
GAMUTS
GEMOTS
GIMELS
GIMMES
GUMBOS
HAMALS
HOMERS
HUMANS
HUMMUS
HUMORS
HUMPHS
JAMUPS
JUMBOS
KEMPIS
KHMERS
KUMISS
LAMEDS
LAMIAS
LAMMAS
LEMANS
LEMMAS
LEMNOS
LEMONS
LEMURS
LIMBOS
LIMBUS
LIMENS
LIMEYS
LIMITS
LUMENS
LYMPHS
MAMBAS
MAMBOS
MAMMAS
MIMEOS
MIMERS
MIMICS
MOMMAS
NAMERS
NIMBUS
NOMADS
NYMETS
NYMPHS
OLMECS
OSMICS
PAMIRS
PAMPAS
RAMETS
RAMIES
RAMOUS
RAMSES
REMANS
REMAPS
REMISS
REMITS
REMOPS
REMOWS
ROMANS
ROMEOS
RUMBAS
RUMENS
RUMORS
RUMPUS
SAMBAS
SOMERS
SUMACS
SUMMAS
SUMUPS
TAMERS
TAMILS
TEMPOS
TEMPTS
TEMPUS
TIMERS
UNMANS
WOMENS
ZAMIAS

•••MS•

AHIMSA
CLUMSY
FLIMSY
SLIMSY
WHIMSY
WHOMSO

•••M•S

ABOMBS
AGAMAS
ALAMOS
ANIMAS
ANIMES
ANIMUS
ARAMIS
AROMAS
BIOMES
BLAMES
BLIMPS
BRUMES
CADMUS
CHAMPS
CHIMES
CHIMPS
CHOMPS
CHUMPS
CLAMPS
CLIMBS
CLIMES
CLOMPS
CLUMPS
COMMAS
COSMOS
CRAMPS
CREMES
CRIMES
CRIMPS
CRUMBS
DEIMOS
DERMIS
DISMES
DOGMAS
DOLMAS
DRAMAS
DROMOS
DUOMOS
EDAMES
ELEMIS
FEMMES
FLAMES
FLUMES
FRAMES
FRUMPS
GAMMAS
GIMMES
GIZMOS
GNOMES
GRAMAS
GRAMPS
GRIMES
GRUMPS
HBOMBS
HERMES
HOLMES
HUMMUS
KERMES
KERMIS
LAMMAS
LEMMAS
LITMUS
LLAMAS
MAGMAS
MAMMAS
MOMMAS
NEUMES
OROMOS
PALMAS
PATMOS
PLUMBS
PLUMES
PLUMPS
PRIMES
PRIMOS
PRIMPS
PRIMUS
PROMOS
RHAMES
RHOMBS
RHUMBS
RHYMES
SCAMPS
SCHMOS
SEAMUS
SHAMES
SHAMUS
SIGMAS
SKIMPS
SLIMES
SLUMPS
SPUMES
STAMPS
STOMAS
STOMPS
STUMPS
SUMMAS
SWAMIS
SWAMPS
THAMES
THEMES
THOMAS
THUMBS
THUMPS
THYMUS
TRAMPS
TROMPS
TRUMPS
WHOMPS

••••MS

ABOHMS
ABRAMS
ABYSMS
ADDAMS
ADEEMS
ALARMS
ALBUMS
ATEAMS
AXIOMS
BEDIMS
BEGUMS
BESOMS
BLOOMS
BRAHMS
BREAMS
BROOMS
CAROMS
CDROMS
CHARMS
CHASMS
CLAIMS
CREAMS
DENIMS
DREAMS
EPROMS
FORUMS
GLEAMS
GLOOMS
GOLEMS
GROOMS
HAKIMS
HAREMS
HAULMS
HBEAMS
IBEAMS
IDIOMS
JORUMS
KHOUMS
KILIMS
LARAMS
MADAMS
MAXIMS
MINIMS
MODEMS
ODIUMS
OGHAMS
PRISMS
PROAMS
PROEMS
PSALMS
QUALMS
REAIMS
REALMS
REARMS
REHEMS
RHEUMS
SCRAMS
SCRIMS
SCRUMS
SEDUMS
SEISMS
SERUMS
SHAWMS
SPASMS
STEAMS
STORMS
STRUMS
SWARMS
THERMS
THRUMS
TOTEMS
UGGAMS
UNARMS
UNJAMS
VENOMS
VROOMS
WHELMS

M•T•••

MATERS
MATEYS
MATHER
MATHIS
MATING
MATINS
MATLIN
MATRIX
MATRON
MATTEA
MATTED
MATTEL
MATTER
MATTES
MATTIE
MATURE
MATZOH
MATZOS
METALS
METATE
METEOR
METERS
METHOD
METHYL
METIER
METING
METOPE
METRES
METRIC
METROS
METTLE
MITERS
MITRAL
MITRED
MITRES
MITTEN
MOTELS
MOTETS
MOTHER
MOTHRA
MOTIFS
MOTILE
MOTION
MOTIVE
MOTLEY
MOTMOT
MOTORS
MOTOWN
MOTTLE
MOTTOS
MUTANT
MUTATE
MUTATO
MUTELY
MUTEST
MUTING
MUTINY
MUTTER
MUTTON
MUTUAL
MYTHIC
MYTHOI
MYTHOL
MYTHOS

M••T••

MADTOM
MAITAI
MAITRE
MALTED
MALTIN
MANTAS
MANTEL
MANTIC
MANTIS
MANTLE
MANTRA
MANTUA
MAOTAI
MARTEL
MARTEN
MARTHA
MARTIN
MARTYR
MASTER
MASTIC
MATTEA
MATTED
MATTEL
MATTER
MATTES
MATTIE
MAYTAG
MEETER
MEETLY
MELTED
MELTON
MENTAL
MENTIS
MENTOR
MERTON
METTLE
MILTIE
MILTON
MINTED
MINTER
MISTED
MISTER
MITTEN
MIXTEC
MOATED
MOLTED
MOLTEN
MOLTER
MOLTKE
MONTEL
MONTES
MONTEZ
MONTHS
MOOTED
MOPTOP
MORTAL
MORTAR
MORTON
MOSTEL
MOSTLY
MOTTLE
MOTTOS
MOUTHS
MOUTHY
MOUTON
MUFTIS
MULTUM
MUNTIN
MUSTER
MUSTNT
MUTTER
MUTTON
MYRTLE
MYSTIC

M•••T•

MAKUTA
MALATE
MALOTI
MAPUTO
MELOTT
MERITS
METATE
MIGHTY
MIKITA
MINUTE
MOIETY
MONETA
MORITA
MORITZ
MOTETS
MOULTS
MOUNTS
MOUNTY
MRMOTO
MULCTS
MULETA
MUTATE
MUTATO

M••••T

MADEIT
MAGNET
MAHOUT
MAKEIT
MALLET
MAOIST
MARGOT
MARIST
MARKET
MARMOT
MASCOT
MAXOUT
MEDLAT
MEERUT
MELOTT
MEREST
MERLOT
MIDGET
MILLET
MINUET
MINUIT
MISFIT
MISHIT
MODELT
MODEST
MOLEST
MOMENT
MONIST
MOPPET
MORANT
MOTMOT
MOZART
MUDCAT
MULLET
MUPPET
MUSCAT
MUSKET
MUSTNT
MUTANT
MUTEST

•MT•••

AMTRAC
AMTRAK
UMTATA

•M•T••

AMATIS
AMATOL
AMSTEL
AMYTAN
DMITRI
EMOTED
EMOTER
EMOTES
EMPTOR
SMITES
SMITHS
SMITHY
SMUTCH
SMUTTY

•M••T•

AMBATO
AMBITS
AMENTS
AMVETS
EMEUTE
EMMETS
EMMETT
IMPUTE
OMERTA
SMALTI
SMALTO
SMARTS
SMARTY
SMELTS
SMOLTS
SMOOTH
SMUTTY
UMTATA

•M•••T

AMIDST
AMOUNT
AMULET
EMMETT
IMARET
IMPACT
IMPART
IMPORT
IMPOST
OMELET
UMLAUT

••MT••

COMTES
SUMTER
TAMTAM
TOMTIT
TOMTOM
YOMTOV

••M•T•

ADMITS
AIMSTO
ALMATY
ARMETS
BEMATA
CAMETO
COMATE
COMETH
COMETO
COMETS
COMITY
DAMATO
DAMITA
DEMITS
DEMOTE
DIMITY
EMMETS
EMMETT
ENMITY
GAMETE
GAMUTS
GEMOTE
GEMOTS
HAMITE
HEMATO
INMATE
IOMOTH
LIMITS
MRMOTO
NAMATH
NEMATO
NIMITZ
NYMETS
RAMATE
RAMETS
REMITS
REMOTE
SAMITE
SEMITE
SOMATA
SOMATO
TEMPTS
TOMATO

••M••T

AIMSAT
ALMOST
ARMLET
ARMPIT
ATMOST
AUMONT
BUMOUT
CAMEAT
CAMLET
CEMENT
COMBAT
COMEAT
COMFIT
COMMIT
COMSAT
DIMOUT
DIMWIT
DUMONT
EGMONT
EMMETT
FOMENT
GAMBIT
GAMEST
GIMLET
HAMLET
INMOST
JUMPAT
KOMBAT
LAMENT
LAMEST
LAMONT
LIMPET
MOMENT
NUMBAT
RAMJET
REMELT
SAMLET
SUMMIT
TAMEST
TOMCAT
TOMTIT
TUMULT
UNMEET
UPMOST
UTMOST
WOMBAT

•••MT•

WARMTH

•••M•T

BONMOT
CERMET
COMMIT
EXEMPT
FERMAT
FORMAT
HAEMAT
HELMET
HELMUT
HERMIT
ILLMET
KERMIT
KISMET
MARMOT
MOTMOT
PELMET
PERMIT
PROMPT
STOMAT
SUBMIT
SUMMIT

••••MT

DREAMT

MU••••

MUCINS
MUCKED
MUCKUP
MUCOSA
MUCOUS
MUDCAT
MUDDED
MUDDER
MUDDLE
MUDEEL
MUDHEN
MUDPIE
MUDRAS
MUFASA
MUFFED
MUFFIN
MUFFLE
MUFTIS
MUGABE
MUGGED
MUGGER
MUGHOS
MUKLUK
MULCTS
MULETA
MULEYS
MULISH
MULLAH
MULLAS
MULLED
MULLER
MULLET
MULTUM
MUMBLE
MUMBLY
MUMMED
MUMMER
MUMPED
MUNCHY
MUNCIE
MUNGOS
MUNICH
MUNTIN
MUPPET
MURALS
MURANO
MURCIA
MURDER
MURIEL
MURINE
MURMUR
MURPHY
MURRAY
MURRES
MURREY
MURROW
MUSCAT
MUSCLE
MUSCLY
MUSERS
MUSEUM
MUSHED
MUSHER
MUSHES
MUSIAL
MUSING
MUSKEG
MUSKET
MUSKIE
MUSKOX
MUSLIM
MUSLIN
MUSSED
MUSSEL
MUSSES
MUSSUP
MUSTER
MUSTNT
MUTANT
MUTATE
MUTATO
MUTELY
MUTEST
MUTING
MUTINY
MUTTER
MUTTON
MUTUAL
MUUMUU
MUZHIK
MUZZED
MUZZES
MUZZLE

M•U•••

MAULED
MAULER
MAUMAU
MAUMEE
MAUNDY
MAURYA
MAUSER
MAUVES
MBUNDU
MOULDS
MOULDY
MOULIN
MOULTS
MOUNDS
MOUNTS
MOUNTY
MOURNS
MOUSED
MOUSER
MOUSES
MOUSEY
MOUSSE
MOUTHS
MOUTHY
MOUTON
MUUMUU

M••U••

MACULA
MADURA
MADURO
MAGUEY
MAKUTA
MANUAL
MANUEL
MAPUTO
MAQUIS
MATURE
MAZUMA
MCHUGH
MCKUEN
MEDUSA
MIFUNE
MIGUEL
MINUET
MINUIT
MINUTE
MISUSE
MIXUPS
MODULE
MODULO
MOGULS
MOHURS
MOPUPS
MSQUAD
MUTUAL

M•••U•

MACOUN
MADEUP
MAGNUM
MAGNUS
MAHOUT
MAIDUS
MAKEUP
MANAUS
MANFUL
MANQUE
MANTUA
MARAUD
MARCUS
MARDUK
MARIUS
MARKUP
MARQUE
MASQUE
MAXOUT
MEDIUM
MEERUT
MESSUP
MINIUM
MISCUE
MISSUS
MOBIUS
MOCKUP
MOPSUP
MOSQUE
MOVEUP
MRBLUE
MUCKUP
MUCOUS
MUKLUK
MULTUM
MURMUR
MUSEUM
MUSSUP
MUUMUU

M••••U

MAKALU
MALIBU
MANCHU
MARILU
MASERU
MAUMAU
MBUNDU
MENJOU
MILIEU
MOLDAU
MOREAU
MUUMUU

•MU•••

AMULET
AMUSED
AMUSES
SMUDGE
SMUDGY
SMUGLY
SMURFS
SMUTCH
SMUTTY

•M•U••

AMBUSH
AMOUNT
AMOURS
AMPULE
AMPULS
EMEUTE
EMQUAD
IMBUED
IMBUES
IMMUNE
IMMUNO
IMMURE
IMPUGN
IMPURE
IMPUTE

•M••U•

AMICUS
AMINUS
BMINUS
CMINUS
DMINUS
IMBRUE
OMASUM
OMNIUM
UMLAUT

•M•••U

AMADOU

••MU••

ARMURE
BEMUSE
CUMULI
CUMULO
DEMURE
DEMURS
EDMUND
FEMURS
GAMUTS
IMMUNE
IMMUNO
IMMURE
JAMUPS
LEMUEL
LEMURS
OSMUND
REMUDA
SAMUEL
SUMUPS
TUMULI
TUMULT

••M•U•

AIMFUL
ARMFUL
ARMOUR
BUMOUT
BUMPUP
CAMEUP
CAMPUS
COMEUP
DAMOUR
DAMSUP
DIMOUT
DIMSUM
DUMDUM
FAMOUS
GUMSUP
HUMBUG
HUMMUS
HUMOUR
JAMSUP
JUMPUP
LAMOUR
LIMBUS
LUMPUR
NIMBUS
OSMIUM
PUMPUP
RAMOUS
RUMOUR
RUMPUS
SUMSUP
TAMMUZ
TEMPUS
WAMPUM
YUMYUM

••M••U

ORMOLU
RAMEAU

•••MU•

ANIMUS
BEAMUP
CADMUS
CLAMUP
DRUMUP
FIRMUP
HELMUT
HORMUZ
HUMMUS
LITMUS
MURMUR
MUUMUU
PRIMUM
PRIMUS
SEAMUS
SHAMUS
TALMUD
TAMMUZ
TEAMUP
THYMUS
WARMUP
WONMUG

•••M•U

MAUMAU
MUUMUU

M•V•••

MAVENS
MOVEIN
MOVEON
MOVERS
MOVEUP
MOVIES
MOVING

M••V••

MARVEL
MARVIN
MAUVES
MELVIL
MELVIN
MELVYN
MERVYN

M•••V•

MOHAVE
MOJAVE
MORAVA
MOSKVA
MOTIVE

M••••V

MOSHAV

•MV•••

AMVETS

•M•V••

BMOVIE

•M•••V

IMPROV

••MV••

HUMVEE

••M•V•

REMOVE

••M••V

YOMTOV

•••M•V

ASIMOV

M•W•••

MEWING
MEWLED
MEWLER
MIWOKS
MOWERS
MOWGLI
MOWING
MYWORD

M••W••

MEOWED
MIDWAY

M•••W•

MACAWS
MALAWI
MOHAWK
MOTOWN

M••••W

MALLOW
MARROW
MCGRAW
MCGREW
MEADOW
MELLOW
MILDEW
MINNOW
MORROW
MOSCOW
MURROW

••MW••
DIMWIT

••M•W•
REMOWN
REMOWS

•••M•W
HAYMOW

M•X•••
MAXENE
MAXIMA
MAXIMS
MAXINE
MAXIXE
MAXOUT
MEXICO
MIXERS
MIXING
MIXTEC
MIXUPS

M••X••
MINXES

M•••X•
MAXIXE

M••••X
MADMAX
MANNIX
MATRIX
MENINX
MUSKOX

•M•••X
SMILAX

••M••X
COMMIX
LUMMOX
TOMMIX

•••M•X
CLIMAX
COMMIX
LUMMOX
MADMAX
TEXMEX
TOMMIX

MY••••
MYELIN
MYGIRL
MYNAHS
MYOHMY
MYOPES
MYOPIA
MYOPIC
MYOSIN
MYOSIS
MYRDAL
MYRIAD
MYRRHS
MYRTLE
MYSELF
MYSORE
MYSTIC
MYTHIC
MYTHOI
MYTHOL
MYTHOS
MYWORD

M•Y•••
MAYANS
MAYBES
MAYDAY
MAYFLY
MAYHAP
MAYHEM
MAYORS
MAYPOP
MAYTAG
MOYERS

M••Y••
MAGYAR
MINYAN
MRHYDE

M•••Y•
MALAYA
MALAYS
MARTYR
MATEYS
MAURYA
MELVYN
MERVYN
METHYL
MONEYS
MORAYS
MOSEYS
MULEYS

M••••Y
MAGUEY
MAINLY
MALADY
MALORY
MANDAY
MANRAY
MARBLY
MARGAY
MARLEY
MARSHY
MASSEY
MAUNDY
MAYDAY
MAYFLY
MAZILY
MEANLY
MEASLY
MEDFLY
MEDLEY
MEEKLY
MEETLY
MELODY
MEMORY
MERELY
MERSEY
MICKEY
MIDDAY
MIDWAY
MIGHTY
MILADY
MILDLY
MILLAY
MINIFY
MISERY
MISLAY
MISSAY
MOBLEY
MODIFY
MOIETY
MONDAY
MONKEY
MONODY
MOONEY
MOPERY
MORLEY
MORNAY
MORPHY
MOSTLY
MOTLEY
MOULDY
MOUNTY
MOUSEY
MOUTHY
MUMBLY
MUNCHY
MURPHY
MURRAY
MURREY
MUSCLY
MUTELY
MUTINY
MYOHMY

•MY•••
AMYTAN
SMYRNA

•M••Y•
EMBAYS
EMBRYO

•M•••Y
AMBERY
EMBODY
EMPERY
EMPLOY
SMARMY
SMARTY
SMEARY
SMELLY
SMILEY
SMIRKY
SMITHY
SMOGGY
SMOKEY
SMUDGY
SMUGLY
SMUTTY

••MY••
YUMYUM

••M•Y•
GAMAYS
LIMEYS
TAMAYO

••M••Y
ALMATY
ARMORY
BOMBAY
BUMBRY
CAMEBY
COMEBY
COMEDY
COMELY
COMITY
COMPLY
DAMPLY
DIMITY
DIMPLY
DUMBLY
ENMITY
FAMILY
GAMELY
GAMILY
HOMELY
HOMILY
HOMINY
HUMBLY
JIMINY
LAMELY
LEMONY
LIMPLY
MEMORY
MUMBLY
NAMELY
NIMBLY
NIMINY
NUMBLY
PIMINY
POMPEY
RAMIFY
RAMSAY
RAMSEY
REMEDY
RIMSKY
ROMANY
ROMNEY
RUMBLY
RUMPLY
SIMONY
SIMPLY
SOMANY
TAMELY
TIMELY
TOMBOY
TUMEFY
WAMBLY
WIMSEY

•••MY•
DAIMYO

•••M•Y
BLIMEY
BRUMBY
CALMLY
CHAMMY
CHUMMY
CLAMMY
CLUMPY
CLUMSY
CRIMPY
CRUMBY
CRUMMY
DISMAY
FIRMLY
FLIMSY
FRUMPY
GLUMLY
GRAMMY
GRIMLY
GRUMPY
NIAMEY
PLUMMY
PRIMLY
QUEMOY
SCUMMY
SEEMLY
SHIMMY
SKIMPY
SLIMLY
SLIMSY
SLUMMY
STIMPY
STUMPY
SWAMPY
TRIMLY
WARMLY
WHAMMY
WHIMSY

••••MY
BIGAMY
BLOOMY
BROOMY
CHAMMY
CHROMY
CHUMMY
CLAMMY
CREAMY
CRUMMY
DREAMY
GLEAMY
GLOOMY
GRAMMY
INFAMY
JEREMY
MYOHMY
PLUMMY
RHEUMY
SCUMMY
SHIMMY
SLUMMY
SMARMY
STEAMY
STORMY
WHAMMY

M•Z•••
MAZERS
MAZIER
MAZILY
MAZOLA
MAZUMA
MEZZOS
MIZENS
MIZZEN
MIZZLE
MOZART
MUZHIK
MUZZED
MUZZES
MUZZLE

M••Z••
MAHZOR
MAIZES
MATZOH
MATZOS
MEZZOS
MIZZEN
MIZZLE
MUZZED
MUZZES
MUZZLE

M••••Z
MILOSZ
MONTEZ
MORITZ

•M•Z••
AMAZED
AMAZES
AMAZON

•M•••Z
AMOSOZ

••M•Z•
LAMAZE

••M••Z
NIMITZ
TAMMUZ

•••M•Z
HORMUZ
TAMMUZ

NA••••
NABBED
NABBER
NABOBS
NABORS
NACHOS
NACRES
NADINE
NADIRS
NAGANO
NAGGED
NAGGER
NAGOYA
NAIADS
NAILED
NAILER
NAILIN
NAIRAS
NAMATH
NAMELY
NAMERS
NAMING
NANNIE
NANOOK
NANSEN
NANTES
NAPERY
NAPIER
NAPKIN
NAPLES
NAPOLI
NAPPED
NAPPER
NAPPES
NAPPIE
NARIAL
NARNIA
NARROW
NARVIK
NARWAL
NASALS
NASCAR
NASDAQ
NASEBY
NASHUA
NASSAU
NASSER
NATANT
NATHAN
NATICK
NATION
NATIVE
NATRON
NATTER
NATURA
NATURE
NAUGHT
NAUSEA
NAUTCH
NAVAHO
NAVAJO
NAVELS
NAVIES
NAWABS
NAYSAY

N•A•••
NEARBY
NEARED
NEARER
NEARLY
NEARTO
NEATEN
NEATER
NEATLY
NIACIN
NIAMEY
NUANCE
NYALAS
NYASSA

N••A••
NAGANO
NAIADS
NAMATH
NASALS
NATANT
NAVAHO
NAVAJO
NAWABS
NEGATE
NEMATO
NEPALI
NEVADA
NEWAGE
NEWARK
NICAEA
NLEAST
NOMADS
NONAGE
NONAME
NONARY
NOSALE
NOTARY
NOTATE
NOVATO
NUTATE

N•••A•
NAIRAS
NARIAL
NARWAL
NASCAR
NASDAQ
NATHAN
NAYSAY
NECTAR
NETMAN
NETPAY
NEUMAN
NEURAL
NEWMAN
NEWMAR
NICEAN
NIIHAU
NILGAI
NINEAM
NINJAS
NIPSAT
NISSAN
NOLEAD
NOLOAD
NONFAT
NOONAN
NORGAY
NORIAS
NORMAL
NORMAN
NORWAY
NOSOAP
NOTBAD
NOUGAT
NUBIAN
NUCHAE
NUCHAL
NULLAH
NUMBAT
NYALAS

N••••A
NAGOYA
NARNIA
NASHUA
NATURA
NAUSEA
NEBULA
NERUDA
NESTEA
NEVADA
NICAEA
NICOLA
NIKITA
NIKOLA
NOOTKA
NOUMEA
NOVENA
NUMINA
NUTRIA
NYASSA

•NA•••
ANACIN
ANADEM
ANALOG
ANANDA
ANATTO
ENABLE
ENACTS
ENAMEL
ENAMOR
ENATES
GNARLS
GNARLY
GNATTY
GNAWED
GNAWER
INAFIX
INAFOG
INAJAM
INANER
INAPET
INARCH
INAROW
INARUT
INAWAY
KNACKS
KNAGGY
KNARRY
KNAVES
ONAGER
SNACKS
SNAFUS
SNAGGY
SNAILS
SNAKED
SNAKES
SNAPAT
SNAPPY
SNAPTO
SNAPUP
SNARED
SNARES
SNARLS
SNARLY
SNATCH
SNATHE
SNATHS
SNAZZY
UNABLE
UNAGED
UNARMS
UNAWED

•N•A••
ANKARA
ANNABA
ANNALS
ANSARA
ANSATE
ANWANG
ANYANG
ENCAGE
ENCAMP
ENCASE
ENDALL
ENDASH
ENFANT
ENGAGE
ENHALO
ENLACE
ENRAGE
ENRAPT
ENTAIL
INCANS
INCASE
INCASH
INDABA
INFACT
INFAMY
INFANT
INHALE
INHALF
INHAND
INHAUL
INLAID
INLAND
INLAWS
INLAYS
INMATE
INNAGE
INNATE
INPART
INSANE
INTACT
INTAKE
INVADE
INVAIN
INWARD
KNEADS
ONCALL
ONEACT
ONHAND
ONLAND
ONSALE
ONTAPE
ONWARD
SNEAKS
SNEAKY
UNBARS
UNCAGE
UNCAPS
UNCASE
UNEASE
UNEASY
UNFAIR
UNHAND
UNIATE
UNIATS
UNJAMS
UNLACE
UNLADE
UNLAID
UNLASH
UNMADE
UNMAKE
UNMANS
UNMASK
UNPACK
UNPAID
UNSAFE
UNSAID
UNSAYS
UNTACK
UNWARY

•N••A•
ANDEAN
ANIMAL
ANIMAS
ANNEAL
ANNUAL
ANORAK
ANSGAR
ANURAN
ANYDAY
ANYWAY
CNIDAE
ENDEAR
ENDMAN
ENGRAM
ENNEAD
ENQUAD
ENTRAP
ENWRAP
INAJAM
INAWAY
INDIAN
INGEAR
INGMAR
INGRAM
INPLAY
INROAD
INSEAM
INSPAN
INSTAL
INSTAR
ONEDAY
ONEMAN
ONEWAY
ONLOAN
SNAPAT
SNOCAT
UNCIAL
UNCLAD
UNDRAW
UNGUAL
UNITAL
UNITAS
UNIVAC
UNLEAD
UNLOAD
UNOCAL
UNREAD
UNREAL
UNSEAL
UNSEAT
UNSNAG
UNSNAP
UNTRAP
UNWRAP

•N•••A
ANANDA
ANCONA
ANDREA
ANEMIA
ANGELA
ANGLIA
ANGOLA
ANGORA
ANITRA
ANKARA
ANNABA
ANNIKA
ANSARA
ENCINA
ENDORA
ENIGMA
INDABA
INDIRA
INTIMA
ONEIDA
PNEUMA

••NA••
ADNATE
AGNATE
ANNABA
ANNALS
BANANA
BINARY
BINATE
BONAMI
BYNAME
CANAAN
CANADA
CANALS
CANAPE
CANARD
CANARY
CONANT
CUNARD
CUNAXA
DANANG
DANAUS
DENALI
DENARY
DINARS
DONALD
DONATE
DUNANT
DYNAMO
DYNAST
ERNANI
FINALE
FINALS
IGNACE
IGNATZ
INNAGE
INNATE
JONAHS
KANAKA
LANAIS
LANARK
LANATE
LENAPE
LINAGE
LUNACY
LUNATE
MANAGE
MANAMA
MANANA
MANAUS
MCNAIR
MENACE
MENADO
MENAGE
MONACO
MONADS
MYNAHS
NONAGE
NONAME
NONARY
ORNATE
OXNARD
PANADA
PANAMA
PENANG
PINATA
RENAIL
RENAME
RENATA
RONALD
SENARY
SENATE
SONANT
SONATA
TANAKA
TANANA
TENACE
TENANT
XANADU
ZENANA
ZONATE

••N•A•
AENEAS
ANNEAL
ANNUAL
BANTAM
BANYAN
BANZAI
BENDAY
BENGAL
BENGAY
BONSAI
BUNYAN
CANAAN
CANCAN
CANNAE
CANTAB
CANVAS
CONFAB
CONGAS
CONMAN
CONRAD
CONTAC
CONWAY
CUNEAL
DANNAY
DENIAL
DENTAL
DONNAS
DUNBAR
DUNCAN
DUNHAM
ENNEAD
EONIAN
FANTAN
FENIAN
FENMAN
FENWAY
FINIAL
FINNAN
FONTAL
GENIAL
GENOAN
GENUAL
GUNMAN
GUNNAR
HANGAR
HANNAH
HENNAS
HINTAT
IONIAN
JINNAH
JUNEAU
JUNTAS
KANSAN
KANSAS
KENYAN
KONRAD
LANDAU
LINEAL
LINEAR
LONGAN
MANDAN
MANDAY
MANIAC
MANIAS
MANRAY
MANTAS
MANUAL
MENIAL
MENSAE
MENSAL
MENSAS
MENTAL
MINOAN
MINYAN
MONDAY
NINEAM
NINJAS
NONFAT
PANDAS
PENMAN
PENNAE
PENPAL
PENTAD
PINDAR
PINEAL
PINNAE
PINNAS
PINOAK
PUNJAB
PUNKAH
QANTAS
QINTAR
RENTAL
RUNSAT
RUNWAY
SANDAL
SENDAK
SENLAC
SENNAS
SINBAD
SINEAD
SINTAX
SONTAG
SUNDAE
SUNDAY
SUNRAY
SUNTAN
SYNTAX
TANKAS
TANOAK
TANOAN
TINCAL
TINCAN
TINEAR
TINHAT
TINMAN
TINPAN
TONGAN
UINTAS
VANDAL
VENIAL
WANTAD
WENTAT
WINKAT
YENTAS
YUNNAN

••N••A
ADNEXA
ANNABA
ANNIKA
ARNICA
BANANA
BANGKA
CANADA
CANOLA
CANOVA
CINEMA
CONCHA
CONTRA
CUNAXA
DUNERA
GENERA
GENEVA
KANAKA
KINEMA
KONICA
LINGUA
LUNULA
MANAMA
MANANA
MANCHA
MANILA
MANTRA
MANTUA
MINIMA
MONERA
MONETA
MONICA
PANADA
PANAMA
PENNIA
PINATA
RENATA
SANCTA
SANDIA
SANDRA
SENECA
SENEGA
SENORA
SENTRA
SONATA
SONOMA
SONORA
TANAKA
TANANA
TANTRA
TUNDRA
TUNICA
WINONA
ZENANA
ZINNIA

•••NA•
ADONAI
AGENAS
ARENAS
ASANAS
ATONAL
AXONAL
BWANAS
CANNAE
CARNAL
CATNAP
COGNAC
DANNAY
DARNAY
DONNAS
EPINAL
FAUNAE
FAUNAL
FAUNAS
FINNAN
GUNNAR
HAINAN
HANNAH
HENNAS
HYENAS
HYMNAL
JINNAH
KARNAK
KAUNAS
KEENAN
KIDNAP
LIANAS
MAENAD
MOLNAR
MORNAY
NOONAN
PENNAE
PINNAE
PINNAS
PLANAR
PUTNAM
REGNAL
REGNAT
REINAS
RHINAL
RUANAS
SAUNAS
SCENAS
SENNAS
SIGNAL
SPINAL
SRANAN
TAINAN
THENAR
TRINAL
UNSNAG
UNSNAP
VARNAS
VEINAL
VERNAL
YUNNAN

•••N•A
AGENDA
AJANTA
AMANDA
AMENRA
ANANDA
BIANCA
BLANCA
BLANDA
BOSNIA
BRENDA
CORNEA
CRANIA
CRENNA
DEANNA
DUENNA
EUPNEA
FAENZA
FRANCA
GLENDA
GLINKA
GOANNA
GUINEA
JOANNA
KAUNDA
KWANZA
LUANDA
NARNIA
OLINDA
PAANGA
PENNIA
QUANTA
QUINOA
RHONDA
RUANDA
RWANDA
SARNIA
SHANIA
SIENNA
STANZA
UGANDA
URANIA
VIENNA
ZINNIA

••••NA
ALUMNA
ANCONA
ARCANA
ARJUNA
ATHENA
BANANA
CABANA
CARINA
CATENA
CESSNA
CORONA
COVINA
CRENNA
DEANNA
DUENNA
ENCINA
ESPANA
FALANA
FARINA
GALENA
GOANNA
GRETNA
GUIANA
GUYANA
HABANA
HAVANA
HELENA
IGUANA
ILEANA
JACANA
JOANNA
KAHUNA
KORUNA
LACUNA
LAGUNA
LAMINA
LATINA
LATONA
LUMINA
MANANA
MARINA
MEDINA
MELINA
MODENA
NOVENA
NUMINA
OKSANA
ORGANA

ORIANA
PARANA
PATINA
PIRANA
POMONA
PRAJNA
PURINA
RAMONA
REGINA
RETINA
ROWENA
ROXANA
RUMINA
SABENA
SALINA
SELENA
SERENA
SHEENA
SIENNA
SMYRNA
STERNA
TANANA
TIRANA
TUCANA
URBANA
VARUNA
VERONA
VICUNA
VIENNA
WINONA
XIMENA
ZENANA

N•B•••
NABBED
NABBER
NABOBS
NABORS
NEBULA
NIBBLE
NOBBLE
NOBLER
NOBLES
NOBODY
NUBBED
NUBBIN
NUBBLE
NUBBLY
NUBIAN
NUBILE

N••B••
NABBED
NABBER
NIBBLE
NIMBLE
NIMBLY
NIMBUS
NOBBLE
NOTBAD
NUBBED
NUBBIN
NUBBLE
NUBBLY
NUMBAT
NUMBED
NUMBER
NUMBLY

N•••B•
NABOBS
NASEBY
NAWABS
NEARBY
NINGBO

•NB•••
ENBLOC
INBORN
INBRED
INBULK
UNBARS
UNBELT
UNBEND
UNBENT
UNBIND
UNBOLT
UNBORN
UNBUSY

•N•B••
ANUBIS
ENABLE
KNOBBY
SNOBBY
SNUBBY
UNABLE

•N••B•
ANNABA
ENROBE
INDABA
INDEBT
KNOBBY
SNOBBY
SNUBBY
UNROBE

••NB••
BONBON
DUNBAR
HENBIT
SINBAD

••N•B•
ANNABA
DANUBE
GONEBY
NINGBO
WENTBY

••N••B
BENUMB
CANTAB
CONFAB
CONJOB
PUNJAB

•••N•B
DIONEB
HOBNOB

N•C•••
NACHOS
NACRES
NECKED
NECTAR
NICAEA
NICEAN
NICELY
NICENE
NICEST
NICETY
NICHES
NICKED
NICKEL
NICKER
NICOLA
NICOLE
NICOLO
NOCENT
NUCHAE
NUCHAL
NUCLEI
NUCLEO

N••C••
NASCAR
NIACIN
NIECES
NONCOM
NOTCHY
NUECES
NUNCIO

N•••C•
NATICK
NAUTCH
NODICE
NOTICE
NOVICE
NUANCE

N••••C
NITRIC
NOETIC
NORDIC

•NC•••
ANCHOR
ANCIEN
ANCONA
ENCAGE
ENCAMP
ENCASE
ENCINA
ENCINO
ENCODE
ENCORE
INCANS
INCASE
INCASH
INCEPT
INCHED
INCHES
INCHON
INCISE
INCITE
INCOME
INCULT
INCURS
INCUSE
ONCALL
UNCAGE
UNCAPS
UNCASE
UNCHIC
UNCIAL
UNCLAD
UNCLES
UNCLOG
UNCOIL
UNCOOL
UNCORK
UNCURL

•N•C••
ANACIN
ANTCOW
ENACTS
KNACKS
KNICKS
KNOCKS
SNACKS
SNICKS
SNOCAT
UNICEF
UNOCAL
VNECKS

•N••C•
ANTICS
ENESCO
ENLACE
ENRICH
ENRICO
ENTICE
INARCH
INDICT
INDUCE
INDUCT
INFACT
INFECT
INJECT
INLUCK
INSECT
INTACT
ONDECK
ONEACT
SNATCH
SNITCH
UNESCO
UNLACE
UNLOCK
UNPACK
UNTACK

•N•••C
ANEMIC
ANGLIC
ANODIC
ANOMIC
ENBLOC
GNOMIC
INSYNC
ONSPEC
UNCHIC
UNIFIC
UNIVAC

••NC••
BONCES
BUNCHE
BUNCHY
BUNCOS
CANCAN
CANCEL
CANCUN
CONCHA
CONCHS
CONCUR
DANCED
DANCER
DANCES
DUNCAN
DUNCES
FENCED
FENCER
FENCES
HINCTY
HONCHO
JUNCOS
LANCED
LANCER
LANCES
LANCET
LUNCHY
MANCHA
MANCHU
MINCED
MINCER
MINCES
MUNCHY
MUNCIE
NONCOM
NUNCIO
OUNCES
PANCHO
PENCEL
PENCIL
PINCER
PONCES
PONCHO
PUNCHY
RANCHO
RANCID
RANCOR
RUNCIE
SANCHO
SANCTA
SYNCED
TINCAL
TINCAN
TINCTS
VINCES
VINCIT
WENCES
WINCED
WINCER
WINCES

••N•C•
ALNICO
ARNICA
CONICS
CONOCO
CYNICS
EUNICE
IGNACE
IONICS
JANICE
KONICA
LUNACY
MENACE
MENSCH
MONACO
MONICA
MUNICH
PANICS
SENECA
SONICS
SUNOCO
TENACE
TONICS
TUNICA
TUNICS
VENICE
ZANUCK

••N••C
CONTAC
FENNEC
FINNIC
MANIAC
MANIOC
MANTIC
PONTIC
RUNDMC
SENLAC
SYNDIC
TANNIC
TENREC
ZENDIC

•••NC•
AGENCY
ATONCE
BIANCA
BLANCA
BLANCH
BLENCH
BOUNCE
BOUNCY
BRANCH
BRONCO
BRONCS
BRUNCH
CHANCE
CHANCY
CHINCH
CLANCY
CLENCH
CLINCH
CRUNCH
DRENCH
EVINCE
FIANCE
FLINCH
FRANCA
FRANCE
FRANCK
FRANCO
FRANCS
FRENCH
GLANCE
GRINCH
HAUNCH
JOUNCE
JOUNCY
LAUNCH
NUANCE
PAUNCH
PLANCK
POUNCE
PRANCE
PRINCE
QUENCH
QUINCE
QUINCY
SCONCE
SEANCE
STANCE
STANCH
STENCH
THENCE
TRANCE
TRENCH
USANCE
WHENCE
WRENCH

•••N•C
ATONIC
BIONIC
CLINIC
COGNAC
CYANIC
EDENIC
ETHNIC
ETONIC
FENNEC
FINNIC
ICONIC
IRENIC
IRONIC
OZONIC
PHONIC
PICNIC
PYKNIC
SCENIC
TANNIC
URANIC

••••NC
FERENC
INSYNC

N•D•••
NADINE
NADIRS
NIDIFY
NODDED
NODDLE
NODICE
NODOFF
NODOSE
NODULE
NUDELY
NUDEST
NUDGED
NUDGER
NUDGES
NUDIST
NUDITY
NUDNIK

N••D••
NASDAQ
NEEDED
NEEDLE
NEEDNT
NODDED
NODDLE
NOODLE
NORDIC

N•••D•
NAIADS
NERUDA
NEVADA
NOBODY
NOMADS

N••••D
NABBED
NAGGED
NAILED
NAPPED
NEARED
NECKED
NEEDED
NEREID
NESTED
NETTED
NICKED
NIMROD
NIPPED
NODDED
NOGOOD
NOISED
NOLEAD
NOLOAD
NOOSED
NOSHED
NOTBAD
NUBBED
NUDGED
NULLED
NUMBED
NURSED
NUTTED

•ND•••
ANDEAN
ANDHOW
ANDREA
ANDREI
ANDRES
ANDREW
ANDREY
ANDROS
ENDALL
ENDASH
ENDEAR
ENDERS
ENDING
ENDIVE
ENDMAN
ENDMEN
ENDORA
ENDOWS
ENDRUN
ENDSUP
ENDUED
ENDUES
ENDURE
ENDURO
ENDUSE
INDABA
INDEBT
INDEED
INDENE
INDENT
INDIAN
INDICT
INDIES
INDIGO
INDIRA
INDITE
INDIUM
INDOOR
INDORE
INDRIS
INDUCE
INDUCT
ONDECK
ONDINE
UNDIES
UNDINE
UNDOER
UNDOES
UNDONE
UNDRAW
UNDULY
UNDYED

•N•D••
ANADEM
ANODES
ANODIC
ANYDAY
CNIDAE
CNIDUS
ONEDAY
ONEDGE
SNIDER
SNYDER

•N••D•
ANANDA
ANHYDR
ENCODE
INSIDE
INVADE
KNEADS
ONEIDA
ONSIDE
SNOODS
UNLADE
UNMADE
UNTIDY

•N•••D
ANELED
ANGLED
ANKLED
ANTEED
ENDUED
ENFOLD
ENGIRD
ENNEAD
ENQUAD
ENSUED
ENURED
ENVIED
GNAWED
INBRED
INCHED
INDEED
INFOLD
INGRID
INHAND
INKIND
INLAID
INLAND
INNEED
INROAD
INTEND
INURED
INWARD
KNIFED
ONHAND
ONHOLD
ONLAND
ONWARD
SNAKED
SNARED
SNIPED
SNORED
SNOWED
UNAGED
UNAWED
UNBEND
UNBIND
UNCLAD
UNDYED
UNFOLD
UNGIRD
UNHAND
UNHEED
UNIPOD
UNITED
UNKIND
UNLAID
UNLEAD
UNLOAD
UNPAID
UNREAD
UNSAID
UNSHED
UNSHOD
UNSOLD
UNTIED
UNTOLD
UNTROD
UNUSED
UNWIND

••ND••
BANDED
BANDIT
BANDOG
BENDAY
BENDED
BENDER
BENDIX
BINDER
BINDUP
BONDED
BUNDLE
CANDID
CANDLE
CANDOR
CINDER
CONDOR
CONDOS
DANDER
DANDIE
DANDLE
DENDRI
DENDRO
DONDER
DUNDEE
FANDOM
FENDED
FENDER
FINDER
FONDER
FONDLE
FONDLY
FONDUE
FUNDED
GANDER
GANDHI
GENDER
GUNDOG
HANDED
HANDEL
HANDIN
HANDLE
HANDON
HANDUP
HINDER
HINDUS
KANDER
KINDER
KINDLE
KINDLY
KINDOF
LANDAU
LANDED
LANDER
LANDHO
LANDIS
LANDON
LANDRY
LENDER
LINDEN
LONDON
LUNDEN
LYNDON
MANDAN
MANDAY
MENDED
MENDEL
MENDER
MENDES
MINDED
MINDER
MONDAY
PANDAS
PANDER
PANDIT
PENDED
PINDAR
PINDUS
PONDER
PUNDIT
RANDOM
RANDRY
RENDER
RONDEL
RONDOS
RUNDLE
RUNDMC
RUNDRY
SANDAL
SANDED
SANDER
SANDIA
SANDRA
SENDAK
SENDER
SENDIN
SENDUP
SONDES
SUNDAE
SUNDAY
SUNDER
SUNDEW
SUNDOG
SUNDRY
SYNDIC
TANDEM
TENDED
TENDER
TENDON
TENDTO
TINDER
TONDOS
TUNDRA
VANDAL
VENDED
VENDEE
VENDOR
WANDER
WENDED
WINDED
WINDER
WINDEX
WINDOM
WINDOW
WINDUP
WONDER
YONDER
ZANDER
ZENDIC
ZENDOS

••N•D•
CANADA
CANIDS
DENUDE
MENADO
MONADS
MONODY
PANADA
RANIDS
SYNODS
XANADU

••N••D
AENEID
ARNOLD
BANDED
BANGED
BANKED
BANNED
BENDED
BINGED
BINNED
BONDED
BONGED
BUNGED
BUNKED
BUNTED
CANARD
CANDID
CANNED
CANOED
CANTED
CENSED
CONFED
CONKED
CONNED
CONOID
CONRAD
CUNARD
DANCED
DENIED
DENNED
DENTED
DINGED
DINNED
DINTED
DONALD
DONNED
DUNKED
DUNNED
ENNEAD
FANGED
FANNED
FENCED
FENDED
FINKED
FINNED
FUNDED
FUNKED
FUNNED
GANGED
GINNED
GONGED
GUNNED
HANDED
HANGED
HENTED
HINGED
HINTED
HONIED
HONKED
HUNTED
INNEED
JINKED
JINXED
JUNKED
KENNED
KINGED
KINKED
KONRAD
LANCED
LANDED
LENSED
LINKED
LONGED
LUNGED
LYNYRD
MANNED
MENDED
MINCED
MINDED
MINTED
MONIED
OINKED
OXNARD
PANNED
PANTED
PENDED
PENNED
PENROD
PENTAD
PINGED
PINKED
PINNED
PONGED
PONGID
PONIED
PUNNED
PUNTED
RANCID
RANGED
RANKED
RANTED
RENTED
RINGED
RINSED
RONALD
SANDED
SENSED
SINBAD
SINEAD
SINGED
SINNED
SUNGOD
SUNNED
SYNCED
TANGED
TANKED
TANNED
TENDED
TENSED
TENTED
TINGED
TINGOD
TINNED
TINTED
VANNED
VENDED
VENTED
WANNED
WANTAD
WANTED
WENDED
WINCED
WINDED
WINGED
WINKED
WONNED
WONTED
YANKED
YENNED
ZINGED
ZONKED

•••ND•
AGENDA
AMANDA
AMENDS
ANANDA
ARENDT
BIONDI
BLANDA
BLENDE
BLENDS
BLINDS
BLONDE
BLONDS
BOUNDS
BRANDO
BRANDS
BRANDT
BRANDX
BRANDY
BRENDA
DIRNDL
EBONDS
ELANDS
EMENDS
FIENDS
FOUNDS
FRONDS
GLANDS
GLENDA
GRANDE
GRANDS
GRINDS
GRUNDY
HOUNDS
HOUNDY
KAUNDA
LUANDA
MAUNDY
MBUNDU
MOUNDS
OLINDA
POUNDS
RHONDA
ROUNDS
RUANDA
RWANDA
SCENDS
SHANDY
SHINDY
SOUNDS
SPENDS
STANDS
TBONDS
TRENDS
TRENDY
UGANDA
UPENDS
VIANDS
WOUNDS
ZOUNDS

•••N•D
ATONED
BANNED
BEANED
BINNED
BRINED
BURNED
CANNED
CLONED
COINED
CONNED
CORNED
CRANED
DAMNED
DARNED
DAWNED
DENNED
DINNED
DONNED
DOWNED
DRONED
DUNNED
DURNED
EARNED
EVENED
FANNED
FAWNED
FINNED
FOINED
FUNNED
GAINED
GINNED
GIRNED
GOUNOD
GOWNED
GUNNED
HORNED
HYMNED
IRONED
JOINED
KEENED
KENNED
KERNED
KILNED
LEANED
LEONID
LIMNED
LOANED
MAENAD
MANNED
MOANED
MOONED
OPENED
OPINED
PAINED
PANNED
PAWNED
PEENED
PENNED
PERNOD
PHONED
PINNED
PLANED
PRUNED
PUNNED
RAINED
REINED
RUINED
SEINED
SHINED
SIGNED
SINNED
SPINED
STONED
SUNNED
TANNED
TINNED
TURNED
TWINED
VANNED
VEINED
WANNED
WARNED
WEANED
WHINED
WONNED
YARNED
YAWNED
YEANED
YENNED

••••ND
ABOUND
ADDEND
ALMOND
APPEND
ARMAND
AROUND
ASCEND
ATHAND
ATTEND
AUFOND
AUGEND
BEHIND
BEYOND
BRIAND
BYHAND
DEFEND
DEMAND
DEMOND
DEPEND
EDMOND
EDMUND
ERRAND
EXPAND
EXPEND
EXTEND
FAGEND
FECUND
FRIEND
GERUND
GROUND
IMPEND
INHAND
INKIND
INLAND
INTEND
ISLAND
JOCUND
LEGEND
LELAND
LEMOND
LIGAND
LOMOND
LOWEND
OBTUND
OFFEND
ONHAND
ONLAND
ORMOND
OSMOND
OSMUND
OSTEND
POLAND
REBEND
REBIND
REFUND
REMAND
REMEND
REMIND
REPAND
RESAND
RESEND
REWIND
RIBAND
ROLAND
ROTUND
SECOND
STRAND
TAGEND
THEEND
UNBEND
UNBIND
UNHAND
UNKIND
UNWIND
UPLAND
UPWIND

NE••••
NEARBY
NEARED
NEARER
NEARLY
NEARTO
NEATEN
NEATER
NEATLY
NEBULA
NECKED
NECTAR
NEEDED
NEEDLE
NEEDNT
NEESON
NEGATE
NEIGHS
NEISSE
NEKTON
NELLIE
NELSON
NEMATO
NENETS
NEPALI
NEPHEW
NEPHRO
NEREID
NEREIS
NEREUS
NEROLI
NERUDA
NERVES
NESSES
NESSIE
NESTEA
NESTED
NESTER
NESTLE
NESTOR
NETHER
NETMAN
NETMEN
NETPAY
NETTED
NETTLE
NETTLY
NETTON
NEUMAN
NEUMES
NEURAL
NEUROL
NEURON
NEUTER
NEVADA
NEVERS
NEVINS
NEVSKY
NEWAGE
NEWARK
NEWELS
NEWEST
NEWISH
NEWLEY
NEWMAN
NEWMAR
NEWTON
NEXTTO

N•E•••
NEEDED
NEEDLE
NEEDNT
NEESON
NIECES
NIELLI
NIELLO
NLEAST
NOESIS
NOETIC
NOEXIT
NUECES

N••E••
NAMELY
NAMERS
NAPERY
NASEBY
NAVELS
NENETS
NEREID
NEREIS
NEREUS
NEVERS
NEWELS
NEWEST
NFLERS
NHLERS
NICEAN
NICELY
NICENE
NICEST
NICETY
NINEAM
NINEPM
NINERS
NINETY
NITERS
NITERY
NLWEST
NOCENT
NOLEAD
NOLENS
NOLESS
NONEGO
NONETS
NOPETS
NOTERS
NOVELS
NOVENA
NUDELY
NUDEST
NUGENT
NUMERO
NYMETS

N•••E•
NABBED
NABBER
NACRES
NAGGED
NAGGER
NAILED
NAILER
NANSEN
NANTES
NAPIER
NAPLES
NAPPED
NAPPER
NAPPES
NASSER
NATTER
NAUSEA
NAVIES
NEARED
NEARER
NEATEN
NEATER
NECKED
NEEDED
NEPHEW
NERVES
NESSES
NESTEA
NESTED
NESTER
NETHER
NETMEN
NETTED
NEUMES
NEUTER
NEWLEY
NGUYEN
NIAMEY
NICAEA
NICHES
NICKED
NICKEL
NICKER
NIECES
NIGHER
NIKKEI
NIPPED
NIPPER
NIPSEY
NISSEN
NITRES
NIXIES
NOBLER
NOBLES
NODDED
NOISED
NOISES
NOONES
NOOSED
NOOSES
NOSHED
NOSHER
NOSHES
NOSIER
NOTYET
NOUMEA
NUBBED
NUCLEI
NUCLEO
NUDGED
NUDGER
NUDGES
NUECES
NUGGET
NULLED
NUMBED
NUMBER
NURSED
NURSER
NURSES
NUTLET
NUTMEG
NUTTED
NUTTER

N••••E
NADINE
NANNIE
NAPPIE
NATIVE
NATURE
NEEDLE
NEGATE
NEISSE
NELLIE
NESSIE
NESTLE
NETTLE
NEWAGE
NIBBLE
NICENE
NICOLE
NIGGLE
NIMBLE
NOBBLE
NODDLE
NODICE
NODOSE
NODULE
NOLOSE
NOMINE
NOMORE
NONAGE
NONAME
NOODLE
NOSALE
NOTATE
NOTICE
NOVICE
NOWISE
NOZZLE
NUANCE
NUBBLE
NUBILE
NUCHAE
NUTATE
NUZZLE

•NE•••
ANELED
ANELES
ANEMIA
ANEMIC
ANERGY
ENERGY
ENESCO
GNEISS
INESSE
KNEADS
KNEELS
KNELLS
ONEACT
ONEDAY
ONEDGE
ONEIDA
ONEILL
ONEMAN
ONETWO
ONEUPS
ONEWAY
PNEUMA
SNEAKS
SNEAKY
SNEERS
SNEERY
SNEEZE
SNEEZY
SNELLS
UNEASE
UNEASY
UNESCO
UNEVEN
VNECKS

•N•E••
ANDEAN
ANGELA
ANGELI
ANGELL
ANGELO
ANGELS
ANGERS
ANNEAL
ANNEXE
ANSELM
ANTEED
ANTERO
ANTEUP
ENDEAR
ENDERS
ENGELS
ENMESH
ENNEAD
ENTERO
ENTERS
INCEPT
INDEBT
INDEED
INDENE
INDENT
INFECT
INFERS
INFEST
INGEAR
INGEST
INHERE
INJECT
INJEST
INKERS
INLETS
INNEED
INNESS
INSEAM
INSECT
INSERT
INSETS
INTEND
INTENS
INTENT
INTERJ
INTERN
INVENT
INVERT
INVEST
KNEELS
ONDECK
ONSETS
SNEERS
SNEERY
SNEEZE
SNEEZY
UNBELT
UNBEND
UNBENT
UNHEED
UNLEAD
UNLESS
UNMEET
UNMESH
UNPEGS
UNPENS
UNREAD
UNREAL
UNREEL
UNREST
UNSEAL
UNSEAT
UNSEEN
UNSEWN
UNSEWS
UNVEIL
UNWELL

•N••E•
ANADEM
ANCIEN
ANDREA
ANDREI
ANDRES
ANDREW
ANDREY
ANELED
ANELES
ANGLED
ANGLER
ANGLES
ANIMES
ANKLED
ANKLES
ANKLET
ANNLEE
ANODES
ANOLES
ANSWER
ANTEED
ANTHEM
ANTHER
ANTLER
ANTRES
CNOTES
ENAMEL
ENATES
ENDMEN
ENDUED
ENDUES
ENSUED
ENSUES
ENTREE
ENURED
ENURES
ENVIED
ENVIER
ENVIES
GNAWED
GNAWER
GNOMES
INANER
INAPET
INBRED
INCHED
INCHES
INDEED
INDIES
INGLES
INGRES
INKIER
INKJET
INKLES
INNEED
INSTEP
INURED
INURES
KNAVES
KNIFED
KNIFES
KNIVES
KNOWER
ONAGER
ONSPEC
ONUSES
ONVIEW
ONYXES
SNAKED
SNAKES
SNARED
SNARES
SNIDER
SNIPED
SNIPER
SNIPES
SNIVEL
SNOPES
SNORED
SNORER
SNORES
SNOWED
SNYDER
TNOTES
UNAGED
UNAWED
UNCLES
UNDIES
UNDOER
UNDOES
UNDYED
UNEVEN
UNFREE
UNGUES
UNHEED
UNICEF
UNISEX
UNITED
UNITER
UNITES
UNMEET
UNOPEN
UNREEL
UNSEEN
UNSHED
UNTIED
UNTIES
UNUSED

•N•••E
ANNEXE
ANNLEE
ANOMIE
ANSATE
ANYONE
CNIDAE
ENABLE
ENCAGE
ENCASE
ENCODE
ENCORE
ENDIVE
ENDURE
ENDUSE
ENGAGE
ENGINE
ENISLE
ENLACE
ENRAGE
ENROBE
ENSILE
ENSURE
ENTICE
ENTIRE
ENTREE
ENZYME
INCASE
INCISE
INCITE
INCOME
INCUSE
INDENE
INDITE
INDORE
INDUCE
INESSE
INFUSE
INHALE
INHERE
INJOKE
INJURE
INLINE
INLOVE
INMATE
INNAGE
INNATE
INOUYE
INSANE
INSIDE
INSOLE
INSURE
INTAKE
INTIME
INTINE
INTONE
INTUNE
INVADE
INVITE
INVOKE
ONDINE
ONEDGE
ONFILE
ONFIRE
ONLINE
ONSALE
ONSIDE
ONSITE
ONTAPE
ONTIME
SNATHE
SNEEZE
SNOOZE
UNABLE
UNCAGE
UNCASE
UNDINE
UNDONE
UNEASE
UNFREE
UNGLUE
UNIATE
UNIQUE
UNLACE
UNLADE
UNLIKE
UNMADE
UNMAKE
UNPILE
UNRIPE
UNROBE
UNSAFE
UNSURE
UNTRUE
UNTUNE
UNWISE
UNWOVE
UNYOKE

••NE••
ADNEXA
AENEAS
AENEID
ANNEAL
ANNEXE
ARNESS
ARNETT
BONERS
BONEUP
CANERS
CINEMA
CONEYS
CUNEAL
DINEIN
DINEON
DINERO
DINERS
DONEES
DONEIN
DONETS
DONEUP
DUNERA
ENNEAD
ERNEST
FINELY
FINERY
FINEST
GENERA
GENETS
GENEVA
GENEVE
GONEBY
GONERS
HONEST
HONEYS
INNEED
INNESS
JUNEAU
KINEMA
LINEAL
LINEAR
LINENS
LINENY
LINERS
LINEUP
LONELY
LONERS
MANEGE
MINERS
MONERA
MONETA
MONEYS
NENETS
NINEAM
NINEPM
NINERS
NINETY
NONEGO
NONETS
ORNERY
OWNERS
PANELS
PINEAL
PINERO
PINERY
RANEES
RENEGE
RENEWS
RONELY
SANELY
SANEST
SENECA
SENEGA
SINEAD
SINEWS
SINEWY
TENENS
TENETS
TINEAR
TONERS
TONEUP
TUNEIN
TUNERS
TUNEUP
VENEER
VENETO
VINERY
WANERS
WINERY

••N•E•
ANNLEE
ARNHEM
BANDED
BANGED
BANGER
BANKED
BANKER
BANNED
BANNER
BANTER
BENDED
BENDER
BINDER
BINGED
BINGES
BINNED
BONCES
BONDED
BONGED
BONIER
BONNES
BONNET
BONZES
BUNGED
BUNGEE
BUNKED
BUNKER
BUNSEN
BUNTED
BUNTER
BUNUEL
CANCEL
CANIER
CANKER
CANNED
CANNEL
CANNER
CANNES
CANOED
CANOES
CANTED
CANTER
CENSED
CENSER
CENSES
CENTER
CINDER
CONFED
CONFER
CONGER
CONIES
CONKED
CONKER
CONMEN
CONNED
CONNER
CONTES
CONVEX
CONVEY
DANCED
DANCER
DANCES
DANDER
DANGER
DANIEL
DANKER
DANNER
DANTES
DENIED
DENIER
DENIES
DENNED
DENSER
DENTED
DENVER
DENZEL
DINGED
DINKEY
DINNED
DINNER
DINTED
DONDER
DONEES
DONKEY
DONNED
DONNEE
DONNER
DUNCES
DUNDEE
DUNKED
DUNKER
DUNNED
FANGED
FANJET
FANNED
FENCED
FENCER
FENCES
FENDED
FENDER
FENMEN
FENNEC
FENNEL
FINDER
FINGER
FINKED
FINNED
FINNEY
FONDER
FUNDED
FUNKED
FUNNED
FUNNEL
GANDER
GANGED
GANGER
GANGES
GANNET
GENDER
GENIES
GENRES
GINGER
GINNED
GONGED
GUNMEN
GUNNED
GUNNEL
GUNNER
GUNTER
HANDED
HANDEL
HANGED
HANGER
HANKER
HANLEY
HANSEL
HENLEY
HENNER
HENTED
HINDER
HINGED
HINGES
HINTED
HINTER
HONIED
HONKED
HONKER
HUNGER
HUNKER
HUNTED
HUNTER
INNEED
JANSEN
JENNER
JENNET
JENNEY
JENSEN
JINKED
JINXED
JINXES
JUNKED
JUNKER
JUNKET
KANDER
KENNED
KENNEL
KENNER
KINDER
KINGED
KINKED
KINSEY
LANCED
LANCER
LANCES
LANCET
LANDED
LANDER
LANIER
LANKER
LENDER
LENSED
LENSES
LENTEN
LINDEN
LINGER
LINIER
LINKED
LINKER
LINNET
LINNEY
LINSEY
LINTEL
LINTER
LONGED
LONGER
LONGES
LUNDEN
LUNGED
LUNGES
LUNKER
LYNLEY
LYNXES
MANGER
MANNED
MANNER
MANSES
MANTEL
MANUEL
MENDED
MENDEL
MENDER
MENDES
MENKEN
MENNEN
MINCED
MINCER
MINCES
MINDED
MINDER
MINKES
MINTED
MINTER
MINUET
MINXES
MONGER
MONIED
MONIES
MONKEY
MONTEL
MONTES
MONTEZ
NANSEN
NANTES
OINKED
OUNCES
PANDER
PANNED
PANNER
PANNES
PANTED
PANZER
PENCEL
PENDED
PENMEN
PENNED
PENNER
PENNEY
PENSEE
PINCER
PINGED
PINIER
PINKED
PINKEN
PINKER
PINNED
PINNER
PINTER
PONCES
PONDER
PONGED
PONGEE
PONIED
PONIES
PONTES
PUNIER
PUNKER
PUNNED
PUNNET
PUNTED
PUNTER
RANEES
RANGED
RANGER
RANGES
RANKED
RANKER
RANTED
RANTER
RENDER
RENNES
RENNET
RENTED
RENTER
RINGED
RINGER
RINSED
RINSES
RONDEL
RUNLET
RUNNEL
RUNNER
SANDED
SANDER
SANGER
SANSEI
SANTEE
SENDER
SENNET
SENSED
SENSEI
SENSES
SINGED
SINGER
SINGES
SINKER
SINNED
SINNER
SINTER
SONDES
SONNET
SUNDER
SUNDEW
SUNKEN
SUNNED
SUNSET
SYNCED
TANDEM
TANGED
TANKED
TANKER
TANNED
TANNER
TANTES
TENDED
TENDER
TENREC
TENSED
TENSER
TENSES
TENTED
TENTER
TINDER
TINGED
TINGES
TINIER
TINKER
TINMEN
TINNED
TINNER
TINSEL
TINTED
TINTER
TONIER
TONNES
TUNNEL
TUNNEY
VANIER
VANNED
VENDED
VENDEE
VENEER
VENTED
VENTER
VENUES
VINCES
VINIER
WANDER
WANIER
WANNED
WANNER
WANTED
WENCES
WENDED
WINCED
WINCER
WINCES
WINDED
WINDER
WINDEX
WINGED
WINGER
WINIER
WINKED
WINKER
WINNER
WINTER
WINZES
WONDER
WONNED
WONTED
WYNTER
YANKED
YANKEE
YENNED
YONDER
ZANDER
ZANIER
ZANIES
ZENGER
ZINGED
ZINGER
ZONKED
ZONKER

••N••E
ADNATE
AGNATE
ANNEXE
ANNLEE
AUNTIE
BANGLE
BINATE
BONNIE
BUNCHE
BUNDLE
BUNGEE
BUNGLE
BYNAME
CANAPE
CANDLE
CANINE
CANNAE
CANTLE
CANUTE
CENOTE
CENTRE
CINQUE
CONNIE
CONTRE
CONURE
DANDIE
DANDLE
DANGLE
DANGME
DANUBE
DENGUE
DENISE
DENOTE
DENUDE
DINGLE
DONATE
DONGLE
DONNEE
DUNDEE
EUNICE
FANNIE
FINALE
FINITE
FONDLE
FONDUE
GANGLE
GANGUE
GENEVE
GENOME
GENTLE
GUNITE
HANDLE
HANKIE
HONORE
IGNACE
IGNITE
IGNORE
INNAGE
INNATE
IONISE
IONIZE
JANGLE
JANICE
JANINE
JENNIE
JINGLE
JUNGLE
JUNKIE
KINDLE
KINGME
LANATE
LANOSE
LENAPE
LENNIE
LENORE
LINAGE
LONGUE
LUNATE
MANAGE
MANEGE
MANGLE
MANQUE
MANTLE
MENACE
MENAGE
MENSAE
MINGLE
MINNIE
MINUTE
MONROE
MUNCIE
NANNIE
NONAGE
NONAME
OENONE
ORNATE
PENNAE
PENSEE
PINITE
PINKIE
PINNAE
PINOLE
PINTLE
PONGEE
PUNKIE
RANKLE
RENAME
RENEGE
RENNIE
RENOTE
RONNIE
RUNCIE
RUNDLE
SANTEE
SENATE
SINGLE
SINISE
SUNDAE

TANGLE TENACE TENURE TINGLE TINKLE TONGUE TONITE VENDEE VENICE VENIRE VENITE VINNIE WANGLE WINKIE WINKLE WINNIE YANKEE ZONATE

•••NE•

AKENES ALINES AMINES ATONED ATONES AZINES BAINES BANNED BANNER BARNES BARNEY BEANED BINNED BIRNEY BONNES BONNET BORNEO BOWNET BRINED BRINES BRUNEI BRUNET BURNED BURNER BURNET BURNEY BYRNES CAGNEY CANNED CANNEL CANNER CANNES CARNES CARNET CARNEY CHANEL CHANEY CHINES CLINES CLONED CLONES COINED COINER CONNED CONNER COONEY CORNEA CORNED CORNEL CORNER CORNET CRANED CRANES CRENEL

CRONES CYGNET DABNEY DAMNED DANNER DARNED DARNEL DARNER DAWNED DENNED DINNED DINNER DIONEB DISNEY DONNED DONNEE DONNER DOWNED DOWNER DOWNEY DRONED DRONER DRONES DUNNED DURNED EARNED EARNER EISNER EUPNEA EVENED EVENER FANNED FAWNED FAWNER FENNEC FENNEL FINNED FINNEY FLYNET FOINED FUNNED FUNNEL GAINED GAINER GANNET GARNER GARNET GINNED GIRNED GOWNED GUINEA GUNNED GUNNEL GUNNER GURNEY HAINES HEANEY HEFNER HENNER HORNED HORNER HORNET HORNEY HYMNED INANER IRENES IRONED IRONER JENNER JENNET JENNEY JITNEY JOINED JOINER

JOYNER KAVNER KEENED KEENEN KEENER KENNED KENNEL KENNER KERNED KERNEL KEYNES KIDNEY KILNED KRONER LEANED LEANER LEONES LERNER LIANES LIENEE LIMNED LIMNER LINNET LINNEY LIONEL LIONET LOANED LOANER LOONEY MAGNET MANNED MANNER MARNER MEANER MENNEN MILNER MOANED MOANER MOINES MOONED MOONEY NOONES OPENED OPENER OPINED OPINER OPINES ORKNEY PAINED PANNED PANNER PANNES PAWNED PAWNEE PAWNER PEENED PENNED PENNER PENNEY PHONED PHONES PHONEY PINNED PINNER PLANED PLANER PLANES PLANET PRUNED PRUNER PRUNES PUNNED PUNNET RADNER

RAINED RAINER RAINES RAINEY REINED REINER RENNES RENNET REUNES RODNEY ROMNEY ROONEY RUINED RUINER RUNNEL RUNNER SCENES SCONES SEINED SEINER SEINES SENNET SHINED SHINER SHINES SIDNEY SIGNED SIGNEE SIGNER SIGNET SIMNEL SINNED SINNER SONNET SOONER SPINED SPINEL SPINES SPINET STONED STONER STONES SUMNER SUNNED SWANEE SYDNEY TANNED TANNER TBONES TEENER TERNES THANES TINNED TINNER TONNES TOWNER TRINES TUNNEL TUNNEY TURNED TURNER TWINED TWINES USENET VAINER VANNED VARNEY VEINED WAGNER WANNED WANNER WAPNER WARNED WARNER

WATNEY WEANED WERNER WHINED WHINER WHINES WHINEY WIENER WINNER WONNED YARNED YAWNED YAWNER YEANED YENNED

•••N•E

ATONCE AVENGE AVENUE BEANIE BERNIE BLENDE BLONDE BONNIE BOUNCE BRONTE BRONZE CANNAE CHANCE CHANGE CONNIE CRINGE DIANNE DIONNE DONNEE EVINCE EVONNE FANNIE FAUNAE FIANCE FLANGE FLENSE FRANCE FRINGE GLANCE GLENNE GRANDE GRANGE GRUNGE GWYNNE JEANNE JENNIE JOANIE JOANNE JOUNCE LAINIE LENNIE LEONIE LIENEE LOONIE LOUNGE MARNIE MEANIE MINNIE NANNIE NUANCE ODENSE ORANGE PAWNEE PENNAE PINNAE PLANTE PLUNGE

POINTE POUNCE PRANCE PRINCE PRYNNE PUENTE QUINCE RENNIE RONNIE SAINTE SCONCE SEANCE SIGNEE SPONGE STANCE SWANEE THENCE TOONIE TOWNIE TRANCE TWINGE USANCE VIENNE VINNIE WEENIE WHENCE WINNIE YVONNE

••••NE

ACHENE ACTONE AFFINE AHERNE ALDINE ALFINE ALKENE ALPINE ANYONE ARCANE ARLENE ARSENE ATHENE ATTUNE BEGONE BEMINE BLAINE BOURNE BOVINE BROWNE BUTANE BUTENE BYGONE BYLINE CANINE CAPONE CELINE CETANE CHAINE COHUNE COSINE DAMONE DAPHNE DAYONE DEBONE DEFINE DEPONE DEVINE DIANNE DIONNE DIVINE DOMINE DWAYNE ELAINE

ELAYNE ENGINE EOCENE EQUINE ERMINE ESSENE ETERNE ETHANE ETHENE EUGENE EVONNE EVZONE FALINE FAMINE FELINE FILENE GAMINE GLENNE GREENE GWYNNE GYRENE HELENE HUMANE IMFINE IMMUNE INDENE INLINE INSANE INTINE INTONE INTUNE IODINE IRLENE IRVINE ISMENE JANINE JEANNE JEJUNE JOANNE JOLENE KALINE KETONE LATENE LEVENE LEVINE LIERNE LUPINE LUPONE LYSINE MALONE MARINE MAXENE MAXINE MIFUNE MODINE MOLINE MURINE NADINE NICENE NOMINE OCTANE OENONE ONDINE ONLINE ORPINE OSCINE PATINE PAVANE PROCNE PRYNNE PUISNE PURINE RACINE RAMONE

RAPINE RATINE RAVINE RECANE REDONE REFINE RELINE REPINE RETENE RETUNE REZONE ROCKNE ROXANE SABINE SALINE SCARNE SELENE SERENE SERINE SHAYNE SHRINE SILONE SIMONE SLOANE SOFINE SOIGNE SPLINE STERNE STRINE SUPINE THRONE TIRANE TISANE TRIUNE TULANE TYRONE UNDINE UNDONE UNTUNE URBANE URSINE VIENNE VISINE WAHINE XYLENE YVONNE

NF••••

NFLERS

N••F••

NONFAT

N•••F•

NIDIFY NODOFF NOTIFY

N••••F

NODOFF

•NF•••

ENFANT ENFOLD INFACT INFAMY INFANT INFECT INFERS INFEST INFIRM INFLOW INFLUX INFOLD INFORM INFULL INFUSE ONFILE ONFIRE ONFOOT UNFAIR UNFITS UNFOLD UNFREE UNFURL

•N•F••

INAFIX INAFOG KNIFED KNIFES SNAFUS SNIFFS SNIFFY SNUFFS SNUFFY UNIFIC

•N••F•

SNIFFS SNIFFY SNUFFS SNUFFY UNSAFE

•N•••F

ENGULF INHALF UNICEF

••NF••

CANFUL CONFAB CONFED CONFER GUNFOR MANFUL NONFAT PANFRY PANFUL RANFOR RUNFOR SINFUL

••N•F•

CANIFF KUNGFU MINIFY RANOFF RUNOFF SENUFO VINIFY

••N••F

CANIFF KINDOF RANOFF RUNOFF

NG••••

NGUYEN

N•G•••

NAGANO NAGGED NAGGER NAGOYA NEGATE NIGGLE NIGHER NIGHTS NIGHTY NOGGIN NOGOOD NUGENT NUGGET

N••G••

NAGGED NAGGER NAUGHT NEIGHS NIGGLE NILGAI NINGBO NOGGIN NORGAY NOUGAT NOUGHT NUDGED NUDGER NUDGES NUGGET

N•••G•

NEWAGE NONAGE NONEGO

N••••G

NAMING NIXING NOSING NOTING NUKING NUTMEG

•NG•••

ANGELA ANGELI ANGELL ANGELO ANGELS ANGERS ANGKOR ANGLED ANGLER ANGLES ANGLIA ANGLIC ANGLOS ANGOLA ANGORA ENGAGE ENGELS ENGINE ENGIRD ENGIRT ENGLUT ENGRAM ENGULF INGEAR INGEST INGLES INGMAR INGOTS INGRAM INGRES INGRID UNGIRD UNGIRT UNGLUE UNGUAL UNGUES UNGUIS

•N•G••

ANSGAR ENIGMA KNAGGY KNIGHT ONAGER SNAGGY SNUGLI SNUGLY UNAGED

•N••G•

ANERGY ENCAGE ENERGY ENGAGE ENOUGH ENRAGE ENSIGN INDIGO INNAGE KNAGGY ONEDGE ONHIGH SNAGGY UNCAGE UNPEGS UNRIGS

•N•••G

ANALOG ANWANG ANYANG ENDING INAFOG INKING INNING UNCLOG UNPLUG UNSNAG UNSUNG

••NG••

BANGED BANGER BANGKA BANGLE BANGOR BANGUI BANGUP BENGAL BENGAY BINGED BINGES BONGED BONGOS BUNGED BUNGEE BUNGLE CONGAS CONGER CONGOU DANGER DANGLE DANGLY DANGME DENGUE DINGED DINGHY DINGLE DINGUS DONGLE FANGED FINGER FUNGUS GANGED GANGER GANGES GANGLE GANGLY GANGUE GANGUP GINGER GONGED GUNGHO HANGAR HANGED HANGER HANGIN HANGON HANGUL HANGUP HINGED HINGES HINGIS HUNGER HUNGIN HUNGON HUNGRY HUNGUP HUNGWU JANGLE JANGLY JINGLE JINGLY JUNGLE JUNGLY KINGED KINGLY KINGME KUNGFU LANGUR LENGTH LINGER LINGUA LONGAN LONGED LONGER LONGES LONGLY LONGUE LUNGED LUNGES MANGER MANGLE MANGOS MINGLE MONGER MONGOL MUNGOS NINGBO PENGHU PINGED PONGED PONGEE PONGID RANGED RANGER RANGES RANGUP RINGED RINGER RINGUP RUNGUP

SANGER SANGTO SINGED SINGER SINGES SINGIN SINGLE SINGLY SINGTO SUNGOD TANGED TANGLE TANGLY TANGOS TANGUY TINGED TINGES TINGLE TINGLY TINGOD TONGAN TONGUE WANGLE WINGED WINGER WINGIT XINGIN YANGON YUNGLO ZENGER ZINGED ZINGER

••N•G•

BENIGN GINKGO GONOGO INNAGE LINAGE MANAGE MANEGE MENAGE NONAGE NONEGO RENEGE SENEGA

••N••G

AWNING BANDOG BENING BONING CANING DANANG DANZIG DINING FINING GUNDOG HONING INNING KENNYG LINING MINING OWNING PENANG PINING SONTAG SUNDOG TONING TUNING VINING WANING WINING WONMUG ZONING

•••NG•

AVENGE BEINGS BOINGO BRINGS CHANGE CLANGS CLINGS CLINGY CRINGE DOINGS DRINGS ERYNGO FLANGE FLINGS FRINGE FRINGY GOINGS GRANGE GRINGO GRUNGE GRUNGY HMONGS ICINGS KIANGS LIANGS LOUNGE OLINGO ORANGE ORANGS ORANGY ORINGS PAANGA PLUNGE PRANGS PRONGS QUANGO SLANGS SLANGY SLINGS SPONGE SPONGY STINGO STINGS STINGY SWINGS SWINGY THINGS THINGY THONGS TWANGS TWANGY TWINGE UBANGI WHANGS WRINGS WRONGS

•••N•G

EGGNOG KENNYG KOENIG STENOG UNSNAG

••••NG

AAHING ABYING ACHING ACTING ADDING AGEING AIDING AILING AIMING AIRING ANWANG ANYANG ARCING ARMING ASKING AWNING BAAING BAKING BALING BARING BARONG BASING BATING BAYING BBKING BELONG BENING BERING BIDING BIKING BITING BLUING BODING BOEING BOGONG BONING BOOING BORING BOWING BOXING BUSING BUTUNG BUYING CAGING CAKING CANING CARING CASING CAVING CAWING CEDING CHIANG CITING CLUING CODING COMING COOING COPING CORING COWING CRYING CUBING CURING DANANG DARING DATING DATONG DAZING DEKING DELONG DEWING DICING DIKING DINING DIVING DOLING DOMING DOPING DOSING DOTING DOZING DRYING DUGONG DUKING DUPING DURING DYEING EALING EARING EASING EATING EBBING EDGING EGGING ENDING EPPING ERRING ERVING EYEING FACING FADING FAKING FARING FAXING FAZING FEEING FETING FIFING FILING FINING FIRING FIXING FLYING FOXING FRYING FUMING FUSING FUZING GAGING GAMING GAPING GATING GAZING GEEING GIBING GIVING GLUING GORING GUYING GYBING HALING HARING HATING HAVING HAWING HAYING HAZING HEWING HEXING HIDING HIEING HIKING HIRING HIVING HOEING HOLING HOMING HONING HOPING HOSING HYPING ICHING IDLING IMPING

INKING
INNING
IRKING
IRVING
JADING
JAPING
JAWING
JIBING
JIVING
JOKING
JUKING
KDLANG
KEYING
KITING
LACING
LADING
LAMING
LAVING
LAWING
LAYING
LAZING
LIKING
LIMING
LINING
LIPENG
LIVING
LOPING
LOSING
LOVING
LOWING
LUBING
LURING
LUTING
MAKING
MATING
MEKONG
METING
MEWING
MIKING
MIMING
MINING
MIRING
MIXING
MOOING
MOPING
MOVING
MOWING
MUSING
MUTING
NAMING
NIXING
NOSING
NOTING
NUKING
OARING
OBLONG
OFFING
OGLING
OILING
OOHING
OOLONG
OOZING
OPTING
ORBING
OUTING
OWNING
PACING
PADANG
PAGING
PAHANG
PALING
PARANG
PARING
PAVING
PAWING
PAYING
PEKING
PENANG
PIKING
PILING
PINING
PIPING
PLYING
POKING
POLING
PORING
POSING
PRYING
PULING
RACING
RAGING
RAKING
RARING
RASING
RATING
RAVING
RAZING
REDING
REHANG
REHUNG
RESING
RICING
RIDING
RILING
RIMING
RISING
RIVING
ROBING
ROPING
ROVING
ROWING
RULING
SARONG
SATANG
SATING
SAVING
SAWING
SAYING
SEEING
SEWING
SHYING
SIDING
SIRING
SITING
SIXING
SIZING
SKIING
SKYING
SLUING
SOLING
SOLONG
SOWING
SPRANG
SPRING
SPRUNG
SPYING
STRING
STRONG
STRUNG
TAKING
TAMING
TAPING
TARING
TAWING
TAXING
TEEING
THRONG
TIDING
TIEING
TILING
TIMING
TIRING
TOEING
TONING
TOTING
TOWING
TOYING
TRUING
TRYING
TUBING
TUNING
TURING
TYPING
UNSUNG
UPPING
URGING
VEXING
VIKING
VINING
VOTING
VOWING
WADING
WAGING
WAKING
WANING
WARING
WAVING
WAXING
WILING
WINING
WIPING
WIRING
WOOING
WOWING
YAWING
YOKING
ZONING

NH••••
NHLERS

N•H•••
NIHILO
NOHITS

N••H••
NACHOS
NASHUA
NATHAN
NEPHEW
NEPHRO
NETHER
NICHES
NIGHER
NIGHTS
NIGHTY
NIIHAU
NOSHED
NOSHER
NOSHES
NOSHOW
NUCHAE
NUCHAL

N•••H•
NAUGHT
NAVAHO
NEIGHS
NINTHS
NORTHS
NOTCHY
NOUGHT
NYMPHS

N••••H
NAMATH
NAUTCH
NEWISH
NULLAH

•NH•••
ANHYDR
ENHALO
INHALE
INHALF
INHAND
INHAUL
INHERE
ONHAND
ONHIGH
ONHOLD
UNHAND
UNHEED
UNHOLY
UNHOOK
UNHURT

•N•H••
ANCHOR
ANDHOW
ANNHON
ANTHEM
ANTHER
ANYHOW
INCHED
INCHES
INCHON
UNCHIC
UNSHED
UNSHOD

•N••H•
KNIGHT
SNATHE
SNATHS

•N•••H
ENDASH
ENMESH
ENOUGH
ENRICH
INARCH
INCASH
INRUSH
INWITH
ONHIGH
ONRUSH
SNATCH
SNITCH
UNLASH
UNMESH
UNWISH

••NH••
ANNHON
ARNHEM
BENHUR
DUNHAM
JANHUS
MENHIR
SENHOR
TINHAT

••N•H•
BUNCHE
BUNCHY
CANTHI
CONCHA
CONCHS
DINGHY
GANDHI
GUNGHO
GUNSHY
HONCHO
HONSHU
JONAHS
LANDHO
LUNCHY
MANCHA
MANCHU
MONTHS
MUNCHY
MYNAHS
NINTHS
PANCHO
PENGHU
PONCHO
PUNCHY
RANCHO
SANCHO
TENTHS
XANTHO

••N••H
BANISH
DANISH
FINISH
HANNAH
JINNAH
LENGTH
MENSCH
MUNICH
ORNITH
PUNISH
PUNKAH
TONISH
VANISH
WINISH
ZENITH

•••N•H
BLANCH
BLENCH
BRANCH
BRUNCH
CHINCH
CLENCH
CLINCH
CRUNCH
DRENCH
FLINCH
FRENCH
GRINCH
HANNAH
HAUNCH
JINNAH
LAUNCH
PAUNCH
PLINTH
QUENCH
STANCH
STENCH
TRENCH
WRENCH

NI••••
NIACIN
NIAMEY
NIBBLE
NICAEA
NICEAN
NICELY
NICENE
NICEST
NICETY
NICHES
NICKED
NICKEL
NICKER
NICOLA
NICOLE
NICOLO
NIDIFY
NIECES
NIELLI
NIELLO
NIGGLE
NIGHER
NIGHTS
NIGHTY
NIHILO
NIIHAU
NIKITA
NIKKEI
NIKOLA
NILGAI
NIMBLE
NIMBLY
NIMBUS
NIMINY
NIMITZ
NIMROD
NINEAM
NINEPM
NINERS
NINETY
NINGBO
NINJAS
NINTHS
NIPPED
NIPPER
NIPPON
NIPPUR
NIPSAT
NIPSEY
NIPUPS
NISSAN
NISSEN
NITERS
NITERY
NITRES
NITRIC
NITWIT
NIXIES
NIXING

N•I•••
NAIADS
NAILED
NAILER
NAILIN
NAIRAS
NEIGHS
NEISSE
NIIHAU
NOIRON
NOISED
NOISES

N••I••
NADINE
NADIRS
NAMING
NAPIER
NARIAL
NATICK
NATION
NATIVE
NAVIES
NEVINS
NEWISH
NIDIFY
NIHILO
NIKITA
NIMINY
NIMITZ
NIXIES
NIXING
NODICE
NOHITS
NOMINE
NORIAS
NOSIER
NOSILY
NOSING
NOTICE
NOTIFY
NOTING
NOTION
NOVICE
NOWISE
NUBIAN
NUBILE
NUDIST
NUDITY
NUKING
NUMINA

N•••I•
NAILIN
NANNIE
NAPKIN
NAPPIE
NARNIA
NARVIK
NELLIE
NEREID
NEREIS
NESSIE
NIACIN
NITRIC
NITWIT
NOESIS
NOETIC
NOEXIT
NOGGIN
NORDIC
NORRIS
NUBBIN
NUDNIK
NUNCIO
NUTKIN
NUTRIA
NYQUIL

N••••I
NAPOLI
NEPALI
NEROLI
NIELLI
NIKKEI
NILGAI
NUCLEI

•NI•••
ANIMAL
ANIMAS
ANIMES
ANIMUS
ANIONS
ANITRA
CNIDAE
CNIDUS
ENIGMA
ENISLE
INIONS
INITIO
KNICKS
KNIFED
KNIFES
KNIGHT
KNIVES
ONIONS
ONIONY
SNICKS
SNIDER
SNIFFS
SNIFFY
SNIPED
SNIPER
SNIPES
SNIPPY
SNITCH
SNIVEL
UNIATE
UNIATS
UNICEF
UNIFIC
UNIONS
UNIPOD
UNIQUE
UNISEX
UNISON
UNISYS
UNITAL
UNITAS
UNITED
UNITER
UNITES
UNIVAC

•N•I••
ANCIEN
ANNIKA
ANOINT
ANTICS
ANVILS
ENCINA
ENCINO
ENDING
ENDIVE
ENGINE
ENGIRD
ENGIRT
ENLIST
ENMITY
ENNIUS
ENRICH
ENRICO
ENSIGN
ENSILE
ENTICE
ENTIRE
ENTITY
ENVIED
ENVIER
ENVIES
GNEISS
INCISE
INCITE
INDIAN
INDICT
INDIES
INDIGO
INDIRA
INDITE
INDIUM
INFIRM
INKIER
INKIND
INKING
INLINE
INNING
INSIDE
INSIST
INSITU
INTIMA
INTIME
INTINE
INUITS
INVITE
INVIVO
INWITH
ONDINE
ONEIDA
ONEILL
ONFILE
ONFIRE
ONHIGH
ONLINE
ONSIDE
ONSITE
ONTIME
ONVIEW
SNAILS
UNBIND
UNCIAL
UNDIES
UNDINE
UNFITS
UNGIRD
UNGIRT
UNKIND
UNKINK
UNLIKE
UNLINK
UNOILY
UNPILE
UNPINS
UNRIGS
UNRIPE
UNTIDY
UNTIED
UNTIES
UNWILY
UNWIND
UNWISE
UNWISH
UNZIPS

•N••I•
ANACIN
ANEMIA
ANEMIC
ANGLIA
ANGLIC
ANNUIT
ANODIC
ANOMIC
ANOMIE
ANTRIM
ANUBIS
ENJOIN
ENOKIS
ENOSIS
ENTAIL
ENVOIS
GNOMIC
GNOSIS
INAFIX
INDRIS
INGRID
INITIO
INLAID
INSTIL
INTUIT
INVAIN
SNOWIN
UNCHIC
UNCOIL
UNFAIR
UNGUIS
UNIFIC
UNKNIT
UNLAID
UNPAID
UNSAID
UNVEIL

•N•••I
ANDREI
ANGELI
ANNULI
SNUGLI

••NI••
ALNICO
AMNION
ANNIKA
ARNICA
AWNING
BANISH
BENIGN
BENING
BENITO
BONIER
BONING
BONITO
BUNION
CANIDS
CANIER
CANIFF
CANINE
CANING
CONICS
CONIES
CONIUM
CYNICS
DANIEL
DANISH
DENIAL
DENIED
DENIER
DENIES
DENIMS
DENIRO
DENISE
DINING
DONITZ
ELNINO
ENNIUS
EONIAN
EUNICE
FANION
FENIAN
FINIAL
FINING
FINISH
FINITE
FINITO
GENIAL
GENIES
GENIUS
GUNITE
HONIED
HONING
IGNITE
INNING
IONIAN
IONICS
IONISE
IONIUM
IONIZE
JANICE
JANINE
JUNIOR
KONICA
LANIER
LENITY
LINIER
LINING
MANIAC
MANIAS
MANILA
MANIOC
MENIAL
MENINX
MINIFY
MINIMA
MINIMS
MINING
MINION
MINIUM
MONICA
MONIED
MONIES
MONISM
MONIST
MUNICH
OMNIUM
ORNITH
OWNING
PANICS
PINIER
PINING
PINION
PINITE
PONIED
PONIES
PUNIER
PUNILY
PUNISH
RANIDS
RUNINS
SANITY
SENIOR
SENITI
SINISE
SONICS
TANIST
TINIER
TINILY
TONICS
TONIER
TONING
TONISH
TONITE
TUNICA
TUNICS
TUNING
VANIER
VANISH
VANITY
VENIAL
VENICE
VENIRE
VENITE
VINIER
VINIFY
VINING
WANIER
WANING
WINIER
WINING
WINISH
ZANIER
ZANIES
ZANILY
ZENITH
ZONING

••N•I•
AENEID
ANNUIT
AUNTIE
BANDIT
BENDIX
BENOIT
BONNIE
BUNYIP
CANDID
CANLIT
CONNIE
CONOID
DANDIE
DANZIG
DENNIS
DENTIL
DENTIN
DINEIN
DONEIN
DUNLIN
FANNIE
FINNIC
HANDIN
HANGIN
HANKIE
HENBIT
HENNIN
HENRIK
HINGIS
HUNGIN
JENNIE
JUNKIE
LANAIS
LANDIS
LANVIN
LENNIE
LENTIL
MANNIX
MANTIC
MANTIS
MCNAIR
MENHIR
MENTIS
MINNIE
MINUIT
MUNCIE
MUNTIN
NANNIE
NUNCIO
PANDIT
PENCIL
PENNIA
PENNIS
PINKIE
PINXIT
PINYIN
PONGID
PONTIC
PUNDIT
PUNKIE
RANCID
RANKIN
RENAIL
RENNIE
RENNIN
RENOIR
RONNIE
RUNCIE
RUNSIN
SANDIA
SANTIR
SENDIN
SENNIT
SENTIN
SINGIN
SINKIN
SUNLIT
SUNNIS
SYNDIC
TANNIC
TANNIN
TENNIS
TENPIN
TONKIN
TONSIL
TUNEIN
VINCIT
VINNIE
WANTIN
WENTIN
WINGIT
WINKIE
WINNIE
WINWIN
XINGIN
ZENDIC
ZINNIA

••N••I
ANNULI
BANGUI
BANZAI
BENONI
BONAMI
BONSAI
CANTHI
CENTRI
DENALI
DENDRI
ERNANI
GANDHI
KINSKI
SANSEI
SENITI
SENSEI
YANQUI

•••NI•
ADONIS
ALANIS
ATONIC
BEANIE
BERNIE
BIONIC
BLINIS
BONNIE
BOSNIA
CATNIP
CHENIN
CLINIC
CONNIE
CRANIA
CRANIO
CRONIN
CYANIC
DARNIT
DENNIS
EDENIC
ETHNIC
ETONIC
FAFNIR
FANNIE
FINNIC
GLYNIS
HENNIN
HORNIN
ICONIC
IRANIS
IRENIC
IRONIC
JENNIE
JOANIE
JOININ
KOENIG
LAINIE
LENNIE
LEONID
LEONIE
LIGNIN
LOONIE
MANNIX
MARNIE
MEANIE
MINNIE
NANNIE
NARNIA
NUDNIK
OMANIS
OZONIC
PARNIS
PENNIA
PENNIS
PERNIO
PHONIC
PICNIC
PYKNIC
REININ
RENNIE
RENNIN
RESNIK
RONNIE
SARNIA
SCENIC
SEENIN
SENNIT
SHANIA
SIGNIN
SUNNIS
TANNIC
TANNIN
TENNIS
TOONIE
TOWNIE
TURNIN
TURNIP
UNKNIT
URANIA
URANIC
VINNIE
WEENIE
WINNIE
ZINNIA

•••N•I
ADONAI
AVANTI
BIONDI
BRUNEI
EVENKI
KERNOI
RIENZI
UBANGI

••••NI
ADJANI
ALUMNI
ARMANI
BENONI
BIKINI
BIMINI
BODONI
BUSONI
CARONI
DOMANI
DOMINI
ERNANI
FULANI
GEMINI
ILLINI
LATINI
MORONI
RAPINI
RIMINI
ROTINI
SILENI
TAHINI
YEMENI
YOGINI

N••J••
NINJAS

N•••J•
NAVAJO

•NJ•••
ANJOUS
ENJOIN
ENJOYS
INJECT
INJEST
INJOKE
INJURE
INJURY
UNJAMS
UNJUST

•N•J••
INAJAM
INKJET

•N•••J
INTERJ

••NJ••
BANJOS
BANJUL
CONJOB
DONJON
FANJET
MENJOU
NINJAS
PUNJAB

•••NJ•
CHONJU

N•K•••
NEKTON
NIKITA
NIKKEI
NIKOLA
NUKING

N••K••
NAPKIN
NECKED
NICKED
NICKEL
NICKER
NIKKEI
NUTKIN

N•••K•
NEVSKY
NOOTKA

N••••K
NANOOK
NARVIK
NATICK
NEWARK
NUDNIK

•NK•••
ANKARA
ANKLED
ANKLES
ANKLET
INKERS
INKIER
INKIND
INKING
INKJET
INKLES
UNKIND
UNKINK
UNKNIT
UNKNOT

•N•K••
ANGKOR
ENOKIS
SNAKED
SNAKES

•N••K•
ANNIKA
INJOKE
INTAKE
INVOKE
KNACKS
KNICKS
KNOCKS
SNACKS
SNEAKS
SNEAKY
SNICKS
SNOOKS
SNOOKY
UNLIKE
UNMAKE
UNYOKE
VNECKS

•N•••K
ANORAK
INBULK
INLUCK
ONDECK
UNCORK

UNHOOK
UNKINK
UNLINK
UNLOCK
UNMASK
UNPACK
UNTACK

••NK••
BANKED
BANKER
BANKON
BUNKED
BUNKER
BUNKOS
BUNKUM
CANKER
CONKED
CONKER
DANKER
DANKLY
DINKEY
DONKEY
DUNKED
DUNKER
FINKED
FUNKED
GINKGO
HANKER
HANKIE
HONKED
HONKER
HUNKER
JINKED
JUNKED
JUNKER
JUNKET
JUNKIE
KINKED
LANKER
LANKLY
LINKED
LINKER
LINKUP
LUNKER
MENKEN
MINKES
MONKEY
OINKED
PINKED
PINKEN
PINKER
PINKIE
PUNKAH
PUNKER
PUNKIE
RANKED
RANKER
RANKIN
RANKLE
RANKLY
SINKER
SINKIN
SUNKEN
TANKAS
TANKED
TANKER
TANKUP
TINKER
TINKLE
TINKLY
TONKIN
WINKAT
WINKED

WINKER
WINKIE
WINKLE
YANKED
YANKEE
ZONKED
ZONKER

••N•K•
ANNIKA
BANGKA
JANSKY
KANAKA
KINSKI
TANAKA

••N••K
HENRIK
LANARK
NANOOK
PINOAK
SENDAK
TANOAK
ZANUCK

•••NK•
BLANKS
BLINKS
BRINKS
CHINKS
CHINKY
CHUNKS
CHUNKY
CLANKS
CLANKY
CLINKS
CLONKS
CLUNKS
CLUNKY
CRANKS
CRANKY
DRINKS
EVENKI
FLANKS
FLUNKS
FLUNKY
FRANKS
GLINKA
PLANKS
PLINKS
PLONKS
PLUNKS
PRANKS
PRINKS
REINKS
SHANKS
SKANKS
SKINKS
SKUNKS
SKUNKY
SLINKS
SLINKY
SPANKS
SPANKY
SPINKS
SPUNKY
STANKY
STINKS
STINKY
SWANKS
SWANKY
THANKS
THINKS
THUNKS

TRUNKS

•••N•K
FRANCK
GDANSK
KARNAK
NUDNIK
PLANCK
RESNIK

••••NK
DEBUNK
DRYINK
EMBANK
PODUNK
REDINK
SHRANK
SHRINK
SHRUNK
UNKINK
UNLINK
UPLINK

NL••••
NLEAST
NLWEST

N•L•••
NELLIE
NELSON
NFLERS
NHLERS
NILGAI
NOLEAD
NOLENS
NOLESS
NOLOAD
NOLOSE
NULLAH
NULLED
NYLONS

N••L••
NAILED
NAILER
NAILIN
NAPLES
NELLIE
NEWLEY
NIELLI
NIELLO
NOBLER
NOBLES
NUCLEI
NUCLEO
NULLAH
NULLED
NUTLET
NYALAS

N•••L•
NAMELY
NAPOLI
NASALS
NAVELS
NEARLY
NEATLY
NEBULA
NEEDLE
NEPALI
NEROLI
NESTLE
NETTLE
NETTLY

NEWELS
NIBBLE
NICELY
NICOLA
NICOLE
NICOLO
NIELLI
NIELLO
NIGGLE
NIHILO
NIKOLA
NIMBLE
NIMBLY
NOBBLE
NODDLE
NODULE
NOODLE
NOSALE
NOSILY
NOVELS
NOZZLE
NUBBLE
NUBBLY
NUBILE
NUDELY
NUMBLY
NUZZLE

N••••L
NARIAL
NARWAL
NEURAL
NEUROL
NICKEL
NORMAL
NUCHAL
NYQUIL

•NL•••
ENLACE
ENLIST
INLAID
INLAND
INLAWS
INLAYS
INLETS
INLINE
INLOVE
INLUCK
ONLAND
ONLINE
ONLOAN
UNLACE
UNLADE
UNLAID
UNLASH
UNLEAD
UNLESS
UNLIKE
UNLINK
UNLOAD
UNLOCK

•N•L••
ANALOG
ANELED
ANELES
ANGLED
ANGLER
ANGLES
ANGLIA
ANGLIC
ANGLOS
ANKLED

ANKLES
ANKLET
ANNLEE
ANOLES
ANTLER
ENBLOC
ENGLUT
INFLOW
INFLUX
INGLES
INKLES
INPLAY
KNELLS
KNOLLS
KNOLLY
SNELLS
UNCLAD
UNCLES
UNCLOG
UNGLUE
UNPLUG

•N••L•
ANGELA
ANGELI
ANGELL
ANGELO
ANGELS
ANGOLA
ANNALS
ANNULI
ANNULS
ANSELM
ANVILS
ENABLE
ENDALL
ENFOLD
ENGELS
ENGULF
ENHALO
ENISLE
ENROLL
ENROLS
ENSILE
GNARLS
GNARLY
INBULK
INCULT
INFOLD
INFULL
INHALE
INHALF
INSOLE
INSULT
KNEELS
KNELLS
KNOLLS
KNOLLY
KNURLS
KNURLY
ONCALL
ONEILL
ONFILE
ONHOLD
ONSALE
SNAILS
SNARLS
SNARLY
SNELLS
SNUGLI
SNUGLY
UNABLE
UNBELT
UNBOLT

UNDULY
UNFOLD
UNHOLY
UNOILY
UNPILE
UNROLL
UNRULY
UNSOLD
UNTOLD
UNWELL
UNWILY

•N•••L
ANGELL
ANIMAL
ANNEAL
ANNUAL
ENAMEL
ENDALL
ENROLL
ENSOUL
ENTAIL
INFULL
INHAUL
INSTAL
INSTIL
ONCALL
ONEILL
SNIVEL
UNCIAL
UNCOIL
UNCOOL
UNCURL
UNFURL
UNGUAL
UNITAL
UNOCAL
UNREAL
UNREEL
UNROLL
UNSEAL
UNVEIL
UNWELL

••NL••
ANNLEE
BANLON
CANLIT
DUNLIN
DUNLOP
HANLEY
HENLEY
KUNLUN
LYNLEY
RUNLET
SENLAC
SUNLIT

••N•L•
ANNALS
ANNULI
ANNULS
ARNOLD
BANGLE
BUNDLE
BUNGLE
CANALS
CANDLE
CANOLA
CANTLE
DANDLE
DANGLE
DANGLY
DANKLY

DENALI
DINGLE
DONALD
DONGLE
FINALE
FINALS
FINELY
FONDLE
FONDLY
GANGLE
GANGLY
GENTLE
GENTLY
HANDLE
JANGLE
JANGLY
JINGLE
JINGLY
JUNGLE
JUNGLY
KINDLE
KINDLY
KINGLY
LANKLY
LONELY
LONGLY
LUNULA
MANGLE
MANILA
MANTLE
MINGLE
PANELS
PENULT
PINOLE
PINTLE
PUNILY
RANKLE
RANKLY
RONALD
RONELY
RUNDLE
SANELY
SINGLE
SINGLY
TANGLE
TANGLY
TINGLE
TINGLY
TINILY
TINKLE
TINKLY
VINYLS
WANGLE
WINKLE
YUNGLO
ZANILY

••N••L
ANNEAL
ANNUAL
BANJUL
BENGAL
BENZOL
BUNUEL
CANCEL
CANFUL
CANNEL
CONSUL
CUNEAL
DANIEL
DENIAL
DENTAL
DENTIL
DENZEL

FENNEL
FINIAL
FONTAL
FUNNEL
GENIAL
GENUAL
GUNNEL
HANDEL
HANGUL
HANSEL
KENNEL
LENTIL
LINEAL
LINTEL
LONNOL
MANFUL
MANTEL
MANUAL
MANUEL
MENDEL
MENIAL
MENSAL
MENTAL
MONGOL
MONTEL
PANFUL
PENCEL
PENCIL
PENPAL
PINEAL
RENAIL
RENTAL
RONDEL
RUNNEL
SANDAL
SINFUL
TINCAL
TINSEL
TONSIL
TUNNEL
VANDAL
VENIAL

•••NL•
EVENLY
GAINLY
KEENLY
LEANLY
LIONLY
MAINLY
MEANLY
OPENLY
THINLY
VAINLY

•••N•L
ATONAL
AXONAL
CANNEL
CARNAL
CHANEL
CORNEL
CRENEL
DARNEL
DIRNDL
EPINAL
FAUNAL
FENNEL
FUNNEL
GUNNEL
HYMNAL
KENNEL
KERNEL
LIONEL

LONNOL
PHENOL
PHENYL
REGNAL
RHINAL
RUNNEL
SIGNAL
SIMNEL
SPINAL
SPINEL
TRINAL
TUNNEL
VEINAL
VERNAL

N•M•••
NAMATH
NAMELY
NAMERS
NAMING
NEMATO
NIMBLE
NIMBLY
NIMBUS
NIMINY
NIMITZ
NIMROD
NOMADS
NOMINE
NOMORE
NUMBAT
NUMBED
NUMBER
NUMBLY
NUMERO
NUMINA
NYMETS
NYMPHS

N••M••
NETMAN
NETMEN
NEUMAN
NEUMES
NEWMAN
NEWMAR
NIAMEY
NORMAL
NORMAN
NOUMEA
NUTMEG

N•••M•
NONAME

N••••M
NINEAM
NINEPM
NONCOM

•NM•••
ENMESH
ENMITY
INMATE
INMOST
UNMADE
UNMAKE
UNMANS
UNMASK
UNMEET
UNMESH
UNMOOR

•N•M••
ANEMIA
ANEMIC
ANIMAL
ANIMAS
ANIMES
ANIMUS
ANOMIC
ANOMIE
ENAMEL
ENAMOR
ENDMAN
ENDMEN
GNOMES
GNOMIC
GNOMON
INGMAR
ONEMAN

•N••M•
ENCAMP
ENIGMA
ENTOMO
ENZYME
INCOME
INFAMY
INTIMA
INTIME
ONTIME
PNEUMA
UNARMS
UNJAMS

•N•••M
ANADEM
ANONYM
ANSELM
ANTHEM
ANTRIM
ANTRUM
ENGRAM
INAJAM
INDIUM
INFIRM
INFORM
INGRAM
INSEAM

••NM••
BONMOT
CONMAN
CONMEN
FENMAN
FENMEN
GUNMAN
GUNMEN
PENMAN
PENMEN
TINMAN
TINMEN
WONMUG

••N•M•
BENUMB
BONAMI
BYNAME
CINEMA
DANGME
DENIMS
DYNAMO
GENOME
KINEMA
KINGME
MANAMA

MINIMA
MINIMS
NONAME
PANAMA
RENAME
RUNDMC
SONOMA
VENOMS

••N••M
ARNHEM
BANTAM
BUNKUM
CONIUM
DUNHAM
FANDOM
HANSOM
IONIUM
MINIUM
MONISM
NINEAM
NINEPM
NONCOM
OMNIUM
RANDOM
RANSOM
TANDEM
WINDOM

•••N•M
ANONYM
BARNUM
EPONYM
FRENUM
MAGNUM
PHENOM
PLENUM
PUTNAM

N•N•••
NANNIE
NANOOK
NANSEN
NANTES
NENETS
NINEAM
NINEPM
NINERS
NINETY
NINGBO
NINJAS
NINTHS
NONAGE
NONAME
NONARY
NONCOM
NONEGO
NONETS
NONFAT
NUNCIO

N••N••
NANNIE
NARNIA
NOONAN
NOONES
NOTNOW
NUANCE
NUDNIK

N•••N•
NADINE
NAGANO
NAMING

NATANT
NEEDNT
NEVINS
NICENE
NIMINY
NIXING
NOCENT
NOLENS
NOMINE
NOSING
NOTING
NOVENA
NUGENT
NUKING
NUMINA
NYLONS

N••••N
NAILIN
NANSEN
NAPKIN
NATHAN
NATION
NATRON
NEATEN
NEESON
NEKTON
NELSON
NETMAN
NETMEN
NETTON
NEUMAN
NEURON
NEWMAN
NEWTON
NGUYEN
NIACIN
NICEAN
NIPPON
NISSAN
NISSEN
NOGGIN
NOIRON
NOONAN
NORMAN
NORTON
NOTION
NUBBIN
NUBIAN
NUTKIN

•NN•••
ANNABA
ANNALS
ANNEAL
ANNEXE
ANNHON
ANNIKA
ANNLEE
ANNOYS
ANNUAL
ANNUIT
ANNULI
ANNULS
ENNEAD
ENNIUS
INNAGE
INNATE
INNEED
INNESS
INNING

•N•N••
ANANDA

ANONYM
INANER
UNKNIT
UNKNOT
UNSNAG
UNSNAP

•N••N•
ANCONA
ANIONS
ANOINT
ANTONY
ANWANG
ANYANG
ANYONE
ENCINA
ENCINO
ENDING
ENFANT
ENGINE
INCANS
INDENE
INDENT
INFANT
INHAND
INIONS
INKIND
INKING
INLAND
INLINE
INNING
INSANE
INSYNC
INTEND
INTENS
INTENT
INTINE
INTONE
INTUNE
INVENT
KNOWNS
ONDINE
ONHAND
ONIONS
ONIONY
ONLAND
ONLINE
UNBEND
UNBENT
UNBIND
UNDINE
UNDONE
UNHAND
UNIONS
UNKIND
UNKINK
UNLINK
UNMANS
UNPENS
UNPINS
UNSUNG
UNTUNE
UNWIND

•N•••N
ANACIN
ANCIEN
ANDEAN
ANNHON
ANTRON
ANURAN
ENDMAN
ENDMEN
ENDRUN

ENJOIN
ENSIGN
GNOMON
INBORN
INCHON
INDIAN
INSPAN
INTERN
INTOWN
INTURN
INVAIN
ONEMAN
ONLOAN
SNOWIN
UNBORN
UNEVEN
UNISON
UNOPEN
UNSEEN
UNSEWN
UNSOWN
UNTORN
UNWORN

••NN••
BANNED
BANNER
BINNED
BONNES
BONNET
BONNIE
CANNAE
CANNED
CANNEL
CANNER
CANNES
CANNON
CANNOT
CONNED
CONNER
CONNIE
CONNOR
DANNAY
DANNER
DENNED
DENNIS
DINNED
DINNER
DONNAS
DONNED
DONNEE
DONNER
DUNNED
FANNED
FANNIE
FENNEC
FENNEL
FINNAN
FINNED
FINNEY
FINNIC
FUNNED
FUNNEL
GANNET
GINNED
GUNNAR
GUNNED
GUNNEL
GUNNER
HANNAH
HENNAS
HENNER
HENNIN
JENNER

JENNET
JENNEY
JENNIE
JINNAH
KENNED
KENNEL
KENNER
KENNYG
LENNIE
LENNON
LENNOX
LINNET
LINNEY
LONNOL
MANNED
MANNER
MANNIX
MENNEN
MINNIE
MINNOW
NANNIE
PANNED
PANNER
PANNES
PENNAE
PENNED
PENNER
PENNEY
PENNIA
PENNIS
PENNON
PINNAE
PINNAS
PINNED
PINNER
PUNNED
PUNNET
RENNES
RENNET
RENNIE
RENNIN
RONNIE
RUNNEL
RUNNER
SANNUP
SENNAS
SENNET
SENNIT
SINNED
SINNER
SONNET
SUNNED
SUNNIS
TANNED
TANNER
TANNIC
TANNIN
TENNIS
TINNED
TINNER
TONNES
TUNNEL
TUNNEY
VANNED
VINNIE
WANNED
WANNER
WINNER
WINNIE
WINNOW
WONNED
YENNED
YUNNAN
ZINNIA

••N•N•
AWNING
BANANA
BENING
BENONI
BONING
CANINE
CANING
CANONS
CONANT
DANANG
DINING
DUNANT
ELNINO
ERNANI
FANONS
FINING
HONING
INNING
JANINE
LINENS
LINENY
LINING
MANANA
MENINX
MINING
OENONE
OWNING
PENANG
PINING
PINONS
RUNINS
RUNONS
SONANT
SUNUNU
TANANA
TENANT
TENENS
TENONS
TONING
TUNING
VINING
WANING
WINING
WINONA
ZENANA
ZONING

••N••N
AMNION
ANNHON
BANKON
BANLON
BANYAN
BENIGN
BENSON
BENTON
BONBON
BONTON
BUNION
BUNSEN
BUNYAN
CANAAN
CANCAN
CANCUN
CANNON
CANTON
CANYON
CONMAN
CONMEN
DANSON
DANTON
DENTIN
DENTON

DINEIN
DINEON
DONEIN
DONJON
DUNCAN
DUNLIN
EONIAN
FANION
FANTAN
FENIAN
FENMAN
FENMEN
FINNAN
GENOAN
GUNMAN
GUNMEN
HANDIN
HANDON
HANGIN
HANGON
HANSON
HENNIN
HENSON
HINTON
HUNGIN
HUNGON
IONIAN
JANSEN
JENSEN
JONSON
KANSAN
KENTON
KENYAN
KUNLUN
LANDON
LANSON
LANVIN
LENNON
LENTEN
LINDEN
LONDON
LONGAN
LUNDEN
LYNDON
MANDAN
MENKEN
MENNEN
MINION
MINOAN
MINYAN
MUNTIN
NANSEN
PENMAN
PENMEN
PENNON
PINION
PINKEN
PINSON
PINYIN
PINYON
PINZON
RANKIN
RENNIN
RENOWN
RUNSIN
RUNSON
RUNYON
SENDIN
SENTIN
SINGIN
SINKIN
SUNKEN
SUNTAN
TANNIN
TANOAN
TENDON
TENPIN
TINCAN
TINMAN
TINMEN
TINPAN
TONGAN
TONKIN
TUNEIN
VANRYN
VINTON
WANTIN
WANTON
WENTIN
WENTON
WINWIN
WONTON
WYNTON
XINGIN
YANGON
YUNNAN

•••NN•

BLENNY
BRANNY
CRANNY
CRENNA
DEANNA
DIANNE
DIONNE
DUENNA
EVONNE
FRANNY
GLENNE
GOANNA
GRANNY
GWYNNE
JEANNE
JOANNA
JOANNE
JOHNNY
PRYNNE
SHANNY
SHINNY
SIENNA
SKINNY
VIENNA
VIENNE
WHINNY
YVONNE

•••N•N

ALANON
CANNON
CHENIN
CRONIN
CRONYN
DAWNON
DOWNON
FINNAN
GAINON
GUENON
HAINAN
HENNIN
HORNIN
IRONON
JOININ
KEENAN
KEENEN
LEANON
LENNON
LIGNIN
MAGNON
MEMNON
MENNEN
MIGNON
NOONAN
PENNON
PHONON
PLANON
REININ
RENNIN
SEENIN
SEWNON
SIGNIN
SIGNON
SRANAN
TAINAN
TANNIN
TURNIN
TURNON
VERNON
YUNNAN

••••NN

EDWYNN
JOHANN
MCCANN
SUSANN

NO••••

NOBBLE
NOBLER
NOBLES
NOBODY
NOCENT
NODDED
NODDLE
NODICE
NODOFF
NODOSE
NODULE
NOESIS
NOETIC
NOEXIT
NOGGIN
NOGOOD
NOHITS
NOIRON
NOISED
NOISES
NOLEAD
NOLENS
NOLESS
NOLOAD
NOLOSE
NOMADS
NOMINE
NOMORE
NONAGE
NONAME
NONARY
NONCOM
NONEGO
NONETS
NONFAT
NOODLE
NOONAN
NOONES
NOOSED
NOOSES
NOOTKA
NOPETS
NORDIC
NORGAY
NORIAS
NORMAL
NORMAN
NORRIS
NORTHS
NORTON
NORWAY
NOSALE
NOSHED
NOSHER
NOSHES
NOSHOW
NOSIER
NOSILY
NOSING
NOSOAP
NOTARY
NOTATE
NOTBAD
NOTCHY
NOTERS
NOTICE
NOTIFY
NOTING
NOTION
NOTNOW
NOTYET
NOUGAT
NOUGHT
NOUMEA
NOVATO
NOVELS
NOVENA
NOVICE
NOWISE
NOZZLE

N•O•••

NOODLE
NOONAN
NOONES
NOOSED
NOOSES
NOOTKA

N••O••

NABOBS
NABORS
NAGOYA
NANOOK
NAPOLI
NEROLI
NICOLA
NICOLE
NICOLO
NIKOLA
NOBODY
NODOFF
NODOSE
NOGOOD
NOLOAD
NOLOSE
NOMORE
NOSOAP
NYLONS

N•••O•

NACHOS
NANOOK
NARROW
NATION
NATRON
NEESON
NEKTON
NELSON
NESTOR
NETTON
NEUROL
NEURON
NEWTON
NIMROD
NIPPON
NOGOOD
NOIRON
NONCOM
NORTON
NOSHOW
NOTION
NOTNOW

N••••O

NAGANO
NAVAHO
NAVAJO
NEARTO
NEMATO
NEPHRO
NEXTTO
NICOLO
NIELLO
NIHILO
NINGBO
NONEGO
NOVATO
NUCLEO
NUMERO
NUNCIO

•NO•••

ANODES
ANODIC
ANOINT
ANOLES
ANOMIC
ANOMIE
ANONYM
ANORAK
CNOTES
ENOKIS
ENOSIS
ENOUGH
GNOMES
GNOMIC
GNOMON
GNOSIS
INOUYE
KNOBBY
KNOCKS
KNOLLS
KNOLLY
KNOTTS
KNOTTY
KNOUTS
KNOWER
KNOWNS
SNOBBY
SNOCAT
SNOODS
SNOOKS
SNOOKY
SNOOPS
SNOOPY
SNOOTS
SNOOTY
SNOOZE
SNOOZY
SNOPES
SNORED
SNORER
SNORES
SNORTS
SNOTTY
SNOUTS
SNOWED
SNOWIN
TNOTES
UNOCAL
UNOILY
UNOPEN

•N•O••

ANCONA
ANGOLA
ANGORA
ANIONS
ANJOUS
ANNOYS
ANTONY
ANYONE
ENCODE
ENCORE
ENDORA
ENDOWS
ENFOLD
ENJOIN
ENJOYS
ENROBE
ENROLL
ENROLS
ENROOT
ENSOUL
ENTOMO
ENVOIS
ENVOYS
INBORN
INCOME
INDOOR
INDORE
INFOLD
INFORM
INGOTS
INIONS
INJOKE
INLOVE
INMOST
INPORT
INPOUR
INROAD
INSOLE
INTONE
INTOTO
INTOWN
INVOKE
ONFOOT
ONHOLD
ONIONS
ONIONY
ONLOAN
ONTOUR
SNOODS
SNOOKS
SNOOKY
SNOOPS
SNOOPY
SNOOTS
SNOOTY
SNOOZE
SNOOZY
UNBOLT
UNBORN
UNCOIL
UNCOOL
UNCORK
UNDOER
UNDOES
UNDONE
UNFOLD
UNHOLY
UNHOOK
UNIONS
UNLOAD
UNLOCK
UNMOOR
UNROBE
UNROLL
UNROOT
UNSOLD
UNSOWN
UNTOLD
UNTORN
UNWORN
UNWOVE
UNYOKE

•N••O•

ANALOG
ANCHOR
ANDHOW
ANDROS
ANGKOR
ANGLOS
ANNHON
ANTCOW
ANTRON
ANYHOW
ENAMOR
ENBLOC
ENROOT
GNOMON
INAFOG
INAROW
INCHON
INDOOR
INFLOW
INTROS
ONFOOT
UNCLOG
UNCOOL
UNHOOK
UNIPOD
UNISON
UNKNOT
UNMOOR
UNROOT
UNSHOD
UNSTOP
UNTROD

•N•••O

ANATTO
ANGELO
ANTERO
ENCINO
ENDURO
ENESCO
ENHALO
ENRICO
ENTERO
ENTOMO
INDIGO
INITIO
INTOTO
INVIVO
ONETWO
SNAPTO
UNESCO

••NO••

ANNOYS
ARNOLD
BENOIT
BENONI
CANOED
CANOES
CANOLA
CANONS
CANOPY
CANOVA
CENOTE
CONOCO
CONOID
DENOTE
DENOVO
DONORS
FANONS
FANOUT
GENOAN
GENOME
GONOGO
HONORE
HONORS
HONOUR
IGNORE
LANOSE
LENORE
MANORS
MINOAN
MINORS
MONODY
NANOOK
OENONE
PANOUT
PINOAK
PINOLE
PINONS
PINOTS
RANOFF
RANOUT
RENOIR
RENOTE
RENOWN
RUNOFF
RUNONS
RUNOUT
SENORA
SENORS
SONOMA
SONORA
SUNOCO
SYNODS
TANOAK
TANOAN
TENONS
TENORS
VENOMS
VENOUS
VINOUS
WINONA
WINOUT
WONOUT

••N•O•

AMNION
ANNHON
BANDOG
BANGOR
BANJOS
BANKON
BANLON
BENSON
BENTON
BENZOL
BONBON
BONGOS
BONMOT
BONTON
BUNCOS
BUNION
BUNKOS
CANDOR
CANNON
CANNOT
CANTON
CANTOR
CANTOS
CANYON
CENSOR
CENTOS
CONDOR
CONDOS
CONGOU
CONJOB
CONNOR
CONROY
CONVOY
DANSON
DANTON
DENTON
DINEON
DONJON
DUNLOP
FANDOM
FANION
GUNDOG
GUNFOR
HANDON
HANGON
HANSOM
HANSON
HENSON
HINTON
HUNGON
JONSON
JUNCOS
JUNIOR
JUNTOS
KANTOR
KENTON
KINDOF
LANDON
LANSON
LENNON
LENNOX
LONDON
LONNOL
LYNDON
MANGOS
MANIOC
MENJOU
MENTOR
MINION
MINNOW
MONGOL
MONROE
MUNGOS
NANOOK
NONCOM
PANTOS
PENNON
PENROD
PINION
PINSON
PINTOS
PINYON
PINZON
RANCOR
RANDOM
RANFOR
RANSOM
RONDOS
RUNFOR
RUNSON
RUNYON
SANTOS
SENHOR
SENIOR
SENSOR
SUNDOG
SUNGOD
TANGOS
TENDON
TENSOR
TINGOD
TINPOT
TONDOS
VENDOR
VINTON
WANTON
WENTON
WINDOM
WINDOW
WINNOW
WINSOR
WONTON
WYNTON
YANGON
ZENDOS

••N••O

ALNICO
BANQUO
BENITO
BONITO
CENTRO
CONOCO
DENDRO
DENIRO
DENOVO
DINERO
DYNAMO
ELNINO
FINITO
GINKGO
GONOGO
GUNGHO
HONCHO
LANDHO
MENADO
MONACO
NINGBO
NONEGO
NUNCIO
PANCHO
PINERO
PONCHO
RANCHO
RUNSTO
SANCHO
SANGTO
SENUFO
SINGTO
SUNOCO
TENDTO
TENUTO
VENETO
WANTTO
XANTHO
YUNGLO

•••NO•

ALANON
AMINOR
BEANOS
BMINOR
BUENOS
CANNON
CANNOT
CARNOT
CHINOS
CMINOR
CONNOR
CPSNOW
DAWNON
DMINOR
DOWNON
EGGNOG
ELINOR
EMINOR
ERENOW
ETHNOS
FMINOR
GAINON
GAYNOR
GMINOR
GOUNOD
GUENON
HOBNOB
HOWNOW
HYPNOS
IRONON
KERNOI
KERNOS
KRONOR
LEANON
LEMNOS
LENNON
LENNOX
LLANOS
LONNOL
MAGNON
MEMNON
MIGNON
MINNOW
NOTNOW
PENNON
PERNOD
PHENOL
PHENOM
PHONON
PHONOS
PIANOS
PLANON
QUINOA
RHINOS
SCHNOZ
SEWNON
SIGNON
SIGNOR
STENOG
STENOS
TAINOS
TURNON
UNKNOT
VERNON
WHYNOT
WINNOW

•••N•O

ALONSO
ALONZO
BOINGO
BORNEO
BRANDO
BRONCO
CRANIO
ERYNGO
EVENSO
FRANCO
GOINTO
GRINGO
LEANTO
ODONTO
OLINGO
OPENTO
PERNIO
PRONTO
QUANGO
SEENTO
SHINTO
SPINTO
STINGO
TURNTO

••••NO

ACTINO
ADRENO
ALBANO
ALBINO
AQUINO
AVERNO
CAMINO
CASINO
CHRONO
CYRANO
DELANO
DIVINO
DOMINO
ECHINO
ELNINO
ENCINO
FRESNO
GITANO
GOLINO
GRODNO
IMMUNO
JOURNO
KIMONO
LADINO
LATINO
LUPINO
MARINO
MELANO
MERINO
MILANO
MORENO
MURANO
NAGANO
ORSINO
PACINO
PEPINO
PISANO
POCONO
ROMANO
SELENO
STERNO
STHENO
TECHNO
TEJANO
TORINO

N•P•••

NAPERY
NAPIER
NAPKIN
NAPLES
NAPOLI
NAPPED
NAPPER
NAPPES
NAPPIE
NEPALI
NEPHEW
NEPHRO
NIPPED
NIPPER
NIPPON
NIPPUR
NIPSAT
NIPSEY
NIPUPS
NOPETS

N••P••

NAPPED
NAPPER
NAPPES
NAPPIE
NETPAY
NIPPED
NIPPER
NIPPON
NIPPUR
NYMPHS

N•••P•

NINEPM
NIPUPS

N••••P

NOSOAP

•NP•••

INPART
INPLAY
INPORT
INPOUR
INPUTS
UNPACK
UNPAID
UNPEGS
UNPENS
UNPILE
UNPINS
UNPLUG

•N•P••

INAPET
INSPAN
ONSPEC
SNAPAT
SNAPPY
SNAPTO
SNAPUP
SNIPED
SNIPER
SNIPES
SNIPPY
SNOPES
UNIPOD
UNOPEN

•N••P•

ENRAPT
INCEPT
ONEUPS
ONTAPE
SNAPPY
SNIPPY
SNOOPS
SNOOPY
UNCAPS
UNRIPE
UNZIPS

•N•••P

ANTEUP
ENCAMP
ENDSUP
ENTRAP
ENWRAP
INSTEP
SNAPUP
UNSNAP
UNSTOP
UNTRAP
UNWRAP

••NP••

PENPAL
TENPIN
TINPAN
TINPOT

••N•P•

CANAPE
CANOPY
LENAPE
NINEPM
PINUPS
RUNUPS
SUNUPS

••N••P

BANGUP
BINDUP
BONEUP
BUNYIP
DONEUP
DUNLOP
GANGUP
HANDUP
HANGUP
HUNGUP
LINEUP
LINKUP
OWNSUP
PENTUP
PONYUP
RANGUP
RINGUP
RUNGUP
RUNSUP
SANNUP
SENDUP
SENTUP
TANKUP
TONEUP
TUNEUP
WENTUP
WINDUP

•••N•P

BURNUP
CATNAP
CATNIP
CHINUP
EVENUP
JOINUP
KIDNAP
OPENUP
PRENUP
SANNUP
SEWNUP
SIGNUP
TURNIP
TURNUP
UNSNAP

N•Q•••

NYQUIL

N••••Q

NASDAQ

•NQ•••

ENQUAD

•N•Q••

UNIQUE

••NQ••

BANQUO
CINQUE
MANQUE
YANQUI

N•R•••

NARIAL
NARNIA
NARROW
NARVIK
NARWAL
NEREID
NEREIS
NEREUS
NEROLI
NERUDA
NERVES
NORDIC
NORGAY
NORIAS
NORMAL
NORMAN
NORRIS
NORTHS
NORTON
NORWAY
NURSED
NURSER
NURSES

N••R••

NACRES
NAIRAS
NARROW
NATRON
NEARBY
NEARED
NEARER
NEARLY
NEARTO
NEURAL
NEUROL
NEURON
NIMROD
NITRES
NITRIC
NOIRON
NORRIS
NUTRIA

N•••R•

NABORS
NADIRS
NAMERS
NAPERY
NATURA
NATURE
NEPHRO
NEVERS
NEWARK
NFLERS
NHLERS
NINERS
NITERS
NITERY
NOMORE
NONARY
NOTARY
NOTERS
NUMERO

N••••R

NABBER
NAGGER
NAILER
NAPIER
NAPPER
NASCAR
NASSER
NATTER
NEARER
NEATER
NECTAR
NESTER
NESTOR
NETHER
NEUTER
NEWMAR
NICKER
NIGHER
NIPPER
NIPPUR
NOBLER
NOSHER
NOSIER
NUDGER
NUMBER
NURSER
NUTTER

•NR•••

ENRAGE
ENRAPT
ENRICH
ENRICO
ENROBE
ENROLL
ENROLS
ENROOT
INROAD
INRUSH
ONRUSH
UNREAD
UNREAL
UNREEL
UNREST
UNRIGS
UNRIPE
UNROBE
UNROLL
UNROOT
UNRULY

•N•R••

ANDREA
ANDREI
ANDRES
ANDREW
ANDREY
ANDROS
ANERGY
ANORAK

ANTRES
ANTRIM
ANTRON
ANTRUM
ANURAN
ENDRUN
ENERGY
ENGRAM
ENTRAP
ENTREE
ENURED
ENURES
ENWRAP
GNARLS
GNARLY
INARCH
INAROW
INARUT
INBRED
INDRIS
INGRAM
INGRES
INGRID
INTROS
INURED
INURES
KNARRY
KNURLS
KNURLY
SNARED
SNARES
SNARLS
SNARLY
SNORED
SNORER
SNORES
SNORTS
UNARMS
UNDRAW
UNFREE
UNTRAP
UNTROD
UNTRUE
UNWRAP

•N••R•
ANGERS
ANGORA
ANITRA
ANKARA
ANSARA
ANTERO
ENCORE
ENDERS
ENDORA
ENDURE
ENDURO
ENGIRD
ENGIRT
ENSURE
ENTERO
ENTERS
ENTIRE
INBORN
INCURS
INDIRA
INDORE
INFERS
INFIRM
INFORM
INHERE
INJURE
INJURY
INKERS
INPART
INPORT
INSERT
INSURE
INTERJ
INTERN
INTURN
INVERT
INWARD
KNARRY
ONFIRE
ONWARD
SNEERS
SNEERY
UNBARS
UNBORN
UNCORK
UNCURL
UNFURL
UNGIRD
UNGIRT
UNHURT
UNSURE
UNTORN
UNWARY
UNWORN

•N•••R
ANCHOR
ANGKOR
ANGLER
ANHYDR
ANSGAR
ANSWER
ANTHER
ANTLER
ENAMOR
ENDEAR
ENVIER
GNAWER
INANER
INDOOR
INGEAR
INGMAR
INKIER
INPOUR
INSTAR
KNOWER
ONAGER
ONTOUR
SNIDER
SNIPER
SNORER
SNYDER
UNDOER
UNFAIR
UNITER
UNMOOR

••NR••
CONRAD
CONROY
GENRES
HENRIK
HENRYV
KONRAD
MANRAY
MONROE
PENROD
SUNRAY
TENREC
VANRYN

••N•R•
BINARY
BONERS
CANARD
CANARY
CANERS
CENTRE
CENTRI
CENTRO
CONTRA
CONTRE
CONURE
CUNARD
DENARY
DENDRI
DENDRO
DENIRO
DINARS
DINERO
DINERS
DONORS
DUNERA
FINERY
GANTRY
GENERA
GENTRY
GONERS
HONORE
HONORS
HUNGRY
IGNORE
LANARK
LANDRY
LENORE
LINERS
LONERS
LYNYRD
MANORS
MANTRA
MINERS
MINORS
MONERA
NINERS
NONARY
ORNERY
OWNERS
OXNARD
PANFRY
PANTRY
PENURY
PINERO
PINERY
RANDRY
RUNDRY
SANDRA
SENARY
SENORA
SENORS
SENTRA
SENTRY
SONORA
SUNDRY
TANTRA
TENORS
TENURE
TONERS
TUNDRA
TUNERS
VENIRE
VINERY
WANERS
WINERY
WINTRY

••N••R
BANGER
BANGOR
BANKER
BANNER
BANTER
BENDER
BENHUR
BINDER
BONIER
BUNKER
BUNTER
CANDOR
CANIER
CANKER
CANNER
CANTER
CANTOR
CENSER
CENSOR
CENTER
CINDER
CONCUR
CONDOR
CONFER
CONGER
CONKER
CONNER
CONNOR
DANCER
DANDER
DANGER
DANKER
DANNER
DENIER
DENSER
DENVER
DINNER
DONDER
DONNER
DUNBAR
DUNKER
FENCER
FENDER
FINDER
FINGER
FONDER
GANDER
GANGER
GENDER
GINGER
GUNFOR
GUNNAR
GUNNER
GUNTER
HANGAR
HANGER
HANKER
HENNER
HINDER
HINTER
HONKER
HONOUR
HUNGER
HUNKER
HUNTER
JENNER
JUNIOR
JUNKER
KANDER
KANTOR
KENNER
KINDER
LANCER
LANDER
LANGUR
LANIER
LANKER
LENDER
LINEAR
LINGER
LINIER
LINKER
LINTER
LONGER
LUNKER
MANGER
MANNER
MCNAIR
MENDER
MENHIR
MENTOR
MINCER
MINDER
MINTER
MONGER
PANDER
PANNER
PANZER
PENNER
PINCER
PINDAR
PINIER
PINKER
PINNER
PINTER
PONDER
PUNIER
PUNKER
PUNTER
QINTAR
RANCOR
RANFOR
RANGER
RANKER
RANTER
RENDER
RENOIR
RENTER
RINGER
RUNFOR
RUNNER
SANDER
SANGER
SANTIR
SENDER
SENHOR
SENIOR
SENSOR
SINGER
SINKER
SINNER
SINTER
SUNDER
TANKER
TANNER
TENDER
TENSER
TENSOR
TENTER
TINDER
TINEAR
TINIER
TINKER
TINNER
TINTER
TONIER
VANIER
VENDOR
VENEER
VENTER
VINIER
WANDER
WANIER
WANNER
WINCER
WINDER
WINGER
WINIER
WINKER
WINNER
WINSOR
WINTER
WONDER
WYNTER
YONDER
ZANDER
ZANIER
ZENGER
ZINGER
ZONKER

•••NR•
AMENRA
OHENRY

•••N•R
AMINOR
BANNER
BMINOR
BURNER
CANNER
CMINOR
COINER
CONNER
CONNOR
CORNER
DANNER
DARNER
DINNER
DMINOR
DONNER
DOWNER
DRONER
EARNER
EISNER
ELINOR
EMINOR
EVENER
FAFNIR
FAWNER
FMINOR
GAINER
GARNER
GAYNOR
GMINOR
GUNNAR
GUNNER
HEFNER
HENNER
HORNER
INANER
IRONER
JENNER
JOINER
JOYNER
KAVNER
KEENER
KENNER
KRONER
KRONOR
KRONUR
LEANER
LERNER
LIMNER
LOANER
MANNER
MARNER
MEANER
MILNER
MOANER
MOLNAR
OPENER
OPINER
PANNER
PAWNER
PENNER
PINNER
PLANAR
PLANER
PRUNER
RADNER
RAINER
REINER
RUINER
RUNNER
SEINER
SHINER
SIGNER
SIGNOR
SINNER
SOONER
STONER
SUMNER
TANNER
TEENER
THENAR
TINNER
TOWNER
TURNER
VAINER
WAGNER
WANNER
WAPNER
WARNER
WERNER
WHINER
WIENER
WINNER
YAWNER

N•S•••
NASALS
NASCAR
NASDAQ
NASEBY
NASHUA
NASSAU
NASSER
NESSES
NESSIE
NESTEA
NESTED
NESTER
NESTLE
NESTOR
NISSAN
NISSEN
NOSALE
NOSHED
NOSHER
NOSHES
NOSHOW
NOSIER
NOSILY
NOSING
NOSOAP

N••S••
NANSEN
NASSAU
NASSER
NAUSEA
NAYSAY
NEESON
NEISSE
NELSON
NESSES
NESSIE
NEVSKY
NIPSAT
NIPSEY
NISSAN
NISSEN
NOESIS
NOISED
NOISES
NOOSED
NOOSES
NURSED
NURSER
NURSES
NYASSA

N•••S•
NEISSE
NEWEST
NEWISH
NICEST
NLEAST
NLWEST
NODOSE
NOLESS
NOLOSE
NOWISE
NUDEST
NUDIST
NYASSA

N••••S
NABOBS
NABORS
NACHOS
NACRES
NADIRS
NAIADS
NAIRAS
NAMERS
NANTES
NAPLES
NAPPES
NASALS
NAVELS
NAVIES
NAWABS
NEIGHS
NENETS
NEREIS
NEREUS
NERVES
NESSES
NEUMES
NEVERS
NEVINS
NEWELS
NFLERS
NHLERS
NICHES
NIECES
NIGHTS
NIMBUS
NINERS
NINJAS
NINTHS
NIPUPS
NITERS
NITRES
NIXIES
NOBLES
NOESIS
NOHITS
NOISES
NOLENS
NOLESS
NOMADS
NONETS
NOONES
NOOSES
NOPETS
NORIAS
NORRIS
NORTHS
NOSHES
NOTERS
NOVELS
NUDGES
NUECES
NURSES
NYALAS
NYLONS
NYMETS
NYMPHS

•NS•••
ANSARA
ANSATE
ANSELM
ANSGAR
ANSWER
ENSIGN
ENSILE
ENSOUL
ENSUED
ENSUES
ENSURE
INSANE
INSEAM
INSECT
INSERT
INSETS
INSIDE
INSIST
INSITU
INSOLE
INSPAN
INSTAL
INSTAR
INSTEP
INSTIL
INSULT
INSURE
INSYNC
ONSALE
ONSETS
ONSIDE
ONSITE
ONSPEC
UNSAFE
UNSAID
UNSAYS
UNSEAL
UNSEAT
UNSEEN
UNSEWN
UNSEWS
UNSHED
UNSHOD
UNSNAG
UNSNAP
UNSOLD
UNSOWN
UNSTOP
UNSUNG
UNSURE

•N•S••
ENDSUP
ENESCO
ENISLE
ENOSIS
GNOSIS
INESSE
ONUSES
UNESCO
UNISEX
UNISON
UNISYS
UNUSED

•N••S•
ENCASE
ENDASH
ENDUSE
ENLIST
ENMESH
GNEISS
INCASE
INCASH
INCISE
INCUSE
INESSE
INFEST
INFUSE
INGEST
INJEST
INMOST
INNESS
INRUSH
INSIST
INVEST
ONRUSH
UNBUSY
UNCASE
UNEASE
UNEASY
UNJUST
UNLASH
UNLESS
UNMASK
UNMESH
UNREST
UNWISE
UNWISH

•N•••S
ANDRES
ANDROS
ANELES
ANGELS
ANGERS
ANGLES
ANGLOS
ANIMAS
ANIMES
ANIMUS
ANIONS
ANJOUS
ANKLES
ANNALS
ANNOYS
ANNULS
ANODES
ANOLES
ANTICS
ANTRES
ANUBIS
ANVILS
CNIDUS
CNOTES
ENACTS
ENATES
ENDERS
ENDOWS
ENDUES
ENGELS
ENJOYS
ENNIUS
ENOKIS
ENOSIS
ENROLS
ENSUES
ENTERS
ENURES
ENVIES
ENVOIS
ENVOYS
GNARLS
GNEISS
GNOMES
GNOSIS
INCANS
INCHES
INCURS
INDIES
INDRIS
INFERS
INGLES
INGOTS
INGRES
INIONS
INKERS
INKLES
INLAWS
INLAYS
INLETS
INNESS
INPUTS
INSETS
INTENS
INTROS
INUITS
INURES
KNACKS
KNAVES
KNEADS
KNEELS
KNELLS
KNICKS
KNIFES
KNIVES
KNOCKS
KNOLLS
KNOTTS
KNOUTS
KNOWNS
KNURLS
ONEUPS
ONIONS
ONSETS
ONUSES
ONYXES
SNACKS
SNAFUS
SNAILS
SNAKES
SNARES
SNARLS
SNATHS
SNEAKS
SNEERS
SNELLS
SNICKS
SNIFFS
SNIPES
SNOODS
SNOOKS
SNOOPS
SNOOTS
SNOPES
SNORES
SNORTS
SNOUTS
SNUFFS
TNOTES
UNARMS
UNBARS
UNCAPS
UNCLES
UNDIES
UNDOES
UNFITS
UNGUES
UNGUIS
UNIATS
UNIONS
UNISYS
UNITAS
UNITES
UNJAMS
UNLESS
UNMANS
UNPEGS
UNPENS
UNPINS
UNRIGS
UNSAYS
UNSEWS
UNTIES
UNZIPS
VNECKS

••NS••
BENSON
BONSAI
BUNSEN
CENSED
CENSER
CENSES
CENSOR
CENSUS
CONSUL
DANSON
DENSER
GUNSHY
HANSEL
HANSOM
HANSON
HENSON
HONSHU
JANSEN
JANSKY
JENSEN
JONSON
KANSAN
KANSAS
KINSEY
KINSKI
LANSON
LENSED
LENSES
LINSEY
MANSES
MENSAE
MENSAL
MENSAS
MENSCH
NANSEN
OWNSUP
PENSEE
PINSON
RANSOM
RINSED
RINSES
RUNSAT
RUNSIN
RUNSON
RUNSTO
RUNSUP
SANSEI
SENSED
SENSEI
SENSES
SENSOR
SUNSET
TENSED
TENSER
TENSES
TENSOR
TINSEL
TONSIL
WINSOR

••N•S•
ARNESS
BANISH
DANISH
DENISE
DYNAST
ERNEST
FINEST
FINISH
HONEST
INNESS
IONISE
LANOSE
MONISM
MONIST
PUNISH
SANEST
SINISE
TANIST
TONISH
VANISH
WINISH

••N••S
AENEAS
ANNALS
ANNOYS
ANNULS
ARNESS
BANJOS
BANTUS
BINGES
BONCES
BONERS
BONGOS
BONNES
BONZES
BUNCOS
BUNKOS
CANALS
CANERS
CANIDS
CANNES
CANOES
CANONS
CANTOS
CANVAS
CENSES
CENSUS
CENTOS
CONCHS
CONDOS
CONEYS
CONGAS
CONICS
CONIES
CONTES
CYNICS
DANAUS
DANCES
DANTES
DENIES
DENIMS
DENNIS
DINARS
DINERS
DINGUS
DONEES
DONETS
DONNAS
DONORS
DONUTS
DUNCES
ENNIUS
FANONS
FENCES
FINALS
FUNGUS
GANGES
GENETS
GENIES
GENIUS
GENRES
GONERS
HENNAS
HINDUS
HINGES
HINGIS
HONEYS
HONORS
INNESS
IONICS
JANHUS
JINXES
JONAHS
JUNCOS
JUNTAS
JUNTOS
KANSAS
LANAIS
LANCES
LANDIS
LENSES
LINENS
LINERS
LONERS
LONGES
LUNGES
LYNXES
MANAUS
MANGOS
MANIAS
MANORS
MANSES
MANTAS
MANTIS
MENDES
MENSAS
MENTIS
MINCES
MINERS
MINIMS
MINKES
MINORS
MINXES
MONADS
MONEYS
MONIES
MONTES
MONTHS
MUNGOS
MYNAHS
NANTES
NENETS
NINERS
NINJAS
NINTHS
NONETS
OUNCES
OWNERS
PANDAS
PANELS
PANICS
PANNES
PANTOS
PENNIS
PINDUS
PINNAS
PINONS
PINOTS
PINTOS
PINUPS
PONCES
PONIES
PONTES
PONTUS
QANTAS
RANEES
RANGES
RANIDS
RENEWS
RENNES
RINSES
RONDOS
RUNINS
RUNONS
RUNUPS
SANTOS
SENNAS
SENORS
SENSES
SINEWS
SINGES
SONDES
SONICS
SUNNIS
SUNUPS
SYNODS
TANGOS
TANKAS
TANTES
TENENS
TENETS
TENNIS
TENONS
TENORS
TENSES
TENTHS
TINCTS
TINGES
TONDOS
TONERS
TONICS
TONNES
TUNERS
TUNICS
UINTAS
VENOMS
VENOUS
VENUES
VINCES
VINOUS
VINYLS
WANERS
WENCES
WINCES
WINZES
YENTAS
ZANIES
ZENDOS

•••NS•
ALONSO
EVENSO
FLENSE
GAINST
GDANSK
ODENSE
TEENSY
WEENSY

•••N•S
ACINUS
ADONIS
AGENAS
AGENTS
AKENES
ALANIS
ALINES
AMENDS
AMENTS
AMINES
AMINUS
ARENAS
ASANAS
ATONES
AZINES
BAINES
BARNES
BEANOS
BEINGS
BLANKS
BLENDS
BLINDS
BLINIS
BLINKS
BLONDS
BLUNTS
BMINUS
BONNES
BOUNDS
BRANDS
BRANTS
BRENTS
BRINES
BRINGS
BRINKS
BRONCS
BRUNTS
BUENOS

BWANAS BYRNES CANNES CARNES CHANTS CHINES CHINKS CHINOS CHUNKS CLANGS CLANKS CLINES CLINGS CLINKS CLONES CLONKS CLONUS CLUNKS CMINUS COUNTS CRANES CRANKS CRONES CRONUS CYGNUS DAUNTS DENNIS DMINUS DOINGS DONNAS DRINGS DRINKS DRONES EBONDS ELANDS EMENDS ERINYS ETHNOS EVENTS FAINTS FAUNAS FAUNUS FEINTS FIENDS FLANKS FLINGS FLINTS FLUNKS FOUNDS FOUNTS FRANCS FRANKS FRONDS FRONTS GIANTS GLANDS GLINTS GLYNIS GOINGS GRANDS GRANTS GRINDS GRUNTS HAINES HAUNTS HENNAS HMONGS HOUNDS HYENAS HYPNOS ICINGS IRANIS IRENES JAUNTS

JOINTS KAUNAS KERNOS KEYNES KIANGS LEMNOS LEONES LIANAS LIANES LIANGS LLANOS MAGNUS MOINES MOUNDS MOUNTS NOONES OMANIS OPINES ORANGS ORANTS ORINGS PAINTS PANNES PARNIS PENNIS PHONES PHONOS PIANOS PINNAS PLANES PLANKS PLANTS PLINKS PLONKS PLUNKS POINTS POUNDS PRANGS PRANKS PRINKS PRINTS PRONGS PRUNES QUINTS RAINES REINAS REINKS RENNES REUNES RHINOS ROUNDS RUANAS SAINTS SAUNAS SCANTS SCENAS SCENDS SCENES SCENTS SCONES SEINES SENNAS SHANKS SHINES SHUNTS SKANKS SKINKS SKUNKS SLANGS SLANTS SLINGS SLINKS SOUNDS SPANKS

SPENDS SPINES SPINKS STANDS STENOS STINGS STINKS STINTS STONES STUNTS SUNNIS SWANKS SWINGS TAINOS TAINTS TAUNTS TBONDS TBONES TENNIS TERNES THANES THANKS THINGS THINKS THONGS THUNKS TONNES TRENDS TRINES TRUNKS TWANGS TWINES UPENDS URANUS VARNAS VAUNTS VIANDS WHANGS WHINES WOUNDS WRINGS WRONGS ZOUNDS

••••NS

ACORNS ADDONS ADORNS ALIENS ALIGNS ALOINS AMIENS ANIONS APRONS ARSONS ARYANS ASIANS ASPENS ATHENS ATKINS AUDENS AUXINS AVIANS AXIONS BAIRNS BARONS BASINS BATONS BEGINS BISONS BOSONS BOSUNS BRAINS BRIANS

BROWNS BRUINS BURINS CABINS CAIRNS CAJUNS CANONS CAPONS CHAINS CHURNS CLEANS CLOWNS CODONS COIGNS COLONS COVENS COWENS COZENS CROONS CROWNS CUTINS DEIGNS DEMONS DIVANS DIZENS DOGONS DOYENS DOZENS DRAINS DROWNS EOSINS FANONS FEIGNS FELONS FLYINS FOEHNS FROWNS FUTONS GAMINS GHAINS GIVENS GLEANS GLUONS GRAINS GREENS GROANS GROINS GYRONS HAVENS HAZANS HELENS HERONS HOGANS HUMANS HURONS INCANS INIONS INTENS IOWANS JAPANS KNOWNS LAPINS LATENS LATINS LEARNS LEMANS LEMONS LIKENS LIMENS LINENS LIVENS LODENS LUDENS LUMENS

LYSINS MASONS MATINS MAVENS MAYANS MELONS MESONS MIZENS MORONS MOURNS MUCINS NEVINS NOLENS NYLONS OCEANS ONIONS ORGANS PAEANS PAEONS PAGANS PARENS PATENS PECANS PEKINS PINONS PISANS PITONS PLAINS PRAWNS PREENS PRIONS PUTONS PYLONS QUEENS QUERNS QUOINS RACONS RAVENS RAYONS RECONS REIGNS REMANS REPINS RERUNS RESINS REWINS RIPENS ROBINS ROMANS ROSINS ROWENS RUBENS RUMENS RUNINS RUNONS SABINS SALONS SARANS SATINS SAXONS SCIONS SCORNS SEDANS SERINS SETINS SEVENS SHEENS SIRENS SITINS SKEANS SKEINS SOLANS SPAWNS SPOONS

SPURNS STAINS STEINS STERNS SWAINS SWOONS TAKINS TALONS TAPINS TAUONS TENENS TENONS TETONS TEXANS THORNS TIEINS TIPINS TITANS TOEINS TOKENS TOXINS TOYONS TRAINS TWEENS UCLANS UHLANS UNIONS UNMANS UNPENS UNPINS UTURNS VALENS VEGANS VIXENS VOLANS VOLENS VSIGNS WAGONS WAKENS WAYANS WIDENS WIZENS WOMENS YEARNS ZAYINS ZAZENS

N•T•••

NATANT NATHAN NATICK NATION NATIVE NATRON NATTER NATURA NATURE NETHER NETMAN NETMEN NETPAY NETTED NETTLE NETTLY NETTON NITERS NITERY NITRES NITRIC NITWIT NOTARY NOTATE NOTBAD NOTCHY

NOTERS NOTICE NOTIFY NOTING NOTION NOTNOW NOTYET NUTATE NUTKIN NUTLET NUTMEG NUTRIA NUTTED NUTTER

N••T••

NANTES NATTER NAUTCH NEATEN NEATER NEATLY NECTAR NEKTON NESTEA NESTED NESTER NESTLE NESTOR NETTED NETTLE NETTLY NETTON NEUTER NEWTON NEXTTO NINTHS NOETIC NOOTKA NORTHS NORTON NUTTED NUTTER

N•••T•

NAMATH NEARTO NEGATE NEMATO NENETS NEXTTO NICETY NIGHTS NIGHTY NIKITA NIMITZ NINETY NOHITS NONETS NOPETS NOTATE NOVATO NUDITY NUTATE NYMETS

N••••T

NATANT NAUGHT NEEDNT NEWEST NICEST NIPSAT NITWIT

NLEAST NLWEST NOCENT NOEXIT NONFAT NOTYET NOUGAT NOUGHT NUDEST NUDIST NUGENT NUGGET NUMBAT NUTLET

•NT•••

ANTCOW ANTEED ANTERO ANTEUP ANTHEM ANTHER ANTICS ANTLER ANTONY ANTRES ANTRIM ANTRON ANTRUM ENTAIL ENTERO ENTERS ENTICE ENTIRE ENTITY ENTOMO ENTRAP ENTREE INTACT INTAKE INTEND INTENS INTENT INTERJ INTERN INTIMA INTIME INTINE INTONE INTOTO INTOWN INTROS INTUIT INTUNE INTURN ONTAPE ONTIME ONTOUR UNTACK UNTIDY UNTIED UNTIES UNTOLD UNTORN UNTRAP UNTROD UNTRUE UNTUNE

•N•T••

ANATTO ANITRA CNOTES ENATES

GNATTY INITIO INSTAL INSTAR INSTEP INSTIL KNOTTS KNOTTY ONETWO SNATCH SNATHE SNATHS SNITCH SNOTTY TNOTES UNITAL UNITAS UNITED UNITER UNITES UNSTOP

•N••T•

ANATTO ANSATE ENACTS ENMITY ENTITY GNATTY INCITE INDITE INGOTS INLETS INMATE INNATE INPUTS INSETS INSITU INTOTO INUITS INVITE INWITH KNOTTS KNOTTY KNOUTS ONSETS ONSITE SNAPTO SNOOTS SNOOTY SNORTS SNOTTY SNOUTS UNFITS UNIATE UNIATS

•N•••T

ANKLET ANNUIT ANOINT ENFANT ENGIRT ENGLUT ENLIST ENRAPT ENROOT INAPET INARUT INCEPT INCULT INDEBT INDENT INDICT

INDUCT INFACT INFANT INFECT INFEST INGEST INJECT INJEST INKJET INMOST INPART INPORT INSECT INSERT INSIST INSULT INTACT INTENT INTUIT INVENT INVERT INVEST KNIGHT ONEACT ONFOOT SNAPAT SNOCAT UNBELT UNBENT UNBOLT UNGIRT UNHURT UNJUST UNKNIT UNKNOT UNMEET UNREST UNROOT UNSEAT

••NT••

AUNTIE BANTAM BANTER BANTUS BENTON BONTON BUNTED BUNTER CANTAB CANTED CANTER CANTHI CANTLE CANTON CANTOR CANTOS CENTER CENTOS CENTRE CENTRI CENTRO CONTAC CONTES CONTRA CONTRE DANTES DANTON DENTAL DENTED DENTIL DENTIN DENTON DINTED

FANTAN FONTAL GANTRY GENTLE GENTLY GENTRY GUNTER HENTED HINTAT HINTED HINTER HINTON HUNTED HUNTER JUNTAS JUNTOS KANTOR KENTON LENTEN LENTIL LINTEL LINTER MANTAS MANTEL MANTIC MANTIS MANTLE MANTRA MANTUA MENTAL MENTIS MENTOR MINTED MINTER MONTEL MONTES MONTEZ MONTHS MUNTIN NANTES NINTHS PANTED PANTOS PANTRY PENTAD PENTUP PINTER PINTLE PINTOS PONTES PONTIC PONTUS PUNTED PUNTER QANTAS QINTAR RANTED RANTER RENTAL RENTED RENTER SANTEE SANTIR SANTOS SENTIN SENTRA SENTRY SENTUP SINTAX SINTER SONTAG SUNTAN SYNTAX TANTES

TANTRA TENTED TENTER TENTHS TINTED TINTER UINTAS VENTED VENTER VINTON WANTAD WANTED WANTIN WANTON WANTTO WENTAT WENTBY WENTIN WENTON WENTUP WINTER WINTRY WONTED WONTON WYNTER WYNTON XANTHO YENTAS

••N•T•

ADNATE AGNATE ARNETT BENITO BINATE BONITO CANUTE CENOTE DENOTE DONATE DONETS DONITZ DONUTS FINITE FINITO GENETS GUNITE HINCTY IGNATZ IGNITE INNATE LANATE LENGTH LENITY LUNATE MINUTE MONETA NENETS NINETY NONETS ORNATE ORNITH PINATA PINITE PINOTS RENATA RENOTE RUNSTO SANCTA SANGTO SANITY SENATE SENITI SINGTO

SONATA TENDTO TENETS TENUTO TINCTS TONITE UINTAS VANITY VENETO VENITE WANTTO ZENITH ZONATE

••N••T

ANNUIT ARNETT BANDIT BENOIT BONMOT BONNET CANLIT CANNOT CONANT DUNANT DYNAST ERNEST FANJET FANOUT FINEST GANNET HENBIT HINTAT HONEST JENNET JUNKET LANCET LINNET MINUET MINUIT MONIST NONFAT PANDIT PANOUT PENULT PINXIT PUNDIT PUNNET RANOUT RENNET RUNLET RUNOUT RUNSAT SANEST SENNET SENNIT SONANT SONNET SUNLIT SUNSET TANIST TENANT TINHAT TINPOT VINCIT WENTAT WINGIT WINKAT WINOUT WONOUT

•••NT•

AGENTS AJANTA AMENTS

AVANTI BLINTZ BLUNTS BOUNTY BRANTS BRENTS BRONTE BRUNTS CHANTS CHINTZ COUNTS COUNTY DAINTY DAUNTS EVENTS FAINTS FEINTS FLINTS FLINTY FOUNTS FRONTS GIANTS GLINTS GOINTO GRANTS GRUNTS HAUNTS JAUNTS JAUNTY JOINTS KOONTZ KRANTZ LEANTO MOUNTS MOUNTY ODONTO OPENTO ORANTS PAINTS PAINTY PLANTE PLANTS PLENTY PLINTH POINTE POINTS POINTY PRINTS PRONTO PUENTE QUANTA QUINTS SAINTE SAINTS SCANTS SCANTY SCENTS SEENTO SHANTY SHINTO SHUNTS SLANTS SPINTO STINTS STUNTS STUNTY TAINTS TAUNTS TURNTO TWENTY VAUNTS

•••N•T

ARENDT

BONNET BOWNET BRANDT BRUNET BURNET CANNOT CAPNUT CARNET CARNOT CORNET CYGNET DARNIT FLYNET GAINST GANNET GARNET HEXNUT HORNET JENNET LINNET LIONET LUGNUT MAGNET PEANUT PIGNUT PLANET PUNNET REGNAT RENNET SENNET SENNIT SIGNET SONNET SPINET UNKNIT UNKNOT USENET WALNUT WHYNOT

••••NT

ABSENT ACCENT ADVENT AGLINT AMOUNT ANOINT ARDENT ARGENT ARPENT ARRANT ASCENT ASLANT ASSENT AUMONT AVAUNT BESANT BEZANT BRYANT CADENT CEDANT CEMENT CLIENT COGENT CONANT COVENT DARENT DECANT DECENT DETENT DISANT DOCENT DOESNT DOPANT

DUMONT DUNANT DUPONT DURANT EGMONT ENFANT ERRANT ESCENT EXEUNT EXTANT EXTENT FLAUNT FLUENT FOMENT FORINT GERENT GERONT HAVENT HLHUNT INDENT INFANT INTENT INVENT LAMENT LAMONT LATENT LEARNT LEVANT LUCENT MOMENT MORANT MUSTNT MUTANT NATANT NEEDNT NOCENT NUGENT OCTANT ORIENT PARENT PATENT PEDANT PLAINT PLIANT POTENT QUAINT REBENT RECANT RECENT REDANT REGENT RELENT REPENT RERENT RESENT RIDENT RODENT SAVANT SECANT SEJANT SILENT SOLENT SONANT SPLINT SPRINT SQUINT TALENT TENANT TRUANT TYRANT UNBENT URGENT UTHANT VACANT

VALENT
VIVANT
VOLANT
WERENT
WISENT

NU••••
NUANCE
NUBBED
NUBBIN
NUBBLE
NUBBLY
NUBIAN
NUBILE
NUCHAE
NUCHAL
NUCLEI
NUCLEO
NUDELY
NUDEST
NUDGED
NUDGER
NUDGES
NUDIST
NUDITY
NUDNIK
NUECES
NUGENT
NUGGET
NUKING
NULLAH
NULLED
NUMBAT
NUMBED
NUMBER
NUMBLY
NUMERO
NUMINA
NUNCIO
NURSED
NURSER
NURSES
NUTATE
NUTKIN
NUTLET
NUTMEG
NUTRIA
NUTTED
NUTTER
NUZZLE

N•U•••
NAUGHT
NAUSEA
NAUTCH
NEUMAN
NEUMES
NEURAL
NEUROL
NEURON
NEUTER
NGUYEN
NOUGAT
NOUGHT
NOUMEA

N••U••
NATURA
NATURE
NEBULA
NERUDA
NIPUPS
NODULE
NYQUIL

N•••U•
NASHUA
NEREUS
NIMBUS
NIPPUR

N••••U
NASSAU
NIIHAU

•NU•••
ANUBIS
ANURAN
ENURED
ENURES
INUITS
INURED
INURES
KNURLS
KNURLY
ONUSES
SNUBBY
SNUFFS
SNUFFY
SNUGLI
SNUGLY
UNUSED

•N•U••
ANNUAL
ANNUIT
ANNULI
ANNULS
ENDUED
ENDUES
ENDURE
ENDURO
ENDUSE
ENGULF
ENOUGH
ENQUAD
ENSUED
ENSUES
ENSURE
INBULK
INCULT
INCURS
INCUSE
INDUCE
INDUCT
INFULL
INFUSE
INJURE
INJURY
INLUCK
INOUYE
INPUTS
INRUSH
INSULT
INSURE
INTUIT
INTUNE
INTURN
KNOUTS
ONEUPS
ONRUSH
PNEUMA
SNOUTS
UNBUSY
UNCURL
UNDULY
UNFURL
UNGUAL
UNGUES
UNGUIS
UNHURT
UNJUST
UNRULY
UNSUNG
UNSURE
UNTUNE

•N••U•
ANIMUS
ANJOUS
ANTEUP
ANTRUM
CNIDUS
ENDRUN
ENDSUP
ENGLUT
ENNIUS
ENSOUL
INARUT
INDIUM
INFLUX
INHAUL
INPOUR
ONTOUR
SNAFUS
SNAPUP
UNGLUE
UNIQUE
UNPLUG
UNTRUE

•N•••U
INSITU

••NU••
ANNUAL
ANNUIT
ANNULI
ANNULS
BENUMB
BUNUEL
CANUTE
CONURE
DANUBE
DENUDE
DONUTS
GENUAL
LUNULA
MANUAL
MANUEL
MINUET
MINUIT
MINUTE
PENULT
PENURY
PINUPS
RUNUPS
SENUFO
SUNUNU
SUNUPS
TENURE
TENUTO
VENUES
ZANUCK

••N•U•
BANGUI
BANGUP
BANJUL
BANQUO
BANTUS
BENHUR
BINDUP
BONEUP
BUNKUM
CANCUN
CANFUL
CENSUS
CINQUE
CONCUR
CONIUM
CONSUL
DANAUS
DENGUE
DINGUS
DONEUP
ENNIUS
FANOUT
FONDUE
FUNGUS
GANGUE
GANGUP
GENIUS
HANDUP
HANGUL
HANGUP
HINDUS
HONOUR
HUNGUP
IONIUM
JANHUS
KUNLUN
LANGUR
LINEUP
LINGUA
LINKUP
LONGUE
MANAUS
MANFUL
MANQUE
MANTUA
MINIUM
OMNIUM
OWNSUP
PANFUL
PANOUT
PENTUP
PINDUS
PONTUS
PONYUP
RANGUP
RANOUT
RINGUP
RUNGUP
RUNOUT
RUNSUP
SANNUP
SENDUP
SENTUP
SINFUL
TANGUY
TANKUP
TONEUP
TONGUE
TUNEUP
VENOUS
VINOUS
WENTUP
WINDUP
WINOUT
WONMUG
WONOUT
YANQUI

••N••U
CONGOU
HONSHU
HUNGWU
JUNEAU
KUNGFU
LANDAU
MANCHU
MENJOU
PENGHU
SUNUNU
XANADU

•••NU•
ACINUS
AMINUS
AVENUE
BARNUM
BMINUS
BURNUP
CAPNUT
CHINUP
CLONUS
CMINUS
CRONUS
CYGNUS
DMINUS
EVENUP
FAUNUS
FRENUM
HEXNUT
JOINUP
KRONUR
LUGNUT
MAGNUM
MAGNUS
OPENUP
PEANUT
PIGNUT
PLENUM
PRENUP
SANNUP
SEWNUP
SIGNUP
TURNUP
URANUS
WALNUT

•••N•U
CHONJU
MBUNDU

••••NU
SUNUNU
VISHNU

N•V•••
NAVAHO
NAVAJO
NAVELS
NAVIES
NEVADA
NEVERS
NEVINS
NEVSKY
NOVATO
NOVELS
NOVENA
NOVICE

N••V••
NARVIK
NERVES

N•••V•
NATIVE

•NV•••
ANVILS
ENVIED
ENVIER
ENVIES
ENVOIS
ENVOYS
INVADE
INVAIN
INVENT
INVERT
INVEST
INVITE
INVIVO
INVOKE
ONVIEW
UNVEIL

•N•V••
KNAVES
KNIVES
SNIVEL
UNEVEN
UNIVAC

•N••V•
ENDIVE
INLOVE
INVIVO
UNWOVE

••NV••
CANVAS
CONVEX
CONVEY
CONVOY
DENVER
LANVIN

••N•V•
CANOVA
DENOVO
GENEVA
GENEVE

••N••V
HENRYV

N•W•••
NAWABS
NEWAGE
NEWARK
NEWELS
NEWEST
NEWISH
NEWLEY
NEWMAN
NEWMAR
NEWTON
NLWEST
NOWISE

N••W••
NARWAL
NITWIT
NORWAY

N••••W
NARROW
NEPHEW
NOSHOW
NOTNOW

•NW•••
ANWANG
ENWRAP
INWARD
INWITH
ONWARD
UNWARY
UNWELL
UNWILY
UNWIND
UNWISE
UNWISH
UNWORN
UNWOVE
UNWRAP

•N•W••
ANSWER
ANYWAY
GNAWED
GNAWER
INAWAY
KNOWER
KNOWNS
ONEWAY
SNOWED
SNOWIN
UNAWED

•N••W•
ENDOWS
INLAWS
INTOWN
ONETWO
UNSEWN
UNSEWS
UNSOWN

•N•••W
ANDHOW
ANDREW
ANTCOW
ANYHOW
INAROW
INFLOW
ONVIEW
UNDRAW

••NW••
CONWAY
FENWAY
RUNWAY
WINWIN

••N•W•
HUNGWU
RENEWS
RENOWN
SINEWS
SINEWY

••N••W
MINNOW
SUNDEW
WINDOW
WINNOW

•••N•W
CPSNOW
ERENOW
HOWNOW
MINNOW
NOTNOW
WINNOW

N•X•••
NEXTTO
NIXIES
NIXING

N••X••
NOEXIT

•N•X••
ONYXES

•N••X•
ANNEXE

•N•••X
INAFIX
INFLUX
UNISEX

••NX••
JINXED
JINXES
LYNXES
MINXES
PINXIT
SKNXXX

••N•X•
ADNEXA
ANNEXE
CUNAXA
SKNXXX

••N••X
BENDIX
CONVEX
LENNOX
MANNIX
MENINX
SINTAX
SKNXXX
SYNTAX
WINDEX

•••N•X
BRANDX
LENNOX
MANNIX

••••NX
LARYNX
MENINX
SPHINX
SYRINX

NY••••
NYALAS
NYASSA
NYLONS
NYMETS
NYMPHS
NYQUIL

N•Y•••
NAYSAY

N••Y••
NGUYEN
NOTYET

N•••Y•
NAGOYA

N••••Y
NAMELY
NAPERY
NASEBY
NAYSAY
NEARBY
NEARLY
NEATLY
NETPAY
NETTLY
NEVSKY
NEWLEY
NIAMEY
NICELY
NICETY
NIDIFY
NIGHTY
NIMBLY
NIMINY
NINETY
NIPSEY
NITERY
NOBODY
NONARY
NORGAY
NORWAY
NOSILY
NOTARY
NOTCHY
NOTIFY
NUBBLY
NUDELY
NUDITY
NUMBLY

•NY•••
ANYANG
ANYDAY
ANYHOW
ANYONE
ANYWAY
ONYXES
SNYDER
UNYOKE

•N•Y••
ANHYDR
ENZYME
INSYNC
UNDYED

•N••Y•
ANNOYS
ANONYM
ENJOYS
ENVOYS
INLAYS
INOUYE
UNISYS
UNSAYS

•N•••Y
ANDREY
ANERGY
ANTONY
ANYDAY
ANYWAY
ENERGY
ENMITY
ENTITY
GNARLY
GNATTY
INAWAY
INFAMY
INJURY
INPLAY
KNAGGY
KNARRY
KNOBBY
KNOLLY
KNOTTY
KNURLY
ONEDAY
ONEWAY
ONIONY
SNAGGY
SNAPPY
SNARLY
SNAZZY
SNEAKY
SNEERY
SNEEZY
SNIFFY
SNIPPY
SNOBBY
SNOOKY
SNOOPY
SNOOTY
SNOOZY
SNOTTY
SNUBBY
SNUFFY
SNUGLY
UNBUSY
UNDULY
UNEASY
UNHOLY
UNOILY
UNRULY
UNTIDY
UNWARY
UNWILY

••NY••
BANYAN
BUNYAN
BUNYIP
CANYON
KENYAN
LYNYRD
MINYAN
PINYIN
PINYON
PONYUP
RUNYON
VINYLS

••N•Y•
ANNOYS
CONEYS
HENRYV
HONEYS
KENNYG
MONEYS
VANRYN

••N••Y
BENDAY
BENGAY
BINARY
BUNCHY
CANARY
CANOPY
CONROY
CONVEY
CONVOY
CONWAY
DANGLY
DANKLY
DANNAY
DENARY
DINGHY
DINKEY
DONKEY
FENWAY
FINELY
FINERY
FINNEY
FONDLY
GANGLY
GANTRY
GENTLY
GENTRY
GONEBY
GUNSHY
HANLEY
HENLEY
HINCTY
HUNGRY
JANGLY
JANSKY
JENNEY
JINGLY
JUNGLY
KINDLY
KINGLY
KINSEY
LANDRY
LANKLY
LENITY
LINENY
LINNEY
LINSEY
LONELY
LONGLY
LUNACY
LUNCHY
LYNLEY
MANDAY
MANRAY
MINIFY
MONDAY
MONKEY
MONODY
MUNCHY
NINETY
NONARY
ORNERY
PANFRY
PANTRY
PENNEY
PENURY
PINERY
PUNCHY
PUNILY
RANDRY
RANKLY
RONELY
RUNDRY
RUNWAY
SANELY
SANITY
SENARY
SENTRY
SINEWY
SINGLY
SUNDAY
SUNDRY
SUNRAY
TANGLY
TANGUY
TINGLY
TINILY
TINKLY
TUNNEY
VANITY
VINERY
VINIFY
WENTBY
WINERY
WINTRY
ZANILY

•••NY•
ANONYM
CRONYN
EPONYM
ERINYS
KENNYG
PHENYL

•••N•Y
AGENCY
BARNEY
BIRNEY
BLENNY
BOUNCY
BOUNTY
BRANDY
BRANNY
BRONZY
BURNEY
CAGNEY
CARNEY
CHANCY
CHANEY
CHINKY
CHUNKY
CLANCY
CLANKY
CLINGY
CLUNKY
COONEY
COUNTY
CRANKY
CRANNY
DABNEY
DAINTY
DANNAY
DARNAY
DISNEY
DOWNEY
EVENLY
FINNEY
FLINTY
FLUNKY
FRANNY
FRENZY
FRINGY
GAINLY
GRANNY
GRUNDY
GRUNGY
GURNEY
HEANEY
HORNEY
HOUNDY
JAUNTY
JENNEY
JITNEY
JOHNNY
JOUNCY
KEENLY
KIDNEY
LEANLY
LINNEY
LIONLY
LOONEY
MAINLY
MAUNDY
MEANLY
MOONEY
MORNAY
MOUNTY
OHENRY
OPENLY
ORANGY
ORKNEY
PAINTY
PENNEY
PHONEY
PLENTY
POINTY
QUINCY
RAINEY
RODNEY
ROMNEY
ROONEY
SCANTY
SHANDY
SHANNY
SHANTY
SHINDY
SHINNY
SIDNEY
SKINNY
SKUNKY
SLANGY
SLINKY
SPANKY
SPONGY
SPUNKY
STANKY
STINGY
STINKY
STUNTY
SWANKY
SWINGY
SYDNEY
TEENSY
THINGY
THINLY
TRENDY
TUNNEY
TWANGY
TWENTY
VAINLY
VARNEY
WATNEY
WEENSY
WHINEY
WHINNY

••••NY
ALBANY
ANTONY
BARONY
BETONY
BLENNY
BOIGNY
BOTANY
BRAINY
BRANNY
BRAWNY
BROWNY
BRYONY
COLONY
CRANNY
CZERNY
DELANY
FELONY
FRANNY
GRAINY
GRANNY
GREENY
GROZNY
HOMINY
JIMINY
JOHNNY
KEARNY
KRASNY
LEMONY
LINENY
LITANY
MUTINY
NIMINY
ONIONY
PIMINY
REDENY
RESINY
ROMANY
ROSINY
SATINY
SAXONY
SHANNY
SHINNY
SIMONY
SKINNY
SOMANY
SPOONY
THORNY
TWEENY
WHINNY

N•Z•••
NOZZLE
NUZZLE

N••Z••
NOZZLE
NUZZLE

N••••Z
NIMITZ

•NZ•••
ENZYME
UNZIPS

•N•Z••
SNAZZY

•N••Z•
SNAZZY
SNEEZE
SNEEZY
SNOOZE
SNOOZY

••NZ••
BANZAI
BENZOL
BONZES
DANZIG
DENZEL
PANZER
PINZON
WINZES

••N•Z•
IONIZE

••N••Z
DONITZ
IGNATZ
MONTEZ

•••NZ•
ALONZO
BRONZE
BRONZY
FAENZA
FRENZY
KWANZA
RIENZI
STANZA

•••N•Z
BLINTZ
CHINTZ
KOONTZ
KRANTZ
SCHNOZ

••••NZ
BRIENZ
DOLENZ
LORENZ

OA••••
OAFISH
OAKLEY
OARING
OATERS
OATIER
OAXACA

O•A•••
OCASEK
OCASEY
OKAPIS
OKAYED
OMAHAN
OMAHAS
OMANIS
OMASUM
ONAGER
OPAQUE
ORACHS
ORACLE
ORALES
ORALLY
ORANGE
ORANGS
ORANGY
ORANTS
ORATED
ORATES
ORATOR
OSAGES
OVALLY
OXALIS
OZARKS

O••A••
OAXACA
OBEAHS
OBLAST
OBLATE
OBTAIN
OCEANS
OCTADS
OCTANE
OCTANT
OCTAVE
OCTAVO
OFLATE
OGHAMS
OGLALA
OKSANA
OLDAGE
OLEARY
OLEATE
ONCALL
ONEACT
ONHAND
ONLAND
ONSALE
ONTAPE
ONWARD
OOLALA
OPIATE
ORBACH
ORDAIN
OREADS
ORGANA
ORGANS
ORGATE
ORIANA
ORNATE
OSCARS
OSHAWA
OSWALD
OTTAVA
OTTAWA
OUTACT
OUTAGE
OUTATE
OXCART
OXNARD
OXTAIL

O•••A•
OBIWAN
OBRIAN
OCREAE
OCULAR
OFFDAY
OGDOAD
OHIOAN
OHYEAH
OILCAN
OILMAN
OILPAN
OLDHAM
OLDHAT
OLDMAN
OLDSAW
OMAHAN
OMAHAS
OMEGAS
ONEDAY
ONEMAN
ONEWAY
ONLOAN
OOMPAH
OPERAS
ORDEAL
ORGEAT
ORPHAN
OSSIAN
OSTEAL
OUTEAT
OUTLAW
OUTLAY
OUTRAN
OVISAC
OVULAR

O••••A
OAXACA
OBELIA

ODESSA ODETTA OEDEMA OGLALA OJIBWA OKSANA OLINDA OLIVIA OMERTA ONEIDA OOLALA OPTIMA OREIDA ORGANA ORIANA ORISSA ORTEGA OSCULA OSHAWA OTTAVA OTTAWA

•OA•••

BOARDS BOASTS BOATED BOATEL BOATER COALER COAPTS COARSE COASTS COATED COATIS COAXED COAXER COAXES DOABLE FOALED FOAMED GOADED GOALIE GOANNA GOATEE GOAWAY GOAWRY HOAGIE HOARDS HOARSE HOAXED HOAXER HOAXES JOANIE JOANNA JOANNE KOALAS LOADED LOADER LOAFED LOAFER LOAMED LOANED LOANER LOATHE LOAVES MOANED MOANER MOATED POACHY ROADIE ROAMED ROAMER ROARED ROARER ROASTS SOAKED SOAKER SOAKUP SOAPED SOAPER SOARED SOARER SOARES SOASTO SOAVES TOAMAN TOASTS TOASTY TOATEE

•O•A••

AODAIS BOGART BONAMI BORAGE BORATE BORAXO BOTANY BOVARY BOYARS COBALT COLADA COMATE CONANT COPAYS CORALS COWARD DOMAIN DOMANI DONALD DONATE DOPANT DORADO DORAGS DORATI DOSAGE DOTAGE DOTARD DOUALA FORAGE FORAYS GOBACK GOCART GODARD GOEASY GOKART GORALS HOBART HODADS HOGANS HOMAGE HORACE HOTAIR HOWARD IODATE IOWANS JOHANN JONAHS KODALY KORATS KOVACS LOBATE LOCALE LOCALS LOCATE LORAIN LOTAHS LOVAGE MOHAIR MOHAVE MOHAWK MOJAVE MOLARS MONACO MONADS MORALE MORALS MORANT MORASS MORAVA MORAYS MOSAIC MOZART NOMADS NONAGE NONAME NONARY NOSALE NOTARY NOTATE NOVATO OOLALA POLAND POMACE POMADE POPART POSADA POTAGE POTASH POTATO ROBALO ROLAND ROMAIC ROMAJI ROMANO ROMANS ROMANY RONALD ROSARY ROTARY ROTATE ROXANA ROXANE ROYALE ROYALS SOCAGE SOLACE SOLANS SOLARS SOMALI SOMANY SOMATA SOMATO SONANT SONATA SOUARI TOBAGO TODATE TOGAED TOKAYS TOMATO TORAHS TOTALS TOWAGE TOWARD VOCALS VOLANS VOLANT VOLARE VOTARY VOYAGE YOUALL ZONATE ZOUAVE

•O••A•

AORTAE AORTAL AORTAS AOUDAD BOBCAT BOMBAY BONSAI BOREAL BOREAS BORMAN BOWMAN BOWOAR BOWSAW BOXCAR COBHAM COBIAS COBRAS COCOAS COEVAL COGNAC COLFAX COLLAR COLMAN COMBAT COMEAT COMMAS COMPAQ COMSAT CONFAB CONGAS CONMAN CONRAD CONTAC CONWAY COOGAN CORBAN CORDAY CORMAN CORRAL COSTAE COSTAL COSTAR COSTAS COTTAS COUGAR COWMAN DOBLAS DOBRAS DOGDAY DOGEAR DOGMAS DOGSAT DOGTAG DOLLAR DOLMAN DOLMAS DONNAS DOODAD DOODAH DORCAS DORIAN DORSAL DOSSAL DOTHAN EOLIAN EONIAN FOETAL FOGHAT FOLIAR FONTAL FORBAD FORMAL FORMAN FORMAT FORTAS FOSSAE FOSSAS FOURAM FOVEAE GOAWAY GOESAT GOSTAG GOTHAM GOTMAD HOOHAH HOOHAS HOOKAH HOORAH HOORAY HOOTAT HOSTAS HOTCAP HOTCAR HOTWAR HOWDAH IONIAN JORDAN JOSIAH JOVIAL JOVIAN KOALAS KODIAK KOMBAT KONRAD KOREAN KORMAN KOUFAX LOGJAM LONGAN LOOFAH LOOFAS LOOKAT LOQUAT LOREAL LOTHAR LOWCAL LOWFAT MOBCAP MOCHAS MOLDAU MOLNAR MOMMAS MONDAY MOOLAH MOREAU MORGAN MORNAY MORTAL MORTAR MOSHAV NOLEAD NOLOAD NONFAT NOONAN NORGAY NORIAS NORMAL NORMAN NORWAY NOSOAP NOTBAD NOUGAT OOMPAH POKEAT POLEAX POLKAS POPLAR POPPAS PORTAL POSTAL RODHAM RODMAN ROSEAU SOCIAL SOLDAN SOLFAS SONTAG SOTHAT SOWHAT TOAMAN TOBIAS TODDAO TODMAN TOECAP TOETAP TOKLAS TOMBAC TOMCAT TONGAN TOOBAD TOPCAT TOPHAT TOREAT TOUCAN TOWCAR VODKAS VOLVAS WOMBAT ZODIAC

•O•••A

BODEGA BOGOTA BORGIA BOSNIA COLADA COLIMA CONCHA CONTRA COPULA CORNEA CORONA CORYZA COULDA COVINA COWPEA DODECA DODOMA DOUALA GOANNA GODIVA GOTCHA HOOPLA HOTTEA JOANNA JOJOBA JOSHUA KONICA KORUNA LOGGIA LOLITA LORICA LOUISA LOYOLA MODELA MODENA MONERA MONETA MONICA MORAVA MORITA MOSKVA MOTHRA NOOTKA NOUMEA NOVENA OOLALA POMONA PORTIA POSADA ROBBIA ROMOLA ROSITA ROSTRA ROWENA ROXANA SOMATA SONATA SONOMA SONORA SOPHIA TOLUCA TOPEKA TOYOTA WOVOKA YORUBA YOYOMA ZOYSIA

••OA••

ABOARD BLOATS BROACH BROADS CHOATE CLOACA CLOAKS CROAKS CROAKY CROATS EBOATS FLOATS FLOATY GLOATS GROANS GROATS PROAMS SHOALS SHOALY SHOATS SKOALS SLOANE STOATS UBOATS

••O•A•

ABORAL ADONAI AGORAE AGORAS ALOHAS ALOMAR AMORAL ANORAK APODAL AROMAS ASOSAN ATONAL AVOWAL AXONAL BAOBAB BHOPAL BIOGAS BIOTAS BROGAN BROKAW CHORAL COOGAN DEODAR DOODAD DOODAH DVORAK FLORAE FLORAL FLORAS GLOBAL HOOHAH HOOHAS HOOKAH HOORAH HOORAY HOOTAT ISOBAR KIOWAS LOOFAH LOOFAS LOOKAT MAOTAI MOOLAH NOONAN PROTAX PROZAC QUOTAS RIOJAS RYOKAN SHOFAR SHORAN SHOTAT SIOUAN SLOGAN SLOVAK SNOCAT STOMAS STOMAT THOMAS THORAX TOOBAD TROCAR TROJAN TWOWAY UNOCAL VIOLAS XHOSAS YEOMAN

••O••A

ABOLLA AEOLIA AMOEBA CHOLLA CHOPRA CLOACA EROICA GLORIA GLOSSA HOOPLA LIOTTA MYOPIA NOOTKA PEORIA PHOBIA QUOKKA QUOTHA RHONDA SCORIA SCOTIA SFORZA SHORTA TROIKA UTOPIA

•••OA•

ABROAD AFLOAT BEMOAN BOWOAR BUROAK BYROAD COCOAS GENOAN INROAD MINOAN NOLOAD NOSOAP OGDOAD OHIOAN ONLOAN PINOAK PTBOAT RECOAT REDOAK RELOAD SAMOAN SILOAM STJOAN TANOAK TANOAN THROAT UNLOAD UPLOAD UPROAR

•••O•A

ANCONA ANGOLA ANGORA AREOLA ARROBA AURORA BAROJA BITOLA BOGOTA BULOVA CANOLA CANOVA CHROMA CIBOLA CORONA CUPOLA DAKOTA DODOMA EIDOLA ENDORA ESPOSA EUBOEA EUDORA EUROPA FEDORA FEMORA JOJOBA JUDOKA LADOGA LAKOTA LAROSA LATONA LATOYA LOYOLA MAZOLA MIMOSA MUCOSA NAGOYA NICOLA NIKOLA PAGODA PALOMA PAYOLA PELOTA POMONA RAMONA RCCOLA REMORA ROMOLA SAMOSA SENORA SEROSA SONOMA SONORA TACOMA TOYOTA VERONA VIGODA WINONA WOVOKA YOYOMA ZADORA

••••OA

BALBOA HIVAOA HULLOA JERBOA LISBOA QUINOA

OB••••

OBEAHS OBELIA OBELUS OBERON OBEYED OBISPO OBITER OBIWAN OBJECT OBLAST OBLATE OBLIGE OBLONG OBOIST OBRIAN OBRIEN OBSESS OBSTET OBTAIN OBTEST OBTUND OBTUSE OBVERT

O•B•••

ORBACH ORBING ORBITS OSBORN OXBOWS

O••B••

OJIBWA OLDBOY ORIBIS OUTBID OUTBOX

O••••B

ODDJOB

•OB•••

BOBBED BOBBER BOBBIE BOBBIN BOBBLE BOBCAT BOBSUP COBALT COBBLE COBHAM COBIAS COBRAS COBURG COBURN COBWEB DOBBER DOBBIN DOBLAS DOBLIN DOBRAS DOBROS DOBSON FOBBED FOBOFF GOBACK GOBBLE GOBIES GOBLET GOBLIN GOBUST HOBART HOBBES HOBBIT HOBBLE HOBNOB HOBOES HOBSON JOBBED JOBBER JOBETH JOBHOP JOBLOT KOBOLD LOBATE LOBBED LOBBER LOBULE MOBBED MOBCAP MOBILE MOBIUS MOBLEY NOBBLE NOBLER NOBLES NOBODY POBOYS ROBALO ROBBED ROBBER ROBBIA ROBBIE ROBERT ROBING ROBINS ROBLES ROBOTS ROBROY ROBSON ROBUST SOBBED SOBBER SOBEIT SOBERS SOBFUL TOBAGO TOBIAS TOBIES TOBOOT TOBRUK WOBBLE WOBBLY YOBBOS

•O•B••

BOBBED BOBBER BOBBIE BOBBIN BOBBLE BOMBAY BOMBED BOMBER BOMBES BONBON BOOBOO BOUBOU BOXBOY COBBLE COMBAT COMBED COMBER COMBES COMBOS CORBAN CORBEL CORBIN COWBOY DOABLE DOBBER DOBBIN DOOBIE DOUBLE DOUBLY DOUBTS FOBBED FOGBOW FOIBLE FORBAD FORBES FORBID GOBBLE GOOBER HOBBES HOBBIT HOBBLE HOMBRE HOTBED HOTBOX JOBBED JOBBER KOMBAT KORBUT LOBBED LOBBER LOMBOK LOWBOY MOBBED MORBID NOBBLE NOTBAD ROBBED ROBBER ROBBIA ROBBIE ROUBLE SOBBED SOBBER SOMBER SOMBRE SORBET SORBIC SOWBUG TOMBAC TOMBOY TOOBAD WOBBLE WOBBLY WOMBAT YOBBOS YOUBET ZOMBIE

•O••B•

COMEBY DOESBY GOESBY GONEBY GOODBY JOJOBA YORUBA

•O•••B

COBWEB CONFAB CONJOB HOBNOB HOTTUB TOPJOB

••OB••

ADOBES BAOBAB BIOBIO BOOBOO DOOBIE GLOBAL GLOBED GLOBES GLOBIN GOOBER IROBOT ISOBAR KNOBBY PHOBIA PHOBIC PHOBOS PROBED PROBER PROBES SLOBBY SNOBBY TOOBAD TWOBIT

••O•B•

ABOMBS AMOEBA CROSBY DROPBY GOODBY HBOMBS KNOBBY PHOEBE RHOMBI RHOMBS SLOBBY SNOBBY

••O••B

BAOBAB DIONEB

•••OB•

AEROBE ARROBA CAROBS DEMOBS ENROBE JACOBI JOJOBA KABOBS KEBOBS MCJOBS NABOBS STROBE THROBS TYCOBB UNROBE

•••O•B

ABSORB ADSORB APLOMB RESORB TYCOBB

••••OB

CONJOB DAYJOB HOBNOB ODDJOB SKIBOB TOPJOB

OC••••

OCASEK OCASEY OCCULT OCCUPY OCCURS OCEANS OCELLI OCELOT OCHERS OCHERY OCHRES OCLOCK OCREAE OCTADS OCTANE OCTANT OCTAVE OCTAVO OCTETS OCTOPI OCTROI OCULAR

O•C•••

OCCULT OCCUPY OCCURS ONCALL OOCYTE ORCHID ORCHIL OSCARS OSCINE OSCULA OXCART

O••C••

OILCAN ORACHS ORACLE OUNCES OUTCRY

O•••C•

OAXACA OBJECT OCLOCK OFFICE OLMECS ONDECK ONEACT OPTICS ORBACH OROZCO OSMICS OUTACT

O••••C

OLDVIC ONSPEC ORPHIC OTITIC OVISAC OXIDIC OZONIC

•OC•••

BOCCIE BOCHCO COCCID COCCUS COCCYX COCHIN COCKED COCKER COCKLE COCOAS COCOON DOCENT DOCILE DOCKED DOCKER DOCKET DOCTOR EOCENE FOCSLE GOCART HOCKED HOCKEY JOCKEY JOCOSE JOCUND LOCALE LOCALS LOCATE LOCKED LOCKER LOCKET LOCKIN LOCKON LOCKUP LOCUST MOCHAS MOCKED MOCKER MOCKUP NOCENT OOCYTE POCKET POCONO ROCHET ROCKED ROCKER ROCKET ROCKNE ROCKYV ROCOCO SOCAGE SOCCER SOCIAL SOCKED SOCKET SOCKIN SOCLES TOCSIN VOCALS

•O•C••

BOBCAT BOCCIE BONCES BOTCHY BOUCLE BOXCAR COCCID COCCUS COCCYX CONCHA CONCHS CONCUR DORCAS FORCED FORCER FORCES GOTCHA HONCHO HOTCAP HOTCAR LOUCHE LOWCAL MOBCAP MOSCOW NONCOM NOTCHY POACHY PONCES PONCHO POUCHY ROSCOE SOCCER TOECAP TOMCAT TOPCAT TORCHY TOUCAN TOUCHE TOUCHY TOWCAR VOICED VOICES YOICKS

•O••C•

BOCHCO BODICE BORSCH BOUNCE BOUNCY COERCE COMICS CONICS CONOCO DODECA GOBACK

HOOTCH HORACE IONICS JOUNCE JOUNCY KONICA KOPECK KOVACS LORICA MODOCS MOHOCK MOLOCH MONACO MONICA NODICE NOTICE NOVICE POLICE POLICY POMACE POUNCE ROCOCO SOLACE SONICS SOURCE TOLUCA TONICS TOPICS TOXICS VOTECH YORICK

•O•••C

AORTIC COGNAC CONTAC COPTIC COSMIC COURIC FORMIC GOTHIC HOMEEC MOSAIC NOETIC NORDIC POETIC PONTIC ROMAIC SORBIC TOLTEC TOMBAC ZODIAC

••OC••

AVOCET BLOCKS BLOCKY CHOCKS CLOCHE CLOCKS CROCKS CROCUS EPOCHS FLOCKS FLOCKY FROCKS GROCER KNOCKS PHOCIS PROCNE SHOCKS SMOCKS SNOCAT STOCKS STOCKY TROCAR TROCHE UNOCAL

••O•C•

ATONCE AVOUCH BLOTCH BROACH BRONCO BRONCS BROOCH CHOICE CLOACA CROUCH EROICA GROUCH HOOTCH OROZCO SCONCE SCORCH SCOTCH SLOUCH SMOOCH STOICS STORCH

••O••C

AEOLIC ANODIC ANOMIC ATOMIC ATONIC BIONIC BIOTIC EROTIC ETONIC EXOTIC FROLIC GNOMIC ICONIC IRONIC MYOPIC OZONIC PHOBIC PHONIC PHOTIC PROZAC TROPIC

•••OC•

BROOCH CONOCO DECOCT DUROCS EDKOCH HAVOCS IDIOCY MODOCS MOHOCK MOLOCH OCLOCK RELOCK ROCOCO SMOOCH SUNOCO UNLOCK VELOCE

•••O•C

ECHOIC HEROIC

••••OC

BELLOC ENBLOC MANIOC TLALOC ZIPLOC

OD••••

ODDEST ODDITY ODDJOB ODDLOT ODDSON ODENSE ODESSA ODETTA ODETTE ODIOUS ODISTS ODIUMS ODONTO ODOURS

O•D•••

ODDEST ODDITY ODDJOB ODDLOT ODDSON OEDEMA OGDOAD OLDAGE OLDBOY OLDEST OLDHAM OLDHAT OLDIES OLDISH OLDMAN OLDMEN OLDPRO OLDSAW OLDVIC ONDECK ONDINE OODLES ORDAIN ORDEAL ORDERS ORDURE

O••D••

OFFDAY ONEDAY ONEDGE OUTDID OXIDES OXIDIC OXYDOL

O•••D•

OCTADS OLINDA ONEIDA ONSIDE OREADS OREIDA OROIDE OVERDO OVIEDO OVOIDS

O••••D

OBEYED OBTUND OFFEND OGDOAD OINKED OKAYED ONHAND ONHOLD ONLAND ONWARD OPENED OPINED ORATED ORCHID ORMOND OSGOOD OSMOND OSMUND OSTEND OSWALD OUSTED OUTBID OUTDID OXFORD OXNARD

•OD•••

AODAIS BODEGA BODICE BODIED BODIES BODILY BODING BODKIN BODONI CODDLE CODERS CODGER CODIFY CODING CODONS DODDER DODECA DODGED DODGER DODGES DODODO DODOES DODOMA FODDER GODARD GODETS GODIVA GODOWN GODSON GODWIN GODWIT HODADS HODGES IODATE IODIDE IODINE IODISE IODIZE KODALY KODIAK LODENS LODGED LODGER LODGES MODELA MODELS MODELT MODEMS MODENA MODERN MODEST MODIFY MODINE MODISH MODOCS MODULE MODULO NODDED NODDLE NODICE NODOFF NODOSE NODULE OODLES PODDED PODIUM PODUNK RODDED RODENT RODEOS RODHAM RODMAN RODNEY SODDED SODDEN SODIUM TODATE TODDAO TODDLE TODMAN VODKAS WODGES YODELS ZODIAC

•O•D••

AOUDAD BOLDER BOLDLY BONDED BOODLE BORDEN BORDER BOUDIN CODDLE COEDIT COLDER COLDLY CONDOR CONDOS COODER CORDAY CORDED CORDON DODDER DOGDAY DOGDOM DONDER DOODAD DOODAH DOODLE FODDER FOLDED FOLDER FOLDUP FONDER FONDLE FONDLY FONDUE FOODIE FORDED GOADED GOLDEN GOLDIE GOODBY GOODEN GOODIE GOODLY GOODOH GORDIE GORDON HOLDEN HOLDER HOLDIN HOLDIT HOLDON HOLDTO HOLDUP HOODED HOODOO HORDES HOTDOG HOWDAH HOYDEN JORDAN LOADED LOADER LONDON LORDED LORDLY LOUDEN LOUDER LOUDLY MOLDAU MOLDED MOLDER MONDAY NODDED NODDLE NOODLE NORDIC PODDED POLDER PONDER POODLE POWDER ROADIE RODDED RONDEL RONDOS SODDED SODDEN SOLDAN SOLDER SOLDON SONDES SORDID TODDAO TODDLE TOEDIN TOLDOF TOLDON TONDOS TOPDOG TOYDOG VOIDED VOODOO WONDER WOODED WOODEN WOODSY WORDED YONDER

•O••D•

BOARDS BOLIDE BORIDE BOUNDS BOVIDS COLADA COMEDY COULDA DODODO DORADO DOSIDO FOUNDS GOURDE GOURDS HOARDS HODADS HOUNDS HOUNDY IODIDE KOMODO MONADS MONODY MOPEDS MOULDS MOULDY MOUNDS NOBODY NOMADS POMADE POSADA POUNDS ROUNDS SOLIDI SOLIDS SOUNDS TOLEDO WORLDS WOUNDS ZOOIDS ZOUNDS

•O•••D

AOUDAD BOATED BOBBED BODIED BOFFED BOGGED BOILED BOLTED BOMBED BONDED BONGED BOOKED BOOMED BOOTED BOPPED BOSSED BOUSED BOWLED COATED COAXED COCCID COCKED COGGED COIFED COILED COINED COMBED CONFED CONKED CONNED CONOID CONRAD COOKED COOLED COOPED COPIED COPPED CORDED CORKED CORNED COSHED COSIED COWARD COWLED COZIED DOCKED DODGED DOFFED DOGGED DOGOOD DOLLED DONALD DONNED DOODAD DOOMED DOSSED DOTARD DOTTED DOUSED DOWNED DOWSED FOALED FOAMED FOBBED FOETID FOGGED FOILED FOINED FOLDED FOOLED FOOTED FORBAD FORBID FORCED FORDED FORGED FORKED FORMED FOULED FOWLED GOADED GODARD GOLFED GONGED GOOFED GOOSED GORGED GOTMAD GOUGED GOUNOD GOWILD GOWNED HOAXED HOCKED HOGGED HONIED HONKED HOODED HOOFED HOOKED HOOPED HOOTED HOPPED HORNED HORRID HORSED HOSTED HOTBED HOTROD HOUSED HOWARD HOWLED JOBBED JOCUND JOGGED JOINED JOLTED JOSHED JOTTED KOBOLD KONRAD LOADED LOAFED LOAMED LOANED LOBBED LOCKED LODGED LOFTED LOGGED LOLLED LOMOND LONGED LOOKED LOOMED LOOPED LOOSED LOOTED LOPPED LORDED LOTTED LOUSED LOWEND MOANED MOATED MOBBED MOCKED MOILED MOLDED MOLTED MONIED MOONED MOORED MOOTED MOPPED MORBID MOSHED MOSSED MOUSED NODDED NOGOOD NOISED NOLEAD NOLOAD NOOSED NOSHED NOTBAD PODDED POISED POLAND POLLED PONGED PONGID PONIED POOHED POOLED POOPED POPPED PORTED POSTED POTTED POURED POUTED ROAMED ROARED ROBBED ROCKED RODDED ROILED ROLAND ROLLED ROMPED RONALD ROOFED ROOKED ROOMED ROOTED ROTTED ROTUND ROUGED ROUSED ROUTED SOAKED SOAPED SOARED SOBBED SOCKED SODDED SOILED SOLOED SOLVED SOPPED SORDID SORTED SOTTED SOURED SOUSED TOGAED TOGGED TOILED TOLLED TOOBAD TOOLED TOOTED TOPPED TOROID TORPID TORRID TOSSED TOTTED TOURED TOUTED TOWARD VOICED VOIDED WOLFED WONNED WONTED WOODED WOOFED WORDED WORKED WORMED YOLKED YOWLED YOYOED ZONKED ZOOMED

••OD••

ABODES ANODES ANODIC APODAL ATODDS AZODYE BOODLE BRODIE CLODDY COODER DEODAR DIODES DOODAD DOODAH DOODLE EPODES ERODED ERODES EXODUS FOODIE FYODOR GEODES GOODBY GOODEN GOODIE GOODLY GOODOH GRODIN GRODNO HOODED HOODOO NOODLE POODLE RHODES SHODDY STODGE STODGY VOODOO WOODED WOODEN WOODSY

••O•D•

AROIDS ATODDS AVOIDS BIONDI BLONDE BLONDS BLOODY BROADS BROODS BROODY CHORDS CLODDY CLOUDS CLOUDY CROWDS DROIDS EBONDS FIORDS FJORDS FLOODS FRONDS IDOIDO ISOLDE LLOYDS OROIDE OVOIDS RHONDA SCOLDS SHODDY SNOODS SWORDS TBONDS ZOOIDS

••O••D

ABOARD ABOUND ADORED AROUND ATONED AVOWED BOOKED BOOMED BOOTED BUOYED CHOKED CHOWED CLONED CLOSED CLOYED COOKED COOLED COOPED CROWED DOODAD DOOMED DRONED ELOPED EMOTED ERODED EVOKED FLORID FLOWED FOOLED FOOTED GAOLED GLOBED GLOVED GLOWED GLOZED GOOFED GOOSED GROPED GROUND HOODED HOOFED HOOKED HOOPED HOOTED IRONED ISOPOD LEONID LOOKED LOOMED LOOPED LOOSED LOOTED MEOWED MOONED MOORED MOOTED NOOSED PHONED PLOWED POOHED POOLED POOPED PROBED PROSED PROVED QUOTED RIOTED ROOFED ROOKED ROOMED ROOTED SCOPED SCORED SHOOED SHORED SHOULD SHOVED SHOWED SLOPED SLOWED SMOKED SNORED SNOWED SPOKED STOKED STOLID STONED STORED STOWED TOOBAD TOOLED TOOTED TROWED WOODED WOOFED ZOOMED

•••OD•

BIPODS BLOODY BROODS BROODY DECODE DEMODE DIPODY DODODO EMBODY ENCODE EPHODS FLOODS KOMODO MELODY MONODY NOBODY PAGODA PARODY RECODE RESODS SARODS SCRODS SNOODS STRODE SYNODS TRIODE VIGODA

•••O•D

ABROAD ACCORD AFFORD AGEOLD ALMOND ARNOLD ATWOOD AUFOND BEHOLD BEYOND BIFOLD BUJOLD BYROAD BYWORD CANOED CONOID CUBOID DADOED DEMOND DEVOID DOGOOD ECHOED EDMOND EDWOOD ELWOOD ENFOLD HALOED HALOID HAROLD HYPOED INFOLD INROAD KAYOED KOBOLD LEMOND LIPOID LOMOND MILORD MYWORD NOGOOD NOLOAD OGDOAD ONHOLD ORMOND OSGOOD OSMOND OXFORD RECORD RELOAD REMOLD RESOLD RETOLD REWORD SECOND SHOOED SHROUD SILOED SOLOED STROUD TOROID UNFOLD UNLOAD UNSOLD UNTOLD UPHOLD UPLOAD VETOED XYLOID YOYOED ZEROED

••••OD

ATWOOD DOGOOD EDWOOD ELWOOD FLYROD GOUNOD HESIOD HOTROD ISOPOD METHOD NIMROD NOGOOD OSGOOD PEAPOD PENROD PEQUOD PERIOD PERNOD RAMROD RESHOD SUNGOD TIEROD TINGOD TRIPOD UNIPOD UNSHOD UNTROD WARGOD

OE••••

OEDEMA OENONE OERTER OEUVRE

O•E•••

OBEAHS OBELIA OBELUS OBERON OBEYED OCEANS OCELLI OCELOT ODENSE ODESSA ODETTA ODETTE OHENRY OKEEFE OKELLY OLEARY OLEATE OLEFIN OLESON OLEVEL OMEGAS OMELET OMERTA ONEACT ONEDAY ONEDGE ONEIDA ONEILL ONEMAN ONETWO ONEUPS ONEWAY OPENED OPENER OPENLY OPENTO OPENUP OPERAS OREADS OREGON OREIDA ORELSE OTELLO OVERDO OVERLY OXEYES

O••E••

OATERS OBJECT OBSESS OBTEST OBVERT OCHERS OCHERY OCREAE OCTETS ODDEST OEDEMA OFFEND OFFERS OGLERS OGRESS OHWELL OHYEAH OILERS OKEEFE OLDEST OLMECS ONDECK ONSETS ORDEAL ORDERS ORGEAT ORIELS ORIENT ORNERY ORRERY ORTEGA ORWELL OSIERS OSSEIN OSSETE OSTEAL OSTEND OSWEGO OTHERS OTTERS OUSELS OUTEAT OUZELS OVIEDO OWLETS OWNERS

O•••E•

OAKLEY OATIER OBEYED OBITER OBRIEN OBSTET OCASEK OCASEY OCHRES OERTER OFFKEY OFFSET OGIVES OILIER OILMEN OINKED OKAYED OLDIES OLDMEN OLEVEL OLIVER OLIVES OMELET ONAGER ONSPEC ONUSES ONVIEW ONYXES OODLES OOZIER OPENED OPENER OPINED OPINER OPINES OPUSES ORALES ORATED ORATES ORGIES

ORIGEN ORKNEY ORTLES ORYXES OSAGES OSPREY OSTLER OUNCES OUSTED OUSTER OUTLET OUTSET OVULES OXEYES OXIDES OXYGEN OYSTER

O••••E

OBLATE OBLIGE OBTUSE OCREAE OCTANE OCTAVE ODENSE ODETTE OENONE OEUVRE OFFICE OFLATE OKEEFE OLDAGE OLEATE ONDINE ONEDGE ONFILE ONFIRE ONLINE ONSALE ONSIDE ONSITE ONTAPE ONTIME OOCYTE OOLITE OPAQUE OPHITE OPIATE OPPOSE ORACLE ORANGE ORDURE ORELSE ORGATE ORIOLE ORNATE OROIDE ORPINE OSCINE OSMOSE OSSETE OTIOSE OTOOLE OUTAGE OUTATE OXLIKE

•OE•••

BOEING COEDIT COELOM COERCE COEVAL DOESBY DOESIN DOESNT DOESUP FOEHNS FOETAL FOETID FOETOR FOETUS GOEASY GOESAT GOESBY GOESIN GOESON GOESUP GOETHE HOEING JOETEX KOENIG NOESIS NOETIC NOEXIT POETIC POETRY SOEURS TOECAP TOEDIN TOEING TOEINS TOESIN TOETAP WOEFUL

•O•E••

BODEGA BOGEYS BOLERO BOLEYN BONERS BONEUP BOPEEP BOREAL BOREAS BOREON BORERS BOREUP BOTELS BOWERS BOWERY BOXERS CODERS COGENT COHEIR COHERE COLEUS COMEAT COMEBY COMEDY COMEIN COMELY COMEON COMERS COMETH COMETO COMETS COMEUP CONEYS COOERS CORERS COSELL COVENS COVENT COVERS COVERT COVETS COVEYS COWENS COWERS COYEST COZENS DOCENT DODECA DOGEAR DOGEYS DOLENZ DONEES DONEIN DONETS DONEUP DOREMI DOSERS DOTELL DOTEON DOVEIN DOWELS DOWERS DOWERY DOYENS DOZENS DOZERS EOCENE FOGEYS FOMENT FOREGO FOREST FOVEAE FOYERS GODETS GOFERS GOLEMS GONEBY GONERS GOVERN GOWEST HOLEUP HOMEEC HOMELY HOMERS HONEST HONEYS HOPERS HOSELS HOTELS HOVELS HOVERS HOVETO HOWELL JOBETH JOKERS JOLENE JOSEPH JOWETT KOPECK KOPEKS KOREAN LODENS LOMEIN LONELY LONERS LOPERS LOREAL LORENZ LOSEIT LOSERS LOVEIN LOVELL LOVELY LOVERS LOVETT LOWELL LOWEND LOWERS LOWERY LOWEST MODELA MODELS MODELT MODEMS MODENA MODERN MODEST MOIETY MOLEST MOMENT MONERA MONETA MONEYS MOPEDS MOPERS MOPERY MOREAU MOREEN MORELS MORENO MOSEYS MOTELS MOTETS MOVEIN MOVEON MOVERS MOVEUP MOWERS MOYERS NOCENT NOLEAD NOLENS NOLESS NONEGO NONETS NOPETS NOTERS NOVELS NOVENA POKEAT POKERS POKERY POKEYS POLEAX POLERS POLEYN POMELO POPEYE POSERS POSEUR POTEEN POTENT POWELL POWERS ROBERT RODENT RODEOS ROGERS ROLEOS ROMEOS ROMERO RONELY ROPEIN ROPERS ROSEAU ROVERS ROWELS ROWENA ROWENS ROWERS SOBEIT SOBERS SOLEIL SOLELY SOLEMN SOLENT SOLERS SOLEUS SOMERS SORELY SOREST SOWERS SOWETO SOXERS TOKENS TOLEDO TONERS TONEUP TOPEKA TOPERS TOREAT TORERO TOREUP TOTEMS TOTERS TOWELS TOWERS TOWERY VOLENS VOTECH VOTEIN VOTERS VOWELS VOWELY VOWERS WOKEUP WOMENS WOOERS WOREON YODELS YOKELS

•O••E•

BOATED BOATEL BOATER BOBBED BOBBER BODIED BODIES BOFFED BOGGED BOGIES BOGLES BOILED BOILER BOITES BOLDER BOLGER BOLTED BOMBED BOMBER BOMBES BONCES BONDED BONGED BONIER BONNES BONNET BONZES BOOKED BOOKER BOOMED BOOMER BOOTED BOOTEE BOOTES BOPEEP BOPPED BOPPER BORDEN BORDER BORNEO BOSKET BOSLEY BOSSED BOSSES BOTHER BOTREE BOULES BOULEZ BOUSED BOUSES BOVVER BOWLED BOWLER BOWLES BOWMEN BOWNET BOWSER BOWYER BOXIER BOXSET COALER COATED COAXED COAXER COAXES COBWEB COCKED COCKER CODGER COFFEE COFFER COGGED COIFED COILED COINED COINER COKIER COLDER COLIES COLLET COLTER COMBED COMBER COMBES COMPEL COMTES CONFED CONFER CONGER CONIES CONKED CONKER CONMEN CONNED CONNER CONTES CONVEX CONVEY COODER COOKED COOKER COOLED COOLER COONEY COOPED COOPER COOTER COPIED COPIER COPIES COPLEY COPPED COPPER COPSES COPTER COQUET CORBEL CORDED CORKED CORKER CORNEA CORNED CORNEL CORNER CORNET CORREL CORSET CORTES CORTEX CORTEZ CORVEE CORVES COSHED COSHES COSIED COSIER COSIES COSSET COTTEN COTTER COULEE COUPES COUTER COWLED COWLEY COWMEN COWPEA COWPER COZIED COZIER COZIES DOBBER DOCKED DOCKER DOCKET DODDER DODGED DODGER DODGES DODOES DOFFED DOGGED DOGGER DOGIES DOGLEG DOLLED DOLMEN DOMREP DONDER DONEES DONKEY DONNED DONNEE DONNER DOOLEY DOOMED DOPIER DORIES DORMER DORSET DORSEY DOSSED DOSSEL DOSSER DOSSES DOTTED DOURER DOUSED DOUSES DOWNED DOWNER DOWNEY DOWSED DOWSER DOWSES DOZIER FOALED FOAMED FOBBED FODDER FOGGED FOGGER FOGIES FOILED FOINED FOKKER FOLDED FOLDER FONDER FOOLED FOOLER FOOTED FOOTER FORBES FORCED FORCER FORCES FORDED FORGED FORGER FORGES FORGET FORKED FORKER FORMED FORMER FORTES FOSSES FOSSEY FOSTER FOULED FOULER FOWLED FOWLER FOWLES FOXIER GOADED GOATEE GOBIES GOBLET GOLDEN GOLFED GOLFER GONGED GOOBER GOODEN GOOFED GOOIER GOOSED GOOSES GOOSEY GOOVER GOPHER GORGED GORGES GORGET GORIER GORSES GOSHEN GOSPEL GOTSET GOTTEN GOUGED GOUGER GOUGES GOULET GOWNED HOAXED HOAXER HOAXES HOBBES HOBOES HOCKED HOCKEY HODGES HOGGED HOGGET HOKIER HOLDEN HOLDER HOLIER HOLLER HOLMES HOMEEC HOMIER HONIED HONKED HONKER HOODED HOOFED HOOFER HOOKED HOOPED HOOPER HOOTED HOOTER HOOVER HOOVES HOPPED HOPPER HORDES HORMEL HORNED HORNER HORNET HORNEY HORSED HORSES HORSEY HOSIER HOSTED HOSTEL HOTBED HOTTEA HOTTER HOUSED HOUSES HOWLED HOWLER HOYDEN JOBBED JOBBER JOCKEY JOETEX JOGGED JOGGER JOINED JOINER JOKIER JOLIET JOLTED JOSHED JOSHES JOSSER JOSSES JOTTED JOULES JOYNER KOHLER KOPJES KOPPEL KOSHER KOTTER LOADED LOADER LOAFED LOAFER LOAMED LOANED LOANER LOAVES LOBBED LOBBER LOCKED LOCKER LOCKET LODGED LODGER LODGES LOFTED LOGGED LOGGER LOGIER LOITER LOLLED LONGED LONGER LONGES LOOIES LOOKED LOOKER LOOMED LOONEY LOOPED LOOPER LOOSED LOOSEN LOOSER LOOSES LOOTED LOOTER LOPPED LOPPER LORDED LORIES LOSSES LOTTED LOUDEN LOUDER LOUPES LOUSED LOUSES LOUVER LOWKEY MOANED MOANER MOATED MOBBED MOBLEY MOCKED MOCKER MOILED MOILER MOINES MOIRES MOLDED MOLDER MOLTED MOLTEN MOLTER MONGER MONIED MONIES MONKEY MONTEL MONTES MONTEZ MOONED MOONEY MOORED MOOTED MOPIER MOPPED MOPPER MOPPET MOREEN MORGEN MORLEY MORSEL MOSHED MOSHER MOSHES MOSLEM MOSSED MOSSES MOSTEL MOTHER MOTLEY MOUSED MOUSER MOUSES MOUSEY MOVIES NOBLER NOBLES NODDED NOISED NOISES NOONES NOOSED NOOSES NOSHED NOSHER NOSHES NOSIER NOTYET NOUMEA OODLES OOZIER POCKET PODDED POGIES POISED POISES POKIER POLDER POLLED POLLEN POLLER POLLEX POMMEE POMMEL POMPEY PONCES PONDER PONGED PONGEE PONIED PONIES PONTES POOHED POOLED POOPED POORER POPPED POPPER POPPET PORKER PORTED PORTER POSHER POSIES POSSES POSSET POSTED POSTER POTEEN POTHER POTTED POTTER POURED POURER POUTED POUTER POWDER ROAMED ROAMER ROARED ROARER ROBBED ROBBER ROBLES ROCHET ROCKED ROCKER ROCKET RODDED RODNEY ROGUES ROHMER ROILED ROLLED ROLLER ROMMEL ROMNEY ROMPED ROMPER RONDEL ROOFED ROOFER ROOKED ROOMED ROOMER ROONEY ROOTED ROOTER ROPIER ROSIER ROSTER ROTTED ROTTEN ROTTER ROUGED ROUGES ROUSED ROUSER ROUSES ROUTED ROUTER ROUTES ROZZER SOAKED SOAKER SOAPED SOAPER SOARED SOARER SOARES SOAVES SOBBED SOBBER SOCCER SOCKED SOCKET SOCLES SODDED SODDEN SOFTEN SOFTER SOILED SOIREE SOLDER SOLOED SOLVED SOLVER SOLVES SOMBER SOMMER SONDES SONNET SOONER SOPPED SORBET SORREL SORTED SORTER SOTTED SOURED SOURER SOUSED SOUSES SOUTER SOVIET TOATEE TOBIES TOFFEE TOGAED TOGGED TOILED TOILER TOILES TOILET TOLLED TOLTEC TONIER TONNES TOOLED TOOTED TOOTER TOPPED TOPPER TOPTEN TOQUES TORIES TORRES TORREY TORTES TOSSED TOSSER TOSSES TOTHER TOTTED TOTTER TOUPEE TOURED TOURER TOUTED TOUTER TOWHEE TOWNER VOGUES VOICED VOICES VOIDED VOILES VOLLEY VORTEX VOSGES WODGES WOHLER WOLFED WOLPER WOLSEY WOLVES WONDER WONNED WONTED WOODED WOODEN WOOFED WOOFER WOOLEN WOOLEY WORDED WORKED WORKER WORMED WORSEN WOWSER YOLKED YONDER YORKER YOUBET YOWLED YOYOED ZONKED ZONKER ZOOMED

•O•••E

AORTAE BOBBIE BOBBLE BOCCIE BODICE BOGGLE BOLIDE BONNIE BOODLE BOOGIE BOOKIE BOOTEE BOOTHE BOOTIE BORAGE BORATE BORIDE BOTREE BOTTLE BOUCLE BOUFFE BOULLE BOUNCE BOURKE BOURNE BOURSE BOVINE BOWTIE COARSE COBBLE COCKLE CODDLE COERCE COFFEE COHERE COHUNE COLLIE COMATE CONNIE CONTRE CONURE COOKIE COOTIE CORVEE COSINE COSTAE COULEE COUPLE COURSE COWRIE COYOTE DOABLE DOCILE DOGGIE DOMINE DONATE DONGLE DONNEE DOOBIE DOODLE DOOGIE DOOZIE DOSAGE DOTAGE DOTTIE DOTTLE DOUBLE EOCENE FOCSLE FOIBLE FOLKIE FONDLE FONDUE FOODIE FOOZLE FORAGE FOSSAE FOVEAE FOZZIE GOALIE GOATEE GOBBLE GOETHE GOGGLE GOHOME GOLDIE GOODIE GOOGLE GORDIE GOURDE HOAGIE HOARSE HOBBLE HOGTIE HOMAGE HOMBRE HONORE HOOPLE HOOPOE HOOTIE HOPPLE HORACE IODATE IODIDE IODINE IODISE IODIZE IOLITE IONISE IONIZE JOANIE JOANNE JOCOSE JOGGLE JOHORE JOLENE JOSTLE JOUNCE KOOKIE LOATHE LOBATE LOBULE LOCALE LOCATE LONGUE LOONIE LOUCHE LOUISE LOUNGE LOUVRE LOVAGE MOBILE MODINE MODULE MOHAVE MOJAVE MOLINE MOLTKE MOMMIE MONROE MORALE MOROSE MOSQUE MOTILE MOTIVE MOTTLE MOUSSE NOBBLE NODDLE NODICE NODOSE NODULE NOLOSE NOMINE NOMORE NONAGE NONAME NOODLE NOSALE NOTATE NOTICE NOVICE NOWISE NOZZLE OOCYTE OOLITE POINTE POLICE POLITE POMACE POMADE POMMEE PONGEE

POODLE
POPEYE
POPPLE
POTAGE
POTPIE
POTTLE
POUNCE
POUSSE
ROADIE
ROBBIE
ROCKNE
ROLLIE
RONNIE
ROOKIE
ROOMIE
ROSCOE
ROTATE
ROUBLE
ROURKE
ROXANE
ROYALE
SOCAGE
SOFINE
SOFTIE
SOIGNE
SOIREE
SOLACE
SOLUTE
SOMBRE
SOOTHE
SOPHIE
SORTIE
SOURCE
TOATEE
TODATE
TODDLE
TOFFEE
TOGGLE
TOLIFE
TONGUE
TONITE
TOONIE
TOOTLE
TOPPLE
TOROSE
TORQUE
TOUCHE
TOUPEE
TOUSLE
TOWAGE
TOWHEE
TOWNIE
VOLARE
VOLUME
VOLUTE
VOTIVE
VOYAGE
WOBBLE
WOOGIE
WOOKIE
YORKIE
ZOMBIE
ZONATE
ZOUAVE

••OE••
AMOEBA
COOERS
PHOEBE
PROEMS
SHOERS
WOOERS

••O•E•
ABODES
ADOBES
ADORED
ADOREE
ADORER
ADORES
AMOLES
ANODES
ANOLES
APOGEE
ATONED
ATONES
AVOCET
AVOWED
AVOWER
AWOKEN
AZORES
BIOMES
BLOKES
BLOOEY
BLOWER
BOOKED
BOOKER
BOOMED
BOOMER
BOOTED
BOOTEE
BOOTES
BROKEN
BROKER
BUOYED
CHOKED
CHOKER
CHOKES
CHOLER
CHORES
CHOSEN
CHOWED
CLONED
CLONES
CLOSED
CLOSER
CLOSES
CLOSET
CLOVEN
CLOVER
CLOVES
CLOYED
CNOTES
COODER
COOKED
COOKER
COOLED
COOLER
COONEY
COOPED
COOPER
COOTER
CRONES
CROWED
CROWER
CROZES
DHOLES
DHOTEL
DIODES
DIONEB
DOOLEY
DOOMED
DRONED
DRONER
DRONES
DROVER
DROVES
ECOLES
ELOPED
ELOPER
ELOPES
EMOTED
EMOTER
EMOTES
EPODES
EPOPEE
ERODED
ERODES
EVOKED
EVOKER
EVOKES
FLOOEY
FLORES
FLORET
FLOWED
FLOWER
FOOLED
FOOLER
FOOTED
FOOTER
FROZEN
GAOLED
GAOLER
GEODES
GLOBED
GLOBES
GLOVED
GLOVER
GLOVES
GLOWED
GLOWER
GLOZED
GLOZES
GNOMES
GOOBER
GOODEN
GOOFED
GOOIER
GOOSED
GOOSES
GOOSEY
GOOVER
GROCER
GROPED
GROPES
GROVEL
GROVER
GROVES
GROWER
HAOLES
HOODED
HOOFED
HOOFER
HOOKED
HOOPED
HOOPER
HOOTED
HOOTER
HOOVER
HOOVES
IMOGEN
IRONED
IRONER
ISOHEL
ISOMER
KJOLEN
KNOWER
KRONER
LEONES
LIONEL
LIONET
LOOIES
LOOKED
LOOKER
LOOMED
LOONEY
LOOPED
LOOPER
LOOSED
LOOSEN
LOOSER
LOOSES
LOOTED
LOOTER
MEOWED
MOONED
MOONEY
MOORED
MOOTED
MYOPES
NOONES
NOOSED
NOOSES
PHONED
PHONES
PHONEY
PHOOEY
PIOLET
PLOVER
PLOWED
PLOWER
POOHED
POOLED
POOPED
POORER
PROBED
PROBER
PROBES
PROLES
PROPEL
PROPER
PROSED
PROSER
PROSES
PROTEI
PROTEM
PROVED
PROVEN
PROVER
PROVES
QUOTED
QUOTER
QUOTES
REOPEN
RHODES
RIOTED
RIOTER
ROOFED
ROOFER
ROOKED
ROOMED
ROOMER
ROONEY
ROOTED
ROOTER
SCONES
SCOPED
SCOPES
SCORED
SCORER
SCORES
SCOTER
SHOLEM
SHOOED
SHORED
SHORES
SHOVED
SHOVEL
SHOVER
SHOVES
SHOWED
SHOWER
SLOPED
SLOPES
SLOVEN
SLOWED
SLOWER
SMOKED
SMOKER
SMOKES
SMOKEY
SNOPES
SNORED
SNORER
SNORES
SNOWED
SOONER
SPOKED
SPOKEN
SPOKES
SPORES
STOKED
STOKER
STOKES
STOLEN
STOLES
STONED
STONER
STONES
STOPES
STORED
STORER
STORES
STOREY
STOVER
STOVES
STOWED
TBONES
THOLES
TNOTES
TOOLED
TOOTED
TOOTER
TROPES
TROPEZ
TROVES
TROWED
TROWEL
TWOFER
UNOPEN
USOPEN
VIOLET
WHOLES
WOODED
WOODEN
WOOFED
WOOFER
WOOLEN
WOOLEY
YEOMEN
ZOOMED

••O••E
ADOREE
AGORAE
ANOMIE
APOGEE
AROUSE
ATONCE
AZODYE
BLONDE
BLOUSE
BMOVIE
BOODLE
BOOGIE
BOOKIE
BOOTEE
BOOTHE
BOOTIE
BRODIE
BROGUE
BRONTE
BRONZE
BROOKE
BROWNE
BROWSE
CHOATE
CHOICE
CHOOSE
CLOCHE
CLOQUE
CLOTHE
COOKIE
COOTIE
CROSSE
CROUSE
CROUTE
DIONNE
DOOBIE
DOODLE
DOOGIE
DOOZIE
DROGUE
DROWSE
ELOISE
EPOPEE
ETOILE
EVOLVE
EVONNE
FLORAE
FOODIE
FOOZLE
GEORGE
GOODIE
GOOGLE
GROOVE
GROSSE
GROUSE
HOOPLE
HOOPOE
HOOTIE
INOUYE
ISOLDE
KOOKIE
LAOTSE
LEONIE
LHOTSE
LOONIE
NOODLE
OROIDE
OTOOLE
PEOPLE
PHOEBE
POODLE
PROCNE
PROPRE
PROWSE
QUOQUE
ROOKIE
ROOMIE
SCONCE
SCOUSE
SHOPPE
SHORTE
SHOWME
SKOKIE
SKOPJE
SLOANE
SNOOZE
SOOTHE
SPONGE
SPOUSE
STODGE
STOGIE
STOLLE
STOOGE
THORPE
TOONIE
TOOTLE
TROCHE
TROMPE
TROUPE
TROUVE
WOOGIE
WOOKIE
YVONNE

•••OE•
BLOOEY
CANOED
CANOES
DADOED
DADOES
DODOES
ECHOED
ECHOES
EDDOES
EUBOEA
FLOOEY
GIJOES
HALOED
HALOES
HEROES
HOBOES
HYPOED
KAYOED
PEKOES
PHLOEM
PHOOEY
REDOES
SHOOED
SILOED
SOLOED
THROES
UNDOER
UNDOES
VETOED
VETOER
VETOES
YOYOED
ZEROED
ZEROES

•••O•E
ACTONE
AEROBE
ALCOVE
ALDOSE
ALGORE
ANYONE
APPOSE
ARIOSE
ASHORE
ASLOPE
ATHOME
BECOME
BEFORE
BEGONE
BEHOVE
BROOKE
BYGONE
BYJOVE
BYROTE
CAJOLE
CAPONE
CAPOTE
CAROLE
CENOTE
CHOOSE
CHROME
COYOTE
CREOLE
DAMONE
DAMORE
DAYONE
DEBONE
DECODE
DEMODE
DEMOTE
DENOTE
DEPONE
DEPOSE
DEVOTE
DIPOLE
EEYORE
ELMORE
ENCODE
ENCORE
ENROBE
EUROPE
EVZONE
EXMORE
EXPOSE
FILOSE
FURORE
GALORE
GEMOTE
GENOME
GOHOME
GROOVE
GYROSE
HONORE
IGNORE
IMPOSE
INCOME
INDORE
INJOKE
INLOVE
INSOLE
INTONE
INVOKE
JAMOKE
JEROME
JOCOSE
JOHORE
KETONE
LAHORE
LANOSE
LENORE
LUPONE
MALONE
MEROPE
METOPE
MOROSE
MYSORE
NICOLE
NODOSE
NOLOSE
NOMORE
OENONE
OPPOSE
ORIOLE
OSMOSE
OTIOSE
OTOOLE
PAROLE
PEYOTE
PILOSE
PINOLE
RADOME
RAMONE
RAMOSE
RECODE
REDONE
REMOTE
REMOVE
RENOTE
REPOSE
RESOLE
REVOKE
REWOVE
REZONE
RIBOSE
RIMOSE
RUGOSE
SALOME
SAVOIE
SETOSE
SHROVE
SILONE
SIMONE
SNOOZE
STOOGE
STROBE
STRODE
STROKE
STROVE
TAGORE
THRONE
THROVE
TOROSE
TRIODE
TYRONE
UGSOME
UNDONE
UNROBE
UNWOVE
UNYOKE
UPROSE
VADOSE
VELOCE
ZYGOTE

••••OE
BIGTOE
CHIGOE
CHILOE
CRUSOE
FAEROE
FELLOE
HOOPOE
MONROE
RESHOE
ROSCOE
TIPTOE
WASHOE

OF••••
OFFDAY
OFFEND
OFFERS
OFFICE
OFFING
OFFISH
OFFKEY
OFFSET
OFLATE

O•F•••
OAFISH
OFFDAY
OFFEND
OFFERS
OFFICE
OFFING
OFFISH
OFFKEY
OFFSET
ONFILE
ONFIRE
ONFOOT
OXFORD

O••F••
OLEFIN
OPTFOR
OUTFIT
OUTFLY
OUTFOX

O•••F•
OKEEFE
OSSIFY

•OF•••
BOFFED
BOFFIN
BOFFOS
COFFEE
COFFER
DOFFED
GOFERS
GOFISH
LOFTED
SOFFIT
SOFINE
SOFTEN
SOFTER
SOFTIE
SOFTLY
TOFFEE

•O•F••
BOFFED
BOFFIN
BOFFOS
BOTFLY
BOUFFE
BOWFIN
BOXFUL
COFFEE
COFFER
COIFED
COLFAX
COMFIT
CONFAB
CONFED
CONFER
DOFFED
DOOFUS
GOLFED
GOLFER
GOOFED
GOOFUP
HOOFED
HOOFER
HOOFIT
JOYFUL
KOUFAX
LOAFED
LOAFER
LOOFAH
LOOFAS
LOWFAT
NONFAT
POPFLY
POTFUL
ROOFED
ROOFER
SOBFUL
SOFFIT
SOLFAS
TOFFEE
WOEFUL
WOLFED
WOOFED
WOOFER

•O••F•
BOUFFE
CODIFY
FOBOFF
GOSOFT
GOTOFF
HOPOFF
LOGOFF
MODIFY
MOTIFS
NODOFF
NOTIFY
POPOFF
TOLIFE
TOPOFF

•O•••F
FOBOFF
GOTOFF
HOPOFF
LOGOFF
NODOFF
POPOFF
SORTOF
TOLDOF
TOPOFF

••OF••
CROFTS
DOOFUS
GOOFED
GOOFUP
HOOFED
HOOFER
HOOFIT
LOOFAH
LOOFAS
PROFIT
ROOFED
ROOFER
SCOFFS
SHOFAR
TWOFER
WOOFED
WOOFER

••O•F•
KLOOFS
PROOFS
SCOFFS
SPOOFS
WHOOFS

•••OF•
BEGOFF
BITOFF
BUGOFF
BUYOFF
CRYOFF
CUTOFF
DIEOFF
DRYOFF
FAROFF
FOBOFF
GETOFF
GOSOFT
GOTOFF
HOPOFF
KLOOFS
LAYOFF
LEDOFF
LETOFF
LOGOFF
NODOFF
PAYOFF
POPOFF
PROOFS
PUTOFF
RANOFF
RIPOFF
RUBOFF
RUNOFF
SAWOFF
SEEOFF
SETOFF
SPOOFS
TAPOFF
TEEOFF
TIPOFF
TOPOFF
WHOOFS

•••O•F
BEGOFF
BEHOOF
BITOFF
BUGOFF
BUYOFF
CRYOFF
CUTOFF
DIEOFF
DRYOFF
FAROFF
FOBOFF
GETOFF
GOTOFF
HOPOFF
LAYOFF
LEDOFF
LETOFF
LOGOFF
NODOFF
PAYOFF
POPOFF
PUTOFF
RANOFF
RIPOFF
RUBOFF
RUDOLF
RUNOFF
SAWOFF
SEEOFF
SETOFF
TAPOFF
TEEOFF
TIPOFF
TOPOFF

••••OF
BEHOOF
HEAROF
HEREOF
KINDOF
RIDSOF
SORTOF
TELLOF
TOLDOF

OG••••
OGDOAD
OGHAMS
OGIVES
OGLALA
OGLERS
OGLING
OGRESS
OGRISH

O•G•••
ORGANA
ORGANS
ORGATE
ORGEAT
ORGIES
OSGOOD
OUGHTS

O••G••
OMEGAS
ONAGER
OREGON
ORIGEN
ORIGIN
OSAGES
OUTGUN
OXYGEN

O•••G•
OBLIGE
OLDAGE
OLINGO
ONEDGE
ONHIGH
OOLOGY
OPPUGN
ORANGE
ORANGS
ORANGY
ORINGS
ORTEGA
OSWEGO
OUTAGE

O••••G
OARING
OBLONG
OFFING
OGLING
OILING
OILRIG
OOHING
OOLONG
OOZING
OPTING
ORBING
OUTING
OWNING

•OG•••
BOGART
BOGEYS
BOGGED
BOGGLE
BOGIES
BOGLES
BOGONG
BOGOTA
COGENT
COGGED
COGITO
COGNAC
DOGDAY
DOGDOM
DOGEAR
DOGEYS
DOGGED
DOGGER
DOGGIE
DOGIES
DOGLEG
DOGMAS
DOGONS
DOGOOD
DOGSAT
DOGSIT
DOGTAG
FOGBOW
FOGEYS
FOGGED
FOGGER
FOGHAT
FOGIES
FOGSIN
FOGSUP
GOGGLE
GOGGLY
HOGANS
HOGGED
HOGGET
HOGTIE
JOGGED
JOGGER
JOGGLE
LOGGED
LOGGER
LOGGIA
LOGIER
LOGILY
LOGION
LOGJAM
LOGOFF
LOGOUT
LOGSIN
LOGSON
MOGULS
NOGGIN
NOGOOD
POGIES
ROGERS
ROGUES
TOGAED
TOGGED
TOGGLE
VOGUES
YOGINI
YOGISM
YOGURT

•O•G••
BOGGED
BOGGLE
BOIGNY
BOLGER
BONGED
BONGOS
BOOGIE
BORGIA
BOUGHS
BOUGHT
CODGER
COGGED
COIGNS
CONGAS
CONGER
CONGOU
COOGAN
CORGIS
COUGAR
COUGHS
DODGED
DODGER
DODGES
DOGGED
DOGGER
DOGGIE
DONGLE
DOOGIE
DOUGHS
DOUGHY
FOGGED
FOGGER
FORGED
FORGER
FORGES
FORGET
FORGOT
FOUGHT
GOGGLE
GOGGLY
GONGED
GOOGLE
GOOGLY
GOOGOL
GOOGOO
GORGED
GORGES
GORGET
GORGON
GOUGED
GOUGER
GOUGES
HOAGIE
HODGES
HOGGED
HOGGET
HOUGHS
JOGGED
JOGGER
JOGGLE
LODGED
LODGER
LODGES
LOGGED
LOGGER
LOGGIA
LONGAN
LONGED
LONGER
LONGES
LONGLY
LONGUE
LOUGHS
MONGER
MONGOL
MORGAN
MORGEN
MOWGLI
NOGGIN
NORGAY
NOUGAT
NOUGHT
PONGED
PONGEE
PONGID
POPGUN
ROTGUT
ROUGED
ROUGES
ROUGHS
ROUGHY
SOIGNE
SOUGHS
SOUGHT
TOGGED
TOGGLE
TONGAN
TONGUE
TOPGUN
TOUGHS
TOUGHY
VOIGHT
VOSGES
WODGES
WOOGIE

•O••G•
BODEGA
BOINGO
BORAGE
COLUGO
COSIGN
DOINGS
DORAGS
DOSAGE
DOTAGE
FORAGE
FOREGO
GOINGS
GONOGO
HOMAGE
LOUNGE
LOVAGE
NONAGE
NONEGO
OOLOGY
POTAGE
SOCAGE
TOBAGO
TOWAGE
VOYAGE

•O•••G
BODING
BOEING
BOGONG
BONING
BOOING
BORING
BOWING
BOXING
COBURG
CODING
COMING
COOING
COPING
CORING
COWING
DOGLEG
DOGTAG
DOLING
DOMING
DOPING
DOSING
DOTING

DOZING
FOXING
GORING
GOSTAG
HOEING
HOLING
HOMING
HONING
HOPING
HOSING
HOTDOG
JOKING
KOENIG
LOPING
LOSING
LOVING
LOWING
MOOING
MOPING
MOVING
MOWING
NOSING
NOTING
OOHING
OOLONG
OOZING
POKING
POLING
PORING
POSING
ROBING
ROPING
ROVING
ROWING
SOLING
SOLONG
SONTAG
SOWBUG
SOWING
TOEING
TONING
TOPDOG
TOTING
TOWING
TOYDOG
TOYING
VOTING
VOWING
WONMUG
WOOING
WOWING
YOKING
ZONING

••OG••

APOGEE
BIOGAS
BOOGIE
BROGAN
BROGUE
CLOGGY
CLOGUP
COOGAN
DOOGIE
DROGUE
FROGGY
GLOGGS
GOOGLE
GOOGLY
GOOGOL
GOOGOO
GROGGY
IMOGEN
ISOGON
SHOGUN
SLOGAN
SMOGGY
STOGIE
TROGON
WOOGIE

••O•G•

CHOUGH
CLOGGY
ELOIGN
ENOUGH
FROGGY
GEORGE
GEORGY
GLOGGS
GROGGY
HMONGS
PLOUGH
PRONGS
SLOUGH
SMOGGY
SPONGE
SPONGY
STODGE
STODGY
STOOGE
THONGS
THOUGH
TROUGH
WRONGS

••O••G

BOOING
COOING
MOOING
PHOTOG
PROLOG
WOOING

•••OG•

BEFOGS
DEFOGS
EULOGY
GONOGO
LADOGA
OOLOGY
STOOGE

•••O•G

ALBORG
BARONG
BELONG
BOGONG
CYBORG
DATONG
DELONG
DUGONG
MEKONG
OBLONG
OOLONG
SARONG
SOLONG
STRONG
THRONG
VYBORG

••••OG

ANALOG
BANDOG
DIALOG
EGGNOG
EPILOG
GASLOG
GUNDOG
HERZOG
HOTDOG
ICEFOG
INAFOG
LAPDOG
LITHOG
PETROG
PHOTOG
PROLOG
PYEDOG
QUAHOG
REDDOG
SAWLOG
SEADOG
STENOG
SUNDOG
TAUTOG
TOPDOG
TOYDOG
UNCLOG

OH••••

OHENRY
OHIOAN
OHWELL
OHYEAH

O•H•••

OCHERS
OCHERY
OCHRES
OGHAMS
ONHAND
ONHIGH
ONHOLD
OOHING
OPHITE
OSHAWA
OTHERS

O••H••

OLDHAM
OLDHAT
OMAHAN
OMAHAS
ORCHID
ORCHIL
ORPHAN
ORPHIC
OUGHTS
OUTHIT

O•••H•

OBEAHS
ORACHS

O••••H

OAFISH
OFFISH
OGRISH
OHYEAH
OLDISH
ONHIGH
ONRUSH
OOLITH
OOMPAH
ORBACH
ORNITH
OWLISH

•OH•••

COHEIR
COHERE
COHORT
COHOST
COHUNE
GOHOME
HOHOHO
JOHANN
JOHNNY
JOHORE
KOHLER
MOHAIR
MOHAVE
MOHAWK
MOHOCK
MOHURS
NOHITS
OOHING
ROHMER
WOHLER
YOHOHO

•O•H••

BOCHCO
BOOHOO
BOTHER
COBHAM
COCHIN
COSHED
COSHES
DOTHAN
FOEHNS
FOGHAT
GOPHER
GOSHEN
GOTHAM
GOTHIC
HOOHAH
HOOHAS
JOBHOP
JOSHED
JOSHES
JOSHUA
KOSHER
LOTHAR
MOCHAS
MOSHAV
MOSHED
MOSHER
MOSHES
MOTHER
MOTHRA
NOSHED
NOSHER
NOSHES
NOSHOW
POOHED
POSHER
POSHLY
POTHER
ROCHET
RODHAM
ROTHKO
SOPHIA
SOPHIE
SOTHAT
SOWHAT
TOPHAT
TOPHUS
TOTHER
TOWHEE
YOOHOO

•O••H•

BOLSHY
BOOTHE
BOOTHS
BOTCHY
BOUGHS
BOUGHT
CONCHA
CONCHS
COUGHS
DOUGHS
DOUGHY
FOUGHT
GOETHE
GOTCHA
HOHOHO
HONCHO
HONSHU
HOUGHS
JONAHS
LOATHE
LOTAHS
LOUCHE
LOUGHS
MONTHS
MORPHO
MORPHS
MORPHY
MOUTHS
MOUTHY
NORTHS
NOTCHY
NOUGHT
POACHY
PONCHO
POUCHY
ROUGHS
ROUGHY
SOOTHE
SOUGHS
SOUGHT
SOUTHS
TOOTHY
TORAHS
TORCHY
TOUCHE
TOUCHY
TOUGHS
TOUGHY
VOIGHT
WORTHS
WORTHY
YOHOHO
YOUTHS

•O•••H

BORSCH
BOYISH
COMETH
COYISH
DOODAH
DOVISH
EOLITH
FOURTH
GOFISH
GOODOH
GOWITH
HOOHAH
HOOKAH
HOORAH
HOOTCH
HOWDAH
IOMOTH
JOBETH
JOSEPH
JOSIAH
LOOFAH
LOWISH
MODISH
MOLOCH
MOOLAH
MOPISH
OOLITH
OOMPAH
POLISH
POTASH
TONISH
VOTECH

••OH••

ABOHMS
ALOHAS
BOOHOO
ELOHIM
HOOHAH
HOOHAS
ISOHEL
MYOHMY
POOHED
YOOHOO

••O•H•

BOOTHE
BOOTHS
BROTHS
CLOCHE
CLOTHE
CLOTHO
CLOTHS
EPOCHS
FROTHS
FROTHY
QUOTHA
SLOSHY
SLOTHS
SOOTHE
TOOTHY
TROCHE
TROPHY
TROTHS

••O••H

ADOLPH
AVOUCH
BLOTCH
BROACH
BROOCH
CHOUGH
CROUCH
DOODAH
ENOUGH
GOODOH
GROUCH
GROWTH
HOOHAH
HOOKAH
HOORAH
HOOTCH
LOOFAH
MOOLAH
PLOUGH
SCORCH
SCOTCH
SLOUCH
SLOUGH
SMOOCH
SMOOTH
STORCH
SWOOSH
THOUGH
TROUGH
WHOOSH

•••OH•

HOHOHO
JAWOHL
MEGOHM
STJOHN
UPJOHN
YOHOHO

•••O•H

BROOCH
BYGOSH
EDKOCH
GALOSH
IOMOTH
KIBOSH
MOLOCH
SMOOCH
SMOOTH
SPLOSH
SWOOSH
WHOOSH
ZEROTH

••••OH

GOODOH
MATZOH
SHILOH

OI••••

OILCAN
OILERS
OILIER
OILILY
OILING
OILMAN
OILMEN
OILPAN
OILRIG
OINKED

O•I•••

OBISPO
OBITER
OBIWAN
ODIOUS
ODISTS
ODIUMS
OGIVES
OHIOAN
OJIBWA
OLINDA
OLINGO
OLIVER
OLIVES
OLIVIA
ONIONS
ONIONY
OPIATE
OPINED
OPINER
OPINES
ORIANA
ORIBIS
ORIELS
ORIENT
ORIGEN
ORIGIN
ORINGS
ORIOLE
ORISON
ORISSA
OSIERS
OSIRIS
OTIOSE
OTITIC
OTITIS
OVIEDO
OVISAC
OXIDES
OXIDIC

O••I••

OAFISH
OARING
OATIER
OBLIGE
OBOIST
OBRIAN
OBRIEN
ODDITY
OFFICE
OFFING
OFFISH
OGLING
OGRISH
OILIER
OILILY
OILING
OLDIES
OLDISH
OMNIUM
ONDINE
ONEIDA
ONEILL
ONFILE
ONFIRE
ONHIGH
ONLINE
ONSIDE
ONSITE
ONTIME
ONVIEW
OOHING
OOLITE
OOLITH
OOZIER
OOZILY
OOZING
OPHITE
OPTICS
OPTIMA
OPTING
OPTION
ORBING
ORBITS
OREIDA
ORGIES
ORNITH
OROIDE
ORPINE
ORSINO
OSCINE
OSMICS
OSMIUM
OSSIAN
OSSIFY
OSTIUM
OUTING
OVOIDS
OWLISH
OWNING
OXLIKE
OXLIPS

O•••I•

OBELIA
OBTAIN
OILRIG
OKAPIS
OLDVIC
OLEFIN
OLIVIA
OMANIS
ORCHID
ORCHIL
ORDAIN
ORIBIS
ORIGIN
ORPHIC
OSIRIS
OSSEIN
OTITIC
OTITIS
OUTBID
OUTDID
OUTFIT
OUTHIT
OUTWIT
OXALIS
OXIDIC
OXTAIL
OZONIC

O••••I

OCELLI
OCTOPI
OCTROI

•OI•••

BOIGNY
BOILED
BOILER
BOINGO
BOITES
COIFED
COIGNS
COILED
COILUP
COINED
COINER
DOINGS
EOIPSO
FOIBLE
FOILED
FOINED
FOISTS
GOINGS
GOINTO
HOISTS
JOINED
JOINER
JOININ
JOINTS
JOINUP
JOISTS
LOITER
MOIETY
MOILED
MOILER
MOINES
MOIRES
NOIRON
NOISED
NOISES
POILUS
POINTE
POINTS
POINTY
POIROT
POISED
POISES
POISON
ROILED
SOIGNE
SOILED
SOIREE
TOILED
TOILER
TOILES
TOILET
VOICED
VOICES
VOIDED
VOIGHT
VOILES
YOICKS

•O•I••

AORIST
BODICE
BODIED
BODIES
BODILY
BODING
BOEING
BOGIES
BOLIDE
BONIER
BONING
BONITO
BOOING
BORIDE
BORING
BOVIDS
BOVINE
BOWING
BOXIER
BOXING
BOYISH
COBIAS
CODIFY
CODING
COGITO
COKIER
COLIES
COLIMA
COMICS
COMING
COMITY
CONICS
CONIES
CONIUM
COOING
COPIED
COPIER
COPIES
COPING
CORING
CORIUM
COSIED
COSIER
COSIES
COSIGN
COSILY
COSINE
COVINA
COWING
COYISH
COZIED
COZIER
COZIES
COZILY
DOCILE
DOGIES
DOLING
DOMINE
DOMING
DOMINI
DOMINO
DONITZ
DOPIER
DOPING
DORIAN
DORIES
DOSIDO
DOSING
DOTING
DOVISH
DOZIER
DOZILY
DOZING
EOLIAN
EOLITH
EONIAN
EOSINS
FOGIES
FOLIAR
FOLIOS
FOLIUM
FORINT
FOXIER
FOXILY
FOXING
GOBIES
GODIVA
GOFISH
GOLINO
GOOIER
GORIER
GORILY
GORING
GOWILD
GOWITH
HOEING
HOKIER
HOLIER
HOLILY
HOLING
HOLISM
HOLIST
HOMIER
HOMILY
HOMING
HOMINY
HONIED
HONING
HOPING
HOSIER
HOSING
IODIDE
IODINE
IODISE
IODIZE
IOLITE
IONIAN
IONICS
IONISE
IONIUM
IONIZE
JOKIER
JOKILY
JOKING
JOLIET
JOLIOT
JOSIAH
JOVIAL
JOVIAN
KODIAK
KONICA
LOGIER
LOGILY
LOGION
LOLITA
LOOIES
LOPING
LORICA
LORIES
LOSING
LOTION
LOUISA
LOUISE
LOVING
LOWING
LOWISH
MOBILE
MOBIUS
MODIFY
MODINE
MODISH
MOLINE
MONICA
MONIED
MONIES
MONISM
MONIST
MOOING
MOPIER
MOPING
MOPISH
MORION
MORITA
MORITZ
MOTIFS
MOTILE
MOTION
MOTIVE
MOVIES
MOVING
MOWING
NODICE
NOHITS
NOMINE
NORIAS
NOSIER
NOSILY
NOSING
NOTICE
NOTIFY
NOTING
NOTION
NOVICE
NOWISE
OOHING
OOLITE
OOLITH
OOZIER
OOZILY
OOZING
PODIUM
POGIES
POKIER
POKILY
POKING
POLICE
POLICY
POLING
POLISH
POLITE
POLITY
PONIED
PONIES
PORING
POSIES
POSING
POSITS
POTION
ROBING
ROBINS
ROPIER
ROPING
ROSIER
ROSILY
ROSINS
ROSINY
ROSITA
ROTINI
ROVING
ROWING
SOCIAL
SODIUM
SOFINE
SOLIDI
SOLIDS
SOLING
SONICS
SOVIET
SOWING
TOBIAS
TOBIES
TOEING
TOEINS
TOLIFE
TONICS
TONIER
TONING
TONISH
TONITE
TOPICS
TORIES
TORINO
TOTING
TOWING
TOXICS
TOXINS
TOYING
VOTING
VOTIVE
VOWING
WOOING
WOWING
YOGINI
YOGISM
YOKING
YORICK
ZODIAC
ZONING
ZOOIDS
ZORILS

•O••I•

AODAIS
AORTIC
BOBBIE
BOBBIN
BOCCIE
BODKIN
BOFFIN
BOLLIX
BONNIE
BOOGIE
BOOKIE
BOOTIE
BORGIA
BOSNIA
BOUDIN
BOWFIN
BOWTIE
COATIS
COCCID
COCHIN
COEDIT
COHEIR
COLLIE
COMEIN
COMFIT
COMMIT
COMMIX
CONNIE
CONOID
COOKIE
COOLIT
COOTIE
COPTIC
CORBIN
CORGIS
COSMIC
COURIC
COUSIN
COWRIE
DOBBIN
DOBLIN
DOESIN
DOGGIE
DOGSIT
DOMAIN
DONEIN
DOOBIE
DOOGIE
DOOZIE
DORRIT
DOTTIE
DOVEIN
FOETID
FOGSIN
FOLKIE
FOODIE
FORBID
FORMIC
FOSSIL
FOZZIE
GOALIE
GOBLIN
GODWIN
GODWIT
GOESIN
GOLDIE
GOODIE
GORDIE
GOSSIP
GOTHIC
GOTOIT
HOAGIE
HOBBIT
HOGTIE
HOLDIN
HOLDIT
HOOFIT
HOOTIE
HOPSIN
HORNIN
HORRID
HOTAIR
HOTTIP
HOURIS
HOWLIN
JOANIE
JOININ
JOPLIN
JOSKIN
KOENIG
KOOKIE
LOCKIN
LOGGIA
LOGSIN
LOMEIN
LOOKIN
LOONIE
LORAIN
LOSEIT
LOSTIT
LOVEIN
MOHAIR
MOMMIE
MORBID
MORRIS
MOSAIC
MOULIN
MOVEIN
NOESIS
NOETIC
NOEXIT
NOGGIN
NORDIC
NORRIS
POETIC
PONGID
PONTIC
POPLIN
POPSIN
PORTIA
POSTIT
POTPIE
POURIN
ROADIE
ROBBIA
ROBBIE
ROLLIE
ROLLIN
ROMAIC
RONNIE
ROOKIE
ROOMIE
ROPEIN
SOBEIT
SOCKIN
SOFFIT
SOFTIE
SOLEIL
SOPHIA
SOPHIE
SORBIC
SORDID
SORTIE
TOCSIN
TOEDIN
TOESIN
TOMLIN
TOMMIX
TOMTIT
TONKIN
TONSIL
TOOKIN
TOOKIT
TOONIE
TOROID
TORPID
TORRID
TOWNIE
VOTEIN
WOOGIE
WOOKIE
WORKIN
YORKIE
ZOMBIE
ZOOMIN
ZOYSIA

•O•••I

BODONI
BONAMI
BONSAI
BORZOI
DOMANI
DOMINI
DORATI
DOREMI
MORONI
MOWGLI
POLLOI
POPULI
POTOSI
ROMAJI
ROTINI
SOLIDI
SOMALI
SOUARI
YOGINI

••OI••

ALOINS
ANOINT
AROIDS
AVOIDS
BOOING
BROILS
CHOICE
CHOIRS
COOING
DROIDS
DROITS
EGOISM
EGOIST
ELOIGN
ELOISE
EROICA
ETOILE
GOOIER
GROINS
IDOIDO
ILOILO
LOOIES
MAOISM
MAOIST
MOOING
OBOIST
OROIDE
OVOIDS
QUOINS
QUOITS
REOILS
SPOILS
SPOILT
STOICS
TAOISM
TAOIST
TROIKA
UNOILY
WOOING
ZOOIDS

••O•I•

ADONIS
AEOLIA
AEOLIC
ANODIC
ANOMIC
ANOMIE
ATOMIC

ATONIC
AZORIN
BIOBIO
BIONIC
BIOTIC
BIOTIN
BLOWIN
BLOWIT
BMOVIE
BOOGIE
BOOKIE
BOOTIE
BRODIE
BROLIN
CHOPIN
CLORIS
CLOVIS
COOKIE
COOLIT
COOTIE
CRONIN
DHOTIS
DIOXIN
DOOBIE
DOOGIE
DOOZIE
DROPIN
DROPIT
ELOHIM
ENOKIS
ENOSIS
EROTIC
ETONIC
EXOTIC
FLORID
FLORIN
FLORIO
FOODIE
FROLIC
GLOBIN
GLORIA
GNOMIC
GNOSIS
GOODIE
GRODIN
HOOFIT
HOOTIE
ICONIC
IGOTIT
ILORIN
IRONIC
KAOLIN
KOOKIE
KUOPIO
LEONID
LEONIE
LOOKIN
LOONIE
MAORIS
MIOSIS
MYOPIA
MYOPIC
MYOSIN
MYOSIS
OZONIC
PEORIA
PHOBIA
PHOBIC
PHOCIS
PHONIC
PHOTIC
PROFIT
PROLIX
PROSIT
ROOKIE
ROOMIE
SCORIA
SCOTIA
SHOJIS
SHOOIN
SHOWIN
SKOKIE
SLOVIK
SNOWIN
STOGIE
STOLID
STOPIN
STOPIT
STOTIN
TOOKIN
TOOKIT
TOONIE
TROPIC
TWOBIT
UTOPIA
VIOLIN
WOOGIE
WOOKIE
ZOOMIN

••O••I
ADONAI
AGOUTI
BIONDI
DROMOI
MAOTAI
PROTEI
RHOMBI
SHORTI
WHOOPI

•••OI•
ADJOIN
ADROIT
ALBOIN
ARTOIS
BELOIT
BENOIT
CONOID
CUBOID
DACOIT
DEVOID
DEVOIR
DUBOIS
ECHOIC
ENJOIN
ENVOIS
GALOIS
GOTOIT
HALOID
HEROIC
LIPOID
MEMOIR
PATOIS
REBOIL
RECOIL
REJOIN
RENOIR
REVOIR
SAVOIE
SAVOIR
SHOOIN
TOROID
UNCOIL
VALOIS
XYLOID
ZEROIN

•••O•I
BENONI
BILOXI
BODONI
BUSONI
CARONI
EPHORI
JACOBI
LUGOSI
MALOTI
MIDORI
MORONI
NAPOLI
NEROLI
OCTOPI
PILOTI
POTOSI
PRIORI
SATORI
TIVOLI
WHOOPI

••••OI
BORZOI
DROMOI
KERNOI
MYTHOI
OCTROI
POLLOI

OJ••••
OJIBWA

O•J•••
OBJECT

O••J••
ODDJOB

•OJ•••
JOJOBA
MOJAVE

•O•J••
BOOJUM
CONJOB
DONJON
KOPJES
LOGJAM
TOPJOB

•O••J•
ROMAJI

••OJ••
BOOJUM
RIOJAS
SHOJIS
STOJKO
TROJAN

••O•J•
CHONJU
SKOPJE

•••OJ•
BAROJA

OK••••
OKAPIS
OKAYED
OKEEFE
OKELLY
OKSANA

O•K•••
OAKLEY
ORKNEY

O••K••
OFFKEY
OINKED

O•••K•
OXLIKE
OZARKS

O••••K
OCASEK
OCLOCK
ONDECK

•OK•••
COKIER
FOKKER
GOKART
HOKIER
JOKERS
JOKIER
JOKILY
JOKING
KOKOMO
POKEAT
POKERS
POKERY
POKEYS
POKIER
POKILY
POKING
TOKAYS
TOKENS
TOKLAS
WOKEUP
YOKELS
YOKING
YOKUTS

•O•K••
BODKIN
BOOKED
BOOKER
BOOKIE
BOSKET
COCKED
COCKER
COCKLE
CONKED
CONKER
COOKED
COOKER
COOKIE
COOKUP
CORKED
CORKER
DOCKED
DOCKER
DOCKET
DONKEY
FOKKER
FOLKIE
FOLKSY
FORKED
FORKER
HOCKED
HOCKEY
HONKED
HONKER
HOOKAH
HOOKED
HOOKUP
JOCKEY
JOSKIN
KOOKIE
LOCKED
LOCKER
LOCKET
LOCKIN
LOCKON
LOCKUP
LOOKAT
LOOKED
LOOKER
LOOKIN
LOOKON
LOOKTO
LOOKUP
LOWKEY
MOCKED
MOCKER
MOCKUP
MONKEY
MOSKVA
POCKET
POLKAS
PORKER
ROCKED
ROCKER
ROCKET
ROCKNE
ROCKYV
ROOKED
ROOKIE
SOAKED
SOAKER
SOAKUP
SOCKED
SOCKET
SOCKIN
TONKIN
TOOKIN
TOOKIT
TOOKON
TOOKTO
TOOKUP
VODKAS
WOOKIE
WORKED
WORKER
WORKIN
WORKON
WORKUP
YOLKED
YORKER
YORKIE
ZONKED
ZONKER

•O••K•
BOURKE
KOPEKS
MOLTKE
NOOTKA
ROTHKO
ROURKE
TOPEKA
WOVOKA
YOICKS

•O•••K
GOBACK
KODIAK
KOPECK
LOMBOK
MOHAWK
MOHOCK
PODUNK
TOBRUK
VOSTOK
YORICK

••OK••
AWOKEN
BLOKES
BOOKED
BOOKER
BOOKIE
BROKAW
BROKEN
BROKER
CHOKED
CHOKER
CHOKES
COOKED
COOKER
COOKIE
COOKUP
ENOKIS
EVOKED
EVOKER
EVOKES
HOOKAH
HOOKED
HOOKUP
KOOKIE
LOOKAT
LOOKED
LOOKER
LOOKIN
LOOKON
LOOKTO
LOOKUP
QUOKKA
ROOKED
ROOKIE
RYOKAN
SKOKIE
SMOKED
SMOKER
SMOKES
SMOKEY
SPOKED
SPOKEN
SPOKES
STOKED
STOKER
STOKES
TOOKIN
TOOKIT
TOOKON
TOOKTO
TOOKUP
WOOKIE

••O•K•
BLOCKS
BLOCKY
BROOKE
BROOKS
BROOKY
CHOCKS
CLOAKS
CLOCKS
CLONKS
CROAKS
CROAKY
CROCKS
CROOKS
FLOCKS
FLOCKY
FROCKS
KIOSKS
KNOCKS
NOOTKA
PLONKS
PROSKY
QUOKKA
SHOCKS
SHOOKS
SMOCKS
SNOOKS
SNOOKY
SPOOKS
SPOOKY
STOCKS
STOCKY
STOJKO
STOOKS
STORKS
TROIKA

••O••K
ANORAK
DVORAK
SLOVAK
SLOVIK

•••OK•
BROOKE
BROOKS
BROOKY
CROOKS
INJOKE
INVOKE
JAMOKE
JUDOKA
MIWOKS
REVOKE
SHOOKS
SNOOKS
SNOOKY
SPOOKS
SPOOKY
STOOKS
STROKE
UNYOKE
WOVOKA
YAPOKS
YUROKS

•••O•K
ATWORK
BETOOK
BUROAK
DRHOOK
FAROUK
MOHOCK
NANOOK
OCLOCK
PINOAK
RECORK
REDOAK
REHOOK
RELOCK
RETOOK
REWORK
TANOAK
UNCORK
UNHOOK
UNLOCK

••••OK
BARTOK
BETOOK
DRHOOK
HICKOK
LOMBOK
NANOOK
REEBOK
REHOOK
RETOOK
RHEBOK
UNHOOK
VOSTOK

OL••••
OLDAGE
OLDBOY
OLDEST
OLDHAM
OLDHAT
OLDIES
OLDISH
OLDMAN
OLDMEN
OLDPRO
OLDSAW
OLDVIC
OLEARY
OLEATE
OLEFIN
OLESON
OLEVEL
OLINDA
OLINGO
OLIVER
OLIVES
OLIVIA
OLMECS

O•L•••
OBLAST
OBLATE
OBLIGE
OBLONG
OCLOCK
OFLATE
OGLALA
OGLERS
OGLING
OILCAN
OILERS
OILIER
OILILY
OILING
OILMAN
OILMEN
OILPAN
OILRIG
ONLAND
ONLINE
ONLOAN
OOLALA
OOLITE
OOLITH
OOLOGY
OOLONG
ORLOPS
OWLETS
OWLISH
OXLIKE
OXLIPS

O••L••
OAKLEY
OBELIA
OBELUS
OCELLI
OCELOT
OCULAR
ODDLOT
OKELLY
OMELET
OODLES
ORALES
ORALLY
ORELSE
ORTLES
OSTLER
OTELLO
OUTLAW
OUTLAY
OUTLET
OVALLY
OVULAR
OVULES
OXALIS

O•••L•
OCCULT
OCELLI
OGLALA
OHWELL
OILILY
OKELLY
ONCALL
ONEILL
ONFILE
ONHOLD
ONSALE
OOLALA
OOZILY
OPENLY
ORACLE
ORALLY
ORIELS
ORIOLE
ORMOLU
ORWELL
OSCULA
OSWALD
OTELLO
OTOOLE
OUSELS
OUTFLY
OUZELS
OVALLY
OVERLY

O••••L
OHWELL
OLEVEL
ONCALL
ONEILL
ORCHIL
ORDEAL
ORWELL
OSTEAL
OXTAIL
OXYDOL

•OL•••
BOLDER
BOLDLY
BOLERO
BOLEYN
BOLGER
BOLIDE
BOLLIX
BOLSHY
BOLTED
BOLTON
COLADA
COLDER
COLDLY
COLEUS
COLFAX
COLIES
COLIMA
COLLAR
COLLET
COLLIE
COLLOP
COLLOQ
COLMAN
COLONS
COLONY
COLORS
COLOUR
COLTER
COLUGO
COLUMN
DOLENZ
DOLING
DOLLAR
DOLLED
DOLLOP
DOLLUP
DOLMAN
DOLMAS
DOLMEN
DOLORS
DOLOUR
EOLIAN
EOLITH
FOLDED
FOLDER
FOLDUP
FOLIAR
FOLIOS
FOLIUM
FOLKIE
FOLKSY
FOLLOW
FOLSOM
GOLDEN
GOLDIE
GOLEMS
GOLFED
GOLFER
GOLINO
GOLLUM
HOLDEN
HOLDER
HOLDIN
HOLDIT
HOLDON
HOLDTO
HOLDUP
HOLEUP
HOLIER
HOLILY
HOLING
HOLISM
HOLIST
HOLLER
HOLLOW
HOLMES
IOLITE
JOLENE
JOLIET
JOLIOT
JOLSON
JOLTED
LOLITA
LOLLED
LOLLOP
MOLARS
MOLDAU
MOLDED
MOLDER
MOLEST
MOLINE
MOLNAR
MOLOCH
MOLOPO
MOLTED
MOLTEN
MOLTER
MOLTKE
NOLEAD
NOLENS
NOLESS
NOLOAD
NOLOSE
OOLALA
OOLITE
OOLITH
OOLOGY
OOLONG
POLAND
POLDER
POLEAX
POLERS
POLEYN
POLICE
POLICY
POLING
POLISH
POLITE
POLITY
POLKAS
POLLED
POLLEN
POLLER
POLLEX
POLLOI
POLLUX
POLPOT
POLYPS
ROLAND
ROLEOS
ROLLED
ROLLER
ROLLIE
ROLLIN
ROLLON
ROLLUP
SOLACE
SOLANS
SOLARS
SOLDAN
SOLDER
SOLDON
SOLEIL
SOLELY
SOLEMN
SOLENT
SOLERS
SOLEUS
SOLFAS
SOLIDI
SOLIDS
SOLING
SOLOED
SOLONG
SOLUTE
SOLVED
SOLVER
SOLVES
TOLDOF
TOLDON
TOLEDO
TOLIFE
TOLLED
TOLTEC
TOLUCA
VOLANS
VOLANT
VOLARE
VOLENS
VOLLEY
VOLUME
VOLUTE
VOLVAS
VOLVOX
WOLFED
WOLPER
WOLSEY
WOLVES
YOLKED

•O•L••
BOGLES
BOILED
BOILER
BOLLIX
BOSLEY
BOULES
BOULEZ
BOULLE
BOWLED
BOWLER
BOWLES
COALER
COELOM
COILED
COILUP
COLLAR
COLLET
COLLIE
COLLOP
COLLOQ
COOLED
COOLER
COOLIT
COOLLY
COPLEY
COULDA
COULEE
COWLED
COWLEY
DOBLAS
DOBLIN
DOGLEG
DOLLAR
DOLLED
DOLLOP
DOLLUP
DOOLEY
FOALED
FOILED
FOLLOW
FOOLED
FOOLER
FOULED
FOULER
FOULLY
FOULUP
FOWLED
FOWLER
FOWLES
GOALIE
GOBLET
GOBLIN
GOLLUM
GOSLOW
GOULET
HOLLER
HOLLOW
HOWLED
HOWLER
HOWLIN
JOBLOT
JOPLIN
JOULES
KOALAS
KOHLER
LOLLED
LOLLOP
MOBLEY
MOILED
MOILER
MOOLAH
MORLEY
MOSLEM
MOTLEY
MOULDS
MOULDY
MOULIN
MOULTS
NOBLER
NOBLES
OODLES
POILUS
POLLED
POLLEN
POLLER
POLLEX
POLLOI
POLLUX
POOLED
POPLAR
POPLIN
POULTS
ROBLES
ROILED
ROLLED
ROLLER
ROLLIE
ROLLIN
ROLLON
ROLLUP
SOCLES
SOILED
TOILED
TOILER
TOILES
TOILET
TOKLAS
TOLLED
TOMLIN
TOOLED
TOOLUP
TOULON
VOILES
VOLLEY
WOHLER
WOOLEN
WOOLEY
WOOLLY
WORLDS
YOWLED

•O••L•
BOBBLE
BODILY
BOGGLE
BOLDLY
BOODLE
BOTELS
BOTFLY
BOTTLE
BOUCLE
BOULLE
COBALT
COBBLE
COCKLE
CODDLE
COLDLY
COMELY
COMPLY
COOLLY
COPULA
CORALS
COSELL
COSILY
COSTLY
COUPLE
COZILY
DOABLE
DOCILE
DONALD
DONGLE
DOODLE
DOTELL
DOTTLE
DOUALA
DOUBLE
DOUBLY
DOURLY
DOWELS
DOZILY
FOCSLE
FOIBLE
FONDLE
FONDLY
FOOZLE
FOULLY
FOXILY
GOBBLE
GOGGLE
GOGGLY
GOODLY
GOOGLE
GOOGLY
GORALS
GORILY
GOWILD
HOBBLE
HOLILY
HOMELY
HOMILY
HOOPLA
HOOPLE
HOPPLE
HOSELS
HOSTLY
HOTELS
HOURLY
HOVELS
HOWELL
JOGGLE
JOKILY
JOSTLE
KOBOLD
KODALY
LOBULE
LOCALE
LOCALS
LOGILY
LONELY
LONGLY
LORDLY
LOUDLY
LOVELL
LOVELY
LOWELL
LOYOLA
MOBILE
MODELA
MODELS
MODELT
MODULE
MODULO
MOGULS
MORALE
MORALS
MORELS
MOSTLY
MOTELS
MOTILE
MOTTLE
MOWGLI
NOBBLE
NODDLE
NODULE
NOODLE
NOSALE
NOSILY
NOVELS
NOZZLE
OOLALA
OOZILY
POKILY
POMELO
POODLE
POORLY
POPFLY
POPPLE
POPULI
PORTLY
POSHLY
POSSLQ
POTTLE
POWELL
ROBALO
ROMOLA
RONALD
RONELY
ROSILY
ROUBLE
ROWELS
ROYALE
ROYALS
SOFTLY
SOLELY
SOMALI
SORELY
SOTOLS
SOURLY
TODDLE
TOGGLE
TOOTLE
TOPPLE
TOTALS
TOUSLE
TOWELS
VOCALS
VOWELS
VOWELY
WOBBLE
WOBBLY
WOOLLY
YODELS
YOKELS
YOUALL
ZORILS

•O•••L
AORTAL
BOATEL
BOREAL
BOXFUL
COEVAL
COMPEL
CONSUL
CORBEL
CORNEL
CORRAL
CORREL
COSELL
COSTAL
DORSAL
DOSSAL
DOSSEL
DOTELL
FOETAL
FONTAL
FORMAL
FOSSIL
GOOGOL
GOSPEL
HORMEL
HOSTEL
HOWELL
JOVIAL
JOYFUL
KOPPEL
LONNOL
LOREAL
LOVELL
LOWCAL
LOWELL
MONGOL
MONTEL
MORSEL
MORTAL
MOSTEL
NORMAL
POMMEL
PORTAL
POSTAL
POTFUL
POWELL
ROMMEL
RONDEL
SOBFUL
SOCIAL
SOLEIL
SORREL
TONSIL
WOEFUL
YOUALL

••OL••
ABOLLA
ADOLPH
AEOLIA
AEOLIC
AEOLUS
AMOLES
ANOLES
APOLLO
ATOLLS
BROLIN

BROLLY
CHOLER
CHOLLA
CHOLOS
COOLED
COOLER
COOLIT
COOLLY
DHOLES
DOOLEY
DROLLS
DROLLY
ECOLES
EVOLVE
FOOLED
FOOLER
FROLIC
GAOLED
GAOLER
HAOLES
ISOLDE
KAOLIN
KJOLEN
KNOLLS
KNOLLY
MOOLAH
PIOLET
POOLED
PROLES
PROLIX
PROLOG
SCOLDS
SHOLEM
SHOLOM
SMOLTS
STOLEN
STOLES
STOLID
STOLLE
STOLON
THOLES
TOOLED
TOOLUP
TROLLS
UBOLTS
VIOLAS
VIOLET
VIOLIN
WHOLES
WHOLLY
WOOLEN
WOOLEY
WOOLLY

••O•L•

ABOLLA
APOLLO
ATOLLS
BOODLE
BROILS
BROLLY
CEORLS
CHOLLA
COOLLY
DOODLE
DROLLS
DROLLY
DROOLS
DROOLY
ETOILE
FOOZLE
GHOULS
GOODLY
GOOGLE
GOOGLY
GROWLS
GROWLY
HOOPLA
HOOPLE
ILOILO
KNOLLS
KNOLLY
LIONLY
NOODLE
OTOOLE
PEOPLE
POODLE
POORLY
PROWLS
REOILS
SCOWLS
SHOALS
SHOALY
SHOULD
SKOALS
SLOWLY
SPOILS
SPOILT
SPOOLS
STOLLE
STOOLS
STOOLY
TOOTLE
TROLLS
TWOPLY
UNOILY
WHOLLY
WHORLS
WOOLLY

••O••L

ABORAL
AMORAL
APODAL
ATONAL
AVOWAL
AXONAL
BHOPAL
CHORAL
DHOTEL
FLORAL
GLOBAL
GOOGOL
GROVEL
ISOHEL
LIONEL
PROPEL
SHOVEL
TROWEL
UNOCAL

•••OL•

AGEOLD
ANGOLA
AREOLA
ARNOLD
BAROLO
BEHOLD
BIFOLD
BITOLA
BUJOLD
CAJOLE
CANOLA
CAROLE
CAROLS
CIBOLA
CREOLE
CUPOLA
DIPOLE
DROOLS
DROOLY
EIDOLA
ENFOLD
ENROLL
ENROLS
ERROLL
EXTOLS
GIGOLO
HAROLD
INFOLD
INSOLE
KOBOLD
LOYOLA
MAZOLA
NAPOLI
NEROLI
NICOLA
NICOLE
NICOLO
NIKOLA
ONHOLD
ORIOLE
ORMOLU
OTOOLE
PAROLE
PAYOLA
PINOLE
RCCOLA
REBOLT
REMOLD
REPOLL
RESOLD
RESOLE
RETOLD
REVOLT
ROMOLA
RUDOLF
SCROLL
SOTOLS
SPOOLS
STOOLS
STOOLY
STROLL
TIVOLI
UNBOLT
UNFOLD
UNHOLY
UNROLL
UNSOLD
UNTOLD
UPHOLD

•••O•L

BEFOUL
ENROLL
ENSOUL
ERROLL
FAZOOL
JAWOHL
MRCOOL
REBOIL
RECOIL
REPOLL
RETOOL
SCHOOL
SCHORL
SCROLL
STROLL
UNCOIL
UNCOOL
UNROLL

••••OL

AMATOL
AMIDOL
BENZOL
CARROL
CRESOL
ETYMOL
FAZOOL
FRIJOL
GAMBOL
GLYCOL
GOOGOL
LONNOL
MONGOL
MRCOOL
MYTHOL
NEUROL
OXYDOL
PATHOL
PATROL
PETROL
PHENOL
PHILOL
PISTOL
RETOOL
SCHOOL
STEROL
SYMBOL
TYDBOL
UNCOOL
WARHOL

OM••••

OMAHAN
OMAHAS
OMANIS
OMASUM
OMEGAS
OMELET
OMERTA
OMNIUM

O•M•••

OLMECS
OOMPAH
ORMOLU
ORMOND
OSMICS
OSMIUM
OSMOND
OSMOSE
OSMUND

O••M••

OILMAN
OILMEN
OLDMAN
OLDMEN
ONEMAN
OROMOS

O•••M•

ODIUMS
OEDEMA
OGHAMS
ONTIME
OPTIMA

O••••M

OLDHAM
OMASUM
OMNIUM
OSMIUM
OSTIUM

•OM•••

BOMBAY
BOMBED
BOMBER
BOMBES
COMATE
COMBAT
COMBED
COMBER
COMBES
COMBOS
COMEAT
COMEBY
COMEDY
COMEIN
COMELY
COMEON
COMERS
COMETH
COMETO
COMETS
COMEUP
COMFIT
COMICS
COMING
COMITY
COMMAS
COMMIT
COMMIX
COMMON
COMPAQ
COMPEL
COMPLY
COMPOS
COMSAT
COMTES
DOMAIN
DOMANI
DOMINE
DOMING
DOMINI
DOMINO
DOMREP
FOMENT
HOMAGE
HOMBRE
HOMEEC
HOMELY
HOMERS
HOMIER
HOMILY
HOMING
HOMINY
IOMOTH
KOMBAT
KOMODO
LOMBOK
LOMEIN
LOMOND
MOMENT
MOMMAS
MOMMIE
NOMADS
NOMINE
NOMORE
OOMPAH
POMACE
POMADE
POMELO
POMMEE
POMMEL
POMONA
POMPEY
POMPOM
POMPON
ROMAIC
ROMAJI
ROMANO
ROMANS
ROMANY
ROMEOS
ROMERO
ROMMEL
ROMNEY
ROMOLA
ROMPED
ROMPER
SOMALI
SOMANY
SOMATA
SOMATO
SOMBER
SOMBRE
SOMERS
SOMMER
TOMATO
TOMBAC
TOMBOY
TOMCAT
TOMLIN
TOMMIX
TOMTIT
TOMTOM
WOMBAT
WOMENS
YOMTOV
ZOMBIE

•O•M••

BONMOT
BOOMED
BOOMER
BORMAN
BOWMAN
BOWMEN
COLMAN
COMMAS
COMMIT
COMMIX
COMMON
CONMAN
CONMEN
CORMAN
COSMIC
COSMOS
COWMAN
COWMEN
DOGMAS
DOLMAN
DOLMAS
DOLMEN
DOOMED
DORMER
FOAMED
FORMAL
FORMAN
FORMAT
FORMED
FORMER
FORMIC
GOTMAD
HOLMES
HORMEL
HORMUZ
KORMAN
LOAMED
LOOMED
MOMMAS
MOMMIE
MORMON
MOTMOT
NORMAL
NORMAN
NOUMEA
POMMEE
POMMEL
ROAMED
ROAMER
RODMAN
ROHMER
ROMMEL
ROOMED
ROOMER
ROOMIE
SOMMER
TOAMAN
TODMAN
TOMMIX
WONMUG
WORMED
ZOOMED
ZOOMIN

•O••M•

BONAMI
COLIMA
COLUMN
DODOMA
DOREMI
FORUMS
GOHOME
GOLEMS
JORUMS
KOKOMO
MODEMS
NONAME
SOLEMN
SONOMA
TOTEMS
VOLUME
YOYOMA

•O•••M

BOOJUM
BOTTOM
COBHAM
COELOM
CONIUM
CORIUM
DOGDOM
DORSUM
FOLIUM
FOLSOM
FOURAM
FOURPM
GOLLUM
GOTHAM
HOLISM
IONIUM
LOGJAM
MONISM
MOSLEM
NONCOM
PODIUM
POMPOM
POSSUM
RODHAM
SODIUM
TOMTOM
YOGISM

••OM••

ABOMBS
ALOMAR
ANOMIC
ANOMIE
AROMAS
ATOMIC
BIOMES
BOOMED
BOOMER
CHOMPS
CLOMPS
DOOMED
DROMOI
DROMOS
DUOMOS
GNOMES
GNOMIC
GNOMON
HBOMBS
ISOMER
LOOMED
OROMOS
PROMOS
PROMPT
RHOMBI
RHOMBS
ROOMED
ROOMER
ROOMIE
STOMAS
STOMAT
STOMPS
THOMAS
TROMPE
TROMPS
WHOMPS
WHOMSO
YEOMAN
YEOMEN
ZOOMED
ZOOMIN

••O•M•

ABOHMS
BLOOMS
BLOOMY
BROOMS
BROOMY
GLOOMS
GLOOMY
GROOMS
KHOUMS
MYOHMY
PROAMS
PROEMS
SHOWME
STORMS
STORMY
VROOMS

••O••M

ANONYM
BOOJUM
EGOISM
ELOHIM
EPONYM
MAOISM
PROTEM
QUORUM
SHOLEM
SHOLOM
TAOISM

•••OM•

APLOMB
ATHOME
AXIOMS
BECOME
BESOMS
BLOOMS
BLOOMY
BROOMS
BROOMY
CAROMS
CDROMS
CHROMA
CHROME
CHROMO
CHROMY
DODOMA
ENTOMO
EPROMS
GENOME
GLOOMS
GLOOMY
GOHOME
GROOMS
IDIOMS
INCOME
JEROME
KOKOMO
PALOMA
RADOME
SALOME
SONOMA
TACOMA
UGSOME
VENOMS
VROOMS
YOYOMA

•••O•M

ABLOOM
DEFORM
INFORM
KABOOM
MEGOHM
PHLOEM
REFORM
SHBOOM
SILOAM

••••OM

ABLOOM
BOTTOM
COELOM
CUSTOM
DIATOM
DOGDOM
FANDOM
FATHOM
FOLSOM
HANSOM
KABOOM
MADTOM
NONCOM
PHENOM
POMPOM
RANDOM
RANSOM
SELDOM
SHALOM
SHBOOM
SHOLOM
SITCOM
SLALOM
TOMTOM
VIACOM
WHILOM
WINDOM
WISDOM

ON••••

ONAGER
ONCALL
ONDECK
ONDINE
ONEACT
ONEDAY
ONEDGE
ONEIDA
ONEILL
ONEMAN
ONETWO
ONEUPS
ONEWAY
ONFILE
ONFIRE
ONFOOT
ONHAND
ONHIGH
ONHOLD
ONIONS
ONIONY
ONLAND
ONLINE
ONLOAN
ONRUSH
ONSALE
ONSETS
ONSIDE
ONSITE
ONSPEC
ONTAPE
ONTIME
ONTOUR
ONUSES
ONVIEW
ONWARD
ONYXES

O•N•••

OENONE
OINKED
OMNIUM
ORNATE
ORNERY
ORNITH
OUNCES
OWNERS
OWNING
OWNSUP
OXNARD

O••N••

ODENSE
ODONTO
OHENRY
OLINDA
OLINGO
OMANIS
OPENED
OPENER
OPENLY
OPENTO
OPENUP
OPINED
OPINER
OPINES
ORANGE
ORANGS
ORANGY
ORANTS
ORINGS
ORKNEY
OZONIC

O•••N•

OARING
OBLONG
OBTUND
OCEANS
OCTANE
OCTANT
OENONE
OFFEND
OFFING
OGLING
OILING
OKSANA
ONDINE
ONHAND
ONIONS
ONIONY
ONLAND
ONLINE
OOHING
OOLONG
OOZING
OPTING
ORBING
ORGANA
ORGANS
ORIANA
ORIENT
ORMOND
ORPINE
ORSINO
OSCINE
OSMOND
OSMUND
OSTEND
OUTING
OWNING

O••••N

OBERON
OBIWAN
OBRIAN
OBRIEN
OBTAIN
ODDSON
OHIOAN
OILCAN
OILMAN
OILMEN
OILPAN
OLDMAN
OLDMEN
OLEFIN
OLESON
OMAHAN
ONEMAN
ONLOAN
OPPUGN
OPTION
ORDAIN
OREGON
ORIGEN
ORIGIN
ORISON
ORPHAN
OSBORN
OSSEIN
OSSIAN
OUTGUN
OUTRAN
OUTRUN
OXYGEN

•ON•••

BONAMI
BONBON
BONCES
BONDED
BONERS
BONEUP
BONGED
BONGOS
BONIER
BONING
BONITO
BONMOT
BONNES
BONNET
BONNIE
BONSAI
BONTON
BONZES
CONANT
CONCHA
CONCHS
CONCUR
CONDOR
CONDOS
CONEYS
CONFAB
CONFED
CONFER
CONGAS
CONGER
CONGOU
CONICS
CONIES
CONIUM
CONJOB
CONKED
CONKER
CONMAN
CONMEN
CONNED
CONNER
CONNIE
CONNOR
CONOCO
CONOID
CONRAD
CONROY
CONSUL
CONTAC
CONTES
CONTRA
CONTRE
CONURE
CONVEX
CONVEY
CONVOY
CONWAY
DONALD
DONATE
DONDER
DONEES
DONEIN
DONETS
DONEUP
DONGLE
DONITZ
DONJON
DONKEY
DONNAS
DONNED
DONNEE
DONNER
DONORS
DONUTS
EONIAN
FONDER
FONDLE
FONDLY
FONDUE
FONTAL
GONEBY
GONERS
GONGED
GONOGO
HONCHO
HONEST
HONEYS
HONIED
HONING
HONKED
HONKER
HONORE
HONORS
HONOUR
HONSHU
IONIAN
IONICS
IONISE
IONIUM
IONIZE
JONAHS
JONSON
KONICA
KONRAD
LONDON
LONELY
LONERS
LONGAN
LONGED
LONGER
LONGES
LONGLY
LONGUE
LONNOL
MONACO
MONADS
MONDAY
MONERA
MONETA
MONEYS
MONGER
MONGOL
MONICA
MONIED
MONIES
MONISM
MONIST
MONKEY
MONODY
MONROE
MONTEL
MONTES
MONTEZ
MONTHS
NONAGE
NONAME
NONARY
NONCOM
NONEGO
NONETS
NONFAT
PONCES
PONCHO
PONDER
PONGED
PONGEE
PONGID
PONIED
PONIES
PONTES
PONTIC
PONTUS
PONYUP
RONALD
RONDEL
RONDOS
RONELY
RONNIE
SONANT
SONATA
SONDES
SONICS
SONNET
SONOMA
SONORA
SONTAG
TONDOS
TONERS
TONEUP
TONGAN
TONGUE
TONICS
TONIER
TONING
TONISH
TONITE
TONKIN
TONNES
TONSIL
WONDER
WONMUG
WONNED
WONOUT
WONTED
WONTON
YONDER
ZONATE
ZONING
ZONKED
ZONKER

•O•N••

BOINGO
BONNES
BONNET
BONNIE
BORNEO
BOSNIA
BOUNCE
BOUNCY
BOUNDS
BOUNTY
BOWNET
COGNAC
COINED
COINER
CONNED
CONNER
CONNIE
CONNOR
COONEY
CORNEA
CORNED
CORNEL
CORNER
CORNET
COUNTS
COUNTY
DOINGS
DONNAS
DONNED
DONNEE
DONNER
DOWNED
DOWNER
DOWNEY
DOWNON
FOINED
FOUNDS
FOUNTS
GOANNA
GOINGS
GOINTO
GOUNOD
GOWNED
HOBNOB
HORNED
HORNER
HORNET
HORNEY
HORNIN
HOUNDS
HOUNDY
HOWNOW
JOANIE
JOANNA
JOANNE
JOHNNY
JOINED
JOINER
JOININ
JOINTS
JOINUP
JOUNCE
JOUNCY
JOYNER
KOENIG
KOONTZ
LOANED
LOANER
LONNOL
LOONEY
LOONIE
LOUNGE
MOANED
MOANER
MOINES
MOLNAR
MOONED
MOONEY
MORNAY
MOUNDS
MOUNTS
MOUNTY
NOONAN
NOONES
NOTNOW
POINTE
POINTS
POINTY
POUNCE
POUNDS
RODNEY
ROMNEY
RONNIE
ROONEY
ROUNDS
SONNET
SOONER
SOUNDS
TONNES
TOONIE
TOWNER
TOWNIE
WONNED
WOUNDS
ZOUNDS

•O••N•

BODING
BODONI
BOEING
BOGONG
BOIGNY
BONING
BOOING
BORING
BOSONS
BOSUNS
BOTANY
BOURNE
BOVINE
BOWING
BOXING
CODING
CODONS
COGENT
COHUNE
COIGNS
COLONS
COLONY
COMING
CONANT
COOING
COPING
CORING
CORONA
COSINE
COVENS
COVENT
COVINA
COWENS
COWING
COZENS
DOCENT
DOESNT
DOGONS
DOLENZ
DOLING
DOMANI
DOMINE
DOMING
DOMINI
DOMINO
DOPANT
DOPING
DOSING
DOTING
DOYENS
DOZENS
DOZING
EOCENE
EOSINS
FOEHNS
FOMENT
FORINT
FOXING
GOANNA
GOLINO
GORING
HOEING
HOGANS
HOLING
HOMING

HOMINY
HONING
HOPING
HOSING
IODINE
IOWANS
JOANNA
JOANNE
JOCUND
JOHANN
JOHNNY
JOKING
JOLENE
JOURNO
KORUNA
LODENS
LOMOND
LOPING
LORENZ
LOSING
LOVING
LOWEND
LOWING
MODENA
MODINE
MOLINE
MOMENT
MOOING
MOPING
MORANT
MORENO
MORONI
MORONS
MOURNS
MOVING
MOWING
NOCENT
NOLENS
NOMINE
NOSING
NOTING
NOVENA
OOHING
OOLONG
OOZING
POCONO
PODUNK
POKING
POLAND
POLING
POMONA
PORING
POSING
POTENT
ROBING
ROBINS
ROCKNE
RODENT
ROLAND
ROMANO
ROMANS
ROMANY
ROPING
ROSINS
ROSINY
ROTINI
ROTUND
ROVING
ROWENA
ROWENS
ROWING
ROXANA
ROXANE
SOFINE

SOIGNE
SOLANS
SOLENT
SOLING
SOLONG
SOMANY
SONANT
SOWING
TOEING
TOEINS
TOKENS
TONING
TORINO
TOTING
TOWING
TOXINS
TOYING
TOYONS
VOLANS
VOLANT
VOLENS
VOTING
VOWING
WOMENS
WOOING
WOWING
YOGINI
YOKING
ZONING

•O•••N
BOBBIN
BODKIN
BOFFIN
BOLEYN
BOLTON
BONBON
BONTON
BORDEN
BOREON
BORMAN
BOSTON
BOUDIN
BOWFIN
BOWMAN
BOWMEN
COBURN
COCHIN
COCOON
COLMAN
COLUMN
COMEIN
COMEON
COMMON
CONMAN
CONMEN
COOGAN
CORBAN
CORBIN
CORDON
CORMAN
COSIGN
COTTEN
COTTON
COUPON
COUSIN
COWMAN
COWMEN
DOBBIN
DOBLIN
DOBSON
DOESIN
DOLMAN
DOLMEN

DOMAIN
DONEIN
DONJON
DORIAN
DOTEON
DOTHAN
DOVEIN
DOWNON
EOLIAN
EONIAN
FOGSIN
FORMAN
GOBLIN
GODOWN
GODSON
GODWIN
GOESIN
GOESON
GOLDEN
GOODEN
GORDON
GORGON
GOSHEN
GOTTEN
GOVERN
HOBSON
HOLDEN
HOLDIN
HOLDON
HOPSIN
HORNIN
HORTON
HOWLIN
HOYDEN
IONIAN
JOHANN
JOININ
JOLSON
JONSON
JOPLIN
JORDAN
JOSKIN
JOVIAN
KOREAN
KORMAN
LOCKIN
LOCKON
LOGION
LOGSIN
LOGSON
LOMEIN
LONDON
LONGAN
LOOKIN
LOOKON
LOOSEN
LORAIN
LOTION
LOUDEN
LOVEIN
MODERN
MOLTEN
MOREEN
MORGAN
MORGEN
MORION
MORMON
MORTON
MOTION
MOTOWN
MOULIN
MOUTON
MOVEIN
MOVEON

NOGGIN
NOIRON
NOONAN
NORMAN
NORTON
NOTION
POISON
POLEYN
POLLEN
POMPON
POPGUN
POPLIN
POPSIN
POSTON
POTEEN
POTION
POURIN
ROBSON
RODMAN
ROLLIN
ROLLON
ROPEIN
ROTTEN
SOCKIN
SODDEN
SOFTEN
SOLDAN
SOLDON
SOLEMN
SOSOON
TOAMAN
TOCSIN
TODMAN
TOEDIN
TOESIN
TOLDON
TOMLIN
TONGAN
TONKIN
TOOKIN
TOOKON
TOPGUN
TOPTEN
TOUCAN
TOULON
VOTEIN
WONTON
WOODEN
WOOLEN
WOREON
WORKIN
WORKON
WORSEN
ZOOMIN

••ON••
ADONAI
ADONIS
ALONSO
ALONZO
ANONYM
ATONAL
ATONCE
ATONED
ATONES
ATONIC
AXONAL
BIONDI
BIONIC
BLONDE
BLONDS
BRONCO
BRONCS
BRONTE

BRONZE
BRONZY
CHONJU
CLONED
CLONES
CLONKS
CLONUS
COONEY
CRONES
CRONIN
CRONUS
CRONYN
DIONEB
DIONNE
DRONED
DRONER
DRONES
EBONDS
EPONYM
ETONIC
EVONNE
FRONDS
FRONTS
HMONGS
ICONIC
IRONED
IRONER
IRONIC
IRONON
KOONTZ
KRONER
KRONOR
KRONUR
LEONES
LEONID
LEONIE
LIONEL
LIONET
LIONLY
LOONEY
LOONIE
MOONED
MOONEY
NOONAN
NOONES
ODONTO
OZONIC
PHONED
PHONES
PHONEY
PHONIC
PHONON
PHONOS
PLONKS
PRONGS
PRONTO
RHONDA
ROONEY
SCONCE
SCONES
SOONER
SPONGE
SPONGY
STONED
STONER
STONES
TBONDS
TBONES
THONGS
TOONIE
WRONGS
YVONNE

••O•N•
ABOUND
ACORNS
ADORNS
ALOINS
AMOUNT
ANOINT
AROUND
BOOING
BROWNE
BROWNS
BROWNY
CLOWNS
COOING
CROONS
CROWNS
DIONNE
DROWNS
EVONNE
FROWNS
GROANS
GRODNO
GROINS
GROUND
GROZNY
KNOWNS
MOOING
PROCNE
QUOINS
SCORNS
SLOANE
SPOONS
SPOONY
SWOONS
THORNS
THORNY
WOOING
YVONNE

••O••N
ASOSAN
AWOKEN
AZORIN
BIOTIN
BLOWIN
BROGAN
BROKEN
BROLIN
CHOPIN
CHOSEN
CLOVEN
COOGAN
CRONIN
CRONYN
CROTON
DIOXIN
DROPIN
ELOIGN
FLORIN
FROZEN
GLOBIN
GNOMON
GOODEN
GRODIN
GROTON
GROWON
ILORIN
IMOGEN
IRONON
ISOGON
KAOLIN
KJOLEN
LOOKIN
LOOKON

LOOSEN
MYOSIN
NOONAN
PHONON
PHOTON
PROTON
PROVEN
REOPEN
RYOKAN
SHOGUN
SHOOIN
SHORAN
SHOWIN
SIOUAN
SLOGAN
SLOVEN
SNOWIN
SPOKEN
STOLEN
STOLON
STOPIN
STOTIN
TOOKIN
TOOKON
TROGON
TROJAN
UNOPEN
USOPEN
VIOLIN
WOODEN
WOOLEN
YEOMAN
YEOMEN
ZOOMIN

•••ON•
ACTONE
ADDONS
ALMOND
ANCONA
ANIONS
ANTONY
ANYONE
APRONS
ARSONS
AUFOND
AUMONT
AXIONS
BARONG
BARONS
BARONY
BATONS
BEGONE
BELONG
BENONI
BETONY
BEYOND
BISONS
BODONI
BOGONG
BOSONS
BRYONY
BUSONI
BYGONE
CANONS
CAPONE
CAPONS
CARONI
CHRONO
CODONS
COLONS
COLONY
CORONA
CROONS

DAMONE
DATONG
DAYONE
DEBONE
DELONG
DEMOND
DEMONS
DEPONE
DOGONS
DUGONG
DUMONT
DUPONT
EDMOND
EGMONT
EVZONE
FANONS
FELONS
FELONY
FUTONS
GERONT
GLUONS
GYRONS
HERONS
HURONS
INIONS
INTONE
KETONE
KIMONO
LAMONT
LATONA
LEMOND
LEMONS
LEMONY
LOMOND
LUPONE
MALONE
MASONS
MEKONG
MELONS
MESONS
MORONI
MORONS
NYLONS
OBLONG
OENONE
ONIONS
ONIONY
OOLONG
ORMOND
OSMOND
PAEONS
PINONS
PITONS
POCONO
POMONA
PRIONS
PUTONS
PYLONS
RACONS
RAMONA
RAMONE
RAYONS
RECONS
REDONE
REZONE
RUNONS
SALONS
SARONG
SAXONS
SAXONY
SCIONS
SECOND
SILONE
SIMONE

SIMONY
SOLONG
SPOONS
SPOONY
STRONG
SWOONS
TALONS
TAUONS
TENONS
TETONS
THRONE
THRONG
TOYONS
TYRONE
UNDONE
UNIONS
VERONA
WAGONS
WINONA

•••O•N
ADJOIN
ALBOIN
ASWOON
BABOON
BEMOAN
BICORN
COCOON
DEHORN
DISOWN
ENJOIN
GENOAN
GODOWN
INBORN
INTOWN
LAGOON
MACOUN
MAROON
MINOAN
MOTOWN
OHIOAN
ONLOAN
OSBORN
REBORN
REJOIN
REMOWN
RENOWN
SALOON
SAMOAN
SHOOIN
SOSOON
STJOAN
STJOHN
SUBORN
TANOAN
THROWN
TYCOON
UNBORN
UNSOWN
UNTORN
UNWORN
UPJOHN
UPTOWN
ZEROIN

••••ON
ACTION
ACTSON
ADDSON
ALANON
ALBION
ALISON
AMAZON
AMNION

ANNHON
ANTRON
ARAGON
ARCHON
ASWOON
AVALON
AVEDON
BABOON
BABSON
BALLON
BANKON
BANLON
BARRON
BARTON
BARYON
BEACON
BEAMON
BEARON
BEATON
BECKON
BENSON
BENTON
BETSON
BIDSON
BILLON
BLAZON
BOLTON
BONBON
BONTON
BOREON
BOSTON
BRETON
BRITON
BRYSON
BUFFON
BUNION
BURTON
BUTTON
CALLON
CAMEON
CAMION
CANNON
CANTON
CANYON
CARBON
CARSON
CARTON
CASTON
CATION
CATTON
CAXTON
CEYLON
CHARON
CHIRON
CHITON
CHYRON
CITRON
CLIPON
COCOON
COMEON
COMMON
CORDON
COTTON
COUPON
CRAYON
CROTON
CURZON
DACRON
DAIKON
DAIMON
DALTON
DAMSON
DANSON
DANTON

DAWNON
DAWSON
DAYTON
DEACON
DEADON
DELEON
DENTON
DIDION
DILLON
DINEON
DOBSON
DONJON
DOTEON
DOWNON
DRAGON
DRAWON
DREWON
EASTON
EDISON
EGGSON
EPHRON
ETYMON
FALCON
FALLON
FANION
FEEDON
FELDON
FELLON
FLACON
FLAGON
FULTON
FUSION
GABION
GAINON
GALLON
GAMMON
GARCON
GARSON
GASCON
GASTON
GETSON
GIBBON
GIBSON
GIDEON
GNOMON
GODSON
GOESON
GORDON
GORGON
GREWON
GRISON
GROTON
GROWON
GUENON
GUIDON
HADRON
HAEMON
HAGDON
HANDON
HANGON
HANSON
HARMON
HARPON
HAVEON
HEADON
HEBRON
HEDRON
HELDON
HENSON
HEREON
HERMON
HESTON
HIERON
HILTON

HINTON
HIREON
HITSON
HOBSON
HOLDON
HORTON
HUDSON
HUNGON
HUSTON
HUTTON
INCHON
IRONON
ISOGON
JARGON
JETSON
JIMSON
JOLSON
JONSON
JUMPON
KEATON
KEEPON
KENTON
KEPTON
KLAXON
KMESON
LAGOON
LAIDON
LANDON
LANSON
LARDON
LARSON
LAWSON
LAWTON
LAYSON
LEADON
LEANON
LEGION
LEMMON
LENNON
LEPTON
LESSON
LETSON
LIPTON
LISBON
LISTON
LIVEON
LOCKON
LOGION
LOGSON
LONDON
LOOKON
LOTION
LYNDON
LYTTON
MACRON
MAGNON
MAMMON
MARION
MARLON
MAROON
MARRON
MATRON
MELLON
MELTON
MEMNON
MERLON
MERTON
MICRON
MIGNON
MILTON
MINION
MORION
MORMON
MORTON

MOTION
MOUTON
MOVEON
MUTTON
NATION
NATRON
NEESON
NEKTON
NELSON
NETTON
NEURON
NEWTON
NIPPON
NOIRON
NORTON
NOTION
OBERON
ODDSON
OLESON
OPTION
OREGON
ORISON
PARDON
PARSON
PARTON
PASSON
PATRON
PATTON
PAXTON
PAYSON
PELION
PENNON
PERSON
PEYTON
PHONON
PHOTON
PICKON
PIGEON
PILEON
PINION
PINSON
PINYON
PINZON
PISTON
PLANON
PLAYON
POISON
POMPON
POSTON
POTION
PREYON
PRISON
PROTON
PULLON
PUSHON
PUTSON
PYTHON
QUEZON
RAMSON
RATION
RATSON
REASON
RECKON
REGION
RESTON
RETTON
REVLON
REVSON
RHYTON
RIBBON
ROBSON
ROLLON
RULEON
RUNSON

RUNYON
SAIGON
SALMON
SALOON
SALTON
SAMSON
SARGON
SARTON
SEASON
SEATON
SERMON
SETSON
SEWNON
SEWSON
SEXTON
SHARON
SHIMON
SIGNON
SIMEON
SIPHON
SITSON
SLIPON
SOLDON
SOSOON
SPURON
STAYON
STEPON
STOLON
STYRON
SUMMON
SUTTON
SYPHON
TACKON
TAKEON
TALION
TARPON
TEFLON
TELLON
TENDON
TEUTON
TIGLON
TOLDON
TOOKON
TOULON
TRIGON
TRITON
TROGON
TRYLON
TUCSON
TURNON
TYCOON
UNISON
VERDON
VERNON
VILLON
VINTON
VISION
WAGGON
WAITON
WALKON
WALTON
WANTON
WATSON
WAYLON
WEAPON
WENTON
WESSON
WILSON
WILTON
WONTON
WOREON
WORKON
WYNTON
YANGON

YAUPON
ZIRCON

OO••••
OOCYTE
OODLES
OOHING
OOLALA
OOLITE
OOLITH
OOLOGY
OOLONG
OOMPAH
OOZIER
OOZILY
OOZING

O•O•••
OBOIST
ODONTO
ODOURS
OPORTO
OROIDE
OROMOS
OROZCO
OTOOLE
OVOIDS
OZONIC

O••O••
OBLONG
OCLOCK
OCTOPI
ODIOUS
OENONE
OGDOAD
OHIOAN
ONFOOT
ONHOLD
ONIONS
ONIONY
ONLOAN
ONTOUR
OOLOGY
OOLONG
OPPOSE
OPTOUT
ORIOLE
ORLOPS
ORMOLU
ORMOND
OSBORN
OSGOOD
OSMOND
OSMOSE
OTIOSE
OTOOLE
OXBOWS
OXFORD

O•••O•
OBERON
OCELOT
OCTROI
ODDJOB
ODDLOT
ODDSON
OLDBOY
OLESON
ONFOOT
OPTFOR
OPTION
ORATOR
OREGON

ORISON
OROMOS
OSGOOD
OUTBOX
OUTFOX
OXYDOL

O••••O
OBISPO
OCTAVO
ODONTO
OLDPRO
OLINGO
ONETWO
OPENTO
OPORTO
OROZCO
ORSINO
OSWEGO
OTELLO
OVERDO
OVIEDO

•OO•••
BOOBOO
BOODLE
BOOGIE
BOOHOO
BOOING
BOOJUM
BOOKED
BOOKER
BOOKIE
BOOMED
BOOMER
BOOSTS
BOOTED
BOOTEE
BOOTES
BOOTHE
BOOTHS
BOOTIE
BOOTSY
BOOTUP
COODER
COOERS
COOGAN
COOING
COOKED
COOKER
COOKIE
COOKUP
COOLED
COOLER
COOLIT
COOLLY
COONEY
COOPED
COOPER
COOPTS
COOPUP
COOTER
COOTIE
DOOBIE
DOODAD
DOODAH
DOODLE
DOOFUS
DOOGIE
DOOLEY
DOOMED
DOOWOP
DOOZIE
FOODIE

FOOLED
FOOLER
FOOTED
FOOTER
FOOZLE
GOOBER
GOODBY
GOODEN
GOODIE
GOODLY
GOODOH
GOOFED
GOOFUP
GOOGLE
GOOGLY
GOOGOL
GOOGOO
GOOIER
GOOSED
GOOSES
GOOSEY
GOOVER
HOODED
HOODOO
HOOFED
HOOFER
HOOFIT
HOOHAH
HOOHAS
HOOKAH
HOOKED
HOOKUP
HOOPED
HOOPER
HOOPLA
HOOPLE
HOOPOE
HOORAH
HOORAY
HOOTAT
HOOTCH
HOOTED
HOOTER
HOOTIE
HOOVER
HOOVES
KOOKIE
KOONTZ
LOOFAH
LOOFAS
LOOIES
LOOKAT
LOOKED
LOOKER
LOOKIN
LOOKON
LOOKTO
LOOKUP
LOOMED
LOONEY
LOONIE
LOOPED
LOOPER
LOOSED
LOOSEN
LOOSER
LOOSES
LOOTED
LOOTER
MOOING
MOOLAH
MOONED
MOONEY
MOORED
MOOTED
NOODLE
NOONAN
NOONES
NOOSED
NOOSES
NOOTKA
POODLE
POOHED
POOLED
POOPED
POORER
POORLY
ROOFED
ROOFER
ROOKED
ROOKIE
ROOMED
ROOMER
ROOMIE
ROONEY
ROOSTS
ROOTED
ROOTER
SOONER
SOOTHE
TOOBAD
TOOKIN
TOOKIT
TOOKON
TOOKTO
TOOKUP
TOOLED
TOOLUP
TOONIE
TOOTED
TOOTER
TOOTHY
TOOTLE
TOOTOO
TOOTSY
VOODOO
WOODED
WOODEN
WOODSY
WOOERS
WOOFED
WOOFER
WOOGIE
WOOING
WOOKIE
WOOLEN
WOOLEY
WOOLLY
YOOHOO
ZOOIDS
ZOOMED
ZOOMIN

•O•O••

BODONI
BOGONG
BOGOTA
BOSONS
BOWOAR
BOWOUT
COCOAS
COCOON
CODONS
COHORT
COHOST
COLONS
COLONY
COLORS
COLOUR
CONOCO
CONOID
COPOUT
CORONA
COYOTE
DODODO
DODOES
DODOMA
DOGONS
DOGOOD
DOLORS
DOLOUR
DONORS
FOBOFF
GODOWN
GOHOME
GONOGO
GOSOFT
GOTOFF
GOTOIT
GOTOUT
HOBOES
HOHOHO
HONORE
HONORS
HONOUR
HOPOFF
IOMOTH
JOCOSE
JOHORE
JOJOBA
JOYOUS
KOBOLD
KOKOMO
KOMODO
KOSOVO
LOGOFF
LOGOUT
LOMOND
LOYOLA
MODOCS
MOHOCK
MOLOCH
MOLOPO
MONODY
MORONI
MORONS
MOROSE
MOTORS
MOTOWN
NOBODY
NODOFF
NODOSE
NOGOOD
NOLOAD
NOLOSE
NOMORE
NOSOAP
OOLOGY
OOLONG
POBOYS
POCONO
POMONA
POPOFF
POPOUT
POROUS
POTOSI
ROBOTS
ROCOCO
ROMOLA
ROTORS
SOLOED
SOLONG
SONOMA
SONORA
SOPORS
SOSOON
SOTOLS
TOBOOT
TOPOFF
TOPOUT
TOROID
TOROSE
TOYONS
TOYOTA
VOROUS
WONOUT
WOVOKA
YOHOHO
YOYOED
YOYOMA

•O••O•

BOFFOS
BOLTON
BONBON
BONGOS
BONMOT
BONTON
BOOBOO
BOOHOO
BOREON
BORROW
BORZOI
BOSTON
BOTTOM
BOUBOU
BOWWOW
BOXBOY
BOXTOP
COCOON
COELOM
COLLOP
COLLOQ
COMBOS
COMEON
COMMON
COMPOS
CONDOR
CONDOS
CONGOU
CONJOB
CONNOR
CONROY
CONVOY
CORDON
COSMOS
COTTON
COUPON
COWBOY
COWPOX
DOBROS
DOBSON
DOCTOR
DOGDOM
DOGOOD
DOLLOP
DONJON
DOOWOP
DOTEON
DOWNON
FOETOR
FOGBOW
FOLIOS
FOLLOW
FOLSOM
FORGOT
GODSON
GOESON
GOODOH
GOOGOL
GOOGOO
GORDON
GORGON
GOSLOW
GOUNOD
HOBNOB
HOBSON
HOLDON
HOLLOW
HOODOO
HOOPOE
HORROR
HORTON
HOTBOX
HOTDOG
HOTPOT
HOTROD
HOWNOW
HOWTOS
JOBHOP
JOBLOT
JOLIOT
JOLSON
JONSON
KOWTOW
LOCKON
LOGION
LOGSON
LOLLOP
LOMBOK
LONDON
LONNOL
LOOKON
LOTION
LOTTOS
LOWBOY
MONGOL
MONROE
MOPTOP
MORION
MORMON
MORROW
MORTON
MOSCOW
MOTION
MOTMOT
MOTTOS
MOUTON
MOVEON
NOGOOD
NOIRON
NONCOM
NORTON
NOSHOW
NOTION
NOTNOW
POIROT
POISON
POLLOI
POLPOT
POMPOM
POMPON
POPTOP
POSTON
POTION
POTTOS
POWWOW
ROBROY
ROBSON
RODEOS
ROLEOS
ROLLON
ROMEOS
RONDOS
ROSCOE
ROSTOV
SOLDON
SORROW
SORTOF
SOSOON
TOBOOT
TOLDOF
TOLDON
TOMBOY
TOMTOM
TONDOS
TOOKON
TOOTOO
TOPDOG
TOPJOB
TORPOR
TORSOS
TOULON
TOYDOG
VOLVOX
VOODOO
VOSTOK
VOXPOP
WONTON
WOREON
WORKON
YOBBOS
YOMTOV
YOOHOO

•O•••O

BOCHCO
BOINGO
BOLERO
BONITO
BOOBOO
BOOHOO
BORAXO
BORNEO
COGITO
COLUGO
COMETO
CONOCO
DODODO
DOMINO
DORADO
DOSIDO
EOIPSO
FOREGO
GOINTO
GOLINO
GONOGO
GOOGOO
HOHOHO
HOLDTO
HONCHO
HOODOO
HOVETO
JOURNO
KOKOMO
KOMODO
KOSOVO
LOOKTO
MODULO
MOLOPO
MONACO
MORENO
MORPHO
NONEGO
NOVATO
POCONO
POMELO
PONCHO
POTATO
ROBALO
ROCOCO
ROMANO
ROMERO
ROTHKO
SOASTO
SOMATO
SOWETO
TOBAGO
TODDAO
TOLEDO
TOMATO
TOOKTO
TOOTOO
TORERO
TORINO
VOODOO
YOHOHO
YOOHOO

••OO••

BLOODY
BLOOEY
BLOOMS
BLOOMY
BLOOPS
BROOCH
BROODS
BROODY
BROOKE
BROOKS
BROOKY
BROOMS
BROOMY
CHOOSE
CHOOSY
CHOOYU
CROOKS
CROONS
DROOLS
DROOLY
DROOPS
DROOPY
FLOODS
FLOOEY
FLOORS
GLOOMS
GLOOMY
GROOMS
GROOVE
GROOVY
KLOOFS
OTOOLE
PHOOEY
PROOFS
SCOOPS
SCOOTS
SHOOED
SHOOIN
SHOOKS
SHOOTS
SLOOPS
SMOOCH
SMOOTH
SNOODS
SNOOKS
SNOOKY
SNOOPS
SNOOPY
SNOOTS
SNOOTY
SNOOZE
SNOOZY
SPOOFS
SPOOKS
SPOOKY
SPOOLS
SPOONS
SPOONY
SPOORS
STOOGE
STOOKS
STOOLS
STOOLY
STOOPS
SWOONS
SWOOPS
SWOOSH
TROOPS
VROOMS
WHOOFS
WHOOPI
WHOOPS
WHOOSH

••O•O•

AGOROT
AMOSOZ
BOOBOO
BOOHOO
CHOLOS
CLOROX
CROTON
DOOWOP
DROMOI
DROMOS
DUOMOS
FYODOR
GNOMON
GOODOH
GOOGOL
GOOGOO
GROTON
GROWON
HOODOO
HOOPOE
IROBOT
IRONON
ISOGON
ISOPOD
KRONOR
LOOKON
OROMOS
PHOBOS
PHONON
PHONOS
PHOTOG
PHOTON
PHOTOS
PROLOG
PROMOS
PROTON
SHOLOM
STOLON
TOOKON
TOOTOO
TROGON
VOODOO
YOOHOO

••O••O

ALONSO
ALONZO
APOLLO
BIOBIO
BLOTTO
BOOBOO
BOOHOO
BRONCO
CLOTHO
FLORIO
GIOTTO
GLOSSO
GOOGOO
GRODNO
GROSSO
GROTTO
HOODOO
IDOIDO
ILOILO
KUOPIO
LOOKTO
ODONTO
OPORTO
OROZCO
PRONTO
SCOTTO
SHORTO
STOJKO
TOOKTO
TOOTOO
TROPPO
VOODOO
WHOMSO
YOOHOO

•••OO•

ABLOOM
ASWOON
ATWOOD
BABOON
BEHOOF
BETOOK
COCOON
DOGOOD
DRHOOK
EDWOOD
ELWOOD
ENROOT
EXMOOR
FAZOOL
FTROOP
GALOOT
IGLOOS
INDOOR
KABOOM
KAZOOS
LAGOON
MAROON
MRCOOL
NANOOK
NOGOOD
ONFOOT
OSGOOD
REBOOT
REHOOK
RETOOK
RETOOL
SALOON
SCHOOL
SCROOP
SHBOOM
SOSOON
TABOOS
TOBOOT
TYCOON
UNCOOL
UNHOOK
UNMOOR
UNROOT
UPROOT
WAHOOS
YAHOOS

•••O•O

ALIOTO
ARIOSO
ARROYO
BAROLO
CHLORO
CHROMO
CHRONO
CONOCO
DENOVO
DESOTO
DEVOTO
DODODO
ENTOMO
ESPOSO
EXVOTO
FLUORO
GIGOLO
GONOGO
HOHOHO
INTOTO
KIMONO
KOKOMO
KOMODO
KOSOVO
MOLOPO
MRMOTO
NICOLO
POCONO
REBOZO
ROCOCO
SUNOCO
YOHOHO

••••OO

AHCHOO
BAMBOO
BOOBOO
BOOHOO
BURGOO
CUCKOO
GOOGOO
HALLOO
HOODOO
KARROO
MCADOO
SCHMOO
TATTOO
TOOTOO
VOODOO
YOOHOO

OP••••

OPAQUE
OPENED
OPENER
OPENLY
OPENTO
OPENUP
OPERAS
OPHITE
OPIATE
OPINED
OPINER
OPINES
OPORTO
OPPOSE
OPPUGN
OPTFOR
OPTICS
OPTIMA
OPTING
OPTION
OPTOUT
OPUSES

O•P•••

OPPOSE
OPPUGN
ORPHAN
ORPHIC
ORPINE
OSPREY

O••P••

OILPAN
OKAPIS
OLDPRO
ONSPEC
OOMPAH
OUTPUT

O•••P•

OBISPO
OCCUPY
OCTOPI
ONEUPS
ONTAPE
ORLOPS
OXLIPS

O••••P

OPENUP
OWNSUP

•OP•••

BOPEEP
BOPPED
BOPPER
COPAYS
COPIED
COPIER
COPIES
COPING
COPLEY
COPOUT
COPPED
COPPER
COPSES
COPTER
COPTIC
COPULA
DOPANT
DOPIER
DOPING
GOPHER
HOPERS
HOPING
HOPOFF
HOPPED
HOPPER
HOPPLE
HOPSIN
HOPSUP
JOPLIN
KOPECK
KOPEKS
KOPJES
KOPPEL
LOPERS
LOPING
LOPPED
LOPPER
MOPEDS
MOPERS
MOPERY
MOPIER
MOPING
MOPISH
MOPPED
MOPPER
MOPPET
MOPSUP
MOPTOP
MOPUPS
NOPETS
POPART
POPEYE
POPFLY
POPGUN
POPLAR
POPLIN
POPOFF
POPOUT
POPPAS
POPPED
POPPER
POPPET
POPPLE
POPSIN
POPSUP
POPTOP
POPULI
POPUPS
ROPEIN
ROPERS
ROPIER
ROPING
SOPHIA
SOPHIE
SOPORS
SOPPED
SOPSUP
TOPCAT
TOPDOG
TOPEKA
TOPERS
TOPGUN
TOPHAT
TOPHUS
TOPICS
TOPJOB
TOPOFF
TOPOUT
TOPPED
TOPPER
TOPPLE
TOPTEN

•O•P••

BOPPED
BOPPER
COAPTS
COMPAQ
COMPEL
COMPLY
COMPOS
COOPED
COOPER
COOPTS
COOPUP
COPPED
COPPER
CORPUS
COUPES
COUPLE
COUPON
COWPEA
COWPER
COWPOX
COYPUS
EOIPSO
GOSPEL
HOOPED
HOOPER
HOOPLA
HOOPLE
HOOPOE
HOPPED
HOPPER
HOPPLE
HOTPOT
KOPPEL
LOOPED
LOOPER
LOPPED
LOPPER
LOUPES
MOPPED
MOPPER
MOPPET
MORPHO
MORPHS
MORPHY
OOMPAH
POLPOT
POMPEY
POMPOM
POMPON
POOPED
POPPAS
POPPED
POPPER
POPPET
POPPLE
POTPIE
ROMPED
ROMPER
SOAPED
SOAPER
SOPPED
SOUPUP
TOPPED
TOPPER
TOPPLE
TORPID
TORPOR
TOUPEE
VOXPOP
WOLPER

•O••P•

FOURPM
JOSEPH
MOLOPO
MOPUPS
POLYPS
POPUPS

•O•••P

BOBSUP
BONEUP
BOOTUP
BOPEEP
BOREUP
BOXTOP
COILUP
COLLOP
COMEUP
COOKUP
COOPUP
DOESUP
DOLLOP
DOLLUP
DOMREP
DONEUP
DOOWOP
FOGSUP
FOLDUP
FOULUP
GOESUP
GOOFUP
GOSSIP
HOLDUP
HOLEUP
HOOKUP
HOPSUP
HOTCAP
HOTTIP
JOBHOP
JOINUP
LOCKUP
LOLLOP
LOOKUP
MOBCAP
MOCKUP
MOPSUP
MOPTOP
MOVEUP
NOSOAP
PONYUP
POPSUP
POPTOP
ROLLUP
SOAKUP
SOPSUP
SOUPUP
TOECAP
TOETAP
TONEUP
TOOKUP
TOOLUP
TOREUP
TOSSUP
TOTSUP
VOXPOP
WOKEUP
WORKUP

••OP••

ADOPTS
BHOPAL
CHOPIN
CHOPPY
CHOPRA
COOPED
COOPER
COOPTS
COOPUP
CROPUP
DROPBY
DROPIN
DROPIT
ELOPED
ELOPER
ELOPES
EPOPEE
FLOPPY
FLOPSY
GLOPPY
GROPED
GROPES
HOOPED
HOOPER
HOOPLA
HOOPLE
HOOPOE
ISOPOD
KUOPIO
LOOPED
LOOPER
MYOPES
MYOPIA
MYOPIC
PEOPLE
POOPED
PROPEL
PROPER
PROPRE
PROPUP
REOPEN
SCOPED
SCOPES
SHOPPE
SKOPJE
SLOPED
SLOPES
SLOPPY
SNOPES
STOPES
STOPIN
STOPIT
STOPUP
TROPES
TROPEZ
TROPHY
TROPIC
TROPPO
TWOPLY
UNOPEN
USOPEN
UTOPIA

••O•P•

ADOLPH
BLOOPS
CHOMPS
CHOPPY
CLOMPS
CROUPY
DROOPS
DROOPY
FLOPPY
GLOPPY
GROUPS
PROMPT
SCOOPS
SHOPPE
SLOOPS
SLOPPY
SNOOPS
SNOOPY
STOMPS
STOOPS
STOUPS
SWOOPS
THORPE
THORPS
TROMPE
TROMPS
TROOPS
TROPPO
TROUPE
WHOMPS
WHOOPI
WHOOPS

••O••P

BLOWUP
BOOTUP
BUOYUP
CLOGUP
COOKUP
COOPUP
CROPUP
DOOWOP
GOOFUP
GROWUP
HOOKUP
LOOKUP
PROPUP
SHOTUP
SHOWUP
SLOWUP
STOPUP
TOOKUP
TOOLUP

•••OP•

ASLOPE
BEBOPS
BLOOPS
CANOPY
CHEOPS
DROOPS
DROOPY
ESTOPS
EUROPA
EUROPE
FSTOPS
GALOPS
JALOPY
MEROPE
METOPE
MOLOPO
OCTOPI
ORLOPS
PELOPS
RECOPY
REMOPS
RETOPS
SCOOPS
SLOOPS
SNOOPS
SNOOPY
STOOPS
STROPS
SWOOPS
SYSOPS
TROOPS
WHOOPI
WHOOPS
WICOPY

•••O•P

FTROOP
NOSOAP
RECOUP
SCROOP

••••OP

BARHOP
BIGTOP
BISHOP
BOXTOP
CARHOP
COLLOP
DETROP
DOLLOP
DOOWOP
DUNLOP

FTROOP
GALLOP
HIPHOP
HYSSOP
JOBHOP
LAPTOP
LOLLOP
MAYPOP
MOPTOP
PEGTOP
POPTOP
RAGMOP
RAGTOP
REDTOP
SCROOP
TIPTOP
UNSTOP
VOXPOP
WALLOP
WETMOP

O••Q••

OPAQUE

•OQ•••

COQUET
LOQUAT
TOQUES

•O•Q••

MOSQUE
TORQUE

•O•••Q

COLLOQ
COMPAQ
POSSLQ

••OQ••

CLOQUE
QUOQUE

••••OQ

COLLOQ

OR••••

ORACHS
ORACLE
ORALES
ORALLY
ORANGE
ORANGS
ORANGY
ORANTS
ORATED
ORATES
ORATOR
ORBACH
ORBING
ORBITS
ORCHID
ORCHIL
ORDAIN
ORDEAL
ORDERS
ORDURE
OREADS
OREGON
OREIDA
ORELSE
ORGANA
ORGANS
ORGATE
ORGEAT
ORGIES
ORIANA
ORIBIS
ORIELS
ORIENT
ORIGEN
ORIGIN
ORINGS
ORIOLE
ORISON
ORISSA
ORKNEY
ORLOPS
ORMOLU
ORMOND
ORNATE
ORNERY
ORNITH
OROIDE
OROMOS
OROZCO
ORPHAN
ORPHIC
ORPINE
ORRERY
ORSINO
ORTEGA
ORTLES
ORWELL
ORYXES

O•R•••

OARING
OBRIAN
OBRIEN
OCREAE
OERTER
OGRESS
OGRISH
ONRUSH
ORRERY

O••R••

OBERON
OCHRES
OCTROI
OILRIG
OMERTA
OPERAS
OPORTO
OSIRIS
OSPREY
OUTRAN
OUTRUN
OVERDO
OVERLY
OZARKS

O•••R•

OATERS
OBVERT
OCCURS
OCHERS
OCHERY
ODOURS
OEUVRE
OFFERS
OGLERS
OHENRY
OILERS
OLDPRO
OLEARY
ONFIRE
ONWARD
ORDERS
ORDURE
ORNERY
ORRERY
OSBORN
OSCARS
OSIERS
OTHERS
OTTERS
OUTCRY
OWNERS
OXCART
OXFORD
OXNARD

O••••R

OATIER
OBITER
OCULAR
OERTER
OILIER
OLIVER
ONAGER
ONTOUR
OOZIER
OPENER
OPINER
OPTFOR
ORATOR
OSTLER
OUSTER
OVULAR
OYSTER

•OR•••

AORIST
AORTAE
AORTAL
AORTAS
AORTIC
BORAGE
BORATE
BORAXO
BORDEN
BORDER
BOREAL
BOREAS
BOREON
BORERS
BOREUP
BORGIA
BORIDE
BORING
BORMAN
BORNEO
BORROW
BORSCH
BORZOI
CORALS
CORBAN
CORBEL
CORBIN
CORDAY
CORDED
CORDON
CORERS
CORGIS
CORING
CORIUM
CORKED
CORKER
CORMAN
CORNEA
CORNED
CORNEL
CORNER
CORNET
CORONA
CORPUS
CORRAL
CORREL
CORSET
CORTES
CORTEX
CORTEZ
CORVEE
CORVES
CORYZA
DORADO
DORAGS
DORATI
DORCAS
DOREMI
DORIAN
DORIES
DORMER
DORRIT
DORSAL
DORSET
DORSEY
DORSUM
FORAGE
FORAYS
FORBAD
FORBES
FORBID
FORCED
FORCER
FORCES
FORDED
FOREGO
FOREST
FORGED
FORGER
FORGES
FORGET
FORGOT
FORINT
FORKED
FORKER
FORMAL
FORMAN
FORMAT
FORMED
FORMER
FORMIC
FORTAS
FORTES
FORUMS
GORALS
GORDIE
GORDON
GORGED
GORGES
GORGET
GORGON
GORIER
GORILY
GORING
GORSES
HORACE
HORDES
HORMEL
HORMUZ
HORNED
HORNER
HORNET
HORNEY
HORNIN
HORRID
HORROR
HORSED
HORSES
HORSEY
HORTON
JORDAN
JORUMS
KORATS
KORBUT
KOREAN
KORMAN
KORUNA
LORAIN
LORDED
LORDLY
LOREAL
LORENZ
LORICA
LORIES
MORALE
MORALS
MORANT
MORASS
MORAVA
MORAYS
MORBID
MOREAU
MOREEN
MORELS
MORENO
MORGAN
MORGEN
MORION
MORITA
MORITZ
MORLEY
MORMON
MORNAY
MORONI
MORONS
MOROSE
MORPHO
MORPHS
MORPHY
MORRIS
MORROW
MORSEL
MORTAL
MORTAR
MORTON
NORDIC
NORGAY
NORIAS
NORMAL
NORMAN
NORRIS
NORTHS
NORTON
NORWAY
PORING
PORKER
POROUS
PORTAL
PORTED
PORTER
PORTIA
PORTLY
SORBET
SORBIC
SORDID
SORELY
SOREST
SORREL
SORROW
SORTED
SORTER
SORTIE
SORTOF
TORAHS
TORCHY
TOREAT
TORERO
TOREUP
TORIES
TORINO
TOROID
TOROSE
TORPID
TORPOR
TORQUE
TORRES
TORREY
TORRID
TORSOS
TORTES
VOROUS
VORTEX
WORDED
WOREON
WORKED
WORKER
WORKIN
WORKON
WORKUP
WORLDS
WORMED
WORSEN
WORSTS
WORTHS
WORTHY
YORICK
YORKER
YORKIE
YORUBA
ZORILS

•O•R••

BOARDS
BORROW
BOTREE
BOURKE
BOURNE
BOURSE
COARSE
COBRAS
COERCE
CONRAD
CONROY
CORRAL
CORREL
COURIC
COURSE
COURTS
COWRIE
DOBRAS
DOBROS
DOMREP
DORRIT
DOURER
DOURLY
FOURAM
FOURPM
FOURTH
GOURDE
GOURDS
HOARDS
HOARSE
HOORAH
HOORAY
HORRID
HORROR
HOTROD
HOURIS
HOURLY
JOURNO
KONRAD
MOIRES
MONROE
MOORED
MORRIS
MORROW
MOURNS
NOIRON
NORRIS
POIROT
POORER
POORLY
POURED
POURER
POURIN
ROARED
ROARER
ROBROY
ROURKE
SOARED
SOARER
SOARES
SOIREE
SORREL
SORROW
SOURCE
SOURED
SOURER
SOURLY
TOBRUK
TORRES
TORREY
TORRID
TOURED
TOURER

•O••R•

BOGART
BOLERO
BONERS
BORERS
BOVARY
BOWERS
BOWERY
BOXERS
BOYARS
COBURG
COBURN
CODERS
COHERE
COHORT
COLORS
COMERS
CONTRA
CONTRE
CONURE
COOERS
CORERS
COVERS
COVERT
COWARD
COWERS
DOLORS
DONORS
DOSERS
DOTARD
DOWERS
DOWERY
DOZERS
FOYERS
GOAWRY
GOCART
GODARD
GOFERS
GOKART
GONERS
GOVERN
HOBART
HOMBRE
HOMERS
HONORE
HONORS
HOPERS
HOVERS
HOWARD
JOHORE
JOKERS
LONERS
LOPERS
LOSERS
LOUVRE
LOVERS
LOWERS
LOWERY
MODERN
MOHURS
MOLARS
MONERA
MOPERS
MOPERY
MOTHRA
MOTORS
MOVERS
MOWERS
MOYERS
MOZART
NOMORE
NONARY
NOTARY
NOTERS
POETRY
POKERS
POKERY
POLERS
POPART
POSERS
POWERS
ROBERT
ROGERS
ROMERO
ROPERS
ROSARY
ROSTRA
ROTARY
ROTORS
ROVERS
ROWERS
SOBERS
SOEURS
SOLARS
SOLERS
SOMBRE
SOMERS
SONORA
SOPORS
SOUARI
SOWERS
SOXERS
TONERS
TOPERS
TORERO
TOTERS
TOWARD
TOWERS
TOWERY
VOLARE
VOTARY
VOTERS
VOWERS
WOOERS
YOGURT

•O•••R

BOATER
BOBBER
BOILER
BOLDER
BOLGER
BOMBER
BONIER
BOOKER
BOOMER
BOPPER
BORDER
BOTHER
BOVVER
BOWLER
BOWOAR
BOWSER
BOWYER
BOXCAR
BOXIER
COALER
COAXER
COCKER
CODGER
COFFER
COHEIR
COINER
COKIER
COLDER
COLLAR
COLOUR
COLTER
COMBER
CONCUR
CONDOR
CONFER
CONGER
CONKER
CONNER
CONNOR
COODER
COOKER
COOLER
COOPER
COOTER
COPIER
COPPER
COPTER
CORKER
CORNER
COSIER
COSTAR
COTTER
COUGAR
COUTER
COWPER
COZIER
DOBBER
DOCKER
DOCTOR
DODDER
DODGER
DOGEAR
DOGGER
DOLLAR
DOLOUR
DONDER
DONNER
DOPIER
DORMER
DOSSER
DOURER
DOWNER
DOWSER
DOZIER
FODDER
FOETOR
FOGGER
FOKKER
FOLDER
FOLIAR
FONDER
FOOLER
FOOTER
FORCER
FORGER
FORKER
FORMER
FOSTER
FOULER
FOWLER
FOXIER
GOLFER
GOOBER
GOOIER
GOOVER
GOPHER
GORIER
GOUGER
HOAXER
HOKIER
HOLDER
HOLIER
HOLLER
HOMIER
HONKER
HONOUR
HOOFER
HOOPER
HOOTER
HOOVER
HOPPER
HORNER
HORROR
HOSIER
HOTAIR
HOTCAR
HOTTER
HOTWAR
HOWLER
JOBBER
JOGGER
JOINER
JOKIER
JOSSER
JOYNER
KOHLER
KOSHER
KOTTER
LOADER
LOAFER
LOANER
LOBBER
LOCKER
LODGER
LOGGER
LOGIER
LOITER
LONGER
LOOKER
LOOPER
LOOSER
LOOTER
LOPPER
LOTHAR
LOUDER
LOUVER
MOANER
MOCKER
MOHAIR
MOILER
MOLDER
MOLNAR
MOLTER
MONGER
MOPIER
MOPPER
MORTAR
MOSHER
MOTHER
MOUSER
NOBLER
NOSHER
NOSIER
OOZIER
POKIER
POLDER
POLLER
PONDER
POORER
POPLAR
POPPER
PORKER
PORTER
POSEUR
POSHER
POSTER
POTHER
POTTER
POURER
POUTER
POWDER
ROAMER
ROARER
ROBBER
ROCKER
ROHMER
ROLLER
ROMPER
ROOFER
ROOMER
ROOTER
ROPIER
ROSIER
ROSTER
ROTTER
ROUSER
ROUTER
ROZZER
SOAKER
SOAPER
SOARER
SOBBER
SOCCER
SOFTER
SOLDER
SOLVER
SOMBER
SOMMER
SOONER
SORTER
SOURER
SOUTER
TOILER
TONIER
TOOTER
TOPPER
TORPOR
TOSSER
TOTHER
TOTTER
TOURER
TOUTER
TOWCAR
TOWNER
WOHLER
WOLPER
WONDER
WOOFER
WORKER
WOWSER
YONDER
YORKER
ZONKER

••OR••

ABORAL
ABORTS
ACORNS
ADORED
ADOREE
ADORER
ADORES
ADORNS
AGORAE
AGORAS
AGOROT
AMORAL
ANORAK
AZORES
AZORIN
CEORLS
CHORAL
CHORDS
CHORES
CHORUS
CLORIS
CLOROX
DVORAK
FIORDS
FJORDS
FLORAE
FLORAL
FLORAS
FLORES
FLORET
FLORID
FLORIN
FLORIO
GEORGE
GEORGY
GLORIA
HOORAH
HOORAY
ILORIN
MAORIS
MOORED
OPORTO
PEORIA
POORER
POORLY
QUORUM
SCORCH
SCORED
SCORER
SCORES
SCORIA
SCORNS
SFORZA
SHORAN
SHORED
SHORES
SHORTA
SHORTE
SHORTI
SHORTO
SHORTS
SHORTU
SHORTY
SKORTS
SNORED
SNORER
SNORES
SNORTS
SPORES
SPORTS
SPORTY
STORCH
STORED
STORER
STORES
STOREY
STORKS
STORMS
STORMY
STORRS
SWORDS
THORAX
THORNS
THORNY
THORPE
THORPS
WHORLS

••O•R•

ABOARD
AMOURS
CHOIRS
CHOPRA
COOERS
FLOORS
FLOURS
FLOURY
ODOURS
PROPRE
SCOURS
SHOERS
SPOORS
STORRS
WOOERS

••O••R

ADORER
ALOMAR
AVOWER
BLOWER
BOOKER
BOOMER
BROKER
CHOKER
CHOLER
CLOSER
CLOVER
COODER
COOKER
COOLER
COOPER
COOTER
CROWER
DEODAR
DRONER
DROVER
ELOPER
EMOTER
EVOKER
FLOWER
FOOLER
FOOTER
FYODOR
GAOLER
GLOVER
GLOWER
GOOBER
GOOIER
GOOVER
GROCER
GROVER
GROWER
HOOFER
HOOPER
HOOTER
HOOVER
IRONER
ISOBAR
ISOMER
KNOWER
KRONER
KRONOR
KRONUR
LOOKER
LOOPER
LOOSER
LOOTER
PLOVER
PLOWER
POORER
PROBER
PROPER
PROSER
PROVER
QUOTER
RIOTER
ROOFER
ROOMER
ROOTER
SCORER
SCOTER
SHOFAR
SHOVER
SHOWER
SLOWER
SMOKER
SNORER
SOONER
STOKER
STONER
STORER
STOVER
TOOTER
TROCAR
TWOFER
WOOFER

•••OR•

ABHORS
ABSORB
ACCORD
ACTORS
ADSORB
AFFORD
ALBORG
ALGORE
ANGORA
ARBORS
ARDORS
ARMORS
ARMORY
ASHORE
ASSORT
ATWORK
AURORA
BEFORE
BICORN
BYWORD
CAVORT
CHLORO
COHORT
COLORS
CYBORG
DAMORE
DECORS
DEFORM
DEHORN
DEPORT
DOLORS
DONORS
EEYORE
EFFORT
ELMORE
ENCORE
ENDORA
EPHORI
EPHORS
ERRORS
ESCORT
EUDORA
EXHORT
EXMORE
EXPORT
EXTORT
FAVORS
FEDORA
FEMORA
FLOORS
FLUORO
FURORE
FURORS
GALORE
GATORS
HONORE
HONORS
HUMORS
IGNORE
IMPORT
INBORN
INDORE
INFORM
INPORT
JOHORE
JURORS
KIDORY
LABORS
LAHORE
LENORE
MAJORS
MALORY
MANORS
MAYORS
MEMORY
MIDORI
MILORD
MINORS
MOTORS
MYSORE
MYWORD
NABORS
NOMORE
OSBORN
OXFORD
PRIORI
PRIORS
PRIORY
RAZORS
REBORN
RECORD
RECORK
REFORM
REMORA
REPORT
RESORB
RESORT
RETORT
REWORD
REWORK
RIGORS
ROTORS
RUMORS
SAPORS
SATORI
SAVORS
SAVORY
SCHORL
SENORA
SENORS
SONORA
SOPORS
SPOORS
SUBORN
TABORS
TAGORE
TENORS
THEORY
TUDORS
TUTORS
UNBORN
UNCORK
UNTORN
UNWORN
VAPORS
VAPORY
VIGORS
VISORS
VYBORG
ZADORA

•••O•R

ARBOUR
ARDOUR
ARMOUR
BOWOAR
COLOUR
DAMOUR
DETOUR
DEVOIR
DEVOUR
DOLOUR
EXMOOR
FAVOUR
HONOUR
HUMOUR
INDOOR
INPOUR
LABOUR
LAMOUR
LATOUR
MEMOIR
ONTOUR
RENOIR
RETOUR

REVOIR
RIGOUR
RUMOUR
SAVOIR
SAVOUR
UNDOER
UNMOOR
UPROAR
VALOUR
VAPOUR
VELOUR
VETOER
VIGOUR

••••OR
AIMFOR
ALLFOR
AMAJOR
AMINOR
ANCHOR
ANGKOR
ASKFOR
AUTHOR
BAILOR
BANGOR
BAYLOR
BETTOR
BMAJOR
BMINOR
CANDOR
CANTOR
CAPTOR
CASTOR
CAWDOR
CENSOR
CHADOR
CLAMOR
CMAJOR
CMINOR
CONDOR
CONNOR
CURSOR
DEBTOR
DMAJOR
DMINOR
DOCTOR
EDITOR
ELINOR
EMAJOR
EMINOR
EMPTOR
ENAMOR
ETUXOR
EXMOOR
FACTOR
FERVOR
FLAVOR
FLEXOR
FMAJOR
FMINOR
FOETOR
FYODOR
GAYNOR
GLAMOR
GMAJOR
GMINOR
GREGOR
GUNFOR
HARBOR
HATHOR
HECTOR
HORROR
INDOOR
ISADOR
JUNIOR
KANTOR
KRONOR
LAYFOR
LECTOR
LESSOR
LICTOR
LIQUOR
LUTHOR
MAHZOR
MENTOR
METEOR
MIRROR
NESTOR
OPTFOR
ORATOR
PALLOR
PARLOR
PASTOR
PAYFOR
PLEXOR
RANCOR
RANFOR
RAPTOR
RECTOR
RHETOR
RUNFOR
SAILOR
SALVOR
SAVIOR
SECTOR
SENHOR
SENIOR
SENSOR
SIGNOR
STATOR
STUPOR
SUCCOR
SUITOR
TAILOR
TAYLOR
TENSOR
TERROR
TORPOR
TREMOR
TREVOR
TRYFOR
TURGOR
UNMOOR
VECTOR
VENDOR
VICTOR
WINSOR

OS••••
OSAGES
OSBORN
OSCARS
OSCINE
OSCULA
OSGOOD
OSHAWA
OSIERS
OSIRIS
OSMICS
OSMIUM
OSMOND
OSMOSE
OSMUND
OSPREY
OSSEIN
OSSETE
OSSIAN
OSSIFY
OSTEAL
OSTEND
OSTIUM
OSTLER
OSWALD
OSWEGO

O•S•••
OBSESS
OBSTET
OKSANA
ONSALE
ONSETS
ONSIDE
ONSITE
ONSPEC
ORSINO
OSSEIN
OSSETE
OSSIAN
OSSIFY
OUSELS
OUSTED
OUSTER
OYSTER

O••S••
OBISPO
OCASEK
OCASEY
ODDSON
ODESSA
ODISTS
OFFSET
OLDSAW
OLESON
OMASUM
ONUSES
OPUSES
ORISON
ORISSA
OUTSET
OVISAC
OWNSUP

O•••S•
OAFISH
OBLAST
OBOIST
OBSESS
OBTEST
OBTUSE
ODDEST
ODENSE
ODESSA
OFFISH
OGRESS
OGRISH
OLDEST
OLDISH
ONRUSH
OPPOSE
ORELSE
ORISSA
OSMOSE
OTIOSE
OWLISH

O••••S
OATERS
OBEAHS
OBELUS
OBSESS
OCCURS
OCEANS
OCHERS
OCHRES
OCTADS
OCTETS
ODIOUS
ODISTS
ODIUMS
ODOURS
OFFERS
OGHAMS
OGIVES
OGLERS
OGRESS
OILERS
OKAPIS
OLDIES
OLIVES
OLMECS
OMAHAS
OMANIS
OMEGAS
ONEUPS
ONIONS
ONSETS
ONUSES
ONYXES
OODLES
OPERAS
OPINES
OPTICS
OPUSES
ORACHS
ORALES
ORANGS
ORANTS
ORATES
ORBITS
ORDERS
OREADS
ORGANS
ORGIES
ORIBIS
ORIELS
ORINGS
ORLOPS
OROMOS
ORTLES
ORYXES
OSAGES
OSCARS
OSIERS
OSIRIS
OSMICS
OTHERS
OTITIS
OTTERS
OUGHTS
OUNCES
OUSELS
OUZELS
OVOIDS
OVULES
OWLETS
OWNERS
OXALIS
OXBOWS
OXEYES
OXIDES
OXLIPS
OZARKS

•OS•••
BOSKET
BOSLEY
BOSNIA
BOSONS
BOSSED
BOSSES
BOSTON
BOSUNS
COSELL
COSHED
COSHES
COSIED
COSIER
COSIES
COSIGN
COSILY
COSINE
COSMIC
COSMOS
COSSET
COSTAE
COSTAL
COSTAR
COSTAS
COSTLY
DOSAGE
DOSERS
DOSIDO
DOSING
DOSSAL
DOSSED
DOSSEL
DOSSER
DOSSES
EOSINS
FOSSAE
FOSSAS
FOSSES
FOSSEY
FOSSIL
FOSTER
GOSHEN
GOSLOW
GOSOFT
GOSPEL
GOSSIP
GOSTAG
HOSELS
HOSIER
HOSING
HOSTAS
HOSTED
HOSTEL
HOSTLY
JOSEPH
JOSHED
JOSHES
JOSHUA
JOSIAH
JOSKIN
JOSSER
JOSSES
JOSTLE
KOSHER
KOSOVO
LOSEIT
LOSERS
LOSING
LOSSES
LOSTIT
MOSAIC
MOSCOW
MOSEYS
MOSHAV
MOSHED
MOSHER
MOSHES
MOSKVA
MOSLEM
MOSQUE
MOSSED
MOSSES
MOSTEL
MOSTLY
NOSALE
NOSHED
NOSHER
NOSHES
NOSHOW
NOSIER
NOSILY
NOSING
NOSOAP
POSADA
POSERS
POSEUR
POSHER
POSHLY
POSIES
POSING
POSITS
POSSES
POSSET
POSSLQ
POSSUM
POSTAL
POSTED
POSTER
POSTIT
POSTON
ROSARY
ROSCOE
ROSEAU
ROSIER
ROSILY
ROSINS
ROSINY
ROSITA
ROSTER
ROSTOV
ROSTRA
SOSOON
TOSSED
TOSSER
TOSSES
TOSSUP
VOSGES
VOSTOK

•O•S••
BOASTS
BOBSUP
BOLSHY
BONSAI
BOOSTS
BORSCH
BOSSED
BOSSES
BOUSED
BOUSES
BOWSAW
BOWSER
BOXSET
COASTS
COMSAT
CONSUL
COPSES
CORSET
COSSET
COUSIN
DOBSON
DOESBY
DOESIN
DOESNT
DOESUP
DOGSAT
DOGSIT
DORSAL
DORSET
DORSEY
DORSUM
DOSSAL
DOSSED
DOSSEL
DOSSER
DOSSES
DOUSED
DOUSES
DOWSED
DOWSER
DOWSES
FOCSLE
FOGSIN
FOGSUP
FOISTS
FOLSOM
FOSSAE
FOSSAS
FOSSES
FOSSEY
FOSSIL
GODSON
GOESAT
GOESBY
GOESIN
GOESON
GOESUP
GOOSED
GOOSES
GOOSEY
GORSES
GOSSIP
GOTSET
HOBSON
HOISTS
HONSHU
HOPSIN
HOPSUP
HORSED
HORSES
HORSEY
HOUSED
HOUSES
JOISTS
JOLSON
JONSON
JOSSER
JOSSES
JOUSTS
LOGSIN
LOGSON
LOOSED
LOOSEN
LOOSER
LOOSES
LOSSES
LOUSED
LOUSES
MOPSUP
MORSEL
MOSSED
MOSSES
MOUSED
MOUSER
MOUSES
MOUSEY
MOUSSE
NOESIS
NOISED
NOISES
NOOSED
NOOSES
POISED
POISES
POISON
POPSIN
POPSUP
POSSES
POSSET
POSSLQ
POSSUM
POUSSE
ROASTS
ROBSON
ROOSTS
ROUSED
ROUSER
ROUSES
ROUSTS
SOASTO
SOPSUP
SOUSED
SOUSES
TOASTS
TOASTY
TOCSIN
TOESIN
TONSIL
TORSOS
TOSSED
TOSSER
TOSSES
TOSSUP
TOTSUP
TOUSLE
WOLSEY
WORSEN
WORSTS
WOWSER
ZOYSIA

•O••S•
AORIST
BOOTSY
BOURSE
BOYISH
COARSE
COHOST
COURSE
COYEST
COYISH
DOVISH
EOIPSO
FOLKSY
FOREST
GOBUST
GOEASY
GOFISH
GOWEST
HOARSE
HOLISM
HOLIST
HONEST
IODISE
IONISE
JOCOSE
LOCUST
LOUISA
LOUISE
LOWEST
LOWISH
MODEST
MODISH
MOLEST
MONISM
MONIST
MOPISH
MORASS
MOROSE
MOUSSE
NODOSE
NOLESS
NOLOSE
NOWISE
POLISH
POTASH
POTOSI
POUSSE
ROBUST
SOREST
TONISH
TOOTSY
TOROSE
WOODSY
YOGISM

•O•••S
AODAIS
AORTAS
BOARDS
BOASTS
BODIES
BOFFOS
BOGEYS
BOGIES
BOGLES
BOITES
BOMBES
BONCES
BONERS
BONGOS
BONNES
BONZES
BOOSTS
BOOTES
BOOTHS
BOREAS
BORERS
BOSONS
BOSSES
BOSUNS
BOTELS
BOUGHS
BOULES
BOUNDS
BOUSES
BOVIDS
BOWERS
BOWLES
BOXERS
BOYARS
COAPTS
COASTS
COATIS
COAXES
COBIAS
COBRAS
COCCUS
COCOAS
CODERS
CODONS
COIGNS
COLEUS
COLIES
COLONS
COLORS
COMBES
COMBOS
COMERS
COMETS
COMICS
COMMAS
COMPOS
COMTES
CONCHS
CONDOS
CONEYS
CONGAS
CONICS
CONIES
CONTES
COOERS
COOPTS
COPAYS
COPIES
COPSES
CORALS
CORERS
CORGIS
CORPUS
CORTES
CORVES
COSHES
COSIES
COSMOS
COSTAS
COTTAS
COUGHS
COUNTS
COUPES
COURTS
COVENS
COVERS
COVETS
COVEYS
COWENS
COWERS
COYPUS
COZENS
COZIES
DOBLAS
DOBRAS
DOBROS
DODGES
DODOES
DOGEYS
DOGIES
DOGMAS
DOGONS
DOINGS
DOLMAS
DOLORS
DONEES
DONETS
DONNAS
DONORS
DONUTS
DOOFUS
DORAGS
DORCAS
DORIES
DOSERS
DOSSES
DOUBTS
DOUGHS
DOUSES
DOWELS
DOWERS
DOWSES
DOYENS
DOZENS
DOZERS
EOSINS
FOEHNS
FOETUS
FOGEYS
FOGIES
FOISTS
FOLIOS
FORAYS
FORBES
FORCES
FORGES
FORTAS
FORTES
FORUMS
FOSSAS
FOSSES
FOUNDS
FOUNTS
FOWLES
FOYERS
GOBIES
GODETS
GOFERS
GOINGS
GOLEMS
GONERS
GOOSES
GORALS
GORGES
GORSES
GOUGES
GOURDS
HOARDS
HOAXES
HOBBES
HOBOES
HODADS
HODGES
HOGANS
HOISTS
HOLMES
HOMERS
HONEYS
HONORS
HOOHAS
HOOVES
HOPERS
HORDES
HORSES
HOSELS
HOSTAS
HOTELS
HOUGHS
HOUNDS
HOURIS
HOUSES
HOVELS
HOVERS
HOWTOS
IONICS
IOWANS
JOINTS
JOISTS
JOKERS
JONAHS
JORUMS
JOSHES
JOSSES
JOULES
JOUSTS
JOYOUS
KOALAS
KOPEKS
KOPJES
KORATS
KOVACS
LOAVES
LOCALS
LODENS
LODGES
LONERS
LONGES
LOOFAS
LOOIES
LOOSES
LOPERS
LORIES
LOSERS
LOSSES
LOTAHS
LOTTOS
LOUGHS
LOUPES
LOUSES
LOVERS
LOWERS
MOBIUS
MOCHAS
MODELS
MODEMS
MODOCS
MOGULS
MOHURS
MOINES
MOIRES
MOLARS
MOMMAS
MONADS
MONEYS
MONIES
MONTES
MONTHS
MOPEDS
MOPERS
MOPUPS
MORALS
MORASS
MORAYS
MORELS
MORONS
MORPHS
MORRIS
MOSEYS
MOSHES
MOSSES
MOTELS
MOTETS
MOTIFS
MOTORS
MOTTOS
MOULDS
MOULTS
MOUNDS
MOUNTS
MOURNS
MOUSES
MOUTHS
MOVERS
MOVIES
MOWERS
MOYERS
NOBLES
NOESIS
NOHITS
NOISES
NOLENS
NOLESS
NOMADS
NONETS
NOONES
NOOSES
NOPETS
NORIAS
NORRIS
NORTHS
NOSHES
NOTERS
NOVELS
OODLES
POBOYS
POGIES
POILUS
POINTS
POISES
POKERS
POKEYS
POLERS
POLKAS
POLYPS
PONCES
PONIES
PONTES
PONTUS
POPPAS
POPUPS
POROUS
POSERS
POSIES
POSITS
POSSES
POTTOS
POULTS
POUNDS
POWERS
ROASTS
ROBINS
ROBLES
ROBOTS
RODEOS
ROGERS
ROGUES
ROLEOS
ROMANS
ROMEOS
RONDOS
ROOSTS
ROPERS
ROSINS
ROTORS
ROUGES
ROUGHS
ROUNDS
ROUSES
ROUSTS
ROUTES
ROVERS
ROWELS
ROWENS
ROWERS
ROYALS
SOARES
SOAVES
SOBERS
SOCLES
SOEURS
SOLANS
SOLARS
SOLERS
SOLEUS
SOLFAS
SOLIDS
SOLVES
SOMERS
SONDES
SONICS
SOPORS
SOTOLS
SOUGHS
SOUNDS
SOUSES
SOUTHS
SOWERS
SOXERS
TOASTS
TOBIAS
TOBIES
TOEINS
TOILES
TOKAYS
TOKENS
TOKLAS
TONDOS
TONERS
TONICS
TONNES
TOPERS
TOPHUS
TOPICS
TOQUES
TORAHS
TORIES
TORRES
TORSOS
TORTES
TOSSES
TOTALS
TOTEMS
TOTERS
TOUGHS
TOWELS
TOWERS
TOXICS
TOXINS
TOYONS
VOCALS
VODKAS
VOGUES
VOICES
VOILES
VOLANS
VOLENS
VOLVAS
VOROUS
VOSGES
VOTERS
VOWELS
VOWERS
WODGES
WOLVES
WOMENS
WOOERS
WORLDS
WORSTS
WORTHS
WOUNDS
YOBBOS
YODELS
YOICKS
YOKELS
YOKUTS
YOUTHS
ZOOIDS
ZORILS
ZOUNDS

••OS••
AMOSOZ
ASOSAN
BOOSTS
CHOSEN
CLOSED
CLOSER
CLOSES
CLOSET
CROSBY
CROSSE
ENOSIS
FLOSSY
FROSTS
FROSTY
GHOSTS
GLOSSA
GLOSSO
GLOSSY
GNOSIS
GOOSED
GOOSES
GOOSEY
GROSSE
GROSSO
GROSZY
KIOSKS
LOOSED
LOOSEN
LOOSER
LOOSES
MIOSIS
MYOSIN
MYOSIS
NOOSED
NOOSES
PROSED
PROSER
PROSES
PROSIT
PROSKY
ROOSTS
SLOSHY
XHOSAS

••O•S•
ALONSO
AROUSE
BLOUSE
BLOWSY
BOOTSY
BROWSE
CHOOSE
CHOOSY
CROSSE
CROUSE
DROWSE
DROWSY
EGOISM
EGOIST
ELOISE
FLOPSY
FLOSSY
GLOSSA
GLOSSO
GLOSSY
GROSSE
GROSSO
GROUSE
LAOTSE
LHOTSE
MAOISM
MAOIST
OBOIST
PROUST
PROWSE
SCOUSE
SPOUSE
SWOOSH
TAOISM
TAOIST
TOOTSY
WHOMSO
WHOOSH
WOODSY

••O••S
ABODES
ABOHMS
ABOMBS
ABORTS
ACORNS
ADOBES
ADONIS
ADOPTS
ADORES
ADORNS
AEOLUS
AGORAS
ALOHAS
ALOINS
AMOLES
AMOURS
ANODES
ANOLES
AROIDS
AROMAS
ATODDS
ATOLLS
ATONES
AVOIDS
AZORES
BIOGAS
BIOMES
BIOTAS
BLOATS
BLOCKS
BLOKES
BLONDS
BLOOMS
BLOOPS
BOOSTS
BOOTES
BOOTHS
BROADS
BROILS
BRONCS
BROODS
BROOKS
BROOMS
BROTHS
BROWNS
CEORLS
CHOCKS
CHOIRS
CHOKES
CHOLOS
CHOMPS
CHORDS
CHORES
CHORUS
CLOAKS

CLOCKS
CLOMPS
CLONES
CLONKS
CLONUS
CLORIS
CLOSES
CLOTHS
CLOUDS
CLOUTS
CLOVES
CLOVIS
CLOWNS
CNOTES
COOERS
COOPTS
CROAKS
CROATS
CROCKS
CROCUS
CROFTS
CRONES
CRONUS
CROOKS
CROONS
CROWDS
CROWNS
CROZES
DHOLES
DHOTIS
DIODES
DOOFUS
DROIDS
DROITS
DROLLS
DROMOS
DRONES
DROOLS
DROOPS
DROVES
DROWNS
DUOMOS
EBOATS
EBONDS
ECOLES
ELOPES
EMOTES
ENOKIS
ENOSIS
EPOCHS
EPODES
ERODES
EVOKES
EXODUS
FIORDS
FJORDS
FLOATS
FLOCKS
FLOODS
FLOORS
FLORAS
FLORES
FLOURS
FLOUTS
FROCKS
FRONDS
FRONTS
FROSTS
FROTHS
FROWNS
GEODES
GHOSTS
GHOULS
GLOATS

GLOBES
GLOGGS
GLOOMS
GLOVES
GLOZES
GNOMES
GNOSIS
GOOSES
GROANS
GROATS
GROINS
GROOMS
GROPES
GROUPS
GROUTS
GROVES
GROWLS
HAOLES
HBOMBS
HMONGS
HOOHAS
HOOVES
KHOUMS
KIOSKS
KIOWAS
KLOOFS
KNOCKS
KNOLLS
KNOTTS
KNOUTS
KNOWNS
LEONES
LLOYDS
LOOFAS
LOOIES
LOOSES
MAORIS
MIOSIS
MYOPES
MYOSIS
NOONES
NOOSES
ODOURS
OROMOS
OVOIDS
PHOBOS
PHOCIS
PHONES
PHONOS
PHOTOS
PLONKS
PROAMS
PROBES
PROEMS
PROLES
PROMOS
PRONGS
PROOFS
PROSES
PROVES
PROWLS
QUOINS
QUOITS
QUOTAS
QUOTES
REOILS
RHODES
RHOMBS
RIOJAS
ROOSTS
SCOFFS
SCOLDS
SCONES
SCOOPS

SCOOTS
SCOPES
SCORES
SCORNS
SCOURS
SCOUTS
SCOWLS
SHOALS
SHOATS
SHOCKS
SHOERS
SHOJIS
SHOOKS
SHOOTS
SHORES
SHORTS
SHOUTS
SHOVES
SKOALS
SKORTS
SLOOPS
SLOPES
SLOTHS
SMOCKS
SMOKES
SMOLTS
SNOODS
SNOOKS
SNOOPS
SNOOTS
SNOPES
SNORES
SNORTS
SNOUTS
SPOILS
SPOKES
SPOOFS
SPOOKS
SPOOLS
SPOONS
SPOORS
SPORES
SPORTS
SPOUTS
STOATS
STOCKS
STOICS
STOKES
STOLES
STOMAS
STOMPS
STONES
STOOKS
STOOLS
STOOPS
STOPES
STORES
STORKS
STORMS
STORRS
STOUPS
STOUTS
STOVES
SWOONS
SWOOPS
SWORDS
TBONDS
TBONES
THOLES
THOMAS
THONGS
THORNS
THORPS
TNOTES

TROLLS
TROMPS
TROOPS
TROPES
TROTHS
TROUTS
TROVES
UBOATS
UBOLTS
VIOLAS
VROOMS
WHOLES
WHOMPS
WHOOFS
WHOOPS
WHORLS
WOOERS
WRONGS
XHOSAS
ZLOTYS
ZOOIDS

•••OS•

ACCOST
ACROSS
ALDOSE
ALMOST
APPOSE
ARGOSY
ARIOSE
ARIOSO
ATCOST
ATMOST
BYGOSH
CHOOSE
CHOOSY
COHOST
DEPOSE
EMBOSS
ESPOSA
ESPOSO
EXPOSE
EXPOST
FILOSE
GALOSH
GYROSE
IMPOSE
IMPOST
INMOST
JOCOSE
KAROSS
KIBOSH
LANOSE
LAROSA
LUGOSI
MILOSZ
MIMOSA
MOROSE
MUCOSA
NODOSE
NOLOSE
OPPOSE
OSMOSE
OTIOSE
PILOSE
POTOSI
RAMOSE
REPOSE
REPOST
RIBOSE
RIMOSE
RUGOSE
SAMOSA
SEROSA
SETOSE
SPLOSH
SWOOSH
TOROSE
UPMOST
UPROSE
UTMOST
VADOSE
WHOOSH

•••O•S

ABBOTS
ABHORS
ACEOUS
ACROSS
ACTORS
ADDONS
ALDOUS
ALLOTS
ALLOWS
ALLOYS
ANIONS
ANJOUS
ANNOYS
APRONS
ARBORS
ARDORS
ARGOTS
ARMORS
ARROWS
ARSONS
ARTOIS
ASCOTS
AUROUS
AXIOMS
AXIONS
BARONS
BATONS
BAYOUS
BEBOPS
BEFOGS
BESOMS
BESOTS
BIGOTS
BIPODS
BISONS
BLOOMS
BLOOPS
BOSONS
BROODS
BROOKS
BROOMS
CAHOWS
CANOES
CANONS
CAPONS
CAROBS
CAROLS
CAROMS
CDROMS
CHEOPS
COCOAS
CODONS
COLONS
COLORS
CROOKS
CROONS
CSPOTS
DADOES
DECORS
DECOYS
DEFOGS
DEMOBS
DEMONS
DEPOTS
DICOTS
DIVOTS
DODOES
DOGONS
DOLORS
DONORS
DROOLS
DROOPS
DUBOIS
DUROCS
ECHOES
EDDOES
ELBOWS
EMBOSS
ENDOWS
ENJOYS
ENROLS
ENVOIS
ENVOYS
EPHODS
EPHORS
EPROMS
ERGOTS
ERRORS
ESTOPS
EXTOLS
FAGOTS
FAMOUS
FANONS
FAVORS
FELONS
FLOODS
FLOORS
FSTOPS
FURORS
FUTONS
GALOIS
GALOPS
GATORS
GEMOTS
GIGOTS
GIJOES
GLOOMS
GLUONS
GRIOTS
GROOMS
GUYOTS
GYRONS
HALOES
HAVOCS
HELOTS
HEROES
HERONS
HOBOES
HONORS
HUMORS
HURONS
IDIOMS
IDIOTS
IGLOOS
INGOTS
INIONS
JABOTS
JOYOUS
JURORS
KABOBS
KAROSS
KAZOOS
KEBOBS
KLOOFS
LABORS
LEMONS
MAJORS
MANORS
MASONS
MAYORS
MCJOBS
MELONS
MESONS
MINORS
MIWOKS
MODOCS
MORONS
MOTORS
MUCOUS
NABOBS
NABORS
NYLONS
ODIOUS
ONIONS
ORLOPS
OXBOWS
PAEONS
PATOIS
PEKOES
PELOPS
PICOTS
PILOTS
PINONS
PINOTS
PITONS
PIVOTS
POBOYS
POROUS
PRIONS
PRIORS
PROOFS
PUTONS
PYLONS
RACONS
RAMOUS
RAYONS
RAZORS
RECONS
REDOES
REMOPS
REMOWS
REPOTS
RESODS
RETOPS
RETOWS
RIGORS
ROBOTS
ROTORS
RUFOUS
RUMORS
RUNONS
SABOTS
SALONS
SAPORS
SARODS
SAVORS
SAXONS
SCIONS
SCOOPS
SCOOTS
SCRODS
SENORS
SEPOYS
SEROUS
SEROWS
SHOOKS
SHOOTS
SLOOPS
SNOODS
SNOOKS
SNOOPS
SNOOTS
SOPORS
SOTOLS
SPOOFS
SPOOKS
SPOOLS
SPOONS
SPOORS
STOOKS
STOOLS
STOOPS
STROPS
SWOONS
SWOOPS
SYNODS
SYSOPS
TABOOS
TABORS
TALONS
TAROTS
TAUONS
TENONS
TENORS
TETONS
THROBS
THROES
THROWS
TOYONS
TROOPS
TUDORS
TUTORS
UNDOES
UNIONS
UPBOWS
VALOIS
VAPORS
VENOMS
VENOUS
VETOES
VIGORS
VINOUS
VISORS
VOROUS
VROOMS
WAGONS
WAHOOS
WHOOFS
WHOOPS
WIDOWS
YAHOOS
YAPOKS
YUROKS
ZEROES

••••OS

ABYDOS
AGGROS
ALAMOS
AMIGOS
ANDROS
ANGLOS
ARCCOS
ASTROS
AUDIOS
AVISOS
BANJOS
BASSOS
BATHOS
BEANOS
BOFFOS
BONGOS
BRAVOS
BRAZOS
BUENOS
BUFFOS
BUNCOS
BUNKOS
BURGOS
BURROS
BUTEOS
CACAOS
CAICOS
CAMEOS
CAMPOS
CANTOS
CARBOS
CARGOS
CARLOS
CELLOS
CENTOS
CERROS
CESTOS
CHINOS
CHOLOS
CISCOS
CLAROS
COMBOS
COMPOS
CONDOS
COSMOS
CREDOS
CURIOS
CUSTOS
CYCLOS
DEIMOS
DEKKOS
DISCOS
DITTOS
DOBROS
DROMOS
DUOMOS
EJIDOS
ETHNOS
FOLIOS
FRITOS
GECKOS
GIZMOS
GUACOS
GUIROS
GUMBOS
HALLOS
HELIOS
HELLOS
HIPPOS
HOWTOS
HUEVOS
HULLOS
HYDROS
HYKSOS
HYPNOS
IGLOOS
INTROS
JUMBOS
JUNCOS
JUNTOS
KAZOOS
KERNOS
LARGOS
LASSOS
LEMNOS
LESBOS
LIMBOS
LITHOS
LLANOS
LOTTOS
MACHOS
MACROS
MAMBOS
MANGOS
MARCOS
MATZOS
METROS
MEZZOS
MICROS
MIMEOS
MOTTOS
MUGHOS
MUNGOS
MYTHOS
NACHOS
OROMOS
PANTOS
PASEOS
PATHOS
PATIOS
PATMOS
PEPLOS
PESTOS
PHAROS
PHILOS
PHOBOS
PHONOS
PHOTOS
PIANOS
PINTOS
POTTOS
PRIMOS
PROMOS
RADIOS
RATIOS
RECTOS
REPROS
RETROS
RHINOS
RODEOS
ROLEOS
ROMEOS
RONDOS
SALVOS
SANTOS
SARGOS
SAYSOS
SCHMOS
SERVOS
SESTOS
SETTOS
SHAKOS
SKIROS
SPIROS
STENOS
TABOOS
TAINOS
TANGOS
TEMPOS
TONDOS
TORSOS
TRIPOS
TURBOS
VERSOS
VIDEOS
VIREOS
WACKOS
WAHOOS
YAHOOS
YOBBOS
ZENDOS

OT••••

OTELLO
OTHERS
OTIOSE
OTITIC
OTITIS
OTOOLE
OTTAVA
OTTAWA
OTTERS

O•T•••

OATERS
OATIER
OBTAIN
OBTEST
OBTUND
OBTUSE
OCTADS
OCTANE
OCTANT
OCTAVE
OCTAVO
OCTETS
OCTOPI
OCTROI
ONTAPE
ONTIME
ONTOUR
OPTFOR
OPTICS
OPTIMA
OPTING
OPTION
OPTOUT
ORTEGA
ORTLES
OSTEAL
OSTEND
OSTIUM
OSTLER
OTTAVA
OTTAWA
OTTERS
OUTACT
OUTAGE
OUTATE
OUTBID
OUTBOX
OUTCRY
OUTDID
OUTEAT
OUTFIT
OUTFLY
OUTFOX
OUTGUN
OUTHIT
OUTING
OUTLAW
OUTLAY
OUTLET
OUTPUT
OUTRAN
OUTRUN
OUTSET
OUTWIT
OXTAIL

O••T••

OBITER
OBSTET
ODETTA
ODETTE
OERTER
ONETWO
ORATED
ORATES
ORATOR
OTITIC
OTITIS
OUSTED
OUSTER
OYSTER

O•••T•

OBLATE
OCTETS
ODDITY
ODETTA
ODETTE
ODISTS
ODONTO
OFLATE
OLEATE
OMERTA
ONSETS
ONSITE
OOCYTE
OOLITE
OOLITH
OPENTO
OPHITE
OPIATE
OPORTO
ORANTS
ORBITS
ORGATE
ORNATE
ORNITH
OSSETE
OUGHTS
OUTATE
OWLETS

O••••T

OBJECT
OBLAST
OBOIST
OBSTET
OBTEST
OBVERT
OCCULT
OCELOT
OCTANT
ODDEST
ODDLOT
OFFSET
OLDEST
OLDHAT
OMELET
ONEACT
ONFOOT
OPTOUT
ORGEAT
ORIENT
OUTACT
OUTEAT
OUTFIT
OUTHIT
OUTLET
OUTPUT
OUTSET
OUTWIT
OXCART

•OT•••

BOTANY
BOTCHY
BOTELS
BOTFLY
BOTHER
BOTREE
BOTTLE
BOTTOM
COTTAS
COTTEN
COTTER
COTTON
DOTAGE
DOTARD
DOTELL
DOTEON
DOTHAN
DOTING
DOTTED
DOTTIE
DOTTLE
GOTCHA
GOTHAM
GOTHIC
GOTMAD
GOTOFF
GOTOIT
GOTOUT
GOTSET
GOTTEN
HOTAIR
HOTBED
HOTBOX
HOTCAP
HOTCAR
HOTDOG
HOTELS
HOTPOT
HOTROD
HOTTEA
HOTTER
HOTTIP
HOTTUB
HOTWAR
JOTTED
KOTTER
LOTAHS
LOTHAR
LOTION
LOTTED
LOTTOS
MOTELS
MOTETS
MOTHER
MOTHRA
MOTIFS
MOTILE
MOTION
MOTIVE
MOTLEY
MOTMOT
MOTORS
MOTOWN
MOTTLE
MOTTOS
NOTARY
NOTATE
NOTBAD
NOTCHY
NOTERS
NOTICE
NOTIFY
NOTING
NOTION
NOTNOW
NOTYET
POTAGE
POTASH
POTATO
POTEEN
POTENT
POTFUL
POTHER
POTION
POTOSI
POTPIE
POTTED
POTTER
POTTLE
POTTOS
ROTARY
ROTATE
ROTGUT
ROTHKO
ROTINI
ROTORS
ROTTED
ROTTEN
ROTTER
ROTUND
SOTHAT
SOTOLS
SOTTED
TOTALS
TOTEMS
TOTERS
TOTHER
TOTING
TOTSUP
TOTTED
TOTTER
VOTARY
VOTECH
VOTEIN
VOTERS
VOTING
VOTIVE

•O•T••

AORTAE
AORTAL
AORTAS
AORTIC
BOATED
BOATEL
BOATER
BOITES
BOLTED
BOLTON
BONTON
BOOTED
BOOTEE
BOOTES
BOOTHE
BOOTHS
BOOTIE
BOOTSY
BOOTUP
BOSTON
BOTTLE
BOTTOM
BOWTIE
BOXTOP
COATED
COATIS
COLTER
COMTES
CONTAC
CONTES
CONTRA
CONTRE
COOTER
COOTIE
COPTER
COPTIC
CORTES
CORTEX
CORTEZ
COSTAE
COSTAL
COSTAR
COSTAS
COSTLY
COTTAS
COTTEN
COTTER
COTTON
COUTER
DOCTOR
DOGTAG
DOTTED
DOTTIE
DOTTLE
FOETAL
FOETID
FOETOR
FOETUS
FONTAL
FOOTED
FOOTER
FORTAS
FORTES
FOSTER
GOATEE
GOETHE
GOSTAG
GOTTEN
HOGTIE
HOOTAT
HOOTCH
HOOTED
HOOTER
HOOTIE
HORTON
HOSTAS
HOSTED
HOSTEL
HOSTLY
HOTTEA
HOTTER
HOTTIP
HOTTUB
HOWTOS
JOETEX
JOLTED
JOSTLE
JOTTED
KOTTER
KOWTOW
LOATHE
LOFTED
LOITER
LOOTED
LOOTER
LOSTIT
LOTTED
LOTTOS
MOATED
MOLTED
MOLTEN
MOLTER
MOLTKE
MONTEL
MONTES
MONTEZ
MONTHS
MOOTED
MOPTOP
MORTAL
MORTAR
MORTON
MOSTEL
MOSTLY
MOTTLE
MOTTOS
MOUTHS
MOUTHY
MOUTON
NOETIC
NOOTKA
NORTHS
NORTON
POETIC
POETRY
PONTES
PONTIC
PONTUS
POPTOP
PORTAL
PORTED
PORTER
PORTIA
PORTLY
POSTAL
POSTED
POSTER
POSTIT
POSTON
POTTED
POTTER
POTTLE
POTTOS
POUTED
POUTER
ROOTED
ROOTER
ROSTER
ROSTOV
ROSTRA
ROTTED
ROTTEN
ROTTER
ROUTED
ROUTER
ROUTES
SOFTEN
SOFTER
SOFTIE
SOFTLY
SONTAG
SOOTHE
SORTED
SORTER
SORTIE
SORTOF
SOTTED
SOUTER
SOUTHS
TOATEE
TOETAP
TOLTEC
TOMTIT
TOMTOM
TOOTED
TOOTER
TOOTHY
TOOTLE
TOOTOO
TOOTSY
TOPTEN
TORTES
TOTTED
TOTTER

TOUTED
TOUTER
VORTEX
VOSTOK
WONTED
WONTON
WORTHS
WORTHY
YOMTOV
YOUTHS

•O••T•

BOASTS
BOGOTA
BONITO
BOOSTS
BORATE
BOUNTY
COAPTS
COASTS
COGITO
COMATE
COMETH
COMETO
COMETS
COMITY
COOPTS
COUNTS
COUNTY
COURTS
COVETS
COYOTE
DONATE
DONETS
DONITZ
DONUTS
DORATI
DOUBTS
EOLITH
FOISTS
FOUNTS
FOURTH
GODETS
GOINTO
GOWITH
HOISTS
HOLDTO
HOVETO
IODATE
IOLITE
IOMOTH
JOBETH
JOINTS
JOISTS
JOUSTS
JOWETT
KOONTZ
KORATS
LOBATE
LOCATE
LOLITA
LOOKTO
LOVETT
MOIETY
MONETA
MORITA
MORITZ
MOTETS
MOULTS
MOUNTS
MOUNTY
NOHITS
NONETS
NOPETS
NOTATE
NOVATO
OOCYTE
OOLITE
OOLITH
POINTE
POINTS
POINTY
POLITE
POLITY
POSITS
POTATO
POULTS
ROASTS
ROBOTS
ROOSTS
ROSITA
ROTATE
ROUSTS
SOASTO
SOLUTE
SOMATA
SOMATO
SONATA
SOWETO
TOASTS
TOASTY
TODATE
TOMATO
TONITE
TOOKTO
TOYOTA
VOLUTE
WORSTS
YOKUTS
ZONATE

•O•••T

AORIST
BOBCAT
BOGART
BONMOT
BONNET
BOSKET
BOUGHT
BOWNET
BOWOUT
BOXSET
COBALT
COEDIT
COGENT
COHORT
COHOST
COLLET
COMBAT
COMEAT
COMFIT
COMMIT
COMSAT
CONANT
COOLIT
COPOUT
COQUET
CORNET
CORSET
COSSET
COVENT
COVERT
COYEST
DOCENT
DOCKET
DOESNT
DOGSAT
DOGSIT
DOPANT
DORRIT
DORSET
FOGHAT
FOMENT
FOREST
FORGET
FORGOT
FORINT
FORMAT
FOUGHT
GOBLET
GOBUST
GOCART
GODWIT
GOESAT
GOKART
GORGET
GOSOFT
GOTOIT
GOTOUT
GOTSET
GOULET
GOWEST
HOBART
HOBBIT
HOGGET
HOLDIT
HOLIST
HONEST
HOOFIT
HOOTAT
HORNET
HOTPOT
JOBLOT
JOLIET
JOLIOT
JOWETT
KOMBAT
KORBUT
LOCKET
LOCUST
LOGOUT
LOOKAT
LOQUAT
LOSEIT
LOSTIT
LOVETT
LOWEST
LOWFAT
MODELT
MODEST
MOLEST
MOMENT
MONIST
MOPPET
MORANT
MOTMOT
MOZART
NOCENT
NOEXIT
NONFAT
NOTYET
NOUGAT
NOUGHT
POCKET
POIROT
POKEAT
POLPOT
POPART
POPOUT
POPPET
POSSET
POSTIT
POTENT
ROBERT
ROBUST
ROCHET
ROCKET
RODENT
ROTGUT
SOBEIT
SOCKET
SOFFIT
SOLENT
SONANT
SONNET
SORBET
SOREST
SOTHAT
SOUGHT
SOVIET
SOWHAT
TOBOOT
TOILET
TOMCAT
TOMTIT
TOOKIT
TOPCAT
TOPHAT
TOPOUT
TOREAT
VOIGHT
VOLANT
WOMBAT
WONOUT
YOGURT
YOUBET

••OT••

BIOTAS
BIOTIC
BIOTIN
BLOTCH
BLOTTO
BLOTTY
BOOTED
BOOTEE
BOOTES
BOOTHE
BOOTHS
BOOTIE
BOOTSY
BOOTUP
BROTHS
CLOTHE
CLOTHO
CLOTHS
CLOTTY
CNOTES
COOTER
COOTIE
CROTON
DHOTEL
DHOTIS
EMOTED
EMOTER
EMOTES
EROTIC
EXOTIC
FOOTED
FOOTER
FROTHS
FROTHY
GIOTTO
GROTON
GROTTO
GROTTY
HOOTAT
HOOTCH
HOOTED
HOOTER
HOOTIE
IGOTIT
KNOTTS
KNOTTY
LAOTSE
LAOTZU
LHOTSE
LIOTTA
LOOTED
LOOTER
MAOTAI
MOOTED
NOOTKA
PHOTIC
PHOTOG
PHOTON
PHOTOS
PLOTTY
PROTAX
PROTEI
PROTEM
PROTON
QUOTAS
QUOTED
QUOTER
QUOTES
QUOTHA
RIOTED
RIOTER
ROOTED
ROOTER
SCOTCH
SCOTER
SCOTIA
SCOTTO
SCOTTY
SHOTAT
SHOTUP
SLOTHS
SNOTTY
SOOTHE
SPOTTY
STOTIN
TNOTES
TOOTED
TOOTER
TOOTHY
TOOTLE
TOOTOO
TOOTSY
TROTHS
ZLOTYS

••O•T•

ABORTS
ADOPTS
AGOUTI
BLOATS
BLOTTO
BLOTTY
BOOSTS
BRONTE
CHOATE
CLOTTY
CLOUTS
COOPTS
CROATS
CROFTS
CROUTE
DROITS
EBOATS
FLOATS
FLOATY
FLOUTS
FRONTS
FROSTS
FROSTY
GHOSTS
GIOTTO
GLOATS
GROATS
GROTTO
GROTTY
GROUTS
GROUTY
GROWTH
KNOTTS
KNOTTY
KNOUTS
KOONTZ
LIOTTA
LOOKTO
ODONTO
OPORTO
PLOTTY
PRONTO
QUOITS
ROOSTS
SCOOTS
SCOTTO
SCOTTY
SCOUTS
SHOATS
SHOOTS
SHORTA
SHORTE
SHORTI
SHORTO
SHORTS
SHORTU
SHORTY
SHOUTS
SKORTS
SMOLTS
SMOOTH
SNOOTS
SNOOTY
SNORTS
SNOTTY
SNOUTS
SPORTS
SPORTY
SPOTTY
SPOUTS
STOATS
STOUTS
TOOKTO
TROUTS
UBOATS
UBOLTS

••O••T

AGOROT
AMOUNT
ANOINT
AVOCET
BLOWIT
CLOSET
COOLIT
DROPIT
EGOIST
FLORET
HOOFIT
HOOTAT
IGOTIT
IROBOT
LIONET
LOOKAT
MAOIST
OBOIST
PIOLET
PROFIT
PROMPT
PROSIT
PROUST
SHOTAT
SNOCAT
SPOILT
STOMAT
STOPIT
TAOIST
TOOKIT
TWOBIT
VIOLET

•••OT•

ABBOTS
ABBOTT
ALCOTT
ALIOTO
ALLOTS
ARGOTS
ASCOTS
BESOTS
BIGOTS
BOGOTA
BYROTE
CAPOTE
CENOTE
COYOTE
CSPOTS
DAKOTA
DEMOTE
DENOTE
DEPOTS
DESOTO
DEVOTE
DEVOTO
DICOTS
DIVOTS
ERGOTS
EXVOTO
FAGOTS
GEMOTE
GEMOTS
GIGOTS
GRIOTS
GUYOTS
HELOTS
IDIOTS
INGOTS
INTOTO
IOMOTH
JABOTS
LAKOTA
MALOTI
MELOTT
MRMOTO
PELOTA
PEYOTE
PICOTS
PILOTI
PILOTS
PINOTS
PIVOTS
REMOTE
RENOTE
REPOTS
ROBOTS
SABOTS
SCOOTS
SHOOTS
SMOOTH
SNOOTS
SNOOTY
TAROTS
TOYOTA
ZEROTH
ZYGOTE

•••O•T

ABBOTT
ACCOST
ACEOUT
ACTOUT
ADROIT
AFLOAT
AIROUT
AJFOYT
ALCOTT
ALLOUT
ALMOST
ASKOUT
ASSORT
ATCOST
ATEOUT
ATMOST
AUMONT
BELOIT
BENOIT
BOWOUT
BUGOUT
BUMOUT
BUYOUT
CAVORT
COHORT
COHOST
COPOUT
CUTOUT
DACOIT
DECOCT
DEPORT
DEVOUT
DIEOUT
DIGOUT
DIMOUT
DRYOUT
DUGOUT
DUMONT
DUPONT
EATOUT
EFFORT
EGMONT
EKEOUT
ENROOT
ESCORT
EXHORT
EXPORT
EXPOST
EXTORT
FANOUT
FAROUT
FLYOUT
GALOOT
GERONT
GETOUT
GOSOFT
GOTOIT
GOTOUT
HIDOUT
HITOUT
ICEOUT
IMPORT
IMPOST
INMOST
INPORT
LAMONT
LAYOUT
LEDOUT
LETOUT
LITOUT
LOGOUT
MAHOUT
MAXOUT
MELOTT
ONFOOT
OPTOUT
PANOUT
PAYOUT
PIGOUT
POPOUT
PTBOAT
PUTOUT
RAGOUT
RANOUT
REBOLT
REBOOT
RECOAT
REPORT
REPOST
RESORT
RETORT
REVOLT
RIPOUT
RUBOUT
RUNOUT
SATOUT
SAWOUT
SEEOUT
SETOUT
SITOUT
SPROUT
TAGOUT
TAPOUT
THROAT
TOBOOT
TOPOUT
TRYOUT
UNBOLT
UNROOT
UPMOST
UPROOT
UTMOST
WAYOUT
WIGOUT
WINOUT
WONOUT
XEDOUT

••••OT

AGOROT
BADLOT
BALLOT
BARDOT
BONMOT
BURBOT
CANNOT
CARLOT
CARNOT
CARROT
DESPOT
DIGLOT
DRYROT
DYELOT
ELLIOT
ENROOT
FORGOT
GALOOT
HERIOT
HOTPOT
IROBOT
JOBLOT
JOLIOT
MARGOT
MARMOT
MASCOT
MERLOT
MOTMOT
OCELOT
ODDLOT
ONFOOT
PARROT
PEQUOT
PERROT
POIROT
POLPOT
REBOOT
REDHOT
RESHOT
SPIGOT
TALBOT
TEAPOT
TINPOT
TOBOOT
TRICOT
TURBOT
UNKNOT
UNROOT
UPROOT
UPSHOT
WHYNOT
ZEALOT

OU••••

OUGHTS
OUNCES
OUSELS
OUSTED
OUSTER
OUTACT
OUTAGE
OUTATE
OUTBID
OUTBOX
OUTCRY
OUTDID
OUTEAT
OUTFIT
OUTFLY
OUTFOX
OUTGUN
OUTHIT
OUTING
OUTLAW
OUTLAY
OUTLET
OUTPUT
OUTRAN
OUTRUN
OUTSET
OUTWIT
OUZELS

O•U•••

OCULAR
OEUVRE
ONUSES
OPUSES
OVULAR
OVULES

O••U••

OBTUND
OBTUSE
OCCULT
OCCUPY
OCCURS
ODIUMS
ODOURS
ONEUPS
ONRUSH
OPPUGN
ORDURE
OSCULA
OSMUND

O•••U•

OBELUS
ODIOUS
OMASUM
OMNIUM
ONTOUR
OPAQUE
OPENUP
OPTOUT
OSMIUM
OSTIUM
OUTGUN
OUTPUT
OUTRUN
OWNSUP

O••••U

ORMOLU

•OU•••

AOUDAD
BOUBOU
BOUCLE
BOUDIN
BOUFFE
BOUGHS
BOUGHT
BOULES
BOULEZ
BOULLE
BOUNCE
BOUNCY
BOUNDS
BOUNTY
BOURKE
BOURNE
BOURSE
BOUSED
BOUSES
COUGAR
COUGHS
COULDA
COULEE
COUNTS
COUNTY
COUPES
COUPLE
COUPON
COURIC
COURSE
COURTS
COUSIN
COUTER
DOUALA
DOUBLE
DOUBLY
DOUBTS
DOUGHS
DOUGHY
DOURER
DOURLY
DOUSED
DOUSES
FOUGHT
FOULED
FOULER
FOULLY
FOULUP
FOUNDS
FOUNTS
FOURAM
FOURPM
FOURTH
GOUGED
GOUGER
GOUGES
GOULET
GOUNOD
GOURDE
GOURDS
HOUGHS
HOUNDS
HOUNDY
HOURIS
HOURLY
HOUSED
HOUSES
JOULES
JOUNCE
JOUNCY
JOURNO
JOUSTS
KOUFAX
LOUCHE
LOUDEN
LOUDER
LOUDLY
LOUGHS
LOUISA
LOUISE
LOUNGE
LOUPES
LOUSED
LOUSES
LOUVER
LOUVRE
MOULDS
MOULDY
MOULIN
MOULTS
MOUNDS
MOUNTS
MOUNTY
MOURNS
MOUSED
MOUSER
MOUSES
MOUSEY
MOUSSE
MOUTHS
MOUTHY
MOUTON
NOUGAT
NOUGHT
NOUMEA
POUCHY
POULTS
POUNCE
POUNDS
POURED
POURER
POURIN
POUSSE
POUTED
POUTER
ROUBLE
ROUGED
ROUGES
ROUGHS
ROUGHY
ROUNDS
ROURKE
ROUSED
ROUSER
ROUSES
ROUSTS
ROUTED
ROUTER
ROUTES
SOUARI
SOUGHS
SOUGHT
SOUNDS
SOUPUP
SOURCE
SOURED
SOURER
SOURLY
SOUSED
SOUSES
SOUTER
SOUTHS
TOUCAN
TOUCHE
TOUCHY
TOUGHS
TOUGHY
TOULON
TOUPEE
TOURED
TOURER
TOUSLE
TOUTED
TOUTER
WOUNDS
YOUALL
YOUBET
YOUTHS
ZOUAVE
ZOUNDS

•O•U••

BOSUNS
COBURG
COBURN
COHUNE
COLUGO
COLUMN
CONURE
COPULA
COQUET
DONUTS
FORUMS
GOBUST
JOCUND
JORUMS
KORUNA
LOBULE
LOCUST
LOQUAT
MODULE
MODULO
MOGULS
MOHURS
MOPUPS
NODULE
PODUNK
POPULI
POPUPS
ROBUST
ROGUES
ROTUND
SOEURS
SOLUTE
TOLUCA
TOQUES
VOGUES
VOLUME
VOLUTE
YOGURT
YOKUTS
YORUBA

•O••U•

BOBSUP
BONEUP
BOOJUM
BOOTUP
BOREUP
BOWOUT
BOXFUL
COCCUS
COILUP
COLEUS
COLOUR
COMEUP
CONCUR
CONIUM
CONSUL
COOKUP
COOPUP
COPOUT
CORIUM
CORPUS
COYPUS
DOESUP
DOLLUP
DOLOUR
DONEUP
DOOFUS
DORSUM
FOETUS
FOGSUP
FOLDUP
FOLIUM
FONDUE
FOULUP
GOESUP
GOLLUM
GOOFUP
GOTOUT
HOLDUP
HOLEUP
HONOUR
HOOKUP
HOPSUP
HORMUZ
HOTTUB
IONIUM
JOINUP
JOSHUA
JOYFUL
JOYOUS
KORBUT
LOCKUP
LOGOUT
LONGUE
LOOKUP
MOBIUS
MOCKUP
MOPSUP
MOSQUE
MOVEUP
PODIUM
POILUS
POLLUX
PONTUS
PONYUP
POPGUN
POPOUT
POPSUP
POROUS
POSEUR
POSSUM
POTFUL
ROLLUP
ROTGUT
SOAKUP
SOBFUL
SODIUM
SOLEUS
SOPSUP
SOUPUP
SOWBUG
TOBRUK
TONEUP
TONGUE
TOOKUP
TOOLUP
TOPGUN
TOPHUS
TOPOUT
TOREUP
TORQUE
TOSSUP
TOTSUP
VOROUS
WOEFUL
WOKEUP
WONMUG
WONOUT
WORKUP

•O•••U

BOUBOU
CONGOU
HONSHU
MOLDAU
MOREAU
ROSEAU

••OU••

ABOUND
AGOUTI
AMOUNT
AMOURS
AROUND
AROUSE
AVOUCH
BLOUSE
CHOUGH
CLOUDS
CLOUDY
CLOUTS
CROUCH
CROUPY
CROUSE
CROUTE
ENOUGH
FLOURS
FLOURY
FLOUTS
GHOULS
GROUCH
GROUND
GROUPS
GROUSE
GROUTS
GROUTY
INOUYE
KHOUMS
KNOUTS
ODOURS
PLOUGH
PROUST
SCOURS
SCOUSE
SCOUTS
SHOULD
SHOUTS
SIOUAN
SLOUCH
SLOUGH
SNOUTS
SPOUSE
SPOUTS
STOUPS
STOUTS
THOUGH
TROUGH
TROUPE
TROUTS
TROUVE

••O•U•

AEOLUS
BLOWUP
BOOJUM
BOOTUP
BROGUE
BUOYUP
CHORUS
CLOGUP
CLONUS
CLOQUE
COOKUP
COOPUP
CROCUS
CRONUS
CROPUP
DOOFUS
DROGUE
EXODUS
GOOFUP
GROWUP
HOOKUP
KRONUR
LOOKUP
PROPUP
QUOQUE
QUORUM
SHOGUN
SHOTUP
SHOWUP
SLOWUP
STOPUP
TOOKUP
TOOLUP

••O••U

CHONJU
CHOOYU
LAOTZU
SHORTU

•••OU•

ACEOUS
ACEOUT
ACTOUT

AIROUT
ALDOUS
ALLOUT
ANJOUS
ARBOUR
ARDOUR
ARMOUR
ASKOUT
ATEOUT
AUROUS
BAYOUS
BEFOUL
BIJOUX
BOWOUT
BUGOUT
BUMOUT
BUYOUT
COLOUR
COPOUT
CUTOUT
DAMOUR
DETOUR
DEVOUR
DEVOUT
DIEOUT
DIGOUT
DIMOUT
DOLOUR
DRYOUT
DUGOUT
EATOUT
EKEOUT
ENSOUL
FAMOUS
FANOUT
FAROUK
FAROUT
FAVOUR
FLYOUT
GETOUT
GOTOUT
HIDOUT
HITOUT
HONOUR
HUMOUR
ICEOUT
INPOUR
JOYOUS
LABOUR
LAMOUR
LATOUR
LAYOUT
LEDOUT
LETOUT
LITOUT
LOGOUT
MACOUN
MAHOUT
MAXOUT
MUCOUS
ODIOUS
ONTOUR
OPTOUT
PANOUT
PAYOUT
PIGOUT
POPOUT
POROUS
PUTOUT
RAGOUT
RAMOUS
RANOUT
RECOUP
RETOUR
RIGOUR
RIPOUT
RUBOUT
RUFOUS
RUMOUR
RUNOUT
SATOUT
SAVOUR
SAWOUT
SEEOUT
SEROUS
SETOUT
SHROUD
SITOUT
SPROUT
STROUD
TAGOUT
TAPOUT
TOPOUT
TRYOUT
VALOUR
VAPOUR
VELOUR
VENOUS
VIGOUR
VINOUS
VOROUS
WAYOUT
WIGOUT
WINOUT
WONOUT
XEDOUT

•••O•U

CHOOYU
ORMOLU

••••OU

ACAJOU
AMADOU
BALLOU
BOUBOU
CACHOU
CONGOU
FUZHOU
HEYYOU
MENJOU
PAILOU

OV••••

OVALLY
OVERDO
OVERLY
OVIEDO
OVISAC
OVOIDS
OVULAR
OVULES

O•V•••

OBVERT
ONVIEW

O••V••

OEUVRE
OGIVES
OLDVIC
OLEVEL
OLIVER
OLIVES
OLIVIA

O•••V•

OCTAVE
OCTAVO
OTTAVA

•OV•••

BOVARY
BOVIDS
BOVINE
BOVVER
COVENS
COVENT
COVERS
COVERT
COVETS
COVEYS
COVINA
DOVEIN
DOVISH
FOVEAE
GOVERN
HOVELS
HOVERS
HOVETO
JOVIAL
JOVIAN
KOVACS
LOVAGE
LOVEIN
LOVELL
LOVELY
LOVERS
LOVETT
LOVING
MOVEIN
MOVEON
MOVERS
MOVEUP
MOVIES
MOVING
NOVATO
NOVELS
NOVENA
NOVICE
ROVERS
ROVING
SOVIET
WOVOKA

•O•V••

BOVVER
COEVAL
CONVEX
CONVEY
CONVOY
CORVEE
CORVES
GOOVER
HOOVER
HOOVES
LOAVES
LOUVER
LOUVRE
SOAVES
SOLVED
SOLVER
SOLVES
VOLVAS
VOLVOX
WOLVES

•O••V•

GODIVA
KOSOVO
MOHAVE
MOJAVE
MORAVA
MOSKVA
MOTIVE
VOTIVE
ZOUAVE

•O•••V

MOSHAV
ROCKYV
ROSTOV
YOMTOV

••OV••

BMOVIE
CLOVEN
CLOVER
CLOVES
CLOVIS
DROVER
DROVES
GLOVED
GLOVER
GLOVES
GOOVER
GROVEL
GROVER
GROVES
HOOVER
HOOVES
PLOVER
PROVED
PROVEN
PROVER
PROVES
SHOVED
SHOVEL
SHOVER
SHOVES
SLOVAK
SLOVEN
SLOVIK
STOVER
STOVES
TROVES

••O•V•

EVOLVE
GROOVE
GROOVY
TROUVE

•••OV•

ALCOVE
BEHOVE
BULOVA
BYJOVE
CANOVA
DENOVO
GROOVE
GROOVY
INLOVE
KOSOVO
REMOVE
REWOVE
SHROVE
STROVE
THROVE
UNWOVE

••••OV

ASIMOV
BRASOV
CHEKOV
IMPROV
KARPOV
PAVLOV
ROSTOV
YOMTOV
ZHUKOV

OW••••

OWLETS
OWLISH
OWNERS
OWNING
OWNSUP

O•W•••

OHWELL
ONWARD
ORWELL
OSWALD
OSWEGO

O••W••

OBIWAN
ONEWAY
OUTWIT

O•••W•

OJIBWA
ONETWO
OSHAWA
OTTAWA
OXBOWS

O••••W

OLDSAW
ONVIEW
OUTLAW

•OW•••

BOWERS
BOWERY
BOWFIN
BOWING
BOWLED
BOWLER
BOWLES
BOWMAN
BOWMEN
BOWNET
BOWOAR
BOWOUT
BOWSAW
BOWSER
BOWTIE
BOWWOW
BOWYER
COWARD
COWBOY
COWENS
COWERS
COWING
COWLED
COWLEY
COWMAN
COWMEN
COWPEA
COWPER
COWPOX
COWRIE
DOWELS
DOWERS
DOWERY
DOWNED
DOWNER
DOWNEY
DOWNON
DOWSED
DOWSER
DOWSES
FOWLED
FOWLER
FOWLES
GOWEST
GOWILD
GOWITH
GOWNED
HOWARD
HOWDAH
HOWELL
HOWLED
HOWLER
HOWLIN
HOWNOW
HOWTOS
IOWANS
JOWETT
KOWTOW
LOWBOY
LOWCAL
LOWELL
LOWEND
LOWERS
LOWERY
LOWEST
LOWFAT
LOWING
LOWISH
LOWKEY
MOWERS
MOWGLI
MOWING
NOWISE
POWDER
POWELL
POWERS
POWWOW
ROWELS
ROWENA
ROWENS
ROWERS
ROWING
SOWBUG
SOWERS
SOWETO
SOWHAT
SOWING
TOWAGE
TOWARD
TOWCAR
TOWELS
TOWERS
TOWERY
TOWHEE
TOWING
TOWNER
TOWNIE
VOWELS
VOWELY
VOWERS
VOWING
WOWING
WOWSER
YOWLED

•O•W••

BOWWOW
COBWEB
CONWAY
DOOWOP
GOAWAY
GOAWRY
GODWIN
GODWIT
HOTWAR
NORWAY
POWWOW

•O••W•

GODOWN
MOHAWK
MOTOWN

•O•••W

BORROW
BOWSAW
BOWWOW
FOGBOW
FOLLOW
GOSLOW
HOLLOW
HOWNOW
KOWTOW
MORROW
MOSCOW
NOSHOW
NOTNOW
POWWOW
SORROW

••OW••

AVOWAL
AVOWED
AVOWER
BLOWER
BLOWIN
BLOWIT
BLOWSY
BLOWUP
BLOWZY
BROWNE
BROWNS
BROWNY
BROWSE
CHOWED
CLOWNS
CROWDS
CROWED
CROWER
CROWNS
DOOWOP
DROWNS
DROWSE
DROWSY
FLOWED
FLOWER
FROWNS
FROWZY
GLOWED
GLOWER
GROWER
GROWLS
GROWLY
GROWON
GROWTH
GROWUP
KIOWAS
KNOWER
KNOWNS
MEOWED
PLOWED
PLOWER
PROWLS
PROWSE
SCOWLS
SHOWED
SHOWER
SHOWIN
SHOWME
SHOWUP
SLOWED
SLOWER
SLOWLY
SLOWUP
SNOWED
SNOWIN
STOWED
TROWED
TROWEL
TWOWAY

••O••W

BROKAW

•••OW•

ALLOWS
ARROWS
CAHOWS
DISOWN
ELBOWS
ENDOWS
GODOWN
INTOWN
MOTOWN
OXBOWS
REMOWN
REMOWS
RENOWN
RETOWS
SEROWS
THROWN
THROWS
UNSOWN
UPBOWS
UPTOWN
WIDOWS

••••OW

ANDHOW
ANTCOW
ANYHOW
BARROW
BELLOW
BESTOW
BILLOW
BORROW
BOWWOW
BURROW
CALLOW
CPSNOW
DARROW
ERENOW
ESCROW
FALLOW
FARLOW
FARROW
FELLOW
FOGBOW
FOLLOW
FURROW
GOSLOW
HALLOW
HARLOW
HARROW
HAYMOW
HOLLOW
HOWNOW
INAROW
INFLOW
KOWTOW
KRAKOW
KUDROW
LAYLOW
LIELOW
MALLOW
MARROW
MEADOW
MELLOW
MINNOW
MORROW
MOSCOW
MURROW
NARROW
NOSHOW
NOTNOW
PESCOW
PILLOW
POWWOW
REPLOW
SALLOW
SEACOW
SHADOW
SKITOW
SORROW
TALLOW
TVSHOW
WALLOW
WILLOW
WINDOW
WINNOW
YARROW
YELLOW

OX••••

OXALIS
OXBOWS
OXCART
OXEYES
OXFORD
OXIDES
OXIDIC
OXLIKE
OXLIPS
OXNARD
OXTAIL
OXYDOL
OXYGEN

O•X•••

OAXACA

O••X••

ONYXES
ORYXES

O••••X

OUTBOX
OUTFOX

•OX•••

BOXBOY
BOXCAR
BOXERS
BOXFUL
BOXIER
BOXING
BOXSET
BOXTOP
FOXIER
FOXILY
FOXING
ROXANA
ROXANE
SOXERS
TOXICS
TOXINS
VOXPOP

•O•X••

COAXED
COAXER
COAXES
HOAXED
HOAXER
HOAXES
NOEXIT

•O••X•

BORAXO

•O•••X

BOLLIX
COCCYX
COLFAX
COMMIX
CONVEX
CORTEX
COWPOX
HOTBOX
JOETEX
KOUFAX
POLEAX
POLLEX
POLLUX
TOMMIX
VOLVOX
VORTEX

••OX••

DIOXIN

••O••X

CLOROX
PROLIX
PROTAX
THORAX

•••OX•

BILOXI

•••O•X

BIJOUX

••••OX

BLUEOX
CHISOX
CLOROX
COWPOX
HATBOX
HOTBOX
ICEBOX
KITFOX
LENNOX
LUMMOX
MUSKOX
OUTBOX
OUTFOX
PAYBOX
REDFOX
REDSOX
SEAFOX
SKYBOX
VOLVOX
WILCOX

OY••••

OYSTER

O•Y•••

OHYEAH
ONYXES
ORYXES
OXYDOL
OXYGEN

O••Y••

OBEYED
OKAYED
OOCYTE
OXEYES

O••••Y

OAKLEY
OCASEY
OCCUPY
OCHERY
ODDITY
OFFDAY
OFFKEY
OHENRY
OILILY
OKELLY
OLDBOY
OLEARY
ONEDAY
ONEWAY
ONIONY
OOLOGY
OOZILY
OPENLY
ORALLY
ORANGY
ORKNEY
ORNERY
ORRERY
OSPREY
OSSIFY
OUTCRY
OUTFLY
OUTLAY
OVALLY
OVERLY

•OY•••

BOYARS
BOYISH
COYEST
COYISH
COYOTE
COYPUS
DOYENS
FOYERS
HOYDEN
JOYFUL
JOYNER
JOYOUS
LOYOLA
MOYERS
ROYALE
ROYALS
TOYDOG
TOYING
TOYONS
TOYOTA
VOYAGE
YOYOED
YOYOMA
ZOYSIA

•O•Y••

BOWYER
CORYZA
NOTYET
OOCYTE
POLYPS
PONYUP

•O••Y•

BOGEYS
BOLEYN
COCCYX
CONEYS
COPAYS
COVEYS
DOGEYS
FOGEYS
FORAYS
HONEYS
MONEYS
MORAYS
MOSEYS
POBOYS
POKEYS
POLEYN
POPEYE
ROCKYV
TOKAYS

•O•••Y

BODILY
BOIGNY
BOLDLY
BOLSHY
BOMBAY
BOOTSY
BOSLEY
BOTANY
BOTCHY
BOTFLY
BOUNCY
BOUNTY
BOVARY
BOWERY
BOXBOY
CODIFY
COLDLY
COLONY
COMEBY
COMEDY
COMELY
COMITY
COMPLY
CONROY
CONVEY
CONVOY
CONWAY
COOLLY
COONEY
COPLEY
CORDAY
COSILY
COSTLY
COUNTY
COWBOY
COWLEY
COZILY
DOESBY
DOGDAY
DONKEY
DOOLEY
DORSEY
DOUBLY
DOUGHY
DOURLY
DOWERY
DOWNEY
DOZILY
FOLKSY
FONDLY
FOSSEY
FOULLY
FOXILY
GOAWAY
GOAWRY
GOEASY
GOESBY
GOGGLY
GONEBY
GOODBY
GOODLY
GOOGLY
GOOSEY
GORILY
HOCKEY
HOLILY
HOMELY
HOMILY
HOMINY
HOORAY
HORNEY
HORSEY
HOSTLY
HOUNDY
HOURLY
JOCKEY
JOHNNY
JOKILY
JOUNCY
KODALY
LOGILY
LONELY
LONGLY
LOONEY
LORDLY
LOUDLY
LOVELY
LOWBOY
LOWERY
LOWKEY
MOBLEY
MODIFY
MOIETY
MONDAY
MONKEY
MONODY
MOONEY
MOPERY
MORLEY
MORNAY
MORPHY
MOSTLY
MOTLEY
MOULDY
MOUNTY
MOUSEY
MOUTHY
NOBODY
NONARY
NORGAY
NORWAY
NOSILY
NOTARY
NOTCHY
NOTIFY
OOLOGY
OOZILY
POACHY
POETRY
POINTY
POKERY
POKILY
POLICY
POLITY
POMPEY
POORLY
POPFLY
PORTLY
POSHLY
POUCHY
ROBROY
RODNEY
ROMANY
ROMNEY
RONELY
ROONEY
ROSARY
ROSILY
ROSINY
ROTARY
ROUGHY
SOFTLY
SOLELY
SOMANY
SORELY
SOURLY
TOASTY
TOMBOY
TOOTHY
TOOTSY
TORCHY
TORREY
TOUCHY
TOUGHY
TOWERY
VOLLEY
VOTARY
VOWELY
WOBBLY
WOLSEY
WOODSY
WOOLEY
WOOLLY
WORTHY

••OY••

BUOYED
BUOYUP
CLOYED
LLOYDS

••O•Y•

ANONYM
AZODYE
CHOOYU
CRONYN
EPONYM
INOUYE
ZLOTYS

••O••Y

BLOCKY
BLOODY
BLOOEY
BLOOMY
BLOTTY
BLOWSY
BLOWZY
BOOTSY
BROLLY
BRONZY
BROODY
BROOKY
BROOMY
BROWNY
CHOOSY
CHOPPY
CLODDY
CLOGGY
CLOTTY
CLOUDY
COOLLY
COONEY
CROAKY
CROSBY
CROUPY
DOOLEY
DROLLY
DROOLY
DROOPY
DROPBY
DROWSY
FLOATY
FLOCKY
FLOOEY
FLOPPY
FLOPSY
FLOSSY
FLOURY
FROGGY
FROSTY
FROTHY
FROWZY
GEORGY
GLOOMY
GLOPPY
GLOSSY
GOODBY
GOODLY
GOOGLY
GOOSEY
GROGGY
GROOVY
GROSZY
GROTTY
GROUTY
GROWLY
GROZNY
HOORAY
KNOBBY
KNOLLY
KNOTTY
LIONLY
LOONEY
MOONEY
MYOHMY
PHONEY
PHOOEY
PLOTTY
POORLY
PROSKY
ROONEY
SCOTTY
SHOALY
SHODDY
SHORTY
SLOBBY
SLOPPY
SLOSHY
SLOWLY
SMOGGY
SMOKEY
SNOBBY
SNOOKY
SNOOPY
SNOOTY
SNOOZY
SNOTTY
SPONGY
SPOOKY
SPOONY
SPORTY
SPOTTY
STOCKY
STODGY
STOOLY
STOREY
STORMY
THORNY
TOOTHY
TOOTSY
TROPHY
TWOPLY
TWOWAY
UNOILY
WHOLLY
WOODSY
WOOLEY
WOOLLY

•••OY•

AJFOYT
ALLOYS
ANNOYS
ARROYO
CHOOYU
DECOYS
ENJOYS
ENVOYS
LATOYA
NAGOYA
POBOYS
SEPOYS

•••O•Y

ANTONY
ARGOSY
ARMORY
BARONY
BETONY
BLOODY
BLOOEY
BLOOMY
BROODY
BROOKY
BROOMY
BRYONY
CANOPY
CHOOSY
CHROMY
COLONY
DIPODY
DROOLY
DROOPY
EMBODY
EULOGY
FELONY
FLOOEY
GLOOMY
GROOVY
IDIOCY
JALOPY
KIDORY
LEMONY
MALORY
MELODY
MEMORY
MONODY
NOBODY
ONIONY

OOLOGY PARODY PHOOEY PRIORY RECOPY SAVORY SAXONY SIMONY SNOOKY SNOOPY SNOOTY SNOOZY SPOOKY SPOONY STOOLY THEORY UNHOLY VAPORY WICOPY

••••OY

BADBOY BATBOY BIGBOY BOXBOY BUSBOY CARBOY CONROY CONVOY COWBOY DAYBOY DELROY DEPLOY EMPLOY FLYBOY KILROY LAZBOY LOWBOY OLDBOY QUEMOY ROBROY STEFOY TEAPOY THETOY TOMBOY

OZ••••

OZARKS OZONIC

O•Z•••

OOZIER OOZILY OOZING OUZELS

O••Z••

OROZCO

•OZ•••

COZENS COZIED COZIER COZIES COZILY DOZENS DOZERS DOZIER DOZILY DOZING FOZZIE MOZART NOZZLE OOZIER OOZILY OOZING ROZZER

•O•Z••

BONZES BORZOI DOOZIE FOOZLE FOZZIE NOZZLE ROZZER

•O••Z•

CORYZA IODIZE IONIZE

•O•••Z

BOULEZ CORTEZ DOLENZ DONITZ HORMUZ KOONTZ LORENZ MONTEZ MORITZ

••OZ••

CROZES DOOZIE FOOZLE FROZEN GLOZED GLOZES GROZNY OROZCO PROZAC

••O•Z•

ALONZO BLOWZY BRONZE BRONZY FROWZY GROSZY LAOTZU SFORZA SNOOZE SNOOZY

••O••Z

AMOSOZ KOONTZ TROPEZ

•••OZ•

REBOZO SNOOZE SNOOZY

•••O•Z

MILOSZ

••••OZ

AMOSOZ SCHNOZ

PA••••

PAANGA PABLUM PACERS PACIFY PACING PACINO PACKED PACKER PACKET PACKUP PACMAN PADANG PADDED PADDER PADDLE PADRES PADUAN PAEANS PAELLA PAEONS PAGANS PAGERS PAGING PAGODA PAHANG PAHARI PAIDIN PAIDUP PAILOU PAINED PAINTS PAINTY PAIRED PAIRUP PAISAS PAIUTE PAJAMA PAKULA PALACE PALAEO PALATE PALEAE PALELY PALEST PALIER PALING PALISH PALLAS PALLED PALLET PALLIA PALLID PALLOR PALMAS PALMED PALMER PALOMA PALPUS PALTER PALTRY PAMELA PAMIRS PAMPAS PAMPER PANADA PANAMA PANCHO PANDAS PANDER PANDIT PANELS PANFRY PANFUL PANICS PANNED PANNER PANNES PANOUT PANTED PANTOS PANTRY PANZER PAPACY PAPAGO PAPAIN PAPAWS PAPAYA PAPERS PAPERY PAPIER PAPPAS PAPPUS PAPUAN PAPYRI PAQUIN PARADE PARANA PARANG PARAPH PARCAE PARCEL PARDON PARENS PARENT PARERS PARETO PAREVE PARGET PARIAH PARING PARISH PARITY PARKAS PARKAY PARKED PARKER PARLAY PARLEY PARLOR PARNIS PARODY PAROLE PARRED PARREL PARRIS PARROT PARSEC PARSED PARSEE PARSER PARSES PARSON PARTED PARTLY PARTON PARULA PARURE PARVIS PASCAL PASEOS PASHAS PASHTO PASSBY PASSED PASSEL PASSER PASSES PASSIM PASSON PASSUP PASTAS PASTED PASTEL PASTES PASTIS PASTOR PASTRY PATACA PATCHY PATENS PATENT PATERS PATHAN PATHOL PATHOS PATINA PATINE PATIOS PATMOS PATOIS PATROL PATRON PATTED PATTEN PATTER PATTON PAUCIS PAULEY PAUNCH PAUPER PAUSED PAUSES PAVANE PAVERS PAVING PAVLOV PAWERS PAWING PAWNED PAWNEE PAWNER PAWPAW PAWSAT PAXTON PAYBOX PAYDAY PAYEES PAYERS PAYFOR PAYING PAYOFF PAYOLA PAYOUT PAYSIN PAYSON PAYSUP

P•A•••

PAANGA PEACHY PEAHEN PEAKED PEALED PEANUT PEAPOD PEARLS PEARLY PEAVEY PHAGES PHAROS PHASED PHASER PHASES PHATIC PIAFFE PIAGET PIANOS PIAZZA PLACED PLACER PLACES PLACET PLACID PLAGAL PLAGES PLAGIO PLAGUE PLAICE PLAIDS PLAINS PLAINT PLAITS PLANAR PLANCK PLANED PLANER PLANES PLANET PLANKS PLANON PLANTE PLANTS PLAQUE PLASHY PLASMA PLASMO PLASTY PLATED PLATEN PLATER PLATES PLATTE PLAYAS PLAYAT PLAYED PLAYER PLAYON PLAYUP PLAZAS POACHY PRAGUE PRAISE PRAJNA PRANCE PRANGS PRANKS PRASES PRATED PRATER PRATES PRAVDA PRAWNS PRAXES PRAXIS PRAYED PRAYER PSALMS

P••A••

PADANG PAEANS PAGANS PAHANG PAHARI PAJAMA PALACE PALAEO PALATE PANADA PANAMA PAPACY PAPAGO PAPAIN PAPAWS PAPAYA PARADE PARANA PARANG PARAPH PATACA PAVANE PECANS PEDALS PEDANT PEDATE PELAGE PENANG PESACH PESAWA PETAIN PETALS PETARD PHIALS PHRASE PICABO PICARA PICARD PICARO PIKAKE PILAFS PILATE PINATA PIPALS PIRACY PIRANA PIRATE PISANO PISANS PIZAZZ PLEACH PLEADS PLEASE PLEATS PLIANT POLAND POMACE POMADE POPART POSADA POTAGE POTASH POTATO PREACH PREAMP PROAMS PTRAPS PURACE PYJAMA

P•••A•

PACMAN PADUAN PAISAS PALEAE PALLAS PALMAS PAMPAS PANDAS PAPPAS PAPUAN PARCAE PARIAH PARKAS PARKAY PARLAY PASCAL PASHAS PASTAS PATHAN PAWPAW PAWSAT PAYDAY PECKAT PEDLAR PEDWAY PEEKAT PEERAT PENMAN PENNAE PENPAL PENTAD PHILAE PHYLAE PICKAT PICKAX PIEMAN PIEPAN PIETAS PILLAR PINDAR PINEAL PINNAE PINNAS PINOAK PISGAH PITMAN PITSAW PIZZAS PLAGAL PLANAR PLAYAS PLAYAT PLAZAS PLEIAD PLEXAL PLICAE PLURAL POKEAT POLEAX POLKAS POPLAR POPPAS PORTAL POSTAL PREFAB PRELAW PREPAY PRETAX PREWAR PRIMAL PROTAX PROZAC PSYWAR PTBOAT PULSAR PUNJAB PUNKAH PURDAH PUTNAM

P••••A

PAANGA PAELLA PAGODA PAJAMA PAKULA PALLIA PALOMA PAMELA PANADA PANAMA PAPAYA PARANA PARULA PATACA PATINA PAYOLA PELOTA PENNIA PEORIA PEPITA PERCHA PERSIA PERUGA PESAWA PESETA PETULA PHOBIA PIAZZA PICARA PINATA PIRANA PLASMA PLEURA PNEUMA POMONA PORTIA POSADA PRAJNA PRAVDA PSYLLA PUEBLA PURINA PYJAMA PYTHIA

•PA•••

APACHE APATHY EPARCH OPAQUE SPACED SPACEK SPACER SPACES SPACEY SPADED SPADER SPADES SPADIX SPAHIS SPALLS SPANKS SPANKY SPARED SPARER SPARES SPARGE SPARKS SPARKY SPARSE SPARTA SPASMS SPATES SPATHE SPAVIN SPAWNS SPAYED UPASES

•P•A••

APIARY APPALL APPALS EPHAHS OPIATE SPEAKS SPEARS SPLASH SPLATS SPLAYS SPRAGS SPRAIN SPRANG SPRATS SPRAWL SPRAYS UPCAST UPDATE UPLAND UPTAKE UPTALK UPWARD

•P••A•

APEMAN APICAL APODAL APPEAL APPEAR APPIAN EPICAL EPINAL IPECAC OPERAS SPICAS SPINAL SPIRAL SPIVAK SPREAD UPBEAT UPLOAD UPROAR

•P•••A

APULIA OPTIMA SPARTA SPIREA

••PA••

ALPACA APPALL APPALS AUPAIR BYPASS BYPAST BYPATH COPAYS DEPART DEPAUL DEPAUW DOPANT ELPASO ESPANA EXPAND IMPACT IMPAIR IMPALA IMPALE IMPART INPART JAPANS LIPASE NEPALI PAPACY PAPAGO PAPAIN PAPAWS PAPAYA PIPALS POPART REPADS REPAID REPAIR REPAND REPAST REPAVE REPAYS RUPAUL SEPALS STPAUL TEPALS UNPACK UNPAID ZAPATA

••P•A•

ALPHAS APPEAL APPEAR APPIAN BYPLAY CAPIAS CAPTAN CUPPAS ESPIAL HEPCAT HEPTAD INPLAY KAPLAN KAPPAS KEPTAT LAPHAM NIPSAT ORPHAN PAPPAS PAPUAN POPLAR POPPAS REPEAL REPEAT REPLAN REPLAY RIPRAP RIPSAW RUPIAH SEPIAS SEPTAL TAPPAN TOPCAT TOPHAT TUPIAN

••P••A

ALPACA ASPERA CAPITA COPULA CUPOLA ESPANA ESPOSA EUPNEA IMPALA LAPUTA PAPAYA PEPITA SOPHIA TEPHRA TOPEKA ZAPATA

•••PA•

BHOPAL CALPAC CARPAL CASPAR COMPAQ CUPPAS DEEPAK FRYPAN GALPAL GASPAR INSPAN JUMPAT KAPPAS KEEPAT KEYPAD MILPAS NETPAY OILPAN OOMPAH PAMPAS PAPPAS PAWPAW PENPAL PIEPAN POPPAS PREPAY SAIPAN SAMPAN SNAPAT STUPAS SUBPAR TAIPAN TAPPAN TARPAN TINPAN TREPAN ZILPAH

•••P•A

CHOPRA COWPEA GRAPPA HOOPLA MYOPIA UTOPIA

••••PA

EUROPA GRAMPA GRAPPA JALAPA SHERPA

P•B•••

PABLUM PEBBLE PEBBLY POBOYS PTBOAT PUBLIC

P••B••

PAYBOX PEBBLE PEBBLY PHOBIA PHOBIC PHOBOS PLEBES PROBED PROBER PROBES PUEBLA PUEBLO

P•••B•

PASSBY PHILBY PHLEBO PHOEBE PICABO PLUMBS PUTSBY

P••••B

PREFAB PUNJAB

•PB•••

UPBEAT UPBOWS

•P••B•

EPHEBE

•P•••B

APLOMB

••P••B

SUPERB TOPJOB

•••PB•

DROPBY

P•C•••

PACERS PACIFY PACING PACINO PACKED PACKER PACKET PACKUP PACMAN PECANS PECKAT PECKED PECTIC PECTIN PICABO PICARA PICARD PICARO PICCHU PICKAT PICKAX PICKED PICKER PICKET PICKLE PICKON PICKUP PICNIC PICOTS PICULS POCKET POCONO PUCKER

P••C••

PANCHO PARCAE PARCEL PASCAL PATCHY PAUCIS PEACHY PENCEL PENCIL PERCHA PESCOW PHOCIS PICCHU PIECED PIECER PIECES PINCER PISCES PITCHY PLACED PLACER PLACES PLACET PLACID PLICAE PLUCKS PLUCKY POACHY PONCES PONCHO POUCHY PRECIS PRICED PRICER PRICES PRICEY PRICKS PROCNE PSYCHE PSYCHO PSYCHS PUNCHY

P•••C•

PALACE PANICS PAPACY PATACA PAUNCH PEERCE PESACH PIERCE PIRACY PLAICE PLANCK PLEACH POLICE POLICY POMACE POUNCE PRANCE PREACH PRINCE PUMICE PURACE PUTSCH

P••••C

PARSEC PECTIC PELVIC PEPTIC PHATIC PHOBIC PHONIC PHOTIC PICNIC POETIC PONTIC PROZAC PUBLIC PYKNIC

•PC•••

UPCAST

•P•C••

APACHE APICAL APICES EPICAL EPOCHS IPECAC SPACED SPACEK SPACER SPACES SPACEY SPECIE SPECKS SPICAS SPICED SPICES

•P••C•

APERCU APIECE EPARCH OPTICS SPEECH SPLICE SPRUCE UPTICK

•P•••C

IPECAC

••PC••

HEPCAT TOPCAT

••P•C•

ALPACA ASPECT ASPICS DEPICT EXPECT IMPACT KOPECK PAPACY TOPICS UNPACK

••P••C

COPTIC CUPRIC ORPHIC PEPTIC SEPTIC ZIPLOC

•••P•C

CALPAC MYOPIC ONSPEC TROPIC

P•D•••

PADANG PADDED PADDER PADDLE PADRES PADUAN PEDALS PEDANT PEDATE PEDDLE PEDLAR PEDWAY PIDGIN PODDED PODIUM PODUNK PUDDLE PUDDLY

P••D••

PADDED PADDER PADDLE PAIDIN PAIDUP PANDAS PANDER PANDIT PARDON PAYDAY PEDDLE PEEDEE PENDED PERDUE PHEDRE PINDAR PINDUS PLEDGE PODDED POLDER PONDER POODLE POWDER PRIDED PRIDES PRUDES PUDDLE PUDDLY PUNDIT PURDAH PURDUE PYEDOG

P•••D•

PAGODA PANADA PARADE PARODY PLAIDS PLEADS POMADE POSADA POUNDS PRAVDA PSEUDO PSEUDS

P••••D

PACKED PADDED PAINED PAIRED PALLED PALLID PALMED PANNED PANTED PARKED

PARRED
PARSED
PARTED
PASSED
PASTED
PATTED
PAUSED
PAWNED
PEAKED
PEALED
PEAPOD
PECKED
PEEKED
PEELED
PEENED
PEEPED
PEERED
PEEVED
PEGGED
PELTED
PENDED
PENNED
PENROD
PENTAD
PEPPED
PEQUOD
PERIOD
PERKED
PERMED
PERNOD
PETARD
PETTED
PHASED
PHONED
PHYSED
PICARD
PICKED
PIECED
PIGGED
PILLED
PINGED
PINKED
PINNED
PIPPED
PIQUED
PITHED
PITIED
PITTED
PLACED
PLACID
PLANED
PLATED
PLAYED
PLEIAD
PLOWED
PLUMED
PODDED
POISED
POLAND
POLLED
PONGED
PONGID
PONIED
POOHED
POOLED
POOPED
POPPED
PORTED
POSTED
POTTED
POURED
POUTED
PRATED
PRAYED
PREMED
PREYED
PRICED
PRIDED
PRIMED
PRIZED
PROBED
PROSED
PROVED
PRUNED
PUFFED
PUGGED
PULLED
PULPED
PULSED
PUMPED
PUNNED
PUNTED
PUREED
PURGED
PURLED
PURRED
PURSED
PUSHED
PUTRID
PUTTED

•PD•••
UPDATE
UPDIKE

•P•D••
APODAL
EPODES
SPADED
SPADER
SPADES
SPADIX
SPEDUP
SPIDER

•P••D•
APHIDS
EPHODS
SPEEDO
SPEEDS
SPEEDY
SPENDS
UPENDS
UPSIDE

•P•••D
APPEND
OPENED
OPINED
SPACED
SPADED
SPARED
SPAYED
SPEWED
SPICED
SPIKED
SPINED
SPIRED
SPITED
SPOKED
SPREAD
SPUMED
UPHELD
UPHOLD
UPLAND
UPLOAD
UPWARD
UPWIND

••PD••
LAPDOG
TOPDOG

••P•D•
BIPEDS
BIPODS
CUPIDS
DIPODY
IMPEDE
LIPIDE
LIPIDS
MOPEDS
RAPIDS
REPADS

••P••D
AMPHID
APPEND
BOPPED
CAPPED
CAPSID
COPIED
COPPED
CUPPED
DAPPED
DEPEND
DIPPED
ESPIED
EXPAND
EXPEND
GAPPED
GIPPED
GYPPED
HAPPED
HEPTAD
HIPPED
HOPPED
HYPOED
IMPEND
LAPPED
LAPSED
LIPOID
LIPPED
LOPPED
MAPPED
MOPPED
NAPPED
NIPPED
PEPPED
PIPPED
POPPED
RAPPED
REPAID
REPAND
RIPPED
SAPPED
SIPPED
SOPPED
SUPPED
TAPPED
TIPPED
TOPPED
UNPAID
YAPPED
YIPPED
ZAPPED
ZIPPED

•••P•D
BEEPED
BOPPED
BUMPED
BURPED
CAMPED
CAPPED
CARPED
CLEPED
COOPED
COPPED
CUPPED
CUSPED
CUSPID
DAMPED
DAPPED
DIPPED
DRAPED
DUMPED
ELAPID
ELOPED
GAPPED
GASPED
GAWPED
GIPPED
GRIPED
GROPED
GULPED
GYPPED
HAPPED
HARPED
HASPED
HEAPED
HELPED
HIPPED
HISPID
HOOPED
HOPPED
HUMPED
ISOPOD
JUMPED
KEYPAD
LAPPED
LEAPED
LIMPED
LIMPID
LIPPED
LISPED
LOOPED
LOPPED
LUMPED
MAPPED
MOPPED
MUMPED
NAPPED
NIPPED
PEAPOD
PEEPED
PEPPED
PIPPED
POOPED
POPPED
PULPED
PUMPED
RAMPED
RAPPED
RASPED
REAPED
RIPPED
ROMPED
RSVPED
SAPPED
SCAPED
SCOPED
SEEPED
SHAPED
SIPPED
SLOPED
SNIPED
SOAPED
SOPPED
STUPID
SUPPED
SWIPED
TAMPED
TAPPED
TEMPED
TIPPED
TOPPED
TORPID
TREPID
TRIPOD
UNIPOD
VAMPED
VESPID
WARPED
WISPED
YAPPED
YAWPED
YELPED
YIPPED
ZAPPED
ZIPPED

PE••••
PEACHY
PEAHEN
PEAKED
PEALED
PEANUT
PEAPOD
PEARLS
PEARLY
PEAVEY
PEBBLE
PEBBLY
PECANS
PECKAT
PECKED
PECTIC
PECTIN
PEDALS
PEDANT
PEDATE
PEDDLE
PEDLAR
PEDWAY
PEEDEE
PEEKAT
PEEKED
PEELED
PEELER
PEENED
PEEPED
PEEPER
PEERAT
PEERCE
PEERED
PEERIN
PEEVED
PEEVES
PEEWEE
PEGGED
PEGLER
PEGTOP
PEKING
PEKINS
PEKOES
PELAGE
PELEUS
PELIKE
PELION
PELLET
PELMET
PELOPS
PELOTA
PELTED
PELTER
PELTRY
PELVIC
PELVIS
PENANG
PENCEL
PENCIL
PENDED
PENGHU
PENMAN
PENMEN
PENNAE
PENNED
PENNER
PENNEY
PENNIA
PENNIS
PENNON
PENPAL
PENROD
PENSEE
PENTAD
PENTUP
PENULT
PENURY
PEOPLE
PEORIA
PEPFUL
PEPINO
PEPITA
PEPLOS
PEPLUM
PEPPED
PEPPER
PEPSIN
PEPSUP
PEPTIC
PEQUOD
PEQUOT
PERCHA
PERDUE
PERILS
PERIOD
PERISH
PERKED
PERKUP
PERMED
PERMIT
PERNIO
PERNOD
PERROT
PERSIA
PERSON
PERTER
PERTLY
PERUGA
PERUKE
PERUSE
PESACH
PESAWA
PESCOW
PESETA
PESTER
PESTLE
PESTOS
PETAIN
PETALS
PETARD
PETERS
PETITE
PETREL
PETRIE
PETROG
PETROL
PETTED
PETTER
PETTIT
PETULA
PEWEES
PEWITS
PEWTER
PEYOTE
PEYTON

P•E•••
PAEANS
PAELLA
PAEONS
PEEDEE
PEEKAT
PEEKED
PEELED
PEELER
PEENED
PEEPED
PEEPER
PEERAT
PEERCE
PEERED
PEERIN
PEEVED
PEEVES
PEEWEE
PHEDRE
PHENOL
PHENOM
PHENYL
PIECED
PIECER
PIECES
PIEMAN
PIEMEN
PIEPAN
PIERCE
PIERRE
PIETAS
PIETER
PIETIN
PIETRO
PLEACH
PLEADS
PLEASE
PLEATS
PLEBES
PLEDGE
PLEIAD
PLENTY
PLENUM
PLEURA
PLEXAL
PLEXOR
PLEXUS
PNEUMA
POETIC
POETRY
PREACH
PREAMP
PRECIS
PREENS
PREFAB
PREFER
PREFIX
PRELAW
PRELIM
PREMED
PREMIE
PRENUP
PREPAY
PREPPY
PRESET
PRESTO
PRETAX
PRETER
PRETTY
PREVIN
PREWAR
PREYED
PREYON
PSEUDO
PSEUDS
PUEBLA
PUEBLO
PUENTE
PUERTO
PYEDOG

P••E••
PACERS
PAGERS
PALEAE
PALELY
PALEST
PAMELA
PANELS
PAPERS
PAPERY
PARENS
PARENT
PARERS
PARETO
PAREVE
PASEOS
PATENS
PATENT
PATERS
PAVERS
PAWERS
PAYEES
PAYERS
PELEUS
PESETA
PETERS
PEWEES
PHLEBO
PHLEGM
PHOEBE
PIGEON
PIKERS
PILEIN
PILEON
PILEUM
PILEUP
PILEUS
PINEAL
PINERO
PINERY
PIPERS
PIPEUP
PIXELS
PLIERS
POKEAT
POKERS
POKERY
POKEYS
POLEAX
POLERS
POLEYN
POMELO
POPEYE
POSERS
POSEUR
POTEEN
POTENT
POWELL
POWERS
PREENS
PRIERS
PRIEST
PROEMS
PUREED
PUREES
PURELY
PUREST

P•••E•
PACKED
PACKER
PACKET
PADDED
PADDER
PADRES
PAINED
PAIRED
PALAEO
PALIER
PALLED
PALLET
PALMED
PALMER
PALTER
PAMPER
PANDER
PANNED
PANNER
PANNES
PANTED
PANZER
PAPIER
PARCEL
PARGET
PARKED
PARKER
PARLEY
PARRED
PARREL
PARSEC
PARSED
PARSEE
PARSER
PARSES
PARTED
PASSED
PASSEL
PASSER
PASSES
PASTED
PASTEL
PASTES
PATTED
PATTEN
PATTER
PAULEY
PAUPER
PAUSED
PAUSES
PAWNED
PAWNEE
PAWNER
PAYEES
PEAHEN
PEAKED
PEALED
PEAVEY
PECKED
PEEDEE
PEEKED
PEELED
PEELER
PEENED
PEEPED
PEEPER
PEERED
PEEVED
PEEVES
PEEWEE
PEGGED
PEGLER
PEKOES
PELLET
PELMET
PELTED
PELTER
PENCEL
PENDED
PENMEN
PENNED
PENNER
PENNEY
PENSEE
PEPPED
PEPPER
PERKED
PERMED
PERTER
PESTER
PETREL
PETTED
PETTER
PEWEES
PEWTER
PFIZER
PHAGES
PHASED
PHASER
PHASES
PHLOEM
PHONED
PHONES
PHONEY
PHOOEY
PHYSED
PIAGET
PICKED
PICKER
PICKET
PIECED
PIECER
PIECES
PIEMEN
PIETER
PIGGED
PIGLET
PIGPEN
PILFER
PILLED
PINCER
PINGED
PINIER
PINKED
PINKEN
PINKER
PINNED
PINNER
PINTER
PIOLET
PIPIER
PIPPED
PIQUED
PIQUES
PIQUET
PISCES
PISTES
PITHED
PITIED
PITIER
PITIES
PITMEN
PITTED
PITTER
PIXIES
PLACED
PLACER
PLACES
PLACET
PLAGES
PLANED
PLANER
PLANES
PLANET
PLATED
PLATEN
PLATER
PLATES
PLAYED
PLAYER
PLEBES
PLOVER
PLOWED
PLOWER
PLUMED
PLUMES
PLUSES
POCKET
PODDED
POGIES
POISED
POISES
POKIER
POLDER
POLLED
POLLEN
POLLER
POLLEX
POMMEE
POMMEL
POMPEY
PONCES
PONDER
PONGED
PONGEE
PONIED
PONIES
PONTES
POOHED
POOLED
POOPED
POORER
POPPED
POPPER
POPPET
PORKER
PORTED
PORTER
POSHER
POSIES
POSSES
POSSET
POSTED
POSTER
POTEEN
POTHER
POTTED
POTTER
POURED
POURER
POUTED
POUTER
POWDER
PRASES
PRATED
PRATER
PRATES
PRAXES
PRAYED
PRAYER
PREFER
PREMED
PRESET
PRETER
PREYED
PRICED
PRICER
PRICES
PRICEY
PRIDED
PRIDES
PRIMED
PRIMER
PRIMES
PRIPET
PRIVET
PRIZED
PRIZES
PROBED
PROBER
PROBES
PROLES
PROPEL
PROPER
PROSED
PROSER
PROSES
PROTEI
PROTEM
PROVED
PROVEN
PROVER
PROVES
PRUDES
PRUNED
PRUNER
PRUNES
PUCKER
PUFFED
PUFFER
PUGGED
PUGREE
PULLED
PULLET
PULLEY
PULPED
PULSED
PULSES
PUMMEL
PUMPED
PUMPER
PUNIER
PUNKER
PUNNED
PUNNET
PUNTED
PUNTER
PUPPET
PUREED
PUREES
PURGED
PURGES
PURLED
PURRED
PURRER
PURSED
PURSER
PURSES
PURVEY
PUSHED
PUSHES
PUSSES
PUTTED
PUTTEE
PUTTER
PYXIES

P••••E
PADDLE
PAIUTE
PALACE
PALATE
PALEAE
PARADE
PARCAE
PAREVE
PAROLE
PARSEE
PARURE
PATINE
PAVANE
PAWNEE
PEBBLE
PEDATE
PEDDLE
PEEDEE
PEERCE
PEEWEE
PELAGE
PELIKE
PENNAE
PENSEE
PEOPLE
PERDUE
PERUKE
PERUSE
PESTLE
PETITE
PETRIE
PEYOTE
PHEDRE
PHILAE
PHOEBE
PHRASE
PHYLAE
PIAFFE
PICKLE
PIERCE
PIERRE
PIFFLE
PIGGIE
PIKAKE
PILATE
PILOSE
PINITE
PINKIE
PINNAE
PINOLE
PINTLE
PIRATE
PLAGUE
PLAICE
PLANTE
PLAQUE
PLATTE
PLEASE
PLEDGE
PLICAE
PLISSE
PLUNGE
POINTE
POLICE
POLITE
POMACE
POMADE
POMMEE
PONGEE
POODLE
POPEYE
POPPLE
POTAGE
POTPIE
POTTLE
POUNCE
POUSSE
PRAGUE
PRAISE
PRANCE
PREMIE
PRINCE
PROCNE
PROPRE
PROWSE
PRYNNE
PSYCHE
PUDDLE
PUENTE
PUGREE
PUISNE
PULQUE
PUMICE
PUNKIE
PURACE
PURDUE
PURFLE
PURINE
PURPLE
PURSUE
PUTTEE
PUZZLE
PYRITE

•PE•••
APEMAN
APEMEN
APERCU
APEXES
IPECAC
KPELLE
OPENED
OPENER
OPENLY
OPENTO
OPENUP
OPERAS
SPEAKS
SPEARS
SPECIE
SPECKS
SPEDUP
SPEECH
SPEEDO
SPEEDS
SPEEDY
SPELLS
SPENDS
SPERRY
SPEWED
UPENDS

•P•E••
APIECE
APPEAL
APPEAR
APPEND
APTEST
EPHEBE
SPEECH
SPEEDO
SPEEDS
SPEEDY
SPHERE
SPHERY
SPIELS
SPIERS
SPLEEN
SPREAD
SPREES
UPBEAT
UPHELD
UPKEEP
UPPERS
UPSETS
UPWELL

•P••E•
APEMEN
APEXES
APICES
APOGEE
APPLES
APPLET
EPODES
EPOPEE
OPENED
OPENER
OPINED
OPINER
OPINES
OPUSES
SPACED
SPACEK
SPACER
SPACES
SPACEY
SPADED
SPADER
SPADES
SPARED
SPARER
SPARES
SPATES
SPAYED
SPEWED
SPICED
SPICES
SPIDER
SPIKED
SPIKER
SPIKES
SPILES
SPINED
SPINEL
SPINES
SPINET
SPIREA
SPIRED
SPIRES
SPITED
SPITES
SPLEEN
SPOKED
SPOKEN
SPOKES
SPORES
SPREES
SPRIER
SPRUES
SPRYER
SPUMED
SPUMES
UPASES
UPKEEP

•P•••E
APACHE
APIECE
APLITE
APOGEE
APPOSE
EPHEBE
EPOPEE
KPELLE
OPAQUE
OPHITE
OPIATE
OPPOSE
SPARGE
SPARSE
SPATHE
SPECIE
SPHERE
SPLICE
SPLINE
SPONGE
SPOUSE
SPRITE
SPRUCE
SPURGE
UPDATE
UPDIKE
UPRISE
UPROSE
UPSIDE
UPTAKE
UPTIME

••PE••
ALPERT
AMPERE
APPEAL
APPEAR
APPEND
ARPENT
ASPECT
ASPENS
ASPERA
BIPEDS
BOPEEP
CAPERS
CUPELS
DEPEND
DUPERY
EMPERY
EXPECT
EXPELS
EXPEND
EXPERT
GAPERS
HOPERS
HYPEUP
IMPEDE
IMPELS
IMPEND
IMPERF

JAPERS JAPERY KOPECK KOPEKS LAPELS LIPENG LOPERS MOPEDS MOPERS MOPERY NAPERY NOPETS PAPERS PAPERY PIPERS PIPEUP POPEYE REPEAL REPEAT REPEGS REPELS REPENT RIPELY RIPENS RIPEST ROPEIN ROPERS RUPEES RUPERT STPETE SUPERB SUPERS TAPERS TEPEES TOPEKA TOPERS TUPELO TYPERS TYPEUP UNPEGS UNPENS UPPERS VIPERS WIPERS WIPEUP

••P•E•

AMPLER APPLES APPLET BOPEEP BOPPED BOPPER CAPLET CAPPED CAPPER CIPHER COPIED COPIER COPIES COPLEY COPPED COPPER COPSES COPTER CUPPED CYPHER DAPPED DAPPER DIPPED DIPPER DOPIER DUPLEX ESPIED ESPIES EUPNEA GAPPED GIPPED GIPPER GOPHER GYPPED GYPPER HAPPED HAPPEN HEPPER HIPPED HIPPER HOPPED HOPPER HYPHEN HYPOED KEPLER KIPPER KOPJES KOPPEL LAPPED LAPPET LAPSED LAPSES LAPTEV LIPPED LOPPED LOPPER MAPLES MAPPED MAPPER MOPIER MOPPED MOPPER MOPPET MUPPET NAPIER NAPLES NAPPED NAPPER NAPPES NEPHEW NIPPED NIPPER NIPSEY OSPREY PAPIER PEPPED PEPPER PIPIER PIPPED POPPED POPPER POPPET PUPPET RAPIER RAPPED RAPPEE RAPPEL RAPPER RIPKEN RIPLEY RIPPED RIPPER ROPIER RUPEES SAPPED SAPPER SEPTET SIPPED SIPPER SIPPET SOPPED SUPPED SUPPER TAPPED TAPPER TAPPET TEPEES TIPPED TIPPER TIPPET TOPPED TOPPER TOPTEN TYPIER WAPNER YAPPED YIPPED YIPPEE ZAPPED ZAPPER ZIPPED ZIPPER

••P••E

ALPINE AMPERE AMPULE APPOSE ASPIRE CAPONE CAPOTE DAPHNE DAPPLE DEPONE DEPOSE DEPUTE DIPOLE EMPIRE EXPIRE EXPOSE FIPPLE HIPPIE HOPPLE IMPALE IMPEDE IMPOSE IMPURE IMPUTE LIPASE LIPIDE LUPINE LUPONE NAPPIE OPPOSE ORPINE POPEYE POPPLE RAPINE RAPPEE REPAVE REPINE REPOSE REPUTE RIPPLE SOPHIE STPETE SUPINE SUPPLE TIPPLE TIPTOE TOPPLE UMPIRE UNPILE YIPPEE YUPPIE

•••PE•

AUSPEX BEEPED BEEPER BOPPED BOPPER BUMPED BUMPER BURPED CAMPED CAMPER CAPPED CAPPER CARPED CARPEL CARPER CARPET CASPER CHAPEL CLEPED COMPEL COOPED COOPER COPPED COPPER COUPES COWPEA COWPER CRAPES CREPES CRIPES CUPPED CUSPED DAMPED DAMPEN DAMPER DAPPED DAPPER DEEPEN DEEPER DIAPER DIPPED DIPPER DISPEL DRAPED DRAPER DRAPES DRUPES DUMPED DUMPER ELOPED ELOPER ELOPES EPOPEE ETAPES GAPPED GASPED GASPER GAWPED GIPPED GIPPER GOSPEL GRAPES GRAPEY GRIPED GRIPER GRIPES GROPED GROPES GULPED GULPER GYPPED GYPPER HAMPER HAPPED HAPPEN HARPED HARPER HASPED HEAPED HELPED HELPER HEPPER HIPPED HIPPER HOOPED HOOPER HOPPED HOPPER HUMPED INAPET JASPER JUMPED JUMPER KEEPER KIPPER KOPPEL LAPPED LAPPET LAUPER LEAPED LEAPER LIMPED LIMPER LIMPET LIPPED LISPED LOOPED LOOPER LOPPED LOPPER LOUPES LUMPED LUMPEN LUMPER MAPPED MAPPER MOPPED MOPPER MOPPET MUMPED MUPPET MYOPES NAPPED NAPPER NAPPES NIPPED NIPPER ONSPEC PAMPER PAUPER PEEPED PEEPER PEPPED PEPPER PIGPEN PIPPED POMPEY POOPED POPPED POPPER POPPET PRIPET PROPEL PROPER PULPED PUMPED PUMPER PUPPET RAMPED RAPPED RAPPEE RAPPEL RAPPER RASPED RASPER REAPED REAPER REOPEN RIPPED RIPPER ROMPED ROMPER RSVPED SAPPED SAPPER SCAPED SCAPES SCOPED SCOPES SEEPED SEMPER SHAPED SHAPER SHAPES SIMPER SIPPED SIPPER SIPPET SLOPED SLOPES SLYPES SNIPED SNIPER SNIPES SNOPES SOAPED SOAPER SOPPED STAPES STIPEL STIPES STOPES STUPES SUPPED SUPPER SWIPED SWIPER SWIPES TAIPEI TAMPED TAMPER TAPPED TAPPER TAPPET TAUPES TEMPED TEMPEH TEMPER TIPPED TIPPER TIPPET TOPPED TOPPER TOUPEE TROPES TROPEZ UNOPEN USOPEN VAMPED VAMPER VESPER WARPED WEEPER WISPED WOLPER YAPPED YAWPED YAWPER YELPED YELPER YIPPED YIPPEE ZAPPED ZAPPER ZIPPED ZIPPER

•••P•E

COUPLE DAPPLE DIEPPE DIMPLE ELAPSE EPOPEE FIPPLE FRAPPE GRIPPE HIPPIE HOOPLE HOOPOE HOPPLE KELPIE KEWPIE MAGPIE MARPLE MUDPIE NAPPIE PEOPLE POPPLE POTPIE PROPRE PURPLE RAPPEE RIMPLE RIPPLE RUMPLE SAMPLE SEMPRE SHOPPE SIMPLE SKOPJE STAPLE STEPPE SUPPLE TEMPLE TIPPLE TOPPLE TOUPEE TRIPLE WEEPIE WIMPLE YIPPEE YUPPIE

••••PE

ASLOPE CANAPE DIEPPE ECTYPE ESCAPE EUROPE FELIPE FRAPPE GRIPPE GUIMPE LENAPE MEROPE METOPE ONTAPE RECIPE RETAPE RETYPE SCRAPE SERAPE SHOPPE STEPPE STRIPE THORPE TROMPE TROUPE UNRIPE

PF••••

PFIZER

P•F•••

PIFFLE PUFFED PUFFER PUFFIN

P••F••

PANFRY PANFUL PAYFOR PEPFUL PIAFFE PIFFLE PILFER POPFLY POTFUL PREFAB PREFER PREFIX PROFIT PUFFED PUFFER PUFFIN PURFLE

P•••F•

PACIFY PAYOFF PIAFFE PILAFS POPOFF PROOFS PURIFY PUTOFF

P••••F

PAYOFF POPOFF PUTOFF

•P•F••

OPTFOR SPIFFS SPIFFY

•P••F•

SPIFFS SPIFFY SPOOFS UPLIFT

••PF••

CAPFUL CUPFUL LAPFUL PEPFUL POPFLY

••P•F•

HOPOFF POPOFF RIPOFF TAPOFF TIPOFF TOPOFF TYPIFY

••P••F

HOPOFF IMPERF POPOFF RIPOFF TAPOFF TIPOFF TOPOFF

•••P•F

STAPUF

P•G•••

PAGANS PAGERS PAGING PAGODA PEGGED PEGLER PEGTOP PIGEON PIGGED PIGGIE PIGLET PIGNUT PIGOUT PIGPEN PIGSTY POGIES PUGGED PUGREE

P••G••

PARGET PEGGED PENGHU PHAGES PIAGET PIDGIN PIGGED PIGGIE PINGED PISGAH PLAGAL PLAGES PLAGIO PLAGUE PLIGHT PLUGIN PONGED PONGEE PONGID POPGUN PRAGUE PUGGED PURGED PURGES

P•••G•

PAANGA PAPAGO PELAGE PERUGA PHLEGM PLEDGE PLOUGH PLUNGE POTAGE PRANGS PRONGS

P••••G

PACING PADANG PAGING PAHANG PALING PARANG PARING PAVING PAWING PAYING PEKING PENANG PETROG PHOTOG PIKING PILING PINING PIPING PLYING POKING POLING PORING POSING PROLOG PRYING PULING PYEDOG

•P•G••

APOGEE SPIGOT

•P••G•

OPPUGN SPARGE SPONGE SPONGY SPRAGS SPRIGS SPURGE

•P•••G

EPILOG EPPING OPTING SPRANG SPRING SPRUNG SPYING UPPING

••PG••

CAPGUN POPGUN TOPGUN

••P•G•

IMPUGN OPPUGN PAPAGO REPEGS REPUGN UNPEGS

••P••G

COPING DOPING DUPING EPPING GAPING HOPING HYPING IMPING JAPING LAPDOG LIPENG LOPING MOPING PIPING ROPING TAPING TOPDOG TYPING UNPLUG UPPING WIPING

PH••••

PHAGES PHAROS PHASED PHASER PHASES PHATIC PHEDRE PHENOL PHENOM PHENYL PHIALS PHILAE PHILBY PHILIP PHILLY PHILOL PHILOS PHLEBO PHLEGM PHLOEM PHOBIA PHOBIC PHOBOS PHOCIS PHOEBE PHONED PHONES PHONEY PHONIC PHONON PHONOS PHOOEY PHOTIC PHOTOG PHOTON PHOTOS PHRASE PHYLAE PHYLLO PHYLUM PHYSED PHYSIO

P•H•••

PAHANG PAHARI

P••H••

PASHAS PASHTO PATHAN PATHOL PATHOS PEAHEN PITHED POOHED POSHER POSHLY POTHER PUSHED PUSHES PUSHON PUSHUP PYTHIA PYTHON

P•••H•

PANCHO PATCHY PEACHY PENGHU PERCHA PICCHU PITCHY PLASHY PLIGHT PLUSHY POACHY PONCHO POUCHY PSYCHE PSYCHO PSYCHS PUNCHY

P••••H

PALISH PARAPH PARIAH PARISH PAUNCH PERISH PESACH PISGAH PLEACH PLINTH PLOUGH POLISH POTASH PREACH PUNISH PUNKAH PURDAH PUTSCH

•PH•••

APHIDS EPHAHS EPHEBE EPHODS EPHORI EPHORS EPHRON OPHITE SPHERE SPHERY SPHINX UPHELD UPHILL UPHOLD

•P•H••

SPAHIS UPSHOT

•P••H•

APACHE APATHY EPHAHS EPOCHS SPATHE UPJOHN

•P•••H

EPARCH SPEECH SPILTH SPLASH SPLOSH UPPISH UPRUSH

••PH••

ALPHAS AMPHID CIPHER CYPHER DAPHNE GOPHER HIPHOP HYPHEN LAPHAM NEPHEW NEPHRO ORPHAN ORPHIC SIPHON SOPHIA SOPHIE SYPHON TEPHRA TOPHAT TOPHUS TYPHUS ZEPHYR

••P•H•

DEPTHS SAPPHO

••P••H

ASPISH BYPATH IMPISH MOPISH RUPIAH UPPISH

•••PH•

ALEPHS DELPHI GLYPHS GRAPHS GRAPHY HUMPHS LYMPHS MORPHO MORPHS MORPHY MURPHY NYMPHS SAPPHO SYLPHS TROPHY

•••P•H

OOMPAH TEMPEH ZILPAH

••••PH

ADOLPH CALIPH CERIPH GUELPH JOSEPH PARAPH SERAPH TERAPH

PI••••

PIAFFE PIAGET PIANOS PIAZZA PICABO PICARA PICARD PICARO PICCHU PICKAT PICKAX PICKED PICKER PICKET PICKLE PICKON PICKUP PICNIC PICOTS PICULS PIDGIN PIECED PIECER PIECES PIEMAN PIEMEN PIEPAN PIERCE PIERRE PIETAS PIETER PIETIN PIETRO PIFFLE PIGEON PIGGED PIGGIE PIGLET PIGNUT PIGOUT PIGPEN PIGSTY PIKAKE PIKERS PIKING PILAFS PILATE PILEIN PILEON PILEUM PILEUP PILEUS PILFER PILING PILLAR PILLED PILLOW PILOSE PILOTI PILOTS PIMINY PINATA PINCER PINDAR PINDUS PINEAL PINERO PINERY PINGED PINIER PINING PINION PINITE PINKED PINKEN PINKER PINKIE PINNAE PINNAS PINNED PINNER PINOAK PINOLE PINONS PINOTS PINSON PINTER PINTLE PINTOS PINUPS PINXIT PINYIN PINYON PINZON PIOLET PIPALS PIPERS PIPEUP PIPIER PIPING PIPITS PIPKIN PIPPED PIPPIN PIQUED PIQUES PIQUET PIRACY PIRANA PIRATE PIRRIP PISANO PISANS PISCES PISGAH PISTES PISTIL PISTOL PISTON PITCHY PITHED PITIED PITIER PITIES PITMAN PITMEN PITONS PITSAW PITTED PITTER PIVOTS PIXELS PIXIES PIZAZZ PIZZAS

P•I•••

PAIDIN PAIDUP PAILOU PAINED PAINTS PAINTY PAIRED PAIRUP PAISAS PAIUTE PFIZER PHIALS PHILAE PHILBY PHILIP PHILLY PHILOL PHILOS PLIANT PLICAE PLIERS PLIGHT PLINKS PLINTH PLISSE POILUS POINTE POINTS POINTY POIROT POISED POISES POISON PRICED PRICER PRICES PRICEY PRICKS PRIDED PRIDES PRIERS PRIEST PRIMAL PRIMED PRIMER PRIMES PRIMLY PRIMOS PRIMPS PRIMUM PRIMUS PRINCE PRINKS PRINTS PRIONS PRIORI PRIORS PRIORY PRIPET PRISMS PRISON PRISSY PRIVET PRIZED PRIZES PUISNE

P••I••

PACIFY PACING PACINO PAGING PALIER

PALING
PALISH
PAMIRS
PANICS
PAPIER
PARIAH
PARING
PARISH
PARITY
PATINA
PATINE
PATIOS
PAVING
PAWING
PAYING
PEKING
PEKINS
PELIKE
PELION
PEPINO
PEPITA
PERILS
PERIOD
PERISH
PETITE
PEWITS
PIKING
PILING
PIMINY
PINIER
PINING
PINION
PINITE
PIPIER
PIPING
PIPITS
PITIED
PITIER
PITIES
PIXIES
PLAICE
PLAIDS
PLAINS
PLAINT
PLAITS
PLEIAD
PLYING
PODIUM
POGIES
POKIER
POKILY
POKING
POLICE
POLICY
POLING
POLISH
POLITE
POLITY
PONIED
PONIES
PORING
POSIES
POSING
POSITS
POTION
PRAISE
PRYING
PULING
PUMICE
PUNIER
PUNILY
PUNISH
PUPILS
PURIFY
PURINA
PURINE
PURISM
PURIST
PURITY
PYRITE
PYXIES

P•••I•
PAIDIN
PALLIA
PALLID
PANDIT
PAPAIN
PAQUIN
PARNIS
PARRIS
PARVIS
PASSIM
PASTIS
PATOIS
PAUCIS
PAYSIN
PECTIC
PECTIN
PEERIN
PELVIC
PELVIS
PENCIL
PENNIA
PENNIS
PEORIA
PEPSIN
PEPTIC
PERMIT
PERNIO
PERSIA
PETAIN
PETRIE
PETTIT
PHATIC
PHILIP
PHOBIA
PHOBIC
PHOCIS
PHONIC
PHOTIC
PHYSIO
PICNIC
PIDGIN
PIETIN
PIGGIE
PILEIN
PINKIE
PINXIT
PINYIN
PIPKIN
PIPPIN
PIRRIP
PISTIL
PLACID
PLAGIO
PLUGIN
POETIC
PONGID
PONTIC
POPLIN
POPSIN
PORTIA
POSTIT
POTPIE
POURIN
PRAXIS
PRECIS
PREFIX
PRELIM
PREMIE
PREVIN
PROFIT
PROLIX
PROSIT
PUBLIC
PUFFIN
PULLIN
PULPIT
PUNDIT
PUNKIE
PURLIN
PUTRID
PUTSIN
PYKNIC
PYTHIA

P••••I
PAHARI
PAPYRI
PILOTI
POLLOI
POPULI
POTOSI
PRIORI
PROTEI

•PI•••
APIARY
APICAL
APICES
APIECE
EPICAL
EPILOG
EPINAL
EPIRUS
OPIATE
OPINED
OPINER
OPINES
SPICAS
SPICED
SPICES
SPIDER
SPIELS
SPIERS
SPIFFS
SPIFFY
SPIGOT
SPIKED
SPIKER
SPIKES
SPILES
SPILLS
SPILTH
SPINAL
SPINED
SPINEL
SPINES
SPINET
SPINKS
SPINTO
SPIRAL
SPIREA
SPIRED
SPIRES
SPIRIT
SPIROS
SPITED
SPITES
SPIVAK
SPIVVY

•P•I••
APHIDS
APLITE
APPIAN
EPPING
OPHITE
OPTICS
OPTIMA
OPTING
OPTION
SPHINX
SPLICE
SPLINE
SPLINT
SPLITS
SPOILS
SPOILT
SPRIER
SPRIGS
SPRING
SPRINT
SPRITE
SPRITS
SPRITZ
SPYING
UPDIKE
UPHILL
UPLIFT
UPLINK
UPPING
UPPISH
UPPITY
UPRISE
UPSIDE
UPTICK
UPTIME
UPWIND

•P••I•
APULIA
SPADIX
SPAHIS
SPAVIN
SPECIE
SPIRIT
SPRAIN

•P•••I
EPHORI

••PI••
ALPINE
APPIAN
ASPICS
ASPIRE
ASPISH
CAPIAS
CAPITA
COPIED
COPIER
COPIES
COPING
CUPIDS
DEPICT
DOPIER
DOPING
DUPING
EMPIRE
EPPING
ESPIAL
ESPIED
ESPIES
EXPIRE
EXPIRY
GAPING
HOPING
HYPING
IMPING
IMPISH
JAPING
LAPINS
LIPIDE
LIPIDS
LOPING
LUPINE
LUPINO
MOPIER
MOPING
MOPISH
NAPIER
ORPINE
PAPIER
PEPINO
PEPITA
PIPIER
PIPING
PIPITS
PUPILS
RAPIDS
RAPIER
RAPINE
RAPINI
REPINE
REPINS
ROPIER
ROPING
RUPIAH
SEPIAS
SUPINE
TAPING
TAPINS
TAPIRS
TIPINS
TOPICS
TUPIAN
TYPIER
TYPIFY
TYPING
TYPIST
UMPIRE
UNPILE
UNPINS
UPPING
UPPISH
UPPITY
WAPITI
WIPING

••P•I•
AMPHID
AUPAIR
CAPRIS
CAPSID
COPTIC
CUPRIC
ESPRIT
HIPPIE
HOPSIN
IMPAIR
JOPLIN
LIPOID
NAPKIN
NAPPIE
ORPHIC
PAPAIN
PEPSIN
PEPTIC
PIPKIN
PIPPIN
POPLIN
POPSIN
REPAID
REPAIR
ROPEIN
SEPTIC
SOPHIA
SOPHIE
TIPSIN
UNPAID
YUPPIE

••P••I
NAPOLI
NEPALI
PAPYRI
POPULI
RAPINI
WAPITI

•••PI•
ARMPIT
CHAPIN
CHIPIN
CHOPIN
CUSPID
DROPIN
DROPIT
ELAPID
HATPIN
HIPPIE
HISPID
JUMPIN
KEEPIN
KELPIE
KEMPIS
KEWPIE
KUOPIO
LIMPID
MAGPIE
MUDPIE
MYOPIA
MYOPIC
NAPPIE
OKAPIS
PIPPIN
POTPIE
PULPIT
RESPIN
SCIPIO
SEEPIN
SKIPIT
SLIPIN
STEPIN
STOPIN
STOPIT
STUPID
TARPIT
TENPIN
TIEPIN
TORPID
TREPID
TROPIC
TURPIN
UTOPIA
VESPID
WEEPIE
YUPPIE

•••P•I
DELPHI
TAIPEI

••••PI
OCTOPI
SCAMPI
WHOOPI

P•J•••
PAJAMA
PYJAMA

P••J••
PRAJNA
PUNJAB

•PJ•••
UPJOHN

••PJ••
KOPJES
TOPJOB

•••PJ•
SKOPJE

P•K•••
PAKULA
PEKING
PEKINS
PEKOES
PIKAKE
PIKERS
PIKING
POKEAT
POKERS
POKERY
POKEYS
POKIER
POKILY
POKING
PYKNIC

P••K••
PACKED
PACKER
PACKET
PACKUP
PARKAS
PARKAY
PARKED
PARKER
PEAKED
PECKAT
PECKED
PEEKAT
PEEKED
PERKED
PERKUP
PICKAT
PICKAX
PICKED
PICKER
PICKET
PICKLE
PICKON
PICKUP
PINKED
PINKEN
PINKER
PINKIE
PIPKIN
POCKET
POLKAS
PORKER
PUCKER
PUNKAH
PUNKER
PUNKIE

P•••K•
PELIKE
PERUKE
PIKAKE
PLANKS
PLINKS
PLONKS
PLUCKS
PLUCKY
PLUNKS
PRANKS
PRICKS
PRINKS
PROSKY

P••••K
PINOAK
PLANCK
PODUNK

•PK•••
UPKEEP

•P•K••
SPIKED
SPIKER
SPIKES
SPOKED
SPOKEN
SPOKES

•P••K•
SPANKS
SPANKY
SPARKS
SPARKY
SPEAKS
SPECKS
SPINKS
SPOOKS
SPOOKY
SPUNKY
UPDIKE
UPTAKE

•P•••K
SPACEK
SPIVAK
UPLINK
UPTALK
UPTICK

••PK••
NAPKIN
PIPKIN
RIPKEN

••P•K•
KOPEKS
TOPEKA
YAPOKS

••P••K
KOPECK
UNPACK

•••P•K
DEEPAK
KUSPUK

PL••••
PLACED
PLACER
PLACES
PLACET
PLACID
PLAGAL
PLAGES
PLAGIO
PLAGUE
PLAICE
PLAIDS
PLAINS
PLAINT
PLAITS
PLANAR
PLANCK
PLANED
PLANER
PLANES
PLANET
PLANKS
PLANON
PLANTE
PLANTS
PLAQUE
PLASHY
PLASMA
PLASMO
PLASTY
PLATED
PLATEN
PLATER
PLATES
PLATTE
PLAYAS
PLAYAT
PLAYED
PLAYER
PLAYON
PLAYUP
PLAZAS
PLEACH
PLEADS
PLEASE
PLEATS
PLEBES
PLEDGE
PLEIAD
PLENTY
PLENUM
PLEURA
PLEXAL
PLEXOR
PLEXUS
PLIANT
PLICAE
PLIERS
PLIGHT
PLINKS
PLINTH
PLISSE
PLONKS
PLOTTY
PLOUGH
PLOVER
PLOWED
PLOWER
PLUCKS
PLUCKY
PLUGIN
PLUMBS
PLUMED
PLUMES
PLUMMY
PLUMPS
PLUNGE
PLUNKS
PLURAL
PLUSES
PLUSHY
PLYING

P•L•••
PALACE
PALAEO
PALATE
PALEAE
PALELY
PALEST
PALIER
PALING
PALISH
PALLAS
PALLED
PALLET
PALLIA
PALLID
PALLOR
PALMAS
PALMED
PALMER
PALOMA
PALPUS
PALTER
PALTRY
PELAGE
PELEUS
PELIKE
PELION
PELLET
PELMET
PELOPS
PELOTA
PELTED
PELTER
PELTRY
PELVIC
PELVIS
PHLEBO
PHLEGM
PHLOEM
PILAFS
PILATE
PILEIN
PILEON
PILEUM
PILEUP
PILEUS
PILFER
PILING
PILLAR
PILLED
PILLOW
PILOSE
PILOTI
PILOTS
POLAND
POLDER
POLEAX
POLERS
POLEYN
POLICE
POLICY
POLING
POLISH
POLITE
POLITY
POLKAS
POLLED
POLLEN
POLLER
POLLEX
POLLOI
POLLUX
POLPOT
POLYPS
PULING
PULLED
PULLET
PULLEY
PULLIN
PULLON
PULLUP
PULPED
PULPIT
PULQUE
PULSAR
PULSED
PULSES
PYLONS

P••L••
PABLUM
PAELLA
PAILOU
PALLAS
PALLED
PALLET
PALLIA
PALLID
PALLOR
PARLAY
PARLEY
PARLOR
PAULEY
PAVLOV
PEALED
PEDLAR
PEELED
PEELER
PEGLER
PELLET
PEPLOS
PEPLUM
PHILAE
PHILBY
PHILIP
PHILLY
PHILOL
PHILOS
PHYLAE
PHYLLO
PHYLUM
PIGLET
PILLAR
PILLED
PILLOW
PIOLET
POILUS
POLLED
POLLEN
POLLER
POLLEX
POLLOI
POLLUX
POOLED
POPLAR
POPLIN
POULTS
PRELAW
PRELIM
PROLES
PROLIX
PROLOG
PSALMS
PSYLLA
PUBLIC
PULLED
PULLET
PULLEY
PULLIN
PULLON
PULLUP
PURLED
PURLIN

P•••L•
PADDLE
PAELLA
PAKULA
PALELY
PAMELA
PANELS
PAROLE
PARTLY
PARULA
PAYOLA
PEARLS
PEARLY
PEBBLE
PEBBLY
PEDALS
PEDDLE
PENULT
PEOPLE
PERILS
PERTLY
PESTLE
PETALS
PETULA
PHIALS
PHILLY
PHYLLO
PICKLE
PICULS
PIFFLE
PINOLE
PINTLE
PIPALS
PIXELS
POKILY
POMELO
POODLE
POORLY
POPFLY
POPPLE
POPULI
PORTLY
POSHLY
POSSLQ
POTTLE
POWELL
PRIMLY
PROWLS
PSYLLA
PUDDLE
PUDDLY
PUEBLA
PUEBLO
PUNILY
PUPILS
PURELY
PURFLE
PURPLE
PURPLY
PUZZLE

P••••L
PANFUL
PARCEL
PARREL
PASCAL
PASSEL
PASTEL
PATHOL
PATROL
PENCEL
PENCIL
PENPAL
PEPFUL
PETREL
PETROL
PHENOL
PHENYL
PHILOL
PINEAL
PISTIL
PISTOL
PLAGAL
PLEXAL
PLURAL
POMMEL
PORTAL
POSTAL
POTFUL
POWELL
PRIMAL
PROPEL
PUMMEL

•PL•••
APLITE
APLOMB
SPLASH
SPLATS
SPLAYS
SPLEEN
SPLICE
SPLINE
SPLINT
SPLITS
SPLOSH
UPLAND
UPLIFT
UPLINK
UPLOAD

•P•L••
APOLLO
APPLES
APPLET
APULIA
EPILOG
KPELLE
SPALLS
SPELLS
SPILES
SPILLS
SPILTH

•P••L•
APOLLO
APPALL
APPALS
KPELLE
OPENLY
SPALLS
SPELLS
SPIELS
SPILLS
SPOILS
SPOILT
SPOOLS
SPRYLY
UPHELD
UPHILL
UPHOLD
UPTALK
UPWELL

•P•••L
APICAL
APODAL
APPALL
APPEAL
EPICAL
EPINAL
SPINAL
SPINEL
SPIRAL
SPRAWL
UPHILL
UPWELL

••PL••
AMPLER
APPLES
APPLET
BYPLAY
CAPLET
COPLEY
DEPLOY
DUPLEX
EMPLOY
INPLAY
JOPLIN
KAPLAN
KEPLER
MAPLES
NAPLES
PEPLOS
PEPLUM
POPLAR
POPLIN
REPLAN
REPLAY
REPLOW
RIPLEY
UNPLUG
ZIPLOC

••P•L•
AMPULE
AMPULS
APPALL
APPALS
COPULA
CUPELS
CUPOLA
DAPPLE
DIPOLE
EXPELS
FIPPLE
HOPPLE
IMPALA
IMPALE
IMPELS
LAPELS
NAPOLI
NEPALI
PIPALS
POPFLY
POPPLE
POPULI
PUPILS
RAPTLY
REPELS
REPOLL
RIPELY
RIPPLE
RIPPLY
SEPALS
SUPPLE
SUPPLY
TEPALS
TIPPLE
TOPPLE
TUPELO
UNPILE

••P••L
APPALL
APPEAL
CAPFUL
CUPFUL
DEPAUL
ESPIAL
KOPPEL
LAPFUL
PEPFUL
RAPPEL
REPEAL
REPOLL
RUPAUL
SEPTAL
STPAUL

•••PL•
COMPLY
COUPLE
DAMPLY
DAPPLE
DEEPLY
DIMPLE
DIMPLY
FIPPLE
HOOPLA
HOOPLE
HOPPLE
LIMPLY
MARPLE
PEOPLE
POPPLE
PURPLE
PURPLY
RIMPLE
RIPPLE
RIPPLY
RUMPLE
RUMPLY
SAMPLE
SIMPLE
SIMPLY
STAPLE
SUPPLE
SUPPLY
TEMPLE
TIPPLE
TOPPLE
TRIPLE
TRIPLY
TWOPLY
WIMPLE

•••P•L
BHOPAL
CARPAL
CARPEL
CHAPEL
COMPEL
DISPEL
GALPAL
GOSPEL
KOPPEL
PENPAL
PROPEL
RAPPEL
STIPEL

P•M•••
PAMELA
PAMIRS
PAMPAS
PAMPER
PIMINY
POMACE
POMADE
POMELO
POMMEE
POMMEL
POMONA
POMPEY
POMPOM
POMPON
PUMICE
PUMMEL
PUMPED
PUMPER
PUMPUP

P••M••
PACMAN
PALMAS
PALMED
PALMER
PATMOS
PELMET
PENMAN
PENMEN
PERMED
PERMIT
PIEMAN
PIEMEN
PITMAN
PITMEN
PLUMBS
PLUMED
PLUMES
PLUMMY
PLUMPS
POMMEE
POMMEL
PREMED
PREMIE
PRIMAL
PRIMED
PRIMER
PRIMES
PRIMLY
PRIMOS
PRIMPS
PRIMUM
PRIMUS
PROMOS
PROMPT
PUMMEL

P•••M•
PAJAMA
PALOMA
PANAMA

PLASMA PLASMO PLUMMY PNEUMA PREAMP PRISMS PROAMS PROEMS PSALMS PYJAMA

P••••M

PABLUM PASSIM PEPLUM PHENOM PHLEGM PHLOEM PHYLUM PILEUM PLENUM PODIUM POMPOM POSSUM PRELIM PRIMUM PROTEM PURISM PUTNAM

•PM•••

UPMOST

•P•M••

APEMAN APEMEN SPUMED SPUMES

•P••M•

APLOMB EPROMS OPTIMA SPASMS UPTIME

•P•••M

EPONYM

••P••M

GYPSUM LAPHAM PEPLUM SEPTUM

•••P•M

POMPOM WAMPUM

••••PM

FIVEPM FOURPM NINEPM

PN••••

PNEUMA

P•N•••

PANADA PANAMA PANCHO PANDAS PANDER PANDIT PANELS PANFRY PANFUL PANICS PANNED PANNER PANNES PANOUT PANTED PANTOS PANTRY PANZER PENANG PENCEL PENCIL PENDED PENGHU PENMAN PENMEN PENNAE PENNED PENNER PENNEY PENNIA PENNIS PENNON PENPAL PENROD PENSEE PENTAD PENTUP PENULT PENURY PINATA PINCER PINDAR PINDUS PINEAL PINERO PINERY PINGED PINIER PINING PINION PINITE PINKED PINKEN PINKER PINKIE PINNAE PINNAS PINNED PINNER PINOAK PINOLE PINONS PINOTS PINSON PINTER PINTLE PINTOS PINUPS PINXIT PINYIN PINYON PINZON PONCES PONCHO PONDER PONGED PONGEE PONGID PONIED PONIES PONTES PONTIC PONTUS PONYUP PUNCHY PUNDIT PUNIER PUNILY PUNISH PUNJAB PUNKAH PUNKER PUNKIE PUNNED PUNNET PUNTED PUNTER

P••N••

PAANGA PAINED PAINTS PAINTY PANNED PANNER PANNES PARNIS PAUNCH PAWNED PAWNEE PAWNER PEANUT PEENED PENNAE PENNED PENNER PENNEY PENNIA PENNIS PENNON PERNIO PERNOD PHENOL PHENOM PHENYL PHONED PHONES PHONEY PHONIC PHONON PHONOS PIANOS PICNIC PIGNUT PINNAE PINNAS PINNED PINNER PLANAR PLANCK PLANED PLANER PLANES PLANET PLANKS PLANON PLANTE PLANTS PLENTY PLENUM PLINKS PLINTH PLONKS PLUNGE PLUNKS POINTE POINTS POINTY POUNCE POUNDS PRANCE PRANGS PRANKS PRENUP PRINCE PRINKS PRINTS PRONGS PRONTO PRUNED PRUNER PRUNES PRYNNE PUENTE PUNNED PUNNET PUTNAM PYKNIC

P•••N•

PACING PACINO PADANG PAEANS PAEONS PAGANS PAGING PAHANG PALING PARANA PARANG PARENS PARENT PARING PATENS PATENT PATINA PATINE PAVANE PAVING PAWING PAYING PECANS PEDANT PEKING PEKINS PENANG PEPINO PIKING PILING PIMINY PINING PINONS PIPING PIRANA PISANO PISANS PITONS PLAINS PLAINT PLIANT PLYING POCONO PODUNK POKING POLAND POLING POMONA PORING POSING POTENT PRAJNA PRAWNS PREENS PRIONS PROCNE PRYING PRYNNE PUISNE PULING PURINA PURINE PUTONS PYLONS

P••••N

PACMAN PADUAN PAIDIN PAPAIN PAPUAN PAQUIN PARDON PARSON PARTON PASSON PATHAN PATRON PATTEN PATTON PAXTON PAYSIN PAYSON PEAHEN PECTIN PEERIN PELION PENMAN PENMEN PENNON PEPSIN PERSON PETAIN PEYTON PHONON PHOTON PICKON PIDGIN PIEMAN PIEMEN PIEPAN PIETIN PIGEON PIGPEN PILEIN PILEON PINION PINKEN PINSON PINYIN PINYON PINZON PIPKIN PIPPIN PISTON PITMAN PITMEN PLANON PLATEN PLAYON PLUGIN POISON POLEYN POLLEN POMPON POPGUN POPLIN POPSIN POSTON POTEEN POTION POURIN PREVIN PREYON PRISON PROTON PROVEN PUFFIN PULLIN PULLON PURLIN PUSHON PUTSIN PUTSON PYTHON

•P•N••

CPSNOW EPINAL EPONYM OPENED OPENER OPENLY OPENTO OPENUP OPINED OPINER OPINES SPANKS SPANKY SPENDS SPINAL SPINED SPINEL SPINES SPINET SPINKS SPINTO SPONGE SPONGY SPUNKY UPENDS

•P••N•

APPEND APRONS EPPING OPTING SPAWNS SPHINX SPLINE SPLINT SPOONS SPOONY SPRANG SPRING SPRINT SPRUNG SPURNS SPYING UPLAND UPLINK UPPING UPWIND

•P•••N

APEMAN APEMEN APPIAN EPHRON OPPUGN OPTION SPAVIN SPLEEN SPOKEN SPRAIN SPURON UPJOHN UPTOWN UPTURN

••PN••

CAPNUT EUPNEA HYPNOS WAPNER

••P•N•

ALPINE APPEND ARPENT ASPENS CAPONE CAPONS COPING DAPHNE DEPEND DEPONE DOPANT DOPING DUPING DUPONT EPPING ESPANA EXPAND EXPEND GAPING HOPING HYPING IMPEND IMPING JAPANS JAPING LAPINS LIPENG LOPING LUPINE LUPINO LUPONE MOPING ORPINE PEPINO PIPING RAPINE RAPINI REPAND REPENT REPINE REPINS RIPENS ROPING SUPINE TAPING TAPINS TIPINS TYPING UNPENS UNPINS UPPING WIPING

••P••N

APPIAN CAPGUN CAPTAN HAPPEN HOPSIN HYPHEN IMPUGN JOPLIN KAPLAN KEPTON LEPTON LIPTON NAPKIN NIPPON OPPUGN ORPHAN PAPAIN PAPUAN PEPSIN PIPKIN PIPPIN POPGUN POPLIN POPSIN REPLAN REPUGN RIPKEN ROPEIN SIPHON SYPHON TAPPAN TIPSIN TOPGUN TOPTEN TUPIAN

•••P•N

CHAPIN CHIPIN CHOPIN CLIPON COUPON DAMPEN DEEPEN DROPIN FRYPAN HAPPEN HARPON HATPIN INSPAN JUMPIN JUMPON KEEPIN KEEPON LUMPEN NIPPON OILPAN PIEPAN PIGPEN PIPPIN POMPON REOPEN RESPIN SAIPAN SAMPAN SEEPIN SLIPIN SLIPON STEPIN STEPON STOPIN TAIPAN TAPPAN TARPAN TARPON TENPIN TIEPIN TINPAN TREPAN TURPIN UNOPEN USOPEN WEAPON YAUPON

PO••••

POACHY POBOYS POCKET POCONO PODDED PODIUM PODUNK POETIC POETRY POGIES POILUS POINTE POINTS POINTY POIROT POISED POISES POISON POKEAT POKERS POKERY POKEYS POKIER POKILY POKING POLAND POLDER POLEAX POLERS POLEYN POLICE POLICY POLING POLISH POLITE POLITY POLKAS POLLED POLLEN POLLER POLLEX POLLOI POLLUX POLPOT POLYPS POMACE POMADE POMELO POMMEE POMMEL POMONA POMPEY POMPOM POMPON PONCES PONCHO PONDER PONGED PONGEE PONGID PONIED PONIES PONTES PONTIC PONTUS PONYUP POODLE POOHED POOLED POOPED POORER POORLY POPART POPEYE POPFLY POPGUN POPLAR POPLIN POPOFF POPOUT POPPAS POPPED POPPER POPPET POPPLE POPSIN POPSUP POPTOP POPULI POPUPS PORING PORKER POROUS PORTAL PORTED PORTER PORTIA PORTLY POSADA POSERS POSEUR POSHER POSHLY POSIES POSING POSITS POSSES POSSET POSSLQ POSSUM POSTAL POSTED POSTER POSTIT POSTON POTAGE POTASH POTATO POTEEN POTENT POTFUL POTHER POTION POTOSI POTPIE POTTED POTTER POTTLE POTTOS POUCHY POULTS POUNCE POUNDS POURED POURER POURIN POUSSE POUTED POUTER POWDER POWELL POWERS POWWOW

P•O•••

PEOPLE PEORIA PHOBIA PHOBIC PHOBOS PHOCIS PHOEBE PHONED PHONES PHONEY PHONIC PHONON PHONOS PHOOEY PHOTIC PHOTOG PHOTON PHOTOS PIOLET PLONKS PLOTTY PLOUGH PLOVER PLOWED PLOWER POODLE POOHED POOLED POOPED POORER POORLY PROAMS PROBED PROBER PROBES PROCNE PROEMS PROFIT PROLES PROLIX PROLOG PROMOS PROMPT PRONGS PRONTO PROOFS PROPEL PROPER PROPRE PROPUP PROSED PROSER PROSES PROSIT PROSKY PROTAX PROTEI PROTEM PROTON PROUST PROVED PROVEN PROVER PROVES PROWLS PROWSE PROZAC

P••O••

PAEONS PAGODA PALOMA PANOUT PARODY PAROLE PATOIS PAYOFF PAYOLA PAYOUT PEKOES PELOPS PELOTA PEYOTE PHLOEM PHOOEY PICOTS PIGOUT PILOSE PILOTI PILOTS PINOAK PINOLE PINONS PINOTS PITONS PIVOTS POBOYS POCONO POMONA POPOFF POPOUT POROUS POTOSI PRIONS PRIORI PRIORS PRIORY PROOFS PTBOAT PUTOFF PUTONS PUTOUT PYLONS

P•••O•

PAILOU PALLOR PANTOS PARDON PARLOR PARROT PARSON PARTON PASEOS PASSON PASTOR PATHOL PATHOS PATIOS PATMOS PATROL PATRON PATTON PAVLOV PAXTON PAYBOX PAYFOR PAYSON PEAPOD PEGTOP PELION PENNON PENROD PEPLOS PEQUOD PEQUOT PERIOD PERNOD PERROT PERSON PESCOW PESTOS PETROG PETROL PEYTON PHAROS PHENOL PHENOM PHILOL PHILOS PHOBOS PHONON PHONOS PHOTOG PHOTON PHOTOS PIANOS PICKON PIGEON PILEON PILLOW PINION PINSON PINTOS PINYON PINZON PISTOL PISTON PLANON PLAYON PLEXOR POIROT POISON POLLOI POLPOT POMPOM POMPON POPTOP POSTON POTION POTTOS POWWOW PREYON PRIMOS PRISON PROLOG PROMOS PROTON PULLON PUSHON PUTSON PYEDOG PYTHON

P••••O

PACINO PALAEO PANCHO PAPAGO PARETO PASHTO PEPINO PERNIO PHLEBO PHYLLO PHYSIO PICABO PICARO PIETRO PINERO PISANO PLAGIO PLASMO POCONO POMELO PONCHO POTATO PRESTO PRONTO PSEUDO PSYCHO PUEBLO PUERTO PUTSTO

•PO•••

APODAL APOGEE APOLLO EPOCHS EPODES EPONYM EPOPEE OPORTO SPOILS SPOILT SPOKED SPOKEN SPOKES SPONGE SPONGY SPOOFS SPOOKS SPOOKY SPOOLS SPOONS SPOONY SPOORS SPORES SPORTS SPORTY SPOTTY SPOUSE SPOUTS

•P•O••

APLOMB APPOSE APRONS EPHODS EPHORI EPHORS EPROMS OPPOSE OPTOUT SPLOSH SPOOFS SPOOKS SPOOKY SPOOLS SPOONS SPOONY SPOORS SPROUT UPBOWS UPHOLD UPJOHN UPLOAD UPMOST UPROAR UPROOT UPROSE UPTOWN

•P••O•

CPSNOW EPHRON EPILOG OPTFOR OPTION SPIGOT SPIROS SPURON UPROOT UPSHOT

•P•••O

APOLLO OPENTO OPORTO SPEEDO SPINTO

••PO••

APPOSE BIPODS CAPONE CAPONS CAPOTE COPOUT CSPOTS CUPOLA DEPONE DEPORT DEPOSE DEPOTS DIPODY DIPOLE DUPONT ESPOSA ESPOSO EXPORT EXPOSE EXPOST HOPOFF HYPOED IMPORT IMPOSE IMPOST INPORT INPOUR LIPOID LUPONE NAPOLI OPPOSE POPOFF POPOUT REPOLL REPORT REPOSE REPOST REPOTS RIPOFF RIPOUT SAPORS SEPOYS SOPORS TAPOFF TAPOUT TIPOFF TOPOFF TOPOUT VAPORS VAPORY VAPOUR YAPOKS

••P•O•

CAPTOR DEPLOY EMPLOY EMPTOR HIPHOP HIPPOS HYPNOS IMPROV KEPTON LAPDOG LAPTOP LEPTON LIPTON MOPTOP NIPPON PEPLOS POPTOP RAPTOR REPLOW REPROS SIPHON SYPHON TIPTOE TIPTOP TOPDOG TOPJOB ZIPLOC

••P••O

ELPASO ESPOSO LUPINO MAPUTO NEPHRO PAPAGO PEPINO SAPPHO TUPELO

•••PO•

CAMPOS CLIPON COMPOS COUPON COWPOX DESPOT HARPON HIPPOS HOOPOE HOTPOT ISOPOD JUMPON KARPOV KEEPON MAYPOP NIPPON PEAPOD POLPOT POMPOM POMPON SLIPON STEPON STUPOR TARPON

TEAPOT TEAPOY TEMPOS TINPOT TORPOR TRIPOD TRIPOS UNIPOD VOXPOP WEAPON YAUPON

•••P•O

ALEPPO ALLPRO BUMPPO CRYPTO EOIPSO KEEPTO KUOPIO MORPHO OLDPRO SAPPHO SCIPIO SNAPTO TROPPO

••••PO

ALEPPO ATEMPO BUMPPO CHEAPO DACAPO KAKAPO MOLOPO OBISPO TROPPO

P•P•••

PAPACY PAPAGO PAPAIN PAPAWS PAPAYA PAPERS PAPERY PAPIER PAPPAS PAPPUS PAPUAN PAPYRI PEPFUL PEPINO PEPITA PEPLOS PEPLUM PEPPED PEPPER PEPSIN PEPSUP PEPTIC PIPALS PIPERS PIPEUP PIPIER PIPING PIPITS PIPKIN PIPPED PIPPIN POPART POPEYE POPFLY POPGUN POPLAR POPLIN POPOFF POPOUT POPPAS POPPED POPPER POPPET POPPLE POPSIN POPSUP POPTOP POPULI POPUPS PUPILS PUPPET

P••P••

PALPUS PAMPAS PAMPER PAPPAS PAPPUS PAUPER PAWPAW PEAPOD PEEPED PEEPER PENPAL PEOPLE PEPPED PEPPER PIEPAN PIGPEN PIPPED PIPPIN POLPOT POMPEY POMPOM POMPON POOPED POPPAS POPPED POPPER POPPET POPPLE POTPIE PREPAY PREPPY PRIPET PROPEL PROPER PROPRE PROPUP PULPED PULPIT PUMPED PUMPER PUMPUP PUPPET PURPLE PURPLY PUTPUT

P•••P•

PARAPH PELOPS PINUPS PLUMPS POLYPS POPUPS PREPPY PRIMPS PROMPT PTRAPS

P••••P

PACKUP PAIDUP PAIRUP PASSUP PAYSUP PEGTOP PENTUP PEPSUP PERKUP PHILIP PICKUP PILEUP PIPEUP PIRRIP PLAYUP PONYUP POPSUP POPTOP PREAMP PRENUP PROPUP PULLUP PUMPUP PUSHUP PUTSUP

•PP•••

APPALL APPALS APPEAL APPEAR APPEND APPIAN APPLES APPLET APPOSE EPPING OPPOSE OPPUGN UPPERS UPPING UPPISH UPPITY

•P•P••

EPOPEE

•P•••P

OPENUP SPEDUP UPKEEP

••PP••

BOPPED BOPPER CAPPED CAPPER COPPED COPPER CUPPAS CUPPED DAPPED DAPPER DAPPLE DIPPED DIPPER FIPPLE GAPPED GIPPED GIPPER GYPPED GYPPER HAPPED HAPPEN HEPPER HIPPED HIPPER HIPPIE HIPPOS HOPPED HOPPER HOPPLE KAPPAS KIPPER KIPPUR KOPPEL LAPPED LAPPET LIPPED LOPPED LOPPER MAPPED MAPPER MOPPED MOPPER MOPPET MUPPET NAPPED NAPPER NAPPES NAPPIE NIPPED NIPPER NIPPON NIPPUR PAPPAS PAPPUS PEPPED PEPPER PIPPED PIPPIN POPPAS POPPED POPPER POPPET POPPLE PUPPET RAPPED RAPPEE RAPPEL RAPPER RIPPED RIPPER RIPPLE RIPPLY SAPPED SAPPER SAPPHO SIPPED SIPPER SIPPET SOPPED SUPPED SUPPER SUPPLE SUPPLY TAPPAN TAPPED TAPPER TAPPET TIPPED TIPPER TIPPET TIPPLE TOPPED TOPPER TOPPLE YAPPED YIPPED YIPPEE YUPPIE ZAPPED ZAPPER ZIPPED ZIPPER

••P•P•

MOPUPS NIPUPS POPUPS TIPUPS

••P••P

BOPEEP HIPHOP HOPSUP HYPEUP KEPTUP LAPSUP LAPTOP MOPSUP MOPTOP PEPSUP PIPEUP POPSUP POPTOP RIPRAP RIPSUP SOPSUP TIPTOP TYPEUP WIPEUP ZIPSUP

•••PP•

ALEPPO BUMPPO CHOPPY DIEPPE DRIPPY FLAPPY FLOPPY FRAPPE GLOPPY GRAPPA GRIPPE PREPPY QUIPPY SHOPPE SKIPPY SLAPPY SLIPPY SLOPPY SNAPPY SNIPPY STEPPE TRAPPY TROPPO WHIPPY

•••P•P

BUMPUP COOPUP CROPUP FLIPUP JUMPUP KEEPUP MAYPOP PROPUP PUMPUP SLAPUP SLIPUP SNAPUP SOUPUP STEPUP STOPUP TRIPUP VOXPOP WHIPUP WRAPUP

••••PP

ALCAPP

P•Q•••

PAQUIN PEQUOD PEQUOT PIQUED PIQUES PIQUET

P••Q••

PLAQUE PULQUE

P••••Q

POSSLQ

•P•Q••

OPAQUE

•••P•Q

COMPAQ

PR••••

PRAGUE PRAISE PRAJNA PRANCE PRANGS PRANKS PRASES PRATED PRATER PRATES PRAVDA PRAWNS PRAXES PRAXIS PRAYED PRAYER PREACH PREAMP PRECIS PREENS PREFAB PREFER PREFIX PRELAW PRELIM PREMED PREMIE PRENUP PREPAY PREPPY PRESET PRESTO PRETAX PRETER PRETTY PREVIN PREWAR PREYED PREYON PRICED PRICER PRICES PRICEY PRICKS PRIDED PRIDES PRIERS PRIEST PRIMAL PRIMED PRIMER PRIMES PRIMLY PRIMOS PRIMPS PRIMUM PRIMUS PRINCE PRINKS PRINTS PRIONS PRIORI PRIORS PRIORY PRIPET PRISMS PRISON PRISSY PRIVET PRIZED PRIZES PROAMS PROBED PROBER PROBES PROCNE PROEMS PROFIT PROLES PROLIX PROLOG PROMOS PROMPT PRONGS PRONTO PROOFS PROPEL PROPER PROPRE PROPUP PROSED PROSER PROSES PROSIT PROSKY PROTAX PROTEI PROTEM PROTON PROUST PROVED PROVEN PROVER PROVES PROWLS PROWSE PROZAC PRUDES PRUNED PRUNER PRUNES PRYING PRYNNE

P•R•••

PARADE PARANA PARANG PARAPH PARCAE PARCEL PARDON PARENS PARENT PARERS PARETO PAREVE PARGET PARIAH PARING PARISH PARITY PARKAS PARKAY PARKED PARKER PARLAY PARLEY PARLOR PARNIS PARODY PAROLE PARRED PARREL PARRIS PARROT PARSEC PARSED PARSEE PARSER PARSES PARSON PARTED PARTLY PARTON PARULA PARURE PARVIS PERCHA PERDUE PERILS PERIOD PERISH PERKED PERKUP PERMED PERMIT PERNIO PERNOD PERROT PERSIA PERSON PERTER PERTLY PERUGA PERUKE PERUSE PHRASE PIRACY PIRANA PIRATE PIRRIP PORING PORKER POROUS PORTAL PORTED PORTER PORTIA PORTLY PTRAPS PURACE PURDAH PURDUE PUREED PUREES PURELY PUREST PURFLE PURGED PURGES PURIFY PURINA PURINE PURISM PURIST PURITY PURLED PURLIN PURPLE PURPLY PURRED PURRER PURSED PURSER PURSES PURSUE PURVEY PYRITE

P••R••

PADRES PAIRED PAIRUP PARRED PARREL PARRIS PARROT PATROL PATRON PEARLS PEARLY PEERAT PEERCE PEERED PEERIN PENROD PEORIA PERROT PETREL PETRIE PETROG PETROL PHAROS PIERCE PIERRE PIRRIP PLURAL POIROT POORER POORLY POURED POURER POURIN PUERTO PUGREE PURRED PURRER PUTRID

P•••R•

PACERS PAGERS PAHARI PALTRY PAMIRS PANFRY PANTRY PAPERS PAPERY PAPYRI PARERS PARURE PASTRY PATERS PAVERS PAWERS PAYERS PELTRY PENURY PETARD PETERS PHEDRE PICARA PICARD PICARO PIERRE PIETRO PIKERS PINERO PINERY PIPERS PLEURA PLIERS POETRY POKERS POKERY POLERS POPART POSERS POWERS PRIERS PRIORI PRIORS PRIORY PROPRE

P••••R

PACKER PADDER PALIER PALLOR PALMER PALTER PAMPER PANDER PANNER PANZER PAPIER PARKER PARLOR PARSER PASSER PASTOR PATTER PAUPER PAWNER PAYFOR PEDLAR PEELER PEEPER PEGLER PELTER PENNER PEPPER PERTER PESTER PETTER PEWTER PFIZER PHASER PICKER PIECER PIETER PILFER PILLAR PINCER PINDAR PINIER PINKER PINNER PINTER PIPIER PITIER PITTER PLACER PLANAR PLANER PLATER PLAYER PLEXOR PLOVER PLOWER POKIER POLDER POLLER PONDER POORER POPLAR POPPER PORKER PORTER POSEUR POSHER POSTER POTHER POTTER POURER POUTER POWDER PRATER PRAYER PREFER PRETER PREWAR PRICER PRIMER PROBER PROPER PROSER PROVER PRUNER PSYWAR PUCKER PUFFER PULSAR PUMPER PUNIER PUNKER PUNTER PURRER PURSER PUTTER

•PR•••

APRONS EPROMS SPRAGS SPRAIN SPRANG SPRATS SPRAWL SPRAYS SPREAD SPREES SPRIER SPRIGS SPRING SPRINT SPRITE SPRITS SPRITZ SPROUT SPRUCE SPRUES SPRUNG SPRYER SPRYLY UPRISE UPROAR UPROOT UPROSE UPRUSH

•P•R••

APERCU EPARCH EPHRON EPIRUS OPERAS OPORTO SPARED SPARER SPARES SPARGE SPARKS SPARKY SPARSE SPARTA SPERRY SPIRAL SPIREA SPIRED SPIRES SPIRIT SPIROS SPORES SPORTS SPORTY SPURGE SPURNS SPURON SPURRY SPURTS

•P••R•

APIARY EPHORI EPHORS SPEARS SPERRY SPHERE SPHERY SPIERS SPOORS SPURRY UPPERS UPTURN UPWARD

•P•••R

APPEAR OPENER OPINER OPTFOR SPACER SPADER SPARER SPIDER SPIKER SPRIER SPRYER UPROAR

••PR••

CAPRIS CUPRIC CYPRUS ESPRIT IMPROV OSPREY REPROS RIPRAP

••P•R•

ALPERT AMPERE ASPERA ASPIRE CAPERS DEPART DEPORT DUPERY EMPERY EMPIRE EXPERT EXPIRE EXPIRY EXPORT GAPERS HOPERS IMPART IMPERF IMPORT IMPURE INPART INPORT JAPERS JAPERY LOPERS MOPERS MOPERY NAPERY NEPHRO PAPERS PAPERY PAPYRI PIPERS POPART REPORT ROPERS RUPERT SAPORS SOPORS SUPERB SUPERS TAPERS TAPIRS TEPHRA TOPERS TYPERS UMPIRE UPPERS VAPORS VAPORY VIPERS WIPERS

••P••R

AMPLER APPEAR AUPAIR BOPPER CAPPER CAPTOR CIPHER COPIER COPPER COPTER CYPHER DAPPER DIPPER DOPIER EMPTOR GIPPER GOPHER GYPPER HEPPER HIPPER HOPPER IMPAIR INPOUR KEPLER KIPPER KIPPUR LOPPER MAPPER MOPIER MOPPER NAPIER NAPPER NIPPER NIPPUR PAPIER PEPPER PIPIER POPLAR POPPER RAPIER RAPPER RAPTOR REPAIR RIPPER ROPIER SAPPER SIPPER SUPPER TAPPER TIPPER TOPPER TYPIER VAPOUR WAPNER ZAPPER ZEPHYR ZIPPER

•••PR•

ALLPRO CHOPRA OLDPRO PROPRE SEMPRE

•••P•R

BEEPER BOPPER BUMPER CAMPER CAPPER CARPER CASPAR CASPER COOPER COPPER COWPER DAMPER DAPPER DEEPER DIAPER DIPPER DRAPER DUMPER ELOPER GASPAR GASPER GIPPER GRIPER GULPER GYPPER HAMPER HARPER HELPER HEPPER HIPPER HOOPER HOPPER JAIPUR JASPER JUMPER KEEPER KIPPER KIPPUR LAUPER LEAPER LIMPER LOOPER LOPPER LUMPER LUMPUR MAPPER MOPPER NAPPER NIPPER NIPPUR PAMPER PAUPER PEEPER PEPPER POPPER PROPER PUMPER RAIPUR RAPPER RASPER REAPER RIPPER ROMPER SAPPER SEMPER SHAPER SIMPER SIPPER SNIPER SOAPER STUPOR SUBPAR SUPPER SWIPER TAMPER TAPPER TEMPER TIPPER TOPPER TORPOR VAMPER VESPER WEEPER WOLPER YAWPER YELPER ZAPPER ZIPPER

PS••••

PSALMS PSEUDO PSEUDS PSYCHE PSYCHO PSYCHS PSYLLA PSYWAR

P•S•••

PASCAL PASEOS PASHAS PASHTO PASSBY PASSED PASSEL PASSER PASSES PASSIM PASSON PASSUP PASTAS PASTED PASTEL PASTES PASTIS PASTOR PASTRY PESACH PESAWA PESCOW PESETA PESTER PESTLE PESTOS PISANO PISANS PISCES PISGAH PISTES PISTIL PISTOL PISTON POSADA POSERS POSEUR POSHER POSHLY POSIES POSING POSITS POSSES POSSET POSSLQ POSSUM POSTAL POSTED POSTER POSTIT POSTON PUSHED PUSHES

PUSHON
PUSHUP
PUSSES

P••S••
PAISAS
PARSEC
PARSED
PARSEE
PARSER
PARSES
PARSON
PASSBY
PASSED
PASSEL
PASSER
PASSES
PASSIM
PASSON
PASSUP
PAUSED
PAUSES
PAWSAT
PAYSIN
PAYSON
PAYSUP
PENSEE
PEPSIN
PEPSUP
PERSIA
PERSON
PHASED
PHASER
PHASES
PHYSED
PHYSIO
PIGSTY
PINSON
PITSAW
PLASHY
PLASMA
PLASMO
PLASTY
PLISSE
PLUSES
PLUSHY
POISED
POISES
POISON
POPSIN
POPSUP
POSSES
POSSET
POSSLQ
POSSUM
POUSSE
PRASES
PRESET
PRESTO
PRISMS
PRISON
PRISSY
PROSED
PROSER
PROSES
PROSIT
PROSKY
PUISNE
PULSAR
PULSED
PULSES
PURSED
PURSER
PURSES
PURSUE
PUSSES
PUTSBY
PUTSCH
PUTSIN
PUTSON
PUTSTO
PUTSUP

P•••S•
PALEST
PALISH
PARISH
PERISH
PERUSE
PHRASE
PILOSE
PLEASE
PLISSE
POLISH
POTASH
POTOSI
POUSSE
PRAISE
PRIEST
PRISSY
PROUST
PROWSE
PUNISH
PUREST
PURISM
PURIST

P••••S
PACERS
PADRES
PAEANS
PAEONS
PAGANS
PAGERS
PAINTS
PAISAS
PALLAS
PALMAS
PALPUS
PAMIRS
PAMPAS
PANDAS
PANELS
PANICS
PANNES
PANTOS
PAPAWS
PAPERS
PAPPAS
PAPPUS
PARENS
PARERS
PARKAS
PARNIS
PARRIS
PARSES
PARVIS
PASEOS
PASHAS
PASSES
PASTAS
PASTES
PASTIS
PATENS
PATERS
PATHOS
PATIOS
PATMOS
PATOIS
PAUCIS
PAUSES
PAVERS
PAWERS
PAYEES
PAYERS
PEARLS
PECANS
PEDALS
PEEVES
PEKINS
PEKOES
PELEUS
PELOPS
PELVIS
PENNIS
PEPLOS
PERILS
PESTOS
PETALS
PETERS
PEWEES
PEWITS
PHAGES
PHAROS
PHASES
PHIALS
PHILOS
PHOBOS
PHOCIS
PHONES
PHONOS
PHOTOS
PIANOS
PICOTS
PICULS
PIECES
PIETAS
PIKERS
PILAFS
PILEUS
PILOTS
PINDUS
PINNAS
PINONS
PINOTS
PINTOS
PINUPS
PIPALS
PIPERS
PIPITS
PIQUES
PISANS
PISCES
PISTES
PITIES
PITONS
PIVOTS
PIXELS
PIXIES
PIZZAS
PLACES
PLAGES
PLAIDS
PLAINS
PLAITS
PLANES
PLANKS
PLANTS
PLATES
PLAYAS
PLAZAS
PLEADS
PLEATS
PLEBES
PLEXUS
PLIERS
PLINKS
PLONKS
PLUCKS
PLUMBS
PLUMES
PLUMPS
PLUNKS
PLUSES
POBOYS
POGIES
POILUS
POINTS
POISES
POKERS
POKEYS
POLERS
POLKAS
POLYPS
PONCES
PONIES
PONTES
PONTUS
POPPAS
POPUPS
POROUS
POSERS
POSIES
POSITS
POSSES
POTTOS
POULTS
POUNDS
POWERS
PRANGS
PRANKS
PRASES
PRATES
PRAWNS
PRAXES
PRAXIS
PRECIS
PREENS
PRICES
PRICKS
PRIDES
PRIERS
PRIMES
PRIMOS
PRIMPS
PRIMUS
PRINKS
PRINTS
PRIONS
PRIORS
PRISMS
PRIZES
PROAMS
PROBES
PROEMS
PROLES
PROMOS
PRONGS
PROOFS
PROSES
PROVES
PROWLS
PRUDES
PRUNES
PSALMS
PSEUDS
PSYCHS
PTRAPS
PULSES
PUPILS
PUREES
PURGES
PURSES
PUSHES
PUSSES
PUTONS
PYLONS
PYXIES

•PS•••
CPSNOW
UPSETS
UPSHOT
UPSIDE

•P•S••
OPUSES
SPASMS
UPASES

•P••S•
APPOSE
APTEST
OPPOSE
SPARSE
SPLASH
SPLOSH
SPOUSE
UPCAST
UPMOST
UPPISH
UPRISE
UPROSE
UPRUSH

•P•••S
APEXES
APHIDS
APICES
APPALS
APPLES
APRONS
EPHAHS
EPHODS
EPHORS
EPIRUS
EPOCHS
EPODES
EPROMS
OPERAS
OPINES
OPTICS
OPUSES
SPACES
SPADES
SPAHIS
SPALLS
SPANKS
SPARES
SPARKS
SPASMS
SPATES
SPAWNS
SPEAKS
SPEARS
SPECKS
SPEEDS
SPELLS
SPENDS
SPICAS
SPICES
SPIELS
SPIERS
SPIFFS
SPIKES
SPILES
SPILLS
SPINES
SPINKS
SPIRES
SPIROS
SPITES
SPLATS
SPLAYS
SPLITS
SPOILS
SPOKES
SPOOFS
SPOOKS
SPOOLS
SPOONS
SPOORS
SPORES
SPORTS
SPOUTS
SPRAGS
SPRATS
SPRAYS
SPREES
SPRIGS
SPRITS
SPRUES
SPUMES
SPURNS
SPURTS
UPASES
UPBOWS
UPENDS
UPPERS
UPSETS

••PS••
CAPSID
COPSES
GYPSUM
HOPSIN
HOPSUP
LAPSED
LAPSES
LAPSUP
MOPSUP
NIPSAT
NIPSEY
PEPSIN
PEPSUP
POPSIN
POPSUP
RIPSAW
RIPSUP
SOPSUP
TIPSIN
ZIPSUP

••P•S•
APPOSE
ASPISH
BYPASS
BYPAST
DEPOSE
ELPASO
ESPOSA
ESPOSO
EXPOSE
EXPOST
IMPISH
IMPOSE
IMPOST
LIPASE
MOPISH
OPPOSE
REPAST
REPOSE
REPOST
RIPEST
TYPIST
UPPISH

••P••S
ALPHAS
AMPULS
APPALS
APPLES
ASPENS
ASPICS
BIPEDS
BIPODS
BYPASS
CAPERS
CAPIAS
CAPONS
CAPRIS
COPAYS
COPIES
COPSES
CSPOTS
CUPELS
CUPIDS
CUPPAS
CYPRUS
DEPOTS
DEPTHS
ESPIES
EXPELS
GAPERS
HIPPOS
HOPERS
HYPNOS
IMPELS
INPUTS
JAPANS
JAPERS
KAPPAS
KOPEKS
KOPJES
LAPELS
LAPINS
LAPSES
LIPIDS
LOPERS
MAPLES
MOPEDS
MOPERS
MOPUPS
NAPLES
NAPPES
NIPUPS
NOPETS
PAPAWS
PAPERS
PAPPAS
PAPPUS
PEPLOS
PIPALS
PIPERS
PIPITS
POPPAS
POPUPS
PUPILS
RAPIDS
REPADS
REPAYS
REPEGS
REPELS
REPINS
REPOTS
REPROS
RIPENS
ROPERS
RUPEES
SAPORS
SEPALS
SEPIAS
SEPOYS
SOPORS
SUPERS
TAPERS
TAPINS
TAPIRS
TEPALS
TEPEES
TIPINS
TIPUPS
TOPERS
TOPHUS
TOPICS
TYPERS
TYPHUS
UNPEGS
UNPENS
UNPINS
UPPERS
VAPORS
VIPERS
WIPERS
YAPOKS

•••PS•
ELAPSE
EOIPSO
FLOPSY

•••P•S
ADAPTS
ADEPTS
ADOPTS
ALEPHS
CAMPOS
CAMPUS
CARPUS
COAPTS
COMPOS
COOPTS
CORPUS
COUPES
COYPUS
CRAPES
CREPES
CRIPES
CRYPTS
CUPPAS
DRAPES
DRUPES
ELOPES
ERUPTS
ETAPES
GLYPHS
GRAPES
GRAPHS
GRIPES
GROPES
HIPPOS
HUMPHS
KAPPAS
KEMPIS
LOUPES
LYMPHS
MILPAS
MORPHS
MYOPES
NAPPES
NYMPHS
OKAPIS
PALPUS
PAMPAS
PAPPAS
PAPPUS
POPPAS
QUIPUS
RUMPUS
SCAPES
SCOPES
SHAPES
SLOPES
SLYPES
SNIPES
SNOPES
STAPES
STIPES
STOPES
STUPAS
STUPES
SWIPES
SYLPHS
TAUPES
TEMPOS
TEMPTS
TEMPUS
TRIPOS
TROPES

••••PS
BEBOPS
BICEPS
BLEEPS
BLIMPS
BLOOPS
CHAMPS
CHEEPS
CHEOPS
CHIMPS
CHIRPS
CHOMPS
CHUMPS
CLAMPS
CLASPS
CLOMPS
CLUMPS
CRAMPS
CREEPS
CRIMPS
CRISPS
CUTUPS
DROOPS
EQUIPS
ESTOPS
FIXUPS
FRUMPS
FSTOPS
GALOPS
GETUPS
GRAMPS
GRASPS
GROUPS
GRUMPS
JAMUPS
JULEPS
LAYUPS
LETUPS
MIXUPS
MOPUPS
NIPUPS
ONEUPS
ORLOPS
OXLIPS
PELOPS
PINUPS
PLUMPS
POLYPS
POPUPS
PRIMPS
PTRAPS
RECAPS
REMAPS
REMOPS
RETAPS
RETOPS
RUNUPS
SCALPS
SCAMPS
SCARPS
SCAUPS
SCOOPS
SCRAPS
SCRIPS
SETUPS
SHARPS
SHEEPS
SITUPS
SKIMPS
SLEEPS
SLOOPS
SLUMPS
SLURPS
SNOOPS
STAMPS
STEEPS
STOMPS
STOOPS
STOUPS
STRAPS
STRIPS
STROPS
STUMPS
SUMUPS
SUNUPS
SWAMPS
SWEEPS
SWOOPS
SYRUPS
SYSOPS
THORPS
THRIPS
THUMPS
TIEUPS
TIPUPS
TRAMPS
TROMPS
TROOPS
TRUMPS
TULIPS
TWERPS
UNCAPS
UNZIPS
USURPS
VCHIPS
WHELPS
WHOMPS
WHOOPS

PT••••
PTBOAT
PTRAPS

P•T•••
PATACA
PATCHY
PATENS
PATENT
PATERS
PATHAN
PATHOL
PATHOS
PATINA
PATINE
PATIOS
PATMOS
PATOIS
PATROL
PATRON
PATTED
PATTEN
PATTER
PATTON
PETAIN
PETALS
PETARD
PETERS
PETITE
PETREL
PETRIE
PETROG
PETROL
PETTED
PETTER
PETTIT
PETULA
PITCHY
PITHED
PITIED
PITIER
PITIES
PITMAN
PITMEN
PITONS
PITSAW
PITTED
PITTER
POTAGE
POTASH
POTATO
POTEEN
POTENT
POTFUL
POTHER
POTION
POTOSI
POTPIE
POTTED
POTTER
POTTLE
POTTOS
PUTNAM
PUTOFF
PUTONS
PUTOUT
PUTPUT
PUTRID
PUTSBY
PUTSCH
PUTSIN
PUTSON
PUTSTO
PUTSUP
PUTTED
PUTTEE
PUTTER
PYTHIA
PYTHON

P••T••
PALTER
PALTRY
PANTED
PANTOS
PANTRY
PARTED
PARTLY
PARTON
PASTAS
PASTED
PASTEL
PASTES
PASTIS
PASTOR
PASTRY
PATTED
PATTEN
PATTER
PATTON
PAXTON
PECTIC
PECTIN
PEGTOP
PELTED
PELTER
PELTRY
PENTAD
PENTUP
PEPTIC
PERTER
PERTLY
PESTER
PESTLE
PESTOS
PETTED
PETTER
PETTIT
PEWTER
PEYTON
PHATIC
PHOTIC
PHOTOG
PHOTON
PHOTOS
PIETAS
PIETER
PIETIN
PIETRO
PINTER
PINTLE
PINTOS
PISTES
PISTIL
PISTOL
PISTON
PITTED
PITTER
PLATED
PLATEN
PLATER
PLATES
PLATTE
PLOTTY
POETIC
POETRY
PONTES
PONTIC
PONTUS
POPTOP
PORTAL
PORTED
PORTER
PORTIA
PORTLY
POSTAL
POSTED
POSTER
POSTIT
POSTON
POTTED
POTTER
POTTLE
POTTOS
POUTED
POUTER
PRATED
PRATER
PRATES
PRETAX
PRETER
PRETTY
PROTAX
PROTEI
PROTEM
PROTON
PUNTED
PUNTER
PUTTED
PUTTEE
PUTTER

P•••T•
PAINTS
PAINTY
PAIUTE
PALATE
PARETO
PARITY
PASHTO
PEDATE
PELOTA
PEPITA
PESETA
PETITE
PEWITS
PEYOTE
PICOTS
PIGSTY
PILATE
PILOTI
PILOTS
PINATA
PINITE
PINOTS
PIPITS
PIRATE
PIVOTS
PLAITS
PLANTE
PLANTS
PLASTY
PLATTE
PLEATS
PLENTY
PLINTH
PLOTTY
POINTE
POINTS
POINTY
POLITE
POLITY
POSITS
POTATO
POULTS
PRESTO
PRETTY
PRINTS
PRONTO
PUENTE
PUERTO
PURITY
PUTSTO
PYRITE

P••••T
PACKET
PALEST
PALLET
PANDIT
PANOUT
PARENT
PARGET
PARROT
PATENT
PAWSAT
PAYOUT
PEANUT
PECKAT
PEDANT
PEEKAT
PEERAT
PELLET
PELMET
PENULT
PEQUOT
PERMIT
PERROT
PETTIT
PIAGET
PICKAT
PICKET
PIGLET
PIGNUT
PIGOUT
PINXIT
PIOLET
PIQUET
PLACET
PLAINT
PLANET
PLAYAT
PLIANT
PLIGHT
POCKET
POIROT
POKEAT
POLPOT
POPART
POPOUT
POPPET
POSSET
POSTIT
POTENT
PRESET
PRIEST
PRIPET
PRIVET
PROFIT
PROMPT
PROSIT
PROUST
PTBOAT
PULLET
PULPIT
PUNDIT
PUNNET
PUPPET
PUREST
PURIST
PUTOUT
PUTPUT

•PT•••
APTEST
OPTFOR
OPTICS
OPTIMA
OPTING
OPTION
OPTOUT
UPTAKE
UPTALK
UPTICK
UPTIME
UPTOWN
UPTURN

•P•T••
APATHY
SPATES
SPATHE
SPITED
SPITES
SPOTTY

•P••T•
APLITE
OPENTO
OPHITE
OPIATE
OPORTO
SPARTA
SPILTH
SPINTO
SPLATS
SPLITS
SPORTS
SPORTY
SPOTTY
SPOUTS
SPRATS
SPRITE
SPRITS
SPRITZ
SPURTS
UPDATE
UPPITY
UPSETS

•P•••T
APPLET
APTEST
OPTOUT
SPIGOT
SPINET
SPIRIT
SPLINT
SPOILT
SPRINT
SPROUT
UPBEAT
UPCAST
UPLIFT
UPMOST
UPROOT
UPSHOT

••PT••
CAPTAN
CAPTOR
COPTER
COPTIC
DEPTHS
EMPTOR
HEPTAD
KEPTAT
KEPTON
KEPTUP
LAPTEV
LAPTOP
LEPTON
LIPTON
MOPTOP
PEPTIC
POPTOP
RAPTLY
RAPTOR
SEPTAL
SEPTET
SEPTIC
SEPTUM
TIPTOE
TIPTOP
TOPTEN

••P•T•
BYPATH
CAPITA
CAPOTE
CSPOTS
DEPOTS
DEPUTE
DEPUTY
IMPUTE
INPUTS
LAPUTA
MAPUTO
NOPETS
PEPITA
PIPITS
REPOTS
REPUTE
STPETE
UPPITY
WAPITI
ZAPATA

••P••T
ALPERT
APPLET
ARPENT
ASPECT
BYPAST
CAPLET
CAPNUT
COPOUT
DEPART
DEPICT
DEPORT
DOPANT
DUPONT
ESPRIT
EXPECT
EXPERT
EXPORT
EXPOST
HEPCAT
IMPACT
IMPART
IMPORT
IMPOST
INPART
INPORT

KEPTAT
LAPPET
MOPPET
MUPPET
NIPSAT
POPART
POPOUT
POPPET
PUPPET
REPAST
REPEAT
REPENT
REPORT
REPOST
RIPEST
RIPOUT
RUPERT
SEPTET
SIPPET
TAPOUT
TAPPET
TIPPET
TOPCAT
TOPHAT
TOPOUT
TYPIST

•••PT•
ADAPTS
ADEPTS
ADOPTS
COAPTS
COOPTS
CRYPTO
CRYPTS
ERUPTS
KEEPTO
SNAPTO
TEMPTS

•••P•T
ARMPIT
CARPET
DESPOT
DROPIT
HOTPOT
INAPET
JUMPAT
KEEPAT
LAPPET
LIMPET
MOPPET
MUPPET
OUTPUT
POLPOT
POPPET
PRIPET
PULPIT
PUPPET
PUTPUT
RAJPUT
SIPPET
SKIPIT
SNAPAT
STOPIT
TAPPET
TARPIT
TEAPOT
TINPOT
TIPPET

••••PT
ABRUPT
ACCEPT
ENRAPT
EXCEPT
EXEMPT
INCEPT
IRRUPT
PROMPT
SCRIPT
SCULPT

PU••••
PUBLIC
PUCKER
PUDDLE
PUDDLY
PUEBLA
PUEBLO
PUENTE
PUERTO
PUFFED
PUFFER
PUFFIN
PUGGED
PUGREE
PUISNE
PULING
PULLED
PULLET
PULLEY
PULLIN
PULLON
PULLUP
PULPED
PULPIT
PULQUE
PULSAR
PULSED
PULSES
PUMICE
PUMMEL
PUMPED
PUMPER
PUMPUP
PUNCHY
PUNDIT
PUNIER
PUNILY
PUNISH
PUNJAB
PUNKAH
PUNKER
PUNKIE
PUNNED
PUNNET
PUNTED
PUNTER
PUPILS
PUPPET
PURACE
PURDAH
PURDUE
PUREED
PUREES
PURELY
PUREST
PURFLE
PURGED
PURGES
PURIFY
PURINA
PURINE
PURISM
PURIST
PURITY
PURLED
PURLIN
PURPLE
PURPLY
PURRED
PURRER
PURSED
PURSER
PURSES
PURSUE
PURVEY
PUSHED
PUSHES
PUSHON
PUSHUP
PUSSES
PUTNAM
PUTOFF
PUTONS
PUTOUT
PUTPUT
PUTRID
PUTSBY
PUTSCH
PUTSIN
PUTSON
PUTSTO
PUTSUP
PUTTED
PUTTEE
PUTTER
PUZZLE

P•U•••
PAUCIS
PAULEY
PAUNCH
PAUPER
PAUSED
PAUSES
PLUCKS
PLUCKY
PLUGIN
PLUMBS
PLUMED
PLUMES
PLUMMY
PLUMPS
PLUNGE
PLUNKS
PLURAL
PLUSES
PLUSHY
POUCHY
POULTS
POUNCE
POUNDS
POURED
POURER
POURIN
POUSSE
POUTED
POUTER
PRUDES
PRUNED
PRUNER
PRUNES

P••U••
PADUAN
PAIUTE
PAKULA
PAPUAN
PAQUIN
PARULA
PARURE
PENULT
PENURY
PEQUOD
PEQUOT
PERUGA
PERUKE
PERUSE
PETULA
PICULS
PINUPS
PIQUED
PIQUES
PIQUET
PLEURA
PLOUGH
PNEUMA
PODUNK
POPULI
POPUPS
PROUST
PSEUDO
PSEUDS

P•••U•
PABLUM
PACKUP
PAIDUP
PAIRUP
PALPUS
PANFUL
PANOUT
PAPPUS
PASSUP
PAYOUT
PAYSUP
PEANUT
PELEUS
PENTUP
PEPFUL
PEPLUM
PEPSUP
PERDUE
PERKUP
PHYLUM
PICKUP
PIGNUT
PIGOUT
PILEUM
PILEUP
PILEUS
PINDUS
PIPEUP
PLAGUE
PLAQUE
PLAYUP
PLENUM
PLEXUS
PODIUM
POILUS
POLLUX
PONTUS
PONYUP
POPGUN
POPOUT
POPSUP
POROUS
POSEUR
POSSUM
POTFUL
PRAGUE
PRENUP
PRIMUM
PRIMUS
PROPUP
PULLUP
PULQUE
PUMPUP
PURDUE
PURSUE
PUSHUP
PUTOUT
PUTPUT
PUTSUP

P••••U
PAILOU
PENGHU
PICCHU

•PU•••
APULIA
OPUSES
SPUMED
SPUMES
SPUNKY
SPURGE
SPURNS
SPURON
SPURRY
SPURTS

•P•U••
OPPUGN
SPOUSE
SPOUTS
SPRUCE
SPRUES
SPRUNG
UPRUSH
UPTURN

•P••U•
EPIRUS
OPAQUE
OPENUP
OPTOUT
SPEDUP
SPROUT

•P•••U
APERCU

••PU••
AMPULE
AMPULS
COPULA
DEPUTE
DEPUTY
IMPUGN
IMPURE
IMPUTE
INPUTS
LAPUTA
MAPUTO
MOPUPS
NIPUPS
OPPUGN
PAPUAN
POPULI
POPUPS
REPUGN
REPUTE
TIPUPS

••P•U•
CAPFUL
CAPGUN
CAPNUT
COPOUT
CUPFUL
CYPRUS
DEPAUL
DEPAUW
GYPSUM
HOPSUP
HYPEUP
INPOUR
KEPTUP
KIPPUR
LAPFUL
LAPSUP
MOPSUP
NIPPUR
PAPPUS
PEPFUL
PEPLUM
PEPSUP
PIPEUP
POPGUN
POPOUT
POPSUP
RIPOUT
RIPSUP
RUPAUL
SEPTUM
SOPSUP
STPAUL
TAPOUT
TOPGUN
TOPHUS
TOPOUT
TYPEUP
TYPHUS
UNPLUG
VAPOUR
WIPEUP
ZIPSUP

•••PU•
BUMPUP
CAMPUS
CARPUS
COOPUP
CORPUS
COYPUS
CROPUP
FLIPUP
JAIPUR
JUMPUP
KEEPUP
KIPPUR
KUSPUK
LUMPUR
NIPPUR
OUTPUT
PALPUS
PAPPUS
PROPUP
PUMPUP
PUTPUT
QUIPUS
RAIPUR
RAJPUT
RUMPUS
SLAPUP
SLIPUP
SNAPUP
SOUPUP
STAPUF
STEPUP
STOPUP
TEMPUS
TRIPUP
WAMPUM
WHIPUP
WRAPUP

P•V•••
PAVANE
PAVERS
PAVING
PAVLOV
PIVOTS

P••V••
PARVIS
PEAVEY
PEEVED
PEEVES
PELVIC
PELVIS
PLOVER
PRAVDA
PREVIN
PRIVET
PROVED
PROVEN
PROVER
PROVES
PURVEY

P•••V•
PAREVE

P••••V
PAVLOV

•P•V••
SPAVIN
SPIVAK
SPIVVY

•P••V•
SPIVVY

••P•V•
REPAVE

••P••V
IMPROV
LAPTEV

•••P•V
KARPOV

P•W•••
PAWERS
PAWING
PAWNED
PAWNEE
PAWNER
PAWPAW
PAWSAT
PEWEES
PEWITS
PEWTER
POWDER
POWELL
POWERS
POWWOW

P••W••
PEDWAY
PEEWEE
PLOWED
PLOWER
POWWOW
PRAWNS
PREWAR
PROWLS
PROWSE
PSYWAR

P•••W•
PAPAWS
PESAWA

P••••W
PAWPAW
PESCOW
PILLOW
PITSAW
POWWOW
PRELAW

•PW•••
UPWARD
UPWELL
UPWIND

•P•W••
SPAWNS
SPEWED

•P••W•
SPRAWL
UPBOWS
UPTOWN

•P•••W
CPSNOW

••P•W•
PAPAWS

••P••W
DEPAUW
NEPHEW
REPLOW
RIPSAW

•••P•W
PAWPAW

P•X•••
PAXTON
PIXELS
PIXIES
PYXIES

P••X••
PINXIT
PLEXAL
PLEXOR
PLEXUS
PRAXES
PRAXIS

P••••X
PAYBOX
PICKAX
POLEAX
POLLEX
POLLUX
PREFIX
PRETAX
PROLIX
PROTAX

•P•X••
APEXES

•P•••X
SPADIX
SPHINX

••P••X
DUPLEX

•••P•X
AUSPEX
COWPOX

PY••••
PYEDOG
PYJAMA
PYKNIC
PYLONS
PYRITE
PYTHIA
PYTHON
PYXIES

P•Y•••
PAYBOX
PAYDAY
PAYEES
PAYERS
PAYFOR
PAYING
PAYOFF
PAYOLA
PAYOUT
PAYSIN
PAYSON
PAYSUP
PEYOTE
PEYTON
PHYLAE
PHYLLO
PHYLUM
PHYSED
PHYSIO
PLYING
PRYING
PRYNNE
PSYCHE
PSYCHO
PSYCHS
PSYLLA
PSYWAR

P••Y••
PAPYRI
PINYIN
PINYON
PLAYAS
PLAYAT
PLAYED
PLAYER
PLAYON
PLAYUP
POLYPS
PONYUP
PRAYED
PRAYER
PREYED
PREYON

P•••Y•
PAPAYA
PHENYL
POBOYS
POKEYS
POLEYN
POPEYE

P••••Y
PACIFY
PAINTY
PALELY
PALTRY
PANFRY
PANTRY
PAPACY
PAPERY
PARITY
PARKAY
PARLAY
PARLEY
PARODY
PARTLY
PASSBY
PASTRY
PATCHY
PAULEY
PAYDAY
PEACHY
PEARLY
PEAVEY
PEBBLY
PEDWAY
PELTRY
PENNEY
PENURY
PERTLY
PHILBY
PHILLY
PHONEY
PHOOEY
PIGSTY
PIMINY
PINERY
PIRACY
PITCHY
PLASHY
PLASTY
PLENTY
PLOTTY
PLUCKY
PLUMMY
PLUSHY
POACHY
POETRY
POINTY
POKERY
POKILY
POLICY
POLITY
POMPEY
POORLY
POPFLY
PORTLY
POSHLY
POUCHY
PREPAY
PREPPY
PRETTY
PRICEY
PRIMLY
PRIORY
PRISSY
PROSKY
PUDDLY
PULLEY
PUNCHY
PUNILY
PURELY
PURIFY
PURITY
PURPLY
PURVEY
PUTSBY

•PY•••
SPYING

•P•Y••
SPAYED
SPRYER
SPRYLY

•P••Y•
EPONYM
SPLAYS
SPRAYS

•P•••Y
APATHY
APIARY
OPENLY
SPACEY
SPANKY
SPARKY
SPEEDY
SPERRY
SPHERY
SPIFFY
SPIVVY
SPONGY
SPOOKY
SPOONY
SPORTY
SPOTTY
SPRYLY
SPUNKY
SPURRY
UPPITY

••PY••
PAPYRI

••P•Y•
COPAYS
PAPAYA
POPEYE
REPAYS
SEPOYS
ZEPHYR

••P••Y
BYPLAY
COPLEY
DEPLOY
DEPUTY
DIPODY
DUPERY
EMPERY
EMPLOY
EXPIRY
INPLAY
JAPERY
MOPERY
NAPERY
NIPSEY
OSPREY
PAPACY
PAPERY
POPFLY
RAPTLY
REPLAY
RIPELY
RIPLEY
RIPPLY
SUPPLY
TYPIFY
UPPITY
VAPORY

•••P•Y
CHOPPY
COMPLY
DAMPLY
DEEPLY
DIMPLY
DRIPPY
DROPBY
FLAPPY
FLOPPY
FLOPSY
GLOPPY
GRAPEY
GRAPHY
LIMPLY
MORPHY
MURPHY
NETPAY
POMPEY
PREPAY
PREPPY
PURPLY
QUIPPY
RIPPLY
RUMPLY
SIMPLY
SKIPPY
SLAPPY
SLIPPY
SLOPPY
SNAPPY
SNIPPY
SUPPLY
TEAPOY
TRAPPY
TRIPLY
TROPHY
TWOPLY
WHIPPY

••••PY
CANOPY
CHIRPY
CHOPPY
CLUMPY
CREEPY
CRIMPY
CRISPY
CROUPY
DRIPPY
DROOPY
FLAPPY
FLOPPY
FRUMPY
GLOPPY
GRUMPY
JALOPY
OCCUPY
PREPPY
QUIPPY
RECOPY
SKIMPY
SKIPPY
SLAPPY
SLEEPY
SLIPPY
SLOPPY
SNAPPY
SNIPPY
SNOOPY
STIMPY
STRIPY
STUMPY
SWAMPY
SYRUPY
TRAPPY
WHIPPY
WICOPY

P•Z•••
PIZAZZ
PIZZAS
PUZZLE

P••Z••
PANZER
PFIZER
PIAZZA
PINZON
PIZZAS
PLAZAS
PRIZED
PRIZES
PROZAC
PUZZLE

P•••Z•
PIAZZA
PIZAZZ

P••••Z
PIZAZZ

•P•••Z
SPRITZ

•••P•Z
TROPEZ

QA••••
QANTAS
QATARI

Q•A•••
QUACKS
QUADRI
QUAFFS
QUAGGA
QUAGGY
QUAHOG
QUAILS
QUAINT
QUAKED
QUAKER
QUAKES
QUALMS
QUANGO
QUANTA
QUARKS
QUARRY
QUARTO
QUARTS
QUARTZ
QUASAR
QUAVER
QUAYLE

Q••A••
QATARI
QUEASY

Q•••A•
QANTAS
QINTAR
QUASAR
QUMRAN
QUOTAS

Q••••A
QUAGGA
QUANTA
QUETTA
QUINOA
QUOKKA
QUOTHA

•Q•A••
AQUATE
EQUALS
EQUATE
SQUABS
SQUADS
SQUALL
SQUARE
SQUASH
SQUATS
SQUAWK

•Q••A•
SQUEAK
SQUEAL

•Q•••A
AQUILA

••Q•A•
EMQUAD
ENQUAD
LOQUAT
MSQUAD

••Q••A
BUQSHA

Q••B••
QUEBEC

•Q••B•
SQUABS
SQUIBB
SQUIBS

•Q•••B
SQUIBB

Q••C••
QUACKS
QUICHE

Q•••C•
QUENCH
QUINCE
QUINCY

Q••••C
QUEBEC

Q••D••
QUADRI
QUIDDE

Q•••D•
QUIDDE

Q••••D
QUAKED
QUEUED
QUOTED

•Q••D•
SQUADS
SQUIDS

••Q••D
EMQUAD
ENQUAD
LIQUID
MSQUAD
PEQUOD
PIQUED

Q•E•••
QUEASY
QUEBEC
QUEENS
QUELLS
QUEMOY
QUENCH
QUERNS
QUESTS
QUETTA
QUEUED
QUEUER
QUEUES
QUEZON
QWERTY

Q••E••
QUEENS
QUIETS

Q•••E•
QUAKED
QUAKER
QUAKES
QUAVER
QUEBEC
QUEUED
QUEUER
QUEUES
QUIRES
QUIVER
QUOTED
QUOTER
QUOTES

Q••••E
QUAYLE
QUICHE
QUIDDE
QUINCE
QUOQUE

•Q•E••
IQTEST
SQUEAK
SQUEAL

•Q•••E
AQUATE
EQUATE
EQUINE
SQUARE
SQUIRE

••Q•E•
COQUET
PIQUED
PIQUES
PIQUET
RAQUEL
SEQUEL
TOQUES
TUQUES

•••Q•E
BARQUE
BASQUE
BISQUE
BRAQUE
CAIQUE
CALQUE
CASQUE
CHEQUE
CINQUE
CIRQUE
CLAQUE
CLIQUE
CLOQUE
CUIQUE
MANQUE
MARQUE
MASQUE
MOSQUE
OPAQUE
PLAQUE
PULQUE
QUOQUE
RISQUE
SACQUE
TORQUE
UBIQUE
UNIQUE

Q••F••
QUAFFS

Q•••F•
QUAFFS

Q••G••
QUAGGA
QUAGGY

Q•••G•
QUAGGA
QUAGGY
QUANGO

Q••••G
QUAHOG

Q••H••
QUAHOG

Q•••H•
QUICHE
QUOTHA

Q••••H
QUENCH
QURUSH

•Q•••H
SQUASH
SQUISH
SQUUSH

••Q•H•
BUQSHA

QI••••
QINTAR
QIVIUT

Q•I•••
QUICHE
QUIDDE
QUIETS
QUILLS
QUILTS
QUINCE
QUINCY
QUINOA
QUINTS
QUIPPY
QUIPUS
QUIRES
QUIRKS
QUIRKY
QUIRTS
QUITIT
QUIVER

Q••I••
QIVIUT
QUAILS
QUAINT
QUOINS
QUOITS

Q•••I•
QUITIT

Q••••I
QATARI
QUADRI

•Q•I••
AQUILA
AQUINO
EQUINE
EQUIPS
EQUITY
SQUIBB
SQUIBS
SQUIDS
SQUILL
SQUINT
SQUIRE
SQUIRM
SQUIRT
SQUISH

••Q•I•
ACQUIT
LIQUID
MAQUIS
NYQUIL
PAQUIN
SEQUIN
YAQUIS

•••QI•
IRAQIS

•••Q•I
SESQUI
YANQUI

Q•K•••
QUAKED
QUAKER
QUAKES
QUOKKA

Q•••K•
QUACKS
QUARKS
QUIRKS
QUIRKY
QUOKKA

•Q•••K
SQUAWK
SQUEAK

Q••L••
QUALMS
QUELLS
QUILLS
QUILTS

Q•••L•
QUAILS
QUAYLE
QUELLS
QUILLS

•Q••L•
AQUILA
EQUALS
SQUALL
SQUILL

•Q•••L
SQUALL
SQUEAL
SQUILL

••Q••L
NYQUIL
RAQUEL
SEQUEL

Q•M•••
QUMRAN

Q••M••
QUEMOY

Q•••M•
QUALMS

Q••••M
QUORUM

•Q•••M
SQUIRM

Q•N•••
QANTAS
QINTAR

Q••N••
QUANGO
QUANTA
QUENCH
QUINCE
QUINCY
QUINOA
QUINTS

Q•••N•
QUAINT
QUEENS
QUERNS
QUOINS

Q••••N
QUEZON
QUMRAN

•Q••N•
AQUINO
EQUINE
SQUINT

••Q••N
PAQUIN
SEQUIN

Q•O•••
QUOINS
QUOITS
QUOKKA
QUOQUE
QUORUM
QUOTAS
QUOTED
QUOTER
QUOTES
QUOTHA

Q•••O•
QUAHOG
QUEMOY
QUEZON
QUINOA

Q••••O
QUANGO
QUARTO

•Q•••O
AQUINO

••Q•O•
LIQUOR
PEQUOD
PEQUOT

•••Q•O
BANQUO

Q••P••
QUIPPY
QUIPUS

Q•••P•
QUIPPY

•Q••P•
EQUIPS

Q••Q••
QUOQUE

••••QQ
ETSEQQ

Q•R•••
QURUSH

Q••R••
QUARKS
QUARRY
QUARTO
QUARTS
QUARTZ
QUERNS
QUIRES
QUIRKS
QUIRKY
QUIRTS
QUMRAN
QUORUM
QWERTY

Q•••R•
QATARI
QUADRI
QUARRY

Q••••R
QINTAR
QUAKER
QUASAR
QUAVER
QUEUER
QUIVER
QUOTER

•Q••R•
SQUARE
SQUIRE
SQUIRM
SQUIRT

••Q••R
LIQUOR

Q••S••
QUASAR
QUESTS

Q•••S•
QUEASY
QURUSH

Q••••S
QANTAS
QUACKS
QUAFFS
QUAILS
QUAKES
QUALMS
QUARKS
QUARTS
QUEENS
QUELLS
QUERNS
QUESTS
QUEUES
QUIETS
QUILLS
QUILTS
QUINTS
QUIPUS
QUIRES
QUIRKS
QUIRTS
QUOINS
QUOITS
QUOTAS
QUOTES

•Q••S•
IQTEST
SQUASH
SQUISH
SQUUSH

•Q•••S
EQUALS
EQUIPS
SQUABS
SQUADS
SQUATS
SQUIBS
SQUIDS

••QS••
BUQSHA

••Q••S
MAQUIS
PIQUES
TOQUES
TUQUES
YAQUIS

•••Q•S
IRAQIS

Q•T•••
QATARI

Q••T••
QANTAS
QINTAR
QUETTA
QUITIT
QUOTAS
QUOTED
QUOTER
QUOTES
QUOTHA

Q•••T•
QUANTA
QUARTO
QUARTS
QUARTZ
QUESTS
QUETTA
QUIETS
QUILTS
QUINTS
QUIRTS
QUOITS
QWERTY

Q••••T
QIVIUT
QUAINT
QUITIT

•QT•••
IQTEST

•Q••T•
AQUATE
EQUATE
EQUITY
SQUATS

•Q•••T
IQTEST
SQUINT
SQUIRT

••Q••T
ACQUIT
COQUET
LOQUAT
PEQUOT
PIQUET

QU••••
QUACKS
QUADRI
QUAFFS
QUAGGA
QUAGGY
QUAHOG
QUAILS
QUAINT
QUAKED
QUAKER
QUAKES
QUALMS
QUANGO
QUANTA
QUARKS
QUARRY
QUARTO
QUARTS
QUARTZ
QUASAR
QUAVER
QUAYLE
QUEASY
QUEBEC
QUEENS
QUELLS
QUEMOY
QUENCH
QUERNS
QUESTS
QUETTA
QUEUED
QUEUER
QUEUES
QUEZON
QUICHE
QUIDDE
QUIETS
QUILLS
QUILTS
QUINCE
QUINCY
QUINOA
QUINTS
QUIPPY
QUIPUS
QUIRES
QUIRKS
QUIRKY
QUIRTS
QUITIT
QUIVER
QUMRAN
QUOINS
QUOITS
QUOKKA
QUOQUE
QUORUM
QUOTAS
QUOTED
QUOTER
QUOTES
QUOTHA
QURUSH

Q•U•••
QUEUED
QUEUER
QUEUES
QURUSH

Q•••U•
QIVIUT
QUIPUS
QUOQUE
QUORUM

•QU•••
AQUATE
AQUILA
AQUINO
EQUALS
EQUATE
EQUINE
EQUIPS
EQUITY
SQUABS
SQUADS
SQUALL
SQUARE
SQUASH
SQUATS
SQUAWK
SQUEAK
SQUEAL
SQUIBB
SQUIBS
SQUIDS
SQUILL
SQUINT
SQUIRE
SQUIRM
SQUIRT
SQUISH
SQUUSH

•Q•U••
SQUUSH

••QU••
ACQUIT
COQUET
EMQUAD
ENQUAD
LIQUID
LIQUOR
LOQUAT
MAQUIS
MSQUAD
NYQUIL
PAQUIN
PEQUOD
PEQUOT
PIQUED
PIQUES
PIQUET
RAQUEL
SEQUEL
SEQUIN
TOQUES
TUQUES
YAQUIS

•••QU•
BANQUO
BARQUE
BASQUE
BISQUE
BRAQUE
CAIQUE
CALQUE
CASQUE
CHEQUE
CINQUE
CIRQUE
CLAQUE
CLIQUE
CLIQUY
CLOQUE
CUIQUE
MANQUE
MARQUE
MASQUE
MOSQUE
OPAQUE
PLAQUE
PULQUE
QUOQUE
RISQUE
SACQUE
SESQUI
TORQUE
UBIQUE
UNIQUE
YANQUI

Q•V•••
QIVIUT

Q••V••
QUAVER
QUIVER

QW••••
QWERTY

•Q••W•
SQUAWK

Q••Y••
QUAYLE

Q••••Y
QUAGGY
QUARRY
QUEASY
QUEMOY
QUINCY
QUIPPY
QUIRKY
QWERTY

•Q•••Y
EQUITY

•••Q•Y
CLIQUY

Q••Z••
QUEZON

Q••••Z
QUARTZ

RA••••
RABATO
RABBET
RABBIS
RABBIT
RABBLE
RABIES
RACEME
RACERS
RACHEL
RACHIS
RACIAL
RACIER
RACILY
RACINE
RACING
RACKED
RACKET
RACKUP
RACONS
RADDLE
RADIAL
RADIAN
RADIOS
RADISH
RADIUM
RADIUS
RADNER
RADOME
RADULA
RAFAEL
RAFFIA
RAFFLE
RAFTED
RAFTER
RAGBAG
RAGGED
RAGING
RAGLAN
RAGMAN
RAGMEN
RAGMOP
RAGOUT
RAGRUG
RAGTAG
RAGTOP
RAHRAH
RAIDED
RAIDER
RAILAT
RAILED
RAILER
RAINED
RAINER
RAINES
RAINEY
RAIPUR
RAISED
RAISER
RAISES
RAISIN
RAJAHS
RAJPUT
RAKEIN
RAKERS
RAKEUP
RAKING
RAKISH
RAMADA
RAMATE
RAMBLA
RAMBLE
RAMEAU
RAMETS
RAMIES
RAMIFY
RAMJET
RAMMED
RAMONA
RAMONE
RAMOSE
RAMOUS
RAMPED
RAMROD
RAMSAY
RAMSES
RAMSEY
RAMSON
RANCHO
RANCID
RANCOR
RANDOM
RANDRY
RANEES
RANFOR
RANGED
RANGER
RANGES
RANGUP
RANIDS
RANKED
RANKER
RANKIN
RANKLE
RANKLY
RANOFF
RANOUT
RANSOM
RANTED
RANTER
RAPIDS
RAPIER
RAPINE
RAPINI
RAPPED
RAPPEE
RAPPEL
RAPPER
RAPTLY
RAPTOR
RAQUEL
RAREFY
RARELY
RAREST
RARIFY
RARING
RARITY
RASCAL
RASERS
RASHAD
RASHER
RASHES
RASHID
RASHLY
RASING
RASPED
RASPER
RASSLE
RASTER
RATEDG
RATEDR
RATEDX
RATELS
RATERS
RATHER
RATIFY
RATINE
RATING
RATION
RATIOS
RATITE
RATLIN
RATSON
RATTAN
RATTED
RATTER
RATTLE
RATTLY
RAVAGE
RAVELS
RAVENS
RAVERS
RAVEUP
RAVINE
RAVING
RAVISH
RAWEGG
RAWEST
RAWISH
RAYGUN
RAYONS
RAZING
RAZORS
RAZZED
RAZZES
RAZZLE

R•A•••
REACTS
READER
READIN
REAGAN
REAIMS
REAIRS
REALER
REALES
REALIA
REALLY
REALMS
REALTY
REAMED
REAMER
REAPED
REAPER
REARED
REARER
REARMS
REARUP
REASON
REATAS
RHABDO
RHAMES
RIALTO
RIATAS
ROADIE
ROAMED
ROAMER
ROARED
ROARER
ROASTS
RRATED
RUANAS
RUANDA
RVALUE
RWANDA
RYAZAN

R••A••
RABATO
RAFAEL
RAJAHS
RAMADA
RAMATE
RAVAGE
REBAGS
REBARS
REBATE
RECALL
RECANE
RECANT
RECAPS
RECAST
REDACT
REDANT
REDATE
REFACE
REGAIN
REGALE
REGARD
REHABS
REHANG
REHASH
RELACE
RELAID
RELATE
RELAYS
REMADE
REMAIL
REMAIN
REMAKE
REMAND
REMANS
REMAPS
REMARK
RENAIL
RENAME
RENATA
REPADS
REPAID
REPAIR
REPAND
REPAST
REPAVE
REPAYS
RERATE
RESALE
RESALT
RESAND
RESAWN
RESAWS
RETAGS
RETAIL
RETAIN
RETAKE
RETAPE
RETAPS
RETARD
RETARS
REVAMP
REWARD
REWARM
REWASH
RIBALD
RIBAND
RITARD
RIVALS
RIYADH
RIYALS
ROBALO
ROLAND
ROMAIC
ROMAJI
ROMANO
ROMANS
ROMANY
RONALD
ROSARY
ROTARY
ROTATE
ROXANA
ROXANE
ROYALE
ROYALS
RUBATI
RUBATO
RUGATE
RUPAUL

R•••A•
RACIAL
RADIAL
RADIAN
RAGBAG
RAGLAN
RAGMAN
RAGTAG
RAHRAH
RAILAT
RAMEAU
RAMSAY
RASCAL
RASHAD
RATTAN
REAGAN
REATAS
RECOAT
REDBAY
REDCAP
REDEAL
REDHAT
REDIAL
REDOAK
REDRAW
REDTAG
REFLAG
REGGAE
REGNAL
REGNAT
REHEAL
REHEAR
REHEAT
REINAS
RELOAD
RENTAL
REPEAL
REPEAT
REPLAN
REPLAY
REREAD
RESEAL
RESEAT
RESEAU
RETEAR
RETIAL
RETRAL
REVEAL
REWRAP
REXCAT
RHINAL
RIATAS
RIOJAS
RIPRAP
RIPSAW
RITUAL
RODHAM
RODMAN
ROSEAU
RUANAS
RUDMAN
RUMBAS
RUNSAT
RUNWAY
RUPIAH
RUTTAN
RYAZAN
RYOKAN

R••••A
RADULA
RAFFIA
RAMADA
RAMBLA
RAMONA
RCCOLA
REALIA
REDSEA
REGINA
REMORA
REMUDA
RENATA
RESEDA
RETINA
RHONDA
RHUMBA
RIVERA
ROBBIA
ROMOLA
ROSITA
ROSTRA
ROWENA
ROXANA
RUANDA
RUMINA
RUSSIA
RWANDA

•RA•••
ARABIA
ARABIC
ARABLE
ARAFAT
ARAGON
ARALIA
ARALLU
ARAMIS
ARARAT
ARAWAK
BRACED
BRACER
BRACES
BRACHY
BRACTS
BRAHMA
BRAHMS
BRAIDS
BRAILA
BRAILS
BRAINS
BRAINY
BRAISE
BRAKED
BRAKES
BRANCH
BRANDO
BRANDS
BRANDT
BRANDX
BRANDY
BRANNY
BRANTS
BRAQUE
BRASHY
BRASOV
BRASSY
BRATSK
BRATTY
BRAVAS
BRAVED
BRAVER
BRAVES
BRAVOS
BRAWLS
BRAWNY
BRAYED
BRAYER
BRAZED
BRAZEN
BRAZER
BRAZES
BRAZIL
BRAZOS
BRAZZA
BRAZZI
CRABBE
CRABBY
CRACKS
CRACKY
CRADLE
CRAFTS
CRAFTY
CRAGGY
CRAKES
CRAMBO
CRAMPS
CRANED
CRANES
CRANIA
CRANIO
CRANKS
CRANKY
CRANNY
CRAPES
CRATED
CRATER
CRATES
CRAVAT
CRAVED
CRAVEN
CRAVER
CRAVES
CRAWLS
CRAWLY
CRAYON
CRAZED
CRAZES
DRABLY
DRACHM
DRAFTS
DRAFTY
DRAGEE
DRAGGY
DRAGIN
DRAGON
DRAILS
DRAINS
DRAKES
DRAMAS
DRAPED
DRAPER
DRAPES
DRAWER
DRAWIN
DRAWLS
DRAWLY
DRAWON
DRAWUP
DRAYED
ERASED
ERASER
ERASES
FRACAS
FRAIDY
FRAISE
FRAMED
FRAMES
FRANCA
FRANCE
FRANCK
FRANCO
FRANCS
FRANKS
FRANNY
FRAPPE
FRASER
FRAUDS
FRAUEN
FRAYED
FRAZER
GRABAT
GRABBY
GRABEN
GRABLE
GRACED
GRACES
GRACIE
GRADEA
GRADED
GRADER
GRADES
GRADIN
GRADUS
GRAECO
GRAFTS
GRAHAM
GRAILS
GRAINS
GRAINY
GRAMAS
GRAMME
GRAMMY
GRAMPA
GRAMPS
GRANDE
GRANDS
GRANGE
GRANNY
GRANTS
GRAPES
GRAPEY
GRAPHS
GRAPHY
GRAPPA
GRASPS
GRASSO
GRASSY
GRATED
GRATER
GRATES
GRATIA
GRATIN
GRATIS
GRAVED
GRAVEL
GRAVEN
GRAVER
GRAVES
GRAVID
GRAYED
GRAYER
GRAYLY
GRAZED
GRAZER
GRAZES
IRANIS
IRAQIS
IRATER
KRAALS
KRAITS
KRAKEN
KRAKOW
KRAMER
KRANTZ
KRASNY
KRATER
ORACHS
ORACLE
ORALES
ORALLY
ORANGE
ORANGS
ORANGY

ORANTS
ORATED
ORATES
ORATOR
PRAGUE
PRAISE
PRAJNA
PRANCE
PRANGS
PRANKS
PRASES
PRATED
PRATER
PRATES
PRAVDA
PRAWNS
PRAXES
PRAXIS
PRAYED
PRAYER
RRATED
SRANAN
TRACED
TRACER
TRACES
TRACEY
TRACHY
TRACKS
TRACTS
TRADED
TRADER
TRADES
TRAGIC
TRAILS
TRAINS
TRAITS
TRAJAN
TRALEE
TRAMPS
TRANCE
TRAPPY
TRASHY
TRAUMA
TRAVEL
TRAVES
TRAVIS
TRAWLS
URACIL
URAEUS
URALIC
URALSK
URANIA
URANIC
URANUS
WRACKS
WRAITH
WRAPUP
WRASSE
WRATHS
WRATHY
XRATED
XRAYED

•R•A••

ARCADE
ARCANA
ARCANE
ARCARO
ARGALI
ARMADA
ARMAGH
ARMAND
ARMANI
ARRACK
ARRANT
ARRAYS
ARVADA
ARYANS
BREACH
BREADS
BREAKS
BREAMS
BREAST
BREATH
BRIAND
BRIANS
BRIARD
BRIARS
BROACH
BROADS
BRYANT
CREAKS
CREAKY
CREAMS
CREAMY
CREASE
CREASY
CREATE
CROAKS
CROAKY
CROATS
DREADS
DREAMS
DREAMT
DREAMY
DREARY
DRYADS
ERGATE
ERHARD
ERNANI
ERRAND
ERRANT
ERRARE
ERRATA
ERSATZ
FREAKS
FREAKY
FRIARS
FRIARY
GREASE
GREASY
GREATS
GREAVE
GROANS
GROATS
KRAALS
ORBACH
ORDAIN
OREADS
ORGANA
ORGANS
ORGATE
ORIANA
ORNATE
PREACH
PREAMP
PROAMS
TREADS
TREATS
TREATY
TRIADS
TRIAGE
TRIALS
TRUANT
URBANA
URBANE
URIALS
WREAKS
WREATH

•R••A•

ARAFAT
ARARAT
ARAWAK
ARCTAN
ARECAS
ARENAS
AROMAS
ARREAR
ARUBAN
BRAVAS
BRIDAL
BROGAN
BROKAW
BRUMAL
BRUTAL
CRAVAT
CRETAN
CRURAL
DRAMAS
FRACAS
FRIDAY
FRUGAL
FRYPAN
GRABAT
GRAHAM
GRAMAS
IRREAL
ORDEAL
ORGEAT
ORPHAN
PREFAB
PRELAW
PREPAY
PRETAX
PREWAR
PRIMAL
PROTAX
PROZAC
SRANAN
TRAJAN
TREPAN
TRIBAL
TRINAL
TROCAR
TROJAN
TRUMAN

•R•••A

ARABIA
ARALIA
ARBELA
ARCANA
AREOLA
ARETHA
ARISTA
ARJUNA
ARMADA
ARNICA
ARRIBA
ARROBA
ARVADA
BRAHMA
BRAILA
BRAZZA
BRENDA
CRANIA
CRENNA
CREUSA
CRIMEA
EROICA
ERRATA
FRANCA
FRESCA
GRADEA
GRAMPA
GRAPPA
GRATIA
GRETNA
OREIDA
ORGANA
ORIANA
ORISSA
ORTEGA
PRAJNA
PRAVDA
TRAUMA
TREDIA
TRICIA
TRISHA
TRIVIA
TROIKA
URANIA
URBANA
URSULA

••RA••

ABRADE
ABRAMS
AERATE
AFRAID
AFRAME
AIRARM
ARRACK
ARRANT
ARRAYS
BERATE
BORAGE
BORATE
BORAXO
CARAFE
CARATS
CERATE
CORALS
CURACY
CURARE
CURATE
CYRANO
DERAIL
DORADO
DORAGS
DORATI
DURANT
ENRAGE
ENRAPT
ERRAND
ERRANT
ERRARE
ERRATA
EURAIL
FARADS
FORAGE
FORAYS
GARAGE
GERAHS
GERALD
GERARD
GIRARD
GORALS
GYRATE
HARALD
HARARE
HARASS
HERALD
HORACE
ISRAEL
JURADO
JURATS
KARATE
KARATS
KERALA
KORATS
KURALT
LARAMS
LORAIN
MARACA
MARAUD
MIRAGE
MORALE
MORALS
MORANT
MORASS
MORAVA
MORAYS
MURALS
MURANO
PARADE
PARANA
PARANG
PARAPH
PHRASE
PIRACY
PIRANA
PIRATE
PTRAPS
PURACE
RERATE
SARANS
SCRAGS
SCRAMS
SCRAPE
SCRAPS
SCRAWL
SERACS
SERAIS
SERAPE
SERAPH
SHRANK
SPRAGS
SPRAIN
SPRANG
SPRATS
SPRAWL
SPRAYS
STRABO
STRADS
STRAFE
STRAIN
STRAIT
STRAKE
STRAND
STRAPS
STRASS
STRATA
STRATI
STRATO
STRAUB
STRAUS
STRAWS
STRAWY
STRAYS
SURAHS
TARAWA
TERAPH
TERATO
THRACE
THRALE
THRALL
THRASH
TIRADE
TIRANA
TIRANE
TORAHS
TYRANT
VIRAGO

••R•A•

ABROAD
ADRIAN
AERIAL
AIRBAG
AIRDAM
AIRMAN
AIRSAC
AIRWAY
AORTAE
AORTAL
AORTAS
ARREAR
ATRIAL
BARCAR
BARKAT
BARMAN
BARTAB
BOREAL
BOREAS
BORMAN
BUREAU
BURGAS
BURLAP
BURMAN
BUROAK
BURSAE
BURSAL
BURSAR
BURSAS
BYROAD
CARMAN
CARNAL
CARPAL
CEREAL
CORBAN
CORDAY
CORMAN
CORRAL
CURIAE
CURIAL
DARNAY
DERMAL
DIRHAM
DORCAS
DORIAN
DORSAL
DURBAN
DURBAR
DURHAM
DURIAN
EARLAP
EARWAX
FARRAH
FARRAR
FERIAL
FERIAS
FERMAT
FIRMAN
FORBAD
FORMAL
FORMAN
FORMAT
FORTAS
GERMAN
HARLAN
HERBAL
HEREAT
HERMAN
HURRAH
HURRAY
INROAD
IRREAL
JARRAH
JORDAN
KARNAK
KARRAS
KERMAN
KIRMAN
KOREAN
KORMAN
KURGAN
LARIAT
LARVAE
LARVAL
LARVAS
LOREAL
MARGAY
MARIAH
MARIAN
MERMAN
MIRIAM
MOREAU
MORGAN
MORNAY
MORTAL
MORTAR
MURRAY
MYRDAL
MYRIAD
NARIAL
NARWAL
NORGAY
NORIAS
NORMAL
NORMAN
NORWAY
OBRIAN
OCREAE
PARCAE
PARIAH
PARKAS
PARKAY
PARLAY
PORTAL
PURDAH
REREAD
SCREAK
SCREAM
SERIAL
SERVAL
SIRDAR
SIRRAH
SPREAD
STREAK
STREAM
STRIAE
SURTAX
SYRIAN
TARMAC
TARPAN
TARSAL
TARTAN
TARTAR
TARZAN
TERRAN
THREAD
THREAT
THROAT
TOREAT
TURBAN
TYRIAN
UGRIAN
UNREAD
UNREAL
UPROAR
VARNAS
VERBAL
VERNAL
WARSAW

••R••A

AFRICA
ARRIBA
ARROBA
AURIGA
AURORA
BARBRA
BAROJA
BERTHA
BORGIA
CARINA
CHROMA
CORNEA
CORONA
CORYZA
DURYEA
EARTHA
ERRATA
EUREKA
EUROPA
FARINA
GARCIA
GURKHA
JERBOA
KARIBA
KERALA
KORUNA
LAROSA
LERIDA
LORICA
MARACA
MARCIA
MARINA
MARISA
MARKKA
MARSHA
MARTHA
MERIDA
MORAVA
MORITA
MURCIA
NARNIA
NERUDA
PARANA
PARULA
PERCHA
PERSIA
PERUGA
PIRANA
PORTIA
PURINA
SARNIA
SERBIA
SERENA
SEROSA
SIRICA
STRATA
TARAWA
TERESA
TIRANA
VARUNA
VERONA
YORUBA
ZAREBA

•••RA•

ABORAL
AFFRAY
AGORAE
AGORAS
AMORAL
AMTRAC
AMTRAK
ANORAK
ANURAN
ARARAT
ASHRAM
ASTRAL
ASTRAY
BETRAY
BEWRAY
BUMRAP
CHIRAC
CHORAL
COBRAS
CONRAD
CORRAL
CRURAL
DEBRAS
DEFRAY
DELRAY
DIGRAM
DOBRAS
DVORAK
ENGRAM
ENTRAP
ENWRAP
ESDRAS
ESTRAY
EXTRAS
FABRAY
FARRAH
FARRAR
FLORAE
FLORAL
FLORAS
FOURAM
GIBRAN
HIJRAH
HOORAH
HOORAY
HURRAH
HURRAY
HYDRAE
HYDRAS
INGRAM
JARRAH
JEERAT
KARRAS
KONRAD
LEERAT
MACRAE
MADRAS
MANRAY
MCGRAW
MIHRAB
MITRAL
MUDRAS
MURRAY
NAIRAS
NEURAL
OPERAS
OUTRAN
PEERAT
PLURAL
QUMRAN
RAHRAH
REDRAW
RETRAL
REWRAP
RIPRAP
SABRAS
SACRAL
SATRAP
SCARAB
SEURAT
SHIRAZ
SHORAN
SIRRAH
SPIRAL
SUDRAS
SUNRAY
SUTRAS
SWARAJ
TAYRAS
TEARAT
TERRAN
TETRAD
TETRAS
THORAX
TIARAS
ULTRAS
UMBRAE
UMBRAL
UMBRAS
UNDRAW
UNTRAP
UNWRAP
ZEBRAS

•••R•A

ANDREA
DHARMA
DJERBA
EGERIA
GLORIA
IBERIA
ICARIA
ISTRIA
LABREA
MAURYA
MCCREA
NUTRIA
OMERTA
PEORIA
SCORIA
SFORZA
SHARIA
SHERPA
SHORTA
SIERRA
SMYRNA
SPARTA
SPIREA
STERNA
STYRIA
TIERRA
UMBRIA

••••RA

AMENRA
AMHARA
ANGORA
ANITRA
ANKARA
ANSARA
ASMARA
ASPERA
AURORA
AYMARA
BARBRA
BIAFRA
CAMERA
CETERA
CHOPRA
CONTRA
DATURA
DUNERA
ELMIRA
ELVIRA
ENDORA
EUDORA
EXEDRA
FEDORA
FEMORA
FULCRA
GEMARA
GENERA
GEZIRA
HEGIRA
INDIRA
KAGERA
MADURA
MANTRA
MEGARA
MONERA
MOTHRA
NATURA
PICARA
PLEURA
REMORA
RIVERA
ROSTRA
SAHARA
SAMARA
SANDRA
SCLERA
SEGURA
SENORA
SENTRA
SIERRA
SISERA
SISTRA
SONORA
TAMARA
TANTRA
TEPHRA
TIERRA
TUNDRA
ZADORA

R•B•••

RABATO
RABBET
RABBIS
RABBIT
RABBLE
RABIES
REBAGS
REBARS
REBATE
REBBES
REBECS
REBELS
REBEND
REBENT
REBIDS
REBIND
REBOIL
REBOLT
REBOOT
REBORN
REBOZO
REBUFF
REBUKE
REBURY
REBUTS
RIBALD
RIBAND
RIBBED
RIBBON
RIBEYE
RIBOSE
ROBALO
ROBBED
ROBBER
ROBBIA
ROBBIE
ROBERT
ROBING
ROBINS
ROBLES
ROBOTS
ROBROY
ROBSON
ROBUST
RUBATI
RUBATO
RUBBED
RUBBER
RUBBLE
RUBBLY
RUBENS
RUBIED
RUBIES
RUBIFY
RUBLES
RUBLEV
RUBOFF
RUBOUT
RUBRIC
RUBSIN

R••B••

RABBET
RABBIS
RABBIT
RABBLE
RAGBAG
RAMBLA
RAMBLE
REBBES
REDBAY
REDBUD
REEBOK
REUBEN
RHABDO
RHEBOK
RIBBED
RIBBON
ROBBED
ROBBER
ROBBIA
ROBBIE
ROUBLE
RUBBED
RUBBER
RUBBLE
RUBBLY
RUMBAS
RUMBLE
RUMBLY

R•••B•

REDUBS
REHABS
RHOMBI
RHOMBS
RHUMBA
RHUMBS

R••••B

RESORB
REVERB

•RB•••

ARBELA
ARBORS
ARBOUR
ERBIUM
MRBLUE
ORBACH
ORBING
ORBITS
URBANA
URBANE

•R•B••

ARABIA
ARABIC
ARABLE
ARUBAN
BRIBED
BRIBES
CRABBE
CRABBY
DRABLY
EREBUS
GRABAT
GRABBY
GRABEN
GRABLE
GREBES
GRUBBY
IROBOT
ORIBIS
PROBED
PROBER
PROBES
TREBEK
TREBLE
TREBLY
TRIBAL
TRIBES

•R••B•

ARDEBS
ARRIBA
ARROBA
BRUMBY
CRABBE
CRABBY
CRAMBO
CROSBY
CRUMBS
CRUMBY
DROPBY
GRABBY
GRUBBY
TRILBY

•R•••B

PREFAB

••RB••

AIRBAG
AIRBUS
BARBED
BARBEL
BARBER
BARBET
BARBIE
BARBRA
BERBER
BURBLE
BURBLY
BURBOT
CARBON
CARBOS
CARBOY
CORBAN
CORBEL
CORBIN
CURBED
DURBAN
DURBAR
DURBIN
FERBER
FORBAD
FORBES
FORBID
GARBED
GARBLE
GERBER
GERBIL
HARBIN
HARBOR
HERBAL
HERBIE
JERBOA
KORBUT
MARBLE
MARBLY
MORBID
SERBIA
SORBET
SORBIC
TURBAN
TURBID
TURBIT
TURBOS
TURBOT
VERBAL
VERBIS
WARBLE

••R•B•

AEROBE
ARRIBA
ARROBA
CARIBE
CARIBS
CAROBS
ENROBE
HARDBY
HEREBY
KARIBA
SCRIBE
SCRUBS
SHRUBS
STRABO
STROBE
THROBS
UNROBE
YORUBA
ZAREBA

••R••B

BARTAB
STRAUB

•••RB•

BLURBS
DJERBA
EXURBS
ITURBI
NEARBY

•••R•B

CHERUB
MIDRIB
MIHRAB
SCARAB
ZAGREB

••••RB

ABSORB
ADSORB
ADVERB
BICARB
RESORB
REVERB
SUBURB
SUPERB

RC••••

RCCOLA

R•C•••

RACEME
RACERS
RACHEL
RACHIS
RACIAL
RACIER
RACILY
RACINE
RACING
RACKED
RACKET
RACKUP
RACONS
RCCOLA
RECALL
RECANE
RECANT
RECAPS
RECAST
RECEDE
RECENT
RECESS
RECIFE
RECIPE
RECITE
RECKON
RECOAT
RECODE
RECOIL
RECONS
RECOPY
RECORD
RECORK
RECOUP
RECTOR
RECTOS
RECTUS
RECURS
RECUSE
RICERS
RICHEN
RICHER
RICHES
RICHIE
RICHLY
RICING
RICKED
RICKEY
ROCHET
ROCKED
ROCKER
ROCKET
ROCKNE
ROCKYV
ROCOCO
RUCHES
RUCKED
RUCKUS

R••C••

RANCHO
RANCID
RANCOR
RASCAL
REACTS
REDCAP
REECHO
RESCUE
REXCAT
ROSCOE
RUNCIE

R•••C•

REBECS
REDACT
REDUCE
REFACE
REJECT
RELACE
RELICS
RELICT
RELOCK
RELUCT
REMICK
RESECT
ROCOCO

R••••C

ROMAIC
RUBRIC
RUNDMC
RUSTIC

•RC•••

ARCADE
ARCANA
ARCANE
ARCARO
ARCCOS
ARCHED
ARCHER
ARCHES
ARCHIE
ARCHLY
ARCHON
ARCING
ARCTAN
ARCTIC
MRCOOL
ORCHID
ORCHIL
URCHIN

•R•C••

ARCCOS
ARECAS
BRACED
BRACER
BRACES
BRACHY
BRACTS
BRECHT
BRICKS
BRICKY
CRACKS
CRACKY
CRECHE

CRICKS
CROCKS
CROCUS
CRUCES
DRACHM
ERECTS
ERUCTS
FRACAS
FROCKS
GRACED
GRACES
GRACIE
GROCER
ORACHS
ORACLE
PRECIS
PRICED
PRICER
PRICES
PRICEY
PRICKS
PROCNE
TRACED
TRACER
TRACES
TRACEY
TRACHY
TRACKS
TRACTS
TRICED
TRICEP
TRICES
TRICHO
TRICIA
TRICKS
TRICKY
TRICOT
TROCAR
TROCHE
TRUCES
TRUCKS
URACIL
WRACKS
WRECKS

•R••C•
ARNICA
ARRACK
BRANCH
BREACH
BREECH
BROACH
BRONCO
BRONCS
BROOCH
BRUNCH
CRISCO
CROUCH
CRUNCH
CRUTCH
DRENCH
DRYICE
EROICA
FRANCA
FRANCE
FRANCK
FRANCO
FRANCS
FRENCH
FRESCA
FRESCO
FRISCO
GRAECO
GREECE
GRINCH
GROUCH
ORBACH
OROZCO
PRANCE
PREACH
PRINCE
TRANCE
TRENCH
WRENCH
WRETCH

•R•••C
ARABIC
ARCTIC
CRITIC
EROTIC
FROLIC
IRENIC
IRIDIC
IRONIC
ORPHIC
PROZAC
TRAGIC
TROPIC
URALIC
URANIC

••RC••
BARCAR
CIRCLE
CIRCUM
CIRCUS
DORCAS
FARCED
FARCES
FARCRY
FORCED
FORCER
FORCES
GARCIA
GARCON
MARCEL
MARCHE
MARCIA
MARCIE
MARCOS
MARCUS
MERCED
MERCER
MURCIA
PARCAE
PARCEL
PERCHA
TERCEL
TERCET
TORCHY
WARCRY
ZIRCON

••R•C•
AFRICA
ARRACK
BARUCH
BORSCH
CURACY
DIRECT
DUROCS
ENRICH
ENRICO
HIRSCH
HORACE
KIRSCH
LORICA
LYRICS
MARACA
PIRACY
PURACE
SERACS
SIRICA
SPRUCE
STRICK
STRICT
STRUCK
THRACE
THRICE
YORICK
ZURICH

••R••C
AIRSAC
AORTIC
BARDIC
FERENC
FERRIC
FORMIC
GARLIC
HEROIC
KARMIC
NORDIC
PARSEC
SORBIC
TARMAC
TURKIC

•••RC•
AMERCE
APERCU
BIERCE
CHURCH
COERCE
EPARCH
EXARCH
FIERCE
INARCH
PEERCE
PIERCE
SCARCE
SCORCH
SEARCH
SMIRCH
SOURCE
STARCH
STORCH
TIERCE

•••R•C
AGARIC
ALARIC
AMTRAC
CEDRIC
CHIRAC
CITRIC
CLERIC
COURIC
CUPRIC
CYMRIC
FABRIC
FERRIC
IATRIC
METRIC
NITRIC
RUBRIC
TENREC
VITRIC

R•D•••
RADDLE
RADIAL
RADIAN
RADIOS
RADISH
RADIUM
RADIUS
RADNER
RADOME
RADULA
REDACT
REDANT
REDATE
REDBAY
REDBUD
REDCAP
REDDEN
REDDER
REDDOG
REDEAL
REDEEM
REDENY
REDEYE
REDFIN
REDFIR
REDFOX
REDGUM
REDHAT
REDHOT
REDIAL
REDING
REDINK
REDOAK
REDOES
REDONE
REDRAW
REDREW
REDSEA
REDSOX
REDTAG
REDTOP
REDUBS
REDUCE
REDYED
REDYES
RIDDED
RIDDEN
RIDDLE
RIDENT
RIDERS
RIDGED
RIDGES
RIDING
RIDLEY
RIDSOF
RODDED
RODENT
RODEOS
RODHAM
RODMAN
RODNEY
RUDDER
RUDDLE
RUDELY
RUDEST
RUDMAN
RUDOLF
RYDELL

R••D••
RADDLE
RAIDED
RAIDER
RANDOM
RANDRY
READER
READIN
REDDEN
REDDER
REDDOG
REEDIT
RENDER
RHODES
RIDDED
RIDDEN
RIDDLE
ROADIE
RODDED
RONDEL
RONDOS
RUDDER
RUDDLE
RUNDLE
RUNDMC
RUNDRY

R•••D•
RAMADA
RANIDS
RAPIDS
RATEDG
RATEDR
RATEDX
REBIDS
RECEDE
RECODE
REMADE
REMEDY
REMUDA
REPADS
RESEDA
RESIDE
RESODS
REWEDS
RHABDO
RHONDA
RIYADH
ROUNDS
RUANDA
RWANDA

R••••D
RACKED
RAFTED
RAGGED
RAIDED
RAILED
RAINED
RAISED
RAMMED
RAMPED
RAMROD
RANCID
RANGED
RANKED
RANTED
RAPPED
RASHAD
RASHID
RASPED
RATTED
RAZZED
REAMED
REAPED
REARED
REBEND
REBIND
RECORD
REDBUD
REDYED
REEFED
REEKED
REELED
REEVED
REFFED
REFUND
REGARD
REHELD
REINED
RELAID
RELIED
RELOAD
REMAND
REMEND
REMIND
REMOLD
RENTED
REPAID
REPAND
REREAD
RESAND
RESEED
RESEND
RESHOD
RESOLD
RESTED
RETARD
RETIED
RETOLD
REUSED
REVVED
REWARD
REWELD
REWIND
REWORD
RHYMED
RIBALD
RIBAND
RIBBED
RICKED
RIDDED
RIDGED
RIFFED
RIFLED
RIFTED
RIGGED
RIMMED
RINGED
RINSED
RIOTED
RIPPED
RISKED
RITARD
ROAMED
ROARED
ROBBED
ROCKED
RODDED
ROILED
ROLAND
ROLLED
ROMPED
RONALD
ROOFED
ROOKED
ROOMED
ROOTED
ROTTED
ROTUND
ROUGED
ROUSED
ROUTED
RRATED
RSVPED
RUBBED
RUBIED
RUCKED
RUFFED
RUGGED
RUINED
RUSHED
RUSTED
RUTTED

•RD•••
ARDEBS
ARDENT
ARDORS
ARDOUR
ORDAIN
ORDEAL
ORDERS
ORDURE

•R•D••
ARIDLY
BRIDAL
BRIDES
BRIDGE
BRIDLE
BRODIE
BRUDER
CRADLE
CREDIT
CREDOS
CRUDDY
CRUDER
DREDGE
DRUDGE
DRYDEN
ERODED
ERODES
FREDDY
FRIDAY
FRIDGE
GRADEA
GRADED
GRADER
GRADES
GRADIN
GRADUS
GRODIN
GRODNO
GRUDGE
IRIDES
IRIDIC
PRIDED
PRIDES
PRUDES
TRADED
TRADER
TRADES
TREDIA
TRUDGE

•R••D•
ARCADE
ARENDT
ARMADA
AROIDS
ARVADA
BRAIDS
BRANDO
BRANDS
BRANDT
BRANDX
BRANDY
BREADS
BREEDS
BRENDA
BROADS
BROODS
BROODY
CREEDS
CROWDS
CRUDDY
DREADS
DROIDS
DRUIDS
DRYADS
FRAIDY
FRAUDS
FREDDY
FRONDS
GRANDE
GRANDS
GREEDY
GRINDS
GRUNDY
MRHYDE
OREADS
OREIDA
OROIDE
PRAVDA
TREADS
TRENDS
TRENDY
TRIADS
TRIODE
URSIDS

•R•••D
ARCHED
ARGUED
ARMAND
ARNOLD
AROUND
BRACED
BRAKED
BRAVED
BRAYED
BRAZED
BREWED
BRIAND
BRIARD
BRIBED
BRIGID
BRINED
BRUXED
CRANED
CRATED
CRAVED
CRAZED
CREWED
CROWED
DRAPED
DRAYED
DRONED
ERASED
ERHARD
ERODED
ERRAND
FRAMED
FRAYED
FRIEND
FRIGID
GRACED
GRADED
GRATED
GRAVED
GRAVID
GRAYED
GRAZED
GREYED
GRIMED
GRIPED
GROPED
GROUND
IRONED
ORATED
ORCHID
ORMOND
PRATED
PRAYED
PREMED
PREYED
PRICED
PRIDED
PRIMED
PRIZED
PROBED
PROSED
PROVED
PRUNED
RRATED
TRACED
TRADED
TREPID
TRICED
TRIFID
TRIPOD
TROWED
XRATED
XRAYED

••RD••
AIRDAM
AIRDRY
BARDIC
BARDOT
BIRDED
BIRDER
BIRDIE
BORDEN
BORDER
BURDEN
CARDED
CARDER
CARDIN
CARDIO
CORDAY
CORDED
CORDON
CURDED
CURDLE
FORDED
GARDEN
GIRDED
GIRDER
GIRDLE
GORDIE
GORDON
HARDBY
HARDEN
HARDER
HARDLY
HARDUP
HERDED
HERDER
HORDES
HURDLE
JORDAN
LARDED
LARDER
LARDON
LORDED
LORDLY
MARDUK
MURDER
MYRDAL
NORDIC
PARDON
PERDUE
PURDAH
PURDUE
SARDIS
SIRDAR
SORDID
VARDEN
VERDIN
VERDON
VERDUN
WARDED
WARDEN
WARDER
WORDED
YARDED

••R•D•
ABRADE
BORIDE
DERIDE
DIRNDL
DORADO
FARADS
JURADO
LAREDO
LERIDA
MERIDA
NERUDA
PARADE
PARODY
SARODS
SCRODS
SHREDS
STRADS
STRIDE
STRODE
TEREDO
TIRADE
WORLDS

••R••D
ABROAD
AFRAID
AGREED
BARBED
BARGED
BARKED
BARRED
BIRDED
BIRLED
BURIED
BURLED
BURNED
BURPED
BURRED
BYROAD
CARDED
CARKED
CARPED
CARTED
CARVED
CERVID
CORDED
CORKED
CORNED
CURBED
CURDED
CURLED
CURRED
CURSED
CURVED
DARNED
DARTED
DURNED
EARNED
ERRAND
FARCED
FARMED
FERVID
FIRMED
FORBAD
FORBID
FORCED
FORDED
FORGED
FORKED
FORMED
FURLED
FURRED
GARBED
GERALD
GERARD
GERUND
GIRARD
GIRDED
GIRNED
GIRTED
GORGED
HARALD
HARKED
HARMED
HAROLD
HARPED
HERALD
HERDED
HORNED
HORRID
HORSED
HURLED
INROAD
JARRED
JERKED
KERNED
LARDED
LARKED
LORDED
LURKED
MARAUD
MARKED
MARLED
MARRED
MERCED
MERGED
MORBID
MYRIAD
NEREID
NURSED
PARKED
PARRED
PARSED
PARTED
PERIOD
PERKED
PERMED
PERNOD
PORTED
PUREED
PURGED
PURLED
PURRED
PURSED
REREAD
SCREED
SERVED
SHREWD
SHROUD
SORDID
SORTED
SPREAD
STRAND
STROUD
SURFED
SURGED
TARRED
TERMED
THREAD
THREED
TOROID
TORPID
TORRID
TURBID
TURFED
TURGID
TURNED
UNREAD
VARIED
VERGED
VERSED
WARDED
WARGOD
WARMED
WARNED
WARPED
WARRED
WORDED
WORKED
WORMED
YARDED
YARNED
YERKED
ZEROED

•••RD•
AWARDS
BEARDS
BOARDS
CHORDS
CIARDI
FIORDS
FJORDS
GOURDE
GOURDS
GUARDS
HAIRDO
HOARDS
LAIRDS
OVERDO
SHARDS
STURDY
SWARDS
SWORDS
TBIRDS
THIRDS
WEIRDO
WEIRDY

•••R•D
ACARID
ADORED
ALFRED
ASTRID
BARRED
BIGRED
BLARED
BURRED
CONRAD
CURRED
ENURED
FAIRED
FEARED
FLARED
FLORID
FLYROD
FURRED
GEARED
GLARED
HAIRED
HATRED
HORRID
HOTROD
HYBRID
INBRED
INGRID
INURED
JARRED
JEERED
KONRAD
LEERED
MADRID
MARRED
MITRED
MOORED
NEARED
NIMROD
PAIRED
PARRED
PEERED
PENROD
POURED
PURRED
PUTRID
RAMROD
REARED
ROARED
SACRED
SAWRED
SCARED
SCORED
SEARED
SEERED
SHARED
SHORED
SNARED
SNORED
SOARED
SOURED
SPARED
SPIRED
STARED
STORED
TARRED
TEARED
TETRAD
TIERED
TIEROD
TITRED
TORRID
TOURED
UNTROD
USERID
VEERED
WARRED
WHERED

••••RD
ABOARD
ABSURD
ACCORD
AFEARD
AFFORD
ASGARD
BAYARD
BRIARD
BYWORD
CANARD
COWARD
CUNARD
DOTARD
EDGARD
EDUARD
EDVARD
EDWARD
ENGIRD
ERHARD
EZZARD
FUGARD
GERARD
GIRARD
GODARD
HAZARD
HOWARD
IDCARD
INWARD
IZZARD
LIZARD
LYNYRD
MILORD
MYWORD
ONWARD
OXFORD
OXNARD
PETARD
PICARD
RECORD
REGARD
RETARD
REWARD
REWORD
RITARD
SEWARD
SIGURD
TABARD
TOWARD
UNGIRD
UPWARD
WIZARD

RE••••
REACTS
READER
READIN
REAGAN
REAIMS
REAIRS
REALER
REALES
REALIA
REALLY
REALMS
REALTY
REAMED
REAMER
REAPED
REAPER
REARED
REARER
REARMS
REARUP
REASON
REATAS
REBAGS
REBARS
REBATE
REBBES
REBECS
REBELS
REBEND
REBENT
REBIDS
REBIND
REBOIL
REBOLT
REBOOT
REBORN
REBOZO
REBUFF
REBUKE
REBURY
REBUTS
RECALL
RECANE
RECANT
RECAPS
RECAST
RECEDE
RECENT
RECESS
RECIFE
RECIPE
RECITE
RECKON
RECOAT
RECODE
RECOIL
RECONS
RECOPY
RECORD
RECORK
RECOUP
RECTOR
RECTOS
RECTUS
RECURS
RECUSE
REDACT
REDANT
REDATE
REDBAY
REDBUD
REDCAP
REDDEN
REDDER
REDDOG
REDEAL
REDEEM
REDENY
REDEYE
REDFIN
REDFIR
REDFOX
REDGUM
REDHAT
REDHOT
REDIAL
REDING
REDINK
REDOAK
REDOES
REDONE
REDRAW
REDREW
REDSEA
REDSOX
REDTAG
REDTOP
REDUBS
REDUCE
REDYED
REDYES
REEBOK
REECHO
REEDIT
REEFED
REEFER
REEKED
REELED
REELIN
REESES
REEVED
REEVES
REFACE
REFERS
REFFED
REFILE
REFILL
REFINE
REFITS
REFLAG
REFLEX
REFLUX
REFORM
REFUEL
REFUGE
REFUND
REFUSE
REFUTE
REGAIN
REGALE
REGARD
REGENT
REGGAE
REGGIE
REGIME
REGINA
REGION
REGIUS
REGLET
REGLUE
REGNAL
REGNAT
REGRET
REHABS
REHANG
REHASH
REHEAL
REHEAR
REHEAT
REHEEL
REHELD
REHEMS
REHIRE
REHOOK
REHUNG
REIGNS
REILLY
REINAS
REINED
REINER
REININ
REINKS
REJECT
REJOIN
REKEYS
RELACE
RELAID
RELATE
RELAYS
RELENT
RELETS
RELEVY
RELICS

RELICT RELIED RELIEF RELIES RELINE RELISH RELIST RELIVE RELOAD RELOCK RELUCT RELUME REMADE REMAIL REMAIN REMAKE REMAND REMANS REMAPS REMARK REMEDY REMELT REMEND REMICK REMIND REMISE REMISS REMITS REMOLD REMOPS REMORA REMOTE REMOVE REMOWN REMOWS REMUDA RENAIL RENAME RENATA RENDER RENEGE RENEWS RENNES RENNET RENNIE RENNIN RENOIR RENOTE RENOWN RENTAL RENTED RENTER REOILS REOPEN REPADS REPAID REPAIR REPAND REPAST REPAVE REPAYS REPEAL REPEAT REPEGS REPELS REPENT REPINE REPINS REPLAN REPLAY REPLOW REPOLL REPORT REPOSE

REPOST REPOTS REPROS REPUGN REPUTE RERATE REREAD RERENT RERUNS RESALE RESALT RESAND RESAWN RESAWS RESCUE RESEAL RESEAT RESEAU RESECT RESEDA RESEED RESEEN RESEES RESELL RESEND RESENT RESETS RESEWN RESEWS RESHES RESHIP RESHOD RESHOE RESHOT RESIDE RESIGN RESILE RESING RESINS RESINY RESIST RESNIK RESODS RESOLD RESOLE RESORB RESORT RESPIN RESTED RESTER RESTON RESTUP RESULT RESUME RETAGS RETAIL RETAIN RETAKE RETAPE RETAPS RETARD RETARS RETEAR RETELL RETENE RETEST RETIAL RETIED RETIES RETILE RETIME RETINA RETIRE RETOLD

RETOOK RETOOL RETOPS RETORT RETOUR RETOWS RETRAL RETRIM RETROS RETTON RETUNE RETURN RETYPE REUBEN REUNES REUSED REUSES REUTER REVAMP REVEAL REVELS REVERB REVERE REVERS REVERT REVETS REVIEW REVILE REVISE REVIVE REVLON REVOIR REVOKE REVOLT REVSON REVSUP REVUES REVVED REWARD REWARM REWASH REWEDS REWELD REWIND REWINS REWIRE REWORD REWORK REWOVE REWRAP REXCAT REZONE

R•E•••

REEBOK REECHO REEDIT REEFED REEFER REEKED REELED REELIN REESES REEVED REEVES RHEBOK RHESUS RHETOR RHEUMS RHEUMY RIENZI RUEFUL

R••E••

RACEME RACERS RAKEIN RAKERS RAKEUP RAMEAU RAMETS RANEES RAREFY RARELY RAREST RASERS RATEDG RATEDR RATEDX RATELS RATERS RAVELS RAVENS RAVERS RAVEUP RAWEGG RAWEST REBECS REBELS REBEND REBENT RECEDE RECENT RECESS REDEAL REDEEM REDENY REDEYE REFERS REGENT REHEAL REHEAR REHEAT REHEEL REHELD REHEMS REJECT REKEYS RELENT RELETS RELEVY REMEDY REMELT REMEND RENEGE RENEWS REPEAL REPEAT REPEGS REPELS REPENT REREAD RERENT RESEAL RESEAT RESEAU RESECT RESEDA RESEED RESEEN RESEES RESELL RESEND RESENT RESETS RESEWN RESEWS

RETEAR RETELL RETENE RETEST REVEAL REVELS REVERB REVERE REVERS REVERT REVETS REWEDS REWELD RIBEYE RICERS RIDENT RIDERS RIFELY RIFEST RILEUP RIPELY RIPENS RIPEST RISERS RIVERA RIVERS RIVETS ROBERT RODENT RODEOS ROGERS ROLEOS ROMEOS ROMERO RONELY ROPEIN ROPERS ROSEAU ROVERS ROWELS ROWENA ROWENS ROWERS RUBENS RUDELY RUDEST RULEON RULERS RUMENS RUPEES RUPERT RYDELL

R•••E•

RABBET RABIES RACHEL RACIER RACKED RACKET RADNER RAFAEL RAFTED RAFTER RAGGED RAGMEN RAIDED RAIDER RAILED RAILER RAINED RAINER RAINES RAINEY

RAISED RAISER RAISES RAMIES RAMJET RAMMED RAMPED RAMSES RAMSEY RANEES RANGED RANGER RANGES RANKED RANKER RANTED RANTER RAPIER RAPPED RAPPEE RAPPEL RAPPER RAQUEL RASHER RASHES RASPED RASPER RASTER RATHER RATTED RATTER RAZZED RAZZES READER REALER REALES REAMED REAMER REAPED REAPER REARED REARER REBBES REDDEN REDDER REDEEM REDOES REDREW REDSEA REDYED REDYES REEFED REEFER REEKED REELED REESES REEVED REEVES REFFED REFLEX REFUEL REGLET REGRET REHEEL REINED REINER RELIED RELIEF RELIES RENDER RENNES RENNET RENTED RENTER

REOPEN RESEED RESEEN RESEES RESHES RESTED RESTER RETIED RETIES REUBEN REUNES REUSED REUSES REUTER REVIEW REVUES REVVED RHAMES RHODES RHYMED RHYMER RHYMES RIBBED RICHEN RICHER RICHES RICKED RICKEY RIDDED RIDDEN RIDGED RIDGES RIDLEY RIFFED RIFLED RIFLER RIFLES RIFTED RIGGED RIGGER RILLES RILLET RIMIER RIMMED RINGED RINGER RINSED RINSES RIOTED RIOTER RIPKEN RIPLEY RIPPED RIPPER RISKED RISKER RITTER ROAMED ROAMER ROARED ROARER ROBBED ROBBER ROBLES ROCHET ROCKED ROCKER ROCKET RODDED RODNEY ROGUES ROHMER ROILED ROLLED

ROLLER ROMMEL ROMNEY ROMPED ROMPER RONDEL ROOFED ROOFER ROOKED ROOMED ROOMER ROONEY ROOTED ROOTER ROPIER ROSIER ROSTER ROTTED ROTTEN ROTTER ROUGED ROUGES ROUSED ROUSER ROUSES ROUTED ROUTER ROUTES ROZZER RRATED RSVPED RUBBED RUBBER RUBIED RUBIES RUBLES RUBLEV RUCHES RUCKED RUDDER RUFFED RUGGED RUINED RUINER RUMMER RUNLET RUNNEL RUNNER RUPEES RUSHED RUSHEE RUSHES RUSSET RUSTED RUTGER RUTTED

R••••E

RABBLE RACEME RACINE RADDLE RADOME RAFFLE RAMATE RAMBLE RAMONE RAMOSE RANKLE RAPINE RAPPEE RASSLE RATINE RATITE

RATTLE RAVAGE RAVINE RAZZLE REBATE REBUKE RECANE RECEDE RECIFE RECIPE RECITE RECODE RECUSE REDATE REDEYE REDONE REDUCE REFACE REFILE REFINE REFUGE REFUSE REFUTE REGALE REGGAE REGGIE REGIME REGLUE REHIRE RELACE RELATE RELINE RELIVE RELUME REMADE REMAKE REMISE REMOTE REMOVE RENAME RENEGE RENNIE RENOTE REPAVE REPINE REPOSE REPUTE RERATE RESALE RESCUE RESHOE RESIDE RESILE RESOLE RESUME RETAKE RETAPE RETENE RETILE RETIME RETIRE RETUNE RETYPE REVERE REVILE REVISE REVIVE REVOKE REWIRE REWOVE REZONE RIBEYE RIBOSE RICHIE

RIDDLE RIFFLE RIMOSE RIMPLE RIPPLE RISQUE ROADIE ROBBIE ROCKNE ROLLIE RONNIE ROOKIE ROOMIE ROSCOE ROTATE ROUBLE ROURKE ROXANE ROYALE RUBBLE RUDDLE RUFFLE RUGATE RUGOSE RUMBLE RUMPLE RUNCIE RUNDLE RUSHEE RUSTLE RUTILE RVALUE

•RE•••

ARECAS ARENAS ARENDT AREOLA ARETES ARETHA AREZZO BREACH BREADS BREAKS BREAMS BREAST BREATH BRECHT BREECH BREEDS BREEZE BREEZY BREMEN BRENDA BRENTS BRETON BREUER BREVES BREVET BREVIS BREWED BREWER BREYER CREAKS CREAKY CREAMS CREAMY CREASE CREASY CREATE CRECHE CREDIT CREDOS CREEDS

CREEKS CREELS CREEPS CREEPY CREMES CRENEL CRENNA CREOLE CREPES CRESOL CRESTS CRETAN CRETIN CREUSA CREWED CREWEL DREADS DREAMS DREAMT DREAMY DREARY DREDGE DRENCH DRESSY DREWIN DREWON DREWUP DREXEL EREBUS ERECTS ERENOW ERESTU FREAKS FREAKY FREDDY FREELY FREEST FREEZE FRENCH FRENUM FRENZY FRESCA FRESCO FRESNO FRETTY GREASE GREASY GREATS GREAVE GREBES GREECE GREEDY GREEKS GREENE GREENS GREENY GREETS GREGOR GREIGE GRETEL GRETNA GREWON GREWUP GREYED GREYER GREYLY IREFUL IRENES IRENIC KRESGE OREADS OREGON OREIDA ORELSE

PREACH PREAMP PRECIS PREENS PREFAB PREFER PREFIX PRELAW PRELIM PREMED PREMIE PRENUP PREPAY PREPPY PRESET PRESTO PRETAX PRETER PRETTY PREVIN PREWAR PREYED PREYON TREADS TREATS TREATY TREBEK TREBLE TREBLY TREDIA TREMOR TRENCH TRENDS TRENDY TREPAN TREPID TREVOR WREAKS WREATH WRECKS WRENCH WRESTS WRETCH

•R•E••

ARBELA ARDEBS ARDENT ARGENT ARLEEN ARLENE ARMETS ARNESS ARNETT ARPENT ARREAR ARREST ARSENE ARTELS ARTERY BREECH BREEDS BREEZE BREEZY BRIEFS BRIENZ BRIERS BRIERY CREEDS CREEKS CREELS CREEPS CREEPY CRIERS

CRUETS CRYERS DRIERS DRIEST DRYERS DRYEST ERNEST FREELY FREEST FREEZE FRIEND FRIERS FRIEZE FRYERS GRAECO GREECE GREEDY GREEKS GREENE GREENS GREENY GREETS GRIEFS GRIEVE GRUELS IRLENE IRREAL ORDEAL ORDERS ORGEAT ORIELS ORIENT ORNERY ORRERY ORTEGA ORWELL PREENS PRIERS PRIEST PROEMS TRIERS TRUEST URAEUS URGENT URGERS URTEXT WRIEST WRYEST

•R••E•

ARCHED ARCHER ARCHES ARETES ARGUED ARGUER ARGUES ARISEN ARISES ARLEEN ARMIES ARMLET ARNHEM ARTIER BRACED BRACER BRACES BRAKED BRAKES BRAVED BRAVER BRAVES BRAYED BRAYER

BRAZED BRAZEN BRAZER BRAZES BREMEN BREUER BREVES BREVET BREWED BREWER BREYER BRIBED BRIBES BRIDES BRINED BRINES BROKEN BROKER BRUDER BRUGES BRULES BRUMES BRUNEI BRUNET BRUTES BRUXED BRUXES CRAKES CRANED CRANES CRAPES CRATED CRATER CRATES CRAVED CRAVEN CRAVER CRAVES CRAZED CRAZES CREMES CRENEL CREPES CREWED CREWEL CRIKEY CRIMEA CRIMES CRIPES CRISES CRONES CROWED CROWER CROZES CRUCES CRUDER CRUSES CRUXES DRAGEE DRAKES DRAPED DRAPER DRAPES DRAWER DRAYED DREXEL DRIVEL DRIVEN DRIVER DRIVES DRONED DRONER DRONES DROVER

DROVES DRUPES DRUZES DRYDEN ERASED ERASER ERASES ERODED ERODES FRAMED FRAMES FRASER FRAUEN FRAYED FRAZER FRISEE FRISES FROZEN GRABEN GRACED GRACES GRADEA GRADED GRADER GRADES GRAPES GRAPEY GRATED GRATER GRATES GRAVED GRAVEL GRAVEN GRAVER GRAVES GRAYED GRAYER GRAZED GRAZER GRAZES GREBES GRETEL GREYED GREYER GRIMED GRIMES GRIPED GRIPER GRIPES GRIVET GROCER GROPED GROPES GROVEL GROVER GROVES GROWER IRATER IRENES IRIDES IRISES IRONED IRONER KRAKEN KRAMER KRATER KRONER KRUGER ORALES ORATED ORATES ORGIES ORIGEN ORKNEY

ORTLES ORYXES PRASES PRATED PRATER PRATES PRAXES PRAYED PRAYER PREFER PREMED PRESET PRETER PREYED PRICED PRICER PRICES PRICEY PRIDED PRIDES PRIMED PRIMER PRIMES PRIPET PRIVET PRIZED PRIZES PROBED PROBER PROBES PROLES PROPEL PROPER PROSED PROSER PROSES PROTEI PROTEM PROVED PROVEN PROVER PROVES PRUDES PRUNED PRUNER PRUNES RRATED TRACED TRACER TRACES TRACEY TRADED TRADER TRADES TRALEE TRAVEL TRAVES TREBEK TRIBES TRICED TRICEP TRICES TRIJET TRIKES TRINES TRITER TRIVET TROPES TROPEZ TROVES TROWED TROWEL TRUCES URUSES

WRITER
WRITES
XRATED
XRAYED

•R•••E

ARABLE
ARCADE
ARCANE
ARCHIE
ARGIVE
ARGYLE
ARIOSE
ARLENE
ARMURE
AROUSE
ARRIVE
ARSENE
BRAISE
BRAQUE
BREEZE
BRIDGE
BRIDLE
BRODIE
BROGUE
BRONTE
BRONZE
BROOKE
BROWNE
BROWSE
BRUISE
CRABBE
CRADLE
CREASE
CREATE
CRECHE
CREOLE
CRINGE
CROSSE
CROUSE
CROUTE
CRUISE
CRUSOE
DRAGEE
DREDGE
DROGUE
DROWSE
DRUDGE
DRYICE
ERGATE
ERMINE
ERRARE
FRAISE
FRANCE
FRAPPE
FREEZE
FRIDGE
FRIEZE
FRINGE
FRISEE
GRABLE
GRACIE
GRAMME
GRANDE
GRANGE
GREASE
GREAVE
GREECE
GREENE
GREIGE
GRIEVE
GRILLE
GRILSE
GRIMKE

GRIPPE
GROOVE
GROSSE
GROUSE
GRUDGE
GRUNGE
IRLENE
IRVINE
KRESGE
MRBLUE
MRHYDE
ORACLE
ORANGE
ORDURE
ORELSE
ORGATE
ORIOLE
ORNATE
OROIDE
ORPINE
PRAGUE
PRAISE
PRANCE
PREMIE
PRINCE
PROCNE
PROPRE
PROWSE
PRYNNE
TRALEE
TRANCE
TREBLE
TRIAGE
TRIFLE
TRIODE
TRIPLE
TRISTE
TRIUNE
TRIXIE
TROCHE
TROMPE
TROUPE
TROUVE
TRUDGE
URBANE
URSINE
WRASSE
WRITHE

••RE••

ADRENO
AFREET
AFRESH
AGREED
AGREES
ARREAR
ARREST
ATREST
ATREUS
AUREUS
BAREGE
BARELY
BAREST
BEREFT
BERETS
BIREME
BOREAL
BOREAS
BOREON
BORERS
BOREUP
BUREAU
CAREEN
CAREER

CARESS
CARETO
CARETS
CEREAL
CEREUS
CORERS
CURERS
DARENT
DARETO
DIRECT
DIRELY
DIREST
DOREMI
DURESS
EGRESS
EGRETS
EUREKA
FARERS
FERENC
FIRERS
FIREUP
FOREGO
FOREST
GARETH
GERENT
GYRENE
HAREMS
HEREAT
HEREBY
HEREIN
HEREOF
HEREON
HERESY
HERETO
HIREON
HIRERS
IRREAL
JEREMY
KAREEM
KOREAN
LAREDO
LOREAL
LORENZ
MERELY
MEREST
MOREAU
MOREEN
MORELS
MORENO
NEREID
NEREIS
NEREUS
OCREAE
OGRESS
ORRERY
PARENS
PARENT
PARERS
PARETO
PAREVE
PUREED
PUREES
PURELY
PUREST
RAREFY
RARELY
RAREST
REREAD
RERENT
SCREAK
SCREAM
SCREED
SCREEN
SCREES

SCREWS
SCREWY
SERENA
SERENE
SHREDS
SHREWD
SHREWS
SIRENS
SORELY
SOREST
SPREAD
SPREES
STREAK
STREAM
STREEP
STREET
STRESS
STREWN
STREWS
SURELY
SUREST
SURETE
SURETY
TEREDO
TERESA
TERETE
TEREUS
THREAD
THREAT
THREED
THREES
THRESH
TOREAT
TORERO
TOREUP
TUREEN
UNREAD
UNREAL
UNREEL
UNREST
VARESE
VEREEN
VIREOS
WERENT
WIRERS
WOREON
YARELY
YAREST
ZAREBA

••R•E•

ADRIEN
AERIES
AFREET
AGREED
AGREES
AIRIER
AIRMEN
BARBED
BARBEL
BARBER
BARBET
BARGED
BARGES
BARKED
BARKER
BARLEY
BARMEN
BARNES
BARNEY
BARRED
BARREL
BARREN
BARRES

BARTER
BERBER
BERGEN
BIRDED
BIRDER
BIRLED
BIRNEY
BORDEN
BORDER
BORNEO
BURDEN
BURGEE
BURGER
BURIED
BURIES
BURLED
BURLEY
BURNED
BURNER
BURNET
BURNEY
BURPED
BURRED
BURSES
BYRNES
CARDED
CARDER
CAREEN
CAREER
CARIES
CARKED
CARMEL
CARMEN
CARNES
CARNET
CARNEY
CARPED
CARPEL
CARPER
CARPET
CARREL
CARREY
CARTED
CARTEL
CARTER
CARTES
CARVED
CARVER
CARVES
CARVEY
CERMET
CORBEL
CORDED
CORKED
CORKER
CORNEA
CORNED
CORNEL
CORNER
CORNET
CORREL
CORSET
CORTES
CORTEX
CORTEZ
CORVEE
CORVES
CURBED
CURDED
CURFEW
CURLED
CURLER
CURLEW
CURLEY

CURRED
CURSED
CURSES
CURTER
CURVED
CURVES
CURVET
DARIEN
DARKEN
DARKER
DARNED
DARNEL
DARNER
DARREN
DARTED
DARTER
DIRGES
DORIES
DORMER
DORSET
DORSEY
DURFEY
DURNED
DURYEA
EARNED
EARNER
EERIER
EYRIES
FARCED
FARCES
FARLEY
FARMED
FARMER
FERBER
FERRER
FERRET
FIRMED
FIRMER
FORBES
FORCED
FORCER
FORCES
FORDED
FORGED
FORGER
FORGES
FORGET
FORKED
FORKER
FORMED
FORMER
FORTES
FURIES
FURLED
FURRED
FURZES
GARBED
GARDEN
GARNER
GARNET
GARRET
GARTER
GARVEY
GERBER
GIRDED
GIRDER
GIRNED
GIRTED
GORGED
GORGES
GORGET
GORIER
GORSES
GURLEY

GURNEY
HARDEN
HARDER
HARKED
HARKEN
HARKER
HARLEM
HARLEY
HARMED
HARPED
HARPER
HARVEY
HERDED
HERDER
HERMES
HEROES
HERSEY
HORDES
HORMEL
HORNED
HORNER
HORNET
HORNEY
HORSED
HORSES
HORSEY
HURLED
HURLER
HURLEY
ISRAEL
JARRED
JERKED
JERSEY
JURIES
KAREEM
KERMES
KERNED
KERNEL
KERSEE
KERSEY
LARDED
LARDER
LARGER
LARGES
LARKED
LARSEN
LERNER
LORDED
LORIES
LURKED
MARCEL
MARGES
MARIEL
MARKED
MARKER
MARKET
MARLED
MARLEE
MARLEY
MARMEE
MARNER
MARRED
MARTEL
MARTEN
MARVEL
MERCED
MERCER
MERGED
MERGER
MERGES
MERKEL
MERMEN
MERSEY
MIRIER

MIRREN
MOREEN
MORGEN
MORLEY
MORSEL
MURDER
MURIEL
MURRES
MURREY
NERVES
NURSED
NURSER
NURSES
OBRIEN
OERTER
PARCEL
PARGET
PARKED
PARKER
PARLEY
PARRED
PARREL
PARSEC
PARSED
PARSEE
PARSER
PARSES
PARTED
PERKED
PERMED
PERTER
PORKER
PORTED
PORTER
PUREED
PUREES
PURGED
PURGES
PURLED
PURRED
PURRER
PURSED
PURSER
PURSES
PURVEY
SARGES
SCREED
SCREEN
SCREES
SERGEI
SERGES
SERIES
SERVED
SERVER
SERVES
SHRIEK
SIRREE
SORBET
SORREL
SORTED
SORTER
SPREES
SPRIER
SPRUES
SPRYER
STREEP
STREET
SURFED
SURFER
SURGED
SURGES
SURREY
SURVEY
TARGES

TARGET
TARRED
TARTER
TERCEL
TERCET
TERKEL
TERMED
TERNES
TERRET
TERSER
THREED
THREES
THROES
TORIES
TORRES
TORREY
TORTES
TUREEN
TURFED
TURKEY
TURNED
TURNER
TURRET
TURVES
UNREEL
VARDEN
VARIED
VARIES
VARLET
VARNEY
VEREEN
VERGED
VERGER
VERGES
VERSED
VERSES
VERTEX
VERVES
VERVET
VORTEX
WARDED
WARDEN
WARDER
WARIER
WARMED
WARMER
WARNED
WARNER
WARPED
WARRED
WARREN
WERFEL
WERNER
WIRIER
WORDED
WORKED
WORKER
WORMED
WORSEN
WURLEY
XERXES
YARDED
YARNED
YERKED
YERKES
YORKER
ZEROED
ZEROES

••R••E

ABRADE
AERATE
AEROBE
AFRAME

AORTAE
ARRIVE
BARBIE
BAREGE
BARITE
BARQUE
BARRIE
BERATE
BERNIE
BERTIE
BIRDIE
BIREME
BORAGE
BORATE
BORIDE
BURBLE
BURGEE
BURGLE
BURSAE
BYROTE
CARAFE
CARIBE
CAROLE
CARRIE
CERATE
CERISE
CERUSE
CHROME
CIRCLE
CIRQUE
CORVEE
CURARE
CURATE
CURDLE
CURIAE
CURULE
DARKLE
DERIDE
DERIVE
DIRIGE
ENRAGE
ENROBE
ERRARE
EUROPE
FERGIE
FERULE
FORAGE
FURORE
GARAGE
GARBLE
GARGLE
GERTIE
GIRDLE
GORDIE
GURGLE
GYRATE
GYRENE
GYROSE
HARARE
HERBIE
HORACE
HURDLE
HURTLE
JEROME
KARATE
KERSEE
KIRTLE
KURILE
LARVAE
MARBLE
MARCHE
MARCIE
MARGIE
MARINE

MARLEE
MARMEE
MARNIE
MARPLE
MARQUE
MEROPE
MIRAGE
MORALE
MOROSE
MURINE
MYRTLE
OCREAE
PARADE
PARCAE
PAREVE
PAROLE
PARSEE
PARURE
PERDUE
PERUKE
PERUSE
PHRASE
PIRATE
PURACE
PURDUE
PURFLE
PURINE
PURPLE
PURSUE
PYRITE
RERATE
SARTRE
SCRAPE
SCRIBE
SERAPE
SERENE
SERINE
SHRIKE
SHRINE
SHRIVE
SHROVE
SIRREE
SORTIE
SPRITE
SPRUCE
STRAFE
STRAKE
STRIAE
STRIDE
STRIFE
STRIKE
STRINE
STRIPE
STRIVE
STROBE
STRODE
STROKE
STROVE
SURETE
TERETE
THRACE
THRALE
THRICE
THRIVE
THRONE
THROVE
TIRADE
TIRANE
TOROSE
TORQUE
TURTLE
TYRONE
UNRIPE
UNROBE

UPRISE
UPROSE
VARESE
VERITE
VIRILE
VIRTUE
WARBLE
YORKIE

•••RE•

ADORED
ADOREE
ADORER
ADORES
AIGRET
ALFRED
ANDREA
ANDREI
ANDRES
ANDREW
ANDREY
ANTRES
AUBREY
AUDREY
AZORES
BARRED
BARREL
BARREN
BARRES
BEARER
BIGRED
BLARED
BLARES
BOTREE
BURRED
CADRES
CARREL
CARREY
CHORES
CLARET
CORREL
CURRED
DAIREN
DARREN
DEARER
DECREE
DEGREE
DOMREP
DOURER
EAGRES
ENTREE
ENURED
ENURES
FAIRED
FAIRER
FEARED
FEARER
FERRER
FERRET
FIBRES
FLARED
FLARES
FLORES
FLORET
FURRED
GARRET
GEARED
GENRES
GLARED
GLARES
HAIRED
HATRED
HEARER
HEBREW

HEDREN
IMARET
INBRED
INGRES
INURED
INURES
JARRED
JAURES
JEERED
JEERER
JUAREZ
LABREA
LABRET
LAUREL
LAUREN
LEERED
LEERER
LEGREE
LEHRER
LITRES
LIVRES
MADRES
MARRED
MCCREA
MCGREW
METRES
MIRREN
MITRED
MITRES
MOIRES
MOORED
MURRES
MURREY
NACRES
NEARED
NEARER
NITRES
OCHRES
OSPREY
PADRES
PAIRED
PARRED
PARREL
PEERED
PETREL
POORER
POURED
POURER
PUGREE
PURRED
PURRER
QUIRES
REARED
REARER
REDREW
REGRET
ROARED
ROARER
SABRES
SACRED
SAUREL
SAWRED
SCARED
SCARER
SCARES
SCORED
SCORER
SCORES
SEARED
SECRET
SEERED
SEVRES
SHARED
SHARER

SHARES
SHEREE
SHIRER
SHIRES
SHORED
SHORES
SIRREE
SNARED
SNARES
SNORED
SNORER
SNORES
SOARED
SOARER
SOARES
SOIREE
SORREL
SOURED
SOURER
SPARED
SPARER
SPARES
SPIREA
SPIRED
SPIRES
SPORES
STARED
STARER
STARES
STEREO
STERES
STORED
STORER
STORES
STOREY
SURREY
TARRED
TEARED
TENREC
TERRET
THERES
TIERED
TITRED
TITRES
TORRES
TORREY
TOURED
TOURER
TUAREG
TURRET
UNFREE
USURER
VEERED
WARRED
WARREN
WEARER
WHERED
WHERES
ZAGREB
ZAIRES

•••R•E

ACCRUE
ADOREE
AGORAE
AHERNE
AMERCE
AVERSE
BARRIE
BEURRE
BIERCE
BOTREE
BOURKE
BOURNE

BOURSE
CARRIE
CHARGE
CHERIE
CLARKE
COARSE
COERCE
COURSE
COWRIE
DEARIE
DEARME
DECREE
DEGREE
DUARTE
ECARTE
EDERLE
EMERGE
ENTREE
ETERNE
FAERIE
FAEROE
FIERCE
FLORAE
GEORGE
GOURDE
GUERRE
HEARYE
HOARSE
HYDRAE
IMBRUE
LAURIE
LEGREE
LIERNE
MACRAE
MONROE
PEERCE
PETRIE
PIERCE
PIERRE
PUGREE
ROURKE
SCARCE
SCARNE
SCURVE
SEARLE
SHEREE
SHORTE
SIRREE
SOIREE
SOURCE
SPARGE
SPARSE
SPURGE
STARVE
STERNE
SWERVE
THORPE
TIERCE
UMBRAE
UNFREE
UNTRUE

••••RE

ABJURE
ADHERE
ADJURE
ADMIRE
AGLARE
ALEGRE
ALGORE
ALLURE
AMPERE
ARMURE
ASHORE

ASPIRE
ASSURE
ATTIRE
BEFORE
BEMIRE
BEURRE
BEWARE
CENTRE
CESARE
CHEVRE
CLAIRE
COHERE
CONTRE
CONURE
CURARE
DAMORE
DEIDRE
DEJURE
DEMURE
DESIRE
EEYORE
ELMORE
EMIGRE
EMPIRE
ENCORE
ENDURE
ENSURE
ENTIRE
ERRARE
EUCHRE
EXMORE
EXPIRE
FIACRE
FIGURE
FURORE
FUTURE
GALORE
GUERRE
HARARE
HOMBRE
HONORE
IGNORE
IMMURE
IMPURE
INDORE
INHERE
INJURE
INSURE
JOHORE
KHAFRE
LAHORE
LENORE
LIGURE
LOUVRE
LUSTRE
MAITRE
MATURE
MEAGRE
MYSORE
NATURE
NOMORE
OEUVRE
ONFIRE
ORDURE
PARURE
PHEDRE
PIERRE
PROPRE
REHIRE
RETIRE
REVERE
REWIRE
SAFIRE
SARTRE

SATIRE SECURE SEMPRE SEVERE SOMBRE SPHERE SQUARE SQUIRE SUTURE TAGORE TENURE THEYRE TIMBRE TULARE TUYERE UMPIRE UNSURE VENIRE VOLARE

R•F•••
RAFAEL RAFFIA RAFFLE RAFTED RAFTER REFACE REFERS REFFED REFILE REFILL REFINE REFITS REFLAG REFLEX REFLUX REFORM REFUEL REFUGE REFUND REFUSE REFUTE RIFELY RIFEST RIFFED RIFFLE RIFIFI RIFLED RIFLER RIFLES RIFTED RUFFED RUFFLE RUFFLY RUFOUS

R••F••
RAFFIA RAFFLE RANFOR REDFIN REDFIR REDFOX REEFED REEFER REFFED RIFFED RIFFLE ROOFED ROOFER RUEFUL RUFFED RUFFLE RUFFLY RUNFOR

R•••F•
RAMIFY RANOFF RAREFY RARIFY RATIFY REBUFF RECIFE RIFIFI RIPOFF RUBIFY RUBOFF RUNOFF

R••••F
RANOFF REBUFF RELIEF RIDSOF RIPOFF RUBOFF RUDOLF RUNOFF

•RF•••
ERFURT

•R•F••
ARAFAT ARMFUL ARTFUL CRAFTS CRAFTY CROFTS DRAFTS DRAFTY DRIFTS DRIFTY DRYFLY GRAFTS GRIFTS IREFUL PREFAB PREFER PREFIX PROFIT TRIFID TRIFLE TRYFOR

•R••F•
ARGUFY BRIEFS CRYOFF DRYOFF GRIEFS PROOFS

•R•••F
CRYOFF DRYOFF

••RF••
BARFLY CARFUL CURFEW DURFEY EARFUL JARFUL PURFLE SURFED SURFER TURFED WERFEL

••R•F•
ADRIFT AERIFY AURIFY BEREFT CARAFE FAROFF PURIFY RAREFY RARIFY SCRUFF SERIFS SHRIFT STRAFE STRIFE TARIFF THRIFT VERIFY

••R••F
CERTIF FAROFF HEREOF SCRUFF SORTOF TARIFF

•••RF•
DWARFS SCARFS SCURFY SMURFS WHARFS

•••R•F
HEAROF SHARIF SHERIF

••••RF
IMPERF

R•G•••
RAGBAG RAGGED RAGING RAGLAN RAGMAN RAGMEN RAGMOP RAGOUT RAGRUG RAGTAG RAGTOP REGAIN REGALE REGARD REGENT REGGAE REGGIE REGIME REGINA REGION REGIUS REGLET REGLUE REGNAL REGNAT REGRET RIGGED RIGGER RIGHTO RIGHTS RIGHTY RIGORS RIGOUR RIGSUP ROGERS ROGUES RUGATE RUGGED RUGOSE

R••G••
RAGGED RANGED RANGER RANGES RANGUP RAYGUN REAGAN REDGUM REGGAE REGGIE REIGNS RIDGED RIDGES RIGGED RIGGER RINGED RINGER RINGUP ROTGUT ROUGED ROUGES ROUGHS ROUGHY RUGGED RUNGUP RUTGER

R•••G•
RAVAGE RAWEGG REBAGS REFUGE RENEGE REPEGS REPUGN RESIGN RETAGS

R••••G
RACING RAGBAG RAGING RAGRUG RAGTAG RAKING RARING RASING RATEDG RATING RAVING RAWEGG RAZING REDDOG REDING REDTAG REFLAG REHANG REHUNG RESING RICING RIDING RILING RIMING RISING RIVING ROBING ROPING ROVING ROWING RULING

•RG•••
ARGALI ARGENT ARGIVE ARGOSY ARGOTS ARGUED ARGUER ARGUES ARGUFY ARGYLE ARGYLL ERGATE ERGOTS ORGANA ORGANS ORGATE ORGEAT ORGIES URGENT URGERS URGING

•R•G••
ARAGON ARIGHT ARTGUM BRIGGS BRIGHT BRIGID BROGAN BROGUE BRUGES CRAGGY DRAGEE DRAGGY DRAGIN DRAGON DROGUE FRIGHT FRIGID FROGGY FRUGAL GREGOR GRIGRI GROGGY KRUGER OREGON ORIGEN ORIGIN PRAGUE TRAGIC TRIGLY TRIGON TROGON WRIGHT

•R••G•
ARMAGH BRIDGE BRIGGS BRINGS CRAGGY CRINGE DRAGGY DREDGE DRINGS DRUDGE ERYNGO FRIDGE FRINGE FRINGY FROGGY GRANGE GREIGE GRINGO GROGGY GRUDGE GRUNGE GRUNGY KRESGE ORANGE ORANGS ORANGY ORINGS ORTEGA PRANGS PRONGS TRIAGE TROUGH TRUDGE WRINGS WRONGS

•R•••G
ARCING ARMING CRYING DRYING ERRING ERVING FRYING IRKING IRVING ORBING PROLOG PRYING TRUING TRYING URGING

••RG••
AIRGUN BARGED BARGES BERGEN BIRGIT BORGIA BURGAS BURGEE BURGER BURGHS BURGLE BURGOO BURGOS CARGOS CORGIS DIRGES FERGIE FERGUS FORGED FORGER FORGES FORGET FORGOT GARGLE GORGED GORGES GORGET GORGON GURGLE JARGON KURGAN LARGER LARGES LARGOS MARGAY MARGES MARGIE MARGIN MARGOT MERGED MERGER MERGES MORGAN MORGEN NORGAY PARGET PURGED PURGES SARGES SARGON SARGOS SERGEI SERGES SERGIO SURGED SURGES TARGES TARGET TURGID TURGOR VERGED VERGER VERGES VIRGIL VIRGIN WARGOD

••R•G•
AURIGA BAREGE BORAGE DIRIGE DIRIGO DORAGS ENRAGE FORAGE FOREGO GARAGE MIRAGE PERUGA SCRAGS SHRUGS SPRAGS SPRIGS UNRIGS VIRAGO

••R••G
AIRBAG AIRING BARING BARONG BERING BORING CARING CORING CURING DARING DURING EARING EARWIG ERRING FARING FIRING GORING HARING HERZOG HIRING LURING MIRING OARING PARANG PARING PORING RARING SARONG SIRING SPRANG SPRING SPRUNG STRING STRONG STRUNG TARING THRONG TIRING TURING WARING WIRING

•••RG•
ANERGY ATERGO CHARGE CLERGY EMERGE ENERGY GEORGE GEORGY SPARGE SPURGE

•••R•G
CATRIG GEHRIG OILRIG PETROG RAGRUG TUAREG

••••RG
ALBORG COBURG CYBORG EDBERG EKBERG SEBERG VYBORG

RH••••
RHABDO RHAMES RHEBOK RHESUS RHETOR RHEUMS RHEUMY RHINAL RHINOS RHODES RHOMBI RHOMBS RHONDA RHUMBA RHUMBS RHYMED RHYMER RHYMES RHYTHM RHYTON

R•H•••
RAHRAH REHABS REHANG REHASH REHEAL REHEAR REHEAT REHEEL REHELD REHEMS REHIRE REHOOK REHUNG ROHMER

R••H••
RACHEL RACHIS RASHAD RASHER RASHES RASHID RASHLY RATHER REDHAT REDHOT RESHES RESHIP RESHOD RESHOE RESHOT RICHEN RICHER RICHES RICHIE RICHLY RIGHTO RIGHTS RIGHTY ROCHET RODHAM ROTHKO RUCHES RUSHED RUSHEE RUSHES

R•••H•
RAJAHS RANCHO REECHO RHYTHM ROUGHS ROUGHY

R••••H
RADISH RAHRAH RAKISH RAVISH RAWISH REHASH RELISH REWASH RIYADH RUPIAH

•RH•••
DRHOOK ERHARD MRHYDE

•R•H••
ARCHED ARCHER ARCHES ARCHIE ARCHLY ARCHON ARNHEM ARTHRO ARTHUR BRAHMA BRAHMS GRAHAM ORCHID ORCHIL ORPHAN ORPHIC URCHIN

•R••H•
ARETHA ARIGHT BRACHY BRASHY BRECHT BRIGHT BROTHS BRUSHY CRECHE DRACHM FRIGHT FROTHS FROTHY GRAPHS GRAPHY ORACHS TRACHY TRASHY TRICHO TRISHA TROCHE TROPHY TROTHS TRUTHS WRATHS WRATHY WRIGHT WRITHE

•R•••H
ARMAGH BRANCH BREACH BREATH BREECH BROACH BROOCH BRUNCH CROUCH CRUNCH CRUTCH DRENCH FRENCH GRINCH GROUCH GROWTH IRTYSH ORBACH ORNITH PREACH TRENCH TROUGH WRAITH WREATH WRENCH WRETCH

••RH••
BARHOP CARHOP DIRHAM DURHAM WARHOL

••R•H•
BERTHA BERTHS BIRTHS BURGHS EARTHA EARTHY FIRTHS GARTHS GERAHS GIRTHS GURKHA MARCHE MARSHA MARSHY MARTHA MORPHO MORPHS MORPHY MURPHY MYRRHS NORTHS PERCHA SURAHS TORAHS TORCHY WORTHS WORTHY

••R••H
AFRESH BARISH BARUCH BORSCH CERIPH ENRICH FARRAH GARETH GARISH HIRSCH HURRAH INRUSH JARRAH KIRSCH MARIAH MARISH OGRISH ONRUSH PARAPH PARIAH PARISH PERISH PURDAH QURUSH SERAPH SIRRAH TERAPH THRASH THRESH THRUSH UPRUSH WARMTH ZEROTH ZURICH

•••RH•
MYRRHS

•••R•H
CHURCH DEARTH EPARCH EXARCH FARRAH FOURTH HEARTH HIJRAH HOORAH HURRAH INARCH JARRAH RAHRAH SCORCH SEARCH SIRRAH SMERSH SMIRCH STARCH STORCH SWARTH

RI••••
RIALTO RIATAS RIBALD RIBAND RIBBED RIBBON RIBEYE RIBOSE RICERS RICHEN RICHER RICHES RICHIE RICHLY RICING RICKED RICKEY RIDDED RIDDEN RIDDLE RIDENT RIDERS RIDGED RIDGES RIDING RIDLEY RIDSOF RIENZI RIFELY RIFEST RIFFED RIFFLE RIFIFI RIFLED RIFLER RIFLES RIFTED RIGGED RIGGER RIGHTO RIGHTS RIGHTY RIGORS RIGOUR RIGSUP RILEUP RILING RILLES RILLET RIMIER RIMING RIMINI RIMMED RIMOSE RIMPLE RIMSKY RINGED RINGER RINGUP RINSED RINSES RIOJAS RIOTED RIOTER RIPELY RIPENS RIPEST RIPKEN RIPLEY RIPOFF RIPOUT RIPPED RIPPER RIPPLE RIPPLY RIPRAP RIPSAW RIPSUP RISERS RISING RISKED RISKER RISQUE RITARD RITTER RITUAL RIVALS RIVERA RIVERS RIVETS RIVING RIYADH RIYALS RIZZIO

R•I•••
RAIDED RAIDER RAILAT RAILED RAILER RAINED RAINER RAINES RAINEY RAIPUR RAISED RAISER RAISES RAISIN REIGNS REILLY REINAS REINED REINER REININ REINKS RHINAL RHINOS ROILED RUINED RUINER

R••I••
RABIES RACIAL RACIER RACILY RACINE RACING RADIAL RADIAN RADIOS RADISH RADIUM RADIUS RAGING RAKING RAKISH RAMIES RAMIFY RANIDS RAPIDS RAPIER RAPINE RAPINI RARIFY RARING RARITY RASING RATIFY RATINE RATING RATION RATIOS RATITE RAVINE RAVING RAVISH RAWISH RAZING REAIMS REAIRS REBIDS REBIND RECIFE RECIPE RECITE REDIAL REDING REDINK REFILE REFILL REFINE REFITS REGIME REGINA REGION REGIUS REHIRE RELICS RELICT RELIED RELIEF RELIES RELINE RELISH RELIST RELIVE REMICK REMIND REMISE REMISS REMITS REOILS REPINE REPINS RESIDE RESIGN RESILE RESING RESINS RESINY RESIST RETIAL RETIED RETIES RETILE RETIME RETINA RETIRE REVIEW REVILE REVISE REVIVE REWIND REWINS REWIRE RICING RIDING RIFIFI RILING RIMIER RIMING RIMINI RISING RIVING ROBING ROBINS ROPIER ROPING ROSIER ROSILY ROSINS ROSINY ROSITA ROTINI ROVING ROWING RUBIED RUBIES RUBIFY RULING RUMINA RUNINS RUPIAH RUTILE

R•••I•
RABBIS RABBIT RACHIS RAFFIA RAISIN RAKEIN RANCID RANKIN RASHID RATLIN READIN REALIA REBOIL RECOIL REDFIN REDFIR REEDIT REELIN REGAIN REGGIE REININ REJOIN RELAID REMAIL REMAIN RENAIL RENNIE RENNIN RENOIR REPAID REPAIR RESHIP RESNIK RESPIN RETAIL RETAIN RETRIM REVOIR RICHIE RIZZIO ROADIE ROBBIA ROBBIE ROLLIE ROLLIN ROMAIC RONNIE ROOKIE ROOMIE ROPEIN RUBRIC RUBSIN RUNCIE RUNSIN RUSKIN RUSSIA RUSTIC

R••••I
RAPINI RHOMBI RIENZI RIFIFI RIMINI ROMAJI ROTINI RUBATI

•RI•••
ARIDLY ARIGHT ARIOSE ARIOSO ARISEN ARISES ARISTA ARISTO BRIAND BRIANS BRIARD BRIARS BRIBED BRIBES BRICKS BRICKY BRIDAL BRIDES BRIDGE

BRIDLE
BRIEFS
BRIENZ
BRIERS
BRIERY
BRIGGS
BRIGHT
BRIGID
BRILLO
BRILLS
BRINED
BRINES
BRINGS
BRINKS
BRITON
CRICKS
CRIERS
CRIKEY
CRIMEA
CRIMES
CRIMPS
CRIMPY
CRINGE
CRIPES
CRISCO
CRISES
CRISIS
CRISPS
CRISPY
CRISTO
CRITIC
DRIERS
DRIEST
DRIFTS
DRIFTY
DRILLS
DRINGS
DRINKS
DRIPPY
DRIVEL
DRIVEN
DRIVER
DRIVES
ERINYS
FRIARS
FRIARY
FRIDAY
FRIDGE
FRIEND
FRIERS
FRIEZE
FRIGHT
FRIGID
FRIJOL
FRILLS
FRILLY
FRINGE
FRINGY
FRISCO
FRISEE
FRISES
FRISKS
FRISKY
FRITOS
FRIZZY
GRIEFS
GRIEVE
GRIFTS
GRIGRI
GRILLE
GRILLS
GRILSE
GRIMED
GRIMES
GRIMKE
GRIMLY
GRINCH
GRINDS
GRINGO
GRIOTS
GRIPED
GRIPER
GRIPES
GRIPPE
GRISLY
GRISON
GRISTS
GRITTY
GRIVET
IRIDES
IRIDIC
IRISES
IRISIN
ORIANA
ORIBIS
ORIELS
ORIENT
ORIGEN
ORIGIN
ORINGS
ORIOLE
ORISON
ORISSA
PRICED
PRICER
PRICES
PRICEY
PRICKS
PRIDED
PRIDES
PRIERS
PRIEST
PRIMAL
PRIMED
PRIMER
PRIMES
PRIMLY
PRIMOS
PRIMPS
PRIMUM
PRIMUS
PRINCE
PRINKS
PRINTS
PRIONS
PRIORI
PRIORS
PRIORY
PRIPET
PRISMS
PRISON
PRISSY
PRIVET
PRIZED
PRIZES
TRIADS
TRIAGE
TRIALS
TRIBAL
TRIBES
TRICED
TRICEP
TRICES
TRICHO
TRICIA
TRICKS
TRICKY
TRICOT
TRIERS
TRIFID
TRIFLE
TRIGLY
TRIGON
TRIJET
TRIKES
TRILBY
TRILLS
TRIMLY
TRINAL
TRINES
TRIODE
TRIPLE
TRIPLY
TRIPOD
TRIPOS
TRIPUP
TRISHA
TRISTE
TRITER
TRITON
TRIUNE
TRIVET
TRIVIA
TRIXIE
URIALS
WRIEST
WRIGHT
WRINGS
WRISTS
WRITER
WRITES
WRITHE

•R•I••

ARCING
ARGIVE
ARLISS
ARMIES
ARMING
ARNICA
AROIDS
ARRIBA
ARRIVE
ARTIER
ARTILY
ARTIST
BRAIDS
BRAILA
BRAILS
BRAINS
BRAINY
BRAISE
BROILS
BRUINS
BRUISE
BRUITS
CRUISE
CRYING
DRAILS
DRAINS
DROIDS
DROITS
DRUIDS
DRYICE
DRYING
DRYINK
ERBIUM
ERMINE
EROICA
ERRING
ERVING
FRAIDY
FRAISE
FRUITS
FRUITY
FRYING
GRAILS
GRAINS
GRAINY
GREIGE
GROINS
IRKING
IRVINE
IRVING
KRAITS
ORBING
ORBITS
OREIDA
ORGIES
ORNITH
OROIDE
ORPINE
ORSINO
PRAISE
PRYING
TRAILS
TRAINS
TRAITS
TROIKA
TRUING
TRUISM
TRYING
URGING
URSIDS
URSINE
WRAITH

•R••I•

ARABIA
ARABIC
ARALIA
ARAMIS
ARCHIE
ARCTIC
ARMPIT
ARTOIS
BRAZIL
BREVIS
BRIGID
BRODIE
BROLIN
CRANIA
CRANIO
CREDIT
CRETIN
CRISIS
CRITIC
CRONIN
DRAGIN
DRAWIN
DREWIN
DROPIN
DROPIT
EROTIC
FRIGID
FROLIC
GRACIE
GRADIN
GRATIA
GRATIN
GRATIS
GRAVID
GRODIN
IRANIS
IRAQIS
IRENIC
IRIDIC
IRISIN
IRONIC
ORCHID
ORCHIL
ORDAIN
ORIBIS
ORIGIN
ORPHIC
PRAXIS
PRECIS
PREFIX
PRELIM
PREMIE
PREVIN
PROFIT
PROLIX
PROSIT
TRAGIC
TRAVIS
TREDIA
TREPID
TRICIA
TRIFID
TRIVIA
TRIXIE
TROPIC
URACIL
URALIC
URANIA
URANIC
URCHIN

•R•••I

ARGALI
ARMANI
BRAZZI
BRUNEI
DROMOI
ERNANI
FRUTTI
GRIGRI
PRIORI
PROTEI

••RI••

ADRIAN
ADRIEN
ADRIFT
AERIAL
AERIES
AERIFY
AERILY
AFRICA
AFRITS
AIRIER
AIRILY
AIRING
AORIST
ARRIBA
ARRIVE
ATRIAL
ATRISK
ATRIUM
AURIFY
AURIGA
BARING
BARISH
BARITE
BARIUM
BERING
BORIDE
BORING
BURIED
BURIES
BURINS
CARIBE
CARIBS
CARIES
CARINA
CARING
CERIPH
CERISE
CERIUM
CHRISM
CORING
CORIUM
CURIAE
CURIAL
CURING
CURIOS
CURIUM
DARIEN
DARING
DARIUS
DERIDE
DERIVE
DIRIGE
DIRIGO
DORIAN
DORIES
DURIAN
DURING
EARING
EERIER
EERILY
ENRICH
ENRICO
ERRING
EYRIES
FARINA
FARING
FERIAL
FERIAS
FERITY
FIRING
FORINT
FURIES
GARISH
GORIER
GORILY
GORING
HARING
HERIOT
HIRING
JURIES
JURIST
KARIBA
KURILE
LARIAT
LERIDA
LORICA
LORIES
LURING
LYRICS
LYRIST
MARIAH
MARIAN
MARIEL
MARIKO
MARILU
MARINA
MARINE
MARINO
MARION
MARISA
MARISH
MARIST
MARIUS
MERIDA
MERINO
MERITS
MIRIAM
MIRIER
MIRING
MORION
MORITA
MORITZ
MURIEL
MURINE
MYRIAD
NARIAL
NORIAS
OARING
OBRIAN
OBRIEN
OGRISH
PARIAH
PARING
PARISH
PARITY
PERILS
PERIOD
PERISH
PORING
PURIFY
PURINA
PURINE
PURISM
PURIST
PURITY
PYRITE
RARIFY
RARING
RARITY
SCRIBE
SCRIMP
SCRIMS
SCRIPS
SCRIPT
SERIAL
SERIES
SERIFS
SERINE
SERINS
SHRIEK
SHRIFT
SHRIKE
SHRILL
SHRIMP
SHRINE
SHRINK
SHRIVE
SIRICA
SIRING
SIRIUS
SPRIER
SPRIGS
SPRING
SPRINT
SPRITE
SPRITS
SPRITZ
STRIAE
STRICK
STRICT
STRIDE
STRIFE
STRIKE
STRINE
STRING
STRIPE
STRIPS
STRIPY
STRIVE
SURIMI
SYRIAN
SYRINX
TARIFF
TARING
THRICE
THRIFT
THRILL
THRIPS
THRIVE
TIRING
TORIES
TORINO
TURING
TYRIAN
UGRIAN
UNRIGS
UNRIPE
UPRISE
VARIED
VARIES
VERIFY
VERILY
VERISM
VERITE
VERITY
VIRILE
WARIER
WARILY
WARING
WIRIER
WIRILY
WIRING
YORICK
ZORILS
ZURICH

••R•I•

ADROIT
AFRAID
AORTIC
BARBIE
BARDIC
BARKIN
BARRIE
BARRIO
BARRIS
BERLIN
BERNIE
BERTIE
BIRDIE
BIRGIT
BORGIA
CARDIN
CARDIO
CARLIN
CARRIE
CERTIF
CERVID
CORBIN
CORGIS
CURTIN
CURTIS
CURTIZ
DARNIT
DARWIN
DERAIL
DERMIS
DERRIS
DORRIT
DURBIN
EARWIG
EURAIL
FERGIE
FERRIC
FERRIS
FERVID
FIRKIN
FORBID
FORMIC
GARCIA
GARLIC
GERBIL
GERTIE
GORDIE
HARBIN
HARLIN
HARRIS
HERBIE
HEREIN
HERMIT
HEROIC
HORNIN
HORRID
JERKIN
KARMIC
KERMIS
KERMIT
LORAIN
MARCIA
MARCIE
MARGIE
MARGIN
MARLIN
MARNIE
MARTIN
MARVIN
MERLIN
MORBID
MORRIS
MURCIA
NARNIA
NARVIK
NEREID
NEREIS
NORDIC
NORRIS
PARNIS
PARRIS
PARVIS
PERMIT
PERNIO
PERSIA
PIRRIP
PORTIA
PURLIN
SARDIS
SARNIA
SERAIS
SERBIA
SERGIO
SERKIN
SORBIC
SORDID
SORTIE
SPRAIN
STRAIN
STRAIT
TARPIT
TOROID
TORPID
TORRID
TURBID
TURBIT
TURGID
TURKIC
TURNIN
TURNIP
TURPIN
VERBIS
VERDIN
VERMIN
VIRGIL
VIRGIN
WORKIN
YORKIE
ZEROIN

••R••I

BORZOI
CARONI
DORATI
DOREMI
KERNOI
MORONI
NEROLI
SERGEI
STRATI
SURIMI

•••RI•

ACARID
AGARIC
ALARIC
ALDRIN
ANTRIM
ASTRID
ATTRIT
AZORIN
BARRIE
BARRIO
BARRIS
CAPRIS
CARRIE
CATRIG
CEDRIC
CHERIE
CITRIC
CLERIC
CLORIS
COURIC
COWRIE
CUPRIC
CYMRIC
DEARIE
DEBRIS
DELRIO
DERRIS
DORRIT
EGERIA
ESPRIT
FABRIC
FAERIE
FERRIC
FERRIS
FIBRIL
FIBRIN
FLORID
FLORIN
FLORIO
GEHRIG
GLORIA
HARRIS
HENRIK
HORRID
HOURIS
HUBRIS
HYBRID
IATRIC
IBERIA
ICARIA
ILORIN
INDRIS
INGRID
ISTRIA
KAURIS
KUKRIS
LAURIE
LIBRIS
MADRID
MAORIS
MATRIX
METRIC
MIDRIB
MORRIS
NITRIC
NORRIS
NUTRIA
OILRIG
OSIRIS
PARRIS
PEERIN
PEORIA
PETRIE
PIRRIP
POURIN
PUTRID
RETRIM
RUBRIC
SCORIA
SHARIA
SHARIF
SHERIF
SPIRIT
STIRIN
STYRIA
TABRIZ
TETRIS
TIGRIS
TORRID
TSURIS
TUGRIK
UMBRIA
USERID
VITRIC

•••R•I

ANDREI
CIARDI
ITURBI
OCTROI
SHORTI
THYRSI

••••RI

ASKARI
BIHARI
CENTRI
DENDRI
DMITRI
EPHORI
GRIGRI
HATARI
HEGARI
HUMERI
JAVARI
LIBERI
MIDORI
PAHARI
PAPYRI
PRIORI
QATARI
QUADRI
SAFARI
SATORI
SOUARI
TISHRI
UAKARI
VIDERI

R•J•••

RAJAHS
RAJPUT
REJECT
REJOIN

R••J••

RAMJET
RIOJAS

R•••J•

ROMAJI

•RJ•••

ARJUNA

•R•J••

FRIJOL
PRAJNA
TRAJAN
TRIJET
TROJAN

••R•J•

BAROJA

•••R•J

SWARAJ

••••RJ

INTERJ

R•K•••

RAKEIN
RAKERS
RAKEUP
RAKING
RAKISH
REKEYS

R••K••

RACKED
RACKET
RACKUP
RANKED
RANKER
RANKIN
RANKLE
RANKLY
RECKON
REEKED
RICKED
RICKEY
RIPKEN
RISKED
RISKER
ROCKED
ROCKER
ROCKET
ROCKNE
ROCKYV
ROOKED
ROOKIE
RUCKED
RUCKUS
RUSKIN
RYOKAN
RYUKYU

R•••K•

REBUKE
REINKS
REMAKE
RETAKE
REVOKE
RIMSKY
ROTHKO
ROURKE

R••••K

RECORK
REDINK
REDOAK
REEBOK
REHOOK
RELOCK
REMARK
REMICK
RESNIK
RETOOK
REWORK
RHEBOK

•RK•••

IRKING
ORKNEY

•R•K••

BRAKED
BRAKES
BROKAW
BROKEN
BROKER
CRAKES
CRIKEY
DRAKES
KRAKEN
KRAKOW
TRIKES

•R••K•

BREAKS
BRICKS
BRICKY
BRINKS
BROOKE
BROOKS
BROOKY
CRACKS
CRACKY
CRANKS
CRANKY
CREAKS
CREAKY
CREEKS
CRICKS
CROAKS
CROAKY
CROCKS
CROOKS
DRINKS
FRANKS
FREAKS
FREAKY
FRISKS
FRISKY
FROCKS
GREEKS
GRIMKE
PRANKS
PRICKS
PRINKS
PROSKY
TRACKS
TRICKS
TRICKY
TROIKA
TRUCKS
TRUNKS
WRACKS
WREAKS
WRECKS

•R•••K

ARAWAK
ARRACK
BRATSK
DRHOOK
DRYINK
FRANCK
TREBEK
URALSK

••RK••

BARKAT
BARKED
BARKER
BARKIN
CARKED
CORKED
CORKER
DARKEN
DARKER
DARKLE
DARKLY
FIRKIN
FORKED
FORKER
GURKHA
HARKED
HARKEN
HARKER
JERKED
JERKIN
LARKED
LURKED
MARKED
MARKER
MARKET
MARKKA
MARKUP
MERKEL
PARKAS
PARKAY
PARKED
PARKER
PERKED
PERKUP
PORKER
SERKIN
TERKEL
TURKEY
TURKIC
WORKED
WORKER
WORKIN
WORKON
WORKUP
YERKED
YERKES
YORKER
YORKIE

••R•K•

EUREKA
MARIKO
MARKKA
PERUKE
SHRIKE
STRAKE
STRIKE
STROKE
YUROKS

••R••K

ARRACK
ATRISK
BARTOK
BUROAK
FAROUK
KARNAK
MARDUK
NARVIK
SCREAK
SHRANK
SHRIEK
SHRINK
SHRUNK
STREAK
STRICK
STRUCK
YORICK

•••RK•

BOURKE
CLARKE
CLERKS
DMARKS
OZARKS
QUARKS
QUIRKS
QUIRKY
ROURKE
SHARKS
SHIRKS
SMIRKS
SMIRKY
SPARKS
SPARKY
STIRKS
STORKS

•••R•K

AMTRAK
ANORAK
DVORAK
HENRIK
TOBRUK
TUGRIK

••••RK

ATWORK
DEBARK
EMBARK
LANARK
NEWARK
RECORK
REMARK
REWORK
STMARK
UNCORK

R•L•••

RELACE
RELAID
RELATE
RELAYS
RELENT
RELETS
RELEVY
RELICS
RELICT
RELIED
RELIEF
RELIES
RELINE
RELISH
RELIST
RELIVE
RELOAD
RELOCK
RELUCT
RELUME
RILEUP
RILING
RILLES
RILLET
ROLAND
ROLEOS
ROLLED
ROLLER
ROLLIE
ROLLIN
ROLLON
ROLLUP
RULEON
RULERS
RULING

R••L••

RAGLAN
RAILAT
RAILED
RAILER
RATLIN
REALER
REALES
REALIA
REALLY
REALMS
REALTY
REELED
REELIN
REFLAG
REFLEX
REFLUX
REGLET
REGLUE
REILLY
REPLAN
REPLAY
REPLOW
REVLON
RIALTO
RIDLEY
RIFLED
RIFLER
RIFLES
RILLES
RILLET
RIPLEY
ROBLES
ROILED
ROLLED
ROLLER
ROLLIE
ROLLIN
ROLLON
ROLLUP
RUBLES
RUBLEV
RUNLET
RVALUE

R•••L•
RABBLE
RACILY
RADDLE
RADULA
RAFFLE
RAMBLA
RAMBLE
RANKLE
RANKLY
RAPTLY
RARELY
RASHLY
RASSLE
RATELS
RATTLE
RATTLY
RAVELS
RAZZLE
RCCOLA
REALLY
REBELS
REBOLT
RECALL
REFILE
REFILL
REGALE
REHELD
REILLY
REMELT
REMOLD
REOILS
REPELS
REPOLL
RESALE
RESALT
RESELL
RESILE
RESOLD
RESOLE
RESULT
RETELL
RETILE
RETOLD
REVELS
REVILE
REVOLT
REWELD
RIBALD
RICHLY
RIDDLE
RIFELY
RIFFLE
RIMPLE
RIPELY
RIPPLE
RIPPLY
RIVALS
RIYALS
ROBALO
ROMOLA
RONALD
RONELY
ROSILY
ROUBLE
ROWELS
ROYALE
ROYALS
RUBBLE
RUBBLY
RUDDLE
RUDELY
RUDOLF
RUFFLE
RUFFLY
RUMBLE
RUMBLY
RUMPLE
RUMPLY
RUNDLE
RUSTLE
RUTILE
RYDELL

R••••L
RACHEL
RACIAL
RADIAL
RAFAEL
RAPPEL
RAQUEL
RASCAL
REBOIL
RECALL
RECOIL
REDEAL
REDIAL
REFILL
REFUEL
REGNAL
REHEAL
REHEEL
REMAIL
RENAIL
RENTAL
REPEAL
REPOLL
RESEAL
RESELL
RETAIL
RETELL
RETIAL
RETOOL
RETRAL
REVEAL
RHINAL
RITUAL
ROMMEL
RONDEL
RUEFUL
RUNNEL
RUPAUL
RYDELL

•RL•••
ARLEEN
ARLENE
ARLISS
IRLENE
ORLOPS

•R•L••
ARALIA
ARALLU
ARMLET
BRILLO
BRILLS
BROLIN
BROLLY
BRULES
DRILLS
DROLLS
DROLLY
FRILLS
FRILLY
FROLIC
GRILLE
GRILLS
GRILSE
MRBLUE
ORALES
ORALLY
ORELSE
ORTLES
PRELAW
PRELIM
PROLES
PROLIX
PROLOG
TRALEE
TRILBY
TRILLS
TROLLS
TRYLON
URALIC
URALSK

•R••L•
ARABLE
ARALLU
ARBELA
ARCHLY
AREOLA
ARGALI
ARGYLE
ARGYLL
ARIDLY
ARNOLD
ARTELS
ARTILY
BRAILA
BRAILS
BRAWLS
BRIDLE
BRILLO
BRILLS
BROILS
BROLLY
CRADLE
CRAWLS
CRAWLY
CREELS
CREOLE
DRABLY
DRAILS
DRAWLS
DRAWLY
DRILLS
DROLLS
DROLLY
DROOLS
DROOLY
DRYFLY
ERROLL
FREELY
FRILLS
FRILLY
GRABLE
GRAILS
GRAYLY
GREYLY
GRILLE
GRILLS
GRIMLY
GRISLY
GROWLS
GROWLY
GRUELS
KRAALS
ORACLE
ORALLY
ORIELS
ORIOLE
ORMOLU
ORWELL
PRIMLY
PROWLS
TRAILS
TRAWLS
TREBLE
TREBLY
TRIALS
TRIFLE
TRIGLY
TRILLS
TRIMLY
TRIPLE
TRIPLY
TROLLS
URIALS
URSULA

•R•••L
ARGYLL
ARMFUL
ARTFUL
BRAZIL
BRIDAL
BRUMAL
BRUTAL
CRENEL
CRESOL
CREWEL
CRURAL
DREXEL
DRIVEL
ERROLL
FRIJOL
FRUGAL
GRAVEL
GRETEL
GROVEL
IREFUL
IRREAL
MRCOOL
ORCHIL
ORDEAL
ORWELL
PRIMAL
PROPEL
TRAVEL
TRIBAL
TRINAL
TROWEL
URACIL

••RL••
BARLEY
BERLIN
BIRLED
BURLAP
BURLED
BURLEY
CARLIN
CARLOS
CARLOT
CURLED
CURLER
CURLEW
CURLEY
CURLUP
EARLAP
FARLEY
FARLOW
FURLED
GARLIC
GURLEY
HARLAN
HARLEM
HARLEY
HARLIN
HARLOW
HURLED
HURLER
HURLEY
MARLED
MARLEE
MARLEY
MARLIN
MARLON
MERLIN
MERLON
MERLOT
MORLEY
PARLAY
PARLEY
PARLOR
PURLED
PURLIN
VARLET
WORLDS
WURLEY

••R•L•
AERILY
AIRILY
BARELY
BARFLY
BAROLO
BURBLE
BURBLY
BURGLE
CAROLE
CAROLS
CIRCLE
CORALS
CURDLE
CURTLY
CURULE
DARKLE
DARKLY
DIRELY
EERILY
ENROLL
ENROLS
ERROLL
FERULE
FIRMLY
GARBLE
GARGLE
GERALD
GIRDLE
GORALS
GORILY
GURGLE
HARALD
HARDLY
HAROLD
HERALD
HURDLE
HURTLE
KERALA
KIRTLE
KURALT
KURILE
LORDLY
MARBLE
MARBLY
MARILU
MARPLE
MERELY
MORALE
MORALS
MORELS
MURALS
MYRTLE
NEROLI
PAROLE
PARTLY
PARULA
PERILS
PERTLY
PORTLY
PURELY
PURFLE
PURPLE
PURPLY
RARELY
SCROLL
SHRILL
SORELY
SPRYLY
STROLL
SURELY
TARTLY
THRALE
THRALL
THRILL
TURTLE
UNROLL
UNRULY
VERILY
VIRILE
WARBLE
WARILY
WARMLY
WIRILY
YARELY
ZORILS

••R••L
AERIAL
AORTAL
ATRIAL
BARBEL
BARREL
BOREAL
BURSAL
CARFUL
CARMEL
CARNAL
CARPAL
CARPEL
CARREL
CARROL
CARTEL
CEREAL
CORBEL
CORNEL
CORRAL
CORREL
CURIAL
DARNEL
DARRYL
DERAIL
DERMAL
DIRNDL
DORSAL
EARFUL
ENROLL
ERROLL
EURAIL
FERIAL
FORMAL
GERBIL
HERBAL
HORMEL
IRREAL
ISRAEL
JARFUL
KERNEL
LARVAL
LOREAL
MARCEL
MARIEL
MARTEL
MARVEL
MERKEL
MORSEL
MORTAL
MURIEL
MYRDAL
NARIAL
NARWAL
NORMAL
PARCEL
PARREL
PORTAL
SCRAWL
SCROLL
SERIAL
SERVAL
SHRILL
SORREL
SPRAWL
STROLL
TARSAL
TERCEL
TERKEL
THRALL
THRILL
UNREAL
UNREEL
UNROLL
VERBAL
VERNAL
VIRGIL
WARHOL
WERFEL

•••RL•
BGIRLS
CEORLS
CHARLY
CHURLS
DEARLY
DOURLY
EBERLY
EDERLE
EVERLY
FAIRLY
GNARLS
GNARLY
HOURLY
KNURLS
KNURLY
NEARLY
OVERLY
PEARLS
PEARLY
POORLY
SEARLE
SKIRLS
SNARLS
SNARLY
SOURLY
SWIRLS
SWIRLY
TWIRLS
WHIRLS
WHIRLY
WHORLS
YEARLY

•••R•L
ABORAL
AMORAL
ASTRAL
BARREL
CARREL
CARROL
CHERYL
CHORAL
CORRAL
CORREL
CRURAL
DARRYL
FIBRIL
FLORAL
LAUREL
MITRAL
NEURAL
NEUROL
PARREL
PATROL
PETREL
PETROL
PLURAL
RETRAL
SACRAL
SAUREL
SHERYL
SORREL
SPIRAL
STEROL
UMBRAL

••••RL
ASWIRL
AWHIRL
MYGIRL
SCHORL
UNCURL
UNFURL

R•M•••
RAMADA
RAMATE
RAMBLA
RAMBLE
RAMEAU
RAMETS
RAMIES
RAMIFY
RAMJET
RAMMED
RAMONA
RAMONE
RAMOSE
RAMOUS
RAMPED
RAMROD
RAMSAY
RAMSES
RAMSEY
RAMSON
REMADE
REMAIL
REMAIN
REMAKE
REMAND
REMANS
REMAPS
REMARK
REMEDY
REMELT
REMEND
REMICK
REMIND
REMISE
REMISS
REMITS
REMOLD
REMOPS
REMORA
REMOTE
REMOVE
REMOWN
REMOWS
REMUDA
RIMIER
RIMING
RIMINI
RIMMED
RIMOSE
RIMPLE
RIMSKY
ROMAIC
ROMAJI
ROMANO
ROMANS
ROMANY
ROMEOS
ROMERO
ROMMEL
ROMNEY
ROMOLA
ROMPED
ROMPER
RUMBAS
RUMBLE
RUMBLY
RUMENS
RUMINA
RUMMER
RUMORS
RUMOUR
RUMPLE
RUMPLY
RUMPUS

R••M••
RAGMAN
RAGMEN
RAGMOP
RAMMED
REAMED
REAMER
RHAMES
RHOMBI
RHOMBS
RHUMBA
RHUMBS
RHYMED
RHYMER
RHYMES
RIMMED
ROAMED
ROAMER
RODMAN
ROHMER
ROMMEL
ROOMED
ROOMER
ROOMIE
RUDMAN
RUMMER

R•••M•
RACEME
RADOME
REAIMS
REALMS
REARMS
REGIME
REHEMS
RELUME
RENAME
RESUME
RETIME
REVAMP
RHEUMS
RHEUMY
RUNDMC

R••••M
RADIUM
RANDOM
RANSOM
REDEEM
REDGUM
REFORM
RETRIM
REWARM
RHYTHM
RODHAM

•RM•••
ARMADA
ARMAGH
ARMAND
ARMANI
ARMETS
ARMFUL
ARMIES
ARMING
ARMLET
ARMORS
ARMORY
ARMOUR
ARMPIT
ARMURE
ERMINE
MRMOTO
ORMOLU
ORMOND

•R•M••
ARAMIS
AROMAS
BREMEN
BRUMAL
BRUMBY
BRUMES
CRAMBO
CRAMPS
CREMES
CRIMEA
CRIMES
CRIMPS
CRIMPY
CRUMBS
CRUMBY
CRUMMY
DRAMAS
DROMOI
DROMOS
DRUMUP
FRAMED
FRAMES
FRUMPS
FRUMPY
GRAMAS
GRAMME
GRAMMY
GRAMPA
GRAMPS
GRIMED
GRIMES
GRIMKE
GRIMLY
GRUMPS
GRUMPY
KRAMER
OROMOS
PREMED
PREMIE
PRIMAL
PRIMED
PRIMER
PRIMES
PRIMLY
PRIMOS
PRIMPS
PRIMUM
PRIMUS
PROMOS
PROMPT
TRAMPS
TREMOR
TRIMLY
TROMPE
TROMPS
TRUMAN
TRUMPS

•R••M•
BRAHMA
BRAHMS
BREAMS
BROOMS
BROOMY
CREAMS
CREAMY
CRUMMY
DREAMS
DREAMT
DREAMY
GRAMME
GRAMMY
GROOMS
PREAMP
PRISMS
PROAMS
PROEMS
TRAUMA
VROOMS

•R•••M
ARNHEM
ARTGUM
DRACHM
ERBIUM
FRENUM
GRAHAM
PRELIM
PRIMUM
PROTEM
TRUISM

••RM••
AIRMAN
AIRMEN
BARMAN
BARMEN
BORMAN
BURMAN
CARMAN
CARMEL
CARMEN
CERMET
CORMAN
DERMAL
DERMIS
DORMER
FARMED
FARMER
FERMAT
FIRMAN
FIRMED
FIRMER
FIRMLY
FIRMUP
FORMAL
FORMAN
FORMAT
FORMED
FORMER
FORMIC
GERMAN
HARMED
HARMON
HERMAN
HERMES
HERMIT
HERMON
HORMEL
HORMUZ
KARMIC
KERMAN
KERMES
KERMIS
KERMIT
KIRMAN
KORMAN
MARMEE
MARMOT
MERMAN
MERMEN
MORMON
MURMUR
NORMAL
NORMAN
PERMED
PERMIT
SERMON
TARMAC
TERMED
VERMIN
WARMED
WARMER
WARMLY
WARMTH
WARMUP
WORMED

••R•M•
ABRAMS
AFRAME
BIREME
CAROMS
CDROMS
CHROMA
CHROME
CHROMO
CHROMY
DOREMI
EPROMS
FORUMS
HAREMS
JEREMY
JEROME
JORUMS
LARAMS
SCRAMS
SCRIMP
SCRIMS
SCRUMS
SERUMS
SHRIMP
STRUMS
SURIMI
THRUMS

••R••M
AIRARM
AIRDAM
ATRIUM
BARIUM
BARNUM
CERIUM
CHRISM
CIRCUM
CORIUM
CURIUM
DIRHAM
DORSUM
DURHAM
HARLEM
KAREEM
MIRIAM
PURISM
SCREAM
STREAM
VERISM

•••RM•
ALARMS
CHARMS
DEARME
DHARMA
REARMS
SMARMY
STORMS
STORMY
SWARMS
THERMO
THERMS
UNARMS

•••R•M
ALARUM
ANTRIM
ANTRUM
ASHRAM
BAYRUM
DIGRAM
ENGRAM
FOURAM
FOURPM
INGRAM
LABRUM
QUORUM
RETRIM
SACRUM
SCARUM

••••RM
AFFIRM
AIRARM
DEFORM
DISARM
INFIRM
INFORM
REFORM
REWARM
SQUIRM

R•N•••
RANCHO
RANCID
RANCOR
RANDOM
RANDRY
RANEES
RANFOR
RANGED
RANGER
RANGES
RANGUP
RANIDS
RANKED
RANKER
RANKIN
RANKLE
RANKLY
RANOFF
RANOUT
RANSOM
RANTED
RANTER
RENAIL
RENAME
RENATA
RENDER
RENEGE
RENEWS
RENNES
RENNET
RENNIE
RENNIN
RENOIR
RENOTE
RENOWN
RENTAL
RENTED
RENTER
RINGED
RINGER
RINGUP
RINSED
RINSES
RONALD
RONDEL
RONDOS
RONELY
RONNIE
RUNCIE
RUNDLE
RUNDMC
RUNDRY
RUNFOR
RUNGUP
RUNINS
RUNLET
RUNNEL
RUNNER
RUNOFF
RUNONS
RUNOUT
RUNSAT
RUNSIN
RUNSON
RUNSTO
RUNSUP
RUNUPS
RUNWAY
RUNYON

R••N••
RADNER
RAINED
RAINER
RAINES
RAINEY
REGNAL
REGNAT
REINAS
REINED
REINER
REININ
REINKS
RENNES
RENNET
RENNIE
RENNIN
RESNIK
REUNES
RHINAL
RHINOS
RHONDA
RIENZI
RODNEY
ROMNEY
RONNIE
ROONEY
ROUNDS
RUANAS
RUANDA
RUINED
RUINER
RUNNEL
RUNNER
RWANDA

R•••N•
RACINE
RACING
RACONS
RAGING
RAKING
RAMONA
RAMONE
RAPINE
RAPINI
RARING
RASING
RATINE
RATING
RAVENS
RAVINE
RAVING
RAYONS
RAZING
REBEND
REBENT
REBIND
RECANE
RECANT
RECENT
RECONS
REDANT
REDENY
REDING
REDINK
REDONE
REFINE
REFUND
REGENT
REGINA
REHANG
REHUNG
REIGNS
RELENT
RELINE
REMAND
REMANS
REMEND
REMIND
REPAND
REPENT
REPINE
REPINS
RERENT
RERUNS
RESAND
RESEND
RESENT
RESING
RESINS
RESINY
RETENE
RETINA
RETUNE
REWIND
REWINS
REZONE
RIBAND
RICING
RIDENT
RIDING
RILING
RIMING
RIMINI
RIPENS
RISING
RIVING
ROBING
ROBINS
ROCKNE
RODENT
ROLAND
ROMANO
ROMANS
ROMANY
ROPING
ROSINS
ROSINY
ROTINI
ROTUND
ROVING
ROWENA
ROWENS
ROWING
ROXANA
ROXANE
RUBENS
RULING
RUMENS
RUMINA
RUNINS
RUNONS

R••••N
RADIAN
RAGLAN
RAGMAN
RAGMEN
RAISIN
RAKEIN
RAMSON
RANKIN
RATION
RATLIN

RATSON RATTAN RAYGUN READIN REAGAN REASON REBORN RECKON REDDEN REDFIN REELIN REGAIN REGION REININ REJOIN REMAIN REMOWN RENNIN RENOWN REOPEN REPLAN REPUGN RESAWN RESEEN RESEWN RESIGN RESPIN RESTON RETAIN RETTON RETURN REUBEN REVLON REVSON RHYTON RIBBON RICHEN RIDDEN RIPKEN ROBSON RODMAN ROLLIN ROLLON ROPEIN ROTTEN RUBSIN RUDMAN RULEON RUNSIN RUNSON RUNYON RUSKIN RUTTAN RYAZAN RYOKAN

•RN•••

ARNESS ARNETT ARNHEM ARNICA ARNOLD ERNANI ERNEST ORNATE ORNERY ORNITH

•R•N••

ARENAS ARENDT BRANCH BRANDO BRANDS BRANDT BRANDX BRANDY BRANNY BRANTS BRENDA BRENTS BRINED BRINES BRINGS BRINKS BRONCO BRONCS BRONTE BRONZE BRONZY BRUNCH BRUNEI BRUNET BRUNTS CRANED CRANES CRANIA CRANIO CRANKS CRANKY CRANNY CRENEL CRENNA CRINGE CRONES CRONIN CRONUS CRONYN CRUNCH DRENCH DRINGS DRINKS DRONED DRONER DRONES ERENOW ERINYS ERYNGO FRANCA FRANCE FRANCK FRANCO FRANCS FRANKS FRANNY FRENCH FRENUM FRENZY FRINGE FRINGY FRONDS FRONTS GRANDE GRANDS GRANGE GRANNY GRANTS GRINCH GRINDS GRINGO GRUNDY GRUNGE GRUNGY GRUNTS IRANIS IRENES IRENIC IRONED IRONER IRONIC IRONON KRANTZ KRONER KRONOR KRONUR ORANGE ORANGS ORANGY ORANTS ORINGS ORKNEY PRANCE PRANGS PRANKS PRENUP PRINCE PRINKS PRINTS PRONGS PRONTO PRUNED PRUNER PRUNES PRYNNE SRANAN TRANCE TRENCH TRENDS TRENDY TRINAL TRINES TRUNKS URANIA URANIC URANUS WRENCH WRINGS WRONGS

•R••N•

ARCANA ARCANE ARCING ARDENT ARGENT ARJUNA ARLENE ARMAND ARMANI ARMING AROUND ARPENT ARRANT ARSENE ARSONS ARYANS BRAINS BRAINY BRANNY BRAWNY BRIAND BRIANS BRIENZ BROWNE BROWNS BROWNY BRUINS BRYANT BRYONY CRANNY CRENNA CROONS CROWNS CRYING DRAINS DROWNS DRYING DRYINK ERMINE ERNANI ERRAND ERRANT ERRING ERVING FRANNY FRESNO FRIEND FROWNS FRYING GRAINS GRAINY GRANNY GREENE GREENS GREENY GRETNA GROANS GRODNO GROINS GROUND GROZNY IRKING IRLENE IRVINE IRVING KRASNY ORBING ORGANA ORGANS ORIANA ORIENT ORMOND ORPINE ORSINO PRAJNA PRAWNS PREENS PRIONS PROCNE PRYING PRYNNE TRAINS TRIUNE TRUANT TRUING TRYING URBANA URBANE URGENT URGING URSINE

•R•••N

ARAGON ARCHON ARCTAN ARISEN ARLEEN ARUBAN BRAZEN BREMEN BRETON BRITON BROGAN BROKEN BROLIN BRYSON CRAVEN CRAYON CRETAN CRETIN CRONIN CRONYN CROTON DRAGIN DRAGON DRAWIN DRAWON DREWIN DREWON DRIVEN DROPIN DRYDEN DRYRUN FRAUEN FROZEN FRYPAN GRABEN GRADIN GRATIN GRAVEN GREWON GRISON GRODIN GROTON GROWON IRISIN IRONON KRAKEN ORDAIN OREGON ORIGEN ORIGIN ORISON ORPHAN PREVIN PREYON PRISON PROTON PROVEN SRANAN TRAJAN TREPAN TRIGON TRITON TROGON TROJAN TRUMAN TRYLON URCHIN

••RN••

BARNES BARNEY BARNUM BERNIE BIRNEY BORNEO BURNED BURNER BURNET BURNEY BURNUP BYRNES CARNAL CARNES CARNET CARNEY CARNOT CORNEA CORNED CORNEL CORNER CORNET DARNAY DARNED DARNEL DARNER DARNIT DIRNDL DURNED EARNED EARNER GARNER GARNET GIRNED GURNEY HORNED HORNER HORNET HORNEY HORNIN KARNAK KERNED KERNEL KERNOI KERNOS LERNER MARNER MARNIE MORNAY NARNIA PARNIS PERNIO PERNOD SARNIA TERNES TURNED TURNER TURNIN TURNIP TURNON TURNTO TURNUP VARNAS VARNEY VERNAL VERNON WARNED WARNER WERNER YARNED

••R•N•

ADRENO AIRING APRONS ARRANT BARING BARONG BARONS BARONY BERING BORING BURINS CARINA CARING CARONI CHRONO CORING CORONA CURING CYRANO DARENT DARING DURANT DURING EARING ERRAND ERRANT ERRING FARINA FARING FERENC FIRING FORINT GERENT GERONT GERUND GORING GYRENE GYRONS HARING HERONS HIRING HURONS KORUNA LARYNX LORENZ LURING MARINA MARINE MARINO MERINO MIRING MORANT MORENO MORONI MORONS MURANO MURINE OARING PARANA PARANG PARENS PARENT PARING PIRANA PORING PURINA PURINE RARING RERENT RERUNS SARANS SARONG SERENA SERENE SERINE SERINS SHRANK SHRINE SHRINK SHRUNK SIRENS SIRING SPRANG SPRING SPRINT SPRUNG STRAND STRINE STRING STRONG STRUNG SYRINX TARING THRONE THRONG TIRANA TIRANE TIRING TORINO TURING TYRANT TYRONE VARUNA VERONA WARING WERENT WIRING

••R••N

ADRIAN ADRIEN AIRGUN AIRMAN AIRMEN BARKIN BARMAN BARMEN BARREN BARRON BARTON BARYON BARZUN BERGEN BERLIN BORDEN BOREON BORMAN BURDEN BURMAN BURTON CARBON CARDIN CAREEN CARLIN CARMAN CARMEN CARSON CARTON CORBAN CORBIN CORDON CORMAN CURTIN CURZON DARIEN DARKEN DARREN DARWIN DORIAN DURBAN DURBIN DURIAN FIRKIN FIRMAN FORMAN GARCON GARDEN GARSON GERMAN GORDON GORGON HARBIN HARDEN HARKEN HARLAN HARLIN HARMON HARPON HEREIN HEREON HERMAN HERMON HIREON HORNIN HORTON JARGON JERKIN JORDAN KERMAN KIRMAN KOREAN KORMAN KURGAN LARDON LARSEN LARSON LORAIN MARGIN MARIAN MARION MARLIN MARLON MAROON MARRON MARTEN MARTIN MARVIN MERLIN MERLON MERMAN MERMEN MERTON MERVYN MIRREN MOREEN MORGAN MORGEN MORION MORMON MORTON NORMAN NORTON OBRIAN OBRIEN PARDON PARSON PARTON PERSON PURLIN SARGON SARTON SCREEN SERKIN SERMON SPRAIN STRAIN STREWN SYRIAN TARPAN TARPON TARTAN TARZAN TERRAN THROWN TURBAN TUREEN TURNIN TURNON TURPIN TYRIAN UGRIAN VARDEN VERDIN VERDON VERDUN VEREEN VERMIN VERNON VIRGIN WARDEN WARREN WOREON WORKIN WORKON WORSEN ZEROIN ZIRCON

•••RN•

ACORNS ADORNS AHERNE AVERNO BAIRNS BOURNE CAIRNS CHURNS CZERNY ETERNE JOURNO KEARNY LEARNS LEARNT LIERNE MOURNS QUERNS SCARNE SCORNS SMYRNA SPURNS STERNA STERNE STERNO STERNS THORNS THORNY UTURNS YEARNS

•••R•N

ALDRIN ANTRON ANURAN AZORIN BARREN BARRON BEARON CHARON CHIRON CHYRON CITRON DACRON DAIREN DARREN DRYRUN ENDRUN EPHRON FIBRIN FLORIN GIBRAN GUDRUN HADRON HEBRON HEDREN HEDRON HIERON ILORIN LAUREN LEBRUN MACRON MARRON MATRON MICRON MIRREN NATRON NEURON NOIRON OBERON OUTRAN OUTRUN PATRON PEERIN POURIN QUMRAN SHARON SHORAN SKIRUN SPURON STIRIN STYRON TERRAN VANRYN WARREN

••••RN

ASTERN AUBURN BICORN CASERN CAVERN COBURN DEHORN EXTERN GOVERN INBORN INTERN INTURN MODERN OSBORN REBORN RETURN SATURN SECERN SEVERN SUBORN TAVERN UNBORN UNTORN UNWORN UPTURN WEBERN WYVERN

RO••••

ROADIE ROAMED ROAMER ROARED ROARER ROASTS ROBALO ROBBED ROBBER ROBBIA ROBBIE ROBERT ROBING ROBINS ROBLES ROBOTS ROBROY ROBSON ROBUST ROCHET ROCKED ROCKER ROCKET ROCKNE ROCKYV ROCOCO RODDED RODENT RODEOS RODHAM RODMAN RODNEY ROGERS ROGUES ROHMER ROILED ROLAND ROLEOS ROLLED ROLLER ROLLIE ROLLIN ROLLON ROLLUP ROMAIC ROMAJI ROMANO ROMANS ROMANY ROMEOS ROMERO ROMMEL ROMNEY ROMOLA ROMPED ROMPER RONALD RONDEL RONDOS RONELY RONNIE ROOFED ROOFER ROOKED ROOKIE ROOMED ROOMER ROOMIE ROONEY ROOSTS ROOTED ROOTER ROPEIN ROPERS ROPIER ROPING ROSARY ROSCOE ROSEAU ROSIER ROSILY ROSINS ROSINY ROSITA ROSTER ROSTOV ROSTRA ROTARY ROTATE ROTGUT ROTHKO ROTINI ROTORS ROTTED ROTTEN ROTTER ROTUND ROUBLE ROUGED ROUGES ROUGHS ROUGHY ROUNDS ROURKE ROUSED ROUSER ROUSES ROUSTS ROUTED ROUTER ROUTES ROVERS ROVING ROWELS ROWENA ROWENS ROWERS ROWING ROXANA ROXANE ROYALE ROYALS ROZZER

R•O•••

REOILS REOPEN RHODES RHOMBI RHOMBS RHONDA RIOJAS RIOTED RIOTER ROOFED ROOFER ROOKED ROOKIE ROOMED ROOMER ROOMIE ROONEY ROOSTS ROOTED ROOTER RYOKAN

R••O••

RACONS RADOME RAGOUT RAMONA RAMONE RAMOSE RAMOUS RANOFF RANOUT RAYONS RAZORS RCCOLA REBOIL REBOLT REBOOT REBORN REBOZO RECOAT RECODE RECOIL RECONS RECOPY RECORD RECORK RECOUP REDOAK REDOES REDONE REFORM REHOOK REJOIN RELOAD RELOCK REMOLD REMOPS REMORA REMOTE REMOVE REMOWN REMOWS RENOIR RENOTE RENOWN REPOLL REPORT REPOSE REPOST REPOTS RESODS RESOLD RESOLE RESORB RESORT RETOLD RETOOK RETOOL RETOPS RETORT RETOUR RETOWS REVOIR REVOKE REVOLT REWORD REWORK REWOVE REZONE RIBOSE RIGORS RIGOUR RIMOSE RIPOFF RIPOUT ROBOTS ROCOCO ROMOLA ROTORS RUBOFF RUBOUT RUDOLF RUFOUS RUGOSE RUMORS RUMOUR RUNOFF RUNONS RUNOUT

R•••O•

RADIOS RAGMOP RAGTOP RAMROD RAMSON RANCOR RANDOM RANFOR RANSOM RAPTOR RATION RATIOS RATSON REASON REBOOT RECKON RECTOR RECTOS REDDOG REDFOX REDHOT REDSOX REDTOP REEBOK REGION REHOOK REPLOW REPROS RESHOD RESHOE RESHOT RESTON RETOOK RETOOL RETROS RETTON REVLON REVSON RHEBOK RHETOR RHINOS RHYTON RIBBON RIDSOF ROBROY ROBSON RODEOS ROLEOS ROLLON ROMEOS RONDOS ROSCOE ROSTOV RULEON RUNFOR RUNSON RUNYON

R••••O

RABATO RANCHO REBOZO REECHO RHABDO RIALTO RIGHTO RIZZIO ROBALO ROCOCO ROMANO ROMERO ROTHKO RUBATO RUNSTO

•RO•••

AROIDS AROMAS AROUND AROUSE BROACH BROADS BRODIE BROGAN BROGUE BROILS BROKAW BROKEN BROKER BROLIN BROLLY BRONCO BRONCS BRONTE BRONZE BRONZY BROOCH BROODS BROODY BROOKE BROOKS BROOKY BROOMS BROOMY BROTHS BROWNE BROWNS BROWNY BROWSE CROAKS CROAKY CROATS CROCKS CROCUS CROFTS CRONES CRONIN CRONUS CRONYN CROOKS CROONS CROPUP CROSBY CROSSE CROTON CROUCH CROUPY CROUSE CROUTE CROWDS CROWED CROWER CROWNS CROZES DROGUE DROIDS DROITS DROLLS DROLLY DROMOI DROMOS DRONED DRONER DRONES DROOLS DROOLY DROOPS DROOPY DROPBY

DROPIN
DROPIT
DROVER
DROVES
DROWNS
DROWSE
DROWSY
ERODED
ERODES
EROICA
EROTIC
FROCKS
FROGGY
FROLIC
FRONDS
FRONTS
FROSTS
FROSTY
FROTHS
FROTHY
FROWNS
FROWZY
FROZEN
GROANS
GROATS
GROCER
GRODIN
GRODNO
GROGGY
GROINS
GROOMS
GROOVE
GROOVY
GROPED
GROPES
GROSSE
GROSSO
GROSZY
GROTON
GROTTO
GROTTY
GROUCH
GROUND
GROUPS
GROUSE
GROUTS
GROUTY
GROVEL
GROVER
GROVES
GROWER
GROWLS
GROWLY
GROWON
GROWTH
GROWUP
GROZNY
IROBOT
IRONED
IRONER
IRONIC
IRONON
KRONER
KRONOR
KRONUR
OROIDE
OROMOS
OROZCO
PROAMS
PROBED
PROBER
PROBES
PROCNE
PROEMS
PROFIT
PROLES
PROLIX
PROLOG
PROMOS
PROMPT
PRONGS
PRONTO
PROOFS
PROPEL
PROPER
PROPRE
PROPUP
PROSED
PROSER
PROSES
PROSIT
PROSKY
PROTAX
PROTEI
PROTEM
PROTON
PROUST
PROVED
PROVEN
PROVER
PROVES
PROWLS
PROWSE
PROZAC
TROCAR
TROCHE
TROGON
TROIKA
TROJAN
TROLLS
TROMPE
TROMPS
TROOPS
TROPES
TROPEZ
TROPHY
TROPIC
TROPPO
TROTHS
TROUGH
TROUPE
TROUTS
TROUVE
TROVES
TROWED
TROWEL
VROOMS
WRONGS

•R•O••
ARBORS
ARBOUR
ARDORS
ARDOUR
AREOLA
ARGOSY
ARGOTS
ARIOSE
ARIOSO
ARMORS
ARMORY
ARMOUR
ARNOLD
ARROBA
ARROWS
ARROYO
ARSONS
ARTOIS
BROOCH
BROODS
BROODY
BROOKE
BROOKS
BROOKY
BROOMS
BROOMY
BRYONY
CREOLE
CROOKS
CROONS
CRYOFF
DRHOOK
DROOLS
DROOLY
DROOPS
DROOPY
DRYOFF
DRYOUT
ERGOTS
ERROLL
ERRORS
GRIOTS
GROOMS
GROOVE
GROOVY
MRCOOL
MRMOTO
ORIOLE
ORLOPS
ORMOLU
ORMOND
PRIONS
PRIORI
PRIORS
PRIORY
PROOFS
TRIODE
TROOPS
TRYOUT
VROOMS

•R••O•
ARAGON
ARCCOS
ARCHON
BRASOV
BRAVOS
BRAZOS
BRETON
BRITON
BRYSON
CRAYON
CREDOS
CRESOL
CROTON
CRUSOE
DRAGON
DRAWON
DREWON
DRHOOK
DROMOI
DROMOS
DRYROT
ERENOW
FRIJOL
FRITOS
GREGOR
GREWON
GRISON
GROTON
GROWON
IROBOT
IRONON
KRAKOW
KRONOR
MRCOOL
ORATOR
OREGON
ORISON
OROMOS
PREYON
PRIMOS
PRISON
PROLOG
PROMOS
PROTON
TREMOR
TREVOR
TRICOT
TRIGON
TRIPOD
TRIPOS
TRITON
TROGON
TRYFOR
TRYLON

•R•••O
ARCARO
AREZZO
ARIOSO
ARISTO
ARROYO
ARTHRO
ARTURO
BRANDO
BRILLO
BRONCO
CRAMBO
CRANIO
CRISCO
CRISTO
CRYPTO
ERYNGO
FRANCO
FRESCO
FRESNO
FRISCO
GRAECO
GRASSO
GRINGO
GRODNO
GROSSO
GROTTO
MRMOTO
OROZCO
ORSINO
PRESTO
PRONTO
TRICHO
TROPPO

••RO••
ABROAD
ACROSS
ADROIT
AEROBE
AIROUT
APRONS
ARROBA
ARROWS
ARROYO
AURORA
AUROUS
BAROJA
BAROLO
BARONG
BARONS
BARONY
BUROAK
BYROAD
BYROTE
CAROBS
CAROLE
CAROLS
CAROMS
CARONI
CDROMS
CHROMA
CHROME
CHROMO
CHROMY
CHRONO
CORONA
DUROCS
ENROBE
ENROLL
ENROLS
ENROOT
EPROMS
ERROLL
ERRORS
EUROPA
EUROPE
FAROFF
FAROUK
FAROUT
FTROOP
FURORE
FURORS
GERONT
GYRONS
GYROSE
HAROLD
HEROES
HEROIC
HERONS
HURONS
INROAD
JEROME
JURORS
KAROSS
LAROSA
MAROON
MEROPE
MORONI
MORONS
MOROSE
NEROLI
PARODY
PAROLE
POROUS
SARODS
SARONG
SCRODS
SCROLL
SCROOP
SEROSA
SEROUS
SEROWS
SHROUD
SHROVE
SPROUT
STROBE
STRODE
STROKE
STROLL
STRONG
STROPS
STROUD
STROVE
TAROTS
THROAT
THROBS
THROES
THRONE
THRONG
THROVE
THROWN
THROWS
TOROID
TOROSE
TYRONE
UNROBE
UNROLL
UNROOT
UPROAR
UPROOT
UPROSE
VERONA
VOROUS
YUROKS
ZEROED
ZEROES
ZEROIN
ZEROTH

••R•O•
BARDOT
BARHOP
BARRON
BARROW
BARTOK
BARTON
BARYON
BOREON
BORROW
BORZOI
BURBOT
BURGOO
BURGOS
BURROS
BURROW
BURTON
CARBON
CARBOS
CARBOY
CARGOS
CARHOP
CARLOS
CARLOT
CARNOT
CARROL
CARROT
CARSON
CARTON
CERROS
CORDON
CURIOS
CURSOR
CURZON
DARROW
ENROOT
FARLOW
FARROW
FERVOR
FORGOT
FTROOP
FURROW
GARCON
GARSON
GORDON
GORGON
HARBOR
HARLOW
HARMON
HARPON
HARROW
HEREOF
HEREON
HERIOT
HERMON
HERZOG
HIREON
HORROR
HORTON
JARGON
JERBOA
KARPOV
KARROO
KERNOI
KERNOS
LARDON
LARGOS
LARSON
MARCOS
MARGOT
MARION
MARLON
MARMOT
MAROON
MARRON
MARROW
MERLON
MERLOT
MERTON
MIRROR
MORION
MORMON
MORROW
MORTON
MURROW
NARROW
NORTON
PARDON
PARLOR
PARROT
PARSON
PARTON
PERIOD
PERNOD
PERROT
PERSON
SARGON
SARGOS
SARTON
SCROOP
SERMON
SERVOS
SORROW
SORTOF
TARPON
TERROR
TORPOR
TORSOS
TURBOS
TURBOT
TURGOR
TURNON
UNROOT
UPROOT
VERDON
VERNON
VERSOS
VIREOS
WARGOD
WARHOL
WOREON
WORKON
YARROW
ZIRCON

••R••O
ADRENO
ARROYO
BAROLO
BARRIO
BORAXO
BORNEO
BURGOO
CARDIO
CARETO
CARUSO
CHROMO
CHRONO
CYRANO
DARETO
DIRIGO
DORADO
ENRICO
FOREGO
HERETO
JURADO
KARROO
LAREDO
MARIKO
MARINO
MERINO
MORENO
MORPHO
MURANO
PARETO
PERNIO
SERGIO
STRABO
STRATO
TERATO
TEREDO
TORERO
TORINO
TURNTO
VIRAGO

•••RO•
AGGROS
AGOROT
ANDROS
ANTRON
ASTROS
BARRON
BARROW
BEARON
BORROW
BURROS
BURROW
CARROL
CARROT
CERROS
CHARON
CHIRON
CHYRON
CITRON
CLAROS
CLOROX
CONROY
DACRON
DARROW
DELROY
DETROP
DOBROS
DRYROT
EPHRON
ESCROW
FAEROE
FARROW
FLYROD
FURROW
GUIROS
HADRON
HARROW
HEAROF
HEBRON
HEDRON
HIERON
HORROR
HOTROD
HYDROS
IMPROV
INAROW
INTROS
KARROO
KILROY
KUDROW
MACRON
MACROS
MARRON
MARROW
MATRON
METROS
MICRON
MICROS
MIRROR
MONROE
MORROW
MURROW
NARROW
NATRON
NEUROL
NEURON
NIMROD
NOIRON
OBERON
OCTROI
PARROT
PATROL
PATRON
PENROD
PERROT
PETROG
PETROL
PHAROS
POIROT
RAMROD
REPROS
RETROS
ROBROY
SHARON
SKIROS
SORROW
SPIROS
SPURON
STEROL
STYRON
TERROR
TIEROD
UNTROD
YARROW

•••R•O
ATERGO
AVERNO
BARRIO
CHARRO
CHURRO
DELRIO
EMBRYO
EVERSO
FLORIO
GEARTO
HAIRDO
JOURNO
KARROO
NEARTO
OPORTO
OVERDO
PUERTO
QUARTO
SHORTO
STEREO
STERNO
THERMO
WEIRDO

••••RO
ALLPRO
ANTERO
ARCARO
ARTHRO
ARTURO
AUSTRO
BISTRO
BOLERO
CAMARO
CASTRO
CENTRO
CHARRO
CHLORO
CHURRO
CICERO
DENDRO
DENIRO
DEXTRO
DINERO
ENDURO
ENTERO
FIGARO
FLUORO
GABBRO
GASTRO
HASBRO
HETERO
JETHRO
MADERO
MADURO
NEPHRO
NUMERO
OLDPRO
PICARO
PIETRO
PINERO
ROMERO
SCLERO
SIDERO
TORERO
VELCRO

R•P•••
RAPIDS
RAPIER
RAPINE
RAPINI
RAPPED
RAPPEE
RAPPEL
RAPPER
RAPTLY
RAPTOR
REPADS
REPAID
REPAIR
REPAND
REPAST
REPAVE
REPAYS
REPEAL
REPEAT
REPEGS
REPELS
REPENT
REPINE
REPINS
REPLAN
REPLAY
REPLOW
REPOLL
REPORT
REPOSE
REPOST
REPOTS
REPROS
REPUGN
REPUTE
RIPELY
RIPENS
RIPEST
RIPKEN
RIPLEY
RIPOFF
RIPOUT
RIPPED
RIPPER
RIPPLE
RIPPLY
RIPRAP
RIPSAW
RIPSUP
ROPEIN
ROPERS
ROPIER
ROPING
RUPAUL
RUPEES
RUPERT
RUPIAH

R••P••
RAIPUR
RAJPUT
RAMPED
RAPPED
RAPPEE
RAPPEL
RAPPER
RASPED
RASPER
REAPED
REAPER
REOPEN
RESPIN
RIMPLE
RIPPED
RIPPER
RIPPLE
RIPPLY
ROMPED
ROMPER
RSVPED
RUMPLE
RUMPLY
RUMPUS

R•••P•
RECAPS
RECIPE
RECOPY
REMAPS
REMOPS
RETAPE
RETAPS
RETOPS
RETYPE
RUNUPS

R••••P
RACKUP
RAGMOP
RAGTOP
RAKEUP
RANGUP
RAVEUP
REARUP
RECOUP
REDCAP
REDTOP
RESHIP
RESTUP
REVAMP
REVSUP
REWRAP
RIGSUP
RILEUP
RINGUP
RIPRAP
RIPSUP
ROLLUP
RUNGUP
RUNSUP

•RP•••
ARPENT
ORPHAN
ORPHIC
ORPINE

•R•P••
ARMPIT
CRAPES
CREPES
CRIPES
CROPUP
CRYPTO
CRYPTS
DRAPED
DRAPER
DRAPES
DRIPPY
DROPBY
DROPIN
DROPIT
DRUPES
ERUPTS
FRAPPE
FRYPAN
GRAPES
GRAPEY
GRAPHS
GRAPHY
GRAPPA
GRIPED
GRIPER
GRIPES
GRIPPE
GROPED
GROPES
PREPAY
PREPPY
PRIPET
PROPEL
PROPER
PROPRE
PROPUP
TRAPPY
TREPAN
TREPID
TRIPLE
TRIPLY
TRIPOD
TRIPOS
TRIPUP
TROPES
TROPEZ
TROPHY
TROPIC
TROPPO
WRAPUP

•R••P•
CRAMPS
CREEPS
CREEPY
CRIMPS
CRIMPY
CRISPS
CRISPY
CROUPY
DRIPPY
DROOPS
DROOPY
FRAPPE
FRUMPS
FRUMPY
GRAMPA
GRAMPS
GRAPPA
GRASPS
GRIPPE
GROUPS
GRUMPS
GRUMPY
IRRUPT
ORLOPS
PREPPY
PRIMPS
PROMPT
TRAMPS
TRAPPY
TROMPE
TROMPS
TROOPS
TROPPO
TROUPE
TRUMPS

•R•••P
CROPUP
DRAWUP
DREWUP
DRUMUP
GREWUP
GROWUP
PREAMP
PRENUP
PROPUP
TRICEP
TRIPUP
WRAPUP

••RP••
BURPED
CARPAL
CARPED
CARPEL
CARPER
CARPET
CARPUS
CORPUS
HARPED
HARPER
HARPON
KARPOV
MARPLE
MORPHO
MORPHS
MORPHY
MURPHY
PURPLE
PURPLY
TARPAN
TARPIT
TARPON
TORPID
TORPOR
TURPIN
WARPED

••R•P•
ABRUPT
CERIPH
ENRAPT
EUROPA
EUROPE
IRRUPT
MEROPE
PARAPH
PTRAPS
SCRAPE
SCRAPS
SCRIPS
SCRIPT
SERAPE
SERAPH
STRAPS
STRIPE
STRIPS
STRIPY
STROPS
SYRUPS
SYRUPY
TERAPH
THRIPS
UNRIPE

••R••P
BARHOP
BOREUP
BURLAP
BURNUP
CARHOP
CURLUP
EARLAP
FIREUP
FIRMUP
FTROOP
HARDUP
LARRUP
MARKUP
PERKUP
PIRRIP
SCRIMP
SCROOP
SHRIMP
STREEP
TOREUP
TURNIP
TURNUP
WARMUP
WORKUP

•••RP•
CHIRPS
CHIRPY
FOURPM
SCARPS
SHARPS
SHERPA
SLURPS
THORPE
THORPS
TWERPS
USURPS

•••R•P
AMERSP
BEARUP
BUMRAP
DETROP
DOMREP
ENTRAP
ENWRAP
FAIRUP
GEARUP
LARRUP
PAIRUP
PIRRIP
REARUP
REWRAP
RIPRAP
SATRAP
STIRUP
TEARUP
UNTRAP
UNWRAP

••••RP
ASHARP
BSHARP
CSHARP
DSHARP
ESCARP
ESHARP
FSHARP
GSHARP

R•Q•••
RAQUEL

R••Q••
RISQUE

•R•Q••
BRAQUE
IRAQIS

••RQ••
BARQUE
CIRQUE
MARQUE
TORQUE

RR••••
RRATED

R•R•••
RAREFY
RARELY
RAREST
RARIFY
RARING
RARITY
RERATE
REREAD
RERENT
RERUNS

R••R••
RAGRUG
RAHRAH
RAMROD
REARED
REARER
REARMS
REARUP
REDRAW
REDREW
REGRET
REPROS
RETRAL
RETRIM
RETROS
REWRAP
RIPRAP
ROARED
ROARER
ROBROY
ROURKE
RUBRIC

R•••R•
RACERS
RAKERS
RANDRY
RASERS
RATERS
RAVERS
RAZORS
REAIRS
REBARS
REBORN
REBURY
RECORD
RECORK
RECURS
REFERS
REFORM
REGARD
REHIRE
REMARK
REMORA
REPORT
RESORB
RESORT
RETARD
RETARS
RETIRE
RETORT
RETURN
REVERB
REVERE
REVERS
REVERT
REWARD
REWARM
REWIRE
REWORD
REWORK
RICERS
RIDERS
RIGORS
RISERS
RITARD
RIVERA
RIVERS
ROBERT
ROGERS

ROMERO
ROPERS
ROSARY
ROSTRA
ROTARY
ROTORS
ROVERS
ROWERS
RULERS
RUMORS
RUNDRY
RUPERT

R••••R

RACIER
RADNER
RAFTER
RAIDER
RAILER
RAINER
RAIPUR
RAISER
RANCOR
RANFOR
RANGER
RANKER
RANTER
RAPIER
RAPPER
RAPTOR
RASHER
RASPER
RASTER
RATEDR
RATHER
RATTER
READER
REALER
REAMER
REAPER
REARER
RECTOR
REDDER
REDFIR
REEFER
REHEAR
REINER
RENDER
RENOIR
RENTER
REPAIR
RESTER
RETEAR
RETOUR
REUTER
REVOIR
RHETOR
RHYMER
RICHER
RIFLER
RIGGER
RIGOUR
RIMIER
RINGER
RIOTER
RIPPER
RISKER
RITTER
ROAMER
ROARER
ROBBER
ROCKER
ROHMER
ROLLER
ROMPER
ROOFER
ROOMER
ROOTER
ROPIER
ROSIER
ROSTER
ROTTER
ROUSER
ROUTER
ROZZER
RUBBER
RUDDER
RUINER
RUMMER
RUMOUR
RUNFOR
RUNNER
RUTGER

•RR•••

ARRACK
ARRANT
ARRAYS
ARREAR
ARREST
ARRIBA
ARRIVE
ARROBA
ARROWS
ARROYO
ERRAND
ERRANT
ERRARE
ERRATA
ERRING
ERROLL
ERRORS
IRREAL
IRRUPT
ORRERY

•R•R••

ARARAT
CRURAL
DRYROT
DRYRUN

•R••R•

ARBORS
ARCARO
ARDORS
ARMORS
ARMORY
ARMURE
ARTERY
ARTHRO
ARTURO
BRIARD
BRIARS
BRIERS
BRIERY
CRIERS
CRYERS
DREARY
DRIERS
DRYERS
ERFURT
ERHARD
ERRARE
ERRORS
FRIARS
FRIARY
FRIERS
FRYERS
GRIGRI
ORDERS
ORDURE
ORNERY
ORRERY
PRIERS
PRIORI
PRIORS
PRIORY
PROPRE
TRIERS
URGERS

•R•••R

ARBOUR
ARCHER
ARDOUR
ARGUER
ARMOUR
ARREAR
ARTHUR
ARTIER
BRACER
BRAVER
BRAYER
BRAZER
BREUER
BREWER
BREYER
BROKER
BRUDER
CRATER
CRAVER
CROWER
CRUDER
DRAPER
DRAWER
DRIVER
DRONER
DROVER
ERASER
FRASER
FRAZER
GRADER
GRATER
GRAVER
GRAYER
GRAZER
GREGOR
GREYER
GRIPER
GROCER
GROVER
GROWER
IRATER
IRONER
KRAMER
KRATER
KRONER
KRONOR
KRONUR
KRUGER
ORATOR
PRATER
PRAYER
PREFER
PRETER
PREWAR
PRICER
PRIMER
PROBER
PROPER
PROSER
PROVER
PRUNER
TRACER
TRADER
TREMOR
TREVOR
TRITER
TROCAR
TRYFOR
WRITER

••RR••

BARRED
BARREL
BARREN
BARRES
BARRIE
BARRIO
BARRIS
BARRON
BARROW
BORROW
BURRED
BURROS
BURROW
CARREL
CARREY
CARRIE
CARROL
CARROT
CERROS
CIRRUS
CORRAL
CORREL
CURRED
DARREN
DARROW
DARRYL
DERRIS
DORRIT
FARRAH
FARRAR
FARROW
FERRER
FERRET
FERRIC
FERRIS
FURRED
FURROW
GARRET
HARRIS
HARROW
HORRID
HORROR
HURRAH
HURRAY
JARRAH
JARRED
KARRAS
KARROO
LARRUP
MARRED
MARRON
MARROW
MIRREN
MIRROR
MORRIS
MORROW
MURRAY
MURRES
MURREY
MURROW
MYRRHS
NARROW
NORRIS
PARRED
PARREL
PARRIS
PARROT
PERROT
PIRRIP
PURRED
PURRER
SIRRAH
SIRREE
SORREL
SORROW
SURREY
TARRED
TERRAN
TERRET
TERROR
TORRES
TORREY
TORRID
TURRET
WARRED
WARREN
YARROW

••R•R•

AIRARM
AIRDRY
AURORA
BARBRA
BORERS
CORERS
CURARE
CURERS
ERRARE
ERRORS
FARCRY
FARERS
FIRERS
FURORE
FURORS
GERARD
GIRARD
HARARE
HIRERS
JURORS
ORRERY
PARERS
PARURE
SARTRE
TORERO
WARCRY
WIRERS

••R••R

AIRIER
ARREAR
BARBER
BARCAR
BARKER
BARTER
BERBER
BIRDER
BORDER
BURGER
BURNER
BURSAR
CARDER
CAREER
CARPER
CARTER
CARVER
CORKER
CORNER
CURLER
CURSOR
CURTER
DARKER
DARNER
DARTER
DORMER
DURBAR
EARNER
EERIER
FARMER
FARRAR
FERBER
FERRER
FERVOR
FIRMER
FORCER
FORGER
FORKER
FORMER
GARNER
GARTER
GERBER
GIRDER
GORIER
HARBOR
HARDER
HARKER
HARPER
HERDER
HORNER
HORROR
HURLER
LARDER
LARGER
LERNER
MARKER
MARNER
MARTYR
MERCER
MERGER
MIRIER
MIRROR
MORTAR
MURDER
MURMUR
NURSER
OERTER
PARKER
PARLOR
PARSER
PERTER
PORKER
PORTER
PURRER
PURSER
SERVER
SIRDAR
SORTER
SPRIER
SPRYER
SURFER
TARTAR
TARTER
TERROR
TERSER
TORPOR
TURGOR
TURNER
UPROAR
VERGER
WARDER
WARIER
WARMER
WARNER
WERNER
WIRIER
WORKER
YORKER

•••RR•

BEURRE
BLURRY
CHARRO
CHERRY
CHIRRS
CHURRO
CHURRS
FLURRY
GHARRY
GUERRE
KNARRY
PIERRE
QUARRY
SCARRY
SCURRY
SHERRY
SHIRRS
SIERRA
SKERRY
SKIRRS
SLURRY
SPERRY
SPURRY
STARRY
STORRS
TIERRA
WHERRY
WHIRRS

•••R•R

ADORER
BEARER
DEARER
DOURER
FAIRER
FARRAR
FEARER
FERRER
HEARER
HORROR
JEERER
LEERER
LEHRER
MIRROR
NEARER
POORER
POURER
PURRER
REARER
ROARER
SCARER
SCORER
SHARER
SHIRER
SNORER
SOARER
SOURER
SPARER
STARER
STORER
TERROR
TOURER
USURER
WEARER

••••RR

LAMARR

RS••••

RSVPED

R•S•••

RASCAL
RASERS
RASHAD
RASHER
RASHES
RASHID
RASHLY
RASING
RASPED
RASPER
RASSLE
RASTER
RESALE
RESALT
RESAND
RESAWN
RESAWS
RESCUE
RESEAL
RESEAT
RESEAU
RESECT
RESEDA
RESEED
RESEEN
RESEES
RESELL
RESEND
RESENT
RESETS
RESEWN
RESEWS
RESHES
RESHIP
RESHOD
RESHOE
RESHOT
RESIDE
RESIGN
RESILE
RESING
RESINS
RESINY
RESIST
RESNIK
RESODS
RESOLD
RESOLE
RESORB
RESORT
RESPIN
RESTED
RESTER
RESTON
RESTUP
RESULT
RESUME
RISERS
RISING
RISKED
RISKER
RISQUE
ROSARY
ROSCOE
ROSEAU
ROSIER
ROSILY
ROSINS
ROSINY
ROSITA
ROSTER
ROSTOV
ROSTRA
RUSHED
RUSHEE
RUSHES
RUSKIN
RUSSET
RUSSIA
RUSTED
RUSTIC
RUSTLE

R••S••

RAISED
RAISER
RAISES
RAISIN
RAMSAY
RAMSES
RAMSEY
RAMSON
RANSOM
RASSLE
RATSON
REASON
REDSEA
REDSOX
REESES
REUSED
REUSES
REVSON
REVSUP
RHESUS
RIDSOF
RIGSUP
RIMSKY
RINSED
RINSES
RIPSAW
RIPSUP
ROASTS
ROBSON
ROOSTS
ROUSED
ROUSER
ROUSES
ROUSTS
RUBSIN
RUNSAT
RUNSIN
RUNSON
RUNSTO
RUNSUP
RUSSET
RUSSIA

R•••S•

RADISH
RAKISH
RAMOSE
RAREST
RAVISH
RAWEST
RAWISH
RECAST
RECESS
RECUSE
REFUSE
REHASH
RELISH
RELIST
REMISE
REMISS
REPAST
REPOSE
REPOST
RESIST
RETEST
REVISE
REWASH
RIBOSE
RIFEST
RIMOSE
RIPEST
ROBUST
RUDEST
RUGOSE

R••••S

RABBIS
RABIES
RACERS
RACHIS
RACONS
RADIOS
RADIUS
RAINES
RAISES
RAJAHS
RAKERS
RAMETS
RAMIES
RAMOUS
RAMSES
RANEES
RANGES
RANIDS
RAPIDS
RASERS
RASHES
RATELS
RATERS
RATIOS
RAVELS
RAVENS
RAVERS
RAYONS
RAZORS
RAZZES
REACTS
REAIMS
REAIRS
REALES
REALMS
REARMS
REATAS
REBAGS
REBARS
REBBES
REBECS
REBELS
REBIDS
REBUTS
RECAPS
RECESS
RECONS
RECTOS
RECTUS
RECURS
REDOES
REDUBS
REDYES
REESES
REEVES
REFERS
REFITS
REGIUS
REHABS
REHEMS
REIGNS
REINAS
REINKS
REKEYS
RELAYS
RELETS
RELICS
RELIES
REMANS
REMAPS
REMISS
REMITS
REMOPS
REMOWS
RENEWS
RENNES
REOILS
REPADS
REPAYS
REPEGS
REPELS
REPINS
REPOTS
REPROS
RERUNS
RESAWS
RESEES
RESETS
RESEWS
RESHES
RESINS
RESODS
RETAGS
RETAPS
RETARS
RETIES
RETOPS
RETOWS
RETROS
REUNES
REUSES
REVELS
REVERS
REVETS
REVUES
REWEDS
REWINS
RHAMES
RHESUS
RHEUMS
RHINOS
RHODES
RHOMBS
RHUMBS
RHYMES
RIATAS
RICERS
RICHES
RIDERS
RIDGES
RIFLES
RIGHTS
RIGORS
RILLES
RINSES
RIOJAS
RIPENS
RISERS
RIVALS
RIVERS
RIVETS
RIYALS
ROASTS
ROBINS
ROBLES
ROBOTS
RODEOS
ROGERS
ROGUES
ROLEOS
ROMANS
ROMEOS
RONDOS
ROOSTS
ROPERS
ROSINS
ROTORS
ROUGES
ROUGHS
ROUNDS
ROUSES
ROUSTS
ROUTES
ROVERS
ROWELS
ROWENS
ROWERS
ROYALS
RUANAS
RUBENS
RUBIES
RUBLES
RUCHES
RUCKUS
RUFOUS
RULERS
RUMBAS
RUMENS
RUMORS
RUMPUS
RUNINS
RUNONS
RUNUPS
RUPEES
RUSHES

•RS•••

ARSENE
ARSONS
ERSATZ
ORSINO
URSIDS
URSINE
URSULA

•R•S••

ARISEN
ARISES
ARISTA
ARISTO
BRASHY
BRASOV
BRASSY
BRUSHY
BRYSON
CRESOL
CRESTS
CRISCO
CRISES
CRISIS
CRISPS
CRISPY
CRISTO
CROSBY
CROSSE
CRUSES
CRUSOE
CRUSTS
CRUSTY
DRESSY
ERASED
ERASER
ERASES
ERESTU
FRASER
FRESCA
FRESCO
FRESNO
FRISCO
FRISEE
FRISES
FRISKS
FRISKY
FROSTS
FROSTY
GRASPS
GRASSO
GRASSY
GRISLY
GRISON
GRISTS
GROSSE
GROSSO
GROSZY
IRISES
IRISIN
KRASNY
KRESGE
ORISON
ORISSA
PRASES
PRESET
PRESTO
PRISMS
PRISON
PRISSY
PROSED
PROSER
PROSES
PROSIT
PROSKY
TRASHY
TRISHA
TRISTE
TRUSTS
TRUSTY
TRYSTS
URUSES
WRASSE
WRESTS
WRISTS

•R••S•

ARGOSY
ARIOSE
ARIOSO
ARLISS
ARNESS
AROUSE
ARREST
ARTIST
BRAISE
BRASSY
BRATSK
BREAST
BROWSE
BRUISE
CREASE
CREASY
CREUSA
CROSSE
CROUSE
CRUISE
DRESSY
DRIEST
DROWSE
DROWSY
DRYEST
ERNEST
FRAISE
FREEST
GRASSO
GRASSY
GREASE
GREASY
GRILSE
GROSSE
GROSSO
GROUSE
IRTYSH
ORELSE
ORISSA
PRAISE
PRIEST
PRISSY
PROUST
PROWSE
TRUEST
TRUISM
URALSK
WRASSE
WRIEST
WRYEST

•R•••S

ARAMIS
ARBORS
ARCCOS
ARCHES
ARDEBS
ARDORS
ARECAS
ARENAS
ARETES
ARGOTS
ARGUES
ARISES
ARLISS
ARMETS
ARMIES
ARMORS
ARNESS
AROIDS
AROMAS
ARRAYS
ARROWS
ARSONS
ARTELS
ARTOIS
ARYANS
BRACES
BRACTS
BRAHMS
BRAIDS
BRAILS
BRAINS
BRAKES
BRANDS
BRANTS
BRAVAS
BRAVES
BRAVOS
BRAWLS
BRAZES
BRAZOS
BREADS
BREAKS
BREAMS
BREEDS
BRENTS
BREVES
BREVIS
BRIANS
BRIARS
BRIBES
BRICKS
BRIDES
BRIEFS
BRIERS
BRIGGS
BRILLS
BRINES
BRINGS
BRINKS
BROADS
BROILS
BRONCS
BROODS
BROOKS
BROOMS
BROTHS
BROWNS
BRUGES
BRUINS
BRUITS
BRULES
BRUMES
BRUNTS
BRUTES
BRUTUS
BRUXES
CRACKS
CRAFTS
CRAKES
CRAMPS
CRANES
CRANKS
CRAPES
CRATES
CRAVES
CRAWLS
CRAZES
CREAKS
CREAMS
CREDOS
CREEDS
CREEKS
CREELS
CREEPS
CREMES
CREPES
CRESTS
CRICKS
CRIERS
CRIMES
CRIMPS
CRIPES
CRISES
CRISIS
CRISPS
CROAKS
CROATS
CROCKS
CROCUS
CROFTS
CRONES
CRONUS
CROOKS
CROONS
CROWDS
CROWNS
CROZES
CRUCES
CRUETS
CRUMBS
CRUSES
CRUSTS
CRUXES
CRYERS
CRYPTS
DRAFTS
DRAILS
DRAINS
DRAKES
DRAMAS
DRAPES
DRAWLS
DREADS
DREAMS
DRIERS
DRIFTS
DRILLS
DRINGS
DRINKS
DRIVES
DROIDS
DROITS
DROLLS
DROMOS
DRONES
DROOLS
DROOPS
DROVES
DROWNS
DRUIDS
DRUPES
DRUZES
DRYADS
DRYERS
ERASES
EREBUS
ERECTS
ERGOTS
ERINYS
ERODES
ERRORS
ERUCTS
ERUPTS
FRACAS
FRAMES
FRANCS
FRANKS
FRAUDS
FREAKS
FRIARS
FRIERS
FRILLS
FRISES
FRISKS
FRITOS
FROCKS
FRONDS
FRONTS
FROSTS
FROTHS
FROWNS
FRUITS
FRUMPS
FRYERS

GRACES
GRADES
GRADUS
GRAFTS
GRAILS
GRAINS
GRAMAS
GRAMPS
GRANDS
GRANTS
GRAPES
GRAPHS
GRASPS
GRATES
GRATIS
GRAVES
GRAZES
GREATS
GREBES
GREEKS
GREENS
GREETS
GRIEFS
GRIFTS
GRILLS
GRIMES
GRINDS
GRIOTS
GRIPES
GRISTS
GROANS
GROATS
GROINS
GROOMS
GROPES
GROUPS
GROUTS
GROVES
GROWLS
GRUELS
GRUMPS
GRUNTS
IRANIS
IRAQIS
IRENES
IRIDES
IRISES
KRAALS
KRAITS
ORACHS
ORALES
ORANGS
ORANTS
ORATES
ORBITS
ORDERS
OREADS
ORGANS
ORGIES
ORIBIS
ORIELS
ORINGS
ORLOPS
OROMOS
ORTLES
ORYXES
PRANGS
PRANKS
PRASES
PRATES
PRAWNS
PRAXES
PRAXIS
PRECIS

PREENS
PRICES
PRICKS
PRIDES
PRIERS
PRIMES
PRIMOS
PRIMPS
PRIMUS
PRINKS
PRINTS
PRIONS
PRIORS
PRISMS
PRIZES
PROAMS
PROBES
PROEMS
PROLES
PROMOS
PRONGS
PROOFS
PROSES
PROVES
PROWLS
PRUDES
PRUNES
TRACES
TRACKS
TRACTS
TRADES
TRAILS
TRAINS
TRAITS
TRAMPS
TRAVES
TRAVIS
TRAWLS
TREADS
TREATS
TRENDS
TRIADS
TRIALS
TRIBES
TRICES
TRICKS
TRIERS
TRIKES
TRILLS
TRINES
TRIPOS
TROLLS
TROMPS
TROOPS
TROPES
TROTHS
TROUTS
TROVES
TRUCES
TRUCKS
TRUMPS
TRUNKS
TRUSTS
TRUTHS
TRYSTS
URAEUS
URANUS
URGERS
URIALS
URSIDS
URUSES
VROOMS
WRACKS
WRATHS

WREAKS
WRECKS
WRESTS
WRINGS
WRISTS
WRITES
WRONGS

••RS••

AIRSAC
BORSCH
BURSAE
BURSAL
BURSAR
BURSAS
BURSES
BURSTS
CARSON
CORSET
CURSED
CURSES
CURSOR
DORSAL
DORSET
DORSEY
DORSUM
FIRSTS
GARSON
GORSES
HERSEY
HIRSCH
HORSED
HORSES
HORSEY
JERSEY
KARSTS
KERSEE
KERSEY
KIRSCH
LARSEN
LARSON
MARSHA
MARSHY
MERSEY
MORSEL
NURSED
NURSER
NURSES
PARSEC
PARSED
PARSEE
PARSER
PARSES
PARSON
PERSIA
PERSON
PURSED
PURSER
PURSES
PURSUE
TARSAL
TARSUS
TERSER
TORSOS
VERSED
VERSES
VERSOS
VERSTS
VERSUS
WARSAW
WORSEN
WORSTS
WURSTS

••R•S•

ACROSS
AFRESH
AORIST
ARREST
ATREST
ATRISK
BAREST
BARISH
CARESS
CARUSO
CERISE
CERUSE
CHRISM
CURTSY
DIREST
DURESS
EGRESS
FOREST
GARISH
GYROSE
HARASS
HERESY
INRUSH
JURIST
KAROSS
LAROSA
LYRIST
MARISA
MARISH
MARIST
MEREST
MORASS
MOROSE
OGRESS
OGRISH
ONRUSH
PARISH
PERISH
PERUSE
PHRASE
PUREST
PURISM
PURIST
QURUSH
RAREST
SEROSA
SOREST
STRASS
STRESS
SUREST
TERESA
THRASH
THRESH
THRUSH
THRUST
TOROSE
UNREST
UPRISE
UPROSE
UPRUSH
VARESE
VERISM
YAREST

••R••S

ABRAMS
ACROSS
AERIES
AFRITS
AGREES
AIRBUS
AORTAS
APRONS

ARRAYS
ARROWS
ATREUS
AUREUS
AUROUS
BARGES
BARNES
BARONS
BARRES
BARRIS
BERETS
BERTHS
BIRTHS
BOREAS
BORERS
BURGAS
BURGHS
BURGOS
BURIES
BURINS
BURROS
BURSAS
BURSES
BURSTS
BYRNES
CARATS
CARBOS
CARESS
CARETS
CARGOS
CARIBS
CARIES
CARLOS
CARNES
CAROBS
CAROLS
CAROMS
CARPUS
CARTES
CARVES
CDROMS
CEREUS
CERROS
CIRCUS
CIRRUS
CORALS
CORERS
CORGIS
CORPUS
CORTES
CORVES
CURERS
CURIOS
CURSES
CURTIS
CURVES
DARIUS
DERMIS
DERRIS
DIRGES
DORAGS
DORCAS
DORIES
DURESS
DUROCS
EGRESS
EGRETS
ENROLS
EPROMS
ERRORS
EYRIES
FARADS
FARCES
FARERS

FERGUS
FERIAS
FERRIS
FIRERS
FIRSTS
FIRTHS
FORAYS
FORBES
FORCES
FORGES
FORTAS
FORTES
FORUMS
FURIES
FURORS
FURZES
GARTHS
GERAHS
GIRTHS
GORALS
GORGES
GORSES
GYRONS
HARASS
HAREMS
HARRIS
HERMES
HEROES
HERONS
HIRERS
HORDES
HORSES
HURONS
JORUMS
JURATS
JURIES
JURORS
KARATS
KAROSS
KARRAS
KARSTS
KERMES
KERMIS
KERNOS
KORATS
LARAMS
LARGES
LARGOS
LARVAS
LORIES
LYRICS
MARCOS
MARCUS
MARGES
MARIUS
MERGES
MERITS
MORALS
MORASS
MORAYS
MORELS
MORONS
MORPHS
MORRIS
MURALS
MURRES
MYRRHS
NEREIS
NEREUS
NERVES
NORIAS
NORRIS
NORTHS
NURSES

OGRESS
PARENS
PARERS
PARKAS
PARNIS
PARRIS
PARSES
PARVIS
PERILS
POROUS
PTRAPS
PUREES
PURGES
PURSES
RERUNS
SARANS
SARDIS
SARGES
SARGOS
SARODS
SCRAGS
SCRAMS
SCRAPS
SCREES
SCREWS
SCRIMS
SCRIPS
SCRODS
SCRUBS
SCRUMS
SERACS
SERAIS
SERGES
SERIES
SERIFS
SERINS
SEROUS
SEROWS
SERUMS
SERVES
SERVOS
SHREDS
SHREWS
SHRUBS
SHRUGS
SIRENS
SIRIUS
SPRAGS
SPRATS
SPRAYS
SPREES
SPRIGS
SPRITS
SPRUES
STRADS
STRAPS
STRASS
STRAUS
STRAWS
STRAYS
STRESS
STREWS
STRIPS
STROPS
STRUMS
STRUTS
SURAHS
SURGES
SYRUPS
TARGES
TAROTS
TARSUS
TEREUS
TERNES

THREES
THRIPS
THROBS
THROES
THROWS
THRUMS
TORAHS
TORIES
TORRES
TORSOS
TORTES
TURBOS
TURVES
UNRIGS
VARIES
VARNAS
VERBIS
VERGES
VERSES
VERSOS
VERSTS
VERSUS
VERVES
VIREOS
VIRTUS
VOROUS
WIRERS
WORLDS
WORSTS
WORTHS
WURSTS
XERXES
YERKES
YUROKS
ZEROES
ZORILS

•••RS•

AMERSP
AVERSE
BOURSE
COARSE
COURSE
EVERSO
HEARST
HOARSE
SMERSH
SPARSE
THIRST
THYRSI

•••R•S

ABORTS
ACARUS
ACORNS
ADORES
ADORNS
AGGROS
AGORAS
ALARMS
ALERTS
ANDRES
ANDROS
ANTRES
ASTROS
AVERTS
AWARDS
AZORES
BAIRNS
BARRES
BARRIS
BEARDS
BGIRLS
BLARES

BLURBS
BLURTS
BOARDS
BURROS
CADRES
CAIRNS
CAPRIS
CEORLS
CERROS
CHARMS
CHARTS
CHIRPS
CHIRRS
CHORDS
CHORES
CHORUS
CHURLS
CHURNS
CHURRS
CIRRUS
CITRUS
CLAROS
CLERKS
CLORIS
COBRAS
COURTS
CYPRUS
DEBRAS
DEBRIS
DERRIS
DMARKS
DOBRAS
DOBROS
DWARFS
EAGRES
ELBRUS
ENURES
EPIRUS
ESDRAS
EVERTS
EXERTS
EXTRAS
EXURBS
FERRIS
FIBRES
FIORDS
FJORDS
FLARES
FLIRTS
FLORAS
FLORES
GENRES
GLARES
GNARLS
GOURDS
GUARDS
GUIROS
HARRIS
HEARTS
HOARDS
HOURIS
HUBRIS
HYDRAS
HYDROS
ICARUS
INDRIS
INGRES
INTROS
INURES
JAURES
KARRAS
KAURIS
KNURLS
KUKRIS

LAIRDS
LEARNS
LIBRIS
LITRES
LIVRES
MACROS
MADRAS
MADRES
MAORIS
METRES
METROS
MICROS
MITRES
MOIRES
MORRIS
MOURNS
MUDRAS
MURRES
MYRRHS
NACRES
NAIRAS
NITRES
NORRIS
OCHRES
OPERAS
OSIRIS
OZARKS
PADRES
PARRIS
PEARLS
PHAROS
QUARKS
QUARTS
QUERNS
QUIRES
QUIRKS
QUIRTS
REARMS
REPROS
RETROS
SABRAS
SABRES
SCARES
SCARFS
SCARPS
SCORES
SCORNS
SEVRES
SHARDS
SHARES
SHARKS
SHARPS
SHIRES
SHIRKS
SHIRRS
SHIRTS
SHORES
SHORTS
SKIRLS
SKIROS
SKIRRS
SKIRTS
SKORTS
SLURPS
SMARTS
SMIRKS
SMURFS
SNARES
SNARLS
SNORES
SNORTS
SOARES
SPARES
SPARKS

SPIRES
SPIROS
SPORES
SPORTS
SPURNS
SPURTS
STARES
STARTS
STERES
STERNS
STIRKS
STORES
STORKS
STORMS
STORRS
SUDRAS
SUTRAS
SWARDS
SWARMS
SWIRLS
SWORDS
TAURUS
TAYRAS
TBIRDS
TETRAS
TETRIS
THERES
THERMS
THIRDS
THORNS
THORPS
TIARAS
TIGRIS
TITRES
TORRES
TSURIS
TWERPS
TWIRLS
ULTRAS
UMBRAS
UNARMS
USURPS
UTURNS
WALRUS
WHARFS
WHERES
WHIRLS
WHIRRS
WHORLS
YEARNS
ZAIRES
ZEBRAS

••••RS

ABHORS
ACTORS
ADDERS
AIDERS
AILERS
ALDERS
ALTARS
ALTERS
AMBERS
AMEERS
AMOURS
ANGERS
ARBORS
ARDORS
ARMORS
ASKERS
ASTERS
ATTARS
AUGERS
AUGURS

BAKERS
BALERS
BIKERS
BITERS
BLEARS
BONERS
BORERS
BOWERS
BOXERS
BOYARS
BRIARS
BRIERS
BUYERS
CABERS
CAGERS
CANERS
CAPERS
CATERS
CAVERS
CEDARS
CHAIRS
CHEERS
CHIRRS
CHOIRS
CHURRS
CIDERS
CIGARS
CITERS
CLEARS
CODERS
COLORS
COMERS
COOERS
CORERS
COVERS
COWERS
CRIERS
CRYERS
CURERS
CYDERS
DATERS
DEBARS
DECORS
DEFERS
DEMURS
DETERS
DICERS
DINARS
DINERS
DIVERS
DIYERS
DOLORS
DONORS
DOSERS
DOWERS
DOZERS
DRIERS
DRYERS
EATERS
EDGARS
EDGERS
EELERS
EIDERS
ELDERS
ELVERS
EMBERS
EMEERS
ENDERS
ENTERS
EPHORS
ERRORS
ESKERS
ESTERS
ETHERS

FAKERS
FAKIRS
FARERS
FAVORS
FEMURS
FEVERS
FIBERS
FIFERS
FILERS
FIRERS
FIVERS
FIXERS
FLAIRS
FLEERS
FLIERS
FLOORS
FLOURS
FLYERS
FOYERS
FRIARS
FRIERS
FRYERS
FURORS
GAPERS
GATERS
GATORS
GIBERS
GIVERS
GLAIRS
GLUERS
GOFERS
GONERS
HALERS
HATERS
HAVERS
HAZERS
HEWERS
HEXERS
HIDERS
HIKERS
HIRERS
HOMERS
HONORS
HOPERS
HOVERS
HUMORS
IDLERS
INCURS
INFERS
INKERS
JAPERS
JIVERS
JOKERS
JURORS
KAFIRS
KEFIRS
KHMERS
KITERS
LABORS
LACERS
LADERS
LAGERS
LAKERS
LASERS
LAVERS
LAYERS
LEMURS
LEVERS
LIFERS
LIGERS
LINERS
LITERS
LIVERS
LONERS

LOPERS
LOSERS
LOVERS
LOWERS
LUGERS
MAJORS
MAKERS
MANORS
MASERS
MATERS
MAYORS
MAZERS
MESSRS
METERS
MILERS
MIMERS
MINERS
MINORS
MISERS
MITERS
MIXERS
MOHURS
MOLARS
MOPERS
MOTORS
MOVERS
MOWERS
MOYERS
MUSERS
NABORS
NADIRS
NAMERS
NEVERS
NFLERS
NHLERS
NINERS
NITERS
NOTERS
OATERS
OCCURS
OCHERS
ODOURS
OFFERS
OGLERS
OILERS
ORDERS
OSCARS
OSIERS
OTHERS
OTTERS
OWNERS
PACERS
PAGERS
PAMIRS
PAPERS
PARERS
PATERS
PAVERS
PAWERS
PAYERS
PETERS
PIKERS
PIPERS
PLIERS
POKERS
POLERS
POSERS
POWERS
PRIERS
PRIORS
RACERS
RAKERS
RASERS
RATERS

RAVERS
RAZORS
REAIRS
REBARS
RECURS
REFERS
RETARS
REVERS
RICERS
RIDERS
RIGORS
RISERS
RIVERS
ROGERS
ROPERS
ROTORS
ROVERS
ROWERS
RULERS
RUMORS
SABERS
SAKERS
SAPORS
SATYRS
SAVERS
SAVORS
SAYERS
SCOURS
SEDERS
SENORS
SEVERS
SEWERS
SHEARS
SHEERS
SHIRRS
SHOERS
SIDERS
SITARS
SIXERS
SIZERS
SKIERS
SKIRRS
SMEARS
SNEERS
SOBERS
SOEURS
SOLARS
SOLERS
SOMERS
SOPORS
SOWERS
SOXERS
SPEARS
SPIERS
SPOORS
STAIRS
STEERS
STORRS
SUGARS
SUPERS
SWEARS
TABORS
TAKERS
TALERS
TAMERS
TAPERS
TAPIRS
TASERS
TATARS
TATERS
TAXERS
TENORS
THEIRS
TIGERS

TILERS
TIMERS
TITERS
TONERS
TOPERS
TOTERS
TOWERS
TRIERS
TUBERS
TUDORS
TUNERS
TUTORS
TYPERS
UDDERS
UIGURS
ULCERS
UMBERS
UNBARS
UPPERS
URGERS
USHERS
UTTERS
VAPORS
VEXERS
VICARS
VIGORS
VIPERS
VISORS
VOTERS
VOWERS
WADERS
WAFERS
WAGERS
WALERS
WANERS
WATERS
WAVERS
WAXERS
WHIRRS
WIPERS
WIRERS
WOOERS

R•T•••

RATEDG
RATEDR
RATEDX
RATELS
RATERS
RATHER
RATIFY
RATINE
RATING
RATION
RATIOS
RATITE
RATLIN
RATSON
RATTAN
RATTED
RATTER
RATTLE
RATTLY
RETAGS
RETAIL
RETAIN
RETAKE
RETAPE
RETAPS
RETARD
RETARS
RETEAR
RETELL
RETENE

RETEST
RETIAL
RETIED
RETIES
RETILE
RETIME
RETINA
RETIRE
RETOLD
RETOOK
RETOOL
RETOPS
RETORT
RETOUR
RETOWS
RETRAL
RETRIM
RETROS
RETTON
RETUNE
RETURN
RETYPE
RITARD
RITTER
RITUAL
ROTARY
ROTATE
ROTGUT
ROTHKO
ROTINI
ROTORS
ROTTED
ROTTEN
ROTTER
ROTUND
RUTGER
RUTILE
RUTTAN
RUTTED

R••T••

RAFTED
RAFTER
RAGTAG
RAGTOP
RANTED
RANTER
RAPTLY
RAPTOR
RASTER
RATTAN
RATTED
RATTER
RATTLE
RATTLY
REATAS
RECTOR
RECTOS
RECTUS
REDTAG
REDTOP
RENTAL
RENTED
RENTER
RESTED
RESTER
RESTON
RESTUP
RETTON
REUTER
RHETOR
RHYTHM
RHYTON
RIATAS
RIFTED
RIOTED
RIOTER
RITTER
ROOTED
ROOTER
ROSTER
ROSTOV
ROSTRA
ROTTED
ROTTEN
ROTTER
ROUTED
ROUTER
ROUTES
RRATED
RUSTED
RUSTIC
RUSTLE
RUTTAN
RUTTED

R•••T•

RABATO
RAMATE
RAMETS
RARITY
RATITE
REACTS
REALTY
REBATE
REBUTS
RECITE
REDATE
REFITS
REFUTE
RELATE
RELETS
REMITS
REMOTE
RENATA
RENOTE
REPOTS
REPUTE
RERATE
RESETS
REVETS
RIALTO
RIGHTO
RIGHTS
RIGHTY
RIVETS
ROASTS
ROBOTS
ROOSTS
ROSITA
ROTATE
ROUSTS
RUBATI
RUBATO
RUGATE
RUNSTO

R••••T

RABBET
RABBIT
RACKET
RAGOUT
RAILAT
RAJPUT
RAMJET
RANOUT
RAREST
RAWEST
REBENT
REBOLT
REBOOT
RECANT
RECAST
RECENT
RECOAT
REDACT
REDANT
REDHAT
REDHOT
REEDIT
REGENT
REGLET
REGNAT
REGRET
REHEAT
REJECT
RELENT
RELICT
RELIST
RELUCT
REMELT
RENNET
REPAST
REPEAT
REPENT
REPORT
REPOST
RERENT
RESALT
RESEAT
RESECT
RESENT
RESHOT
RESIST
RESORT
RESULT
RETEST
RETORT
REVERT
REVOLT
REXCAT
RIDENT
RIFEST
RILLET
RIPEST
RIPOUT
ROBERT
ROBUST
ROCHET
ROCKET
RODENT
ROTGUT
RUBOUT
RUDEST
RUNLET
RUNOUT
RUNSAT
RUPERT
RUSSET

•RT•••

ARTELS
ARTERY
ARTFUL
ARTGUM
ARTHRO
ARTHUR
ARTIER
ARTILY
ARTIST
ARTOIS
ARTURO
IRTYSH
ORTEGA
ORTLES
URTEXT

•R•T••

ARCTAN
ARCTIC
ARETES
ARETHA
BRATSK
BRATTY
BRETON
BRITON
BROTHS
BRUTAL
BRUTES
BRUTUS
CRATED
CRATER
CRATES
CRETAN
CRETIN
CRITIC
CROTON
CRUTCH
EROTIC
FRETTY
FRITOS
FROTHS
FROTHY
FRUTTI
GRATED
GRATER
GRATES
GRATIA
GRATIN
GRATIS
GRETEL
GRETNA
GRITTY
GROTON
GROTTO
GROTTY
IRATER
KRATER
ORATED
ORATES
ORATOR
PRATED
PRATER
PRATES
PRETAX
PRETER
PRETTY
PROTAX
PROTEI
PROTEM
PROTON
RRATED
TRITER
TRITON
TROTHS
TRUTHS
WRATHS
WRATHY
WRETCH
WRITER
WRITES
WRITHE
XRATED

•R••T•

ARGOTS
ARISTA
ARISTO
ARMETS
ARNETT
BRACTS
BRANTS
BRATTY
BREATH
BRENTS
BRONTE
BRUITS
BRUNTS
CRAFTS
CRAFTY
CREATE
CRESTS
CRISTO
CROATS
CROFTS
CROUTE
CRUETS
CRUSTS
CRUSTY
CRYPTO
CRYPTS
DRAFTS
DRAFTY
DRIFTS
DRIFTY
DROITS
ERECTS
ERESTU
ERGATE
ERGOTS
ERRATA
ERSATZ
ERUCTS
ERUPTS
FRETTY
FRONTS
FROSTS
FROSTY
FRUITS
FRUITY
FRUTTI
GRAFTS
GRANTS
GREATS
GREETS
GRIFTS
GRIOTS
GRISTS
GRITTY
GROATS
GROTTO
GROTTY
GROUTS
GROUTY
GROWTH
GRUNTS
KRAITS
KRANTZ
MRMOTO
ORANTS
ORBITS
ORGATE
ORNATE
ORNITH
PRESTO
PRETTY
PRINTS
PRONTO
TRACTS
TRAITS
TREATS
TREATY
TRISTE
TROUTS
TRUSTS
TRUSTY
TRYSTS
WRAITH
WREATH
WRESTS
WRISTS

•R•••T

ARAFAT
ARARAT
ARDENT
ARENDT
ARGENT
ARIGHT
ARMLET
ARMPIT
ARNETT
ARPENT
ARRANT
ARREST
ARTIST
BRANDT
BREAST
BRECHT
BREVET
BRIGHT
BRUNET
BRYANT
CRAVAT
CREDIT
DREAMT
DRIEST
DROPIT
DRYEST
DRYOUT
DRYROT
ERFURT
ERNEST
ERRANT
FREEST
FRIGHT
GRABAT
GRIVET
IROBOT
IRRUPT
ORGEAT
ORIENT
PRESET
PRIEST
PRIPET
PRIVET
PROFIT
PROMPT
PROSIT
PROUST
TRICOT
TRIJET
TRIVET
TRUANT
TRUEST
TRYOUT
URGENT
URTEXT
WRIEST
WRIGHT
WRYEST

••RT••

AORTAE
AORTAL
AORTAS
AORTIC
BARTAB
BARTER
BARTOK
BARTON
BERTHA
BERTHS
BERTIE
BIRTHS
BURTON
CARTED
CARTEL
CARTER
CARTES
CARTON
CERTIF
CORTES
CORTEX
CORTEZ
CURTER
CURTIN
CURTIS
CURTIZ
CURTLY
CURTSY
DARTED
DARTER
EARTHA
EARTHY
FIRTHS
FORTAS
FORTES
GARTER
GARTHS
GERTIE
GIRTED
GIRTHS
HORTON
HURTLE
KIRTLE
MARTEL
MARTEN
MARTHA
MARTIN
MARTYR
MERTON
MORTAL
MORTAR
MORTON
MYRTLE
NORTHS
NORTON
OERTER
PARTED
PARTLY
PARTON
PERTER
PERTLY
PORTAL
PORTED
PORTER
PORTIA
PORTLY
SARTON
SARTRE
SORTED
SORTER
SORTIE
SORTOF
SURTAX
TARTAN
TARTAR
TARTER
TARTLY
TORTES
TURTLE
VERTEX
VIRTUE
VIRTUS
VORTEX
WORTHS
WORTHY

••R•T•

AERATE
AFRITS
BARITE
BERATE
BERETS
BORATE
BURSTS
BYROTE
CARATS
CARETO
CARETS
CERATE
CURATE
DARETO
DORATI
EGRETS
ERRATA
FERITY
FIRSTS
GARETH
GYRATE
HERETO
JURATS
KARATE
KARATS
KARSTS
KORATS
MERITS
MORITA
MORITZ
PARETO
PARITY
PIRATE
PURITY
PYRITE
RARITY
RERATE
SPRATS
SPRITE
SPRITS
SPRITZ
STRATA
STRATI
STRATO
STRUTS
SURETE
SURETY
TAROTS
TERATO
TERETE
TURNTO
VERITE
VERITY
VERSTS
WARMTH
WORSTS
WURSTS
ZEROTH

••R••T

ABRUPT
ADRIFT
ADROIT
AFREET
AIROUT
AORIST
ARRANT
ARREST
ATREST
BARBET
BARDOT
BAREST
BARKAT
BEREFT
BIRGIT
BURBOT
BURNET
CARLOT
CARNET
CARNOT
CARPET
CARROT
CERMET
CORNET
CORSET
CURVET
DARENT
DARNIT
DIRECT
DIREST
DORRIT
DORSET
DURANT
ENRAPT
ENROOT
ERRANT
FAROUT
FERMAT
FERRET
FOREST
FORGET
FORGOT
FORINT
FORMAT
GARNET
GARRET
GERENT
GERONT
GORGET
HEREAT
HERIOT
HERMIT
HORNET
IRRUPT
JURIST
KERMIT
KORBUT
KURALT
LARIAT
LYRIST
MARGOT
MARIST
MARKET
MARMOT
MEREST
MERLOT
MORANT
PARENT
PARGET
PARROT
PERMIT
PERROT
PUREST
PURIST
RAREST
RERENT
SCRIPT
SHRIFT
SORBET
SOREST
SPRINT
SPROUT
STRAIT
STREET
STRICT
SUREST
TARGET
TARPIT
TERCET
TERRET
THREAT
THRIFT
THROAT
THRUST
TOREAT
TURBIT
TURBOT
TURRET
TYRANT
UNREST
UNROOT
UPROOT
VARLET
VERVET
WERENT
YAREST

•••RT•

ABORTS
ALERTS
AVERTS
BLURTS
CHARTS
CHERTY
COURTS
DEARTH
DUARTE
ECARTE
EVERTS
EXERTS
FLIRTS
FLIRTY
FOURTH
GEARTO
HEARTH
HEARTS
HEARTY
NEARTO
OMERTA
OPORTO
PUERTO
QUARTO
QUARTS
QUARTZ
QUIRTS
QWERTY
SHIRTS
SHIRTY
SHORTA
SHORTE
SHORTI
SHORTO
SHORTS
SHORTU
SHORTY
SKIRTS
SKORTS
SMARTS
SMARTY
SNORTS
SPARTA
SPORTS
SPORTY
SPURTS
STARTS
SWARTH
THIRTY

•••R•T

AGOROT
AIGRET
ARARAT
ATTRIT
BEIRUT
CARROT
CLARET
DORRIT
DRYROT
ESPRIT
FERRET
FLORET
GARRET
HEARST
IMARET
INARUT
JEERAT
LABRET
LEARNT
LEERAT
MEERUT
PARROT
PEERAT
PERROT
POIROT
REGRET
SECRET
SEURAT
SPIRIT
TEARAT
TERRET
THIRST
TURRET

••••RT

ADVERT
ALBERT
ALHIRT
ALPERT
ASSERT
ASSORT
BOGART
CAVORT
COHORT
COVERT
DEPART
DEPORT
DESERT
DIVERT
EFFORT
EGBERT
ELBERT
ENGIRT
ERFURT
ESCORT
EXHORT
EXPERT
EXPORT
EXSERT
EXTORT
GOCART
GOKART
HOBART
HUBERT
IMPART
IMPORT
INPART
INPORT
INSERT
INVERT
MOZART
OBVERT
OXCART
POPART
REPORT
RESORT
RETORT
REVERT
ROBERT
RUPERT
SQUIRT
STUART
THWART
TSHIRT
UNGIRT
UNHURT
YOGURT

RU••••

RUANAS
RUANDA
RUBATI
RUBATO
RUBBED
RUBBER
RUBBLE
RUBBLY
RUBENS
RUBIED
RUBIES
RUBIFY
RUBLES
RUBLEV
RUBOFF
RUBOUT
RUBRIC
RUBSIN
RUCHES
RUCKED
RUCKUS
RUDDER
RUDDLE
RUDELY
RUDEST
RUDMAN
RUDOLF
RUEFUL
RUFFED
RUFFLE
RUFFLY
RUFOUS
RUGATE
RUGGED
RUGOSE
RUINED
RUINER
RULEON
RULERS
RULING
RUMBAS
RUMBLE
RUMBLY
RUMENS
RUMINA
RUMMER
RUMORS
RUMOUR
RUMPLE
RUMPLY
RUMPUS
RUNCIE
RUNDLE
RUNDMC
RUNDRY
RUNFOR
RUNGUP
RUNINS
RUNLET
RUNNEL
RUNNER
RUNOFF
RUNONS
RUNOUT
RUNSAT
RUNSIN
RUNSON
RUNSTO
RUNSUP
RUNUPS
RUNWAY
RUNYON
RUPAUL
RUPEES
RUPERT
RUPIAH
RUSHED
RUSHEE
RUSHES
RUSKIN
RUSSET
RUSSIA
RUSTED
RUSTIC
RUSTLE
RUTGER
RUTILE
RUTTAN
RUTTED

R•U•••

REUBEN
REUNES
REUSED
REUSES
REUTER
RHUMBA
RHUMBS
ROUBLE
ROUGED
ROUGES
ROUGHS
ROUGHY
ROUNDS
ROURKE
ROUSED
ROUSER
ROUSES
ROUSTS
ROUTED
ROUTER
ROUTES
RYUKYU

R••U••

RADULA
RAQUEL
REBUFF
REBUKE
REBURY
REBUTS
RECURS
RECUSE
REDUBS
REDUCE
REFUEL
REFUGE
REFUND
REFUSE
REFUTE
REHUNG
RELUCT
RELUME
REMUDA
REPUGN
REPUTE
RERUNS
RESULT
RESUME
RETUNE
RETURN
REVUES
RHEUMS
RHEUMY
RITUAL
ROBUST
ROGUES
ROTUND
RUNUPS

R•••U•

RACKUP
RADIUM
RADIUS
RAGOUT
RAGRUG
RAIPUR
RAJPUT
RAKEUP
RAMOUS
RANGUP
RANOUT
RAVEUP
RAYGUN
REARUP
RECOUP
RECTUS
REDBUD
REDGUM
REFLUX
REGIUS
REGLUE
RESCUE
RESTUP
RETOUR
REVSUP
RHESUS
RIGOUR
RIGSUP
RILEUP
RINGUP
RIPOUT
RIPSUP
RISQUE
ROLLUP
ROTGUT
RUBOUT
RUCKUS
RUEFUL
RUFOUS
RUMOUR
RUMPUS
RUNGUP
RUNOUT
RUNSUP
RUPAUL
RVALUE

R••••U

RAMEAU
RESEAU
ROSEAU
RYUKYU

•RU•••

ARUBAN
BRUDER
BRUGES
BRUINS
BRUISE
BRUITS
BRULES
BRUMAL
BRUMBY
BRUMES
BRUNCH
BRUNEI
BRUNET
BRUNTS
BRUSHY
BRUTAL
BRUTES
BRUTUS
BRUXED
BRUXES
CRUCES
CRUDDY
CRUDER
CRUETS
CRUISE
CRUMBS
CRUMBY
CRUMMY
CRUNCH
CRURAL
CRUSES
CRUSOE
CRUSTS
CRUSTY
CRUTCH
CRUXES
DRUDGE
DRUIDS
DRUMUP
DRUPES
DRUZES
ERUCTS
ERUPTS
FRUGAL
FRUITS
FRUITY
FRUMPS
FRUMPY
FRUTTI
GRUBBY
GRUDGE
GRUELS
GRUMPS
GRUMPY
GRUNDY
GRUNGE
GRUNGY
GRUNTS
KRUGER
PRUDES
PRUNED
PRUNER
PRUNES
TRUANT
TRUCES
TRUCKS
TRUDGE
TRUEST
TRUING
TRUISM
TRUMAN
TRUMPS
TRUNKS
TRUSTS
TRUSTY
TRUTHS
URUSES

•R•U••

ARGUED
ARGUER
ARGUES
ARGUFY
ARJUNA
ARMURE
AROUND
AROUSE
ARTURO
BREUER
CREUSA
CROUCH
CROUPY
CROUSE
CROUTE
ERFURT
FRAUDS
FRAUEN
GROUCH
GROUND
GROUPS
GROUSE
GROUTS
GROUTY
IRRUPT
ORDURE
PROUST
TRAUMA
TRIUNE
TROUGH
TROUPE
TROUTS
TROUVE
URSULA

•R••U•

ARBOUR
ARDOUR
ARMFUL
ARMOUR
ARTFUL
ARTGUM
ARTHUR
BRAQUE
BROGUE
BRUTUS
CROCUS
CRONUS
CROPUP
DRAWUP
DREWUP
DROGUE
DRUMUP
DRYOUT
DRYRUN
ERBIUM
EREBUS
FRENUM
GRADUS
GREWUP
GROWUP
IREFUL

KRONUR
MRBLUE
PRAGUE
PRENUP
PRIMUM
PRIMUS
PROPUP
TRIPUP
TRYOUT
URAEUS
URANUS
WRAPUP

•R•••U
ARALLU
ERESTU
ORMOLU

••RU••
ABRUPT
BARUCH
CARUSO
CERUSE
CURULE
FERULE
FORUMS
GERUND
INRUSH
IRRUPT
JORUMS
KORUNA
NERUDA
ONRUSH
PARULA
PARURE
PERUGA
PERUKE
PERUSE
QURUSH
RERUNS
SCRUBS
SCRUFF
SCRUMS
SERUMS
SHRUBS
SHRUGS
SHRUNK
SPRUCE
SPRUES
SPRUNG
STRUCK
STRUMS
STRUNG
STRUTS
SYRUPS
SYRUPY
THRUMS
THRUSH
THRUST
UNRULY
UPRUSH
VARUNA
YORUBA

••R•U•
AIRBUS
AIRGUN
AIROUT
ATREUS
ATRIUM
AUREUS
AUROUS
BARIUM
BARNUM
BARQUE
BARZUN
BOREUP
BURNUP
CARFUL
CARPUS
CEREUS
CERIUM
CIRCUM
CIRCUS
CIRQUE
CIRRUS
CORIUM
CORPUS
CURIUM
CURLUP
DARIUS
DORSUM
EARFUL
FAROUK
FAROUT
FERGUS
FIREUP
FIRMUP
HARDUP
HORMUZ
JARFUL
KORBUT
LARRUP
MARAUD
MARCUS
MARDUK
MARIUS
MARKUP
MARQUE
MURMUR
NEREUS
PERDUE
PERKUP
POROUS
PURDUE
PURSUE
SEROUS
SHROUD
SIRIUS
SPROUT
STRAUB
STRAUS
STROUD
TARSUS
TEREUS
TOREUP
TORQUE
TURNUP
VERDUN
VERSUS
VIRTUE
VIRTUS
VOROUS
WARMUP
WORKUP

••R••U
BUREAU
MARILU
MOREAU

•••RU•
ACARUS
ACCRUE
ALARUM
ANTRUM
BAYRUM
BEARUP
BEIRUT
CHERUB
CHORUS
CIRRUS
CITRUS
CYPRUS
DRYRUN
ELBRUS
ENDRUN
EPIRUS
FAIRUP
GEARUP
GUDRUN
ICARUS
IMBRUE
INARUT
LABRUM
LARRUP
LEBRUN
MEERUT
OUTRUN
PAIRUP
QUORUM
RAGRUG
REARUP
SACRUM
SCARUM
SKIRUN
STIRUP
TAURUS
TEARUP
TOBRUK
UNTRUE
WALRUS

•••R•U
APERCU
SHORTU

••••RU
HALERU
JABIRU
MASERU
SUBARU

RV••••
RVALUE

R•V•••
RAVAGE
RAVELS
RAVENS
RAVERS
RAVEUP
RAVINE
RAVING
RAVISH
REVAMP
REVEAL
REVELS
REVERB
REVERE
REVERS
REVERT
REVETS
REVIEW
REVILE
REVISE
REVIVE
REVLON
REVOIR
REVOKE
REVOLT
REVSON
REVSUP
REVUES
REVVED
RIVALS
RIVERA
RIVERS
RIVETS
RIVING
ROVERS
ROVING
RSVPED

R••V••
REEVED
REEVES
REVVED

R•••V•
RELEVY
RELIVE
REMOVE
REPAVE
REVIVE
REWOVE

R••••V
ROCKYV
ROSTOV
RUBLEV

•RV•••
ARVADA
ERVING
IRVINE
IRVING

•R•V••
BRAVAS
BRAVED
BRAVER
BRAVES
BRAVOS
BREVES
BREVET
BREVIS
CRAVAT
CRAVED
CRAVEN
CRAVER
CRAVES
DRIVEL
DRIVEN
DRIVER
DRIVES
DROVER
DROVES
GRAVED
GRAVEL
GRAVEN
GRAVER
GRAVES
GRAVID
GRIVET
GROVEL
GROVER
GROVES
PRAVDA
PREVIN
PRIVET
PROVED
PROVEN
PROVER
PROVES
TRAVEL
TRAVES
TRAVIS
TREVOR
TRIVET
TRIVIA
TROVES

•R••V•
ARGIVE
ARRIVE
GREAVE
GRIEVE
GROOVE
GROOVY
TROUVE

•R•••V
BRASOV

••RV••
CARVED
CARVER
CARVES
CARVEY
CERVID
CORVEE
CORVES
CURVED
CURVES
CURVET
FERVID
FERVOR
GARVEY
HARVEY
LARVAE
LARVAL
LARVAS
MARVEL
MARVIN
MERVYN
NARVIK
NERVES
PARVIS
PURVEY
SERVAL
SERVED
SERVER
SERVES
SERVOS
SURVEY
TURVES
VERVES
VERVET

••R•V•
ARRIVE
DERIVE
MORAVA
PAREVE
SHRIVE
SHROVE
STRIVE
STROVE
THRIVE
THROVE

••R••V
KARPOV

•••RV•
SCURVE
SCURVY
STARVE
SWERVE

•••R•V
HENRYV
IMPROV

RW••••
RWANDA

R•W•••
RAWEGG
RAWEST
RAWISH
REWARD
REWARM
REWASH
REWEDS
REWELD
REWIND
REWINS
REWIRE
REWORD
REWORK
REWOVE
REWRAP
ROWELS
ROWENA
ROWENS
ROWERS
ROWING

R••W••
RUNWAY

R•••W•
REMOWN
REMOWS
RENEWS
RENOWN
RESAWN
RESAWS
RESEWN
RESEWS
RETOWS

R••••W
REDRAW
REDREW
REPLOW
REVIEW
RIPSAW

•RW•••
ORWELL

•R•W••
ARAWAK
BRAWLS
BRAWNY
BREWED
BREWER
BROWNE
BROWNS
BROWNY
BROWSE
CRAWLS
CRAWLY
CREWED
CREWEL
CROWDS
CROWED
CROWER
CROWNS
DRAWER
DRAWIN
DRAWLS
DRAWLY
DRAWON
DRAWUP
DREWIN
DREWON
DREWUP
DROWNS
DROWSE
DROWSY
FROWNS
FROWZY
GREWON
GREWUP
GROWER
GROWLS
GROWLY
GROWON
GROWTH
GROWUP
PRAWNS
PREWAR
PROWLS
PROWSE
TRAWLS
TROWED
TROWEL

•R••W•
ARROWS

•R•••W
BROKAW
ERENOW
KRAKOW
PRELAW

••RW••
AIRWAY
DARWIN
EARWAX
EARWIG
NARWAL
NORWAY

••R•W•
ARROWS
SCRAWL
SCREWS
SCREWY
SEROWS
SHREWD
SHREWS
SPRAWL
STRAWS
STRAWY
STREWN
STREWS
TARAWA
THROWN
THROWS

••R••W
BARROW
BORROW
BURROW
CURFEW
CURLEW
DARROW
FARLOW
FARROW
FURROW
HARLOW
HARROW
MARROW
MORROW
MURROW
NARROW
SORROW
WARSAW
YARROW

•••R•W
ANDREW
BARROW
BORROW
BURROW
DARROW
ESCROW
FARROW
FURROW
HARROW
HEBREW
INAROW
KUDROW
MARROW
MCGRAW
MCGREW
MORROW
MURROW
NARROW
REDRAW
REDREW
SORROW
UNDRAW
YARROW

R•X•••
REXCAT
ROXANA
ROXANE

R••••X
RATEDX
REDFOX
REDSOX
REFLEX
REFLUX

•R•X••
BRUXED
BRUXES
CRUXES
DREXEL
ORYXES
PRAXES
PRAXIS
TRIXIE

•R••X•
URTEXT

•R•••X
BRANDX
PREFIX
PRETAX
PROLIX
PROTAX

••RX••
XERXES

••R•X•
BORAXO

••R••X
CORTEX
EARWAX
LARYNX
SURTAX
SYRINX
VERTEX
VORTEX

•••R•X
CLOROX
MATRIX
THORAX

RY••••
RYAZAN
RYDELL
RYOKAN
RYUKYU

R•Y•••
RAYGUN
RAYONS
RHYMED
RHYMER
RHYMES
RHYTHM
RHYTON
RIYADH
RIYALS
ROYALE
ROYALS

R••Y••
REDYED
REDYES
RETYPE
RUNYON

R•••Y•
REDEYE
REKEYS
RELAYS
REPAYS
RIBEYE
ROCKYV
RYUKYU

R••••Y
RACILY
RAINEY
RAMIFY
RAMSAY
RAMSEY
RANDRY
RANKLY
RAPTLY
RAREFY
RARELY
RARIFY
RARITY
RASHLY
RATIFY
RATTLY
REALLY
REALTY
REBURY
RECOPY
REDBAY
REDENY
REILLY
RELEVY
REMEDY
REPLAY
RESINY
RHEUMY
RICHLY
RICKEY
RIDLEY
RIFELY
RIGHTY
RIMSKY
RIPELY
RIPLEY
RIPPLY
ROBROY
RODNEY
ROMANY
ROMNEY
RONELY
ROONEY
ROSARY
ROSILY
ROSINY
ROTARY
ROUGHY
RUBBLY
RUBIFY
RUDELY
RUFFLY
RUMBLY
RUMPLY
RUNDRY
RUNWAY

•RY•••
ARYANS
BRYANT
BRYONY
BRYSON
CRYERS
CRYING
CRYOFF
CRYPTO
CRYPTS
DRYADS
DRYDEN
DRYERS
DRYEST
DRYFLY
DRYICE
DRYING
DRYINK
DRYOFF
DRYOUT
DRYROT
DRYRUN
ERYNGO
FRYERS
FRYING
FRYPAN
ORYXES
PRYING
PRYNNE
TRYFOR
TRYING
TRYLON
TRYOUT
TRYSTS
WRYEST

•R•Y••
ARGYLE
ARGYLL
BRAYED
BRAYER
BREYER
CRAYON
DRAYED
FRAYED
GRAYED
GRAYER
GRAYLY
GREYED
GREYER
GREYLY
IRTYSH
MRHYDE
PRAYED
PRAYER
PREYED
PREYON
XRAYED

•R••Y•
ARRAYS
ARROYO
CRONYN
ERINYS

•R•••Y
ARCHLY
ARGOSY
ARGUFY
ARIDLY
ARMORY
ARTERY
ARTILY
BRACHY
BRAINY
BRANDY
BRANNY
BRASHY
BRASSY
BRATTY
BRAWNY
BREEZY
BRICKY
BRIERY
BROLLY
BRONZY
BROODY
BROOKY
BROOMY
BROWNY
BRUMBY
BRUSHY
BRYONY
CRABBY
CRACKY
CRAFTY
CRAGGY
CRANKY
CRANNY
CRAWLY
CREAKY
CREAMY
CREASY
CREEPY
CRIKEY
CRIMPY
CRISPY
CROAKY
CROSBY
CROUPY
CRUDDY
CRUMBY
CRUMMY
CRUSTY
DRABLY
DRAFTY
DRAGGY
DRAWLY
DREAMY
DREARY
DRESSY
DRIFTY
DRIPPY
DROLLY
DROOLY
DROOPY
DROPBY
DROWSY
DRYFLY
FRAIDY
FRANNY
FREAKY
FREDDY
FREELY
FRENZY
FRETTY
FRIARY
FRIDAY
FRILLY
FRINGY
FRISKY
FRIZZY
FROGGY
FROSTY
FROTHY
FROWZY
FRUITY
FRUMPY
GRABBY
GRAINY
GRAMMY
GRANNY
GRAPEY
GRAPHY
GRASSY
GRAYLY
GREASY
GREEDY
GREENY
GREYLY
GRIMLY
GRISLY
GRITTY
GROGGY
GROOVY
GROSZY
GROTTY
GROUTY
GROWLY
GROZNY
GRUBBY
GRUMPY
GRUNDY
GRUNGY
KRASNY
ORALLY
ORANGY
ORKNEY
ORNERY
ORRERY
PREPAY
PREPPY
PRETTY
PRICEY
PRIMLY
PRIORY
PRISSY
PROSKY
TRACEY
TRACHY
TRAPPY
TRASHY
TREATY
TREBLY
TRENDY
TRICKY
TRIGLY
TRILBY
TRIMLY
TRIPLY
TROPHY
TRUSTY
WRATHY

••RY••
BARYON
CORYZA
DURYEA
LARYNX
SPRYER
SPRYLY

••R•Y•
ARRAYS
ARROYO
DARRYL
FORAYS
MARTYR
MERVYN
MORAYS
SPRAYS
STRAYS

••R••Y
AERIFY
AERILY
AIRDRY
AIRILY
AIRWAY
AURIFY
BARELY
BARFLY
BARLEY
BARNEY
BARONY
BIRNEY
BURBLY
BURLEY
BURNEY
CARBOY
CARNEY
CARREY
CARVEY
CHROMY
CORDAY
CURACY
CURLEY
CURTLY
CURTSY
DARKLY
DARNAY
DIRELY
DORSEY
DURFEY
EARTHY
EERILY
FARCRY
FARLEY
FERITY
FIRMLY
GARVEY
GORILY
GURLEY
GURNEY
HARDBY
HARDLY
HARLEY
HARVEY
HEREBY
HERESY
HERSEY
HORNEY
HORSEY
HURLEY
HURRAY
JEREMY
JERSEY
KERSEY
LORDLY
MARBLY
MARGAY
MARLEY
MARSHY
MERELY
MERSEY
MORLEY
MORNAY
MORPHY
MURPHY
MURRAY
MURREY
NORGAY
NORWAY
ORRERY
PARITY
PARKAY
PARLAY
PARLEY
PARODY
PARTLY
PERTLY
PIRACY
PORTLY
PURELY
PURIFY
PURITY
PURPLY
PURVEY
RAREFY
RARELY
RARIFY
RARITY
SCREWY
SORELY
SPRYLY
STRAWY
STRIPY
SURELY
SURETY
SURREY
SURVEY
SYRUPY
TARTLY
TORCHY
TORREY
TURKEY
UNRULY
VARNEY
VERIFY
VERILY
VERITY
WARCRY
WARILY
WARMLY
WIRILY
WORTHY
WURLEY
YARELY

•••RY•
CHERYL
DARRYL
EMBRYO
HEARYE
HENRYV
MAURYA
SHERYL
VANRYN

•••R•Y
AFFRAY
ANDREY
ANERGY
ASTRAY
AUBREY
AUDREY
BETRAY
BEWRAY
BLURRY
CARREY
CHARLY
CHERRY
CHERTY
CHIRPY
CLERGY
CONROY
CZERNY
DEARLY
DEFRAY
DELRAY
DELROY
DOURLY
EBERLY
ENERGY
ESTRAY
EVERLY
FABRAY
FAIRLY
FLIRTY
FLURRY
GEORGY
GHARRY
GNARLY
HEARTY
HOORAY
HOURLY
HURRAY
KEARNY
KILROY
KNARRY
KNURLY
MANRAY
MURRAY
MURREY
NEARBY
NEARLY
OSPREY
OVERLY
PEARLY
POORLY
QUARRY
QUIRKY
QWERTY
ROBROY
SCARRY
SCURFY
SCURRY
SCURVY
SHERRY
SHIRTY
SHORTY
SKERRY
SLURRY
SMARMY
SMARTY
SMIRKY
SNARLY
SOURLY
SPARKY
SPERRY
SPORTY
SPURRY
STARRY
STOREY
STORMY
STURDY
SUNRAY
SURREY
SWIRLY
THIRTY
THORNY
TORREY
WEIRDY
WHERRY
WHIRLY
YEARLY

••••RY
AIRDRY
AMBERY
APIARY
ARMORY
ARTERY
ASBURY
AUGURY
AVIARY
AWEARY
BAKERY
BELFRY
BINARY
BLEARY
BLURRY
BOVARY
BOWERY
BRIERY
BUMBRY
CANARY
CELERY
CHEERY
CHERRY
DATARY
DENARY
DESCRY
DESTRY
DOWERY
DREARY
DUPERY
EATERY
ELLERY
EMPERY
EXPIRY
FAKERY
FARCRY
FINERY
FLEURY
FLOURY
FLURRY
FRIARY
GANTRY
GENTRY
GHARRY
GLAIRY
GOAWRY
GUITRY
HILARY
HUNGRY
INJURY
JAPERY
KIDORY
KNARRY
LANDRY

LIVERY LOWERY LUXURY MALORY MEMORY MISERY MOPERY NAPERY NITERY NONARY NOTARY OCHERY OHENRY OLEARY ORNERY ORRERY OUTCRY PALTRY PANFRY PANTRY PAPERY PASTRY PELTRY PENURY PINERY POETRY POKERY PRIORY QUARRY RANDRY REBURY ROSARY ROTARY RUNDRY SALARY SAVORY SCARRY SCURRY SENARY SENTRY SEVERY SHERRY SKERRY SLURRY SMEARY SNEERY SPERRY SPHERY SPURRY STARRY SUGARY SULTRY SUNDRY TAWDRY THEORY TOWERY UNWARY VAGARY VALERY VAPORY VESTRY VINERY VOTARY WAFERY WARCRY WATERY WAVERY WHERRY WINERY WINTRY

R•Z•••

RAZING RAZORS RAZZED RAZZES RAZZLE REZONE RIZZIO ROZZER

R••Z••

RAZZED RAZZES RAZZLE RIZZIO ROZZER RYAZAN

R•••Z•

REBOZO RIENZI

•R•Z••

AREZZO BRAZED BRAZEN BRAZER BRAZES BRAZIL BRAZOS BRAZZA BRAZZI CRAZED CRAZES CROZES DRUZES FRAZER FRIZZY FROZEN GRAZED GRAZER GRAZES GROZNY OROZCO PRIZED PRIZES PROZAC

•R••Z•

AREZZO BRAZZA BRAZZI BREEZE BREEZY BRONZE BRONZY FREEZE FRENZY FRIEZE FRIZZY FROWZY GROSZY

•R•••Z

BRIENZ ERSATZ KRANTZ TROPEZ

••RZ••

BARZUN BORZOI CURZON FURZES HERZOG TARZAN

••R•Z•

CORYZA

••R••Z

CORTEZ CURTIZ HORMUZ LORENZ MORITZ SPRITZ

•••RZ•

SFORZA

•••R•Z

JUAREZ QUARTZ SHIRAZ TABRIZ

SA••••

SABATO SABENA SABERS SABINE SABINS SABLES SABOTS SABRAS SABRES SACHEM SACHET SACKED SACKER SACQUE SACRAL SACRED SACRUM SADDAM SADDEN SADDER SADDLE SADHES SADHUS SAFARI SAFELY SAFEST SAFETY SAFIRE SAGELY SAGEST SAGGED SAHARA SAHIBS SAIGAS SAIGON SAILED SAILOR SAINTE SAINTS SAIPAN SAKERS SALAAM SALADO SALADS SALALS SALAMI SALARY SALIFY SALINA SALINE SALISH SALIVA SALLET SALLOW SALMAN SALMON SALOME SALONS SALOON SALSAS SALTED SALTEN SALTER SALTON SALTUM SALUKI SALUTE SALVED SALVER SALVES SALVIA SALVOR SALVOS SALYUT SAMARA SAMBAL SAMBAR SAMBAS SAMECH SAMEKH SAMIAM SAMITE SAMLET SAMMIE SAMOAN SAMOSA SAMPAN SAMPLE SAMSON SAMUEL SANCHO SANCTA SANDAL SANDED SANDER SANDIA SANDRA SANELY SANEST SANGER SANGTO SANITY SANNUP SANSEI SANTEE SANTIR SANTOS SAPORS SAPPED SAPPER SAPPHO SARANS SARDIS SARGES SARGON SARGOS SARNIA SARODS SARONG SARTON SARTRE SASEBO SASHAY SASHED SASHES SASSED SASSER SASSES SATANG SATEEN SATING SATINS SATINY SATIRE SATORI SATOUT SATRAP SATURN SATYRS SAUCED SAUCER SAUCES SAUDIS SAUGER SAULTS SAUNAS SAUREL SAUTES SAVAGE SAVAII SAVANT SAVATE SAVERS SAVEUP SAVING SAVIOR SAVOIE SAVOIR SAVORS SAVORY SAVOUR SAWFIT SAWING SAWLOG SAWOFF SAWOUT SAWRED SAWYER SAXONS SAXONY SAYERS SAYING SAYLES SAYSOS SAYYES SAYYID

S•A•••

SCABBY SCALAR SCALDS SCALED SCALER SCALES SCALIA SCALPS SCAMPI SCAMPS SCANTS SCANTY SCAPED SCAPES SCARAB SCARCE SCARED SCARER SCARES SCARFS SCARNE SCARPS SCARRY SCARUM SCATHE SCATTY SCAUPS SEABAG SEABED SEABEE SEACOW SEADOG SEAFAN SEAFOX SEAGAL SEALAB SEALED SEALER SEALUP SEAMAN SEAMED SEAMEN SEAMUS SEANCE SEARCH SEARED SEARLE SEASON SEATED SEATER SEATON SEAWAY SHABAN SHABBY SHACKS SHADED SHADES SHADOW SHAFTS SHAGGY SHAKEN SHAKER SHAKES SHAKOS SHAKTI SHALES SHALEY SHALLY SHALOM SHAMAN SHAMED SHAMES SHAMIR SHAMUS SHANDY SHANIA SHANKS SHANNY SHANTY SHAPED SHAPER SHAPES SHARDS SHARED SHARER SHARES SHARIA SHARIF SHARKS SHARON SHARPS SHASTA SHAVED SHAVEN SHAVER SHAVES SHAWLS SHAWMS SHAYNE SHAZAM SKALDS SKANKS SKATED SKATER SKATES SLACKS SLAGGY SLAKED SLAKES SLALOM SLANGS SLANGY SLANTS SLAPPY SLAPUP SLATED SLATER SLATES SLAVED SLAVER SLAVES SLAVEY SLAVIC SLAYED SLAYER SMACKS SMALLS SMALTI SMALTO SMARMY SMARTS SMARTY SNACKS SNAFUS SNAGGY SNAILS SNAKED SNAKES SNAPAT SNAPPY SNAPTO SNAPUP SNARED SNARES SNARLS SNARLY SNATCH SNATHE SNATHS SNAZZY SOAKED SOAKER SOAKUP SOAPED SOAPER SOARED SOARER SOARES SOASTO SOAVES SPACED SPACEK SPACER SPACES SPACEY SPADED SPADER SPADES SPADIX SPAHIS SPALLS SPANKS SPANKY SPARED SPARER SPARES SPARGE SPARKS SPARKY SPARSE SPARTA SPASMS SPATES SPATHE SPAVIN SPAWNS SPAYED SRANAN STABAT STABLE STABLY STACEY STACKS STACTE STADIA STAFFS STAGED STAGER STAGES STAINS STAIRS STAKED STAKES STALAG STALED STALER STALES STALIN STALKS STALKY STALLS STAMEN STAMPS STANCE STANCH STANDS STANKY STANZA STAPES STAPLE STAPUF STARCH STARED STARER STARES STARRY STARTS STARVE STASES STASIS STATED STATEN STATER STATES STATIC STATOR STATUE STATUS STAVED STAVES STAYED STAYON STAYUP SUAVER SWABBY SWAGED SWAGES SWAINS SWALES SWAMIS SWAMPS SWAMPY SWANEE SWANKS SWANKY SWARAJ SWARDS SWARMS SWARTH SWATCH SWATHE SWATHS SWAYED SWAYER SWAYZE SWAZIS

S••A••

SABATO SAFARI SAHARA SALAAM SALADO SALADS SALALS SALAMI SALARY SAMARA SARANS SATANG SAVAGE SAVAII SAVANT SAVATE SCLAFF SCRAGS SCRAMS SCRAPE SCRAPS SCRAWL SECANT SEDAKA SEDANS SEDATE SEJANT SENARY SENATE SEPALS SERACS SERAIS SERAPE SERAPH SESAME SEWAGE SEWARD SHEAFS SHEARS SHEATH SHEAVE SHOALS SHOALY SHOATS SHRANK SILAGE SISALS SITARS SIWASH SKEANS SKOALS SLEAVE SLEAZE SLEAZY SLOANE SMEARS SMEARY SNEAKS SNEAKY SOCAGE SOLACE SOLANS SOLARS SOMALI SOMANY SOMATA SOMATO SONANT SONATA SOUARI SPEAKS SPEARS SPLASH SPLATS SPLAYS SPRAGS SPRAIN SPRANG SPRATS SPRAWL SPRAYS SQUABS SQUADS SQUALL SQUARE SQUASH SQUATS SQUAWK STEADS STEADY STEAKS STEALS STEAMS STEAMY STMALO STMARK STOATS STPAUL STRABO STRADS STRAFE STRAIN STRAIT STRAKE STRAND STRAPS STRASS STRATA STRATI STRATO STRAUB STRAUS STRAWS STRAWY STRAYS STUART SUBARU SUGARS SUGARY SUMACS SURAHS SUSANN SWEARS SWEATS SWEATY

S•••A•

SABRAS SACRAL SADDAM SAIGAS SAIPAN SALAAM SALMAN SALSAS SAMBAL SAMBAR SAMBAS SAMIAM SAMOAN SAMPAN SANDAL SASHAY SATRAP SAUNAS SCALAR SCARAB SCENAS SCHWAB SCHWAS SCREAK SCREAM SCUBAS SEABAG SEAFAN SEAGAL SEALAB SEAMAN SEAWAY SEESAW SENDAK SENLAC SENNAS SEPIAS SEPTAL SERIAL SERVAL SETSAT SEURAT SGTMAJ SHABAN SHAMAN SHAZAM SHEVAT SHIKAR SHIRAZ SHOFAR SHORAN SHOTAT SIGMAS SIGNAL SILOAM SILVAS SIMIAN SINBAD SINEAD SINTAX SIOUAN SIRDAR SIRRAH SKYCAP SKYLAB SKYWAY SLEZAK SLOGAN SLOVAK SMILAX SNAPAT SNOCAT SOCIAL SOLDAN SOLFAS SONTAG SOTHAT SOWHAT SPICAS SPINAL SPIRAL SPIVAK SPREAD SQUEAK SQUEAL SRANAN STABAT STALAG STEFAN STELAE STELAR STJOAN STOMAS STOMAT STREAK STREAM STRIAE STUPAS SUBPAR SUBWAY SUCHAS SUCKAS SUDRAS SUKKAH SULTAN SUMMAE SUMMAS SUNDAE SUNDAY SUNRAY SUNTAN SURTAX SUTRAS SWARAJ SYLVAN SYNTAX SYRIAN

S••••A

SABENA SAHARA SALINA SALIVA SALVIA SAMARA SAMOSA SANCTA SANDIA SANDRA SARNIA SCALIA SCHEMA SCLERA SCORIA SCOTIA SCYLLA SEDAKA SEGURA SELENA SENECA SENEGA SENORA SENTRA SERBIA SERENA SEROSA SFORZA SHANIA SHARIA SHASTA SHEENA SHEILA SHERPA SHORTA SIENNA SIERRA SIESTA SILICA SIRICA SISERA SISTRA SMYRNA SOMATA SONATA SONOMA SONORA SOPHIA SPARTA SPIREA STADIA STANZA STELLA STERNA STIGMA STRATA STYRIA SYLVIA

•SA•••

ASANAS ISABEL ISADOR ISAIAH OSAGES PSALMS USABLE USABLY USAGES USANCE ZSAZSA

•S•A••

ASGARD ASHARP ASIANS ASKARI ASLANT ASMARA ASSAIL ASSAYS BSHARP CSHARP DSHARP ESCAPE ESCARP ESHARP ESPANA ESSAYS ESTATE FSHARP GSHARP GSTAAD ISLAND ISRAEL OSCARS OSHAWA OSWALD USMAIL USUALS

•S••A•

ASANAS ASCHAM ASHCAN ASHLAR ASHRAM ASOSAN ASTRAL ASTRAY ESDRAS ESPIAL ESTRAY GSTAAD ISAIAH ISHTAR ISOBAR MSQUAD OSSIAN OSTEAL PSYWAR

•S•••A

ASMARA ASPERA ESPANA ESPOSA ISCHIA ISTRIA OSCULA OSHAWA PSYLLA ZSAZSA

••SA••

ALSACE ANSARA ANSATE ASSAIL ASSAYS BASALT BESANT CASABA CASALS CASAVA CESARE CUSACK DESALT DISANT DISARM DOSAGE ERSATZ ESSAYS INSANE LESAGE LUSAKA MASADA MASAIS MESABI MOSAIC NASALS NOSALE OKSANA ONSALE PESACH PESAWA PISANO PISANS POSADA RESALE RESALT RESAND RESAWN RESAWS ROSARY SESAME SISALS SUSANN TISANE UNSAFE UNSAID UNSAYS VISAED VISAGE WASABI

••S•A•

ABSCAM ANSGAR BISCAY BISSAU BUSBAR BUSMAN CASBAH CASPAR CASUAL CESTAS COSTAE COSTAL COSTAR COSTAS CUSHAW DESMAN DISBAR DISMAL DISMAY DISTAL DOSSAL FESTAL FESTAS FISCAL FOSSAE FOSSAS GASBAG GASCAP GASMAN GASPAR GOSTAG GUSTAV HASSAM HASSAN HISSAT HOSTAS HUSSAR INSEAM INSPAN INSTAL INSTAR JOSIAH KASBAH KASDAN LASCAR LESTAT MESCAL MISHAP MISLAY MISSAL MISSAY MOSHAV MUSCAT MUSIAL NASCAR NASDAQ NASSAU NISSAN NOSOAP OSSIAN PASCAL PASHAS PASTAS PISGAH POSTAL RASCAL RASHAD RESEAL RESEAT RESEAU ROSEAU SASHAY TASMAN TESLAS TESTAE TUSCAN TUSSAH UNSEAL UNSEAT UNSNAG UNSNAP VASLAV VASSAL VASSAR VESTAL VESTAS VISTAS VISUAL WYSTAN YESMAN

••S••A

ANSARA BOSNIA BUSHWA CASABA CASAVA CASSIA CESSNA DESICA FASCIA HESTIA JASCHA JOSHUA KESHIA LISBOA LUSAKA MASADA MISCHA MOSKVA NASHUA NESTEA OKSANA PESAWA PESETA POSADA RESEDA ROSITA ROSTRA RUSSIA SISERA SISTRA URSULA

•••SA•

ACTSAS AIMSAT AIRSAC ASOSAN BALSAM BISSAU BONSAI BOWSAW BURSAE BURSAL BURSAR

BURSAS CAESAR CAUSAL COMSAT DOGSAT DORSAL DOSSAL EATSAT FAISAL FOSSAE FOSSAS GETSAT GOESAT HASSAM HASSAN HAUSAS HISSAT HUSSAR ILLSAY JETSAM JIGSAW KANSAN KANSAS LETSAT MENSAE MENSAL MENSAS MILSAP MISSAL MISSAY NASSAU NAYSAY NIPSAT NISSAN OLDSAW OVISAC PAISAS PAWSAT PITSAW PULSAR QUASAR RAMSAY RIPSAW RUNSAT SALSAS SEESAW SETSAT TARSAL TULSAN TUSSAH VASSAL VASSAR WARSAW WAUSAU XHOSAS

•••S•A

ALASKA ALYSSA ARISTA AVESTA AYESHA BUQSHA CASSIA CESSNA CUESTA EDESSA EGESTA ELISHA ELISSA FIESTA FRESCA GEISHA GLOSSA ILESHA ITASCA MARSHA MIASMA NAUSEA NYASSA ODESSA ORISSA PERSIA PLASMA REDSEA RUSSIA SHASTA SIESTA THESEA TRISHA VAISYA VIZSLA ZOYSIA

••••SA

AHIMSA ALYSSA CREUSA EDESSA ELISSA ESPOSA GLOSSA LAMESA LAROSA LOUISA MARISA MEDUSA MIMOSA MUCOSA MUFASA NYASSA ODESSA ORISSA SAMOSA SEROSA TERESA WALESA ZSAZSA

S•B•••

SABATO SABENA SABERS SABINE SABINS SABLES SABOTS SABRAS SABRES SEBERG SHBOOM SIBYLS SOBBED SOBBER SOBEIT SOBERS SOBFUL SUBARU SUBBED SUBDEB SUBDUE SUBGUM SUBITO SUBLET SUBMIT SUBORN SUBPAR SUBSET SUBTLE SUBTLY SUBURB SUBWAY

S••B••

SAMBAL SAMBAR SAMBAS SCABBY SCUBAS SEABAG SEABED SEABEE SERBIA SHABAN SHABBY SIMBEL SINBAD SKIBOB SKYBOX SLOBBY SNOBBY SNUBBY SOBBED SOBBER SOMBER SOMBRE SORBET SORBIC SOWBUG STABAT STABLE STABLY STUBBY SUBBED SWABBY SYMBOL

S•••B•

SAHIBS SASEBO SCABBY SCRIBE SCRUBS SETSBY SHABBY SHRUBS SITSBY SLOBBY SNOBBY SNUBBY SQUABS SQUIBB SQUIBS STRABO STROBE STUBBY SWABBY

S••••B

SCARAB SCHWAB SEALAB SKIBOB SKYLAB SQUIBB STRAUB SUBDEB SUBURB SUPERB

•SB•••

ASBURY OSBORN

•S•B••

ISABEL ISOBAR USABLE USABLY

••SB••

BUSBAR BUSBOY CASBAH DISBAR GASBAG HASBRO KASBAH LESBOS LISBOA LISBON

••S•B•

CASABA MESABI NASEBY PASSBY SASEBO WASABI

••S••B

ABSORB ADSORB RESORB

•••SB•

CROSBY DOESBY GATSBY GETSBY GOESBY LAYSBY LETSBE PASSBY PUTSBY SETSBY SITSBY THISBE

SC••••

SCABBY SCALAR SCALDS SCALED SCALER SCALES SCALIA SCALPS SCAMPI SCAMPS SCANTS SCANTY SCAPED SCAPES SCARAB SCARCE SCARED SCARER SCARES SCARFS SCARNE SCARPS SCARRY SCARUM SCATHE SCATTY SCAUPS SCENAS SCENDS SCENES SCENIC SCENTS SCHELL SCHEMA SCHEME SCHICK SCHIFF SCHISM SCHIST SCHIZY SCHLEP SCHMOO SCHMOS SCHNOZ SCHOOL SCHORL SCHULZ SCHUSS SCHWAB SCHWAS SCIFIS SCIONS SCIPIO SCLAFF SCLERA SCLERO SCOFFS SCOLDS SCONCE SCONES SCOOPS SCOOTS SCOPED SCOPES SCORCH SCORED SCORER SCORES SCORIA SCORNS SCOTCH SCOTER SCOTIA SCOTTO SCOTTY SCOURS SCOUSE SCOUTS SCOWLS SCRAGS SCRAMS SCRAPE SCRAPS SCRAWL SCREAK SCREAM SCREED SCREEN SCREES SCREWS SCREWY SCRIBE SCRIMP SCRIMS SCRIPS SCRIPT SCRODS SCROLL SCROOP SCRUBS SCRUFF SCRUMS SCUBAS SCUFFS SCULLS SCULLY SCULPT SCUMMY SCURFY SCURRY SCURVE SCURVY SCUTCH SCUTES SCUZZY SCYLLA SCYTHE

S•C•••

SACHEM SACHET SACKED SACKER SACQUE SACRAL SACRED SACRUM SECANT SECEDE SECERN SECKEL SECOND SECRET SECTOR SECURE SICCED SICILY SICKEN SICKER SICKLE SICKLY SOCAGE SOCCER SOCIAL SOCKED SOCKET SOCKIN SOCLES SUCCES SUCCOR SUCHAS SUCKAS SUCKED SUCKER SUCKIN

S••C••

SANCHO SANCTA SAUCED SAUCER SAUCES SEACOW SEICHE SHACKS SHOCKS SHUCKS SICCED SIECLE SITCOM SKYCAP SLACKS SLICED SLICER SLICES SLICKS SMACKS SMOCKS SNACKS SNICKS SNOCAT SOCCER SPACED SPACEK SPACER SPACES SPACEY SPECIE SPECKS SPICAS SPICED SPICES STACEY STACKS STACTE STICKS STICKY STOCKS STOCKY STUCCO SUCCES SUCCOR SULCUS SYNCED

S•••C•

SAMECH SCARCE SCHICK SCONCE SCORCH SCOTCH SCUTCH SEANCE SEARCH SEDUCE SELECT SENECA SERACS SHTICK SILICA SIRICA SKETCH SKITCH SLOUCH SLUICE SMIRCH SMOOCH SMUTCH SNATCH SNITCH SOLACE SONICS SOURCE SPEECH SPLICE SPRUCE STANCE STANCH STARCH STENCH STITCH STOICS STORCH STRICK STRICT STRUCK STUCCO SUMACS SUNOCO SWATCH SWITCH

S••••C

SCENIC SENLAC SEPTIC SLAVIC SORBIC STATIC STIVIC SYNDIC

•SC•••

ASCEND ASCENT ASCHAM ASCOTS ESCAPE ESCARP ESCENT ESCHER ESCHEW ESCORT ESCROW ESCUDO ISCHIA OSCARS OSCINE OSCULA

•S•C••

ASHCAN PSYCHE PSYCHO PSYCHS

•S••C•

ASDICS ASPECT ASPICS OSMICS USANCE

••SC••

ABSCAM BISCAY CISCOS DESCRY DISCOS DISCUS FASCES FASCIA FESCUE FISCAL GASCAP GASCON JASCHA LASCAR MASCOT MESCAL MISCHA MISCUE MOSCOW MUSCAT MUSCLE MUSCLY NASCAR PASCAL PESCOW PISCES RASCAL RESCUE ROSCOE TUSCAN VISCID

••S•C•

ALSACE BASICS BISECT CUSACK DESICA INSECT PESACH RESECT

••S••C

COSMIC FISTIC FUSTIC GESTIC INSYNC MASTIC MOSAIC MYSTIC ONSPEC RUSTIC

•••SC•

BORSCH CRISCO ENESCO FIASCO FRESCA FRESCO FRISCO HIRSCH ITASCA KIRSCH KITSCH MENSCH PUTSCH UNESCO

•••S•C

AIRSAC ECESIC OVISAC PARSEC

S•D•••

SADDAM SADDEN SADDER SADDLE SADHES SADHUS SEDAKA SEDANS SEDATE SEDERS SEDGES SEDILE SEDUCE SEDUMS SIDDUR SIDERO SIDERS SIDING SIDLED SIDLES SIDNEY SODDED SODDEN SODIUM SUDDEN SUDRAS SUDSED SUDSES SYDNEY

S••D••

SADDAM SADDEN SADDER SADDLE SANDAL SANDED SANDER SANDIA SANDRA SARDIS SAUDIS SEADOG SEEDED SEEDER SEIDEL SELDOM SENDAK SENDER SENDIN SENDUP SHADED SHADES SHADOW SHODDY SIDDUR SIRDAR SKIDDY SLEDGE SLIDER SLIDES SLIDIN SLUDGE SLUDGY SMUDGE SMUDGY SNIDER SNYDER SODDED SODDEN SOLDAN SOLDER SOLDON SONDES SORDID SPADED SPADER SPADES SPADIX SPEDUP SPIDER STADIA STODGE STODGY STUDIO SUBDEB SUBDUE SUDDEN SUEDES SUNDAE SUNDAY SUNDER SUNDEW SUNDOG SUNDRY SWEDEN SWEDES SYNDIC

S•••D•

SALADO SALADS SARODS SCALDS SCENDS SCOLDS SCRODS SECEDE SHANDY SHARDS SHEEDY SHINDY SHODDY SHREDS SKALDS SKIDDY SNOODS SOLIDI SOLIDS SOUNDS SPEEDO SPEEDS SPEEDY SPENDS SQUADS SQUIDS STANDS STEADS STEADY STEEDS STRADS STRIDE STRODE STURDY SWARDS SWORDS SYNODS

S••••D

SACKED SACRED SAGGED SAILED SALTED SALVED SANDED SAPPED SASHED SASSED SAUCED SAWRED SAYYID SCALED SCAPED SCARED SCOPED SCORED SCREED SEABED SEALED SEAMED SEARED SEATED SECOND SEEDED SEEMED SEEPED SEERED SEGUED SEINED SEIZED SENSED SERVED SEWARD SHADED SHAMED SHAPED SHARED SHAVED SHIELD SHINED SHOOED SHORED SHOULD SHOVED SHOWED SHREWD SHROUD SICCED SIDLED SIEGED SIEVED SIFTED SIGHED SIGNED SIGURD SILKED SILOED SILTED SINBAD SINEAD SINGED SINNED SIPPED SKATED SKEWED SKIVED SLAKED SLATED SLAVED SLAYED SLEWED SLICED SLIMED SLOPED SLOWED SMILED SMOKED SNAKED SNARED SNIPED SNORED SNOWED SOAKED SOAPED SOARED SOBBED SOCKED SODDED SOILED SOLOED SOLVED SOPPED SORDID SORTED SOTTED SOURED SOUSED SPACED SPADED SPARED SPAYED SPEWED SPICED SPIKED SPINED SPIRED SPITED SPOKED SPREAD SPUMED STAGED STAKED STALED STARED STATED STAVED STAYED STEWED STOKED STOLID STONED STORED STOWED STRAND STROUD STUPID STYLED SUBBED SUCKED SUDSED SUITED SULKED SUMMED SUNGOD SUNNED SUPPED SURFED SURGED SUSSED SWAGED SWAYED SWIPED SYNCED

•SD•••

ASDICS ESDRAS

•S•D••

ASIDES BSIDES ISADOR USEDTO USEDUP

•S••D•

ESCUDO ISOLDE PSEUDO PSEUDS

•S•••D

ASCEND ASGARD ASTRID ESPIED GSTAAD ISLAND ISOPOD ISSUED MSQUAD OSGOOD OSMOND OSMUND OSTEND OSWALD RSVPED USERID

••SD••

KASDAN MISDID NASDAQ WISDOM

••S•D•

BESIDE DOSIDO INSIDE MASADA ONSIDE POSADA RESEDA RESIDE RESODS UPSIDE URSIDS

••S••D

ABSURD ATSTUD AXSEED BASHED BASKED BASTED BESTED BOSSED BUSHED BUSIED BUSKED BUSSED BUSTED CASHED CESSED COSHED COSIED CUSPED CUSPID CUSSED DASHED DISHED DISKED DISSED DOSSED DUSTED ENSUED FASTED FESSED FISHED FISTED FUSSED GASHED GASPED GASSED GUSHED GUSTED HASHED HASPED HESIOD HISPID HISSED HOSTED HUSHED HUSKED ISSUED JESTED JOSHED KISSED LASHED LASTED LISPED LISTED LUSTED MASHED MASKED MASSED MESHED MESSED MISDID MISLED MISSED MISTED MOSHED MOSSED MUSHED MUSSED NESTED NOSHED OUSTED PASSED PASTED POSTED PUSHED RASHAD RASHID RASPED RESAND RESEED RESEND RESHOD RESOLD RESTED RISKED RUSHED RUSTED SASHED SASSED SUSSED TASKED TASTED TESTED TOSSED TUSKED UNSAID UNSHED UNSHOD UNSOLD VESPID VESTED VISAED VISCID WASHED WASTED WISHED WISPED YESSED ZESTED

•••S•D

ABASED ABUSED AMUSED BIASED BOSSED BOUSED BUSSED CAPSID CAUSED CEASED CENSED CESSED CHASED CLOSED CURSED CUSSED DISSED DOSSED DOUSED DOWSED ERASED FESSED FUSSED GASSED GOOSED HISSED HORSED HOUSED KISSED LAPSED LEASED LENSED LOOSED LOUSED MASSED MESSED MISSED MOSSED MOUSED MUSSED NOISED NOOSED NURSED PARSED PASSED PAUSED PHASED PHYSED POISED PROSED PULSED PURSED RAISED REUSED RINSED ROUSED SASSED SENSED SOUSED SUDSED SUSSED TEASED TENSED TOSSED UNUSED VERSED YESSED

SE••••

SEABAG SEABED SEABEE SEACOW SEADOG SEAFAN SEAFOX SEAGAL SEALAB SEALED SEALER SEALUP SEAMAN SEAMED SEAMEN SEAMUS SEANCE SEARCH SEARED SEARLE SEASON SEATED SEATER

SEATON
SEAWAY
SEBERG
SECANT
SECEDE
SECERN
SECKEL
SECOND
SECRET
SECTOR
SECURE
SEDAKA
SEDANS
SEDATE
SEDERS
SEDGES
SEDILE
SEDUCE
SEDUMS
SEEDED
SEEDER
SEEFIT
SEEGER
SEEING
SEEKER
SEELEY
SEEMED
SEEMLY
SEENIN
SEENTO
SEEOFF
SEEOUT
SEEPED
SEEPIN
SEERED
SEESAW
SEESIN
SEESTO
SEETHE
SEGUED
SEGUES
SEGURA
SEICHE
SEIDEL
SEINED
SEINER
SEINES
SEISMO
SEISMS
SEIZED
SEIZER
SEIZES
SEJANT
SELDOM
SELECT
SELENA
SELENE
SELENO
SELJUK
SELLER
SELVES
SEMELE
SEMITE
SEMPER
SEMPRE
SENARY
SENATE
SENDAK
SENDER
SENDIN
SENDUP
SENECA
SENEGA
SENHOR

SENIOR
SENITI
SENLAC
SENNAS
SENNET
SENNIT
SENORA
SENORS
SENSED
SENSEI
SENSES
SENSOR
SENTIN
SENTRA
SENTRY
SENTUP
SENUFO
SEPALS
SEPIAS
SEPOYS
SEPTAL
SEPTET
SEPTIC
SEPTUM
SEQUEL
SEQUIN
SERACS
SERAIS
SERAPE
SERAPH
SERBIA
SERENA
SERENE
SERGEI
SERGES
SERGIO
SERIAL
SERIES
SERIFS
SERINE
SERINS
SERKIN
SERMON
SEROSA
SEROUS
SEROWS
SERUMS
SERVAL
SERVED
SERVER
SERVES
SERVOS
SESAME
SESQUI
SESTET
SESTOS
SETINS
SETOFF
SETOSE
SETOUT
SETSAT
SETSBY
SETSIN
SETSON
SETSUP
SETTEE
SETTER
SETTLE
SETTOS
SETUPS
SEURAT
SEVENS
SEVERE
SEVERN

SEVERS
SEVERY
SEVRES
SEWAGE
SEWARD
SEWELL
SEWERS
SEWING
SEWNON
SEWNUP
SEWSON
SEWSUP
SEXIER
SEXILY
SEXIST
SEXTET
SEXTON

S•E•••

SCENAS
SCENDS
SCENES
SCENIC
SCENTS
SEEDED
SEEDER
SEEFIT
SEEGER
SEEING
SEEKER
SEELEY
SEEMED
SEEMLY
SEENIN
SEENTO
SEEOFF
SEEOUT
SEEPED
SEEPIN
SEERED
SEESAW
SEESIN
SEESTO
SEETHE
SHEAFS
SHEARS
SHEATH
SHEAVE
SHEEDY
SHEEHY
SHEENA
SHEENS
SHEEPS
SHEERS
SHEETS
SHEIKS
SHEILA
SHEKEL
SHELLS
SHELLY
SHELTY
SHELVE
SHEREE
SHERIF
SHERPA
SHERRY
SHERYL
SHEVAT
SIECLE
SIEGED
SIEGEL
SIEGES
SIENNA
SIERRA

SIESTA
SIEVED
SIEVES
SKEANS
SKEINS
SKERRY
SKETCH
SKEWED
SKEWER
SLEAVE
SLEAZE
SLEAZY
SLEDGE
SLEEKS
SLEEKY
SLEEPS
SLEEPY
SLEETS
SLEETY
SLEEVE
SLEIGH
SLEUTH
SLEWED
SLEZAK
SMEARS
SMEARY
SMELLS
SMELLY
SMELTS
SMERSH
SNEAKS
SNEAKY
SNEERS
SNEERY
SNEEZE
SNEEZY
SNELLS
SOEURS
SPEAKS
SPEARS
SPECIE
SPECKS
SPEDUP
SPEECH
SPEEDO
SPEEDS
SPEEDY
SPELLS
SPENDS
SPERRY
SPEWED
STEADS
STEADY
STEAKS
STEALS
STEAMS
STEAMY
STEEDS
STEELE
STEELS
STEELY
STEEPS
STEERS
STEEVE
STEFAN
STEFFI
STEFOY
STEINS
STELAE
STELAR
STELES
STELLA
STELMO
STENCH

STENOG
STENOS
STEPIN
STEPON
STEPPE
STEPUP
STEREO
STERES
STERNA
STERNE
STERNO
STERNS
STEROL
STEVEN
STEVIE
STEWED
STEWER
SUEDES
SVELTE
SWEARS
SWEATS
SWEATY
SWEDEN
SWEDES
SWEEPS
SWEETS
SWELLS
SWERVE

S••E••

SABENA
SABERS
SAFELY
SAFEST
SAFETY
SAGELY
SAGEST
SAKERS
SAMECH
SAMEKH
SANELY
SANEST
SASEBO
SATEEN
SAVERS
SAVEUP
SAYERS
SCHELL
SCHEMA
SCHEME
SCLERA
SCLERO
SCREAK
SCREAM
SCREED
SCREEN
SCREES
SCREWS
SCREWY
SEBERG
SECEDE
SECERN
SEDERS
SELECT
SELENA
SELENE
SELENO
SEMELE
SENECA
SENEGA
SERENA
SERENE
SEVENS
SEVERE

SEVERN
SEVERS
SEVERY
SEWELL
SEWERS
SHEEDY
SHEEHY
SHEENA
SHEENS
SHEEPS
SHEERS
SHEETS
SHIELD
SHIEST
SHOERS
SHREDS
SHREWD
SHREWS
SHTETL
SHYEST
SIDERO
SIDERS
SILENI
SILENT
SIMEON
SINEAD
SINEWS
SINEWY
SIRENS
SISERA
SIXERS
SIZERS
SIZEUP
SKIERS
SLEEKS
SLEEKY
SLEEPS
SLEEPY
SLEETS
SLEETY
SLEEVE
SLIEST
SLYEST
SNEERS
SNEERY
SNEEZE
SNEEZY
SOBEIT
SOBERS
SOLEIL
SOLELY
SOLEMN
SOLENT
SOLERS
SOLEUS
SOMERS
SORELY
SOREST
SOWERS
SOWETO
SOXERS
SPEECH
SPEEDO
SPEEDS
SPEEDY
SPHERE
SPHERY
SPIELS
SPIERS
SPLEEN
SPREAD
SPREES
SQUEAK
SQUEAL

STEEDS
STEELE
STEELS
STEELY
STEEPS
STEERS
STEEVE
STHENO
STPETE
STREAK
STREAM
STREEP
STREET
STRESS
STREWN
STREWS
SUPERB
SUPERS
SURELY
SUREST
SURETE
SURETY
SWEEPS
SWEETS

S•••E•

SABLES
SABRES
SACHEM
SACHET
SACKED
SACKER
SACRED
SADDEN
SADDER
SADHES
SAGGED
SAILED
SALLET
SALTED
SALTEN
SALTER
SALVED
SALVER
SALVES
SAMLET
SAMUEL
SANDED
SANDER
SANGER
SANSEI
SANTEE
SAPPED
SAPPER
SARGES
SASHED
SASHES
SASSED
SASSER
SASSES
SATEEN
SAUCED
SAUCER
SAUCES
SAUGER
SAUREL
SAUTES
SAWRED
SAWYER
SAYLES
SAYYES
SCALED
SCALER
SCALES

SCAPED
SCAPES
SCARED
SCARER
SCARES
SCENES
SCHLEP
SCONES
SCOPED
SCOPES
SCORED
SCORER
SCORES
SCOTER
SCREED
SCREEN
SCREES
SCUTES
SEABED
SEABEE
SEALED
SEALER
SEAMED
SEAMEN
SEARED
SEATED
SEATER
SECKEL
SECRET
SEDGES
SEEDED
SEEDER
SEEGER
SEEKER
SEELEY
SEEMED
SEEPED
SEERED
SEGUED
SEGUES
SEIDEL
SEINED
SEINER
SEINES
SEIZED
SEIZER
SEIZES
SELLER
SELVES
SEMPER
SENDER
SENNET
SENSED
SENSEI
SENSES
SEPTET
SEQUEL
SERGEI
SERGES
SERIES
SERVED
SERVER
SERVES
SESTET
SETTEE
SETTER
SEVRES
SEXIER
SEXTET
SHADED
SHADES
SHAKEN
SHAKER
SHAKES

SHALES
SHALEY
SHAMED
SHAMES
SHAPED
SHAPER
SHAPES
SHARED
SHARER
SHARES
SHAVED
SHAVEN
SHAVER
SHAVES
SHEKEL
SHEREE
SHINED
SHINER
SHINES
SHIRER
SHIRES
SHIVER
SHOLEM
SHOOED
SHORED
SHORES
SHOVED
SHOVEL
SHOVER
SHOVES
SHOWED
SHOWER
SHRIEK
SICCED
SICKEN
SICKER
SIDLED
SIDLES
SIDNEY
SIEGED
SIEGEL
SIEGES
SIEVED
SIEVES
SIFTED
SIFTER
SIGHED
SIGHER
SIGNED
SIGNEE
SIGNER
SIGNET
SILKED
SILKEN
SILOED
SILTED
SILVER
SIMBEL
SIMMER
SIMNEL
SIMPER
SINGED
SINGER
SINGES
SINKER
SINNED
SINNER
SINTER
SIPPED
SIPPER
SIPPET
SIRREE
SISKEL
SISLER

SISLEY
SISTER
SITTER
SKATED
SKATER
SKATES
SKEWED
SKEWER
SKIVED
SKIVER
SKIVES
SLAKED
SLAKES
SLATED
SLATER
SLATES
SLAVED
SLAVER
SLAVES
SLAVEY
SLAYED
SLAYER
SLEWED
SLICED
SLICER
SLICES
SLIDER
SLIDES
SLIMED
SLIMES
SLIVER
SLOPED
SLOPES
SLOVEN
SLOWED
SLOWER
SLYPES
SMILED
SMILER
SMILES
SMILEY
SMITES
SMOKED
SMOKER
SMOKES
SMOKEY
SNAKED
SNAKES
SNARED
SNARES
SNIDER
SNIPED
SNIPER
SNIPES
SNIVEL
SNOPES
SNORED
SNORER
SNORES
SNOWED
SNYDER
SOAKED
SOAKER
SOAPED
SOAPER
SOARED
SOARER
SOARES
SOAVES
SOBBED
SOBBER
SOCCER
SOCKED
SOCKET

SOCLES
SODDED
SODDEN
SOFTEN
SOFTER
SOILED
SOIREE
SOLDER
SOLOED
SOLVED
SOLVER
SOLVES
SOMBER
SOMMER
SONDES
SONNET
SOONER
SOPPED
SORBET
SORREL
SORTED
SORTER
SOTTED
SOURED
SOURER
SOUSED
SOUSES
SOUTER
SOVIET
SPACED
SPACEK
SPACER
SPACES
SPACEY
SPADED
SPADER
SPADES
SPARED
SPARER
SPARES
SPATES
SPAYED
SPEWED
SPICED
SPICES
SPIDER
SPIKED
SPIKER
SPIKES
SPILES
SPINED
SPINEL
SPINES
SPINET
SPIREA
SPIRED
SPIRES
SPITED
SPITES
SPLEEN
SPOKED
SPOKEN
SPOKES
SPORES
SPREES
SPRIER
SPRUES
SPRYER
SPUMED
SPUMES
STACEY
STAGED
STAGER
STAGES

STAKED
STAKES
STALED
STALER
STALES
STAMEN
STAPES
STARED
STARER
STARES
STASES
STATED
STATEN
STATER
STATES
STAVED
STAVES
STAYED
STELES
STEREO
STERES
STEVEN
STEWED
STEWER
STILES
STIPEL
STIPES
STIVER
STOKED
STOKER
STOKES
STOLEN
STOLES
STONED
STONER
STONES
STOPES
STORED
STORER
STORES
STOREY
STOVER
STOVES
STOWED
STREEP
STREET
STUMER
STUPES
STYLED
STYLER
STYLES
STYLET
SUAVER
SUBBED
SUBDEB
SUBLET
SUBSET
SUCCES
SUCKED
SUCKER
SUDDEN
SUDSED
SUDSES
SUEDES
SUFFER
SUITED
SUITES
SULKED
SULKER
SULLEN
SUMMED
SUMMER
SUMNER
SUMTER

SUNDER
SUNDEW
SUNKEN
SUNNED
SUNSET
SUPPED
SUPPER
SURFED
SURFER
SURGED
SURGES
SURREY
SURVEY
SUSIEQ
SUSSED
SUSSES
SUSSEX
SUTLER
SUTTER
SWAGED
SWAGES
SWALES
SWANEE
SWAYED
SWAYER
SWEDEN
SWEDES
SWIPED
SWIPER
SWIPES
SWIVEL
SWIVET
SYDNEY
SYNCED
SYSTEM

S••••E

SABINE
SACQUE
SADDLE
SAFIRE
SAINTE
SALINE
SALOME
SALUTE
SAMITE
SAMMIE
SAMPLE
SANTEE
SARTRE
SATIRE
SAVAGE
SAVATE
SAVOIE
SCARCE
SCARNE
SCATHE
SCHEME
SCONCE
SCOUSE
SCRAPE
SCRIBE
SCURVE
SCYTHE
SEABEE
SEANCE
SEARLE
SECEDE
SECURE
SEDATE
SEDILE
SEDUCE
SEETHE
SEICHE

SELENE
SEMELE
SEMITE
SEMPRE
SENATE
SERAPE
SERENE
SERINE
SESAME
SETOSE
SETTEE
SETTLE
SEVERE
SEWAGE
SHAYNE
SHEAVE
SHELVE
SHEREE
SHIITE
SHOPPE
SHORTE
SHOWME
SHRIKE
SHRINE
SHRIVE
SHROVE
SICKLE
SIECLE
SIGNEE
SILAGE
SILONE
SIMILE
SIMONE
SIMPLE
SINGLE
SINISE
SIRREE
SIZZLE
SKOKIE
SKOPJE
SLEAVE
SLEAZE
SLEDGE
SLEEVE
SLOANE
SLUDGE
SLUICE
SMUDGE
SNATHE
SNEEZE
SNOOZE
SOCAGE
SOFINE
SOFTIE
SOIGNE
SOIREE
SOLACE
SOLUTE
SOMBRE
SOOTHE
SOPHIE
SORTIE
SOURCE
SPARGE
SPARSE
SPATHE
SPECIE
SPHERE
SPLICE
SPLINE
SPONGE
SPOUSE
SPRITE
SPRUCE

SPURGE
SQUARE
SQUIRE
STABLE
STACTE
STANCE
STAPLE
STARVE
STATUE
STEELE
STEEVE
STELAE
STEPPE
STERNE
STEVIE
STIFLE
STLUKE
STODGE
STOGIE
STOLLE
STOOGE
STPETE
STRAFE
STRAKE
STRIAE
STRIDE
STRIFE
STRIKE
STRINE
STRIPE
STRIVE
STROBE
STRODE
STROKE
STROVE
STYMIE
SUBDUE
SUBTLE
SUISSE
SUMMAE
SUNDAE
SUPINE
SUPPLE
SURETE
SUTURE
SVELTE
SWANEE
SWATHE
SWAYZE
SWERVE

•SE•••

ASEITY
ASEVER
ISELIN
ISEULT
PSEUDO
PSEUDS
TSETSE
USEDTO
USEDUP
USEFUL
USENET
USERID
USESUP

•S•E••

ASCEND
ASCENT
ASKERS
ASLEEP
ASPECT
ASPENS
ASPERA

ASSENT
ASSERT
ASSESS
ASSETS
ASTERN
ASTERS
ASWELL
ESCENT
ESKERS
ESSENE
ESTEEM
ESTERS
ISLETS
ISMENE
OSIERS
OSSEIN
OSSETE
OSTEAL
OSTEND
OSWEGO
USHERS

•S••E•

ASEVER
ASHIER
ASHLEY
ASIDES
ASLEEP
BSIDES
ESCHER
ESCHEW
ESPIED
ESPIES
ESTEEM
ESTHER
ISABEL
ISOHEL
ISOMER
ISRAEL
ISSUED
ISSUER
ISSUES
ISTLES
OSAGES
OSPREY
OSTLER
RSVPED
USAGES
USENET
USOPEN
USURER
VSIXES

•S•••E

ASHORE
ASLOPE
ASPIRE
ASSIZE
ASSUME
ASSURE
ASTUTE
ESCAPE
ESSENE
ESTATE
ISMENE
ISOLDE
OSCINE
OSMOSE
OSSETE
PSYCHE
TSETSE
USABLE
USANCE

••SE••

ABSENT ANSELM ARSENE ASSENT ASSERT ASSESS ASSETS AXSEED BASELY BASEST BESETS BISECT CASEFY CASERN COSELL DESERT DOSERS EASEIN EASELS EASEUP EDSELS ESSENE ETSEQQ EXSERT FUSEES HOSELS INSEAM INSECT INSERT INSETS ITSELF JASEYS JOSEPH LASERS LOSEIT LOSERS MASERS MASERU MISERS MISERY MOSEYS MUSERS MUSEUM MYSELF NASEBY OBSESS ONSETS OSSEIN OSSETE OUSELS PASEOS PESETA POSERS POSEUR RASERS RESEAL RESEAT RESEAU RESECT RESEDA RESEED RESEEN RESEES RESELL RESEND RESENT RESETS RESEWN RESEWS RISERS ROSEAU SASEBO SISERA TASERS TVSETS UNSEAL UNSEAT UNSEEN UNSEWN UNSEWS UPSETS WISELY WISENT WISEST WISETO WISEUP

••S•E•

AISLES AMSTEL ANSWER AUSPEX AUSTEN AXSEED BASHED BASHES BASKED BASKET BASSES BASSET BASTED BASTER BASTES BESSER BESTED BISSET BOSKET BOSLEY BOSSED BOSSES BUSHED BUSHEL BUSHES BUSIED BUSIER BUSIES BUSKED BUSMEN BUSSED BUSSES BUSTED BUSTER CASHED CASHES CASHEW CASPER CASTER CASTES CESSED CESSES CISKEI COSHED COSHES COSIED COSIER COSIES COSSET CUSPED CUSSED CUSSES CUSTER DASHED DASHER DASHES DISHED DISHES DISKED DISMES DISNEY DISPEL DISSED DOSSED DOSSEL DOSSER DOSSES DUSTED DUSTER EASIER EASTER EISNER ENSUED ENSUES FASCES FASTED FASTEN FASTER FESSED FESSES FESTER FISHED FISHER FISHES FISTED FOSSES FOSSEY FOSTER FUSEES FUSSED FUSSES GASHED GASHES GASJET GASKET GASMEN GASPED GASPER GASSED GASSER GASSES GESTES GOSHEN GOSPEL GUSHED GUSHER GUSHES GUSSET GUSTED HASHED HASHES HASPED HASTEN HASTES HESTER HISSED HISSER HISSES HOSIER HOSTED HOSTEL HUSHED HUSHES HUSKED HUSKER HUSSEY IJSSEL INSTEP ISSUED ISSUER ISSUES JASPER JESSEL JESTED JESTER JOSHED JOSHES JOSSER JOSSES JUSTER KISLEV KISMET KISSED KISSER KISSES KOSHER LASHED LASHER LASHES LASSEN LASSER LASSES LASTED LASTEX LESLEY LESSEE LESSEN LESSER LESTER LISLES LISPED LISTED LISTEE LISTEL LISTEN LISTER LOSSES LUSHER LUSTED LUSTER MASHED MASHER MASHES MASKED MASKER MASSED MASSES MASSEY MASTER MESHED MESHES MESMER MESSED MESSES MISLED MISSED MISSES MISTED MISTER MOSHED MOSHER MOSHES MOSLEM MOSSED MOSSES MOSTEL MUSHED MUSHER MUSHES MUSKEG MUSKET MUSSED MUSSEL MUSSES MUSTER NASSER NESSES NESTEA NESTED NESTER NISSEN NOSHED NOSHER NOSHES NOSIER OBSTET ONSPEC OUSTED OUSTER OYSTER PASSED PASSEL PASSER PASSES PASTED PASTEL PASTES PESTER PISCES PISTES POSHER POSIES POSSES POSSET POSTED POSTER PUSHED PUSHES PUSSES RASHER RASHES RASPED RASPER RASTER RESEED RESEEN RESEES RESHES RESTED RESTER RISKED RISKER ROSIER ROSTER RUSHED RUSHEE RUSHES RUSSET RUSTED SASHED SASHES SASSED SASSER SASSES SESTET SISKEL SISLER SISLEY SISTER SUSIEQ SUSSED SUSSES SUSSEX SYSTEM TASKED TASSEL TASSES TASTED TASTER TASTES TESTED TESTEE TESTER TOSSED TOSSER TOSSES TUSKED TUSKER ULSTER UNSEEN UNSHED VASTER VESPER VESSEL VESTED VESTEE VISAED VOSGES WASHED WASHER WASHES WASTED WASTER WASTES WESLEY WESSEX WISHED WISHER WISHES WISPED WISTER WUSSES XYSTER YASSER YESMEN YESSED YESSES YESTER ZESTED

••S••E

ALSACE ANSATE ARSENE ASSIZE ASSUME ASSURE AUSSIE BASQUE BESIDE BESSIE BISQUE BUSTLE BYSSHE CASQUE CASTLE CESARE COSINE COSTAE DESIRE DISUSE DOSAGE ENSILE ENSURE ESSENE FESCUE FOSSAE HASSLE HUSTLE INSANE INSIDE INSOLE INSURE JESSIE JOSTLE KISHKE LASSIE LESAGE LESLIE LESSEE LISTEE LUSTRE LYSINE MASHIE MASQUE MISCUE MISUSE MOSQUE MUSCLE MUSKIE MYSORE NESSIE NESTLE NOSALE ONSALE ONSIDE ONSITE OSSETE PESTLE RASSLE RESALE RESCUE RESHOE RESIDE RESILE RESOLE RESUME RISQUE ROSCOE RUSHEE RUSTLE SESAME TESSIE TESTAE TESTEE TISANE TISSUE TUSSLE UGSOME UNSAFE UNSURE UPSIDE URSINE VESTEE VISAGE VISINE WASHOE

•••SE•

ABASED ABASES ABUSED ABUSER ABUSES ALLSET AMUSED AMUSES ARISEN ARISES BASSES BASSET BESSER BETSEY BIASED BIASES BISSET BOSSED BOSSES BOUSED BOUSES BOWSER BOXSET BUNSEN BURSES BUSSED BUSSES CAUSED CAUSES CEASED CEASES CENSED CENSER CENSES CESSED CESSES CHASED CHASER CHASES CHISEL CHOSEN CLOSED CLOSER CLOSES CLOSET COPSES CORSET COSSET CRISES CRUSES CURSED CURSES CUSSED CUSSES DAISES DAMSEL DENSER DIESEL DIESES DILSEY DISSED DORSET DORSEY DOSSED DOSSEL DOSSER DOSSES DOUSED DOUSES DOWSED DOWSER DOWSES ELYSEE ERASED ERASER ERASES FALSER FESSED FESSES FOSSES FOSSEY FRASER FRISEE FRISES FUSSED FUSSES GASSED GASSER GASSES GEISEL GELSEY GETSET GEYSER GLASER GOOSED GOOSES GOOSEY GORSES GOTSET GUISES GUSSET HALSEY HANSEL HAWSER HAWSES HERSEY HISSED HISSER HISSES HORSED HORSES HORSEY HOUSED HOUSES HUSSEY IBISES IJSSEL IRISES JANSEN JENSEN JERSEY JESSEL JETSET JOSSER JOSSES KAISER KELSEY KERSEE KERSEY KINSEY KISSED KISSER KISSES LAPSED LAPSES LARSEN LASSEN LASSER LASSES LEASED LEASER LEASES LENSED LENSES LESSEE LESSEN LESSER LINSEY LOOSED LOOSEN LOOSER LOOSES LOSSES LOUSED LOUSES MADSEN MANSES MASSED MASSES MASSEY MAUSER MERSEY MESSED MESSES MISSED MISSES MORSEL MOSSED MOSSES MOUSED MOUSER MOUSES MOUSEY MUSSED MUSSEL MUSSES NANSEN NASSER NAUSEA NESSES NIPSEY NISSEN NOISED NOISES NOOSED NOOSES NURSED NURSER NURSES OCASEK OCASEY OFFSET ONUSES OPUSES OUTSET PARSEC PARSED PARSEE PARSER PARSES PASSED PASSEL PASSER PASSES PAUSED PAUSES PENSEE PHASED PHASER PHASES PHYSED PLUSES POISED POISES POSSES POSSET PRASES PRESET PROSED PROSER PROSES PULSED PULSES PURSED PURSER PURSES PUSSES RAISED RAISER RAISES RAMSES RAMSEY REDSEA REESES REUSED REUSES RINSED RINSES ROUSED ROUSER ROUSES RUSSET SANSEI SASSED SASSER SASSES SENSED SENSEI SENSES SOUSED SOUSES STASES SUBSET SUDSED SUDSES SUNSET SUSSED SUSSES SUSSEX TASSEL TASSES TEASED TEASEL TEASER TEASES TEASET TENSED TENSER TENSES TERSER THESEA THESES TINSEL TOSSED TOSSER TOSSES UKASES UNISEX UNUSED UPASES URUSES VERSED VERSES VESSEL WEASEL WESSEX WIESEL WIMSEY WOLSEY WORSEN WOWSER WUSSES YASSER YESSED YESSES

•••S•E

ABESSE ADESTE AUSSIE BESSIE BURSAE BYSSHE CHASSE CHASTE CROSSE CRUSOE CUISSE ELYSEE ENISLE FOCSLE FOSSAE FRISEE GROSSE HASSLE INESSE JESSIE KERSEE KRESGE LASSIE LESSEE LETSBE MAISIE MENSAE MOUSSE NEISSE NESSIE PARSEE PENSEE PLISSE POUSSE PUISNE PURSUE RASSLE SUISSE TESSIE THISBE TISSUE TOUSLE TRISTE TUSSLE WRASSE

••••SE

ABESSE ACCUSE ADVISE ALDOSE APPOSE ARIOSE AROUSE ATEASE AVERSE AVULSE BEMUSE BETISE BLAISE BLOUSE BOURSE BRAISE BROWSE BRUISE CAMISE CAYUSE CERISE CERUSE CHAISE CHASSE CHEESE CHOOSE CLAUSE CLEESE COARSE COURSE CREASE CROSSE CROUSE CRUISE CUISSE DEBASE DEFUSE DEMISE DENISE DEPOSE DEVISE DISUSE DROWSE EFFUSE ELAPSE ELOISE ENCASE ENDUSE EVULSE EXCISE EXCUSE EXPOSE FILOSE FLENSE FRAISE GREASE GRILSE GROSSE GROUSE GYROSE HOARSE ILLUSE IMPOSE INCASE INCISE INCUSE INESSE INFUSE IODISE IONISE JOCOSE LANOSE LAOTSE LHOTSE LIAISE LIPASE LOUISE MISUSE MOROSE MOUSSE NEISSE NODOSE NOLOSE NOWISE OBTUSE ODENSE OPPOSE ORELSE OSMOSE OTIOSE PERUSE PHRASE PILOSE PLEASE PLISSE POUSSE PRAISE PROWSE RAMOSE RECUSE REFUSE REMISE REPOSE REVISE RIBOSE RIMOSE RUGOSE SCOUSE SETOSE SINISE SPARSE SPOUSE SUISSE TALESE TOROSE TSETSE UNCASE UNEASE UNWISE UPRISE UPROSE VADOSE VALISE VARESE WRASSE ZYMASE

SF••••

SFORZA

S•F•••

SAFARI SAFELY SAFEST SAFETY SAFIRE SIFTED SIFTER SOFFIT SOFINE SOFTEN SOFTER SOFTIE SOFTLY SUFFER SUFFIX SUFISM

S••F••

SAWFIT SCIFIS SCOFFS SCUFFS SEAFAN SEAFOX SEEFIT SHAFTS SHIFTS SHIFTY SHOFAR SINFUL SKIFFS SNAFUS SNIFFS SNIFFY SNUFFS SNUFFY SOBFUL SOFFIT SOLFAS SPIFFS SPIFFY STAFFS STEFAN STEFFI STEFOY STIFFS STIFLE STUFFS STUFFY SUFFER SUFFIX SULFUR SURFED SURFER SWIFTS

S•••F•

SALIFY SAWOFF SCARFS SCHIFF SCLAFF SCOFFS SCRUFF SCUFFS SCURFY SEEOFF SENUFO SERIFS SETOFF SHEAFS SHRIFT SKIFFS SMURFS SNIFFS SNIFFY SNUFFS SNUFFY SPIFFS SPIFFY SPOOFS STAFFS STEFFI STIFFS STRAFE STRIFE STUFFS STUFFY

S••••F

SAWOFF SCHIFF SCLAFF SCRUFF SEEOFF SETOFF SHARIF SHERIF SORTOF STAPUF

•S•F••

ASKFOR USEFUL

•S••F•

OSSIFY

••SF••

MISFIT

••S•F•

BASIFY CASEFY GASIFY GOSOFT OSSIFY UNSAFE

••S••F

ITSELF MASSIF MYSELF

•••S•F

MASSIF RIDSOF

SG••••

SGTMAJ

S•G•••

SAGELY SAGEST SAGGED SEGUED SEGUES SEGURA SIGHED SIGHER SIGHTS SIGILS SIGMAS SIGNAL SIGNED SIGNEE SIGNER SIGNET SIGNIN SIGNON SIGNOR SIGNUP SIGURD SUGARS SUGARY

S••G••

SAGGED SAIGAS SAIGON SANGER SANGTO SARGES SARGON SARGOS SAUGER SEAGAL SEDGES SEEGER SERGEI SERGES SERGIO SHAGGY SHOGUN SIEGED SIEGEL SIEGES SINGED SINGER SINGES SINGIN SINGLE SINGLY SINGTO SIXGUN SLAGGY SLIGHT SLOGAN SLUGGO SMOGGY SMUGLY SNAGGY SNUGLI SNUGLY SOIGNE SOUGHS SOUGHT SPIGOT STAGED STAGER STAGES STIGMA STOGIE SUBGUM SUNGOD SURGED SURGES SWAGED SWAGES

S•••G•
SAVAGE
SCRAGS
SENEGA
SEWAGE
SHAGGY
SHRUGS
SILAGE
SLAGGY
SLANGS
SLANGY
SLEDGE
SLEIGH
SLINGS
SLOUGH
SLUDGE
SLUDGY
SLUGGO
SMOGGY
SMUDGE
SMUDGY
SNAGGY
SOCAGE
SPARGE
SPONGE
SPONGY
SPRAGS
SPRIGS
SPURGE
STINGO
STINGS
STINGY
STODGE
STODGY
STOOGE
SWINGS
SWINGY
SYZYGY

S••••G
SARONG
SATANG
SATING
SAVING
SAWING
SAWLOG
SAYING
SEABAG
SEADOG
SEBERG
SEEING
SEWING
SHYING
SIDING
SIRING
SITING
SIXING
SIZING
SKIING
SKYING
SLUING
SOLING
SOLONG
SONTAG
SOWBUG
SOWING
SPRANG
SPRING
SPRUNG
SPYING
STALAG
STENOG
STRING
STRONG
STRUNG
SUNDOG

•SG•••
ASGARD
OSGOOD

•S•G••
ISOGON
OSAGES
USAGES
VSIGNS

•S••G•
ASSIGN
OSWEGO

•S•••G
ASKING

••SG••
ANSGAR
PISGAH
VOSGES

••S•G•
ASSIGN
COSIGN
DESIGN
DOSAGE
ENSIGN
LESAGE
RESIGN
VISAGE

••S••G
BASING
BUSING
CASING
DOSING
EASING
FUSING
GASBAG
GASLOG
GOSTAG
HOSING
LOSING
MUSING
MUSKEG
NOSING
POSING
RASING
RESING
RISING
UNSNAG
UNSUNG

•••SG•
KRESGE
LETSGO

SH••••
SHABAN
SHABBY
SHACKS
SHADED
SHADES
SHADOW
SHAFTS
SHAGGY
SHAKEN
SHAKER
SHAKES
SHAKOS
SHAKTI
SHALES
SHALEY
SHALLY
SHALOM
SHAMAN
SHAMED
SHAMES
SHAMIR
SHAMUS
SHANDY
SHANIA
SHANKS
SHANNY
SHANTY
SHAPED
SHAPER
SHAPES
SHARDS
SHARED
SHARER
SHARES
SHARIA
SHARIF
SHARKS
SHARON
SHARPS
SHASTA
SHAVED
SHAVEN
SHAVER
SHAVES
SHAWLS
SHAWMS
SHAYNE
SHAZAM
SHBOOM
SHEAFS
SHEARS
SHEATH
SHEAVE
SHEEDY
SHEEHY
SHEENA
SHEENS
SHEEPS
SHEERS
SHEETS
SHEIKS
SHEILA
SHEKEL
SHELLS
SHELLY
SHELTY
SHELVE
SHEREE
SHERIF
SHERPA
SHERRY
SHERYL
SHEVAT
SHIELD
SHIEST
SHIFTS
SHIFTY
SHIISM
SHIITE
SHIKAR
SHILLS
SHILLY
SHILOH
SHIMMY
SHIMON
SHINDY
SHINED
SHINER
SHINES
SHINNY
SHINTO
SHIRAZ
SHIRER
SHIRES
SHIRKS
SHIRRS
SHIRTS
SHIRTY
SHIVER
SHOALS
SHOALY
SHOATS
SHOCKS
SHODDY
SHOERS
SHOFAR
SHOGUN
SHOJIS
SHOLEM
SHOLOM
SHOOED
SHOOIN
SHOOKS
SHOOTS
SHOPPE
SHORAN
SHORED
SHORES
SHORTA
SHORTE
SHORTI
SHORTO
SHORTS
SHORTU
SHORTY
SHOTAT
SHOTUP
SHOULD
SHOUTS
SHOVED
SHOVEL
SHOVER
SHOVES
SHOWED
SHOWER
SHOWIN
SHOWME
SHOWUP
SHRANK
SHREDS
SHREWD
SHREWS
SHRIEK
SHRIFT
SHRIKE
SHRILL
SHRIMP
SHRINE
SHRINK
SHRIVE
SHROUD
SHROVE
SHRUBS
SHRUGS
SHRUNK
SHTETL
SHTICK
SHUCKS
SHUNTS
SHUTIN
SHUTUP
SHYEST
SHYING

S•H•••
SAHARA
SAHIBS
SCHELL
SCHEMA
SCHEME
SCHICK
SCHIFF
SCHISM
SCHIST
SCHIZY
SCHLEP
SCHMOO
SCHMOS
SCHNOZ
SCHOOL
SCHORL
SCHULZ
SCHUSS
SCHWAB
SCHWAS
SPHERE
SPHERY
SPHINX
STHENO

S••H••
SACHEM
SACHET
SADHES
SADHUS
SASHAY
SASHED
SASHES
SENHOR
SIGHED
SIGHER
SIGHTS
SIPHON
SOPHIA
SOPHIE
SOTHAT
SOWHAT
SPAHIS
SUCHAS
SYPHON

S•••H•
SANCHO
SAPPHO
SCATHE
SCYTHE
SEETHE
SEICHE
SHEEHY
SIXTHS
SLIGHT
SLITHY
SLOSHY
SLOTHS
SLUSHY
SMITHS
SMITHY
SNATHE
SNATHS
SOOTHE
SOUGHS
SOUGHT
SOUTHS
SPATHE
STITHY
STJOHN
SURAHS
SWATHE
SWATHS
SYLPHS

S••••H
SALISH
SAMECH
SAMEKH
SCORCH
SCOTCH
SCUTCH
SEARCH
SERAPH
SHEATH
SHILOH
SIRRAH
SIWASH
SKETCH
SKITCH
SLEIGH
SLEUTH
SLOUCH
SLOUGH
SMERSH
SMIRCH
SMOOCH
SMOOTH
SMUTCH
SNATCH
SNITCH
SPEECH
SPILTH
SPLASH
SPLOSH
SQUASH
SQUISH
SQUUSH
STANCH
STARCH
STENCH
STITCH
STORCH
SUKKAH
SWARTH
SWATCH
SWITCH
SWOOSH

•SH•••
ASHARP
ASHCAN
ASHIER
ASHLAR
ASHLEY
ASHORE
ASHRAM
BSHARP
CSHARP
DSHARP
ESHARP
FSHARP
GSHARP
ISHTAR
OSHAWA
TSHIRT
USHERS

•S•H••
ASCHAM
ESCHER
ESCHEW
ESTHER
ISCHIA
ISOHEL
ISTHMI

•S••H•
PSYCHE
PSYCHO
PSYCHS

•S•••H
ASPISH
ISAIAH

••SH••
BASHED
BASHES
BISHOP
BUSHED
BUSHEL
BUSHES
BUSHWA
CASHED
CASHES
CASHEW
CASHIN
COSHED
COSHES
CUSHAW
DASHED
DASHER
DASHES
DASHIS
DISHED
DISHES
FISHED
FISHER
FISHES
GASHED
GASHES
GOSHEN
GUSHED
GUSHER
GUSHES
HASHED
HASHES
HUSHED
HUSHES
JOSHED
JOSHES
JOSHUA
KESHIA
KISHKE
KOSHER
LASHED
LASHER
LASHES
LASHIO
LASHUP
LUSHER
LUSHLY
MASHED
MASHER
MASHES
MASHIE
MESHED
MESHES
MISHAP
MISHIT
MOSHAV
MOSHED
MOSHER
MOSHES
MUSHED
MUSHER
MUSHES
NASHUA
NOSHED
NOSHER
NOSHES
NOSHOW
PASHAS
PASHTO
POSHER
POSHLY
PUSHED
PUSHES
PUSHON
PUSHUP
RASHAD
RASHER
RASHES
RASHID
RASHLY
RESHES
RESHIP
RESHOD
RESHOE
RESHOT
RUSHED
RUSHEE
RUSHES
SASHAY
SASHED
SASHES
TISHRI
TVSHOW
UNSHED
UNSHOD
UPSHOT
VASHTI
VISHNU
WASHED
WASHER
WASHES
WASHOE
WASHUP
WISHED
WISHER
WISHES

••S•H•
BYSSHE
JASCHA
MISCHA

••S••H
CASBAH
JOSEPH
JOSIAH
KASBAH
PESACH
PISGAH
TUSSAH

•••SH•
AYESHA
BOLSHY
BRASHY
BRUSHY
BUQSHA
BYSSHE
ELISHA
FLASHY
FLESHY
GEISHA
GUNSHY
HONSHU
ILESHA
KYUSHU
MARSHA
MARSHY
PLASHY
PLUSHY
SLOSHY
SLUSHY
TRASHY
TRISHA

•••S•H
BORSCH
HIRSCH
KIRSCH
KITSCH
MENSCH
PUTSCH
TUSSAH

••••SH
ABLUSH
AFRESH
AGUISH
AMBUSH
ASPISH
BANISH
BARISH
BLUISH
BOYISH
BYGOSH
CALASH
COYISH
DANISH
DOVISH
DUDISH
ELFISH
ELVISH
EMDASH
ENDASH
ENMESH
FAMISH
FETISH
FINISH
GALOSH
GARISH
GOFISH
IMPISH
INCASH
INRUSH
IRTYSH
JADISH
JEWISH
JUTISH
KIBOSH
LAGASH
LATISH
LAVISH
LOWISH
MARISH
MODISH
MOPISH
MULISH
NEWISH
OAFISH
OFFISH
OGRISH
OLDISH
ONRUSH
OWLISH
PALISH
PARISH
PERISH
POLISH
POTASH
PUNISH
QURUSH
RADISH
RAKISH
RAVISH
RAWISH
REHASH
RELISH
REWASH
SALISH
SIWASH
SMERSH
SPLASH
SPLOSH
SQUASH
SQUISH
SQUUSH
SWOOSH
THRASH
THRESH
THRUSH
TONISH
UNLASH
UNMESH
UNWISH
UPPISH
UPRUSH
VANISH
WABASH
WHOOSH
WIDISH
WINISH

SI••••
SIBYLS
SICCED
SICILY
SICKEN
SICKER
SICKLE
SICKLY
SIDDUR
SIDERO
SIDERS
SIDING
SIDLED
SIDLES
SIDNEY
SIECLE
SIEGED
SIEGEL
SIEGES
SIENNA
SIERRA
SIESTA
SIEVED
SIEVES
SIFTED
SIFTER
SIGHED
SIGHER
SIGHTS
SIGILS
SIGMAS
SIGNAL
SIGNED
SIGNEE
SIGNER
SIGNET
SIGNIN
SIGNON
SIGNOR
SIGNUP
SIGURD
SIKKIM
SILAGE
SILENI
SILENT
SILICA
SILKED
SILKEN
SILOAM
SILOED
SILONE
SILTED
SILVAS
SILVER
SIMBEL
SIMEON
SIMIAN
SIMILE
SIMMER
SIMNEL
SIMONE
SIMONY
SIMPER
SIMPLE
SIMPLY
SINBAD
SINEAD
SINEWS
SINEWY
SINFUL
SINGED
SINGER
SINGES
SINGIN
SINGLE
SINGLY
SINGTO
SINISE
SINKER
SINKIN
SINNED
SINNER
SINTAX
SINTER
SIOUAN
SIPHON
SIPPED
SIPPER
SIPPET
SIRDAR
SIRENS
SIRICA
SIRING
SIRIUS
SIRRAH
SIRREE
SISALS
SISERA
SISKEL
SISKIN
SISLER
SISLEY
SISTER
SISTRA
SITARS
SITCOM
SITING
SITINS
SITOUT
SITSBY
SITSIN
SITSON
SITSUP
SITTER
SITUPS
SIWASH
SIXERS
SIXGUN
SIXING
SIXTHS
SIXTUS
SIZERS
SIZEUP
SIZING
SIZZLE

S•I•••
SAIGAS
SAIGON
SAILED
SAILOR
SAINTE
SAINTS
SAIPAN
SCIFIS
SCIONS
SCIPIO
SEICHE
SEIDEL
SEINED
SEINER
SEINES
SEISMO
SEISMS
SEIZED
SEIZER
SEIZES
SHIELD
SHIEST
SHIFTS
SHIFTY
SHIISM
SHIITE
SHIKAR
SHILLS
SHILLY
SHILOH
SHIMMY
SHIMON
SHINDY
SHINED
SHINER
SHINES
SHINNY
SHINTO
SHIRAZ
SHIRER
SHIRES
SHIRKS
SHIRRS
SHIRTS
SHIRTY
SHIVER
SKIBOB
SKIDDY
SKIERS
SKIFFS
SKIING
SKILLS
SKIMPS
SKIMPY
SKINKS
SKINNY
SKIPIT
SKIPPY
SKIRLS
SKIROS
SKIRRS
SKIRTS
SKIRUN
SKITCH
SKITOW
SKIVED
SKIVER
SKIVES
SKIVVY
SLICED
SLICER
SLICES
SLICKS
SLIDER
SLIDES
SLIDIN
SLIEST
SLIGHT
SLIMED
SLIMES
SLIMLY
SLIMSY
SLINGS
SLINKS
SLINKY
SLIPIN
SLIPON
SLIPPY
SLIPUP
SLITHY
SLITTY
SLIVER
SMILAX
SMILED
SMILER
SMILES
SMILEY
SMILIN
SMIRCH
SMIRKS
SMIRKY
SMITES
SMITHS
SMITHY
SNICKS
SNIDER
SNIFFS
SNIFFY
SNIPED
SNIPER
SNIPES
SNIPPY
SNITCH
SNIVEL
SOIGNE
SOILED
SOIREE
SPICAS
SPICED
SPICES
SPIDER
SPIELS
SPIERS
SPIFFS
SPIFFY
SPIGOT
SPIKED
SPIKER
SPIKES
SPILES
SPILLS
SPILTH
SPINAL
SPINED
SPINEL
SPINES
SPINET
SPINKS
SPINTO
SPIRAL
SPIREA
SPIRED
SPIRES
SPIRIT
SPIROS
SPITED
SPITES
SPIVAK
SPIVVY
STICKS
STICKY
STIFFS
STIFLE
STIGMA
STILES
STILLS
STILLY
STILTS
STIMPY
STINGO
STINGS
STINGY
STINKS
STINKY
STINTS
STIPEL
STIPES
STIRIN
STIRKS
STIRUP
STITCH
STITHY
STIVER
STIVIC
SUISSE
SUITED
SUITES
SUITOR
SUITUP
SWIFTS
SWILLS
SWINGS
SWINGY
SWIPED
SWIPER
SWIPES
SWIRLS
SWIRLY
SWITCH
SWIVEL
SWIVET

S••I••
SABINE
SABINS
SAFIRE
SAHIBS
SALIFY
SALINA
SALINE
SALISH
SALIVA
SAMIAM
SAMITE
SANITY
SATING
SATINS
SATINY
SATIRE
SAVING
SAVIOR
SAWING
SAYING
SCHICK
SCHIFF
SCHISM
SCHIST
SCHIZY
SCRIBE
SCRIMP
SCRIMS
SCRIPS
SCRIPT
SEDILE
SEEING
SEMITE
SENIOR
SENITI
SEPIAS
SERIAL
SERIES
SERIFS
SERINE
SERINS
SETINS
SEWING
SEXIER
SEXILY
SEXIST
SHEIKS
SHEILA
SHIISM
SHIITE
SHRIEK
SHRIFT
SHRIKE
SHRILL
SHRIMP
SHRINE
SHRINK
SHRIVE
SHTICK
SHYING
SICILY
SIDING
SIGILS
SILICA
SIMIAN
SIMILE
SINISE
SIRICA
SIRING
SIRIUS
SITING
SITINS
SIXING
SIZING
SKEINS
SKIING
SKYING
SLEIGH
SLUICE
SLUING
SNAILS
SOCIAL
SODIUM
SOFINE
SOLIDI
SOLIDS
SOLING
SONICS
SOVIET
SOWING
SPHINX
SPLICE
SPLINE
SPLINT
SPLITS
SPOILS
SPOILT
SPRIER
SPRIGS
SPRING
SPRINT
SPRITE
SPRITS
SPRITZ
SPYING
SQUIBB
SQUIBS
SQUIDS
SQUILL
SQUINT
SQUIRE
SQUIRM
SQUIRT
SQUISH
STAINS
STAIRS
STEINS
STOICS
STRIAE
STRICK
STRICT
STRIDE
STRIFE
STRIKE
STRINE
STRING
STRIPE
STRIPS
STRIPY
STRIVE
SUBITO
SUFISM
SUPINE
SURIMI
SUSIEQ
SWAINS
SYRIAN
SYRINX

S•••I•
SALVIA
SAMMIE
SANDIA
SANTIR
SARDIS
SARNIA
SAUDIS
SAVAII
SAVOIE
SAVOIR
SAWFIT
SAYYID
SCALIA
SCENIC
SCIFIS
SCIPIO
SCORIA
SCOTIA
SEEFIT
SEENIN
SEEPIN
SEESIN
SENDIN
SENNIT

SENTIN
SEPTIC
SEQUIN
SERAIS
SERBIA
SERGIO
SERKIN
SETSIN
SHAMIR
SHANIA
SHARIA
SHARIF
SHERIF
SHOJIS
SHOOIN
SHOWIN
SHUTIN
SIGNIN
SIKKIM
SINGIN
SINKIN
SISKIN
SITSIN
SKIPIT
SKOKIE
SLAVIC
SLIDIN
SLIPIN
SLOVIK
SMILIN
SNOWIN
SOBEIT
SOCKIN
SOFFIT
SOFTIE
SOLEIL
SOPHIA
SOPHIE
SORBIC
SORDID
SORTIE
SPADIX
SPAHIS
SPAVIN
SPECIE
SPIRIT
SPRAIN
STADIA
STALIN
STASIS
STATIC
STEPIN
STEVIE
STIRIN
STIVIC
STOGIE
STOLID
STOPIN
STOPIT
STOTIN
STRAIN
STRAIT
STUDIO
STUPID
STYMIE
STYRIA
SUBMIT
SUCKIN
SUFFIX
SUMMIT
SUNLIT
SUNNIS
SUSLIK
SWAMIS
SWAZIS
SYLVIA
SYNDIC

S••••I

SAFARI
SALAMI
SALUKI
SANSEI
SATORI
SAVAII
SCAMPI
SENITI
SENSEI
SERGEI
SESQUI
SHAKTI
SHORTI
SILENI
SMALTI
SNUGLI
SOLIDI
SOMALI
SOUARI
STEFFI
STRATI
SURIMI
SUZUKI

•SI•••

ASIANS
ASIDES
ASIMOV
BSIDES
OSIERS
OSIRIS
VSIGNS
VSIXES

•S•I••

ASDICS
ASEITY
ASHIER
ASKING
ASPICS
ASPIRE
ASPISH
ASSIGN
ASSISI
ASSIST
ASSIZE
ASWIRL
ESKIMO
ESPIAL
ESPIED
ESPIES
GSUITS
ISAIAH
OSCINE
OSMICS
OSMIUM
OSSIAN
OSSIFY
OSTIUM
TSHIRT

•S••I•

ASKSIN
ASSAIL
ASTRID
ESPRIT
ISCHIA
ISELIN
ISTRIA
OSIRIS
OSSEIN
TSURIS
USERID
USMAIL

•S•••I

ASKARI
ASSISI
ISTHMI

••SI••

ASSIGN
ASSISI
ASSIST
ASSIZE
BASICS
BASIFY
BASING
BASINS
BESIDE
BUSIED
BUSIER
BUSIES
BUSILY
BUSING
CASING
CASINO
CESIUM
COSIED
COSIER
COSIES
COSIGN
COSILY
COSINE
DESICA
DESIGN
DESILU
DESIRE
DESIST
DOSIDO
DOSING
EASIER
EASILY
EASING
ENSIGN
ENSILE
EOSINS
FUSILS
FUSING
FUSION
GASIFY
HESIOD
HOSIER
HOSING
INSIDE
INSIST
INSITU
JOSIAH
LOSING
LYSINE
LYSINS
MUSIAL
MUSING
NOSIER
NOSILY
NOSING
ONSIDE
ONSITE
ORSINO
OSSIAN
OSSIFY
POSIES
POSING
POSITS
RASING
RESIDE
RESIGN
RESILE
RESING
RESINS
RESINY
RESIST
RISING
ROSIER
ROSILY
ROSINS
ROSINY
ROSITA
SUSIEQ
UPSIDE
URSIDS
URSINE
VISINE
VISION
VISITS

••S•I•

ASSAIL
AUSSIE
AUSTIN
BESSIE
BESTIR
BOSNIA
BUSKIN
BUSTIN
CASHIN
CASSIA
CASSIO
CASSIS
COSMIC
CUSPID
CUSTIS
DASHIS
DASSIN
DISTIL
DUSTIN
EASEIN
FASCIA
FISTIC
FOSSIL
FUSTIC
GASKIN
GASLIT
GESTIC
GOSSIP
HESTIA
HISPID
INSTIL
JESSIE
JESUIT
JOSKIN
JUSTIN
KESHIA
LASHIO
LASSIE
LESLIE
LOSEIT
LOSTIT
MASAIS
MASHIE
MASSIF
MASTIC
MISDID
MISFIT
MISHIT
MISSIS
MOSAIC
MUSKIE
MUSLIM
MUSLIN
MYSTIC
NESSIE
OSSEIN
PASSIM
PASTIS
PISTIL
POSTIT
RASHID
RESHIP
RESNIK
RESPIN
RUSKIN
RUSSIA
RUSTIC
SISKIN
SUSLIK
TESSIE
UNSAID
VESPID
VISCID
WESKIT
YESSIR

••S••I

ASSISI
BUSONI
CISKEI
MESABI
SESQUI
TISHRI
VASHTI
WASABI

•••SI•

ADDSIN
ASKSIN
AUSSIE
BAGSIT
BESSIE
BIDSIN
CAPSID
CASSIA
CASSIO
CASSIS
COUSIN
CRISIS
CUTSIN
DASSIN
DEASIL
DIESIS
DIGSIN
DOESIN
DOGSIT
EATSIN
ECESIC
ECESIS
ENOSIS
FITSIN
FOGSIN
FOSSIL
GETSIN
GETSIT
GNOSIS
GOESIN
GOSSIP
HEMSIN
HITSIT
HOPSIN
ICESIN
IRISIN
JAMSIN
JESSIE
KEYSIN
LASSIE
LAYSIN
LETSIN
LIESIN
LOGSIN
MAISIE
MASSIF
MIOSIS
MISSIS
MYOSIN
MYOSIS
NESSIE
NOESIS
PASSIM
PAYSIN
PEPSIN
PERSIA
PHYSIO
POPSIN
PROSIT
PUTSIN
RAISIN
RUBSIN
RUNSIN
RUSSIA
SEESIN
SETSIN
SITSIN
STASIS
TESSIE
THESIS
THESIX
TIESIN
TILSIT
TIPSIN
TMESIS
TOCSIN
TOESIN
TONSIL
YESSIR
ZOYSIA

•••S•I

AGASSI
BONSAI
JETSKI
KINSKI
SANSEI
SENSEI

••••SI

AGASSI
ASSISI
CHUHSI
DALASI
KWEISI
LUGOSI
POTOSI
THYRSI
TZUHSI
WATUSI

S•J•••

SEJANT
STJOAN
STJOHN

S••J••

SELJUK
SHOJIS
STOJKO

S•••J•

SKOPJE

S••••J

SGTMAJ
SWARAJ

••SJ••

GASJET

SK••••

SKALDS
SKANKS
SKATED
SKATER
SKATES
SKEANS
SKEINS
SKERRY
SKETCH
SKEWED
SKEWER
SKIBOB
SKIDDY
SKIERS
SKIFFS
SKIING
SKILLS
SKIMPS
SKIMPY
SKINKS
SKINNY
SKIPIT
SKIPPY
SKIRLS
SKIROS
SKIRRS
SKIRTS
SKIRUN
SKITCH
SKITOW
SKIVED
SKIVER
SKIVES
SKIVVY
SKNXXX
SKOALS
SKOKIE
SKOPJE
SKORTS
SKULKS
SKULLS
SKUNKS
SKUNKY
SKYBOX
SKYCAP
SKYING
SKYLAB
SKYWAY

S•K•••

SAKERS
SIKKIM
SUKKAH

S••K••

SACKED
SACKER
SECKEL
SEEKER
SERKIN
SHAKEN
SHAKER
SHAKES
SHAKOS
SHAKTI
SHEKEL
SHIKAR
SICKEN
SICKER
SICKLE
SICKLY
SIKKIM
SILKED
SILKEN
SINKER
SINKIN
SISKEL
SISKIN
SKOKIE
SLAKED
SLAKES
SMOKED
SMOKER
SMOKES
SMOKEY
SNAKED
SNAKES
SOAKED
SOAKER
SOAKUP
SOCKED
SOCKET
SOCKIN
SPIKED
SPIKER
SPIKES
SPOKED
SPOKEN
SPOKES
STAKED
STAKES
STOKED
STOKER
STOKES
SUCKAS
SUCKED
SUCKER
SUCKIN
SUKKAH
SULKED
SULKER
SUNKEN

S•••K•

SALUKI
SAMEKH
SEDAKA
SHACKS
SHANKS
SHARKS
SHEIKS
SHIRKS
SHOCKS
SHOOKS
SHRIKE
SHUCKS
SKANKS
SKINKS
SKULKS
SKUNKS
SKUNKY
SLACKS
SLEEKS
SLEEKY
SLICKS
SLINKS
SLINKY
SMACKS
SMIRKS
SMIRKY
SMOCKS
SNACKS
SNEAKS
SNEAKY
SNICKS
SNOOKS
SNOOKY
SPANKS
SPANKY
SPARKS
SPARKY
SPEAKS
SPECKS
SPINKS
SPOOKS
SPOOKY
SPUNKY
STACKS
STALKS
STALKY
STANKY
STEAKS
STICKS
STICKY
STINKS
STINKY
STIRKS
STLUKE
STOCKS
STOCKY
STOJKO
STOOKS
STORKS
STRAKE
STRIKE
STROKE
SUZUKI
SWANKS
SWANKY

S••••K

SCHICK
SCREAK
SELJUK
SENDAK
SHRANK
SHRIEK
SHRINK
SHRUNK
SHTICK
SLEZAK
SLOVAK
SLOVIK
SPACEK
SPIVAK
SQUAWK
SQUEAK
STMARK
STREAK
STRICK
STRUCK
SUSLIK

•SK•••

ASKARI
ASKERS
ASKFOR
ASKING
ASKOUT
ASKSIN
ESKERS
ESKIMO

••SK••

BASKED
BASKET
BOSKET
BUSKED
BUSKIN
CISKEI
DISKED
GASKET
GASKIN
HUSKED
HUSKER
JOSKIN
MASKED
MASKER
MOSKVA
MUSKEG
MUSKET
MUSKIE
MUSKOX
RISKED
RISKER
RUSKIN
SISKEL
SISKIN
TASKED
TUSKED
TUSKER
WESKIT

••S•K•

KISHKE
LUSAKA

••S••K

CUSACK
KUSPUK
RESNIK
SUSLIK
VOSTOK

•••SK•

ALASKA
FLASKS
FRISKS
FRISKY
JANSKY
JETSKI
KINSKI
KIOSKS
NEVSKY
PROSKY
RIMSKY
WHISKS
WHISKY

•••S•K

OCASEK

••••SK

ATRISK
BRATSK
DAMASK
GDANSK
UNMASK
URALSK

SL••••

SLACKS
SLAGGY
SLAKED
SLAKES
SLALOM
SLANGS
SLANGY
SLANTS
SLAPPY
SLAPUP
SLATED
SLATER
SLATES
SLAVED
SLAVER
SLAVES
SLAVEY
SLAVIC
SLAYED
SLAYER
SLEAVE
SLEAZE
SLEAZY
SLEDGE
SLEEKS
SLEEKY
SLEEPS
SLEEPY
SLEETS
SLEETY
SLEEVE
SLEIGH
SLEUTH
SLEWED
SLEZAK
SLICED
SLICER
SLICES
SLICKS
SLIDER
SLIDES
SLIDIN
SLIEST
SLIGHT
SLIMED
SLIMES
SLIMLY
SLIMSY
SLINGS
SLINKS
SLINKY
SLIPIN
SLIPON
SLIPPY
SLIPUP
SLITHY
SLITTY
SLIVER
SLOANE
SLOBBY
SLOGAN
SLOOPS
SLOPED
SLOPES
SLOPPY
SLOSHY
SLOTHS
SLOUCH
SLOUGH
SLOVAK
SLOVEN
SLOVIK
SLOWED
SLOWER
SLOWLY
SLOWUP
SLUDGE
SLUDGY
SLUGGO
SLUICE
SLUING
SLUMMY
SLUMPS
SLURPS
SLURRY
SLUSHY
SLYEST
SLYPES

S•L•••

SALAAM
SALADO
SALADS
SALALS
SALAMI
SALARY
SALIFY
SALINA
SALINE
SALISH
SALIVA
SALLET
SALLOW
SALMAN
SALMON
SALOME
SALONS
SALOON
SALSAS
SALTED
SALTEN
SALTER
SALTON
SALTUM
SALUKI
SALUTE
SALVED
SALVER
SALVES
SALVIA
SALVOR
SALVOS
SALYUT
SCLAFF
SCLERA
SCLERO
SELDOM
SELECT
SELENA
SELENE
SELENO
SELJUK
SELLER
SELVES
SILAGE
SILENI
SILENT
SILICA
SILKED
SILKEN
SILOAM
SILOED
SILONE
SILTED
SILVAS
SILVER
SOLACE
SOLANS
SOLARS
SOLDAN
SOLDER
SOLDON
SOLEIL
SOLELY
SOLEMN
SOLENT
SOLERS
SOLEUS
SOLFAS
SOLIDI
SOLIDS
SOLING
SOLOED
SOLONG
SOLUTE
SOLVED
SOLVER
SOLVES
SPLASH
SPLATS
SPLAYS
SPLEEN
SPLICE
SPLINE
SPLINT
SPLITS
SPLOSH
STLUKE
SULCUS
SULFUR
SULKED
SULKER
SULLEN
SULTAN
SULTRY
SYLPHS
SYLVAN
SYLVIA

S••L••

SABLES
SAILED
SAILOR
SALLET
SALLOW
SAMLET
SAULTS
SAWLOG
SAYLES
SCALAR
SCALDS
SCALED
SCALER
SCALES
SCALIA
SCALPS
SCHLEP
SCOLDS
SCULLS
SCULLY
SCULPT
SCYLLA
SEALAB
SEALED
SEALER
SEALUP
SEELEY
SELLER
SENLAC
SHALES
SHALEY
SHALLY
SHALOM
SHELLS
SHELLY
SHELTY
SHELVE
SHILLS
SHILLY
SHILOH
SHOLEM
SHOLOM
SIDLED
SIDLES
SISLER
SISLEY
SKALDS
SKILLS
SKULKS
SKULLS
SKYLAB
SLALOM
SMALLS
SMALTI
SMALTO
SMELLS
SMELLY
SMELTS
SMILAX
SMILED
SMILER
SMILES
SMILEY
SMILIN
SMOLTS
SNELLS
SOCLES
SOILED
SPALLS
SPELLS
SPILES
SPILLS
SPILTH
STALAG
STALED
STALER
STALES
STALIN
STALKS
STALKY
STALLS
STELAE
STELAR
STELES
STELLA
STELMO
STILES
STILLS
STILLY
STILTS
STOLEN
STOLES
STOLID
STOLLE
STOLON
STULLS
STYLED
STYLER
STYLES
STYLET
STYLUS
SUBLET
SULLEN
SUNLIT
SUSLIK
SUTLER
SVELTE
SWALES
SWELLS
SWILLS

S•••L•

SADDLE
SAFELY
SAGELY
SALALS
SAMPLE
SANELY
SCHELL
SCHULZ
SCOWLS
SCROLL
SCULLS
SCULLY
SCYLLA
SEARLE
SEDILE
SEEMLY
SEMELE
SEPALS
SETTLE
SEWELL
SEXILY
SHALLY
SHAWLS
SHEILA
SHELLS
SHELLY
SHIELD
SHILLS
SHILLY
SHOALS
SHOALY
SHOULD
SHRILL
SIBYLS
SICILY
SICKLE
SICKLY
SIECLE
SIGILS
SIMILE
SIMPLE
SIMPLY
SINGLE
SINGLY
SISALS
SIZZLE
SKILLS
SKIRLS
SKOALS
SKULLS
SLIMLY
SLOWLY
SMALLS
SMELLS
SMELLY
SMUGLY
SNAILS
SNARLS
SNARLY
SNELLS
SNUGLI
SNUGLY
SOFTLY
SOLELY
SOMALI
SORELY
SOTOLS
SOURLY
SPALLS
SPELLS
SPIELS
SPILLS
SPOILS
SPOILT
SPOOLS
SPRYLY
SQUALL
SQUILL
STABLE
STABLY
STALLS
STAPLE
STEALS
STEELE
STEELS
STEELY
STELLA
STIFLE
STILLS
STILLY
STMALO
STOLLE
STOOLS
STOOLY
STROLL
STULLS
SUBTLE
SUBTLY
SUPPLE
SUPPLY
SURELY
SWELLS
SWILLS
SWIRLS
SWIRLY

S••••L

SACRAL
SAMBAL
SAMUEL
SANDAL
SAUREL
SCHELL
SCHOOL
SCHORL
SCRAWL
SCROLL
SEAGAL
SECKEL
SEIDEL
SEPTAL
SEQUEL
SERIAL
SERVAL
SEWELL
SHEKEL
SHERYL
SHOVEL
SHRILL
SHTETL
SIEGEL
SIGNAL
SIMBEL
SIMNEL
SINFUL
SISKEL
SNIVEL
SOBFUL
SOCIAL
SOLEIL
SORREL
SPINAL
SPINEL
SPIRAL
SPRAWL
SQUALL
SQUEAL

SQUILL
STEROL
STIPEL
STPAUL
STROLL
SWIVEL
SYMBOL

•SL•••
ASLANT
ASLEEP
ASLOPE
ISLAND
ISLETS

•S•L••
ASHLAR
ASHLEY
ASYLUM
ISELIN
ISOLDE
ISTLES
OSTLER
PSALMS
PSYLLA

•S••L•
ASWELL
ISEULT
OSCULA
OSWALD
PSYLLA
USABLE
USABLY
USUALS

•S•••L
ASSAIL
ASTRAL
ASWELL
ASWIRL
ESPIAL
ISABEL
ISOHEL
ISRAEL
OSTEAL
USEFUL
USMAIL

••SL••
AISLES
BOSLEY
GASLIT
GASLOG
GOSLOW
KISLEV
LESLEY
LESLIE
LISLES
MISLAY
MISLED
MOSLEM
MUSLIM
MUSLIN
SISLER
SISLEY
SUSLIK
TESLAS
VASLAV
WESLEY

••S•L•
ANSELM
BASALT
BASELY
BASSLY
BUSILY
BUSTLE
CASALS
CASTLE
COSELL
COSILY
COSTLY
DESALT
DESILU
EASELS
EASILY
EDSELS
ENSILE
FUSILS
HASSLE
HOSELS
HOSTLY
HUSTLE
INSOLE
INSULT
ITSELF
JOSTLE
JUSTLY
LASTLY
LUSHLY
MOSTLY
MUSCLE
MUSCLY
MYSELF
NASALS
NESTLE
NOSALE
NOSILY
ONSALE
OUSELS
PESTLE
POSHLY
POSSLQ
RASHLY
RASSLE
RESALE
RESALT
RESELL
RESILE
RESOLD
RESOLE
RESULT
ROSILY
RUSTLE
SISALS
TUSSLE
UNSOLD
URSULA
VASTLY
WISELY

••S••L
AMSTEL
ASSAIL
BUSHEL
CASUAL
COSELL
COSTAL
DISMAL
DISPEL
DISTAL
DISTIL
DOSSAL
DOSSEL
ENSOUL
FESTAL
FISCAL
FOSSIL
GOSPEL
HOSTEL
IJSSEL
INSTAL
INSTIL
JESSEL
LISTEL
MESCAL
MISSAL
MOSTEL
MUSIAL
MUSSEL
PASCAL
PASSEL
PASTEL
PISTIL
PISTOL
POSTAL
RASCAL
RESEAL
RESELL
SISKEL
TASSEL
UNSEAL
VASSAL
VESSEL
VESTAL
VISUAL

•••SL•
BASSLY
ENISLE
FOCSLE
GRISLY
HASSLE
MEASLY
POSSLQ
RASSLE
THUSLY
TOUSLE
TUSSLE
VIZSLA

•••S•L
BURSAL
CAUSAL
CHISEL
CONSUL
CRESOL
DAMSEL
DEASIL
DIESEL
DORSAL
DOSSAL
DOSSEL
FAISAL
FOSSIL
GEISEL
HANSEL
IJSSEL
JESSEL
MENSAL
MISSAL
MORSEL
MUSSEL
PASSEL
TARSAL
TASSEL
TEASEL
TINSEL
TONSIL
VASSAL
VESSEL
WEASEL
WIESEL

SM••••
SMACKS
SMALLS
SMALTI
SMALTO
SMARMY
SMARTS
SMARTY
SMEARS
SMEARY
SMELLS
SMELLY
SMELTS
SMERSH
SMILAX
SMILED
SMILER
SMILES
SMILEY
SMILIN
SMIRCH
SMIRKS
SMIRKY
SMITES
SMITHS
SMITHY
SMOCKS
SMOGGY
SMOKED
SMOKER
SMOKES
SMOKEY
SMOLTS
SMOOCH
SMOOTH
SMUDGE
SMUDGY
SMUGLY
SMURFS
SMUTCH
SMUTTY
SMYRNA

S•M•••
SAMARA
SAMBAL
SAMBAR
SAMBAS
SAMECH
SAMEKH
SAMIAM
SAMITE
SAMLET
SAMMIE
SAMOAN
SAMOSA
SAMPAN
SAMPLE
SAMSON
SAMUEL
SEMELE
SEMITE
SEMPER
SEMPRE
SIMBEL
SIMEON
SIMIAN
SIMILE
SIMMER
SIMNEL
SIMONE
SIMONY
SIMPER
SIMPLE
SIMPLY
SOMALI
SOMANY
SOMATA
SOMATO
SOMBER
SOMBRE
SOMERS
SOMMER
STMALO
STMARK
SUMACS
SUMMAE
SUMMAS
SUMMED
SUMMER
SUMMIT
SUMMON
SUMNER
SUMSUP
SUMTER
SUMUPS
SYMBOL

S••M••
SALMAN
SALMON
SAMMIE
SCAMPI
SCAMPS
SCHMOO
SCHMOS
SCUMMY
SEAMAN
SEAMED
SEAMEN
SEAMUS
SEEMED
SEEMLY
SERMON
SGTMAJ
SHAMAN
SHAMED
SHAMES
SHAMIR
SHAMUS
SHIMMY
SHIMON
SIGMAS
SIMMER
SKIMPS
SKIMPY
SLIMED
SLIMES
SLIMLY
SLIMSY
SLUMMY
SLUMPS
SOMMER
SPUMED
SPUMES
STAMEN
STAMPS
STIMPY
STOMAS
STOMAT
STOMPS
STUMER
STUMPS
STUMPY
STYMIE
SUBMIT
SUMMAE
SUMMAS
SUMMED
SUMMER
SUMMIT
SUMMON
SWAMIS
SWAMPS
SWAMPY

S•••M•
SALAMI
SALOME
SCHEMA
SCHEME
SCRAMS
SCRIMP
SCRIMS
SCRUMS
SCUMMY
SEDUMS
SEISMO
SEISMS
SERUMS
SESAME
SHAWMS
SHIMMY
SHOWME
SHRIMP
SLUMMY
SMARMY
SOLEMN
SONOMA
SPASMS
STEAMS
STEAMY
STELMO
STIGMA
STORMS
STORMY
STRUMS
SURIMI
SWARMS

S••••M
SACHEM
SACRUM
SADDAM
SALAAM
SALTUM
SAMIAM
SCARUM
SCHISM
SCREAM
SELDOM
SEPTUM
SHALOM
SHAZAM
SHBOOM
SHIISM
SHOLEM
SHOLOM
SIKKIM
SILOAM
SITCOM
SLALOM
SODIUM
SQUIRM
STREAM
SUBGUM
SUFISM
SYSTEM

•SM•••
ASMARA
ISMENE
OSMICS
OSMIUM
OSMOND
OSMOSE
OSMUND
USMAIL

•S•M••
ASIMOV
ISOMER

•S••M•
ASSUME
ESKIMO
ISTHMI
PSALMS

•S•••M
ASCHAM
ASHRAM
ASYLUM
ESTEEM
OSMIUM
OSTIUM

••SM••
BUSMAN
BUSMEN
COSMIC
COSMOS
DESMAN
DISMAL
DISMAY
DISMES
GASMAN
GASMEN
KISMET
MESMER
TASMAN
YESMAN
YESMEN

••S•M•
ASSUME
BESOMS
RESUME
SESAME
UGSOME

••S••M
ABSCAM
ANSELM
CESIUM
CUSTOM
DISARM
HASSAM
INSEAM
MOSLEM
MUSEUM
MUSLIM
PASSIM
POSSUM
SYSTEM
WISDOM

•••SM•
ABYSMS
CHASMS
MIASMA
PLASMA
PLASMO
PRISMS
SEISMO
SEISMS
SPASMS

•••S•M
BALSAM
DIMSUM
DORSUM
FOLSOM
GYPSUM
HANSOM
HASSAM
JETSAM
OMASUM
PASSIM
POSSUM
RANSOM

••••SM
AGEISM
CHRISM
CUBISM
EGOISM
HOLISM
MAOISM
MONISM
PURISM
SCHISM
SHIISM
SUFISM
TAOISM
THEISM
TRUISM
VERISM
YOGISM

SN••••
SNACKS
SNAFUS
SNAGGY
SNAILS
SNAKED
SNAKES
SNAPAT
SNAPPY
SNAPTO
SNAPUP
SNARED
SNARES
SNARLS
SNARLY
SNATCH
SNATHE
SNATHS
SNAZZY
SNEAKS
SNEAKY
SNEERS
SNEERY
SNEEZE
SNEEZY
SNELLS
SNICKS
SNIDER
SNIFFS
SNIFFY
SNIPED
SNIPER
SNIPES
SNIPPY
SNITCH
SNIVEL
SNOBBY
SNOCAT
SNOODS
SNOOKS
SNOOKY
SNOOPS
SNOOPY
SNOOTS
SNOOTY
SNOOZE
SNOOZY
SNOPES
SNORED
SNORER
SNORES
SNORTS
SNOTTY
SNOUTS
SNOWED
SNOWIN
SNUBBY
SNUFFS
SNUFFY
SNUGLI
SNUGLY
SNYDER

S•N•••
SANCHO
SANCTA
SANDAL
SANDED
SANDER
SANDIA
SANDRA
SANELY
SANEST
SANGER
SANGTO
SANITY
SANNUP
SANSEI
SANTEE
SANTIR
SANTOS
SENARY
SENATE
SENDAK
SENDER
SENDIN
SENDUP
SENECA
SENEGA
SENHOR
SENIOR
SENITI
SENLAC
SENNAS
SENNET
SENNIT
SENORA
SENORS
SENSED
SENSEI
SENSES
SENSOR
SENTIN
SENTRA
SENTRY
SENTUP
SENUFO
SINBAD
SINEAD
SINEWS
SINEWY
SINFUL
SINGED
SINGER
SINGES
SINGIN
SINGLE
SINGLY
SINGTO
SINISE
SINKER
SINKIN
SINNED
SINNER
SINTAX
SINTER
SKNXXX
SONANT
SONATA
SONDES
SONICS
SONNET
SONOMA
SONORA
SONTAG
SUNDAE
SUNDAY
SUNDER
SUNDEW
SUNDOG
SUNDRY
SUNGOD
SUNKEN
SUNLIT
SUNNED
SUNNIS
SUNOCO
SUNRAY
SUNSET
SUNTAN
SUNUNU
SUNUPS
SYNCED
SYNDIC
SYNODS
SYNTAX

S••N••
SAINTE
SAINTS
SANNUP
SARNIA
SAUNAS
SCANTS
SCANTY
SCENAS
SCENDS
SCENES
SCENIC
SCENTS
SCHNOZ
SCONCE
SCONES
SEANCE
SEENIN
SEENTO
SEINED
SEINER
SEINES
SENNAS
SENNET
SENNIT
SEWNON
SEWNUP
SHANDY
SHANIA
SHANKS
SHANNY
SHANTY
SHINDY
SHINED
SHINER
SHINES
SHINNY
SHINTO
SHUNTS
SIDNEY
SIENNA
SIGNAL
SIGNED
SIGNEE
SIGNER
SIGNET
SIGNIN
SIGNON
SIGNOR
SIGNUP
SIMNEL
SINNED
SINNER
SKANKS
SKINKS
SKINNY
SKUNKS
SKUNKY
SLANGS
SLANGY
SLANTS
SLINGS
SLINKS
SLINKY
SONNET
SOONER
SOUNDS
SPANKS
SPANKY
SPENDS
SPINAL
SPINED
SPINEL
SPINES
SPINET
SPINKS
SPINTO
SPONGE
SPONGY
SPUNKY
SRANAN
STANCE
STANCH
STANDS
STANKY
STANZA
STENCH
STENOG
STENOS
STINGO
STINGS
STINGY
STINKS
STINKY
STINTS
STONED
STONER
STONES
STUNTS
STUNTY
SUMNER
SUNNED
SUNNIS
SWANEE
SWANKS
SWANKY
SWINGS
SWINGY
SYDNEY

S•••N•
SABENA
SABINE
SABINS
SALINA
SALINE
SALONS
SARANS
SARONG
SATANG
SATING
SATINS
SATINY
SAVANT
SAVING
SAWING
SAXONS
SAXONY
SAYING
SCARNE
SCIONS
SCORNS
SECANT
SECOND
SEDANS
SEEING
SEJANT
SELENA
SELENE
SELENO
SERENA
SERENE
SERINE
SERINS
SETINS
SEVENS
SEWING
SHANNY
SHAYNE
SHEENA
SHEENS
SHINNY
SHRANK
SHRINE
SHRINK
SHRUNK
SHYING
SIDING
SIENNA
SILENI
SILENT
SILONE
SIMONE
SIMONY
SIRENS
SIRING
SITING
SITINS
SIXING
SIZING
SKEANS
SKEINS
SKIING
SKINNY
SKYING
SLOANE
SLUING
SMYRNA
SOFINE
SOIGNE
SOLANS
SOLENT
SOLING
SOLONG
SOMANY
SONANT
SOWING
SPAWNS
SPHINX
SPLINE
SPLINT
SPOONS
SPOONY
SPRANG
SPRING
SPRINT
SPRUNG
SPURNS
SPYING
SQUINT
STAINS
STEINS
STERNA
STERNE
STERNO
STERNS
STHENO
STRAND
STRINE
STRING
STRONG
STRUNG
SUNUNU
SUPINE
SUSANN
SWAINS
SWOONS
SYRINX

S••••N
SADDEN
SAIGON
SAIPAN
SALMAN
SALMON
SALOON
SALTEN
SALTON
SAMOAN
SAMPAN
SAMSON
SARGON
SARTON
SATEEN
SATURN
SCREEN
SEAFAN
SEAMAN
SEAMEN
SEASON
SEATON
SECERN
SEENIN
SEEPIN
SEESIN
SENDIN
SENTIN
SEQUIN
SERKIN
SERMON
SETSIN
SETSON
SEVERN
SEWNON
SEWSON
SEXTON
SHABAN
SHAKEN
SHAMAN
SHARON
SHAVEN
SHIMON
SHOGUN
SHOOIN
SHORAN
SHOWIN
SHUTIN
SICKEN
SIGNIN
SIGNON
SILKEN
SIMEON
SIMIAN
SINGIN
SINKIN
SIOUAN
SIPHON
SISKIN
SITSIN
SITSON
SIXGUN
SKIRUN
SLIDIN
SLIPIN
SLIPON
SLOGAN
SLOVEN
SMILIN
SNOWIN
SOCKIN
SODDEN
SOFTEN
SOLDAN
SOLDON
SOLEMN
SOSOON
SPAVIN
SPLEEN
SPOKEN
SPRAIN
SPURON
SRANAN
STALIN
STAMEN
STATEN
STAYON
STEFAN
STEPIN
STEPON
STEVEN
STIRIN
STJOAN
STJOHN
STOLEN
STOLON
STOPIN
STOTIN
STRAIN
STREWN
STYRON
SUBORN
SUCKIN
SUDDEN
SULLEN
SULTAN
SUMMON
SUNKEN
SUNTAN
SUSANN
SUTTON
SWEDEN
SYLVAN
SYPHON
SYRIAN

•S•N••
ASANAS
USANCE
USENET

•S••N•
ASCEND
ASCENT
ASIANS
ASKING
ASLANT
ASPENS
ASSENT
ESCENT
ESPANA
ESSENE
ISLAND
ISMENE
OSCINE
OSMOND
OSMUND
OSTEND
VSIGNS

•S•••N
ASHCAN
ASKSIN
ASOSAN
ASSIGN
ASTERN
ASWOON
ISELIN
ISOGON
OSBORN
OSSEIN
OSSIAN
USOPEN

••SN••
BOSNIA
CPSNOW
DISNEY
EISNER
RESNIK
UNSNAG
UNSNAP

••S•N•
ABSENT
ARSENE
ARSONS
ASSENT
BASING
BASINS
BESANT
BISONS
BOSONS
BOSUNS
BUSING
BUSONI
CASING
CASINO
CESSNA
COSINE
DISANT
DOSING
EASING
EOSINS
ESSENE
FUSING
HOSING
INSANE
INSYNC
LOSING
LYSINE
LYSINS
MASONS
MESONS
MUSING
MUSTNT
NOSING
OKSANA
ORSINO
PISANO
PISANS
POSING
RASING
RESAND
RESEND
RESENT
RESING
RESINS
RESINY
RISING
ROSINS
ROSINY
SUSANN
TISANE
UNSUNG
URSINE
VISHNU
VISINE
WISENT

••S••N
ASSIGN
AUSTEN
AUSTIN
BOSTON
BUSKIN
BUSMAN
BUSMEN
BUSTIN
CASERN
CASHIN
CASTON
COSIGN
DASSIN
DESIGN
DESMAN
DISOWN
DUSTIN
EASEIN
EASTON
ENSIGN
FASTEN
FUSION
GASCON
GASKIN
GASMAN
GASMEN
GASTON
GOSHEN
HASSAN
HASTEN
HESTON
HUSTON

INSPAN
JOSKIN
JUSTIN
KASDAN
LASSEN
LESSEN
LESSON
LISBON
LISTEN
LISTON
MUSLIN
NISSAN
NISSEN
OSSEIN
OSSIAN
PASSON
PISTON
POSTON
PUSHON
RESAWN
RESEEN
RESEWN
RESIGN
RESPIN
RESTON
RUSKIN
SISKIN
SOSOON
SUSANN
TASMAN
TUSCAN
UNSEEN
UNSEWN
UNSOWN
VISION
WESSON
WYSTAN
YESMAN
YESMEN

•••SN•
CESSNA
DOESNT
FRESNO
KRASNY
PUISNE

•••S•N
ACTSON
ADDSIN
ADDSON
ALISON
ARISEN
ASKSIN
ASOSAN
BABSON
BENSON
BETSON
BIDSIN
BIDSON
BRYSON
BUNSEN
CARSON
CHOSEN
COUSIN
CUTSIN
DAMSON
DANSON
DASSIN
DATSUN
DAWSON
DIGSIN
DOBSON
DOESIN
EATSIN
EDISON
EGGSON
FITSIN
FOGSIN
GARSON
GETSIN
GETSON
GIBSON
GODSON
GOESIN
GOESON
GRISON
HANSON
HASSAN
HEMSIN
HENSON
HITSON
HOBSON
HOPSIN
HUDSON
ICESIN
IRISIN
JAMSIN
JANSEN
JENSEN
JETSON
JIMSON
JOLSON
JONSON
KANSAN
KEYSIN
KMESON
LANSON
LARSEN
LARSON
LASSEN
LAWSON
LAYSIN
LAYSON
LESSEN
LESSON
LETSIN
LETSON
LIESIN
LOGSIN
LOGSON
LOOSEN
MADSEN
MYOSIN
NANSEN
NEESON
NELSON
NISSAN
NISSEN
ODDSON
OLESON
ORISON
PARSON
PASSON
PAYSIN
PAYSON
PEPSIN
PERSON
PINSON
POISON
POPSIN
PRISON
PUTSIN
PUTSON
RAISIN
RAMSON
RATSON
REASON
REVSON
ROBSON
RUBSIN
RUNSIN
RUNSON
SAMSON
SEASON
SEESIN
SETSIN
SETSON
SEWSON
SITSIN
SITSON
TIESIN
TIPSIN
TOCSIN
TOESIN
TUCSON
TULSAN
UNISON
WATSON
WESSON
WILSON
WORSEN

SO••••
SOAKED
SOAKER
SOAKUP
SOAPED
SOAPER
SOARED
SOARER
SOARES
SOASTO
SOAVES
SOBBED
SOBBER
SOBEIT
SOBERS
SOBFUL
SOCAGE
SOCCER
SOCIAL
SOCKED
SOCKET
SOCKIN
SOCLES
SODDED
SODDEN
SODIUM
SOEURS
SOFFIT
SOFINE
SOFTEN
SOFTER
SOFTIE
SOFTLY
SOIGNE
SOILED
SOIREE
SOLACE
SOLANS
SOLARS
SOLDAN
SOLDER
SOLDON
SOLEIL
SOLELY
SOLEMN
SOLENT
SOLERS
SOLEUS
SOLFAS
SOLIDI
SOLIDS
SOLING
SOLOED
SOLONG
SOLUTE
SOLVED
SOLVER
SOLVES
SOMALI
SOMANY
SOMATA
SOMATO
SOMBER
SOMBRE
SOMERS
SOMMER
SONANT
SONATA
SONDES
SONICS
SONNET
SONOMA
SONORA
SONTAG
SOONER
SOOTHE
SOPHIA
SOPHIE
SOPORS
SOPPED
SOPSUP
SORBET
SORBIC
SORDID
SORELY
SOREST
SORREL
SORROW
SORTED
SORTER
SORTIE
SORTOF
SOSOON
SOTHAT
SOTOLS
SOTTED
SOUARI
SOUGHS
SOUGHT
SOUNDS
SOUPUP
SOURCE
SOURED
SOURER
SOURLY
SOUSED
SOUSES
SOUTER
SOUTHS
SOVIET
SOWBUG
SOWERS
SOWETO
SOWHAT
SOWING
SOXERS

S•O•••
SCOFFS
SCOLDS
SCONCE
SCONES
SCOOPS
SCOOTS
SCOPED
SCOPES
SCORCH
SCORED
SCORER
SCORES
SCORIA
SCORNS
SCOTCH
SCOTER
SCOTIA
SCOTTO
SCOTTY
SCOURS
SCOUSE
SCOUTS
SCOWLS
SFORZA
SHOALS
SHOALY
SHOATS
SHOCKS
SHODDY
SHOERS
SHOFAR
SHOGUN
SHOJIS
SHOLEM
SHOLOM
SHOOED
SHOOIN
SHOOKS
SHOOTS
SHOPPE
SHORAN
SHORED
SHORES
SHORTA
SHORTE
SHORTI
SHORTO
SHORTS
SHORTU
SHORTY
SHOTAT
SHOTUP
SHOULD
SHOUTS
SHOVED
SHOVEL
SHOVER
SHOVES
SHOWED
SHOWER
SHOWIN
SHOWME
SHOWUP
SIOUAN
SKOALS
SKOKIE
SKOPJE
SKORTS
SLOANE
SLOBBY
SLOGAN
SLOOPS
SLOPED
SLOPES
SLOPPY
SLOSHY
SLOTHS
SLOUCH
SLOUGH
SLOVAK
SLOVEN
SLOVIK
SLOWED
SLOWER
SLOWLY
SLOWUP
SMOCKS
SMOGGY
SMOKED
SMOKER
SMOKES
SMOKEY
SMOLTS
SMOOCH
SMOOTH
SNOBBY
SNOCAT
SNOODS
SNOOKS
SNOOKY
SNOOPS
SNOOPY
SNOOTS
SNOOTY
SNOOZE
SNOOZY
SNOPES
SNORED
SNORER
SNORES
SNORTS
SNOTTY
SNOUTS
SNOWED
SNOWIN
SOONER
SOOTHE
SPOILS
SPOILT
SPOKED
SPOKEN
SPOKES
SPONGE
SPONGY
SPOOFS
SPOOKS
SPOOKY
SPOOLS
SPOONS
SPOONY
SPOORS
SPORES
SPORTS
SPORTY
SPOTTY
SPOUSE
SPOUTS
STOATS
STOCKS
STOCKY
STODGE
STODGY
STOGIE
STOICS
STOJKO
STOKED
STOKER
STOKES
STOLEN
STOLES
STOLID
STOLLE
STOLON
STOMAS
STOMAT
STOMPS
STONED
STONER
STONES
STOOGE
STOOKS
STOOLS
STOOLY
STOOPS
STOPES
STOPIN
STOPIT
STOPUP
STORCH
STORED
STORER
STORES
STOREY
STORKS
STORMS
STORMY
STORRS
STOTIN
STOUPS
STOUTS
STOVER
STOVES
STOWED
SWOONS
SWOOPS
SWOOSH
SWORDS

S••O••
SABOTS
SALOME
SALONS
SALOON
SAMOAN
SAMOSA
SAPORS
SARODS
SARONG
SATORI
SATOUT
SAVOIE
SAVOIR
SAVORS
SAVORY
SAVOUR
SAWOFF
SAWOUT
SAXONS
SAXONY
SCHOOL
SCHORL
SCIONS
SCOOPS
SCOOTS
SCRODS
SCROLL
SCROOP
SECOND
SEEOFF
SEEOUT
SENORA
SENORS
SEPOYS
SEROSA
SEROUS
SEROWS
SETOFF
SETOSE
SETOUT
SHBOOM
SHOOED
SHOOIN
SHOOKS
SHOOTS
SHROUD
SHROVE
SILOAM
SILOED
SILONE
SIMONE
SIMONY
SITOUT
SLOOPS
SMOOCH
SMOOTH
SNOODS
SNOOKS
SNOOKY
SNOOPS
SNOOPY
SNOOTS
SNOOTY
SNOOZE
SNOOZY
SOLOED
SOLONG
SONOMA
SONORA
SOPORS
SOSOON
SOTOLS
SPLOSH
SPOOFS
SPOOKS
SPOOKY
SPOOLS
SPOONS
SPOONY
SPOORS
SPROUT
STJOAN
STJOHN
STOOGE
STOOKS
STOOLS
STOOLY
STOOPS
STROBE
STRODE
STROKE
STROLL
STRONG
STROPS
STROUD
STROVE
SUBORN
SUNOCO
SWOONS
SWOOPS
SWOOSH
SYNODS
SYSOPS

S•••O•
SAIGON
SAILOR
SALLOW
SALMON
SALOON
SALTON
SALVOR
SALVOS
SAMSON
SANTOS
SARGON
SARGOS
SARTON
SAVIOR
SAWLOG
SAYSOS
SCHMOO
SCHMOS
SCHNOZ
SCHOOL
SCROOP
SEACOW
SEADOG
SEAFOX
SEASON
SEATON
SECTOR
SELDOM
SENHOR
SENIOR
SENSOR
SERMON
SERVOS
SESTOS
SETSON
SETTOS
SEWNON
SEWSON
SEXTON
SHADOW
SHAKOS
SHALOM
SHARON
SHBOOM
SHILOH
SHIMON
SHOLOM
SIGNON
SIGNOR
SIMEON
SIPHON
SITCOM
SITSON
SKIBOB
SKIROS
SKITOW
SKYBOX
SLALOM
SLIPON
SOLDON
SORROW
SORTOF
SOSOON
SPIGOT
SPIROS
SPURON
STATOR
STAYON
STEFOY
STENOG
STENOS
STEPON
STEROL
STOLON
STUPOR
STYRON
SUCCOR
SUITOR
SUMMON
SUNDOG
SUNGOD
SUTTON
SYMBOL
SYPHON

S••••O
SABATO
SALADO
SANCHO
SANGTO
SAPPHO
SASEBO
SCHMOO
SCIPIO
SCLERO
SCOTTO
SEENTO
SEESTO
SEISMO
SELENO
SENUFO
SERGIO
SHINTO
SHORTO
SIDERO
SINGTO
SLUGGO
SMALTO
SNAPTO
SOASTO
SOMATO
SOWETO
SPEEDO
SPINTO
STELMO
STEREO
STERNO
STHENO
STINGO
STMALO
STOJKO
STRABO
STRATO
STUCCO
STUDIO
SUBITO
SUNOCO

•SO•••
ASOSAN
ISOBAR
ISOGON
ISOHEL
ISOLDE
ISOMER
ISOPOD
USOPEN

•S•O••
ASCOTS
ASHORE
ASKOUT
ASLOPE
ASSORT
ASWOON
CSPOTS
ESCORT
ESPOSA
ESPOSO
ESTOPS
FSTOPS
OSBORN
OSGOOD
OSMOND
OSMOSE

•S••O•
ASIMOV
ASKFOR
ASTROS
ASWOON
ESCROW
ISADOR
ISOGON
ISOPOD
OSGOOD

•S•••O
ESCUDO
ESKIMO
ESPOSO
OSWEGO
PSEUDO
PSYCHO
USEDTO

••SO••
ABSORB
ADSORB
ARSONS
ASSORT
BESOMS
BESOTS
BISONS
BOSONS
BUSONI
DESOTO
DISOWN
ENSOUL
GOSOFT
INSOLE
KOSOVO
MASONS
MESONS
MYSORE
NOSOAP
RESODS
RESOLD
RESOLE
RESORB
RESORT
SOSOON
SYSOPS
UGSOME
UNSOLD
UNSOWN
VISORS

••S•O•
BASSOS
BESTOW
BISHOP
BOSTON
BUSBOY
CASTON
CASTOR
CESTOS
CISCOS
COSMOS
CPSNOW
CUSTOM
CUSTOS
DESPOT
DISCOS
EASTON
FUSION
GASCON
GASLOG
GASTON
GOSLOW
HESIOD
HESTON
HUSTON
HYSSOP
LASSOS
LESBOS
LESSON
LESSOR
LISBOA
LISBON
LISTON
MASCOT
MOSCOW
MUSKOX
NESTOR
NOSHOW
PASEOS
PASSON
PASTOR
PESCOW
PESTOS
PISTOL
PISTON
POSTON
PUSHON
RESHOD
RESHOE
RESHOT
RESTON
ROSCOE
ROSTOV
SESTOS
SOSOON
TVSHOW
UNSHOD
UNSTOP
UPSHOT
VISION
VOSTOK
WASHOE
WESSON
WISDOM

••S••O
AUSTRO
BISTRO
CASINO
CASSIO
CASTRO
DESOTO
DOSIDO
GASTRO
HASBRO
KOSOVO
LASHIO
ORSINO
PASHTO
PISANO
SASEBO
WISETO

•••SO•
ACTSON
ADDSON
ALISON
AMOSOZ
AVISOS
BABSON
BASSOS
BENSON
BETSON
BIDSON
BRASOV
BRYSON
CARSON
CENSOR
CHISOX
CRESOL
CRUSOE
CURSOR
DAMSON
DANSON
DAWSON
DOBSON
EDISON
EGGSON
FOLSOM
GARSON
GETSON
GIBSON
GODSON
GOESON
GRISON
HANSOM
HANSON
HENSON
HITSON
HOBSON
HUDSON
HYKSOS
HYSSOP
JETSON
JIMSON
JOLSON
JONSON
KMESON
LANSON
LARSON
LASSOS
LAWSON
LAYSON
LESSON
LESSOR
LETSON
LOGSON
NEESON
NELSON
ODDSON
OLESON
ORISON
PARSON
PASSON
PAYSON
PERSON
PINSON
POISON
PRISON
PUTSON
RAMSON
RANSOM
RATSON
REASON
REDSOX
REVSON
RIDSOF
ROBSON
RUNSON
SAMSON
SAYSOS
SEASON
SENSOR
SETSON
SEWSON
SITSON
TENSOR
TORSOS
TUCSON
UNISON
VERSOS
WATSON
WESSON
WILSON
WINSOR

•••S•O
ADDSTO
AIMSTO
ARISTO
CASSIO
CRISCO
CRISTO
ENESCO
FIASCO
FRESCO
FRESNO
FRISCO
GETSTO
GLOSSO
GRASSO
GROSSO
LAYSTO
LETSGO
LIESTO
OBISPO
PHYSIO
PLASMO
PRESTO
PUTSTO
RUNSTO
SEESTO
SEISMO
SOASTO
TIESTO
UNESCO

••••SO
ALONSO
ARIOSO
CARUSO
ELPASO
EOIPSO
ESPOSO
EVENSO
EVERSO
GLOSSO
GRASSO
GROSSO
WHOMSO

SP••••
SPACED
SPACEK
SPACER
SPACES
SPACEY
SPADED
SPADER
SPADES
SPADIX
SPAHIS
SPALLS
SPANKS
SPANKY
SPARED
SPARER
SPARES
SPARGE
SPARKS
SPARKY
SPARSE
SPARTA
SPASMS
SPATES
SPATHE
SPAVIN
SPAWNS
SPAYED
SPEAKS
SPEARS
SPECIE
SPECKS
SPEDUP
SPEECH
SPEEDO
SPEEDS
SPEEDY
SPELLS
SPENDS
SPERRY
SPEWED
SPHERE
SPHERY
SPHINX
SPICAS
SPICED
SPICES
SPIDER
SPIELS
SPIERS
SPIFFS
SPIFFY
SPIGOT
SPIKED
SPIKER
SPIKES
SPILES
SPILLS
SPILTH
SPINAL
SPINED
SPINEL
SPINES
SPINET
SPINKS
SPINTO
SPIRAL
SPIREA
SPIRED
SPIRES
SPIRIT
SPIROS
SPITED
SPITES
SPIVAK
SPIVVY
SPLASH
SPLATS
SPLAYS
SPLEEN
SPLICE
SPLINE
SPLINT
SPLITS
SPLOSH
SPOILS
SPOILT
SPOKED
SPOKEN
SPOKES
SPONGE
SPONGY
SPOOFS
SPOOKS
SPOOKY
SPOOLS
SPOONS
SPOONY
SPOORS
SPORES
SPORTS
SPORTY
SPOTTY
SPOUSE
SPOUTS
SPRAGS
SPRAIN
SPRANG
SPRATS
SPRAWL
SPRAYS
SPREAD
SPREES
SPRIER
SPRIGS
SPRING
SPRINT
SPRITE
SPRITS
SPRITZ
SPROUT
SPRUCE
SPRUES
SPRUNG
SPRYER
SPRYLY
SPUMED
SPUMES
SPUNKY
SPURGE
SPURNS
SPURON
SPURRY
SPURTS
SPYING

S•P•••
SAPORS
SAPPED
SAPPER
SAPPHO
SEPALS
SEPIAS
SEPOYS
SEPTAL
SEPTET
SEPTIC
SEPTUM
SIPHON
SIPPED
SIPPER
SIPPET
SOPHIA
SOPHIE
SOPORS
SOPPED
SOPSUP
STPAUL
STPETE
SUPERB
SUPERS
SUPINE
SUPPED
SUPPER
SUPPLE
SUPPLY
SYPHON

S••P••
SAIPAN
SAMPAN

SAMPLE
SAPPED
SAPPER
SAPPHO
SCAPED
SCAPES
SCIPIO
SCOPED
SCOPES
SEEPED
SEEPIN
SEMPER
SEMPRE
SHAPED
SHAPER
SHAPES
SHOPPE
SIMPER
SIMPLE
SIMPLY
SIPPED
SIPPER
SIPPET
SKIPIT
SKIPPY
SKOPJE
SLAPPY
SLAPUP
SLIPIN
SLIPON
SLIPPY
SLIPUP
SLOPED
SLOPES
SLOPPY
SLYPES
SNAPAT
SNAPPY
SNAPTO
SNAPUP
SNIPED
SNIPER
SNIPES
SNIPPY
SNOPES
SOAPED
SOAPER
SOPPED
SOUPUP
STAPES
STAPLE
STAPUF
STEPIN
STEPON
STEPPE
STEPUP
STIPEL
STIPES
STOPES
STOPIN
STOPIT
STOPUP
STUPAS
STUPES
STUPID
STUPOR
SUBPAR
SUPPED
SUPPER
SUPPLE
SUPPLY
SWIPED
SWIPER
SWIPES
SYLPHS

S•••P•
SCALPS
SCAMPI
SCAMPS
SCARPS
SCAUPS
SCOOPS
SCRAPE
SCRAPS
SCRIPS
SCRIPT
SCULPT
SERAPE
SERAPH
SETUPS
SHARPS
SHEEPS
SHERPA
SHOPPE
SITUPS
SKIMPS
SKIMPY
SKIPPY
SLAPPY
SLEEPS
SLEEPY
SLIPPY
SLOOPS
SLOPPY
SLUMPS
SLURPS
SNAPPY
SNIPPY
SNOOPS
SNOOPY
STAMPS
STEEPS
STEPPE
STIMPY
STOMPS
STOOPS
STOUPS
STRAPS
STRIPE
STRIPS
STRIPY
STROPS
STUMPS
STUMPY
SUMUPS
SUNUPS
SWAMPS
SWAMPY
SWEEPS
SWOOPS
SYRUPS
SYRUPY
SYSOPS

S••••P
SANNUP
SATRAP
SAVEUP
SCHLEP
SCRIMP
SCROOP
SEALUP
SENDUP
SENTUP
SETSUP
SEWNUP
SEWSUP
SHOTUP
SHOWUP
SHRIMP
SHUTUP
SIGNUP
SITSUP
SIZEUP
SKYCAP
SLAPUP
SLIPUP
SLOWUP
SNAPUP
SOAKUP
SOPSUP
SOUPUP
SPEDUP
STAYUP
STEPUP
STIRUP
STOPUP
STREEP
SUITUP
SUMSUP

•SP•••
ASPECT
ASPENS
ASPERA
ASPICS
ASPIRE
ASPISH
CSPOTS
ESPANA
ESPIAL
ESPIED
ESPIES
ESPOSA
ESPOSO
ESPRIT
OSPREY

•S•P••
ISOPOD
RSVPED
USOPEN

•S••P•
ASLOPE
ESCAPE
ESTOPS
FSTOPS
USURPS

•S•••P
ASHARP
ASLEEP
BSHARP
CSHARP
DSHARP
ESCARP
ESHARP
FSHARP
GSHARP
USEDUP
USESUP

••SP••
AUSPEX
CASPAR
CASPER
CUSPED
CUSPID
DESPOT
DISPEL
GASPAR
GASPED
GASPER
GOSPEL
HASPED
HISPID
INSPAN
JASPER
KUSPUK
LISPED
ONSPEC
RASPED
RASPER
RESPIN
VESPER
VESPID
WISPED

••S•P•
JOSEPH
SYSOPS

••S••P
BISHOP
DUSTUP
EASEUP
FESSUP
GASCAP
GOSSIP
HYSSOP
INSTEP
LASHUP
MESSUP
MISHAP
MUSSUP
NOSOAP
PASSUP
PUSHUP
RESHIP
RESTUP
TOSSUP
UNSNAP
UNSTOP
WASHUP
WISEUP

•••SP•
CLASPS
CRISPS
CRISPY
GRASPS
OBISPO

•••S•P
ACESUP
ACTSUP
ADDSUP
BIDSUP
BOBSUP
BUYSUP
CATSUP
CUTSUP
DAMSUP
DIGSUP
DOESUP
EATSUP
ENDSUP
FESSUP
FOGSUP
GETSUP
GOESUP
GOSSIP
GUMSUP
HITSUP
HOPSUP
HYSSOP
ICESUP
JAMSUP
KEYSUP
LAPSUP
LAYSUP
LETSUP
MESSUP
MILSAP
MOPSUP
MUSSUP
OWNSUP
PASSUP
PAYSUP
PEPSUP
POPSUP
PUTSUP
REVSUP
RIGSUP
RIPSUP
RUNSUP
SETSUP
SEWSUP
SITSUP
SOPSUP
SUMSUP
TAGSUP
TEESUP
TIESUP
TOSSUP
TOTSUP
USESUP
WADSUP
ZIPSUP

••••SP
AMERSP

SQ••••
SQUABS
SQUADS
SQUALL
SQUARE
SQUASH
SQUATS
SQUAWK
SQUEAK
SQUEAL
SQUIBB
SQUIBS
SQUIDS
SQUILL
SQUINT
SQUIRE
SQUIRM
SQUIRT
SQUISH
SQUUSH

S•Q•••
SEQUEL
SEQUIN

S••Q••
SACQUE
SESQUI

S••••Q
SUSIEQ

•SQ•••
MSQUAD

••SQ••
BASQUE
BISQUE
CASQUE
MASQUE
MOSQUE
RISQUE
SESQUI

••S•Q•
ETSEQQ

••S••Q
ETSEQQ
NASDAQ
POSSLQ
SUSIEQ

•••S•Q
POSSLQ

SR••••
SRANAN

S•R•••
SARANS
SARDIS
SARGES
SARGON
SARGOS
SARNIA
SARODS
SARONG
SARTON
SARTRE
SCRAGS
SCRAMS
SCRAPE
SCRAPS
SCRAWL
SCREAK
SCREAM
SCREED
SCREEN
SCREES
SCREWS
SCREWY
SCRIBE
SCRIMP
SCRIMS
SCRIPS
SCRIPT
SCRODS
SCROLL
SCROOP
SCRUBS
SCRUFF
SCRUMS
SERACS
SERAIS
SERAPE
SERAPH
SERBIA
SERENA
SERENE
SERGEI
SERGES
SERGIO
SERIAL
SERIES
SERIFS
SERINE
SERINS
SERKIN
SERMON
SEROSA
SEROUS
SEROWS
SERUMS
SERVAL
SERVED
SERVER
SERVES
SERVOS
SHRANK
SHREDS
SHREWD
SHREWS
SHRIEK
SHRIFT
SHRIKE
SHRILL
SHRIMP
SHRINE
SHRINK
SHRIVE
SHROUD
SHROVE
SHRUBS
SHRUGS
SHRUNK
SIRDAR
SIRENS
SIRICA
SIRING
SIRIUS
SIRRAH
SIRREE
SORBET
SORBIC
SORDID
SORELY
SOREST
SORREL
SORROW
SORTED
SORTER
SORTIE
SORTOF
SPRAGS
SPRAIN
SPRANG
SPRATS
SPRAWL
SPRAYS
SPREAD
SPREES
SPRIER
SPRIGS
SPRING
SPRINT
SPRITE
SPRITS
SPRITZ
SPROUT
SPRUCE
SPRUES
SPRUNG
SPRYER
SPRYLY
STRABO
STRADS
STRAFE
STRAIN
STRAIT
STRAKE
STRAND
STRAPS
STRASS
STRATA
STRATI
STRATO
STRAUB
STRAUS
STRAWS
STRAWY
STRAYS
STREAK
STREAM
STREEP
STREET
STRESS
STREWN
STREWS
STRIAE
STRICK
STRICT
STRIDE
STRIFE
STRIKE
STRINE
STRING
STRIPE
STRIPS
STRIPY
STRIVE
STROBE
STRODE
STROKE
STROLL
STRONG
STROPS
STROUD
STROVE
STRUCK
STRUMS
STRUNG
STRUTS
SURAHS
SURELY
SUREST
SURETE
SURETY
SURFED
SURFER
SURGED
SURGES
SURIMI
SURREY
SURTAX
SURVEY
SYRIAN
SYRINX
SYRUPS
SYRUPY

S••R••
SABRAS
SABRES
SACRAL
SACRED
SACRUM
SATRAP
SAUREL
SAWRED
SCARAB
SCARCE
SCARED
SCARER
SCARES
SCARFS
SCARNE
SCARPS
SCARRY
SCARUM
SCORCH
SCORED
SCORER
SCORES
SCORIA
SCORNS
SCURFY
SCURRY
SCURVE
SCURVY
SEARCH
SEARED
SEARLE
SECRET
SEERED
SEURAT
SEVRES
SFORZA
SHARDS
SHARED
SHARER
SHARES
SHARIA
SHARIF
SHARKS
SHARON
SHARPS
SHEREE
SHERIF
SHERPA
SHERRY
SHERYL
SHIRAZ
SHIRER
SHIRES
SHIRKS
SHIRRS
SHIRTS
SHIRTY
SHORAN
SHORED
SHORES
SHORTA
SHORTE
SHORTI
SHORTO
SHORTS
SHORTU
SHORTY
SIERRA
SIRRAH
SIRREE
SKERRY
SKIRLS
SKIROS
SKIRRS
SKIRTS
SKIRUN
SKORTS
SLURPS
SLURRY
SMARMY
SMARTS
SMARTY
SMERSH
SMIRCH
SMIRKS
SMIRKY
SMURFS
SMYRNA
SNARED
SNARES
SNARLS
SNARLY
SNORED
SNORER
SNORES
SNORTS
SOARED
SOARER
SOARES
SOIREE
SORREL
SORROW
SOURCE
SOURED
SOURER
SOURLY
SPARED
SPARER
SPARES
SPARGE
SPARKS
SPARKY
SPARSE
SPARTA
SPERRY
SPIRAL
SPIREA
SPIRED
SPIRES
SPIRIT
SPIROS
SPORES
SPORTS
SPORTY
SPURGE
SPURNS
SPURON
SPURRY
SPURTS
STARCH
STARED
STARER
STARES
STARRY
STARTS
STARVE
STEREO
STERES
STERNA
STERNE
STERNO
STERNS
STEROL
STIRIN
STIRKS
STIRUP
STORCH
STORED
STORER
STORES
STOREY
STORKS
STORMS
STORMY
STORRS
STURDY
STYRIA
STYRON
SUDRAS
SUNRAY
SURREY
SUTRAS
SWARAJ
SWARDS
SWARMS
SWARTH
SWERVE
SWIRLS
SWIRLY
SWORDS

S•••R•
SABERS
SAFARI
SAFIRE
SAHARA
SAKERS
SALARY
SAMARA
SANDRA
SAPORS
SARTRE
SATIRE
SATORI
SATURN
SATYRS
SAVERS
SAVORS
SAVORY
SAYERS
SCARRY
SCHORL
SCLERA
SCLERO
SCOURS
SCURRY
SEBERG
SECERN
SECURE
SEDERS
SEGURA
SEMPRE
SENARY
SENORA
SENORS
SENTRA
SENTRY
SEVERE
SEVERN
SEVERS
SEVERY
SEWARD
SEWERS
SHEARS
SHEERS
SHERRY
SHIRRS
SHOERS
SIDERO
SIDERS
SIERRA
SIGURD
SISERA
SISTRA
SITARS
SIXERS
SIZERS
SKERRY
SKIERS
SKIRRS
SLURRY
SMEARS
SMEARY
SNEERS
SNEERY
SOBERS
SOEURS
SOLARS
SOLERS
SOMBRE
SOMERS
SONORA
SOPORS
SOUARI
SOWERS
SOXERS
SPEARS
SPERRY
SPHERE
SPHERY
SPIERS
SPOORS
SPURRY
SQUARE
SQUIRE
SQUIRM
SQUIRT
STAIRS
STARRY
STEERS
STMARK
STORRS
STUART
SUBARU
SUBORN
SUBURB
SUGARS
SUGARY
SULTRY
SUNDRY
SUPERB
SUPERS
SUTURE
SWEARS

S••••R
SACKER
SADDER
SAILOR
SALTER
SALVER
SALVOR
SAMBAR
SANDER
SANGER
SANTIR
SAPPER
SASSER
SAUCER
SAUGER
SAVIOR
SAVOIR
SAVOUR
SAWYER
SCALAR
SCALER
SCARER
SCORER
SCOTER
SEALER
SEATER
SECTOR
SEEDER
SEEGER
SEEKER
SEINER
SEIZER
SELLER
SEMPER
SENDER
SENHOR
SENIOR
SENSOR
SERVER
SETTER
SEXIER
SHAKER
SHAMIR
SHAPER
SHARER
SHAVER
SHIKAR
SHINER
SHIRER
SHIVER
SHOFAR
SHOVER
SHOWER
SICKER
SIDDUR
SIFTER
SIGHER
SIGNER
SIGNOR
SILVER
SIMMER
SIMPER
SINGER
SINKER
SINNER
SINTER
SIPPER
SIRDAR
SISLER
SISTER
SITTER
SKATER
SKEWER
SKIVER
SLATER
SLAVER
SLAYER
SLICER
SLIDER
SLIVER
SLOWER
SMILER
SMOKER
SNIDER
SNIPER
SNORER
SNYDER
SOAKER
SOAPER
SOARER
SOBBER
SOCCER
SOFTER
SOLDER
SOLVER
SOMBER
SOMMER
SOONER
SORTER
SOURER
SOUTER
SPACER
SPADER
SPARER
SPIDER
SPIKER
SPRIER
SPRYER
STAGER
STALER
STARER
STATER
STATOR
STELAR
STEWER
STIVER
STOKER
STONER
STORER
STOVER
STUMER
STUPOR
STYLER
SUAVER
SUBPAR
SUCCOR
SUCKER
SUFFER
SUITOR
SULFUR
SULKER
SUMMER
SUMNER
SUMTER
SUNDER
SUPPER
SURFER
SUTLER
SUTTER
SWAYER
SWIPER

•SR•••
ISRAEL

•S•R••
ASHRAM
ASTRAL
ASTRAY
ASTRID
ASTROS
ESCROW
ESDRAS
ESPRIT
ESTRAY
ISTRIA
OSIRIS
OSPREY
TSURIS
USERID
USURER
USURPS

•S••R•
ASBURY
ASGARD
ASHARP
ASHORE
ASKARI
ASKERS
ASMARA
ASPERA
ASPIRE
ASSERT
ASSORT
ASSURE
ASTERN
ASTERS
ASWIRL
BSHARP
CSHARP
DSHARP
ESCARP
ESCORT
ESHARP
ESKERS
ESTERS
FSHARP
GSHARP
OSBORN
OSCARS
OSIERS
TSHIRT
USHERS

•S•••R
ASEVER
ASHIER
ASHLAR
ASKFOR
ESCHER
ESTHER
ISADOR
ISHTAR
ISOBAR
ISOMER
ISSUER
OSTLER
PSYWAR
USURER

••S•R•
ABSORB
ABSURD
ADSORB
ANSARA
ASSERT
ASSORT
ASSURE
AUSTRO
BISTRO
CASERN
CASTRO
CESARE
DESCRY
DESERT
DESIRE
DESTRY
DISARM
DOSERS
ENSURE
EXSERT
GASTRO
HASBRO
INSERT
INSURE
LASERS
LOSERS
LUSTRE
MASERS
MASERU
MESSRS
MISERS
MISERY
MUSERS
MYSORE
PASTRY
POSERS
RASERS
RESORB
RESORT
RISERS
ROSARY
ROSTRA
SISERA
SISTRA
TASERS
TISHRI
UNSURE
VESTRY
VISORS

••S••R
ANSGAR
ANSWER
BASTER
BESSER
BESTIR
BUSBAR
BUSIER
BUSTER
CASPAR
CASPER
CASTER
CASTOR
COSIER
COSTAR
CUSTER
DASHER
DISBAR
DOSSER
DUSTER
EASIER
EASTER
EISNER
FASTER
FESTER
FISHER
FOSTER
GASPAR
GASPER
GASSER
GUSHER
HESTER
HISSER
HOSIER
HUSKER
HUSSAR
INSTAR
ISSUER
JASPER
JESTER
JOSSER
JUSTER
KISSER
KOSHER
LASCAR
LASHER
LASSER
LESSER
LESSOR
LESTER
LISTER
LUSHER
LUSTER
MASHER
MASKER
MASTER
MESMER
MISTER
MOSHER
MUSHER
MUSTER
NASCAR
NASSER
NESTER
NESTOR
NOSHER
NOSIER
OUSTER
OYSTER
PASSER

PASTOR
PESTER
POSEUR
POSHER
POSTER
RASHER
RASPER
RASTER
RESTER
RISKER
ROSIER
ROSTER
SASSER
SISLER
SISTER
TASTER
TESTER
TOSSER
TUSKER
ULSTER
VASSAR
VASTER
VESPER
WASHER
WASTER
WISHER
WISTER
XYSTER
YASSER
YESSIR
YESTER

•••SR•

MESSRS

•••S•R

ABUSER
BESSER
BIGSUR
BOWSER
BURSAR
CAESAR
CENSER
CENSOR
CHASER
CLOSER
CURSOR
DENSER
DOSSER
DOWSER
ERASER
FALSER
FRASER
GASSER
GEYSER
GLASER
HAWSER
HISSER
HUSSAR
JOSSER
KAISER
KISSER
LASSER
LEASER
LESSER
LESSOR
LOOSER
MAUSER
MOUSER
NASSER
NURSER
PARSER
PASSER
PHASER
PROSER
PULSAR
PURSER
QUASAR
RAISER
ROUSER
SASSER
SENSOR
TEASER
TENSER
TENSOR
TERSER
TOSSER
VASSAR
WINSOR
WOWSER
YASSER
YESSIR

S•S•••

SASEBO
SASHAY
SASHED
SASHES
SASSED
SASSER
SASSES
SESAME
SESQUI
SESTET
SESTOS
SISALS
SISERA
SISKEL
SISKIN
SISLER
SISLEY
SISTER
SISTRA
SOSOON
SUSANN
SUSIEQ
SUSLIK
SUSSED
SUSSES
SUSSEX
SYSOPS
SYSTEM

S••S••

SALSAS
SAMSON
SANSEI
SASSED
SASSER
SASSES
SAYSOS
SEASON
SEESAW
SEESIN
SEESTO
SEISMO
SEISMS
SENSED
SENSEI
SENSES
SENSOR
SETSAT
SETSBY
SETSIN
SETSON
SETSUP
SEWSON
SEWSUP
SHASTA
SIESTA
SITSBY
SITSIN
SITSON
SITSUP
SLOSHY
SLUSHY
SOASTO
SOPSUP
SOUSED
SOUSES
SPASMS
STASES
STASIS
SUBSET
SUDSED
SUDSES
SUISSE
SUMSUP
SUNSET
SUSSED
SUSSES
SUSSEX

S•••S•

SAFEST
SAGEST
SALISH
SAMOSA
SANEST
SCHISM
SCHIST
SCHUSS
SCOUSE
SEROSA
SETOSE
SEXIST
SHIEST
SHIISM
SHYEST
SINISE
SIWASH
SLIEST
SLIMSY
SLYEST
SMERSH
SOREST
SPARSE
SPLASH
SPLOSH
SPOUSE
SQUASH
SQUISH
SQUUSH
STRASS
STRESS
SUFISM
SUISSE
SUREST
SWOOSH

S••••S

SABERS
SABINS
SABLES
SABOTS
SABRAS
SABRES
SADHES
SADHUS
SAHIBS
SAIGAS
SAINTS
SAKERS
SALADS
SALALS
SALONS
SALSAS
SALVES
SALVOS
SAMBAS
SANTOS
SAPORS
SARANS
SARDIS
SARGES
SARGOS
SARODS
SASHES
SASSES
SATINS
SATYRS
SAUCES
SAUDIS
SAULTS
SAUNAS
SAUTES
SAVERS
SAVORS
SAXONS
SAYERS
SAYLES
SAYSOS
SAYYES
SCALDS
SCALES
SCALPS
SCAMPS
SCANTS
SCAPES
SCARES
SCARFS
SCARPS
SCAUPS
SCENAS
SCENDS
SCENES
SCENTS
SCHMOS
SCHUSS
SCHWAS
SCIFIS
SCIONS
SCOFFS
SCOLDS
SCONES
SCOOPS
SCOOTS
SCOPES
SCORES
SCORNS
SCOURS
SCOUTS
SCOWLS
SCRAGS
SCRAMS
SCRAPS
SCREES
SCREWS
SCRIMS
SCRIPS
SCRODS
SCRUBS
SCRUMS
SCUBAS
SCUFFS
SCULLS
SCUTES
SEAMUS
SEDANS
SEDERS
SEDGES
SEDUMS
SEGUES
SEINES
SEISMS
SEIZES
SELVES
SENNAS
SENORS
SENSES
SEPALS
SEPIAS
SEPOYS
SERACS
SERAIS
SERGES
SERIES
SERIFS
SERINS
SEROUS
SEROWS
SERUMS
SERVES
SERVOS
SESTOS
SETINS
SETTOS
SETUPS
SEVENS
SEVERS
SEVRES
SEWERS
SHACKS
SHADES
SHAFTS
SHAKES
SHAKOS
SHALES
SHAMES
SHAMUS
SHANKS
SHAPES
SHARDS
SHARES
SHARKS
SHARPS
SHAVES
SHAWLS
SHAWMS
SHEAFS
SHEARS
SHEENS
SHEEPS
SHEERS
SHEETS
SHEIKS
SHELLS
SHIFTS
SHILLS
SHINES
SHIRES
SHIRKS
SHIRRS
SHIRTS
SHOALS
SHOATS
SHOCKS
SHOERS
SHOJIS
SHOOKS
SHOOTS
SHORES
SHORTS
SHOUTS
SHOVES
SHREDS
SHREWS
SHRUBS
SHRUGS
SHUCKS
SHUNTS
SIBYLS
SIDERS
SIDLES
SIEGES
SIEVES
SIGHTS
SIGILS
SIGMAS
SILVAS
SINEWS
SINGES
SIRENS
SIRIUS
SISALS
SITARS
SITINS
SITUPS
SIXERS
SIXTHS
SIXTUS
SIZERS
SKALDS
SKANKS
SKATES
SKEANS
SKEINS
SKIERS
SKIFFS
SKILLS
SKIMPS
SKINKS
SKIRLS
SKIROS
SKIRRS
SKIRTS
SKIVES
SKOALS
SKORTS
SKULKS
SKULLS
SKUNKS
SLACKS
SLAKES
SLANGS
SLANTS
SLATES
SLAVES
SLEEKS
SLEEPS
SLEETS
SLICES
SLICKS
SLIDES
SLIMES
SLINGS
SLINKS
SLOOPS
SLOPES
SLOTHS
SLUMPS
SLURPS
SLYPES
SMACKS
SMALLS
SMARTS
SMEARS
SMELLS
SMELTS
SMILES
SMIRKS
SMITES
SMITHS
SMOCKS
SMOKES
SMOLTS
SMURFS
SNACKS
SNAFUS
SNAILS
SNAKES
SNARES
SNARLS
SNATHS
SNEAKS
SNEERS
SNELLS
SNICKS
SNIFFS
SNIPES
SNOODS
SNOOKS
SNOOPS
SNOOTS
SNOPES
SNORES
SNORTS
SNOUTS
SNUFFS
SOARES
SOAVES
SOBERS
SOCLES
SOEURS
SOLANS
SOLARS
SOLERS
SOLEUS
SOLFAS
SOLIDS
SOLVES
SOMERS
SONDES
SONICS
SOPORS
SOTOLS
SOUGHS
SOUNDS
SOUSES
SOUTHS
SOWERS
SOXERS
SPACES
SPADES
SPAHIS
SPALLS
SPANKS
SPARES
SPARKS
SPASMS
SPATES
SPAWNS
SPEAKS
SPEARS
SPECKS
SPEEDS
SPELLS
SPENDS
SPICAS
SPICES
SPIELS
SPIERS
SPIFFS
SPIKES
SPILES
SPILLS
SPINES
SPINKS
SPIRES
SPIROS
SPITES
SPLATS
SPLAYS
SPLITS
SPOILS
SPOKES
SPOOFS
SPOOKS
SPOOLS
SPOONS
SPOORS
SPORES
SPORTS
SPOUTS
SPRAGS
SPRATS
SPRAYS
SPREES
SPRIGS
SPRITS
SPRUES
SPUMES
SPURNS
SPURTS
SQUABS
SQUADS
SQUATS
SQUIBS
SQUIDS
STACKS
STAFFS
STAGES
STAINS
STAIRS
STAKES
STALES
STALKS
STALLS
STAMPS
STANDS
STAPES
STARES
STARTS
STASES
STASIS
STATES
STATUS
STAVES
STEADS
STEAKS
STEALS
STEAMS
STEEDS
STEELS
STEEPS
STEERS
STEINS
STELES
STENOS
STERES
STERNS
STICKS
STIFFS
STILES
STILLS
STILTS
STINGS
STINKS
STINTS
STIPES
STIRKS
STOATS
STOCKS
STOICS
STOKES
STOLES
STOMAS
STOMPS
STONES
STOOKS
STOOLS
STOOPS
STOPES
STORES
STORKS
STORMS
STORRS
STOUPS
STOUTS
STOVES
STRADS
STRAPS
STRASS
STRAUS
STRAWS
STRAYS
STRESS
STREWS
STRIPS
STROPS
STRUMS
STRUTS
STUFFS
STULLS
STUMPS
STUNTS
STUPAS
STUPES
STYLES
STYLUS
SUCCES
SUCHAS
SUCKAS
SUDRAS
SUDSES
SUEDES
SUGARS
SUITES
SULCUS
SUMACS
SUMMAS
SUMUPS
SUNNIS
SUNUPS
SUPERS
SURAHS
SURGES
SUSSES
SUTRAS
SWAGES
SWAINS
SWALES
SWAMIS
SWAMPS
SWANKS
SWARDS
SWARMS
SWATHS
SWAZIS
SWEARS
SWEATS
SWEDES
SWEEPS
SWEETS
SWELLS
SWIFTS
SWILLS
SWINGS
SWIPES
SWIRLS
SWOONS
SWOOPS
SWORDS
SYLPHS
SYNODS
SYRUPS
SYSOPS

•SS•••

ASSAIL
ASSAYS
ASSENT
ASSERT
ASSESS
ASSETS
ASSIGN
ASSISI
ASSIST
ASSIZE
ASSORT
ASSUME
ASSURE
ESSAYS
ESSENE
ISSUED
ISSUER
ISSUES
OSSEIN
OSSETE
OSSIAN
OSSIFY

•S•S••

ASKSIN
ASOSAN
USESUP

•S••S•

ASPISH
ASSESS
ASSISI
ASSIST
ESPOSA
ESPOSO
OSMOSE
TSETSE
ZSAZSA

•S•••S

ASANAS
ASCOTS
ASDICS
ASIANS
ASIDES
ASKERS
ASPENS
ASPICS
ASSAYS
ASSESS
ASSETS
ASTERS
ASTROS
BSIDES
CSPOTS
ESDRAS
ESKERS
ESPIES
ESSAYS
ESTERS
ESTOPS
FSTOPS
GSUITS
ISLETS
ISSUES
ISTLES
OSAGES
OSCARS
OSIERS
OSIRIS
OSMICS
PSALMS
PSEUDS
PSYCHS
USAGES
USHERS
USUALS
USURPS
VSIGNS
VSIXES

••SS••

AUSSIE
BASSES
BASSET
BASSLY
BASSOS
BESSER
BESSIE
BISSAU
BISSET
BOSSED
BOSSES
BUSSED
BUSSES
BYSSHE
BYSSUS
CASSIA
CASSIO
CASSIS
CESSED
CESSES
CESSNA
COSSET
CUSSED
CUSSES
DASSIN
DISSED
DOSSAL
DOSSED
DOSSEL
DOSSER
DOSSES
FESSED
FESSES
FESSUP
FOSSAE
FOSSAS
FOSSES
FOSSEY
FOSSIL
FUSSED
FUSSES
GASSED
GASSER
GASSES
GOSSIP
GUSSET
HASSAM
HASSAN
HASSLE
HISSAT
HISSED
HISSER
HISSES
HUSSAR
HUSSEY
HYSSOP
IJSSEL
JESSEL
JESSIE
JOSSER
JOSSES
KISSED
KISSER
KISSES
LASSEN
LASSER
LASSES
LASSIE
LASSOS
LESSEE
LESSEN
LESSER
LESSON
LESSOR
LOSSES
MASSED
MASSES
MASSEY
MASSIF
MESSED
MESSES
MESSRS
MESSUP
MISSAL
MISSAY
MISSED
MISSES
MISSIS
MISSUS
MOSSED
MOSSES
MUSSED
MUSSEL
MUSSES
MUSSUP
NASSAU
NASSER
NESSES
NESSIE
NISSAN
NISSEN
PASSBY
PASSED
PASSEL
PASSER
PASSES
PASSIM
PASSON
PASSUP
POSSES
POSSET
POSSLQ
POSSUM
PUSSES
RASSLE
RUSSET
RUSSIA
SASSED
SASSER
SASSES
SUSSED
SUSSES
SUSSEX
TASSEL
TASSES
TESSIE
TISSUE
TOSSED
TOSSER
TOSSES
TOSSUP
TUSSAH
TUSSLE
VASSAL
VASSAR
VESSEL
WESSEX
WESSON
WUSSES
YASSER
YESSED
YESSES
YESSIR

••S•S•

ASSESS
ASSISI
ASSIST
BASEST
DESIST
DISUSE
INSIST
MISUSE
OBSESS
RESIST
WISEST

••S••S

AISLES
ARSONS
ASSAYS
ASSESS
ASSETS
BASHES
BASICS
BASINS
BASSES
BASSOS
BASTES
BESETS
BESOMS
BESOTS
BISONS
BOSONS
BOSSES
BOSUNS
BUSHES
BUSIES
BUSSES
BYSSUS
CASALS
CASHES
CASSIS
CASTES
CESSES
CESTAS
CESTOS
CESTUS
CISCOS
COSHES
COSIES
COSMOS
COSTAS
CUSSES
CUSTIS
CUSTOS
DASHES
DASHIS
DISCOS
DISCUS
DISHES
DISMES
DOSERS
DOSSES
EASELS
EDSELS
ENSUES
EOSINS
ESSAYS
FASCES
FESSES
FESTAS
FESTUS
FISHES
FOSSAS
FOSSES
FUSEES
FUSILS
FUSSES
GASHES
GASSES
GESTES
GUSHES
HASHES
HASTES
HISSES
HOSELS
HOSTAS
HUSHES
INSETS
ISSUES
JASEYS
JOSHES
JOSSES
KISSES
LASERS
LASHES
LASSES
LASSOS
LESBOS
LISLES
LOSERS
LOSSES
LYSINS
MASAIS
MASERS
MASHES
MASONS
MASSES
MESHES
MESONS
MESSES
MESSRS
MISERS
MISSES
MISSIS
MISSUS
MOSEYS
MOSHES
MOSSES
MUSERS
MUSHES
MUSSES
NASALS
NESSES
NOSHES
OBSESS
ONSETS
OUSELS
PASEOS
PASHAS
PASSES
PASTAS
PASTES
PASTIS
PESTOS
PISANS
PISCES
PISTES
POSERS
POSIES
POSITS
POSSES
PUSHES
PUSSES
RASERS
RASHES
RESAWS
RESEES
RESETS
RESEWS
RESHES
RESINS
RESODS
RISERS
ROSINS
RUSHES
SASHES
SASSES
SESTOS
SISALS
SUSSES
SYSOPS
TASERS
TASSES
TASTES
TESLAS
TOSSES
TVSETS
UNSAYS
UNSEWS
UPSETS
URSIDS
VESTAS
VISITS
VISORS
VISTAS
VOSGES
WASHES
WASTES
WISHES
WUSSES
YESSES

•••SS•

ABESSE
AGASSI
ALYSSA
BRASSY
CHASSE
CLASSY
CROSSE
CUISSE
DRESSY
EDESSA
ELISSA
FLOSSY
GLASSY
GLOSSA
GLOSSO
GLOSSY
GRASSO
GRASSY
GROSSE
GROSSO
INESSE
MOUSSE
NEISSE
NYASSA
ODESSA
ORISSA
PLISSE
POUSSE
PRISSY
SUISSE
WRASSE

•••S•S

ABASES
ABUSES
ABYSMS
ACTSAS
AMUSES
ARISES
ATESTS
AVISOS
BASSES
BASSOS
BEASTS
BIASES
BLASTS
BOASTS
BOOSTS
BOSSES
BOUSES
BURSAS
BURSES
BURSTS
BUSSES
BYSSUS
CASSIS
CAUSES
CEASES
CENSES
CENSUS
CESSES
CHASES
CHASMS
CHESTS
CLASPS
CLOSES
COASTS
COPSES
CRESTS
CRISES
CRISIS
CRISPS
CRUSES
CRUSTS
CURSES
CUSSES
DAISES
DEISTS
DIESES
DIESIS
DOSSES
DOUSES
DOWSES
ECESIS
EGESTS
ENOSIS
ERASES

EXISTS
FEASTS
FESSES
FIRSTS
FLASKS
FOISTS
FOSSAS
FOSSES
FRISES
FRISKS
FROSTS
FUSSES
GASSES
GHOSTS
GNOSIS
GOOSES
GORSES
GRASPS
GRISTS
GUESTS
GUISES
HAUSAS
HAWSES
HEISTS
HISSES
HOISTS
HORSES
HOUSES
HYKSOS
IBISES
IRISES
JOISTS
JOSSES
JOUSTS
KANSAS
KARSTS
KIOSKS
KISSES
LAPSES
LASSES
LASSOS
LEASES
LENSES
LOOSES
LOSSES
LOUSES
MANSES
MASSES
MENSAS
MESSES
MESSRS
MIOSIS
MISSES
MISSIS
MISSUS
MOSSES
MOUSES
MUSSES
MYOSIS
NESSES
NOESIS
NOISES
NOOSES
NURSES
ODISTS
ONUSES
OPUSES
PAISAS
PARSES
PASSES
PAUSES
PHASES
PLUSES
POISES

POSSES
PRASES
PRISMS
PROSES
PULSES
PURSES
PUSSES
QUESTS
RAISES
RAMSES
REESES
REUSES
RHESUS
RINSES
ROASTS
ROOSTS
ROUSES
ROUSTS
SALSAS
SASSES
SAYSOS
SEISMS
SENSES
SOUSES
SPASMS
STASES
STASIS
SUDSES
SUSSES
TARSUS
TASSES
TEASES
TENSES
THESES
THESIS
TMESIS
TOASTS
TORSOS
TOSSES
TRUSTS
TRYSTS
TWISTS
UKASES
UNISYS
UPASES
URUSES
VERSES
VERSOS
VERSTS
VERSUS
WAISTS
WHISKS
WORSTS
WRESTS
WRISTS
WURSTS
WUSSES
XHOSAS
YEASTS
YESSES

••••SS

ABBESS
ACCESS
ACROSS
ADMASS
ARLISS
ARNESS
ASSESS
BYPASS
CARESS
DURESS
EGRESS
EMBOSS
EXCESS
GNEISS
HARASS
INNESS
KAROSS
KUMISS
MORASS
NOLESS
OBSESS
OGRESS
RECESS
REMISS
SCHUSS
STRASS
STRESS
UNLESS

ST••••

STABAT
STABLE
STABLY
STACEY
STACKS
STACTE
STADIA
STAFFS
STAGED
STAGER
STAGES
STAINS
STAIRS
STAKED
STAKES
STALAG
STALED
STALER
STALES
STALIN
STALKS
STALKY
STALLS
STAMEN
STAMPS
STANCE
STANCH
STANDS
STANKY
STANZA
STAPES
STAPLE
STAPUF
STARCH
STARED
STARER
STARES
STARRY
STARTS
STARVE
STASES
STASIS
STATED
STATEN
STATER
STATES
STATIC
STATOR
STATUE
STATUS
STAVED
STAVES
STAYED
STAYON
STAYUP
STEADS
STEADY
STEAKS
STEALS
STEAMS
STEAMY
STEEDS
STEELE
STEELS
STEELY
STEEPS
STEERS
STEEVE
STEFAN
STEFFI
STEFOY
STEINS
STELAE
STELAR
STELES
STELLA
STELMO
STENCH
STENOG
STENOS
STEPIN
STEPON
STEPPE
STEPUP
STEREO
STERES
STERNA
STERNE
STERNO
STERNS
STEROL
STEVEN
STEVIE
STEWED
STEWER
STHENO
STICKS
STICKY
STIFFS
STIFLE
STIGMA
STILES
STILLS
STILLY
STILTS
STIMPY
STINGO
STINGS
STINGY
STINKS
STINKY
STINTS
STIPEL
STIPES
STIRIN
STIRKS
STIRUP
STITCH
STITHY
STIVER
STIVIC
STJOAN
STJOHN
STLUKE
STMALO
STMARK
STOATS
STOCKS
STOCKY
STODGE
STODGY
STOGIE
STOICS
STOJKO
STOKED
STOKER
STOKES
STOLEN
STOLES
STOLID
STOLLE
STOLON
STOMAS
STOMAT
STOMPS
STONED
STONER
STONES
STOOGE
STOOKS
STOOLS
STOOLY
STOOPS
STOPES
STOPIN
STOPIT
STOPUP
STORCH
STORED
STORER
STORES
STOREY
STORKS
STORMS
STORMY
STORRS
STOTIN
STOUPS
STOUTS
STOVER
STOVES
STOWED
STPAUL
STPETE
STRABO
STRADS
STRAFE
STRAIN
STRAIT
STRAKE
STRAND
STRAPS
STRASS
STRATA
STRATI
STRATO
STRAUB
STRAUS
STRAWS
STRAWY
STRAYS
STREAK
STREAM
STREEP
STREET
STRESS
STREWN
STREWS
STRIAE
STRICK
STRICT
STRIDE
STRIFE
STRIKE
STRINE
STRING
STRIPE
STRIPS
STRIPY
STRIVE
STROBE
STRODE
STROKE
STROLL
STRONG
STROPS
STROUD
STROVE
STRUCK
STRUMS
STRUNG
STRUTS
STUART
STUBBY
STUCCO
STUDIO
STUFFS
STUFFY
STULLS
STUMER
STUMPS
STUMPY
STUNTS
STUNTY
STUPAS
STUPES
STUPID
STUPOR
STURDY
STYLED
STYLER
STYLES
STYLET
STYLUS
STYMIE
STYRIA
STYRON

S•T•••

SATANG
SATEEN
SATING
SATINS
SATINY
SATIRE
SATORI
SATOUT
SATRAP
SATURN
SATYRS
SETINS
SETOFF
SETOSE
SETOUT
SETSAT
SETSBY
SETSIN
SETSON
SETSUP
SETTEE
SETTER
SETTLE
SETTOS
SETUPS
SGTMAJ
SHTETL
SHTICK
SITARS
SITCOM
SITING
SITINS
SITOUT
SITSBY
SITSIN
SITSON
SITSUP
SITTER
SITUPS
SOTHAT
SOTOLS
SOTTED
SUTLER
SUTRAS
SUTTER
SUTTON
SUTURE

S••T••

SALTED
SALTEN
SALTER
SALTON
SALTUM
SANTEE
SANTIR
SANTOS
SARTON
SARTRE
SAUTES
SCATHE
SCATTY
SCOTCH
SCOTER
SCOTIA
SCOTTO
SCOTTY
SCUTCH
SCUTES
SCYTHE
SEATED
SEATER
SEATON
SECTOR
SEETHE
SENTIN
SENTRA
SENTRY
SENTUP
SEPTAL
SEPTET
SEPTIC
SEPTUM
SESTET
SESTOS
SETTEE
SETTER
SETTLE
SETTOS
SEXTET
SEXTON
SHOTAT
SHOTUP
SHUTIN
SHUTUP
SIFTED
SIFTER
SILTED
SINTAX
SINTER
SISTER
SISTRA
SITTER
SIXTHS
SIXTUS
SKATED
SKATER
SKATES
SKETCH
SKITCH
SKITOW
SLATED
SLATER
SLATES
SLITHY
SLITTY
SLOTHS
SMITES
SMITHS
SMITHY
SMUTCH
SMUTTY
SNATCH
SNATHE
SNATHS
SNITCH
SNOTTY
SOFTEN
SOFTER
SOFTIE
SOFTLY
SONTAG
SOOTHE
SORTED
SORTER
SORTIE
SORTOF
SOTTED
SOUTER
SOUTHS
SPATES
SPATHE
SPITED
SPITES
SPOTTY
STATED
STATEN
STATER
STATES
STATIC
STATOR
STATUE
STATUS
STITCH
STITHY
STOTIN
SUBTLE
SUBTLY
SUITED
SUITES
SUITOR
SUITUP
SULTAN
SULTRY
SUMTER
SUNTAN
SURTAX
SUTTER
SUTTON
SWATCH
SWATHE
SWATHS
SWITCH
SYNTAX
SYSTEM

S•••T•

SABATO
SABOTS
SAFETY
SAINTE
SAINTS
SALUTE
SAMITE
SANCTA
SANGTO
SANITY
SAULTS
SAVATE
SCANTS
SCANTY
SCATTY
SCENTS
SCOOTS
SCOTTO
SCOTTY
SCOUTS
SEDATE
SEENTO
SEESTO
SEMITE
SENATE
SENITI
SHAFTS
SHAKTI
SHANTY
SHASTA
SHEATH
SHEETS
SHELTY
SHIFTS
SHIFTY
SHIITE
SHINTO
SHIRTS
SHIRTY
SHOATS
SHOOTS
SHORTA
SHORTE
SHORTI
SHORTO
SHORTS
SHORTU
SHORTY
SHOUTS
SHTETL
SHUNTS
SIESTA
SIGHTS
SINGTO
SKIRTS
SKORTS
SLANTS
SLEETS
SLEETY
SLEUTH
SLITTY
SMALTI
SMALTO
SMARTS
SMARTY
SMELTS
SMOLTS
SMOOTH
SMUTTY
SNAPTO
SNOOTS
SNOOTY
SNORTS
SNOTTY
SNOUTS
SOASTO
SOLUTE
SOMATA
SOMATO
SONATA
SOWETO
SPARTA
SPILTH
SPINTO
SPLATS
SPLITS
SPORTS
SPORTY
SPOTTY
SPOUTS
SPRATS
SPRITE
SPRITS
SPRITZ
SPURTS
SQUATS
STACTE
STARTS
STILTS
STINTS
STOATS
STOUTS
STPETE
STRATA
STRATI
STRATO
STRUTS
STUNTS
STUNTY
SUBITO
SURETE
SURETY
SVELTE
SWARTH
SWEATS
SWEATY
SWEETS
SWIFTS

S••••T

SACHET
SAFEST
SAGEST
SALLET
SALYUT
SAMLET
SANEST
SATOUT
SAVANT
SAWFIT
SAWOUT
SCHIST
SCRIPT
SCULPT
SECANT
SECRET
SEEFIT
SEEOUT
SEJANT
SELECT
SENNET
SENNIT
SEPTET
SESTET
SETOUT
SETSAT
SEURAT
SEXIST
SEXTET
SHEVAT
SHIEST
SHOTAT
SHRIFT
SHYEST
SIGNET
SILENT
SIPPET
SITOUT
SKIPIT
SLIEST
SLIGHT
SLYEST
SNAPAT
SNOCAT
SOBEIT
SOCKET
SOFFIT
SOLENT
SONANT
SONNET
SORBET
SOREST
SOTHAT
SOUGHT
SOVIET
SOWHAT
SPIGOT
SPINET
SPIRIT
SPLINT
SPOILT
SPRINT
SPROUT
SQUINT
SQUIRT
STABAT
STOMAT
STOPIT
STRAIT
STREET
STRICT
STUART
STYLET
SUBLET
SUBMIT
SUBSET
SUMMIT
SUNLIT
SUNSET
SUREST
SWIVET

•ST•••

ASTERN
ASTERS
ASTRAL
ASTRAY
ASTRID
ASTROS
ASTUTE
ESTATE
ESTEEM
ESTERS
ESTHER
ESTOPS
ESTRAY
FSTOPS
GSTAAD
ISTHMI
ISTLES
ISTRIA
OSTEAL
OSTEND
OSTIUM
OSTLER

•S•T••

ISHTAR
TSETSE

•S••T•

ASCOTS
ASEITY
ASSETS
ASTUTE
CSPOTS
ESTATE
GSUITS
ISLETS
OSSETE
USEDTO

•S•••T

ASCENT
ASKOUT
ASLANT
ASPECT
ASSENT
ASSERT
ASSIST
ASSORT
ESCENT
ESCORT
ESPRIT
ISEULT
TSHIRT
USENET

••ST••

AMSTEL
ATSTUD
AUSTEN
AUSTIN
AUSTRO
BASTED
BASTER
BASTES
BESTED
BESTIR
BESTOW
BISTRO
BOSTON
BUSTED
BUSTER
BUSTIN
BUSTLE
CASTER
CASTES
CASTLE
CASTON
CASTOR
CASTRO
CESTAS
CESTOS
CESTUS
COSTAE
COSTAL
COSTAR
COSTAS
COSTLY
CUSTER
CUSTIS
CUSTOM
CUSTOS
DESTRY
DISTAL
DISTIL
DUSTED
DUSTER
DUSTIN
DUSTUP
EASTER
EASTON
FASTED
FASTEN
FASTER
FESTAL
FESTAS
FESTER
FESTUS
FISTED
FISTIC
FOSTER
FUSTIC
GASTON
GASTRO
GESTES
GESTIC
GOSTAG
GUSTAV
GUSTED
HASTEN
HASTES
HESTER
HESTIA
HESTON
HOSTAS
HOSTED
HOSTEL
HOSTLY
HUSTLE
HUSTON
INSTAL
INSTAR
INSTEP
INSTIL
JESTED
JESTER
JOSTLE
JUSTER
JUSTIN
JUSTLY
LASTED
LASTEX
LASTLY
LESTAT
LESTER
LISTED
LISTEE
LISTEL
LISTEN
LISTER
LISTON
LOSTIT
LUSTED
LUSTER
LUSTRE
MASTER
MASTIC
MISTED
MISTER
MOSTEL
MOSTLY
MUSTER
MUSTNT
MYSTIC
NESTEA
NESTED
NESTER
NESTLE
NESTOR
OBSTET
OUSTED
OUSTER
OYSTER
PASTAS
PASTED
PASTEL
PASTES
PASTIS
PASTOR
PASTRY
PESTER
PESTLE
PESTOS
PISTES
PISTIL
PISTOL
PISTON
POSTAL
POSTED
POSTER
POSTIT
POSTON
RASTER
RESTED
RESTER
RESTON
RESTUP
ROSTER
ROSTOV
ROSTRA
RUSTED
RUSTIC
RUSTLE
SESTET
SESTOS
SISTER
SISTRA
SYSTEM
TASTED
TASTER
TASTES
TESTAE
TESTED
TESTEE
TESTER
ULSTER
UNSTOP
VASTER
VASTLY
VESTAL
VESTAS
VESTED
VESTEE
VESTRY
VISTAS
VOSTOK
WASTED
WASTER
WASTES
WISTER
WYSTAN
XYSTER
YESTER
ZESTED

••S•T•

ANSATE
ASSETS
BESETS
BESOTS
DESOTO
ERSATZ
INSETS
INSITU
ONSETS
ONSITE
OSSETE
PASHTO
PESETA
POSITS
RESETS
ROSITA
TVSETS
UPSETS
VASHTI
VISITS
WISETO

••S••T

ABSENT
ASSENT
ASSERT
ASSIST
ASSORT
BASALT
BASEST
BASKET
BASSET
BESANT
BISECT
BISSET
BOSKET
COSSET
DESALT
DESERT
DESIST
DESPOT
DISANT
EXSERT
GASJET
GASKET
GASLIT
GOSOFT
GUSSET
HISSAT
INSECT
INSERT
INSIST
INSULT
JESUIT
KISMET
LESTAT
LOSEIT
LOSTIT
MASCOT
MISFIT
MISHIT
MUSCAT
MUSKET
MUSTNT
OBSTET
POSSET
POSTIT
RESALT
RESEAT
RESECT
RESENT
RESHOT
RESIST
RESORT
RESULT
RUSSET
SESTET
UNSEAT
UPSHOT
WESKIT
WISENT
WISEST

•••ST•

ADDSTO
ADESTE
AIMSTO
ARISTA
ARISTO
ATESTS
AVESTA
BEASTS
BLASTS
BOASTS
BOOSTS
BURSTS
CHASTE
CHESTS
CHESTY
COASTS
CRESTS
CRISTO
CRUSTS
CRUSTY
CUESTA
DEISTS
EGESTA
EGESTS
ERESTU
EXISTS
FEASTS
FEISTY
FIESTA
FIRSTS
FOISTS
FROSTS
FROSTY
GETSTO
GHOSTS
GRISTS
GUESTS
HEISTS
HOISTS
JOISTS
JOUSTS
KARSTS
LAYSTO
LIESTO
ODISTS
PIGSTY
PLASTY
PRESTO
PUTSTO
QUESTS
ROASTS
ROOSTS
ROUSTS
RUNSTO
SEESTO
SHASTA
SIESTA
SOASTO
TIESTO
TOASTS
TOASTY
TRISTE
TRUSTS
TRUSTY
TRYSTS
TWISTS
TWISTY
VERSTS
WAISTS

WORSTS
WRESTS
WRISTS
WURSTS
YEASTS
YEASTY

•••S•T
AIMSAT
ALLSET
BAGSIT
BASSET
BISSET
BOXSET
CLOSET
COMSAT
CORSET
COSSET
DOESNT
DOGSAT
DOGSIT
DORSET
EATSAT
GETSAT
GETSET
GETSIT
GOESAT
GOTSET
GUSSET
HISSAT
HITSIT
JETSET
LETSAT
NIPSAT
OFFSET
OUTSET
PAWSAT
POSSET
PRESET
PROSIT
RUNSAT
RUSSET
SETSAT
SUBSET
SUNSET
TEASET
TILSIT

••••ST
ABLEST
ACCOST
ADJUST
AGEIST
AGHAST
ALEAST
ALMOST
ALWEST
AMIDST
AORIST
APTEST
ARREST
ARTIST
ASSIST
ATBEST
ATCOST
ATLAST
ATMOST
ATREST
ATTEST
AUGUST
BAREST
BASEST
BEHEST
BLUEST
BREAST
BYPAST
COHOST
COYEST
CUBIST
CUTEST
DEGUST
DELIST
DESIST
DETEST
DEVEST
DIGEST
DIREST
DIVEST
DRIEST
DRYEST
DYNAST
EGOIST
ELDEST
ENLIST
ERNEST
EXPOST
FEWEST
FEYEST
FINEST
FOREST
FREEST
GAINST
GAMEST
GAYEST
GOBUST
GOWEST
HALEST
HEARST
HOLIST
HONEST
HUGEST
ICIEST
IDLEST
ILLEST
IMPOST
INFEST
INGEST
INJEST
INMOST
INSIST
INVEST
IQTEST
JURIST
KLEIST
LAMEST
LATEST
LAXEST
LEGIST
LOCUST
LOWEST
LUTIST
LYRIST
MAOIST
MARIST
MEREST
MODEST
MOLEST
MONIST
MUTEST
NEWEST
NICEST
NLEAST
NLWEST
NUDEST
NUDIST
OBLAST
OBOIST
OBTEST
ODDEST
OLDEST
PALEST
PRIEST
PROUST
PUREST
PURIST
RAREST
RAWEST
RECAST
RELIST
REPAST
REPOST
RESIST
RETEST
RIFEST
RIPEST
ROBUST
RUDEST
SAFEST
SAGEST
SANEST
SCHIST
SEXIST
SHIEST
SHYEST
SLIEST
SLYEST
SOREST
SUREST
TAMEST
TANIST
TAOIST
THEIST
THIRST
THRUST
TRUEST
TUBIST
TWEEST
TYPIST
UNJUST
UNREST
UPCAST
UPMOST
UTMOST
VILEST
WHILST
WIDEST
WISEST
WRIEST
WRYEST
YAREST

SU••••
SUAVER
SUBARU
SUBBED
SUBDEB
SUBDUE
SUBGUM
SUBITO
SUBLET
SUBMIT
SUBORN
SUBPAR
SUBSET
SUBTLE
SUBTLY
SUBURB
SUBWAY
SUCCES
SUCCOR
SUCHAS
SUCKAS
SUCKED
SUCKER
SUCKIN
SUDDEN
SUDRAS
SUDSED
SUDSES
SUEDES
SUFFER
SUFFIX
SUFISM
SUGARS
SUGARY
SUISSE
SUITED
SUITES
SUITOR
SUITUP
SUKKAH
SULCUS
SULFUR
SULKED
SULKER
SULLEN
SULTAN
SULTRY
SUMACS
SUMMAE
SUMMAS
SUMMED
SUMMER
SUMMIT
SUMMON
SUMNER
SUMSUP
SUMTER
SUMUPS
SUNDAE
SUNDAY
SUNDER
SUNDEW
SUNDOG
SUNDRY
SUNGOD
SUNKEN
SUNLIT
SUNNED
SUNNIS
SUNOCO
SUNRAY
SUNSET
SUNTAN
SUNUNU
SUNUPS
SUPERB
SUPERS
SUPINE
SUPPED
SUPPER
SUPPLE
SUPPLY
SURAHS
SURELY
SUREST
SURETE
SURETY
SURFED
SURFER
SURGED
SURGES
SURIMI
SURREY
SURTAX
SURVEY
SUSANN
SUSIEQ
SUSLIK
SUSSED
SUSSES
SUSSEX
SUTLER
SUTRAS
SUTTER
SUTTON
SUTURE
SUZUKI

S•U•••
SAUCED
SAUCER
SAUCES
SAUDIS
SAUGER
SAULTS
SAUNAS
SAUREL
SAUTES
SCUBAS
SCUFFS
SCULLS
SCULLY
SCULPT
SCUMMY
SCURFY
SCURRY
SCURVE
SCURVY
SCUTCH
SCUTES
SCUZZY
SEURAT
SHUCKS
SHUNTS
SHUTIN
SHUTUP
SKULKS
SKULLS
SKUNKS
SKUNKY
SLUDGE
SLUDGY
SLUGGO
SLUICE
SLUING
SLUMMY
SLUMPS
SLURPS
SLURRY
SLUSHY
SMUDGE
SMUDGY
SMUGLY
SMURFS
SMUTCH
SMUTTY
SNUBBY
SNUFFS
SNUFFY
SNUGLI
SNUGLY
SOUARI
SOUGHS
SOUGHT
SOUNDS
SOUPUP
SOURCE
SOURED
SOURER
SOURLY
SOUSED
SOUSES
SOUTER
SOUTHS
SPUMED
SPUMES
SPUNKY
SPURGE
SPURNS
SPURON
SPURRY
SPURTS
SQUABS
SQUADS
SQUALL
SQUARE
SQUASH
SQUATS
SQUAWK
SQUEAK
SQUEAL
SQUIBB
SQUIBS
SQUIDS
SQUILL
SQUINT
SQUIRE
SQUIRM
SQUIRT
SQUISH
SQUUSH
STUART
STUBBY
STUCCO
STUDIO
STUFFS
STUFFY
STULLS
STUMER
STUMPS
STUMPY
STUNTS
STUNTY
STUPAS
STUPES
STUPID
STUPOR
STURDY

S••U••
SALUKI
SALUTE
SAMUEL
SATURN
SCAUPS
SCHULZ
SCHUSS
SCOURS
SCOUSE
SCOUTS
SCRUBS
SCRUFF
SCRUMS
SECURE
SEDUCE
SEDUMS
SEGUED
SEGUES
SEGURA
SENUFO
SEQUEL
SEQUIN
SERUMS
SETUPS
SHOULD
SHOUTS
SHRUBS
SHRUGS
SHRUNK
SIGURD
SIOUAN
SITUPS
SLEUTH
SLOUCH
SLOUGH
SNOUTS
SOEURS
SOLUTE
SPOUSE
SPOUTS
SPRUCE
SPRUES
SPRUNG
SQUUSH
STLUKE
STOUPS
STOUTS
STRUCK
STRUMS
STRUNG
STRUTS
SUBURB
SUMUPS
SUNUNU
SUNUPS
SUTURE
SUZUKI
SYRUPS
SYRUPY

S•••U•
SACQUE
SACRUM
SADHUS
SALTUM
SALYUT
SANNUP
SATOUT
SAVEUP
SAVOUR
SAWOUT
SCARUM
SEALUP
SEAMUS
SEEOUT
SELJUK
SENDUP
SENTUP
SEPTUM
SEROUS
SESQUI
SETOUT
SETSUP
SEWNUP
SEWSUP
SHAMUS
SHOGUN
SHOTUP
SHOWUP
SHROUD
SHUTUP
SIDDUR
SIGNUP
SINFUL
SIRIUS
SITOUT
SITSUP
SIXGUN
SIXTUS
SIZEUP
SKIRUN
SLAPUP
SLIPUP
SLOWUP
SNAFUS
SNAPUP
SOAKUP
SOBFUL
SODIUM
SOLEUS
SOPSUP
SOUPUP
SOWBUG
SPEDUP
SPROUT
STAPUF
STATUE
STATUS
STAYUP
STEPUP
STIRUP
STOPUP
STPAUL
STRAUB
STRAUS
STROUD
STYLUS
SUBDUE
SUBGUM
SUITUP
SULCUS
SULFUR
SUMSUP

S••••U
SHORTU
SUBARU
SUNUNU

•SU•••
GSUITS
TSURIS
USUALS
USURER
USURPS

•S•U••
ASBURY
ASSUME
ASSURE
ASTUTE
ESCUDO
ISEULT
ISSUED
ISSUER
ISSUES
MSQUAD
OSCULA
OSMUND
PSEUDO
PSEUDS

•S••U•
ASKOUT
ASYLUM
OSMIUM
OSTIUM
USEDUP
USEFUL
USESUP

••SU••
ABSURD
ASSUME
ASSURE
BOSUNS
CASUAL
DISUSE
ENSUED
ENSUES
ENSURE
INSULT
INSURE
ISSUED
ISSUER
ISSUES
JESUIT
MISUSE
RESULT
RESUME
UNSUNG
UNSURE
URSULA
VISUAL

••S•U•
ATSTUD
BASQUE
BISQUE
BYSSUS
CASQUE
CESIUM
CESTUS
DISCUS
DUSTUP
EASEUP
ENSOUL
FESCUE
FESSUP
FESTUS
JOSHUA
KUSPUK
LASHUP
MASQUE
MESSUP
MISCUE
MISSUS
MOSQUE
MUSEUM
MUSSUP
NASHUA
PASSUP
POSEUR
POSSUM
PUSHUP
RESCUE
RESTUP
RISQUE
SESQUI
TISSUE
TOSSUP
WASHUP
WISEUP

••S••U
BISSAU
DESILU
INSITU
MASERU
NASSAU
RESEAU
ROSEAU
VISHNU

•••SU•
ACESUP
ACTSUP
ADDSUP
BIDSUP
BIGSUR
BOBSUP
BUYSUP
BYSSUS
CATSUP
CENSUS
CONSUL
CUTSUP
DAMSUP
DATSUN
DIGSUP
DIMSUM
DOESUP
DORSUM
EATSUP
ENDSUP
FESSUP
FOGSUP
GETSUP
GOESUP
GUMSUP
GYPSUM
HITSUP
HOPSUP
ICESUP
JAMSUP
KEYSUP
LAPSUP
LAYSUP
LETSUP
MESSUP
MISSUS
MOPSUP
MUSSUP
OMASUM
OWNSUP
PASSUP
PAYSUP
PEPSUP
POPSUP
POSSUM
PURSUE
PUTSUP
REVSUP
RHESUS
RIGSUP
RIPSUP
RUNSUP
SETSUP
SEWSUP
SITSUP
SOPSUP
SUMSUP
TAGSUP
TARSUS
TEESUP
TIESUP
TISSUE
TOSSUP
TOTSUP
USESUP
VERSUS
WADSUP
ZIPSUP

•••S•U
BISSAU
ERESTU
HONSHU
KYUSHU
NASSAU
WAUSAU

••••SU
HAVASU

SV••••
SVELTE

S•V•••
SAVAGE
SAVAII
SAVANT
SAVATE
SAVERS
SAVEUP
SAVING
SAVIOR
SAVOIE
SAVOIR
SAVORS
SAVORY
SAVOUR
SEVENS
SEVERE
SEVERN
SEVERS
SEVERY
SEVRES
SOVIET

S••V••
SALVED
SALVER
SALVES
SALVIA
SALVOR
SALVOS
SELVES
SERVAL
SERVED
SERVER
SERVES
SERVOS
SHAVED
SHAVEN
SHAVER
SHAVES
SHEVAT
SHIVER
SHOVED
SHOVEL
SHOVER
SHOVES
SIEVED
SIEVES
SILVAS
SILVER
SKIVED
SKIVER
SKIVES
SKIVVY
SLAVED
SLAVER
SLAVES
SLAVEY
SLAVIC
SLIVER
SLOVAK
SLOVEN
SLOVIK
SNIVEL
SOAVES
SOLVED
SOLVER
SOLVES
SPAVIN
SPIVAK
SPIVVY
STAVED
STAVES
STEVEN
STEVIE
STIVER
STIVIC
STOVER
STOVES
SUAVER
SURVEY
SWIVEL
SWIVET
SYLVAN
SYLVIA

S•••V•
SALIVA
SCURVE
SCURVY
SHEAVE
SHELVE
SHRIVE
SHROVE
SKIVVY
SLEAVE
SLEEVE
SPIVVY
STARVE
STEEVE
STRIVE
STROVE
SWERVE

•SV•••
RSVPED

•S•V••
ASEVER

•S•••V
ASIMOV

••S•V•
CASAVA
KOSOVO
MOSKVA

••S••V
GUSTAV
KISLEV
MOSHAV
ROSTOV
VASLAV

•••S•V
BRASOV

SW••••
SWABBY
SWAGED
SWAGES
SWAINS
SWALES
SWAMIS
SWAMPS
SWAMPY
SWANEE
SWANKS
SWANKY
SWARAJ
SWARDS
SWARMS
SWARTH
SWATCH
SWATHE
SWATHS
SWAYED
SWAYER
SWAYZE
SWAZIS
SWEARS
SWEATS
SWEATY
SWEDEN
SWEDES
SWEEPS
SWEETS
SWELLS
SWERVE
SWIFTS
SWILLS
SWINGS
SWINGY
SWIPED
SWIPER
SWIPES
SWIRLS
SWIRLY
SWITCH
SWIVEL
SWIVET
SWOONS
SWOOPS
SWOOSH
SWORDS

S•W•••
SAWFIT
SAWING
SAWLOG
SAWOFF
SAWOUT
SAWRED
SAWYER
SEWAGE
SEWARD
SEWELL
SEWERS
SEWING
SEWNON
SEWNUP
SEWSON
SEWSUP
SIWASH
SOWBUG
SOWERS
SOWETO
SOWHAT
SOWING

S••W••
SCHWAB
SCHWAS
SCOWLS
SEAWAY
SHAWLS
SHAWMS
SHOWED
SHOWER
SHOWIN
SHOWME
SHOWUP
SKEWED
SKEWER
SKYWAY
SLEWED
SLOWED
SLOWER
SLOWLY
SLOWUP
SNOWED
SNOWIN
SPAWNS
SPEWED
STEWED
STEWER
STOWED
SUBWAY

S•••W•
SCRAWL
SCREWS
SCREWY
SEROWS
SHREWD
SHREWS
SINEWS
SINEWY
SPRAWL
SQUAWK
STRAWS
STRAWY
STREWN
STREWS

S••••W
SALLOW
SEACOW
SEESAW
SHADOW
SKITOW
SORROW
SUNDEW

•SW•••
ASWELL
ASWIRL
ASWOON
OSWALD
OSWEGO

•S•W••
PSYWAR

•S••W•
OSHAWA

•S•••W
ESCHEW
ESCROW

••SW••
ANSWER

••S•W•
BUSHWA
DISOWN
PESAWA
RESAWN
RESAWS
RESEWN
RESEWS
UNSEWN
UNSEWS
UNSOWN

••S••W
BESTOW
CASHEW
CPSNOW
CUSHAW
GOSLOW
MOSCOW
NOSHOW
PESCOW
TVSHOW

•••S•W
BOWSAW
JIGSAW
OLDSAW
PITSAW
RIPSAW
SEESAW
WARSAW

S•X•••
SAXONS
SAXONY
SEXIER
SEXILY
SEXIST
SEXTET
SEXTON
SIXERS
SIXGUN
SIXING
SIXTHS
SIXTUS
SOXERS

S••X••
SKNXXX

S•••X•
SKNXXX

S••••X
SEAFOX
SINTAX
SKNXXX
SKYBOX
SMILAX
SPADIX
SPHINX
SUFFIX
SURTAX
SUSSEX
SYNTAX
SYRINX

•S•X••
VSIXES

••S••X
AUSPEX
LASTEX
MUSKOX
SUSSEX
WESSEX

•••S•X
CHISOX
REDSOX
SUSSEX
THESIX
UNISEX
WESSEX

SY••••
SYDNEY
SYLPHS
SYLVAN
SYLVIA
SYMBOL
SYNCED
SYNDIC
SYNODS
SYNTAX
SYPHON
SYRIAN
SYRINX
SYRUPS
SYRUPY
SYSOPS
SYSTEM
SYZYGY

S•Y•••
SAYERS
SAYING
SAYLES
SAYSOS
SAYYES
SAYYID
SCYLLA
SCYTHE
SHYEST
SHYING
SKYBOX
SKYCAP
SKYING
SKYLAB
SKYWAY
SLYEST
SLYPES
SMYRNA
SNYDER
SPYING
STYLED
STYLER
STYLES
STYLET
STYLUS
STYMIE
STYRIA
STYRON

S••Y••
SALYUT
SATYRS
SAWYER
SAYYES
SAYYID
SHAYNE
SIBYLS
SLAYED
SLAYER
SPAYED
SPRYER
SPRYLY
STAYED
STAYON
STAYUP
SWAYED
SWAYER
SWAYZE
SYZYGY

S•••Y•
SEPOYS
SHERYL
SPLAYS

SPRAYS
STRAYS

S••••Y
SAFELY
SAFETY
SAGELY
SALARY
SALIFY
SANELY
SANITY
SASHAY
SATINY
SAVORY
SAXONY
SCABBY
SCANTY
SCARRY
SCATTY
SCHIZY
SCOTTY
SCREWY
SCULLY
SCUMMY
SCURFY
SCURRY
SCURVY
SCUZZY
SEAWAY
SEELEY
SEEMLY
SENARY
SENTRY
SETSBY
SEVERY
SEXILY
SHABBY
SHAGGY
SHALEY
SHALLY
SHANDY
SHANNY
SHANTY
SHEEDY
SHEEHY
SHELLY
SHELTY
SHERRY
SHIFTY
SHILLY
SHIMMY
SHINDY
SHINNY
SHIRTY
SHOALY
SHODDY
SHORTY
SICILY
SICKLY
SIDNEY
SIMONY
SIMPLY
SINEWY
SINGLY
SISLEY
SITSBY
SKERRY
SKIDDY
SKIMPY
SKINNY
SKIPPY
SKIVVY
SKUNKY
SKYWAY
SLAGGY
SLANGY
SLAPPY
SLAVEY
SLEAZY
SLEEKY
SLEEPY
SLEETY
SLIMLY
SLIMSY
SLINKY
SLIPPY
SLITHY
SLITTY
SLOBBY
SLOPPY
SLOSHY
SLOWLY
SLUDGY
SLUMMY
SLURRY
SLUSHY
SMARMY
SMARTY
SMEARY
SMELLY
SMILEY
SMIRKY
SMITHY
SMOGGY
SMOKEY
SMUDGY
SMUGLY
SMUTTY
SNAGGY
SNAPPY
SNARLY
SNAZZY
SNEAKY
SNEERY
SNEEZY
SNIFFY
SNIPPY
SNOBBY
SNOOKY
SNOOPY
SNOOTY
SNOOZY
SNOTTY
SNUBBY
SNUFFY
SNUGLY
SOFTLY
SOLELY
SOMANY
SORELY
SOURLY
SPACEY
SPANKY
SPARKY
SPEEDY
SPERRY
SPHERY
SPIFFY
SPIVVY
SPONGY
SPOOKY
SPOONY
SPORTY
SPOTTY
SPRYLY
SPUNKY
SPURRY
STABLY
STACEY
STALKY
STANKY
STARRY
STEADY
STEAMY
STEELY
STEFOY
STICKY
STILLY
STIMPY
STINGY
STINKY
STITHY
STOCKY
STODGY
STOOLY
STOREY
STORMY
STRAWY
STRIPY
STUBBY
STUFFY
STUMPY
STUNTY
STURDY
SUBTLY
SUBWAY
SUGARY
SULTRY
SUNDAY
SUNDRY
SUNRAY
SUPPLY
SURELY
SURETY
SURREY
SURVEY
SWABBY
SWAMPY
SWANKY
SWEATY
SWINGY
SWIRLY
SYDNEY
SYRUPY
SYZYGY

•SY•••
ASYLUM
PSYCHE
PSYCHO
PSYCHS
PSYLLA
PSYWAR

•S••Y•
ASSAYS
ESSAYS

•S•••Y
ASBURY
ASEITY
ASHLEY
ASTRAY
ESTRAY
OSPREY
OSSIFY
USABLY

••SY••
INSYNC

••S•Y•
ASSAYS
ESSAYS
JASEYS
MOSEYS
UNSAYS

••S••Y
BASELY
BASIFY
BASSLY
BISCAY
BOSLEY
BUSBOY
BUSILY
CASEFY
COSILY
COSTLY
DESCRY
DESTRY
DISMAY
DISNEY
EASILY
FOSSEY
GASIFY
HOSTLY
HUSSEY
JUSTLY
LASTLY
LESLEY
LUSHLY
MASSEY
MISERY
MISLAY
MISSAY
MOSTLY
MUSCLY
NASEBY
NOSILY
OSSIFY
PASSBY
PASTRY
POSHLY
RASHLY
RESINY
ROSARY
ROSILY
ROSINY
SASHAY
SISLEY
VASTLY
VESTRY
WESLEY
WISELY

•••SY•
UNISYS
VAISYA

•••S•Y
BASSLY
BETSEY
BOLSHY
BRASHY
BRASSY
BRUSHY
CHESTY
CLASSY
CRISPY
CROSBY
CRUSTY
DILSEY
DOESBY
DORSEY
DRESSY
FEISTY
FLASHY
FLESHY
FLOSSY
FOSSEY
FRISKY
FROSTY
GATSBY
GELSEY
GETSBY
GLASSY
GLOSSY
GOESBY
GOOSEY
GRASSY
GRISLY
GROSZY
GUNSHY
HALSEY
HERSEY
HORSEY
HUSSEY
ILLSAY
JANSKY
JERSEY
KELSEY
KERSEY
KINSEY
KRASNY
LAYSBY
LINSEY
MARSHY
MASSEY
MEASLY
MERSEY
MISSAY
MOUSEY
NAYSAY
NEVSKY
NIPSEY
OCASEY
PASSBY
PIGSTY
PLASHY
PLASTY
PLUSHY
PRISSY
PROSKY
PUTSBY
RAMSAY
RAMSEY
RIMSKY
SETSBY
SITSBY
SLOSHY
SLUSHY
THUSLY
TOASTY
TRASHY
TRUSTY
TWISTY
WHISKY
WIMSEY
WOLSEY
YEASTY

••••SY
ARGOSY
BEKESY
BLOWSY
BLUESY
BOOTSY
BRASSY
CHEESY
CHOOSY
CLASSY
CLUMSY
CREASY
CURTSY
CUTESY
DRESSY
DROWSY
FLIMSY
FLOPSY
FLOSSY
FOLKSY
GLASSY
GLOSSY
GOEASY
GRASSY
GREASY
HERESY
PRISSY
QUEASY
SLIMSY
TEENSY
TOOTSY
UNBUSY
UNEASY
WEENSY
WHIMSY
WOODSY

S•Z•••
SIZERS
SIZEUP
SIZING
SIZZLE
SUZUKI
SYZYGY

S••Z••
SCUZZY
SEIZED
SEIZER
SEIZES
SHAZAM
SIZZLE
SLEZAK
SNAZZY
SWAZIS

S•••Z•
SCHIZY
SCUZZY
SFORZA
SLEAZE
SLEAZY
SNAZZY
SNEEZE
SNEEZY
SNOOZE
SNOOZY
STANZA
SWAYZE

S••••Z
SCHNOZ
SCHULZ
SHIRAZ
SPRITZ

•S•Z••
ZSAZSA

•S••Z•
ASSIZE

••S•Z•
ASSIZE

••S••Z
ERSATZ

•••SZ•
GROSZY

•••S•Z
AMOSOZ

••••SZ
KUVASZ
MILOSZ

TA••••
TABARD
TABBED
TABLAS
TABLED
TABLES
TABLET
TABOOS
TABORS
TABRIZ
TABULA
TACKED
TACKER
TACKLE
TACKON
TACOMA
TACTIC
TAGDAY
TAGEND
TAGGED
TAGORE
TAGOUT
TAGSUP
TAHINI
TAHITI
TAICHI
TAIGAS
TAILED
TAILLE
TAILOR
TAINAN
TAINOS
TAINTS
TAIPAN
TAIPEI
TAIWAN
TAKEIN
TAKEON
TAKERS
TAKETH
TAKETO
TAKEUP
TAKING
TAKINS
TALBOT
TALCED
TALCUM
TALENT
TALERS
TALESE
TALION
TALKAT
TALKED
TALKER
TALKIE
TALKTO
TALKUP
TALLER
TALLOW
TALMUD
TALONS
TAMALE
TAMARA
TAMAYO
TAMELY
TAMERS
TAMEST
TAMILS
TAMING
TAMMUZ
TAMPED
TAMPER
TAMTAM
TANAKA
TANANA
TANDEM
TANGED
TANGLE
TANGLY
TANGOS
TANGUY
TANIST
TANKAS
TANKED
TANKER
TANKUP
TANNED
TANNER
TANNIC
TANNIN
TANOAK
TANOAN
TANTES
TANTRA
TAOISM
TAOIST
TAPERS
TAPING
TAPINS
TAPIRS
TAPOFF
TAPOUT
TAPPAN
TAPPED
TAPPER
TAPPET
TARAWA
TARGES
TARGET
TARIFF
TARING
TARMAC
TAROTS
TARPAN
TARPIT
TARPON
TARRED
TARSAL
TARSUS
TARTAN
TARTAR
TARTER
TARTLY
TARZAN
TASERS
TASKED
TASMAN
TASSEL
TASSES
TASTED
TASTER
TASTES
TATAMI
TATARS
TATERS
TATTED
TATTER
TATTLE
TATTOO
TAUGHT
TAUNTS
TAUONS
TAUPES
TAURUS
TAUTEN
TAUTER
TAUTLY
TAUTOG
TAVERN
TAWDRY
TAWING
TAXERS
TAXIED
TAXIES
TAXING
TAXMAN
TAXMEN
TAYLOR
TAYRAS
TAZZAS

T•A•••
TEABAG
TEACUP
TEAMED
TEAMUP
TEAPOT
TEAPOY
TEARAT
TEARED
TEARUP
TEASED
TEASEL
TEASER
TEASES
TEASET
THALER
THALES
THALIA
THAMES
THANES
THANKS
THATCH
THATIS
THATLL
THAWED
THAYER
TIARAS
TLALOC
TOAMAN
TOASTS
TOASTY
TOATEE
TRACED
TRACER
TRACES
TRACEY
TRACHY
TRACKS
TRACTS
TRADED
TRADER
TRADES
TRAGIC
TRAILS
TRAINS
TRAITS
TRAJAN
TRALEE
TRAMPS
TRANCE
TRAPPY
TRASHY
TRAUMA
TRAVEL
TRAVES
TRAVIS
TRAWLS
TUAREG
TWANGS
TWANGY

T••A••
TABARD
TAMALE
TAMARA
TAMAYO
TANAKA
TANANA
TARAWA
TATAMI
TATARS
TEJANO
TENACE
TENANT
TEPALS
TERAPH
TERATO
TEXACO
TEXANS
THRACE
THRALE
THRALL
THRASH
THWACK
THWART
TICALS
TILAKS
TIRADE
TIRANA
TIRANE
TISANE
TITANS
TOBAGO
TODATE
TOGAED
TOKAYS
TOMATO
TORAHS
TOTALS
TOWAGE
TOWARD
TREADS
TREATS
TREATY
TRIADS
TRIAGE
TRIALS
TRUANT
TUBATE
TUCANA
TULANE
TULARE
TUVALU
TWEAKS
TYBALT
TYRANT

T•••A•
TABLAS
TAGDAY
TAIGAS
TAINAN
TAIPAN
TAIWAN
TALKAT
TAMTAM
TANKAS
TANOAK
TANOAN
TAPPAN
TARMAC
TARPAN
TARSAL
TARTAN
TARTAR
TARZAN
TASMAN
TAXMAN
TAYRAS
TAZZAS
TEABAG
TEARAT
TERRAN
TESLAS
TESTAE
TETRAD
TETRAS
THECAE
THECAL
THEHAJ
THENAR
THETAS
THOMAS
THORAX
THREAD
THREAT
THROAT
THUJAS
TIARAS
TIBIAE
TIBIAL
TIBIAS
TICTAC
TIMBAL
TINCAL
TINCAN
TINEAR
TINHAT
TINMAN
TINPAN
TITIAN
TOAMAN
TOBIAS
TODDAO
TODMAN
TOECAP
TOETAP
TOKLAS
TOMBAC
TOMCAT
TONGAN
TOOBAD
TOPCAT
TOPHAT
TOREAT
TOUCAN
TOWCAR
TRAJAN
TREPAN
TRIBAL
TRINAL
TROCAR
TROJAN
TRUMAN
TUBMAN
TULSAN
TUPIAN
TURBAN
TUSCAN
TUSSAH
TWOWAY
TYRIAN

T••••A
TABULA
TACOMA
TAMARA
TANAKA
TANANA
TANTRA
TARAWA
TEPHRA
TERESA
THALIA
THELMA
THESEA
TIERRA
TIRANA
TOLUCA
TOPEKA
TOYOTA
TRAUMA
TREDIA
TRICIA
TRISHA
TRIVIA
TROIKA
TUCANA
TUNDRA
TUNICA

•TA•••
ATAMAN
ETALIA
ETALII
ETAPES
ITALIA
ITALIC
ITASCA
STABAT
STABLE
STABLY
STACEY
STACKS
STACTE
STADIA
STAFFS
STAGED
STAGER
STAGES
STAINS
STAIRS
STAKED
STAKES
STALAG
STALED
STALER
STALES
STALIN
STALKS
STALKY
STALLS
STAMEN
STAMPS
STANCE
STANCH
STANDS
STANKY
STANZA
STAPES
STAPLE
STAPUF
STARCH
STARED
STARER
STARES
STARRY
STARTS
STARVE
STASES
STASIS
STATED
STATEN
STATER
STATES
STATIC
STATOR
STATUE
STATUS
STAVED
STAVES
STAYED
STAYON
STAYUP
UTAHAN

•T•A••
ATBATS
ATEAMS
ATEASE
ATHAND
ATLAST
ATLATL
ATTACH
ATTACK
ATTAIN
ATTARS
ETHANE
ITHACA
ITHAKI
OTTAVA
OTTAWA
PTRAPS
STEADS
STEADY
STEAKS
STEALS
STEAMS
STEAMY
STMALO
STMARK
STOATS
STPAUL
STRABO
STRADS
STRAFE
STRAIN
STRAIT
STRAKE
STRAND
STRAPS
STRASS
STRATA
STRATI
STRATO
STRAUB
STRAUS
STRAWS
STRAWY
STRAYS
STUART
UTHANT

•T••A•
ATAMAN
ATONAL
ATRIAL
ATTHAT
ITZHAK
PTBOAT
STABAT
STALAG
STEFAN
STELAE
STELAR
STJOAN
STOMAS
STOMAT
STREAK
STREAM
STRIAE
STUPAS
UTAHAN

•T•••A
ATHENA
ATTICA
ATTILA
ETALIA
ITALIA
ITASCA
ITHACA
OTTAVA
OTTAWA
STADIA
STANZA
STELLA
STERNA
STIGMA
STRATA
STYRIA
UTOPIA

••TA••
ALTAIC
ALTAIR
ALTARS
ATTACH
ATTACK
ATTAIN
ATTARS
BATAAN
BETAKE
BOTANY
BUTANE
BYTALK
CETANE
CITATO
DATARY
DETACH
DETAIL
DETAIN
DOTAGE
DOTARD
ENTAIL
ESTATE
EUTAXY
EXTANT
FATALE
GITANO
GSTAAD
HATARI
HOTAIR
IDTAGS
INTACT
INTAKE
LITANY
LOTAHS
METALS
METATE
MUTANT
MUTATE
MUTATO
NATANT
NOTARY
NOTATE
NUTATE
OBTAIN
OCTADS
OCTANE
OCTANT
OCTAVE
OCTAVO
ONTAPE
OTTAVA
OTTAWA
OUTACT
OUTAGE
OUTATE
OXTAIL
PATACA
PETAIN
PETALS
PETARD
POTAGE
POTASH
POTATO
QATARI
RETAGS
RETAIL
RETAIN
RETAKE
RETAPE
RETAPS
RETARD
RETARS
RITARD
ROTARY
ROTATE
SATANG
SITARS
TATAMI
TATARS
TITANS
TOTALS
UMTATA
UNTACK
UPTAKE
UPTALK
VITALE
VITALS
VOTARY

••T•A•
ACTSAS
ACTUAL
ALTMAN
AMTRAC
AMTRAK
ASTRAL
ASTRAY
ATTHAT
BATAAN
BATEAU
BATMAN
BATYAM
BETRAY
BETTAS
BITMAP
CATHAY
CATNAP
COTTAS
DOTHAN
EATSAT
ENTRAP
ESTRAY
EXTRAS
FATCAT
FATWAS
GATEAU
GETMAD
GETSAT
GOTHAM
GOTMAD
GSTAAD
GUTTAE
HETMAN
HITMAN
HOTCAP
HOTCAR
HOTWAR
JETLAG
JETSAM
JETWAY
KATMAI
KITBAG
KITKAT
LETHAL
LETSAT
LOTHAR
MITRAL
MUTUAL
NATHAN
NETMAN
NETPAY
NOTBAD
OSTEAL
OUTEAT
OUTLAW
OUTLAY
OUTRAN
PATHAN
PITMAN
PITSAW
PUTNAM
RATTAN
RETEAR
RETIAL
RETRAL
RITUAL
RUTTAN
SATRAP
SETSAT
SGTMAJ
SOTHAT
SUTRAS
TETRAD
TETRAS
TITIAN
ULTRAS
UNTRAP
WETBAR
WITHAL

••T••A
ALTHEA
ALTIMA
ATTICA
ATTILA
BETCHA
BITOLA
CATENA
CETERA

DATURA
FATIMA
GOTCHA
HOTTEA
INTIMA
ISTRIA
LATINA
LATONA
LATOYA
LATVIA
MATTEA
MOTHRA
NATURA
NUTRIA
OPTIMA
ORTEGA
OTTAVA
OTTAWA
PATACA
PATINA
PETULA
PYTHIA
RETINA
ULTIMA
UMTATA

•••TA•
ACETAL
AKITAS
ALATAU
AMYTAN
AORTAE
AORTAL
AORTAS
ARCTAN
AVATAR
BANTAM
BARTAB
BETTAS
BHUTAN
BIOTAS
BRUTAL
CAFTAN
CANTAB
CAPTAN
CESTAS
CONTAC
COSTAE
COSTAL
COSTAR
COSTAS
COTTAS
CRETAN
DELTAS
DENTAL
DIKTAT
DISTAL
DOGTAG
DUCTAL
FANTAN
FESTAL
FESTAS
FOETAL
FONTAL
FORTAS
GOSTAG
GUITAR
GUSTAV
GUTTAE
HEPTAD
HIATAL
HINTAT
HOOTAT
HOSTAS
HYETAL
INSTAL
INSTAR
ISHTAR
JUNTAS
KEPTAT
LESTAT
MAITAI
MANTAS
MAOTAI
MAYTAG
MENTAL
MORTAL
MORTAR
NECTAR
PASTAS
PENTAD
PIETAS
PORTAL
POSTAL
PRETAX
PROTAX
QANTAS
QINTAR
QUOTAS
RAGTAG
RATTAN
REATAS
REDTAG
RENTAL
RIATAS
RUTTAN
SEPTAL
SHOTAT
SINTAX
SONTAG
SULTAN
SUNTAN
SURTAX
SYNTAX
TAMTAM
TARTAN
TARTAR
TESTAE
THETAS
TICTAC
TOETAP
UINTAS
UNITAL
UNITAS
VESTAL
VESTAS
VISTAS
WANTAD
WENTAT
WYSTAN
YENTAS

•••T•A
AGATHA
ANITRA
ARETHA
BERTHA
CONTRA
EARTHA
GRATIA
GRETNA
HESTIA
HOTTEA
LIOTTA
MANTRA
MANTUA
MARTHA
MATTEA
NESTEA
NOOTKA
ODETTA
PORTIA
QUETTA
QUOTHA
ROSTRA
SCOTIA
SENTRA
SISTRA
TANTRA

••••TA
AJANTA
ARISTA
AVESTA
BALATA
BEMATA
BOGOTA
CAPITA
CUESTA
DAKOTA
DAMITA
EGESTA
EJECTA
ERRATA
EXACTA
FAJITA
FIESTA
GALATA
LAKOTA
LAPUTA
LIOTTA
LOLITA
MAKUTA
MIKITA
MONETA
MORITA
MULETA
NIKITA
ODETTA
OMERTA
PELOTA
PEPITA
PESETA
PINATA
QUANTA
QUETTA
RENATA
ROSITA
SANCTA
SHASTA
SHORTA
SIESTA
SOMATA
SONATA
SPARTA
STRATA
TOYOTA
UMTATA
YUKATA
ZAPATA

TB••••
TBILLS
TBIRDS
TBONDS
TBONES

T•B•••
TABARD
TABBED
TABLAS
TABLED
TABLES
TABLET
TABOOS
TABORS
TABRIZ
TABULA
TIBIAE
TIBIAL
TIBIAS
TOBAGO
TOBIAS
TOBIES
TOBOOT
TOBRUK
TUBATE
TUBBED
TUBERS
TUBING
TUBIST
TUBMAN
TYBALT

T••B••
TABBED
TALBOT
TEABAG
THEBES
TIDBIT
TIMBAL
TIMBER
TIMBRE
TITBIT
TOMBAC
TOMBOY
TOOBAD
TREBEK
TREBLE
TREBLY
TRIBAL
TRIBES
TUBBED
TUMBLE
TURBAN
TURBID
TURBIT
TURBOS
TURBOT
TWOBIT
TYDBOL

T•••B•
THISBE
THROBS
THUMBS
TRILBY
TYCOBB

T••••B
THEWEB
TOPJOB
TYCOBB

•TB•••
ATBATS
ATBEST
PTBOAT

•T•B••
STABAT
STABLE
STABLY
STUBBY

•T••B•
ITURBI
STRABO
STROBE
STUBBY

•T•••B
STRAUB

••TB••
BATBOY
HATBOX
HOTBED
HOTBOX
KITBAG
NOTBAD
OUTBID
OUTBOX
TITBIT
WETBAR

••T•B•
GATSBY
GETSBY
LETSBE
PUTSBY
SETSBY
SITSBY

••T••B
HOTTUB

•••TB•
WENTBY

•••T•B
BARTAB
CANTAB
HOTTUB

T•C•••
TACKED
TACKER
TACKLE
TACKON
TACOMA
TACTIC
TECHIE
TECHNO
TICALS
TICKED
TICKER
TICKET
TICKLE
TICKLY
TICTAC
TOCSIN
TUCANA
TUCHUN
TUCKED
TUCKER
TUCKET
TUCKIN
TUCSON
TYCOBB
TYCOON

T••C••
TAICHI
TALCED
TALCUM
TEACUP
TERCEL
TERCET
TETCHY
THECAE
THECAL
THICKE
TINCAL
TINCAN
TINCTS
TOECAP
TOMCAT
TOPCAT
TORCHY
TOUCAN
TOUCHE
TOUCHY
TOWCAR
TRACED
TRACER
TRACES
TRACEY
TRACHY
TRACKS
TRACTS
TRICED
TRICEP
TRICES
TRICHO
TRICIA
TRICKS
TRICKY
TRICOT
TROCAR
TROCHE
TRUCES
TRUCKS
TUSCAN

T•••C•
TENACE
TEXACO
THATCH
THENCE
THRACE
THRICE
THWACK
TIERCE
TOLUCA
TONICS
TOPICS
TOXICS
TRANCE
TRENCH
TUNICA
TUNICS
TWITCH

T••••C
TACTIC
TANNIC
TARMAC
TENREC
THETIC
TICTAC
TLALOC
TOLTEC
TOMBAC
TRAGIC
TROPIC
TURKIC

•TC•••
ATCOST
ETCHED
ETCHER
ETCHES
ITCHED
ITCHES

•T•C••
STACEY
STACKS
STACTE
STICKS
STICKY
STOCKS
STOCKY
STUCCO

•T••C•
ATONCE
ATTACH
ATTACK
ATTICA
ATTICS
ETHICS
ITASCA
ITHACA
STANCE
STANCH
STARCH
STENCH
STITCH
STOICS
STORCH
STRICK
STRICT
STRUCK
STUCCO

•T•••C
ATOMIC
ATONIC
ETHNIC
ETONIC
ITALIC
OTITIC
STATIC
STIVIC

••TC••
ANTCOW
BETCHA
BOTCHY
CATCHY
FATCAT
GOTCHA
HOTCAP
HOTCAR
LITCHI
NOTCHY
OUTCRY
PATCHY
PITCHY
SITCOM
TETCHY
WITCHY

••T•C•
ANTICS
ATTACH
ATTACK
ATTICA
ATTICS
AZTECS
DETACH
DETECT
ENTICE
HITECH
INTACT
KITSCH
NATICK
NOTICE
OPTICS
OUTACT
PATACA
PUTSCH
SHTICK
UNTACK
UPTICK
VOTECH

••T••C
ALTAIC
AMTRAC
CITRIC
GOTHIC
IATRIC
LITHIC
METRIC
MYTHIC
NITRIC
VITRIC

•••TC•
BLOTCH
CLUTCH
CRUTCH
FLETCH
FLITCH
GLITCH
HOOTCH
KLATCH
KVETCH
NAUTCH
SCOTCH
SCUTCH
SKETCH
SKITCH
SMUTCH
SNATCH
SNITCH
STITCH
SWATCH
SWITCH
THATCH
TWITCH
WRETCH

•••T•C
ACETIC
AORTIC
ARCTIC
BALTIC
BIOTIC
CELTIC
CONTAC
COPTIC
CRITIC
CULTIC
DELTIC
EROTIC
EXOTIC
FISTIC
FUSTIC
GESTIC
HECTIC
LACTIC
MANTIC
MASTIC
MIXTEC
MYSTIC
NOETIC
OTITIC
PECTIC
PEPTIC
PHATIC
PHOTIC
POETIC
PONTIC
RUSTIC
SEPTIC
STATIC
TACTIC
THETIC
TICTAC
TOLTEC

T•D•••
TEDDED
TEDDER
TEDEUM
TEDIUM
TEDKEY
TIDBIT
TIDDLY
TIDIED
TIDIER
TIDIES
TIDILY
TIDING
TIDYUP
TODATE
TODDAO
TODDLE
TODMAN
TUDORS
TYDBOL

T••D••
TAGDAY
TANDEM
TAWDRY
TEDDED
TEDDER
TEEDUP
TENDED
TENDER
TENDON
TENDTO
TIDDLY
TIEDIN
TIEDTO
TIEDUP
TIEDYE
TILDEN
TILDES
TINDER
TODDAO
TODDLE
TOEDIN
TOLDOF
TOLDON
TONDOS
TOPDOG
TOYDOG
TRADED
TRADER
TRADES
TREDIA
TRUDGE
TUNDRA

T•••D•
TBIRDS
TBONDS
TELEDU
TEREDO
THIRDS
TIRADE
TOLEDO
TREADS
TRENDS
TRENDY
TRIADS
TRIODE
TUXEDO
TWEEDS
TWEEDY

T••••D
TABARD
TABBED
TABLED
TACKED
TAGEND
TAGGED
TAILED
TALCED
TALKED
TALMUD
TAMPED
TANGED
TANKED
TANNED
TAPPED
TARRED
TASKED
TASTED
TATTED
TAXIED
TEAMED
TEARED
TEASED
TEDDED
TEEMED
TEHEED
TEMPED
TENDED
TENSED
TENTED
TERMED
TESTED
TETRAD
THAWED
THEEND
THEFED
THEKID
THEMED
THREAD
THREED
TICKED
TIDIED
TIERED
TIEROD
TIFFED
TILLED
TILTED
TINGED
TINGOD
TINNED
TINTED
TIPPED
TITHED
TITLED
TITRED
TOGAED
TOGGED
TOILED
TOLLED
TOOBAD
TOOLED
TOOTED
TOPPED
TOROID
TORPID
TORRID
TOSSED
TOTTED
TOURED
TOUTED
TOWARD
TRACED
TRADED
TREPID
TRICED
TRIFID
TRIPOD
TROWED
TUBBED
TUCKED
TUFTED
TUGGED
TUMMED
TURBID
TURFED
TURGID
TURNED
TUSKED
TUTUED
TWINED

•T•D••
ATODDS
ETUDES
STADIA
STODGE
STODGY
STUDIO

•T••D•
ATODDS
STANDS
STEADS
STEADY
STEEDS
STRADS
STRIDE
STRODE
STURDY

•T•••D
ATHAND
ATONED
ATSTUD
ATTEND
ATWOOD
ETCHED
ITCHED
STAGED
STAKED
STALED
STARED
STATED
STAVED
STAYED
STEWED
STOKED
STOLID
STONED
STORED
STOWED
STRAND
STROUD
STUPID
STYLED

••TD••
HOTDOG
OUTDID

••T•D•
BETIDE
OCTADS
RATEDG
RATEDR
RATEDX
UNTIDY

••T••D
ANTEED
ASTRID
ATTEND
BATHED
BATTED
BITTED
BUTTED
CATTED
DOTARD
DOTTED
EXTEND
FATTED
FITTED
FUTZED
GETMAD
GOTMAD
GSTAAD
GUTTED
HATRED
HATTED
HOTBED
HOTROD
HUTTED
INTEND
JETTED
JOTTED
JUTTED
LATHED
LETTED
LOTTED
MATTED
METHOD
MITRED
NETTED
NOTBAD
NUTTED
OBTUND
OSTEND
OUTBID
OUTDID
PATTED
PETARD
PETTED
PITHED
PITIED
PITTED
POTTED
PUTRID
PUTTED
RATTED
RETARD
RETIED
RETOLD
RITARD
ROTTED
ROTUND
RUTTED
SOTTED
TATTED
TETRAD
TITHED
TITLED
TITRED
TOTTED
TUTUED
UNTIED
UNTOLD
UNTROD
VATTED
VETOED
VETTED
WETTED
WITHED
WITTED

•••T•D
ABATED
ALATED
ATSTUD
BAITED
BASTED
BATTED
BELTED
BESTED
BITTED
BOATED
BOLTED
BOOTED
BUNTED
BUSTED
BUTTED
CANTED
CARTED
CATTED
CHUTED
COATED
CRATED
DARTED
DENTED
DIETED
DINTED
DOTTED
DUSTED
EDITED
ELATED
ELUTED
EMOTED
EXITED
FASTED
FATTED
FELTED
FISTED
FITTED
FLUTED
FOETID
FOOTED
GAITED
GIFTED
GIRTED
GRATED
GUSTED
GUTTED
HAFTED
HALTED
HATTED
HEATED
HEFTED
HENTED
HEPTAD
HINTED
HOOTED
HOSTED
HUNTED
HUTTED
JESTED
JETTED
JILTED
JOLTED
JOTTED
JUTTED
KILTED
LASTED
LETTED
LIFTED
LILTED
LISTED
LOFTED
LOOTED
LOTTED
LUSTED
MALTED
MATTED
MELTED
MINTED
MISTED
MOATED
MOLTED
MOOTED
NESTED
NETTED
NUTTED
ORATED
OUSTED
PANTED
PARTED
PASTED
PATTED
PELTED
PENTAD
PETTED
PITTED
PLATED
PORTED
POSTED
POTTED
POUTED
PRATED
PUNTED
PUTTED
QUOTED
RAFTED
RANTED
RATTED
RENTED
RESTED
RIFTED
RIOTED
ROOTED
ROTTED
ROUTED
RRATED
RUSTED
RUTTED
SALTED
SEATED
SIFTED
SILTED
SKATED
SLATED
SORTED
SOTTED
SPITED
STATED
SUITED
TASTED
TATTED
TENTED
TESTED
TILTED
TINTED
TOOTED
TOTTED
TOUTED
TUFTED
UNITED
VATTED
VENTED
VESTED
VETTED
WAFTED
WAITED
WANTAD
WANTED
WASTED
WELTED
WETTED
WILTED
WITTED
WONTED
XRATED
ZESTED

TE••••
TEABAG
TEACUP
TEAMED
TEAMUP
TEAPOT
TEAPOY
TEARAT
TEARED
TEARUP
TEASED
TEASEL
TEASER
TEASES
TEASET
TECHIE
TECHNO
TEDDED
TEDDER
TEDEUM
TEDIUM
TEDKEY
TEEDUP
TEEHEE
TEEING
TEEMED
TEENER
TEENSY
TEEOFF
TEESUP
TEETER
TEETHE
TEEVEE
TEFLON
TEHEED
TEHEES
TEJANO
TELEDU
TELLER
TELLOF
TELLON
TELUGU
TEMPED
TEMPEH
TEMPER
TEMPLE
TEMPOS
TEMPTS
TEMPUS
TENACE
TENANT
TENDED
TENDER
TENDON
TENDTO
TENENS
TENETS
TENNIS
TENONS
TENORS
TENPIN
TENREC
TENSED
TENSER
TENSES
TENSOR
TENTED
TENTER
TENTHS
TENURE
TENUTO
TEPALS
TEPEES
TEPHRA
TERAPH
TERATO
TERCEL
TERCET
TEREDO
TERESA
TERETE
TEREUS
TERKEL
TERMED
TERNES
TERRAN
TERRET
TERROR
TERSER
TESLAS
TESSIE
TESTAE
TESTED
TESTEE
TESTER
TETCHY
TETHER
TETHYS
TETONS
TETRAD
TETRAS
TETRIS
TETZEL
TEUTON
TEXACO
TEXANS
TEXMEX

T•E•••
TEEDUP
TEEHEE
TEEING
TEEMED
TEENER
TEENSY
TEEOFF
TEESUP
TEETER
TEETHE
TEEVEE
THEBES
THECAE
THECAL
THEEND
THEFED

THEFLY
THEFTS
THEHAJ
THEIRS
THEISM
THEIST
THEKID
THELIP
THELMA
THEMED
THEMES
THENAR
THENCE
THEORY
THERES
THERMO
THERMS
THESEA
THESES
THESIS
THESIX
THETAS
THETIC
THETIS
THETOY
THEWEB
THEWIZ
THEYLL
THEYRE
THEYVE
TIEDIN
TIEDTO
TIEDUP
TIEDYE
TIEING
TIEINS
TIEPIN
TIERCE
TIERED
TIEROD
TIERRA
TIESIN
TIESTO
TIESUP
TIEUPS
TMESIS
TOECAP
TOEDIN
TOEING
TOEINS
TOESIN
TOETAP
TREADS
TREATS
TREATY
TREBEK
TREBLE
TREBLY
TREDIA
TREMOR
TRENCH
TRENDS
TRENDY
TREPAN
TREPID
TREVOR
TSETSE
TWEAKS
TWEEDS
TWEEDY
TWEENS
TWEENY
TWEEST
TWEETS
TWEETY
TWEEZE
TWELVE
TWENTY
TWERPS

T••E••

TAGEND
TAKEIN
TAKEON
TAKERS
TAKETH
TAKETO
TAKEUP
TALENT
TALERS
TALESE
TAMELY
TAMERS
TAMEST
TAPERS
TASERS
TATERS
TAVERN
TAXERS
TEDEUM
TEHEED
TEHEES
TELEDU
TENENS
TENETS
TEPEES
TEREDO
TERESA
TERETE
TEREUS
THEEND
THIEVE
THREAD
THREAT
THREED
THREES
THRESH
TIGERS
TILERS
TIMELY
TIMERS
TINEAR
TITERS
TOKENS
TOLEDO
TONERS
TONEUP
TOPEKA
TOPERS
TOREAT
TORERO
TOREUP
TOTEMS
TOTERS
TOWELS
TOWERS
TOWERY
TRIERS
TRUEST
TUBERS
TUMEFY
TUNEIN
TUNERS
TUNEUP
TUPELO
TUREEN
TUXEDO
TUYERE
TVSETS
TWEEDS
TWEEDY
TWEENS
TWEENY
TWEEST
TWEETS
TWEETY
TWEEZE
TYPERS
TYPEUP

T•••E•

TABBED
TABLED
TABLES
TABLET
TACKED
TACKER
TAGGED
TAILED
TAIPEI
TALCED
TALKED
TALKER
TALLER
TAMPED
TAMPER
TANDEM
TANGED
TANKED
TANKER
TANNED
TANNER
TANTES
TAPPED
TAPPER
TAPPET
TARGES
TARGET
TARRED
TARTER
TASKED
TASSEL
TASSES
TASTED
TASTER
TASTES
TATTED
TATTER
TAUPES
TAUTEN
TAUTER
TAXIED
TAXIES
TAXMEN
TBONES
TEAMED
TEARED
TEASED
TEASEL
TEASER
TEASES
TEASET
TEDDED
TEDDER
TEDKEY
TEEHEE
TEEMED
TEENER
TEETER
TEEVEE
TEHEED
TEHEES
TELLER
TEMPED
TEMPEH
TEMPER
TENDED
TENDER
TENREC
TENSED
TENSER
TENSES
TENTED
TENTER
TEPEES
TERCEL
TERCET
TERKEL
TERMED
TERNES
TERRET
TERSER
TESTED
TESTEE
TESTER
TETHER
TETZEL
TEXMEX
THALER
THALES
THAMES
THANES
THAWED
THAYER
THEBES
THEFED
THEMED
THEMES
THERES
THESEA
THESES
THEWEB
THOLES
THREED
THREES
THROES
TICKED
TICKER
TICKET
TIDIED
TIDIER
TIDIES
TIERED
TIFFED
TIGGER
TILDEN
TILDES
TILLED
TILLER
TILTED
TILTER
TIMBER
TINDER
TINGED
TINGES
TINIER
TINKER
TINMEN
TINNED
TINNER
TINSEL
TINTED
TINTER
TIPPED
TIPPER
TIPPET
TITFER
TITHED
TITHER
TITHES
TITLED
TITLES
TITRED
TITRES
TITTER
TNOTES
TOATEE
TOBIES
TOFFEE
TOGAED
TOGGED
TOILED
TOILER
TOILES
TOILET
TOLLED
TOLTEC
TONIER
TONNES
TOOLED
TOOTED
TOOTER
TOPPED
TOPPER
TOPTEN
TOQUES
TORIES
TORRES
TORREY
TORTES
TOSSED
TOSSER
TOSSES
TOTHER
TOTTED
TOTTER
TOUPEE
TOURED
TOURER
TOUTED
TOUTER
TOWHEE
TOWNER
TRACED
TRACER
TRACES
TRACEY
TRADED
TRADER
TRADES
TRALEE
TRAVEL
TRAVES
TREBEK
TRIBES
TRICED
TRICEP
TRICES
TRIJET
TRIKES
TRINES
TRITER
TRIVET
TROPES
TROPEZ
TROVES
TROWED
TROWEL
TRUCES
TUAREG
TUBBED
TUCKED
TUCKER
TUCKET
TUFFET
TUFTED
TUGGED
TUGGER
TULLES
TUMMED
TUNNEL
TUNNEY
TUQUES
TUREEN
TURFED
TURKEY
TURNED
TURNER
TURRET
TURVES
TUSKED
TUSKER
TUTUED
TWINED
TWINES
TWOFER
TYPIER

T••••E

TACKLE
TAGORE
TAILLE
TALESE
TALKIE
TAMALE
TANGLE
TATTLE
TECHIE
TEEHEE
TEETHE
TEEVEE
TEMPLE
TENACE
TENURE
TERETE
TESSIE
TESTAE
TESTEE
THECAE
THENCE
THEYRE
THEYVE
THICKE
THIEVE
THISBE
THORPE
THRACE
THRALE
THRICE
THRIVE
THRONE
THROVE
TIBIAE
TICKLE
TIEDYE
TIERCE
TILLIE
TIMBRE
TINGLE
TINKLE
TIPPLE
TIPTOE
TIRADE
TIRANE
TISANE
TISSUE
TITTLE
TOATEE
TODATE
TODDLE
TOFFEE
TOGGLE
TOLIFE
TONGUE
TONITE
TOONIE
TOOTLE
TOPPLE
TOROSE
TORQUE
TOUCHE
TOUPEE
TOUSLE
TOWAGE
TOWHEE
TOWNIE
TRALEE
TRANCE
TREBLE
TRIAGE
TRIFLE
TRIODE
TRIPLE
TRISTE
TRIUNE
TRIXIE
TROCHE
TROMPE
TROUPE
TROUVE
TRUDGE
TSETSE
TUBATE
TUILLE
TULANE
TULARE
TUMBLE
TURTLE
TUSSLE
TUYERE
TWEEZE
TWELVE
TWINGE
TYRONE

•TE•••

ATEAMS
ATEASE
ATEMPO
ATEOUT
ATERGO
ATESTS
ETERNE
OTELLO
STEADS
STEADY
STEAKS
STEALS
STEAMS
STEAMY
STEEDS
STEELE
STEELS
STEELY
STEEPS
STEERS
STEEVE
STEFAN
STEFFI
STEFOY
STEINS
STELAE
STELAR
STELES
STELLA
STELMO
STENCH
STENOG
STENOS
STEPIN
STEPON
STEPPE
STEPUP
STEREO
STERES
STERNA
STERNE
STERNO
STERNS
STEROL
STEVEN
STEVIE
STEWED
STEWER

•T•E••

ATBEST
ATHENA
ATHENE
ATHENS
ATREST
ATREUS
ATTEND
ATTEST
ETHENE
ETHERS
ETSEQQ
ITSELF
OTHERS
OTTERS
STEEDS
STEELE
STEELS
STEELY
STEEPS
STEERS
STEEVE
STHENO
STPETE
STREAK
STREAM
STREEP
STREET
STRESS
STREWN
STREWS
UTTERS

•T••E•

ATONED
ATONES
ATTLEE
ETAPES
ETCHED
ETCHER
ETCHES
ETUDES
ITCHED
ITCHES
STACEY
STAGED
STAGER
STAGES
STAKED
STAKES
STALED
STALER
STALES
STAMEN
STAPES
STARED
STARER
STARES
STASES
STATED
STATEN
STATER
STATES
STAVED
STAVES
STAYED
STELES
STEREO
STERES
STEVEN
STEWED
STEWER
STILES
STIPEL
STIPES
STIVER
STOKED
STOKER
STOKES
STOLEN
STOLES
STONED
STONER
STONES
STOPES
STORED
STORER
STORES
STOREY
STOVER
STOVES
STOWED
STREEP
STREET
STUMER
STUPES
STYLED
STYLER
STYLES
STYLET

•T•••E

ATEASE
ATHENE
ATHOME
ATONCE
ATTIRE
ATTLEE
ATTUNE
ETERNE
ETHANE
ETHENE
ETOILE
OTIOSE
OTOOLE
STABLE
STACTE
STANCE
STAPLE
STARVE
STATUE
STEELE
STEEVE
STELAE
STEPPE
STERNE
STEVIE
STIFLE
STLUKE
STODGE
STOGIE
STOLLE
STOOGE
STPETE
STRAFE
STRAKE
STRIAE
STRIDE
STRIFE
STRIKE
STRINE
STRIPE
STRIVE
STROBE
STRODE
STROKE
STROVE
STYMIE

••TE••

ALTERS
ANTEED
ANTERO
ANTEUP
APTEST
ARTELS
ARTERY
ASTERN
ASTERS
ATTEND
ATTEST
AUTEUR
AZTECS
BATEAU
BETELS
BITERS
BOTELS
BUTENE
BUTEOS
CATENA
CATERS
CETERA
CITERS
CUTELY
CUTEST
CUTESY
DATERS
DETECT
DETENT
DETERS
DETEST
DOTELL
DOTEON
EATERS
EATERY
ENTERO
ENTERS
ESTEEM
ESTERS
EXTEND
EXTENT
EXTERN
GATEAU
GATERS
HATERS
HETERO
HITECH
HOTELS
INTEND
INTENS
INTENT
INTERJ
INTERN
IQTEST
KITERS
LATEEN
LATELY
LATENE
LATENS
LATENT
LATEST
LITERS
MATERS
MATEYS
METEOR
METERS
MITERS
MOTELS
MOTETS
MUTELY
MUTEST
NITERS
NITERY
NOTERS
OATERS
OBTEST
OCTETS
ORTEGA
OSTEAL
OSTEND
OTTERS
OUTEAT
PATENS
PATENT
PATERS
PETERS
POTEEN
POTENT
RATEDG
RATEDR
RATEDX
RATELS
RATERS
RETEAR
RETELL
RETENE
RETEST
SATEEN
SHTETL
TATERS
TITERS
TOTEMS
TOTERS
URTEXT
UTTERS
VOTECH
VOTEIN
VOTERS
WATERS
WATERY

••T•E•

AETHER
ALTHEA
ANTEED
ANTHEM
ANTHER
ANTLER
ANTRES
ARTIER
ATTLEE
BATHED
BATHER
BATHES
BATMEN
BATTED
BATTEL
BATTEN
BATTER
BETHEL
BETSEY
BETTER
BITTED
BITTEN
BITTER
BOTHER
BOTREE
BUTLER
BUTTED
BUTTER
BUTTES
CATHER
CATTED
CITIES
COTTEN
COTTER
CUTIES
CUTLER
CUTLET
CUTTER
DITHER
DITZES
DOTTED
DUTIES
EITHER
ENTREE
ESTEEM
ESTHER
FATHER
FATTED
FATTEN
FATTER
FETTER
FITTED
FITTER
FUTZED
FUTZES
GATHER
GETSET
GETTER
GOTSET
GOTTEN
GUTTED
GUTTER
HATRED
HATTED
HATTER
HITHER
HITMEN
HITTER
HOTBED
HOTTEA
HOTTER
HUTTED
ISTLES
JETSET
JETTED
JITNEY
JITTER
JOTTED
JUTTED
KITTEN
KOTTER
LATEEN
LATHED
LATHER
LATHES
LATKES
LATTEN
LATTER
LETTED
LETTER
LITRES
LITTER
LOTTED
LUTHER
LUTZES
MATHER
MATTEA
MATTED
MATTEL
MATTER
MATTES
METIER
METRES
MITRED
MITRES
MITTEN
MOTHER
MOTLEY
MUTTER
NATTER
NETHER
NETMEN
NETTED
NITRES
NOTYET
NUTLET
NUTMEG
NUTTED
NUTTER
OATIER
ORTLES
OSTLER
OUTLET
OUTSET
PATTED
PATTEN
PATTER
PETREL
PETTED
PETTER
PITHED
PITIED
PITIER
PITIES
PITMEN
PITTED
PITTER
POTEEN
POTHER
POTTED
POTTER
PUTTED
PUTTEE
PUTTER
RATHER
RATTED
RATTER
RETIED
RETIES
RITTER
ROTTED
ROTTEN
ROTTER
RUTGER
RUTTED
SATEEN
SETTEE
SETTER
SITTER
SOTTED
SUTLER
SUTTER
TATTED
TATTER
TETHER
TETZEL
TITFER
TITHED
TITHER
TITHES
TITLED
TITLES
TITRED
TITRES
TITTER
TOTHER
TOTTED
TOTTER
TUTUED
UNTIED
UNTIES
VATTED
VETOED
VETOER
VETOES
VETTED
WATNEY
WETHER
WETTED
WETTER
WITHED
WITHER
WITHES
WITTED
ZITHER

••T••E

ACTIVE
ACTONE
ASTUTE
ATTIRE
ATTLEE
ATTUNE
BATTLE
BATTUE
BETAKE
BETIDE
BETISE
BOTREE
BOTTLE
BUTANE
BUTENE
CATTLE
CETANE
DATIVE
DOTAGE
DOTTIE
DOTTLE
ECTYPE
ENTICE
ENTIRE
ENTREE
ESTATE
FATALE
FETTLE
FUTILE
FUTURE
GUTTAE
HATTIE
HETTIE
INTAKE
INTIME
INTINE
INTONE
INTUNE
KATHIE
KETONE
KETTLE
LATENE
LETSBE
LITTLE
MATTIE
MATURE
METATE
METOPE
METTLE
MOTILE
MOTIVE
MOTTLE
MUTATE
NATIVE
NATURE
NETTLE
NOTATE
NOTICE
NUTATE
OBTUSE
OCTANE
OCTAVE
ONTAPE
ONTIME
OUTAGE
OUTATE
PATINE
PETITE
PETRIE
POTAGE
POTPIE
POTTLE
PUTTEE
RATINE
RATITE
RATTLE
RETAKE
RETAPE
RETENE
RETILE
RETIME
RETIRE
RETUNE
RETYPE
ROTATE
RUTILE
SATIRE
SETOSE
SETTEE
SETTLE
SUTURE
TATTLE
TITTLE
UNTRUE
UNTUNE
UPTAKE
UPTIME
VITALE
VOTIVE
WATTLE

•••TE•

ABATED
ABATES
AEETES
AGATES
ALATED
ALITER
AMSTEL
ARETES
AUSTEN
BAITED
BANTER
BARTER
BASTED
BASTER
BASTES
BATTED
BATTEL
BATTEN
BATTER
BAXTER
BEATEN
BEATER
BELTED
BESTED
BETTER
BIGTEN
BITTED
BITTEN
BITTER
BOATED
BOATEL
BOATER
BOITES
BOLTED
BOOTED
BOOTEE
BOOTES
BRUTES
BUNTED
BUNTER
BUSTED
BUSTER
BUTTED
BUTTER
BUTTES
CANTED
CANTER
CARTED
CARTEL
CARTER
CARTES
CASTER
CASTES
CATTED
CENTER
CHUTED
CHUTES
CNOTES
COATED
COLTER
COMTES
CONTES
COOTER
COPTER
CORTES
CORTEX
CORTEZ
COTTEN
COTTER
COUTER
CRATED
CRATER
CRATES
CURTER
CUSTER
CUTTER
DAFTER
DANTES

DARTED
DARTER
DEFTER
DENTED
DEXTER
DHOTEL
DIETED
DIETER
DINTED
DOTTED
DUSTED
DUSTER
EASTER
EDITED
ELATED
ELATER
ELATES
ELITES
ELUTED
ELUTES
EMOTED
EMOTER
EMOTES
ENATES
EXETER
EXITED
FALTER
FASTED
FASTEN
FASTER
FATTED
FATTEN
FATTER
FELTED
FESTER
FETTER
FILTER
FISTED
FITTED
FITTER
FLUTED
FLUTES
FLUTEY
FOOTED
FOOTER
FORTES
FOSTER
GAITED
GAITER
GARTER
GESTES
GETTER
GIFTED
GIRTED
GLUTEI
GLUTEN
GLUTES
GOATEE
GOTTEN
GRATED
GRATER
GRATES
GRETEL
GUNTER
GUSTED
GUTTED
GUTTER
HAFTED
HALTED
HALTER
HASTEN
HASTES
HATTED
HATTER
HEATED
HEATER
HEFTED
HELTER
HENTED
HESTER
HINTED
HINTER
HITTER
HOOTED
HOOTER
HOSTED
HOSTEL
HOTTEA
HOTTER
HUNTED
HUNTER
HUTTED
INSTEP
IRATER
JEETER
JESTED
JESTER
JETTED
JILTED
JITTER
JOETEX
JOLTED
JOTTED
JUSTER
JUTTED
KEITEL
KILTED
KILTER
KITTEN
KOTTER
KRATER
LAPTEV
LASTED
LASTEX
LATTEN
LATTER
LECTER
LENTEN
LESTER
LETTED
LETTER
LIFTED
LIFTER
LILTED
LINTEL
LINTER
LISTED
LISTEE
LISTEL
LISTEN
LISTER
LITTER
LOFTED
LOITER
LOOTED
LOOTER
LOTTED
LUSTED
LUSTER
MALTED
MANTEL
MARTEL
MARTEN
MASTER
MATTEA
MATTED
MATTEL
MATTER
MATTES
MEETER
MELTED
MINTED
MINTER
MISTED
MISTER
MITTEN
MIXTEC
MOATED
MOLTED
MOLTEN
MOLTER
MONTEL
MONTES
MONTEZ
MOOTED
MOSTEL
MUSTER
MUTTER
NANTES
NATTER
NEATEN
NEATER
NESTEA
NESTED
NESTER
NETTED
NEUTER
NUTTED
NUTTER
OBITER
OBSTET
OERTER
ORATED
ORATES
OUSTED
OUSTER
OYSTER
PALTER
PANTED
PARTED
PASTED
PASTEL
PASTES
PATTED
PATTEN
PATTER
PELTED
PELTER
PERTER
PESTER
PETTED
PETTER
PEWTER
PIETER
PINTER
PISTES
PITTED
PITTER
PLATED
PLATEN
PLATER
PLATES
PONTES
PORTED
PORTER
POSTED
POSTER
POTTED
POTTER
POUTED
POUTER
PRATED
PRATER
PRATES
PRETER
PROTEI
PROTEM
PUNTED
PUNTER
PUTTED
PUTTEE
PUTTER
QUOTED
QUOTER
QUOTES
RAFTED
RAFTER
RANTED
RANTER
RASTER
RATTED
RATTER
RENTED
RENTER
RESTED
RESTER
REUTER
RIFTED
RIOTED
RIOTER
RITTER
ROOTED
ROOTER
ROSTER
ROTTED
ROTTEN
ROTTER
ROUTED
ROUTER
ROUTES
RRATED
RUSTED
RUTTED
SALTED
SALTEN
SALTER
SANTEE
SAUTES
SCOTER
SCUTES
SEATED
SEATER
SEPTET
SESTET
SETTEE
SETTER
SEXTET
SIFTED
SIFTER
SILTED
SINTER
SISTER
SITTER
SKATED
SKATER
SKATES
SLATED
SLATER
SLATES
SMITES
SOFTEN
SOFTER
SORTED
SORTER
SOTTED
SOUTER
SPATES
SPITED
SPITES
STATED
STATEN
STATER
STATES
SUITED
SUITES
SUMTER
SUTTER
SYSTEM
TANTES
TARTER
TASTED
TASTER
TASTES
TATTED
TATTER
TAUTEN
TAUTER
TEETER
TENTED
TENTER
TESTED
TESTEE
TESTER
TILTED
TILTER
TINTED
TINTER
TITTER
TNOTES
TOATEE
TOLTEC
TOOTED
TOOTER
TOPTEN
TORTES
TOTTED
TOTTER
TOUTED
TOUTER
TRITER
TUFTED
ULSTER
UNITED
UNITER
UNITES
VASTER
VATTED
VENTED
VENTER
VERTEX
VESTED
VESTEE
VETTED
VORTEX
WAFTED
WAITED
WAITER
WALTER
WANTED
WASTED
WASTER
WASTES
WELTED
WELTER
WETTED
WETTER
WHITEN
WHITER
WHITES
WILTED
WINTER
WISTER
WITTED
WONTED
WRITER
WRITES
WYNTER
XRATED
XYSTER
YESTER
ZESTED

•••T•E

AORTAE
AUNTIE
BATTLE
BATTUE
BEATLE
BEETLE
BERTIE
BIGTOE
BLITHE
BLYTHE
BOOTEE
BOOTHE
BOOTIE
BOTTLE
BOWTIE
BUSTLE
CANTLE
CASTLE
CATTLE
CENTRE
CLOTHE
CONTRE
COOTIE
COSTAE
DOTTIE
DOTTLE
FETTLE
GENTLE
GERTIE
GOATEE
GOETHE
GUTTAE
HATTIE
HETTIE
HOGTIE
HOOTIE
HURTLE
HUSTLE
JOSTLE
KETTLE
KILTIE
KIRTLE
LAOTSE
LEFTIE
LHOTSE
LISTEE
LITTLE
LOATHE
LUSTRE
MAITRE
MANTLE
MATTIE
METTLE
MILTIE
MOLTKE
MOTTLE
MYRTLE
NESTLE
NETTLE
ODETTE
PESTLE
PINTLE
PLATTE
POTTLE
PUTTEE
RATTLE
RUSTLE
SANTEE
SARTRE
SCATHE
SCYTHE
SEETHE
SETTEE
SETTLE
SNATHE
SOFTIE
SOOTHE
SORTIE
SPATHE
STATUE
SUBTLE
SWATHE
TATTLE
TEETHE
TESTAE
TESTEE
TIPTOE
TITTLE
TOATEE
TOOTLE
TSETSE
TURTLE
VESTEE
VIRTUE
WATTLE
WHATVE
WRITHE
YVETTE

••••TE

ABLATE
ACUATE
ADESTE
ADNATE
AERATE
AGNATE
ANSATE
APLITE
AQUATE
ASTUTE
AVIATE
BARITE
BERATE
BINATE
BORATE
BRONTE
BYROTE
CANUTE
CAPOTE
CENOTE
CERATE
CHASTE
CHOATE
COMATE
COYOTE
CREATE
CROUTE
CURATE
DEBATE
DELATE
DELETE
DEMOTE
DENOTE
DEPUTE
DEVOTE
DILATE
DILUTE
DONATE
DUARTE
ECARTE
EFFETE
EMEUTE
EQUATE
ERGATE
ESTATE
EXCITE
FICHTE
FINITE
FIXATE
GAMETE
GEMOTE
GUNITE
GYRATE
HALITE
HAMITE
HECATE
IDEATE
IGNITE
IMPUTE
INCITE
INDITE
INMATE
INNATE
INVITE
IODATE
IOLITE
KARATE
LANATE
LEGATE
LEVITE
LIGATE
LOBATE
LOCATE
LUCITE
LUNATE
LUXATE
MALATE
METATE
MINUTE
MUTATE
NEGATE
NOTATE
NUTATE
OBLATE
ODETTE
OFLATE
OLEATE
ONSITE
OOCYTE
OOLITE
OPHITE
OPIATE
ORGATE
ORNATE
OSSETE
OUTATE
PAIUTE
PALATE
PEDATE
PETITE
PEYOTE
PILATE
PINITE
PIRATE
PLANTE
PLATTE
POINTE
POLITE
PUENTE
PYRITE
RAMATE
RATITE
REBATE
RECITE
REDATE
REFUTE
RELATE
REMOTE
RENOTE
REPUTE
RERATE
ROTATE
RUGATE
SAINTE
SALUTE
SAMITE
SAVATE
SEDATE
SEMITE
SENATE
SHIITE
SHORTE
SOLUTE
SPRITE
STACTE
STPETE
SURETE
SVELTE
TERETE
TODATE
TONITE
TRISTE
TUBATE
UNIATE
UPDATE
VACATE
VENITE
VERITE
VOLUTE
YVETTE
ZONATE
ZYGOTE

T•F•••

TEFLON
TIFFED
TIFFIN
TOFFEE
TUFFET
TUFTED

T••F••

THEFED
THEFLY
THEFTS
TIFFED
TIFFIN
TITFER
TOFFEE
TRIFID
TRIFLE
TRYFOR
TUFFET
TURFED
TWOFER

T•••F•

TAPOFF
TARIFF
TEEOFF
THRIFT
TIPOFF
TOLIFE
TOPOFF
TUMEFY
TYPIFY

T••••F

TAPOFF
TARIFF
TEEOFF
TELLOF
TIPOFF
TOLDOF
TOPOFF

•T•F••

STAFFS
STEFAN
STEFFI
STEFOY
STIFFS
STIFLE
STUFFS
STUFFY

•T••F•

STAFFS
STEFFI
STIFFS
STRAFE
STRIFE
STUFFS
STUFFY

•T•••F

ITSELF
STAPUF

••TF••

ARTFUL
BOTFLY
FITFUL
HATFUL
KITFOX
LETFLY
OPTFOR
OUTFIT
OUTFLY
OUTFOX
POTFUL
TITFER
VATFUL
WETFLY

••T•F•

BITOFF
CITIFY
CUTOFF
GETOFF
GOTOFF
LETOFF
MOTIFS
NOTIFY
PUTOFF
RATIFY
SETOFF

••T••F

BITOFF
CUTOFF
GETOFF
GOTOFF
LETOFF
PUTOFF
SETOFF

•••T•F

CERTIF
SORTOF
WHATIF

T•G•••

TAGDAY
TAGEND
TAGGED
TAGORE
TAGOUT
TAGSUP
TIGERS
TIGGER
TIGHTS
TIGLON
TIGRIS
TOGAED
TOGGED
TOGGLE
TUGGED
TUGGER
TUGRIK

T••G••

TAGGED
TAIGAS
TANGED
TANGLE
TANGLY
TANGOS
TANGUY
TARGES
TARGET
TAUGHT
THIGHS
TIGGER
TINGED
TINGES
TINGLE
TINGLY
TINGOD
TOGGED
TOGGLE
TONGAN
TONGUE
TOPGUN
TOUGHS
TOUGHY
TRAGIC
TRIGLY
TRIGON
TROGON
TUGGED
TUGGER
TURGID
TURGOR
TWIGGY

T•••G•

TELUGU
THINGS
THINGY
THONGS
THOUGH
TOBAGO
TOWAGE
TRIAGE
TROUGH
TRUDGE
TWANGS
TWANGY
TWIGGY
TWINGE

T••••G

TAKING
TAMING
TAPING
TARING
TAUTOG
TAWING
TAXING
TEABAG
TEEING
THRONG
TIDING
TIEING
TILING
TIMING
TIRING
TOEING
TONING
TOPDOG
TOTING
TOWING
TOYDOG
TOYING
TRUING
TRYING
TUAREG
TUBING
TUNING
TURING
TYPING

•T•G••

STAGED
STAGER
STAGES
STIGMA
STOGIE

•T••G•

ATERGO
STINGO
STINGS
STINGY
STODGE
STODGY
STOOGE

•T•••G

STALAG
STENOG
STRING
STRONG
STRUNG

••TG••

ARTGUM
CATGUT
JETGUN
OUTGUN
ROTGUT
RUTGER

••T•G•

DOTAGE
IDTAGS
LATIGO
LETSGO
ORTEGA
OUTAGE
POTAGE
RETAGS

••T••G

ACTING
BATING
BITING
BUTUNG
CATRIG
CITING
DATING
DATONG
DOTING
EATING
FETING
GATING
HATING
HOTDOG
JETLAG
KITBAG
KITING
LITHOG
LUTING
MATING
METING
MUTING
NOTING
NUTMEG
OPTING
OUTING
PETROG
RATEDG
RATING
SATANG
SATING
SITING
TOTING
VOTING
WETTIG

•••T•G

DOGTAG
GOSTAG
MAYTAG
PHOTOG
RAGTAG
REDTAG
SONTAG
TAUTOG
WETTIG
ZAFTIG

TH••••

THALER
THALES
THALIA
THAMES
THANES
THANKS
THATCH
THATIS
THATLL
THAWED
THAYER
THEBES
THECAE
THECAL
THEEND
THEFED
THEFLY
THEFTS
THEHAJ
THEIRS
THEISM
THEIST
THEKID
THELIP
THELMA
THEMED
THEMES
THENAR
THENCE
THEORY
THERES
THERMO
THERMS
THESEA
THESES
THESIS
THESIX
THETAS
THETIC
THETIS
THETOY
THEWEB
THEWIZ
THEYLL
THEYRE
THEYVE
THICKE
THIEVE
THIGHS
THILLS
THINGS
THINGY
THINKS
THINLY
THIRDS
THIRST
THIRTY
THISBE
THOLES
THOMAS
THONGS
THORAX
THORNS
THORNY
THORPE
THORPS
THOUGH
THRACE
THRALE
THRALL
THRASH
THREAD
THREAT
THREED
THREES
THRESH
THRICE
THRIFT
THRILL
THRIPS
THRIVE
THROAT
THROBS
THROES
THRONE
THRONG
THROVE
THROWN
THROWS
THRUMS
THRUSH
THRUST
THUJAS
THUMBS
THUMPS
THUNKS
THUSLY
THWACK
THWART
THYMUS
THYRSI

T•H•••

TAHINI
TAHITI
TEHEED
TEHEES
TSHIRT

T••H••

TECHIE
TECHNO
TEEHEE
TEPHRA
TETHER
TETHYS
THEHAJ
TIGHTS
TINHAT
TISHRI
TITHED
TITHER
TITHES
TOPHAT
TOPHUS
TOTHER
TOWHEE
TUCHUN
TVSHOW
TYPHUS
TZUHSI

T•••H•

TAICHI
TAUGHT
TEETHE
TENTHS
TETCHY
THIGHS
TOOTHY
TORAHS
TORCHY
TOUCHE
TOUCHY
TOUGHS
TOUGHY
TRACHY
TRASHY
TRICHO
TRISHA
TROCHE
TROPHY
TROTHS
TRUTHS

T••••H

TAKETH
TEMPEH
TERAPH
THATCH
THOUGH
THRASH
THRESH
THRUSH
TONISH
TRENCH
TROUGH
TUSSAH
TWITCH

•TH•••

ATHAND
ATHENA
ATHENE
ATHENS
ATHOME
ETHANE
ETHENE
ETHERS
ETHICS
ETHNIC
ETHNOS
ITHACA
ITHAKI
OTHERS
STHENO
UTHANT

•T•H••

ATTHAT
ETCHED
ETCHER
ETCHES
ITCHED
ITCHES
ITZHAK
UTAHAN

•T••H•

STITHY
STJOHN

•T•••H

ATTACH
STANCH
STARCH
STENCH
STITCH
STORCH

••TH••

AETHER
ALTHEA
ANTHEM
ANTHER
ARTHRO
ARTHUR
ATTHAT
AUTHOR
BATHED
BATHER
BATHES
BATHOS
BETHEL
BOTHER
CATHAY
CATHER
DITHER
DOTHAN
EITHER
ESTHER
FATHER
FATHOM
GATHER
GOTHAM
GOTHIC
HATHOR
HITHER
ISTHMI
JETHRO
KATHIE
LATHED
LATHER
LATHES
LETHAL
LITHIC
LITHOG
LITHOS

LOTHAR LUTHER LUTHOR MATHER MATHIS METHOD METHYL MOTHER MOTHRA MYTHIC MYTHOI MYTHOL MYTHOS NATHAN NETHER OUTHIT PATHAN PATHOL PATHOS PITHED POTHER PYTHIA PYTHON RATHER ROTHKO SOTHAT TETHER TETHYS TITHED TITHER TITHES TOTHER WETHER WITHAL WITHED WITHER WITHES WITHIN WITHIT ZITHER

••T•H•

BETCHA BOTCHY CATCHY GOTCHA LITCHI LOTAHS NOTCHY PATCHY PITCHY TETCHY WITCHY

••T••H

ATTACH DETACH FETISH HITECH IRTYSH JUTISH KITSCH LATISH MATZOH POTASH PUTSCH VOTECH

•••TH•

AGATHA APATHY ARETHA BERTHA BERTHS BIRTHS BLITHE BLYTHE BOOTHE BOOTHS BROTHS CANTHI CHETHS CLOTHE CLOTHO CLOTHS DEPTHS EARTHA EARTHY FAITHS FIFTHS FILTHY FIRTHS FROTHS FROTHY GARTHS GIRTHS GOETHE HEATHS HEATHY ICHTHY LOATHE MARTHA MONTHS MOUTHS MOUTHY NINTHS NORTHS QUOTHA RHYTHM SCATHE SCYTHE SEETHE SIXTHS SLITHY SLOTHS SMITHS SMITHY SNATHE SNATHS SOOTHE SOUTHS SPATHE STITHY SWATHE SWATHS TEETHE TENTHS TOOTHY TROTHS TRUTHS WIDTHS WORTHS WORTHY WRATHS WRATHY WRITHE XANTHO YOUTHS

•••T•H

BLOTCH CLUTCH CRUTCH FLETCH FLITCH GLITCH HOOTCH KLATCH KVETCH NAUTCH SCOTCH SCUTCH SKETCH SKITCH SMUTCH SNATCH SNITCH STITCH SWATCH SWITCH THATCH TWITCH WRETCH

••••TH

BREATH BYPATH COMETH DALETH DEARTH DULUTH EIGHTH EOLITH FOURTH GARETH GOWITH GROWTH HEALTH HEARTH INWITH IOMOTH JOBETH JUDITH LENGTH LILITH NAMATH OOLITH ORNITH PLINTH SHEATH SLEUTH SMOOTH SPILTH SWARTH TAKETH WARMTH WEALTH WRAITH WREATH ZENITH ZEROTH ZIZITH

TI••••

TIARAS TIBIAE TIBIAL TIBIAS TICALS TICKED TICKER TICKET TICKLE TICKLY TICTAC TIDBIT TIDDLY TIDIED TIDIER TIDIES TIDILY TIDING TIDYUP TIEDIN TIEDTO TIEDUP TIEDYE TIEING TIEINS TIEPIN TIERCE TIERED TIEROD TIERRA TIESIN TIESTO TIESUP TIEUPS TIFFED TIFFIN TIGERS TIGGER TIGHTS TIGLON TIGRIS TILAKS TILDEN TILDES TILERS TILING TILLED TILLER TILLIE TILLIS TILSIT TILTED TILTER TIMBAL TIMBER TIMBRE TIMELY TIMERS TIMING TINCAL TINCAN TINCTS TINDER TINEAR TINGED TINGES TINGLE TINGLY TINGOD TINHAT TINIER TINILY TINKER TINKLE TINKLY TINMAN TINMEN TINNED TINNER TINPAN TINPOT TINSEL TINTED TINTER TIPINS TIPOFF TIPPED TIPPER TIPPET TIPPLE TIPSIN TIPTOE TIPTOP TIPUPS TIRADE TIRANA TIRANE TIRING TISANE TISHRI TISSUE TITANS TITBIT TITERS TITFER TITHED TITHER TITHES TITIAN TITLED TITLES TITRED TITRES TITTER TITTLE TITTUP TIVOLI

T•I•••

TAICHI TAIGAS TAILED TAILLE TAILOR TAINAN TAINOS TAINTS TAIPAN TAIPEI TAIWAN TBILLS TBIRDS THICKE THIEVE THIGHS THILLS THINGS THINGY THINKS THINLY THIRDS THIRST THIRTY THISBE TOILED TOILER TOILES TOILET TRIADS TRIAGE TRIALS TRIBAL TRIBES TRICED TRICEP TRICES TRICHO TRICIA TRICKS TRICKY TRICOT TRIERS TRIFID TRIFLE TRIGLY TRIGON TRIJET TRIKES TRILBY TRILLS TRIMLY TRINAL TRINES TRIODE TRIPLE TRIPLY TRIPOD TRIPOS TRIPUP TRISHA TRISTE TRITER TRITON TRIUNE TRIVET TRIVIA TRIXIE TUILLE TWIGGY TWILIT TWILLS TWINED TWINES TWINGE TWIRLS TWISTS TWISTY TWITCH TWITTY

T••I••

TAHINI TAHITI TAKING TAKINS TALION TAMILS TAMING TANIST TAOISM TAOIST TAPING TAPINS TAPIRS TARIFF TARING TAWING TAXIED TAXIES TAXING TEDIUM TEEING THEIRS THEISM THEIST THRICE THRIFT THRILL THRIPS THRIVE TIBIAE TIBIAL TIBIAS TIDIED TIDIER TIDIES TIDILY TIDING TIEING TIEINS TILING TIMING TINIER TINILY TIPINS TIRING TITIAN TOBIAS TOBIES TOEING TOEINS TOLIFE TONICS TONIER TONING TONISH TONITE TOPICS TORIES TORINO TOTING TOWING TOXICS TOXINS TOYING TRAILS TRAINS TRAITS TROIKA TRUING TRUISM TRYING TSHIRT TUBING TUBIST TULIPS TUNICA TUNICS TUNING TUPIAN TURING TYPIER TYPIFY TYPING TYPIST TYRIAN

T•••I•

TABRIZ TACTIC TAKEIN TALKIE TANNIC TANNIN TARPIT TECHIE TENNIS TENPIN TESSIE TETRIS THALIA THATIS THEKID THELIP THESIS THESIX THETIC THETIS THEWIZ TIDBIT TIEDIN TIEPIN TIESIN TIFFIN TIGRIS TILLIE TILLIS TILSIT TIPSIN TITBIT TMESIS TOCSIN TOEDIN TOESIN TOMLIN TOMMIX TOMTIT TONKIN TONSIL TOOKIN TOOKIT TOONIE TOROID TORPID TORRID TOWNIE TRAGIC TRAVIS TREDIA TREPID TRICIA TRIFID TRIVIA TRIXIE TROPIC TSURIS TUCKIN TUGRIK TUNEIN TURBID TURBIT TURGID TURKIC TURNIN TURNIP TURPIN TWILIT TWOBIT

T••••I

TAHINI TAHITI TAICHI TAIPEI TATAMI THYRSI TISHRI TIVOLI TUMULI TZUHSI

•TI•••

OTIOSE OTITIC OTITIS STICKS STICKY STIFFS STIFLE STIGMA STILES STILLS STILLY STILTS STIMPY STINGO STINGS STINGY STINKS STINKY STINTS STIPEL STIPES STIRIN STIRKS STIRUP STITCH STITHY STIVER STIVIC

•T•I••

ATKINS ATRIAL ATRISK ATRIUM ATTICA ATTICS ATTILA ATTIRE ATWILL ETHICS ETOILE STAINS STAIRS STEINS STOICS STRIAE STRICK STRICT STRIDE STRIFE STRIKE STRINE STRING STRIPE STRIPS STRIPY STRIVE

•T••I•

ATOMIC ATONIC ATTAIN ATTRIT ETALIA ETALII ETHNIC ETONIC ITALIA ITALIC OTITIC OTITIS STADIA STALIN STASIS STATIC STEPIN STEVIE STIRIN STIVIC STOGIE STOLID STOPIN STOPIT STOTIN STRAIN STRAIT STUDIO STUPID STYMIE STYRIA UTOPIA

•T•••I

ETALII ITHAKI ITURBI STEFFI STRATI

••TI••

ACTIII ACTING ACTINO ACTION ACTIUM ACTIVE ALTIMA ALTIUS ANTICS ARTIER ARTILY ARTIST ATTICA ATTICS ATTILA ATTIRE BATIKS BATING BETIDE BETISE BITING CATION CITIES CITIFY CITING CITIUS CUTIES CUTINS DATING DATIVE DOTING DUTIES EATING ENTICE ENTIRE ENTITY FATIMA FETING FETISH FUTILE GATING HATING INTIMA INTIME INTINE JUTISH KITING LATIGO LATINA LATINI LATINO LATINS LATISH LATIUM LOTION LUTING LUTIST MATING MATINS METIER METING MOTIFS MOTILE MOTION MOTIVE MUTING MUTINY NATICK NATION NATIVE NOTICE NOTIFY NOTING NOTION OATIER ONTIME OPTICS OPTIMA OPTING OPTION OSTIUM OUTING PATINA PATINE PATIOS PETITE PITIED PITIER PITIES POTION RATIFY RATINE RATING RATION RATIOS RATITE RETIAL RETIED RETIES RETILE RETIME RETINA RETIRE ROTINI RUTILE SATING SATINS SATINY SATIRE SETINS SHTICK SITING SITINS TITIAN TOTING ULTIMA ULTIMO UNTIDY UNTIED UNTIES UPTICK UPTIME VOTING VOTIVE

••T•I•

ACTIII ALTAIC ALTAIR ANTRIM ARTOIS ASTRID ATTAIN ATTRIT BUTTIN CATKIN CATNIP CATRIG CITRIC CUTSIN DETAIL DETAIN DOTTIE EATSIN ENTAIL FITSIN GATLIN GETSIN GETSIT GOTHIC GOTOIT HATPIN HATTIE HETTIE HITSIT HOTAIR HOTTIP IATRIC INTUIT ISTRIA KATHIE LATVIA LETSIN LITHIC MATHIS MATLIN MATRIX MATTIE METRIC MYTHIC NITRIC NITWIT NUTKIN NUTRIA OBTAIN OUTBID OUTDID OUTFIT OUTHIT OUTWIT OXTAIL PATOIS PETAIN PETRIE PETTIT POTPIE PUTRID PUTSIN PYTHIA RATLIN RETAIL RETAIN RETRIM SETSIN SITSIN TETRIS TITBIT VITRIC VOTEIN WETTIG WITHIN WITHIT

••T••I

ACTIII BATUMI HATARI ISTHMI JETSKI KATMAI LATINI LITCHI MYTHOI OCTOPI OCTROI POTOSI QATARI ROTINI SATORI TATAMI WATUSI

•••TI•

ABATIS ACETIC AMATIS AORTIC ARCTIC AUNTIE AUSTIN BALTIC BEATIT BERTIE BESTIR BIOTIC BIOTIN BOOTIE BOWTIE BUSTIN BUTTIN CELTIC CERTIF CHITIN COATIS COOTIE COPTIC CRETIN CRITIC CULTIC CURTIN CURTIS CURTIZ CUSTIS DELTIC DENTIL DENTIN DHOTIS DISTIL DOTTIE DUSTIN EDITIO EROTIC EXOTIC FISTIC FOETID FUSTIC GERTIE GESTIC GRATIA GRATIN GRATIS HATTIE HECTIC HESTIA HETTIE HOGTIE HOOTIE HOTTIP IGETIT IGOTIT INITIO INSTIL JUSTIN KILTIE LACTIC LEFTIE LEFTIN LENTIL LOSTIT MALTIN MANTIC MANTIS MARTIN MASTIC MATTIE MENTIS MILTIE MUFTIS MUNTIN MYSTIC NOETIC OTITIC OTITIS PASTIS PECTIC PECTIN PEPTIC PETTIT PHATIC PHOTIC PIETIN PISTIL POETIC PONTIC PORTIA POSTIT QUITIT RUSTIC SANTIR SCOTIA SENTIN SEPTIC SHUTIN SOFTIE SORTIE STATIC STOTIN TACTIC THATIS THETIC THETIS TOMTIT VICTIM VICTIS WANTIN WENTIN WETTIG WHATIF ZAFTIG

•••T•I

CANTHI CENTRI DMITRI FRUTTI GLUTEI MAITAI MAOTAI PROTEI

••••TI

AGOUTI AVANTI BHAKTI DORATI FRUTTI GELATI MALOTI PILOTI RUBATI SENITI SHAKTI SHORTI SMALTI STRATI TAHITI VASHTI WAPITI

T•J•••

TEJANO

T••J••

THUJAS TOPJOB TRAJAN TRIJET TROJAN

T••••J

THEHAJ

•TJ•••

STJOAN STJOHN

•T•J••

STOJKO

••T••J

INTERJ SGTMAJ

T•K•••

TAKEIN TAKEON TAKERS TAKETH TAKETO TAKEUP TAKING TAKINS TOKAYS TOKENS TOKLAS

T••K••

TACKED TACKER TACKLE TACKON TALKAT TALKED TALKER TALKIE TALKTO TALKUP TANKAS TANKED TANKER TANKUP TASKED TEDKEY TERKEL THEKID TICKED TICKER TICKET TICKLE TICKLY TINKER TINKLE TINKLY TONKIN TOOKIN TOOKIT TOOKON TOOKTO TOOKUP TRIKES TUCKED TUCKER TUCKET TUCKIN TURKEY TURKIC TUSKED TUSKER

T•••K•

TANAKA THANKS THICKE THINKS THUNKS TILAKS TOPEKA TRACKS TRICKS TRICKY TROIKA TRUCKS TRUNKS TWEAKS

T••••K

TANOAK THWACK TOBRUK TREBEK TUGRIK

•TK•••

ATKINS

•T•K••

STAKED STAKES STOKED STOKER STOKES

•T••K•

ITHAKI STACKS STALKS STALKY STANKY STEAKS STICKS STICKY STINKS STINKY STIRKS STLUKE STOCKS STOCKY STOJKO STOOKS STORKS STRAKE STRIKE STROKE

•T•••K

ATRISK ATTACK ATWORK

ITZHAK
STMARK
STREAK
STRICK
STRUCK

••TK••

CATKIN
KITKAT
LATKES
NUTKIN

••T•K•

BATIKS
BETAKE
INTAKE
JETSKI
RETAKE
ROTHKO
UPTAKE

••T••K

AMTRAK
ATTACK
BETOOK
BYTALK
NATICK
RETOOK
SHTICK
UNTACK
UPTALK
UPTICK

•••TK•

MOLTKE
NOOTKA

•••T•K

BARTOK
BRATSK
VOSTOK

TL••••

TLALOC

T•L•••

TALBOT
TALCED
TALCUM
TALENT
TALERS
TALESE
TALION
TALKAT
TALKED
TALKER
TALKIE
TALKTO
TALKUP
TALLER
TALLOW
TALMUD
TALONS
TELEDU
TELLER
TELLOF
TELLON
TELUGU
TILAKS
TILDEN
TILDES
TILERS
TILING
TILLED
TILLER
TILLIE
TILLIS
TILSIT
TILTED
TILTER
TOLDOF
TOLDON
TOLEDO
TOLIFE
TOLLED
TOLTEC
TOLUCA
TULANE
TULARE
TULIPS
TULLES
TULSAN

T••L••

TABLAS
TABLED
TABLES
TABLET
TAILED
TAILLE
TAILOR
TALLER
TALLOW
TAYLOR
TBILLS
TEFLON
TELLER
TELLOF
TELLON
TESLAS
THALER
THALES
THALIA
THELIP
THELMA
THILLS
THOLES
TIGLON
TILLED
TILLER
TILLIE
TILLIS
TITLED
TITLES
TLALOC
TOILED
TOILER
TOILES
TOILET
TOKLAS
TOLLED
TOMLIN
TOOLED
TOOLUP
TOULON
TRALEE
TRILBY
TRILLS
TROLLS
TRYLON
TUILLE
TULLES
TWELVE
TWILIT
TWILLS

T•••L•

TABULA
TACKLE
TAILLE
TAMALE
TAMELY
TAMILS
TANGLE
TANGLY
TARTLY
TATTLE
TAUTLY
TBILLS
TEMPLE
TEPALS
THATLL
THEFLY
THEYLL
THILLS
THINLY
THRALE
THRALL
THRILL
THUSLY
TICALS
TICKLE
TICKLY
TIDDLY
TIDILY
TIMELY
TINGLE
TINGLY
TINILY
TINKLE
TINKLY
TIPPLE
TITTLE
TIVOLI
TODDLE
TOGGLE
TOOTLE
TOPPLE
TOTALS
TOUSLE
TOWELS
TRAILS
TRAWLS
TREBLE
TREBLY
TRIALS
TRIFLE
TRIGLY
TRILLS
TRIMLY
TRIPLE
TRIPLY
TROLLS
TUILLE
TUMBLE
TUMULI
TUMULT
TUPELO
TURTLE
TUSSLE
TUVALU
TWILLS
TWIRLS
TWOPLY
TYBALT

T••••L

TARSAL
TASSEL
TEASEL
TERCEL
TERKEL
TETZEL
THATLL
THECAL
THEYLL
THRALL
THRILL
TIBIAL
TIMBAL
TINCAL
TINSEL
TONSIL
TRAVEL
TRIBAL
TRINAL
TROWEL
TUNNEL
TYDBOL

•TL•••

ATLAST
ATLATL
STLUKE

•T•L••

ATOLLS
ATTLEE
ETALIA
ETALII
ITALIA
ITALIC
OTELLO
STALAG
STALED
STALER
STALES
STALIN
STALKS
STALKY
STALLS
STELAE
STELAR
STELES
STELLA
STELMO
STILES
STILLS
STILLY
STILTS
STOLEN
STOLES
STOLID
STOLLE
STOLON
STULLS
STYLED
STYLER
STYLES
STYLET
STYLUS

•T••L•

ATOLLS
ATTILA
ATWILL
ETOILE
ITSELF
OTELLO
OTOOLE
STABLE
STABLY
STALLS
STAPLE
STEALS
STEELE
STEELS
STEELY
STELLA
STIFLE
STILLS
STILLY
STMALO
STOLLE
STOOLS
STOOLY
STROLL
STULLS

•T•••L

ATLATL
ATONAL
ATRIAL
ATWILL
ETYMOL
STEROL
STIPEL
STPAUL
STROLL

••TL••

ANTLER
ATTLEE
BUTLER
CUTLER
CUTLET
GATLIN
ISTLES
JETLAG
MATLIN
MOTLEY
NUTLET
ORTLES
OSTLER
OUTLAW
OUTLAY
OUTLET
RATLIN
SUTLER
TITLED
TITLES

••T•L•

ARTELS
ARTILY
ATTILA
BATTLE
BETELS
BITOLA
BOTELS
BOTFLY
BOTTLE
BYTALK
CATTLE
CUTELY
DOTELL
DOTTLE
EXTOLS
FATALE
FETTLE
FUTILE
HOTELS
KETTLE
LATELY
LETFLY
LITTLE
METALS
METTLE
MOTELS
MOTILE
MOTTLE
MUTELY
NETTLE
NETTLY
OUTFLY
PETALS
PETULA
POTTLE
RATELS
RATTLE
RATTLY
RETELL
RETILE
RETOLD
RUTILE
SETTLE
SOTOLS
TATTLE
TITTLE
TOTALS
UNTOLD
UPTALK
VITALE
VITALS
WATTLE
WETFLY

••T••L

ACTUAL
ARTFUL
ASTRAL
BATTEL
BETHEL
DETAIL
DOTELL
ENTAIL
FITFUL
HATFUL
LETHAL
MATTEL
METHYL
MITRAL
MUTUAL
MYTHOL
OSTEAL
OXTAIL
PATHOL
PATROL
PETREL
PETROL
POTFUL
RETAIL
RETELL
RETIAL
RETOOL
RETRAL
RITUAL
SHTETL
TETZEL
VATFUL
WITHAL

•••TL•

BATTLE
BEATLE
BEETLE
BOTTLE
BUSTLE
CANTLE
CASTLE
CATTLE
COSTLY
CURTLY
DAFTLY
DEFTLY
DOTTLE
FEATLY
FETTLE
FLATLY
GENTLE
GENTLY
HOSTLY
HURTLE
HUSTLE
JOSTLE
JUSTLY
KETTLE
KIRTLE
LASTLY
LITTLE
MANTLE
MEETLY
METTLE
MOSTLY
MOTTLE
MYRTLE
NEATLY
NESTLE
NETTLE
NETTLY
PARTLY
PERTLY
PESTLE
PINTLE
PORTLY
POTTLE
RAPTLY
RATTLE
RATTLY
RUSTLE
SETTLE
SOFTLY
SUBTLE
SUBTLY
TARTLY
TATTLE
TAUTLY
THATLL
TITTLE
TOOTLE
TURTLE
VASTLY
WATTLE
WHATLL

•••T•L

ACETAL
ACETYL
AMATOL
AMSTEL
AORTAL
BATTEL
BOATEL
BRUTAL
CARTEL
COSTAL
DACTYL
DENTAL
DENTIL
DHOTEL
DISTAL
DISTIL
DUCTAL
FESTAL
FOETAL
FONTAL
GRETEL
HIATAL
HOSTEL
HYETAL
INSTAL
INSTIL
KEITEL
LENTIL
LINTEL
LISTEL
MANTEL
MARTEL
MATTEL
MENTAL
MONTEL
MORTAL
MOSTEL
PASTEL
PISTIL
PISTOL
PORTAL
POSTAL
RENTAL
SEPTAL
THATLL
UNITAL
VESTAL
WHATLL

••••TL

ATLATL
SHTETL

TM••••

TMESIS

T•M•••

TAMALE
TAMARA
TAMAYO
TAMELY
TAMERS
TAMEST
TAMILS
TAMING
TAMMUZ
TAMPED
TAMPER
TAMTAM
TEMPED
TEMPEH
TEMPER
TEMPLE
TEMPOS
TEMPTS
TEMPUS
TIMBAL
TIMBER
TIMBRE
TIMELY
TIMERS
TIMING
TOMATO
TOMBAC
TOMBOY
TOMCAT
TOMLIN
TOMMIX
TOMTIT
TOMTOM
TUMBLE
TUMEFY
TUMMED
TUMULI
TUMULT

T••M••

TALMUD
TAMMUZ
TARMAC
TASMAN
TAXMAN
TAXMEN
TEAMED
TEAMUP
TEEMED
TERMED
TEXMEX
THAMES
THEMED
THEMES
THOMAS
THUMBS
THUMPS
THYMUS
TINMAN
TINMEN
TOAMAN
TODMAN
TOMMIX
TRAMPS
TREMOR
TRIMLY
TROMPE
TROMPS
TRUMAN
TRUMPS
TUBMAN
TUMMED

T•••M•

TACOMA
TATAMI
THELMA
THERMO
THERMS
THRUMS
TOTEMS
TRAUMA

T••••M

TALCUM
TAMTAM
TANDEM
TAOISM
TEDEUM
TEDIUM
THEISM
TOMTOM
TRUISM

•TM•••

ATMOST
STMALO
STMARK
UTMOST

•T•M••

ATAMAN
ATEMPO
ATOMIC
ETYMOL
ETYMON
STAMEN
STAMPS
STIMPY
STOMAS
STOMAT
STOMPS
STUMER
STUMPS
STUMPY
STYMIE

•T••M•

ATEAMS
ATHOME
STEAMS
STEAMY
STELMO
STIGMA
STORMS
STORMY
STRUMS

•T•••M

ATRIUM
STREAM

••TM••

ALTMAN
BATMAN
BATMEN
BITMAP
GETMAD
GOTMAD
HETMAN
HITMAN
HITMEN
KATMAI
LITMUS
MOTMOT
NETMAN
NETMEN
NUTMEG
PATMOS
PITMAN
PITMEN
SGTMAJ
WETMOP

••T•M•

ALTIMA
AUTUMN
BATUMI
ENTOMO
FATIMA
INTIMA
INTIME
ISTHMI
ONTIME
OPTIMA
RETIME
TATAMI
TOTEMS
ULTIMA
ULTIMO
UPTIME

••T••M

ACTIUM
ANTHEM
ANTRIM
ANTRUM
ARTGUM
BATYAM
BOTTOM
ESTEEM
FATHOM
GOTHAM
JETSAM
LATIUM
OSTIUM
PUTNAM
RETRIM
SITCOM

•••T•M

ADYTUM
BANTAM
BOTTOM
CUSTOM
DIATOM
DICTUM
MADTOM
MULTUM
PROTEM
RHYTHM
SALTUM
SEPTUM
SYSTEM
TAMTAM
TOMTOM
VICTIM

TN••••

TNOTES

T•N•••

TANAKA
TANANA
TANDEM
TANGED
TANGLE
TANGLY
TANGOS
TANGUY
TANIST
TANKAS
TANKED
TANKER
TANKUP
TANNED
TANNER
TANNIC
TANNIN
TANOAK
TANOAN
TANTES
TANTRA
TENACE
TENANT
TENDED
TENDER
TENDON
TENDTO
TENENS
TENETS
TENNIS
TENONS
TENORS
TENPIN
TENREC
TENSED
TENSER
TENSES
TENSOR
TENTED
TENTER
TENTHS
TENURE
TENUTO
TINCAL
TINCAN
TINCTS
TINDER
TINEAR
TINGED
TINGES
TINGLE
TINGLY
TINGOD
TINHAT
TINIER
TINILY
TINKER
TINKLE
TINKLY
TINMAN
TINMEN
TINNED
TINNER
TINPAN
TINPOT
TINSEL
TINTED
TINTER
TONDOS
TONERS
TONEUP
TONGAN
TONGUE
TONICS
TONIER
TONING
TONISH
TONITE
TONKIN
TONNES
TONSIL
TUNDRA
TUNEIN
TUNERS
TUNEUP
TUNICA
TUNICS
TUNING
TUNNEL
TUNNEY

T••N••

TAINAN
TAINOS
TAINTS
TANNED
TANNER
TANNIC
TANNIN
TAUNTS
TBONDS
TBONES
TEENER
TEENSY
TENNIS
TERNES
THANES
THANKS
THENAR
THENCE
THINGS
THINGY
THINKS
THINLY
THONGS
THUNKS
TINNED
TINNER
TONNES
TOONIE
TOWNER
TOWNIE
TRANCE
TRENCH
TRENDS
TRENDY
TRINAL
TRINES
TRUNKS
TUNNEL
TUNNEY
TURNED
TURNER
TURNIN
TURNIP
TURNON
TURNTO
TURNUP
TWANGS
TWANGY
TWENTY
TWINED
TWINES
TWINGE

T•••N•

TAGEND
TAHINI
TAKING
TAKINS
TALENT
TALONS
TAMING
TANANA
TAPING
TAPINS
TARING
TAUONS
TAWING
TAXING
TECHNO
TEEING
TEJANO
TENANT
TENENS
TENONS
TETONS
TEXANS
THEEND
THORNS
THORNY
THRONE
THRONG
TIDING
TIEING
TIEINS
TILING
TIMING
TIPINS
TIRANA
TIRANE
TIRING
TISANE
TITANS
TOEING
TOEINS
TOKENS
TONING
TORINO
TOTING
TOWING
TOXINS
TOYING
TOYONS
TRAINS
TRIUNE
TRUANT
TRUING
TRYING
TUBING
TUCANA
TULANE
TUNING
TURING
TWEENS
TWEENY
TYPING
TYRANT
TYRONE

T••••N

TACKON
TAINAN
TAIPAN
TAIWAN
TAKEIN
TAKEON
TALION
TANNIN
TANOAN
TAPPAN
TARPAN
TARPON
TARTAN
TARZAN
TASMAN
TAUTEN
TAVERN
TAXMAN
TAXMEN
TEFLON
TELLON
TENDON
TENPIN
TERRAN
TEUTON
THROWN
TIEDIN
TIEPIN
TIESIN
TIFFIN
TIGLON
TILDEN
TINCAN
TINMAN
TINMEN
TINPAN
TIPSIN
TITIAN
TOAMAN
TOCSIN
TODMAN
TOEDIN
TOESIN
TOLDON
TOMLIN
TONGAN
TONKIN
TOOKIN
TOOKON
TOPGUN
TOPTEN
TOUCAN
TOULON
TRAJAN
TREPAN
TRIGON
TRITON
TROGON
TROJAN
TRUMAN
TRYLON
TUBMAN
TUCHUN
TUCKIN
TUCSON
TULSAN
TUNEIN
TUPIAN
TURBAN
TUREEN
TURNIN
TURNON
TURPIN
TUSCAN
TYCOON
TYRIAN

•T•N••

ATONAL
ATONCE
ATONED
ATONES
ATONIC
ETHNIC
ETHNOS
ETONIC
STANCE
STANCH
STANDS
STANKY
STANZA
STENCH
STENOG
STENOS
STINGO
STINGS
STINGY
STINKS
STINKY
STINTS
STONED
STONER
STONES
STUNTS
STUNTY

•T••N•

ATHAND
ATHENA
ATHENE
ATHENS
ATKINS
ATTEND
ATTUNE
ETERNE
ETHANE
ETHENE
STAINS
STEINS
STERNA
STERNE
STERNO
STERNS
STHENO
STRAND
STRINE
STRING
STRONG
STRUNG
UTHANT
UTURNS

•T•••N

ATAMAN
ATTAIN
ETYMON
STALIN
STAMEN
STATEN
STAYON
STEFAN
STEPIN
STEPON
STEVEN
STIRIN
STJOAN
STJOHN
STOLEN
STOLON
STOPIN
STOTIN
STRAIN
STREWN
STYRON
UTAHAN

••TN••

CATNAP
CATNIP
JITNEY
NOTNOW
PUTNAM
WATNEY

••T•N•

ACTING
ACTINO
ACTONE
ANTONY
ATTEND
ATTUNE
BATING
BATONS
BETONY
BITING
BOTANY
BUTANE
BUTENE
BUTUNG
CATENA
CETANE
CITING
CUTINS
DATING
DATONG
DETENT
DOTING
EATING
EXTANT
EXTEND
EXTENT
FETING
FUTONS
GATING
GITANO
HATING
INTEND
INTENS
INTENT
INTINE
INTONE
INTUNE
KETONE
KITING
LATENE
LATENS
LATENT
LATINA

LATINI
LATINO
LATINS
LATONA
LITANY
LUTING
MATING
MATINS
METING
MUTANT
MUTING
MUTINY
NATANT
NOTING
OBTUND
OCTANE
OCTANT
OPTING
OSTEND
OUTING
PATENS
PATENT
PATINA
PATINE
PITONS
POTENT
PUTONS
RATINE
RATING
RETENE
RETINA
RETUNE
ROTINI
ROTUND
SATANG
SATING
SATINS
SATINY
SETINS
SITING
SITINS
TETONS
TITANS
TOTING
UNTUNE
VOTING

••T••N

ACTION
ACTSON
ALTMAN
ANTRON
ASTERN
ATTAIN
AUTUMN
BATAAN
BATMAN
BATMEN
BATTEN
BETSON
BITTEN
BUTTIN
BUTTON
CATION
CATKIN
CATTON
CITRON
COTTEN
COTTON
CUTSIN
DATSUN
DETAIN
DOTEON
DOTHAN
EATSIN
EXTERN
FATTEN
FITSIN
GATLIN
GETSIN
GETSON
GOTTEN
HATPIN
HETMAN
HITMAN
HITMEN
HITSON
HUTTON
INTERN
INTOWN
INTURN
JETGUN
JETSON
KITTEN
LATEEN
LATTEN
LETSIN
LETSON
LOTION
LYTTON
MATLIN
MATRON
MITTEN
MOTION
MOTOWN
MUTTON
NATHAN
NATION
NATRON
NETMAN
NETMEN
NETTON
NOTION
NUTKIN
OBTAIN
OPTION
OUTGUN
OUTRAN
OUTRUN
PATHAN
PATRON
PATTEN
PATTON
PETAIN
PITMAN
PITMEN
POTEEN
POTION
PUTSIN
PUTSON
PYTHON
RATION
RATLIN
RATSON
RATTAN
RETAIN
RETTON
RETURN
ROTTEN
RUTTAN
SATEEN
SATURN
SETSIN
SETSON
SITSIN
SITSON
SUTTON
TITIAN
UNTORN
UPTOWN
UPTURN
VOTEIN
WATSON
WITHIN

•••TN•

GRETNA
MUSTNT

•••T•N

AMYTAN
ARCTAN
AUSTEN
AUSTIN
BARTON
BATTEN
BEATEN
BEATON
BENTON
BHUTAN
BIGTEN
BIOTIN
BITTEN
BOLTON
BONTON
BOSTON
BRETON
BRITON
BURTON
BUSTIN
BUTTIN
BUTTON
CAFTAN
CANTON
CAPTAN
CARTON
CASTON
CATTON
CAXTON
CHITIN
CHITON
COTTEN
COTTON
CRETAN
CRETIN
CROTON
CURTIN
DALTON
DANTON
DAYTON
DENTIN
DENTON
DUSTIN
EASTON
FANTAN
FASTEN
FATTEN
FULTON
GASTON
GLUTEN
GOTTEN
GRATIN
GROTON
HASTEN
HESTON
HILTON
HINTON
HORTON
HUSTON
HUTTON
JUSTIN
KEATON
KENTON
KEPTON
KITTEN
LATTEN
LAWTON
LEFTIN
LENTEN
LEPTON
LIPTON
LISTEN
LISTON
LYTTON
MALTIN
MARTEN
MARTIN
MELTON
MERTON
MILTON
MITTEN
MOLTEN
MORTON
MOUTON
MUNTIN
MUTTON
NEATEN
NEKTON
NETTON
NEWTON
NORTON
PARTON
PATTEN
PATTON
PAXTON
PECTIN
PEYTON
PHOTON
PIETIN
PISTON
PLATEN
POSTON
PROTON
RATTAN
RESTON
RETTON
RHYTON
ROTTEN
RUTTAN
SALTEN
SALTON
SARTON
SEATON
SENTIN
SEXTON
SHUTIN
SOFTEN
STATEN
STOTIN
SULTAN
SUNTAN
SUTTON
TARTAN
TAUTEN
TEUTON
TOPTEN
TRITON
VINTON
WAITON
WALTON
WANTIN
WANTON
WENTIN
WENTON
WHITEN
WILTON
WONTON
WYNTON
WYSTAN

TO••••

TOAMAN
TOASTS
TOASTY
TOATEE
TOBAGO
TOBIAS
TOBIES
TOBOOT
TOBRUK
TOCSIN
TODATE
TODDAO
TODDLE
TODMAN
TOECAP
TOEDIN
TOEING
TOEINS
TOESIN
TOETAP
TOFFEE
TOGAED
TOGGED
TOGGLE
TOILED
TOILER
TOILES
TOILET
TOKAYS
TOKENS
TOKLAS
TOLDOF
TOLDON
TOLEDO
TOLIFE
TOLLED
TOLTEC
TOLUCA
TOMATO
TOMBAC
TOMBOY
TOMCAT
TOMLIN
TOMMIX
TOMTIT
TOMTOM
TONDOS
TONERS
TONEUP
TONGAN
TONGUE
TONICS
TONIER
TONING
TONISH
TONITE
TONKIN
TONNES
TONSIL
TOOBAD
TOOKIN
TOOKIT
TOOKON
TOOKTO
TOOKUP
TOOLED
TOOLUP
TOONIE
TOOTED
TOOTER
TOOTHY
TOOTLE
TOOTOO
TOOTSY
TOPCAT
TOPDOG
TOPEKA
TOPERS
TOPGUN
TOPHAT
TOPHUS
TOPICS
TOPJOB
TOPOFF
TOPOUT
TOPPED
TOPPER
TOPPLE
TOPTEN
TOQUES
TORAHS
TORCHY
TOREAT
TORERO
TOREUP
TORIES
TORINO
TOROID
TOROSE
TORPID
TORPOR
TORQUE
TORRES
TORREY
TORRID
TORSOS
TORTES
TOSSED
TOSSER
TOSSES
TOSSUP
TOTALS
TOTEMS
TOTERS
TOTHER
TOTING
TOTSUP
TOTTED
TOTTER
TOUCAN
TOUCHE
TOUCHY
TOUGHS
TOUGHY
TOULON
TOUPEE
TOURED
TOURER
TOUSLE
TOUTED
TOUTER
TOWAGE
TOWARD
TOWCAR
TOWELS
TOWERS
TOWERY
TOWHEE
TOWING
TOWNER
TOWNIE
TOXICS
TOXINS
TOYDOG
TOYING
TOYONS
TOYOTA

T•O•••

TAOISM
TAOIST
TBONDS
TBONES
THOLES
THOMAS
THONGS
THORAX
THORNS
THORNY
THORPE
THORPS
THOUGH
TNOTES
TOOBAD
TOOKIN
TOOKIT
TOOKON
TOOKTO
TOOKUP
TOOLED
TOOLUP
TOONIE
TOOTED
TOOTER
TOOTHY
TOOTLE
TOOTOO
TOOTSY
TROCAR
TROCHE
TROGON
TROIKA
TROJAN
TROLLS
TROMPE
TROMPS
TROOPS
TROPES
TROPEZ
TROPHY
TROPIC
TROPPO
TROTHS
TROUGH
TROUPE
TROUTS
TROUVE
TROVES
TROWED
TROWEL
TWOBIT
TWOFER
TWOPLY
TWOWAY

T••O••

TABOOS
TABORS
TACOMA
TAGORE
TAGOUT
TALONS
TANOAK
TANOAN
TAPOFF
TAPOUT
TAROTS
TAUONS
TEEOFF
TENONS
TENORS
TETONS
THEORY
THROAT
THROBS
THROES
THRONE
THRONG
THROVE
THROWN
THROWS
TIPOFF
TIVOLI
TOBOOT
TOPOFF
TOPOUT
TOROID
TOROSE
TOYONS
TOYOTA
TRIODE
TROOPS
TRYOUT
TUDORS
TUTORS
TYCOBB
TYCOON
TYRONE

T•••O•

TABOOS
TACKON
TAILOR
TAINOS
TAKEON
TALBOT
TALION
TALLOW
TANGOS
TARPON
TATTOO
TAUTOG
TAYLOR
TEAPOT
TEAPOY
TEFLON
TELLOF
TELLON
TEMPOS
TENDON
TENSOR
TERROR
TEUTON
THETOY
TIEROD
TIGLON
TINGOD
TINPOT
TIPTOE
TIPTOP
TLALOC
TOBOOT
TOLDOF
TOLDON
TOMBOY
TOMTOM
TONDOS
TOOKON
TOOTOO
TOPDOG
TOPJOB
TORPOR
TORSOS
TOULON
TOYDOG
TREMOR
TREVOR
TRICOT
TRIGON
TRIPOD
TRIPOS
TRITON
TROGON
TRYFOR
TRYLON
TUCSON
TURBOS
TURBOT
TURGOR
TURNON
TVSHOW
TYCOON
TYDBOL

T••••O

TAKETO
TALKTO
TAMAYO
TATTOO
TECHNO
TEJANO
TENDTO
TENUTO
TERATO
TEREDO
TEXACO
THERMO
TIEDTO
TIESTO
TOBAGO
TODDAO
TOLEDO
TOMATO
TOOKTO
TOOTOO
TORERO
TORINO
TRICHO
TROPPO
TUPELO
TURNTO
TUXEDO

•TO•••

ATODDS
ATOLLS
ATOMIC
ATONAL
ATONCE
ATONED
ATONES
ATONIC
ETOILE
ETONIC
OTOOLE
STOATS
STOCKS
STOCKY
STODGE
STODGY
STOGIE
STOICS
STOJKO
STOKED
STOKER
STOKES
STOLEN
STOLES
STOLID
STOLLE
STOLON
STOMAS
STOMAT
STOMPS
STONED
STONER
STONES
STOOGE
STOOKS
STOOLS
STOOLY
STOOPS
STOPES
STOPIN
STOPIT
STOPUP
STORCH
STORED
STORER
STORES
STOREY
STORKS
STORMS
STORMY
STORRS
STOTIN
STOUPS
STOUTS
STOVER
STOVES
STOWED
UTOPIA

•T•O••

ATCOST
ATEOUT
ATHOME
ATMOST
ATWOOD
ATWORK
FTROOP
FSTOPS
OTIOSE
OTOOLE
PTBOAT
STJOAN
STJOHN
STOOGE
STOOKS
STOOLS
STOOLY
STOOPS
STROBE
STRODE
STROKE
STROLL
STRONG
STROPS
STROUD
STROVE
UTMOST

•T••O•

ATWOOD
ETHNOS
ETUXOR
ETYMOL
ETYMON
FTROOP
STATOR
STAYON
STEFOY
STENOG
STENOS
STEPON
STEROL
STOLON
STUPOR
STYRON

•T•••O

ATEMPO
ATERGO
OTELLO
STELMO
STEREO
STERNO
STHENO
STINGO
STMALO
STOJKO
STRABO
STRATO
STUCCO
STUDIO

••TO••

ACTONE
ACTORS
ACTOUT
ANTONY
ARTOIS
BATONS
BETONY
BETOOK
BITOFF
BITOLA
CUTOFF
CUTOUT
DATONG
DETOUR
EATOUT
ENTOMO
ESTOPS
EXTOLS
EXTORT
FSTOPS
FUTONS
GATORS
GETOFF
GETOUT
GOTOFF
GOTOIT
GOTOUT
HITOUT
INTONE
INTOTO
INTOWN
KETONE
LATONA
LATOUR
LATOYA
LETOFF
LETOUT
LITOUT
METOPE
MOTORS
MOTOWN
OCTOPI
ONTOUR
OPTOUT
PATOIS
PITONS
POTOSI
PUTOFF
PUTONS
PUTOUT
RETOLD
RETOOK
RETOOL
RETOPS
RETORT
RETOUR
RETOWS
ROTORS
SATORI
SATOUT
SETOFF
SETOSE
SETOUT
SITOUT
SOTOLS
TETONS
TUTORS
UNTOLD
UNTORN
UPTOWN
VETOED
VETOER
VETOES

••T•O•

ACTION
ACTSON
ANTCOW
ANTRON
ASTROS
AUTHOR
BATBOY
BATHOS
BETOOK
BETSON
BETTOR
BOTTOM
BUTEOS
BUTTON
CATION
CATTON
CITRON
COTTON
DETROP
DITTOS
DOTEON
FATHOM
GETSON
HATBOX
HATHOR
HITSON
HOTBOX
HOTDOG
HOTPOT
HOTROD
HUTTON
INTROS
JETSON
KITFOX
LETSON
LITHOG
LITHOS
LOTION
LOTTOS
LUTHOR
LYTTON
MATRON
MATZOH
MATZOS
METEOR
METHOD
METROS
MOTION
MOTMOT
MOTTOS
MUTTON
MYTHOI
MYTHOL
MYTHOS
NATION
NATRON
NETTON
NOTION
NOTNOW
OCTROI
OPTFOR
OPTION
OUTBOX
OUTFOX
PATHOL
PATHOS
PATIOS
PATMOS
PATROL
PATRON
PATTON
PETROG
PETROL
POTION
POTTOS
PUTSON
PYTHON
RATION
RATIOS
RATSON
RETOOK
RETOOL
RETROS
RETTON
SETSON
SETTOS
SITCOM
SITSON
SUTTON
TATTOO
UNTROD
WATSON
WETMOP

••T••O

ACTINO
ACTTWO
ANTERO
ARTHRO
ARTURO
CITATO
ENTERO
ENTOMO
GETSTO
GITANO
HETERO
INTOTO
JETHRO
LATIGO
LATINO
LETSGO
MUTATO
OCTAVO
POTATO
PUTSTO
ROTHKO
TATTOO
ULTIMO

•••TO•

AMATOL
BARTOK
BARTON
BEATON
BENTON
BESTOW
BETTOR
BIGTOE
BIGTOP
BOLTON
BONTON
BOSTON
BOTTOM
BOXTOP
BRETON
BRITON
BURTON
BUTTON
CANTON
CANTOR
CANTOS
CAPTOR
CARTON
CASTON
CASTOR
CATTON
CAXTON
CENTOS
CESTOS
CHITON
COTTON
CROTON
CUSTOM
CUSTOS
DALTON
DANTON
DAYTON
DEBTOR
DENTON
DIATOM
DITTOS
DOCTOR
EASTON
EDITOR
EMPTOR
FACTOR
FOETOR
FRITOS
FULTON
GASTON
GROTON
HECTOR
HESTON
HILTON
HINTON
HORTON
HOWTOS
HUSTON
HUTTON
JUNTOS
KANTOR
KEATON
KENTON
KEPTON
KOWTOW
LAPTOP
LAWTON
LECTOR
LEPTON
LICTOR
LIPTON
LISTON
LOTTOS
LYTTON
MADTOM
MELTON
MENTOR
MERTON
MILTON
MOPTOP
MORTON
MOTTOS
MOUTON
MUTTON
NEKTON
NESTOR
NETTON
NEWTON
NORTON
ORATOR
PANTOS
PARTON
PASTOR
PATTON
PAXTON
PEGTOP
PESTOS
PEYTON
PHOTOG
PHOTON
PHOTOS
PINTOS
PISTOL
PISTON
POPTOP
POSTON
POTTOS
PROTON
RAGTOP
RAPTOR
RECTOR
RECTOS
REDTOP
RESTON
RETTON
RHETOR
RHYTON
ROSTOV
SALTON
SANTOS
SARTON
SEATON
SECTOR
SESTOS
SETTOS
SEXTON
SKITOW
SORTOF
STATOR
SUITOR
SUTTON
TATTOO
TAUTOG
TEUTON
THETOY
TIPTOE
TIPTOP
TOMTOM
TOOTOO
TRITON
UNSTOP
VECTOR
VICTOR
VINTON
VOSTOK
WAITON
WALTON
WANTON
WENTON
WILTON
WONTON
WYNTON
YOMTOV

•••T•O

ACTTWO
ANATTO
AUSTRO
BHUTTO
BISTRO
BLOTTO
CASTRO
CENTRO
CLOTHO
DEXTRO
EDITIO
GASTRO
GHETTO
GIOTTO
GROTTO
INITIO
NEXTTO
ONETWO
PIETRO
SCOTTO
TATTOO
TOOTOO
WANTTO
XANTHO

••••TO

ADDSTO
AIMSTO
ALECTO
ALIOTO
AMBATO
ANATTO
ARISTO
BENITO
BHUTTO
BLOTTO
BONITO
CAMETO
CARETO
CITATO
COGITO
COMETO
CRISTO
CRYPTO
DAMATO
DARETO
DESOTO
DEVITO
DEVOTO
EXACTO
EXVOTO
FALLTO
FELLTO
FINITO
GEARTO
GELATO
GETSTO
GHETTO
GIOTTO
GIVETO
GOINTO
GROTTO
HELDTO
HEMATO
HERETO
HOLDTO

HOVETO INTOTO KEEPTO LAIDTO LAYSTO LEADTO LEANTO LEGATO LIESTO LOOKTO MAPUTO MRMOTO MUTATO NEARTO NEMATO NEXTTO NOVATO ODONTO OPENTO OPORTO PARETO PASHTO POTATO PRESTO PRONTO PUERTO PUTSTO QUARTO RABATO RIALTO RIGHTO RUBATO RUNSTO SABATO SANGTO SCOTTO SEENTO SEESTO SHINTO SHORTO SINGTO SMALTO SNAPTO SOASTO SOMATO SOWETO SPINTO STRATO SUBITO TAKETO TALKTO TENDTO TENUTO TERATO TIEDTO TIESTO TOMATO TOOKTO TURNTO USEDTO VENETO WANTTO WISETO

T•P•••

TAPERS TAPING TAPINS TAPIRS TAPOFF TAPOUT TAPPAN TAPPED TAPPER TAPPET TEPALS TEPEES TEPHRA TIPINS TIPOFF TIPPED TIPPER TIPPET TIPPLE TIPSIN TIPTOE TIPTOP TIPUPS TOPCAT TOPDOG TOPEKA TOPERS TOPGUN TOPHAT TOPHUS TOPICS TOPJOB TOPOFF TOPOUT TOPPED TOPPER TOPPLE TOPTEN TUPELO TUPIAN TYPERS TYPEUP TYPHUS TYPIER TYPIFY TYPING TYPIST

T••P••

TAIPAN TAIPEI TAMPED TAMPER TAPPAN TAPPED TAPPER TAPPET TARPAN TARPIT TARPON TAUPES TEAPOT TEAPOY TEMPED TEMPEH TEMPER TEMPLE TEMPOS TEMPTS TEMPUS TENPIN TIEPIN TINPAN TINPOT TIPPED TIPPER TIPPET TIPPLE TOPPED TOPPER TOPPLE TORPID TORPOR TOUPEE TRAPPY TREPAN TREPID TRIPLE TRIPLY TRIPOD TRIPOS TRIPUP TROPES TROPEZ TROPHY TROPIC TROPPO TURPIN TWOPLY

T•••P•

TERAPH THORPE THORPS THRIPS THUMPS TIEUPS TIPUPS TRAMPS TRAPPY TROMPE TROMPS TROOPS TROPPO TROUPE TRUMPS TULIPS TWERPS

T••••P

TAGSUP TAKEUP TALKUP TANKUP TEACUP TEAMUP TEARUP TEEDUP TEESUP THELIP TIDYUP TIEDUP TIESUP TIPTOP TITTUP TOECAP TOETAP TONEUP TOOKUP TOOLUP TOREUP TOSSUP TOTSUP TRICEP TRIPUP TUNEUP TURNIP TURNUP TYPEUP

•TP•••

STPAUL STPETE

•T•P••

ETAPES STAPES STAPLE STAPUF STEPIN STEPON STEPPE STEPUP STIPEL STIPES STOPES STOPIN STOPIT STOPUP STUPAS STUPES STUPID STUPOR UTOPIA

•T••P•

ATEMPO PTRAPS STAMPS STEEPS STEPPE STIMPY STOMPS STOOPS STOUPS STRAPS STRIPE STRIPS STRIPY STROPS STUMPS STUMPY

•T•••P

FTROOP STAYUP STEPUP STIRUP STOPUP STREEP

••TP••

HATPIN HOTPOT NETPAY OUTPUT POTPIE PUTPUT

••T•P•

CUTUPS ECTYPE ESTOPS FSTOPS GETUPS LETUPS METOPE OCTOPI ONTAPE RETAPE RETAPS RETOPS RETYPE SETUPS SITUPS

••T••P

ACTSUP ANTEUP BITMAP CATNAP CATNIP CATSUP CUTSUP DETROP EATSUP ENTRAP GETSUP HITSUP HOTCAP HOTTIP LETSUP PUTSUP SATRAP SETSUP SITSUP TITTUP TOTSUP UNTRAP WETMOP

•••T•P

BEATUP BIGTOP BOOTUP BOXTOP CHATUP DUSTUP HEATUP HOTTIP INSTEP KEPTUP LAPTOP LIFTUP MOPTOP PEGTOP PENTUP POPTOP RAGTOP REDTOP RESTUP SENTUP SHOTUP SHUTUP SUITUP TIPTOP TITTUP TOETAP UNSTOP WAITUP WENTUP

T•Q•••

TOQUES TUQUES

T••Q••

TORQUE

•T••Q•

ETSEQQ

•T•••Q

ETSEQQ

TR••••

TRACED TRACER TRACES TRACEY TRACHY TRACKS TRACTS TRADED TRADER TRADES TRAGIC TRAILS TRAINS TRAITS TRAJAN TRALEE TRAMPS TRANCE TRAPPY TRASHY TRAUMA TRAVEL TRAVES TRAVIS TRAWLS TREADS TREATS TREATY TREBEK TREBLE TREBLY TREDIA TREMOR TRENCH TRENDS TRENDY TREPAN TREPID TREVOR TRIADS TRIAGE TRIALS TRIBAL TRIBES TRICED TRICEP TRICES TRICHO TRICIA TRICKS TRICKY TRICOT TRIERS TRIFID TRIFLE TRIGLY TRIGON TRIJET TRIKES TRILBY TRILLS TRIMLY TRINAL TRINES TRIODE TRIPLE TRIPLY TRIPOD TRIPOS TRIPUP TRISHA TRISTE TRITER TRITON TRIUNE TRIVET TRIVIA TRIXIE TROCAR TROCHE TROGON TROIKA TROJAN TROLLS TROMPE TROMPS TROOPS TROPES TROPEZ TROPHY TROPIC TROPPO TROTHS TROUGH TROUPE TROUTS TROUVE TROVES TROWED TROWEL TRUANT TRUCES TRUCKS TRUDGE TRUEST TRUING TRUISM TRUMAN TRUMPS TRUNKS TRUSTS TRUSTY TRUTHS TRYFOR TRYING TRYLON TRYOUT TRYSTS

T•R•••

TARAWA TARGES TARGET TARIFF TARING TARMAC TAROTS TARPAN TARPIT TARPON TARRED TARSAL TARSUS TARTAN TARTAR TARTER TARTLY TARZAN TERAPH TERATO TERCEL TERCET TEREDO TERESA TERETE TEREUS TERKEL TERMED TERNES TERRAN TERRET TERROR TERSER THRACE THRALE THRALL THRASH THREAD THREAT THREED THREES THRESH THRICE THRIFT THRILL THRIPS THRIVE THROAT THROBS THROES THRONE THRONG THROVE THROWN THROWS THRUMS THRUSH THRUST TIRADE TIRANA TIRANE TIRING TORAHS TORCHY TOREAT TORERO TOREUP TORIES TORINO TOROID TOROSE TORPID TORPOR TORQUE TORRES TORREY TORRID TORSOS TORTES TURBAN TURBID TURBIT TURBOS TURBOT TUREEN TURFED TURGID TURGOR TURING TURKEY TURKIC TURNED TURNER TURNIN TURNIP TURNON TURNTO TURNUP TURPIN TURRET TURTLE TURVES TYRANT TYRIAN TYRONE

T••R••

TABRIZ TARRED TAURUS TAYRAS TBIRDS TEARAT TEARED TEARUP TENREC TERRAN TERRET TERROR TETRAD TETRAS TETRIS THERES THERMO THERMS THIRDS THIRST THIRTY THORAX THORNS THORNY THORPE THORPS THYRSI TIARAS TIERCE TIERED TIEROD TIERRA TIGRIS TITRED TITRES TOBRUK TORRES TORREY TORRID TOURED TOURER TSURIS TUAREG TUGRIK TURRET TWERPS TWIRLS

T•••R•

TABARD TABORS TAGORE TAKERS TALERS TAMARA TAMERS TANTRA TAPERS TAPIRS TASERS TATARS TATERS TAVERN TAWDRY TAXERS TENORS TENURE TEPHRA THEIRS THEORY THEYRE THWART TIERRA TIGERS TILERS TIMBRE TIMERS TISHRI TITERS TONERS TOPERS TORERO TOTERS TOWARD TOWERS TOWERY TRIERS TSHIRT TUBERS TUDORS TULARE TUNDRA TUNERS TUTORS TUYERE TYPERS

T••••R

TACKER TAILOR TALKER TALLER TAMPER TANKER TANNER TAPPER TARTAR TARTER TASTER TATTER TAUTER TAYLOR TEASER TEDDER TEENER TEETER TELLER TEMPER TENDER TENSER TENSOR TENTER TERROR TERSER TESTER TETHER THALER THAYER THENAR TICKER TIDIER TIGGER TILLER TILTER TIMBER TINDER TINEAR TINIER TINKER TINNER TINTER TIPPER TITFER TITHER TITTER TOILER TONIER TOOTER TOPPER TORPOR TOSSER TOTHER TOTTER TOURER TOUTER TOWCAR TOWNER TRACER TRADER TREMOR TREVOR TRITER TROCAR TRYFOR TUCKER TUGGER TURGOR TURNER TUSKER TWOFER TYPIER

•TR•••

ATREST ATREUS ATRIAL ATRISK ATRIUM FTROOP PTRAPS STRABO STRADS STRAFE STRAIN STRAIT STRAKE STRAND STRAPS STRASS STRATA STRATI STRATO STRAUB STRAUS STRAWS STRAWY STRAYS STREAK STREAM STREEP STREET STRESS STREWN STREWS STRIAE STRICK STRICT STRIDE STRIFE STRIKE STRINE STRING STRIPE STRIPS STRIPY STRIVE STROBE STRODE STROKE STROLL STRONG STROPS STROUD STROVE STRUCK STRUMS STRUNG STRUTS

•T•R••

ATERGO ATTRIT ETERNE ITURBI STARCH STARED STARER STARES STARRY STARTS STARVE STEREO STERES STERNA STERNE STERNO STERNS STEROL STIRIN STIRKS STIRUP STORCH STORED STORER STORES STOREY STORKS STORMS STORMY STORRS STURDY STYRIA STYRON UTURNS

•T••R•

ATTARS ATTIRE ATWORK ETHERS OTHERS OTTERS STAIRS STARRY STEERS STMARK STORRS STUART UTTERS

•T•••R

ETCHER ETUXOR STAGER STALER STARER STATER STATOR STELAR STEWER STIVER STOKER STONER STORER STOVER STUMER STUPOR STYLER

••TR••

AMTRAC AMTRAK ANTRES ANTRIM ANTRON ANTRUM ASTRAL ASTRAY ASTRID ASTROS ATTRIT BETRAY BOTREE CATRIG CITRIC CITRON CITRUS DETROP ENTRAP ENTREE ESTRAY EXTRAS HATRED HOTROD IATRIC INTROS ISTRIA LITRES MATRIX MATRON METRES METRIC METROS MITRAL MITRED MITRES NATRON NITRES NITRIC NUTRIA OCTROI OUTRAN OUTRUN PATROL PATRON PETREL PETRIE PETROG PETROL PUTRID RETRAL RETRIM RETROS SATRAP SUTRAS TETRAD TETRAS TETRIS TITRED TITRES ULTRAS UNTRAP UNTROD UNTRUE VITRIC

••T•R•

ACTORS ALTARS ALTERS ANTERO ARTERY ARTHRO ARTURO ASTERN ASTERS ATTARS ATTIRE BITERS CATERS CETERA CITERS DATARY DATERS DATURA DETERS DOTARD EATERS EATERY ENTERO ENTERS ENTIRE ESTERS EXTERN EXTORT FUTURE GATERS GATORS HATARI HATERS HETERO INTERJ INTERN INTURN JETHRO KITERS LITERS MATERS MATURE METERS MITERS MOTHRA MOTORS NATURA NATURE NITERS NITERY NOTARY NOTERS OATERS OTTERS OUTCRY PATERS PETARD PETERS QATARI RATERS RETARD RETARS RETIRE RETORT RETURN RITARD ROTARY ROTORS SATIRE SATORI SATURN SATYRS SITARS SUTURE TATARS TATERS TITERS TOTERS TUTORS UNTORN UPTURN UTTERS VOTARY VOTERS WATERS WATERY

••T••R

AETHER ALTAIR ANTHER ANTLER ARTHUR ARTIER AUTEUR AUTHOR BATHER BATTER BETTER BETTOR BITTER BOTHER BUTLER BUTTER CATHER COTTER CUTLER CUTTER DETOUR DITHER EITHER ESTHER FATHER FATTER FETTER FITTER GATHER GETTER GUTTER HATHOR HATTER HITHER HITTER HOTAIR HOTCAR HOTTER HOTWAR JITTER KOTTER LATHER LATOUR LATTER LETTER LITTER LOTHAR LUTHER LUTHOR MATHER MATTER METEOR METIER MOTHER MUTTER NATTER NETHER NUTTER OATIER ONTOUR OPTFOR OSTLER PATTER PETTER PITIER PITTER POTHER POTTER PUTTER RATEDR RATHER RATTER RETEAR RETOUR RITTER ROTTER RUTGER SETTER SITTER SUTLER SUTTER TATTER TETHER TITFER TITHER TITTER TOTHER TOTTER VETOER WETBAR WETHER WETTER WITHER ZITHER

•••TR•

ANITRA AUSTRO BISTRO CASTRO CENTRE CENTRI CENTRO CONTRA CONTRE DESTRY DEXTRO DMITRI GANTRY GASTRO GENTRY GUITRY LUSTRE MAITRE MANTRA PALTRY PANTRY PASTRY PELTRY PIETRO POETRY ROSTRA SARTRE SENTRA SENTRY SISTRA SULTRY TANTRA VESTRY WINTRY

•••T•R

ALITER AVATAR BANTER BARTER BASTER BATTER BAXTER BEATER

BESTIR
BETTER
BETTOR
BITTER
BOATER
BUNTER
BUSTER
BUTTER
CANTER
CANTOR
CAPTOR
CARTER
CASTER
CASTOR
CENTER
COLTER
COOTER
COPTER
COSTAR
COTTER
COUTER
CRATER
CURTER
CUSTER
CUTTER
DAFTER
DARTER
DEBTOR
DEFTER
DEXTER
DIETER
DOCTOR
DUSTER
EASTER
EDITOR
ELATER
EMOTER
EMPTOR
EXETER
FACTOR
FALTER
FASTER
FATTER
FESTER
FETTER
FILTER
FITTER
FOETOR
FOOTER
FOSTER
GAITER
GARTER
GETTER
GRATER
GUITAR
GUNTER
GUTTER
HALTER
HATTER
HEATER
HECTOR
HELTER
HESTER
HINTER
HITTER
HOOTER
HOTTER
HUNTER
INSTAR
IRATER
ISHTAR
JEETER
JESTER
JITTER
JUSTER
KANTOR
KILTER
KOTTER
KRATER
KULTUR
LATTER
LECTER
LECTOR
LESTER
LETTER
LICTOR
LIFTER
LINTER
LISTER
LITTER
LOITER
LOOTER
LUSTER
MARTYR
MASTER
MATTER
MEETER
MENTOR
MINTER
MISTER
MOLTER
MORTAR
MUSTER
MUTTER
NATTER
NEATER
NECTAR
NESTER
NESTOR
NEUTER
NUTTER
OBITER
OERTER
ORATOR
OUSTER
OYSTER
PALTER
PASTOR
PATTER
PELTER
PERTER
PESTER
PETTER
PEWTER
PIETER
PINTER
PITTER
PLATER
PORTER
POSTER
POTTER
POUTER
PRATER
PRETER
PUNTER
PUTTER
QINTAR
QUOTER
RAFTER
RANTER
RAPTOR
RASTER
RATTER
RECTOR
RENTER
RESTER
REUTER
RHETOR
RIOTER
RITTER
ROOTER
ROSTER
ROTTER
ROUTER
SALTER
SANTIR
SCOTER
SEATER
SECTOR
SETTER
SIFTER
SINTER
SISTER
SITTER
SKATER
SLATER
SOFTER
SORTER
SOUTER
STATER
STATOR
SUITOR
SUMTER
SUTTER
TARTAR
TARTER
TASTER
TATTER
TAUTER
TEETER
TENTER
TESTER
TILTER
TINTER
TITTER
TOOTER
TOTTER
TOUTER
TRITER
ULSTER
UNITER
VASTER
VECTOR
VENTER
VICTOR
WAITER
WALTER
WASTER
WELTER
WETTER
WHITER
WINTER
WISTER
WRITER
WYNTER
XYSTER
YESTER

TS••••

TSETSE
TSHIRT
TSURIS

T•S•••

TASERS
TASKED
TASMAN
TASSEL
TASSES
TASTED
TASTER
TASTES
TESLAS
TESSIE
TESTAE
TESTED
TESTEE
TESTER
TISANE
TISHRI
TISSUE
TOSSED
TOSSER
TOSSES
TOSSUP
TUSCAN
TUSKED
TUSKER
TUSSAH
TUSSLE
TVSETS
TVSHOW

T••S••

TAGSUP
TARSAL
TARSUS
TASSEL
TASSES
TEASED
TEASEL
TEASER
TEASES
TEASET
TEESUP
TENSED
TENSER
TENSES
TENSOR
TERSER
TESSIE
THESEA
THESES
THESIS
THESIX
THISBE
THUSLY
TIESIN
TIESTO
TIESUP
TILSIT
TINSEL
TIPSIN
TISSUE
TMESIS
TOASTS
TOASTY
TOCSIN
TOESIN
TONSIL
TORSOS
TOSSED
TOSSER
TOSSES
TOSSUP
TOTSUP
TOUSLE
TRASHY
TRISHA
TRISTE
TRUSTS
TRUSTY
TRYSTS
TUCSON
TULSAN
TUSSAH
TUSSLE
TWISTS
TWISTY

T•••S•

TALESE
TAMEST
TANIST
TAOISM
TAOIST
TEENSY
TERESA
THEISM
THEIST
THIRST
THRASH
THRESH
THRUSH
THRUST
THYRSI
TONISH
TOOTSY
TOROSE
TRUEST
TRUISM
TSETSE
TUBIST
TWEEST
TYPIST
TZUHSI

T••••S

TABLAS
TABLES
TABOOS
TABORS
TAIGAS
TAINOS
TAINTS
TAKERS
TAKINS
TALERS
TALONS
TAMERS
TAMILS
TANGOS
TANKAS
TANTES
TAPERS
TAPINS
TAPIRS
TARGES
TAROTS
TARSUS
TASERS
TASSES
TASTES
TATARS
TATERS
TAUNTS
TAUONS
TAUPES
TAURUS
TAXERS
TAXIES
TAYRAS
TAZZAS
TBILLS
TBIRDS
TBONDS
TBONES
TEASES
TEHEES
TEMPOS
TEMPTS
TEMPUS
TENENS
TENETS
TENNIS
TENONS
TENORS
TENSES
TENTHS
TEPALS
TEPEES
TEREUS
TERNES
TESLAS
TETHYS
TETONS
TETRAS
TETRIS
TEXANS
THALES
THAMES
THANES
THANKS
THATIS
THEBES
THEFTS
THEIRS
THEMES
THERES
THERMS
THESES
THESIS
THETAS
THETIS
THIGHS
THILLS
THINGS
THINKS
THIRDS
THOLES
THOMAS
THONGS
THORNS
THORPS
THREES
THRIPS
THROBS
THROES
THROWS
THRUMS
THUJAS
THUMBS
THUMPS
THUNKS
THYMUS
TIARAS
TIBIAS
TICALS
TIDIES
TIEINS
TIEUPS
TIGERS
TIGHTS
TIGRIS
TILAKS
TILDES
TILERS
TILLIS
TIMERS
TINCTS
TINGES
TIPINS
TIPUPS
TITANS
TITERS
TITHES
TITLES
TITRES
TMESIS
TNOTES
TOASTS
TOBIAS
TOBIES
TOEINS
TOILES
TOKAYS
TOKENS
TOKLAS
TONDOS
TONERS
TONICS
TONNES
TOPERS
TOPHUS
TOPICS
TOQUES
TORAHS
TORIES
TORRES
TORSOS
TORTES
TOSSES
TOTALS
TOTEMS
TOTERS
TOUGHS
TOWELS
TOWERS
TOXICS
TOXINS
TOYONS
TRACES
TRACKS
TRACTS
TRADES
TRAILS
TRAINS
TRAITS
TRAMPS
TRAVES
TRAVIS
TRAWLS
TREADS
TREATS
TRENDS
TRIADS
TRIALS
TRIBES
TRICES
TRICKS
TRIERS
TRIKES
TRILLS
TRINES
TRIPOS
TROLLS
TROMPS
TROOPS
TROPES
TROTHS
TROUTS
TROVES
TRUCES
TRUCKS
TRUMPS
TRUNKS
TRUSTS
TRUTHS
TRYSTS
TSURIS
TUBERS
TUDORS
TULIPS
TULLES
TUNERS
TUNICS
TUQUES
TURBOS
TURVES
TUTORS
TVSETS
TWANGS
TWEAKS
TWEEDS
TWEENS
TWEETS
TWERPS
TWILLS
TWINES
TWIRLS
TWISTS
TYPERS
TYPHUS

•TS•••

ATSTUD
ETSEQQ
ITSELF

•T•S••

ATESTS
ITASCA
STASES
STASIS

•T••S•

ATBEST
ATCOST
ATEASE
ATLAST
ATMOST
ATREST
ATRISK
ATTEST
OTIOSE
STRASS
STRESS
UTMOST

•T•••S

ATBATS
ATEAMS
ATESTS
ATHENS
ATKINS
ATODDS
ATOLLS
ATONES
ATREUS
ATTARS
ATTICS
ETAPES
ETCHES
ETHERS
ETHICS
ETHNOS
ETUDES
ITCHES
OTHERS
OTITIS
OTTERS
PTRAPS
STACKS
STAFFS
STAGES
STAINS
STAIRS
STAKES
STALES
STALKS
STALLS
STAMPS
STANDS
STAPES
STARES
STARTS
STASES
STASIS
STATES
STATUS
STAVES
STEADS
STEAKS
STEALS
STEAMS
STEEDS
STEELS
STEEPS
STEERS
STEINS
STELES
STENOS
STERES
STERNS
STICKS
STIFFS
STILES
STILLS
STILTS
STINGS
STINKS
STINTS
STIPES
STIRKS
STOATS
STOCKS
STOICS
STOKES
STOLES
STOMAS
STOMPS
STONES
STOOKS
STOOLS
STOOPS
STOPES
STORES
STORKS
STORMS
STORRS
STOUPS
STOUTS
STOVES
STRADS
STRAPS
STRASS
STRAUS
STRAWS
STRAYS
STRESS
STREWS
STRIPS
STROPS
STRUMS
STRUTS
STUFFS
STULLS
STUMPS
STUNTS
STUPAS
STUPES
STYLES
STYLUS
UTTERS
UTURNS

••TS••

ACTSAS
ACTSON
ACTSUP
BETSEY
BETSON
CATSUP
CUTSIN
CUTSUP
DATSUN
EATSAT
EATSIN
EATSUP
FITSIN
GATSBY
GETSAT
GETSBY
GETSET
GETSIN
GETSIT
GETSON
GETSTO
GETSUP
GOTSET
HITSIT
HITSON
HITSUP
JETSAM
JETSET
JETSKI
JETSON
KITSCH
LETSAT
LETSBE
LETSGO
LETSIN
LETSON
LETSUP
OUTSET
PITSAW
PUTSBY
PUTSCH
PUTSIN
PUTSON
PUTSTO
PUTSUP
RATSON
SETSAT
SETSBY
SETSIN
SETSON
SETSUP
SITSBY
SITSIN
SITSON
SITSUP
TOTSUP
WATSON

••T•S•

APTEST
ARTIST
ATTEST
BETISE
CUTEST
CUTESY
DETEST
FETISH
IQTEST
IRTYSH
JUTISH
LATEST
LATISH
LUTIST
MUTEST
OBTEST
OBTUSE
POTASH
POTOSI
RETEST
SETOSE
WATUSI

••T••S

ACTORS
ACTSAS
ALTARS
ALTERS
ALTIUS
ANTICS
ANTRES
ARTELS
ARTOIS
ASTERS
ASTROS
ATTARS
ATTICS
AZTECS
BATHES
BATHOS
BATIKS
BATONS
BETELS
BETTAS
BITERS
BOTELS
BUTEOS
BUTTES
BUTUTS
CATERS
CITERS
CITIES
CITIUS
CITRUS
COTTAS
CUTIES
CUTINS
CUTUPS
DATERS
DETERS
DITTOS
DITZES
DUTIES
EATERS
ENTERS
ESTERS
ESTOPS
EXTOLS
EXTRAS
FATWAS
FSTOPS
FUTONS
FUTZES
GATERS
GATORS
GETUPS
HATERS
HOTELS
IDTAGS
INTENS
INTROS
ISTLES
KITERS
LATENS
LATHES
LATINS
LATKES
LETUPS
LITERS
LITHOS
LITMUS
LITRES
LOTAHS
LOTTOS
LUTZES
MATERS
MATEYS
MATHIS
MATINS
MATTES
MATZOS
METALS
METERS
METRES
METROS
MITERS
MITRES
MOTELS
MOTETS
MOTIFS
MOTORS
MOTTOS
MYTHOS
NITERS
NITRES
NOTERS
OATERS
OCTADS
OCTETS
OPTICS
ORTLES
OTTERS
PATENS
PATERS
PATHOS
PATIOS
PATMOS
PATOIS
PETALS
PETERS
PITIES
PITONS
POTTOS
PUTONS
RATELS
RATERS
RATIOS
RETAGS
RETAPS
RETARS
RETIES
RETOPS
RETOWS
RETROS
ROTORS
SATINS
SATYRS
SETINS
SETTOS
SETUPS
SITARS
SITINS
SITUPS
SOTOLS
SUTRAS
TATARS
TATERS
TETHYS
TETONS
TETRAS
TETRIS
TITANS
TITERS
TITHES
TITLES
TITRES
TOTALS
TOTEMS
TOTERS
TUTORS
ULTRAS
UNTIES
UTTERS
VETOES
VITALS
VOTERS
WATERS
WITHES

•••TS•

BOOTSY
BRATSK
CURTSY
LAOTSE
LHOTSE
TOOTSY
TSETSE

•••T•S

ABATES
ABATIS
AEETES
AGATES
AKITAS
AMATIS
AORTAS
ARETES
BANTUS
BASTES
BERTHS
BETTAS
BIOTAS
BIRTHS
BOITES
BOOTES
BOOTHS
BROTHS
BRUTES
BRUTUS
BUTTES
CACTUS
CANTOS
CARTES
CASTES
CENTOS
CESTAS
CESTOS
CESTUS
CHETHS
CHUTES
CLOTHS
CNOTES
COATIS
COMTES
CONTES
CORTES
COSTAS
COTTAS
CRATES
CURTIS
CUSTIS
CUSTOS
DANTES
DELTAS
DEPTHS
DHOTIS
DICTUS
DITTOS
ELATES
ELITES
ELUTES
EMOTES
ENATES
FAITHS
FESTAS
FESTUS
FIFTHS
FIRTHS
FLUTES
FOETUS
FORTAS
FORTES
FRITOS
FROTHS
GARTHS
GESTES
GIRTHS
GLUTES
GRATES
GRATIS
HASTES
HEATHS
HIATUS
HOSTAS
HOWTOS
JUNTAS
JUNTOS
KNOTTS
LOTTOS
MANTAS
MANTIS
MATTES
MENTIS
MONTES
MONTHS
MOTTOS
MOUTHS
MUFTIS
NANTES
NINTHS
NORTHS
ORATES
OTITIS
PANTOS
PASTAS
PASTES
PASTIS
PESTOS
PHOTOS
PIETAS
PINTOS
PISTES
PLATES
PONTES
PONTUS
POTTOS
PRATES
QANTAS
QUOTAS
QUOTES
REATAS
RECTOS
RECTUS
RIATAS
ROUTES
SANTOS
SAUTES
SCUTES
SESTOS
SETTOS
SIXTHS
SIXTUS
SKATES
SLATES
SLOTHS
SMITES
SMITHS
SNATHS
SOUTHS
SPATES
SPITES
STATES
STATUS
SUITES
SWATHS
TANTES
TASTES
TENTHS
THATIS
THETAS
THETIS
TNOTES
TORTES
TROTHS
TRUTHS
UINTAS
UNITAS
UNITES
VESTAS
VICTIS
VIRTUS
VISTAS
WASTES
WHITES
WIDTHS
WORTHS
WRATHS
WRITES
YENTAS
YOUTHS
ZLOTYS

••••TS

ABBOTS
ABORTS
ADAPTS
ADEPTS
ADMITS
ADOPTS
ADULTS
AFLATS
AFRITS
AGENTS
AGLETS
ALERTS
ALEUTS
ALLOTS
AMBITS
AMENTS
AMVETS
ARGOTS
ARMETS
ASCOTS
ASSETS
ATBATS
ATESTS
AUDITS
AUGHTS
AVERTS
AWAITS
BEASTS
BEAUTS
BEFITS
BEGETS
BERETS
BESETS
BESOTS
BIGHTS
BIGOTS
BLASTS
BLEATS
BLOATS
BLUETS
BLUNTS
BLURTS
BOASTS
BOOSTS
BRACTS
BRANTS
BRENTS
BRUITS
BRUNTS
BURSTS
BUTUTS
CADETS
CARATS
CARETS
CHANTS
CHARTS
CHEATS
CHESTS
CIVETS
CLEATS
CLEFTS
CLOUTS
COAPTS
COASTS
COMETS
COOPTS
COUNTS
COURTS
COVETS
CRAFTS
CRESTS
CROATS
CROFTS
CRUETS
CRUSTS
CRYPTS
CSPOTS
CUBITS
CULETS
DAUNTS
DAVITS
DEBITS
DEBUTS
DEFATS
DEISTS
DELFTS
DEMITS
DEPOTS
DICOTS
DIGITS
DIVOTS
DIXITS
DONETS
DONUTS
DOUBTS

DRAFTS
DRIFTS
DROITS
DUCATS
DUVETS
EBOATS
ECLATS
EDICTS
EFLATS
EGESTS
EGRETS
EIGHTS
EJECTS
ELECTS
EMMETS
ENACTS
ERECTS
ERGOTS
ERUCTS
ERUPTS
EVENTS
EVERTS
EVICTS
EXACTS
EXALTS
EXERTS
EXISTS
EXULTS
FACETS
FAGOTS
FAINTS
FAULTS
FEASTS
FEINTS
FIGHTS
FILETS
FIRSTS
FLEETS
FLINTS
FLIRTS
FLOATS
FLOUTS
FOISTS
FOUNTS
FRONTS
FROSTS
FRUITS
GAMUTS
GEMOTS
GENETS
GHOSTS
GIANTS
GIGOTS
GLINTS
GLOATS
GODETS
GRAFTS
GRANTS
GREATS
GREETS
GRIFTS
GRIOTS
GRISTS
GROATS
GROUTS
GRUNTS
GSUITS
GUESTS
GUYOTS
HABITS
HAUNTS
HEARTS
HEISTS
HELOTS
HOISTS
IDIOTS
INGOTS
INLETS
INPUTS
INSETS
INUITS
ISLETS
JABOTS
JAUNTS
JOINTS
JOISTS
JOUSTS
JURATS
KARATS
KARSTS
KNOTTS
KNOUTS
KORATS
KRAITS
LIEUTS
LIGHTS
LIMITS
MERITS
MOTETS
MOULTS
MOUNTS
MULCTS
NENETS
NIGHTS
NOHITS
NONETS
NOPETS
NYMETS
OCTETS
ODISTS
ONSETS
ORANTS
ORBITS
OUGHTS
OWLETS
PAINTS
PEWITS
PICOTS
PILOTS
PINOTS
PIPITS
PIVOTS
PLAITS
PLANTS
PLEATS
POINTS
POSITS
POULTS
PRINTS
QUARTS
QUESTS
QUIETS
QUILTS
QUINTS
QUIRTS
QUOITS
RAMETS
REACTS
REBUTS
REFITS
RELETS
REMITS
REPOTS
RESETS
REVETS
RIGHTS
RIVETS
ROASTS
ROBOTS
ROOSTS
ROUSTS
SABOTS
SAINTS
SAULTS
SCANTS
SCENTS
SCOOTS
SCOUTS
SHAFTS
SHEETS
SHIFTS
SHIRTS
SHOATS
SHOOTS
SHORTS
SHOUTS
SHUNTS
SIGHTS
SKIRTS
SKORTS
SLANTS
SLEETS
SMARTS
SMELTS
SMOLTS
SNOOTS
SNORTS
SNOUTS
SPLATS
SPLITS
SPORTS
SPOUTS
SPRATS
SPRITS
SPURTS
SQUATS
STARTS
STILTS
STINTS
STOATS
STOUTS
STRUTS
STUNTS
SWEATS
SWEETS
SWIFTS
TAINTS
TAROTS
TAUNTS
TEMPTS
TENETS
THEFTS
TIGHTS
TINCTS
TOASTS
TRACTS
TRAITS
TREATS
TROUTS
TRUSTS
TRYSTS
TVSETS
TWEETS
TWISTS
UBOATS
UBOLTS
UNFITS
UNIATS
UPSETS
VALETS
VAULTS
VAUNTS
VELDTS
VERSTS
VISITS
WAISTS
WHEATS
WIGHTS
WORSTS
WRESTS
WRISTS
WURSTS
YACHTS
YAKUTS
YEASTS
YOKUTS
ZIBETS

T•T•••
TATAMI
TATARS
TATERS
TATTED
TATTER
TATTLE
TATTOO
TETCHY
TETHER
TETHYS
TETONS
TETRAD
TETRAS
TETRIS
TETZEL
TITANS
TITBIT
TITERS
TITFER
TITHED
TITHER
TITHES
TITIAN
TITLED
TITLES
TITRED
TITRES
TITTER
TITTLE
TITTUP
TOTALS
TOTEMS
TOTERS
TOTHER
TOTING
TOTSUP
TOTTED
TOTTER
TUTORS
TUTTUT
TUTUED

T••T••
TACTIC
TAMTAM
TANTES
TANTRA
TARTAN
TARTAR
TARTER
TARTLY
TASTED
TASTER
TASTES
TATTED
TATTER
TATTLE
TATTOO
TAUTEN
TAUTER
TAUTLY
TAUTOG
TEETER
TEETHE
TENTED
TENTER
TENTHS
TESTAE
TESTED
TESTEE
TESTER
TEUTON
THATCH
THATIS
THATLL
THETAS
THETIC
THETIS
THETOY
TICTAC
TILTED
TILTER
TINTED
TINTER
TIPTOE
TIPTOP
TITTER
TITTLE
TITTUP
TNOTES
TOATEE
TOETAP
TOLTEC
TOMTIT
TOMTOM
TOOTED
TOOTER
TOOTHY
TOOTLE
TOOTOO
TOOTSY
TOPTEN
TORTES
TOTTED
TOTTER
TOUTED
TOUTER
TRITER
TRITON
TROTHS
TRUTHS
TSETSE
TUFTED
TURTLE
TUTTUT
TWITCH
TWITTY

T•••T•
TAHITI
TAINTS
TAKETH
TAKETO
TALKTO
TAROTS
TAUNTS
TEMPTS
TENDTO
TENETS
TENUTO
TERATO
TERETE
THEFTS
THIRTY
TIEDTO
TIESTO
TIGHTS
TINCTS
TOASTS
TOASTY
TODATE
TOMATO
TONITE
TOOKTO
TOYOTA
TRACTS
TRAITS
TREATS
TREATY
TRISTE
TROUTS
TRUSTS
TRUSTY
TRYSTS
TUBATE
TURNTO
TVSETS
TWEETS
TWEETY
TWENTY
TWISTS
TWISTY
TWITTY

T••••T
TABLET
TAGOUT
TALBOT
TALENT
TALKAT
TAMEST
TANIST
TAOIST
TAPOUT
TAPPET
TARGET
TARPIT
TAUGHT
TEAPOT
TEARAT
TEASET
TENANT
TERCET
TERRET
THEIST
THIRST
THREAT
THRIFT
THROAT
THRUST
THWART
TICKET
TIDBIT
TILSIT
TINHAT
TINPOT
TIPPET
TITBIT
TOBOOT
TOILET
TOMCAT
TOMTIT
TOOKIT
TOPCAT
TOPHAT
TOPOUT
TOREAT
TRICOT
TRIJET
TRIVET
TRUANT
TRUEST
TRYOUT
TSHIRT
TUBIST
TUCKET
TUFFET
TUMULT
TURBIT
TURBOT
TURRET
TUTTUT
TWEEST
TWILIT
TWOBIT
TYBALT
TYPIST
TYRANT

•TT•••
ATTACH
ATTACK
ATTAIN
ATTARS
ATTEND
ATTEST
ATTHAT
ATTICA
ATTICS
ATTILA
ATTIRE
ATTLEE
ATTRIT
ATTUNE
OTTAVA
OTTAWA
OTTERS
UTTERS

•T•T••
ATSTUD
OTITIC
OTITIS
STATED
STATEN
STATER
STATES
STATIC
STATOR
STATUE
STATUS
STITCH
STITHY
STOTIN

•T••T•
ATBATS
ATESTS
ATLATL
STACTE
STARTS
STILTS
STINTS
STOATS
STOUTS
STPETE
STRATA
STRATI
STRATO
STRUTS
STUNTS
STUNTY

•T•••T
ATBEST
ATCOST
ATEOUT
ATLAST
ATMOST
ATREST
ATTEST
ATTHAT
ATTRIT
PTBOAT
STABAT
STOMAT
STOPIT
STRAIT
STREET
STRICT
STUART
STYLET
UTHANT
UTMOST

••TT••
ACTTWO
BATTED
BATTEL
BATTEN
BATTER
BATTLE
BATTUE
BETTAS
BETTER
BETTOR
BITTED
BITTEN
BITTER
BOTTLE
BOTTOM
BUTTED
BUTTER
BUTTES
BUTTIN
BUTTON
CATTED
CATTLE
CATTON
COTTAS
COTTEN
COTTER
COTTON
CUTTER
DITTOS
DOTTED
DOTTIE
DOTTLE
FATTED
FATTEN
FATTER
FETTER
FETTLE
FITTED
FITTER
GETTER
GOTTEN
GUTTAE
GUTTED
GUTTER
HATTED
HATTER
HATTIE
HETTIE
HITTER
HOTTEA
HOTTER
HOTTIP
HOTTUB
HUTTED
HUTTON
JETTED
JITTER
JOTTED
JUTTED
KETTLE
KITTEN
KOTTER
LATTEN
LATTER
LETTED
LETTER
LITTER
LITTLE
LOTTED
LOTTOS
LYTTON
MATTEA
MATTED
MATTEL
MATTER
MATTES
MATTIE
METTLE
MITTEN
MOTTLE
MOTTOS
MUTTER
MUTTON
NATTER
NETTED
NETTLE
NETTLY
NETTON
NUTTED
NUTTER
PATTED
PATTEN
PATTER
PATTON
PETTED
PETTER
PETTIT
PITTED
PITTER
POTTED
POTTER
POTTLE
POTTOS
PUTTED
PUTTEE
PUTTER
RATTAN
RATTED
RATTER
RATTLE
RATTLY
RETTON
RITTER
ROTTED
ROTTEN
ROTTER
RUTTAN
RUTTED
SETTEE
SETTER
SETTLE
SETTOS
SITTER
SOTTED
SUTTER
SUTTON
TATTED
TATTER
TATTLE
TATTOO
TITTER
TITTLE
TITTUP
TOTTED
TOTTER
TUTTUT
VATTED
VETTED
WATTLE
WETTED
WETTER
WETTIG
WITTED

••T•T•
ASTUTE
BUTUTS
CITATO
ENTITY
ESTATE
GETSTO
INTOTO
METATE
MOTETS
MUTATE
MUTATO
NOTATE
NUTATE
OCTETS
OUTATE
PETITE
POTATO
PUTSTO
RATITE
ROTATE
SHTETL
UMTATA

••T••T
ACTOUT
APTEST
ARTIST
ATTEST
ATTHAT
ATTRIT
CATGUT
CUTEST
CUTLET
CUTOUT
DETECT
DETENT
DETEST
EATOUT
EATSAT
EXTANT
EXTENT
EXTORT
FATCAT
GETOUT
GETSAT
GETSET
GETSIT
GOTOIT
GOTOUT
GOTSET
HITOUT
HITSIT
HOTPOT
INTACT
INTENT
INTUIT
IQTEST
JETSET
KITKAT
LATENT
LATEST
LETOUT
LETSAT
LITOUT
LUTIST
MOTMOT
MUTANT
MUTEST
NATANT
NITWIT
NOTYET
NUTLET
OBTEST
OCTANT
OPTOUT
OUTACT
OUTEAT
OUTFIT
OUTHIT
OUTLET
OUTPUT
OUTSET
OUTWIT
PATENT
PETTIT
POTENT
PUTOUT
PUTPUT
RETEST
RETORT
ROTGUT
SATOUT
SETOUT
SETSAT
SITOUT
SOTHAT
TITBIT
TUTTUT
URTEXT
WITHIT

•••TT•
ANATTO
BEATTY
BHUTTO
BLATTY
BLOTTO
BLOTTY
BRATTY
CHATTY
CLOTTY
FRETTY
FRUTTI
GHETTO
GIOTTO
GNATTY
GRITTY
GROTTO
GROTTY
KNOTTS
KNOTTY
LIOTTA
NEXTTO
ODETTA
ODETTE
PLATTE
PLOTTY
PRETTY
QUETTA
SCATTY
SCOTTO
SCOTTY
SLITTY
SMUTTY
SNOTTY
SPOTTY
TWITTY
WANTTO
WHITTY
YVETTE

•••T•T
BEATIT
DIKTAT
HINTAT
HOOTAT
IGETIT
IGOTIT
KEPTAT
LESTAT
LOSTIT
MUSTNT
OBSTET
PETTIT
POSTIT
QUITIT
SEPTET
SESTET
SEXTET
SHOTAT
TOMTIT
TUTTUT
WENTAT

••••TT
ABBOTT
ALCOTT
ARNETT
CAVETT
DEWITT
EMMETT
JEWETT
JOWETT
LOVETT
MELOTT

TU••••
TUAREG
TUBATE
TUBBED
TUBERS
TUBING
TUBIST
TUBMAN
TUCANA
TUCHUN
TUCKED
TUCKER
TUCKET
TUCKIN
TUCSON
TUDORS
TUFFET
TUFTED
TUGGED
TUGGER
TUGRIK
TUILLE
TULANE
TULARE
TULIPS
TULLES
TULSAN
TUMBLE
TUMEFY
TUMMED
TUMULI
TUMULT
TUNDRA
TUNEIN
TUNERS
TUNEUP
TUNICA
TUNICS
TUNING
TUNNEL
TUNNEY
TUPELO
TUPIAN
TUQUES
TURBAN
TURBID
TURBIT
TURBOS
TURBOT
TUREEN
TURFED
TURGID
TURGOR
TURING
TURKEY
TURKIC
TURNED
TURNER
TURNIN
TURNIP
TURNON
TURNTO
TURNUP
TURPIN
TURRET
TURTLE
TURVES
TUSCAN
TUSKED
TUSKER
TUSSAH
TUSSLE
TUTORS
TUTTUT
TUTUED
TUVALU
TUXEDO
TUYERE

T•U•••
TAUGHT
TAUNTS
TAUONS
TAUPES
TAURUS
TAUTEN
TAUTER
TAUTLY
TAUTOG
TEUTON
THUJAS
THUMBS
THUMPS
THUNKS
THUSLY
TOUCAN
TOUCHE
TOUCHY
TOUGHS
TOUGHY
TOULON
TOUPEE
TOURED
TOURER
TOUSLE
TOUTED
TOUTER
TRUANT
TRUCES
TRUCKS
TRUDGE
TRUEST
TRUING
TRUISM
TRUMAN
TRUMPS
TRUNKS
TRUSTS
TRUSTY
TRUTHS
TSURIS
TZUHSI

T••U••
TABULA
TELUGU
TENURE
TENUTO
THOUGH
THRUMS
THRUSH
THRUST
TIEUPS
TIPUPS
TOLUCA
TOQUES
TRAUMA
TRIUNE
TROUGH
TROUPE
TROUTS
TROUVE
TUMULI
TUMULT
TUQUES
TUTUED

T•••U•
TAGOUT
TAGSUP
TAKEUP
TALCUM
TALKUP
TALMUD
TAMMUZ
TANGUY
TANKUP
TAPOUT
TARSUS
TAURUS
TEACUP
TEAMUP
TEARUP
TEDEUM
TEDIUM
TEEDUP
TEESUP
TEMPUS
TEREUS
THYMUS
TIDYUP
TIEDUP
TIESUP
TISSUE
TITTUP
TOBRUK
TONEUP
TONGUE
TOOKUP
TOOLUP
TOPGUN
TOPHUS
TOPOUT
TOREUP
TORQUE
TOSSUP
TOTSUP
TRIPUP
TRYOUT
TUCHUN
TUNEUP
TURNUP
TUTTUT
TYPEUP
TYPHUS

T••••U
TELEDU
TELUGU
TUVALU

•TU•••
ETUDES
ETUXOR
ITURBI
STUART
STUBBY
STUCCO
STUDIO
STUFFS
STUFFY
STULLS
STUMER
STUMPS
STUMPY
STUNTS
STUNTY
STUPAS
STUPES
STUPID
STUPOR
STURDY
UTURNS

•T•U••
ATTUNE
STLUKE
STOUPS
STOUTS
STRUCK
STRUMS
STRUNG
STRUTS

•T••U•
ATEOUT
ATREUS
ATRIUM
ATSTUD
STAPUF
STATUE
STATUS
STAYUP
STEPUP
STIRUP
STOPUP
STPAUL
STRAUB
STRAUS
STROUD
STYLUS

••TU••
ACTUAL
ARTURO
ASTUTE
ATTUNE
AUTUMN
BATUMI
BUTUNG
BUTUTS
CUTUPS
DATURA
FUTURE
GETUPS
INTUIT
INTUNE
INTURN
LETUPS
MATURE
MUTUAL
NATURA
NATURE
OBTUND
OBTUSE
PETULA
RETUNE
RETURN
RITUAL
ROTUND
SATURN
SETUPS
SITUPS
SUTURE
TUTUED
UNTUNE
UPTURN
WATUSI

••T•U•
ACTIUM
ACTOUT
ACTSUP
ALTIUS
ANTEUP
ANTRUM
ARTFUL
ARTGUM
ARTHUR
AUTEUR
BATTUE
CATGUT
CATSUP
CITIUS
CITRUS
CUTOUT
CUTSUP
DATSUN
DETOUR
EATOUT
EATSUP
FITFUL
GETOUT
GETSUP
GOTOUT
HATFUL
HITOUT
HITSUP

HOTTUB
JETGUN
LATIUM
LATOUR
LETOUT
LETSUP
LITMUS
LITOUT
ONTOUR
OPTOUT
OSTIUM
OUTGUN
OUTPUT
OUTRUN
POTFUL
PUTOUT
PUTPUT
PUTSUP
RETOUR
ROTGUT
SATOUT
SETOUT
SETSUP
SITOUT
SITSUP
TITTUP
TOTSUP
TUTTUT
UNTRUE
VATFUL

••T••U
BATEAU
GATEAU

•••TU•
ADYTUM
ATSTUD
BANTUS
BATTUE
BEATUP
BOOTUP
BRUTUS
CACTUS
CESTUS
CHATUP
DICTUM
DICTUS
DUSTUP
FESTUS
FOETUS
HEATUP
HIATUS
HOTTUB
KEPTUP
KULTUR
LIFTUP
MANTUA
MULTUM
PENTUP
PONTUS
RECTUS
RESTUP
SALTUM
SENTUP
SEPTUM
SHOTUP
SHUTUP
SIXTUS
STATUE
STATUS
SUITUP
TITTUP
TUTTUT

VIRTUE
VIRTUS
WAITUP
WENTUP

•••T•U
ALATAU
LAOTZU

••••TU
ERESTU
INSITU
SHORTU

TV••••
TVSETS
TVSHOW

T•V•••
TAVERN
TIVOLI
TUVALU

T••V••
TEEVEE
TRAVEL
TRAVES
TRAVIS
TREVOR
TRIVET
TRIVIA
TROVES
TURVES

T•••V•
THEYVE
THIEVE
THRIVE
THROVE
TROUVE
TWELVE

•T•V••
STAVED
STAVES
STEVEN
STEVIE
STIVER
STIVIC
STOVER
STOVES

•T••V•
OTTAVA
STARVE
STEEVE
STRIVE
STROVE

••TV••
LATVIA

••T•V•
ACTIVE
DATIVE
MOTIVE
NATIVE
OCTAVE
OCTAVO
OTTAVA
VOTIVE

•••TV•
WHATVE

•••T•V
GUSTAV
LAPTEV
ROSTOV
YOMTOV

TW••••
TWANGS
TWANGY
TWEAKS
TWEEDS
TWEEDY
TWEENS
TWEENY
TWEEST
TWEETS
TWEETY
TWEEZE
TWELVE
TWENTY
TWERPS
TWIGGY
TWILIT
TWILLS
TWINED
TWINES
TWINGE
TWIRLS
TWISTS
TWISTY
TWITCH
TWITTY
TWOBIT
TWOFER
TWOPLY
TWOWAY

T•W•••
TAWDRY
TAWING
THWACK
THWART
TOWAGE
TOWARD
TOWCAR
TOWELS
TOWERS
TOWERY
TOWHEE
TOWING
TOWNER
TOWNIE

T••W••
TAIWAN
THAWED
THEWEB
THEWIZ
TRAWLS
TROWED
TROWEL
TWOWAY

T•••W•
TARAWA
THROWN
THROWS

T••••W
TALLOW
TVSHOW

•TW•••
ATWILL

ATWOOD
ATWORK

•T•W••
STEWED
STEWER
STOWED

•T••W•
OTTAWA
STRAWS
STRAWY
STREWN
STREWS

••TW••
FATWAS
HOTWAR
JETWAY
NITWIT
OUTWIT

••T•W•
ACTTWO
INTOWN
MOTOWN
OTTAWA
RETOWS
UPTOWN

••T••W
ANTCOW
NOTNOW
OUTLAW
PITSAW

•••TW•
ACTTWO
ONETWO

•••T•W
BESTOW
KOWTOW
SKITOW

T•X•••
TAXERS
TAXIED
TAXIES
TAXING
TAXMAN
TAXMEN
TEXACO
TEXANS
TEXMEX
TOXICS
TOXINS
TUXEDO

T••X••
TRIXIE

T••••X
TEXMEX
THESIX
THORAX
TOMMIX

•T•X••
ETUXOR

••T•X•
EUTAXY
URTEXT

••T••X
HATBOX
HOTBOX
KITFOX
MATRIX
OUTBOX
OUTFOX
RATEDX

•••T•X
CORTEX
JOETEX
LASTEX
PRETAX
PROTAX
SINTAX
SURTAX
SYNTAX
VERTEX
VORTEX

TY••••
TYBALT
TYCOBB
TYCOON
TYDBOL
TYPERS
TYPEUP
TYPHUS
TYPIER
TYPIFY
TYPING
TYPIST
TYRANT
TYRIAN
TYRONE

T•Y•••
TAYLOR
TAYRAS
THYMUS
THYRSI
TOYDOG
TOYING
TOYONS
TOYOTA
TRYFOR
TRYING
TRYLON
TRYOUT
TRYSTS
TUYERE

T••Y••
THAYER
THEYLL
THEYRE
THEYVE
TIDYUP

T•••Y•
TAMAYO
TETHYS
TIEDYE
TOKAYS

T••••Y
TAGDAY
TAMELY
TANGLY
TANGUY
TARTLY
TAUTLY
TAWDRY

TEAPOY
TEDKEY
TEENSY
TETCHY
THEFLY
THEORY
THETOY
THINGY
THINLY
THIRTY
THORNY
THUSLY
TICKLY
TIDDLY
TIDILY
TIMELY
TINGLY
TINILY
TINKLY
TOASTY
TOMBOY
TOOTHY
TOOTSY
TORCHY
TORREY
TOUCHY
TOUGHY
TOWERY
TRACEY
TRACHY
TRAPPY
TRASHY
TREATY
TREBLY
TRENDY
TRICKY
TRIGLY
TRILBY
TRIMLY
TRIPLY
TROPHY
TRUSTY
TUMEFY
TUNNEY
TURKEY
TWANGY
TWEEDY
TWEENY
TWEETY
TWENTY
TWIGGY
TWISTY
TWITTY
TWOPLY
TWOWAY
TYPIFY

•TY•••
ETYMOL
ETYMON
STYLED
STYLER
STYLES
STYLET
STYLUS
STYMIE
STYRIA
STYRON

•T•Y••
STAYED
STAYON
STAYUP

•T••Y•
STRAYS

•T•••Y
STABLY
STACEY
STALKY
STANKY
STARRY
STEADY
STEAMY
STEELY
STEFOY
STICKY
STILLY
STIMPY
STINGY
STINKY
STITHY
STOCKY
STODGY
STOOLY
STOREY
STORMY
STRAWY
STRIPY
STUBBY
STUFFY
STUMPY
STUNTY
STURDY

••TY••
BATYAM
ECTYPE
IRTYSH
NOTYET
RETYPE
SATYRS

••T•Y•
LATOYA
MATEYS
METHYL
TETHYS

••T••Y
ANTONY
ARTERY
ARTILY
ASTRAY
BATBOY
BETONY
BETRAY
BETSEY
BOTANY
BOTCHY
BOTFLY
CATCHY
CATHAY
CITIFY
CUTELY
CUTESY
DATARY
EATERY
ENTITY
ESTRAY
EUTAXY
GATSBY
GETSBY
JETWAY
JITNEY
LATELY
LETFLY
LITANY
MOTLEY
MUTELY
MUTINY
NETPAY
NETTLY
NITERY
NOTARY
NOTCHY
NOTIFY
OUTCRY
OUTFLY
OUTLAY
PATCHY
PITCHY
PUTSBY
RATIFY
RATTLY
ROTARY
SATINY
SETSBY
SITSBY
TETCHY
UNTIDY
VOTARY
WATERY
WATNEY
WETFLY
WITCHY

•••TY•
ACETYL
DACTYL
MARTYR
ZLOTYS

•••T•Y
APATHY
BEATTY
BLATTY
BLOTTY
BOOTSY
BRATTY
CHATTY
CLOTTY
COSTLY
CURTLY
CURTSY
DAFTLY
DEFTLY
DESTRY
EARTHY
FEATLY
FILTHY
FLATLY
FLUTEY
FRETTY
FROTHY
GANTRY
GENTLY
GENTRY
GLITZY
GNATTY
GRITTY
GROTTY
GUITRY
HEATHY
HOSTLY
ICHTHY
JUSTLY
KLUTZY
KNOTTY
LASTLY
MEETLY
MOSTLY
MOUTHY
NEATLY
NETTLY
PALTRY
PANTRY
PARTLY
PASTRY
PELTRY
PERTLY
PLOTTY
POETRY
PORTLY
PRETTY
RAPTLY
RATTLY
SCATTY
SCOTTY
SENTRY
SLITHY
SLITTY
SMITHY
SMUTTY
SNOTTY
SOFTLY
SPOTTY
STITHY
SUBTLY
SULTRY
TARTLY
TAUTLY
THETOY
TOOTHY
TOOTSY
TWITTY
VASTLY
VESTRY
WENTBY
WHITTY
WINTRY
WORTHY
WRATHY

••••TY
ACUITY
ALMATY
ASEITY
BEATTY
BEAUTY
BLATTY
BLOTTY
BOUNTY
BRATTY
CAVITY
CHATTY
CHERTY
CHESTY
CLOTTY
COMITY
COUNTY
CRAFTY
CRUSTY
DAINTY
DEPUTY
DIMITY
DRAFTY
DRIFTY
EIGHTY
ENMITY
ENTITY
EQUITY
FAULTY
FAWLTY
FEALTY
FEISTY
FERITY
FIXITY
FLINTY
FLIRTY
FLOATY
FRETTY
FROSTY
FRUITY
GAIETY
GNATTY
GRITTY
GROTTY
GROUTY
GUILTY
HEARTY
HINCTY
JAUNTY
KNOTTY
LAXITY
LEALTY
LENITY
LEVITY
MIGHTY
MOIETY
MOUNTY
NICETY
NIGHTY
NINETY
NUDITY
ODDITY
PAINTY
PARITY
PIGSTY
PLASTY
PLENTY
PLOTTY
POINTY
POLITY
PRETTY
PURITY
QWERTY
RARITY
REALTY
RIGHTY
SAFETY
SANITY
SCANTY
SCATTY
SCOTTY
SHANTY
SHELTY
SHIFTY
SHIRTY
SHORTY
SLEETY
SLITTY
SMARTY
SMUTTY
SNOOTY
SNOTTY
SPORTY
SPOTTY
STUNTY
SURETY
SWEATY
THIRTY
TOASTY
TREATY
TRUSTY
TWEETY
TWENTY
TWISTY
TWITTY
UBIETY
UPPITY
VANITY
VAULTY
VERITY
WHITTY
YEASTY

TZ••••
TZUHSI

T•Z•••
TAZZAS

T••Z••
TARZAN
TAZZAS
TETZEL

T•••Z•
TWEEZE

T••••Z
TABRIZ
TAMMUZ
THEWIZ
TROPEZ

•TZ•••
ITZHAK

•T••Z•
STANZA

••TZ••
DITZES
FUTZED
FUTZES
LUTZES
MATZOH
MATZOS
TETZEL

•••TZ•
GLITZY
KLUTZY
LAOTZU

•••T•Z
CORTEZ
CURTIZ
MONTEZ

••••TZ
BLINTZ
CHINTZ
DONITZ
ERSATZ
IGNATZ
KIBITZ
KOONTZ
KRANTZ
MORITZ
NIMITZ
QUARTZ
SPRITZ

UA••••
UAKARI

U•A•••
UBANGI
UGANDA
UKASES
UNABLE
UNAGED
UNARMS
UNAWED
UPASES
URACIL
URAEUS
URALIC
URALSK
URANIA
URANIC
URANUS
USABLE
USABLY
USAGES
USANCE
UTAHAN
UVALUE

U••A••
UAKARI
UBOATS
UCLANS
UGGAMS
UHLANS
UJJAIN
ULLAGE
UMIAKS
UMLAUT
UMTATA
UNBARS
UNCAGE
UNCAPS
UNCASE
UNEASE
UNEASY
UNFAIR
UNHAND
UNIATE
UNIATS
UNJAMS
UNLACE
UNLADE
UNLAID
UNLASH
UNMADE
UNMAKE
UNMANS
UNMASK
UNPACK
UNPAID
UNSAFE
UNSAID
UNSAYS
UNTACK
UNWARY
UPCAST
UPDATE
UPLAND
UPTAKE
UPTALK
UPWARD
URBANA
URBANE
URIALS
USMAIL
USUALS
UTHANT

U•••A•
UGRIAN
UINTAS
ULLMAN
ULTRAS
UMBRAE
UMBRAL
UMBRAS
UNCIAL
UNCLAD
UNDRAW
UNGUAL
UNITAL
UNITAS
UNIVAC
UNLEAD
UNLOAD
UNOCAL
UNREAD
UNREAL
UNSEAL
UNSEAT
UNSNAG
UNSNAP
UNTRAP
UNWRAP
UPBEAT
UPLOAD
UPROAR
UTAHAN
UVULAE
UVULAR
UVULAS
UZZIAH

U••••A
UGANDA
ULTIMA
UMBRIA
UMTATA
URANIA
URBANA
URSULA
UTOPIA

•UA•••
DUALLY
DUARTE
GUACOS
GUARDS
GUAVAS
JUAREZ
LUANDA
NUANCE
QUACKS
QUADRI
QUAFFS
QUAGGA
QUAGGY
QUAHOG
QUAILS
QUAINT
QUAKED
QUAKER
QUAKES
QUALMS
QUANGO
QUANTA
QUARKS
QUARRY
QUARTO
QUARTS
QUARTZ
QUASAR
QUAVER
QUAYLE
RUANAS
RUANDA
SUAVER
TUAREG

•U•A••
AUBADE
AUFAIT
AULAIT
AUPAIR
BUTANE
CUBAGE
CUIABA
CUNARD
CUNAXA
CURACY
CURARE
CURATE
CUSACK
DUCATS
DUNANT
DURANT
DUVALL
EURAIL
EUTAXY
FUGARD
FULANI
GUIANA
GULAGS
GUYANA
HUMANE
HUMANS
JUDAEA
JUDAIC
JUMADA
JURADO
JURATS
KULAKS
KURALT
KUVASZ
KUWAIT
LUNACY
LUNATE
LUSAKA
LUXATE
MUFASA
MUGABE
MURALS
MURANO
MUTANT
MUTATE
MUTATO
NUTATE
OUTACT
OUTAGE
OUTATE
PURACE
QUEASY
RUBATI
RUBATO
RUGATE
RUPAUL
SUBARU
SUGARS
SUGARY
SUMACS
SURAHS
SUSANN
TUBATE
TUCANA
TULANE
TULARE
TUVALU
YUKATA
YUKAWA

•U••A•
AUDIAL
AUGEAN
BUCCAL
BUCHAN
BULGAR
BULLAE
BUMRAP
BUNYAN
BUREAU
BURGAS
BURLAP
BURMAN
BUROAK
BURSAE
BURSAL
BURSAR
BURSAS
BUSBAR
BUSMAN
CUNEAL
CUPPAS
CURIAE
CURIAL
CUSHAW
DUCTAL
DUNBAR
DUNCAN
DUNHAM
DURBAN
DURBAR
DURHAM
DURIAN
FUJIAN
FULMAR
GUAVAS
GUFFAW
GUITAR
GULLAH
GUNMAN
GUNNAR
GUSTAV
GUTTAE
HUBCAP
HURRAH
HURRAY
HUSSAR
HUZZAH
HUZZAS
JUBBAH
JULIAN
JUMPAT
JUNEAU
JUNTAS
KUBLAI
KURGAN
LUCIAN
LUMBAR
MUDCAT
MUDRAS
MULLAH
MULLAS
MURRAY
MUSCAT
MUSIAL
MUTUAL
NUBIAN
NUCHAE
NUCHAL
NULLAH
NUMBAT
OUTEAT
OUTLAW
OUTLAY
OUTRAN
PULSAR
PUNJAB
PUNKAH
PURDAH
PUTNAM
QUASAR
QUMRAN
QUOTAS
RUANAS
RUDMAN
RUMBAS
RUNSAT
RUNWAY
RUPIAH
RUTTAN
SUBPAR
SUBWAY
SUCHAS
SUCKAS
SUDRAS
SUKKAH
SULTAN
SUMMAE
SUMMAS
SUNDAE
SUNDAY
SUNRAY
SUNTAN
SURTAX
SUTRAS
TUBMAN
TULSAN
TUPIAN
TURBAN
TUSCAN
TUSSAH
VULCAN
VULGAR
YUCCAS
YUNNAN

•U•••A
AURIGA
AURORA
BUDDHA
BULOVA
BUQSHA
BUSHWA
CUESTA
CUIABA
CUNAXA
CUPOLA
DUENNA
DULLEA
DUNERA
DURYEA
EUBOEA
EUDORA
EUPNEA
EUREKA
EUROPA
FULCRA
GUIANA
GUINEA
GURKHA
GUYANA
HULLOA
JUDAEA
JUDOKA
JUMADA
LUANDA
LUMINA
LUNULA

LUSAKA MUCOSA MUFASA MULETA MURCIA NUMINA NUTRIA PUEBLA PURINA QUAGGA QUANTA QUETTA QUINOA QUOKKA QUOTHA RUANDA RUMINA RUSSIA TUCANA TUNDRA TUNICA YUKATA YUKAWA

••UA••

ACUATE AKUAKU AQUATE DOUALA EDUARD EQUALS EQUATE IGUACU IGUANA SOUARI SQUABS SQUADS SQUALL SQUARE SQUASH SQUATS SQUAWK STUART TRUANT USUALS YOUALL ZOUAVE

••U•A•

ALULAE ALULAR ANURAN AOUDAD ARUBAN BEULAH BHUTAN BRUMAL BRUTAL CAUDAL CAUSAL CHUKAR CIUDAD COUGAR CRURAL FAUNAE FAUNAL FAUNAS FEUDAL FOURAM FRUGAL HAUSAS KAUNAS KOUFAX MAUMAU NEUMAN NEURAL NOUGAT OCULAR OVULAR PLURAL SAUNAS SCUBAS SEURAT SQUEAK SQUEAL STUPAS THUJAS TOUCAN TRUMAN UVULAE UVULAR UVULAS WAUSAU

••U••A

ALUMNA APULIA AQUILA CHUKKA COULDA DOUALA IGUANA KAUNDA LOUISA MAURYA NAUSEA NOUMEA RHUMBA ZEUGMA

•••UA•

ACTUAL ANNUAL CAGUAS CASUAL EMQUAD ENQUAD GENUAL JAGUAR LEHUAS LOQUAT MANUAL MSQUAD MUTUAL PADUAN PAPUAN RITUAL SIOUAN UNGUAL VISUAL

•••U•A

ARJUNA BAKULA BELUGA CAYUGA COPULA CREUSA DATURA FACULA FIBULA HECUBA KAHUNA KORUNA LACUNA LAGUNA LAPUTA LIGULA LUNULA MACULA MADURA MAKUTA MAZUMA MEDUSA NATURA NEBULA NERUDA OSCULA PAKULA PARULA PERUGA PETULA PLEURA PNEUMA RADULA REMUDA SEGURA TABULA TOLUCA TRAUMA URSULA VARUNA VICUNA YAKUZA YORUBA

••••UA

JOSHUA KAHLUA KAILUA LINGUA MANTUA NASHUA

UB••••

UBANGI UBIETY UBIQUE UBOATS UBOLTS

U•B•••

UMBELS UMBERS UMBRAE UMBRAL UMBRAS UMBRIA UNBARS UNBELT UNBEND UNBENT UNBIND UNBOLT UNBORN UNBUSY UPBEAT UPBOWS URBANA URBANE UZBEKS

U••B••

UNABLE USABLE USABLY

U•••B•

UNROBE

•UB•••

AUBADE AUBREY AUBURN BUBBLE BUBBLY CUBAGE CUBEBS CUBICS CUBING CUBISM CUBIST CUBITS CUBOID DUBBED DUBBIN DUBCEK DUBLIN DUBOIS EUBOEA FUBBED HUBBLE HUBBLY HUBBUB HUBCAP HUBERT HUBRIS JUBBAH KUBLAI LUBBER LUBECK LUBING LUBLIN NUBBED NUBBIN NUBBLE NUBBLY NUBIAN NUBILE PUBLIC RUBATI RUBATO RUBBED RUBBER RUBBLE RUBBLY RUBENS RUBIED RUBIES RUBIFY RUBLES RUBLEV RUBOFF RUBOUT RUBRIC RUBSIN SUBARU SUBBED SUBDEB SUBDUE SUBGUM SUBITO SUBLET SUBMIT SUBORN SUBPAR SUBSET SUBTLE SUBTLY SUBURB SUBWAY TUBATE TUBBED TUBERS TUBING TUBIST TUBMAN

•U•B••

BUBBLE BUBBLY BULBIL BULBUL BUMBLE BUMBRY BURBLE BURBLY BURBOT BUSBAR BUSBOY CUMBER CURBED DUBBED DUBBIN DUMBER DUMBLY DUNBAR DURBAN DURBAR DURBIN FUBBED FUMBLE GUMBEL GUMBOS HUBBLE HUBBLY HUBBUB HUMBLE HUMBLY HUMBUG JUBBAH JUMBLE JUMBOS LUBBER LUMBAR LUMBER MUMBLE MUMBLY NUBBED NUBBIN NUBBLE NUBBLY NUMBAT NUMBED NUMBER NUMBLY OUTBID OUTBOX PUEBLA PUEBLO QUEBEC RUBBED RUBBER RUBBLE RUBBLY RUMBAS RUMBLE RUMBLY SUBBED TUBBED TUMBLE TURBAN TURBID TURBIT TURBOS TURBOT

•U••B•

CUBEBS CUIABA JUJUBE MUGABE PUTSBY

•U•••B

HUBBUB PUNJAB SUBDEB SUBURB SUPERB

••UB••

ANUBIS ARUBAN BAUBLE BOUBOU CHUBBY CLUBBY DAUBED DAUBER DAUBES DOUBLE DOUBLY DOUBTS GRUBBY REUBEN ROUBLE SCUBAS SNUBBY STUBBY YOUBET

••U•B•

BLURBS BRUMBY CHUBBY CLUBBY CRUMBS CRUMBY EXURBS GRUBBY ITURBI PLUMBS RHUMBA RHUMBS SNUBBY SQUABS SQUIBB SQUIBS STUBBY THUMBS

••U••B

SQUIBB

•••UB•

DANUBE HECUBA JUJUBE REDUBS SCRUBS SHRUBS YORUBA

•••U•B

BENUMB SUBURB

••••UB

BEDAUB CHERUB HOTTUB HUBBUB STRAUB

UC••••

UCLANS

U•C•••

ULCERS UNCAGE UNCAPS UNCASE UNCHIC UNCIAL UNCLAD UNCLES UNCLOG UNCOIL UNCOOL UNCORK UNCURL UPCAST URCHIN

U••C••

UNICEF UNOCAL URACIL

U•••C•

UNESCO UNLACE UNLOCK UNPACK UNTACK UPTICK USANCE

U••••C

UNCHIC UNIFIC UNIVAC URALIC URANIC

•UC•••

BUCCAL BUCHAN BUCKED BUCKET BUCKLE BUCKUP CUCKOO DUCATS DUCHIN DUCKED DUCTAL EUCHRE EUCLID KUCHEN LUCENT LUCIAN LUCITE LUCIUS LUCKED MUCINS MUCKED MUCKUP MUCOSA MUCOUS NUCHAE NUCHAL NUCLEI NUCLEO PUCKER RUCHES RUCKED RUCKUS SUCCES SUCCOR SUCHAS SUCKAS SUCKED SUCKER SUCKIN TUCANA TUCHUN TUCKED TUCKER TUCKET TUCKIN TUCSON YUCCAS

•U•C••

BUCCAL BUNCHE BUNCHY BUNCOS DUBCEK DULCET DUNCAN DUNCES FULCRA GUACOS HUBCAP JUICED JUICER JUICES JUNCOS LUNCHY MUDCAT MULCTS MUNCHY MUNCIE MURCIA MUSCAT MUSCLE MUSCLY NUECES NUNCIO OUNCES OUTCRY PUNCHY QUACKS QUICHE RUNCIE SUCCES SUCCOR SULCUS TUSCAN VULCAN YUCCAS

•U••C•

CUBICS CURACY CUSACK DUROCS EUNICE LUBECK LUNACY MUNICH NUANCE OUTACT PUMICE PURACE PUTSCH QUENCH QUINCE QUINCY SUMACS SUNOCO TUNICA TUNICS ZURICH

•U•••C

CULTIC CUPRIC FUSTIC JUDAIC PUBLIC QUEBEC RUBRIC RUNDMC RUSTIC TURKIC

••UC••

BAUCIS BOUCLE CAUCHO CAUCHY CAUCUS CHUCKS CLUCKS CRUCES DEUCED DEUCES EDUCED EDUCES ERUCTS FAUCES FAUCET GAUCHE GAUCHO LOUCHE PAUCIS PLUCKS PLUCKY POUCHY SAUCED SAUCER SAUCES SHUCKS STUCCO TOUCAN TOUCHE TOUCHY TRUCES TRUCKS

••U•C•

BOUNCE BOUNCY BRUNCH CHURCH CLUTCH CRUNCH CRUTCH HAUNCH IGUACU JOUNCE JOUNCY LAUNCH NAUTCH PAUNCH POUNCE SCUTCH SLUICE SMUTCH SOURCE STUCCO

••U••C

COURIC

•••UC•

ABDUCT ADDUCE ADDUCT AVOUCH BARUCH CROUCH DEDUCE DEDUCT GROUCH INDUCE INDUCT INLUCK REDUCE RELUCT SEDUCE SLOUCH SPRUCE STRUCK TOLUCA ZANUCK

UD••••

UDDERS

U•D•••

UDDERS UNDIES UNDINE UNDOER UNDOES UNDONE UNDRAW UNDULY UNDYED UPDATE UPDIKE

U••D••

USEDTO USEDUP

U•••D•

UGANDA UNLADE UNMADE UNTIDY UPENDS UPSIDE URSIDS

U••••D

UNAGED UNAWED UNBEND UNBIND UNCLAD UNDYED UNFOLD UNGIRD UNHAND UNHEED UNIPOD UNITED UNKIND UNLAID UNLEAD UNLOAD UNPAID UNREAD UNSAID UNSHED UNSHOD UNSOLD UNTIED UNTOLD UNTROD UNUSED UNWIND UPHELD UPHOLD UPLAND UPLOAD UPWARD UPWIND USERID

•UD•••

AUDENS AUDIAL AUDILE AUDIOS AUDITS AUDREY BUDDED BUDDHA BUDGED BUDGES BUDGET BUDGIE CUDDLE CUDDLY CUDGEL DUDEEN DUDISH DUDLEY EUDORA FUDDLE FUDGED FUDGES GUDRUN HUDDLE HUDSON JUDAEA JUDAIC JUDDER JUDGED JUDGES JUDITH JUDOKA KUDROW KUDZUS LUDDEN LUDENS LUDLUM LUDWIG MUDCAT MUDDED MUDDER MUDDLE MUDEEL MUDHEN MUDPIE MUDRAS NUDELY NUDEST NUDGED NUDGER NUDGES NUDIST NUDITY NUDNIK PUDDLE PUDDLY RUDDER RUDDLE RUDELY RUDEST RUDMAN RUDOLF SUDDEN SUDRAS SUDSED SUDSES TUDORS

•U•D••

BUDDED BUDDHA BUNDLE BURDEN CUDDLE CUDDLY CURDED CURDLE DUMDUM DUNDEE FUDDLE FUNDED GUIDED GUIDES GUIDON GUNDOG HUDDLE HURDLE JUDDER LUDDEN LUNDEN MUDDED MUDDER MUDDLE MURDER OUTDID PUDDLE PUDDLY PUNDIT PURDAH PURDUE QUADRI QUIDDE RUDDER RUDDLE RUNDLE RUNDMC RUNDRY SUBDEB SUBDUE SUDDEN SUEDES SUNDAE SUNDAY SUNDER SUNDEW SUNDOG SUNDRY TUNDRA ZUIDER

•U••D•

AUBADE BUILDS CUPIDS GUARDS GUILDS JUMADA JURADO LUANDA QUIDDE RUANDA TUXEDO

•U•••D

AUFOND AUGEND BUCKED BUDDED BUDGED BUFFED BUGGED BUGLED BUJOLD BULGED BULKED BULLED BUMMED BUMPED BUNGED BUNKED BUNTED BUOYED BURIED BURLED BURNED BURPED BURRED BUSHED BUSIED BUSKED BUSSED BUSTED BUTTED BUZZED CUBOID CUFFED CULLED CUNARD CUPPED CURBED CURDED CURLED CURRED CURSED CURVED CUSPED CUSPID CUSSED DUBBED DUCKED DUELED DULLED DUMPED DUNKED DUNNED DURNED DUSTED EUCLID FUBBED FUDGED FUELED FUGARD FUNDED FUNKED FUNNED FURLED FURRED FUSSED FUTZED FUZZED GUIDED GULFED GULLED GULPED GUMMED GUNNED GUSHED GUSTED GUTTED HUFFED HUGGED HULKED HULLED HUMMED HUMPED HUNTED HURLED HUSHED HUSKED HUTTED JUDGED JUGGED JUICED JUMPED JUNKED JUTTED LUCKED LUFFED LUGGED LULLED LUMPED LUNGED LURKED LUSTED MUCKED MUDDED MUFFED MUGGED MULLED MUMMED MUMPED MUSHED MUSSED MUZZED NUBBED NUDGED NULLED NUMBED NURSED NUTTED OUSTED OUTBID OUTDID PUFFED PUGGED PULLED PULPED PULSED PUMPED PUNNED PUNTED PUREED PURGED PURLED PURRED PURSED PUSHED PUTRID PUTTED QUAKED QUEUED QUOTED RUBBED RUBIED RUCKED RUFFED RUGGED RUINED RUSHED RUSTED RUTTED SUBBED SUCKED SUDSED SUITED SULKED SUMMED SUNGOD SUNNED SUPPED SURFED SURGED SUSSED TUBBED TUCKED TUFTED TUGGED TUMMED TURBID TURFED TURGID TURNED TUSKED TUTUED YUKKED

••UD••

AOUDAD BOUDIN BRUDER CAUDAL CAUDEX CAUDLE CIUDAD CRUDDY CRUDER DRUDGE ELUDED ELUDER ELUDES ETUDES EXUDED EXUDES FEUDAL FEUDED GRUDGE KLUDGE LAUDED LAUDER LOUDEN LOUDER LOUDLY PRUDES SAUDIS SLUDGE SLUDGY SMUDGE SMUDGY STUDIO TRUDGE

••U•D•

BOUNDS COULDA CRUDDY DRUIDS FLUIDS FOUNDS GOURDE GOURDS GRUNDY HOUNDS HOUNDY KAUNDA MAUNDY MBUNDU MOULDS MOULDY MOUNDS POUNDS ROUNDS SOUNDS SQUADS SQUIDS STURDY WOUNDS ZOUNDS

••U••D

ABUSED AMUSED AOUDAD BOUSED BRUXED CAUSED CHUTED CIUDAD DAUBED DEUCED DOUSED EDUARD EDUCED ELUDED ELUTED ENURED EXUDED FEUDED FLUTED FLUXED FOULED GAUGED GAUMED GOUGED GOUNOD HAULED HOUSED INURED LAUDED LOUSED MAULED MOUSED PAUSED PLUMED POURED POUTED PRUNED REUSED ROUGED ROUSED ROUTED SAUCED SOURED SOUSED SPUMED STUPID TOURED TOUTED UNUSED

•••UD•

ALLUDE CLAUDE CLOUDS CLOUDY DELUDE DENUDE ESCUDO

FRAUDS
NERUDA
PSEUDO
PSEUDS
REMUDA
YEHUDI

•••U•D

ABOUND
ABSURD
ARGUED
AROUND
EDMUND
EMQUAD
ENDUED
ENQUAD
ENSUED
FECUND
GERUND
GROUND
IMBUED
ISSUED
JOCUND
LIQUID
MSQUAD
OBTUND
OSMUND
PEQUOD
PIQUED
QUEUED
REFUND
ROTUND
SEGUED
SHOULD
SIGURD
TUTUED
VALUED

••••UD

ATSTUD
MARAUD
REDBUD
SHROUD
STROUD
TALMUD

U•E•••

UNEASE
UNEASY
UNESCO
UNEVEN
UPENDS
USEDTO
USEDUP
USEFUL
USENET
USERID
USESUP

U••E••

UBIETY
UDDERS
ULCERS
UMBELS
UMBERS
UNBELT
UNBEND
UNBENT
UNHEED
UNLEAD
UNLESS
UNMEET
UNMESH
UNPEGS
UNPENS
UNREAD
UNREAL
UNREEL
UNREST
UNSEAL
UNSEAT
UNSEEN
UNSEWN
UNSEWS
UNVEIL
UNWELL
UPBEAT
UPHELD
UPKEEP
UPPERS
UPSETS
UPWELL
URAEUS
URGENT
URGERS
URTEXT
USHERS
UTTERS
UZBEKS

U•••E•

UGLIER
UGLIES
UKASES
ULSTER
UNAGED
UNAWED
UNCLES
UNDIES
UNDOER
UNDOES
UNDYED
UNEVEN
UNFREE
UNGUES
UNHEED
UNICEF
UNISEX
UNITED
UNITER
UNITES
UNMEET
UNOPEN
UNREEL
UNSEEN
UNSHED
UNTIED
UNTIES
UNUSED
UPASES
UPKEEP
URUSES
USAGES
USENET
USOPEN
USURER

U••••E

UBIQUE
UGSOME
ULLAGE
UMBRAE
UMPIRE
UNABLE
UNCAGE
UNCASE
UNDINE
UNDONE
UNEASE
UNFREE
UNGLUE
UNIATE
UNIQUE
UNLACE
UNLADE
UNLIKE
UNMADE
UNMAKE
UNPILE
UNRIPE
UNROBE
UNSAFE
UNSURE
UNTRUE
UNTUNE
UNWISE
UNWOVE
UNYOKE
UPDATE
UPDIKE
UPRISE
UPROSE
UPSIDE
UPTAKE
UPTIME
URBANE
URSINE
USABLE
USANCE
UVALUE
UVULAE

•UE•••

BUENOS
CUESTA
DUELED
DUELER
DUELLO
DUENNA
FUELED
FUELER
GUELPH
GUENON
GUERRE
GUESTS
HUEVOS
NUECES
PUEBLA
PUEBLO
PUENTE
PUERTO
QUEASY
QUEBEC
QUEENS
QUELLS
QUEMOY
QUENCH
QUERNS
QUESTS
QUETTA
QUEUED
QUEUER
QUEUES
QUEZON
RUEFUL
SUEDES

•U•E••

AUDENS
AUGEAN
AUGEND
AUGERS
AUREUS
AUTEUR
BUREAU
BUTENE
BUTEOS
BUYERS
CUBEBS
CULETS
CUNEAL
CUPELS
CURERS
CUTELY
CUTEST
CUTESY
CUVEES
DUDEEN
DUNERA
DUPERY
DURESS
DUVETS
EUGENE
EUREKA
FUSEES
FUZEES
HUBERT
HUGELY
HUGEST
HUMERI
JULEPS
JUNEAU
LUBECK
LUCENT
LUDENS
LUGERS
LUMENS
MUDEEL
MULETA
MULEYS
MUSERS
MUSEUM
MUTELY
MUTEST
NUDELY
NUDEST
NUGENT
NUMERO
OUSELS
OUTEAT
OUZELS
PUREED
PUREES
PURELY
PUREST
QUEENS
QUIETS
RUBENS
RUDELY
RUDEST
RULEON
RULERS
RUMENS
RUPEES
RUPERT
SUPERB
SUPERS
SURELY
SUREST
SURETE
SURETY
TUBERS
TUMEFY
TUNEIN
TUNERS
TUNEUP
TUPELO
TUREEN
TUXEDO
TUYERE

•U••E•

AUBREY
AUDREY
AUKLET
AUSPEX
AUSTEN
BUCKED
BUCKET
BUDDED
BUDGED
BUDGES
BUDGET
BUFFED
BUFFER
BUFFET
BUGGED
BUGLED
BUGLER
BUGLES
BULGED
BULGES
BULKED
BULLED
BULLET
BULWER
BUMMED
BUMMER
BUMPED
BUMPER
BUNGED
BUNGEE
BUNKED
BUNKER
BUNSEN
BUNTED
BUNTER
BUNUEL
BUOYED
BURDEN
BURGEE
BURGER
BURIED
BURIES
BURLED
BURLEY
BURNED
BURNER
BURNET
BURNEY
BURPED
BURRED
BURSES
BUSHED
BUSHEL
BUSHES
BUSIED
BUSIER
BUSIES
BUSKED
BUSMEN
BUSSED
BUSSES
BUSTED
BUSTER
BUTLER
BUTTED
BUTTER
BUTTES
BUZZED
BUZZER
BUZZES
CUDGEL
CUFFED
CULLED
CULLEN
CULLER
CULLET
CULVER
CUMBER
CUPPED
CURBED
CURDED
CURFEW
CURLED
CURLER
CURLEW
CURLEY
CURRED
CURSED
CURSES
CURTER
CURVED
CURVES
CURVET
CUSPED
CUSSED
CUSSES
CUSTER
CUTIES
CUTLER
CUTLET
CUTTER
CUVEES
DUBBED
DUBCEK
DUCKED
DUDEEN
DUDLEY
DUELED
DUELER
DUFFEL
DUFFER
DUIKER
DULCET
DULLEA
DULLED
DULLER
DULLES
DUMBER
DUMPED
DUMPER
DUNCES
DUNDEE
DUNKED
DUNKER
DUNNED
DUPLEX
DURFEY
DURNED
DURYEA
DUSTED
DUSTER
DUTIES
EUBOEA
EUPNEA
FUBBED
FUDGED
FUDGES
FUELED
FUELER
FUGUES
FULLER
FUMIER
FUNDED
FUNKED
FUNNED
FUNNEL
FURIES
FURLED
FURRED
FURZES
FUSEES
FUSSED
FUSSES
FUTZED
FUTZES
FUZEES
FUZZED
FUZZES
GUIDED
GUIDES
GUILES
GUINEA
GUISES
GULFED
GULLED
GULLET
GULPED
GULPER
GUMBEL
GUMMED
GUNMEN
GUNNED
GUNNEL
GUNNER
GUNTER
GURLEY
GURNEY
GUSHED
GUSHER
GUSHES
GUSSET
GUSTED
GUTTED
GUTTER
HUFFED
HUGGED
HUGGER
HUGHES
HULKED
HULLED
HULLER
HUMMED
HUMMER
HUMPED
HUMVEE
HUNGER
HUNKER
HUNTED
HUNTER
HURLED
HURLER
HURLEY
HUSHED
HUSHES
HUSKED
HUSKER
HUSSEY
HUTTED
HUXLEY
JUAREZ
JUDAEA
JUDDER
JUDGED
JUDGES
JUGGED
JUICED
JUICER
JUICES
JULIET
JUMPED
JUMPER
JUNKED
JUNKER
JUNKET
JURIES
JUSTER
JUTTED
KUCHEN
KUMMEL
LUBBER
LUCKED
LUDDEN
LUFFED
LUGGED
LUGGER
LULLED
LUMBER
LUMPED
LUMPEN
LUMPER
LUNDEN
LUNGED
LUNGES
LUNKER
LURKED
LUSHER
LUSTED
LUSTER
LUTHER
LUTZES
MUCKED
MUDDED
MUDDER
MUDEEL
MUDHEN
MUFFED
MUGGED
MUGGER
MULLED
MULLER
MULLET
MUMMED
MUMMER
MUMPED
MUPPET
MURDER
MURIEL
MURRES
MURREY
MUSHED
MUSHER
MUSHES
MUSKEG
MUSKET
MUSSED
MUSSEL
MUSSES
MUSTER
MUTTER
MUZZED
MUZZES
NUBBED
NUCLEI
NUCLEO
NUDGED
NUDGER
NUDGES
NUECES
NUGGET
NULLED
NUMBED
NUMBER
NURSED
NURSER
NURSES
NUTLET
NUTMEG
NUTTED
NUTTER
OUNCES
OUSTED
OUSTER
OUTLET
OUTSET
PUCKER
PUFFED
PUFFER
PUGGED
PUGREE
PULLED
PULLET
PULLEY
PULPED
PULSED
PULSES
PUMMEL
PUMPED
PUMPER
PUNIER
PUNKER
PUNNED
PUNNET
PUNTED
PUNTER
PUPPET
PUREED
PUREES
PURGED
PURGES
PURLED
PURRED
PURRER
PURSED
PURSER
PURSES
PURVEY
PUSHED
PUSHES
PUSSES
PUTTED
PUTTEE
PUTTER
QUAKED
QUAKER
QUAKES
QUAVER
QUEBEC
QUEUED
QUEUER
QUEUES
QUIRES
QUIVER
QUOTED
QUOTER
QUOTES
RUBBED
RUBBER
RUBIED
RUBIES
RUBLES
RUBLEV
RUCHES
RUCKED
RUDDER
RUFFED
RUGGED
RUINED
RUINER
RUMMER
RUNLET
RUNNEL
RUNNER
RUPEES
RUSHED
RUSHEE
RUSHES
RUSSET
RUSTED
RUTGER
RUTTED
SUAVER
SUBBED
SUBDEB
SUBLET
SUBSET
SUCCES
SUCKED
SUCKER
SUDDEN
SUDSED
SUDSES
SUEDES
SUFFER
SUITED
SUITES
SULKED
SULKER
SULLEN
SUMMED
SUMMER
SUMNER
SUMTER
SUNDER
SUNDEW
SUNKEN
SUNNED
SUNSET
SUPPED
SUPPER
SURFED
SURFER
SURGED
SURGES
SURREY
SURVEY
SUSIEQ
SUSSED
SUSSES
SUSSEX
SUTLER
SUTTER
TUAREG
TUBBED
TUCKED
TUCKER
TUCKET
TUFFET
TUFTED
TUGGED
TUGGER
TULLES
TUMMED
TUNNEL
TUNNEY
TUQUES
TUREEN
TURFED
TURKEY
TURNED
TURNER
TURRET
TURVES
TUSKED
TUSKER
TUTUED
WURLEY
WUSSES
YUKKED
ZUIDER

•U•••E

AUBADE
AUDILE
AUNTIE
AUSSIE
BUBBLE
BUCKLE
BUDGIE
BULLAE
BUMBLE
BUNCHE
BUNDLE
BUNGEE
BUNGLE
BURBLE
BURGEE
BURGLE
BURSAE
BUSTLE
BUTANE
BUTENE
CUBAGE
CUDDLE
CUIQUE
CUISSE
CURARE
CURATE
CURDLE
CURIAE
CURULE
DUARTE
DUNDEE
EUCHRE
EUGENE
EUNICE
EUROPE
FUDDLE
FUMBLE
FURORE
FUTILE
FUTURE
GUERRE
GUIMPE
GUNITE
GURGLE
GUTTAE
GUZZLE
HUBBLE
HUDDLE
HUMANE
HUMBLE
HUMVEE
HURDLE
HURTLE
HUSTLE
JUGGLE
JUJUBE
JUMBLE
JUNGLE
JUNKIE
KURILE
LUCITE
LUNATE
LUPINE
LUPONE
LUSTRE
LUXATE
MUDDLE
MUDPIE
MUFFLE
MUGABE
MUMBLE
MUNCIE
MURINE
MUSCLE
MUSKIE
MUTATE
MUZZLE
NUANCE
NUBBLE
NUBILE
NUCHAE
NUTATE
NUZZLE
OUTAGE
OUTATE
PUDDLE
PUENTE
PUGREE
PUISNE
PULQUE
PUMICE
PUNKIE
PURACE
PURDUE
PURFLE
PURINE
PURPLE
PURSUE
PUTTEE
PUZZLE
QUAYLE
QUICHE
QUIDDE
QUINCE
QUOQUE
RUBBLE
RUDDLE
RUFFLE
RUGATE
RUGOSE
RUMBLE
RUMPLE
RUNCIE
RUNDLE
RUSHEE
RUSTLE
RUTILE
SUBDUE
SUBTLE
SUISSE
SUMMAE
SUNDAE
SUPINE
SUPPLE
SURETE
SUTURE
TUBATE
TUILLE
TULANE
TULARE
TUMBLE
TURTLE
TUSSLE
TUYERE
YUPPIE

••UE••

BLUELY
BLUEOX
BLUEST
BLUESY
BLUETS
BLUEYS
CLUEIN
CRUETS
FLUENT
GLUERS
GRUELS
SQUEAK
SQUEAL
TRUEST

••U•E•

ABUSED
ABUSER
ABUSES
ACUMEN
AMULET
AMUSED
AMUSES
BOULES
BOULEZ
BOUSED
BOUSES
BRUDER
BRUGES
BRULES
BRUMES
BRUNEI
BRUNET
BRUTES
BRUXED
BRUXES
CAUDEX
CAUSED
CAUSES
CHUTED
CHUTES
COULEE
COUPES
COUTER
CRUCES
CRUDER
CRUSES
CRUXES
DAUBED
DAUBER
DAUBES
DEUCED
DEUCES
DOURER
DOUSED
DOUSES
DRUPES
DRUZES
EDUCED
EDUCES
ELUDED
ELUDER
ELUDES
ELUTED
ELUTES
ENURED
ENURES
ETUDES
EXUDED
EXUDES
FAUCES
FAUCET
FEUDED
FLUKES
FLUKEY
FLUMES
FLUTED
FLUTES
FLUTEY
FLUXED
FLUXES
FOULED
FOULER
GAUGED
GAUGER
GAUGES
GAUMED
GAUZES
GLUIER
GLUTEI
GLUTEN
GLUTES
GOUGED
GOUGER
GOUGES
GOULET
HAULED
HAULER
HOUSED
HOUSES
INURED
INURES
JAURES
JOULES
KRUGER
LAUDED
LAUDER
LAUPER
LAUREL
LAUREN
LOUDEN
LOUDER
LOUPES
LOUSED
LOUSES
LOUVER
MAULED
MAULER
MAUMEE
MAUSER
MAUVES
MOUSED
MOUSER
MOUSES
MOUSEY
NAUSEA
NEUMES
NEUTER
NGUYEN
NOUMEA
ONUSES
OPUSES
OVULES
PAULEY
PAUPER
PAUSED
PAUSES
PLUMED
PLUMES
PLUSES
POURED
POURER
POUTED
POUTER
PRUDES
PRUNED
PRUNER
PRUNES
REUBEN
REUNES
REUSED
REUSES
REUTER
ROUGED
ROUGES
ROUSED
ROUSER
ROUSES
ROUTED
ROUTER
ROUTES
SAUCED
SAUCER
SAUCES
SAUGER
SAUREL
SAUTES
SCUTES
SOURED
SOURER
SOUSED
SOUSES
SOUTER
SPUMED
SPUMES
STUMER
STUPES
TAUPES
TAUTEN
TAUTER
TOUPEE
TOURED
TOURER
TOUTED
TOUTER
TRUCES
UNUSED
URUSES
USURER
YOUBET

••U••E

ACUATE
ALULAE
AQUATE
AVULSE
BAUBLE
BEURRE
BOUCLE
BOUFFE
BOULLE
BOUNCE
BOURKE
BOURNE
BOURSE
BRUISE
CAUDLE
COULEE
COUPLE
COURSE
CRUISE
CRUSOE
DOUBLE
DRUDGE
EQUATE
EQUINE
EVULSE
FAUNAE
GAUCHE
GOURDE
GRUDGE
GRUNGE
JOUNCE
KLUDGE
LAURIE
LOUCHE
LOUISE
LOUNGE
LOUVRE
MAUMEE
MOUSSE
OEUVRE
PLUNGE
POUNCE
POUSSE
ROUBLE
ROURKE
SCURVE
SLUDGE
SLUICE
SMUDGE
SOURCE
SPURGE
SQUARE
SQUIRE
TOUCHE
TOUPEE
TOUSLE
TRUDGE
UVULAE
ZOUAVE

•••UE•

ARGUED
ARGUER
ARGUES
BREUER
BUNUEL
COQUET
ENDUED
ENDUES
ENSUED
ENSUES
FRAUEN
FUGUES
GIGUES
IMBUED
IMBUES
ISSUED
ISSUER
ISSUES
LEMUEL
MAGUEY
MANUEL
MCKUEN
MIGUEL
MINUET
PIQUED
PIQUES
PIQUET
QUEUED
QUEUER
QUEUES
RAQUEL
REFUEL
REVUES
ROGUES
SAMUEL
SEGUED
SEGUES
SEQUEL
SPRUES
TOQUES
TUQUES
TUTUED

UNGUES
VAGUER
VALUED
VALUES
VENUES
VOGUES

•••U•E
ABJURE
ACCUSE
ADDUCE
ADJURE
ALLUDE
ALLURE
AMPULE
ARMURE
AROUSE
ASSUME
ASSURE
ASTUTE
ATTUNE
BEMUSE
BLOUSE
CANUTE
CAYUSE
CERUSE
CLAUDE
CLAUSE
COHUNE
CONURE
CROUSE
CROUTE
CURULE
DANUBE
DEDUCE
DEFUSE
DEJURE
DELUDE
DELUGE
DELUXE
DEMURE
DENUDE
DEPUTE
DILUTE
DISUSE
EFFUSE
EMEUTE
ENDURE
ENDUSE
ENSURE
EXCUSE
FERULE
FIGURE
FUTURE
GROUSE
ILLUME
ILLUSE
IMMUNE
IMMURE
IMPURE
IMPUTE
INCUSE
INDUCE
INFUSE
INJURE
INOUYE
INSURE
INTUNE
JEJUNE
JUJUBE
LEGUME
LIGURE
LOBULE
MATURE
MIFUNE
MINUTE
MISUSE
MODULE
NATURE
NODULE
OBTUSE
ORDURE
PAIUTE
PARURE
PERUKE
PERUSE
REBUKE
RECUSE
REDUCE
REFUGE
REFUSE
REFUTE
RELUME
REPUTE
RESUME
RETUNE
SALUTE
SCOUSE
SECURE
SEDUCE
SOLUTE
SPOUSE
SPRUCE
STLUKE
SUTURE
TENURE
TRIUNE
TROUPE
TROUVE
UNSURE
UNTUNE
VOLUME
VOLUTE

••••UE
ACCRUE
AVENUE
BARQUE
BASQUE
BATTUE
BISQUE
BRAQUE
BROGUE
CAIQUE
CALQUE
CASQUE
CHEQUE
CINQUE
CIRQUE
CLAQUE
CLIQUE
CLOQUE
CUIQUE
DENGUE
DROGUE
FESCUE
FONDUE
GANGUE
IMBRUE
LEAGUE
LONGUE
MANQUE
MARQUE
MASQUE
MISCUE
MOSQUE
MRBLUE
OPAQUE
PERDUE
PLAGUE
PLAQUE
PRAGUE
PULQUE
PURDUE
PURSUE
QUOQUE
REGLUE
RESCUE
RISQUE
RVALUE
SACQUE
STATUE
SUBDUE
TISSUE
TONGUE
TORQUE
UBIQUE
UNGLUE
UNIQUE
UNTRUE
UVALUE
VIRTUE

U•F•••
UNFAIR
UNFITS
UNFOLD
UNFREE
UNFURL

U••F••
UNIFIC
USEFUL

U•••F•
UGLIFY
UNSAFE
UPLIFT

U••••F
UNICEF

•UF•••
AUFAIT
AUFOND
BUFFED
BUFFER
BUFFET
BUFFON
BUFFOS
CUFFED
DUFFEL
DUFFER
GUFFAW
HUFFED
LUFFED
MUFASA
MUFFED
MUFFIN
MUFFLE
MUFTIS
PUFFED
PUFFER
PUFFIN
RUFFED
RUFFLE
RUFFLY
RUFOUS
SUFFER
SUFFIX
SUFISM
TUFFET
TUFTED

•U•F••
BUFFED
BUFFER
BUFFET
BUFFON
BUFFOS
CUFFED
CUPFUL
CURFEW
DUFFEL
DUFFER
DURFEY
FULFIL
GUFFAW
GULFED
GUNFOR
HUFFED
JUGFUL
LUFFED
MUFFED
MUFFIN
MUFFLE
OUTFIT
OUTFLY
OUTFOX
PUFFED
PUFFER
PUFFIN
PURFLE
QUAFFS
RUEFUL
RUFFED
RUFFLE
RUFFLY
RUNFOR
SUFFER
SUFFIX
SULFUR
SURFED
SURFER
TUFFET
TURFED

•U••F•
AURIFY
BUGOFF
BUYOFF
CUTOFF
KUNGFU
PURIFY
PUTOFF
QUAFFS
RUBIFY
RUBOFF
RUNOFF
TUMEFY

•U•••F
BUGOFF
BUYOFF
CUTOFF
PUTOFF
RUBOFF
RUDOLF
RUNOFF

••UF••
BLUFFS
BOUFFE
CHUFFY
FLUFFS
FLUFFY
KOUFAX
SCUFFS
SNUFFS
SNUFFY
STUFFS
STUFFY

••U•F•
BLUFFS
BOUFFE
CHUFFY
FLUFFS
FLUFFY
SCUFFS
SCURFY
SMURFS
SNUFFS
SNUFFY
STUFFS
STUFFY

•••UF•
ARGUFY
REBUFF
SCRUFF
SENUFO

•••U•F
ENGULF
REBUFF
SCRUFF

••••UF
STAPUF

UG••••
UGANDA
UGGAMS
UGLIER
UGLIES
UGLIFY
UGLILY
UGRIAN
UGSOME

U•G•••
UGGAMS
UIGURS
UNGIRD
UNGIRT
UNGLUE
UNGUAL
UNGUES
UNGUIS
URGENT
URGERS
URGING

U••G••
UNAGED
USAGES

U•••G•
UBANGI
ULLAGE
UNCAGE
UNPEGS
UNRIGS

U••••G
UNCLOG
UNPLUG
UNSNAG
UNSUNG
UPPING
URGING

•UG•••
AUGEAN
AUGEND
AUGERS
AUGHTS
AUGURS
AUGURY
AUGUST
BUGGED
BUGLED
BUGLER
BUGLES
BUGOFF
BUGOUT
DUGONG
DUGOUT
EUGENE
FUGARD
FUGUES
HUGELY
HUGEST
HUGGED
HUGGER
HUGHES
JUGFUL
JUGGED
JUGGLE
LUGERS
LUGGED
LUGGER
LUGNUT
LUGOSI
MUGABE
MUGGED
MUGGER
MUGHOS
NUGENT
NUGGET
OUGHTS
PUGGED
PUGREE
RUGATE
RUGGED
RUGOSE
SUGARS
SUGARY
TUGGED
TUGGER
TUGRIK

•U•G••
BUDGED
BUDGES
BUDGET
BUDGIE
BUGGED
BULGAR
BULGED
BULGES
BULGUR
BUNGED
BUNGEE
BUNGLE
BURGAS
BURGEE
BURGER
BURGHS
BURGLE
BURGOO
BURGOS
CUDGEL
FUDGED
FUDGES
FUNGUS
GUNGHO
GURGLE
HUGGED
HUGGER
HUNGER
HUNGIN
HUNGON
HUNGRY
HUNGUP
HUNGWU
JUDGED
JUDGES
JUGGED
JUGGLE
JUNGLE
JUNGLY
KUNGFU
KURGAN
LUGGED
LUGGER
LUNGED
LUNGES
MUGGED
MUGGER
MUNGOS
NUDGED
NUDGER
NUDGES
NUGGET
OUTGUN
PUGGED
PURGED
PURGES
QUAGGA
QUAGGY
RUGGED
RUNGUP
RUTGER
SUBGUM
SUNGOD
SURGED
SURGES
TUGGED
TUGGER
TURGID
TURGOR
VULGAR
YUNGLO

•U••G•
AURIGA
CUBAGE
EULOGY
GULAGS
OUTAGE
QUAGGA
QUAGGY
QUANGO

•U•••G
BUSING
BUTUNG
BUYING
CUBING
CURING
DUGONG
DUKING
DUPING
DURING
FUMING
FUSING
FUZING
GUNDOG
GUYING
HUMBUG
JUKING
LUBING
LUDWIG
LURING
LUTING
MUSING
MUSKEG
MUTING
NUKING
NUTMEG
OUTING
PULING
QUAHOG
RULING
SUNDOG
TUAREG
TUBING
TUNING
TURING

••UG••
BOUGHS
BOUGHT
BRUGES
CAUGHT
COUGAR
COUGHS
DOUGHS
DOUGHY
FOUGHT
FRUGAL
GAUGED
GAUGER
GAUGES
GOUGED
GOUGER
GOUGES
HOUGHS
KRUGER
LAUGHS
LOUGHS
NAUGHT
NOUGAT
NOUGHT
PLUGIN
ROUGED
ROUGES
ROUGHS
ROUGHY
SAUGER
SLUGGO
SMUGLY
SNUGLI
SNUGLY
SOUGHS
SOUGHT
TAUGHT
TOUGHS
TOUGHY
VAUGHN
ZEUGMA

••U•G•
DRUDGE
GRUDGE
GRUNGE
GRUNGY
KLUDGE
LOUNGE
PLUNGE
SLUDGE
SLUDGY
SLUGGO
SMUDGE
SMUDGY
SPURGE
TRUDGE

••U••G
BLUING
CLUING
GLUING
SLUING
TAUTOG
TRUING

•••UG•
BELUGA
CAYUGA
CHOUGH
COLUGO
DEBUGS
DELUGE
ENOUGH
IMPUGN
MCHUGH
OPPUGN
PERUGA
PLOUGH
REFUGE
REPUGN
SHRUGS
SLOUGH
TELUGU
THOUGH
TROUGH

•••U•G
BUTUNG
COBURG
REHUNG
SPRUNG
STRUNG
UNSUNG

••••UG
BEDBUG
HUMBUG
RAGRUG
SOWBUG
UNPLUG
WONMUG

UH••••
UHLANS

U•H•••
UNHAND
UNHEED
UNHOLY
UNHOOK
UNHURT
UPHELD
UPHILL
UPHOLD
USHERS
UTHANT

U••H••
UNCHIC
UNSHED
UNSHOD
UPSHOT
URCHIN
UTAHAN

U•••H•
UPJOHN

U••••H
UNLASH
UNMESH
UNWISH
UPPISH
UPRUSH
UZZIAH

•U•H••
AUGHTS
AUTHOR
BUCHAN
BUSHED
BUSHEL
BUSHES
BUSHWA
CUSHAW
DUCHIN
DUNHAM
DURHAM
EUCHRE
FUZHOU
GUSHED
GUSHER
GUSHES
HUGHES
HUSHED
HUSHES
KUCHEN
LUSHER
LUSHLY
LUTHER
LUTHOR
MUDHEN
MUGHOS
MUSHED
MUSHER
MUSHES
MUZHIK
NUCHAE
NUCHAL
OUGHTS
OUTHIT
PUSHED
PUSHES
PUSHON
PUSHUP
QUAHOG
RUCHES
RUSHED
RUSHEE
RUSHES
SUCHAS
TUCHUN

•U••H•
BUDDHA
BUNCHE
BUNCHY
BUQSHA
BURGHS
GUNGHO
GUNSHY
GURKHA
HUMPHS
LUNCHY
MUNCHY
MURPHY
PUNCHY
QUICHE
QUOTHA
SURAHS

•U•••H
DUDISH
DULUTH
GUELPH
GULLAH
HURRAH
HUZZAH
JUBBAH
JUDITH
JUTISH
MULISH
MULLAH
MUNICH
NULLAH
PUNISH
PUNKAH
PURDAH
PUTSCH
QUENCH
QURUSH
RUPIAH
SUKKAH
TUSSAH
ZURICH

••UH••
CHUHSI
TZUHSI

••U•H•
BOUGHS
BOUGHT
BRUSHY
CAUCHO
CAUCHY
CAUGHT
COUGHS
DOUGHS
DOUGHY
FOUGHT
GAUCHE
GAUCHO
HOUGHS
KYUSHU
LAUGHS
LOUCHE
LOUGHS
MOUTHS
MOUTHY
NAUGHT
NOUGHT
PLUSHY
POUCHY
ROUGHS
ROUGHY
SLUSHY
SOUGHS
SOUGHT
SOUTHS
TAUGHT
TOUCHE
TOUCHY
TOUGHS
TOUGHY
TRUTHS
VAUGHN
YOUTHS

••U••H
AGUISH
BEULAH
BLUISH
BRUNCH
CHURCH
CLUTCH
CRUNCH
CRUTCH
FOURTH
HAUNCH
LAUNCH
NAUTCH
PAUNCH
SCUTCH
SMUTCH
SQUASH
SQUISH
SQUUSH

•••U•H
ABLUSH
AMBUSH
AVOUCH
BARUCH
CHOUGH
CROUCH
DULUTH
ENOUGH
GROUCH
INRUSH
MCHUGH
ONRUSH
PLOUGH
QURUSH
SLEUTH
SLOUCH
SLOUGH
SQUUSH
THOUGH
THRUSH
TROUGH
UPRUSH

UI••••
UIGURS
UINTAS

U•I•••
UBIETY
UBIQUE
UMIAKS
UNIATE
UNIATS
UNICEF
UNIFIC
UNIONS
UNIPOD
UNIQUE
UNISEX
UNISON
UNISYS
UNITAL
UNITAS
UNITED
UNITER
UNITES
UNIVAC
URIALS

U••I••
UGLIER
UGLIES
UGLIFY
UGLILY
UGRIAN
ULTIMA
ULTIMO
UMPIRE
UNBIND
UNCIAL
UNDIES
UNDINE
UNFITS
UNGIRD
UNGIRT
UNKIND
UNKINK
UNLIKE
UNLINK
UNOILY
UNPILE
UNPINS
UNRIGS
UNRIPE
UNTIDY
UNTIED
UNTIES
UNWILY
UNWIND
UNWISE
UNWISH
UNZIPS
UPDIKE
UPHILL
UPLIFT
UPLINK
UPPING
UPPISH
UPPITY
UPRISE
UPSIDE
UPTICK
UPTIME
UPWIND
URGING
URSIDS
URSINE
UZZIAH

U•••I•
UJJAIN
UMBRIA
UNCHIC
UNCOIL
UNFAIR
UNGUIS
UNIFIC
UNKNIT
UNLAID
UNPAID
UNSAID
UNVEIL
URACIL
URALIC
URANIA
URANIC
URCHIN
USERID
USMAIL
UTOPIA

U••••I
UAKARI
UBANGI

•UI•••
BUILDS
CUIABA
CUIQUE
CUISSE
DUIKER
GUIANA
GUIDED
GUIDES
GUIDON
GUILDS
GUILES
GUILTY
GUIMPE
GUINEA
GUIROS
GUISES
GUITAR
GUITRY
JUICED
JUICER
JUICES
PUISNE
QUICHE
QUIDDE
QUIETS
QUILLS
QUILTS
QUINCE
QUINCY
QUINOA
QUINTS
QUIPPY
QUIPUS
QUIRES
QUIRKS
QUIRKY
QUIRTS
QUITIT
QUIVER
RUINED
RUINER
SUISSE
SUITED
SUITES
SUITOR
SUITUP
TUILLE
ZUIDER

•U•I••
AUDIAL
AUDILE
AUDIOS
AUDITS
AURIFY
AURIGA
AUXINS
BUNION
BURIED
BURIES
BURINS
BUSIED
BUSIER
BUSIES
BUSILY
BUSING
BUYING
CUBICS
CUBING
CUBISM
CUBIST
CUBITS
CUPIDS
CURIAE
CURIAL
CURING
CURIOS
CURIUM
CUTIES
CUTINS
DUDISH
DUKING
DUPING
DURIAN
DURING
DUTIES
EUNICE
FUJIAN
FUMIER
FUMING
FURIES
FUSILS
FUSING
FUSION
FUTILE
FUZING
GUNITE
GUYING
JUDITH
JUKING
JULIAN
JULIET
JULIUS
JUNIOR
JURIES
JURIST
JUTISH
KUMISS
KURILE
LUBING
LUCIAN
LUCITE
LUCIUS
LUMINA
LUPINE
LUPINO
LURING
LUTING
LUTIST
MUCINS
MULISH
MUNICH
MURIEL
MURINE
MUSIAL
MUSING
MUTING
MUTINY
NUBIAN
NUBILE
NUDIST
NUDITY
NUKING
NUMINA
OUTING
PULING
PUMICE
PUNIER
PUNILY
PUNISH
PUPILS
PURIFY
PURINA
PURINE
PURISM
PURIST
PURITY
QUAILS
QUAINT
QUOINS
QUOITS
RUBIED
RUBIES
RUBIFY
RULING
RUMINA
RUNINS
RUPIAH
RUTILE
SUBITO
SUFISM
SUPINE
SURIMI
SUSIEQ
TUBING
TUBIST
TULIPS
TUNICA
TUNICS
TUNING
TUPIAN
TURING
ZURICH

•U••I•
AUFAIT
AULAIT
AUNTIE
AUPAIR
AUSSIE
AUSTIN
BUDGIE
BULBIL
BUNYIP
BUSKIN
BUSTIN
BUTTIN
CUBOID
CULKIN
CULLIS
CULTIC
CUPRIC
CURTIN
CURTIS
CURTIZ
CUSPID
CUSTIS
CUTSIN
DUBBIN
DUBLIN
DUBOIS
DUCHIN
DUNLIN
DURBIN
DUSTIN
EUCLID
EURAIL
FULFIL
FUSTIC
HUBRIS
HUNGIN
JUDAIC
JUMPIN
JUNKIE
JUSTIN
KUKRIS
KUOPIO
KUWAIT
LUBLIN
LUDWIG
MUDPIE
MUFFIN
MUFTIS
MUNCIE
MUNTIN

MURCIA
MUSKIE
MUSLIM
MUSLIN
MUZHIK
NUBBIN
NUDNIK
NUNCIO
NUTKIN
NUTRIA
OUTBID
OUTDID
OUTFIT
OUTHIT
OUTWIT
PUBLIC
PUFFIN
PULLIN
PULPIT
PUNDIT
PUNKIE
PURLIN
PUTRID
PUTSIN
QUITIT
RUBRIC
RUBSIN
RUNCIE
RUNSIN
RUSKIN
RUSSIA
RUSTIC
SUBMIT
SUCKIN
SUFFIX
SUMMIT
SUNLIT
SUNNIS
SUSLIK
TUCKIN
TUGRIK
TUNEIN
TURBID
TURBIT
TURGID
TURKIC
TURNIN
TURNIP
TURPIN
YUPPIE

•U•••I

BUSONI
CUMULI
FULANI
HUMERI
KUBLAI
LUGOSI
NUCLEI
QUADRI
RUBATI
SURIMI
SUZUKI
TUMULI

••UI••

ACUITY
AGUISH
AQUILA
AQUINO
BLUING
BLUISH
BRUINS
BRUISE
BRUITS
CLUING
CRUISE
DRUIDS
EQUINE
EQUIPS
EQUITY
FLUIDS
FRUITS
FRUITY
GLUIER
GLUING
GSUITS
INUITS
LOUISA
LOUISE
SLUICE
SLUING
SQUIBB
SQUIBS
SQUIDS
SQUILL
SQUINT
SQUIRE
SQUIRM
SQUIRT
SQUISH
TRUING
TRUISM

••U•I•

ABUKIR
ANUBIS
APULIA
BAUCIS
BOUDIN
CLUEIN
COURIC
COUSIN
HOURIS
KAURIS
LAURIE
MOULIN
PAUCIS
PLUGIN
POURIN
SAUDIS
SHUTIN
STUDIO
STUPID
TSURIS
ZEUXIS

••U••I

ALUMNI
BRUNEI
CHUHSI
FRUTTI
GLUTEI
ITURBI
SNUGLI
SOUARI
TZUHSI

•••UI•

ACQUIT
ALCUIN
ANNUIT
BAGUIO
INTUIT
JESUIT
LEGUIN
LIQUID
MAQUIS
MINUIT
NYQUIL
PAQUIN
SEQUIN
UNGUIS
YAQUIS

•••U•I

ADZUKI
AGOUTI
ANNULI
BATUMI
CUMULI
KABUKI
LAZULI
POPULI
SALUKI
SUZUKI
TUMULI
WATUSI
YEHUDI

••••UI

BANGUI
SESQUI
YANQUI

UJ••••

UJJAIN

U•J•••

UJJAIN
UNJAMS
UNJUST
UPJOHN

•UJ•••

BUJOLD
FUJIAN
JUJUBE

•U•J••

PUNJAB

••UJ••

THUJAS

UK••••

UKASES

U•K•••

UAKARI
UNKIND
UNKINK
UNKNIT
UNKNOT
UPKEEP

U•••K•

UMIAKS
UNLIKE
UNMAKE
UNYOKE
UPDIKE
UPTAKE
UZBEKS

U••••K

UNCORK
UNHOOK
UNKINK
UNLINK
UNLOCK
UNMASK
UNPACK
UNTACK
UPLINK
UPTALK
UPTICK
URALSK

•UK•••

AUKLET
DUKING
JUKING
KUKRIS
MUKLUK
NUKING
SUKKAH
YUKATA
YUKAWA
YUKKED

•U•K••

BUCKED
BUCKET
BUCKLE
BUCKUP
BULKED
BUNKED
BUNKER
BUNKOS
BUNKUM
BUSKED
BUSKIN
CUCKOO
CULKIN
DUCKED
DUIKER
DUNKED
DUNKER
FUNKED
GURKHA
HULKED
HUNKER
HUSKED
HUSKER
JUNKED
JUNKER
JUNKET
JUNKIE
LUCKED
LUNKER
LURKED
MUCKED
MUCKUP
MUSKEG
MUSKET
MUSKIE
MUSKOX
NUTKIN
PUCKER
PUNKAH
PUNKER
PUNKIE
QUAKED
QUAKER
QUAKES
QUOKKA
RUCKED
RUCKUS
RUSKIN
SUCKAS
SUCKED
SUCKER
SUCKIN
SUKKAH
SULKED
SULKER
SUNKEN
TUCKED
TUCKER
TUCKET
TUCKIN
TURKEY
TURKIC
TUSKED
TUSKER
YUKKED

•U••K•

EUREKA
JUDOKA
KULAKS
LUSAKA
QUACKS
QUARKS
QUIRKS
QUIRKY
QUOKKA
SUZUKI
YUROKS

•U•••K

BUROAK
CUSACK
DUBCEK
KUSPUK
LUBECK
MUKLUK
MUZHIK
NUDNIK
SUSLIK
TUGRIK

••UK••

ABUKIR
CHUKAR
CHUKKA
FLUKES
FLUKEY
RYUKYU
ZHUKOV

••U•K•

AKUAKU
BAULKS
BOURKE
CAULKS
CHUCKS
CHUKKA
CHUNKS
CHUNKY
CLUCKS
CLUNKS
CLUNKY
FLUNKS
FLUNKY
PLUCKS
PLUCKY
PLUNKS
ROURKE
SHUCKS
SKULKS
SKUNKS
SKUNKY
SPUNKY
THUNKS
TRUCKS
TRUNKS

••U••K

SQUAWK
SQUEAK

•••UK•

ADZUKI
KABUKI
PERUKE
REBUKE
SALUKI
STLUKE
SUZUKI

•••U•K

DEBUNK
INBULK
INLUCK
PODUNK
SHRUNK
STRUCK
ZANUCK

••••UK

DYBBUK
FAROUK
KUSPUK
MARDUK
MUKLUK
SELJUK
TOBRUK

UL••••

ULCERS
ULLAGE
ULLMAN
ULSTER
ULTIMA
ULTIMO
ULTRAS

U•L•••

UCLANS
UGLIER
UGLIES
UGLIFY
UGLILY
UHLANS
ULLAGE
ULLMAN
UMLAUT
UNLACE
UNLADE
UNLAID
UNLASH
UNLEAD
UNLESS
UNLIKE
UNLINK
UNLOAD
UNLOCK
UPLAND
UPLIFT
UPLINK
UPLOAD

U••L••

UBOLTS
UNCLAD
UNCLES
UNCLOG
UNGLUE
UNPLUG
URALIC
URALSK
UVALUE
UVULAE
UVULAR
UVULAS

U•••L•

UGLILY
UMBELS
UNABLE
UNBELT
UNBOLT
UNDULY
UNFOLD
UNHOLY
UNOILY
UNPILE
UNROLL
UNRULY
UNSOLD
UNTOLD
UNWELL
UNWILY
UPHELD
UPHILL
UPHOLD
UPTALK
UPWELL
URIALS
URSULA
USABLE
USABLY
USUALS

U••••L

UMBRAL
UNCIAL
UNCOIL
UNCOOL
UNCURL
UNFURL
UNGUAL
UNITAL
UNOCAL
UNREAL
UNREEL
UNROLL
UNSEAL
UNVEIL
UNWELL
UPHILL
UPWELL
URACIL
USEFUL
USMAIL

•UL•••

AULAIT
BULBIL
BULBUL
BULGAR
BULGED
BULGES
BULGUR
BULKED
BULLAE
BULLED
BULLET
BULOVA
BULWER
CULETS
CULKIN
CULLED
CULLEN
CULLER
CULLET
CULLIS
CULTIC
CULVER
DULCET
DULLEA
DULLED
DULLER
DULLES
DULUTH
EULOGY
FULANI
FULCRA
FULFIL
FULLER
FULMAR
FULTON
GULAGS
GULFED
GULLAH
GULLED
GULLET
GULPED
GULPER
HULKED
HULLED
HULLER
HULLOA
HULLOS
JULEPS
JULIAN
JULIET
JULIUS
KULAKS
KULTUR
LULLED
MULCTS
MULETA
MULEYS
MULISH
MULLAH
MULLAS
MULLED
MULLER
MULLET
MULTUM
NULLAH
NULLED
PULING
PULLED
PULLET
PULLEY
PULLIN
PULLON
PULLUP
PULPED
PULPIT
PULQUE
PULSAR
PULSED
PULSES
RULEON
RULERS
RULING
SULCUS
SULFUR
SULKED
SULKER
SULLEN
SULTAN
SULTRY
TULANE
TULARE
TULIPS
TULLES
TULSAN
VULCAN
VULGAR

•U•L••

AUKLET
BUGLED
BUGLER
BUGLES
BUILDS
BULLAE
BULLED
BULLET
BURLAP
BURLED
BURLEY
BUTLER
CULLED
CULLEN
CULLER
CULLET
CULLIS
CURLED
CURLER
CURLEW
CURLEY
CURLUP
CUTLER
CUTLET
DUALLY
DUBLIN
DUDLEY
DUELED
DUELER
DUELLO
DULLEA
DULLED
DULLER
DULLES
DUNLIN
DUNLOP
DUPLEX
EUCLID
FUELED
FUELER
FULLER
FURLED
GUELPH
GUILDS
GUILES
GUILTY
GULLAH
GULLED
GULLET
GURLEY
HULLED
HULLER
HULLOA
HULLOS
HURLED
HURLER
HURLEY
HUXLEY
KUBLAI
KUNLUN
LUBLIN
LUDLUM
LULLED
MUKLUK
MULLAH
MULLAS
MULLED
MULLER
MULLET
MUSLIM
MUSLIN
NUCLEI
NUCLEO
NULLAH
NULLED
NUTLET
OUTLAW
OUTLAY
OUTLET
PUBLIC
PULLED
PULLET
PULLEY
PULLIN
PULLON
PULLUP
PURLED
PURLIN
QUALMS
QUELLS
QUILLS
QUILTS
RUBLES
RUBLEV
RUNLET
SUBLET
SULLEN
SUNLIT
SUSLIK
SUTLER
TUILLE
TULLES
WURLEY

•U••L•

AUDILE
BUBBLE
BUBBLY
BUCKLE
BUJOLD
BUMBLE
BUNDLE
BUNGLE
BURBLE
BURBLY
BURGLE
BUSILY
BUSTLE
CUDDLE
CUDDLY
CUMULI
CUMULO
CUPELS
CUPOLA
CURDLE
CURTLY
CURULE
CUTELY
DUALLY
DUELLO
DUMBLY
DUVALL
FUDDLE
FUMBLE
FUSILS
FUTILE
GURGLE
GUZZLE
HUBBLE
HUBBLY
HUDDLE
HUGELY
HUMBLE
HUMBLY
HURDLE
HURTLE
HUSTLE
JUGGLE
JUMBLE
JUNGLE
JUNGLY
JUSTLY
KURALT
KURILE
LUNULA
LUSHLY
MUDDLE
MUFFLE
MUMBLE
MUMBLY
MURALS
MUSCLE
MUSCLY
MUTELY
MUZZLE
NUBBLE
NUBBLY
NUBILE
NUDELY
NUMBLY
NUZZLE
OUSELS
OUTFLY
OUZELS
PUDDLE
PUDDLY
PUEBLA
PUEBLO
PUNILY
PUPILS
PURELY
PURFLE
PURPLE
PURPLY
PUZZLE
QUAILS
QUAYLE
QUELLS
QUILLS
RUBBLE
RUBBLY
RUDDLE
RUDELY
RUDOLF
RUFFLE
RUFFLY
RUMBLE
RUMBLY
RUMPLE
RUMPLY
RUNDLE
RUSTLE
RUTILE
SUBTLE
SUBTLY
SUPPLE
SUPPLY
SURELY
TUILLE
TUMBLE
TUMULI
TUMULT
TUPELO
TURTLE
TUSSLE
TUVALU
YUNGLO

•U•••L

AUDIAL
BUCCAL
BULBIL
BULBUL
BUNUEL
BURSAL
BUSHEL
CUDGEL
CUNEAL
CUPFUL
CURIAL
DUCTAL
DUFFEL
DUVALL
EURAIL
FULFIL
FUNNEL
GUMBEL
GUNNEL
JUGFUL
KUMMEL
MUDEEL
MURIEL
MUSIAL
MUSSEL
MUTUAL
NUCHAL
PUMMEL
RUEFUL
RUNNEL
RUPAUL
TUNNEL

••UL••

ADULTS
ALULAE
ALULAR
AMULET
APULIA
AVULSE
BAULKS
BEULAH
BOULES
BOULEZ
BOULLE
BRULES
CAULKS
COULDA
COULEE
EVULSE
EXULTS
FAULTS
FAULTY
FOULED
FOULER
FOULLY
FOULUP
GOULET
HAULED
HAULER
HAULMS
HAULUP
JOULES
MAULED
MAULER
MOULDS
MOULDY
MOULIN
MOULTS
OCULAR
OVULAR
OVULES
PAULEY
POULTS
SAULTS
SCULLS
SCULLY
SCULPT
SKULKS
SKULLS
STULLS
TOULON
UVULAE
UVULAR
UVULAS
VAULTS
VAULTY

••U•L•

AQUILA
BAUBLE
BLUELY
BOUCLE
BOULLE
CAUDLE
CHURLS
COUPLE
DOUALA
DOUBLE
DOUBLY
DOURLY
EQUALS
FOULLY
GLUMLY
GRUELS
HOURLY
KNURLS
KNURLY
LOUDLY
ROUBLE
SCULLS
SCULLY
SKULLS
SMUGLY
SNUGLI
SNUGLY
SOURLY
SQUALL
SQUILL
STULLS
TAUTLY
THUSLY
TOUSLE
USUALS
YOUALL

••U••L

BRUMAL
BRUTAL
CAUDAL
CAUSAL
CRURAL
FAUNAL
FEUDAL
FRUGAL
LAUREL
NEURAL
NEUROL
PLURAL
SAUREL
SQUALL
SQUEAL
SQUILL
YOUALL

•••UL•

AMPULE
AMPULS
ANNULI
ANNULS
BABULS
BAKULA
COPULA
CUMULI
CUMULO
CURULE
ENGULF
FACULA
FERULE
FIBULA
GHOULS
INBULK
INCULT
INFULL
INSULT
ISEULT
LAZULI
LIGULA
LOBULE
LUNULA
MACULA
MODULE
MODULO
MOGULS
NEBULA
NODULE
OCCULT
OSCULA
PAKULA
PARULA
PENULT
PETULA
PICULS
POPULI
RADULA
RESULT
SCHULZ
SHOULD
TABULA
TUMULI
TUMULT
UNDULY
UNRULY
URSULA

•••U•L

ACTUAL
ANNUAL
BUNUEL
CASUAL
GENUAL
INFULL
LEMUEL
MANUAL
MANUEL
MIGUEL
MUTUAL
NYQUIL
RAQUEL
REFUEL
RITUAL
SAMUEL
SEQUEL
UNCURL
UNFURL
UNGUAL
VISUAL

••••UL

AIDFUL
AIMFUL
ARMFUL
ARTFUL
BAGFUL
BANJUL
BEFOUL
BOXFUL
BULBUL
CANFUL
CAPFUL
CARFUL
CONSUL
CUPFUL
DEPAUL
EARFUL
ENSOUL
EYEFUL
FITFUL
HANGUL
HATFUL
INHAUL
IREFUL
JARFUL
JOYFUL
JUGFUL
LAPFUL
LAWFUL
MANFUL
PANFUL
PEPFUL
POTFUL
RUEFUL
RUPAUL
SINFUL
SOBFUL
STPAUL
USEFUL
VATFUL
WILFUL
WOEFUL

UM••••

UMBELS
UMBERS
UMBRAE
UMBRAL
UMBRAS
UMBRIA
UMIAKS
UMLAUT
UMPIRE
UMTATA

U•M•••

UNMADE
UNMAKE
UNMANS
UNMASK
UNMEET
UNMESH
UNMOOR
UPMOST
USMAIL
UTMOST

U••M••

ULLMAN

U•••M•

UGGAMS
UGSOME
ULTIMA
ULTIMO
UNARMS
UNJAMS
UPTIME

•UM•••

AUMONT
BUMBLE
BUMBRY
BUMMED
BUMMER
BUMOUT
BUMPED
BUMPER
BUMPPO
BUMPUP
BUMRAP
CUMBER
CUMULI
CUMULO
DUMBER
DUMBLY
DUMDUM
DUMONT
DUMPED
DUMPER
FUMBLE
FUMIER
FUMING
GUMBEL
GUMBOS
GUMMED
GUMSUP
HUMANE
HUMANS
HUMBLE
HUMBLY
HUMBUG
HUMERI
HUMMED
HUMMER
HUMMUS
HUMORS
HUMOUR
HUMPED
HUMPHS
HUMVEE
JUMADA
JUMBLE
JUMBOS
JUMPAT
JUMPED
JUMPER
JUMPIN
JUMPON
JUMPUP
KUMISS
KUMMEL
LUMBAR
LUMBER
LUMENS
LUMINA
LUMMOX
LUMPED
LUMPEN
LUMPER
LUMPUR
MUMBLE
MUMBLY
MUMMED
MUMMER
MUMPED
NUMBAT
NUMBED

NUMBER
NUMBLY
NUMERO
NUMINA
PUMICE
PUMMEL
PUMPED
PUMPER
PUMPUP
QUMRAN
RUMBAS
RUMBLE
RUMBLY
RUMENS
RUMINA
RUMMER
RUMORS
RUMOUR
RUMPLE
RUMPLY
RUMPUS
SUMACS
SUMMAE
SUMMAS
SUMMED
SUMMER
SUMMIT
SUMMON
SUMNER
SUMSUP
SUMTER
SUMUPS
TUMBLE
TUMEFY
TUMMED
TUMULI
TUMULT
YUMYUM

•U•M••
BUMMED
BUMMER
BURMAN
BUSMAN
BUSMEN
DUOMOS
FULMAR
GUIMPE
GUMMED
GUNMAN
GUNMEN
HUMMED
HUMMER
HUMMUS
KUMMEL
LUMMOX
MUMMED
MUMMER
MURMUR
MUUMUU
NUTMEG
PUMMEL
QUEMOY
RUDMAN
RUMMER
SUBMIT
SUMMAE
SUMMAS
SUMMED
SUMMER
SUMMIT
SUMMON
TUBMAN
TUMMED

•U••M•
AUTUMN
QUALMS
RUNDMC
SURIMI

•U•••M
BUNKUM
CUBISM
CURIUM
CUSTOM
DUMDUM
DUNHAM
DURHAM
LUDLUM
MULTUM
MUSEUM
MUSLIM
PURISM
PUTNAM
QUORUM
SUBGUM
SUFISM
YUMYUM

••UM••
ACUMEN
ALUMNA
ALUMNI
BRUMAL
BRUMBY
BRUMES
CHUMMY
CHUMPS
CLUMPS
CLUMPY
CLUMSY
CRUMBS
CRUMBY
CRUMMY
DRUMUP
FLUMES
FRUMPS
FRUMPY
GAUMED
GLUMLY
GRUMPS
GRUMPY
MAUMAU
MAUMEE
MUUMUU
NEUMAN
NEUMES
NOUMEA
PLUMBS
PLUMED
PLUMES
PLUMMY
PLUMPS
RHUMBA
RHUMBS
SCUMMY
SLUMMY
SLUMPS
SPUMED
SPUMES
STUMER
STUMPS
STUMPY
THUMBS
THUMPS
TRUMAN
TRUMPS

••U•M•
CHUMMY
CRUMMY
HAULMS
PLUMMY
SCUMMY
SLUMMY
ZEUGMA

••U••M
FOURAM
FOURPM
SQUIRM
TRUISM

•••UM•
ALBUMS
ASSUME
AUTUMN
BATUMI
BEGUMS
BENUMB
COLUMN
FORUMS
GAZUMP
ILLUME
JORUMS
KHOUMS
LEGUME
MAZUMA
ODIUMS
PNEUMA
RELUME
RESUME
RHEUMS
RHEUMY
SCRUMS
SEDUMS
SERUMS
STRUMS
THRUMS
TRAUMA
VOLUME

•••U•M
VACUUM

••••UM
ACTIUM
ADYTUM
ALARUM
ALLIUM
ANTRUM
ARTGUM
ASYLUM
ATRIUM
BARIUM
BARNUM
BAYRUM
BEEGUM
BOOJUM
BUNKUM
CERIUM
CESIUM
CILIUM
CIRCUM
CONIUM
CORIUM
CURIUM
DICTUM
DIMSUM
DORSUM
DUMDUM
ERBIUM
FAIYUM
FOLIUM
FRENUM
GOLLUM
GYPSUM
HELIUM
INDIUM
IONIUM
LABRUM
LATIUM
LUDLUM
LYCEUM
MAGNUM
MEDIUM
MINIUM
MULTUM
MUSEUM
OMASUM
OMNIUM
OSMIUM
OSTIUM
PABLUM
PEPLUM
PHYLUM
PILEUM
PLENUM
PODIUM
POSSUM
PRIMUM
QUORUM
RADIUM
REDGUM
SACRUM
SALTUM
SCARUM
SEPTUM
SODIUM
SUBGUM
TALCUM
TEDEUM
TEDIUM
VACUUM
VALIUM
VELLUM
WAMPUM
YUMYUM

UN••••
UNABLE
UNAGED
UNARMS
UNAWED
UNBARS
UNBELT
UNBEND
UNBENT
UNBIND
UNBOLT
UNBORN
UNBUSY
UNCAGE
UNCAPS
UNCASE
UNCHIC
UNCIAL
UNCLAD
UNCLES
UNCLOG
UNCOIL
UNCOOL
UNCORK
UNCURL
UNDIES
UNDINE
UNDOER
UNDOES
UNDONE
UNDRAW
UNDULY
UNDYED
UNEASE
UNEASY
UNESCO
UNEVEN
UNFAIR
UNFITS
UNFOLD
UNFREE
UNFURL
UNGIRD
UNGIRT
UNGLUE
UNGUAL
UNGUES
UNGUIS
UNHAND
UNHEED
UNHOLY
UNHOOK
UNHURT
UNIATE
UNIATS
UNICEF
UNIFIC
UNIONS
UNIPOD
UNIQUE
UNISEX
UNISON
UNISYS
UNITAL
UNITAS
UNITED
UNITER
UNITES
UNIVAC
UNJAMS
UNJUST
UNKIND
UNKINK
UNKNIT
UNKNOT
UNLACE
UNLADE
UNLAID
UNLASH
UNLEAD
UNLESS
UNLIKE
UNLINK
UNLOAD
UNLOCK
UNMADE
UNMAKE
UNMANS
UNMASK
UNMEET
UNMESH
UNMOOR
UNOCAL
UNOILY
UNOPEN
UNPACK
UNPAID
UNPEGS
UNPENS
UNPILE
UNPINS
UNPLUG
UNREAD
UNREAL
UNREEL
UNREST
UNRIGS
UNRIPE
UNROBE
UNROLL
UNROOT
UNRULY
UNSAFE
UNSAID
UNSAYS
UNSEAL
UNSEAT
UNSEEN
UNSEWN
UNSEWS
UNSHED
UNSHOD
UNSNAG
UNSNAP
UNSOLD
UNSOWN
UNSTOP
UNSUNG
UNSURE
UNTACK
UNTIDY
UNTIED
UNTIES
UNTOLD
UNTORN
UNTRAP
UNTROD
UNTRUE
UNTUNE
UNUSED
UNVEIL
UNWARY
UNWELL
UNWILY
UNWIND
UNWISE
UNWISH
UNWORN
UNWOVE
UNWRAP
UNYOKE
UNZIPS

U•N•••
UINTAS

U••N••
UBANGI
UGANDA
UNKNIT
UNKNOT
UNSNAG
UNSNAP
UPENDS
URANIA
URANIC
URANUS
USANCE
USENET

U•••N•
UCLANS
UHLANS
UNBEND
UNBENT
UNBIND
UNDINE
UNDONE
UNHAND
UNIONS
UNKIND
UNKINK
UNLINK
UNMANS
UNPENS
UNPINS
UNSUNG
UNTUNE
UNWIND
UPLAND
UPLINK
UPPING
UPWIND
URBANA
URBANE
URGENT
URGING
URSINE
UTHANT
UTURNS

U••••N
UGRIAN
UJJAIN
ULLMAN
UNBORN
UNEVEN
UNISON
UNOPEN
UNSEEN
UNSEWN
UNSOWN
UNTORN
UNWORN
UPJOHN
UPTOWN
UPTURN
URCHIN
USOPEN
UTAHAN

•UN•••
AUNTIE
BUNCHE
BUNCHY
BUNCOS
BUNDLE
BUNGED
BUNGEE
BUNGLE
BUNION
BUNKED
BUNKER
BUNKOS
BUNKUM
BUNSEN
BUNTED
BUNTER
BUNUEL
BUNYAN
BUNYIP
CUNARD
CUNAXA
CUNEAL
DUNANT
DUNBAR
DUNCAN
DUNCES
DUNDEE
DUNERA
DUNHAM
DUNKED
DUNKER
DUNLIN
DUNLOP
DUNNED
EUNICE
FUNDED
FUNGUS
FUNKED
FUNNED
FUNNEL
GUNDOG
GUNFOR
GUNGHO
GUNITE
GUNMAN
GUNMEN
GUNNAR
GUNNED
GUNNEL
GUNNER
GUNSHY
GUNTER
HUNGER
HUNGIN
HUNGON
HUNGRY
HUNGUP
HUNGWU
HUNKER
HUNTED
HUNTER
JUNCOS
JUNEAU
JUNGLE
JUNGLY
JUNIOR
JUNKED
JUNKER
JUNKET
JUNKIE
JUNTAS
JUNTOS
KUNGFU
KUNLUN
LUNACY
LUNATE
LUNCHY
LUNDEN
LUNGED
LUNGES
LUNKER
LUNULA
MUNCHY
MUNCIE
MUNGOS
MUNICH
MUNTIN
NUNCIO
OUNCES
PUNCHY
PUNDIT
PUNIER
PUNILY
PUNISH
PUNJAB
PUNKAH
PUNKER
PUNKIE
PUNNED
PUNNET
PUNTED
PUNTER
RUNCIE
RUNDLE
RUNDMC
RUNDRY
RUNFOR
RUNGUP
RUNINS
RUNLET
RUNNEL
RUNNER
RUNOFF
RUNONS
RUNOUT
RUNSAT
RUNSIN
RUNSON
RUNSTO
RUNSUP
RUNUPS
RUNWAY
RUNYON
SUNDAE
SUNDAY
SUNDER
SUNDEW
SUNDOG
SUNDRY
SUNGOD
SUNKEN
SUNLIT
SUNNED
SUNNIS
SUNOCO
SUNRAY
SUNSET
SUNTAN
SUNUNU
SUNUPS
TUNDRA
TUNEIN
TUNERS
TUNEUP
TUNICA
TUNICS
TUNING
TUNNEL
TUNNEY
YUNGLO
YUNNAN

•U•N••
BUENOS
BURNED
BURNER
BURNET
BURNEY
BURNUP
DUENNA
DUNNED
DURNED
EUPNEA
FUNNED
FUNNEL
GUENON
GUINEA
GUNNAR
GUNNED
GUNNEL
GUNNER
GURNEY
LUANDA
LUGNUT
NUANCE
NUDNIK
PUENTE
PUNNED
PUNNET
PUTNAM
QUANGO
QUANTA
QUENCH
QUINCE
QUINCY
QUINOA
QUINTS
RUANAS
RUANDA
RUINED
RUINER
RUNNEL
RUNNER
SUMNER
SUNNED
SUNNIS
TUNNEL
TUNNEY
TURNED
TURNER
TURNIN
TURNIP
TURNON
TURNTO
TURNUP
YUNNAN

•U••N•
AUDENS
AUFOND
AUGEND
AUMONT
AUXINS
BURINS
BUSING
BUSONI
BUTANE
BUTENE
BUTUNG
BUYING
CUBING
CURING
CUTINS
DUENNA
DUGONG
DUKING
DUMONT
DUNANT
DUPING
DUPONT
DURANT
DURING
EUGENE
FULANI
FUMING
FUSING
FUTONS
FUZING
GUIANA
GUYANA
GUYING
HUMANE
HUMANS
HURONS
JUKING
LUBING
LUCENT
LUDENS
LUMENS
LUMINA
LUPINE
LUPINO
LUPONE
LURING
LUTING
MUCINS
MURANO
MURINE
MUSING
MUSTNT
MUTANT
MUTING
MUTINY
NUGENT
NUKING
NUMINA
OUTING
PUISNE
PULING
PURINA
PURINE
PUTONS
QUAINT
QUEENS
QUERNS
QUOINS
RUBENS
RULING
RUMENS
RUMINA
RUNINS
RUNONS
SUNUNU
SUPINE
SUSANN
TUBING
TUCANA
TULANE
TUNING
TURING

•U•••N
AUBURN
AUGEAN
AUSTEN
AUSTIN
AUTUMN
BUCHAN
BUFFON
BUNION
BUNSEN
BUNYAN
BURDEN
BURMAN
BURTON
BUSKIN
BUSMAN
BUSMEN
BUSTIN
BUTTIN
BUTTON
CULKIN
CULLEN
CURTIN
CURZON
CUTSIN
DUBBIN
DUBLIN
DUCHIN
DUDEEN
DUNCAN
DUNLIN
DURBAN
DURBIN
DURIAN
DUSTIN
FUJIAN
FULTON
FUSION
GUDRUN
GUENON
GUIDON
GUNMAN
GUNMEN
HUDSON
HUNGIN
HUNGON
HUSTON
HUTTON
JULIAN
JUMPIN
JUMPON
JUSTIN
KUCHEN
KUNLUN
KURGAN
LUBLIN
LUCIAN
LUDDEN
LUMPEN
LUNDEN
MUDHEN
MUFFIN
MUNTIN
MUSLIN
MUTTON
NUBBIN
NUBIAN
NUTKIN
OUTGUN
OUTRAN
OUTRUN
PUFFIN
PULLIN
PULLON
PURLIN
PUSHON
PUTSIN
PUTSON
QUEZON
QUMRAN
RUBSIN
RUDMAN
RULEON
RUNSIN
RUNSON
RUNYON
RUSKIN
RUTTAN
SUBORN
SUCKIN
SUDDEN
SULLEN
SULTAN
SUMMON
SUNKEN
SUNTAN
SUSANN
SUTTON
TUBMAN
TUCHUN
TUCKIN
TUCSON
TULSAN
TUNEIN
TUPIAN
TURBAN
TUREEN
TURNIN
TURNON
TURPIN
TUSCAN
VULCAN
YUNNAN

••UN••
BLUNTS
BOUNCE
BOUNCY
BOUNDS
BOUNTY
BRUNCH
BRUNEI
BRUNET
BRUNTS
CHUNKS
CHUNKY
CLUNKS
CLUNKY
COUNTS
COUNTY
CRUNCH
DAUNTS
FAUNAE
FAUNAL
FAUNAS
FAUNUS
FLUNKS
FLUNKY
FOUNDS
FOUNTS
GOUNOD
GRUNDY
GRUNGE
GRUNGY
GRUNTS
HAUNCH
HAUNTS
HOUNDS
HOUNDY
JAUNTS
JAUNTY
JOUNCE
JOUNCY
KAUNAS
KAUNDA
LAUNCH
LOUNGE
MAUNDY
MBUNDU
MOUNDS
MOUNTS
MOUNTY
PAUNCH
PLUNGE
PLUNKS
POUNCE
POUNDS
PRUNED
PRUNER
PRUNES
REUNES
ROUNDS
SAUNAS
SHUNTS
SKUNKS
SKUNKY
SOUNDS
SPUNKY
STUNTS
STUNTY
TAUNTS
THUNKS
TRUNKS
VAUNTS
WOUNDS
ZOUNDS

••U•N•
ALUMNA
ALUMNI
AQUINO
BLUING
BOURNE
BRUINS
CHURNS
CLUING
EQUINE
GLUING
GLUONS
IGUANA
JOURNO
MOURNS
SLUING
SPURNS
SQUINT
TAUONS
TRUANT
TRUING
UTURNS

••U••N
ACUMEN
ANURAN
ARUBAN
BHUTAN
BOUDIN
CLUEIN
COUPON
COUSIN
GLUTEN
LAUREN
LOUDEN
MOULIN
MOUTON
NEUMAN
NEURON
NGUYEN
PLUGIN
POURIN
REUBEN
SHUTIN
SPURON
TAUTEN
TEUTON
TOUCAN
TOULON
TRUMAN
VAUGHN
YAUPON

•••UN•
ABOUND
AMOUNT
ARJUNA
AROUND
ATTUNE
AVAUNT
BOSUNS
BUTUNG
CAJUNS
COHUNE
DEBUNK
EDMUND
EXEUNT
FECUND
FLAUNT
GERUND
GROUND
HLHUNT
IMMUNE
IMMUNO
INTUNE
JEJUNE
JOCUND
KAHUNA
KORUNA
LACUNA
LAGUNA
MIFUNE
OBTUND
OSMUND
PODUNK
REFUND
REHUNG
RERUNS
RETUNE
ROTUND
SHRUNK
SPRUNG
STRUNG
SUNUNU
TRIUNE
UNSUNG
UNTUNE
VARUNA
VICUNA

•••U•N
ALCUIN
AUBURN
AUTUMN
COBURN
COLUMN
FRAUEN
IMPUGN
INTURN
LEGUIN
MCKUEN
OPPUGN
PADUAN
PAPUAN
PAQUIN
REPUGN
RETURN
SATURN
SEQUIN
SIOUAN
UPTURN

••••UN
AIRGUN
BARZUN
BIGGUN
CANCUN
CAPGUN
DATSUN
DRYRUN
ENDRUN
GUDRUN
JETGUN
KUNLUN
LEBRUN
MACOUN
OUTGUN
OUTRUN
POPGUN
RAYGUN
SHOGUN
SIXGUN
SKIRUN
TOPGUN
TUCHUN
VERDUN

U•O•••
UBOATS
UBOLTS
UNOCAL
UNOILY
UNOPEN
USOPEN
UTOPIA

U••O••
UGSOME
UNBOLT
UNBORN
UNCOIL
UNCOOL
UNCORK
UNDOER
UNDOES
UNDONE
UNFOLD
UNHOLY
UNHOOK
UNIONS
UNLOAD
UNLOCK
UNMOOR
UNROBE
UNROLL
UNROOT
UNSOLD
UNSOWN
UNTOLD
UNTORN
UNWORN
UNWOVE
UNYOKE
UPBOWS
UPHOLD
UPJOHN
UPLOAD
UPMOST
UPROAR
UPROOT
UPROSE
UPTOWN
UTMOST

U•••O•
UNCLOG
UNCOOL
UNHOOK
UNIPOD
UNISON
UNKNOT
UNMOOR
UNROOT
UNSHOD
UNSTOP
UNTROD
UPROOT
UPSHOT

U••••O
ULTIMO
UNESCO
USEDTO

•UO•••
BUOYED
BUOYUP
DUOMOS
KUOPIO
QUOINS
QUOITS
QUOKKA
QUOQUE
QUORUM
QUOTAS
QUOTED
QUOTER
QUOTES
QUOTHA

•U•O••
AUFOND
AUMONT
AURORA
AUROUS
BUGOFF
BUGOUT
BUJOLD
BULOVA
BUMOUT
BUROAK
BUSONI
BUYOFF
BUYOUT
CUBOID
CUPOLA
CUTOFF
CUTOUT
DUBOIS
DUGONG
DUGOUT
DUMONT
DUPONT
DUROCS
EUBOEA
EUDORA
EULOGY
EUROPA
EUROPE
FURORE
FURORS
FUTONS
GUYOTS
HUMORS
HUMOUR
HURONS
JUDOKA
JURORS
LUGOSI
LUPONE
MUCOSA
MUCOUS
PUTOFF
PUTONS
PUTOUT
RUBOFF
RUBOUT
RUDOLF
RUFOUS
RUGOSE
RUMORS
RUMOUR
RUNOFF
RUNONS
RUNOUT
SUBORN
SUNOCO
TUDORS
TUTORS
YUROKS

•U••O•
AUDIOS
AUTHOR
BUENOS
BUFFON
BUFFOS
BUNCOS
BUNION
BUNKOS
BURBOT
BURGOO
BURGOS
BURROS
BURROW
BURTON
BUSBOY
BUTEOS
BUTTON
CUCKOO
CURIOS
CURSOR
CURZON
CUSTOM
CUSTOS
DUNLOP
DUOMOS
FULTON
FURROW
FUSION
FUZHOU
GUACOS
GUENON
GUIDON
GUIROS
GUMBOS
GUNDOG
GUNFOR
HUDSON
HUEVOS
HULLOA
HULLOS
HUNGON
HUSTON
HUTTON
JUMBOS
JUMPON
JUNCOS
JUNIOR
JUNTOS
KUDROW
LUMMOX
LUTHOR
MUGHOS
MUNGOS
MURROW
MUSKOX
MUTTON
OUTBOX
OUTFOX
PULLON
PUSHON
PUTSON
QUAHOG
QUEMOY
QUEZON
QUINOA
RULEON
RUNFOR
RUNSON
RUNYON
SUCCOR
SUITOR
SUMMON
SUNDOG
SUNGOD
SUTTON
TUCSON
TURBOS
TURBOT
TURGOR
TURNON

•U•••O
AUSTRO
BUMPPO
BURGOO
CUCKOO
CUMULO
DUELLO
GUNGHO
JURADO
KUOPIO
LUPINO
MURANO
MUTATO
NUCLEO
NUMERO
NUNCIO
PUEBLO
PUERTO
PUTSTO
QUANGO
QUARTO
RUBATO
RUNSTO
SUBITO
SUNOCO
TUPELO
TURNTO
TUXEDO
YUNGLO

••UO••
FLUORO
GLUONS
TAUONS

••U•O•
BLUEOX
BOUBOU
COUPON
CRUSOE
ETUXOR
GOUNOD
MOUTON
NEUROL
NEURON
SPURON
STUPOR
TAUTOG
TEUTON
TOULON
YAUPON
ZHUKOV

••U••O
AQUINO
BHUTTO
CAUCHO
CHURRO
FLUORO
GAUCHO
JOURNO
SLUGGO
STUCCO
STUDIO

•••UO•
LIQUOR
PEQUOD
PEQUOT

•••U•O
ARTURO
BAGUIO
CARUSO
COLUGO
CUMULO
ENDURO
ESCUDO
IMMUNO
MADURO
MAPUTO
MODULO
PSEUDO
SENUFO
TENUTO

••••UO
BANQUO

UP••••
UPASES
UPBEAT
UPBOWS
UPCAST
UPDATE
UPDIKE
UPENDS
UPHELD
UPHILL
UPHOLD
UPJOHN
UPKEEP
UPLAND
UPLIFT
UPLINK
UPLOAD
UPMOST
UPPERS
UPPING
UPPISH
UPPITY
UPRISE
UPROAR
UPROOT
UPROSE
UPRUSH
UPSETS
UPSHOT
UPSIDE
UPTAKE
UPTALK
UPTICK
UPTIME
UPTOWN
UPTURN
UPWARD
UPWELL
UPWIND

U•P•••
UMPIRE
UNPACK
UNPAID
UNPEGS
UNPENS
UNPILE
UNPINS
UNPLUG
UPPERS
UPPING
UPPISH
UPPITY

U••P••
UNIPOD
UNOPEN
USOPEN
UTOPIA

U•••P•
UNCAPS
UNRIPE
UNZIPS
USURPS

U••••P
UNSNAP
UNSTOP
UNTRAP
UNWRAP
UPKEEP
USEDUP
USESUP

•UP•••
AUPAIR
CUPELS
CUPFUL
CUPIDS
CUPOLA
CUPPAS
CUPPED
CUPRIC
DUPERY
DUPING
DUPLEX
DUPONT
EUPNEA
LUPINE
LUPINO
LUPONE
MUPPET
PUPILS
PUPPET
RUPAUL
RUPEES
RUPERT
RUPIAH
SUPERB
SUPERS
SUPINE
SUPPED
SUPPER
SUPPLE
SUPPLY
TUPELO
TUPIAN
YUPPIE

•U•P••
AUSPEX
BUMPED
BUMPER
BUMPPO
BUMPUP
BURPED
CUPPAS
CUPPED
CUSPED
CUSPID
DUMPED
DUMPER
GULPED
GULPER
HUMPED
HUMPHS
JUMPAT
JUMPED
JUMPER
JUMPIN
JUMPON
JUMPUP
KUOPIO
KUSPUK
LUMPED
LUMPEN
LUMPER
LUMPUR
MUDPIE
MUMPED
MUPPET
MURPHY
OUTPUT
PULPED
PULPIT
PUMPED
PUMPER
PUMPUP
PUPPET
PURPLE
PURPLY
PUTPUT
QUIPPY
QUIPUS
RUMPLE
RUMPLY
RUMPUS
SUBPAR
SUPPED
SUPPER
SUPPLE
SUPPLY
TURPIN
YUPPIE

•U••P•
BUMPPO
CUTUPS
EUROPA
EUROPE
GUELPH
GUIMPE
JULEPS
QUIPPY
RUNUPS
SUMUPS
SUNUPS
TULIPS

•U•••P
BUCKUP
BUMPUP
BUMRAP
BUNYIP
BUOYUP
BURLAP
BURNUP
BUYSUP
CURLUP
CUTSUP
DUNLOP
DUSTUP
GUMSUP
HUBCAP
HUNGUP
JUMPUP
MUCKUP
MUSSUP
PULLUP
PUMPUP
PUSHUP
PUTSUP
RUNGUP
RUNSUP
SUITUP
SUMSUP
TUNEUP
TURNIP
TURNUP

••UP••
COUPES
COUPLE
COUPON
DRUPES
ERUPTS
LAUPER
LOUPES
PAUPER
SOUPUP
STUPAS
STUPES
STUPID
STUPOR
TAUPES
TOUPEE
YAUPON

••U•P•
CHUMPS
CLUMPS
CLUMPY
EQUIPS
FOURPM
FRUMPS
FRUMPY
GRUMPS
GRUMPY
PLUMPS
SCULPT
SLUMPS
SLURPS
STUMPS
STUMPY
THUMPS
TRUMPS
USURPS

••U••P
DRUMUP
FOULUP
HAULUP
SHUTUP
SOUPUP

•••UP•
ABRUPT
CROUPY
CUTUPS
FIXUPS
GETUPS
GROUPS
IRRUPT
JAMUPS
LAYUPS
LETUPS
MIXUPS
MOPUPS
NIPUPS
OCCUPY
ONEUPS
PINUPS
POPUPS
RUNUPS
SCAUPS
SETUPS
SITUPS
STOUPS
SUMUPS
SUNUPS
SYRUPS
SYRUPY
TIEUPS
TIPUPS
TROUPE

•••U•P
GAZUMP

••••UP
ACESUP
ACTSUP
ADDSUP
ANTEUP
BACKUP
BALLUP
BANGUP
BEADUP
BEAMUP
BEARUP
BEATUP
BEEFUP
BIDSUP
BINDUP
BLEWUP
BLOWUP
BOBSUP
BONEUP
BOOTUP
BOREUP
BUCKUP
BUMPUP
BUOYUP
BURNUP
BUYSUP
CALLUP
CAMEUP
CATSUP
CHATUP
CHEWUP
CHINUP
CLAMUP
CLOGUP
COILUP
COMEUP
COOKUP
COOPUP
CROPUP
CURLUP
CUTSUP
DAMSUP
DIALUP
DIGSUP
DOESUP
DOLLUP
DONEUP
DRAWUP
DREWUP
DRUMUP
DUSTUP
EASEUP
EATSUP
EGGCUP
ENDSUP
EVENUP
EYECUP
FACEUP
FAIRUP
FESSUP
FILLUP
FIREUP
FIRMUP
FLIPUP
FOGSUP
FOLDUP
FOULUP
GALLUP
GANGUP
GAVEUP
GEARUP
GETSUP
GIVEUP
GOESUP
GOOFUP
GREWUP
GROWUP
GUMSUP
HANDUP
HANGUP
HARDUP
HAULUP
HEADUP
HEATUP
HELDUP
HICCUP
HIGHUP
HIKEUP
HITSUP
HOLDUP
HOLEUP
HOOKUP
HOPSUP
HUNGUP
HYPEUP
ICEDUP
ICESUP
JACKUP
JAMSUP
JAZZUP
JOINUP
JUMPUP
KEEPUP
KEPTUP
KEYSUP
KICKUP
LACEUP
LAIDUP
LAPSUP
LARRUP
LASHUP
LAYSUP
LEADUP
LETSUP
LIFTUP
LINEUP
LINKUP
LOCKUP
LOOKUP
MADEUP
MAKEUP
MARKUP
MESSUP
MOCKUP
MOPSUP
MOVEUP
MUCKUP
MUSSUP
OPENUP
OWNSUP
PACKUP
PAIDUP
PAIRUP
PASSUP
PAYSUP
PENTUP
PEPSUP
PERKUP
PICKUP
PILEUP
PIPEUP
PLAYUP
PONYUP
POPSUP
PRENUP
PROPUP
PULLUP
PUMPUP
PUSHUP
PUTSUP
RACKUP
RAKEUP
RANGUP
RAVEUP
REARUP
RECOUP
RESTUP
REVSUP
RIGSUP
RILEUP
RINGUP
RIPSUP
ROLLUP
RUNGUP
RUNSUP
SANNUP
SAVEUP
SEALUP
SENDUP
SENTUP
SETSUP
SEWNUP
SEWSUP
SHOTUP
SHOWUP
SHUTUP
SIGNUP
SITSUP
SIZEUP
SLAPUP
SLIPUP
SLOWUP
SNAPUP
SOAKUP
SOPSUP
SOUPUP
SPEDUP
STAYUP
STEPUP
STIRUP
STOPUP
SUITUP
SUMSUP
TAGSUP
TAKEUP
TALKUP
TANKUP
TEACUP
TEAMUP
TEARUP
TEEDUP
TEESUP
TIDYUP
TIEDUP
TIESUP
TITTUP
TONEUP
TOOKUP
TOOLUP
TOREUP
TOSSUP
TOTSUP
TRIPUP
TUNEUP
TURNUP
TYPEUP
USEDUP
USESUP
WADSUP
WAITUP
WAKEUP
WALKUP
WALLUP
WARMUP
WASHUP
WELLUP
WENTUP
WHIPUP
WINDUP
WIPEUP
WISEUP
WOKEUP
WORKUP
WRAPUP
ZIPSUP

U••Q••
UBIQUE
UNIQUE

•UQ•••
BUQSHA
TUQUES

•U•Q••
CUIQUE
PULQUE
QUOQUE

•U•••Q
SUSIEQ

UR••••
URACIL
URAEUS
URALIC
URALSK
URANIA
URANIC
URANUS
URBANA
URBANE
URCHIN
URGENT
URGERS
URGING
URIALS
URSIDS
URSINE
URSULA
URTEXT
URUSES

U•R•••
UGRIAN
UNREAD
UNREAL
UNREEL
UNREST
UNRIGS
UNRIPE
UNROBE
UNROLL
UNROOT
UNRULY
UPRISE
UPROAR
UPROOT
UPROSE
UPRUSH

U••R••
ULTRAS
UMBRAE
UMBRAL
UMBRAS
UMBRIA
UNARMS
UNDRAW
UNFREE
UNTRAP
UNTROD
UNTRUE
UNWRAP
USERID
USURER
USURPS
UTURNS

U•••R•
UAKARI
UDDERS
UIGURS
ULCERS
UMBERS
UMPIRE
UNBARS
UNBORN
UNCORK
UNCURL
UNFURL
UNGIRD
UNGIRT
UNHURT
UNSURE
UNTORN
UNWARY
UNWORN
UPPERS
UPTURN
UPWARD
URGERS
USHERS
UTTERS

U••••R
UGLIER
ULSTER
UNDOER
UNFAIR
UNITER
UNMOOR
UPROAR
USURER
UVULAR

•UR•••
AUREUS
AURIFY
AURIGA
AURORA
AUROUS
BURBLE
BURBLY
BURBOT
BURDEN
BUREAU
BURGAS
BURGEE
BURGER
BURGHS
BURGLE
BURGOO
BURGOS
BURIED
BURIES
BURINS
BURLAP
BURLED
BURLEY
BURMAN
BURNED
BURNER
BURNET
BURNEY
BURNUP
BUROAK
BURPED
BURRED
BURROS
BURROW
BURSAE
BURSAL
BURSAR
BURSAS
BURSES
BURSTS
BURTON
CURACY
CURARE
CURATE
CURBED
CURDED
CURDLE
CURERS
CURFEW
CURIAE
CURIAL
CURING
CURIOS
CURIUM
CURLED
CURLER
CURLEW
CURLEY
CURLUP
CURRED
CURSED
CURSES
CURSOR
CURTER
CURTIN
CURTIS
CURTIZ
CURTLY
CURTSY
CURULE
CURVED
CURVES
CURVET
CURZON
DURANT
DURBAN
DURBAR
DURBIN
DURESS
DURFEY
DURHAM
DURIAN
DURING
DURNED
DUROCS
DURYEA
EURAIL
EUREKA
EUROPA
EUROPE
FURIES
FURLED
FURORE
FURORS
FURRED
FURROW
FURZES
GURGLE
GURKHA
GURLEY
GURNEY
HURDLE
HURLED
HURLER
HURLEY
HURONS
HURRAH
HURRAY
HURTLE
JURADO
JURATS
JURIES
JURIST
JURORS
KURALT
KURGAN
KURILE
LURING
LURKED
MURALS
MURANO
MURCIA
MURDER
MURIEL
MURINE
MURMUR
MURPHY
MURRAY
MURRES
MURREY
MURROW
NURSED
NURSER
NURSES
PURACE
PURDAH
PURDUE
PUREED
PUREES
PURELY
PUREST
PURFLE
PURGED
PURGES
PURIFY
PURINA
PURINE
PURISM
PURIST
PURITY
PURLED
PURLIN
PURPLE
PURPLY
PURRED
PURRER
PURSED
PURSER
PURSES
PURSUE
PURVEY
QURUSH
SURAHS
SURELY
SUREST
SURETE
SURETY
SURFED
SURFER
SURGED
SURGES
SURIMI
SURREY
SURTAX
SURVEY
TURBAN
TURBID
TURBIT
TURBOS
TURBOT
TUREEN
TURFED
TURGID
TURGOR
TURING
TURKEY
TURKIC
TURNED
TURNER
TURNIN
TURNIP
TURNON
TURNTO
TURNUP
TURPIN
TURRET
TURTLE
TURVES
WURLEY
WURSTS
YUROKS
ZURICH

•U•R••
AUBREY
AUDREY
BUMRAP
BURRED
BURROS
BURROW
CUPRIC
CURRED
DUARTE
FURRED
FURROW
GUARDS
GUDRUN
GUERRE
GUIROS
HUBRIS
HURRAH
HURRAY
JUAREZ
KUDROW
KUKRIS
MUDRAS
MURRAY
MURRES
MURREY
MURROW
NUTRIA
OUTRAN
OUTRUN
PUERTO
PUGREE
PURRED
PURRER
PUTRID
QUARKS
QUARRY
QUARTO
QUARTS
QUARTZ
QUERNS
QUIRES
QUIRKS
QUIRKY
QUIRTS
QUMRAN
QUORUM
RUBRIC
SUDRAS
SUNRAY
SURREY
SUTRAS
TUAREG
TUGRIK
TURRET

•U••R•
AUBURN
AUGERS
AUGURS
AUGURY
AURORA
AUSTRO
BUMBRY
BUYERS
CUNARD
CURARE
CURERS
DUNERA
DUPERY
EUCHRE
EUDORA
FUGARD
FULCRA
FURORE
FURORS
FUTURE
GUERRE
GUITRY
HUBERT
HUMERI
HUMORS
HUNGRY
JURORS
LUGERS
LUSTRE
LUXURY
MUSERS
NUMERO
OUTCRY
QUADRI
QUARRY
RULERS
RUMORS
RUNDRY
RUPERT

SUBARU SUBORN SUBURB SUGARS SUGARY SULTRY SUNDRY SUPERB SUPERS SUTURE TUBERS TUDORS TULARE TUNDRA TUNERS TUTORS TUYERE

•U•••R

AUPAIR AUTEUR AUTHOR BUFFER BUGLER BULGAR BULGUR BULWER BUMMER BUMPER BUNKER BUNTER BURGER BURNER BURSAR BUSBAR BUSIER BUSTER BUTLER BUTTER BUZZER CULLER CULVER CUMBER CURLER CURSOR CURTER CUSTER CUTLER CUTTER DUELER DUFFER DUIKER DULLER DUMBER DUMPER DUNBAR DUNKER DURBAR DUSTER FUELER FULLER FULMAR FUMIER GUITAR GULPER GUNFOR GUNNAR GUNNER GUNTER GUSHER GUTTER HUGGER HULLER HUMMER HUMOUR HUNGER HUNKER HUNTER HURLER HUSKER HUSSAR JUDDER JUICER JUMPER JUNIOR JUNKER JUSTER KULTUR LUBBER LUGGER LUMBAR LUMBER LUMPER LUMPUR LUNKER LUSHER LUSTER LUTHER LUTHOR MUDDER MUGGER MULLER MUMMER MURDER MURMUR MUSHER MUSTER MUTTER NUDGER NUMBER NURSER NUTTER OUSTER PUCKER PUFFER PULSAR PUMPER PUNIER PUNKER PUNTER PURRER PURSER PUTTER QUAKER QUASAR QUAVER QUEUER QUIVER QUOTER RUBBER RUDDER RUINER RUMMER RUMOUR RUNFOR RUNNER RUTGER SUAVER SUBPAR SUCCOR SUCKER SUFFER SUITOR SULFUR SULKER SUMMER SUMNER SUMTER SUNDER SUPPER SURFER SUTLER SUTTER TUCKER TUGGER TURGOR TURNER TUSKER VULGAR ZUIDER

••UR••

ANURAN BEURRE BLURBS BLURRY BLURTS BOURKE BOURNE BOURSE CHURCH CHURLS CHURNS CHURRO CHURRS COURIC COURSE COURTS CRURAL DOURER DOURLY ENURED ENURES EXURBS FLURRY FOURAM FOURPM FOURTH GOURDE GOURDS HOURIS HOURLY INURED INURES ITURBI JAURES JOURNO KAURIS KNURLS KNURLY LAUREL LAUREN LAURIE MAURYA MOURNS NEURAL NEUROL NEURON PLURAL POURED POURER POURIN ROURKE SAUREL SCURFY SCURRY SCURVE SCURVY SEURAT SLURPS SLURRY SMURFS SOURCE SOURED SOURER SOURLY SPURGE SPURNS SPURON SPURRY SPURTS STURDY TAURUS TOURED TOURER TSURIS USURER USURPS UTURNS

••U•R•

BEURRE BLURRY CHURRO CHURRS EDUARD FLUORO FLURRY GLUERS LOUVRE OEUVRE SCURRY SLURRY SOUARI SPURRY SQUARE SQUIRE SQUIRM SQUIRT STUART

••U••R

ABUKIR ABUSER ALULAR BRUDER CHUKAR COUGAR COUTER CRUDER DAUBER DOURER ELUDER ETUXOR FOULER GAUGER GLUIER GOUGER HAULER KRUGER LAUDER LAUPER LOUDER LOUVER MAULER MAUSER MOUSER NEUTER OCULAR OVULAR PAUPER POURER POUTER PRUNER REUTER ROUSER ROUTER SAUCER SAUGER SOURER SOUTER STUMER STUPOR TAUTER TOURER TOUTER USURER UVULAR

•••UR•

ABJURE ABSURD ADJURE ALLURE AMOURS ARMURE ARTURO ASBURY ASSURE AUBURN AUGURS AUGURY COBURG COBURN CONURE DATURA DEJURE DEMURE DEMURS ENDURE ENDURO ENSURE ERFURT FEMURS FIGURE FLEURY FLOURS FLOURY FUTURE IMMURE IMPURE INCURS INJURE INJURY INSURE INTURN LEMURS LIGURE LUXURY MADURA MADURO MATURE MOHURS NATURA NATURE OCCURS ODOURS ORDURE PARURE PENURY PLEURA REBURY RECURS RETURN SATURN SCOURS SECURE SEGURA SIGURD SOEURS SUBURB SUTURE TENURE UIGURS UNCURL UNFURL UNHURT UNSURE UPTURN YOGURT

•••U•R

ARGUER BREUER ISSUER JAGUAR LIQUOR QUEUER VAGUER

••••UR

ARBOUR ARDOUR ARMOUR ARTHUR AUTEUR BENHUR BIGSUR BULGUR COLOUR CONCUR DAMOUR DETOUR DEVOUR DOLOUR FAVOUR HONOUR HUMOUR INPOUR JAIPUR KIPPUR KRONUR KULTUR LABOUR LAMOUR LANGUR LATOUR LUMPUR MURMUR NIPPUR ONTOUR POSEUR RAIPUR RETOUR RIGOUR RUMOUR SAVOUR SIDDUR SULFUR VALOUR VAPOUR VELOUR VIGOUR WILBUR

US••••

USABLE USABLY USAGES USANCE USEDTO USEDUP USEFUL USENET USERID USESUP USHERS USMAIL USOPEN USUALS USURER USURPS

U•S•••

UGSOME ULSTER UNSAFE UNSAID UNSAYS UNSEAL UNSEAT UNSEEN UNSEWN UNSEWS UNSHED UNSHOD UNSNAG UNSNAP UNSOLD UNSOWN UNSTOP UNSUNG UNSURE UPSETS UPSHOT UPSIDE URSIDS URSINE URSULA

U••S••

UKASES UNESCO UNISEX UNISON UNISYS UNUSED UPASES URUSES USESUP

U•••S•

UNBUSY UNCASE UNEASE UNEASY UNJUST UNLASH UNLESS UNMASK UNMESH UNREST UNWISE UNWISH UPCAST UPMOST UPPISH UPRISE UPROSE UPRUSH URALSK UTMOST

U••••S

UBOATS UBOLTS UCLANS UDDERS UGGAMS UGLIES UHLANS UIGURS UINTAS UKASES ULCERS ULTRAS UMBELS UMBERS UMBRAS UMIAKS UNARMS UNBARS UNCAPS UNCLES UNDIES UNDOES UNFITS UNGUES UNGUIS UNIATS UNIONS UNISYS UNITAS UNITES UNJAMS UNLESS UNMANS UNPEGS UNPENS UNPINS UNRIGS UNSAYS UNSEWS UNTIES UNZIPS UPASES UPBOWS UPENDS UPPERS UPSETS URAEUS URANUS URGERS URIALS URSIDS URUSES USAGES USHERS USUALS USURPS UTTERS UTURNS UVULAS UZBEKS

•US•••

AUSPEX AUSSIE AUSTEN AUSTIN AUSTRO BUSBAR BUSBOY BUSHED BUSHEL BUSHES BUSHWA BUSIED BUSIER BUSIES BUSILY BUSING BUSKED BUSKIN BUSMAN BUSMEN BUSONI BUSSED BUSSES BUSTED BUSTER BUSTIN BUSTLE CUSACK CUSHAW CUSPED CUSPID CUSSED CUSSES CUSTER CUSTIS CUSTOM CUSTOS DUSTED DUSTER DUSTIN DUSTUP FUSEES FUSILS FUSING FUSION FUSSED FUSSES FUSTIC GUSHED GUSHER GUSHES GUSSET GUSTAV GUSTED HUSHED HUSHES HUSKED HUSKER HUSSAR HUSSEY HUSTLE HUSTON JUSTER JUSTIN JUSTLY KUSPUK LUSAKA LUSHER LUSHLY LUSTED LUSTER LUSTRE MUSCAT MUSCLE MUSCLY MUSERS MUSEUM MUSHED MUSHER MUSHES MUSIAL MUSING MUSKEG MUSKET MUSKIE MUSKOX MUSLIM MUSLIN MUSSED MUSSEL MUSSES MUSSUP MUSTER MUSTNT OUSELS OUSTED OUSTER PUSHED PUSHES PUSHON PUSHUP PUSSES RUSHED RUSHEE RUSHES RUSKIN RUSSET RUSSIA RUSTED RUSTIC RUSTLE SUSANN SUSIEQ SUSLIK SUSSED SUSSES SUSSEX TUSCAN TUSKED TUSKER TUSSAH TUSSLE WUSSES

•U•S••

AUSSIE BUNSEN BUQSHA BURSAE BURSAL BURSAR BURSAS BURSES BURSTS BUSSED BUSSES BUYSUP CUESTA CUISSE CURSED CURSES CURSOR CUSSED CUSSES CUTSIN CUTSUP FUSSED FUSSES GUESTS GUISES GUMSUP GUNSHY GUSSET HUDSON HUSSAR HUSSEY MUSSED MUSSEL MUSSES MUSSUP NURSED NURSER NURSES OUTSET PUISNE PULSAR PULSED PULSES PURSED PURSER PURSES PURSUE PUSSES PUTSBY PUTSCH PUTSIN PUTSON PUTSTO PUTSUP QUASAR QUESTS RUBSIN RUNSAT RUNSIN RUNSON RUNSTO RUNSUP RUSSET RUSSIA SUBSET SUDSED SUDSES SUISSE SUMSUP SUNSET SUSSED SUSSES SUSSEX TUCSON TULSAN TUSSAH TUSSLE WURSTS WUSSES

•U••S•

AUGUST CUBISM CUBIST CUISSE CURTSY CUTEST CUTESY DUDISH DURESS HUGEST JURIST JUTISH KUMISS KUVASZ LUGOSI LUTIST MUCOSA MUFASA MULISH MUTEST NUDEST NUDIST PUNISH PUREST PURISM PURIST QUEASY QURUSH RUDEST RUGOSE SUFISM SUISSE SUREST TUBIST

•U•••S

AUDENS AUDIOS AUDITS AUGERS AUGHTS AUGURS AUREUS AUROUS AUXINS BUDGES BUENOS BUFFOS BUGLES BUILDS BULGES BUNCOS BUNKOS BURGAS BURGHS BURGOS BURIES BURINS BURROS BURSAS BURSES BURSTS BUSHES BUSIES BUSSES BUTEOS BUTTES BUTUTS BUYERS BUZZES CUBEBS CUBICS CUBITS CULETS CULLIS CUPELS CUPIDS CUPPAS CURERS CURIOS CURSES CURTIS CURVES CUSSES CUSTIS CUSTOS CUTIES CUTINS CUTUPS CUVEES DUBOIS DUCATS DULLES DUNCES DUOMOS DURESS DUROCS DUTIES DUVETS FUDGES FUGUES FUNGUS FURIES FURORS FURZES FUSEES FUSILS FUSSES FUTONS FUTZES FUZEES FUZZES GUACOS GUARDS GUAVAS GUESTS GUIDES GUILDS GUILES GUIROS GUISES GULAGS GUMBOS GUSHES GUYOTS HUBRIS HUEVOS HUGHES HULLOS HUMANS HUMMUS HUMORS HUMPHS HURONS HUSHES HUZZAS JUDGES JUICES JULEPS JULIUS JUMBOS JUNCOS JUNTAS JUNTOS JURATS JURIES JURORS KUDZUS KUKRIS KULAKS KUMISS LUCIUS LUDENS LUGERS LUMENS LUNGES LUTZES MUCINS MUCOUS MUDRAS MUFTIS MUGHOS MULCTS MULEYS MULLAS MUNGOS MURALS MURRES MUSERS MUSHES MUSSES MUZZES NUDGES NUECES NURSES OUGHTS OUNCES OUSELS OUZELS PULSES PUPILS PUREES PURGES PURSES PUSHES PUSSES PUTONS QUACKS QUAFFS QUAILS QUAKES QUALMS QUARKS QUARTS QUEENS QUELLS QUERNS QUESTS QUEUES QUIETS QUILLS QUILTS QUINTS QUIPUS QUIRES QUIRKS QUIRTS QUOINS QUOITS QUOTAS QUOTES RUANAS RUBENS RUBIES RUBLES RUCHES RUCKUS RUFOUS RULERS RUMBAS RUMENS RUMORS RUMPUS RUNINS RUNONS RUNUPS RUPEES RUSHES SUCCES SUCHAS SUCKAS SUDRAS SUDSES SUEDES SUGARS SUITES SULCUS SUMACS SUMMAS SUMUPS SUNNIS SUNUPS SUPERS SURAHS SURGES SUSSES SUTRAS TUBERS TUDORS TULIPS TULLES TUNERS TUNICS TUQUES TURBOS TURVES TUTORS WURSTS WUSSES YUCCAS YUROKS

••US••

ABUSED ABUSER ABUSES AMUSED AMUSES BOUSED BOUSES BRUSHY CAUSAL CAUSED CAUSES COUSIN CRUSES CRUSOE CRUSTS CRUSTY DOUSED DOUSES HAUSAS HOUSED HOUSES JOUSTS KYUSHU LOUSED LOUSES MAUSER MOUSED MOUSER MOUSES MOUSEY MOUSSE NAUSEA ONUSES OPUSES PAUSED PAUSES PLUSES PLUSHY POUSSE REUSED REUSES ROUSED ROUSER ROUSES ROUSTS SLUSHY SOUSED SOUSES THUSLY TOUSLE TRUSTS TRUSTY UNUSED URUSES WAUSAU

••U•S•

AGUISH AVULSE BLUEST BLUESY BLUISH BOURSE BRUISE CHUHSI CLUMSY COURSE CRUISE EVULSE LOUISA LOUISE MOUSSE POUSSE SQUASH SQUISH SQUUSH TRUEST TRUISM TZUHSI

••U••S

ABUSES ADULTS AMUSES ANUBIS BAUCIS BAULKS BLUETS BLUEYS BLUFFS BLUNTS BLURBS BLURTS BOUGHS BOULES BOUNDS BOUSES BRUGES BRUINS BRUITS BRULES BRUMES BRUNTS BRUTES BRUTUS BRUXES CAUCUS CAULKS CAUSES CHUCKS CHUMPS CHUNKS CHURLS CHURNS CHURRS CHUTES CLUCKS CLUMPS CLUNKS COUGHS COUNTS COUPES COURTS CRUCES CRUETS CRUMBS CRUSES CRUSTS CRUXES DAUBES DAUNTS DEUCES DOUBTS DOUGHS DOUSES DRUIDS DRUPES DRUZES EDUCES

ELUDES
ELUTES
ENURES
EQUALS
EQUIPS
ERUCTS
ERUPTS
ETUDES
EXUDES
EXULTS
EXURBS
FAUCES
FAULTS
FAUNAS
FAUNUS
FLUFFS
FLUIDS
FLUKES
FLUMES
FLUNKS
FLUTES
FLUXES
FOUNDS
FOUNTS
FRUITS
FRUMPS
GAUGES
GAUZES
GLUERS
GLUONS
GLUTES
GOUGES
GOURDS
GRUELS
GRUMPS
GRUNTS
GSUITS
HAULMS
HAUNTS
HAUSAS
HOUGHS
HOUNDS
HOURIS
HOUSES
INUITS
INURES
JAUNTS
JAURES
JOULES
JOUSTS
KAUNAS
KAURIS
KNURLS
LAUGHS
LOUGHS
LOUPES
LOUSES
MAUVES
MOULDS
MOULTS
MOUNDS
MOUNTS
MOURNS
MOUSES
MOUTHS
NEUMES
ONUSES
OPUSES
OVULES
PAUCIS
PAUSES
PLUCKS
PLUMBS
PLUMES
PLUMPS
PLUNKS
PLUSES
POULTS
POUNDS
PRUDES
PRUNES
REUNES
REUSES
RHUMBS
ROUGES
ROUGHS
ROUNDS
ROUSES
ROUSTS
ROUTES
SAUCES
SAUDIS
SAULTS
SAUNAS
SAUTES
SCUBAS
SCUFFS
SCULLS
SCUTES
SHUCKS
SHUNTS
SKULKS
SKULLS
SKUNKS
SLUMPS
SLURPS
SMURFS
SNUFFS
SOUGHS
SOUNDS
SOUSES
SOUTHS
SPUMES
SPURNS
SPURTS
SQUABS
SQUADS
SQUATS
SQUIBS
SQUIDS
STUFFS
STULLS
STUMPS
STUNTS
STUPAS
STUPES
TAUNTS
TAUONS
TAUPES
TAURUS
THUJAS
THUMBS
THUMPS
THUNKS
TOUGHS
TRUCES
TRUCKS
TRUMPS
TRUNKS
TRUSTS
TRUTHS
TSURIS
URUSES
USUALS
USURPS
UTURNS
UVULAS
VAULTS
VAUNTS
WOUNDS
YOUTHS
ZEUXIS
ZOUNDS

•••US•

ABLUSH
ACCUSE
ADJUST
AMBUSH
AROUSE
AUGUST
BEMUSE
BLOUSE
CARUSO
CAYUSE
CERUSE
CLAUSE
CREUSA
CROUSE
DEFUSE
DEGUST
DISUSE
EFFUSE
ENDUSE
EXCUSE
GOBUST
GROUSE
ILLUSE
INCUSE
INFUSE
INRUSH
LOCUST
MEDUSA
MISUSE
OBTUSE
ONRUSH
PERUSE
PROUST
QURUSH
RECUSE
REFUSE
ROBUST
SCHUSS
SCOUSE
SPOUSE
SQUUSH
THRUSH
THRUST
UNBUSY
UNJUST
UPRUSH
WATUSI

•••U•S

ALBUMS
ALEUTS
AMOURS
AMPULS
ANNULS
ARGUES
AUGURS
BABULS
BEAUTS
BEGUMS
BOSUNS
BUTUTS
CAGUAS
CAJUNS
CLOUDS
CLOUTS
CUTUPS
DEBUGS
DEBUTS
DEMURS
DONUTS
ENDUES
ENSUES
FEMURS
FIXUPS
FLOURS
FLOUTS
FORUMS
FRAUDS
FUGUES
GAMUTS
GETUPS
GHOULS
GIGUES
GROUPS
GROUTS
IMBUES
INCURS
INPUTS
ISSUES
JAMUPS
JORUMS
KHOUMS
KNOUTS
LAYUPS
LEHUAS
LEMURS
LETUPS
LIEUTS
MAQUIS
MIXUPS
MOGULS
MOHURS
MOPUPS
NIPUPS
OCCURS
ODIUMS
ODOURS
ONEUPS
PICULS
PINUPS
PIQUES
POPUPS
PSEUDS
QUEUES
REBUTS
RECURS
REDUBS
RERUNS
REVUES
RHEUMS
ROGUES
RUNUPS
SCAUPS
SCHUSS
SCOURS
SCOUTS
SCRUBS
SCRUMS
SEDUMS
SEGUES
SERUMS
SETUPS
SHOUTS
SHRUBS
SHRUGS
SITUPS
SNOUTS
SOEURS
SPOUTS
SPRUES
STOUPS
STOUTS
STRUMS
STRUTS
SUMUPS
SUNUPS
SYRUPS
THRUMS
TIEUPS
TIPUPS
TOQUES
TROUTS
TUQUES
UIGURS
UNGUES
UNGUIS
VALUES
VENUES
VOGUES
YAKUTS
YAQUIS
YOKUTS

••••US

ABACUS
ACARUS
ACEOUS
ACINUS
ADIEUS
AEOLUS
AIRBUS
ALDOUS
ALTIUS
AMICUS
AMINUS
ANIMUS
ANJOUS
ATREUS
AUREUS
AUROUS
BACKUS
BANTUS
BAYOUS
BMINUS
BRUTUS
BYSSUS
CACTUS
CADMUS
CALLUS
CAMPUS
CARPUS
CAUCUS
CENSUS
CEREUS
CESTUS
CHIAUS
CHORUS
CIRCUS
CIRRUS
CITIUS
CITRUS
CLONUS
CMINUS
CNIDUS
COCCUS
COLEUS
CORPUS
COYPUS
CROCUS
CRONUS
CYGNUS
CYPRUS
DANAUS
DARIUS
DELIUS
DICTUS
DINGUS
DISCUS
DMINUS
DOOFUS
ELBRUS
ENNIUS
EPIRUS
EREBUS
EXODUS
FAMOUS
FAUNUS
FERGUS
FESTUS
FICHUS
FILIUS
FOETUS
FUNGUS
GENIUS
GRADUS
HAIKUS
HIATUS
HINDUS
HUMMUS
ICARUS
JANHUS
JOYOUS
JULIUS
KUDZUS
LIMBUS
LITMUS
LUCIUS
MAGNUS
MAIDUS
MANAUS
MARCUS
MARIUS
MISSUS
MOBIUS
MUCOUS
NEREUS
NIMBUS
OBELUS
ODIOUS
PALPUS
PAPPUS
PELEUS
PILEUS
PINDUS
PLEXUS
POILUS
PONTUS
POROUS
PRIMUS
QUIPUS
RADIUS
RAMOUS
RECTUS
REGIUS
RHESUS
RUCKUS
RUFOUS
RUMPUS
SADHUS
SEAMUS
SEROUS
SHAMUS
SIRIUS
SIXTUS
SNAFUS
SOLEUS
STATUS
STRAUS
STYLUS
SULCUS
TARSUS
TAURUS
TEMPUS
TEREUS
THYMUS
TOPHUS
TYPHUS
URAEUS
URANUS
VENOUS
VERSUS
VILLUS
VINOUS
VIRTUS
VOROUS
WALRUS

UT••••

UTAHAN
UTHANT
UTMOST
UTOPIA
UTTERS
UTURNS

U•T•••

ULTIMA
ULTIMO
ULTRAS
UMTATA
UNTACK
UNTIDY
UNTIED
UNTIES
UNTOLD
UNTORN
UNTRAP
UNTROD
UNTRUE
UNTUNE
UPTAKE
UPTALK
UPTICK
UPTIME
UPTOWN
UPTURN
URTEXT
UTTERS

U••T••

UINTAS
ULSTER
UNITAL
UNITAS
UNITED
UNITER
UNITES
UNSTOP

U•••T•

UBIETY
UBOATS
UBOLTS
UMTATA
UNFITS
UNIATE
UNIATS
UPDATE
UPPITY
UPSETS
USEDTO

U••••T

UMLAUT
UNBELT
UNBENT
UNBOLT
UNGIRT
UNHURT
UNJUST
UNKNIT
UNKNOT
UNMEET
UNREST
UNROOT
UNSEAT
UPBEAT
UPCAST
UPLIFT
UPMOST
UPROOT
UPSHOT
URGENT
URTEXT
USENET
UTHANT
UTMOST

•UT•••

AUTEUR
AUTHOR
AUTUMN
BUTANE
BUTENE
BUTEOS
BUTLER
BUTTED
BUTTER
BUTTES
BUTTIN
BUTTON
BUTUNG
BUTUTS
CUTELY
CUTEST
CUTESY
CUTIES
CUTINS
CUTLER
CUTLET
CUTOFF
CUTOUT
CUTSIN
CUTSUP
CUTTER
CUTUPS
DUTIES
EUTAXY
FUTILE
FUTONS
FUTURE
FUTZED
FUTZES
GUTTAE
GUTTED
GUTTER
HUTTED
HUTTON
JUTISH
JUTTED
LUTHER
LUTHOR
LUTING
LUTIST
LUTZES
MUTANT
MUTATE
MUTATO
MUTELY
MUTEST
MUTING
MUTINY
MUTTER
MUTTON
MUTUAL
NUTATE
NUTKIN
NUTLET
NUTMEG
NUTRIA
NUTTED
NUTTER
OUTACT
OUTAGE
OUTATE
OUTBID
OUTBOX
OUTCRY
OUTDID
OUTEAT
OUTFIT
OUTFLY
OUTFOX
OUTGUN
OUTHIT
OUTING
OUTLAW
OUTLAY
OUTLET
OUTPUT
OUTRAN
OUTRUN
OUTSET
OUTWIT
PUTNAM
PUTOFF
PUTONS
PUTOUT
PUTPUT
PUTRID
PUTSBY
PUTSCH
PUTSIN
PUTSON
PUTSTO
PUTSUP
PUTTED
PUTTEE
PUTTER
RUTGER
RUTILE
RUTTAN
RUTTED
SUTLER
SUTRAS
SUTTER
SUTTON
SUTURE
TUTORS
TUTTUT
TUTUED

•U•T••

AUNTIE
AUSTEN
AUSTIN
AUSTRO
BUNTED
BUNTER
BURTON
BUSTED
BUSTER
BUSTIN
BUSTLE
BUTTED
BUTTER
BUTTES
BUTTIN
BUTTON
CULTIC
CURTER
CURTIN
CURTIS
CURTIZ
CURTLY
CURTSY
CUSTER
CUSTIS
CUSTOM
CUSTOS
CUTTER
DUCTAL
DUSTED
DUSTER
DUSTIN
DUSTUP
FULTON
FUSTIC
GUITAR
GUITRY
GUNTER
GUSTAV
GUSTED
GUTTAE
GUTTED
GUTTER
HUNTED
HUNTER
HURTLE
HUSTLE
HUSTON
HUTTED
HUTTON
JUNTAS
JUNTOS
JUSTER
JUSTIN
JUSTLY
JUTTED
KULTUR
LUSTED
LUSTER
LUSTRE
MUFTIS
MULTUM
MUNTIN
MUSTER
MUSTNT
MUTTER
MUTTON
NUTTED
NUTTER
OUSTED
OUSTER
PUNTED
PUNTER
PUTTED
PUTTEE
PUTTER
QUETTA
QUITIT
QUOTAS
QUOTED
QUOTER
QUOTES
QUOTHA
RUSTED
RUSTIC
RUSTLE
RUTTAN
RUTTED
SUBTLE
SUBTLY
SUITED
SUITES
SUITOR
SUITUP
SULTAN
SULTRY
SUMTER
SUNTAN
SURTAX
SUTTER
SUTTON
TUFTED
TURTLE
TUTTUT

•U••T•

AUDITS
AUGHTS
BURSTS
BUTUTS
CUBITS
CUESTA
CULETS
CURATE
DUARTE
DUCATS
DULUTH
DUVETS
GUESTS
GUILTY
GUNITE
GUYOTS
JUDITH
JURATS
LUCITE
LUNATE
LUXATE
MULCTS
MULETA
MUTATE
MUTATO
NUDITY
NUTATE
OUGHTS
OUTATE
PUENTE
PUERTO
PURITY
PUTSTO
QUANTA
QUARTO
QUARTS
QUARTZ
QUESTS
QUETTA
QUIETS
QUILTS
QUINTS
QUIRTS
QUOITS
RUBATI
RUBATO
RUGATE
RUNSTO
SUBITO
SURETE
SURETY
TUBATE
TURNTO
WURSTS
YUKATA

•U•••T

AUFAIT
AUGUST
AUKLET
AULAIT
AUMONT
BUCKET
BUDGET
BUFFET
BUGOUT
BULLET
BUMOUT
BURBOT
BURNET
BUYOUT
CUBIST
CULLET
CURVET
CUTEST
CUTLET
CUTOUT
DUGOUT
DULCET
DUMONT
DUNANT
DUPONT
DURANT
GULLET
GUSSET
HUBERT
HUGEST
JULIET
JUMPAT
JUNKET
JURIST
KURALT
KUWAIT
LUCENT
LUGNUT
LUTIST
MUDCAT
MULLET
MUPPET
MUSCAT
MUSKET
MUSTNT
MUTANT
MUTEST
NUDEST
NUDIST
NUGENT
NUGGET
NUMBAT
NUTLET
OUTACT
OUTEAT
OUTFIT
OUTHIT
OUTLET
OUTPUT
OUTSET
OUTWIT
PULLET
PULPIT
PUNDIT
PUNNET
PUPPET
PUREST
PURIST
PUTOUT
PUTPUT
QUAINT
QUITIT
RUBOUT
RUDEST
RUNLET
RUNOUT
RUNSAT
RUPERT
RUSSET
SUBLET
SUBMIT
SUBSET
SUMMIT
SUNLIT
SUNSET
SUREST
TUBIST
TUCKET
TUFFET
TUMULT
TURBIT
TURBOT
TURRET
TUTTUT

••UT••

BHUTAN
BHUTTO
BRUTAL
BRUTES
BRUTUS
CHUTED
CHUTES
CLUTCH
COUTER
CRUTCH
ELUTED
ELUTES
FLUTED
FLUTES
FLUTEY
FRUTTI
GLUTEI
GLUTEN
GLUTES
KLUTZY
MOUTHS
MOUTHY
MOUTON
NAUTCH
NEUTER
POUTED
POUTER
REUTER
ROUTED
ROUTER
ROUTES
SAUTES
SCUTCH
SCUTES
SHUTIN
SHUTUP
SMUTCH
SMUTTY
SOUTER
SOUTHS
TAUTEN
TAUTER
TAUTLY
TAUTOG
TEUTON
TOUTED
TOUTER
TRUTHS
YOUTHS

••U•T•

ACUATE
ACUITY
ADULTS
AQUATE
BHUTTO
BLUETS
BLUNTS
BLURTS
BOUNTY
BRUITS
BRUNTS
COUNTS
COUNTY
COURTS
CRUETS
CRUSTS
CRUSTY
DAUNTS
DOUBTS
EQUATE
EQUITY
ERUCTS
ERUPTS
EXULTS
FAULTS
FAULTY
FOUNTS
FOURTH
FRUITS
FRUITY
FRUTTI
GRUNTS
GSUITS
HAUNTS
INUITS
JAUNTS
JAUNTY
JOUSTS
MOULTS
MOUNTS
MOUNTY
POULTS
ROUSTS
SAULTS
SHUNTS
SMUTTY
SPURTS
SQUATS
STUNTS
STUNTY
TAUNTS
TRUSTS
TRUSTY
VAULTS
VAULTY
VAUNTS

••U••T

AMULET
BLUEST
BOUGHT
BRUNET
CAUGHT
FAUCET
FLUENT
FOUGHT
GOULET
NAUGHT
NOUGAT
NOUGHT
SCULPT
SEURAT
SOUGHT
SQUINT
SQUIRT
STUART
TAUGHT
TRUANT
TRUEST
YOUBET

•••UT•

AGOUTI
ALEUTS
ASTUTE
BEAUTS
BEAUTY
BUTUTS
CANUTE
CLOUTS
CROUTE
DEBUTS
DEPUTE
DEPUTY
DILUTE
DONUTS
DULUTH
EMEUTE
FLOUTS
GAMUTS
GROUTS
GROUTY
IMPUTE
INPUTS
KNOUTS
LAPUTA
LIEUTS
MAKUTA
MAPUTO
MINUTE
PAIUTE
REBUTS
REFUTE
REPUTE
SALUTE
SCOUTS
SHOUTS
SLEUTH
SNOUTS
SOLUTE
SPOUTS
STOUTS
STRUTS
TENUTO
TROUTS
VOLUTE
YAKUTS
YOKUTS

•••U•T

ABDUCT
ABRUPT
ACQUIT
ADDUCT
ADJUST
AMOUNT
ANNUIT
AUGUST
AVAUNT
COQUET
DEDUCT
DEGUST
ERFURT
EXEUNT
FLAUNT
GOBUST
HLHUNT
INCULT
INDUCT
INSULT
INTUIT
IRRUPT
ISEULT
JESUIT
LOCUST
LOQUAT
MINUET
MINUIT
OCCULT
PENULT
PEQUOT
PIQUET
PROUST
RELUCT
RESULT
ROBUST
THRUST
TUMULT
UNHURT
UNJUST
YOGURT

••••UT

ABLAUT
ACEOUT
ACTOUT
AIROUT
ALLBUT
ALLOUT
ASKOUT
ATEOUT
BEIRUT
BOWOUT
BUGOUT
BUMOUT
BUYOUT
CAPNUT
CATGUT
COPOUT
CUTOUT
DEVOUT
DIEOUT
DIGOUT
DIMOUT
DRYOUT
DUGOUT
EATOUT
EKEOUT
ENGLUT
FANOUT
FAROUT
FLYOUT
GETOUT
GOTOUT
HELMUT
HEXNUT
HIDOUT
HITOUT
ICEOUT
INARUT
KORBUT
LAYOUT
LEDOUT
LETOUT
LITOUT

LOGOUT
LUGNUT
MAHOUT
MAXOUT
MEERUT
OPTOUT
OUTPUT
PANOUT
PAYOUT
PEANUT
PIGNUT
PIGOUT
POPOUT
PUTOUT
PUTPUT
QIVIUT
RAGOUT
RAJPUT
RANOUT
RIPOUT
ROTGUT
RUBOUT
RUNOUT
SALYUT
SATOUT
SAWOUT
SEEOUT
SETOUT
SITOUT
SPROUT
TAGOUT
TAPOUT
TOPOUT
TRYOUT
TUTTUT
UMLAUT
WALNUT
WAYOUT
WIGOUT
WINOUT
WONOUT
XEDOUT

U•U•••
UNUSED
URUSES
USUALS
USURER
USURPS
UTURNS
UVULAE
UVULAR
UVULAS

U••U••
UIGURS
UNBUSY
UNCURL
UNDULY
UNFURL
UNGUAL
UNGUES
UNGUIS
UNHURT
UNJUST
UNRULY
UNSUNG
UNSURE
UNTUNE
UPRUSH
UPTURN
URSULA

U•••U•
UBIQUE
UMLAUT
UNGLUE
UNIQUE
UNPLUG
UNTRUE
URAEUS
URANUS
USEDUP
USEFUL
USESUP
UVALUE

•UU•••
MUUMUU

•U•U••
AUBURN
AUGURS
AUGURY
AUGUST
AUTUMN
BUNUEL
BUTUNG
BUTUTS
CUMULI
CUMULO
CURULE
CUTUPS
DULUTH
FUGUES
FUTURE
JUJUBE
LUNULA
LUXURY
MUTUAL
QUEUED
QUEUER
QUEUES
QURUSH
RUNUPS
SUBURB
SUMUPS
SUNUNU
SUNUPS
SUTURE
SUZUKI
TUMULI
TUMULT
TUQUES
TUTUED

•U••U•
AUREUS
AUROUS
AUTEUR
BUCKUP
BUGOUT
BULBUL
BULGUR
BUMOUT
BUMPUP
BUNKUM
BUOYUP
BURNUP
BUYOUT
BUYSUP
CUIQUE
CUPFUL
CURIUM
CURLUP
CUTOUT
CUTSUP
DUGOUT
DUMDUM
DUSTUP
FUNGUS
GUDRUN
GUMSUP
HUBBUB
HUMBUG
HUMMUS
HUMOUR
HUNGUP
JUGFUL
JULIUS
JUMPUP
KUDZUS
KULTUR
KUNLUN
KUSPUK
LUCIUS
LUDLUM
LUGNUT
LUMPUR
MUCKUP
MUCOUS
MUKLUK
MULTUM
MURMUR
MUSEUM
MUSSUP
MUUMUU
OUTGUN
OUTPUT
OUTRUN
PULLUP
PULQUE
PUMPUP
PURDUE
PURSUE
PUSHUP
PUTOUT
PUTPUT
PUTSUP
QUIPUS
QUOQUE
QUORUM
RUBOUT
RUCKUS
RUEFUL
RUFOUS
RUMOUR
RUMPUS
RUNGUP
RUNOUT
RUNSUP
RUPAUL
SUBDUE
SUBGUM
SUITUP
SULCUS
SULFUR
SUMSUP
TUCHUN
TUNEUP
TURNUP
TUTTUT
YUMYUM

•U•••U
BUREAU
FUZHOU
HUNGWU
JUNEAU
KUNGFU
MUUMUU
SUBARU
SUNUNU
TUVALU

••UU••
SQUUSH

••U•U•
BRUTUS
CAUCUS
DRUMUP
FAUNUS
FOULUP
HAULUP
MUUMUU
SHUTUP
SOUPUP
TAURUS

••U••U
AKUAKU
BOUBOU
IGUACU
KYUSHU
MAUMAU
MBUNDU
MUUMUU
RYUKYU
WAUSAU

•••UU•
VACUUM

•••U•U
KIKUYU
SUNUNU
TELUGU

••••UU
MUUMUU

UV••••
UVALUE
UVULAE
UVULAR
UVULAS

U•V•••
UNVEIL

U••V••
UNEVEN
UNIVAC

U•••V•
UNWOVE

•UV•••
CUVEES
DUVALL
DUVETS
KUVASZ
TUVALU

•U•V••
CULVER
CURVED
CURVES
CURVET
GUAVAS
HUEVOS
HUMVEE
PURVEY
QUAVER
QUIVER
SUAVER
SURVEY
TURVES

•U••V•
BULOVA

•U•••V
GUSTAV
RUBLEV

••UV••
LOUVER
LOUVRE
MAUVES
OEUVRE

••U•V•
SCURVE
SCURVY
ZOUAVE

••U••V
ZHUKOV

•••UV•
TROUVE

U•W•••
UNWARY
UNWELL
UNWILY
UNWIND
UNWISE
UNWISH
UNWORN
UNWOVE
UNWRAP
UPWARD
UPWELL
UPWIND

U••W••
UNAWED

U•••W•
UNSEWN
UNSEWS
UNSOWN
UPBOWS
UPTOWN

U••••W
UNDRAW

•UW•••
KUWAIT

•U•W••
BULWER
LUDWIG
OUTWIT
RUNWAY
SUBWAY

•U••W•
BUSHWA
HUNGWU
YUKAWA

•U•••W
BURROW
CURFEW
CURLEW
CUSHAW
FURROW
GUFFAW
KUDROW
MURROW
OUTLAW
SUNDEW

••U•W•
SQUAWK

••••UW
DEPAUW

U•••X•
URTEXT

U••••X
UNISEX

•UX•••
AUXINS
HUXLEY
LUXATE
LUXURY
TUXEDO

•U••X•
CUNAXA
EUTAXY

•U•••X
AUSPEX
DUPLEX
LUMMOX
MUSKOX
OUTBOX
OUTFOX
SUFFIX
SURTAX
SUSSEX

••UX••
BRUXED
BRUXES
CRUXES
ETUXOR
FLUXED
FLUXES
ZEUXIS

••U••X
BLUEOX
CAUDEX
KOUFAX

•••UX•
DELUXE

••••UX
ADIEUX
BAYEUX
BIJOUX
EFFLUX
HALLUX
INFLUX
POLLUX
REFLUX

U•Y•••
UNYOKE

U••Y••
UNDYED

U•••Y•
UNISYS
UNSAYS

U••••Y
UBIETY
UGLIFY
UGLILY
UNBUSY
UNDULY
UNEASY
UNHOLY
UNOILY
UNRULY
UNTIDY
UNWARY
UNWILY
UPPITY
USABLY

•UY•••
BUYERS
BUYING
BUYOFF
BUYOUT
BUYSUP
GUYANA
GUYING
GUYOTS
TUYERE

•U•Y••
BUNYAN
BUNYIP
BUOYED
BUOYUP
DURYEA
QUAYLE
RUNYON
YUMYUM

•U••Y•
MULEYS

•U•••Y
AUBREY
AUDREY
AUGURY
AURIFY
BUBBLY
BUMBRY
BUNCHY
BURBLY
BURLEY
BURNEY
BUSBOY
BUSILY
CUDDLY
CURACY
CURLEY
CURTLY
CURTSY
CUTELY
CUTESY
DUALLY
DUDLEY
DUMBLY
DUPERY
DURFEY
EULOGY
EUTAXY
GUILTY
GUITRY
GUNSHY
GURLEY
GURNEY
HUBBLY
HUGELY
HUMBLY
HUNGRY
HURLEY
HURRAY
HUSSEY
HUXLEY
JUNGLY
JUSTLY
LUNACY
LUNCHY
LUSHLY
LUXURY
MUMBLY
MUNCHY
MURPHY
MURRAY
MURREY
MUSCLY
MUTELY
MUTINY
NUBBLY
NUDELY
NUDITY
NUMBLY
OUTCRY
OUTFLY
OUTLAY
PUDDLY
PULLEY
PUNCHY
PUNILY
PURELY
PURIFY
PURITY
PURPLY
PURVEY
PUTSBY
QUAGGY
QUARRY
QUEASY
QUEMOY
QUINCY
QUIPPY
QUIRKY
RUBBLY
RUBIFY
RUDELY
RUFFLY
RUMBLY
RUMPLY
RUNDRY
RUNWAY
SUBTLY
SUBWAY
SUGARY
SULTRY
SUNDAY
SUNDRY
SUNRAY
SUPPLY
SURELY
SURETY
SURREY
SURVEY
TUMEFY
TUNNEY
TURKEY
WURLEY

••UY••
NGUYEN

••U•Y•
BLUEYS
MAURYA
RYUKYU

••U••Y
ACUITY
BLUELY
BLUESY
BLURRY
BOUNCY
BOUNTY
BRUMBY
BRUSHY
CAUCHY
CHUBBY
CHUFFY
CHUMMY
CHUNKY
CLUBBY
CLUMPY
CLUMSY
CLUNKY
COUNTY
CRUDDY
CRUMBY
CRUMMY
CRUSTY
DOUBLY
DOUGHY
DOURLY
EQUITY
FAULTY
FLUFFY
FLUKEY
FLUNKY
FLURRY
FLUTEY
FOULLY
FRUITY
FRUMPY
GLUMLY
GRUBBY
GRUMPY
GRUNDY
GRUNGY
HOUNDY
HOURLY
JAUNTY
JOUNCY
KLUTZY
KNURLY
LOUDLY
MAUNDY
MOULDY
MOUNTY
MOUSEY
MOUTHY
PAULEY
PLUCKY
PLUMMY
PLUSHY
POUCHY
ROUGHY
SCULLY
SCUMMY
SCURFY
SCURRY
SCURVY
SCUZZY
SKUNKY
SLUDGY
SLUMMY
SLURRY
SLUSHY
SMUDGY
SMUGLY
SMUTTY
SNUBBY
SNUFFY
SNUGLY
SOURLY
SPUNKY
SPURRY
STUBBY
STUFFY
STUMPY
STUNTY
STURDY
TAUTLY
THUSLY
TOUCHY
TOUGHY
TRUSTY
VAULTY

•••UY•
INOUYE
KIKUYU

•••U•Y
ARGUFY
ASBURY
AUGURY
BEAUTY
CLOUDY
CROUPY
DEPUTY
FLEURY
FLOURY
GROUTY
INJURY
LUXURY
MAGUEY
OCCUPY
PENURY
REBURY
RHEUMY
SYRUPY
UNBUSY
UNDULY
UNRULY

••••UY
BADGUY
CLIQUY
GILGUY
TANGUY

UZ••••
UZBEKS
UZZIAH

U•Z•••
UNZIPS
UZZIAH

•UZ•••
BUZZED
BUZZER
BUZZES
FUZEES
FUZHOU
FUZING
FUZZED
FUZZES
GUZZLE
HUZZAH
HUZZAS
MUZHIK
MUZZED
MUZZES
MUZZLE
NUZZLE
OUZELS
PUZZLE
SUZUKI

•U•Z••
BUZZED
BUZZER
BUZZES
CURZON
FURZES
FUTZED
FUTZES
FUZZED
FUZZES
GUZZLE
HUZZAH
HUZZAS
KUDZUS
LUTZES
MUZZED
MUZZES
MUZZLE
NUZZLE
PUZZLE
QUEZON

•U•••Z
CURTIZ
JUAREZ
KUVASZ
QUARTZ

••UZ••
DRUZES
GAUZES
SCUZZY

••U•Z•
KLUTZY
SCUZZY

••U••Z
BOULEZ

•••UZ•
YAKUZA

•••U•Z
SCHULZ

••••UZ
HORMUZ
TAMMUZ

VA••••
VACANT
VACATE
VACHEL
VACLAV
VACUUM
VADOSE
VAGARY
VAGUER
VAINER
VAINLY
VAISYA
VALDEZ
VALENS
VALENT
VALERY
VALETS
VALISE
VALIUM
VALLEE
VALLEY
VALOIS
VALOUR
VALUED
VALUES
VALVED
VALVES
VAMPED
VAMPER
VANDAL
VANIER
VANISH
VANITY
VANNED
VANRYN
VAPORS
VAPORY
VAPOUR
VARDEN
VARESE
VARIED
VARIES
VARLET
VARNAS
VARNEY
VARUNA
VASHTI
VASLAV
VASSAL
VASSAR
VASTER
VASTLY
VATFUL
VATTED
VAUGHN
VAULTS
VAULTY
VAUNTS

V•A•••
VIABLE
VIABLY
VIACOM
VIANDS

V••A••
VACANT
VACATE
VAGARY
VEGANS
VICARS
VIRAGO
VISAED
VISAGE
VITALE
VITALS
VIVACE
VIVANT
VOCALS
VOLANS
VOLANT
VOLARE
VOTARY
VOYAGE

V•••A•
VACLAV
VANDAL
VARNAS
VASLAV
VASSAL
VASSAR
VEEJAY
VEINAL
VENIAL
VERBAL
VERNAL
VESTAL
VESTAS
VILLAS
VIOLAS
VISTAS
VISUAL
VIVIAN
VODKAS
VOLVAS
VULCAN
VULGAR

V••••A
VAISYA
VARUNA
VERONA
VICUNA
VIENNA
VIGODA
VIZSLA

•VA•••
AVAILS
AVALON
AVANTI
AVATAR
AVAUNT
EVADED
EVADER
EVADES
OVALLY
RVALUE
UVALUE

•V•A••
AVIANS
AVIARY
AVIATE

•V••A•
AVATAR
AVOWAL
DVORAK
OVISAC
OVULAR
UVULAE
UVULAR
UVULAS

•V•••A
AVESTA

••VA••
ARVADA
BOVARY
DIVANS
DUVALL
EDVARD
HAVANA
HAVASU
HIVAOA
INVADE
INVAIN
JAVARI
KOVACS
KUVASZ
LAVABO
LAVAGE
LEVANT
LOVAGE
NAVAHO
NAVAJO
NEVADA
NOVATO
PAVANE
RAVAGE
REVAMP
RIVALS
SAVAGE
SAVAII
SAVANT
SAVATE
TUVALU
VIVACE
VIVANT

••V•A•
CAVEAT
CAVIAR
FIVEAM
FOVEAE
GAVIAL
HAVEAT
JOVIAL
JOVIAN
KEVLAR
REVEAL
VIVIAN

••V••A
ARVADA
COVINA
ELVIRA
HAVANA
HIVAOA
NEVADA
NOVENA
RIVERA
WOVOKA

•••VA•
BRAVAS
CANVAS
CHEVAL
COEVAL
CRAVAT
GUAVAS
HALVAH
LARVAE
LARVAL
LARVAS
LEKVAR
SERVAL
SHEVAT
SILVAS
SLOVAK
SPIVAK
SYLVAN
UNIVAC
VOLVAS

•••V•A
FLAVIA
LATVIA
OLIVIA
PRAVDA
SALVIA
SYLVIA
TRIVIA

••••VA
BULOVA
CANOVA
CASAVA
GENEVA
GODIVA
MORAVA
MOSKVA
OTTAVA
SALIVA

V•B•••
VEBLEN
VYBORG

V••B••
VERBAL
VERBIS
VIABLE
VIABLY

••V•B•
LAVABO

••V••B
ADVERB
REVERB

VC••••
VCHIPS

V•C•••
VACANT
VACATE
VACHEL
VACLAV
VACUUM
VECTOR
VICARS
VICTIM
VICTIS
VICTOR
VICUNA
VOCALS

V••C••
VELCRO
VIACOM
VINCES
VINCIT
VISCID
VNECKS
VOICED
VOICES
VULCAN

V•••C•
VELOCE
VENICE
VIVACE
VOTECH

V••••C
VITRIC

•V•C••
AVOCET
EVICTS

•V••C•
AVOUCH
EVINCE
KVETCH

•V•••C
OVISAC

••V•C•
ADVICE
CIVICS
DEVICE
HAVOCS
KOVACS
NOVICE
VIVACE

•••V•C
OLDVIC
PELVIC
SLAVIC
STIVIC
UNIVAC

V•D•••
VADOSE
VEDDER
VIDEOS
VIDERI
VODKAS

V••D••
VALDEZ
VANDAL
VARDEN
VEDDER
VELDTS
VENDED
VENDEE
VENDOR
VERDIN
VERDON
VERDUN
VOIDED
VOODOO

V•••D•
VIANDS
VIGODA

V••••D
VALUED
VALVED
VAMPED
VANNED
VARIED
VATTED
VEERED
VEGGED
VEILED
VEINED
VENDED
VENTED
VERGED
VERSED
VESPID
VESTED
VETOED
VETTED
VIEWED
VISAED
VISCID
VOICED
VOIDED

•V•D••
AVEDON
AVIDLY
EVADED
EVADER
EVADES

•V••D•
AVOIDS
OVERDO
OVIEDO
OVOIDS

•V•••D
AVOWED
EVADED
EVENED
EVOKED

••V•D•
ARVADA
BOVIDS
DIVIDE
INVADE
NEVADA

••V••D
DEVOID
EDVARD
ENVIED
LEVEED
LEVIED
REVVED
RSVPED

•••VD•
PRAVDA

•••V•D
BRAVED
CALVED
CARVED
CERVID
CRAVED
CURVED
DELVED
FERVID
GLOVED
GRAVED
GRAVID
HALVED
HEAVED
KIDVID
LEAVED
PEEVED
PROVED
REEVED
REVVED
SALVED
SERVED
SHAVED
SHOVED
SIEVED
SKIVED
SLAVED
SOLVED
STAVED
VALVED
WAIVED
WEAVED

VE••••
VEBLEN
VECTOR
VEDDER
VEEJAY
VEERED
VEGANS
VEGGED
VEGGIE
VEIGHT
VEILED
VEINAL
VEINED
VELCRO
VELDTS
VELLUM
VELOCE
VELOUR
VELVET
VENDED
VENDEE
VENDOR
VENEER
VENETO
VENIAL
VENICE
VENIRE
VENITE
VENOMS
VENOUS
VENTED
VENTER
VENUES
VERBAL
VERBIS
VERDIN
VERDON
VERDUN
VEREEN
VERGED
VERGER
VERGES
VERIFY
VERILY
VERISM
VERITE
VERITY
VERMIN
VERNAL
VERNON
VERONA
VERSED
VERSES
VERSOS
VERSTS
VERSUS
VERTEX
VERVES
VERVET
VESPER
VESPID
VESSEL
VESTAL
VESTAS
VESTED
VESTEE
VESTRY
VETOED
VETOER
VETOES
VETTED
VEXERS
VEXING

V•E•••
VEEJAY
VEERED
VIENNA
VIENNE
VIEWED
VIEWER
VNECKS

V••E••
VALENS
VALENT
VALERY
VALETS
VARESE
VENEER
VENETO
VEREEN
VEXERS
VIDEOS
VIDERI
VILELY
VILEST
VINERY
VIPERS
VIREOS
VIXENS
VOLENS
VOTECH
VOTEIN
VOTERS
VOWELS
VOWELY
VOWERS

V•••E•
VACHEL
VAGUER
VAINER
VALDEZ
VALLEE
VALLEY
VALUED
VALUES
VALVED
VALVES
VAMPED
VAMPER
VANIER
VANNED
VARDEN
VARIED
VARIES
VARLET
VARNEY
VASTER
VATTED
VEBLEN
VEDDER
VEERED
VEGGED
VEILED
VEINED
VELVET
VENDED
VENDEE
VENEER
VENTED
VENTER
VENUES
VEREEN
VERGED
VERGER
VERGES
VERSED
VERSES
VERTEX
VERVES
VERVET
VESPER
VESSEL
VESTED
VESTEE
VETOED
VETOER
VETOES
VETTED
VIEWED
VIEWER
VINCES
VINIER
VIOLET
VISAED
VIVIEN
VIZIER
VOGUES
VOICED
VOICES
VOIDED
VOILES
VOLLEY
VORTEX
VOSGES
VSIXES

V••••E
VACATE
VADOSE
VALISE
VALLEE
VARESE
VEGGIE
VELOCE
VENDEE
VENICE
VENIRE
VENITE
VERITE
VESTEE
VIABLE
VIENNE
VINNIE
VIRILE
VIRTUE
VISAGE
VISINE
VITALE
VIVACE
VOLARE
VOLUME
VOLUTE
VOTIVE
VOYAGE

•VE•••
AVEDON
AVENGE
AVENUE
AVERNO
AVERSE
AVERTS
AVESTA
EVELYN
EVENED
EVENER
EVENKI
EVENLY
EVENSO
EVENTS
EVENUP
EVERLY
EVERSO
EVERTS
KVELLS
KVETCH
OVERDO
OVERLY
SVELTE
YVETTE

•V•E••
OVIEDO
TVSETS

•V••E•
AVOCET
AVOWED
AVOWER
EVADED
EVADER
EVADES
EVENED
EVENER
EVILER
EVOKED
EVOKER
EVOKES
OVULES

•V•••E
AVENGE
AVENUE
AVERSE
AVIATE
AVULSE
EVINCE
EVOLVE
EVONNE
EVULSE
EVZONE
RVALUE
SVELTE
UVALUE
UVULAE
YVETTE
YVONNE

••VE••
ADVENT
ADVERB
ADVERT
AMVETS
BEVELS
CAVEAT
CAVEIN
CAVELL
CAVERN
CAVERS
CAVETT
CIVETS
COVENS
COVENT
COVERS
COVERT
COVETS
COVEYS
CUVEES
DEVEIN
DEVEST
DIVEIN
DIVERS
DIVERT
DIVEST
DOVEIN
DUVETS
ELVERS
FEVERS
FIVEAM
FIVEPM
FIVERS
FIVEWS
FOVEAE
GAVEIN
GAVELS
GAVEUP
GIVEIN
GIVENS
GIVERS
GIVETO
GIVEUP
GOVERN
HAVEAT
HAVENS
HAVENT
HAVEON
HAVERS
HOVELS
HOVERS
HOVETO
INVENT
INVERT
INVEST
JIVERS
KEVELS
LAVERS
LEVEED
LEVEES
LEVELS
LEVENE
LEVERS
LIVEIN
LIVELY
LIVENS
LIVEON
LIVERS
LIVERY
LOVEIN
LOVELL
LOVELY
LOVERS
LOVETT
MAVENS
MOVEIN
MOVEON
MOVERS
MOVEUP
NAVELS
NEVERS
NOVELS
NOVENA
OBVERT
PAVERS
RAVELS
RAVENS
RAVERS
RAVEUP
REVEAL
REVELS
REVERB
REVERE
REVERS
REVERT
REVETS
RIVERA
RIVERS
RIVETS
ROVERS
SAVERS
SAVEUP
SEVENS
SEVERE
SEVERN
SEVERS
SEVERY
TAVERN
UNVEIL
WAVEIN
WAVERS
WAVERY
WYVERN

••V•E•
BEVIES
BOVVER
CUVEES
DAVIES
ENVIED
ENVIER
ENVIES
JAVIER
JIVIER
KAVNER
LEVEED
LEVEES
LEVIED
LEVIER
LEVIES
LIVRES
MOVIES
NAVIES
ONVIEW
REVIEW
REVUES
REVVED
RSVPED
SEVRES
SOVIET
VIVIEN
WAVIER
XAVIER

••V••E
ADVICE
ADVISE
BOVINE
DEVICE
DEVINE
DEVISE
DEVOTE
DIVIDE
DIVINE
FOVEAE
INVADE
INVITE
INVOKE
IRVINE
LAVAGE
LEVENE
LEVINE
LEVITE
LOVAGE
NOVICE
PAVANE
RAVAGE
RAVINE
REVERE
REVILE
REVISE
REVIVE
REVOKE
SAVAGE
SAVATE
SAVOIE
SEVERE
VIVACE

•••VE•
AGAVES
ALEVEL
ALFVEN
ASEVER
BEAVER
BEEVES
BOVVER
BRAVED
BRAVER
BRAVES
BREVES
BREVET
CALVED
CALVES
CARVED
CARVER
CARVES
CARVEY
CHAVEZ
CHEVET
CHIVES
CLAVES
CLEVER
CLEVES
CLOVEN
CLOVER
CLOVES
CONVEX
CONVEY
CORVEE
CORVES
CRAVED
CRAVEN
CRAVER
CRAVES
CULVER
CURVED
CURVES
CURVET
DELVED
DELVER
DELVES
DENVER
DRIVEL
DRIVEN
DRIVER
DRIVES
DROVER
DROVES
ELEVEN
ELEVES
GARVEY
GLOVED
GLOVER
GLOVES
GOOVER
GRAVED
GRAVEL
GRAVEN
GRAVER
GRAVES
GRIVET
GROVEL
GROVER
GROVES
HALVED
HALVES
HARVEY
HEAVED
HEAVEN
HEAVER
HEAVES
HELVES
HOOVER
HOOVES
HUMVEE
JAYVEE
JEEVES
KNAVES
KNIVES
LEAVED
LEAVEN
LEAVES
LOAVES
LOUVER
MARVEL
MAUVES
NERVES
OGIVES
OLEVEL
OLIVER
OLIVES
PEAVEY
PEEVED
PEEVES
PLOVER
PRIVET
PROVED
PROVEN
PROVER
PROVES
PURVEY
QUAVER
QUIVER
REEVED
REEVES
REVVED
SALVED
SALVER
SALVES
SELVES
SERVED
SERVER
SERVES
SHAVED
SHAVEN
SHAVER
SHAVES
SHIVER
SHOVED
SHOVEL
SHOVER
SHOVES
SIEVED
SIEVES
SILVER
SKIVED
SKIVER
SKIVES
SLAVED
SLAVER
SLAVES
SLAVEY
SLIVER
SLOVEN
SNIVEL
SOAVES
SOLVED
SOLVER
SOLVES
STAVED
STAVES
STEVEN
STIVER
STOVER
STOVES
SUAVER
SURVEY
SWIVEL
SWIVET
TEEVEE
TRAVEL
TRAVES
TRIVET
TROVES
TURVES
UNEVEN
VALVED
VALVES
VELVET
VERVES
VERVET
WAIVED
WAIVER
WAIVES
WEAVED
WEAVER
WEAVES
WOLVES

•••V•E
BMOVIE
CHEVRE
CORVEE
HUMVEE
JAYVEE
LARVAE
LOUVRE
OEUVRE
STEVIE
TEEVEE

••••VE
ACTIVE
ALCOVE
ARGIVE
ARRIVE
BEHAVE
BEHOVE
BYJOVE
CLEAVE
DATIVE
DERIVE
ENDIVE
EVOLVE
GENEVE
GREAVE
GRIEVE
GROOVE
INLOVE
MOHAVE
MOJAVE
MOTIVE
NATIVE
OCTAVE
PAREVE
RELIVE
REMOVE
REPAVE
REVIVE
REWOVE
SCURVE
SHEAVE
SHELVE
SHRIVE
SHROVE
SLEAVE
SLEEVE
STARVE
STEEVE
STRIVE
STROVE
SWERVE
THEYVE
THIEVE
THRIVE
THROVE
TROUVE
TWELVE
UNWOVE
VOTIVE
WHATVE
ZOUAVE

V••F••
VATFUL

V•••F•
VERIFY
VILIFY
VINIFY
VIVIFY

••V•F•
VIVIFY

V•G•••
VAGARY
VAGUER
VEGANS
VEGGED
VEGGIE
VIGILS
VIGODA
VIGORS
VIGOUR
VOGUES

V••G••
VAUGHN
VEGGED
VEGGIE
VEIGHT
VERGED
VERGER
VERGES
VIRGIL
VIRGIN
VOIGHT
VOSGES
VSIGNS
VULGAR

V•••G•
VIRAGO
VISAGE
VOYAGE

V••••G
VEXING
VIKING
VINING
VOTING
VOWING
VYBORG

•V••G•
AVENGE

••V•G•
LAVAGE
LOVAGE
RAVAGE
SAVAGE

••V••G
CAVING
DIVING
ERVING
GIVING
HAVING
HIVING
IRVING
JIVING
LAVING
LIVING
LOVING
MOVING
PAVING
RAVING
RIVING
ROVING
SAVING
WAVING

V•H•••
VCHIPS

V••H••
VACHEL
VASHTI
VISHNU

V•••H•
VAUGHN
VEIGHT
VOIGHT

V••••H
VANISH
VOTECH

•V•H••
TVSHOW

•V•••H
AVOUCH
KVETCH

••V•H•
NAVAHO

••V••H
DOVISH
ELVISH
LAVISH
RAVISH

•••V•H
HALVAH

VI••••
VIABLE
VIABLY
VIACOM
VIANDS
VICARS
VICTIM
VICTIS
VICTOR
VICUNA
VIDEOS
VIDERI
VIENNA
VIENNE
VIEWED
VIEWER
VIGILS
VIGODA
VIGORS
VIGOUR
VIKING
VILELY
VILEST
VILIFY
VILLAS
VILLON
VILLUS
VINCES
VINCIT
VINERY
VINIER
VINIFY
VINING
VINNIE
VINOUS
VINTON
VINYLS
VIOLAS
VIOLET
VIOLIN
VIPERS
VIRAGO
VIREOS
VIRGIL
VIRGIN
VIRILE
VIRTUE
VIRTUS
VISAED
VISAGE
VISCID
VISHNU
VISINE
VISION
VISITS
VISORS
VISTAS
VISUAL
VITALE
VITALS
VITRIC
VIVACE
VIVANT
VIVIAN
VIVIEN
VIVIFY
VIXENS
VIZIER
VIZSLA

V•I•••
VAINER
VAINLY
VAISYA
VEIGHT
VEILED
VEINAL
VEINED
VOICED
VOICES
VOIDED
VOIGHT
VOILES
VSIGNS
VSIXES

V••I••
VALISE
VALIUM
VANIER
VANISH
VANITY
VARIED
VARIES
VCHIPS
VENIAL
VENICE
VENIRE
VENITE
VERIFY
VERILY
VERISM
VERITE
VERITY
VEXING
VIGILS
VIKING
VILIFY
VINIER
VINIFY
VINING
VIRILE
VISINE
VISION
VISITS
VIVIAN
VIVIEN
VIVIFY
VIZIER
VOTING
VOTIVE
VOWING

V•••I•
VALOIS
VEGGIE
VERBIS
VERDIN
VERMIN
VESPID
VICTIM
VICTIS
VINCIT
VINNIE
VIOLIN
VIRGIL
VIRGIN
VISCID
VITRIC
VOTEIN

V••••I
VASHTI
VIDERI

•VI•••
AVIANS
AVIARY
AVIATE
AVIDLY
AVISOS
EVICTS
EVILER
EVILLY
EVINCE
OVIEDO
OVISAC

•V•I••
AVAILS
AVOIDS
OVOIDS

•V•••I
AVANTI
EVENKI

••VI••
ADVICE
ADVISE
ANVILS
BEVIES
BOVIDS
BOVINE
CAVIAR
CAVILS
CAVING
CAVITY
CIVICS
COVINA
DAVIES
DAVITS
DEVICE
DEVILS
DEVINE
DEVISE
DEVITO
DIVIDE
DIVINE
DIVING
DIVINO
DOVISH
ELVIRA
ELVISH
ENVIED
ENVIER
ENVIES
ERVING
GAVIAL
GIVING
HAVING
HIVING
INVITE
INVIVO
IRVINE
IRVING
JAVIER
JIVIER
JIVING
JOVIAL
JOVIAN
LAVING
LAVISH
LEVIED
LEVIER
LEVIES
LEVINE
LEVITE
LEVITY
LIVING
LOVING
MOVIES
MOVING
NAVIES
NEVINS
NOVICE
ONVIEW
PAVING
QIVIUT
RAVINE
RAVING
RAVISH
REVIEW
REVILE
REVISE
REVIVE
RIVING
ROVING
SAVING
SAVIOR
SOVIET
VIVIAN
VIVIEN
VIVIFY
WAVIER
WAVILY
WAVING
XAVIER

••V•I•
CAVEIN
DEVEIN
DEVOID
DEVOIR
DIVEIN
DOVEIN
ENVOIS
GAVEIN
GIVEIN
INVAIN
LIVEIN
LOVEIN
MOVEIN
REVOIR
SAVAII
SAVOIE
SAVOIR
UNVEIL
WAVEIN

••V••I
JAVARI
SAVAII
TIVOLI

•••VI•
BEAVIS
BMOVIE
BREVIS
CALVIN
CERVID
CLAVIN
CLEVIS
CLOVIS
FERVID
FLAVIA
GRAVID
KELVIN
KIDVID
LANVIN
LATVIA
MARVIN
MELVIL
MELVIN
NARVIK
OLDVIC
OLIVIA
PARVIS
PELVIC
PELVIS
PREVIN
SALVIA
SLAVIC
SLOVIK
SPAVIN
STEVIE
STIVIC
SYLVIA
TRAVIS
TRIVIA
WEEVIL

V••J••
VEEJAY

••V•J•
NAVAJO

V•K•••
VIKING

V••K••
VODKAS

V•••K•
VNECKS

V••••K
VOSTOK

•V•K••
EVOKED
EVOKER
EVOKES

•V••K•
EVENKI

•V•••K
DVORAK

••V•K•
INVOKE
NEVSKY
REVOKE
WOVOKA

•••V•K
NARVIK
SLOVAK
SLOVIK
SPIVAK

V•L•••
VALDEZ
VALENS
VALENT
VALERY
VALETS
VALISE
VALIUM
VALLEE
VALLEY
VALOIS
VALOUR
VALUED
VALUES
VALVED
VALVES
VELCRO
VELDTS
VELLUM
VELOCE
VELOUR
VELVET
VILELY
VILEST
VILIFY
VILLAS
VILLON
VILLUS
VOLANS
VOLANT
VOLARE
VOLENS
VOLLEY
VOLUME
VOLUTE
VOLVAS
VOLVOX
VULCAN
VULGAR

V••L••
VACLAV
VALLEE
VALLEY
VARLET
VASLAV
VAULTS
VAULTY
VEBLEN
VEILED
VELLUM
VILLAS
VILLON
VILLUS
VIOLAS
VIOLET
VIOLIN
VOILES
VOLLEY

V•••L•
VAINLY
VASTLY
VERILY
VIABLE
VIABLY
VIGILS
VILELY
VINYLS
VIRILE
VITALE
VITALS
VIZSLA
VOCALS
VOWELS
VOWELY

V••••L
VACHEL
VANDAL
VASSAL
VATFUL
VEINAL
VENIAL
VERBAL
VERNAL
VESSEL
VESTAL
VIRGIL
VISUAL

•V•L••
AVALON
AVULSE
EVELYN
EVILER
EVILLY
EVOLVE
EVULSE
KVELLS
OVALLY
OVULAR
OVULES
RVALUE
SVELTE
UVALUE
UVULAE
UVULAR
UVULAS

•V••L•
AVAILS
AVIDLY
EVENLY
EVERLY
EVILLY
KVELLS
OVALLY
OVERLY

•V•••L
AVOWAL

••VL••
KEVLAR
PAVLOV
REVLON

••V•L•
ANVILS
BEVELS
CAVELL
CAVILS
DEVILS
DUVALL
GAVELS
HOVELS
KEVELS
LEVELS
LIVELY
LOVELL
LOVELY
NAVELS
NOVELS
RAVELS
REVELS
REVILE
REVOLT
RIVALS
TIVOLI
TUVALU
WAVILY

••V••L
CAVELL
DUVALL
GAVIAL
JOVIAL
LOVELL
REVEAL
UNVEIL

•••V•L
ALEVEL
CHEVAL
COEVAL
DRIVEL
GRAVEL
GROVEL
LARVAL
MARVEL
MELVIL
OLEVEL
SERVAL
SHOVEL
SNIVEL
SWIVEL
TRAVEL
WEEVIL

V•M•••
VAMPED
VAMPER

V••M••
VERMIN

V•••M•
VENOMS
VOLUME
VROOMS

V••••M
VACUUM
VALIUM
VELLUM
VERISM
VIACOM
VICTIM

••V•M•
REVAMP

••V••M
FIVEAM
FIVEPM

VN••••
VNECKS

V•N•••
VANDAL
VANIER
VANISH
VANITY
VANNED
VANRYN
VENDED
VENDEE
VENDOR
VENEER
VENETO
VENIAL
VENICE
VENIRE
VENITE
VENOMS
VENOUS
VENTED
VENTER
VENUES
VINCES
VINCIT
VINERY
VINIER
VINIFY
VINING
VINNIE
VINOUS
VINTON
VINYLS

V••N••
VAINER
VAINLY
VANNED
VARNAS
VARNEY
VAUNTS
VEINAL
VEINED
VERNAL
VERNON
VIANDS
VIENNA
VIENNE
VINNIE

V•••N•
VACANT
VALENS
VALENT
VARUNA
VEGANS
VERONA
VEXING
VICUNA
VIENNA
VIENNE
VIKING
VINING
VISHNU
VISINE
VIVANT
VIXENS
VOLANS
VOLANT
VOLENS
VOTING
VOWING
VSIGNS

V••••N
VANRYN
VARDEN
VAUGHN
VEBLEN
VERDIN
VERDON
VERDUN
VEREEN
VERMIN
VERNON
VILLON
VINTON
VIOLIN
VIRGIN
VISION
VIVIAN
VIVIEN
VOTEIN
VULCAN

•V•N••
AVANTI
AVENGE
AVENUE
EVENED
EVENER
EVENKI
EVENLY
EVENSO
EVENTS
EVENUP
EVINCE
EVONNE
YVONNE

•V••N•
AVAUNT
AVERNO
AVIANS
EVONNE
EVZONE
YVONNE

•V•••N
AVALON
AVEDON
EVELYN

••VN••
KAVNER

••V•N•
ADVENT
BOVINE
CAVING
COVENS
COVENT
COVINA
DEVINE
DIVANS
DIVINE
DIVING
DIVINO
ERVING
GIVENS
GIVING
HAVANA
HAVENS
HAVENT
HAVING
HIVING
INVENT
IRVINE
IRVING
JIVING
LAVING
LEVANT
LEVENE
LEVINE
LIVENS
LIVING
LOVING
MAVENS
MOVING
NEVINS
NOVENA
PAVANE
PAVING
RAVENS
RAVINE
RAVING
RIVING
ROVING
SAVANT
SAVING
SEVENS
VIVANT
WAVING

••V••N
CAVEIN
CAVERN
DEVEIN
DIVEIN
DOVEIN
GAVEIN
GIVEIN
GOVERN
HAVEON
INVAIN
JOVIAN
LIVEIN
LIVEON
LOVEIN
MOVEIN
MOVEON
REVLON
REVSON
SEVERN
TAVERN
VIVIAN
VIVIEN
WAVEIN
WYVERN

•••V•N
ALFVEN
CALVIN
CLAVIN
CLOVEN
CRAVEN
DRIVEN
ELEVEN
GRAVEN
HEAVEN
KELVIN
LANVIN
LEAVEN
MARVIN
MELVIN
MELVYN
MERVYN
PREVIN
PROVEN
SHAVEN
SLOVEN
SPAVIN
STEVEN
SYLVAN
UNEVEN

VO••••
VOCALS
VODKAS
VOGUES
VOICED
VOICES
VOIDED
VOIGHT
VOILES
VOLANS
VOLANT
VOLARE
VOLENS
VOLLEY
VOLUME
VOLUTE
VOLVAS
VOLVOX
VOODOO
VOROUS
VORTEX
VOSGES
VOSTOK
VOTARY
VOTECH
VOTEIN
VOTERS
VOTING
VOTIVE
VOWELS
VOWELY
VOWERS
VOWING
VOXPOP
VOYAGE

V•O•••
VIOLAS
VIOLET
VIOLIN
VOODOO
VROOMS

V••O••
VADOSE
VALOIS
VALOUR
VAPORS
VAPORY
VAPOUR
VELOCE
VELOUR
VENOMS
VENOUS
VERONA
VETOED
VETOER
VETOES
VIGODA
VIGORS
VIGOUR
VINOUS
VISORS
VOROUS
VROOMS
VYBORG

V•••O•
VECTOR
VENDOR
VERDON
VERNON
VERSOS
VIACOM
VICTOR
VIDEOS
VILLON
VINTON
VIREOS
VISION
VOLVOX
VOODOO
VOSTOK
VOXPOP

V••••O
VELCRO
VENETO
VIRAGO
VOODOO

•VO•••
AVOCET
AVOIDS
AVOUCH
AVOWAL
AVOWED
AVOWER
DVORAK
EVOKED
EVOKER
EVOKES
EVOLVE
EVONNE
OVOIDS
YVONNE

•V•O••
EVZONE

•V••O•
AVALON
AVEDON
AVISOS
TVSHOW

•V•••O
AVERNO
EVENSO
EVERSO
OVERDO
OVIEDO

••VO••
CAVORT
DEVOID
DEVOIR
DEVOTE
DEVOTO
DEVOUR
DEVOUT
DIVOTS
ENVOIS
ENVOYS
EXVOTO
FAVORS
FAVOUR
HAVOCS
INVOKE
PIVOTS
REVOIR
REVOKE
REVOLT
SAVOIE
SAVOIR
SAVORS
SAVORY
SAVOUR
TIVOLI
WOVOKA

••V•O•
HAVEON
HIVAOA
LIVEON
MOVEON
PAVLOV
REVLON
REVSON
SAVIOR

••V••O
DEVITO
DEVOTO
DIVINO
EXVOTO
GIVETO
HOVETO
INVIVO
LAVABO
NAVAHO
NAVAJO
NOVATO

•••VO•
BRAVOS
CONVOY
FERVOR
FLAVOR
HUEVOS
SALVOR
SALVOS
SERVOS
TREVOR
VOLVOX

••••VO
DENOVO
INVIVO
KOSOVO
OCTAVO

V•P•••
VAPORS
VAPORY
VAPOUR
VIPERS

V••P••
VAMPED
VAMPER
VESPER
VESPID
VOXPOP

V•••P•
VCHIPS

V••••P
VOXPOP

•V•••P
EVENUP

••VP••
RSVPED

••V•P•
FIVEPM

••V••P
GAVEUP
GIVEUP
MOVEUP
RAVEUP
REVAMP
REVSUP
SAVEUP

VR••••
VROOMS

V•R•••
VARDEN
VARESE
VARIED
VARIES
VARLET
VARNAS
VARNEY
VARUNA
VERBAL
VERBIS
VERDIN
VERDON
VERDUN
VEREEN
VERGED
VERGER
VERGES
VERIFY
VERILY
VERISM
VERITE
VERITY
VERMIN
VERNAL
VERNON
VERONA
VERSED
VERSES
VERSOS
VERSTS
VERSUS
VERTEX
VERVES
VERVET
VIRAGO
VIREOS
VIRGIL
VIRGIN
VIRILE
VIRTUE
VIRTUS
VOROUS
VORTEX

V••R••
VANRYN
VEERED
VITRIC

V•••R•
VAGARY
VALERY
VAPORS
VAPORY
VELCRO
VENIRE
VESTRY
VEXERS
VICARS
VIDERI
VIGORS
VINERY
VIPERS
VISORS
VOLARE
VOTARY
VOTERS
VOWERS
VYBORG

V••••R
VAGUER
VAINER
VALOUR
VAMPER
VANIER
VAPOUR
VASSAR
VASTER
VECTOR
VEDDER
VELOUR
VENDOR
VENEER
VENTER
VERGER
VESPER
VETOER
VICTOR
VIEWER
VIGOUR
VINIER
VIZIER
VULGAR

•V•R••
AVERNO
AVERSE
AVERTS
DVORAK
EVERLY
EVERSO
EVERTS
OVERDO
OVERLY

•V••R•
AVIARY

•V•••R
AVATAR
AVOWER
EVADER
EVENER
EVILER
EVOKER
OVULAR
UVULAR

••VR••
LIVRES
SEVRES

••V•R•
ADVERB
ADVERT
BOVARY
CAVERN
CAVERS
CAVORT
COVERS
COVERT
DIVERS
DIVERT
EDVARD
ELVERS
ELVIRA
FAVORS
FEVERS
FIVERS
GIVERS
GOVERN
HAVERS
HOVERS
INVERT
JAVARI
JIVERS
LAVERS
LEVERS
LIVERS
LIVERY
LOVERS
MOVERS
NEVERS
OBVERT
PAVERS
RAVERS
REVERB
REVERE
REVERS
REVERT
RIVERA
RIVERS
ROVERS
SAVERS
SAVORS
SAVORY
SEVERE
SEVERN
SEVERS
SEVERY
TAVERN
WAVERS
WAVERY
WYVERN

••V••R
BOVVER
CAVIAR
DEVOIR
DEVOUR
ENVIER
FAVOUR
JAVIER
JIVIER
KAVNER
KEVLAR
LEVIER
REVOIR
SAVIOR
SAVOIR
SAVOUR
WAVIER
XAVIER

•••VR•
CHEVRE
LOUVRE
OEUVRE

•••V•R
ASEVER
BEAVER
BOVVER
BRAVER
CARVER
CLEVER
CLOVER
CRAVER
CULVER
DELVER
DENVER
DRIVER
DROVER
FERVOR
FLAVOR
GLOVER
GOOVER
GRAVER
GROVER
HEAVER
HOOVER
LEKVAR
LOUVER
OLIVER
PLOVER
PROVER
QUAVER
QUIVER
SALVER
SALVOR
SERVER
SHAVER
SHIVER
SHOVER
SILVER
SKIVER
SLAVER
SLIVER
SOLVER
STIVER
STOVER
SUAVER
TREVOR
WAIVER
WEAVER

VS••••
VSIGNS
VSIXES

V•S•••
VASHTI
VASLAV
VASSAL
VASSAR
VASTER
VASTLY
VESPER
VESPID
VESSEL
VESTAL
VESTAS
VESTED
VESTEE
VESTRY
VISAED
VISAGE
VISCID
VISHNU
VISINE
VISION
VISITS
VISORS
VISTAS
VISUAL
VOSGES
VOSTOK

V••S••
VAISYA
VASSAL
VASSAR
VERSED
VERSES
VERSOS
VERSTS
VERSUS
VESSEL
VIZSLA

V•••S•
VADOSE
VALISE
VANISH
VARESE
VERISM
VILEST

V••••S
VALENS
VALETS
VALOIS
VALUES
VALVES
VAPORS
VARIES
VARNAS
VAULTS
VAUNTS
VCHIPS
VEGANS
VELDTS
VENOMS
VENOUS
VENUES
VERBIS
VERGES
VERSES
VERSOS
VERSTS
VERSUS
VERVES
VESTAS
VETOES
VEXERS
VIANDS
VICARS
VICTIS
VIDEOS
VIGILS
VIGORS
VILLAS
VILLUS
VINCES
VINOUS
VINYLS
VIOLAS
VIPERS
VIREOS
VIRTUS
VISITS
VISORS
VISTAS
VITALS
VIXENS
VNECKS
VOCALS
VODKAS
VOGUES
VOICES
VOILES
VOLANS
VOLENS
VOLVAS
VOROUS
VOSGES
VOTERS
VOWELS
VOWERS
VROOMS
VSIGNS
VSIXES

•VS•••
TVSETS
TVSHOW

•V•S••
AVESTA
AVISOS
OVISAC

•V••S•
AVERSE
AVULSE
EVENSO
EVERSO
EVULSE

•V•••S
AVAILS
AVERTS
AVIANS
AVISOS
AVOIDS
EVADES
EVENTS
EVERTS
EVICTS
EVOKES
KVELLS
OVOIDS
OVULES
TVSETS
UVULAS

••VS••
NEVSKY
REVSON
REVSUP

••V•S•
ADVISE
DEVEST
DEVISE
DIVEST
DOVISH
ELVISH
HAVASU
INVEST
KUVASZ
LAVISH
RAVISH
REVISE

••V••S
AMVETS
ANVILS
BEVELS
BEVIES
BOVIDS
CAVERS
CAVILS
CIVETS
CIVICS
COVENS
COVERS
COVETS
COVEYS
CUVEES
DAVIES
DAVITS
DEVILS
DIVANS
DIVERS
DIVOTS
DUVETS
ELVERS
ENVIES
ENVOIS
ENVOYS
FAVORS
FEVERS
FIVERS
FIVEWS
GAVELS
GIVENS
GIVERS
HAVENS
HAVERS
HAVOCS
HOVELS
HOVERS
JIVERS
KEVELS
KOVACS
LAVERS
LEVEES
LEVELS
LEVERS
LEVIES
LIVENS
LIVERS
LIVRES
LOVERS
MAVENS
MOVERS
MOVIES
NAVELS
NAVIES
NEVERS
NEVINS
NOVELS
PAVERS
PIVOTS

RAVELS
RAVENS
RAVERS
REVELS
REVERS
REVETS
REVUES
RIVALS
RIVERS
RIVETS
ROVERS
SAVERS
SAVORS
SEVENS
SEVERS
SEVRES
WAVERS

•••V•S
AGAVES
BEAVIS
BEEVES
BRAVAS
BRAVES
BRAVOS
BREVES
BREVIS
CALVES
CANVAS
CARVES
CHIVES
CLAVES
CLEVES
CLEVIS
CLOVES
CLOVIS
CORVES
CRAVES
CURVES
DELVES
DRIVES
DROVES
ELEVES
GLOVES
GRAVES
GROVES
GUAVAS
HALVES
HEAVES
HELVES
HOOVES
HUEVOS
JEEVES
KNAVES
KNIVES
LARVAS
LEAVES
LOAVES
MAUVES
NERVES
OGIVES
OLIVES
PARVIS
PEEVES
PELVIS
PROVES
REEVES
SALVES
SALVOS
SELVES
SERVES
SERVOS
SHAVES
SHOVES
SIEVES
SILVAS
SKIVES
SLAVES
SOAVES
SOLVES
STAVES
STOVES
TRAVES
TRAVIS
TROVES
TURVES
VALVES
VERVES
VOLVAS
WAIVES
WEAVES
WOLVES

V•T•••
VATFUL
VATTED
VETOED
VETOER
VETOES
VETTED
VITALE
VITALS
VITRIC
VOTARY
VOTECH
VOTEIN
VOTERS
VOTING
VOTIVE

V••T••
VASTER
VASTLY
VATTED
VECTOR
VENTED
VENTER
VERTEX
VESTAL
VESTAS
VESTED
VESTEE
VESTRY
VETTED
VICTIM
VICTIS
VICTOR
VINTON
VIRTUE
VIRTUS
VISTAS
VORTEX
VOSTOK

V•••T•
VACATE
VALETS
VANITY
VASHTI
VAULTS
VAULTY
VAUNTS
VELDTS
VENETO
VENITE
VERITE
VERITY
VERSTS
VISITS
VOLUTE

V••••T
VACANT
VALENT
VARLET
VEIGHT
VELVET
VERVET
VILEST
VINCIT
VIOLET
VIVANT
VOIGHT
VOLANT

•V•T••
AVATAR
KVETCH
YVETTE

•V••T•
AVANTI
AVERTS
AVESTA
AVIATE
EVENTS
EVERTS
EVICTS
SVELTE
TVSETS
YVETTE

•V•••T
AVAUNT
AVOCET

••V•T•
AMVETS
CAVETT
CAVITY
CIVETS
COVETS
DAVITS
DEVITO
DEVOTE
DEVOTO
DIVOTS
DUVETS
EXVOTO
GIVETO
HOVETO
INVITE
LEVITE
LEVITY
LOVETT
NOVATO
PIVOTS
REVETS
RIVETS
SAVATE

••V••T
ADVENT
ADVERT
CAVEAT
CAVETT
CAVORT
COVENT
COVERT
DEVEST
DEVOUT
DIVERT
DIVEST
HAVEAT
HAVENT
INVENT
INVERT
INVEST
LEVANT
LOVETT
OBVERT
QIVIUT
REVERT
REVOLT
SAVANT
SOVIET
VIVANT

•••V•T
BREVET
CHEVET
CRAVAT
CURVET
GRIVET
PRIVET
SHEVAT
SWIVET
TRIVET
VELVET
VERVET

VU••••
VULCAN
VULGAR

V•U•••
VAUGHN
VAULTS
VAULTY
VAUNTS

V••U••
VACUUM
VAGUER
VALUED
VALUES
VARUNA
VENUES
VICUNA
VISUAL
VOGUES
VOLUME
VOLUTE

V•••U•
VACUUM
VALIUM
VALOUR
VAPOUR
VATFUL
VELLUM
VELOUR
VENOUS
VERDUN
VERSUS
VIGOUR
VILLUS
VINOUS
VIRTUE
VIRTUS
VOROUS

V••••U
VISHNU

•VU•••
AVULSE
EVULSE
OVULAR
OVULES
UVULAE
UVULAR
UVULAS

•V•U••
AVAUNT
AVOUCH

•V••U•
AVENUE
EVENUP
RVALUE
UVALUE

••VU••
REVUES

••V•U•
DEVOUR
DEVOUT
FAVOUR
GAVEUP
GIVEUP
MOVEUP
QIVIUT
RAVEUP
REVSUP
SAVEUP
SAVOUR

••V••U
HAVASU
TUVALU

••••VU
DEJAVU

V•V•••
VIVACE
VIVANT
VIVIAN
VIVIEN
VIVIFY

V••V••
VALVED
VALVES
VELVET
VERVES
VERVET
VOLVAS
VOLVOX

V•••V•
VOTIVE

V••••V
VACLAV
VASLAV

•V••V•
EVOLVE

••VV••
BOVVER
REVVED

••V•V•
INVIVO
REVIVE

••V••V
PAVLOV

•••VV•
SKIVVY
SPIVVY

V•W•••
VOWELS
VOWELY
VOWERS
VOWING

V••W••
VIEWED
VIEWER

•V•W••
AVOWAL
AVOWED
AVOWER

•V•••W
TVSHOW

••V•W•
FIVEWS

••V••W
ONVIEW
REVIEW

V•X•••
VEXERS
VEXING
VIXENS
VOXPOP

V••X••
VSIXES

V••••X
VERTEX
VOLVOX
VORTEX

•••V•X
CONVEX
VOLVOX

VY••••
VYBORG

V•Y•••
VOYAGE

V••Y••
VINYLS

V•••Y•
VAISYA
VANRYN

V••••Y
VAGARY
VAINLY
VALERY
VALLEY
VANITY
VAPORY
VARNEY
VASTLY
VAULTY
VEEJAY
VERIFY
VERILY
VERITY
VESTRY
VIABLY
VILELY
VILIFY
VINERY
VINIFY
VIVIFY
VOLLEY
VOTARY
VOWELY

•V••Y•
EVELYN

•V•••Y
AVIARY
AVIDLY
EVENLY
EVERLY
EVILLY
OVALLY
OVERLY

••V•Y•
COVEYS
ENVOYS

••V••Y
BOVARY
CAVITY
LEVITY
LIVELY
LIVERY
LOVELY
NEVSKY
SAVORY
SEVERY
VIVIFY
WAVERY
WAVILY

•••VY•
MELVYN
MERVYN

•••V•Y
CARVEY
CONVEY
CONVOY
GARVEY
HARVEY
PEAVEY
PURVEY
SKIVVY
SLAVEY
SPIVVY
SURVEY

••••VY
GROOVY
HALEVY
RELEVY
SCURVY
SKIVVY
SPIVVY

V•Z•••
VIZIER
VIZSLA

V••••Z
VALDEZ

•VZ•••
EVZONE

••V••Z
KUVASZ

•••V•Z
CHAVEZ

WA••••
WABASH
WACKOS
WADDED
WADDLE
WADDLY
WADEIN
WADERS
WADING
WADSUP
WAFERS
WAFERY
WAFFLE
WAFFLY
WAFTED
WAGERS
WAGGED
WAGGLE
WAGGLY
WAGGON
WAGING
WAGNER
WAGONS
WAHINE
WAHOOS
WAHWAH
WAILED
WAILER
WAISTS
WAITED
WAITER
WAITON
WAITUP
WAIVED
WAIVER
WAIVES
WAKENS
WAKEUP
WAKING
WALDEN
WALERS
WALESA
WALKED
WALKEN
WALKER
WALKIE
WALKIN
WALKON
WALKUP
WALLED
WALLER
WALLET
WALLIS
WALLOP
WALLOW
WALLUP
WALNUT
WALRUS
WALTER
WALTON
WAMBLE
WAMBLY
WAMPUM
WANDER
WANERS
WANGLE
WANIER
WANING
WANNED
WANNER
WANTAD
WANTED
WANTIN
WANTON
WANTTO
WAPITI
WAPNER
WARBLE
WARCRY
WARDED
WARDEN
WARDER
WARGOD
WARHOL
WARIER
WARILY
WARING
WARMED
WARMER
WARMLY
WARMTH
WARMUP
WARNED
WARNER
WARPED
WARRED
WARREN
WARSAW
WASABI
WASHED
WASHER
WASHES
WASHOE
WASHUP
WASTED
WASTER
WASTES
WATERS
WATERY
WATNEY
WATSON
WATTLE
WATUSI
WAUSAU
WAVEIN
WAVERS
WAVERY
WAVIER
WAVILY
WAVING
WAXERS
WAXIER
WAXILY
WAXING
WAYANS
WAYLAY
WAYLON
WAYOUT

W•A•••
WEAKEN
WEAKER
WEAKLY
WEALTH
WEANED
WEAPON
WEARER
WEASEL
WEAVED
WEAVER
WEAVES
WHACKS
WHACKY
WHALER
WHALES
WHAMMO
WHAMMY
WHANGS
WHARFS
WHATIF
WHATLL
WHATVE
WRACKS
WRAITH
WRAPUP
WRASSE
WRATHS
WRATHY

W••A••
WABASH
WASABI
WAYANS
WHEALS
WHEATS
WIZARD
WREAKS
WREATH

W•••A•
WAHWAH
WANTAD
WARSAW
WAUSAU
WAYLAY
WEIMAR
WENTAT
WETBAR
WHYDAH
WICCAN
WIGWAG
WIGWAM
WINKAT
WITHAL
WOMBAT
WYSTAN

W••••A
WALESA
WINONA
WOVOKA

•WA•••
AWAITS
AWAKED
AWAKEN
AWAKES
AWARDS
BWANAS
DWARFS
DWAYNE
KWACHA
KWANZA
RWANDA
SWABBY
SWAGED
SWAGES
SWAINS
SWALES
SWAMIS
SWAMPS
SWAMPY
SWANEE
SWANKS
SWANKY
SWARAJ
SWARDS
SWARMS
SWARTH
SWATCH
SWATHE
SWATHS
SWAYED
SWAYER
SWAYZE
SWAZIS
TWANGS
TWANGY

•W•A••
AWEARY
SWEARS
SWEATS
SWEATY
TWEAKS

•W••A•
BWANAS
SWARAJ
TWOWAY

•W•••A
KWACHA
KWANZA
RWANDA

••WA••
ALWAYS
ANWANG
BEWAIL
BEWARE
BYWAYS
COWARD
EDWARD
GAWAIN
HAWAII
HOWARD
INWARD
IOWANS
KUWAIT
NAWABS
NEWAGE
NEWARK
ONWARD
OSWALD
REWARD
REWARM
REWASH
SEWAGE
SEWARD
SIWASH
THWACK
THWART
TOWAGE
TOWARD
UNWARY
UPWARD

••W•A•
BEWRAY
BOWMAN
BOWOAR
BOWSAW
COWMAN
DEWLAP
ENWRAP
GEWGAW
HAWHAW
HOWDAH
LAWMAN
LOWCAL
LOWFAT
NEWMAN
NEWMAR
PAWPAW
PAWSAT
REWRAP
SOWHAT
TOWCAR
UNWRAP

••W••A
COWPEA
ROWENA

•••WA•
AIRWAY
ANYWAY
ARAWAK
AVOWAL
CONWAY
EARWAX
FATWAS
FENWAY
FLEWAT
FLYWAY
GALWAY
GOAWAY
HOTWAR
INAWAY
JETWAY
KEYWAY
KIOWAS
LEEWAY
MIDWAY
NARWAL
NORWAY
OBIWAN
ONEWAY
PEDWAY
PREWAR
PSYWAR
RUNWAY
SCHWAB
SCHWAS
SEAWAY
SKYWAY
SUBWAY
TAIWAN
TWOWAY
WAHWAH
WIGWAG
WIGWAM

••••WA
BUSHWA
OJIBWA
OSHAWA
OTTAWA
PESAWA
TARAWA
YUKAWA

W•B•••
WABASH
WEBBED
WEBBER
WEBERN
WOBBLE
WOBBLY

W••B••
WAMBLE
WAMBLY
WARBLE
WEBBED
WEBBER
WETBAR
WILBUR
WIMBLE
WOBBLE
WOBBLY
WOMBAT

W•••B•
WASABI
WENTBY

•W•B••
SWABBY
TWOBIT

•W••B•
DWEEBS
SWABBY

••WB••
COWBOY
LOWBOY
SOWBUG

••W•B•
NAWABS

•••W•B
COBWEB
SCHWAB
THEWEB

W•C•••
WACKOS
WICCAN
WICKED
WICKER
WICKET
WICOPY

W••C••
WARCRY
WENCES
WHACKS
WHACKY
WICCAN
WILCOX
WINCED
WINCER
WINCES
WITCHY
WRACKS
WRECKS

W•••C•
WHENCE
WRENCH
WRETCH

•W•C••
KWACHA

•W••C•
SWATCH
SWITCH
TWITCH

••WC••
LOWCAL
TOWCAR

••W•C•
THWACK

W•D•••
WADDED
WADDLE
WADDLY
WADEIN
WADERS
WADING
WADSUP
WEDDED
WEDELN
WEDGED
WEDGES
WEDGIE
WIDELY
WIDENS
WIDEST
WIDGET
WIDISH
WIDOWS
WIDTHS
WODGES

W••D••
WADDED
WADDLE
WADDLY
WALDEN
WANDER
WARDED
WARDEN
WARDER
WEDDED
WEEDED
WEEDER
WELDED
WELDER
WENDED
WHYDAH
WILDER
WILDLY
WINDED
WINDER
WINDEX
WINDOM
WINDOW
WINDUP
WISDOM
WONDER
WOODED
WOODEN
WOODSY
WORDED

W•••D•
WEIRDO
WEIRDY
WIELDS
WORLDS
WOUNDS

W••••D
WADDED
WAFTED
WAGGED
WAILED
WAITED
WAIVED
WALKED
WALLED
WANNED
WANTAD
WANTED
WARDED
WARGOD
WARMED
WARNED
WARPED
WARRED
WASHED
WASTED
WEANED
WEAVED
WEBBED
WEDDED
WEDGED
WEEDED
WELDED
WELLED
WELTED
WENDED
WETTED
WHERED
WHILED
WHINED
WICKED
WIGGED
WILLED
WILTED
WINCED
WINDED
WINGED
WINKED
WISHED
WISPED
WITHED
WITTED
WIZARD
WOLFED
WONNED
WONTED
WOODED
WOOFED
WORDED
WORKED
WORMED

•W•D••
AWEDLY
SWEDEN
SWEDES

•W••D•
AWARDS
RWANDA
SWARDS
SWORDS
TWEEDS
TWEEDY

•W•••D
AWAKED
SWAGED
SWAYED
SWIPED
TWINED

••WD••
CAWDOR
DAWDLE
HOWDAH
LEWDER
LEWDLY
POWDER
TAWDRY

••W•D•
REWEDS

••W••D
ATWOOD
BAWLED
BOWLED
BYWORD
COWARD
COWLED
DAWNED
DOWNED
DOWSED
EDWARD
EDWOOD
ELWOOD
FAWNED
FOWLED
GAWKED
GAWPED
GOWILD
GOWNED
HAWKED
HOWARD
HOWLED
INWARD
LOWEND
MEWLED
MYWORD
ONWARD
OSWALD
PAWNED
REWARD
REWELD
REWIND
REWORD
SAWRED
SEWARD
TOWARD
UNWIND
UPWARD
UPWIND
YAWNED
YAWPED
YOWLED

•••WD•
CROWDS

•••W•D
AVOWED
BREWED
CHEWED
CHOWED
CLAWED
CLEWED
CREWED
CROWED
FLAWED
FLOWED
GLOWED
GNAWED
MEOWED
PLOWED
SHOWED
SKEWED
SLEWED
SLOWED

SNOWED
SPEWED
STEWED
STOWED
THAWED
TROWED
UNAWED
VIEWED

••••WD
SHREWD

WE••••
WEAKEN
WEAKER
WEAKLY
WEALTH
WEANED
WEAPON
WEARER
WEASEL
WEAVED
WEAVER
WEAVES
WEBBED
WEBBER
WEBERN
WEDDED
WEDELN
WEDGED
WEDGES
WEDGIE
WEEDED
WEEDER
WEEKLY
WEENIE
WEENSY
WEEPER
WEEPIE
WEEVIL
WEIGHS
WEIGHT
WEIMAR
WEIRDO
WEIRDY
WELDED
WELDER
WELKIN
WELLED
WELLER
WELLES
WELLUP
WELTED
WELTER
WENCES
WENDED
WENTAT
WENTBY
WENTIN
WENTON
WENTUP
WERENT
WERFEL
WERNER
WESKIT
WESLEY
WESSEX
WESSON
WETBAR
WETFLY
WETHER
WETMOP
WETTED
WETTER
WETTIG

W•E•••
WEEDED
WEEDER
WEEKLY
WEENIE
WEENSY
WEEPER
WEEPIE
WEEVIL
WHEALS
WHEATS
WHEELS
WHEEZE
WHEEZY
WHELKS
WHELMS
WHELPS
WHENCE
WHERED
WHERES
WHERRY
WIELDS
WIENER
WIESEL
WOEFUL
WREAKS
WREATH
WRECKS
WRENCH
WRESTS
WRETCH

W••E••
WADEIN
WADERS
WAFERS
WAFERY
WAGERS
WAKENS
WAKEUP
WALERS
WALESA
WANERS
WATERS
WATERY
WAVEIN
WAVERS
WAVERY
WAXERS
WEBERN
WEDELN
WERENT
WHEELS
WHEEZE
WHEEZY
WIDELY
WIDENS
WIDEST
WIFELY
WINERY
WIPERS
WIPEUP
WIRERS
WISELY
WISENT
WISEST
WISETO
WISEUP
WIZENS
WOKEUP
WOMENS
WOOERS
WOREON
WRIEST
WRYEST
WYVERN

W•••E•
WADDED
WAFTED
WAGGED
WAGNER
WAILED
WAILER
WAITED
WAITER
WAIVED
WAIVER
WAIVES
WALDEN
WALKED
WALKEN
WALKER
WALLED
WALLER
WALLET
WALTER
WANDER
WANIER
WANNED
WANNER
WANTED
WAPNER
WARDED
WARDEN
WARDER
WARIER
WARMED
WARMER
WARNED
WARNER
WARPED
WARRED
WARREN
WASHED
WASHER
WASHES
WASTED
WASTER
WASTES
WATNEY
WAVIER
WAXIER
WEAKEN
WEAKER
WEANED
WEARER
WEASEL
WEAVED
WEAVER
WEAVES
WEBBED
WEBBER
WEDDED
WEDGED
WEDGES
WEEDED
WEEDER
WEEPER
WELDED
WELDER
WELLED
WELLER
WELLES
WELTED
WELTER
WENCES
WENDED
WERFEL
WERNER
WESLEY
WESSEX
WETHER
WETTED
WETTER
WHALER
WHALES
WHERED
WHERES
WHILED
WHILES
WHINED
WHINER
WHINES
WHINEY
WHITEN
WHITER
WHITES
WHOLES
WICKED
WICKER
WICKET
WIDGET
WIENER
WIESEL
WIGGED
WIGLET
WILDER
WILIER
WILKES
WILLED
WILLEM
WILLET
WILTED
WIMSEY
WINCED
WINCER
WINCES
WINDED
WINDER
WINDEX
WINGED
WINGER
WINIER
WINKED
WINKER
WINNER
WINTER
WINZES
WIRIER
WISHED
WISHER
WISHES
WISPED
WISTER
WITHED
WITHER
WITHES
WITTED
WODGES
WOHLER
WOLFED
WOLPER
WOLSEY
WOLVES
WONDER
WONNED
WONTED
WOODED
WOODEN
WOOFED
WOOFER
WOOLEN
WOOLEY
WORDED
WORKED
WORKER
WORMED
WORSEN
WOWSER
WRITER
WRITES
WURLEY
WUSSES
WYNTER

W••••E
WADDLE
WAFFLE
WAGGLE
WAHINE
WALKIE
WAMBLE
WANGLE
WARBLE
WASHOE
WATTLE
WEDGIE
WEENIE
WEEPIE
WHATVE
WHEEZE
WHENCE
WIGGLE
WILLIE
WIMBLE
WIMPLE
WINKIE
WINKLE
WINNIE
WOBBLE
WOOGIE
WOOKIE
WRASSE
WRITHE

•WE•••
AWEARY
AWEDLY
AWEIGH
DWEEBS
DWELLS
KWEISI
QWERTY
SWEARS
SWEATS
SWEATY
SWEDEN
SWEDES
SWEEPS
SWEETS
SWELLS
SWERVE
TWEAKS
TWEEDS
TWEEDY
TWEENS
TWEENY
TWEEST
TWEETS
TWEETY
TWEEZE
TWELVE
TWENTY
TWERPS

•W•E••
DWEEBS
OWLETS
OWNERS
SWEEPS
SWEETS
TWEEDS
TWEEDY
TWEENS
TWEENY
TWEEST
TWEETS
TWEETY
TWEEZE

•W••E•
AWAKED
AWAKEN
AWAKES
AWOKEN
SWAGED
SWAGES
SWALES
SWANEE
SWAYED
SWAYER
SWEDEN
SWEDES
SWIPED
SWIPER
SWIPES
SWIVEL
SWIVET
TWINED
TWINES
TWOFER

•W•••E
AWHILE
DWAYNE
GWYNNE
SWANEE
SWATHE
SWAYZE
SWERVE
TWEEZE
TWELVE
TWINGE

••WE••
ADWEEK
ALWEST
ASWELL
BOWERS
BOWERY
COWENS
COWERS
DOWELS
DOWERS
DOWERY
FEWEST
GOWEST
HEWERS
HOWELL
JEWELS
JEWETT
JOWETT
LOWELL
LOWEND
LOWERS
LOWERY
LOWEST
MOWERS
NEWELS
NEWEST
NLWEST
OHWELL
ORWELL
OSWEGO
PAWERS
PEWEES
POWELL
POWERS
RAWEGG
RAWEST
REWEDS
REWELD
ROWELS
ROWENA
ROWENS
ROWERS
SEWELL
SEWERS
SOWERS
SOWETO
TOWELS
TOWERS
TOWERY
UNWELL
UPWELL
VOWELS
VOWELY
VOWERS

••W•E•
ADWEEK
BAWLED
BAWLER
BOWLED
BOWLER
BOWLES
BOWMEN
BOWNET
BOWSER
BOWYER
COWLED
COWLEY
COWMEN
COWPEA
COWPER
DAWNED
DEWIER
DOWNED
DOWNER
DOWNEY
DOWSED
DOWSER
DOWSES
FAWKES
FAWNED
FAWNER
FOWLED
FOWLER
FOWLES
GAWKED
GAWKER
GAWPED
GOWNED
HAWKED
HAWKER
HAWSER
HAWSES
HOWLED
HOWLER
LAWMEN
LAWYER
LEWDER
LOWKEY
MEWLED
MEWLER
NEWLEY
PAWNED
PAWNEE
PAWNER
PEWEES
PEWTER
POWDER
SAWRED
SAWYER
TOWHEE
TOWNER
WOWSER
YAWNED
YAWNER
YAWPED
YAWPER
YOWLED

••W••E
BEWARE
BOWTIE
COWRIE
DAWDLE
EXWIFE
KEWPIE
NEWAGE
NOWISE
PAWNEE
REWIRE
REWOVE
SEWAGE
TOWAGE
TOWHEE
TOWNIE
UNWISE
UNWOVE

•••WE•
ALLWET
ANSWER
AVOWED
AVOWER
BLOWER
BREWED
BREWER
BULWER
CHEWED
CHEWER
CHOWED
CLAWED
CLAWER
CLEWED
COBWEB
CREWED
CREWEL
CROWED
CROWER
DRAWER
FLAWED
FLOWED
FLOWER
GLOWED
GLOWER
GNAWED
GNAWER
GROWER
KNOWER
MEOWED
PEEWEE
PLOWED
PLOWER
SHOWED
SHOWER
SKEWED
SKEWER
SLEWED
SLOWED
SLOWER
SNOWED
SPEWED
STEWED
STEWER
STOWED
THAWED
THEWEB
TROWED
TROWEL
UNAWED
VIEWED
VIEWER
YAHWEH

•••W•E
BROWNE
BROWSE
DROWSE
PEEWEE
PROWSE
SHOWME

W•F•••
WAFERS
WAFERY
WAFFLE
WAFFLY
WAFTED
WIFELY

W••F••
WAFFLE
WAFFLY
WERFEL
WETFLY
WHIFFS
WILFUL
WOEFUL
WOLFED
WOOFED
WOOFER

W•••F•
WHARFS
WHIFFS
WHOOFS

W••••F
WHATIF

•W•F••
SWIFTS
TWOFER

•W••F•
DWARFS

••WF••
BOWFIN
LAWFUL
LOWFAT
SAWFIT

••W•F•
EXWIFE
SAWOFF

••W••F
SAWOFF

W•G•••
WAGERS
WAGGED
WAGGLE
WAGGLY
WAGGON
WAGING
WAGNER
WAGONS
WIGGED
WIGGLE
WIGGLY
WIGHTS
WIGLET
WIGOUT
WIGWAG
WIGWAM

W••G••
WAGGED
WAGGLE
WAGGLY
WAGGON
WANGLE
WARGOD
WEDGED
WEDGES
WEDGIE
WEIGHS
WEIGHT
WIDGET
WIGGED
WIGGLE
WIGGLY
WINGED
WINGER
WINGIT
WODGES
WOOGIE
WRIGHT

W•••G•
WHANGS
WRINGS
WRONGS

W••••G
WADING
WAGING
WAKING
WANING
WARING
WAVING
WAXING
WETTIG
WIGWAG
WILING
WINING
WIPING
WIRING
WONMUG
WOOING
WOWING

•W•G••
DWIGHT
SWAGED
SWAGES
TWIGGY

•W••G•
AWEIGH
SWINGS
SWINGY
TWANGS
TWANGY
TWIGGY
TWINGE

•W•••G
AWNING
OWNING

••WG••
GEWGAW
MOWGLI

••W•G•
NEWAGE
OSWEGO
RAWEGG
SEWAGE
TOWAGE

••W••G
ANWANG
BOWING
CAWING
COWING
DEWING
HAWING
HEWING
JAWING
LAWING
LOWING
MEWING
MOWING
PAWING
RAWEGG
ROWING
SAWING
SAWLOG
SEWING
SOWBUG
SOWING
TAWING
TOWING
VOWING
WOWING
YAWING

•••W•G
BIGWIG
EARWIG
LUDWIG
WIGWAG

WH••••
WHACKS
WHACKY
WHALER
WHALES
WHAMMO
WHAMMY
WHANGS
WHARFS
WHATIF
WHATLL
WHATVE
WHEALS
WHEATS
WHEELS
WHEEZE
WHEEZY
WHELKS
WHELMS
WHELPS
WHENCE
WHERED
WHERES
WHERRY
WHIFFS
WHILED
WHILES
WHILOM
WHILST
WHIMSY
WHINED
WHINER
WHINES
WHINEY
WHINNY
WHIPPY
WHIPUP
WHIRLS
WHIRLY
WHIRRS
WHISKS
WHISKY
WHITEN
WHITER
WHITES
WHITTY
WHIZZO
WHOLES
WHOLLY
WHOMPS
WHOMSO
WHOOFS
WHOOPI
WHOOPS
WHOOSH
WHORLS
WHYDAH
WHYNOT

W•H•••
WAHINE
WAHOOS
WAHWAH
WOHLER

W••H••
WARHOL
WASHED
WASHER
WASHES
WASHOE
WASHUP
WETHER
WIGHTS
WISHED
WISHER
WISHES
WITHAL
WITHED
WITHER
WITHES
WITHIN
WITHIT

W•••H•
WEIGHS
WEIGHT
WIDTHS
WITCHY
WORTHS
WORTHY
WRATHS
WRATHY
WRIGHT
WRITHE

W••••H
WABASH
WAHWAH
WARMTH
WEALTH
WHOOSH
WHYDAH
WIDISH
WINISH
WRAITH
WREATH
WRENCH
WRETCH

•WH•••
AWHILE
AWHIRL

•W••H•
DWIGHT
KWACHA
SWATHE
SWATHS

•W•••H
AWEIGH
OWLISH
SWARTH
SWATCH
SWITCH
SWOOSH
TWITCH

••WH••
HAWHAW
SOWHAT
TOWHEE

••W•H•
JAWOHL

••W••H
GOWITH
HOWDAH
INWITH
JEWISH
LOWISH
NEWISH
RAWISH
REWASH
SIWASH
UNWISH

•••W•H
GROWTH
WAHWAH
YAHWEH

WI••••
WICCAN
WICKED
WICKER
WICKET
WICOPY
WIDELY
WIDENS
WIDEST
WIDGET
WIDISH
WIDOWS
WIDTHS
WIELDS
WIENER
WIESEL
WIFELY
WIGGED
WIGGLE
WIGGLY
WIGHTS
WIGLET
WIGOUT
WIGWAG
WIGWAM
WILBUR
WILCOX
WILDER
WILDLY
WILFUL
WILIER
WILILY
WILING
WILKES
WILLED
WILLEM
WILLET
WILLIE
WILLIS
WILLOW
WILSON
WILTED
WILTON
WIMBLE
WIMPLE
WIMSEY
WINCED
WINCER
WINCES
WINDED
WINDER
WINDEX
WINDOM
WINDOW
WINDUP
WINERY
WINGED
WINGER
WINGIT
WINIER
WINING
WINISH
WINKAT
WINKED
WINKER
WINKIE
WINKLE
WINNER
WINNIE
WINNOW
WINONA
WINOUT
WINSOR
WINTER
WINTRY
WINWIN
WINZES
WIPERS
WIPEUP
WIPING
WIRERS
WIRIER
WIRILY
WIRING
WISDOM
WISELY
WISENT
WISEST
WISETO
WISEUP
WISHED
WISHER
WISHES
WISPED
WISTER
WITCHY
WITHAL
WITHED
WITHER
WITHES
WITHIN
WITHIT
WITTED
WIZARD
WIZENS

W•I•••
WAILED
WAILER
WAISTS
WAITED
WAITER
WAITON
WAITUP
WAIVED
WAIVER
WAIVES
WEIGHS
WEIGHT
WEIMAR
WEIRDO
WEIRDY
WHIFFS
WHILED
WHILES
WHILOM
WHILST
WHIMSY
WHINED
WHINER
WHINES
WHINEY
WHINNY
WHIPPY
WHIPUP
WHIRLS
WHIRLY
WHIRRS
WHISKS
WHISKY
WHITEN
WHITER
WHITES
WHITTY
WHIZZO
WRIEST
WRIGHT
WRINGS
WRISTS
WRITER
WRITES
WRITHE

W••I••
WADING
WAGING
WAHINE
WAKING
WANIER
WANING
WAPITI
WARIER
WARILY
WARING
WAVIER
WAVILY
WAVING
WAXIER
WAXILY
WAXING
WIDISH
WILIER
WILILY
WILING
WINIER
WINING
WINISH
WIPING
WIRIER
WIRILY
WIRING
WOOING
WOWING
WRAITH

W•••I•
WADEIN
WALKIE
WALKIN
WALLIS
WANTIN
WAVEIN
WEDGIE
WEENIE
WEEPIE
WEEVIL
WELKIN
WENTIN
WESKIT
WETTIG
WHATIF
WILLIE
WILLIS
WINGIT
WINKIE
WINNIE
WINWIN
WITHIN
WITHIT
WOOGIE
WOOKIE
WORKIN

W••••I
WAPITI
WASABI
WATUSI
WHOOPI

•WI•••
DWIGHT
SWIFTS
SWILLS
SWINGS
SWINGY
SWIPED
SWIPER
SWIPES
SWIRLS
SWIRLY
SWITCH
SWIVEL
SWIVET

TWIGGY
TWILIT
TWILLS
TWINED
TWINES
TWINGE
TWIRLS
TWISTS
TWISTY
TWITCH
TWITTY

•W•I••
AWAITS
AWEIGH
AWHILE
AWHIRL
AWNING
KWEISI
OWLISH
OWNING
SWAINS

•W••I•
SWAMIS
SWAZIS
TWILIT
TWOBIT

•W•••I
KWEISI

••WI••
ASWIRL
ATWILL
BOWING
CAWING
COWING
DEWIER
DEWILY
DEWING
DEWITT
EXWIFE
GOWILD
GOWITH
HAWING
HEWING
INWITH
JAWING
JEWISH
LAWING
LOWING
LOWISH
MEWING
MOWING
NEWISH
NOWISE
PAWING
PEWITS
RAWISH
REWIND
REWINS
REWIRE
ROWING
SAWING
SEWING
SOWING
TAWING
TOWING
UNWILY
UNWIND
UNWISE
UNWISH
UPWIND
VOWING
WOWING
YAWING

••W•I•
BEWAIL
BOWFIN
BOWTIE
COWRIE
GAWAIN
HAWAII
HOWLIN
KEWPIE
KUWAIT
SAWFIT
TOWNIE

••W••I
HAWAII
MOWGLI

•••WI•
BIGWIG
BLEWIT
BLOWIN
BLOWIT
DARWIN
DIMWIT
DRAWIN
DREWIN
EARWIG
FLEWIN
GODWIN
GODWIT
LUDWIG
NITWIT
OUTWIT
SHOWIN
SNOWIN
THEWIZ
WINWIN

••••WI
MALAWI

•W•••J
SWARAJ

W•K•••
WAKENS
WAKEUP
WAKING
WOKEUP

W••K••
WACKOS
WALKED
WALKEN
WALKER
WALKIE
WALKIN
WALKON
WALKUP
WEAKEN
WEAKER
WEAKLY
WEEKLY
WELKIN
WESKIT
WICKED
WICKER
WICKET
WILKES
WINKAT
WINKED
WINKER
WINKIE
WINKLE
WOOKIE
WORKED
WORKER
WORKIN
WORKON
WORKUP

W•••K•
WHACKS
WHACKY
WHELKS
WHISKS
WHISKY
WOVOKA
WRACKS
WREAKS
WRECKS

•W•K••
AWAKED
AWAKEN
AWAKES
AWOKEN

•W••K•
SWANKS
SWANKY
TWEAKS

••WK••
FAWKES
GAWKED
GAWKER
HAWKED
HAWKER
LOWKEY

••W•K•
MIWOKS

••W••K
ADWEEK
ATWORK
NEWARK
REWORK
THWACK

•••W•K
ARAWAK

••••WK
MOHAWK
SQUAWK

W•L•••
WALDEN
WALERS
WALESA
WALKED
WALKEN
WALKER
WALKIE
WALKIN
WALKON
WALKUP
WALLED
WALLER
WALLET
WALLIS
WALLOP
WALLOW
WALLUP
WALNUT
WALRUS
WALTER
WALTON
WELDED
WELDER
WELKIN
WELLED
WELLER
WELLES
WELLUP
WELTED
WELTER
WILBUR
WILCOX
WILDER
WILDLY
WILFUL
WILIER
WILILY
WILING
WILKES
WILLED
WILLEM
WILLET
WILLIE
WILLIS
WILLOW
WILSON
WILTED
WILTON
WOLFED
WOLPER
WOLSEY
WOLVES

W••L••
WAILED
WAILER
WALLED
WALLER
WALLET
WALLIS
WALLOP
WALLOW
WALLUP
WAYLAY
WAYLON
WEALTH
WELLED
WELLER
WELLES
WELLUP
WESLEY
WHALER
WHALES
WHELKS
WHELMS
WHELPS
WHILED
WHILES
WHILOM
WHILST
WHOLES
WHOLLY
WIELDS
WIGLET
WILLED
WILLEM
WILLET
WILLIE
WILLIS
WILLOW
WOHLER
WOOLEN
WOOLEY
WOOLLY
WORLDS
WURLEY

W•••L•
WADDLE
WADDLY
WAFFLE
WAFFLY
WAGGLE
WAGGLY
WAMBLE
WAMBLY
WANGLE
WARBLE
WARILY
WARMLY
WATTLE
WAVILY
WAXILY
WEAKLY
WEDELN
WEEKLY
WETFLY
WHATLL
WHEALS
WHEELS
WHIRLS
WHIRLY
WHOLLY
WHORLS
WIDELY
WIFELY
WIGGLE
WIGGLY
WILDLY
WILILY
WIMBLE
WIMPLE
WINKLE
WIRILY
WISELY
WOBBLE
WOBBLY
WOOLLY

W••••L
WARHOL
WEASEL
WEEVIL
WERFEL
WHATLL
WIESEL
WILFUL
WITHAL
WOEFUL

•WL•••
OWLETS
OWLISH

•W•L••
DWELLS
SWALES
SWELLS
SWILLS
TWELVE
TWILIT
TWILLS

•W••L•
AWEDLY
AWHILE
DWELLS
SWELLS
SWILLS
SWIRLS
SWIRLY
TWILLS
TWIRLS
TWOPLY

•W•••L
AWHIRL
SWIVEL

••WL••
BAWLED
BAWLER
BOWLED
BOWLER
BOWLES
COWLED
COWLEY
DEWLAP
FAWLTY
FOWLED
FOWLER
FOWLES
HOWLED
HOWLER
HOWLIN
MEWLED
MEWLER
NEWLEY
SAWLOG
YOWLED

••W•L•
ASWELL
ATWILL
DAWDLE
DEWILY
DOWELS
GOWILD
HOWELL
JEWELS
LEWDLY
LOWELL
MOWGLI
NEWELS
OHWELL
ORWELL
OSWALD
POWELL
REWELD
ROWELS
SEWELL
TOWELS
UNWELL
UNWILY
UPWELL
VOWELS
VOWELY

••W••L
ASWELL
ASWIRL
ATWILL
BEWAIL
HOWELL
JAWOHL
LAWFUL
LOWCAL
LOWELL
OHWELL
ORWELL
POWELL
SEWELL
UNWELL
UPWELL

•••WL•
BRAWLS
CRAWLS
CRAWLY
DRAWLS
DRAWLY
GROWLS
GROWLY
PROWLS
SCOWLS
SHAWLS
SLOWLY
TRAWLS

•••W•L
AVOWAL
CREWEL
NARWAL
TROWEL

••••WL
SCRAWL
SPRAWL

W•M•••
WAMBLE
WAMBLY
WAMPUM
WIMBLE
WIMPLE
WIMSEY
WOMBAT
WOMENS

W••M••
WARMED
WARMER
WARMLY
WARMTH
WARMUP
WEIMAR
WETMOP
WHAMMO
WHAMMY
WHIMSY
WHOMPS
WHOMSO
WONMUG
WORMED

W•••M•
WHAMMO
WHAMMY
WHELMS

W••••M
WAMPUM
WHILOM
WIGWAM
WILLEM
WINDOM
WISDOM

•W•M••
SWAMIS
SWAMPS
SWAMPY

•W••M•
SWARMS

••WM••
BOWMAN
BOWMEN
COWMAN
COWMEN
LAWMAN
LAWMEN
NEWMAN
NEWMAR

••W••M
REWARM

•••WM•
SHAWMS
SHOWME

•••W•M
WIGWAM

W•N•••
WANDER
WANERS
WANGLE
WANIER
WANING
WANNED
WANNER
WANTAD
WANTED
WANTIN
WANTON
WANTTO
WENCES
WENDED
WENTAT
WENTBY
WENTIN
WENTON
WENTUP
WINCED
WINCER
WINCES
WINDED
WINDER
WINDEX
WINDOM
WINDOW
WINDUP
WINERY
WINGED
WINGER
WINGIT
WINIER
WINING
WINISH
WINKAT
WINKED
WINKER
WINKIE
WINKLE
WINNER
WINNIE
WINNOW
WINONA
WINOUT
WINSOR
WINTER
WINTRY
WINWIN
WINZES
WONDER
WONMUG
WONNED
WONOUT
WONTED
WONTON
WYNTER
WYNTON

W••N••
WAGNER
WALNUT
WANNED
WANNER
WAPNER
WARNED
WARNER
WATNEY
WEANED
WEENIE
WEENSY
WERNER
WHANGS
WHENCE
WHINED
WHINER
WHINES
WHINEY
WHINNY
WHYNOT
WIENER
WINNER
WINNIE
WINNOW
WONNED
WOUNDS
WRENCH
WRINGS
WRONGS

W•••N•
WADING
WAGING
WAGONS
WAHINE
WAKENS
WAKING
WANING
WARING
WAVING
WAXING
WAYANS
WERENT
WHINNY
WIDENS
WILING
WINING
WINONA
WIPING
WIRING
WISENT
WIZENS
WOMENS
WOOING
WOWING

W••••N
WADEIN
WAGGON
WAITON
WALDEN
WALKEN
WALKIN
WALKON
WALTON
WANTIN
WANTON
WARDEN
WARREN
WATSON
WAVEIN
WAYLON
WEAKEN
WEAPON
WEBERN
WEDELN
WELKIN
WENTIN
WENTON
WESSON
WHITEN
WICCAN
WILSON
WILTON
WINWIN
WITHIN
WONTON
WOODEN
WOOLEN
WOREON
WORKIN
WORKON
WORSEN
WYNTON
WYSTAN
WYVERN

•WN•••
AWNING
OWNERS
OWNING
OWNSUP

•W•N••
BWANAS
GWYNNE
KWANZA
RWANDA
SWANEE
SWANKS
SWANKY
SWINGS
SWINGY
TWANGS
TWANGY
TWENTY
TWINED
TWINES
TWINGE

•W••N•
AWNING
DWAYNE
GWYNNE
OWNING
SWAINS
SWOONS
TWEENS
TWEENY

•W•••N
AWAKEN
AWOKEN
SWEDEN

••WN••
BOWNET
DAWNED
DAWNON
DOWNED
DOWNER
DOWNEY
DOWNON
FAWNED
FAWNER
GOWNED
HOWNOW
PAWNED
PAWNEE
PAWNER
SEWNON
SEWNUP
TOWNER
TOWNIE
YAWNED
YAWNER

••W•N•
ANWANG
BOWING
CAWING
COWENS
COWING
DEWING
EDWYNN
HAWING
HEWING
IOWANS
JAWING
LAWING
LOWEND
LOWING
MEWING
MOWING
PAWING
REWIND
REWINS
ROWENA
ROWENS
ROWING
SAWING
SEWING
SOWING
TAWING
TOWING
UNWIND
UPWIND
VOWING
WOWING
YAWING

••W••N
ASWOON
BOWFIN
BOWMAN
BOWMEN
COWMAN
COWMEN
DAWNON
DAWSON
DOWNON
EDWYNN
GAWAIN
HOWLIN
LAWMAN
LAWMEN
LAWSON
LAWTON
NEWMAN
NEWTON
SEWNON
SEWSON
UNWORN

•••WN•
BRAWNY
BROWNE
BROWNS
BROWNY
CLOWNS
CROWNS
DROWNS
FROWNS
KNOWNS
PRAWNS
SPAWNS

•••W•N
BLOWIN
DARWIN
DRAWIN
DRAWON
DREWIN
DREWON
FLEWIN
GODWIN
GREWON
GROWON
OBIWAN
SHOWIN
SNOWIN
TAIWAN
WINWIN

••••WN
DISOWN
GODOWN
INTOWN
MOTOWN
REMOWN
RENOWN
RESAWN
RESEWN
STREWN
THROWN
UNSEWN
UNSOWN
UPTOWN

WO••••
WOBBLE
WOBBLY
WODGES
WOEFUL
WOHLER
WOKEUP
WOLFED
WOLPER
WOLSEY
WOLVES
WOMBAT
WOMENS
WONDER
WONMUG
WONNED
WONOUT
WONTED
WONTON
WOODED
WOODEN
WOODSY
WOOERS
WOOFED
WOOFER
WOOGIE
WOOING
WOOKIE
WOOLEN
WOOLEY
WOOLLY
WORDED
WOREON
WORKED
WORKER
WORKIN
WORKON
WORKUP
WORLDS
WORMED
WORSEN
WORSTS
WORTHS
WORTHY
WOUNDS
WOVOKA
WOWING
WOWSER

W•O•••
WHOLES
WHOLLY
WHOMPS
WHOMSO
WHOOFS
WHOOPI
WHOOPS
WHOOSH
WHORLS
WOODED
WOODEN
WOODSY
WOOERS
WOOFED
WOOFER
WOOGIE
WOOING
WOOKIE
WOOLEN
WOOLEY
WOOLLY
WRONGS

W••O••
WAGONS
WAHOOS
WAYOUT
WHOOFS
WHOOPI
WHOOPS
WHOOSH
WICOPY
WIDOWS
WIGOUT
WINONA
WINOUT
WONOUT
WOVOKA

W•••O•
WACKOS
WAGGON
WAHOOS
WAITON
WALKON
WALLOP
WALLOW
WALTON
WANTON
WARGOD
WARHOL
WASHOE
WATSON
WAYLON
WEAPON
WENTON
WESSON
WETMOP
WHILOM
WHYNOT
WILCOX
WILLOW
WILSON
WILTON
WINDOM
WINDOW
WINNOW
WINSOR
WISDOM
WONTON
WOREON
WORKON
WYNTON

W••••O
WANTTO
WEIRDO
WHAMMO
WHIZZO
WHOMSO
WISETO

•WO•••
AWOKEN
SWOONS
SWOOPS
SWOOSH
SWORDS
TWOBIT
TWOFER
TWOPLY
TWOWAY

•W•O••
SWOONS
SWOOPS
SWOOSH

••WO••
ASWOON
ATWOOD
ATWORK
BOWOAR
BOWOUT
BYWORD
EDWOOD
ELWOOD
JAWOHL
MIWOKS
MYWORD
REWORD
REWORK
REWOVE
SAWOFF
SAWOUT
UNWORN
UNWOVE

••W•O•
ASWOON
ATWOOD
BOWWOW
CAWDOR
COWBOY
COWPOX
DAWNON
DAWSON
DOWNON
EDWOOD
ELWOOD
HOWNOW
HOWTOS
KOWTOW
LAWSON
LAWTON
LOWBOY
NEWTON
POWWOW
SAWLOG
SEWNON
SEWSON

••W••O
OSWEGO
SOWETO

•••WO•
BOWWOW
DOOWOP
DRAWON
DREWON
GREWON
GROWON
POWWOW

••••WO
ACTTWO
ONETWO

W•P•••
WAPITI
WAPNER
WIPERS
WIPEUP
WIPING

W••P••
WAMPUM
WARPED
WEAPON
WEEPER
WEEPIE
WHIPPY
WHIPUP
WIMPLE
WISPED
WOLPER
WRAPUP

W•••P•
WHELPS
WHIPPY
WHOMPS
WHOOPI
WHOOPS
WICOPY

W••••P
WADSUP
WAITUP
WAKEUP
WALKUP
WALLOP
WALLUP
WARMUP
WASHUP
WELLUP
WENTUP
WETMOP
WHIPUP
WINDUP
WIPEUP
WISEUP
WOKEUP
WORKUP
WRAPUP

•W•P••
SWIPED
SWIPER
SWIPES
TWOPLY

•W••P•
SWAMPS
SWAMPY
SWEEPS
SWOOPS
TWERPS

•W•••P
OWNSUP

••WP••
COWPEA
COWPER
COWPOX
GAWPED
KEWPIE
PAWPAW
YAWPED
YAWPER

••W••P
DEWLAP
ENWRAP
REWRAP
SEWNUP
SEWSUP
UNWRAP

•••W•P
BLEWUP
BLOWUP
CHEWUP
DOOWOP
DRAWUP
DREWUP
GREWUP
GROWUP
SHOWUP
SLOWUP

WR••••
WRACKS
WRAITH
WRAPUP
WRASSE
WRATHS
WRATHY
WREAKS
WREATH
WRECKS
WRENCH
WRESTS
WRETCH
WRIEST
WRIGHT
WRINGS
WRISTS

WRITER
WRITES
WRITHE
WRONGS
WRYEST

W•R•••
WARBLE
WARCRY
WARDED
WARDEN
WARDER
WARGOD
WARHOL
WARIER
WARILY
WARING
WARMED
WARMER
WARMLY
WARMTH
WARMUP
WARNED
WARNER
WARPED
WARRED
WARREN
WARSAW
WERENT
WERFEL
WERNER
WIRERS
WIRIER
WIRILY
WIRING
WORDED
WOREON
WORKED
WORKER
WORKIN
WORKON
WORKUP
WORLDS
WORMED
WORSEN
WORSTS
WORTHS
WORTHY
WURLEY
WURSTS

W••R••
WALRUS
WARRED
WARREN
WEARER
WEIRDO
WEIRDY
WHARFS
WHERED
WHERES
WHERRY
WHIRLS
WHIRLY
WHIRRS
WHORLS

W•••R•
WADERS
WAFERS
WAFERY
WAGERS
WALERS
WANERS
WARCRY
WATERS
WATERY
WAVERS
WAVERY
WAXERS
WEBERN
WHERRY
WHIRRS
WINERY
WINTRY
WIPERS
WIRERS
WIZARD
WOOERS
WYVERN

W••••R
WAGNER
WAILER
WAITER
WAIVER
WALKER
WALLER
WALTER
WANDER
WANIER
WANNER
WAPNER
WARDER
WARIER
WARMER
WARNER
WASHER
WASTER
WAVIER
WAXIER
WEAKER
WEARER
WEAVER
WEBBER
WEEDER
WEEPER
WEIMAR
WELDER
WELLER
WELTER
WERNER
WETBAR
WETHER
WETTER
WHALER
WHINER
WHITER
WICKER
WIENER
WILBUR
WILDER
WILIER
WINCER
WINDER
WINGER
WINIER
WINKER
WINNER
WINSOR
WINTER
WIRIER
WISHER
WISTER
WITHER
WOHLER
WOLPER
WONDER
WOOFER
WORKER
WOWSER
WRITER
WYNTER

•W•R••
AWARDS
DWARFS
QWERTY
SWARAJ
SWARDS
SWARMS
SWARTH
SWERVE
SWIRLS
SWIRLY
SWORDS
TWERPS
TWIRLS

•W••R•
AWEARY
AWHIRL
OWNERS
SWEARS

•W•••R
SWAYER
SWIPER
TWOFER

••WR••
BEWRAY
COWRIE
ENWRAP
REWRAP
SAWRED
UNWRAP

••W•R•
ASWIRL
ATWORK
BEWARE
BOWERS
BOWERY
BYWORD
COWARD
COWERS
DOWERS
DOWERY
EDWARD
HEWERS
HOWARD
INWARD
LOWERS
LOWERY
MOWERS
MYWORD
NEWARK
ONWARD
PAWERS
POWERS
REWARD
REWARM
REWIRE
REWORD
REWORK
ROWERS
SEWARD
SEWERS
SOWERS
TAWDRY
THWART
TOWARD
TOWERS
TOWERY
UNWARY
UNWORN
UPWARD
VOWERS

••W••R
BAWLER
BOWLER
BOWOAR
BOWSER
BOWYER
CAWDOR
COWPER
DEWIER
DOWNER
DOWSER
FAWNER
FOWLER
GAWKER
HAWKER
HAWSER
HOWLER
LAWYER
LEWDER
MEWLER
NEWMAR
PAWNER
PEWTER
POWDER
SAWYER
TOWCAR
TOWNER
WOWSER
YAWNER
YAWPER

•••WR•
GOAWRY

•••W•R
ANSWER
AVOWER
BLOWER
BREWER
BULWER
CHEWER
CLAWER
CROWER
DRAWER
FLOWER
GLOWER
GNAWER
GROWER
HOTWAR
KNOWER
PLOWER
PREWAR
PSYWAR
SHOWER
SKEWER
SLOWER
STEWER
VIEWER

W•S•••
WASABI
WASHED
WASHER
WASHES
WASHOE
WASHUP
WASTED
WASTER
WASTES
WESKIT
WESLEY
WESSEX
WESSON
WISDOM
WISELY
WISENT
WISEST
WISETO
WISEUP
WISHED
WISHER
WISHES
WISPED
WISTER
WUSSES
WYSTAN

W••S••
WADSUP
WAISTS
WARSAW
WATSON
WAUSAU
WEASEL
WESSEX
WESSON
WHISKS
WHISKY
WIESEL
WILSON
WIMSEY
WINSOR
WOLSEY
WORSEN
WORSTS
WOWSER
WRASSE
WRESTS
WRISTS
WURSTS
WUSSES

W•••S•
WABASH
WALESA
WATUSI
WEENSY
WHILST
WHIMSY
WHOMSO
WHOOSH
WIDEST
WIDISH
WINISH
WISEST
WOODSY
WRASSE
WRIEST
WRYEST

W••••S
WACKOS
WADERS
WAFERS
WAGERS
WAGONS
WAHOOS
WAISTS
WAIVES
WAKENS
WALERS
WALLIS
WALRUS
WANERS
WASHES
WASTES
WATERS
WAVERS
WAXERS
WAYANS
WEAVES
WEDGES
WEIGHS
WELLES
WENCES
WHACKS
WHALES
WHANGS
WHARFS
WHEALS
WHEATS
WHEELS
WHELKS
WHELMS
WHELPS
WHERES
WHIFFS
WHILES
WHINES
WHIRLS
WHIRRS
WHISKS
WHITES
WHOLES
WHOMPS
WHOOFS
WHOOPS
WHORLS
WIDENS
WIDOWS
WIDTHS
WIELDS
WIGHTS
WILKES
WILLIS
WINCES
WINZES
WIPERS
WIRERS
WISHES
WITHES
WIZENS
WODGES
WOLVES
WOMENS
WOOERS
WORLDS
WORSTS
WORTHS
WOUNDS
WRACKS
WRATHS
WREAKS
WRECKS
WRESTS
WRINGS
WRISTS
WRITES
WRONGS
WURSTS
WUSSES

•W•S••
OWNSUP
TWISTS
TWISTY

•W••S•
KWEISI
OWLISH
SWOOSH
TWEEST

•W•••S
AWAITS
AWAKES
AWARDS
BWANAS
DWARFS
DWEEBS
DWELLS
OWLETS
OWNERS
SWAGES
SWAINS
SWALES
SWAMIS
SWAMPS
SWANKS
SWARDS
SWARMS
SWATHS
SWAZIS
SWEARS
SWEATS
SWEDES
SWEEPS
SWEETS
SWELLS
SWIFTS
SWILLS
SWINGS
SWIPES
SWIRLS
SWOONS
SWOOPS
SWORDS
TWANGS
TWEAKS
TWEEDS
TWEENS
TWEETS
TWERPS
TWILLS
TWINES
TWIRLS
TWISTS

••WS••
BOWSAW
BOWSER
DAWSON
DOWSED
DOWSER
DOWSES
HAWSER
HAWSES
LAWSON
PAWSAT
SEWSON
SEWSUP
WOWSER

••W•S•
ALWEST
FEWEST
GOWEST
JEWISH
LOWEST
LOWISH
NEWEST
NEWISH
NLWEST
NOWISE
RAWEST
RAWISH
REWASH
SIWASH
UNWISE
UNWISH

••W••S
ALWAYS
BOWERS
BOWLES
BYWAYS
COWENS
COWERS
DOWELS
DOWERS
DOWSES
FAWKES
FOWLES
HAWSES
HEWERS
HOWTOS
IOWANS
JEWELS
LOWERS
MIWOKS
MOWERS
NAWABS
NEWELS
PAWERS
PEWEES
PEWITS
POWERS
REWEDS
REWINS
ROWELS
ROWENS
ROWERS
SEWERS
SOWERS
TOWELS
TOWERS
VOWELS
VOWERS

•••WS•
BLOWSY
BROWSE
DROWSE
DROWSY
PROWSE

•••W•S
BRAWLS
BROWNS
CLOWNS
CRAWLS
CROWDS
CROWNS
DRAWLS
DROWNS
FATWAS
FROWNS
GROWLS
KIOWAS
KNOWNS
PRAWNS
PROWLS
SCHWAS
SCOWLS
SHAWLS
SHAWMS
SPAWNS
TRAWLS

••••WS
ALLOWS
ARROWS
BEDEWS
BYLAWS
CAHOWS
ELBOWS
ENDOWS
FIVEWS
INLAWS
MACAWS
OXBOWS
PAPAWS
REMOWS
RENEWS
RESAWS
RESEWS
RETOWS
SCREWS
SEROWS
SHREWS
SINEWS
STRAWS
STREWS
THROWS
UNSEWS
UPBOWS
WIDOWS

W•T•••
WATERS
WATERY
WATNEY
WATSON
WATTLE
WATUSI
WETBAR
WETFLY
WETHER
WETMOP
WETTED
WETTER
WETTIG
WITCHY
WITHAL
WITHED
WITHER
WITHES
WITHIN
WITHIT
WITTED

W••T••
WAFTED
WAITED
WAITER
WAITON
WAITUP
WALTER
WALTON
WANTAD
WANTED
WANTIN
WANTON
WANTTO
WASTED
WASTER
WASTES
WATTLE
WELTED
WELTER
WENTAT
WENTBY
WENTIN
WENTON
WENTUP
WETTED
WETTER
WETTIG
WHATIF
WHATLL
WHATVE
WHITEN
WHITER
WHITES
WHITTY
WIDTHS
WILTED
WILTON
WINTER
WINTRY
WISTER
WITTED
WONTED
WONTON
WORTHS
WORTHY
WRATHS
WRATHY
WRETCH
WRITER
WRITES
WRITHE
WYNTER
WYNTON
WYSTAN

W•••T•
WAISTS
WANTTO
WAPITI
WARMTH
WEALTH
WHEATS
WHITTY
WIGHTS
WISETO
WORSTS
WRAITH
WREATH
WRESTS
WRISTS
WURSTS

W••••T
WALLET
WALNUT
WAYOUT
WEIGHT
WENTAT
WERENT
WESKIT
WHILST
WHYNOT
WICKET
WIDEST
WIDGET
WIGLET
WIGOUT
WILLET
WINGIT
WINKAT
WINOUT
WISENT
WISEST
WITHIT
WOMBAT
WONOUT
WRIEST
WRIGHT
WRYEST

•W•T••
SWATCH
SWATHE
SWATHS
SWITCH
TWITCH
TWITTY

•W••T•
AWAITS
OWLETS
QWERTY
SWARTH
SWEATS
SWEATY
SWEETS
SWIFTS
TWEETS
TWEETY
TWENTY
TWISTS
TWISTY
TWITTY

•W•••T
DWIGHT
SWIVET
TWEEST
TWILIT
TWOBIT

••WT••
BOWTIE
HOWTOS
KOWTOW
LAWTON
NEWTON
PEWTER

••W•T•
DEWITT
FAWLTY
GOWITH
INWITH
JEWETT
JOWETT
PEWITS
SOWETO

••W••T
ALWEST
BOWNET
BOWOUT
DEWITT
FEWEST
GOWEST
JEWETT
JOWETT
KUWAIT
LOWEST
LOWFAT
NEWEST
NLWEST
PAWSAT
RAWEST
SAWFIT
SAWOUT
SOWHAT
THWART

•••WT•
GROWTH

•••W•T
ALLWET
BLEWIT
BLOWIT
DIMWIT
FLEWAT
GODWIT
NITWIT
OUTWIT

WU••••
WURLEY
WURSTS
WUSSES

W•U•••
WAUSAU
WOUNDS

W••U••
WATUSI

W•••U•
WADSUP
WAITUP
WAKEUP
WALKUP
WALLUP
WALNUT
WALRUS
WAMPUM
WARMUP
WASHUP
WAYOUT
WELLUP
WENTUP
WHIPUP
WIGOUT
WILBUR
WILFUL
WINDUP
WINOUT
WIPEUP
WISEUP
WOEFUL
WOKEUP
WONMUG
WONOUT
WORKUP
WRAPUP

W••••U
WAUSAU

•W••U•
OWNSUP

••W•U•
BOWOUT
LAWFUL
SAWOUT
SEWNUP
SEWSUP
SOWBUG

•••WU•
BLEWUP
BLOWUP
CHEWUP
DRAWUP
DREWUP
GREWUP
GROWUP
SHOWUP
SLOWUP

••••WU
HUNGWU

W•V•••
WAVEIN
WAVERS
WAVERY
WAVIER
WAVILY
WAVING
WOVOKA
WYVERN

W••V••
WAIVED
WAIVER
WAIVES
WEAVED
WEAVER
WEAVES
WEEVIL
WOLVES

W•••V•
WHATVE

•W•V••
SWIVEL
SWIVET

•W••V•
SWERVE
TWELVE

••W•V•
REWOVE
UNWOVE

W•W•••
WOWING
WOWSER

W••W••
WAHWAH
WIGWAG
WIGWAM
WINWIN

W•••W•
WIDOWS

W••••W
WALLOW
WARSAW
WILLOW
WINDOW
WINNOW

•W•W••
TWOWAY

••WW••
BOWWOW
POWWOW

••W••W
BOWSAW
BOWWOW
GEWGAW
HAWHAW
HOWNOW
KOWTOW
PAWPAW
POWWOW

•••W•W
BOWWOW
POWWOW

W•X•••
WAXERS
WAXIER
WAXILY
WAXING

W••••X
WESSEX
WILCOX
WINDEX

••W••X
COWPOX

•••W•X
EARWAX

WY••••
WYNTER
WYNTON
WYSTAN
WYVERN

W•Y•••
WAYANS
WAYLAY
WAYLON
WAYOUT
WHYDAH
WHYNOT
WRYEST

W••••Y
WADDLY
WAFERY
WAFFLY
WAGGLY
WAMBLY
WARCRY
WARILY
WARMLY
WATERY
WATNEY
WAVERY
WAVILY
WAXILY
WAYLAY
WEAKLY
WEEKLY
WEENSY
WEIRDY
WENTBY
WESLEY
WETFLY
WHACKY
WHAMMY
WHEEZY
WHERRY
WHIMSY
WHINEY
WHINNY
WHIPPY
WHIRLY
WHISKY
WHITTY
WHOLLY
WICOPY
WIDELY
WIFELY
WIGGLY
WILDLY
WILILY
WIMSEY
WINERY
WINTRY
WIRILY
WISELY
WITCHY
WOBBLY
WOLSEY
WOODSY
WOOLEY
WOOLLY
WORTHY
WRATHY
WURLEY

•WY•••
GWYNNE

•W•Y••
DWAYNE
SWAYED
SWAYER
SWAYZE

•W•••Y
AWEARY
AWEDLY
QWERTY
SWABBY
SWAMPY
SWANKY
SWEATY
SWINGY
SWIRLY
TWANGY
TWEEDY
TWEENY
TWEETY
TWENTY
TWIGGY
TWISTY
TWITTY
TWOPLY
TWOWAY

••WY••
BOWYER
EDWYNN
LAWYER
SAWYER

••W•Y•
ALWAYS
BYWAYS

••W••Y
BEWRAY
BOWERY
COWBOY
COWLEY
DEWILY
DOWERY
DOWNEY
FAWLTY
LEWDLY
LOWBOY
LOWERY
LOWKEY
NEWLEY
TAWDRY
TOWERY
UNWARY
UNWILY
VOWELY

•••W•Y
AIRWAY
ANYWAY
BLOWSY
BLOWZY
BRAWNY
BROWNY
CONWAY
CRAWLY
DRAWLY
DROWSY
FENWAY
FLYWAY
FROWZY
GALWAY
GOAWAY
GOAWRY
GROWLY
INAWAY
JETWAY
KEYWAY
LEEWAY
MIDWAY
NORWAY
ONEWAY
PEDWAY
RUNWAY
SEAWAY
SKYWAY
SLOWLY
SUBWAY
TWOWAY

••••WY
SCREWY
SINEWY
STRAWY

W•Z•••
WIZARD
WIZENS

W••Z••
WHIZZO
WINZES

W•••Z•
WHEEZE
WHEEZY
WHIZZO

•W•Z••
SWAZIS

•W••Z•
KWANZA
SWAYZE
TWEEZE

•••WZ•
BLOWZY
FROWZY

•••W•Z
THEWIZ

XA••••
XANADU
XANTHO
XAVIER

X•A•••
XIAMEN
XRATED
XRAYED

X••A••
XANADU

X•••A•
XHOSAS

X••••A
XIMENA

•XA•••
EXACTA
EXACTO
EXACTS
EXALTS
EXARCH
OXALIS

•X•A••
EXHALE
EXPAND
EXTANT
OXCART
OXNARD
OXTAIL

•X••A•
AXONAL
EXTRAS

•X•••A
AXILLA
EXACTA
EXEDRA

••XA••
FIXATE
HEXADS
LUXATE
OAXACA
ROXANA
ROXANE
TEXACO
TEXANS

••X•A•
BOXCAR
REXCAT
TAXMAN

••X••A
LEXICA
MAXIMA
OAXACA
ROXANA

•••XA•
PLEXAL

•••X•A
ALEXIA

••••XA
ADNEXA
CUNAXA

X•B•••
XEBECS

•XB•••
OXBOWS

•X••B•
EXURBS

••XB••
BOXBOY

X•••C•
XEBECS

•XC•••
EXCEED
EXCELS
EXCEPT
EXCESS
EXCISE
EXCITE
EXCUSE
OXCART

•X•C••
EXACTA
EXACTO
EXACTS

•X••C•
EXARCH
EXPECT

•X•••C
EXILIC
EXOTIC
OXIDIC

••XC••
BOXCAR
REXCAT

••X•C•
LEXICA
MEXICO
OAXACA
TEXACO
TOXICS

••X••C
MIXTEC

X•D•••
XEDOUT

X•••D•
XANADU

X••••D
XRATED
XRAYED
XYLOID

•X•D••
EXEDRA
EXODUS
EXUDED
EXUDES
OXIDES
OXIDIC
OXYDOL

•X•••D
AXSEED
EXCEED
EXILED
EXITED
EXPAND
EXPEND
EXTEND
EXUDED
OXFORD
OXNARD

••X•D•
HEXADS
TUXEDO

••X••D
TAXIED

•••X•D
BRUXED
COAXED
FLEXED
FLUXED
HOAXED
JINXED

XE••••
XEBECS
XEDOUT
XERXES

X••E••
XEBECS
XIMENA
XYLENE

X•••E•
XAVIER
XERXES
XFILES
XIAMEN
XRATED
XRAYED
XYSTER

X••••E
XYLENE

•XE•••
EXEDRA
EXEMPT
EXERTS
EXETER
EXEUNT
OXEYES

•X•E••
AXSEED
EXCEED
EXCELS
EXCEPT
EXCESS
EXLEGE
EXPECT
EXPELS
EXPEND
EXPERT
EXSERT
EXTEND
EXTENT
EXTERN

•X••E•
AXSEED
EXCEED
EXETER
EXILED
EXILES
EXITED
EXUDED
EXUDES
OXEYES
OXIDES
OXYGEN

•X•••E
AXLIKE
EXCISE
EXCITE
EXCUSE
EXHALE
EXLEGE
EXMORE
EXPIRE
EXPOSE
EXWIFE
OXLIKE

••XE••
BOXERS
FIXERS
HEXERS
LAXEST
LEXEME
MAXENE
MIXERS
PIXELS
SIXERS
SOXERS
TAXERS
TUXEDO
VEXERS
VIXENS
WAXERS

••X•E•
BAXTER
BOXIER
BOXSET
DEXTER
FOXIER
HUXLEY
MIXTEC
NIXIES
PIXIES
PYXIES
SEXIER
SEXTET
TAXIED
TAXIES
TAXMEN
TEXMEX
WAXIER

••X••E
FIXATE
LEXEME
LUXATE
MAXENE
MAXINE
MAXIXE
ROXANE

•••XE•
ALEXEI
APEXES
BLIXEN
BRUXED
BRUXES
CALXES
COAXED
COAXER
COAXES
CRUXES
DREXEL
FLAXEN
FLAXES
FLEXED
FLEXES
FLUXED
FLUXES
HOAXED
HOAXER
HOAXES
IBEXES
ILEXES
JINXED
JINXES
LYNXES
MINXES
ONYXES
ORYXES
PRAXES
VSIXES
XERXES

•••X•E
TRIXIE

••••XE
ANNEXE
DELUXE
MAXIXE

XF••••
XFILES

•XF•••
OXFORD

•X••F•
EXWIFE

••XF••
BOXFUL

X••G••
XINGIN

•X•G••
OXYGEN

•X••G•
EXLEGE

••XG••
SIXGUN

••X••G
BOXING
FAXING
FIXING
FOXING
HEXING
MIXING
NIXING
SIXING
TAXING
VEXING
WAXING

XH••••
XHOSAS

X•••H•
XANTHO

•XH•••
EXHALE
EXHORT

•X•••H
EXARCH

••X•H•
SIXTHS

XI••••
XIAMEN
XIMENA
XINGIN

X•I•••
XFILES

X••I••
XAVIER

X•••I•
XINGIN
XYLOID

•XI•••
AXILLA
AXIOMS
AXIONS
EXILED
EXILES
EXILIC
EXISTS
EXITED
OXIDES
OXIDIC

•X•I••
AXLIKE
EXCISE
EXCITE
EXPIRE
EXPIRY
EXWIFE
OXLIKE
OXLIPS

•X••I•
EXILIC
EXOTIC
OXALIS
OXIDIC
OXTAIL

••XI••
AUXINS
BOXIER
BOXING
DIXITS
FAXING
FIXING
FIXITY
FOXIER
FOXILY
FOXING
HEXING
LAXITY
LEXICA
MAXIMA
MAXIMS
MAXINE
MAXIXE
MEXICO
MIXING
NIXIES
NIXING
PIXIES
PYXIES
SEXIER
SEXILY
SEXIST
SIXING
TAXIED
TAXIES
TAXING
TOXICS
TOXINS
VEXING
WAXIER
WAXILY
WAXING

•••XI•
ALEXIA
ALEXIS
DIOXIN
ELIXIR
NOEXIT
PINXIT
PRAXIS
TRIXIE
ZEUXIS

•••X•I
ALEXEI

••••XI
BILOXI

•X••K•
AXLIKE
OXLIKE

X•L•••
XYLENE
XYLOID

X••L••
XFILES

•XL•••
AXLIKE
EXLEGE
OXLIKE
OXLIPS

•X•L••
AXILLA
EXALTS
EXILED
EXILES
EXILIC
EXULTS
OXALIS

•X••L•
AXILLA
EXCELS
EXHALE
EXPELS
EXTOLS

•X•••L
AXONAL
OXTAIL
OXYDOL

••XL••
HUXLEY

••X•L•
FOXILY
PIXELS
SEXILY
WAXILY

••X••L
BOXFUL

•••X•L
DREXEL
PLEXAL

X•M•••
XIMENA

X••M••
XIAMEN

•XM•••
EXMOOR
EXMORE

•X•M••
EXEMPT

•X••M•
AXIOMS

••XM••
TAXMAN
TAXMEN
TEXMEX

••X•M•
LEXEME
MAXIMA
MAXIMS

X•N•••
XANADU
XANTHO
XINGIN

X•••N•
XIMENA
XYLENE

X••••N
XIAMEN
XINGIN

•XN•••
OXNARD

•X•N••
AXONAL

•X••N•
AXIONS
EXEUNT
EXPAND
EXPEND
EXTANT
EXTEND
EXTENT

•X•••N
EXTERN
OXYGEN

••XN••
HEXNUT

••X•N•
AUXINS
BOXING
FAXING
FIXING
FOXING
HEXING
MAXENE
MAXINE
MIXING
NIXING
ROXANA
ROXANE
SAXONS
SAXONY
SIXING
TAXING
TEXANS
TOXINS
VEXING
VIXENS
WAXING

••X••N
CAXTON
PAXTON
SEXTON
SIXGUN
TAXMAN
TAXMEN

•••X•N
BLIXEN
DIOXIN
FLAXEN
KLAXON

X•O•••
XHOSAS

X••O••
XEDOUT
XYLOID

X••••O
XANTHO

•XO•••
AXONAL
EXODUS
EXOTIC

•X•O••
AXIOMS
AXIONS
EXHORT
EXMOOR
EXMORE
EXPORT
EXPOSE
EXPOST
EXTOLS
EXTORT
EXVOTO
OXBOWS
OXFORD

•X••O•
EXMOOR
OXYDOL

•X•••O
EXACTO
EXVOTO

••XO••
MAXOUT
SAXONS
SAXONY

••X•O•
BOXBOY
BOXTOP
CAXTON
PAXTON
SEXTON
VOXPOP

••X••O
DEXTRO
MEXICO
NEXTTO
TEXACO
TUXEDO

•••XO•
ETUXOR
FLEXOR
KLAXON
PLEXOR

••••XO
BORAXO

•XP•••
EXPAND
EXPECT
EXPELS
EXPEND
EXPERT
EXPIRE
EXPIRY
EXPORT
EXPOSE
EXPOST

•X••P•
EXCEPT
EXEMPT
OXLIPS

••XP••
VOXPOP

••X•P•
FIXUPS
MIXUPS

••X••P
BOXTOP
VOXPOP

XR••••
XRATED
XRAYED

X•R•••
XERXES

X••••R
XAVIER
XYSTER

•X•R••
EXARCH
EXERTS
EXTRAS
EXURBS

•X••R•
EXEDRA
EXHORT
EXMORE
EXPERT
EXPIRE
EXPIRY
EXPORT
EXSERT
EXTERN
EXTORT
OXCART
OXFORD
OXNARD

•X•••R
EXETER
EXMOOR

••X•R•
BOXERS
DEXTRO
FIXERS
HEXERS
LUXURY
MIXERS
SIXERS
SOXERS
TAXERS
VEXERS
WAXERS

••X••R
BAXTER
BOXCAR
BOXIER
DEXTER
FOXIER
SEXIER
WAXIER

•••X•R
COAXER
ELIXIR
ETUXOR
FLEXOR
HOAXER
PLEXOR

X•S•••
XYSTER

X••S••
XHOSAS

X••••S
XEBECS
XERXES
XFILES
XHOSAS

•XS•••
AXSEED
EXSERT

•X•S••
EXISTS

•X••S•
EXCESS
EXCISE
EXCUSE
EXPOSE
EXPOST

•X•••S
AXIOMS
AXIONS
EXACTS
EXALTS
EXCELS
EXCESS
EXERTS
EXILES
EXISTS
EXODUS
EXPELS
EXTOLS
EXTRAS
EXUDES
EXULTS
EXURBS
OXALIS
OXBOWS
OXEYES
OXIDES
OXLIPS

••XS••
BOXSET

••X•S•
LAXEST
SEXIST

••X••S
AUXINS
BOXERS
DIXITS
FIXERS
FIXUPS
HEXADS
HEXERS
MAXIMS
MIXERS
MIXUPS
NIXIES
PIXELS
PIXIES
PYXIES
SAXONS
SIXERS
SIXTHS
SIXTUS
SOXERS
TAXERS
TAXIES
TEXANS
TOXICS
TOXINS
VEXERS
VIXENS
WAXERS

•••X•S
ALEXIS
APEXES
BRUXES
CALXES
COAXES
CRUXES
FLAXES
FLEXES
FLUXES
HOAXES
IBEXES
ILEXES
JINXES
LYNXES
MINXES
ONYXES
ORYXES
PLEXUS
PRAXES
PRAXIS
VSIXES
XERXES
ZEUXIS

X••T••
XANTHO
XRATED
XYSTER

X••••T
XEDOUT

•XT•••
EXTANT
EXTEND
EXTENT
EXTERN
EXTOLS
EXTORT
EXTRAS
OXTAIL

•X•T••
EXETER
EXITED
EXOTIC

•X••T•
EXACTA
EXACTO
EXACTS
EXALTS
EXCITE
EXERTS
EXISTS
EXULTS
EXVOTO

•X•••T
EXCEPT
EXEMPT
EXEUNT
EXHORT
EXPECT
EXPERT
EXPORT
EXPOST
EXSERT
EXTANT
EXTENT
EXTORT
OXCART

••XT••
BAXTER
BOXTOP
CAXTON
DEXTER
DEXTRO
MIXTEC
NEXTTO
PAXTON
SEXTET
SEXTON
SIXTHS
SIXTUS

••X•T•
DIXITS
FIXATE
FIXITY
LAXITY
LUXATE
NEXTTO

••X••T
BOXSET
HEXNUT
LAXEST
MAXOUT
REXCAT
SEXIST
SEXTET

•••X•T
NOEXIT
PINXIT

••••XT
URTEXT

X•••U•
XEDOUT

X••••U
XANADU

•XU•••
EXUDED
EXUDES
EXULTS
EXURBS

•X•U••
EXCUSE
EXEUNT

•X••U•
EXODUS

••XU••
FIXUPS
LUXURY
MIXUPS

••X•U•
BOXFUL
HEXNUT
MAXOUT
SIXGUN
SIXTUS

•••XU•
PLEXUS

X•V•••
XAVIER

•XV•••
EXVOTO

•XW•••
EXWIFE

•X••W•
OXBOWS

X••X••
XERXES

••X•X•
MAXIXE

••X••X
TEXMEX

•••XX•
SKNXXX

•••X•X
SKNXXX

••••XX
SKNXXX

XY••••
XYLENE
XYLOID
XYSTER

X••Y••
XRAYED

•XY•••
OXYDOL
OXYGEN

•X•Y••
OXEYES

•X•••Y
EXPIRY

••X••Y
BOXBOY
FIXITY
FOXILY
HUXLEY
LAXITY
LUXURY
SAXONY
SEXILY
WAXILY

••••XY
EUTAXY
GALAXY

YA••••
YABBER
YACHTS
YACKED
YAHOOS
YAHWEH
YAKIMA
YAKKED
YAKKER
YAKUTS
YAKUZA
YALIES
YAMAHA
YAMMER
YANGON
YANKED
YANKEE
YANQUI
YAPOKS
YAPPED
YAQUIS
YARDED
YARELY
YAREST
YARNED
YARROW
YASSER
YAUPON
YAWING
YAWNED
YAWNER
YAWPED
YAWPER

Y•A•••
YEAGER
YEANED
YEARLY
YEARNS
YEASTS
YEASTY

Y••A••
YAMAHA
YOUALL
YUKATA
YUKAWA

Y•••A•
YENTAS
YEOMAN
YESMAN
YUCCAS
YUNNAN

Y••••A
YAKIMA
YAKUZA
YAMAHA
YORUBA
YOYOMA
YUKATA
YUKAWA

•YA•••
CYANIC
DYADIC
HYADES
KYACKS
NYALAS
NYASSA
RYAZAN

•Y•A••
AYEAYE
AYMARA
BYHAND
BYLAWS
BYNAME
BYPASS
BYPAST
BYPATH
BYTALK
BYWAYS
CYCADS

CYRANO
DYNAMO
DYNAST
GYRATE
MYNAHS
PYJAMA
TYBALT
TYRANT
ZYMASE

•Y••A•
BYPLAY
BYROAD
CYCLAS
CYMBAL
GYMBAG
HYDRAE
HYDRAS
HYENAS
HYETAL
HYMNAL
MYRDAL
MYRIAD
NYALAS
RYAZAN
RYOKAN
SYLVAN
SYNTAX
SYRIAN
TYRIAN
WYSTAN

•Y•••A
AYESHA
AYMARA
MYOPIA
NYASSA
PYJAMA
PYTHIA
SYLVIA

••YA••
ANYANG
ARYANS
BAYARD
BOYARS
BRYANT
DRYADS
GAYALS
GUYANA
KAYAKS
MAYANS
RIYADH
RIYALS
ROYALE
ROYALS
VOYAGE
WAYANS

••Y•A•
AMYTAN
ANYDAY
ANYWAY
CAYMAN
FLYMAN
FLYWAY
FRYPAN
HEYDAY
KEYPAD
KEYWAY
LAYMAN
MAYDAY
MAYHAP
MAYTAG
NAYSAY
OHYEAH
PAYDAY
PHYLAE
PSYWAR
SKYCAP
SKYLAB
SKYWAY
TAYRAS
WAYLAY
WHYDAH

••Y••A
ALYSSA
CAYUGA
GUYANA
LOYOLA
PAYOLA
PSYLLA
SCYLLA
SMYRNA
STYRIA
TOYOTA
YOYOMA
ZOYSIA

•••YA•
BANYAN
BATYAM
BUNYAN
GALYAK
KENYAN
LIBYAN
MAGYAR
MINYAN
PLAYAS
PLAYAT

•••Y•A
CORYZA
DURYEA

••••YA
LATOYA
MALAYA
MAURYA
NAGOYA
PAPAYA
VAISYA

Y•B•••
YABBER
YOBBOS

Y••B••
YABBER
YOBBOS
YOUBET

Y•••B•
YORUBA

•YB•••
CYBELE
CYBILL
CYBORG
DYBBUK
GYBING
HYBRID
TYBALT
VYBORG

•Y•B••
BYEBYE
CYMBAL
DYBBUK
GYMBAG
SYMBOL
TYDBOL

•Y••B•
TYCOBB

•Y•••B
TYCOBB

••YB••
DAYBED
DAYBOY
FLYBOY
FLYBYS
KHYBER
LAYBYS
MAYBES
PAYBOX
SKYBOX

••Y•B•
LAYSBY

••Y••B
DAYJOB
SKYLAB

Y•C•••
YACHTS
YACKED
YUCCAS

Y••C••
YOICKS
YUCCAS

Y•••C•
YORICK

•YC•••
CYCADS
CYCLAS
CYCLED
CYCLER
CYCLES
CYCLIC
CYCLOS
LYCEES
LYCEUM
TYCOBB
TYCOON

•Y•C••
EYECUP
KYACKS
SYNCED

•Y••C•
CYNICS
LYRICS
ZYDECO

•Y•••C
CYANIC
CYCLIC
CYMRIC
DYADIC
MYOPIC
MYSTIC
MYTHIC
PYKNIC
SYNDIC

••YC••
GLYCOL
JAYCEE
PSYCHE
PSYCHO
PSYCHS
SKYCAP

••Y•C•
DRYICE

•••Y•C
INSYNC

Y•D•••
YODELS

Y••D••
YARDED
YONDER

Y•••D•
YEHUDI
YIELDS

Y••••D
YACKED
YAKKED
YANKED
YAPPED
YARDED
YARNED
YAWNED
YAWPED
YEANED
YELLED
YELPED
YENNED
YERKED
YESSED
YIPPED
YOLKED
YOWLED
YOYOED
YUKKED

•YD•••
CYDERS
HYDRAE
HYDRAS
HYDROS
RYDELL
SYDNEY
TYDBOL
ZYDECO

•Y•D••
DYADIC
FYODOR
HYADES
LYNDON
MYRDAL
PYEDOG
SYNDIC

•Y••D•
CYCADS
SYNODS

•Y•••D
BYHAND
BYROAD
BYWORD
CYCLED
EYELID
GYPPED
HYBRID
HYMNED
HYPOED
LYNYRD
MYRIAD
MYWORD
SYNCED
XYLOID

••YD••
ABYDOS
ANYDAY
DRYDEN
HAYDEN
HEYDAY
HOYDEN
LEYDEN
MAYDAY
OXYDOL
PAYDAY
SNYDER
TOYDOG
WHYDAH

••Y•D•
DRYADS
RIYADH

••Y••D
BAYARD
BEYOND
DAYBED
FLYROD
KAYOED
KEYPAD
PHYSED
RHYMED
SAYYID
STYLED
YOYOED

•••YD•
ALKYDS
ANHYDR
LLOYDS
MRHYDE

•••Y•D
BRAYED
BUOYED
CLOYED
DRAYED
FLAYED
FLEYED
FRAYED
GRAYED
GREYED
LYNYRD
OBEYED
OKAYED
PLAYED
PRAYED
PREYED
REDYED
SAYYID
SLAYED
SPAYED
STAYED
SWAYED
UNDYED
XRAYED

YE••••
YEAGER
YEANED
YEARLY
YEARNS
YEASTS
YEASTY
YEHUDI
YELLED
YELLER
YELLOW
YELPED
YELPER
YEMENI
YENNED
YENTAS
YEOMAN
YEOMEN
YERKED
YERKES
YESMAN
YESMEN
YESSED
YESSES
YESSIR
YESTER

Y•E•••
YIELDS
YVETTE

Y••E••
YARELY
YAREST
YEMENI
YODELS
YOKELS

Y•••E•
YABBER
YACKED
YAHWEH
YAKKED
YAKKER
YALIES
YAMMER
YANKED
YANKEE
YAPPED
YARDED
YARNED
YASSER
YAWNED
YAWNER
YAWPED
YAWPER
YEAGER
YEANED
YELLED
YELLER
YELPED
YELPER
YENNED
YEOMEN
YERKED
YERKES
YESMEN
YESSED
YESSES
YESTER
YIPPED
YIPPEE
YOLKED
YONDER
YORKER
YOUBET
YOWLED
YOYOED
YUKKED

Y••••E
YANKEE
YIPPEE
YORKIE
YUPPIE
YVETTE
YVONNE

•YE•••
AYEAYE
AYESHA
BYEBYE
DYEING
DYELOT
EYECUP
EYEFUL
EYEING
EYELET
EYELID
HYENAS
HYETAL
MYELIN
PYEDOG

•Y•E••
CYBELE
CYDERS
GYRENE
HYPEUP
LYCEES
LYCEUM
MYSELF
NYMETS
RYDELL
TYPERS
TYPEUP
WYVERN
XYLENE
ZYDECO

•Y••E•
BYRNES
CYCLED
CYCLER
CYCLES
CYGNET
CYPHER
EYELET
EYRIES
GYPPED
GYPPER
HYADES
HYMNED
HYPHEN
HYPOED
LYCEES
LYNLEY
LYNXES
MYOPES
OYSTER
PYXIES
SYDNEY
SYNCED
SYSTEM
TYPIER
WYNTER
XYSTER

•Y•••E
AYEAYE
BYEBYE
BYGONE
BYJOVE
BYLINE
BYNAME
BYROTE
BYSSHE
CYBELE
GYRATE
GYRENE
GYROSE
HYDRAE
LYSINE
MYRTLE
MYSORE
PYRITE
TYRONE
XYLENE
ZYGOTE
ZYMASE

••YE••
BAYEUX
BUYERS
COYEST
CRYERS
DIYERS
DOYENS
DRYERS
DRYEST
FEYEST
FLYERS
FOYERS
FRYERS
GAYEST
LAYERS
MOYERS
OHYEAH
PAYEES
PAYERS
SAYERS
SHYEST
SLYEST
TUYERE
WRYEST

••Y•E•
DAYBED
DRYDEN
ELYSEE
FLYMEN
FLYNET
GEYSER
HAYDEN
HAYLEY
HOYDEN
JAYCEE
JAYVEE
JOYNER
KAYOED
KEYNES
KHYBER
LAYMEN
LEYDEN
MAYBES
MAYHEM
ONYXES
ORYXES
OXYGEN
PAYEES
PHYSED
RHYMED
RHYMER
RHYMES
SAYLES
SAYYES
SLYPES
SNYDER
STYLED
STYLER
STYLES
STYLET
YOYOED

••Y••E
ANYONE
BLYTHE
CAYUSE
COYOTE
DAYONE
DRYICE
EEYORE
ELYSEE
GWYNNE
JAYCEE
JAYVEE
PEYOTE
PHYLAE
PRYNNE
PSYCHE
ROYALE
SCYTHE
STYMIE
TUYERE
UNYOKE
VOYAGE

•••YE•
BOWYER
BRAYED
BRAYER
BREYER
BUOYED
CLAYEY
CLOYED
DLAYER
DRAYED
DURYEA
ELAYER
FLAYED
FLAYER
FLEYED
FRAYED
GRAYED
GRAYER
GREYED
GREYER
LAWYER
NGUYEN
NOTYET
OBEYED
OKAYED
OXEYES
PLAYED
PLAYER
PRAYED
PRAYER
PREYED
REDYED
REDYES
SAWYER
SAYYES
SLAYED
SLAYER
SPAYED
SPRYER
STAYED
SWAYED
SWAYER
THAYER
UNDYED
XRAYED

•••Y•E
ARGYLE
DWAYNE
ECTYPE
ELAYNE
ENZYME
MRHYDE
OOCYTE
QUAYLE
RETYPE
SHAYNE
SWAYZE
THEYRE
THEYVE

••••YE
AYEAYE
AZODYE
BYEBYE
HEARYE
INOUYE
POPEYE
REDEYE
RIBEYE
TIEDYE

•Y•F••
EYEFUL

•Y••F•
TYPIFY

•Y•••F
MYSELF

••YF••
DRYFLY
JOYFUL
LAYFOR
MAYFLY
PAYFOR
TRYFOR

••Y•F•
BUYOFF
CRYOFF
DRYOFF
LAYOFF
PAYOFF

••Y••F
BUYOFF
CRYOFF
DRYOFF
LAYOFF
PAYOFF

Y•G•••
YOGINI
YOGISM
YOGURT

Y••G••
YANGON
YEAGER
YUNGLO

Y••••G
YAWING
YOKING

•YG•••
BYGONE
BYGOSH
CYGNET
CYGNUS
MYGIRL
ZYGOTE

•Y••G•
SYZYGY

•Y•••G
CYBORG
DYEING
EYEING
GYBING
GYMBAG
HYPING
PYEDOG
TYPING
VYBORG

••YG••
DAYGLO
OXYGEN
RAYGUN

••Y•G•
CAYUGA
ERYNGO
VOYAGE

••Y••G
ABYING
ANYANG
BAYING
BUYING
CRYING
DRYING
FLYING
FRYING
GUYING
HAYING
KEYING
LAYING
MAYTAG
PAYING
PLYING
PRYING
SAYING
SHYING
SKYING
SPYING
TOYDOG
TOYING
TRYING

•••YG•
SYZYGY

••••YG
KENNYG

Y•H•••
YAHOOS
YAHWEH
YEHUDI
YOHOHO

Y••H••
YACHTS
YOOHOO

Y•••H•
YAMAHA
YOHOHO
YOUTHS

Y••••H
YAHWEH

•YH•••
BYHAND

•Y•H••
CYPHER
HYPHEN
MYOHMY
MYTHIC
MYTHOI
MYTHOL
MYTHOS
PYTHIA
PYTHON
SYPHON
TYPHUS

•Y••H•
AYESHA
BYSSHE
KYUSHU
LYMPHS
MYNAHS
MYRRHS
NYMPHS
SYLPHS

•Y•••H
BYGOSH
BYPATH

••YH••
ANYHOW
MAYHAP
MAYHEM

••Y•H•
BLYTHE
GLYPHS
PSYCHE
PSYCHO
PSYCHS
RHYTHM
SCYTHE

••Y••H
BOYISH
COYISH
OHYEAH
RIYADH
WHYDAH

•••Y•H
IRTYSH

YI••••
YIELDS
YIPPED
YIPPEE

Y•I•••
YOICKS

Y••I••
YAKIMA
YALIES
YAWING
YOGINI
YOGISM
YOKING
YORICK

Y•••I•
YAQUIS
YESSIR
YORKIE
YUPPIE

Y••••I
YANQUI
YEHUDI
YEMENI
YOGINI

•Y•I••
BYLINE
CYBILL
CYNICS
DYEING
EYEING
EYRIES
GYBING
HYPING
LYRICS
LYRIST
LYSINE
LYSINS
MYGIRL
MYRIAD
PYRITE
PYXIES
SYRIAN
SYRINX
TYPIER
TYPIFY
TYPING
TYPIST
TYRIAN

•Y••I•
CYANIC
CYCLIC
CYMRIC
DYADIC
EYELID
HYBRID
MYELIN
MYOPIA
MYOPIC
MYOSIN
MYOSIS
MYSTIC
MYTHIC
NYQUIL
PYKNIC
PYTHIA
SYLVIA
SYNDIC
XYLOID

•Y•••I
MYTHOI

••YI••
ABYING
BAYING
BOYISH
BUYING
COYISH
CRYING
DRYICE
DRYING
DRYINK
FLYING
FLYINS
FRYING
GUYING
HAYING
KEYING
LAYING
PAYING
PLYING
PRYING
SAYING
SHYING
SKYING
SPYING
TOYING
TRYING
ZAYINS

••Y•I•
DAYLIT
GLYNIS
KEYSIN
LAYSIN
PAYSIN
PHYSIO
SAYYID
STYMIE
STYRIA
ZOYSIA

••Y••I
THYRSI

•••YI•
BUNYIP
PINYIN
SAYYID

•••Y•I
PAPYRI

•YJ•••
BYJOVE
PYJAMA

••YJ••
DAYJOB

Y•K•••
YAKIMA
YAKKED
YAKKER
YAKUTS
YAKUZA
YOKELS
YOKING
YOKUTS
YUKATA
YUKAWA
YUKKED

Y••K••
YACKED
YAKKED
YAKKER
YANKED
YANKEE
YERKED
YERKES
YOLKED
YORKER
YORKIE
YUKKED

Y•••K•
YAPOKS
YOICKS
YUROKS

Y••••K
YORICK

•YK•••
HYKSOS
PYKNIC

•Y•K••
RYOKAN
RYUKYU

•Y••K•
KYACKS

•Y•••K
BYTALK
DYBBUK

••Y•K•
KAYAKS
UNYOKE

••Y••K
DRYINK

•••Y•K
GALYAK

Y•L•••
YALIES
YELLED
YELLER
YELLOW
YELPED
YELPER
YOLKED

Y••L••
YELLED
YELLER
YELLOW
YIELDS
YOWLED

Y•••L•
YARELY
YEARLY
YODELS
YOKELS
YOUALL
YUNGLO

Y••••L
YOUALL

•YL•••
BYLAWS
BYLINE
NYLONS
PYLONS
SYLPHS
SYLVAN
SYLVIA
XYLENE
XYLOID

•Y•L••
BYPLAY
CYCLAS
CYCLED
CYCLER
CYCLES
CYCLIC
CYCLOS
DYELOT
EYELET
EYELID
LYNLEY
MYELIN
NYALAS

•Y••L•
BYTALK
CYBELE
CYBILL
MYRTLE
MYSELF
RYDELL
TYBALT

•Y•••L
CYBILL
CYMBAL
EYEFUL
HYETAL
HYMNAL
MYGIRL
MYRDAL
MYTHOL
NYQUIL
RYDELL
SYMBOL
TYDBOL

••YL••
ASYLUM
BAYLOR
CEYLON
DAYLIT
HAYLEY
IDYLLS
LAYLOW
PHYLAE
PHYLLO
PHYLUM
PSYLLA
SAYLES
SCYLLA
SKYLAB
STYLED
STYLER
STYLES
STYLET
STYLUS
TAYLOR
TRYLON
WAYLAY
WAYLON

••Y•L•
DAYGLO
DRYFLY
GAYALS
IDYLLS
LOYOLA
MAYFLY
PAYOLA

PHYLLO
PSYLLA
RIYALS
ROYALE
ROYALS
SCYLLA

••Y••L
ETYMOL
GLYCOL
JOYFUL
OXYDOL

•••YL•
ALKYLS
ARGYLE
ARGYLL
GRAYLY
GREYLY
JEKYLL
QUAYLE
SIBYLS
SPRYLY
THEYLL
VINYLS

•••Y•L
ARGYLL
JEKYLL
THEYLL

••••YL
ACETYL
CHERYL
DACTYL
DARRYL
METHYL
PHENYL
SHERYL

Y•M•••
YAMAHA
YAMMER
YEMENI
YOMTOV
YUMYUM

Y••M••
YAMMER
YEOMAN
YEOMEN
YESMAN
YESMEN

Y•••M•
YAKIMA
YOYOMA

Y••••M
YOGISM
YUMYUM

•YM•••
AYMARA
CYMBAL
CYMRIC
GYMBAG
HYMNAL
HYMNED
LYMPHS
NYMETS
NYMPHS
SYMBOL
ZYMASE

•Y••M•
BYNAME
DYNAMO
MYOHMY
PYJAMA

•Y•••M
GYPSUM
LYCEUM
SYSTEM

••YM••
CAYMAN
ETYMOL
ETYMON
FLYMAN
FLYMEN
HAYMOW
LAYMAN
LAYMEN
RHYMED
RHYMER
RHYMES
STYMIE
THYMUS

••Y•M•
ABYSMS
YOYOMA

••Y••M
ADYTUM
ASYLUM
BAYRUM
MAYHEM
PHYLUM
RHYTHM

•••YM•
ENZYME

•••Y•M
BATYAM
FAIYUM
YUMYUM

••••YM
ANONYM
EPONYM

Y•N•••
YANGON
YANKED
YANKEE
YANQUI
YENNED
YENTAS
YONDER
YUNGLO
YUNNAN

Y••N••
YARNED
YAWNED
YAWNER
YEANED
YENNED
YUNNAN
YVONNE

Y•••N•
YAWING
YEARNS
YEMENI
YOGINI
YOKING
YVONNE

Y••••N
YANGON
YAUPON
YEOMAN
YEOMEN
YESMAN
YESMEN
YUNNAN

•YN•••
BYNAME
CYNICS
DYNAMO
DYNAST
LYNDON
LYNLEY
LYNXES
LYNYRD
MYNAHS
SYNCED
SYNDIC
SYNODS
SYNTAX
WYNTER
WYNTON

•Y•N••
BYRNES
CYANIC
CYGNET
CYGNUS
HYENAS
HYMNAL
HYMNED
HYPNOS
PYKNIC
SYDNEY

•Y••N•
BYGONE
BYHAND
BYLINE
CYRANO
DYEING
EYEING
GYBING
GYRENE
GYRONS
HYPING
LYSINE
LYSINS
NYLONS
PYLONS
SYRINX
TYPING
TYRANT
TYRONE
XYLENE

•Y•••N
HYPHEN
LYNDON
LYTTON
MYELIN
MYOSIN
PYTHON
RYAZAN
RYOKAN
SYLVAN
SYPHON
SYRIAN
TYCOON
TYRIAN
WYNTON
WYSTAN
WYVERN

••YN••
ERYNGO
FLYNET
GAYNOR
GLYNIS
GWYNNE
JOYNER
KEYNES
PRYNNE
WHYNOT

••Y•N•
ABYING
ANYANG
ANYONE
ARYANS
BAYING
BEYOND
BRYANT
BRYONY
BUYING
CRYING
DAYONE
DOYENS
DRYING
DRYINK
FLYING
FLYINS
FRYING
GUYANA
GUYING
GWYNNE
HAYING
KEYING
LAYING
MAYANS
PAYING
PLYING
PRYING
PRYNNE
RAYONS
SAYING
SHYING
SKYING
SMYRNA
SPYING
TOYING
TOYONS
TRYING
WAYANS
ZAYINS

••Y••N
AMYTAN
BRYSON
CAYMAN
CEYLON
CHYRON
DAYTON
DRYDEN
DRYRUN
ETYMON
FLYMAN
FLYMEN
FRYPAN
HAYDEN
HOYDEN
KEYSIN
LAYMAN
LAYMEN
LAYSIN
LAYSON
LEYDEN
OXYGEN
PAYSIN
PAYSON
PEYTON
RAYGUN
RHYTON
STYRON
TRYLON
WAYLON

•••YN•
DWAYNE
EDWYNN
ELAYNE
INSYNC
LARYNX
SHAYNE

•••Y•N
BANYAN
BARYON
BUNYAN
CANYON
CRAYON
EDWYNN
KENYAN
LIBYAN
MINYAN
NGUYEN
PINYIN
PINYON
PLAYON
PREYON
RUNYON
STAYON

••••YN
BOLEYN
CRONYN
EVELYN
JACLYN
MELVYN
MERVYN
POLEYN
VANRYN

YO••••
YOBBOS
YODELS
YOGINI
YOGISM
YOGURT
YOHOHO
YOICKS
YOKELS
YOKING
YOKUTS
YOLKED
YOMTOV
YONDER
YOOHOO
YORICK
YORKER
YORKIE
YORUBA
YOUALL
YOUBET
YOUTHS
YOWLED
YOYOED
YOYOMA

Y•O•••
YEOMAN
YEOMEN
YOOHOO
YVONNE

Y••O••
YAHOOS
YAPOKS
YOHOHO
YOYOED
YOYOMA
YUROKS

Y•••O•
YAHOOS
YANGON
YARROW
YAUPON
YELLOW
YOBBOS
YOMTOV
YOOHOO

Y••••O
YOHOHO
YOOHOO
YUNGLO

•YO•••
FYODOR
MYOHMY
MYOPES
MYOPIA
MYOPIC
MYOSIN
MYOSIS
RYOKAN

•Y•O••
BYGONE
BYGOSH
BYJOVE
BYROAD
BYROTE
BYWORD
CYBORG
GYRONS
GYROSE
HYPOED
MYSORE
MYWORD
NYLONS
PYLONS
SYNODS
SYSOPS
TYCOBB
TYCOON
TYRONE
VYBORG
XYLOID
ZYGOTE

•Y••O•
CYCLOS
DYELOT
FYODOR
HYDROS
HYKSOS
HYPNOS
HYSSOP
LYNDON
LYTTON
MYTHOI
MYTHOL
MYTHOS
PYEDOG
PYTHON
SYMBOL
SYPHON
TYCOON
TYDBOL
WYNTON

•Y•••O
CYRANO
DYNAMO
ZYDECO

••YO••
ANYONE
BAYOUS
BEYOND
BRYONY
BUYOFF
BUYOUT
COYOTE
CRYOFF
DAYONE
DRYOFF
DRYOUT
EEYORE
FLYOUT
GUYOTS
JOYOUS
KAYOED
LAYOFF
LAYOUT
LOYOLA
MAYORS
PAYOFF
PAYOLA
PAYOUT
PEYOTE
RAYONS
TOYONS
TOYOTA
TRYOUT
UNYOKE
WAYOUT
YOYOED
YOYOMA

••Y•O•
ABYDOS
ANYHOW
BAYLOR
BRYSON
CEYLON
CHYRON
DAYBOY
DAYJOB
DAYTON
DRYROT
ETYMOL
ETYMON
FLYBOY
FLYROD
GAYNOR
GLYCOL
HAYMOW
HEYYOU
LAYFOR
LAYLOW
LAYSON
MAYPOP
OXYDOL
PAYBOX
PAYFOR
PAYSON
PEYTON
RHYTON
SAYSOS
SKYBOX
STYRON
TAYLOR
TOYDOG
TRYFOR
TRYLON
WAYLON
WHYNOT

••Y••O
CRYPTO
DAYGLO
ERYNGO
LAYSTO
PHYLLO
PHYSIO
PSYCHO

•••YO•
BARYON
CANYON
CRAYON
HEYYOU
PINYON
PLAYON
PREYON
RUNYON
STAYON

••••YO
ARROYO
DADDYO
DAIMYO
EMBRYO
TAMAYO

Y•P•••
YAPOKS
YAPPED
YIPPED
YIPPEE
YUPPIE

Y••P••
YAPPED
YAUPON
YAWPED
YAWPER
YELPED
YELPER
YIPPED
YIPPEE
YUPPIE

•YP•••
BYPASS
BYPAST
BYPATH
BYPLAY
CYPHER
CYPRUS
GYPPED
GYPPER
GYPSUM
HYPEUP
HYPHEN
HYPING
HYPNOS
HYPOED
SYPHON
TYPERS
TYPEUP
TYPHUS
TYPIER
TYPIFY
TYPING
TYPIST

•Y•P••
GYPPED
GYPPER
LYMPHS
MYOPES
MYOPIA
MYOPIC
NYMPHS
SYLPHS

•Y••P•
SYRUPS
SYRUPY
SYSOPS

•Y•••P
EYECUP
HYPEUP
HYSSOP
TYPEUP

••YP••
COYPUS
CRYPTO
CRYPTS
FRYPAN
GLYPHS
KEYPAD
MAYPOP
SLYPES

••Y•P•
LAYUPS

••Y••P
BUYSUP
KEYSUP
LAYSUP
MAYHAP
MAYPOP
PAYSUP
SKYCAP

•••YP•
ECTYPE
POLYPS
RETYPE

•••Y•P
BUNYIP
BUOYUP
PLAYUP
PONYUP
STAYUP
TIDYUP

Y•Q•••
YAQUIS

Y••Q••
YANQUI

•YQ•••
NYQUIL

Y•R•••
YARDED
YARELY
YAREST
YARNED
YARROW
YERKED
YERKES
YORICK
YORKER
YORKIE
YORUBA
YUROKS

Y••R••
YARROW
YEARLY
YEARNS

Y•••R•
YOGURT

Y••••R
YABBER
YAKKER
YAMMER
YASSER
YAWNER
YAWPER
YEAGER
YELLER
YELPER
YESSIR
YESTER
YONDER
YORKER

•YR•••
BYRNES
BYROAD
BYROTE
CYRANO
EYRIES
GYRATE
GYRENE
GYRONS
GYROSE
LYRICS
LYRIST
MYRDAL
MYRIAD
MYRRHS
MYRTLE
PYRITE
SYRIAN
SYRINX
SYRUPS
SYRUPY
TYRANT
TYRIAN
TYRONE

•Y•R••
CYMRIC
CYPRUS
HYBRID
HYDRAE
HYDRAS
HYDROS
MYRRHS

•Y••R•
AYMARA
BYWORD
CYBORG
CYDERS
LYNYRD
MYGIRL
MYSORE
MYWORD
TYPERS
VYBORG
WYVERN

•Y•••R
CYCLER
CYPHER
FYODOR
GYPPER
OYSTER
TYPIER
WYNTER
XYSTER

••YR••
BAYRUM
CHYRON
DRYROT
DRYRUN
FLYROD
SMYRNA
STYRIA
STYRON
TAYRAS
THYRSI

••Y•R•
BAYARD
BOYARS
BUYERS
CRYERS
DIYERS
DRYERS
EEYORE
FLYERS
FOYERS
FRYERS
LAYERS
MAYORS
MOYERS
PAYERS
SAYERS
TUYERE

••Y••R
BAYLOR
GAYNOR
GEYSER
JOYNER
KHYBER
LAYFOR
PAYFOR
PSYWAR
RHYMER
SNYDER
STYLER
TAYLOR
TRYFOR

•••YR•
LYNYRD
PAPYRI
SATYRS
THEYRE

•••Y•R
ANHYDR
BOWYER
BRAYER
BREYER
DLAYER
ELAYER
FLAYER
GRAYER
GREYER
LAWYER
MAGYAR
PLAYER
PRAYER
SAWYER
SLAYER
SPRYER
SWAYER
THAYER

••••YR
MARTYR
ZEPHYR

Y•S•••
YASSER
YESMAN
YESMEN
YESSED
YESSES
YESSIR
YESTER

Y••S••
YASSER
YEASTS
YEASTY
YESSED
YESSES
YESSIR

Y•••S•
YAREST
YOGISM

Y••••S
YACHTS
YAHOOS
YAKUTS
YALIES
YAPOKS
YAQUIS
YEARNS
YEASTS
YENTAS
YERKES
YESSES
YIELDS
YOBBOS
YODELS
YOICKS
YOKELS
YOKUTS
YOUTHS
YUCCAS
YUROKS

•YS•••
BYSSHE
BYSSUS
HYSSOP
LYSINE
LYSINS
MYSELF
MYSORE
MYSTIC
OYSTER
SYSOPS
SYSTEM
WYSTAN
XYSTER

•Y•S••
AYESHA
BYSSHE
BYSSUS
GYPSUM
HYKSOS
HYSSOP
KYUSHU
MYOSIN
MYOSIS
NYASSA

•Y••S•
BYGOSH
BYPASS
BYPAST
DYNAST
GYROSE
LYRIST
NYASSA
TYPIST
ZYMASE

•Y•••S
BYLAWS
BYPASS
BYRNES
BYSSUS
BYWAYS
CYCADS
CYCLAS
CYCLES
CYCLOS
CYDERS
CYGNUS
CYNICS
CYPRUS
EYRIES
GYRONS
HYADES
HYDRAS
HYDROS
HYENAS
HYKSOS
HYPNOS
KYACKS
LYCEES
LYMPHS
LYNXES
LYRICS
LYSINS
MYNAHS
MYOPES
MYOSIS
MYRRHS
MYTHOS
NYALAS
NYLONS
NYMETS
NYMPHS
PYLONS
PYXIES
SYLPHS
SYNODS
SYRUPS
SYSOPS
TYPERS
TYPHUS

••YS••
ABYSMS
ALYSSA
BRYSON
BUYSUP
ELYSEE
GEYSER
KEYSIN
KEYSUP
LAYSBY
LAYSIN
LAYSON
LAYSTO
LAYSUP
NAYSAY
PAYSIN
PAYSON
PAYSUP
PHYSED
PHYSIO
SAYSOS
TRYSTS
ZOYSIA

••Y•S•
ALYSSA
BOYISH
CAYUSE
COYEST
COYISH
DRYEST
FEYEST
GAYEST
SHYEST
SLYEST
THYRSI
WRYEST

••Y••S
ABYDOS
ABYSMS
ARYANS
BAYOUS
BOYARS
BUYERS
COYPUS
CRYERS
CRYPTS
DIYERS
DOYENS
DRYADS
DRYERS
FLYBYS
FLYERS
FLYINS
FOYERS
FRYERS
GAYALS
GLYNIS
GLYPHS
GUYOTS
IDYLLS
JOYOUS
KAYAKS
KEYNES
LAYBYS
LAYERS
LAYUPS
MAYANS
MAYBES
MAYORS
MOYERS
ONYXES
ORYXES
PAYEES
PAYERS
PSYCHS
RAYONS
RHYMES
RIYALS
ROYALS
SAYERS
SAYLES
SAYSOS
SAYYES
SLYPES
STYLES
STYLUS
TAYRAS
THYMUS
TOYONS
TRYSTS
WAYANS
ZAYINS

•••YS•
IRTYSH

•••Y•S
ALKYDS
ALKYLS
LLOYDS
OXEYES
PLAYAS
POLYPS
REDYES
SATYRS
SAYYES
SIBYLS
VINYLS

••••YS
ABBEYS
ALLAYS
ALLEYS
ALLOYS
ALWAYS
ANNOYS
ARRAYS
ASSAYS
BELAYS
BLUEYS
BOGEYS
BYWAYS
CONEYS
COPAYS
COVEYS
DECAYS
DECOYS
DELAYS
DOGEYS
EMBAYS
ENJOYS
ENVOYS
ERINYS
ESSAYS
FLYBYS
FOGEYS
FORAYS
GAMAYS
GLADYS
HONEYS
INLAYS
JASEYS
LAYBYS
LIEBYS
LIMEYS
MALAYS
MATEYS
MONEYS
MORAYS
MOSEYS
MULEYS
POBOYS
POKEYS
REKEYS
RELAYS
REPAYS
SEPOYS
SPLAYS
SPRAYS
STRAYS
TETHYS
TOKAYS
UNISYS
UNSAYS
ZLOTYS

Y••T••
YENTAS
YESTER
YOMTOV
YOUTHS
YVETTE

Y•••T•
YACHTS
YAKUTS
YEASTS
YEASTY
YOKUTS
YUKATA
YVETTE

Y••••T
YAREST
YOGURT
YOUBET

•YT•••
BYTALK
LYTTON
MYTHIC
MYTHOI
MYTHOL
MYTHOS
PYTHIA
PYTHON

•Y•T••
HYETAL
LYTTON
MYRTLE
MYSTIC
OYSTER
SYNTAX
SYSTEM
WYNTER
WYNTON
WYSTAN
XYSTER

•Y••T•
BYPATH
BYROTE
GYRATE
NYMETS
PYRITE
ZYGOTE

•Y••T
BYPAST CYGNET DYELOT DYNAST EYELET LYRIST TYBALT TYPIST TYRANT

••YT••
ADYTUM AMYTAN BLYTHE DAYTON MAYTAG PEYTON RHYTHM RHYTON SCYTHE

••Y•T•
COYOTE CRYPTO CRYPTS GUYOTS LAYSTO PEYOTE TOYOTA TRYSTS

••Y••T
BRYANT BUYOUT COYEST DAYLIT DRYEST DRYOUT DRYROT FEYEST FLYNET FLYOUT GAYEST LAYOUT PAYOUT SHYEST SLYEST STYLET TRYOUT WAYOUT WHYNOT WRYEST

•••YT•
OOCYTE

•••Y•T
NOTYET PLAYAT SALYUT

••••YT
AJFOYT

YU••••
YUCCAS YUKATA YUKAWA YUKKED YUMYUM YUNGLO YUNNAN YUPPIE YUROKS

Y•U•••
YAUPON YOUALL YOUBET YOUTHS

Y••U••
YAKUTS YAKUZA YAQUIS YEHUDI YOGURT YOKUTS YORUBA

Y•••U•
YANQUI YUMYUM

•YU•••
KYUSHU RYUKYU

•Y•U••
NYQUIL SYRUPS SYRUPY

•Y••U•
BYSSUS CYGNUS CYPRUS DYBBUK EYECUP EYEFUL GYPSUM HYPEUP LYCEUM TYPEUP TYPHUS

•Y•••U
KYUSHU RYUKYU

••YU••
CAYUGA CAYUSE LAYUPS

••Y•U•
ADYTUM ASYLUM BAYEUX BAYOUS BAYRUM BUYOUT BUYSUP COYPUS DRYOUT DRYRUN FLYOUT JOYFUL JOYOUS KEYSUP LAYOUT LAYSUP PAYOUT PAYSUP PHYLUM RAYGUN STYLUS THYMUS TRYOUT WAYOUT

••Y••U
HEYYOU

•••YU•
BUOYUP FAIYUM PLAYUP PONYUP SALYUT STAYUP TIDYUP YUMYUM

•••Y•U
HEYYOU

••••YU
CHOOYU KIKUYU RYUKYU

YV••••
YVETTE YVONNE

Y••••V
YOMTOV

•YV•••
WYVERN

•Y•V••
SYLVAN SYLVIA

•Y••V•
BYJOVE

••YV••
JAYVEE

•••YV•
THEYVE

••••YV
HENRYV ROCKYV

Y•W•••
YAWING YAWNED YAWNER YAWPED YAWPER YOWLED

Y••W••
YAHWEH

Y•••W•
YUKAWA

Y••••W
YARROW YELLOW

•YW•••
BYWAYS BYWORD MYWORD

•Y••W•
BYLAWS

••YW••
ANYWAY FLYWAY KEYWAY PSYWAR SKYWAY

••Y••W
ANYHOW HAYMOW LAYLOW

•YX•••
PYXIES

•Y•X••
LYNXES

•Y•••X
SYNTAX SYRINX

••YX••
ONYXES ORYXES

••Y••X
BAYEUX PAYBOX SKYBOX

•••Y•X
LARYNX

••••YX
COCCYX

Y•Y•••
YOYOED YOYOMA

Y••Y••
YUMYUM

Y••••Y
YARELY YEARLY YEASTY

•Y•Y••
LYNYRD SYZYGY

•Y••Y•
AYEAYE BYEBYE BYWAYS RYUKYU

•Y•••Y
BYPLAY LYNLEY MYOHMY SYDNEY SYRUPY SYZYGY TYPIFY

••YY••
HEYYOU SAYYES SAYYID

••Y•Y•
FLYBYS LAYBYS

••Y••Y
ANYDAY ANYWAY BRYONY DAYBOY DRYFLY FLYBOY FLYWAY HAYLEY HEYDAY KEYWAY LAYSBY MAYDAY MAYFLY NAYSAY PAYDAY SKYWAY WAYLAY

•••Y•Y
CLAYEY GRAYLY GREYLY SPRYLY SYZYGY

Y•••Z•
YAKUZA

•YZ•••
SYZYGY

•Y•Z••
RYAZAN

•••YZ•
CORYZA SWAYZE

ZA••••
ZADDIK ZADORA ZAFFER ZAFTIG ZAGGED ZAGREB ZAIRES ZAMBIA ZAMIAS ZANDER ZANIER ZANIES ZANILY ZANUCK ZAPATA ZAPPED ZAPPER ZAREBA ZAYINS ZAZENS

Z•A•••
ZEALOT ZSAZSA

Z••A••
ZAPATA ZENANA ZONATE ZOUAVE ZYMASE

Z•••A•
ZAMIAS ZEBRAS ZEDBAR ZEEMAN ZIGZAG ZILPAH ZODIAC

Z••••A
ZADORA ZAMBIA ZAPATA ZAREBA ZENANA ZEUGMA ZINNIA ZOYSIA ZSAZSA

•ZA•••
AZALEA IZABAL OZARKS

•Z•A••
EZZARD IZZARD

•Z••A•
IZABAL UZZIAH

•Z•••A
AZALEA

••ZA••
BAZAAR BEZANT EZZARD HAZANS HAZARD IZZARD KAZAKH KAZAKS LIZARD MOZART PIZAZZ WIZARD

••Z•A•
BAZAAR FEZZAN HUZZAH HUZZAS ITZHAK PIZZAS TAZZAS UZZIAH

••Z••A
GEZIRA MAZOLA MAZUMA VIZSLA

•••ZA•
BAIZAS BALZAC BANZAI FEZZAN HUZZAH HUZZAS PIZZAS PLAZAS PROZAC RYAZAN SHAZAM SLEZAK TARZAN TAZZAS ZIGZAG

•••Z•A
BRAZZA PIAZZA ZSAZSA

••••ZA
BRAZZA CORYZA FAENZA KWANZA PIAZZA SFORZA STANZA YAKUZA

Z•B•••
ZEBRAS ZIBETS

Z••B••
ZAMBIA ZEDBAR ZOMBIE

Z•••B•
ZAREBA

Z••••B
ZAGREB

•ZB•••
UZBEKS

•Z•B••
IZABAL

••ZB••
LAZBOY

••Z•B•
GAZEBO

Z••C••
ZIRCON

Z•••C•
ZANUCK ZURICH ZYDECO

Z••••C
ZENDIC ZIPLOC ZODIAC

•Z•C••
CZECHS

•Z••C•
AZTECS

•Z•••C
OZONIC

•••ZC•
OROZCO

•••Z•C
BALZAC PROZAC

Z•D•••
ZADDIK ZADORA ZEDBAR ZODIAC ZYDECO

Z••D••
ZADDIK ZANDER ZENDIC ZENDOS ZUIDER

Z•••D•
ZOOIDS ZOUNDS

Z••••D
ZAGGED ZAPPED ZEROED ZESTED ZIGGED ZINGED ZIPPED ZONKED ZOOMED

•Z•D••
AZIDES AZODYE

•Z•••D
EZZARD IZZARD

••Z••D
BUZZED COZIED EZZARD FIZZED FUZZED HAZARD IZZARD JAZZED LIZARD MUZZED RAZZED WIZARD

•••Z•D
AMAZED BLAZED BRAZED BUZZED CRAZED FIZZED FUTZED FUZZED GLAZED GLOZED GRAZED JAZZED MUZZED PRIZED RAZZED SEIZED

ZE••••
ZEALOT ZEBRAS ZEDBAR ZEEMAN ZENANA ZENDIC ZENDOS ZENGER ZENITH ZEPHYR ZEROED ZEROES ZEROIN ZEROTH ZESTED ZEUGMA ZEUXIS

Z•E•••
ZEEMAN

Z••E••
ZAREBA ZAZENS ZIBETS ZYDECO

Z•••E•
ZAFFER ZAGGED ZAGREB ZAIRES ZANDER ZANIER ZANIES ZAPPED ZAPPER ZENGER ZEROED ZEROES ZESTED ZIGGED ZIMMER ZINGED ZINGER ZIPPED ZIPPER ZITHER ZONKED ZONKER ZOOMED ZUIDER

Z••••E
ZOMBIE ZONATE ZOUAVE ZYGOTE ZYMASE

•ZE•••
CZECHS CZERNY

•Z•E••
AZTECS UZBEKS

•Z••E•
AZALEA AZIDES AZINES AZORES

•Z•••E
AZODYE

••ZE••
BEZELS COZENS DIZENS DOZENS DOZERS FUZEES GAZEBO HAZELS HAZERS MAZERS MIZENS OUZELS SIZERS SIZEUP WIZENS ZAZENS

••Z•E•
BUZZED BUZZER BUZZES COZIED COZIER COZIES DOZIER FEZZES FIZZED FIZZES FUZEES FUZZED FUZZES HAZIER JAZZED JAZZES LAZIER MAZIER MIZZEN MUZZED MUZZES OOZIER RAZZED RAZZES ROZZER VIZIER

••Z••E
DAZZLE ENZYME EVZONE FIZZLE FOZZIE GUZZLE LIZZIE MIZZLE MUZZLE NOZZLE NUZZLE PUZZLE RAZZLE REZONE SIZZLE

•••ZE•
AMAZED AMAZES BLAZED BLAZER BLAZES BONZES BRAZED BRAZEN BRAZER BRAZES BUZZED BUZZER BUZZES CRAZED CRAZES CROZES DENZEL DITZES DRUZES FEZZES FIZZED FIZZES FRAZER FROZEN FURZES FUTZED FUTZES FUZZED FUZZES GAUZES GEEZER GLAZED GLAZER GLAZES GLOZED GLOZES GRAZED GRAZER GRAZES JAZZED JAZZES LUTZES MAIZES MIZZEN MUZZED MUZZES PANZER PFIZER PRIZED PRIZES RAZZED RAZZES ROZZER SEIZED SEIZER SEIZES TETZEL WINZES

•••Z•E
DAZZLE DOOZIE FIZZLE FOOZLE FOZZIE GUZZLE LIZZIE MIZZLE MUZZLE NOZZLE NUZZLE PUZZLE RAZZLE SIZZLE

••••ZE
ABLAZE ASSIZE BEDAZE BELIZE BREEZE BRONZE FREEZE FRIEZE IODIZE IONIZE LAMAZE SLEAZE SNEEZE SNOOZE SWAYZE TWEEZE WHEEZE

Z•F•••
ZAFFER ZAFTIG

Z••F••
ZAFFER

Z•G•••
ZAGGED ZAGREB ZIGGED ZIGZAG ZYGOTE

Z••G••
ZAGGED ZENGER ZEUGMA ZIGGED ZINGED ZINGER

Z••••G
ZAFTIG ZIGZAG ZONING

••ZG••
FIZGIG

••Z•G•
SYZYGY

••Z••G
DAZING DOZING FAZING FIZGIG FUZING GAZING HAZING LAZING OOZING RAZING SIZING

•••Z•G
DANZIG HERZOG ZIGZAG

ZH••••
ZHUKOV

Z••H••
ZEPHYR ZITHER

Z••••H
ZENITH ZEROTH ZILPAH ZIZITH ZURICH

•Z•H••
TZUHSI

•Z••H•
CZECHS

•Z•••H
UZZIAH

••ZH••
FUZHOU ITZHAK MUZHIK

••Z••H
HUZZAH KAZAKH UZZIAH ZIZITH

•••Z•H
HUZZAH MATZOH

ZI••••
ZIBETS ZIGGED ZIGZAG ZILPAH ZIMMER ZINGED ZINGER ZINNIA ZIPLOC ZIPPED ZIPPER ZIPSUP ZIRCON ZITHER ZIZITH

Z•I•••
ZAIRES ZUIDER

Z••I••
ZAMIAS ZANIER ZANIES ZANILY ZAYINS ZENITH ZIZITH ZODIAC ZONING ZOOIDS ZORILS ZURICH

Z•••I•
ZADDIK ZAFTIG ZAMBIA ZENDIC ZEROIN ZEUXIS ZINNIA ZOMBIE ZOOMIN ZOYSIA

•ZI•••
AZIDES AZINES

•Z•I••
UZZIAH

•Z••I•
AZORIN OZONIC

•Z•••I
TZUHSI

••ZI••
COZIED COZIER COZIES COZILY DAZING DOZIER DOZILY DOZING FAZING FUZING GAZING GEZIRA HAZIER HAZILY HAZING LAZIER LAZILY LAZING MAZIER MAZILY OOZIER OOZILY OOZING RAZING SIZING UNZIPS UZZIAH VIZIER ZIZITH

••Z•I•
FIZGIG FOZZIE LIZZIE MUZHIK RIZZIO

••Z••I
ADZUKI LAZULI SUZUKI

•••ZI•
BRAZIL DANZIG DOOZIE FOZZIE GHAZIS LIZZIE RIZZIO SWAZIS

•••Z•I
BANZAI BORZOI BRAZZI

••••ZI
BRAZZI RIENZI

Z••K••
ZHUKOV ZONKED ZONKER

Z••••K
ZADDIK ZANUCK

•Z••K•
OZARKS UZBEKS

••Z•K•
ADZUKI KAZAKH KAZAKS SUZUKI

••Z••K
ITZHAK MUZHIK

•••Z•K
SLEZAK

ZL••••
ZLOTYS

Z•L•••
ZILPAH

Z••L••
ZEALOT ZIPLOC

Z•••L•
ZANILY ZORILS

•Z•L••
AZALEA

•Z•••L
IZABAL

••Z•L•
BEZELS COZILY DAZZLE DOZILY FIZZLE GUZZLE HAZELS HAZILY LAZILY LAZULI MAZILY MAZOLA MIZZLE MUZZLE NOZZLE NUZZLE OOZILY OUZELS PUZZLE RAZZLE SIZZLE VIZSLA

••Z••L
FAZOOL

•••ZL•
DAZZLE FIZZLE FOOZLE GUZZLE MIZZLE MUZZLE NOZZLE NUZZLE PUZZLE RAZZLE SIZZLE

•••Z•L
BENZOL BRAZIL DENZEL TETZEL

Z•M•••
ZAMBIA ZAMIAS ZIMMER ZOMBIE ZYMASE

Z••M••
ZEEMAN ZIMMER ZOOMED ZOOMIN

Z•••M•
ZEUGMA

••ZM••
GIZMOS

••Z•M•
ENZYME GAZUMP MAZUMA

•••Z•M
SHAZAM

Z•N•••
ZANDER ZANIER ZANIES ZANILY ZANUCK ZENANA ZENDIC ZENDOS ZENGER ZENITH ZINGED ZINGER ZINNIA ZONATE ZONING ZONKED ZONKER

Z••N••
ZINNIA
ZOUNDS

Z•••N•
ZAYINS
ZAZENS
ZENANA
ZONING

Z••••N
ZEEMAN
ZEROIN
ZIRCON
ZOOMIN

•Z•N••
AZINES
OZONIC

•Z••N•
CZERNY

•Z•••N
AZORIN

••Z•N•
BEZANT
COZENS
DAZING
DIZENS
DOZENS
DOZING
EVZONE
FAZING
FUZING
GAZING
HAZANS
HAZING
LAZING
MIZENS
OOZING
RAZING
REZONE
SIZING
WIZENS
ZAZENS

••Z••N
FEZZAN
MIZZEN

•••ZN•
GROZNY

•••Z•N
AMAZON
BARZUN
BLAZON
BRAZEN
CURZON
FEZZAN
FROZEN
MIZZEN
PINZON
QUEZON
RYAZAN
TARZAN

ZO••••
ZODIAC
ZOMBIE
ZONATE
ZONING
ZONKED
ZONKER
ZOOIDS
ZOOMED
ZOOMIN
ZORILS
ZOUAVE
ZOUNDS
ZOYSIA

Z•O•••
ZLOTYS
ZOOIDS
ZOOMED
ZOOMIN

Z••O••
ZADORA
ZEROED
ZEROES
ZEROIN
ZEROTH
ZYGOTE

Z•••O•
ZEALOT
ZENDOS
ZHUKOV
ZIPLOC
ZIRCON

Z••••O
ZYDECO

•ZO•••
AZODYE
AZORES
AZORIN
OZONIC

••ZO••
EVZONE
FAZOOL
KAZOOS
MAZOLA
RAZORS
REZONE

••Z•O•
FAZOOL
FUZHOU
GIZMOS
KAZOOS
LAZBOY
MEZZOS

••Z••O
GAZEBO
RIZZIO

•••ZO•
AMAZON
BENZOL
BLAZON
BORZOI
BRAZOS
CURZON
HERZOG
MAHZOR
MATZOH
MATZOS
MEZZOS
PINZON
QUEZON

•••Z•O
AREZZO
OROZCO
RIZZIO
WHIZZO

••••ZO
ALONZO
AREZZO
REBOZO
WHIZZO

Z•P•••
ZAPATA
ZAPPED
ZAPPER
ZEPHYR
ZIPLOC
ZIPPED
ZIPPER
ZIPSUP

Z••P••
ZAPPED
ZAPPER
ZILPAH
ZIPPED
ZIPPER

Z••••P
ZIPSUP

••Z•P•
UNZIPS

••Z••P
GAZUMP
JAZZUP
SIZEUP

•••Z•P
JAZZUP

Z•R•••
ZAREBA
ZEROED
ZEROES
ZEROIN
ZEROTH
ZIRCON
ZORILS
ZURICH

Z••R••
ZAGREB
ZAIRES
ZEBRAS

Z•••R•
ZADORA

Z••••R
ZAFFER
ZANDER
ZANIER
ZAPPER
ZEDBAR
ZENGER
ZEPHYR
ZIMMER
ZINGER
ZIPPER
ZITHER
ZONKER
ZUIDER

•Z•R••
AZORES
AZORIN
CZERNY
OZARKS

•Z••R•
EZZARD
IZZARD

••Z•R•
DOZERS
EZZARD
GEZIRA
HAZARD
HAZERS
IZZARD
LIZARD
MAZERS
MOZART
RAZORS
SIZERS
WIZARD

••Z••R
BAZAAR
BUZZER
COZIER
DOZIER
HAZIER
LAZIER
MAZIER
OOZIER
ROZZER
VIZIER

•••Z•R
BLAZER
BRAZER
BUZZER
FRAZER
GEEZER
GLAZER
GRAZER
MAHZOR
PANZER
PFIZER
ROZZER
SEIZER

ZS••••
ZSAZSA

Z•S•••
ZESTED

Z••S••
ZIPSUP
ZOYSIA

Z•••S•
ZSAZSA
ZYMASE

Z••••S
ZAIRES
ZAMIAS
ZANIES
ZAYINS
ZAZENS
ZEBRAS
ZENDOS
ZEROES
ZEUXIS
ZIBETS
ZLOTYS
ZOOIDS
ZORILS
ZOUNDS

•Z••S•
TZUHSI

•Z•••S
AZIDES
AZINES
AZORES
AZTECS
CZECHS
OZARKS
UZBEKS

••ZS••
VIZSLA

••Z••S
BEZELS
BUZZES
COZENS
COZIES
DIZENS
DOZENS
DOZERS
FEZZES
FIZZES
FUZEES
FUZZES
GIZMOS
HAZANS
HAZELS
HAZERS
HUZZAS
JAZZES
KAZAKS
KAZOOS
MAZERS
MEZZOS
MIZENS
MUZZES
OUZELS
PIZZAS
RAZORS
RAZZES
SIZERS
TAZZAS
UNZIPS
WIZENS
ZAZENS

•••ZS•
ZSAZSA

•••Z•S
AMAZES
BAIZAS
BLAZES
BONZES
BRAZES
BRAZOS
BUZZES
CRAZES
CROZES
DITZES
DRUZES
FEZZES
FIZZES
FURZES
FUTZES
FUZZES
GAUZES
GHAZIS
GLAZES
GLOZES
GRAZES
HUZZAS
JAZZES
KUDZUS
LUTZES
MAIZES
MATZOS
MEZZOS
MUZZES
PIZZAS
PLAZAS
PRIZES
RAZZES
SEIZES
SWAZIS
TAZZAS
WINZES

Z•T•••
ZITHER

Z••T••
ZAFTIG
ZESTED
ZLOTYS

Z•••T•
ZAPATA
ZENITH
ZEROTH
ZIBETS
ZIZITH
ZONATE
ZYGOTE

Z••••T
ZEALOT

•ZT•••
AZTECS

••Z•T•
ZIZITH

••Z••T
BEZANT
MOZART

ZU••••
ZUIDER
ZURICH

Z•U•••
ZEUGMA
ZEUXIS
ZHUKOV
ZOUAVE
ZOUNDS

Z••U••
ZANUCK

Z•••U•
ZIPSUP

•ZU•••
TZUHSI

••ZU••
ADZUKI
GAZUMP
LAZULI
MAZUMA
SUZUKI

••Z•U•
JAZZUP
SIZEUP

••Z••U
FUZHOU

•••ZU•
BARZUN
JAZZUP
KUDZUS

••••ZU
LAOTZU

Z•••V•
ZOUAVE

Z••••V
ZHUKOV

Z••X••
ZEUXIS

ZY••••
ZYDECO
ZYGOTE
ZYMASE

Z•Y•••
ZAYINS
ZOYSIA

Z•••Y•
ZEPHYR
ZLOTYS

Z••••Y
ZANILY

•Z••Y•
AZODYE

•Z•••Y
CZERNY

••ZY••
ENZYME
SYZYGY

••Z••Y
COZILY
DOZILY
HAZILY
LAZBOY
LAZILY
MAZILY
OOZILY
SYZYGY

•••Z•Y
FRIZZY
GROZNY
SCUZZY
SNAZZY

••••ZY
BLOWZY
BREEZY
BRONZY
FRENZY
FRIZZY
FROWZY
GLITZY
GROSZY
KLUTZY
SCHIZY
SCUZZY
SLEAZY
SNAZZY
SNEEZY
SNOOZY
WHEEZY

Z•Z•••
ZAZENS
ZIZITH

Z••Z••
ZIGZAG
ZSAZSA

•ZZ•••
EZZARD
IZZARD
UZZIAH

••ZZ••
BUZZED
BUZZER
BUZZES
DAZZLE
FEZZAN
FEZZES
FIZZED
FIZZES
FIZZLE
FOZZIE
FUZZED
FUZZES
GUZZLE
HUZZAH
HUZZAS
JAZZED
JAZZES
JAZZUP
LIZZIE
MEZZOS
MIZZEN
MIZZLE
MUZZED
MUZZES
MUZZLE
NOZZLE
NUZZLE
PIZZAS
PUZZLE
RAZZED
RAZZES
RAZZLE
RIZZIO
ROZZER
SIZZLE
TAZZAS

••Z•Z•
PIZAZZ

••Z••Z
PIZAZZ

•••ZZ•
AREZZO
BRAZZA
BRAZZI
FRIZZY
PIAZZA
SCUZZY
SNAZZY
WHIZZO

••••ZZ
PIZAZZ

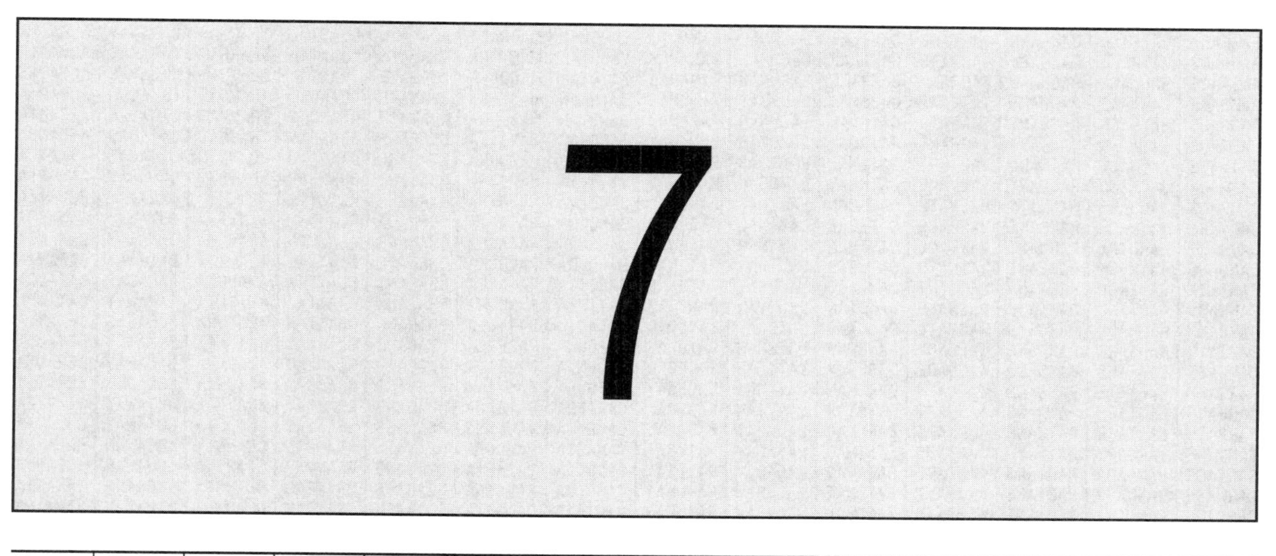

AA•••••
AAMILNE

A•A••••
ABALONE
ABANDON
ABASHED
ABASHES
ABASING
ABATING
ACACIAS
ACADEME
ACADEMY
ACADIAN
ACANTHI
ACARIDS
ADAGIOS
ADAMANT
ADAMITE
ADAMSON
ADAPTED
ADAPTER
ADAPTOR
AGAINST
AGAKHAN
AGARICS
AGASSIZ
AJACCIO
ALABAMA
ALADDIN
ALAKING
ALAMEDA
ALAMEIN
ALAMODE
ALARCON
ALARMED
ALARMER
ALARUMS
ALASKAN
AMADEUS
AMALGAM
AMAPOLA
AMASSED
AMASSER
AMASSES
AMATEUR
AMATIVE
AMATORY
AMAZING
AMAZONS
ANADEMS
ANAEMIA
ANAEMIC
ANAGRAM
ANAHEIM
ANAHUAC
ANALOGS
ANALOGY
ANALYSE
ANALYST
ANALYZE
ANANIAS
ANAPEST
ANARCHY
ANASAZI
ANATOLE
ANATOMY
APACHES
APATITE
ARABIAN
ARACHNE
ARAFURA
ARALSEA
ARAMAIC
ARAMEAN
ARAPAHO
ARAWAKS
ASARULE
ATACAMA
ATALOSS
ATAMANS
ATATURK
ATAVISM
ATAVIST
AVAILED
AVARICE
AVATARS
AWAITED
AWAKENS
AWAKING
AWARDED
AWARDEE
AWARDER
AWAREOF
AZALEAS

A••A•••
ABLATED
ABLATES
ABLAUTS
ABNAKIS
ABRADED
ABRADER
ABRADES
ABRAHAM
ABSALOM
ACHATES
ACKACKS
ACTABLE
ACTAEON
ADDABLE
ADVANCE
AERATED
AERATES
AERATOR
AFFABLE
AFFABLY
AFFAIRE
AFFAIRS
AFRAMES
AGNATES
AGRAFFE
AHEADOF
ALBANIA
ALCAZAR
ALFALFA
ALIASES
ALKALIS
ALLAYED
ALLAYER
ALMAATA
ALMADEN
ALMANAC
ALPACAS
ALSATIA
ALVAREZ
AMHARIC
AMIABLE
AMIABLY
AMRADIO
ANDANTE
ANNABEL
ANNALEE
ANNATTO
ANTACID
ANTAEUS
ANTARES
APPALLS
APPARAT
APPAREL
AQUARIA
AQUATIC
AQUAVIT
ARCADES
ARCADIA
ARCANUM
AREARUG
AREAWAY
ARIADNE
ARMADAS
ARRAIGN
ARRANGE
ARRASES
ARRAYED
ASFARAS
ASHAMED
ASHANTI
ASIATIC
ASKANCE
ASSAILS
ASSAULT
ASSAYED
ASSAYER
ASTAIRE
ASTARTE
ATFAULT
ATLANTA
ATLARGE
ATLASES
ATLATLS
ATTABOY
ATTACHE
ATTACKS
ATTAINS
AUBADES
AUPAIRS
AURALEE
AURALLY
AUTARKY
AVIANCA
AVIATED
AVIATES
AVIATOR
AXIALLY
AYEAYES

A•••A••
ABELARD
ABENAKI
ABEYANT
ABIGAIL
ABREAST
ABSTAIN
ABUBAKR
ACCLAIM
ACETATE
ACREAGE
ACTUARY
ACTUATE
ADAMANT
ADONAIS
ADULATE
AERIALS
AFFRAYS
AFGHANI
AFGHANS
AGESAGO
AGITATE
AGITATO
AIRBAGS
AIRBALL
AIRBASE
AIRDAMS
AIRDATE
AIRFARE
AIRLANE
AIRMADA
AIRMAIL
AIRMASS
AIRRAID
AIRSACS
AIRTAXI
AIRWAVE
AIRWAYS
ALABAMA
ALIBABA
ALIDADE
ALLEARS
ALLHAIL
ALMAATA
ALOHAOE
ALREADY
AMYLASE
ANASAZI
ANDEANS
ANIMALS
ANIMATE
ANIMATO
ANNEALS
ANNUALS
ANOMALY
ANORAKS
ANTFARM
ANTIART
AOUDADS
APPEALS
APPEARS
APPEASE
APPLAUD
ARAMAIC
ARAPAHO
ARAWAKS
ARCHAIC
ARCLAMP
ARIKARA
ARMBAND
ARMYANT
ARREARS
ARTWARE
ASHCANS
ASHLAND
ASHLARS
ASHRAMS
ASPHALT
ASSUAGE
ATACAMA
ATAMANS
ATHEART
ATHWART
ATLEAST
ATPEACE
ATSTAKE
ATTRACT
AUREATE
AVATARS
AVERAGE
AVOCADO
AVOWALS
AWKWARD
AYNRAND

A••••A•
ABRAHAM
ABUTTAL
ABYSMAL
ACACIAS
ACADIAN
ACCRUAL
ACROBAT
ADMIRAL
ADRENAL
AEOLIAN
AEROBAT
AFRICAN
AGAKHAN
AGENDAS
AIMEDAT
AIRBOAT
AIRHEAD
AIRPLAY
ALASKAN
ALCAZAR
ALLHEAL
ALLOWAY
ALLSTAR
ALMANAC
ALPACAS
ALSORAN
ALTOSAX
ALUMNAE
ALUMNAL
ALYKHAN
AMALGAM
AMISTAD
AMOEBAE
AMOEBAS
AMSCRAY
ANAGRAM
ANAHUAC
ANANIAS
ANDREAS
ANGOLAN
ANGORAS
ANGULAR
ANNULAR
ANTBEAR
ANTITAX
ANTIWAR
ANYROAD
APPARAT
APTERAL
AQUINAS
ARABIAN
ARAMEAN
ARCHWAY
AREAWAY
AREOLAE
AREOLAR
AREOLAS
ARISTAE
ARISTAS
ARMADAS
ARMLOAD
ARNICAS
AROUSAL
ARRIVAL
ARROBAS
ARSENAL
ARTISAN
ASFARAS
ASHTRAY
ASOCIAL
ASSEGAI
ASTOLAT
ASUSUAL
AUGURAL
AURORAE
AURORAL
AURORAS
AUSTRAL
AUTOMAT
AXILLAE
AZALEAS
AZTECAN

A•••••A
ABEXTRA
ABINTRA
ACEROLA
ADDENDA
AGRIPPA
AIRMADA
ALABAMA
ALAMEDA
ALBANIA
ALBERTA
ALFALFA
ALFORJA
ALGEBRA
ALGERIA
ALIBABA
ALLUVIA
ALMAATA
ALSATIA
ALTOONA
ALYOSHA
AMAPOLA
AMERICA
AMERIKA
AMMONIA
AMNESIA
AMPHORA
ANAEMIA
ANDORRA
ANOSMIA
ANTENNA
ANTIGUA
ANTONIA
APHELIA
AQUARIA
ARAFURA
ARALSEA
ARCADIA
ARIETTA
ARIKARA
ARIZONA
ARMENIA
ARUGULA
ASSYRIA
ASTORIA
ATACAMA
ATLANTA
AUGUSTA
AUREOLA
AUSTRIA
AVIANCA
AVONLEA

•AA••••
HAARLEM
LAAGERS
PAANGAS

•A•A•••
BABALOO
BABASSU
BACALAO
BACARDI
BAHAMAS
BALANCE
BALATON
BANALLY
BANANAS
BARANOF
BASALLY
BASALTS
BAVARIA
BAZAARS
CABALAS
CABANAS
CABARET
CACANNY
CANAPES
CANARDS
CANASTA
CAPABLE
CAPABLY
CAPAPIE
CARABAO
CARACAL
CARACAS
CARAFES
CARAMBA
CARAMEL
CARAMIA
CARAVAN
CARAVEL
CARAWAY
CASABAS
CASAVAS
CATALAN
CATALOG
CATALPA
CATAWBA
CAVALRY
DADAISM
DADAIST
DAMAGED
DAMAGES
DAMASKS
DATASET
EARACHE
EATABLE
EATAWAY
FABARES
FACADES
FALAFEL
FANATIC
FARADAY
FARAWAY
GAGARIN
GALAGOS
GALAHAD
GALATEA
GALATIA
GARAGED
GARAGES
HAVARTI
HAZARDS
JACANAS
JAIALAI
JAKARTA
JAMAICA
JANACEK
JAVAMAN
KANAKAS
KARACHI
KARAJAN
KARAKUL
KARAKUM
KARAOKE
KARASEA
KAYAKED
KAYAKER
KAZAKHS
LABAMBA
LAFARGE
LALAKER
LALANNE
LAMAISM
LAMAIST
LAMARCK
LAPALMA
LARAINE
LARAMIE
LASAGNA
LASAGNE
LASALLE
LAVALSE
LAYAWAY
LAZARUS
MACABRE
MACADAM
MACAQUE
MADAMEX
MAHALIA
MAHARIS
MAHATMA
MALABAR
MALACCA
MALACHI
MALAISE
MALAMUD
MALAYAN
MANACLE
MANAGED
MANAGER
MANAGES
MANAGUA
MANANAS
MANATEE
MARABOU
MARACAS
MARAUDS
MASARYK
MATADOR
MAYALIN
NAIADES
NANAIMO
NASALLY
NATALIA
NATALIE
NATASHA
NAVAHOS
NAVAJOS
NAVARRE
PAJAMAS
PALACES
PALADIN
PALANCE
PALATAL
PALATES
PALAVER
PALAZZI
PALAZZO
PANACEA
PANACHE
PANADAS
PANAMAS
PANARAB
PAPADOC
PAPAGOS
PAPAYAS
PARABLE
PARADED
PARADES
PARADOX
PARAGON
PARAPET
PARAPHS
PARASOL
PARATUS
PATACAS
PAVANES
PAYABLE
QATARIS
RAMADAN
RAMADAS
RANAWAY
RAPANUI
RATABLE
RATAFIA
RATATAT
RAVAGED
RAVAGER
RAVAGES
SAFARIS
SAHARAN
SALAAMS
SALABLE
SALADIN
SALAMIS
SALAZAR
SAMARIA
SARACEN
SARALEE
SARANAC
SARAWAK
SARAZEN
SAVABLE
SAVAGED
SAVAGER
SAVAGES
SAVALAS
SAVANNA
SAVANTS
SAVARIN
TABARDS
TABASCO
TAGALOG
TALARIA
TAMABLE
TAMALES
TAMARIN
TANAGER
TARANTO
TATAMIS
TAXABLE
VACANCY
VACATED
VACATES
VALANCE
WASATCH
ZAPATEO

•A••A••
BABBAGE
BAGGAGE
BAHRAIN
BAKLAVA
BALKANS
BALLADE
BALLADS
BALLARD
BALLAST
BALSAMS
BANDAGE
BANDAID
BANDANA
BANTAMS
BANYANS
BAOBABS
BARBARA
BARBARY
BARCARS
BARGAIN
BARMAID
BARNABY
BARNARD
BARRACK
BARRAGE
BARTABS
BARWARE

BATEAUX
BAUHAUS
BAZAARS
CABBAGE
CAESARS
CAFTANS
CAIMANS
CALGARY
CALPACS
CALVARY
CAMPARI
CANCANS
CANTATA
CANVASS
CAPEANN
CAPTAIN
CARCASE
CARCASS
CARFARE
CARPALS
CARPARK
CARTAGE
CARWASH
CASCADE
CASCARA
CASSATT
CASSAVA
CASUALS
CATCALL
CATHAIR
CATNAPS
CATTAIL
CATWALK
CAVEATS
CAVIARS
CAYMANS
DABHAND
DAMMARS
DASTARD
DAYCAMP
DAYCARE
DAYMARE
EARHART
EARMARK
FACIALS
FALLACY
FANFARE
FANMAIL
FANTAIL
FANTASY
FAREAST
FARRAGO
FATBACK
FATCATS
GAGLAWS
GALLANT
GALPALS
GALVANI
GAMBADO
GARBAGE
GARLAND
GASBAGS
GASCAPS
GASMAIN
GATEAUX
GAUTAMA
GAVIALS
HAEMATO
HAGGARD
HALVAHS
HALYARD
HANGARS
HANSARP
HARVARD
HATBAND
HATRACK
HAULAGE
HAWHAWS
HAYRACK
HAYWARD
JACKALS
JACKASS
JAGUARS
JAMPACK
JANUARY
JAYWALK
JAZZAGE
KAFTANS
KAMPALA
KANSANS
LABIALS
LABIATE
LACTASE
LACTATE
LAGGARD
LAMBADA
LANDAUS
LANTANA
LANYARD
LAPLACE
LAPLAND
LAPLATA
LARIATS
LASCALA
LASCAUX
LAYBACK
MACRAME
MADCAPS
MAENADS
MAGNANI
MAGNATE
MAGYARS
MAITAIS
MALEATE
MALLARD
MALRAUX
MAMMALS
MANDALA
MANDANS
MANDATE
MANDAYS
MANIACS
MANMADE
MANSARD
MANUALS
MARCATO
MARGATE
MARGAUX
MARGAYS
MARIANA
MARMARA
MARSALA
MARYANN
MASCARA
MASSAGE
MASTABA
MAUMAUS
MAXBAER
MAYDAYS
MAYFAIR
MAYNARD
NAHUATL
NARRATE
NARWALS
NASTASE
NAYSAID
NAYSAYS
OAKLAND
OAKLAWN
PACKAGE
PACKARD
PADUANS
PAGEANT
PAHLAVI
PAISANO
PALMARY
PALMATE
PANCAKE
PAPUANS
PARFAIT
PARIAHS
PARKADE
PARLAYS
PARTAKE
PASSADO
PASSAGE
PAWPAWS
PAYCASH
PAYDAYS
RADIALS
RADIANS
RADIANT
RADIATE
RAGBAGS
RAGLANS
RAMPAGE
RAMPANT
RAMPART
RANDALL
RANLATE
RANSACK
RAPHAEL
RASCALS
RATPACK
RATRACE
RATTAIL
RATTANS
RAWDATA
SABBATH
SADSACK
SAGUARO
SALAAMS
SALVAGE
SAMBAED
SAMBALS
SAMBARS
SAMOANS
SAMPANS
SAMSARA
SANDALS
SANTAFE
SANTANA
SAPSAGO
SARCASM
SASHAYS
SATIATE
SATRAPS
SAUSAGE
TAGGANT
TAGSALE
TAIPANS
TAKEAIM
TAMBALA
TAMMANY
TAMTAMS
TANKARD
TANOAKS
TANTARA
TARBABY
TARMACS
TARSALS
TARTANS
TARTARE
TARTARS
TARZANA
TATIANA
TAXRATE
VAGRANT
VALIANT
VALUATE
VALVATE
VANDALS
VANTAGE
VANUATU
VARIANT
VASSALS
WAGTAIL
WALLABY
WALLACE
WALLACH
WALMART
WANNABE
WANTADS
WARFARE
WARGAME
WARPATH
WARRANT
WASSAIL
WASTAGE
WATTAGE
WAYLAID
WAYLAYS
WAYWARD
YARDAGE
YARDARM
ZACHARY

•A•••A•

BABYSAT
BACALAO
BACKBAY
BAGHDAD
BAHAMAS
BALBOAS
BALIHAI
BANANAS
BANDSAW
BARKSAT
BARSOAP
BASEMAN
BASEPAY
BATEMAN
BATHMAT
BATSMAN
BAYLEAF
CABALAS
CABANAS
CADDOAN
CALIBAN
CAMERAS
CAPITAL
CAPITAN
CAPSHAW
CAPSTAN
CARABAO
CARACAL
CARACAS
CARAVAN
CARAWAY
CARCOAT
CARDIAC
CARINAS
CARLOAD
CARSEAT
CASABAS
CASAVAS
CASELAW
CASHBAR
CASPIAN
CASSIAS
CATALAN
CATBOAT
CATENAE
CATHEAD
CATSCAN
CATSPAW
CAVEMAN
CAYUGAS
DAHLIAS
DAKOTAN
DAKOTAS
DANELAW
DARESAY
DARKMAN
DAYSTAR
EARFLAP
EASTMAN
EATAWAY
EATENAT
FACTUAL
FACULAE
FADIMAN
FAIRWAY
FAJITAS
FARADAY
FARAWAY
FASCIAS
FATHEAD
FAUXPAS
FAYWRAY
GAINSAY
GALAHAD
GAMBIAN
GAMELAW
GANGSAW
GANGWAY
GATEMAN
GATEWAY
GAVEWAY
HABITAT
HACKMAN
HACKSAW
HADRIAN
HAITIAN
HALFDAN
HALFWAY
HALIFAX
HALLWAY
HANDBAG
HANDCAR
HANDSAW
HANGMAN
HANUKAH
HARDHAT
HARDPAN
HARTMAN
JACANAS
JACKDAW
JACKTAR
JAIALAI
JANEWAY
JAVAMAN
JAZZMAN
KAHUNAS
KANAKAS
KARAJAN
KAUFMAN
LABCOAT
LACHLAN
LACTEAL
LACUNAE
LACUNAL
LACUNAS
LADYDAY
LAGUNAS
LAKOTAS
LAMBDAS
LAMBEAU
LAMINAE
LAMINAL
LAMINAR
LAMINAS
LANDSAT
LAOTIAN
LATERAL
LATERAN
LATIFAH
LATINAS
LATVIAN
LAUGHAT
LAYAWAY
MACADAM
MACGRAW
MACULAE
MADEHAY
MADEPAR
MADEWAY
MADIGAN
MAGICAL
MAILBAG
MAILCAR
MAKEHAY
MAKEPAR
MAKEWAY
MALABAR
MALAYAN
MALLRAT
MANANAS
MANOWAR
MANTRAP
MANTRAS
MANXCAT
MANXMAN
MANYEAR
MARACAS
MARCEAU
MARINAS
MARITAL
MARKHAM
MARKKAA
MARSHAL
MARTIAL
MARTIAN
MARYKAY
MATEWAN
MATHIAS
MATTHAU
MAUGHAM
MAXIMAL
MAYORAL
NAMEDAY
NAMETAG
NARWHAL
NATURAL
OAKLEAF
OATMEAL
PAANGAS
PACECAR
PACKRAT
PADUCAH
PAGODAS
PAJAMAS
PALATAL
PALOMAR
PANADAS
PANAMAS
PANARAB
PANCHAX
PAPAYAS
PARKWAY
PARTIAL
PARTWAY
PASCHAL
PATACAS
PATHWAY
PATINAS
PATRIAL
PAWEDAT
PAYLOAD
PAYOLAS
RACECAR
RACEWAY
RADICAL
RADULAE
RAILSAT
RAILWAY
RAINHAT
RAINMAN
RAMADAN
RAMADAS
RAMBEAU
RANAWAY
RAREGAS
RARITAN
RATATAT
RATTRAP
RAWDEAL
RAYOVAC
SAGINAW
SAHARAN
SALAZAR
SALINAS
SALVIAS
SAMEDAY
SAMOVAR
SAMPRAS
SAMURAI
SANDBAG
SANDBAR
SANDMAN
SANJUAN
SARANAC
SARAWAK
SAROYAN
SASHBAR
SAURIAN
SAVALAS
TABLEAU
TABULAR
TAGTEAM
TALKSAT
TANGRAM
TAPEMAN
TASHMAN
TAXICAB
TAXIMAN
TAXIWAY
VALJEAN
VATICAN
VAUGHAN
WALKMAN
WALKWAY
WASHRAG
WATTEAU
WAXBEAN
XANTHAN
YAKIMAS
YAKUZAS
YARDMAN
YASHMAK
ZAIREAN
ZAIRIAN
ZAMBIAN
ZAREBAS

•A••••A

BAKLAVA
BANDANA
BARBARA
BARBUDA
BARETTA
BATISTA
BAVARIA
BAZOOKA
CADENZA
CAESURA
CALDERA
CAMELIA
CANASTA
CANDELA
CANDIDA
CANTATA
CANTINA
CAPELLA
CARAMBA
CARAMIA
CARIOCA
CARNERA
CASCARA
CASSAVA
CATALPA
CATAWBA
DAYTONA
GALATEA
GALATIA
GANGLIA
GANGSTA
GAUTAMA
IACOCCA
JAKARTA
JAMAICA
KACHINA
KAMPALA
KARASEA
LABAMBA
LAJOLLA
LAMBADA
LAMOTTA
LANTANA
LAPALMA
LAPLATA
LASAGNA
LASCALA
LASORDA
LATOSCA
LAVINIA
MACHINA
MADEIRA
MADONNA
MAGENTA
MAHALIA
MAHATMA
MAJORCA
MALACCA
MANAGUA
MANDALA
MANDELA
MARIANA
MARIMBA
MARKKAA
MARKOVA
MARMARA
MARSALA
MARTINA
MASCARA
MASTABA
MATILDA
MAXILLA
MAZURKA
NAMIBIA
NAPHTHA
NATALIA
NATASHA
PALOOKA
PANACEA
PANDORA
PAPILLA
PAPRIKA
PARTITA
PASTINA
PATELLA
PAULINA
PAVLOVA
RATAFIA
RAVENNA
RAWDATA
SABRINA
SALSODA
SAMARIA
SAMSARA
SANGRIA
SANTANA
SATSUMA
SAVANNA
TABITHA
TAFFETA
TALARIA
TAMBALA
TANTARA
TAPIOCA
TARZANA
TATIANA
VAMPIRA
VANESSA
VANILLA

••AA•••

ELAAIUN

••A•A••

ADAMANT
ALABAMA
ANASAZI
ARAMAIC
ARAPAHO
ARAWAKS
ATACAMA
ATAMANS
AVATARS
BLATANT
BRANAGH
BRAVADO
CHAGALL
CHAPATI
CHARADE
CRAVATS
DEADAIR
DRAYAGE
EMANANT
EMANATE
GRAHAME
GRAHAMS
GRANADA
GRANARY
GUANACO
GUARANI
HEALALL
IMAMATE
INADAZE
JEANARP
KLAMATH
LEAFAGE
LEAKAGE
MBABANE
NIAGARA
OCANADA
ONADARE
ONADATE
PEASANT
PHALANX
PHARAOH
PLACARD
PLACATE
PLAYACT
QUASARS
REAMASS
REAVAIL
SCALARS
SCARABS
SEABAGS
SEABASS
SEAFANS
SEAGATE
SEALABS
SEALANE
SEALANT
SEASALT
SEAWALL
SEAWARD
SEAWAYS
SHALALA
SHAMANS
SHANANA
STALAGS
TEABAGS
TEABALL
TEACAKE
TEACART
TRALALA
TRAVAIL
UNAWARE
UTAHANS
ZEALAND

••A••A•

ACACIAS
ACADIAN
AGAKHAN
ALASKAN
AMALGAM
ANAGRAM
ANAHUAC
ANANIAS
ARABIAN
ARAMEAN
AZALEAS
BEANBAG
BEARCAT
BEARPAW
BOATMAN
BRAHMAN
BRAHMAS
CHACHAS
CHAPEAU
CHAPMAN
CHATEAU
CHATHAM
COALCAR
COALGAS
COALTAR
COASTAL
COAXIAL
CRANIAL
CRAWDAD
CZARDAS
DEADPAN
DIAGRAM
DRAWBAR
EXACTAS
FLAGDAY
FLAGMAN
FLATCAR
FLATTAX
FRACTAL
GHANIAN
GLACIAL
GOAHEAD
GRABBAG
GRABSAT
GRACIAS
GRADUAL
GRAMMAR
GRAMPAS
GRANDAM
GRAPPAS
GRATIAS
GRAYJAY
GRAYLAG
HEADMAN
HEADWAY
HEARSAY
HIALEAH
IDAHOAN
INAHEAP
IRANIAN
ITALIAN
KHAYYAM
KWACHAS
KWANZAS
MIAMIAN
MIAMIAS
MIAOYAO
MIASMAS
MUAMMAR
MYANMAR
OBADIAH
ONATEAR
PAANGAS
PEABEAN
PEACOAT
PHARLAP
PIAZZAS
PLANTAR
PLASMAS
PLATEAU
PLAYSAT
QUAGGAS
ROADMAP
ROADWAY
RUANDAN
RWANDAN
SCANDAL
SEAGRAM
SEASTAR
SHANKAR
SHAWWAL
SNAPSAT
SPARTAN
SPATIAL
STANZAS
STAREAT
STARMAN
STARMAP
TEALEAF
TEARGAS
TEARSAT
TEATRAY
TRAMCAR
TRAMPAS
TRAUMAS
UGANDAN
YEATEAM

••A•••A

ALABAMA
ALAMEDA
AMAPOLA
ANAEMIA
ARAFURA
ARALSEA
ATACAMA
BLACULA
BRAVURA
CLAUDIA
CRAYOLA
CZARINA
DEADSEA
DRACHMA
DRACULA
GRANADA
GRANDMA
GRANDPA
GRANOLA
IPANEMA
ISADORA
NIAGARA
OCANADA
OCARINA
PHAEDRA
SCAPULA
SHALALA
SHANANA
SPATULA
STAMINA
SWANSEA
TRACHEA
TRALALA
TSARINA
TZARINA
ULANOVA

•••AA••

ALMAATA
BAZAARS
SALAAMS

•••A•A•

ABRAHAM
ALCAZAR
ALMANAC
ALPACAS
APPARAT
AREAWAY
ARMADAS
ASFARAS
BACALAO
BAHAMAS
BANANAS
BENATAR
BETAMAX
BETARAY
BROADAX
CABALAS
CABANAS
CARABAO
CARACAL
CARACAS
CARAVAN
CARAWAY
CASABAS
CASAVAS
CATALAN
CICADAE
CICADAS
CLOACAE
CLOACAS
CURACAO
CUTAWAY
DUNAWAY
EATAWAY
FARADAY
FARAWAY
FLEABAG
FLYAWAY
GALAHAD
GELADAS
GETAWAY
GOTAWAY
IDEAMAN
IGUANAS
IMPALAS
ITHACAN
JACANAS
JAIALAI
JAVAMAN
JICAMAS
KANAKAS
KARAJAN
LAYAWAY
MACADAM
MALABAR
MALAYAN
MANANAS
MARACAS
MIRAMAR
MIRAMAX
MUBARAK
NEVADAN
OGLALAS
OTTAWAS
PAJAMAS
PALATAL
PANADAS
PANAMAS
PANARAB
PAPAYAS
PATACAS
PESAWAS
PHRASAL
PINATAS
PITAPAT
POSADAS
PUTAWAY
PYJAMAS
RAMADAN
RAMADAS
RANAWAY
RATATAT
RUNAWAY
SAHARAN
SALAZAR
SARANAC
SARAWAK
SAVALAS
SONATAS
SWEARAT
TOWAWAY
YUCATAN
ZENANAS

•••A••A

ALBANIA
ALFALFA
ALMAATA
ALSATIA
AQUARIA
ARCADIA
ATLANTA
AVIANCA
BAVARIA
BONANZA
CANASTA
CARAMBA
CARAMIA
CATALPA
CATAWBA
CROATIA
DEFALLA
DEPALMA
EURASIA
GALATEA
GALATIA
HOSANNA
INFANTA
JAKARTA
JAMAICA
JOCASTA
JOHANNA
KARASEA
KILAUEA
LABAMBA
LAPALMA
LASAGNA
MAHALIA
MAHATMA
MALACCA
MANAGUA
MIRANDA
MORAVIA
NATALIA
NATASHA
OCEANIA
OCTAVIA
ORGANZA
PANACEA
PIRANHA
RATAFIA
REDALGA
REGALIA
REGATTA
ROMANIA
ROSANNA
SAMARIA
SAVANNA
SEDALIA
SINATRA
SOLARIA
SOMALIA
SUMATRA
SUSANNA
TALARIA
TITANIA
VEDANTA
VERANDA
VIDALIA
VISALIA

••••AA•

ROLVAAG
YESMAAM

••••A•A

AIRMADA
ALABAMA
ALIBABA
ALMAATA

ARIKARA
ATACAMA
BAKLAVA
BANDANA
BARBARA
BOKHARA
CANTATA
CASCARA
CASSAVA
CHICANA
DIORAMA
DOGMATA
ESTRADA
GAUTAMA
GRANADA
GRENADA
GUEVARA
HONIARA
IKEBANA
INDIANA
JULIANA
KAMPALA
LAMBADA
LANTANA
LAPLATA
LASCALA
MANDALA
MARIANA
MARMARA
MARSALA
MASCARA
MASTABA
MESSALA
MOMBASA
MONTANA
MORGANA
MUSTAFA
NIAGARA
NIRVANA
OCANADA
OKINAWA
OOHLALA
OVIPARA
PRORATA
RAWDATA
SAMSARA
SANTANA
SHALALA
SHANANA
SMETANA
STOMATA
SULTANA
TAMBALA
TANTARA
TARZANA
TATIANA
TIJUANA
TOCCATA
TOSTADA
TRALALA
TYMPANA
UPPSALA

•••••AA
MARKKAA
RUFIYAA

AB•••••
ABALONE
ABANDON
ABASHED
ABASHES
ABASING
ABATING
ABBOTCY
ABDOMEN
ABDUCTS
ABELARD
ABENAKI
ABETTED
ABETTOR
ABEXTRA
ABEYANT
ABIDEBY
ABIDING
ABIGAIL
ABILENE
ABILITY
ABINTRA
ABITIBI
ABJURED
ABJURES
ABLATED
ABLATES
ABLAUTS
ABNAKIS
ABOLISH
ABORTED
ABOUGHT
ABOUNDS
ABRADED
ABRADER
ABRADES
ABRAHAM
ABREAST
ABRIDGE
ABRUZZI
ABSALOM
ABSCOND
ABSENCE
ABSENTS
ABSOLUT
ABSOLVE
ABSORBS
ABSTAIN
ABUBAKR
ABUSERS
ABUSING
ABUSIVE
ABUTTAL
ABUTTED
ABYSMAL
ABYSSES

A•B••••
ABBOTCY
ALBANIA
ALBEDOS
ALBENIZ
ALBERTA
ALBERTO
ALBINOS
ALBUMEN
ALBUMIN
ALBUNDY
AMBIENT
AMBLERS
AMBLING
AMBRIES
AMBROSE
ARBITER
ARBORED
ARBOURS
ARBUTUS
AUBADES
AUBURNS

A••B•••
ABUBAKR
AIRBAGS
AIRBALL
AIRBASE
AIRBOAT
ALABAMA
ALIBABA
AMIBLUE
ANTBEAR
ANYBODY
ARABIAN
ARMBAND
ASHBURY

A•••B••
ACERBIC
ACROBAT
ACTABLE
ADDABLE
ADDIBLE
AEROBAT
AEROBES
AEROBIC
AFFABLE
AFFABLY
ALEMBIC
ALGEBRA
AMIABLE
AMIABLY
AMOEBAE
AMOEBAS
AMOEBIC
ANNABEL
ANTIBES
ARROBAS
ATTABOY
AUDIBLE
AUDIBLY
AUDUBON

A••••B•
ABIDEBY
ABITIBI
ABSORBS
ADSORBS
ADVERBS
ALIBABA
ALLENBY
ARECIBO
ASCRIBE

•AB••••
BABALOO
BABASSU
BABBAGE
BABBITT
BABBLED
BABBLES
BABETTE
BABOONS
BABYING
BABYISH
BABYLON
BABYSAT
BABYSIT
CABALAS
CABANAS
CABARET
CABBAGE
CABBIES
CABINET
CABLERS
CABLETV
CABLING
CABOOSE
CABRINI
DABBING
DABBLED
DABBLER
DABBLES
DABHAND
FABARES
FABERGE
FABLERS
FABRICS
GABBERS
GABBIER
GABBING
GABBLED
GABBLES
GABBROS
GABFEST
GABRIEL
HABITAT
HABITED
HABITUE
JABBERS
JABBING
JABIRUS
KABUKIS
LABAMBA
LABCOAT
LABELED
LABELER
LABELLE
LABIALS
LABIATE
LABORED
LABORER
LABOURS
LABRETS
NABBERS
NABBING
NABISCO
NABOKOV
PABLUMS
PABULUM
RABBETS
RABBITS
RABBITT
RABBLES
RABIDLY
SABBATH
SABINES
SABRINA
TABARDS
TABASCO
TABBIES
TABBING
TABITHA
TABLEAU
TABLETS
TABLING
TABLOID
TABORET
TABULAR
YABBERS

•A•B•••
BABBAGE
BABBITT
BABBLED
BABBLES
BADBOYS
BALBOAS
BAMBINO
BAMBOOS
BAOBABS
BARBARA
BARBARY
BARBELL
BARBELS
BARBERS
BARBING
BARBUDA
BATBOYS
BAUBLES
CABBAGE
CABBIES
CADBURY
CAMBERS
CAMBIUM
CAMBRIC
CARBIDE
CARBINE
CARBONS
CARBOYS
CATBERT
CATBIRD
CATBOAT
DABBING
DABBLED
DABBLER
DABBLES
DANBURY
DARBIES
DASBOOT
DAUBERS
DAUBING
DAYBEDS
DAYBOOK
DAYBOYS
FANBELT
FATBACK
GABBERS
GABBIER
GABBING
GABBLED
GABBLES
GABBROS
GAMBADO
GAMBIAN
GAMBITS
GAMBLED
GAMBLER
GAMBLES
GAMBOLS
GAMBREL
GARBAGE
GARBING
GARBLED
GARBLES
GASBAGS
HAMBURG
HARBORS
HARBOUR
HARBURG
HASBEEN
HATBAND
HAUBERK
JABBERS
JABBING
JAWBONE
JAYBIRD
LAMBADA
LAMBDAS
LAMBEAU
LAMBENT
LAMBERT
LAPBELT
LAYBACK
MACBETH
MAMBOED
MARBLED
MARBLES
MAXBAER
MAXBORN
NABBERS
NABBING
PARBOIL
RABBETS
RABBITS
RABBITT
RABBLES
RAGBAGS
RAMBEAU
RAMBLED
RAMBLER
RAMBLES
RATBERT
RAYBURN
SABBATH
SAMBAED
SAMBALS
SAMBARS
SAWBUCK
TABBIES
TABBING
TAMBALA
TAMBOUR
TARBABY
TARBELL
WAMBLED
WAMBLES
WARBLED
WARBLER
WARBLES
WAXBEAN
WAYBILL
YABBERS
ZAMBEZI
ZAMBIAN
ZAMBONI

•A••B••
BACKBAY
BACKBIT
BALLBOY
BANDBOX
CALIBAN
CALIBER
CALIBRE
CALLBOX
CAPABLE
CAPABLY
CARABAO
CARIBES
CARIBOU
CASABAS
CASHBAR
CASHBOX
EATABLE
GAZEBOS
HALIBUT
HANDBAG
HAUTBOY
JACOBIN
LADYBUG
MACABRE
MAILBAG
MAILBOX
MALABAR
MARABOU
NAMIBIA
PAGEBOY
PARABLE
PAYABLE
RAINBOW
RAREBIT
RATABLE
SALABLE
SALTBOX
SANDBAG
SANDBAR
SANDBOX
SANIBEL
SASHBAR
SAVABLE
TALKBIG
TAMABLE
TAXABLE
ZAREBAS

•A•••B•
BAOBABS
BARNABY
BARTABS
CARAMBA
CATAWBA
DAYJOBS
EARLOBE
LABAMBA
LAPROBE
MADLIBS
MARIMBA
MASTABA
NAIROBI
TARBABY
WALLABY
WANNABE

•A••••B
BACKRUB
BATHTUB
FANCLUB
PANARAB
TAXICAB
WASHTUB

••AB•••
ALABAMA
ARABIAN
BLABBED
BLABBER
CHABLIS
CLABBER
CRABBED
CRABBER
DIABOLI
DRABBER
ENABLED
ENABLES
GOABOUT
GRABBAG
GRABBED
GRABBER
GRABSAT
MBABANE
PEABEAN
PEABODY
SEABAGS
SEABASS
SEABEDS
SEABEES
SEABIRD
SEABLUE
SEABORG
SLABBED
STABBED
STABILE
STABLED
STABLER
STABLES
SWABBED
TEABAGS
TEABALL
TRABERT

••A•B••
BEANBAG
BLABBED
BLABBER
BRAMBLE
BRAMBLY
CHAMBER
CLABBER
CLAMBER
COALBIN
CRABBED
CRABBER
DRABBER
DRAWBAR
FLAMBED
FLAMBES
FLATBED
GEARBOX
GRABBAG
GRABBED
GRABBER
PEATBOG
PLAYBOY
ROADBED
SHAMBLE
SLABBED
SOAPBOX
STABBED
SWABBED

••A••B•
BYANDBY
PLACEBO
SCARABS
SEALABS
STANDBY

••A•••B
BEARCUB

•••AB••
ACTABLE
ADDABLE
AFFABLE
AFFABLY
AMIABLE
AMIABLY
ANNABEL
ATTABOY
BELABOR
BUGABOO
BUYABLE
CAPABLE
CAPABLY
CARABAO
CASABAS
CITABLE
COHABIT
DISABLE
DURABLE
DURABLY
EATABLE
EQUABLE
EQUABLY
FIXABLE
FLEABAG
FRIABLE
HIRABLE
ICHABOD
INHABIT
LIEABED
LIKABLE
LIVABLE
LOVABLE
LOVABLY
MACABRE
MALABAR
MARABOU
MINABLE
MIXABLE
MOVABLE
MOVABLY
MUTABLE
MUTABLY
NOTABIT
NOTABLE
NOTABLY
PARABLE
PAYABLE
PLIABLE
PLIABLY
POTABLE
RATABLE
SALABLE
SAVABLE
SEEABLE
SIZABLE
SIZABLY
SOFABED
TAMABLE
TAXABLE
TENABLE
TENABLY
USEABLE

•••A•B•
BEDAUBS
CARAMBA
CATAWBA
LABAMBA
MOGAMBO
SWEARBY

•••A••B
PANARAB

••••AB•
ALIBABA
BAOBABS
BARNABY
BARTABS
CONFABS
CRYBABY
HUSHABY
LULLABY
MASTABA
PREFABS
PUNJABI
SCARABS
SEALABS
SYLLABI
TARBABY
THEBABE
WALLABY
WANNABE

••••A•B
RHUBARB

•••••AB
CHEMLAB
GODTHAB
MINICAB
PANARAB
PEDICAB
PULLTAB
TAXICAB

AC•••••
ACACIAS
ACADEME
ACADEMY
ACADIAN
ACANTHI
ACARIDS
ACCEDED
ACCEDER
ACCEDES
ACCENTS
ACCEPTS
ACCLAIM
ACCORDS
ACCOSTS
ACCOUNT
ACCRETE
ACCRUAL
ACCRUED
ACCRUES
ACCURST
ACCUSED
ACCUSER
ACCUSES
ACEDOUT
ACERBIC
ACEROLA
ACEROSE
ACESOUT
ACETATE
ACETONE
ACHATES
ACHENES
ACHERON
ACHESON
ACHIEST
ACHIEVE
ACHTUNG
ACIDIFY
ACIDITY
ACKACKS
ACOLYTE
ACONITE
ACQUIRE
ACQUITS
ACREAGE
ACRIDLY
ACROBAT
ACRONYM
ACRYLIC
ACTABLE
ACTAEON
ACTEDON
ACTEDUP
ACTFIVE
ACTFOUR
ACTINIC
ACTIONS
ACTIVES
ACTRESS
ACTSOUT
ACTUARY
ACTUATE
ACTUPON
ACUMENS
ACUTELY

A•C••••
ACCEDED
ACCEDER
ACCEDES
ACCENTS
ACCEPTS
ACCLAIM
ACCORDS
ACCOSTS
ACCOUNT
ACCRETE
ACCRUAL
ACCRUED
ACCRUES
ACCURST
ACCUSED
ACCUSER
ACCUSES
ALCAZAR
ALCHEMY
ALCOHOL
ALCOVES
ANCHORS
ANCHOVY
ANCIENT
ARCADES
ARCADIA
ARCANUM
ARCHAIC
ARCHERS
ARCHERY
ARCHING
ARCHIVE
ARCHONS
ARCHWAY
ARCLAMP
ARCSINE
ASCENDS
ASCENTS
ASCETIC
ASCRIBE
AUCTION

A••C•••
ABSCOND
ACACIAS
AIRCOOL
AIRCREW
AITCHES
AJACCIO
AMSCRAY
ANTCOWS
APACHES
APOCOPE
ARACHNE
ARECIBO
ASHCANS
ASOCIAL
ATACAMA
ATECROW
AVOCADO
AVOCETS

A•••C••
ABDUCTS
ACKACKS
ADDUCED
ADDUCES
ADDUCTS
AFFECTS
AFRICAN
AJACCIO
ALARCON
ALENCON
ALPACAS
AMERCED
AMERCES
ANARCHY
ANTACID
APERCUS
APRICOT
ARNICAS
ARTICLE
ASPECTS
ATTACHE
ATTACKS
ATTICUS
ATTUCKS
AURICLE
AUROCHS
AZTECAN

A••••C•
ABBOTCY
ABSENCE
ADJUNCT
ADVANCE
AFFLICT
AGARICS
AIRLOCK
AIRSACS
AIRSOCK
ALDRICH
AMERICA
ANTIOCH
ARDENCY
ARMLOCK
ARTDECO
ASKANCE
ATPEACE
ATTRACT
AUSPICE
AVARICE
AVIANCA

A•••••C
ACERBIC
ACRYLIC
ACTINIC
AELFRIC
AEROBIC
ALEMBIC
ALMANAC
AMHARIC
AMOEBIC
ANAEMIC
ANAHUAC
ANGELIC
ANOSMIC
AQUATIC
ARAMAIC
ARCHAIC
ARSENIC
ASCETIC
ASEPTIC
ASIATIC

•AC••••
BACALAO
BACARDI
BACCHUS
BACHING
BACILLI
BACKBAY
BACKBIT
BACKEND
BACKERS
BACKHOE
BACKING
BACKLIT
BACKLOG
BACKOFF
BACKOUT
BACKRUB
BACKSIN
BACKSUP
BACKUPS
CACANNY
CACHETS
CACHING
CACHOUS
CACKLED
CACKLER
CACKLES
DACTYLS
FACADES
FACEOFF
FACETED
FACIALS
FACINGS
FACTFUL
FACTION
FACTOID
FACTORS
FACTORY
FACTUAL
FACULAE
FACULTY
HACKERS
HACKETT
HACKIES
HACKING
HACKLED
HACKLES
HACKMAN
HACKNEY
HACKSAW
IACOCCA
JACANAS
JACCUSE
JACINTH
JACKALS
JACKASS
JACKDAW
JACKETS
JACKEYS
JACKIES
JACKING
JACKPOT
JACKSON
JACKSUP
JACKTAR
JACOBIN
JACONET
JACQUES
JACUZZI
KACHINA
LACEDUP
LACESUP
LACHLAN
LACIEST
LACINGS
LACKEYS
LACKING
LACONIC
LACOSTE
LACQUER
LACTASE
LACTATE
LACTEAL
LACTOSE
LACUNAE
LACUNAL
LACUNAS
MACABRE
MACADAM
MACAQUE
MACBETH
MACDUFF
MACGRAW
MACHETE
MACHINA
MACHINE
MACRAME
MACRONS
MACULAE
NACELLE
PACECAR
PACHISI
PACIFIC
PACKAGE
PACKARD
PACKERS
PACKETS
PACKICE
PACKING
PACKRAT
PACKSUP
RACCOON
RACECAR
RACEMES
RACEWAY
RACIEST
RACKETS
RACKING
RACKSUP
RACQUET
SACHEMS
SACHETS
SACKERS
SACKFUL
SACKING
SACKOUT
SACLIKE
SACQUES
TACITLY
TACITUS
TACKERS
TACKIER
TACKILY
TACKING
TACKLED
TACKLER
TACKLES
TACKSON
TACTFUL
TACTICS
TACTILE
VACANCY
VACATED
VACATES
VACCINE
VACUITY
VACUOLE
VACUOUS
VACUUMS
WACKIER
WACKILY
YACHTED
YACKING
ZACHARY

•A•C•••
BACCHUS

BALCONY
BARCARS
BARCODE
BATCHED
BATCHES
BAYCITY
CALCIFY
CALCITE
CALCIUM
CANCANS
CANCELS
CARCASE
CARCASS
CARCOAT
CASCADE
CASCARA
CATCALL
CATCHER
CATCHES
CATCHON
CATCHUP
DANCERS
DANCING
DAYCAMP
DAYCARE
EATCROW
FALCONS
FANCIED
FANCIER
FANCIES
FANCIFY
FANCILY
FANCLUB
FARCING
FASCIAS
FATCATS
FATCITY
FAUCETS
FAWCETT
GARCONS
GASCAPS
GASCONS
GASCONY
GAUCHER
GAUCHOS
HALCYON
HANCOCK
HATCHED
HATCHER
HATCHES
HATCHET
JACCUSE
JAYCEES
LABCOAT
LANCERS
LANCETS
LAOCOON
LARCENY
LARCHES
LASCALA
LASCAUX
LATCHED
LATCHES
MADCAPS
MADCHEN
MALCOLM
MANCINI
MARCATO
MARCEAU
MARCELS
MARCHED
MARCHER
MARCHES
MARCHON
MARCONI
MASCARA
MASCOTS
MATCHED
MATCHES
MATCHUP
NASCENT
NATCHEZ
PANCAKE
PANCHAX
PARCELS
PARCHED
PARCHES
PASCHAL
PATCHED
PATCHES
PATCHUP
PAUCITY
PAYCASH
RACCOON
RANCHED
RANCHER
RANCHES
RANCHOS
RANCOUR
RASCALS
RATCHET
RAUCOUS
SALCHOW
SANCTUM
SARCASM
SATCHEL
SATCHMO
SAUCERS
SAUCIER
SAUCILY
TALCUMS
VACCINE
WALCOTT
WATCHED
WATCHER
WATCHES
WATCHIT
WAYCOOL

•A••C••

CADUCEI
CALICES
CALICOS
CALYCES
CAPECOD
CARACAL
CARACAS
CASHCOW
CATSCAN
EARACHE
HAIRCUT
HANDCAR
HARICOT
IACOCCA
JANACEK
KARACHI
LATICES
MAGICAL
MAILCAR
MALACCA
MALACHI
MANACLE
MANXCAT
MARACAS
PACECAR
PADUCAH
PALACES
PANACEA
PANACHE
PANICKY
PANICLE
PATACAS
PAUNCHY
RACECAR
RADICAL
RADICES
RADICLE
SAMECHS
SARACEN
TAXICAB
VATICAN

•A•••C•

BALANCE
BANNOCK
BARRACK
CADENCE
CADENCY
CALPACS
CALTECH
CANDICE
CANSECO
CAPRICE
CARIOCA
CARRICK
CASSOCK
DAVINCI
EARLOCK
FABRICS
FAIENCE
FALLACY
FATBACK
GARRICK
HADDOCK
HAMHOCK
HAMMOCK
HANCOCK
HASSOCK
HATRACK
HAYRACK
IACOCCA
JALISCO
JAMAICA
JAMPACK
JANNOCK
LAMARCK
LAPLACE
LATENCY
LATOSCA
LATTICE
LAYBACK
MAFFICK
MAJORCA
MALACCA
MANIACS
MANIOCS
MASTICS
MATLOCK
MATTOCK
MAURICE
NABISCO
OARLOCK
PACKICE
PADDOCK
PADLOCK
PALANCE
PANDECT
PARSECS
PATRICE
PATRICK
RANSACK
RATPACK
RATRACE
SADSACK
SAWBUCK
TABASCO
TACTICS
TAMPICO
TAPIOCA
TARMACS
VACANCY
VALANCE
VALENCE
VALENCY
VANDYCK
VANEYCK
WALLACE
WALLACH
WARLOCK
WARWICK
WASATCH

•A••••C

BALDRIC
CALORIC
CAMBRIC
CANONIC
CARDIAC
CAUSTIC
FANATIC
GASTRIC
HAMITIC
HASIDIC
LACONIC
LAENNEC
LAUTREC
MALEFIC
MANTRIC
MASONIC
PACIFIC
PAPADOC
RAYKROC
RAYOVAC
SARANAC
SATIRIC
XANTHIC
ZAPOTEC

••AC•••

ACACIAS
AJACCIO
APACHES
ARACHNE
ATACAMA
BEACHED
BEACHES
BEACONS
BLACKED
BLACKEN
BLACKER
BLACKIE
BLACKLY
BLACULA
BRACERO
BRACERS
BRACEUP
BRACING
BRACKEN
BRACKET
CHACHAS
CLACKED
COACHED
COACHES
CRACKED
CRACKER
CRACKLE
CRACKLY
CRACKUP
DEACONS
DRACHMA
DRACHMS
DRACULA
EDACITY
ENACTED
ENACTOR
EVACUEE
EXACTAS
EXACTED
EXACTER
EXACTLY
EXACTOR
FIACRES
FLACCID
FLACONS
FRACTAL
GIACOMO
GLACEED
GLACIAL
GLACIER
GRACIAS
GRACILE
GRACING
GRACKLE
JOACHIM
KNACKER
KWACHAS
LEACHED
LEACHES
LEACOCK
LOACHES
OPACITY
ORACLES
PEACHED
PEACHES
PEACOAT
PEACOCK
PLACARD
PLACATE
PLACEBO
PLACERS
PLACIDO
PLACING
PLACKET
POACHED
POACHER
POACHES
QUACKED
REACHED
REACHES
REACTED
REACTOR
REACTTO
ROACHED
ROACHES
SEACOWS
SHACKLE
SLACKED
SLACKEN
SLACKER
SLACKLY
SMACKED
SMACKER
SNACKED
SNACKER
SPACERS
SPACIER
SPACING
SPACKLE
STACKED
STACKUP
TEACAKE
TEACART
TEACHER
TEACHES
TEACHIN
TEACUPS
TRACERS
TRACERY
TRACHEA
TRACING
TRACKED
TRACKER
TRACTOR
WHACKED
WRACKED

••A•C••

AJACCIO
ALARCON
ANARCHY
BEARCAT
BEARCUB
BLANCHE
CHANCED
CHANCEL
CHANCER
CHANCES
CHAUCER
COALCAR
EPARCHS
EPARCHY
EXARCHS
FIANCEE
FIANCES
FIASCOS
FLACCID
FLATCAR
FRANCES
FRANCIS
GLANCED
GLANCES
NUANCED
NUANCES
PLAICES
PRANCED
PRANCER
PRANCES
SCARCER
SEANCES
STANCES
STARCHY
THATCHY
TRAMCAR
TRANCES

••A••C•

AGARICS
AVARICE
CHALICE
CLARICE
DIALECT
GUANACO
ITALICS
KLATSCH
LEACOCK
PEACOCK
PLAYACT
SEASICK
STATICE
STATICS
STAUNCH
TRADUCE
UNAVOCE
VIADUCT

••A•••C

ANAEMIC
ANAHUAC
ARAMAIC
CHAOTIC
CLASSIC
DRASTIC
EDAPHIC
ELASTIC
FRANTIC
GRAPHIC
JEANLUC
MIASMIC
PLASTIC
STANNIC
TRAFFIC

•••AC••

ACKACKS
ALPACAS
ANTACID
ATTACHE
ATTACKS
BORACIC
CARACAL
CARACAS
CLOACAE
CLOACAS
CURACAO
DEBACLE
DEFACED
DEFACES
DEFACTO
DIDACTS
EARACHE
EFFACED
EFFACES
ENLACED
ENLACES
EXFACTO
GOUACHE
HIBACHI
HIJACKS
HITACHI
HYRACES
IMPACTS
INVACUO
ITHACAN
JANACEK
KARACHI
KOLACKY
MALACCA
MALACHI
MANACLE
MARACAS
MENACED
MENACES
MIRACLE
OUTACTS
PALACES
PANACEA
PANACHE
PATACAS
PREACHY
REDACTS
REFACED
REFACES
RELACED
RELACES
SARACEN
SOLACES
TENACES
THWACKS
TOBACCO
TREACLE
TREACLY
UNLACED
UNLACES
UNPACKS
UNTACKS

•••A•C•

ADVANCE
ASKANCE
AVIANCA
BALANCE
BELASCO
DEBAUCH
DURANCE
ENHANCE
ERRANCY
FINANCE
INFANCY
JAMAICA
LAMARCK
MALACCA
MONARCH
MOSAICS
PALANCE
PENANCE
PLIANCY
ROMANCE
SCRATCH
TABASCO
TENANCY
TOBACCO
TRUANCY
UNLATCH
VACANCY
VALANCE
WASATCH

•••A••C

ALMANAC
AMHARIC
AQUATIC
ASIATIC
BORACIC
CERAMIC
DYNAMIC
ERRATIC
FANATIC
HEPATIC
ISLAMIC
LUNATIC
NOMADIC
OCEANIC
ORGANIC
PAPADOC
PELAGIC
PIRATIC
SARANAC
SOMATIC
TITANIC
VOCALIC

••••AC•

AIRSACS
ATPEACE
ATTRACT
BARRACK
CALPACS
COGNACS
COMPACT
CONTACT
COSSACK
CUTBACK
DETRACT
DOGFACE
EMBRACE
EXTRACT
FALLACY
FATBACK
FURNACE
GETBACK
GOTBACK
GRIMACE
GUANACO
HATRACK
HAYRACK
HOGBACK
ICEPACK
IMPEACH
INEXACT
INPEACE
INPLACE
JAMPACK
LAPLACE
LAYBACK
MANIACS
MICMACS
MUDPACK
ONTRACK
OUTBACK
OUTFACE
OUTPACE
OUTRACE
OVERACT
OVISACS
PINNACE
PLAYACT
POLLACK
PREFACE
PRIMACY
PRIVACY
RANSACK
RATPACK
RATRACE
REENACT
REFRACT
REPLACE
RETEACH
RETRACE
RETRACK
RETRACT
RIOTACT
RUNBACK
SADSACK
SETBACK
SIXPACK
SKIRACK
SKYJACK
SPINACH
STOMACH
SURFACE
TARMACS
TEDMACK
TERRACE
TICTACS
TIERACK
TIETACK
TINTACK
TOURACO
UNSTACK
WALLACE
WALLACH
ZODIACS

••••A•C

ARAMAIC
ARCHAIC
DELTAIC
HEBRAIC
PROSAIC
VOLTAIC

•••••AC

ALMANAC
ANAHUAC
BIVOUAC
CARDIAC
ELEGIAC
KEROUAC
MEDEVAC
PONTIAC
POTOMAC
RAYOVAC
SARANAC
SHELLAC

AD•••••

ADAGIOS
ADAMANT
ADAMITE
ADAMSON
ADAPTED
ADAPTER
ADAPTOR
ADDABLE
ADDEDIN
ADDEDON
ADDEDTO
ADDEDUP
ADDENDA
ADDENDS
ADDIBLE
ADDISON
ADDLING
ADDONTO
ADDRESS
ADDUCED
ADDUCES
ADDUCTS
ADDUPTO
ADELINE
ADENINE
ADEPTLY
ADFINEM
ADHERED
ADHERES
ADIPOSE
ADJOINS
ADJOURN
ADJUDGE
ADJUNCT
ADJURED
ADJURES
ADJUSTS
ADMIRAL
ADMIRED
ADMIRER
ADMIRES
ADMITTO
ADMIXED
ADMIXES
ADOLPHE
ADONAIS
ADOPTED
ADOPTEE
ADOPTER
ADORERS
ADORING
ADORNED
ADORNER
ADRENAL
ADSORBS
ADULATE
ADULTLY
ADVANCE
ADVENTS
ADVERBS
ADVERSE
ADVERTS
ADVISED
ADVISER
ADVISES
ADVISOR

A•D••••

ABDOMEN
ABDUCTS
ADDABLE
ADDEDIN
ADDEDON
ADDEDTO
ADDEDUP
ADDENDA
ADDENDS
ADDIBLE
ADDISON
ADDLING
ADDONTO
ADDRESS
ADDUCED
ADDUCES
ADDUCTS
ADDUPTO
AEDILES
AIDLESS
ALDENTE
ALDRICH
ANDANTE
ANDEANS
ANDIRON
ANDORRA
ANDOVER
ANDREAS
ANDRESS
ANDREWS
ANDROID
ANDSOON
ARDENCY
ARDMORE
ARDOURS
ARDUOUS
AUDIBLE
AUDIBLY
AUDILES
AUDITED
AUDITOR
AUDUBON

A••D•••

ABIDEBY
ABIDING
ACADEME
ACADEMY
ACADIAN
ACEDOUT
ACIDIFY
ACIDITY
AIRDAMS
AIRDATE
AIRDROP
ALADDIN
ALIDADE
AMADEUS
ANADEMS
ANODISE
ANODIZE
ANODYNE
AOUDADS
ARIDEST
ARIDITY
ARTDECO
AVIDITY
AZODYES

A•••D••

ABANDON
ABRADED
ABRADER
ABRADES
ABRIDGE
ACCEDED
ACCEDER
ACCEDES
ACRIDLY
ACTEDON
ACTEDUP
ADDEDIN
ADDEDON
ADDEDTO
ADDEDUP
ADJUDGE
AGENDAS
AHEADOF
AIMEDAT
AIMEDTO
ALADDIN
ALBEDOS
ALLUDED
ALLUDES
ALMADEN
AMENDED
AMRADIO
ANTEDUP
APSIDES
ARCADES
ARCADIA
ARIADNE
ARLEDGE
ARMADAS
ASKEDIN
ASUNDER
AUBADES
AVOIDED
AWARDED
AWARDEE
AWARDER

A••••D•

ABOUNDS
ACARIDS
ACCORDS
ADDENDA
ADDENDS
AFFORDS
AIRMADA
ALAMEDA
ALAMODE
ALBUNDY
ALFREDO
ALIDADE
ALLENDE
ALMONDS
ALREADY
ANYBODY
AOUDADS
APPENDS
ASCENDS
ASTRIDE
ATTENDS
AUGENDS
AVOCADO
AXSEEDS

A•••••D

ABASHED
ABELARD
ABETTED
ABJURED
ABLATED
ABORTED
ABRADED
ABSCOND
ABUTTED
ACCEDED
ACCRUED
ACCUSED
ADAPTED
ADDUCED
ADHERED
ADJURED
ADMIRED
ADMIXED
ADOPTED
ADORNED
ADVISED
AERATED
AFFIXED
AGROUND
AIRHEAD
AIRRAID
ALARMED
ALERTED
ALIGNED
ALLAYED
ALLEGED
ALLOWED
ALLOYED
ALLTOLD
ALLUDED
ALLURED
ALTERED
AMASSED
AMENDED
AMERCED
AMERIND
AMISTAD
ANDROID
ANEROID
ANGERED
ANISEED
ANNELID
ANNEXED
ANNOYED
ANTACID
ANYROAD
APPLAUD
APPLIED
APPOSED
APRONED
ARBORED
ARMBAND
ARMLOAD
ARMORED
AROUSED
ARRAYED
ARRIVED
ASHAMED
ASHFORD
ASHLAND
ASPIRED
ASSAYED
ASSUMED
ASSURED
ASTOUND
ATTIRED
ATTUNED
AUDITED
AUGURED
AVAILED
AVENGED
AVERRED
AVERTED
AVIATED
AVOIDED
AVULSED
AWAITED
AWARDED
AWKWARD
AYKROYD
AYNRAND

•AD••••

BADBOYS
BADDEST
BADDIES
BADDISH
BADEGGS
BADGERS
BADGUYS
BADNESS
CADBURY
CADDIED
CADDIES
CADDISH
CADDOAN
CADENCE
CADENCY
CADENZA
CADETTE
CADGERS
CADGING
CADMIUM
CADUCEI
DADAISM
DADAIST
DADDIES
FADDISH
FADDISM
FADDIST
FADEDIN
FADEINS
FADEOUT
FADESIN
FADIMAN
FADLIKE
GADDERS
GADDING
GADGETS
GADGETY
GADSDEN
HADDOCK
HADRIAN
JADEDLY
JADEITE
KADDISH
LADDERS
LADDIES
LADDISH
LADINOS
LADLERS
LADLING
LADYBUG
LADYDAY
LADYISH
MADAMEX
MADCAPS
MADCHEN
MADDENS

MADDERS
MADDEST
MADDING
MADDISH
MADEFOR
MADEHAY
MADEIRA
MADEOFF
MADEOUT
MADEPAR
MADEWAY
MADIGAN
MADISON
MADLIBS
MADNESS
MADONNA
PADDERS
PADDIES
PADDING
PADDLED
PADDLER
PADDLES
PADDOCK
PADLOCK
PADRONE
PADRONI
PADUANS
PADUCAH
RADDLED
RADDLES
RADIALS
RADIANS
RADIANT
RADIATE
RADICAL
RADICES
RADICLE
RADIOED
RADIXES
RADOMES
RADULAE
SADDENS
SADDEST
SADDLED
SADDLER
SADDLES
SADNESS
SADSACK
TADPOLE
WADDIES
WADDING
WADDLED
WADDLER
WADDLES
WADEDIN
WADESIN

•A•D•••

BADDEST
BADDIES
BADDISH
BALDEST
BALDING
BALDISH
BALDRIC
BALDWIN
BANDAGE
BANDAID
BANDANA
BANDBOX
BANDIED
BANDIES
BANDING
BANDITO
BANDITS
BANDSAW
BARDISH
BAWDIER
BAWDILY
CADDIED
CADDIES
CADDISH
CADDOAN
CALDERA
CALDRON
CANDELA
CANDICE
CANDIDA
CANDIDE
CANDIDS
CANDIED
CANDIES
CANDLES
CANDOUR
CARDERS
CARDIAC
CARDING
CARDOZO
CAUDLES
DADDIES
DANDERS
DANDIER
DANDIES
DANDIFY
DANDLED
DANDLES
DAWDLED
DAWDLER
DAWDLES
EARDROP
EARDRUM
FADDISH
FADDISM
FADDIST
GADDERS
GADDING
GANDERS
GARDENS
GARDNER
GAUDIER
GAUDILY
HADDOCK
HAGDONS
HANDBAG
HANDCAR
HANDFED
HANDFUL
HANDGUN
HANDIER
HANDILY
HANDING
HANDLED
HANDLER
HANDLES
HANDOFF
HANDOUT
HANDSAW
HANDSET
HANDSIN
HANDSON
HANDSUP
HARDENS
HARDEST
HARDHAT
HARDHIT
HARDIER
HARDILY
HARDING
HARDPAN
HARDPUT
HARDSET
HARDTOP
HARDWON
KADDISH
LADDERS
LADDIES
LADDISH
LAIDFOR
LAIDLOW
LAIDOFF
LAIDOUT
LANDAUS
LANDERS
LANDING
LANDSAT
LAPDOGS
LARDERS
LARDIER
LARDING
LARDNER
LARDONS
LAUDING
LAYDOWN
MACDUFF
MADDENS
MADDERS
MADDEST
MADDING
MADDISH
MAIDENS
MAIDISH
MANDALA
MANDANS
MANDATE
MANDAYS
MANDELA
MAUDLIN
MAYDAYS
PADDERS
PADDIES
PADDING
PADDLED
PADDLER
PADDLES
PADDOCK
PAIDFOR
PAIDOFF
PAIDOUT
PANDECT
PANDERS
PANDITS
PANDORA
PARDNER
PARDONS
PAYDAYS
PAYDIRT
RADDLED
RADDLES
RAGDOLL
RAIDERS
RAIDING
RANDALL
RANDIER
RANDOWN
RAWDATA
RAWDEAL
SADDENS
SADDEST
SADDLED
SADDLER
SADDLES
SANDALS
SANDBAG
SANDBAR
SANDBOX
SANDERS
SANDFLY
SANDHOG
SANDIER
SANDING
SANDLOT
SANDMAN
SANDMEN
SARDINE
SATDOWN
SAWDUST
TANDEMS
TARDIER
TARDILY
VANDALS
VANDINE
VANDYCK
VANDYKE
WADDIES
WADDING
WADDLED
WADDLER
WADDLES
WALDORF
WANDERS
WARDENS
WARDERS
WARDING
WARDOFF
YARDAGE
YARDARM
YARDMAN
YARDMEN
ZANDERS

•A••D••

BAGHDAD
CAMEDUE
CAVEDIN
DATEDLY
DAZEDLY
EARLDOM
EASEDIN
EASEDUP
FACADES
FADEDIN
FARADAY
GADSDEN
HAIRDOS
HAIRDYE
HALFDAN
HALIDES
HANGDOG
HASIDIC
HASIDIM
JACKDAW
JADEDLY
JANEDOE
KATYDID
LACEDUP
LADYDAY
LAMBDAS
LAMEDHS
LANGDON
LAUNDER
LAUNDRY
MACADAM
MALODOR
MATADOR
MAULDIN
MAUNDER
NAIADES
NAKEDLY
NAMEDAY
PAGODAS
PALADIN
PALEDRY
PANADAS
PAPADOC
PARADED
PARADES
PARADOX
PASTDUE
PAWEDAT
RABIDLY
RAKEDIN
RAKEDUP
RAMADAN
RAMADAS
RAPIDER
RAPIDLY
SALADIN
SAMEDAY
SAVEDUP
VALIDLY
VAPIDLY
WADEDIN
WAVEDIN

•A•••D•

BACARDI
BALLADE
BALLADS
BARBUDA
BARCODE
CALENDS
CANARDS
CANDIDA
CANDIDE
CANDIDS
CAPSIDS
CARBIDE
CASCADE
CASSIDY
CATHODE
DAYBEDS
FAGENDS
GAMBADO
HAYRIDE
HAZARDS
LAMBADA
LASORDA
MAENADS
MAKESDO
MALTEDS
MANMADE
MARAUDS
MATILDA
PARKADE
PASSADO
RAGGEDY
RAMRODS
RAWHIDE
SALSODA
SAYYIDS
TABARDS
TAGENDS
WANTADS
WARGODS
WAYSIDE
YAOUNDE

•A••••D

BABBLED
BACKEND
BAFFLED
BAGHDAD
BAGNOLD
BALLARD
BANDAID
BANDIED
BARMAID
BARNARD
BARTEND
BATCHED
BATIKED
BATTLED
BAULKED
CACKLED
CADDIED
CAJOLED
CAMEOED
CANDIED
CAPECOD
CAPERED
CARLOAD
CAROLED
CAROMED
CAROTID
CARRIED
CASQUED
CASTLED
CATBIRD
CATERED
CATFOOD
CATHEAD
CAULKED
CAVILED
DABBLED
DABHAND
DAGWOOD
DALLIED
DAMAGED
DANDLED
DANGLED
DAPPLED
DASTARD
DAUNTED
DAWDLED
DAZZLED
EASTEND
FACETED
FACTOID
FAGOTED
FAINTED
FANCIED
FATHEAD
FAULTED
FAVORED
GABBLED
GALAHAD
GAMBLED
GANGLED
GARAGED
GARBLED
GARGLED
GARLAND
GAVELED
HABITED
HACKLED
HAGGARD
HAGGLED
HALYARD
HAMMOND
HANDFED
HANDLED
HARRIED
HARVARD
HASSLED
HATBAND
HATCHED
HAUNTED
HAVERED
HAYSEED
HAYWARD
JANGLED
JAUNTED
JAYBIRD
KATYDID
KAYAKED
LABELED
LABORED
LAGGARD
LANFORD
LANGUID
LANYARD
LAPELED
LAPLAND
LASSOED
LATCHED
LAUGHED
LAWFORD
LAYERED
MAITRED
MAJORED
MALAMUD
MALLARD
MAMBOED
MANAGED
MANFRED
MANGLED
MANHOOD
MANKIND
MANSARD
MANTLED
MARBLED
MARCHED
MARRIED
MASTOID
MATCHED
MATURED
MAYNARD
NATURED
NAYSAID
OAKLAND
PACKARD
PADDLED
PAINTED
PANELED
PAPERED
PARADED
PARCHED
PAROLED
PARRIED
PARTIED
PATCHED
PAYLOAD
RADDLED
RADIOED
RAFFLED
RAGWEED
RALLIED
RAMBLED
RANCHED
RANKLED
RASSLED
RATTLED
RAVAGED
RAVELED
RAVENED
RAYMOND
RAZORED
SADDLED
SAINTED
SALLIED
SALUTED
SAMBAED
SAMOYED
SAMPLED
SANFORD
SAUTEED
SAVAGED
SAVORED
SAWWOOD
TABLOID
TACKLED
TAILEND
TAINTED
TALLIED
TALONED
TANGLED
TANGOED
TANKARD
TAPERED
TARRIED
TATTLED
TAUNTED
VACATED
VAULTED
VAUNTED
WADDLED
WAFFLED
WAGERED
WAGGLED
WAKENED
WALTZED
WAMBLED
WANGLED
WARBLED
WARLORD
WATCHED
WATERED
WAVERED
WAYLAID
WAYWARD
YACHTED

••AD•••

ACADEME
ACADEMY
ACADIAN
ALADDIN
AMADEUS
ANADEMS
BEADIER
BEADING
BEADLES
BEADSUP
BLADDER
BLADERS
BLADING
BRADLEE
BRADLEY
CRADLED
CRADLES
DEADAIR
DEADEND
DEADENS
DEADEYE
DEADPAN
DEADSEA
DEADSET
DIADEMS
EVADERS
EVADING
GLADDEN
GLADDER
GLADEYE
GOADING
GRADERS
GRADING
GRADUAL
HEADERS
HEADIER
HEADILY
HEADING
HEADMAN
HEADMEN
HEADOFF
HEADOUT
HEADPIN
HEADSET
HEADSIN
HEADSUP
HEADWAY
INADAZE
ISADORA
LEADERS
LEADIER
LEADING
LEADINS
LEADOFF
LEADOUT
LEADSIN
LEADSON
LEADSTO
LEADSUP
LOADERS
LOADING
MEADOWS
MEADOWY
OBADIAH
ONADARE
ONADATE
ONADIET
READERS
READIED
READIER
READIES
READILY
READING
READMIT
READOUT
READSIN
ROADBED
ROADHOG
ROADIES
ROADMAP
ROADWAY
SEADOGS
SEADUTY
SHADIER
SHADILY
SHADING
SHADOOF
SHADOWS
SHADOWY
SPADERS
SPADING
STADIUM
SWADDLE
TOADIED
TOADIES
TOADISH
TRADEIN
TRADEON
TRADERS
TRADEUP
TRADING
TRADUCE
TWADDLE
VIADUCT

••A•D••

ABANDON
ALADDIN
AWARDED
AWARDEE
AWARDER
BEARDED
BLADDER
BLANDER
BLANDLY
BOARDED
BOARDER
BRAIDED
BRAIDER
BRANDED
BRANDER
BRANDON
BYANDBY
CLAUDIA
CLAUDIO
CRAWDAD
CZARDAS
CZARDOM
EVANDER
FLAGDAY
GLADDEN
GLADDER
GRANDAM
GRANDEE
GRANDER
GRANDLY
GRANDMA
GRANDPA
GUARDED
GUARDEE
HEARDOF
HOARDED
HOARDER
LEANDER
MEANDER
ONANDON
PHAEDRA
PLAUDIT
PLAYDOH
PSANDQS
RUANDAN
RWANDAN
SCALDED
SCANDAL
SHAHDOM
SLANDER
SOANDSO
SPANDEX
STAIDER
STAIDLY
STANDBY
STANDEE
STANDIN
STANDON
STANDUP
STARDOM
SWADDLE
TWADDLE
UGANDAN
UNAIDED
WHAUDEN
WYANDOT

••A••D•

ACARIDS
ALAMEDA
ALAMODE
BRAVADO
CHARADE
ELAPIDS
GRANADA
OCANADA
PEABODY
PEAPODS
PLACIDO
SEABEDS
SEASIDE
TRAGEDY

••A•••D

ABASHED
ADAPTED
ALARMED
AMASSED
AVAILED
AWAITED
AWARDED
BEACHED
BEARDED
BIASSED
BLABBED
BLACKED
BLANKED
BLASTED
BLATTED
BOARDED
BOASTED
BRAGGED
BRAIDED
BRAINED
BRAISED
BRANDED
BRAWLED
CHAINED
CHAIRED
CHALKED
CHAMPED
CHANCED
CHANGED
CHANTED
CHAPPED
CHARGED
CHARMED
CHARRED
CHARTED
CHATTED
CLACKED
CLAIMED
CLAMMED
CLAMPED
CLANGED
CLANKED
CLAPPED
CLASHED
CLASPED
CLASSED
COACHED
COASTED
CRABBED
CRACKED
CRADLED
CRAFTED
CRAMMED
CRAMPED
CRANKED
CRASHED
CRAWDAD
CRAWLED
DEADEND
DIAMOND
DRAFTED
DRAGGED
DRAINED
DRATTED
DRAWLED
DWARFED
ELAPSED
EMAILED
ENABLED
ENACTED
EXACTED
EXALTED
FEASTED
FLACCID
FLAGGED
FLAILED
FLAMBED
FLANKED
FLAPPED
FLASHED
FLATBED
FLATTED
FRANKED
GLACEED
GLAIRED
GLANCED
GLASSED
GNARLED
GNARRED
GNASHED
GOAHEAD
GOATEED
GRABBED
GRAFTED
GRAINED
GRANTED
GRAPHED
GRASPED
GRASSED
GUARDED
HEARTED
HOARDED
INAWORD
LEACHED
LEARNED
LEASHED
LIAISED
LOATHED
NUANCED
PEACHED
PEARLED
PLACARD
PLAGUED
PLAITED
PLANKED
PLANNED
PLANTED
PLASHED
POACHED
PRAISED
PRANCED
PRANGED
PRANKED
PSALMED
QUACKED
QUAFFED
QUAILED
QUASHED
REACHED
REACTED
READIED
REAIMED
REAIRED
REAREND
REARMED
ROACHED
ROADBED
ROASTED
SCALDED
SCALPED
SCAMMED
SCAMPED
SCANNED
SCANTED
SCARFED
SCARPED
SCARRED
SCATHED
SCATTED
SEABIRD
SEAFOOD
SEAWARD
SEAWEED
SHAFTED
SHAGGED
SHAMMED
SHANKED
SHARPED
SKANKED
SLABBED
SLACKED
SLAMMED
SLANTED
SLAPPED
SLASHED
SLATTED
SMACKED
SMARTED
SMASHED
SNACKED
SNAFUED
SNAGGED
SNAPPED
SNARLED
SPALLED
SPAMMED
SPANKED
SPANNED
SPARGED
SPARKED
SPARRED
SPATTED
SPAWNED
STABBED
STABLED
STACKED
STAFFED
STAGGED
STAINED
STALKED
STALLED
STAMPED
STAPLED
STARRED
STARTED
STARVED
STASHED
SWABBED
SWAMPED
SWANKED
SWAPPED
SWARMED
SWATHED
SWATTED
THANKED
TOADIED
TOASTED
TRACKED
TRAILED
TRAINED
TRAMPED
TRAPPED
TRASHED
TRAWLED
TWANGED
UNAIDED
UNAIMED
UNAIRED
UNARMED
UNASKED
WEARIED
WHACKED
WHAMMED
WHANGED
WHARFED
WRACKED
WRAPPED
YEAREND
YEARNED
ZEALAND

•••AD••

ABRADED
ABRADER
ABRADES
AHEADOF
ALMADEN
AMRADIO
ARCADES
ARCADIA
ARIADNE
ARMADAS
AUBADES
BREADED
BREADTH
BROADAX
BROADEN
BROADER
BROADLY
CBRADIO
CELADON
CICADAE
CICADAS
CITADEL
DECADES
DREADED
ECUADOR
FACADES
FARADAY
FMRADIO
GELADAS
INVADED
INVADER
INVADES
KNEADED
KNEADER
MACADAM
MATADOR
MIKADOS
MIRADOR
NAIADES
NEVADAN
NOMADIC
PALADIN
PANADAS
PAPADOC
PARADED
PARADES
PARADOX
PICADOR
PLEADED
PLEADER
POMADED

POMADES
POSADAS
RAMADAN
RAMADAS
SALADIN
TIRADES
TREADED
TREADER
TREADLE
UNLADES

•••A•D•

BACARDI
BOIARDO
BRIARDS
CANARDS
COWARDS
DEMANDS
DOTARDS
EDWARDS
ENGARDE
ERRANDS
EXPANDS
GERALDO
HAZARDS
HERALDS
HOWARDS
IDCARDS
INNARDS
INWARDS
ISLANDS
IZZARDS
LIGANDS
LIZARDS
MARAUDS
MIRANDA
NOCANDO
ONWARDS
ORGANDY
ORLANDO
ORMANDY
PETARDS
PICARDY
REGARDS
REMANDS
RENARDS
RESANDS
RETARDS
REWARDS
RIBANDS
RICARDO
ROBARDS
ROLAIDS
STRANDS
TABARDS
TOWARDS
UNHANDS
UNHANDY
UPLANDS
UPWARDS
VERANDA
VIVALDI
WCHANDY
WIZARDS

•••A••D

ABLATED
ABRADED
AERATED
ALLAYED
ANTACID
ARRAYED
ASHAMED
ASSAYED
AVIATED
BEHAVED
BELATED
BELAYED
BERATED
BLEARED
BLEATED
BLOATED
BREADED
CEDARED
CHEATED
CLEANED
CLEARED
CLEAVED
CLOAKED
CREAKED
CREAMED
CREASED
CREATED
CROAKED
DAMAGED
DEBASED
DEBATED
DECAPOD
DECAYED
DEFACED
DEFAMED
DELAYED
DILATED
DONATED
DREADED
DREAMED
EFFACED
EMBAYED
ENCAGED
ENCASED
ENGAGED
ENLACED
ENRAGED
EQUALED
EQUATED
ESCAPED
ESSAYED
EXHALED
FIXATED
FLOATED
FORAGED
FREAKED
GALAHAD
GARAGED
GLEAMED
GLEANED
GLOATED
GREASED
GROANED
GYRATED
ICHABOD
IDEATED
IMPALED
INCASED
INHALED
INVADED
INVALID
KAYAKED
KNEADED
LIEABED
LIGATED
LOCATED
LUXATED
MALAMUD
MANAGED
MEDALED
MENACED
MUTATED
NEGATED
NOTATED
NUTATED
OCEANID
PARADED
PEDALED
PETALED
PHRASED
PIRATED
PLEADED
PLEASED
PLEATED
POMADED
PYRAMID
RAVAGED
REBATED
RECANED
REDATED
REFACED
REGALED
RELACED
RELATED
RELAXED
RELAYED
RENAMED
REPAVED
RERATED
RESAWED
RETAPED
RETAXED
REWAXED
RIVALED
ROTATED
SAVAGED
SCRAPED
SEDATED
SHEARED
SHEAVED
SMEARED
SNEAKED
SOFABED
SPEARED
SPLAYED
SPRAYED
SQUALID
SQUARED
STEAMED
STRAFED
STRAYED
SUGARED
SWEATED
TOTALED
TREADED
TREATED
TWEAKED
UNBAKED
UNCAGED
UNCASED
UNDATED
UNFAZED
UNLACED
UNNAMED
UNPAVED
UNRATED
UNSATED
UNTAMED
UNTAPED
UPDATED
VACATED
VOYAGED
WREAKED

••••AD•

AIRMADA
ALIDADE
ALREADY
AOUDADS
AVOCADO
BALLADE
BALLADS
BEHEADS
BRAVADO
BRIGADE
BROCADE
BYROADS
CASCADE
CHARADE
COCKADE
COMRADE
CRUSADE
CRUSADO
CRUZADO
DEGRADE
DOODADS
ENNEADS
ESTRADA
FORBADE
GAMBADO
GRANADA
GRENADA
GRENADE
HEPTADS
HUNYADY
INROADS
KEYPADS
LAMBADA
LIMEADE
MAENADS
MANMADE
MYRIADS
OCANADA
OGDOADS
PARKADE
PASSADO
PENTADS
PERVADE
REGRADE
RELOADS
REREADS
RETRADE
ROULADE
SPREADS
TETRADS
THREADS
THREADY
TORNADO
TOSTADA
UNLOADS
UNREADY
UPGRADE
UPLOADS
WANTADS

••••A•D

ABELARD
AIRRAID
APPLAUD
ARMBAND
ASHLAND
AWKWARD
AYNRAND
BALLARD
BANDAID
BARMAID
BARNARD
BERNARD
BIGBAND
BOMBARD
BRIGAND
BUSTARD
BUZZARD
COLLARD
COMMAND
CONGAED
COPLAND
COWHAND
CUECARD
CUSTARD
DABHAND
DASTARD
DEFRAUD
DIEHARD
DILLARD
DISBAND
DISCARD
DULLARD
EDOUARD
EMERALD
ENGLAND
FINLAND
FORWARD
FOULARD
FROWARD
GARLAND
GIZZARD
GODDARD
GOTLAND
HAGGARD
HALYARD
HARVARD
HATBAND
HAYWARD
HENNAED
HOLLAND
HUBBARD
HUSBAND
IBNSAUD
ICELAND
INBOARD
IRELAND
JUGBAND
JUTLAND
KEYCARD
KOOLAID
LAGGARD
LANYARD
LAPLAND
LEEWARD
LEGRAND
LEONARD
LEOPARD
LEOTARD
LOLLARD
LOMBARD
LOWLAND
LOWPAID
MALLARD
MANSARD
MAYNARD
MERMAID
MIDLAND
MILHAUD
MILLAND
MILLARD
MISLAID
MISSAID
MONTAND
MUSTARD
NAYSAID
NIGGARD
NORMAND
OAKLAND
OFFHAND
OLDHAND
OLDMAID
ONBOARD
ONGUARD
OPERAND
ORCHARD
OUTLAID
OUTLAND
OUTWARD
PACKARD
PEPPARD
PICCARD
PIEBALD
PLACARD
POLKAED
PONIARD
PREPAID
REHEARD
REYNARD
RICHARD
RIMBAUD
ROSTAND
RUDYARD
RUMBAED
SAMBAED
SEAWARD
SHEPARD
SKYWARD
STEWARD
SUNMAID
TANKARD
TOYLAND
TUSSAUD
UNHEARD
UPBRAID
WAYLAID
WAYWARD
WELLAND
WETLAND
WILLARD
WOODARD
ZEALAND

•••••AD

AIRHEAD
AMISTAD
ANYROAD
ARMLOAD
BAGHDAD
BIGHEAD
CARLOAD
CATHEAD
CRAWDAD
EGGHEAD
FATHEAD
FOOTPAD
GALAHAD
GOAHEAD
GOESBAD
HELIPAD
HOTHEAD
INSTEAD
JUGHEAD
KNEEPAD
LIKEMAD
LILYPAD
LIPREAD
LOWROAD
MISLEAD
MISREAD
NOTEPAD
OFFLOAD
OFFROAD
PAYLOAD
PINHEAD
PRELOAD
REDHEAD
RETREAD
SOLEDAD
SUBHEAD
TOWHEAD
WENTBAD

AE•••••

AEDILES
AELFRIC
AEOLIAN
AERATED
AERATES
AERATOR
AERIALS
AERIEST
AEROBAT
AEROBES
AEROBIC
AEROSOL
AETHERS

A•E••••

ABELARD
ABENAKI
ABETTED
ABETTOR
ABEXTRA
ABEYANT
ACEDOUT
ACERBIC
ACEROLA
ACEROSE
ACESOUT
ACETATE
ACETONE
ADELINE
ADENINE
ADEPTLY
AGEISTS
AGELESS
AGENDAS
AGESAGO
AHEADOF
ALEMBIC
ALENCON
ALERTED
ALERTER
ALERTLY
ALEWIFE
AMENDED
AMENITY
AMERCED
AMERCES
AMERICA
AMERIGO
AMERIKA
AMERIND
ANELING
ANEMONE
ANEROID
APELIKE
APERCUS
APERIES
AREARUG
AREAWAY
ARECIBO
AREOLAE
AREOLAR
AREOLAS
ARETINO
ASEPSIS
ASEPTIC
ATECROW
ATELIER
AVENGED
AVENGER
AVENGES
AVENUES
AVERAGE
AVERRED
AVERTED
AWELESS
AWESOME
AYEAYES

A••E•••

ABREAST
ABSENCE
ABSENTS
ACCEDED
ACCEDER
ACCEDES
ACCENTS
ACCEPTS
ACHENES
ACHERON
ACHESON
ACREAGE
ACTEDON
ACTEDUP
ADDEDIN
ADDEDON
ADDEDTO
ADDEDUP
ADDENDA
ADDENDS
ADHERED
ADHERES
ADRENAL
ADVENTS
ADVERBS
ADVERSE
ADVERTS
AFFECTS
AFREETS
AGREETO
AILERON
AIMEDAT
AIMEDTO
ALBEDOS
ALBENIZ
ALBERTA
ALBERTO
ALDENTE
ALGEBRA
ALGERIA
ALIENEE
ALIENOR
ALKENES
ALLEARS
ALLEGED
ALLEGER
ALLEGES
ALLEGRO
ALLELES
ALLENBY
ALLENDE
ALLERGY
ALLEYES
ALREADY
ALTERED
ALTERER
ALVEOLI
AMHERST
AMMETER
AMNESIA
AMNESTY
AMOEBAE
AMOEBAS
AMOEBIC
AMPERES
ANAEMIA
ANAEMIC
ANDEANS
ANGELES
ANGELIC
ANGELOU
ANGELUS
ANGERED
ANNEALS
ANNELID
ANNETTE
ANNEXED
ANNEXES
ANTEDUP
ANTEING
ANTENNA
ANTESUP
APHELIA
APHESES
APLENTY
APPEALS
APPEARS
APPEASE
APPENDS
APTERAL
AQUEOUS
ARDENCY
ARIETTA
ARLEDGE
ARMENIA
ARPENTS
ARREARS
ARRESTS
ARSENAL
ARSENIC
ARSENIO
ARTEMIS
ARTEMUS
ASCENDS
ASCENTS
ASCETIC
ASKEDIN
ASPECTS
ASPERSE
ASSEGAI
ASSENTS
ASSERTS
ATHEART
ATHEISM
ATHEIST
ATLEAST
ATPEACE
ATTEMPT
ATTENDS
ATTESTS
AUGENDS
AUREATE
AUREOLA
AUREOLE
AUTEURS
AXSEEDS
AZTECAN

A•••E••

ABIDEBY
ABILENE
ABUSERS
ACADEME
ACADEMY
ACCRETE
ACHIEST
ACHIEVE
ACTAEON
ACTRESS
ACUMENS
ACUTELY
ADDRESS
ADORERS
AERIEST
AETHERS
AFREETS
AGELESS
AGGRESS
AGILELY
AGREETO
AIDLESS
AIGRETS
AILMENT
AIMLESS
AIRHEAD
AIRIEST
AIRLESS
ALAMEDA
ALAMEIN
ALCHEMY
ALFIERI
ALFREDO
ALGIERS
ALIMENT
ALLHEAL
ALLHERE
AMADEUS
AMATEUR
AMBIENT
AMBLERS
AMPLEST
AMULETS
ANADEMS
ANAHEIM
ANAPEST
ANCIENT
ANDREAS
ANDRESS
ANDREWS
ANGLERS
ANISEED
ANKLETS
ANSWERS
ANTAEUS
ANTBEAR
ANTHEMS
ANTHERS
ANTLERS
ANTWERP
ANXIETY
APOGEES
APPLETS
APTNESS
ARAMEAN
ARCHERS
ARCHERY
ARGUERS
ARIDEST
ARMLESS
ARMLETS
ARMREST
ARRIERE
ARTDECO
ARTIEST
ARTLESS
ASHIEST
ASHLESS
ATHLETE
AUGMENT
AUKLETS
AUSTERE
AVOCETS
AVOWERS
AWAKENS
AWAREOF
AWELESS
AWNLESS
AXSEEDS
AZALEAS

A••••E•

ABASHED
ABASHES
ABDOMEN
ABETTED
ABJURED
ABJURES
ABLATED
ABLATES
ABORTED
ABRADED
ABRADER
ABRADES
ABUTTED
ABYSSES
ACCEDED
ACCEDER
ACCEDES
ACCRUED
ACCRUES
ACCUSED
ACCUSER
ACCUSES
ACHATES
ACHENES
ACTIVES
ADAPTED
ADAPTER
ADDUCED
ADDUCES
ADFINEM
ADHERED
ADHERES
ADJURED
ADJURES
ADMIRED
ADMIRER
ADMIRES
ADMIXED
ADMIXES
ADOPTED
ADOPTEE
ADOPTER
ADORNED
ADORNER
ADVISED
ADVISER
ADVISES
AEDILES
AERATED
AERATES
AEROBES
AFFINES
AFFIXED
AFFIXES
AFRAMES
AGNATES
AGNOMEN
AIRCREW
AITCHES
ALARMED
ALARMER
ALBUMEN
ALCOVES
ALERTED
ALERTER
ALIASES
ALIENEE
ALIGNED
ALIGNER
ALKENES
ALLAYED
ALLAYER
ALLEGED
ALLEGER
ALLEGES
ALLELES
ALLEYES
ALLOVER
ALLOWED
ALLOYED
ALLUDED
ALLUDES
ALLURED
ALLURES
ALMADEN
ALTERED
ALTERER
ALUNSER
ALVAREZ
AMASSED
AMASSER
AMASSES
AMBRIES
AMENDED
AMERCED
AMERCES
AMMETER
AMPERES
AMPULES
ANDOVER
ANGELES
ANGERED
ANGRIER
ANISEED
ANNABEL
ANNALEE
ANNEXED
ANNEXES
ANNOYED
ANOMIES
ANOTHER
ANTARES
ANTIBES
ANTIGEN
ANTSIER
ANYONES
APACHES
APERIES
APHESES
APOGEES
APOTHEM
APPAREL
APPLIED
APPLIES
APPOSED
APPOSES
APRONED
APSIDES
AQUIFER
AQUIVER
ARALSEA
ARBITER
ARBORED
ARCADES
ARGIVES
ARGYLES
ARMORED
ARMORER
ARMURES
AROUSED
AROUSES
ARRASES
ARRAYED
ARRISES
ARRIVED
ARRIVER
ARRIVES
ARTSIER
ASHAMED
ASPIRED
ASPIRER
ASPIRES
ASSAYED
ASSAYER
ASSIZES
ASSUMED
ASSUMES
ASSURED
ASSURES
ASUNDER
ATELIER
ATHOMES
ATLASES
ATOMIES
ATONIES
ATTIMES
ATTIRED
ATTIRES
ATTUNED
ATTUNES
AUBADES
AUDILES
AUDITED
AUGURED
AUNTIES
AURALEE
AUSSIES
AVAILED
AVENGED
AVENGER
AVENGES
AVENUES
AVERRED
AVERTED
AVIATED
AVIATES
AVOIDED
AVONLEA
AVULSED
AVULSES
AWAITED
AWARDED
AWARDEE
AWARDER
AYEAYES
AZODYES

A•••••E

AAMILNE
ABALONE
ABILENE
ABRIDGE
ABSENCE
ABSOLVE
ABUSIVE
ACADEME
ACCRETE
ACEROSE
ACETATE
ACETONE
ACHIEVE
ACOLYTE
ACONITE
ACQUIRE
ACREAGE
ACTABLE
ACTFIVE
ACTUATE
ADAMITE
ADDABLE
ADDIBLE
ADELINE
ADENINE
ADIPOSE
ADJUDGE
ADOLPHE
ADOPTEE
ADULATE
ADVANCE
ADVERSE
AFFABLE
AFFAIRE
AGITATE
AGONISE
AGONIZE
AGRAFFE
AIRBASE
AIRDATE
AIRFARE
AIRHOLE
AIRLANE
AIRLIKE
AIRLINE
AIRMILE
AIRTIME
AIRWAVE
ALAMODE
ALDENTE
ALEWIFE
ALIDADE
ALIENEE
ALLENDE
ALLGONE
ALLHERE
ALLOFME
ALLTIME
ALOHAOE
ALUMNAE
AMATIVE
AMBROSE
AMIABLE
AMIBLUE
AMOEBAE
AMPOULE
AMYLASE
ANALYSE
ANALYZE
ANATOLE
ANDANTE
ANEMONE
ANILINE
ANIMATE
ANNALEE
ANNETTE
ANODISE
ANODIZE
ANODYNE
ANTIQUE
ANTLIKE
ANTOINE
ANYMORE

ANYTIME
APATITE
APELIKE
APOCOPE
APOSTLE
APPEASE
APPRISE
APPRIZE
APPROVE
ARACHNE
ARCHIVE
ARCSINE
ARDMORE
AREOLAE
ARGONNE
ARIADNE
ARISTAE
ARLEDGE
ARMHOLE
ARMLIKE
ARMOIRE
ARRANGE
ARRIERE
ARTICLE
ARTISTE
ARTWARE
ASARULE
ASCRIBE
ASININE
ASKANCE
ASPERSE
ASSLIKE
ASSUAGE
ASTAIRE
ASTARTE
ASTRIDE
ATHLETE
ATINGLE
ATISSUE
ATLARGE
ATOMISE
ATOMIZE
ATPEACE
ATSTAKE
ATTACHE
ATTRITE
AUDIBLE
AUGUSTE
AURALEE
AUREATE
AUREOLE
AURICLE
AURORAE
AUSPICE
AUSTERE
AVARICE
AVERAGE
AWARDEE
AWESOME
AXILLAE
AZURITE

•AE••••

CAESARS
CAESIUM
CAESURA
FAERIES
HAEMATO
JAEGERS
LAENNEC
LAERTES
MAENADS
MAESTRI
MAESTRO
MAEWEST

•A•E•••

BABETTE
BADEGGS
BAKEOFF
BALEENS
BALEFUL
BANEFUL
BARENTS
BARETTA
BASEHIT
BASEMAN
BASEMEN
BASENJI
BASEPAY
BATEAUX
BATEMAN
CADENCE
CADENCY
CADENZA
CADETTE
CAKEMIX
CALENDS
CAMEDUE
CAMELIA
CAMELOT
CAMEOED
CAMEOFF
CAMEOUT
CAMERAS
CAMERON
CAPEANN
CAPECOD
CAPELET
CAPELLA
CAPERED
CAREENS
CAREERS
CAREFOR
CAREFUL
CASELAW
CASERNE
CASERNS
CATENAE
CATERED
CATERER
CATERTO
CAVEATS
CAVEDIN
CAVEINS
CAVEMAN
CAVEMEN
CAVERNS
CAVESIN
CAVETTO
CAYENNE
DALETHS
DANELAW
DAREFUL
DARESAY
DARESTO
DATEDLY
DAZEDLY
EAGERER
EAGERLY
EASEDIN
EASEDUP
EASEFUL
EASEOFF
EASEOUT
EASESIN
EASESUP
EATENAT
EATENUP
FABERGE
FACEOFF
FACETED
FADEDIN
FADEINS
FADEOUT
FADESIN
FAGENDS
FAIENCE
FAKEFUR
FAREAST
FATEFUL
GAMELAW
GAMETES
GASEOUS
GATEAUX
GATELEG
GATEMAN
GATEMEN
GATEWAY
GAVELED
GAVEOFF
GAVEOUT
GAVEWAY
GAZEBOS
GAZELLE
GAZETTE
HAMELIN
HAPENNY
HATEFUL
HAVENOT
HAVERED
JADEDLY
JADEITE
JAMESON
JANEDOE
JANEWAY
JAVELIN
LABELED
LABELER
LABELLE
LACEDUP
LACESUP
LAMEDHS
LAMENTS
LAPELED
LATEENS
LATENCY
LATENTS
LATERAL
LATERAN
LATERON
LATEXES
LAVERNE
LAYERED
LAYETTE
MADEFOR
MADEHAY
MADEIRA
MADEOFF
MADEOUT
MADEPAR
MADEWAY
MAGENTA
MAJESTE
MAJESTY
MAJEURE
MAKEFOR
MAKEHAY
MAKEOFF
MAKEOUT
MAKEPAR
MAKESDO
MAKESIT
MAKESUP
MAKEUPS
MAKEWAY
MALEATE
MALEFIC
MANEGES
MARENGO
MATELOT
MATEWAN
NACELLE
NAKEDLY
NAMEDAY
NAMETAG
NANETTE
PACECAR
PAGEANT
PAGEBOY
PAGEFUL
PALEDRY
PALERMO
PALETTE
PANELED
PAPEETE
PAPERED
PAPERER
PARENTS
PATELLA
PATENTS
PATERNO
PAWEDAT
RACECAR
RACEMES
RACEWAY
RAGEFUL
RAKEDIN
RAKEDUP
RAKEOFF
RAKESIN
RAKESUP
RALEIGH
RAMEKIN
RAMESES
RAREBIT
RAREGAS
RAVELED
RAVENED
RAVENNA
RAVEUPS
RAWEGGS
SAGEHEN
SALERNO
SAMECHS
SAMEDAY
SATEENS
SAVEDUP
SAVELOY
SAVESUP
TAGENDS
TAKEAIM
TAKENIN
TAKENON
TAKEOFF
TAKEONE
TAKEOUT
TAKESIN
TAKESON
TAKESTO
TAKESUP
TAKETEN
TALENTS
TAPEMAN
TAPEMEN
TAPERED
TAVERNS
VALENCE
VALENCY
VALERIE
VANESSA
VANEYCK
WADEDIN
WADESIN
WAGERED
WAGERER
WAKEFUL
WAKENED
WAKENER
WAKESUP
WATERED
WATERER
WAVEDIN
WAVELET
WAVEOFF
WAVERED
WAVERER
WAVESIN
ZAREBAS

•A••E••

BACKEND
BACKERS
BADDEST
BADGERS
BADNESS
BAGGERS
BAILEES
BAILERS
BAILEYS
BALDEST
BALEENS
BALLETS
BANKERS
BANNERS
BANTERS
BARBELL
BARBELS
BARBERS
BARGEIN
BARKEEP
BARKERS
BARLESS
BARLEYS
BARNEYS
BARRELS
BARRENS
BARRETT
BARTEND
BARTERS
BASKETS
BASSETS
BASTERS
BATHERS
BATTELS
BATTENS
BATTERS
BATTERY
BAWLERS
BAYLEAF
CABLERS
CABLETV
CACHETS
CADGERS
CAGIEST
CAHIERS
CAKIEST
CALDERA
CALLERS
CALMEST
CALTECH
CALVERT
CAMBERS
CAMPERS
CANCELS
CANDELA
CANIEST
CANKERS
CANNERS
CANNERY
CANSECO
CANTEEN
CANTERS
CAPLESS
CAPLETS
CAPPERS
CARDERS
CAREENS
CAREERS
CARLESS
CARNERA
CARNETS
CARPELS
CARPERS
CARPETS
CARRELS
CARSEAT
CARTELS
CARTERS
CARVERS
CASHEWS
CASTERS
CATBERT
CATHEAD
CATSEYE
DAFTEST
DAGGERS
DAMPENS
DAMPERS
DAMPEST
DAMSELS
DANCERS
DANDERS
DANGERS
DANIELS
DANKEST
DANSEUR
DARKENS
DARKEST
DARLENE
DARNERS
DARTERS
DASHERS
DAUBERS
DAYBEDS
EAGLETS
EARLESS
EARNERS
EARNEST
EASIEST
EASTEND
EASTERN
EASTERS
FABLERS
FAIREST
FALSELY
FALSEST
FALTERS
FALWELL
FANBELT
FANJETS
FARLEFT
FARMERS
FARMERY
FARWEST
FASTENS
FASTEST
FATHEAD
FATHERS
FATLESS
FATNESS
FATTENS
FATTEST
FAUCETS
FAWCETT
FAWNERS
GABBERS
GABFEST
GADDERS
GADGETS
GADGETY
GAFFERS
GAINERS
GAITERS
GALLEON
GALLERY
GALLEYS
GAMIEST
GAMMERS
GANDERS
GANGERS
GANNETS
GANNETT
GAOLERS
GAPLESS
GARDENS
GARMENT
GARNERS
GARNETS
GARRETS
GARRETT
GARTERS
GASJETS
GASKETS
GASLESS
GASPERS
GASSERS
GATHERS
GAUGERS
GAWKERS
HACKERS
HACKETT
HALTERS
HAMLETS
HAMMERS
HAMMETT
HAMPERS
HANGERS
HANKERS
HAPLESS
HAPPENS
HARDENS
HARDEST
HARKENS
HARNESS
HARPERS
HARVEST
HASBEEN
HASTENS
HATLESS
HATTERS
HAUBERK
HAULERS
HAUTEUR
HAWKERS
HAWKEYE
HAWSERS
HAYSEED
HAZIEST
JABBERS
JACKETS
JACKEYS
JAEGERS
JAGLESS
JAILERS
JAMMERS
JAPHETH
JARLESS
JASPERS
JAWLESS
JAYCEES
JAYLENO
JAYVEES
KAISERS
LAAGERS
LABRETS
LACIEST
LACKEYS
LACTEAL
LADDERS
LADLERS
LAGGERS
LAKIEST
LAMBEAU
LAMBENT
LAMBERT
LANCERS
LANCETS
LANDERS
LANKEST
LANTERN
LAPBELT
LAPPETS
LARCENY
LARDERS
LARGELY
LARGESS
LARGEST
LASHERS
LATEENS
LATHERS
LATHERY
LATTENS
LAURELS
LAURENT
LAWLESS
LAWYERS
LAXNESS
LAZIEST
MACBETH
MACHETE
MADDENS
MADDERS
MADDEST
MADNESS
MAEWEST
MAGNETO
MAGNETS
MAGUEYS
MAIDENS
MAILERS
MALLETS
MALTEDS
MALTESE
MANDELA
MANGERS
MANLESS
MANNERS
MANTELS
MANYEAR
MAPPERS
MARCEAU
MARCELS
MARKERS
MARKETS
MARLENE
MARTENS
MARVELS
MASHERS
MASKERS
MASSEUR
MASTERS
MASTERY
MATHERS
MATHEWS
MATLESS
MATTERS
MAUREEN
MAXWELL
MAYHEMS
MAZIEST
NABBERS
NAILERS
NAIVELY
NAIVETE
NAIVETY
NANKEEN
NAPLESS
NAPPERS
NASCENT
NATTERS
OAKFERN
OAKLEAF
OARLESS
OATMEAL
PACKERS
PACKETS
PADDERS
PALIEST
PALLETS
PALTERS
PAMPERS
PANDECT
PANDERS
PANNERS
PANZERS
PAPEETE
PARCELS
PARGETS
PARLEYS
PARSECS
PARSEES
PARSERS
PARVENU
PASSELS
PASSERS
PASSEUL
PASTELS
PASTERN
PASTEUP
PASTEUR
PATIENT
PATNESS
PATTENS
PATTERN
PATTERS
PAUPERS
PAWNEES
PAWNERS
PAYMENT
RABBETS
RACIEST
RACKETS
RAFTERS
RAGGEDY
RAGWEED
RAIDERS
RAILERS
RAIMENT
RAISERS
RAISEUP
RAMBEAU
RAMJETS
RANGERS
RANKERS
RANKEST
RANTERS
RAPIERS
RAPPELS
RAPPERS
RASHERS
RASHEST
RASPERS
RASTERS
RATBERT
RATTERS
RAWDEAL
RAWNESS
SACHEMS
SACHETS
SACKERS
SADDENS
SADDEST
SADNESS
SALIENT
SALIERI
SALLETS
SALTERS
SALVERS
SAMLETS
SANDERS
SANREMO
SAPIENS
SAPIENT
SAPLESS
SAPPERS
SARGENT
SASSERS
SATEENS
SATIETY
SAUCERS
SAUTEED
SAWYERS
TABLEAU
TABLETS
TACKERS
TAFFETA
TAGTEAM
TAILEND
TALKERS
TALLEST
TAMPERS
TANDEMS
TANGELO
TANGENT
TANGERE
TANKERS
TANNERS
TANNERY
TANNEST
TAPPERS
TAPPETS
TARBELL
TARGETS
TARHEEL
TARTEST
TASSELS
TASTERS
TATTERS
TAUTENS
TAUTEST
TAXLESS
VAGUELY
VAGUEST
VAINEST
VALJEAN
VALLEJO
VALLEYS
VAMPERS
VAQUERO
VARIETY
VARLETS
VASTEST
WAGGERY
WAILERS
WAITERS
WAIVERS
WALKERS
WALLETS
WALLEYE
WALTERS
WANDERS
WANIEST
WANNESS
WANNEST
WARDENS
WARDERS
WARIEST
WARLESS
WARMEST
WARRENS
WASHERS
WASTERS
WATTEAU
WAVIEST
WAXBEAN
WAXIEST
WAYLESS
YABBERS
YAKKERS
YAMMERS
YANKEES
YAPPERS
YAWNERS
YAWPERS
ZAFFERS
ZAIREAN
ZAMBEZI
ZANDERS
ZANIEST
ZAPPERS

•A•••E•

BABBLED
BABBLES
BADDIES
BAFFLED
BAFFLER
BAFFLES
BAGGIER
BAGGIES
BAILEES
BAINTER
BALKIER
BALMIER
BALONEY
BANDIED
BANDIES
BANGLES
BANJOES
BANQUET
BANSHEE
BARKEEP
BARKIER
BARKLEY
BARMIER
BARONET
BARRIER
BASEMEN
BASQUES
BATCHED
BATCHES
BATIKED
BATSMEN
BATTIER
BATTLED
BATTLER
BATTLES
BATTUES
BAUBLES
BAULKED
BAWDIER
BAYONET
CABARET
CABBIES
CABINET
CACKLED
CACKLER
CACKLES
CADDIED
CADDIES
CADUCEI
CAIQUES
CAJOLED
CAJOLER
CAJOLES
CALIBER
CALICES
CALIPER
CALOMEL
CALUMET
CALYCES
CALYXES
CAMEOED
CAMISES
CAMPIER
CANAPES
CANDIED
CANDIES
CANDLES
CANINES
CANNIER
CANTEEN
CANTLES
CAPELET
CAPERED
CAPULET
CARAFES
CARAMEL
CARAVEL
CARGOES
CARIBES
CARNIES
CAROLED
CAROLER
CAROMED
CARRIED
CARRIER
CARRIES
CARTIER
CASHIER
CASQUED
CASQUES
CASTLED
CASTLES
CATCHER
CATCHES
CATERED
CATERER
CATTIER
CAUDLES
CAULKED
CAULKER
CAVEMEN
CAVILED
CAVILER
CAYUSES
DABBLED
DABBLER
DABBLES
DADDIES
DAFFIER
DAHOMEY
DAILIES
DAIMLER
DAIRIES
DAISIES
DALLIED
DALLIER
DALLIES
DALTREY
DAMAGED
DAMAGES
DANDIER
DANDIES
DANDLED
DANDLES
DANGLED
DANGLER
DANGLES
DAPPLED
DAPPLES
DARBIES
DARNLEY
DATASET
DAUMIER
DAUNTED
DAWDLED
DAWDLER
DAWDLES
DAZZLED
DAZZLER
DAZZLES
EAGERER
EARLIER
EARTHEN
FABARES
FACADES
FACETED
FAERIES
FAGOTED
FAINTED
FAINTER
FAIRIES
FALAFEL
FAMINES
FANCIED
FANCIER
FANCIES
FARRIER
FARTHER
FATTIER
FAULTED
FAVORED
GABBIER
GABBLED
GABBLES
GABRIEL
GADSDEN
GAGGLES
GAGSTER
GALATEA
GALILEE
GALILEI
GALILEO
GAMBLED
GAMBLER
GAMBLES
GAMBREL
GAMETES
GAMINES
GAMMIER
GANGLED
GANTLET
GARAGED
GARAGES
GARBLED
GARBLES
GARDNER
GARGLED
GARGLES
GASSIER
GATELEG
GATEMEN
GAUCHER
GAUDIER
GAUNTER
GAUZIER
GAVELED
GAWKIER
HAARLEM
HABITED
HACKIES
HACKLED
HACKLES
HACKNEY
HAGGLED
HAGGLER
HAGGLES
HAIRIER
HAIRNET
HALIDES
HALITES
HALOGEN
HAMITES
HAMMIER
HAMSTER
HANDFED
HANDIER
HANDLED
HANDLER
HANDLES
HANDSET
HANGMEN
HANGTEN
HANKIES
HANOVER
HAPPIER
HARDIER
HARDSET
HARPIES
HARRIED
HARRIER
HARRIES
HARRIET
HARSHEN
HARSHER
HASBEEN
HASSLED
HASSLES
HASTIER
HATCHED
HATCHER
HATCHES
HATCHET
HAUNTED

HAVERED
HAYSEED
JACKIES
JACONET
JACQUES
JAGGIER
JAGGIES
JAMMIER
JANACEK
JANGLED
JANGLES
JANSSEN
JANVIER
JAUNTED
JAYCEES
JAYVEES
JAZZIER
JAZZMEN
KAISHEK
KARASEA
KAYAKED
KAYAKER
LABELED
LABELER
LABORED
LABORER
LACQUER
LADDIES
LAENNEC
LAERTES
LAISSEZ
LALAKER
LAMPREY
LANGLEY
LANKIER
LAPELED
LARCHES
LARDIER
LARDNER
LASSIES
LASSOED
LASSOER
LASSOES
LATCHED
LATCHES
LATEXES
LATICES
LAUGHED
LAUGHER
LAUNDER
LAUTREC
LAYERED
LAYOPEN
LAYOVER
MADAMEX
MADCHEN
MAGPIES
MAHONEY
MAIGRET
MAITRED
MAJORED
MALMSEY
MALTIER
MAMBOED
MANAGED
MANAGER
MANAGES
MANATEE
MANEGES
MANFRED
MANGIER
MANGLED
MANGLES
MANGOES
MANLIER
MANTLED
MANTLES
MANXMEN
MARBLED
MARBLES
MARCHED
MARCHER
MARCHES
MARGRET
MARINER
MARINES
MARQUEE
MARQUES
MARQUEZ
MARRIED
MARRIES
MARSHES
MASHIES
MASQUES
MASSIER
MATCHED
MATCHES
MATINEE
MATTHEW
MATURED
MATURER
MATURES
MAUNDER
MAUREEN
MAXBAER
MAYTREE
NAGGIER
NAIADES
NAILSET
NANKEEN
NANNIES
NAPPIES
NARTHEX
NASTIER
NATCHEZ
NATIVES
NATTIER
NATURED
NATURES
NAVVIES
OAKTREE
PADDIES
PADDLED
PADDLER
PADDLES
PAINTED
PAINTER
PAISLEY
PAIUTES
PALACES
PALATES
PALAVER
PALFREY
PALJOEY
PALLIER
PALMIER
PANACEA
PANELED
PANNIER
PANSIES
PANTHER
PAPERED
PAPERER
PARADED
PARADES
PARAPET
PARCHED
PARCHES
PARDNER
PAROLED
PAROLEE
PAROLES
PARQUET
PARRIED
PARRIER
PARRIES
PARSEES
PARSLEY
PARTIED
PARTIER
PARTIES
PARTNER
PARURES
PASSKEY
PASTIER
PATCHED
PATCHES
PATSIES
PATTIES
PAULSEN
PAVANES
PAWKIER
PAWNEES
RABBLES
RACEMES
RACQUET
RADDLED
RADDLES
RADICES
RADIOED
RADIXES
RADOMES
RAFFLED
RAFFLER
RAFFLES
RAGWEED
RAINIER
RALLIED
RALLIER
RALLIES
RAMBLED
RAMBLER
RAMBLES
RAMESES
RANCHED
RANCHER
RANCHES
RANDIER
RANGIER
RANKLED
RANKLES
RANOVER
RAPHAEL
RAPIDER
RAPINES
RASPIER
RASSLED
RASSLES
RATCHET
RATITES
RATTIER
RATTLED
RATTLER
RATTLES
RAVAGED
RAVAGER
RAVAGES
RAVELED
RAVENED
RAVINES
RAZORED
SABINES
SACQUES
SADDLED
SADDLER
SADDLES
SAGEHEN
SAGGIER
SAINTED
SALLIED
SALLIES
SALTIER
SALUTED
SALUTES
SALVOES
SAMBAED
SAMISEN
SAMITES
SAMOYED
SAMPLED
SAMPLER
SAMPLES
SANDIER
SANDMEN
SANIBEL
SAPPIER
SARACEN
SARALEE
SARAZEN
SARKIER
SASSIER
SASSIES
SATCHEL
SATINET
SATIRES
SAUCIER
SAUNTER
SAUTEED
SAVAGED
SAVAGER
SAVAGES
SAVORED
SAVVIER
SAYWHEN
TABBIES
TABORET
TACKIER
TACKLED
TACKLER
TACKLES
TAFFIES
TAILLES
TAINTED
TAKETEN
TALKIER
TALKIES
TALLIED
TALLIER
TALLIES
TALONED
TALUSES
TAMALES
TANAGER
TANGIER
TANGLED
TANGLES
TANGOED
TANSIES
TAPEMEN
TAPERED
TAPSTER
TARDIER
TARHEEL
TARRIED
TARRIER
TARRIES
TARSIER
TASTIER
TATTIER
TATTLED
TATTLER
TATTLES
TAUNTED
TAWNIER
TAXFREE
TAXIMEN
VACATED
VACATES
VALISES
VASTIER
VAULTED
VAULTER
VAUNTED
VAUNTER
WACKIER
WADDIES
WADDLED
WADDLER
WADDLES
WAFFLED
WAFFLER
WAFFLES
WAGERED
WAGERER
WAGGLED
WAGGLES
WAGONER
WAHINES
WAKENED
WAKENER
WALTZED
WALTZER
WALTZES
WAMBLED
WAMBLES
WANGLED
WANGLER
WANGLES
WARBLED
WARBLER
WARBLES
WARTIER
WASHIER
WASPIER
WASTREL
WATCHED
WATCHER
WATCHES
WATERED
WATERER
WATTLES
WAVELET
WAVERED
WAVERER
YACHTED
YAHTZEE
YANKEES
YARDMEN
ZAPATEO
ZAPOTEC
ZAPPIER
ZATOPEK

•A••••E

AAMILNE
BABBAGE
BABETTE
BACKHOE
BAGGAGE
BAGLIKE
BAGPIPE
BALANCE
BALLADE
BANDAGE
BANSHEE
BAPTISE
BAPTIZE
BARCODE
BARNONE
BAROQUE
BARRAGE
BARWARE
BATISTE
BATLIKE
BAUXITE
CABBAGE
CABOOSE
CADENCE
CADETTE
CALCITE
CALIBRE
CALORIE
CALZONE
CAMEDUE
CAMILLE
CANDICE
CANDIDE
CANZONE
CAPABLE
CAPAPIE
CAPRICE
CAPSIZE
CAPSULE
CAPTIVE
CAPTURE
CARBIDE
CARBINE
CARCASE
CARFARE
CARLYLE
CARMINE
CAROUSE
CARTAGE
CASCADE
CASERNE
CASTILE
CATENAE
CATHODE
CATLIKE
CATSEYE
CAYENNE
DARLENE
DASYURE
DAYCARE
DAYMARE
DAYTIME
EARACHE
EARLIKE
EARLOBE
EATABLE
FABERGE
FACULAE
FADLIKE
FAIENCE
FAILURE
FANFARE
FANLIKE
FANZINE
FARGONE
FASTONE
FATIGUE
FATLIKE
GAGLINE
GAGRULE
GALILEE
GARBAGE
GARONNE
GAVOTTE
GAZELLE
GAZETTE
HABITUE
HAGLIKE
HAIRDYE
HATLIKE
HAULAGE
HAWKEYE
HAYRIDE
HAYWIRE
JACCUSE
JADEITE
JAMLIKE
JANEDOE
JASMINE
JAWBONE
JAWLIKE
JAWLINE
JAZZAGE
KARAOKE
LABELLE
LABIATE
LACOSTE
LACTASE
LACTATE
LACTOSE
LACUNAE
LAFARGE
LAFITTE
LALANNE
LALIQUE
LAMINAE
LAPLACE
LAPORTE
LAPROBE
LARAINE
LARAMIE
LASAGNE
LASALLE
LATTICE
LAVALSE
LAVERNE
LAWLIKE
LAYETTE
MACABRE
MACAQUE
MACHETE
MACHINE
MACRAME
MACULAE
MAGNATE
MAGUIRE
MAJESTE
MAJEURE
MALAISE
MALEATE
MALTESE
MALTOSE
MANACLE
MANATEE
MANDATE
MANHOLE
MANIPLE
MANLIKE
MANMADE
MARGATE
MARLENE
MARLOWE
MARQUEE
MARRYME
MASSAGE
MASSIVE
MATINEE
MATISSE
MAURICE
MAYPOLE
MAYTIME
MAYTREE
MAYWINE
NACELLE
NAIVETE
NANETTE
NAPTIME
NARRATE
NASTASE
NATALIE
NAVARRE
OAKLIKE
OAKTREE
OARLIKE
OATLIKE
PACKAGE
PACKICE
PADRONE
PALANCE
PALETTE
PALMATE
PANACHE
PANCAKE
PANICLE
PANPIPE
PANURGE
PAPEETE
PAPLIKE
PAPOOSE
PARABLE
PARKADE
PAROLEE
PARTAKE
PARTITE
PASSAGE
PASSIVE
PASTDUE
PASTIME
PASTURE
PATRICE
PAULINE
PAYABLE
RADIATE
RADICLE
RADULAE
RAGTIME
RAMLIKE
RAMPAGE
RANLATE
RAPTURE
RATABLE
RATHOLE
RATLIKE
RATLINE
RATRACE
RAWHIDE
RAYLIKE
SACLIKE
SALABLE
SALTINE
SALVAGE
SANJOSE
SANTAFE
SAOTOME
SARALEE
SARDINE
SATIATE
SAUSAGE
SAVABLE
SAWLIKE
TACTILE
TADPOLE
TAGLIKE
TAGLINE
TAGSALE
TAKEONE
TAMABLE
TANGERE
TANLINE
TARTARE
TAURINE
TAXABLE
TAXFREE
TAXRATE
VACCINE
VACUOLE
VALANCE
VALENCE
VALERIE
VALUATE
VALVATE
VAMOOSE
VAMPIRE
VANDINE
VANDYKE
VANTAGE
WALLACE
WALLEYE
WALPOLE
WANNABE
WARFARE
WARGAME
WARLIKE
WARTIME
WARZONE
WASTAGE
WATTAGE
WAXLIKE
WAYSIDE
YAHTZEE
YANGTZE
YAOUNDE
YARDAGE

••AE•••

ANAEMIA
ANAEMIC
PHAEDRA
PHAETON
PRAETOR

••A•E••

ACADEME
ACADEMY
ALAMEDA
ALAMEIN
AMADEUS
AMATEUR
ANADEMS
ANAHEIM
ANAPEST
ARAMEAN
AWAKENS
AWAREOF
AZALEAS
BEAKERS
BEANERY
BEARERS
BEATERS
BEAVERS
BLADERS
BLAZERS
BOATELS
BOATERS
BRACERO
BRACERS
BRACEUP
BRALESS
BRAVELY
BRAVERY
BRAVEST
BRAYERS
CHALETS
CHAPEAU
CHAPELS
CHASERS
CHATEAU
CLARETS
CLAVELL
CLAWERS
COALERS
COAXERS
CRATERS
CRAVENS
CRAVERS
DEADEND
DEADENS
DEADEYE
DEAFENS
DEAFEST
DEALERS
DEANERY
DEAREST
DIADEMS
DIALECT
DIALERS
DIAPERS
DRAPERS
DRAPERY
DRAWERS
ELATERS
ENAMELS
ERASERS
ETAGERE
EVADERS
FEARERS
FLAKERS
FLANEUR
FLAREUP
FRAMEUP
GLACEED
GLADEYE
GLAZERS
GNAWERS
GOAHEAD
GOATEED
GOATEES
GRADERS
GRATERS
GRAVELS
GRAVELY
GRAVERS
GRAVEST
GRAYEST
GRAZERS
HEADERS
HEALERS
HEARERS
HEATERS
HEAVEHO
HEAVENS
HEAVERS
HEAVETO
HIALEAH
HOAXERS
IMAGERS
IMAGERY
IMARETS
INAHEAP
INAMESS
INANELY
INANEST
INAWEOF
IPANEMA
IRATELY
IRATEST
KNAVERY
KRATERS
LAAGERS
LEADERS
LEAKERS
LEANERS
LEANEST
LEAPERS
LEASERS
LEAVEIN
LEAVENS
LOADERS
LOAFERS
LOANERS
MEANEST
MOANERS
NEAREST
NEATENS
NEATEST
ONAGERS
ONATEAR
PEABEAN
PEAHENS
PEAVEYS
PHASEIN
PHASERS
PLACEBO
PLACERS
PLANERS
PLANETS
PLATEAU
PLATENS
PLATERS
PLAYERS
PRATERS
PRAYERS
QUAKERS
QUAVERS
QUAVERY
READERS
REAGENT
REAMERS
REAPERS
REAREND
REARERS
ROAMERS
ROARERS
SCALENE
SCALERS
SCARERS
SCAREUP
SEABEDS
SEABEES
SEALEGS
SEALERS
SEATERS
SEAWEED
SHAKERS
SHAKEUP
SHAPELY
SHAPERS
SHAPEUP
SHAREIN
SHARERS
SHAVERS
SIAMESE
SKATERS
SLAVERS
SLAVERY
SLAVEYS
SLAYERS
SOAKERS
SOAPERS
SOARERS
SPACERS
SPADERS
SPARELY
SPAREST
STAGERS
STALELY
STALEST
STAMENS
STAREAT
STARERS
STARETS
STATELY
SUAVELY
SUAVEST
SWAYERS
TEALEAF
TEALESS
TEASELS
TEASERS
TEASETS
THALERS
TRABERT
TRACERS
TRACERY
TRADEIN
TRADEON
TRADERS
TRADEUP
TRAGEDY
TRAPEZE
TRAVELS
TRAVERS
TUAREGS
WEAKENS
WEAKEST
WEARERS
WEASELS
WEAVERS
WHALERS
YEAREND
YEATEAM

••A••E•

ABASHED
ABASHES
ADAPTED
ADAPTER
ALARMED
ALARMER
AMASSED
AMASSER
AMASSES
APACHES
ARALSEA
AVAILED
AWAITED
AWARDED
AWARDEE
AWARDER
BEACHED
BEACHES
BEADIER
BEADLES
BEAGLES
BEAMIER
BEANIES
BEARDED
BEATLES
BIALIES
BIASSED
BLABBED
BLABBER
BLACKED
BLACKEN
BLACKER
BLADDER
BLANDER
BLANKED
BLANKER
BLANKET
BLARNEY
BLASTED
BLASTER
BLATHER
BLATTED
BOARDED
BOARDER
BOASTED
BOASTER
BOATMEN
BRACKEN
BRACKET
BRADLEE
BRADLEY
BRAGGED
BRAGGER
BRAIDED
BRAIDER
BRAINED
BRAISED
BRAISES
BRANDED
BRANDER
BRASHER
BRASSES
BRAVOES
BRAWLED
BRAWLER
BRAZIER
CHAINED
CHAIRED
CHAISES
CHALKED
CHAMBER
CHAMFER
CHAMPED
CHANCED
CHANCEL
CHANCER
CHANCES
CHANGED
CHANGER
CHANGES
CHANNEL
CHANTED
CHANTER
CHANTEY
CHAPLET
CHAPMEN
CHAPPED
CHAPTER
CHARGED
CHARGER
CHARGES
CHARIER
CHARLES
CHARLEY
CHARMED
CHARMER
CHARRED
CHARTED
CHARTER
CHASSES
CHASTEN
CHASTER
CHATTED
CHATTEL
CHATTER
CHAUCER
CLABBER
CLACKED
CLAIMED
CLAIMER
CLAMBER
CLAMMED
CLAMMER
CLAMPED
CLANGED
CLANKED
CLAPPED
CLAPPER
CLAQUES
CLASHED
CLASHES
CLASPED
CLASSED
CLASSES
CLATTER
CLAUSES
CLAVIER
CLAYIER
COACHED
COACHES
COARSEN
COARSER
COASTED
COASTER
CRABBED
CRABBER
CRACKED
CRACKER
CRADLED
CRADLES
CRAFTED
CRAFTER
CRAMMED
CRAMMER
CRAMPED
CRANKED
CRASHED
CRASHES
CRASSER
CRAWLED
CRAWLER
CRAZIER
CRAZIES
DEADSEA
DEADSET
DEARIES
DIARIES
DRABBER
DRAFTED
DRAFTEE
DRAGGED
DRAGGER
DRAGNET
DRAINED
DRAINER
DRATTED
DRAWLED
DWARFED
DWARVES

EDASNER
ELAPSED
ELAPSES
EMAILED
EMANUEL
ENABLED
ENABLES
ENACTED
EPAULET
EVACUEE
EVANDER
EVANGEL
EXACTED
EXACTER
EXALTED
FEASTED
FEATHER
FIACRES
FIANCEE
FIANCES
FLAGGED
FLAGMEN
FLAILED
FLAKIER
FLAMBED
FLAMBES
FLAMIER
FLANGES
FLANKED
FLANKER
FLANNEL
FLAPPED
FLAPPER
FLASHED
FLASHER
FLASHES
FLATBED
FLATLET
FLATTED
FLATTEN
FLATTER
FLAXIER
FOAMIER
FRAILER
FRAISES
FRANCES
FRANKED
FRANKEN
FRANKER
FRAPPES
FRASIER
FRAWLEY
FRAZIER
GLACEED
GLACIER
GLADDEN
GLADDER
GLAIRED
GLANCED
GLANCES
GLASSED
GLASSES
GLAZIER
GNARLED
GNARRED
GNASHED
GNASHES
GOAFTER
GOALIES
GOATEED
GOATEES
GRABBED
GRABBER
GRAFTED
GRAINED
GRAMMER
GRAMMES
GRANDEE
GRANDER
GRANGER
GRANGES
GRANTED
GRANTEE
GRAPHED
GRAPIER
GRAPNEL
GRASPED
GRASSED
GRASSES
GRAVIES
GUARDED
GUARDEE
HAARLEM
HEADIER
HEADMEN
HEADSET
HEARKEN
HEARTED
HEARTEN
HEATHEN
HEATHER
HEATTER
HEAVIER
HEAVIES
HOAGIES
HOARDED
HOARDER
HOARIER
HOARSEN
HOARSER
IMAGOES
INAPTER
INASTEW
KEARNEY
KNACKER
LEACHED
LEACHES
LEADIER
LEAFIER
LEAFLET
LEAGUES
LEAKIER
LEANDER
LEARIER
LEARJET
LEARNED
LEARNER
LEASHED
LEASHES
LEATHER
LIAISED
LIAISES
LOACHES
LOAMIER
LOATHED
LOATHES
MEALIER
MEALIES
MEANDER
MEANIES
MEASLES
MEATIER
NUANCED
NUANCES
ONADIET
OPAQUES
ORACLES
ORANGES
ORANGEY
PEACHED
PEACHES
PEARLED
PEATIER
PIASTER
PLACKET
PLAGUED
PLAGUES
PLAICES
PLAINER
PLAITED
PLANKED
PLANNED
PLANNER
PLANTED
PLANTER
PLAQUES
PLASHED
PLASHES
PLASTER
PLATIER
PLATTER
PLAYLET
PLAYPEN
POACHED
POACHER
POACHES
PRAISED
PRAISER
PRAISES
PRANCED
PRANCER
PRANCES
PRANGED
PRANKED
PSALMED
PSALTER
QUACKED
QUAFFED
QUAFFER
QUAILED
QUAKIER
QUARREL
QUARTER
QUARTET
QUASHED
QUASHES
REACHED
REACHES
REACTED
READIED
READIER
READIES
REAIMED
REAIRED
REARMED
ROACHED
ROACHES
ROADBED
ROADIES
ROASTED
ROASTER
SCALDED
SCALIER
SCALPED
SCALPEL
SCALPER
SCAMMED
SCAMPED
SCAMPER
SCANNED
SCANNER
SCANTED
SCANTER
SCARCER
SCARFED
SCARIER
SCARLET
SCARPED
SCARPER
SCARRED
SCARVES
SCATHED
SCATHES
SCATTED
SCATTER
SEABEES
SEAMIER
SEANCES
SEAWEED
SHADIER
SHAFFER
SHAFTED
SHAGGED
SHAKIER
SHAKOES
SHAMMED
SHANKED
SHANTEY
SHAPLEY
SHARKEY
SHARPED
SHARPEI
SHARPEN
SHARPER
SHATNER
SHATTER
SHAWNEE
SKANKED
SKANKER
SLABBED
SLACKED
SLACKEN
SLACKER
SLAMMED
SLAMMER
SLANDER
SLANTED
SLAPPED
SLASHED
SLASHER
SLASHES
SLATHER
SLATIER
SLATTED
SMACKED
SMACKER
SMALLER
SMARTED
SMARTEN
SMARTER
SMASHED
SMASHER
SMASHES
SMATTER
SNACKED
SNACKER
SNAFUED
SNAGGED
SNAKIER
SNAPPED
SNAPPER
SNARLED
SOAPIER
SPACIER
SPALLED
SPAMMED
SPAMMER
SPANDEX
SPANIEL
SPANKED
SPANKER
SPANNED
SPANNER
SPARGED
SPARGES
SPARKED
SPARRED
SPARSER
SPATTED
SPATTER
SPAWNED
STABBED
STABLED
STABLER
STABLES
STACKED
STAFFED
STAFFER
STAGGED
STAGGER
STAGIER
STAIDER
STAINED
STAINER
STALKED
STALKER
STALLED
STAMMER
STAMPED
STANCES
STANDEE
STANLEE
STANLEY
STAPLED
STAPLER
STAPLES
STARKER
STARLET
STARRED
STARTED
STARTER
STARVED
STARVES
STASHED
STASHES
STASSEN
STATUES
SWABBED
SWAGGER
SWALLET
SWAMPED
SWANKED
SWANKER
SWANSEA
SWAPPED
SWAPPER
SWARMED
SWATHED
SWATHES
SWATTED
SWATTER
TEACHER
TEACHES
TEARIER
TEATREE
THANKED
TOADIED
TOADIES
TOASTED
TOASTER
TRACHEA
TRACKED
TRACKER
TRAILED
TRAILER
TRAINED
TRAINEE
TRAINER
TRAMMEL
TRAMPED
TRANCES
TRAPPED
TRAPPER
TRASHED
TRASHES
TRAWLED
TRAWLER
TWANGED
UNAIDED
UNAIMED
UNAIRED
UNARMED
UNASKED
UPATREE
VEALIER
WEARIED
WEARIER
WEARIES
WEATHER
WHACKED
WHAMMED
WHANGED
WHARFED
WHARVES
WHAUDEN
WRACKED
WRAPPED
WRAPPER
YEARNED
YEARNER

••A•••E

ABALONE
ACADEME
ADAMITE
ALAMODE
AMATIVE
ANALYSE
ANALYZE
ANATOLE
APATITE
ARACHNE
ASARULE
AVARICE
AWARDEE
BEASTIE
BEATSME
BEATTIE
BLACKIE
BLANCHE
BRADLEE
BRAILLE
BRAMBLE
BRASSIE
BYANOSE
CHALICE
CHAPPIE
CHARADE
CHARLIE
CLARICE
CRACKLE
CRAPPIE
DEADEYE
DRAFTEE
DRAYAGE
EGALITE
EMANATE
ERASURE
ETAGERE
ETAMINE
EVACUEE
EVASIVE
EXAMINE
EXAMPLE
FEATURE
FIANCEE
FRAGILE
FRANKIE
FRAZZLE
GLADEYE
GRACILE
GRACKLE
GRAHAME
GRANDEE
GRANITE
GRANTEE
GRANULE
GRAPPLE
GRAVURE
GUANINE
GUARDEE
HYALINE
IMAGINE
IMAMATE
INADAZE
IVANHOE
JEANNIE
LEAFAGE
LEAKAGE
MBABANE
MEASURE
ONADARE
ONADATE
OPALINE
PEALIKE
PIASTRE
PLACATE
PRAIRIE
PRALINE
PRATTLE
REALISE
REALIZE
REARGUE
ROANOKE
SCALENE
SEABLUE
SEAFIRE
SEAGATE
SEALANE
SEASIDE
SEATTLE
SHACKLE
SHAMBLE
SHAWNEE
SIAMESE
SNAFFLE
SNAPPLE
SPACKLE
SPANGLE
SPARKLE
STABILE
STANDEE
STANLEE
STARTLE
STATICE
STATURE
STATUTE
SWADDLE
TEACAKE
TEAROSE
TEATIME
TEATREE
TRADUCE
TRAINEE
TRAIPSE
TRAMPLE
TRAPEZE
TWADDLE
ULALUME
UNALIKE
UNAVOCE
UNAWARE
UPATREE
URANITE
WRANGLE

•••AE••

ACTAEON
ANTAEUS
ISRAELI
PIRAEUS

•••A•E•

ABLATED
ABLATES
ABRADED
ABRADER
ABRADES
ACHATES
AERATED
AERATES
AFRAMES
AGNATES
ALIASES
ALLAYED
ALLAYER
ALMADEN
ALVAREZ
ANNABEL
ANNALEE
ANTARES
APPAREL
ARCADES
ARRASES
ARRAYED
ASHAMED
ASSAYED
ASSAYER
ATLASES
AUBADES
AURALEE
AVIATED
AVIATES
AYEAYES
BEHAVED
BEHAVES
BELATED
BELAYED
BERATED
BERATES
BETAKEN
BETAKES
BLEAKER
BLEARED
BLEATED
BLOATED
BORATES
BREADED
BREAKER
BROADEN
BROADER
CABARET
CANAPES
CARAFES
CARAMEL
CARAVEL
CEDARED
CHEAPEN
CHEAPER
CHEATED
CHEATER
CITADEL
CLEANED
CLEANER
CLEARED
CLEARER
CLEAVED
CLEAVER
CLEAVES
CLOAKED
CREAKED
CREAMED
CREAMER
CREASED
CREASES
CREATED
CREATES
CROAKED
CURATES
DAMAGED
DAMAGES
DATASET
DEBAKEY
DEBASED
DEBASES
DEBATED
DEBATER
DEBATES
DECADES
DECAYED
DEFACED
DEFACES
DEFAMED
DEFAMES
DELANEY
DELAYED
DELAYER
DILATED
DILATES
DONATED
DONATES
DOSAGES
DOWAGER
DREADED
DREAMED
DREAMER
EFFACED
EFFACES
EMBAYED
EMPANEL
ENCAGED
ENCAGES
ENCASED
ENCASES
ENGAGED
ENGAGES
ENLACED
ENLACES
ENRAGED
ENRAGES
EQUALED
EQUATED
EQUATES
ERGATES
ESCAPED
ESCAPEE
ESCAPES
ESSAYED
ESTATES
EXHALED
EXHALES
FABARES
FACADES
FALAFEL
FEMALES
FINALES
FIXATED
FIXATES
FLOATED
FLOATER
FORAGED
FORAGER
FORAGES
FREAKED
GALATEA
GARAGED
GARAGES
GLEAMED
GLEANED
GLEANER
GLOATED
GREASED
GREASER
GREASES
GREATER
GREAVES
GROANED
GROANER
GYRATED
GYRATES
HYRACES
HYRAXES
ICEAGES
ICEAXES
IDEAMEN
IDEATED
IDEATES
IMPALED
IMPALES
IMPANEL
INCASED
INCASES
INHALED
INHALER
INHALES
INMATES
INTAKES
INVADED
INVADER
INVADES
IODATES
JANACEK
KARASEA
KAYAKED
KAYAKER
KILAUEA
KNEADED
KNEADER
LALAKER
LEGATEE
LEGATES
LIEABED
LIGATED
LIGATES
LINAGES
LOCALES
LOCATED
LOCATER
LOCATES
LUXATED
LUXATES
MADAMEX
MANAGED
MANAGER
MANAGES
MANATEE
MEDALED
MENACED
MENACES
MENAGES
METATES
MINARET
MIRAGES
MORALES
MUTAGEN
MUTATED
MUTATES
NAIADES
NEGATED
NEGATER
NEGATES
NEWAGER
NOGALES
NONAGES
NOTATED
NOTATES
NUTATED
NUTATES
OBLATES
OCTANES
OCTAVES
OLEATES
OPIATES
ORGATES
OUTAGES
PALACES
PALATES
PALAVER
PANACEA
PARADED
PARADES
PARAPET
PAVANES
PDJAMES
PEDALED
PELAGES
PENATES
PETALED
PHRASED
PHRASES
PIRATED
PIRATES
PLEADED
PLEADER
PLEASED
PLEASER
PLEASES
PLEATED
POMADED
POMADES
POTAGES
PUTAMEN
RAVAGED
RAVAGER
RAVAGES
REBATED
REBATES
RECANED
RECANES
REDATED
REDATES
REFACED
REFACES
REGALED
REGALES
RELACED
RELACES
RELATED
RELATES
RELAXED
RELAXES
RELAYED
REMAKES
RENAMED
RENAMES
REPAPER
REPAVED
REPAVES
RERATED
RERATES
RESALES
RESAWED
RETAKEN
RETAKES
RETAPED
RETAPES
RETAXED
RETAXES
REWAXED
REWAXES
RIVALED
ROTATED
ROTATES
SARACEN
SARALEE
SARAZEN
SAVAGED
SAVAGER
SAVAGES
SCRAPED
SCRAPER
SCRAPES
SEDATED
SEDATER
SEDATES
SENATES
SERAPES
SESAMES
SHEARED
SHEARER
SHEAVED
SHEAVES
SMEARED
SNEAKED
SNEAKER
SOFABED
SOLACES
SPEAKER
SPEARED
SPLAYED
SPRAYED
SPRAYER
SQUARED
SQUARER
SQUARES
STEAMED
STEAMER
STRAFED
STRAFES
STRAYED
SUGARED
SWEARER
SWEATED
SWEATER
TAMALES
TANAGER
TENACES
THEATER
TIRADES
TISANES
TOPAZES
TOTALED
TREADED
TREADER
TREATED
TWEAKED
UNBAKED
UNCAGED
UNCAGES
UNCASED
UNCASES
UNDATED
UNEATEN
UNFAZED
UNLACED
UNLACES
UNLADES
UNMAKES
UNNAMED
UNPAVED
UNRATED
UNRAVEL
UNSATED
UNTAMED
UNTAPED
UPDATED
UPDATES
UPTAKES
URBANER
VACATED
VACATES
VISAGES
VOYAGED
VOYAGER
VOYAGES
WREAKED
ZAPATEO
ZOUAVES

•••A••E

ACTABLE
ADDABLE
ADVANCE
AFFABLE
AFFAIRE
AGRAFFE
AMIABLE
ANDANTE
ANNALEE
ARIADNE
ARRANGE
ASKANCE
ASTAIRE
ASTARTE
ATLARGE
ATTACHE
AURALEE
BALANCE
BECAUSE
BIVALVE
BIZARRE
BREATHE
BUYABLE
CAPABLE
CAPAPIE
CEZANNE
CHEAPIE
CICADAE
CITABLE
CLEANSE
CLOACAE
DEBACLE
DEBARGE
DEFARGE
DEVALUE
DISABLE
DONAHUE
DURABLE
DURANCE
DURANTE
EARACHE
EATABLE
ENGARDE
ENHANCE
ENLARGE
ENMASSE
EQUABLE
ESCAPEE
EXPANSE
EXPARTE
FINAGLE
FINANCE
FIXABLE
FRIABLE
GIRAFFE
GOUACHE
HILAIRE
HIRABLE
IMPASSE
INHASTE
KARAOKE
LAFARGE
LALANNE
LARAINE
LARAMIE
LASAGNE
LASALLE
LAVALSE
LECARRE
LEGATEE
LEHAVRE
LIKABLE
LIVABLE
LOVABLE
MACABRE
MACAQUE
MALAISE
MANACLE
MANATEE
MELANGE
MELANIE
MINABLE
MIRACLE
MIXABLE
MORAINE
MOVABLE
MUTABLE
NATALIE
NAVARRE
NOTABLE
PALANCE
PANACHE
PARABLE
PAYABLE
PENANCE
PICANTE
PLIABLE
POTABLE
RATABLE
REBASTE
RELAPSE
REPASTE
RERAISE
REVALUE
ROGAINE
ROMAINE

ROMANCE
ROSALIE
ROSANNE
ROXANNE
ROYALWE
SALABLE
SARALEE
SAVABLE
SEEABLE
SHEATHE
SIZABLE
STRANGE
STRASSE
SUSANNE
SUZANNE
SYNAPSE
TAMABLE
TAXABLE
TENABLE
THEATRE
TREACLE
TREADLE
UKRAINE
UPRAISE
USEABLE
VALANCE
WREATHE

••••AE•

CONGAED
HENNAED
ISHMAEL
MAXBAER
MICHAEL
POLKAED
RAPHAEL
RUMBAED
SAMBAED
SUNDAES

••••A•E

ACETATE
ACREAGE
ACTUATE
ADULATE
AGITATE
AIRBASE
AIRDATE
AIRFARE
AIRLANE
AIRWAVE
ALIDADE
ALOHAOE
AMYLASE
ANIMATE
APPEASE
ARTWARE
ASSUAGE
ATPEACE
ATSTAKE
AUREATE
AVERAGE
BABBAGE
BAGGAGE
BALLADE
BANDAGE
BARRAGE
BARWARE
BELDAME
BELTANE
BEREAVE
BIGGAME
BIGNAME
BIPLANE
BONDAGE
BRIGADE
BROCADE
BROMATE
BUSFARE
CABBAGE
CARCASE
CARFARE
CARTAGE
CASCADE
CHARADE
CHORALE
CILIATE
CITRATE
CLIMATE
COCKADE
COGNATE
COINAGE
COLGATE
COLLAGE
COLLATE
COMPARE
COMRADE
CONCAVE
CONGAME
CORDAGE
CORDATE
CORKAGE
CORSAGE
COTTAGE
COURAGE
CRUSADE
CUPCAKE
CUTRATE
DAYCARE
DAYMARE
DECLARE
DEFLATE
DEGRADE
DENTATE
DEPLANE
DEPRAVE
DEVIATE
DICTATE
DISEASE
DOCKAGE
DOGBANE
DOGFACE
DRAYAGE
DUEDATE
EDUCATE
EGGCASE
ELEVATE
EMANATE
EMBRACE
EMIRATE
EMULATE
ENCLAVE
ENDGAME
ENGRAVE
ENPLANE
ENSLAVE
ENSNARE
EXPIATE
FANFARE
FERRATE
FOLIAGE
FOLIATE
FOOTAGE
FORBADE
FORGAVE
FORSAKE
FORSALE
FRIGATE
FROMAGE
FURNACE
GARBAGE
GERMANE
GESTATE
GOESAPE
GRAHAME
GRENADE
GRIMACE
GUNWALE
HAULAGE
HECTARE
HENBANE
HERBAGE
HOECAKE
HOSTAGE
HOTCAKE
HOVLANE
HYDRATE
IMAMATE
IMITATE
INADAZE
INFLAME
INFLATE
INGRATE
INPEACE
INPHASE
INPLACE
INSCAPE
INSHAPE
INSTATE
IRONAGE
ISOLATE
ITERATE
JAZZAGE
KILDARE
LABIATE
LACTASE
LACTATE
LAPLACE
LEAFAGE
LEAKAGE
LIMEADE
LINEAGE
LINEATE
LINKAGE
LUGGAGE
MACRAME
MAGNATE
MALEATE
MANDATE
MANMADE
MARGATE
MASSAGE
MBABANE
MEDIATE
MESSAGE
METHANE
MIGRATE
MILEAGE
MISDATE
MISMATE
MISNAME
MISTAKE
MONDALE
MONTAGE
MONTANE
MOORAGE
MOULAGE
MUNDANE
NARRATE
NASTASE
NEONATE
NESCAFE
NEWGATE
NEWWAVE
NITRATE
OBVIATE
OFFBASE
OILCAKE
ONADARE
ONADATE
ONELANE
ONLEAVE
ONSTAGE
OPERATE
OUTFACE
OUTPACE
OUTRACE
OUTRAGE
OUTTAKE
OVERAGE
OVERATE
OVERAWE
OXIDASE
PACKAGE
PALMATE
PANCAKE
PARKADE
PARTAKE
PASSAGE
PEERAGE
PELTATE
PENNAME
PENNATE
PEONAGE
PERCALE
PERVADE
PETNAME
PICKAXE
PILLAGE
PINNACE
PINNATE
PINWALE
PLACATE
PLUMAGE
POLEAXE
PORTAGE
POSTAGE
POTTAGE
PREDATE
PREFACE
PRELATE
PREPARE
PRESAGE
PRESALE
PRETAPE
PRIMATE
PRIVATE
PROBATE
PROFANE
PROPANE
PRORATE
PULSATE
RADIATE
RAMPAGE
RANLATE
RATRACE
RECLAME
REDTAPE
REFRAME
REGRADE
RELEASE
REPLACE
REPLATE
RESCALE
RESTAGE
RESTATE
RETRACE
RETRADE
REWEAVE
RIBCAGE
ROSEATE
ROULADE
RUMMAGE
RUNLATE
SALVAGE
SANTAFE
SATIATE
SAUSAGE
SEAGATE
SEALANE
SELVAGE
SENSATE
SERIATE
SERRATE
SINKAGE
SITUATE
SORBATE
SOUTANE
SPOKANE
STORAGE
STRIATE
SUCRASE
SULFATE
SURFACE
SURNAME
TAGSALE
TARTARE
TAXRATE
TEACAKE
TEENAGE
TERNATE
TERRACE
THEBABE
TILLAGE
TIMBALE
TINWARE
TITRATE
TONNAGE
TOSCALE
TOSPARE
TSQUARE
TWOBASE
TWOLANE
ULULATE
UMBRAGE
UNAWARE
UNCRATE
UNDRAPE
UNWEAVE
UPGRADE
UPSCALE
UPSTAGE
UPSTATE
VALUATE
VALVATE
VANTAGE
VIBRATE
VILLAGE
VINTAGE
VIOLATE
VITIATE
VOLTAGE
VULGATE
WALLACE
WANNABE
WARFARE
WARGAME
WASTAGE
WATTAGE
WEBPAGE
WELFARE
WENTAPE
YARDAGE

•••••AE

ALUMNAE
AMOEBAE
AREOLAE
ARISTAE
AURORAE
AXILLAE
CATENAE
CICADAE
CLOACAE
COPULAE
CORONAE
FACULAE
FIBULAE
GLOSSAE
LACUNAE
LAMINAE
LORICAE
MACULAE
MEDUSAE
NEBULAE
RADULAE
RETINAE

AF•••••

AFFABLE
AFFABLY
AFFAIRE
AFFAIRS
AFFECTS
AFFINES
AFFIRMS
AFFIXED
AFFIXES
AFFLICT
AFFORDS
AFFRAYS
AFFRONT
AFGHANI
AFGHANS
AFRAMES
AFREETS
AFRICAN

A•F••••

ADFINEM
AFFABLE
AFFABLY
AFFAIRE
AFFAIRS
AFFECTS
AFFINES
AFFIRMS
AFFIXED
AFFIXES
AFFLICT
AFFORDS
AFFRAYS
AFFRONT
ALFALFA
ALFIERI
ALFONSO
ALFORJA
ALFREDO
ASFARAS
ATFAULT
AWFULLY

A••F•••

ACTFIVE
ACTFOUR
AELFRIC
AIRFARE
AIRFLOW
AIRFOIL
ANTFARM
ARAFURA
ARMFULS
ARTFILM
ARTFORM
ASHFORD
ASOFNOW

A•••F••

AGRAFFE
AIMSFOR
ALLOFME
ALOOFLY
ANTIFOG
AQUIFER
ASKSFOR

A••••F•

ACIDIFY
AGRAFFE
AIRLIFT
ALEWIFE
ALFALFA
AMPLIFY

A•••••F

AHEADOF
AIRWOLF
AWAREOF

•AF••••

BAFFLED
BAFFLER
BAFFLES
CAFTANS
DAFFIER
DAFFILY
DAFFING
DAFTEST
GAFFERS
GAFFING
HAFNIUM
HAFTING
KAFFIRS
KAFTANS
LAFARGE
LAFITTE
MAFFICK
RAFFISH
RAFFLED
RAFFLER
RAFFLES
RAFTERS
RAFTING
SAFARIS
SAFFRON
TAFFETA
TAFFIES
WAFFLED
WAFFLER
WAFFLES
WAFTING
ZAFFERS

•A•F•••

BAFFLED
BAFFLER
BAFFLES
BAGFULS
BALFOUR
CANFULS
CAPFULS
CARFARE
CARFULS
CATFISH
CATFOOD
DAFFIER
DAFFILY
DAFFING
EARFLAP
EARFULS
FANFARE
GABFEST
GAFFERS
GAFFING
HALFDAN
HALFWAY
HALFWIT
HAYFORK
JARFULS
KAFFIRS
KAUFMAN
LANFORD
LAPFULS
LAWFORD
MAFFICK
MANFRED
MAYFAIR
OAKFERN
PALFREY
PANFISH
PANFULS
PARFAIT
RAFFISH
RAFFLED
RAFFLER
RAFFLES
RATFINK
SAFFRON
SANFORD
SAWFISH
TAFFETA
TAFFIES
TAXFREE
VATFULS
WAFFLED
WAFFLER
WAFFLES
WARFARE
ZAFFERS

•A••F••

BALEFUL
BANEFUL
BASHFUL
CALLFOR
CARAFES
CAREFOR
CAREFUL
DAREFUL
EASEFUL
FACTFUL
FAKEFUR
FALAFEL
FALLFOR
FATEFUL
GAINFUL
HALIFAX
HANDFED
HANDFUL
HARMFUL
HATEFUL
LAIDFOR
LATIFAH
LAYOFFS
LAYSFOR
MADEFOR
MAKEFOR
MALEFIC
PACIFIC
PAGEFUL
PAIDFOR
PAILFUL
PAINFUL
PASSFOR
PAYOFFS
PAYSFOR
RAGEFUL
RATAFIA
SACKFUL
SANDFLY
TACTFUL
TAILFIN
TANKFUL
TARIFFS
WAILFUL
WAITFOR
WAKEFUL
YAWNFUL

•A•••F•

BACKOFF
BAILIFF
BAKEOFF
CALCIFY
CALLOFF
CAMEOFF
CASTOFF
DANDIFY
DASHOFF
EARMUFF
EASEOFF
EASYOFF
FACEOFF
FAIROFF
FALLOFF
FALSIFY
FANCIFY
FARLEFT
GAVEOFF
HANDOFF
HANGOFF
HAULOFF
HAYLOFT
KARLOFF
LAIDOFF
LAYOFFS
LAYSOFF
MACDUFF
MADEOFF
MAGNIFY
MAKEOFF
MARKOFF
MASSIFS
MASTIFF
PAIDOFF
PAIROFF
PALMOFF
PASSOFF
PAWNOFF
PAYOFFS
PAYSOFF
RAKEOFF
RANGOFF
SALSIFY
SANTAFE
SATISFY
TAILOFF
TAKEOFF
TAPSOFF
TARIFFS
WARDOFF
WASHOFF
WAVEOFF

•A••••F

BACKOFF
BAILIFF
BAKEOFF
BARANOF
BAYLEAF
CALLOFF
CAMEOFF
CASTOFF
DASHOFF
EARMUFF
EASEOFF
EASYOFF
FACEOFF
FAIROFF
FALLOFF
GAVEOFF
HANDOFF
HANGOFF
HAULOFF
KARLOFF
LAIDOFF
LAYSOFF
MACDUFF
MADEOFF
MAKEOFF
MARKOFF
MASTIFF
OAKLEAF
PAIDOFF
PAIROFF
PALMOFF
PASSOFF
PAWNOFF
PAYSOFF
RAKEOFF
RANGOFF
TAILOFF
TAKEOFF
TAPSOFF
WALDORF
WARDOFF
WASHOFF
WAVEOFF

••AF•••

ARAFURA
CHAFING
CRAFTED
CRAFTER
CRAFTSY
DEAFENS
DEAFEST
DRAFTED
DRAFTEE
GOAFTER
GRAFTED
GRAFTON
LEAFAGE
LEAFIER
LEAFING
LEAFLET
LOAFERS
LOAFING
PEAFOWL
QUAFFED
QUAFFER
REAFFIX
SEAFANS
SEAFIRE
SEAFOOD
SHAFFER
SHAFTED
SNAFFLE
SNAFUED
STAFFED
STAFFER
TRAFFIC

••A•F••

CHAMFER
DWARFED
FEARFUL
HEATFUL
MOANFUL
PLAYFUL
PRAYFOR
QUAFFED
QUAFFER
REAFFIX
SCARFED
SHAFFER
SNAFFLE
STAFFED
STAFFER
TEARFUL
TRAFFIC
TRAYFUL
UNAWFUL
WHARFED
WHATFOR

••A••F•

BEAROFF
BEATIFY
CLARIFY
GRATIFY
HEADOFF
LEADOFF
PLAYOFF
QUALIFY
SCARIFY
SEALOFF
TEAROFF
WEAROFF

••A•••F

AWAREOF
BEAROFF
HEADOFF
HEARDOF
HEARSOF
INAWEOF
LEADOFF
PLAYOFF
SEALOFF
SEAWOLF
SHADOOF
TEALEAF
TEAROFF
WEAROFF

•••AF••

AGRAFFE
CARAFES
FALAFEL
GIRAFFE
RATAFIA
STRAFED
STRAFES

•••A•F•

AGRAFFE
ALFALFA
GIRAFFE

•••A••F

AHEADOF
BARANOF
BYWAYOF
SPEAKOF

••••AF•

DISTAFF
ENGRAFT
MUSTAFA
NESCAFE
SANTAFE
UPDRAFT

••••A•F

DISTAFF

•••••AF

BAYLEAF
FIGLEAF
FLYLEAF
OAKLEAF
TEALEAF

AG•••••

AGAINST
AGAKHAN
AGARICS
AGASSIZ
AGEISTS
AGELESS
AGENDAS
AGESAGO
AGGRESS
AGILELY
AGILITY
AGITATE
AGITATO
AGNATES
AGNOMEN
AGONISE
AGONIST
AGONIZE
AGOUTIS
AGRAFFE
AGREETO
AGRIPPA
AGROUND

A•G••••

AFGHANI
AFGHANS
AGGRESS
AIGRETS
ALGEBRA
ALGERIA
ALGIERS
ANGELES
ANGELIC
ANGELOU
ANGELUS
ANGERED
ANGLERS
ANGLING
ANGOLAN
ANGORAS
ANGRIER
ANGRILY
ANGULAR
ARGIVES
ARGONNE
ARGUERS
ARGUING
ARGYLES
AUGENDS
AUGMENT
AUGURAL
AUGURED
AUGUSTA
AUGUSTE

A••G•••

ABIGAIL
ADAGIOS
AIRGUNS
ALIGHTS
ALIGNED
ALIGNER
ALLGONE
ANAGRAM
APOGEES
ARUGULA
AVIGNON

A•••G••

ABOUGHT
ALLEGED
ALLEGER
ALLEGES
ALLEGRO
ALRIGHT
AMALGAM
AMONGST
ANTIGEN
ANTIGUA
ASSEGAI
ASSIGNS
ATINGLE
AVENGED
AVENGER
AVENGES

A••••G•

ABRIDGE
ACREAGE
ADJUDGE
AGESAGO
AIRBAGS
AIRINGS
ALLERGY
AMERIGO
ANALOGS
ANALOGY
APOLOGY
ARLEDGE
ARRAIGN
ARRANGE
ASSUAGE
ATLARGE
AVERAGE
AWNINGS

A•••••G

ABASING
ABATING
ABIDING
ABUSING
ACHTUNG
ADDLING
ADORING
ALAKING
ALINING
ALLYING
AMAZING
AMBLING
AMUSING
ANELING
ANGLING
ANTEING
ANTIFOG
ANTILOG
ARCHING
AREARUG
ARGUING
ARISING
ARTSONG
ATONING
AVOWING
AWAKING

•AG••••

BAGFULS
BAGGAGE
BAGGERS
BAGGIER
BAGGIES
BAGGILY
BAGGING
BAGHDAD
BAGLIKE
BAGNOLD
BAGPIPE
CAGIEST
DAGGERS
DAGWOOD
EAGERER
EAGERLY
EAGLETS
EAGLING
FAGENDS
FAGGING
FAGOTED
GAGARIN
GAGGING
GAGGLES
GAGLAWS
GAGLINE
GAGRULE
GAGSTER
HAGDONS
HAGGARD
HAGGISH
HAGGLED
HAGGLER
HAGGLES
HAGLIKE
JAGGIER
JAGGIES
JAGGING
JAGLESS
JAGUARS
LAGGARD
LAGGERS
LAGGING
LAGOONS
LAGUNAS
MAGENTA
MAGICAL
MAGINOT
MAGNANI
MAGNATE
MAGNETO
MAGNETS
MAGNIFY
MAGNUMS
MAGPIES
MAGUEYS

MAGUIRE
MAGYARS
NAGGIER
NAGGING
NAGGISH
PAGEANT
PAGEBOY
PAGEFUL
PAGODAS
RAGBAGS
RAGDOLL
RAGEFUL
RAGGEDY
RAGGING
RAGLANS
RAGMOPS
RAGOUTS
RAGRUGS
RAGTIME
RAGTOPS
RAGWEED
SAGEHEN
SAGGIER
SAGGING
SAGINAW
SAGUARO
TAGALOG
TAGENDS
TAGGANT
TAGGING
TAGLIKE
TAGLINE
TAGSALE
TAGSOUT
TAGTEAM
VAGRANT
VAGUELY
VAGUEST
WAGERED
WAGERER
WAGGERY
WAGGING
WAGGISH
WAGGLED
WAGGLES
WAGGONS
WAGONER
WAGTAIL
ZAGGING

•A•G•••
BADGERS
BADGUYS
BAGGAGE
BAGGERS
BAGGIER
BAGGIES
BAGGILY
BAGGING
BANGING
BANGKOK
BANGLES
BANGSUP
BARGAIN
BARGEIN
BARGING
BATGIRL
CADGERS
CADGING
CALGARY
CAPGUNS
CARGOES
DAGGERS
DANGERS
DANGLED
DANGLER
DANGLES
FAGGING
FARGONE
GADGETS
GADGETY
GAGGING
GAGGLES
GANGERS
GANGING
GANGLED
GANGLIA
GANGSAW
GANGSTA
GANGSUP
GANGTOK
GANGWAY
GARGLED
GARGLES
GAUGERS
GAUGING
GAUGUIN
HAGGARD
HAGGISH
HAGGLED
HAGGLER
HAGGLES
HANGARS
HANGDOG
HANGERS
HANGING
HANGMAN
HANGMEN
HANGOFF
HANGOUT
HANGSIN
HANGSON
HANGSUP
HANGTEN
HANGUPS
HAUGHTY
JAEGERS
JAGGIER
JAGGIES
JAGGING
JANGLED
JANGLES
JARGONS
JARGONY
LAAGERS
LAGGARD
LAGGERS
LAGGING
LANGDON
LANGLEY
LANGTRY
LANGUID
LANGUOR
LANGURS
LARGELY
LARGESS
LARGEST
LARGISH
LAUGHAT
LAUGHED
LAUGHER
LAUGHIN
MACGRAW
MAIGRET
MANGERS
MANGIER
MANGLED
MANGLES
MANGOES
MARGATE
MARGAUX
MARGAYS
MARGINS
MARGRET
MAUGHAM
NAGGIER
NAGGING
NAGGISH
NAUGHTS
NAUGHTY
PARGETS
RAGGEDY
RAGGING
RANGERS
RANGIER
RANGING
RANGOFF
RANGOON
RANGOUT
RAYGUNS
SAGGIER
SAGGING
SANGOUT
SANGRIA
SARGENT
TAGGANT
TAGGING
TANGELO
TANGENT
TANGERE
TANGIER
TANGLED
TANGLES
TANGOED
TANGRAM
TARGETS
VANGOGH
VAUGHAN
WAGGERY
WAGGING
WAGGISH
WAGGLED
WAGGLES
WAGGONS
WANGLED
WANGLER
WANGLES
WARGAME
WARGODS
YANGTZE
ZAGGING

•A••G••
BADEGGS
CAYUGAS
DAMAGED
DAMAGES
FALLGUY
FATIGUE
GALAGOS
GARAGED
GARAGES
HALOGEN
HANDGUN
LASAGNA
LASAGNE
MADIGAN
MALIGNS
MANAGED
MANAGER
MANAGES
MANAGUA
MANEGES
PAANGAS
PAPAGOS
PARAGON
RAREGAS
RAVAGED
RAVAGER
RAVAGES
RAWEGGS
SAVAGED
SAVAGER
SAVAGES
TANAGER

•A•••G•
BABBAGE
BADEGGS
BAGGAGE
BANDAGE
BARONGS
BARRAGE
CABBAGE
CARTAGE
CASINGS
EARWIGS
FABERGE
FACINGS
FARRAGO
GARBAGE
GASBAGS
GASLOGS
HAULAGE
HAZINGS
JAZZAGE
LACINGS
LAFARGE
LAPDOGS
MAKINGS
MARENGO
MASSAGE
PACKAGE
PANURGE
PARINGS
PASSAGE
RAGBAGS
RAGRUGS
RALEIGH
RAMPAGE
RATINGS
RAVINGS
RAWEGGS
SALVAGE
SAPSAGO
SARONGS
SAUSAGE
SAVINGS
SAWLOGS
SAYINGS
TAPINGS
VANGOGH
VANTAGE
WASTAGE
WATTAGE
YARDAGE

•A••••G
BABYING
BACHING
BACKING
BACKLOG
BAGGING
BAILING
BAITING
BALDING
BALKING
BANDING
BANGING
BANKING
BANNING
BARBING
BARGING
BARKING
BARRING
BASHING
BASKING
BASTING
BATHING
BATTING
BATWING
BAWLING
CABLING
CACHING
CADGING
CALKING
CALLING
CALMING
CALVING
CAMPING
CANNING
CANTING
CAPPING
CARDING
CARKING
CARPING
CARTING
CARVING
CASHING
CASTING
CATALOG
CATTING
CAUSING
DABBING
DAFFING
DAMMING
DAMNING
DAMPING
DANCING
DAPPING
DARLING
DARNING
DARTING
DASHING
DAUBING
DAWNING
DAYLONG
EAGLING
EARNING
EARPLUG
EARRING
FAGGING
FAILING
FAIRING
FALLING
FANNING
FARCING
FARMING
FASTING
FAWNING
GABBING
GADDING
GAFFING
GAGGING
GAINING
GAITING
GALLING
GAMMING
GANGING
GAOLING
GAPPING
GARBING
GASHING
GASPING
GATELEG
GATLING
GAUGING
GAUMING
GAWKING
GAWPING
HACKING
HAFTING
HAILING
HALOING
HALTING
HALVING
HAMBURG
HAMMING
HANDBAG
HANDING
HANGDOG
HANGING
HAPPING
HARBURG
HARDING
HARKING
HARMING
HARPING
HASHING
HASPING
HASTING
HATTING
HAULING
HAWKING
JABBING
JACKING
JAGGING
JAILING
JAMMING
JARRING
JAZZING
KAYOING
LACKING
LADLING
LADYBUG
LAGGING
LAMMING
LANDING
LANSING
LAPPING
LAPSING
LAPWING
LARDING
LASHING
LASTING
LATHING
LAUDING
MADDING
MAILBAG
MAILING
MALTING
MANNING
MAPPING
MARKING
MARRING
MASHING
MASKING
MASSING
MATTING
MAULING
NABBING
NAGGING
NAILING
NAMETAG
NAPPING
PACKING
PADDING
PAIRING
PALLING
PALMING
PANNING
PANTING
PARKING
PARRING
PARSING
PARTING
PASSING
PASTING
PATTING
PAULING
PAUSING
PAWNING
RACKING
RAFTING
RAGGING
RAIDING
RAILING
RAINING
RAISING
RAMMING
RANGING
RANKING
RANTING
RAPPING
RASPING
RATTING
RAZZING
SACKING
SAGGING
SAILING
SALTING
SALVING
SAMSUNG
SANDBAG
SANDHOG
SANDING
SAPLING
SAPPING
SASSING
TABBING
TABLING
TACKING
TAGALOG
TAGGING
TAILING
TALKBIG
TALKING
TAMPING
TANKING
TANNING
TAPPING
TARRING
TASKING
TASTING
TATTING
TAXIING
VALUING
VAMPING
VARYING
VATTING
WADDING
WAFTING
WAGGING
WAILING
WAITING
WAIVING
WALKING
WALLING
WANTING
WARDING
WARMING
WARNING
WARPING
WARRING
WARTHOG
WASHING
WASHRAG
WASTING
WAXWING
YACKING
YAKKING
YANKING
YAPPING
YARNING
YAWNING
YAWPING
ZAGGING
ZAPPING

••AG•••
ADAGIOS
ANAGRAM
BEAGLES
BRAGGED
BRAGGER
CHAGALL
CHAGRIN
DIAGRAM
DRAGGED
DRAGGER
DRAGNET
DRAGONS
DRAGOON
DRAGOUT
DRAGSIN
DRAGSON
ETAGERE
FLAGDAY
FLAGGED
FLAGMAN
FLAGMEN
FLAGONS
FRAGILE
HOAGIES
IMAGERS
IMAGERY
IMAGINE
IMAGING
IMAGOES
LAAGERS
LEAGUES
NIAGARA
ONAGERS
PLAGUED
PLAGUES
QUAGGAS
REAGENT
SEAGATE
SEAGIRT
SEAGRAM
SEAGULL
SHAGGED
SNAGGED
STAGERS
STAGGED
STAGGER
STAGIER
STAGILY
STAGING
SWAGGER
TRAGEDY

••A•G••
AMALGAM
BRAGGED
BRAGGER
CHANGED
CHANGER
CHANGES
CHARGED
CHARGER
CHARGES
CLANGED
CLANGOR
COALGAS
DRAGGED
DRAGGER
DRAUGHT
EVANGEL
FLAGGED
FLANGES
FRAUGHT
GLASGOW
GRANGER
GRANGES
GUARGUM
ORANGES
ORANGEY
PAANGAS
PRANGED
QUAGGAS
QUANGOS
REARGUE
SHAGGED
SHANGRI
SNAGGED
SPANGLE
SPANGLY
SPARGED
SPARGES
STAGGED
STAGGER
SWAGGER
TEARGAS
TWANGED
WHANGED
WRANGLE

••A••G•
ANALOGS
ANALOGY
BRANAGH
DIALOGS
DRAYAGE
LEAFAGE
LEAKAGE
QUAHOGS
SEABAGS
SEADOGS
SEALEGS
STALAGS
TEABAGS
TUAREGS

••A•••G
ABASING
ABATING
ALAKING
AMAZING
AWAKING
BEADING
BEAMING
BEANBAG
BEANING
BEARHUG
BEARING
BEATING
BIASING
BLADING
BLAMING
BLARING
BLAZING
BOATING
BRACING
BRAKING
BRAVING
BRAYING
BRAZING
CEASING
CHAFING
CHASING
CLAWING
COATING
COAXING
CRANING
CRATING
CRAVING
CRAZING
DEALING
DIALING
DRAPING
DRAWING
DRAYING
ELATING
ERASING
EVADING
FEARING
FLAKING
FLAMING
FLARING
FLAWING
FLAYING
FOALING
FOAMING
FRAMING
FRAYING
GEARING
GLARING
GLAZING
GNAWING
GOADING
GOALONG
GRABBAG
GRACING
GRADING
GRATING
GRAVING
GRAYING
GRAYLAG
GRAZING
HEADING
HEALING
HEAPING
HEARING
HEATING
HEAVING
HOAXING
IMAGING
LEADING
LEAFING
LEAKING
LEANING
LEAPING
LEASING
LEAVING
LOADING
LOAFING
LOAMING
LOANING
MEANING
MOANING
NEARING
OKAYING
ORATING
PEAKING
PEALING
PEATBOG
PHASING
PLACING
PLANING
PLATING
PLAYING
PRATING
PRAYING
QUAKING
READING
REAMING
REAPING
REARING
ROADHOG
ROAMING
ROARING
SCALING
SCARING
SEABORG
SEALING
SEAMING
SEARING
SEASLUG
SEATING
SHADING
SHAKING
SHAMING
SHAPING
SHARING
SHAVING
SKATING
SLAKING
SLATING
SLAVING
SNAKING
SNARING
SOAKING
SOAPING
SOARING
SPACING
SPADING
SPARING
SPAYING
STAGING
STAKING
STARING
STATING
STAVING
STAYING
SWAYING
TEAMING
TEARING
TEASING
THAWING
TRACING
TRADING
WEANING
WEARING
WEAVING
WHALING
XRATING
XRAYING
YEANING

•••AG••
DAMAGED
DAMAGES
DECAGON
DOSAGES
DOWAGER
ENCAGED
ENCAGES
ENGAGED
ENGAGES
ENRAGED
ENRAGES
FINAGLE
FORAGED
FORAGER
FORAGES
GALAGOS
GARAGED
GARAGES
HEXAGON
ICEAGES
LASAGNA
LASAGNE
LINAGES
MANAGED
MANAGER
MANAGES
MANAGUA
MENAGES
MIRAGES
MRMAGOO
MUTAGEN
NEWAGER
NONAGES
NONAGON
OCTAGON
OUTAGES
PAPAGOS
PARAGON
PELAGES
PELAGIC
POTAGES
RAVAGED
RAVAGER
RAVAGES
SAVAGED
SAVAGER
SAVAGES
SCRAGGY
TANAGER
UNCAGED
UNCAGES
VIRAGOS
VISAGES
VOYAGED
VOYAGER
VOYAGES

•••A•G•
ARRAIGN
ARRANGE
ATLARGE
DEBARGE
DEFARGE
DURANGO
EMBARGO
ENLARGE
HIDALGO
LAFARGE
MELANGE
REDALGA
REHANGS
SCRAGGY
STRANGE

•••A••G
AREARUG
CATALOG
DECALOG
FLEABAG
RDLAING
TAGALOG
VISAING

••••AG•
ACREAGE
AGESAGO
AIRBAGS
ASSUAGE
AVERAGE
BABBAGE
BAGGAGE
BANDAGE
BARRAGE
BONDAGE
BRANAGH
CABBAGE
CARTAGE
CHICAGO
COINAGE
COLLAGE
CORDAGE
CORKAGE
CORSAGE
COTTAGE
COURAGE
DOCKAGE
DOGTAGS
DRAYAGE
FARRAGO
FOLIAGE
FOOTAGE
FROMAGE
GARBAGE
GASBAGS
GYMBAGS
HAULAGE
HERBAGE
HOSTAGE
ICEBAGS
IRONAGE
JAZZAGE
KITBAGS
LEAFAGE
LEAKAGE
LINEAGE
LINKAGE
LONGAGO
LUGGAGE
LUMBAGO
MASSAGE
MESSAGE
MILEAGE
MONTAGE
MOORAGE
MOULAGE
ONSTAGE
OUTRAGE
OVERAGE
PACKAGE
PASSAGE
PEERAGE
PEONAGE
PILLAGE
PLUMAGE
PORTAGE
POSTAGE
POTTAGE
PRESAGE
RAGBAGS
RAMPAGE
REFLAGS
RESTAGE
RIBCAGE
RUMMAGE
SALVAGE
SAPSAGO
SAUSAGE
SEABAGS
SELVAGE
SINKAGE
STALAGS
STORAGE
TEABAGS
TEENAGE
TILLAGE
TONNAGE
UMBRAGE
UNSNAGS
UPSTAGE
VANTAGE
VILLAGE
VINTAGE
VOLTAGE
WASTAGE
WATTAGE
WEBPAGE
WIGWAGS
YARDAGE
ZHIVAGO
ZIGZAGS

••••A•G
BIGBANG
MUSTANG
OURGANG
ROLVAAG
SHEBANG

•••••AG
BEANBAG
BELTBAG
DISHRAG
FEEDBAG
FLEABAG
GRABBAG
GRAYLAG
HANDBAG
MAILBAG
NAMETAG
NOSEBAG
POSTBAG
REDFLAG
ROLVAAG
SANDBAG
TIMELAG
TOTEBAG
WASHRAG
WINDBAG

AH•••••
AHEADOF

A•H••••
ACHATES
ACHENES
ACHERON
ACHESON
ACHIEST
ACHIEVE
ACHTUNG
ADHERED
ADHERES
AMHARIC
AMHERST
APHELIA

APHESES ASHAMED ASHANTI ASHBURY ASHCANS ASHFORD ASHIEST ASHLAND ASHLARS ASHLESS ASHRAMS ASHTRAY ATHEART ATHEISM ATHEIST ATHIRST ATHLETE ATHOMES ATHWART

A••H•••

AETHERS AFGHANI AFGHANS AIRHEAD AIRHOLE AKIHITO ALCHEMY ALLHAIL ALLHEAL ALLHERE ALOHAOE AMPHORA ANAHEIM ANAHUAC ANCHORS ANCHOVY ANTHEMS ANTHERS ANTHILL ANTHONY ARCHAIC ARCHERS ARCHERY ARCHING ARCHIVE ARCHONS ARCHWAY ARMHOLE ASPHALT AUTHORS

A•••H••

ABASHED ABASHES ABRAHAM AGAKHAN AIRSHIP AIRSHOW AITCHES ALCOHOL ALIGHTS ALYKHAN ANOTHER APACHES APISHLY APOTHEM ARACHNE

A••••H•

ABOUGHT ACANTHI ADOLPHE ALRIGHT ALYOSHA ANARCHY ARAPAHO ATROPHY ATTACHE AUROCHS

A•••••H

ABOLISH ALDRICH ALWORTH ANOUILH ANTIOCH AZIMUTH

•AH••••

BAHAMAS BAHRAIN CAHIERS CAHOOTS DAHLIAS DAHOMEY HAHNIUM KAHUNAS MAHALIA MAHARIS MAHATMA MAHONEY MAHOUTS NAHUATL PAHLAVI SAHARAN WAHINES YAHTZEE

•A•H•••

BACHING BAGHDAD BARHOPS BASHFUL BASHING BATHERS BATHING BATHMAT BATHOIL BATHTUB BAUHAUS CACHETS CACHING CACHOUS CALHOUN CARHOPS CASHBAR CASHBOX CASHCOW CASHEWS CASHIER CASHING CASHOUT CATHAIR CATHEAD CATHODE DABHAND DAPHNIS DASHERS DASHIKI DASHING DASHOFF EARHART FASHION FATHEAD FATHERS FATHOMS GASHING GATHERS HAMHOCK HASHING HAWHAWS JAPHETH KACHINA KASHMIR KATHRYN LACHLAN LASHERS LASHING LASHUPS LATHERS LATHERY LATHING MACHETE MACHINA MACHINE MANHOLE MANHOOD MANHOUR MANHUNT MASHERS MASHIES MASHING MATHERS MATHEWS MATHIAS MAYHEMS NAPHTHA PACHISI PATHWAY RAPHAEL RASHERS RASHEST RATHOLE RAWHIDE SACHEMS SACHETS SAMHILL SASHAYS SASHBAR SASHIMI SAXHORN TARHEEL TASHLIN TASHMAN WASHERS WASHIER WASHING WASHOFF WASHOUT WASHRAG WASHTUB WASHUPS YACHTED YASHMAK ZACHARY

•A••H••

BACCHUS BACKHOE BALIHAI BANSHEE BASEHIT BATCHED BATCHES CAMPHOR CAPSHAW CATCHER CATCHES CATCHON CATCHUP CATSHOW DAUPHIN EARSHOT EARTHEN EARTHLY FARTHER GALAHAD GASOHOL GAUCHER GAUCHOS HARDHAT HARDHIT HARSHEN HARSHER HARSHLY HATCHED HATCHER HATCHES HATCHET HAUGHTY KAISHEK LAKSHMI LARCHES LATCHED LATCHES LAUGHAT LAUGHED LAUGHER LAUGHIN MADCHEN MADEHAY MAKEHAY MALTHUS MARCHED MARCHER MARCHES MARCHON MARKHAM MARKHOR MARSHAL MARSHES MATCHED MATCHES MATCHUP MATTHAU MATTHEW MAUGHAM NARTHEX NARWHAL NATCHEZ NAUGHTS NAUGHTY NAVAHOS PANCHAX PANTHER PARCHED PARCHES PASCHAL PATCHED PATCHES PATCHUP RAINHAT RANCHED RANCHER RANCHES RANCHOS RATCHET SAGEHEN SALCHOW SANDHOG SATCHEL SATCHMO SAYWHEN VAUGHAN WARSHIP WARTHOG WATCHED WATCHER WATCHES WATCHIT XANTHAN XANTHIC

•A•••H•

CALIPHS DALETHS EARACHE HALVAHS KARACHI KAZAKHS LAMEDHS MALACHI MATZOHS NAPHTHA NATASHA PANACHE PARAPHS PARIAHS PAUNCHY SAMECHS TABITHA TALLYHO

•A••••H

BABYISH BADDISH BALDISH BARDISH CADDISH CALTECH CARWASH CATFISH CATTISH DAMPISH DARKISH DAWKISH FADDISH FAIRISH FATTISH GALUMPH GARNISH GAULISH GAWKISH HAGGISH HANUKAH HAWKISH JACINTH JAPHETH KADDISH LADDISH LADYISH LAPPISH LARGISH LARKISH LATIFAH LAZYISH MACBETH MADDISH MAIDISH MAMMOTH MANNISH MAWKISH NAGGISH PADUCAH PANFISH PARRISH PAYCASH RAFFISH RALEIGH RAMMISH RANKISH RASPISH RATTISH SABBATH SALTISH SAWFISH TALLISH TANNISH TARNISH TARTISH VAMPISH VANGOGH VARNISH WAGGISH WALLACH WANNISH WARMISH WARPATH WASATCH WASPISH ZANYISH

••AH•••

ANAHEIM ANAHUAC BRAHMAN BRAHMAS BRAHMIN GOAHEAD GRAHAME GRAHAMS IDAHOAN INAHEAP PEAHENS QUAHOGS SHAHDOM SWAHILI UTAHANS

••A•H••

ABASHED ABASHES AGAKHAN APACHES ARACHNE BEACHED BEACHES BEARHUG BLATHER BRASHER BRASHLY CHACHAS CHATHAM CLASHED CLASHES COACHED COACHES CRASHED CRASHES DRACHMA DRACHMS EDAPHIC FEATHER FLASHED FLASHER FLASHES GNASHED GNASHES GRAPHED GRAPHIC HEATHEN HEATHER IVANHOE JOACHIM KWACHAS LEACHED LEACHES LEASHED LEASHES LEATHER LOACHES LOATHED LOATHES PEACHED PEACHES PLASHED PLASHES POACHED POACHER POACHES QUASHED QUASHES REACHED REACHES ROACHED ROACHES ROADHOG SCATHED SCATHES SLASHED SLASHER SLASHES SLATHER SMASHED SMASHER SMASHES SMASHUP STASHED STASHES SWATHED SWATHES TEACHER TEACHES TEACHIN TEASHOP TRACHEA TRASHED TRASHES WEATHER

••A••H•

ACANTHI ANARCHY ARAPAHO BLANCHE DEARTHS DRAUGHT EPARCHS EPARCHY EXARCHS FRAUGHT HEALTHY HEARTHS HEAVEHO STARCHY SWARTHY THATCHY WEALTHY WRAITHS

••A•••H

BEAMISH BEARISH BEAUISH BOARISH BRANAGH CLAYISH EVANISH GOATISH GRAYISH HIALEAH INARUSH KLAMATH KLATSCH KNAVISH OBADIAH PEAKISH PHARAOH PLANISH PLAYDOH SLAVISH SPANISH STAUNCH TOADISH WEAKISH

•••AH••

ABRAHAM DONAHUE GALAHAD MCMAHON MEGAHIT NAVAHOS

•••A•H•

ATTACHE BREATHE BREATHS BREATHY BYPATHS EARACHE EMPATHY GOUACHE HIBACHI HITACHI KARACHI KAZAKHS MALACHI NATASHA PANACHE PARAPHS PIRANHA PREACHY SERAPHS SHEATHE SHEATHS SPLASHY TERAPHS WREATHE WREATHS

•••A••H

BREADTH DEBAUCH HOGARTH MONARCH ROMANSH SCRATCH STEALTH UNEARTH UNLATCH WASATCH

••••AH•

ARAPAHO DOODAHS FELLAHS GULLAHS HALVAHS HOOHAHS HOOKAHS HOWDAHS HURRAHS HUZZAHS LOOFAHS MULLAHS NULLAHS OOMPAHS PARIAHS PUNKAHS PURDAHS RUPIAHS WHYDAHS

••••A•H

BENEATH BONEASH BRANAGH CARWASH DIGRAPH EYELASH EYEWASH GOLIATH GOULASH HOGWASH IMPEACH JETWASH KLAMATH NEWMATH PAYCASH PHARAOH PREWASH RETEACH SABBATH SPINACH STOMACH SUNBATH TOWPATH UNLEASH WALLACH WARPATH

•••••AH

CHEETAH DEBORAH DELILAH HANUKAH HIALEAH LATIFAH MENORAH MESSIAH MITZVAH OBADIAH PADUCAH POOHBAH REBEKAH

AI•••••

AIDLESS AIGRETS AILERON AILMENT AIMEDAT AIMEDTO AIMLESS AIMSFOR AIRBAGS AIRBALL AIRBASE AIRBOAT AIRCOOL AIRCREW AIRDAMS AIRDATE AIRDROP AIRFARE AIRFLOW AIRFOIL AIRGUNS AIRHEAD AIRHOLE AIRIEST AIRINGS AIRKISS AIRLANE AIRLESS AIRLIFT AIRLIKE AIRLINE AIRLOCK AIRMADA AIRMAIL AIRMASS AIRMILE AIRPLAY AIRPORT AIRPUMP AIRRAID AIRSACS AIRSHIP AIRSHOW AIRSOCK AIRSOUT AIRTAXI AIRTIME AIRWAVE AIRWAYS AIRWOLF AITCHES

A•I••••

ABIDEBY ABIDING ABIGAIL ABILENE ABILITY ABINTRA ABITIBI ACIDIFY ACIDITY ADIPOSE AGILELY AGILITY AGITATE AGITATO AKIHITO ALIASES ALIBABA ALIDADE ALIENEE ALIENOR ALIGHTS ALIGNED ALIGNER ALIMENT ALIMONY ALINING AMIABLE AMIABLY AMIBLUE AMISTAD ANILINE ANIMALS ANIMATE ANIMATO ANIMISM ANIMIST ANISEED ANISTON APISHLY ARIADNE ARIDEST ARIDITY ARIETTA ARIKARA ARIOSOS ARIOSTO ARISING ARISTAE ARISTAS ARISTOS ARIZONA ASIATIC ASININE ATINGLE ATISSUE AVIANCA AVIATED AVIATES AVIATOR AVIDITY AVIGNON AXIALLY AXILLAE AZIMUTH

A••I•••

AAMILNE ABRIDGE ACHIEST ACHIEVE ACRIDLY ACTINIC ACTIONS ACTIVES ADDIBLE ADDISON ADFINEM ADMIRAL ADMIRED ADMIRER ADMIRES ADMITTO ADMIXED ADMIXES ADVISED ADVISER ADVISES ADVISOR AEDILES AERIALS AERIEST AFFINES AFFIRMS AFFIXED AFFIXES AFRICAN AGAINST AGEISTS AGRIPPA AIRIEST AIRINGS ALBINOS ALFIERI ALGIERS ALLISON ALRIGHT AMBIENT AMNIONS ANCIENT ANDIRON ANOINTS ANTIART ANTIBES ANTIFOG ANTIGEN ANTIGUA ANTILOG ANTIOCH ANTIQUE ANTITAX ANTIWAR ANXIETY ANXIOUS AORISTS APRICOT APRIORI APSIDES AQUIFER AQUINAS AQUIVER ARBITER ARGIVES ARNICAS ARRIERE ARRISES ARRIVAL ARRIVED ARRIVER ARRIVES ARTICLE ARTIEST ARTISAN ARTISTE ARTISTS ASHIEST ASPIRED ASPIRER ASPIRES ASPIRIN ASSIGNS ASSISTS ASSIZES ATHIRST ATRIUMS ATTICUS ATTIMES ATTIRED ATTIRES AUDIBLE AUDIBLY AUDILES AUDITED AUDITOR AURICLE AVAILED AVOIDED AWAITED AWNINGS

A•••I••

ABASING ABATING ABIDING ABILITY ABITIBI ABOLISH ABUSING ABUSIVE ACACIAS ACADIAN ACARIDS ACIDIFY ACIDITY ACONITE ACQUIRE ACQUITS ACTFIVE ADAGIOS ADAMITE ADDLING ADELINE ADENINE ADJOINS ADORING AEOLIAN AFFAIRE AFFAIRS AFFLICT AGARICS AGILITY AGONISE AGONIST AGONIZE AIRKISS AIRLIFT AIRLIKE AIRLINE AIRMILE AIRTIME AKIHITO ALAKING ALDRICH ALEWIFE ALINING ALLTIME ALLYING AMATIVE AMAZING AMBLING AMBRIES AMENITY AMERICA AMERIGO AMERIKA AMERIND AMPLIFY AMUSING ANANIAS ANELING ANGLING ANGRIER ANGRILY ANILINE ANIMISM ANIMIST ANNUITY ANODISE ANODIZE ANOMIES ANOUILH ANTEING ANTHILL ANTLIKE ANTLION ANTOINE ANTSIER ANYTIME APATITE APELIKE APERIES APPLIED APPLIES APPOINT APPRISE APPRIZE ARABIAN ARCHING ARCHIVE ARCSINE ARECIBO ARETINO ARGUING ARIDITY ARISING ARMLIKE ARMOIRE ARMPITS ARRAIGN ARTFILM ARTSIER ASCRIBE ASININE ASOCIAL ASSAILS ASSLIKE ASTAIRE ASTRIDE ATAVISM ATAVIST ATELIER ATHEISM ATHEIST ATOMIES ATOMISE ATOMIZE ATONIES ATONING ATTAINS ATTRITE ATTRITS AUCTION AUNTIES AUPAIRS AUSPICE AUSSIES AVARICE AVIDITY AVOWING AWAKING AZURITE

A••••I•

ABIGAIL ABNAKIS ABSTAIN ACCLAIM ACERBIC ACRYLIC ACTINIC ADDEDIN ADONAIS AELFRIC AEROBIC AGASSIZ AGOUTIS AIRFOIL AIRMAIL AIRRAID AIRSHIP AJACCIO ALADDIN ALAMEIN ALBANIA ALBENIZ ALBUMIN ALEMBIC ALGERIA ALKALIS ALLHAIL ALLUVIA ALSATIA AMHARIC AMMONIA AMNESIA

AMOEBIC
AMRADIO
ANAEMIA
ANAEMIC
ANAHEIM
ANDROID
ANEROID
ANGELIC
ANNELID
ANOSMIA
ANOSMIC
ANTACID
ANTONIA
ANTONIN
ANTONIO
APHELIA
AQUARIA
AQUATIC
AQUAVIT
ARAMAIC
ARCADIA
ARCHAIC
ARMENIA
ARSENIC
ARSENIO
ARTEMIS
ASCETIC
ASEPSIS
ASEPTIC
ASIATIC
ASKEDIN
ASPIRIN
ASSYRIA
ASTORIA
AUSTRIA

A•••••I

ABENAKI
ABITIBI
ABRUZZI
ACANTHI
AFGHANI
AIRTAXI
ALFIERI
ALVEOLI
ANASAZI
APRIORI
ASHANTI
ASSEGAI

•AI••••

BAILEES
BAILERS
BAILEYS
BAILIFF
BAILING
BAILORS
BAILOUT
BAINTER
BAITING
CAIMANS
CAIQUES
CAISSON
DAILIES
DAIMLER
DAIMONS
DAIRIES
DAISIES
FAIENCE
FAILING
FAILURE
FAINTED
FAINTER
FAINTLY
FAIREST
FAIRIES
FAIRING
FAIRISH
FAIROFF
FAIRSUP
FAIRWAY
GAINERS
GAINFUL
GAINING
GAINSAY
GAINSON
GAITERS
GAITING
HAILING
HAIRCUT
HAIRDOS
HAIRDYE
HAIRIER
HAIRNET
HAIRPIN
HAITIAN
JAIALAI
JAILERS
JAILING
KAISERS
KAISHEK
LAIDFOR
LAIDLOW
LAIDOFF
LAIDOUT
LAISSEZ
MAIDENS
MAIDISH
MAIGRET
MAILBAG
MAILBOX
MAILCAR
MAILERS
MAILING
MAILLOT
MAILOUT
MAILSIN
MAINTOP
MAITAIS
MAITRED
NAIADES
NAILERS
NAILING
NAILSET
NAILSIN
NAIROBI
NAIVELY
NAIVETE
NAIVETY
PAIDFOR
PAIDOFF
PAIDOUT
PAILFUL
PAILOUS
PAINFUL
PAINTED
PAINTER
PAIRING
PAIROFF
PAIRSUP
PAISANO
PAISLEY
PAIUTES
RAIDERS
RAIDING
RAILERS
RAILING
RAILSAT
RAILWAY
RAIMENT
RAINBOW
RAINHAT
RAINIER
RAINILY
RAINING
RAINMAN
RAINOUT
RAISERS
RAISEUP
RAISING
RAISINS
SAILING
SAILORS
SAINTED
SAINTLY
TAILEND
TAILFIN
TAILING
TAILLES
TAILOFF
TAILORS
TAINTED
TAIPANS
VAINEST
WAIKIKI
WAILERS
WAILFUL
WAILING
WAITERS
WAITFOR
WAITING
WAITOUT
WAITRON
WAITSON
WAITSUP
WAIVERS
WAIVING
ZAIREAN
ZAIRIAN

•A•I•••

AAMILNE
BACILLI
BALIHAI
BATIKED
BATISTA
BATISTE
CABINET
CAGIEST
CAHIERS
CAKIEST
CALIBAN
CALIBER
CALIBRE
CALICES
CALICOS
CALIPER
CALIPHS
CAMILLE
CAMISES
CANIEST
CANINES
CAPITAL
CAPITAN
CAPITOL
CARIBES
CARIBOU
CARINAS
CARIOCA
CASINGS
CASINOS
CATIONS
CAVIARS
CAVILED
CAVILER
DANIELS
DAVINCI
EASIEST
FACIALS
FACINGS
FADIMAN
FAJITAS
FAMINES
FANIONS
FATIGUE
GALILEE
GALILEI
GALILEO
GAMIEST
GAMINES
GAVIALS
HABITAT
HABITED
HABITUE
HALIBUT
HALIDES
HALIFAX
HALITES
HAMITES
HAMITIC
HAMITUP
HARICOT
HASIDIC
HASIDIM
HAZIEST
HAZINGS
JABIRUS
JACINTH
JALISCO
JANITOR
LABIALS
LABIATE
LACIEST
LACINGS
LADINOS
LAFITTE
LAKIEST
LALIQUE
LAMINAE
LAMINAL
LAMINAR
LAMINAS
LARIATS
LATICES
LATIFAH
LATINAS
LATINOS
LAVINIA
LAYINTO
LAYITON
LAZIEST
MADIGAN
MADISON
MAGICAL
MAGINOT
MAKINGS
MALIGNS
MANIACS
MANILOW
MANIOCS
MANIPLE
MANITOU
MAOISTS
MARIANA
MARILYN
MARIMBA
MARINAS
MARINER
MARINES
MARITAL
MATILDA
MATINEE
MATISSE
MAXILLA
MAXIMAL
MAXIMUM
MAXIMUS
MAZIEST
NABISCO
NAMIBIA
NATIONS
NATIVES
PACIFIC
PALIEST
PANICKY
PANICLE
PAPILLA
PARIAHS
PARINGS
PATIENT
PATINAS
PAVIOUR
RABIDLY
RACIEST
RADIALS
RADIANS
RADIANT
RADIATE
RADICAL
RADICES
RADICLE
RADIOED
RADIXES
RAMINTO
RANINTO
RAPIDER
RAPIDLY
RAPIERS
RAPINES
RARITAN
RATINGS
RATIONS
RATITES
RAVINES
RAVINGS
RAVIOLI
SABINES
SAGINAW
SALIENT
SALIERI
SALINAS
SAMISEN
SAMITES
SANIBEL
SAPIENS
SAPIENT
SATIATE
SATIETY
SATINET
SATIRES
SATIRIC
SATISFY
SAVINGS
SAVIORS
SAVIOUR
SAYINGS
TABITHA
TACITLY
TACITUS
TAOISTS
TAPINGS
TAPINTO
TAPIOCA
TARIFFS
TATIANA
TAXICAB
TAXIING
TAXIMAN
TAXIMEN
TAXIWAY
VALIANT
VALIDLY
VALISES
VANILLA
VANILLI
VAPIDLY
VARIANT
VARIETY
VARIOUS
VATICAN
WAHINES
WANIEST
WAPITIS
WARIEST
WAVIEST
WAXIEST
YAKIMAS
ZANIEST

•A••I••

BABBITT
BABYING
BABYISH
BACHING
BACKING
BADDIES
BADDISH
BAGGIER
BAGGIES
BAGGILY
BAGGING
BAGLIKE
BAGPIPE
BAILIFF
BAILING
BAITING
BALDING
BALDISH
BALKIER
BALKILY
BALKING
BALMIER
BALMILY
BAMBINO
BANDIED
BANDIES
BANDING
BANDITO
BANDITS
BANGING
BANKING
BANNING
BAPTISE
BAPTISM
BAPTIST
BAPTIZE
BARBING
BARDISH
BARGING
BARKIER
BARKING
BARMIER
BARRIER
BARRING
BARRIOS
BASHING
BASKING
BASSIST
BASTING
BASTION
BATGIRL
BATHING
BATLIKE
BATTIER
BATTING
BATWING
BAUXITE
BAWDIER
BAWDILY
BAWLING
BAYCITY
CABBIES
CABLING
CABRINI
CACHING
CADDIED
CADDIES
CADDISH
CADGING
CADMIUM
CAESIUM
CALCIFY
CALCITE
CALCIUM
CALKING
CALKINS
CALLING
CALLINS
CALMING
CALVING
CAMBIUM
CAMPIER
CAMPILY
CAMPING
CAMPION
CANDICE
CANDIDA
CANDIDE
CANDIDS
CANDIED
CANDIES
CANNIER
CANNILY
CANNING
CANTILY
CANTINA
CANTING
CAPPING
CAPRICE
CAPSIDS
CAPSIZE
CAPTION
CAPTIVE
CARBIDE
CARBINE
CARDIAC
CARDING
CARKING
CARMINE
CARNIES
CARPING
CARRICK
CARRIED
CARRIER
CARRIES
CARRION
CARTIER
CARTING
CARVING
CASHIER
CASHING
CASPIAN
CASSIAS
CASSIDY
CASSINI
CASSINO
CASSIUS
CASTILE
CASTING
CATBIRD
CATFISH
CATKINS
CATLIKE
CATNIPS
CATTIER
CATTILY
CATTING
CATTISH
CAUSING
CAUTION
CAVEINS
DABBING
DADAISM
DADAIST
DADDIES
DAFFIER
DAFFILY
DAFFING
DAHLIAS
DAILIES
DAIRIES
DAISIES
DALLIED
DALLIER
DALLIES
DAMMING
DAMNING
DAMPING
DAMPISH
DANCING
DANDIER
DANDIES
DANDIFY
DAPPING
DARBIES
DARKISH
DARLING
DARNING
DARTING
DASHIKI
DASHING
DAUBING
DAUMIER
DAWKISH
DAWNING
DAYLILY
DAYSINN
DAYTIME
EAGLING
EARLIER
EARLIKE
EARNING
EARRING
EARWIGS
FABRICS
FACTION
FADDISH
FADDISM
FADDIST
FADEINS
FADLIKE
FAERIES
FAGGING
FAILING
FAIRIES
FAIRING
FAIRISH
FALLING
FALSIFY
FALSITY
FANCIED
FANCIER
FANCIES
FANCIFY
FANCILY
FANLIKE
FANNING
FANZINE
FARCING
FARMING
FARRIER
FASCIAS
FASHION
FASTING
FATCITY
FATLIKE
FATTIER
FATTILY
FATTISH
FATUITY
FAUVISM
FAUVIST
FAWNING
GABBIER
GABBING
GABRIEL
GADDING
GAFFING
GAGGING
GAGLINE
GAINING
GAITING
GALLING
GALLIUM
GAMBIAN
GAMBITS
GAMMIER
GAMMING
GANGING
GAOLING
GAPPING
GARBING
GARNISH
GARRICK
GASHING
GASKINS
GASPING
GASSIER
GATLING
GAUDIER
GAUDILY
GAUGING
GAULISH
GAUMING
GAUZIER
GAUZILY
GAWKIER
GAWKILY
GAWKING
GAWKISH
GAWPING
HACKIES
HACKING
HADRIAN
HAFNIUM
HAFTING
HAGGISH
HAGLIKE
HAHNIUM
HAILING
HAIRIER
HAITIAN
HALOING
HALTING
HALVING
HAMMIER
HAMMILY
HAMMING
HANDIER
HANDILY
HANDING
HANGING
HANKIES
HAPPIER
HAPPILY
HAPPING
HARDIER
HARDILY
HARDING
HARKING
HARMING
HARPIES
HARPING
HARPIST
HARRIED
HARRIER
HARRIES
HARRIET
HASHING
HASPING
HASTIER
HASTILY
HASTING
HATLIKE
HATPINS
HATTING
HAULING
HAWKING
HAWKINS
HAWKISH
HAYRIDE
HAYWIRE
JABBING
JACKIES
JACKING
JADEITE
JAGGIER
JAGGIES
JAGGING
JAILING
JAMAICA
JAMLIKE
JAMMIER
JAMMING
JANVIER
JARRING
JASMINE
JAWLIKE
JAWLINE
JAYBIRD
JAZZIER
JAZZILY
JAZZING
KACHINA
KADDISH
KAFFIRS
KAYOING
LACKING
LADDIES
LADDISH
LADLING
LADYISH
LAGGING
LAMAISM
LAMAIST
LAMMING
LANDING
LANKIER
LANKILY
LANSING
LAOTIAN
LAPPING
LAPPISH
LAPSING
LAPWING
LARAINE
LARDIER
LARDING
LARGISH
LARKISH
LASHING
LASSIES
LASTING
LATHING
LATTICE
LATVIAN
LAUDING
LAWLIKE
LAZYISH
MACHINA
MACHINE
MADDING
MADDISH
MADEIRA
MADLIBS
MAFFICK
MAGNIFY
MAGPIES
MAGUIRE
MAIDISH
MAILING
MALAISE
MALKINS
MALTIER
MALTING
MANCINI
MANGIER
MANKIND
MANLIER
MANLIKE
MANNING
MANNISH
MANSION
MAPPING
MARGINS
MARKING
MARLINS
MARMION
MARRIED
MARRIES
MARRING
MARTIAL
MARTIAN
MARTINA
MARTINI
MARTINO
MARTINS
MARXISM
MARXIST
MASHIES
MASHING
MASKING
MASSIER
MASSIFS
MASSING
MASSIVE
MASTICS
MASTIFF
MATHIAS
MATTING
MAULING
MAURICE
MAWKISH
MAYTIME
MAYWINE
NABBING
NAGGIER
NAGGING
NAGGISH
NAILING
NANAIMO
NANNIES
NAPKINS
NAPPIES
NAPPING
NAPTIME
NASTIER
NASTILY
NATRIUM
NATTIER
NATTILY
NAVVIES
OAKLIKE
OARLIKE
OATLIKE
PACHISI
PACKICE
PACKING
PADDIES
PADDING
PAIRING
PALLIER
PALLING
PALLIUM
PALMIER
PALMING
PALMIST
PANDITS
PANFISH
PANNIER
PANNING
PANPIPE
PANSIES
PANTING
PAPLIKE
PAPRIKA
PARKING
PARRIED
PARRIER
PARRIES
PARRING
PARRISH
PARSING
PARTIAL
PARTIED
PARTIER
PARTIES
PARTING
PARTITA
PARTITE
PASSING
PASSION
PASSIVE
PASTIER
PASTIME
PASTINA
PASTING
PATRIAL
PATRICE
PATRICK
PATRIOT
PATSIES
PATTIES
PATTING
PAUCITY
PAULINA
PAULINE
PAULING
PAULIST
PAUSING
PAWKIER
PAWNING
PAYDIRT
RABBITS
RABBITT
RACKING
RAFFISH
RAFTING
RAGGING
RAGTIME
RAIDING
RAILING
RAINIER
RAINILY
RAINING
RAISING
RAISINS
RALEIGH
RALLIED
RALLIER
RALLIES
RAMLIKE
RAMMING
RAMMISH
RANDIER
RANGIER
RANGING
RANKING
RANKISH
RANRIOT
RANTING
RAPPING
RASPIER
RASPING
RASPISH
RATFINK
RATLIKE
RATLINE
RATTIER
RATTING
RATTISH
RAWHIDE
RAWSILK
RAYLIKE
RAZZING
SABRINA
SACKING
SACLIKE
SAGGIER
SAGGING
SAILING
SALLIED
SALLIES
SALSIFY
SALTIER
SALTILY
SALTINE
SALTING
SALTISH
SALVIAS
SALVING
SAMHILL
SANDIER
SANDING
SANTINI
SANTIRS
SAPLING
SAPPIER
SAPPILY
SAPPING
SARDINE
SARKIER
SASHIMI
SASSIER
SASSIES
SASSILY
SASSING
SAUCIER
SAUCILY
SAURIAN
SAVVIER
SAVVILY
SAWFISH
SAWLIKE
SAWMILL
SAYYIDS
TABBIES
TABBING
TABLING
TACKIER
TACKILY
TACKING
TACTICS
TACTILE
TAFFIES
TAGGING
TAGLIKE
TAGLINE
TAILING
TALKIER
TALKIES
TALKING
TALLIED
TALLIER
TALLIES
TALLINN
TALLISH
TAMPICO
TAMPING
TANGIER
TANKING
TANLINE
TANNING
TANNINS
TANNISH
TANSIES
TANTIVY
TAPPING
TARDIER
TARDILY
TARNISH
TARPITS
TARRIED
TARRIER
TARRIES
TARRING
TARSIER
TARTISH
TASKING
TASTIER
TASTILY
TASTING
TATTIER
TATTILY
TATTING
TAURINE

TAWNIER
TAWNILY
TAXIING
VACCINE
VACUITY
VALUING
VAMPING
VAMPIRA
VAMPIRE
VAMPISH
VANDINE
VARMINT
VARNISH
VARSITY
VARYING
VASTIER
VATTING
WACKIER
WACKILY
WADDIES
WADDING
WAFTING
WAGGING
WAGGISH
WAIKIKI
WAILING
WAITING
WAIVING
WALKING
WALKINS
WALLING
WANNISH
WANTING
WARDING
WARLIKE
WARMING
WARMISH
WARNING
WARPING
WARRING
WARRIOR
WARTIER
WARTIME
WARWICK
WASHIER
WASHING
WASPIER
WASPILY
WASPISH
WASTING
WAXLIKE
WAXWING
WAYBILL
WAYSIDE
YACKING
YAKKING
YANKING
YAPPING
YARNING
YAWNING
YAWPING
ZAGGING
ZAIRIAN
ZAMBIAN
ZANYISH
ZAPPIER
ZAPPING

•A••I•

BABYSIT
BACKBIT
BACKLIT
BACKSIN
BAHRAIN
BALDRIC
BALDWIN
BANDAID
BARGAIN
BARGEIN
BARMAID
BASEHIT
BATHOIL
BAVARIA
CAKEMIX
CALLSIN
CALORIC
CALORIE
CAMBRIC
CAMELIA
CANONIC
CANTRIP
CAPAPIE
CAPTAIN
CARAMIA
CAROTID
CATHAIR
CATSUIT
CATTAIL
CAUSTIC
CAVEDIN
CAVESIN
DAPHNIS
DAUPHIN
DAYTRIP
EASEDIN
EASESIN
FACTOID
FADEDIN
FADESIN
FALLSIN
FANATIC
FANMAIL
FANTAIL
GAGARIN
GALATIA
GANGLIA
GASMAIN
GASTRIC
GAUGUIN
HAIRPIN
HALFWIT
HAMELIN
HAMITIC
HANDSIN
HANGSIN
HARDHIT
HASIDIC
HASIDIM
JACOBIN
JAVELIN
KABUKIS
KASHMIR
KATYDID
LACONIC
LAMPOIL
LANGUID
LANOLIN
LARAMIE
LAUGHIN
LAVINIA
LAWSUIT
MAHALIA
MAHARIS
MAILSIN
MAITAIS
MAKESIT
MALEFIC
MANTRIC
MANUMIT
MARQUIS
MASONIC
MASTOID
MAUDLIN
MAULDIN
MAUROIS
MAYALIN
MAYFAIR
NAILSIN
NAMIBIA
NATALIA
NATALIE
NAYSAID
PACIFIC
PALADIN
PALMOIL
PARBOIL
PARFAIT
PARSNIP
QATARIS
RAKEDIN
RAKESIN
RAMEKIN
RAREBIT
RATAFIA
RATTAIL
SAFARIS
SALADIN
SALAMIS
SALUKIS
SAMARIA
SANGRIA
SANLUIS
SATIRIC
SAVARIN
TABLOID
TAILFIN
TAKEAIM
TAKENIN
TAKESIN
TALARIA
TALKBIG
TAMARIN
TASHLIN
TATAMIS
VALERIE
WADEDIN
WADESIN
WAGTAIL
WANTSIN
WAPITIS
WARSHIP
WASSAIL
WATCHIT
WAVEDIN
WAVESIN
WAYLAID
XANTHIC
YANQUIS

•A••••I

BACARDI
BACILLI
BALIHAI
BASENJI
CABRINI
CADUCEI
CAMPARI
CANNOLI
CASSINI
DASHIKI
DAVINCI
GALILEI
GALVANI
HAVARTI
JACUZZI
JAIALAI
KARACHI
KAROLYI
LAKSHMI
MAESTRI
MAGNANI
MALACHI
MANCINI
MARCONI
MARTINI
NAIROBI
PACHISI
PADRONI
PAHLAVI
PALAZZI
RAPANUI
RAVIOLI
SALIERI
SAMURAI
SANTINI
SASHIMI
VANILLI
WAIKIKI
ZAMBEZI
ZAMBONI

••AI•••

AGAINST
AVAILED
AWAITED
BRAIDED
BRAIDER
BRAILLE
BRAINED
BRAISED
BRAISES
CHAINED
CHAIRED
CHAISES
CLAIMED
CLAIMER
CLAIROL
DRAINED
DRAINER
EMAILED
FLAILED
FRAILER
FRAILLY
FRAILTY
FRAISES
GLAIRED
GRAINED
LIAISED
LIAISES
LIAISON
PLAICES
PLAINER
PLAINLY
PLAINTS
PLAITED
PRAIRIE
PRAISED
PRAISER
PRAISES
QUAILED
REAIMED
REAIRED
STAIDER
STAIDLY
STAINED
STAINER
TRAILED
TRAILER
TRAINED
TRAINEE
TRAINER
TRAIPSE
TRAITOR
UNAIDED
UNAIMED
UNAIRED
WRAITHS

••A•I••

ABASING
ABATING
ACACIAS
ACADIAN
ACARIDS
ADAGIOS
ADAMITE
AGARICS
ALAKING
AMATIVE
AMAZING
ANANIAS
APATITE
ARABIAN
ATAVISM
ATAVIST
AVARICE
AWAKING
BEADIER
BEADING
BEAMIER
BEAMING
BEAMISH
BEANIES
BEANING
BEARING
BEARISH
BEATIFY
BEATING
BEAUISH
BIALIES
BIASING
BLADING
BLAMING
BLARING
BLAZING
BOARISH
BOATING
BRACING
BRAKING
BRAVING
BRAYING
BRAZIER
BRAZING
CEASING
CHAFING
CHALICE
CHARIER
CHARILY
CHARIOT
CHARITY
CHASING
CLARICE
CLARIFY
CLARION
CLARITY
CLAVIER
CLAWING
CLAYIER
CLAYISH
COATING
COAXIAL
COAXING
CRANIAL
CRANING
CRANIUM
CRATING
CRAVING
CRAZIER
CRAZIES
CRAZILY
CRAZING
CZARINA
CZARISM
CZARIST
DEALING
DEARIES
DIALING
DIARIES
DRAPING
DRAWING
DRAYING
DUALITY
EDACITY
EGALITE
ELAAIUN
ELAPIDS
ELATING
ELATION
ERASING
ETAMINE
EVADING
EVANISH
EVASION
EVASIVE
EXAMINE
EXANIMO
FEARING
FLAKIER
FLAKILY
FLAKING
FLAMIER
FLAMING
FLARING
FLAWING
FLAXIER
FLAYING
FOALING
FOAMIER
FOAMILY
FOAMING
FRAGILE
FRAMING
FRASIER
FRAYING
FRAZIER
GEARING
GHANIAN
GLACIAL
GLACIER
GLARING
GLAZIER
GLAZING
GNAWING
GOADING
GOALIES
GOATISH
GRACIAS
GRACILE
GRACING
GRADING
GRANITE
GRAPIER
GRATIAS
GRATIFY
GRATING
GRAVIES
GRAVING
GRAVITY
GRAYING
GRAYISH
GRAZING
GUANINE
HEADIER
HEADILY
HEADING
HEALING
HEAPING
HEARING
HEATING
HEAVIER
HEAVIES
HEAVILY
HEAVING
HOAGIES
HOARIER
HOARILY
HOAXING
HYALINE
IMAGINE
IMAGING
INANITY
IRANIAN
ITALIAN
ITALICS
KNAVISH
KRATION
LEADIER
LEADING
LEADINS
LEAFIER
LEAFING
LEAKIER
LEAKING
LEANING
LEAPING
LEARIER
LEASING
LEAVING
LOADING
LOAFING
LOAMIER
LOAMING
LOANING
MEALIER
MEALIES
MEANIES
MEANING
MEATIER
MEATILY
MIAMIAN
MIAMIAS
MOANING
NEARING
OBADIAH
OCARINA
OKAYING
ONADIET
OPACITY
OPALINE
ORATING
ORATION
OVATION
PEAKING
PEAKISH
PEALIKE
PEALING
PEATIER
PHASING
PIANISM
PIANIST
PLACIDO
PLACING
PLANING
PLANISH
PLATIER
PLATING
PLAYING
PRALINE
PRATING
PRAYING
QUAKIER
QUAKILY
QUAKING
QUALIFY
QUALITY
READIED
READIER
READIES
READILY
READING
REALISE
REALISM
REALIST
REALITY
REALIZE
REAMING
REAPING
REARING
ROADIES
ROAMING
ROARING
SCALIER
SCALING
SCARIER
SCARIFY
SCARILY
SCARING
SEABIRD
SEAFIRE
SEAGIRT
SEALILY
SEALING
SEALION
SEAMIER
SEAMING
SEARING
SEASICK
SEASIDE
SEATING
SHADIER
SHADILY
SHADING
SHAKIER
SHAKILY
SHAKING
SHAMING
SHAPING
SHAPIRO
SHARING
SHAVING
SKATING
SLAKING
SLATIER
SLATING
SLAVING
SLAVISH
SNAKIER
SNAKILY
SNAKING
SNARING
SOAKING
SOAPIER
SOAPILY
SOAPING
SOARING
SPACIER
SPACING
SPADING
SPANIEL
SPANISH
SPARING
SPATIAL
SPAVINS
SPAYING
STABILE
STADIUM
STAGIER
STAGILY
STAGING
STAKING
STAMINA
STARING
STATICE
STATICS
STATING
STATION
STATIST
STAVING
STAYING
SUASION
SUAVITY
SWAHILI
SWAYING
TEAMING
TEARIER
TEARILY
TEARING
TEASING
TEATIME
THAWING
TOADIED
TOADIES
TOADISH
TRACING
TRADING
TSARINA
TSARIST
TZARINA
UNALIKE
URANITE
URANIUM
VEALIER
WEAKISH
WEANING
WEARIED
WEARIER
WEARIES
WEARILY
WEARING
WEAVING
WHALING
XRATING
XRAYING
YEANING

••A••I•

AGASSIZ
AJACCIO
ALADDIN
ALAMEIN
ANAEMIA
ANAEMIC
ANAHEIM
ARAMAIC
BEASTIE
BEATNIK
BEATRIX
BEATSIT
BEATTIE
BLACKIE
BRAHMIN
BRASSIE
CHABLIS
CHAGRIN
CHAMOIS
CHAOTIC
CHAPLIN
CHAPPIE
CHARLIE
CHARMIN
CHASSIS
CLASSIC
CLAUDIA
CLAUDIO
COALBIN
COALOIL
CRAPPIE
DEADAIR
DEALSIN
DEALTIN
DEARSIR
DRAGSIN
DRASTIC
DRAWNIN
DRAWSIN
EDAPHIC
ELASTIC
FLACCID
FRANCIS
FRANKIE
FRANTIC
GRAPHIC
HEADPIN
HEADSIN
INASNIT
INASPIN
JEANNIE
JOACHIM
JOAQUIN
LEADSIN
LEAVEIN
MIASMIC
ONASSIS
PHASEIN
PLASTIC
PLAUDIT
PRAIRIE
READMIT
READSIN
REAFFIX
REAVAIL
SHAREIN
STANDIN
STANNIC
STARLIT
TEACHIN
THATSIT
TIANJIN
TRADEIN
TRAFFIC
TRANSIT
TRAVAIL
TRAVOIS

••A•••I

ACANTHI
ANASAZI
CHAPATI
DIABOLI
GUARANI
PLATYPI
SHANGRI
SHARPEI
SHASTRI
SWAHILI

•••AI••

AFFAIRE
AFFAIRS
ARRAIGN
ASSAILS
ASTAIRE
ATTAINS
AUPAIRS
BEWAILS
DADAISM
DADAIST
DERAILS
DETAILS
DETAINS
DOMAINS
ECLAIRS
ELAAIUN
ENTAILS
GERAINT
HILAIRE
IMPAIRS
JAMAICA
JUDAISM
KUWAITI
LAMAISM
LAMAIST
LARAINE
MALAISE
MOHAIRS
MORAINE
MOSAICS
NANAIMO
OBTAINS
ORDAINS
RDLAING
REGAINS
REMAILS
REMAINS
RENAILS
REPAINT
REPAIRS
RERAISE
RETAILS
RETAINS
ROGAINE
ROLAIDS
ROMAINE
SPRAINS
STRAINS
STRAITS
TUBAIST
UKRAINE
UPRAISE
VISAING

•••A•I•

ABNAKIS
ALBANIA
ALKALIS
ALSATIA
AMHARIC
AMRADIO
ANTACID
AQUARIA
AQUATIC
AQUAVIT
ARCADIA
ASIATIC
BAVARIA
BENAZIR
BORACIC
BREAKIN
CAPAPIE
CARAMIA
CBRADIO
CERAMIC
CHEAPIE
CHEATIN
COHABIT
CROATIA
DENARII
DUKAKIS
DYNAMIC
ERRATIC
EURASIA
FANATIC
FLEAPIT
FMRADIO
GAGARIN
GALATIA
GELATIN
GELATIS
HEPARIN
HEPATIC
HORATIO
IDIAMIN
INHABIT
INVALID
ISLAMIC
KERATIN
KIWANIS
LARAMIE
LUNATIC
MAHALIA
MAHARIS
MAYALIN
MCGAVIN
MEGAHIT
MELANIE
MELANIN
MORANIS
MORAVIA
NATALIA
NATALIE
NEPALIS
NOMADIC
NOTABIT
OCEANIA
OCEANIC
OCEANID
OCTAVIA
ONTARIO
ORGANIC
PALADIN
PELAGIC
PIRATIC
POLARIS
PYRAMID
QATARIS
RATAFIA
REGALIA
ROMANIA
ROSALIE
ROSARIO
SAFARIS
SALADIN
SALAMIS
SAMARIA
SAVARIN
SEDALIA
SERAPIS
SNEAKIN
SOLARIA
SOMALIA
SOMALIS
SOMATIC
SQUALID
SWEARIN
TALARIA
TAMARIN
TATAMIS
TELAVIV
TITANIA
TITANIC
VIDALIA
VISALIA
VISAVIS
VITAMIN
VOCALIC

•••A••I

ASHANTI
BACARDI
CHIANTI
DENARII
HAVARTI
HIBACHI
HITACHI
ISRAELI
JAIALAI
JUMANJI
KARACHI
KUWAITI
MALACHI
PALAZZI
PULASKI
RAPANUI
SCHATZI
VIVALDI

••••AI•

ABIGAIL
ABSTAIN
ACCLAIM
ADONAIS
AIRMAIL
AIRRAID
ALLHAIL
ARAMAIC
ARCHAIC
BAHRAIN
BANDAID
BARGAIN
BARMAID
BIDFAIR
BOBTAIL
BRITAIN
CAPTAIN
CATHAIR
CATTAIL
CERTAIN
COCHAIR
CONTAIN
CORSAIR
COSTAIN
CURTAIL
CURTAIN
DEADAIR
DECLAIM
DELTAIC
DESPAIR
DETRAIN
DISDAIN
ENCHAIN
ENTRAIN
EXCLAIM
EXPLAIN
FANMAIL
FANTAIL
FOXTAIL
FUNFAIR
GASMAIN
HEBRAIC
HOBNAIL
INGRAIN
KOOLAID
LOWPAID
MAITAIS
MAYFAIR
MERMAID
MIKHAIL
MISLAID
MISSAID
NAYSAID
OLDMAID
OPENAIR
OUTLAID
PARFAIT
PERTAIN
PIGTAIL
PINTAIL
PREPAID
PREVAIL
PROSAIC
RATTAIL
REAVAIL
RECLAIM
REDHAIR
REFRAIN
RESTAIN
RETRAIN
SETSAIL
SUNMAID
SUSTAIN
TAKEAIM
TERRAIN
THINAIR
TOENAIL
TOPSAIL
TRAVAIL
TREMAIN
UNCHAIN
UPBRAID
VILLAIN
VOLTAIC
WAGTAIL
WASSAIL
WAYLAID

••••A•I

ABENAKI
AFGHANI
AIRTAXI
ANASAZI
BENGALI
CAMPARI
CHAPATI
FERRARI
GALVANI
GOURAMI
GUARANI
MAGNANI
MONTANI
OMPHALI
ORIGAMI
PAHLAVI
PUNJABI
SHIKARI
SYLLABI
TOPKAPI

TSUNAMI
TYMPANI

•••••AI
ASSEGAI
BALIHAI
HYUNDAI
JAIALAI
KUTENAI
MOLOKAI
NIKOLAI
OLDUVAI
SAMURAI

AJ•••••
AJACCIO

A•J••••
ABJURED
ABJURES
ADJOINS
ADJOURN
ADJUDGE
ADJUNCT
ADJURED
ADJURES
ADJUSTS

A••••J•
ALFORJA

•AJ••••
CAJOLED
CAJOLER
CAJOLES
FAJITAS
LAJOLLA
MAJESTE
MAJESTY
MAJEURE
MAJORCA
MAJORED
PAJAMAS
RAJPUTS

•A•J•••
BANJOES
DAYJOBS
FANJETS
GASJETS
PALJOEY
RAMJETS
SANJOSE
SANJUAN
VALJEAN

•A••J••
KARAJAN
NAVAJOS

•A•••J•
BASENJI
VALLEJO

••A•J••
GRAYJAY
LEARJET
TIANJIN

•••AJ••
KARAJAN
NAVAJOS

•••A•J•
JUMANJI

AK•••••
AKIHITO

A•K••••
ACKACKS
ALKALIS
ALKENES
ANKLETS
ASKANCE
ASKEDIN
ASKSFOR
ASKSOUT
AUKLETS
AWKWARD
AYKROYD

A••K•••
AGAKHAN
AIRKISS
ALAKING
ALYKHAN
ARIKARA
AWAKENS
AWAKING

A•••K••
ABNAKIS
ALASKAN

A••••K•
ABENAKI
ABUBAKR
ACKACKS
AIRLIKE
AMERIKA
ANORAKS
ANTLIKE
APELIKE
ARAWAKS
ARMLIKE
ASSLIKE
ATSTAKE
ATTACKS
ATTUCKS
AUTARKY

A•••••K
AIRLOCK
AIRSOCK
ARMLOCK
ARTWORK
ATATURK

•AK••••
BAKEOFF
BAKLAVA
CAKEMIX
CAKIEST
DAKOTAN
DAKOTAS
FAKEFUR
JAKARTA
LAKIEST
LAKOTAS
LAKSHMI
MAKEFOR
MAKEHAY
MAKEOFF
MAKEOUT
MAKEPAR
MAKESDO
MAKESIT
MAKESUP
MAKEUPS
MAKEWAY
MAKINGS
NAKEDLY
OAKFERN
OAKLAND
OAKLAWN
OAKLEAF
OAKLIKE
OAKMOSS
OAKTREE
RAKEDIN
RAKEDUP
RAKEOFF
RAKESIN
RAKESUP
TAKEAIM
TAKENIN
TAKENON
TAKEOFF
TAKEONE
TAKEOUT
TAKESIN
TAKESON
TAKESTO
TAKESUP
TAKETEN
WAKEFUL
WAKENED
WAKENER
WAKESUP
YAKIMAS
YAKKERS
YAKKING
YAKUTSK
YAKUZAS

•A•K•••
BACKBAY
BACKBIT
BACKEND
BACKERS
BACKHOE
BACKING
BACKLIT
BACKLOG
BACKOFF
BACKOUT
BACKRUB
BACKSIN
BACKSUP
BACKUPS
BALKANS
BALKIER
BALKILY
BALKING
BANKERS
BANKING
BANKSON
BARKEEP
BARKERS
BARKIER
BARKING
BARKLEY
BARKSAT
BASKETS
BASKING
CACKLED
CACKLER
CACKLES
CALKING
CALKINS
CANKERS
CARKING
CATKINS
DANKEST
DARKENS
DARKEST
DARKISH
DARKMAN
DAWKISH
GASKETS
GASKINS
GAWKERS
GAWKIER
GAWKILY
GAWKING
GAWKISH
HACKERS
HACKETT
HACKIES
HACKING
HACKLED
HACKLES
HACKMAN
HACKNEY
HACKSAW
HANKERS
HANKIES
HARKENS
HARKING
HAWKERS
HAWKEYE
HAWKING
HAWKINS
HAWKISH
JACKALS
JACKASS
JACKDAW
JACKETS
JACKEYS
JACKIES
JACKING
JACKPOT
JACKSON
JACKSUP
JACKTAR
LACKEYS
LACKING
LANKEST
LANKIER
LANKILY
LARKISH
MALKINS
MANKIND
MARKERS
MARKETS
MARKHAM
MARKHOR
MARKING
MARKKAA
MARKOFF
MARKOVA
MARKSUP
MARKUPS
MASKERS
MASKING
MAWKISH
NANKEEN
NAPKINS
PACKAGE
PACKARD
PACKERS
PACKETS
PACKICE
PACKING
PACKRAT
PACKSUP
PARKADE
PARKING
PARKWAY
PAWKIER
RACKETS
RACKING
RACKSUP
RANKERS
RANKEST
RANKING
RANKISH
RANKLED
RANKLES
RAYKROC
SACKERS
SACKFUL
SACKING
SACKOUT
SARKIER
TACKERS
TACKIER
TACKILY
TACKING
TACKLED
TACKLER
TACKLES
TACKSON
TALKBIG
TALKERS
TALKIER
TALKIES
TALKING
TALKOUT
TALKSAT
TALKSTO
TALKSUP
TANKARD
TANKERS
TANKFUL
TANKING
TANKSUP
TANKTOP
TASKING
WACKIER
WACKILY
WAIKIKI
WALKERS
WALKING
WALKINS
WALKMAN
WALKONS
WALKOUT
WALKSON
WALKUPS
WALKWAY
YACKING
YAKKERS
YAKKING
YANKEES
YANKING
YANKTON

•A••K••
BANGKOK
BATIKED
BAULKED
CAULKED
CAULKER
HANUKAH
KABUKIS
KANAKAS
KARAKUL
KARAKUM
KAYAKED
KAYAKER
KAZAKHS
LALAKER
MARKKAA
MARYKAY
NABOKOV
PASSKEY
RAMEKIN
SALUKIS

•A•••K•
BAGLIKE
BATLIKE
BAZOOKA
CATLIKE
DAMASKS
DASHIKI
EARLIKE
FADLIKE
FANLIKE
FATLIKE
HAGLIKE
HATLIKE
JAMLIKE
JAWLIKE
KARAOKE
LAWLIKE
MANLIKE
MAZURKA
OAKLIKE
OARLIKE
OATLIKE
PALOOKA
PANCAKE
PANICKY
PAPLIKE
PAPRIKA
PARTAKE
RAMLIKE
RATLIKE
RAYLIKE
SACLIKE
SAWLIKE
TAGLIKE
TANOAKS
VANDYKE
WAIKIKI
WARLIKE
WAXLIKE

•A••••K
BANGKOK
BANNOCK
BARRACK
CARPARK
CARRICK
CASSOCK
CATWALK
DAYBOOK
EARLOCK
EARMARK
FATBACK
GANGTOK
GARRICK
HADDOCK
HAMHOCK
HAMMOCK
HANCOCK
HASSOCK
HATRACK
HAUBERK
HAYFORK
HAYRACK
JAMPACK
JANACEK
JANNOCK
JAYWALK
KAISHEK
LAMARCK
LAYBACK
MAFFICK
MASARYK
MATLOCK
MATTOCK
OARLOCK
PADDOCK
PADLOCK
PARTOOK
PATRICK
RANSACK
RATFINK
RATPACK
RAWSILK
SADSACK
SARAWAK
SAWBUCK
VANDYCK
VANEYCK
WARLOCK
WARWICK
WAXWORK
YAKUTSK
YASHMAK
ZATOPEK

••AK•••
AGAKHAN
ALAKING
AWAKENS
AWAKING
BEAKERS
BRAKING
FLAKERS
FLAKIER
FLAKILY
FLAKING
LEAKAGE
LEAKERS
LEAKIER
LEAKING
PEAKING
PEAKISH
QUAKERS
QUAKIER
QUAKILY
QUAKING
SHAKERS
SHAKEUP
SHAKIER
SHAKILY
SHAKING
SHAKOES
SLAKING
SNAKIER
SNAKILY
SNAKING
SOAKERS
SOAKING
SOAKSUP
STAKING
WEAKENS
WEAKEST
WEAKISH

••A•K••
ALASKAN
BLACKED
BLACKEN
BLACKER
BLACKIE
BLACKLY
BLANKED
BLANKER
BLANKET
BLANKLY
BRACKEN
BRACKET
CHALKED
CHALKUP
CLACKED
CLANKED
CRACKED
CRACKER
CRACKLE
CRACKLY
CRACKUP
CRANKED
CRANKUP
FLANKED
FLANKER
FRANKED
FRANKEN
FRANKER
FRANKIE
FRANKLY
FRANKOZ
GRACKLE
HEARKEN
KNACKER
PLACKET
PLANKED
PRANKED
QUACKED
SHACKLE
SHANKAR
SHANKED
SHARKEY
SKANKED
SKANKER
SLACKED
SLACKEN
SLACKER
SLACKLY
SMACKED
SMACKER
SNACKED
SNACKER
SPACKLE
SPANKED
SPANKER
SPARKED
SPARKLE
STACKED
STACKUP
STALKED
STALKER
STARKER
STARKLY
SWANKED
SWANKER
THANKED
TRACKED
TRACKER
UNASKED
WHACKED
WRACKED

••A••K•
ARAWAKS
PEALIKE
ROANOKE
SPASSKY
TEACAKE
UNALIKE

••A•••K
ATATURK
BEATNIK
LEACOCK
PEACOCK
SEASICK

•••AK••
ABNAKIS
BELAKUN
BETAKEN
BETAKES
BLEAKER
BLEAKLY
BREAKER
BREAKIN
BREAKUP
CLOAKED
CONAKRY
CREAKED
CROAKED
DEBAKEY
DUKAKIS
FREAKED
INTAKES
KANAKAS
KARAKUL
KARAKUM
KAYAKED
KAYAKER
KAZAKHS
LALAKER
REMAKES
RETAKEN
RETAKES
SNEAKED
SNEAKER
SNEAKIN
SPEAKER
SPEAKOF
SPEAKUP
TWEAKED
UNBAKED
UNMAKES
UPTAKES
WREAKED

•••A•K•
ACKACKS
ATTACKS
AUTARKY
DAMASKS
DEBARKS
EMBANKS
EMBARKS
HIJACKS
KARAOKE
KOLACKY
MOHAWKS
PULASKI
REMARKS
SQUAWKS
SQUAWKY
THWACKS
UNMASKS
UNPACKS
UNTACKS

•••A••K
JANACEK
LAMARCK
MASARYK
MUBARAK
RUNAMOK
SARAWAK

••••AK•
ABENAKI
ABUBAKR
ANORAKS
ARAWAKS
ATSTAKE
BUROAKS
CUPCAKE
FORSAKE
HOECAKE
HOTCAKE
KODIAKS
MISTAKE
OILCAKE
OUTTAKE
PANCAKE
PARTAKE
PINOAKS
REDOAKS
SCREAKS
SLOVAKS
SQUEAKS
SQUEAKY
STREAKS
STREAKY
TANOAKS
TEACAKE

••••A•K
BARRACK
BIGTALK
BULWARK
BURBANK
CARPARK
CATWALK
COSSACK
CUTBACK
DENMARK
EARMARK
EYEBANK
FATBACK
FOGBANK
GETBACK
GOSHAWK
GOTBACK
HATRACK
HAYRACK
HOGBACK
HOLYARK
ICEPACK
JAMPACK
JAYWALK
JOBBANK
LAYBACK
MUDPACK
ONTRACK
OUTBACK
OUTRANK
OUTTALK
PEPTALK
POLLACK
RANSACK
RATPACK
RECHALK
RETRACK
RUNBACK
SADSACK
SETBACK
SIXPACK
SKIMASK
SKIRACK
SKYJACK
SKYLARK
TEDMACK
TIERACK
TIETACK
TINTACK
UNSTACK
UPQUARK
WIDMARK

•••••AK
BESPEAK
HOLMOAK
LIVEOAK
MUBARAK
OFFPEAK
PRESOAK
SARAWAK
UNCLOAK
WOZNIAK
YASHMAK
YITZHAK

AL•••••
ALABAMA
ALADDIN
ALAKING
ALAMEDA
ALAMEIN
ALAMODE
ALARCON
ALARMED
ALARMER
ALARUMS
ALASKAN
ALBANIA
ALBEDOS
ALBENIZ
ALBERTA
ALBERTO
ALBINOS
ALBUMEN
ALBUMIN
ALBUNDY
ALCAZAR
ALCHEMY
ALCOHOL
ALCOVES
ALDENTE
ALDRICH
ALEMBIC
ALENCON
ALERTED
ALERTER
ALERTLY
ALEWIFE
ALFALFA
ALFIERI
ALFONSO
ALFORJA
ALFREDO
ALGEBRA
ALGERIA
ALGIERS
ALIASES
ALIBABA
ALIDADE
ALIENEE
ALIENOR
ALIGHTS
ALIGNED
ALIGNER
ALIMENT
ALIMONY
ALINING
ALKALIS
ALKENES
ALLAYED
ALLAYER
ALLEARS
ALLEGED
ALLEGER
ALLEGES
ALLEGRO
ALLELES
ALLENBY
ALLENDE
ALLERGY
ALLEYES
ALLGONE
ALLHAIL
ALLHEAL
ALLHERE
ALLISON
ALLOFME
ALLOVER
ALLOWAY
ALLOWED
ALLOYED
ALLSTAR
ALLSTON
ALLTIME
ALLTOLD
ALLUDED
ALLUDES
ALLURED
ALLURES
ALLUVIA
ALLYING
ALLYSON
ALMAATA
ALMADEN
ALMANAC
ALMONDS
ALOHAOE
ALOOFLY
ALPACAS
ALREADY
ALRIGHT
ALSATIA
ALSORAN
ALTERED
ALTERER
ALTOONA
ALTOSAX
ALUMNAE
ALUMNAL
ALUMNUS
ALUNSER
ALVAREZ
ALVEOLI
ALWORTH
ALYKHAN
ALYOSHA
ALYSSUM

A•L••••
ABLATED
ABLATES
ABLAUTS
AELFRIC
AILERON
AILMENT
ALLAYED
ALLAYER
ALLEARS
ALLEGED
ALLEGER
ALLEGES
ALLEGRO
ALLELES
ALLENBY
ALLENDE
ALLERGY
ALLEYES
ALLGONE
ALLHAIL
ALLHEAL
ALLHERE
ALLISON
ALLOFME
ALLOVER
ALLOWAY
ALLOWED
ALLOYED
ALLSTAR
ALLSTON
ALLTIME
ALLTOLD
ALLUDED
ALLUDES
ALLURED
ALLURES
ALLUVIA
ALLYING
ALLYSON
APLENTY
ARLEDGE
ATLANTA
ATLARGE
ATLASES
ATLATLS
ATLEAST

A••L•••
ABALONE
ABELARD
ABILENE
ABILITY
ABOLISH
ACCLAIM
ACOLYTE
ADDLING
ADELINE
ADOLPHE
ADULATE
ADULTLY
AEOLIAN
AFFLICT
AGELESS
AGILELY
AGILITY
AIDLESS
AIMLESS
AIRLANE
AIRLESS
AIRLIFT
AIRLIKE
AIRLINE
AIRLOCK
AMALGAM
AMBLERS
AMBLING
AMPLEST
AMPLIFY
AMULETS
AMYLASE
ANALOGS
ANALOGY
ANALYSE
ANALYST
ANALYZE
ANELING
ANGLERS
ANGLING
ANILINE
ANKLETS
ANTLERS
ANTLIKE
ANTLION
APELIKE
APOLOGY
APPLAUD
APPLETS
APPLIED
APPLIES
ARALSEA
ARCLAMP
ARMLESS
ARMLETS
ARMLIKE
ARMLOAD
ARMLOCK
ARTLESS
ASHLAND
ASHLARS
ASHLESS
ASSLIKE
ASYLUMS
ATALOSS
ATELIER
ATHLETE
AUKLETS
AVULSED
AVULSES
AWELESS
AWNLESS
AXILLAE
AXOLOTL
AZALEAS

A•••L••
AAMILNE
ABSALOM
ABSOLUT
ABSOLVE
ACRYLIC
AEDILES
AIRFLOW
AIRPLAY
ALFALFA
ALKALIS
ALLELES
AMIBLUE
AMPULES
ANGELES
ANGELIC
ANGELOU
ANGELUS
ANGOLAN
ANGULAR
ANNALEE
ANNELID
ANNULAR
ANNULUS
ANTILOG
APHELIA
APPALLS
AREOLAE
AREOLAR
AREOLAS

ARGYLES
ASTOLAT
AUDILES
AURALEE
AURALLY
AVAILED
AVONLEA
AWFULLY
AXIALLY
AXILLAE

A••••L•

ACEROLA
ACRIDLY
ACTABLE
ACUTELY
ADDABLE
ADDIBLE
ADEPTLY
ADULTLY
AERIALS
AFFABLE
AFFABLY
AGILELY
AIRBALL
AIRHOLE
AIRMILE
AIRWOLF
ALERTLY
ALLTOLD
ALOOFLY
ALVEOLI
AMAPOLA
AMIABLE
AMIABLY
AMPOULE
ANATOLE
ANGRILY
ANIMALS
ANNEALS
ANNUALS
ANOMALY
ANOUILH
ANTHILL
APISHLY
APOSTLE
APPALLS
APPEALS
ARMFULS
ARMHOLE
ARTFILM
ARTICLE
ARUGULA
ASARULE
ASPHALT
ASSAILS
ASSAULT
ATFAULT
ATINGLE
ATLATLS
AUDIBLE
AUDIBLY
AURALLY
AUREOLA
AUREOLE
AURICLE
AVOWALS
AWFULLY
AXIALLY

A•••••L

ABIGAIL
ABUTTAL
ABYSMAL
ACCRUAL
ADMIRAL
ADRENAL
AEROSOL
AIRBALL
AIRCOOL
AIRFOIL
AIRMAIL
ALCOHOL
ALLHAIL
ALLHEAL
ALUMNAL
ANNABEL
ANTHILL
APPAREL
APTERAL
AROUSAL
ARRIVAL
ARSENAL
ASOCIAL
ASUSUAL
AUGURAL
AURORAL
AUSTRAL
AXOLOTL

•AL••••

BALANCE
BALATON
BALBOAS
BALCONY
BALDEST
BALDING
BALDISH
BALDRIC
BALDWIN
BALEENS
BALEFUL
BALFOUR
BALIHAI
BALKANS
BALKIER
BALKILY
BALKING
BALLADE
BALLADS
BALLARD
BALLAST
BALLBOY
BALLETS
BALLOON
BALLOTS
BALLSUP
BALMIER
BALMILY
BALONEY
BALSAMS
CALCIFY
CALCITE
CALCIUM
CALDERA
CALDRON
CALENDS
CALGARY
CALHOUN
CALIBAN
CALIBER
CALIBRE
CALICES
CALICOS
CALIPER
CALIPHS
CALKING
CALKINS
CALLBOX
CALLERS
CALLFOR
CALLING
CALLINS
CALLOFF
CALLOUS
CALLOUT
CALLSIN
CALLSON
CALLSUP
CALMEST
CALMING
CALOMEL
CALORIC
CALORIE
CALPACS
CALTECH
CALUMET
CALUMNY
CALVARY
CALVERT
CALVING
CALYCES
CALYPSO
CALYXES
CALZONE
DALETHS
DALLIED
DALLIER
DALLIES
DALTREY
FALAFEL
FALCONS
FALLACY
FALLFOR
FALLGUY
FALLING
FALLOFF
FALLOUT
FALLOWS
FALLSIN
FALLSON
FALLSTO
FALSELY
FALSEST
FALSIFY
FALSITY
FALTERS
FALWELL
GALAGOS
GALAHAD
GALATEA
GALATIA
GALILEE
GALILEI
GALILEO
GALLANT
GALLEON
GALLERY
GALLEYS
GALLING
GALLIUM
GALLONS
GALLOPS
GALOOTS
GALPALS
GALUMPH
GALVANI
HALCYON
HALFDAN
HALFWAY
HALFWIT
HALIBUT
HALIDES
HALIFAX
HALITES
HALLOWS
HALLWAY
HALOGEN
HALOING
HALSTON
HALTERS
HALTING
HALVAHS
HALVING
HALYARD
JALISCO
LALAKER
LALANNE
LALIQUE
MALABAR
MALACCA
MALACHI
MALAISE
MALAMUD
MALAYAN
MALCOLM
MALEATE
MALEFIC
MALIGNS
MALKINS
MALLARD
MALLETS
MALLOWS
MALLRAT
MALMSEY
MALODOR
MALRAUX
MALTEDS
MALTESE
MALTHUS
MALTIER
MALTING
MALTOSE
PALACES
PALADIN
PALANCE
PALATAL
PALATES
PALAVER
PALAZZI
PALAZZO
PALEDRY
PALERMO
PALETTE
PALFREY
PALIEST
PALJOEY
PALLETS
PALLIER
PALLING
PALLIUM
PALLORS
PALMARY
PALMATE
PALMIER
PALMING
PALMIST
PALMOFF
PALMOIL
PALMTOP
PALOMAR
PALOOKA
PALTERS
PALTROW
RALEIGH
RALLIED
RALLIER
RALLIES
RALLYTO
RALSTON
SALAAMS
SALABLE
SALADIN
SALAMIS
SALAZAR
SALCHOW
SALERNO
SALIENT
SALIERI
SALINAS
SALLETS
SALLIED
SALLIES
SALLOWS
SALMONS
SALOONS
SALSIFY
SALSODA
SALTBOX
SALTERS
SALTIER
SALTILY
SALTINE
SALTING
SALTISH
SALUKIS
SALUTED
SALUTES
SALVAGE
SALVERS
SALVIAS
SALVING
SALVOES
SALVORS
TALARIA
TALCUMS
TALENTS
TALKBIG
TALKERS
TALKIER
TALKIES
TALKING
TALKOUT
TALKSAT
TALKSTO
TALKSUP
TALLEST
TALLIED
TALLIER
TALLIES
TALLINN
TALLISH
TALLOWS
TALLYHO
TALLYUP
TALONED
TALUSES
VALANCE
VALENCE
VALENCY
VALERIE
VALIANT
VALIDLY
VALISES
VALJEAN
VALLEJO
VALLEYS
VALOURS
VALUATE
VALUING
VALVATE
WALCOTT
WALDORF
WALKERS
WALKING
WALKINS
WALKMAN
WALKONS
WALKOUT
WALKSON
WALKUPS
WALKWAY
WALLABY
WALLACE
WALLACH
WALLETS
WALLEYE
WALLING
WALLOON
WALLOPS
WALLOWS
WALLSUP
WALMART
WALNUTS
WALPOLE
WALSTON
WALTERS
WALTZED
WALTZER
WALTZES

•A•L•••

BAGLIKE
BAILEES
BAILERS
BAILEYS
BAILIFF
BAILING
BAILORS
BAILOUT
BAKLAVA
BALLADE
BALLADS
BALLARD
BALLAST
BALLBOY
BALLETS
BALLOON
BALLOTS
BALLSUP
BARLESS
BARLEYS
BATLIKE
BAULKED
BAWLERS
BAWLING
BAWLOUT
BAYLEAF
CABLERS
CABLETV
CABLING
CALLBOX
CALLERS
CALLFOR
CALLING
CALLINS
CALLOFF
CALLOUS
CALLOUT
CALLSIN
CALLSON
CALLSUP
CAPLESS
CAPLETS
CARLESS
CARLOAD
CARLSON
CARLTON
CARLYLE
CATLIKE
CAULKED
CAULKER
DAHLIAS
DAILIES
DALLIED
DALLIER
DALLIES
DARLENE
DARLING
DAYLILY
DAYLONG
EAGLETS
EAGLING
EARLDOM
EARLESS
EARLIER
EARLIKE
EARLOBE
EARLOCK
EARLYON
FABLERS
FADLIKE
FAILING
FAILURE
FALLACY
FALLFOR
FALLGUY
FALLING
FALLOFF
FALLOUT
FALLOWS
FALLSIN
FALLSON
FALLSTO
FANLIKE
FARLEFT
FATLESS
FATLIKE
FAULTED
GAGLAWS
GAGLINE
GALLANT
GALLEON
GALLERY
GALLEYS
GALLING
GALLIUM
GALLONS
GALLOPS
GAOLERS
GAOLING
GAPLESS
GARLAND
GASLESS
GASLOGS
GATLING
GAULISH
HAGLIKE
HAILING
HALLOWS
HALLWAY
HAMLETS
HAPLESS
HATLESS
HATLIKE
HAULAGE
HAULERS
HAULING
HAULOFF
HAULSUP
HAYLOFT
JAGLESS
JAILERS
JAILING
JAMLIKE
JARLESS
JAWLESS
JAWLIKE
JAWLINE
JAYLENO
KARLOFF
LADLERS
LADLING
LAPLACE
LAPLAND
LAPLATA
LAWLESS
LAWLIKE
MADLIBS
MAILBAG
MAILBOX
MAILCAR
MAILERS
MAILING
MAILLOT
MAILOUT
MAILSIN
MALLARD
MALLETS
MALLOWS
MALLRAT
MANLESS
MANLIER
MANLIKE
MARLENE
MARLINS
MARLOWE
MATLESS
MATLOCK
MAULDIN
MAULING
NAILERS
NAILING
NAILSET
NAILSIN
NAPLESS
OAKLAND
OAKLAWN
OAKLEAF
OAKLIKE
OARLESS
OARLIKE
OARLOCK
OATLIKE
PABLUMS
PADLOCK
PAHLAVI
PAILFUL
PAILOUS
PALLETS
PALLIER
PALLING
PALLIUM
PALLORS
PAPLIKE
PARLAYS
PARLEYS
PARLORS
PARLOUR
PARLOUS
PAULINA
PAULINE
PAULING
PAULIST
PAULSEN
PAVLOVA
PAYLOAD
RAGLANS
RAILERS
RAILING
RAILSAT
RAILWAY
RALLIED
RALLIER
RALLIES
RALLYTO
RAMLIKE
RANLATE
RATLIKE
RATLINE
RAYLIKE
SACLIKE
SAILING
SAILORS
SALLETS
SALLIED
SALLIES
SALLOWS
SAMLETS
SANLUIS
SAPLESS
SAPLING
SAWLIKE
SAWLOGS
TABLEAU
TABLETS
TABLING
TABLOID
TAGLIKE
TAGLINE
TAILEND
TAILFIN
TAILING
TAILLES
TAILOFF
TAILORS
TALLEST
TALLIED
TALLIER
TALLIES
TALLINN
TALLISH
TALLOWS
TALLYHO
TALLYUP
TANLINE
TAXLESS
VALLEJO
VALLEYS
VARLETS
VAULTED
VAULTER
WAILERS
WAILFUL
WAILING
WALLABY
WALLACE
WALLACH
WALLETS
WALLEYE
WALLING
WALLOON
WALLOPS
WALLOWS
WALLSUP
WARLESS
WARLIKE
WARLOCK
WARLORD
WAXLIKE
WAYLAID
WAYLAYS
WAYLESS

•A••L••

AAMILNE
BABALOO
BABBLED
BABBLER
BABBLES
BABYLON
BACALAO
BACILLI
BACKLIT
BACKLOG
BAFFLED
BAFFLER
BAFFLES
BANALLY
BANGLES
BARKLEY
BASALLY
BASALTS
BATTLED
BATTLER
BATTLES
BAUBLES
CABALAS
CACKLED
CACKLER
CACKLES
CAJOLED
CAJOLER
CAJOLES
CAMELIA
CAMELOT
CAMILLE
CANDLES
CANTLES
CAPELET
CAPELLA
CAPULET
CAROLED
CAROLER
CAROLUS
CAROLYN
CASELAW
CASTLED
CASTLES
CATALAN
CATALOG
CATALPA
CAUDLES
CAVALRY
CAVILED
CAVILER
DABBLED
DABBLER
DABBLES
DAIMLER
DANDLED
DANDLES
DANELAW
DANGLED
DANGLER
DANGLES
DAPPLED
DAPPLES
DARNLEY
DAWDLED
DAWDLER
DAWDLES
DAZZLED
DAZZLER
DAZZLES
EARFLAP
EARPLUG
FACULAE
FACULTY
FAMULUS
FANCLUB
GABBLED
GABBLES
GAGGLES
GALILEE
GALILEI
GALILEO
GAMBLED
GAMBLER
GAMBLES
GAMELAW
GANGLED
GANGLIA
GANTLET
GARBLED
GARBLES
GARGLED
GARGLES
GATELEG
GAVELED
GAZELLE
HAARLEM
HACKLED
HACKLES
HAGGLED
HAGGLER
HAGGLES
HAMELIN
HANDLED
HANDLER
HANDLES
HASSLED
HASSLES
JAIALAI
JANGLED
JANGLES
JAVELIN
KAROLYI
LABELED
LABELER
LABELLE
LACHLAN
LAIDLOW
LAJOLLA
LANGLEY
LANOLIN
LAPALMA
LAPELED
LASALLE
LAVALSE
LAYSLOW
MACULAE
MAHALIA
MAILLOT
MANGLED
MANGLES
MANILOW
MANTLED
MANTLES
MARBLED
MARBLES
MARILYN
MARYLOU
MATELOT
MATILDA
MAUDLIN
MAXILLA
MAYALIN
NACELLE
NASALLY
NATALIA
NATALIE
PABULUM
PADDLED
PADDLER
PADDLES
PAISLEY
PANELED
PAPILLA
PAROLED
PAROLEE
PAROLES
PARSLEY
PATELLA
PAYOLAS
RABBLES
RADDLED
RADDLES
RADULAE
RAFFLED
RAFFLER
RAFFLES
RAMBLED
RAMBLER
RAMBLES
RANKLED
RANKLES
RASSLED
RASSLES
RATTLED
RATTLER
RATTLES
RAVELED
SADDLED
SADDLER
SADDLES
SAMPLED
SAMPLER
SAMPLES
SANDLOT
SARALEE
SAVALAS
SAVELOY
TABULAR
TACKLED
TACKLER
TACKLES
TAGALOG
TAILLES
TAMALES
TANGLED
TANGLES
TASHLIN
TATTLED
TATTLER
TATTLES
VANILLA
VANILLI
WADDLED
WADDLER
WADDLES
WAFFLED
WAFFLER
WAFFLES
WAGGLED
WAGGLES
WAMBLED
WAMBLES
WANGLED
WANGLER
WANGLES
WARBLED
WARBLER
WARBLES
WATTLES
WAVELET

•A•••L•

BACILLI
BAGFULS
BAGGILY
BAGNOLD
BALKILY
BALMILY
BANALLY
BARBELL
BARBELS
BARRELS
BASALLY
BATTELS
BAWDILY
CAMILLE
CAMPILY
CANCELS
CANDELA
CANFULS
CANNILY
CANNOLI
CANTILY
CAPABLE
CAPABLY
CAPELLA
CAPFULS
CAPSULE
CARFULS
CARLYLE
CARPALS
CARPELS
CARRELS
CARROLL
CARTELS
CASTILE
CASUALS
CATCALL
CATTILY
CATWALK
DACTYLS
DAFFILY
DAMSELS
DANIELS
DATEDLY
DAYLILY
DAZEDLY
EAGERLY
EARFULS
EARTHLY
EATABLE
FACIALS
FAINTLY
FALSELY
FALWELL
FANBELT
FANCILY
FATTILY
GAGRULE
GALPALS
GAMBOLS
GAUDILY
GAUNTLY
GAUZILY
GAVIALS
GAWKILY
GAZELLE
HAMMILY
HANDILY
HANSOLO
HAPPILY
HARDILY
HARSHLY
HASTILY
JACKALS
JADEDLY
JARFULS
JAYWALK
JAZZILY
KAMPALA
LABELLE
LABIALS
LAJOLLA
LANKILY
LAPBELT
LAPFULS
LARGELY
LASALLE
LASCALA
LAURELS
MALCOLM
MAMMALS
MANACLE
MANDALA
MANDELA
MANHOLE
MANIPLE
MANTELS
MANUALS
MARCELS
MARSALA
MARVELS
MAXILLA
MAXWELL
MAYPOLE
NACELLE
NAIVELY
NAKEDLY
NARWALS
NASALLY
NASTILY
NATTILY
PANFULS
PANICLE
PANOPLY
PAPILLA
PARABLE
PARCELS
PASSELS
PASTELS
PATELLA
PATROLS
PAYABLE
PAYROLL
RABIDLY
RADIALS
RADICLE
RAGDOLL
RAINILY
RANDALL
RAPIDLY
RAPPELS
RASCALS
RATABLE
RATHOLE
RAVIOLI
RAWSILK
SAINTLY
SALABLE
SALTILY
SAMBALS

SAMHILL
SANDALS
SANDFLY
SAPPILY
SASSILY
SAUCILY
SAVABLE
SAVVILY
SAWMILL
TACITLY
TACKILY
TACTILE
TADPOLE
TAGSALE
TAMABLE
TAMBALA
TANGELO
TARBELL
TARDILY
TARSALS
TASSELS
TASTILY
TATTILY
TAWNILY
TAXABLE
VACUOLE
VAGUELY
VALIDLY
VANDALS
VANILLA
VANILLI
VAPIDLY
VASSALS
VATFULS
WACKILY
WALPOLE
WASPILY
WAYBILL

•A•••L

BALEFUL
BANEFUL
BARBELL
BARNOWL
BASHFUL
BATGIRL
BATHOIL
CALOMEL
CAPITAL
CAPITOL
CARACAL
CARAMEL
CARAVEL
CAREFUL
CARPOOL
CARROLL
CATCALL
CATTAIL
DAREFUL
EASEFUL
FACTFUL
FACTUAL
FALAFEL
FALWELL
FANMAIL
FANTAIL
FATEFUL
GABRIEL
GAINFUL
GAMBREL
GASOHOL
HANDFUL
HARMFUL
HATEFUL
KARAKUL
LACTEAL
LACUNAL
LAMINAL
LAMPOIL
LATERAL
MAGICAL
MARITAL
MARSHAL
MARTIAL
MAXIMAL
MAXWELL
MAYORAL
NAHUATL
NARWHAL
NATURAL
OATMEAL
PAGEFUL
PAILFUL
PAINFUL
PALATAL
PALMOIL
PARASOL
PARBOIL
PARTIAL
PASCHAL
PASSEUL
PATRIAL
PAYROLL
RADICAL
RAGDOLL
RAGEFUL
RANDALL
RAPHAEL
RATTAIL
RAWDEAL
SACKFUL
SAMHILL
SANIBEL
SATCHEL
SAWMILL
TACTFUL
TANKFUL
TARBELL
TARHEEL
VANPOOL
WAGTAIL
WAILFUL
WAKEFUL
WASSAIL
WASTREL
WAYBILL
WAYCOOL
YAWNFUL

••AL•••

ABALONE
AMALGAM
ANALOGS
ANALOGY
ANALYSE
ANALYST
ANALYZE
ARALSEA
ATALOSS
AZALEAS
BIALIES
BRALESS
CHALETS
CHALICE
CHALKED
CHALKUP
CHALONS
COALBIN
COALCAR
COALERS
COALGAS
COALOIL
COALTAR
DEALERS
DEALING
DEALOUT
DEALSIN
DEALTIN
DIALECT
DIALERS
DIALING
DIALOGS
DUALITY
EGALITE
EXALTED
FOALING
GOALIES
GOALONG
HEALALL
HEALERS
HEALING
HEALTHY
HIALEAH
HYALINE
ITALIAN
ITALICS
JEALOUS
MEALIER
MEALIES
OPALINE
PEALIKE
PEALING
PHALANX
PRALINE
PSALMED
PSALTER
QUALIFY
QUALITY
REALISE
REALISM
REALIST
REALITY
REALIZE
REALTOR
SCALARS
SCALDED
SCALENE
SCALERS
SCALIER
SCALING
SCALLOP
SCALPED
SCALPEL
SCALPER
SEALABS
SEALANE
SEALANT
SEALEGS
SEALERS
SEALILY
SEALING
SEALION
SEALOFF
SEALSUP
SHALALA
SHALLOT
SHALLOW
SHALOMS
SLALOMS
SMALLER
SMALTOS
SPALLED
STALAGS
STALELY
STALEST
STALKED
STALKER
STALLED
SWALLET
SWALLOW
TEALEAF
TEALESS
THALERS
TRALALA
ULALUME
UNALIKE
VEALIER
WEALTHY
WHALERS
WHALING
ZEALAND
ZEALOTS
ZEALOUS

••A•L••

AVAILED
BEADLES
BEAGLES
BEATLES
BRADLEE
BRADLEY
BRAILLE
BRAWLED
BRAWLER
CHABLIS
CHAPLET
CHAPLIN
CHARLES
CHARLEY
CHARLIE
CRADLED
CRADLES
CRAWLED
CRAWLER
DRAWLED
EMAILED
ENABLED
ENABLES
EPAULET
FIATLUX
FLAILED
FLATLET
FRAILER
FRAILLY
FRAILTY
FRAWLEY
GNARLED
GRAYLAG
HAARLEM
JEANLUC
LEAFLET
MEASLES
ORACLES
PEARLED
PHARLAP
PLAYLET
QUAILED
SCALLOP
SCARLET
SEABLUE
SEASLUG
SHALLOT
SHALLOW
SHAPLEY
SMALLER
SNARLED
SPALLED
STABLED
STABLER
STABLES
STALLED
STANLEE
STANLEY
STAPLED
STAPLER
STAPLES
STARLET
STARLIT
SWALLET
SWALLOW
TRAILED
TRAILER
TRAWLED
TRAWLER

••A••L•

AMAPOLA
ANATOLE
ASARULE
BEASTLY
BLACKLY
BLACULA
BLANDLY
BLANKLY
BOATELS
BRAILLE
BRAMBLE
BRAMBLY
BRASHLY
BRAVELY
CHAGALL
CHAPELS
CHARILY
CLAVELL
CRACKLE
CRACKLY
CRASSLY
CRAYOLA
CRAZILY
DIABOLI
DRACULA
ENAMELS
EXACTLY
EXAMPLE
FLAKILY
FOAMILY
FRAGILE
FRAILLY
FRANKLY
FRAZZLE
GHASTLY
GRACILE
GRACKLE
GRANDLY
GRANOLA
GRANULE
GRAPPLE
GRAVELS
GRAVELY
HEADILY
HEALALL
HEAVILY
HOARILY
INANELY
INAPTLY
IRATELY
MEATILY
ONAROLL
PLAINLY
PRATTLE
QUAKILY
READILY
RIANTLY
SCANTLY
SCAPULA
SCARILY
SEAGULL
SEALILY
SEASALT
SEATTLE
SEAWALL
SEAWOLF
SHACKLE
SHADILY
SHAKILY
SHALALA
SHAMBLE
SHAPELY
SHARPLY
SLACKLY
SMARTLY
SNAFFLE
SNAKILY
SNAPPLE
SOAPILY
SPACKLE
SPANGLE
SPANGLY
SPARELY
SPARKLE
SPATULA
STABILE
STAGILY
STAIDLY
STALELY
STARKLY
STARTLE
STATELY
SUAVELY
SWADDLE
SWAHILI
TEABALL
TEARILY
TEASELS
TRALALA
TRAMPLE
TRAVELS
TWADDLE
UNAPTLY
WEARILY
WEASELS
WRANGLE

••A•••L

CHAGALL
CHANCEL
CHANNEL
CHATTEL
CLAIROL
CLAVELL
COALOIL
COASTAL
COAXIAL
CRANIAL
EMANUEL
EVANGEL
FEARFUL
FLANNEL
FRACTAL
GLACIAL
GRADUAL
GRAPNEL
HEALALL
HEATFUL
MOANFUL
ONAROLL
PEAFOWL
PLAYFUL
QUARREL
REAVAIL
SCALPEL
SCANDAL
SEAGULL
SEAWALL
SHAWWAL
SPANIEL
SPATIAL
TEABALL
TEARFUL
TRAMMEL
TRAVAIL
TRAYFUL
UNAWFUL

•••AL••

ABSALOM
ALFALFA
ALKALIS
ANNALEE
APPALLS
AURALEE
AURALLY
AXIALLY
BABALOO
BACALAO
BANALLY
BASALLY
BASALTS
BECALMS
BEFALLS
BIVALVE
BUGALOO
CABALAS
CATALAN
CATALOG
CATALPA
CAVALRY
DECALOG
DEDALUS
DEFALLA
DEPALMA
DESALTS
DEVALUE
EQUALED
EQUALLY
EXHALED
EXHALES
FEMALES
FINALES
FINALLY
GERALDO
HERALDS
HIDALGO
IDEALLY
IMPALAS
IMPALED
IMPALES
INGALLS
INHALED
INHALER
INHALES
INVALID
JAIALAI
LAPALMA
LASALLE
LAVALSE
LEGALLY
LOCALES
LOCALLY
LOYALLY
LOYALTY
MAHALIA
MAYALIN
MCCALLS
MEDALED
MISALLY
MORALES
MORALLY
NASALLY
NATALIA
NATALIE
NEPALIS
NOGALES
OGLALAS
PEDALED
PENALTY
PETALED
RECALLS
REDALGA
REGALED
REGALES
REGALIA
REGALLY
RESALES
RESALTS
REVALUE
RIVALED
RIVALRY
ROSALIE
ROYALLY
ROYALTY
ROYALWE
RURALLY
SARALEE
SAVALAS
SEDALIA
SOMALIA
SOMALIS
SQUALID
SQUALLS
SQUALOR
STEALTH
TAGALOG
TAMALES
THRALLS
TONALLY
TOTALED
TOTALLY
USUALLY
VENALLY
VIDALIA
VISALIA
VITALLY
VIVALDI
VOCALIC
VOCALLY
ZONALLY

•••A•L•

ACTABLE
ADDABLE
AFFABLE
AFFABLY
AMIABLE
AMIABLY
APPALLS
ASSAILS
ASSAULT
ATFAULT
ATLATLS
AURALLY
AXIALLY
BANALLY
BASALLY
BEFALLS
BEWAILS
BLEAKLY
BROADLY
BUYABLE
CAPABLE
CAPABLY
CHEAPLY
CITABLE
CLEANLY
CLEARLY
DEBACLE
DECARLO
DEFALLA
DEFAULT
DERAILS
DETAILS
DISABLE
DURABLE
DURABLY
EATABLE
ENTAILS
EQUABLE
EQUABLY
EQUALLY
FINAGLE
FINALLY
FIXABLE
FRIABLE
GREATLY
HIRABLE
HUMANLY
IDEALLY
INGALLS
INHAULS
ISRAELI
LASALLE
LEGALLY
LIKABLE
LIVABLE
LOCALLY
LOVABLE
LOVABLY
LOYALLY
MANACLE
MCCALLS
MINABLE
MIRACLE
MISALLY
MIXABLE
MORALLY
MOVABLE
MOVABLY
MUTABLE
MUTABLY
NASALLY
NOFAULT
NOTABLE
NOTABLY
PARABLE
PAYABLE
PLIABLE
PLIABLY
POTABLE
RATABLE
RECALLS
REGALLY
REMAILS
RENAILS
RENAULT
RETAILS
ROYALLY
RURALLY
SALABLE
SAVABLE
SCRAWLS
SCRAWLY
SEEABLE
SIZABLE
SIZABLY
SPRAWLS
SQUALLS
SQUATLY
TAMABLE
TAXABLE
TENABLE
TENABLY
THRALLS
TONALLY
TOTALLY
TREACLE
TREACLY
TREADLE
USEABLE
USUALLY
VENALLY
VITALLY
VOCALLY
WOMANLY
ZONALLY

•••A••L

ANNABEL
APPAREL
BUTANOL
CARACAL
CARAMEL
CARAVEL
CITADEL
EMPANEL
ESPANOL
ETHANOL
FALAFEL
GIRASOL
IMPANEL
KARAKUL
PALATAL
PARASOL
PHRASAL
UNRAVEL

••••AL•

AERIALS
AIRBALL
ANIMALS
ANNEALS
ANNUALS
ANOMALY
APPEALS
ASPHALT
AVOWALS
BEEBALM
BEEFALO
BENGALI
BENGALS
BIGTALK
BRIDALS
BUFFALO
CARPALS
CASUALS
CATCALL
CATWALK
CEMBALO
CEREALS
CHAGALL
CHORALE
CHORALS
COEVALS
CORRALS
CUEBALL
CUREALL
CYMBALS
DENIALS
DORSALS
DOSSALS
DRYWALL
EMERALD
ESPIALS
EYEBALL
FACIALS
FINIALS
FLYBALL
FORMALS
FORSALE
FURBALL
GALPALS
GAVIALS
GESTALT
GIMBALS
GOODALL
GUMBALL
GUNWALE
HEALALL
HERBALS
HYMNALS
INSTALL
INSTALS
JACKALS
JAYWALK
KAMPALA
KENDALL
KIMBALL
LABIALS
LASCALA
LIPBALM
LOWBALL
MAMMALS
MANDALA
MANUALS
MARSALA
MENIALS
MESCALS
MESSALA
MISCALL
MISSALS
MONDALE
MORTALS
MUTUALS
NARWALS
NORMALS
ODDBALL
OMPHALI
OOHLALA
ORDEALS
OUTTALK
OVERALL
PENPALS
PEPTALK
PERCALE
PIEBALD
PINBALL
PINWALE
PITFALL
PLURALS
PORTALS
PRESALE
RADIALS
RANDALL
RASCALS
RECHALK
REDEALS
REDEALT
REDIALS
REHEALS
RENTALS
REPEALS
RESCALE
RESEALS
REVEALS
RITUALS
SAMBALS
SANDALS
SEASALT
SEAWALL
SERIALS
SERVALS
SHALALA
SIGNALS
SOCIALS
SPIRALS
SQUEALS
TAGSALE
TAMBALA
TARSALS
TEABALL
TELLALL
TIMBALE
TIMBALS
TOSCALE
TRALALA
UNCIALS
UNSEALS
UPPSALA
UPSCALE
VANDALS
VASSALS
VERBALS
VISUALS

••••A•L

ABIGAIL
AIRBALL
AIRMAIL
ALLHAIL
BOBTAIL
CATCALL
CATTAIL
CHAGALL
CUEBALL
CUREALL
CURTAIL
DRYWALL
ENSNARL
EYEBALL
FANMAIL
FANTAIL
FLYBALL
FOXTAIL
FURBALL
GOODALL
GUMBALL
HEALALL
HOBNAIL
INSTALL
ISHMAEL
KENDALL
KIMBALL
LESPAUL
LOWBALL
MICHAEL
MIKHAIL
MISCALL
NAHUATL
ODDBALL
OVERALL
PIGTAIL
PINBALL
PINTAIL
PITFALL
PREVAIL
RANDALL
RAPHAEL
RATTAIL
REAVAIL
SEAWALL
SETSAIL
TEABALL
TELLALL
TOENAIL
TOPSAIL
TRAVAIL
UNSNARL
WAGTAIL
WASSAIL

•••••AL

ABUTTAL
ABYSMAL
ACCRUAL
ADMIRAL
ADRENAL
ALLHEAL
ALUMNAL
APTERAL
AROUSAL
ARRIVAL
ARSENAL
ASOCIAL
ASUSUAL
AUGURAL
AURORAL
AUSTRAL
BESTIAL
BIFOCAL
BIGDEAL
BIMODAL
BIPEDAL
CAPITAL
CARACAL
CENTRAL
CHLORAL
COASTAL
COAXIAL
COEQUAL
COMICAL
CONCEAL
CONGEAL
CONICAL
CORDIAL
CORNEAL
CRANIAL
CRUCIAL
CRYSTAL
CYNICAL
DECIMAL
DEPOSAL
DIGITAL
DIURNAL
DONEGAL
ENTHRAL
EPOCHAL
ESTIVAL
ETERNAL
ETHICAL
FACTUAL
FEDERAL
FEMORAL
FLUVIAL
FORREAL
FRACTAL
FRONTAL
FUNCHAL
FURSEAL
GENERAL
GETREAL
GLACIAL
GLOTTAL
GRADUAL
HELICAL
HUMERAL
ILLEGAL
IMMORAL
INITIAL
JOURNAL
JUVENAL
LACTEAL
LACUNAL
LAMINAL
LATERAL
LEXICAL
LIBERAL
LINGUAL
LITERAL
LOGICAL
LYRICAL
MAGICAL
MARITAL
MARSHAL
MARTIAL
MAXIMAL
MAYORAL
MEDICAL
MINERAL
MINIMAL
MISDEAL
MISDIAL
MISTRAL
MUSICAL
NARWHAL
NATURAL
NEUTRAL
NEWDEAL
NOMINAL
NUMERAL
NUPTIAL
OATMEAL
OEDIPAL
ONTRIAL
OPTICAL
OPTIMAL
ORBITAL
ORDINAL
OVOIDAL
PALATAL
PARTIAL
PASCHAL
PATRIAL
PERUSAL
PHRASAL
PIVOTAL
PLUVIAL
QUETZAL
RADICAL
RAWDEAL
RECITAL
REFUSAL
REMOVAL
RENEWAL
RETINAL
RETRIAL
REVIVAL
RORQUAL

SCANDAL
SEMINAL
SENEGAL
SENSUAL
SEVERAL
SHAWWAL
SORORAL
SPATIAL
SPECIAL
SPOUSAL
STERNAL
STOICAL
SUNDIAL
SURREAL
SYNODAL
TERTIAL
TEXTUAL
THERMAL
TOPICAL
TRIVIAL
TRUCIAL
TYPICAL
UNEQUAL
UNUSUAL
UXORIAL
VEGETAL
VENTRAL
VICTUAL
VIRTUAL
WOLFGAL

AM•••••

AMADEUS
AMALGAM
AMAPOLA
AMASSED
AMASSER
AMASSES
AMATEUR
AMATIVE
AMATORY
AMAZING
AMAZONS
AMBIENT
AMBLERS
AMBLING
AMBRIES
AMBROSE
AMENDED
AMENITY
AMERCED
AMERCES
AMERICA
AMERIGO
AMERIKA
AMERIND
AMHARIC
AMHERST
AMIABLE
AMIABLY
AMIBLUE
AMISTAD
AMMETER
AMMONIA
AMNESIA
AMNESTY
AMNIONS
AMOEBAE
AMOEBAS
AMOEBIC
AMONGST
AMOROUS
AMOUNTS
AMPERES
AMPHORA
AMPLEST
AMPLIFY
AMPOULE
AMPULES
AMRADIO
AMSCRAY
AMULETS
AMUSING
AMYLASE

A•M••••

AAMILNE
ADMIRAL
ADMIRED
ADMIRER
ADMIRES
ADMITTO
ADMIXED
ADMIXES
AIMEDAT
AIMEDTO
AIMLESS
AIMSFOR
ALMAATA
ALMADEN
ALMANAC
ALMONDS
AMMETER
AMMONIA
ARMADAS
ARMBAND
ARMENIA
ARMFULS
ARMHOLE
ARMLESS
ARMLETS
ARMLIKE
ARMLOAD
ARMLOCK
ARMOIRE
ARMORED
ARMORER
ARMOURS
ARMOURY
ARMPITS
ARMREST
ARMURES
ARMYANT

A••M•••

ACUMENS
ADAMANT
ADAMITE
ADAMSON
AILMENT
AIRMADA
AIRMAIL
AIRMASS
AIRMILE
ALAMEDA
ALAMEIN
ALAMODE
ALEMBIC
ALIMENT
ALIMONY
ALUMNAE
ALUMNAL
ALUMNUS
ANEMONE
ANIMALS
ANIMATE
ANIMATO
ANIMISM
ANIMIST
ANOMALY
ANOMIES
ANYMORE
ARAMAIC
ARAMEAN
ARDMORE
ATAMANS
ATOMIES
ATOMISE
ATOMIZE
AUGMENT
AZIMUTH

A•••M••

ABDOMEN
ABYSMAL
AFRAMES
AGNOMEN
ALARMED
ALARMER
ALBUMEN
ALBUMIN
ANAEMIA
ANAEMIC
ANOSMIA
ANOSMIC
ARTEMIS
ARTEMUS
ASHAMED
ASSUMED
ASSUMES
ATHOMES
ATTEMPT
ATTIMES
AUTOMAT
AUTUMNS

A••••M•

ACADEME
ACADEMY
AFFIRMS
AIRDAMS
AIRPUMP
AIRTIME
ALABAMA
ALARUMS
ALCHEMY
ALLOFME
ALLTIME
ANADEMS
ANATOMY
ANONYMS
ANTHEMS
ANYTIME
ARCLAMP
ASHRAMS
ASYLUMS
ATACAMA
ATRIUMS
AWESOME

A•••••M

ABRAHAM
ABSALOM
ACCLAIM
ACRONYM
ADFINEM
ALYSSUM
AMALGAM
ANAGRAM
ANAHEIM
ANIMISM
ANTFARM
ANTONYM
APOTHEM
ARCANUM
ARTFILM
ARTFORM
ATAVISM
ATHEISM

•AM••••

AAMILNE
BAMBINO
BAMBOOS
CAMBERS
CAMBIUM
CAMBRIC
CAMEDUE
CAMELIA
CAMELOT
CAMEOED
CAMEOFF
CAMEOUT
CAMERAS
CAMERON
CAMILLE
CAMISES
CAMPARI
CAMPERS
CAMPHOR
CAMPIER
CAMPILY
CAMPING
CAMPION
CAMPOUT
DAMAGED
DAMAGES
DAMASKS
DAMMARS
DAMMING
DAMNING
DAMPENS
DAMPERS
DAMPEST
DAMPING
DAMPISH
DAMSELS
DAMSONS
FAMINES
FAMULUS
GAMBADO
GAMBIAN
GAMBITS
GAMBLED
GAMBLER
GAMBLES
GAMBOLS
GAMBREL
GAMELAW
GAMETES
GAMIEST
GAMINES
GAMMERS
GAMMIER
GAMMING
GAMMONS
HAMBURG
HAMELIN
HAMHOCK
HAMITES
HAMITIC
HAMITUP
HAMLETS
HAMMERS
HAMMETT
HAMMIER
HAMMILY
HAMMING
HAMMOCK
HAMMOND
HAMPERS
HAMPTON
HAMSTER
JAMAICA
JAMESON
JAMLIKE
JAMMERS
JAMMIER
JAMMING
JAMPACK
KAMPALA
LAMAISM
LAMAIST
LAMARCK
LAMBADA
LAMBDAS
LAMBEAU
LAMBENT
LAMBERT
LAMEDHS
LAMENTS
LAMINAE
LAMINAL
LAMINAR
LAMINAS
LAMMING
LAMOTTA
LAMPOIL
LAMPOON
LAMPREY
MAMBOED
MAMMALS
MAMMOTH
NAMEDAY
NAMETAG
NAMIBIA
PAMPERS
RAMADAN
RAMADAS
RAMBEAU
RAMBLED
RAMBLER
RAMBLES
RAMEKIN
RAMESES
RAMINTO
RAMJETS
RAMLIKE
RAMMING
RAMMISH
RAMPAGE
RAMPANT
RAMPART
RAMRODS
SAMARIA
SAMBAED
SAMBALS
SAMBARS
SAMECHS
SAMEDAY
SAMHILL
SAMISEN
SAMITES
SAMLETS
SAMOANS
SAMOVAR
SAMOYED
SAMPANS
SAMPLED
SAMPLER
SAMPLES
SAMPRAS
SAMPSON
SAMSARA
SAMSUNG
SAMURAI
TAMABLE
TAMALES
TAMARIN
TAMBALA
TAMBOUR
TAMMANY
TAMPERS
TAMPICO
TAMPING
TAMTAMS
VAMOOSE
VAMPERS
VAMPING
VAMPIRA
VAMPIRE
VAMPISH
WAMBLED
WAMBLES
YAMMERS
ZAMBEZI
ZAMBIAN
ZAMBONI

•A•M•••

BALMIER
BALMILY
BARMAID
BARMIER
CADMIUM
CAIMANS
CALMEST
CALMING
CARMINE
CAYMANS
DAIMLER
DAIMONS
DAMMARS
DAMMING
DAUMIER
DAYMARE
EARMARK
EARMUFF
FANMAIL
FARMERS
FARMERY
FARMING
FARMOUT
GAMMERS
GAMMIER
GAMMING
GAMMONS
GARMENT
GASMAIN
GAUMING
HAEMATO
HAMMERS
HAMMETT
HAMMIER
HAMMILY
HAMMING
HAMMOCK
HAMMOND
HARMFUL
HARMING
HARMONY
HAYMOWS
JAMMERS
JAMMIER
JAMMING
JASMINE
LAMMING
MALMSEY
MAMMALS
MAMMOTH
MANMADE
MARMARA
MARMION
MARMOTS
MAUMAUS
OAKMOSS
OATMEAL
PALMARY
PALMATE
PALMIER
PALMING
PALMIST
PALMOFF
PALMOIL
PALMTOP
PAYMENT
RAGMOPS
RAIMENT
RAMMING
RAMMISH
RAYMOND
SALMONS
SAWMILL
TAMMANY
TARMACS
VARMINT
WALMART
WARMEST
WARMING
WARMISH
WARMSUP
WARMUPS
YAMMERS

•A••M••

BAHAMAS
BASEMAN
BASEMEN
BATEMAN
BATHMAT
BATSMAN
BATSMEN
CAKEMIX
CALOMEL
CALUMET
CALUMNY
CARAMBA
CARAMEL
CARAMIA
CAROMED
CAVEMAN
CAVEMEN
DAHOMEY
DARKMAN
EASTMAN
FADIMAN
GALUMPH
GATEMAN
GATEMEN
GAZUMPS
HACKMAN
HANGMAN
HANGMEN
HARTMAN
JAVAMAN
JAZZMAN
JAZZMEN
KASHMIR
KAUFMAN
LABAMBA
LARAMIE
MADAMEX
MALAMUD
MANUMIT
MANXMAN
MANXMEN
MARIMBA
MAXIMAL
MAXIMUM
MAXIMUS
PAJAMAS
PALOMAR
PANAMAS
RACEMES
RADOMES
RAINMAN
SALAMIS
SANDMAN
SANDMEN
TAPEMAN
TAPEMEN
TASHMAN
TATAMIS
TAXIMAN
TAXIMEN
WALKMAN
YAKIMAS
YARDMAN
YARDMEN
YASHMAK

•A•••M•

BALSAMS
BANTAMS
DAYCAMP
DAYTIME
FATHOMS
GASPUMP
GAUTAMA
HANSOMS
LAKSHMI
LAPALMA
MACRAME
MAGNUMS
MAHATMA
MARRYME
MAYHEMS
MAYTIME
NANAIMO
NAPTIME
PABLUMS
PALERMO
PASTIME
RAGTIME
RANSOMS
SACHEMS
SALAAMS
SANREMO
SAOTOME
SASHIMI
SATCHMO
SATSUMA
TALCUMS
TAMTAMS
TANDEMS
VACUUMS
WARGAME
WARTIME

•A••••M

BAPTISM
BARROOM
CADMIUM
CAESIUM
CALCIUM
CAMBIUM
DADAISM
DAYROOM
EARDRUM
EARLDOM
FADDISM
FAUVISM
GALLIUM
HAARLEM
HAFNIUM
HAHNIUM
HASIDIM
KARAKUM
LAMAISM
MACADAM
MALCOLM
MARKHAM
MARXISM
MAUGHAM
MAXIMUM
NATRIUM
PABULUM
PALLIUM
SANCTUM
SARCASM
TAGTEAM
TAKEAIM
TANGRAM
TANTRUM
TAPROOM
YARDARM

••AM•••

ADAMANT
ADAMITE
ADAMSON
ALAMEDA
ALAMEIN
ALAMODE
ARAMAIC
ARAMEAN
ATAMANS
BEAMIER
BEAMING
BEAMISH
BEAMSUP
BLAMING
BRAMBLE
BRAMBLY
CHAMBER
CHAMFER
CHAMOIS
CHAMPED
CLAMBER
CLAMMED
CLAMMER
CLAMORS
CLAMOUR
CLAMPED
CLAMSUP
CRAMMED
CRAMMER
CRAMPED
CRAMPON
DIAMOND
ENAMELS
ENAMORS
ENAMOUR
ETAMINE
EXAMINE
EXAMPLE
FLAMBED
FLAMBES
FLAMIER
FLAMING
FOAMIER
FOAMILY
FOAMING
FRAMEUP
FRAMING
GLAMOUR
GRAMMAR
GRAMMER
GRAMMES
GRAMMYS
GRAMPAS
GRAMPUS
IMAMATE
INAMESS
KLAMATH
LOAMIER
LOAMING
MIAMIAN
MIAMIAS
MUAMMAR
REAMASS
REAMERS
REAMING
ROAMERS
ROAMING
SCAMMED
SCAMPED
SCAMPER
SEAMIER
SEAMING
SEAMOSS
SHAMANS
SHAMBLE
SHAMING
SHAMMED
SHAMPOO
SIAMESE
SLAMMED
SLAMMER
SPAMMED
SPAMMER
STAMENS
STAMINA
STAMMER
STAMPED
SWAMPED
TEAMING
TEAMSUP
TRAMCAR
TRAMMEL
TRAMPAS
TRAMPED
TRAMPLE
UNAMUNO
WHAMMED

••A•M••

ALARMED
ALARMER
ANAEMIA
ANAEMIC
BOATMAN
BOATMEN
BRAHMAN
BRAHMAS
BRAHMIN
CHAPMAN
CHAPMEN
CHARMED
CHARMER
CHARMIN
CLAIMED
CLAIMER
CLAMMED
CLAMMER
CRAMMED
CRAMMER
ERASMUS
FLAGMAN
FLAGMEN
GRAMMAR
GRAMMER
GRAMMES
GRAMMYS
HEADMAN
HEADMEN
MIASMAS
MIASMIC
MUAMMAR
MYANMAR
PLASMAS
PSALMED
READMIT
REAIMED
REARMED
ROADMAP
SCAMMED
SHAMMED
SLAMMED
SLAMMER
SPAMMED
SPAMMER
STAMMER
STARMAN
STARMAP
SWARMED
TRAMMEL
TRAUMAS
UNAIMED
UNARMED
WHAMMED

••A••M•

ACADEME
ACADEMY
ALABAMA
ALARUMS
ANADEMS
ANATOMY
ATACAMA
BEATSME
DIADEMS
DIATOMS
DRACHMA
DRACHMS
EXANIMO
GIACOMO
GRAHAME
GRAHAMS
GRANDMA
IPANEMA
SHALOMS
SLALOMS
TEATIME
ULALUME

••A•••M

AMALGAM
ANAGRAM
ANAHEIM
ATAVISM
CHATHAM
CRANIUM
CZARDOM
CZARISM
DIAGRAM
GRANDAM
GUARGUM
HAARLEM
JOACHIM
KHAYYAM
PHANTOM
PIANISM
QUANTUM
REALISM
SEAGRAM
SHAHDOM
STADIUM
STARDOM
TEAROOM
TRANSOM
URANIUM
YEATEAM

•••AM••

AFRAMES
ASHAMED
BAHAMAS
BETAMAX
CARAMBA
CARAMEL
CARAMIA
CCLAMPS
CERAMIC
CREAMED
CREAMER
DECAMPS
DEFAMED
DEFAMES
DREAMED
DREAMER
DREAMON
DREAMUP
DYNAMIC
DYNAMOS
ENCAMPS
GLEAMED
IDEAMAN
IDEAMEN
IDIAMIN
ISLAMIC
JAVAMAN
JICAMAS
LABAMBA
LARAMIE
MADAMEX
MALAMUD
MIRAMAR
MIRAMAX
MOGAMBO
MYMAMMY
PAJAMAS
PANAMAS
PDJAMES
PREAMPS
PUTAMEN
PYJAMAS
PYRAMID
PYRAMUS
RENAMED
RENAMES
REVAMPS
RUNAMOK
SALAMIS
SESAMES
STEAMED
STEAMER
TATAMIS
UNNAMED
UNTAMED
VITAMIN

•••A•M•

BECALMS
DEPALMA
DISARMS
LAPALMA
MAHATMA
MYMAMMY
NANAIMO
REWARMS
SALAAMS

•••A••M

ABRAHAM
ABSALOM
ARCANUM
DADAISM
ERRATUM
HUMANUM
JUDAISM
KARAKUM
LAMAISM
MACADAM
ORGANUM
STRATUM

••••AM•

AIRDAMS
ALABAMA
ARCLAMP
ASHRAMS
ATACAMA
BALSAMS
BANTAMS
BEDLAMP
BELDAME
BELDAMS
BELLAMY
BIGGAME
BIGNAME
CONGAME
DAYCAMP
DIGRAMS
DIORAMA
ENDGAME
ENGRAMS
GAUTAMA
GOURAMI
GRAHAME
GRAHAMS
INFLAME
INSEAMS
JIMJAMS
LOGJAMS
MACRAME
MISNAME
OFFRAMP
OILLAMP
ORIGAMI
PENNAME
PETNAME
RECLAME
REFRAME
RESTAMP
SALAAMS
SCREAMS
STREAMS
SUNLAMP
SURNAME
TAMTAMS
TSUNAMI
WARGAME
WIGWAMS

••••A•M

ACCLAIM
ANTFARM
BEEBALM
DECLAIM
EXCLAIM
FIREARM
FOREARM
LIPBALM
LONGARM
RECLAIM
SARCASM
SIDEARM
TAKEAIM
TONEARM
YARDARM
YESMAAM

•••••AM

ABRAHAM
AMALGAM
ANAGRAM
BEECHAM
BENTHAM
BINGHAM
BRIGHAM
BUCKRAM
CHATHAM
CULTJAM
DIAGRAM
EIGHTAM
EPIGRAM
FLOTSAM
FORDHAM
GINGHAM
GLORIAM
GRANDAM
GRISHAM
KETCHAM
KHAYYAM
LOWBEAM
MACADAM
MARKHAM
MAUGHAM
MILLDAM
MINICAM
NEEDHAM
POTSDAM
PROGRAM
SEAGRAM
SEVENAM
SUNBEAM
SURINAM
TAGTEAM
TANGRAM
THREEAM
TRIGRAM
VIETNAM
WILLIAM
WOLFRAM
YEATEAM
YESMAAM

AN•••••

ANADEMS
ANAEMIA
ANAEMIC
ANAGRAM
ANAHEIM
ANAHUAC
ANALOGS

ANALOGY
ANALYSE
ANALYST
ANALYZE
ANANIAS
ANAPEST
ANARCHY
ANASAZI
ANATOLE
ANATOMY
ANCHORS
ANCHOVY
ANCIENT
ANDANTE
ANDEANS
ANDIRON
ANDORRA
ANDOVER
ANDREAS
ANDRESS
ANDREWS
ANDROID
ANDSOON
ANELING
ANEMONE
ANEROID
ANGELES
ANGELIC
ANGELOU
ANGELUS
ANGERED
ANGLERS
ANGLING
ANGOLAN
ANGORAS
ANGRIER
ANGRILY
ANGULAR
ANILINE
ANIMALS
ANIMATE
ANIMATO
ANIMISM
ANIMIST
ANISEED
ANISTON
ANKLETS
ANNABEL
ANNALEE
ANNATTO
ANNEALS
ANNELID
ANNETTE
ANNEXED
ANNEXES
ANNOYED
ANNUALS
ANNUITY
ANNULAR
ANNULUS
ANODISE
ANODIZE
ANODYNE
ANOINTS
ANOMALY
ANOMIES
ANONYMS
ANORAKS
ANOSMIA
ANOSMIC
ANOTHER
ANOUILH
ANSWERS
ANTACID
ANTAEUS
ANTARES
ANTBEAR
ANTCOWS
ANTEDUP
ANTEING
ANTENNA
ANTESUP
ANTFARM
ANTHEMS
ANTHERS
ANTHILL
ANTHONY
ANTIART
ANTIBES
ANTIFOG
ANTIGEN
ANTIGUA
ANTILOG
ANTIOCH
ANTIQUE
ANTITAX
ANTIWAR
ANTLERS
ANTLIKE
ANTLION
ANTOINE
ANTONIA
ANTONIN
ANTONIO
ANTONYM
ANTSIER
ANTWERP
ANXIETY
ANXIOUS
ANYBODY
ANYMORE
ANYONES
ANYROAD
ANYTIME

A•N••••

ABNAKIS
AGNATES
AGNOMEN
AMNESIA
AMNESTY
AMNIONS
ANNABEL
ANNALEE
ANNATTO
ANNEALS
ANNELID
ANNETTE
ANNEXED
ANNEXES
ANNOYED
ANNUALS
ANNUITY
ANNULAR
ANNULUS
ARNICAS
AUNTIES
AWNINGS
AWNLESS
AYNRAND

A••N•••

ABANDON
ABENAKI
ABINTRA
ACANTHI
ACONITE
ADENINE
ADONAIS
AGENDAS
AGONISE
AGONIST
AGONIZE
ALENCON
ALINING
ALUNSER
AMENDED
AMENITY
AMONGST
ANANIAS
ANONYMS
APTNESS
ASININE
ASUNDER
ATINGLE
ATONIES
ATONING
AVENGED
AVENGER
AVENGES
AVENUES
AVONLEA

A•••N••

ABOUNDS
ABSENCE
ABSENTS
ACCENTS
ACHENES
ACRONYM
ACTINIC
ADDENDA
ADDENDS
ADDONTO
ADFINEM
ADJUNCT
ADORNED
ADORNER
ADRENAL
ADVANCE
ADVENTS
AFFINES
AGAINST
AIRINGS
ALBANIA
ALBENIZ
ALBINOS
ALBUNDY
ALDENTE
ALFONSO
ALIENEE
ALIENOR
ALIGNED
ALIGNER
ALKENES
ALLENBY
ALLENDE
ALMANAC
ALMONDS
ALUMNAE
ALUMNAL
ALUMNUS
AMMONIA
AMOUNTS
ANDANTE
ANOINTS
ANTENNA
ANTONIA
ANTONIN
ANTONIO
ANTONYM
ANYONES
APLENTY
APPENDS
APRONED
AQUINAS
ARCANUM
ARDENCY
ARGONNE
ARMENIA
ARPENTS
ARRANGE
ARSENAL
ARSENIC
ARSENIO
ASCENDS
ASCENTS
ASHANTI
ASKANCE
ASOFNOW
ASSENTS
ATLANTA
ATTENDS
ATTUNED
ATTUNES
AUGENDS
AVIANCA
AVIGNON
AWNINGS

A••••N•

AAMILNE
ABALONE
ABASING
ABATING
ABEYANT
ABIDING
ABILENE
ABSCOND
ABUSING
ACCOUNT
ACETONE
ACHTUNG
ACTIONS
ACUMENS
ADAMANT
ADDLING
ADELINE
ADENINE
ADJOINS
ADORING
AFFRONT
AFGHANI
AFGHANS
AGROUND
AILMENT
AIRGUNS
AIRLANE
AIRLINE
ALAKING
ALIMENT
ALIMONY
ALINING
ALLGONE
ALLYING
ALTOONA
AMAZING
AMAZONS
AMBIENT
AMBLING
AMERIND
AMNIONS
AMUSING
ANCIENT
ANDEANS
ANELING
ANEMONE
ANGLING
ANILINE
ANODYNE
ANTEING
ANTENNA
ANTHONY
ANTOINE
APPOINT
ARACHNE
ARCHING
ARCHONS
ARCSINE
ARETINO
ARGONNE
ARGUING
ARIADNE
ARISING
ARIZONA
ARMBAND
ARMYANT
ARTSONG
ASHCANS
ASHLAND
ASININE
ASSIGNS
ASTOUND
ATAMANS
ATONING
ATTAINS
AUBURNS
AUGMENT
AUTUMNS
AVOWING
AWAKENS
AWAKING
AYNRAND

A••••••N

ABANDON
ABDOMEN
ABSTAIN
ACADIAN
ACHERON
ACHESON
ACTAEON
ACTEDON
ACTUPON
ADAMSON
ADDEDIN
ADDEDON
ADDISON
ADJOURN
AEOLIAN
AFRICAN
AGAKHAN
AGNOMEN
AILERON
ALADDIN
ALAMEIN
ALARCON
ALASKAN
ALBUMEN
ALBUMIN
ALENCON
ALLISON
ALLSTON
ALLYSON
ALMADEN
ALSORAN
ALYKHAN
ANDIRON
ANDSOON
ANGOLAN
ANISTON
ANTIGEN
ANTLION
ANTONIN
ARABIAN
ARAMEAN
ARRAIGN
ARTISAN
ASKEDIN
ASPIRIN
AUCTION
AUDUBON
AVIGNON
AZTECAN

•AN••••

BANALLY
BANANAS
BANDAGE
BANDAID
BANDANA
BANDBOX
BANDIED
BANDIES
BANDING
BANDITO
BANDITS
BANDSAW
BANEFUL
BANGING
BANGKOK
BANGLES
BANGSUP
BANJOES
BANKERS
BANKING
BANKSON
BANNERS
BANNING
BANNOCK
BANQUET
BANSHEE
BANTAMS
BANTERS
BANYANS
CANAPES
CANARDS
CANASTA
CANCANS
CANCELS
CANDELA
CANDICE
CANDIDA
CANDIDE
CANDIDS
CANDIED
CANDIES
CANDLES
CANDOUR
CANFULS
CANIEST
CANINES
CANKERS
CANNERS
CANNERY
CANNIER
CANNILY
CANNING
CANNOLI
CANNONS
CANONIC
CANOPUS
CANSECO
CANTATA
CANTEEN
CANTERS
CANTILY
CANTINA
CANTING
CANTLES
CANTONS
CANTORS
CANTRIP
CANVASS
CANYONS
CANZONE
DANBURY
DANCERS
DANCING
DANDERS
DANDIER
DANDIES
DANDIFY
DANDLED
DANDLES
DANELAW
DANGERS
DANGLED
DANGLER
DANGLES
DANIELS
DANKEST
DANSEUR
FANATIC
FANBELT
FANCIED
FANCIER
FANCIES
FANCIFY
FANCILY
FANCLUB
FANFARE
FANIONS
FANJETS
FANLIKE
FANMAIL
FANNING
FANOUTS
FANSOUT
FANTAIL
FANTASY
FANZINE
GANDERS
GANGERS
GANGING
GANGLED
GANGLIA
GANGSAW
GANGSTA
GANGSUP
GANGTOK
GANGWAY
GANNETS
GANNETT
GANTLET
HANCOCK
HANDBAG
HANDCAR
HANDFED
HANDFUL
HANDGUN
HANDIER
HANDILY
HANDING
HANDLED
HANDLER
HANDLES
HANDOFF
HANDOUT
HANDSAW
HANDSET
HANDSIN
HANDSON
HANDSUP
HANGARS
HANGDOG
HANGERS
HANGING
HANGMAN
HANGMEN
HANGOFF
HANGOUT
HANGSIN
HANGSON
HANGSUP
HANGTEN
HANGUPS
HANKERS
HANKIES
HANOVER
HANSARP
HANSOLO
HANSOMS
HANUKAH
JANACEK
JANEDOE
JANEWAY
JANGLED
JANGLES
JANITOR
JANNOCK
JANSSEN
JANUARY
JANVIER
KANAKAS
KANSANS
LANCERS
LANCETS
LANDAUS
LANDERS
LANDING
LANDSAT
LANFORD
LANGDON
LANGLEY
LANGTRY
LANGUID
LANGUOR
LANGURS
LANKEST
LANKIER
LANKILY
LANOLIN
LANSING
LANTANA
LANTERN
LANYARD
MANACLE
MANAGED
MANAGER
MANAGES
MANAGUA
MANANAS
MANATEE
MANCINI
MANDALA
MANDANS
MANDATE
MANDAYS
MANDELA
MANEGES
MANFRED
MANGERS
MANGIER
MANGLED
MANGLES
MANGOES
MANHOLE
MANHOOD
MANHOUR
MANHUNT
MANIACS
MANILOW
MANIOCS
MANIPLE
MANITOU
MANKIND
MANLESS
MANLIER
MANLIKE
MANMADE
MANNERS
MANNING
MANNISH
MANOWAR
MANSARD
MANSION
MANTELS
MANTLED
MANTLES
MANTRAP
MANTRAS
MANTRIC
MANUALS
MANUMIT
MANXCAT
MANXMAN
MANXMEN
MANYEAR
NANAIMO
NANETTE
NANKEEN
NANNIES
PANACEA
PANACHE
PANADAS
PANAMAS
PANARAB
PANCAKE
PANCHAX
PANDECT
PANDERS
PANDITS
PANDORA
PANELED
PANFISH
PANFULS
PANICKY
PANICLE
PANNERS
PANNIER
PANNING
PANOPLY
PANPIPE
PANSIES
PANSOUT
PANTHER
PANTING
PANURGE
PANZERS
RANAWAY
RANCHED
RANCHER
RANCHES
RANCHOS
RANCOUR
RANDALL
RANDIER
RANDOWN
RANGERS
RANGIER
RANGING
RANGOFF
RANGOON
RANGOUT
RANINTO
RANKERS
RANKEST
RANKING
RANKISH
RANKLED
RANKLES
RANLATE
RANOVER
RANRIOT
RANSACK
RANSOMS
RANTERS
RANTING
SANCTUM
SANDALS
SANDBAG
SANDBAR
SANDBOX
SANDERS
SANDFLY
SANDHOG
SANDIER
SANDING
SANDLOT
SANDMAN
SANDMEN
SANFORD
SANGOUT
SANGRIA
SANIBEL
SANJOSE
SANJUAN
SANLUIS
SANREMO
SANTAFE
SANTANA
SANTINI
SANTIRS
TANAGER
TANDEMS
TANGELO
TANGENT
TANGERE
TANGIER
TANGLED
TANGLES
TANGOED
TANGRAM
TANKARD
TANKERS
TANKFUL
TANKING
TANKSUP
TANKTOP
TANLINE
TANNERS
TANNERY
TANNEST
TANNING
TANNINS
TANNISH
TANOAKS
TANSIES
TANTARA
TANTIVY
TANTRUM
VANDALS
VANDINE
VANDYCK
VANDYKE
VANESSA
VANEYCK
VANGOGH
VANILLA
VANILLI
VANPOOL
VANTAGE
VANUATU
WANDERS
WANGLED
WANGLER
WANGLES
WANIEST
WANNABE
WANNESS
WANNEST
WANNISH
WANTADS
WANTING
WANTOUT
WANTSIN
WANTSTO
XANTHAN
XANTHIC
YANGTZE
YANKEES
YANKING
YANKTON
YANQUIS
ZANDERS
ZANIEST
ZANYISH

•A•N•••

BADNESS
BAGNOLD
BAINTER
BANNERS
BANNING
BANNOCK
BARNABY
BARNARD
BARNEYS
BARNONE
BARNOWL
CANNERS
CANNERY
CANNIER
CANNILY
CANNING
CANNOLI
CANNONS
CAPNUTS
CARNERA
CARNETS
CARNIES
CATNAPS
CATNIPS
DAMNING
DARNERS
DARNING
DARNLEY
DAUNTED
DAWNING
DAWNSON
EARNERS
EARNEST
EARNING
FAINTED
FAINTER
FAINTLY
FANNING
FATNESS
FAWNERS
FAWNING
GAINERS
GAINFUL
GAINING
GAINSAY
GAINSON
GANNETS
GANNETT
GARNERS
GARNETS
GARNISH
GAUNTER
GAUNTLY
HAFNIUM
HAHNIUM
HARNESS
HAUNTED
JANNOCK
JAUNTED
LAENNEC
LAUNDER
LAUNDRY
LAXNESS
MADNESS
MAENADS
MAGNANI
MAGNATE
MAGNETO
MAGNETS
MAGNIFY
MAGNUMS
MAINTOP
MANNERS
MANNING
MANNISH
MAUNDER
MAYNARD
NANNIES
PAANGAS
PAINFUL
PAINTED
PAINTER
PANNERS
PANNIER
PANNING
PATNESS
PAUNCHY
PAWNEES
PAWNERS
PAWNING
PAWNOFF
RAINBOW
RAINHAT
RAINIER
RAINILY
RAINING
RAINMAN
RAINOUT
RAWNESS
SADNESS
SAINTED
SAINTLY
SAUNTER
TAINTED
TANNERS
TANNERY
TANNEST
TANNING
TANNINS
TANNISH
TARNISH
TAUNTED
TAWNIER
TAWNILY
VAINEST
VARNISH
VAUNTED
VAUNTER
WALNUTS
WANNABE
WANNESS
WANNEST
WANNISH
WARNING
YARNING
YAWNERS
YAWNFUL
YAWNING

•A••N••

BALANCE
BALONEY
BANANAS
BARANOF
BARENTS
BARONET
BARONGS
BASENJI
BAYONET
CABANAS
CABINET
CACANNY
CADENCE
CADENCY
CADENZA
CALENDS
CANINES
CANONIC
CARINAS
CASINGS
CASINOS
CATENAE
CAYENNE
DAPHNIS
DAVINCI
EATENAT
EATENUP
FACINGS
FAGENDS
FAIENCE
FAMINES
GAMINES
GARDNER
GARONNE
HACKNEY
HAIRNET
HAPENNY
HAVENOT
HAZINGS
JACANAS
JACINTH
JACONET
KAHUNAS
LACINGS
LACONIC
LACUNAE
LACUNAL
LACUNAS
LADINOS
LAENNEC
LAGUNAS
LALANNE
LAMENTS
LAMINAE
LAMINAL
LAMINAR
LAMINAS
LARDNER
LATENCY
LATENTS
LATINAS
LATINOS
LAVINIA
LAYINTO
MADONNA
MAGENTA
MAGINOT
MAHONEY
MAKINGS
MANANAS
MARENGO
MARINAS
MARINER
MARINES
MASONIC
MASONRY
MATINEE
PALANCE
PARDNER
PARENTS
PARINGS
PARSNIP
PARTNER
PATENTS
PATINAS
PAVANES
RAMINTO
RANINTO
RAPANUI
RAPINES
RATINGS
RAVENED
RAVENNA
RAVINES
RAVINGS
SABINES
SAGINAW
SALINAS
SARANAC
SARONGS
SATINET
SAVANNA
SAVANTS
SAVINGS
SAYINGS
TAGENDS
TAKENIN
TAKENON
TALENTS
TALONED
TAPINGS
TAPINTO
TARANTO
VACANCY
VALANCE
VALENCE
VALENCY
WAGONER
WAHINES
WAKENED
WAKENER
YAOUNDE

•A•••N•

AAMILNE
BABOONS

BABYING
BACHING
BACKEND
BACKING
BAGGING
BAILING
BAITING
BALCONY
BALDING
BALEENS
BALKANS
BALKING
BAMBINO
BANDANA
BANDING
BANGING
BANKING
BANNING
BANYANS
BARBING
BARGING
BARKING
BARNONE
BARRENS
BARRING
BARTEND
BARYONS
BASHING
BASKING
BASTING
BATHING
BATTENS
BATTING
BATWING
BAWLING
CABLING
CABRINI
CACANNY
CACHING
CADGING
CAFTANS
CAIMANS
CALKING
CALKINS
CALLING
CALLINS
CALMING
CALUMNY
CALVING
CALZONE
CAMPING
CANCANS
CANNING
CANNONS
CANTINA
CANTING
CANTONS
CANYONS
CANZONE
CAPEANN
CAPGUNS
CAPPING
CARBINE
CARBONS
CARDING
CAREENS
CARKING
CARMINE
CARPING
CARTING
CARTONS
CARVING
CASERNE
CASERNS
CASHING
CASSINI
CASSINO
CASTING
CATIONS
CATKINS
CATTING
CAUSING
CAVEINS
CAVERNS
CAYENNE
CAYMANS
DABBING
DABHAND
DAFFING
DAIMONS
DAMMING
DAMNING
DAMPENS
DAMPING
DAMSONS
DANCING
DAPPING
DARKENS
DARLENE
DARLING
DARNING
DARTING
DASHING
DAUBING
DAWNING
DAYLONG
DAYSINN
DAYTONA
EAGLING
EARNING
EARRING
EASTEND
FADEINS
FAGGING
FAILING
FAIRING
FALCONS
FALLING
FANIONS
FANNING
FANZINE
FARCING
FARGONE
FARMING
FASTENS
FASTING
FASTONE
FATTENS
FAWNING
GABBING
GADDING
GAFFING
GAGGING
GAGLINE
GAINING
GAITING
GALLANT
GALLING
GALLONS
GALVANI
GAMMING
GAMMONS
GANGING
GAOLING
GAPPING
GARBING
GARCONS
GARDENS
GARLAND
GARMENT
GARONNE
GASCONS
GASCONY
GASHING
GASKINS
GASPING
GATLING
GAUGING
GAUMING
GAWKING
GAWPING
HACKING
HAFTING
HAGDONS
HAILING
HALOING
HALTING
HALVING
HAMMING
HAMMOND
HANDING
HANGING
HAPENNY
HAPPENS
HAPPING
HARDENS
HARDING
HARKENS
HARKING
HARMING
HARMONY
HARPING
HASHING
HASPING
HASTENS
HASTING
HATBAND
HATPINS
HATTING
HAULING
HAWKING
HAWKINS
JABBING
JACKING
JAGGING
JAILING
JAMMING
JARGONS
JARGONY
JARRING
JASMINE
JAWBONE
JAWLINE
JAYLENO
JAZZING
KACHINA
KAFTANS
KANSANS
KAYOING
LACKING
LADLING
LAGGING
LAGOONS
LALANNE
LAMBENT
LAMMING
LANDING
LANSING
LANTANA
LAPLAND
LAPPING
LAPSING
LAPWING
LARAINE
LARCENY
LARDING
LARDONS
LASAGNA
LASAGNE
LASHING
LASTING
LATEENS
LATHING
LATTENS
LAUDING
LAURENT
LAVERNE
MACHINA
MACHINE
MACRONS
MADDENS
MADDING
MADONNA
MAGNANI
MAIDENS
MAILING
MALIGNS
MALKINS
MALTING
MANCINI
MANDANS
MANHUNT
MANKIND
MANNING
MAPPING
MARCONI
MARGINS
MARIANA
MARKING
MARLENE
MARLINS
MAROONS
MARRING
MARTENS
MARTINA
MARTINI
MARTINO
MARTINS
MARYANN
MASHING
MASKING
MASSING
MATRONS
MATTING
MAULING
MAYWINE
NABBING
NAGGING
NAILING
NAPKINS
NAPPING
NASCENT
NATIONS
OAKLAND
PACKING
PADDING
PADRONE
PADRONI
PADUANS
PAGEANT
PAIRING
PAISANO
PALLING
PALMING
PANNING
PANTING
PAPUANS
PARDONS
PARKING
PARRING
PARSING
PARSONS
PARTING
PARVENU
PASSING
PASTINA
PASTING
PATERNO
PATIENT
PATRONS
PATTENS
PATTING
PAULINA
PAULINE
PAULING
PAUSING
PAWNING
PAYMENT
RACKING
RADIANS
RADIANT
RAFTING
RAGGING
RAGLANS
RAIDING
RAILING
RAIMENT
RAINING
RAISING
RAISINS
RAMMING
RAMPANT
RANGING
RANKING
RANTING
RAPPING
RASPING
RATFINK
RATIONS
RATLINE
RATTANS
RATTING
RAVENNA
RAYGUNS
RAYMOND
RAZZING
SABRINA
SACKING
SADDENS
SAGGING
SAILING
SALERNO
SALIENT
SALMONS
SALOONS
SALTINE
SALTING
SALVING
SAMOANS
SAMPANS
SAMSUNG
SANDING
SANTANA
SANTINI
SAPIENS
SAPIENT
SAPLING
SAPPING
SARDINE
SARGENT
SASSING
SATEENS
SAVANNA
TABBING
TABLING
TACKING
TAGGANT
TAGGING
TAGLINE
TAILEND
TAILING
TAIPANS
TAKEONE
TALKING
TALLINN
TAMMANY
TAMPING
TANGENT
TANKING
TANLINE
TANNING
TANNINS
TAPPING
TARPONS
TARRING
TARTANS
TARZANA
TASKING
TASTING
TATIANA
TATTING
TAURINE
TAUTENS
TAVERNS
TAXIING
VACCINE
VAGRANT
VALIANT
VALUING
VAMPING
VANDINE
VARIANT
VARMINT
VARYING
VATTING
WADDING
WAFTING
WAGGING
WAGGONS
WAILING
WAITING
WAIVING
WALKING
WALKINS
WALKONS
WALLING
WANTING
WARDENS
WARDING
WARMING
WARNING
WARPING
WARRANT
WARRENS
WARRING
WARZONE
WASHING
WASTING
WAXWING
YACKING
YAKKING
YANKING
YAPPING
YARNING
YAUPONS
YAWNING
YAWPING
ZAGGING
ZAMBONI
ZAPPING

•A••••N

BABYLON
BACKSIN
BAHRAIN
BALATON
BALDWIN
BALLOON
BANKSON
BARGAIN
BARGEIN
BASEMAN
BASEMEN
BASSOON
BASTION
BATEMAN
BATSMAN
BATSMEN
CADDOAN
CAISSON
CALDRON
CALHOUN
CALIBAN
CALLSIN
CALLSON
CAMERON
CAMPION
CANTEEN
CAPEANN
CAPITAN
CAPSTAN
CAPTAIN
CAPTION
CARAVAN
CARLSON
CARLTON
CAROLYN
CARRION
CARRYON
CARTOON
CASPIAN
CATALAN
CATCHON
CATSCAN
CAUTION
CAVEDIN
CAVEMAN
CAVEMEN
CAVESIN
DAKOTAN
DARKMAN
DAUPHIN
DAWNSON
DAYSINN
EARLYON
EARTHEN
EASEDIN
EASESIN
EASTERN
EASTMAN
FACTION
FADEDIN
FADESIN
FADIMAN
FALLSIN
FALLSON
FASHION
GADSDEN
GAGARIN
GAINSON
GALLEON
GAMBIAN
GASMAIN
GATEMAN
GATEMEN
GAUGUIN
HACKMAN
HADRIAN
HAIRPIN
HAITIAN
HALCYON
HALFDAN
HALOGEN
HALSTON
HAMELIN
HAMPTON
HANDGUN
HANDSIN
HANDSON
HANGMAN
HANGMEN
HANGSIN
HANGSON
HANGTEN
HARDPAN
HARDWON
HARPOON
HARPSON
HARSHEN
HARTMAN
HASBEEN
JACKSON
JACOBIN
JAMESON
JANSSEN
JAVAMAN
JAVELIN
JAZZMAN
JAZZMEN
KARAJAN
KATHRYN
KAUFMAN
LACHLAN
LAMPOON
LANGDON
LANOLIN
LANTERN
LAOCOON
LAOTIAN
LATERAN
LATERON
LATVIAN
LAUGHIN
LAYDOWN
LAYITON
LAYOPEN
MADCHEN
MADIGAN
MADISON
MAILSIN
MALAYAN
MANSION
MANXMAN
MANXMEN
MARCHON
MARILYN
MARMION
MARTIAN
MARYANN
MATEWAN
MAUDLIN
MAULDIN
MAUREEN
MAXBORN
MAYALIN
NAILSIN
NANKEEN
OAKFERN
OAKLAWN
PALADIN
PARAGON
PASSION
PASTERN
PATROON
PATTERN
PAULSEN
RACCOON
RAINMAN
RAKEDIN
RAKESIN
RALSTON
RAMADAN
RAMEKIN
RANDOWN
RANGOON
RARITAN
RAYBURN
SAFFRON
SAGEHEN
SAHARAN
SALADIN
SAMISEN
SAMPSON
SANDMAN
SANDMEN
SANJUAN
SARACEN
SARAZEN
SAROYAN
SASSOON
SATDOWN
SAURIAN
SAVARIN
SAXHORN
SAYWHEN
TACKSON
TAILFIN
TAKENIN
TAKENON
TAKESIN
TAKESON
TAKETEN
TALLINN
TAMARIN
TAPEMAN
TAPEMEN
TASHLIN
TASHMAN
TAXIMAN
TAXIMEN
VALJEAN
VATICAN
VAUGHAN
WADEDIN
WADESIN
WAITRON
WAITSON
WALKMAN
WALKSON
WALLOON
WALSTON
WANTSIN
WAVEDIN
WAVESIN
WAXBEAN
WAYWORN
XANTHAN
YANKTON
YARDMAN
YARDMEN
ZAIREAN
ZAIRIAN
ZAMBIAN

••AN•••

ABANDON
ACANTHI
ANANIAS
BEANBAG
BEANERY
BEANIES
BEANING
BLANCHE
BLANDER
BLANDLY
BLANKED
BLANKER
BLANKET
BLANKLY
BRANAGH
BRANDED
BRANDER
BRANDON
BRANSON
BYANDBY
BYANOSE
CHANCED
CHANCEL
CHANCER
CHANCES
CHANGED
CHANGER
CHANGES
CHANNEL
CHANSON
CHANTED
CHANTER
CHANTEY
CLANGED
CLANGOR
CLANKED
CRANIAL
CRANING
CRANIUM
CRANKED
CRANKUP
DEANERY
EMANANT
EMANATE
EMANUEL
EVANDER
EVANGEL
EVANISH
EXANIMO
FIANCEE
FIANCES
FLANEUR
FLANGES
FLANKED
FLANKER
FLANNEL
FRANCES
FRANCIS
FRANKED
FRANKEN
FRANKER
FRANKIE
FRANKLY
FRANKOZ
FRANTIC
GHANIAN
GLANCED
GLANCES
GRANADA
GRANARY
GRANDAM
GRANDEE
GRANDER
GRANDLY
GRANDMA
GRANDPA
GRANGER
GRANGES
GRANITE
GRANOLA
GRANTED
GRANTEE
GRANTOR
GRANULE
GUANACO
GUANINE
INANELY
INANEST
INANITY
IPANEMA
IRANIAN
IVANHOE
IVANOVO
JEANARP
JEANLUC
JEANNIE
KWANZAS
LEANDER
LEANERS
LEANEST
LEANING
LEANSON
LEANTOS
LOANERS
LOANING
MEANDER
MEANEST
MEANIES
MEANING
MOANERS
MOANFUL
MOANING
MYANMAR
NUANCED
NUANCES
OCANADA
ONANDON
ORANGES
ORANGEY
PAANGAS
PEANUTS
PHANTOM
PIANISM
PIANIST
PLANERS
PLANETS
PLANING
PLANISH
PLANKED
PLANNED
PLANNER
PLANOUT
PLANSON
PLANTAR
PLANTED
PLANTER
PRANCED
PRANCER
PRANCES
PRANGED
PRANKED
PSANDQS
QUANGOS
QUANTUM
RIANTLY
ROANOKE
RUANDAN
RWANDAN
SCANDAL
SCANNED
SCANNER
SCANTED
SCANTER
SCANTLY
SEANCES
SHANANA
SHANGRI
SHANKAR
SHANKED
SHANNON
SHANTEY
SKANKED
SKANKER
SLANDER
SLANTED
SOANDSO
SPANDEX
SPANGLE
SPANGLY
SPANIEL
SPANISH
SPANKED
SPANKER
SPANNED
SPANNER
STANCES
STANDBY
STANDEE
STANDIN
STANDON
STANDUP
STANLEE
STANLEY
STANNIC
STANTON
STANZAS
SWANKED
SWANKER
SWANSEA
SWANSON
THANKED
TIANJIN
TRANCES
TRANSIT
TRANSOM
TWANGED
UGANDAN
ULANOVA
URANITE
URANIUM
WEANING
WHANGED
WRANGLE
WYANDOT
YEANING

••A•N••

AGAINST
BEATNIK
BLARNEY
BRAINED
CHAINED
CHANNEL
DRAGNET
DRAINED
DRAINER
DRAWNIN
DRAWNON
DRAWNUP
EDASNER
FLANNEL
FLAUNTS
FLAUNTY
GRAINED
GRAPNEL
INASNIT
JEANNIE
KEARNEY
LEARNED
LEARNER
PLAINER
PLAINLY
PLAINTS
PLANNED
PLANNER
SCANNED
SCANNER
SHANNON
SHATNER
SHAWNEE
SPANNED
SPANNER
SPAWNED
STAINED
STAINER
STANNIC
STAUNCH
TRAINED
TRAINEE
TRAINER
WHATNOT
YEARNED
YEARNER

••A••N•

ABALONE
ABASING
ABATING
ADAMANT
ALAKING
AMAZING
AMAZONS
ARACHNE
ATAMANS
AWAKENS
AWAKING
BEACONS
BEADING
BEAMING
BEANING
BEARING
BEATING
BIASING
BLADING
BLAMING
BLARING
BLATANT
BLAZING
BLAZONS
BOATING
BRACING
BRAKING
BRAVING
BRAYING
BRAZING
CEASING
CHAFING
CHALONS
CHASING
CLAWING
COATING
COAXING
CRANING
CRATING
CRAVENS
CRAVING
CRAYONS
CRAZING
CZARINA
DEACONS
DEADEND
DEADENS
DEAFENS
DEALING
DIALING
DIAMOND
DRAGONS
DRAPING
DRAWING
DRAYING
ELATING
EMANANT
ERASING
ETAMINE
EVADING
EXAMINE
FEARING
FLACONS
FLAGONS
FLAKING
FLAMING
FLARING
FLAWING
FLAYING
FOALING
FOAMING
FRAMING
FRAYING
GEARING
GLARING
GLAZING
GNAWING
GOADING
GOALONG
GRACING
GRADING
GRATING
GRAVING
GRAYING
GRAZING
GUANINE
GUARANI
HEADING
HEALING
HEAPING
HEARING
HEATING
HEAVENS
HEAVING
HOAXING
HYALINE
IMAGINE
IMAGING
KLAXONS
LEADING
LEADINS
LEAFING
LEAKING
LEANING
LEAPING
LEASING

LEAVENS
LEAVING
LOADING
LOAFING
LOAMING
LOANING
MBABANE
MEANING
MOANING
NEARING
NEATENS
OCARINA
OKAYING
OPALINE
ORATING
PEAHENS
PEAKING
PEALING
PEASANT
PHALANX
PHARYNX
PHASING
PLACING
PLANING
PLATENS
PLATING
PLAYING
PRALINE
PRATING
PRAYING
QUAKING
READING
REAGENT
REAMING
REAPING
REAREND
REARING
REASONS
ROAMING
ROARING
SCALENE
SCALING
SCARING
SEAFANS
SEALANE
SEALANT
SEALING
SEAMING
SEARING
SEASONS
SEATING
SHADING
SHAKING
SHAMANS
SHAMING
SHANANA
SHAPING
SHARING
SHAVING
SKATING
SLAKING
SLATING
SLAVING
SNAKING
SNAPONS
SNARING
SOAKING
SOAPING
SOARING
SPACING
SPADING
SPARING
SPAVINS
SPAYING
STAGING
STAKING
STAMENS
STAMINA
STARING
STATING
STAVING
STAYING
SWAYING
TEAMING
TEARING
TEASING
THAWING
TRACING
TRADING
TSARINA
TZARINA
UNAMUNO
UTAHANS
WEAKENS
WEANING
WEAPONS
WEARING
WEAVING
WHALING
XRATING
XRAYING
YEANING
YEAREND
ZEALAND

••A•••N

ABANDON
ACADIAN
ADAMSON
AGAKHAN
ALADDIN
ALAMEIN
ALARCON
ALASKAN
ARABIAN
ARAMEAN
BEARSON
BLACKEN
BOATMAN
BOATMEN
BRACKEN
BRAHMAN
BRAHMIN
BRANDON
BRANSON
BRAXTON
CHAGRIN
CHANSON
CHAPLIN
CHAPMAN
CHAPMEN
CHARMIN
CHASTEN
CLAPTON
CLARION
CLAYTON
COALBIN
COARSEN
CRAMPON
DEADPAN
DEALSIN
DEALTIN
DRAGOON
DRAGSIN
DRAGSON
DRAWNIN
DRAWNON
DRAWSIN
DRAWSON
ELAAIUN
ELATION
EVASION
FLAGMAN
FLAGMEN
FLATTEN
FRANKEN
GHANIAN
GLADDEN
GRAFTON
GRAYSON
HEADMAN
HEADMEN
HEADPIN
HEADSIN
HEARKEN
HEARTEN
HEATHEN
HOARSEN
IDAHOAN
INASPIN
IRANIAN
ITALIAN
JOAQUIN
KRATION
LEADSIN
LEADSON
LEANSON
LEAVEIN
LIAISON
MIAMIAN
ONANDON
ORATION
OVATION
PEABEAN
PEARSON
PHAETON
PHASEIN
PLANSON
PLATOON
PLAYPEN
PLAYSON
READSIN
RUANDAN
RWANDAN
SEALION
SHANNON
SHAREIN
SHARPEN
SLACKEN
SLAYTON
SMARTEN
SPARTAN
STANDIN
STANDON
STANTON
STARMAN
STASSEN
STATION
SUASION
SWANSON
TEACHIN
TIANJIN
TRADEIN
TRADEON
UGANDAN
WHARTON
WHAUDEN

•••AN••

ADVANCE
ALBANIA
ALMANAC
ANDANTE
ARCANUM
ARRANGE
ASHANTI
ASKANCE
ATLANTA
AVIANCA
BALANCE
BANANAS
BARANOF
BONANZA
BUTANOL
CABANAS
CACANNY
CEZANNE
CHIANTI
CLEANED
CLEANER
CLEANLY
CLEANSE
CLEANUP
DECANTS
DELANEY
DEMANDS
DOPANTS
DURANCE
DURANGO
DURANTE
ELEANOR
EMBANKS
EMPANEL
ENHANCE
ERRANCY
ERRANDS
ESPANOL
ETHANOL
EXPANDS
EXPANSE
FINANCE
GLEANED
GLEANER
GROANED
GROANER
HOSANNA
HUMANLY
HUMANUM
IGUANAS
IMPANEL
INCANTS
INFANCY
INFANTA
INFANTS
ISLANDS
JACANAS
JOHANNA
JUMANJI
KIWANIS
LALANNE
LEBANON
LEPANTO
LEVANTS
LIGANDS
MANANAS
MELANGE
MELANIE
MELANIN
MIRANDA
MORANIS
MUTANTS
NOCANDO
OCEANIA
OCEANIC
OCEANID
OCEANUS
OCTANES
OCTANTS
ORGANDY
ORGANIC
ORGANON
ORGANUM
ORGANZA
ORLANDO
ORMANDY
OTRANTO
PALANCE
PAVANES
PEDANTS
PENANCE
PICANTE
PIRANHA
PLIANCY
RAPANUI
RECANED
RECANES
RECANTS
REDANTS
REHANGS
REMANDS
RESANDS
RIBANDS
ROMANCE
ROMANIA
ROMANOV
ROMANSH
ROSANNA
ROSANNE
ROXANNE
SARANAC
SAVANNA
SAVANTS
SECANTS
SQUANTO
STRANDS
STRANGE
SUSANNA
SUSANNE
SUZANNE
TARANTO
TENANCY
TENANTS
TETANUS
TISANES
TITANIA
TITANIC
TRUANCY
TRUANTS
TYRANNY
TYRANTS
ULYANOV
UNCANNY
UNHANDS
UNHANDY
UPLANDS
URBANER
VACANCY
VALANCE
VEDANTA
VERANDA
WCHANDY
WOMANLY
ZENANAS

•••A•N•

ARIADNE
ATTAINS
CACANNY
CEZANNE
DETAINS
DOMAINS
GERAINT
HOSANNA
JOHANNA
LALANNE
LARAINE
LASAGNA
LASAGNE
LOCARNO
MORAINE
OBTAINS
ORDAINS
RDLAING
REGAINS
REMAINS
REPAINT
RETAINS
ROGAINE
ROMAINE
ROSANNA
ROSANNE
ROXANNE
SAVANNA
SCRAWNY
SPRAINS
STRAINS
SUKARNO
SUSANNA
SUSANNE
SUZANNE
TYRANNY
UKRAINE
UNCANNY
VISAING

•••A••N

ACTAEON
ALMADEN
ARRAIGN
BALATON
BELAKUN
BETAKEN
BREAKIN
BROADEN
CARAVAN
CATALAN
CELADON
CHEAPEN
CHEATIN
CLEAVON
CORAZON
DECAGON
DREAMON
ELAAIUN
GAGARIN
GELATIN
GLEASON
HEPARIN
HEXAGON
IDEAMAN
IDEAMEN
IDIAMIN
ITHACAN
JAVAMAN
KARAJAN
KERATIN
LEBANON
LEBARON
MALAYAN
MAYALIN
MCGAVIN
MCMAHON
MELANIN
MUTAGEN
NEVADAN
NONAGON
OCTAGON
ORGANON
PALADIN
PARAGON
PUTAMEN
RAMADAN
RETAKEN
SAHARAN
SALADIN
SARACEN
SARAZEN
SAVARIN
SNEAKIN
SWEARIN
TAMARIN
TREASON
UNEATEN
VITAMIN
WHEATON
YUCATAN

••••AN•

ABEYANT
ADAMANT
AFGHANI
AFGHANS
AIRLANE
ANDEANS
ARMBAND
ARMYANT
ASHCANS
ASHLAND
ATAMANS
AYNRAND
BALKANS
BANDANA
BANYANS
BELTANE
BEMOANS
BETHANY
BIGBAND
BIGBANG
BIPLANE
BLATANT
BOITANO
BRIGAND
BROGANS
BUOYANT
BURBANK
BURMANS
CAFTANS
CAIMANS
CANCANS
CAPEANN
CAYMANS
CEBUANO
CHICANA
CHICANO
CINZANO
COMMAND
COMPANY
COOLANT
COPLAND
COURANT
COWHAND
CRETANS
CURRANT
DABHAND
DEFIANT
DEMEANS
DEPLANE
DESCANT
DEVIANT
DISBAND
DISTANT
DITTANY
DOGBANE
DOLMANS
DORMANT
ELEGANT
EMANANT
ENCHANT
ENGLAND
ENPLANE
ENTRANT
ETCHANT
EYEBANK
FENIANS
FIJIANS
FINLAND
FIREANT
FOGBANK
FONDANT
FRYPANS
GALLANT
GALVANI
GARLAND
GERMANE
GERMANS
GERMANY
GOTLAND
GUARANI
HATBAND
HENBANE
HERMANN
HETMANS
HISPANO
HOLLAND
HOVLANE
HUSBAND
HYDRANT
ICELAND
IKEBANA
ILOCANO
IMPLANT
INDIANA
INDIANS
INSPANS
INSTANT
IRELAND
ITERANT
JOBBANK
JUGBAND
JULIANA
JUTLAND
KAFTANS
KANSANS
KENYANS
KIRMANS
KOREANS
LANTANA
LAPLAND
LEGRAND
LENFANT
LIBYANS
LOWLAND
LUCIANO
MAGNANI
MANDANS
MARIANA
MARYANN
MBABANE
MEDIANS
MEDIANT
METHANE
MIDLAND
MIGRANT
MILLAND
MINOANS
MINYANS
MONTANA
MONTAND
MONTANE
MONTANI
MORDANT
MORGANA
MORGANS
MUNDANE
MUSTANG
NIRVANA
NITTANY
NORMAND
NORMANS
NUBIANS
OAKLAND
OFFHAND
OHIOANS
OILCANS
OILPANS
OLDHAND
ONELANE
OPERAND
OREGANO
ORLEANS
ORPHANS
OURGANG
OUTLAND
OUTRANK
OXIDANT
PADUANS
PAGEANT
PAISANO
PAPUANS
PEASANT
PECCANT
PENDANT
PENNANT
PHALANX
PIEPANS
PIQUANT
POMPANO
PROFANE
PROPANE
RADIANS
RADIANT
RAGLANS
RAMPANT
RATTANS
REGNANT
RELIANT
REMNANT
REPLANS
REPLANT
ROSTAND
SAMOANS
SAMPANS
SANTANA
SEAFANS
SEALANE
SEALANT
SERVANT
SEXTANS
SEXTANT
SHAMANS
SHANANA
SHEBANG
SIMIANS
SIOUANS
SLOGANS
SMETANA
SOPRANO
SOUTANE
SPIRANT
SPOKANE
SULTANA
SULTANS
SUNTANS
SYLVANS
SYRIANS
TAGGANT
TAIPANS
TAMMANY
TARTANS
TARZANA
TATIANA
TIFFANY
TIJUANA
TINCANS
TONGANS
TOUCANS
TOYLAND
TREPANS
TROJANS
TULSANS
TURBANS
TUSCANY
TWOLANE
TYMPANA
TYMPANI
ULLMANN
ULULANT
USGRANT
UTAHANS
VAGRANT
VALIANT
VARIANT
VERDANT
VIBRANT
VOLCANO
VULCANS
WARRANT
WELLAND
WETLAND
YOUMANS
ZEALAND

••••A•N

ABSTAIN
BAHRAIN
BARGAIN
BRITAIN
CAPEANN
CAPTAIN
CERTAIN
CONTAIN
COSTAIN
CURTAIN
DETRAIN
DISDAIN
ENCHAIN
ENTRAIN
EXPLAIN
GASMAIN
HERMANN
INGRAIN
MARYANN
OAKLAWN
PERTAIN
PREDAWN
REDRAWN
REFRAIN
RELEARN
RESTAIN
RETRAIN
SUSTAIN
TERRAIN
TREMAIN
ULLMANN
UNCHAIN
UNDRAWN
UNLEARN
VILLAIN

•••••AN

ACADIAN
AEOLIAN
AFRICAN
AGAKHAN
ALASKAN
ALSORAN
ALYKHAN
ANGOLAN
ARABIAN
ARAMEAN
ARTISAN
AZTECAN
BASEMAN
BATEMAN
BATSMAN
BELGIAN
BELLMAN
BERGMAN
BESTMAN
BIRDMAN
BKLIBAN
BOATMAN
BONDMAN
BOOLEAN
BRAHMAN
BRENDAN
BRENNAN
BROSNAN
BUSHMAN
BYREMAN
CADDOAN
CALIBAN
CAPITAN
CAPSTAN
CARAVAN
CASPIAN
CATALAN
CATSCAN
CAVEMAN
CHAPMAN
CHILEAN
COCHRAN
COLEMAN
CREWMAN
CRIMEAN
DAKOTAN
DARKMAN
DEADPAN
DISHPAN
DONJUAN
DONOVAN
DOORMAN
DRIPPAN
DRISTAN
DUSTMAN
DUSTPAN
EASTMAN
ELYSIAN
ETESIAN
ETONIAN
EXURBAN
FADIMAN
FELDMAN
FEYNMAN
FIREMAN
FLAGMAN
FOOTMAN
FOREMAN
FORERAN
FORTRAN
FREEMAN
FRIEDAN
FRISIAN
FROGMAN
FUSTIAN
GAMBIAN
GATEMAN
GENTIAN
GHANIAN
GILLIAN
GOODMAN
GORDIAN
GRECIAN
HACKMAN
HADRIAN
HAITIAN
HALFDAN
HANGMAN
HARDPAN
HARTMAN
HEADMAN
HEISMAN
HELLMAN
HESHVAN
HESSIAN
HICKMAN
HOFFMAN
HOUSMAN
IBERIAN
IDAHOAN
IDEAMAN
INHUMAN
IRANIAN
IRONMAN
ITALIAN
ITHACAN
JAVAMAN
JAZZMAN
JILLIAN
JOURDAN
JUNKMAN
KARAJAN
KAUFMAN
KEESHAN
KINGMAN
KINSMAN
KLUGMAN
LACHLAN
LAOTIAN
LATERAN
LATVIAN
LILLIAN
LINEMAN
LOCOMAN
MADIGAN
MALAYAN
MANXMAN
MARTIAN
MATEWAN
MCLUHAN
MEGRYAN
MEXICAN
MIAMIAN
MILKMAN
MINIVAN
MOHICAN
MRCLEAN
NEVADAN
NEWSMAN
ORPHEAN
ORTOLAN
OTTOMAN
OVERRAN
OXONIAN
PEABEAN
PELICAN
PEMICAN
PERLMAN
PERSIAN
PIKEMAN
PITTMAN
PLOWMAN
PORTMAN
POSTMAN
PROPMAN
PROTEAN
PULLMAN
PURITAN
PYTHIAN
RAINMAN
RAMADAN
RARITAN
RECLEAN
REITMAN
REPOMAN
RICHMAN
RICKMAN
ROMULAN
RUANDAN
RUFFIAN
RUSSIAN
RWANDAN
SAHARAN
SANDMAN
SANJUAN
SAROYAN
SAURIAN
SERBIAN
SHERMAN
SHIPMAN
SHOWMAN
SICHUAN
SIDEMAN
SIOBHAN
SNOWMAN
SOYBEAN
SPARTAN
SPORRAN
STARMAN
STYGIAN
STYRIAN
SYNGMAN
TAPEMAN
TASHMAN
TAXIMAN
TEHERAN
TELERAN
TESTBAN
THURMAN
TIBETAN
TRISTAN
TUCHMAN
UGANDAN
UMBRIAN
UNCLEAN
UTOPIAN
VALJEAN
VATICAN
VAUGHAN
VETERAN
VIRGOAN
WALKMAN
WAXBEAN
WELLMAN
WHITMAN
WISEMAN
WOLFMAN
WORKMAN
XANTHAN
YARDMAN
YEREVAN
YUCATAN
ZAIREAN
ZAIRIAN
ZAMBIAN

AO•••••

AORISTS
AOUDADS

A•O••••

ABOLISH
ABORTED
ABOUGHT
ABOUNDS
ACOLYTE
ACONITE
ADOLPHE
ADONAIS
ADOPTED
ADOPTEE
ADOPTER
ADORERS
ADORING
ADORNED
ADORNER
AEOLIAN
AGONISE
AGONIST
AGONIZE
AGOUTIS
ALOHAOE
ALOOFLY
AMOEBAE
AMOEBAS
AMOEBIC
AMONGST
AMOROUS
AMOUNTS
ANODISE
ANODIZE
ANODYNE
ANOINTS
ANOMALY
ANOMIES
ANONYMS
ANORAKS
ANOSMIA
ANOSMIC
ANOTHER
ANOUILH
APOCOPE
APOGEES
APOLOGY
APOSTLE
APOTHEM
AROUSAL
AROUSED
AROUSES
ASOCIAL
ASOFNOW
ATOMIES
ATOMISE
ATOMIZE
ATONIES
ATONING

AVOCADO
AVOCETS
AVOIDED
AVONLEA
AVOWALS
AVOWERS
AVOWING
AXOLOTL
AZODYES

A••O•••

ABBOTCY
ABDOMEN
ABSOLUT
ABSOLVE
ABSORBS
ACCORDS
ACCOSTS
ACCOUNT
ACROBAT
ACRONYM
ADDONTO
ADJOINS
ADJOURN
ADSORBS
AEROBAT
AEROBES
AEROBIC
AEROSOL
AFFORDS
AGNOMEN
AGROUND
ALCOHOL
ALCOVES
ALFONSO
ALFORJA
ALLOFME
ALLOVER
ALLOWAY
ALLOWED
ALLOYED
ALMONDS
ALOOFLY
ALSORAN
ALTOONA
ALTOSAX
ALWORTH
ALYOSHA
AMMONIA
AMPOULE
ANDORRA
ANDOVER
ANGOLAN
ANGORAS
ANNOYED
ANTOINE
ANTONIA
ANTONIN
ANTONIO
ANTONYM
ANYONES
APPOINT
APPOSED
APPOSES
APRONED
APROPOS
ARBORED
ARBOURS
ARDOURS
AREOLAE
AREOLAR
AREOLAS
ARGONNE
ARIOSOS
ARIOSTO
ARMOIRE
ARMORED
ARMORER
ARMOURS
ARMOURY
ARROBAS
ARROYOS
ASSORTS
ASTOLAT
ASTORIA
ASTOUND
ATHOMES
ATROPHY
ATWORST
AUROCHS
AURORAE
AURORAL
AURORAS
AUTOMAT

A•••O••

ABALONE
ABSCOND
ACEDOUT
ACEROLA
ACEROSE
ACESOUT
ACETONE
ACTFOUR
ACTIONS
ACTSOUT
ADIPOSE
AFFRONT
AIRBOAT
AIRCOOL
AIRFOIL
AIRHOLE
AIRLOCK
AIRPORT
AIRSOCK
AIRSOUT
AIRWOLF
ALAMODE
ALIMONY
ALLGONE
ALLTOLD
ALTOONA
ALVEOLI
AMAPOLA
AMATORY
AMAZONS
AMBROSE
AMNIONS
AMOROUS
AMPHORA
ANALOGS
ANALOGY
ANATOLE
ANATOMY
ANCHORS
ANCHOVY
ANDROID
ANDSOON
ANEMONE
ANEROID
ANTCOWS
ANTHONY
ANTIOCH
ANXIOUS
ANYBODY
ANYMORE
ANYROAD
APOCOPE
APOLOGY
APPROVE
APRIORI
AQUEOUS
ARCHONS
ARDMORE
ARDUOUS
ARIZONA
ARMHOLE
ARMLOAD
ARMLOCK
ARTFORM
ARTSONG
ARTWORK
ASHFORD
ASKSOUT
ATALOSS
AUREOLA
AUREOLE
AUTHORS
AWESOME
AXOLOTL
AYKROYD

A••••O•

ABANDON
ABETTOR
ABSALOM
ACHERON
ACHESON
ACTAEON
ACTEDON
ACTUPON
ADAGIOS
ADAMSON
ADAPTOR
ADDEDON
ADDISON
ADVISOR
AERATOR
AEROSOL
AHEADOF
AILERON
AIMSFOR
AIRCOOL
AIRDROP
AIRFLOW
AIRSHOW
ALARCON
ALBEDOS
ALBINOS
ALCOHOL
ALENCON
ALIENOR
ALLISON
ALLSTON
ALLYSON
ALOHAOE
ANDIRON
ANDSOON
ANGELOU
ANISTON
ANTIFOG
ANTILOG
ANTLION
APRICOT
APROPOS
ARIOSOS
ARISTOS
ARROYOS
ASKSFOR
ASOFNOW
ATECROW
ATTABOY
AUCTION
AUDITOR
AUDUBON
AVIATOR
AVIGNON
AWAREOF

A•••••O

ADDEDTO
ADDONTO
ADDUPTO
ADMITTO
AGESAGO
AGITATO
AGREETO
AIMEDTO
AJACCIO
AKIHITO
ALBERTO
ALFONSO
ALFREDO
ALLEGRO
AMERIGO
AMRADIO
ANIMATO
ANNATTO
ANTONIO
ARAPAHO
ARECIBO
ARETINO
ARIOSTO
ARSENIO
ARTDECO
AVOCADO

•AO••••

BAOBABS
GAOLERS
GAOLING
LAOCOON
LAOTIAN
MAOISTS
SAOTOME
TAOISTS
YAOUNDE

•A•O•••

BABOONS
BALONEY
BARONET
BARONGS
BAROQUE
BAYONET
BAZOOKA
CABOOSE
CAHOOTS
CAJOLED
CAJOLER
CAJOLES
CALOMEL
CALORIC
CALORIE
CANONIC
CANOPUS
CAROLED
CAROLER
CAROLUS
CAROLYN
CAROMED
CAROTID
CAROUSE
CAVORTS
DAHOMEY
DAKOTAN
DAKOTAS
FAGOTED
FANOUTS
FAVORED
FAVOURS
GALOOTS
GARONNE
GASOHOL
GAVOTTE
HALOGEN
HALOING
HANOVER
IACOCCA
JACOBIN
JACONET
KAROLYI
KAYOING
LABORED
LABORER
LABOURS
LACONIC
LACOSTE
LAGOONS
LAJOLLA
LAKOTAS
LAMOTTA
LANOLIN
LAPORTE
LASORDA
LATOSCA
LAYOFFS
LAYOPEN
LAYOUTS
LAYOVER
MADONNA
MAHONEY
MAHOUTS
MAJORCA
MAJORED
MALODOR
MANOWAR
MAROONS
MASONIC
MASONRY
MAYORAL
NABOKOV
PAGODAS
PALOMAR
PALOOKA
PANOPLY
PAPOOSE
PAROLED
PAROLEE
PAROLES
PAYOFFS
PAYOLAS
PAYOUTS
RADOMES
RAGOUTS
RANOVER
RAYOVAC
RAZORED
SALOONS
SAMOANS
SAMOVAR
SAMOYED
SARONGS
SAROYAN
SAVORED
SAVOURS
SAVOURY
TABORET
TALONED
TANOAKS
VALOURS
VAMOOSE
VAPOURS
WAGONER
ZAPOTEC
ZATOPEK

•A••O••

BABOONS
BACKOFF
BACKOUT
BADBOYS
BAGNOLD
BAILORS
BAILOUT
BAKEOFF
BALBOAS
BALCONY
BALFOUR
BALLOON
BALLOTS
BAMBOOS
BANJOES
BANNOCK
BARCODE
BARHOPS
BARNONE
BARNOWL
BARROOM
BARROWS
BARSOAP
BARYONS
BASSOON
BATBOYS
BATHOIL
BAWLOUT
BAZOOKA
CABOOSE
CACHOUS
CADDOAN
CAHOOTS
CALHOUN
CALLOFF
CALLOUS
CALLOUT
CALZONE
CAMEOED
CAMEOFF
CAMEOUT
CAMPOUT
CANDOUR
CANNOLI
CANNONS
CANTONS
CANTORS
CANYONS
CANZONE
CAPTORS
CARBONS
CARBOYS
CARCOAT
CARDOZO
CARGOES
CARHOPS
CARIOCA
CARLOAD
CARPOOL
CARPORT
CARROLL
CARROTS
CARTONS
CARTOON
CASHOUT
CASSOCK
CASTOFF
CASTOUT
CATBOAT
CATFOOD
CATHODE
CATIONS
DAGWOOD
DAIMONS
DAMSONS
DASBOOT
DASHOFF
DAYBOOK
DAYBOYS
DAYJOBS
DAYLONG
DAYROOM
DAYTONA
EARLOBE
EARLOCK
EASEOFF
EASEOUT
EASYOFF
EATSOUT
FACEOFF
FACTOID
FACTORS
FACTORY
FADEOUT
FAIROFF
FALCONS
FALLOFF
FALLOUT
FALLOWS
FANIONS
FANSOUT
FARGONE
FARMOUT
FARROWS
FASTONE
FATHOMS
FATUOUS
GALLONS
GALLOPS
GALOOTS
GAMBOLS
GAMMONS
GARCONS
GASCONS
GASCONY
GASEOUS
GASLOGS
GAVEOFF
GAVEOUT
HADDOCK
HAGDONS
HALLOWS
HAMHOCK
HAMMOCK
HAMMOND
HANCOCK
HANDOFF
HANDOUT
HANGOFF
HANGOUT
HANSOLO
HANSOMS
HARBORS
HARBOUR
HARMONY
HARPOON
HARROWS
HASSOCK
HAULOFF
HAYFORK
HAYLOFT
HAYMOWS
JANNOCK
JARGONS
JARGONY
JAWBONE
KARAOKE
KARLOFF
LABCOAT
LACTOSE
LAGOONS
LAIDOFF
LAIDOUT
LAMPOIL
LAMPOON
LANFORD
LAOCOON
LAPDOGS
LAPROBE
LAPTOPS
LARDONS
LASSOED
LASSOER
LASSOES
LASTORY
LAWFORD
LAYDOWN
LAYSOFF
LAYSOUT
MACRONS
MADEOFF
MADEOUT
MAILOUT
MAKEOFF
MAKEOUT
MALCOLM
MALLOWS
MALTOSE
MAMBOED
MAMMOTH
MANGOES
MANHOLE
MANHOOD
MANHOUR
MANIOCS
MARCONI
MARKOFF
MARKOVA
MARLOWE
MARMOTS
MAROONS
MARROWS
MASCOTS
MASTOID
MATLOCK
MATRONS
MATTOCK
MATZOHS
MAUROIS
MAXBORN
MAYPOLE
NAIROBI
NARROWS
NATIONS
OAKMOSS
OARLOCK
PADDOCK
PADLOCK
PADRONE
PADRONI
PAIDOFF
PAIDOUT
PAILOUS
PAIROFF
PALJOEY
PALLORS
PALMOFF
PALMOIL
PALOOKA
PANDORA
PANSOUT
PAPOOSE
PARBOIL
PARDONS
PARLORS
PARLOUR
PARLOUS
PARROTS
PARSONS
PARTOOK
PARTOUT
PASSOFF
PASSOUT
PASTORS
PATROLS
PATRONS
PATROON
PAVIOUR
PAVLOVA
PAWNOFF
PAYLOAD
PAYROLL
PAYSOFF
PAYSOUT
RACCOON
RADIOED
RAGDOLL
RAGMOPS
RAGTOPS
RAINOUT
RAKEOFF
RAMRODS
RANCOUR
RANDOWN
RANGOFF
RANGOON
RANGOUT
RANSOMS
RAPPORT
RAPTORS
RATHOLE
RATIONS
RAUCOUS
RAVIOLI
RAYMOND
SACKOUT
SAILORS
SALLOWS
SALMONS
SALOONS
SALSODA
SALVOES
SALVORS
SANFORD
SANGOUT
SANJOSE
SAOTOME
SAPPORO
SASSOON
SATDOWN
SAVIORS
SAVIOUR
SAWLOGS
SAWWOOD
SAXHORN
TABLOID
TADPOLE
TAGSOUT
TAILOFF
TAILORS
TAKEOFF
TAKEONE
TAKEOUT
TALKOUT
TALLOWS
TAMBOUR
TANGOED
TAPIOCA
TAPROOM
TAPROOT
TAPSOFF
TAPSOUT
TARPONS
TATTOOS
VACUOLE
VACUOUS
VAMOOSE
VANGOGH
VANPOOL
VARIOUS
WAGGONS
WAITOUT
WALCOTT
WALDORF
WALKONS
WALKOUT
WALLOON
WALLOPS
WALLOWS
WALPOLE
WANTOUT
WARDOFF
WARGODS
WARLOCK
WARLORD
WARZONE
WASHOFF
WASHOUT
WAVEOFF
WAXWORK
WAYCOOL
WAYWORN
YARROWS
YAUPONS
ZAMBONI

•A•••O•

BABALOO
BABYLON
BACKHOE
BACKLOG
BALATON
BALLBOY
BALLOON
BAMBOOS
BANDBOX
BANGKOK
BANKSON
BARANOF
BARRIOS
BARROOM
BARSTOW
BASSOON
BASTION
CAISSON
CALDRON
CALICOS
CALLBOX
CALLFOR
CALLSON
CAMELOT
CAMERON
CAMPHOR
CAMPION
CAPECOD
CAPITOL
CAPTION
CAREFOR
CARIBOU
CARLSON
CARLTON
CARPOOL
CARRION
CARRYON
CARTOON
CASHBOX
CASHCOW
CASINOS
CATALOG
CATCHON
CATFOOD
CATSHOW
CAUTION
DAGWOOD
DASBOOT
DAWNSON
DAYBOOK
DAYROOM
EARDROP
EARLDOM
EARLYON
EARSHOT
EATCROW
FACTION
FALLFOR
FALLSON
FASHION
GABBROS
GAINSON
GALAGOS
GALLEON
GANGTOK
GASOHOL
GAUCHOS
GAZEBOS
HAIRDOS
HALCYON
HALSTON
HAMPTON
HANDSON
HANGDOG
HANGSON
HARDTOP
HARDWON
HARICOT
HARPOON
HARPSON
HAUTBOY
HAVENOT
JACKPOT
JACKSON
JAMESON
JANEDOE
JANITOR
LADINOS
LAIDFOR
LAIDLOW
LAMPOON
LANGDON
LANGUOR
LAOCOON
LATERON
LATINOS
LAYITON
LAYSFOR
LAYSLOW
MADEFOR
MADISON
MAGINOT
MAILBOX
MAILLOT
MAINTOP
MAKEFOR
MALODOR
MANHOOD
MANILOW
MANITOU
MANSION
MARABOU
MARCHON
MARKHOR
MARMION
MARYLOU
MATADOR
MATELOT
NABOKOV
NAVAHOS
NAVAJOS
PAGEBOY
PAIDFOR
PALMTOP
PALTROW
PAPADOC
PAPAGOS
PARADOX
PARAGON
PARASOL
PARTOOK
PASSFOR
PASSION
PATRIOT
PATROON
PAYSFOR
RACCOON
RAINBOW
RALSTON
RANCHOS
RANGOON
RANRIOT
RAYKROC
SAFFRON
SALCHOW
SALTBOX
SAMPSON
SANDBOX
SANDHOG
SANDLOT
SASSOON
SAVELOY
SAWWOOD
TACKSON
TAGALOG
TAKENON
TAKESON
TANKTOP
TAPROOM
TAPROOT
TATTOOS
VANPOOL
WAITFOR
WAITRON
WAITSON
WALKSON
WALLOON
WALSTON
WARRIOR
WARTHOG
WAYCOOL
YANKTON

•A••••O

BABALOO
BACALAO
BAMBINO
BANDITO
CALYPSO
CANSECO
CARABAO
CARDOZO
CASSINO
CATERTO
CAVETTO
DARESTO
FALLSTO
FARRAGO
GALILEO
GAMBADO
HAEMATO
HANSOLO
JALISCO
JAYLENO
LAYINTO
MAESTRO
MAGNETO
MAKESDO
MARCATO
MARENGO
MARTINO
NABISCO
NANAIMO
PAISANO
PALAZZO
PALERMO
PASSADO
PATERNO
RALLYTO
RAMINTO
RANINTO
SAGUARO
SALERNO
SANREMO
SAPPORO
SAPSAGO
SATCHMO
TABASCO
TAKESTO
TALKSTO
TALLYHO
TAMPICO
TANGELO
TAPINTO
TARANTO
VALLEJO
VAQUERO
WANTSTO
ZAPATEO

••AO•••

CHAOTIC
MIAOYAO

••A•O••

ABALONE
ALAMODE
AMAPOLA
AMATORY
AMAZONS
ANALOGS
ANALOGY
ANATOLE
ANATOMY
ATALOSS
BEACONS
BEAROFF
BEAROUT
BEATOUT
BLAZONS
BRAVOES
BYANOSE
CHALONS
CHAMOIS
CLAMORS
CLAMOUR
COALOIL
CRAYOLA
CRAYONS
DEACONS
DEALOUT
DIABOLI
DIALOGS
DIAMOND
DIATOMS
DRAGONS
DRAGOON
DRAGOUT
DRAWOUT
ENAMORS
ENAMOUR
FLACONS
FLAGONS
FLATOUT
FLAVORS
FLAVOUR
GIACOMO
GLAMOUR
GOABOUT
GOALONG
GRANOLA
HEADOFF
HEADOUT
HEAROUT
IDAHOAN
IMAGOES
INAWORD
ISADORA
IVANOVO
JEALOUS
KLAXONS
LEACOCK
LEADOFF
LEADOUT
MEADOWS
MEADOWY
OFASORT
ONAROLL
ORATORS
ORATORY
PEABODY
PEACOAT
PEACOCK
PEAFOWL
PEAPODS
PEASOUP
PLANOUT
PLATOON
PLAYOFF
PLAYOUT
QUAHOGS
READOUT
REASONS
ROANOKE
SEABORG
SEACOWS
SEADOGS
SEAFOOD
SEALOFF
SEAMOSS
SEAPORT

SEASONS
SEAWOLF
SHADOOF
SHADOWS
SHADOWY
SHAKOES
SHALOMS
SLALOMS
SNAPONS
STATORS
TEAPOTS
TEAPOYS
TEAROFF
TEAROOM
TEAROSE
TEAROUT
TRAVOIS
ULANOVA
UNAVOCE
WEAPONS
WEAROFF
WEAROUT
ZEALOTS
ZEALOUS

••A••O•

ABANDON
ADAGIOS
ADAMSON
ADAPTOR
ALARCON
AWAREOF
BEARSON
BRANDON
BRANSON
BRAXTON
CHANSON
CHARIOT
CLAIROL
CLANGOR
CLAPTON
CLARION
CLAYTON
CRAMPON
CZARDOM
DRAGOON
DRAGSON
DRAWNON
DRAWSON
ELATION
ENACTOR
EVASION
EXACTOR
FIASCOS
FLATTOP
FRANKOZ
GEARBOX
GLASGOW
GRAFTON
GRANTOR
GRAYSON
HEARDOF
HEARSOF
INASPOT
INAWEOF
IVANHOE
KRATION
LEADSON
LEANSON
LEANTOS
LIAISON
NEARYOU
ONANDON
ORATION
OVATION
PEARSON
PEATBOG
PHAETON
PHANTOM
PHARAOH
PLANSON
PLATOON
PLAYBOY
PLAYDOH
PLAYSON
PRAETOR
PRAYFOR
QUANGOS
QUARTOS
REACTOR
REALTOR
ROADHOG
SCALLOP
SEAFOOD
SEALION
SHADOOF
SHAHDOM
SHALLOT
SHALLOW
SHAMPOO
SHANNON
SLAYTON
SMALTOS
SOAPBOX
SPARROW
STANDON
STANTON
STARDOM
STATION
SUASION
SWALLOW
SWANSON
TEAROOM
TEASHOP
TRACTOR
TRADEON
TRAITOR
TRANSOM
WHARTON
WHATFOR
WHATNOT
WYANDOT

••A•••O

AJACCIO
ARAPAHO
BRACERO
BRAVADO
CLAUDIO
EXANIMO
GEARSTO
GIACOMO
GUANACO
HEAVEHO
HEAVETO
IVANOVO
LEADSTO
MIAOYAO
PLACEBO
PLACIDO
PRAYSTO
REACTTO
SHAMPOO
SHAPIRO
SNAPSTO
SOANDSO
UNAMUNO

•••AO••

KARAOKE

•••A•O•

ABSALOM
ACTAEON
AERATOR
AHEADOF
ATTABOY
AVIATOR
BABALOO
BALATON
BARANOF
BELABOR
BUGABOO
BUGALOO
BUTANOL
BYWAYOF
CATALOG
CELADON
CLEAVON
CORAZON
CREATOR
CURATOR
DECAGON
DECALOG
DECAPOD
DISAVOW
DONATOR
DREAMON
DYNAMOS
ECUADOR
ELEANOR
EQUATOR
ESPANOL
ETHANOL
GALAGOS
GIRASOL
GLEASON
GYRATOR
HEXAGON
ICHABOD
INFAVOR
LEBANON
LEBARON
LEGATOS
LOCATOR
MARABOU
MATADOR
MCMAHON
MIKADOS
MIRADOR
MRMAGOO
NAVAHOS
NAVAJOS
NEGATOR
NONAGON
OCTAGON
OCTAVOS
ORGANON
PAPADOC
PAPAGOS
PARADOX
PARAGON
PARASOL
PICADOR
PICAROS
ROMANOV
ROTATOR
RUBATOS
RUNAMOK
SENATOR
SODAPOP
SPEAKOF
SQUALOR
TAGALOG
TREASON
ULYANOV
VIRAGOS
WHEATON

•••A••O

AMRADIO
ANNATTO
BABALOO
BACALAO
BELASCO
BOIARDO
BUGABOO
BUGALOO
CARABAO
CBRADIO
CURACAO
DECARLO
DEFACTO
DURANGO
EMBARGO
ESPARTO
EXFACTO
FMRADIO
GERALDO
HIDALGO
HORATIO
IMPASTO
INVACUO
LEPANTO
LOCARNO
MOGAMBO
MRMAGOO
NANAIMO
NOCANDO
NOVARRO
ONTARIO
ORLANDO
OTRANTO
PALAZZO
PICASSO
PIZARRO
RICARDO
ROSARIO
SQUANTO
SUHARTO
SUKARNO
SWEARTO
TABASCO
TARANTO
TOBACCO
ZAPATEO

••••AO•

ALOHAOE
PHARAOH

••••A•O

AGESAGO
AGITATO
ANIMATO
ARAPAHO
AVOCADO
BEEFALO
BOITANO
BRAVADO
BUFFALO
CEBUANO
CEMBALO
CENTAVO
CHICAGO
CHICANO
CINZANO
CRUSADO
CRUZADO
FARRAGO
FERRARO
GAMBADO
GENNARO
GUANACO
HAEMATO
HISPANO
ILOCANO
LONGAGO
LUCIANO
LUMBAGO
MARCATO
OREGANO
PAISANO
PASSADO
POMPANO
SAGUARO
SAPSAGO
SFUMATO
SOPRANO
TORNADO
TOURACO
VIBRATO
VOLCANO
ZHIVAGO

•••••AO

BACALAO
CARABAO
CURACAO
LINBIAO
LINPIAO
MIAOYAO
QINGDAO

AP•••••

APACHES
APATITE
APELIKE
APERCUS
APERIES
APHELIA
APHESES
APISHLY
APLENTY
APOCOPE
APOGEES
APOLOGY
APOSTLE
APOTHEM
APPALLS
APPARAT
APPAREL
APPEALS
APPEARS
APPEASE
APPENDS
APPLAUD
APPLETS
APPLIED
APPLIES
APPOINT
APPOSED
APPOSES
APPRISE
APPRIZE
APPROVE
APRICOT
APRIORI
APRONED
APROPOS
APSIDES
APTERAL
APTNESS

A•P••••

ALPACAS
AMPERES
AMPHORA
AMPLEST
AMPLIFY
AMPOULE
AMPULES
APPALLS
APPARAT
APPAREL
APPEALS
APPEARS
APPEASE
APPENDS
APPLAUD
APPLETS
APPLIED
APPLIES
APPOINT
APPOSED
APPOSES
APPRISE
APPRIZE
APPROVE
ARPENTS
ASPECTS
ASPERSE
ASPHALT
ASPIRED
ASPIRER
ASPIRES
ASPIRIN
ATPEACE
AUPAIRS

A••P•••

ADAPTED
ADAPTER
ADAPTOR
ADEPTLY
ADIPOSE
ADOPTED
ADOPTEE
ADOPTER
AIRPLAY
AIRPORT
AIRPUMP
AMAPOLA
ANAPEST
ARAPAHO
ARMPITS
ASEPSIS
ASEPTIC
AUSPICE

A•••P••

ACCEPTS
ACTUPON
ADDUPTO
ADOLPHE
AGRIPPA
APROPOS
ATROPHY

A••••P•

AGRIPPA
APOCOPE
ATTEMPT

A•••••P

ACTEDUP
ADDEDUP
AIRDROP
AIRPUMP
AIRSHIP
ANTEDUP
ANTESUP
ANTWERP
ARCLAMP

•AP••••

BAPTISE
BAPTISM
BAPTIST
BAPTIZE
CAPABLE
CAPABLY
CAPAPIE
CAPEANN
CAPECOD
CAPELET
CAPELLA
CAPERED
CAPFULS
CAPGUNS
CAPITAL
CAPITAN
CAPITOL
CAPLESS
CAPLETS
CAPNUTS
CAPPERS
CAPPING
CAPRICE
CAPSHAW
CAPSIDS
CAPSIZE
CAPSTAN
CAPSULE
CAPTAIN
CAPTION
CAPTIVE
CAPTORS
CAPTURE
CAPULET
DAPHNIS
DAPPING
DAPPLED
DAPPLES
GAPLESS
GAPPING
HAPENNY
HAPLESS
HAPPENS
HAPPIER
HAPPILY
HAPPING
JAPHETH
LAPALMA
LAPBELT
LAPDOGS
LAPELED
LAPFULS
LAPLACE
LAPLAND
LAPLATA
LAPORTE
LAPPETS
LAPPING
LAPPISH
LAPROBE
LAPSING
LAPTOPS
LAPWING
MAPPERS
MAPPING
NAPHTHA
NAPKINS
NAPLESS
NAPPERS
NAPPIES
NAPPING
NAPTIME
PAPADOC
PAPAGOS
PAPAYAS
PAPEETE
PAPERED
PAPERER
PAPILLA
PAPLIKE
PAPOOSE
PAPRIKA
PAPUANS
PAPYRUS
RAPANUI
RAPHAEL
RAPIDER
RAPIDLY
RAPIERS
RAPINES
RAPPELS
RAPPERS
RAPPING
RAPPORT
RAPTORS
RAPTURE
SAPIENS
SAPIENT
SAPLESS
SAPLING
SAPPERS
SAPPIER
SAPPILY
SAPPING
SAPPORO
SAPSAGO
TAPEMAN
TAPEMEN
TAPERED
TAPINGS
TAPINTO
TAPIOCA
TAPPERS
TAPPETS
TAPPING
TAPROOM
TAPROOT
TAPSOFF
TAPSOUT
TAPSTER
VAPIDLY
VAPOURS
WAPITIS
YAPPERS
YAPPING
ZAPATEO
ZAPOTEC
ZAPPERS
ZAPPIER
ZAPPING

•A•P•••

BAGPIPE
CALPACS
CAMPARI
CAMPERS
CAMPHOR
CAMPIER
CAMPILY
CAMPING
CAMPION
CAMPOUT
CAPPERS
CAPPING
CARPALS
CARPARK
CARPELS
CARPERS
CARPETS
CARPING
CARPOOL
CARPORT
CASPIAN
DAMPENS
DAMPERS
DAMPEST
DAMPING
DAMPISH
DAPPING
DAPPLED
DAPPLES
DAUPHIN
EARPLUG
GALPALS
GAPPING
GASPERS
GASPING
GASPUMP
GAWPING
HAMPERS
HAMPTON
HAPPENS
HAPPIER
HAPPILY
HAPPING
HARPERS
HARPIES
HARPING
HARPIST
HARPOON
HARPSON
HASPING
HATPINS
JAMPACK
JASPERS
KAMPALA
LAMPOIL
LAMPOON
LAMPREY
LAPPETS
LAPPING
LAPPISH
MAGPIES
MAPPERS
MAPPING
MAYPOLE
NAPPERS
NAPPIES
NAPPING
PAMPERS
PANPIPE
PAUPERS
PAWPAWS
RAJPUTS
RAMPAGE
RAMPANT
RAMPART
RAPPELS
RAPPERS
RAPPING
RAPPORT
RASPERS
RASPIER
RASPING
RASPISH
RATPACK
SAMPANS
SAMPLED
SAMPLER
SAMPLES
SAMPRAS
SAMPSON
SAPPERS
SAPPIER
SAPPILY
SAPPING
SAPPORO
TADPOLE
TAIPANS
TAMPERS
TAMPICO
TAMPING
TAPPERS
TAPPETS
TAPPING
TARPITS
TARPONS
VAMPERS
VAMPING
VAMPIRA
VAMPIRE
VAMPISH
VANPOOL
WALPOLE
WARPATH
WARPING
WASPIER
WASPILY
WASPISH
YAPPERS
YAPPING
YAUPONS
YAWPERS
YAWPING
ZAPPERS
ZAPPIER
ZAPPING

•A••P••

BASEPAY
CALIPER
CALIPHS
CALYPSO
CANAPES
CANOPUS
CAPAPIE
CATSPAW
FAUXPAS
HAIRPIN
HARDPAN
HARDPUT
JACKPOT
LAYOPEN
MADEPAR
MAKEPAR
MANIPLE
PANOPLY
PARAPET
PARAPHS
ZATOPEK

•A•••P•

BACKUPS
BAGPIPE
BARHOPS
CARHOPS
CATALPA
CATNAPS
CATNIPS
GALLOPS
GALUMPH
GASCAPS
GAZUMPS
HANGUPS
LAPTOPS
LARRUPS
LASHUPS
MADCAPS
MAKEUPS
MARKUPS
PANPIPE
RAGMOPS
RAGTOPS
RAVEUPS
SATRAPS
WALKUPS
WALLOPS
WARMUPS
WASHUPS

•A••••P

BACKSUP
BALLSUP
BANGSUP
BARKEEP
BARSOAP
CALLSUP
CANTRIP
CATCHUP
DAYCAMP
DAYTRIP
EARDROP
EARFLAP
EASEDUP
EASESUP
EATENUP
FAIRSUP
GANGSUP
GASPUMP
HAMITUP
HANDSUP
HANGSUP
HANSARP
HARDTOP
HAULSUP
JACKSUP
LACEDUP
LACESUP
MAINTOP
MAKESUP
MANTRAP
MARKSUP
MATCHUP
PACKSUP
PAIRSUP
PALMTOP
PARSNIP
PASTEUP
PATCHUP
RACKSUP
RAISEUP
RAKEDUP
RAKESUP
RATTRAP
SAVEDUP
SAVESUP
TAKESUP
TALKSUP
TALLYUP
TANKSUP
TANKTOP
WAITSUP
WAKESUP
WALLSUP
WARMSUP
WARSHIP

••AP•••

ADAPTED
ADAPTER
ADAPTOR
AMAPOLA
ANAPEST
ARAPAHO
CHAPATI
CHAPEAU
CHAPELS
CHAPLET
CHAPLIN
CHAPMAN
CHAPMEN
CHAPPED
CHAPPIE
CHAPTER
CLAPPED
CLAPPER
CLAPTON
CRAPPIE
DIAPERS
DRAPERS
DRAPERY
DRAPING
EDAPHIC
ELAPIDS
ELAPSED
ELAPSES
FLAPPED
FLAPPER
FRAPPES
GRAPHED
GRAPHIC
GRAPIER
GRAPNEL
GRAPPAS
GRAPPLE
HEAPING
INAPTER
INAPTLY
LEAPERS
LEAPING
PEAPODS
REAPERS
REAPING
SCAPULA
SEAPORT
SHAPELY
SHAPERS
SHAPEUP
SHAPING
SHAPIRO
SHAPLEY
SLAPPED
SNAPONS
SNAPPED
SNAPPER
SNAPPLE
SNAPSAT
SNAPSTO
SNAPSUP
SOAPBOX
SOAPERS
SOAPIER
SOAPILY
SOAPING
STAPLED
STAPLER
STAPLES
SWAPPED
SWAPPER
TEAPOTS
TEAPOYS
TRAPEZE
TRAPPED
TRAPPER
UNAPTLY
WEAPONS
WRAPPED
WRAPPER
WRAPSUP
WRAPUPS

••A•P••

BEARPAW
CHAMPED
CHAPPED
CHAPPIE
CLAMPED
CLAPPED
CLAPPER
CLASPED
CRAMPED
CRAMPON
CRAPPIE
DEADPAN
EXAMPLE
FLAPPED
FLAPPER
FRAPPES
GRAMPAS
GRAMPUS
GRAPPAS
GRAPPLE
GRASPED
HEADPIN
INASPIN
INASPOT
PLAYPEN
SCALPED
SCALPEL
SCALPER
SCAMPED
SCAMPER
SCARPED
SCARPER
SHAMPOO
SHARPED
SHARPEI
SHARPEN
SHARPER
SHARPLY
SLAPPED
SNAPPED
SNAPPER
SNAPPLE
STAMPED
STAYPUT
SWAMPED
SWAPPED
SWAPPER
TRAIPSE
TRAMPAS
TRAMPED
TRAMPLE
TRAPPED
TRAPPER
WRAPPED
WRAPPER

••A••P•

GRANDPA
PLATYPI
TEACUPS
WRAPUPS

••A•••P

BEADSUP
BEAMSUP
BEARSUP
BEATSUP
BRACEUP
CHALKUP
CHATSUP
CLAMSUP
CRACKUP
CRANKUP
DRAWNUP
DRAWSUP
FLAREUP
FLATTOP
FRAMEUP
GEARSUP
HEADSUP
HEATSUP
INAHEAP
JEANARP
LEADSUP
PEASOUP
PHARLAP
PLAYSUP
REARSUP
ROADMAP
SCALLOP
SCAREUP
SEALSUP
SHAKEUP
SHAPEUP
SMASHUP
SNAPSUP
SOAKSUP
STACKUP
STANDUP
STARMAP
STARTUP
STAYSUP
TEAMSUP
TEARSUP
TEASHOP
TRADEUP
WRAPSUP

•••AP••

CANAPES
CAPAPIE
CHEAPEN
CHEAPER
CHEAPIE
CHEAPLY
DECAPOD
ESCAPED
ESCAPEE
ESCAPES
FLEAPIT
PARAPET
PARAPHS
PITAPAT
RELAPSE
REPAPER
RETAPED
RETAPES
SCRAPED

SCRAPER
SCRAPES
SCRAPPY
SERAPES
SERAPHS
SERAPIS
SODAPOP
SYNAPSE
TERAPHS
UNHAPPY
UNTAPED

•••A•P•
CATALPA
CCLAMPS
DECAMPS
ENCAMPS
ESCARPS
PREAMPS
REVAMPS
SCRAPPY
UNHAPPY

•••A••P
BREAKUP
CLEANUP
CLEARUP
DREAMUP
SODAPOP
SPEAKUP

••••AP•
BITMAPS
BUMRAPS
BURLAPS
CATNAPS
DEWLAPS
DIGRAPH
ENTRAPS
ENWRAPS
GASCAPS
GOESAPE
HOTCAPS
HUBCAPS
ICECAPS
INSCAPE
INSHAPE
KIDNAPS
MADCAPS
MISHAPS
MOBCAPS
PERHAPS
PRETAPE
REDCAPS
REDTAPE
REWRAPS
RIPRAPS
SATRAPS
SCHNAPS
SKYCAPS
THERAPY
TOECAPS
TOETAPS
TOPKAPI
UNDRAPE
UNSNAPS
UNTRAPS
UNWRAPS
WENTAPE

••••A•P
ARCLAMP
BEDLAMP
DAYCAMP
HANSARP
JEANARP
OFFRAMP
OILLAMP
RESTAMP
SUNLAMP
UNCLASP

•••••AP
BARSOAP
EARFLAP
FLYTRAP
GIDDYAP
HEELTAP
INAHEAP
INKYCAP
KNEECAP
MANTRAP
MEDIGAP
OLDCHAP
OVERLAP
PHARLAP
PINESAP
RATTRAP
ROADMAP
SNOWCAP
STARMAP
STOPGAP
UNSTRAP
WINESAP
WIRETAP

AQ•••••
AQUARIA
AQUATIC
AQUAVIT
AQUEOUS
AQUIFER
AQUINAS
AQUIVER

A•Q••••
ACQUIRE
ACQUITS

A•••Q••
ANTIQUE

•AQ••••
VAQUERO

•A•Q•••
BANQUET
BASQUES
CAIQUES
CASQUED
CASQUES
JACQUES
LACQUER
MARQUEE
MARQUES
MARQUEZ
MARQUIS
MASQUES
PARQUET
RACQUET
SACQUES
YANQUIS

•A••Q••
BAROQUE
LALIQUE
MACAQUE

••AQ•••
CLAQUES
JOAQUIN
OPAQUES
PLAQUES

••A••Q•
PSANDQS

•••AQ••
MACAQUE

AR•••••
ARABIAN
ARACHNE
ARAFURA
ARALSEA
ARAMAIC
ARAMEAN
ARAPAHO
ARAWAKS
ARBITER
ARBORED
ARBOURS
ARBUTUS
ARCADES
ARCADIA
ARCANUM
ARCHAIC
ARCHERS
ARCHERY
ARCHING
ARCHIVE
ARCHONS
ARCHWAY
ARCLAMP
ARCSINE
ARDENCY
ARDMORE
ARDOURS
ARDUOUS
AREARUG
AREAWAY
ARECIBO
AREOLAE
AREOLAR
AREOLAS
ARETINO
ARGIVES
ARGONNE
ARGUERS
ARGUING
ARGYLES
ARIADNE
ARIDEST
ARIDITY
ARIETTA
ARIKARA
ARIOSOS
ARIOSTO
ARISING
ARISTAE
ARISTAS
ARISTOS
ARIZONA
ARLEDGE
ARMADAS
ARMBAND
ARMENIA
ARMFULS
ARMHOLE
ARMLESS
ARMLETS
ARMLIKE
ARMLOAD
ARMLOCK
ARMOIRE
ARMORED
ARMORER
ARMOURS
ARMOURY
ARMPITS
ARMREST
ARMURES
ARMYANT
ARNICAS
AROUSAL
AROUSED
AROUSES
ARPENTS
ARRAIGN
ARRANGE
ARRASES
ARRAYED
ARREARS
ARRESTS
ARRIERE
ARRISES
ARRIVAL
ARRIVED
ARRIVER
ARRIVES
ARROBAS
ARROYOS
ARSENAL
ARSENIC
ARSENIO
ARTDECO
ARTEMIS
ARTEMUS
ARTFILM
ARTFORM
ARTICLE
ARTIEST
ARTISAN
ARTISTE
ARTISTS
ARTLESS
ARTSIER
ARTSONG
ARTWARE
ARTWORK
ARUGULA

A•R••••
ABRADED
ABRADER
ABRADES
ABRAHAM
ABREAST
ABRIDGE
ABRUZZI
ACREAGE
ACRIDLY
ACROBAT
ACRONYM
ACRYLIC
ADRENAL
AERATED
AERATES
AERATOR
AERIALS
AERIEST
AEROBAT
AEROBES
AEROBIC
AEROSOL
AFRAMES
AFREETS
AFRICAN
AGRAFFE
AGREETO
AGRIPPA
AGROUND
AIRBAGS
AIRBALL
AIRBASE
AIRBOAT
AIRCOOL
AIRCREW
AIRDAMS
AIRDATE
AIRDROP
AIRFARE
AIRFLOW
AIRFOIL
AIRGUNS
AIRHEAD
AIRHOLE
AIRIEST
AIRINGS
AIRKISS
AIRLANE
AIRLESS
AIRLIFT
AIRLIKE
AIRLINE
AIRLOCK
AIRMADA
AIRMAIL
AIRMASS
AIRMILE
AIRPLAY
AIRPORT
AIRPUMP
AIRRAID
AIRSACS
AIRSHIP
AIRSHOW
AIRSOCK
AIRSOUT
AIRTAXI
AIRTIME
AIRWAVE
AIRWAYS
AIRWOLF
ALREADY
ALRIGHT
AMRADIO
AORISTS
APRICOT
APRIORI
APRONED
APROPOS
ARRAIGN
ARRANGE
ARRASES
ARRAYED
ARREARS
ARRESTS
ARRIERE
ARRISES
ARRIVAL
ARRIVED
ARRIVER
ARRIVES
ARROBAS
ARROYOS
ATRIUMS
ATROPHY
AURALEE
AURALLY
AUREATE
AUREOLA
AUREOLE
AURICLE
AUROCHS
AURORAE
AURORAL
AURORAS

A••R•••
ABORTED
ACARIDS
ACCRETE
ACCRUAL
ACCRUED
ACCRUES
ACERBIC
ACEROLA
ACEROSE
ACTRESS
ADDRESS
ADORERS
ADORING
ADORNED
ADORNER
AFFRAYS
AFFRONT
AGARICS
AGGRESS
AIGRETS
AIRRAID
ALARCON
ALARMED
ALARMER
ALARUMS
ALDRICH
ALERTED
ALERTER
ALERTLY
ALFREDO
AMBRIES
AMBROSE
AMERCED
AMERCES
AMERICA
AMERIGO
AMERIKA
AMERIND
AMOROUS
ANARCHY
ANDREAS
ANDRESS
ANDREWS
ANDROID
ANEROID
ANGRIER
ANGRILY
ANORAKS
ANYROAD
APERCUS
APERIES
APPRISE
APPRIZE
APPROVE
ARMREST
ASARULE
ASCRIBE
ASHRAMS
ASTRIDE
ATTRACT
ATTRITE
ATTRITS
AVARICE
AVERAGE
AVERRED
AVERTED
AWARDED
AWARDEE
AWARDER
AWAREOF
AYKROYD
AYNRAND
AZURITE

A•••R••
ABJURED
ABJURES
ABSORBS
ACCORDS
ACCURST
ACHERON
ADHERED
ADHERES
ADJURED
ADJURES
ADMIRAL
ADMIRED
ADMIRER
ADMIRES
ADSORBS
ADVERBS
ADVERSE
ADVERTS
AELFRIC
AFFIRMS
AFFORDS
AILERON
AIRCREW
AIRDROP
ALBERTA
ALBERTO
ALFORJA
ALGERIA
ALLERGY
ALLURED
ALLURES
ALSORAN
ALTERED
ALTERER
ALVAREZ
ALWORTH
AMHARIC
AMHERST
AMPERES
AMSCRAY
ANAGRAM
ANDIRON
ANDORRA
ANGERED
ANGORAS
ANTARES
APPARAT
APPAREL
APTERAL
AQUARIA
ARBORED
AREARUG
ARMORED
ARMORER
ARMURES
ASFARAS
ASHTRAY
ASPERSE
ASPIRED
ASPIRER
ASPIRES
ASPIRIN
ASSERTS
ASSORTS
ASSURED
ASSURES
ASSYRIA
ASTARTE
ASTORIA
ATECROW
ATHIRST
ATLARGE
ATTIRED
ATTIRES
ATWORST
AUBURNS
AUGURAL
AUGURED
AURORAE
AURORAL
AURORAS
AUSTRAL
AUSTRIA
AUTARKY
AVERRED

A••••R•
ABELARD
ABEXTRA
ABINTRA
ABUSERS
ACQUIRE
ACTUARY
ADJOURN
ADORERS
AETHERS
AFFAIRE
AFFAIRS
AIRFARE
AIRPORT
ALFIERI
ALGEBRA
ALGIERS
ALLEARS
ALLEGRO
ALLHERE
AMATORY
AMBLERS
AMPHORA
ANCHORS
ANDORRA
ANGLERS
ANSWERS
ANTFARM
ANTHERS
ANTIART
ANTLERS
ANTWERP
ANYMORE
APPEARS
APRIORI
ARAFURA
ARBOURS
ARCHERS
ARCHERY
ARDMORE
ARDOURS
ARGUERS
ARIKARA
ARMOIRE
ARMOURS
ARMOURY
ARREARS
ARRIERE
ARTFORM
ARTWARE
ARTWORK
ASHBURY
ASHFORD
ASHLARS
ASTAIRE
ATATURK
ATHEART
ATHWART
AUPAIRS
AUSTERE
AUTEURS
AUTHORS
AVATARS
AVOWERS
AWKWARD

A•••••R
ABETTOR
ABRADER
ABUBAKR
ACCEDER
ACCUSER
ACTFOUR
ADAPTER
ADAPTOR
ADMIRER
ADOPTER
ADORNER
ADVISER
ADVISOR
AERATOR
AIMSFOR
ALARMER
ALCAZAR
ALERTER
ALIENOR
ALIGNER
ALLAYER
ALLEGER
ALLOVER
ALLSTAR
ALTERER
ALUNSER
AMASSER
AMATEUR
AMMETER
ANDOVER
ANGRIER
ANGULAR
ANNULAR
ANOTHER
ANTBEAR
ANTIWAR
ANTSIER
AQUIFER
AQUIVER
ARBITER
AREOLAR
ARMORER
ARRIVER
ARTSIER
ASKSFOR
ASPIRER
ASSAYER
ASUNDER
ATELIER
AUDITOR
AVENGER
AVIATOR
AWARDER

•AR••••
BARANOF
BARBARA
BARBARY
BARBELL
BARBELS
BARBERS
BARBING
BARBUDA
BARCARS
BARCODE
BARDISH
BARENTS
BARETTA
BARGAIN
BARGEIN
BARGING
BARHOPS
BARKEEP
BARKERS
BARKIER
BARKING
BARKLEY
BARKSAT
BARLESS
BARLEYS
BARMAID
BARMIER
BARNABY
BARNARD
BARNEYS
BARNONE
BARNOWL
BARONET
BARONGS
BAROQUE
BARRACK
BARRAGE
BARRELS
BARRENS
BARRETT
BARRIER
BARRING
BARRIOS
BARROOM
BARROWS
BARSOAP
BARSTOW
BARTABS
BARTEND
BARTERS
BARWARE
BARYONS
CARABAO
CARACAL
CARACAS
CARAFES
CARAMBA
CARAMEL
CARAMIA
CARAVAN
CARAVEL
CARAWAY
CARBIDE
CARBINE
CARBONS
CARBOYS
CARCASE
CARCASS
CARCOAT
CARDERS
CARDIAC
CARDING
CARDOZO
CAREENS
CAREERS
CAREFOR
CAREFUL
CARFARE
CARFULS
CARGOES
CARHOPS
CARIBES
CARIBOU
CARINAS
CARIOCA
CARKING
CARLESS
CARLOAD
CARLSON
CARLTON
CARLYLE
CARMINE
CARNERA
CARNETS
CARNIES
CAROLED
CAROLER
CAROLUS
CAROLYN
CAROMED
CAROTID
CAROUSE
CARPALS
CARPARK
CARPELS
CARPERS
CARPETS
CARPING
CARPOOL
CARPORT
CARRELS
CARRICK
CARRIED
CARRIER
CARRIES
CARRION
CARROLL
CARROTS
CARRYON
CARSEAT
CARTAGE
CARTELS
CARTERS
CARTIER
CARTING
CARTONS
CARTOON
CARVERS
CARVING
CARWASH
DARBIES
DAREFUL
DARESAY
DARESTO
DARKENS
DARKEST
DARKISH
DARKMAN
DARLENE
DARLING
DARNERS
DARNING
DARNLEY
DARTERS
DARTING
EARACHE
EARDROP
EARDRUM
EARFLAP
EARFULS
EARHART
EARLDOM
EARLESS
EARLIER
EARLIKE
EARLOBE
EARLOCK
EARLYON
EARMARK
EARMUFF
EARNERS
EARNEST
EARNING
EARPLUG
EARRING
EARSHOT
EARTHEN
EARTHLY
EARWIGS
FARADAY
FARAWAY
FARCING
FAREAST
FARGONE
FARLEFT
FARMERS
FARMERY
FARMING
FARMOUT
FARRAGO
FARRIER
FARROWS
FARTHER
FARWEST
GARAGED
GARAGES
GARBAGE
GARBING
GARBLED
GARBLES
GARCONS
GARDENS
GARDNER
GARGLED
GARGLES
GARLAND
GARMENT
GARNERS
GARNETS
GARNISH
GARONNE
GARRETS
GARRETT
GARRICK
GARTERS
HARBORS
HARBOUR
HARBURG
HARDENS
HARDEST
HARDHAT
HARDHIT
HARDIER
HARDILY
HARDING
HARDPAN
HARDPUT
HARDSET
HARDTOP
HARDWON
HARICOT
HARKENS
HARKING
HARMFUL
HARMING
HARMONY
HARNESS
HARPERS
HARPIES
HARPING
HARPIST
HARPOON
HARPSON
HARRIED
HARRIER
HARRIES
HARRIET
HARROWS
HARSHEN
HARSHER
HARSHLY
HARTMAN
HARVARD
HARVEST
JARFULS
JARGONS
JARGONY
JARLESS
JARRING
KARACHI
KARAJAN
KARAKUL
KARAKUM
KARAOKE
KARASEA
KARLOFF
KAROLYI
LARAINE
LARAMIE
LARCENY
LARCHES
LARDERS
LARDIER
LARDING
LARDNER
LARDONS
LARGELY
LARGESS
LARGEST
LARGISH
LARIATS
LARKISH
LARRUPS
MARABOU
MARACAS
MARAUDS
MARBLED
MARBLES
MARCATO
MARCEAU
MARCELS
MARCHED
MARCHER
MARCHES
MARCHON
MARCONI
MARENGO
MARGATE
MARGAUX
MARGAYS
MARGINS
MARGRET
MARIANA
MARILYN
MARIMBA
MARINAS
MARINER
MARINES
MARITAL
MARKERS
MARKETS
MARKHAM
MARKHOR
MARKING
MARKKAA
MARKOFF
MARKOVA
MARKSUP
MARKUPS
MARLENE
MARLINS
MARLOWE
MARMARA
MARMION
MARMOTS
MAROONS
MARQUEE
MARQUES
MARQUEZ
MARQUIS
MARRIED
MARRIES
MARRING
MARROWS
MARRYME
MARSALA
MARSHAL
MARSHES
MARTENS
MARTIAL
MARTIAN
MARTINA
MARTINI
MARTINO
MARTINS
MARTYRS
MARVELS
MARXISM
MARXIST
MARYANN
MARYKAY
MARYLOU
NARRATE
NARROWS
NARTHEX
NARWALS
NARWHAL
OARLESS
OARLIKE
OARLOCK
PARABLE
PARADED
PARADES
PARADOX
PARAGON
PARAPET
PARAPHS
PARASOL
PARATUS
PARBOIL
PARCELS
PARCHED
PARCHES
PARDNER
PARDONS
PARENTS
PARFAIT
PARGETS
PARIAHS
PARINGS
PARKADE
PARKING
PARKWAY

PARLAYS
PARLEYS
PARLORS
PARLOUR
PARLOUS
PAROLED
PAROLEE
PAROLES
PARQUET
PARRIED
PARRIER
PARRIES
PARRING
PARRISH
PARROTS
PARSECS
PARSEES
PARSERS
PARSING
PARSLEY
PARSNIP
PARSONS
PARTAKE
PARTIAL
PARTIED
PARTIER
PARTIES
PARTING
PARTITA
PARTITE
PARTNER
PARTOOK
PARTOUT
PARTWAY
PARURES
PARVENU
RAREBIT
RAREGAS
RARITAN
SARACEN
SARALEE
SARANAC
SARAWAK
SARAZEN
SARCASM
SARDINE
SARGENT
SARKIER
SARONGS
SAROYAN
TARANTO
TARBABY
TARBELL
TARDIER
TARDILY
TARGETS
TARHEEL
TARIFFS
TARMACS
TARNISH
TARPITS
TARPONS
TARRIED
TARRIER
TARRIES
TARRING
TARSALS
TARSIER
TARTANS
TARTARE
TARTARS
TARTEST
TARTISH
TARZANA

VARIANT
VARIETY
VARIOUS
VARLETS
VARMINT
VARNISH
VARSITY
VARYING
WARBLED
WARBLER
WARBLES
WARDENS
WARDERS
WARDING
WARDOFF
WARFARE
WARGAME
WARGODS
WARIEST
WARLESS
WARLIKE
WARLOCK
WARLORD
WARMEST
WARMING
WARMISH
WARMSUP
WARMUPS
WARNING
WARPATH
WARPING
WARRANT
WARRENS
WARRING
WARRIOR
WARSHIP
WARTHOG
WARTIER
WARTIME
WARWICK
WARZONE
YARDAGE
YARDARM
YARDMAN
YARDMEN
YARNING
YARROWS
ZAREBAS

•A•R•••

BAHRAIN
BARRACK
BARRAGE
BARRELS
BARRENS
BARRETT
BARRIER
BARRING
BARRIOS
BARROOM
BARROWS
CABRINI
CAPRICE
CARRELS
CARRICK
CARRIED
CARRIER
CARRIES
CARRION
CARROLL
CARROTS
CARRYON
DAIRIES
DAYROOM

EARRING
FABRICS
FAERIES
FAIREST
FAIRIES
FAIRING
FAIRISH
FAIROFF
FAIRSUP
FAIRWAY
FARRAGO
FARRIER
FARROWS
GABRIEL
GAGRULE
GARRETS
GARRETT
GARRICK
HAARLEM
HADRIAN
HAIRCUT
HAIRDOS
HAIRDYE
HAIRIER
HAIRNET
HAIRPIN
HARRIED
HARRIER
HARRIES
HARRIET
HARROWS
HATRACK
HAYRACK
HAYRIDE
JARRING
LABRETS
LAERTES
LAPROBE
LARRUPS
LAURELS
LAURENT
MACRAME
MACRONS
MALRAUX
MARRIED
MARRIES
MARRING
MARROWS
MARRYME
MATRONS
MAUREEN
MAURICE
MAUROIS
NAIROBI
NARRATE
NARROWS
NATRIUM
PADRONE
PADRONI
PAIRING
PAIROFF
PAIRSUP
PAPRIKA
PARRIED
PARRIER
PARRIES
PARRING
PARRISH
PARROTS
PATRIAL
PATRICE
PATRICK
PATRIOT
PATROLS

PATRONS
PATROON
PAYROLL
RAGRUGS
RAMRODS
RANRIOT
RATRACE
SABRINA
SANREMO
SATRAPS
SAURIAN
TAPROOM
TAPROOT
TARRIED
TARRIER
TARRIES
TARRING
TAURINE
TAXRATE
VAGRANT
WARRANT
WARRENS
WARRING
WARRIOR
YARROWS
ZAIREAN
ZAIRIAN

•A••R••

BACARDI
BACKRUB
BALDRIC
BAVARIA
CABARET
CALDRON
CALORIC
CALORIE
CAMBRIC
CAMERAS
CAMERON
CANARDS
CANTRIP
CAPERED
CASERNE
CASERNS
CATERED
CATERER
CATERTO
CAVERNS
CAVORTS
DALTREY
DAYTRIP
EAGERER
EAGERLY
EARDROP
EARDRUM
EATCROW
FABARES
FABERGE
FAVORED
FAYWRAY
GABBROS
GAGARIN
GAMBREL
GASTRIC
HAVARTI
HAVERED
HAZARDS
JABIRUS
JAKARTA
KATHRYN
LABORED
LABORER
LAFARGE

LAMARCK
LAMPREY
LAPORTE
LASORDA
LATERAL
LATERAN
LATERON
LAUTREC
LAVERNE
LAYERED
LAZARUS
MACGRAW
MAHARIS
MAIGRET
MAITRED
MAJORCA
MAJORED
MALLRAT
MANFRED
MANTRAP
MANTRAS
MANTRIC
MARGRET
MASARYK
MATURED
MATURER
MATURES
MAYORAL
MAYTREE
MAZURKA
NATURAL
NATURED
NATURES
NAVARRE
OAKTREE
PACKRAT
PALERMO
PALFREY
PALTROW
PANARAB
PANURGE
PAPERED
PAPERER
PAPYRUS
PARURES
PATERNO
QATARIS
RATTRAP
RAYKROC
RAZORED
SAFARIS
SAFFRON
SAHARAN
SALERNO
SAMARIA
SAMPRAS
SAMURAI
SANGRIA
SATIRES
SATIRIC
SAVARIN
SAVORED
TABARDS
TABORET
TALARIA
TAMARIN
TANGRAM
TANTRUM
TAPERED
TAVERNS
TAXFREE
VALERIE
WAGERED
WAGERER

WAITRON
WASHRAG
WASTREL
WATERED
WATERER
WAVERED
WAVERER

•A•••R•

BACKERS
BADGERS
BAGGERS
BAILERS
BAILORS
BALLARD
BANKERS
BANNERS
BANTERS
BARBARA
BARBARY
BARBERS
BARCARS
BARKERS
BARNARD
BARTERS
BARWARE
BASTERS
BATGIRL
BATHERS
BATTERS
BATTERY
BAWLERS
BAZAARS
CABLERS
CADBURY
CADGERS
CAESARS
CAESURA
CAHIERS
CALDERA
CALGARY
CALIBRE
CALLERS
CALVARY
CALVERT
CAMBERS
CAMPARI
CAMPERS
CANKERS
CANNERS
CANNERY
CANTERS
CANTORS
CAPPERS
CAPTORS
CAPTURE
CARDERS
CAREERS
CARFARE
CARNERA
CARPARK
CARPERS
CARPORT
CARTERS
CARVERS
CASCARA
CASTERS
CATBERT
CATBIRD
CAVALRY
CAVIARS
DAGGERS
DAMMARS
DAMPERS

DANBURY
DANCERS
DANDERS
DANGERS
DARNERS
DARTERS
DASHERS
DASTARD
DASYURE
DAUBERS
DAYCARE
DAYMARE
EARHART
EARMARK
EARNERS
EASTERN
EASTERS
FABLERS
FACTORS
FACTORY
FAILURE
FALTERS
FANFARE
FARMERS
FARMERY
FATHERS
FAVOURS
FAWNERS
GABBERS
GADDERS
GAFFERS
GAINERS
GAITERS
GALLERY
GAMMERS
GANDERS
GANGERS
GAOLERS
GARNERS
GARTERS
GASPERS
GASSERS
GATHERS
GAUGERS
GAWKERS
HACKERS
HAGGARD
HALTERS
HALYARD
HAMBURG
HAMMERS
HAMPERS
HANGARS
HANGERS
HANKERS
HANSARP
HARBORS
HARBURG
HARPERS
HARVARD
HATTERS
HAUBERK
HAULERS
HAWKERS
HAWSERS
HAYFORK
HAYWARD
HAYWIRE
JABBERS
JAEGERS
JAGUARS
JAILERS
JAMMERS
JANUARY

JASPERS
JAYBIRD
KAFFIRS
KAISERS
LAAGERS
LABOURS
LADDERS
LADLERS
LAGGARD
LAGGERS
LAMBERT
LANCERS
LANDERS
LANFORD
LANGTRY
LANGURS
LANTERN
LANYARD
LARDERS
LASHERS
LASTORY
LATHERS
LATHERY
LAUNDRY
LAWFORD
LAWYERS
MACABRE
MADDERS
MADEIRA
MAESTRI
MAESTRO
MAGUIRE
MAGYARS
MAILERS
MAJEURE
MALLARD
MANGERS
MANNERS
MANSARD
MAPPERS
MARKERS
MARMARA
MARTYRS
MASCARA
MASHERS
MASKERS
MASONRY
MASTERS
MASTERY
MATHERS
MATTERS
MAXBORN
MAYNARD
NABBERS
NAILERS
NAPPERS
NATTERS
NAVARRE
OAKFERN
PACKARD
PACKERS
PADDERS
PALEDRY
PALLORS
PALMARY
PALTERS
PAMPERS
PANDERS
PANDORA
PANNERS
PANZERS
PARLORS
PARSERS
PASSERS

PASTERN
PASTORS
PASTURE
PATTERN
PATTERS
PAUPERS
PAWNERS
PAYDIRT
RAFTERS
RAIDERS
RAILERS
RAISERS
RAMPART
RANGERS
RANKERS
RANTERS
RAPIERS
RAPPERS
RAPPORT
RAPTORS
RAPTURE
RASHERS
RASPERS
RASTERS
RATBERT
RATTERS
RAYBURN
SACKERS
SAGUARO
SAILORS
SALIERI
SALTERS
SALVERS
SALVORS
SAMBARS
SAMSARA
SANDERS
SANFORD
SANTIRS
SAPPERS
SAPPORO
SASSERS
SAUCERS
SAVIORS
SAVOURS
SAVOURY
SAWYERS
SAXHORN
TACKERS
TAILORS
TALKERS
TAMPERS
TANGERE
TANKARD
TANKERS
TANNERS
TANNERY
TANTARA
TAPPERS
TARTARE
TARTARS
TASTERS
TATTERS
VALOURS
VAMPERS
VAMPIRA
VAMPIRE
VAPOURS
VAQUERO
WAGGERY
WAILERS
WAITERS
WAIVERS
WALDORF

WALKERS
WALMART
WALTERS
WANDERS
WARDERS
WARFARE
WARLORD
WASHERS
WASTERS
WAXWORK
WAYWARD
WAYWORN
YABBERS
YAKKERS
YAMMERS
YAPPERS
YARDARM
YAWNERS
YAWPERS
ZACHARY
ZAFFERS
ZANDERS
ZAPPERS

•A••••R

BAFFLER
BAGGIER
BAINTER
BALFOUR
BALKIER
BALMIER
BARKIER
BARMIER
BARRIER
BATTIER
BATTLER
BAWDIER
CACKLER
CAJOLER
CALIBER
CALIPER
CALLFOR
CAMPHOR
CAMPIER
CANDOUR
CANNIER
CAREFOR
CAROLER
CARRIER
CARTIER
CASHBAR
CASHIER
CATCHER
CATERER
CATHAIR
CATTIER
CAULKER
CAVILER
DABBLER
DAFFIER
DAIMLER
DALLIER
DANDIER
DANGLER
DANSEUR
DAUMIER
DAWDLER
DAYSTAR
DAZZLER
EAGERER
EARLIER
FAINTER
FAKEFUR
FALLFOR

FANCIER
FARRIER
FARTHER
FATTIER
GABBIER
GAGSTER
GAMBLER
GAMMIER
GARDNER
GASSIER
GAUCHER
GAUDIER
GAUNTER
GAUZIER
GAWKIER
HAGGLER
HAIRIER
HAMMIER
HAMSTER
HANDCAR
HANDIER
HANDLER
HANOVER
HAPPIER
HARBOUR
HARDIER
HARRIER
HARSHER
HASTIER
HATCHER
HAUTEUR
JACKTAR
JAGGIER
JAMMIER
JANITOR
JANVIER
JAZZIER
KASHMIR
KAYAKER
LABELER
LABORER
LACQUER
LAIDFOR
LALAKER
LAMINAR
LANGUOR
LANKIER
LARDIER
LARDNER
LASSOER
LAUGHER
LAUNDER
LAYOVER
LAYSFOR
MADEFOR
MADEPAR
MAILCAR
MAKEFOR
MAKEPAR
MALABAR
MALODOR
MALTIER
MANAGER
MANGIER
MANHOUR
MANLIER
MANOWAR
MANYEAR
MARCHER
MARINER
MARKHOR
MASSEUR
MASSIER
MATADOR

MATURER
MAUNDER
MAXBAER
MAYFAIR
NAGGIER
NASTIER
NATTIER
PACECAR
PADDLER
PAIDFOR
PAINTER
PALAVER
PALLIER
PALMIER
PALOMAR
PANNIER
PANTHER
PAPERER
PARDNER
PARLOUR
PARRIER
PARTIER
PARTNER
PASSFOR
PASTEUR
PASTIER
PAVIOUR
PAWKIER
PAYSFOR
RACECAR
RAFFLER
RAINIER
RALLIER
RAMBLER
RANCHER
RANCOUR
RANDIER
RANGIER
RANOVER
RAPIDER
RASPIER
RATTIER
RATTLER
RAVAGER
SADDLER
SAGGIER
SALAZAR
SALTIER
SAMOVAR
SAMPLER
SANDBAR
SANDIER
SAPPIER
SARKIER
SASHBAR
SASSIER
SAUCIER
SAUNTER
SAVAGER
SAVIOUR
SAVVIER
TABULAR
TACKIER
TACKLER
TALKIER
TALLIER
TAMBOUR
TANAGER
TANGIER
TAPSTER
TARDIER
TARRIER
TARSIER
TASTIER

TATTIER
TATTLER
TAWNIER
VASTIER
VAULTER
VAUNTER
WACKIER
WADDLER
WAFFLER
WAGERER
WAGONER
WAITFOR
WAKENER
WALTZER
WANGLER
WARBLER
WARRIOR
WARTIER
WASHIER
WASPIER
WATCHER
WATERER
WAVERER
ZAPPIER

••AR•••

ACARIDS
AGARICS
ALARCON
ALARMED
ALARMER
ALARUMS
ANARCHY
ASARULE
AVARICE
AWARDED
AWARDEE
AWARDER
AWAREOF
BEARCAT
BEARCUB
BEARDED
BEARERS
BEARHUG
BEARING
BEARISH
BEAROFF
BEAROUT
BEARPAW
BEARSON
BEARSUP
BLARING
BLARNEY
BOARDED
BOARDER
BOARISH
CHARADE
CHARGED
CHARGER
CHARGES
CHARIER
CHARILY
CHARIOT
CHARITY
CHARLES
CHARLEY
CHARLIE
CHARMED
CHARMER
CHARMIN
CHARRED
CHARTED
CHARTER
CLARETS

CLARICE
CLARIFY
CLARION
CLARITY
COARSEN
COARSER
CZARDAS
CZARDOM
CZARINA
CZARISM
CZARIST
DEAREST
DEARIES
DEARSIR
DEARTHS
DIARIES
DWARFED
DWARVES
EPARCHS
EPARCHY
EXARCHS
FEARERS
FEARFUL
FEARING
FLAREUP
FLARING
GEARBOX
GEARING
GEARSTO
GEARSUP
GLARING
GNARLED
GNARRED
GUARANI
GUARDED
GUARDEE
GUARGUM
HAARLEM
HEARDOF
HEARERS
HEARING
HEARKEN
HEAROUT
HEARSAY
HEARSOF
HEARTED
HEARTEN
HEARTHS
HOARDED
HOARDER
HOARIER
HOARILY
HOARSEN
HOARSER
IMARETS
INARUSH
KEARNEY
LEARIER
LEARJET
LEARNED
LEARNER
NEAREST
NEARING
NEARYOU
OCARINA
ONAROLL
PEARLED
PEARSON
PHARAOH
PHARLAP
PHARYNX
QUARREL
QUARTER
QUARTET

QUARTOS
REAREND
REARERS
REARGUE
REARING
REARMED
REARSUP
ROARERS
ROARING
SCARABS
SCARCER
SCARERS
SCAREUP
SCARFED
SCARIER
SCARIFY
SCARILY
SCARING
SCARLET
SCARPED
SCARPER
SCARRED
SCARVES
SEARING
SHAREIN
SHARERS
SHARING
SHARKEY
SHARPED
SHARPEI
SHARPEN
SHARPER
SHARPLY
SMARTED
SMARTEN
SMARTER
SMARTLY
SNARING
SNARLED
SOARERS
SOARING
SPARELY
SPAREST
SPARGED
SPARGES
SPARING
SPARKED
SPARKLE
SPARRED
SPARROW
SPARSER
SPARTAN
STARCHY
STARDOM
STAREAT
STARERS
STARETS
STARING
STARKER
STARKLY
STARLET
STARLIT
STARMAN
STARMAP
STARRED
STARTED
STARTER
STARTLE
STARTUP
STARVED
STARVES
SWARMED
SWARTHY
TEARFUL
TEARGAS
TEARIER
TEARILY
TEARING
TEAROFF
TEAROOM
TEAROSE
TEAROUT
TEARSAT
TEARSUP
TSARINA
TSARIST
TUAREGS
TZARINA
UNARMED
WEARERS
WEARIED
WEARIER
WEARIES
WEARILY
WEARING
WEAROFF
WEAROUT
WHARFED
WHARTON
WHARVES
YEAREND
YEARNED
YEARNER

••A•R••

ANAGRAM
BEATRIX
CHAGRIN
CHAIRED
CHARRED
CLAIROL
DIAGRAM
FIACRES
GLAIRED
GNARRED
PRAIRIE
QUARREL
REAIRED
SCARRED
SEAGRAM
SPARRED
SPARROW
STARRED
TEATRAY
TEATREE
UNAIRED
UPATREE

••A••R•

AMATORY
ARAFURA
ATATURK
AVATARS
BEAKERS
BEANERY
BEARERS
BEATERS
BEAVERS
BLADERS
BLAZERS
BOATERS
BRACERO
BRACERS
BRAVERY
BRAVURA
BRAYERS
CHASERS
CLAMORS
CLAWERS
COALERS
COAXERS
CRATERS
CRAVERS
DEALERS
DEANERY
DIALERS
DIAPERS
DRAPERS
DRAPERY
DRAWERS
ELATERS
ENAMORS
ERASERS
ERASURE
ETAGERE
EVADERS
FEARERS
FEATURE
FLAKERS
FLAVORS
GLAZERS
GNAWERS
GRADERS
GRANARY
GRATERS
GRAVERS
GRAVURE
GRAZERS
HEADERS
HEALERS
HEARERS
HEATERS
HEAVERS
HOAXERS
IMAGERS
IMAGERY
INAWORD
ISADORA
JEANARP
KNAVERY
KRATERS
LAAGERS
LEADERS
LEAKERS
LEANERS
LEAPERS
LEASERS
LOADERS
LOAFERS
LOANERS
MEASURE
MOANERS
NIAGARA
OFASORT
ONADARE
ONAGERS
ORATORS
ORATORY
PHAEDRA
PHASERS
PIASTRE
PLACARD
PLACERS
PLANERS
PLATERS
PLAYERS
PRATERS
PRAYERS
QUAKERS
QUASARS
QUAVERS
QUAVERY
READERS
REAMERS
REAPERS
REARERS
ROAMERS
ROARERS
SCALARS
SCALERS
SCARERS
SEABIRD
SEABORG
SEAFIRE
SEAGIRT
SEALERS
SEAPORT
SEATERS
SEAWARD
SHAKERS
SHANGRI
SHAPERS
SHAPIRO
SHARERS
SHASTRI
SHAVERS
SKATERS
SLAVERS
SLAVERY
SLAYERS
SOAKERS
SOAPERS
SOARERS
SPACERS
SPADERS
STAGERS
STARERS
STATORS
STATURE
SWAYERS
TEACART
TEASERS
THALERS
TRABERT
TRACERS
TRACERY
TRADERS
TRAVERS
UNAWARE
WEARERS
WEAVERS
WHALERS

••A•••R

ADAPTER
ADAPTOR
ALARMER
AMASSER
AMATEUR
AWARDER
BEADIER
BEAMIER
BLABBER
BLACKER
BLADDER
BLANDER
BLANKER
BLASTER
BLATHER
BOARDER
BOASTER
BRAGGER
BRAIDER
BRANDER
BRASHER
BRAWLER
BRAZIER
CHAMBER
CHAMFER
CHANCER
CHANGER
CHANTER
CHAPTER
CHARGER
CHARIER
CHARMER
CHARTER
CHASTER
CHATTER
CHAUCER
CLABBER
CLAIMER
CLAMBER
CLAMMER
CLAMOUR
CLANGOR
CLAPPER
CLATTER
CLAVIER
CLAYIER
COALCAR
COALTAR
COARSER
COASTER
CRABBER
CRACKER
CRAFTER
CRAMMER
CRASSER
CRAWLER
CRAZIER
DEADAIR
DEARSIR
DRABBER
DRAGGER
DRAINER
DRAWBAR
EDASNER
ENACTOR
ENAMOUR
EVANDER
EXACTER
EXACTOR
FEATHER
FLAKIER
FLAMIER
FLANEUR
FLANKER
FLAPPER
FLASHER
FLATCAR
FLATTER
FLAVOUR
FLAXIER
FOAMIER
FRAILER
FRANKER
FRASIER
FRAZIER
GLACIER
GLADDER
GLAMOUR
GLAZIER
GOAFTER
GRABBER
GRAMMAR
GRAMMER
GRANDER
GRANGER
GRANTOR
GRAPIER
HEADIER
HEATHER
HEATTER
HEAVIER
HOARDER
HOARIER
HOARSER
INAPTER
KNACKER
LEADIER
LEAFIER
LEAKIER
LEANDER
LEARIER
LEARNER
LEATHER
LOAMIER
MEALIER
MEANDER
MEATIER
MUAMMAR
MYANMAR
ONATEAR
PEATIER
PIASTER
PLAINER
PLANNER
PLANTAR
PLANTER
PLASTER
PLATIER
PLATTER
POACHER
PRAETOR
PRAISER
PRANCER
PRAYFOR
PSALTER
QUAFFER
QUAKIER
QUARTER
REACTOR
READIER
REALTOR
ROASTER
SCALIER
SCALPER
SCAMPER
SCANNER
SCANTER
SCARCER
SCARIER
SCARPER
SCATTER
SEAMIER
SEASTAR
SHADIER
SHAFFER
SHAKIER
SHANKAR
SHARPER
SHATNER
SHATTER
SKANKER
SLACKER
SLAMMER
SLANDER
SLASHER
SLATHER
SLATIER
SMACKER
SMALLER
SMARTER
SMASHER
SMATTER
SNACKER
SNAKIER
SNAPPER
SOAPIER
SPACIER
SPAMMER
SPANKER
SPANNER
SPARSER
SPATTER
STABLER
STAFFER
STAGGER
STAGIER
STAIDER
STAINER
STALKER
STAMMER
STAPLER
STARKER
STARTER
SWAGGER
SWANKER
SWAPPER
SWATTER
TEACHER
TEARIER
TOASTER
TRACKER
TRACTOR
TRAILER
TRAINER
TRAITOR
TRAMCAR
TRAPPER
TRAWLER
VEALIER
WEARIER
WEATHER
WHATFOR
WRAPPER
YEARNER

•••AR••

ALVAREZ
AMHARIC
ANTARES
APPARAT
APPAREL
AQUARIA
AREARUG
ASFARAS
ASTARTE
ATLARGE
AUTARKY
BACARDI
BAVARIA
BETARAY
BIZARRE
BLEARED
BOIARDO
BRIARDS
CABARET
CANARDS
CEDARED
CLEARED
CLEARER
CLEARLY
CLEARUP
COWARDS
DEBARGE
DEBARKS
DECARLO
DEFARGE
DENARII
DEPARTS
DISARMS
DOTARDS
DUBARRY
EDWARDS
EMBARGO
EMBARKS
ENGARDE
ENLARGE
ESCARPS
ESPARTO
EXPARTE
FABARES
GAGARIN
GOCARTS
GOKARTS
HAVARTI
HAZARDS
HEPARIN
HOGARTH
HOWARDS
IDCARDS
IMPARTS
INNARDS
INWARDS
IZZARDS
JAKARTA
LAFARGE
LAMARCK
LAZARUS
LEBARON
LECARRE
LIZARDS
LOCARNO
MAHARIS
MASARYK
MINARET
MONARCH
MUBARAK
NAVARRE
NOVARRO
ONTARIO
ONWARDS
OXCARTS
PANARAB
PETARDS
PICARDY
PICAROS
PIZARRO
POLARIS
QATARIS
REGARDS
REMARKS
REMARRY
RENARDS
RETARDS
REWARDS
REWARMS
RICARDO
ROBARDS
ROSARIO
SAFARIS
SAHARAN
SAMARIA
SAVARIN
SHEARED
SHEARER
SMEARED
SOLARIA
SPEARED
SQUARED
SQUARER
SQUARES
SUGARED
SUHARTO
SUKARNO
SWEARAT
SWEARBY
SWEARER
SWEARIN
SWEARTO
TABARDS
TALARIA
TAMARIN
THWARTS
TOWARDS
UNEARTH
UPWARDS
WIZARDS

•••A•R•

AFFAIRE
AFFAIRS
ASTAIRE
AUPAIRS
BAZAARS
BIZARRE
CAVALRY
CONAKRY
DUBARRY
ECLAIRS
HILAIRE
IMPAIRS
LECARRE
LEHAVRE
MACABRE
MOHAIRS
NAVARRE
NOVARRO
PIZARRO
REMARRY
REPAIRS
RIVALRY
SINATRA
SUMATRA
THEATRE

•••A••R

ABRADER
AERATOR
ALCAZAR
ALLAYER
ASSAYER
AVIATOR
BELABOR
BENATAR
BENAZIR
BLEAKER
BREAKER
BROADER
CHEAPER
CHEATER
CLEANER
CLEARER
CLEAVER
CREAMER
CREATOR
CURATOR
DEBATER
DECATUR
DELAYER
DONATOR
DOWAGER
DREAMER
ECUADOR
ELEANOR
EQUATOR
FLOATER
FORAGER
GLEANER
GREASER
GREATER
GROANER
GYRATOR
INFAVOR
INHALER
INVADER
KAYAKER
KNEADER
LALAKER
LOCATER
LOCATOR
MALABAR
MANAGER
MATADOR
MIRADOR
NEGATER
NEGATOR
NEWAGER
PALAVER
PICADOR
PLEADER
PLEASER
RAVAGER
REPAPER
ROTATOR
SALAZAR
SAVAGER
SCRAPER
SEDATER
SENATOR
SHEARER
SNEAKER
SPEAKER
SPRAYER
SQUALOR
SQUARER
STEAMER
SWEARER
SWEATER
TANAGER
THEATER
TREADER
URBANER
VOYAGER

••••AR•

ABELARD
ACTUARY
AIRFARE
ALLEARS
ANTFARM
ANTIART
APPEARS
ARIKARA
ARREARS
ARTWARE
ASHLARS
ATHEART
ATHWART
AVATARS
AWKWARD
BALLARD
BARBARA
BARBARY
BARCARS
BARNARD
BARWARE
BAZAARS
BEGGARS
BERNARD
BITPART
BOKHARA
BOMBARD
BOXCARS
BULGARS
BULWARK
BURSARS
BURSARY
BUSFARE
BUSTARD
BUZZARD
BYHEART
CAESARS
CALGARY
CALVARY
CAMPARI
CARFARE
CARPARK
CASCARA
CAVIARS
CELLARS
CLIPART
COLLARD
COLLARS
COMPARE
COSTARS
COUGARS
CUECARD
CUSTARD
DAMMARS
DASTARD
DAYCARE
DAYMARE
DECLARE
DENMARK
DEODARS
DIEHARD
DIETARY
DILLARD
DISBARS
DISCARD
DOGCART
DOGEARS
DOLLARS
DULLARD
EARHART
EARMARK
ECKHART
EDOUARD
ELKHART
ENDEARS
ENSNARE
ENSNARL
ESTUARY
FANFARE
FERRARI
FERRARO
FINEART
FIREARM
FOLKART
FOREARM
FORWARD
FOULARD
FROWARD
GENNARO
GIZZARD
GODDARD
GRANARY
GUEVARA
GUITARS
HAGGARD
HALYARD
HANGARS
HANSARP
HARVARD
HAYWARD
HECTARE
HILLARY
HOLYARK
HONIARA
HOTCARS
HOTWARS
HUBBARD
HUNGARY
HUSSARS
INBOARD
INSTARS
INTEARS
ISOBARS
JAGUARS
JANUARY
JEANARP
JUNKART
KEYCARD
KILDARE
LAGGARD
LANYARD
LEEWARD
LEKVARS
LEONARD
LEOPARD
LEOTARD
LIBRARY
LOLLARD
LOMBARD
LONGARM
LUMBARS
MAGYARS
MALLARD
MANSARD
MARMARA
MASCARA
MAYNARD
MILLARD
MORTARS
MUSTARD
NECTARS
NEWHART
NIAGARA
NIGGARD
ONADARE
ONBOARD
ONGUARD
ORCHARD
OUTWARD
OVIPARA
PACKARD
PALMARY
PECCARY
PEDLARS
PEPPARD
PICCARD
PILLARS
PLACARD
PLENARY
PONIARD
POPLARS
POPTART
PREPARE
PRIMARY
PULSARS
QINTARS
QUASARS
QUINARY
RAMPART
REHEARD
REHEARS
RELEARN
RESTART
RETEARS
RETIARY
REYNARD
RHUBARB
RICHARD
RUDYARD
SAGUARO
SAMBARS
SAMSARA
SCALARS
SEAWARD
SHEPARD
SHIKARI
SHOFARS
SIDEARM
SKYLARK
SKYWARD
STEWARD
STEWART
SUMMARY
TANKARD
TANTARA
TARTARE
TARTARS
TEACART
TERNARY
THECARS
THENARS
TINEARS
TINWARE
TONEARM
TOPIARY
TOSPARE
TOWCARS
TRENARY
TROCARS
TSQUARE
UNAWARE
UNHEARD
UNITARY
UNLEARN
UNSNARL
UPQUARK
UPROARS
UPSTART
WALMART
WARFARE
WAYWARD
WELFARE
WETBARS
WIDMARK
WILLARD
WOODARD
YARDARM
ZACHARY
ZEDBARS

••••A•R

ABUBAKR
BIDFAIR
CATHAIR
CENTAUR
COCHAIR
CORSAIR
DEADAIR
DESPAIR
FUNFAIR
MAXBAER
MAYFAIR
OPENAIR
REDHAIR
THINAIR

•••••AR

ALCAZAR
ALLSTAR
ANGULAR
ANNULAR
ANTBEAR
ANTIWAR
AREOLAR
BELLJAR
BENATAR
BESMEAR
BIPOLAR
BOERWAR
BOLIVAR
BUGBEAR
BURGLAR
CASHBAR
CHEDDAR
CLUBCAR
COALCAR
COALTAR
COLDWAR
CROWBAR
DAYSTAR
DIPOLAR
DOGSTAR
DRAWBAR
FERNBAR
FLATCAR
FORBEAR
GOODBAR
GRAMMAR
HANDCAR
HOLYWAR
INGEMAR
INSOFAR
INSULAR
JACKTAR
JOCULAR
JUGULAR
LAMINAR
LOWGEAR
MADEPAR
MAILCAR
MAKEPAR
MALABAR
MANOWAR
MANYEAR
MIDYEAR
MIRAMAR
MISHEAR
MODULAR
MUAMMAR
MYANMAR
NEBULAR
NEWYEAR
NODULAR
NUCLEAR
NYUNGAR
OFFYEAR
ONATEAR
ONESTAR
OPENBAR
OUTWEAR
PACECAR
PALOMAR
PINETAR
PLANTAR
POLECAR
POPULAR
POSTWAR

RACECAR
REDSTAR
REGULAR
ROLLBAR
SALAZAR
SAMOVAR
SANDBAR
SASHBAR
SCHOLAR
SEASTAR
SECULAR
SEMINAR
SHANKAR
SIDEBAR
SIDECAR
SIMILAR
SKIWEAR
SLOTCAR
STELLAR
TABULAR
TELSTAR
TEMPLAR
THUSFAR
TINSTAR
TITULAR
TRAMCAR
TRISTAR
TUBULAR
TURFWAR
TUTELAR
TWOSTAR
UNCLEAR
UPTOPAR
VINEGAR
WINEBAR
YESDEAR

AS•••••

ASARULE
ASCENDS
ASCENTS
ASCETIC
ASCRIBE
ASEPSIS
ASEPTIC
ASFARAS
ASHAMED
ASHANTI
ASHBURY
ASHCANS
ASHFORD
ASHIEST
ASHLAND
ASHLARS
ASHLESS
ASHRAMS
ASHTRAY
ASIATIC
ASININE
ASKANCE
ASKEDIN
ASKSFOR
ASKSOUT
ASOCIAL
ASOFNOW
ASPECTS
ASPERSE
ASPHALT
ASPIRED
ASPIRER
ASPIRES
ASPIRIN
ASSAILS
ASSAULT
ASSAYED
ASSAYER
ASSEGAI
ASSENTS
ASSERTS
ASSIGNS
ASSISTS
ASSIZES
ASSLIKE
ASSORTS
ASSUAGE
ASSUMED
ASSUMES
ASSURED
ASSURES
ASSYRIA
ASTAIRE
ASTARTE
ASTOLAT
ASTORIA
ASTOUND
ASTRIDE
ASUNDER
ASUSUAL
ASYLUMS

A•S••••

ABSALOM
ABSCOND
ABSENCE
ABSENTS
ABSOLUT
ABSOLVE
ABSORBS
ABSTAIN
ADSORBS
ALSATIA
ALSORAN
AMSCRAY
ANSWERS
APSIDES
ARSENAL
ARSENIC
ARSENIO
ASSAILS
ASSAULT
ASSAYED
ASSAYER
ASSEGAI
ASSENTS
ASSERTS
ASSIGNS
ASSISTS
ASSIZES
ASSLIKE
ASSORTS
ASSUAGE
ASSUMED
ASSUMES
ASSURED
ASSURES
ASSYRIA
ATSTAKE
AUSPICE
AUSSIES
AUSTERE
AUSTRAL
AUSTRIA
AXSEEDS

A••S•••

ABASHED
ABASHES
ABASING
ABUSERS
ABUSING
ABUSIVE
ABYSMAL
ABYSSES
ACESOUT
ACTSOUT
AGASSIZ
AGESAGO
AIMSFOR
AIRSACS
AIRSHIP
AIRSHOW
AIRSOCK
AIRSOUT
ALASKAN
ALLSTAR
ALLSTON
ALYSSUM
AMASSED
AMASSER
AMASSES
AMISTAD
AMUSING
ANASAZI
ANDSOON
ANISEED
ANISTON
ANOSMIA
ANOSMIC
ANTSIER
APISHLY
APOSTLE
ARCSINE
ARISING
ARISTAE
ARISTAS
ARISTOS
ARTSIER
ARTSONG
ASKSFOR
ASKSOUT
ASUSUAL
ATISSUE
AUSSIES
AWESOME

A•••S••

ABYSSES
ACCOSTS
ACCUSED
ACCUSER
ACCUSES
ACHESON
ADAMSON
ADDISON
ADJUSTS
ADVISED
ADVISER
ADVISES
ADVISOR
AEROSOL
AGASSIZ
AGEISTS
ALIASES
ALLISON
ALLYSON
ALTOSAX
ALUNSER
ALYOSHA
ALYSSUM
AMASSED
AMASSER
AMASSES
AMNESIA
AMNESTY
ANTESUP
AORISTS
APHESES
APPOSED
APPOSES
ARALSEA
ARIOSOS
ARIOSTO
AROUSAL
AROUSED
AROUSES
ARRASES
ARRESTS
ARRISES
ARTISAN
ARTISTE
ARTISTS
ASEPSIS
ASSISTS
ATISSUE
ATLASES
ATTESTS
AUGUSTA
AUGUSTE
AVULSED
AVULSES

A••••S•

ABOLISH
ABREAST
ACCURST
ACEROSE
ACHIEST
ACTRESS
ADDRESS
ADIPOSE
ADVERSE
AERIEST
AGAINST
AGELESS
AGGRESS
AGONISE
AGONIST
AIDLESS
AIMLESS
AIRBASE
AIRIEST
AIRKISS
AIRLESS
AIRMASS
ALFONSO
AMBROSE
AMHERST
AMONGST
AMPLEST
AMYLASE
ANALYSE
ANALYST
ANAPEST
ANDRESS
ANIMISM
ANIMIST
ANODISE
APPEASE
APPRISE
APTNESS
ARIDEST
ARMLESS
ARMREST
ARTIEST
ARTLESS
ASHIEST
ASHLESS
ASPERSE
ATALOSS
ATAVISM
ATAVIST
ATHEISM
ATHEIST
ATHIRST
ATLEAST
ATOMISE
ATWORST
AWELESS
AWNLESS

A•••••S

ABASHES
ABDUCTS
ABJURES
ABLATES
ABLAUTS
ABNAKIS
ABOUNDS
ABRADES
ABSENTS
ABSORBS
ABUSERS
ABYSSES
ACACIAS
ACARIDS
ACCEDES
ACCENTS
ACCEPTS
ACCORDS
ACCOSTS
ACCRUES
ACCUSES
ACHATES
ACHENES
ACKACKS
ACQUITS
ACTIONS
ACTIVES
ACTRESS
ACUMENS
ADAGIOS
ADDENDS
ADDRESS
ADDUCES
ADDUCTS
ADHERES
ADJOINS
ADJURES
ADJUSTS
ADMIRES
ADMIXES
ADONAIS
ADORERS
ADSORBS
ADVENTS
ADVERBS
ADVERTS
ADVISES
AEDILES
AERATES
AERIALS
AEROBES
AETHERS
AFFAIRS
AFFECTS
AFFINES
AFFIRMS
AFFIXES
AFFORDS
AFFRAYS
AFGHANS
AFRAMES
AFREETS
AGARICS
AGEISTS
AGELESS
AGENDAS
AGGRESS
AGNATES
AGOUTIS
AIDLESS
AIGRETS
AIMLESS
AIRBAGS
AIRDAMS
AIRGUNS
AIRINGS
AIRKISS
AIRLESS
AIRMASS
AIRSACS
AIRWAYS
AITCHES
ALARUMS
ALBEDOS
ALBINOS
ALCOVES
ALGIERS
ALIASES
ALIGHTS
ALKALIS
ALKENES
ALLEARS
ALLEGES
ALLELES
ALLEYES
ALLUDES
ALLURES
ALMONDS
ALPACAS
ALUMNUS
AMADEUS
AMASSES
AMAZONS
AMBLERS
AMBRIES
AMERCES
AMNIONS
AMOEBAS
AMOROUS
AMOUNTS
AMPERES
AMPULES
AMULETS
ANADEMS
ANALOGS
ANANIAS
ANCHORS
ANDEANS
ANDREAS
ANDRESS
ANDREWS
ANGELES
ANGELUS
ANGLERS
ANGORAS
ANIMALS
ANKLETS
ANNEALS
ANNEXES
ANNUALS
ANNULUS
ANOINTS
ANOMIES
ANONYMS
ANORAKS
ANSWERS
ANTAEUS
ANTARES
ANTCOWS
ANTHEMS
ANTHERS
ANTIBES
ANTLERS
ANXIOUS
ANYONES
AORISTS
AOUDADS
APACHES
APERCUS
APERIES
APHESES
APOGEES
APPALLS
APPEALS
APPEARS
APPENDS
APPLETS
APPLIES
APPOSES
APROPOS
APSIDES
APTNESS
AQUEOUS
AQUINAS
ARAWAKS
ARBOURS
ARBUTUS
ARCADES
ARCHERS
ARCHONS
ARDOURS
ARDUOUS
AREOLAS
ARGIVES
ARGUERS
ARGYLES
ARIOSOS
ARISTAS
ARISTOS
ARMADAS
ARMFULS
ARMLESS
ARMLETS
ARMOURS
ARMPITS
ARMURES
ARNICAS
AROUSES
ARPENTS
ARRASES
ARREARS
ARRESTS
ARRISES
ARRIVES
ARROBAS
ARROYOS
ARTEMIS
ARTEMUS
ARTISTS
ARTLESS
ASCENDS
ASCENTS
ASEPSIS
ASFARAS
ASHCANS
ASHLARS
ASHLESS
ASHRAMS
ASPECTS
ASPIRES
ASSAILS
ASSENTS
ASSERTS
ASSIGNS
ASSISTS
ASSIZES
ASSORTS
ASSUMES
ASSURES
ASYLUMS
ATALOSS
ATAMANS
ATHOMES
ATLASES
ATLATLS
ATOMIES
ATONIES
ATRIUMS
ATTACKS
ATTAINS
ATTENDS
ATTESTS
ATTICUS
ATTIMES
ATTIRES
ATTRITS
ATTUCKS
ATTUNES
AUBADES
AUBURNS
AUDILES
AUGENDS
AUKLETS
AUNTIES
AUPAIRS
AUROCHS
AURORAS
AUSSIES
AUTEURS
AUTHORS
AUTUMNS
AVATARS
AVENGES
AVENUES
AVIATES
AVOCETS
AVOWALS
AVOWERS
AVULSES
AWAKENS
AWELESS
AWNINGS
AWNLESS
AXSEEDS
AYEAYES
AZALEAS
AZODYES

•AS••••

BASALLY
BASALTS
BASEHIT
BASEMAN
BASEMEN
BASENJI
BASEPAY
BASHFUL
BASHING
BASKETS
BASKING
BASQUES
BASSETS
BASSIST
BASSOON
BASTERS
BASTING
BASTION
CASABAS
CASAVAS
CASCADE
CASCARA
CASELAW
CASERNE
CASERNS
CASHBAR
CASHBOX
CASHCOW
CASHEWS
CASHIER
CASHING
CASHOUT
CASINGS
CASINOS
CASPIAN
CASQUED
CASQUES
CASSATT
CASSAVA
CASSIAS
CASSIDY
CASSINI
CASSINO
CASSIUS
CASSOCK
CASTERS
CASTILE
CASTING
CASTLED
CASTLES
CASTOFF
CASTOUT
CASUALS
DASBOOT
DASHERS
DASHIKI
DASHING
DASHOFF
DASTARD
DASYURE
EASEDIN
EASEDUP
EASEFUL
EASEOFF
EASEOUT
EASESIN
EASESUP
EASIEST
EASTEND
EASTERN
EASTERS
EASTMAN
EASYOFF
FASCIAS
FASHION
FASTENS
FASTEST
FASTING
FASTONE
GASBAGS
GASCAPS
GASCONS
GASCONY
GASEOUS
GASHING
GASJETS
GASKETS
GASKINS
GASLESS
GASLOGS
GASMAIN
GASOHOL
GASPERS
GASPING
GASPUMP
GASSERS
GASSIER
GASTRIC
HASBEEN
HASHING
HASIDIC
HASIDIM
HASPING
HASSLED
HASSLES
HASSOCK
HASTENS
HASTIER
HASTILY
HASTING
JASMINE
JASPERS
KASHMIR
LASAGNA
LASAGNE
LASALLE
LASCALA
LASCAUX
LASHERS
LASHING
LASHUPS
LASORDA
LASSIES
LASSOED
LASSOER
LASSOES
LASTING
LASTORY
MASARYK
MASCARA
MASCOTS
MASHERS
MASHIES
MASHING
MASKERS
MASKING
MASONIC
MASONRY
MASQUES
MASSAGE
MASSEUR
MASSIER
MASSIFS
MASSING
MASSIVE
MASTABA
MASTERS
MASTERY
MASTICS
MASTIFF
MASTOID
NASALLY
NASCENT
NASTASE
NASTIER
NASTILY
PASCHAL
PASSADO
PASSAGE
PASSELS
PASSERS
PASSEUL
PASSFOR
PASSING
PASSION
PASSIVE
PASSKEY
PASSOFF
PASSOUT
PASTDUE
PASTELS
PASTERN
PASTEUP
PASTEUR
PASTIER
PASTIME
PASTINA
PASTING
PASTORS
PASTURE
RASCALS
RASHERS
RASHEST
RASPERS
RASPIER
RASPING
RASPISH
RASSLED
RASSLES
RASTERS
SASHAYS
SASHBAR
SASHIMI
SASSERS
SASSIER
SASSIES
SASSILY
SASSING
SASSOON
TASHLIN
TASHMAN
TASKING
TASSELS
TASTERS
TASTIER
TASTILY
TASTING
VASSALS
VASTEST
VASTIER
WASATCH
WASHERS
WASHIER
WASHING
WASHOFF
WASHOUT
WASHRAG
WASHTUB
WASHUPS
WASPIER
WASPILY
WASPISH
WASSAIL
WASTAGE
WASTERS
WASTING
WASTREL
YASHMAK

•A•S•••

BALSAMS
BANSHEE
BARSOAP
BARSTOW
BASSETS
BASSIST
BASSOON
BATSMAN
BATSMEN
CAESARS
CAESIUM
CAESURA
CAISSON
CANSECO
CAPSHAW
CAPSIDS
CAPSIZE
CAPSTAN
CAPSULE
CARSEAT
CASSATT
CASSAVA
CASSIAS
CASSIDY
CASSINI
CASSINO
CASSIUS
CASSOCK
CATSCAN
CATSEYE
CATSHOW
CATSPAW
CATSUIT
CAUSING
CAUSTIC
DAISIES
DAMSELS
DAMSONS
DANSEUR
DAYSINN
DAYSTAR
EARSHOT
EATSOUT
FALSELY
FALSEST
FALSIFY
FALSITY
FANSOUT
FAUSTUS
GADSDEN
GAGSTER
GASSERS
GASSIER
HALSTON
HAMSTER
HANSARP
HANSOLO
HANSOMS
HARSHEN
HARSHER
HARSHLY
HASSLED
HASSLES
HASSOCK
HAWSERS
HAYSEED
JANSSEN
KAISERS
KAISHEK
KANSANS
LAISSEZ
LAKSHMI
LANSING
LAPSING
LASSIES
LASSOED
LASSOER
LASSOES
LAWSUIT
LAYSFOR
LAYSLOW
LAYSOFF
LAYSOUT
MAESTRI
MAESTRO
MANSARD
MANSION
MARSALA
MARSHAL
MARSHES
MASSAGE
MASSEUR
MASSIER
MASSIFS
MASSING
MASSIVE
NAYSAID
NAYSAYS
PAISANO
PAISLEY
PANSIES
PANSOUT
PARSECS
PARSEES
PARSERS
PARSING
PARSLEY
PARSNIP
PARSONS
PASSADO
PASSAGE
PASSELS
PASSERS
PASSEUL
PASSFOR
PASSING
PASSION
PASSIVE
PASSKEY
PASSOFF
PASSOUT
PATSIES
PAUSING
PAYSFOR
PAYSOFF
PAYSOUT
RAISERS
RAISEUP
RAISING
RAISINS
RALSTON
RANSACK
RANSOMS
RASSLED
RASSLES
RAWSILK
SADSACK
SALSIFY
SALSODA
SAMSARA
SAMSUNG
SAPSAGO
SASSERS
SASSIER
SASSIES
SASSILY
SASSING
SASSOON
SATSUMA
SAUSAGE
TAGSALE
TAGSOUT
TANSIES
TAPSOFF
TAPSOUT
TAPSTER
TARSALS
TARSIER
TASSELS
VARSITY
VASSALS
WALSTON
WARSHIP
WASSAIL
WAYSIDE

•A••S••

BABASSU
BABYSAT
BABYSIT
BACKSIN
BACKSUP
BALLSUP
BANDSAW
BANGSUP
BANKSON
BARKSAT
BATISTA
BATISTE
CAISSON
CALLSIN
CALLSON
CALLSUP
CAMISES
CANASTA
CARLSON
CAVESIN
CAYUSES
DAMASKS
DARESAY
DARESTO
DATASET
DAWNSON
EASESIN
EASESUP
FADESIN
FAIRSUP
FALLSIN
FALLSON
FALLSTO
GAINSAY
GAINSON
GANGSAW
GANGSTA
GANGSUP
HACKSAW
HANDSAW
HANDSET
HANDSIN
HANDSON
HANDSUP
HANGSIN
HANGSON
HANGSUP
HARDSET
HARPSON
HAULSUP
JACKSON
JACKSUP
JALISCO
JAMESON
JANSSEN
KARASEA
LACESUP
LACOSTE
LAISSEZ

LANDSAT
LATOSCA
MADISON
MAILSIN
MAJESTE
MAJESTY
MAKESDO
MAKESIT
MAKESUP
MALMSEY
MAOISTS
MARKSUP
MATISSE
NABISCO
NAILSET
NAILSIN
NATASHA
PACKSUP
PAIRSUP
PARASOL
PAULSEN
RACKSUP
RAILSAT
RAKESIN
RAKESUP
RAMESES
SAMISEN
SAMPSON
SATISFY
SAVESUP
TABASCO
TACKSON
TAKESIN
TAKESON
TAKESTO
TAKESUP
TALKSAT
TALKSTO
TALKSUP
TALUSES
TANKSUP
TAOISTS
VALISES
VANESSA
WADESIN
WAITSON
WAITSUP
WAKESUP
WALKSON
WALLSUP
WANTSIN
WANTSTO
WARMSUP
WAVESIN

•A••S•

BABASSU
BABYISH
BADDEST
BADDISH
BADNESS
BALDEST
BALDISH
BALLAST
BAPTISE
BAPTISM
BAPTIST
BARDISH
BARLESS
BASSIST
CABOOSE
CADDISH
CAGIEST
CAKIEST
CALMEST
CALYPSO
CANIEST
CANVASS
CAPLESS
CARCASE
CARCASS
CARLESS
CAROUSE
CARWASH
CATFISH
CATTISH
DADAISM
DADAIST
DAFTEST
DAMPEST
DAMPISH
DANKEST
DARKEST
DARKISH
DAWKISH
EARLESS
EARNEST
EASIEST
FADDISH
FADDISM
FADDIST
FAIREST
FAIRISH
FALSEST
FANTASY
FAREAST
FARWEST
FASTEST
FATLESS
FATNESS
FATTEST
FATTISH
FAUVISM
FAUVIST
GABFEST
GAMIEST
GAPLESS
GARNISH
GASLESS
GAULISH
GAWKISH
HAGGISH
HAPLESS
HARDEST
HARNESS
HARPIST
HARVEST
HATLESS
HAWKISH
HAZIEST
JACCUSE
JACKASS
JAGLESS
JARLESS
JAWLESS
KADDISH
LACIEST
LACTASE
LACTOSE
LADDISH
LADYISH
LAKIEST
LAMAISM
LAMAIST
LANKEST
LAPPISH
LARGESS
LARGEST
LARGISH
LARKISH
LAVALSE
LAWLESS
LAXNESS
LAZIEST
LAZYISH
MADDEST
MADDISH
MADNESS
MAEWEST
MAIDISH
MALAISE
MALTESE
MALTOSE
MANLESS
MANNISH
MARXISM
MARXIST
MATISSE
MATLESS
MAWKISH
MAZIEST
NAGGISH
NAPLESS
NASTASE
OAKMOSS
OARLESS
PACHISI
PALIEST
PALMIST
PANFISH
PAPOOSE
PARRISH
PATNESS
PAULIST
PAYCASH
RACIEST
RAFFISH
RAMMISH
RANKEST
RANKISH
RASHEST
RASPISH
RATTISH
RAWNESS
SADDEST
SADNESS
SALTISH
SANJOSE
SAPLESS
SARCASM
SAWDUST
SAWFISH
TALLEST
TALLISH
TANNEST
TANNISH
TARNISH
TARTEST
TARTISH
TAUTEST
TAXLESS
VAGUEST
VAINEST
VAMOOSE
VAMPISH
VANESSA
VARNISH
VASTEST
WAGGISH
WANIEST
WANNESS
WANNEST
WANNISH
WARIEST
WARLESS
WARMEST
WARMISH
WASPISH
WAVIEST
WAXIEST
WAYLESS
YAKUTSK
ZANIEST
ZANYISH

•A••••S

BABBLES
BABOONS
BACCHUS
BACKERS
BACKUPS
BADBOYS
BADDIES
BADEGGS
BADGERS
BADGUYS
BADNESS
BAFFLES
BAGFULS
BAGGERS
BAGGIES
BAHAMAS
BAILEES
BAILERS
BAILEYS
BAILORS
BALBOAS
BALEENS
BALKANS
BALLADS
BALLETS
BALLOTS
BALSAMS
BAMBOOS
BANANAS
BANDIES
BANDITS
BANGLES
BANJOES
BANKERS
BANNERS
BANTAMS
BANTERS
BANYANS
BAOBABS
BARBELS
BARBERS
BARCARS
BARENTS
BARHOPS
BARKERS
BARLESS
BARLEYS
BARNEYS
BARONGS
BARRELS
BARRENS
BARRIOS
BARROWS
BARTABS
BARTERS
BARYONS
BASALTS
BASKETS
BASQUES
BASSETS
BASTERS
BATBOYS
BATCHES
BATHERS
BATTELS
BATTENS
BATTERS
BATTLES
BATTUES
BAUBLES
BAUHAUS
BAWLERS
BAZAARS
CABALAS
CABANAS
CABBIES
CABLERS
CACHETS
CACHOUS
CACKLES
CADDIES
CADGERS
CAESARS
CAFTANS
CAHIERS
CAHOOTS
CAIMANS
CAIQUES
CAJOLES
CALENDS
CALICES
CALICOS
CALIPHS
CALKINS
CALLERS
CALLINS
CALLOUS
CALPACS
CALYCES
CALYXES
CAMBERS
CAMERAS
CAMISES
CAMPERS
CANAPES
CANARDS
CANCANS
CANCELS
CANDIDS
CANDIES
CANDLES
CANFULS
CANINES
CANKERS
CANNERS
CANNONS
CANOPUS
CANTERS
CANTLES
CANTONS
CANTORS
CANVASS
CANYONS
CAPFULS
CAPGUNS
CAPLESS
CAPLETS
CAPNUTS
CAPPERS
CAPSIDS
CAPTORS
CARACAS
CARAFES
CARBONS
CARBOYS
CARCASS
CARDERS
CAREENS
CAREERS
CARFULS
CARGOES
CARHOPS
CARIBES
CARINAS
CARLESS
CARNETS
CARNIES
CAROLUS
CARPALS
CARPELS
CARPERS
CARPETS
CARRELS
CARRIES
CARROTS
CARTELS
CARTERS
CARTONS
CARVERS
CASABAS
CASAVAS
CASERNS
CASHEWS
CASINGS
CASINOS
CASQUES
CASSIAS
CASSIUS
CASTERS
CASTLES
CASUALS
CATCHES
CATIONS
CATKINS
CATNAPS
CATNIPS
CAUDLES
CAVEATS
CAVEINS
CAVERNS
CAVIARS
CAVORTS
CAYMANS
CAYUGAS
CAYUSES
DABBLES
DACTYLS
DADDIES
DAGGERS
DAHLIAS
DAILIES
DAIMONS
DAIRIES
DAISIES
DAKOTAS
DALETHS
DALLIES
DAMAGES
DAMASKS
DAMMARS
DAMPENS
DAMPERS
DAMSELS
DAMSONS
DANCERS
DANDERS
DANDIES
DANDLES
DANGERS
DANGLES
DANIELS
DAPHNIS
DAPPLES
DARBIES
DARKENS
DARNERS
DARTERS
DASHERS
DAUBERS
DAWDLES
DAYBEDS
DAYBOYS
DAYJOBS
DAZZLES
EAGLETS
EARFULS
EARLESS
EARNERS
EARWIGS
EASTERS
FABARES
FABLERS
FABRICS
FACADES
FACIALS
FACINGS
FACTORS
FADEINS
FAERIES
FAGENDS
FAIRIES
FAJITAS
FALCONS
FALLOWS
FALTERS
FAMINES
FAMULUS
FANCIES
FANIONS
FANJETS
FANOUTS
FARMERS
FARROWS
FASCIAS
FASTENS
FATCATS
FATHERS
FATHOMS
FATLESS
FATNESS
FATTENS
FATUOUS
FAUCETS
FAUSTUS
FAUXPAS
FAVOURS
FAWNERS
GABBERS
GABBLES
GABBROS
GADDERS
GADGETS
GAFFERS
GAGGLES
GAGLAWS
GAINERS
GAITERS
GALAGOS
GALLEYS
GALLONS
GALLOPS
GALOOTS
GALPALS
GAMBITS
GAMBLES
GAMBOLS
GAMETES
GAMINES
GAMMERS
GAMMONS
GANDERS
GANGERS
GANNETS
GAOLERS
GAPLESS
GARAGES
GARBLES
GARCONS
GARDENS
GARGLES
GARNERS
GARNETS
GARRETS
GARTERS
GASBAGS
GASCAPS
GASCONS
GASEOUS
GASJETS
GASKETS
GASKINS
GASLESS
GASLOGS
GASPERS
GASSERS
GATHERS
GAUCHOS
GAUGERS
GAVIALS
GAWKERS
GAZEBOS
GAZUMPS
HACKERS
HACKIES
HACKLES
HAGDONS
HAGGLES
HAIRDOS
HALIDES
HALITES
HALLOWS
HALTERS
HALVAHS
HAMITES
HAMLETS
HAMMERS
HAMPERS
HANDLES
HANGARS
HANGERS
HANGUPS
HANKERS
HANKIES
HANSOMS
HAPLESS
HAPPENS
HARBORS
HARDENS
HARKENS
HARNESS
HARPERS
HARPIES
HARRIES
HARROWS
HASSLES
HASTENS
HATCHES
HATLESS
HATPINS
HATTERS
HAULERS
HAWHAWS
HAWKERS
HAWKINS
HAWSERS
HAYMOWS
HAZARDS
HAZINGS
JABBERS
JABIRUS
JACANAS
JACKALS
JACKASS
JACKETS
JACKEYS
JACKIES
JACQUES
JAEGERS
JAGGIES
JAGLESS
JAGUARS
JAILERS
JAMMERS
JANGLES
JARFULS
JARGONS
JARLESS
JASPERS
JAWLESS
JAYCEES
JAYVEES
KABUKIS
KAFFIRS
KAFTANS
KAHUNAS
KAISERS
KANAKAS
KANSANS
KAZAKHS
LAAGERS
LABIALS
LABOURS
LABRETS
LACINGS
LACKEYS
LACUNAS
LADDERS
LADDIES
LADINOS
LADLERS
LAERTES
LAGGERS
LAGOONS
LAGUNAS
LAKOTAS
LAMBDAS
LAMEDHS
LAMENTS
LAMINAS
LANCERS
LANCETS
LANDAUS
LANDERS
LANGURS
LAPDOGS
LAPFULS
LAPPETS
LAPTOPS
LARCHES
LARDERS
LARDONS
LARGESS
LARIATS
LARRUPS
LASHERS
LASHUPS
LASSIES
LASSOES
LATCHES
LATEENS
LATENTS
LATEXES
LATHERS
LATICES
LATINAS
LATINOS
LATTENS
LAURELS
LAWLESS
LAWYERS
LAXNESS
LAYOFFS
LAYOUTS
LAZARUS
MACRONS
MADCAPS
MADDENS
MADDERS
MADLIBS
MADNESS
MAENADS
MAGNETS
MAGNUMS
MAGPIES
MAGUEYS
MAGYARS
MAHARIS
MAHOUTS
MAIDENS
MAILERS
MAITAIS
MAKEUPS
MAKINGS
MALIGNS
MALKINS
MALLETS
MALLOWS
MALTEDS
MALTHUS
MAMMALS
MANAGES
MANANAS
MANDANS
MANDAYS
MANEGES
MANGERS
MANGLES
MANGOES
MANIACS
MANIOCS
MANLESS
MANNERS
MANTELS
MANTLES
MANTRAS
MANUALS
MAOISTS
MAPPERS
MARACAS
MARAUDS
MARBLES
MARCELS
MARCHES
MARGAYS
MARGINS
MARINAS
MARINES
MARKERS
MARKETS
MARKUPS
MARLINS
MARMOTS
MAROONS
MARQUES
MARQUIS
MARRIES
MARROWS
MARSHES
MARTENS
MARTINS
MARTYRS
MARVELS
MASCOTS
MASHERS
MASHIES
MASKERS
MASQUES
MASSIFS
MASTERS
MASTICS
MATCHES
MATHERS
MATHEWS
MATHIAS
MATLESS
MATRONS
MATTERS
MATURES
MATZOHS
MAUMAUS
MAUROIS
MAXIMUS
MAYDAYS
MAYHEMS
NABBERS
NAIADES
NAILERS
NANNIES
NAPKINS
NAPLESS
NAPPERS
NAPPIES
NARROWS
NARWALS
NATIONS
NATIVES
NATTERS
NATURES
NAUGHTS
NAVAHOS
NAVAJOS
NAVVIES
NAYSAYS
OAKMOSS
OARLESS
PAANGAS
PABLUMS
PACKERS
PACKETS
PADDERS
PADDIES
PADDLES
PADUANS
PAGODAS
PAILOUS
PAIUTES
PAJAMAS
PALACES
PALATES
PALLETS
PALLORS
PALTERS
PAMPERS
PANADAS
PANAMAS
PANDERS
PANDITS
PANFULS
PANNERS
PANSIES
PANZERS
PAPAGOS
PAPAYAS
PAPUANS
PAPYRUS
PARADES
PARAPHS
PARATUS
PARCELS
PARCHES
PARDONS
PARENTS
PARGETS
PARIAHS
PARINGS
PARLAYS
PARLEYS
PARLORS
PARLOUS
PAROLES
PARRIES
PARROTS
PARSECS
PARSEES
PARSERS
PARSONS
PARTIES
PARURES
PASSELS
PASSERS
PASTELS
PASTORS
PATACAS
PATCHES
PATENTS
PATINAS
PATNESS
PATROLS
PATRONS
PATSIES
PATTENS
PATTERS
PATTIES
PAUPERS
PAVANES
PAWNEES
PAWNERS
PAWPAWS
PAYDAYS
PAYOFFS
PAYOLAS
PAYOUTS
QATARIS
RABBETS
RABBITS
RABBLES
RACEMES
RACKETS
RADDLES
RADIALS
RADIANS
RADICES
RADIXES
RADOMES
RAFFLES
RAFTERS
RAGBAGS
RAGLANS
RAGMOPS
RAGOUTS
RAGRUGS
RAGTOPS
RAIDERS
RAILERS
RAISERS
RAISINS
RAJPUTS
RALLIES
RAMADAS
RAMBLES
RAMESES
RAMJETS
RAMRODS
RANCHES
RANCHOS
RANGERS
RANKERS
RANKLES
RANSOMS
RANTERS
RAPIERS
RAPINES
RAPPELS
RAPPERS
RAPTORS
RAREGAS
RASCALS
RASHERS
RASPERS
RASSLES
RASTERS
RATINGS
RATIONS
RATITES
RATTANS
RATTERS
RATTLES
RAUCOUS
RAVAGES
RAVEUPS
RAVINES
RAVINGS
RAWEGGS
RAWNESS
RAYGUNS
SABINES
SACHEMS
SACHETS
SACKERS
SACQUES
SADDENS
SADDLES
SADNESS
SAFARIS
SAILORS
SALAAMS
SALAMIS
SALINAS
SALLETS
SALLIES
SALLOWS
SALMONS
SALOONS
SALTERS
SALUKIS
SALUTES
SALVERS
SALVIAS
SALVOES
SALVORS
SAMBALS
SAMBARS
SAMECHS
SAMITES
SAMLETS
SAMOANS
SAMPANS
SAMPLES
SAMPRAS
SANDALS
SANDERS
SANLUIS
SANTIRS
SAPIENS
SAPLESS
SAPPERS
SARONGS
SASHAYS
SASSERS
SASSIES
SATEENS
SATIRES
SATRAPS
SAUCERS
SAVAGES
SAVALAS
SAVANTS
SAVINGS
SAVIORS
SAVOURS
SAWLOGS
SAWYERS
SAYINGS
SAYYIDS
TABARDS
TABBIES
TABLETS
TACITUS
TACKERS
TACKLES
TACTICS
TAFFIES
TAGENDS
TAILLES
TAILORS
TAIPANS
TALCUMS
TALENTS
TALKERS
TALKIES
TALLIES
TALLOWS
TALUSES
TAMALES
TAMPERS
TAMTAMS
TANDEMS
TANGLES
TANKERS
TANNERS
TANNINS
TANOAKS
TANSIES
TAOISTS
TAPINGS
TAPPERS
TAPPETS
TARGETS
TARIFFS
TARMACS

TARPITS
TARPONS
TARRIES
TARSALS
TARTANS
TARTARS
TASSELS
TASTERS
TATAMIS
TATTERS
TATTLES
TATTOOS
TAUTENS
TAVERNS
TAXLESS
VACATES
VACUOUS
VACUUMS
VALISES
VALLEYS
VALOURS
VAMPERS
VANDALS
VAPOURS
VARIOUS
VARLETS
VASSALS
VATFULS
WADDIES
WADDLES
WAFFLES
WAGGLES
WAGGONS
WAHINES
WAILERS
WAITERS
WAIVERS
WALKERS
WALKINS
WALKONS
WALKUPS
WALLETS
WALLOPS
WALLOWS
WALNUTS
WALTERS
WALTZES
WAMBLES
WANDERS
WANGLES
WANNESS
WANTADS
WAPITIS
WARBLES
WARDENS
WARDERS
WARGODS
WARLESS
WARMUPS
WARRENS
WASHERS
WASHUPS
WASTERS
WATCHES
WATTLES
WAYLAYS
WAYLESS
YABBERS
YAKIMAS
YAKKERS
YAKUZAS
YAMMERS
YANKEES
YANQUIS
YAPPERS
YARROWS
YAUPONS
YAWNERS
YAWPERS
ZAFFERS
ZANDERS
ZAPPERS
ZAREBAS

••AS•••

ABASHED
ABASHES
ABASING
AGASSIZ
ALASKAN
AMASSED
AMASSER
AMASSES
ANASAZI
BEASTIE
BEASTLY
BIASING
BIASSED
BLASTED
BLASTER
BOASTED
BOASTER
BRASHER
BRASHLY
BRASSES
BRASSIE
CEASING
CHASERS
CHASING
CHASSES
CHASSIS
CHASTEN
CHASTER
CLASHED
CLASHES
CLASPED
CLASSED
CLASSES
CLASSIC
COASTAL
COASTED
COASTER
CRASHED
CRASHES
CRASSER
CRASSLY
CRASSUS
DRASTIC
EDASNER
ELASTIC
ERASERS
ERASING
ERASMUS
ERASURE
EVASION
EVASIVE
FEASTED
FIASCOS
FLASHED
FLASHER
FLASHES
FRASIER
GHASTLY
GLASGOW
GLASSED
GLASSES
GNASHED
GNASHES
GRASPED
GRASSED
GRASSES
INASNIT
INASPIN
INASPOT
INASTEW
LEASERS
LEASHED
LEASHES
LEASING
MEASLES
MEASURE
MIASMAS
MIASMIC
OFASORT
ONASSIS
PEASANT
PEASOUP
PHASEIN
PHASERS
PHASING
PIASTER
PIASTRE
PLASHED
PLASHES
PLASMAS
PLASTER
PLASTIC
QUASARS
QUASHED
QUASHES
REASONS
ROASTED
ROASTER
SEASALT
SEASICK
SEASIDE
SEASLUG
SEASONS
SEASTAR
SHASTRI
SLASHED
SLASHER
SLASHES
SMASHED
SMASHER
SMASHES
SMASHUP
SPASSKY
STASHED
STASHES
STASSEN
SUASION
TEASELS
TEASERS
TEASETS
TEASHOP
TEASING
TOASTED
TOASTER
TRASHED
TRASHES
UNASKED
WEASELS

••A•S••

ADAMSON
AGASSIZ
AMASSED
AMASSER
AMASSES
ARALSEA
BEADSUP
BEAMSUP
BEARSON
BEARSUP
BEATSIT
BEATSME
BEATSUP
BIASSED
BRAISED
BRAISES
BRANSON
BRASSES
BRASSIE
CHAISES
CHANSON
CHASSES
CHASSIS
CHATSUP
CLAMSUP
CLASSED
CLASSES
CLASSIC
CLAUSES
COARSEN
COARSER
CRASSER
CRASSLY
CRASSUS
DEADSEA
DEADSET
DEALSIN
DEARSIR
DRAGSIN
DRAGSON
DRAWSIN
DRAWSON
DRAWSUP
ELAPSED
ELAPSES
FRAISES
GEARSTO
GEARSUP
GLASSED
GLASSES
GRABSAT
GRASSED
GRASSES
GRAYSON
HEADSET
HEADSIN
HEADSUP
HEARSAY
HEARSOF
HEATSUP
HOARSEN
HOARSER
KLATSCH
LEADSIN
LEADSON
LEADSTO
LEADSUP
LEANSON
LIAISED
LIAISES
LIAISON
ONASSIS
PEARSON
PLANSON
PLAYSAT
PLAYSON
PLAYSUP
PRAISED
PRAISER
PRAISES
PRAYSTO
READSIN
REARSUP
SEALSUP
SNAPSAT
SNAPSTO
SNAPSUP
SOAKSUP
SPARSER
SPASSKY
STASSEN
STAYSUP
SWANSEA
SWANSON
TEAMSUP
TEARSAT
TEARSUP
THATSIT
TRANSIT
TRANSOM
WRAPSUP

••A••S•

AGAINST
ANALYSE
ANALYST
ANAPEST
ATALOSS
ATAVISM
ATAVIST
BEAMISH
BEARISH
BEAUISH
BOARISH
BRALESS
BRAVEST
BYANOSE
CLAYISH
CRAFTSY
CZARISM
CZARIST
DEAFEST
DEAREST
EVANISH
GOATISH
GRAVEST
GRAYEST
GRAYISH
INAMESS
INANEST
INARUSH
IRATEST
KNAVISH
LEANEST
MEANEST
NEAREST
NEATEST
PEAKISH
PIANISM
PIANIST
PLANISH
REALISE
REALISM
REALIST
REAMASS
SEABASS
SEAMOSS
SIAMESE
SLAVISH
SOANDSO
SPANISH
SPAREST
STALEST
STATIST
SUAVEST
TEALESS
TEAROSE
TOADISH
TRAIPSE
TSARIST
WEAKEST
WEAKISH

••A•••S

ABASHES
ACACIAS
ACARIDS
ADAGIOS
AGARICS
ALARUMS
AMADEUS
AMASSES
AMAZONS
ANADEMS
ANALOGS
ANANIAS
APACHES
ARAWAKS
ATALOSS
ATAMANS
AVATARS
AWAKENS
AZALEAS
BEACHES
BEACONS
BEADLES
BEAGLES
BEAKERS
BEANIES
BEARERS
BEATERS
BEATLES
BEAVERS
BIALIES
BLADERS
BLAZERS
BLAZONS
BOATELS
BOATERS
BRACERS
BRAHMAS
BRAISES
BRALESS
BRASSES
BRAVOES
BRAYERS
CHABLIS
CHACHAS
CHAISES
CHALETS
CHALONS
CHAMOIS
CHANCES
CHANGES
CHAPELS
CHARGES
CHARLES
CHASERS
CHASSES
CHASSIS
CLAMORS
CLAQUES
CLARETS
CLASHES
CLASSES
CLAUSES
CLAWERS
COACHES
COALERS
COALGAS
COAXERS
CRADLES
CRASHES
CRASSUS
CRATERS
CRAVATS
CRAVENS
CRAVERS
CRAYONS
CRAZIES
CZARDAS
DEACONS
DEADENS
DEAFENS
DEALERS
DEARIES
DEARTHS
DIADEMS
DIALERS
DIALOGS
DIAPERS
DIARIES
DIATOMS
DRACHMS
DRAGONS
DRAPERS
DRAWERS
DWARVES
ELAPIDS
ELAPSES
ELATERS
ENABLES
ENAMELS
ENAMORS
EPARCHS
ERASERS
ERASMUS
EVADERS
EXACTAS
EXARCHS
FEARERS
FIACRES
FIANCES
FIASCOS
FLACONS
FLAGONS
FLAKERS
FLAMBES
FLANGES
FLASHES
FLAUNTS
FLAVORS
FRAISES
FRANCES
FRANCIS
FRAPPES
GLANCES
GLASSES
GLAZERS
GNASHES
GNAWERS
GOALIES
GOATEES
GRACIAS
GRADERS
GRAHAMS
GRAMMES
GRAMMYS
GRAMPAS
GRAMPUS
GRANGES
GRAPPAS
GRASSES
GRATERS
GRATIAS
GRAVELS
GRAVERS
GRAVIES
GRAZERS
HEADERS
HEALERS
HEARERS
HEARTHS
HEATERS
HEAVENS
HEAVERS
HEAVIES
HOAGIES
HOAXERS
IMAGERS
IMAGOES
IMARETS
INAMESS
ITALICS
JEALOUS
KLAXONS
KRATERS
KWACHAS
KWANZAS
LAAGERS
LEACHES
LEADERS
LEADINS
LEAGUES
LEAKERS
LEANERS
LEANTOS
LEAPERS
LEASERS
LEASHES
LEAVENS
LIAISES
LOACHES
LOADERS
LOAFERS
LOANERS
LOATHES
MEADOWS
MEALIES
MEANIES
MEASLES
MIAMIAS
MIASMAS
MOANERS
NEATENS
NUANCES
ONAGERS
ONASSIS
OPAQUES
ORACLES
ORANGES
ORATORS
PAANGAS
PEACHES
PEAHENS
PEANUTS
PEAPODS
PEAVEYS
PHASERS
PIAZZAS
PLACERS
PLAGUES
PLAICES
PLAINTS
PLANERS
PLANETS
PLAQUES
PLASHES
PLASMAS
PLATENS
PLATERS
PLAUTUS
PLAYERS
POACHES
PRAISES
PRANCES
PRATERS
PRAYERS
PSANDQS
QUAGGAS
QUAHOGS
QUAKERS
QUANGOS
QUARTOS
QUASARS
QUASHES
QUAVERS
REACHES
READERS
READIES
REAMASS
REAMERS
REAPERS
REARERS
REASONS
ROACHES
ROADIES
ROAMERS
ROARERS
SCALARS
SCALERS
SCARABS
SCARERS
SCARVES
SCATHES
SEABAGS
SEABASS
SEABEDS
SEABEES
SEACOWS
SEADOGS
SEAFANS
SEALABS
SEALEGS
SEALERS
SEAMOSS
SEANCES
SEASONS
SEATERS
SEAWAYS
SHADOWS
SHAKERS
SHAKOES
SHALOMS
SHAMANS
SHAPERS
SHARERS
SHAVERS
SKATERS
SLALOMS
SLASHES
SLAVERS
SLAVEYS
SLAYERS
SMALTOS
SMASHES
SNAPONS
SOAKERS
SOAPERS
SOARERS
SPACERS
SPADERS
SPARGES
SPAVINS
STABLES
STAGERS
STALAGS
STAMENS
STANCES
STANZAS
STAPLES
STARERS
STARETS
STARVES
STASHES
STATICS
STATORS
STATUES
SWATHES
SWAYERS
TEABAGS
TEACHES
TEACUPS
TEALESS
TEAPOTS
TEAPOYS
TEARGAS
TEASELS
TEASERS
TEASETS
THALERS
TOADIES
TRACERS
TRADERS
TRAMPAS
TRANCES
TRASHES
TRAUMAS
TRAVELS
TRAVERS
TRAVOIS
TUAREGS
UTAHANS
WEAKENS
WEAPONS
WEARERS
WEARIES
WEASELS
WEAVERS
WHALERS
WHARVES
WRAITHS
WRAPUPS
ZEALOTS
ZEALOUS

•••AS••

ALIASES
ARRASES
ATLASES
BABASSU
BELASCO
BREASTS
CANASTA
CREASED
CREASES
DAMASKS
DATASET
DEBASED
DEBASES
DYNASTS
DYNASTY
EMBASSY
ENCASED
ENCASES
ENMASSE
EURASIA
GIRASOL
GLEASON
GREASED
GREASER
GREASES
IMPASSE
IMPASTO
INCASED
INCASES
INHASTE
JOCASTA
KARASEA
NATASHA
OBLASTS
PARASOL
PEGASUS
PHRASAL
PHRASED
PHRASES
PICASSO
PLEASED
PLEASER
PLEASES
PULASKI
REBASTE
RECASTS
REPASTE
REPASTS
SPLASHY
STRASSE
TABASCO
TREASON
UNCASED
UNCASES
UNMASKS

•••A•S•

BABASSU
BECAUSE
CLEANSE
DADAISM
DADAIST
DEGAUSS
EMBASSY
ENMASSE
EXHAUST
EXPANSE
IMPASSE
JUDAISM
KOMATSU
LAMAISM
LAMAIST
LAVALSE
MALAISE
PICASSO
RELAPSE
RERAISE
ROMANSH
SHIATSU
STRASSE
STRAUSS
SYNAPSE
TUBAIST
UPRAISE

•••A••S

ABLATES
ABLAUTS
ABNAKIS
ABRADES
ACHATES
ACKACKS
AERATES
AFFAIRS
AFRAMES
AGNATES
ALIASES
ALKALIS
ALPACAS
ANTAEUS
ANTARES
APPALLS
ARCADES
ARMADAS
ARRASES
ASFARAS
ASSAILS
ATLASES
ATLATLS
ATTACKS
ATTAINS
AUBADES
AUPAIRS
AVIATES
AYEAYES
BAHAMAS
BANANAS
BASALTS
BAZAARS
BECALMS
BEDAUBS
BEFALLS
BEHAVES
BERATES
BETAKES
BEWAILS
BORATES
BREASTS
BREATHS
BRIARDS
BYPATHS
CABALAS
CABANAS
CANAPES
CANARDS
CARACAS
CARAFES
CASABAS
CASAVAS
CCLAMPS
CICADAS
CLEAVES
CLOACAS
COWARDS
CREASES
CREATES
CURATES
DAMAGES
DAMASKS
DEBARKS
DEBASES
DEBATES
DECADES
DECAMPS
DECANTS
DEDALUS
DEFACES
DEFAMES
DEGAUSS
DEMANDS
DEPARTS
DERAILS
DESALTS
DETAILS
DETAINS
DIDACTS
DILATES
DISARMS
DOMAINS
DONATES
DOPANTS
DOSAGES
DOTARDS
DUKAKIS
DYNAMOS
DYNASTS
ECLAIRS
EDWARDS
EFFACES
EMBANKS
EMBARKS
ENCAGES
ENCAMPS
ENCASES
ENGAGES
ENLACES
ENRAGES
ENTAILS
EQUATES
ERGATES
ERRANDS
ESCAPES
ESCARPS
ESTATES
EXHALES
EXPANDS
FABARES
FACADES
FEMALES
FINALES
FIXATES
FORAGES
GALAGOS
GARAGES
GELADAS
GELATIS
GOCARTS
GOKARTS
GREASES
GREAVES
GYRATES
HAZARDS
HERALDS
HIJACKS
HOWARDS
HYRACES
HYRAXES
ICEAGES
ICEAXES
IDCARDS
IDEATES
IGUANAS
IMPACTS
IMPAIRS
IMPALAS
IMPALES
IMPARTS
INCANTS
INCASES
INFANTS
INGALLS
INHALES
INHAULS
INMATES
INNARDS
INTAKES
INVADES
INWARDS
IODATES
ISLANDS
IZZARDS
JACANAS
JICAMAS
KANAKAS
KAZAKHS
KIWANIS
LAZARUS
LEGATES
LEGATOS
LEVANTS
LIGANDS
LIGATES
LINAGES
LIZARDS
LOCALES
LOCATES
LUXATES
MAHARIS
MANAGES
MANANAS
MARACAS
MARAUDS
MCCALLS
MENACES
MENAGES
METATES
MIKADOS
MIRAGES
MOHAIRS
MOHAWKS
MORALES
MORANIS
MOSAICS
MUTANTS
MUTATES
NAIADES
NAVAHOS
NAVAJOS
NEGATES
NEPALIS
NOGALES
NONAGES
NOTATES
NUTATES
OBLASTS
OBLATES
OBTAINS
OCEANUS
OCTANES
OCTANTS
OCTAVES
OCTAVOS
OGLALAS
OLEATES
ONWARDS
OPIATES
ORDAINS
ORGATES
OTTAWAS
OUTACTS
OUTAGES
OXCARTS
PAJAMAS
PALACES
PALATES
PANADAS
PANAMAS
PAPAGOS
PAPAYAS
PARADES
PARAPHS
PARATUS
PATACAS
PAVANES

PDJAMES
PEDANTS
PEGASUS
PELAGES
PENATES
PESAWAS
PETARDS
PHRASES
PICAROS
PINATAS
PIRAEUS
PIRATES
PLEASES
POLARIS
POMADES
POSADAS
POTAGES
PREAMPS
PYJAMAS
PYRAMUS
QATARIS
RAMADAS
RAVAGES
REBATES
RECALLS
RECANES
RECANTS
RECASTS
REDACTS
REDANTS
REDATES
REFACES
REGAINS
REGALES
REGARDS
REHANGS
RELACES
RELATES
RELAXES
REMAILS
REMAINS
REMAKES
REMANDS
REMARKS
RENAILS
RENAMES
RENARDS
REPAIRS
REPASTS
REPAVES
RERATES
RESALES
RESALTS
RESANDS
RETAILS
RETAINS
RETAKES
RETAPES
RETARDS
RETAXES
REVAMPS
REWARDS
REWARMS
REWAXES
RIBANDS
ROBARDS
ROLAIDS
ROTATES
RUBATOS
SAFARIS
SALAAMS
SALAMIS
SAVAGES
SAVALAS
SAVANTS
SCRAPES
SCRAWLS
SECANTS
SEDATES
SENATES
SERAPES
SERAPHS
SERAPIS
SESAMES
SHEATHS
SHEAVES
SOLACES
SOMALIS
SONATAS
SPRAINS
SPRAWLS
SQUALLS
SQUARES
SQUAWKS
STRAFES
STRAINS
STRAITS
STRANDS
STRATUS
STRAUSS
TABARDS
TAMALES
TATAMIS
TENACES
TENANTS
TERAPHS
TETANUS
THRALLS
THWACKS
THWARTS
TIRADES
TISANES
TOPAZES
TOWARDS
TRUANTS
TYRANTS
UMLAUTS
UNCAGES
UNCASES
UNHANDS
UNLACES
UNLADES
UNMAKES
UNMASKS
UNPACKS
UNTACKS
UPDATES
UPLANDS
UPTAKES
UPWARDS
VACATES
VIRAGOS
VISAGES
VISAVIS
VOYAGES
WIZARDS
WREATHS
ZENANAS
ZOUAVES

••••AS•

ABREAST
AIRBASE
AIRMASS
AMYLASE
APPEASE
ATLEAST
BALLAST
BELFAST
BIOMASS
BOMBAST
BONEASH
CANVASS
CARCASE
CARCASS
CARWASH
COMPASS
CUIRASS
CUTLASS
DECLASS
DISEASE
ECSTASY
EGGCASE
EYELASH
EYEWASH
FANTASY
FAREAST
FLYCAST
FLYPAST
GOULASH
GYMNAST
HOGWASH
INPHASE
JACKASS
JETWASH
LACTASE
MIDEAST
MISCAST
MOMBASA
NASTASE
OFFBASE
OUTCAST
OUTLAST
OXIDASE
PAYCASH
PRECAST
PREWASH
REAMASS
RELEASE
SARCASM
SEABASS
SKIMASK
SUCRASE
SURPASS
TOPMAST
TWOBASE
UNCLASP
UNLEASH

••••A•S

ADONAIS
AERIALS
AFFRAYS
AFGHANS
AIRBAGS
AIRDAMS
AIRMASS
AIRSACS
AIRWAYS
ALLEARS
ANDEANS
ANIMALS
ANNEALS
ANNUALS
ANORAKS
AOUDADS
APPEALS
APPEARS
ARAWAKS
ARREARS
ASHCANS
ASHLARS
ASHRAMS
ATAMANS
AVATARS
AVOWALS
BALKANS
BALLADS
BALSAMS
BANTAMS
BANYANS
BAOBABS
BARCARS
BARTABS
BAUHAUS
BAZAARS
BEGGARS
BEHEADS
BELDAMS
BEMOANS
BENGALS
BETRAYS
BIOMASS
BITMAPS
BOBCATS
BOWSAWS
BOXCARS
BRIDALS
BROGANS
BULGARS
BUMRAPS
BUREAUS
BURLAPS
BURMANS
BUROAKS
BURSARS
BYPLAYS
BYROADS
CAESARS
CAFTANS
CAIMANS
CALPACS
CANCANS
CANVASS
CARCASS
CARPALS
CASUALS
CATNAPS
CAVEATS
CAVIARS
CAYMANS
CELLARS
CEREALS
CHORALS
COEVALS
COGNACS
COLLARS
COMBATS
COMPASS
CONFABS
CORRALS
COSTARS
COUGARS
CRAVATS
CRETANS
CUIRASS
CUSHAWS
CUTLASS
CYMBALS
DAMMARS
DECLASS
DEEJAYS
DEFEATS
DEFRAYS
DEMEANS
DENIALS
DEODARS
DEWLAPS
DIGRAMS
DIKTATS
DISBARS
DISMAYS
DOGDAYS
DOGEARS
DOGTAGS
DOLLARS
DOLMANS
DOODADS
DOODAHS
DORSALS
DOSSALS
ENDEARS
ENDWAYS
ENGRAMS
ENNEADS
ENTRAPS
ENWRAPS
ESPIALS
ESTRAYS
FACIALS
FATCATS
FELLAHS
FENIANS
FIJIANS
FINIALS
FLYWAYS
FORMALS
FORMATS
FRIDAYS
FRYPANS
GAGLAWS
GALPALS
GASBAGS
GASCAPS
GAVIALS
GEEGAWS
GERMANS
GEWGAWS
GIMBALS
GRAHAMS
GUFFAWS
GUITARS
GULLAHS
GYMBAGS
HALVAHS
HANGARS
HAWHAWS
HEEHAWS
HEPCATS
HEPTADS
HERBALS
HETMANS
HEYDAYS
HOOHAHS
HOOKAHS
HOTCAPS
HOTCARS
HOTWARS
HOWDAHS
HUBCAPS
HURRAHS
HUSSARS
HUZZAHS
HYMNALS
ICEBAGS
ICECAPS
INDIANS
INROADS
INSEAMS
INSPANS
INSTALS
INSTARS
INTEARS
ISOBARS
JACKALS
JACKASS
JAGUARS
JETWAYS
JIGSAWS
JIMJAMS
KAFTANS
KANSANS
KENYANS
KEYPADS
KIDNAPS
KIRMANS
KITBAGS
KODIAKS
KOREANS
LABIALS
LANDAUS
LARIATS
LEKVARS
LIBYANS
LOGJAMS
LOOFAHS
LOQUATS
LUMBARS
MADCAPS
MAENADS
MAGYARS
MAITAIS
MAMMALS
MANDANS
MANDAYS
MANIACS
MANUALS
MARGAYS
MAUMAUS
MAYDAYS
MEDIANS
MENIALS
MESCALS
MICMACS
MIDDAYS
MIDWAYS
MINOANS
MINYANS
MISHAPS
MISLAYS
MISSALS
MISSAYS
MOBCAPS
MONDAYS
MORGANS
MORTALS
MORTARS
MUDCATS
MULLAHS
MUSCATS
MUTUALS
MYRIADS
NARWALS
NAYSAYS
NECTARS
NORMALS
NORMANS
NOUGATS
NUBIANS
NULLAHS
NUMBATS
OGDOADS
OHIOANS
OILCANS
OILPANS
OLDDAYS
OLDSAWS
OOMPAHS
ORDEALS
ORGEATS
ORLEANS
ORPHANS
OUTEATS
OUTLAWS
OUTLAYS
OVISACS
PADUANS
PAPUANS
PARIAHS
PARLAYS
PAWPAWS
PAYDAYS
PEDLARS
PEDWAYS
PENPALS
PENTADS
PERHAPS
PIEPANS
PILLARS
PINOAKS
PITSAWS
PLURALS
POPLARS
PORTALS
PREFABS
PREPAYS
PTBOATS
PULSARS
PUNKAHS
PURDAHS
QINTARS
QUASARS
RADIALS
RADIANS
RAGBAGS
RAGLANS
RASCALS
RATTANS
REAMASS
RECOATS
REDCAPS
REDEALS
REDHATS
REDIALS
REDOAKS
REDRAWS
REFLAGS
REHEALS
REHEARS
REHEATS
RELOADS
RENTALS
REPEALS
REPEATS
REPLANS
REPLAYS
REREADS
RESEALS
RESEATS
RETEARS
REVEALS
REWRAPS
REXCATS
RIPRAPS
RIPSAWS
RITUALS
RUNWAYS
RUPIAHS
SALAAMS
SAMBALS
SAMBARS
SAMOANS
SAMPANS
SANDALS
SASHAYS
SATRAPS
SCALARS
SCARABS
SCHNAPS
SCREAKS
SCREAMS
SEABAGS
SEABASS
SEAFANS
SEALABS
SEAWAYS
SEESAWS
SERIALS
SERVALS
SEXTANS
SHAMANS
SHOFARS
SIGNALS
SIMIANS
SIOUANS
SKYCAPS
SKYWAYS
SLOGANS
SLOVAKS
SNOCATS
SOCIALS
SPIRALS
SPREADS
SQUEAKS
SQUEALS
STALAGS
STREAKS
STREAMS
SUBWAYS
SULTANS
SUNDAES
SUNDAYS
SUNRAYS
SUNTANS
SURPASS
SYLVANS
SYRIANS
TAIPANS
TAMTAMS
TANOAKS
TARMACS
TARSALS
TARTANS
TARTARS
TEABAGS
TETRADS
THECARS
THENARS
THREADS
THREATS
THROATS
TICTACS
TIMBALS
TINCANS
TINEARS
TINHATS
TOECAPS
TOETAPS
TOMCATS
TONGANS
TOPHATS
TOUCANS
TOWCARS
TREPANS
TROCARS
TROJANS
TULSANS
TURBANS
UNCIALS
UNLOADS
UNSEALS
UNSEATS
UNSNAGS
UNSNAPS
UNTRAPS
UNWRAPS
UPBEATS
UPLOADS
UPROARS
UTAHANS
VANDALS
VASSALS
VEEJAYS
VERBALS
VISUALS
VULCANS
WANTADS
WAYLAYS
WETBARS
WHYDAHS
WIGWAGS
WIGWAMS
WOMBATS
YOUMANS
ZEDBARS
ZIGZAGS
ZODIACS

•••••AS

ACACIAS
AGENDAS
ALPACAS
AMOEBAS
ANANIAS
ANDREAS
ANGORAS
AQUINAS
AREOLAS
ARISTAS
ARMADAS
ARNICAS
ARROBAS
ASFARAS
AURORAS
AZALEAS
BAHAMAS
BALBOAS
BANANAS
BODEGAS
BRAHMAS
BUDDHAS
CABALAS
CABANAS
CAMERAS
CARACAS
CARINAS
CASABAS
CASAVAS
CASSIAS
CAYUGAS
CHACHAS
CHOLLAS
CHUKKAS
CICADAS
CINEMAS
CLOACAS
COALGAS
CONTRAS
COPULAS
CORNEAS
CORONAS
COWPEAS
CUPOLAS
CZARDAS
DAHLIAS
DAKOTAS
DOUGLAS
DUENNAS
ENCINAS
ENIGMAS
ESPOSAS
EXACTAS
FAJITAS
FASCIAS
FAUXPAS
FEDORAS
FIBULAS
FIESTAS
GEISHAS
GELADAS
GILBLAS
GLORIAS
GOTCHAS
GRACIAS
GRAMPAS
GRAPPAS
GRATIAS
GUINEAS
GURKHAS
HEGIRAS
HOOPLAS
HULLOAS
IGUANAS
IMPALAS
JACANAS
JERBOAS
JICAMAS
KAHUNAS
KANAKAS
KINEMAS
KORUNAS
KWACHAS
KWANZAS
LACUNAS
LAGUNAS
LAKOTAS
LAMBDAS
LAMINAS
LATINAS
LOGGIAS
MANANAS
MANTRAS
MARACAS
MARINAS
MATHIAS
MEDUSAS
MIAMIAS
MIASMAS
MIMOSAS
MITHRAS
MODELAS
MULETAS
NEBULAS
NICOLAS
NOVENAS
NUTRIAS
OGLALAS
OJIBWAS
ONEIDAS
OTTAWAS
PAANGAS
PAGODAS
PAJAMAS
PANADAS
PANAMAS
PAPAYAS
PATACAS
PATINAS
PAYOLAS
PELOTAS
PESAWAS
PESETAS
PHIDIAS
PHINEAS
PHOBIAS
PIAZZAS
PINATAS
PINCHAS
PLASMAS
POSADAS
PYJAMAS
PYTHIAS
QUAGGAS
QUINOAS
QUOKKAS
RAMADAS
RAREGAS
REMORAS
REMUDAS
RETINAS
RHUMBAS
SALINAS
SALVIAS
SAMPRAS
SAVALAS
SCHEMAS
SCLERAS
SENECAS
SENORAS
SHEILAS
SHERPAS
SIENNAS
SIERRAS
SIESTAS
SILICAS
SONATAS
SPIREAS
STANZAS
STIGMAS
TEARGAS
TRAMPAS
TRAUMAS
TROIKAS
TUNDRAS
ULTIMAS
UTOPIAS
VERITAS
VICUNAS
VIZSLAS
WHEREAS
YAKIMAS
YAKUZAS
ZAREBAS
ZENANAS
ZEUGMAS
ZINNIAS
ZOYSIAS

AT•••••

ATACAMA
ATALOSS
ATAMANS
ATATURK
ATAVISM
ATAVIST
ATECROW
ATELIER
ATFAULT
ATHEART
ATHEISM
ATHEIST
ATHIRST
ATHLETE
ATHOMES
ATHWART
ATINGLE
ATISSUE
ATLANTA
ATLARGE
ATLASES
ATLATLS
ATLEAST
ATOMIES
ATOMISE
ATOMIZE
ATONIES
ATONING
ATPEACE
ATRIUMS
ATROPHY
ATSTAKE
ATTABOY
ATTACHE
ATTACKS
ATTAINS
ATTEMPT
ATTENDS
ATTESTS
ATTICUS
ATTIMES
ATTIRED
ATTIRES
ATTRACT
ATTRITE
ATTRITS
ATTUCKS
ATTUNED
ATTUNES
ATWORST

A•T••••

ACTABLE
ACTAEON
ACTEDON
ACTEDUP
ACTFIVE
ACTFOUR
ACTINIC
ACTIONS
ACTIVES
ACTRESS
ACTSOUT
ACTUARY
ACTUATE
ACTUPON
AETHERS
AITCHES
ALTERED
ALTERER
ALTOONA
ALTOSAX
ANTACID
ANTAEUS
ANTARES
ANTBEAR
ANTCOWS
ANTEDUP
ANTEING
ANTENNA
ANTESUP
ANTFARM
ANTHEMS
ANTHERS
ANTHILL
ANTHONY
ANTIART
ANTIBES
ANTIFOG
ANTIGEN
ANTIGUA
ANTILOG
ANTIOCH
ANTIQUE
ANTITAX
ANTIWAR
ANTLERS
ANTLIKE
ANTLION
ANTOINE
ANTONIA
ANTONIN
ANTONIO
ANTONYM
ANTSIER
ANTWERP
APTERAL
APTNESS
ARTDECO
ARTEMIS
ARTEMUS
ARTFILM
ARTFORM
ARTICLE
ARTIEST
ARTISAN
ARTISTE
ARTISTS
ARTLESS
ARTSIER
ARTSONG
ARTWARE
ARTWORK
ASTAIRE
ASTARTE
ASTOLAT
ASTORIA
ASTOUND
ASTRIDE
ATTABOY
ATTACHE
ATTACKS
ATTAINS
ATTEMPT
ATTENDS
ATTESTS
ATTICUS
ATTIMES
ATTIRED
ATTIRES
ATTRACT
ATTRITE
ATTRITS
ATTUCKS
ATTUNED
ATTUNES
AUTARKY
AUTEURS
AUTHORS
AUTOMAT
AUTUMNS
AZTECAN

A••T•••

ABATING
ABETTED
ABETTOR
ABITIBI
ABSTAIN
ABUTTAL
ABUTTED
ACETATE
ACETONE
ACHTUNG
ACUTELY
AGITATE
AGITATO
AIRTAXI
AIRTIME
ALLTIME
ALLTOLD
AMATEUR
AMATIVE
AMATORY
ANATOLE
ANATOMY
ANOTHER
ANYTIME
APATITE
APOTHEM
ARETINO
ASHTRAY
ATATURK
ATSTAKE
AUCTION
AUNTIES
AUSTERE
AUSTRAL
AUSTRIA
AVATARS

A•••T••

ABBOTCY
ABETTED
ABETTOR
ABEXTRA
ABINTRA
ABLATED
ABLATES
ABORTED
ABUTTAL
ABUTTED
ACANTHI
ACHATES
ADAPTED
ADAPTER
ADAPTOR
ADEPTLY
ADMITTO
ADOPTED
ADOPTEE
ADOPTER
ADULTLY
AERATED
AERATES
AERATOR
AGNATES
AGOUTIS
ALERTED
ALERTER
ALERTLY
ALLSTAR
ALLSTON
ALSATIA
AMISTAD
AMMETER
ANISTON

ANNATTO
ANNETTE
ANTITAX
APOSTLE
AQUATIC
ARBITER
ARBUTUS
ARIETTA
ARISTAE
ARISTAS
ARISTOS
ASCETIC
ASEPTIC
ASIATIC
ATLATLS
AUDITED
AUDITOR
AVERTED
AVIATED
AVIATES
AVIATOR
AWAITED

A••••T•

ABDUCTS
ABILITY
ABLAUTS
ABSENTS
ACCENTS
ACCEPTS
ACCOSTS
ACCRETE
ACETATE
ACIDITY
ACOLYTE
ACONITE
ACQUITS
ACTUATE
ADAMITE
ADDEDTO
ADDONTO
ADDUCTS
ADDUPTO
ADJUSTS
ADMITTO
ADULATE
ADVENTS
ADVERTS
AFFECTS
AFREETS
AGEISTS
AGILITY
AGITATE
AGITATO
AGREETO
AIGRETS
AIMEDTO
AIRDATE
AKIHITO
ALBERTA
ALBERTO
ALDENTE
ALIGHTS
ALMAATA
ALWORTH
AMENITY
AMNESTY
AMOUNTS
AMULETS
ANDANTE
ANIMATE
ANIMATO
ANKLETS
ANNATTO
ANNETTE
ANNUITY
ANOINTS
ANXIETY
AORISTS
APATITE
APLENTY
APPLETS
ARIDITY
ARIETTA
ARIOSTO
ARMLETS
ARMPITS
ARPENTS
ARRESTS
ARTISTE
ARTISTS
ASCENTS
ASHANTI
ASPECTS
ASSENTS
ASSERTS
ASSISTS
ASSORTS
ASTARTE
ATHLETE
ATLANTA
ATTESTS
ATTRITE
ATTRITS
AUGUSTA
AUGUSTE
AUKLETS
AUREATE
AVIDITY
AVOCETS
AXOLOTL
AZIMUTH
AZURITE

A•••••T

ABEYANT
ABOUGHT
ABREAST
ABSOLUT
ACCOUNT
ACCURST
ACEDOUT
ACESOUT
ACHIEST
ACROBAT
ACTSOUT
ADAMANT
ADJUNCT
AERIEST
AEROBAT
AFFLICT
AFFRONT
AGAINST
AGONIST
AILMENT
AIMEDAT
AIRBOAT
AIRIEST
AIRLIFT
AIRPORT
AIRSOUT
ALIMENT
ALRIGHT
AMBIENT
AMHERST
AMONGST
AMPLEST
ANALYST
ANAPEST
ANCIENT
ANIMIST
ANTIART
APPARAT
APPOINT
APRICOT
AQUAVIT
ARIDEST
ARMREST
ARMYANT
ARTIEST
ASHIEST
ASKSOUT
ASPHALT
ASSAULT
ASTOLAT
ATAVIST
ATFAULT
ATHEART
ATHEIST
ATHIRST
ATHWART
ATLEAST
ATTEMPT
ATTRACT
ATWORST
AUGMENT
AUTOMAT

•AT••••

BATBOYS
BATCHED
BATCHES
BATEAUX
BATEMAN
BATGIRL
BATHERS
BATHING
BATHMAT
BATHOIL
BATHTUB
BATIKED
BATISTA
BATISTE
BATLIKE
BATSMAN
BATSMEN
BATTELS
BATTENS
BATTERS
BATTERY
BATTIER
BATTING
BATTLED
BATTLER
BATTLES
BATTUES
BATWING
CATALAN
CATALOG
CATALPA
CATAWBA
CATBERT
CATBIRD
CATBOAT
CATCALL
CATCHER
CATCHES
CATCHON
CATCHUP
CATENAE
CATERED
CATERER
CATERTO
CATFISH
CATFOOD
CATHAIR
CATHEAD
CATHODE
CATIONS
CATKINS
CATLIKE
CATNAPS
CATNIPS
CATSCAN
CATSEYE
CATSHOW
CATSPAW
CATSUIT
CATTAIL
CATTIER
CATTILY
CATTING
CATTISH
CATWALK
DATASET
DATEDLY
EATABLE
EATAWAY
EATCROW
EATENAT
EATENUP
EATSOUT
FATBACK
FATCATS
FATCITY
FATEFUL
FATHEAD
FATHERS
FATHOMS
FATIGUE
FATLESS
FATLIKE
FATNESS
FATTENS
FATTEST
FATTIER
FATTILY
FATTISH
FATUITY
FATUOUS
GATEAUX
GATELEG
GATEMAN
GATEMEN
GATEWAY
GATHERS
GATLING
HATBAND
HATCHED
HATCHER
HATCHES
HATCHET
HATEFUL
HATLESS
HATLIKE
HATPINS
HATRACK
HATTERS
HATTING
KATHRYN
KATYDID
LATCHED
LATCHES
LATEENS
LATENCY
LATENTS
LATERAL
LATERAN
LATERON
LATEXES
LATHERS
LATHERY
LATHING
LATICES
LATIFAH
LATINAS
LATINOS
LATOSCA
LATTENS
LATTICE
LATVIAN
MATADOR
MATCHED
MATCHES
MATCHUP
MATELOT
MATEWAN
MATHERS
MATHEWS
MATHIAS
MATILDA
MATINEE
MATISSE
MATLESS
MATLOCK
MATRONS
MATTERS
MATTHAU
MATTHEW
MATTING
MATTOCK
MATURED
MATURER
MATURES
MATZOHS
NATALIA
NATALIE
NATASHA
NATCHEZ
NATIONS
NATIVES
NATRIUM
NATTERS
NATTIER
NATTILY
NATURAL
NATURED
NATURES
OATLIKE
OATMEAL
PATACAS
PATCHED
PATCHES
PATCHUP
PATELLA
PATENTS
PATERNO
PATHWAY
PATIENT
PATINAS
PATNESS
PATRIAL
PATRICE
PATRICK
PATRIOT
PATROLS
PATRONS
PATROON
PATSIES
PATTENS
PATTERN
PATTERS
PATTIES
PATTING
QATARIS
RATABLE
RATAFIA
RATATAT
RATBERT
RATCHET
RATFINK
RATHOLE
RATINGS
RATIONS
RATITES
RATLIKE
RATLINE
RATPACK
RATRACE
RATTAIL
RATTANS
RATTERS
RATTIER
RATTING
RATTISH
RATTLED
RATTLER
RATTLES
RATTRAP
SATCHEL
SATCHMO
SATDOWN
SATEENS
SATIATE
SATIETY
SATINET
SATIRES
SATIRIC
SATISFY
SATRAPS
SATSUMA
TATAMIS
TATIANA
TATTERS
TATTIER
TATTILY
TATTING
TATTLED
TATTLER
TATTLES
TATTOOS
VATFULS
VATICAN
VATTING
WATCHED
WATCHER
WATCHES
WATCHIT
WATERED
WATERER
WATTAGE
WATTEAU
WATTLES
ZATOPEK

•A•T•••

BAITING
BANTAMS
BANTERS
BAPTISE
BAPTISM
BAPTIST
BAPTIZE
BARTABS
BARTEND
BARTERS
BASTERS
BASTING
BASTION
BATTELS
BATTENS
BATTERS
BATTERY
BATTIER
BATTING
BATTLED
BATTLER
BATTLES
BATTUES
CAFTANS
CALTECH
CANTATA
CANTEEN
CANTERS
CANTILY
CANTINA
CANTING
CANTLES
CANTONS
CANTORS
CANTRIP
CAPTAIN
CAPTION
CAPTIVE
CAPTORS
CAPTURE
CARTAGE
CARTELS
CARTERS
CARTIER
CARTING
CARTONS
CARTOON
CASTERS
CASTILE
CASTING
CASTLED
CASTLES
CASTOFF
CASTOUT
CATTAIL
CATTIER
CATTILY
CATTING
CATTISH
CAUTION
DACTYLS
DAFTEST
DALTREY
DARTERS
DARTING
DASTARD
DAYTIME
DAYTONA
DAYTRIP
EARTHEN
EARTHLY
EASTEND
EASTERN
EASTERS
EASTMAN
FACTFUL
FACTION
FACTOID
FACTORS
FACTORY
FACTUAL
FALTERS
FANTAIL
FANTASY
FARTHER
FASTENS
FASTEST
FASTING
FASTONE
FATTENS
FATTEST
FATTIER
FATTILY
FATTISH
GAITERS
GAITING
GANTLET
GARTERS
GASTRIC
GAUTAMA
HAFTING
HAITIAN
HALTERS
HALTING
HARTMAN
HASTENS
HASTIER
HASTILY
HASTING
HATTERS
HATTING
HAUTBOY
HAUTEUR
KAFTANS
LACTASE
LACTATE
LACTEAL
LACTOSE
LANTANA
LANTERN
LAOTIAN
LAPTOPS
LASTING
LASTORY
LATTENS
LATTICE
LAUTREC
MAITAIS
MAITRED
MALTEDS
MALTESE
MALTHUS
MALTIER
MALTING
MALTOSE
MANTELS
MANTLED
MANTLES
MANTRAP
MANTRAS
MANTRIC
MARTENS
MARTIAL
MARTIAN
MARTINA
MARTINI
MARTINO
MARTINS
MARTYRS
MASTABA
MASTERS
MASTERY
MASTICS
MASTIFF
MASTOID
MATTERS
MATTHAU
MATTHEW
MATTING
MATTOCK
MAYTIME
MAYTREE
NAPTIME
NARTHEX
NASTASE
NASTIER
NASTILY
NATTERS
NATTIER
NATTILY
OAKTREE
PALTERS
PALTROW
PANTHER
PANTING
PARTAKE
PARTIAL
PARTIED
PARTIER
PARTIES
PARTING
PARTITA
PARTITE
PARTNER
PARTOOK
PARTOUT
PARTWAY
PASTDUE
PASTELS
PASTERN
PASTEUP
PASTEUR
PASTIER
PASTIME
PASTINA
PASTING
PASTORS
PASTURE
PATTENS
PATTERN
PATTERS
PATTIES
PATTING
RAFTERS
RAFTING
RAGTIME
RAGTOPS
RANTERS
RANTING
RAPTORS
RAPTURE
RASTERS
RATTAIL
RATTANS
RATTERS
RATTIER
RATTING
RATTISH
RATTLED
RATTLER
RATTLES
RATTRAP
SALTBOX
SALTERS
SALTIER
SALTILY
SALTINE
SALTING
SALTISH
SANTAFE
SANTANA
SANTINI
SANTIRS
SAOTOME
SAUTEED
TACTFUL
TACTICS
TACTILE
TAGTEAM
TAMTAMS
TANTARA
TANTIVY
TANTRUM
TARTANS
TARTARE
TARTARS
TARTEST
TARTISH
TASTERS
TASTIER
TASTILY
TASTING
TATTERS
TATTIER
TATTILY
TATTING
TATTLED
TATTLER
TATTLES
TATTOOS
TAUTENS
TAUTEST
VANTAGE
VASTEST
VASTIER
VATTING
WAFTING
WAGTAIL
WAITERS
WAITFOR
WAITING
WAITOUT
WAITRON
WAITSON
WAITSUP
WALTERS
WALTZED
WALTZER
WALTZES
WANTADS
WANTING
WANTOUT
WANTSIN
WANTSTO
WARTHOG
WARTIER
WARTIME
WASTAGE
WASTERS
WASTING
WASTREL
WATTAGE
WATTEAU
WATTLES
XANTHAN
XANTHIC
YAHTZEE

•A••T••

BABETTE
BAINTER
BALATON
BARETTA
BARSTOW
BATHTUB
CADETTE
CAPITAL
CAPITAN
CAPITOL
CAPSTAN
CARLTON
CAROTID
CAUSTIC
CAVETTO
DAKOTAN
DAKOTAS
DALETHS
DAUNTED
DAYSTAR
FACETED
FAGOTED
FAINTED
FAINTER
FAINTLY
FAJITAS
FANATIC
FAULTED
FAUSTUS
GAGSTER
GALATEA
GALATIA
GAMETES
GANGTOK
GAUNTER
GAUNTLY
GAVOTTE
GAZETTE
HABITAT
HABITED
HABITUE
HALITES
HALSTON
HAMITES
HAMITIC
HAMITUP
HAMPTON
HAMSTER
HANGTEN
HARDTOP
HAUNTED
JACKTAR
JANITOR
JAUNTED
LAERTES
LAFITTE
LAKOTAS
LAMOTTA
LANGTRY
LAYETTE
LAYITON
MAESTRI
MAESTRO
MAHATMA
MAINTOP
MANATEE
MANITOU
MARITAL
NAMETAG
NANETTE
NAPHTHA
PAINTED
PAINTER
PAIUTES
PALATAL
PALATES
PALETTE
PALMTOP
PARATUS
RALSTON
RARITAN
RATATAT
RATITES
SAINTED
SAINTLY
SALUTED
SALUTES
SAMITES
SANCTUM
SAUNTER
TABITHA
TACITLY
TACITUS
TAINTED
TAKETEN
TANKTOP
TAPSTER
TAUNTED
VACATED
VACATES
VAULTED
VAULTER
VAUNTED
VAUNTER
WALSTON
WAPITIS
WASATCH
WASHTUB
YACHTED
YAKUTSK
YANGTZE
YANKTON
ZAPATEO
ZAPOTEC

•A•••T•

BABBITT
BABETTE
BALLETS
BALLOTS
BANDITO
BANDITS
BARENTS
BARETTA
BARRETT
BASALTS
BASKETS
BASSETS
BATISTA
BATISTE
BAUXITE
BAYCITY
CABLETV
CACHETS
CADETTE
CAHOOTS
CALCITE
CANASTA
CANTATA
CAPLETS
CAPNUTS
CARNETS
CARPETS
CARROTS
CASSATT
CATERTO
CAVEATS
CAVETTO
CAVORTS
DARESTO
EAGLETS
FACULTY
FALLSTO
FALSITY
FANJETS
FANOUTS
FATCATS
FATCITY
FATUITY
FAUCETS
FAWCETT
GADGETS
GADGETY
GALOOTS
GAMBITS
GANGSTA
GANNETS
GANNETT
GARNETS
GARRETS
GARRETT
GASJETS
GASKETS
GAVOTTE
GAZETTE
HACKETT
HAEMATO
HAMLETS
HAMMETT
HAUGHTY
HAVARTI
JACINTH
JACKETS
JADEITE
JAKARTA
JAPHETH
LABIATE
LABRETS
LACOSTE
LACTATE
LAFITTE
LAMENTS
LAMOTTA
LANCETS
LAPLATA
LAPORTE
LAPPETS
LARIATS
LATENTS
LAYETTE
LAYINTO
LAYOUTS
MACBETH
MACHETE
MAGENTA
MAGNATE
MAGNETO
MAGNETS
MAHOUTS
MAJESTE
MAJESTY
MALEATE
MALLETS
MAMMOTH
MANDATE
MAOISTS
MARCATO
MARGATE
MARKETS
MARMOTS
MASCOTS
NAHUATL
NAIVETE
NAIVETY
NANETTE
NARRATE
NAUGHTS
NAUGHTY
PACKETS
PALETTE
PALLETS
PALMATE
PANDITS
PAPEETE
PARENTS
PARGETS
PARROTS
PARTITA
PARTITE
PATENTS
PAUCITY
PAYOUTS
RABBETS
RABBITS
RABBITT
RACKETS
RADIATE
RAGOUTS
RAJPUTS
RALLYTO
RAMINTO
RAMJETS
RANINTO
RANLATE
RAWDATA
SABBATH
SACHETS
SALLETS
SAMLETS
SATIATE
SATIETY
SAVANTS
TABLETS
TAFFETA
TAKESTO
TALENTS
TALKSTO
TAOISTS
TAPINTO
TAPPETS
TARANTO
TARGETS
TARPITS
TAXRATE
VACUITY
VALUATE
VALVATE
VANUATU
VARIETY
VARLETS
VARSITY
WALCOTT
WALLETS
WALNUTS
WANTSTO
WARPATH

•A••••T

BABBITT
BABYSAT
BABYSIT
BACKBIT
BACKLIT
BACKOUT
BADDEST
BAILOUT
BALDEST
BALLAST
BANQUET
BAPTIST
BARKSAT

BARONET
BARRETT
BASEHIT
BASSIST
BATHMAT
BAWLOUT
BAYONET
CABARET
CABINET
CAGIEST
CAKIEST
CALLOUT
CALMEST
CALUMET
CALVERT
CAMELOT
CAMEOUT
CAMPOUT
CANIEST
CAPELET
CAPULET
CARCOAT
CARPORT
CARSEAT
CASHOUT
CASSATT
CASTOUT
CATBERT
CATBOAT
CATSUIT
DADAIST
DAFTEST
DAMPEST
DANKEST
DARKEST
DASBOOT
DATASET
EARHART
EARNEST
EARSHOT
EASEOUT
EASIEST
EATENAT
EATSOUT
FADDIST
FADEOUT
FAIREST
FALLOUT
FALSEST
FANBELT
FANSOUT
FAREAST
FARLEFT
FARMOUT
FARWEST
FASTEST
FATTEST
FAUVIST
FAWCETT
GABFEST
GALLANT
GAMIEST
GANNETT
GANTLET
GARMENT
GARRETT
GAVEOUT
HABITAT
HACKETT
HAIRCUT
HAIRNET
HALFWIT
HALIBUT
HAMMETT
HANDOUT
HANDSET
HANGOUT
HARDEST
HARDHAT
HARDHIT
HARDPUT
HARDSET
HARICOT
HARPIST
HARRIET
HARVEST
HATCHET
HAVENOT
HAYLOFT
HAZIEST
JACKPOT
JACONET
LABCOAT
LACIEST
LAIDOUT
LAKIEST
LAMAIST
LAMBENT
LAMBERT
LANDSAT
LANKEST
LAPBELT
LARGEST
LAUGHAT
LAURENT
LAWSUIT
LAYSOUT
LAZIEST
MADDEST
MADEOUT
MAEWEST
MAGINOT
MAIGRET
MAILLOT
MAILOUT
MAKEOUT
MAKESIT
MALLRAT
MANHUNT
MANUMIT
MANXCAT
MARGRET
MARXIST
MATELOT
MAZIEST
NAILSET
NASCENT
PACKRAT
PAGEANT
PAIDOUT
PALIEST
PALMIST
PANDECT
PANSOUT
PARAPET
PARFAIT
PARQUET
PARTOUT
PASSOUT
PATIENT
PATRIOT
PAULIST
PAWEDAT
PAYDIRT
PAYMENT
PAYSOUT
RABBITT
RACIEST
RACQUET
RADIANT
RAILSAT
RAIMENT
RAINHAT
RAINOUT
RAMPANT
RAMPART
RANGOUT
RANKEST
RANRIOT
RAPPORT
RAREBIT
RASHEST
RATATAT
RATBERT
RATCHET
SACKOUT
SADDEST
SALIENT
SANDLOT
SANGOUT
SAPIENT
SARGENT
SATINET
SAWDUST
TABORET
TAGGANT
TAGSOUT
TAKEOUT
TALKOUT
TALKSAT
TALLEST
TANGENT
TANNEST
TAPROOT
TAPSOUT
TARTEST
TAUTEST
VAGRANT
VAGUEST
VAINEST
VALIANT
VARIANT
VARMINT
VASTEST
WAITOUT
WALCOTT
WALKOUT
WALMART
WANIEST
WANNEST
WANTOUT
WARIEST
WARMEST
WARRANT
WASHOUT
WATCHIT
WAVELET
WAVIEST
WAXIEST
ZANIEST

••AT•••

ABATING
AMATEUR
AMATIVE
AMATORY
ANATOLE
ANATOMY
APATITE
ATATURK
AVATARS
BEATERS
BEATIFY
BEATING
BEATLES
BEATNIK
BEATOUT
BEATRIX
BEATSIT
BEATSME
BEATSUP
BEATTIE
BLATANT
BLATHER
BLATTED
BOATELS
BOATERS
BOATING
BOATMAN
BOATMEN
CHATEAU
CHATHAM
CHATSUP
CHATTED
CHATTEL
CHATTER
CLATTER
COATING
CRATERS
CRATING
DIATOMS
DRATTED
ELATERS
ELATING
ELATION
FEATHER
FEATURE
FIATLUX
FLATBED
FLATCAR
FLATLET
FLATOUT
FLATTAX
FLATTED
FLATTEN
FLATTER
FLATTOP
GOATEED
GOATEES
GOATISH
GRATERS
GRATIAS
GRATIFY
GRATING
HEATERS
HEATFUL
HEATHEN
HEATHER
HEATING
HEATSUP
HEATTER
IRATELY
IRATEST
KLATSCH
KRATERS
KRATION
LEATHER
LOATHED
LOATHES
MEATIER
MEATILY
NEATENS
NEATEST
ONATEAR
ORATING
ORATION
ORATORS
ORATORY
OVATION
PEATBOG
PEATIER
PLATEAU
PLATENS
PLATERS
PLATIER
PLATING
PLATOON
PLATTER
PLATYPI
PRATERS
PRATING
PRATTLE
SCATHED
SCATHES
SCATTED
SCATTER
SEATERS
SEATING
SEATTLE
SHATNER
SHATTER
SKATERS
SKATING
SLATHER
SLATIER
SLATING
SLATTED
SMATTER
SPATIAL
SPATTED
SPATTER
SPATULA
STATELY
STATICE
STATICS
STATING
STATION
STATIST
STATORS
STATUES
STATURE
STATUTE
SWATHED
SWATHES
SWATTED
SWATTER
TEATIME
TEATRAY
TEATREE
THATCHY
THATSIT
UPATREE
WEATHER
WHATFOR
WHATNOT
XRATING
YEATEAM

••A•T••

ACANTHI
ADAPTED
ADAPTER
ADAPTOR
AWAITED
BEASTIE
BEASTLY
BEATTIE
BLASTED
BLASTER
BLATTED
BOASTED
BOASTER
BRAXTON
CHANTED
CHANTER
CHANTEY
CHAOTIC
CHAPTER
CHARTED
CHARTER
CHASTEN
CHASTER
CHATTED
CHATTEL
CHATTER
CLAPTON
CLATTER
CLAYTON
COALTAR
COASTAL
COASTED
COASTER
CRAFTED
CRAFTER
CRAFTSY
DEALTIN
DEARTHS
DRAFTED
DRAFTEE
DRASTIC
DRATTED
ELASTIC
ENACTED
ENACTOR
EXACTAS
EXACTED
EXACTER
EXACTLY
EXACTOR
EXALTED
FEASTED
FLATTAX
FLATTED
FLATTEN
FLATTER
FLATTOP
FRACTAL
FRANTIC
GHASTLY
GOAFTER
GRAFTED
GRAFTON
GRANTED
GRANTEE
GRANTOR
HEALTHY
HEARTED
HEARTEN
HEARTHS
HEATTER
INAPTER
INAPTLY
INASTEW
LEANTOS
PHAETON
PHANTOM
PIASTER
PIASTRE
PLAITED
PLANTAR
PLANTED
PLANTER
PLASTER
PLASTIC
PLATTER
PLAUTUS
PRAETOR
PRATTLE
PSALTER
QUANTUM
QUARTER
QUARTET
QUARTOS
REACTED
REACTOR
REACTTO
REALTOR
RIANTLY
ROASTED
ROASTER
SCANTED
SCANTER
SCANTLY
SCATTED
SCATTER
SEASTAR
SEATTLE
SHAFTED
SHANTEY
SHASTRI
SHATTER
SLANTED
SLATTED
SLAYTON
SMALTOS
SMARTED
SMARTEN
SMARTER
SMARTLY
SMATTER
SPARTAN
SPATTED
SPATTER
STANTON
STARTED
STARTER
STARTLE
STARTUP
SWARTHY
SWATTED
SWATTER
TOASTED
TOASTER
TRACTOR
TRAITOR
UNAPTLY
WEALTHY
WHARTON
WRAITHS

••A••T•

ADAMITE
APATITE
CHALETS
CHAPATI
CHARITY
CLARETS
CLARITY
CRAVATS
DUALITY
EDACITY
EGALITE
EMANATE
FLAUNTS
FLAUNTY
FRAILTY
GEARSTO
GRANITE
GRAVITY
HEAVETO
IMAMATE
IMARETS
INANITY
KLAMATH
LEADSTO
ONADATE
OPACITY
PEANUTS
PLACATE
PLAINTS
PLANETS
PRAYSTO
QUALITY
REACTTO
REALITY
SEADUTY
SEAGATE
SNAPSTO
STARETS
STATUTE
SUAVITY
TEAPOTS
TEASETS
URANITE
ZEALOTS

••A•••T

ADAMANT
AGAINST
ANALYST
ANAPEST
ATAVIST
BEARCAT
BEAROUT
BEATOUT
BEATSIT
BLANKET
BLATANT
BRACKET
BRAVEST
CHAPLET
CHARIOT
CZARIST
DEADSET
DEAFEST
DEALOUT
DEAREST
DIALECT
DRAGNET
DRAGOUT
DRAUGHT
DRAWOUT
EMANANT
EPAULET
FLATLET
FLATOUT
FRAUGHT
GOABOUT
GRABSAT
GRAVEST
GRAYEST
HEADOUT
HEADSET
HEAROUT
INANEST
INASNIT
INASPOT
IRATEST
LEADOUT
LEAFLET
LEANEST
LEARJET
MEANEST
NEAREST
NEATEST
OFASORT
ONADIET
PEACOAT
PEASANT
PIANIST
PLACKET
PLANOUT
PLAUDIT
PLAYACT
PLAYLET
PLAYOUT
PLAYSAT
QUARTET
READMIT
READOUT
REAGENT
REALIST
SCARLET
SEAGIRT
SEALANT
SEAPORT
SEASALT
SHALLOT
SNAPSAT
SPAREST
STALEST
STAREAT
STARLET
STARLIT
STATIST
STAYPUT
SUAVEST
SWALLET
TEACART
TEAROUT
TEARSAT
THATSIT
TRABERT
TRANSIT
TSARIST
VIADUCT
WEAKEST
WEAROUT
WHATNOT
WYANDOT

•••AT••

ABLATED
ABLATES
ACHATES
AERATED
AERATES
AERATOR
AGNATES
ALSATIA
ANNATTO
AQUATIC
ASIATIC
ATLATLS
AVIATED
AVIATES
AVIATOR
BALATON
BELATED
BENATAR
BERATED
BERATES
BLEATED
BLOATED
BORATES
BREATHE
BREATHS
BREATHY
BYPATHS
CHEATED
CHEATER
CHEATIN
CREATED
CREATES
CREATOR
CROATIA
CURATES
CURATOR
DEBATED
DEBATER
DEBATES
DECATUR
DILATED
DILATES
DONATED
DONATES
DONATOR
EMPATHY
EQUATED
EQUATES
EQUATOR
ERGATES
ERRATIC
ERRATUM
ESTATES
FANATIC
FIXATED
FIXATES
FLOATED
FLOATER
GALATEA
GALATIA
GELATIN
GELATIS
GLOATED
GREATER
GREATLY
GYRATED
GYRATES
GYRATOR
HEPATIC
HORATIO
IDEATED
IDEATES
INMATES
IODATES
KERATIN
KOMATSU
LEGATEE
LEGATES
LEGATOS
LIGATED
LIGATES
LOCATED
LOCATER
LOCATES
LOCATOR
LUNATIC
LUXATED
LUXATES
MAHATMA
MANATEE
METATES
MUTATED
MUTATES
NEGATED
NEGATER
NEGATES
NEGATOR
NOTATED
NOTATES
NUTATED
NUTATES
OBLATES
OLEATES
OPIATES
ORGATES
PALATAL
PALATES
PARATUS
PENATES
PINATAS
PIRATED
PIRATES
PIRATIC
PLEATED
RATATAT
REBATED
REBATES
REDATED
REDATES
REGATTA
RELATED
RELATES
RERATED
RERATES
ROTATED
ROTATES
ROTATOR
RUBATOS
SCHATZI
SCRATCH
SEDATED
SEDATER
SEDATES
SENATES
SENATOR
SHEATHE
SHEATHS
SHIATSU
SINATRA
SOMATIC
SONATAS
SQUATLY
SQUATTY
STRATUM
STRATUS
SUMATRA
SWEATED
SWEATER
THEATER
THEATRE
TREATED
UNDATED
UNEATEN
UNLATCH
UNRATED
UNSATED
UPDATED
UPDATES
VACATED
VACATES
WASATCH
WHEATON
WREATHE
WREATHS
YUCATAN
ZAPATEO

•••A•T•

ABLAUTS
ALMAATA
ANDANTE
ANNATTO
ASHANTI
ASTARTE
ATLANTA
BASALTS
BREADTH
BREASTS
CANASTA
CHIANTI
DECANTS
DEFACTO
DEPARTS
DESALTS
DIDACTS
DOPANTS
DURANTE
DYNASTS
DYNASTY
ESPARTO
EXFACTO
EXPARTE
GOCARTS
GOKARTS
HAVARTI
HOGARTH
IMPACTS
IMPARTS
IMPASTO
INCANTS
INFANTA
INFANTS
INHASTE
JAKARTA
JOCASTA
KUWAITI
LEPANTO
LEVANTS
LOYALTY
MUTANTS
OBLASTS
OCTANTS
OTRANTO
OUTACTS
OXCARTS
PEDANTS
PENALTY
PICANTE
REBASTE
RECANTS
RECASTS
REDACTS
REDANTS
REGATTA
REPASTE
REPASTS
RESALTS
ROYALTY
SAVANTS
SECANTS
SQUANTO
SQUATTY
STEALTH
STRAITS
SUHARTO
SWEARTO
TARANTO
TENANTS
THWARTS
TRUANTS
TYRANTS
UMLAUTS
UNEARTH
VEDANTA

•••A••T

APPARAT
AQUAVIT
ASSAULT
ATFAULT
CABARET
COHABIT
DADAIST
DATASET
DEFAULT
EXHAUST
FLEAPIT
GERAINT
INHABIT
LAMAIST
MEGAHIT
MINARET
NOFAULT
NOTABIT
PARAPET
PITAPAT
RATATAT
RENAULT
REPAINT
SWEARAT
TUBAIST

••••AT•

ACETATE
ACTUATE
ADULATE
AGITATE
AGITATO
AIRDATE
ALMAATA
ANIMATE
ANIMATO
AUREATE
BENEATH
BOBCATS
BROMATE
CANTATA
CASSATT
CAVEATS
CHAPATI
CILIATE
CITRATE
CLIMATE
COGNATE
COLGATE
COLLATE
COMBATS
CORDATE
CRAVATS
CUTRATE
DEFEATS
DEFLATE
DENTATE
DEVIATE
DICTATE
DIKTATS
DOGMATA
DUEDATE
EDUCATE
ELEVATE
EMANATE
EMIRATE
EMULATE
EXPIATE
FATCATS
FERRATE
FOLIATE
FORMATS
FRIGATE
GESTATE
GOLIATH
HAEMATO
HEPCATS
HYDRATE
IMAMATE
IMITATE
INFLATE
INGRATE
INSTATE
ISOLATE
ITERATE
KKKKATY
KLAMATH
LABIATE
LACTATE
LAPLATA
LARIATS
LINEATE
LOQUATS
MAGNATE
MALEATE
MANDATE
MARCATO
MARGATE
MEDIATE
MIGRATE
MISDATE
MISMATE
MUDCATS
MUSCATS
NAHUATL
NARRATE
NEONATE
NEWGATE
NEWMATH
NITRATE
NOUGATS
NUMBATS
OBVIATE
ONADATE
OPERATE
ORGEATS
OUTEATS
OVERATE
PALMATE
PELTATE
PENNATE
PINNATE
PLACATE
PREDATE
PRELATE
PRIMATE
PRIVATE
PROBATE
PRORATA
PRORATE
PTBOATS
PULSATE
RADIATE
RANLATE
RAWDATA
RECOATS
REDHATS
REHEATS
REPEATS
REPLATE
RESEATS
RESTATE
REXCATS
ROSEATE
RUNLATE
SABBATH
SATIATE

SEAGATE
SENSATE
SERIATE
SERRATE
SFUMATO
SITUATE
SNOCATS
SORBATE
STOMATA
STRIATE
SULFATE
SUNBATH
TAXRATE
TERNATE
THREATS
THROATS
THROATY
TINHATS
TITRATE
TOCCATA
TOMCATS
TOPHATS
TOWPATH
ULULATE
UNCRATE
UNSEATS
UPBEATS
UPSTATE
VALUATE
VALVATE
VANUATU
VIBRATE
VIBRATO
VIOLATE
VITIATE
VULGATE
WARPATH
WOMBATS
ZERMATT

••••A•T

ABEYANT
ABREAST
ADAMANT
ANTIART
ARMYANT
ASPHALT
ATHEART
ATHWART
ATLEAST
ATTRACT
BALLAST
BELFAST
BITPART
BLATANT
BOMBAST
BUOYANT
BYHEART
CASSATT
CLIPART
COMPACT
CONTACT
COOLANT
COURANT
CURRANT
DEFIANT
DESCANT
DETRACT
DEVIANT
DISTANT
DOGCART
DORMANT
EARHART
ECKHART
ELEGANT
ELKHART
EMANANT
ENCHANT
ENGRAFT
ENTRANT
ETCHANT
EXTRACT
FAREAST
FINEART
FIREANT
FLYCAST
FLYPAST
FOLKART
FONDANT
GALLANT
GESTALT
GYMNAST
HYDRANT
IMPLANT
INEXACT
INSTANT
ITERANT
JUNKART
LENFANT
MEDIANT
MIDEAST
MIGRANT
MISCAST
MORDANT
NEWHART
OUTCAST
OUTLAST
OVERACT
OXIDANT
PAGEANT
PARFAIT
PEASANT
PECCANT
PENDANT
PENNANT
PIQUANT
PLAYACT
POPTART
PRECAST
RADIANT
RAMPANT
RAMPART
REDEALT
REENACT
REFRACT
REGNANT
RELIANT
REMNANT
REPLANT
RESTART
RETRACT
RIOTACT
SEALANT
SEASALT
SERVANT
SEXTANT
SPIRANT
STEWART
TAGGANT
TEACART
TOPMAST
ULULANT
UPDRAFT
UPSTART
USGRANT
VAGRANT
VALIANT
VARIANT
VERDANT
VIBRANT
WALMART
WARRANT
ZERMATT

•••••AT

ACROBAT
AEROBAT
AIMEDAT
AIRBOAT
APPARAT
ASTOLAT
AUTOMAT
BABYSAT
BARKSAT
BATHMAT
BEARCAT
BLINKAT
BODYFAT
BOXSEAT
CARCOAT
CARSEAT
CATBOAT
COMESAT
COONCAT
COPYCAT
DEEPFAT
DINGBAT
DOORMAT
DOWNPAT
DRIVEAT
EATENAT
ENTREAT
ESCHEAT
FLIESAT
FLOWNAT
FROWNAT
GOINGAT
GRABSAT
GUNBOAT
HABITAT
HARDHAT
HELLCAT
HIGHHAT
HINTSAT
HOOTSAT
HOTSEAT
ICEBOAT
JEERSAT
JETBOAT
JUMPSAT
KEEPSAT
KINGRAT
KUMQUAT
LABCOAT
LANDSAT
LAUGHAT
LEERSAT
LOOKSAT
LUNGEAT
MALLRAT
MANXCAT
MUSKRAT
NOSWEAT
NUTMEAT
OFFBEAT
OVEREAT
PACKRAT
PAWEDAT
PEACOAT
PECKSAT
PEEKSAT
PEERSAT
PICKSAT
PITAPAT
PLAYSAT
POKEDAT
POKESAT
POLECAT
PREHEAT
RAILSAT
RAINHAT
RATATAT
REDCOAT
REDHEAT
REDMEAT
RETREAT
RICERAT
ROWBOAT
SHOOTAT
SILKHAT
SNAPSAT
SNEERAT
SNIFFAT
SNIPEAT
SNOWCAT
STAREAT
SURCOAT
SWEARAT
SWOREAT
TALKSAT
TEARSAT
THEREAT
TOPCOAT
TREERAT
TUGBOAT
WHEREAT
WILDCAT
WINKSAT
YELLSAT

AU•••••

AUBADES
AUBURNS
AUCTION
AUDIBLE
AUDIBLY
AUDILES
AUDITED
AUDITOR
AUDUBON
AUGENDS
AUGMENT
AUGURAL
AUGURED
AUGUSTA
AUGUSTE
AUKLETS
AUNTIES
AUPAIRS
AURALEE
AURALLY
AUREATE
AUREOLA
AUREOLE
AURICLE
AUROCHS
AURORAE
AURORAL
AURORAS
AUSPICE
AUSSIES
AUSTERE
AUSTRAL
AUSTRIA
AUTARKY
AUTEURS
AUTHORS
AUTOMAT
AUTUMNS

A•U••••

ABUBAKR
ABUSERS
ABUSING
ABUSIVE
ABUTTAL
ABUTTED
ACUMENS
ACUTELY
ADULATE
ADULTLY
ALUMNAE
ALUMNAL
ALUMNUS
ALUNSER
AMULETS
AMUSING
AOUDADS
AQUARIA
AQUATIC
AQUAVIT
AQUEOUS
AQUIFER
AQUINAS
AQUIVER
ARUGULA
ASUNDER
ASUSUAL
AVULSED
AVULSES
AZURITE

A••U•••

ABDUCTS
ABJURED
ABJURES
ABOUGHT
ABOUNDS
ABRUZZI
ACCURST
ACCUSED
ACCUSER
ACCUSES
ACQUIRE
ACQUITS
ACTUARY
ACTUATE
ACTUPON
ADDUCED
ADDUCES
ADDUCTS
ADDUPTO
ADJUDGE
ADJUNCT
ADJURED
ADJURES
ADJUSTS
AGOUTIS
ALBUMEN
ALBUMIN
ALBUNDY
ALLUDED
ALLUDES
ALLURED
ALLURES
ALLUVIA
AMOUNTS
AMPULES
ANGULAR
ANNUALS
ANNUITY
ANNULAR
ANNULUS
ANOUILH
ARBUTUS
ARDUOUS
ARGUERS
ARGUING
ARMURES
AROUSAL
AROUSED
AROUSES
ASSUAGE
ASSUMED
ASSUMES
ASSURED
ASSURES
ATTUCKS
ATTUNED
ATTUNES
AUBURNS
AUDUBON
AUGURAL
AUGURED
AUGUSTA
AUGUSTE
AUTUMNS
AWFULLY

A•••U••

ABLAUTS
ACCOUNT
ACCRUAL
ACCRUED
ACCRUES
ACHTUNG
ADJOURN
AGROUND
AIRGUNS
AIRPUMP
ALARUMS
AMPOULE
ANAHUAC
ARAFURA
ARBOURS
ARDOURS
ARMFULS
ARMOURS
ARMOURY
ARUGULA
ASARULE
ASHBURY
ASSAULT
ASTOUND
ASUSUAL
ASYLUMS
ATATURK
ATFAULT
ATRIUMS
AUTEURS
AVENUES
AZIMUTH

A••••U•

ABSOLUT
ACEDOUT
ACESOUT
ACTEDUP
ACTFOUR
ACTSOUT
ADDEDUP
AIRSOUT
ALUMNUS
ALYSSUM
AMADEUS
AMATEUR
AMIBLUE
AMOROUS
ANGELUS
ANNULUS
ANTAEUS
ANTEDUP
ANTESUP
ANTIGUA
ANTIQUE
ANXIOUS
APERCUS
APPLAUD
AQUEOUS
ARBUTUS
ARCANUM
ARDUOUS
AREARUG
ARTEMUS
ASKSOUT
ATISSUE
ATTICUS

A•••••U

ANGELOU

•AU••••

BAUBLES
BAUHAUS
BAULKED
BAUXITE
CAUDLES
CAULKED
CAULKER
CAUSING
CAUSTIC
CAUTION
DAUBERS
DAUBING
DAUMIER
DAUNTED
DAUPHIN
FAUCETS
FAULTED
FAUSTUS
FAUVISM
FAUVIST
FAUXPAS
GAUCHER
GAUCHOS
GAUDIER
GAUDILY
GAUGERS
GAUGING
GAUGUIN
GAULISH
GAUMING
GAUNTER
GAUNTLY
GAUTAMA
GAUZIER
GAUZILY
HAUBERK
HAUGHTY
HAULAGE
HAULERS
HAULING
HAULOFF
HAULSUP
HAUNTED
HAUTBOY
HAUTEUR
JAUNTED
KAUFMAN
LAUDING
LAUGHAT
LAUGHED
LAUGHER
LAUGHIN
LAUNDER
LAUNDRY
LAURELS
LAURENT
LAUTREC
MAUDLIN
MAUGHAM
MAULDIN
MAULING
MAUMAUS
MAUNDER
MAUREEN
MAURICE
MAUROIS
NAUGHTS
NAUGHTY
PAUCITY
PAULINA
PAULINE
PAULING
PAULIST
PAULSEN
PAUNCHY
PAUPERS
PAUSING
RAUCOUS
SAUCERS
SAUCIER
SAUCILY
SAUNTER
SAURIAN
SAUSAGE
SAUTEED
TAUNTED
TAURINE
TAUTENS
TAUTEST
VAUGHAN
VAULTED
VAULTER
VAUNTED
VAUNTER
YAUPONS

•A•U•••

CADUCEI
CALUMET
CALUMNY
CAPULET
CASUALS
CAYUGAS
CAYUSES
FACULAE
FACULTY
FAMULUS
FATUITY
FATUOUS
GALUMPH
GAZUMPS
HANUKAH
JACUZZI
JAGUARS
JANUARY
KABUKIS
KAHUNAS
LACUNAE
LACUNAL
LACUNAS
LAGUNAS
MACULAE
MAGUEYS
MAGUIRE
MANUALS
MANUMIT
MATURED
MATURER
MATURES
MAZURKA
NAHUATL
NATURAL
NATURED
NATURES
PABULUM
PADUANS
PADUCAH
PAIUTES
PANURGE
PAPUANS
PARURES
RADULAE
SAGUARO
SALUKIS
SALUTED
SALUTES
SAMURAI
TABULAR
TALUSES
VACUITY
VACUOLE
VACUOUS
VACUUMS
VAGUELY
VAGUEST
VALUATE
VALUING
VANUATU
VAQUERO
YAKUTSK
YAKUZAS
YAOUNDE

•A••U••

BACKUPS
BADGUYS
BAGFULS
BANQUET
BARBUDA
BASQUES
BATTUES
CADBURY
CAESURA
CAIQUES
CANFULS
CAPFULS
CAPGUNS
CAPNUTS
CAPSULE
CAPTURE
CARFULS
CAROUSE
CASQUED
CASQUES
CATSUIT
DANBURY
DASYURE
EARFULS
EARMUFF
FACTUAL
FAILURE
FANOUTS
FAVOURS
GAGRULE
GASPUMP
GAUGUIN
HAMBURG
HANGUPS
HARBURG
JACCUSE
JACQUES
JARFULS
LABOURS
LACQUER
LANGUID
LANGUOR
LANGURS
LAPFULS
LARRUPS
LASHUPS
LAWSUIT
LAYOUTS
MACDUFF
MAGNUMS
MAHOUTS
MAJEURE
MAKEUPS
MANHUNT
MARAUDS
MARKUPS
MARQUEE
MARQUES
MARQUEZ
MARQUIS
MASQUES
PABLUMS
PANFULS
PARQUET
PASTURE
PAYOUTS
RACQUET
RAGOUTS
RAGRUGS
RAJPUTS
RAPTURE
RAVEUPS
RAYBURN
RAYGUNS
SACQUES
SAMSUNG
SANJUAN
SANLUIS
SATSUMA
SAVOURS
SAVOURY
SAWBUCK
SAWDUST
TALCUMS
VACUUMS
VALOURS
VAPOURS
VATFULS
WALKUPS
WALNUTS
WARMUPS
WASHUPS
YANQUIS

•A•••U•

BACCHUS
BACKOUT
BACKRUB
BACKSUP
BAILOUT
BALEFUL
BALFOUR
BALLSUP
BANEFUL
BANGSUP
BAROQUE
BASHFUL
BATEAUX
BATHTUB
BAUHAUS
BAWLOUT
CACHOUS
CADMIUM
CAESIUM
CALCIUM
CALHOUN
CALLOUS
CALLOUT
CALLSUP
CAMBIUM
CAMEDUE
CAMEOUT
CAMPOUT
CANDOUR
CANOPUS
CAREFUL
CAROLUS
CASHOUT
CASSIUS
CASTOUT
CATCHUP
DANSEUR
DAREFUL
EARDRUM
EARPLUG
EASEDUP
EASEFUL
EASEOUT
EASESUP
EATENUP
EATSOUT
FACTFUL
FADEOUT
FAIRSUP
FAKEFUR
FALLGUY
FALLOUT
FAMULUS
FANCLUB
FANSOUT
FARMOUT
FATEFUL
FATIGUE
FATUOUS
FAUSTUS
GAINFUL
GALLIUM
GANGSUP
GASEOUS
GATEAUX
GAVEOUT
HABITUE
HAFNIUM
HAHNIUM
HAIRCUT
HALIBUT
HAMITUP
HANDFUL
HANDGUN
HANDOUT
HANDSUP
HANGOUT
HANGSUP
HARBOUR
HARDPUT
HARMFUL
HATEFUL
HAULSUP
HAUTEUR
JABIRUS
JACKSUP
KARAKUL
KARAKUM
LACEDUP
LACESUP
LADYBUG
LAIDOUT
LALIQUE
LANDAUS
LASCAUX
LAYSOUT
LAZARUS
MACAQUE
MADEOUT
MAILOUT
MAKEOUT
MAKESUP
MALAMUD
MALRAUX
MALTHUS
MANAGUA
MANHOUR
MARGAUX
MARKSUP
MASSEUR
MATCHUP
MAUMAUS
MAXIMUM
MAXIMUS
NATRIUM
PABULUM
PACKSUP
PAGEFUL
PAIDOUT
PAILFUL
PAILOUS
PAINFUL
PAIRSUP
PALLIUM
PANSOUT
PAPYRUS
PARATUS
PARLOUR
PARLOUS
PARTOUT
PASSEUL
PASSOUT
PASTDUE
PASTEUP
PASTEUR
PATCHUP
PAVIOUR
PAYSOUT
RACKSUP
RAGEFUL
RAINOUT
RAISEUP
RAKEDUP
RAKESUP
RANCOUR
RANGOUT
RAPANUI
RAUCOUS
SACKFUL
SACKOUT
SANCTUM
SANGOUT
SAVEDUP
SAVESUP
SAVIOUR
TACITUS
TACTFUL
TAGSOUT
TAKEOUT
TAKESUP
TALKOUT
TALKSUP
TALLYUP
TAMBOUR
TANKFUL
TANKSUP
TANTRUM
TAPSOUT
VACUOUS
VARIOUS
WAILFUL
WAITOUT
WAITSUP
WAKEFUL
WAKESUP
WALKOUT
WALLSUP
WANTOUT
WARMSUP
WASHOUT
WASHTUB
YAWNFUL

•A••••U

BABASSU
CARIBOU
LAMBEAU
MANITOU
MARABOU
MARCEAU
MARYLOU
MATTHAU
PARVENU
RAMBEAU
TABLEAU
VANUATU
WATTEAU

••AU•••

BEAUISH
CHAUCER
CLAUDIA
CLAUDIO
CLAUSES
DRAUGHT
EPAULET
FLAUNTS
FLAUNTY
FRAUGHT
PLAUDIT
PLAUTUS
STAUNCH
TRAUMAS
WHAUDEN

••A•U••

ALARUMS
ANAHUAC
ARAFURA
ASARULE
ATATURK
BLACULA
BRAVURA
CLAQUES
DRACULA
EMANUEL
ERASURE
EVACUEE
FEATURE
GRADUAL
GRANULE
GRAVURE
INARUSH
JOAQUIN
LEAGUES
MEASURE
OPAQUES
PEANUTS
PLAGUED
PLAGUES
PLAQUES
SCAPULA
SEADUTY
SEAGULL
SNAFUED
SPATULA
STATUES
STATURE
STATUTE
TEACUPS
TRADUCE
ULALUME
UNAMUNO
VIADUCT
WRAPUPS

••A••U•

AMADEUS
AMATEUR
BEADSUP
BEAMSUP
BEARCUB
BEARHUG
BEAROUT
BEARSUP
BEATOUT
BEATSUP
BRACEUP
CHALKUP
CHATSUP
CLAMOUR
CLAMSUP
CRACKUP
CRANIUM
CRANKUP
CRASSUS
DEALOUT
DRAGOUT
DRAWNUP
DRAWOUT
DRAWSUP
ELAAIUN
ENAMOUR
ERASMUS
FEARFUL
FIATLUX
FLANEUR
FLAREUP
FLATOUT
FLAVOUR
FRAMEUP
GEARSUP
GLAMOUR
GOABOUT
GRAMPUS
GUARGUM
HEADOUT
HEADSUP
HEAROUT
HEATFUL
HEATSUP
JEALOUS
JEANLUC
LEADOUT
LEADSUP

MOANFUL
PEASOUP
PLANOUT
PLAUTUS
PLAYFUL
PLAYOUT
PLAYSUP
QUANTUM
READOUT
REARGUE
REARSUP
SCAREUP
SEABLUE
SEALSUP
SEASLUG
SHAKEUP
SHAPEUP
SMASHUP
SNAPSUP
SOAKSUP
STACKUP
STADIUM
STANDUP
STARTUP
STAYPUT
STAYSUP
TEAMSUP
TEARFUL
TEAROUT
TEARSUP
TRADEUP
TRAYFUL
UNAWFUL
URANIUM
WEAROUT
WRAPSUP
ZEALOUS

••A•••U
CHAPEAU
CHATEAU
NEARYOU
PLATEAU

•••AU••
ABLAUTS
ASSAULT
ATFAULT
BECAUSE
BEDAUBS
DEBAUCH
DEFAULT
DEGAUSS
EXHAUST
INHAULS
KILAUEA
MARAUDS
NOFAULT
RENAULT
STRAUSS
UMLAUTS

•••A•U•
ANTAEUS
ARCANUM
AREARUG
BELAKUN
BREAKUP
CLEANUP
CLEARUP
DECATUR
DEDALUS
DEVALUE
DONAHUE
DREAMUP
ELAAIUN
ERRATUM
HUMANUM
INVACUO
KARAKUL
KARAKUM
LAZARUS
MACAQUE
MALAMUD
MANAGUA
OCEANUS
ORGANUM
PARATUS
PEGASUS
PIRAEUS
PYRAMUS
RAPANUI
REVALUE
SPEAKUP
STRATUM
STRATUS
TETANUS

•••A••U
BABASSU
KOMATSU
MARABOU
SHIATSU

••••AU•
APPLAUD
BATEAUX
BAUHAUS
BUREAUS
CENTAUR
DEFRAUD
GATEAUX
IBNSAUD
LANDAUS
LASCAUX
LESPAUL
MALRAUX
MARGAUX
MAUMAUS
MILHAUD
RIMBAUD
TUSSAUD

••••A•U
VANUATU

•••••AU
CHAPEAU
CHATEAU
COCTEAU
FRENEAU
HOFBRAU
LAMBEAU
MARCEAU
MATTHAU
NOUVEAU
PLATEAU
RAMBEAU
RONDEAU
TABLEAU
THOREAU
TONNEAU
TRUDEAU
WATTEAU

AV•••••
AVAILED
AVARICE
AVATARS
AVENGED
AVENGER
AVENGES
AVENUES
AVERAGE
AVERRED
AVERTED
AVIANCA
AVIATED
AVIATES
AVIATOR
AVIDITY
AVIGNON
AVOCADO
AVOCETS
AVOIDED
AVONLEA
AVOWALS
AVOWERS
AVOWING
AVULSED
AVULSES

A•V••••
ADVANCE
ADVENTS
ADVERBS
ADVERSE
ADVERTS
ADVISED
ADVISER
ADVISES
ADVISOR
ALVAREZ
ALVEOLI

A••V•••
ATAVISM
ATAVIST

A•••V••
ACTIVES
ALCOVES
ALLOVER
ALLUVIA
ANDOVER
AQUAVIT
AQUIVER
ARGIVES
ARRIVAL
ARRIVED
ARRIVER
ARRIVES

A••••V•
ABSOLVE
ABUSIVE
ACHIEVE
ACTFIVE
AIRWAVE
AMATIVE
ANCHOVY
APPROVE
ARCHIVE

•AV••••
BAVARIA
CAVALRY
CAVEATS
CAVEDIN
CAVEINS
CAVEMAN
CAVEMEN
CAVERNS
CAVESIN
CAVETTO
CAVIARS
CAVILED
CAVILER
CAVORTS
DAVINCI
FAVORED
FAVOURS
GAVELED
GAVEOFF
GAVEOUT
GAVEWAY
GAVIALS
GAVOTTE
HAVARTI
HAVENOT
HAVERED
JAVAMAN
JAVELIN
LAVALSE
LAVERNE
LAVINIA
NAVAHOS
NAVAJOS
NAVARRE
NAVVIES
PAVANES
PAVIOUR
PAVLOVA
RAVAGED
RAVAGER
RAVAGES
RAVELED
RAVENED
RAVENNA
RAVEUPS
RAVINES
RAVINGS
RAVIOLI
SAVABLE
SAVAGED
SAVAGER
SAVAGES
SAVALAS
SAVANNA
SAVANTS
SAVARIN
SAVEDUP
SAVELOY
SAVESUP
SAVINGS
SAVIORS
SAVIOUR
SAVORED
SAVOURS
SAVOURY
SAVVIER
SAVVILY
TAVERNS
WAVEDIN
WAVELET
WAVEOFF
WAVERED
WAVERER
WAVESIN
WAVIEST

•A•V•••
CALVARY
CALVERT
CALVING
CANVASS
CARVERS
CARVING
FAUVISM
FAUVIST
GALVANI
HALVAHS
HALVING
HARVARD
HARVEST
JANVIER
JAYVEES
LATVIAN
MARVELS
NAIVELY
NAIVETE
NAIVETY
NAVVIES
PARVENU
SALVAGE
SALVERS
SALVIAS
SALVING
SALVOES
SALVORS
SAVVIER
SAVVILY
VALVATE
WAIVERS
WAIVING

•A••V••
CARAVAN
CARAVEL
CASAVAS
HANOVER
LAYOVER
NATIVES
PALAVER
RANOVER
RAYOVAC
SAMOVAR

•A•••V•
BAKLAVA
CAPTIVE
CASSAVA
MARKOVA
MASSIVE
PAHLAVI
PASSIVE
PAVLOVA
TANTIVY

•A••••V
CABLETV
NABOKOV

••AV•••
ATAVISM
ATAVIST
BEAVERS
BRAVADO
BRAVELY
BRAVERY
BRAVEST
BRAVING
BRAVOES
BRAVURA
CLAVELL
CLAVIER
CRAVATS
CRAVENS
CRAVERS
CRAVING
FLAVORS
FLAVOUR
GRAVELS
GRAVELY
GRAVERS
GRAVEST
GRAVIES
GRAVING
GRAVITY
GRAVURE
HEAVEHO
HEAVENS
HEAVERS
HEAVETO
HEAVIER
HEAVIES
HEAVILY
HEAVING
KNAVERY
KNAVISH
LEAVEIN
LEAVENS
LEAVING
PEAVEYS
QUAVERS
QUAVERY
REAVAIL
SHAVERS
SHAVING
SLAVERS
SLAVERY
SLAVEYS
SLAVING
SLAVISH
SPAVINS
STAVING
SUAVELY
SUAVEST
SUAVITY
TRAVAIL
TRAVELS
TRAVERS
TRAVOIS
UNAVOCE
WEAVERS
WEAVING

••A•V••
DWARVES
SCARVES
STARVED
STARVES
WHARVES

••A••V•
AMATIVE
EVASIVE
IVANOVO
ULANOVA

•••AV••
AQUAVIT
BEHAVED
BEHAVES
CARAVAN
CARAVEL
CASAVAS
CLEAVED
CLEAVER
CLEAVES
CLEAVON
DISAVOW
GREAVES
INFAVOR
LEHAVRE
MCGAVIN
MORAVIA
OCTAVES
OCTAVIA
OCTAVOS
PALAVER
REPAVED
REPAVES
SHEAVED
SHEAVES
TELAVIV
UNPAVED
UNRAVEL
VISAVIS
ZOUAVES

•••A•V•
BIVALVE

•••A••V
ROMANOV
TELAVIV
ULYANOV

••••AV•
AIRWAVE
BAKLAVA
BEREAVE
CASSAVA
CENTAVO
CONCAVE
DEPRAVE
ENCLAVE
ENGRAVE
ENSLAVE
FORGAVE
NEWWAVE
ONLEAVE
PAHLAVI
REWEAVE
UNWEAVE

AW•••••
AWAITED
AWAKENS
AWAKING
AWARDED
AWARDEE
AWARDER
AWAREOF
AWELESS
AWESOME
AWFULLY
AWKWARD
AWNINGS
AWNLESS

A•W••••
ALWORTH
ATWORST

A••W•••
AIRWAVE
AIRWAYS
AIRWOLF
ALEWIFE
ANSWERS
ANTWERP
ARAWAKS
ARTWARE
ARTWORK
ATHWART
AVOWALS
AVOWERS
AVOWING
AWKWARD

A•••W••
ALLOWAY
ALLOWED
ANTIWAR
ARCHWAY
AREAWAY

A••••W•
ANDREWS
ANTCOWS

A•••••W
AIRCREW
AIRFLOW
AIRSHOW
ASOFNOW
ATECROW

•AW••••
BAWDIER
BAWDILY
BAWLERS
BAWLING
BAWLOUT
DAWDLED
DAWDLER
DAWDLES
DAWKISH
DAWNING
DAWNSON
FAWCETT
FAWNERS
FAWNING
GAWKERS
GAWKIER
GAWKILY
GAWKING
GAWKISH
GAWPING
HAWHAWS
HAWKERS
HAWKEYE
HAWKING
HAWKINS
HAWKISH
HAWSERS
JAWBONE
JAWLESS
JAWLIKE
JAWLINE
LAWFORD
LAWLESS
LAWLIKE
LAWSUIT
LAWYERS
MAWKISH
PAWEDAT
PAWKIER
PAWNEES
PAWNERS
PAWNING
PAWNOFF
PAWPAWS
RAWDATA
RAWDEAL
RAWEGGS
RAWHIDE
RAWNESS
RAWSILK
SAWBUCK
SAWDUST
SAWFISH
SAWLIKE
SAWLOGS
SAWMILL
SAWWOOD
SAWYERS
TAWNIER
TAWNILY
YAWNERS
YAWNFUL
YAWNING
YAWPERS
YAWPING

•A•W•••
BARWARE
BATWING
CARWASH
CATWALK
DAGWOOD
EARWIGS
FALWELL
FARWEST
FAYWRAY
HAYWARD
HAYWIRE
JAYWALK
LAPWING
MAEWEST
MAXWELL
MAYWINE
NARWALS
NARWHAL
RAGWEED
SAWWOOD
SAYWHEN
WARWICK
WAXWING
WAXWORK
WAYWARD
WAYWORN

•A••W••
BALDWIN
CARAWAY
CATAWBA
EATAWAY
FAIRWAY
FARAWAY
GANGWAY
GATEWAY
GAVEWAY
HALFWAY
HALFWIT
HALLWAY
HARDWON
JANEWAY
LAYAWAY
MADEWAY
MAKEWAY
MANOWAR
MATEWAN
PARKWAY
PARTWAY
PATHWAY
RACEWAY
RAILWAY
RANAWAY
SARAWAK
TAXIWAY
WALKWAY

•A•••W•
BARNOWL
BARROWS
CASHEWS
FALLOWS
FARROWS
GAGLAWS
HALLOWS
HARROWS
HAWHAWS
HAYMOWS
LAYDOWN
MALLOWS
MARLOWE
MARROWS
MATHEWS
NARROWS
OAKLAWN
PAWPAWS
RANDOWN
SALLOWS
SATDOWN
TALLOWS
WALLOWS
YARROWS

•A••••W
BANDSAW
BARSTOW
CAPSHAW
CASELAW
CASHCOW
CATSHOW
CATSPAW
DANELAW
EATCROW
GAMELAW
GANGSAW
HACKSAW
HANDSAW
JACKDAW
LAIDLOW
LAYSLOW
MACGRAW
MANILOW
MATTHEW
PALTROW
RAINBOW
SAGINAW
SALCHOW

••AW•••
ARAWAKS
BRAWLED
BRAWLER
CLAWERS
CLAWING
CRAWDAD
CRAWLED
CRAWLER
DRAWBAR
DRAWERS
DRAWING
DRAWLED
DRAWNIN
DRAWNON
DRAWNUP
DRAWOUT
DRAWSIN
DRAWSON
DRAWSUP
FLAWING
FRAWLEY
GNAWERS
GNAWING
INAWEOF
INAWORD
SEAWALL
SEAWARD
SEAWAYS
SEAWEED
SEAWOLF
SHAWNEE
SHAWWAL
SPAWNED
THAWING
TRAWLED
TRAWLER
UNAWARE
UNAWFUL

••A•W••
HEADWAY
ROADWAY
SHAWWAL

••A••W•
MEADOWS
MEADOWY
PEAFOWL
SEACOWS
SHADOWS
SHADOWY

••A•••W
BEARPAW
GLASGOW
INASTEW
SHALLOW
SPARROW
SWALLOW

•••AW••
AREAWAY
CARAWAY
CATAWBA
CUTAWAY
DUNAWAY
EATAWAY
FARAWAY
FLYAWAY
GETAWAY
GOTAWAY
LAYAWAY
MOHAWKS
OTTAWAS
PESAWAS
PUTAWAY
RANAWAY
RESAWED
RUNAWAY
SARAWAK
SCRAWLS
SCRAWLY
SCRAWNY
SPRAWLS
SQUAWKS
SQUAWKY
TOWAWAY

•••A•W•
ROYALWE

•••A••W
DISAVOW

••••AW•
BOWSAWS
CUSHAWS
GAGLAWS
GEEGAWS
GEWGAWS
GOSHAWK
GUFFAWS
HAWHAWS
HEEHAWS
JIGSAWS
OAKLAWN
OKINAWA
OLDSAWS
OUTLAWS
OVERAWE
PAWPAWS
PITSAWS
PREDAWN
REDRAWN
REDRAWS
RIPSAWS
SEESAWS
UNDRAWN

•••••AW
BANDSAW
BEARPAW
BLUELAW
BUCKSAW
BUZZSAW
CAPSHAW
CASELAW
CATSPAW
CHOCTAW
DANELAW
DEWCLAW
FOREPAW
FORESAW
FRETSAW
GAMELAW
GANGSAW
HACKSAW
HANDSAW
JACKDAW
MACGRAW
OUTDRAW
OVERSAW
SAGINAW
TRISHAW
WHIPSAW

AX•••••
AXIALLY
AXILLAE
AXOLOTL
AXSEEDS

A•X••••
ANXIETY
ANXIOUS

A••X•••
ABEXTRA

A•••X••
ADMIXED
ADMIXES
AFFIXED
AFFIXES
ANNEXED
ANNEXES

A••••X•
AIRTAXI

A•••••X
ALTOSAX
ANTITAX

•AX••••
LAXNESS
MAXBAER
MAXBORN
MAXILLA
MAXIMAL
MAXIMUM
MAXIMUS
MAXWELL
SAXHORN
TAXABLE
TAXFREE
TAXICAB
TAXIING
TAXIMAN
TAXIMEN
TAXIWAY
TAXLESS
TAXRATE
WAXBEAN
WAXIEST
WAXLIKE
WAXWING
WAXWORK

•A•X•••
BAUXITE
FAUXPAS
MANXCAT
MANXMAN
MANXMEN
MARXISM
MARXIST

•A••X••
CALYXES
LATEXES
RADIXES

•A••••X
BANDBOX
BATEAUX
CAKEMIX
CALLBOX
CASHBOX
GATEAUX
HALIFAX
LASCAUX
MADAMEX
MAILBOX
MALRAUX
MARGAUX
NARTHEX
PANCHAX
PARADOX
SALTBOX
SANDBOX

••AX•••
BRAXTON
COAXERS
COAXIAL
COAXING
FLAXIER
HOAXERS
HOAXING
KLAXONS

••A•••X
BEATRIX
FIATLUX
FLATTAX
GEARBOX
PHALANX
PHARYNX
REAFFIX
SOAPBOX
SPANDEX

•••AX••
HYRAXES
ICEAXES
RELAXED
RELAXES
RETAXED
RETAXES
REWAXED
REWAXES

•••A••X
BETAMAX
BROADAX
MADAMEX
MIRAMAX
PARADOX

••••AX•
AIRTAXI
PICKAXE
POLEAXE

••••A•X
BATEAUX
GATEAUX
LASCAUX
MALRAUX
MARGAUX
PHALANX

•••••AX
ALTOSAX
ANTITAX
BEESWAX
BETAMAX
BROADAX
CINEMAX
FLATTAX
HALIFAX
MIRAMAX
OVERTAX
PANCHAX
POLLTAX

AY•••••
AYEAYES
AYKROYD
AYNRAND

A•Y••••
ABYSMAL
ABYSSES
ALYKHAN
ALYOSHA
ALYSSUM
AMYLASE
ANYBODY
ANYMORE
ANYONES
ANYROAD
ANYTIME
ASYLUMS

A••Y•••
ABEYANT

ACRYLIC
ALLYING
ALLYSON
ARGYLES
ARMYANT
ASSYRIA

A•••Y••
ACOLYTE
ALLAYED
ALLAYER
ALLEYES
ALLOYED
ANALYSE
ANALYST
ANALYZE
ANNOYED
ANODYNE
ANONYMS
ARRAYED
ARROYOS
ASSAYED
ASSAYER
AYEAYES
AZODYES

A••••Y•
ACRONYM
AFFRAYS
AIRWAYS
ANTONYM
AYKROYD

A•••••Y
ABBOTCY
ABIDEBY
ABILITY
ACADEMY
ACIDIFY
ACIDITY
ACRIDLY
ACTUARY
ACUTELY
ADEPTLY
ADULTLY
AFFABLY
AGILELY
AGILITY
AIRPLAY
ALBUNDY
ALCHEMY
ALERTLY
ALIMONY
ALLENBY
ALLERGY
ALLOWAY
ALOOFLY
ALREADY
AMATORY
AMENITY
AMIABLY
AMNESTY
AMPLIFY
AMSCRAY
ANALOGY
ANARCHY
ANATOMY
ANCHOVY
ANGRILY
ANNUITY
ANOMALY
ANTHONY
ANXIETY
ANYBODY
APISHLY
APLENTY
APOLOGY
ARCHERY
ARCHWAY
ARDENCY
AREAWAY
ARIDITY
ARMOURY
ASHBURY
ASHTRAY
ATROPHY
ATTABOY
AUDIBLY
AURALLY
AUTARKY
AVIDITY
AWFULLY
AXIALLY

•AY••••
BAYCITY
BAYLEAF
BAYONET
CAYENNE
CAYMANS
CAYUGAS
CAYUSES
DAYBEDS
DAYBOOK
DAYBOYS
DAYCAMP
DAYCARE
DAYJOBS
DAYLILY
DAYLONG
DAYMARE
DAYROOM
DAYSINN
DAYSTAR
DAYTIME
DAYTONA
DAYTRIP
FAYWRAY
HAYFORK
HAYLOFT
HAYMOWS
HAYRACK
HAYRIDE
HAYSEED
HAYWARD
HAYWIRE
JAYBIRD
JAYCEES
JAYLENO
JAYVEES
JAYWALK
KAYAKED
KAYAKER
KAYOING
LAYAWAY
LAYBACK
LAYDOWN
LAYERED
LAYETTE
LAYINTO
LAYITON
LAYOFFS
LAYOPEN
LAYOUTS
LAYOVER
LAYSFOR
LAYSLOW
LAYSOFF
LAYSOUT
MAYALIN
MAYDAYS
MAYFAIR
MAYHEMS
MAYNARD
MAYORAL
MAYPOLE
MAYTIME
MAYTREE
MAYWINE
NAYSAID
NAYSAYS
PAYABLE
PAYCASH
PAYDAYS
PAYDIRT
PAYLOAD
PAYMENT
PAYOFFS
PAYOLAS
PAYOUTS
PAYROLL
PAYSFOR
PAYSOFF
PAYSOUT
RAYBURN
RAYGUNS
RAYKROC
RAYLIKE
RAYMOND
RAYOVAC
SAYINGS
SAYWHEN
SAYYIDS
WAYBILL
WAYCOOL
WAYLAID
WAYLAYS
WAYLESS
WAYSIDE
WAYWARD
WAYWORN

•A•Y•••
BABYING
BABYISH
BABYLON
BABYSAT
BABYSIT
BANYANS
BARYONS
CALYCES
CALYPSO
CALYXES
CANYONS
DASYURE
EASYOFF
HALYARD
KATYDID
LADYBUG
LADYDAY
LADYISH
LANYARD
LAWYERS
LAZYISH
MAGYARS
MANYEAR
MARYANN
MARYKAY
MARYLOU
PAPYRUS
SAWYERS
SAYYIDS
VARYING
ZANYISH

•A••Y••
CARLYLE
CARRYON
DACTYLS
EARLYON
HALCYON
MALAYAN
MARRYME
MARTYRS
PAPAYAS
RALLYTO
SAMOYED
SAROYAN
TALLYHO
TALLYUP
VANDYCK
VANDYKE
VANEYCK

•A•••Y•
BADBOYS
BADGUYS
BAILEYS
BARLEYS
BARNEYS
BATBOYS
CARBOYS
CAROLYN
CATSEYE
DAYBOYS
GALLEYS
HAIRDYE
HAWKEYE
JACKEYS
KAROLYI
KATHRYN
LACKEYS
MAGUEYS
MANDAYS
MARGAYS
MARILYN
MASARYK
MAYDAYS
NAYSAYS
PARLAYS
PARLEYS
PAYDAYS
SASHAYS
VALLEYS
WALLEYE
WAYLAYS

•A••••Y
BACKBAY
BAGGILY
BALCONY
BALKILY
BALLBOY
BALMILY
BALONEY
BANALLY
BARBARY
BARKLEY
BARNABY
BASALLY
BASEPAY
BATTERY
BAWDILY
BAYCITY
CACANNY
CADBURY
CADENCY
CALCIFY
CALGARY
CALUMNY
CALVARY
CAMPILY
CANNERY
CANNILY
CANTILY
CAPABLY
CARAWAY
CASSIDY
CATTILY
CAVALRY
DAFFILY
DAHOMEY
DALTREY
DANBURY
DANDIFY
DARESAY
DARNLEY
DATEDLY
DAYLILY
DAZEDLY
EAGERLY
EARTHLY
EATAWAY
FACTORY
FACULTY
FAINTLY
FAIRWAY
FALLACY
FALLGUY
FALSELY
FALSIFY
FALSITY
FANCIFY
FANCILY
FANTASY
FARADAY
FARAWAY
FARMERY
FATCITY
FATTILY
FATUITY
FAYWRAY
GADGETY
GAINSAY
GALLERY
GANGWAY
GASCONY
GATEWAY
GAUDILY
GAUNTLY
GAUZILY
GAVEWAY
GAWKILY
HACKNEY
HALFWAY
HALLWAY
HAMMILY
HANDILY
HAPENNY
HAPPILY
HARDILY
HARMONY
HARSHLY
HASTILY
HAUGHTY
HAUTBOY
JADEDLY
JANEWAY
JANUARY
JARGONY
JAZZILY
LADYDAY
LAMPREY
LANGLEY
LANGTRY
LANKILY
LARCENY
LARGELY
LASTORY
LATENCY
LATHERY
LAUNDRY
LAYAWAY
MADEHAY
MADEWAY
MAGNIFY
MAHONEY
MAJESTY
MAKEHAY
MAKEWAY
MALMSEY
MARYKAY
MASONRY
MASTERY
NAIVELY
NAIVETY
NAKEDLY
NAMEDAY
NASALLY
NASTILY
NATTILY
NAUGHTY
PAGEBOY
PAISLEY
PALEDRY
PALFREY
PALJOEY
PALMARY
PANICKY
PANOPLY
PARKWAY
PARSLEY
PARTWAY
PASSKEY
PATHWAY
PAUCITY
PAUNCHY
RABIDLY
RACEWAY
RAGGEDY
RAILWAY
RAINILY
RANAWAY
RAPIDLY
SAINTLY
SALSIFY
SALTILY
SAMEDAY
SANDFLY
SAPPILY
SASSILY
SATIETY
SATISFY
SAUCILY
SAVELOY
SAVOURY
SAVVILY
TACITLY
TACKILY
TAMMANY
TANNERY
TANTIVY
TARBABY
TARDILY
TASTILY
TATTILY
TAWNILY
TAXIWAY
VACANCY
VACUITY
VAGUELY
VALENCY
VALIDLY
VAPIDLY
VARIETY
VARSITY
WACKILY
WAGGERY
WALKWAY
WALLABY
WASPILY
ZACHARY

••AY•••
BRAYERS
BRAYING
CLAYIER
CLAYISH
CLAYTON
CRAYOLA
CRAYONS
DRAYAGE
DRAYING
FLAYING
FRAYING
GRAYEST
GRAYING
GRAYISH
GRAYJAY
GRAYLAG
GRAYSON
KHAYYAM
OKAYING
PLAYACT
PLAYBOY
PLAYDOH
PLAYERS
PLAYFUL
PLAYING
PLAYLET
PLAYOFF
PLAYOUT
PLAYPEN
PLAYSAT
PLAYSON
PLAYSUP
PRAYERS
PRAYFOR
PRAYING
PRAYSTO
SLAYERS
SLAYTON
SPAYING
STAYING
STAYPUT
STAYSUP
SWAYERS
SWAYING
TRAYFUL
XRAYING

••A•Y••
ANALYSE
ANALYST
ANALYZE
KHAYYAM
MIAOYAO
NEARYOU
PHARYNX
PLATYPI

••A••Y•
DEADEYE
GLADEYE
GRAMMYS
PEAVEYS
SEAWAYS
SLAVEYS
TEAPOYS

••A•••Y
ACADEMY
AMATORY
ANALOGY
ANARCHY
ANATOMY
BEANERY
BEASTLY
BEATIFY
BLACKLY
BLANDLY
BLANKLY
BLARNEY
BRADLEY
BRAMBLY
BRASHLY
BRAVELY
BRAVERY
BYANDBY
CHANTEY
CHARILY
CHARITY
CHARLEY
CLARIFY
CLARITY
CRACKLY
CRAFTSY
CRASSLY
CRAZILY
DEANERY
DRAPERY
DUALITY
EDACITY
EPARCHY
EXACTLY
FLAGDAY
FLAKILY
FLAUNTY
FOAMILY
FRAILLY
FRAILTY
FRANKLY
FRAWLEY
GHASTLY
GRANARY
GRANDLY
GRATIFY
GRAVELY
GRAVITY
GRAYJAY
HEADILY
HEADWAY
HEALTHY
HEARSAY
HEAVILY
HOARILY
IMAGERY
INANELY
INANITY
INAPTLY
IRATELY
KEARNEY
KNAVERY
MEADOWY
MEATILY
OPACITY
ORANGEY
ORATORY
PEABODY
PLAINLY
PLAYBOY
QUAKILY
QUALIFY
QUALITY
QUAVERY
READILY
REALITY
RIANTLY
ROADWAY
SCANTLY
SCARIFY
SCARILY
SEADUTY
SEALILY
SHADILY
SHADOWY
SHAKILY
SHANTEY
SHAPELY
SHAPLEY
SHARKEY
SHARPLY
SLACKLY
SLAVERY
SMARTLY
SNAKILY
SOAPILY
SPANGLY
SPARELY
SPASSKY
STAGILY
STAIDLY
STALELY
STANDBY
STANLEY
STARCHY
STARKLY
STATELY
SUAVELY
SUAVITY
SWARTHY
TEARILY
TEATRAY
THATCHY
TRACERY
TRAGEDY
UNAPTLY
WEALTHY
WEARILY

•••AY••
ALLAYED
ALLAYER
ARRAYED
ASSAYED
ASSAYER
AYEAYES
BELAYED
BYWAYOF
DECAYED
DELAYED
DELAYER
EMBAYED
ESSAYED
MALAYAN
PAPAYAS
RELAYED
SPLAYED
SPRAYED
SPRAYER
STRAYED

•••A•Y•
MASARYK

•••A••Y
AFFABLY
AMIABLY
AREAWAY
ATTABOY
AURALLY
AUTARKY
AXIALLY
BANALLY
BASALLY
BETARAY
BLEAKLY
BREATHY
BROADLY
CACANNY
CAPABLY
CARAWAY
CAVALRY
CHEAPLY
CLEANLY
CLEARLY
CONAKRY
CUTAWAY
DEBAKEY
DELANEY
DUBARRY
DUNAWAY
DURABLY
DYNASTY
EATAWAY
EMBASSY
EMPATHY
EQUABLY
EQUALLY
ERRANCY
FARADAY
FARAWAY
FINALLY
FLYAWAY
GETAWAY
GOTAWAY
GREATLY
HUMANLY
IDEALLY
INFANCY
KOLACKY
LAYAWAY
LEGALLY
LOCALLY
LOVABLY
LOYALLY
LOYALTY
MISALLY
MORALLY
MOVABLY
MUTABLY
MYMAMMY
NASALLY
NOTABLY
ORGANDY
ORMANDY
PENALTY
PICARDY
PLIABLY
PLIANCY
PREACHY
PUTAWAY
RANAWAY
REGALLY
REMARRY
RIVALRY
ROYALLY
ROYALTY
RUNAWAY
RURALLY
SCRAGGY
SCRAPPY
SCRAWLY
SCRAWNY
SIZABLY
SPLASHY
SQUATLY
SQUATTY
SQUAWKY
SWEARBY
TENABLY
TENANCY
TONALLY
TOTALLY
TOWAWAY
TREACLY
TRUANCY
TYRANNY
UNCANNY
UNHANDY
UNHAPPY
USUALLY
VACANCY
VENALLY
VITALLY
VOCALLY
WCHANDY
WOMANLY
ZONALLY

••••AY•
AFFRAYS
AIRWAYS
BETRAYS
BYPLAYS
DEEJAYS
DEFRAYS
DISMAYS
DOGDAYS
ENDWAYS
ESTRAYS
FLYWAYS
FRIDAYS
HEYDAYS
JETWAYS
MANDAYS
MARGAYS
MAYDAYS
MIDDAYS
MIDWAYS
MISLAYS
MISSAYS
MONDAYS
NAYSAYS
OLDDAYS
OUTLAYS
PARLAYS
PAYDAYS
PEDWAYS
PREPAYS
REPLAYS
RUNWAYS
SASHAYS
SEAWAYS
SKYWAYS
SUBWAYS
SUNDAYS
SUNRAYS
VEEJAYS
WAYLAYS

••••A•Y
ACTUARY
ALREADY
ANOMALY
BARBARY
BARNABY
BELLAMY
BETHANY
BURSARY
CALGARY
CALVARY
COMPANY
CRYBABY
DIETARY
DITTANY
ECSTASY
ESTUARY
FALLACY
FANTASY
GERMANY
GRANARY
HILLARY
HUNGARY
HUNYADY
HUSHABY
JANUARY
KKKKATY
LIBRARY
LULLABY
NITTANY
PALMARY
PECCARY
PLENARY
PRIMACY
PRIMARY
PRIVACY
QUINARY
RETIARY
SQUEAKY
STREAKY
SUMMARY
TAMMANY
TARBABY
TERNARY
THERAPY
THREADY
THROATY
TIFFANY
TOPIARY
TRENARY
TUSCANY
UNITARY
UNREADY
WALLABY
ZACHARY

•••••AY
AIRPLAY
ALLOWAY
AMSCRAY
ARCHWAY
AREAWAY
ASHTRAY
BACKBAY
BASEPAY
BELTWAY
BETARAY
BIKEWAY
BLUEJAY
CARAWAY
CUTAWAY
DARESAY
DISPLAY
DOORWAY
DUNAWAY
EATAWAY
ENDPLAY
FAIRWAY
FARADAY
FARAWAY
FAYWRAY
FLAGDAY
FLYAWAY
FOLKWAY
FOOTWAY
FOURWAY
FREEWAY
GAINSAY
GANGWAY
GATEWAY
GAVEWAY
GETAWAY
GIVEWAY
GOTAWAY
GRAYJAY
GUNPLAY
HALFWAY
HALLWAY
HEADWAY
HEARSAY
HIGHDAY
HIGHWAY
HOLIDAY
HOLYDAY
INNOWAY
JANEWAY
JOHNGAY
JOHNJAY
LADYDAY
LAYAWAY
LINDSAY
MADEHAY
MADEWAY
MAKEHAY
MAKEWAY
MARYKAY
MISPLAY
NAMEDAY
NEWSDAY
NOONDAY
NOSEGAY
OJIBWAY
OUTPLAY
OVERLAY
PARKWAY
PARTWAY
PATHWAY
PORTRAY
PUTAWAY
RACEWAY
RAILWAY
RANAWAY
RIDGWAY
ROADWAY
ROSEBAY
RUNAWAY
SAMEDAY
SICKBAY
SICKDAY
SICKPAY
SNOWDAY
SOMEDAY
SOMEWAY
TAXIWAY
TEATRAY
THRUWAY
TOLLWAY
TOWAWAY
TUESDAY
URUGUAY
WALKWAY
WEEKDAY
WORKDAY

AZ•••••
AZALEAS
AZIMUTH
AZODYES
AZTECAN
AZURITE

A••Z•••
AMAZING
AMAZONS
ARIZONA

A•••Z••
ABRUZZI
ALCAZAR
ASSIZES

A••••Z•
ABRUZZI
AGONIZE
ANALYZE
ANASAZI
ANODIZE
APPRIZE
ATOMIZE

A•••••Z
AGASSIZ
ALBENIZ
ALVAREZ

•AZ••••
BAZAARS
BAZOOKA
DAZEDLY
DAZZLED
DAZZLER
DAZZLES
GAZEBOS
GAZELLE
GAZETTE
GAZUMPS
HAZARDS
HAZIEST
HAZINGS
JAZZAGE
JAZZIER
JAZZILY
JAZZING
JAZZMAN
JAZZMEN
KAZAKHS
LAZARUS
LAZIEST
LAZYISH
MAZIEST
MAZURKA
RAZORED
RAZZING

•A•Z•••
CALZONE
CANZONE
DAZZLED
DAZZLER
DAZZLES
FANZINE
GAUZIER
GAUZILY
JAZZAGE
JAZZIER
JAZZILY
JAZZING
JAZZMAN
JAZZMEN
MATZOHS
PANZERS
RAZZING
TARZANA
WARZONE

•A••Z••
JACUZZI
PALAZZI
PALAZZO
SALAZAR
SARAZEN
WALTZED
WALTZER
WALTZES
YAHTZEE
YAKUZAS

•A•••Z•
BAPTIZE
CADENZA
CAPSIZE
CARDOZO
JACUZZI
PALAZZI
PALAZZO
YANGTZE
ZAMBEZI

•A••••Z
LAISSEZ
MARQUEZ
NATCHEZ

••AZ•••
AMAZING
AMAZONS
BLAZERS
BLAZING
BLAZONS
BRAZIER
BRAZING
CRAZIER
CRAZIES
CRAZILY
CRAZING
FRAZIER
FRAZZLE
GLAZERS
GLAZIER
GLAZING
GRAZERS
GRAZING
PIAZZAS

••A•Z••
FRAZZLE
KWANZAS
PIAZZAS
STANZAS

••A••Z•
ANALYZE
ANASAZI
INADAZE
REALIZE
TRAPEZE

••A•••Z
AGASSIZ
FRANKOZ

•••AZ••
ALCAZAR
BENAZIR
CORAZON
PALAZZI
PALAZZO
SALAZAR
SARAZEN
TOPAZES
UNFAZED

•••A•Z•
BONANZA
ORGANZA
PALAZZI
PALAZZO
SCHATZI

•••A••Z
ALVAREZ

••••AZ•
ANASAZI
INADAZE
PIZZAZZ

••••A•Z
PIZZAZZ

BA•••••
BABALOO
BABASSU
BABBAGE
BABBITT
BABBLED
BABBLES
BABETTE
BABOONS
BABYING
BABYISH
BABYLON
BABYSAT
BABYSIT
BACALAO
BACARDI
BACCHUS
BACHING
BACILLI
BACKBAY
BACKBIT
BACKEND
BACKERS
BACKHOE
BACKING
BACKLIT
BACKLOG
BACKOFF
BACKOUT
BACKRUB
BACKSIN
BACKSUP
BACKUPS
BADBOYS
BADDEST
BADDIES
BADDISH
BADEGGS
BADGERS
BADGUYS
BADNESS
BAFFLED
BAFFLER
BAFFLES
BAGFULS
BAGGAGE
BAGGERS
BAGGIER
BAGGIES
BAGGILY
BAGGING
BAGHDAD
BAGLIKE
BAGNOLD
BAGPIPE
BAHAMAS
BAHRAIN
BAILEES
BAILERS
BAILEYS
BAILIFF
BAILING
BAILORS
BAILOUT
BAINTER
BAITING
BAKEOFF
BAKLAVA
BALANCE
BALATON
BALBOAS
BALCONY
BALDEST
BALDING
BALDISH
BALDRIC
BALDWIN
BALEENS
BALEFUL
BALFOUR
BALIHAI
BALKANS
BALKIER
BALKILY
BALKING
BALLADE
BALLADS
BALLARD
BALLAST
BALLBOY
BALLETS
BALLOON
BALLOTS
BALLSUP
BALMIER
BALMILY
BALONEY
BALSAMS
BAMBINO
BAMBOOS
BANALLY
BANANAS
BANDAGE
BANDAID
BANDANA
BANDBOX
BANDIED
BANDIES
BANDING
BANDITO
BANDITS
BANDSAW
BANEFUL
BANGING
BANGKOK
BANGLES
BANGSUP
BANJOES
BANKERS
BANKING
BANKSON
BANNERS
BANNING
BANNOCK
BANQUET
BANSHEE
BANTAMS
BANTERS
BANYANS
BAOBABS
BAPTISE
BAPTISM
BAPTIST
BAPTIZE
BARANOF
BARBARA
BARBARY
BARBELL
BARBELS
BARBERS
BARBING
BARBUDA
BARCARS
BARCODE
BARDISH
BARENTS
BARETTA
BARGAIN
BARGEIN
BARGING
BARHOPS
BARKEEP
BARKERS
BARKIER
BARKING
BARKLEY
BARKSAT
BARLESS
BARLEYS
BARMAID
BARMIER
BARNABY
BARNARD
BARNEYS
BARNONE
BARNOWL
BARONET
BARONGS
BAROQUE
BARRACK
BARRAGE
BARRELS
BARRENS
BARRETT
BARRIER
BARRING
BARRIOS
BARROOM
BARROWS
BARSOAP
BARSTOW
BARTABS
BARTEND
BARTERS
BARWARE
BARYONS
BASALLY
BASALTS
BASEHIT
BASEMAN
BASEMEN
BASENJI
BASEPAY
BASHFUL
BASHING
BASKETS
BASKING
BASQUES
BASSETS
BASSIST
BASSOON
BASTERS
BASTING
BASTION
BATBOYS
BATCHED
BATCHES
BATEAUX
BATEMAN
BATGIRL
BATHERS
BATHING
BATHMAT
BATHOIL
BATHTUB
BATIKED
BATISTA
BATISTE
BATLIKE
BATSMAN
BATSMEN
BATTELS
BATTENS
BATTERS
BATTERY
BATTIER
BATTING
BATTLED
BATTLER
BATTLES
BATTUES
BATWING
BAUBLES
BAUHAUS
BAULKED
BAUXITE
BAVARIA
BAWDIER
BAWDILY
BAWLERS
BAWLING
BAWLOUT
BAYCITY
BAYLEAF
BAYONET
BAZAARS
BAZOOKA

B•A••••
BEACHED
BEACHES
BEACONS
BEADIER
BEADING
BEADLES
BEADSUP
BEAGLES
BEAKERS
BEAMIER
BEAMING
BEAMISH
BEAMSUP
BEANBAG
BEANERY
BEANIES
BEANING
BEARCAT
BEARCUB
BEARDED
BEARERS
BEARHUG
BEARING
BEARISH
BEAROFF
BEAROUT
BEARPAW
BEARSON
BEARSUP
BEASTIE
BEASTLY
BEATERS
BEATIFY
BEATING
BEATLES
BEATNIK
BEATOUT
BEATRIX
BEATSIT
BEATSME
BEATSUP
BEATTIE
BEAUISH
BEAVERS
BIALIES
BIASING
BIASSED
BLABBED
BLABBER
BLACKED
BLACKEN
BLACKER
BLACKIE
BLACKLY
BLACULA
BLADDER
BLADERS
BLADING
BLAMING
BLANCHE
BLANDER
BLANDLY
BLANKED
BLANKER
BLANKET
BLANKLY
BLARING
BLARNEY
BLASTED
BLASTER
BLATANT
BLATHER
BLATTED
BLAZERS
BLAZING
BLAZONS
BOARDED
BOARDER
BOARISH
BOASTED
BOASTER
BOATELS
BOATERS
BOATING
BOATMAN
BOATMEN
BRACERO
BRACERS
BRACEUP
BRACING
BRACKEN
BRACKET
BRADLEE
BRADLEY
BRAGGED
BRAGGER
BRAHMAN
BRAHMAS
BRAHMIN
BRAIDED
BRAIDER
BRAILLE
BRAINED
BRAISED
BRAISES
BRAKING
BRALESS
BRAMBLE
BRAMBLY
BRANAGH
BRANDED
BRANDER
BRANDON
BRANSON
BRASHER
BRASHLY
BRASSES
BRASSIE
BRAVADO
BRAVELY
BRAVERY
BRAVEST
BRAVING
BRAVOES
BRAVURA
BRAWLED
BRAWLER
BRAXTON
BRAYERS
BRAYING
BRAZIER
BRAZING
BYANDBY
BYANOSE

B••A•••
BABALOO
BABASSU
BACALAO
BACARDI
BAHAMAS
BALANCE
BALATON
BANALLY
BANANAS
BARANOF
BASALLY
BASALTS
BAVARIA
BAZAARS
BECALMS
BECAUSE
BEDAUBS
BEFALLS
BEHAVED
BEHAVES
BELABOR
BELAKUN
BELASCO
BELATED
BELAYED
BENATAR
BENAZIR
BERATED
BERATES
BETAKEN
BETAKES
BETAMAX
BETARAY
BEWAILS
BIVALVE
BIZARRE
BLEAKER
BLEAKLY
BLEARED
BLEATED
BLOATED
BOIARDO
BONANZA
BORACIC
BORATES
BREADED
BREADTH
BREAKER
BREAKIN
BREAKUP
BREASTS
BREATHE
BREATHS
BREATHY
BRIARDS
BROADAX
BROADEN
BROADER
BROADLY
BUGABOO
BUGALOO
BUTANOL
BUYABLE
BYPATHS
BYWAYOF

B•••A••
BABBAGE
BAGGAGE
BAHRAIN
BAKLAVA
BALKANS
BALLADE
BALLADS
BALLARD
BALLAST
BALSAMS
BANDAGE
BANDAID
BANDANA
BANTAMS
BANYANS
BAOBABS
BARBARA
BARBARY
BARCARS
BARGAIN
BARMAID
BARNABY
BARNARD
BARRACK
BARRAGE
BARTABS
BARWARE
BATEAUX
BAUHAUS
BAZAARS
BEDLAMP
BEEBALM
BEEFALO
BEGGARS
BEHEADS
BELDAME
BELDAMS
BELFAST
BELLAMY
BELTANE
BEMOANS
BENEATH
BENGALI
BENGALS
BEREAVE
BERNARD
BETHANY
BETRAYS
BIDFAIR
BIGBAND
BIGBANG
BIGGAME
BIGNAME
BIGTALK
BIOMASS
BIPLANE
BITMAPS
BITPART
BLATANT
BOBCATS
BOBTAIL
BOITANO
BOKHARA
BOMBARD
BOMBAST
BONDAGE
BONEASH
BOWSAWS
BOXCARS
BRANAGH
BRAVADO
BRIDALS
BRIGADE
BRIGAND
BRITAIN
BROCADE
BROGANS
BROMATE
BUFFALO
BULGARS
BULWARK
BUMRAPS
BUOYANT
BURBANK
BUREAUS
BURLAPS
BURMANS
BUROAKS
BURSARS
BURSARY
BUSFARE
BUSTARD
BUZZARD
BYHEART
BYPLAYS
BYROADS

B••••A•
BABYSAT
BACALAO
BACKBAY
BAGHDAD
BAHAMAS
BALBOAS
BALIHAI
BANANAS
BANDSAW
BARKSAT
BARSOAP
BASEMAN
BASEPAY
BATEMAN
BATHMAT
BATSMAN
BAYLEAF
BEANBAG
BEARCAT
BEARPAW
BEECHAM
BEESWAX
BELGIAN
BELLJAR
BELLMAN
BELTBAG
BELTWAY
BENATAR
BENTHAM
BERGMAN
BESMEAR
BESPEAK
BESTIAL
BESTMAN
BETAMAX
BETARAY
BIFOCAL
BIGDEAL
BIGHEAD
BIKEWAY
BIMODAL
BINGHAM
BIPEDAL
BIPOLAR
BIRDMAN
BIVOUAC
BKLIBAN
BLINKAT
BLUEJAY
BLUELAW
BOATMAN
BODEGAS
BODYFAT
BOERWAR
BOLIVAR
BONDMAN
BOOLEAN
BOXSEAT
BRAHMAN
BRAHMAS
BRENDAN
BRENNAN
BRIGHAM
BROADAX
BROSNAN
BUCKRAM
BUCKSAW
BUDDHAS
BUGBEAR
BURGLAR
BUSHMAN
BUZZSAW
BYREMAN

B•••••A
BAKLAVA
BANDANA
BARBARA
BARBUDA
BARETTA
BATISTA
BAVARIA
BAZOOKA
BEDELIA
BEEFTEA
BEGONIA
BEGORRA
BELINDA
BERETTA
BERMUDA
BIRETTA
BLACULA
BOBVILA
BOHEMIA
BOKHARA
BOLIVIA
BOLOGNA
BONANZA
BOOTHIA
BOTHNIA
BRAVURA
BURKINA

•BA••••
ABALONE
ABANDON
ABASHED
ABASHES
ABASING
ABATING
MBABANE
OBADIAH

•B•A•••
ABLATED
ABLATES
ABLAUTS
ABNAKIS
ABRADED
ABRADER
ABRADES
ABRAHAM
ABSALOM
CBRADIO
OBLASTS
OBLATES
OBTAINS

•B••A••
ABELARD
ABENAKI
ABEYANT
ABIGAIL
ABREAST
ABSTAIN
ABUBAKR
IBNSAUD
MBABANE
OBVIATE

•B•••A•
ABRAHAM
ABUTTAL
ABYSMAL
IBERIAN
OBADIAH

•B••••A
ABEXTRA
ABINTRA

••BA•••
ALBANIA
AUBADES
BABALOO
BABASSU
CABALAS
CABANAS
CABARET
DEBACLE
DEBAKEY
DEBARGE
DEBARKS
DEBASED
DEBASES
DEBATED
DEBATER
DEBATES
DEBAUCH
DUBARRY
EMBANKS
EMBARGO
EMBARKS
EMBASSY
EMBAYED
FABARES
HIBACHI
LABAMBA
LEBANON
LEBARON
MUBARAK
REBASTE
REBATED
REBATES
RIBANDS
ROBARDS
RUBATOS
TABARDS
TABASCO
TOBACCO
TUBAIST
UNBAKED
URBANER

••B•A••
BABBAGE
BOBCATS
BOBTAIL
CABBAGE
CEBUANO
DABHAND
EMBRACE
HEBRAIC
HOBNAIL
HUBBARD
HUBCAPS
INBOARD
JOBBANK
LABIALS
LABIATE
LIBRARY
LIBYANS
MOBCAPS
NUBIANS
ONBOARD
PTBOATS
RIBCAGE
SABBATH
SUBWAYS
UMBRAGE
UPBEATS
UPBRAID
VIBRANT
VIBRATE
VIBRATO
WEBPAGE

••B••A•
BABYSAT
CABALAS
CABANAS
DEBORAH
FIBULAE
FIBULAS
HABITAT
LABCOAT
LIBERAL
MUBARAK
NEBULAE
NEBULAR
NEBULAS
ORBITAL
REBEKAH
SUBHEAD
TABLEAU
TABULAR
TIBETAN
TUBULAR
UMBRIAN

••B•••A
ALBANIA
ALBERTA
BOBVILA
CIBORIA
LABAMBA
LIBERIA
REBECCA
ROBERTA
ROBUSTA
SABRINA
SIBERIA
SUBROSA
TABITHA

•••BA••
ABUBAKR
AIRBAGS
AIRBALL
AIRBASE
ALABAMA
ALIBABA
ARMBAND
BABBAGE
BAOBABS
BARBARA
BARBARY
BEEBALM
BIGBAND
BIGBANG
BOMBARD
BOMBAST
BURBANK
CABBAGE
CEMBALO
COMBATS
CRYBABY
CUEBALL
CUTBACK
CYMBALS
DISBAND
DISBARS
DOGBANE
EYEBALL
EYEBANK
FATBACK
FLYBALL
FOGBANK
FORBADE
FURBALL
GAMBADO
GARBAGE
GASBAGS
GETBACK
GIMBALS
GOTBACK
GUMBALL
GYMBAGS
HATBAND
HENBANE
HERBAGE
HERBALS
HOGBACK
HUBBARD
HUSBAND
ICEBAGS
IKEBANA
ISOBARS
JOBBANK
JUGBAND
KIMBALL
KITBAGS
LAMBADA
LAYBACK
LIPBALM
LOMBARD
LOWBALL
LUMBAGO
LUMBARS
MAXBAER
MBABANE
MOMBASA
NUMBATS
ODDBALL
OFFBASE
OUTBACK
PIEBALD
PINBALL
PROBATE
RAGBAGS
RHUBARB
RIMBAUD
RUMBAED
RUNBACK
SABBATH
SAMBAED
SAMBALS
SAMBARS
SEABAGS
SEABASS
SETBACK
SHEBANG
SORBATE
SUNBATH
TAMBALA
TARBABY
TEABAGS
TEABALL
THEBABE
TIMBALE
TIMBALS
TURBANS
TWOBASE
VERBALS
WETBARS
WOMBATS
ZEDBARS

•••B•A•
AIRBOAT
ANTBEAR
ARABIAN
BALBOAS
BUGBEAR
CATBOAT
CLUBCAR
FORBEAR
GAMBIAN
GILBLAS
GRABBAG
GRABSAT
GUNBOAT
HOFBRAU
ICEBOAT
JERBOAS
JETBOAT
LAMBDAS
LAMBEAU
LINBIAO
LOWBEAM
OFFBEAT
OJIBWAS
OJIBWAY
PEABEAN
PHOBIAS
RAMBEAU
ROWBOAT
SERBIAN
SIOBHAN
SOYBEAN
SUNBEAM
TUGBOAT
WAXBEAN
ZAMBIAN

•••B••A
ALABAMA
ALIBABA
BARBARA
BARBUDA
HERBTEA
IKEBANA
LAMBADA
MOMBASA
TAMBALA
TOMBOLA
VERBENA

••••BA•
ACROBAT
AEROBAT
AMOEBAE
AMOEBAS
ARROBAS
BACKBAY
BEANBAG
BELTBAG
BKLIBAN
CALIBAN
CARABAO
CASABAS
CASHBAR
CROWBAR
DINGBAT
DRAWBAR
EXURBAN
FEEDBAG
FERNBAR
FLEABAG
GOESBAD
GOODBAR
GRABBAG
HANDBAG
MAILBAG
MALABAR
NOSEBAG
OPENBAR
POOHBAH
POSTBAG
RHUMBAS
ROLLBAR
ROSEBAY
SANDBAG
SANDBAR
SASHBAR
SICKBAY
SIDEBAR
TESTBAN
TOTEBAG
WENTBAD
WINDBAG
WINEBAR
ZAREBAS

••••B•A
ALGEBRA
CEREBRA
CULEBRA
EXURBIA
NAMIBIA
ZENOBIA

•••••BA
ALIBABA
CARAMBA
CATAWBA
CORDOBA
LABAMBA
MARIMBA
MASTABA
TOSHIBA

B•B••••
BABALOO
BABASSU
BABBAGE
BABBITT
BABBLED
BABBLES
BABETTE
BABOONS
BABYING
BABYISH
BABYLON
BABYSAT
BABYSIT
BIBELOT
BIBLESS
BIBLIKE
BOBBERS
BOBBIES
BOBBING
BOBBINS
BOBBLED
BOBBLES
BOBCATS
BOBDOLE
BOBHOPE
BOBSLED
BOBTAIL
BOBVILA
BUBBLED
BUBBLES

B••B•••
BABBAGE
BABBITT
BABBLED
BABBLES
BADBOYS
BALBOAS
BAMBINO
BAMBOOS
BAOBABS
BARBARA
BARBARY
BARBELL
BARBELS
BARBERS
BARBING
BARBUDA
BATBOYS
BAUBLES
BEDBUGS
BEEBALM
BERBERS
BIGBAND
BIGBANG
BIGBEND
BIGBIRD
BIGBOYS
BILBIES
BILBOES
BLABBED
BLABBER
BLUBBER
BOBBERS
BOBBIES
BOBBING
BOBBINS
BOBBLED
BOBBLES
BOMBARD
BOMBAST
BOMBECK
BOMBERS
BOMBING
BONBONS
BOOBIES
BOOBOOS
BRIBERY
BRIBING
BRUBECK
BUBBLED
BUBBLES
BUGBEAR
BULBLET
BULBOUS
BULBULS
BUMBLED
BUMBLER
BUMBLES
BURBANK
BURBLED
BURBLES
BURBOTS
BUSBIES
BUSBOYS

B•••B••
BACKBAY
BACKBIT
BALLBOY
BANDBOX
BEANBAG
BELABOR
BELLBOY
BELTBAG
BESTBOY
BKLIBAN
BLABBED
BLABBER
BLUBBER
BLUEBOY
BOOMBOX
BOURBON
BRAMBLE
BRAMBLY
BUGABOO
BUNKBED
BUYABLE

B••••B•
BAOBABS
BARNABY
BARTABS
BEDAUBS
BENUMBS
BYANDBY
BYTHEBY

B•••••B
BACKRUB
BATHTUB
BEARCUB

•BB••••
ABBOTCY
EBBTIDE

•B•B•••
ABUBAKR
MBABANE

•B•••B•
ABIDEBY
ABITIBI
ABSORBS

••BB•••
BABBAGE
BABBITT
BABBLED
BABBLES
BOBBERS
BOBBIES
BOBBING
BOBBINS
BOBBLED
BOBBLES
BUBBLED
BUBBLES
CABBAGE
CABBIES
COBBLED
COBBLER
COBBLES
CUBBIES
CUBBISH
DABBING
DABBLED
DABBLER
DABBLES
DIBBLED
DIBBLES
DOBBIES
DOBBINS
DUBBERS
DUBBING
DYBBUKS
FIBBERS
FIBBING
FOBBING
FUBBING
GABBERS
GABBIER
GABBING
GABBLED
GABBLES
GABBROS
GIBBERS
GIBBETS
GIBBING
GIBBONS
GIBBOUS
GOBBLED
GOBBLER
GOBBLES
HOBBIES
HOBBITS
HOBBLED
HOBBLES
HUBBARD
HUBBELL
HUBBIES
HUBBUBS
JABBERS
JABBING
JIBBING
JIBBOOM
JOBBANK
JOBBERS
JOBBERY
JOBBING
KIBBLED
KIBBLES
KIBBUTZ
LIBBERS
LIBBING
LOBBERS
LOBBIED
LOBBIES
LOBBING
LOBBYER
LUBBERS
LUBBOCK
MOBBING
MOBBISH
NABBERS
NABBING
NEBBISH
NIBBLED
NIBBLER
NIBBLES
NOBBIER
NOBBLED
NOBBLER
NOBBLES
NUBBIER
NUBBINS
NUBBLES
PEBBLED
PEBBLES
RABBETS
RABBITS
RABBITT
RABBLES
RIBBIES
RIBBING
RIBBONS
ROBBERS
ROBBERY
ROBBING
ROBBINS
RUBBERS
RUBBERY
RUBBING
RUBBISH
RUBBLES
SABBATH
SOBBERS
SOBBING
SUBBING
TABBIES
TABBING
TUBBIER
WEBBIER
WEBBING
WOBBLED
WOBBLES
YABBERS

••B•B••
IMBIBED
IMBIBES

••B••B•
COBWEBS
HOBNOBS
HUBBUBS
LABAMBA
SUBDEBS
SUBURBS

••B•••B
LUBEJOB

•••BB••
BLABBED
BLABBER
BLUBBER
CLABBER
CLOBBER
CLUBBED
CRABBED
CRABBER
CRIBBED
DRABBER
DRIBBLE
DRUBBED
FLUBBED
FLUBBER
GLIBBER
GRABBAG
GRABBED
GRABBER
GRUBBED
KNOBBED
QUIBBLE
SLABBED
SLOBBER
SNUBBED
STABBED
STUBBED
STUBBLE
STUBBLY
SWABBED
SWOBBED

•••B•B•
ALIBABA
BAOBABS
CRYBABY
HUBBUBS
SKIBOBS
TARBABY
THEBABE

•••B••B
DIMBULB
RHUBARB
THEBLOB

••••BB•
ENTEBBE
SCRUBBY
SHRUBBY

B•C••••
BACALAO
BACARDI
BACCHUS
BACHING
BACILLI
BACKBAY
BACKBIT
BACKEND
BACKERS
BACKHOE
BACKING
BACKLIT
BACKLOG
BACKOFF
BACKOUT
BACKRUB
BACKSIN
BACKSUP
BACKUPS
BECALMS
BECAUSE
BECKETT
BECKONS
BECLOUD
BECOMES
BICKERS
BICOLOR
BICYCLE
BSCHOOL
BUCKETS
BUCKEYE
BUCKING
BUCKLED
BUCKLER
BUCKLES
BUCKLEY
BUCKOES
BUCKRAM
BUCKSAW
BUCKSUP
BUCOLIC

B••C•••
BACCHUS
BALCONY
BARCARS
BARCODE
BATCHED
BATCHES
BAYCITY
BEACHED
BEACHES
BEACONS
BEECHAM
BEECHER
BEECHES
BELCHED
BELCHES
BENCHED
BENCHES
BIOCHIP
BIRCHED
BIRCHES
BISCUIT
BLACKED
BLACKEN
BLACKER
BLACKIE
BLACKLY
BLACULA
BLOCKED
BLOCKER
BOBCATS
BOKCHOY
BOTCHED
BOTCHES
BOTCHUP
BOXCARS
BOYCOTT
BRACERO
BRACERS
BRACEUP
BRACING
BRACKEN
BRACKET
BRICKED
BROCADE
BUNCHED
BUNCHES
BUNCOED
BUTCHER

B•••C••
BEARCAT
BEARCUB
BEDECKS
BICYCLE
BIFOCAL
BINOCHE
BISECTS
BLANCHE
BLOTCHY
BODICES
BORACIC
BORSCHT
BOUNCED
BOUNCER
BOUNCES
BRIOCHE
BRONCHI
BRONCOS

B••••C•
BALANCE
BANNOCK
BARRACK
BEDROCK
BELASCO
BERNICE
BESEECH
BEWITCH
BIONICS
BOMBECK
BRUBECK
BULLOCK
BURDOCK
BYFORCE

B•••••C
BALDRIC
BIVOUAC
BORACIC
BUCOLIC

•B•C•••
ABSCOND
OBSCENE
OBSCURE

•B••C••
ABDUCTS
OBJECTS

•B•••C•
ABBOTCY
ABSENCE

••BC•••
BOBCATS
HUBCAPS
LABCOAT
MOBCAPS
RIBCAGE

••B•C••
CUBICLE
DEBACLE
HIBACHI
REBECCA
ROBOCOP
RUBICON
TOBACCO

••B••C•
ABBOTCY
DEBAUCH
DEBOUCH
EMBRACE
FABRICS
KUBRICK
LUBBOCK
NABISCO
NIBLICK
PUBLICS
REBECCA
RUBRICS
SUBJECT
SUBVOCE
TABASCO
TOBACCO
UNBLOCK

••B•••C
HEBRAIC
ROBOTIC

•••BC••
CLUBCAR
CURBCUT

•••B•C•
BOMBECK
BRUBECK
CUTBACK
FATBACK
GETBACK
GOTBACK
HOGBACK
LAYBACK
LUBBOCK
OUTBACK
PHOBICS
ROEBUCK
RUNBACK
SAWBUCK
SETBACK

•••B••C
CAMBRIC

••••B•C
ACERBIC
AEROBIC
ALEMBIC
AMOEBIC

B•D••••
BADBOYS
BADDEST
BADDIES
BADDISH
BADEGGS
BADGERS
BADGUYS
BADNESS
BEDAUBS
BEDBUGS
BEDDING
BEDDOWN
BEDECKS
BEDELIA
BEDEVIL
BEDEWED
BEDIZEN
BEDLAMP
BEDLESS
BEDLIKE
BEDOUIN
BEDPOST
BEDREST
BEDROCK
BEDROLL
BEDROOM
BEDSIDE
BEDTIME
BIDDERS
BIDDIES
BIDDING
BIDFAIR
BODEGAS
BODEREK
BODICES
BODKINS
BODYFAT
BUDDHAS
BUDDIES
BUDDING
BUDDYUP
BUDGETS
BUDGIES
BUDGING
BUDLESS
BUDLIKE

B••D•••
BADDEST
BADDIES
BADDISH
BALDEST
BALDING
BALDISH
BALDRIC
BALDWIN
BANDAGE
BANDAID
BANDANA
BANDBOX
BANDIED
BANDIES
BANDING
BANDITO
BANDITS
BANDSAW
BARDISH
BAWDIER
BAWDILY
BEADIER
BEADING
BEADLES
BEADSUP
BEDDING
BEDDOWN
BELDAME
BELDAMS
BENDERS
BENDIER
BENDIGO
BENDING
BIDDERS
BIDDIES
BIDDING
BIGDEAL
BINDERS
BINDERY
BINDING
BINDSUP
BIRDDOG
BIRDERS
BIRDIED
BIRDIES
BIRDING
BIRDMAN
BIRDMEN
BLADDER
BLADERS
BLADING
BOBDOLE
BOGDOWN
BOLDEST
BONDAGE
BONDING
BONDMAN
BONDMEN
BOODLES
BORDERS
BOUDOIR
BOWDLER
BRADLEE
BRADLEY
BRIDALS
BRIDGED
BRIDGES
BRIDGET
BRIDLED
BRIDLES
BUDDHAS
BUDDIES
BUDDING
BUDDYUP
BUNDLED
BUNDLES
BURDENS
BURDOCK

B•••D••
BAGHDAD
BEARDED
BERIDOF
BESIDES
BETIDED
BETIDES
BIMODAL
BIPEDAL
BIRDDOG
BLADDER
BLANDER
BLANDLY
BLENDED
BLENDER
BLINDED
BLINDER
BLINDLY
BLONDER
BLONDES
BLONDIE
BLOODED
BLOWDRY
BLUNDER
BOARDED
BOARDER
BOLIDES
BONEDRY
BONEDUP
BOREDOM
BORODIN
BOULDER
BOUNDED
BOUNDER
BOUNDUP
BOXEDIN
BOXEDUP
BRAIDED
BRAIDER
BRANDED
BRANDER
BRANDON
BREADED
BREADTH
BREEDER
BRENDAN
BRINDLE
BROADAX
BROADEN
BROADER
BROADLY
BROODED
BROODER
BUILDER
BUILDIN
BUILDUP
BULLDOG
BYANDBY

B••••D•
BACARDI
BALLADE
BALLADS
BARBUDA
BARCODE
BEDSIDE
BEHEADS
BEHOLDS
BELINDA
BERMUDA
BOIARDO
BRAVADO
BRIARDS
BRIGADE
BROCADE
BROMIDE
BUSHIDO
BYROADS
BYWORDS

B•••••D
BABBLED
BACKEND
BAFFLED
BAGHDAD
BAGNOLD
BALLARD
BANDAID
BANDIED
BARMAID
BARNARD
BARTEND
BATCHED
BATIKED
BATTLED
BAULKED
BEACHED
BEARDED
BECLOUD
BEDEWED
BEHAVED
BEHOVED
BELATED
BELAYED
BELCHED
BELLIED
BELOVED
BEMIRED
BEMUSED
BENCHED
BERATED
BERNARD
BERRIED
BERTHED
BETIDED
BEVELED
BIASSED
BIGBAND
BIGBEND
BIGBIRD
BIGHEAD
BIGOTED
BIRCHED
BIRDIED
BIRTHED
BLABBED
BLACKED
BLANKED
BLASTED
BLATTED
BLEARED
BLEATED
BLEEPED
BLENDED
BLESSED
BLINDED
BLINKED
BLIPPED
BLITZED
BLOATED
BLOCKED
BLOODED
BLOOMED
BLOOPED
BLOTTED
BLOUSED
BLUFFED
BLUNTED
BLURRED
BLURTED
BLUSHED
BOARDED
BOASTED
BOBBLED
BOBSLED
BOGEYED
BOGGLED
BOMBARD
BOOGIED
BOOKEND
BOOSTED
BOTCHED
BOTTLED
BOUNCED
BOUNDED
BOWERED
BOXWOOD
BOYHOOD
BRAGGED
BRAIDED
BRAINED
BRAISED
BRANDED
BRAWLED
BREADED
BREEZED
BRICKED
BRIDGED
BRIDLED
BRIEFED
BRIGAND
BRIMMED
BROILED
BRONZED
BROODED
BROOKED
BROWNED
BROWSED
BRUISED
BRUITED
BRUSHED
BUBBLED
BUCKLED
BUGEYED
BULLIED
BUMBLED
BUNCHED
BUNCOED
BUNDLED
BUNGLED
BUNKBED
BUNKOED
BURBLED
BURGLED
BUSTARD
BUSTLED
BUZZARD
BYLINED

•BD••••
ABDOMEN
ABDUCTS

•B•D•••
ABIDEBY
ABIDING
OBADIAH

•B••D••
ABANDON
ABRADED
ABRADER
ABRADES
ABRIDGE
CBRADIO

•B•••D•
ABOUNDS
EBBTIDE
OBTRUDE
OBTUNDS

•B••••D
ABASHED
ABELARD
ABETTED
ABJURED
ABLATED
ABORTED
ABRADED
ABSCOND
ABUTTED

IBNSAUD
OBLIGED

••BD•••

BOBDOLE
RUBDOWN
SUBDEBS
SUBDUED
SUBDUER
SUBDUES

••B•D••

ALBEDOS
AUBADES
LIBIDOS
NOBODYS
RABIDLY

••B••D•

ALBUNDY
EBBTIDE
HYBRIDS
KOBOLDS
REBENDS
REBINDS
RIBANDS
ROBARDS
SUBSIDE
SUBSIDY
TABARDS
UNBENDS
UNBINDS

••B•••D

ARBORED
BABBLED
BOBBLED
BOBSLED
BUBBLED
COBBLED
DABBLED
DABHAND
DEBASED
DEBATED
DEBITED
DEBONED
DEBUTED
DIBBLED
ELBOWED
EMBAYED
GABBLED
GOBBLED
HABITED
HOBBLED
HUBBARD
IMBIBED
IMBRUED
INBOARD
INBOUND
INBREED
KIBBLED
LABELED
LABORED
LIBELED
LOBBIED
NIBBLED
NOBBLED
ONBOARD
ORBITED
OXBLOOD
PEBBLED
REBATED
REBOUND
REBUILD
REBUKED
SOBERED
SUBDUED
SUBHEAD
SUBTEND
TABLOID
UNBAKED
UNBOUND
UNBOWED
UNBOXED
UPBRAID
WEBTOED
WOBBLED

•••BD••

LAMBDAS

•••B•D•

ANYBODY
BARBUDA
CARBIDE
DAYBEDS
FORBADE
FORBIDS
GAMBADO
HOTBEDS
LAMBADA
OUTBIDS
PEABODY
REDBUDS
SEABEDS

•••B••D

ARMBAND
BABBLED
BIGBAND
BIGBEND
BIGBIRD
BLABBED
BOBBLED
BOMBARD
BUBBLED
BUMBLED
BURBLED
CATBIRD
CLUBBED
COBBLED
COWBIRD
CRABBED
CRIBBED
DABBLED
DIBBLED
DISBAND
DOUBLED
DOUBTED
DRUBBED
ENABLED
FLUBBED
FUMBLED
GABBLED
GAMBLED
GARBLED
GOBBLED
GRABBED
GRUBBED
HATBAND
HOBBLED
HUBBARD
HUMBLED
HUSBAND
ILLBRED
JAYBIRD
JUGBAND
JUMBLED
KIBBLED
KNOBBED
LOBBIED
LOMBARD
LOWBRED
MAMBOED
MARBLED
MUMBLED
NIBBLED
NOBBLED
PEBBLED
PIEBALD
PREBEND
RAMBLED
REDBIRD
RIMBAUD
RUMBAED
RUMBLED
SAMBAED
SEABIRD
SLABBED
SNUBBED
STABBED
STABLED
STUBBED
SWABBED
SWOBBED
TREBLED
TUMBLED
WAMBLED
WARBLED
WIMBLED
WOBBLED

••••B•D

BLABBED
BUNKBED
CLIMBED
CLUBBED
CRABBED
CRIBBED
DRUBBED
ENROBED
FLAMBED
FLATBED
FLUBBED
GOESBAD
GRABBED
GRUBBED
ICHABOD
IMBIBED
KNOBBED
LIEABED
PLUMBED
ROADBED
ROSEBUD
SEEDBED
SLABBED
SNUBBED
SOFABED
STABBED
STUBBED
SWABBED
SWOBBED
THUMBED
TWINBED
UNROBED
WENTBAD

BE•••••

BEACHED
BEACHES
BEACONS
BEADIER
BEADING
BEADLES
BEADSUP
BEAGLES
BEAKERS
BEAMIER
BEAMING
BEAMISH
BEAMSUP
BEANBAG
BEANERY
BEANIES
BEANING
BEARCAT
BEARCUB
BEARDED
BEARERS
BEARHUG
BEARING
BEARISH
BEAROFF
BEAROUT
BEARPAW
BEARSON
BEARSUP
BEASTIE
BEASTLY
BEATERS
BEATIFY
BEATING
BEATLES
BEATNIK
BEATOUT
BEATRIX
BEATSIT
BEATSME
BEATSUP
BEATTIE
BEAUISH
BEAVERS
BECALMS
BECAUSE
BECKETT
BECKONS
BECLOUD
BECOMES
BEDAUBS
BEDBUGS
BEDDING
BEDDOWN
BEDECKS
BEDELIA
BEDEVIL
BEDEWED
BEDIZEN
BEDLAMP
BEDLESS
BEDLIKE
BEDOUIN
BEDPOST
BEDREST
BEDROCK
BEDROLL
BEDROOM
BEDSIDE
BEDTIME
BEEBALM
BEECHAM
BEECHER
BEECHES
BEEFALO
BEEFIER
BEEFING
BEEFSUP
BEEFTEA
BEEGEES
BEEGUMS
BEEHIVE
BEELIKE
BEELINE
BEEPERS
BEEPING
BEERIER
BEESWAX
BEETLES
BEFALLS
BEFOULS
BEGGARS
BEGGING
BEGONIA
BEGORRA
BEGRIME
BEGSOFF
BEGUILE
BEGUINE
BEHAVED
BEHAVES
BEHEADS
BEHESTS
BEHOLDS
BEHOOVE
BEHOVED
BEHOVES
BEIJING
BELABOR
BELAKUN
BELASCO
BELATED
BELAYED
BELCHED
BELCHES
BELDAME
BELDAMS
BELFAST
BELGIAN
BELGIUM
BELIEFS
BELIEVE
BELINDA
BELLAMY
BELLBOY
BELLEEK
BELLHOP
BELLIED
BELLIES
BELLING
BELLINI
BELLJAR
BELLMAN
BELLMEN
BELLOWS
BELLYUP
BELMONT
BELONGS
BELOVED
BELTANE
BELTBAG
BELTING
BELTWAY
BELUSHI
BELYING
BEMIRED
BEMIRES
BEMOANS
BEMUSED
BEMUSES
BENATAR
BENAZIR
BENCHED
BENCHES
BENDERS
BENDIER
BENDIGO
BENDING
BENEATH
BENEFIT
BENELUX
BENGALI
BENGALS
BENISON
BENNETT
BENTHAM
BENTLEY
BENTSEN
BENUMBS
BENZENE
BEOWULF
BEQUEST
BERATED
BERATES
BERBERS
BEREAVE
BERETTA
BERGERE
BERGMAN
BERGSON
BERIDOF
BERLIOZ
BERLITZ
BERMEJO
BERMUDA
BERNARD
BERNESE
BERNICE
BERNSEN
BERRIED
BERRIES
BERSERK
BERTHED
BERTOLT
BESEECH
BESEEMS
BESIDES
BESIEGE
BESMEAR
BESPEAK
BESPOKE
BESTBOY
BESTIAL
BESTING
BESTIRS
BESTMAN
BESTMEN
BESTOWS
BESTREW
BETAKEN
BETAKES
BETAMAX
BETARAY
BETHANY
BETHELS
BETHINK
BETIDED
BETIDES
BETIMES
BETISES
BETOKEN
BETRAYS
BETROTH
BETTERS
BETTING
BETTORS
BETWEEN
BETWIXT
BEVELED
BEVERLY
BEWAILS
BEWITCH
BEZIERS
BEZIQUE

B•E••••

BEEBALM
BEECHAM
BEECHER
BEECHES
BEEFALO
BEEFIER
BEEFING
BEEFSUP
BEEFTEA
BEEGEES
BEEGUMS
BEEHIVE
BEELIKE
BEELINE
BEEPERS
BEEPING
BEERIER
BEESWAX
BEETLES
BIENTOT
BLEAKER
BLEAKLY
BLEARED
BLEATED
BLEEPED
BLEEPER
BLEMISH
BLENDED
BLENDER
BLERIOT
BLESSED
BLESSES
BLEWOFF
BLEWOUT
BOERWAR
BREADED
BREADTH
BREAKER
BREAKIN
BREAKUP
BREASTS
BREATHE
BREATHS
BREATHY
BREEDER
BREEZED
BREEZES
BRENDAN
BRENNAN
BRENNER
BRERFOX
BRESLIN
BRETONS
BREVETS
BREVITY
BREWERS
BREWERY
BREWING

B••E•••

BABETTE
BADEGGS
BAKEOFF
BALEENS
BALEFUL
BANEFUL
BARENTS
BARETTA
BASEHIT
BASEMAN
BASEMEN
BASENJI
BASEPAY
BATEAUX
BATEMAN
BEDECKS
BEDELIA
BEDEVIL
BEDEWED
BEHEADS
BEHESTS
BENEATH
BENEFIT
BENELUX
BEREAVE
BERETTA
BESEECH
BESEEMS
BEVELED
BEVERLY
BIBELOT
BIGELOW
BIGEYES
BIKEWAY
BILEVEL
BIPEDAL
BIREMES
BIRETTA
BISECTS
BITEOFF
BLEEPED
BLEEPER
BLUEBOY
BLUEFIN
BLUEFOX
BLUEGUM
BLUEING
BLUEISH
BLUEJAY
BLUELAW
BLUESKY
BODEGAS
BODEREK
BOGEYED
BOHEMIA
BOLEROS
BONEASH
BONEDRY
BONEDUP
BONESET
BONESUP
BOREDOM
BOREOUT
BOWERED
BOXEDIN
BOXEDUP
BOXESIN
BOXESUP
BREEDER
BREEZED
BREEZES
BRIEFED
BRIEFER
BRIEFLY
BRUEGEL
BUGEYED
BUREAUS
BURETTE
BYHEART
BYREMAN
BYREMEN

B•••E••

BACKEND
BACKERS
BADDEST
BADGERS
BADNESS
BAGGERS
BAILEES
BAILERS
BAILEYS
BALDEST
BALEENS
BALLETS
BANKERS
BANNERS
BANTERS
BARBELL
BARBELS
BARBERS
BARGEIN
BARKEEP
BARKERS
BARLESS
BARLEYS
BARNEYS
BARRELS
BARRENS
BARRETT
BARTEND
BARTERS
BASKETS
BASSETS
BASTERS
BATHERS
BATTELS
BATTENS
BATTERS
BATTERY
BAWLERS
BAYLEAF
BEAKERS
BEANERY
BEARERS
BEATERS
BEAVERS
BECKETT
BEDLESS
BEDREST
BEEGEES
BEEPERS
BELIEFS
BELIEVE
BELLEEK
BENDERS
BENNETT
BENZENE
BEQUEST
BERBERS
BERGERE
BERMEJO
BERNESE
BERSERK
BESEECH
BESEEMS
BESIEGE
BESMEAR
BESPEAK
BETHELS
BETTERS
BETWEEN
BEZIERS
BIBLESS
BICKERS
BIDDERS
BIGBEND
BIGDEAL
BIGFEET
BIGGERS
BIGGEST
BIGHEAD
BIGNESS
BILLETS
BINDERS
BINDERY
BIOGENY
BIRDERS
BITLESS
BITTERN
BITTERS
BLADERS
BLAZERS
BLOWERS
BOATELS
BOATERS
BOBBERS
BOILERS
BOLDEST
BOMBECK
BOMBERS
BONIEST
BONKERS
BONNETS
BOOKEND
BOOLEAN
BOOMERS
BOOTEES
BOPPERS
BORDERS
BORNEUP
BOSKETS
BOSWELL
BOTHERS
BOVVERS
BOWLERS
BOWLESS
BOWYERS
BOXIEST
BOXSEAT
BRACERO
BRACERS
BRACEUP
BRALESS
BRAVELY
BRAVERY
BRAVEST
BRAYERS
BREVETS
BREWERS
BREWERY
BRIBERY
BROKEIN
BROKERS
BROKEUP
BRUBECK
BRUNETS
BRUTELY
BUCKETS
BUCKEYE
BUDGETS
BUDLESS
BUFFERS
BUFFETS
BUFFETT
BUGBEAR
BUGLERS
BULLETS
BUMMERS
BUMPERS
BUNGEES
BUNKERS
BURDENS
BURGEES
BURGEON
BURGERS
BURGESS
BURMESE
BURNERS
BURNETT
BUSHELS
BUSIEST
BUSTERS
BUTLERS
BUTTERS
BUTTERY
BUZZERS
BYTHEBY

B••••E•

BABBLED
BABBLES
BADDIES
BAFFLED
BAFFLER
BAFFLES
BAGGIER
BAGGIES
BAILEES
BAINTER
BALKIER
BALMIER
BALONEY
BANDIED
BANDIES
BANGLES
BANJOES
BANQUET
BANSHEE
BARKEEP
BARKIER
BARKLEY
BARMIER
BARONET
BARRIER
BASEMEN
BASQUES
BATCHED
BATCHES
BATIKED
BATSMEN
BATTIER
BATTLED
BATTLER
BATTLES
BATTUES
BAUBLES
BAULKED
BAWDIER
BAYONET
BEACHED
BEACHES
BEADIER
BEADLES
BEAGLES
BEAMIER
BEANIES
BEARDED
BEATLES
BECOMES
BEDEWED
BEDIZEN
BEECHER
BEECHES
BEEFIER
BEEFTEA
BEEGEES
BEERIER
BEETLES
BEHAVED
BEHAVES
BEHOVED
BEHOVES
BELATED
BELAYED
BELCHED
BELCHES
BELLEEK
BELLIED
BELLIES
BELLMEN
BELOVED
BEMIRED
BEMIRES
BEMUSED
BEMUSES
BENCHED
BENCHES
BENDIER
BENTLEY
BENTSEN
BERATED
BERATES
BERNSEN
BERRIED
BERRIES
BERTHED
BESIDES
BESTMEN
BESTREW
BETAKEN
BETAKES
BETIDED
BETIDES
BETIMES
BETISES
BETOKEN
BETWEEN
BEVELED
BIALIES
BIASSED
BIDDIES
BIGEYES
BIGFEET
BIGGIES
BIGLIES
BIGOSES
BIGOTED
BIGTOES
BILBIES
BILBOES
BILEVEL
BILGIER
BILLIES
BINGOES
BIRCHED
BIRCHES
BIRDIED
BIRDIES
BIRDMEN
BIREMES
BIRTHED
BISQUES
BITSIER
BITTIER
BITUMEN
BLABBED
BLABBER
BLACKED
BLACKEN
BLACKER
BLADDER
BLANDER
BLANKED
BLANKER
BLANKET
BLARNEY
BLASTED
BLASTER
BLATHER
BLATTED
BLEAKER
BLEARED
BLEATED
BLEEPED
BLEEPER
BLENDED
BLENDER
BLESSED
BLESSES
BLINDED
BLINDER
BLINKED
BLINKER
BLIPPED
BLISTER
BLITHER
BLITZED
BLITZEN
BLITZES
BLOATED
BLOCKED
BLOCKER
BLONDER
BLONDES
BLOODED
BLOOMED
BLOOMER
BLOOPED
BLOOPER
BLOTTED
BLOTTER
BLOUSED
BLOUSES
BLOWIER
BLUBBER
BLUFFED
BLUFFER
BLUNDER
BLUNTED
BLUNTER
BLURRED
BLURTED
BLUSHED
BLUSHER
BLUSHES
BLUSTER
BMOVIES
BOARDED
BOARDER
BOASTED
BOASTER
BOATMEN
BOBBIES
BOBBLED
BOBBLES
BOBSLED
BODEREK
BODICES
BOGEYED
BOGGIER
BOGGLED
BOGGLER
BOGGLES
BOLIDES
BOLSTER
BOLUSES
BONDMEN
BONESET
BONGOES
BONNIER
BONUSES
BOOBIES
BOODLES
BOOGIED
BOOGIES
BOOKIES
BOOKLET
BOOMIER
BOONIES
BOOSLER
BOOSTED
BOOSTER
BOOTEES
BOOTIES
BOOTLEG
BORATES
BOSKIER
BOSSIER
BOTCHED
BOTCHES
BOTTLED
BOTTLER
BOTTLES
BOULDER
BOULLES
BOUNCED
BOUNCER
BOUNCES
BOUNDED
BOUNDER
BOUQUET
BOURREE
BOURSES
BOVINES
BOWDLER
BOWERED
BOWTIES
BOXSTEP
BRACKEN
BRACKET
BRADLEE
BRADLEY
BRAGGED
BRAGGER
BRAIDED
BRAIDER
BRAINED
BRAISED
BRAISES
BRANDED
BRANDER
BRASHER
BRASSES
BRAVOES
BRAWLED
BRAWLER
BRAZIER
BREADED
BREAKER
BREEDER
BREEZED

BREEZES
BRENNER
BRICKED
BRIDGED
BRIDGES
BRIDGET
BRIDLED
BRIDLES
BRIEFED
BRIEFER
BRIMLEY
BRIMMED
BRINGER
BRINIER
BRIQUET
BRISKER
BRISKET
BRITTEN
BROADEN
BROADER
BROGUES
BROILED
BROILER
BRONZED
BRONZES
BROODED
BROODER
BROOKED
BROTHER
BROWNED
BROWNER
BROWSED
BROWSER
BROWSES
BRUEGEL
BRUISED
BRUISER
BRUISES
BRUITED
BRUMMEL
BRUSHED
BRUSHES
BRYNNER
BUBBLED
BUBBLES
BUCKLED
BUCKLER
BUCKLES
BUCKLEY
BUCKOES
BUDDIES
BUDGIES
BUGEYED
BUGFREE
BUGGIER
BUGGIES
BUILDER
BULBLET
BULGIER
BULKIER
BULLIED
BULLIES
BULLPEN
BUMBLED
BUMBLER
BUMBLES
BUMPIER
BUNCHED
BUNCHES
BUNCOED
BUNDLED
BUNDLES
BUNGEES
BUNGLED

BUNGLER
BUNGLES
BUNKBED
BUNKOED
BUNNIES
BURBLED
BURBLES
BURGEES
BURGHER
BURGLED
BURGLES
BURLIER
BUSBIES
BUSHIER
BUSHMEN
BUSTLED
BUSTLES
BUTCHER
BUTTIES
BYGONES
BYLINED
BYLINES
BYREMEN

B•••••E

BABBAGE
BABETTE
BACKHOE
BAGGAGE
BAGLIKE
BAGPIPE
BALANCE
BALLADE
BANDAGE
BANSHEE
BAPTISE
BAPTIZE
BARCODE
BARNONE
BAROQUE
BARRAGE
BARWARE
BATISTE
BATLIKE
BAUXITE
BEASTIE
BEATSME
BEATTIE
BECAUSE
BEDLIKE
BEDSIDE
BEDTIME
BEEHIVE
BEELIKE
BEELINE
BEGRIME
BEGUILE
BEGUINE
BEHOOVE
BELDAME
BELIEVE
BELTANE
BENZENE
BEREAVE
BERGERE
BERNESE
BERNICE
BESIEGE
BESPOKE
BEZIQUE
BIBLIKE
BICYCLE
BIGGAME
BIGNAME

BIGTIME
BINOCHE
BIPLANE
BIVALVE
BIZARRE
BLACKIE
BLANCHE
BLONDIE
BOBDOLE
BOBHOPE
BOGHOLE
BOLOTIE
BONDAGE
BONFIRE
BOURREE
BOWLIKE
BOWLINE
BOXKITE
BOXLIKE
BRADLEE
BRAILLE
BRAMBLE
BRASSIE
BREATHE
BRIGADE
BRINDLE
BRIOCHE
BRISTLE
BRITTLE
BROCADE
BROMATE
BROMIDE
BROMINE
BROWNIE
BRUSQUE
BUCKEYE
BUDLIKE
BUGFREE
BURETTE
BURMESE
BUSFARE
BUSLINE
BUYABLE
BUYTIME
BYANOSE
BYFORCE

•BE••••

ABELARD
ABENAKI
ABETTED
ABETTOR
ABEXTRA
ABEYANT
IBERIAN
OBELISK
OBERLIN
OBEYING

•B•E•••

ABREAST
ABSENCE
ABSENTS
OBJECTS
OBSERVE
OBVERSE
OBVERTS

•B••E••

ABIDEBY
ABILENE
ABUSERS
OBSCENE

•B•••E•

ABASHED
ABASHES
ABDOMEN
ABETTED
ABJURED
ABJURES
ABLATED
ABLATES
ABORTED
ABRADED
ABRADER
ABRADES
ABUTTED
ABYSSES
EBONIES
OBLATES
OBLIGED
OBLIGES
OBTUSER

•B••••E

ABALONE
ABILENE
ABRIDGE
ABSENCE
ABSOLVE
ABUSIVE
EBBTIDE
EBONITE
EBWHITE
MBABANE
OBLIQUE
OBSCENE
OBSCURE
OBSERVE
OBTRUDE
OBVERSE
OBVIATE

••BE•••

ALBEDOS
ALBENIZ
ALBERTA
ALBERTO
BABETTE
BIBELOT
DEBEERS
FABERGE
LABELED
LABELER
LABELLE
LIBELED
LIBELER
LIBERAL
LIBERIA
LIBERTY
LUBEJOB
PUBERTY
REBECCA
REBEKAH
REBENDS
RIBEYES
ROBERTA
ROBERTO
ROBERTS
ROBESON
SIBERIA
SOBERED
SOBERER
SOBERLY
TIBETAN
UMBERTO
UNBENDS

UPBEATS
WOBEGON

••B•E••

AMBIENT
AMBLERS
BIBLESS
BOBBERS
CABLERS
CABLETV
COBWEBS
DEBEERS
DUBBERS
DUBIETY
EMBLEMS
FABLERS
FIBBERS
GABBERS
GABFEST
GIBBERS
GIBBETS
GIBLETS
GOBLETS
HEBREWS
HUBBELL
INBREED
JABBERS
JOBBERS
JOBBERY
JOBLESS
KOBLENZ
LABRETS
LIBBERS
LOBBERS
LUBBERS
NABBERS
NOBLEST
ORBLESS
RABBETS
RIBLESS
ROBBERS
ROBBERY
RUBBERS
RUBBERY
SOBBERS
SUBDEBS
SUBHEAD
SUBJECT
SUBLETS
SUBSETS
SUBTEND
SUBTEXT
SUBVERT
SUBZERO
TABLEAU
TABLETS
UNBLEST
WEBFEET
WEBLESS
YABBERS

••B••E•

ALBUMEN
AMBRIES
ARBITER
ARBORED
AUBADES
BABBLED
BABBLES
BOBBIES
BOBBLED
BOBBLES
BOBSLED
BUBBLED

BUBBLES
CABARET
CABBIES
CABINET
COBBLED
COBBLER
COBBLES
CUBBIES
DABBLED
DABBLER
DABBLES
DEBAKEY
DEBASED
DEBASES
DEBATED
DEBATER
DEBATES
DEBITED
DEBONED
DEBONES
DEBRIEF
DEBUTED
DIBBLED
DIBBLES
DOBBIES
ELBOWED
EMBAYED
FABARES
FUBSIER
GABBIER
GABBLED
GABBLES
GABRIEL
GIBLUES
GOBBLED
GOBBLER
GOBBLES
HABITED
HOBBIES
HOBBLED
HOBBLES
HOBOKEN
HUBBIES
IMBIBED
IMBIBES
IMBRUED
IMBRUES
INBOXES
INBREED
INBRIEF
JUBILEE
KIBBLED
KIBBLES
LABELED
LABELER
LABORED
LABORER
LIBELED
LIBELER
LOBBIED
LOBBIES
LOBBYER
LOBSTER
LOBULES
MOBILES
MOBSTER
MRBONES
NIBBLED
NIBBLER
NIBBLES
NOBBIER
NOBBLED
NOBBLER
NOBBLES

NUBBIER
NUBBLES
ORBITED
ORBITER
PEBBLED
PEBBLES
POBOXES
RABBLES
REBATED
REBATES
REBUKED
REBUKES
REBUSES
RIBBIES
RIBEYES
RUBBLES
SABINES
SOBERED
SOBERER
SUBDUED
SUBDUER
SUBDUES
SUBTLER
TABBIES
TABORET
TUBBIER
UNBAKED
UNBOWED
UNBOXED
UNBOXES
URBANER
WEBBIER
WEBFEET
WEBSTER
WEBTOED
WOBBLED
WOBBLES

••B•••E

AMBROSE
BABBAGE
BABETTE
BIBLIKE
BOBDOLE
BOBHOPE
CABBAGE
CABOOSE
CUBICLE
DEBACLE
DEBARGE
DUBUQUE
EBBTIDE
EMBRACE
FABERGE
FEBRILE
FIBULAE
GOBROKE
HABITUE
JUBILEE
LABELLE
LABIATE
NEBULAE
NIBLIKE
ORBLIKE
OSBORNE
REBASTE
RIBCAGE
RIBLIKE
ROBLOWE
SUBLIME
SUBSIDE
SUBSUME
SUBVOCE
TUBLIKE

UMBRAGE
UPBORNE
VIBRATE
WEBLIKE
WEBPAGE
WEBSITE

•••BE••

ANTBEAR
BARBELL
BARBELS
BARBERS
BERBERS
BIGBEND
BOBBERS
BOMBECK
BOMBERS
BRIBERY
BRUBECK
BUGBEAR
CAMBERS
CATBERT
COLBERT
COMBERS
CORBELS
CORBETT
COWBELL
DAUBERS
DAYBEDS
DILBERT
DOGBERT
DUBBERS
DUMBEST
FANBELT
FIBBERS
FILBERT
FORBEAR
GABBERS
GIBBERS
GIBBETS
GILBERT
GOOBERS
HASBEEN
HAUBERK
HERBERT
HOLBEIN
HOTBEDS
HOWBEIT
HUBBELL
ICEBEER
ICEBERG
JABBERS
JOBBERS
JOBBERY
LAMBEAU
LAMBENT
LAMBERT
LAPBELT
LIBBERS
LIMBERS
LOBBERS
LOWBEAM
LUBBERS
LUMBERS
MACBETH
MEMBERS
NABBERS
NEWBERY
NORBERT
NUMBERS
NUMBEST
OFFBEAT
PEABEAN
PREBEND

PROBERS
RABBETS
RAMBEAU
RATBERT
REUBENS
ROBBERS
ROBBERY
RUBBERS
RUBBERY
SEABEDS
SEABEES
SHUBERT
SOBBERS
SORBETS
SOYBEAN
SUNBEAM
SUNBELT
TARBELL
TIMBERS
TRABERT
VERBENA
WAXBEAN
YABBERS
ZAMBEZI

•••B•E•

BABBLED
BABBLES
BAUBLES
BILBIES
BILBOES
BLABBED
BLABBER
BLUBBER
BOBBIES
BOBBLED
BOBBLES
BOOBIES
BUBBLED
BUBBLES
BULBLET
BUMBLED
BUMBLER
BUMBLES
BURBLED
BURBLES
BUSBIES
CABBIES
CLABBER
CLOBBER
CLUBBED
COBBLED
COBBLER
COBBLES
CRABBED
CRABBER
CRIBBED
CUBBIES
DABBLED
DABBLER
DABBLES
DARBIES
DERBIES
DIBBLED
DIBBLES
DOBBIES
DOUBLED
DOUBLES
DOUBLET
DOUBLEU
DOUBTED
DOUBTER
DRABBER
DRIBLET

DRUBBED
EDIBLES
ENABLED
ENABLES
FEEBLER
FLUBBED
FLUBBER
FOIBLES
FUMBLED
FUMBLER
FUMBLES
GABBIER
GABBLED
GABBLES
GAMBLED
GAMBLER
GAMBLES
GAMBREL
GARBLED
GARBLES
GLIBBER
GOBBLED
GOBBLER
GOBBLES
GRABBED
GRABBER
GRUBBED
HASBEEN
HERBIER
HERBTEA
HOBBIES
HOBBLED
HOBBLES
HOMBRES
HUBBIES
HUMBLED
HUMBLER
HUMBLES
ICEBEER
ILLBRED
JEEBIES
JUMBLED
JUMBLES
KEEBLER
KIBBLED
KIBBLES
KNOBBED
LOBBIED
LOBBIES
LOBBYER
LOOBIES
LOWBRED
MAMBOED
MARBLED
MARBLES
MAXBAER
MUMBLED
MUMBLER
MUMBLES
NIBBLED
NIBBLER
NIBBLES
NIMBLER
NOBBIER
NOBBLED
NOBBLER
NOBBLES
NUBBIER
NUBBLES
PEBBLED
PEBBLES
PROBLEM
RABBLES
RAMBLED

RAMBLER
RAMBLES
RIBBIES
ROUBLES
RUBBLES
RUMBAED
RUMBLED
RUMBLES
SAMBAED
SEABEES
SLABBED
SLOBBER
SNUBBED
STABBED
STABLED
STABLER
STABLES
STUBBED
SWABBED
SWOBBED
TABBIES
TIMBRES
TREBLED
TREBLES
TUBBIER
TUMBLED
TUMBLER
TUMBLES
TUMBREL
WAMBLED
WAMBLES
WARBLED
WARBLER
WARBLES
WEBBIER
WIMBLED
WIMBLES
WOBBLED
WOBBLES
ZOMBIES

•••B••E

AIRBASE
AMIBLUE
BABBAGE
CABBAGE
CARBIDE
CARBINE
COMBINE
DOGBANE
DRIBBLE
FORBADE
FORBORE
GARBAGE
GLOBULE
HENBANE
HERBAGE
HIPBONE
ICEBLUE
JAWBONE
MBABANE
OFFBASE
PROBATE
QUIBBLE
SEABLUE
SKYBLUE
SORBATE
STABILE
STUBBLE
THEBABE
TIMBALE
TRIBUNE
TRIBUTE
TURBINE

TWOBASE
VERBOSE

••••BE•

AEROBES
ANNABEL
ANTIBES
BLABBED
BLABBER
BLUBBER
BUNKBED
CALIBER
CARIBES
CELEBES
CHAMBER
CLABBER
CLAMBER
CLIMBED
CLIMBER
CLOBBER
CLUBBED
CRABBED
CRABBER
CRIBBED
DECIBEL
DELIBES
DISOBEY
DRABBER
DRUBBED
ENROBED
ENROBES
FLAMBED
FLAMBES
FLATBED
FLUBBED
FLUBBER
FNUMBER
FREEBEE
FRISBEE
GLIBBER
GRABBED
GRABBER
GRUBBED
IMBIBED
IMBIBES
JEZEBEL
JUJUBES
KNOBBED
LIEABED
OCTOBER
PHOEBES
PLUMBED
PLUMBER
ROADBED
SANIBEL
SCRIBES
SEEDBED
SHERBET
SIDEBET
SLABBED
SLOBBER
SLUMBER
SNUBBED
SOFABED
STABBED
STEUBEN
STROBES
STUBBED
SWABBED
SWOBBED
THUMBED
THURBER
TOYNBEE
TWINBED

UNROBED
UNROBES

••••B•E

ACTABLE
ADDABLE
ADDIBLE
AFFABLE
AMIABLE
AMOEBAE
AUDIBLE
BRAMBLE
BUYABLE
CALIBRE
CAPABLE
CELEBRE
CITABLE
CRUMBLE
DISABLE
DRIBBLE
DURABLE
EATABLE
ENNOBLE
ENTEBBE
EQUABLE
FIXABLE
FREEBEE
FREEBIE
FRIABLE
FRISBEE
GOODBYE
GRUMBLE
HIRABLE
IGNOBLE
LEGIBLE
LIKABLE
LIVABLE
LOVABLE
MACABRE
MINABLE
MIXABLE
MOVABLE
MUTABLE
NOTABLE
PARABLE
PAYABLE
PLIABLE
POTABLE
QUIBBLE
RATABLE
RISIBLE
SALABLE
SAVABLE
SEEABLE
SHAMBLE
SIZABLE
SOLUBLE
STUBBLE
STUMBLE
TAMABLE
TAXABLE
TENABLE
THIMBLE
TOYNBEE
TREMBLE
TROUBLE
USEABLE
VISIBLE
VOLUBLE

•••••BE

ASCRIBE
DISROBE
EARLOBE

ENTEBBE
ICECUBE
LAPROBE
LETITBE
MICROBE
THEBABE
WANNABE
WOULDBE

B•F••••

BAFFLED
BAFFLER
BAFFLES
BEFALLS
BEFOULS
BIFOCAL
BOFFINS
BUFFALO
BUFFERS
BUFFETS
BUFFETT
BUFFING
BUFFOON
BYFORCE

B••F•••

BAFFLED
BAFFLER
BAFFLES
BAGFULS
BALFOUR
BEEFALO
BEEFIER
BEEFING
BEEFSUP
BEEFTEA
BELFAST
BIDFAIR
BIGFEET
BIGFOOT
BLUFFED
BLUFFER
BLUFFLY
BOFFINS
BONFIRE
BOWFINS
BOXFULS
BUFFALO
BUFFERS
BUFFETS
BUFFETT
BUFFING
BUFFOON
BUGFREE
BUSFARE

B•••F••

BALEFUL
BANEFUL
BASHFUL
BENEFIT
BLOWFLY
BLUEFIN
BLUEFOX
BLUFFED
BLUFFER
BLUFFLY
BODYFAT
BOWLFUL
BRERFOX
BRIEFED
BRIEFER
BRIEFLY
BRIMFUL

B••••F•
BACKOFF
BAILIFF
BAKEOFF
BEAROFF
BEATIFY
BEGSOFF
BELIEFS
BITEOFF
BLEWOFF
BLOWOFF
BUGSOFF
BUYSOFF
BUZZOFF

B•••••F
BACKOFF
BAILIFF
BAKEOFF
BARANOF
BAYLEAF
BEAROFF
BEGSOFF
BEOWULF
BERIDOF
BITEOFF
BLEWOFF
BLOWOFF
BUGSOFF
BUYSOFF
BUZZOFF
BYWAYOF

••BF•••
GABFEST
WEBFEET
WEBFOOT

••B•F••
REBUFFS

••B••F•
FOBSOFF
REBUFFS
RUBSOFF

••B•••F
DEBRIEF
FOBSOFF
INBRIEF
RUBSOFF

•••B•F•
ZOMBIFY

B•G••••
BAGFULS
BAGGAGE
BAGGERS
BAGGIER
BAGGIES
BAGGILY
BAGGING
BAGHDAD
BAGLIKE
BAGNOLD
BAGPIPE
BEGGARS
BEGGING
BEGONIA
BEGORRA
BEGRIME
BEGSOFF
BEGUILE
BEGUINE
BIGBAND
BIGBANG
BIGBEND
BIGBIRD
BIGBOYS
BIGDEAL
BIGELOW
BIGEYES
BIGFEET
BIGFOOT
BIGGAME
BIGGERS
BIGGEST
BIGGIES
BIGGISH
BIGGUNS
BIGHEAD
BIGHORN
BIGJOHN
BIGLIES
BIGNAME
BIGNESS
BIGOSES
BIGOTED
BIGOTRY
BIGSHOT
BIGTALK
BIGTIME
BIGTOES
BIGTOPS
BIGWIGS
BOGDOWN
BOGEYED
BOGGIER
BOGGING
BOGGISH
BOGGLED
BOGGLER
BOGGLES
BOGHOLE
BUGABOO
BUGALOO
BUGBEAR
BUGEYED
BUGFREE
BUGGIER
BUGGIES
BUGGING
BUGLERS
BUGLING
BUGSOFF
BUGSOUT
BYGOLLY
BYGONES

B••G•••
BADGERS
BADGUYS
BAGGAGE
BAGGERS
BAGGIER
BAGGIES
BAGGILY
BAGGING
BANGING
BANGKOK
BANGLES
BANGSUP
BARGAIN
BARGEIN
BARGING
BATGIRL
BEAGLES
BEEGEES
BEEGUMS
BEGGARS
BEGGING
BELGIAN
BELGIUM
BENGALI
BENGALS
BERGERE
BERGMAN
BERGSON
BIGGAME
BIGGERS
BIGGEST
BIGGIES
BIGGISH
BIGGUNS
BILGIER
BINGHAM
BINGING
BINGOES
BIOGENY
BLIGHTS
BLIGHTY
BOGGIER
BOGGING
BOGGISH
BOGGLED
BOGGLER
BOGGLES
BONGING
BONGOES
BOOGIED
BOOGIES
BRAGGED
BRAGGER
BRIGADE
BRIGAND
BRIGHAM
BROGANS
BROGUES
BUDGETS
BUDGIES
BUDGING
BUGGIER
BUGGIES
BUGGING
BULGARS
BULGHUR
BULGIER
BULGING
BUNGEES
BUNGING
BUNGLED
BUNGLER
BUNGLES
BURGEES
BURGEON
BURGERS
BURGESS
BURGHER
BURGLAR
BURGLED
BURGLES
BURGOOS
BUSGIRL

B•••G••
BADEGGS
BLOWGUN
BLUEGUM
BODEGAS
BOLOGNA
BRAGGED
BRAGGER
BRIDGED
BRIDGES
BRIDGET
BRINGER
BRINGIN
BRINGON
BRINGTO
BRINGUP
BROUGHT
BRUEGEL
BURPGUN

B••••G•
BABBAGE
BADEGGS
BAGGAGE
BANDAGE
BARONGS
BARRAGE
BEDBUGS
BELONGS
BENDIGO
BESIEGE
BIGWIGS
BIOLOGY
BONDAGE
BOROUGH
BRANAGH

B•••••G
BABYING
BACHING
BACKING
BACKLOG
BAGGING
BAILING
BAITING
BALDING
BALKING
BANDING
BANGING
BANKING
BANNING
BARBING
BARGING
BARKING
BARRING
BASHING
BASKING
BASTING
BATHING
BATTING
BATWING
BAWLING
BEADING
BEAMING
BEANBAG
BEANING
BEARHUG
BEARING
BEATING
BEDDING
BEEFING
BEEPING
BEGGING
BEIJING
BELLING
BELTBAG
BELTING
BELYING
BENDING
BESTING
BETTING
BIASING
BIDDING
BIGBANG
BILKING
BILLING
BINDING
BINGING
BINNING
BIRDDOG
BIRDING
BIRLING
BITTING
BLADING
BLAMING
BLARING
BLAZING
BLOWING
BLUEING
BOATING
BOBBING
BOGGING
BOILING
BOLTING
BOMBING
BONDING
BONGING
BOOKING
BOOMING
BOOTING
BOOTLEG
BOPPING
BOSSING
BOUSING
BOWLING
BRACING
BRAKING
BRAVING
BRAYING
BRAZING
BREWING
BRIBING
BRINING
BRUXING
BUCKING
BUDDING
BUDGING
BUFFING
BUGGING
BUGLING
BULGING
BULKING
BULLDOG
BULLING
BUMMING
BUMPING
BUNGING
BUNKING
BUNTING
BUOYING
BURLING
BURNING
BURPING
BURYING
BUSHHOG
BUSHING
BUSHPIG
BUSKING
BUSSING
BUSTING
BUSYING
BUTTING
BUZZING

•B•G•••
ABIGAIL

•B••G••
ABOUGHT
OBLIGED
OBLIGES

•B•••G•
ABRIDGE
OBLONGS

•B••••G
ABASING
ABATING
ABIDING
ABUSING
OBEYING

••B•G••
WOBEGON

••B••G•
BABBAGE
CABBAGE
CYBORGS
DEBARGE
EMBARGO
FABERGE
RIBCAGE
UMBRAGE
WEBPAGE

••B•••G
AMBLING
BABYING
BOBBING
CABLING
DABBING
DUBBING
FIBBING
FOBBING
FUBBING
GABBING
GIBBING
HOBOING
IMBUING
JABBING
JIBBING
JOBBING
LIBBING
LOBBING
MOBBING
NABBING
RIBBING
ROBBING
RUBBING
SIBLING
SOBBING
SUBBING
TABBING
TABLING
WEBBING

•••B•G•
AIRBAGS
BABBAGE
BEDBUGS
CABBAGE
GARBAGE
GASBAGS
GYMBAGS
HERBAGE
HUMBUGS
ICEBAGS
KITBAGS
LUMBAGO
RAGBAGS
SEABAGS
SOWBUGS
TEABAGS

•••B••G
BARBING
BIGBANG
BOBBING
BOMBING
BRIBING
COMBING
CURBING
DABBING
DAUBING
DUBBING
DUMBING
FIBBING
FOBBING
FUBBING
GABBING
GARBING
GIBBING
GLOBING
GRABBAG
HAMBURG
HARBURG
HOMBURG
ICEBERG
JABBING
JIBBING
JOBBING
LIBBING
LIMBING
LOBBING
MOBBING
NABBING
NUMBING
PROBING
RIBBING
ROBBING
RUBBING
SEABORG
SHEBANG
SOBBING
SUBBING
TABBING
WEBBING

••••B•G
BEANBAG
BELTBAG
FEEDBAG
FIREBUG
FLEABAG
GOLDBUG
GRABBAG
HANDBAG
JUNEBUG
LADYBUG
LOVEBUG
MAILBAG
NOSEBAG
OVERBIG
PEATBOG
PILLBUG
POSTBAG
SANDBAG
TALKBIG
TOTEBAG
WINDBAG

B•H••••
BAHAMAS
BAHRAIN
BEHAVED
BEHAVES
BEHEADS
BEHESTS
BEHOLDS
BEHOOVE
BEHOVED
BEHOVES
BOHEMIA
BYHEART

B••H•••
BACHING
BAGHDAD
BARHOPS
BASHFUL
BASHING
BATHERS
BATHING
BATHMAT
BATHOIL
BATHTUB
BAUHAUS
BEEHIVE
BETHANY
BETHELS
BETHINK
BIGHEAD
BIGHORN
BISHOPS
BOBHOPE
BOGHOLE
BOKHARA
BOOHOOS
BOTHERS
BOTHNIA
BOYHOOD
BRAHMAN
BRAHMAS
BRAHMIN
BSCHOOL
BUSHELS
BUSHHOG
BUSHIDO
BUSHIER
BUSHILY
BUSHING
BUSHMAN
BUSHMEN
BUSHPIG
BYTHEBY

B•••H••
BACCHUS
BACKHOE
BALIHAI
BANSHEE
BASEHIT
BATCHED
BATCHES
BEACHED
BEACHES
BEARHUG
BEECHAM
BEECHER
BEECHES
BELCHED
BELCHES
BELLHOP
BENCHED
BENCHES
BENTHAM
BERTHED
BIGSHOT
BINGHAM
BIOCHIP
BIRCHED
BIRCHES
BIRTHED
BLATHER
BLIGHTS
BLIGHTY
BLITHER
BLUSHED
BLUSHER
BLUSHES
BLUSHON
BOKCHOY
BOLSHOI
BOOTHIA
BOTCHED
BOTCHES
BOTCHUP
BRASHER
BRASHLY
BRIGHAM
BROTHER
BRUSHED
BRUSHES
BRUSHUP
BUDDHAS
BULGHUR
BUNCHED
BUNCHES
BURGHER
BUSHHOG
BUTCHER

B••••H•
BELUSHI
BIGJOHN
BINOCHE
BLANCHE
BLOTCHY
BORSCHT
BREATHE
BREATHS
BREATHY
BRIOCHE
BRONCHI
BROUGHT
BYPATHS

B•••••H
BABYISH
BADDISH
BALDISH
BARDISH
BEAMISH
BEARISH
BEAUISH
BENEATH
BESEECH
BETROTH
BEWITCH
BIGGISH
BISMUTH
BLEMISH
BLUEISH
BOARISH
BOGGISH
BONEASH
BOOKISH
BOORISH
BOROUGH
BRANAGH
BREADTH
BRINISH
BRITISH
BRUTISH
BULLISH
BULRUSH
BUMRUSH
BURNISH

•B•H•••
EBWHITE

•B••H••
ABASHED
ABASHES
ABRAHAM

•B•••H•
ABOUGHT

•B••••H
ABOLISH
OBADIAH

••BH•••
BOBHOPE
DABHAND
JOBHOPS
JOBHUNT
NOBHILL
SUBHEAD

••B••H•
HIBACHI
TABITHA

••B•••H
BABYISH
CUBBISH
DEBAUCH
DEBORAH
DEBOUCH
MOBBISH
NEBBISH
PUBLISH
REBEKAH
REBIRTH
RUBBISH
SABBATH

•••BH••
SIOBHAN

•••B•H•
NIEBUHR

•••B••H
CUBBISH
FURBISH
MACBETH
MOBBISH
NEBBISH
RUBBISH
SABBATH
SUNBATH

••••B•H
POOHBAH

BI•••••
BIALIES
BIASING
BIASSED
BIBELOT
BIBLESS
BIBLIKE
BICKERS
BICOLOR
BICYCLE
BIDDERS
BIDDIES
BIDDING
BIDFAIR
BIENTOT
BIFOCAL
BIGBAND
BIGBANG
BIGBEND
BIGBIRD
BIGBOYS
BIGDEAL
BIGELOW
BIGEYES
BIGFEET
BIGFOOT
BIGGAME
BIGGERS
BIGGEST
BIGGIES
BIGGISH
BIGGUNS
BIGHEAD
BIGHORN
BIGJOHN
BIGLIES
BIGNAME
BIGNESS
BIGOSES
BIGOTED
BIGOTRY
BIGSHOT
BIGTALK
BIGTIME
BIGTOES
BIGTOPS
BIGWIGS
BIKEWAY
BIKINIS
BILBIES
BILBOES
BILEVEL
BILGIER
BILIOUS
BILKING
BILLETS
BILLIES
BILLING
BILLION
BILLOWS
BILLOWY
BIMODAL
BINDERS
BINDERY
BINDING
BINDSUP
BINGHAM
BINGING
BINGOES
BINNING
BINOCHE
BIOCHIP
BIOGENY
BIOLOGY
BIOMASS
BIONICS
BIPEDAL
BIPLANE
BIPOLAR
BIRCHED
BIRCHES
BIRDDOG
BIRDERS
BIRDIED
BIRDIES
BIRDING
BIRDMAN
BIRDMEN
BIREMES
BIRETTA
BIRLING
BIRTHED
BISCUIT
BISECTS
BISHOPS
BISMUTH
BISQUES
BISTROS
BITEOFF
BITLESS
BITMAPS
BITPART
BITSIER
BITTERN
BITTERS
BITTIER
BITTING
BITUMEN
BIVALVE
BIVOUAC
BIZARRE

B•I••••
BAILEES
BAILERS
BAILEYS
BAILIFF
BAILING
BAILORS
BAILOUT
BAINTER
BAITING
BEIJING
BLIGHTS
BLIGHTY
BLINDED
BLINDER
BLINDLY
BLINKAT
BLINKED
BLINKER
BLIPPED
BLISTER
BLITHER
BLITZED
BLITZEN
BLITZES
BOIARDO
BOILERS
BOILING
BOITANO
BRIARDS
BRIBERY
BRIBING
BRICKED
BRIDALS
BRIDGED
BRIDGES
BRIDGET
BRIDLED
BRIDLES
BRIEFED
BRIEFER
BRIEFLY
BRIGADE
BRIGAND
BRIGHAM
BRIMFUL
BRIMLEY
BRIMMED
BRINDLE
BRINGER
BRINGIN
BRINGON
BRINGTO
BRINGUP
BRINIER
BRINING
BRINISH
BRIOCHE
BRIQUET
BRISKER
BRISKET
BRISKLY
BRISTLE
BRISTLY
BRISTOL
BRITAIN
BRITISH
BRITONS
BRITTEN
BRITTLE
BRITTON
BUILDER
BUILDIN
BUILDUP
BUILTIN
BUILTUP

B••I•••
BACILLI
BALIHAI
BATIKED
BATISTA
BATISTE
BEDIZEN
BELIEFS
BELIEVE
BELINDA
BEMIRED
BEMIRES
BENISON
BERIDOF
BESIDES
BESIEGE
BETIDED
BETIDES
BETIMES
BETISES
BEWITCH
BEZIERS
BEZIQUE
BIKINIS
BILIOUS
BKLIBAN
BODICES
BOLIDES
BOLIVAR
BOLIVIA
BONIEST
BONITOS
BOVINES
BOXIEST
BRAIDED
BRAIDER
BRAILLE
BRAINED
BRAISED
BRAISES
BROILED
BROILER
BRUISED
BRUISER
BRUISES
BRUITED
BUNIONS
BUSIEST
BYLINED
BYLINES

B•••I••
BABBITT
BABYING
BABYISH
BACHING
BACKING
BADDIES
BADDISH
BAGGIER
BAGGIES
BAGGILY
BAGGING
BAGLIKE
BAGPIPE
BAILIFF
BAILING
BAITING
BALDING
BALDISH
BALKIER
BALKILY
BALKING
BALMIER
BALMILY
BAMBINO
BANDIED
BANDIES
BANDING
BANDITO
BANDITS
BANGING
BANKING
BANNING
BAPTISE
BAPTISM
BAPTIST
BAPTIZE
BARBING
BARDISH
BARGING
BARKIER
BARKING
BARMIER
BARRIER
BARRING
BARRIOS
BASHING
BASKING
BASSIST
BASTING
BASTION
BATGIRL
BATHING
BATLIKE
BATTIER
BATTING
BATWING
BAUXITE
BAWDIER
BAWDILY

BAWLING
BAYCITY
BEADIER
BEADING
BEAMIER
BEAMING
BEAMISH
BEANIES
BEANING
BEARING
BEARISH
BEATIFY
BEATING
BEAUISH
BEDDING
BEDLIKE
BEDSIDE
BEDTIME
BEEFIER
BEEFING
BEEHIVE
BEELIKE
BEELINE
BEEPING
BEERIER
BEGGING
BEGRIME
BEGUILE
BEGUINE
BEIJING
BELGIAN
BELGIUM
BELLIED
BELLIES
BELLING
BELLINI
BELTING
BELYING
BENDIER
BENDIGO
BENDING
BERLIOZ
BERLITZ
BERNICE
BERRIED
BERRIES
BESTIAL
BESTING
BESTIRS
BETHINK
BETTING
BETWIXT
BEWAILS
BIALIES
BIASING
BIBLIKE
BIDDIES
BIDDING
BIGBIRD
BIGGIES
BIGGISH
BIGLIES
BIGTIME
BIGWIGS
BILBIES
BILGIER
BILKING
BILLIES
BILLING
BILLION
BINDING
BINGING
BINNING
BIONICS
BIRDIED
BIRDIES
BIRDING
BIRLING
BITSIER
BITTIER
BITTING
BLADING
BLAMING
BLARING
BLAZING
BLEMISH
BLERIOT
BLOWIER
BLOWING
BLUEING
BLUEISH
BMOVIES
BOARISH
BOATING
BOBBIES
BOBBING
BOBBINS
BOBVILA
BODKINS
BOFFINS
BOGGIER
BOGGING
BOGGISH
BOILING
BOLTING
BOMBING
BONDING
BONFIRE
BONGING
BONNIER
BONNILY
BOOBIES
BOOGIED
BOOGIES
BOOKIES
BOOKING
BOOKISH
BOOMIER
BOOMING
BOONIES
BOORISH
BOOTIES
BOOTING
BOPPING
BOSKIER
BOSSIER
BOSSILY
BOSSING
BOUSING
BOWFINS
BOWLIKE
BOWLINE
BOWLING
BOWTIES
BOXKITE
BOXLIKE
BRACING
BRAKING
BRAVING
BRAYING
BRAZIER
BRAZING
BREVITY
BREWING
BRIBING
BRINIER
BRINING
BRINISH
BRITISH
BROMIDE
BROMINE
BRUTISH
BRUXING
BUCKING
BUDDIES
BUDDING
BUDGIES
BUDGING
BUDLIKE
BUFFING
BUGGIER
BUGGIES
BUGGING
BUGLING
BULGIER
BULGING
BULKIER
BULKING
BULLIED
BULLIES
BULLING
BULLION
BULLISH
BULLITT
BUMMING
BUMPIER
BUMPILY
BUMPING
BUNGING
BUNKING
BUNNIES
BUNTING
BUNYIPS
BUOYING
BURKINA
BURLIER
BURLING
BURNING
BURNISH
BURPING
BURRITO
BURYING
BUSBIES
BUSGIRL
BUSHIDO
BUSHIER
BUSHILY
BUSHING
BUSKING
BUSKINS
BUSLINE
BUSSING
BUSTING
BUSYING
BUTTIES
BUTTING
BUYTIME
BUZZING

B••••l•

BABYSIT
BACKBIT
BACKLIT
BACKSIN
BAHRAIN
BALDRIC
BALDWIN
BANDAID
BARGAIN
BARGEIN
BARMAID
BASEHIT
BATHOIL
BAVARIA
BEASTIE
BEATNIK
BEATRIX
BEATSIT
BEATTIE
BEDELIA
BEDEVIL
BEDOUIN
BEGONIA
BENAZIR
BENEFIT
BIDFAIR
BIKINIS
BIOCHIP
BISCUIT
BLACKIE
BLONDIE
BLOWSIN
BLOWSIT
BLUEFIN
BOBTAIL
BOHEMIA
BOLIVIA
BOLOTIE
BONSOIR
BOOTHIA
BORACIC
BORODIN
BORZOIS
BOTHNIA
BOUDOIR
BOXEDIN
BOXESIN
BRAHMIN
BRASSIE
BREAKIN
BRESLIN
BRINGIN
BRITAIN
BROKEIN
BROWNIE
BUCOLIC
BUILDIN
BUILTIN
BUMPKIN
BUSHPIG
BUTTSIN

B•••••l

BACARDI
BACILLI
BALIHAI
BASENJI
BELLINI
BELUSHI
BENGALI
BOLSHOI
BONJOVI
BRONCHI

•Bl••••

ABIDEBY
ABIDING
ABIGAIL
ABILENE
ABILITY
ABINTRA
ABITIBI
TBILISI

•B•l•••

ABRIDGE
OBLIGED
OBLIGES
OBLIQUE
OBOISTS
OBVIATE
OBVIOUS

•B••l••

ABASING
ABATING
ABIDING
ABILITY
ABITIBI
ABOLISH
ABUSING
ABUSIVE
EBBTIDE
EBONIES
EBONITE
EBWHITE
IBERIAN
OBADIAH
OBELISK
OBEYING
OBTAINS
TBILISI

•B•••l•

ABIGAIL
ABNAKIS
ABSTAIN
CBRADIO
OBERLIN

•B••••l

ABENAKI
ABITIBI
ABRUZZI
TBILISI

••Bl•••

ALBINOS
AMBIENT
ARBITER
CABINET
CUBICLE
CUBISTS
DEBITED
DUBIETY
DUBIOUS
HABITAT
HABITED
HABITUE
IMBIBED
IMBIBES
JABIRUS
JUBILEE
LABIALS
LABIATE
LIBIDOS
MOBILES
NABISCO
NUBIANS
ORBISON
ORBITAL
ORBITED
ORBITER
RABIDLY
REBINDS
REBIRTH
RUBICON
RUBITIN
SABINES
TABITHA
TUBISTS
UNBINDS

••B•l••

AMBLING
AMBRIES
BABBITT
BABYING
BABYISH
BIBLIKE
BOBBIES
BOBBING
BOBBINS
BOBVILA
CABBIES
CABLING
CABRINI
CUBBIES
CUBBISH
DABBING
DEBRIEF
DOBBIES
DOBBINS
DUBBING
EBBTIDE
FABRICS
FEBRILE
FIBBING
FIBRILS
FIBRINS
FOBBING
FUBBING
FUBSIER
GABBIER
GABBING
GABRIEL
GIBBING
GOBLINS
HOBBIES
HOBBITS
HOBOING
HUBBIES
HYBRIDS
IMBUING
INBRIEF
JABBING
JIBBING
JOBBING
KUBRICK
LIBBING
LOBBIED
LOBBIES
LOBBING
MOBBING
MOBBISH
NABBING
NEBBISH
NIBLICK
NIBLIKE
NOBBIER
NOBHILL
NUBBIER
NUBBINS
ORBLIKE
PUBLICS
PUBLISH
RABBITS
RABBITT
REBOILS
REBUILD
REBUILT
RIBBIES
RIBBING
RIBLIKE
ROBBING
ROBBINS
RUBBING
RUBBISH
RUBRICS
SABRINA
SIBLING
SOBBING
SUBBING
SUBLIME
SUBMITS
SUBSIDE
SUBSIDY
SUBSIST
TABBIES
TABBING
TABLING
TUBAIST
TUBBIER
TUBLIKE
UMBRIAN
WEBBIER
WEBBING
WEBLIKE
WEBSITE

••B••l•

ALBANIA
ALBENIZ
ALBUMIN
BABYSIT
BOBTAIL
CIBORIA
EMBROIL
HEBRAIC
HOBNAIL
KABUKIS
LIBERIA
ROBOTIC
RUBITIN
SIBERIA
SUBJOIN
SUBSOIL
SUBUNIT
TABLOID
UPBRAID

••B•••l

CABRINI
HIBACHI

•••Bl••

ARABIAN
BABBITT
BAMBINO
BARBING
BIGBIRD
BILBIES
BOBBIES
BOBBING
BOBBINS
BOMBING
BOOBIES
BRIBING
BUSBIES
CABBIES
CAMBIUM
CARBIDE
CARBINE
CATBIRD
COMBINE
COMBING
COWBIRD
CUBBIES
CUBBISH
CURBING
DABBING
DARBIES
DAUBING
DERBIES
DOBBIES
DOBBINS
DUBBING
DUMBING
FIBBING
FOBBING
FORBIDS
FUBBING
FURBISH
GABBIER
GABBING
GAMBIAN
GAMBITS
GARBING
GERBILS
GIBBING
GLOBING
HENBITS
HERBIER
HOBBIES
HOBBITS
HUBBIES
JABBING
JAYBIRD
JEEBIES
JIBBING
JOBBING
LIBBING
LIMBING
LINBIAO
LOBBIED
LOBBIES
LOBBING
LOOBIES
MOBBING
MOBBISH
NABBING
NEBBISH
NIOBIUM
NOBBIER
NUBBIER
NUBBINS
NUMBING
OUTBIDS
PHOBIAS
PHOBICS
PROBING
PROBITY
RABBITS
RABBITT
REDBIRD
RIBBIES
RIBBING
ROBBING
ROBBINS
RUBBING
RUBBISH
SEABIRD
SERBIAN
SOBBING
STABILE
SUBBING
TABBIES
TABBING
TERBIUM
TIDBITS
TITBITS
TUBBIER
TURBINE
TURBITS
TWOBITS
WAYBILL
WEBBIER
WEBBING
ZAMBIAN
ZOMBIES
ZOMBIFY

•••B•l•

CAMBRIC
CHABLIS
CONBRIO
HOLBEIN
HOWBEIT
LEIBNIZ
PARBOIL

•••B••l

DIABOLI
ZAMBEZI
ZAMBONI

••••Bl•

ACERBIC
AEROBIC
ALEMBIC
AMOEBIC
BACKBIT
COALBIN
COHABIT
DUSTBIN
EXHIBIT
EXURBIA
FREEBIE
INHABIT
INHIBIT
INORBIT
JACOBIN
NAMIBIA
NOTABIT
OVERBIG
PHILBIN
RAREBIT
SHOWBIZ
TALKBIG
ZENOBIA

•••••Bl

ABITIBI
NAIROBI
PUNJABI
SYLLABI

B••J•••

BANJOES
BEIJING
BIGJOHN
BONJOUR
BONJOVI

B•••J••

BELLJAR
BLUEJAY

B••••J•

BASENJI
BERMEJO

•BJ••••

ABJURED
ABJURES
OBJECTS

••BJ•••

SUBJECT
SUBJOIN

••B•J••

LUBEJOB

BK•••••

BKLIBAN

B•K••••

BAKEOFF
BAKLAVA
BIKEWAY
BIKINIS
BOKCHOY
BOKHARA

B••K•••

BACKBAY
BACKBIT
BACKEND
BACKERS
BACKHOE
BACKING
BACKLIT
BACKLOG
BACKOFF
BACKOUT
BACKRUB
BACKSIN
BACKSUP
BACKUPS
BALKANS
BALKIER
BALKILY
BALKING
BANKERS
BANKING
BANKSON
BARKEEP
BARKERS
BARKIER
BARKING
BARKLEY
BARKSAT
BASKETS
BASKING
BEAKERS
BECKETT
BECKONS
BICKERS
BILKING
BODKINS
BONKERS
BOOKEND
BOOKIES
BOOKING
BOOKISH
BOOKLET
BOSKETS
BOSKIER
BOWKNOT
BOXKITE
BRAKING
BROKEIN
BROKERS
BROKEUP
BUCKETS
BUCKEYE
BUCKING
BUCKLED
BUCKLER
BUCKLES
BUCKLEY
BUCKOES
BUCKRAM
BUCKSAW
BUCKSUP
BULKIER
BULKING
BUNKBED
BUNKERS
BUNKING
BUNKOED
BURKINA
BUSKING
BUSKINS

B•••K••

BANGKOK
BATIKED
BAULKED
BELAKUN
BETAKEN
BETAKES
BETOKEN
BLACKED
BLACKEN
BLACKER
BLACKIE
BLACKLY
BLANKED
BLANKER
BLANKET
BLANKLY
BLEAKER
BLEAKLY
BLINKAT
BLINKED
BLINKER
BLOCKED
BLOCKER
BRACKEN
BRACKET
BREAKER
BREAKIN
BREAKUP
BRICKED
BRISKER
BRISKET
BRISKLY
BROOKED
BUMPKIN

B••••K•

BAGLIKE
BATLIKE
BAZOOKA
BEDECKS
BEDLIKE
BEELIKE
BESPOKE
BIBLIKE
BLUESKY
BOWLIKE
BOXLIKE
BUDLIKE
BUROAKS

B•••••K

BANGKOK
BANNOCK
BARRACK
BEATNIK
BEDROCK
BELLEEK
BERSERK
BESPEAK
BETHINK
BIGTALK
BODEREK
BOMBECK
BRUBECK
BULLOCK
BULWARK
BURBANK
BURDOCK

•B••K••

ABNAKIS

•B•••K•

ABENAKI
ABUBAKR

•B••••K

OBELISK

••B•K••

DEBAKEY
HOBOKEN
KABUKIS
NABOKOV
REBEKAH
REBUKED
REBUKES
UNBAKED

••B••K•

BIBLIKE
DEBARKS
DEBUNKS
DYBBUKS
EMBANKS
EMBARKS
GOBROKE
NIBLIKE
ORBLIKE
RIBLIKE
TUBLIKE
WEBLIKE

••B•••K

JOBBANK
KUBRICK
LUBBOCK
MUBARAK
NIBLICK
UNBLOCK

•••B•K•

ABUBAKR
DYBBUKS
RHEBOKS

•••B••K

BOMBECK
BRUBECK
BURBANK
CUTBACK
DAYBOOK
EYEBANK
FATBACK
FOGBANK
GETBACK
GOTBACK
HAUBERK
HOGBACK
JOBBANK
LAYBACK
LOGBOOK
LUBBOCK
OUTBACK
REDBOOK
ROEBUCK
RUNBACK
SAWBUCK
SETBACK

••••B•K

GEMSBOK

BL•••••

BLABBED
BLABBER
BLACKED
BLACKEN
BLACKER
BLACKIE
BLACKLY
BLACULA
BLADDER
BLADERS
BLADING
BLAMING
BLANCHE
BLANDER
BLANDLY
BLANKED
BLANKER
BLANKET
BLANKLY
BLARING
BLARNEY
BLASTED
BLASTER
BLATANT
BLATHER
BLATTED
BLAZERS
BLAZING
BLAZONS
BLEAKER
BLEAKLY
BLEARED
BLEATED
BLEEPED
BLEEPER
BLEMISH
BLENDED
BLENDER
BLERIOT
BLESSED
BLESSES
BLEWOFF
BLEWOUT
BLIGHTS
BLIGHTY
BLINDED
BLINDER
BLINDLY
BLINKAT
BLINKED
BLINKER
BLIPPED
BLISTER
BLITHER
BLITZED
BLITZEN
BLITZES
BLOATED
BLOCKED
BLOCKER
BLONDER
BLONDES
BLONDIE
BLOODED
BLOOMED
BLOOMER
BLOOPED
BLOOPER
BLOSSOM
BLOTCHY
BLOTOUT
BLOTTED
BLOTTER
BLOUSED
BLOUSES
BLOUSON
BLOWDRY
BLOWERS
BLOWFLY
BLOWGUN
BLOWIER
BLOWING
BLOWNUP
BLOWOFF
BLOWOUT
BLOWSIN
BLOWSIT
BLOWSUP
BLOWUPS
BLUBBER
BLUEBOY
BLUEFIN
BLUEFOX
BLUEGUM
BLUEING
BLUEISH
BLUEJAY
BLUELAW
BLUESKY
BLUFFED
BLUFFER
BLUFFLY
BLUNDER
BLUNTED
BLUNTER
BLUNTLY
BLURRED
BLURTED
BLUSHED
BLUSHER
BLUSHES
BLUSHON
BLUSTER

B•L••••

BALANCE
BALATON
BALBOAS
BALCONY
BALDEST
BALDING
BALDISH
BALDRIC
BALDWIN
BALEENS
BALEFUL
BALFOUR
BALIHAI
BALKANS
BALKIER
BALKILY
BALKING
BALLADE
BALLADS
BALLARD
BALLAST

BALLBOY
BALLETS
BALLOON
BALLOTS
BALLSUP
BALMIER
BALMILY
BALONEY
BALSAMS
BELABOR
BELAKUN
BELASCO
BELATED
BELAYED
BELCHED
BELCHES
BELDAME
BELDAMS
BELFAST
BELGIAN
BELGIUM
BELIEFS
BELIEVE
BELINDA
BELLAMY
BELLBOY
BELLEEK
BELLHOP
BELLIED
BELLIES
BELLING
BELLINI
BELLJAR
BELLMAN
BELLMEN
BELLOWS
BELLYUP
BELMONT
BELONGS
BELOVED
BELTANE
BELTBAG
BELTING
BELTWAY
BELUSHI
BELYING
BILBIES
BILBOES
BILEVEL
BILGIER
BILIOUS
BILKING
BILLETS
BILLIES
BILLING
BILLION
BILLOWS
BILLOWY
BKLIBAN
BOLDEST
BOLEROS
BOLIDES
BOLIVAR
BOLIVIA
BOLOGNA
BOLOTIE
BOLSHOI
BOLSTER
BOLTING
BOLUSES
BULBLET
BULBOUS
BULBULS
BULGARS
BULGHUR
BULGIER
BULGING
BULKIER
BULKING
BULLDOG
BULLETS
BULLIED
BULLIES
BULLING
BULLION
BULLISH
BULLITT
BULLOCK
BULLPEN
BULLRUN
BULRUSH
BULWARK
BYLINED
BYLINES

B••L•••

BAGLIKE
BAILEES
BAILERS
BAILEYS
BAILIFF
BAILING
BAILORS
BAILOUT
BAKLAVA
BALLADE
BALLADS
BALLARD
BALLAST
BALLBOY
BALLETS
BALLOON
BALLOTS
BALLSUP
BARLESS
BARLEYS
BATLIKE
BAULKED
BAWLERS
BAWLING
BAWLOUT
BAYLEAF
BECLOUD
BEDLAMP
BEDLESS
BEDLIKE
BEELIKE
BEELINE
BELLAMY
BELLBOY
BELLEEK
BELLHOP
BELLIED
BELLIES
BELLING
BELLINI
BELLJAR
BELLMAN
BELLMEN
BELLOWS
BELLYUP
BERLIOZ
BERLITZ
BIALIES
BIBLESS
BIBLIKE
BIGLIES
BILLETS
BILLIES
BILLING
BILLION
BILLOWS
BILLOWY
BIOLOGY
BIPLANE
BIRLING
BITLESS
BOILERS
BOILING
BOOLEAN
BOULDER
BOULLES
BOWLERS
BOWLESS
BOWLFUL
BOWLIKE
BOWLINE
BOWLING
BOXLIKE
BRALESS
BUDLESS
BUDLIKE
BUGLERS
BUGLING
BUILDER
BUILDIN
BUILDUP
BUILTIN
BUILTUP
BULLDOG
BULLETS
BULLIED
BULLIES
BULLING
BULLION
BULLISH
BULLITT
BULLOCK
BULLPEN
BULLRUN
BURLAPS
BURLIER
BURLING
BUSLINE
BUTLERS
BYPLAYS

B•••L••

BABALOO
BABBLED
BABBLES
BABYLON
BACALAO
BACILLI
BACKLIT
BACKLOG
BAFFLED
BAFFLER
BAFFLES
BANALLY
BANGLES
BARKLEY
BASALLY
BASALTS
BATTLED
BATTLER
BATTLES
BAUBLES
BEADLES
BEAGLES
BEATLES
BECALMS
BEDELIA
BEETLES
BEFALLS
BEHOLDS
BENELUX
BENTLEY
BEVELED
BIBELOT
BICOLOR
BIGELOW
BIPOLAR
BIVALVE
BLUELAW
BOBBLED
BOBBLES
BOBSLED
BOGGLED
BOGGLER
BOGGLES
BOODLES
BOOKLET
BOOSLER
BOOTLEG
BOTTLED
BOTTLER
BOTTLES
BOULLES
BOWDLER
BRADLEE
BRADLEY
BRAILLE
BRAWLED
BRAWLER
BRESLIN
BRIDLED
BRIDLES
BRIMLEY
BROILED
BROILER
BUBBLED
BUBBLES
BUCKLED
BUCKLER
BUCKLES
BUCKLEY
BUCOLIC
BUGALOO
BULBLET
BUMBLED
BUMBLER
BUMBLES
BUNDLED
BUNDLES
BUNGLED
BUNGLER
BUNGLES
BURBLED
BURBLES
BURGLAR
BURGLED
BURGLES
BUSTLED
BUSTLES
BYGOLLY

B••••L•

BACILLI
BAGFULS
BAGGILY
BAGNOLD
BALKILY
BALMILY
BANALLY
BARBELL
BARBELS
BARRELS
BASALLY
BATTELS
BAWDILY
BEASTLY
BEDROLL
BEEBALM
BEEFALO
BEFALLS
BEFOULS
BEGUILE
BENGALI
BENGALS
BEOWULF
BERTOLT
BETHELS
BEVERLY
BEWAILS
BICYCLE
BIGTALK
BLACKLY
BLACULA
BLANDLY
BLANKLY
BLEAKLY
BLINDLY
BLOWFLY
BLUFFLY
BLUNTLY
BOATELS
BOBDOLE
BOBVILA
BOGHOLE
BONNILY
BOSSILY
BOSWELL
BOXFULS
BRAILLE
BRAMBLE
BRAMBLY
BRASHLY
BRAVELY
BRIDALS
BRIEFLY
BRINDLE
BRISKLY
BRISTLE
BRISTLY
BRITTLE
BROADLY
BRUTELY
BUFFALO
BULBULS
BUMPILY
BUSHELS
BUSHILY
BUYABLE
BYGOLLY

B•••••L

BALEFUL
BANEFUL
BARBELL
BARNOWL
BASHFUL
BATGIRL
BATHOIL
BEDEVIL
BEDROLL
BESTIAL
BIFOCAL
BIGDEAL
BILEVEL
BIMODAL
BIPEDAL
BOBTAIL
BOSWELL
BOWLFUL
BRIMFUL
BRISTOL
BRUEGEL
BRUMMEL
BSCHOOL
BUSGIRL
BUTANOL

•BL••••

ABLATED
ABLATES
ABLAUTS
OBLASTS
OBLATES
OBLIGED
OBLIGES
OBLIQUE
OBLONGS
OBLOQUY

•B•L•••

ABALONE
ABELARD
ABILENE
ABILITY
ABOLISH
OBELISK
TBILISI

•B••L••

ABSALOM
ABSOLUT
ABSOLVE
OBERLIN

•B••••L

ABIGAIL
ABUTTAL
ABYSMAL

••BL•••

AMBLERS
AMBLING
BIBLESS
BIBLIKE
CABLERS
CABLETV
CABLING
EMBLEMS
FABLERS
GIBLETS
GIBLUES
GOBLETS
GOBLINS
INBLOOM
JOBLESS
JOBLOTS
KOBLENZ
NIBLICK
NIBLIKE
NOBLEST
ORBLESS
ORBLIKE
OXBLOOD
PABLUMS
PUBLICS
PUBLISH
REBLOOM
RIBLESS
RIBLIKE
ROBLOWE
SIBLING
SUBLETS
SUBLIME
TABLEAU
TABLETS
TABLING
TABLOID
TUBLIKE
UNBLEST
UNBLOCK
WEBLESS
WEBLIKE

••B•L••

BABALOO
BABBLED
BABBLES
BABYLON
BIBELOT
BOBBLED
BOBBLES
BOBSLED
BUBBLED
BUBBLES
CABALAS
COBBLED
COBBLER
COBBLES
DABBLED
DABBLER
DABBLES
DIBBLED
DIBBLES
FIBULAE
FIBULAS
GABBLED
GABBLES
GOBBLED
GOBBLER
GOBBLES
HOBBLED
HOBBLES
JUBILEE
KIBBLED
KIBBLES
KOBOLDS
LABELED
LABELER
LABELLE
LIBELED
LIBELER
LOBULES
MOBILES
NEBULAE
NEBULAR
NEBULAS
NIBBLED
NIBBLER
NIBBLES
NOBBLED
NOBBLER
NOBBLES
NUBBLES
PABULUM
PEBBLED
PEBBLES
RABBLES
REBOLTS
RUBBLES
SUBPLOT
SUBTLER
TABULAR
TUBULAR
UNBOLTS
WOBBLED
WOBBLES
ZEBULON

••B••L•

BOBDOLE
BOBVILA
CUBICLE
DEBACLE
FEBRILE
FIBRILS
HUBBELL
LABELLE
LABIALS
NOBHILL
RABIDLY
REBOILS
REBUILD
REBUILT
SOBERLY

••B•••L

BOBTAIL
EMBROIL
GABRIEL
HOBNAIL
HUBBELL
LIBERAL
NOBHILL
ORBITAL
SUBSOIL

•••BL••

AMIBLUE
BABBLED
BABBLES
BAUBLES
BOBBLED
BOBBLES
BUBBLED
BUBBLES
BULBLET
BUMBLED
BUMBLER
BUMBLES
BURBLED
BURBLES
CHABLIS
COBBLED
COBBLER
COBBLES
DABBLED
DABBLER
DABBLES
DIBBLED
DIBBLES
DOUBLED
DOUBLES
DOUBLET
DOUBLEU
DRIBLET
EDIBLES
ENABLED
ENABLES
FEEBLER
FOIBLES
FUMBLED
FUMBLER
FUMBLES
GABBLED
GABBLES
GAMBLED
GAMBLER
GAMBLES
GARBLED
GARBLES
GILBLAS
GOBBLED
GOBBLER
GOBBLES
HOBBLED
HOBBLES
HUMBLED
HUMBLER
HUMBLES
ICEBLUE
INKBLOT
JOEBLOW
JUMBLED
JUMBLES
KEEBLER
KIBBLED
KIBBLES
LOWBLOW
MARBLED
MARBLES
MUMBLED
MUMBLER
MUMBLES
NIBBLED
NIBBLER
NIBBLES
NIMBLER
NOBBLED
NOBBLER
NOBBLES
NUBBLES
PEBBLED
PEBBLES
PROBLEM
PUEBLOS
RABBLES
RAMBLED
RAMBLER
RAMBLES
ROUBLES
RUBBLES
RUMBLED
RUMBLES
SEABLUE
SKYBLUE
STABLED
STABLER
STABLES
TEMBLOR
THEBLOB
TREBLED
TREBLES
TUMBLED
TUMBLER
TUMBLES
WAMBLED
WAMBLES
WARBLED
WARBLER
WARBLES
WIMBLED
WIMBLES
WOBBLED
WOBBLES

•••B•L•

AIRBALL
BARBELL
BARBELS
BEEBALM
BULBULS
CEMBALO
CORBELS
COWBELL
CUEBALL
CYMBALS
DIABOLI
DIMBULB
DRIBBLE
EYEBALL
EYEBOLT
FANBELT
FLYBALL
FURBALL
GAMBOLS
GERBILS
GIMBALS
GLOBULE
GUMBALL
HERBALS
HUBBELL
KIMBALL
LAPBELT
LIPBALM
LOWBALL
ODDBALL
PIEBALD
PINBALL
PITBULL
QUIBBLE
SAMBALS
STABILE
STUBBLE
STUBBLY
SUNBELT
SYMBOLS
TAMBALA
TARBELL
TEABALL
TIMBALE
TIMBALS
TOMBOLA
VERBALS
WAYBILL

•••B••L

AIRBALL
BARBELL
COWBELL
CUEBALL
EYEBALL
FLYBALL
FURBALL
GAMBREL
GUMBALL
HUBBELL
KIMBALL
LOWBALL
ODDBALL
PARBOIL
PINBALL
PITBULL
SUNBOWL
TARBELL
TEABALL
TUMBREL
WAYBILL

••••BL•

ACTABLE
ADDABLE
ADDIBLE
AFFABLE
AFFABLY
AMIABLE
AMIABLY
AUDIBLE
AUDIBLY
BRAMBLE
BRAMBLY
BUYABLE
CAPABLE
CAPABLY
CITABLE
CRUMBLE
CRUMBLY
DISABLE
DRIBBLE
DURABLE
DURABLY
EATABLE
ENNOBLE
EQUABLE
EQUABLY
FIXABLE
FRIABLE
GRUMBLE
GRUMBLY
HIRABLE
IGNOBLE
IGNOBLY
LEGIBLE
LEGIBLY
LIKABLE
LIVABLE
LOVABLE
LOVABLY
MINABLE
MIXABLE
MOVABLE
MOVABLY
MUTABLE
MUTABLY
NOTABLE
NOTABLY
PARABLE
PAYABLE
PLIABLE
PLIABLY
POTABLE
QUIBBLE
RATABLE
RISIBLE
RISIBLY
SALABLE
SAVABLE
SEEABLE
SHAMBLE
SIZABLE
SIZABLY
SOLUBLE
STUBBLE
STUBBLY
STUMBLE
TAMABLE
TAXABLE
TENABLE
TENABLY
THIMBLE
TREMBLE
TREMBLY
TROUBLE
USEABLE
VISIBLE
VISIBLY
VOLUBLE
VOLUBLY

••••B•L

ANNABEL
DECIBEL
JEZEBEL
SANIBEL

BM•••••

BMOVIES

B•M••••

BAMBINO
BAMBOOS
BEMIRED
BEMIRES
BEMOANS
BEMUSED
BEMUSES
BIMODAL
BOMBARD
BOMBAST
BOMBECK
BOMBERS
BOMBING
BUMBLED
BUMBLER
BUMBLES
BUMMERS
BUMMING
BUMPERS
BUMPIER
BUMPILY
BUMPING
BUMPKIN
BUMPSUP
BUMRAPS
BUMRUSH
BUMSOUT

B••M•••

BALMIER
BALMILY
BARMAID
BARMIER
BEAMIER
BEAMING
BEAMISH
BEAMSUP
BELMONT
BERMEJO
BERMUDA
BESMEAR
BIOMASS
BISMUTH
BITMAPS
BLAMING
BLEMISH
BONMOTS
BOOMBOX
BOOMERS
BOOMIER
BOOMING
BRAMBLE
BRAMBLY
BRIMFUL
BRIMLEY
BRIMMED
BROMATE
BROMIDE
BROMINE
BRUMMEL
BUMMERS
BUMMING
BURMANS
BURMESE

B•••M••

BAHAMAS
BASEMAN
BASEMEN
BATEMAN
BATHMAT
BATSMAN
BATSMEN
BECOMES
BELLMAN
BELLMEN
BENUMBS
BERGMAN
BESTMAN
BESTMEN
BETAMAX
BETIMES
BIRDMAN
BIRDMEN
BIREMES
BITUMEN
BLOOMED
BLOOMER
BOATMAN
BOATMEN
BOHEMIA
BONDMAN
BONDMEN
BRAHMAN
BRAHMAS
BRAHMIN
BRIMMED
BRUMMEL
BUSHMAN
BUSHMEN
BYREMAN
BYREMEN

B••••M•

BALSAMS
BANTAMS
BEATSME
BECALMS
BEDLAMP
BEDTIME
BEEGUMS
BEGRIME
BELDAME
BELDAMS
BELLAMY
BESEEMS
BIGGAME
BIGNAME
BIGTIME
BOTTOMS
BUYTIME

B•••••M

BAPTISM
BARROOM
BEDROOM
BEEBALM
BEECHAM
BELGIUM
BENTHAM
BINGHAM
BLOSSOM
BLUEGUM
BOREDOM
BOXROOM
BRIGHAM
BUCKRAM

•B••M••

ABDOMEN
ABYSMAL

•B••••M

ABRAHAM
ABSALOM

••BM•••

SUBMITS

••B•M••

ALBUMEN
ALBUMIN
LABAMBA

••B••M•

EMBLEMS
PABLUMS
SUBLIME
SUBSUME

••B•••M

INBLOOM
JIBBOOM
PABULUM
REBLOOM

•••B•M•

ALABAMA

•••B••M

BEEBALM
CAMBIUM
JIBBOOM
LIPBALM
LOWBEAM
NIOBIUM
PROBLEM
SUNBEAM
TERBIUM

B•N••••

BANALLY
BANANAS
BANDAGE
BANDAID
BANDANA
BANDBOX
BANDIED
BANDIES
BANDING
BANDITO
BANDITS
BANDSAW
BANEFUL
BANGING
BANGKOK
BANGLES
BANGSUP
BANJOES
BANKERS
BANKING
BANKSON
BANNERS
BANNING
BANNOCK
BANQUET
BANSHEE
BANTAMS
BANTERS
BANYANS
BENATAR
BENAZIR

BENCHED
BENCHES
BENDERS
BENDIER
BENDIGO
BENDING
BENEATH
BENEFIT
BENELUX
BENGALI
BENGALS
BENISON
BENNETT
BENTHAM
BENTLEY
BENTSEN
BENUMBS
BENZENE
BINDERS
BINDERY
BINDING
BINDSUP
BINGHAM
BINGING
BINGOES
BINNING
BINOCHE
BONANZA
BONBONS
BONDAGE
BONDING
BONDMAN
BONDMEN
BONEASH
BONEDRY
BONEDUP
BONESET
BONESUP
BONFIRE
BONGING
BONGOES
BONIEST
BONITOS
BONJOUR
BONJOVI
BONKERS
BONMOTS
BONNETS
BONNIER
BONNILY
BONSOIR
BONUSES
BUNCHED
BUNCHES
BUNCOED
BUNDLED
BUNDLES
BUNGEES
BUNGING
BUNGLED
BUNGLER
BUNGLES
BUNIONS
BUNKBED
BUNKERS
BUNKING
BUNKOED
BUNNIES
BUNTING
BUNYIPS

B••N•••

BADNESS
BAGNOLD
BAINTER
BANNERS
BANNING
BANNOCK
BARNABY
BARNARD
BARNEYS
BARNONE
BARNOWL
BEANBAG
BEANERY
BEANIES
BEANING
BENNETT
BERNARD
BERNESE
BERNICE
BERNSEN
BIENTOT
BIGNAME
BIGNESS
BINNING
BIONICS
BLANCHE
BLANDER
BLANDLY
BLANKED
BLANKER
BLANKET
BLANKLY
BLENDED
BLENDER
BLINDED
BLINDER
BLINDLY
BLINKAT
BLINKED
BLINKER
BLONDER
BLONDES
BLONDIE
BLUNDER
BLUNTED
BLUNTER
BLUNTLY
BONNETS
BONNIER
BONNILY
BOONIES
BORNEUP
BOUNCED
BOUNCER
BOUNCES
BOUNDED
BOUNDER
BOUNDUP
BRANAGH
BRANDED
BRANDER
BRANDON
BRANSON
BRENDAN
BRENNAN
BRENNER
BRINDLE
BRINGER
BRINGIN
BRINGON
BRINGTO
BRINGUP
BRINIER
BRINING
BRINISH
BRONCHI
BRONCOS
BRONSON
BRONZED
BRONZES
BRUNETS
BRYNNER
BUNNIES
BURNERS
BURNETT
BURNING
BURNISH
BURNOUT
BURNSUP
BURNTUP
BYANDBY
BYANOSE

B•••N••

BALANCE
BALONEY
BANANAS
BARANOF
BARENTS
BARONET
BARONGS
BASENJI
BAYONET
BEATNIK
BEGONIA
BELINDA
BELONGS
BIKINIS
BLARNEY
BLOWNUP
BONANZA
BOTHNIA
BOVINES
BOWKNOT
BRAINED
BRENNAN
BRENNER
BROSNAN
BROWNED
BROWNER
BROWNIE
BRYNNER
BUTANOL
BYGONES
BYLINED
BYLINES

B••••N•

BABOONS
BABYING
BACHING
BACKEND
BACKING
BAGGING
BAILING
BAITING
BALCONY
BALDING
BALEENS
BALKANS
BALKING
BAMBINO
BANDANA
BANDING
BANGING
BANKING
BANNING
BANYANS
BARBING
BARGING
BARKING
BARNONE
BARRENS
BARRING
BARTEND
BARYONS
BASHING
BASKING
BASTING
BATHING
BATTENS
BATTING
BATWING
BAWLING
BEACONS
BEADING
BEAMING
BEANING
BEARING
BEATING
BECKONS
BEDDING
BEEFING
BEELINE
BEEPING
BEGGING
BEGUINE
BEIJING
BELLING
BELLINI
BELMONT
BELTANE
BELTING
BELYING
BEMOANS
BENDING
BENZENE
BESTING
BETHANY
BETHINK
BETTING
BIASING
BIDDING
BIGBAND
BIGBANG
BIGBEND
BIGGUNS
BILKING
BILLING
BINDING
BINGING
BINNING
BIOGENY
BIPLANE
BIRDING
BIRLING
BITTING
BLADING
BLAMING
BLARING
BLATANT
BLAZING
BLAZONS
BLOWING
BLUEING
BOATING
BOBBING
BOBBINS
BODKINS
BOFFINS
BOGGING
BOILING
BOITANO
BOLOGNA
BOLTING
BOMBING
BONBONS
BONDING
BONGING
BOOKEND
BOOKING
BOOMING
BOOTING
BOPPING
BOSSING
BOUSING
BOWFINS
BOWLINE
BOWLING
BRACING
BRAKING
BRAVING
BRAYING
BRAZING
BRETONS
BREWING
BRIBING
BRIGAND
BRINING
BRITONS
BROGANS
BROMINE
BRUXING
BUCKING
BUDDING
BUDGING
BUFFING
BUGGING
BUGLING
BULGING
BULKING
BULLING
BUMMING
BUMPING
BUNGING
BUNIONS
BUNKING
BUNTING
BUOYANT
BUOYING
BURBANK
BURDENS
BURKINA
BURLING
BURMANS
BURNING
BURPING
BURYING
BUSHING
BUSKING
BUSKINS
BUSLINE
BUSSING
BUSTING
BUSYING
BUTTING
BUTTONS
BUZZING
BYTURNS

B•••••N

BABYLON
BACKSIN
BAHRAIN
BALATON
BALDWIN
BALLOON
BANKSON
BARGAIN
BARGEIN
BASEMAN
BASEMEN
BASSOON
BASTION
BATEMAN
BATSMAN
BATSMEN
BEARSON
BEDDOWN
BEDIZEN
BEDOUIN
BELAKUN
BELGIAN
BELLMAN
BELLMEN
BENISON
BENTSEN
BERGMAN
BERGSON
BERNSEN
BESTMAN
BESTMEN
BETAKEN
BETOKEN
BETWEEN
BIGHORN
BIGJOHN
BILLION
BIRDMAN
BIRDMEN
BITTERN
BITUMEN
BKLIBAN
BLACKEN
BLITZEN
BLOUSON
BLOWGUN
BLOWSIN
BLUEFIN
BLUSHON
BOATMAN
BOATMEN
BOGDOWN
BONDMAN
BONDMEN
BOOLEAN
BORODIN
BOURBON
BOXEDIN
BOXESIN
BRACKEN
BRAHMAN
BRAHMIN
BRANDON
BRANSON
BRAXTON
BREAKIN
BRENDAN
BRENNAN
BRESLIN
BRINGIN
BRINGON
BRITAIN
BRITTEN
BRITTON
BROADEN
BROKEIN
BRONSON
BROSNAN
BUFFOON
BUILDIN
BUILTIN
BULLION
BULLPEN
BULLRUN
BUMPKIN
BURGEON
BURPGUN
BURSTYN
BUSHMAN
BUSHMEN
BUTTSIN
BYREMAN
BYREMEN

•BN••••

ABNAKIS
IBNSAUD

•B•N•••

ABANDON
ABENAKI
ABINTRA
EBONIES
EBONITE

•B••N••

ABOUNDS
ABSENCE
ABSENTS
OBLONGS
OBTUNDS

•B•••N•

ABALONE
ABASING
ABATING
ABEYANT
ABIDING
ABILENE
ABSCOND
ABUSING
MBABANE
OBEYING
OBSCENE
OBTAINS

•B••••N

ABANDON
ABDOMEN
ABSTAIN
IBERIAN
OBERLIN

••BN•••

HOBNAIL
HOBNOBS

••B•N••

ALBANIA
ALBENIZ
ALBINOS
ALBUNDY
CABANAS
CABINET
DEBONED
DEBONES
DEBUNKS
EMBANKS
LEBANON
MRBONES
REBENDS
REBINDS
RIBANDS
SABINES
SUBUNIT
UNBENDS
UNBINDS
URBANER

••B••N•

AMBIENT
AMBLING
AUBURNS
BABOONS
BABYING
BOBBING
BOBBINS
CABLING
CABRINI
CEBUANO
DABBING
DABHAND
DOBBINS
DUBBING
FIBBING
FIBRINS
FOBBING
FUBBING
GABBING
GIBBING
GIBBONS
GOBLINS
HOBOING
IMBUING
INBOUND
JABBING
JIBBING
JOBBANK
JOBBING
JOBHUNT
KOBLENZ
LIBBING
LIBYANS
LOBBING
MOBBING
NABBING
NUBBINS
NUBIANS
OSBORNE
REBOUND
RIBBING
RIBBONS
ROBBING
ROBBINS
RUBBING
SABRINA
SIBLING
SOBBING
SUBBING
SUBORNS
SUBTEND
TABBING
TABLING
UNBOUND
UPBORNE
VIBRANT
WEBBING

••B•••N

ALBUMEN
ALBUMIN
BABYLON
HOBOKEN
LEBANON
LEBARON
ORBISON
ROBESON
RUBDOWN
RUBICON
RUBITIN
SUBJOIN
TIBETAN
UMBRIAN
WOBEGON
ZEBULON

•••BN••

LEIBNIZ

•••B•N•

ARMBAND
BAMBINO
BARBING
BIGBAND
BIGBANG
BIGBEND
BOBBING
BOBBINS
BOMBING
BONBONS
BRIBING
BURBANK
CARBINE
CARBONS
COMBINE
COMBING
CUIBONO
CURBING
DABBING
DAUBING
DISBAND
DOBBINS
DOGBANE
DUBBING
DUMBING
EYEBANK
FIBBING
FOBBING
FOGBANK
FUBBING
GABBING
GARBING
GIBBING
GIBBONS
GLOBING
HATBAND
HENBANE
HIPBONE
HUSBAND
IKEBANA
JABBING
JAWBONE
JIBBING
JOBBANK
JOBBING
JUGBAND
LAMBENT
LIBBING
LIMBING
LOBBING
MBABANE
MOBBING
NABBING
NUBBINS
NUMBING
PREBEND
PROBING
PROBONO
REUBENS
RIBBING
RIBBONS
ROBBING
ROBBINS
RUBBING
SHEBANG
SOBBING
SUBBING
TABBING
TRIBUNE
TURBANS
TURBINE
VERBENA
WEBBING
ZAMBONI

•••B••N

ARABIAN
CLIBURN
COGBURN
GAMBIAN
HASBEEN
HEPBURN
HOLBEIN
LOWBORN
MAXBORN
NEWBORN
PEABEAN
RAYBURN
SERBIAN
SIOBHAN
SOYBEAN
SUNBURN
WAXBEAN
ZAMBIAN

••••B•N

AUDUBON
BKLIBAN
BOURBON
CALIBAN
COALBIN
DUSTBIN
EXURBAN
JACOBIN
PHILBIN
STEUBEN
TESTBAN

BO•••••

BOARDED
BOARDER
BOARISH
BOASTED
BOASTER
BOATELS
BOATERS
BOATING
BOATMAN
BOATMEN
BOBBERS
BOBBIES
BOBBING
BOBBINS
BOBBLED
BOBBLES
BOBCATS
BOBDOLE
BOBHOPE
BOBSLED
BOBTAIL
BOBVILA
BODEGAS
BODEREK
BODICES
BODKINS
BODYFAT
BOERWAR
BOFFINS
BOGDOWN
BOGEYED
BOGGIER
BOGGING
BOGGISH
BOGGLED
BOGGLER
BOGGLES
BOGHOLE
BOHEMIA
BOIARDO
BOILERS
BOILING
BOITANO
BOKCHOY
BOKHARA
BOLDEST
BOLEROS
BOLIDES
BOLIVAR
BOLIVIA
BOLOGNA
BOLOTIE
BOLSHOI
BOLSTER
BOLTING
BOLUSES
BOMBARD
BOMBAST
BOMBECK
BOMBERS
BOMBING
BONANZA
BONBONS
BONDAGE
BONDING
BONDMAN
BONDMEN
BONEASH
BONEDRY
BONEDUP
BONESET
BONESUP
BONFIRE
BONGING
BONGOES
BONIEST
BONITOS
BONJOUR
BONJOVI
BONKERS
BONMOTS
BONNETS
BONNIER
BONNILY
BONSOIR
BONUSES
BOOBIES
BOOBOOS
BOODLES
BOOGIED
BOOGIES
BOOHOOS
BOOKEND
BOOKIES
BOOKING
BOOKISH
BOOKLET
BOOLEAN
BOOMBOX
BOOMERS
BOOMIER
BOOMING
BOONIES
BOORISH
BOOSLER
BOOSTED
BOOSTER
BOOSTUP
BOOTEES
BOOTHIA
BOOTIES
BOOTING
BOOTLEG
BOOTOUT
BOOTSUP
BOPPERS
BOPPING
BORACIC
BORATES
BORDERS
BOREDOM
BOREOUT
BORNEUP
BORODIN
BOROUGH
BORROWS
BORSCHT
BORZOIS
BOSKETS
BOSKIER
BOSSIER
BOSSILY
BOSSING
BOSWELL
BOTCHED
BOTCHES
BOTCHUP
BOTHERS
BOTHNIA
BOTTLED
BOTTLER
BOTTLES
BOTTOMS
BOUDOIR
BOULDER
BOULLES
BOUNCED
BOUNCER
BOUNCES
BOUNDED
BOUNDER
BOUNDUP
BOUQUET
BOURBON
BOURREE
BOURSES
BOUSING
BOUTROS
BOVINES
BOVVERS
BOWDLER
BOWERED
BOWFINS
BOWKNOT
BOWLERS
BOWLESS
BOWLFUL
BOWLIKE
BOWLINE
BOWLING
BOWSAWS
BOWSOUT
BOWTIES
BOWWOWS
BOWYERS
BOXCARS
BOXEDIN
BOXEDUP
BOXESIN
BOXESUP
BOXFULS
BOXIEST
BOXKITE
BOXLIKE
BOXROOM
BOXSEAT
BOXSTEP
BOXTOPS
BOXWOOD
BOYCOTT
BOYHOOD

B•O••••

BAOBABS
BEOWULF
BIOCHIP
BIOGENY
BIOLOGY
BIOMASS
BIONICS
BLOATED
BLOCKED
BLOCKER
BLONDER
BLONDES
BLONDIE
BLOODED
BLOOMED
BLOOMER
BLOOPED
BLOOPER
BLOSSOM
BLOTCHY
BLOTOUT
BLOTTED
BLOTTER
BLOUSED
BLOUSES
BLOUSON
BLOWDRY
BLOWERS
BLOWFLY
BLOWGUN
BLOWIER
BLOWING
BLOWNUP
BLOWOFF
BLOWOUT
BLOWSIN
BLOWSIT
BLOWSUP
BLOWUPS
BMOVIES
BOOBIES
BOOBOOS
BOODLES
BOOGIED
BOOGIES
BOOHOOS
BOOKEND
BOOKIES
BOOKING
BOOKISH
BOOKLET
BOOLEAN
BOOMBOX
BOOMERS
BOOMIER
BOOMING
BOONIES
BOORISH
BOOSLER
BOOSTED
BOOSTER
BOOSTUP
BOOTEES
BOOTHIA
BOOTIES
BOOTING
BOOTLEG
BOOTOUT
BOOTSUP
BROADAX
BROADEN
BROADER
BROADLY
BROCADE
BROGANS
BROGUES
BROILED
BROILER
BROKEIN
BROKERS
BROKEUP
BROMATE
BROMIDE
BROMINE
BRONCHI
BRONCOS
BRONSON
BRONZED
BRONZES
BROODED
BROODER
BROOKED
BROSNAN
BROTHER
BROUGHT
BROWNED
BROWNER
BROWNIE
BROWSED
BROWSER
BROWSES
BUOYANT
BUOYING
BUOYSUP

B••O•••

BABOONS
BALONEY
BARONET
BARONGS
BAROQUE
BAYONET
BAZOOKA
BECOMES
BEDOUIN
BEFOULS
BEGONIA
BEGORRA
BEHOLDS
BEHOOVE
BEHOVED
BEHOVES
BELONGS
BELOVED
BEMOANS
BETOKEN
BICOLOR
BIFOCAL
BIGOSES
BIGOTED
BIGOTRY

BIMODAL
BINOCHE
BIPOLAR
BIVOUAC
BLOODED
BLOOMED
BLOOMER
BLOOPED
BLOOPER
BOLOGNA
BOLOTIE
BORODIN
BOROUGH
BRIOCHE
BROODED
BROODER
BROOKED
BUCOLIC
BUROAKS
BUYOUTS
BYFORCE
BYGOLLY
BYGONES
BYROADS
BYWORDS

B•••O••

BABOONS
BACKOFF
BACKOUT
BADBOYS
BAGNOLD
BAILORS
BAILOUT
BAKEOFF
BALBOAS
BALCONY
BALFOUR
BALLOON
BALLOTS
BAMBOOS
BANJOES
BANNOCK
BARCODE
BARHOPS
BARNONE
BARNOWL
BARROOM
BARROWS
BARSOAP
BARYONS
BASSOON
BATBOYS
BATHOIL
BAWLOUT
BAZOOKA
BEACONS
BEAROFF
BEAROUT
BEATOUT
BECKONS
BECLOUD
BEDDOWN
BEDPOST
BEDROCK
BEDROLL
BEDROOM
BEGSOFF
BEHOOVE
BELLOWS
BELMONT
BERTOLT
BESPOKE
BESTOWS
BETROTH
BETTORS
BIGBOYS
BIGFOOT
BIGHORN
BIGJOHN
BIGTOES
BIGTOPS
BILBOES
BILIOUS
BILLOWS
BILLOWY
BINGOES
BIOLOGY
BISHOPS
BITEOFF
BLAZONS
BLEWOFF
BLEWOUT
BLOTOUT
BLOWOFF
BLOWOUT
BOBDOLE
BOBHOPE
BOGDOWN
BOGHOLE
BONBONS
BONGOES
BONJOUR
BONJOVI
BONMOTS
BONSOIR
BOOBOOS
BOOHOOS
BOOTOUT
BOREOUT
BORROWS
BORZOIS
BOTTOMS
BOUDOIR
BOWSOUT
BOWWOWS
BOXROOM
BOXTOPS
BOXWOOD
BOYCOTT
BOYHOOD
BRAVOES
BRETONS
BRITONS
BSCHOOL
BUCKOES
BUFFOON
BUGSOFF
BUGSOUT
BULBOUS
BULLOCK
BUMSOUT
BUNCOED
BUNIONS
BUNKOED
BURBOTS
BURDOCK
BURGOOS
BURNOUT
BURROWS
BUSBOYS
BUSTOUT
BUTTONS
BUTTOUT
BUYSOFF
BUYSOUT
BUZZOFF
BYANOSE

B••••O•

BABALOO
BABYLON
BACKHOE
BACKLOG
BALATON
BALLBOY
BALLOON
BAMBOOS
BANDBOX
BANGKOK
BANKSON
BARANOF
BARRIOS
BARROOM
BARSTOW
BASSOON
BASTION
BEARSON
BEDROOM
BELABOR
BELLBOY
BELLHOP
BENISON
BERGSON
BERIDOF
BERLIOZ
BESTBOY
BIBELOT
BICOLOR
BIENTOT
BIGELOW
BIGFOOT
BIGSHOT
BILLION
BIRDDOG
BISTROS
BLERIOT
BLOSSOM
BLOUSON
BLUEBOY
BLUEFOX
BLUSHON
BOKCHOY
BOLEROS
BOLSHOI
BONITOS
BOOBOOS
BOOHOOS
BOOMBOX
BOREDOM
BOURBON
BOUTROS
BOWKNOT
BOXROOM
BOXWOOD
BOYHOOD
BRANDON
BRANSON
BRAXTON
BRERFOX
BRINGON
BRISTOL
BRITTON
BRONCOS
BRONSON
BSCHOOL
BUFFOON
BUGABOO
BUGALOO
BULLDOG
BULLION
BURGEON
BURGOOS
BUSHHOG
BUSSTOP
BUTANOL
BYWAYOF

B•••••O

BABALOO
BACALAO
BAMBINO
BANDITO
BEEFALO
BELASCO
BENDIGO
BERMEJO
BOIARDO
BOITANO
BRACERO
BRAVADO
BRINGTO
BUFFALO
BUGABOO
BUGALOO
BURRITO
BUSHIDO

•BO••••

ABOLISH
ABORTED
ABOUGHT
ABOUNDS
EBONIES
EBONITE
OBOISTS

•B•O•••

ABBOTCY
ABDOMEN
ABSOLUT
ABSOLVE
ABSORBS
OBLONGS
OBLOQUY

•B••O••

ABALONE
ABSCOND
OBVIOUS

•B•••O•

ABANDON
ABETTOR
ABSALOM

•B••••O

CBRADIO

••BO•••

ABBOTCY
ARBORED
ARBOURS
BABOONS
CABOOSE
CIBORIA
CYBORGS
DEBONED
DEBONES
DEBORAH
DEBOUCH
ELBOWED
HOBOING
HOBOKEN
INBOARD
INBOUND
INBOXES
KOBOLDS
LABORED
LABORER
LABOURS
MRBONES
NABOKOV
NOBODYS
ONBOARD
OSBORNE
POBOXES
PTBOATS
REBOILS
REBOLTS
REBOOTS
REBOUND
REBOZOS
ROBOCOP
ROBOTIC
SUBORNS
TABORET
UNBOLTS
UNBOUND
UNBOWED
UNBOXED
UNBOXES
UPBORNE

••B•O••

AMBROSE
BABOONS
BOBDOLE
BOBHOPE
CABOOSE
DEBTORS
DUBIOUS
EMBROIL
FIBROUS
FOBSOFF
GIBBONS
GIBBOUS
GOBROKE
HOBNOBS
INBLOOM
JIBBOOM
JOBHOPS
JOBLOTS
LABCOAT
LUBBOCK
OXBLOOD
REBLOOM
REBOOTS
RIBBONS
ROBLOWE
ROBROYS
RUBDOWN
RUBSOFF
RUBSOUT
SUBJOIN
SUBROSA
SUBSOIL
SUBVOCE
TABLOID
UNBLOCK
WEBFOOT
WEBTOED

••B••O•

ALBEDOS
ALBINOS
BABALOO
BABYLON
BIBELOT
EMBRYOS
GABBROS
INBLOOM
JIBBOOM
LEBANON
LEBARON
LIBIDOS
LUBEJOB
NABOKOV
ORBISON
OXBLOOD
REBLOOM
REBOZOS
ROBESON
ROBOCOP
RUBATOS
RUBICON
SUBPLOT
WEBFOOT
WOBEGON
ZEBULON

••B•••O

ALBERTO
BABALOO
CEBUANO
EMBARGO
NABISCO
ROBERTO
SUBZERO
TABASCO
TOBACCO
UMBERTO
VIBRATO

•••BO••

AIRBOAT
ANYBODY
BADBOYS
BALBOAS
BAMBOOS
BATBOYS
BIGBOYS
BILBOES
BONBONS
BOOBOOS
BULBOUS
BURBOTS
BUSBOYS
CARBONS
CARBOYS
CATBOAT
COWBOYS
CUIBONO
DASBOOT
DAYBOOK
DAYBOYS
DIABOLI
EYEBOLT
FLYBOYS
FOGBOWS
FORBORE
GAMBOLS
GIBBONS
GIBBOUS
GOABOUT
GUNBOAT
HARBORS
HARBOUR
HIPBONE
HIPBOOT
ICEBOAT
JAWBONE
JERBOAS
JETBOAT
JIBBOOM
LOGBOOK
LOWBORN
LOWBOYS
LUBBOCK
MAMBOED
MAXBORN
NEWBORN
PARBOIL
PEABODY
PITBOSS
PROBONO
REDBOOK
RHEBOKS
RIBBONS
ROWBOAT
SEABORG
SKIBOBS
SKIBOOT
SUNBOWL
SYMBOLS
TAMBOUR
TOMBOLA
TOMBOYS
TUGBOAT
TURBOTS
VERBOSE
ZAMBONI

•••B•O•

BAMBOOS
BOOBOOS
DASBOOT
DAYBOOK
EYEBROW
GABBROS
HIPBOOT
INKBLOT
JIBBOOM
JOEBLOW
LOGBOOK
LOWBLOW
LOWBROW
PUEBLOS
REDBOOK
SKIBOOT
TEMBLOR
THEBLOB

•••B••O

BAMBINO
CEMBALO
CONBRIO
CUIBONO
GAMBADO
LINBIAO
LUMBAGO
PROBONO

••••BO•

ATTABOY
AUDUBON
BALLBOY
BANDBOX
BELABOR
BELLBOY
BESTBOY
BLUEBOY
BOOMBOX
BOURBON
BUGABOO
CALLBOX
CARIBOU
CASHBOX
COPYBOY
DOWNBOW
FIREBOX
GAZEBOS
GEARBOX
GEMSBOK
HAUTBOY
HIGHBOY
HOMEBOY
ICHABOD
JUKEBOX
LOCKBOX
LONGBOW
MAILBOX
MARABOU
NEWSBOY
PAGEBOY
PEATBOG
PILLBOX
PLAYBOY
PLOWBOY
POORBOX
POORBOY
POSTBOX
RAINBOW
SALTBOX
SANDBOX
SHOEBOX
SOAPBOX
TOOLBOX

••••B•O

BUGABOO
CARABAO

•••••BO

ARECIBO
COLUMBO
MOGAMBO
PLACEBO
RIOLOBO

B•P••••

BAPTISE
BAPTISM
BAPTIST
BAPTIZE
BIPEDAL
BIPLANE
BIPOLAR
BOPPERS
BOPPING
BYPATHS
BYPLAYS

B••P•••

BAGPIPE
BEDPOST
BEEPERS
BEEPING
BESPEAK
BESPOKE
BITPART
BLIPPED
BOPPERS
BOPPING
BUMPERS
BUMPIER
BUMPILY
BUMPING
BUMPKIN
BUMPSUP
BURPGUN
BURPING

B•••P••

BASEPAY
BEARPAW
BLEEPED
BLEEPER
BLIPPED
BLOOPED
BLOOPER
BULLPEN
BUSHPIG

B••••P•

BACKUPS
BAGPIPE
BARHOPS
BIGTOPS
BISHOPS
BITMAPS
BLOWUPS
BOBHOPE
BOXTOPS
BUMRAPS
BUNYIPS
BURLAPS

B•••••P

BACKSUP
BALLSUP
BANGSUP
BARKEEP
BARSOAP
BEADSUP
BEAMSUP
BEARSUP
BEATSUP
BEDLAMP
BEEFSUP
BELLHOP
BELLYUP
BINDSUP
BIOCHIP
BLOWNUP
BLOWSUP
BONEDUP
BONESUP
BOOSTUP
BOOTSUP
BORNEUP
BOTCHUP
BOUNDUP
BOXEDUP
BOXESUP
BOXSTEP
BRACEUP
BREAKUP
BRINGUP
BROKEUP
BRUSHUP
BUCKSUP
BUDDYUP
BUILDUP
BUILTUP
BUMPSUP
BUOYSUP
BURNSUP
BURNTUP
BUSSTOP

••BP•••

SUBPLOT
WEBPAGE

••B••P•

BOBHOPE

HUBCAPS
JOBHOPS
MOBCAPS

••B•••P

ROBOCOP

••••B•P

SCRUBUP

B•Q••••

BEQUEST

B••Q•••

BANQUET
BASQUES
BISQUES
BOUQUET
BRIQUET

B•••Q••

BAROQUE
BEZIQUE
BRUSQUE

•B••Q••

OBLIQUE
OBLOQUY

••B•Q••

DUBUQUE

BR•••••

BRACERO
BRACERS
BRACEUP
BRACING
BRACKEN
BRACKET
BRADLEE
BRADLEY
BRAGGED
BRAGGER
BRAHMAN
BRAHMAS
BRAHMIN
BRAIDED
BRAIDER
BRAILLE
BRAINED
BRAISED
BRAISES
BRAKING
BRALESS
BRAMBLE
BRAMBLY
BRANAGH
BRANDED
BRANDER
BRANDON
BRANSON
BRASHER
BRASHLY
BRASSES
BRASSIE
BRAVADO
BRAVELY
BRAVERY
BRAVEST
BRAVING
BRAVOES
BRAVURA
BRAWLED
BRAWLER
BRAXTON
BRAYERS
BRAYING
BRAZIER
BRAZING
BREADED
BREADTH
BREAKER
BREAKIN
BREAKUP
BREASTS
BREATHE
BREATHS
BREATHY
BREEDER
BREEZED
BREEZES
BRENDAN
BRENNAN
BRENNER
BRERFOX
BRESLIN
BRETONS
BREVETS
BREVITY
BREWERS
BREWERY
BREWING
BRIARDS
BRIBERY
BRIBING
BRICKED
BRIDALS
BRIDGED
BRIDGES
BRIDGET
BRIDLED
BRIDLES
BRIEFED
BRIEFER
BRIEFLY
BRIGADE
BRIGAND
BRIGHAM
BRIMFUL
BRIMLEY
BRIMMED
BRINDLE
BRINGER
BRINGIN
BRINGON
BRINGTO
BRINGUP
BRINIER
BRINING
BRINISH
BRIOCHE
BRIQUET
BRISKER
BRISKET
BRISKLY
BRISTLE
BRISTLY
BRISTOL
BRITAIN
BRITISH
BRITONS
BRITTEN
BRITTLE
BRITTON
BROADAX
BROADEN
BROADER
BROADLY
BROCADE
BROGANS
BROGUES
BROILED
BROILER
BROKEIN
BROKERS
BROKEUP
BROMATE
BROMIDE
BROMINE
BRONCHI
BRONCOS
BRONSON
BRONZED
BRONZES
BROODED
BROODER
BROOKED
BROSNAN
BROTHER
BROUGHT
BROWNED
BROWNER
BROWNIE
BROWSED
BROWSER
BROWSES
BRUBECK
BRUEGEL
BRUISED
BRUISER
BRUISES
BRUITED
BRUMMEL
BRUNETS
BRUSHED
BRUSHES
BRUSHUP
BRUSQUE
BRUTELY
BRUTISH
BRUXING
BRYNNER

B•R••••

BARANOF
BARBARA
BARBARY
BARBELL
BARBELS
BARBERS
BARBING
BARBUDA
BARCARS
BARCODE
BARDISH
BARENTS
BARETTA
BARGAIN
BARGEIN
BARGING
BARHOPS
BARKEEP
BARKERS
BARKIER
BARKING
BARKLEY
BARKSAT
BARLESS
BARLEYS
BARMAID
BARMIER
BARNABY
BARNARD
BARNEYS
BARNONE
BARNOWL
BARONET
BARONGS
BAROQUE
BARRACK
BARRAGE
BARRELS
BARRENS
BARRETT
BARRIER
BARRING
BARRIOS
BARROOM
BARROWS
BARSOAP
BARSTOW
BARTABS
BARTEND
BARTERS
BARWARE
BARYONS
BERATED
BERATES
BERBERS
BEREAVE
BERETTA
BERGERE
BERGMAN
BERGSON
BERIDOF
BERLIOZ
BERLITZ
BERMEJO
BERMUDA
BERNARD
BERNESE
BERNICE
BERNSEN
BERRIED
BERRIES
BERSERK
BERTHED
BERTOLT
BIRCHED
BIRCHES
BIRDDOG
BIRDERS
BIRDIED
BIRDIES
BIRDING
BIRDMAN
BIRDMEN
BIREMES
BIRETTA
BIRLING
BIRTHED
BORACIC
BORATES
BORDERS
BOREDOM
BOREOUT
BORNEUP
BORODIN
BOROUGH
BORROWS
BORSCHT
BORZOIS
BURBANK
BURBLED
BURBLES
BURBOTS
BURDENS
BURDOCK
BUREAUS
BURETTE
BURGEES
BURGEON
BURGERS
BURGESS
BURGHER
BURGLAR
BURGLED
BURGLES
BURGOOS
BURKINA
BURLAPS
BURLIER
BURLING
BURMANS
BURMESE
BURNERS
BURNETT
BURNING
BURNISH
BURNOUT
BURNSUP
BURNTUP
BUROAKS
BURPGUN
BURPING
BURRITO
BURROWS
BURSARS
BURSARY
BURSTYN
BURYING
BYREMAN
BYREMEN
BYROADS

B••R•••

BAHRAIN
BARRACK
BARRAGE
BARRELS
BARRENS
BARRETT
BARRIER
BARRING
BARRIOS
BARROOM
BARROWS
BEARCAT
BEARCUB
BEARDED
BEARERS
BEARHUG
BEARING
BEARISH
BEAROFF
BEAROUT
BEARPAW
BEARSON
BEARSUP
BEDREST
BEDROCK
BEDROLL
BEDROOM
BEERIER
BEGRIME
BERRIED
BERRIES
BETRAYS
BETROTH
BLARING

BLARNEY
BLERIOT
BLURRED
BLURTED
BOARDED
BOARDER
BOARISH
BOERWAR
BOORISH
BORROWS
BOURBON
BOURREE
BOURSES
BOXROOM
BRERFOX
BULRUSH
BUMRAPS
BUMRUSH
BURRITO
BURROWS

B•••R••

BACARDI
BACKRUB
BALDRIC
BAVARIA
BEATRIX
BEGORRA
BEMIRED
BEMIRES
BESTREW
BETARAY
BEVERLY
BISTROS
BIZARRE
BLEARED
BLURRED
BODEREK
BOIARDO
BOLEROS
BOURREE
BOUTROS
BOWERED
BRIARDS
BUCKRAM
BUGFREE
BULLRUN
BYFORCE
BYTURNS
BYWORDS

B••••R•

BACKERS
BADGERS
BAGGERS
BAILERS
BAILORS
BALLARD
BANKERS
BANNERS
BANTERS
BARBARA
BARBARY
BARBERS
BARCARS
BARKERS
BARNARD
BARTERS
BARWARE
BASTERS
BATGIRL
BATHERS
BATTERS
BATTERY
BAWLERS
BAZAARS
BEAKERS
BEANERY
BEARERS
BEATERS
BEAVERS
BEEPERS
BEGGARS
BEGORRA
BENDERS
BERBERS
BERGERE
BERNARD
BERSERK
BESTIRS
BETTERS
BETTORS
BEZIERS
BICKERS
BIDDERS
BIGBIRD
BIGGERS
BIGHORN
BIGOTRY
BINDERS
BINDERY
BIRDERS
BITPART
BITTERN
BITTERS
BIZARRE
BLADERS
BLAZERS
BLOWDRY
BLOWERS
BOATERS
BOBBERS
BOILERS
BOKHARA
BOMBARD
BOMBERS
BONEDRY
BONFIRE
BONKERS
BOOMERS
BOPPERS
BORDERS
BOTHERS
BOVVERS
BOWLERS
BOWYERS
BOXCARS
BRACERO
BRACERS
BRAVERY
BRAVURA
BRAYERS
BREWERS
BREWERY
BRIBERY
BROKERS
BUFFERS
BUGLERS
BULGARS
BULWARK
BUMMERS
BUMPERS
BUNKERS
BURGERS
BURNERS
BURSARS
BURSARY
BUSFARE
BUSGIRL
BUSTARD
BUSTERS
BUTLERS
BUTTERS
BUTTERY
BUZZARD
BUZZERS
BYHEART

B•••••R

BAFFLER
BAGGIER
BAINTER
BALFOUR
BALKIER
BALMIER
BARKIER
BARMIER
BARRIER
BATTIER
BATTLER
BAWDIER
BEADIER
BEAMIER
BEECHER
BEEFIER
BEERIER
BELABOR
BELLJAR
BENATAR
BENAZIR
BENDIER
BESMEAR
BICOLOR
BIDFAIR
BILGIER
BIPOLAR
BITSIER
BITTIER
BLABBER
BLACKER
BLADDER
BLANDER
BLANKER
BLASTER
BLATHER
BLEAKER
BLEEPER
BLENDER
BLINDER
BLINKER
BLISTER
BLITHER
BLOCKER
BLONDER
BLOOMER
BLOOPER
BLOTTER
BLOWIER
BLUBBER
BLUFFER
BLUNDER
BLUNTER
BLUSHER
BLUSTER
BOARDER
BOASTER
BOERWAR
BOGGIER
BOGGLER
BOLIVAR
BOLSTER
BONJOUR
BONNIER
BONSOIR
BOOMIER
BOOSLER
BOOSTER
BOSKIER
BOSSIER
BOTTLER
BOUDOIR
BOULDER
BOUNCER
BOUNDER
BOWDLER
BRAGGER
BRAIDER
BRANDER
BRASHER
BRAWLER
BRAZIER
BREAKER
BREEDER
BRENNER
BRIEFER
BRINGER
BRINIER
BRISKER
BROADER
BROILER
BROODER
BROTHER
BROWNER
BROWSER
BRUISER
BRYNNER
BUCKLER
BUGBEAR
BUGGIER
BUILDER
BULGHUR
BULGIER
BULKIER
BUMBLER
BUMPIER
BUNGLER
BURGHER
BURGLAR
BURLIER
BUSHIER
BUTCHER

•BR••••

ABRADED
ABRADER
ABRADES
ABRAHAM
ABREAST
ABRIDGE
ABRUZZI
CBRADIO

•B•R•••

ABORTED
IBERIAN
OBERLIN
OBTRUDE

•B••R••

ABJURED
ABJURES
ABSORBS
OBSERVE
OBVERSE
OBVERTS

•B•••R•

ABELARD
ABEXTRA
ABINTRA
ABUSERS
OBSCURE

•B••••R

ABETTOR
ABRADER
ABUBAKR
OBTUSER

••BR•••

AMBRIES
AMBROSE
CABRINI
DEBRIEF
EMBRACE
EMBROIL
EMBRYOS
FABRICS
FEBRILE
FIBRILS
FIBRINS
FIBROUS
GABRIEL
GOBROKE
HEBRAIC
HEBREWS
HYBRIDS
IMBRUED
IMBRUES
INBREED
INBRIEF
KUBRICK
LABRETS
LIBRARY
ROBROYS
RUBRICS
SABRINA
SUBROSA
UMBRAGE
UMBRIAN
UPBRAID
VIBRANT
VIBRATE
VIBRATO

••B•R••

ALBERTA
ALBERTO
ARBORED
AUBURNS
CABARET
CIBORIA
CYBORGS
DEBARGE
DEBARKS
DEBORAH
DUBARRY
EMBARGO
EMBARKS
FABARES
FABERGE
GABBROS
JABIRUS
LABORED
LABORER
LEBARON
LIBERAL
LIBERIA
LIBERTY
MUBARAK
OSBORNE
PUBERTY
REBIRTH
ROBARDS
ROBERTA
ROBERTO
ROBERTS
SIBERIA
SOBERED
SOBERER
SOBERLY
SUBORNS
SUBURBS
TABARDS
TABORET
UMBERTO
UPBORNE

••B••R•

AMBLERS
ARBOURS
BOBBERS
CABLERS
DEBEERS
DEBTORS
DUBARRY
DUBBERS
FABLERS
FIBBERS
GABBERS
GIBBERS
HUBBARD
INBOARD
JABBERS
JOBBERS
JOBBERY
LABOURS
LIBBERS
LIBRARY
LOBBERS
LUBBERS
NABBERS
ONBOARD
ROBBERS
ROBBERY
RUBBERS
RUBBERY
SOBBERS
SUBVERT
SUBZERO
YABBERS

••B•••R

ARBITER
COBBLER
DABBLER
DEBATER
FUBSIER
GABBIER
GOBBLER
LABELER
LABORER
LIBELER
LOBBYER
LOBSTER
MOBSTER
NEBULAR
NIBBLER
NOBBIER
NOBBLER
NUBBIER
ORBITER
SOBERER
SUBDUER
SUBTLER
TABULAR
TUBBIER
TUBULAR
URBANER
WEBBIER
WEBSTER

•••BR••

CAMBRIC
CONBRIO
EYEBROW
GABBROS
GAMBREL
HOFBRAU
HOMBRES
ILLBRED
LOWBRED
LOWBROW
TIMBRES
TUMBREL

•••B•R•

ASHBURY
BARBARA
BARBARY
BARBERS
BIGBIRD
BOBBERS
BOMBARD
BOMBERS
BRIBERY
CADBURY
CAMBERS
CATBERT
CATBIRD
CLIBURN
COGBURN
COLBERT
COMBERS
COWBIRD
DANBURY
DAUBERS
DILBERT
DISBARS
DOGBERT
DUBBERS
FIBBERS
FILBERT
FORBORE
GABBERS
GIBBERS
GILBERT
GOOBERS
HAMBURG
HARBORS
HARBURG
HAUBERK
HEPBURN
HERBERT
HOMBURG
HUBBARD
ICEBERG
ISOBARS
JABBERS
JAYBIRD
JOBBERS
JOBBERY
LAMBERT
LIBBERS
LIMBERS
LOBBERS
LOMBARD
LOWBORN
LUBBERS
LUMBARS
LUMBERS
MAXBORN
MEMBERS
NABBERS
NEWBERY
NEWBORN
NORBERT
NUMBERS
PROBERS
RATBERT
RAYBURN
REDBIRD
RHUBARB
ROBBERS
ROBBERY
RUBBERS
RUBBERY
SAMBARS
SEABIRD
SEABORG
SHUBERT
SOBBERS
SUDBURY
SUNBURN
TIMBERS
TRABERT
WETBARS
YABBERS
ZEDBARS

•••B••R

ABUBAKR
ANTBEAR
BLABBER
BLUBBER
BUGBEAR
BUMBLER
CLABBER
CLOBBER
CLUBCAR
COBBLER
CRABBER
DABBLER
DOUBTER
DRABBER
FEEBLER
FLUBBER
FORBEAR
FUMBLER
GABBIER
GAMBLER
GLIBBER
GOBBLER
GRABBER
HARBOUR
HERBIER
HUMBLER
ICEBEER
KEEBLER
LOBBYER
MAXBAER
MUMBLER
NIBBLER
NIEBUHR
NIMBLER
NOBBIER
NOBBLER
NUBBIER
RAMBLER
SLOBBER
STABLER
TAMBOUR
TEMBLOR
TUBBIER
TUMBLER
WARBLER
WEBBIER

••••BR•

ALGEBRA
CALIBRE
CELEBRE
CEREBRA
CULEBRA
MACABRE

••••B•R

BELABOR
BLABBER
BLUBBER
CALIBER
CASHBAR
CHAMBER
CLABBER
CLAMBER
CLIMBER
CLOBBER
CRABBER
CROWBAR
DRABBER
DRAWBAR
FERNBAR
FLUBBER
FNUMBER
GLIBBER
GOODBAR
GRABBER
MALABAR
OCTOBER
OPENBAR
PLUMBER
ROLLBAR
SANDBAR
SASHBAR
SIDEBAR
SLOBBER
SLUMBER
THURBER
WINEBAR

BS•••••

BSCHOOL

B•S••••

BASALLY
BASALTS
BASEHIT
BASEMAN
BASEMEN
BASENJI
BASEPAY
BASHFUL
BASHING
BASKETS
BASKING
BASQUES
BASSETS
BASSIST
BASSOON
BASTERS
BASTING
BASTION
BESEECH
BESEEMS
BESIDES
BESIEGE
BESMEAR
BESPEAK
BESPOKE
BESTBOY
BESTIAL
BESTING
BESTIRS
BESTMAN
BESTMEN
BESTOWS
BESTREW
BISCUIT
BISECTS
BISHOPS
BISMUTH
BISQUES
BISTROS
BOSKETS
BOSKIER
BOSSIER
BOSSILY
BOSSING
BOSWELL
BUSBIES
BUSBOYS
BUSFARE
BUSGIRL
BUSHELS
BUSHHOG
BUSHIDO
BUSHIER
BUSHILY
BUSHING
BUSHMAN
BUSHMEN
BUSHPIG
BUSIEST
BUSKING
BUSKINS
BUSLINE
BUSSING
BUSSTOP
BUSTARD
BUSTERS
BUSTING
BUSTLED
BUSTLES
BUSTOUT
BUSYING

B••S•••

BALSAMS
BANSHEE
BARSOAP
BARSTOW
BASSETS
BASSIST
BASSOON
BATSMAN
BATSMEN
BEASTIE
BEASTLY
BEDSIDE
BEESWAX
BEGSOFF
BERSERK
BIASING
BIASSED
BIGSHOT
BITSIER
BLASTED
BLASTER
BLESSED
BLESSES
BLISTER
BLOSSOM
BLUSHED
BLUSHER
BLUSHES
BLUSHON
BLUSTER
BOASTED
BOASTER
BOBSLED
BOLSHOI
BOLSTER
BONSOIR
BOOSLER
BOOSTED
BOOSTER
BOOSTUP
BORSCHT
BOSSIER
BOSSILY
BOSSING
BOUSING
BOWSAWS
BOWSOUT
BOXSEAT
BOXSTEP
BRASHER
BRASHLY
BRASSES
BRASSIE
BRESLIN
BRISKER
BRISKET
BRISKLY
BRISTLE
BRISTLY
BRISTOL
BROSNAN
BRUSHED
BRUSHES
BRUSHUP
BRUSQUE
BUGSOFF
BUGSOUT
BUMSOUT
BURSARS
BURSARY
BURSTYN
BUSSING
BUSSTOP
BUYSOFF
BUYSOUT

B•••S••

BABASSU
BABYSAT
BABYSIT
BACKSIN
BACKSUP
BALLSUP
BANDSAW
BANGSUP
BANKSON
BARKSAT
BATISTA
BATISTE
BEADSUP
BEAMSUP
BEARSON
BEARSUP
BEATSIT
BEATSME
BEATSUP
BEEFSUP
BEHESTS
BELASCO
BELUSHI
BEMUSED
BEMUSES
BENISON
BENTSEN
BERGSON
BERNSEN
BETISES
BIASSED
BIGOSES
BINDSUP
BLESSED
BLESSES
BLOSSOM
BLOUSED
BLOUSES
BLOUSON
BLOWSIN
BLOWSIT
BLOWSUP
BLUESKY
BOLUSES
BONESET
BONESUP
BONUSES
BOOTSUP
BOURSES
BOXESIN
BOXESUP
BRAISED
BRAISES
BRANSON
BRASSES
BRASSIE
BREASTS
BRONSON
BROWSED
BROWSER
BROWSES
BRUISED
BRUISER
BRUISES
BUCKSAW
BUCKSUP
BUMPSUP
BUOYSUP
BURNSUP
BUTTSIN
BUZZSAW

B••••S•

BABASSU
BABYISH
BADDEST
BADDISH
BADNESS
BALDEST
BALDISH
BALLAST
BAPTISE
BAPTISM
BAPTIST
BARDISH
BARLESS
BASSIST
BEAMISH
BEARISH
BEAUISH
BECAUSE
BEDLESS
BEDPOST
BEDREST
BELFAST
BEQUEST
BERNESE
BIBLESS
BIGGEST
BIGGISH
BIGNESS
BIOMASS
BITLESS
BLEMISH
BLUEISH
BOARISH
BOGGISH
BOLDEST
BOMBAST
BONEASH
BONIEST
BOOKISH
BOORISH
BOWLESS
BOXIEST
BRALESS
BRAVEST
BRINISH
BRITISH
BRUTISH
BUDLESS
BULLISH
BULRUSH
BUMRUSH
BURGESS
BURMESE
BURNISH
BUSIEST
BYANOSE

B•••••S

BABBLES
BABOONS
BACCHUS
BACKERS
BACKUPS
BADBOYS
BADDIES
BADEGGS
BADGERS
BADGUYS
BADNESS
BAFFLES
BAGFULS
BAGGERS
BAGGIES
BAHAMAS
BAILEES
BAILERS
BAILEYS
BAILORS
BALBOAS
BALEENS
BALKANS
BALLADS
BALLETS
BALLOTS
BALSAMS
BAMBOOS
BANANAS
BANDIES
BANDITS
BANGLES
BANJOES
BANKERS
BANNERS
BANTAMS
BANTERS
BANYANS
BAOBABS
BARBELS
BARBERS
BARCARS
BARENTS
BARHOPS
BARKERS
BARLESS
BARLEYS
BARNEYS
BARONGS
BARRELS
BARRENS
BARRIOS
BARROWS
BARTABS
BARTERS
BARYONS
BASALTS
BASKETS
BASQUES
BASSETS
BASTERS
BATBOYS
BATCHES
BATHERS
BATTELS
BATTENS
BATTERS
BATTLES
BATTUES
BAUBLES
BAUHAUS
BAWLERS
BAZAARS
BEACHES
BEACONS
BEADLES
BEAGLES
BEAKERS
BEANIES
BEARERS
BEATERS
BEATLES
BEAVERS
BECALMS
BECKONS
BECOMES
BEDAUBS
BEDBUGS
BEDECKS
BEDLESS
BEECHES
BEEGEES
BEEGUMS
BEEPERS
BEETLES
BEFALLS
BEFOULS
BEGGARS
BEHAVES
BEHEADS
BEHESTS
BEHOLDS
BEHOVES
BELCHES
BELDAMS
BELIEFS
BELLIES
BELLOWS
BELONGS
BEMIRES

BEMOANS
BEMUSES
BENCHES
BENDERS
BENGALS
BENUMBS
BERATES
BERBERS
BERRIES
BESEEMS
BESIDES
BESTIRS
BESTOWS
BETAKES
BETHELS
BETIDES
BETIMES
BETISES
BETRAYS
BETTERS
BETTORS
BEWAILS
BEZIERS
BIALIES
BIBLESS
BICKERS
BIDDERS
BIDDIES
BIGBOYS
BIGEYES
BIGGERS
BIGGIES
BIGGUNS
BIGLIES
BIGNESS
BIGOSES
BIGTOES
BIGTOPS
BIGWIGS
BIKINIS
BILBIES
BILBOES
BILIOUS
BILLETS
BILLIES
BILLOWS
BINDERS
BINGOES
BIOMASS
BIONICS
BIRCHES
BIRDERS
BIRDIES
BIREMES
BISECTS
BISHOPS
BISQUES
BISTROS
BITLESS
BITMAPS
BITTERS
BLADERS
BLAZERS
BLAZONS
BLESSES
BLIGHTS
BLITZES
BLONDES
BLOUSES
BLOWERS
BLOWUPS
BLUSHES
BMOVIES
BOATELS
BOATERS
BOBBERS
BOBBIES
BOBBINS
BOBBLES
BOBCATS
BODEGAS
BODICES
BODKINS
BOFFINS
BOGGLES
BOILERS
BOLEROS
BOLIDES
BOLUSES
BOMBERS
BONBONS
BONGOES
BONITOS
BONKERS
BONMOTS
BONNETS
BONUSES
BOOBIES
BOOBOOS
BOODLES
BOOGIES
BOOHOOS
BOOKIES
BOOMERS
BOONIES
BOOTEES
BOOTIES
BOPPERS
BORATES
BORDERS
BORROWS
BORZOIS
BOSKETS
BOTCHES
BOTHERS
BOTTLES
BOTTOMS
BOULLES
BOUNCES
BOURSES
BOUTROS
BOVINES
BOVVERS
BOWFINS
BOWLERS
BOWLESS
BOWSAWS
BOWTIES
BOWWOWS
BOWYERS
BOXCARS
BOXFULS
BOXTOPS
BRACERS
BRAHMAS
BRAISES
BRALESS
BRASSES
BRAVOES
BRAYERS
BREASTS
BREATHS
BREEZES
BRETONS
BREVETS
BREWERS
BRIARDS
BRIDALS
BRIDGES
BRIDLES
BRITONS
BROGANS
BROGUES
BROKERS
BRONCOS
BRONZES
BROWSES
BRUISES
BRUNETS
BRUSHES
BUBBLES
BUCKETS
BUCKLES
BUCKOES
BUDDHAS
BUDDIES
BUDGETS
BUDGIES
BUDLESS
BUFFERS
BUFFETS
BUGGIES
BUGLERS
BULBOUS
BULBULS
BULGARS
BULLETS
BULLIES
BUMBLES
BUMMERS
BUMPERS
BUMRAPS
BUNCHES
BUNDLES
BUNGEES
BUNGLES
BUNIONS
BUNKERS
BUNNIES
BUNYIPS
BURBLES
BURBOTS
BURDENS
BUREAUS
BURGEES
BURGERS
BURGESS
BURGLES
BURGOOS
BURLAPS
BURMANS
BURNERS
BUROAKS
BURROWS
BURSARS
BUSBIES
BUSBOYS
BUSHELS
BUSKINS
BUSTERS
BUSTLES
BUTLERS
BUTTERS
BUTTIES
BUTTONS
BUYOUTS
BUZZERS
BYGONES
BYLINES
BYPATHS
BYPLAYS
BYROADS
BYTURNS
BYWORDS

•BS••••

ABSALOM
ABSCOND
ABSENCE
ABSENTS
ABSOLUT
ABSOLVE
ABSORBS
ABSTAIN
OBSCENE
OBSCURE
OBSERVE

•B•S•••

ABASHED
ABASHES
ABASING
ABUSERS
ABUSING
ABUSIVE
ABYSMAL
ABYSSES
IBNSAUD

•B••S••

ABYSSES
OBLASTS
OBOISTS
OBTUSER

•B•••S•

ABOLISH
ABREAST
OBELISK
OBVERSE
TBILISI

•B••••S

ABASHES
ABDUCTS
ABJURES
ABLATES
ABLAUTS
ABNAKIS
ABOUNDS
ABRADES
ABSENTS
ABSORBS
ABUSERS
ABYSSES
EBONIES
OBJECTS
OBLASTS
OBLATES
OBLIGES
OBLONGS
OBOISTS
OBTAINS
OBTUNDS
OBVERTS
OBVIOUS

••BS•••

BOBSLED
FOBSOFF
FUBSIER
LOBSTER
MOBSTER
RUBSOFF
RUBSOUT
SUBSETS
SUBSIDE
SUBSIDY
SUBSIST
SUBSOIL
SUBSUME
WEBSITE
WEBSTER

••B•S••

BABASSU
BABYSAT
BABYSIT
CUBISTS
DEBASED
DEBASES
DEBUSSY
EMBASSY
NABISCO
ORBISON
REBASTE
REBUSES
ROBESON
ROBUSTA
TABASCO
TUBISTS

••B••S•

AMBROSE
BABASSU
BABYISH
BIBLESS
CABOOSE
CUBBISH
DEBUSSY
EMBASSY
GABFEST
JOBLESS
MOBBISH
NEBBISH
NOBLEST
ORBLESS
PUBLISH
RIBLESS
RUBBISH
SUBROSA
SUBSIST
TUBAIST
UNBLEST
WEBLESS

••B•••S

ALBEDOS
ALBINOS
AMBLERS
AMBRIES
ARBOURS
ARBUTUS
AUBADES
AUBURNS
BABBLES
BABOONS
BIBLESS
BOBBERS
BOBBIES
BOBBINS
BOBBLES
BOBCATS
BUBBLES
CABALAS
CABANAS
CABBIES
CABLERS
COBBLES
COBWEBS
CUBBIES
CUBISTS
CYBORGS
DABBLES
DEBARKS
DEBASES
DEBATES
DEBEERS
DEBONES
DEBTORS
DEBUNKS
DIBBLES
DOBBIES
DOBBINS
DUBBERS
DUBIOUS
DYBBUKS
EMBANKS
EMBARKS
EMBLEMS
EMBRYOS
FABARES
FABLERS
FABRICS
FIBBERS
FIBRILS
FIBRINS
FIBROUS
FIBULAS
GABBERS
GABBLES
GABBROS
GIBBERS
GIBBETS
GIBBONS
GIBBOUS
GIBLETS
GIBLUES
GOBBLES
GOBLETS
GOBLINS
HEBREWS
HOBBIES
HOBBITS
HOBBLES
HOBNOBS
HUBBIES
HUBBUBS
HUBCAPS
HYBRIDS
IMBIBES
IMBRUES
INBOXES
JABBERS
JABIRUS
JOBBERS
JOBHOPS
JOBLESS
JOBLOTS
KABUKIS
KIBBLES
KOBOLDS
LABIALS
LABOURS
LABRETS
LIBBERS
LIBIDOS
LIBYANS
LOBBERS
LOBBIES
LOBULES
LUBBERS
MOBCAPS
MOBILES
MRBONES
NABBERS
NEBULAS
NIBBLES
NOBBLES
NOBODYS
NUBBINS
NUBBLES
NUBIANS
ORBLESS
PABLUMS
PEBBLES
POBOXES
PTBOATS
PUBLICS
RABBETS
RABBITS
RABBLES
REBATES
REBENDS
REBINDS
REBOILS
REBOLTS
REBOOTS
REBOZOS
REBUFFS
REBUKES
REBUSES
RIBANDS
RIBBIES
RIBBONS
RIBEYES
RIBLESS
ROBARDS
ROBBERS
ROBBINS
ROBERTS
ROBROYS
RUBATOS
RUBBERS
RUBBLES
RUBRICS
SABINES
SOBBERS
SUBDEBS
SUBDUES
SUBLETS
SUBMITS
SUBORNS
SUBSETS
SUBURBS
SUBWAYS
TABARDS
TABBIES
TABLETS
TUBISTS
UNBENDS
UNBINDS
UNBOLTS
UNBOXES
UPBEATS
WEBLESS
WOBBLES
YABBERS

•••BS••

GRABSAT

•••B•S•

AIRBASE
BOMBAST
COMBUST
CUBBISH
DUMBEST
FURBISH
MOBBISH
MOMBASA
NEBBISH
NUMBEST
OFFBASE
PITBOSS
RUBBISH
SEABASS
TWOBASE
VERBOSE

•••B••S

AIRBAGS
BABBLES
BADBOYS
BALBOAS
BAMBOOS
BAOBABS
BARBELS
BARBERS
BATBOYS
BAUBLES
BEDBUGS
BERBERS
BIGBOYS
BILBIES
BILBOES
BOBBERS
BOBBIES
BOBBINS
BOBBLES
BOMBERS
BONBONS
BOOBIES
BOOBOOS
BUBBLES
BULBOUS
BULBULS
BUMBLES
BURBLES
BURBOTS
BUSBIES
BUSBOYS
CABBIES
CAMBERS
CARBONS
CARBOYS
CHABLIS
COBBLES
COMBATS
COMBERS
CORBELS
COWBOYS
CUBBIES
CYMBALS
DABBLES
DARBIES
DAUBERS
DAYBEDS
DAYBOYS
DERBIES
DIBBLES
DISBARS
DOBBIES
DOBBINS
DOUBLES
DUBBERS
DYBBUKS
EDIBLES
ENABLES
FIBBERS
FLYBOYS
FOGBOWS
FOIBLES
FORBIDS
FUMBLES
GABBERS
GABBLES
GABBROS
GAMBITS
GAMBLES
GAMBOLS
GARBLES
GASBAGS
GERBILS
GIBBERS
GIBBETS
GIBBONS
GIBBOUS
GILBLAS
GIMBALS
GOBBLES
GOOBERS
GYMBAGS
HARBORS
HENBITS
HERBALS
HOBBIES
HOBBITS
HOBBLES
HOMBRES
HOTBEDS
HUBBIES
HUBBUBS
HUMBLES
HUMBUGS
ICEBAGS
ISOBARS
JABBERS
JEEBIES
JERBOAS
JOBBERS
JUMBLES
KIBBLES
KITBAGS
LAMBDAS
LIBBERS
LIMBERS
LOBBERS
LOBBIES
LOOBIES
LOWBOYS
LUBBERS
LUMBARS
LUMBERS
MARBLES
MEMBERS
MUMBLES
NABBERS
NIBBLES
NOBBLES
NUBBINS
NUBBLES
NUMBATS
NUMBERS
OJIBWAS
OUTBIDS
PEBBLES
PHOBIAS
PHOBICS
PITBOSS
PROBERS
PUEBLOS
RABBETS
RABBITS
RABBLES
RAGBAGS
RAMBLES
REDBUDS
REUBENS
RHEBOKS
RIBBIES
RIBBONS
ROBBERS
ROBBINS
ROUBLES
RUBBERS
RUBBLES
RUMBLES
SAMBALS
SAMBARS
SEABAGS
SEABASS
SEABEDS
SEABEES
SKIBOBS
SOBBERS
SORBETS
SOWBUGS
STABLES
SYMBOLS
TABBIES
TEABAGS
TIDBITS
TIMBALS
TIMBERS
TIMBRES
TITBITS
TOMBOYS
TREBLES
TUMBLES
TURBANS
TURBITS
TURBOTS
TWOBITS
VERBALS
WAMBLES
WARBLES
WETBARS
WIMBLES
WOBBLES
WOMBATS
YABBERS
ZEDBARS
ZOMBIES

••••B•S

AEROBES
AMOEBAS
ANTIBES
ARROBAS
CARIBES
CASABAS
CELEBES
COLOBUS
DELIBES
ENROBES
FLAMBES
GAZEBOS
GOODBYS
IMBIBES
JUJUBES
MINIBUS
OMNIBUS
PHOEBES
PHOEBUS
RHOMBUS
RHUMBAS
SCRIBES
STROBES
UNROBES
VIRIBUS
ZAREBAS

•••••BS

ABSORBS
ADSORBS
ADVERBS
BAOBABS
BARTABS
BEDAUBS
BENUMBS
CHERUBS
COBWEBS
CONFABS
CONJOBS
DAYJOBS
HOBNOBS
HOTTUBS
HUBBUBS
MADLIBS
MIDRIBS
ODDJOBS
PREFABS
RESORBS
REVERBS
SCARABS
SEALABS
SKIBOBS
SUBDEBS
SUBURBS

B•T••••

BATBOYS
BATCHED
BATCHES
BATEAUX
BATEMAN
BATGIRL
BATHERS
BATHING
BATHMAT
BATHOIL
BATHTUB
BATIKED
BATISTA
BATISTE
BATLIKE
BATSMAN
BATSMEN
BATTELS
BATTENS
BATTERS
BATTERY
BATTIER
BATTING
BATTLED
BATTLER
BATTLES
BATTUES
BATWING
BETAKEN
BETAKES
BETAMAX
BETARAY
BETHANY
BETHELS
BETHINK
BETIDED
BETIDES
BETIMES
BETISES
BETOKEN
BETRAYS
BETROTH
BETTERS
BETTING
BETTORS
BETWEEN
BETWIXT
BITEOFF
BITLESS
BITMAPS
BITPART
BITSIER
BITTERN
BITTERS
BITTIER
BITTING
BITUMEN
BOTCHED
BOTCHES
BOTCHUP
BOTHERS
BOTHNIA
BOTTLED
BOTTLER
BOTTLES
BOTTOMS
BUTANOL
BUTCHER
BUTLERS
BUTTERS
BUTTERY
BUTTIES
BUTTING
BUTTONS
BUTTOUT
BUTTSIN
BYTHEBY
BYTURNS

B••T•••

BAITING
BANTAMS
BANTERS
BAPTISE
BAPTISM
BAPTIST
BAPTIZE
BARTABS
BARTEND
BARTERS
BASTERS
BASTING
BASTION
BATTELS
BATTENS
BATTERS
BATTERY
BATTIER
BATTING
BATTLED
BATTLER
BATTLES
BATTUES
BEATERS
BEATIFY
BEATING
BEATLES
BEATNIK
BEATOUT
BEATRIX
BEATSIT
BEATSME
BEATSUP
BEATTIE
BEDTIME
BEETLES
BELTANE
BELTBAG
BELTING
BELTWAY
BENTHAM
BENTLEY
BENTSEN
BERTHED
BERTOLT
BESTBOY
BESTIAL
BESTING
BESTIRS
BESTMAN
BESTMEN
BESTOWS
BESTREW
BETTERS
BETTING
BETTORS
BIGTALK
BIGTIME
BIGTOES
BIGTOPS
BIRTHED
BISTROS
BITTERN
BITTERS
BITTIER
BITTING
BLATANT
BLATHER
BLATTED
BLITHER
BLITZED
BLITZEN
BLITZES
BLOTCHY
BLOTOUT
BLOTTED
BLOTTER
BOATELS
BOATERS
BOATING
BOATMAN
BOATMEN
BOBTAIL
BOITANO
BOLTING
BOOTEES
BOOTHIA
BOOTIES
BOOTING
BOOTLEG
BOOTOUT
BOOTSUP
BOTTLED
BOTTLER
BOTTLES
BOTTOMS
BOUTROS
BOWTIES
BOXTOPS
BRETONS
BRITAIN
BRITISH
BRITONS
BRITTEN
BRITTLE
BRITTON
BROTHER
BRUTELY
BRUTISH
BUNTING
BUSTARD
BUSTERS
BUSTING
BUSTLED
BUSTLES
BUSTOUT
BUTTERS
BUTTERY
BUTTIES
BUTTING
BUTTONS
BUTTOUT
BUTTSIN
BUYTIME

B•••T••

BABETTE
BAINTER
BALATON
BARETTA
BARSTOW
BATHTUB
BEASTIE
BEASTLY
BEATTIE
BEEFTEA
BELATED
BENATAR
BERATED
BERATES
BERETTA
BEWITCH
BIENTOT
BIGOTED
BIGOTRY
BIRETTA
BLASTED
BLASTER
BLATTED
BLEATED
BLISTER
BLOATED
BLOTTED
BLOTTER
BLUNTED
BLUNTER
BLUNTLY
BLURTED
BLUSTER
BOASTED
BOASTER
BOLOTIE
BOLSTER
BONITOS
BOOSTED
BOOSTER
BOOSTUP
BORATES
BOXSTEP
BRAXTON
BREATHE
BREATHS
BREATHY
BRISTLE
BRISTLY
BRISTOL
BRITTEN
BRITTLE
BRITTON
BRUITED
BUILTIN
BUILTUP
BURETTE
BURNTUP

BURSTYN
BUSSTOP
BYPATHS

B••••T•

BABBITT
BABETTE
BALLETS
BALLOTS
BANDITO
BANDITS
BARENTS
BARETTA
BARRETT
BASALTS
BASKETS
BASSETS
BATISTA
BATISTE
BAUXITE
BAYCITY
BECKETT
BEHESTS
BENEATH
BENNETT
BERETTA
BERLITZ
BETROTH
BILLETS
BIRETTA
BISECTS
BISMUTH
BLIGHTS
BLIGHTY
BOBCATS
BONMOTS
BONNETS
BOSKETS
BOXKITE
BOYCOTT
BREADTH
BREASTS
BREVETS
BREVITY
BRINGTO
BROMATE
BRUNETS
BUCKETS
BUDGETS
BUFFETS
BUFFETT
BULLETS
BULLITT
BURBOTS
BURETTE
BURNETT
BURRITO
BUYOUTS

B•••••T

BABBITT
BABYSAT
BABYSIT
BACKBIT
BACKLIT
BACKOUT
BADDEST
BAILOUT
BALDEST
BALLAST
BANQUET
BAPTIST
BARKSAT
BARONET
BARRETT
BASEHIT
BASSIST
BATHMAT
BAWLOUT
BAYONET
BEARCAT
BEAROUT
BEATOUT
BEATSIT
BECKETT
BEDPOST
BEDREST
BELFAST
BELMONT
BENEFIT
BENNETT
BEQUEST
BERTOLT
BETWIXT
BIBELOT
BIENTOT
BIGFEET
BIGFOOT
BIGGEST
BIGSHOT
BISCUIT
BITPART
BLANKET
BLATANT
BLERIOT
BLEWOUT
BLINKAT
BLOTOUT
BLOWOUT
BLOWSIT
BODYFAT
BOLDEST
BOMBAST
BONESET
BONIEST
BOOKLET
BOOTOUT
BOREOUT
BORSCHT
BOUQUET
BOWKNOT
BOWSOUT
BOXIEST
BOXSEAT
BOYCOTT
BRACKET
BRAVEST
BRIDGET
BRIQUET
BRISKET
BROUGHT
BUFFETT
BUGSOUT
BULBLET
BULLITT
BUMSOUT
BUOYANT
BURNETT
BURNOUT
BUSIEST
BUSTOUT
BUTTOUT
BUYSOUT
BYHEART

•BT••••

OBTAINS
OBTRUDE
OBTUNDS
OBTUSER

•B•T•••

ABATING
ABETTED
ABETTOR
ABITIBI
ABSTAIN
ABUTTAL
ABUTTED
EBBTIDE

•B••T••

ABBOTCY
ABETTED
ABETTOR
ABEXTRA
ABINTRA
ABLATED
ABLATES
ABORTED
ABUTTAL
ABUTTED
OBLATES

•B•••T•

ABDUCTS
ABILITY
ABLAUTS
ABSENTS
EBONITE
EBWHITE
OBJECTS
OBLASTS
OBOISTS
OBVERTS
OBVIATE

•B••••T

ABEYANT
ABOUGHT
ABREAST
ABSOLUT

••BT•••

BOBTAIL
DEBTORS
EBBTIDE
SUBTEND
SUBTEXT
SUBTLER
WEBTOED

••B•T••

ABBOTCY
ARBITER
ARBUTUS
BABETTE
DEBATED
DEBATER
DEBATES
DEBITED
DEBUTED
HABITAT
HABITED
HABITUE
LOBSTER
MOBSTER
ORBITAL
ORBITED
ORBITER
REBATED
REBATES
ROBOTIC
RUBATOS
RUBITIN
TABITHA
TIBETAN
WEBSTER

••B••T•

ALBERTA
ALBERTO
BABBITT
BABETTE
BOBCATS
CABLETV
CUBISTS
DUBIETY
GIBBETS
GIBLETS
GOBLETS
HOBBITS
JOBLOTS
KIBBUTZ
LABIATE
LABRETS
LIBERTY
PTBOATS
PUBERTY
RABBETS
RABBITS
RABBITT
REBASTE
REBIRTH
REBOLTS
REBOOTS
ROBERTA
ROBERTO
ROBERTS
ROBUSTA
SABBATH
SUBLETS
SUBMITS
SUBSETS
TABLETS
TUBISTS
UMBERTO
UNBOLTS
UPBEATS
VIBRATE
VIBRATO
WEBSITE

••B•••T

AMBIENT
BABBITT
BABYSAT
BABYSIT
BIBELOT
CABARET
CABINET
GABFEST
HABITAT
JOBHUNT
LABCOAT
NOBLEST
RABBITT
REBUILT
RUBSOUT
SUBJECT
SUBPLOT
SUBSIST
SUBTEXT
SUBUNIT
SUBVERT
TABORET
TUBAIST
UNBLEST
VIBRANT
WEBFEET
WEBFOOT

•••BT••

DOUBTED
DOUBTER
HERBTEA

•••B•T•

BABBITT
BURBOTS
COMBATS
CORBETT
GAMBITS
GIBBETS
HENBITS
HOBBITS
KIBBUTZ
MACBETH
NUMBATS
PROBATE
PROBITY
RABBETS
RABBITS
RABBITT
SABBATH
SORBATE
SORBETS
SUNBATH
TIDBITS
TITBITS
TRIBUTE
TURBITS
TURBOTS
TWOBITS
WOMBATS

•••B••T

AIRBOAT
BABBITT
BOMBAST
BULBLET
CATBERT
CATBOAT
COLBERT
COMBUST
CORBETT
CURBCUT
DASBOOT
DILBERT
DOGBERT
DOUBLET
DRIBLET
DUMBEST
EYEBOLT
FANBELT
FILBERT
GILBERT
GOABOUT
GRABSAT
GUNBOAT
HERBERT
HIPBOOT
HOWBEIT
ICEBOAT
INKBLOT
JETBOAT
LAMBENT
LAMBERT
LAPBELT
NORBERT
NUMBEST
OFFBEAT
RABBITT
RATBERT
ROWBOAT
SHUBERT
SKIBOOT
SUNBELT
TRABERT
TUGBOAT

••••B•T

ACROBAT
AEROBAT
BACKBIT
COHABIT
DINGBAT
EXHIBIT
HALIBUT
INHABIT
INHIBIT
INORBIT
NOTABIT
RAREBIT
SHERBET
SIDEBET

•••••BT

INDOUBT
NODOUBT
REDOUBT

BU•••••

BUBBLED
BUBBLES
BUCKETS
BUCKEYE
BUCKING
BUCKLED
BUCKLER
BUCKLES
BUCKLEY
BUCKOES
BUCKRAM
BUCKSAW
BUCKSUP
BUCOLIC
BUDDHAS
BUDDIES
BUDDING
BUDDYUP
BUDGETS
BUDGIES
BUDGING
BUDLESS
BUDLIKE
BUFFALO
BUFFERS
BUFFETS
BUFFETT
BUFFING
BUFFOON
BUGABOO
BUGALOO
BUGBEAR
BUGEYED
BUGFREE
BUGGIER
BUGGIES
BUGGING
BUGLERS
BUGLING
BUGSOFF
BUGSOUT
BUILDER
BUILDIN
BUILDUP
BUILTIN
BUILTUP
BULBLET
BULBOUS
BULBULS
BULGARS
BULGHUR
BULGIER
BULGING
BULKIER
BULKING
BULLDOG
BULLETS
BULLIED
BULLIES
BULLING
BULLION
BULLISH
BULLITT
BULLOCK
BULLPEN
BULLRUN
BULRUSH
BULWARK
BUMBLED
BUMBLER
BUMBLES
BUMMERS
BUMMING
BUMPERS
BUMPIER
BUMPILY
BUMPING
BUMPKIN
BUMPSUP
BUMRAPS
BUMRUSH
BUMSOUT
BUNCHED
BUNCHES
BUNCOED
BUNDLED
BUNDLES
BUNGEES
BUNGING
BUNGLED
BUNGLER
BUNGLES
BUNIONS
BUNKBED
BUNKERS
BUNKING
BUNKOED
BUNNIES
BUNTING
BUNYIPS
BUOYANT
BUOYING
BUOYSUP
BURBANK
BURBLED
BURBLES
BURBOTS
BURDENS
BURDOCK
BUREAUS
BURETTE
BURGEES
BURGEON
BURGERS
BURGESS
BURGHER
BURGLAR
BURGLED
BURGLES
BURGOOS
BURKINA
BURLAPS
BURLIER
BURLING
BURMANS
BURMESE
BURNERS
BURNETT
BURNING
BURNISH
BURNOUT
BURNSUP
BURNTUP
BUROAKS
BURPGUN
BURPING
BURRITO
BURROWS
BURSARS
BURSARY
BURSTYN
BURYING
BUSBIES
BUSBOYS
BUSFARE
BUSGIRL
BUSHELS
BUSHHOG
BUSHIDO
BUSHIER
BUSHILY
BUSHING
BUSHMAN
BUSHMEN
BUSHPIG
BUSIEST
BUSKING
BUSKINS
BUSLINE
BUSSING
BUSSTOP
BUSTARD
BUSTERS
BUSTING
BUSTLED
BUSTLES
BUSTOUT
BUSYING
BUTANOL
BUTCHER
BUTLERS
BUTTERS
BUTTERY
BUTTIES
BUTTING
BUTTONS
BUTTOUT
BUTTSIN
BUYABLE
BUYOUTS
BUYSOFF
BUYSOUT
BUYTIME
BUZZARD
BUZZERS
BUZZING
BUZZOFF
BUZZSAW

B•U••••

BAUBLES
BAUHAUS
BAULKED
BAUXITE
BLUBBER
BLUEBOY
BLUEFIN
BLUEFOX
BLUEGUM
BLUEING
BLUEISH
BLUEJAY
BLUELAW
BLUESKY
BLUFFED
BLUFFER
BLUFFLY
BLUNDER
BLUNTED
BLUNTER
BLUNTLY
BLURRED
BLURTED
BLUSHED
BLUSHER
BLUSHES
BLUSHON
BLUSTER
BOUDOIR
BOULDER
BOULLES
BOUNCED
BOUNCER
BOUNCES
BOUNDED
BOUNDER
BOUNDUP
BOUQUET
BOURBON
BOURREE
BOURSES
BOUSING
BOUTROS
BRUBECK
BRUEGEL
BRUISED
BRUISER
BRUISES
BRUITED
BRUMMEL
BRUNETS
BRUSHED
BRUSHES
BRUSHUP
BRUSQUE
BRUTELY
BRUTISH
BRUXING

B••U•••

BEAUISH
BEGUILE
BEGUINE
BELUSHI
BEMUSED
BEMUSES
BENUMBS
BEQUEST
BITUMEN
BLOUSED
BLOUSES
BLOUSON
BOLUSES
BONUSES
BROUGHT
BYTURNS

B•••U••

BACKUPS
BADGUYS
BAGFULS
BANQUET
BARBUDA
BASQUES
BATTUES
BECAUSE
BEDAUBS
BEDBUGS
BEDOUIN
BEEGUMS
BEFOULS
BEOWULF
BERMUDA
BIGGUNS
BISCUIT
BISMUTH
BISQUES
BIVOUAC
BLACULA
BLOWUPS
BOROUGH
BOUQUET
BOXFULS
BRAVURA
BRIQUET
BROGUES
BULBULS
BULRUSH
BUMRUSH
BUYOUTS

B••••U•

BACCHUS
BACKOUT
BACKRUB
BACKSUP
BAILOUT
BALEFUL
BALFOUR
BALLSUP
BANEFUL
BANGSUP
BAROQUE
BASHFUL
BATEAUX
BATHTUB
BAUHAUS
BAWLOUT
BEADSUP
BEAMSUP
BEARCUB
BEARHUG
BEAROUT
BEARSUP
BEATOUT
BEATSUP
BECLOUD
BEEFSUP
BELAKUN
BELGIUM
BELLYUP
BENELUX
BEZIQUE
BILIOUS
BINDSUP
BLEWOUT
BLOTOUT
BLOWGUN
BLOWNUP
BLOWOUT
BLOWSUP
BLUEGUM
BONEDUP
BONESUP
BONJOUR
BOOSTUP
BOOTOUT
BOOTSUP
BOREOUT
BORNEUP
BOTCHUP
BOUNDUP
BOWLFUL
BOWSOUT
BOXEDUP
BOXESUP
BRACEUP
BREAKUP
BRIMFUL
BRINGUP
BROKEUP
BRUSHUP
BRUSQUE
BUCKSUP
BUDDYUP
BUGSOUT
BUILDUP
BUILTUP
BULBOUS
BULGHUR
BULLRUN
BUMPSUP
BUMSOUT
BUOYSUP
BUREAUS
BURNOUT
BURNSUP
BURNTUP
BURPGUN
BUSTOUT
BUTTOUT
BUYSOUT

B•••••U

BABASSU

•BU••••

ABUBAKR
ABUSERS
ABUSING
ABUSIVE
ABUTTAL
ABUTTED

•B•U•••

ABDUCTS
ABJURED
ABJURES
ABOUGHT
ABOUNDS
ABRUZZI
OBTUNDS
OBTUSER

•B••U••

ABLAUTS
OBSCURE
OBTRUDE

•B•••U•

ABSOLUT
IBNSAUD
OBLIQUE
OBLOQUY
OBVIOUS

••BU•••

ALBUMEN
ALBUMIN
ALBUNDY
ARBUTUS
AUBURNS
CEBUANO
DEBUNKS
DEBUSSY
DEBUTED
DUBUQUE
FIBULAE
FIBULAS
IMBUING
KABUKIS
LOBULES
NEBULAE
NEBULAR
NEBULAS
PABULUM
REBUFFS
REBUILD
REBUILT
REBUKED
REBUKES
REBUSES
ROBUSTA
SUBUNIT
SUBURBS
TABULAR
TUBULAR
ZEBULON

••B•U••

ARBOURS
DEBAUCH
DEBOUCH
DYBBUKS
GIBLUES
HUBBUBS
IMBRUED
IMBRUES
INBOUND
JOBHUNT
KIBBUTZ
LABOURS
PABLUMS
REBOUND
SUBDUED
SUBDUER
SUBDUES
SUBSUME
UNBOUND

••B••U•

ARBUTUS
DUBIOUS
DUBUQUE
FIBROUS
GIBBOUS
HABITUE
JABIRUS
PABULUM
RUBSOUT

••B•••U

BABASSU
TABLEAU

•••BU••

ASHBURY
BARBUDA
BEDBUGS
BULBULS
CADBURY
CLIBURN
COGBURN
COMBUST
DANBURY
DIMBULB
DYBBUKS
GLOBULE
HAMBURG
HARBURG
HEPBURN
HOMBURG
HUBBUBS
HUMBUGS
KIBBUTZ
NIEBUHR
PITBULL
RAYBURN
REDBUDS
ROEBUCK
SAWBUCK
SOWBUGS
SUDBURY
SUNBURN
TRIBUNE
TRIBUTE

•••B•U•

AMIBLUE
BULBOUS
CAMBIUM
CURBCUT
GIBBOUS
GOABOUT
HARBOUR
ICEBLUE
NIOBIUM
RIMBAUD
SEABLUE
SKYBLUE
TAMBOUR
TERBIUM

•••B••U

DOUBLEU
HOFBRAU
LAMBEAU
RAMBEAU

••••BU•

COLOBUS
FIREBUG
GOLDBUG
HALIBUT
JUNEBUG
LADYBUG
LOVEBUG
MINIBUS
OMNIBUS
OVERBUY
PHOEBUS
PILLBUG
RHOMBUS
ROSEBUD
SCRUBUP
VIRIBUS

••••B•U

CARIBOU
MARABOU

B•V••••

BAVARIA
BEVELED
BEVERLY
BIVALVE
BIVOUAC
BOVINES
BOVVERS

B••V•••

BEAVERS
BMOVIES
BOBVILA
BOVVERS
BRAVADO
BRAVELY
BRAVERY
BRAVEST
BRAVING
BRAVOES
BRAVURA
BREVETS
BREVITY

B•••V••

BEDEVIL
BEHAVED
BEHAVES
BEHOVED
BEHOVES
BELOVED
BILEVEL
BOLIVAR
BOLIVIA

B••••V•

BAKLAVA
BEEHIVE
BEHOOVE
BELIEVE
BEREAVE
BIVALVE
BONJOVI

•BV••••

OBVERSE
OBVERTS
OBVIATE
OBVIOUS

•B•••V•

ABSOLVE
ABUSIVE
OBSERVE

••BV•••

BOBVILA
SUBVERT
SUBVOCE

••B•••V

CABLETV
NABOKOV

B•W••••

BAWDIER
BAWDILY
BAWLERS
BAWLING
BAWLOUT
BEWAILS
BEWITCH

BOWDLER
BOWERED
BOWFINS
BOWKNOT
BOWLERS
BOWLESS
BOWLFUL
BOWLIKE
BOWLINE
BOWLING
BOWSAWS
BOWSOUT
BOWTIES
BOWWOWS
BOWYERS
BYWAYOF
BYWORDS

B••W•••
BARWARE
BATWING
BEOWULF
BETWEEN
BETWIXT
BIGWIGS
BLEWOFF
BLEWOUT
BLOWDRY
BLOWERS
BLOWFLY
BLOWGUN
BLOWIER
BLOWING
BLOWNUP
BLOWOFF
BLOWOUT
BLOWSIN
BLOWSIT
BLOWSUP
BLOWUPS
BOSWELL
BOWWOWS
BOXWOOD
BRAWLED
BRAWLER
BREWERS
BREWERY
BREWING
BROWNED
BROWNER
BROWNIE
BROWSED
BROWSER
BROWSES
BULWARK

B•••W••
BALDWIN
BEDEWED
BEESWAX
BELTWAY
BIKEWAY
BOERWAR

B••••W•
BARNOWL
BARROWS
BEDDOWN
BELLOWS
BESTOWS
BILLOWS
BILLOWY
BOGDOWN
BORROWS
BOWSAWS
BOWWOWS
BURROWS

B•••••W
BANDSAW
BARSTOW
BEARPAW
BESTREW
BIGELOW
BLUELAW
BUCKSAW
BUZZSAW

•BW••••
EBWHITE

••BW•••
COBWEBS
SUBWAYS

••B•W••
ELBOWED
UNBOWED

••B••W•
HEBREWS
ROBLOWE
RUBDOWN

•••BW••
OJIBWAS
OJIBWAY

•••B•W•
FOGBOWS
SUNBOWL

•••B••W
EYEBROW
JOEBLOW
LOWBLOW
LOWBROW

••••B•W
DOWNBOW
LONGBOW
RAINBOW

B•X••••
BOXCARS
BOXEDIN
BOXEDUP
BOXESIN
BOXESUP
BOXFULS
BOXIEST
BOXKITE
BOXLIKE
BOXROOM
BOXSEAT
BOXSTEP
BOXTOPS
BOXWOOD

B••X•••
BAUXITE
BRAXTON
BRUXING

B••••X•
BETWIXT

B•••••X
BANDBOX
BATEAUX
BEATRIX
BEESWAX
BENELUX
BETAMAX
BLUEFOX
BOOMBOX
BRERFOX
BROADAX

•B•X•••
ABEXTRA

••B•X••
INBOXES
POBOXES
UNBOXED
UNBOXES

••B••X•
SUBTEXT

••••B•X
BANDBOX
BOOMBOX
CALLBOX
CASHBOX
FIREBOX
GEARBOX
JUKEBOX
LOCKBOX
MAILBOX
PILLBOX
POORBOX
POSTBOX
SALTBOX
SANDBOX
SHOEBOX
SOAPBOX
TOOLBOX

BY•••••
BYANDBY
BYANOSE
BYFORCE
BYGOLLY
BYGONES
BYHEART
BYLINED
BYLINES
BYPATHS
BYPLAYS
BYREMAN
BYREMEN
BYROADS
BYTHEBY
BYTURNS
BYWAYOF
BYWORDS

B•Y••••
BAYCITY
BAYLEAF
BAYONET
BOYCOTT
BOYHOOD
BRYNNER
BUYABLE
BUYOUTS
BUYSOFF
BUYSOUT
BUYTIME

B••Y•••
BABYING
BABYISH
BABYLON
BABYSAT
BABYSIT
BANYANS
BARYONS
BELYING
BICYCLE
BODYFAT
BOWYERS
BRAYERS
BRAYING
BUNYIPS
BUOYANT
BUOYING
BUOYSUP
BURYING
BUSYING

B•••Y••
BELAYED
BELLYUP
BIGEYES
BOGEYED
BUDDYUP
BUGEYED
BYWAYOF

B••••Y•
BADBOYS
BADGUYS
BAILEYS
BARLEYS
BARNEYS
BATBOYS
BETRAYS
BIGBOYS
BUCKEYE
BURSTYN
BUSBOYS
BYPLAYS

B•••••Y
BACKBAY
BAGGILY
BALCONY
BALKILY
BALLBOY
BALMILY
BALONEY
BANALLY
BARBARY
BARKLEY
BARNABY
BASALLY
BASEPAY
BATTERY
BAWDILY
BAYCITY
BEANERY
BEASTLY
BEATIFY
BELLAMY
BELLBOY
BELTWAY
BENTLEY
BESTBOY
BETARAY
BETHANY
BEVERLY
BIGOTRY
BIKEWAY
BILLOWY
BINDERY
BIOGENY
BIOLOGY
BLACKLY
BLANDLY
BLANKLY
BLARNEY
BLEAKLY
BLIGHTY
BLINDLY
BLOTCHY
BLOWDRY
BLOWFLY
BLUEBOY
BLUEJAY
BLUESKY
BLUFFLY
BLUNTLY
BOKCHOY
BONEDRY
BONNILY
BOSSILY
BRADLEY
BRAMBLY
BRASHLY
BRAVELY
BRAVERY
BREATHY
BREVITY
BREWERY
BRIBERY
BRIEFLY
BRIMLEY
BRISKLY
BRISTLY
BROADLY
BRUTELY
BUCKLEY
BUMPILY
BURSARY
BUSHILY
BUTTERY
BYANDBY
BYGOLLY
BYTHEBY

•BY••••
ABYSMAL
ABYSSES

•B•Y•••
ABEYANT
OBEYING

•B••••Y
ABBOTCY
ABIDEBY
ABILITY
OBLOQUY

••BY•••
BABYING
BABYISH
BABYLON
BABYSAT
BABYSIT
LIBYANS

••B•Y••
EMBAYED
EMBRYOS
LOBBYER
RIBEYES

••B••Y•
NOBODYS
ROBROYS
SUBWAYS

••B•••Y
ABBOTCY
ALBUNDY
DEBAKEY
DEBUSSY
DUBARRY
DUBIETY
EMBASSY
JOBBERY
LIBERTY
LIBRARY
PUBERTY
RABIDLY
ROBBERY
RUBBERY
SOBERLY
SUBSIDY

•••BY••
LOBBYER

•••B•Y•
BADBOYS
BATBOYS
BIGBOYS
BUSBOYS
CARBOYS
COWBOYS
DAYBOYS
FLYBOYS
LOWBOYS
TOMBOYS

•••B••Y
ANYBODY
ASHBURY
BARBARY
BRIBERY
CADBURY
CRYBABY
DANBURY
JOBBERY
NEWBERY
OJIBWAY
PEABODY
PROBITY
ROBBERY
RUBBERY
STUBBLY
SUDBURY
TARBABY
ZOMBIFY

••••BY•
GOODBYE
GOODBYS

••••B•Y
AFFABLY
AMIABLY
ATTABOY
AUDIBLY
BACKBAY
BALLBOY
BELLBOY
BESTBOY
BLUEBOY
BRAMBLY
CAPABLY
COPYBOY
CRUMBLY
DISOBEY
DURABLY
EQUABLY
GRUMBLY
HAUTBOY
HIGHBOY
HOMEBOY
IGNOBLY
LEGIBLY
LOVABLY
MOVABLY
MUTABLY
NEWSBOY
NOTABLY
OVERBUY
PAGEBOY
PLAYBOY
PLIABLY
PLOWBOY
POORBOY
RISIBLY
ROSEBAY
SCRUBBY
SHRUBBY
SICKBAY
SIZABLY
STUBBLY
TENABLY
TREMBLY
VISIBLY
VOLUBLY

•••••BY
ABIDEBY
ALLENBY
BARNABY
BYANDBY
BYTHEBY
CLOSEBY
COMESBY
CRYBABY
DROPSBY
GOINGBY
HORNSBY
HUSHABY
LULLABY
MORESBY
SCRUBBY
SHRUBBY
STANDBY
STOODBY
SWEARBY
SWINGBY
SWOREBY
TARBABY
THEREBY
WALLABY
WHEREBY

B•Z••••
BAZAARS
BAZOOKA
BEZIERS
BEZIQUE
BIZARRE
BUZZARD
BUZZERS
BUZZING
BUZZOFF
BUZZSAW

B••Z•••
BENZENE
BLAZERS
BLAZING
BLAZONS
BORZOIS
BRAZIER
BRAZING
BUZZARD
BUZZERS
BUZZING
BUZZOFF
BUZZSAW

B•••Z••
BEDIZEN
BENAZIR
BLITZED
BLITZEN
BLITZES
BREEZED
BREEZES
BRONZED
BRONZES

B••••Z•
BAPTIZE
BONANZA

B•••••Z
BERLIOZ
BERLITZ

•B••Z••
ABRUZZI

•B•••Z•
ABRUZZI

••BZ•••
SUBZERO

••B•Z••
REBOZOS

••B•••Z
ALBENIZ
KIBBUTZ
KOBLENZ

•••B•Z•
ZAMBEZI

•••B••Z
KIBBUTZ
LEIBNIZ

••••B•Z
SHOWBIZ

CA•••••
CABALAS
CABANAS
CABARET
CABBAGE
CABBIES
CABINET
CABLERS
CABLETV
CABLING
CABOOSE
CABRINI
CACANNY
CACHETS
CACHING
CACHOUS
CACKLED
CACKLER
CACKLES
CADBURY
CADDIED
CADDIES
CADDISH
CADDOAN
CADENCE
CADENCY
CADENZA
CADETTE
CADGERS
CADGING
CADMIUM
CADUCEI
CAESARS
CAESIUM
CAESURA
CAFTANS
CAGIEST
CAHIERS
CAHOOTS
CAIMANS
CAIQUES
CAISSON
CAJOLED
CAJOLER
CAJOLES
CAKEMIX
CAKIEST
CALCIFY
CALCITE
CALCIUM
CALDERA
CALDRON
CALENDS
CALGARY
CALHOUN
CALIBAN
CALIBER
CALIBRE
CALICES
CALICOS
CALIPER
CALIPHS
CALKING
CALKINS
CALLBOX
CALLERS
CALLFOR
CALLING
CALLINS
CALLOFF
CALLOUS
CALLOUT
CALLSIN
CALLSON
CALLSUP
CALMEST
CALMING
CALOMEL
CALORIC
CALORIE
CALPACS
CALTECH
CALUMET
CALUMNY
CALVARY
CALVERT
CALVING
CALYCES
CALYPSO
CALYXES
CALZONE
CAMBERS
CAMBIUM
CAMBRIC
CAMEDUE
CAMELIA
CAMELOT
CAMEOED
CAMEOFF
CAMEOUT
CAMERAS
CAMERON
CAMILLE
CAMISES
CAMPARI
CAMPERS
CAMPHOR
CAMPIER
CAMPILY
CAMPING
CAMPION
CAMPOUT
CANAPES
CANARDS
CANASTA
CANCANS
CANCELS
CANDELA
CANDICE
CANDIDA
CANDIDE
CANDIDS
CANDIED
CANDIES
CANDLES
CANDOUR
CANFULS
CANIEST
CANINES
CANKERS
CANNERS
CANNERY
CANNIER
CANNILY
CANNING
CANNOLI
CANNONS
CANONIC
CANOPUS
CANSECO
CANTATA
CANTEEN
CANTERS
CANTILY
CANTINA
CANTING
CANTLES
CANTONS
CANTORS
CANTRIP
CANVASS
CANYONS
CANZONE
CAPABLE
CAPABLY
CAPAPIE
CAPEANN
CAPECOD
CAPELET
CAPELLA
CAPERED
CAPFULS
CAPGUNS
CAPITAL
CAPITAN
CAPITOL
CAPLESS
CAPLETS
CAPNUTS
CAPPERS
CAPPING
CAPRICE
CAPSHAW
CAPSIDS
CAPSIZE
CAPSTAN
CAPSULE
CAPTAIN
CAPTION
CAPTIVE
CAPTORS
CAPTURE
CAPULET
CARABAO
CARACAL
CARACAS
CARAFES
CARAMBA
CARAMEL
CARAMIA
CARAVAN
CARAVEL
CARAWAY
CARBIDE
CARBINE
CARBONS
CARBOYS
CARCASE
CARCASS
CARCOAT
CARDERS
CARDIAC
CARDING
CARDOZO
CAREENS
CAREERS
CAREFOR
CAREFUL
CARFARE
CARFULS
CARGOES
CARHOPS
CARIBES
CARIBOU
CARINAS
CARIOCA
CARKING
CARLESS
CARLOAD
CARLSON
CARLTON
CARLYLE
CARMINE
CARNERA
CARNETS
CARNIES
CAROLED
CAROLER
CAROLUS
CAROLYN
CAROMED
CAROTID
CAROUSE
CARPALS
CARPARK
CARPELS
CARPERS
CARPETS
CARPING
CARPOOL
CARPORT
CARRELS
CARRICK
CARRIED
CARRIER
CARRIES
CARRION
CARROLL
CARROTS
CARRYON
CARSEAT
CARTAGE
CARTELS
CARTERS
CARTIER
CARTING
CARTONS
CARTOON
CARVERS
CARVING
CARWASH
CASABAS
CASAVAS
CASCADE
CASCARA
CASELAW
CASERNE
CASERNS
CASHBAR
CASHBOX
CASHCOW
CASHEWS
CASHIER
CASHING
CASHOUT
CASINGS
CASINOS
CASPIAN
CASQUED
CASQUES
CASSATT
CASSAVA
CASSIAS
CASSIDY
CASSINI
CASSINO
CASSIUS
CASSOCK
CASTERS
CASTILE
CASTING
CASTLED
CASTLES
CASTOFF
CASTOUT
CASUALS
CATALAN
CATALOG
CATALPA
CATAWBA
CATBERT
CATBIRD
CATBOAT
CATCALL
CATCHER
CATCHES
CATCHON
CATCHUP
CATENAE
CATERED
CATERER
CATERTO
CATFISH
CATFOOD
CATHAIR
CATHEAD
CATHODE
CATIONS
CATKINS
CATLIKE
CATNAPS
CATNIPS
CATSCAN
CATSEYE
CATSHOW
CATSPAW
CATSUIT
CATTAIL
CATTIER
CATTILY
CATTING
CATTISH
CATWALK
CAUDLES
CAULKED
CAULKER
CAUSING
CAUSTIC
CAUTION
CAVALRY
CAVEATS
CAVEDIN
CAVEINS
CAVEMAN
CAVEMEN
CAVERNS
CAVESIN
CAVETTO
CAVIARS
CAVILED
CAVILER
CAVORTS
CAYENNE
CAYMANS
CAYUGAS
CAYUSES

C•A••••
CEASING
CHABLIS
CHACHAS
CHAFING
CHAGALL
CHAGRIN
CHAINED
CHAIRED
CHAISES
CHALETS
CHALICE
CHALKED
CHALKUP
CHALONS
CHAMBER
CHAMFER
CHAMOIS
CHAMPED
CHANCED
CHANCEL
CHANCER
CHANCES
CHANGED
CHANGER
CHANGES
CHANNEL
CHANSON
CHANTED
CHANTER
CHANTEY
CHAOTIC
CHAPATI
CHAPEAU
CHAPELS
CHAPLET
CHAPLIN
CHAPMAN
CHAPMEN
CHAPPED
CHAPPIE
CHAPTER
CHARADE
CHARGED
CHARGER
CHARGES
CHARIER
CHARILY
CHARIOT
CHARITY
CHARLES
CHARLEY
CHARLIE
CHARMED
CHARMER
CHARMIN
CHARRED
CHARTED
CHARTER
CHASERS
CHASING
CHASSES
CHASSIS
CHASTEN
CHASTER
CHATEAU
CHATHAM
CHATSUP
CHATTED
CHATTEL
CHATTER
CHAUCER
CLABBER
CLACKED
CLAIMED
CLAIMER
CLAIROL
CLAMBER
CLAMMED
CLAMMER
CLAMORS
CLAMOUR
CLAMPED
CLAMSUP
CLANGED
CLANGOR
CLANKED
CLAPPED
CLAPPER
CLAPTON
CLAQUES
CLARETS
CLARICE
CLARIFY
CLARION
CLARITY
CLASHED
CLASHES
CLASPED
CLASSED
CLASSES

CLASSIC
CLATTER
CLAUDIA
CLAUDIO
CLAUSES
CLAVELL
CLAVIER
CLAWERS
CLAWING
CLAYIER
CLAYISH
CLAYTON
COACHED
COACHES
COALBIN
COALCAR
COALERS
COALGAS
COALOIL
COALTAR
COARSEN
COARSER
COASTAL
COASTED
COASTER
COATING
COAXERS
COAXIAL
COAXING
CRABBED
CRABBER
CRACKED
CRACKER
CRACKLE
CRACKLY
CRACKUP
CRADLED
CRADLES
CRAFTED
CRAFTER
CRAFTSY
CRAMMED
CRAMMER
CRAMPED
CRAMPON
CRANIAL
CRANING
CRANIUM
CRANKED
CRANKUP
CRAPPIE
CRASHED
CRASHES
CRASSER
CRASSLY
CRASSUS
CRATERS
CRATING
CRAVATS
CRAVENS
CRAVERS
CRAVING
CRAWDAD
CRAWLED
CRAWLER
CRAYOLA
CRAYONS
CRAZIER
CRAZIES
CRAZILY
CRAZING
CZARDAS
CZARDOM
CZARINA
CZARISM
CZARIST

C••A•••

CABALAS
CABANAS
CABARET
CACANNY
CANAPES
CANARDS
CANASTA
CAPABLE
CAPABLY
CAPAPIE
CARABAO
CARACAL
CARACAS
CARAFES
CARAMBA
CARAMEL
CARAMIA
CARAVAN
CARAVEL
CARAWAY
CASABAS
CASAVAS
CATALAN
CATALOG
CATALPA
CATAWBA
CAVALRY
CBRADIO
CCLAMPS
CEDARED
CELADON
CERAMIC
CEZANNE
CHEAPEN
CHEAPER
CHEAPIE
CHEAPLY
CHEATED
CHEATER
CHEATIN
CHIANTI
CICADAE
CICADAS
CITABLE
CITADEL
CLEANED
CLEANER
CLEANLY
CLEANSE
CLEANUP
CLEARED
CLEARER
CLEARLY
CLEARUP
CLEAVED
CLEAVER
CLEAVES
CLEAVON
CLOACAE
CLOACAS
CLOAKED
COHABIT
CONAKRY
CORAZON
COWARDS
CREAKED
CREAMED
CREAMER
CREASED
CREASES
CREATED
CREATES
CREATOR
CROAKED
CROATIA
CURACAO
CURATES
CURATOR
CUTAWAY

C•••A••

CABBAGE
CAESARS
CAFTANS
CAIMANS
CALGARY
CALPACS
CALVARY
CAMPARI
CANCANS
CANTATA
CANVASS
CAPEANN
CAPTAIN
CARCASE
CARCASS
CARFARE
CARPALS
CARPARK
CARTAGE
CARWASH
CASCADE
CASCARA
CASSATT
CASSAVA
CASUALS
CATCALL
CATHAIR
CATNAPS
CATTAIL
CATWALK
CAVEATS
CAVIARS
CAYMANS
CEBUANO
CELLARS
CEMBALO
CENTAUR
CENTAVO
CEREALS
CERTAIN
CHAGALL
CHAPATI
CHARADE
CHICAGO
CHICANA
CHICANO
CHORALE
CHORALS
CILIATE
CINZANO
CITRATE
CLIMATE
CLIPART
COCHAIR
COCKADE
COEVALS
COGNACS
COGNATE
COINAGE
COLGATE
COLLAGE
COLLARD
COLLARS
COLLATE
COMBATS
COMMAND
COMPACT
COMPANY
COMPARE
COMPASS
COMRADE
CONCAVE
CONFABS
CONGAED
CONGAME
CONTACT
CONTAIN
COOLANT
COPLAND
CORDAGE
CORDATE
CORKAGE
CORRALS
CORSAGE
CORSAIR
COSSACK
COSTAIN
COSTARS
COTTAGE
COUGARS
COURAGE
COURANT
COWHAND
CRAVATS
CRETANS
CRUSADE
CRUSADO
CRUZADO
CRYBABY
CUEBALL
CUECARD
CUIRASS
CUPCAKE
CUREALL
CURRANT
CURTAIL
CURTAIN
CUSHAWS
CUSTARD
CUTBACK
CUTLASS
CUTRATE
CYMBALS

C••••A•

CABALAS
CABANAS
CADDOAN
CALIBAN
CAMERAS
CAPITAL
CAPITAN
CAPSHAW
CAPSTAN
CARABAO
CARACAL
CARACAS
CARAVAN
CARAWAY
CARCOAT
CARDIAC
CARINAS
CARLOAD
CARSEAT
CASABAS
CASAVAS
CASELAW
CASHBAR
CASPIAN
CASSIAS
CATALAN
CATBOAT
CATENAE
CATHEAD
CATSCAN
CATSPAW
CAVEMAN
CAYUGAS
CENTRAL
CHACHAS
CHAPEAU
CHAPMAN
CHATEAU
CHATHAM
CHEDDAR
CHEETAH
CHEMLAB
CHILEAN
CHLORAL
CHOCTAW
CHOLLAS
CHUKKAS
CICADAE
CICADAS
CINEMAS
CINEMAX
CLOACAE
CLOACAS
CLUBCAR
COALCAR
COALGAS
COALTAR
COASTAL
COAXIAL
COCHRAN
COCTEAU
COEQUAL
COLDWAR
COLEMAN
COMESAT
COMICAL
CONCEAL
CONGEAL
CONICAL
CONTRAS
COONCAT
COPULAE
COPULAS
COPYCAT
CORDIAL
CORNEAL
CORNEAS
CORONAE
CORONAS
COWPEAS
CRANIAL
CRAWDAD
CREWMAN
CRIMEAN
CROWBAR
CRUCIAL
CRYSTAL
CULTJAM
CUPOLAS
CURACAO
CUTAWAY
CYNICAL
CZARDAS

C•••••A

CADENZA
CAESURA
CALDERA
CAMELIA
CANASTA
CANDELA
CANDIDA
CANTATA
CANTINA
CAPELLA
CARAMBA
CARAMIA
CARIOCA
CARNERA
CASCARA
CASSAVA
CATALPA
CATAWBA
CECILIA
CEDILLA
CELESTA
CEREBRA
CHELSEA
CHICANA
CHIMERA
CIBORIA
CLAUDIA
COCHLEA
CONDITA
COPPOLA
CORDOBA
CORETTA
COROLLA
CORRIDA
CORSICA
CRAYOLA
CREMONA
CROATIA
CULEBRA
CYNTHIA
CZARINA

•CA••••

ACACIAS
ACADEME
ACADEMY
ACADIAN
ACANTHI
ACARIDS
OCANADA
OCARINA
SCALARS
SCALDED
SCALENE
SCALERS
SCALIER
SCALING
SCALLOP
SCALPED
SCALPEL
SCALPER
SCAMMED
SCAMPED
SCAMPER
SCANDAL
SCANNED
SCANNER
SCANTED
SCANTER
SCANTLY
SCAPULA
SCARABS
SCARCER
SCARERS
SCAREUP
SCARFED
SCARIER
SCARIFY
SCARILY
SCARING
SCARLET
SCARPED
SCARPER
SCARRED
SCARVES
SCATHED
SCATHES
SCATTED
SCATTER

•C•A•••

ACHATES
ACKACKS
ACTABLE
ACTAEON
CCLAMPS
ECLAIRS
ECUADOR
ICEAGES
ICEAXES
ICHABOD
MCCALLS
MCGAVIN
MCMAHON
OCEANIA
OCEANIC
OCEANID
OCEANUS
OCTAGON
OCTANES
OCTANTS
OCTAVES
OCTAVIA
OCTAVOS
SCHATZI
SCRAGGY
SCRAPED
SCRAPER
SCRAPES
SCRAPPY
SCRATCH
SCRAWLS
SCRAWLY
SCRAWNY
WCHANDY

•C••A••

ACCLAIM
ACETATE
ACREAGE
ACTUARY
ACTUATE
ECKHART
ECSTASY
ICEBAGS
ICECAPS
ICELAND
ICEPACK
OCANADA
SCALARS
SCARABS
SCHNAPS
SCREAKS
SCREAMS

•C•••A•

ACACIAS
ACADIAN
ACCRUAL
ACROBAT
ICEBOAT
MCLUHAN
SCANDAL
SCHEMAS
SCHOLAR
SCLERAS

•C••••A

ACEROLA
ECHIDNA
ICEDTEA
OCANADA
OCARINA
OCEANIA
OCTAVIA
SCAPULA
SCHIRRA
SCIORRA

••CA•••

ALCAZAR
ARCADES
ARCADIA
ARCANUM
BACALAO
BACARDI
BECALMS
BECAUSE
CACANNY
CICADAE
CICADAS
DECADES
DECAGON
DECALOG
DECAMPS
DECANTS
DECAPOD
DECARLO
DECATUR
DECAYED
ENCAGED
ENCAGES
ENCAMPS
ENCASED
ENCASES
ESCAPED
ESCAPEE
ESCAPES
ESCARPS
FACADES
GOCARTS
IDCARDS
INCANTS
INCASED
INCASES
JACANAS
JICAMAS
JOCASTA
LECARRE
LOCALES
LOCALLY
LOCARNO
LOCATED
LOCATER
LOCATES
LOCATOR
MACABRE
MACADAM
MACAQUE
MCCALLS
NOCANDO
OXCARTS
PICADOR
PICANTE
PICARDY
PICAROS
PICASSO
RECALLS
RECANED
RECANES
RECANTS
RECASTS
RICARDO
SECANTS
UNCAGED
UNCAGES
UNCANNY
UNCASED
UNCASES
VACANCY
VACATED
VACATES
VOCALIC
VOCALLY
YUCATAN

••C•A••

ACCLAIM
ARCHAIC
ARCLAMP
COCHAIR
COCKADE
DECLAIM
DECLARE
DECLASS
DICTATE
DOCKAGE
ENCHAIN
ENCHANT
ENCLAVE
ETCHANT
EXCLAIM
FACIALS
HECTARE
JACKALS
JACKASS
LACTASE
LACTATE
LUCIANO
MACRAME
MICHAEL
MICMACS
NECTARS
ORCHARD
PACKAGE
PACKARD
PECCANT
PECCARY
PICCARD
PICKAXE
RECHALK
RECLAIM
RECLAME
RECOATS
RICHARD
SOCIALS
SUCRASE
TICTACS
TOCCATA
UNCHAIN
UNCIALS
UNCLASP
UNCRATE
ZACHARY

••C••A•

ACCRUAL
ALCAZAR
ARCHWAY
BACALAO
BACKBAY
BUCKRAM
BUCKSAW
CICADAE
CICADAS
COCHRAN
COCTEAU
DECIMAL
ENCINAS
ESCHEAT
FACTUAL
FACULAE
HACKMAN
HACKSAW
HICKMAN
JACANAS
JACKDAW
JACKTAR
JICAMAS
JOCULAR
LACHLAN
LACTEAL
LACUNAE
LACUNAL
LACUNAS
LOCOMAN
MACADAM
MACGRAW
MACULAE
MRCLEAN
NICOLAS
NUCLEAR
PACECAR
PACKRAT
PECKSAT
PICKSAT
RACECAR
RACEWAY
RECITAL
RECLEAN
RICERAT
RICHMAN
RICKMAN
SECULAR
SICHUAN
SICKBAY
SICKDAY
SICKPAY
TUCHMAN
UNCLEAN
UNCLEAR
UNCLOAK
VICTUAL
VICUNAS
YUCATAN

••C•••A

ARCADIA
CECILIA
COCHLEA
ENCOMIA
FUCHSIA
IACOCCA
JOCASTA
KACHINA
MACHINA
NICOSIA
OSCEOLA
RICKSHA
RICOTTA
TOCCATA
WICHITA

•••CA••

ASHCANS
ATACAMA
AVOCADO
BARCARS
BOBCATS
BOXCARS
BROCADE
CANCANS
CARCASE
CARCASS
CASCADE
CASCARA
CATCALL
CHICAGO
CHICANA
CHICANO
CONCAVE
CUECARD
CUPCAKE
DAYCAMP
DAYCARE
DESCANT
DISCARD
DOGCART
EDUCATE
EGGCASE
FATCATS
FLYCAST
GASCAPS
HEPCATS
HOECAKE
HOTCAKE
HOTCAPS
HOTCARS
HUBCAPS
ICECAPS
ILOCANO
INSCAPE
KEYCARD
LASCALA
LASCAUX
MADCAPS
MARCATO
MASCARA
MESCALS
MISCALL
MISCAST
MOBCAPS
MUDCATS
MUSCATS
NESCAFE
OILCAKE
OILCANS
OUTCAST
PANCAKE
PAYCASH
PECCANT
PECCARY
PERCALE
PICCARD
PLACARD
PLACATE
PRECAST
RASCALS
REDCAPS
RESCALE
REXCATS
RIBCAGE
SARCASM
SKYCAPS
SNOCATS
TEACAKE
TEACART
THECARS
TINCANS
TOCCATA
TOECAPS
TOMCATS
TOSCALE
TOUCANS
TOWCARS
TROCARS
TUSCANY
UPSCALE
VOLCANO
VULCANS

•••C•A•

ACACIAS
AMSCRAY
ASOCIAL
BEECHAM
CARCOAT
CHACHAS
CHOCTAW
CONCEAL
CRUCIAL
DEWCLAW
EPOCHAL
EXACTAS
FASCIAS
FRACTAL
FUNCHAL
GLACIAL
GOTCHAS
GRACIAS
GRECIAN
KETCHAM
KWACHAS
LABCOAT
MARCEAU
OLDCHAP
PANCHAX
PASCHAL
PEACOAT
PINCHAS
REDCOAT
SPECIAL
SURCOAT
TOPCOAT
TRUCIAL

•••C••A

ATACAMA
BLACULA
CASCARA
CHICANA
DRACHMA
DRACULA
ELECTRA
INOCULA
LASCALA
MASCARA
PLECTRA
QUECHUA
SPECTRA
TOCCATA
TRACHEA
VISCERA

••••CA•

AFRICAN
ALPACAS
ARNICAS
AZTECAN
BEARCAT
BIFOCAL
CARACAL
CARACAS
CATSCAN
CLOACAE
CLOACAS
CLUBCAR
COALCAR
COMICAL
CONICAL
COONCAT
COPYCAT
CURACAO
CYNICAL
ETHICAL
FLATCAR
HANDCAR
HELICAL
HELLCAT
INKYCAP
ITHACAN
KNEECAP
LEXICAL
LOGICAL
LORICAE
LYRICAL
MAGICAL
MAILCAR
MANXCAT
MARACAS
MEDICAL
MEXICAN
MINICAB
MINICAM
MOHICAN
MUSICAL
OPTICAL
PACECAR
PADUCAH
PATACAS
PEDICAB
PELICAN
PEMICAN
POLECAR
POLECAT
RACECAR
RADICAL
SENECAS
SIDECAR
SILICAS
SLOTCAR
SNOWCAP
SNOWCAT
STOICAL
TAXICAB
TOPICAL
TRAMCAR
TYPICAL
VATICAN
WILDCAT

••••C•A

FELICIA
FELUCCA
IACOCCA
INDICIA
MALACCA
PANACEA
REBECCA
STLUCIA

•••••CA

AMERICA
AVIANCA
CARIOCA
CORSICA
EROTICA
EXOTICA
FELUCCA
FORMICA
IACOCCA
JAMAICA
JESSICA
LATOSCA
MAJORCA
MALACCA
MINORCA
REBECCA
REPLICA
TAPIOCA

CB•••••

CBRADIO

C•B••••

CABALAS
CABANAS
CABARET
CABBAGE
CABBIES
CABINET
CABLERS
CABLETV
CABLING
CABOOSE
CABRINI
CEBUANO
CIBORIA
COBBLED
COBBLER
COBBLES
COBWEBS
CUBBIES
CUBBISH
CUBICLE
CUBISTS
CYBORGS

C••B•••

CABBAGE
CABBIES
CADBURY
CAMBERS
CAMBIUM
CAMBRIC
CARBIDE
CARBINE
CARBONS
CARBOYS
CATBERT
CATBIRD
CATBOAT
CEMBALO
CHABLIS
CLABBER
CLIBURN
CLOBBER
CLUBBED
CLUBCAR
COBBLED
COBBLER
COBBLES
COGBURN
COLBERT
COMBATS
COMBERS
COMBINE

COMBING
COMBUST
CONBRIO
CORBELS
CORBETT
COWBELL
COWBIRD
COWBOYS
CRABBED
CRABBER
CRIBBED
CRYBABY
CUBBIES
CUBBISH
CUEBALL
CUIBONO
CURBCUT
CURBING
CUTBACK
CYMBALS

C•••B••
CALIBAN
CALIBER
CALIBRE
CALLBOX
CAPABLE
CAPABLY
CARABAO
CARIBES
CARIBOU
CASABAS
CASHBAR
CASHBOX
CELEBES
CELEBRE
CEREBRA
CHAMBER
CITABLE
CLABBER
CLAMBER
CLIMBED
CLIMBER
CLOBBER
CLUBBED
COALBIN
COHABIT
COLOBUS
COPYBOY
CRABBED
CRABBER
CRIBBED
CROWBAR
CRUMBLE
CRUMBLY
CULEBRA

C••••B•
CARAMBA
CATAWBA
CHERUBS
CLOSEBY
COBWEBS
COLUMBO
COMESBY
CONFABS
CONJOBS
CORDOBA
CRYBABY

C•••••B
CHEMLAB
CORNCOB
COULOMB
COXCOMB

•C•B•••
ICEBAGS
ICEBEER
ICEBERG
ICEBLUE
ICEBOAT

•C••B••
ACERBIC
ACROBAT
ACTABLE
ICHABOD
OCTOBER
SCRIBES
SCRUBBY
SCRUBUP

•C•••B•
ICECUBE
SCARABS
SCRUBBY

••CB•••
MACBETH

••C•B••
BACKBAY
BACKBIT
DECIBEL
JACOBIN
LOCKBOX
MACABRE
SICKBAY

••C••B•
ASCRIBE
MICROBE

••C•••B
BACKRUB
SUCCUMB

•••C•B•
ARECIBO
ICECUBE
PLACEBO

•••C••B
COXCOMB
FANCLUB
HOTCOMB
KEYCLUB
SUCCUMB

••••C•B
BEARCUB
CORNCOB
LIONCUB
MINICAB
PEDICAB
TAXICAB

CC•••••
CCLAMPS
CCRIDER

C•C••••
CACANNY
CACHETS
CACHING
CACHOUS
CACKLED
CACKLER
CACKLES
CECILIA
CICADAE
CICADAS
COCHAIR
COCHERE
COCHISE
COCHLEA
COCHRAN
COCKADE
COCKERS
COCKIER
COCKILY
COCKING
COCKISH
COCKLES
COCKNEY
COCKPIT
COCKSHY
COCONUT
COCOONS
COCTEAU
CUCKOOS
CYCLERS
CYCLING
CYCLIST
CYCLONE
CYCLOPS

C••C•••
CALCIFY
CALCITE
CALCIUM
CANCANS
CANCELS
CARCASE
CARCASS
CARCOAT
CASCADE
CASCARA
CATCALL
CATCHER
CATCHES
CATCHON
CATCHUP
CHACHAS
CHECHEN
CHECKED
CHECKER
CHECKIN
CHECKUP
CHICAGO
CHICANA
CHICANO
CHICHEN
CHICKEN
CHICORY
CHOCTAW
CHUCKED
CHUCKLE
CINCHED
CINCHES
CIRCLED
CIRCLES
CIRCLET
CIRCUIT
CIRCUSY
CLACKED
CLICHES
CLICKED
CLOCHES
CLOCKED
CLOCKER
CLOCKIN
CLUCKED
COACHED
COACHES
CONCAVE
CONCEAL
CONCEDE
CONCEIT
CONCEPT
CONCERN
CONCERT
CONCHES
CONCISE
CONCOCT
CONCORD
CONCURS
COUCHED
COUCHES
COXCOMB
CRACKED
CRACKER
CRACKLE
CRACKLY
CRACKUP
CRECHES
CRICKED
CRICKET
CROCHET
CRUCIAL
CRUCIFY
CUECARD
CUPCAKE

C•••C••
CADUCEI
CALICES
CALICOS
CALYCES
CAPECOD
CARACAL
CARACAS
CASHCOW
CATSCAN
CHANCED
CHANCEL
CHANCER
CHANCES
CHAUCER
CHOICER
CHOICES
CLOACAE
CLOACAS
CLUBCAR
COALCAR
CODICES
CODICIL
COERCED
COERCER
COERCES
COLDCUT
COMICAL
CONICAL
COONCAT
COPYCAT
CORNCOB
COUNCIL
CREWCUT
CRUNCHY
CUBICLE
CURACAO
CURBCUT
CUTICLE
CYNICAL

C••••C•
CADENCE
CADENCY
CALPACS
CALTECH
CANDICE
CANSECO
CAPRICE
CARIOCA
CARRICK
CASSOCK
CELTICS
CHALICE
CHIRICO
CLARICE
CLERICS
CLINICS
COGENCY
COGNACS
COLLECT
COMPACT
CONCOCT
CONDUCE
CONDUCT
CONNECT
CONNICK
CONTACT
CONVICT
COPPICE
CORNICE
CORRECT
CORSICA
COSSACK
COWLICK
CREVICE
CRITICS
CUTBACK

C•••••C
CALORIC
CAMBRIC
CANONIC
CARDIAC
CAUSTIC
CENTRIC
CERAMIC
CHAOTIC
CHRONIC
CLASSIC
COMEDIC
CRYPTIC

•CC••••
ACCEDED
ACCEDER
ACCEDES
ACCENTS
ACCEPTS
ACCLAIM
ACCORDS
ACCOSTS
ACCOUNT
ACCRETE
ACCRUAL
ACCRUED
ACCRUES
ACCURST
ACCUSED
ACCUSER
ACCUSES
MCCALLS
MCCLOUD
MCCLURE
OCCIPUT
OCCLUDE
OCCULTS
UCCELLO

•C•C•••
ACACIAS
ICECAPS
ICECOLD
ICECUBE
ICICLES

•C••C••
ACKACKS
SCARCER
SCONCES

•C•••C•
ICEPACK
ICEPICK
SCHLOCK
SCIENCE
SCRATCH
SCREECH
SCRUNCH

•C••••C
ACERBIC
ACRYLIC
ACTINIC
OCEANIC
SCEPTIC

••CC•••
BACCHUS
HICCUPS
JACCUSE
NICCOLO
PECCANT
PECCARY
PICCARD
PICCOLO
PUCCINI
RACCOON
SICCING
SUCCEED
SUCCESS
SUCCORS
SUCCOUR
SUCCUMB
TOCCATA
VACCINE

••C•C••
BICYCLE
DECOCTS
IACOCCA
PACECAR
RACECAR
RECYCLE

••C••C•
DECENCY
IACOCCA
LICENCE
LUCENCY
MICMACS
PACKICE
PICNICS
RECENCY
RECHECK
SECRECY
TACTICS
TICTACS
VACANCY

••C•••C
ARCHAIC
ASCETIC
BUCOLIC
LACONIC
NUCLEIC
PACIFIC
VOCALIC

•••CC••
AJACCIO
FLACCID
GNOCCHI
REOCCUR
SPECCED
STUCCOS

•••C•C•
CONCOCT
HANCOCK
LEACOCK
PEACOCK
PETCOCK

•••C••C
PSYCHIC

••••CC•
FELUCCA
IACOCCA
MALACCA
MOROCCO
REBECCA
SIROCCO
TOBACCO

••••C•C
BORACIC

C•D••••
CADBURY
CADDIED
CADDIES
CADDISH
CADDOAN
CADENCE
CADENCY
CADENZA
CADETTE
CADGERS
CADGING
CADMIUM
CADUCEI
CEDARED
CEDILLA
CODDLED
CODDLER
CODDLES
CODEINE
CODFISH
CODGERS
CODICES
CODICIL
CUDDIES
CUDDLED
CUDDLES
CUDGELS

C••D•••
CADDIED
CADDIES
CADDISH
CADDOAN
CALDERA
CALDRON
CANDELA
CANDICE
CANDIDA
CANDIDE
CANDIDS
CANDIED
CANDIES
CANDLES
CANDOUR
CARDERS
CARDIAC
CARDING
CARDOZO
CAUDLES
CHEDDAR
CHIDERS
CHIDING
CINDERS
CINDERY
CODDLED
CODDLER
CODDLES
COEDITS
COLDCUT
COLDEST
COLDISH
COLDWAR
CONDEMN
CONDIGN
CONDITA
CONDOLE
CONDONE
CONDORS
CONDUCE
CONDUCT
CONDUIT
CORDAGE
CORDATE
CORDELL
CORDERO
CORDIAL
CORDING
CORDITE
CORDOBA
CORDONS
CRADLED
CRADLES
CREDITS
CRUDELY
CRUDEST
CRUDITY
CUDDIES
CUDDLED
CUDDLES
CURDIER
CURDING
CURDLED
CURDLES
CUTDOWN

C•••D••
CAMEDUE
CAVEDIN
CBRADIO
CCRIDER
CELADON
CHEDDAR
CHOWDER
CICADAE
CICADAS
CITADEL
CLAUDIA
CLAUDIO
CLOUDED
CLOWDER
CLUEDIN
COMEDIC
COMEDUE
CORNDOG
COULDNT
CRAWDAD
CROWDED
CZARDAS
CZARDOM

C••••D•
CALENDS
CANARDS
CANDIDA
CANDIDE
CANDIDS
CAPSIDS
CARBIDE
CASCADE
CASSIDY
CATHODE
CERVIDS
CHARADE
COCKADE
COLLIDE
COLLODI
COLLUDE
COMMODE
COMRADE
CONCEDE
CONFIDE
CONOIDS
CORRIDA
CORRODE
COWARDS
COWHIDE
CRUSADE
CRUSADO
CRUZADO
CUSPIDS
CUSTODY

C•••••D
CACKLED
CADDIED
CAJOLED
CAMEOED
CANDIED
CAPECOD
CAPERED
CARLOAD
CAROLED
CAROMED
CAROTID
CARRIED
CASQUED
CASTLED
CATBIRD
CATERED
CATFOOD
CATHEAD
CAULKED
CAVILED
CEDARED
CENTRED
CHAINED
CHAIRED
CHALKED
CHAMPED
CHANCED
CHANGED
CHANTED
CHAPPED
CHARGED
CHARMED
CHARRED
CHARTED
CHATTED
CHEATED
CHECKED
CHEEPED
CHEERED
CHEVIED
CHILLED
CHINKED
CHINNED
CHIPPED
CHIRPED
CHOMPED
CHOPPED
CHUCKED
CHUGGED
CHUMMED
CHURNED
CINCHED
CIRCLED
CLACKED
CLAIMED
CLAMMED
CLAMPED
CLANGED
CLANKED
CLAPPED
CLASHED
CLASPED
CLASSED
CLEANED
CLEARED
CLEAVED
CLERKED
CLICKED
CLIMBED
CLINKED
CLIPPED
CLOAKED
CLOCKED
CLOGGED
CLOMPED
CLOPPED
CLOTHED
CLOTTED
CLOUDED
CLOUTED
CLOWNED
CLUBBED
CLUCKED
CLUMPED
CLUNKED
COACHED
COASTED
COBBLED
CODDLED
COERCED
COHERED
COLLARD
COLLOID
COLORED
COMMAND
COMMEND
CONCORD
CONGAED
CONRIED
CONTEND
COOPTED
COPLAND
CORNFED
COUCHED
COUGHED
COUNTED
COUPLED
COURSED
COURTED
COVERED
COVETED
COWBIRD
COWERED
COWHAND
COWHERD
COZENED
CRABBED
CRACKED
CRADLED
CRAFTED
CRAMMED
CRAMPED
CRANKED
CRASHED
CRAWDAD
CRAWLED
CREAKED
CREAMED
CREASED
CREATED
CREEPED
CRESTED
CRIBBED
CRICKED
CRIMPED
CRINGED
CRINOID
CRISPED
CROAKED
CROOKED
CROONED
CROPPED
CROSSED
CROWDED
CROWNED
CRUISED
CRUSHED
CRUSTED
CUDDLED
CUECARD
CULLIED
CURDLED
CURRIED
CUSTARD

•CD••••
ECDYSES
ECDYSIS

•C•D•••
ACADEME
ACADEMY
ACADIAN
ACEDOUT
ACIDIFY
ACIDITY
ICEDOUT
ICEDTEA
SCUDDED

•C••D••
ACCEDED
ACCEDER
ACCEDES
ACRIDLY
ACTEDON
ACTEDUP
CCRIDER
ECHIDNA
ECUADOR
SCALDED
SCANDAL
SCENDED
SCOLDED
SCOLDER
SCUDDED

•C•••D•
ACARIDS
ACCORDS
OCANADA
OCCLUDE
SCHMIDT
SCREEDS
WCHANDY

•C••••D
ACCEDED
ACCRUED
ACCUSED
ICECOLD
ICELAND
ICHABOD
MCCLOUD
OCEANID
OCTOPOD
SCALDED
SCALPED
SCAMMED
SCAMPED
SCANNED
SCANTED
SCARFED
SCARPED
SCARRED
SCATHED
SCATTED
SCENDED
SCENTED
SCHEMED
SCOFFED
SCOLDED
SCOOPED
SCOOTED
SCORNED
SCOURED
SCOUTED
SCOWLED
SCRAPED
SCREWED
SCUDDED
SCUFFED
SCULLED
SCYTHED

••CD•••
MACDUFF

••C•D••
ACCEDED
ACCEDER
ACCEDES
ARCADES
ARCADIA
CICADAE
CICADAS
DECADES
DECIDED
DECIDES
DECODED
DECODER
DECODES
ENCODED
ENCODER
ENCODES
ESCUDOS
FACADES
INCUDES
JACKDAW
LACEDUP
LUCIDLY
MACADAM
PICADOR
RECEDED
RECEDES
RECODED
RECODES
SECEDED
SECEDER
SECEDES
SICKDAY

••C••D•
ACCORDS
ASCENDS
BACARDI
COCKADE
EXCEEDS
EXCLUDE
IDCARDS
INCLUDE
NOCANDO
NUCLIDE
OCCLUDE
ORCHIDS
PICARDY
RECORDS
RICARDO
SECLUDE
SECONDS

••C•••D
ACCEDED
ACCRUED
ACCUSED
BACKEND
BECLOUD
BUCKLED
CACKLED
DECAPOD
DECAYED
DECIDED
DECODED
DECOYED
DECREED
DECRIED
ENCAGED
ENCASED
ENCODED
ESCAPED
EUCHRED
EXCISED
EXCITED
EXCUSED
FACETED
FACTOID
FOCUSED
HACKLED
HECKLED
INCASED
INCISED
INCITED
LOCATED
MCCLOUD
ORCHARD
PACKARD
PICCARD
PICKLED
RECANED
RECEDED
RECITED
RECODED
RECUSED
RICHARD
SECEDED
SECURED
SUCCEED
TACKLED
TICKLED
UNCAGED
UNCASED
VACATED
YACHTED

•••C•D•
AVOCADO
BARCODE
BROCADE
CASCADE
CONCEDE
PLACIDO
PRECEDE
ZIPCODE

•••C••D
ABSCOND
BATCHED
BEACHED
BELCHED
BENCHED
BIRCHED
BLACKED
BLOCKED
BOTCHED
BRICKED
BUNCHED
BUNCOED
CHECKED
CHUCKED
CINCHED
CIRCLED
CLACKED
CLICKED
CLOCKED
CLUCKED
COACHED
CONCORD
COUCHED
CRACKED
CRICKED
CUECARD
DESCEND
DISCARD
DISCOED
DISCORD
DITCHED
EJECTED
ELECTED
ENACTED
ERECTED
ERUCTED
EVICTED
EXACTED
FANCIED
FETCHED
FILCHED
FLACCID
FLECKED
FLICKED

FLOCKED
FROCKED
GLACEED
HATCHED
HITCHED
HUNCHED
ICECOLD
KEYCARD
KNOCKED
LATCHED
LEACHED
LEECHED
LUNCHED
LURCHED
MARCHED
MATCHED
MISCUED
MOOCHED
MULCHED
MULCTED
MUNCHED
MUSCLED
NOTCHED
PARCHED
PATCHED
PEACHED
PERCHED
PICCARD
PINCHED
PITCHED
PLACARD
PLUCKED
POACHED
POUCHED
PRICKED
PROCEED
PSYCHED
PUNCHED
QUACKED
RANCHED
REACHED
REACTED
RESCIND
RESCUED
RIPCORD
ROACHED
SHOCKED
SHUCKED
SLACKED
SLICKED
SMACKED
SNACKED
SPECCED
SPECKED
STACKED
STOCKED
SUCCEED
SYNCHED
TETCHED
TORCHED
TOUCHED
TRACKED
TRICKED
TRUCKED
VOUCHED
WATCHED
WELCHED
WHACKED
WINCHED
WRACKED
WRECKED

••••C•D

ADDUCED
AMERCED
ANTACID
BOUNCED
CAPECOD
CHANCED
COERCED
DEDUCED
DEFACED
EFFACED
ENLACED
ENTICED
EVINCED
FLACCID
FLEECED
GLANCED
INDUCED
JOUNCED
MENACED
NOTICED
NUANCED
PIERCED
POLICED
POUNCED
PRANCED
REDUCED
REFACED
RELACED
SEDUCED
SLUICED
SOURCED
SPECCED
SPLICED
SPRUCED
UNLACED

CE•••••

CEASING
CEBUANO
CECILIA
CEDARED
CEDILLA
CEILING
CELADON
CELEBES
CELEBRE
CELESTA
CELESTE
CELLARS
CELLINI
CELLIST
CELSIUS
CELTICS
CEMBALO
CEMENTS
CENSERS
CENSING
CENSORS
CENSURE
CENTAUR
CENTAVO
CENTERS
CENTIME
CENTIMO
CENTRAL
CENTRED
CENTRES
CENTRIC
CENTURY
CEPHEUS
CERAMIC
CEREALS
CEREBRA
CERIPHS
CERTAIN
CERTIFY
CERUMEN
CERVIDS
CESSING
CESSION
CETERIS
CEZANNE

C•E••••

CAESARS
CAESIUM
CAESURA
CHEAPEN
CHEAPER
CHEAPIE
CHEAPLY
CHEATED
CHEATER
CHEATIN
CHECHEN
CHECKED
CHECKER
CHECKIN
CHECKUP
CHEDDAR
CHEEPED
CHEERED
CHEERIO
CHEERUP
CHEESES
CHEETAH
CHEETOS
CHEEVER
CHEKHOV
CHELSEA
CHEMISE
CHEMIST
CHEMLAB
CHENIER
CHEQUER
CHEQUES
CHERISH
CHEROOT
CHERUBS
CHERVIL
CHESTER
CHETRUM
CHEVIED
CHEVIES
CHEVIOT
CHEVRES
CHEVRON
CHEWERS
CHEWIER
CHEWING
CHEWOUT
CHEWSUP
CHEWTOY
CLEANED
CLEANER
CLEANLY
CLEANSE
CLEANUP
CLEARED
CLEARER
CLEARLY
CLEARUP
CLEAVED
CLEAVER
CLEAVES
CLEAVON
CLEMENS
CLEMENT
CLEMSON
CLERICS
CLERISY
CLERKED
COEDITS
COEPTIS
COEQUAL
COERCED
COERCER
COERCES
COEVALS
COEXIST
CREAKED
CREAMED
CREAMER
CREASED
CREASES
CREATED
CREATES
CREATOR
CRECHES
CREDITS
CREEPED
CREEPER
CREEPUP
CREMONA
CRENELS
CREOLES
CREOSOL
CRESSES
CRESTED
CRETANS
CRETINS
CREVICE
CREWCUT
CREWELS
CREWING
CREWMAN
CREWMEN
CUEBALL
CUECARD

C••E•••

CADENCE
CADENCY
CADENZA
CADETTE
CAKEMIX
CALENDS
CAMEDUE
CAMELIA
CAMELOT
CAMEOED
CAMEOFF
CAMEOUT
CAMERAS
CAMERON
CAPEANN
CAPECOD
CAPELET
CAPELLA
CAPERED
CAREENS
CAREERS
CAREFOR
CAREFUL
CASELAW
CASERNE
CASERNS
CATENAE
CATERED
CATERER
CATERTO
CAVEATS
CAVEDIN
CAVEINS
CAVEMAN
CAVEMEN
CAVERNS
CAVESIN
CAVETTO
CAYENNE
CELEBES
CELEBRE
CELESTA
CELESTE
CEMENTS
CEREALS
CEREBRA
CETERIS
CHEEPED
CHEERED
CHEERIO
CHEERUP
CHEESES
CHEETAH
CHEETOS
CHEEVER
CHIEFLY
CINEMAS
CINEMAX
CLIENTS
CLUEDIN
CLUEING
CLUESIN
CODEINE
COGENCY
COHEIRS
COHERED
COHERES
COLEMAN
COLETTE
COMEDIC
COMEDUE
COMEOFF
COMEONS
COMEOUT
COMESAT
COMESBY
COMESIN
COMESON
COMESTO
COMESUP
CORELLI
CORETTA
COTERIE
COVERED
COVERUP
COVETED
COWERED
COZENED
CREEPED
CREEPER
CREEPUP
CROESUS
CRUELER
CRUELLY
CRUELTY
CSLEWIS
CULEBRA
CUREALL

C•••E••

CABLERS
CABLETV
CACHETS
CADGERS
CAGIEST
CAHIERS
CAKIEST
CALDERA
CALLERS
CALMEST
CALTECH
CALVERT
CAMBERS
CAMPERS
CANCELS
CANDELA
CANIEST
CANKERS
CANNERS
CANNERY
CANSECO
CANTEEN
CANTERS
CAPLESS
CAPLETS
CAPPERS
CARDERS
CAREENS
CAREERS
CARLESS
CARNERA
CARNETS
CARPELS
CARPERS
CARPETS
CARRELS
CARSEAT
CARTELS
CARTERS
CARVERS
CASHEWS
CASTERS
CATBERT
CATHEAD
CATSEYE
CENSERS
CENTERS
CEPHEUS
CHALETS
CHAPEAU
CHAPELS
CHASERS
CHATEAU
CHEWERS
CHIDERS
CHILEAN
CHIMERA
CHINESE
CHISELS
CHOKERS
CHOKEUP
CINDERS
CINDERY
CIPHERS
CISTERN
CLARETS
CLAVELL
CLAWERS
CLEMENS
CLEMENT
CLORETS
CLOSEBY
CLOSEIN
CLOSELY
CLOSEST
CLOSETS
CLOSEUP
CLOVERS
COALERS
COAXERS
COBWEBS
COCHERE
COCKERS
COCTEAU
CODGERS
COFFEES
COFFERS
COINERS
COKIEST
COLBERT
COLDEST
COLLECT
COLLEEN
COLLEGE
COLLETS
COMBERS
COMMEND
COMMENT
COMPEER
COMPELS
COMPERE
COMPETE
CONCEAL
CONCEDE
CONCEIT
CONCEPT
CONCERN
CONCERT
CONDEMN
CONFERS
CONFESS
CONGEAL
CONGERS
CONGEST
CONKERS
CONNECT
CONNERY
CONSENT
CONTEMN
CONTEND
CONTENT
CONTEST
CONTEXT
CONVENE
CONVENT
CONVERT
CONVEYS
COOKERS
COOKERY
COOLERS
COOLEST
COOPERS
COPIERS
COPPERS
COPPERY
COPTERS
CORBELS
CORBETT
CORDELL
CORDERO
CORKERS
CORNEAL
CORNEAS
CORNELL
CORNERS
CORNETS
CORRECT
CORSETS
CORTEGE
COSIEST
COSSETS
COTTERS
COULEES
COWBELL
COWHERD
COWPEAS
COYNESS
COZIEST
COZZENS
CRATERS
CRAVENS
CRAVERS
CRENELS
CREWELS
CRIMEAN
CROWERS
CRUDELY
CRUDEST
CUDGELS
CULLERS
CULVERS
CULVERT
CURFEWS
CURLERS
CURLEWS
CURRENT
CURTEST
CURVETS
CUTLERS
CUTLERY
CUTLETS
CUTTERS
CYCLERS
CYGNETS
CYPHERS
CYPRESS

C••••E•

CABARET
CABBIES
CABINET
CACKLED
CACKLER
CACKLES
CADDIED
CADDIES
CADUCEI
CAIQUES
CAJOLED
CAJOLER
CAJOLES
CALIBER
CALICES
CALIPER
CALOMEL
CALUMET
CALYCES
CALYXES
CAMEOED
CAMISES
CAMPIER
CANAPES
CANDIED
CANDIES
CANDLES
CANINES
CANNIER
CANTEEN
CANTLES
CAPELET
CAPERED
CAPULET
CARAFES
CARAMEL
CARAVEL
CARGOES
CARIBES
CARNIES
CAROLED
CAROLER
CAROMED
CARRIED
CARRIER
CARRIES
CARTIER
CASHIER
CASQUED
CASQUES
CASTLED
CASTLES
CATCHER
CATCHES
CATERED
CATERER
CATTIER
CAUDLES
CAULKED
CAULKER
CAVEMEN
CAVILED
CAVILER
CAYUSES
CCRIDER
CEDARED
CELEBES
CENTRED
CENTRES
CERUMEN
CHAINED
CHAIRED
CHAISES
CHALKED
CHAMBER
CHAMFER
CHAMPED
CHANCED
CHANCEL
CHANCER
CHANCES
CHANGED
CHANGER
CHANGES
CHANNEL
CHANTED
CHANTER
CHANTEY
CHAPLET
CHAPMEN
CHAPPED
CHAPTER
CHARGED
CHARGER
CHARGES
CHARIER
CHARLES
CHARLEY
CHARMED
CHARMER
CHARRED
CHARTED
CHARTER
CHASSES
CHASTEN
CHASTER
CHATTED
CHATTEL
CHATTER
CHAUCER
CHEAPEN
CHEAPER
CHEATED
CHEATER
CHECHEN
CHECKED
CHECKER
CHEEPED
CHEERED
CHEESES
CHEEVER
CHELSEA
CHENIER
CHEQUER
CHEQUES
CHESTER
CHEVIED
CHEVIES
CHEVRES
CHEWIER
CHICHEN
CHICKEN
CHIGGER
CHIGOES
CHILIES
CHILLED
CHILLER
CHIMNEY
CHINKED
CHINNED
CHIPPED
CHIPPER
CHIRPED
CHITTER
CHOICER
CHOICES
CHOKIER
CHOMPED
CHOOSER
CHOOSES
CHOPPED
CHOPPER
CHOWDER
CHROMES
CHUCKED
CHUGGED
CHUKKER
CHUMMED
CHUNNEL
CHUNTER
CHURNED
CHUTNEY
CINCHED
CINCHES
CIRCLED
CIRCLES
CIRCLET
CIRQUES
CITADEL
CITIZEN
CITROEN
CIVVIES
CLABBER
CLACKED
CLAIMED
CLAIMER
CLAMBER
CLAMMED
CLAMMER
CLAMPED
CLANGED
CLANKED
CLAPPED
CLAPPER
CLAQUES
CLASHED
CLASHES
CLASPED
CLASSED
CLASSES
CLATTER
CLAUSES
CLAVIER
CLAYIER
CLEANED
CLEANER
CLEARED
CLEARER
CLEAVED
CLEAVER
CLEAVES
CLERKED
CLICHES
CLICKED
CLIMBED
CLIMBER
CLINKED
CLINKER
CLIPPED
CLIPPER
CLIQUES
CLIQUEY
CLOAKED
CLOBBER
CLOCHES
CLOCKED
CLOCKER
CLOGGED
CLOMPED
CLOONEY
CLOPPED
CLOQUES
CLOTHED
CLOTHES
CLOTTED
CLOUDED
CLOUTED
CLOWDER
CLOWNED
CLUBBED
CLUCKED
CLUMPED
CLUNKED
CLUNKER
CLUSTER
CLUTTER
CNTOWER
COACHED
COACHES
COARSEN
COARSER
COASTED
COASTER
COBBLED
COBBLER
COBBLES
COCHLEA
COCKIER
COCKLES
COCKNEY
CODDLED
CODDLER
CODDLES
CODICES
COERCED
COERCER
COERCES
COFFEES
COHERED
COHERES
COLLEEN
COLLIER
COLLIES
COLLYER
COLONEL
COLONES
COLORED
COMFIER
COMFREY
COMPEER
COMPLEX
CONCHES
CONGAED
CONIFER
CONQUER
CONRIED
CONURES
COOKIES
COOPTED
COOTIES
CORKIER
CORNFED
CORNIER
CORONET
COSINES
COSTNER
COUCHED
COUCHES
COUGHED
COULEES
COULTER
COUNSEL
COUNTED
COUNTER
COUPLED
COUPLES
COUPLET
COURIER
COURSED
COURSER
COURSES
COURTED
COVERED
COVETED
COWERED
COWRIES
COYOTES
COZENED
COZUMEL
CRABBED
CRABBER
CRACKED
CRACKER
CRADLED
CRADLES
CRAFTED
CRAFTER
CRAMMED
CRAMMER
CRAMPED
CRANKED
CRASHED
CRASHES
CRASSER
CRAWLED
CRAWLER
CRAZIER
CRAZIES
CREAKED
CREAMED
CREAMER
CREASED
CREASES
CREATED
CREATES
CRECHES
CREEPED
CREEPER
CREOLES
CRESSES
CRESTED
CREWMEN
CRIBBED
CRICKED
CRICKET
CRIMPED
CRIMPER
CRINGED
CRINGES
CRISPED
CRISPER
CRITTER
CROAKED
CROCHET
CROFTER
CRONIES
CROOKED
CROONED
CROONER
CROPPED
CROPPER
CROQUET
CROSIER
CROSSED
CROSSER
CROSSES
CROWDED
CROWNED
CRUELER
CRUISED
CRUISER
CRUISES
CRULLER
CRUMPET
CRUSHED
CRUSHER
CRUSHES
CRUSTED
CRYOGEN
CUBBIES
CUDDIES
CUDDLED
CUDDLES
CULLIED
CULLIES
CURATES
CURDIER
CURDLED
CURDLES
CURLIER
CURRIED
CURRIER
CURRIES
CURTSEY
CURVIER
CUSHIER
CUSSLER

C•••••E

CABBAGE
CABOOSE
CADENCE
CADETTE
CALCITE
CALIBRE
CALORIE
CALZONE
CAMEDUE
CAMILLE
CANDICE
CANDIDE
CANZONE
CAPABLE
CAPAPIE
CAPRICE
CAPSIZE
CAPSULE
CAPTIVE
CAPTURE
CARBIDE
CARBINE
CARCASE
CARFARE
CARLYLE
CARMINE
CAROUSE
CARTAGE
CASCADE
CASERNE
CASTILE
CATENAE
CATHODE
CATLIKE
CATSEYE
CAYENNE
CELEBRE
CELESTE
CENSURE
CENTIME
CEZANNE
CHALICE
CHAPPIE
CHARADE
CHARLIE
CHEAPIE
CHEMISE
CHINESE
CHOLINE
CHORALE
CHORINE
CHORTLE
CHUCKLE
CICADAE
CILIATE
CITABLE
CITRATE
CITRINE
CLARICE
CLEANSE
CLIMATE
CLOACAE
CLOSURE
CLOTURE
COCHERE
COCHISE
COCKADE
CODEINE
COGNATE
COINAGE
COLETTE
COLGATE
COLLAGE
COLLATE
COLLEGE
COLLIDE
COLLUDE
COLOGNE
COMBINE
COMEDUE
COMIQUE
COMMODE
COMMOVE
COMMUNE
COMMUTE

COMPARE
COMPERE
COMPETE
COMPILE
COMPOSE
COMPOTE
COMPUTE
COMRADE
CONCAVE
CONCEDE
CONCISE
CONDOLE
CONDONE
CONDUCE
CONFIDE
CONFINE
CONFUSE
CONFUTE
CONGAME
CONJURE
CONNIVE
CONNOTE
CONSOLE
CONSUME
CONTUSE
CONVENE
CONVOKE
COPPICE
COPULAE
CORDAGE
CORDATE
CORDITE
CORKAGE
CORNICE
CORONAE
CORRODE
CORSAGE
CORTEGE
COSTUME
COTERIE
COTTAGE
COURAGE
COUTURE
COWHIDE
COWLIKE
COWPOKE
CRACKLE
CRAPPIE
CREVICE
CRINKLE
CRUMBLE
CRUMPLE
CRUSADE
CUBICLE
CUISINE
CULOTTE
CULTURE
CUPCAKE
CUPLIKE
CURLIKE
CURSIVE
CUTICLE
CUTRATE
CUTTIME
CYCLONE

•CE••••

ACEDOUT
ACERBIC
ACEROLA
ACEROSE
ACESOUT
ACETATE
ACETONE
ICEAGES
ICEAXES
ICEBAGS
ICEBEER
ICEBERG
ICEBLUE
ICEBOAT
ICECAPS
ICECOLD
ICECUBE
ICEDOUT
ICEDTEA
ICEFLOE
ICEFOGS
ICEFREE
ICELAND
ICELESS
ICELIKE
ICEMILK
ICEPACK
ICEPICK
ICERINK
ICESHOW
ICESOUT
MCENROE
OCEANIA
OCEANIC
OCEANID
OCEANUS
OCELLUS
OCELOTS
SCENDED
SCENERY
SCENTED
SCEPTER
SCEPTIC
SCEPTRE

•C•E•••

ACCEDED
ACCEDER
ACCEDES
ACCENTS
ACCEPTS
ACHENES
ACHERON
ACHESON
ACREAGE
ACTEDON
ACTEDUP
ECHELON
MCHENRY
SCHEMAS
SCHEMED
SCHEMER
SCHEMES
SCHERZI
SCHERZO
SCIENCE
SCLERAS
SCREAKS
SCREAMS
SCREECH
SCREEDS
SCREENS
SCREWED
SCREWUP
UCCELLO

•C••E••

ACADEME
ACADEMY
ACCRETE
ACHIEST
ACHIEVE
ACTAEON
ACTRESS
ACUMENS
ACUTELY
ICEBEER
ICEBERG
ICELESS
ICINESS
ICKIEST
MCQUEEN
NCWYETH
SCALENE
SCALERS
SCARERS
SCAREUP
SCENERY
SCHLEPP
SCHLEPS
SCHMEER
SCORERS
SCOTERS
SCREECH
SCREEDS
SCREENS

•C•••E•

ACCEDED
ACCEDER
ACCEDES
ACCRUED
ACCRUES
ACCUSED
ACCUSER
ACCUSES
ACHATES
ACHENES
ACTIVES
CCRIDER
ECDYSES
ECTYPES
ICEAGES
ICEAXES
ICEBEER
ICEDTEA
ICEFREE
ICICLES
MCQUEEN
OCTANES
OCTAVES
OCTOBER
SCALDED
SCALIER
SCALPED
SCALPEL
SCALPER
SCAMMED
SCAMPED
SCAMPER
SCANNED
SCANNER
SCANTED
SCANTER
SCARCER
SCARFED
SCARIER
SCARLET
SCARPED
SCARPER
SCARRED
SCARVES
SCATHED
SCATHES
SCATTED
SCATTER
SCENDED
SCENTED
SCEPTER
SCHEMED
SCHEMER
SCHEMES
SCHMEER
SCHMOES
SCOFFED
SCOFFER
SCOLDED
SCOLDER
SCONCES
SCOOPED
SCOOPER
SCOOTED
SCOOTER
SCORNED
SCORNER
SCOURED
SCOURER
SCOUSES
SCOUTED
SCOUTER
SCOWLED
SCOWLER
SCRAPED
SCRAPER
SCRAPES
SCREWED
SCRIBES
SCRIVEN
SCUDDED
SCUFFED
SCULLED
SCULLER
SCUPPER
SCURVES
SCYTHED
SCYTHES

•C••••E

ACADEME
ACCRETE
ACEROSE
ACETATE
ACETONE
ACHIEVE
ACOLYTE
ACONITE
ACQUIRE
ACREAGE
ACTABLE
ACTFIVE
ACTUATE
ECLIPSE
ECLOGUE
ICEBLUE
ICECUBE
ICEFLOE
ICEFREE
ICELIKE
MCCLURE
MCENROE
MCGUIRE
MCSWINE
OCCLUDE
OCTUPLE
SCALENE
SCEPTRE
SCIENCE
SCOTTIE
SCOURGE
SCROOGE
SCRUPLE
SCUFFLE
SCUTTLE

••CE•••

ACCEDED
ACCEDER
ACCEDES
ACCENTS
ACCEPTS
ASCENDS
ASCENTS
ASCETIC
DECEITS
DECEIVE
DECENCY
DOCENTS
EXCEEDS
EXCEPTS
EXCERPT
FACEOFF
FACETED
INCENSE
INCEPTS
LACEDUP
LACESUP
LICENCE
LICENSE
LUCENCY
LUCERNE
LYCEUMS
NACELLE
OSCEOLA
PACECAR
RACECAR
RACEMES
RACEWAY
RECEDED
RECEDES
RECEIPT
RECEIVE
RECENCY
RICERAT
SECEDED
SECEDER
SECEDES
UCCELLO
VICEROY

••C•E••

ACCRETE
ALCHEMY
ANCIENT
ARCHERS
ARCHERY
BACKEND
BACKERS
BECKETT
BICKERS
BUCKETS
BUCKEYE
CACHETS
COCHERE
COCKERS
COCTEAU
CYCLERS
DECREED
DECREES
DICIEST
DICKENS
DICKERS
DICKEYS
DOCKERS
DOCKETS
DUCHESS
ESCHEAT
ESCHEWS
ETCHERS
EXCEEDS
EXCRETE
HACKERS
HACKETT
IPCRESS
JACKETS
JACKEYS
JOCKEYS
KICKERS
KUCHENS
LACIEST
LACKEYS
LACTEAL
LECTERN
LICHENS
LOCKERS
LOCKETS
MACBETH
MACHETE
MICHELE
MICKEYS
MOCKERS
MOCKERY
MRCLEAN
NECKERS
NICKELS
NICKERS
NUCLEAR
NUCLEIC
NUCLEON
NUCLEUS
PACKERS
PACKETS
PICKENS
PICKERS
PICKETS
PICKETT
POCKETS
PUCKERS
PUCKETT
RACIEST
RACKETS
RECHECK
RECLEAN
RICHEST
RICKETY
RICKEYS
ROCHETS
ROCKERS
ROCKERY
ROCKETS
SACHEMS
SACHETS
SACKERS
SECKELS
SECRECY
SECRETE
SECRETS
SICKENS
SICKEST
SOCIETY
SOCKETS
SOCKEYE
SUCCEED
SUCCESS
SUCKERS
TACKERS
TICKERS
TICKETS
TICKETY
TUCKERS
UNCLEAN
UNCLEAR
WICKERS
WICKETS
WYCHELM

••C••E•

ACCEDED
ACCEDER
ACCEDES
ACCRUED
ACCRUES
ACCUSED
ACCUSER
ACCUSES
ALCOVES
ARCADES
BECOMES
BUCKLED
BUCKLER
BUCKLES
BUCKLEY
BUCKOES
CACKLED
CACKLER
CACKLES
COCHLEA
COCKIER
COCKLES
COCKNEY
DECADES
DECAYED
DECIBEL
DECIDED
DECIDES
DECKLES
DECODED
DECODER
DECODES
DECOYED
DECREED
DECREES
DECRIED
DECRIER
DECRIES
DICKIES
DUCHIES
DUCKIER
ENCAGED
ENCAGES
ENCASED
ENCASES
ENCODED
ENCODER
ENCODES
ENCORES
ESCAPED
ESCAPEE
ESCAPES
EUCHRED
EUCHRES
EXCISED
EXCISES
EXCITED
EXCITES
EXCUSED
EXCUSES
FACADES
FACETED
FICKLER
FICUSES
FOCSLES
FOCUSED
FOCUSES
GECKOES
HACKIES
HACKLED
HACKLES
HACKNEY
HECKLED
HECKLER
HECKLES
INCASED
INCASES
INCISED
INCISES
INCITED
INCITER
INCITES
INCOMES
INCUDES
ITCHIER
JACKIES
JACONET
JACQUES
KICKIER
LACQUER
LOCALES
LOCATED
LOCATER
LOCATES
LOCOMEN
LUCIFER
LUCKIER
MICHAEL
MUCKIER
OOCYTES
OSCINES
PECKIER
PICKIER
PICKLED
PICKLES
RACEMES
RACQUET
RECANED
RECANES
RECEDED
RECEDES
RECIPES
RECITED
RECITER
RECITES
RECODED
RECODES
RECOVER
RECUSED
RECUSES
RICHTER
RICKLES
ROCKIER
ROCKIES
SACQUES
SECEDED
SECEDER
SECEDES
SECURED
SECURER
SECURES
SICKLES
SUCCEED
TACKIER
TACKLED
TACKLER
TACKLES
TECHIER
TECHIES
TICKLED
TICKLER
TICKLES
UNCAGED
UNCAGES
UNCASED
UNCASES
UNCOVER
VACATED
VACATES
WACKIER
YACHTED
YUCKIER

••C•••E

ACCRETE
ARCHIVE
ARCSINE
ASCRIBE
BACKHOE
BECAUSE
BICYCLE
BUCKEYE
CICADAE
COCHERE
COCHISE
COCKADE
CYCLONE
DECEIVE
DECLARE
DECLINE
DICTATE
DOCKAGE
DUCTILE
ENCLAVE
ENCLOSE
ESCAPEE
EXCLUDE
EXCRETE
FACULAE
FICTIVE
HECTARE
INCENSE
INCLINE
INCLOSE
INCLUDE
JACCUSE
LACOSTE
LACTASE
LACTATE
LACTOSE
LACUNAE
LECARRE
LECTURE
LICENCE
LICENSE
LUCERNE
LUCILLE
MACABRE
MACAQUE
MACHETE
MACHINE
MACRAME
MACULAE
MCCLURE
MICHELE
MICROBE
NACELLE
NECKTIE
NUCLIDE
OCCLUDE
PACKAGE
PACKICE
PICANTE
PICKAXE
PICTURE
RECEIVE
RECHOSE
RECLAME
RECLINE
RECLUSE
RECYCLE
SACLIKE
SECLUDE
SECRETE
SOCKEYE
SUCRASE
SUCROSE
TACTILE
UNCLOSE
UNCRATE
UPCLOSE
VACCINE
VACUOLE

•••CE••

AVOCETS
BRACERO
BRACERS
BRACEUP
CANCELS
CONCEAL
CONCEDE
CONCEIT
CONCEPT
CONCERN
CONCERT
DANCERS
DEICERS
DESCEND
DESCENT
DIOCESE
DISCERN
DRYCELL
EPICENE
FAUCETS
FAWCETT
FENCERS
FORCEPS
FORCERS
GLACEED
GROCERS
GROCERY
JAYCEES
JUICERS
JUICEUP
LANCERS
LANCETS
LARCENY
MARCEAU
MARCELS
MERCERS
MERCERY
MINCERS
MIOCENE
NASCENT
OBSCENE
PARCELS
PERCENT
PIECERS
PINCERS
PLACEBO
PLACERS
PRECEDE
PRECEPT
PRICERS
PROCEED
PROCESS
PURCELL
REDCELL
REDCENT
SAUCERS
SINCERE
SLICERS
SORCERY
SPACERS
SPICERY
SPICEUP
SUCCEED
SUCCESS
TENCENT
TERCELS
TERCETS
TRACERS
TRACERY
TRICEPS
VINCENT
VISCERA
WETCELL
WINCERS

•••C•E•

AIRCREW
AITCHES
APACHES
BATCHED
BATCHES
BEACHED
BEACHES
BEECHER
BEECHES
BELCHED
BELCHES
BENCHED
BENCHES
BIRCHED
BIRCHES
BLACKED
BLACKEN
BLACKER
BLOCKED
BLOCKER
BOTCHED
BOTCHES
BRACKEN
BRACKET
BRICKED
BUNCHED
BUNCHES
BUNCOED
BUTCHER
CATCHER
CATCHES
CHECHEN
CHECKED
CHECKER
CHICHEN
CHICKEN
CHUCKED
CINCHED
CINCHES
CIRCLED
CIRCLES
CIRCLET
CLACKED
CLICHES
CLICKED
CLOCHES
CLOCKED
CLOCKER
CLUCKED
COACHED
COACHES
CONCHES
COUCHED
COUCHES
CRACKED
CRACKER
CRECHES
CRICKED
CRICKET
CROCHET
DISCOED
DITCHED
DITCHES
DRUCKER
EJECTED
ELECTED
ELECTEE
ENACTED
ERECTED
ERECTER
ERUCTED
EVACUEE
EVICTED
EXACTED
EXACTER
FANCIED
FANCIER
FANCIES
FESCUES
FETCHED
FETCHES
FIACRES
FILCHED
FILCHER
FILCHES
FINCHES
FISCHER
FITCHES
FLECHES
FLECKED
FLICKED
FLICKER
FLOCKED
FROCKED
GAUCHER
GLACEED
GLACIER
GULCHES
HATCHED
HATCHER
HATCHES
HATCHET
HITCHED
HITCHER
HITCHES
HUNCHED
HUNCHES
HUTCHES
ICICLES
JAYCEES
JIMCHEE
JUICIER
JUNCOES
KETCHES
KIMCHEE
KITCHEN
KNACKER
KNOCKED
KNOCKER
LARCHES
LATCHED
LATCHES
LEACHED
LEACHES
LEECHED
LEECHES
LOACHES
LUNCHED
LUNCHES
LURCHED
LURCHES
MADCHEN
MARCHED
MARCHER
MARCHES
MATCHED
MATCHES
MENCKEN
MERCIES
MISCUED
MISCUES
MOOCHED
MOOCHER
MOOCHES
MULCHED
MULCHES
MULCTED
MUNCHED
MUNCHER
MUNCHES
MUSCLED
MUSCLES
NATCHEZ
NOTCHED
NOTCHES
ORACLES
PARCHED
PARCHES
PATCHED
PATCHES
PEACHED
PEACHES
PERCHED
PERCHES
PINCHED
PINCHER
PINCHES
PITCHED
PITCHER
PITCHES
PLACKET
PLUCKED
POACHED
POACHER
POACHES
POOCHES
PORCHES
POUCHED
POUCHES
PRICIER
PRICKED
PROCEED
PSYCHED
PSYCHES
PUNCHED
PUNCHER
PUNCHES
QUACKED
QUICHES
QUICKEN
QUICKER
RANCHED
RANCHER
RANCHES
RATCHET
REACHED
REACHES
REACTED
RESCUED
RESCUER
RESCUES
ROACHED
ROACHES
SATCHEL
SAUCIER
SEICHES
SHOCKED
SHOCKER
SHUCKED
SHUCKER
SLACKED
SLACKEN
SLACKER
SLICKED
SLICKER
SMACKED
SMACKER
SNACKED
SNACKER
SNICKER
SPACIER
SPECCED
SPECIES
SPECKED
SPECTER
SPICIER
STACKED
STICHES
STICKER
STOCKED
SUCCEED
SYNCHED
SYNCHES
TEACHER
TEACHES
TEICHER
TETCHED
THICKEN
THICKER
THICKET
TORCHED
TORCHES
TOUCHED
TOUCHES
TRACHEA
TRACKED
TRACKER
TRICKED
TRICKER
TROCHEE
TROCHES
TRUCKED
TRUCKEE
TRUCKER
UNSCREW
VETCHES
VOUCHED
VOUCHER
VOUCHES
WATCHED
WATCHER
WATCHES
WELCHED
WELCHES
WENCHES
WHACKED
WINCHED
WINCHES
WITCHES
WRACKED
WRECKED
WRECKER

ZILCHES

•••C••E

APOCOPE
ARACHNE
BARCODE
BLACKIE
BROCADE
CALCITE
CARCASE
CASCADE
CHUCKLE
CONCAVE
CONCEDE
CONCISE
CRACKLE
CUPCAKE
DAYCARE
DIOCESE
EDUCATE
EGGCASE
ELECTEE
EPICENE
EPICURE
EVACUEE
EXECUTE
FRECKLE
FRICKIE
GLUCOSE
GRACILE
GRACKLE
HERCULE
HOECAKE
HOTCAKE
HOWCOME
ICECUBE
INSCAPE
JACCUSE
JIMCHEE
KIMCHEE
KNUCKLE
LEUCINE
MIOCENE
NESCAFE
OBSCENE
OBSCURE
OILCAKE
OUTCOME
PANCAKE
PERCALE
PISCINE
PLACATE
PORCINE
PRECEDE
PRECISE
PRICKLE
PROCURE
QUICKIE
RESCALE
RIBCAGE
SHACKLE
SINCERE
SNOCONE
SPACKLE
SPECKLE
SPECTRE
TEACAKE
TOSCALE
TRICKLE
TROCHEE
TRUCKEE
TRUCKLE
UPSCALE
VACCINE
WELCOME
ZIPCODE

••••CE•

ADDUCED
ADDUCES
AMERCED
AMERCES
BODICES
BOUNCED
BOUNCER
BOUNCES
CADUCEI
CALICES
CALYCES
CHANCED
CHANCEL
CHANCER
CHANCES
CHAUCER
CHOICER
CHOICES
CODICES
COERCED
COERCER
COERCES
DEDUCED
DEDUCES
DEFACED
DEFACES
DEVICES
EFFACED
EFFACES
ENLACED
ENLACES
ENTICED
ENTICER
ENTICES
EVINCED
EVINCES
FIANCEE
FIANCES
FIERCER
FLEECED
FLEECES
FRANCES
GLANCED
GLANCES
HELICES
HYRACES
INDICES
INDUCED
INDUCER
INDUCES
JANACEK
JOUNCED
JOUNCES
LATICES
MENACED
MENACES
NOTICED
NOTICES
NOVICES
NUANCED
NUANCES
OFFICER
OFFICES
PALACES
PANACEA
PEDICEL
PIERCED
PIERCES
PLAICES
POLICED
POLICES
POUNCED
POUNCER
POUNCES
PRANCED
PRANCER
PRANCES
PRINCES
PUMICES
QUINCES
RADICES
REDUCED
REDUCER
REDUCES
REFACED
REFACES
RELACED
RELACES
SARACEN
SCARCER
SCONCES
SEANCES
SEDUCED
SEDUCER
SEDUCES
SLUICED
SLUICES
SOLACES
SOURCED
SOURCES
SPECCED
SPENCER
SPLICED
SPLICER
SPLICES
SPRUCED
SPRUCER
SPRUCES
STANCES
TENACES
TRANCES
UNLACED
UNLACES

••••C•E

ARTICLE
ATTACHE
AURICLE
BICYCLE
BINOCHE
BLANCHE
BRIOCHE
CLOACAE
CUBICLE
CUTICLE
DEBACLE
EARACHE
FIANCEE
GOUACHE
LORICAE
MANACLE
MIRACLE
MONOCLE
OSSICLE
PANACHE
PANICLE
PEDICLE
PENUCHE
PINOCLE
PORSCHE
RADICLE
RECYCLE
RETICLE
TREACLE
TUNICLE
VEHICLE

•••••CE

ABSENCE
ADVANCE
ASKANCE
ATPEACE
AUSPICE
AVARICE
BALANCE
BERNICE
BYFORCE
CADENCE
CANDICE
CAPRICE
CHALICE
CLARICE
CONDUCE
COPPICE
CORNICE
CREVICE
DEFENCE
DEHISCE
DIVORCE
DNOTICE
DOGFACE
DORMICE
DURANCE
EDIFICE
EMBRACE
ENFORCE
ENHANCE
ENOUNCE
ESSENCE
FAIENCE
FINANCE
FLOUNCE
FURNACE
GRIMACE
HOSPICE
INFORCE
INPEACE
INPLACE
INVOICE
JUSTICE
LAPLACE
LATTICE
LETTUCE
LICENCE
MAURICE
OFFENCE
ORIFICE
OUTFACE
OUTPACE
OUTRACE
PACKICE
PALANCE
PATRICE
PENANCE
PINNACE
PREFACE
PRODUCE
RATRACE
REJOICE
REPLACE
REPRICE
RETRACE
REVOICE
ROMANCE
SCIENCE
SERVICE
SILENCE
STATICE
SUBVOCE
SUFFICE
SURFACE
TERENCE
TERRACE
THINICE
TITMICE
TRADUCE
TROUNCE
UNAVOCE
VALANCE
VALENCE
WALLACE

C•F••••

CAFTANS
COFFEES
COFFERS
CUFFING

C••F•••

CANFULS
CAPFULS
CARFARE
CARFULS
CATFISH
CATFOOD
CHAFING
CHIFFON
CLIFTON
CODFISH
COFFEES
COFFERS
COIFING
COMFIER
COMFITS
COMFORT
COMFREY
CONFABS
CONFERS
CONFESS
CONFIDE
CONFINE
CONFIRM
CONFORM
CONFUSE
CONFUTE
CRAFTED
CRAFTER
CRAFTSY
CROFTER
CUFFING
CUPFULS
CURFEWS

C•••F••

CALLFOR
CARAFES
CAREFOR
CAREFUL
CHAMFER
CHIEFLY
CHIFFON
CONIFER
CORNFED
CUTOFFS

C••••F•

CALCIFY
CALLOFF
CAMEOFF
CASTOFF
CERTIFY
CLARIFY
COMEOFF
CONNIFF
COOKOFF
CRUCIFY
CUTOFFS
CUTSOFF

C•••••F

CALLOFF
CAMEOFF
CASTOFF
COMEOFF
CONNIFF
COOKOFF
CRYWOLF
CUTSOFF

•C•F•••

ACTFIVE
ACTFOUR
ICEFLOE
ICEFOGS
ICEFREE
SCOFFED
SCOFFER
SCUFFED
SCUFFLE

•C••F••

SCARFED
SCOFFED
SCOFFER
SCRUFFS
SCRUFFY
SCUFFED
SCUFFLE

•C•••F•

ACIDIFY
SCARIFY
SCRUFFS
SCRUFFY

••C•F••

FACTFUL
LUCIFER
PACIFIC
SACKFUL
TACTFUL

••C••F•

BACKOFF
FACEOFF
KICKOFF
MACDUFF
PICKOFF
RECTIFY
TICKOFF

••C•••F

BACKOFF
FACEOFF
KICKOFF
MACDUFF
PICKOFF
TICKOFF

•••C•F•

CALCIFY
CRUCIFY
DULCIFY
FANCIFY
NESCAFE
SPECIFY

C•G••••

CAGIEST
COGBURN
COGENCY
COGNACS
COGNATE
CYGNETS

C••G•••

CADGERS
CADGING
CALGARY
CAPGUNS
CARGOES
CHAGALL
CHAGRIN
CHIGGER
CHIGNON
CHIGOES
CHUGGED
CLOGGED
CLOGSUP
CODGERS
COLGATE
CONGAED
CONGAME
CONGEAL
CONGERS
CONGEST
COUGARS
COUGHED
COUGHUP
COWGIRL
CUDGELS

C•••G••

CAYUGAS
CHANGED
CHANGER
CHANGES
CHARGED
CHARGER
CHARGES
CHIGGER
CHUGGED
CLANGED
CLANGOR
CLOGGED
COALGAS
COLOGNE
COSIGNS
CRINGED
CRINGES
CRYOGEN

C••••G•

CABBAGE
CARTAGE
CASINGS
CHICAGO
COINAGE
COLLAGE
COLLEGE
COMINGS
CONDIGN
CONSIGN
CORDAGE
CORKAGE
CORSAGE
CORTEGE
COTTAGE
COURAGE
CYBORGS

C•••••G

CABLING
CACHING
CADGING
CALKING
CALLING
CALMING
CALVING
CAMPING
CANNING
CANTING
CAPPING
CARDING
CARKING
CARPING
CARTING
CARVING
CASHING
CASTING
CATALOG
CATTING
CAUSING
CEASING
CEILING
CENSING
CESSING
CHAFING
CHASING
CHEWING
CHIDING
CHIMING
CLAWING
CLONING
CLOSING
CLOYING
CLUEING
COATING
COAXING
COCKING
COIFING
COILING
COINING
COMBING
CONKING
CONNING
COOKING
COOLING
COOPING
COPPING
COPYING
CORDING
CORKING
CORNDOG
CORNING
COSHING
COSTING
COWLING
COZYING
CRANING
CRATING
CRAVING
CRAZING
CREWING
CROWING
CUFFING
CULLING
CUNNING
CUPPING
CURBING
CURDING
CURLING
CURSING
CURVING
CUSHING
CUSSING
CUTTING
CYCLING
CYYOUNG

•CG••••

MCGAVIN
MCGUIRE

•C••G••

ECLOGUE
ICEAGES
ICINGIN
ICINGUP
OCTAGON
SCRAGGY

•C•••G•

ACREAGE
ECOLOGY
ICEBAGS
ICEFOGS
SCOURGE
SCRAGGY
SCROOGE

•C••••G

ACHTUNG
ECHOING
ICEBERG
SCALING
SCARING
SCOPING
SCORING

••CG•••

MACGRAW

••C•G••

DECAGON
ENCAGED
ENCAGES
UNCAGED
UNCAGES

••C••G•

DOCKAGE
FACINGS
LACINGS
PACKAGE
UNCLOGS

••C•••G

ARCHING
BACHING
BACKING
BACKLOG
BUCKING
CACHING
COCKING
CYCLING
DECALOG
DECKING
DOCKING
DUCKING
DUCTING
ETCHING
HACKING
HOCKING
INCHING
ITCHING
JACKING
KICKING
LACKING
LICKING
LOCKING
LUCKING
MOCKING
MUCKING
NECKING
NICKING
PACKING
PECKING
PICKING
RACKING
ROCKING
RUCHING
RUCKING
SACKING
SICCING
SOCKING
SUCKING
TACKING
TICKING
TUCKING
YACKING

•••C•G•

CHICAGO
RIBCAGE

•••C••G

BRACING
DANCING
DEICING
EDUCING
FARCING
FENCING
FORCING
GRACING
JUICING
MINCING
PIECING
PLACING
PRICING
SICCING
SLICING
SPACING
SPECING
SPICING
SYNCING
TRACING
VOICING
WINCING

CH•••••

CHABLIS
CHACHAS
CHAFING
CHAGALL
CHAGRIN
CHAINED
CHAIRED
CHAISES
CHALETS
CHALICE
CHALKED
CHALKUP
CHALONS
CHAMBER
CHAMFER
CHAMOIS
CHAMPED
CHANCED
CHANCEL
CHANCER
CHANCES
CHANGED
CHANGER
CHANGES
CHANNEL
CHANSON
CHANTED
CHANTER
CHANTEY
CHAOTIC
CHAPATI
CHAPEAU
CHAPELS
CHAPLET
CHAPLIN
CHAPMAN
CHAPMEN
CHAPPED
CHAPPIE
CHAPTER
CHARADE
CHARGED
CHARGER
CHARGES
CHARIER
CHARILY
CHARIOT
CHARITY
CHARLES
CHARLEY
CHARLIE
CHARMED
CHARMER
CHARMIN
CHARRED
CHARTED
CHARTER
CHASERS
CHASING
CHASSES
CHASSIS
CHASTEN
CHASTER
CHATEAU
CHATHAM
CHATSUP
CHATTED
CHATTEL
CHATTER
CHAUCER
CHEAPEN
CHEAPER
CHEAPIE
CHEAPLY
CHEATED
CHEATER
CHEATIN
CHECHEN
CHECKED
CHECKER
CHECKIN
CHECKUP
CHEDDAR
CHEEPED
CHEERED
CHEERIO
CHEERUP
CHEESES
CHEETAH
CHEETOS
CHEEVER
CHEKHOV
CHELSEA
CHEMISE
CHEMIST
CHEMLAB
CHENIER
CHEQUER
CHEQUES
CHERISH
CHEROOT
CHERUBS
CHERVIL
CHESTER
CHETRUM
CHEVIED
CHEVIES
CHEVIOT
CHEVRES
CHEVRON
CHEWERS
CHEWIER
CHEWING
CHEWOUT
CHEWSUP
CHEWTOY
CHIANTI
CHICAGO
CHICANA
CHICANO
CHICHEN
CHICKEN
CHICORY
CHIDERS
CHIDING
CHIEFLY
CHIFFON
CHIGGER
CHIGNON
CHIGOES
CHILEAN
CHILIES
CHILLED
CHILLER
CHIMERA
CHIMING
CHIMNEY
CHINESE
CHINKED
CHINNED
CHINOOK
CHINTZY
CHINUPS
CHIPPED
CHIPPER
CHIPSIN
CHIRICO
CHIRPED
CHISELS
CHITTER
CHLORAL
CHOCTAW
CHOICER
CHOICES
CHOKERS
CHOKEUP
CHOKIER
CHOLINE
CHOLLAS
CHOMPED
CHOMSKY
CHOOSER
CHOOSES
CHOPPED
CHOPPER
CHORALE
CHORALS
CHORINE
CHORIZO
CHORTLE
CHOWDER
CHRISMS
CHRISTI
CHRISTO
CHRISTY
CHROMES
CHRONIC
CHUCKED
CHUCKLE
CHUGGED
CHUKKAS
CHUKKER
CHUMMED
CHUNNEL
CHUNTER
CHURNED
CHUTNEY

C•H••••

CAHIERS
CAHOOTS
COHABIT
COHEIRS
COHERED
COHERES
COHORTS
COHOSTS

C••H•••

CACHETS
CACHING
CACHOUS
CALHOUN
CARHOPS
CASHBAR
CASHBOX
CASHCOW
CASHEWS
CASHIER
CASHING
CASHOUT
CATHAIR
CATHEAD
CATHODE
CEPHEUS
CIPHERS
COCHAIR
COCHERE
COCHISE
COCHLEA
COCHRAN
COSHING
COWHAND
COWHERD
COWHIDE
CUSHAWS
CUSHIER
CUSHING
CUSHION
CYPHERS

C•••H••

CAMPHOR
CAPSHAW
CATCHER
CATCHES
CATCHON
CATCHUP
CATSHOW
CHACHAS
CHATHAM
CHECHEN
CHEKHOV
CHICHEN
CINCHED
CINCHES
CLASHED
CLASHES
CLICHES
CLOCHES
CLOTHED
CLOTHES
COACHED
COACHES
CONCHES
COUCHED
COUCHES
COUGHED
COUGHUP
CRASHED
CRASHES
CRECHES
CROCHET
CRUSHED
CRUSHER
CRUSHES
CYNTHIA

C••••H•

CALIPHS
CERIPHS
COCKSHY
CRUNCHY

C•••••H

CADDISH
CALTECH
CARWASH
CATFISH
CATTISH
CHEETAH
CHERISH
CLAYISH
COCKISH
CODFISH
COLDISH
COLTISH
COOLISH
CORINTH
CORNISH
CRONISH
CUBBISH
CULTISH
CURRISH

•CH••••

ACHATES
ACHENES
ACHERON
ACHESON
ACHIEST
ACHIEVE
ACHTUNG
ECHELON
ECHIDNA
ECHINUS
ECHOING
ICHABOD
MCHENRY
SCHATZI
SCHEMAS
SCHEMED
SCHEMER
SCHEMES
SCHERZI
SCHERZO
SCHIRRA
SCHISMS

SCHLEPP
SCHLEPS
SCHLOCK
SCHMEER
SCHMIDT
SCHMOES
SCHMOOS
SCHNAPS
SCHOLAR
SCHOOLS
SCHULTZ
SCHWINN
WCHANDY

•C•H•••

ECKHART

•C••H••

ICESHOW
MCLUHAN
MCMAHON
SCATHED
SCATHES
SCYTHED
SCYTHES

•C•••H•

ACANTHI

•C••••H

NCWYETH
SCRATCH
SCREECH
SCRUNCH

••CH•••

ALCHEMY
ANCHORS
ANCHOVY
ARCHAIC
ARCHERS
ARCHERY
ARCHING
ARCHIVE
ARCHONS
ARCHWAY
BACHING
BSCHOOL
CACHETS
CACHING
CACHOUS
COCHAIR
COCHERE
COCHISE
COCHLEA
COCHRAN
DUCHESS
DUCHIES
ENCHAIN
ENCHANT
ESCHEAT
ESCHEWS
ETCHANT
ETCHERS
ETCHING
EUCHRED
EUCHRES
FUCHSIA
INCHING
ITCHIER
ITCHING
KACHINA
KUCHENS
LACHLAN
LICHENS
MACHETE
MACHINA
MACHINE
MICHAEL
MICHELE
MRCHIPS
NICHOLS
ORCHARD
ORCHIDS
PACHISI
RECHALK
RECHECK
RECHOSE
RICHARD
RICHEST
RICHMAN
RICHTER
ROCHETS
RUCHING
SACHEMS
SACHETS
SICHUAN
TECHIER
TECHIES
TUCHMAN
UNCHAIN
URCHINS
WICHITA
WYCHELM
YACHTED
ZACHARY

••C•H••

ALCOHOL
BACCHUS
BACKHOE

••C••H•

COCKSHY
RICKSHA

••C•••H

COCKISH
JACINTH
MACBETH
PECKISH
PICTISH
PUCKISH
SICKISH
UNCOUTH

•••CH••

AITCHES
APACHES
ARACHNE
BACCHUS
BATCHED
BATCHES
BEACHED
BEACHES
BEECHAM
BEECHER
BEECHES
BELCHED
BELCHES
BENCHED
BENCHES
BIOCHIP
BIRCHED
BIRCHES
BOKCHOY
BOTCHED
BOTCHES
BOTCHUP
BUNCHED
BUNCHES
BUTCHER
CATCHER
CATCHES
CATCHON
CATCHUP
CHACHAS
CHECHEN
CHICHEN
CINCHED
CINCHES
CLICHES
CLOCHES
COACHED
COACHES
CONCHES
COUCHED
COUCHES
CRECHES
CROCHET
DITCHED
DITCHES
DOGCHOW
DRACHMA
DRACHMS
EPOCHAL
FETCHED
FETCHES
FILCHED
FILCHER
FILCHES
FINCHES
FISCHER
FITCHES
FLECHES
FUNCHAL
GAUCHER
GAUCHOS
GOTCHAS
GULCHES
HATCHED
HATCHER
HATCHES
HATCHET
HITCHED
HITCHER
HITCHES
HONCHOS
HUNCHED
HUNCHES
HUTCHES
JIMCHEE
JOACHIM
KERCHOO
KETCHAM
KETCHES
KETCHUP
KIMCHEE
KINCHIN
KITCHEN
KUTCHIN
KWACHAS
LARCHES
LATCHED
LATCHES
LEACHED
LEACHES
LEECHED
LEECHES
LITCHIS
LOACHES
LUNCHED
LUNCHES
LURCHED
LURCHES
MADCHEN
MARCHED
MARCHER
MARCHES
MARCHON
MATCHED
MATCHES
MATCHUP
MITCHUM
MOOCHED
MOOCHER
MOOCHES
MULCHED
MULCHES
MUNCHED
MUNCHER
MUNCHES
NATCHEZ
NOTCHED
NOTCHES
OLDCHAP
PANCHAX
PARCHED
PARCHES
PASCHAL
PATCHED
PATCHES
PATCHUP
PEACHED
PEACHES
PERCHED
PERCHES
PINCHAS
PINCHED
PINCHER
PINCHES
PITCHED
PITCHER
PITCHES
PITCHIN
POACHED
POACHER
POACHES
PONCHOS
POOCHES
PORCHES
POUCHED
POUCHES
PSYCHED
PSYCHES
PSYCHIC
PSYCHUP
PUNCHED
PUNCHER
PUNCHES
PUNCHIN
PUNCHUP
PYNCHON
QUECHUA
QUICHES
RANCHED
RANCHER
RANCHES
RANCHOS
RATCHET
REACHED
REACHES
ROACHED
ROACHES
SALCHOW
SATCHEL
SATCHMO
SEICHES
STICHES
SYNCHED
SYNCHES
TEACHER
TEACHES
TEACHIN
TEICHER
TETCHED
TORCHED
TORCHES
TOUCHED
TOUCHES
TOUCHON
TOUCHUP
TRACHEA
TROCHEE
TROCHES
VETCHES
VOUCHED
VOUCHER
VOUCHES
WATCHED
WATCHER
WATCHES
WATCHIT
WELCHED
WELCHES
WENCHES
WINCHED
WINCHES
WITCHES
ZILCHES

•••C•H•

GNOCCHI

•••C••H

DUNCISH
PAYCASH

••••CH•

ANARCHY
ATTACHE
AUROCHS
BINOCHE
BLANCHE
BLOTCHY
BORSCHT
BRIOCHE
BRONCHI
CRUNCHY
EARACHE
EPARCHS
EPARCHY
EXARCHS
GNOCCHI
GOUACHE
GROUCHO
GROUCHY
HIBACHI
HITACHI
JERICHO
KARACHI
KITSCHY
MALACHI
MOLOCHS
NOGUCHI
PANACHE
PAUNCHY
PENUCHE
PORSCHE
PREACHY
SAMECHS
SKETCHY
SLOUCHY
SNITCHY
STARCHY
THATCHY
TWITCHY
UTRECHT
VOTECHS

••••C•H

PADUCAH

•••••CH

ALDRICH
ANTIOCH
BESEECH
BEWITCH
CALTECH
DEBAUCH
DEBOUCH
DIPTYCH
EHRLICH
GODUTCH
IMPEACH
INDUTCH
IPSWICH
KLATSCH
LOWTECH
MONARCH
MURDOCH
OSTRICH
RETEACH
RETOUCH
SCRATCH
SCREECH
SCRUNCH
SPINACH
SPLOTCH
SQUELCH
SQUINCH
STAUNCH
STOMACH
STRETCH
UNHITCH
UNLATCH
WALLACH
WASATCH

CI•••••

CIBORIA
CICADAE
CICADAS
CILIATE
CINCHED
CINCHES
CINDERS
CINDERY
CINEMAS
CINEMAX
CINZANO
CIPHERS
CIRCLED
CIRCLES
CIRCLET
CIRCUIT
CIRCUSY
CIRQUES
CISTERN
CITABLE
CITADEL
CITIZEN
CITRATE
CITRINE
CITROEN
CITRONS
CITROUS
CIVILLY
CIVVIES

C•I••••

CAIMANS
CAIQUES
CAISSON
CEILING
CHIANTI
CHICAGO
CHICANA
CHICANO
CHICHEN
CHICKEN
CHICORY
CHIDERS
CHIDING
CHIEFLY
CHIFFON
CHIGGER
CHIGNON
CHIGOES
CHILEAN
CHILIES
CHILLED
CHILLER
CHIMERA
CHIMING
CHIMNEY
CHINESE
CHINKED
CHINNED
CHINOOK
CHINTZY
CHINUPS
CHIPPED
CHIPPER
CHIPSIN
CHIRICO
CHIRPED
CHISELS
CHITTER
CLIBURN
CLICHES
CLICKED
CLIENTS
CLIFTON
CLIMATE
CLIMBED
CLIMBER
CLINICS
CLINKED
CLINKER
CLINTON
CLIPART
CLIPONS
CLIPPED
CLIPPER
CLIQUES
CLIQUEY
COIFING
COILING
COILSUP
COINAGE
COINERS
COINING
CRIBBED
CRICKED
CRICKET
CRIMEAN
CRIMPED
CRIMPER
CRIMSON
CRINGED
CRINGES
CRINKLE
CRINKLY
CRINOID
CRIOLLO
CRISPED
CRISPER
CRISPIN
CRISPLY
CRISPUS
CRITICS
CRITTER
CUIBONO
CUIRASS
CUISINE

C••I•••

CABINET
CAGIEST
CAHIERS
CAKIEST
CALIBAN
CALIBER
CALIBRE
CALICES
CALICOS
CALIPER
CALIPHS
CAMILLE
CAMISES
CANIEST
CANINES
CAPITAL
CAPITAN
CAPITOL
CARIBES
CARIBOU
CARINAS
CARIOCA
CASINGS
CASINOS
CATIONS
CAVIARS
CAVILED
CAVILER
CCRIDER
CECILIA
CEDILLA
CERIPHS
CHAINED
CHAIRED
CHAISES
CHOICER
CHOICES
CHRISMS
CHRISTI
CHRISTO
CHRISTY
CILIATE
CITIZEN
CIVILLY
CLAIMED
CLAIMER
CLAIROL
CODICES
CODICIL
COKIEST
COMICAL
COMINGS
COMIQUE
CONICAL
CONIFER
COPIERS
COPILOT
COPIOUS
CORINTH
COSIEST
COSIGNS
COSINES
COZIEST
CRUISED
CRUISER
CRUISES
CUBICLE
CUBISTS
CURIOUS
CUTICLE
CUTINTO
CYNICAL

C•••I••

CABBIES
CABLING
CABRINI
CACHING
CADDIED
CADDIES
CADDISH
CADGING
CADMIUM
CAESIUM
CALCIFY
CALCITE
CALCIUM
CALKING
CALKINS
CALLING
CALLINS
CALMING
CALVING
CAMBIUM
CAMPIER
CAMPILY
CAMPING
CAMPION
CANDICE
CANDIDA
CANDIDE
CANDIDS
CANDIED
CANDIES
CANNIER
CANNILY
CANNING
CANTILY
CANTINA
CANTING
CAPPING
CAPRICE
CAPSIDS
CAPSIZE
CAPTION
CAPTIVE
CARBIDE
CARBINE
CARDIAC
CARDING
CARKING
CARMINE
CARNIES
CARPING
CARRICK
CARRIED
CARRIER
CARRIES
CARRION
CARTIER
CARTING
CARVING
CASHIER
CASHING
CASPIAN
CASSIAS
CASSIDY
CASSINI
CASSINO
CASSIUS
CASTILE
CASTING
CATBIRD
CATFISH
CATKINS
CATLIKE
CATNIPS
CATTIER
CATTILY
CATTING
CATTISH
CAUSING
CAUTION
CAVEINS
CEASING
CEILING
CELLINI
CELLIST
CELSIUS
CELTICS
CENSING
CENTIME
CENTIMO
CERTIFY
CERVIDS
CESSING
CESSION
CHAFING
CHALICE
CHARIER
CHARILY
CHARIOT
CHARITY
CHASING
CHEMISE
CHEMIST
CHENIER
CHERISH
CHEVIED
CHEVIES
CHEVIOT
CHEWIER
CHEWING
CHIDING
CHILIES
CHIMING
CHIRICO
CHOKIER
CHOLINE
CHORINE
CHORIZO
CITRINE
CIVVIES
CLARICE
CLARIFY
CLARION
CLARITY
CLAVIER
CLAWING
CLAYIER
CLAYISH
CLERICS
CLERISY
CLINICS
CLONING
CLOSING
CLOYING
CLUEING
COATING
COAXIAL
COAXING
COCHISE
COCKIER
COCKILY
COCKING
COCKISH
CODEINE
CODFISH
COEDITS
COEXIST
COHEIRS
COIFING
COILING
COINING
COLDISH
COLLIDE
COLLIER
COLLIES
COLLINS
COLTISH
COMBINE
COMBING
COMFIER
COMFITS
COMMITS
COMPILE
CONCISE
CONDIGN
CONDITA
CONFIDE
CONFINE
CONFIRM
CONKING
CONNICK
CONNIFF
CONNING
CONNIVE
CONOIDS
CONRIED
CONSIGN
CONSIST
CONVICT
COOKIES
COOKING
COOLING
COOLISH
COOPING
COOTIES
COPPICE
COPPING
COPYING
COPYIST
CORDIAL
CORDING
CORDITE
CORKIER
CORKING
CORNICE
CORNIER
CORNILY
CORNING
CORNISH
CORRIDA
CORSICA
COSHING
COSTING
COURIER
COUSINS
COWBIRD
COWGIRL
COWHIDE
COWLICK
COWLIKE
COWLING
COWRIES
COZYING
CRANIAL
CRANING
CRANIUM
CRATING
CRAVING
CRAZIER
CRAZIES
CRAZILY
CRAZING
CREDITS
CRETINS
CREVICE
CREWING
CRITICS
CRONIES
CRONISH
CROSIER
CROWING
CRUCIAL
CRUCIFY
CRUDITY
CUBBIES
CUBBISH
CUDDIES
CUFFING
CUISINE
CULLIED
CULLIES
CULLING
CULTISH
CULTISM
CULTIST
CUNNING
CUPLIKE
CUPPING
CURBING
CURDIER
CURDING
CURLIER
CURLIKE
CURLING
CURRIED
CURRIER
CURRIES
CURRISH
CURSING
CURSIVE
CURTISS
CURVIER
CURVING
CUSHIER
CUSHING
CUSHION
CUSPIDS
CUSSING
CUTTIME
CUTTING
CYCLING
CYCLIST
CYPRIOT
CZARINA
CZARISM
CZARIST

C••••I•

CAKEMIX
CALLSIN
CALORIC
CALORIE
CAMBRIC
CAMELIA
CANONIC
CANTRIP
CAPAPIE
CAPTAIN
CARAMIA
CAROTID
CATHAIR
CATSUIT
CATTAIL
CAUSTIC
CAVEDIN
CAVESIN
CBRADIO
CECILIA
CENTRIC
CERAMIC
CERTAIN
CETERIS
CHABLIS
CHAGRIN
CHAMOIS
CHAOTIC
CHAPLIN
CHAPPIE
CHARLIE
CHARMIN
CHASSIS
CHEAPIE
CHEATIN
CHECKIN
CHEERIO
CHERVIL
CHIPSIN
CHRONIC
CIBORIA
CIRCUIT
CLASSIC
CLAUDIA
CLAUDIO
CLOCKIN
CLOSEIN
CLUEDIN
CLUESIN
COALBIN
COALOIL
COCHAIR
COCKPIT
CODICIL
COEPTIS
COHABIT
COLLOID
COMEDIC
COMESIN
CONBRIO
CONCEIT
CONDUIT
CONJOIN
CONTAIN
COOLSIT
CORNOIL
CORSAIR
COSTAIN
COTERIE
COUNCIL
COWSLIP
CRAPPIE
CRINOID
CRISPIN
CROATIA
CRYPTIC
CSLEWIS
CULPRIT
CURTAIL
CURTAIN
CYNTHIA

C•••••I

CABRINI
CADUCEI
CAMPARI
CANNOLI
CASSINI
CELLINI
CHAPATI
CHIANTI
CHRISTI
COLLODI
COLOSSI
CORELLI

•CI••••

ACIDIFY
ACIDITY
ICICLES
ICINESS
ICINGIN
ICINGUP
SCIENCE
SCIORRA
SCISSOR

•C•I•••

ACHIEST
ACHIEVE
ACRIDLY
ACTINIC
ACTIONS
ACTIVES
CCRIDER
ECHIDNA
ECHINUS
ECLIPSE
ICKIEST
OCCIPUT
SCHIRRA
SCHISMS
SCRIBES
SCRIMPS
SCRIMPY
SCRIPPS
SCRIPTS
SCRIVEN

•C••I••

ACACIAS
ACADIAN
ACARIDS
ACIDIFY
ACIDITY
ACONITE
ACQUIRE
ACQUITS
ACTFIVE
ECHOING
ECLAIRS
ICELIKE
ICEMILK
ICEPICK
ICERINK
MCGUIRE
MCSWINE

OCARINA
OCULIST
SCALIER
SCALING
SCARIER
SCARIFY
SCARILY
SCARING
SCHMIDT
SCHWINN
SCOPING
SCORING

•C•••I•

ACCLAIM
ACERBIC
ACRYLIC
ACTINIC
ECDYSIS
ICINGIN
MCGAVIN
OCEANIA
OCEANIC
OCEANID
OCTAVIA
OCTROIS
SCEPTIC
SCORPIO
SCOTTIE

•C••••I

ACANTHI
SCHATZI
SCHERZI

••CI•••

ANCIENT
BACILLI
CECILIA
DECIBEL
DECIDED
DECIDES
DECIMAL
DICIEST
ENCINAS
EXCISED
EXCISES
EXCITED
EXCITES
FACIALS
FACINGS
INCIPIT
INCISED
INCISES
INCISOR
INCITED
INCITER
INCITES
INCIVIL
JACINTH
LACIEST
LACINGS
LICITLY
LUCIANO
LUCIDLY
LUCIFER
LUCILLE
OCCIPUT
OSCINES
PACIFIC
RACIEST
RECIPES
RECITAL
RECITED
RECITER
RECITES
SOCIALS
SOCIETY
TACITLY
TACITUS
UNCIALS
UNCIVIL
VICIOUS

••C•I••

ARCHING
ARCHIVE
ARCSINE
ASCRIBE
AUCTION
BACHING
BACKING
BUCKING
CACHING
COCHISE
COCKIER
COCKILY
COCKING
COCKISH
CYCLING
CYCLIST
DECEITS
DECEIVE
DECKING
DECLINE
DECRIED
DECRIER
DECRIES
DICKIES
DICTION
DOCKING
DUCHIES
DUCKIER
DUCKING
DUCTILE
DUCTING
ETCHING
FACTION
FICTION
FICTIVE
HACKIES
HACKING
HOCKING
INCHING
INCLINE
ITCHIER
ITCHING
JACKIES
JACKING
KACHINA
KICKIER
KICKING
LACKING
LICKING
LOCKING
LOCKINS
LUCKIER
LUCKILY
LUCKING
MACHINA
MACHINE
MOCKING
MRCHIPS
MUCKIER
MUCKILY
MUCKING
NECKING
NICKING
NUCLIDE
ORCHIDS
PACHISI
PACKICE
PACKING
PECKIER
PECKING
PECKISH
PECTINS
PICKIER
PICKING
PICNICS
PICTISH
PUCCINI
PUCKISH
RACKING
RECEIPT
RECEIVE
RECLINE
RECOILS
RECTIFY
ROCKIER
ROCKIES
ROCKING
RUCHING
RUCKING
RUCTION
SACKING
SACLIKE
SECTION
SICCING
SICKISH
SOCKING
SUCKING
SUCTION
TACKIER
TACKILY
TACKING
TACTICS
TACTILE
TECHIER
TECHIES
TICKING
TOCSINS
TUCKING
UNCOILS
UNCTION
URCHINS
VACCINE
VACUITY
VICTIMS
WACKIER
WACKILY
WICHITA
WICKIUP
YACKING
YUCKIER

••C••I•

ACCLAIM
ARCADIA
ARCHAIC
ASCETIC
BACKBIT
BACKLIT
BACKSIN
BUCOLIC
CECILIA
COCHAIR
COCKPIT
DECLAIM
DUCKPIN
ENCHAIN
ENCOMIA
EXCLAIM
FACTOID
FUCHSIA
INCIPIT
INCIVIL
JACOBIN
KICKSIN
LACONIC
NECKTIE
NICOSIA
NUCLEIC
PACIFIC
RECLAIM
RECRUIT
ROCKYII
ROCKYIV
SOCKSIN
STCROIX
SUCKSIN
TUCKSIN
UNCHAIN
UNCIVIL
VOCALIC

••C•••I

BACARDI
BACILLI
JACUZZI
PACHISI
PUCCINI
ROCKYII

•••CI••

ACACIAS
ARECIBO
ASOCIAL
BAYCITY
BRACING
CALCIFY
CALCITE
CALCIUM
CONCISE
CRUCIAL
CRUCIFY
DANCING
DEICING
DULCIFY
DUNCISH
EDACITY
EDUCING
ELICITS
FANCIED
FANCIER
FANCIES
FANCIFY
FANCILY
FARCING
FASCIAS
FATCITY
FENCING
FORCING
GLACIAL
GLACIER
GRACIAS
GRACILE
GRACING
GRECIAN
JUICIER
JUICILY
JUICING
LEUCINE
MANCINI
MERCIES
MINCING
NUNCIOS
OPACITY
PAUCITY
PENCILS
PIECING
PISCINE
PLACIDO
PLACING
PORCINE
PRECISE
PRICIER
PRICING
PUCCINI
RESCIND
SAUCIER
SAUCILY
SICCING
SLICING
SPACIER
SPACING
SPECIAL
SPECIES
SPECIFY
SPECING
SPICIER
SPICILY
SPICING
SUNCITY
SYNCING
TRACING
TRUCIAL
VACCINE
VOICING
WINCING

•••C•I•

AJACCIO
BIOCHIP
BISCUIT
BLACKIE
CHECKIN
CIRCUIT
CLOCKIN
CONCEIT
FLACCID
FRICKIE
JOACHIM
KINCHIN
KUTCHIN
LITCHIS
LITCRIT
PITCHIN
PSYCHIC
PUNCHIN
QUICKIE
TEACHIN
TIECLIP
WATCHIT

•••C••I

GNOCCHI
MANCINI
MARCONI
PUCCINI

••••CI•

AJACCIO
ANTACID
BORACIC
CODICIL
COUNCIL
DEFICIT
FELICIA
FLACCID
FRANCIS
ILLICIT
INDICIA
SOLICIT
STENCIL
STLUCIA

••••C•I

BRONCHI
CADUCEI
DELICTI
GNOCCHI
HIBACHI
HITACHI
KARACHI
MALACHI
NOGUCHI

•••••CI

DAVINCI
MENISCI

C•J••••

CAJOLED
CAJOLER
CAJOLES

C••J•••

CONJOBS
CONJOIN
CONJURE

C•••J••

CULTJAM

••C•••J

LLCOOLJ

C•K••••

CAKEMIX
CAKIEST
COKIEST

C••K•••

CACKLED
CACKLER
CACKLES
CALKING
CALKINS
CANKERS
CARKING
CATKINS
CHEKHOV
CHOKERS
CHOKEUP
CHOKIER
CHUKKAS
CHUKKER
COCKADE
COCKERS
COCKIER
COCKILY
COCKING
COCKISH
COCKLES
COCKNEY
COCKPIT
COCKSHY
CONKERS
CONKING
CONKOUT
COOKERS
COOKERY
COOKIES
COOKING
COOKOFF
COOKOUT
COOKSUP
COOKTOP
CORKAGE
CORKERS
CORKIER
CORKING
CUCKOOS

C•••K••

CAULKED
CAULKER
CHALKED
CHALKUP
CHECKED
CHECKER
CHECKIN
CHECKUP
CHICKEN
CHINKED
CHUCKED
CHUCKLE
CHUKKAS
CHUKKER
CLACKED
CLANKED
CLERKED
CLICKED
CLINKED
CLINKER
CLOAKED
CLOCKED
CLOCKER
CLOCKIN
CLUCKED
CLUNKED
CLUNKER
CONAKRY
CRACKED
CRACKER
CRACKLE
CRACKLY
CRACKUP
CRANKED
CRANKUP
CREAKED
CRICKED
CRICKET
CRINKLE
CRINKLY
CROAKED
CROOKED

C••••K•

CATLIKE
CHOMSKY
CONVOKE
COWLIKE
COWPOKE
CUPCAKE
CUPLIKE
CURLIKE

C•••••K

CARPARK
CARRICK
CASSOCK
CATWALK
CHINOOK
CONNICK
COSSACK
COWLICK
CUTBACK

•CK••••

ACKACKS
ECKHART
ICKIEST

•C•••K•

ACKACKS
ICELIKE
SCREAKS

•C••••K

ICEMILK
ICEPACK
ICEPICK
ICERINK
SCHLOCK

••CK•••

BACKBAY
BACKBIT
BACKEND
BACKERS
BACKHOE
BACKING
BACKLIT
BACKLOG
BACKOFF
BACKOUT
BACKRUB
BACKSIN
BACKSUP
BACKUPS
BECKETT
BECKONS
BICKERS
BUCKETS
BUCKEYE
BUCKING
BUCKLED
BUCKLER
BUCKLES
BUCKLEY
BUCKOES
BUCKRAM
BUCKSAW
BUCKSUP
CACKLED
CACKLER
CACKLES
COCKADE
COCKERS
COCKIER
COCKILY
COCKING
COCKISH
COCKLES
COCKNEY
COCKPIT
COCKSHY
CUCKOOS
DECKING
DECKLES
DECKOUT
DICKENS
DICKERS
DICKEYS
DICKIES
DOCKAGE
DOCKERS
DOCKETS
DOCKING
DUCKIER
DUCKING
DUCKPIN
FICKLER
GECKOES
HACKERS
HACKETT
HACKIES
HACKING
HACKLED
HACKLES
HACKMAN
HACKNEY
HACKSAW
HECKLED
HECKLER
HECKLES
HICKMAN
HICKORY
HOCKING
JACKALS
JACKASS
JACKDAW
JACKETS
JACKEYS
JACKIES
JACKING
JACKPOT
JACKSON
JACKSUP
JACKTAR
JOCKEYS
KICKERS
KICKIER
KICKING
KICKOFF
KICKOUT
KICKSIN
KICKSUP
KICKUPS
LACKEYS
LACKING
LICKING
LOCKBOX
LOCKERS
LOCKETS
LOCKING
LOCKINS
LOCKNUT
LOCKOUT
LOCKSON
LOCKSUP
LOCKUPS
LUCKIER
LUCKILY
LUCKING
LUCKOUT
MICKEYS
MOCKERS
MOCKERY
MOCKING
MOCKUPS
MUCKIER
MUCKILY
MUCKING
MUCKSUP
NECKERS
NECKING
NECKTIE
NICKELS
NICKERS
NICKING
PACKAGE
PACKARD
PACKERS
PACKETS
PACKICE
PACKING
PACKRAT
PACKSUP
PECKIER
PECKING
PECKISH
PECKSAT
PICKAXE
PICKENS
PICKERS
PICKETS
PICKETT
PICKIER
PICKING
PICKLED
PICKLES
PICKOFF
PICKOUT
PICKSAT
PICKSON
PICKSUP
PICKUPS
POCKETS
PUCKERS
PUCKETT
PUCKISH
RACKETS
RACKING
RACKSUP
RECKONS
RICKETY
RICKEYS
RICKLES
RICKMAN
RICKSHA
ROCKERS
ROCKERY
ROCKETS
ROCKIER
ROCKIES
ROCKING
ROCKYII
ROCKYIV
RUCKING
SACKERS
SACKFUL
SACKING
SACKOUT
SECKELS
SICKBAY
SICKDAY
SICKENS
SICKEST
SICKISH
SICKLES
SICKOUT
SICKPAY
SOCKETS
SOCKEYE
SOCKING
SOCKSIN
SUCKERS
SUCKING
SUCKSIN
TACKERS
TACKIER
TACKILY
TACKING
TACKLED
TACKLER
TACKLES
TACKSON
TICKERS
TICKETS
TICKETY
TICKING
TICKLED
TICKLER
TICKLES
TICKOFF
TUCKERS
TUCKING
TUCKSIN
WACKIER
WACKILY
WICKERS
WICKETS
WICKIUP
YACKING
YUCKIER

••C••K•

RECORKS
SACLIKE
UNCORKS

••C•••K

RECHALK
RECHECK
UNCLOAK

•••CK••

BLACKED
BLACKEN
BLACKER
BLACKIE
BLACKLY
BLOCKED
BLOCKER
BRACKEN
BRACKET
BRICKED
CHECKED
CHECKER
CHECKIN
CHECKUP
CHICKEN
CHUCKED
CHUCKLE
CLACKED
CLICKED
CLOCKED
CLOCKER
CLOCKIN
CLUCKED
CRACKED
CRACKER
CRACKLE
CRACKLY
CRACKUP
CRICKED
CRICKET
DRUCKER
FLECKED
FLICKED
FLICKER
FLOCKED
FLOCKTO
FRECKLE
FRECKLY
FRICKIE
FROCKED
GRACKLE
IRECKON
KNACKER
KNOCKED
KNOCKER
KNUCKLE
MENCKEN
PLACKET
PLUCKED
PRICKED
PRICKLE
PRICKLY
QUACKED
QUICKEN
QUICKER
QUICKIE
QUICKLY
SHACKLE
SHOCKED
SHOCKER
SHUCKED
SHUCKER
SLACKED
SLACKEN
SLACKER
SLACKLY
SLICKED
SLICKER
SLICKLY
SMACKED
SMACKER
SNACKED
SNACKER
SNICKER
SPACKLE
SPECKED
SPECKLE
STACKED
STACKUP
STICKER
STICKTO
STICKUP
STOCKED
STOCKUP
STUCKTO
STUCKUP
THICKEN
THICKER
THICKET
THICKLY
TRACKED
TRACKER
TRICKED
TRICKER
TRICKLE
TRUCKED
TRUCKEE
TRUCKER
TRUCKLE
WHACKED
WRACKED
WRECKED
WRECKER

•••C•K•

CUPCAKE
HOECAKE
HOTCAKE
OILCAKE
PANCAKE
TEACAKE

•••C••K

FRYCOOK
HANCOCK
LEACOCK
PEACOCK
PETCOCK
PRECOOK

••••CK•

ACKACKS
ATTACKS
ATTUCKS
BEDECKS
FINICKY
HIJACKS
KOLACKY
KOPECKS
PANICKY
RELOCKS
SHTICKS
THWACKS
UNLOCKS
UNLUCKY
UNPACKS
UNTACKS
UPTICKS

••••C•K

JANACEK

•••••CK

AIRLOCK
AIRSOCK
ARMLOCK
BANNOCK
BARRACK
BEDROCK
BOMBECK
BRUBECK
BULLOCK
BURDOCK
CARRICK
CASSOCK
CONNICK
COSSACK
COWLICK
CUTBACK
DEFROCK
DERRICK
DRSPOCK
DRYDOCK
DUNNOCK
EARLOCK
FATBACK
FETLOCK
FOSDICK
GARRICK
GETBACK
GIMMICK
GOTBACK
GUNLOCK
HADDOCK
HAMHOCK
HAMMOCK
HANCOCK
HASSOCK
HATRACK
HAYRACK
HEMLOCK
HENPECK
HILLOCK
HOGBACK
HUMMOCK
ICEPACK
ICEPICK
INSTOCK
JAMPACK
JANNOCK
JONNICK
KUBRICK
LAMARCK
LAYBACK
LEACOCK
LOWNECK
LUBBOCK
MAFFICK
MATLOCK
MATTOCK
MRSPOCK
MUDPACK
NIBLICK
NITPICK
OARLOCK
OLDNICK
ONTRACK
OUTBACK
PADDOCK
PADLOCK
PATRICK
PEACOCK
PETCOCK
PETROCK
POLLACK
POLLOCK
POTLUCK
RANSACK
RATPACK
RECHECK
RESTOCK
RETRACK
RIDDICK
ROEBUCK
ROLLICK
RUNBACK
SADSACK
SAWBUCK
SCHLOCK
SEASICK
SELLECK
SETBACK
SHYLOCK
SIXPACK
SKIRACK
SKYJACK
SUNDECK
TEDMACK
TIERACK
TIETACK
TINTACK
TOPKICK
TUSSOCK
UNBLOCK
UNFROCK
UNSTACK
UNSTICK
UNSTUCK
VANDYCK
VANEYCK
VEENECK
WARLOCK
WARWICK
WEDLOCK
WOZZECK

CL•••••

CLABBER
CLACKED
CLAIMED
CLAIMER
CLAIROL
CLAMBER
CLAMMED
CLAMMER
CLAMORS

CLAMOUR
CLAMPED
CLAMSUP
CLANGED
CLANGOR
CLANKED
CLAPPED
CLAPPER
CLAPTON
CLAQUES
CLARETS
CLARICE
CLARIFY
CLARION
CLARITY
CLASHED
CLASHES
CLASPED
CLASSED
CLASSES
CLASSIC
CLATTER
CLAUDIA
CLAUDIO
CLAUSES
CLAVELL
CLAVIER
CLAWERS
CLAWING
CLAYIER
CLAYISH
CLAYTON
CLEANED
CLEANER
CLEANLY
CLEANSE
CLEANUP
CLEARED
CLEARER
CLEARLY
CLEARUP
CLEAVED
CLEAVER
CLEAVES
CLEAVON
CLEMENS
CLEMENT
CLEMSON
CLERICS
CLERISY
CLERKED
CLIBURN
CLICHES
CLICKED
CLIENTS
CLIFTON
CLIMATE
CLIMBED
CLIMBER
CLINICS
CLINKED
CLINKER
CLINTON
CLIPART
CLIPONS
CLIPPED
CLIPPER
CLIQUES
CLIQUEY
CLOACAE
CLOACAS
CLOAKED
CLOBBER
CLOCHES
CLOCKED
CLOCKER
CLOCKIN
CLOGGED
CLOGSUP
CLOMPED
CLONING
CLOONEY
CLOPPED
CLOQUES
CLORETS
CLOSEBY
CLOSEIN
CLOSELY
CLOSEST
CLOSETS
CLOSEUP
CLOSING
CLOSURE
CLOTHED
CLOTHES
CLOTTED
CLOTURE
CLOUDED
CLOUTED
CLOVERS
CLOWDER
CLOWNED
CLOYING
CLUBBED
CLUBCAR
CLUCKED
CLUEDIN
CLUEING
CLUESIN
CLUMPED
CLUNKED
CLUNKER
CLUSTER
CLUTTER

C•L••••

CALCIFY
CALCITE
CALCIUM
CALDERA
CALDRON
CALENDS
CALGARY
CALHOUN
CALIBAN
CALIBER
CALIBRE
CALICES
CALICOS
CALIPER
CALIPHS
CALKING
CALKINS
CALLBOX
CALLERS
CALLFOR
CALLING
CALLINS
CALLOFF
CALLOUS
CALLOUT
CALLSIN
CALLSON
CALLSUP
CALMEST
CALMING
CALOMEL
CALORIC
CALORIE
CALPACS
CALTECH
CALUMET
CALUMNY
CALVARY
CALVERT
CALVING
CALYCES
CALYPSO
CALYXES
CALZONE
CCLAMPS
CELADON
CELEBES
CELEBRE
CELESTA
CELESTE
CELLARS
CELLINI
CELLIST
CELSIUS
CELTICS
CHLORAL
CILIATE
COLBERT
COLDCUT
COLDEST
COLDISH
COLDWAR
COLEMAN
COLETTE
COLGATE
COLLAGE
COLLARD
COLLARS
COLLATE
COLLECT
COLLEEN
COLLEGE
COLLETS
COLLIDE
COLLIER
COLLIES
COLLINS
COLLODI
COLLOID
COLLOPS
COLLUDE
COLLYER
COLOBUS
COLOGNE
COLONEL
COLONES
COLORED
COLOSSI
COLOURS
COLTISH
COLUMBO
COLUMNS
CSLEWIS
CULEBRA
CULLERS
CULLIED
CULLIES
CULLING
CULOTTE
CULPRIT
CULTISH
CULTISM
CULTIST
CULTJAM
CULTURE
CULVERS
CULVERT

C••L•••

CABLERS
CABLETV
CABLING
CALLBOX
CALLERS
CALLFOR
CALLING
CALLINS
CALLOFF
CALLOUS
CALLOUT
CALLSIN
CALLSON
CALLSUP
CAPLESS
CAPLETS
CARLESS
CARLOAD
CARLSON
CARLTON
CARLYLE
CATLIKE
CAULKED
CAULKER
CEILING
CELLARS
CELLINI
CELLIST
CHALETS
CHALICE
CHALKED
CHALKUP
CHALONS
CHELSEA
CHILEAN
CHILIES
CHILLED
CHILLER
CHOLINE
CHOLLAS
COALBIN
COALCAR
COALERS
COALGAS
COALOIL
COALTAR
COILING
COILSUP
COLLAGE
COLLARD
COLLARS
COLLATE
COLLECT
COLLEEN
COLLEGE
COLLETS
COLLIDE
COLLIER
COLLIES
COLLINS
COLLODI
COLLOID
COLLOPS
COLLUDE
COLLYER
COOLANT
COOLERS
COOLEST
COOLING
COOLISH
COOLSIT
COPLAND
COULDNT
COULEES
COULOMB
COULTER
COWLICK
COWLIKE
COWLING
CRULLER
CULLERS
CULLIED
CULLIES
CULLING
CUPLIKE
CURLERS
CURLEWS
CURLIER
CURLIKE
CURLING
CURLSUP
CUTLASS
CUTLERS
CUTLERY
CUTLETS
CYCLERS
CYCLING
CYCLIST
CYCLONE
CYCLOPS

C•••L••

CABALAS
CACKLED
CACKLER
CACKLES
CAJOLED
CAJOLER
CAJOLES
CAMELIA
CAMELOT
CAMILLE
CANDLES
CANTLES
CAPELET
CAPELLA
CAPULET
CAROLED
CAROLER
CAROLUS
CAROLYN
CASELAW
CASTLED
CASTLES
CATALAN
CATALOG
CATALPA
CAUDLES
CAVALRY
CAVILED
CAVILER
CECILIA
CEDILLA
CHABLIS
CHAPLET
CHAPLIN
CHARLES
CHARLEY
CHARLIE
CHEMLAB
CHILLED
CHILLER
CHOLLAS
CIRCLED
CIRCLES
CIRCLET
CIVILLY
COBBLED
COBBLER
COBBLES
COCHLEA
COCKLES
CODDLED
CODDLER
CODDLES
COMPLEX
COPILOT
COPULAE
COPULAS
CORELLI
COROLLA
COUPLED
COUPLES
COUPLET
COWSLIP
CRADLED
CRADLES
CRAWLED
CRAWLER
CREOLES
CRIOLLO
CRUELER
CRUELLY
CRUELTY
CRULLER
CUDDLED
CUDDLES
CUMULUS
CUPOLAS
CURDLED
CURDLES
CUSSLER

C••••L•

CAMILLE
CAMPILY
CANCELS
CANDELA
CANFULS
CANNILY
CANNOLI
CANTILY
CAPABLE
CAPABLY
CAPFULS
CAPSULE
CARFULS
CARLYLE
CARPALS
CARPELS
CARRELS
CARROLL
CARTELS
CASTILE
CASUALS
CATCALL
CATTILY
CATWALK
CEDILLA
CEMBALO
CEREALS
CHAGALL
CHAPELS
CHARILY
CHEAPLY
CHIEFLY
CHISELS
CHORALE
CHORALS
CHORTLE
CHUCKLE
CITABLE
CIVILLY
CLAVELL
CLEANLY
CLEARLY
CLOSELY
COCKILY
COEVALS
COMPELS
COMPILE
CONDOLE
CONSOLE
CONSULS
CONSULT
COPPOLA
CORBELS
CORDELL
CORELLI
CORNELL
CORNILY
COROLLA
CORRALS
COURTLY
COWBELL
CRACKLE
CRACKLY
CRASSLY
CRAYOLA
CRAZILY
CRENELS
CREWELS
CRINKLE
CRINKLY
CRIOLLO
CRISPLY
CROSSLY
CRUDELY
CRUELLY
CRUMBLE
CRUMBLY
CRUMPLE
CRUMPLY
CRYWOLF
CUBICLE
CUDGELS
CUEBALL
CUPFULS
CUREALL
CUTICLE
CYMBALS

C•••••L

CALOMEL
CAPITAL
CAPITOL
CARACAL
CARAMEL
CARAVEL
CAREFUL
CARPOOL
CARROLL
CATCALL
CATTAIL
CENTRAL
CHAGALL
CHANCEL
CHANNEL
CHATTEL
CHERVIL
CHLORAL
CHUNNEL
CITADEL
CLAIROL
CLAVELL
COALOIL
COASTAL
COAXIAL
CODICIL
COEQUAL
COLONEL
COMICAL
CONCEAL
CONGEAL
CONICAL
CONTROL
CORDELL
CORDIAL
CORNEAL
CORNELL
CORNOIL
COUNCIL
COUNSEL
COWBELL
COWGIRL
COZUMEL
CRANIAL
CREOSOL
CRUCIAL
CRYSTAL
CUEBALL
CUREALL
CURTAIL
CYNICAL

•CL••••

CCLAMPS
ECLAIRS
ECLIPSE
ECLOGUE
MCLUHAN
SCLERAS

•C•L•••

ACCLAIM
ACOLYTE
ECOLOGY
ICELAND
ICELESS
ICELIKE
MCCLOUD
MCCLURE
OCCLUDE
OCELLUS
OCELOTS
OCULIST
SCALARS
SCALDED
SCALENE
SCALERS
SCALIER
SCALING
SCALLOP
SCALPED
SCALPEL
SCALPER
SCHLEPP
SCHLEPS
SCHLOCK
SCOLDED
SCOLDER
SCULLED
SCULLER
SCULPTS

•C••L••

ACRYLIC
ECHELON
ICEBLUE
ICEFLOE
ICICLES
MCCALLS
OCCULTS
OCELLUS
SCALLOP
SCARLET
SCHOLAR
SCHULTZ
SCOWLED
SCOWLER
SCROLLS
SCULLED
SCULLER
UCCELLO

•C•••L•

ACEROLA
ACRIDLY
ACTABLE
ACUTELY
ICECOLD
ICEMILK
MCCALLS
OCTUPLE
SCANTLY
SCAPULA
SCARILY
SCHOOLS
SCRAWLS
SCRAWLY
SCROLLS
SCRUPLE
SCUFFLE
SCUTTLE
UCCELLO

•C••••L

ACCRUAL
SCALPEL
SCANDAL

••CL•••

ACCLAIM
ARCLAMP
BECLOUD
CYCLERS
CYCLING
CYCLIST
CYCLONE
CYCLOPS
DECLAIM
DECLARE
DECLASS
DECLINE
ENCLAVE
ENCLOSE
EXCLAIM
EXCLUDE
INCLINE
INCLOSE
INCLUDE
MCCLOUD
MCCLURE
MRCLEAN
NUCLEAR
NUCLEIC
NUCLEON
NUCLEUS
NUCLIDE
OCCLUDE
RECLAIM
RECLAME
RECLEAN
RECLINE
RECLUSE
SACLIKE
SECLUDE
UNCLASP
UNCLEAN
UNCLEAR
UNCLOAK
UNCLOGS
UNCLOSE
UPCLOSE

••C•L••

BACALAO
BACILLI
BACKLIT
BACKLOG
BECALMS
BICOLOR
BUCKLED
BUCKLER
BUCKLES
BUCKLEY
BUCOLIC
CACKLED
CACKLER
CACKLES
CECILIA
COCHLEA
COCKLES
DECALOG
DECKLES
FACULAE
FACULTY
FICKLER
FOCSLES
HACKLED
HACKLES
HECKLED
HECKLER
HECKLES
JOCULAR
LACHLAN
LOCALES
LOCALLY
LUCILLE
MACULAE
MCCALLS
NACELLE
NICOLAS
OCCULTS
PICKLED
PICKLES
RECALLS
RECOLOR
RICKLES
SECULAR
SICKLES
TACKLED
TACKLER
TACKLES
TICKLED
TICKLER
TICKLES
UCCELLO
VOCALIC
VOCALLY

••C••L•

BACILLI
BICYCLE
COCKILY
DACTYLS
DECARLO
DUCTILE
FACIALS
JACKALS
LICITLY
LLCOOLJ
LOCALLY
LUCIDLY
LUCILLE
LUCKILY
MCCALLS
MICHELE
MUCKILY
NACELLE
NICCOLO
NICHOLS
NICKELS
OSCEOLA
PICCOLO
RECALLS
RECHALK
RECOILS
RECYCLE
SECKELS
SOCIALS
TACITLY
TACKILY
TACTILE
UCCELLO
UNCIALS
UNCOILS
UNCURLS
VACUOLE
VOCALLY
WACKILY
WYCHELM

••C•••L

ACCRUAL
ALCOHOL
BSCHOOL
DECIBEL
DECIMAL
FACTFUL
FACTUAL
INCIVIL
LACTEAL
LACUNAL
MICHAEL
RECITAL
SACKFUL
TACTFUL
UNCIVIL
VICTUAL

•••CL••

CIRCLED
CIRCLES
CIRCLET
DEWCLAW
FANCLUB
ICICLES
KEYCLUB
MUSCLED
MUSCLES
ORACLES
TIECLIP

•••C•L•

BLACKLY
BLACULA
CANCELS
CATCALL
CHUCKLE
CRACKLE
CRACKLY
DRACULA
DRYCELL
ERECTLY
EXACTLY
FANCILY
FRECKLE
FRECKLY
GRACILE
GRACKLE
HERCULE
ICECOLD
INOCULA
JUICILY
KNUCKLE
LASCALA
LINCOLN
MALCOLM
MARCELS
MESCALS
MISCALL
NICCOLO
PARCELS
PENCILS
PERCALE
PICCOLO
PRICKLE
PRICKLY
PURCELL
QUICKLY
RASCALS
REDCELL
RESCALE
SAUCILY
SHACKLE
SLACKLY
SLICKLY
SPACKLE
SPECKLE
SPICILY
TERCELS
THICKLY
TOSCALE
TRICKLE
TRUCKLE
UPSCALE
WETCELL

•••C••L

AIRCOOL
ASOCIAL
CATCALL
CONCEAL
CRUCIAL
DRYCELL
EPOCHAL
FRACTAL
FUNCHAL
GLACIAL
MISCALL
PASCHAL
PINCURL
PRECOOL
PURCELL
REDCELL
SATCHEL
SPECIAL
TRUCIAL
WAYCOOL
WETCELL

••••CL•

ARTICLE
AURICLE
BICYCLE
CUBICLE
CUTICLE
DEBACLE
MANACLE
MIRACLE
MONOCLE
OSSICLE
PANICLE
PEDICLE
PINOCLE
RADICLE
RECYCLE
RETICLE
TREACLE
TREACLY
TUNICLE
VEHICLE

••••C•L

BIFOCAL
CARACAL
CHANCEL
CODICIL
COMICAL
CONICAL
COUNCIL
CYNICAL
ETHICAL
HELICAL
LEXICAL
LOGICAL
LYRICAL
MAGICAL
MEDICAL
MUSICAL
OPTICAL
PEDICEL
RADICAL
STENCIL
STOICAL
TOPICAL
TYPICAL

C•M••••

CAMBERS
CAMBIUM
CAMBRIC
CAMEDUE
CAMELIA
CAMELOT
CAMEOED
CAMEOFF
CAMEOUT
CAMERAS
CAMERON
CAMILLE
CAMISES
CAMPARI
CAMPERS
CAMPHOR
CAMPIER
CAMPILY
CAMPING
CAMPION
CAMPOUT
CEMBALO
CEMENTS
COMBATS
COMBERS
COMBINE
COMBING
COMBUST
COMEDIC
COMEDUE
COMEOFF
COMEONS
COMEOUT
COMESAT
COMESBY
COMESIN
COMESON
COMESTO
COMESUP
COMFIER
COMFITS
COMFORT
COMFREY
COMICAL
COMINGS
COMIQUE
COMMAND
COMMEND
COMMENT
COMMITS
COMMODE
COMMONS
COMMOVE
COMMUNE
COMMUTE
COMOROS
COMPACT
COMPANY
COMPARE
COMPASS
COMPEER
COMPELS
COMPERE
COMPETE
COMPILE
COMPLEX
COMPORT
COMPOSE
COMPOST
COMPOTE
COMPUTE
COMRADE
CUMULUS
CYMBALS

C••M•••

CADMIUM
CAIMANS
CALMEST
CALMING
CARMINE
CAYMANS
CHAMBER
CHAMFER
CHAMOIS
CHAMPED
CHEMISE
CHEMIST
CHEMLAB
CHIMERA
CHIMING
CHIMNEY
CHOMPED
CHOMSKY
CHUMMED
CLAMBER
CLAMMED
CLAMMER
CLAMORS
CLAMOUR

CLAMPED
CLAMSUP
CLEMENS
CLEMENT
CLEMSON
CLIMATE
CLIMBED
CLIMBER
CLOMPED
CLUMPED
COMMAND
COMMEND
COMMENT
COMMITS
COMMODE
COMMONS
COMMOVE
COMMUNE
COMMUTE
CONMOTO
CRAMMED
CRAMMER
CRAMPED
CRAMPON
CREMONA
CRIMEAN
CRIMPED
CRIMPER
CRIMSON
CRUMBLE
CRUMBLY
CRUMPET
CRUMPLE
CRUMPLY

C•••M••
CAKEMIX
CALOMEL
CALUMET
CALUMNY
CARAMBA
CARAMEL
CARAMIA
CAROMED
CAVEMAN
CAVEMEN
CCLAMPS
CERAMIC
CERUMEN
CHAPMAN
CHAPMEN
CHARMED
CHARMER
CHARMIN
CHROMES
CHUMMED
CINEMAS
CINEMAX
CLAIMED
CLAIMER
CLAMMED
CLAMMER
COLEMAN
COLUMBO
COLUMNS
COZUMEL
CRAMMED
CRAMMER
CREAMED
CREAMER
CREWMAN
CREWMEN

C••••M•
CENTIME
CENTIMO
CHRISMS
CONDEMN
CONGAME
CONSUME
CONTEMN
COSTUME
COULOMB
COXCOMB
CUSTOMS
CUTTIME

C•••••M
CADMIUM
CAESIUM
CALCIUM
CAMBIUM
CHATHAM
CHETRUM
CONFIRM
CONFORM
CRANIUM
CULTISM
CULTJAM
CZARDOM
CZARISM

•CM••••
MCMAHON

•C•M•••
ACUMENS
ICEMILK
SCAMMED
SCAMPED
SCAMPER
SCHMEER
SCHMIDT
SCHMOES
SCHMOOS

•C••M••
CCLAMPS
SCAMMED
SCHEMAS
SCHEMED
SCHEMER
SCHEMES
SCRIMPS
SCRIMPY
SCRUMMY

•C•••M•
ACADEME
ACADEMY
ECONOMY
SCHISMS
SCREAMS
SCRUMMY

•C••••M
ACCLAIM
ACRONYM

••CM•••
MICMACS

••C•M••
BECOMES
DECAMPS
DECIMAL
ENCAMPS
ENCOMIA
HACKMAN
HICKMAN
INCOMES
JICAMAS
LOCOMAN
LOCOMEN
RACEMES
RICHMAN
RICKMAN
TUCHMAN

••C••M•
ALCHEMY
ARCLAMP
BECALMS
DICTUMS
LYCEUMS
MACRAME
RECLAME
SACHEMS
SUCCUMB
VACUUMS
VICTIMS

••C•••M
ACCLAIM
ARCANUM
BUCKRAM
DECLAIM
DECORUM
EXCLAIM
MACADAM
RECLAIM
RECROOM
WYCHELM

•••C•M•
ATACAMA
COXCOMB
DAYCAMP
DRACHMA
DRACHMS
GIACOMO
HOTCOMB
HOWCOME
NONCOMS
OUTCOME
SATCHMO
SITCOMS
SUCCUMB
TALCUMS
WELCOME

•••C••M
BEECHAM
CALCIUM
FULCRUM
JOACHIM
KETCHAM
MALCOLM
MITCHUM
SANCTUM
SARCASM

••••C•M
MINICAM
MODICUM

CN•••••
CNTOWER

C•N••••
CANAPES
CANARDS
CANASTA
CANCANS
CANCELS
CANDELA
CANDICE
CANDIDA
CANDIDE
CANDIDS
CANDIED
CANDIES
CANDLES
CANDOUR
CANFULS
CANIEST
CANINES
CANKERS
CANNERS
CANNERY
CANNIER
CANNILY
CANNING
CANNOLI
CANNONS
CANONIC
CANOPUS
CANSECO
CANTATA
CANTEEN
CANTERS
CANTILY
CANTINA
CANTING
CANTLES
CANTONS
CANTORS
CANTRIP
CANVASS
CANYONS
CANZONE
CENSERS
CENSING
CENSORS
CENSURE
CENTAUR
CENTAVO
CENTERS
CENTIME
CENTIMO
CENTRAL
CENTRED
CENTRES
CENTRIC
CENTURY
CINCHED
CINCHES
CINDERS
CINDERY
CINEMAS
CINEMAX
CINZANO
CONAKRY
CONBRIO
CONCAVE
CONCEAL
CONCEDE
CONCEIT
CONCEPT
CONCERN
CONCERT
CONCHES
CONCISE
CONCOCT
CONCORD
CONCURS
CONDEMN
CONDIGN
CONDITA
CONDOLE
CONDONE
CONDORS
CONDUCE
CONDUCT
CONDUIT
CONFABS
CONFERS
CONFESS
CONFIDE
CONFINE
CONFIRM
CONFORM
CONFUSE
CONFUTE
CONGAED
CONGAME
CONGEAL
CONGERS
CONGEST
CONICAL
CONIFER
CONJOBS
CONJOIN
CONJURE
CONKERS
CONKING
CONKOUT
CONMOTO
CONNECT
CONNERY
CONNICK
CONNIFF
CONNING
CONNIVE
CONNORS
CONNOTE
CONOIDS
CONQUER
CONRIED
CONSENT
CONSIGN
CONSIST
CONSOLE
CONSORT
CONSULS
CONSULT
CONSUME
CONTACT
CONTAIN
CONTEMN
CONTEND
CONTENT
CONTEST
CONTEXT
CONTORT
CONTOUR
CONTRAS
CONTROL
CONTUSE
CONURES
CONVENE
CONVENT
CONVERT
CONVEYS
CONVICT
CONVOKE
CONVOYS
CUNNING
CYNICAL
CYNTHIA

C••N•••
CANNERS
CANNERY
CANNIER
CANNILY
CANNING
CANNOLI
CANNONS
CAPNUTS
CARNERA
CARNETS
CARNIES
CATNAPS
CATNIPS
CHANCED
CHANCEL
CHANCER
CHANCES
CHANGED
CHANGER
CHANGES
CHANNEL
CHANSON
CHANTED
CHANTER
CHANTEY
CHENIER
CHINESE
CHINKED
CHINNED
CHINOOK
CHINTZY
CHINUPS
CHUNNEL
CHUNTER
CLANGED
CLANGOR
CLANKED
CLINICS
CLINKED
CLINKER
CLINTON
CLONING
CLUNKED
CLUNKER
COGNACS
COGNATE
COINAGE
COINERS
COINING
CONNECT
CONNERY
CONNICK
CONNIFF
CONNING
CONNIVE
CONNORS
CONNOTE
COONCAT
CORNCOB
CORNDOG
CORNEAL
CORNEAS
CORNELL
CORNERS
CORNETS
CORNFED
CORNICE
CORNIER
CORNILY
CORNING
CORNISH
CORNOIL
CORNROW
COUNCIL
COUNSEL
COUNTED
COUNTER
COUNTON
COUNTRY
COYNESS
CRANIAL
CRANING
CRANIUM
CRANKED
CRANKUP
CRENELS
CRINGED
CRINGES
CRINKLE
CRINKLY
CRINOID
CRONIES
CRONISH
CRUNCHY
CUNNING
CYGNETS

C•••N••
CABANAS
CABINET
CACANNY
CADENCE
CADENCY
CADENZA
CALENDS
CANINES
CANONIC
CARINAS
CASINGS
CASINOS
CATENAE
CAYENNE
CEMENTS
CEZANNE
CHAINED
CHANNEL
CHIANTI
CHIGNON
CHIMNEY
CHINNED
CHRONIC
CHUNNEL
CHURNED
CHUTNEY
CLEANED
CLEANER
CLEANLY
CLEANSE
CLEANUP
CLIENTS
CLOONEY
CLOWNED
COCKNEY
COCONUT
COGENCY
COLONEL
COLONES
COMINGS
CORINTH
CORONAE
CORONAS
CORONET
COSINES
COSTNER
COZENED
CROONED
CROONER
CROWNED
CUTINTO

C••••N•
CABLING
CABRINI
CACANNY
CACHING
CADGING
CAFTANS
CAIMANS
CALKING
CALKINS
CALLING
CALLINS
CALMING
CALUMNY
CALVING
CALZONE
CAMPING
CANCANS
CANNING
CANNONS
CANTINA
CANTING
CANTONS
CANYONS
CANZONE
CAPEANN
CAPGUNS
CAPPING
CARBINE
CARBONS
CARDING
CAREENS
CARKING
CARMINE
CARPING
CARTING
CARTONS
CARVING
CASERNE
CASERNS
CASHING
CASSINI
CASSINO
CASTING
CATIONS
CATKINS
CATTING
CAUSING
CAVEINS
CAVERNS
CAYENNE
CAYMANS
CEASING
CEBUANO
CEILING
CELLINI
CENSING
CESSING
CEZANNE
CHAFING
CHALONS
CHASING
CHEWING
CHICANA
CHICANO
CHIDING
CHIMING
CHOLINE
CHORINE
CINZANO
CITRINE
CITRONS
CLAWING
CLEMENS
CLEMENT
CLIPONS
CLONING
CLOSING
CLOYING
CLUEING
COATING
COAXING
COCKING
COCOONS
CODEINE
COIFING
COILING
COINING
COLLINS
COLOGNE
COLUMNS
COMBINE
COMBING
COMEONS
COMMAND
COMMEND
COMMENT
COMMONS
COMMUNE
COMPANY
CONDONE
CONFINE
CONKING
CONNING
CONSENT
CONTEND
CONTENT
CONVENE
CONVENT
COOKING
COOLANT
COOLING
COOPING
COPLAND
COPPING
COPYING
CORDING
CORDONS
CORKING
CORNING
COSHING
COSIGNS
COSTING
COTTONS
COTTONY
COULDNT
COUPONS
COURANT
COUSINS
COWHAND
COWLING
COWPONY
COZYING
COZZENS
CRANING
CRATING
CRAVENS
CRAVING
CRAYONS
CRAZING
CREMONA
CRETANS
CRETINS
CREWING
CROWING
CUFFING
CUIBONO
CUISINE
CULLING
CUNNING
CUPPING
CURBING
CURDING
CURLING
CURRANT
CURRENT
CURSING
CURVING
CUSHING
CUSSING
CUTTING
CYCLING
CYCLONE
CYYOUNG
CZARINA

C•••••N
CADDOAN
CAISSON
CALDRON
CALHOUN
CALIBAN
CALLSIN
CALLSON
CAMERON
CAMPION
CANTEEN
CAPEANN
CAPITAN
CAPSTAN
CAPTAIN
CAPTION
CARAVAN
CARLSON
CARLTON
CAROLYN
CARRION
CARRYON
CARTOON
CASPIAN
CATALAN
CATCHON
CATSCAN
CAUTION
CAVEDIN
CAVEMAN
CAVEMEN
CAVESIN
CELADON
CERTAIN
CERUMEN
CESSION
CHAGRIN
CHANSON
CHAPLIN
CHAPMAN
CHAPMEN
CHARMIN
CHASTEN
CHEAPEN
CHEATIN
CHECHEN
CHECKIN
CHEVRON
CHICHEN
CHICKEN
CHIFFON
CHIGNON
CHILEAN
CHIPSIN
CISTERN
CITIZEN
CITROEN
CLAPTON
CLARION
CLAYTON
CLEAVON
CLEMSON
CLIBURN
CLIFTON
CLINTON
CLOCKIN
CLOSEIN
CLUEDIN
CLUESIN
COALBIN
COARSEN
COCHRAN
COGBURN
COLEMAN
COLLEEN
COMESIN
COMESON
CONCERN
CONDEMN
CONDIGN
CONJOIN
CONSIGN
CONTAIN
CONTEMN
CORAZON
COSTAIN
COUNTON
COWTOWN
CRAMPON
CREWMAN
CREWMEN
CRIMEAN
CRIMSON
CRISPIN
CROUTON
CRYOGEN
CURTAIN
CUSHION
CUTDOWN

•C•N•••
ACANTHI
ACONITE
ECONOMY
ICINESS
ICINGIN
ICINGUP
MCENROE
OCANADA
OCONNOR
SCANDAL
SCANNED
SCANNER
SCANTED
SCANTER
SCANTLY
SCENDED
SCENERY
SCENTED
SCHNAPS
SCONCES

•C••N••
ACCENTS
ACHENES
ACRONYM
ACTINIC
ECHINUS
MCHENRY
OCEANIA
OCEANIC
OCEANID
OCEANUS
OCONNOR
OCTANES
OCTANTS
SCANNED
SCANNER
SCIENCE
SCORNED
SCORNER
SCRUNCH
WCHANDY

•C•••N•
ACCOUNT
ACETONE
ACHTUNG
ACTIONS
ACUMENS
ECHIDNA
ECHOING
ICELAND
ICERINK
MCSWINE
OCARINA
SCALENE
SCALING
SCARING
SCHWINN
SCOPING
SCORING
SCRAWNY
SCREENS

•C••••N
ACADIAN
ACHERON
ACHESON
ACTAEON
ACTEDON
ACTUPON
ECHELON
ICINGIN
MCGAVIN
MCLUHAN
MCMAHON
MCQUEEN
OCTAGON
SCHWINN
SCRIVEN

••CN•••
PICNICS

••C•N••
ACCENTS
ARCANUM
ASCENDS
ASCENTS
CACANNY
COCKNEY
COCONUT
DECANTS
DECENCY
DOCENTS
ENCINAS
FACINGS
HACKNEY
INCANTS
INCENSE
JACANAS
JACINTH
JACONET
LACINGS
LACONIC
LACUNAE
LACUNAL
LACUNAS
LICENCE
LICENSE
LOCKNUT
LUCENCY
NOCANDO
OSCINES
PICANTE
POCONOS
RECANED
RECANES
RECANTS
RECENCY
SECANTS
SECONDS
UNCANNY
VACANCY
VICUNAS

••C••N•
ACCOUNT
ANCIENT
ARCHING
ARCHONS
ARCSINE
BACHING
BACKEND
BACKING
BECKONS
BUCKING
CACANNY
CACHING
COCKING
COCOONS
CYCLING
CYCLONE
DECKING
DECLINE
DICKENS
DOCKING
DUCKING
DUCTING
ENCHANT
ETCHANT
ETCHING
HACKING
HOCKING
INCHING
INCLINE
ITCHING
JACKING
KACHINA
KICKING
KUCHENS
LACKING
LICHENS
LICKING
LOCARNO
LOCKING
LOCKINS
LUCERNE
LUCIANO
LUCKING
MACHINA
MACHINE
MACRONS
MICRONS
MOCKING
MUCKING
NECKING
NICKING
PACKING
PECCANT
PECKING
PECTINS
PICKENS
PICKING
PUCCINI
RACKING
RECKONS
RECLINE
RECOUNT
ROCKING
RUCHING
RUCKING
SACKING
SICCING
SICKENS
SOCKING
SUCKING
TACKING
TICKING
TOCSINS
TUCKING
TYCOONS
UNCANNY
URCHINS
VACCINE
YACKING

••C•••N
AUCTION
BACKSIN
COCHRAN
DECAGON
DICTION
DUCKPIN
ENCHAIN
FACTION
FICTION
HACKMAN
HICKMAN
JACKSON
JACOBIN
KICKSIN
LACHLAN
LECTERN
LOCKSON
LOCOMAN
LOCOMEN
MRCLEAN
NOCTURN
NUCLEON
PICKSON
RACCOON
RECLEAN
RICHMAN
RICKMAN
RUCTION
SECTION
SICHUAN
SOCKSIN
SUCKSIN
SUCTION
TACKSON
TUCHMAN
TUCKSIN
UNCHAIN
UNCLEAN

UNCTION
YUCATAN

•••C•N•

ABSCOND
ARACHNE
ASHCANS
BALCONY
BEACONS
BRACING
CANCANS
CHICANA
CHICANO
DANCING
DEACONS
DEICING
DESCANT
DESCEND
DESCENT
EDUCING
EPICENE
FALCONS
FARCING
FENCING
FLACONS
FORCING
GARCONS
GASCONS
GASCONY
GRACING
ILOCANO
JUICING
LARCENY
LEUCINE
MANCINI
MARCONI
MINCING
MIOCENE
NASCENT
OBSCENE
OILCANS
PECCANT
PERCENT
PIECING
PISCINE
PLACING
PORCINE
PRICING
PUCCINI
REDCENT
RESCIND
SICCING
SLICING
SNOCONE
SPACING
SPECING
SPICING
SYNCING
TENCENT
TINCANS
TOUCANS
TRACING
TUSCANY
VACCINE
VINCENT
VOICING
VOLCANO
VULCANS
WINCING
ZIRCONS

•••C••N

BLACKEN
BRACKEN
CATCHON
CHECHEN
CHECKIN
CHICHEN
CHICKEN
CLOCKIN
CONCERN
DISCERN
ERICSON
GRECIAN
HALCYON
IRECKON
KINCHIN
KITCHEN
KUTCHIN
LAOCOON
LINCOLN
MADCHEN
MARCHON
MENCKEN
OMICRON
PITCHIN
POPCORN
PROCYON
PUNCHIN
PYNCHON
QUICKEN
RACCOON
SLACKEN
TEACHIN
THICKEN
TOUCHON
TRICORN
UNICORN

••••C•N

AFRICAN
ALARCON
ALENCON
AZTECAN
CATSCAN
HELICON
ITHACAN
LEXICON
MEXICAN
MOHICAN
PELICAN
PEMICAN
RUBICON
SARACEN
SILICON
SOUPCON
VATICAN

CO•••••

COACHED
COACHES
COALBIN
COALCAR
COALERS
COALGAS
COALOIL
COALTAR
COARSEN
COARSER
COASTAL
COASTED
COASTER
COATING
COAXERS
COAXIAL
COAXING
COBBLED
COBBLER
COBBLES
COBWEBS
COCHAIR
COCHERE
COCHISE
COCHLEA
COCHRAN
COCKADE
COCKERS
COCKIER
COCKILY
COCKING
COCKISH
COCKLES
COCKNEY
COCKPIT
COCKSHY
COCONUT
COCOONS
COCTEAU
CODDLED
CODDLER
CODDLES
CODEINE
CODFISH
CODGERS
CODICES
CODICIL
COEDITS
COEPTIS
COEQUAL
COERCED
COERCER
COERCES
COEVALS
COEXIST
COFFEES
COFFERS
COGBURN
COGENCY
COGNACS
COGNATE
COHABIT
COHEIRS
COHERED
COHERES
COHORTS
COHOSTS
COIFING
COILING
COILSUP
COINAGE
COINERS
COINING
COKIEST
COLBERT
COLDCUT
COLDEST
COLDISH
COLDWAR
COLEMAN
COLETTE
COLGATE
COLLAGE
COLLARD
COLLARS
COLLATE
COLLECT
COLLEEN
COLLEGE
COLLETS
COLLIDE
COLLIER
COLLIES
COLLINS
COLLODI
COLLOID
COLLOPS
COLLUDE
COLLYER
COLOBUS
COLOGNE
COLONEL
COLONES
COLORED
COLOSSI
COLOURS
COLTISH
COLUMBO
COLUMNS
COMBATS
COMBERS
COMBINE
COMBING
COMBUST
COMEDIC
COMEDUE
COMEOFF
COMEONS
COMEOUT
COMESAT
COMESBY
COMESIN
COMESON
COMESTO
COMESUP
COMFIER
COMFITS
COMFORT
COMFREY
COMICAL
COMINGS
COMIQUE
COMMAND
COMMEND
COMMENT
COMMITS
COMMODE
COMMONS
COMMOVE
COMMUNE
COMMUTE
COMOROS
COMPACT
COMPANY
COMPARE
COMPASS
COMPEER
COMPELS
COMPERE
COMPETE
COMPILE
COMPLEX
COMPORT
COMPOSE
COMPOST
COMPOTE
COMPUTE
COMRADE
CONAKRY
CONBRIO
CONCAVE
CONCEAL
CONCEDE
CONCEIT
CONCEPT
CONCERN
CONCERT
CONCHES
CONCISE
CONCOCT
CONCORD
CONCURS
CONDEMN
CONDIGN
CONDITA
CONDOLE
CONDONE
CONDORS
CONDUCE
CONDUCT
CONDUIT
CONFABS
CONFERS
CONFESS
CONFIDE
CONFINE
CONFIRM
CONFORM
CONFUSE
CONFUTE
CONGAED
CONGAME
CONGEAL
CONGERS
CONGEST
CONICAL
CONIFER
CONJOBS
CONJOIN
CONJURE
CONKERS
CONKING
CONKOUT
CONMOTO
CONNECT
CONNERY
CONNICK
CONNIFF
CONNING
CONNIVE
CONNORS
CONNOTE
CONOIDS
CONQUER
CONRIED
CONSENT
CONSIGN
CONSIST
CONSOLE
CONSORT
CONSULS
CONSULT
CONSUME
CONTACT
CONTAIN
CONTEMN
CONTEND
CONTENT
CONTEST
CONTEXT
CONTORT
CONTOUR
CONTRAS
CONTROL
CONTUSE
CONURES
CONVENE
CONVENT
CONVERT
CONVEYS
CONVICT
CONVOKE
CONVOYS
COOKERS
COOKERY
COOKIES
COOKING
COOKOFF
COOKOUT
COOKSUP
COOKTOP
COOLANT
COOLERS
COOLEST
COOLING
COOLISH
COOLSIT
COONCAT
COOPERS
COOPING
COOPSUP
COOPTED
COOTIES
COPIERS
COPILOT
COPIOUS
COPLAND
COPOUTS
COPPERS
COPPERY
COPPICE
COPPING
COPPOLA
COPSOUT
COPTERS
COPULAE
COPULAS
COPYBOY
COPYCAT
COPYING
COPYIST
CORAZON
CORBELS
CORBETT
CORDAGE
CORDATE
CORDELL
CORDERO
CORDIAL
CORDING
CORDITE
CORDOBA
CORDONS
CORELLI
CORETTA
CORINTH
CORKAGE
CORKERS
CORKIER
CORKING
CORNCOB
CORNDOG
CORNEAL
CORNEAS
CORNELL
CORNERS
CORNETS
CORNFED
CORNICE
CORNIER
CORNILY
CORNING
CORNISH
CORNOIL
CORNROW
COROLLA
CORONAE
CORONAS
CORONET
CORRALS
CORRECT
CORRIDA
CORRODE
CORRUPT
CORSAGE
CORSAIR
CORSETS
CORSICA
CORTEGE
COSHING
COSIEST
COSIGNS
COSINES
COSSACK
COSSETS
COSTAIN
COSTARS
COSTING
COSTNER
COSTUME
COTERIE
COTTAGE
COTTERS
COTTONS
COTTONY
COUCHED
COUCHES
COUGARS
COUGHED
COUGHUP
COULDNT
COULEES
COULOMB
COULTER
COUNCIL
COUNSEL
COUNTED
COUNTER
COUNTON
COUNTRY
COUPLED
COUPLES
COUPLET
COUPONS
COURAGE
COURANT
COURIER
COURSED
COURSER
COURSES
COURTED
COURTLY
COUSINS
COUTURE
COVERED
COVERUP
COVETED
COWARDS
COWBELL
COWBIRD
COWBOYS
COWERED
COWGIRL
COWHAND
COWHERD
COWHIDE
COWLICK
COWLIKE
COWLING
COWPEAS
COWPOKE
COWPONY
COWRIES
COWSLIP
COWTOWN
COXCOMB
COYNESS
COYOTES
COZENED
COZIEST
COZUMEL
COZYING
COZZENS

C•O••••

CHOCTAW
CHOICER
CHOICES
CHOKERS
CHOKEUP
CHOKIER
CHOLINE
CHOLLAS
CHOMPED
CHOMSKY
CHOOSER
CHOOSES
CHOPPED
CHOPPER
CHORALE
CHORALS
CHORINE
CHORIZO
CHORTLE
CHOWDER
CLOACAE
CLOACAS
CLOAKED
CLOBBER
CLOCHES
CLOCKED
CLOCKER
CLOCKIN
CLOGGED
CLOGSUP
CLOMPED
CLONING
CLOONEY
CLOPPED
CLOQUES
CLORETS
CLOSEBY
CLOSEIN
CLOSELY
CLOSEST
CLOSETS
CLOSEUP
CLOSING
CLOSURE
CLOTHED
CLOTHES
CLOTTED
CLOTURE
CLOUDED
CLOUTED
CLOVERS
CLOWDER
CLOWNED
CLOYING
COOKERS
COOKERY
COOKIES
COOKING
COOKOFF
COOKOUT
COOKSUP
COOKTOP
COOLANT
COOLERS
COOLEST
COOLING
COOLISH
COOLSIT
COONCAT
COOPERS
COOPING
COOPSUP
COOPTED
COOTIES
CROAKED
CROATIA
CROCHET
CROESUS
CROFTER
CRONIES
CRONISH
CROOKED
CROONED
CROONER
CROPPED
CROPPER
CROPSUP
CROQUET
CROSIER
CROSSED
CROSSER
CROSSES
CROSSLY
CROSSUP
CROUTON
CROWBAR
CROWDED
CROWERS
CROWING
CROWNED

C••O•••

CABOOSE
CAHOOTS
CAJOLED
CAJOLER
CAJOLES
CALOMEL
CALORIC
CALORIE
CANONIC
CANOPUS
CAROLED
CAROLER
CAROLUS
CAROLYN
CAROMED
CAROTID
CAROUSE
CAVORTS
CHAOTIC
CHLORAL
CHOOSER
CHOOSES
CHROMES
CHRONIC
CIBORIA
CLOONEY
CNTOWER
COCONUT
COCOONS
COHORTS
COHOSTS
COLOBUS
COLOGNE
COLONEL
COLONES
COLORED
COLOSSI
COLOURS
COMOROS
CONOIDS
COPOUTS
COROLLA
CORONAE
CORONAS
CORONET
COYOTES
CREOLES
CREOSOL
CRIOLLO
CROOKED
CROONED
CROONER
CRYOGEN
CULOTTE
CUPOLAS
CUTOFFS
CUTOUTS
CYBORGS
CYYOUNG

C•••O••

CABOOSE
CACHOUS
CADDOAN
CAHOOTS
CALHOUN
CALLOFF
CALLOUS
CALLOUT
CALZONE
CAMEOED
CAMEOFF
CAMEOUT
CAMPOUT
CANDOUR
CANNOLI
CANNONS
CANTONS
CANTORS
CANYONS
CANZONE
CAPTORS
CARBONS
CARBOYS
CARCOAT
CARDOZO
CARGOES
CARHOPS
CARIOCA
CARLOAD
CARPOOL
CARPORT
CARROLL
CARROTS
CARTONS
CARTOON
CASHOUT
CASSOCK
CASTOFF
CASTOUT
CATBOAT
CATFOOD
CATHODE
CATIONS
CENSORS
CHALONS
CHAMOIS
CHEROOT
CHEWOUT
CHICORY
CHIGOES
CHINOOK
CITROEN
CITRONS
CITROUS
CLAMORS
CLAMOUR
CLIPONS
COALOIL
COCOONS
COLLODI
COLLOID
COLLOPS
COMEOFF
COMEONS
COMEOUT
COMFORT
COMMODE
COMMONS
COMMOVE
COMPORT
COMPOSE
COMPOST
COMPOTE
CONCOCT
CONCORD
CONDOLE
CONDONE
CONDORS
CONFORM
CONJOBS
CONJOIN
CONKOUT
CONMOTO
CONNORS
CONNOTE
CONSOLE
CONSORT
CONTORT
CONTOUR
CONVOKE
CONVOYS
COOKOFF
COOKOUT
COPIOUS
COPPOLA
COPSOUT
CORDOBA
CORDONS
CORNOIL
CORRODE
COTTONS
COTTONY
COULOMB
COUPONS
COWBOYS
COWPOKE
COWPONY
COWTOWN
COXCOMB
CRAYOLA
CRAYONS
CREMONA
CRINOID
CRYWOLF
CUCKOOS
CUIBONO
CURIOUS
CURSORS
CURSORY
CUSTODY
CUSTOMS
CUTDOWN
CUTSOFF
CUTSOUT
CYCLONE
CYCLOPS

C••••O•

CAISSON
CALDRON
CALICOS
CALLBOX
CALLFOR
CALLSON
CAMELOT
CAMERON
CAMPHOR
CAMPION
CAPECOD
CAPITOL
CAPTION
CAREFOR
CARIBOU
CARLSON
CARLTON
CARPOOL
CARRION
CARRYON
CARTOON
CASHBOX
CASHCOW
CASINOS
CATALOG
CATCHON
CATFOOD
CATSHOW
CAUTION
CELADON
CESSION
CHANSON
CHARIOT
CHEETOS
CHEKHOV
CHEROOT
CHEVIOT
CHEVRON
CHEWTOY
CHIFFON
CHIGNON
CHINOOK
CLAIROL
CLANGOR
CLAPTON
CLARION
CLAYTON
CLEAVON
CLEMSON
CLIFTON
CLINTON
COMESON
COMOROS
CONTROL
COOKTOP
COPILOT
COPYBOY
CORAZON
CORNCOB
CORNDOG
CORNROW
COUNTON
CRAMPON
CREATOR
CREOSOL
CRIMSON
CROUTON
CRYPTOS
CUCKOOS
CURATOR
CUSHION
CYPRIOT
CZARDOM

C•••••O

CALYPSO
CANSECO
CARABAO
CARDOZO
CASSINO
CATERTO
CAVETTO
CBRADIO
CEBUANO
CEMBALO
CENTAVO
CENTIMO
CHEERIO
CHICAGO
CHICANO
CHIRICO
CHORIZO
CHRISTO
CINZANO
CLAUDIO
COLUMBO
COMESTO
CONBRIO
CONMOTO
CORDERO
CRIOLLO
CRUSADO
CRUZADO
CUIBONO
CURACAO
CUTINTO

•CO••••

ACOLYTE
ACONITE
ECOLOGY
ECONOMY
OCONNOR
SCOFFED
SCOFFER
SCOLDED
SCOLDER
SCONCES
SCOOPED
SCOOPER
SCOOTED
SCOOTER
SCOPING
SCORERS
SCORING
SCORNED
SCORNER
SCORPIO
SCOTERS
SCOTTIE
SCOURED
SCOURER
SCOURGE
SCOUSES
SCOUTED
SCOUTER
SCOWLED
SCOWLER

•C•O•••

ACCORDS
ACCOSTS
ACCOUNT
ACROBAT
ACRONYM
ECHOING
ECLOGUE
OCTOBER
OCTOPOD
OCTOPUS
SCHOLAR
SCHOOLS
SCIORRA
SCOOPED
SCOOPER
SCOOTED
SCOOTER
SCROLLS
SCROOGE

•C••O••

ACEDOUT
ACEROLA
ACEROSE
ACESOUT
ACETONE
ACTFOUR
ACTIONS
ACTSOUT
ECOLOGY
ECONOMY
ICEBOAT
ICECOLD
ICEDOUT
ICEFOGS
ICESOUT
MCCLOUD
OCELOTS
OCTROIS
SCHLOCK
SCHMOES
SCHMOOS
SCHOOLS
SCROOGE

•C•••O•

ACHERON
ACHESON
ACTAEON
ACTEDON
ACTUPON
ECHELON
ECUADOR
ICEFLOE
ICESHOW
ICHABOD
MCENROE
MCMAHON
OCONNOR
OCTAGON
OCTAVOS
OCTOPOD
SCALLOP
SCHMOOS
SCISSOR

•C••••O

SCHERZO
SCORPIO
UCCELLO

••CO•••
ACCORDS
ACCOSTS
ACCOUNT
ALCOHOL
ALCOVES
BECOMES
BICOLOR
BUCOLIC
COCONUT
COCOONS
DECOCTS
DECODED
DECODER
DECODES
DECORUM
DECOYED
ENCODED
ENCODER
ENCODES
ENCOMIA
ENCORES
ESCORTS
IACOCCA
INCOMES
JACOBIN
JACONET
LACONIC
LACOSTE
LLCOOLJ
LOCOMAN
LOCOMEN
NICOLAS
NICOSIA
POCONOS
RECOATS
RECODED
RECODES
RECOILS
RECOLOR
RECORDS
RECORKS
RECOUNT
RECOUPS
RECOVER
RICOTTA
SECONDS
TYCOONS
UNCOILS
UNCORKS
UNCOUTH
UNCOVER

••C•O••
ANCHORS
ANCHOVY
ARCHONS
BACKOFF
BACKOUT
BECKONS
BECLOUD
BSCHOOL
BUCKOES
CACHOUS
COCOONS
CUCKOOS
CYCLONE
CYCLOPS
DECKOUT
DOCTORS
ENCLOSE
ESCROWS
FACEOFF
FACTOID
FACTORS
FACTORY
GECKOES
HECTORS
HICKORY
INCLOSE
KICKOFF
KICKOUT
LACTOSE
LECTORS
LICTORS
LLCOOLJ
LOCKOUT
LUCKOUT
MACRONS
MCCLOUD
MICROBE
MICRONS
NICCOLO
NICHOLS
NOCUOUS
OSCEOLA
PICCOLO
PICKOFF
PICKOUT
RACCOON
RECHOSE
RECKONS
RECROOM
RECROSS
RECTORS
RECTORY
SACKOUT
SECTORS
SICKOUT
STCROIX
SUCCORS
SUCCOUR
SUCROSE
TICKOFF
TYCOONS
UNCLOAK
UNCLOGS
UNCLOSE
UPCLOSE
VACUOLE
VACUOUS
VECTORS
VICIOUS
VICTORS
VICTORY

••C••O•
ALCOHOL
AUCTION
BACKHOE
BACKLOG
BICOLOR
BSCHOOL
CUCKOOS
DECAGON
DECALOG
DECAPOD
DICTION
ESCUDOS
FACTION
FICTION
INCISOR
JACKPOT
JACKSON
LOCATOR
LOCKBOX
LOCKSON
NUCLEON
PICADOR
PICAROS
PICKSON
POCONOS
RACCOON
RECOLOR
RECROOM
RUCTION
SECTION
SUCTION
TACKSON
UNCTION
VICEROY

••C•••O
BACALAO
DECARLO
LOCARNO
LUCIANO
NICCOLO
NOCANDO
PICASSO
PICCOLO
RICARDO
UCCELLO

•••CO••
ABSCOND
AIRCOOL
ANTCOWS
APOCOPE
BALCONY
BARCODE
BEACONS
BOYCOTT
BUNCOED
CARCOAT
CHICORY
CONCOCT
CONCORD
COXCOMB
DEACONS
DISCOED
DISCORD
FALCONS
FLACONS
FRYCOOK
GARCONS
GASCONS
GASCONY
GIACOMO
GLUCOSE
HANCOCK
HENCOOP
HOTCOMB
HOWCOME
ICECOLD
JUNCOES
LABCOAT
LAOCOON
LEACOCK
LINCOLN
LOWCOST
MALCOLM
MARCONI
MASCOTS
MUSCOVY
NICCOLO
NONCOMS
OUTCOME
PEACOAT
PEACOCK
PETCOCK
PICCOLO
PISCOPO
POPCORN
PRECOOK
PRECOOL
RACCOON
RANCOUR
RAUCOUS
REDCOAT
RIPCORD
SEACOWS
SITCOMS
SNOCONE
SUCCORS
SUCCOUR
SURCOAT
TOPCOAT
TRICORN
TRICOTS
UNICORN
VISCOUS
WALCOTT
WAYCOOL
WELCOME
ZIPCODE
ZIRCONS

•••C•O•
AIRCOOL
ATECROW
BOKCHOY
CATCHON
DOGCHOW
EATCROW
ELECTOR
ENACTOR
ERECTOR
ERICSON
EXACTOR
FRYCOOK
GAUCHOS
HALCYON
HENCOOP
HONCHOS
IRECKON
KERCHOO
LAOCOON
MARCHON
NUNCIOS
OMICRON
OUTCROP
PONCHOS
PRECOOK
PRECOOL
PROCTOR
PROCYON
PYNCHON
RACCOON
RANCHOS
REACTOR
SALCHOW
SPECTOR
STUCCOS
THECROW
TOUCHON
TRACTOR
WAYCOOL

•••C••O
AJACCIO
ARECIBO
AVOCADO
BRACERO
CHICAGO
CHICANO
ELECTRO
FLOCKTO
GIACOMO
ILOCANO
KERCHOO
MARCATO
NICCOLO
PICCOLO
PISCOPO
PLACEBO
PLACIDO
REACTTO
SATCHMO
STICKTO
STUCKTO
VOLCANO

••••CO•
ALARCON
ALENCON
APRICOT
BRONCOS
CALICOS
CAPECOD
CASHCOW
CORNCOB
DOVECOT
FIASCOS
FRESCOS
HARICOT
HELICON
HOLYCOW
LEXICON
MEDICOS
MILKCOW
MONOCOT
ROBOCOP
RUBICON
SILICON
SOUPCON
STUCCOS
TIMECOP
ZYDECOS

••••C•O
AJACCIO
CURACAO
DEFACTO
EXFACTO
GROUCHO
INVACUO
JERICHO
MOROCCO
SIROCCO
TOBACCO

•••••CO
ARTDECO
BELASCO
CANSECO
CHIRICO
ELGRECO
GUANACO
IONESCO
JALISCO
MOROCCO
NABISCO
NORELCO
ORINOCO
PIMLICO
PORTICO
SERPICO
SIROCCO
SUOLOCO
TABASCO
TAMPICO
TOBACCO
TOURACO

C•P••••
CAPABLE
CAPABLY
CAPAPIE
CAPEANN
CAPECOD
CAPELET
CAPELLA
CAPERED
CAPFULS
CAPGUNS
CAPITAL
CAPITAN
CAPITOL
CAPLESS
CAPLETS
CAPNUTS
CAPPERS
CAPPING
CAPRICE
CAPSHAW
CAPSIDS
CAPSIZE
CAPSTAN
CAPSULE
CAPTAIN
CAPTION
CAPTIVE
CAPTORS
CAPTURE
CAPULET
CEPHEUS
CIPHERS
COPIERS
COPILOT
COPIOUS
COPLAND
COPOUTS
COPPERS
COPPERY
COPPICE
COPPING
COPPOLA
COPSOUT
COPTERS
COPULAE
COPULAS
COPYBOY
COPYCAT
COPYING
COPYIST
CUPCAKE
CUPFULS
CUPLIKE
CUPOLAS
CUPPING
CYPHERS
CYPRESS
CYPRIOT

C••P•••
CALPACS
CAMPARI
CAMPERS
CAMPHOR
CAMPIER
CAMPILY
CAMPING
CAMPION
CAMPOUT
CAPPERS
CAPPING
CARPALS
CARPARK
CARPELS
CARPERS
CARPETS
CARPING
CARPOOL
CARPORT
CASPIAN
CHAPATI
CHAPEAU
CHAPELS
CHAPLET
CHAPLIN
CHAPMAN
CHAPMEN
CHAPPED
CHAPPIE
CHAPTER
CHIPPED
CHIPPER
CHIPSIN
CHOPPED
CHOPPER
CLAPPED
CLAPPER
CLAPTON
CLIPART
CLIPONS
CLIPPED
CLIPPER
CLOPPED
COEPTIS
COMPACT
COMPANY
COMPARE
COMPASS
COMPEER
COMPELS
COMPERE
COMPETE
COMPILE
COMPLEX
COMPORT
COMPOSE
COMPOST
COMPOTE
COMPUTE
COOPERS
COOPING
COOPSUP
COOPTED
COPPERS
COPPERY
COPPICE
COPPING
COPPOLA
COUPLED
COUPLES
COUPLET
COUPONS
COWPEAS
COWPOKE
COWPONY
CRAPPIE
CROPPED
CROPPER
CROPSUP
CRYPTIC
CRYPTOS
CULPRIT
CUPPING
CUSPIDS

C•••P••
CALIPER
CALIPHS
CALYPSO
CANAPES
CANOPUS
CAPAPIE
CATSPAW
CERIPHS
CHAMPED
CHAPPED
CHAPPIE
CHEAPEN
CHEAPER
CHEAPIE
CHEAPLY
CHEEPED
CHIPPED
CHIPPER
CHIRPED
CHOMPED
CHOPPED
CHOPPER
CLAMPED
CLAPPED
CLAPPER
CLASPED
CLIPPED
CLIPPER
CLOMPED
CLOPPED
CLUMPED
COCKPIT
CRAMPED
CRAMPON
CRAPPIE
CREEPED
CREEPER
CREEPUP
CRIMPED
CRIMPER
CRISPED
CRISPER
CRISPIN
CRISPLY
CRISPUS
CROPPED
CROPPER
CRUMPET
CRUMPLE
CRUMPLY

C••••P•
CARHOPS
CATALPA
CATNAPS
CATNIPS
CCLAMPS
CHINUPS
COLLOPS
CONCEPT
CORRUPT
CYCLOPS

C•••••P
CALLSUP
CANTRIP
CATCHUP
CHALKUP
CHATSUP
CHECKUP
CHEERUP
CHEWSUP
CHOKEUP
CLAMSUP
CLEANUP
CLEARUP
CLOGSUP
CLOSEUP
COILSUP
COMESUP
COOKSUP
COOKTOP
COOPSUP
COUGHUP
COVERUP
COWSLIP
CRACKUP
CRANKUP
CREEPUP
CROPSUP
CROSSUP
CURLSUP

•C•P•••
ICEPACK
ICEPICK
SCAPULA
SCEPTER
SCEPTIC
SCEPTRE
SCOPING
SCUPPER

•C••P••
ACCEPTS
ACTUPON
ECLIPSE
ECTYPES
OCCIPUT
OCTOPOD
OCTOPUS
OCTUPLE
SCALPED
SCALPEL
SCALPER
SCAMPED
SCAMPER
SCARPED
SCARPER
SCOOPED
SCOOPER
SCORPIO
SCRAPED
SCRAPER
SCRAPES
SCRAPPY
SCRIPPS
SCRIPTS
SCRUPLE
SCULPTS
SCUPPER

•C•••P•
CCLAMPS
ICECAPS
SCHLEPP
SCHLEPS
SCHNAPS
SCRAPPY
SCRIMPS
SCRIMPY
SCRIPPS

•C••••P
ACTEDUP
ICINGUP
SCALLOP
SCAREUP
SCHLEPP
SCREWUP
SCRUBUP

••C•P••
ACCEPTS
COCKPIT
DECAPOD
DUCKPIN
ESCAPED
ESCAPEE
ESCAPES
EXCEPTS
INCEPTS
INCIPIT
JACKPOT
OCCIPUT
RECIPES
SICKPAY

••C••P•
BACKUPS
CYCLOPS
DECAMPS
DECRYPT
ENCAMPS
ENCRYPT
ESCARPS
EXCERPT
HICCUPS
KICKUPS
LOCKUPS
MOCKUPS
MRCHIPS
PICKUPS
RECEIPT
RECOUPS

••C•••P
ARCLAMP
BACKSUP
BUCKSUP
JACKSUP
KICKSUP
LACEDUP
LACESUP
LOCKSUP
MUCKSUP
PACKSUP
PICKSUP
RACKSUP
UNCLASP
WICKIUP

•••C•P•
APOCOPE
CONCEPT
EGGCUPS
EYECUPS
FORCEPS
GASCAPS
HICCUPS
HOTCAPS
HUBCAPS
ICECAPS
INSCAPE
MADCAPS
MOBCAPS
PISCOPO
PRECEPT
REDCAPS
SKYCAPS
TEACUPS
TOECAPS
TRICEPS

•••C••P
BIOCHIP
BOTCHUP
BRACEUP
CATCHUP
CHECKUP
CRACKUP
DAYCAMP
HENCOOP
JUICEUP
KETCHUP
MATCHUP
OLDCHAP
OUTCROP
PATCHUP
PSYCHUP
PUNCHUP
SPICEUP
STACKUP
STICKUP
STOCKUP
STUCKUP
TIECLIP
TOUCHUP

••••C•P
INKYCAP
KNEECAP
ROBOCOP
SNOWCAP
TIMECOP

C••Q•••
CAIQUES
CASQUED
CASQUES
CHEQUER
CHEQUES
CIRQUES
CLAQUES
CLIQUES
CLIQUEY
CLOQUES
COEQUAL
CONQUER
CROQUET

C•••Q••
COMIQUE

•CQ••••
ACQUIRE
ACQUITS
MCQUEEN

••CQ•••
JACQUES
LACQUER
RACQUET
SACQUES

••C•Q••
MACAQUE

CR•••••
CRABBED
CRABBER
CRACKED
CRACKER
CRACKLE
CRACKLY
CRACKUP
CRADLED
CRADLES
CRAFTED
CRAFTER
CRAFTSY
CRAMMED
CRAMMER
CRAMPED
CRAMPON
CRANIAL
CRANING
CRANIUM
CRANKED
CRANKUP
CRAPPIE
CRASHED
CRASHES
CRASSER
CRASSLY
CRASSUS
CRATERS
CRATING
CRAVATS
CRAVENS
CRAVERS
CRAVING
CRAWDAD
CRAWLED
CRAWLER
CRAYOLA
CRAYONS
CRAZIER
CRAZIES
CRAZILY
CRAZING
CREAKED
CREAMED
CREAMER
CREASED
CREASES
CREATED
CREATES
CREATOR
CRECHES
CREDITS
CREEPED
CREEPER
CREEPUP
CREMONA
CRENELS
CREOLES
CREOSOL
CRESSES
CRESTED
CRETANS
CRETINS
CREVICE
CREWCUT
CREWELS
CREWING
CREWMAN
CREWMEN
CRIBBED
CRICKED
CRICKET
CRIMEAN
CRIMPED
CRIMPER
CRIMSON
CRINGED
CRINGES
CRINKLE
CRINKLY
CRINOID
CRIOLLO
CRISPED
CRISPER
CRISPIN
CRISPLY
CRISPUS
CRITICS
CRITTER
CROAKED
CROATIA
CROCHET
CROESUS
CROFTER
CRONIES
CRONISH
CROOKED
CROONED
CROONER
CROPPED
CROPPER
CROPSUP
CROQUET
CROSIER
CROSSED
CROSSER
CROSSES
CROSSLY
CROSSUP
CROUTON
CROWBAR
CROWDED
CROWERS
CROWING
CROWNED
CRUCIAL
CRUCIFY
CRUDELY
CRUDEST
CRUDITY
CRUELER
CRUELLY
CRUELTY
CRUISED
CRUISER
CRUISES
CRULLER
CRUMBLE
CRUMBLY
CRUMPET
CRUMPLE
CRUMPLY
CRUNCHY
CRUSADE
CRUSADO
CRUSHED
CRUSHER
CRUSHES
CRUSTED
CRUZADO
CRYBABY
CRYOGEN
CRYPTIC
CRYPTOS
CRYSTAL
CRYWOLF

C•R••••
CARABAO
CARACAL
CARACAS
CARAFES
CARAMBA
CARAMEL
CARAMIA
CARAVAN
CARAVEL
CARAWAY
CARBIDE
CARBINE
CARBONS
CARBOYS
CARCASE
CARCASS
CARCOAT
CARDERS
CARDIAC
CARDING
CARDOZO
CAREENS
CAREERS
CAREFOR
CAREFUL
CARFARE
CARFULS
CARGOES
CARHOPS
CARIBES
CARIBOU
CARINAS
CARIOCA
CARKING
CARLESS
CARLOAD
CARLSON
CARLTON
CARLYLE
CARMINE
CARNERA
CARNETS
CARNIES
CAROLED
CAROLER
CAROLUS
CAROLYN
CAROMED
CAROTID
CAROUSE
CARPALS
CARPARK
CARPELS
CARPERS
CARPETS
CARPING
CARPOOL
CARPORT
CARRELS
CARRICK
CARRIED
CARRIER
CARRIES
CARRION
CARROLL
CARROTS
CARRYON
CARSEAT
CARTAGE
CARTELS
CARTERS
CARTIER
CARTING
CARTONS
CARTOON
CARVERS

CARVING
CARWASH
CBRADIO
CCRIDER
CERAMIC
CEREALS
CEREBRA
CERIPHS
CERTAIN
CERTIFY
CERUMEN
CERVIDS
CHRISMS
CHRISTI
CHRISTO
CHRISTY
CHROMES
CHRONIC
CIRCLED
CIRCLES
CIRCLET
CIRCUIT
CIRCUSY
CIRQUES
CORAZON
CORBELS
CORBETT
CORDAGE
CORDATE
CORDELL
CORDERO
CORDIAL
CORDING
CORDITE
CORDOBA
CORDONS
CORELLI
CORETTA
CORINTH
CORKAGE
CORKERS
CORKIER
CORKING
CORNCOB
CORNDOG
CORNEAL
CORNEAS
CORNELL
CORNERS
CORNETS
CORNFED
CORNICE
CORNIER
CORNILY
CORNING
CORNISH
CORNOIL
CORNROW
COROLLA
CORONAE
CORONAS
CORONET
CORRALS
CORRECT
CORRIDA
CORRODE
CORRUPT
CORSAGE
CORSAIR
CORSETS
CORSICA
CORTEGE
CURACAO
CURATES
CURATOR
CURBCUT
CURBING
CURDIER
CURDING
CURDLED
CURDLES
CUREALL
CURFEWS
CURIOUS
CURLERS
CURLEWS
CURLIER
CURLIKE
CURLING
CURLSUP
CURRANT
CURRENT
CURRIED
CURRIER
CURRIES
CURRISH
CURSING
CURSIVE
CURSORS
CURSORY
CURTAIL
CURTAIN
CURTEST
CURTISS
CURTSEY
CURVETS
CURVIER
CURVING

C••R•••

CABRINI
CAPRICE
CARRELS
CARRICK
CARRIED
CARRIER
CARRIES
CARRION
CARROLL
CARROTS
CARRYON
CHARADE
CHARGED
CHARGER
CHARGES
CHARIER
CHARILY
CHARIOT
CHARITY
CHARLES
CHARLEY
CHARLIE
CHARMED
CHARMER
CHARMIN
CHARRED
CHARTED
CHARTER
CHERISH
CHEROOT
CHERUBS
CHERVIL
CHIRICO
CHIRPED
CHORALE
CHORALS
CHORINE
CHORIZO
CHORTLE
CHURNED
CITRATE
CITRINE
CITROEN
CITRONS
CITROUS
CLARETS
CLARICE
CLARIFY
CLARION
CLARITY
CLERICS
CLERISY
CLERKED
CLORETS
COARSEN
COARSER
COERCED
COERCER
COERCES
COMRADE
CONRIED
CORRALS
CORRECT
CORRIDA
CORRODE
CORRUPT
COURAGE
COURANT
COURIER
COURSED
COURSER
COURSES
COURTED
COURTLY
COWRIES
CUIRASS
CURRANT
CURRENT
CURRIED
CURRIER
CURRIES
CURRISH
CUTRATE
CYPRESS
CYPRIOT
CZARDAS
CZARDOM
CZARINA
CZARISM
CZARIST

C•••R••

CABARET
CALDRON
CALORIC
CALORIE
CAMBRIC
CAMERAS
CAMERON
CANARDS
CANTRIP
CAPERED
CASERNE
CASERNS
CATERED
CATERER
CATERTO
CAVERNS
CAVORTS
CEDARED
CENTRAL
CENTRED
CENTRES
CENTRIC
CETERIS
CHAGRIN
CHAIRED
CHARRED
CHEERED
CHEERIO
CHEERUP
CHETRUM
CHEVRES
CHEVRON
CHLORAL
CIBORIA
CLAIROL
CLEARED
CLEARER
CLEARLY
CLEARUP
COCHRAN
COHERED
COHERES
COHORTS
COLORED
COMFREY
COMOROS
CONBRIO
CONTRAS
CONTROL
CONURES
CORNROW
COTERIE
COVERED
COVERUP
COWARDS
COWERED
CULPRIT
CYBORGS

C••••R•

CABLERS
CADBURY
CADGERS
CAESARS
CAESURA
CAHIERS
CALDERA
CALGARY
CALIBRE
CALLERS
CALVARY
CALVERT
CAMBERS
CAMPARI
CAMPERS
CANKERS
CANNERS
CANNERY
CANTERS
CANTORS
CAPPERS
CAPTORS
CAPTURE
CARDERS
CAREERS
CARFARE
CARNERA
CARPARK
CARPERS
CARPORT
CARTERS
CARVERS
CASCARA
CASTERS
CATBERT
CATBIRD
CAVALRY
CAVIARS
CELEBRE
CELLARS
CENSERS
CENSORS
CENSURE
CENTERS
CENTURY
CEREBRA
CHASERS
CHEWERS
CHICORY
CHIDERS
CHIMERA
CHOKERS
CINDERS
CINDERY
CIPHERS
CISTERN
CLAMORS
CLAWERS
CLIBURN
CLIPART
CLOSURE
CLOTURE
CLOVERS
COALERS
COAXERS
COCHERE
COCKERS
CODGERS
COFFERS
COGBURN
COHEIRS
COINERS
COLBERT
COLLARD
COLLARS
COLOURS
COMBERS
COMFORT
COMPARE
COMPERE
COMPORT
CONAKRY
CONCERN
CONCERT
CONCORD
CONCURS
CONDORS
CONFERS
CONFIRM
CONFORM
CONGERS
CONJURE
CONKERS
CONNERY
CONNORS
CONSORT
CONTORT
CONVERT
COOKERS
COOKERY
COOLERS
COOPERS
COPIERS
COPPERS
COPPERY
COPTERS
CORDERO
CORKERS
CORNERS
COSTARS
COTTERS
COUGARS
COUNTRY
COUTURE
COWBIRD
COWGIRL
COWHERD
CRATERS
CRAVERS
CROWERS
CUECARD
CULEBRA
CULLERS
CULTURE
CULVERS
CULVERT
CURLERS
CURSORS
CURSORY
CUSTARD
CUTLERS
CUTLERY
CUTTERS
CYCLERS
CYPHERS

C•••••R

CACKLER
CAJOLER
CALIBER
CALIPER
CALLFOR
CAMPHOR
CAMPIER
CANDOUR
CANNIER
CAREFOR
CAROLER
CARRIER
CARTIER
CASHBAR
CASHIER
CATCHER
CATERER
CATHAIR
CATTIER
CAULKER
CAVILER
CCRIDER
CENTAUR
CHAMBER
CHAMFER
CHANCER
CHANGER
CHANTER
CHAPTER
CHARGER
CHARIER
CHARMER
CHARTER
CHASTER
CHATTER
CHAUCER
CHEAPER
CHEATER
CHECKER
CHEDDAR
CHEEVER
CHENIER
CHEQUER
CHESTER
CHEWIER
CHIGGER
CHILLER
CHIPPER
CHITTER
CHOICER
CHOKIER
CHOOSER
CHOPPER
CHOWDER
CHUKKER
CHUNTER
CLABBER
CLAIMER
CLAMBER
CLAMMER
CLAMOUR
CLANGOR
CLAPPER
CLATTER
CLAVIER
CLAYIER
CLEANER
CLEARER
CLEAVER
CLIMBER
CLINKER
CLIPPER
CLOBBER
CLOCKER
CLOWDER
CLUBCAR
CLUNKER
CLUSTER
CLUTTER
CNTOWER
COALCAR
COALTAR
COARSER
COASTER
COBBLER
COCHAIR
COCKIER
CODDLER
COERCER
COLDWAR
COLLIER
COLLYER
COMFIER
COMPEER
CONIFER
CONQUER
CONTOUR
CORKIER
CORNIER
CORSAIR
COSTNER
COULTER
COUNTER
COURIER
COURSER
CRABBER
CRACKER
CRAFTER
CRAMMER
CRASSER
CRAWLER
CRAZIER
CREAMER
CREATOR
CREEPER
CRIMPER
CRISPER
CRITTER
CROFTER
CROONER
CROPPER
CROSIER
CROSSER
CROWBAR
CRUELER
CRUISER
CRULLER
CRUSHER
CURATOR
CURDIER
CURLIER
CURRIER
CURVIER
CUSHIER
CUSSLER

•CR••••

ACREAGE
ACRIDLY
ACROBAT
ACRONYM
ACRYLIC
CCRIDER
SCRAGGY
SCRAPED
SCRAPER
SCRAPES
SCRAPPY
SCRATCH
SCRAWLS
SCRAWLY
SCRAWNY
SCREAKS
SCREAMS
SCREECH
SCREEDS
SCREENS
SCREWED
SCREWUP
SCRIBES
SCRIMPS
SCRIMPY
SCRIPPS
SCRIPTS
SCRIVEN
SCROLLS
SCROOGE
SCRUBBY
SCRUBUP
SCRUFFS
SCRUFFY
SCRUMMY
SCRUNCH
SCRUPLE

•C•R•••

ACARIDS
ACCRETE
ACCRUAL
ACCRUED
ACCRUES
ACERBIC
ACEROLA
ACEROSE
ACTRESS
ICERINK
OCARINA
OCTROIS
SCARABS
SCARCER
SCARERS
SCAREUP
SCARFED
SCARIER
SCARIFY
SCARILY
SCARING
SCARLET
SCARPED
SCARPER
SCARRED
SCARVES
SCORERS
SCORING
SCORNED
SCORNER
SCORPIO
SCURVES

•C••R••

ACCORDS
ACCURST
ACHERON
ICEFREE
MCENROE
SCARRED
SCHERZI
SCHERZO
SCHIRRA
SCIORRA
SCLERAS
SCOURED
SCOURER
SCOURGE

•C•••R•

ACQUIRE
ACTUARY
ECKHART
ECLAIRS
ICEBERG
MCCLURE
MCGUIRE
MCHENRY
SCALARS
SCALERS
SCARERS
SCENERY
SCEPTRE
SCHIRRA
SCIORRA
SCORERS
SCOTERS

•C••••R

ACCEDER
ACCUSER
ACTFOUR
CCRIDER
ECUADOR
ICEBEER
OCONNOR
OCTOBER
SCALIER
SCALPER
SCAMPER
SCANNER
SCANTER
SCARCER
SCARIER
SCARPER
SCATTER
SCEPTER
SCHEMER
SCHMEER
SCHOLAR
SCISSOR
SCOFFER
SCOLDER
SCOOPER
SCOOTER
SCORNER
SCOURER
SCOUTER
SCOWLER
SCRAPER
SCULLER
SCUPPER

••CR•••

ACCRETE
ACCRUAL
ACCRUED
ACCRUES
ASCRIBE
DECREED
DECREES
DECRIED
DECRIER
DECRIES
DECRYPT
ENCRUST
ENCRYPT
ESCROWS
EXCRETE
IPCRESS
MACRAME
MACRONS
MICROBE
MICRONS
RECROOM
RECROSS
RECRUIT
SECRECY
SECRETE
SECRETS
STCROIX
SUCRASE
SUCROSE
UNCRATE

••C•R••

ACCORDS
ACCURST
BACARDI
BACKRUB
BUCKRAM
COCHRAN
DECARLO
DECORUM
ENCORES
ESCARPS
ESCORTS
EUCHRED
EUCHRES
EXCERPT
GOCARTS
IDCARDS
LECARRE
LOCARNO
LUCERNE
MACGRAW
OXCARTS
PACKRAT
PICARDY
PICAROS
RECORDS
RECORKS
RICARDO
RICERAT
SECURED
SECURER
SECURES
UNCORKS
UNCURLS
VICEROY

••C••R•

ANCHORS
ARCHERS
ARCHERY
BACKERS
BICKERS
COCHERE
COCKERS
CYCLERS
DECLARE
DICKERS
DOCKERS
DOCTORS
ETCHERS
FACTORS
FACTORY
HACKERS
HECTARE
HECTORS
HICKORY
KICKERS
LECARRE
LECTERN
LECTORS
LECTURE
LICTORS
LOCKERS
MACABRE
MCCLURE
MOCKERS
MOCKERY
NECKERS
NECTARS
NICKERS
NOCTURN
ORCHARD
PACKARD
PACKERS
PECCARY
PICCARD
PICKERS
PICTURE
PUCKERS
RECTORS
RECTORY
RICHARD
ROCKERS
ROCKERY
SACKERS
SECTORS
SUCCORS
SUCKERS
TACKERS
TICKERS
TUCKERS
VECTORS
VICTORS
VICTORY
WICKERS
ZACHARY

••C•••R

ACCEDER
ACCUSER
ALCAZAR
BICOLOR
BUCKLER
CACKLER
COCHAIR
COCKIER
DECATUR
DECODER
DECRIER
DUCKIER
ENCODER
FICKLER
HECKLER
INCISOR
INCITER
ITCHIER
JACKTAR
JOCULAR
KICKIER
LACQUER
LOCATER
LOCATOR
LUCIFER
LUCKIER
MUCKIER
NUCLEAR
PACECAR
PECKIER
PICADOR
PICKIER
RACECAR
RECITER
RECOLOR
RECOVER
RICHTER
ROCKIER
SECEDER
SECULAR
SECURER
SUCCOUR
TACKIER
TACKLER
TECHIER
TICKLER
UNCLEAR
UNCOVER
WACKIER
YUCKIER

•••CR••

AIRCREW
AMSCRAY
ATECROW
EATCROW
FIACRES
FULCRUM
LITCRIT
OMICRON
OUTCROP
THECROW
UNSCREW

•••C•R•

BARCARS
BOXCARS
BRACERO
BRACERS
CASCARA
CHICORY
CONCERN
CONCERT
CONCORD
CONCURS
CUECARD
DANCERS
DAYCARE
DEICERS
DISCARD
DISCERN
DISCORD
DOGCART
ELECTRA
ELECTRO
EPICURE
FENCERS
FORCERS
GROCERS
GROCERY
HOTCARS
JUICERS
KEYCARD
LANCERS
MASCARA
MERCERS
MERCERY
MERCURY
MINCERS
OBSCURE
PECCARY
PICCARD
PIECERS
PINCERS
PINCURL
PLACARD
PLACERS
PLECTRA
POPCORN
PRICERS
PROCURE
RIPCORD
SAUCERS
SINCERE
SLICERS
SORCERY
SPACERS
SPECTRA
SPECTRE
SPICERY
SUCCORS
TEACART
THECARS
TOWCARS
TRACERS
TRACERY
TRICORN
TROCARS
UNICORN
VISCERA
WINCERS

•••C••R

BEECHER
BLACKER
BLOCKER
BUTCHER
CATCHER
CHECKER
CLOCKER
CRACKER
DRUCKER
ELECTOR
ENACTOR
ERECTER
ERECTOR
EXACTER
EXACTOR
FANCIER
FILCHER
FISCHER
FLICKER
GAUCHER
GLACIER
HATCHER
HITCHER
JUICIER
KNACKER
KNOCKER
MARCHER
MOOCHER
MUNCHER
PINCHER
PITCHER
POACHER
PRICIER
PROCTOR
PUNCHER
QUICKER
RANCHER
RANCOUR
REACTOR
REOCCUR
RESCUER
SAUCIER
SHOCKER
SHUCKER
SLACKER
SLICKER
SMACKER
SNACKER
SNICKER
SPACIER
SPECTER
SPECTOR
SPICIER
STICKER
SUCCOUR
TEACHER
TEICHER
THICKER
TRACKER
TRACTOR
TRICKER
TRUCKER
VOUCHER
WATCHER
WRECKER

••••CR•

MIMICRY

••••C•R

BOUNCER
CHANCER
CHAUCER
CHOICER
CLUBCAR
COALCAR
COERCER
ENTICER
FIERCER
FLATCAR
HANDCAR
INDUCER
MAILCAR
OFFICER
PACECAR
POLECAR
POUNCER
PRANCER
RACECAR
REDUCER
REOCCUR
SCARCER
SEDUCER
SIDECAR
SLOTCAR

SPENCER
SPLICER
SPRUCER
TRAMCAR

CS•••••

CSLEWIS

C•S••••

CASABAS
CASAVAS
CASCADE
CASCARA
CASELAW
CASERNE
CASERNS
CASHBAR
CASHBOX
CASHCOW
CASHEWS
CASHIER
CASHING
CASHOUT
CASINGS
CASINOS
CASPIAN
CASQUED
CASQUES
CASSATT
CASSAVA
CASSIAS
CASSIDY
CASSINI
CASSINO
CASSIUS
CASSOCK
CASTERS
CASTILE
CASTING
CASTLED
CASTLES
CASTOFF
CASTOUT
CASUALS
CESSING
CESSION
CISTERN
COSHING
COSIEST
COSIGNS
COSINES
COSSACK
COSSETS
COSTAIN
COSTARS
COSTING
COSTNER
COSTUME
CUSHAWS
CUSHIER
CUSHING
CUSHION
CUSPIDS
CUSSING
CUSSLER
CUSTARD
CUSTODY
CUSTOMS

C••S•••

CAESARS
CAESIUM
CAESURA
CAISSON
CANSECO
CAPSHAW
CAPSIDS
CAPSIZE
CAPSTAN
CAPSULE
CARSEAT
CASSATT
CASSAVA
CASSIAS
CASSIDY
CASSINI
CASSINO
CASSIUS
CASSOCK
CATSCAN
CATSEYE
CATSHOW
CATSPAW
CATSUIT
CAUSING
CAUSTIC
CEASING
CELSIUS
CENSERS
CENSING
CENSORS
CENSURE
CESSING
CESSION
CHASERS
CHASING
CHASSES
CHASSIS
CHASTEN
CHASTER
CHESTER
CHISELS
CLASHED
CLASHES
CLASPED
CLASSED
CLASSES
CLASSIC
CLOSEBY
CLOSEIN
CLOSELY
CLOSEST
CLOSETS
CLOSEUP
CLOSING
CLOSURE
CLUSTER
COASTAL
COASTED
COASTER
CONSENT
CONSIGN
CONSIST
CONSOLE
CONSORT
CONSULS
CONSULT
CONSUME
COPSOUT
CORSAGE
CORSAIR
CORSETS
CORSICA
COSSACK
COSSETS
COUSINS
COWSLIP
CRASHED
CRASHES
CRASSER
CRASSLY
CRASSUS
CRESSES
CRESTED
CRISPED
CRISPER
CRISPIN
CRISPLY
CRISPUS
CROSIER
CROSSED
CROSSER
CROSSES
CROSSLY
CROSSUP
CRUSADE
CRUSADO
CRUSHED
CRUSHER
CRUSHES
CRUSTED
CRYSTAL
CUISINE
CURSING
CURSIVE
CURSORS
CURSORY
CUSSING
CUSSLER
CUTSOFF
CUTSOUT

C•••S••

CAISSON
CALLSIN
CALLSON
CALLSUP
CAMISES
CANASTA
CARLSON
CAVESIN
CAYUSES
CELESTA
CELESTE
CHAISES
CHANSON
CHASSES
CHASSIS
CHATSUP
CHEESES
CHELSEA
CHEWSUP
CHIPSIN
CHOMSKY
CHOOSER
CHOOSES
CHRISMS
CHRISTI
CHRISTO
CHRISTY
CLAMSUP
CLASSED
CLASSES
CLASSIC
CLAUSES
CLEMSON
CLOGSUP
CLUESIN
COARSEN
COARSER
COCKSHY
COHOSTS
COILSUP
COLOSSI
COMESAT
COMESBY
COMESIN
COMESON
COMESTO
COMESUP
COOKSUP
COOLSIT
COOPSUP
COUNSEL
COURSED
COURSER
COURSES
CRASSER
CRASSLY
CRASSUS
CREASED
CREASES
CREOSOL
CRESSES
CRIMSON
CROESUS
CROPSUP
CROSSED
CROSSER
CROSSES
CROSSLY
CROSSUP
CRUISED
CRUISER
CRUISES
CUBISTS
CURLSUP
CURTSEY

C••••S•

CABOOSE
CADDISH
CAGIEST
CAKIEST
CALMEST
CALYPSO
CANIEST
CANVASS
CAPLESS
CARCASE
CARCASS
CARLESS
CAROUSE
CARWASH
CATFISH
CATTISH
CELLIST
CHEMISE
CHEMIST
CHERISH
CHINESE
CIRCUSY
CLAYISH
CLEANSE
CLERISY
CLOSEST
COCHISE
COCKISH
CODFISH
COEXIST
COKIEST
COLDEST
COLDISH
COLOSSI
COLTISH
COMBUST
COMPASS
COMPOSE
COMPOST
CONCISE
CONFESS
CONFUSE
CONGEST
CONSIST
CONTEST
CONTUSE
COOLEST
COOLISH
COPYIST
CORNISH
COSIEST
COYNESS
COZIEST
CRAFTSY
CRONISH
CRUDEST
CUBBISH
CUIRASS
CULTISH
CULTISM
CULTIST
CURRISH
CURTEST
CURTISS
CUTLASS
CYCLIST
CYPRESS
CZARISM
CZARIST

C•••••S

CABALAS
CABANAS
CABBIES
CABLERS
CACHETS
CACHOUS
CACKLES
CADDIES
CADGERS
CAESARS
CAFTANS
CAHIERS
CAHOOTS
CAIMANS
CAIQUES
CAJOLES
CALENDS
CALICES
CALICOS
CALIPHS
CALKINS
CALLERS
CALLINS
CALLOUS
CALPACS
CALYCES
CALYXES
CAMBERS
CAMERAS
CAMISES
CAMPERS
CANAPES
CANARDS
CANCANS
CANCELS
CANDIDS
CANDIES
CANDLES
CANFULS
CANINES
CANKERS
CANNERS
CANNONS
CANOPUS
CANTERS
CANTLES
CANTONS
CANTORS
CANVASS
CANYONS
CAPFULS
CAPGUNS
CAPLESS
CAPLETS
CAPNUTS
CAPPERS
CAPSIDS
CAPTORS
CARACAS
CARAFES
CARBONS
CARBOYS
CARCASS
CARDERS
CAREENS
CAREERS
CARFULS
CARGOES
CARHOPS
CARIBES
CARINAS
CARLESS
CARNETS
CARNIES
CAROLUS
CARPALS
CARPELS
CARPERS
CARPETS
CARRELS
CARRIES
CARROTS
CARTELS
CARTERS
CARTONS
CARVERS
CASABAS
CASAVAS
CASERNS
CASHEWS
CASINGS
CASINOS
CASQUES
CASSIAS
CASSIUS
CASTERS
CASTLES
CASUALS
CATCHES
CATIONS
CATKINS
CATNAPS
CATNIPS
CAUDLES
CAVEATS
CAVEINS
CAVERNS
CAVIARS
CAVORTS
CAYMANS
CAYUGAS
CAYUSES
CCLAMPS
CELEBES
CELLARS
CELSIUS
CELTICS
CEMENTS
CENSERS
CENSORS
CENTERS
CENTRES
CEPHEUS
CEREALS
CERIPHS
CERVIDS
CETERIS
CHABLIS
CHACHAS
CHAISES
CHALETS
CHALONS
CHAMOIS
CHANCES
CHANGES
CHAPELS
CHARGES
CHARLES
CHASERS
CHASSES
CHASSIS
CHEESES
CHEETOS
CHEQUES
CHERUBS
CHEVIES
CHEVRES
CHEWERS
CHIDERS
CHIGOES
CHILIES
CHINUPS
CHISELS
CHOICES
CHOKERS
CHOLLAS
CHOOSES
CHORALS
CHRISMS
CHROMES
CHUKKAS
CICADAS
CINCHES
CINDERS
CINEMAS
CIPHERS
CIRCLES
CIRQUES
CITRONS
CITROUS
CIVVIES
CLAMORS
CLAQUES
CLARETS
CLASHES
CLASSES
CLAUSES
CLAWERS
CLEAVES
CLEMENS
CLERICS
CLICHES
CLIENTS
CLINICS
CLIPONS
CLIQUES
CLOACAS
CLOCHES
CLOQUES
CLORETS
CLOSETS
CLOTHES
CLOVERS
COACHES
COALERS
COALGAS
COAXERS
COBBLES
COBWEBS
COCKERS
COCKLES
COCOONS
CODDLES
CODGERS
CODICES
COEDITS
COEPTIS
COERCES
COEVALS
COFFEES
COFFERS
COGNACS
COHEIRS
COHERES
COHORTS
COHOSTS
COINERS
COLLARS
COLLETS
COLLIES
COLLINS
COLLOPS
COLOBUS
COLONES
COLOURS
COLUMNS
COMBATS
COMBERS
COMEONS
COMFITS
COMINGS
COMMITS
COMMONS
COMOROS
COMPASS
COMPELS
CONCHES
CONCURS
CONDORS
CONFABS
CONFERS
CONFESS
CONGERS
CONJOBS
CONKERS
CONNORS
CONOIDS
CONSULS
CONTRAS
CONURES
CONVEYS
CONVOYS
COOKERS
COOKIES
COOLERS
COOPERS
COOTIES
COPIERS
COPIOUS
COPOUTS
COPPERS
COPTERS
COPULAS
CORBELS
CORDONS
CORKERS
CORNEAS
CORNERS
CORNETS
CORONAS
CORRALS
CORSETS
COSIGNS
COSINES
COSSETS
COSTARS
COTTERS
COTTONS
COUCHES
COUGARS
COULEES
COUPLES
COUPONS
COURSES
COUSINS
COWARDS
COWBOYS
COWPEAS
COWRIES
COYNESS
COYOTES
COZZENS
CRADLES
CRASHES
CRASSUS
CRATERS
CRAVATS
CRAVENS
CRAVERS
CRAYONS
CRAZIES
CREASES
CREATES
CRECHES
CREDITS
CRENELS
CREOLES
CRESSES
CRETANS
CRETINS
CREWELS
CRINGES
CRISPUS
CRITICS
CROESUS
CRONIES
CROSSES
CROWERS
CRUISES
CRUSHES
CRYPTOS
CSLEWIS
CUBBIES
CUBISTS
CUCKOOS
CUDDIES
CUDDLES
CUDGELS
CUIRASS
CULLERS
CULLIES
CULVERS
CUMULUS
CUPFULS
CUPOLAS
CURATES
CURDLES
CURFEWS
CURIOUS
CURLERS
CURLEWS
CURRIES
CURSORS
CURTISS
CURVETS
CUSHAWS
CUSPIDS
CUSTOMS
CUTLASS
CUTLERS
CUTLETS
CUTOFFS
CUTOUTS
CUTTERS
CYBORGS
CYCLERS
CYCLOPS
CYGNETS
CYMBALS
CYPHERS
CYPRESS
CZARDAS

•CS••••

ECSTASY
MCSWINE

•C•S•••

ACESOUT
ACTSOUT
ICESHOW
ICESOUT
SCISSOR

•C••S••

ACCOSTS
ACCUSED
ACCUSER
ACCUSES
ACHESON
ECDYSES
ECDYSIS
SCHISMS
SCISSOR
SCOUSES

•C•••S•

ACCURST
ACEROSE
ACHIEST
ACTRESS
ECLIPSE
ECSTASY
ICELESS
ICINESS
ICKIEST
OCULIST

•C••••S

ACACIAS
ACARIDS
ACCEDES
ACCENTS
ACCEPTS
ACCORDS
ACCOSTS
ACCRUES
ACCUSES
ACHATES
ACHENES
ACKACKS
ACQUITS
ACTIONS
ACTIVES
ACTRESS
ACUMENS
CCLAMPS
ECDYSES
ECDYSIS
ECHINUS
ECLAIRS
ECTYPES
ICEAGES
ICEAXES
ICEBAGS
ICECAPS
ICEFOGS
ICELESS
ICICLES
ICINESS
MCCALLS
OCCULTS
OCEANUS
OCELLUS
OCELOTS
OCTANES
OCTANTS
OCTAVES
OCTAVOS
OCTOPUS
OCTROIS
SCALARS
SCALERS
SCARABS
SCARERS
SCARVES
SCATHES
SCHEMAS
SCHEMES
SCHISMS
SCHLEPS
SCHMOES
SCHMOOS
SCHNAPS
SCHOOLS
SCLERAS
SCONCES
SCORERS
SCOTERS
SCOUSES
SCRAPES
SCRAWLS
SCREAKS
SCREAMS
SCREEDS
SCREENS
SCRIBES
SCRIMPS
SCRIPPS
SCRIPTS
SCROLLS
SCRUFFS
SCULPTS
SCURVES
SCYTHES

••CS•••

ARCSINE
FOCSLES
TOCSINS

••C•S••

ACCOSTS
ACCUSED
ACCUSER
ACCUSES
BACKSIN
BACKSUP
BUCKSAW
BUCKSUP
COCKSHY
ENCASED
ENCASES
EXCISED
EXCISES
EXCUSED
EXCUSES
FICUSES
FOCUSED
FOCUSES
FUCHSIA
HACKSAW
INCASED
INCASES
INCISED
INCISES
INCISOR
JACKSON
JACKSUP
JOCASTA
KICKSIN
KICKSUP
LACESUP
LACOSTE
LOCKSON
LOCKSUP
LOCUSTS
MUCKSUP
NICOSIA
PACKSUP
PECKSAT
PICASSO
PICKSAT
PICKSON
PICKSUP
RACKSUP
RECASTS
RECUSED
RECUSES
RICKSHA
SOCKSIN
SUCKSIN
TACKSON
TUCKSIN
UNCASED
UNCASES

••C••S•

ACCURST
BECAUSE
COCHISE
COCKISH
CYCLIST
DECLASS
DICIEST
DUCHESS
ENCLOSE
ENCRUST
INCENSE
INCLOSE
IPCRESS
JACCUSE
JACKASS
LACIEST
LACTASE
LACTOSE
LICENSE
PACHISI
PECKISH
PICASSO
PICTISH
PUCKISH
RACIEST
RECHOSE
RECLUSE
RECROSS
RICHEST
SICKEST
SICKISH
SUCCESS
SUCRASE
SUCROSE
UNCLASP
UNCLOSE
UPCLOSE

••C•••S

ACCEDES
ACCENTS
ACCEPTS
ACCORDS
ACCOSTS
ACCRUES
ACCUSES
ALCOVES
ANCHORS
ARCADES
ARCHERS
ARCHONS
ASCENDS
ASCENTS
BACCHUS
BACKERS
BACKUPS
BECALMS
BECKONS
BECOMES
BICKERS
BUCKETS
BUCKLES
BUCKOES
CACHETS
CACHOUS
CACKLES
CICADAS
COCKERS
COCKLES
COCOONS
CUCKOOS
CYCLERS
CYCLOPS
DACTYLS
DECADES
DECAMPS
DECANTS
DECEITS
DECIDES
DECKLES
DECLASS
DECOCTS
DECODES
DECREES
DECRIES
DICKENS
DICKERS
DICKEYS
DICKIES
DICTUMS
DOCENTS
DOCKERS
DOCKETS
DOCTORS
DUCHESS
DUCHIES
ENCAGES
ENCAMPS
ENCASES
ENCINAS
ENCODES
ENCORES
ESCAPES
ESCARPS
ESCHEWS
ESCORTS
ESCROWS
ESCUDOS
ETCHERS
EUCHRES
EXCEEDS
EXCEPTS
EXCISES
EXCITES
EXCUSES
FACADES
FACIALS
FACINGS
FACTORS
FICUSES
FOCSLES
FOCUSES
GECKOES
GOCARTS
HACKERS
HACKIES
HACKLES
HECKLES
HECTORS
HICCUPS
IDCARDS
INCANTS
INCASES
INCEPTS
INCISES
INCITES
INCOMES
INCUDES
IPCRESS
JACANAS
JACKALS
JACKASS
JACKETS
JACKEYS
JACKIES
JACQUES
JICAMAS
JOCKEYS
KICKERS
KICKUPS
KUCHENS
LACINGS
LACKEYS
LACUNAS
LECTORS
LICHENS
LICTORS
LOCALES
LOCATES
LOCKERS
LOCKETS
LOCKINS
LOCKUPS
LOCUSTS
LYCEUMS
MACRONS
MCCALLS

MICKEYS
MICMACS
MICRONS
MOCKERS
MOCKUPS
MRCHIPS
NECKERS
NECTARS
NICHOLS
NICKELS
NICKERS
NICOLAS
NOCUOUS
NUCLEUS
OCCULTS
OOCYTES
ORCHIDS
OSCINES
OXCARTS
PACKERS
PACKETS
PECTINS
PICAROS
PICKENS
PICKERS
PICKETS
PICKLES
PICKUPS
PICNICS
POCKETS
POCONOS
PUCKERS
RACEMES
RACKETS
RECALLS
RECANES
RECANTS
RECASTS
RECEDES
RECIPES
RECITES
RECKONS
RECOATS
RECODES
RECOILS
RECORDS
RECORKS
RECOUPS
RECROSS
RECTORS
RECUSES
RICKEYS
RICKLES
ROCHETS
ROCKERS
ROCKETS
ROCKIES
SACHEMS
SACHETS
SACKERS
SACQUES
SECANTS
SECEDES
SECKELS
SECONDS
SECRETS
SECTORS
SECURES
SICKENS
SICKLES
SOCIALS
SOCKETS
SUCCESS
SUCCORS
SUCKERS
TACITUS
TACKERS
TACKLES
TACTICS
TECHIES
TICKERS
TICKETS
TICKLES
TICTACS
TOCSINS
TUCKERS
TYCOONS
UNCAGES
UNCASES
UNCIALS
UNCLOGS
UNCOILS
UNCORKS
UNCURLS
URCHINS
VACATES
VACUOUS
VACUUMS
VECTORS
VICIOUS
VICTIMS
VICTORS
VICUNAS
WICKERS
WICKETS

•••CS••

ERICSON

•••C•S•

CARCASE
CARCASS
CIRCUSY
CONCISE
DIOCESE
DISCUSS
DUNCISH
EGGCASE
FLYCAST
GLUCOSE
JACCUSE
LOWCOST
MISCAST
OUTCAST
PAYCASH
PRECAST
PRECISE
PROCESS
SARCASM
SUCCESS

•••C••S

ACACIAS
AITCHES
ANTCOWS
APACHES
ASHCANS
AVOCETS
BACCHUS
BARCARS
BATCHES
BEACHES
BEACONS
BEECHES
BELCHES
BENCHES
BIRCHES
BOBCATS
BOTCHES
BOXCARS
BRACERS
BUNCHES
CANCANS
CANCELS
CARCASS
CATCHES
CHACHAS
CINCHES
CIRCLES
CLICHES
CLOCHES
COACHES
CONCHES
CONCURS
COUCHES
CRECHES
DANCERS
DEACONS
DEICERS
DISCUSS
DITCHES
DRACHMS
EGGCUPS
ELICITS
EXACTAS
EYECUPS
FALCONS
FANCIES
FASCIAS
FATCATS
FAUCETS
FENCERS
FESCUES
FETCHES
FIACRES
FILCHES
FINCHES
FITCHES
FLACONS
FLECHES
FORCEPS
FORCERS
GARCONS
GASCAPS
GASCONS
GAUCHOS
GOTCHAS
GRACIAS
GROCERS
GULCHES
HATCHES
HEPCATS
HICCUPS
HITCHES
HONCHOS
HOTCAPS
HOTCARS
HUBCAPS
HUNCHES
HUTCHES
ICECAPS
ICICLES
JAYCEES
JUICERS
JUNCOES
KETCHES
KWACHAS
LANCERS
LANCETS
LARCHES
LATCHES
LEACHES
LEECHES
LITCHIS
LOACHES
LUNCHES
LURCHES
MADCAPS
MARCELS
MARCHES
MASCOTS
MATCHES
MERCERS
MERCIES
MESCALS
MINCERS
MISCUES
MOBCAPS
MOOCHES
MUDCATS
MULCHES
MUNCHES
MUSCATS
MUSCLES
NONCOMS
NOTCHES
NUNCIOS
OILCANS
ORACLES
PARCELS
PARCHES
PATCHES
PEACHES
PENCILS
PERCHES
PIECERS
PINCERS
PINCHAS
PINCHES
PITCHES
PLACERS
POACHES
PONCHOS
POOCHES
PORCHES
POUCHES
PRICERS
PROCESS
PSYCHES
PUNCHES
QUICHES
RANCHES
RANCHOS
RASCALS
RAUCOUS
REACHES
REDCAPS
RESCUES
REXCATS
ROACHES
SAUCERS
SEACOWS
SEICHES
SITCOMS
SKYCAPS
SLICERS
SNOCATS
SPACERS
SPECIES
STICHES
STUCCOS
SUCCESS
SUCCORS
SYNCHES
TALCUMS
TEACHES
TEACUPS
TERCELS
TERCETS
THECARS
TINCANS
TOECAPS
TOMCATS
TORCHES
TOUCANS
TOUCHES
TOWCARS
TRACERS
TRICEPS
TRICOTS
TROCARS
TROCHES
VETCHES
VISCOUS
VOUCHES
VULCANS
WATCHES
WELCHES
WENCHES
WINCERS
WINCHES
WITCHES
ZILCHES
ZIRCONS

••••C•S

ABDUCTS
ACKACKS
ADDUCES
ADDUCTS
AFFECTS
ALPACAS
AMERCES
APERCUS
ARNICAS
ASPECTS
ATTACKS
ATTICUS
ATTUCKS
AUROCHS
BEDECKS
BISECTS
BODICES
BOUNCES
BRONCOS
CALICES
CALICOS
CALYCES
CARACAS
CHANCES
CHOICES
CLOACAS
CODICES
COERCES
DECOCTS
DEDUCES
DEDUCTS
DEFACES
DEFECTS
DEJECTS
DELICTS
DEPICTS
DETECTS
DEVICES
DIDACTS
DIRECTS
EFFACES
EFFECTS
ENLACES
ENTICES
EPARCHS
EVINCES
EXARCHS
EXPECTS
FIANCES
FIASCOS
FLEECES
FRANCES
FRANCIS
FRESCOS
GLANCES
HELICES
HIJACKS
HYRACES
IMPACTS
INDICES
INDICTS
INDUCES
INDUCTS
INFECTS
INFOCUS
INJECTS
INSECTS
JOUNCES
KOPECKS
LATICES
MARACAS
MEDICOS
MENACES
MOLOCHS
NOTICES
NOVICES
NUANCES
OBJECTS
OFFICES
OUTACTS
PALACES
PATACAS
PIERCES
PLAICES
POLICES
POUNCES
PRANCES
PRINCES
PUMICES
QUINCES
RADICES
REDACTS
REDUCES
REFACES
REFOCUS
REJECTS
RELACES
RELICTS
RELOCKS
RELUCTS
RESECTS
SAMECHS
SCONCES
SEANCES
SEDUCES
SELECTS
SENECAS
SHTICKS
SILICAS
SLUICES
SOLACES
SOURCES
SPLICES
SPRUCES
STANCES
STUCCOS
TENACES
THWACKS
TRANCES
UNLACES
UNLOCKS
UNPACKS
UNTACKS
UPTICKS
VOTECHS
ZYDECOS

•••••CS

AGARICS
AIRSACS
BIONICS
CALPACS
CELTICS
CLERICS
CLINICS
COGNACS
CRITICS
ETHNICS
EXOTICS
FABRICS
FROLICS
FUSTICS
GOTHICS
HEROICS
ITALICS
MANIACS
MANIOCS
MASTICS
METRICS
MICMACS
MOSAICS
MYSTICS
NOETICS
NORDICS
OVISACS
PARSECS
PHOBICS
PHONICS
PHOTICS
PHYSICS
PICNICS
POETICS
PUBLICS
RUBRICS
RUSTICS
STATICS
TACTICS
TARMACS
TENRECS
TICTACS
TOLTECS
TROPICS
ZODIACS

C•T••••

CATALAN
CATALOG
CATALPA
CATAWBA
CATBERT
CATBIRD
CATBOAT
CATCALL
CATCHER
CATCHES
CATCHON
CATCHUP
CATENAE
CATERED
CATERER
CATERTO
CATFISH
CATFOOD
CATHAIR
CATHEAD
CATHODE
CATIONS
CATKINS
CATLIKE
CATNAPS
CATNIPS
CATSCAN
CATSEYE
CATSHOW
CATSPAW
CATSUIT
CATTAIL
CATTIER
CATTILY
CATTING
CATTISH
CATWALK
CETERIS
CITABLE
CITADEL
CITIZEN
CITRATE
CITRINE
CITROEN
CITRONS
CITROUS
CNTOWER
COTERIE
COTTAGE
COTTERS
COTTONS
COTTONY
CUTAWAY
CUTBACK
CUTDOWN
CUTICLE
CUTINTO
CUTLASS
CUTLERS
CUTLERY
CUTLETS
CUTOFFS
CUTOUTS
CUTRATE
CUTSOFF
CUTSOUT
CUTTERS
CUTTIME
CUTTING

C••T•••

CAFTANS
CALTECH
CANTATA
CANTEEN
CANTERS
CANTILY
CANTINA
CANTING
CANTLES
CANTONS
CANTORS
CANTRIP
CAPTAIN
CAPTION
CAPTIVE
CAPTORS
CAPTURE
CARTAGE
CARTELS
CARTERS
CARTIER
CARTING
CARTONS
CARTOON
CASTERS
CASTILE
CASTING
CASTLED
CASTLES
CASTOFF
CASTOUT
CATTAIL
CATTIER
CATTILY
CATTING
CATTISH
CAUTION
CELTICS
CENTAUR
CENTAVO
CENTERS
CENTIME
CENTIMO
CENTRAL
CENTRED
CENTRES
CENTRIC
CENTURY
CERTAIN
CERTIFY
CHATEAU
CHATHAM
CHATSUP
CHATTED
CHATTEL
CHATTER
CHETRUM
CHITTER
CHUTNEY
CISTERN
CLATTER
CLOTHED
CLOTHES
CLOTTED
CLOTURE
CLUTTER
COATING
COCTEAU
COLTISH
CONTACT
CONTAIN
CONTEMN
CONTEND
CONTENT
CONTEST
CONTEXT
CONTORT
CONTOUR
CONTRAS
CONTROL
CONTUSE
COOTIES
COPTERS
CORTEGE
COSTAIN
COSTARS
COSTING
COSTNER
COSTUME
COTTAGE
COTTERS
COTTONS
COTTONY
COUTURE
COWTOWN
CRATERS
CRATING
CRETANS
CRETINS
CRITICS
CRITTER
CULTISH
CULTISM
CULTIST
CULTJAM
CULTURE
CURTAIL
CURTAIN
CURTEST
CURTISS
CURTSEY
CUSTARD
CUSTODY
CUSTOMS
CUTTERS
CUTTIME
CUTTING
CYNTHIA

C•••T••

CADETTE
CAPITAL
CAPITAN
CAPITOL
CAPSTAN
CARLTON
CAROTID
CAUSTIC
CAVETTO
CHANTED
CHANTER
CHANTEY
CHAOTIC
CHAPTER
CHARTED
CHARTER
CHASTEN
CHASTER
CHATTED
CHATTEL
CHATTER
CHEATED
CHEATER
CHEATIN
CHEETAH
CHEETOS
CHESTER
CHEWTOY
CHINTZY
CHITTER
CHOCTAW
CHORTLE
CHUNTER
CLAPTON
CLATTER
CLAYTON
CLIFTON
CLINTON
CLOTTED
CLOUTED
CLUSTER
CLUTTER
COALTAR
COASTAL
COASTED
COASTER
COEPTIS
COLETTE
COOKTOP
COOPTED
CORETTA
COULTER
COUNTED
COUNTER
COUNTON
COUNTRY
COURTED
COURTLY
COVETED
COYOTES
CRAFTED
CRAFTER
CRAFTSY
CREATED
CREATES
CREATOR
CRESTED
CRITTER
CROATIA
CROFTER
CROUTON
CRUSTED
CRYPTIC
CRYPTOS
CRYSTAL
CULOTTE
CURATES
CURATOR

C••••T•

CABLETV
CACHETS
CADETTE
CAHOOTS
CALCITE
CANASTA
CANTATA
CAPLETS
CAPNUTS
CARNETS
CARPETS
CARROTS
CASSATT
CATERTO
CAVEATS
CAVETTO
CAVORTS
CELESTA
CELESTE
CEMENTS
CHALETS
CHAPATI
CHARITY
CHIANTI
CHRISTI
CHRISTO
CHRISTY
CILIATE
CITRATE
CLARETS
CLARITY
CLIENTS
CLIMATE
CLORETS
CLOSETS
COEDITS
COGNATE
COHORTS
COHOSTS
COLETTE
COLGATE
COLLATE
COLLETS
COMBATS
COMESTO
COMFITS
COMMITS
COMMUTE
COMPETE
COMPOTE
COMPUTE
CONDITA
CONFUTE
CONMOTO
CONNOTE
COPOUTS
CORBETT
CORDATE
CORDITE
CORETTA
CORINTH
CORNETS
CORSETS
COSSETS
CRAVATS
CREDITS
CRUDITY
CRUELTY
CUBISTS
CULOTTE
CURVETS
CUTINTO
CUTLETS
CUTOUTS
CUTRATE
CYGNETS

C•••••T

CABARET
CABINET
CAGIEST
CAKIEST
CALLOUT
CALMEST
CALUMET
CALVERT
CAMELOT
CAMEOUT
CAMPOUT
CANIEST
CAPELET
CAPULET
CARCOAT
CARPORT
CARSEAT
CASHOUT
CASSATT
CASTOUT
CATBERT
CATBOAT
CATSUIT
CELLIST
CHAPLET
CHARIOT
CHEMIST
CHEROOT
CHEVIOT
CHEWOUT
CIRCLET
CIRCUIT
CLEMENT
CLIPART
CLOSEST
COCKPIT
COCONUT
COEXIST
COHABIT
COKIEST
COLBERT
COLDCUT
COLDEST
COLLECT
COMBUST
COMEOUT
COMESAT
COMFORT
COMMENT
COMPACT
COMPORT
COMPOST
CONCEIT
CONCEPT
CONCERT
CONCOCT
CONDUCT
CONDUIT
CONGEST
CONKOUT
CONNECT
CONSENT
CONSIST
CONSORT
CONSULT
CONTACT
CONTENT
CONTEST
CONTEXT
CONTORT
CONVENT
CONVERT
CONVICT
COOKOUT
COOLANT
COOLEST
COOLSIT
COONCAT
COPILOT
COPSOUT
COPYCAT
COPYIST
CORBETT
CORONET
CORRECT
CORRUPT
COSIEST
COULDNT
COUPLET
COURANT
COZIEST
CREWCUT
CRICKET
CROCHET
CROQUET
CRUDEST
CRUMPET
CULPRIT
CULTIST
CULVERT
CURBCUT
CURRANT
CURRENT
CURTEST
CUTSOUT
CYCLIST
CYPRIOT
CZARIST

•CT••••

ACTABLE
ACTAEON
ACTEDON
ACTEDUP
ACTFIVE
ACTFOUR
ACTINIC
ACTIONS
ACTIVES
ACTRESS
ACTSOUT
ACTUARY
ACTUATE
ACTUPON
ECTYPES
OCTAGON
OCTANES
OCTANTS
OCTAVES
OCTAVIA
OCTAVOS
OCTOBER
OCTOPOD
OCTOPUS
OCTROIS
OCTUPLE

•C•T•••

ACETATE
ACETONE
ACHTUNG
ACUTELY
ECSTASY
SCATHED
SCATHES
SCATTED
SCATTER
SCOTERS
SCOTTIE
SCUTTLE
SCYTHED
SCYTHES

•C••T••

ACANTHI
ACHATES
ICEDTEA
SCANTED
SCANTER
SCANTLY
SCATTED
SCATTER
SCENTED
SCEPTER
SCEPTIC
SCEPTRE
SCHATZI
SCOOTED
SCOOTER
SCOTTIE
SCOUTED
SCOUTER
SCRATCH
SCUTTLE

•C•••T•

ACCENTS
ACCEPTS
ACCOSTS
ACCRETE
ACETATE
ACIDITY
ACOLYTE
ACONITE
ACQUITS
ACTUATE

NCWYETH
OCCULTS
OCELOTS
OCTANTS
SCHULTZ
SCRIPTS
SCULPTS

•C••••T
ACCOUNT
ACCURST
ACEDOUT
ACESOUT
ACHIEST
ACROBAT
ACTSOUT
ECKHART
ICEBOAT
ICEDOUT
ICESOUT
ICKIEST
OCCIPUT
OCULIST
SCARLET
SCHMIDT

••CT•••
AUCTION
COCTEAU
DACTYLS
DICTATE
DICTION
DICTUMS
DOCTORS
DUCTILE
DUCTING
FACTFUL
FACTION
FACTOID
FACTORS
FACTORY
FACTUAL
FICTION
FICTIVE
HECTARE
HECTORS
LACTASE
LACTATE
LACTEAL
LACTOSE
LECTERN
LECTORS
LECTURE
LICTORS
NECTARS
NOCTURN
PECTINS
PICTISH
PICTURE
RECTIFY
RECTORS
RECTORY
RUCTION
SECTION
SECTORS
SUCTION
TACTFUL
TACTICS
TACTILE
TICTACS
UNCTION
VECTORS
VICTIMS
VICTORS
VICTORY
VICTUAL

••C•T••
ASCETIC
DECATUR
EXCITED
EXCITES
FACETED
INCITED
INCITER
INCITES
JACKTAR
LICITLY
LOCATED
LOCATER
LOCATES
LOCATOR
NECKTIE
OOCYTES
RECITAL
RECITED
RECITER
RECITES
RICHTER
RICOTTA
TACITLY
TACITUS
VACATED
VACATES
YACHTED
YUCATAN

••C••T•
ACCENTS
ACCEPTS
ACCOSTS
ACCRETE
ASCENTS
BECKETT
BUCKETS
CACHETS
DECANTS
DECEITS
DECOCTS
DICTATE
DOCENTS
DOCKETS
ESCORTS
EXCEPTS
EXCRETE
FACULTY
GOCARTS
HACKETT
INCANTS
INCEPTS
JACINTH
JACKETS
JOCASTA
LACOSTE
LACTATE
LOCKETS
LOCUSTS
MACBETH
MACHETE
OCCULTS
OXCARTS
PACKETS
PICANTE
PICKETS
PICKETT
POCKETS
PUCKETT
RACKETS
RECANTS
RECASTS
RECOATS
RICKETY
RICOTTA
ROCHETS
ROCKETS
SACHETS
SECANTS
SECRETE
SECRETS
SOCIETY
SOCKETS
TICKETS
TICKETY
TOCCATA
UNCOUTH
UNCRATE
VACUITY
WICHITA
WICKETS

••C•••T
ACCOUNT
ACCURST
ANCIENT
BACKBIT
BACKLIT
BACKOUT
BECKETT
COCKPIT
COCONUT
CYCLIST
DECKOUT
DECRYPT
DICIEST
ENCHANT
ENCRUST
ENCRYPT
ESCHEAT
ETCHANT
EXCERPT
HACKETT
INCIPIT
JACKPOT
JACONET
KICKOUT
LACIEST
LOCKNUT
LOCKOUT
LUCKOUT
OCCIPUT
PACKRAT
PECCANT
PECKSAT
PICKETT
PICKOUT
PICKSAT
PUCKETT
RACIEST
RACQUET
RECEIPT
RECOUNT
RECRUIT
RICERAT
RICHEST
SACKOUT
SICKEST
SICKOUT

•••CT••
CHOCTAW
EJECTED
ELECTED
ELECTEE
ELECTOR
ELECTRA
ELECTRO
ENACTED
ENACTOR
ERECTED
ERECTER
ERECTLY
ERECTOR
ERUCTED
EVICTED
EXACTAS
EXACTED
EXACTER
EXACTLY
EXACTOR
FRACTAL
MULCTED
PLECTRA
PROCTOR
REACTED
REACTOR
REACTTO
SANCTUM
SPECTER
SPECTOR
SPECTRA
SPECTRE
TRACTOR

•••C•T•
AVOCETS
BAYCITY
BOBCATS
BOYCOTT
CALCITE
EDACITY
EDUCATE
ELICITS
EXECUTE
FATCATS
FATCITY
FAUCETS
FAWCETT
FLOCKTO
HEPCATS
LANCETS
MARCATO
MASCOTS
MUDCATS
MUSCATS
OPACITY
PAUCITY
PLACATE
REACTTO
REXCATS
SNOCATS
STICKTO
STUCKTO
SUNCITY
TERCETS
TOCCATA
TOMCATS
TRICOTS
WALCOTT

•••C••T
BISCUIT
BOYCOTT
BRACKET
CARCOAT
CIRCLET
CIRCUIT
CONCEIT
CONCEPT
CONCERT
CONCOCT
CRICKET
CROCHET
DESCANT
DESCENT
DOGCART
FAWCETT
FLYCAST
HATCHET
LABCOAT
LITCRIT
LOWCOST
MISCAST
NASCENT
OUTCAST
PEACOAT
PECCANT
PERCENT
PLACKET
PRECAST
PRECEPT
RATCHET
REDCENT
REDCOAT
SURCOAT
TEACART
TENCENT
THICKET
TOPCOAT
VINCENT
WALCOTT
WATCHIT

••••CT•
ABDUCTS
ADDUCTS
AFFECTS
ASPECTS
BISECTS
DECOCTS
DEDUCTS
DEFACTO
DEFECTS
DEJECTS
DELICTI
DELICTS
DEPICTS
DETECTS
DIDACTS
DIRECTS
EFFECTS
EXFACTO
EXPECTS
IMPACTS
INDICTS
INDUCTS
INFECTS
INJECTS
INSECTS
OBJECTS
OUTACTS
REDACTS
REJECTS
RELICTS
RELUCTS
RESECTS
SELECTS

••••C•T
APRICOT
BEARCAT
BORSCHT
COLDCUT
COONCAT
COPYCAT
CREWCUT
CURBCUT
DEFICIT
DOVECOT
HAIRCUT
HARICOT
HELLCAT
ILLICIT
JUMPCUT
MANXCAT
MONOCOT
POLECAT
SNOWCAT
SOLICIT
UTRECHT
WILDCAT
WOODCUT

•••••CT
ADJUNCT
AFFLICT
ATTRACT
COLLECT
COMPACT
CONCOCT
CONDUCT
CONNECT
CONTACT
CONVICT
CORRECT
DEFLECT
DEFUNCT
DETRACT
DIALECT
DISSECT
EXTINCT
EXTRACT
INEXACT
INFLECT
INFLICT
INSPECT
NEGLECT
OVERACT
PANDECT
PERFECT
PLAYACT
PREDICT
PREFECT
PRODUCT
PROJECT
PROTECT
REELECT
REENACT
REFLECT
REFRACT
RESPECT
RETRACT
RIOTACT
SUBJECT
SUSPECT
TRISECT
VERDICT
VIADUCT

CU•••••
CUBBIES
CUBBISH
CUBICLE
CUBISTS
CUCKOOS
CUDDIES
CUDDLED
CUDDLES
CUDGELS
CUEBALL
CUECARD
CUFFING
CUIBONO
CUIRASS
CUISINE
CULEBRA
CULLERS
CULLIED
CULLIES
CULLING
CULOTTE
CULPRIT
CULTISH
CULTISM
CULTIST
CULTJAM
CULTURE
CULVERS
CULVERT
CUMULUS
CUNNING
CUPCAKE
CUPFULS
CUPLIKE
CUPOLAS
CUPPING
CURACAO
CURATES
CURATOR
CURBCUT
CURBING
CURDIER
CURDING
CURDLED
CURDLES
CUREALL
CURFEWS
CURIOUS
CURLERS
CURLEWS
CURLIER
CURLIKE
CURLING
CURLSUP
CURRANT
CURRENT
CURRIED
CURRIER
CURRIES
CURRISH
CURSING
CURSIVE
CURSORS
CURSORY
CURTAIL
CURTAIN
CURTEST
CURTISS
CURTSEY
CURVETS
CURVIER
CURVING
CUSHAWS
CUSHIER
CUSHING
CUSHION
CUSPIDS
CUSSING
CUSSLER
CUSTARD
CUSTODY
CUSTOMS
CUTAWAY
CUTBACK
CUTDOWN
CUTICLE
CUTINTO
CUTLASS
CUTLERS
CUTLERY
CUTLETS
CUTOFFS
CUTOUTS
CUTRATE
CUTSOFF
CUTSOUT
CUTTERS
CUTTIME
CUTTING

C•U••••
CAUDLES
CAULKED
CAULKER
CAUSING
CAUSTIC
CAUTION
CHUCKED
CHUCKLE
CHUGGED
CHUKKAS
CHUKKER
CHUMMED
CHUNNEL
CHUNTER
CHURNED
CHUTNEY
CLUBBED
CLUBCAR
CLUCKED
CLUEDIN
CLUEING
CLUESIN
CLUMPED
CLUNKED
CLUNKER
CLUSTER
CLUTTER
COUCHED
COUCHES
COUGARS
COUGHED
COUGHUP
COULDNT
COULEES
COULOMB
COULTER
COUNCIL
COUNSEL
COUNTED
COUNTER
COUNTON
COUNTRY
COUPLED
COUPLES
COUPLET
COUPONS
COURAGE
COURANT
COURIER
COURSED
COURSER
COURSES
COURTED
COURTLY
COUSINS
COUTURE
CRUCIAL
CRUCIFY
CRUDELY
CRUDEST
CRUDITY
CRUELER
CRUELLY
CRUELTY
CRUISED
CRUISER
CRUISES
CRULLER
CRUMBLE
CRUMBLY
CRUMPET
CRUMPLE
CRUMPLY
CRUNCHY
CRUSADE
CRUSADO
CRUSHED
CRUSHER
CRUSHES
CRUSTED
CRUZADO

C••U•••
CADUCEI
CALUMET
CALUMNY
CAPULET
CASUALS
CAYUGAS
CAYUSES
CEBUANO
CERUMEN
CHAUCER
CLAUDIA
CLAUDIO
CLAUSES
CLOUDED
CLOUTED
COLUMBO
COLUMNS
CONURES
COPULAE
COPULAS
COZUMEL
CROUTON
CUMULUS

C•••U••
CADBURY
CAESURA
CAIQUES
CANFULS
CAPFULS
CAPGUNS
CAPNUTS
CAPSULE
CAPTURE
CARFULS
CAROUSE
CASQUED
CASQUES
CATSUIT
CENSURE
CENTURY
CHEQUER
CHEQUES
CHERUBS
CHINUPS
CIRCUIT
CIRCUSY
CIRQUES
CLAQUES
CLIBURN
CLIQUES
CLIQUEY
CLOQUES
CLOSURE
CLOTURE
COEQUAL
COGBURN
COLLUDE
COLOURS
COMBUST
COMMUNE
COMMUTE
COMPUTE
CONCURS
CONDUCE
CONDUCT
CONDUIT
CONFUSE
CONFUTE
CONJURE
CONQUER
CONSULS
CONSULT
CONSUME
CONTUSE
COPOUTS
CORRUPT
COSTUME
COUTURE
CROQUET
CULTURE
CUPFULS
CUTOUTS
CYYOUNG

C••••U•
CACHOUS
CADMIUM
CAESIUM
CALCIUM
CALHOUN
CALLOUS
CALLOUT
CALLSUP
CAMBIUM
CAMEDUE
CAMEOUT
CAMPOUT
CANDOUR
CANOPUS
CAREFUL
CAROLUS
CASHOUT
CASSIUS
CASTOUT
CATCHUP
CELSIUS
CENTAUR
CEPHEUS
CHALKUP
CHATSUP
CHECKUP
CHEERUP
CHETRUM
CHEWOUT
CHEWSUP
CHOKEUP
CITROUS
CLAMOUR
CLAMSUP
CLEANUP
CLEARUP
CLOGSUP
CLOSEUP
COCONUT
COILSUP
COLDCUT
COLOBUS
COMEDUE
COMEOUT
COMESUP
COMIQUE
CONKOUT
CONTOUR
COOKOUT
COOKSUP
COOPSUP
COPIOUS
COPSOUT
COUGHUP
COVERUP
CRACKUP
CRANIUM
CRANKUP
CRASSUS
CREEPUP
CREWCUT
CRISPUS
CROESUS
CROPSUP
CROSSUP
CUMULUS
CURBCUT
CURIOUS
CURLSUP
CUTSOUT

C•••••U
CARIBOU
CHAPEAU
CHATEAU
COCTEAU

•CU••••
ACUMENS
ACUTELY
ECUADOR
OCULIST
SCUDDED
SCUFFED
SCUFFLE
SCULLED
SCULLER
SCULPTS
SCUPPER
SCURVES
SCUTTLE

•C•U•••
ACCURST
ACCUSED
ACCUSER
ACCUSES
ACQUIRE
ACQUITS
ACTUARY
ACTUATE
ACTUPON
MCGUIRE
MCLUHAN
MCQUEEN
OCCULTS
OCTUPLE
SCHULTZ
SCOURED
SCOURER
SCOURGE
SCOUSES
SCOUTED
SCOUTER
SCRUBBY
SCRUBUP
SCRUFFS
SCRUFFY
SCRUMMY
SCRUNCH
SCRUPLE

•C••U••
ACCOUNT
ACCRUAL
ACCRUED
ACCRUES
ACHTUNG
ICECUBE
MCCLURE
OCCLUDE
SCAPULA

•C•••U•
ACEDOUT
ACESOUT
ACTEDUP
ACTFOUR
ACTSOUT
ECHINUS
ECLOGUE
ICEBLUE
ICEDOUT
ICESOUT
ICINGUP
MCCLOUD
OCCIPUT
OCEANUS
OCELLUS
OCTOPUS
SCAREUP
SCREWUP
SCRUBUP

••CU•••
ACCURST
ACCUSED
ACCUSER
ACCUSES
ESCUDOS
EXCUSED
EXCUSES
FACULAE
FACULTY
FICUSES
FOCUSED
FOCUSES
INCUDES
JACUZZI
JOCULAR
LACUNAE
LACUNAL
LACUNAS
LOCUSTS
MACULAE
NOCUOUS
OCCULTS
RECUSED
RECUSES
SECULAR
SECURED
SECURER
SECURES
UNCURLS
VACUITY
VACUOLE
VACUOUS
VACUUMS
VICUNAS

••C•U••
ACCOUNT
ACCRUAL
ACCRUED
ACCRUES
BACKUPS
BECAUSE
DICTUMS
ENCRUST
EXCLUDE
FACTUAL
HICCUPS
INCLUDE
JACCUSE
JACQUES
KICKUPS
LACQUER
LECTURE
LOCKUPS
LYCEUMS
MACDUFF
MCCLURE
MOCKUPS
NOCTURN
OCCLUDE
PICKUPS
PICTURE
RACQUET
RECLUSE
RECOUNT
RECOUPS
RECRUIT
SACQUES
SECLUDE
SICHUAN
SUCCUMB
UNCOUTH
VACUUMS
VICTUAL

••C••U•
ARCANUM
BACCHUS
BACKOUT
BACKRUB
BACKSUP
BECLOUD
BUCKSUP
CACHOUS
COCONUT
DECATUR
DECKOUT
DECORUM
FACTFUL
JACKSUP
KICKOUT
KICKSUP
LACEDUP
LACESUP
LOCKNUT
LOCKOUT
LOCKSUP
LUCKOUT
MACAQUE
MCCLOUD
MUCKSUP
NOCUOUS
NUCLEUS
OCCIPUT
PACKSUP
PICKOUT
PICKSUP
RACKSUP
SACKFUL
SACKOUT
SICKOUT
SUCCOUR
TACITUS
TACTFUL
VACUOUS
VICIOUS
WICKIUP

••C•••U
COCTEAU

•••CU••
BISCUIT
BLACULA
CIRCUIT
CIRCUSY
CONCURS
DISCUSS
DRACULA
EGGCUPS
EPICURE
EVACUEE
EXECUTE
EYECUPS
FESCUES
HERCULE
HICCUPS
ICECUBE
INOCULA
JACCUSE
MERCURY
MISCUED
MISCUES
OBSCURE
PINCURL
PROCURE
RESCUED
RESCUER
RESCUES
SUCCUMB
TALCUMS
TEACUPS

•••C•U•
BACCHUS
BOTCHUP
BRACEUP
CALCIUM
CATCHUP
CHECKUP
CRACKUP
FANCLUB
FULCRUM
JUICEUP
KETCHUP
KEYCLUB
LASCAUX
MATCHUP
MITCHUM
PATCHUP
PSYCHUP
PUNCHUP

QUECHUA
RANCOUR
RAUCOUS
REOCCUR
SANCTUM
SPICEUP
STACKUP
STICKUP
STOCKUP
STUCKUP
SUCCOUR
TOUCHUP
VISCOUS

•••C••U
MARCEAU

••••CU•
APERCUS
ATTICUS
BEARCUB
COLDCUT
CREWCUT
CURBCUT
HAIRCUT
INFOCUS
INVACUO
JUMPCUT
LIONCUB
MODICUM
REFOCUS
REOCCUR
WOODCUT

•••••CU
ILIESCU

C•V••••
CAVALRY
CAVEATS
CAVEDIN
CAVEINS
CAVEMAN
CAVEMEN
CAVERNS
CAVESIN
CAVETTO
CAVIARS
CAVILED
CAVILER
CAVORTS
CIVILLY
CIVVIES
COVERED
COVERUP
COVETED

C••V•••
CALVARY
CALVERT
CALVING
CANVASS
CARVERS
CARVING
CERVIDS
CHEVIED
CHEVIES
CHEVIOT
CHEVRES
CHEVRON
CIVVIES
CLAVELL
CLAVIER
CLOVERS
COEVALS
CONVENE
CONVENT
CONVERT
CONVEYS
CONVICT
CONVOKE
CONVOYS
CRAVATS
CRAVENS
CRAVERS
CRAVING
CREVICE
CULVERS
CULVERT
CURVETS
CURVIER
CURVING

C•••V••
CARAVAN
CARAVEL
CASAVAS
CHEEVER
CHERVIL
CLEAVED
CLEAVER
CLEAVES
CLEAVON

C••••V•
CAPTIVE
CASSAVA
CENTAVO
COMMOVE
CONCAVE
CONNIVE
CURSIVE

C•••••V
CABLETV
CHEKHOV

•C••V••
ACTIVES
MCGAVIN
OCTAVES
OCTAVIA
OCTAVOS
SCARVES
SCRIVEN
SCURVES

•C•••V•
ACHIEVE
ACTFIVE

••C•V••
ALCOVES
INCIVIL
RECOVER
UNCIVIL
UNCOVER

••C••V•
ANCHOVY
ARCHIVE
DECEIVE
ENCLAVE
FICTIVE
RECEIVE

••C•••V
ROCKYIV

•••C•V•
CONCAVE
MUSCOVY

C•W••••
COWARDS
COWBELL
COWBIRD
COWBOYS
COWERED
COWGIRL
COWHAND
COWHERD
COWHIDE
COWLICK
COWLIKE
COWLING
COWPEAS
COWPOKE
COWPONY
COWRIES
COWSLIP
COWTOWN

C••W•••
CARWASH
CATWALK
CHEWERS
CHEWIER
CHEWING
CHEWOUT
CHEWSUP
CHEWTOY
CHOWDER
CLAWERS
CLAWING
CLOWDER
CLOWNED
COBWEBS
CRAWDAD
CRAWLED
CRAWLER
CREWCUT
CREWELS
CREWING
CREWMAN
CREWMEN
CROWBAR
CROWDED
CROWERS
CROWING
CROWNED
CRYWOLF

C•••W••
CARAWAY
CATAWBA
CNTOWER
COLDWAR
CSLEWIS
CUTAWAY

C••••W•
CASHEWS
COWTOWN
CURFEWS
CURLEWS
CUSHAWS
CUTDOWN

C•••••W
CAPSHAW
CASELAW
CASHCOW
CATSHOW
CATSPAW
CHOCTAW
CORNROW

•CW••••
NCWYETH

•C•W•••
MCSWINE
SCHWINN
SCOWLED
SCOWLER

•C••W••
SCRAWLS
SCRAWLY
SCRAWNY
SCREWED
SCREWUP

•C••••W
ICESHOW

••C•W••
ARCHWAY
RACEWAY

••C••W•
ESCHEWS
ESCROWS

••C•••W
BUCKSAW
HACKSAW
JACKDAW
MACGRAW

•••C•W•
ANTCOWS
SEACOWS

•••C••W
AIRCREW
ATECROW
CHOCTAW
DEWCLAW
DOGCHOW
EATCROW
SALCHOW
THECROW
UNSCREW

••••C•W
CASHCOW
HOLYCOW
MILKCOW

C•X••••
COXCOMB

C••X•••
COAXERS
COAXIAL
COAXING
COEXIST

C•••X••
CALYXES

C••••X•
CONTEXT

C•••••X
CAKEMIX
CALLBOX
CASHBOX
CINEMAX
COMPLEX

•C••X••
ICEAXES

••C••X•
PICKAXE

••C•••X
LOCKBOX
STCROIX

•••C••X
LASCAUX
PANCHAX

CY•••••
CYBORGS
CYCLERS
CYCLING
CYCLIST
CYCLONE
CYCLOPS
CYGNETS
CYMBALS
CYNICAL
CYNTHIA
CYPHERS
CYPRESS
CYPRIOT
CYYOUNG

C•Y••••
CAYENNE
CAYMANS
CAYUGAS
CAYUSES
COYNESS
COYOTES
CRYBABY
CRYOGEN
CRYPTIC
CRYPTOS
CRYSTAL
CRYWOLF
CYYOUNG

C••Y•••
CALYCES
CALYPSO
CALYXES
CANYONS
CLAYIER
CLAYISH
CLAYTON
CLOYING
COPYBOY
COPYCAT
COPYING
COPYIST
COZYING
CRAYOLA
CRAYONS

C•••Y••
CARLYLE
CARRYON
COLLYER

C••••Y•
CARBOYS
CAROLYN
CATSEYE
CONVEYS
CONVOYS
COWBOYS

C•••••Y
CACANNY
CADBURY
CADENCY
CALCIFY
CALGARY
CALUMNY
CALVARY
CAMPILY
CANNERY
CANNILY
CANTILY
CAPABLY
CARAWAY
CASSIDY
CATTILY
CAVALRY
CENTURY
CERTIFY
CHANTEY
CHARILY
CHARITY
CHARLEY
CHEAPLY
CHEWTOY
CHICORY
CHIEFLY
CHIMNEY
CHINTZY
CHOMSKY
CHRISTY
CHUTNEY
CINDERY
CIRCUSY
CIVILLY
CLARIFY
CLARITY
CLEANLY
CLEARLY
CLERISY
CLIQUEY
CLOONEY
CLOSEBY
CLOSELY
COCKILY
COCKNEY
COCKSHY
COGENCY
COMESBY
COMFREY
COMPANY
CONAKRY
CONNERY
COOKERY
COPPERY
COPYBOY
CORNILY
COTTONY
COUNTRY
COURTLY
COWPONY
CRACKLY
CRAFTSY
CRASSLY
CRAZILY
CRINKLY
CRISPLY
CROSSLY
CRUCIFY
CRUDELY
CRUDITY
CRUELLY
CRUELTY
CRUMBLY
CRUMPLY
CRUNCHY
CRYBABY
CURSORY
CURTSEY
CUSTODY
CUTAWAY
CUTLERY

•CY••••
SCYTHED
SCYTHES

•C•Y•••
ACRYLIC
ECDYSES
ECDYSIS
ECTYPES
NCWYETH

•C••Y••
ACOLYTE

•C•••Y•
ACRONYM

•C••••Y
ACADEMY
ACIDIFY
ACIDITY
ACRIDLY
ACTUARY
ACUTELY
ECOLOGY
ECONOMY
ECSTASY
MCHENRY
SCANTLY
SCARIFY
SCARILY
SCENERY
SCRAGGY
SCRAPPY
SCRAWLY
SCRAWNY
SCRIMPY
SCRUBBY
SCRUFFY
SCRUMMY
WCHANDY

••CY•••
BICYCLE
OOCYTES
RECYCLE

••C•Y••
DACTYLS
DECAYED
DECOYED
DECRYPT
ENCRYPT
ROCKYII
ROCKYIV

••C••Y•
BUCKEYE
DICKEYS
JACKEYS
JOCKEYS
LACKEYS
MICKEYS
RICKEYS
SOCKEYE

••C•••Y
ALCHEMY
ANCHOVY
ARCHERY
ARCHWAY
BACKBAY
BUCKLEY
CACANNY
COCKILY
COCKNEY
COCKSHY
DECENCY
FACTORY
FACULTY
HACKNEY
HICKORY
LICITLY
LOCALLY
LUCENCY
LUCIDLY
LUCKILY
MOCKERY
MUCKILY
PECCARY
PICARDY
RACEWAY
RECENCY
RECTIFY
RECTORY
RICKETY
ROCKERY
SECRECY
SICKBAY
SICKDAY
SICKPAY
SOCIETY
TACITLY
TACKILY
TICKETY
UNCANNY
VACANCY
VACUITY
VICEROY
VICTORY
VOCALLY
WACKILY
ZACHARY

•••CY••
HALCYON
PROCYON

•••C••Y
AMSCRAY
BALCONY
BAYCITY
BLACKLY
BOKCHOY
CALCIFY
CHICORY
CIRCUSY
CRACKLY
CRUCIFY
DULCIFY
EDACITY
ERECTLY
EXACTLY
FANCIFY
FANCILY
FATCITY
FRECKLY
GASCONY
GROCERY
JUICILY
LARCENY
MERCERY
MERCURY
MUSCOVY
OPACITY
PAUCITY
PECCARY
PRICKLY
QUICKLY
SAUCILY
SLACKLY
SLICKLY
SORCERY
SPECIFY
SPICERY
SPICILY
SUNCITY
THICKLY
TRACERY
TUSCANY

••••C•Y
ANARCHY
BLOTCHY
CRUNCHY
EPARCHY
FINICKY
GROUCHY
KITSCHY
KOLACKY
MIMICRY
PANICKY
PAUNCHY
PREACHY
SKETCHY
SLOUCHY
SNITCHY
STARCHY
THATCHY
TREACLY
TWITCHY
UNLUCKY

•••••CY
ABBOTCY
ARDENCY
CADENCY
COGENCY
DECENCY
ERRANCY
FALLACY
FLOUNCY
FLUENCY
INFANCY
LATENCY
LUCENCY
PLIANCY
POTENCY
PRIMACY
PRIVACY
PUDENCY
RECENCY
REGENCY
SECRECY
TENANCY
TRUANCY
URGENCY
VACANCY
VALENCY

CZ•••••
CZARDAS
CZARDOM
CZARINA
CZARISM
CZARIST

C•Z••••
CEZANNE
COZENED
COZIEST
COZUMEL
COZYING
COZZENS

C••Z•••
CALZONE
CANZONE
CINZANO
COZZENS
CRAZIER
CRAZIES
CRAZILY
CRAZING
CRUZADO

C•••Z••
CITIZEN
CORAZON

C••••Z•
CADENZA
CAPSIZE
CARDOZO
CHINTZY
CHORIZO

•C•••Z•
SCHATZI
SCHERZI
SCHERZO

•C••••Z
SCHULTZ

••C•Z••
ALCAZAR
JACUZZI

••C••Z•
JACUZZI

•••C••Z
NATCHEZ

DA•••••
DABBING
DABBLED
DABBLER
DABBLES
DABHAND
DACTYLS
DADAISM
DADAIST
DADDIES
DAFFIER
DAFFILY
DAFFING
DAFTEST
DAGGERS
DAGWOOD
DAHLIAS
DAHOMEY
DAILIES
DAIMLER
DAIMONS
DAIRIES
DAISIES
DAKOTAN
DAKOTAS
DALETHS
DALLIED
DALLIER
DALLIES
DALTREY
DAMAGED
DAMAGES
DAMASKS
DAMMARS
DAMMING
DAMNING
DAMPENS
DAMPERS
DAMPEST
DAMPING
DAMPISH
DAMSELS
DAMSONS
DANBURY
DANCERS
DANCING
DANDERS
DANDIER
DANDIES
DANDIFY
DANDLED
DANDLES
DANELAW
DANGERS
DANGLED
DANGLER
DANGLES
DANIELS
DANKEST
DANSEUR
DAPHNIS
DAPPING
DAPPLED
DAPPLES
DARBIES
DAREFUL
DARESAY
DARESTO
DARKENS
DARKEST
DARKISH
DARKMAN
DARLENE
DARLING
DARNERS
DARNING
DARNLEY
DARTERS
DARTING
DASBOOT
DASHERS
DASHIKI
DASHING
DASHOFF
DASTARD
DASYURE
DATASET
DATEDLY
DAUBERS
DAUBING
DAUMIER
DAUNTED
DAUPHIN
DAVINCI
DAWDLED
DAWDLER
DAWDLES
DAWKISH
DAWNING
DAWNSON
DAYBEDS
DAYBOOK
DAYBOYS
DAYCAMP
DAYCARE
DAYJOBS
DAYLILY
DAYLONG
DAYMARE
DAYROOM
DAYSINN
DAYSTAR
DAYTIME
DAYTONA
DAYTRIP
DAZEDLY
DAZZLED
DAZZLER
DAZZLES

D•A••••
DEACONS
DEADAIR
DEADEND
DEADENS
DEADEYE
DEADPAN
DEADSEA
DEADSET
DEAFENS
DEAFEST
DEALERS
DEALING
DEALOUT
DEALSIN
DEALTIN
DEANERY
DEAREST
DEARIES
DEARSIR
DEARTHS
DIABOLI
DIADEMS
DIAGRAM
DIALECT
DIALERS
DIALING
DIALOGS
DIAMOND
DIAPERS
DIARIES
DIATOMS
DRABBER
DRACHMA
DRACHMS
DRACULA
DRAFTED
DRAFTEE
DRAGGED
DRAGGER
DRAGNET
DRAGONS
DRAGOON
DRAGOUT
DRAGSIN
DRAGSON
DRAINED
DRAINER
DRAPERS
DRAPERY
DRAPING
DRASTIC
DRATTED
DRAUGHT
DRAWBAR
DRAWERS
DRAWING
DRAWLED
DRAWNIN
DRAWNON
DRAWNUP
DRAWOUT
DRAWSIN
DRAWSON
DRAWSUP
DRAYAGE
DRAYING
DUALITY
DWARFED
DWARVES

D••A•••
DADAISM
DADAIST
DAMAGED
DAMAGES
DAMASKS
DATASET
DEBACLE
DEBAKEY
DEBARGE
DEBARKS
DEBASED
DEBASES
DEBATED
DEBATER
DEBATES
DEBAUCH
DECADES
DECAGON
DECALOG
DECAMPS
DECANTS
DECAPOD
DECARLO
DECATUR
DECAYED
DEDALUS
DEFACED
DEFACES
DEFACTO
DEFALLA
DEFAMED
DEFAMES
DEFARGE
DEFAULT
DEGAUSS
DELANEY
DELAYED
DELAYER
DEMANDS
DENARII
DEPALMA
DEPARTS
DERAILS
DESALTS
DETAILS
DETAINS
DEVALUE
DIDACTS
DILATED
DILATES
DISABLE
DISARMS
DISAVOW
DOMAINS
DONAHUE
DONATED
DONATES
DONATOR
DOPANTS
DOSAGES
DOTARDS
DOWAGER
DREADED
DREAMED
DREAMER
DREAMON
DREAMUP
DUBARRY
DUKAKIS
DUNAWAY
DURABLE
DURABLY
DURANCE
DURANGO
DURANTE
DYNAMIC
DYNAMOS
DYNASTS
DYNASTY

D•••A••
DABHAND
DAMMARS
DASTARD
DAYCAMP
DAYCARE
DAYMARE
DEADAIR
DECLAIM
DECLARE
DECLASS
DEEJAYS
DEFEATS
DEFIANT
DEFLATE
DEFRAUD
DEFRAYS
DEGRADE
DELTAIC
DEMEANS
DENIALS
DENMARK
DENTATE
DEODARS
DEPLANE
DEPRAVE
DESCANT
DESPAIR
DETRACT
DETRAIN
DEVIANT
DEVIATE
DEWLAPS
DICTATE
DIEHARD
DIETARY
DIGRAMS

DIGRAPH
DIKTATS
DILLARD
DIORAMA
DISBAND
DISBARS
DISCARD
DISDAIN
DISEASE
DISMAYS
DISTAFF
DISTANT
DITTANY
DOCKAGE
DOGBANE
DOGCART
DOGDAYS
DOGEARS
DOGFACE
DOGMATA
DOGTAGS
DOLLARS
DOLMANS
DOODADS
DOODAHS
DORMANT
DORSALS
DOSSALS
DRAYAGE
DRYWALL
DUEDATE
DULLARD

D••••A•

DAHLIAS
DAKOTAN
DAKOTAS
DANELAW
DARESAY
DARKMAN
DAYSTAR
DEADPAN
DEBORAH
DECIMAL
DEEPFAT
DELILAH
DEPOSAL
DEWCLAW
DIAGRAM
DIGITAL
DINGBAT
DIPOLAR
DISHPAN
DISHRAG
DISPLAY
DIURNAL
DOGSTAR
DONEGAL
DONJUAN
DONOVAN
DOORMAN
DOORMAT
DOORWAY
DOUGLAS
DOWNPAT
DRAWBAR
DRIPPAN
DRISTAN
DRIVEAT
DUENNAS
DUNAWAY
DUSTMAN
DUSTPAN

D•••••A

DAYTONA
DEADSEA
DEEPSEA
DEFALLA
DELIRIA
DEPALMA
DILEMMA
DIORAMA
DIPLOMA
DOGMATA
DRACHMA
DRACULA
DUODENA
DYKSTRA

•DA••••

ADAGIOS
ADAMANT
ADAMITE
ADAMSON
ADAPTED
ADAPTER
ADAPTOR
EDACITY
EDAPHIC
EDASNER
IDAHOAN

•D•A•••

ADDABLE
ADVANCE
EDWARDS
IDCARDS
IDEALLY
IDEAMAN
IDEAMEN
IDEATED
IDEATES
IDIAMIN
PDJAMES
RDLAING

•D••A••

ADAMANT
ADONAIS
ADULATE
EDOUARD
EDUCATE
ODDBALL

•D•••A•

ADMIRAL
ADRENAL
IDAHOAN
IDEAMAN

•D••••A

ADDENDA

••DA•••

ADDABLE
ANDANTE
BEDAUBS
CEDARED
DADAISM
DADAIST
DEDALUS
DIDACTS
HIDALGO
IODATES
JUDAISM
MADAMEX
MEDALED
ORDAINS
PEDALED
PEDANTS
REDACTS
REDALGA
REDANTS
REDATED
REDATES
SEDALIA
SEDATED
SEDATER
SEDATES
SODAPOP
UNDATED
UPDATED
UPDATES
VEDANTA
VIDALIA

••D•A••

ANDEANS
BEDLAMP
BIDFAIR
ENDEARS
ENDGAME
ENDWAYS
GODDARD
HYDRANT
HYDRATE
INDIANA
INDIANS
KIDNAPS
KODIAKS
MADCAPS
MEDIANS
MEDIANT
MEDIATE
MIDDAYS
MIDEAST
MIDLAND
MIDWAYS
MUDCATS
MUDPACK
ODDBALL
OGDOADS
OLDDAYS
OLDHAND
OLDMAID
OLDSAWS
ORDEALS
PADUANS
PEDLARS
PEDWAYS
RADIALS
RADIANS
RADIANT
RADIATE
REDCAPS
REDEALS
REDEALT
REDHAIR
REDHATS
REDIALS
REDOAKS
REDRAWN
REDRAWS
REDTAPE
RUDYARD
SADSACK
SIDEARM
TEDMACK
UNDRAPE
UNDRAWN
UPDRAFT
WIDMARK
ZEDBARS
ZODIACS

••D••A•

ANDREAS
BODEGAS
BODYFAT
BUDDHAS
CADDOAN
ENDPLAY
FADIMAN
FEDERAL
FEDORAS
GIDDYAP
GODTHAB
HADRIAN
LADYDAY
MADEHAY
MADEPAR
MADEWAY
MADIGAN
MEDEVAC
MEDICAL
MEDIGAP
MEDUSAE
MEDUSAS
MIDYEAR
MODELAS
MODULAR
NODULAR
OEDIPAL
OLDCHAP
OLDUVAI
ORDINAL
PADUCAH
PEDICAB
RADICAL
RADULAE
REDCOAT
REDFLAG
REDHEAD
REDHEAT
REDMEAT
REDSTAR
RIDGWAY
SIDEBAR
SIDECAR
SIDEMAN

••D•••A

ADDENDA
ANDORRA
BEDELIA
CADENZA
CEDILLA
INDIANA
INDICIA
KEDROVA
MADEIRA
MADONNA
MEDULLA
PODRIDA
REDALGA
SEDALIA
VEDANTA
VIDALIA

•••DA••

AIRDAMS
AIRDATE
ALIDADE
AOUDADS
BANDAGE
BANDAID
BANDANA
BELDAME
BELDAMS
BONDAGE
BRIDALS
CORDAGE
CORDATE
DEADAIR
DEODARS
DISDAIN
DOGDAYS
DOODADS
DOODAHS
DUEDATE
FONDANT
FRIDAYS
GODDARD
GOODALL
HEYDAYS
HOWDAHS
INADAZE
KENDALL
KILDARE
LANDAUS
MANDALA
MANDANS
MANDATE
MANDAYS
MAYDAYS
MIDDAYS
MISDATE
MONDALE
MONDAYS
MORDANT
MUNDANE
OLDDAYS
ONADARE
ONADATE
OXIDANT
OXIDASE
PAYDAYS
PENDANT
PREDATE
PREDAWN
PURDAHS
RANDALL
RAWDATA
SANDALS
SUNDAES
SUNDAYS
VANDALS
VERDANT
WHYDAHS
WOODARD
YARDAGE
YARDARM

•••D•A•

ACADIAN
BANDSAW
BIGDEAL
BIRDMAN
BONDMAN
BUDDHAS
CADDOAN
CARDIAC
CHEDDAR
COLDWAR
CORDIAL
DEADPAN
FEEDBAG
FELDMAN
FORDHAM
GIDDYAP
GOODBAR
GOODMAN
GORDIAN
GRADUAL
HANDBAG
HANDCAR
HANDSAW
HARDHAT
HARDPAN
HEADMAN
HEADWAY
LANDSAT
LINDSAY
MISDEAL
MISDIAL
NEEDHAM
NEWDEAL
OBADIAH
OUTDRAW
PHIDIAS
RAWDEAL
ROADMAP
ROADWAY
RONDEAU
SANDBAG
SANDBAR
SANDMAN
SUNDIAL
TRUDEAU
TUNDRAS
WILDCAT
WINDBAG
YARDMAN
YESDEAR

•••D••A

BANDANA
CALDERA
CANDELA
CANDIDA
CONDITA
CORDOBA
DEADSEA
DUODENA
GONDOLA
ICEDTEA
ISADORA
MANDALA
MANDELA
MENDOZA
MOLDOVA
PANDORA
RAWDATA

••••DA•

AGENDAS
AIMEDAT
ARMADAS
BAGHDAD
BIMODAL
BIPEDAL
BRENDAN
BROADAX
CHEDDAR
CICADAE
CICADAS
CRAWDAD
CZARDAS
FARADAY
FLAGDAY
FRIEDAN
GELADAS
GRANDAM
HALFDAN
HIGHDAY
HOLIDAY
HOLYDAY
HYUNDAI
JACKDAW
JOURDAN
LADYDAY
LAMBDAS
MACADAM
MILLDAM
NAMEDAY
NEVADAN
NEWSDAY
NOONDAY
ONEIDAS
OVOIDAL
PAGODAS
PANADAS
PAWEDAT
POKEDAT
POSADAS
POTSDAM
QINGDAO
RAMADAN
RAMADAS
REMUDAS
RUANDAN
RWANDAN
SAMEDAY
SCANDAL
SICKDAY
SNOWDAY
SOLEDAD
SOMEDAY
SYNODAL
TUESDAY
UGANDAN
WEEKDAY
WORKDAY

••••D•A

ARCADIA
CLAUDIA
ECHIDNA
GRANDMA
GRANDPA
JUNKDNA
PHAEDRA

•••••DA

ADDENDA
AIRMADA
ALAMEDA
BARBUDA
BELINDA
BERMUDA
CANDIDA
CORRIDA
ESTRADA
FLORIDA
GRANADA
GRENADA
LAMBADA
LASORDA
MATILDA
MELINDA
MIRANDA
OCANADA
PODRIDA
RIGVEDA
ROTUNDA
SALSODA
SHOULDA
TOSTADA
VERANDA

D•B••••

DABBING
DABBLED
DABBLER
DABBLES
DABHAND
DEBACLE
DEBAKEY
DEBARGE
DEBARKS
DEBASED
DEBASES
DEBATED
DEBATER
DEBATES
DEBAUCH
DEBEERS
DEBITED
DEBONED
DEBONES
DEBORAH
DEBOUCH
DEBRIEF
DEBTORS
DEBUNKS
DEBUSSY
DEBUTED
DIBBLED
DIBBLES
DOBBIES
DOBBINS
DUBARRY
DUBBERS
DUBBING
DUBIETY
DUBIOUS
DUBUQUE
DYBBUKS

D••B•••

DABBING
DABBLED
DABBLER
DABBLES
DANBURY
DARBIES
DASBOOT
DAUBERS
DAUBING
DAYBEDS
DAYBOOK
DAYBOYS
DERBIES
DIABOLI
DIBBLED
DIBBLES
DILBERT
DIMBULB
DISBAND
DISBARS
DOBBIES
DOBBINS
DOGBANE
DOGBERT
DOUBLED
DOUBLES
DOUBLET
DOUBLEU
DOUBTED
DOUBTER
DRABBER
DRIBBLE
DRIBLET
DRUBBED
DUBBERS
DUBBING
DUMBEST
DUMBING
DYBBUKS

D•••B••

DECIBEL
DELIBES
DINGBAT
DISABLE
DISOBEY
DOWNBOW
DRABBER
DRAWBAR
DRIBBLE
DRUBBED
DURABLE
DURABLY
DUSTBIN

D••••B•

DAYJOBS
DISROBE
DROPSBY

D•••••B

DIMBULB
DISTURB

•D•B•••

EDIBLES
ODDBALL

•D••B••

ADDABLE
ADDIBLE

•D•••B•

ADSORBS
ADVERBS
ODDJOBS

••DB•••

BADBOYS
BEDBUGS
CADBURY
ODDBALL
REDBIRD
REDBOOK
REDBUDS
SUDBURY
TIDBITS
ZEDBARS

••D•B••

ADDABLE
ADDIBLE
AUDIBLE
AUDIBLY
AUDUBON
LADYBUG
SIDEBAR
SIDEBET

••D••B•

BEDAUBS
INDOUBT
MADLIBS
MIDRIBS
NODOUBT
ODDJOBS
REDOUBT

••D•••B

GODTHAB
PEDICAB

•••DB••

BANDBOX
FEEDBAG
GOLDBUG
GOODBAR
GOODBYE
GOODBYS
HANDBAG
ROADBED
SANDBAG
SANDBAR
SANDBOX
SEEDBED
WINDBAG

•••D•B•

ABIDEBY
CORDOBA
SUBDEBS

•••D••B

FOODWEB
GOODJOB

••••DB•

BYANDBY
STANDBY
STOODBY
WOULDBE

••••D•B

OVERDUB

D•C••••

DACTYLS
DECADES
DECAGON
DECALOG
DECAMPS
DECANTS
DECAPOD
DECARLO
DECATUR
DECAYED
DECEITS
DECEIVE
DECENCY
DECIBEL
DECIDED
DECIDES
DECIMAL
DECKING
DECKLES
DECKOUT
DECLAIM
DECLARE
DECLASS
DECLINE
DECOCTS
DECODED
DECODER
DECODES
DECORUM
DECOYED
DECREED
DECREES
DECRIED
DECRIER
DECRIES
DECRYPT
DICIEST
DICKENS
DICKERS
DICKEYS
DICKIES
DICTATE
DICTION
DICTUMS
DOCENTS
DOCKAGE
DOCKERS
DOCKETS
DOCKING
DOCTORS
DUCHESS
DUCHIES
DUCKIER
DUCKING
DUCKPIN
DUCTILE
DUCTING

D••C•••

DANCERS
DANCING
DAYCAMP
DAYCARE
DEACONS
DEICERS
DEICING
DESCANT
DESCEND
DESCENT
DEWCLAW
DIOCESE
DISCARD
DISCERN
DISCOED
DISCORD
DISCUSS
DITCHED
DITCHES
DOGCART
DOGCHOW
DRACHMA
DRACHMS
DRACULA
DRUCKER
DRYCELL
DULCIFY
DUNCISH

D•••C••

DEBACLE
DECOCTS
DEDUCED
DEDUCES
DEDUCTS
DEFACED
DEFACES
DEFACTO
DEFECTS
DEFICIT
DEJECTS
DELICTI
DELICTS
DEPICTS
DETECTS
DEVICES
DIDACTS
DIRECTS
DOVECOT

D••••C•

DAVINCI
DEBAUCH
DEBOUCH
DECENCY
DEFENCE
DEFLECT
DEFROCK
DEFUNCT
DEHISCE
DERRICK
DETRACT
DIALECT
DIPTYCH
DISSECT
DIVORCE
DNOTICE
DOGFACE
DORMICE
DRSPOCK
DRYDOCK
DUNNOCK
DURANCE

D•••••C

DELPHIC
DELTAIC
DEMONIC
DRASTIC
DYNAMIC

•DC••••

IDCARDS

•D•C•••

EDACITY
EDUCATE
EDUCING

•D••C••

ADDUCED
ADDUCES
ADDUCTS

•D•••C•

ADJUNCT
ADVANCE
EDIFICE

•D••••C

EDAPHIC
IDENTIC
IDIOTIC
IDYLLIC

••DC•••

MADCAPS
MADCHEN
MUDCATS
OLDCHAP
REDCAPS
REDCELL
REDCENT
REDCOAT

••D•C••

ABDUCTS
ADDUCED
ADDUCES
ADDUCTS
BEDECKS
BODICES
CADUCEI
CODICES
CODICIL
DEDUCED
DEDUCES
DEDUCTS
DIDACTS
INDICES
INDICIA
INDICTS
INDUCED
INDUCER
INDUCES
INDUCTS
MEDICAL
MEDICOS
MODICUM
PADUCAH
PEDICAB
PEDICEL
PEDICLE
RADICAL
RADICES
RADICLE
REDACTS
REDUCED
REDUCER
REDUCES
SEDUCED
SEDUCER
SEDUCES
SIDECAR
ZYDECOS

••D••C•

ALDRICH
ARDENCY
BEDROCK
CADENCE
CADENCY
GODUTCH
HADDOCK
INDUTCH
MUDPACK
OLDNICK
PADDOCK
PADLOCK
PUDENCY
RIDDICK
SADSACK
TEDMACK
WEDLOCK
ZODIACS

••D•••C

ENDEMIC
MEDEVAC
MIDDLEC

•••DC••

COLDCUT
HANDCAR
WILDCAT
WOODCUT

•••D•C•

ARTDECO
BURDOCK
CANDICE
CONDUCE
CONDUCT
DRYDOCK
FOSDICK
HADDOCK
MURDOCH
NORDICS
PADDOCK
PANDECT
PREDICT
PRODUCE
PRODUCT
RIDDICK
SUNDECK
TRADUCE
VANDYCK
VERDICT
VIADUCT

•••D••C

BALDRIC
CARDIAC
FREDRIC
MIDDLEC

••••D•C

COMEDIC
HASIDIC
JURIDIC
MELODIC
MONODIC
NOMADIC
PAPADOC
SYNODIC

D•D••••

DADAISM
DADAIST
DADDIES
DEDALUS
DEDUCED
DEDUCES
DEDUCTS
DIDACTS
DIDDLED
DIDDLES
DIDDLEY
DIDEROT
DIDGOOD
DIDOVER
DODDERS
DODGERS
DODGIER
DODGING
DODGSON
DUDEDUP
DUDGEON

D••D•••

DADDIES
DANDERS
DANDIER
DANDIES
DANDIFY
DANDLED
DANDLES
DAWDLED
DAWDLER
DAWDLES
DEADAIR
DEADEND
DEADENS
DEADEYE
DEADPAN
DEADSEA
DEADSET
DEEDING
DENDRON
DEODARS

DEWDROP
DIADEMS
DIDDLED
DIDDLES
DIDDLEY
DIEDOFF
DIEDOUT
DIEDOWN
DIKDIKS
DISDAIN
DODDERS
DOGDAYS
DOODADS
DOODAHS
DOODLED
DOODLER
DOODLES
DOWDIER
DOWDILY
DREDGED
DREDGER
DREDGES
DRUDGED
DRUDGES
DRYDOCK
DUEDATE
DUMDUMS
DUODENA

D•••D••

DATEDLY
DAZEDLY
DECADES
DECIDED
DECIDES
DECODED
DECODER
DECODES
DELUDED
DELUDES
DENUDED
DENUDES
DERIDED
DERIDES
DINEDIN
DINEDON
DIRNDLS
DIVIDED
DIVIDER
DIVIDES
DOORDIE
DOSIDOS
DOTEDON
DREADED
DREIDEL
DRESDEN
DRIEDUP
DRIPDRY
DUDEDUP
DUKEDOM
DWINDLE

D••••D•

DAYBEDS
DEFENDS
DEGRADE
DEMANDS
DEPENDS
DIOMEDE
DIOXIDE
DOODADS
DOTARDS

D•••••D

DABBLED
DABHAND
DAGWOOD
DALLIED
DAMAGED
DANDLED
DANGLED
DAPPLED
DASTARD
DAUNTED
DAWDLED
DAZZLED
DEADEND
DEBASED
DEBATED
DEBITED
DEBONED
DEBUTED
DECAPOD
DECAYED
DECIDED
DECODED
DECOYED
DECREED
DECRIED
DEDUCED
DEEPEND
DEFACED
DEFAMED
DEFILED
DEFINED
DEFRAUD
DEFUSED
DEIFIED
DEIGNED
DELAYED
DELETED
DELTOID
DELUDED
DELUGED
DEMIGOD
DEMISED
DEMOTED
DENOTED
DENUDED
DEPONED
DEPOSED
DEPUTED
DERIDED
DERIVED
DESCEND
DESIRED
DESMOND
DEVILED
DEVISED
DEVOTED
DIAMOND
DIBBLED
DIDDLED
DIDGOOD
DIEHARD
DILATED
DILLARD
DILUTED
DIMPLED
DIPLOID
DIRTIED
DISBAND
DISCARD
DISCOED
DISCORD
DISTEND
DISUSED
DITCHED
DITTOED
DIVIDED
DIVINED
DIVVIED
DIZENED
DIZZIED
DOGFOOD
DOGSLED
DOGWOOD
DOLLIED
DONATED
DOODLED
DOUBLED
DOUBTED
DOWERED
DRAFTED
DRAGGED
DRAINED
DRATTED
DRAWLED
DREADED
DREAMED
DREDGED
DRESSED
DRIFTED
DRILLED
DRIPPED
DROOLED
DROOPED
DROPPED
DROWNED
DROWSED
DRUBBED
DRUDGED
DRUGGED
DRUMMED
DRYEYED
DULLARD
DUMMIED
DWARFED
DWELLED

•DD••••

ADDABLE
ADDEDIN
ADDEDON
ADDEDTO
ADDEDUP
ADDENDA
ADDENDS
ADDIBLE
ADDISON
ADDLING
ADDONTO
ADDRESS
ADDUCED
ADDUCES
ADDUCTS
ADDUPTO
EDDYING
ODDBALL
ODDJOBS
ODDLOTS
ODDMENT
ODDNESS

•D••D••

ADDEDIN
ADDEDON
ADDEDTO
ADDEDUP
ADJUDGE
EDGEDIN

•D•••D•

ADDENDA
ADDENDS
EDWARDS
IDCARDS

•D••••D

ADAPTED
ADDUCED
ADHERED
ADJURED
ADMIRED
ADMIXED
ADOPTED
ADORNED
ADVISED
EDIFIED
EDOUARD
IDEATED

••DD•••

BADDEST
BADDIES
BADDISH
BEDDING
BEDDOWN
BIDDERS
BIDDIES
BIDDING
BUDDHAS
BUDDIES
BUDDING
BUDDYUP
CADDIED
CADDIES
CADDISH
CADDOAN
CODDLED
CODDLER
CODDLES
CUDDIES
CUDDLED
CUDDLES
DADDIES
DIDDLED
DIDDLES
DIDDLEY
DODDERS
FADDISH
FADDISM
FADDIST
FIDDLED
FIDDLER
FIDDLES
FODDERS
FUDDLED
FUDDLES
GADDERS
GADDING
GIDDIER
GIDDILY
GIDDYAP
GIDDYUP
GODDARD
GODDESS
HADDOCK
HEDDLES
HUDDLED
HUDDLES
JUDDERS
KADDISH
KIDDERS
KIDDIES
KIDDING
KIDDISH
LADDERS
LADDIES
LADDISH
LUDDITE
MADDENS
MADDERS
MADDEST
MADDING
MADDISH
MEDDLED
MEDDLER
MEDDLES
MIDDAYS
MIDDENS
MIDDIES
MIDDLEC
MIDDLES
MUDDERS
MUDDIED
MUDDIER
MUDDIES
MUDDILY
MUDDLED
MUDDLER
MUDDLES
NEDDIES
NODDERS
NODDING
OLDDAYS
PADDERS
PADDIES
PADDING
PADDLED
PADDLER
PADDLES
PADDOCK
PEDDLED
PEDDLER
PEDDLES
PUDDING
PUDDLED
PUDDLES
RADDLED
RADDLES
REDDEER
REDDENS
REDDEST
REDDING
REDDISH
REDDOGS
RIDDICK
RIDDING
RIDDLED
RIDDLER
RIDDLES
RODDING
RUDDERS
RUDDIER
RUDDILY
SADDENS
SADDEST
SADDLED
SADDLER
SADDLES
SODDIER
SODDIES
SODDING
TEDDERS
TEDDIES
TEDDING
TODDIES
TODDLED
TODDLER
TODDLES
WADDIES
WADDING
WADDLED
WADDLER
WADDLES
WEDDING
YIDDISH

••D•D••

ADDEDIN
ADDEDON
ADDEDTO
ADDEDUP
DUDEDUP
ENDEDUP
FADEDIN
GADSDEN
IODIDES
JADEDLY
LADYDAY
WADEDIN

••D••D•

ADDENDA
ADDENDS
BEDSIDE
MRDEEDS
OGDOADS
PODRIDA
REDBUDS
UNDERDO

••D•••D

ADDUCED
ANDROID
AUDITED
BEDEWED
CADDIED
CEDARED
CODDLED
CUDDLED
DEDUCED
DIDDLED
DIDGOOD
ENDOWED
ENDURED
FIDDLED
FUDDLED
GODDARD
GODSEND
HUDDLED
INDEXED
INDITED
INDUCED
IODISED
IODIZED
MEDALED
MEDDLED
MIDLAND
MODELED
MUDDIED
MUDDLED
OLDGOLD
OLDHAND
OLDMAID
ORDERED
PADDLED
PEDALED
PEDDLED
PUDDLED
RADDLED
RADIOED
REDATED
REDBIRD
REDEYED
REDFORD
REDHEAD
REDOUND
REDUCED
REDWOOD
RIDDLED
RUDYARD
SADDLED
SEDATED
SEDUCED
TODDLED
UNDATED
UPDATED
WADDLED
WIDENED
WIDOWED
YODELED

•••DD••

ALADDIN
BIRDDOG
BLADDER
CHEDDAR
FREDDIE
GLADDEN
GLADDER
GRIDDED
GRIDDER
GRIDDLE
PLODDED
PLODDER
PRODDED
PRODDER
SCUDDED
SHODDEN
SHUDDER
SKIDDED
SKIDDER
SKIDDOO
SLEDDED
SLEDDER
SLEDDOG
STUDDED
SWADDLE
THUDDED
TRODDEN
TWADDLE
TWIDDLE

•••D•D•

ALIDADE
AOUDADS
CANDIDA
CANDIDE
CANDIDS
DOODADS

•••D••D

BANDAID
BANDIED
BIRDIED
BRIDGED
BRIDLED
BUNDLED
CADDIED
CANDIED
CODDLED
CRADLED
CUDDLED
CURDLED
DANDLED
DAWDLED
DEADEND
DIDDLED
DOODLED
DREDGED
DRUDGED
FIDDLED
FLEDGED
FONDLED
FUDDLED
GIRDLED
GODDARD
GRIDDED
GRUDGED
HANDFED
HANDLED
HUDDLED
HUNDRED
HURDLED
KINDLED
KINDRED
LINDIED
MEDDLED
MILDRED
MISDEED
MORDRED
MUDDIED
MUDDLED
NEEDLED
PADDLED
PEDDLED
PLEDGED
PLODDED
PRODDED
PUDDLED
RADDLED
READIED
RIDDLED
ROADBED
SADDLED
SCUDDED
SEEDBED
SEEDPOD
SKIDDED
SLEDDED
SMUDGED
STUDDED
STUDIED
SUBDUED
THUDDED
TIEDYED
TOADIED
TODDLED
TRUDGED
WADDLED
WOODARD

••••DD•

MEGIDDO

••••D•D

ABRADED
ACCEDED
ALLUDED
AMENDED
AVOIDED
AWARDED
BAGHDAD
BEARDED
BETIDED
BLENDED
BLINDED
BLOODED
BOARDED
BOUNDED
BRAIDED
BRANDED
BREADED
BROODED
CLOUDED
CRAWDAD
CROWDED
DECIDED
DECODED
DELUDED
DENUDED
DERIDED
DIVIDED
DREADED
EMENDED
ENCODED
FIELDED
FLOODED
FOUNDED
GRIDDED
GUARDED
HOARDED
HOUNDED
ILLUDED
IMPEDED
INVADED
KATYDID
KNEADED
MOULDED
MOUNDED
OVERDID
PARADED
PLEADED
PLODDED
POMADED
POUNDED
PRODDED
RECEDED
RECODED
RESIDED
ROUNDED
SCALDED
SCENDED
SCOLDED
SCUDDED
SECEDED
SKIDDED
SLEDDED
SOLEDAD
SOUNDED
SPEEDED
STUDDED
THUDDED
TREADED
TRENDED
UNAIDED
UNENDED
UPENDED
WIELDED
WOUNDED
YIELDED

DE•••••

DEACONS
DEADAIR
DEADEND
DEADENS
DEADEYE
DEADPAN
DEADSEA
DEADSET
DEAFENS
DEAFEST
DEALERS
DEALING
DEALOUT
DEALSIN
DEALTIN
DEANERY
DEAREST
DEARIES
DEARSIR
DEARTHS
DEBACLE
DEBAKEY
DEBARGE
DEBARKS
DEBASED
DEBASES
DEBATED
DEBATER
DEBATES
DEBAUCH
DEBEERS
DEBITED
DEBONED
DEBONES
DEBORAH
DEBOUCH
DEBRIEF
DEBTORS
DEBUNKS
DEBUSSY
DEBUTED
DECADES
DECAGON
DECALOG
DECAMPS
DECANTS
DECAPOD
DECARLO
DECATUR
DECAYED
DECEITS
DECEIVE
DECENCY
DECIBEL
DECIDED
DECIDES
DECIMAL
DECKING
DECKLES
DECKOUT
DECLAIM
DECLARE
DECLASS
DECLINE
DECOCTS
DECODED
DECODER
DECODES
DECORUM
DECOYED
DECREED
DECREES
DECRIED
DECRIER
DECRIES
DECRYPT
DEDALUS
DEDUCED
DEDUCES
DEDUCTS
DEEDING
DEEJAYS
DEEMING
DEEPEND
DEEPENS
DEEPEST
DEEPFAT
DEEPFRY
DEEPSEA
DEEPSET
DEEPSIX
DEERFLY
DEFACED
DEFACES
DEFACTO
DEFALLA
DEFAMED
DEFAMES
DEFARGE
DEFAULT
DEFEATS
DEFECTS
DEFENCE
DEFENDS
DEFENSE
DEFIANT
DEFICIT
DEFILED
DEFILER
DEFILES
DEFINED
DEFINES
DEFLATE
DEFLECT
DEFORMS
DEFRAUD
DEFRAYS
DEFROCK
DEFROST
DEFTEST
DEFUNCT
DEFUSED
DEFUSES
DEFYING
DEGAUSS
DEGRADE
DEGREES
DEGUSTS
DEHISCE
DEHORNS
DEICERS
DEICING
DEIFIED
DEIFIES
DEIGNED
DEITIES
DEJECTS
DEKLERK
DELANEY
DELAYED
DELAYER
DELEING
DELETED
DELETES
DELIBES
DELICTI
DELICTS
DELIGHT
DELILAH
DELIMIT
DELIRIA
DELISTS
DELIVER
DELPHIC
DELTAIC
DELTOID
DELUDED
DELUDES
DELUGED
DELUGES
DELUISE
DELVERS
DELVING
DEMANDS
DEMEANS
DEMERIT
DEMEROL
DEMESNE
DEMETER
DEMIGOD
DEMILLE
DEMISED
DEMISES
DEMONIC
DEMOTED
DEMOTES
DEMPSEY
DEMURER
DENARII
DENDRON
DENEUVE
DENIALS
DENIERS
DENIZEN
DENMARK
DENNEHY
DENOTED
DENOTES
DENSELY
DENSEST
DENSITY
DENTATE
DENTINE
DENTING
DENTIST
DENTURE
DENUDED
DENUDES
DENYING
DEODARS
DEPALMA
DEPARTS
DEPENDS
DEPICTS
DEPLANE
DEPLETE
DEPLORE
DEPLOYS
DEPONED
DEPONES
DEPORTS
DEPOSAL
DEPOSED
DEPOSER
DEPOSES
DEPOSIT
DEPRAVE
DEPRESS
DEPRIVE
DEPUTED
DEPUTES
DERAILS
DERBIES
DERIDED
DERIDES
DERIVED
DERIVES
DERNIER
DERRICK
DERRING
DERVISH
DESALTS
DESCANT
DESCEND
DESCENT
DESERTS
DESERVE
DESIGNS
DESIRED
DESIREE
DESIRES
DESISTS
DESKSET
DESKTOP
DESMOND
DESOTOS
DESPAIR
DESPISE
DESPITE
DESPOIL
DESPOTS
DESSERT
DESTINE
DESTINY
DESTROY
DETAILS
DETAINS
DETECTS
DETENTE
DETESTS
DETOURS
DETRACT
DETRAIN
DETROIT
DEUTERO
DEVALUE
DEVEINS
DEVELOP
DEVIANT
DEVIATE
DEVICES
DEVILED
DEVILLE
DEVILRY
DEVIOUS
DEVISED
DEVISES
DEVOLVE
DEVOTED
DEVOTEE
DEVOTES
DEVOURS
DEVRIES
DEWCLAW
DEWDROP
DEWLAPS
DEWLESS
DEWLINE
DEXTRIN

D•E••••

DEEDING
DEEJAYS
DEEMING
DEEPEND
DEEPENS
DEEPEST
DEEPFAT
DEEPFRY
DEEPSEA
DEEPSET
DEEPSIX
DEERFLY
DIEDOFF
DIEDOUT
DIEDOWN
DIEHARD
DIESELS
DIESOFF
DIESOUT
DIETARY
DIETERS
DIETING
DOESKIN
DREADED
DREAMED
DREAMER
DREAMON
DREAMUP
DREDGED
DREDGER
DREDGES
DREIDEL
DREISER
DRESDEN
DRESSED
DRESSER
DRESSES
DRESSUP
DREWOUT
DREYFUS
DUEDATE
DUELERS
DUELING
DUELIST
DUENNAS
DWEEZIL
DWELLED
DWELLER

D••E•••

DALETHS
DANELAW
DAREFUL
DARESAY
DARESTO
DATEDLY
DAZEDLY
DEBEERS
DECEITS
DECEIVE
DECENCY
DEFEATS
DEFECTS
DEFENCE
DEFENDS
DEFENSE
DEJECTS
DELEING
DELETED
DELETES
DEMEANS
DEMERIT
DEMEROL
DEMESNE
DEMETER
DENEUVE
DEPENDS
DESERTS
DESERVE
DETECTS
DETENTE
DETESTS
DEVEINS
DEVELOP
DIDEROT
DIGESTS
DILEMMA
DINEDIN
DINEDON
DINESEN

DINESIN
DINESON
DINETTE
DIRECTS
DIREFUL
DISEASE
DIVERGE
DIVERSE
DIVERTS
DIVESIN
DIVESTS
DIZENED
DOCENTS
DOGEARS
DOLEFUL
DOLEOUT
DONEFOR
DONEGAL
DOPEOUT
DOTEDON
DOTESON
DOVECOT
DOWERED
DOYENNE
DOZENTH
DOZEOFF
DRIEDUP
DRIESUP
DRSEUSS
DRYEYED
DUDEDUP
DUKEDOM
DUTEOUS
DWEEZIL

D•••E••

DAFTEST
DAGGERS
DAMPENS
DAMPERS
DAMPEST
DAMSELS
DANCERS
DANDERS
DANGERS
DANIELS
DANKEST
DANSEUR
DARKENS
DARKEST
DARLENE
DARNERS
DARTERS
DASHERS
DAUBERS
DAYBEDS
DEADEND
DEADENS
DEADEYE
DEAFENS
DEAFEST
DEALERS
DEANERY
DEAREST
DEBEERS
DECREED
DECREES
DEEPEND
DEEPENS
DEEPEST
DEFLECT
DEFTEST
DEGREES
DEICERS
DEKLERK
DELVERS
DENIERS
DENNEHY
DENSELY
DENSEST
DEPLETE
DEPRESS
DESCEND
DESCENT
DESSERT
DEUTERO
DEWLESS
DIADEMS
DIALECT
DIALERS
DIAPERS
DICIEST
DICKENS
DICKERS
DICKEYS
DIESELS
DIETERS
DIFFERS
DIGGERS
DIGRESS
DILBERT
DIMMERS
DIMMEST
DIMNESS
DINNERS
DIOCESE
DIOMEDE
DIPPERS
DISCERN
DISPELS
DISSECT
DISSENT
DISTEND
DITHERS
DITHERY
DOCKERS
DOCKETS
DODDERS
DODGERS
DOGBERT
DOGLEGS
DOGLESS
DOLMENS
DONKEYS
DOPIEST
DORMERS
DORSETT
DOSSERS
DOUREST
DOWNERS
DOWSERS
DOZIEST
DRAPERS
DRAPERY
DRAWERS
DRIVEAT
DRIVEIN
DRIVELS
DRIVERS
DRIVEUP
DRONERS
DROVERS
DRYCELL
DRYNESS
DRYWELL
DUBBERS
DUBIETY
DUCHESS
DUDGEON
DUELERS
DUFFELS
DUFFERS
DULLEST
DUMBEST
DUNGEON
DUNKERS
DUODENA
DURRELL
DUSTERS

D••••E•

DABBLED
DABBLER
DABBLES
DADDIES
DAFFIER
DAHOMEY
DAILIES
DAIMLER
DAIRIES
DAISIES
DALLIED
DALLIER
DALLIES
DALTREY
DAMAGED
DAMAGES
DANDIER
DANDIES
DANDLED
DANDLES
DANGLED
DANGLER
DANGLES
DAPPLED
DAPPLES
DARBIES
DARNLEY
DATASET
DAUMIER
DAUNTED
DAWDLED
DAWDLER
DAWDLES
DAZZLED
DAZZLER
DAZZLES
DEADSEA
DEADSET
DEARIES
DEBAKEY
DEBASED
DEBASES
DEBATED
DEBATER
DEBATES
DEBITED
DEBONED
DEBONES
DEBRIEF
DEBUTED
DECADES
DECAYED
DECIBEL
DECIDED
DECIDES
DECKLES
DECODED
DECODER
DECODES
DECOYED
DECREED
DECREES
DECRIED
DECRIER
DECRIES
DEDUCED
DEDUCES
DEEPSEA
DEEPSET
DEFACED
DEFACES
DEFAMED
DEFAMES
DEFILED
DEFILER
DEFILES
DEFINED
DEFINES
DEFUSED
DEFUSES
DEGREES
DEIFIED
DEIFIES
DEIGNED
DEITIES
DELANEY
DELAYED
DELAYER
DELETED
DELETES
DELIBES
DELIVER
DELUDED
DELUDES
DELUGED
DELUGES
DEMETER
DEMISED
DEMISES
DEMOTED
DEMOTES
DEMPSEY
DEMURER
DENIZEN
DENOTED
DENOTES
DENUDED
DENUDES
DEPONED
DEPONES
DEPOSED
DEPOSER
DEPOSES
DEPUTED
DEPUTES
DERBIES
DERIDED
DERIDES
DERIVED
DERIVES
DERNIER
DESIRED
DESIREE
DESIRES
DESKSET
DEVICES
DEVILED
DEVISED
DEVISES
DEVOTED
DEVOTEE
DEVOTES
DEVRIES
DIARIES
DIBBLED
DIBBLES
DICKIES
DIDDLED
DIDDLES
DIDDLEY
DIDOVER
DILATED
DILATES
DILLIES
DILUTED
DILUTER
DILUTES
DIMPLED
DIMPLES
DINESEN
DINGIER
DINGLES
DINGOES
DINKIER
DINKIES
DIOPTER
DIPOLES
DIPPIER
DIRTIED
DIRTIER
DIRTIES
DISCOED
DISHIER
DISOBEY
DISUSED
DITCHED
DITCHES
DITSIER
DITTIES
DITTOED
DITZIER
DIVIDED
DIVIDER
DIVIDES
DIVINED
DIVINER
DIVINES
DIVVIED
DIVVIES
DIZENED
DIZZIED
DIZZIER
DIZZIES
DOBBIES
DODGIER
DOGGIER
DOGGIES
DOGSLED
DOILIES
DOLLIED
DOLLIES
DOLORES
DONATED
DONATES
DONGLES
DOODLED
DOODLER
DOODLES
DOORMEN
DOOZIES
DOPPLER
DOSAGES
DOSSIER
DOTTIER
DOTTLES
DOUBLED
DOUBLES
DOUBLET
DOUBLEU
DOUBTED
DOUBTER
DOWAGER
DOWDIER
DOWERED
DOWNIER
DOWRIES
DRABBER
DRAFTED
DRAFTEE
DRAGGED
DRAGGER
DRAGNET
DRAINED
DRAINER
DRATTED
DRAWLED
DREADED
DREAMED
DREAMER
DREDGED
DREDGER
DREDGES
DREIDEL
DREISER
DRESDEN
DRESSED
DRESSER
DRESSES
DRIBLET
DRIFTED
DRIFTER
DRILLED
DRILLER
DRINKER
DRIPPED
DROLLER
DROOLED
DROOLER
DROOPED
DROPLET
DROPPED
DROPPER
DROWNED
DROWSED
DROWSES
DRUBBED
DRUCKER
DRUDGED
DRUDGES
DRUGGED
DRUMMED
DRUMMER
DRYEYED
DUCHIES
DUCKIER
DUMMIED
DUMMIES
DUMPIER
DUSKIER
DUSTIER
DUSTMEN
DWARFED
DWARVES
DWELLED
DWELLER

D•••••E

DARLENE
DASYURE
DAYCARE
DAYMARE
DAYTIME
DEADEYE
DEBACLE
DEBARGE
DECEIVE
DECLARE
DECLINE
DEFARGE
DEFENCE
DEFENSE
DEFLATE
DEGRADE
DEHISCE
DELUISE
DEMESNE
DEMILLE
DENEUVE
DENTATE
DENTINE
DENTURE
DEPLANE
DEPLETE
DEPLORE
DEPRAVE
DEPRIVE
DESERVE
DESIREE
DESPISE
DESPITE
DESTINE
DETENTE
DEVALUE
DEVIATE
DEVILLE
DEVOLVE
DEVOTEE
DEWLINE
DHURRIE
DICTATE
DIFFUSE
DINETTE
DIOCESE
DIOMEDE
DIOXIDE
DISABLE
DISEASE
DISLIKE
DISPOSE
DISPUTE
DISROBE
DIVERGE
DIVERSE
DIVORCE
DIVULGE
DNOTICE
DOCKAGE
DOGBANE
DOGFACE
DOGGONE
DOGLIKE
DONAHUE
DONJOSE
DOORDIE
DORMICE
DOTLIKE
DOYENNE
DRAFTEE
DRAYAGE
DRIBBLE
DRIZZLE
DRYHOLE
DUBUQUE
DUCTILE
DUEDATE
DURABLE
DURANCE
DURANTE
DWINDLE

•DE••••

ADELINE
ADENINE
ADEPTLY
IDEALLY
IDEAMAN
IDEAMEN
IDEATED
IDEATES
IDENTIC

•D•E•••

ADDEDIN
ADDEDON
ADDEDTO
ADDEDUP
ADDENDA
ADDENDS
ADHERED
ADHERES
ADRENAL
ADVENTS
ADVERBS
ADVERSE
ADVERTS
EDGEDIN
EDGEOUT
EDGESIN

•D••E••

ADDRESS
ADORERS
EDGIEST
ODDMENT
ODDNESS

•D•••E•

ADAPTED
ADAPTER
ADDUCED
ADDUCES
ADFINEM
ADHERED
ADHERES
ADJURED
ADJURES
ADMIRED
ADMIRER
ADMIRES
ADMIXED
ADMIXES
ADOPTED
ADOPTEE
ADOPTER
ADORNED
ADORNER
ADVISED
ADVISER
ADVISES
EDASNER
EDIBLES
EDIFIED
EDIFIES
IDEAMEN
IDEATED
IDEATES
ODYSSEY
PDJAMES

•D••••E

ADAMITE
ADDABLE
ADDIBLE
ADELINE
ADENINE
ADIPOSE
ADJUDGE
ADOLPHE
ADOPTEE
ADULATE
ADVANCE
ADVERSE
EDIFICE
EDUCATE
IDOLISE
IDOLIZE

••DE•••

ADDEDIN
ADDEDON
ADDEDTO
ADDEDUP
ADDENDA
ADDENDS
ALDENTE
ANDEANS
ARDENCY
BADEGGS
BEDECKS
BEDELIA
BEDEVIL
BEDEWED
BODEGAS
BODEREK
CADENCE
CADENCY
CADENZA
CADETTE
CODEINE
DIDEROT
DUDEDUP
ELDERLY
ENDEARS
ENDEDUP
ENDEMIC
FADEDIN
FADEINS
FADEOUT
FADESIN
FEDERAL
FIDELIO
FIDELIS
GIDEONS
HIDEOUS
HIDEOUT
INDENTS
INDEPTH
INDEXED
INDEXES
JADEDLY
JADEITE
MADEFOR
MADEHAY
MADEIRA
MADEOFF
MADEOUT
MADEPAR
MADEWAY
MEDEVAC
MIDEAST
MODELAS
MODELED
MODELER
MODELTS
MODERNS
MODESTO
MODESTY
MRDEEDS
MUDEELS
ORDEALS
ORDERED
ORDERER
ORDERLY
PUDENCY
REDEALS
REDEALT
REDEEMS
REDEYED
REDEYES
RIDEOFF
RIDEOUT
RODENTS
RODEOFF
RODEOUT
SIDEARM
SIDEBAR
SIDEBET
SIDECAR
SIDEMAN
SIDEMEN
STDENIS
UNDERDO
UNDERGO
WADEDIN
WADESIN
WIDENED
YODELED
YODELER
ZYDECOS

••D•E••

ADDRESS
AIDLESS
ANDREAS
ANDRESS
ANDREWS
BADDEST
BADGERS
BADNESS
BEDLESS
BEDREST
BIDDERS
BUDGETS
BUDLESS
CADGERS
CODGERS
CUDGELS
DODDERS
DODGERS
DUDGEON
ENDLESS
FIDGETS
FIDGETY
FODDERS
GADDERS
GADGETS
GADGETY
GODDESS
GODLESS
GODSEND
HEDGERS
INDWELL
JUDDERS
KIDDERS
KIDNEYS
LADDERS
LADLERS
LEDGERS
LIDLESS
LODGERS
MADDENS
MADDERS
MADDEST
MADNESS
MEDLEYS
MIDDENS
MIDGETS
MIDTERM
MIDWEEK
MIDWEST
MIDYEAR
MRDEEDS
MUDDERS
MUDEELS
MUDHENS
NODDERS
NUDGERS
ODDMENT
ODDNESS
OLDNESS
OLDNEWS
OLDWEST
PADDERS
PIDGEON
REDCELL
REDCENT
REDDEER
REDDENS
REDDEST
REDEEMS
REDHEAD
REDHEAT
REDMEAT
REDNESS
REDRESS
RODGERS
RODLESS
RUDDERS
SADDENS
SADDEST
SADNESS
SODLESS
TEDDERS
TIDIEST
UNDRESS
WIDGEON
WIDGETS

••D••E•

ABDOMEN
ADDUCED
ADDUCES
AEDILES
ANDOVER
AUDILES
AUDITED
BADDIES
BEDEWED
BEDIZEN
BIDDIES
BODEREK
BODICES
BUDDIES
BUDGIES
CADDIED
CADDIES
CADUCEI
CEDARED
CODDLED
CODDLER
CODDLES
CODICES
CUDDIES
CUDDLED
CUDDLES
DADDIES
DEDUCED
DEDUCES
DIDDLED
DIDDLES
DIDDLEY
DIDOVER
DODGIER
ECDYSES
ENDIVES
ENDOWED
ENDURED
ENDURES
ENDUSER
ENDUSES
FIDDLED
FIDDLER
FIDDLES
FUDDLED
FUDDLES
GADSDEN
GIDDIER
GODFREY
GODLIER
HEDDLES
HEDGIER
HUDDLED
HUDDLES
INDEXED
INDEXES
INDICES
INDITED
INDITES
INDUCED
INDUCER
INDUCES
IODATES
IODIDES
IODISED
IODISES
IODIZED
IODIZES
KIDDIES
LADDIES
LEDGIER
MADAMEX
MADCHEN
MEDALED
MEDDLED
MEDDLER
MEDDLES
MIDDIES
MIDDLEC
MIDDLES
MIDWEEK
MODELED
MODELER
MODULES
MUDDIED
MUDDIER
MUDDIES
MUDDLED
MUDDLER
MUDDLES
MUDPIES
NEDDIES
NODULES
OLDSTER
ORDERED
ORDERER
ORDINES
PADDIES
PADDLED
PADDLER
PADDLES
PEDALED
PEDDLED
PEDDLER
PEDDLES
PEDICEL
PODGIER
PUDDLED
PUDDLES
PUDGIER
RADDLED
RADDLES
RADICES
RADIOED
RADIXES
RADOMES
REDATED
REDATES
REDDEER
REDEYED
REDEYES
REDUCED
REDUCER
REDUCES
RIDDLED
RIDDLER
RIDDLES
RIDGIER
RUDDIER
SADDLED
SADDLER
SADDLES
SEDATED
SEDATER
SEDATES
SEDGIER
SEDUCED
SEDUCER
SEDUCES
SIDEBET
SIDEMEN
SODDIER
SODDIES
SUDSIER
TEDDIES
TODDIES
TODDLED
TODDLER
TODDLES
UNDATED
UPDATED
UPDATES
WADDIES
WADDLED
WADDLER
WADDLES
WEDGIER
WEDGIES
WIDENED
WIDOWED
WIDOWER
YODELED
YODELER

••D•••E

ADDABLE
ADDIBLE
ALDENTE
ANDANTE
ARDMORE
AUDIBLE
BEDLIKE
BEDSIDE
BEDTIME
BUDLIKE
CADENCE
CADETTE
CODEINE
ENDGAME
ENDORSE
ENDWISE
ENDZONE
FADLIKE
GODLIKE
HYDRATE
INDORSE
INDULGE
JADEITE
KIDLIKE
LUDDITE
MEDIATE
MEDUSAE
MIDLIFE
MIDLINE
MIDRISE
MIDSIZE
MIDWIFE
MODISTE
OLDLINE
OLDROSE
OLDTIME
PADRONE
PEDICLE
PODLIKE
RADIATE
RADICLE
RADULAE
REDLINE
REDPINE
REDROSE
REDTAPE
REDWINE
RODLIKE
TADPOLE
UNDRAPE

•••DE••

ABIDEBY
ACADEME
ACADEMY
AMADEUS
ANADEMS
ARIDEST
ARTDECO
BADDEST
BALDEST
BENDERS
BIDDERS
BIGDEAL
BINDERS
BINDERY
BIRDERS
BLADERS
BOLDEST
BORDERS
BURDENS
CALDERA
CANDELA
CARDERS
CHIDERS
CINDERS
CINDERY
COLDEST
CONDEMN
CORDELL
CORDERO

CRUDELY
CRUDEST
DANDERS
DEADEND
DEADENS
DEADEYE
DIADEMS
DODDERS
DUODENA
ERODENT
EVADERS
EVIDENT
FEEDERS
FENDERS
FINDERS
FODDERS
FOLDERS
FONDEST
GADDERS
GANDERS
GARDENS
GENDERS
GEODESY
GILDERS
GIRDERS
GLADEYE
GLIDERS
GODDESS
GOODEGG
GRADERS
HARDENS
HARDEST
HEADERS
HERDERS
HINDERS
HOLDERS
HOYDENS
JUDDERS
KIDDERS
KINDEST
LADDERS
LANDERS
LARDERS
LEADERS
LENDERS
LEWDEST
LINDENS
LOADERS
LOUDEST
MADDENS
MADDERS
MADDEST
MAIDENS
MANDELA
MENDERS
MIDDENS
MILDEST
MILDEWS
MILDEWY
MINDERS
MISDEAL
MISDEED
MOLDERS
MORDENT
MUDDERS
MURDERS
NEWDEAL
NODDERS
PADDERS
PANDECT
PANDERS
PENDENT
POLDERS
PONDERS
POWDERS
POWDERY
PRUDENT
PRUDERY
RAIDERS
RAWDEAL
READERS
REDDEER
REDDENS
REDDEST
RENDERS
ROEDEER
RONDEAU
RONDELS
RUDDERS
RUNDEEP
SADDENS
SADDEST
SANDERS
SEEDERS
SEIDELS
SENDERS
SLIDEIN
SLIDERS
SNIDELY
SNIDEST
SOLDERS
SPADERS
SPIDERS
SPIDERY
STUDENT
SUBDEBS
SUNDECK
SUNDERS
SUNDEWS
TANDEMS
TEDDERS
TENDERS
THEDEEP
TINDERS
TRADEIN
TRADEON
TRADERS
TRADEUP
TRIDENT
TRUDEAU
WANDERS
WARDENS
WARDERS
WEEDERS
WELDERS
WENDELL
WENDERS
WILDEST
WINDERS
WONDERS
YESDEAR
ZANDERS

•••D•E•

AZODYES
BADDIES
BANDIED
BANDIES
BAWDIER
BEADIER
BEADLES
BENDIER
BIDDIES
BIRDIED
BIRDIES
BIRDMEN
BLADDER
BONDMEN
BOODLES
BOWDLER
BRADLEE
BRADLEY
BRIDGED
BRIDGES
BRIDGET
BRIDLED
BRIDLES
BUDDIES
BUNDLED
BUNDLES
CADDIED
CADDIES
CANDIED
CANDIES
CANDLES
CAUDLES
CODDLED
CODDLER
CODDLES
CRADLED
CRADLES
CUDDIES
CUDDLED
CUDDLES
CURDIER
CURDLED
CURDLES
DADDIES
DANDIER
DANDIES
DANDLED
DANDLES
DAWDLED
DAWDLER
DAWDLES
DEADSEA
DEADSET
DIDDLED
DIDDLES
DIDDLEY
DOODLED
DOODLER
DOODLES
DOWDIER
DREDGED
DREDGER
DREDGES
DRUDGED
DRUDGES
FIDDLED
FIDDLER
FIDDLES
FIEDLER
FLEDGED
FLEDGES
FONDLED
FONDLES
FONDUES
FOODIES
FOODWEB
FRIDGES
FUDDLED
FUDDLES
GARDNER
GAUDIER
GIDDIER
GIRDLED
GIRDLES
GLADDEN
GLADDER
GOODIES
GOODMEN
GRIDDED
GRIDDER
GRODIER
GRUDGED
GRUDGES
HANDFED
HANDIER
HANDLED
HANDLER
HANDLES
HANDSET
HARDIER
HARDSET
HEADIER
HEADMEN
HEADSET
HEDDLES
HUDDLED
HUDDLES
HUNDRED
HURDLED
HURDLER
HURDLES
ICEDTEA
KIDDIES
KINDLED
KINDLES
KINDRED
KLUDGES
LADDIES
LARDIER
LARDNER
LEADIER
LINDIED
LINDIES
LINDSEY
MEDDLED
MEDDLER
MEDDLES
MIDDIES
MIDDLEC
MIDDLES
MILDRED
MINDSET
MISDEED
MISDOES
MOLDIER
MOODIER
MORDRED
MUDDIED
MUDDIER
MUDDIES
MUDDLED
MUDDLER
MUDDLES
NEDDIES
NEEDIER
NEEDLED
NEEDLES
NERDIER
NOODLES
ONADIET
OUTDOES
OUTDREW
PADDIES
PADDLED
PADDLER
PADDLES
PARDNER
PEDDLED
PEDDLER
PEDDLES
PERDIEM
PLEDGED
PLEDGEE
PLEDGER
PLEDGES
PLODDED
PLODDER
POODLES
PRODDED
PRODDER
PUDDLED
PUDDLES
RADDLED
RADDLES
RANDIER
READIED
READIER
READIES
REDDEER
REEDIER
RIDDLED
RIDDLER
RIDDLES
ROADBED
ROADIES
ROEDEER
ROWDIER
ROWDIES
RUDDIER
RUNDEEP
RUNDLES
SADDLED
SADDLER
SADDLES
SANDIER
SANDMEN
SCUDDED
SEEDBED
SEEDIER
SHADIER
SHODDEN
SHUDDER
SKIDDED
SKIDDER
SLEDDED
SLEDDER
SLEDGES
SLUDGES
SMIDGEN
SMUDGED
SMUDGES
SODDIER
SODDIES
SOLDIER
STUDDED
STUDIED
STUDIES
SUBDUED
SUBDUER
SUBDUES
SUNDAES
TARDIER
TEDDIES
THEDEEP
THUDDED
TIEDYED
TIEDYES
TOADIED
TOADIES
TODDIES
TODDLED
TODDLER
TODDLES
TRODDEN
TRUDGED
TRUDGER
TRUDGES
WADDIES
WADDLED
WADDLER
WADDLES
WEEDIER
WINDIER
WOODIER
WOODIES
WORDIER
YARDMEN

•••D••E

ACADEME
AIRDATE
ALIDADE
ANODISE
ANODIZE
ANODYNE
BANDAGE
BELDAME
BOBDOLE
BONDAGE
BRADLEE
CANDICE
CANDIDE
CONDOLE
CONDONE
CONDUCE
CORDAGE
CORDATE
CORDITE
DEADEYE
DUEDATE
ERUDITE
FREDDIE
GLADEYE
GOODBYE
GOODJOE
GOODONE
GRIDDLE
INADAZE
KILDARE
LUDDITE
MANDATE
MISDATE
MISDONE
MONDALE
MUNDANE
ONADARE
ONADATE
OUTDONE
OXIDASE
OXIDISE
OXIDIZE
PLEDGEE
PREDATE
PRODUCE
PRUDHOE
SARDINE
SKYDIVE
SWADDLE
TRADUCE
TWADDLE
TWIDDLE
VANDINE
VANDYKE
VERDURE
WILDONE
WORDONE
YARDAGE

••••DE•

ABRADED
ABRADER
ABRADES
ACCEDED
ACCEDER
ACCEDES
ALLUDED
ALLUDES
ALMADEN
AMENDED
APSIDES
ARCADES
ASUNDER
AUBADES
AVOIDED
AWARDED
AWARDEE
AWARDER
BEARDED
BESIDES
BETIDED
BETIDES
BLADDER
BLANDER
BLENDED
BLENDER
BLINDED
BLINDER
BLONDER
BLONDES
BLOODED
BLUNDER
BOARDED
BOARDER
BOLIDES
BOULDER
BOUNDED
BOUNDER
BRAIDED
BRAIDER
BRANDED
BRANDER
BREADED
BREEDER
BROADEN
BROADER
BROODED
BROODER
BUILDER
CCRIDER
CHOWDER
CITADEL
CLOUDED
CLOWDER
CROWDED
DECADES
DECIDED
DECIDES
DECODED
DECODER
DECODES
DELUDED
DELUDES
DENUDED
DENUDES
DERIDED
DERIDES
DIVIDED
DIVIDER
DIVIDES
DREADED
DREIDEL
DRESDEN
EMENDED
EMENDER
ENCODED
ENCODER
ENCODES
EVANDER
FACADES
FIELDED
FIELDER
FLOODED
FOUNDED
FOUNDER
GADSDEN
GLADDEN
GLADDER
GOUNDER
GOURDES
GRANDEE
GRANDER
GRENDEL
GRIDDED
GRIDDER
GRINDER
GUARDED
GUARDEE
GUILDER
HALIDES
HOARDED
HOARDER
HOUNDED
ILLUDED
ILLUDES
IMPEDED
IMPEDES
INCUDES
INFIDEL
INSIDER
INSIDES
INVADED
INVADER
INVADES
IODIDES
JOINDER
KNEADED
KNEADER
LAUNDER
LEANDER
LIPIDES
LOURDES
MAUNDER
MEANDER
MOULDED
MOULDER
MOUNDED
NAIADES
ONORDER
ONSIDES
PARADED
PARADES
PLEADED
PLEADER
PLODDED
PLODDER
PLUNDER
POMADED
POMADES
POUNDED
POUNDER
PRODDED
PRODDER
PROUDER
PYXIDES
RAPIDER
RECEDED
RECEDES
RECODED
RECODES
REMODEL
REORDER
RESIDED
RESIDES
ROLODEX
ROUNDED
ROUNDER
SCALDED
SCENDED
SCOLDED
SCOLDER
SCUDDED
SECEDED
SECEDER
SECEDES
SHODDEN
SHUDDER
SKIDDED
SKIDDER
SLANDER
SLEDDED
SLEDDER
SLENDER
SMOLDER
SOLIDER
SOUNDED
SOUNDER
SPANDEX
SPEEDED
SPEEDER
SPENDER
SPONDEE
STAIDER
STANDEE
STRIDER
STRIDES
STRUDEL
STUDDED
THUDDED
THUNDER
TIMIDER
TIRADES
TIREDER
TOORDER
TOTIDEM
TREADED
TREADER
TRENDED
TRIODES
TRODDEN
UNAIDED
UNENDED
UNLADES
UPENDED
VIVIDER
WEIRDER
WHAUDEN
WIELDED
WOUNDED
YIELDED

••••D•E

ABRIDGE
ADJUDGE
ARIADNE
ARLEDGE
AWARDEE
BLONDIE
BRINDLE
CAMEDUE
CICADAE
COMEDUE
DOORDIE
DWINDLE
FREDDIE
GEORDIE
GRANDEE
GRIDDLE
GUARDEE
HAIRDYE
JANEDOE
JOHNDOE
OVERDUE
PASTDUE
RESIDUE
RUSHDIE
SINEDIE
SPINDLE
SPONDEE
STANDEE
SWADDLE
SWINDLE
TREADLE
TRUNDLE
TWADDLE
TWIDDLE
WHEEDLE
WOULDBE

•••••DE

ALAMODE
ALIDADE
ALLENDE
ASTRIDE
BALLADE
BARCODE
BEDSIDE
BRIGADE
BROCADE
BROMIDE
CANDIDE
CARBIDE
CASCADE
CATHODE
CHARADE
COCKADE
COLLIDE
COLLUDE
COMMODE
COMRADE
CONCEDE
CONFIDE
CORRODE
COWHIDE
CRUSADE
DEGRADE
DIOMEDE
DIOXIDE
EBBTIDE
ENGARDE
EPISODE
EXCLUDE
EXPLODE
EXTRUDE
FORBADE
GIRONDE
GRENADE
HAYRIDE
HEYJUDE
IMPLODE
INCLUDE
INTRUDE
JOYRIDE
LEETIDE
LEMONDE
LIMEADE
LOWTIDE
MANMADE
NITRIDE
NUCLIDE
OBTRUDE
OCCLUDE
OFFSIDE
OUTSIDE
PARKADE
PEPTIDE
PERVADE
PRECEDE
PRELUDE
PRESIDE
PROVIDE
RAWHIDE
REGRADE
RETRADE
RIPTIDE
ROULADE
SEASIDE
SECLUDE
SUBSIDE
SULFIDE
TOPSIDE
TVGUIDE
UPGRADE
WAYSIDE
YAOUNDE
ZIPCODE

D•F••••

DAFFIER
DAFFILY
DAFFING
DAFTEST
DEFACED
DEFACES
DEFACTO
DEFALLA
DEFAMED
DEFAMES
DEFARGE
DEFAULT
DEFEATS
DEFECTS
DEFENCE
DEFENDS
DEFENSE
DEFIANT
DEFICIT
DEFILED
DEFILER
DEFILES
DEFINED
DEFINES
DEFLATE
DEFLECT
DEFORMS
DEFRAUD
DEFRAYS
DEFROCK
DEFROST
DEFTEST
DEFUNCT
DEFUSED
DEFUSES
DEFYING
DIFFERS
DIFFUSE
DOFFING
DUFFELS
DUFFERS

D••F•••

DAFFIER
DAFFILY
DAFFING
DEAFENS
DEAFEST
DEIFIED
DEIFIES
DIFFERS
DIFFUSE
DOFFING
DOGFACE
DOGFISH
DOGFOOD
DRAFTED
DRAFTEE
DRIFTED
DRIFTER
DUFFELS
DUFFERS

D•••F••

DAREFUL
DEEPFAT
DEEPFRY
DEERFLY
DIREFUL
DISHFUL
DOLEFUL
DONEFOR
DOOMFUL
DREYFUS
DUTIFUL
DWARFED

D••••F•

DANDIFY
DASHOFF
DIEDOFF
DIESOFF
DIGNIFY
DISTAFF
DOZEOFF
DROPOFF
DULCIFY
DUSTOFF

D•••••F

DASHOFF
DEBRIEF
DIEDOFF
DIESOFF
DISTAFF
DOZEOFF
DROPOFF
DUSTOFF

•DF••••

ADFINEM

•D•F•••

EDIFICE
EDIFIED
EDIFIES

•D••F••

ODORFUL

••DF•••

BIDFAIR
CODFISH
GODFREY
OLDFOGY
REDFINS
REDFIRS
REDFLAG
REDFORD

••D•F••

BODYFAT
MADEFOR

••D••F•

MADEOFF
MIDLIFE
MIDRIFF
MIDWIFE
NODSOFF
RIDEOFF
RODEOFF
RODOLFO
UPDRAFT

••D•••F

MADEOFF
MIDRIFF
NODSOFF
REDWOLF
RIDEOFF
RODEOFF

•••DF••

HANDFED
HANDFUL
HEEDFUL
LAIDFOR
MINDFUL
NEEDFUL
PAIDFOR
SANDFLY
SENDFOR

•••D•F•

ACIDIFY
DANDIFY
DIEDOFF
HANDOFF
HEADOFF
HELDOFF
HOLDOFF
LAIDOFF
LEADOFF
MACDUFF
PAIDOFF
SENDOFF
SOLDOFF
TEEDOFF
TOLDOFF
WARDOFF

•••D••F

DIEDOFF
HANDOFF
HEADOFF
HELDOFF
HOLDOFF
LAIDOFF
LEADOFF
MACDUFF
PAIDOFF
SENDOFF
SHADOOF
SOLDOFF
TEEDOFF
TOLDOFF
WALDORF
WARDOFF

••••D•F

AHEADOF
BERIDOF
HEARDOF
TIREDOF

D•G••••

DAGGERS
DAGWOOD
DEGAUSS
DEGRADE
DEGREES
DEGUSTS
DIGESTS
DIGGERS
DIGGING
DIGITAL
DIGNIFY
DIGNITY
DIGRAMS
DIGRAPH
DIGRESS
DIGSOUT
DOGBANE
DOGBERT
DOGCART
DOGCHOW
DOGDAYS
DOGEARS
DOGFACE
DOGFISH
DOGFOOD
DOGGIER
DOGGIES
DOGGING
DOGGISH
DOGGONE
DOGLEGS
DOGLESS
DOGLIKE
DOGMATA
DOGSHOW
DOGSITS
DOGSLED
DOGSTAR
DOGTAGS
DOGTROT
DOGWOOD
DUGONGS
DUGOUTS

D••G•••

DAGGERS
DANGERS
DANGLED
DANGLER
DANGLES
DEIGNED
DIAGRAM
DIDGOOD
DIGGERS
DIGGING
DINGBAT
DINGIER
DINGILY
DINGING
DINGLES
DINGOES
DISGUST
DODGERS
DODGIER
DODGING
DODGSON
DOGGIER

DOGGIES
DOGGING
DOGGISH
DOGGONE
DONGLES
DOUGHTY
DOUGLAS
DRAGGED
DRAGGER
DRAGNET
DRAGONS
DRAGOON
DRAGOUT
DRAGSIN
DRAGSON
DRUGGED
DUDGEON
DUNGEON

D•••G••
DAMAGED
DAMAGES
DECAGON
DELIGHT
DELUGED
DELUGES
DEMIGOD
DESIGNS
DOINGIN
DOINGUP
DONEGAL
DOSAGES
DOWAGER
DRAGGED
DRAGGER
DRAUGHT
DREDGED
DREDGER
DREDGES
DROUGHT
DRUDGED
DRUDGES
DRUGGED

D••••G•
DEBARGE
DEFARGE
DIALOGS
DIVERGE
DIVULGE
DOCKAGE
DOGLEGS
DOGTAGS
DOMINGO
DRAYAGE
DUGONGS
DURANGO

D•••••G
DABBING
DAFFING
DAMMING
DAMNING
DAMPING
DANCING
DAPPING
DARLING
DARNING
DARTING
DASHING
DAUBING
DAWNING
DAYLONG
DEALING
DECALOG
DECKING
DEEDING
DEEMING
DEFYING
DEICING
DELEING
DELVING
DENTING
DENYING
DERRING
DIALING
DIETING
DIGGING
DIMMING
DINGING
DIPPING
DISHING
DISHRAG
DISSING
DOCKING
DODGING
DOFFING
DOGGING
DOLLING
DONKING
DONNING
DOOMING
DOTTING
DOUSING
DOWNING
DOWSING
DRAPING
DRAWING
DRAYING
DRIVING
DRONING
DUBBING
DUCKING
DUCTING
DUELING
DULLING
DUMBING
DUMPING
DUNKING
DUNNING
DURNING
DUSTING

•DG••••
EDGEDIN
EDGEOUT
EDGESIN
EDGIEST
EDGINGS

•D•G•••
ADAGIOS

•D•••G•
ADJUDGE
EDGINGS

•D••••G
ADDLING
ADORING
EDDYING
EDITING
EDUCING
RDLAING

••DG•••
BADGERS
BADGUYS
BUDGETS
BUDGIES
BUDGING
CADGERS
CADGING
CODGERS
CUDGELS
DIDGOOD
DODGERS
DODGIER
DODGING
DODGSON
DUDGEON
ENDGAME
FIDGETS
FIDGETY
FUDGING
GADGETS
GADGETY
HEDGERS
HEDGIER
HEDGING
JUDGING
LEDGERS
LEDGIER
LODGERS
LODGING
MIDGETS
NUDGERS
NUDGING
OLDGOLD
PIDGEON
PIDGINS
PODGIER
PODGILY
PUDGIER
PUDGILY
REDGUMS
RIDGIER
RIDGING
RIDGWAY
RODGERS
SEDGIER
WEDGIER
WEDGIES
WEDGING
WIDGEON
WIDGETS

••D•G••
BADEGGS
BODEGAS
INDIGOS
MADIGAN
MEDIGAP

••D••G•
BADEGGS
BEDBUGS
ENDINGS
HIDALGO
HIDINGS
INDULGE
OLDFOGY
REDALGA
REDDOGS
SIDINGS
TIDINGS
UNDERGO

••D•••G
ADDLING
BEDDING
BIDDING
BUDDING
BUDGING
CADGING
DODGING
EDDYING
ENDUING
FUDGING
GADDING
HEDGING
JUDGING
KIDDING
LADLING
LADYBUG
LODGING
MADDING
NODDING
NUDGING
PADDING
PUDDING
REDDING
REDFLAG
REDOING
REDWING
RIDDING
RIDGING
RODDING
SIDLING
SODDING
SUDSING
TEDDING
TIDYING
UNDOING
UNDYING
WADDING
WEDDING
WEDGING

•••DG••
BRIDGED
BRIDGES
BRIDGET
DREDGED
DREDGER
DREDGES
DRUDGED
DRUDGES
FLEDGED
FLEDGES
FRIDGES
GRUDGED
GRUDGES
HANDGUN
KLUDGES
PLEDGED
PLEDGEE
PLEDGER
PLEDGES
SLEDGES
SLUDGES
SMIDGEN
SMUDGED
SMUDGES
TRUDGED
TRUDGER
TRUDGES

•••D•G•
BANDAGE
BENDIGO
BONDAGE
CONDIGN
CORDAGE
GOODEGG
GUNDOGS
HOTDOGS
LAPDOGS
PRODIGY
PYEDOGS
REDDOGS
SEADOGS
SUNDOGS
TOPDOGS
TOYDOGS
VERDUGO
YARDAGE

•••D••G
ABIDING
BALDING
BANDING
BEADING
BEDDING
BENDING
BIDDING
BINDING
BIRDDOG
BIRDING
BLADING
BONDING
BUDDING
CARDING
CHIDING
CORDING
CURDING
DEEDING
ELIDING
ELUDING
ERODING
EVADING
EXUDING
FEEDBAG
FEEDING
FENDING
FEUDING
FINDING
FOLDING
FORDING
FUNDING
GADDING
GELDING
GILDING
GIRDING
GLIDING
GOADING
GOLDBUG
GOLDING
GOODEGG
GOODING
GRADING
GUIDING
HANDBAG
HANDING
HARDING
HEADING
HEEDING
HERDING
HOLDING
KIDDING
LANDING
LARDING
LAUDING
LEADING
LENDING
LOADING
LORDING
MADDING
MELDING
MENDING
MINDING
MOLDING
NEEDING
NODDING
PADDING
PENDING
PRIDING
PUDDING
RAIDING
READING
REDDING
REEDING
RENDING
RIDDING
ROADHOG
RODDING
SANDBAG
SANDHOG
SANDING
SEEDING
SENDING
SHADING
SLEDDOG
SLIDING
SODDING
SPADING
TEDDING
TENDING
TRADING
VENDING
VOIDING
WADDING
WARDING
WEDDING
WEEDING
WELDING
WENDING
WILDING
WINDBAG
WINDING
WORDING

••••DG•
ABRIDGE
ADJUDGE
ARLEDGE

••••D•G
BIRDDOG
BULLDOG
CORNDOG
FIREDOG
HANGDOG
MOONDOG
SHINDIG
SHOWDOG
SLEDDOG

DH•••••
DHURRIE

D•H••••
DAHLIAS
DAHOMEY
DEHISCE
DEHORNS

D••H•••
DABHAND
DAPHNIS
DASHERS
DASHIKI
DASHING
DASHOFF
DIEHARD
DISHFUL
DISHIER
DISHING
DISHOUT
DISHPAN
DISHRAG
DITHERS
DITHERY
DRYHOLE
DUCHESS
DUCHIES

D•••H••
DAUPHIN
DELPHIC
DITCHED
DITCHES
DOGCHOW
DOGSHOW
DOLPHIN
DONAHUE
DOUGHTY
DRACHMA
DRACHMS
DROSHKY

D••••H•
DALETHS
DEARTHS
DELIGHT
DENNEHY
DOODAHS
DOROTHY
DRAUGHT
DROUGHT

D•••••H
DAMPISH
DARKISH
DAWKISH
DEBAUCH
DEBORAH
DEBOUCH
DELILAH
DERVISH
DIGRAPH
DIPTYCH
DOGFISH
DOGGISH
DOLLISH
DOLTISH
DONNISH
DOZENTH
DRONISH
DULLISH
DUMPISH
DUNCISH
DUSKISH

•DH••••
ADHERED
ADHERES

•D•H•••
IDAHOAN

•D••H••
EDAPHIC

•D•••H•
ADOLPHE

••DH•••
MUDHENS
OLDHAND
REDHAIR
REDHATS
REDHEAD
REDHEAT
REDHOTS

••D•H••
BUDDHAS
GODTHAB
MADCHEN
MADEHAY
OLDCHAP

••D•••H
ALDRICH
BADDISH
CADDISH
CODFISH
FADDISH
GODUTCH
INDEPTH
INDUTCH
KADDISH
KIDDISH
LADDISH
LADYISH
MADDISH
PADUCAH
REDDISH
RUDOLPH
YIDDISH

•••DH••
BUDDHAS
FORDHAM
HARDHAT
HARDHIT
NEEDHAM
PRUDHOE
ROADHOG
SANDHOG

•••D•H•
DOODAHS
HOWDAHS
PURDAHS
WHYDAHS

•••D••H
BADDISH
BALDISH
BARDISH
CADDISH
COLDISH
FADDISH
GOODISH
KADDISH
KIDDISH
KURDISH
LADDISH
LOUDISH
MADDISH
MAIDISH
MURDOCH
OBADIAH
PRUDISH
REDDISH
SWEDISH
TOADISH
WENDISH
WILDISH
YIDDISH

••••DH•
LAMEDHS

••••D•H
BREADTH
PLAYDOH

DI•••••
DIABOLI
DIADEMS
DIAGRAM
DIALECT
DIALERS
DIALING
DIALOGS
DIAMOND
DIAPERS
DIARIES
DIATOMS
DIBBLED
DIBBLES
DICIEST
DICKENS
DICKERS
DICKEYS
DICKIES
DICTATE
DICTION
DICTUMS
DIDACTS
DIDDLED
DIDDLES
DIDDLEY
DIDEROT
DIDGOOD
DIDOVER
DIEDOFF
DIEDOUT
DIEDOWN
DIEHARD
DIESELS
DIESOFF
DIESOUT
DIETARY
DIETERS
DIETING
DIFFERS
DIFFUSE
DIGESTS
DIGGERS
DIGGING
DIGITAL
DIGNIFY
DIGNITY
DIGRAMS
DIGRAPH
DIGRESS
DIGSOUT
DIKDIKS
DIKTATS
DILATED
DILATES
DILBERT
DILEMMA
DILLARD
DILLIES
DILUTED
DILUTER
DILUTES
DIMBULB
DIMITRI
DIMMERS
DIMMEST
DIMMING
DIMNESS
DIMOUTS
DIMPLED
DIMPLES
DIMWITS
DINEDIN
DINEDON
DINESEN
DINESIN
DINESON
DINETTE
DINGBAT
DINGIER
DINGILY
DINGING
DINGLES
DINGOES
DINKIER
DINKIES
DINMONT
DINNERS
DIOCESE
DIOMEDE
DIOPTER
DIORAMA
DIOXIDE
DIPLOID
DIPLOMA
DIPOLAR
DIPOLES
DIPPERS
DIPPIER
DIPPING
DIPTYCH
DIRECTS
DIREFUL
DIRNDLS
DIRTIED
DIRTIER
DIRTIES
DIRTILY
DISABLE
DISARMS
DISAVOW
DISBAND
DISBARS
DISCARD
DISCERN
DISCOED
DISCORD
DISCUSS
DISDAIN
DISEASE
DISGUST
DISHFUL
DISHIER
DISHING
DISHOUT
DISHPAN
DISHRAG
DISJOIN
DISLIKE
DISMAYS
DISMISS
DISOBEY
DISOWNS
DISPELS
DISPLAY
DISPORT
DISPOSE
DISPUTE
DISROBE
DISRUPT
DISSECT
DISSENT
DISSING
DISTAFF
DISTANT
DISTEND
DISTILL
DISTILS
DISTORT
DISTURB
DISUSED
DITCHED
DITCHES
DITHERS
DITHERY
DITSIER
DITTANY
DITTIES
DITTOED
DITZIER
DIURNAL
DIVERGE
DIVERSE
DIVERTS
DIVESIN
DIVESTS
DIVIDED
DIVIDER
DIVIDES
DIVINED
DIVINER
DIVINES
DIVINUM
DIVISOR
DIVORCE
DIVULGE
DIVVIED
DIVVIES
DIZENED
DIZZIED
DIZZIER
DIZZIES
DIZZILY

D•I••••
DAILIES
DAIMLER
DAIMONS
DAIRIES
DAISIES
DEICERS
DEICING
DEIFIED
DEIFIES
DEIGNED
DEITIES
DOILIES
DOINGIN
DOINGUP
DRIBBLE
DRIBLET
DRIEDUP
DRIESUP
DRIFTED
DRIFTER
DRILLED
DRILLER
DRINKER
DRIPDRY
DRIPPAN
DRIPPED
DRISTAN
DRIVEAT
DRIVEIN
DRIVELS
DRIVERS
DRIVEUP
DRIVING
DRIZZLE
DRIZZLY
DWINDLE

D••I•••
DANIELS
DAVINCI
DEBITED
DECIBEL
DECIDED
DECIDES
DECIMAL
DEFIANT
DEFICIT
DEFILED
DEFILER
DEFILES
DEFINED
DEFINES
DEHISCE
DELIBES
DELICTI
DELICTS
DELIGHT
DELILAH
DELIMIT
DELIRIA
DELISTS
DELIVER
DEMIGOD
DEMILLE
DEMISED
DEMISES
DENIALS
DENIERS
DENIZEN
DEPICTS
DERIDED
DERIDES
DERIVED
DERIVES
DESIGNS
DESIRED
DESIREE
DESIRES
DESISTS
DEVIANT
DEVIATE
DEVICES
DEVILED
DEVILLE
DEVILRY
DEVIOUS
DEVISED
DEVISES
DICIEST
DIGITAL
DIMITRI
DIVIDED
DIVIDER
DIVIDES
DIVINED
DIVINER
DIVINES
DIVINUM
DIVISOR
DOMINGO
DOMINOS
DOMINUS
DONIMUS
DOPIEST
DORITOS
DOSIDOS
DOZIEST
DRAINED
DRAINER
DREIDEL
DREISER
DUBIETY
DUBIOUS
DUTIFUL

D•••I••
DABBING
DADAISM
DADAIST
DADDIES
DAFFIER
DAFFILY
DAFFING
DAHLIAS
DAILIES
DAIRIES
DAISIES
DALLIED
DALLIER
DALLIES
DAMMING
DAMNING
DAMPING
DAMPISH
DANCING
DANDIER
DANDIES
DANDIFY
DAPPING
DARBIES
DARKISH
DARLING
DARNING
DARTING
DASHIKI
DASHING
DAUBING
DAUMIER
DAWKISH
DAWNING
DAYLILY
DAYSINN
DAYTIME
DEALING
DEARIES
DEBRIEF
DECEITS
DECEIVE
DECKING
DECLINE
DECRIED
DECRIER
DECRIES
DEEDING
DEEMING
DEFYING
DEICING
DEIFIED
DEIFIES
DEITIES
DELEING
DELUISE
DELVING
DENSITY
DENTINE
DENTING
DENTIST
DENYING
DEPRIVE
DERAILS
DERBIES
DERNIER
DERRICK
DERRING
DERVISH
DESPISE
DESPITE
DESTINE
DESTINY
DETAILS
DETAINS
DEVEINS
DEVRIES
DEWLINE
DIALING
DIARIES
DICKIES
DICTION
DIETING
DIGGING
DIGNIFY
DIGNITY
DIKDIKS
DILLIES
DIMMING
DIMWITS
DINGIER
DINGILY
DINGING
DINKIER
DINKIES
DIOXIDE
DIPPIER
DIPPING
DIRTIED
DIRTIER
DIRTIES
DIRTILY
DISHIER
DISHING
DISLIKE
DISMISS
DISSING
DISTILL
DISTILS
DITSIER
DITTIES
DITZIER
DIVVIED
DIVVIES
DIZZIED
DIZZIER
DIZZIES
DIZZILY
DNOTICE
DOBBIES
DOBBINS
DOCKING
DODGIER
DODGING
DOFFING
DOGFISH
DOGGIER
DOGGIES
DOGGING
DOGGISH
DOGLIKE
DOGSITS
DOILIES
DOLLIED

DOLLIES
DOLLING
DOLLISH
DOLTISH
DOMAINS
DONKING
DONNING
DONNISH
DOOMING
DOOZIES
DORMICE
DOSSIER
DOTLIKE
DOTTIER
DOTTILY
DOTTING
DOUSING
DOWDIER
DOWDILY
DOWNIER
DOWNING
DOWRIES
DOWSING
DRAPING
DRAWING
DRAYING
DRIVING
DRONING
DRONISH
DROPINS
DUALITY
DUBBING
DUCHIES
DUCKIER
DUCKING
DUCTILE
DUCTING
DUELING
DUELIST
DULCIFY
DULLING
DULLISH
DUMBING
DUMMIED
DUMMIES
DUMPIER
DUMPING
DUMPISH
DUNCISH
DUNKING
DUNKIRK
DUNLINS
DUNNING
DURNING
DUSKIER
DUSKILY
DUSKISH
DUSTIER
DUSTILY
DUSTING

D••••I•
DAPHNIS
DAUPHIN
DAYTRIP
DEADAIR
DEALSIN
DEALTIN
DEARSIR
DECLAIM
DEEPSIX
DEFICIT
DELIMIT
DELIRIA
DELPHIC
DELTAIC
DELTOID
DEMERIT
DEMONIC
DENARII
DEPOSIT
DESPAIR
DESPOIL
DETRAIN
DETROIT
DEXTRIN
DHURRIE
DINEDIN
DINESIN
DIPLOID
DISDAIN
DISJOIN
DIVESIN
DOESKIN
DOINGIN
DOLPHIN
DOORDIE
DRAGSIN
DRASTIC
DRAWNIN
DRAWSIN
DRIVEIN
DROPSIN
DRUMLIN
DRYSUIT
DUCKPIN
DUKAKIS
DUSTBIN
DWEEZIL
DYNAMIC

D•••••I
DASHIKI
DAVINCI
DELICTI
DENARII
DIABOLI
DIMITRI

•DI••••
ADIPOSE
EDIBLES
EDIFICE
EDIFIED
EDIFIES
EDITING
EDITION
EDITORS
EDITOUT
IDIAMIN
IDIOTIC

•D•I•••
ADDIBLE
ADDISON
ADFINEM
ADMIRAL
ADMIRED
ADMIRER
ADMIRES
ADMITTO
ADMIXED
ADMIXES
ADVISED
ADVISER
ADVISES
ADVISOR
EDGIEST
EDGINGS

•D••I••
ADAGIOS
ADAMITE
ADDLING
ADELINE
ADENINE
ADJOINS
ADORING
EDACITY
EDDYING
EDIFICE
EDIFIED
EDIFIES
EDITING
EDITION
EDUCING
IDOLISE
IDOLIZE
RDLAING

•D•••I•
ADDEDIN
ADONAIS
EDAPHIC
EDGEDIN
EDGESIN
IDENTIC
IDIAMIN
IDIOTIC
IDYLLIC

••DI•••
ADDIBLE
ADDISON
AEDILES
ANDIRON
AUDIBLE
AUDIBLY
AUDILES
AUDITED
AUDITOR
BEDIZEN
BODICES
CEDILLA
CODICES
CODICIL
ENDINGS
ENDIVES
FADIMAN
HIDINGS
INDIANA
INDIANS
INDICES
INDICIA
INDICTS
INDIGOS
INDITED
INDITES
IODIDES
IODISED
IODISES
IODIZED
IODIZES
KODIAKS
LADINOS
MADIGAN
MADISON
MEDIANS
MEDIANT
MEDIATE
MEDICAL
MEDICOS
MEDIGAP
MEDIUMS
MODICUM
MODISTE
NUDISTS
OEDIPAL
OEDIPUS
ORDINAL
ORDINES
PEDICAB
PEDICEL
PEDICLE
PODIUMS
RADIALS
RADIANS
RADIANT
RADIATE
RADICAL
RADICES
RADICLE
RADIOED
RADIXES
REDIALS
SIDINGS
TEDIOUS
TEDIUMS
TIDIEST
TIDINGS
ZODIACS

••D•I••
ADDLING
ALDRICH
BADDIES
BADDISH
BEDDING
BEDLIKE
BEDSIDE
BEDTIME
BIDDIES
BIDDING
BODKINS
BUDDIES
BUDDING
BUDGIES
BUDGING
BUDLIKE
CADDIED
CADDIES
CADDISH
CADGING
CADMIUM
CODEINE
CODFISH
CUDDIES
DADAISM
DADAIST
DADDIES
DODGIER
DODGING
EDDYING
ENDUING
ENDWISE
FADDISH
FADDISM
FADDIST
FADEINS
FADLIKE
FUDGING
GADDING
GIDDIER
GIDDILY
GODLIER
GODLIKE
GODWITS
HADRIAN
HEDGIER
HEDGING
JADEITE
JUDAISM
JUDGING
JUDOIST
KADDISH
KIDDIES
KIDDING
KIDDISH
KIDLIKE
LADDIES
LADDISH
LADLING
LADYISH
LEDGIER
LODGING
LUDDITE
MADDING
MADDISH
MADEIRA
MADLIBS
MIDDIES
MIDLIFE
MIDLINE
MIDRIBS
MIDRIFF
MIDRISE
MIDSIZE
MIDWIFE
MUDDIED
MUDDIER
MUDDIES
MUDDILY
MUDPIES
NEDDIES
NODDING
NUDGING
NUDNIKS
OLDLINE
OLDNICK
OLDTIME
ORDAINS
PADDIES
PADDING
PIDGINS
PODGIER
PODGILY
PODLIKE
PODRIDA
PUDDING
PUDGIER
PUDGILY
REDBIRD
REDDING
REDDISH
REDFINS
REDFIRS
REDLINE
REDOING
REDPINE
REDWINE
REDWING
RIDDICK
RIDDING
RIDGIER
RIDGING
RODDING
RODLIKE
RUDDIER
RUDDILY
SEDGIER
SIDLING
SODDIER
SODDIES
SODDING
SUDSIER
SUDSING
TEDDIES
TEDDING
TIDBITS
TIDYING
TODDIES
UNDOING
UNDYING
WADDIES
WADDING
WEDDING
WEDGIER
WEDGIES
WEDGING
YIDDISH

••D••I•
ADDEDIN
ANDROID
BEDELIA
BEDEVIL
BEDOUIN
BIDFAIR
CODICIL
ECDYSIS
ENDEMIC
FADEDIN
FADESIN
FIDELIO
FIDELIS
INDICIA
KIDSKIN
OLDMAID
REDHAIR
SEDALIA
STDENIS
VIDALIA
WADEDIN
WADESIN

••D•••I
CADUCEI
OLDUVAI
PADRONI

•••DI••
ABIDING
ACADIAN
ACIDIFY
ACIDITY
ANODISE
ANODIZE
ARIDITY
AVIDITY
BADDIES
BADDISH
BALDING
BALDISH
BANDIED
BANDIES
BANDING
BANDITO
BANDITS
BARDISH
BAWDIER
BAWDILY
BEADIER
BEADING
BEDDING
BENDIER
BENDIGO
BENDING
BIDDIES
BIDDING
BINDING
BIRDIED
BIRDIES
BIRDING
BLADING
BONDING
BUDDIES
BUDDING
CADDIED
CADDIES
CADDISH
CANDICE
CANDIDA
CANDIDE
CANDIDS
CANDIED
CANDIES
CARDIAC
CARDING
CHIDING
COEDITS
COLDISH
CONDIGN
CONDITA
CORDIAL
CORDING
CORDITE
CREDITS
CRUDITY
CUDDIES
CURDIER
CURDING
DADDIES
DANDIER
DANDIES
DANDIFY
DEEDING
DIKDIKS
DOWDIER
DOWDILY
ELIDING
ELUDING
ERODING
ERUDITE
EVADING
EXUDING
FADDISH
FADDISM
FADDIST
FEEDING
FENDING
FEUDING
FINDING
FOLDING
FOODIES
FORDING
FOSDICK
FUNDING
GADDING
GAUDIER
GAUDILY
GELDING
GIDDIER
GIDDILY
GILDING
GIRDING
GLIDING
GOADING
GOLDING
GOODIES
GOODING
GOODISH
GORDIAN
GRADING
GRODIER
GUIDING
HANDIER
HANDILY
HANDING
HARDIER
HARDILY
HARDING
HEADIER
HEADILY
HEADING
HEEDING
HERDING
HOLDING
HOUDINI
IRIDIUM
KADDISH
KIDDIES
KIDDING
KIDDISH
KURDISH
LADDIES
LADDISH
LANDING
LARDIER
LARDING
LAUDING
LEADIER
LEADING
LEADINS
LENDING
LINDIED
LINDIES
LOADING
LORDING
LOUDISH
LUDDITE
MADDING
MADDISH
MAIDISH
MELDING
MENDING
MIDDIES
MINDING
MISDIAL
MOLDIER
MOLDING
MOODIER
MOODILY
MUDDIED
MUDDIER
MUDDIES
MUDDILY
NEDDIES
NEEDIER
NEEDILY
NEEDING
NERDIER
NODDING
NORDICS
OBADIAH
ONADIET
OXIDISE
OXIDIZE
PADDIES
PADDING
PANDITS
PAYDIRT
PENDING
PERDIEM
PHIDIAS
PREDICT
PRIDING
PRODIGY
PRUDISH
PUDDING
PUNDITS
RAIDING
RANDIER
READIED
READIER
READIES
READILY
READING
REDDING
REDDISH
REEDIER
REEDING
REEDITS
RENDING
RHODIUM
RIDDICK
RIDDING
ROADIES
RODDING
ROWDIER
ROWDIES
ROWDILY
RUDDIER
RUDDILY
SANDIER
SANDING
SARDINE
SEEDIER
SEEDILY
SEEDING
SENDING
SHADIER
SHADILY
SHADING
SKYDIVE
SLIDING
SODDIER
SODDIES
SODDING
SOLDIER
SORDINI
SORDINO
SPADING
STADIUM
STUDIED
STUDIES
STUDIOS
SUNDIAL
SWEDISH
TARDIER
TARDILY
TEDDIES
TEDDING
TENDING
TOADIED
TOADIES
TOADISH
TODDIES
TRADING
VANDINE
VENDING
VERDICT
VOIDING
WADDIES
WADDING
WARDING
WEDDING
WEEDIER
WEEDILY
WEEDING
WELDING
WENDING
WENDISH
WILDING
WILDISH
WINDIER
WINDILY
WINDING
WOODIER
WOODIES
WORDIER
WORDILY
WORDING
YIDDISH

•••D•I•
ALADDIN
BALDRIC
BALDWIN
BANDAID
BOUDOIR
CONDUIT
DEADAIR
DISDAIN
FREDDIE
FREDRIC
GOODWIN
HANDSIN
HARDHIT
HEADPIN
HEADSIN
HENDRIX
HOLDSIN
LEADSIN
LORDJIM
MAUDLIN
READMIT
READSIN
SENDSIN
SLIDEIN
TENDRIL
TRADEIN

•••D••I
HOUDINI
SORDINI

••••DI•
ADDEDIN
ALADDIN
AMRADIO
ARCADIA
ASKEDIN
BLONDIE
BORODIN
BOXEDIN
BUILDIN
CAVEDIN
CBRADIO
CLAUDIA
CLAUDIO
CLUEDIN
COMEDIC
DINEDIN
DOORDIE
EASEDIN
EDGEDIN
FADEDIN
FMRADIO
FREDDIE
GEORDIE
HASIDIC
HASIDIM
JURIDIC
KATYDID
KEYEDIN
LIVEDIN
MAULDIN
MELODIC
MIXEDIN
MONODIC
MOVEDIN
NOMADIC
OVERDID
PALADIN
PILEDIN
PLAUDIT
RAKEDIN
ROPEDIN
RUSHDIE
SALADIN
SHINDIG
SINEDIE
STANDIN
STOODIN
SYNODIC
TUNEDIN
VOTEDIN
WADEDIN
WAVEDIN

••••D•I
HYUNDAI

•••••DI
BACARDI
COLLODI
EFFENDI
VIVALDI
VIVENDI

D•J••••
DEJECTS

D••J•••
DAYJOBS
DEEJAYS
DISJOIN
DONJONS
DONJOSE
DONJUAN

•DJ••••
ADJOINS
ADJOURN
ADJUDGE
ADJUNCT
ADJURED
ADJURES
ADJUSTS
PDJAMES

•D•J•••
ODDJOBS

••DJ•••
ODDJOBS

•••DJ••
GOODJOB
GOODJOE
LORDJIM

D•K••••
DAKOTAN
DAKOTAS
DEKLERK
DIKDIKS
DIKTATS
DUKAKIS
DUKEDOM
DYKSTRA

D••K•••
DANKEST
DARKENS
DARKEST
DARKISH
DARKMAN
DAWKISH
DECKING
DECKLES
DECKOUT
DESKSET
DESKTOP
DICKENS
DICKERS
DICKEYS
DICKIES
DINKIER
DINKIES
DOCKAGE
DOCKERS
DOCKETS
DOCKING
DONKEYS
DONKING
DUCKIER
DUCKING
DUCKPIN
DUNKERS
DUNKING
DUNKIRK
DUSKIER
DUSKILY
DUSKISH

D•••K••
DEBAKEY
DOESKIN
DRINKER
DRUCKER
DUKAKIS

D••••K•
DAMASKS
DASHIKI
DEBARKS
DEBUNKS
DIKDIKS
DISLIKE
DOGLIKE
DOTLIKE
DROSHKY
DYBBUKS

D•••••K
DAYBOOK
DEFROCK
DEKLERK
DENMARK
DERRICK
DMYTRYK
DRSPOCK
DRYDOCK
DUNKIRK
DUNNOCK

••DK•••
BODKINS

••D•K••
KIDSKIN

••D••K•
BEDECKS
BEDLIKE
BUDLIKE
FADLIKE
GODLIKE
KIDLIKE
KODIAKS
NUDNIKS
PODLIKE
REDOAKS
RODLIKE

••D•••K
BEDROCK
BODEREK
HADDOCK
MIDWEEK
MUDPACK
OLDNICK
PADDOCK
PADLOCK
REDBOOK
RIDDICK
SADSACK
TEDMACK
WEDLOCK
WIDMARK

•••D•K•
DIKDIKS
VANDYKE

•••D••K
BURDOCK
DRYDOCK
FOSDICK
HADDOCK
PADDOCK
RIDDICK
SUNDECK
VANDYCK

D•L••••
DALETHS
DALLIED
DALLIER
DALLIES
DALTREY
DELANEY
DELAYED
DELAYER
DELEING
DELETED
DELETES
DELIBES
DELICTI
DELICTS
DELIGHT
DELILAH
DELIMIT
DELIRIA
DELISTS
DELIVER
DELPHIC
DELTAIC
DELTOID
DELUDED
DELUDES
DELUGED
DELUGES
DELUISE
DELVERS
DELVING
DILATED
DILATES
DILBERT
DILEMMA
DILLARD
DILLIES
DILUTED
DILUTER
DILUTES
DOLEFUL
DOLEOUT
DOLLARS
DOLLIED
DOLLIES
DOLLING
DOLLISH
DOLLOPS
DOLLSUP
DOLMANS
DOLMENS
DOLORES
DOLOURS
DOLPHIN
DOLTISH
DULCIFY
DULLARD
DULLEST
DULLING
DULLISH

D••L•••
DAHLIAS
DAILIES
DALLIED
DALLIER
DALLIES
DARLENE
DARLING
DAYLILY
DAYLONG
DEALERS
DEALING
DEALOUT
DEALSIN
DEALTIN
DECLAIM
DECLARE
DECLASS
DECLINE
DEFLATE
DEFLECT
DEKLERK
DEPLANE
DEPLETE
DEPLORE
DEPLOYS
DEWLAPS
DEWLESS
DEWLINE
DIALECT
DIALERS
DIALING
DIALOGS
DILLARD
DILLIES
DIPLOID
DIPLOMA
DISLIKE

DOGLEGS
DOGLESS
DOGLIKE
DOILIES
DOLLARS
DOLLIED
DOLLIES
DOLLING
DOLLISH
DOLLOPS
DOLLSUP
DOTLIKE
DRILLED
DRILLER
DROLLER
DUALITY
DUELERS
DUELING
DUELIST
DULLARD
DULLEST
DULLING
DULLISH
DUNLINS
DWELLED
DWELLER

D•••L••

DABBLED
DABBLER
DABBLES
DAIMLER
DANDLED
DANDLES
DANELAW
DANGLED
DANGLER
DANGLES
DAPPLED
DAPPLES
DARNLEY
DAWDLED
DAWDLER
DAWDLES
DAZZLED
DAZZLER
DAZZLES
DECALOG
DECKLES
DEDALUS
DEFALLA
DEFILED
DEFILER
DEFILES
DELILAH
DEMILLE
DEPALMA
DESALTS
DEVALUE
DEVELOP
DEVILED
DEVILLE
DEVILRY
DEVOLVE
DEWCLAW
DIBBLED
DIBBLES
DIDDLED
DIDDLES
DIDDLEY
DIMPLED
DIMPLES
DINGLES
DIPOLAR
DIPOLES
DISPLAY
DIVULGE
DOGSLED
DONGLES
DOODLED
DOODLER
DOODLES
DOPPLER
DOTTLES
DOUBLED
DOUBLES
DOUBLET
DOUBLEU
DOUGLAS
DRAWLED
DRIBLET
DRILLED
DRILLER
DROLLER
DROOLED
DROOLER
DROPLET
DRUMLIN
DWELLED
DWELLER

D••••L•

DACTYLS
DAFFILY
DAMSELS
DANIELS
DATEDLY
DAYLILY
DAZEDLY
DEBACLE
DECARLO
DEERFLY
DEFALLA
DEFAULT
DEMILLE
DENIALS
DENSELY
DERAILS
DETAILS
DEVILLE
DIABOLI
DIESELS
DIMBULB
DINGILY
DIRNDLS
DIRTILY
DISABLE
DISPELS
DISTILL
DISTILS
DIZZILY
DORSALS
DOSSALS
DOTTILY
DOWDILY
DRACULA
DRIBBLE
DRIVELS
DRIZZLE
DRIZZLY
DRYCELL
DRYHOLE
DRYWALL
DRYWELL
DUCTILE
DUFFELS
DURABLE
DURABLY
DURRELL
DUSKILY
DUSTILY
DWINDLE

D•••••L

DAREFUL
DECIBEL
DECIMAL
DEMEROL
DEPOSAL
DESPOIL
DIGITAL
DIREFUL
DISHFUL
DISTILL
DIURNAL
DOLEFUL
DONEGAL
DOOMFUL
DREIDEL
DRYCELL
DRYWALL
DRYWELL
DURRELL
DUTIFUL
DWEEZIL

•DL••••

RDLAING

•D•L•••

ADDLING
ADELINE
ADOLPHE
ADULATE
ADULTLY
IDOLISE
IDOLIZE
IDYLLIC
ODDLOTS

•D••L••

EDIBLES
IDEALLY
IDYLLIC

•D•••L•

ADDABLE
ADDIBLE
ADEPTLY
ADULTLY
IDEALLY
ODDBALL

•D••••L

ADMIRAL
ADRENAL
ODDBALL
ODORFUL

••DL•••

ADDLING
AIDLESS
BEDLAMP
BEDLESS
BEDLIKE
BUDLESS
BUDLIKE
ENDLESS
FADLIKE
GODLESS
GODLIER
GODLIKE
KIDLIKE
LADLERS
LADLING
LIDLESS
MADLIBS
MEDLEYS
MIDLAND
MIDLIFE
MIDLINE
ODDLOTS
OLDLINE
PADLOCK
PEDLARS
PODLIKE
REDLINE
RODLESS
RODLIKE
SIDLING
SODLESS
WEDLOCK

••D•L••

AEDILES
AUDILES
BEDELIA
CEDILLA
CODDLED
CODDLER
CODDLES
CUDDLED
CUDDLES
DEDALUS
DIDDLED
DIDDLES
DIDDLEY
ENDPLAY
FIDDLED
FIDDLER
FIDDLES
FIDELIO
FIDELIS
FUDDLED
FUDDLES
HEDDLES
HIDALGO
HUDDLED
HUDDLES
INDULGE
MEDALED
MEDDLED
MEDDLER
MEDDLES
MEDULLA
MIDDLEC
MIDDLES
MODELAS
MODELED
MODELER
MODELTS
MODULAR
MODULES
MUDDLED
MUDDLER
MUDDLES
NODULAR
NODULES
PADDLED
PADDLER
PADDLES
PEDALED
PEDDLED
PEDDLER
PEDDLES
PUDDLED
PUDDLES
RADDLED
RADDLES
RADULAE
REDALGA
REDFLAG
RIDDLED
RIDDLER
RIDDLES
RODOLFO
RUDOLPH
SADDLED
SADDLER
SADDLES
SEDALIA
TODDLED
TODDLER
TODDLES
VIDALIA
WADDLED
WADDLER
WADDLES
YODELED
YODELER

••D••L•

ADDABLE
ADDIBLE
AUDIBLE
AUDIBLY
BEDROLL
CEDILLA
CUDGELS
ELDERLY
GIDDILY
INDWELL
JADEDLY
MEDULLA
MUDDILY
MUDEELS
ODDBALL
OLDGOLD
ORDEALS
ORDERLY
PEDICLE
PODGILY
PUDGILY
RADIALS
RADICLE
REDCELL
REDEALS
REDEALT
REDIALS
REDPOLL
REDWOLF
RUDDILY
TADPOLE

••D•••L

BEDEVIL
BEDROLL
CODICIL
FEDERAL
INDWELL
MEDICAL
ODDBALL
OEDIPAL
ORDINAL
PEDICEL
RADICAL
REDCELL
REDPOLL

•••DL••

BEADLES
BOODLES
BOWDLER
BRADLEE
BRADLEY
BRIDLED
BRIDLES
BUNDLED
BUNDLES
CANDLES
CAUDLES
CODDLED
CODDLER
CODDLES
CRADLED
CRADLES
CUDDLED
CUDDLES
CURDLED
CURDLES
DANDLED
DANDLES
DAWDLED
DAWDLER
DAWDLES
DIDDLED
DIDDLES
DIDDLEY
DOODLED
DOODLER
DOODLES
FEEDLOT
FIDDLED
FIDDLER
FIDDLES
FIEDLER
FONDLED
FONDLES
FUDDLED
FUDDLES
GIRDLED
GIRDLES
HANDLED
HANDLER
HANDLES
HEDDLES
HOODLUM
HUDDLED
HUDDLES
HURDLED
HURDLER
HURDLES
KINDLED
KINDLES
LAIDLOW
MAUDLIN
MEDDLED
MEDDLER
MEDDLES
MIDDLEC
MIDDLES
MUDDLED
MUDDLER
MUDDLES
NEEDLED
NEEDLES
NOODLES
PADDLED
PADDLER
PADDLES
PEDDLED
PEDDLER
PEDDLES
POODLES
PUDDLED
PUDDLES
RADDLED
RADDLES
RIDDLED
RIDDLER
RIDDLES
RUNDLES
SADDLED
SADDLER
SADDLES
SANDLOT
TODDLED
TODDLER
TODDLES
WADDLED
WADDLER
WADDLES
WOODLOT

•••D•L•

BAWDILY
BOBDOLE
BRIDALS
CANDELA
CONDOLE
CORDELL
CRUDELY
DOWDILY
GAUDILY
GIDDILY
GONDOLA
GOODALL
GRIDDLE
HANDILY
HARDILY
HEADILY
KENDALL
MANDALA
MANDELA
MONDALE
MOODILY
MUDDILY
NEEDILY
RAGDOLL
RANDALL
READILY
RONDELS
ROWDILY
RUDDILY
SANDALS
SANDFLY
SEEDILY
SEIDELS
SHADILY
SNIDELY
SWADDLE
TARDILY
TWADDLE
TWIDDLE
VANDALS
WEEDILY
WENDELL
WINDILY
WORDILY

•••D••L

BIGDEAL
CORDELL
CORDIAL
GOODALL
GRADUAL
HANDFUL
HEEDFUL
KENDALL
MINDFUL
MISDEAL
MISDIAL
NEEDFUL
NEWDEAL
RAGDOLL
RANDALL
RAWDEAL
SUNDIAL
TENDRIL
WENDELL

••••DL•

ACRIDLY
BLANDLY
BLINDLY
BRINDLE
BROADLY
DATEDLY
DAZEDLY
DIRNDLS
DWINDLE
FETIDLY
FIXEDLY
FLUIDLY
GELIDLY
GRANDLY
GRIDDLE
HUMIDLY
JADEDLY
LIVIDLY
LUCIDLY
LURIDLY
NAKEDLY
NOTEDLY
PROUDLY
RABIDLY
RAPIDLY
RIGIDLY
ROUNDLY
SOLIDLY
SOUNDLY
SPINDLE
SPINDLY
STAIDLY
SWADDLE
SWINDLE
TEPIDLY
THIRDLY
TIMIDLY
TIREDLY
TREADLE
TRUNDLE
TWADDLE
TWIDDLE
UNGODLY
VALIDLY
VAPIDLY
VEXEDLY
VIVIDLY
WEIRDLY
WHEEDLE
WORLDLY

••••D•L

BIMODAL
BIPEDAL
CITADEL
DREIDEL
GRENDEL
INFIDEL
OVOIDAL
REMODEL
SCANDAL
STRUDEL
SYNODAL

DM•••••

DMYTRYK

D•M••••

DAMAGED
DAMAGES
DAMASKS
DAMMARS
DAMMING
DAMNING
DAMPENS
DAMPERS
DAMPEST
DAMPING
DAMPISH
DAMSELS
DAMSONS
DEMANDS
DEMEANS
DEMERIT
DEMEROL
DEMESNE
DEMETER
DEMIGOD
DEMILLE
DEMISED
DEMISES
DEMONIC
DEMOTED
DEMOTES
DEMPSEY
DEMURER
DIMBULB
DIMITRI
DIMMERS
DIMMEST
DIMMING
DIMNESS
DIMOUTS
DIMPLED
DIMPLES
DIMWITS
DOMAINS
DOMINGO
DOMINOS
DOMINUS
DUMBEST
DUMBING
DUMDUMS
DUMMIED
DUMMIES
DUMMYUP
DUMPIER
DUMPING
DUMPISH

D••M•••

DAIMLER
DAIMONS
DAMMARS
DAMMING
DAUMIER
DAYMARE
DEEMING
DENMARK
DESMOND
DIAMOND
DIMMERS
DIMMEST
DIMMING
DINMONT
DIOMEDE
DISMAYS
DISMISS
DOGMATA
DOLMANS
DOLMENS
DOOMFUL
DOOMING
DORMANT
DORMERS
DORMICE
DRUMLIN
DRUMMED
DRUMMER
DRUMSUP
DUMMIED
DUMMIES
DUMMYUP

D•••M••

DAHOMEY
DARKMAN
DECAMPS
DECIMAL
DEFAMED
DEFAMES
DELIMIT
DILEMMA
DONIMUS
DOORMAN
DOORMAT
DOORMEN
DREAMED
DREAMER
DREAMON
DREAMUP
DRUMMED
DRUMMER
DUSTMAN
DUSTMEN
DUSTMOP
DYNAMIC
DYNAMOS

D••••M•

DAYCAMP
DAYTIME
DEFORMS
DEPALMA
DIADEMS
DIATOMS
DICTUMS
DIGRAMS
DILEMMA
DIORAMA
DIPLOMA
DISARMS
DRACHMA
DRACHMS
DUMDUMS

D•••••M

DADAISM
DAYROOM
DECLAIM
DECORUM
DIAGRAM
DIVINUM
DUKEDOM

•DM••••

ADMIRAL
ADMIRED
ADMIRER
ADMIRES
ADMITTO
ADMIXED
ADMIXES

•D•M•••

ADAMANT
ADAMITE
ADAMSON
ODDMENT

•D••M••

IDEAMAN
IDEAMEN
IDIAMIN
PDJAMES

•D••••M

ADFINEM

••DM•••

ARDMORE
CADMIUM
ENDMOST
MIDMOST
ODDMENT
OLDMAID
OLDMOON
REDMEAT
TEDMACK
WIDMARK

••D•M••

ABDOMEN
ENDEMIC
FADIMAN
MADAMEX
RADOMES
SIDEMAN
SIDEMEN

••D••M•

BEDLAMP
BEDTIME
ENDGAME
MEDIUMS
OLDTIME
PODIUMS
REDEEMS
REDGUMS
TEDIUMS

••D•••M

BEDROOM
CADMIUM
DADAISM
FADDISM
JUDAISM
MIDTERM
MODICUM
SIDEARM

•••DM••

BIRDMAN
BIRDMEN
BONDMAN
BONDMEN
FELDMAN
GOODMAN
GOODMEN
HEADMAN
HEADMEN
READMIT
ROADMAP
SANDMAN
SANDMEN
YARDMAN
YARDMEN

•••D•M•

ACADEME
ACADEMY
AIRDAMS
ANADEMS
BELDAME
BELDAMS
CONDEMN
DIADEMS
DUMDUMS
TANDEMS

•••D••M

EARDRUM
FADDISM
FORDHAM
HOODLUM
HUMDRUM
IRIDIUM
LORDJIM
NEEDHAM
PERDIEM
RHODIUM
STADIUM
YARDARM

••••DM•

GRANDMA

••••D•M

BOREDOM
CZARDOM
DUKEDOM
EARLDOM
FIEFDOM
FREEDOM
GRANDAM
HASIDIM
KINGDOM
MACADAM
MILLDAM
POTSDAM
SERFDOM
SHAHDOM
STARDOM
TOTIDEM

DN•••••

DNOTICE

D•N••••

DANBURY
DANCERS
DANCING
DANDERS
DANDIER
DANDIES
DANDIFY
DANDLED
DANDLES
DANELAW
DANGERS
DANGLED
DANGLER
DANGLES
DANIELS
DANKEST
DANSEUR
DENARII
DENDRON
DENEUVE
DENIALS
DENIERS
DENIZEN
DENMARK
DENNEHY
DENOTED
DENOTES
DENSELY
DENSEST
DENSITY
DENTATE
DENTINE
DENTING
DENTIST
DENTURE
DENUDED
DENUDES
DENYING
DINEDIN
DINEDON
DINESEN
DINESIN
DINESON
DINETTE
DINGBAT
DINGIER
DINGILY
DINGING
DINGLES
DINGOES
DINKIER
DINKIES
DINMONT
DINNERS
DONAHUE
DONATED
DONATES
DONATOR
DONEFOR
DONEGAL
DONGLES
DONIMUS
DONJONS
DONJOSE
DONJUAN
DONKEYS
DONKING
DONNING
DONNISH
DONOVAN
DUNAWAY
DUNCISH
DUNGEON
DUNKERS
DUNKING
DUNKIRK
DUNLINS
DUNNING
DUNNOCK
DYNAMIC
DYNAMOS
DYNASTS
DYNASTY

D••N•••

DAMNING
DARNERS
DARNING
DARNLEY
DAUNTED
DAWNING
DAWNSON
DEANERY
DENNEHY
DERNIER
DIGNIFY
DIGNITY
DIMNESS
DINNERS
DIRNDLS
DOINGIN
DOINGUP
DONNING
DONNISH
DOWNBOW
DOWNERS
DOWNIER
DOWNING
DOWNPAT
DRINKER
DRONERS
DRONING
DRONISH
DRYNESS
DUENNAS
DUNNING
DUNNOCK
DURNING
DWINDLE

D•••N••

DAPHNIS
DAVINCI
DEBONED
DEBONES
DEBUNKS
DECANTS
DECENCY
DEFENCE
DEFENDS
DEFENSE
DEFINED
DEFINES
DEFUNCT
DEIGNED
DELANEY
DEMANDS
DEMONIC
DEPENDS
DEPONED
DEPONES
DETENTE
DIURNAL
DIVINED
DIVINER
DIVINES
DIVINUM
DIZENED
DOCENTS
DOMINGO
DOMINOS
DOMINUS
DOPANTS
DOYENNE
DOZENTH
DRAGNET
DRAINED
DRAINER
DRAWNIN
DRAWNON
DRAWNUP
DROWNED
DUENNAS
DUGONGS

DURANCE
DURANGO
DURANTE

D••••N•
DABBING
DABHAND
DAFFING
DAIMONS
DAMMING
DAMNING
DAMPENS
DAMPING
DAMSONS
DANCING
DAPPING
DARKENS
DARLENE
DARLING
DARNING
DARTING
DASHING
DAUBING
DAWNING
DAYLONG
DAYSINN
DAYTONA
DEACONS
DEADEND
DEADENS
DEAFENS
DEALING
DECKING
DECLINE
DEEDING
DEEMING
DEEPEND
DEEPENS
DEFIANT
DEFYING
DEHORNS
DEICING
DELEING
DELVING
DEMEANS
DEMESNE
DENTINE
DENTING
DENYING
DEPLANE
DERRING
DESCANT
DESCEND
DESCENT
DESIGNS
DESMOND
DESTINE
DESTINY
DETAINS
DEVEINS
DEVIANT
DEWLINE
DIALING
DIAMOND
DICKENS
DIETING
DIGGING
DIMMING
DINGING
DINMONT
DIPPING
DISBAND
DISHING
DISOWNS
DISSENT
DISSING
DISTANT
DISTEND
DITTANY
DOBBINS
DOCKING
DODGING
DOFFING
DOGBANE
DOGGING
DOGGONE
DOLLING
DOLMANS
DOLMENS
DOMAINS
DONJONS
DONKING
DONNING
DOOMING
DORMANT
DOTTING
DOUSING
DOWNING
DOWSING
DOYENNE
DRAGONS
DRAPING
DRAWING
DRAYING
DRIVING
DRONING
DROPINS
DRYRUNS
DUBBING
DUCKING
DUCTING
DUELING
DULLING
DUMBING
DUMPING
DUNKING
DUNLINS
DUNNING
DUODENA
DURNING
DUSTING

D•••••N
DAKOTAN
DARKMAN
DAUPHIN
DAWNSON
DAYSINN
DEADPAN
DEALSIN
DEALTIN
DECAGON
DENDRON
DENIZEN
DETRAIN
DEXTRIN
DICTION
DIEDOWN
DINEDIN
DINEDON
DINESEN
DINESIN
DINESON
DISCERN
DISDAIN
DISHPAN
DISJOIN
DIVESIN
DODGSON
DOESKIN
DOINGIN
DOLPHIN
DONJUAN
DONOVAN
DOORMAN
DOORMEN
DOTEDON
DOTESON
DRAGOON
DRAGSIN
DRAGSON
DRAWNIN
DRAWNON
DRAWSIN
DRAWSON
DREAMON
DRESDEN
DRIPPAN
DRISTAN
DRIVEIN
DROPSIN
DRUMLIN
DUCKPIN
DUDGEON
DUNGEON
DUSTBIN
DUSTMAN
DUSTMEN
DUSTPAN

•D•N•••
ADENINE
ADONAIS
IDENTIC
ODDNESS

•D••N••
ADDENDA
ADDENDS
ADDONTO
ADFINEM
ADJUNCT
ADORNED
ADORNER
ADRENAL
ADVANCE
ADVENTS
EDASNER
EDGINGS

•D•••N•
ADAMANT
ADDLING
ADELINE
ADENINE
ADJOINS
ADORING
EDDYING
EDITING
EDUCING
ODDMENT
RDLAING

•D••••N
ADAMSON
ADDEDIN
ADDEDON
ADDISON
ADJOURN
EDGEDIN
EDGESIN
EDITION
IDAHOAN
IDEAMAN
IDEAMEN
IDIAMIN

••DN•••
BADNESS
KIDNAPS
KIDNEYS
MADNESS
NUDNIKS
ODDNESS
OLDNESS
OLDNEWS
OLDNICK
REDNESS
SADNESS

••D•N••
ADDENDA
ADDENDS
ADDONTO
ALDENTE
ANDANTE
ARDENCY
CADENCE
CADENCY
CADENZA
ENDINGS
GODUNOV
HIDINGS
INDENTS
LADINOS
MADONNA
ORDINAL
ORDINES
PEDANTS
PUDENCY
REDANTS
RODENTS
SIDINGS
STDENIS
TIDINGS
VEDANTA
WIDENED

••D••N•
ADDLING
ANDEANS
BEDDING
BIDDING
BODKINS
BUDDING
BUDGING
CADGING
CODEINE
DODGING
EDDYING
ENDRUNS
ENDUING
ENDZONE
FADEINS
FUDGING
GADDING
GIDEONS
GODSEND
GODSONS
HEDGING
HYDRANT
INDIANA
INDIANS
JUDGING
KIDDING
LADLING
LODGING
MADDENS
MADDING
MADONNA
MEDIANS
MEDIANT
MIDDENS
MIDLAND
MIDLINE
MODERNS
MUDHENS
NODDING
NUDGING
ODDMENT
OLDHAND
OLDLINE
ORDAINS
PADDING
PADRONE
PADRONI
PADUANS
PIDGINS
PUDDING
RADIANS
RADIANT
REDCENT
REDDENS
REDDING
REDFINS
REDLINE
REDOING
REDOUND
REDPINE
REDWINE
REDWING
RIDDING
RIDGING
RODDING
SADDENS
SIDLING
SODDING
SUDSING
TEDDING
TIDYING
UNDOING
UNDYING
WADDING
WEDDING
WEDGING

••D•••N
ABDOMEN
ADDEDIN
ADDEDON
ADDISON
ANDIRON
ANDSOON
AUDUBON
BEDDOWN
BEDIZEN
BEDOUIN
CADDOAN
DODGSON
DUDGEON
FADEDIN
FADESIN
FADIMAN
GADSDEN
HADRIAN
KIDSKIN
MADCHEN
MADIGAN
MADISON
MIDTOWN
OLDMOON
PIDGEON
REDRAWN
SIDEMAN
SIDEMEN
UNDRAWN
WADEDIN
WADESIN
WIDGEON

•••DN••
GARDNER
LARDNER
PARDNER

•••D•N•
ABIDING
ANODYNE
BALDING
BANDANA
BANDING
BEADING
BEDDING
BENDING
BIDDING
BINDING
BIRDING
BLADING
BONDING
BUDDING
BURDENS
CARDING
CHIDING
CONDONE
CORDING
CORDONS
CURDING
DEADEND
DEADENS
DEEDING
DUODENA
ELIDING
ELUDING
ERODENT
ERODING
EVADING
EVIDENT
EXUDING
FEEDING
FENDING
FEUDING
FINDING
FOLDING
FONDANT
FORDING
FUNDING
GADDING
GARDENS
GELDING
GILDING
GIRDING
GLIDING
GOADING
GOLDING
GOODING
GOODONE
GRADING
GUIDING
GUIDONS
HAGDONS
HANDING
HARDENS
HARDING
HEADING
HEEDING
HERDING
HOLDING
HOUDINI
HOYDENS
KIDDING
LANDING
LARDING
LARDONS
LAUDING
LEADING
LEADINS
LENDING
LINDENS
LOADING
LORDING
MADDENS
MADDING
MAIDENS
MANDANS
MELDING
MENDING
MIDDENS
MINDING
MISDONE
MOLDING
MORDANT
MORDENT
MUNDANE
NEEDING
NODDING
OUTDONE
OXIDANT
PADDING
PARDONS
PENDANT
PENDENT
PENDING
PRIDING
PRUDENT
PUDDING
RAIDING
READING
REDDENS
REDDING
REEDING
RENDING
RIDDING
RODDING
SADDENS
SANDING
SARDINE
SEEDING
SENDING
SHADING
SLIDING
SODDING
SORDINI
SORDINO
SPADING
STUDENT
TEDDING
TENDING
TENDONS
TRADING
TRIDENT
VANDINE
VENDING
VERDANT
VOIDING
WADDING
WARDENS
WARDING
WEDDING
WEEDING
WELDING
WENDING
WILDING
WILDONE
WINDING
WORDING
WORDONE

•••D••N
ACADIAN
ALADDIN
BALDWIN
BEDDOWN
BIRDMAN
BIRDMEN
BOGDOWN
BONDMAN
BONDMEN
CADDOAN
CALDRON
CONDEMN
CONDIGN
CUTDOWN
DEADPAN
DENDRON
DIEDOWN
DISDAIN
FEEDSON
FELDMAN
GETDOWN
GLADDEN
GOLDWYN
GOODMAN
GOODMEN
GOODSON
GOODWIN
GORDIAN
GOTDOWN
HANDGUN
HANDSIN
HANDSON
HARDPAN
HARDWON
HEADMAN
HEADMEN
HEADPIN
HEADSIN
HOEDOWN
HOLDSIN
HOLDSON
LAYDOWN
LEADSIN
LEADSON
LETDOWN
LIEDOWN
LOWDOWN
MAUDLIN
MOWDOWN
PINDOWN
PREDAWN
PUTDOWN
RANDOWN
READSIN
RUBDOWN
RUNDOWN
SANDMAN
SANDMEN
SATDOWN
SENDSIN
SETDOWN
SHODDEN
SITDOWN
SLIDEIN
SMIDGEN
SUNDOWN
TIEDOWN
TOPDOWN
TRADEIN
TRADEON
TRODDEN
YARDMAN
YARDMEN

••••DN•
ARIADNE
COULDNT
ECHIDNA
JUNKDNA
WOULDNT

••••D•N
ABANDON
ACTEDON
ADDEDIN
ADDEDON
ALADDIN
ALMADEN
ASKEDIN
BORODIN
BOXEDIN
BRANDON
BRENDAN
BROADEN
BUILDIN
CAVEDIN
CELADON
CLUEDIN
DINEDIN
DINEDON
DOTEDON
DRESDEN
EASEDIN
EDGEDIN
EGGEDON
FADEDIN
FRIEDAN
GADSDEN
GLADDEN
GLUEDON
HALFDAN
JOURDAN
KEYEDIN
LANGDON
LIVEDIN
LIVEDON
MAULDIN
MIXEDIN
MOVEDIN
MOVEDON
NEVADAN
ONANDON
PALADIN
PILEDIN
PILEDON
RAKEDIN
RAMADAN
ROPEDIN
ROUNDON
RUANDAN
RWANDAN
SALADIN
SEWEDON
SHELDON
SHODDEN
SNOWDON
SPIEDON
STANDIN
STANDON
STOODIN
TRIEDON
TRODDEN
TUNEDIN
UGANDAN
VOTEDIN
WADEDIN
WAVEDIN
WHAUDEN

DO•••••
DOBBIES
DOBBINS
DOCENTS
DOCKAGE
DOCKERS
DOCKETS
DOCKING
DOCTORS
DODDERS
DODGERS
DODGIER
DODGING
DODGSON
DOESKIN
DOFFING
DOGBANE
DOGBERT
DOGCART
DOGCHOW
DOGDAYS
DOGEARS
DOGFACE
DOGFISH
DOGFOOD
DOGGIER
DOGGIES
DOGGING
DOGGISH
DOGGONE
DOGLEGS
DOGLESS
DOGLIKE
DOGMATA
DOGSHOW
DOGSITS
DOGSLED
DOGSTAR
DOGTAGS
DOGTROT
DOGWOOD
DOILIES
DOINGIN
DOINGUP
DOLEFUL
DOLEOUT
DOLLARS
DOLLIED
DOLLIES
DOLLING
DOLLISH
DOLLOPS
DOLLSUP
DOLMANS
DOLMENS
DOLORES
DOLOURS
DOLPHIN
DOLTISH
DOMAINS
DOMINGO
DOMINOS
DOMINUS
DONAHUE
DONATED
DONATES
DONATOR
DONEFOR
DONEGAL
DONGLES
DONIMUS
DONJONS
DONJOSE
DONJUAN
DONKEYS
DONKING
DONNING
DONNISH
DONOVAN
DOODADS
DOODAHS
DOODLED
DOODLER
DOODLES
DOOMFUL
DOOMING
DOORDIE
DOORMAN
DOORMAT
DOORMEN
DOORWAY
DOOZIES
DOPANTS
DOPEOUT
DOPIEST
DOPPLER
DORITOS
DORMANT
DORMERS
DORMICE
DOROTHY
DORSALS
DORSETT
DOSAGES
DOSIDOS
DOSSALS
DOSSERS
DOSSIER
DOTARDS
DOTEDON
DOTESON
DOTLIKE
DOTTIER
DOTTILY
DOTTING
DOTTLES
DOUBLED
DOUBLES
DOUBLET
DOUBLEU
DOUBTED
DOUBTER
DOUGHTY
DOUGLAS
DOUREST
DOUSING
DOVECOT
DOWAGER
DOWDIER
DOWDILY
DOWERED
DOWNBOW
DOWNERS
DOWNIER
DOWNING
DOWNPAT
DOWRIES
DOWSERS
DOWSING
DOYENNE
DOZENTH
DOZEOFF
DOZIEST

D•O••••
DEODARS
DIOCESE
DIOMEDE
DIOPTER
DIORAMA
DIOXIDE
DNOTICE
DOODADS
DOODAHS
DOODLED
DOODLER
DOODLES
DOOMFUL
DOOMING
DOORDIE
DOORMAN
DOORMAT
DOORMEN
DOORWAY
DOOZIES
DROLLER
DRONERS
DRONING
DRONISH
DROOLED
DROOLER
DROOPED
DROPINS
DROPLET
DROPOFF
DROPOUT
DROPPED
DROPPER
DROPSBY
DROPSIN
DROSHKY
DROUGHT
DROVERS
DROWNED
DROWSED
DROWSES
DUODENA

D••O•••
DAHOMEY
DAKOTAN
DAKOTAS
DEBONED
DEBONES
DEBORAH
DEBOUCH
DECOCTS
DECODED
DECODER
DECODES
DECORUM
DECOYED
DEFORMS
DEHORNS
DEMONIC
DEMOTED
DEMOTES
DENOTED
DENOTES
DEPONED
DEPONES
DEPORTS
DEPOSAL
DEPOSED
DEPOSER
DEPOSES
DEPOSIT
DESOTOS
DETOURS
DEVOLVE
DEVOTED
DEVOTEE
DEVOTES
DEVOURS
DIDOVER
DIMOUTS
DIPOLAR
DIPOLES
DISOBEY
DISOWNS
DIVORCE
DOLORES
DOLOURS
DONOVAN
DOROTHY
DROOLED
DROOLER
DROOPED
DUGONGS
DUGOUTS

D•••O••
DAGWOOD
DAIMONS
DAMSONS
DASBOOT
DASHOFF
DAYBOOK
DAYBOYS
DAYJOBS
DAYLONG
DAYROOM
DAYTONA
DEACONS
DEALOUT
DEBTORS
DECKOUT
DEFROCK
DEFROST
DELTOID
DEPLORE
DEPLOYS
DESMOND
DESPOIL
DESPOTS
DETROIT
DEVIOUS
DIABOLI
DIALOGS
DIAMOND
DIATOMS
DIDGOOD
DIEDOFF
DIEDOUT
DIEDOWN
DIESOFF
DIESOUT
DIGSOUT
DINGOES
DINMONT
DIPLOID
DIPLOMA
DISCOED
DISCORD
DISHOUT
DISJOIN
DISPORT
DISPOSE
DISROBE
DISTORT
DITTOED
DOCTORS
DOGFOOD
DOGGONE
DOGWOOD
DOLEOUT
DOLLOPS
DONJONS
DONJOSE
DOPEOUT
DOZEOFF
DRAGONS
DRAGOON
DRAGOUT
DRAWOUT
DREWOUT
DROPOFF
DROPOUT
DRSPOCK
DRYDOCK
DRYHOLE
DRYROTS
DUBIOUS
DUNNOCK
DUSTOFF
DUTEOUS

D••••O•
DAGWOOD
DASBOOT
DAWNSON
DAYBOOK
DAYROOM
DECAGON
DECALOG
DECAPOD
DEMEROL
DEMIGOD
DENDRON
DESKTOP
DESOTOS
DESTROY
DEVELOP
DEWDROP
DICTION
DIDEROT
DIDGOOD
DINEDON
DINESON
DISAVOW
DIVISOR
DODGSON
DOGCHOW
DOGFOOD
DOGSHOW
DOGTROT
DOGWOOD
DOMINOS
DONATOR
DONEFOR
DORITOS
DOSIDOS
DOTEDON
DOTESON
DOVECOT
DOWNBOW
DRAGOON
DRAGSON
DRAWNON

DRAWSON
DREAMON
DUDGEON
DUKEDOM
DUNGEON
DUSTMOP
DYNAMOS

D•••••O
DARESTO
DECARLO
DEFACTO
DEUTERO
DOMINGO
DURANGO

•DO••••
ADOLPHE
ADONAIS
ADOPTED
ADOPTEE
ADOPTER
ADORERS
ADORING
ADORNED
ADORNER
EDOUARD
IDOLISE
IDOLIZE
ODORFUL
ODOROUS

•D•O•••
ADDONTO
ADJOINS
ADJOURN
ADSORBS
IDIOTIC

•D••O••
ADIPOSE
EDGEOUT
EDITORS
EDITOUT
IDAHOAN
ODDJOBS
ODDLOTS
ODOROUS

•D•••O•
ADAGIOS
ADAMSON
ADAPTOR
ADDEDON
ADDISON
ADVISOR
EDITION

•D••••O
ADDEDTO
ADDONTO
ADDUPTO
ADMITTO

••DO•••
ABDOMEN
ADDONTO
ANDORRA
ANDOVER
ARDOURS
BEDOUIN
DIDOVER
ENDORSE
ENDOWED
FEDORAS
INDOORS
INDORSE
INDOUBT
JUDOIST
MADONNA
NODOUBT
OGDOADS
RADOMES
REDOAKS
REDOING
REDOUBT
REDOUND
RIDOTTO
RODOLFO
RUDOLPH
UNDOING
WIDOWED
WIDOWER

••D•O••
ANDROID
ANDSOON
ARDMORE
ARDUOUS
BADBOYS
BEDDOWN
BEDPOST
BEDROCK
BEDROLL
BEDROOM
CADDOAN
DIDGOOD
ENDMOST
ENDZONE
FADEOUT
GIDEONS
GODSONS
HADDOCK
HIDEOUS
HIDEOUT
HYDROUS
INDOORS
KEDROVA
MADEOFF
MADEOUT
MIDMOST
MIDTOWN
NODSOFF
ODDJOBS
ODDLOTS
OLDFOGY
OLDGOLD
OLDMOON
OLDROSE
PADDOCK
PADLOCK
PADRONE
PADRONI
RADIOED
REDBOOK
REDCOAT
REDDOGS
REDFORD
REDHOTS
REDPOLL
REDROSE
REDTOPS
REDWOLF
REDWOOD
RIDEOFF
RIDEOUT
RODEOFF
RODEOUT
TADPOLE
TEDIOUS
WEDLOCK

••D••O•
ADDEDON
ADDISON
ANDIRON
ANDSOON
AUDITOR
AUDUBON
BEDROOM
DIDEROT
DIDGOOD
DODGSON
DUDGEON
ENDUROS
GODUNOV
INDIGOS
LADINOS
MADEFOR
MADISON
MEDICOS
OLDMOON
OLDPROS
PIDGEON
REDBOOK
REDSPOT
REDWOOD
SODAPOP
WIDGEON
ZYDECOS

••D•••O
ADDEDTO
ADDONTO
ADDUPTO
FIDELIO
HIDALGO
LEDUPTO
MODESTO
RIDOTTO
RODOLFO
UNDERDO
UNDERGO

•••DO••
ACEDOUT
BEDDOWN
BOBDOLE
BOGDOWN
BOUDOIR
BURDOCK
CADDOAN
CANDOUR
CARDOZO
CONDOLE
CONDONE
CONDORS
CORDOBA
CORDONS
CUTDOWN
DIEDOFF
DIEDOUT
DIEDOWN
DRYDOCK
EKEDOUT
FINDOUT
FOLDOUT
GETDOWN
GONDOLA
GOODONE
GOTDOWN
GUIDONS
GUNDOGS
HADDOCK
HAGDONS
HANDOFF
HANDOUT
HEADOFF
HEADOUT
HELDOFF
HELDOUT
HOEDOWN
HOLDOFF
HOLDOUT
HOODOOS
HOTDOGS
ICEDOUT
ISADORA
LAIDOFF
LAIDOUT
LAPDOGS
LARDONS
LAYDOWN
LEADOFF
LEADOUT
LETDOWN
LIEDOWN
LOWDOWN
MEADOWS
MEADOWY
MENDOZA
MISDOES
MISDONE
MOLDOVA
MOWDOWN
MURDOCH
OUTDOES
OUTDONE
OUTDOOR
PADDOCK
PAIDOFF
PAIDOUT
PANDORA
PARDONS
PINDOWN
PUTDOWN
PYEDOGS
RAGDOLL
RANDOWN
READOUT
REDDOGS
RUBDOWN
RUNDOWN
SATDOWN
SEADOGS
SENDOFF
SENDOUT
SETDOWN
SHADOOF
SHADOWS
SHADOWY
SITDOWN
SOLDOFF
SOLDOUT
SUNDOGS
SUNDOWN
TEEDOFF
TENDONS
TIEDOWN
TOLDOFF
TOPDOGS
TOPDOWN
TOYDOGS
VENDORS
VERDOUX
VOODOOS
WALDORF
WARDOFF
WEEDOUT
WILDONE
WINDOWS
WORDONE

•••D•O•
AIRDROP
BANDBOX
BIRDDOG
CALDRON
DENDRON
DEWDROP
EARDROP
FEEDLOT
FEEDSON
GOODJOB
GOODJOE
GOODSON
GUMDROP
HANDSON
HARDTOP
HARDWON
HOLDSON
HOODOOS
LAIDFOR
LAIDLOW
LEADSON
OUTDOOR
PAIDFOR
PRUDHOE
ROADHOG
SANDBOX
SANDHOG
SANDLOT
SEEDPOD
SENDFOR
SHADOOF
SKIDDOO
SKIDROW
SLEDDOG
STUDIOS
TRADEON
VOODOOS
WINDROW
WINDSOR
WOODLOT
WOODROW

•••D••O
ARTDECO
BANDITO
BENDIGO
CARDOZO
CORDERO
HOLDSTO
LEADSTO
SKIDDOO
SORDINO
TENDSTO
VERDUGO

••••DO•
ABANDON
ACTEDON
ADDEDON
AHEADOF
ALBEDOS
BERIDOF
BIRDDOG
BOREDOM
BRANDON
BULLDOG
CELADON
CORNDOG
CZARDOM
DINEDON
DOSIDOS
DOTEDON
DUKEDOM
EARLDOM
ECUADOR
EGGEDON
ESCUDOS
FIEFDOM
FIREDOG
FREEDOM
GLUEDON
HAIRDOS
HANGDOG
HEARDOF
HUMIDOR
JANEDOE
JOHNDOE
KINGDOM
LANGDON
LIBIDOS
LIVEDON
MALODOR
MATADOR
MIKADOS
MIRADOR
MOONDOG
MOVEDON
ONANDON
PAPADOC
PARADOX
PERIDOT
PICADOR
PILEDON
PLAYDOH
REREDOS
ROUNDON
SERFDOM
SEWEDON
SHAHDOM
SHELDON
SHOWDOG
SKIDDOO
SLEDDOG
SNOWDON
SPEEDOS
SPIEDON
STANDON
STARDOM
TEREDOS
TIREDOF
TRIEDON
TUXEDOS
WEIRDOS
WYANDOT

••••D•O
ADDEDTO
AIMEDTO
AMRADIO
CBRADIO
CLAUDIO
FMRADIO
MEGIDDO
QINGDAO
SKIDDOO
SOANDSO

•••••DO
ALFREDO
AVOCADO
BOIARDO
BRAVADO
BUSHIDO
CRUSADO
CRUZADO
GAMBADO
GERALDO
MAKESDO
MEGIDDO
NOCANDO
ORLANDO
PASSADO
PLACIDO
RICARDO
TESTUDO
TORNADO
TORPEDO
UNDERDO

D•P••••
DAPHNIS
DAPPING
DAPPLED
DAPPLES
DEPALMA
DEPARTS
DEPENDS
DEPICTS
DEPLANE
DEPLETE
DEPLORE
DEPLOYS
DEPONED
DEPONES
DEPORTS
DEPOSAL
DEPOSED
DEPOSER
DEPOSES
DEPOSIT
DEPRAVE
DEPRESS
DEPRIVE
DEPUTED
DEPUTES
DIPLOID
DIPLOMA
DIPOLAR
DIPOLES
DIPPERS
DIPPIER
DIPPING
DIPTYCH
DOPANTS
DOPEOUT
DOPIEST
DOPPLER

D••P•••
DAMPENS
DAMPERS
DAMPEST
DAMPING
DAMPISH
DAPPING
DAPPLED
DAPPLES
DAUPHIN
DEEPEND
DEEPENS
DEEPEST
DEEPFAT
DEEPFRY
DEEPSEA
DEEPSET
DEEPSIX
DELPHIC
DEMPSEY
DESPAIR
DESPISE
DESPITE
DESPOIL
DESPOTS
DIAPERS
DIMPLED
DIMPLES
DIOPTER
DIPPERS
DIPPIER
DIPPING
DISPELS
DISPLAY
DISPORT
DISPOSE
DISPUTE
DOLPHIN
DOPPLER
DRAPERS
DRAPERY
DRAPING
DRIPDRY
DRIPPAN
DRIPPED
DROPINS
DROPLET
DROPOFF
DROPOUT
DROPPED
DROPPER
DROPSBY
DROPSIN
DRSPOCK
DUMPIER
DUMPING
DUMPISH

D•••P••
DEADPAN
DECAPOD
DISHPAN
DOWNPAT
DRIPPAN
DRIPPED
DROOPED
DROPPED
DROPPER
DUCKPIN
DUSTPAN

D••••P•
DECAMPS
DECRYPT
DEWLAPS
DIGRAPH
DISRUPT
DOLLOPS
DUSTUPS

D•••••P
DAYCAMP
DAYTRIP
DESKTOP
DEVELOP
DEWDROP
DOINGUP
DOLLSUP
DRAWNUP
DRAWSUP
DREAMUP
DRESSUP
DRIEDUP
DRIESUP
DRIVEUP
DRUMSUP
DUDEDUP
DUMMYUP
DUSTMOP

•D•P•••
ADAPTED
ADAPTER
ADAPTOR
ADEPTLY
ADIPOSE
ADOPTED
ADOPTEE
ADOPTER
EDAPHIC

•D••P••
ADDUPTO
ADOLPHE

•D••••P
ADDEDUP

••DP•••
BEDPOST
ENDPLAY
MUDPACK
MUDPIES
OLDPROS
REDPINE
REDPOLL
TADPOLE

••D•P••
ADDUPTO
INDEPTH
LEDUPTO
MADEPAR
OEDIPAL
OEDIPUS
REDSPOT
SODAPOP

••D••P•
KIDNAPS
MADCAPS
REDCAPS
REDTAPE
REDTOPS
RUDOLPH
UNDRAPE

••D•••P
ADDEDUP
BEDLAMP
BUDDYUP
DUDEDUP
ENDEDUP
GIDDYAP
GIDDYUP
MEDIGAP
OLDCHAP
SODAPOP

•••DP••
DEADPAN
HARDPAN
HARDPUT
HEADPIN
SEEDPOD

•••D•P•
FOLDUPS
HOLDUPS
SENDUPS
WINDUPS

•••D••P
AIRDROP
BEADSUP
BINDSUP
BUDDYUP
DEWDROP
EARDROP
FOLDSUP
GIDDYAP
GIDDYUP
GUMDROP
HANDSUP
HARDTOP
HEADSUP
HOLDSUP
LEADSUP
ROADMAP
RUNDEEP
SENDSUP
THEDEEP
TRADEUP
WINDSUP

••••DP•
GRANDPA

••••D•P
ACTEDUP
ADDEDUP
ANTEDUP
BONEDUP
BOUNDUP
BOXEDUP
BUILDUP
DRIEDUP
DUDEDUP
EASEDUP
ENDEDUP
FIREDUP
FIXEDUP
HIKEDUP
HOLEDUP
HYPEDUP
KEYEDUP
LACEDUP
LINEDUP
MIXEDUP
MOVEDUP
OWNEDUP
PILEDUP
PIPEDUP
RAKEDUP
ROUNDUP
SAVEDUP
SEWEDUP
SIZEDUP
SPEEDUP
STANDUP
STOODUP
TONEDUP
TUNEDUP
TYPEDUP
WIPEDUP
WISEDUP
WOUNDUP

D•••Q••
DUBUQUE

••••DQ•
PSANDQS

DR•••••
DRABBER
DRACHMA
DRACHMS
DRACULA
DRAFTED
DRAFTEE
DRAGGED
DRAGGER
DRAGNET
DRAGONS
DRAGOON
DRAGOUT
DRAGSIN
DRAGSON
DRAINED
DRAINER
DRAPERS
DRAPERY
DRAPING
DRASTIC
DRATTED
DRAUGHT
DRAWBAR
DRAWERS
DRAWING
DRAWLED
DRAWNIN
DRAWNON
DRAWNUP
DRAWOUT
DRAWSIN
DRAWSON
DRAWSUP
DRAYAGE
DRAYING
DREADED
DREAMED
DREAMER
DREAMON
DREAMUP
DREDGED
DREDGER
DREDGES
DREIDEL
DREISER
DRESDEN
DRESSED
DRESSER
DRESSES
DRESSUP
DREWOUT
DREYFUS
DRIBBLE
DRIBLET
DRIEDUP
DRIESUP
DRIFTED
DRIFTER
DRILLED
DRILLER
DRINKER
DRIPDRY
DRIPPAN
DRIPPED
DRISTAN
DRIVEAT
DRIVEIN
DRIVELS
DRIVERS
DRIVEUP
DRIVING
DRIZZLE
DRIZZLY
DROLLER
DRONERS
DRONING
DRONISH
DROOLED
DROOLER
DROOPED
DROPINS
DROPLET
DROPOFF
DROPOUT
DROPPED
DROPPER
DROPSBY
DROPSIN
DROSHKY
DROUGHT
DROVERS
DROWNED
DROWSED
DROWSES
DRSEUSS
DRSPOCK
DRUBBED
DRUCKER
DRUDGED
DRUDGES
DRUGGED
DRUMLIN
DRUMMED
DRUMMER
DRUMSUP
DRYCELL
DRYDOCK
DRYEYED
DRYHOLE
DRYNESS
DRYROTS
DRYRUNS
DRYSUIT
DRYWALL
DRYWELL

D•R••••
DARBIES
DAREFUL
DARESAY
DARESTO
DARKENS
DARKEST
DARKISH
DARKMAN
DARLENE
DARLING
DARNERS
DARNING
DARNLEY
DARTERS
DARTING
DERAILS
DERBIES
DERIDED
DERIDES
DERIVED
DERIVES
DERNIER
DERRICK
DERRING
DERVISH
DIRECTS
DIREFUL
DIRNDLS
DIRTIED
DIRTIER
DIRTIES
DIRTILY
DORITOS
DORMANT
DORMERS
DORMICE
DOROTHY
DORSALS
DORSETT
DURABLE
DURABLY
DURANCE
DURANGO
DURANTE
DURNING
DURRELL

D••R•••
DAIRIES
DAYROOM
DEAREST
DEARIES
DEARSIR
DEARTHS
DEBRIEF
DECREED
DECREES
DECRIED
DECRIER
DECRIES
DECRYPT
DEERFLY
DEFRAUD
DEFRAYS
DEFROCK
DEFROST
DEGRADE
DEGREES
DEPRAVE
DEPRESS
DEPRIVE
DERRICK
DERRING
DETRACT
DETRAIN
DETROIT
DEVRIES
DHURRIE
DIARIES
DIGRAMS
DIGRAPH
DIGRESS
DIORAMA
DISROBE
DISRUPT
DIURNAL
DOORDIE
DOORMAN
DOORMAT
DOORMEN
DOORWAY
DOUREST
DOWRIES
DRYROTS
DRYRUNS
DURRELL
DWARFED
DWARVES

D•••R••
DALTREY
DAYTRIP
DEBARGE
DEBARKS
DEBORAH
DECARLO
DECORUM
DEFARGE
DEFORMS
DEHORNS
DELIRIA
DEMERIT
DEMEROL
DEMURER
DENARII
DENDRON
DEPARTS
DEPORTS
DESERTS
DESERVE
DESIRED
DESIREE
DESIRES
DESTROY
DEWDROP
DEXTRIN
DHURRIE
DIAGRAM
DIDEROT
DISARMS
DISHRAG
DIVERGE
DIVERSE
DIVERTS
DIVORCE
DMYTRYK
DOGTROT
DOLORES
DOTARDS
DOWERED
DUBARRY

D••••R•
DAGGERS
DAMMARS
DAMPERS
DANBURY
DANCERS
DANDERS
DANGERS
DARNERS
DARTERS
DASHERS
DASTARD
DASYURE
DAUBERS
DAYCARE
DAYMARE
DEALERS
DEANERY
DEBEERS
DEBTORS
DECLARE
DEEPFRY
DEICERS
DEKLERK
DELVERS
DENIERS
DENMARK
DENTURE
DEODARS
DEPLORE
DESSERT

DETOURS
DEUTERO
DEVILRY
DEVOURS
DIALERS
DIAPERS
DICKERS
DIEHARD
DIETARY
DIETERS
DIFFERS
DIGGERS
DILBERT
DILLARD
DIMITRI
DIMMERS
DINNERS
DIPPERS
DISBARS
DISCARD
DISCERN
DISCORD
DISPORT
DISTORT
DISTURB
DITHERS
DITHERY
DOCKERS
DOCTORS
DODDERS
DODGERS
DOGBERT
DOGCART
DOGEARS
DOLLARS
DOLOURS
DORMERS
DOSSERS
DOWNERS
DOWSERS
DRAPERS
DRAPERY
DRAWERS
DRIPDRY
DRIVERS
DRONERS
DROVERS
DUBARRY
DUBBERS
DUELERS
DUFFERS
DULLARD
DUNKERS
DUNKIRK
DUSTERS
DYKSTRA

D•••••R
DABBLER
DAFFIER
DAIMLER
DALLIER
DANDIER
DANGLER
DANSEUR
DAUMIER
DAWDLER
DAYSTAR
DAZZLER
DEADAIR
DEARSIR
DEBATER
DECATUR
DECODER
DECRIER
DEFILER
DELAYER
DELIVER
DEMETER
DEMURER
DEPOSER
DERNIER
DESPAIR
DIDOVER
DILUTER
DINGIER
DINKIER
DIOPTER
DIPOLAR
DIPPIER
DIRTIER
DISHIER
DITSIER
DITZIER
DIVIDER
DIVINER
DIVISOR
DIZZIER
DODGIER
DOGGIER
DOGSTAR
DONATOR
DONEFOR
DOODLER
DOPPLER
DOSSIER
DOTTIER
DOUBTER
DOWAGER
DOWDIER
DOWNIER
DRABBER
DRAGGER
DRAINER
DRAWBAR
DREAMER
DREDGER
DREISER
DRESSER
DRIFTER
DRILLER
DRINKER
DROLLER
DROOLER
DROPPER
DRUCKER
DRUMMER
DUCKIER
DUMPIER
DUSKIER
DUSTIER
DWELLER

•DR••••
ADRENAL

•D•R•••
ADDRESS
ADORERS
ADORING
ADORNED
ADORNER
ODORFUL
ODOROUS

•D••R••
ADHERED
ADHERES
ADJURED
ADJURES
ADMIRAL
ADMIRED
ADMIRER
ADMIRES
ADSORBS
ADVERBS
ADVERSE
ADVERTS
EDWARDS
IDCARDS

•D•••R•
ADJOURN
ADORERS
EDITORS
EDOUARD

•D••••R
ADAPTER
ADAPTOR
ADMIRER
ADOPTER
ADORNER
ADVISER
ADVISOR
EDASNER

••DR•••
ADDRESS
ALDRICH
ANDREAS
ANDRESS
ANDREWS
ANDROID
BEDREST
BEDROCK
BEDROLL
BEDROOM
ENDRUNS
HADRIAN
HYDRANT
HYDRATE
HYDROUS
KEDROVA
MIDRIBS
MIDRIFF
MIDRISE
OLDROSE
PADRONE
PADRONI
PODRIDA
REDRAWN
REDRAWS
REDRESS
REDROSE
UNDRAPE
UNDRAWN
UNDRESS
UPDRAFT

••D•R••
ANDIRON
ANDORRA
BODEREK
CEDARED
DIDEROT
ELDERLY
ENDORSE
ENDURED
ENDURES
ENDUROS
FEDERAL
FEDORAS
GODFREY
INDORSE
MODERNS
OLDPROS
ORDERED
ORDERER
ORDERLY
UNDERDO
UNDERGO

••D••R•
ANDORRA
ARDMORE
ARDOURS
BADGERS
BIDDERS
CADBURY
CADGERS
CODGERS
DODDERS
DODGERS
ENDEARS
FODDERS
GADDERS
GODDARD
HEDGERS
INDOORS
JUDDERS
KIDDERS
LADDERS
LADLERS
LEDGERS
LODGERS
MADDERS
MADEIRA
MIDTERM
MUDDERS
NODDERS
NUDGERS
PADDERS
PEDLARS
REDBIRD
REDFIRS
REDFORD
RODGERS
RUDDERS
RUDYARD
SIDEARM
SUDBURY
TEDDERS
WIDMARK
ZEDBARS

••D•••R
ANDOVER
AUDITOR
BIDFAIR
CODDLER
DIDOVER
DODGIER
ENDUSER
FIDDLER
GIDDIER
GODLIER
HEDGIER
INDUCER
LEDGIER
MADEFOR
MADEPAR
MEDDLER
MIDYEAR
MODELER
MODULAR
MUDDIER
MUDDLER
NODULAR
OLDSTER
ORDERER
PADDLER
PEDDLER
PODGIER
PUDGIER
REDDEER
REDHAIR
REDSTAR
REDUCER
RIDDLER
RIDGIER
RUDDIER
SADDLER
SEDATER
SEDGIER
SEDUCER
SIDEBAR
SIDECAR
SODDIER
SUDSIER
TODDLER
WADDLER
WEDGIER
WIDOWER
YODELER

•••DR••
AIRDROP
BALDRIC
CALDRON
DENDRON
DEWDROP
EARDROP
EARDRUM
FREDRIC
GUMDROP
HENDRIX
HUMDRUM
HUNDRED
KINDRED
MILDRED
MORDRED
OUTDRAW
OUTDREW
SKIDROW
TENDRIL
TUNDRAS
WINDROW
WOODROW

•••D•R•
BENDERS
BIDDERS
BINDERS
BINDERY
BIRDERS
BLADERS
BORDERS
CALDERA
CARDERS
CHIDERS
CINDERS
CINDERY
CONDORS
CORDERO
DANDERS
DEODARS
DODDERS
EVADERS
FEEDERS
FENDERS
FINDERS
FODDERS
FOLDERS
GADDERS
GANDERS
GENDERS
GILDERS
GIRDERS
GLIDERS
GODDARD
GRADERS
HEADERS
HERDERS
HINDERS
HOLDERS
ISADORA
JUDDERS
KIDDERS
KILDARE
LADDERS
LANDERS
LARDERS
LEADERS
LENDERS
LOADERS
MADDERS
MENDERS
MINDERS
MOLDERS
MUDDERS
MURDERS
NODDERS
ONADARE
PADDERS
PANDERS
PANDORA
PAYDIRT
POLDERS
PONDERS
POWDERS
POWDERY
PRUDERY
RAIDERS
READERS
RENDERS
RUDDERS
SANDERS
SEEDERS
SENDERS
SLIDERS
SOLDERS
SPADERS
SPIDERS
SPIDERY
SUNDERS
TEDDERS
TENDERS
TINDERS
TRADERS
VENDORS
VERDURE
WALDORF
WANDERS
WARDERS
WEEDERS
WELDERS
WENDERS
WINDERS
WONDERS
WOODARD
YARDARM
ZANDERS

•••D••R
BAWDIER
BEADIER
BENDIER
BLADDER
BOUDOIR
BOWDLER
CANDOUR
CHEDDAR
CODDLER
COLDWAR
CURDIER
DANDIER
DAWDLER
DEADAIR
DOODLER
DOWDIER
DREDGER
FIDDLER
FIEDLER
GARDNER
GAUDIER
GIDDIER
GLADDER
GOODBAR
GRIDDER
GRODIER
HANDCAR
HANDIER
HANDLER
HARDIER
HEADIER
HURDLER
LAIDFOR
LARDIER
LARDNER
LEADIER
MEDDLER
MOLDIER
MOODIER
MUDDIER
MUDDLER
NEEDIER
NERDIER
OUTDOOR
PADDLER
PAIDFOR
PARDNER
PEDDLER
PLEDGER
PLODDER
PRODDER
RANDIER
READIER
REDDEER
REEDIER
RIDDLER
ROEDEER
ROWDIER
RUDDIER
SADDLER
SANDBAR
SANDIER
SEEDIER
SENDFOR
SHADIER
SHUDDER
SKIDDER
SLEDDER
SODDIER
SOLDIER
SUBDUER
TARDIER
TODDLER
TRUDGER
WADDLER
WEEDIER
WINDIER
WINDSOR
WOODIER
WORDIER
YESDEAR

••••DR•
BLOWDRY
BONEDRY
DRIPDRY
FOUNDRY
LAUNDRY
PALEDRY
PHAEDRA
RUNSDRY
SPINDRY

••••D•R
ABRADER
ACCEDER
ASUNDER
AWARDER
BLADDER
BLANDER
BLENDER
BLINDER
BLONDER
BLUNDER
BOARDER
BOULDER
BOUNDER
BRAIDER
BRANDER
BREEDER
BROADER
BROODER
BUILDER
CCRIDER
CHEDDAR
CHOWDER
CLOWDER
DECODER
DIVIDER
ECUADOR
EMENDER
ENCODER
EVANDER
FIELDER
FOUNDER
GLADDER
GOUNDER
GRANDER
GRIDDER
GRINDER
GUILDER
HOARDER
HUMIDOR
INSIDER
INVADER
JOINDER
KNEADER
LAUNDER
LEANDER
MALODOR
MATADOR
MAUNDER
MEANDER
MIRADOR
MOULDER
ONORDER
PICADOR
PLEADER
PLODDER
PLUNDER
POUNDER
PRODDER
PROUDER
RAPIDER
REORDER
ROUNDER
SCOLDER
SECEDER
SHUDDER
SKIDDER
SLANDER
SLEDDER
SLENDER
SMOLDER
SOLIDER
SOUNDER
SPEEDER
SPENDER
STAIDER
STRIDER
THUNDER
TIMIDER
TIREDER
TOORDER
TREADER
VIVIDER
WEIRDER

D•S••••
DASBOOT
DASHERS
DASHIKI
DASHING
DASHOFF
DASTARD
DASYURE
DESALTS
DESCANT
DESCEND
DESCENT
DESERTS
DESERVE
DESIGNS
DESIRED
DESIREE
DESIRES
DESISTS
DESKSET
DESKTOP
DESMOND
DESOTOS
DESPAIR
DESPISE
DESPITE
DESPOIL
DESPOTS
DESSERT
DESTINE
DESTINY
DESTROY
DISABLE
DISARMS
DISAVOW
DISBAND
DISBARS
DISCARD
DISCERN
DISCOED
DISCORD
DISCUSS
DISDAIN
DISEASE
DISGUST
DISHFUL
DISHIER
DISHING
DISHOUT
DISHPAN
DISHRAG
DISJOIN
DISLIKE
DISMAYS
DISMISS
DISOBEY
DISOWNS
DISPELS
DISPLAY
DISPORT
DISPOSE
DISPUTE
DISROBE
DISRUPT
DISSECT
DISSENT
DISSING
DISTAFF
DISTANT
DISTEND
DISTILL
DISTILS
DISTORT
DISTURB
DISUSED
DOSAGES
DOSIDOS
DOSSALS
DOSSERS
DOSSIER
DRSEUSS
DRSPOCK
DUSKIER
DUSKILY
DUSKISH
DUSTBIN
DUSTERS
DUSTIER
DUSTILY
DUSTING
DUSTMAN
DUSTMEN
DUSTMOP
DUSTOFF
DUSTPAN
DUSTUPS

D••S•••
DAISIES
DAMSELS
DAMSONS
DANSEUR
DAYSINN
DAYSTAR
DENSELY
DENSEST
DENSITY
DESSERT
DIESELS
DIESOFF
DIESOUT
DIGSOUT
DISSECT
DISSENT
DISSING
DITSIER
DOESKIN
DOGSHOW
DOGSITS
DOGSLED
DOGSTAR
DORSALS
DORSETT
DOSSALS
DOSSERS
DOSSIER
DOUSING
DOWSERS
DOWSING
DRASTIC
DRESDEN
DRESSED
DRESSER
DRESSES
DRESSUP
DRISTAN
DROSHKY
DRYSUIT
DYKSTRA

D•••S••
DAMASKS
DARESAY
DARESTO
DATASET
DAWNSON
DEADSEA
DEADSET
DEALSIN
DEARSIR
DEBASED
DEBASES
DEBUSSY
DEEPSEA
DEEPSET
DEEPSIX
DEFUSED
DEFUSES
DEGUSTS
DEHISCE
DELISTS
DEMESNE
DEMISED
DEMISES
DEMPSEY
DEPOSAL
DEPOSED
DEPOSER
DEPOSES
DEPOSIT
DESISTS
DESKSET
DETESTS
DEVISED
DEVISES
DIGESTS
DINESEN
DINESIN
DINESON
DISUSED
DIVESIN
DIVESTS
DIVISOR
DODGSON
DOLLSUP
DOTESON
DRAGSIN
DRAGSON
DRAWSIN
DRAWSON
DRAWSUP
DREISER
DRESSED
DRESSER
DRESSES
DRESSUP
DRIESUP
DROPSBY
DROPSIN
DROWSED
DROWSES
DRUMSUP
DYNASTS
DYNASTY

D••••S•
DADAISM
DADAIST
DAFTEST
DAMPEST
DAMPISH
DANKEST
DARKEST
DARKISH
DAWKISH
DEAFEST
DEAREST
DEBUSSY
DECLASS
DEEPEST
DEFENSE
DEFROST
DEFTEST
DEGAUSS
DELUISE
DENSEST
DENTIST
DEPRESS
DERVISH
DESPISE
DEWLESS
DICIEST
DIFFUSE
DIGRESS
DIMMEST
DIMNESS
DIOCESE
DISCUSS
DISEASE
DISGUST
DISMISS
DISPOSE
DIVERSE
DOGFISH
DOGGISH
DOGLESS
DOLLISH
DOLTISH
DONJOSE
DONNISH
DOPIEST
DOUREST
DOZIEST
DRONISH
DRSEUSS
DRYNESS
DUCHESS
DUELIST
DULLEST
DULLISH
DUMBEST
DUMPISH
DUNCISH
DUSKISH

D•••••S
DABBLES
DACTYLS
DADDIES
DAGGERS
DAHLIAS
DAILIES
DAIMONS
DAIRIES
DAISIES
DAKOTAS
DALETHS
DALLIES
DAMAGES
DAMASKS
DAMMARS
DAMPENS
DAMPERS
DAMSELS
DAMSONS
DANCERS
DANDERS
DANDIES
DANDLES
DANGERS
DANGLES
DANIELS
DAPHNIS
DAPPLES
DARBIES
DARKENS
DARNERS
DARTERS
DASHERS
DAUBERS
DAWDLES
DAYBEDS
DAYBOYS
DAYJOBS
DAZZLES
DEACONS
DEADENS
DEAFENS
DEALERS
DEARIES
DEARTHS
DEBARKS
DEBASES
DEBATES
DEBEERS
DEBONES
DEBTORS
DEBUNKS
DECADES
DECAMPS
DECANTS
DECEITS
DECIDES
DECKLES
DECLASS
DECOCTS
DECODES
DECREES
DECRIES
DEDALUS
DEDUCES
DEDUCTS
DEEJAYS
DEEPENS
DEFACES
DEFAMES
DEFEATS
DEFECTS
DEFENDS
DEFILES
DEFINES
DEFORMS
DEFRAYS
DEFUSES
DEGAUSS
DEGREES
DEGUSTS
DEHORNS
DEICERS
DEIFIES
DEITIES
DEJECTS
DELETES
DELIBES
DELICTS
DELISTS
DELUDES
DELUGES
DELVERS
DEMANDS
DEMEANS
DEMISES
DEMOTES
DENIALS
DENIERS
DENOTES
DENUDES
DEODARS
DEPARTS
DEPENDS
DEPICTS
DEPLOYS
DEPONES
DEPORTS
DEPOSES
DEPRESS
DEPUTES
DERAILS
DERBIES
DERIDES
DERIVES
DESALTS
DESERTS
DESIGNS
DESIRES
DESISTS
DESOTOS
DESPOTS
DETAILS
DETAINS
DETECTS
DETESTS
DETOURS
DEVEINS
DEVICES
DEVIOUS
DEVISES
DEVOTES
DEVOURS
DEVRIES
DEWLAPS
DEWLESS
DIADEMS
DIALERS
DIALOGS
DIAPERS
DIARIES
DIATOMS
DIBBLES
DICKENS
DICKERS
DICKEYS
DICKIES

DICTUMS
DIDACTS
DIDDLES
DIESELS
DIETERS
DIFFERS
DIGESTS
DIGGERS
DIGRAMS
DIGRESS
DIKDIKS
DIKTATS
DILATES
DILLIES
DILUTES
DIMMERS
DIMNESS
DIMOUTS
DIMPLES
DIMWITS
DINGLES
DINGOES
DINKIES
DINNERS
DIPOLES
DIPPERS
DIRECTS
DIRNDLS
DIRTIES
DISARMS
DISBARS
DISCUSS
DISMAYS
DISMISS
DISOWNS
DISPELS
DISTILS
DITCHES
DITHERS
DITTIES
DIVERTS
DIVESTS
DIVIDES
DIVINES
DIVVIES
DIZZIES
DOBBIES
DOBBINS
DOCENTS
DOCKERS
DOCKETS
DOCTORS
DODDERS
DODGERS
DOGDAYS
DOGEARS
DOGGIES
DOGLEGS
DOGLESS
DOGSITS
DOGTAGS
DOILIES
DOLLARS
DOLLIES
DOLLOPS
DOLMANS
DOLMENS
DOLORES
DOLOURS
DOMAINS
DOMINOS
DOMINUS
DONATES
DONGLES
DONIMUS
DONJONS
DONKEYS
DOODADS
DOODAHS
DOODLES
DOOZIES
DOPANTS
DORITOS
DORMERS
DORSALS
DOSAGES
DOSIDOS
DOSSALS
DOSSERS
DOTARDS
DOTTLES
DOUBLES
DOUGLAS
DOWNERS
DOWRIES
DOWSERS
DRACHMS
DRAGONS
DRAPERS
DRAWERS
DREDGES
DRESSES
DREYFUS
DRIVELS
DRIVERS
DRONERS
DROPINS
DROVERS
DROWSES
DRSEUSS
DRUDGES
DRYNESS
DRYROTS
DRYRUNS
DUBBERS
DUBIOUS
DUCHESS
DUCHIES
DUELERS
DUENNAS
DUFFELS
DUFFERS
DUGONGS
DUGOUTS
DUKAKIS
DUMDUMS
DUMMIES
DUNKERS
DUNLINS
DUSTERS
DUSTUPS
DUTEOUS
DWARVES
DYBBUKS
DYNAMOS
DYNASTS

•DS••••

ADSORBS

•D•S•••

EDASNER
ODYSSEY

•D••S••

ADAMSON
ADDISON
ADJUSTS
ADVISED
ADVISER
ADVISES
ADVISOR
EDGESIN
ODYSSEY

•D•••S•

ADDRESS
ADIPOSE
ADVERSE
EDGIEST
IDOLISE
ODDNESS

•D••••S

ADAGIOS
ADDENDS
ADDRESS
ADDUCES
ADDUCTS
ADHERES
ADJOINS
ADJURES
ADJUSTS
ADMIRES
ADMIXES
ADONAIS
ADORERS
ADSORBS
ADVENTS
ADVERBS
ADVERTS
ADVISES
EDGINGS
EDIBLES
EDIFIES
EDITORS
EDWARDS
IDCARDS
IDEATES
ODDJOBS
ODDLOTS
ODDNESS
ODOROUS
PDJAMES

••DS•••

ANDSOON
BEDSIDE
GADSDEN
GODSEND
GODSONS
KIDSKIN
MIDSIZE
NODSOFF
OLDSAWS
OLDSTER
REDSPOT
REDSTAR
SADSACK
SUDSIER
SUDSING

••D•S••

ADDISON
DODGSON
ECDYSES
ECDYSIS
ENDUSER
ENDUSES
FADESIN
IODISED
IODISES
MADISON
MEDUSAE
MEDUSAS
MODESTO
MODESTY
MODISTE
NUDISTS
WADESIN

••D••S•

ADDRESS
AIDLESS
ANDRESS
BADDEST
BADDISH
BADNESS
BEDLESS
BEDPOST
BEDREST
BUDLESS
CADDISH
CODFISH
DADAISM
DADAIST
ENDLESS
ENDMOST
ENDORSE
ENDWISE
FADDISH
FADDISM
FADDIST
GODDESS
GODLESS
INDORSE
JUDAISM
JUDOIST
KADDISH
KIDDISH
LADDISH
LADYISH
LIDLESS
MADDEST
MADDISH
MADNESS
MIDEAST
MIDMOST
MIDRISE
MIDWEST
ODDNESS
OLDNESS
OLDROSE
OLDWEST
REDDEST
REDDISH
REDNESS
REDRESS
REDROSE
RODLESS
SADDEST
SADNESS
SODLESS
TIDIEST
UNDRESS
YIDDISH

••D•••S

ABDUCTS
ADDENDS
ADDRESS
ADDUCES
ADDUCTS
AEDILES
AIDLESS
ANDEANS
ANDREAS
ANDRESS
ANDREWS
ARDOURS
ARDUOUS
AUDILES
BADBOYS
BADDIES
BADEGGS
BADGERS
BADGUYS
BADNESS
BEDAUBS
BEDBUGS
BEDECKS
BEDLESS
BIDDERS
BIDDIES
BODEGAS
BODICES
BODKINS
BUDDHAS
BUDDIES
BUDGETS
BUDGIES
BUDLESS
CADDIES
CADGERS
CODDLES
CODGERS
CODICES
CUDDIES
CUDDLES
CUDGELS
DADDIES
DEDALUS
DEDUCES
DEDUCTS
DIDACTS
DIDDLES
DODDERS
DODGERS
ECDYSES
ECDYSIS
ENDEARS
ENDINGS
ENDIVES
ENDLESS
ENDRUNS
ENDURES
ENDUROS
ENDUSES
ENDWAYS
FADEINS
FEDORAS
FIDDLES
FIDELIS
FIDGETS
FODDERS
FUDDLES
GADDERS
GADGETS
GIDEONS
GODDESS
GODLESS
GODSONS
GODWITS
HEDDLES
HEDGERS
HIDEOUS
HIDINGS
HUDDLES
HYDROUS
INDENTS
INDEXES
INDIANS
INDICES
INDICTS
INDIGOS
INDITES
INDOORS
INDUCES
INDUCTS
IODATES
IODIDES
IODISES
IODIZES
JUDDERS
KIDDERS
KIDDIES
KIDNAPS
KIDNEYS
KODIAKS
LADDERS
LADDIES
LADINOS
LADLERS
LEDGERS
LIDLESS
LODGERS
MADCAPS
MADDENS
MADDERS
MADLIBS
MADNESS
MEDDLES
MEDIANS
MEDICOS
MEDIUMS
MEDLEYS
MEDUSAS
MIDDAYS
MIDDENS
MIDDIES
MIDDLES
MIDGETS
MIDRIBS
MIDWAYS
MODELAS
MODELTS
MODERNS
MODULES
MRDEEDS
MUDCATS
MUDDERS
MUDDIES
MUDDLES
MUDEELS
MUDHENS
MUDPIES
NEDDIES
NODDERS
NODULES
NUDGERS
NUDISTS
NUDNIKS
ODDJOBS
ODDLOTS
ODDNESS
OEDIPUS
OGDOADS
OLDDAYS
OLDNESS
OLDNEWS
OLDPROS
OLDSAWS
ORDAINS
ORDEALS
ORDINES
PADDERS
PADDIES
PADDLES
PADUANS
PEDANTS
PEDDLES
PEDLARS
PEDWAYS
PIDGINS
PODIUMS
PUDDLES
RADDLES
RADIALS
RADIANS
RADICES
RADIXES
RADOMES
REDACTS
REDANTS
REDATES
REDBUDS
REDCAPS
REDDENS
REDDOGS
REDEALS
REDEEMS
REDEYES
REDFINS
REDFIRS
REDGUMS
REDHATS
REDHOTS
REDIALS
REDNESS
REDOAKS
REDRAWS
REDRESS
REDTOPS
REDUCES
RIDDLES
RODENTS
RODGERS
RODLESS
RUDDERS
SADDENS
SADDLES
SADNESS
SEDATES
SEDUCES
SIDINGS
SODDIES
SODLESS
STDENIS
TEDDERS
TEDDIES
TEDIOUS
TEDIUMS
TIDBITS
TIDINGS
TODDIES
TODDLES
UNDRESS
UPDATES
WADDIES
WADDLES
WEDGIES
WIDGETS
ZEDBARS
ZODIACS
ZYDECOS

•••DS••

BANDSAW
BEADSUP
BINDSUP
DEADSEA
DEADSET
FEEDSON
FOLDSUP
GOODSON
HANDSAW
HANDSET
HANDSIN
HANDSON
HANDSUP
HARDSET
HEADSET
HEADSIN
HEADSUP
HOLDSIN
HOLDSON
HOLDSTO
HOLDSUP
LANDSAT
LEADSIN
LEADSON
LEADSTO
LEADSUP
LINDSAY
LINDSEY
MINDSET
READSIN
SENDSIN
SENDSUP
TENDSTO
WINDSOR
WINDSUP

•••D•S•

ANODISE
ARIDEST
BADDEST
BADDISH
BALDEST
BALDISH
BARDISH
BOLDEST
CADDISH
COLDEST
COLDISH
CRUDEST
FADDISH
FADDISM
FADDIST
FONDEST
GEODESY
GODDESS
GOODISH
HARDEST
KADDISH
KIDDISH
KINDEST
KURDISH
LADDISH
LEWDEST
LOUDEST
LOUDISH
MADDEST
MADDISH
MAIDISH
MILDEST
OXIDASE
OXIDISE
PRUDISH
REDDEST
REDDISH
SADDEST
SAWDUST
SNIDEST
SWEDISH
TOADISH
WENDISH
WILDEST
WILDISH
YIDDISH

•••D••S

AIRDAMS
AMADEUS
ANADEMS
AOUDADS
AZODYES
BADDIES
BANDIES
BANDITS
BEADLES
BELDAMS
BENDERS
BIDDERS
BIDDIES
BINDERS
BIRDERS
BIRDIES
BLADERS
BOODLES
BORDERS
BRIDALS
BRIDGES
BRIDLES
BUDDHAS
BUDDIES
BUNDLES
BURDENS
CADDIES
CANDIDS
CANDIES
CANDLES
CARDERS
CAUDLES
CHIDERS
CINDERS
CODDLES
COEDITS
CONDORS
CORDONS
CRADLES
CREDITS
CUDDIES
CUDDLES
CURDLES
DADDIES
DANDERS
DANDIES
DANDLES
DAWDLES
DEADENS
DEODARS
DIADEMS
DIDDLES
DIKDIKS
DODDERS
DOGDAYS
DOODADS
DOODAHS
DOODLES
DREDGES
DRUDGES
DUMDUMS
EVADERS
FEEDERS
FENDERS
FIDDLES
FINDERS
FLEDGES
FODDERS
FOLDERS
FOLDUPS
FONDLES
FONDUES
FOODIES
FRIDAYS
FRIDGES
FUDDLES
GADDERS
GANDERS
GARDENS
GENDERS
GILDERS
GIRDERS
GIRDLES
GLIDERS
GODDESS
GOODBYS
GOODIES
GRADERS
GRUDGES
GUIDONS
GUNDOGS
HAGDONS
HANDLES
HARDENS
HEADERS
HEDDLES
HERDERS
HEYDAYS
HINDERS
HOLDERS
HOLDUPS
HOODOOS
HOTDOGS
HOWDAHS
HOYDENS
HUDDLES
HURDLES
JUDDERS
KIDDERS
KIDDIES
KINDLES
KLUDGES
LADDERS
LADDIES
LANDAUS
LANDERS
LAPDOGS
LARDERS
LARDONS
LEADERS
LEADINS
LENDERS
LINDENS
LINDIES
LOADERS
MADDENS
MADDERS
MAIDENS
MANDANS
MANDAYS
MAYDAYS
MEADOWS
MEDDLES
MENDERS
MIDDAYS
MIDDENS
MIDDIES
MIDDLES
MILDEWS
MINDERS
MISDOES
MOLDERS
MONDAYS
MUDDERS
MUDDIES
MUDDLES
MURDERS
NEDDIES
NEEDLES
NODDERS
NOODLES
NORDICS
OLDDAYS
OUTDOES
PADDERS
PADDIES
PADDLES
PANDERS
PANDITS
PARDONS
PAYDAYS
PEDDLES
PHIDIAS
PLEDGES
POLDERS
PONDERS
POODLES
POWDERS
PUDDLES
PUNDITS
PURDAHS
PYEDOGS
RADDLES
RAIDERS
READERS
READIES
REDDENS
REDDOGS
REEDITS
RENDERS
RIDDLES
ROADIES
RONDELS
ROWDIES
RUDDERS
RUNDLES
SADDENS
SADDLES
SANDALS
SANDERS
SEADOGS
SEEDERS
SEIDELS
SENDERS
SENDUPS
SHADOWS
SLEDGES
SLIDERS
SLUDGES
SMUDGES
SODDIES
SOLDERS
SPADERS
SPIDERS
STUDIES
STUDIOS
SUBDEBS
SUBDUES
SUNDAES
SUNDAYS
SUNDERS
SUNDEWS
SUNDOGS
TANDEMS
TEDDERS
TEDDIES
TENDERS
TENDONS
TIEDYES
TINDERS
TOADIES
TODDIES
TODDLES
TOPDOGS
TOYDOGS
TRADERS
TRUDGES
TUNDRAS
VANDALS
VENDORS
VOODOOS
WADDIES
WADDLES
WANDERS
WARDENS
WARDERS
WEEDERS
WELDERS
WENDERS
WHYDAHS
WINDERS
WINDOWS
WINDUPS
WONDERS
WOODIES
ZANDERS

••••DS•

SOANDSO

••••D•S

ABRADES
ACCEDES
AGENDAS
ALBEDOS
ALLUDES
APSIDES
ARCADES
ARMADAS
AUBADES
BESIDES
BETIDES
BLONDES
BOLIDES
CICADAS
CZARDAS
DECADES
DECIDES
DECODES
DELUDES
DENUDES
DERIDES
DIRNDLS
DIVIDES
DOSIDOS
ENCODES
ESCUDOS
FACADES
GELADAS
GOURDES
HAIRDOS
HALIDES
ILLUDES
IMPEDES
INCUDES
INSIDES
INVADES
IODIDES
LAMBDAS
LAMEDHS
LIBIDOS
LIPIDES
LOURDES
MIKADOS
NAIADES
NOBODYS
ONEIDAS
ONSIDES
PAGODAS
PANADAS
PARADES
POMADES
POSADAS
PSANDQS
PYXIDES
RAMADAS
RECEDES
RECODES
REMUDAS
REREDOS
RESIDES
SECEDES
SPEEDOS
STRIDES
TEREDOS
TIRADES
TRIODES
TUXEDOS
UNLADES
WEIRDOS

•••••DS

ABOUNDS
ACARIDS
ACCORDS
ADDENDS
AFFORDS
ALMONDS
AOUDADS
APPENDS
ASCENDS
ATTENDS
AUGENDS
AXSEEDS
BALLADS
BEHEADS
BEHOLDS
BRIARDS
BYROADS
BYWORDS
CALENDS
CANARDS
CANDIDS
CAPSIDS
CERVIDS
CONOIDS
COWARDS
CUSPIDS
DAYBEDS
DEFENDS
DEMANDS
DEPENDS
DOODADS
DOTARDS
EDWARDS
ELAPIDS
ENFOLDS
ENGIRDS
ENNEADS
ERRANDS
EXCEEDS
EXPANDS
EXPENDS
EXTENDS
EYELIDS
FAGENDS
FLYRODS
FORBIDS
FRIENDS
GERUNDS
GROUNDS
HAZARDS
HEPTADS
HERALDS
HOTBEDS
HOTRODS
HOWARDS
HYBRIDS
IDCARDS
IMPENDS
INNARDS
INROADS
INTENDS
INWARDS
ISLANDS
ISOPODS
IZZARDS
KEYPADS
KOBOLDS
LEGENDS
LEONIDS
LIGANDS
LIQUIDS
LIZARDS
MAENADS
MALTEDS
MARAUDS
METHODS
MILORDS
MRDEEDS
MYRIADS
NEREIDS
NIMRODS
OBTUNDS
OFFENDS
OGDOADS
ONWARDS
ORCHIDS
OUTBIDS
OXFORDS
PEAPODS
PENTADS
PERIODS
PETARDS
PONGIDS
PREMEDS
RAMRODS
REBENDS
REBINDS
RECORDS
REDBUDS
REFUNDS
REGARDS
RELOADS
REMANDS
REMENDS
REMINDS
REMOLDS
RENARDS
REREADS
RESANDS
RESEEDS
RESENDS
RETARDS

REWARDS
REWELDS
REWINDS
REWORDS
RIBANDS
ROBARDS
ROLAIDS
SAYYIDS
SCREEDS
SEABEDS
SECONDS
SHIELDS
SHROUDS
SPREADS
STRANDS
SUNGODS
TABARDS
TAGENDS
TETRADS
THREADS
TIERODS
TOROIDS
TOWARDS
TRIPODS
UNBENDS
UNBINDS
UNFOLDS
UNGIRDS
UNHANDS
UNIPODS
UNLOADS
UNWINDS
UPHOLDS
UPLANDS
UPLOADS
UPWARDS
USERIDS
VESPIDS
WANTADS
WARGODS
WIZARDS

D•T••••

DATASET
DATEDLY
DETAILS
DETAINS
DETECTS
DETENTE
DETESTS
DETOURS
DETRACT
DETRAIN
DETROIT
DITCHED
DITCHES
DITHERS
DITHERY
DITSIER
DITTANY
DITTIES
DITTOED
DITZIER
DOTARDS
DOTEDON
DOTESON
DOTLIKE
DOTTIER
DOTTILY
DOTTING
DOTTLES
DUTEOUS
DUTIFUL

D••T•••

DACTYLS
DAFTEST
DALTREY
DARTERS
DARTING
DASTARD
DAYTIME
DAYTONA
DAYTRIP
DEBTORS
DEFTEST
DEITIES
DELTAIC
DELTOID
DENTATE
DENTINE
DENTING
DENTIST
DENTURE
DESTINE
DESTINY
DESTROY
DEUTERO
DEXTRIN
DIATOMS
DICTATE
DICTION
DICTUMS
DIETARY
DIETERS
DIETING
DIKTATS
DIPTYCH
DIRTIED
DIRTIER
DIRTIES
DIRTILY
DISTAFF
DISTANT
DISTEND
DISTILL
DISTILS
DISTORT
DISTURB
DITTANY
DITTIES
DITTOED
DMYTRYK
DNOTICE
DOCTORS
DOGTAGS
DOGTROT
DOLTISH
DOTTIER
DOTTILY
DOTTING
DOTTLES
DRATTED
DUCTILE
DUCTING
DUSTBIN
DUSTERS
DUSTIER
DUSTILY
DUSTING
DUSTMAN
DUSTMEN
DUSTMOP
DUSTOFF
DUSTPAN
DUSTUPS

D•••T••

DAKOTAN
DAKOTAS
DALETHS
DAUNTED
DAYSTAR
DEALTIN
DEARTHS
DEBATED
DEBATER
DEBATES
DEBITED
DEBUTED
DECATUR
DELETED
DELETES
DEMETER
DEMOTED
DEMOTES
DENOTED
DENOTES
DEPUTED
DEPUTES
DESKTOP
DESOTOS
DEVOTED
DEVOTEE
DEVOTES
DIGITAL
DILATED
DILATES
DILUTED
DILUTER
DILUTES
DIMITRI
DINETTE
DIOPTER
DOGSTAR
DONATED
DONATES
DONATOR
DORITOS
DOROTHY
DOUBTED
DOUBTER
DRAFTED
DRAFTEE
DRASTIC
DRATTED
DRIFTED
DRIFTER
DRISTAN
DYKSTRA

D••••T•

DARESTO
DECANTS
DECEITS
DECOCTS
DEDUCTS
DEFACTO
DEFEATS
DEFECTS
DEFLATE
DEGUSTS
DEJECTS
DELICTI
DELICTS
DELISTS
DENSITY
DENTATE
DEPARTS
DEPICTS
DEPLETE
DEPORTS
DESALTS
DESERTS
DESISTS
DESPITE
DESPOTS
DETECTS
DETENTE
DETESTS
DEVIATE
DICTATE
DIDACTS
DIGESTS
DIGNITY
DIKTATS
DIMOUTS
DIMWITS
DINETTE
DIRECTS
DISPUTE
DIVERTS
DIVESTS
DOCENTS
DOCKETS
DOGMATA
DOGSITS
DOPANTS
DORSETT
DOUGHTY
DOZENTH
DRYROTS
DUALITY
DUBIETY
DUEDATE
DUGOUTS
DURANTE
DYNASTS
DYNASTY

D•••••T

DADAIST
DAFTEST
DAMPEST
DANKEST
DARKEST
DASBOOT
DATASET
DEADSET
DEAFEST
DEALOUT
DEAREST
DECKOUT
DECRYPT
DEEPEST
DEEPFAT
DEEPSET
DEFAULT
DEFIANT
DEFICIT
DEFLECT
DEFROST
DEFTEST
DEFUNCT
DELIGHT
DELIMIT
DEMERIT
DENSEST
DENTIST
DEPOSIT
DESCANT
DESCENT
DESKSET
DESSERT
DETRACT
DETROIT
DEVIANT
DIALECT
DICIEST
DIDEROT
DIEDOUT
DIESOUT
DIGSOUT
DILBERT
DIMMEST
DINGBAT
DINMONT
DISGUST
DISHOUT
DISPORT
DISRUPT
DISSECT
DISSENT
DISTANT
DISTORT
DOGBERT
DOGCART
DOGTROT
DOLEOUT
DOORMAT
DOPEOUT
DOPIEST
DORMANT
DORSETT
DOUBLET
DOUREST
DOVECOT
DOWNPAT
DOZIEST
DRAGNET
DRAGOUT
DRAUGHT
DRAWOUT
DREWOUT
DRIBLET
DRIVEAT
DROPLET
DROPOUT
DROUGHT
DRYSUIT
DUELIST
DULLEST
DUMBEST

•D•T•••

EDITING
EDITION
EDITORS
EDITOUT

•D••T••

ADAPTED
ADAPTER
ADAPTOR
ADEPTLY
ADMITTO
ADOPTED
ADOPTEE
ADOPTER
ADULTLY
IDEATED
IDEATES
IDENTIC
IDIOTIC

•D•••T•

ADAMITE
ADDEDTO
ADDONTO
ADDUCTS
ADDUPTO
ADJUSTS
ADMITTO
ADULATE
ADVENTS
ADVERTS
EDACITY
EDUCATE
ODDLOTS

•D••••T

ADAMANT
ADJUNCT
EDGEOUT
EDGIEST
EDITOUT
ODDMENT

••DT•••

BEDTIME
GODTHAB
MIDTERM
MIDTOWN
OLDTIME
REDTAPE
REDTOPS

••D•T••

AUDITED
AUDITOR
CADETTE
GODUTCH
INDITED
INDITES
INDUTCH
IODATES
OLDSTER
REDATED
REDATES
REDSTAR
RIDOTTO
SEDATED
SEDATER
SEDATES
UNDATED
UPDATED
UPDATES

••D••T•

ABDUCTS
ADDEDTO
ADDONTO
ADDUCTS
ADDUPTO
ALDENTE
ANDANTE
BUDGETS
CADETTE
DEDUCTS
DIDACTS
FIDGETS
FIDGETY
GADGETS
GADGETY
GODWITS
HYDRATE
INDENTS
INDEPTH
INDICTS
INDUCTS
JADEITE
LEDUPTO
LUDDITE
MEDIATE
MIDGETS
MODELTS
MODESTO
MODESTY
MODISTE
MUDCATS
NUDISTS
ODDLOTS
PEDANTS
RADIATE
REDACTS
REDANTS
REDHATS
REDHOTS
RIDOTTO
RODENTS
TIDBITS
VEDANTA
WIDGETS

••D•••T

BADDEST
BEDPOST
BEDREST
BODYFAT
DADAIST
DIDEROT
ENDMOST
FADDIST
FADEOUT
HIDEOUT
HYDRANT
INDOUBT
JUDOIST
MADDEST
MADEOUT
MEDIANT
MIDEAST
MIDMOST
MIDWEST
NODOUBT
ODDMENT
OLDWEST
RADIANT
REDCENT
REDCOAT
REDDEST
REDEALT
REDHEAT
REDMEAT
REDOUBT
REDSPOT
RIDEOUT
RODEOUT
SADDEST
SIDEBET
TIDIEST
UPDRAFT

•••DT••

HARDTOP
ICEDTEA

•••D•T•

ACIDITY
AIRDATE
ARIDITY
AVIDITY
BANDITO
BANDITS
COEDITS
CONDITA
CORDATE
CORDITE
CREDITS
CRUDITY
DUEDATE
ERUDITE
HOLDSTO
LEADSTO
LUDDITE
MANDATE
MISDATE
OFFDUTY
ONADATE
PANDITS
PREDATE
PUNDITS
RAWDATA
REEDITS
SEADUTY
TENDSTO

•••D••T

ACEDOUT
ARIDEST
BADDEST
BALDEST
BOLDEST
BRIDGET
COLDCUT
COLDEST
CONDUCT
CONDUIT
CRUDEST
DEADSET
DIEDOUT
EKEDOUT
ERODENT
EVIDENT
FADDIST
FEEDLOT
FINDOUT
FOLDOUT
FONDANT
FONDEST
HANDOUT
HANDSET
HARDEST
HARDHAT
HARDHIT
HARDPUT
HARDSET
HEADOUT
HEADSET
HELDOUT
HOLDOUT
ICEDOUT
KINDEST
LAIDOUT
LANDSAT
LEADOUT
LEWDEST
LOUDEST
MADDEST
MILDEST
MINDSET
MORDANT
MORDENT
ONADIET
OXIDANT
PAIDOUT
PANDECT
PAYDIRT
PENDANT
PENDENT
PREDICT
PRODUCT
PRUDENT
READMIT
READOUT
REDDEST
SADDEST
SANDLOT
SAWDUST
SENDOUT
SNIDEST
SOLDOUT
STUDENT
TRIDENT
VERDANT
VERDICT
VIADUCT
WEEDOUT
WILDCAT
WILDEST
WOODCUT
WOODLOT

••••DT•

ADDEDTO
AIMEDTO
BREADTH

••••D•T

AIMEDAT
COULDNT
PAWEDAT
PERIDOT
PLAUDIT
POKEDAT
WOULDNT
WYANDOT

•••••DT

SCHMIDT

DU•••••

DUALITY
DUBARRY
DUBBERS
DUBBING
DUBIETY
DUBIOUS
DUBUQUE
DUCHESS
DUCHIES
DUCKIER
DUCKING
DUCKPIN
DUCTILE
DUCTING
DUDEDUP
DUDGEON
DUEDATE
DUELERS
DUELING
DUELIST
DUENNAS
DUFFELS
DUFFERS
DUGONGS
DUGOUTS
DUKAKIS
DUKEDOM
DULCIFY
DULLARD
DULLEST
DULLING
DULLISH
DUMBEST
DUMBING
DUMDUMS
DUMMIED
DUMMIES
DUMMYUP
DUMPIER
DUMPING
DUMPISH
DUNAWAY
DUNCISH
DUNGEON
DUNKERS
DUNKING
DUNKIRK
DUNLINS
DUNNING
DUNNOCK
DUODENA
DURABLE
DURABLY
DURANCE
DURANGO
DURANTE
DURNING
DURRELL
DUSKIER
DUSKILY
DUSKISH
DUSTBIN
DUSTERS
DUSTIER
DUSTILY
DUSTING
DUSTMAN
DUSTMEN
DUSTMOP
DUSTOFF
DUSTPAN
DUSTUPS
DUTEOUS
DUTIFUL

D•U••••

DAUBERS
DAUBING
DAUMIER
DAUNTED
DAUPHIN
DEUTERO
DHURRIE
DIURNAL
DOUBLED
DOUBLES
DOUBLET
DOUBLEU
DOUBTED
DOUBTER
DOUGHTY
DOUGLAS
DOUREST
DOUSING
DRUBBED
DRUCKER
DRUDGED
DRUDGES
DRUGGED
DRUMLIN
DRUMMED
DRUMMER
DRUMSUP

D••U•••

DEBUNKS
DEBUSSY
DEBUTED
DEDUCED
DEDUCES
DEDUCTS
DEFUNCT
DEFUSED
DEFUSES
DEGUSTS
DELUDED
DELUDES
DELUGED
DELUGES
DELUISE
DEMURER
DENUDED
DENUDES
DEPUTED
DEPUTES
DILUTED
DILUTER
DILUTES
DISUSED
DIVULGE
DRAUGHT
DROUGHT
DUBUQUE

D•••U••

DANBURY
DASYURE
DEBAUCH
DEBOUCH
DEFAULT
DEGAUSS
DENEUVE
DENTURE
DETOURS
DEVOURS
DICTUMS
DIFFUSE
DIMBULB
DIMOUTS
DISCUSS
DISGUST
DISPUTE
DISRUPT
DISTURB
DOLOURS
DONJUAN
DRACULA
DRSEUSS
DRYRUNS
DRYSUIT
DUGOUTS
DUMDUMS
DUSTUPS
DYBBUKS

D••••U•

DANSEUR
DAREFUL
DEALOUT
DECATUR
DECKOUT
DECORUM
DEDALUS
DEFRAUD
DEVALUE
DEVIOUS
DIEDOUT
DIESOUT
DIGSOUT
DIREFUL
DISHFUL
DISHOUT
DIVINUM
DOINGUP
DOLEFUL
DOLEOUT
DOLLSUP
DOMINUS
DONAHUE
DONIMUS
DOOMFUL
DOPEOUT
DRAGOUT
DRAWNUP
DRAWOUT
DRAWSUP
DREAMUP
DRESSUP
DREWOUT
DREYFUS
DRIEDUP
DRIESUP
DRIVEUP
DROPOUT
DRUMSUP
DUBIOUS
DUBUQUE
DUDEDUP
DUMMYUP
DUTEOUS
DUTIFUL

D•••••U

DOUBLEU

•DU••••

ADULATE
ADULTLY
EDUCATE
EDUCING

•D•U•••

ADDUCED
ADDUCES
ADDUCTS
ADDUPTO
ADJUDGE
ADJUNCT
ADJURED
ADJURES
ADJUSTS
EDOUARD

•D••U••

ADJOURN

•D•••U•

ADDEDUP
EDGEOUT
EDITOUT
ODORFUL
ODOROUS

••DU•••

ABDUCTS
ADDUCED
ADDUCES
ADDUCTS
ADDUPTO
ARDUOUS
AUDUBON
CADUCEI
DEDUCED
DEDUCES
DEDUCTS
ENDUING
ENDURED
ENDURES
ENDUROS
ENDUSER
ENDUSES
GODUNOV
GODUTCH
INDUCED
INDUCER
INDUCES
INDUCTS
INDULGE
INDUTCH
LEDUPTO
MEDULLA
MEDUSAE
MEDUSAS
MODULAR
MODULES
NODULAR
NODULES
OLDUVAI
PADUANS
PADUCAH
RADULAE
REDUCED
REDUCER
REDUCES
SEDUCED
SEDUCER
SEDUCES

••D•U••

ARDOURS
BADGUYS
BEDAUBS
BEDBUGS
BEDOUIN
CADBURY
ENDRUNS
INDOUBT
MEDIUMS
NODOUBT
PODIUMS
REDBUDS
REDGUMS
REDOUBT
REDOUND
SUDBURY
TEDIUMS

••D••U•

ADDEDUP
ARDUOUS
BUDDYUP
CADMIUM
DEDALUS
DUDEDUP
ENDEDUP
FADEOUT
GIDDYUP
HIDEOUS
HIDEOUT
HYDROUS
LADYBUG
MADEOUT
MODICUM
OEDIPUS
RIDEOUT
RODEOUT
TEDIOUS

•••DU••

CONDUCE
CONDUCT
CONDUIT
DUMDUMS
FOLDUPS
FONDUES
GRADUAL
HOLDUPS
MACDUFF
OFFDUTY
PRODUCE
PRODUCT
SAWDUST
SEADUTY
SENDUPS
SUBDUED
SUBDUER
SUBDUES
TRADUCE
VERDUGO
VERDURE
VIADUCT
WINDUPS

•••D•U•

ACEDOUT
AMADEUS
BEADSUP
BINDSUP
BUDDYUP
CANDOUR
COLDCUT
DIEDOUT
EARDRUM
EKEDOUT
FINDOUT
FOLDOUT
FOLDSUP
GIDDYUP
GOLDBUG
HANDFUL
HANDGUN
HANDOUT
HANDSUP
HARDPUT
HEADOUT
HEADSUP
HEEDFUL
HELDOUT
HOLDOUT
HOLDSUP
HOODLUM
HUMDRUM
ICEDOUT
IRIDIUM
LAIDOUT
LANDAUS
LEADOUT
LEADSUP
MINDFUL
NEEDFUL
PAIDOUT
READOUT
RHODIUM
SENDOUT
SENDSUP
SOLDOUT
STADIUM
TRADEUP
VERDOUX
WEEDOUT
WINDSUP
WOODCUT

•••D••U
RONDEAU
TRUDEAU

••••DU•
ACTEDUP
ADDEDUP
ANTEDUP
BONEDUP
BOUNDUP
BOXEDUP
BUILDUP
CAMEDUE
COMEDUE
DRIEDUP
DUDEDUP
EASEDUP
ENDEDUP
FIREDUP
FIXEDUP
HIKEDUP
HOLEDUP
HYPEDUP
KEYEDUP
LACEDUP
LINEDUP
MIXEDUP
MOVEDUP
OVERDUB
OVERDUE
OWNEDUP
PASTDUE
PILEDUP
PIPEDUP
RAKEDUP
RESIDUE
ROUNDUP
SAVEDUP
SEWEDUP
SIZEDUP
SPEEDUP
STANDUP
STOODUP
TONEDUP
TUNEDUP
TYPEDUP
WIPEDUP
WISEDUP
WOUNDUP

D•V••••
DAVINCI
DEVALUE
DEVEINS
DEVELOP
DEVIANT
DEVIATE
DEVICES
DEVILED
DEVILLE
DEVILRY
DEVIOUS
DEVISED
DEVISES
DEVOLVE
DEVOTED
DEVOTEE
DEVOTES
DEVOURS
DEVRIES
DIVERGE
DIVERSE
DIVERTS
DIVESIN
DIVESTS
DIVIDED
DIVIDER
DIVIDES
DIVINED
DIVINER
DIVINES
DIVINUM
DIVISOR
DIVORCE
DIVULGE
DIVVIED
DIVVIES
DOVECOT

D••V•••
DELVERS
DELVING
DERVISH
DIVVIED
DIVVIES
DRIVEAT
DRIVEIN
DRIVELS
DRIVERS
DRIVEUP
DRIVING
DROVERS

D•••V••
DELIVER
DERIVED
DERIVES
DIDOVER
DISAVOW
DONOVAN
DWARVES

D••••V•
DECEIVE
DENEUVE
DEPRAVE
DEPRIVE
DESERVE
DEVOLVE

•DV••••
ADVANCE
ADVENTS
ADVERBS
ADVERSE
ADVERTS
ADVISED
ADVISER
ADVISES
ADVISOR

••D•V••
ANDOVER
BEDEVIL
DIDOVER
ENDIVES
MEDEVAC
OLDUVAI

••D••V•
KEDROVA

••D•••V
GODUNOV

•••D•V•
MOLDOVA
SKYDIVE

DW•••••
DWARFED
DWARVES
DWEEZIL
DWELLED
DWELLER
DWINDLE

D•W••••
DAWDLED
DAWDLER
DAWDLES
DAWKISH
DAWNING
DAWNSON
DEWCLAW
DEWDROP
DEWLAPS
DEWLESS
DEWLINE
DOWAGER
DOWDIER
DOWDILY
DOWERED
DOWNBOW
DOWNERS
DOWNIER
DOWNING
DOWNPAT
DOWRIES
DOWSERS
DOWSING

D••W•••
DAGWOOD
DIMWITS
DOGWOOD
DRAWBAR
DRAWERS
DRAWING
DRAWLED
DRAWNIN
DRAWNON
DRAWNUP
DRAWOUT
DRAWSIN
DRAWSON
DRAWSUP
DREWOUT
DROWNED
DROWSED
DROWSES
DRYWALL
DRYWELL

D•••W••
DISOWNS
DOORWAY
DUNAWAY

D••••W•
DIEDOWN

D•••••W
DANELAW
DEWCLAW
DISAVOW
DOGCHOW
DOGSHOW
DOWNBOW

•DW••••
EDWARDS

••DW•••
ENDWAYS
ENDWISE
GODWITS
INDWELL
MIDWAYS
MIDWEEK
MIDWEST
MIDWIFE
OLDWEST
PEDWAYS
REDWINE
REDWING
REDWOLF
REDWOOD

••D•W••
BEDEWED
ENDOWED
MADEWAY
RIDGWAY
WIDOWED
WIDOWER

••D••W•
ANDREWS
BEDDOWN
MIDTOWN
OLDNEWS
OLDSAWS
REDRAWN
REDRAWS
UNDRAWN

•••DW••
BALDWIN
COLDWAR
FOODWEB
GOLDWYN
GOODWIN
HARDWON
HEADWAY
ROADWAY

•••D•W•
BEDDOWN
BOGDOWN
CUTDOWN
DIEDOWN
GETDOWN
GOTDOWN
HOEDOWN
LAYDOWN
LETDOWN
LIEDOWN
LOWDOWN
MEADOWS
MEADOWY
MILDEWS
MILDEWY
MOWDOWN
PINDOWN
PREDAWN
PUTDOWN
RANDOWN
RUBDOWN
RUNDOWN
SATDOWN
SETDOWN
SHADOWS
SHADOWY
SITDOWN
SUNDEWS
SUNDOWN
TIEDOWN
TOPDOWN
WINDOWS

•••D••W
BANDSAW
HANDSAW
LAIDLOW
OUTDRAW
OUTDREW
SKIDROW
WINDROW
WOODROW

••••D•W
JACKDAW

D•X••••
DEXTRIN

D••X•••
DIOXIDE

D•••••X
DEEPSIX

•D••X••
ADMIXED
ADMIXES

••D•X••
INDEXED
INDEXES
RADIXES

••D•••X
MADAMEX

•••D••X
BANDBOX
HENDRIX
SANDBOX
VERDOUX

••••D•X
BROADAX
PARADOX
ROLODEX
SPANDEX

DY•••••
DYBBUKS
DYKSTRA
DYNAMIC
DYNAMOS
DYNASTS
DYNASTY

D•Y••••
DAYBEDS
DAYBOOK
DAYBOYS
DAYCAMP
DAYCARE
DAYJOBS
DAYLILY
DAYLONG
DAYMARE
DAYROOM
DAYSINN
DAYSTAR
DAYTIME
DAYTONA
DAYTRIP
DMYTRYK
DOYENNE
DRYCELL
DRYDOCK
DRYEYED
DRYHOLE
DRYNESS
DRYROTS
DRYRUNS
DRYSUIT
DRYWALL
DRYWELL

D••Y•••
DASYURE
DEFYING
DENYING
DRAYAGE
DRAYING
DREYFUS

D•••Y••
DACTYLS
DECAYED
DECOYED
DECRYPT
DELAYED
DELAYER
DIPTYCH
DRYEYED
DUMMYUP

D••••Y•
DAYBOYS
DEADEYE
DEEJAYS
DEFRAYS
DEPLOYS
DICKEYS
DISMAYS
DMYTRYK
DOGDAYS
DONKEYS

D•••••Y
DAFFILY
DAHOMEY
DALTREY
DANBURY
DANDIFY
DARESAY
DARNLEY
DATEDLY
DAYLILY
DAZEDLY
DEANERY
DEBAKEY
DEBUSSY
DECENCY
DEEPFRY
DEERFLY
DELANEY
DEMPSEY
DENNEHY
DENSELY
DENSITY
DESTINY
DESTROY
DEVILRY
DIDDLEY
DIETARY
DIGNIFY
DIGNITY
DINGILY
DIRTILY
DISOBEY
DISPLAY
DITHERY
DITTANY
DIZZILY
DOORWAY
DOROTHY
DOTTILY
DOUGHTY
DOWDILY
DRAPERY
DRIPDRY
DRIZZLY
DROPSBY
DROSHKY
DUALITY
DUBARRY
DUBIETY
DULCIFY
DUNAWAY
DURABLY
DUSKILY
DUSTILY
DYNASTY

•DY••••
IDYLLIC
ODYSSEY

•D•Y•••
EDDYING

•D••••Y
ADEPTLY
ADULTLY
EDACITY
IDEALLY
ODYSSEY

••DY•••
BODYFAT
ECDYSES
ECDYSIS
EDDYING
LADYBUG
LADYDAY
LADYISH
MIDYEAR
RUDYARD
TIDYING
UNDYING

••D•Y••
BUDDYUP
GIDDYAP
GIDDYUP
REDEYED
REDEYES

••D••Y•
BADBOYS
BADGUYS
ENDWAYS
KIDNEYS
MEDLEYS
MIDDAYS
MIDWAYS
OLDDAYS
PEDWAYS

••D•••Y
ARDENCY
AUDIBLY
CADBURY
CADENCY
DIDDLEY
ELDERLY
ENDPLAY
FIDGETY
GADGETY
GIDDILY
GODFREY
JADEDLY
LADYDAY
MADEHAY
MADEWAY
MODESTY
MUDDILY
OLDFOGY
ORDERLY
PODGILY
PUDENCY
PUDGILY
RIDGWAY
RUDDILY
SUDBURY

•••DY••
ANODYNE
AZODYES
BUDDYUP
GIDDYAP
GIDDYUP
TIEDYED
TIEDYES
VANDYCK
VANDYKE

•••D•Y•
DEADEYE
DOGDAYS
FRIDAYS
GLADEYE
GOLDWYN
GOODBYE
GOODBYS
HEYDAYS
MANDAYS
MAYDAYS
MIDDAYS
MONDAYS
OLDDAYS
PAYDAYS
SUNDAYS

•••D••Y
ABIDEBY
ACADEMY
ACIDIFY
ACIDITY
ARIDITY
AVIDITY
BAWDILY
BINDERY
BRADLEY
CINDERY
CRUDELY
CRUDITY
DANDIFY
DIDDLEY
DOWDILY
GAUDILY
GEODESY
GIDDILY
HANDILY
HARDILY
HEADILY
HEADWAY
LINDSAY
LINDSEY
MEADOWY
MILDEWY
MOODILY
MUDDILY
NEEDILY
OFFDUTY
POWDERY
PRODIGY
PRUDERY
READILY
ROADWAY
ROWDILY
RUDDILY
SANDFLY
SEADUTY
SEEDILY
SHADILY
SHADOWY
SNIDELY
SPIDERY
TARDILY
WEEDILY
WINDILY
WORDILY

••••DY•
HAIRDYE
NOBODYS

••••D•Y
ACRIDLY
BLANDLY
BLINDLY
BLOWDRY
BONEDRY
BROADLY
BYANDBY
DATEDLY
DAZEDLY
DRIPDRY
FARADAY
FETIDLY
FIXEDLY
FLAGDAY
FLUIDLY
FOUNDRY
GELIDLY
GRANDLY
HIGHDAY
HOLIDAY
HOLYDAY
HUMIDLY
JADEDLY
LADYDAY
LAUNDRY
LIVIDLY
LUCIDLY
LURIDLY
NAKEDLY
NAMEDAY
NEWSDAY
NOONDAY
NOTEDLY
PALEDRY
PROUDLY
RABIDLY
RAPIDLY
RIGIDLY
ROUNDLY
RUNSDRY
SAMEDAY
SICKDAY
SNOWDAY
SOLIDLY
SOMEDAY
SOUNDLY
SPINDLY
SPINDRY
STAIDLY
STANDBY
STOODBY
TEPIDLY
THIRDLY
TIMIDLY
TIREDLY
TUESDAY
UNGODLY
VALIDLY
VAPIDLY
VEXEDLY
VIVIDLY
WEEKDAY
WEIRDLY
WORKDAY
WORLDLY

•••••DY
ALBUNDY
ALREADY
ANYBODY
CASSIDY
CUSTODY
HUNYADY
HYMNODY
KENNEDY
ORGANDY
ORMANDY
PEABODY
PERFIDY
PICARDY
PROSODY
RAGGEDY
SUBSIDY
THREADY
TRAGEDY
UNHANDY
UNREADY
WCHANDY

D•Z••••
DAZEDLY
DAZZLED
DAZZLER
DAZZLES
DIZENED
DIZZIED
DIZZIER
DIZZIES
DIZZILY
DOZENTH
DOZEOFF
DOZIEST

D••Z•••
DAZZLED
DAZZLER
DAZZLES
DITZIER
DIZZIED
DIZZIER
DIZZIES
DIZZILY
DOOZIES
DRIZZLE
DRIZZLY

D•••Z••
DENIZEN
DRIZZLE
DRIZZLY
DWEEZIL

•D•••Z•
IDOLIZE

••DZ•••
ENDZONE

••D•Z••
BEDIZEN
IODIZED
IODIZES

••D••Z•
CADENZA
MIDSIZE

•••D•Z•
ANODIZE
CARDOZO
INADAZE
MENDOZA
OXIDIZE

EA•••••
EAGERER
EAGERLY
EAGLETS
EAGLING
EARACHE
EARDROP
EARDRUM
EARFLAP
EARFULS
EARHART
EARLDOM
EARLESS
EARLIER
EARLIKE
EARLOBE
EARLOCK
EARLYON
EARMARK
EARMUFF
EARNERS
EARNEST
EARNING
EARPLUG
EARRING
EARSHOT
EARTHEN
EARTHLY
EARWIGS
EASEDIN
EASEDUP
EASEFUL
EASEOFF
EASEOUT
EASESIN
EASESUP
EASIEST
EASTEND
EASTERN
EASTERS
EASTMAN
EASYOFF
EATABLE
EATAWAY
EATCROW
EATENAT
EATENUP
EATSOUT

E•A••••
EDACITY
EDAPHIC
EDASNER
EGALITE
ELAAIUN
ELAPIDS
ELAPSED
ELAPSES
ELASTIC
ELATERS
ELATING
ELATION
EMAILED
EMANANT
EMANATE
EMANUEL
ENABLED
ENABLES
ENACTED
ENACTOR
ENAMELS
ENAMORS
ENAMOUR
EPARCHS
EPARCHY
EPAULET
ERASERS
ERASING
ERASMUS
ERASURE
ETAGERE
ETAMINE
EVACUEE
EVADERS
EVADING
EVANDER
EVANGEL
EVANISH
EVASION
EVASIVE
EXACTAS
EXACTED
EXACTER
EXACTLY
EXACTOR
EXALTED
EXAMINE
EXAMPLE
EXANIMO
EXARCHS

E••A•••
EARACHE
EATABLE
EATAWAY
ECLAIRS
ECUADOR
EDWARDS
EFFACED
EFFACES
ELAAIUN
ELEANOR
EMBANKS
EMBARGO
EMBARKS
EMBASSY
EMBAYED
EMPANEL
EMPATHY
ENCAGED
ENCAGES
ENCAMPS
ENCASED
ENCASES
ENGAGED
ENGAGES
ENGARDE
ENHANCE
ENLACED
ENLACES
ENLARGE
ENMASSE
ENRAGED
ENRAGES
ENTAILS
EQUABLE
EQUABLY
EQUALED
EQUALLY
EQUATED
EQUATES
EQUATOR
ERGATES
ERRANCY
ERRANDS
ERRATIC
ERRATUM
ESCAPED
ESCAPEE
ESCAPES
ESCARPS
ESPANOL
ESPARTO
ESSAYED
ESTATES
ETHANOL
EURASIA
EXFACTO
EXHALED
EXHALES
EXHAUST
EXPANDS
EXPANSE
EXPARTE

E•••A••
EARHART
EARMARK
ECKHART
ECSTASY
EDOUARD
EDUCATE
EGGCASE
ELEGANT
ELEVATE
ELKHART
EMANANT
EMANATE
EMBRACE
EMERALD
EMIRATE
EMULATE
ENCHAIN
ENCHANT
ENCLAVE
ENDEARS
ENDGAME
ENDWAYS
ENGLAND
ENGRAFT
ENGRAMS
ENGRAVE
ENNEADS
ENPLANE
ENSLAVE
ENSNARE
ENSNARL
ENTRAIN
ENTRANT
ENTRAPS
ENWRAPS
ESPIALS
ESTRADA
ESTRAYS
ESTUARY
ETCHANT
EXCLAIM
EXPIATE
EXPLAIN
EXTRACT
EYEBALL
EYEBANK
EYELASH
EYEWASH

E••••A•
EARFLAP
EASTMAN
EATAWAY
EATENAT
EGGHEAD
EIGHTAM
ELEGIAC
ELYSIAN
ENCINAS
ENDPLAY
ENIGMAS
ENTHRAL
ENTREAT
EPIGRAM
EPOCHAL
ESCHEAT
ESPOSAS
ESTIVAL
ETERNAL
ETESIAN
ETHICAL
ETONIAN
EXACTAS
EXURBAN

E•••••A
ECHIDNA
ELECTRA
ELEKTRA
EMERITA
EMPORIA
ENCOMIA
ERITREA
EROTICA
ESTONIA
ESTRADA
ETRURIA
EURASIA
EXOTICA
EXURBIA

•EA••••
BEACHED
BEACHES
BEACONS
BEADIER
BEADING
BEADLES
BEADSUP
BEAGLES
BEAKERS
BEAMIER

BEAMING
BEAMISH
BEAMSUP
BEANBAG
BEANERY
BEANIES
BEANING
BEARCAT
BEARCUB
BEARDED
BEARERS
BEARHUG
BEARING
BEARISH
BEAROFF
BEAROUT
BEARPAW
BEARSON
BEARSUP
BEASTIE
BEASTLY
BEATERS
BEATIFY
BEATING
BEATLES
BEATNIK
BEATOUT
BEATRIX
BEATSIT
BEATSME
BEATSUP
BEATTIE
BEAUISH
BEAVERS
CEASING
DEACONS
DEADAIR
DEADEND
DEADENS
DEADEYE
DEADPAN
DEADSEA
DEADSET
DEAFENS
DEAFEST
DEALERS
DEALING
DEALOUT
DEALSIN
DEALTIN
DEANERY
DEAREST
DEARIES
DEARSIR
DEARTHS
FEARERS
FEARFUL
FEARING
FEASTED
FEATHER
FEATURE
GEARBOX
GEARING
GEARSTO
GEARSUP
HEADERS
HEADIER
HEADILY
HEADING
HEADMAN
HEADMEN
HEADOFF
HEADOUT
HEADPIN
HEADSET
HEADSIN
HEADSUP
HEADWAY
HEALALL
HEALERS
HEALING
HEALTHY
HEAPING
HEARDOF
HEARERS
HEARING
HEARKEN
HEAROUT
HEARSAY
HEARSOF
HEARTED
HEARTEN
HEARTHS
HEATERS
HEATFUL
HEATHEN
HEATHER
HEATING
HEATSUP
HEATTER
HEAVEHO
HEAVENS
HEAVERS
HEAVETO
HEAVIER
HEAVIES
HEAVILY
HEAVING
JEALOUS
JEANARP
JEANLUC
JEANNIE
KEARNEY
LEACHED
LEACHES
LEACOCK
LEADERS
LEADIER
LEADING
LEADINS
LEADOFF
LEADOUT
LEADSIN
LEADSON
LEADSTO
LEADSUP
LEAFAGE
LEAFIER
LEAFING
LEAFLET
LEAGUES
LEAKAGE
LEAKERS
LEAKIER
LEAKING
LEANDER
LEANERS
LEANEST
LEANING
LEANSON
LEANTOS
LEAPERS
LEAPING
LEARIER
LEARJET
LEARNED
LEARNER
LEASERS
LEASHED
LEASHES
LEASING
LEATHER
LEAVEIN
LEAVENS
LEAVING
MEADOWS
MEADOWY
MEALIER
MEALIES
MEANDER
MEANEST
MEANIES
MEANING
MEASLES
MEASURE
MEATIER
MEATILY
NEAREST
NEARING
NEARYOU
NEATENS
NEATEST
PEABEAN
PEABODY
PEACHED
PEACHES
PEACOAT
PEACOCK
PEAFOWL
PEAHENS
PEAKING
PEAKISH
PEALIKE
PEALING
PEANUTS
PEAPODS
PEARLED
PEARSON
PEASANT
PEASOUP
PEATBOG
PEATIER
PEAVEYS
REACHED
REACHES
REACTED
REACTOR
REACTTO
READERS
READIED
READIER
READIES
READILY
READING
READMIT
READOUT
READSIN
REAFFIX
REAGENT
REAIMED
REAIRED
REALISE
REALISM
REALIST
REALITY
REALIZE
REALTOR
REAMASS
REAMERS
REAMING
REAPERS
REAPING
REAREND
REARERS
REARGUE
REARING
REARMED
REARSUP
REASONS
REAVAIL
SEABAGS
SEABASS
SEABEDS
SEABEES
SEABIRD
SEABLUE
SEABORG
SEACOWS
SEADOGS
SEADUTY
SEAFANS
SEAFIRE
SEAFOOD
SEAGATE
SEAGIRT
SEAGRAM
SEAGULL
SEALABS
SEALANE
SEALANT
SEALEGS
SEALERS
SEALILY
SEALING
SEALION
SEALOFF
SEALSUP
SEAMIER
SEAMING
SEAMOSS
SEANCES
SEAPORT
SEARING
SEASALT
SEASICK
SEASIDE
SEASLUG
SEASONS
SEASTAR
SEATERS
SEATING
SEATTLE
SEAWALL
SEAWARD
SEAWAYS
SEAWEED
SEAWOLF
TEABAGS
TEABALL
TEACAKE
TEACART
TEACHER
TEACHES
TEACHIN
TEACUPS
TEALEAF
TEALESS
TEAMING
TEAMSUP
TEAPOTS
TEAPOYS
TEARFUL
TEARGAS
TEARIER
TEARILY
TEARING
TEAROFF
TEAROOM
TEAROSE
TEAROUT
TEARSAT
TEARSUP
TEASELS
TEASERS
TEASETS
TEASHOP
TEASING
TEATIME
TEATRAY
TEATREE
VEALIER
WEAKENS
WEAKEST
WEAKISH
WEALTHY
WEANING
WEAPONS
WEARERS
WEARIED
WEARIER
WEARIES
WEARILY
WEARING
WEAROFF
WEAROUT
WEASELS
WEATHER
WEAVERS
WEAVING
YEANING
YEAREND
YEARNED
YEARNER
YEATEAM
ZEALAND
ZEALOTS
ZEALOUS

•E•A•••

AERATED
AERATES
AERATOR
BECALMS
BECAUSE
BEDAUBS
BEFALLS
BEHAVED
BEHAVES
BELABOR
BELAKUN
BELASCO
BELATED
BELAYED
BENATAR
BENAZIR
BERATED
BERATES
BETAKEN
BETAKES
BETAMAX
BETARAY
BEWAILS
CEDARED
CELADON
CERAMIC
CEZANNE
DEBACLE
DEBAKEY
DEBARGE
DEBARKS
DEBASED
DEBASES
DEBATED
DEBATER
DEBATES
DEBAUCH
DECADES
DECAGON
DECALOG
DECAMPS
DECANTS
DECAPOD
DECARLO
DECATUR
DECAYED
DEDALUS
DEFACED
DEFACES
DEFACTO
DEFALLA
DEFAMED
DEFAMES
DEFARGE
DEFAULT
DEGAUSS
DELANEY
DELAYED
DELAYER
DEMANDS
DENARII
DEPALMA
DEPARTS
DERAILS
DESALTS
DETAILS
DETAINS
DEVALUE
FEMALES
GELADAS
GELATIN
GELATIS
GERAINT
GERALDO
GETAWAY
HEPARIN
HEPATIC
HERALDS
HEXAGON
KERATIN
LEBANON
LEBARON
LECARRE
LEGALLY
LEGATEE
LEGATES
LEGATOS
LEHAVRE
LEPANTO
LEVANTS
MEDALED
MEGAHIT
MELANGE
MELANIE
MELANIN
MENACED
MENACES
MENAGES
METATES
NEGATED
NEGATER
NEGATES
NEGATOR
NEPALIS
NEVADAN
NEWAGER
PEDALED
PEDANTS
PEGASUS
PELAGES
PELAGIC
PENALTY
PENANCE
PENATES
PESAWAS
PETALED
PETARDS
REBASTE
REBATED
REBATES
RECALLS
RECANED
RECANES
RECANTS
RECASTS
REDACTS
REDALGA
REDANTS
REDATED
REDATES
REFACED
REFACES
REGAINS
REGALED
REGALES
REGALIA
REGALLY
REGARDS
REGATTA
REHANGS
RELACED
RELACES
RELAPSE
RELATED
RELATES
RELAXED
RELAXES
RELAYED
REMAILS
REMAINS
REMAKES
REMANDS
REMARKS
REMARRY
RENAILS
RENAMED
RENAMES
RENARDS
RENAULT
REPAINT
REPAIRS
REPAPER
REPASTE
REPASTS
REPAVED
REPAVES
RERAISE
RERATED
RERATES
RESALES
RESALTS
RESANDS
RESAWED
RETAILS
RETAINS
RETAKEN
RETAKES
RETAPED
RETAPES
RETARDS
RETAXED
RETAXES
REVALUE
REVAMPS
REWARDS
REWARMS
REWAXED
REWAXES
SECANTS
SEDALIA
SEDATED
SEDATER
SEDATES
SEEABLE
SENATES
SENATOR
SERAPES
SERAPHS
SERAPIS
SESAMES
TELAVIV
TENABLE
TENABLY
TENACES
TENANCY
TENANTS
TERAPHS
TETANUS
VEDANTA
VENALLY
VERANDA
ZENANAS

•E••A••

AERIALS
BEDLAMP
BEEBALM
BEEFALO
BEGGARS
BEHEADS
BELDAME
BELDAMS
BELFAST
BELLAMY
BELTANE
BEMOANS
BENEATH
BENGALI
BENGALS
BEREAVE
BERNARD
BETHANY
BETRAYS
CEBUANO
CELLARS
CEMBALO
CENTAUR
CENTAVO
CEREALS
CERTAIN
DEADAIR
DECLAIM
DECLARE
DECLASS
DEEJAYS
DEFEATS
DEFIANT
DEFLATE
DEFRAUD
DEFRAYS
DEGRADE
DELTAIC
DEMEANS
DENIALS
DENMARK
DENTATE
DEODARS
DEPLANE
DEPRAVE
DESCANT
DESPAIR
DETRACT
DETRAIN
DEVIANT
DEVIATE
DEWLAPS
FELLAHS
FENIANS
FERRARI
FERRARO
FERRATE
GEEGAWS
GENNARO
GERMANE
GERMANS
GERMANY
GESTALT
GESTATE
GETBACK
GEWGAWS
HEALALL
HEBRAIC
HECTARE
HEEHAWS
HENBANE
HENNAED
HEPCATS
HEPTADS
HERBAGE
HERBALS
HERMANN
HETMANS
HEYDAYS
JEANARP
JETWASH
JETWAYS
KENDALL
KENYANS
KEYCARD
KEYPADS
LEAFAGE
LEAKAGE
LEEWARD
LEGRAND
LEKVARS
LENFANT
LEONARD
LEOPARD
LEOTARD
LESPAUL
MEDIANS
MEDIANT
MEDIATE
MENIALS
MERMAID
MESCALS
MESSAGE
MESSALA
METHANE
NECTARS
NEONATE
NESCAFE
NEWGATE
NEWHART
NEWMATH
NEWWAVE
PEASANT
PECCANT
PECCARY
PEDLARS
PEDWAYS
PEERAGE
PELTATE
PENDANT
PENNAME
PENNANT
PENNATE
PENPALS
PENTADS
PEONAGE
PEPPARD
PEPTALK
PERCALE
PERHAPS
PERTAIN
PERVADE
PETNAME
REAMASS
REAVAIL
RECHALK
RECLAIM
RECLAME
RECOATS
REDCAPS
REDEALS
REDEALT
REDHAIR
REDHATS
REDIALS
REDOAKS
REDRAWN
REDRAWS
REDTAPE
REENACT
REFLAGS
REFRACT
REFRAIN
REFRAME
REGNANT
REGRADE
REHEALS
REHEARD
REHEARS
REHEATS
RELEARN
RELEASE
RELIANT
RELOADS
REMNANT
RENTALS
REPEALS
REPEATS
REPLACE
REPLANS
REPLANT
REPLATE
REPLAYS
REREADS
RESCALE
RESEALS
RESEATS
RESTAGE
RESTAIN
RESTAMP
RESTART
RESTATE
RETEACH
RETEARS
RETIARY
RETRACE
RETRACK
RETRACT
RETRADE
RETRAIN
REVEALS
REWEAVE
REWRAPS
REXCATS
REYNARD
SEABAGS
SEABASS
SEAFANS
SEAGATE
SEALABS
SEALANE
SEALANT
SEASALT
SEAWALL
SEAWARD
SEAWAYS
SEESAWS
SELVAGE
SENSATE
SERIALS
SERIATE
SERRATE
SERVALS
SERVANT
SETBACK
SETSAIL
SEXTANS
SEXTANT
TEABAGS
TEABALL
TEACAKE
TEACART
TEDMACK
TEENAGE
TELLALL
TERNARY
TERNATE
TERRACE
TERRAIN
TETRADS
VEEJAYS
VERBALS
VERDANT
WEBPAGE
WELFARE
WELLAND
WENTAPE
WETBARS
WETLAND
YESMAAM
ZEALAND
ZEDBARS
ZERMATT

•E•••A•

AEOLIAN
AEROBAT
BEANBAG
BEARCAT
BEARPAW
BEECHAM
BEESWAX
BELGIAN
BELLJAR
BELLMAN
BELTBAG
BELTWAY
BENATAR
BENTHAM
BERGMAN
BESMEAR
BESPEAK
BESTIAL
BESTMAN
BETAMAX
BETARAY
CENTRAL
DEADPAN
DEBORAH
DECIMAL
DEEPFAT
DELILAH
DEPOSAL
DEWCLAW
FEDERAL
FEDORAS
FEEDBAG
FELDMAN
FEMORAL
FERNBAR
FEYNMAN
GEISHAS
GELADAS
GENERAL
GENTIAN
GETAWAY
GETREAL
HEADMAN
HEADWAY
HEARSAY
HEELTAP
HEGIRAS
HEISMAN
HELICAL
HELIPAD
HELLCAT
HELLMAN
HESHVAN
HESSIAN
JEERSAT
JERBOAS
JETBOAT
KEEPSAT
KEESHAN
KEROUAC
KETCHAM
LEERSAT
LEXICAL
MEDEVAC
MEDICAL
MEDIGAP
MEDUSAE
MEDUSAS
MEGRYAN
MENORAH
MESSIAH
MEXICAN
NEBULAE
NEBULAR
NEBULAS
NEEDHAM
NEUTRAL
NEVADAN
NEWDEAL
NEWSDAY
NEWSMAN
NEWYEAR
OEDIPAL
PEABEAN
PEACOAT
PECKSAT
PEDICAB
PEEKSAT
PEERSAT
PELICAN
PELOTAS
PEMICAN
PERLMAN
PERSIAN
PERUSAL
PESAWAS
PESETAS
REBEKAH
RECITAL
RECLEAN
REDCOAT
REDFLAG
REDHEAD
REDHEAT
REDMEAT
REDSTAR
REFUSAL
REGULAR
REITMAN
REMORAS
REMOVAL
REMUDAS
RENEWAL
REPOMAN
RETINAE
RETINAL
RETINAS
RETREAD
RETREAT
RETRIAL
REVIVAL
SEAGRAM
SEASTAR
SECULAR
SEMINAL
SEMINAR
SENECAS
SENEGAL
SENORAS
SENSUAL
SERBIAN
SEVENAM
SEVERAL
TEALEAF
TEARGAS
TEARSAT
TEATRAY
TEHERAN
TELERAN
TELSTAR
TEMPLAR
TERTIAL
TESTBAN
TEXTUAL
VEGETAL
VENTRAL
VERITAS
VETERAN
WEEKDAY
WELLMAN
WENTBAD
YEATEAM
YELLSAT
YEREVAN
YESDEAR
YESMAAM
ZENANAS
ZEUGMAS

•E••••A

BEDELIA
BEEFTEA
BEGONIA
BEGORRA
BELINDA
BERETTA
BERMUDA
CECILIA
CEDILLA
CELESTA
CEREBRA
DEADSEA
DEEPSEA
DEFALLA
DELIRIA
DEPALMA
FELICIA
FELUCCA
FESTIVA
GEORGIA
HERBTEA
JESSICA
KEDROVA
KENOSHA
LEMPIRA
LEONORA
LETITIA
MEDULLA
MELINDA
MELISSA
MENDOZA
MESSALA
MESSINA
MESTIZA
PERGOLA
PERSONA
PETUNIA
REBECCA
REDALGA
REGALIA
REGATTA
REPLICA
RETSINA
SEDALIA
SEGOVIA
SEQUOIA
SESTINA
TEMPERA
TEMPURA
TEQUILA
TESSERA
VEDANTA
VENTURA
VERANDA
VERBENA
YESHIVA
ZENOBIA

••EA•••

AHEADOF
AREARUG
AREAWAY
AYEAYES
BLEAKER
BLEAKLY
BLEARED
BLEATED
BREADED
BREADTH
BREAKER
BREAKIN
BREAKUP
BREASTS
BREATHE
BREATHS
BREATHY
CHEAPEN
CHEAPER

CHEAPIE
CHEAPLY
CHEATED
CHEATER
CHEATIN
CLEANED
CLEANER
CLEANLY
CLEANSE
CLEANUP
CLEARED
CLEARER
CLEARLY
CLEARUP
CLEAVED
CLEAVER
CLEAVES
CLEAVON
CREAKED
CREAMED
CREAMER
CREASED
CREASES
CREATED
CREATES
CREATOR
DREADED
DREAMED
DREAMER
DREAMON
DREAMUP
ELEANOR
FLEABAG
FLEAPIT
FREAKED
GLEAMED
GLEANED
GLEANER
GLEASON
GREASED
GREASER
GREASES
GREATER
GREATLY
GREAVES
ICEAGES
ICEAXES
IDEALLY
IDEAMAN
IDEAMEN
IDEATED
IDEATES
KNEADED
KNEADER
LIEABED
OCEANIA
OCEANIC
OCEANID
OCEANUS
OLEATES
PLEADED
PLEADER
PLEASED
PLEASER
PLEASES
PLEATED
PREACHY
PREAMPS
SEEABLE
SHEARED
SHEARER
SHEATHE
SHEATHS
SHEAVED

SHEAVES
SMEARED
SNEAKED
SNEAKER
SNEAKIN
SPEAKER
SPEAKOF
SPEAKUP
SPEARED
STEALTH
STEAMED
STEAMER
SWEARAT
SWEARBY
SWEARER
SWEARIN
SWEARTO
SWEATED
SWEATER
THEATER
THEATRE
TREACLE
TREACLY
TREADED
TREADER
TREADLE
TREASON
TREATED
TWEAKED
UNEARTH
UNEATEN
USEABLE
WHEATON
WREAKED
WREATHE
WREATHS

••E•A••
ABELARD
ABENAKI
ABEYANT
ACETATE
AGESAGO
AVERAGE
BEEBALM
BEEFALO
CAESARS
COEVALS
CRETANS
CUEBALL
CUECARD
DEEJAYS
DIEHARD
DIETARY
DUEDATE
ELEGANT
ELEVATE
EMERALD
EYEBALL
EYEBANK
EYELASH
EYEWASH
GEEGAWS
GOESAPE
GRENADA
GRENADE
GUEVARA
HAEMATO
HEEHAWS
HOECAKE
ICEBAGS
ICECAPS
ICELAND
ICEPACK

IKEBANA
INEXACT
IRELAND
ITERANT
ITERATE
LEEWARD
MAENADS
ONELANE
OPENAIR
OPERAND
OPERATE
OREGANO
OVERACT
OVERAGE
OVERALL
OVERATE
OVERAWE
PEERAGE
PIEBALD
PIEPANS
PLENARY
PRECAST
PREDATE
PREDAWN
PREFABS
PREFACE
PRELATE
PREPAID
PREPARE
PREPAYS
PRESAGE
PRESALE
PRETAPE
PREVAIL
PREWASH
REENACT
SEESAWS
SHEBANG
SHEPARD
SMETANA
STEWARD
STEWART
TEENAGE
THEBABE
THECARS
THENARS
THERAPY
TIERACK
TIETACK
TOECAPS
TOENAIL
TOETAPS
TREMAIN
TRENARY
TREPANS
VEEJAYS

••E••A•
AGENDAS
AREAWAY
AREOLAE
AREOLAR
AREOLAS
BEECHAM
BEESWAX
BOERWAR
BRENDAN
BRENNAN
CHEDDAR
CHEETAH
CHEMLAB
COEQUAL
CREWMAN
DEEPFAT

DUENNAS
ELEGIAC
ETERNAL
ETESIAN
FEEDBAG
FIESTAS
FLEABAG
FREEMAN
FREEWAY
FRENEAU
FRETSAW
GOESBAD
GRECIAN
HEELTAP
IBERIAN
ICEBOAT
IDEAMAN
JEERSAT
KEEPSAT
KEESHAN
KNEECAP
KNEEPAD
LEERSAT
NEEDHAM
ONEIDAS
ONESTAR
OPENBAR
OVEREAT
OVERLAP
OVERLAY
OVERRAN
OVERSAW
OVERTAX
PEEKSAT
PEERSAT
PREHEAT
PRELOAD
PRESOAK
QUETZAL
SHEILAS
SHELLAC
SHERMAN
SHERPAS
SIENNAS
SIERRAS
SIESTAS
SNEERAT
SPECIAL
STELLAR
STERNAL
SWEARAT
THEREAT
THERMAL
TREERAT
TUESDAY
UNEQUAL
VIETNAM
WEEKDAY
WHEREAS
WHEREAT

••E•••A
ABEXTRA
ACEROLA
AMERICA
AMERIKA
BEEFTEA
CAESURA
CHELSEA
CREMONA
DEEPSEA
ELECTRA
ELEKTRA
EMERITA

FREESIA
GRENADA
GUEVARA
ICEDTEA
IKEBANA
INERTIA
OCEANIA
OLESTRA
OPENSEA
OVERSEA
PLECTRA
QUECHUA
SMETANA
SPECTRA
THERESA

•••EA••
ABREAST
ACREAGE
ALLEARS
ALREADY
ANDEANS
ANNEALS
APPEALS
APPEARS
APPEASE
ARREARS
ATHEART
ATLEAST
ATPEACE
AUREATE
BATEAUX
BEHEADS
BENEATH
BEREAVE
BONEASH
BUREAUS
BYHEART
CAPEANN
CAVEATS
CEREALS
CUREALL
DEFEATS
DEMEANS
DISEASE
DOGEARS
ENDEARS
ENNEADS
FAREAST
FINEART
FIREANT
FIREARM
FOREARM
GATEAUX
IMPEACH
INPEACE
INSEAMS
INTEARS
KOREANS
LIMEADE
LINEAGE
LINEATE
MALEATE
MIDEAST
MILEAGE
ONLEAVE
ORDEALS
ORGEATS
ORLEANS
OUTEATS
PAGEANT
POLEAXE
REDEALS
REDEALT

REHEALS
REHEARD
REHEARS
REHEATS
RELEARN
RELEASE
REPEALS
REPEATS
REREADS
RESEALS
RESEATS
RETEACH
RETEARS
REVEALS
REWEAVE
ROSEATE
SCREAKS
SCREAMS
SIDEARM
SPREADS
SQUEAKS
SQUEAKY
SQUEALS
STREAKS
STREAKY
STREAMS
TAKEAIM
THREADS
THREADY
THREATS
TINEARS
TONEARM
UNHEARD
UNLEARN
UNLEASH
UNREADY
UNSEALS
UNSEATS
UNWEAVE
UPBEATS

•••E•A•
ADRENAL
AIMEDAT
AMOEBAE
AMOEBAS
APTERAL
ARSENAL
ASSEGAI
AZTECAN
BASEMAN
BASEPAY
BATEMAN
BIKEWAY
BIPEDAL
BLUEJAY
BLUELAW
BODEGAS
BYREMAN
CAMERAS
CASELAW
CATENAE
CAVEMAN
CHEETAH
CINEMAS
CINEMAX
COLEMAN
COMESAT
DANELAW
DARESAY
DONEGAL
EATENAT
FEDERAL
FIREMAN

FLIESAT
FOREMAN
FOREPAW
FORERAN
FORESAW
FREEMAN
FREEWAY
FRIEDAN
GAMELAW
GATEMAN
GATEWAY
GAVEWAY
GENERAL
GIVEWAY
HUMERAL
ILLEGAL
INGEMAR
JANEWAY
JUVENAL
KINEMAS
KNEECAP
KNEEPAD
KUTENAI
LATERAL
LATERAN
LIBERAL
LIKEMAD
LINEMAN
LITERAL
LIVEOAK
MADEHAY
MADEPAR
MADEWAY
MAKEHAY
MAKEPAR
MAKEWAY
MATEWAN
MEDEVAC
MINERAL
MODELAS
MULETAS
NAMEDAY
NAMETAG
NOSEBAG
NOSEGAY
NOTEPAD
NOVENAS
NUMERAL
PACECAR
PAWEDAT
PESETAS
PIKEMAN
PINESAP
PINETAR
POKEDAT
POKESAT
POLECAR
POLECAT
RACECAR
RACEWAY
RAREGAS
REBEKAH
RENEWAL
RICERAT
ROSEBAY
SAMEDAY
SCHEMAS
SCLERAS
SENECAS
SENEGAL
SEVENAM
SEVERAL
SIDEBAR
SIDECAR

SIDEMAN
SNEERAT
SOLEDAD
SOMEDAY
SOMEWAY
TAPEMAN
TEHERAN
TELERAN
THREEAM
TIBETAN
TIMELAG
TOTEBAG
TREERAT
TUTELAR
VEGETAL
VETERAN
VINEGAR
WINEBAR
WINESAP
WIRETAP
WISEMAN
YEREVAN
ZAREBAS

•••E••A
ADDENDA
ALBERTA
ALGEBRA
ALGERIA
AMNESIA
ANAEMIA
ANTENNA
APHELIA
ARIETTA
ARMENIA
AUREOLA
BARETTA
BEDELIA
BERETTA
BIRETTA
BOHEMIA
CADENZA
CAMELIA
CAPELLA
CELESTA
CEREBRA
CORETTA
CULEBRA
DILEMMA
FREESIA
INTEGRA
LIBERIA
LORETTA
LOUELLA
MADEIRA
MAGENTA
MINERVA
NIGERIA
NOVELLA
OPHELIA
OSCEOLA
PATELLA
PHAEDRA
PIPEMMA
POLENTA
RAVENNA
REBECCA
ROBERTA
ROSETTA
SIBERIA
SILESIA
VANESSA

••••EA•
AIRHEAD
ALLHEAL
ANDREAS
ANTBEAR
ARAMEAN
AZALEAS
BAYLEAF
BESMEAR
BESPEAK
BIGDEAL
BIGHEAD
BOOLEAN
BOXSEAT
BUGBEAR
CARSEAT
CATHEAD
CHAPEAU
CHATEAU
CHILEAN
COCTEAU
CONCEAL
CONGEAL
CORNEAL
CORNEAS
COWPEAS
CRIMEAN
DRIVEAT
EGGHEAD
ENTREAT
ESCHEAT
FATHEAD
FIGLEAF
FLYLEAF
FORBEAR
FORREAL
FRENEAU
FURSEAL
GETREAL
GOAHEAD
GUINEAS
HIALEAH
HOTHEAD
HOTSEAT
INAHEAP
INSTEAD
JUGHEAD
LACTEAL
LAMBEAU
LIPREAD
LOWBEAM
LOWGEAR
LUNGEAT
MANYEAR
MARCEAU
MIDYEAR
MISDEAL
MISHEAR
MISLEAD
MISREAD
MRCLEAN
NEWDEAL
NEWYEAR
NOSWEAT
NOUVEAU
NUCLEAR
NUTMEAT
OAKLEAF
OATMEAL
OFFBEAT
OFFPEAK
OFFYEAR
ONATEAR
ORPHEAN

OUTWEAR
OVEREAT
PEABEAN
PHINEAS
PINHEAD
PLATEAU
PREHEAT
PROTEAN
RAMBEAU
RAWDEAL
RECLEAN
REDHEAD
REDHEAT
REDMEAT
RETREAD
RETREAT
RONDEAU
SKIWEAR
SNIPEAT
SOYBEAN
SPIREAS
STAREAT
SUBHEAD
SUNBEAM
SURREAL
SWOREAT
TABLEAU
TAGTEAM
TEALEAF
THEREAT
THOREAU
THREEAM
TONNEAU
TOWHEAD
TRUDEAU
UNCLEAN
UNCLEAR
VALJEAN
WATTEAU
WAXBEAN
WHEREAS
WHEREAT
YEATEAM
YESDEAR
ZAIREAN

••••E•A
ALAMEDA
CALDERA
CANDELA
CARNERA
CHIMERA
DUODENA
HYGIEIA
IPANEMA
MANDELA
NORIEGA
NOXZEMA
POMPEIA
PORSENA
RIGVEDA
RIVIERA
TAFFETA
TEMPERA
TESSERA
THERESA
VERBENA
VISCERA
WOOMERA

•••••EA
ARALSEA
AVONLEA
BEEFTEA

CHELSEA
COCHLEA
DEADSEA
DEEPSEA
ERITREA
GALATEA
HERBTEA
HIGHTEA
ICEDTEA
KARASEA
KILAUEA
OPENSEA
OVERSEA
PANACEA
ROSSSEA
SNOWPEA
SULUSEA
SWANSEA
TRACHEA

EB•••••
EBBTIDE
EBONIES
EBONITE
EBWHITE

E•B••••
EBBTIDE
ELBOWED
EMBANKS
EMBARGO
EMBARKS
EMBASSY
EMBAYED
EMBLEMS
EMBRACE
EMBROIL
EMBRYOS

E••B•••
EDIBLES
ENABLED
ENABLES
EYEBALL
EYEBANK
EYEBOLT
EYEBROW

E•••B••
EATABLE
ENNOBLE
ENROBED
ENROBES
ENTEBBE
EQUABLE
EQUABLY
EXHIBIT
EXURBAN
EXURBIA

E••••B•
EARLOBE
ENTEBBE

•EB••••
CEBUANO
DEBACLE
DEBAKEY
DEBARGE
DEBARKS
DEBASED
DEBASES
DEBATED
DEBATER

DEBATES
DEBAUCH
DEBEERS
DEBITED
DEBONED
DEBONES
DEBORAH
DEBOUCH
DEBRIEF
DEBTORS
DEBUNKS
DEBUSSY
DEBUTED
FEBRILE
HEBRAIC
HEBREWS
LEBANON
LEBARON
NEBBISH
NEBULAE
NEBULAR
NEBULAS
PEBBLED
PEBBLES
REBASTE
REBATED
REBATES
REBECCA
REBEKAH
REBENDS
REBINDS
REBIRTH
REBLOOM
REBOILS
REBOLTS
REBOOTS
REBOUND
REBOZOS
REBUFFS
REBUILD
REBUILT
REBUKED
REBUKES
REBUSES
WEBBIER
WEBBING
WEBFEET
WEBFOOT
WEBLESS
WEBLIKE
WEBPAGE
WEBSITE
WEBSTER
WEBTOED
ZEBULON

•E•B•••
BEDBUGS
BEEBALM
BERBERS
CEMBALO
DERBIES
FEEBLER
GERBILS
GETBACK
HENBANE
HENBITS
HEPBURN
HERBAGE
HERBALS
HERBERT
HERBIER
HERBTEA
JEEBIES

JERBOAS
JETBOAT
KEEBLER
LEIBNIZ
MEMBERS
NEBBISH
NEWBERY
NEWBORN
PEABEAN
PEABODY
PEBBLED
PEBBLES
REDBIRD
REDBOOK
REDBUDS
REUBENS
SEABAGS
SEABASS
SEABEDS
SEABEES
SEABIRD
SEABLUE
SEABORG
SERBIAN
SETBACK
TEABAGS
TEABALL
TEMBLOR
TERBIUM
VERBALS
VERBENA
VERBOSE
WEBBIER
WEBBING
WETBARS
ZEDBARS

•E••B••
AEROBAT
AEROBES
AEROBIC
BEANBAG
BELABOR
BELLBOY
BELTBAG
BESTBOY
CELEBES
CELEBRE
CEREBRA
DECIBEL
DELIBES
FEEDBAG
FERNBAR
GEARBOX
GEMSBOK
JEZEBEL
LEGIBLE
LEGIBLY
NEWSBOY
PEATBOG
SEEABLE
SEEDBED
TENABLE
TENABLY
TESTBAN
WENTBAD
ZENOBIA

•E•••B•
BEDAUBS
BENUMBS
LETITBE
REDOUBT
RESORBS

REVERBS
SEALABS

•E••••B
BEARCUB
KEYCLUB
PEDICAB
PERTURB

••EB•••
BEEBALM
CUEBALL
EYEBALL
EYEBANK
EYEBOLT
EYEBROW
FEEBLER
ICEBAGS
ICEBEER
ICEBERG
ICEBLUE
ICEBOAT
IKEBANA
JEEBIES
JOEBLOW
KEEBLER
NIEBUHR
PIEBALD
PREBEND
PUEBLOS
RHEBOKS
ROEBUCK
SHEBANG
THEBABE
THEBLOB
TREBLED
TREBLES

••E•B••
ACERBIC
ALEMBIC
FEEDBAG
FLEABAG
FREEBEE
FREEBIE
GOESBAD
LIEABED
OPENBAR
OVERBIG
OVERBUY
SEEABLE
SEEDBED
SHERBET
STEUBEN
TREMBLE
TREMBLY
USEABLE

••E••B•
ARECIBO
CHERUBS
ICECUBE
PREFABS
SWEARBY
THEBABE
THEREBY
WHEREBY

••E•••B
CHEMLAB
OVERDUB
THEBLOB

•••EB••
ALGEBRA AMOEBAE AMOEBAS AMOEBIC BLUEBOY CELEBES CELEBRE CEREBRA CULEBRA ENTEBBE FIREBOX FIREBUG FREEBEE FREEBIE GAZEBOS HOMEBOY JEZEBEL JUKEBOX JUNEBUG LOVEBUG NOSEBAG PAGEBOY PHOEBES PHOEBUS RAREBIT ROSEBAY ROSEBUD SHOEBOX SIDEBAR SIDEBET TOTEBAG WINEBAR ZAREBAS

•••E•B•
ADVERBS ALLENBY COMESBY ENTEBBE MORESBY REVERBS

•••E••B
LUBEJOB NOSEJOB

••••EB•
ABIDEBY BYTHEBY CLOSEBY COBWEBS PLACEBO SUBDEBS SWOREBY THEREBY WHEREBY

••••E•B
POTHERB PROVERB

•••••EB
FOODWEB

EC•••••
ECDYSES ECDYSIS ECHELON ECHIDNA ECHINUS ECHOING ECKHART ECLAIRS ECLIPSE ECLOGUE ECOLOGY ECONOMY ECSTASY ECTYPES ECUADOR

E•C••••
ENCAGED ENCAGES ENCAMPS ENCASED ENCASES ENCHAIN ENCHANT ENCINAS ENCLAVE ENCLOSE ENCODED ENCODER ENCODES ENCOMIA ENCORES ENCRUST ENCRYPT ESCAPED ESCAPEE ESCAPES ESCARPS ESCHEAT ESCHEWS ESCORTS ESCROWS ESCUDOS ETCHANT ETCHERS ETCHING EUCHRED EUCHRES EXCEEDS EXCEPTS EXCERPT EXCISED EXCISES EXCITED EXCITES EXCLAIM EXCLUDE EXCRETE EXCUSED EXCUSES

E••C•••
EATCROW EDACITY EDUCATE EDUCING EGGCASE EGGCUPS EJECTED ELECTED ELECTEE ELECTOR ELECTRA ELECTRO ELICITS ENACTED ENACTOR EPICENE EPICURE EPOCHAL ERECTED ERECTER ERECTLY ERECTOR ERICSON ERUCTED EVACUEE EVICTED EXACTAS EXACTED EXACTER EXACTLY EXACTOR EXECUTE EYECUPS

E•••C••
EARACHE EFFACED EFFACES EFFECTS ENLACED ENLACES ENTICED ENTICER ENTICES EPARCHS EPARCHY ETHICAL EVINCED EVINCES EXARCHS EXFACTO EXPECTS

E••••C•
EARLOCK EDIFICE EHRLICH ELGRECO EMBRACE ENFORCE ENHANCE ENOUNCE EROTICA ERRANCY ESSENCE ETHNICS EXOTICA EXOTICS EXTINCT EXTRACT

E•••••C
EDAPHIC ELASTIC ELEGIAC ENDEMIC ERISTIC ERRATIC

•EC••••
BECALMS BECAUSE BECKETT BECKONS BECLOUD BECOMES CECILIA DECADES DECAGON DECALOG DECAMPS DECANTS DECAPOD DECARLO DECATUR DECAYED DECEITS DECEIVE DECENCY DECIBEL DECIDED DECIDES DECIMAL DECKING DECKLES DECKOUT DECLAIM DECLARE DECLASS DECLINE DECOCTS DECODED DECODER DECODES DECORUM DECOYED DECREED DECREES DECRIED DECRIER DECRIES DECRYPT GECKOES HECKLED HECKLER HECKLES HECTARE HECTORS LECARRE LECTERN LECTORS LECTURE NECKERS NECKING NECKTIE NECTARS PECCANT PECCARY PECKIER PECKING PECKISH PECKSAT PECTINS RECALLS RECANED RECANES RECANTS RECASTS RECEDED RECEDES RECEIPT RECEIVE RECENCY RECHALK RECHECK RECHOSE RECIPES RECITAL RECITED RECITER RECITES RECKONS RECLAIM RECLAME RECLEAN RECLINE RECLUSE RECOATS RECODED RECODES RECOILS RECOLOR RECORDS RECORKS RECOUNT RECOUPS RECOVER RECROOM RECROSS RECRUIT RECTIFY RECTORS RECTORY RECUSED RECUSES RECYCLE SECANTS SECEDED SECEDER SECEDES SECKELS SECLUDE SECONDS SECRECY SECRETE SECRETS SECTION SECTORS SECULAR SECURED SECURER SECURES TECHIER TECHIES VECTORS

•E•C•••
BEACHED BEACHES BEACONS BEECHAM BEECHER BEECHES BELCHED BELCHES BENCHED BENCHES DEACONS DEICERS DEICING DESCANT DESCEND DESCENT DEWCLAW FENCERS FENCING FESCUES FETCHED FETCHES HENCOOP HEPCATS HERCULE KERCHOO KETCHAM KETCHES KETCHUP KEYCARD KEYCLUB LEACHED LEACHES LEACOCK LEECHED LEECHES LEUCINE MENCKEN MERCERS MERCERY MERCIES MERCURY MESCALS NESCAFE PEACHED PEACHES PEACOAT PEACOCK PECCANT PECCARY PENCILS PERCALE PERCENT PERCHED PERCHES PETCOCK REACHED REACHES REACTED REACTOR REACTTO REDCAPS REDCELL REDCENT REDCOAT REOCCUR RESCALE RESCIND RESCUED RESCUER RESCUES REXCATS SEACOWS SEICHES TEACAKE TEACART TEACHER TEACHES TEACHIN TEACUPS TEICHER TENCENT TERCELS TERCETS TETCHED VETCHES WELCHED WELCHES WELCOME WENCHES WETCELL

•E••C••
BEARCAT BEARCUB BEDECKS DEBACLE DECOCTS DEDUCED DEDUCES DEDUCTS DEFACED DEFACES DEFACTO DEFECTS DEFICIT DEJECTS DELICTI DELICTS DEPICTS DETECTS DEVICES FELICIA FELUCCA HELICAL HELICES HELICON HELLCAT JERICHO LEXICAL LEXICON MEDICAL MEDICOS MENACED MENACES MEXICAN PEDICAB PEDICEL PEDICLE PELICAN PEMICAN PENUCHE REBECCA RECYCLE REDACTS REDUCED REDUCER REDUCES REFACED REFACES REFOCUS REJECTS RELACED RELACES RELICTS RELOCKS RELUCTS REOCCUR RESECTS RETICLE SEANCES SEDUCED SEDUCER SEDUCES SELECTS SENECAS TENACES VEHICLE

•E•••C•
BEDROCK BELASCO BERNICE BESEECH BEWITCH CELTICS DEBAUCH DEBOUCH DECENCY DEFENCE DEFLECT DEFROCK DEFUNCT DEHISCE DERRICK DETRACT FELUCCA FETLOCK GETBACK HEMLOCK HENPECK HEROICS JESSICA LEACOCK LETTUCE MENISCI METRICS NEGLECT PEACOCK PENANCE PERFECT PETCOCK PETROCK REBECCA RECENCY RECHECK REELECT REENACT REFLECT REFRACT REGENCY REJOICE REPLACE REPLICA REPRICE RESPECT RESTOCK RETEACH RETOUCH RETRACE RETRACK RETRACT REVOICE SEASICK SECRECY SELLECK SERPICO SERVICE SETBACK TEDMACK TENANCY TENRECS TERENCE TERRACE VEENECK VERDICT WEDLOCK

•E••••C
AELFRIC AEROBIC CENTRIC CERAMIC DELPHIC DELTAIC DEMONIC GENERIC GENETIC HEBRAIC HEPATIC HERETIC JEANLUC KEROUAC MEDEVAC MEIOTIC MELODIC PELAGIC SEISMIC SELENIC SEMITIC

••EC•••
ARECIBO ATECROW BEECHAM BEECHER BEECHES CHECHEN CHECKED CHECKER CHECKIN CHECKUP CRECHES CUECARD EJECTED ELECTED ELECTEE ELECTOR ELECTRA ELECTRO ERECTED ERECTER ERECTLY ERECTOR EXECUTE EYECUPS FLECHES FLECKED FRECKLE FRECKLY GRECIAN HOECAKE ICECAPS ICECOLD ICECUBE IRECKON LEECHED LEECHES PIECERS PIECING PLECTRA PRECAST PRECEDE PRECEPT PRECISE PRECOOK PRECOOL QUECHUA SPECCED SPECIAL SPECIES SPECIFY SPECING SPECKED SPECKLE SPECTER SPECTOR SPECTRA SPECTRE THECARS THECROW TIECLIP TOECAPS WRECKED WRECKER

••E•C••
ALENCON AMERCED AMERCES APERCUS COERCED COERCER COERCES CREWCUT FIERCER FLEECED FLEECES FRESCOS KNEECAP PIERCED PIERCES PREACHY SKETCHY SPECCED SPENCER STENCIL TREACLE TREACLY

••E••C•
AMERICA CLERICS CREVICE ICEPACK ICEPICK INEXACT NOETICS OVERACT POETICS PREDICT PREFACE PREFECT REELECT REENACT ROEBUCK TIERACK TIETACK VEENECK

••E•••C
ACERBIC ALEMBIC ASEPTIC ELEGIAC FREDRIC IDENTIC LAENNEC OCEANIC SCEPTIC SHELLAC SKEPTIC

•••EC••
AFFECTS ASPECTS AZTECAN BEDECKS BISECTS CAPECOD DEFECTS DEJECTS DETECTS DIRECTS DOVECOT EFFECTS EXPECTS FLEECED FLEECES INFECTS INJECTS INSECTS KNEECAP KOPECKS OBJECTS PACECAR POLECAR POLECAT RACECAR REBECCA REJECTS RESECTS SAMECHS SELECTS SENECAS SIDECAR TIMECOP UTRECHT VOTECHS ZYDECOS

•••E•C•
ABSENCE ARDENCY ATPEACE BESEECH CADENCE CADENCY COGENCY DECENCY DEFENCE ESSENCE FAIENCE FLUENCY ILIESCU IMPEACH INPEACE IONESCO LATENCY LICENCE LUCENCY NORELCO OFFENCE POTENCY PUDENCY REBECCA RECENCY REGENCY RETEACH SCIENCE SCREECH SILENCE SQUELCH STRETCH TERENCE URGENCY VALENCE VALENCY VANEYCK

•••E••C
AMOEBIC ANAEMIC ANGELIC ARSENIC ASCETIC COMEDIC ENDEMIC GENERIC GENETIC HERETIC HOMERIC KINETIC MALEFIC MEDEVAC MIMETIC NUMERIC PHRENIC POLEMIC SELENIC TONELOC TOTEMIC

••••EC•
ARTDECO BESEECH BOMBECK BRUBECK CALTECH CANSECO COLLECT CONNECT CORRECT DEFLECT DIALECT DISSECT ELGRECO HENPECK INFLECT INSPECT LOWNECK LOWTECH NEGLECT PANDECT PARSECS PERFECT PREFECT PROJECT PROTECT RECHECK REELECT REFLECT RESPECT SCREECH SECRECY SELLECK SUBJECT SUNDECK SUSPECT TENRECS TOLTECS TRISECT VEENECK WOZZECK

••••E•C
NUCLEIC POULENC

•••••EC
LAENNEC LAUTREC MIDDLEC ZAPOTEC

ED•••••
EDACITY EDAPHIC EDASNER EDDYING EDGEDIN EDGEOUT EDGESIN EDGIEST EDGINGS EDIBLES EDIFICE EDIFIED EDIFIES EDITING EDITION EDITORS EDITOUT EDOUARD EDUCATE EDUCING EDWARDS

E•D••••
ECDYSES ECDYSIS EDDYING ELDERLY ENDEARS ENDEDUP ENDEMIC ENDGAME ENDINGS ENDIVES ENDLESS ENDMOST ENDORSE ENDOWED ENDPLAY ENDRUNS ENDUING ENDURED ENDURES ENDUROS ENDUSER ENDUSES ENDWAYS ENDWISE ENDZONE

E••D•••
EARDROP EARDRUM EKEDOUT ELIDING ELUDING ERODENT ERODING ERUDITE EVADERS EVADING EVIDENT EXUDING

E•••D••
EARLDOM EASEDIN EASEDUP ECHIDNA ECUADOR EDGEDIN EGGEDON EMENDED EMENDER ENCODED ENCODER ENCODES ENDEDUP ESCUDOS EVANDER

E••••D•
EBBTIDE EDWARDS EFFENDI ELAPIDS ENFOLDS ENGARDE ENGIRDS ENNEADS EPISODE ERRANDS ESTRADA EXCEEDS EXCLUDE EXPANDS EXPENDS EXPLODE EXTENDS EXTRUDE EYELIDS

E•••••D
EASTEND EDIFIED EDOUARD EFFACED EFFUSED EGESTED EGGHEAD EJECTED ELAPSED ELBOWED ELECTED EMAILED EMBAYED EMENDED EMERALD EMERGED EMERSED EMITTED EMPTIED ENABLED ENACTED ENCAGED ENCASED ENCODED ENDOWED ENDURED ENGAGED ENGLAND ENGLUND ENISLED ENJOYED ENLACED ENRAGED ENROBED ENSILED ENSKIED ENSURED ENTERED ENTICED EQUALED EQUATED ERECTED ERUCTED ERUPTED ESCAPED ESSAYED EUCHRED EVERTED EVICTED EVINCED EVOLVED EVULSED EXACTED EXALTED EXCISED EXCITED EXCUSED EXERTED EXHALED EXISTED EXPIRED EXPOSED EXPOUND EXULTED

•ED••••
AEDILES BEDAUBS BEDBUGS BEDDING BEDDOWN BEDECKS BEDELIA

BEDEVIL
BEDEWED
BEDIZEN
BEDLAMP
BEDLESS
BEDLIKE
BEDOUIN
BEDPOST
BEDREST
BEDROCK
BEDROLL
BEDROOM
BEDSIDE
BEDTIME
CEDARED
CEDILLA
DEDALUS
DEDUCED
DEDUCES
DEDUCTS
FEDERAL
FEDORAS
HEDDLES
HEDGERS
HEDGIER
HEDGING
KEDROVA
LEDGERS
LEDGIER
LEDUPTO
MEDALED
MEDDLED
MEDDLER
MEDDLES
MEDEVAC
MEDIANS
MEDIANT
MEDIATE
MEDICAL
MEDICOS
MEDIGAP
MEDIUMS
MEDLEYS
MEDULLA
MEDUSAE
MEDUSAS
NEDDIES
OEDIPAL
OEDIPUS
PEDALED
PEDANTS
PEDDLED
PEDDLER
PEDDLES
PEDICAB
PEDICEL
PEDICLE
PEDLARS
PEDWAYS
REDACTS
REDALGA
REDANTS
REDATED
REDATES
REDBIRD
REDBOOK
REDBUDS
REDCAPS
REDCELL
REDCENT
REDCOAT
REDDEER
REDDENS
REDDEST

REDDING
REDDISH
REDDOGS
REDEALS
REDEALT
REDEEMS
REDEYED
REDEYES
REDFINS
REDFIRS
REDFLAG
REDFORD
REDGUMS
REDHAIR
REDHATS
REDHEAD
REDHEAT
REDHOTS
REDIALS
REDLINE
REDMEAT
REDNESS
REDOAKS
REDOING
REDOUBT
REDOUND
REDPINE
REDPOLL
REDRAWN
REDRAWS
REDRESS
REDROSE
REDSPOT
REDSTAR
REDTAPE
REDTOPS
REDUCED
REDUCER
REDUCES
REDWINE
REDWING
REDWOLF
REDWOOD
SEDALIA
SEDATED
SEDATER
SEDATES
SEDGIER
SEDUCED
SEDUCER
SEDUCES
TEDDERS
TEDDIES
TEDDING
TEDIOUS
TEDIUMS
TEDMACK
VEDANTA
WEDDING
WEDGIER
WEDGIES
WEDGING
WEDLOCK
ZEDBARS

•E•D•••

BEADIER
BEADING
BEADLES
BEADSUP
BEDDING
BEDDOWN
BELDAME
BELDAMS

BENDERS
BENDIER
BENDIGO
BENDING
DEADAIR
DEADEND
DEADENS
DEADEYE
DEADPAN
DEADSEA
DEADSET
DEEDING
DENDRON
DEODARS
DEWDROP
FEEDBAG
FEEDERS
FEEDING
FEEDLOT
FEEDSON
FELDMAN
FENDERS
FENDING
FEUDING
GELDING
GENDERS
GEODESY
GETDOWN
HEADERS
HEADIER
HEADILY
HEADING
HEADMAN
HEADMEN
HEADOFF
HEADOUT
HEADPIN
HEADSET
HEADSIN
HEADSUP
HEADWAY
HEDDLES
HEEDFUL
HEEDING
HELDOFF
HELDOUT
HENDRIX
HERDERS
HERDING
HEYDAYS
KENDALL
LEADERS
LEADIER
LEADING
LEADINS
LEADOFF
LEADOUT
LEADSIN
LEADSON
LEADSTO
LEADSUP
LENDERS
LENDING
LETDOWN
LEWDEST
MEADOWS
MEADOWY
MEDDLED
MEDDLER
MEDDLES
MELDING
MENDERS
MENDING
MENDOZA

NEDDIES
NEEDFUL
NEEDHAM
NEEDIER
NEEDILY
NEEDING
NEEDLED
NEEDLES
NERDIER
NEWDEAL
PEDDLED
PEDDLER
PEDDLES
PENDANT
PENDENT
PENDING
PERDIEM
READERS
READIED
READIER
READIES
READILY
READING
READMIT
READOUT
READSIN
REDDEER
REDDENS
REDDEST
REDDING
REDDISH
REDDOGS
REEDIER
REEDING
REEDITS
RENDERS
RENDING
SEADOGS
SEADUTY
SEEDBED
SEEDERS
SEEDIER
SEEDILY
SEEDING
SEEDPOD
SEIDELS
SENDERS
SENDFOR
SENDING
SENDOFF
SENDOUT
SENDSIN
SENDSUP
SENDUPS
SETDOWN
TEDDERS
TEDDIES
TEDDING
TEEDOFF
TENDERS
TENDING
TENDONS
TENDRIL
TENDSTO
VENDING
VENDORS
VERDANT
VERDICT
VERDOUX
VERDUGO
VERDURE
WEDDING
WEEDERS
WEEDIER

WEEDILY
WEEDING
WEEDOUT
WELDERS
WELDING
WENDELL
WENDERS
WENDING
WENDISH
YESDEAR

•E••D••

BEARDED
BERIDOF
BESIDES
BETIDED
BETIDES
CELADON
DECADES
DECIDED
DECIDES
DECODED
DECODER
DECODES
DELUDED
DELUDES
DENUDED
DENUDES
DERIDED
DERIDES
FETIDLY
GELADAS
GELIDLY
GEORDIE
HEARDOF
KEYEDIN
KEYEDUP
LEANDER
MEANDER
MEGIDDO
MELODIC
NEVADAN
NEWSDAY
PERIDOT
RECEDED
RECEDES
RECODED
RECODES
REMODEL
REMUDAS
REORDER
REREDOS
RESIDED
RESIDES
RESIDUE
SECEDED
SECEDER
SECEDES
SERFDOM
SEWEDON
SEWEDUP
TEPIDLY
TEREDOS
VEXEDLY
WEEKDAY
WEIRDER
WEIRDLY
WEIRDOS

•E•••D•

BEDSIDE
BEHEADS
BEHOLDS
BELINDA

BERMUDA
CERVIDS
DEFENDS
DEGRADE
DEMANDS
DEPENDS
GERALDO
GERUNDS
HEPTADS
HERALDS
HEYJUDE
KENNEDY
KEYPADS
LEETIDE
LEGENDS
LEMONDE
LEONIDS
MEGIDDO
MELINDA
METHODS
NEREIDS
PEABODY
PEAPODS
PENTADS
PEPTIDE
PERFIDY
PERIODS
PERVADE
PETARDS
REBENDS
REBINDS
RECORDS
REDBUDS
REFUNDS
REGARDS
REGRADE
RELOADS
REMANDS
REMENDS
REMINDS
REMOLDS
RENARDS
REREADS
RESANDS
RESEEDS
RESENDS
RETARDS
RETRADE
REWARDS
REWELDS
REWINDS
REWORDS
SEABEDS
SEASIDE
SECLUDE
SECONDS
TESTUDO
TETRADS
VERANDA
VESPIDS

•E••••D

AERATED
BEACHED
BEARDED
BECLOUD
BEDEWED
BEHAVED
BEHOVED
BELATED
BELAYED
BELCHED
BELLIED
BELOVED

BEMIRED
BEMUSED
BENCHED
BERATED
BERNARD
BERRIED
BERTHED
BETIDED
BEVELED
CEDARED
CENTRED
DEADEND
DEBASED
DEBATED
DEBITED
DEBONED
DEBUTED
DECAPOD
DECAYED
DECIDED
DECODED
DECOYED
DECREED
DECRIED
DEDUCED
DEEPEND
DEFACED
DEFAMED
DEFILED
DEFINED
DEFRAUD
DEFUSED
DEIFIED
DEIGNED
DELAYED
DELETED
DELTOID
DELUDED
DELUGED
DEMIGOD
DEMISED
DEMOTED
DENOTED
DENUDED
DEPONED
DEPOSED
DEPUTED
DERIDED
DERIVED
DESCEND
DESIRED
DESMOND
DEVILED
DEVISED
DEVOTED
FEASTED
FEIGNED
FEINTED
FERRIED
FETCHED
GENTLED
HEARTED
HECKLED
HEISTED
HELIPAD
HENNAED
HEYWOOD
JELLIED
JEMMIED
JEWELED
KEYCARD
KEYWORD
LEACHED
LEARNED

LEASHED
LEECHED
LEEWARD
LEGRAND
LEONARD
LEOPARD
LEOPOLD
LEOTARD
LEVELED
LEVERED
MEDALED
MEDDLED
MENACED
MERITED
MERMAID
METERED
NEEDLED
NEGATED
NEIGHED
NESTLED
NETTLED
PEACHED
PEARLED
PEBBLED
PEDALED
PEDDLED
PEOPLED
PEPPARD
PERCHED
PERSEID
PERUSED
PESTLED
PETALED
PETERED
REACHED
REACTED
READIED
REAIMED
REAIRED
REAREND
REARMED
REBATED
REBOUND
REBUILD
REBUKED
RECANED
RECEDED
RECITED
RECODED
RECUSED
REDATED
REDBIRD
REDEYED
REDFORD
REDHEAD
REDOUND
REDUCED
REDWOOD
REFACED
REFILED
REFINED
REFRIED
REFUSED
REFUTED
REGALED
REGLUED
REHEARD
REHIRED
REIFIED
REIGNED
REINKED
REKEYED
RELACED
RELATED

RELAXED
RELAYED
RELINED
RELIVED
RELUMED
REMIXED
REMOVED
REMOWED
RENAMED
RENEGED
RENEWED
RENOTED
REOILED
REPAVED
REPINED
REPLIED
REPOSED
REPUTED
RERATED
RESAWED
RESCIND
RESCUED
RESIDED
RESILED
RESOLED
RESOUND
RESPOND
RESUMED
RETAPED
RETAXED
RETILED
RETIMED
RETIRED
RETOWED
RETREAD
RETRIED
RETUNED
RETYPED
REUPPED
REVELED
REVERED
REVILED
REVISED
REVIVED
REVOKED
REWAXED
REWIRED
REWOUND
REYNARD
REZONED
SEABIRD
SEAFOOD
SEAWARD
SEAWEED
SECEDED
SECURED
SEDATED
SEDUCED
SEEDBED
SEEDPOD
SEESRED
SEETHED
SERRIED
SETTLED
SEVERED
TEETHED
TELEXED
TEMPTED
TENFOLD
TENONED
TENURED
TETCHED
WEARIED
WEBTOED

WEEKEND
WEIGHED
WELCHED
WELLAND
WELLFED
WENTBAD
WESTEND
WETLAND
YEAREND
YEARNED
ZEALAND

••ED•••

ACEDOUT
CHEDDAR
COEDITS
CREDITS
DEEDING
DIEDOFF
DIEDOUT
DIEDOWN
DREDGED
DREDGER
DREDGES
DUEDATE
EKEDOUT
FEEDBAG
FEEDERS
FEEDING
FEEDLOT
FEEDSON
FIEDLER
FLEDGED
FLEDGES
FREDDIE
FREDRIC
HEEDFUL
HEEDING
HOEDOWN
ICEDOUT
ICEDTEA
LIEDOWN
NEEDFUL
NEEDHAM
NEEDIER
NEEDILY
NEEDING
NEEDLED
NEEDLES
PLEDGED
PLEDGEE
PLEDGER
PLEDGES
PREDATE
PREDAWN
PREDICT
PYEDOGS
REEDIER
REEDING
REEDITS
ROEDEER
SEEDBED
SEEDERS
SEEDIER
SEEDILY
SEEDING
SEEDPOD
SLEDDED
SLEDDER
SLEDDOG
SLEDGES
SWEDISH
TEEDOFF
THEDEEP

TIEDOWN
TIEDYED
TIEDYES
WEEDERS
WEEDIER
WEEDILY
WEEDING
WEEDOUT

••E•D••

AGENDAS
AHEADOF
AMENDED
BLENDED
BLENDER
BREADED
BREADTH
BREEDER
BRENDAN
CHEDDAR
DREADED
DREIDEL
DRESDEN
EMENDED
EMENDER
FIEFDOM
FIELDED
FIELDER
FREDDIE
FREEDOM
GRENDEL
KNEADED
KNEADER
ONEIDAS
OVERDID
OVERDUB
OVERDUE
PLEADED
PLEADER
SCENDED
SHELDON
SLEDDED
SLEDDER
SLEDDOG
SLENDER
SPEEDED
SPEEDER
SPEEDOS
SPEEDUP
SPENDER
TREADED
TREADER
TREADLE
TRENDED
TUESDAY
UNENDED
UPENDED
WEEKDAY
WHEEDLE
WIELDED
YIELDED

••E••D•

EYELIDS
GRENADA
GRENADE
LEETIDE
MAENADS
PRECEDE
PRELUDE
PREMEDS
PRESIDE
TIERODS
USERIDS

••E•••D

ABELARD
ABETTED
ALERTED
AMENDED
AMERCED
AMERIND
ANEROID
AVENGED
AVERRED
AVERTED
BLEARED
BLEATED
BLEEPED
BLENDED
BLESSED
BREADED
BREEZED
CHEATED
CHECKED
CHEEPED
CHEERED
CHEVIED
CLEANED
CLEARED
CLEAVED
CLERKED
COERCED
CREAKED
CREAMED
CREASED
CREATED
CREEPED
CRESTED
CUECARD
DEEPEND
DIEHARD
DREADED
DREAMED
DREDGED
DRESSED
DWELLED
EGESTED
EJECTED
ELECTED
EMENDED
EMERALD
EMERGED
EMERSED
ERECTED
EVERTED
EXERTED
FIELDED
FLECKED
FLEDGED
FLEECED
FLENSED
FLESHED
FREAKED
FRETTED
FUELLED
FUELROD
GIELGUD
GLEAMED
GLEANED
GOESBAD
GREASED
GREENED
GREETED
GUESSED
GUESTED
ICECOLD
ICELAND
IDEATED

IRELAND
KNEADED
KNEELED
KNEEPAD
KNELLED
LEECHED
LEEWARD
LIEABED
NEEDLED
OCEANID
ONEEYED
OPENEND
OPERAND
OVERDID
PIEBALD
PIERCED
PLEADED
PLEASED
PLEATED
PLEDGED
PREBEND
PREENED
PRELOAD
PREPAID
PRESSED
PRETEND
QUEERED
QUELLED
QUERIED
QUESTED
SCENDED
SCENTED
SEEDBED
SEEDPOD
SEESRED
SEETHED
SHEARED
SHEAVED
SHEERED
SHEETED
SHELLED
SHELVED
SHEPARD
SLEDDED
SLEEKED
SLEETED
SMEARED
SMELLED
SMELTED
SNEAKED
SNEERED
SNEEZED
SPEARED
SPECCED
SPECKED
SPEEDED
SPELLED
STEAMED
STEELED
STEEPED
STEERED
STEMMED
STEPPED
STEROID
STETTED
STEWARD
SWEATED
SWELLED
SWERVED
TEETHED
TIEDYED
TOEHOLD
TREADED
TREATED

TREBLED
TREKKED
TRENDED
TWEAKED
TWEETED
TWEEZED
UNENDED
UPENDED
WEEKEND
WHEELED
WHEEZED
WHELMED
WHELPED
WHETTED
WIELDED
WREAKED
WRECKED
WRESTED
YIELDED

•••ED••

ACCEDED
ACCEDER
ACCEDES
ACTEDON
ACTEDUP
ADDEDIN
ADDEDON
ADDEDTO
ADDEDUP
AIMEDAT
AIMEDTO
ALBEDOS
ANTEDUP
ARLEDGE
ASKEDIN
BIPEDAL
BONEDRY
BONEDUP
BOREDOM
BOXEDIN
BOXEDUP
BREEDER
CAMEDUE
CAVEDIN
CLUEDIN
COMEDIC
COMEDUE
DATEDLY
DAZEDLY
DINEDIN
DINEDON
DOTEDON
DRIEDUP
DUDEDUP
DUKEDOM
EASEDIN
EASEDUP
EDGEDIN
EGGEDON
ENDEDUP
FADEDIN
FIREDOG
FIREDUP
FIXEDLY
FIXEDUP
FREEDOM
FRIEDAN
GLUEDON
HIKEDUP
HOLEDUP
HYPEDUP
IMPEDED
IMPEDES

JADEDLY
JANEDOE
KEYEDIN
KEYEDUP
LACEDUP
LAMEDHS
LINEDUP
LIVEDIN
LIVEDON
MIXEDIN
MIXEDUP
MOVEDIN
MOVEDON
MOVEDUP
NAKEDLY
NAMEDAY
NOTEDLY
OWNEDUP
PALEDRY
PAWEDAT
PHAEDRA
PILEDIN
PILEDON
PILEDUP
PIPEDUP
POKEDAT
RAKEDIN
RAKEDUP
RECEDED
RECEDES
REREDOS
ROPEDIN
SAMEDAY
SAVEDUP
SECEDED
SECEDER
SECEDES
SEWEDON
SEWEDUP
SINEDIE
SIZEDUP
SOLEDAD
SOMEDAY
SPEEDED
SPEEDER
SPEEDOS
SPEEDUP
SPIEDON
TEREDOS
TIREDER
TIREDLY
TIREDOF
TONEDUP
TRIEDON
TUNEDIN
TUNEDUP
TUXEDOS
TYPEDUP
VEXEDLY
VOTEDIN
WADEDIN
WAVEDIN
WHEEDLE
WIPEDUP
WISEDUP

•••E•D•

ADDENDA
ADDENDS
ALLENDE
ALREADY
APPENDS
ASCENDS
ATTENDS
AUGENDS
AXSEEDS
BEHEADS
CALENDS
DEFENDS
DEPENDS
EFFENDI
ENNEADS
EXCEEDS
EXPENDS
EXTENDS
FAGENDS
FRIENDS
IMPENDS
INTENDS
LEGENDS
LIMEADE
MAKESDO
MRDEEDS
NEREIDS
OFFENDS
REBENDS
REMENDS
REREADS
RESEEDS
RESENDS
REWELDS
SCREEDS
SHIELDS
SPREADS
TAGENDS
THREADS
THREADY
UNBENDS
UNDERDO
UNREADY
VIVENDI

•••E••D

ACCEDED
ADHERED
ALLEGED
ALTERED
ANGERED
ANNELID
ANNEXED
BEDEWED
BEVELED
BLEEPED
BOGEYED
BOWERED
BREEZED
BRIEFED
BUGEYED
CAMEOED
CAPECOD
CAPERED
CATERED
CHEEPED
CHEERED
COHERED
COVERED
COVETED
COWERED
COZENED
CREEPED
DELETED
DIZENED
DOWERED
DRYEYED
ENTERED
FACETED
FLEECED
GAVELED
GREENED
GREETED
GRIEVED
HAVERED
HOMERED
HONEYED
HOVERED
IMPEDED
INDEXED
INHERED
JEWELED
KNEELED
KNEEPAD
LABELED
LAPELED
LAYERED
LEVELED
LEVERED
LIBELED
LIKEMAD
LIKENED
LIVENED
LOWERED
METERED
MITERED
MODELED
MONEYED
MOSEYED
NOTEPAD
OFFERED
ONEEYED
ORDERED
OSIERED
OSTEOID
PANELED
PAPERED
PETERED
POPEYED
POWERED
PREENED
QUEERED
QUIETED
RAVELED
RAVENED
RECEDED
REDEYED
REHEARD
REKEYED
RENEGED
RENEWED
REVELED
REVERED
RIPENED
RIVETED
ROSEBUD
ROSERED
SCHEMED
SCREWED
SECEDED
SEVERED
SHEERED
SHEETED
SLEEKED
SLEETED
SNEERED
SNEEZED
SOBERED
SOLEDAD
SPEEDED
SPIELED
STEELED
STEEPED
STEERED
STREWED
TAPERED
TELEXED
THIEVED
TOKENED
TOWELED
TOWERED
TWEETED
TWEEZED
UNHEARD
UNSEWED
USHERED
UTTERED
WAGERED
WAKENED
WATERED
WAVERED
WHEELED
WHEEZED
WIDENED
WINERED
WIZENED
YODELED

••••ED•

ALAMEDA
ALFREDO
AXSEEDS
CONCEDE
DAYBEDS
DIOMEDE
EXCEEDS
HOTBEDS
KENNEDY
MALTEDS
MRDEEDS
PRECEDE
PREMEDS
RAGGEDY
RESEEDS
RIGVEDA
SCREEDS
SEABEDS
TORPEDO
TRAGEDY

••••E•D

AIRHEAD
ANISEED
BACKEND
BARTEND
BIGBEND
BIGHEAD
BOOKEND
CATHEAD
COMMEND
CONTEND
COWHERD
DEADEND
DECREED
DEEPEND
DESCEND
DISTEND
EASTEND
EGGHEAD
FATHEAD
FORFEND
GLACEED
GOAHEAD
GOATEED
GODSEND
HAYSEED
HIGHEND
HOTHEAD
INBREED
INFIELD
INSTEAD
JUGHEAD
LINSEED
LIPREAD
MILLEND
MINUEND
MISDEED
MISLEAD
MISREAD
OPENEND
PERSEID
PINHEAD
PORTEND
PREBEND
PRETEND
PROCEED
RAGWEED
REAREND
REDHEAD
RETREAD
SAUTEED
SEAWEED
STIPEND
SUBHEAD
SUBTEND
SUCCEED
SUSPEND
TAILEND
TOWHEAD
WEEKEND
WESTEND
YEAREND

•••••ED

ABASHED
ABETTED
ABJURED
ABLATED
ABORTED
ABRADED
ABUTTED
ACCEDED
ACCRUED
ACCUSED
ADAPTED
ADDUCED
ADHERED
ADJURED
ADMIRED
ADMIXED
ADOPTED
ADORNED
ADVISED
AERATED
AFFIXED
ALARMED
ALERTED
ALIGNED
ALLAYED
ALLEGED
ALLOWED
ALLOYED
ALLUDED
ALLURED
ALTERED
AMASSED
AMENDED
AMERCED
ANGERED
ANISEED
ANNEXED
ANNOYED
APPLIED
APPOSED
APRONED
ARBORED
ARMORED
AROUSED
ARRAYED
ARRIVED
ASHAMED
ASPIRED
ASSAYED
ASSUMED
ASSURED
ATTIRED
ATTUNED
AUDITED
AUGURED
AVAILED
AVENGED
AVERRED
AVERTED
AVIATED
AVOIDED
AVULSED
AWAITED
AWARDED
BABBLED
BAFFLED
BANDIED
BATCHED
BATIKED
BATTLED
BAULKED
BEACHED
BEARDED
BEDEWED
BEHAVED
BEHOVED
BELATED
BELAYED
BELCHED
BELLIED
BELOVED
BEMIRED
BEMUSED
BENCHED
BERATED
BERRIED
BERTHED
BETIDED
BEVELED
BIASSED
BIGOTED
BIRCHED
BIRDIED
BIRTHED
BLABBED
BLACKED
BLANKED
BLASTED
BLATTED
BLEARED
BLEATED
BLEEPED
BLENDED
BLESSED
BLINDED
BLINKED
BLIPPED
BLITZED
BLOATED
BLOCKED
BLOODED
BLOOMED
BLOOPED
BLOTTED
BLOUSED
BLUFFED
BLUNTED
BLURRED
BLURTED
BLUSHED
BOARDED
BOASTED
BOBBLED
BOBSLED
BOGEYED
BOGGLED
BOOGIED
BOOSTED
BOTCHED
BOTTLED
BOUNCED
BOUNDED
BOWERED
BRAGGED
BRAIDED
BRAINED
BRAISED
BRANDED
BRAWLED
BREADED
BREEZED
BRICKED
BRIDGED
BRIDLED
BRIEFED
BRIMMED
BROILED
BRONZED
BROODED
BROOKED
BROWNED
BROWSED
BRUISED
BRUITED
BRUSHED
BUBBLED
BUCKLED
BUGEYED
BULLIED
BUMBLED
BUNCHED
BUNCOED
BUNDLED
BUNGLED
BUNKBED
BUNKOED
BURBLED
BURGLED
BUSTLED
BYLINED
CACKLED
CADDIED
CAJOLED
CAMEOED
CANDIED
CAPERED
CAROLED
CAROMED
CARRIED
CASQUED
CASTLED
CATERED
CAULKED
CAVILED
CEDARED
CENTRED
CHAINED
CHAIRED
CHALKED
CHAMPED
CHANCED
CHANGED
CHANTED
CHAPPED
CHARGED
CHARMED
CHARRED
CHARTED
CHATTED
CHEATED
CHECKED
CHEEPED
CHEERED
CHEVIED
CHILLED
CHINKED
CHINNED
CHIPPED
CHIRPED
CHOMPED
CHOPPED
CHUCKED
CHUGGED
CHUMMED
CHURNED
CINCHED
CIRCLED
CLACKED
CLAIMED
CLAMMED
CLAMPED
CLANGED
CLANKED
CLAPPED
CLASHED
CLASPED
CLASSED
CLEANED
CLEARED
CLEAVED
CLERKED
CLICKED
CLIMBED
CLINKED
CLIPPED
CLOAKED
CLOCKED
CLOGGED
CLOMPED
CLOPPED
CLOTHED
CLOTTED
CLOUDED
CLOUTED
CLOWNED
CLUBBED
CLUCKED
CLUMPED
CLUNKED
COACHED
COASTED
COBBLED
CODDLED
COERCED
COHERED
COLORED
CONGAED
CONRIED
COOPTED
CORNFED
COUCHED
COUGHED
COUNTED
COUPLED
COURSED
COURTED
COVERED
COVETED
COWERED
COZENED
CRABBED
CRACKED
CRADLED
CRAFTED
CRAMMED
CRAMPED
CRANKED
CRASHED
CRAWLED
CREAKED
CREAMED
CREASED
CREATED
CREEPED
CRESTED
CRIBBED
CRICKED
CRIMPED
CRINGED
CRISPED
CROAKED
CROOKED
CROONED
CROPPED
CROSSED
CROWDED
CROWNED
CRUISED
CRUSHED
CRUSTED
CUDDLED
CULLIED
CURDLED
CURRIED
DABBLED
DALLIED
DAMAGED
DANDLED
DANGLED
DAPPLED
DAUNTED
DAWDLED
DAZZLED
DEBASED
DEBATED
DEBITED
DEBONED
DEBUTED
DECAYED
DECIDED
DECODED
DECOYED
DECREED
DECRIED
DEDUCED
DEFACED
DEFAMED
DEFILED
DEFINED
DEFUSED
DEIFIED
DEIGNED
DELAYED
DELETED
DELUDED
DELUGED
DEMISED
DEMOTED
DENOTED
DENUDED
DEPONED
DEPOSED
DEPUTED
DERIDED
DERIVED
DESIRED
DEVILED
DEVISED
DEVOTED
DIBBLED
DIDDLED
DILATED
DILUTED
DIMPLED
DIRTIED
DISCOED
DISUSED
DITCHED
DITTOED
DIVIDED
DIVINED
DIVVIED
DIZENED
DIZZIED
DOGSLED
DOLLIED
DONATED
DOODLED
DOUBLED
DOUBTED
DOWERED
DRAFTED
DRAGGED
DRAINED
DRATTED
DRAWLED
DREADED
DREAMED
DREDGED
DRESSED
DRIFTED
DRILLED
DRIPPED
DROOLED
DROOPED
DROPPED
DROWNED
DROWSED
DRUBBED
DRUDGED
DRUGGED
DRUMMED
DRYEYED
DUMMIED
DWARFED
DWELLED
EDIFIED
EFFACED
EFFUSED
EGESTED
EJECTED
ELAPSED
ELBOWED
ELECTED
EMAILED
EMBAYED
EMENDED
EMERGED
EMERSED
EMITTED
EMPTIED
ENABLED
ENACTED
ENCAGED
ENCASED
ENCODED
ENDOWED
ENDURED
ENGAGED
ENISLED
ENJOYED
ENLACED
ENRAGED
ENROBED
ENSILED
ENSKIED
ENSURED
ENTERED
ENTICED
EQUALED
EQUATED
ERECTED
ERUCTED
ERUPTED
ESCAPED
ESSAYED
EUCHRED
EVERTED
EVICTED
EVINCED
EVOLVED
EVULSED
EXACTED
EXALTED
EXCISED
EXCITED
EXCUSED
EXERTED
EXHALED
EXISTED
EXPIRED
EXPOSED
EXULTED
FACETED
FAGOTED
FAINTED
FANCIED
FAULTED
FAVORED
FEASTED
FEIGNED
FEINTED
FERRIED
FETCHED
FIDDLED
FIELDED
FIGURED
FILCHED
FIXATED
FIZZLED
FLAGGED
FLAILED
FLAMBED
FLANKED
FLAPPED
FLASHED
FLATBED
FLATTED
FLECKED
FLEDGED
FLEECED
FLENSED
FLESHED
FLICKED
FLIPPED
FLIRTED
FLITTED
FLOATED
FLOCKED
FLOGGED
FLOODED
FLOORED
FLOPPED
FLOSSED
FLOURED
FLOUTED
FLUBBED
FLUFFED
FLUNKED
FLUSHED
FOCUSED
FOISTED
FONDLED
FOOZLED
FORAGED
FOUNDED
FRANKED
FREAKED
FRETTED
FRILLED
FRINGED
FRISKED
FRITTED
FRIZZED
FROCKED
FRONTED
FROSTED
FROTHED
FROWNED
FRUITED
FUDDLED
FUELLED
FUMBLED
GABBLED
GAMBLED
GANGLED
GARAGED
GARBLED
GARGLED
GAVELED
GENTLED
GHOSTED
GIGGLED
GIRDLED
GLACEED
GLAIRED
GLANCED
GLASSED
GLEAMED
GLEANED
GLINTED
GLITZED
GLOATED
GLOMMED
GLOOMED
GLORIED
GLOSSED
GLUGGED
GLUTTED
GNARLED
GNARRED
GNASHED
GOATEED
GOBBLED
GOGGLED
GRABBED
GRAFTED
GRAINED
GRANTED
GRAPHED
GRASPED
GRASSED
GREASED
GREENED
GREETED
GRIDDED
GRIEVED
GRILLED
GRINNED
GRIPPED
GRITTED
GROANED
GROOMED
GROOVED
GROSSED
GROUPED
GROUSED
GROUTED
GROWLED
GRUBBED
GRUDGED
GRUMPED
GRUNTED
GUARDED
GUESSED
GUESTED
GURGLED
GUSSIED
GUZZLED
GYRATED
HABITED
HACKLED
HAGGLED
HANDFED
HANDLED
HARRIED
HASSLED
HATCHED
HAUNTED
HAVERED
HAYSEED
HEARTED
HECKLED
HEISTED
HENNAED
HIGGLED
HITCHED
HOARDED
HOBBLED
HOGTIED
HOISTED
HOMERED
HONEYED
HONORED
HOPPLED
HOUGHED
HOUNDED
HOVERED
HUDDLED
HULLOED
HUMBLED
HUMORED
HUNCHED
HUNDRED
HURDLED
HURRIED
HURTLED
HUSTLED
IDEATED
IGNITED
IGNORED
ILLBRED
ILLUDED
ILLUMED
ILLUSED
IMBIBED
IMBRUED
IMMIXED
IMMURED
IMPALED
IMPEDED
IMPLIED
IMPOSED
IMPUTED
INBREED
INCASED
INCISED
INCITED
INDEXED
INDITED
INDUCED
INFUSED
INHALED
INHERED
INJURED
INSURED
INTONED
INVADED
INVITED
INVOKED
IODISED
IODIZED
IONISED
IONIZED
JANGLED
JAUNTED
JELLIED
JEMMIED
JEWELED
JIGGLED
JIMMIED
JINGLED
JOGGLED
JOINTED
JOISTED
JOLLIED
JOSTLED
JOUNCED
JOUSTED
JUGGLED
JUMBLED
JUTTIED
KAYAKED
KIBBLED
KINDLED
KINDRED
KNEADED
KNEELED
KNELLED
KNITTED
KNOBBED
KNOCKED
KNOTTED
KNOUTED
KNURLED
LABELED
LABORED
LAPELED
LASSOED
LATCHED
LAUGHED
LAYERED
LEACHED
LEARNED
LEASHED

LEECHED
LEVELED
LEVERED
LIAISED
LIBELED
LIEABED
LIGATED
LIGHTED
LIKENED
LIMITED
LINDIED
LINSEED
LIVENED
LOATHED
LOBBIED
LOCATED
LOUNGED
LOUVRED
LOWBRED
LOWERED
LUNCHED
LURCHED
LUSTRED
LUXATED
MAITRED
MAJORED
MAMBOED
MANAGED
MANFRED
MANGLED
MANTLED
MARBLED
MARCHED
MARRIED
MATCHED
MATURED
MEDALED
MEDDLED
MENACED
MERITED
METERED
MILDRED
MINGLED
MINORED
MISCUED
MISDEED
MISUSED
MITERED
MIZZLED
MODELED
MONEYED
MOOCHED
MORDRED
MORPHED
MOSEYED
MOTORED
MOTTLED
MOULDED
MOULTED
MOUNDED
MOUNTED
MOURNED
MOUSSED
MOUTHED
MUDDIED
MUDDLED
MUFFLED
MULCHED
MULCTED
MUMBLED
MUNCHED
MUSCLED
MUTATED
MUZZLED

NATURED
NEEDLED
NEGATED
NEIGHED
NESTLED
NETTLED
NIBBLED
NIGGLED
NOBBLED
NOTATED
NOTCHED
NOTICED
NUANCED
NUTATED
NUZZLED
OBLIGED
OFFERED
OMITTED
ONEEYED
OPPOSED
ORBITED
ORDERED
OSIERED
OSMOSED
PADDLED
PAINTED
PANELED
PAPERED
PARADED
PARCHED
PAROLED
PARRIED
PARTIED
PATCHED
PEACHED
PEARLED
PEBBLED
PEDALED
PEDDLED
PEOPLED
PERCHED
PERUSED
PESTLED
PETALED
PETERED
PHOTOED
PHRASED
PICKLED
PIERCED
PIFFLED
PILOTED
PINCHED
PIRATED
PITCHED
PIVOTED
PLAGUED
PLAITED
PLANKED
PLANNED
PLANTED
PLASHED
PLEADED
PLEASED
PLEATED
PLEDGED
PLINKED
PLODDED
PLOPPED
PLOTTED
PLUCKED
PLUGGED
PLUMBED
PLUMPED
PLUNGED

PLUNKED
POACHED
POINTED
POLICED
POLKAED
POMADED
POPEYED
POPPLED
POSITED
POUCHED
POUNCED
POUNDED
POWERED
PRAISED
PRANCED
PRANGED
PRANKED
PREENED
PRESSED
PRICKED
PRIMPED
PRINKED
PRINTED
PROCEED
PRODDED
PROGGED
PRONGED
PROOFED
PROPPED
PROWLED
PSALMED
PSYCHED
PUDDLED
PUNCHED
PURFLED
PURPLED
PURSUED
PUTTIED
PUZZLED
QUACKED
QUAFFED
QUAILED
QUASHED
QUEERED
QUELLED
QUERIED
QUESTED
QUIETED
QUILLED
QUILTED
QUIPPED
QUIZZED
RADDLED
RADIOED
RAFFLED
RAGWEED
RALLIED
RAMBLED
RANCHED
RANKLED
RASSLED
RATTLED
RAVAGED
RAVELED
RAVENED
RAZORED
REACHED
REACTED
READIED
REAIMED
REAIRED
REARMED
REBATED
REBUKED

RECANED
RECEDED
RECITED
RECODED
RECUSED
REDATED
REDEYED
REDUCED
REFACED
REFILED
REFINED
REFRIED
REFUSED
REFUTED
REGALED
REGLUED
REHIRED
REIFIED
REIGNED
REINKED
REKEYED
RELACED
RELATED
RELAXED
RELAYED
RELINED
RELIVED
RELUMED
REMIXED
REMOVED
REMOWED
RENAMED
RENEGED
RENEWED
RENOTED
REOILED
REPAVED
REPINED
REPLIED
REPOSED
REPUTED
RERATED
RESAWED
RESCUED
RESIDED
RESILED
RESOLED
RESUMED
RETAPED
RETAXED
RETILED
RETIMED
RETIRED
RETOWED
RETRIED
RETUNED
RETYPED
REUPPED
REVELED
REVERED
REVILED
REVISED
REVIVED
REVOKED
REWAXED
REWIRED
REZONED
RIDDLED
RIFFLED
RIGHTED
RIMPLED
RIPENED
RIPPLED
RIVALED

RIVETED
ROACHED
ROADBED
ROASTED
ROOSTED
ROSERED
ROTATED
ROUGHED
ROUNDED
ROUSTED
RUFFLED
RUMBAED
RUMBLED
RUMORED
RUMPLED
RUSTLED
SADDLED
SAINTED
SALLIED
SALUTED
SAMBAED
SAMOYED
SAMPLED
SAUTEED
SAVAGED
SAVORED
SCALDED
SCALPED
SCAMMED
SCAMPED
SCANNED
SCANTED
SCARFED
SCARPED
SCARRED
SCATHED
SCATTED
SCENDED
SCENTED
SCHEMED
SCOFFED
SCOLDED
SCOOPED
SCOOTED
SCORNED
SCOURED
SCOUTED
SCOWLED
SCRAPED
SCREWED
SCUDDED
SCUFFED
SCULLED
SCYTHED
SEAWEED
SECEDED
SECURED
SEDATED
SEDUCED
SEEDBED
SEESRED
SEETHED
SERRIED
SETTLED
SEVERED
SHAFTED
SHAGGED
SHAMMED
SHANKED
SHARPED
SHEARED
SHEAVED
SHEERED
SHEETED

SHELLED
SHELVED
SHIFTED
SHILLED
SHINNED
SHIPPED
SHIRKED
SHIRRED
SHOCKED
SHOPPED
SHORTED
SHOUTED
SHUCKED
SHUNNED
SHUNTED
SHUSHED
SIGHTED
SINGLED
SIZZLED
SKANKED
SKIDDED
SKILLED
SKIMMED
SKIMPED
SKINNED
SKIPPED
SKIRLED
SKIRRED
SKIRTED
SKULKED
SKUNKED
SLABBED
SLACKED
SLAMMED
SLANTED
SLAPPED
SLASHED
SLATTED
SLEDDED
SLEEKED
SLEETED
SLICKED
SLIMMED
SLINKED
SLIPPED
SLOGGED
SLOPPED
SLOSHED
SLOTTED
SLUGGED
SLUICED
SLUMMED
SLUMPED
SLURPED
SLURRED
SMACKED
SMARTED
SMASHED
SMEARED
SMELLED
SMELTED
SMIRKED
SMUDGED
SNACKED
SNAFUED
SNAGGED
SNAPPED
SNARLED
SNEAKED
SNEERED
SNEEZED
SNIFFED
SNIPPED
SNOGGED

SNOOPED
SNOOTED
SNOOZED
SNORTED
SNUBBED
SNUFFED
SOBERED
SOFABED
SOOTHED
SORTIED
SOUGHED
SOUNDED
SOURCED
SPALLED
SPAMMED
SPANKED
SPANNED
SPARGED
SPARKED
SPARRED
SPATTED
SPAWNED
SPEARED
SPECCED
SPECKED
SPEEDED
SPELLED
SPIELED
SPILLED
SPLAYED
SPLICED
SPOILED
SPONGED
SPOOFED
SPOOKED
SPOOLED
SPOONED
SPORTED
SPOTTED
SPOUTED
SPRAYED
SPRUCED
SPURNED
SPURRED
SPURTED
SQUARED
SQUIRED
STABBED
STABLED
STACKED
STAFFED
STAGGED
STAINED
STALKED
STALLED
STAMPED
STAPLED
STARRED
STARTED
STARVED
STASHED
STEAMED
STEELED
STEEPED
STEERED
STEMMED
STEPPED
STETTED
STIFFED
STIFLED
STILLED
STILTED
STINTED
STIRRED

STOCKED
STOMPED
STOOKED
STOOPED
STOPPED
STORIED
STORMED
STRAFED
STRAYED
STREWED
STRIPED
STRIVED
STROKED
STUBBED
STUDDED
STUDIED
STUFFED
STUMPED
STUNNED
STUNTED
STYMIED
SUBDUED
SUCCEED
SUGARED
SULLIED
SUTURED
SWABBED
SWAMPED
SWANKED
SWAPPED
SWARMED
SWATHED
SWATTED
SWEATED
SWELLED
SWERVED
SWIGGED
SWILLED
SWIRLED
SWISHED
SWOBBED
SWOONED
SWOOPED
SWOPPED
SYNCHED
TACKLED
TAINTED
TALLIED
TALONED
TANGLED
TANGOED
TAPERED
TARRIED
TATTLED
TAUNTED
TEETHED
TELEXED
TEMPTED
TENONED
TENURED
TETCHED
THANKED
THIEVED
THINNED
THRIVED
THUDDED
THUMBED
THUMPED
TICKLED
TIEDYED
TINGLED
TINKLED
TIPPLED
TIPTOED

TOADIED
TOASTED
TODDLED
TOGGLED
TOKENED
TONGUED
TOOTHED
TOOTLED
TOPPLED
TORCHED
TOTALED
TOUCHED
TOUSLED
TOWELED
TOWERED
TRACKED
TRAILED
TRAINED
TRAMPED
TRAPPED
TRASHED
TRAWLED
TREADED
TREATED
TREBLED
TREKKED
TRENDED
TRICKED
TRIFLED
TRIGGED
TRILLED
TRIMMED
TRIPLED
TRIPPED
TROLLED
TROOPED
TROTHED
TROTTED
TRUCKED
TRUDGED
TRUMPED
TRUSSED
TRUSTED
TRYSTED
TUMBLED
TURTLED
TUSSLED
TUTORED
TWANGED
TWEAKED
TWEETED
TWEEZED
TWILLED
TWINBED
TWINGED
TWINNED
TWIRLED
TWISTED
TWITTED
UMPIRED
UNAIDED
UNAIMED
UNAIRED
UNARMED
UNASKED
UNBAKED
UNBOWED
UNBOXED
UNCAGED
UNCASED
UNDATED
UNENDED
UNFAZED
UNFIXED

UNGLUED
UNIFIED
UNLACED
UNLIKED
UNLINED
UNLOVED
UNMOVED
UNNAMED
UNOILED
UNPAVED
UNPILED
UNRATED
UNROBED
UNSATED
UNSEWED
UNTAMED
UNTAPED
UNTRIED
UNTUNED
UNYOKED
UNZONED
UPDATED
UPENDED
USHERED
USURPED
UTTERED
VACATED
VAULTED
VAUNTED
VISITED
VOUCHED
VOYAGED
WADDLED
WAFFLED
WAGERED
WAGGLED
WAKENED
WALTZED
WAMBLED
WANGLED
WARBLED
WATCHED
WATERED
WAVERED
WEARIED
WEBTOED
WEIGHED
WELCHED
WELLFED
WHACKED
WHAMMED
WHANGED
WHARFED
WHEELED
WHEEZED
WHELMED
WHELPED
WHETTED
WHIFFED
WHIPPED
WHIRLED
WHIRRED
WHISHED
WHISKED
WHIZZED
WHOMPED
WHOOPED
WHOPPED
WHORLED
WHUPPED
WIDENED
WIDOWED
WIELDED
WIGGLED

WIMBLED
WIMPLED
WINCHED
WINERED
WINKLED
WIZENED
WOBBLED
WORRIED
WORSTED
WOUNDED
WRACKED
WRAPPED
WREAKED
WRECKED
WRESTED
WRITHED
WRONGED
YACHTED
YEARNED
YIELDED
YODELED

EE•••••

EELIEST
EELLIKE
EELSKIN
EERIEST

E•E••••

EGESTED
EJECTED
EKEDOUT
EKESOUT
ELEANOR
ELECTED
ELECTEE
ELECTOR
ELECTRA
ELECTRO
ELEGANT
ELEGIAC
ELEGIES
ELEGIST
ELEISON
ELEKTRA
ELEMENT
ELEVATE
ELEVENS
EMENDED
EMENDER
EMERALD
EMERGED
EMERGES
EMERITA
EMERITI
EMERSED
EMERSON
ENEMIES
EPEEIST
EPERGNE
ERECTED
ERECTER
ERECTLY
ERECTOR
ERELONG
EREMITE
EREWHON
ETERNAL
ETESIAN
EVENEST
EVENING
EVENKIS
EVENOUT
EVENSUP
EVEREST
EVERETT
EVERTED
EXECUTE
EXEMPLI
EXEMPTS
EXERTED
EYEBALL
EYEBANK
EYEBOLT
EYEBROW
EYECUPS
EYEFULS
EYEHOLE
EYELASH
EYELESS
EYELETS
EYELIDS
EYELIKE
EYESHOT
EYESORE
EYEWASH
EZEKIEL

E••E•••

EAGERER
EAGERLY
EASEDIN
EASEDUP
EASEFUL
EASEOFF
EASEOUT
EASESIN
EASESUP
EATENAT
EATENUP
ECHELON
EDGEDIN
EDGEOUT
EDGESIN
EFFECTS
EFFENDI
EGGEDON
ELDERLY
EMPEROR
ENDEARS
ENDEDUP
ENDEMIC
ENNEADS
ENTEBBE
ENTENTE
ENTERED
ENTERON
ENVELOP
EPEEIST
EQUERRY
ERNESTO
ESSENCE
ESSENES
ESTEEMS
ESTELLE
ESTEVEZ
ETIENNE
EUGENIE
EUTERPE
EXCEEDS
EXCEPTS
EXCERPT
EXPECTS
EXPENDS
EXPENSE
EXPERTS
EXSERTS
EXTENDS
EXTENTS
EXTERNS

E•••E••

EAGLETS
EARLESS
EARNERS
EARNEST
EASIEST
EASTEND
EASTERN
EASTERS
EDGIEST
EELIEST
EERIEST
EGGHEAD
EGGIEST
EGGLESS
ELATERS
ELEMENT
ELEVENS
ELGRECO
ELOPERS
ELYSEES
EMBLEMS
EMINENT
EMOTERS
EMPRESS
ENAMELS
ENDLESS
ENTREAT
ENTREES
ENVIERS
EPICENE
EPIGENE
EPOPEES
EPSTEIN
ERASERS
ERODENT
EROSELY
ESCHEAT
ESCHEWS
ESOTERY
ESTEEMS
ESTHETE
ETAGERE
ETCHERS
EVADERS
EVENEST
EVEREST
EVERETT
EVIDENT
EVILEST
EVILEYE
EVOKERS
EXCEEDS
EXCRETE
EXIGENT
EXPRESS
EXTREME
EXUPERY
EYELESS
EYELETS

E••••E•

EAGERER
EARLIER
EARTHEN
EBONIES
ECDYSES
ECTYPES
EDASNER
EDIBLES
EDIFIED
EDIFIES
EFFACED
EFFACES
EFFUSED
EFFUSES
EGESTED
EJECTED
ELAPSED
ELAPSES
ELBOWED
ELECTED
ELECTEE
ELEGIES
ELMTREE
ELYSEES
EMAILED
EMANUEL
EMBAYED
EMENDED
EMENDER
EMERGED
EMERGES
EMERSED
EMIGRES
EMITTED
EMITTER
EMPANEL
EMPIRES
EMPOWER
EMPTIED
EMPTIER
EMPTIES
ENABLED
ENABLES
ENACTED
ENCAGED
ENCAGES
ENCASED
ENCASES
ENCODED
ENCODER
ENCODES
ENCORES
ENDIVES
ENDOWED
ENDURED
ENDURES
ENDUSER
ENDUSES
ENEMIES
ENGAGED
ENGAGES
ENGINES
ENISLED
ENISLES
ENJOYED
ENLACED
ENLACES
ENLIVEN
ENRAGED
ENRAGES
ENROBED
ENROBES
ENSILED
ENSILES
ENSKIED
ENSKIES
ENSURED
ENSURES
ENTERED
ENTICED
ENTICER
ENTICES
ENTREES

ENTRIES
ENZYMES
EPAULET
EPITHET
EPOPEES
EPOXIES
EQUALED
EQUATED
EQUATES
EQUINES
ERECTED
ERECTER
ERGATES
ERITREA
ERMINES
ERUCTED
ERUPTED
ESCAPED
ESCAPEE
ESCAPES
ESSAYED
ESSENES
ESTATES
ESTEVEZ
ETOILES
EUCHRED
EUCHRES
EVACUEE
EVANDER
EVANGEL
EVERTED
EVICTED
EVILLER
EVINCED
EVINCES
EVOLVED
EVOLVES
EVULSED
EVULSES
EVZONES
EXACTED
EXACTER
EXALTED
EXCISED
EXCISES
EXCITED
EXCITES
EXCUSED
EXCUSES
EXERTED
EXHALED
EXHALES
EXISTED
EXPIRED
EXPIRES
EXPOSED
EXPOSES
EXULTED
EXWIVES
EZEKIEL

E•••••E

EARACHE
EARLIKE
EARLOBE
EATABLE
EBBTIDE
EBONITE
EBWHITE
ECLIPSE
ECLOGUE
EDIFICE
EDUCATE
EELLIKE
EGALITE
EGGCASE
ELECTEE
ELEVATE
ELFLIKE
ELLIPSE
ELMTREE
ELUSIVE
EMANATE
EMBRACE
EMIRATE
EMOTIVE
EMPLOYE
EMULATE
ENCLAVE
ENCLOSE
ENDGAME
ENDORSE
ENDWISE
ENDZONE
ENFORCE
ENGARDE
ENGORGE
ENGRAVE
ENHANCE
ENLARGE
ENMASSE
ENNOBLE
ENOUNCE
ENPLANE
ENQUIRE
ENROUTE
ENSLAVE
ENSNARE
ENSUITE
ENTEBBE
ENTENTE
ENTHUSE
ENTITLE
ENTWINE
EPERGNE
EPICENE
EPICURE
EPIGENE
EPIGONE
EPISODE
EPISTLE
EPITOME
EQUABLE
ERASURE
EREMITE
EROSIVE
ERSKINE
ERUDITE
ESCAPEE
ESPOUSE
ESQUIRE
ESSENCE
ESTELLE
ESTHETE
ETAGERE
ETAMINE
ETIENNE
EUGENIE
EUTERPE
EVACUEE
EVASIVE
EVILEYE
EXAMINE
EXAMPLE
EXCLUDE
EXCRETE
EXECUTE
EXPANSE
EXPARTE
EXPENSE
EXPIATE
EXPLODE
EXPLORE
EXPUNGE
EXTREME
EXTRUDE
EYEHOLE
EYELIKE
EYESORE

•EE••••

BEEBALM
BEECHAM
BEECHER
BEECHES
BEEFALO
BEEFIER
BEEFING
BEEFSUP
BEEFTEA
BEEGEES
BEEGUMS
BEEHIVE
BEELIKE
BEELINE
BEEPERS
BEEPING
BEERIER
BEESWAX
BEETLES
DEEDING
DEEJAYS
DEEMING
DEEPEND
DEEPENS
DEEPEST
DEEPFAT
DEEPFRY
DEEPSEA
DEEPSET
DEEPSIX
DEERFLY
FEEBLER
FEEDBAG
FEEDERS
FEEDING
FEEDLOT
FEEDSON
FEELERS
FEELESS
FEELFOR
FEELING
FEELOUT
GEEGAWS
GEEKIER
GEEWHIZ
GEEZERS
HEEDFUL
HEEDING
HEEHAWS
HEELERS
HEELING
HEELTAP
JEEBIES
JEEPNEY
JEERERS
JEERING
JEERSAT
KEEBLER
KEELING
KEENERS
KEENEST
KEENING
KEEPERS
KEEPING
KEEPOFF
KEEPSAT
KEEPSIN
KEEPSON
KEEPSTO
KEEPSUP
KEESHAN
LEECHED
LEECHES
LEERERS
LEERIER
LEERILY
LEERING
LEERSAT
LEETIDE
LEEWARD
MEEKEST
MEETING
NEEDFUL
NEEDHAM
NEEDIER
NEEDILY
NEEDING
NEEDLED
NEEDLES
PEEKERS
PEEKING
PEEKOUT
PEEKSAT
PEELERS
PEELING
PEELOFF
PEEPERS
PEEPING
PEEPLES
PEERAGE
PEERESS
PEERING
PEEROUT
PEERSAT
PEERSIN
PEEVING
PEEVISH
PEEWEES
REEDIER
REEDING
REEDITS
REEFERS
REEFING
REEKING
REELECT
REELING
REELOFF
REELSIN
REENACT
REENTER
REENTRY
SEEABLE
SEEDBED
SEEDERS
SEEDIER
SEEDILY
SEEDING
SEEDPOD
SEEHERE
SEEKERS
SEEKING
SEEKOUT
SEEMING
SEENFIT
SEENOFF
SEENOUT
SEEPIER
SEEPING
SEEPSIN
SEERESS
SEESAWS
SEESFIT
SEESOFF
SEESOUT
SEESRED
SEETHED
SEETHES
SEETOIT
TEEDOFF
TEEMING
TEENAGE
TEENERS
TEENIER
TEEPEES
TEESOFF
TEETERS
TEETHED
TEETHER
TEETHES
TEETIME
VEEJAYS
VEENECK
VEERIES
VEERING
WEEDERS
WEEDIER
WEEDILY
WEEDING
WEEDOUT
WEEKDAY
WEEKEND
WEENIER
WEENIES
WEEPERS
WEEPIER
WEEPIES
WEEPING
WEEVILS

•E•E•••

BEDECKS
BEDELIA
BEDEVIL
BEDEWED
BEHEADS
BEHESTS
BENEATH
BENEFIT
BENELUX
BEREAVE
BERETTA
BESEECH
BESEEMS
BEVELED
BEVERLY
CELEBES
CELEBRE
CELESTA
CELESTE
CEMENTS
CEREALS
CEREBRA
CETERIS
DEBEERS
DECEITS
DECEIVE
DECENCY
DEFEATS
DEFECTS
DEFENCE
DEFENDS
DEFENSE
DEJECTS
DELEING
DELETED
DELETES
DEMEANS
DEMERIT
DEMEROL
DEMESNE
DEMETER
DENEUVE
DEPENDS
DESERTS
DESERVE
DETECTS
DETENTE
DETESTS
DEVEINS
DEVELOP
FEDERAL
GENERAL
GENERIC
GENERIS
GENESEE
GENESES
GENESIS
GENETIC
GERENTS
GETEVEN
HERETIC
JEWELED
JEWELER
JEWELRY
JEZEBEL
KEYEDIN
KEYEDUP
LEGENDS
LEVELED
LEVELER
LEVELLY
LEVERED
LEVERET
LEXEMES
MEDEVAC
MEMENTO
METEORS
METEOUT
METERED
NEMEROV
NEMESES
NEMESIS
NEREIDS
PESETAS
PETERED
REBECCA
REBEKAH
REBENDS
RECEDED
RECEDES
RECEIPT
RECEIVE
RECENCY
REDEALS
REDEALT
REDEEMS
REDEYED
REDEYES
REFEREE
REFERTO
REGENCY
REGENTS
REHEALS
REHEARD
REHEARS
REHEATS
REHEELS
REJECTS
REKEYED
RELEARN
RELEASE
RELENTS
REMELTS
REMENDS
RENEGED
RENEGER
RENEGES
RENEGUE
RENEWAL
RENEWED
RENEWER
REPEALS
REPEATS
REPENTS
REREADS
REREDOS
RERENTS
RESEALS
RESEATS
RESECTS
RESEEDS
RESELLS
RESENDS
RESENTS
RESERVE
RETEACH
RETEARS
RETELLS
RETESTS
REVEALS
REVELED
REVELER
REVELRY
REVENGE
REVENUE
REVERBS
REVERED
REVERES
REVERIE
REVERSE
REVERTS
REWEAVE
REWELDS
SECEDED
SECEDER
SECEDES
SELECTS
SELENIC
SENECAS
SENEGAL
SERENER
SEVENAM
SEVENPM
SEVENTH
SEVENTY
SEVENUP
SEVERAL
SEVERED
SEVERER
SEWEDON
SEWEDUP
TEHERAN
TELERAN
TELEXED
TELEXES
TEREDOS
TERENCE
VEGETAL
VENEERS
VETERAN
VEXEDLY
YEMENIS
YEREVAN

•E••E••

AERIEST
AETHERS
BEAKERS
BEANERY
BEARERS
BEATERS
BEAVERS
BECKETT
BEDLESS
BEDREST
BEEGEES
BEEPERS
BELIEFS
BELIEVE
BELLEEK
BENDERS
BENNETT
BENZENE
BEQUEST
BERBERS
BERGERE
BERMEJO
BERNESE
BERSERK
BESEECH
BESEEMS
BESIEGE
BESMEAR
BESPEAK
BETHELS
BETTERS
BETWEEN
BEZIERS
CENSERS
CENTERS
CEPHEUS
DEADEND
DEADENS
DEADEYE
DEAFENS
DEAFEST
DEALERS
DEANERY
DEAREST
DEBEERS
DECREED
DECREES
DEEPEND
DEEPENS
DEEPEST
DEFLECT
DEFTEST
DEGREES
DEICERS
DEKLERK
DELVERS
DENIERS
DENNEHY
DENSELY
DENSEST
DEPLETE
DEPRESS
DESCEND
DESCENT
DESSERT
DEUTERO
DEWLESS
EELIEST
EERIEST
FEARERS
FEEDERS
FEELERS
FEELESS
FELLERS
FENCERS
FENDERS
FERMENT
FERRETS
FERVENT
FESTERS
FETTERS
GEEZERS
GEMLESS
GENDERS
GENOESE
GENTEEL
GEODESY
GETREAL
GETWELL
GEYSERS
HEADERS
HEALERS
HEARERS
HEATERS
HEAVEHO
HEAVENS
HEAVERS
HEAVETO
HEBREWS
HEDGERS
HEELERS
HEIFERS
HEIFETZ
HEIRESS
HELLENE
HELLERS
HELMETS
HELPERS
HEMMERS
HENNERY
HENPECK
HEPPEST
HERBERT
HERDERS
HERSELF
HEWLETT
JEERERS
JEFFERS
JENNETS
JERSEYS
JESTERS
KEENERS
KEENEST
KEEPERS
KEGLERS
KENNEDY
KENNELS
KENNETH
KERNELS
KEYLESS
KEYWEST
LEADERS
LEAKERS
LEANERS
LEANEST
LEAPERS
LEASERS
LEAVEIN
LEAVENS
LECTERN
LEDGERS
LEERERS
LEGLESS
LEMIEUX
LENDERS
LENIENT
LESSEES
LESSENS
LETTERS
LEVIERS
LEWDEST
MEANEST
MEDLEYS
MEEKEST
MEMBERS
MENDERS
MERCERS
MERCERY
MERGERS
METIERS
MEWLERS
NEAREST
NEATENS
NEATEST
NECKERS
NEGLECT
NEPHEWS
NESTEGG
NESTERS
NEWBERY
NEWDEAL
NEWLEFT
NEWNESS
NEWYEAR
PEABEAN
PEAHENS
PEAVEYS
PEEKERS
PEELERS
PEEPERS
PEERESS
PEEWEES
PEGLESS
PELLETS
PELTERS
PENDENT
PENNERS
PENSEES
PEPPERS
PEPPERY
PERCENT
PERFECT
PERSEID
PERSEUS
PERTEST
PESTERS
PETRELS
PETTERS
PEUGEOT
READERS
REAGENT
REAMERS
REAPERS
REAREND
REARERS
RECHECK
RECLEAN
REDCELL
REDCENT
REDDEER
REDDENS
REDDEST
REDEEMS
REDHEAD
REDHEAT
REDMEAT
REDNESS
REDRESS
REEFERS
REELECT
REFLECT
REFRESH
REFUELS
REGLETS
REGRESS
REGRETS
REHEELS
RELIEFS
RELIEVE
RELIEVO
RELLENO
RENDERS
RENTERS
REOPENS
REPLETE
REPRESS
REQUEST
RESEEDS
RESPECT
RESTERS
RETREAD
RETREAT
REUBENS
REUTERS
REVIEWS
SEABEDS
SEABEES
SEALEGS
SEALERS
SEATERS
SEAWEED
SECKELS
SECRECY
SECRETE
SECRETS
SEEDERS
SEEHERE
SEEKERS
SEERESS
SEGMENT
SEIDELS
SEINERS
SEIZERS
SELLECK
SELLERS
SENDERS
SENNETT
SEPTETS
SEQUELS
SERPENT
SERVERS
SERVERY
SERVEUP
SESTETS
SETTEES
SETTERS
SEXIEST
SEXTETS
TEALEAF
TEALESS
TEASELS
TEASERS
TEASETS
TEDDERS
TEENERS
TEEPEES
TEETERS
TELLERS
TEMPEHS
TEMPERA
TEMPERS
TEMPEST
TENCENT
TENDERS
TENNERS
TENRECS
TENSELY
TENSEST
TENSEUP
TENTERS
TERCELS
TERCETS
TERRENE
TERRETS
TERSELY
TERSEST
TESSERA
TESTEES
TESTERS
TETHERS
VEENECK
VELVETS
VELVETY
VENEERS
VENTERS
VERBENA
VERGERS
VERMEER
VERMEIL
VERVETS
VESPERS
VESSELS
VESTEES
VETOERS
WEAKENS
WEAKEST
WEARERS
WEASELS
WEAVERS
WEBFEET
WEBLESS
WEEDERS
WEEKEND
WEEPERS
WELDERS
WELTERS
WENDELL
WENDERS
WESTEND
WESTERN
WETCELL
WETHERS
WETNESS
WETTEST
YEAREND
YEATEAM
YELLERS
YELPERS
YESDEAR
YEVGENY

•E•••E•

AEDILES
AERATED
AERATES
AEROBES
BEACHED
BEACHES
BEADIER
BEADLES
BEAGLES
BEAMIER
BEANIES
BEARDED
BEATLES
BECOMES
BEDEWED
BEDIZEN
BEECHER
BEECHES
BEEFIER
BEEFTEA
BEEGEES
BEERIER
BEETLES
BEHAVED
BEHAVES
BEHOVED
BEHOVES
BELATED
BELAYED
BELCHED
BELCHES
BELLEEK
BELLIED
BELLIES
BELLMEN
BELOVED
BEMIRED
BEMIRES
BEMUSED
BEMUSES
BENCHED
BENCHES
BENDIER
BENTLEY
BENTSEN
BERATED
BERATES
BERNSEN
BERRIED
BERRIES
BERTHED
BESIDES
BESTMEN
BESTREW
BETAKEN
BETAKES
BETIDED
BETIDES
BETIMES
BETISES
BETOKEN
BETWEEN
BEVELED
CEDARED
CELEBES
CENTRED
CENTRES
CERUMEN
DEADSEA
DEADSET
DEARIES
DEBAKEY
DEBASED
DEBASES
DEBATED
DEBATER
DEBATES
DEBITED
DEBONED
DEBONES
DEBRIEF
DEBUTED
DECADES
DECAYED
DECIBEL
DECIDED
DECIDES
DECKLES
DECODED
DECODER
DECODES
DECOYED
DECREED
DECREES
DECRIED
DECRIER
DECRIES
DEDUCED
DEDUCES
DEEPSEA
DEEPSET
DEFACED
DEFACES
DEFAMED
DEFAMES
DEFILED
DEFILER
DEFILES
DEFINED
DEFINES
DEFUSED
DEFUSES
DEGREES
DEIFIED
DEIFIES
DEIGNED
DEITIES
DELANEY
DELAYED
DELAYER
DELETED
DELETES
DELIBES
DELIVER
DELUDED
DELUDES
DELUGED
DELUGES
DEMETER
DEMISED
DEMISES
DEMOTED
DEMOTES
DEMPSEY
DEMURER
DENIZEN
DENOTED
DENOTES
DENUDED
DENUDES
DEPONED
DEPONES
DEPOSED
DEPOSER
DEPOSES
DEPUTED
DEPUTES
DERBIES
DERIDED
DERIDES
DERIVED
DERIVES
DERNIER
DESIRED
DESIREE
DESIRES
DESKSET
DEVICES

DEVILED DEVISED DEVISES DEVOTED DEVOTEE DEVOTES DEVRIES FEASTED FEATHER FEEBLER FEIFFER FEIGNED FEINTED FELINES FELLIES FEMALES FENNIER FERNIER FERRIED FERRIES FERULES FESCUES FETCHED FETCHES FETTLES GECKOES GEEKIER GEMMIER GEMOTES GENESEE GENESES GENOMES GENTEEL GENTLED GENTLER GENTLES GEORGES GERMIER GESSOES GETEVEN GETOVER GETSSET HEADIER HEADMEN HEADSET HEARKEN HEARTED HEARTEN HEATHEN HEATHER HEATTER HEAVIER HEAVIES HECKLED HECKLER HECKLES HEDDLES HEDGIER HEFTIER HEISTED HELICES HELIXES HEMSLEY HENNAED HERBIER HERBTEA HERSHEY JEEBIES JEEPNEY JEFFREY JELLIED JELLIES JEMMIED JEMMIES

JENNIES JERKIER JETTIES JEWELED JEWELER JEZEBEL KEARNEY KEEBLER KELPIES KESTREL KETCHES KETONES KETTLES KEWPIES LEACHED LEACHES LEADIER LEAFIER LEAFLET LEAGUES LEAKIER LEANDER LEARIER LEARJET LEARNED LEARNER LEASHED LEASHES LEATHER LEDGIER LEECHED LEECHES LEERIER LEFTIES LEGATEE LEGATES LEGGIER LEGUMES LEISTER LEPPIES LESSEES LETSSEE LETTRES LEVELED LEVELER LEVERED LEVERET LEVITES LEXEMES MEALIER MEALIES MEANDER MEANIES MEASLES MEATIER MEDALED MEDDLED MEDDLER MEDDLES MEINIES MEIOSES MEISSEN MEISTER MEMOREX MENACED MENACES MENAGES MENCKEN MENZIES MERCIES MERIMEE MERITED MERRIER MESHIER

MESSIER METATES METERED METOOER METTLES NEDDIES NEEDIER NEEDLED NEEDLES NEGATED NEGATER NEGATES NEIGHED NEITHER NEMESES NERDIER NERVIER NESTLED NESTLER NESTLES NETIZEN NETTLED NETTLES NEWAGER NEWSIER NEWSIES NEWSMEN NEXUSES OEUVRES PEACHED PEACHES PEARLED PEATIER PEBBLED PEBBLES PECKIER PEDALED PEDDLED PEDDLER PEDDLES PEDICEL PEEPLES PEEWEES PELAGES PENATES PENNIES PENSEES PEONIES PEOPLED PEOPLES PEPPIER PERCHED PERCHES PERDIEM PERIGEE PERKIER PERPLEX PERRIER PERUKES PERUSED PERUSER PERUSES PESKIER PESTLED PESTLES PETALED PETERED PETITES PETTIER REACHED REACHES REACTED READIED READIER

READIES REAIMED REAIRED REARMED REBATED REBATES REBUKED REBUKES REBUSES RECANED RECANES RECEDED RECEDES RECIPES RECITED RECITER RECITES RECODED RECODES RECOVER RECUSED RECUSES REDATED REDATES REDDEER REDEYED REDEYES REDUCED REDUCER REDUCES REEDIER REENTER REFACED REFACES REFEREE REFILED REFILES REFINED REFINER REFINES REFIRES REFRIED REFRIES REFUGEE REFUGES REFUSED REFUSER REFUSES REFUTED REFUTER REFUTES REGALED REGALES REGIMEN REGIMES REGLUED REGLUES REHIRED REHIRES REIFIED REIFIES REIGNED REINKED REKEYED RELACED RELACES RELATED RELATES RELAXED RELAXES RELAYED RELINED RELINES RELIVED

RELIVES RELUMED RELUMES REMAKES REMIGES REMIXED REMIXES REMODEL REMOTER REMOTES REMOVED REMOVER REMOVES REMOWED RENAMED RENAMES RENEGED RENEGER RENEGES RENEWED RENEWER RENOTED RENOTES REOILED REORDER REPAPER REPAVED REPAVES REPINED REPINES REPLIED REPLIES REPOSED REPOSES REPUTED REPUTES REQUIEM RERATED RERATES RESALES RESAWED RESCUED RESCUER RESCUES RESHOES RESIDED RESIDES RESILED RESILES RESOLED RESOLES RESUMED RESUMES RETAKEN RETAKES RETAPED RETAPES RETAXED RETAXES RETILED RETILES RETIMED RETIMES RETIRED RETIREE RETIRES RETOWED RETRIED RETRIES RETUNED RETUNES RETYPED RETYPES REUPPED

REUTHER REVELED REVELER REVERED REVERES REVILED REVILES REVISED REVISER REVISES REVIVED REVIVES REVOKED REVOKES REWAXED REWAXES REWIRED REWIRES REWOVEN REZONED REZONES SEABEES SEAMIER SEANCES SEAWEED SECEDED SECEDER SECEDES SECURED SECURER SECURES SEDATED SEDATER SEDATES SEDGIER SEDUCED SEDUCER SEDUCES SEEDBED SEEDIER SEEPIER SEESRED SEETHED SEETHES SEICHES SELTZER SEMITES SENATES SENORES SERAPES SERENER SERRIED SESAMES SETTEES SETTLED SETTLER SETTLES SEVERED SEVERER TEACHER TEACHES TEARIER TEATREE TECHIER TECHIES TEDDIES TEENIER TEEPEES TEETHED TEETHER TEETHES TEICHER TELEXED TELEXES

TELLIES TEMPLES TEMPTED TEMPTER TENACES TENNIEL TENONED TENURED TENURES TERRIER TERRIES TESTEES TESTIER TETCHED VEALIER VEERIES VEGGIES VEINIER VERMEER VERNIER VESTEES VETCHES WEARIED WEARIER WEARIES WEATHER WEBBIER WEBFEET WEBSTER WEBTOED WEDGIER WEDGIES WEEDIER WEENIER WEENIES WEEPIER WEEPIES WEIGHED WEIRDER WELCHED WELCHES WELLFED WELLSET WENCHES WERNHER WERTHER YEARNED YEARNER ZESTIER

•E••••E

BEASTIE BEATSME BEATTIE BECAUSE BEDLIKE BEDSIDE BEDTIME BEEHIVE BEELIKE BEELINE BEGRIME BEGUILE BEGUINE BEHOOVE BELDAME BELIEVE BELTANE BENZENE BEREAVE BERGERE BERNESE BERNICE BESIEGE

BESPOKE BEZIQUE CELEBRE CELESTE CENSURE CENTIME CEZANNE DEADEYE DEBACLE DEBARGE DECEIVE DECLARE DECLINE DEFARGE DEFENCE DEFENSE DEFLATE DEGRADE DEHISCE DELUISE DEMESNE DEMILLE DENEUVE DENTATE DENTINE DENTURE DEPLANE DEPLETE DEPLORE DEPRAVE DEPRIVE DESERVE DESIREE DESPISE DESPITE DESTINE DETENTE DEVALUE DEVIATE DEVILLE DEVOLVE DEVOTEE DEWLINE EELLIKE FEATURE FEBRILE FERRATE FERRITE FERRULE FERTILE FESTIVE GEFILTE GEMLIKE GENESEE GENOESE GENTILE GENUINE GEORDIE GERMANE GESTATE GESTURE HECTARE HELLENE HELOISE HEMLINE HENBANE HENLIKE HERBAGE HERCULE HEROINE HEYJUDE JEANNIE KEYHOLE KEYLIME

KEYNOTE LEAFAGE LEAKAGE LECARRE LECTURE LEETIDE LEGATEE LEGIBLE LEGLIKE LEHAVRE LEISURE LEMONDE LEONINE LETITBE LETSSEE LETTUCE LEUCINE MEASURE MEDIATE MEDUSAE MELANGE MELANIE MELROSE MEMOIRE MERIMEE MESSAGE METHANE NEBULAE NECKTIE NEONATE NEPTUNE NESCAFE NETLIKE NETSUKE NEURONE NEVILLE NEWGATE NEWWAVE PEALIKE PEDICLE PEERAGE PEGLIKE PELISSE PELTATE PENANCE PENLIKE PENNAME PENNATE PENSIVE PENUCHE PEONAGE PEPTIDE PERCALE PERFUME PERIGEE PERJURE PERLITE PERVADE PETIOLE PETNAME REALISE REALIZE REARGUE REBASTE RECEIVE RECHOSE RECLAME RECLINE RECLUSE RECYCLE REDLINE REDPINE REDROSE REDTAPE

REDWINE REFEREE REFRAME REFUGEE REGRADE REISSUE REJOICE RELAPSE RELEASE RELIEVE REMORSE RENEGUE REPASTE REPLACE REPLATE REPLETE REPRICE REPRISE REPROVE REPTILE REPULSE REQUIRE REQUITE RERAISE RERINSE REROUTE RESCALE RESERVE RESIDUE RESOLVE RESPIRE RESPITE RESTAGE RESTATE RESTIVE RESTORE RESTYLE RESURGE RETICLE RETINAE RETINUE RETIREE RETITLE RETRACE RETRADE REUNITE REVALUE REVENGE REVENUE REVERIE REVERSE REVOICE REVOLVE REWEAVE REWRITE REWROTE SEABLUE SEAFIRE SEAGATE SEALANE SEASIDE SEATTLE SECLUDE SECRETE SEEABLE SEEHERE SELVAGE SENSATE SERIATE SERRATE SERVICE SERVILE SESSILE SETLINE

SEVIGNE SEVILLE TEACAKE TEAROSE TEATIME TEATREE TEENAGE TEETIME TEKTITE TENABLE TENSILE TENSIVE TERENCE TERHUNE TERMITE TERNATE TERRACE TERRENE TEXTILE TEXTURE VEHICLE VENTURE VERBOSE VERDURE VESTIGE VESTURE WEBLIKE WEBPAGE WEBSITE WELCOME WELFARE WENTAPE

••EE•••

BLEEPED BLEEPER BREEDER BREEZED BREEZES CHEEPED CHEERED CHEERIO CHEERUP CHEESES CHEETAH CHEETOS CHEEVER CREEPED CREEPER CREEPUP DWEEZIL EPEEIST FLEECED FLEECES FLEEING FLEETER FLEETLY FREEBEE FREEBIE FREEDOM FREEING FREEMAN FREEMEN FREESIA FREEWAY FREEZER FREEZES GLEEFUL GREELEY GREENED GREENER GREETED GREETER KLEENEX

KNEECAP KNEEING KNEELED KNEELER KNEEPAD KNEESUP OKEEFFE ONEEYED PREEMIE PREEMPT PREENED PREENER QUEENLY QUEERED QUEERER QUEERLY SHEERED SHEERER SHEERLY SHEETED SKEETER SKEEZIX SLEEKED SLEEKEN SLEEKER SLEEKLY SLEEPER SLEEPIN SLEEPON SLEETED SLEEVES SNEERAT SNEERED SNEERER SNEEZED SNEEZER SNEEZES SPEEDED SPEEDER SPEEDOS SPEEDUP STEELED STEELER STEELIE STEEPED STEEPEN STEEPER STEEPLE STEEPLY STEERED STEERER SWEENEY SWEEPER SWEEPUP SWEETEN SWEETER SWEETIE SWEETLY SWEETON TREEING TREERAT TREETOP TWEETED TWEETER TWEEZED TWEEZES WHEEDLE WHEELED WHEELER WHEELIE WHEEZED WHEEZER WHEEZES

••E•E••

AGELESS AWELESS BEEGEES BEEPERS BREVETS BREWERS BREWERY CHEWERS CLEMENS CLEMENT CRENELS CREWELS DEEPEND DEEPENS DEEPEST DIESELS DIETERS DUELERS ELEMENT ELEVENS EVENEST EVEREST EVERETT EYELESS EYELETS FEEDERS FEELERS FEELESS FRENEAU FUELERS GEEZERS GREYEST HEELERS HUELESS ICEBEER ICEBERG ICELESS IRELESS JAEGERS JEERERS KEENERS KEENEST KEEPERS LEERERS LIENEES MAEWEST MEEKEST OMELETS ONENESS ONESELF OPENEND OPENERS OVEREAT PEEKERS PEELERS PEEPERS PEERESS PEEWEES PIECERS PREBEND PRECEDE PRECEPT PREFECT PREFERS PREHEAT PREMEDS PRESELL PRESENT PRESETS PRETEEN PRETEND PRETEST PRETEXT

PREVENT QUEUERS QUEUEUP REEFERS REELECT ROEDEER SCENERY SEEDERS SEEHERE SEEKERS SEERESS SHEKELS SKEWERS STEREOS STEVENS STEWERS TEENERS TEEPEES TEETERS THEDEEP THEREAT THEREBY THEREIN THERELL THEREOF THEREON THERESA THERETO THESEUS TIELESS TOELESS USELESS VEENECK VIEWERS WEEDERS WEEKEND WEEPERS WHEREAS WHEREAT WHEREBY WHEREIN WHERELL WHEREOF WHERERE WHERETO WHEREVE WIENERS

••E••E•

ABETTED ALERTED ALERTER AMENDED AMERCED AMERCES APERIES ATELIER AVENGED AVENGER AVENGES AVENUES AVERRED AVERTED AYEAYES BEECHER BEECHES BEEFIER BEEFTEA BEEGEES BEERIER BEETLES BLEAKER BLEARED BLEATED

BLEEPED
BLEEPER
BLENDED
BLENDER
BLESSED
BLESSES
BREADED
BREAKER
BREEDER
BREEZED
BREEZES
BRENNER
CHEAPEN
CHEAPER
CHEATED
CHEATER
CHECHEN
CHECKED
CHECKER
CHEEPED
CHEERED
CHEESES
CHEEVER
CHELSEA
CHENIER
CHEQUER
CHEQUES
CHESTER
CHEVIED
CHEVIES
CHEVRES
CHEWIER
CLEANED
CLEANER
CLEARED
CLEARER
CLEAVED
CLEAVER
CLEAVES
CLERKED
COERCED
COERCER
COERCES
CREAKED
CREAMED
CREAMER
CREASED
CREASES
CREATED
CREATES
CRECHES
CREEPED
CREEPER
CREOLES
CRESSES
CRESTED
CREWMEN
DEEPSEA
DEEPSET
DREADED
DREAMED
DREAMER
DREDGED
DREDGER
DREDGES
DREIDEL
DREISER
DRESDEN
DRESSED
DRESSER
DRESSES
DWELLED
DWELLER
EGESTED
EJECTED
ELECTED
ELECTEE
ELEGIES
EMENDED
EMENDER
EMERGED
EMERGES
EMERSED
ENEMIES
ERECTED
ERECTER
EVERTED
EXERTED
EZEKIEL
FAERIES
FEEBLER
FIEDLER
FIELDED
FIELDER
FIENNES
FIERCER
FIERIER
FLECHES
FLECKED
FLEDGED
FLEDGES
FLEECED
FLEECES
FLEETER
FLENSED
FLENSES
FLESHED
FLESHES
FLEXNER
FREAKED
FREEBEE
FREEMEN
FREEZER
FREEZES
FRESHEN
FRESHER
FRESHET
FRETTED
FUELLED
GEEKIER
GLEAMED
GLEANED
GLEANER
GREASED
GREASER
GREASES
GREATER
GREAVES
GREELEY
GREENED
GREENER
GREETED
GREETER
GRENDEL
GREYHEN
GUESSED
GUESSER
GUESSES
GUESTED
ICEAGES
ICEAXES
ICEBEER
ICEDTEA
ICEFREE
IDEAMEN
IDEATED
IDEATES
JEEBIES
JEEPNEY
KEEBLER
KLEENEX
KNEADED
KNEADER
KNEELED
KNEELER
KNELLED
KNESSET
LAENNEC
LAERTES
LEECHED
LEECHES
LEERIER
LIEABED
LIENEES
LIEOVER
LIERNES
LOESSER
LOESSES
NEEDIER
NEEDLED
NEEDLES
NIELSEN
OLEATES
ONEEYED
ONESTEP
OPENSEA
ORESTES
OVERSEA
OVERSEE
PEEPLES
PEEWEES
PIERCED
PIERCES
PIETIES
PLEADED
PLEADER
PLEASED
PLEASER
PLEASES
PLEATED
PLEDGED
PLEDGEE
PLEDGER
PLEDGES
PREENED
PREENER
PREMIER
PREQUEL
PRESLEY
PRESSED
PRESSER
PRESSES
PRETEEN
PRETZEL
PREVIEW
PREXIES
QUEERED
QUEERER
QUELLED
QUERIED
QUERIER
QUERIES
QUESTED
REEDIER
REENTER
ROEDEER
SCENDED
SCENTED
SCEPTER
SEEDBED
SEEDIER
SEEPIER
SEESRED
SEETHED
SEETHES
SHEARED
SHEARER
SHEAVED
SHEAVES
SHEERED
SHEERER
SHEETED
SHELLED
SHELLER
SHELLEY
SHELTER
SHELVED
SHELVES
SHERBET
SKEETER
SKELTER
SLEDDED
SLEDDER
SLEDGES
SLEEKED
SLEEKEN
SLEEKER
SLEEPER
SLEETED
SLEEVES
SLENDER
SMEARED
SMELLED
SMELTED
SMELTER
SNEAKED
SNEAKER
SNEERED
SNEERER
SNEEZED
SNEEZER
SNEEZES
SNELLEN
SPEAKER
SPEARED
SPECCED
SPECIES
SPECKED
SPECTER
SPEEDED
SPEEDER
SPELLED
SPELLER
SPENCER
SPENDER
SPENSER
STEAMED
STEAMER
STEELED
STEELER
STEEPED
STEEPEN
STEEPER
STEERED
STEERER
STEIGER
STEINEM
STEINER
STEMMED
STENGEL
STEPHEN
STEPPED
STEPPER
STEPPES
STERNER
STETTED
STEUBEN
SVELTER
SWEARER
SWEATED
SWEATER
SWEENEY
SWEEPER
SWEETEN
SWEETER
SWELLED
SWELTER
SWERVED
SWERVES
TEENIER
TEEPEES
TEETHED
TEETHER
TEETHES
THEATER
THEDEEP
THEOMEN
THEOREM
THEWIER
TIEDYED
TIEDYES
TIERNEY
TREADED
TREADER
TREATED
TREBLED
TREBLES
TREKKED
TREKKER
TRENDED
TRESSES
TSETSES
TWEAKED
TWEETED
TWEETER
TWEEZED
TWEEZES
TWELVES
UNEATEN
UNENDED
UPENDED
VEERIES
VIEWIER
WEEDIER
WEENIER
WEENIES
WEEPIER
WEEPIES
WHEELED
WHEELER
WHEEZED
WHEEZER
WHEEZES
WHELMED
WHELPED
WHETHER
WHETTED
WIELDED
WIENIES
WREAKED
WRECKED
WRECKER
WRESTED
YIELDED
ZOELLER

••E•••E

ACEROSE
ACETATE
ACETONE
ADELINE
ADENINE
ALEWIFE
ANEMONE
APELIKE
AREOLAE
AVERAGE
AWESOME
BEEHIVE
BEELIKE
BEELINE
BREATHE
CHEAPIE
CHEMISE
CLEANSE
CREVICE
DUEDATE
ELECTEE
ELEVATE
EPERGNE
EREMITE
EXECUTE
EYEHOLE
EYELIKE
EYESORE
FRECKLE
FREDDIE
FREEBEE
FREEBIE
GOESAPE
GRENADE
HOECAKE
ICEBLUE
ICECUBE
ICEFLOE
ICEFREE
ICELIKE
ITEMISE
ITEMIZE
ITERATE
LEETIDE
MCENROE
OKEEFFE
ONELANE
ONENOTE
ONETIME
OPENTOE
OPERATE
OPEROSE
OVERAGE
OVERATE
OVERAWE
OVERDUE
OVERLIE
OVERSEE
OVERUSE
PEERAGE
PIELIKE
PLEDGEE
PRECEDE
PRECISE
PREDATE
PREEMIE
PREFACE
PRELATE
PRELUDE
PREMISE
PREPARE
PREPPIE
PRESAGE
PRESALE
PRESIDE
PRESUME
PRETAPE
PUERILE
SCEPTRE
SEEABLE
SEEHERE
SHEATHE
SHELTIE
SPECKLE
SPECTRE
STEELIE
STEEPLE
STERILE
SWEETIE
TEENAGE
TEETIME
THEATRE
THEBABE
TIELINE
TOELIKE
TOESHOE
TREACLE
TREADLE
TREKKIE
TREMBLE
TRESTLE
USEABLE
WHEEDLE
WHEELIE
WHERERE
WHEREVE
WOEISME
WREATHE
WRESTLE

•••EE••

AFREETS
AGREETO
AXSEEDS
BALEENS
BESEECH
BESEEMS
CAREENS
CAREERS
DEBEERS
ESTEEMS
EXCEEDS
LATEENS
MRDEEDS
MUDEELS
NOSEEUM
PAPEETE
REDEEMS
REHEELS
RESEEDS
SATEENS
SCREECH
SCREEDS
SCREENS
SPLEENS
SQUEEZE
STREETS
THREEAM
THREEPM
THREERS
TUREENS
UNREELS
VENEERS

•••E•E•

ACCEDED
ACCEDER
ACCEDES
ACHENES
ADHERED
ADHERES
ALIENEE
ALKENES
ALLEGED
ALLEGER
ALLEGES
ALLELES
ALLEYES
ALTERED
ALTERER
AMMETER
AMPERES
ANGELES
ANGERED
ANNEXED
ANNEXES
APHESES
BASEMEN
BEDEWED
BEVELED
BIGEYES
BILEVEL
BIREMES
BLEEPED
BLEEPER
BODEREK
BOGEYED
BONESET
BOWERED
BREEDER
BREEZED
BREEZES
BRIEFED
BRIEFER
BRUEGEL
BUGEYED
BYREMEN
CAMEOED
CAPELET
CAPERED
CATERED
CATERER
CAVEMEN
CELEBES
CHEEPED
CHEERED
CHEESES
CHEEVER
COHERED
COHERES
COVERED
COVETED
COWERED
COZENED
CREEPED
CREEPER
CRUELER
DELETED
DELETES
DEMETER
DINESEN
DIZENED
DOWERED
DRYEYED
EAGERER
ENTERED
ESSENES
ESTEVEZ
FACETED
FILENES
FIREMEN
FLEECED
FLEECES
FLEETER
FORELEG
FOREMEN
FORESEE
FOREVER
FREEBEE
FREEMEN
FREEZER
FREEZES
FRIEZES
GAMETES
GATELEG
GATEMEN
GAVELED
GENESEE
GENESES
GETEVEN
GORETEX
GOTEVEN
GREELEY
GREENED
GREENER
GREETED
GREETER
GRIEVED
GRIEVER
GRIEVES
GYRENES
HAVERED
HOMERED
HONEYED
HOVERED
HOVERER
HOWEVER
IMPEDED
IMPEDES
INDEXED
INDEXES
INHERED
INHERES
INTEGER
JEWELED
JEWELER
JEZEBEL
JIMENEZ
JONESES
KLEENEX
KNEELED
KNEELER
KNIEVEL
LABELED
LABELER
LAPELED
LATEXES
LAYERED
LEVELED
LEVELER
LEVERED
LEVERET
LEXEMES
LIBELED
LIBELER
LIFENET
LIKENED
LIKENEW
LINEMEN
LIVENED
LORELEI
LOWERED
MANEGES
METERED
MITERED
MODELED
MODELER
MONEYED
MOSEYED
NEMESES
NINEVEH
NUREYEV
OFFERED
OFFERER
OFTENER
ONEEYED
ORDERED
ORDERER
OSIERED
PANELED
PAPERED
PAPERER
PETERED
PHOEBES
PIKEMEN
POPEYED
POWERED
PREENED
PREENER
QUEERED
QUEERER
QUIETED
QUIETEN
QUIETER
RACEMES
RAMESES
RAVELED
RAVENED
RECEDED
RECEDES
REDEYED
REDEYES
REFEREE
REKEYED
RENEGED
RENEGER
RENEGES
RENEWED
RENEWER
REVELED
REVELER
REVERED
REVERES
RIBEYES
RIPENED
RIVETED
RIVETER
ROSERED
SAGEHEN
SCHEMED
SCHEMER
SCHEMES
SCREWED
SECEDED
SECEDER
SECEDES
SERENER
SEVERED
SEVERER
SHEERED
SHEERER
SHEETED
SIDEBET
SIDEMEN
SKEETER
SLEEKED
SLEEKEN
SLEEKER
SLEEPER
SLEETED
SLEEVES
SNEERED
SNEERER
SNEEZED
SNEEZER
SNEEZES
SOBERED
SOBERER
SPEEDED
SPEEDER
SPHERES
SPIEGEL
SPIELED
SPIELER
STEELED
STEELER
STEEPED
STEEPEN
STEEPER
STEERED
STEERER
STIEGEL
STPETER
STREWED
STREWER
SWEENEY
SWEEPER
SWEETEN
SWEETER
TAKETEN
TAPEMEN
TAPERED
TELEXED
TELEXES
THIEVED
THIEVES
TIREDER
TOKENED
TOWELED
TOWERED
TWEETED
TWEETER
TWEEZED
TWEEZES
TYPESET
UNSEWED
USHERED
UTTERED
UTTERER
WAGERED
WAGERER
WAKENED
WAKENER
WATERED
WATERER
WAVELET
WAVERED
WAVERER
WHEELED
WHEELER
WHEEZED
WHEEZER
WHEEZES
WHOEVER
WIDENED
WINERED
WISEMEN
WIZENED
YODELED
YODELER

•••E••E

ABSENCE
ACREAGE
ADVERSE
ALDENTE
ALIENEE
ALLENDE
AMOEBAE
ANNETTE
APPEASE
ARLEDGE
ASPERSE
ATPEACE
AUREATE
AUREOLE
BABETTE
BEREAVE
BURETTE
CADENCE
CADETTE
CAMEDUE
CASERNE
CATENAE
CAYENNE
CELEBRE
CELESTE
CODEINE
COLETTE
COMEDUE
COTERIE
DECEIVE
DEFENCE
DEFENSE
DEMESNE
DENEUVE
DESERVE
DETENTE
DINETTE
DISEASE
DIVERGE
DIVERSE
DOYENNE
ENTEBBE
ENTENTE
ESSENCE
ESTELLE
ETIENNE
EUGENIE
EUTERPE
EXPENSE
FABERGE
FAIENCE
FINESSE
FIRENZE
FORESEE
FREEBEE
FREEBIE
GAZELLE
GAZETTE
GENESEE
GISELLE
IMMENSE
IMMERSE
INCENSE
INGENUE
INPEACE
INTENSE
INTERSE
INVERSE
JADEITE
JANEDOE
LABELLE
LAVERNE
LAYETTE
LICENCE
LICENSE
LIMEADE
LINEAGE
LINEATE
LISENTE
LIVEONE
LOZENGE
LUCERNE
MAJESTE
MAJEURE
MALEATE
MILEAGE
MOSELLE
MUSETTE
NACELLE
NANETTE
NOVELLE
OBSERVE
OBVERSE
OFFENCE
OFFENSE
OKEEFFE
ONLEAVE
ONSERVE
ORIENTE
ORNETTE
PALETTE
PAPEETE
PIPETTE
POLEAXE
PREEMIE
RECEIVE
REFEREE
RELEASE
RENEGUE
RESERVE
REVENGE
REVENUE
REVERIE
REVERSE
REWEAVE
ROSEATE
ROSELLE
ROSETTE
ROZELLE
SCIENCE
SILENCE
SINEDIE
SOMEONE
SQUEEZE
STEELIE
STEEPLE
SUZETTE
SWEETIE
TAKEONE
TERENCE
TRIESTE
UNNERVE
UNWEAVE
VALENCE
VALERIE
WHEEDLE
WHEELIE
WYNETTE

••••EE•

ANISEED
APOGEES
BAILEES
BARKEEP
BEEGEES
BELLEEK
BETWEEN
BIGFEET
BOOTEES
BUNGEES
BURGEES
CANTEEN
COFFEES
COLLEEN
COMPEER
COULEES
DECREED
DECREES
DEGREES
ELYSEES
ENTREES
EPOPEES
FIFTEEN
GENTEEL
GLACEED
GOATEED
GOATEES
HASBEEN
HAYSEED
HUMVEES
ICEBEER
INBREED
JAYCEES
JAYVEES
LESSEES
LIENEES
LINSEED
LISTEES
LOWHEEL
MAUREEN
MCQUEEN
MIDWEEK
MISDEED
MONKEES
MYNHEER
NANKEEN
PARSEES
PAWNEES
PEEWEES
PENSEES
PIONEER
PONGEES
PRETEEN
PROCEED
PUGREES
PUTTEES
RAGWEED
REDDEER
ROEDEER
RUNDEEP
RUSHEES
SAUTEED
SCHMEER
SEABEES
SEAWEED
SETTEES
SIGNEES
SIXTEEN
SOIREES
SUCCEED
TARHEEL
TEEPEES
TESTEES
THEDEEP
TOFFEES
TOUPEES
TOWHEES
UMPTEEN
UPSWEEP
USSTEEL
VERMEER
VESTEES
WEBFEET
YANKEES

••••E•E

ABILENE

ACADEME
ACCRETE
ACHIEVE
ALLHERE
ARRIERE
ATHLETE
AUSTERE
BELIEVE
BENZENE
BERGERE
BERNESE
BESIEGE
BUCKEYE
BURMESE
CATSEYE
CHINESE
COCHERE
COLLEGE
COMPERE
COMPETE
CONCEDE
CONVENE
CORTEGE
DARLENE
DEADEYE
DEPLETE
DIOCESE
DIOMEDE
EPICENE
EPIGENE
ESTHETE
ETAGERE
EVILEYE
EXCRETE
EXTREME
FISHEYE
GENOESE
GLADEYE
GRUYERE
HAWKEYE
HELLENE
HITHERE
HYGIENE
IMOGENE
LUMIERE
MACHETE
MALTESE
MARLENE
MICHELE
MIOCENE
MOLIERE
NAIVETE
NOWHERE
OBSCENE
PAPEETE
PHONEME
PRECEDE
PROTEGE
RELIEVE
REPLETE
RIVIERE
SCALENE
SECRETE
SEEHERE
SHUTEYE
SIAMESE
SINCERE
SLOVENE
SOCKEYE
SOLFEGE
SOSUEME
SOTHERE
SQUEEZE
STYRENE
SUPREME
TANGERE
TERRENE
TOLUENE
TRAPEZE
TRIREME
UKULELE
WALLEYE
WHERERE
WHEREVE

•••••EE

ADOPTEE
ALIENEE
ANNALEE
AURALEE
AWARDEE
BANSHEE
BOURREE
BRADLEE
BUGFREE
DESIREE
DEVOTEE
DRAFTEE
ELECTEE
ELMTREE
ESCAPEE
EVACUEE
FIANCEE
FORESEE
FORFREE
FREEBEE
FRISBEE
GALILEE
GENESEE
GOLFTEE
GRANDEE
GRANTEE
GUARDEE
GUMTREE
HOLYSEE
HONOREE
ICEFREE
JIMCHEE
JUBILEE
KIMCHEE
LEGATEE
LETSSEE
LOOKSEE
MANATEE
MARQUEE
MATINEE
MAYTREE
MERIMEE
MUSTSEE
NOMINEE
OAKTREE
OVERSEE
PAROLEE
PERIGEE
PLEDGEE
PRITHEE
REFEREE
REFUGEE
RETIREE
SARALEE
SHAWNEE
SOIGNEE
SPONDEE
STANDEE
STANLEE
TAXFREE
TEATREE
TOYNBEE
TRAINEE
TROCHEE
TRUCKEE
TRUSTEE
UPATREE
WHOOPEE
YAHTZEE

EF•••••

EFFACED
EFFACES
EFFECTS
EFFENDI
EFFORTS
EFFUSED
EFFUSES

E•F••••

EFFACED
EFFACES
EFFECTS
EFFENDI
EFFORTS
EFFUSED
EFFUSES
ELFLIKE
ENFOLDS
ENFORCE
EXFACTO

E••F•••

EARFLAP
EARFULS
EDIFICE
EDIFIED
EDIFIES
EYEFULS

E•••F••

EASEFUL

E••••F•

EARMUFF
EASEOFF
EASYOFF
ENGRAFT
ENGULFS

E•••••F

EARMUFF
EASEOFF
EASYOFF

•EF••••

BEFALLS
BEFOULS
DEFACED
DEFACES
DEFACTO
DEFALLA
DEFAMED
DEFAMES
DEFARGE
DEFAULT
DEFEATS
DEFECTS
DEFENCE
DEFENDS
DEFENSE
DEFIANT
DEFICIT
DEFILED
DEFILER
DEFILES
DEFINED
DEFINES
DEFLATE
DEFLECT
DEFORMS
DEFRAUD
DEFRAYS
DEFROCK
DEFROST
DEFTEST
DEFUNCT
DEFUSED
DEFUSES
DEFYING
GEFILTE
HEFTIER
HEFTILY
HEFTING
JEFFERS
JEFFREY
LEFTIES
LEFTIST
LEFTOFF
LEFTOUT
REFACED
REFACES
REFEREE
REFERTO
REFFING
REFILED
REFILES
REFILLS
REFILMS
REFINED
REFINER
REFINES
REFIRES
REFLAGS
REFLECT
REFOCUS
REFORMS
REFRACT
REFRAIN
REFRAME
REFRESH
REFRIED
REFRIES
REFUELS
REFUGEE
REFUGES
REFUNDS
REFUSAL
REFUSED
REFUSER
REFUSES
REFUTED
REFUTER
REFUTES

•E•F•••

AELFRIC
BEEFALO
BEEFIER
BEEFING
BEEFSUP
BEEFTEA
BELFAST
DEAFENS
DEAFEST
DEIFIED
DEIFIES
FEIFFER
HEIFERS
HEIFETZ
JEFFERS
JEFFREY
LEAFAGE
LEAFIER
LEAFING
LEAFLET
LENFANT
MENFOLK
PEAFOWL
PERFECT
PERFIDY
PERFORM
PERFUME
REAFFIX
REDFINS
REDFIRS
REDFLAG
REDFORD
REEFERS
REEFING
REFFING
REIFIED
REIFIES
SEAFANS
SEAFIRE
SEAFOOD
SELFISH
SERFDOM
TENFOLD
TENFOUR
WEBFEET
WEBFOOT
WELFARE

•E••F••

BENEFIT
DEEPFAT
DEEPFRY
DEERFLY
FEARFUL
FEELFOR
FEIFFER
FELLFOR
FELTFOR
HEATFUL
HEEDFUL
HELPFUL
LETSFLY
NEEDFUL
REAFFIX
REBUFFS
RESTFUL
SEENFIT
SEESFIT
SELLFOR
SENDFOR
SENTFOR
SENUFOS
TEARFUL
TESTFLY
WELLFED
WENTFOR
ZESTFUL

•E•••F•

BEAROFF
BEATIFY
BEGSOFF
BELIEFS
CERTIFY
FELLOFF
GETSOFF
HEADOFF
HELDOFF
KEEPOFF
KEPTOFF
LEADOFF
LEFTOFF
LETSOFF
NESCAFE
NEWLEFT
PEELOFF
PETRIFY
REBUFFS
RECTIFY
REELOFF
RELIEFS
REUNIFY
SEALOFF
SEENOFF
SEESOFF
SELLOFF
SENDOFF
SENTOFF
SETSOFF
TEAROFF
TEEDOFF
TEESOFF
TELLOFF
TERRIFY
TESTIFY
VERSIFY
WEAROFF
WELLOFF
WENTOFF

•E••••F

BEAROFF
BEGSOFF
BEOWULF
BERIDOF
DEBRIEF
FELLOFF
GETSOFF
HEADOFF
HEARDOF
HEARSOF
HELDOFF
KEEPOFF
KEPTOFF
LEADOFF
LEFTOFF
LETSOFF
NETSURF
PEELOFF
REDWOLF
REELOFF
REPROOF
SEALOFF
SEAWOLF
SEENOFF
SEESOFF
SELLOFF
SENDOFF
SENTOFF
SETSOFF
TEALEAF
TEAROFF
TEEDOFF
TEESOFF
TELLOFF
TELLSOF
WEAROFF
WELLOFF
WENTOFF

••EF•••

BEEFALO
BEEFIER
BEEFING
BEEFSUP
BEEFTEA
EYEFULS
FIEFDOM
ICEFLOE
ICEFOGS
ICEFREE
OLEFINS
PREFABS
PREFACE
PREFECT
PREFERS
REEFERS
REEFING
THEFIRM
THEFONZ
TREFOIL

••E•F••

BRERFOX
DEEPFAT
DEEPFRY
DEERFLY
DREYFUS
FEELFOR
FRETFUL
GLEEFUL
GOESFOR
HEEDFUL
NEEDFUL
OKEEFFE
OVERFLY
SEENFIT
SEESFIT
TWELFTH

••E••F•

ALEWIFE
BLEWOFF
DIEDOFF
DIESOFF
GOESOFF
KEEPOFF
OKEEFFE
PEELOFF
REELOFF
SEENOFF
SEESOFF
SHERIFF
SPECIFY
TEEDOFF
TEESOFF

••E•••F

AHEADOF
BLEWOFF
DIEDOFF
DIESOFF
GOESOFF
KEEPOFF
ONESELF
PEELOFF
REELOFF
SEENOFF
SEESOFF
SHERIFF
SHEWOLF
SPEAKOF
TEEDOFF
TEESOFF
THEREOF
WHEREOF

•••EF••

BALEFUL
BANEFUL
BENEFIT
BLUEFIN
BLUEFOX
BRIEFED
BRIEFER
BRIEFLY
CAREFOR
CAREFUL
CHIEFLY
DAREFUL
DIREFUL
DOLEFUL
DONEFOR
EASEFUL
FAKEFUR
FATEFUL
FIREFLY
GLEEFUL
HATEFUL
HOPEFUL
LIFEFUL
MADEFOR
MAKEFOR
MALEFIC
MUSEFUL
OKEEFFE
PAGEFUL
PINEFOR
PIPEFUL
POKEFUN
RAGEFUL
TUNEFUL
VOTEFOR
WAKEFUL

•••E•F•

BAKEOFF
BITEOFF
CAMEOFF
COMEOFF
DOZEOFF
EASEOFF
FACEOFF
FIREOFF
GAVEOFF
GIVEOFF
MADEOFF
MAKEOFF
OKEEFFE
RAKEOFF
RIDEOFF
RODEOFF
TAKEOFF
TIMEOFF
TOREOFF
WAVEOFF
WOREOFF

•••E••F

BAKEOFF
BITEOFF
CAMEOFF
COMEOFF
DOZEOFF
EASEOFF
FACEOFF
FIREOFF
GAVEOFF
GIVEOFF
MADEOFF
MAKEOFF
RAKEOFF
RIDEOFF
RODEOFF
TAKEOFF
TIMEOFF
TIREDOF
TOREOFF
WAVEOFF
WOREOFF

••••EF•

BELIEFS
FARLEFT
LIQUEFY
NEWLEFT
RELIEFS
STUPEFY

••••E•F

AWAREOF
BAYLEAF
FIGLEAF
FLYLEAF
HERSELF
HIMSELF
INAWEOF
NONSELF
OAKLEAF
ONESELF
OURSELF
SPOKEOF
TEALEAF
THEREOF
THYSELF
WHEREOF

•••••EF

DEBRIEF
INBRIEF

EG•••••

EGALITE
EGESTED
EGGCASE
EGGCUPS
EGGEDON
EGGHEAD
EGGIEST
EGGLESS
EGGNOGS
EGGROLL
EGOISTS
EGOTISM
EGOTIST
EGOTRIP

E•G••••

EAGERER
EAGERLY
EAGLETS
EAGLING
EDGEDIN
EDGEOUT
EDGESIN
EDGIEST
EDGINGS
EGGCASE
EGGCUPS
EGGEDON
EGGHEAD
EGGIEST
EGGLESS
EGGNOGS
EGGROLL
EIGHTAM
EIGHTHS
EIGHTPM
ELGRECO
ENGAGED
ENGAGES
ENGARDE
ENGINES
ENGIRDS
ENGLAND
ENGLISH
ENGLUND
ENGORGE
ENGRAFT
ENGRAMS
ENGRAVE
ENGROSS
ENGULFS
ERGATES
EUGENIE

E••G•••

ELEGANT
ELEGIAC
ELEGIES
ELEGIST
EMIGRES
ENDGAME
ENIGMAS
EPIGENE
EPIGONE
EPIGRAM
ETAGERE
EXIGENT

E•••G••

ECLOGUE
ELOIGNS
EMERGED
EMERGES
ENCAGED
ENCAGES
ENGAGED
ENGAGES
ENRAGED
ENRAGES
ENSIGNS
EPERGNE
EVANGEL

E••••G•

EARWIGS
ECOLOGY
EDGINGS
EGGNOGS
EMBARGO
ENDINGS
ENGORGE
ENLARGE
EPILOGS
EXPUNGE

E•••••G

EAGLING
EARNING
EARPLUG
EARRING
ECHOING
EDDYING
EDITING
EDUCING
ELATING
ELIDING
ELOPING
ELUDING
ELUTING
EMOTING
ENDUING
ENSUING
ENURING
ENVYING
ERASING
ERELONG
ERODING
ESPYING
ETCHING
EVADING
EVENING
EVOKING
EXILING
EXITING
EXUDING

•EG••••

BEGGARS
BEGGING
BEGONIA
BEGORRA
BEGRIME
BEGSOFF
BEGUILE
BEGUINE
DEGAUSS
DEGRADE
DEGREES
DEGUSTS
HEGIRAS
KEGLERS
LEGALLY
LEGATEE
LEGATES
LEGATOS
LEGENDS
LEGGIER
LEGGING
LEGHORN
LEGIBLE
LEGIBLY
LEGIONS
LEGISTS
LEGLESS
LEGLIKE
LEGPULL
LEGRAND
LEGROOM
LEGUMES
LEGWORK
MEGAHIT
MEGIDDO
MEGOHMS
MEGRIMS
MEGRYAN
NEGATED
NEGATER
NEGATES
NEGATOR
NEGLECT
PEGASUS
PEGGING
PEGLESS
PEGLIKE
PEGTOPS
REGAINS
REGALED
REGALES
REGALIA
REGALLY
REGARDS
REGATTA
REGENCY
REGENTS
REGIMEN
REGIMES
REGIONS
REGLETS
REGLUED
REGLUES
REGNANT
REGRADE
REGRESS
REGRETS
REGROUP
REGULAR
REGULUS
SEGMENT
SEGOVIA
VEGETAL
VEGGIES
VEGGING

•E•G•••

BEAGLES
BEEGEES
BEEGUMS
BEGGARS
BEGGING
BELGIAN
BELGIUM
BENGALI
BENGALS
BERGERE
BERGMAN
BERGSON
DEIGNED
FEIGNED
GEEGAWS
GENGHIS
GEWGAWS
HEDGERS
HEDGIER
HEDGING
HEIGHHO
HEIGHTS
JETGUNS
KEYGRIP
LEAGUES
LEDGERS
LEDGIER
LEGGIER
LEGGING
LENGTHS
LENGTHY
MERGERS
MERGING
NEIGHED
NEWGATE
PEGGING
PENGUIN
PERGOLA
PEUGEOT
REAGENT
REDGUMS
REIGNED
SEAGATE
SEAGIRT
SEAGRAM
SEAGULL
SEDGIER
VEGGIES
VEGGING
VEIGHTS
VERGERS
VERGING
WEDGIER
WEDGIES
WEDGING
WEIGHED
WEIGHIN
WEIGHTS
WEIGHTY
YEVGENY
ZEUGMAS

•E••G••

DECAGON
DELIGHT
DELUGED
DELUGES
DEMIGOD
DESIGNS
GEORGES
GEORGIA
HEXAGON
MEDIGAP
MENAGES
NEWAGER
PELAGES
PELAGIC
PERIGEE
REARGUE
REFUGEE
REFUGES
RELIGHT
REMIGES
RENEGED
RENEGER
RENEGES
RENEGUE
REPUGNS
RESIGNS
SENEGAL
SEVIGNE
TEARGAS

•E•••G•

BEDBUGS
BELONGS
BENDIGO
BESIEGE
DEBARGE
DEFARGE
GEOLOGY
HERBAGE
HEXSIGN
KELLOGG
LEAFAGE
LEAKAGE
LENTIGO
MELANGE
MESSAGE
NESTEGG
PEERAGE
PEONAGE
REDALGA
REDDOGS
REFLAGS
REHANGS
RESINGS
RESTAGE
RESURGE
REVENGE
SEABAGS
SEADOGS
SEALEGS
SELVAGE
TEABAGS
TEENAGE
VERDUGO
VERTIGO
VESTIGE
WEBPAGE

•E••••G

BEADING
BEAMING
BEANBAG
BEANING
BEARHUG
BEARING
BEATING
BEDDING
BEEFING
BEEPING
BEGGING
BEIJING
BELLING
BELTBAG
BELTING
BELYING
BENDING
BESTING
BETTING
CEASING
CEILING
CENSING
CESSING
DEALING
DECALOG
DECKING
DEEDING
DEEMING
DEFYING
DEICING
DELEING
DELVING
DENTING
DENYING
DERRING
FEARING
FEEDBAG
FEEDING
FEELING
FELLING
FENCING
FENDING
FESSING
FEUDING
GEARING
GELDING
GELLING
GETTING
HEADING
HEALING
HEAPING
HEARING
HEATING
HEAVING
HEDGING
HEEDING
HEELING
HEFTING
HELMING
HELPING
HEMMING
HENTING
HERDING
HERRING

JEERING
JELLING
JERKING
JESTING
JETTING
KEELING
KEENING
KEEPING
KELLOGG
KERNING
KEYRING
LEADING
LEAFING
LEAKING
LEANING
LEAPING
LEASING
LEAVING
LEERING
LEGGING
LEIPZIG
LEMMING
LENDING
LESSING
LETTING
LEVYING
MEANING
MEETING
MELDING
MELTING
MENDING
MEOWING
MERGING
MESHING
MESSING
MEWLING
NEARING
NECKING
NEEDING
NESTEGG
NESTING
NETTING
PEAKING
PEALING
PEATBOG
PECKING
PEEKING
PEELING
PEEPING
PEERING
PEEVING
PEGGING
PELTING
PENDING
PENNING
PEPPING
PERKING
PERMING
PETTING
READING
REAMING
REAPING
REARING
REDDING
REDFLAG
REDOING
REDWING
REEDING
REEFING
REEKING
REELING
REFFING
REINING
RELYING
RENDING
RENTING
RESTING
REVVING
SEABORG
SEALING
SEAMING
SEARING
SEASLUG
SEATING
SEEDING
SEEKING
SEEMING
SEEPING
SEINING
SEIZING
SELLING
SEMILOG
SENDING
SENSING
SERLING
SERVING
SETTING
TEAMING
TEARING
TEASING
TEDDING
TEEMING
TELLING
TENDING
TENSING
TENTING
TENZING
TERMING
TESTING
VEERING
VEGGING
VEILING
VEINING
VENDING
VENTING
VERGING
VESTING
VETOING
VETTING
WEANING
WEARING
WEAVING
WEBBING
WEDDING
WEDGING
WEEDING
WEEPING
WELDING
WELLING
WELTING
WENDING
WETTING
YEANING
YELLING
YELPING
YERKING
YESSING
ZEITUNG
ZEROING

••EG•••
BEEGEES
BEEGUMS
ELEGANT
ELEGIAC
ELEGIES
ELEGIST
GEEGAWS
GREGORY
JAEGERS
OREGANO

••E•G••
AVENGED
AVENGER
AVENGES
DREDGED
DREDGER
DREDGES
EMERGED
EMERGES
EPERGNE
FLEDGED
FLEDGES
FREIGHT
GIELGUD
ICEAGES
PLEDGED
PLEDGEE
PLEDGER
PLEDGES
SLEDGES
SLEIGHS
SLEIGHT
STEIGER
STENGEL
XHEIGHT

••E••G•
AGESAGO
AMERIGO
AVERAGE
ICEBAGS
ICEFOGS
OVERAGE
PEERAGE
PRESAGE
PYEDOGS
TEENAGE
THEURGY

••E•••G
ANELING
AREARUG
BEEFING
BEEPING
BREWING
CHEWING
CREWING
DEEDING
DEEMING
DIETING
DUELING
ERELONG
EVENING
FEEDBAG
FEEDING
FEELING
FLEABAG
FLEEING
FLEMING
FLEXING
FLEYING
FREEING
FUELING
GREYING
HEEDING
HEELING
ICEBERG
JEERING
JREWING
KEELING
KEENING
KEEPING
KNEEING
LEERING
MEETING
NEEDING
OBEYING
OPENING
OVERBIG
PEEKING
PEELING
PEEPING
PEERING
PEEVING
PFENNIG
PIECING
QUEUING
REEDING
REEFING
REEKING
REELING
SEEDING
SEEKING
SEEMING
SEEPING
SHEBANG
SKEWING
SLEDDOG
SPECING
SPEWING
STEWING
TEEMING
TIERING
TREEING
VEERING
VIEWING
WEEDING
WEEPING

•••EG••
ALLEGED
ALLEGER
ALLEGES
ALLEGRO
ASSEGAI
BADEGGS
BLUEGUM
BODEGAS
BRUEGEL
DONEGAL
ILLEGAL
INTEGER
INTEGRA
MANEGES
NOSEGAY
RAREGAS
RAWEGGS
RENEGED
RENEGER
RENEGES
RENEGUE
SENEGAL
SLOEGIN
SPIEGEL
STIEGEL
VINEGAR
WISEGUY
WOBEGON

•••E•G•
ACREAGE
ALLERGY
ARLEDGE
BADEGGS
DIVERGE
FABERGE
FOREIGN
INVEIGH
LINEAGE
LOZENGE
MARENGO
MILEAGE
RALEIGH
RAWEGGS
REVENGE
SYNERGY
UNDERGO

•••E••G
ANTEING
BLUEING
CLUEING
DELEING
FIREBUG
FIREDOG
FLEEING
FORELEG
FREEING
GATELEG
JUNEBUG
KNEEING
LOVEBUG
NAMETAG
NOSEBAG
SHOEING
TIMELAG
TOTEBAG
TREEING
TRUEING
YULELOG

••••EG•
BESIEGE
COLLEGE
CORTEGE
DOGLEGS
GOODEGG
MONTEGO
MUSKEGS
NESTEGG
NORIEGA
NUTMEGS
ONTHEGO
PROTEGE
SEALEGS
SOLFEGE
TUAREGS

••••E•G
GINSENG
GOODEGG
ICEBERG
NESTEGG

•••••EG
BOOTLEG
FORELEG
GATELEG

EH•••••
EHRLICH

E•H••••
ECHELON
ECHIDNA
ECHINUS
ECHOING
ENHANCE
ETHANOL
ETHICAL
ETHNICS
EXHALED
EXHALES
EXHAUST
EXHIBIT
EXHORTS

E••H•••
EARHART
EBWHITE
ECKHART
EGGHEAD
EIGHTAM
EIGHTHS
EIGHTPM
ELKHART
ENCHAIN
ENCHANT
ENTHRAL
ENTHUSE
ESCHEAT
ESCHEWS
ESTHETE
ETCHANT
ETCHERS
ETCHING
EUCHRED
EUCHRES
EUPHONY
EYEHOLE

E•••H••
EARSHOT
EARTHEN
EARTHLY
EDAPHIC
EPITHET
EPOCHAL
EREWHON
EYESHOT

E••••H•
EARACHE
EIGHTHS
EMPATHY
EOLITHS
EPARCHS
EPARCHY
EXARCHS

E•••••H
EHRLICH
ENGLISH
EVANISH
EYELASH
EYEWASH

•EH••••
BEHAVED
BEHAVES
BEHEADS
BEHESTS
BEHOLDS
BEHOOVE
BEHOVED
BEHOVES
DEHISCE
DEHORNS
LEHAVRE
REHANGS
REHEALS
REHEARD
REHEARS
REHEATS
REHEELS
REHIRED
REHIRES
REHOOKS
TEHERAN
VEHICLE

•E•H•••
AETHERS
BEEHIVE
BETHANY
BETHELS
BETHINK
CEPHEUS
HEEHAWS
HESHVAN
KEYHOLE
LEGHORN
MENHIRS
MESHIER
MESHING
METHANE
METHODS
NEPHEWS
NEWHART
PEAHENS
PERHAPS
RECHALK
RECHECK
RECHOSE
REDHAIR
REDHATS
REDHEAD
REDHEAT
REDHOTS
RESHIPS
RESHOES
RESHOOT
RETHINK
SEEHERE
TECHIER
TECHIES
TERHUNE
TETHERS
WETHERS
YESHIVA
ZEPHYRS

•E••H••
BEACHED
BEACHES
BEARHUG
BEECHAM
BEECHER
BEECHES
BELCHED
BELCHES
BELLHOP
BENCHED
BENCHES
BENTHAM
BERTHED
DELPHIC
FEATHER
FETCHED
FETCHES
GEEWHIZ
GEISHAS
GENGHIS
HEATHEN
HEATHER
HEIGHHO
HEIGHTS
HERSHEY
KEESHAN
KERCHOO
KETCHAM
KETCHES
KETCHUP
LEACHED
LEACHES
LEASHED
LEASHES
LEATHER
LEECHED
LEECHES
MEGAHIT
MEGOHMS
MEMPHIS
MENTHOL
MENUHIN
NEEDHAM
NEIGHED
NEITHER
PEACHED
PEACHES
PERCHED
PERCHES
REACHED
REACHES
REUTHER
SEETHED
SEETHES
SEICHES
TEACHER
TEACHES
TEACHIN
TEASHOP
TEETHED
TEETHER
TEETHES
TEICHER
TENTHLY
TETCHED
VEIGHTS
VETCHES
WEATHER
WEIGHED
WEIGHIN
WEIGHTS
WEIGHTY
WELCHED
WELCHES
WENCHES
WERNHER
WERTHER

•E•••H•
BELUSHI
CERIPHS
DEARTHS
DELIGHT
DENNEHY
FELLAHS
HEALTHY
HEARTHS
HEAVEHO
HEIGHHO
JERICHO
KENOSHA
LENGTHS
LENGTHY
LESOTHO
PENUCHE
RELIGHT
SERAPHS
TEMPEHS
TERAPHS
WEALTHY
ZENITHS

•E••••H
BEAMISH
BEARISH
BEAUISH
BENEATH
BESEECH
BETROTH
BEWITCH
DEBAUCH
DEBORAH
DEBOUCH
DELILAH
DERVISH
HELLISH
HENNISH
JETWASH
KENNETH
KENTISH
LETTISH
MENORAH
MESSIAH
NEBBISH
NEOLITH
NESMITH
NEWMATH
PEAKISH
PECKISH
PEEVISH
PELTISH
PERKISH
PETTISH
REBEKAH
REBIRTH
REDDISH
REFRESH
RETEACH
RETOUCH
SELFISH
SEVENTH
WEAKISH
WENDISH
WETTISH
YERKISH

••EH•••
BEEHIVE
DIEHARD
EYEHOLE
HEEHAWS
JOEHILL
PREHEAT
SEEHERE
TOEHOLD

••E•H••
BEECHAM
BEECHER
BEECHES
CHECHEN
CHEKHOV
CRECHES
EREWHON
EYESHOT
FLECHES
FLESHED
FLESHES
FLESHLY
FRESHEN
FRESHER
FRESHET
FRESHLY
GEEWHIZ
GREYHEN
ICESHOW
KEESHAN
LEECHED
LEECHES
NEEDHAM
ONESHOT
QUECHUA
SEETHED
SEETHES
STEPHEN
TEETHED
TEETHER
TEETHES
TOESHOE
WHETHER

••E••H•
BREATHE
BREATHS
BREATHY
FREIGHT
GUELPHS
NIEBUHR
PREACHY
SHEATHE
SHEATHS
SHEIKHS
SKETCHY
SLEIGHS
SLEIGHT
SLEUTHS
WREATHE
WREATHS
XHEIGHT

••E•••H
BLEMISH
BREADTH
CHEETAH
CHERISH
EYELASH
EYEWASH
FLEMISH
GREYISH
PEEVISH
PREWASH
RHENISH
STEALTH
SWEDISH
TWELFTH
UNEARTH
WHEYISH

•••EH••
BASEHIT
MADEHAY
MAKEHAY
SAGEHEN
SOMEHOW

•••E•H•
DALETHS
LAMEDHS
SAMECHS
UTRECHT
VOTECHS

•••E••H
BENEATH
BESEECH
BLUEISH
BONEASH
CHEETAH
DOZENTH
IMPEACH
INDEPTH
INVEIGH
NINEVEH
OGREISH
RALEIGH
REBEKAH
RETEACH
SCREECH
SEVENTH
SQUELCH
STRETCH
UNLEASH

••••EH•
DENNEHY
HEAVEHO
TEMPEHS

••••E•H
BESEECH
CALTECH
GWYNETH
HIALEAH
JAPHETH
KENNETH
LOWTECH
MACBETH
NCWYETH
REFRESH
SCREECH

•••••EH
NINEVEH

EI•••••
EIGHTAM
EIGHTHS
EIGHTPM

E•I••••
EDIBLES
EDIFICE
EDIFIED
EDIFIES
EDITING
EDITION
EDITORS
EDITOUT
ELICITS
ELIDING
ELISION
ELITISM
ELITIST
ELIXIRS
EMIGRES
EMINENT
EMIRATE
EMITTED
EMITTER
ENIGMAS
ENISLED
ENISLES
EPICENE
EPICURE
EPIGENE
EPIGONE
EPIGRAM
EPILOGS
EPISODE
EPISTLE
EPITHET
EPITOME
ERICSON
ERISTIC
ERITREA
ETIENNE
EVICTED
EVIDENT
EVILEST
EVILEYE
EVILLER
EVINCED
EVINCES
EXIGENT
EXILING
EXISTED
EXITING

E••I•••
EASIEST
ECHIDNA
ECHINUS
ECLIPSE
EDGIEST
EDGINGS
EELIEST
EERIEST
EGGIEST
EGOISTS
ELEISON
ELLIOTT
ELLIPSE
ELLISON
ELMISTI
ELOIGNS
EMAILED
EMPIRES
ENCINAS
ENDINGS
ENDIVES
ENGINES
ENGIRDS
ENLISTS
ENLIVEN
ENSIGNS
ENSILED
ENSILES
ENTICED
ENTICER
ENTICES
ENTITLE
ENVIERS
ENVIOUS
EOLITHS
EPSILON
EQUINES
EQUINOX
ERMINES
ESKIMOS
ESPIALS
ESTIVAL
ETHICAL
ETOILES
EXCISED
EXCISES
EXCITED
EXCITES
EXHIBIT
EXPIATE
EXPIRED
EXPIRES
EXTINCT
EXWIVES

E•••I••
EAGLING
EARLIER
EARLIKE
EARNING
EARRING
EARWIGS
EBBTIDE
EBONIES
EBONITE
EBWHITE
ECHOING
ECLAIRS
EDACITY
EDDYING
EDIFICE
EDIFIED
EDIFIES
EDITING
EDITION
EDUCING
EELLIKE
EGALITE
EGOTISM
EGOTIST
EHRLICH
ELAAIUN
ELAPIDS
ELATING
ELATION
ELEGIAC
ELEGIES
ELEGIST
ELFLIKE
ELICITS
ELIDING
ELISION
ELITISM
ELITIST
ELIXIRS
ELOPING
ELUDING
ELUSIVE
ELUTING
ELUTION
ELUVIUM
ELYSIAN
ELYSIUM
EMERITA
EMERITI
EMOTING
EMOTION
EMOTIVE
EMPTIED
EMPTIER
EMPTIES
EMPTILY
ENDUING
ENDWISE
ENEMIES
ENGLISH
ENJOINS
ENQUIRE
ENQUIRY
ENSKIED
ENSKIES
ENSUING
ENSUITE
ENTAILS
ENTRIES
ENTWINE
ENURING
ENVYING
EPEEIST
EPOXIES
ERASING
EREMITE
ERODING
EROSION
EROSIVE
EROTICA
ERSKINE
ERUDITE
ESPYING
ESQUIRE
ETAMINE
ETCHING
ETESIAN
ETHNICS
ETONIAN
EVADING
EVANISH
EVASION
EVASIVE
EVENING
EVOKING
EXAMINE
EXANIMO
EXILING
EXITING
EXOTICA
EXOTICS
EXUDING
EYELIDS
EYELIKE
EZEKIEL

E••••I•
EASEDIN
EASESIN
ECDYSIS
EDAPHIC
EDGEDIN
EDGESIN
EELSKIN
EGOTRIP
ELASTIC
EMBROIL
EMPORIA
ENCHAIN
ENCOMIA
ENDEMIC
ENTRAIN
EPSTEIN
ERISTIC
ERRATIC
ESTONIA
ESTORIL
ETRURIA
EUGENIE
EURASIA
EVENKIS
EXCLAIM
EXHIBIT
EXPLAIN
EXPLOIT
EXURBIA

E•••••I
EFFENDI
ELMISTI
EMERITI
EXEMPLI

•EI••••
BEIJING
CEILING
DEICERS

DEICING
DEIFIED
DEIFIES
DEIGNED
DEITIES
FEIFFER
FEIGNED
FEINTED
GEISHAS
HEIFERS
HEIFETZ
HEIGHHO
HEIGHTS
HEINOUS
HEIRESS
HEISMAN
HEISTED
KEILLOR
LEIBNIZ
LEIPZIG
LEISTER
LEISURE
MEINIES
MEIOSES
MEIOSIS
MEIOTIC
MEISSEN
MEISTER
NEIGHED
NEITHER
REIFIED
REIFIES
REIGNED
REINING
REINKED
REINSIN
REISSUE
REITMAN
SEICHES
SEIDELS
SEINERS
SEINING
SEISMIC
SEIZERS
SEIZING
TEICHER
VEIGHTS
VEILING
VEINIER
VEINING
WEIGHED
WEIGHIN
WEIGHTS
WEIGHTY
WEIRDER
WEIRDLY
WEIRDOS
ZEITUNG

•E•I•••

AEDILES
AERIALS
AERIEST
BEDIZEN
BELIEFS
BELIEVE
BELINDA
BEMIRED
BEMIRES
BENISON
BERIDOF
BESIDES
BESIEGE
BETIDED
BETIDES
BETIMES
BETISES
BEWITCH
BEZIERS
BEZIQUE
CECILIA
CEDILLA
CERIPHS
DEBITED
DECIBEL
DECIDED
DECIDES
DECIMAL
DEFIANT
DEFICIT
DEFILED
DEFILER
DEFILES
DEFINED
DEFINES
DEHISCE
DELIBES
DELICTI
DELICTS
DELIGHT
DELILAH
DELIMIT
DELIRIA
DELISTS
DELIVER
DEMIGOD
DEMILLE
DEMISED
DEMISES
DENIALS
DENIERS
DENIZEN
DEPICTS
DERIDED
DERIDES
DERIVED
DERIVES
DESIGNS
DESIRED
DESIREE
DESIRES
DESISTS
DEVIANT
DEVIATE
DEVICES
DEVILED
DEVILLE
DEVILRY
DEVIOUS
DEVISED
DEVISES
EELIEST
EERIEST
FELICIA
FELINES
FENIANS
FETIDLY
GEFILTE
GELIDLY
GERITOL
GETINTO
GETITON
HEGIRAS
HELICAL
HELICES
HELICON
HELIPAD
HELIXES
JERICHO
JEWISON
LEGIBLE
LEGIBLY
LEGIONS
LEGISTS
LEMIEUX
LENIENT
LETINON
LETITBE
LETITIA
LEVIERS
LEVITES
LEXICAL
LEXICON
MEDIANS
MEDIANT
MEDIATE
MEDICAL
MEDICOS
MEDIGAP
MEDIUMS
MEGIDDO
MELINDA
MELISSA
MENIALS
MENISCI
MERIMEE
MERINOS
MERITED
METIERS
MEXICAN
NETIZEN
NEVILLE
OEDIPAL
OEDIPUS
PEDICAB
PEDICEL
PEDICLE
PELICAN
PELISSE
PEMICAN
PERIDOT
PERIGEE
PERIODS
PETIOLE
PETITES
REAIMED
REAIRED
REBINDS
REBIRTH
RECIPES
RECITAL
RECITED
RECITER
RECITES
REDIALS
REFILED
REFILES
REFILLS
REFILMS
REFINED
REFINER
REFINES
REFIRES
REGIMEN
REGIMES
REGIONS
REHIRED
REHIRES
RELIANT
RELICTS
RELIEFS
RELIEVE
RELIEVO
RELIGHT
RELINED
RELINES
RELISTS
RELIVED
RELIVES
REMIGES
REMINDS
REMIXED
REMIXES
REOILED
REPINED
REPINES
RERINSE
RESIDED
RESIDES
RESIDUE
RESIGNS
RESILED
RESILES
RESINGS
RESISTS
RETIARY
RETICLE
RETILED
RETILES
RETIMED
RETIMES
RETINAE
RETINAL
RETINAS
RETINUE
RETIRED
RETIREE
RETIRES
RETITLE
REVIEWS
REVILED
REVILES
REVISED
REVISER
REVISES
REVISIT
REVIVAL
REVIVED
REVIVES
REWINDS
REWIRED
REWIRES
SEMILOG
SEMINAL
SEMINAR
SEMIPRO
SEMITES
SEMITIC
SENIORS
SERIALS
SERIATE
SERIOUS
SETINTO
SEVIGNE
SEVILLE
SEXIEST
SEXISTS
TEDIOUS
TEDIUMS
TEPIDLY
VEHICLE
VENISON
VERISMO
VERITAS
ZENITHS

•E••I••

AEOLIAN
BEADIER
BEADING
BEAMIER
BEAMING
BEAMISH
BEANIES
BEANING
BEARING
BEARISH
BEATIFY
BEATING
BEAUISH
BEDDING
BEDLIKE
BEDSIDE
BEDTIME
BEEFIER
BEEFING
BEEHIVE
BEELIKE
BEELINE
BEEPING
BEERIER
BEGGING
BEGRIME
BEGUILE
BEGUINE
BEIJING
BELGIAN
BELGIUM
BELLIED
BELLIES
BELLING
BELLINI
BELTING
BELYING
BENDIER
BENDIGO
BENDING
BERLIOZ
BERLITZ
BERNICE
BERRIED
BERRIES
BESTIAL
BESTING
BESTIRS
BETHINK
BETTING
BETWIXT
BEWAILS
CEASING
CEILING
CELLINI
CELLIST
CELSIUS
CELTICS
CENSING
CENTIME
CENTIMO
CERTIFY
CERVIDS
CESSING
CESSION
DEALING
DEARIES
DEBRIEF
DECEITS
DECEIVE
DECKING
DECLINE
DECRIED
DECRIER
DECRIES
DEEDING
DEEMING
DEFYING
DEICING
DEIFIED
DEIFIES
DEITIES
DELEING
DELUISE
DELVING
DENSITY
DENTINE
DENTING
DENTIST
DENYING
DEPRIVE
DERAILS
DERBIES
DERNIER
DERRICK
DERRING
DERVISH
DESPISE
DESPITE
DESTINE
DESTINY
DETAILS
DETAINS
DEVEINS
DEVRIES
DEWLINE
EELLIKE
FEARING
FEBRILE
FEEDING
FEELING
FELLIES
FELLING
FELLINI
FENCING
FENDING
FENNIER
FERMIUM
FERNIER
FERRIED
FERRIES
FERRITE
FERTILE
FESSING
FESTIVA
FESTIVE
FEUDING
GEARING
GEEKIER
GELDING
GELLING
GEMLIKE
GEMMIER
GENTIAN
GENTILE
GENUINE
GERAINT
GERBILS
GERMIER
GETTING
HEADIER
HEADILY
HEADING
HEALING
HEAPING
HEARING
HEATING
HEAVIER
HEAVIES
HEAVILY
HEAVING
HEDGIER
HEDGING
HEEDING
HEELING
HEFTIER
HEFTILY
HEFTING
HELLION
HELLISH
HELMING
HELOISE
HELPING
HEMLINE
HEMMING
HENBITS
HENLIKE
HENNISH
HENTING
HERBIER
HERDING
HERMITS
HEROICS
HEROINE
HEROISM
HERRING
HERRIOT
HESSIAN
HEXSIGN
JEEBIES
JEERING
JELLIED
JELLIES
JELLING
JEMMIED
JEMMIES
JENNIES
JERKIER
JERKILY
JERKING
JERKINS
JESSICA
JESTING
JESUITS
JETTIES
JETTING
KEELING
KEENING
KEEPING
KELPIES
KENTISH
KERNING
KEWPIES
KEYLIME
KEYRING
LEADIER
LEADING
LEADINS
LEAFIER
LEAFING
LEAKIER
LEAKING
LEANING
LEAPING
LEARIER
LEASING
LEAVING
LEDGIER
LEERIER
LEERILY
LEERING
LEETIDE
LEFTIES
LEFTIST
LEGGIER
LEGGING
LEGLIKE
LEMMING
LEMPIRA
LENDING
LENTIGO
LENTILS
LEONIDS
LEONINE
LEPPIES
LESSING
LETTING
LETTISH
LEUCINE
LEVYING
MEALIER
MEALIES
MEANIES
MEANING
MEATIER
MEATILY
MEETING
MEGRIMS
MEINIES
MELDING
MELTING
MEMOIRE
MEMOIRS
MENDING
MENHIRS
MENTION
MENZIES
MEOWING
MERCIES
MERGING
MERRIER
MERRILL
MERRILY
MESHIER
MESHING
MESSIAH
MESSIER
MESSILY
MESSINA
MESSING
MESTIZA
MESTIZO
METRICS
MEWLING
NEARING
NEBBISH
NECKING
NEDDIES
NEEDIER
NEEDILY
NEEDING
NEOLITH
NERDIER
NEREIDS
NERVIER
NERVILY
NESMITH
NESTING
NETLIKE
NETTING
NEWSIER
NEWSIES
PEAKING
PEAKISH
PEALIKE
PEALING
PEATIER
PECKIER
PECKING
PECKISH
PECTINS
PEEKING
PEELING
PEEPING
PEERING
PEEVING
PEEVISH
PEGGING
PEGLIKE
PELTING
PELTISH
PENCILS
PENDING
PENLIKE
PENNIES
PENNING
PENSION
PENSIVE
PENTIUM
PEONIES
PEPPIER
PEPPILY
PEPPING
PEPSINS
PEPTIDE
PERDIEM
PERFIDY
PERKIER
PERKILY
PERKING
PERKINS
PERKISH
PERLITE
PERMING
PERMITS
PERRIER
PERSIAN
PERSIST
PERSIUS
PESKIER
PESKILY
PETRIFY
PETTIER
PETTILY
PETTING
PETTISH
READIED
READIER
READIES
READILY
READING
REALISE
REALISM
REALIST
REALITY
REALIZE
REAMING
REAPING
REARING
REBOILS
REBUILD
REBUILT
RECEIPT
RECEIVE
RECLINE
RECOILS
RECTIFY
REDBIRD
REDDING
REDDISH
REDFINS
REDFIRS
REDLINE
REDOING
REDPINE
REDWINE
REDWING
REEDIER
REEDING
REEDITS
REEFING
REEKING
REELING
REFFING
REFRIED
REFRIES
REGAINS
REIFIED
REIFIES
REINING
REJOICE
REJOINS
RELYING
REMAILS
REMAINS
RENAILS
RENDING
RENNINS
RENTING
REPAINT
REPAIRS
REPLICA
REPLIED
REPLIES
REPRICE
REPRINT
REPRISE
REPTILE
REQUIEM
REQUIRE
REQUITE
RERAISE
RESCIND
RESHIPS
RESPINS
RESPIRE
RESPITE
RESTING
RESTIVE
RETAILS
RETAINS
RETHINK
RETRIAL
RETRIED
RETRIES
RETRIMS
RETSINA
REUNIFY
REUNION
REUNITE
REVOICE
REVVING
REWRITE
SEABIRD
SEAFIRE
SEAGIRT
SEALILY
SEALING
SEALION
SEAMIER
SEAMING
SEARING
SEASICK
SEASIDE
SEATING
SECTION
SEDGIER
SEEDIER
SEEDILY
SEEDING
SEEKING
SEEMING
SEEPIER
SEEPING
SEINING
SEIZING
SELFISH
SELKIRK
SELLING
SENDING
SENSING
SEQUINS
SERBIAN
SERLING
SERPICO
SERRIED
SERVICE
SERVILE
SERVING
SESSILE
SESSION
SESTINA
SETLINE
SETTING
TEAMING
TEARIER
TEARILY
TEARING
TEASING
TEATIME
TECHIER
TECHIES
TEDDIES
TEDDING
TEEMING
TEENIER
TEETIME
TEKTITE
TELLIES
TELLING
TENDING
TENNIEL
TENPINS
TENSILE
TENSING
TENSION
TENSIVE
TENTING
TENUITY
TENZING
TEQUILA
TERBIUM
TERMING
TERMINI
TERMITE
TERRIER
TERRIES
TERRIFY
TERTIAL
TESTIER
TESTIFY
TESTILY
TESTING
TEXTILE
VEALIER
VEERIES
VEERING
VEGGIES
VEGGING
VEILING
VEINIER
VEINING
VENDING
VENTING
VERDICT
VERGING
VERNIER
VERSIFY
VERSION
VERTIGO
VESPIDS
VESTIGE
VESTING
VETOING
VETTING
WEAKISH
WEANING
WEARIED
WEARIER
WEARIES
WEARILY
WEARING
WEAVING
WEBBIER
WEBBING
WEBLIKE
WEBSITE
WEDDING
WEDGIER
WEDGIES
WEDGING
WEEDIER
WEEDILY
WEEDING
WEENIER
WEENIES
WEEPIER
WEEPIES
WEEPING
WEEVILS
WELDING
WELKINS
WELLING
WELTING
WENDING
WENDISH
WESKITS
WETTING
WETTISH
YEANING
YELLING
YELPING
YERKING
YERKISH
YESHIVA
YESSING
ZEROING
ZESTIER

•E•••I•

AELFRIC
AEROBIC
BEASTIE
BEATNIK
BEATRIX
BEATSIT
BEATTIE
BEDELIA
BEDEVIL
BEDOUIN
BEGONIA
BENAZIR
BENEFIT
CECILIA
CENTRIC
CERAMIC
CERTAIN
CETERIS
DEADAIR
DEALSIN
DEALTIN
DEARSIR
DECLAIM
DEEPSIX
DEFICIT
DELIMIT
DELIRIA
DELPHIC
DELTAIC
DELTOID
DEMERIT
DEMONIC
DENARII
DEPOSIT
DESPAIR
DESPOIL
DETRAIN
DETROIT
DEXTRIN
EELSKIN
FELICIA
GEEWHIZ
GELATIN
GELATIS
GENERIC
GENERIS
GENESIS
GENETIC
GENGHIS
GEORDIE
GEORGIA
HEADPIN
HEADSIN
HEBRAIC
HENDRIX
HENRYIV
HEPARIN
HEPATIC
HERETIC
JEANNIE
JETSKIS
KEEPSIN
KERATIN
KEYEDIN
KEYGRIP
LEADSIN
LEAVEIN
LEIBNIZ
LEIPZIG
LETITIA
LETSLIP
MEGAHIT
MEIOSIS
MEIOTIC
MELANIE
MELANIN
MELODIC
MEMPHIS
MENUHIN
MERMAID
MESSKIT
NECKTIE
NEMESIS
NEPALIS
PEERSIN
PELAGIC
PENGUIN
PERSEID
PERTAIN
PETUNIA
READMIT
READSIN
REAFFIX
REAVAIL
RECLAIM
RECRUIT
REDHAIR
REELSIN
REFRAIN
REGALIA
REINSIN
RESTAIN
RETRAIN
REVERIE
REVISIT
SEDALIA
SEENFIT
SEEPSIN
SEESFIT
SEETOIT
SEGOVIA
SEISMIC
SELENIC
SEMITIC
SENDSIN
SEQUOIA
SERAPIS
SETSAIL
TEACHIN
TELAVIV
TENDRIL
TERRAIN
VERMEIL
WEIGHIN
WETSUIT
YELTSIN
YEMENIS
ZENOBIA

•E••••I

BELLINI
BELUSHI
BENGALI
CELLINI
DELICTI
DENARII
FELLINI
FERRARI
MENISCI
MENOTTI
TERMINI

••EI•••

AGEISTS
DREIDEL
DREISER
ELEISON
FREIGHT
ONEIDAS
ONEIRON
SHEIKHS
SHEILAS
SLEIGHS
SLEIGHT
STEIGER
STEINEM
STEINER
THEISTS
TIEINTO

WOEISME
XHEIGHT

••E•I••
ADELINE
ADENINE
ALEWIFE
AMENITY
AMERICA
AMERIGO
AMERIKA
AMERIND
ANELING
APELIKE
APERIES
ARECIBO
ARETINO
ATELIER
BEEFIER
BEEFING
BEEHIVE
BEELIKE
BEELINE
BEEPING
BEERIER
BLEMISH
BLERIOT
BREVITY
BREWING
CAESIUM
CHEMISE
CHEMIST
CHENIER
CHERISH
CHEVIED
CHEVIES
CHEVIOT
CHEWIER
CHEWING
CLERICS
CLERISY
COEDITS
COEXIST
CREDITS
CRETINS
CREVICE
CREWING
DEEDING
DEEMING
DIETING
DUELING
DUELIST
ELEGIAC
ELEGIES
ELEGIST
EMERITA
EMERITI
ENEMIES
EPEEIST
EREMITE
ETESIAN
EVENING
EYELIDS
EYELIKE
EZEKIEL
FAERIES
FEEDING
FEELING
FIERIER
FIERILY
FLEEING
FLEMING
FLEMISH
FLEXING
FLEYING
FREEING
FUELING
GEEKIER
GRECIAN
GREYING
GREYISH
HEEDING
HEELING
IBERIAN
ICELIKE
ICEMILK
ICEPICK
ICERINK
ITEMISE
ITEMIZE
JEEBIES
JEERING
JOEHILL
JREWING
KEELING
KEENING
KEEPING
KNEEING
LEERIER
LEERILY
LEERING
LEETIDE
MEETING
NEEDIER
NEEDILY
NEEDING
NOETICS
OBELISK
OBEYING
OLEFINS
OLEMISS
ONETIME
OPENING
PEEKING
PEELING
PEEPING
PEERING
PEEVING
PEEVISH
PIECING
PIELIKE
PIETIES
PIETINS
PIETISM
PIETIST
POETICS
PRECISE
PREDICT
PRELIMS
PREMIER
PREMISE
PREMISS
PREMIUM
PRESIDE
PREVIEW
PREXIES
PUERILE
QUERIED
QUERIER
QUERIES
QUERIST
QUEUING
REEDIER
REEDING
REEDITS
REEFING
REEKING
REELING
RHENISH
RHENIUM
SEEDIER
SEEDILY
SEEDING
SEEKING
SEEMING
SEEPIER
SEEPING
SHERIFF
SKEWING
SPECIAL
SPECIES
SPECIFY
SPECING
SPEWING
STEPINS
STERILE
STEWING
SWEDISH
TEEMING
TEENIER
TEETIME
THEFIRM
THEPITS
THEWIER
TIELINE
TIEPINS
TIERING
TOELIKE
TREEING
TREVINO
TSELIOT
USERIDS
VEERIES
VEERING
VIEWIER
VIEWING
WEEDIER
WEEDILY
WEEDING
WEENIER
WEENIES
WEEPIER
WEEPIES
WEEPING
WEEVILS
WHEYISH
WIENIES

••E••I•
ACERBIC
ALEMBIC
ANEROID
ASEPSIS
ASEPTIC
BREAKIN
BRESLIN
CHEAPIE
CHEATIN
CHECKIN
CHEERIO
CHERVIL
COEPTIS
DEEPSIX
DOESKIN
DWEEZIL
EVENKIS
FLEAPIT
FREDDIE
FREDRIC
FREEBIE
FREESIA
FUELOIL
GEEWHIZ
GHERKIN
GREMLIN
IDENTIC
INERTIA
KEEPSIN
KREMLIN
MUEZZIN
OBERLIN
OCEANIA
OCEANIC
OCEANID
OPENAIR
OPENPIT
OVERBIG
OVERDID
OVERLIE
PEERSIN
PFENNIG
PREEMIE
PREPAID
PREPPIE
PREVAIL
QUENTIN
REELSIN
SCEPTIC
SEENFIT
SEEPSIN
SEESFIT
SEETOIT
SHELTIE
SHERWIN
SKEEZIX
SKEPTIC
SLEEPIN
SLEPTIN
SNEAKIN
STEELIE
STENCIL
STEPSIN
STEROID
SWEARIN
SWEETIE
THEREIN
THESPIS
TIECLIP
TOENAIL
TREFOIL
TREKKIE
TRELLIS
TREMAIN
UTENSIL
WHEELIE
WHEREIN

••E•••I
ABENAKI
EMERITI
EXEMPLI
MAESTRI

•••EI••
ANTEING
ATHEISM
ATHEIST
BLUEING
BLUEISH
CAVEINS
CLUEING
CODEINE
COHEIRS
DECEITS
DECEIVE
DELEING
DEVEINS
EPEEIST
FADEINS
FLEEING
FOREIGN
FREEING
INVEIGH
JADEITE
KNEEING
LOVEINS
MADEIRA
NEREIDS
OGREISH
RALEIGH
RECEIPT
RECEIVE
SHOEING
TREEING
TRUEING
UNVEILS

•••E•I•
ADDEDIN
ALBENIZ
ALGERIA
AMNESIA
AMOEBIC
ANAEMIA
ANAEMIC
ANGELIC
ANNELID
APHELIA
ARMENIA
ARSENIC
ARSENIO
ARTEMIS
ASCETIC
ASKEDIN
BASEHIT
BEDELIA
BEDEVIL
BENEFIT
BLUEFIN
BOHEMIA
BOXEDIN
BOXESIN
CAKEMIX
CAMELIA
CAVEDIN
CAVESIN
CETERIS
CHEERIO
CLUEDIN
CLUESIN
COMEDIC
COMESIN
COTERIE
CSLEWIS
DEMERIT
DINEDIN
DINESIN
DIVESIN
DWEEZIL
EASEDIN
EASESIN
EDGEDIN
EDGESIN
ENDEMIC
EUGENIE
FADEDIN
FADESIN
FIDELIO
FIDELIS
FIRELIT
FLIESIN
FREEBIE
FREESIA
GENERIC
GENERIS
GENESIS
GENETIC
GIVENIN
GIVESIN
GONERIL
HAMELIN
HERETIC
HOMERIC
IMPERIL
INHERIT
INTERIM
JAVELIN
KEYEDIN
KINETIC
LIBERIA
LIVEDIN
LIVESIN
LOSESIT
MAKESIT
MALEFIC
MIMESIS
MIMETIC
MIXEDIN
MIXESIN
MOVEDIN
MOVESIN
NEMESIS
NIGERIA
NINEPIN
NUMERIC
OPHELIA
OSTEOID
PHOENIX
PHRENIC
PILEDIN
PILESIN
POLEMIC
PREEMIE
RAKEDIN
RAKESIN
RAMEKIN
RAREBIT
REVERIE
ROPEDIN
ROPESIN
ROSEOIL
SELENIC
SIBERIA
SILESIA
SINEDIE
SKEEZIX
SLEEPIN
SLOEGIN
STDENIS
STEELIE
SWEETIE
TAKEAIM
TAKENIN
TAKESIN
THREWIN
TOTEMIC
TUNEDIN
TUNESIN
VALERIE
VOTEDIN
VOTESIN
WADEDIN
WADESIN
WAVEDIN
WAVESIN
WHEELIE
YEMENIS

•••E••I
ALVEOLI
ASSEGAI
BASENJI
CORELLI
EFFENDI
KUTENAI
LORELEI
SCHERZI
VIVENDI

••••EI•
ALAMEIN
ANAHEIM
BARGEIN
BROKEIN
CLOSEIN
CONCEIT
DRIVEIN
EPSTEIN
FORFEIT
HOLBEIN
HOWBEIT
HUSSEIN
HYGIEIA
LEAVEIN
MULLEIN
NUCLEIC
PERSEID
PHASEIN
POMPEIA
POMPEII
PROTEIN
SHAREIN
SLIDEIN
SURFEIT
SWOREIN
THEREIN
TRADEIN
VERMEIL
VILLEIN
WHEREIN
WRITEIN
WROTEIN

••••E•I
ALFIERI
ISRAELI
POMPEII
SALIERI
ZAMBEZI

•••••EI
CADUCEI
GALILEI
LORELEI
SHARPEI

EJ•••••
EJECTED

E•J••••
ENJOINS
ENJOYED

•EJ••••
DEJECTS
JEJUNUM
REJECTS
REJOICE
REJOINS

•E•J•••
BEIJING
DEEJAYS
HEYJUDE
PERJURE
PERJURY
VEEJAYS

•E••J••
BELLJAR
LEARJET

•E•••J•
BERMEJO

••EJ•••
DEEJAYS
VEEJAYS

••E•J••
OVERJOY

•••EJ••
BLUEJAY
LUBEJOB
NOSEJOB

•••E•J•
BASENJI

••••EJ•
BERMEJO
VALLEJO

EK•••••
EKEDOUT
EKESOUT

E•K••••
ECKHART
ELKHART
ESKIMOS

E••K•••
ELEKTRA
ENSKIED
ENSKIES
ERSKINE
EVOKERS
EVOKING
EZEKIEL

E•••K••
EELSKIN
EVENKIS

E••••K•
EARLIKE
EELLIKE
ELFLIKE
EMBANKS
EMBARKS
EXWORKS
EYELIKE

E•••••K
EARLOCK
EARMARK
EYEBANK

•EK••••
DEKLERK
LEKVARS
REKEYED
TEKTITE

•E•K•••
BEAKERS
BECKETT
BECKONS
DECKING
DECKLES
DECKOUT
DESKSET
DESKTOP
GECKOES
GEEKIER
HECKLED
HECKLER
HECKLES
JERKIER
JERKILY
JERKING
JERKINS
LEAKAGE
LEAKERS
LEAKIER
LEAKING
MEEKEST
NECKERS
NECKING
NECKTIE
PEAKING
PEAKISH
PECKIER
PECKING
PECKISH
PECKSAT
PEEKERS
PEEKING
PEEKOUT
PEEKSAT
PERKIER
PERKILY
PERKING
PERKINS
PERKISH
PERKSUP
PESKIER
PESKILY
RECKONS
REEKING
SECKELS
SEEKERS
SEEKING
SEEKOUT
SELKIRK
WEAKENS
WEAKEST
WEAKISH
WEEKDAY
WEEKEND
WELKINS
WESKITS
YERKING
YERKISH

•E••K••
BELAKUN
BETAKEN
BETAKES
BETOKEN
DEBAKEY
EELSKIN
HEARKEN
JETSKIS
MENCKEN
MESSKIT
PERUKES
REBEKAH
REBUKED
REBUKES
REINKED
REMAKES
RETAKEN
RETAKES
REVOKED
REVOKES

•E•••K•
BEDECKS
BEDLIKE
BEELIKE
BESPOKE
DEBARKS
DEBUNKS
EELLIKE
GEMLIKE
HENLIKE
LEGLIKE
NETLIKE
NETSUKE
PEALIKE
PEGLIKE
PENLIKE
RECORKS
REDOAKS
REHOOKS
RELOCKS
REMARKS
REWORKS
TEACAKE
WEBLIKE

•E••••K
BEATNIK
BEDROCK
BELLEEK
BERSERK
BESPEAK
BETHINK
DEFROCK
DEKLERK
DENMARK
DERRICK
FETLOCK
GEMSBOK
GETBACK
HEMLOCK
HENPECK
LEACOCK
LEGWORK
MENFOLK
NETWORK
NEWLOOK
NEWYORK
PEACOCK
PEPTALK
PETCOCK
PETROCK
RECHALK
RECHECK
REDBOOK
RESTOCK
RETHINK
RETRACK
SEASICK
SELKIRK
SELLECK
SETBACK
TEDMACK
VEENECK
WEDLOCK

••EK•••
CHEKHOV
ELEKTRA
EZEKIEL
GEEKIER
MEEKEST
PEEKERS
PEEKING
PEEKOUT
PEEKSAT
REEKING
SEEKERS
SEEKING
SEEKOUT
SHEKELS
TREKKED
TREKKER
TREKKIE
WEEKDAY
WEEKEND

••E•K••
BLEAKER
BLEAKLY
BREAKER
BREAKIN
BREAKUP
CHECKED
CHECKER
CHECKIN
CHECKUP
CLERKED
CREAKED
DOESKIN
EVENKIS
FLECKED
FREAKED
FRECKLE
FRECKLY
GHERKIN
IRECKON
SHEIKHS
SLEEKED
SLEEKEN
SLEEKER
SLEEKLY
SNEAKED
SNEAKER
SNEAKIN
SPEAKER
SPEAKOF
SPEAKUP
SPECKED
SPECKLE
TREKKED
TREKKER
TREKKIE
TWEAKED
WREAKED
WRECKED
WRECKER

••E••K•
ABENAKI
AMERIKA
APELIKE
BEELIKE
EYELIKE
GRETZKY
HOECAKE
ICELIKE
PIELIKE
RHEBOKS
TOELIKE

••E•••K
EYEBANK
ICEMILK
ICEPACK
ICEPICK
ICERINK
OBELISK
PRECOOK
PRESOAK
ROEBUCK
SPELUNK
TIERACK
TIETACK
VEENECK

•••EK••
RAMEKIN
REBEKAH
SLEEKED
SLEEKEN
SLEEKER
SLEEKLY

•••E•K•
BEDECKS
BLUESKY
KOPECKS
LYSENKO
SCREAKS
SQUEAKS
SQUEAKY
STREAKS
STREAKY

•••E••K
BODEREK
LIVEOAK
VANEYCK

••••EK•
SHRIEKS

••••E•K
BELLEEK
BERSERK
BESPEAK
BOMBECK
BRUBECK
DEKLERK
HAUBERK
HENPECK
LOWNECK
MIDWEEK
OFFPEAK
RECHECK
SELLECK
SUNDECK
VEENECK
WOZZECK

•••••EK
BELLEEK
BODEREK
JANACEK
KAISHEK
MIDWEEK
ZATOPEK

EL•••••
ELAAIUN
ELAPIDS
ELAPSED
ELAPSES
ELASTIC
ELATERS
ELATING
ELATION
ELBOWED
ELDERLY
ELEANOR
ELECTED
ELECTEE
ELECTOR
ELECTRA
ELECTRO
ELEGANT
ELEGIAC
ELEGIES
ELEGIST
ELEISON
ELEKTRA
ELEMENT
ELEVATE
ELEVENS
ELFLIKE
ELGRECO
ELICITS
ELIDING
ELISION
ELITISM
ELITIST
ELIXIRS
ELKHART
ELLIOTT
ELLIPSE
ELLISON
ELMISTI
ELMTREE
ELOIGNS
ELOPERS
ELOPING
ELUDING
ELUSIVE
ELUSORY
ELUTING
ELUTION
ELUVIUM
ELYSEES
ELYSIAN
ELYSIUM

E•L••••
ECLAIRS
ECLIPSE
ECLOGUE
EELIEST
EELLIKE
EELSKIN
ELLIOTT
ELLIPSE
ELLISON
ENLACED
ENLACES
ENLARGE
ENLISTS
ENLIVEN
EOLITHS

E••L•••
EAGLETS
EAGLING
EARLDOM
EARLESS
EARLIER
EARLIKE
EARLOBE
EARLOCK
EARLYON
ECOLOGY
EELLIKE
EGALITE
EGGLESS
EHRLICH
ELFLIKE
EMBLEMS
EMPLOYE
EMPLOYS
EMULATE
ENCLAVE
ENCLOSE
ENDLESS
ENGLAND
ENGLISH
ENGLUND
ENPLANE
ENSLAVE
EPILOGS
ERELONG
EVILEST
EVILEYE
EVILLER
EVOLVED
EVOLVES
EVULSED
EVULSES
EXALTED
EXCLAIM
EXCLUDE
EXILING
EXPLAIN
EXPLODE
EXPLOIT
EXPLORE
EXULTED
EYELASH
EYELESS
EYELETS
EYELIDS
EYELIKE

E•••L••
EARFLAP
EARPLUG
ECHELON
EDIBLES
EMAILED
EMMYLOU
ENABLED
ENABLES
ENDPLAY
ENFOLDS
ENGULFS
ENISLED
ENISLES
ENROLLS
ENSILED
ENSILES
ENVELOP
EPAULET
EPSILON
EQUALED
EQUALLY
ESTELLE
ETOILES
EVILLER
EXHALED

EXHALES

E••••L•

EAGERLY
EARFULS
EARTHLY
EATABLE
EGGROLL
ELDERLY
EMERALD
EMPTILY
ENAMELS
ENNOBLE
ENROLLS
ENSOULS
ENTAILS
ENTITLE
EPISTLE
EQUABLE
EQUABLY
EQUALLY
ERECTLY
EROSELY
ESPIALS
ESTELLE
EXACTLY
EXAMPLE
EXEMPLI
EYEBALL
EYEBOLT
EYEFULS
EYEHOLE

E•••••L

EASEFUL
EGGROLL
EMANUEL
EMBROIL
EMPANEL
ENSNARL
ENTHRAL
EPOCHAL
ESPANOL
ESTIVAL
ESTORIL
ETERNAL
ETHANOL
ETHICAL
EVANGEL
EYEBALL
EZEKIEL

•EL••••

AELFRIC
BELABOR
BELAKUN
BELASCO
BELATED
BELAYED
BELCHED
BELCHES
BELDAME
BELDAMS
BELFAST
BELGIAN
BELGIUM
BELIEFS
BELIEVE
BELINDA
BELLAMY
BELLBOY
BELLEEK
BELLHOP
BELLIED
BELLIES
BELLING
BELLINI
BELLJAR
BELLMAN
BELLMEN
BELLOWS
BELLYUP
BELMONT
BELONGS
BELOVED
BELTANE
BELTBAG
BELTING
BELTWAY
BELUSHI
BELYING
CELADON
CELEBES
CELEBRE
CELESTA
CELESTE
CELLARS
CELLINI
CELLIST
CELSIUS
CELTICS
DELANEY
DELAYED
DELAYER
DELEING
DELETED
DELETES
DELIBES
DELICTI
DELICTS
DELIGHT
DELILAH
DELIMIT
DELIRIA
DELISTS
DELIVER
DELPHIC
DELTAIC
DELTOID
DELUDED
DELUDES
DELUGED
DELUGES
DELUISE
DELVERS
DELVING
EELIEST
EELLIKE
EELSKIN
FELDMAN
FELICIA
FELINES
FELLAHS
FELLERS
FELLFOR
FELLIES
FELLING
FELLINI
FELLOFF
FELLOUT
FELLOWS
FELTFOR
FELTOUT
FELUCCA
GELADAS
GELATIN
GELATIS
GELDING
GELIDLY
GELLING
HELDOFF
HELDOUT
HELICAL
HELICES
HELICON
HELIPAD
HELIXES
HELLCAT
HELLENE
HELLERS
HELLION
HELLISH
HELLMAN
HELMETS
HELMING
HELOISE
HELOTRY
HELPERS
HELPFUL
HELPING
HELPOUT
JELLIED
JELLIES
JELLING
KELLOGG
KELPIES
MELANGE
MELANIE
MELANIN
MELDING
MELINDA
MELISSA
MELLOWS
MELODIC
MELROSE
MELTING
NELSONS
PELAGES
PELAGIC
PELICAN
PELISSE
PELLETS
PELOTAS
PELTATE
PELTERS
PELTING
PELTISH
RELACED
RELACES
RELAPSE
RELATED
RELATES
RELAXED
RELAXES
RELAYED
RELEARN
RELEASE
RELENTS
RELIANT
RELICTS
RELIEFS
RELIEVE
RELIEVO
RELIGHT
RELINED
RELINES
RELISTS
RELIVED
RELIVES
RELLENO
RELOADS
RELOCKS
RELUCTS
RELUMED
RELUMES
RELYING
SELECTS
SELENIC
SELFISH
SELKIRK
SELLECK
SELLERS
SELLFOR
SELLING
SELLOFF
SELLOUT
SELTZER
SELVAGE
TELAVIV
TELERAN
TELEXED
TELEXES
TELLALL
TELLERS
TELLIES
TELLING
TELLOFF
TELLSOF
TELLSON
TELSTAR
VELLUMS
VELOURS
VELVETS
VELVETY
WELCHED
WELCHES
WELCOME
WELDERS
WELDING
WELFARE
WELKINS
WELLAND
WELLFED
WELLING
WELLMAN
WELLOFF
WELLRUN
WELLSET
WELLSUP
WELTERS
WELTING
YELLERS
YELLING
YELLOWS
YELLOWY
YELLSAT
YELPERS
YELPING
YELTSIN

•E•L•••

AEOLIAN
BECLOUD
BEDLAMP
BEDLESS
BEDLIKE
BEELIKE
BEELINE
BELLAMY
BELLBOY
BELLEEK
BELLHOP
BELLIED
BELLIES
BELLING
BELLINI
BELLJAR
BELLMAN
BELLMEN
BELLOWS
BELLYUP
BERLIOZ
BERLITZ
CEILING
CELLARS
CELLINI
CELLIST
DEALERS
DEALING
DEALOUT
DEALSIN
DEALTIN
DECLAIM
DECLARE
DECLASS
DECLINE
DEFLATE
DEFLECT
DEKLERK
DEPLANE
DEPLETE
DEPLORE
DEPLOYS
DEWLAPS
DEWLESS
DEWLINE
EELLIKE
FEELERS
FEELESS
FEELFOR
FEELING
FEELOUT
FELLAHS
FELLERS
FELLFOR
FELLIES
FELLING
FELLINI
FELLOFF
FELLOUT
FELLOWS
FETLOCK
GELLING
GEMLESS
GEMLIKE
GEOLOGY
GETLOST
HEALALL
HEALERS
HEALING
HEALTHY
HEELERS
HEELING
HEELTAP
HELLCAT
HELLENE
HELLERS
HELLION
HELLISH
HELLMAN
HEMLINE
HEMLOCK
HENLIKE
HEWLETT
JEALOUS
JELLIED
JELLIES
JELLING
KEELING
KEGLERS
KEILLOR
KELLOGG
KEYLESS
KEYLIME
LEGLESS
LEGLIKE
MEALIER
MEALIES
MEDLEYS
MELLOWS
MERLOTS
MEWLERS
MEWLING
NEGLECT
NEOLITH
NETLIKE
NEWLEFT
NEWLOOK
PEALIKE
PEALING
PEDLARS
PEELERS
PEELING
PEELOFF
PEGLESS
PEGLIKE
PELLETS
PENLIKE
PEPLUMS
PERLITE
PERLMAN
REALISE
REALISM
REALIST
REALITY
REALIZE
REALTOR
REBLOOM
RECLAIM
RECLAME
RECLEAN
RECLINE
RECLUSE
REDLINE
REELECT
REELING
REELOFF
REELSIN
REFLAGS
REFLECT
REGLETS
REGLUED
REGLUES
RELLENO
REPLACE
REPLANS
REPLANT
REPLATE
REPLAYS
REPLETE
REPLICA
REPLIED
REPLIES
REPLOWS
SEALABS
SEALANE
SEALANT
SEALEGS
SEALERS
SEALILY
SEALING
SEALION
SEALOFF
SEALSUP
SECLUDE
SELLECK
SELLERS
SELLFOR
SELLING
SELLOFF
SELLOUT
SERLING
SETLINE
TEALEAF
TEALESS
TELLALL
TELLERS
TELLIES
TELLING
TELLOFF
TELLSOF
TELLSON
VEALIER
VEILING
VELLUMS
WEALTHY
WEBLESS
WEBLIKE
WEDLOCK
WELLAND
WELLFED
WELLING
WELLMAN
WELLOFF
WELLRUN
WELLSET
WELLSUP
WETLAND
YELLERS
YELLING
YELLOWS
YELLOWY
YELLSAT
ZEALAND
ZEALOTS
ZEALOUS

•E••L••

AEDILES
BEADLES
BEAGLES
BEATLES
BECALMS
BEDELIA
BEETLES
BEFALLS
BEHOLDS
BENELUX
BENTLEY
BEVELED
CECILIA
CEDILLA
DECALOG
DECKLES
DEDALUS
DEFALLA
DEFILED
DEFILER
DEFILES
DELILAH
DEMILLE
DEPALMA
DESALTS
DEVALUE
DEVELOP
DEVILED
DEVILLE
DEVILRY
DEVOLVE
DEWCLAW
FEEBLER
FEEDLOT
FEMALES
FERULES
FETTLES
GEFILTE
GENTLED
GENTLER
GENTLES
GERALDO
HECKLED
HECKLER
HECKLES
HEDDLES
HEMSLEY
HERALDS
JEANLUC
JEWELED
JEWELER
JEWELRY
KEEBLER
KEILLOR
KERPLOP
KETTLES
KEYCLUB
LEAFLET
LEGALLY
LETSLIP
LEVELED
LEVELER
LEVELLY
MEASLES
MEDALED
MEDDLED
MEDDLER
MEDDLES
MEDULLA
METTLES
NEBULAE
NEBULAR
NEBULAS
NEEDLED
NEEDLES
NEPALIS
NESTLED
NESTLER
NESTLES
NETTLED
NETTLES
NEVILLE
PEARLED
PEBBLED
PEBBLES
PEDALED
PEDDLED
PEDDLER
PEDDLES
PEEPLES
PENALTY
PENULTS
PEOPLED
PEOPLES
PERPLEX
PESTLED
PESTLES
PETALED
REBOLTS
RECALLS
RECOLOR
REDALGA
REDFLAG
REFILED
REFILES
REFILLS
REFILMS
REGALED
REGALES
REGALIA
REGALLY
REGULAR
REGULUS
REMELTS
REMOLDS
REOILED
REPOLLS
REPULSE
RESALES
RESALTS
RESELLS
RESILED
RESILES
RESOLED
RESOLES
RESOLVE
RESULTS
RETELLS
RETILED
RETILES
REVALUE
REVELED
REVELER
REVELRY
REVILED
REVILES
REVOLTS
REVOLVE
REWELDS
SEABLUE
SEASLUG
SECULAR
SEDALIA
SEMILOG
SETTLED
SETTLER
SETTLES
SEVILLE
TEMBLOR
TEMPLAR
TEMPLES
VENALLY
ZEBULON

•E•••L•

AERIALS
BEASTLY
BEDROLL
BEEBALM
BEEFALO
BEFALLS
BEFOULS
BEGUILE
BENGALI
BENGALS
BEOWULF
BERTOLT
BETHELS
BEVERLY
BEWAILS
CEDILLA
CEMBALO
CEREALS
DEBACLE
DECARLO
DEERFLY
DEFALLA
DEFAULT
DEMILLE
DENIALS
DENSELY
DERAILS
DETAILS
DEVILLE
FEBRILE
FERRULE
FERTILE
FETIDLY
GELIDLY
GENTILE
GERBILS
GESTALT
GETWELL
HEADILY
HEALALL
HEAVILY
HEFTILY
HERBALS
HERCULE
HERSELF
JERKILY
KENDALL
KENNELS
KERNELS
KEYHOLE
LEERILY
LEGALLY
LEGIBLE
LEGIBLY
LEGPULL
LENTILS
LEOPOLD
LETSFLY
LEVELLY
MEATILY
MEDULLA
MENFOLK
MENIALS
MERRILL
MERRILY
MESCALS
MESSALA
MESSILY
NEEDILY
NERVILY
NEVILLE
PEDICLE
PENCILS
PENPALS
PEPPILY
PEPTALK
PERCALE
PERGOLA
PERKILY
PESKILY
PETIOLE
PETRELS
PETROLS
PETTILY
READILY
REBOILS
REBUILD
REBUILT
RECALLS
RECHALK
RECOILS
RECYCLE
REDCELL
REDEALS
REDEALT
REDIALS
REDPOLL
REDWOLF
REFILLS
REFUELS
REGALLY
REHEALS
REHEELS
REMAILS
RENAILS
RENAULT
RENTALS
REPEALS
REPOLLS
REPTILE
RESCALE
RESEALS
RESELLS
RESTYLE
RETAILS
RETELLS
RETICLE
RETITLE
RETOOLS
REVEALS
SEAGULL
SEALILY
SEASALT
SEATTLE
SEAWALL
SEAWOLF
SECKELS
SEEABLE
SEEDILY
SEIDELS
SEQUELS
SERIALS
SERVALS
SERVILE
SESSILE
SEVILLE
TEABALL
TEARILY
TEASELS
TELLALL
TENABLE
TENABLY
TENFOLD
TENSELY
TENSILE
TENTHLY
TEPIDLY
TEQUILA
TERCELS
TERSELY
TESTFLY
TESTILY
TEXTILE
VEHICLE
VENALLY
VERBALS
VESSELS
VEXEDLY
WEARILY
WEASELS
WEEDILY
WEEVILS
WEIRDLY
WENDELL
WETCELL

•E••••L

AEROSOL
BEDEVIL
BEDROLL
BESTIAL
CENTRAL
DECIBEL
DECIMAL
DEMEROL
DEPOSAL
DESPOIL
FEARFUL
FEDERAL
FEMORAL
GENERAL
GENTEEL
GERITOL
GETREAL
GETWELL
HEALALL
HEATFUL
HEEDFUL
HELICAL
HELPFUL
JEZEBEL
KENDALL
KESTREL
LEGPULL
LESPAUL
LEXICAL
MEDICAL
MENTHOL
MERRILL
NEEDFUL
NEUTRAL
NEWDEAL
OEDIPAL
PEAFOWL
PEDICEL
PERUSAL
REAVAIL
RECITAL
REDCELL
REDPOLL
REFUSAL
REMODEL
REMOVAL
RENEWAL
RESTFUL
RETINAL
RETRIAL
REVIVAL
SEAGULL
SEAWALL
SEMINAL
SENEGAL
SENSUAL
SETSAIL
SEVERAL
TEABALL
TEARFUL
TELLALL
TENDRIL
TENNIEL
TERTIAL
TEXTUAL
VEGETAL
VENTRAL
VERMEIL
WENDELL
WETCELL
ZESTFUL

••EL•••

ABELARD
ADELINE
AGELESS
ANELING
APELIKE
ATELIER
AWELESS
BEELIKE
BEELINE
CHELSEA
DUELERS
DUELING
DUELIST
DWELLED
DWELLER
ERELONG
EYELASH
EYELESS
EYELETS
EYELIDS
EYELIKE
FEELERS
FEELESS
FEELFOR
FEELING
FEELOUT
FIELDED
FIELDER
FUELERS
FUELING
FUELLED
FUELOIL
FUELROD
GIELGUD
GUELPHS
HEELERS
HEELING
HEELTAP
HUELESS
ICELAND
ICELESS
ICELIKE
IRELAND
IRELESS
KEELING
KNELLED
NIELSEN
OBELISK
OCELLUS
OCELOTS
OMELETS
ONELANE
PEELERS
PEELING
PEELOFF
PIELIKE
PRELATE
PRELIMS
PRELOAD
PRELUDE
QUELLED
REELECT
REELING
REELOFF
REELSIN
SHELDON
SHELLAC
SHELLED
SHELLER
SHELLEY
SHELTER
SHELTIE
SHELTON
SHELVED
SHELVES
SKELTER
SKELTON
SMELLED
SMELTED
SMELTER
SNELLEN
SPELLED
SPELLER
SPELUNK
STELLAR
SVELTER
SWELLED
SWELLUP
SWELTER
SWELTRY
TIELESS
TIELINE
TOELESS
TOELIKE
TOELOOP
TRELLIS
TSELIOT
TWELFTH
TWELVES
USELESS
WHELMED
WHELPED
WIELDED
YIELDED
ZOELLER

••E•L••

AREOLAE
AREOLAR
AREOLAS
BEETLES
BRESLIN
CHEMLAB
CREOLES
DWELLED
DWELLER
FEEBLER
FEEDLOT
FIEDLER
FUELLED
GREELEY
GREMLIN
ICEBLUE
ICEFLOE
IDEALLY
JOEBLOW
KEEBLER
KNEELED
KNEELER
KNELLED
KREMLIN
LIESLOW
NEEDLED
NEEDLES
OBERLIN
OCELLUS
OVERLAP
OVERLAY
OVERLIE
PEEPLES
PRESLEY
PUEBLOS
QUELLED
SHEILAS
SHELLAC
SHELLED
SHELLER
SHELLEY
SMELLED
SNELLEN
SPELLED
SPELLER
STEALTH

STEELED
STEELER
STEELIE
STELLAR
SWELLED
SWELLUP
THEBLOB
TIECLIP
TREBLED
TREBLES
TRELLIS
WHEELED
WHEELER
WHEELIE
ZOELLER

••E••L•

ACEROLA
ADEPTLY
ALERTLY
BEEBALM
BEEFALO
BLEAKLY
CHEAPLY
CLEANLY
CLEARLY
COEVALS
CRENELS
CREWELS
CUEBALL
DEERFLY
DIESELS
EMERALD
ERECTLY
EXEMPLI
EYEBALL
EYEBOLT
EYEFULS
EYEHOLE
FIERILY
FLEETLY
FLESHLY
FRECKLE
FRECKLY
FRESHLY
GREATLY
ICECOLD
ICEMILK
IDEALLY
INEPTLY
INERTLY
JOEHILL
LEERILY
NEEDILY
ONESELF
OVERALL
OVERFLY
OVERTLY
PHENOLS
PIEBALD
PRESALE
PRESELL
PUERILE
QUEENLY
QUEERLY
SEEABLE
SEEDILY
SHEERLY
SHEKELS
SHEWOLF
SLEEKLY
SPECKLE
STEEPLE
STEEPLY
STERILE
STERNLY
STEROLS
SWEETLY
THERELL
TIEPOLO
TOEHOLD
TREACLE
TREACLY
TREADLE
TREMBLE
TREMBLY
TREMOLO
TRESTLE
USEABLE
WEEDILY
WEEVILS
WHEEDLE
WHERELL
WRESTLE

••E•••L

CHERVIL
COEQUAL
CREOSOL
CUEBALL
DREIDEL
DWEEZIL
ETERNAL
EYEBALL
EZEKIEL
FRETFUL
FUELOIL
GLEEFUL
GRENDEL
HEEDFUL
JOEHILL
NEEDFUL
OVERALL
PRECOOL
PREQUEL
PRESELL
PRETZEL
PREVAIL
QUETZAL
SPECIAL
STENCIL
STENGEL
STERNAL
THERELL
THERMAL
TOENAIL
TREFOIL
UNEQUAL
UTENSIL
WHERELL

•••EL••

ALLELES
ANGELES
ANGELIC
ANGELOU
ANGELUS
ANNELID
APHELIA
BEDELIA
BENELUX
BEVELED
BIBELOT
BIGELOW
BLUELAW
CAMELIA
CAMELOT
CAPELET
CAPELLA
CASELAW
CORELLI
CRUELER
CRUELLY
CRUELTY
DANELAW
DEVELOP
ECHELON
ENVELOP
ESTELLE
FIDELIO
FIDELIS
FIRELIT
FORELEG
GAMELAW
GATELEG
GAVELED
GAZELLE
GISELLE
GREELEY
HAMELIN
HGWELLS
HOWELLS
JAVELIN
JEWELED
JEWELER
JEWELRY
KNEELED
KNEELER
LABELED
LABELER
LABELLE
LAPELED
LEVELED
LEVELER
LEVELLY
LIBELED
LIBELER
LORELEI
LOUELLA
MATELOT
MODELAS
MODELED
MODELER
MODELTS
MORELLO
MOSELLE
NACELLE
NORELCO
NOVELLA
NOVELLE
NOVELTY
OPHELIA
OTHELLO
PANELED
PATELLA
POMELOS
RAVELED
REMELTS
RESELLS
RETELLS
REVELED
REVELER
REVELRY
REWELDS
ROSELLE
ROZELLE
SAVELOY
SHIELDS
SPIELED
SPIELER
SQUELCH
STEELED
STEELER
STEELIE
TIMELAG
TONELOC
TOWELED
TUPELOS
TUTELAR
UCCELLO
WAVELET
WHEELED
WHEELER
WHEELIE
YODELED
YODELER
YULELOG

•••E•L•

ALVEOLI
ANNEALS
APPEALS
AUREOLA
AUREOLE
BEVERLY
BRIEFLY
CAPELLA
CEREALS
CHIEFLY
CORELLI
CRUELLY
CUREALL
DATEDLY
DAZEDLY
EAGERLY
ELDERLY
ESTELLE
FIREFLY
FIXEDLY
FLEETLY
GAZELLE
GISELLE
HGWELLS
HOWELLS
JADEDLY
LABELLE
LEVELLY
LOUELLA
LOVERLY
MISERLY
MORELLO
MOSELLE
MUDEELS
NACELLE
NAKEDLY
NOTEDLY
NOVELLA
NOVELLE
ORDEALS
ORDERLY
OSCEOLA
OTHELLO
PATELLA
QUEENLY
QUEERLY
QUIETLY
REDEALS
REDEALT
REHEALS
REHEELS
REPEALS
RESEALS
RESELLS
RETELLS
REVEALS
ROSELLE
ROZELLE
SHEERLY
SLEEKLY
SOBERLY
SQUEALS
STEEPLE
STEEPLY
SWEETLY
TIREDLY
UCCELLO
UNREELS
UNSEALS
UNVEILS
UTTERLY
VEXEDLY
WHEEDLE

•••E••L

ADRENAL
APTERAL
ARSENAL
BALEFUL
BANEFUL
BEDEVIL
BILEVEL
BIPEDAL
BRUEGEL
CAREFUL
CUREALL
DAREFUL
DEMEROL
DIREFUL
DOLEFUL
DONEGAL
DWEEZIL
EASEFUL
FATEFUL
FEDERAL
GENERAL
GLEEFUL
GONERIL
HATEFUL
HOPEFUL
HUMERAL
ILLEGAL
IMPERIL
JEZEBEL
JUVENAL
KNIEVEL
LATERAL
LIBERAL
LIFEFUL
LITERAL
MINERAL
MUSEFUL
NUMERAL
PAGEFUL
PIPEFUL
RAGEFUL
RENEWAL
ROSEOIL
SENEGAL
SEVERAL
SPIEGEL
STIEGEL
TUNEFUL
TYLENOL
VEGETAL
WAKEFUL

••••EL•

ACUTELY
AGILELY
BARBELL
BARBELS
BARRELS
BATTELS
BETHELS
BOATELS
BOSWELL
BRAVELY
BRUTELY
BUSHELS
CANCELS
CANDELA
CARPELS
CARRELS
CARTELS
CHAPELS
CHISELS
CLAVELL
CLOSELY
COMPELS
CORBELS
CORDELL
CORNELL
COWBELL
CRENELS
CREWELS
CRUDELY
CUDGELS
DAMSELS
DANIELS
DENSELY
DIESELS
DISPELS
DRIVELS
DRYCELL
DRYWELL
DUFFELS
DURRELL
ENAMELS
EROSELY
FALSELY
FALWELL
FANBELT
FUNNELS
GETWELL
GOSPELS
GOTWELL
GRAVELS
GRAVELY
GROVELS
GUNNELS
HERSELF
HIMSELF
HOSTELS
HUBBELL
INANELY
INDWELL
INFIELD
INKWELL
IRATELY
ISOHELS
ISRAELI
KENNELS
KERNELS
LAPBELT
LARGELY
LAURELS
LINTELS
LISTELS
LITHELY
LOOSELY
MANDELA
MANTELS
MARCELS
MARVELS
MAXWELL
MICHELE
MORSELS
MUDEELS
MUSSELS
NAIVELY
NICKELS
NONSELF
NOTWELL
OILWELL
ONESELF
OURSELF
OUTSELL
PARCELS
PASSELS
PASTELS
PETRELS
POMMELS
PRESELL
PRONELY
PROPELS
PUMMELS
PURCELL
RAPPELS
REDCELL
REFUELS
REHEELS
RONDELS
ROSWELL
RUNNELS
RUSSELL
SECKELS
SEIDELS
SEQUELS
SHAPELY
SHEKELS
SHOVELS
SITWELL
SNIDELY
SNIVELS
SORRELS
SPARELY
SPINELS
STALELY
STATELY
STOKELY
SUAVELY
SUNBELT
SWIVELS
TANGELO
TARBELL
TASSELS
TEASELS
TENSELY
TERCELS
TERSELY
THERELL
THYSELF
TINSELS
TRAVELS
TRITELY
TROWELS
TUNNELS
UKULELE
UNREELS
VAGUELY
VESSELS
WEASELS
WENDELL
WETCELL
WHERELL
WILHELM
WYCHELM

••••E•L

ALLHEAL
BARBELL
BIGDEAL
BOSWELL
CLAVELL
CONCEAL
CONGEAL
CORDELL
CORNEAL
CORNELL
COWBELL
DRYCELL
DRYWELL
DURRELL
FALWELL
FORREAL
FURSEAL
GENTEEL
GETREAL
GETWELL
GOTWELL
HUBBELL
INDWELL
INKWELL
LACTEAL
LOWHEEL
MAXWELL
MISDEAL
NEWDEAL
NOTWELL
OATMEAL
OILWELL
OUTSELL
PASSEUL
PRESELL
PURCELL
RAWDEAL
REDCELL
ROSWELL
RUSSELL
SITWELL
SURREAL
TARBELL
TARHEEL
THERELL
USSTEEL
VERMEIL
WENDELL
WETCELL
WHERELL

•••••EL

ANNABEL
APPAREL
BILEVEL
BRUEGEL
BRUMMEL
CALOMEL
CARAMEL
CARAVEL
CHANCEL
CHANNEL
CHATTEL
CHUNNEL
CITADEL
COLONEL
COUNSEL
COZUMEL
DECIBEL
DREIDEL
EMANUEL
EMPANEL
EVANGEL
EZEKIEL
FALAFEL
FLANNEL
GABRIEL
GAMBREL
GENTEEL
GRAPNEL
GRENDEL
IMPANEL
INFIDEL
ISHMAEL
JEZEBEL
KESTREL
KNIEVEL
LOWHEEL
MICHAEL
MONGREL
PEDICEL
PREQUEL
PRETZEL
QUARREL
RAPHAEL
REMODEL
SANIBEL
SATCHEL
SCALPEL
SHRIVEL
SNORKEL
SPANIEL
SPIEGEL
STENGEL
STIEGEL
STRUDEL
SYNFUEL
TARHEEL
TENNIEL
TRAMMEL
TUMBREL
UNRAVEL
USSTEEL
WASTREL

EM•••••

EMAILED
EMANANT
EMANATE
EMANUEL
EMBANKS
EMBARGO
EMBARKS
EMBASSY
EMBAYED
EMBLEMS
EMBRACE
EMBROIL
EMBRYOS
EMENDED
EMENDER
EMERALD
EMERGED
EMERGES
EMERITA
EMERITI
EMERSED
EMERSON
EMIGRES
EMINENT
EMIRATE
EMITTED
EMITTER
EMMYLOU
EMOTERS
EMOTING
EMOTION
EMOTIVE
EMPANEL
EMPATHY
EMPEROR
EMPIRES
EMPLOYE
EMPLOYS
EMPORIA
EMPOWER
EMPRESS
EMPTIED
EMPTIER
EMPTIES
EMPTILY
EMULATE

E•M••••

ELMISTI
ELMTREE
EMMYLOU
ENMASSE
ERMINES

E••M•••

EARMARK
EARMUFF
ELEMENT
ENAMELS
ENAMORS
ENAMOUR
ENDMOST
ENEMIES
EREMITE
ETAMINE
EXAMINE
EXAMPLE
EXEMPLI
EXEMPTS

E•••M••

EASTMAN
ENCAMPS
ENCOMIA
ENDEMIC
ENIGMAS
ENZYMES
ERASMUS
ESKIMOS

E••••M•

ECONOMY
EMBLEMS
ENDGAME
ENGRAMS
EPITOME
EPONYMS
EPONYMY
ESTEEMS
EXANIMO
EXTREME

E•••••M

EARDRUM
EARLDOM
EGOTISM
EIGHTAM
EIGHTPM
ELITISM
ELUVIUM
ELYSIUM
EPIGRAM
ERRATUM
EXCLAIM

•EM••••

BEMIRED
BEMIRES
BEMOANS
BEMUSED
BEMUSES
CEMBALO
CEMENTS
DEMANDS
DEMEANS
DEMERIT
DEMEROL
DEMESNE
DEMETER
DEMIGOD
DEMILLE
DEMISED
DEMISES
DEMONIC
DEMOTED
DEMOTES
DEMPSEY
DEMURER
FEMALES
FEMORAL
GEMLESS
GEMLIKE
GEMMIER
GEMOTES
GEMSBOK
HEMLINE
HEMLOCK
HEMMERS
HEMMING
HEMSLEY
JEMMIED
JEMMIES
LEMIEUX
LEMMING
LEMONDE
LEMPIRA
MEMBERS
MEMENTO
MEMOIRE
MEMOIRS
MEMOREX
MEMPHIS
NEMEROV
NEMESES
NEMESIS
PEMICAN
REMAILS
REMAINS
REMAKES
REMANDS
REMARKS
REMARRY
REMELTS
REMENDS
REMIGES
REMINDS
REMIXED
REMIXES
REMNANT
REMODEL
REMOLDS
REMORAS
REMORSE
REMOTER
REMOTES
REMOUNT
REMOVAL
REMOVED
REMOVER
REMOVES
REMOWED
REMUDAS
SEMILOG
SEMINAL
SEMINAR
SEMIPRO
SEMITES
SEMITIC
TEMBLOR
TEMPEHS
TEMPERA
TEMPERS
TEMPEST
TEMPLAR
TEMPLES
TEMPTED
TEMPTER
TEMPURA
YEMENIS
ZEMSTVO

•E•M•••

BEAMIER
BEAMING
BEAMISH
BEAMSUP
BELMONT
BERMEJO
BERMUDA
BESMEAR
DEEMING
DENMARK
DESMOND
FERMENT
FERMIUM
GEMMIER
GERMANE
GERMANS
GERMANY
GERMIER
HELMETS
HELMING
HEMMERS
HEMMING
HERMANN
HERMITS
HETMANS
JEMMIED
JEMMIES
LEMMING
MERMAID
NESMITH
NEWMATH
NEWMOON
NEWMOWN
PERMING
PERMITS
REAMASS
REAMERS
REAMING
REDMEAT
SEAMIER
SEAMING
SEAMOSS
SEEMING
SEGMENT
SERMONS
SEYMOUR
TEAMING
TEAMSUP
TEDMACK
TEEMING
TERMING
TERMINI
TERMITE
VERMEER
VERMEIL
VERMONT
WETMOPS
YESMAAM
ZERMATT

•E••M••

BECOMES
BELLMAN
BELLMEN
BENUMBS
BERGMAN
BESTMAN
BESTMEN
BETAMAX
BETIMES
CERAMIC
CERUMEN
DECAMPS
DECIMAL
DEFAMED
DEFAMES
DELIMIT
FELDMAN
FEYNMAN
GENOMES
HEADMAN
HEADMEN
HEISMAN
HELLMAN
LEGUMES
LEXEMES
MERIMEE
NEWSMAN
NEWSMEN
PERLMAN
READMIT
REAIMED
REARMED
REGIMEN
REGIMES
REITMAN
RELUMED
RELUMES
RENAMED
RENAMES
REPOMAN
RESUMED
RESUMES
RETIMED
RETIMES
REVAMPS
SEISMIC
SESAMES
WELLMAN
ZEUGMAS

•E•••M•

BEATSME
BECALMS
BEDLAMP
BEDTIME
BEEGUMS
BEGRIME
BELDAME
BELDAMS
BELLAMY
BESEEMS
CENTIME
CENTIMO
DEFORMS
DEPALMA
KEYLIME
MEDIUMS
MEGOHMS
MEGRIMS
PENNAME
PEPLUMS
PERFUME
PETNAME
RECLAME
REDEEMS
REDGUMS
REFILMS
REFORMS
REFRAME
RESTAMP
RETRIMS
REWARMS
TEATIME
TEDIUMS
TEETIME
VELLUMS
VERISMO
WELCOME

•E••••M

BEDROOM
BEEBALM
BEECHAM
BELGIUM
BENTHAM
DECLAIM
DECORUM
FERMIUM
HEROISM
JEJUNUM
KETCHAM
LEGROOM
NEEDHAM
PENTIUM
PERDIEM
PERFORM
REALISM
REBLOOM
RECLAIM
RECROOM
REQUIEM
SEAGRAM
SERFDOM
SEVENAM
SEVENPM
TEAROOM
TERBIUM
YEATEAM
YESMAAM
ZEROSUM

••EM•••

ALEMBIC
ANEMONE
BLEMISH
CHEMISE
CHEMIST
CHEMLAB
CLEMENS
CLEMENT
CLEMSON
CREMONA
DEEMING
ELEMENT
ENEMIES
EREMITE
EXEMPLI
EXEMPTS

FLEMING
FLEMISH
FREMONT
GREMLIN
HAEMATO
ICEMILK
ITEMISE
ITEMIZE
KREMLIN
OLEMISS
PREMEDS
PREMIER
PREMISE
PREMISS
PREMIUM
SEEMING
STEMMED
TEEMING
TREMAIN
TREMBLE
TREMBLY
TREMOLO
TREMORS

••E•M••

CREAMED
CREAMER
CREWMAN
CREWMEN
DREAMED
DREAMER
DREAMON
DREAMUP
FREEMAN
FREEMEN
GLEAMED
IDEAMAN
IDEAMEN
PREAMPS
PREEMIE
PREEMPT
SHERMAN
STEAMED
STEAMER
STEMMED
THEOMEN
THERMAL
THERMOS
WHELMED

••E••M•

AWESOME
BEEGUMS
ONETIME
PHENOMS
PLENUMS
PRELIMS
PRESUME
TEETIME
WOEISME

••E•••M

BEEBALM
BEECHAM
CAESIUM
CHETRUM
FIEFDOM
FREEDOM
NEEDHAM
OMENTUM
PIETISM
PREMIUM
RHENIUM
STEINEM
STERNUM
THEFIRM
THEOREM
VIETNAM

•••EM••

ANAEMIA
ANAEMIC
ARTEMIS
ARTEMUS
ATTEMPT
BASEMAN
BASEMEN
BATEMAN
BIREMES
BOHEMIA
BYREMAN
BYREMEN
CAKEMIX
CAVEMAN
CAVEMEN
CINEMAS
CINEMAX
COLEMAN
DILEMMA
ENDEMIC
FIREMAN
FIREMEN
FOREMAN
FOREMEN
FREEMAN
FREEMEN
GATEMAN
GATEMEN
INGEMAR
KINEMAS
LEXEMES
LIKEMAD
LINEMAN
LINEMEN
PIKEMAN
PIKEMEN
PIPEMMA
POLEMIC
PREEMIE
PREEMPT
RACEMES
SCHEMAS
SCHEMED
SCHEMER
SCHEMES
SIDEMAN
SIDEMEN
TAPEMAN
TAPEMEN
TOTEMIC
UNKEMPT
UPTEMPO
WISEMAN
WISEMEN

•••E•M•

BESEEMS
DILEMMA
ESTEEMS
INSEAMS
LYCEUMS
MUSEUMS
PALERMO
PIPEMMA
REDEEMS
SCREAMS
STREAMS

•••E••M

ATHEISM
BLUEGUM
BOREDOM
DUKEDOM
FIREARM
FOREARM
FREEDOM
INTERIM
NOSEEUM
PINETUM
SEVENAM
SEVENPM
SIDEARM
TAKEAIM
THREEAM
THREEPM
TONEARM

••••EM•

ACADEME
ACADEMY
ALCHEMY
ANADEMS
ANTHEMS
BESEEMS
CONDEMN
CONTEMN
DIADEMS
EMBLEMS
ESTEEMS
EXTREME
IPANEMA
MAYHEMS
MOSLEMS
NOXZEMA
PHONEME
PTOLEMY
REDEEMS
SACHEMS
SANREMO
SOSUEME
SUPREME
SUPREMO
SYSTEMS
TANDEMS
TRIREME

••••E•M

ANAHEIM
LOWBEAM
MIDTERM
NOSEEUM
SUNBEAM
TAGTEAM
THREEAM
THREEPM
WILHELM
WYCHELM
YEATEAM

•••••EM

ADFINEM
APOTHEM
HAARLEM
PERDIEM
PROBLEM
REQUIEM
STEINEM
THEOREM
TOTIDEM

EN•••••

ENABLED
ENABLES
ENACTED
ENACTOR
ENAMELS
ENAMORS
ENAMOUR
ENCAGED
ENCAGES
ENCAMPS
ENCASED
ENCASES
ENCHAIN
ENCHANT
ENCINAS
ENCLAVE
ENCLOSE
ENCODED
ENCODER
ENCODES
ENCOMIA
ENCORES
ENCRUST
ENCRYPT
ENDEARS
ENDEDUP
ENDEMIC
ENDGAME
ENDINGS
ENDIVES
ENDLESS
ENDMOST
ENDORSE
ENDOWED
ENDPLAY
ENDRUNS
ENDUING
ENDURED
ENDURES
ENDUROS
ENDUSER
ENDUSES
ENDWAYS
ENDWISE
ENDZONE
ENEMIES
ENFOLDS
ENFORCE
ENGAGED
ENGAGES
ENGARDE
ENGINES
ENGIRDS
ENGLAND
ENGLISH
ENGLUND
ENGORGE
ENGRAFT
ENGRAMS
ENGRAVE
ENGROSS
ENGULFS
ENHANCE
ENIGMAS
ENISLED
ENISLES
ENJOINS
ENJOYED
ENLACED
ENLACES
ENLARGE
ENLISTS
ENLIVEN
ENMASSE
ENNEADS
ENNOBLE
ENOUNCE
ENPLANE
ENQUIRE
ENQUIRY
ENRAGED
ENRAGES
ENROBED
ENROBES
ENROLLS
ENROOTS
ENROUTE
ENSIGNS
ENSILED
ENSILES
ENSKIED
ENSKIES
ENSLAVE
ENSNARE
ENSNARL
ENSOULS
ENSUING
ENSUITE
ENSURED
ENSURES
ENTAILS
ENTEBBE
ENTENTE
ENTERED
ENTERON
ENTHRAL
ENTHUSE
ENTICED
ENTICER
ENTICES
ENTITLE
ENTRAIN
ENTRANT
ENTRAPS
ENTREAT
ENTREES
ENTRIES
ENTROPY
ENTRUST
ENTWINE
ENURING
ENVELOP
ENVIERS
ENVIOUS
ENVYING
ENWRAPS
ENZYMES

E•N••••

ENNEADS
ENNOBLE
ERNESTO

E••N•••

EARNERS
EARNEST
EARNING
EBONIES
EBONITE
ECONOMY
EGGNOGS
EMANANT
EMANATE
EMANUEL
EMENDED
EMENDER
EMINENT
ENSNARE
ENSNARL
EPONYMS
EPONYMY
ETHNICS
ETONIAN
EVANDER
EVANGEL
EVANISH
EVENEST
EVENING
EVENKIS
EVENOUT
EVENSUP
EVINCED
EVINCES
EXANIMO

E•••N••

EATENAT
EATENUP
ECHINUS
EDASNER
EDGINGS
EFFENDI
ELEANOR
EMBANKS
EMPANEL
ENCINAS
ENDINGS
ENGINES
ENHANCE
ENOUNCE
ENTENTE
EQUINES
EQUINOX
ERMINES
ERRANCY
ERRANDS
ESPANOL
ESSENCE
ESSENES
ESTONIA
ETERNAL
ETHANOL
ETIENNE
EUGENIE
EVZONES
EXPANDS
EXPANSE
EXPENDS
EXPENSE
EXPUNGE
EXTENDS
EXTENTS
EXTINCT

E••••N•

EAGLING
EARNING
EARRING
EASTEND
ECHIDNA
ECHOING
EDDYING
EDITING
EDUCING
ELATING
ELEGANT
ELEMENT
ELEVENS
ELIDING
ELOIGNS
ELOPING
ELUDING
ELUTING
EMANANT
EMINENT
EMOTING
ENCHANT
ENDRUNS
ENDUING
ENDZONE
ENGLAND
ENGLUND
ENJOINS
ENPLANE
ENSIGNS
ENSUING
ENTRANT
ENTWINE
ENURING
ENVYING
EPERGNE
EPICENE
EPIGENE
EPIGONE
ERASING
ERELONG
ERODENT
ERODING
ERSKINE
ESPYING
ETAMINE
ETCHANT
ETCHING
ETIENNE
EUPHONY
EVADING
EVENING
EVIDENT
EVOKING
EXAMINE
EXIGENT
EXILING
EXITING
EXPOUND
EXTERNS
EXUDING
EYEBANK

E•••••N

EARLYON
EARTHEN
EASEDIN
EASESIN
EASTERN
EASTMAN
ECHELON
EDGEDIN
EDGESIN
EDITION
EELSKIN
EGGEDON
ELAAIUN
ELATION
ELEISON
ELISION
ELLISON
ELUTION
ELYSIAN
EMERSON
EMOTION
ENCHAIN
ENLIVEN
ENTERON
ENTRAIN
EPSILON
EPSTEIN
EREWHON
ERICSON
EROSION
ETESIAN
ETONIAN
EVASION
EXPLAIN
EXURBAN

•EN••••

BENATAR
BENAZIR
BENCHED
BENCHES
BENDERS
BENDIER
BENDIGO
BENDING
BENEATH
BENEFIT
BENELUX
BENGALI
BENGALS
BENISON
BENNETT
BENTHAM
BENTLEY
BENTSEN
BENUMBS
BENZENE
CENSERS
CENSING
CENSORS
CENSURE
CENTAUR
CENTAVO
CENTERS
CENTIME
CENTIMO
CENTRAL
CENTRED
CENTRES
CENTRIC
CENTURY
DENARII
DENDRON
DENEUVE
DENIALS
DENIERS
DENIZEN
DENMARK
DENNEHY
DENOTED
DENOTES
DENSELY
DENSEST
DENSITY
DENTATE
DENTINE
DENTING
DENTIST
DENTURE
DENUDED
DENUDES
DENYING
FENCERS
FENCING
FENDERS
FENDING
FENIANS
FENNIER
GENDERS
GENERAL
GENERIC
GENERIS
GENESEE
GENESES
GENESIS
GENETIC
GENGHIS
GENNARO
GENOESE
GENOMES
GENTEEL
GENTIAN
GENTILE
GENTLED
GENTLER
GENTLES
GENUINE
HENBANE
HENBITS
HENCOOP
HENDRIX
HENLIKE
HENNAED
HENNERY
HENNISH
HENPECK
HENRYIV
HENTING
JENNETS
JENNIES
KENDALL
KENNEDY
KENNELS
KENNETH
KENOSHA
KENTISH
KENYANS
LENDERS
LENDING
LENFANT
LENGTHS
LENGTHY
LENIENT
LENTIGO
LENTILS
MENACED
MENACES
MENAGES
MENCKEN
MENDERS
MENDING
MENDOZA
MENFOLK
MENHIRS
MENIALS
MENISCI
MENORAH
MENOTTI
MENTHOL
MENTION
MENTORS
MENUHIN
MENZIES
PENALTY
PENANCE
PENATES
PENCILS
PENDANT
PENDENT
PENDING
PENGUIN
PENLIKE
PENNAME
PENNANT
PENNATE
PENNERS
PENNIES
PENNING
PENNONS
PENPALS
PENSEES
PENSION
PENSIVE
PENTADS
PENTIUM
PENUCHE
PENULTS
RENAILS
RENAMED
RENAMES
RENARDS
RENAULT
RENDERS
RENDING
RENEGED
RENEGER
RENEGES
RENEGUE
RENEWAL
RENEWED
RENEWER
RENNINS
RENOTED
RENOTES
RENTALS
RENTERS
RENTING
SENATES
SENATOR
SENDERS
SENDFOR
SENDING
SENDOFF
SENDOUT
SENDSIN
SENDSUP
SENDUPS
SENECAS
SENEGAL
SENIORS
SENNETT
SENORAS
SENORES
SENSATE
SENSING
SENSORS
SENSORY
SENSUAL
SENTFOR
SENTOFF
SENTOUT
SENUFOS
TENABLE
TENABLY
TENACES
TENANCY
TENANTS
TENCENT
TENDERS
TENDING
TENDONS
TENDRIL
TENDSTO
TENFOLD
TENFOUR
TENNERS
TENNIEL
TENONED
TENPINS
TENRECS
TENSELY
TENSEST
TENSEUP
TENSILE
TENSING
TENSION
TENSIVE
TENSORS
TENSPOT
TENTERS
TENTHLY
TENTING
TENUITY
TENUOUS
TENURED
TENURES
TENZING
VENALLY
VENDING
VENDORS
VENEERS
VENISON
VENTERS
VENTING
VENTRAL
VENTURA
VENTURE
WENCHES
WENDELL
WENDERS
WENDING
WENDISH
WENTAPE
WENTBAD
WENTFOR
WENTOFF
WENTOUT
ZENANAS
ZENITHS
ZENOBIA

•E•N•••

BEANBAG
BEANERY
BEANIES
BEANING
BENNETT
BERNARD
BERNESE
BERNICE
BERNSEN
DEANERY
DENNEHY
DERNIER
FEINTED
FENNIER
FERNBAR
FERNIER
FEYNMAN
GENNARO
HEINOUS
HENNAED
HENNERY
HENNISH
HEXNUTS
JEANARP
JEANLUC
JEANNIE
JENNETS
JENNIES
KEENERS
KEENEST
KEENING
KENNEDY
KENNELS
KENNETH
KERNELS
KERNING
KEYNOTE
LEANDER
LEANERS
LEANEST
LEANING
LEANSON
LEANTOS
LEONARD
LEONIDS
LEONINE
LEONORA
MEANDER
MEANEST
MEANIES
MEANING
MEINIES
NEONATE
NEWNESS
PEANUTS
PENNAME
PENNANT
PENNATE
PENNERS
PENNIES
PENNING
PENNONS
PEONAGE
PEONIES
PETNAME
REDNESS
REENACT
REENTER
REENTRY
REGNANT
REINING
REINKED
REINSIN
REMNANT
RENNINS
REUNIFY
REUNION
REUNITE
REYNARD
SEANCES
SEENFIT
SEENOFF
SEENOUT
SEINERS
SEINING
SENNETT
TEENAGE
TEENERS
TEENIER
TENNERS
TENNIEL
TERNARY
TERNATE
VEENECK
VEINIER
VEINING
VERNIER
WEANING
WEENIER
WEENIES
WERNHER
WETNESS
YEANING

•E••N••

BEATNIK
BEGONIA
BELINDA
BELONGS
CEMENTS
CEZANNE
DEBONED
DEBONES
DEBUNKS
DECANTS
DECENCY
DEFENCE
DEFENDS
DEFENSE
DEFINED
DEFINES
DEFUNCT
DEIGNED
DELANEY
DEMANDS
DEMONIC
DEPENDS
DEPONED
DEPONES
DETENTE
FEIGNED
FELINES
GERENTS
GERUNDS
GETINTO
JEANNIE
JEEPNEY
JEJUNUM
KEARNEY
KETONES
LEARNED
LEARNER
LEBANON
LEGENDS
LEIBNIZ
LEMONDE
LEPANTO
LETINON
LEVANTS
MELANGE
MELANIE
MELANIN
MELINDA
MEMENTO
MERINOS
PEDANTS
PENANCE
PETUNIA
REBENDS
REBINDS
RECANED
RECANES
RECANTS
RECENCY
REDANTS
REFINED
REFINER
REFINES
REFUNDS
REGENCY
REGENTS
REHANGS
REIGNED
RELENTS
RELINED
RELINES
REMANDS
REMENDS
REMINDS
REPENTS
REPINED
REPINES
RERENTS
RERINSE
RESANDS
RESENDS
RESENTS
RESINGS
RETINAE
RETINAL
RETINAS
RETINUE
RETUNED
RETUNES
REVENGE
REVENUE
REWINDS
REZONED
REZONES
SECANTS
SECONDS
SELENIC
SEMINAL
SEMINAR
SERENER
SETINTO
SEVENAM
SEVENPM
SEVENTH
SEVENTY
SEVENUP
TENANCY
TENANTS
TENONED
TERENCE
TETANUS
VEDANTA
VERANDA
YEARNED
YEARNER
YEMENIS
ZENANAS

•E•••N•

BEACONS
BEADING
BEAMING
BEANING
BEARING
BEATING
BECKONS
BEDDING
BEEFING
BEELINE
BEEPING
BEGGING
BEGUINE
BEIJING
BELLING
BELLINI
BELMONT
BELTANE
BELTING
BELYING
BEMOANS
BENDING
BENZENE
BESTING
BETHANY
BETHINK
BETTING
CEASING
CEBUANO
CEILING

CELLINI
CENSING
CESSING
CEZANNE
DEACONS
DEADEND
DEADENS
DEAFENS
DEALING
DECKING
DECLINE
DEEDING
DEEMING
DEEPEND
DEEPENS
DEFIANT
DEFYING
DEHORNS
DEICING
DELEING
DELVING
DEMEANS
DEMESNE
DENTINE
DENTING
DENYING
DEPLANE
DERRING
DESCANT
DESCEND
DESCENT
DESIGNS
DESMOND
DESTINE
DESTINY
DETAINS
DEVEINS
DEVIANT
DEWLINE
FEARING
FEEDING
FEELING
FELLING
FELLINI
FENCING
FENDING
FENIANS
FERMENT
FERVENT
FESSING
FEUDING
GEARING
GELDING
GELLING
GENUINE
GERAINT
GERMANE
GERMANS
GERMANY
GETTING
HEADING
HEALING
HEAPING
HEARING
HEATING
HEAVENS
HEAVING
HEDGING
HEEDING
HEELING
HEFTING
HELLENE
HELMING
HELPING
HEMLINE
HEMMING
HENBANE
HENTING
HERDING
HERMANN
HEROINE
HERRING
HETMANS
JEERING
JELLING
JERKING
JERKINS
JESTING
JETGUNS
JETSONS
JETTING
KEELING
KEENING
KEEPING
KENYANS
KERNING
KEYRING
LEADING
LEADINS
LEAFING
LEAKING
LEANING
LEAPING
LEASING
LEAVENS
LEAVING
LEERING
LEGGING
LEGIONS
LEGRAND
LEMMING
LENDING
LENFANT
LENIENT
LEONINE
LEPTONS
LESSENS
LESSING
LESSONS
LETTING
LEUCINE
LEVYING
MEANING
MEDIANS
MEDIANT
MEETING
MELDING
MELTING
MENDING
MEOWING
MERGING
MESHING
MESSINA
MESSING
METHANE
MEWLING
NEARING
NEATENS
NECKING
NEEDING
NELSONS
NEPTUNE
NESTING
NETTING
NEURONE
NEURONS
NEWTONS
PEAHENS
PEAKING
PEALING
PEASANT
PECCANT
PECKING
PECTINS
PEEKING
PEELING
PEEPING
PEERING
PEEVING
PEGGING
PELTING
PENDANT
PENDENT
PENDING
PENNANT
PENNING
PENNONS
PEPPING
PEPSINS
PERCENT
PERKING
PERKINS
PERMING
PERSONA
PERSONS
PETTING
READING
REAGENT
REAMING
REAPING
REAREND
REARING
REASONS
REBOUND
RECKONS
RECLINE
RECOUNT
REDCENT
REDDENS
REDDING
REDFINS
REDLINE
REDOING
REDOUND
REDPINE
REDWINE
REDWING
REEDING
REEFING
REEKING
REELING
REFFING
REGAINS
REGIONS
REGNANT
REINING
REJOINS
RELIANT
RELLENO
RELYING
REMAINS
REMNANT
REMOUNT
RENDING
RENNINS
RENTING
REOPENS
REPAINT
REPLANS
REPLANT
REPRINT
REPUGNS
RESCIND
RESIGNS
RESOUND
RESPINS
RESPOND
RESTING
RETAINS
RETHINK
RETSINA
RETURNS
REUBENS
REVVING
REWOUND
SEAFANS
SEALANE
SEALANT
SEALING
SEAMING
SEARING
SEASONS
SEATING
SEEDING
SEEKING
SEEMING
SEEPING
SEGMENT
SEINING
SEIZING
SELLING
SENDING
SENSING
SEQUINS
SERLING
SERMONS
SERPENT
SERVANT
SERVING
SESTINA
SETLINE
SETTING
SEVIGNE
SEXTANS
SEXTANT
SEXTONS
TEAMING
TEARING
TEASING
TEDDING
TEEMING
TELLING
TENCENT
TENDING
TENDONS
TENPINS
TENSING
TENTING
TENZING
TERHUNE
TERMING
TERMINI
TERRENE
TESTING
TEUTONS
VEERING
VEGGING
VEILING
VEINING
VENDING
VENTING
VERBENA
VERDANT
VERGING
VERMONT
VESTING
VETOING
VETTING
WEAKENS
WEANING
WEAPONS
WEARING
WEAVING
WEBBING
WEDDING
WEDGING
WEEDING
WEEKEND
WEEPING
WELDING
WELKINS
WELLAND
WELLING
WELTING
WENDING
WESTEND
WETLAND
WETTING
YEANING
YEAREND
YELLING
YELPING
YERKING
YESSING
YEVGENY
ZEALAND
ZEITUNG
ZEROING

•E••••N

AEOLIAN
BEARSON
BEDDOWN
BEDIZEN
BEDOUIN
BELAKUN
BELGIAN
BELLMAN
BELLMEN
BENISON
BENTSEN
BERGMAN
BERGSON
BERNSEN
BESTMAN
BESTMEN
BETAKEN
BETOKEN
BETWEEN
CELADON
CERTAIN
CERUMEN
CESSION
DEADPAN
DEALSIN
DEALTIN
DECAGON
DENDRON
DENIZEN
DETRAIN
DEXTRIN
EELSKIN
FEEDSON
FELDMAN
FESTOON
FEYNMAN
GELATIN
GENTIAN
GETDOWN
GETEVEN
GETITON
HEADMAN
HEADMEN
HEADPIN
HEADSIN
HEARKEN
HEARTEN
HEATHEN
HEISMAN
HELICON
HELLION
HELLMAN
HEPARIN
HEPBURN
HERMANN
HESHVAN
HESSIAN
HEXAGON
HEXSIGN
JEWISON
KEEPSIN
KEEPSON
KEESHAN
KERATIN
KEYEDIN
LEADSIN
LEADSON
LEANSON
LEAVEIN
LEBANON
LEBARON
LECTERN
LEGHORN
LETDOWN
LETINON
LETUPON
LEXICON
MEGRYAN
MEISSEN
MELANIN
MENCKEN
MENTION
MENUHIN
MEXICAN
NETIZEN
NEUTRON
NEVADAN
NEWBORN
NEWMOON
NEWMOWN
NEWSMAN
NEWSMEN
NEWTOWN
PEABEAN
PEARSON
PEERSIN
PELICAN
PEMICAN
PENGUIN
PENSION
PERLMAN
PERSIAN
PERTAIN
READSIN
RECLEAN
REDRAWN
REELSIN
REFRAIN
REGIMEN
REINSIN
REITMAN
RELEARN
REPOMAN
RESTAIN
RETAKEN
RETRAIN
REUNION
REWOVEN
SEALION
SECTION
SEEPSIN
SENDSIN
SERBIAN
SESSION
SETDOWN
SETUPON
SEWEDON
TEACHIN
TEHERAN
TELERAN
TELLSON
TENSION
TERRAIN
TESTBAN
VENISON
VERSION
VETERAN
WEIGHIN
WELLMAN
WELLRUN
WESTERN
YELTSIN
YEREVAN
ZEBULON

••EN•••

ABENAKI
ADENINE
AGENDAS
ALENCON
AMENDED
AMENITY
AVENGED
AVENGER
AVENGES
AVENUES
BIENTOT
BLENDED
BLENDER
BRENDAN
BRENNAN
BRENNER
CHENIER
CRENELS
DUENNAS
EMENDED
EMENDER
EVENEST
EVENING
EVENKIS
EVENOUT
EVENSUP
FIENNES
FLENSED
FLENSES
FRENEAU
GRENADA
GRENADE
GRENDEL
IDENTIC
KEENERS
KEENEST
KEENING
LAENNEC
LIENEES
MAENADS
MCENROE
OMENTUM
ONENESS
ONENOTE
OPENAIR
OPENBAR
OPENEND
OPENERS
OPENING
OPENPIT
OPENSEA
OPENSUP
OPENTOE
PFENNIG
PHENOLS
PHENOMS
PLENARY
PLENUMS
PRENUPS
QUENTIN
REENACT
REENTER
REENTRY
RHENISH
RHENIUM
SCENDED
SCENERY
SCENTED
SEENFIT
SEENOFF
SEENOUT
SIENNAS
SLENDER
SPENCER
SPENDER
SPENSER
STENCIL
STENGEL
STENTOR
TEENAGE
TEENERS
TEENIER
THENARS
TOENAIL
TRENARY
TRENDED
TRENTON
UNENDED
UPENDED
UTENSIL
VEENECK
WEENIER
WEENIES
WIENERS
WIENIES

••E•N••

BRENNAN
BRENNER
CLEANED
CLEANER
CLEANLY
CLEANSE
CLEANUP
DUENNAS
ELEANOR
ETERNAL
FIENNES
FLEXNER
GLEANED
GLEANER
GREENED
GREENER
JEEPNEY
KLEENEX
LAENNEC
LIERNES
OCEANIA
OCEANIC
OCEANID
OCEANUS
PFENNIG
PREENED
PREENER
QUEENLY
SIENNAS
STEINEM
STEINER
STERNAL
STERNER
STERNLY
STERNUM
SWEENEY
TIEINTO
TIERNEY
VIETNAM

••E••N•

ABEYANT
ACETONE
ADELINE
ADENINE
AMERIND
ANELING
ANEMONE
ARETINO
BEEFING
BEELINE
BEEPING
BRETONS
BREWING
CHEWING
CLEMENS
CLEMENT
CREMONA
CRETANS
CRETINS
CREWING
DEEDING
DEEMING
DEEPEND
DEEPENS
DIETING
DUELING
ELEGANT
ELEMENT
ELEVENS
EPERGNE
ERELONG
EVENING
EYEBANK
FEEDING
FEELING
FLEEING
FLEMING
FLEXING
FLEYING
FREEING
FREMONT
FUELING
GREYING
HEEDING
HEELING
ICELAND
ICERINK
IKEBANA
IRELAND
ITERANT
JEERING
JREWING
KEELING
KEENING
KEEPING
KMESONS
KNEEING
LEERING
MEETING
NEEDING
OBEYING
OLEFINS
ONELANE
OPENEND
OPENING
OPERAND
OREGANO
PEEKING
PEELING
PEEPING
PEERING
PEEVING
PIECING
PIEPANS
PIETINS
PREBEND
PRESENT
PRETEND
PREVENT
QUEUING
REEDING
REEFING
REEKING
REELING
SEEDING
SEEKING
SEEMING
SEEPING
SHEBANG
SKEWING
SMETANA
SPECING
SPELUNK
SPEWING
STEPINS
STEVENS
STEWING
TEEMING
THEFONZ
TIELINE
TIEPINS
TIERING
TREEING
TREPANS
TREVINO
VEERING
VIEWING
WEEDING
WEEKEND
WEEPING

••E•••N

ALENCON
BREAKIN
BRENDAN
BRENNAN
BRESLIN
CHEAPEN
CHEATIN
CHECHEN
CHECKIN
CHEVRON
CLEAVON
CLEMSON
CREWMAN
CREWMEN
DIEDOWN
DOESKIN
DREAMON
DRESDEN
ELEISON
EMERSON
EREWHON
ETESIAN
FEEDSON
FREEMAN
FREEMEN
FRESHEN
GHERKIN
GLEASON
GRECIAN
GREMLIN
GREYHEN
HOEDOWN
IBERIAN
IDEAMAN
IDEAMEN
IRECKON
KEEPSIN
KEEPSON
KEESHAN
KREMLIN
LIEDOWN
MUEZZIN
NIELSEN
OBERLIN
ONEIRON
OVERRAN
OVERRUN
PEERSIN
PREDAWN
PRESSON
PRESTON
PRETEEN
PREYSON
QUENTIN
REELSIN
SEEPSIN
SHELDON
SHELTON
SHERMAN
SHERWIN
SKELTON
SLEEKEN
SLEEPIN
SLEEPON
SLEPTIN
SLEPTON
SNEAKIN
SNELLEN
STEEPEN
STEPHEN
STEPSIN
STEPSON
STETSON
STEUBEN
SWEARIN
SWEETEN
SWEETON
THEOMEN
THEREIN
THEREON
TIEDOWN
TREASON
TREMAIN
TRENTON
UNEATEN
WHEATON
WHEREIN

•••EN••

ABSENCE
ABSENTS
ACCENTS
ACHENES
ADDENDA
ADDENDS
ADRENAL
ADVENTS
ALBENIZ
ALDENTE
ALIENEE
ALIENOR
ALKENES
ALLENBY
ALLENDE
ANTENNA
APLENTY
APPENDS
ARDENCY
ARMENIA
ARPENTS
ARSENAL
ARSENIC
ARSENIO
ASCENDS
ASCENTS
ASSENTS
ATTENDS
AUGENDS
BARENTS
BASENJI
CADENCE
CADENCY
CADENZA
CALENDS
CATENAE
CAYENNE
CEMENTS
CLIENTS
COGENCY
COZENED
DECENCY
DEFENCE
DEFENDS
DEFENSE
DEPENDS
DETENTE
DIZENED
DOCENTS
DOYENNE
DOZENTH
EATENAT
EATENUP
EFFENDI
ENTENTE
ESSENCE
ESSENES
ETIENNE
EUGENIE
EXPENDS
EXPENSE
EXTENDS
EXTENTS
FAGENDS
FAIENCE
FILENES
FIRENZE
FLUENCY
FOMENTS
FRIENDS
GERENTS
GIVENIN
GIVENTO
GIVENUP
GREENED
GREENER
GYRENES
HAPENNY
HAVENOT
IMMENSE
IMPENDS
INCENSE
INDENTS
INGENUE
INTENDS
INTENSE
INTENTS
INVENTS
JIMENEZ
JUVENAL
KLEENEX
KUTENAI
LAMENTS
LATENCY
LATENTS
LEGENDS
LICENCE
LICENSE
LIFENET
LIKENED
LIKENEW
LISENTE
LIVENED
LORENZO
LOZENGE
LUCENCY
LYSENKO
MAGENTA
MARENGO
MCHENRY
MEMENTO
MOMENTS
NOVENAS
OFFENCE
OFFENDS
OFFENSE
OFTENER
ORIENTE
ORIENTS
PARENTS
PATENTS
PHOENIX
PHRENIC
PIMENTO
PINENUT
POLENTA
POTENCY
PREENED
PREENER
PUDENCY
QUEENLY
RAVENED
RAVENNA
REBENDS
RECENCY
REGENCY
REGENTS
RELENTS
REMENDS
REPENTS
RERENTS
RESENDS
RESENTS
REVENGE
REVENUE
RIPENED
RODENTS
SCIENCE
SELENIC
SERENER
SEVENAM
SEVENPM
SEVENTH
SEVENTY
SEVENUP
SILENCE
SILENTS
SIMENON
STDENIS
SWEENEY
TAGENDS
TAKENIN
TAKENON
TALENTS
TERENCE
TOKENED
TYLENOL
UNBENDS
URGENCY
VALENCE
VALENCY
VIVENDI
WAKENED
WAKENER
WIDENED
WIZENED
WOKENUP
YEMENIS

•••E•N•

ANDEANS
ANTEING
ANTENNA
BALEENS
BLUEING
CAPEANN
CAREENS
CASERNE
CASERNS
CAVEINS
CAVERNS
CAYENNE
CLUEING
CODEINE
COMEONS
DELEING
DEMEANS
DEMESNE
DEVEINS
DOYENNE
ETIENNE
EXTERNS
FADEINS
FIREANT
FLEEING
FREEING
GIDEONS
GOVERNS
HAPENNY
INFERNO
INTERNS
KNEEING
KOREANS
LATEENS
LAVERNE
LIVEONE
LOVEINS
LUCERNE
MODERNS
ORLEANS
PAGEANT

PATERNO
PIGEONS
RAVENNA
SALERNO
SATEENS
SCREENS
SHOEING
SOMEONE
SPLEENS
TAKEONE
TAVERNS
TREEING
TRUEING
TUREENS
WYVERNS

•••E••N

ACHERON
ACHESON
ACTEDON
ADDEDIN
ADDEDON
AILERON
ASKEDIN
AZTECAN
BASEMAN
BASEMEN
BATEMAN
BLUEFIN
BOXEDIN
BOXESIN
BYREMAN
BYREMEN
CAMERON
CAPEANN
CAVEDIN
CAVEMAN
CAVEMEN
CAVESIN
CLUEDIN
CLUESIN
COLEMAN
COMESIN
COMESON
DINEDIN
DINEDON
DINESEN
DINESIN
DINESON
DIVESIN
DOTEDON
DOTESON
EASEDIN
EASESIN
ECHELON
EDGEDIN
EDGESIN
EGGEDON
ENTERON
FADEDIN
FADESIN
FIREMAN
FIREMEN
FLIESIN
FOREIGN
FOREMAN
FOREMEN
FORERAN
FORERUN
FREEMAN
FREEMEN
FRIEDAN
GATEMAN
GATEMEN
GETEVEN
GIVENIN
GIVESIN
GLUEDON
GLUESON
GOTEVEN
HAMELIN
HIRESON
HOMERUN
JAMESON
JAVELIN
KEYEDIN
LATERAN
LATERON
LINEMAN
LINEMEN
LIVEDIN
LIVEDON
LIVESIN
LIVESON
MATEWAN
MIXEDIN
MIXESIN
MOVEDIN
MOVEDON
MOVESIN
MOVESON
MUMESON
NINEPIN
PHAETON
PIKEMAN
PIKEMEN
PILEDIN
PILEDON
PILESIN
PILESON
PIMESON
POKEFUN
QUIETEN
RAKEDIN
RAKESIN
RAMEKIN
RELEARN
ROBESON
ROPEDIN
ROPESIN
RULESON
SAGEHEN
SEWEDON
SIDEMAN
SIDEMEN
SIMENON
SLEEKEN
SLEEPIN
SLEEPON
SLOEGIN
SPIEDON
SPIESON
STEEPEN
SWEETEN
SWEETON
TAKENIN
TAKENON
TAKESIN
TAKESON
TAKETEN
TAPEMAN
TAPEMEN
TEHERAN
TELERAN
THREWIN
TIBETAN
TRIEDON
TRIESON
TUNEDIN
TUNESIN
UNLEARN
VETERAN
VOTEDIN
VOTESIN
WADEDIN
WADESIN
WAVEDIN
WAVESIN
WISEMAN
WISEMEN
WOBEGON
YEREVAN

••••EN•

ABILENE
ACUMENS
AILMENT
ALIMENT
AMBIENT
ANCIENT
AUGMENT
AWAKENS
BACKEND
BALEENS
BARRENS
BARTEND
BATTENS
BENZENE
BIGBEND
BIOGENY
BOOKEND
BURDENS
CAREENS
CLEMENS
CLEMENT
COMMEND
COMMENT
CONSENT
CONTEND
CONTENT
CONVENE
CONVENT
COZZENS
CRAVENS
CURRENT
DAMPENS
DARKENS
DARLENE
DEADEND
DEADENS
DEAFENS
DEEPEND
DEEPENS
DESCEND
DESCENT
DICKENS
DISSENT
DISTEND
DOLMENS
DUODENA
EASTEND
ELEMENT
ELEVENS
EMINENT
EPICENE
EPIGENE
ERODENT
EVIDENT
EXIGENT
FASTENS
FATTENS
FERMENT
FERVENT
FIGMENT
FORFEND
FORRENT
FORWENT
FULGENT
GARDENS
GARMENT
GINSENG
GODSEND
HAPPENS
HARDENS
HARKENS
HASTENS
HEAVENS
HELLENE
HIGHEND
HOYDENS
HUYGENS
HYGIENE
HYPHENS
IMOGENE
JAYLENO
KITTENS
KOBLENZ
KUCHENS
LAMBENT
LARCENY
LATEENS
LATTENS
LAURENT
LEAVENS
LENIENT
LESSENS
LICHENS
LINDENS
LISTENS
LOOSENS
MADDENS
MAIDENS
MARLENE
MARTENS
MIDDENS
MILLEND
MINUEND
MIOCENE
MITTENS
MIZZENS
MORDENT
MUDHENS
NASCENT
NEATENS
OBSCENE
ODDMENT
OPENEND
OPULENT
OROGENY
PARVENU
PATIENT
PATTENS
PAYMENT
PEAHENS
PENDENT
PERCENT
PICKENS
PIGMENT
PIGPENS
PLATENS
POLLENS
PORSENA
PORTEND
PORTENT
POULENC
PREBEND
PRESENT
PRETEND
PREVENT
PROGENY
PRUDENT
PUNGENT
PUPTENT
RAIMENT
REAGENT
REAREND
REDCENT
REDDENS
RELLENO
REOPENS
REUBENS
RIPIENO
SADDENS
SALIENT
SAPIENS
SAPIENT
SARGENT
SATEENS
SCALENE
SCREENS
SEGMENT
SERPENT
SICKENS
SLOVENE
SLOVENS
SOFTENS
SOLVENT
SPLEENS
STAMENS
STEVENS
STIPEND
STUDENT
STYRENE
SUBTEND
SUSPEND
TAILEND
TANGENT
TAUTENS
TENCENT
TERRENE
TOLUENE
TORMENT
TORRENS
TORRENT
TRIDENT
TUREENS
UNGUENT
UNSPENT
USOPENS
VERBENA
VINCENT
VIOLENT
WARDENS
WARRENS
WEAKENS
WEEKEND
WESTEND
WHITENS
WOOLENS
WORSENS
YEAREND
YEVGENY

••••E•N

ACTAEON
ALAMEIN
ARAMEAN
BARGEIN
BETWEEN
BITTERN
BOOLEAN
BROKEIN
BURGEON
CANTEEN
CHILEAN
CISTERN
CLOSEIN
COLLEEN
CONCERN
CONDEMN
CONTEMN
CRIMEAN
DISCERN
DRIVEIN
DUDGEON
DUNGEON
EASTERN
EPSTEIN
FIFTEEN
FONTEYN
GALLEON
HASBEEN
HOLBEIN
HUSSEIN
LANTERN
LEAVEIN
LECTERN
MAUREEN
MCQUEEN
MRCLEAN
MULLEIN
NANKEEN
NUCLEON
OAKFERN
ORPHEAN
PASTERN
PATTERN
PEABEAN
PHASEIN
PIDGEON
POSTERN
PRETEEN
PROTEAN
PROTEIN
RECLEAN
SHAREIN
SIXTEEN
SLIDEIN
SOTHERN
SOYBEAN
SURGEON
SWOREIN
THEREIN
THEREON
TINTERN
TRADEIN
TRADEON
UMPTEEN
UNCLEAN
VALJEAN
VILLEIN
WAXBEAN
WESTERN
WHEREIN
WIDGEON
WRITEIN
WROTEIN
ZAIREAN

•••••EN

ABDOMEN
AGNOMEN
ALBUMEN
ALMADEN
ANTIGEN
BASEMEN
BATSMEN
BEDIZEN
BELLMEN
BENTSEN
BERNSEN
BESTMEN
BETAKEN
BETOKEN
BETWEEN
BIRDMEN
BITUMEN
BLACKEN
BLITZEN
BOATMEN
BONDMEN
BRACKEN
BRITTEN
BROADEN
BULLPEN
BUSHMEN
BYREMEN
CANTEEN
CAVEMEN
CERUMEN
CHAPMEN
CHASTEN
CHEAPEN
CHECHEN
CHICHEN
CHICKEN
CITIZEN
CITROEN
COARSEN
COLLEEN
CREWMEN
CRYOGEN
DENIZEN
DINESEN
DOORMEN
DRESDEN
DUSTMEN
EARTHEN
ENLIVEN
FIFTEEN
FIREMEN
FLAGMEN
FLATTEN
FOOTMEN
FOREMEN
FRANKEN
FREEMEN
FRESHEN
FROGMEN
GADSDEN
GATEMEN
GETEVEN
GLADDEN
GLISTEN
GOODMEN
GOTEVEN
GREYHEN
HALOGEN
HANGMEN
HANGTEN
HARSHEN
HASBEEN
HEADMEN
HEARKEN
HEARTEN
HEATHEN
HOARSEN
HOBOKEN
IDEAMEN
IRONMEN
JANSSEN
JAZZMEN
KINSMEN
KITCHEN
LAYOPEN
LIGHTEN
LINEMEN
LOCOMEN
MADCHEN
MANXMEN
MAUREEN
MCQUEEN
MEISSEN
MENCKEN
MILKMEN
MOISTEN
MOORHEN
MUTAGEN
NANKEEN
NETIZEN
NEWSMEN
NIELSEN
PAULSEN
PIKEMEN
PLAYPEN
PLOWMEN
POSTMEN
PRETEEN
PROPMEN
PUTAMEN
QUICKEN
QUIETEN
REGIMEN
RETAKEN
REWOVEN
RONTGEN
ROUGHEN
SAGEHEN
SAMISEN
SANDMEN
SARACEN
SARAZEN
SAYWHEN
SCRIVEN
SHARPEN
SHIPMEN
SHODDEN
SHORTEN
SHOWMEN
SIDEMEN
SIXTEEN
SLACKEN
SLEEKEN
SMARTEN
SMIDGEN
SMITTEN
SNELLEN
SNOWMEN
STASSEN
STEEPEN
STEPHEN
STEUBEN
STIFFEN
STOLLEN
STOUTEN
STRIVEN
SWEETEN
SWOLLEN
SWONKEN
TAKETEN
TAPEMEN
TAXIMEN
THEOMEN
THICKEN
TIGHTEN
TOLKIEN
TOOKTEN
TOUGHEN
TRODDEN
UMPTEEN
UNEATEN
UNWOVEN
UPRISEN
WHAUDEN
WISEMEN
WOLFMEN
WOOLLEN
WORKMEN
WRITTEN
YARDMEN

EO•••••

EOLITHS

E•O••••

EBONIES
EBONITE
ECOLOGY
ECONOMY
EDOUARD
EGOISTS
EGOTISM
EGOTIST
EGOTRIP
ELOIGNS
ELOPERS
ELOPING
EMOTERS
EMOTING
EMOTION
EMOTIVE
ENOUNCE
EPOCHAL
EPONYMS
EPONYMY
EPOPEES
EPOXIES
ERODENT
ERODING
EROSELY
EROSION
EROSIVE
EROTICA
ESOTERY
ETOILES
ETONIAN
EVOKERS
EVOKING
EVOLVED
EVOLVES
EXOTICA
EXOTICS

E••O•••

ECHOING
ECLOGUE
EFFORTS
ELBOWED
EMPORIA
EMPOWER
ENCODED
ENCODER
ENCODES
ENCOMIA
ENCORES
ENDORSE
ENDOWED
ENFOLDS
ENFORCE
ENGORGE
ENJOINS
ENJOYED
ENNOBLE
ENROBED
ENROBES
ENROLLS
ENROOTS
ENROUTE
ENSOULS
ESCORTS
ESPOSAS
ESPOSOS
ESPOUSE
ESTONIA
ESTORIL
EVZONES
EXHORTS
EXPORTS
EXPOSED
EXPOSES
EXPOUND
EXTORTS
EXWORKS

E•••O••

EARLOBE
EARLOCK
EASEOFF
EASEOUT
EASYOFF
EATSOUT
ECOLOGY
ECONOMY
EDGEOUT
EDITORS
EDITOUT
EGGNOGS
EGGROLL
EKEDOUT
EKESOUT
ELLIOTT
ELUSORY
EMBROIL
EMPLOYE
EMPLOYS
ENAMORS
ENAMOUR
ENCLOSE
ENDMOST
ENDZONE
ENGROSS
ENROOTS
ENTROPY
ENVIOUS
EPIGONE
EPILOGS
EPISODE
EPITOME
ERELONG
ESCROWS
EUPHONY
EVENOUT
EXPLODE
EXPLOIT
EXPLORE
EYEBOLT
EYEHOLE
EYESORE

E••••O•

EARDROP
EARLDOM
EARLYON
EARSHOT
EATCROW
ECHELON
ECUADOR
EDITION
EGGEDON
ELATION
ELEANOR
ELECTOR
ELEISON
ELISION
ELLISON
ELUTION
EMBRYOS
EMERSON
EMMYLOU
EMOTION
EMPEROR
ENACTOR
ENDUROS
ENTERON
ENVELOP
EPSILON
EQUATOR
EQUINOX
ERECTOR
EREWHON
ERICSON
EROSION
ESCUDOS
ESKIMOS
ESPANOL
ESPOSOS
ETHANOL
EVASION
EXACTOR
EYEBROW
EYESHOT

E•••••O

ELECTRO
ELGRECO
EMBARGO
ERNESTO
ESPARTO
EXANIMO
EXFACTO

•EO••••

AEOLIAN
BEOWULF
DEODARS
GEODESY
GEOLOGY
GEORDIE
GEORGES
GEORGIA
LEONARD
LEONIDS
LEONINE
LEONORA
LEOPARD
LEOPOLD
LEOTARD
MEOWING
NEOLITH
NEONATE
PEONAGE
PEONIES
PEOPLED
PEOPLES
REOCCUR
REOILED
REOPENS
REORDER

•E•O•••

AEROBAT
AEROBES
AEROBIC
AEROSOL
BECOMES
BEDOUIN
BEFOULS
BEGONIA
BEGORRA
BEHOLDS
BEHOOVE
BEHOVED
BEHOVES
BELONGS
BELOVED
BEMOANS
BETOKEN
DEBONED
DEBONES
DEBORAH
DEBOUCH
DECOCTS
DECODED
DECODER
DECODES
DECORUM
DECOYED
DEFORMS
DEHORNS
DEMONIC
DEMOTED
DEMOTES
DENOTED
DENOTES
DEPONED
DEPONES
DEPORTS
DEPOSAL
DEPOSED
DEPOSER
DEPOSES
DEPOSIT
DESOTOS
DETOURS
DEVOLVE
DEVOTED
DEVOTEE
DEVOTES
DEVOURS
FEDORAS
FEMORAL
GEMOTES
GENOESE
GENOMES
GETOVER
HELOISE
HELOTRY
HEROICS
HEROINE
HEROISM
KENOSHA
KEROUAC
KETONES
LEMONDE
LESOTHO
MEGOHMS
MEIOSES
MEIOSIS
MEIOTIC
MELODIC
MEMOIRE
MEMOIRS
MEMOREX
MENORAH
MENOTTI
METOOER
PELOTAS
REBOILS
REBOLTS
REBOOTS
REBOUND
REBOZOS
RECOATS
RECODED
RECODES
RECOILS
RECOLOR
RECORDS
RECORKS
RECOUNT
RECOUPS
RECOVER
REDOAKS
REDOING
REDOUBT
REDOUND
REFOCUS
REFORMS
REHOOKS
REJOICE
REJOINS
RELOADS
RELOCKS
REMODEL
REMOLDS
REMORAS
REMORSE
REMOTER
REMOTES
REMOUNT
REMOVAL
REMOVED
REMOVER
REMOVES
REMOWED
RENOTED
RENOTES
REPOLLS
REPOMAN
REPORTS
REPOSED
REPOSES
REROUTE
RESOLED
RESOLES
RESOLVE
RESORBS
RESORTS
RESOUND
RETOOLS
RETORTS
RETOUCH
RETOURS
RETOWED
REVOICE
REVOKED
REVOKES
REVOLTS
REVOLVE
REWORDS
REWORKS
REWOUND
REWOVEN
REZONED
REZONES
SECONDS
SEGOVIA
SENORAS
SENORES
TENONED
VELOURS
VETOERS
VETOING
ZENOBIA
ZEROING
ZEROSUM

•E••O••

BEACONS
BEAROFF
BEAROUT
BEATOUT
BECKONS
BECLOUD
BEDDOWN
BEDPOST
BEDROCK
BEDROLL
BEDROOM
BEGSOFF
BEHOOVE
BELLOWS
BELMONT
BERTOLT
BESPOKE
BESTOWS
BETROTH
BETTORS
CENSORS
DEACONS
DEALOUT
DEBTORS
DECKOUT
DEFROCK
DEFROST
DELTOID
DEPLORE
DEPLOYS
DESMOND
DESPOIL
DESPOTS
DETROIT
DEVIOUS
FEELOUT
FELLOFF
FELLOUT
FELLOWS
FELTOUT
FERROUS
FERVORS
FERVOUR
FESTOON
FETLOCK
GECKOES
GEOLOGY
GESSOES
GETDOWN
GETLOST
GETSOFF
GETSOUT
HEADOFF
HEADOUT
HEAROUT
HECTORS
HEINOUS

HELDOFF
HELDOUT
HELPOUT
HEMLOCK
HENCOOP
HEYWOOD
JEALOUS
JERBOAS
JETBOAT
JETPORT
JETSONS
KEDROVA
KEEPOFF
KELLOGG
KEPTOFF
KEPTOUT
KEYHOLE
KEYNOTE
KEYWORD
LEACOCK
LEADOFF
LEADOUT
LECTORS
LEFTOFF
LEFTOUT
LEGHORN
LEGIONS
LEGROOM
LEGWORK
LEONORA
LEOPOLD
LEPTONS
LESSONS
LESSORS
LETDOWN
LETSOFF
LETSOUT
MEADOWS
MEADOWY
MELLOWS
MELROSE
MENDOZA
MENFOLK
MENTORS
MERLOTS
METEORS
METEOUT
METHODS
METOOER
NELSONS
NERVOUS
NETWORK
NEURONE
NEURONS
NEWBORN
NEWLOOK
NEWMOON
NEWMOWN
NEWPORT
NEWTONS
NEWTOWN
NEWYORK
PEABODY
PEACOAT
PEACOCK
PEAFOWL
PEAPODS
PEASOUP
PEEKOUT
PEELOFF
PEEROUT
PEGTOPS
PENNONS
PEQUOTS
PERFORM
PERGOLA
PERIODS
PERSONA
PERSONS
PETCOCK
PETIOLE
PETROCK
PETROLS
PETROUS
READOUT
REASONS
REBLOOM
REBOOTS
RECHOSE
RECKONS
RECROOM
RECROSS
RECTORS
RECTORY
REDBOOK
REDCOAT
REDDOGS
REDFORD
REDHOTS
REDPOLL
REDROSE
REDTOPS
REDWOLF
REDWOOD
REELOFF
REGIONS
REGROUP
REHOOKS
REPLOWS
REPROOF
REPROVE
RESHOES
RESHOOT
RESPOND
RESTOCK
RESTORE
RETOOLS
REWROTE
SEABORG
SEACOWS
SEADOGS
SEAFOOD
SEALOFF
SEAMOSS
SEAPORT
SEASONS
SEAWOLF
SECTORS
SEEKOUT
SEENOFF
SEENOUT
SEESOFF
SEESOUT
SEETOIT
SELLOFF
SELLOUT
SENDOFF
SENDOUT
SENIORS
SENSORS
SENSORY
SENTOFF
SENTOUT
SEQUOIA
SERIOUS
SERMONS
SETDOWN
SETSOFF
SETSOUT
SEXTONS
SEYMOUR
TEAPOTS
TEAPOYS
TEAROFF
TEAROOM
TEAROSE
TEAROUT
TEDIOUS
TEEDOFF
TEESOFF
TELLOFF
TENDONS
TENFOLD
TENFOUR
TENSORS
TENUOUS
TERRORS
TESTOUT
TEUTONS
VECTORS
VENDORS
VERBOSE
VERDOUX
VERMONT
WEAPONS
WEAROFF
WEAROUT
WEBFOOT
WEBTOED
WEDLOCK
WEEDOUT
WELCOME
WELLOFF
WENTOFF
WENTOUT
WETMOPS
YELLOWS
YELLOWY
ZEALOTS
ZEALOUS

•E•••O•

AERATOR
AEROSOL
BEARSON
BEDROOM
BELABOR
BELLBOY
BELLHOP
BENISON
BERGSON
BERIDOF
BERLIOZ
BESTBOY
CELADON
CESSION
DECAGON
DECALOG
DECAPOD
DEMEROL
DEMIGOD
DENDRON
DESKTOP
DESOTOS
DESTROY
DEVELOP
DEWDROP
FEEDLOT
FEEDSON
FEELFOR
FELLFOR
FELTFOR
FESTOON
GEARBOX
GEMSBOK
GERITOL
GETITON
HEARDOF
HEARSOF
HELICON
HELLION
HENCOOP
HERRIOT
HEXAGON
HEYWOOD
JEWISON
KEEPSON
KEILLOR
KERCHOO
KERPLOP
LEADSON
LEANSON
LEANTOS
LEBANON
LEBARON
LEGATOS
LEGROOM
LETINON
LETUPON
LEXICON
MEDICOS
MENTHOL
MENTION
MERINOS
NEARYOU
NEGATOR
NEMEROV
NEUTRON
NEWLOOK
NEWMOON
NEWSBOY
PEARSON
PEATBOG
PENSION
PERIDOT
PEUGEOT
REACTOR
REALTOR
REBLOOM
REBOZOS
RECOLOR
RECROOM
REDBOOK
REDSPOT
REDWOOD
REPROOF
REREDOS
RESHOOT
REUNION
SEAFOOD
SEALION
SECTION
SEEDPOD
SELLFOR
SEMILOG
SENATOR
SENDFOR
SENTFOR
SENUFOS
SERFDOM
SESSION
SETUPON
SEWEDON
TEAROOM
TEASHOP
TELLSOF
TELLSON
TEMBLOR
TENSION
TENSPOT
TEREDOS
VENISON
VERSION
WEBFOOT
WEIRDOS
WENTFOR
ZEBULON

•E••••O

BEEFALO
BELASCO
BENDIGO
BERMEJO
CEBUANO
CEMBALO
CENTAVO
CENTIMO
DECARLO
DEFACTO
DEUTERO
FERRARO
GEARSTO
GENNARO
GERALDO
GETINTO
HEAVEHO
HEAVETO
HEIGHHO
JERICHO
KEEPSTO
KERCHOO
LEADSTO
LEDUPTO
LENTIGO
LEPANTO
LESOTHO
MEGIDDO
MEMENTO
MESTIZO
REACTTO
REFERTO
RELIEVO
RELLENO
SEMIPRO
SERPICO
SETINTO
TENDSTO
TESTUDO
VERDUGO
VERISMO
VERTIGO
ZEMSTVO

••EO•••

AREOLAE
AREOLAR
AREOLAS
CREOLES
CREOSOL
LIEOVER
THEOMEN
THEOREM

••E•O••

ACEDOUT
ACEROLA
ACEROSE
ACESOUT
ACETONE
ANEMONE
ANEROID
AWESOME
BLEWOFF
BLEWOUT
BRETONS
CHEROOT
CHEWOUT
CREMONA
DIEDOFF
DIEDOUT
DIEDOWN
DIESOFF
DIESOUT
DREWOUT
EKEDOUT
EKESOUT
ERELONG
EVENOUT
EYEBOLT
EYEHOLE
EYESORE
FEELOUT
FLEXORS
FREMONT
FUELOIL
GOESOFF
GOESOUT
GREGORY
HOEDOWN
ICEBOAT
ICECOLD
ICEDOUT
ICEFOGS
ICESOUT
KEEPOFF
KMESONS
LIEDOWN
OCELOTS
ONENOTE
ONEROUS
OPEROSE
PEEKOUT
PEELOFF
PEEROUT
PHENOLS
PHENOMS
PLEXORS
PRECOOK
PRECOOL
PRELOAD
PRESOAK
PRESORT
PYEDOGS
REELOFF
RHEBOKS
RHETORS
SEEKOUT
SEENOFF
SEENOUT
SEESOFF
SEESOUT
SEETOIT
SHEWOLF
STEPOUT
STEROID
STEROLS
TEEDOFF
TEESOFF
THEFONZ
THEROUX
TIEDOWN
TIEPOLO
TIERODS
TOEHOLD
TOELOOP
TREFOIL
TREMOLO
TREMORS
WEEDOUT

••E••O•

ABETTOR
AHEADOF
ALENCON
ATECROW
BIENTOT
BLERIOT
BRERFOX
CHEETOS
CHEKHOV
CHEROOT
CHEVIOT
CHEVRON
CHEWTOY
CLEAVON
CLEMSON
CREATOR
CREOSOL
DREAMON
ELEANOR
ELECTOR
ELEISON
EMERSON
ERECTOR
EREWHON
EYEBROW
EYESHOT
FEEDLOT
FEEDSON
FEELFOR
FIEFDOM
FREEDOM
FRESCOS
FUELROD
GHETTOS
GLEASON
GOESFOR
ICEFLOE
ICESHOW
INERROR
IRECKON
JOEBLOW
KEEPSON
LIESLOW
MCENROE
ONEIRON
ONESHOT
OPENTOE
OVERJOY
PIERROT
PRECOOK
PRECOOL
PRESSON
PRESTON
PRESTOS
PREYSON
PUEBLOS
SEEDPOD
SHELDON
SHELTON
SKELTON
SLEDDOG
SLEEPON
SLEPTON
SPEAKOF
SPECTOR
SPEEDOS
STENTOR
STEPSON
STEREOS
STETSON
SWEETON
THEBLOB
THECROW
THEREOF
THEREON
THERMOS
TOELOOP
TOESHOE
TREASON
TREETOP
TRENTON
TSELIOT
WHEATON
WHEREOF

••E•••O

AGESAGO
AMERIGO
ARECIBO
ARETINO
BEEFALO
CHEERIO
ELECTRO
HAEMATO
KEEPSTO
MAESTRO
OREGANO
SWEARTO
THERETO
TIEINTO
TIEPOLO
TREMOLO
TREVINO
WHERETO

•••EO••

ALVEOLI
AQUEOUS
AUREOLA
AUREOLE
BAKEOFF
BITEOFF
BOREOUT
CAMEOED
CAMEOFF
CAMEOUT
COMEOFF
COMEONS
COMEOUT
DOLEOUT
DOPEOUT
DOZEOFF
DUTEOUS
EASEOFF
EASEOUT
EDGEOUT
FACEOFF
FADEOUT
FIREOFF
GASEOUS
GAVEOFF
GAVEOUT
GIDEONS
GIVEOFF
GIVEOUT
HIDEOUS
HIDEOUT
HOLEOUT
IGNEOUS
LIVEOAK
LIVEONE
LIVEOUT
LOSEOUT
MADEOFF
MADEOUT
MAKEOFF
MAKEOUT
METEORS
METEOUT
MOVEOUT
NOSEOUT
OSCEOLA
OSSEOUS
OSTEOID
PIGEONS
PITEOUS
RAKEOFF
RIDEOFF
RIDEOUT
RODEOFF
RODEOUT
ROSEOIL
RULEOUT
SOMEONE
TAKEOFF
TAKEONE
TAKEOUT
TIMEOFF
TIMEOUT
TIREOUT
TOREOFF
TOREOUT
TUNEOUT
VOTEOUT
WAVEOFF
WIPEOUT
WOREOFF
WOREOUT

•••E•O•

ACHERON
ACHESON
ACTEDON
ADDEDON
AILERON
ALBEDOS
ALIENOR
ANGELOU
BIBELOT
BIGELOW
BLUEBOY
BLUEFOX
BOLEROS
BOREDOM
CAMELOT
CAMERON
CAPECOD
CAREFOR
CHEETOS
COMESON
DEMEROL
DEVELOP
DIDEROT
DINEDON
DINESON
DONEFOR
DOTEDON
DOTESON
DOVECOT
DUKEDOM
ECHELON
EGGEDON
EMPEROR
ENTERON
ENVELOP
FIREBOX
FIREDOG
FREEDOM
GAZEBOS
GLUEDON
GLUESON
HAVENOT
HIRESON
HOMEBOY
JAMESON
JANEDOE
JUKEBOX
LATERON
LIVEDON
LIVESON
LUBEJOB
MADEFOR
MAKEFOR
MATELOT
MOVEDON
MOVESON
MUMESON
NEMEROV
NOSEJOB
PAGEBOY
PHAETON
PILEDON
PILESON
PIMESON
PINEFOR
POMELOS
PRAETOR
REREDOS
ROBESON
ROPETOW
RULESON
SAVELOY
SEWEDON
SHOEBOX
SIMENON
SLEEPON
SOMEHOW
SPEEDOS
SPIEDON
SPIESON
SWEETON
TAKENON
TAKESON
TEREDOS
TIMECOP
TIREDOF
TONELOC
TONEROW
TOREROS
TREETOP
TRIEDON
TRIESON
TUPELOS
TUXEDOS
TYLENOL
VICEROY
VOTEFOR
WOBEGON
YULELOG
ZYDECOS

•••E••O

ADDEDTO
AGREETO
AIMEDTO
ALBERTO
ALLEGRO
ARSENIO
CATERTO
CAVETTO
CHEERIO
COMESTO
DARESTO
ERNESTO
FIDELIO
GIVENTO
GIVESTO
INFERNO
INPETTO
IONESCO
LORENZO
LYSENKO
MAKESDO
MARENGO
MEMENTO
MODESTO
MORELLO
NORELCO
OTHELLO
PALERMO
PATERNO
PIMENTO
REFERTO
ROBERTO
SALERNO
SCHERZO
STRETTO
TAKESTO
UCCELLO
UMBERTO
UNDERDO
UNDERGO
UPTEMPO

••••EO•

ACTAEON
AWAREOF
BURGEON
DUDGEON
DUNGEON
GALLEON
INAWEOF
NUCLEON
PEUGEOT
PIDGEON
SPOKEOF
STEREOS
SURGEON
THEREOF
THEREON
TRADEON
WHEREOF
WIDGEON

••••E•O

AGREETO
ALFREDO
ARTDECO
BERMEJO
BRACERO
CANSECO
CORDERO
DEUTERO
ELGRECO
HEAVEHO
HEAVETO
JAYLENO
MAGNETO
MONTEGO
MONTERO
NONZERO
ONTHEGO
PLACEBO
RELIEVO
RELLENO
RIPIENO
SANREMO
SUBZERO
SUPREMO
TANGELO
THERETO
TORPEDO
VALLEJO
VAQUERO
WHERETO
WRITETO
WROTETO

•••••EO

GALILEO
ZAPATEO

EP•••••

EPARCHS
EPARCHY
EPAULET
EPEEIST
EPERGNE
EPICENE
EPICURE
EPIGENE
EPIGONE
EPIGRAM
EPILOGS
EPISODE
EPISTLE
EPITHET
EPITOME
EPOCHAL
EPONYMS
EPONYMY
EPOPEES
EPOXIES
EPSILON
EPSTEIN

E•P••••

EMPANEL
EMPATHY
EMPEROR
EMPIRES
EMPLOYE
EMPLOYS
EMPORIA
EMPOWER
EMPRESS
EMPTIED
EMPTIER
EMPTIES
EMPTILY
ENPLANE
ESPANOL
ESPARTO
ESPIALS
ESPOSAS
ESPOSOS
ESPOUSE
ESPYING
EUPHONY
EXPANDS
EXPANSE
EXPARTE
EXPECTS
EXPENDS
EXPENSE
EXPERTS
EXPIATE
EXPIRED
EXPIRES
EXPLAIN
EXPLODE
EXPLOIT
EXPLORE
EXPORTS
EXPOSED
EXPOSES
EXPOUND
EXPRESS
EXPUNGE

E••P•••

EARPLUG
EDAPHIC
ELAPIDS
ELAPSED
ELAPSES
ELOPERS
ELOPING
ENDPLAY
EPOPEES
ERUPTED
EXUPERY

E•••P••

ECLIPSE
ECTYPES
ELLIPSE
ESCAPED
ESCAPEE
ESCAPES
EXAMPLE
EXCEPTS
EXEMPLI
EXEMPTS

E••••P•

EGGCUPS
EIGHTPM
ENCAMPS
ENCRYPT
ENTRAPS
ENTROPY
ENWRAPS
ESCARPS
EUTERPE
EXCERPT
EYECUPS

E•••••P

EARDROP
EARFLAP
EASEDUP
EASESUP
EATENUP
EGOTRIP
ENDEDUP
ENVELOP
EVENSUP

•EP••••

CEPHEUS
DEPALMA
DEPARTS
DEPENDS
DEPICTS
DEPLANE
DEPLETE
DEPLORE
DEPLOYS
DEPONED
DEPONES
DEPORTS
DEPOSAL
DEPOSED
DEPOSER
DEPOSES
DEPOSIT
DEPRAVE
DEPRESS
DEPRIVE
DEPUTED
DEPUTES
HEPARIN
HEPATIC
HEPBURN
HEPCATS
HEPPEST
HEPTADS
KEPTOFF
KEPTOUT
LEPANTO
LEPPIES
LEPTONS
NEPALIS
NEPHEWS
NEPTUNE
PEPLUMS
PEPPARD
PEPPERS
PEPPERY
PEPPIER
PEPPILY
PEPPING
PEPSINS
PEPTALK
PEPTIDE
REPAINT
REPAIRS
REPAPER
REPASTE
REPASTS
REPAVED
REPAVES
REPEALS
REPEATS
REPENTS
REPINED
REPINES
REPLACE
REPLANS
REPLANT
REPLATE
REPLAYS
REPLETE
REPLICA
REPLIED
REPLIES
REPLOWS
REPOLLS
REPOMAN
REPORTS
REPOSED
REPOSES
REPRESS
REPRICE
REPRINT
REPRISE
REPROOF
REPROVE
REPTILE
REPUGNS
REPULSE
REPUTED
REPUTES
SEPTETS

TEPIDLY
ZEPHYRS

•E•P•••
BEDPOST
BEEPERS
BEEPING
BESPEAK
BESPOKE
DEEPEND
DEEPENS
DEEPEST
DEEPFAT
DEEPFRY
DEEPSEA
DEEPSET
DEEPSIX
DELPHIC
DEMPSEY
DESPAIR
DESPISE
DESPITE
DESPOIL
DESPOTS
HEAPING
HELPERS
HELPFUL
HELPING
HELPOUT
HENPECK
HEPPEST
JEEPNEY
JETPORT
KEEPERS
KEEPING
KEEPOFF
KEEPSAT
KEEPSIN
KEEPSON
KEEPSTO
KEEPSUP
KELPIES
KERPLOP
KEWPIES
KEYPADS
LEAPERS
LEAPING
LEGPULL
LEIPZIG
LEMPIRA
LEOPARD
LEOPOLD
LEPPIES
LESPAUL
MEMPHIS
NEWPORT
PEAPODS
PEEPERS
PEEPING
PEEPLES
PENPALS
PEOPLED
PEOPLES
PEPPARD
PEPPERS
PEPPERY
PEPPIER
PEPPILY
PEPPING
PERPLEX
REAPERS
REAPING
REDPINE
REDPOLL
REOPENS
RESPECT
RESPINS
RESPIRE
RESPITE
RESPOND
REUPPED
SEAPORT
SEEPIER
SEEPING
SEEPSIN
SERPENT
SERPICO
TEAPOTS
TEAPOYS
TEEPEES
TEMPEHS
TEMPERA
TEMPERS
TEMPEST
TEMPLAR
TEMPLES
TEMPTED
TEMPTER
TEMPURA
TENPINS
VESPERS
VESPIDS
WEAPONS
WEBPAGE
WEEPERS
WEEPIER
WEEPIES
WEEPING
YELPERS
YELPING

•E••P••
BEARPAW
CERIPHS
DEADPAN
DECAPOD
HEADPIN
HELIPAD
LEDUPTO
LETUPON
OEDIPAL
OEDIPUS
RECIPES
REDSPOT
RELAPSE
REPAPER
RETAPED
RETAPES
RETYPED
RETYPES
REUPPED
SEEDPOD
SEMIPRO
SERAPES
SERAPHS
SERAPIS
SETUPON
TENSPOT
TERAPHS

•E•••P•
DECAMPS
DECRYPT
DEWLAPS
PEGTOPS
PERHAPS
RECEIPT
RECOUPS
REDCAPS
REDTAPE
REDTOPS
RESHIPS
REVAMPS
REWRAPS
SENDUPS
SEVENPM
TEACUPS
WENTAPE
WETMOPS

•E••••P
BEADSUP
BEAMSUP
BEARSUP
BEATSUP
BEDLAMP
BEEFSUP
BELLHOP
BELLYUP
DESKTOP
DEVELOP
DEWDROP
GEARSUP
HEADSUP
HEATSUP
HEELTAP
HENCOOP
JEANARP
KEEPSUP
KERPLOP
KETCHUP
KEYEDUP
KEYGRIP
LEADSUP
LETSLIP
MEDIGAP
PEASOUP
PERKSUP
REARSUP
REGROUP
RESTAMP
RESTSUP
SEALSUP
SENDSUP
SERVEUP
SEVENUP
SEWEDUP
TEAMSUP
TEARSUP
TEASHOP
TENSEUP
WELLSUP

••EP•••
ADEPTLY
ASEPSIS
ASEPTIC
BEEPERS
BEEPING
COEPTIS
DEEPEND
DEEPENS
DEEPEST
DEEPFAT
DEEPFRY
DEEPSEA
DEEPSET
DEEPSIX
ICEPACK
ICEPICK
INEPTLY
JEEPNEY
KEEPERS
KEEPING
KEEPOFF
KEEPSAT
KEEPSIN
KEEPSON
KEEPSTO
KEEPSUP
PEEPERS
PEEPING
PEEPLES
PIEPANS
PREPAID
PREPARE
PREPAYS
PREPPIE
SCEPTER
SCEPTIC
SCEPTRE
SEEPIER
SEEPING
SEEPSIN
SHEPARD
SKEPTIC
SLEPTIN
SLEPTON
STEPHEN
STEPINS
STEPOUT
STEPPED
STEPPER
STEPPES
STEPSIN
STEPSON
STEPSUP
STEPUPS
SWEPTUP
TEEPEES
THEPITS
TIEPINS
TIEPOLO
TREPANS
WEEPERS
WEEPIER
WEEPIES
WEEPING

••E•P••
BLEEPED
BLEEPER
CHEAPEN
CHEAPER
CHEAPIE
CHEAPLY
CHEEPED
CREEPED
CREEPER
CREEPUP
EXEMPLI
EXEMPTS
FLEAPIT
GUELPHS
KNEEPAD
OPENPIT
PREPPIE
SEEDPOD
SHERPAS
SLEEPER
SLEEPIN
SLEEPON
STEEPED
STEEPEN
STEEPER
STEEPLE
STEEPLY
STEPPED
STEPPER
STEPPES
SWEEPER
SWEEPUP
THESPIS
WHELPED

••E••P•
EYECUPS
GOESAPE
ICECAPS
PREAMPS
PRECEPT
PREEMPT
PRENUPS
PRETAPE
STEPUPS
THERAPY
TOECAPS
TOETAPS

••E•••P
BEEFSUP
BREAKUP
CHECKUP
CHEERUP
CHEWSUP
CLEANUP
CLEARUP
CREEPUP
DREAMUP
DRESSUP
EVENSUP
HEELTAP
KEEPSUP
KNEECAP
KNEESUP
ONESTEP
OPENSUP
OVERLAP
PRESSUP
QUEUEUP
SPEAKUP
SPEEDUP
STEPSUP
SWEEPUP
SWELLUP
SWEPTUP
THEDEEP
TIECLIP
TOELOOP
TREETOP

•••EP••
ACCEPTS
BASEPAY
BLEEPED
BLEEPER
CHEEPED
CREEPED
CREEPER
CREEPUP
EXCEPTS
FOREPAW
INCEPTS
INDEPTH
KNEEPAD
MADEPAR
MAKEPAR
NINEPIN
NOTEPAD
SLEEPER
SLEEPIN
SLEEPON
STEEPED
STEEPEN
STEEPER
STEEPLE
STEEPLY
SWEEPER
SWEEPUP

•••E•P•
ATTEMPT
EUTERPE
EXCERPT
GIVEUPS
LINEUPS
MAKEUPS
PILEUPS
PREEMPT
RAVEUPS
RECEIPT
SEVENPM
THREEPM
TUNEUPS
UNKEMPT
UPTEMPO

•••E••P
ACTEDUP
ADDEDUP
ANTEDUP
ANTESUP
BONEDUP
BONESUP
BOXEDUP
BOXESUP
CHEERUP
COMESUP
COVERUP
CREEPUP
DEVELOP
DRIEDUP
DRIESUP
DUDEDUP
EASEDUP
EASESUP
EATENUP
ENDEDUP
ENVELOP
FIREDUP
FIRESUP
FIXEDUP
FIXESUP
GIVENUP
GIVESUP
HIKEDUP
HIKESUP
HOLEDUP
HOLESUP
HYPEDUP
HYPESUP
KEYEDUP
KNEECAP
KNEESUP
LACEDUP
LACESUP
LINEDUP
LINESUP
MAKESUP
MIXEDUP
MIXESUP
MOVEDUP
MOVESUP
OWNEDUP
PILEDUP
PILESUP
PINESAP
PIPEDUP
PIPESUP
RAKEDUP
RAKESUP
RILESUP
SAVEDUP
SAVESUP
SCREWUP
SEVENUP
SEWEDUP
SIZEDUP
SIZESUP
SPEEDUP
SWEEPUP
TAKESUP
TIMECOP
TIMESUP
TONEDUP
TONESUP
TREETOP
TUNEDUP
TUNESUP
TYPEDUP
TYPESUP
WAKESUP
WINESAP
WIPEDUP
WIPESUP
WIRETAP
WISEDUP
WISESUP
WOKENUP

••••EP•
CONCEPT
FORCEPS
INSTEPS
PRECEPT
SCHLEPP
SCHLEPS
THREEPM
TRICEPS
UNSWEPT
UPSWEPT

••••E•P
ANTWERP
BARKEEP
BORNEUP
BRACEUP
BROKEUP
CHOKEUP
CLOSEUP
DRIVEUP
FLAREUP
FRAMEUP
IGIVEUP
INAHEAP
JUICEUP
LOUSEUP
PASTEUP
QUEUEUP
RAISEUP
RUNDEEP
SCAREUP
SCHLEPP
SERVEUP
SHAKEUP
SHAPEUP
SPICEUP
SPOKEUP
STOREUP
TENSEUP
THEDEEP
TRADEUP
UPSWEEP
WRITEUP
WROTEUP

•••••EP
BARKEEP
BOXSTEP
MISSTEP
ONESTEP
OUTSTEP
RUNDEEP
THEDEEP
TWOSTEP
UPSWEEP

EQ•••••
EQUABLE
EQUABLY
EQUALED
EQUALLY
EQUATED
EQUATES
EQUATOR
EQUERRY
EQUINES
EQUINOX

E•Q••••
ENQUIRE
ENQUIRY
ESQUIRE

•EQ••••
BEQUEST
PEQUOTS
REQUEST
REQUIEM
REQUIRE
REQUITE
SEQUELS
SEQUINS
SEQUOIA
TEQUILA

•E••Q••
BEZIQUE

••EQ•••
CHEQUER
CHEQUES
COEQUAL
PREQUEL
UNEQUAL

••••EQ•
ONTHEQT

ER•••••
ERASERS
ERASING
ERASMUS
ERASURE
ERECTED
ERECTER
ERECTLY
ERECTOR
ERELONG
EREMITE
EREWHON
ERGATES
ERICSON
ERISTIC
ERITREA
ERMINES
ERNESTO
ERODENT
ERODING
EROSELY
EROSION
EROSIVE
EROTICA
ERRANCY
ERRANDS
ERRATIC
ERRATUM
ERSKINE
ERUCTED
ERUDITE
ERUPTED

E•R••••
EARACHE
EARDROP
EARDRUM
EARFLAP
EARFULS
EARHART
EARLDOM
EARLESS
EARLIER
EARLIKE
EARLOBE
EARLOCK
EARLYON
EARMARK
EARMUFF
EARNERS
EARNEST
EARNING
EARPLUG
EARRING
EARSHOT
EARTHEN
EARTHLY
EARWIGS
EERIEST
EHRLICH
ENRAGED
ENRAGES
ENROBED
ENROBES
ENROLLS
ENROOTS
ENROUTE
ERRANCY
ERRANDS
ERRATIC
ERRATUM
ETRURIA
EURASIA

E••R•••
EARRING
EGGROLL
ELGRECO
EMBRACE
EMBROIL
EMBRYOS
EMERALD
EMERGED
EMERGES
EMERITA
EMERITI
EMERSED
EMERSON
EMIRATE
EMPRESS
ENCRUST
ENCRYPT
ENDRUNS
ENGRAFT
ENGRAMS
ENGRAVE
ENGROSS
ENTRAIN
ENTRANT
ENTRAPS
ENTREAT
ENTREES
ENTRIES
ENTROPY
ENTRUST
ENURING
ENWRAPS
EPARCHS
EPARCHY
EPERGNE
ESCROWS
ESTRADA
ESTRAYS
ETERNAL
EVEREST
EVERETT
EVERTED
EXARCHS
EXCRETE
EXERTED
EXPRESS
EXTRACT
EXTREME
EXTRUDE
EXURBAN
EXURBIA

E•••R••
EAGERER
EAGERLY
EARDROP
EARDRUM
EATCROW
EDWARDS
EFFORTS
EGOTRIP
ELDERLY
ELMTREE
EMBARGO
EMBARKS
EMIGRES
EMPEROR
EMPIRES
EMPORIA
ENCORES
ENDORSE
ENDURED
ENDURES
ENDUROS
ENFORCE
ENGARDE
ENGIRDS
ENGORGE
ENLARGE
ENSURED
ENSURES
ENTERED
ENTERON
ENTHRAL
EPIGRAM
EQUERRY
ERITREA
ESCARPS
ESCORTS
ESPARTO
ESTORIL
ETRURIA
EUCHRED
EUCHRES
EUTERPE
EXCERPT
EXHORTS
EXPARTE
EXPERTS
EXPIRED
EXPIRES
EXPORTS
EXSERTS
EXTERNS
EXTORTS
EXWORKS
EYEBROW

E••••R•
EARHART
EARMARK
EARNERS
EASTERN
EASTERS
ECKHART
ECLAIRS
EDITORS
EDOUARD
ELATERS
ELECTRA
ELECTRO
ELEKTRA
ELIXIRS
ELKHART
ELOPERS
ELUSORY
EMOTERS
ENAMORS
ENDEARS
ENQUIRE
ENQUIRY
ENSNARE
ENSNARL
ENVIERS
EPICURE
EQUERRY
ERASERS
ERASURE
ESOTERY
ESQUIRE
ESTUARY
ETAGERE
ETCHERS
EVADERS
EVOKERS
EXPLORE
EXUPERY
EYESORE

E•••••R
EAGERER
EARLIER
ECUADOR
EDASNER
ELEANOR
ELECTOR
EMENDER
EMITTER
EMPEROR
EMPOWER
EMPTIER
ENACTOR
ENAMOUR
ENCODER
ENDUSER
ENTICER
EQUATOR
ERECTER
ERECTOR
EVANDER
EVILLER
EXACTER
EXACTOR

•ER••••
AERATED
AERATES
AERATOR
AERIALS
AERIEST
AEROBAT
AEROBES
AEROBIC
AEROSOL
BERATED
BERATES
BERBERS
BEREAVE
BERETTA
BERGERE
BERGMAN
BERGSON
BERIDOF
BERLIOZ
BERLITZ
BERMEJO
BERMUDA
BERNARD
BERNESE
BERNICE
BERNSEN
BERRIED
BERRIES
BERSERK
BERTHED
BERTOLT
CERAMIC
CEREALS
CEREBRA
CERIPHS
CERTAIN
CERTIFY
CERUMEN
CERVIDS
DERAILS
DERBIES
DERIDED
DERIDES
DERIVED
DERIVES
DERNIER
DERRICK
DERRING
DERVISH
EERIEST
FERMENT
FERMIUM
FERNBAR
FERNIER
FERRARI
FERRARO
FERRATE
FERRETS
FERRIED
FERRIES
FERRITE
FERROUS
FERRULE
FERTILE
FERULES
FERVENT
FERVORS
FERVOUR
GERAINT
GERALDO
GERBILS
GERENTS
GERITOL
GERMANE
GERMANS
GERMANY
GERMIER
GERUNDS
HERALDS
HERBAGE
HERBALS
HERBERT
HERBIER
HERBTEA
HERCULE
HERDERS
HERDING
HERETIC
HERMANN
HERMITS
HEROICS
HEROINE
HEROISM
HERRING
HERRIOT
HERSELF
HERSHEY
JERBOAS
JERICHO
JERKIER
JERKILY
JERKING
JERKINS
JERSEYS
KERATIN
KERCHOO
KERNELS
KERNING
KEROUAC
KERPLOP
MERCERS
MERCERY
MERCIES
MERCURY
MERGERS
MERGING
MERIMEE
MERINOS
MERITED
MERLOTS
MERMAID
MERRIER
MERRILL
MERRILY
NERDIER
NEREIDS
NERVIER
NERVILY
NERVOUS
PERCALE
PERCENT
PERCHED
PERCHES
PERDIEM
PERFECT
PERFIDY
PERFORM
PERFUME
PERGOLA
PERHAPS
PERIDOT
PERIGEE
PERIODS
PERJURE
PERJURY
PERKIER
PERKILY
PERKING
PERKINS
PERKISH
PERKSUP
PERLITE
PERLMAN
PERMING
PERMITS
PERPLEX
PERRIER
PERSEID
PERSEUS
PERSIAN
PERSIST
PERSIUS
PERSONA
PERSONS
PERTAIN
PERTEST
PERTURB
PERUKES
PERUSAL
PERUSED
PERUSER
PERUSES
PERVADE
RERAISE
RERATED
RERATES
REREADS
REREDOS
RERENTS
RERINSE
REROUTE
SERAPES
SERAPHS
SERAPIS
SERBIAN
SERENER
SERFDOM
SERIALS
SERIATE
SERIOUS
SERLING
SERMONS
SERPENT
SERPICO
SERRATE
SERRIED
SERVALS
SERVANT
SERVERS
SERVERY
SERVEUP
SERVICE
SERVILE
SERVING
TERAPHS
TERBIUM
TERCELS

TERCETS
TEREDOS
TERENCE
TERHUNE
TERMING
TERMINI
TERMITE
TERNARY
TERNATE
TERRACE
TERRAIN
TERRENE
TERRETS
TERRIER
TERRIES
TERRIFY
TERRORS
TERSELY
TERSEST
TERTIAL
VERANDA
VERBALS
VERBENA
VERBOSE
VERDANT
VERDICT
VERDOUX
VERDUGO
VERDURE
VERGERS
VERGING
VERISMO
VERITAS
VERMEER
VERMEIL
VERMONT
VERNIER
VERSIFY
VERSION
VERTIGO
VERVETS
WERNHER
WERTHER
YEREVAN
YERKING
YERKISH
ZERMATT
ZEROING
ZEROSUM

•E•R•••

BEARCAT
BEARCUB
BEARDED
BEARERS
BEARHUG
BEARING
BEARISH
BEAROFF
BEAROUT
BEARPAW
BEARSON
BEARSUP
BEDREST
BEDROCK
BEDROLL
BEDROOM
BEERIER
BEGRIME
BERRIED
BERRIES
BETRAYS
BETROTH
DEAREST
DEARIES
DEARSIR
DEARTHS
DEBRIEF
DECREED
DECREES
DECRIED
DECRIER
DECRIES
DECRYPT
DEERFLY
DEFRAUD
DEFRAYS
DEFROCK
DEFROST
DEGRADE
DEGREES
DEPRAVE
DEPRESS
DEPRIVE
DERRICK
DERRING
DETRACT
DETRAIN
DETROIT
DEVRIES
FEARERS
FEARFUL
FEARING
FEBRILE
FERRARI
FERRARO
FERRATE
FERRETS
FERRIED
FERRIES
FERRITE
FERROUS
FERRULE
GEARBOX
GEARING
GEARSTO
GEARSUP
GEORDIE
GEORGES
GEORGIA
GETREAL
HEARDOF
HEARERS
HEARING
HEARKEN
HEAROUT
HEARSAY
HEARSOF
HEARTED
HEARTEN
HEARTHS
HEBRAIC
HEBREWS
HEIRESS
HENRYIV
HERRING
HERRIOT
JEERERS
JEERING
JEERSAT
KEARNEY
KEDROVA
KEYRING
LEARIER
LEARJET
LEARNED
LEARNER
LEERERS
LEERIER
LEERILY
LEERING
LEERSAT
LEGRAND
LEGROOM
MEGRIMS
MEGRYAN
MELROSE
MERRIER
MERRILL
MERRILY
METRICS
NEAREST
NEARING
NEARYOU
NEURONE
NEURONS
PEARLED
PEARSON
PEERAGE
PEERESS
PEERING
PEEROUT
PEERSAT
PEERSIN
PERRIER
PETRELS
PETRIFY
PETROCK
PETROLS
PETROUS
REAREND
REARERS
REARGUE
REARING
REARMED
REARSUP
RECROOM
RECROSS
RECRUIT
REDRAWN
REDRAWS
REDRESS
REDROSE
REFRACT
REFRAIN
REFRAME
REFRESH
REFRIED
REFRIES
REGRADE
REGRESS
REGRETS
REGROUP
REORDER
REPRESS
REPRICE
REPRINT
REPRISE
REPROOF
REPROVE
RETRACE
RETRACK
RETRACT
RETRADE
RETRAIN
RETREAD
RETREAT
RETRIAL
RETRIED
RETRIES
RETRIMS
REWRAPS
REWRITE
REWROTE
SEARING
SECRECY
SECRETE
SECRETS
SEERESS
SERRATE
SERRIED
TEARFUL
TEARGAS
TEARIER
TEARILY
TEARING
TEAROFF
TEAROOM
TEAROSE
TEAROUT
TEARSAT
TEARSUP
TENRECS
TERRACE
TERRAIN
TERRENE
TERRETS
TERRIER
TERRIES
TERRIFY
TERRORS
TETRADS
VEERIES
VEERING
WEARERS
WEARIED
WEARIER
WEARIES
WEARILY
WEARING
WEAROFF
WEAROUT
WEIRDER
WEIRDLY
WEIRDOS
YEAREND
YEARNED
YEARNER

•E••R••

AELFRIC
BEATRIX
BEGORRA
BEMIRED
BEMIRES
BESTREW
BETARAY
BEVERLY
CEDARED
CENTRAL
CENTRED
CENTRES
CENTRIC
CETERIS
DEBARGE
DEBARKS
DEBORAH
DECARLO
DECORUM
DEFARGE
DEFORMS
DEHORNS
DELIRIA
DEMERIT
DEMEROL
DEMURER
DENARII
DENDRON
DEPARTS
DEPORTS
DESERTS
DESERVE
DESIRED
DESIREE
DESIRES
DESTROY
DEWDROP
DEXTRIN
FEDERAL
FEDORAS
FEMORAL
GENERAL
GENERIC
GENERIS
HEGIRAS
HENDRIX
HEPARIN
JEFFREY
KESTREL
KEYGRIP
LEBARON
LECARRE
LETTRES
LEVERED
LEVERET
MEMOREX
MENORAH
METERED
NEMEROV
NEUTRAL
NEUTRON
OEUVRES
PETARDS
PETERED
REAIRED
REBIRTH
RECORDS
RECORKS
REFEREE
REFERTO
REFIRES
REFORMS
REGARDS
REHIRED
REHIRES
REMARKS
REMARRY
REMORAS
REMORSE
RENARDS
REPORTS
RESERVE
RESORBS
RESORTS
RESURGE
RETARDS
RETIRED
RETIREE
RETIRES
RETORTS
RETURNS
REVERBS
REVERED
REVERES
REVERIE
REVERSE
REVERTS
REWARDS
REWARMS
REWIRED
REWIRES
REWORDS
REWORKS
SEAGRAM
SECURED
SECURER
SECURES
SEESRED
SENORAS
SENORES
SEVERAL
SEVERED
SEVERER
TEATRAY
TEATREE
TEHERAN
TELERAN
TENDRIL
TENURED
TENURES
VENTRAL
VETERAN
WELLRUN

•E•••R•

AETHERS
BEAKERS
BEANERY
BEARERS
BEATERS
BEAVERS
BEEPERS
BEGGARS
BEGORRA
BENDERS
BERBERS
BERGERE
BERNARD
BERSERK
BESTIRS
BETTERS
BETTORS
BEZIERS
CELEBRE
CELLARS
CENSERS
CENSORS
CENSURE
CENTERS
CENTURY
CEREBRA
DEALERS
DEANERY
DEBEERS
DEBTORS
DECLARE
DEEPFRY
DEICERS
DEKLERK
DELVERS
DENIERS
DENMARK
DENTURE
DEODARS
DEPLORE
DESSERT
DETOURS
DEUTERO
DEVILRY
DEVOURS
FEARERS
FEATURE
FEEDERS
FEELERS
FELLERS
FENCERS
FENDERS
FERRARI
FERRARO
FERVORS
FESTERS
FETTERS
GEEZERS
GENDERS
GENNARO
GESTURE
GEYSERS
HEADERS
HEALERS
HEARERS
HEATERS
HEAVERS
HECTARE
HECTORS
HEDGERS
HEELERS
HEIFERS
HELLERS
HELOTRY
HELPERS
HEMMERS
HENNERY
HEPBURN
HERBERT
HERDERS
JEANARP
JEERERS
JEFFERS
JESTERS
JETPORT
JEWELRY
KEENERS
KEEPERS
KEGLERS
KEYCARD
KEYWORD
LEADERS
LEAKERS
LEANERS
LEAPERS
LEASERS
LECARRE
LECTERN
LECTORS
LECTURE
LEDGERS
LEERERS
LEEWARD
LEGHORN
LEGWORK
LEHAVRE
LEISURE
LEKVARS
LEMPIRA
LENDERS
LEONARD
LEONORA
LEOPARD
LEOTARD
LESSORS
LETTERS
LEVIERS
MEASURE
MEMBERS
MEMOIRE
MEMOIRS
MENDERS
MENHIRS
MENTORS
MERCERS
MERCERY
MERCURY
MERGERS
METEORS
METIERS
MEWLERS
NECKERS
NECTARS
NESTERS
NETSURF
NETWORK
NEWBERY
NEWBORN
NEWHART
NEWPORT
NEWYORK
PECCARY
PEDLARS
PEEKERS
PEELERS
PEEPERS
PELTERS
PENNERS
PEPPARD
PEPPERS
PEPPERY
PERFORM
PERJURE
PERJURY
PERTURB
PESTERS
PETTERS
READERS
REAMERS
REAPERS
REARERS
RECTORS
RECTORY
REDBIRD
REDFIRS
REDFORD
REEFERS
REENTRY
REHEARD
REHEARS
RELEARN
REMARRY
RENDERS
RENTERS
REPAIRS
REQUIRE
RESPIRE
RESTART
RESTERS
RESTORE
RETEARS
RETIARY
RETOURS
REUTERS
REVELRY
REYNARD
SEABIRD
SEABORG
SEAFIRE
SEAGIRT
SEALERS
SEAPORT
SEATERS
SEAWARD
SECTORS
SEEDERS
SEEHERE
SEEKERS
SEINERS
SEIZERS
SELKIRK
SELLERS
SEMIPRO
SENDERS
SENIORS
SENSORS
SENSORY
SERVERS
SERVERY
SETTERS
TEACART
TEASERS
TEDDERS
TEENERS
TEETERS
TELLERS
TEMPERA
TEMPERS
TEMPURA
TENDERS
TENNERS
TENSORS
TENTERS
TERNARY
TERRORS
TESSERA
TESTERS
TETHERS
TEXTURE
VECTORS
VELOURS
VENDORS
VENEERS
VENTERS
VENTURA
VENTURE
VERDURE
VERGERS
VESPERS
VESTURE
VETOERS
WEARERS
WEAVERS
WEEDERS
WEEPERS
WELDERS
WELFARE
WELTERS
WENDERS
WESTERN
WETBARS
WETHERS
YELLERS
YELPERS
ZEDBARS
ZEPHYRS

•E••••R

AERATOR
BEADIER
BEAMIER
BEECHER
BEEFIER
BEERIER
BELABOR
BELLJAR
BENATAR
BENAZIR
BENDIER
BESMEAR
CENTAUR
DEADAIR
DEARSIR
DEBATER
DECATUR
DECODER
DECRIER
DEFILER
DELAYER
DELIVER
DEMETER
DEMURER
DEPOSER
DERNIER
DESPAIR
FEATHER
FEEBLER
FEELFOR
FEIFFER
FELLFOR
FELTFOR
FENNIER
FERNBAR
FERNIER
FERVOUR
GEEKIER
GEMMIER
GENTLER
GERMIER
GETOVER
HEADIER
HEATHER
HEATTER
HEAVIER
HECKLER
HEDGIER
HEFTIER
HERBIER
JERKIER
JEWELER
KEEBLER
KEILLOR
LEADIER
LEAFIER
LEAKIER
LEANDER
LEARIER
LEARNER
LEATHER
LEDGIER
LEERIER
LEGGIER
LEISTER
LEVELER
MEALIER
MEANDER
MEATIER
MEDDLER
MEISTER
MERRIER
MESHIER
MESSIER
METOOER
NEBULAR
NEEDIER
NEGATER
NEGATOR
NEITHER
NERDIER
NERVIER
NESTLER
NEWAGER
NEWSIER
NEWYEAR
PEATIER
PECKIER
PEDDLER
PEPPIER
PERKIER
PERRIER
PERUSER
PESKIER
PETTIER
REACTOR
READIER
REALTOR
RECITER
RECOLOR
RECOVER
REDDEER
REDHAIR
REDSTAR
REDUCER
REEDIER
REENTER
REFINER
REFUSER
REFUTER
REGULAR
REMOTER
REMOVER
RENEGER
RENEWER
REOCCUR
REORDER
REPAPER
RESCUER
REUTHER
REVELER
REVISER
SEAMIER
SEASTAR
SECEDER
SECULAR
SECURER
SEDATER
SEDGIER
SEDUCER
SEEDIER
SEEPIER
SELLFOR
SELTZER
SEMINAR
SENATOR
SENDFOR
SENTFOR
SERENER
SETTLER
SEVERER
SEYMOUR
TEACHER
TEARIER
TECHIER
TEENIER
TEETHER
TEICHER
TELSTAR
TEMBLOR
TEMPLAR
TEMPTER
TENFOUR
TERRIER
TESTIER
VEALIER
VEINIER
VERMEER
VERNIER
WEARIER
WEATHER
WEBBIER
WEBSTER
WEDGIER
WEEDIER
WEENIER
WEEPIER
WEIRDER
WENTFOR
WERNHER
WERTHER
YEARNER
YESDEAR
ZESTIER

••ER•••

ACERBIC
ACEROLA
ACEROSE
ALERTED
ALERTER
ALERTLY
AMERCED
AMERCES
AMERICA
AMERIGO
AMERIKA
AMERIND
ANEROID
APERCUS
APERIES
AVERAGE
AVERRED
AVERTED
BEERIER
BLERIOT
BOERWAR
BRERFOX
CHERISH
CHEROOT
CHERUBS
CHERVIL
CLERICS
CLERISY
CLERKED
COERCED
COERCER
COERCES
DEERFLY
EMERALD
EMERGED
EMERGES
EMERITA
EMERITI
EMERSED
EMERSON
EPERGNE
ETERNAL
EVEREST
EVERETT
EVERTED
EXERTED
FAERIES
FIERCER
FIERIER
FIERILY
GHERKIN
IBERIAN
ICERINK
INERROR
INERTIA
INERTLY
ITERANT
ITERATE
JEERERS
JEERING
JEERSAT
LAERTES
LEERERS
LEERIER
LEERILY
LEERING
LEERSAT
LIERNES
OBERLIN
ONEROUS
OPERAND
OPERATE
OPEROSE
OVERACT
OVERAGE
OVERALL
OVERATE
OVERAWE
OVERBIG
OVERBUY
OVERDID
OVERDUB
OVERDUE
OVEREAT
OVERFLY
OVERJOY
OVERLAP
OVERLAY
OVERLIE
OVERRAN
OVERRUN
OVERSAW
OVERSEA
OVERSEE
OVERTAX
OVERTLY
OVERUSE
PEERAGE
PEERESS
PEERING
PEEROUT
PEERSAT
PEERSIN
PIERCED
PIERCES
PIERROT
PUERILE
QUERIED
QUERIER
QUERIES
QUERIST
SEERESS
SHERBET
SHERIFF
SHERMAN
SHERPAS
SHERWIN
SIERRAS
STEREOS
STERILE
STERNAL
STERNER
STERNLY
STERNUM
STEROID
STEROLS
SWERVED
SWERVES
THERAPY
THEREAT
THEREBY
THEREIN
THERELL
THEREOF
THEREON
THERESA
THERETO
THERMAL
THERMOS
THEROUX
TIERACK
TIERING
TIERNEY
TIERODS
USERIDS
VEERIES
VEERING
WHEREAS
WHEREAT
WHEREBY
WHEREIN
WHERELL
WHEREOF
WHERERE
WHERETO
WHEREVE

••E•R••

AREARUG
ATECROW
AVERRED
BLEARED
CHEERED
CHEERIO
CHEERUP
CHETRUM
CHEVRES
CHEVRON
CLEARED
CLEARER
CLEARLY
CLEARUP
EYEBROW
FREDRIC
FUELROD
ICEFREE
INERROR
MCENROE
ONEIRON
OVERRAN
OVERRUN
PIERROT
QUEERED
QUEERER
QUEERLY
SEESRED
SHEARED
SHEARER
SHEERED
SHEERER
SHEERLY
SIERRAS
SMEARED
SNEERAT
SNEERED
SNEERER
SPEARED
STEERED
STEERER
SWEARAT
SWEARBY
SWEARER
SWEARIN
SWEARTO
THECROW
THEOREM
THEURGY

TREERAT
UNEARTH

••E••R•
ABELARD
ABEXTRA
BEEPERS
BREWERS
BREWERY
CAESARS
CAESURA
CHEWERS
CUECARD
DEEPFRY
DIEHARD
DIETARY
DIETERS
DUELERS
ELECTRA
ELECTRO
ELEKTRA
EYESORE
FEEDERS
FEELERS
FLEXORS
FUELERS
GEEZERS
GREGORY
GUEVARA
HEELERS
ICEBERG
JAEGERS
JEERERS
KEENERS
KEEPERS
LEERERS
LEEWARD
MAESTRI
MAESTRO
OLESTRA
OPENERS
PEEKERS
PEELERS
PEEPERS
PIECERS
PLECTRA
PLENARY
PLEXORS
PREFERS
PREPARE
PRESORT
QUEUERS
REEFERS
REENTRY
RHETORS
SCENERY
SCEPTRE
SEEDERS
SEEHERE
SEEKERS
SHEPARD
SKEWERS
SPECTRA
SPECTRE
STEWARD
STEWART
STEWERS
SWELTRY
TEENERS
TEETERS
THEATRE
THECARS
THEFIRM
THENARS
TREMORS
TRENARY
VIEWERS
WEEDERS
WEEPERS
WHERERE
WIENERS

••E•••R
ABETTOR
ALERTER
AREOLAR
ATELIER
AVENGER
BEECHER
BEEFIER
BEERIER
BLEAKER
BLEEPER
BLENDER
BOERWAR
BREAKER
BREEDER
BRENNER
CHEAPER
CHEATER
CHECKER
CHEDDAR
CHEEVER
CHENIER
CHEQUER
CHESTER
CHEWIER
CLEANER
CLEARER
CLEAVER
COERCER
CREAMER
CREATOR
CREEPER
DREAMER
DREDGER
DREISER
DRESSER
DWELLER
ELEANOR
ELECTOR
EMENDER
ERECTER
ERECTOR
FEEBLER
FEELFOR
FIEDLER
FIELDER
FIERCER
FIERIER
FLEETER
FLEXNER
FREEZER
FRESHER
GEEKIER
GLEANER
GOESFOR
GREASER
GREATER
GREENER
GREETER
GUESSER
ICEBEER
INERROR
KEEBLER
KNEADER
KNEELER
LEERIER
LIEOVER
LOESSER
NEEDIER
NIEBUHR
ONESTAR
OPENAIR
OPENBAR
PLEADER
PLEASER
PLEDGER
PREENER
PREMIER
PRESSER
QUEERER
QUERIER
REEDIER
REENTER
ROEDEER
SCEPTER
SEEDIER
SEEPIER
SHEARER
SHEERER
SHELLER
SHELTER
SKEETER
SKELTER
SLEDDER
SLEEKER
SLEEPER
SLENDER
SMELTER
SNEAKER
SNEERER
SNEEZER
SPEAKER
SPECTER
SPECTOR
SPEEDER
SPELLER
SPENCER
SPENDER
SPENSER
STEAMER
STEELER
STEEPER
STEERER
STEIGER
STEINER
STELLAR
STENTOR
STEPPER
STERNER
SVELTER
SWEARER
SWEATER
SWEEPER
SWEETER
SWELTER
TEENIER
TEETHER
THEATER
THEWIER
TREADER
TREKKER
TWEETER
VIEWIER
WEEDIER
WEENIER
WEEPIER
WHEELER
WHEEZER
WHETHER
WRECKER
ZOELLER

•••ER••
ACHERON
ADHERED
ADHERES
ADVERBS
ADVERSE
ADVERTS
AILERON
ALBERTA
ALBERTO
ALGERIA
ALLERGY
ALTERED
ALTERER
AMHERST
AMPERES
ANGERED
APTERAL
ASPERSE
ASSERTS
BEVERLY
BODEREK
BOLEROS
BOWERED
CAMERAS
CAMERON
CAPERED
CASERNE
CASERNS
CATERED
CATERER
CATERTO
CAVERNS
CETERIS
CHEERED
CHEERIO
CHEERUP
COHERED
COHERES
COTERIE
COVERED
COVERUP
COWERED
DEMERIT
DEMEROL
DESERTS
DESERVE
DIDEROT
DIVERGE
DIVERSE
DIVERTS
DOWERED
EAGERER
EAGERLY
ELDERLY
EMPEROR
ENTERED
ENTERON
EQUERRY
EUTERPE
EXCERPT
EXPERTS
EXSERTS
EXTERNS
FABERGE
FEDERAL
FORERAN
FORERUN
GENERAL
GENERIC
GENERIS
GONERIL
GOVERNS
HAVERED
HOMERED
HOMERIC
HOMERUN
HOVERED
HOVERER
HUMERAL
HUMERUS
IMMERSE
IMPERIL
INFERNO
INHERED
INHERES
INHERIT
INSERTS
INTERIM
INTERNS
INTERSE
INVERSE
INVERTS
LATERAL
LATERAN
LATERON
LAVERNE
LAYERED
LEVERED
LEVERET
LIBERAL
LIBERIA
LIBERTY
LITERAL
LOVERLY
LOWERED
LUCERNE
METERED
MINERAL
MINERVA
MISERLY
MITERED
MODERNS
NEMEROV
NIGERIA
NUMERAL
NUMERIC
OBSERVE
OBVERSE
OBVERTS
OFFERED
OFFERER
ONSERVE
ORDERED
ORDERER
ORDERLY
OSIERED
PALERMO
PAPERED
PAPERER
PATERNO
PETERED
POVERTY
POWERED
PUBERTY
QUEERED
QUEERER
QUEERLY
REFEREE
REFERTO
RESERVE
REVERBS
REVERED
REVERES
REVERIE
REVERSE
REVERTS
RICERAT
ROBERTA
ROBERTO
ROBERTS
ROSERED
SALERNO
SCHERZI
SCHERZO
SCLERAS
SEVERAL
SEVERED
SEVERER
SHEERED
SHEERER
SHEERLY
SIBERIA
SNEERAT
SNEERED
SNEERER
SOBERED
SOBERER
SOBERLY
SPHERES
STEERED
STEERER
SYNERGY
TAPERED
TAVERNS
TEHERAN
TELERAN
TONEROW
TOREROS
TOWERED
TREERAT
UMBERTO
UNDERDO
UNDERGO
UNNERVE
USHERED
UTTERED
UTTERER
UTTERLY
VALERIE
VETERAN
VICEROY
WAGERED
WAGERER
WATERED
WATERER
WAVERED
WAVERER
WINERED
WYVERNS

•••E•R•
ALGEBRA
ALLEARS
ALLEGRO
APPEARS
ARREARS
ATHEART
AUTEURS
BONEDRY
BYHEART
CAREERS
CELEBRE
CEREBRA
COHEIRS
CULEBRA
DEBEERS
DOGEARS
ENDEARS
EQUERRY
FINEART
FIREARM
FOREARM
INTEARS
INTEGRA
JEWELRY
MADEIRA
MAJEURE
MCHENRY
METEORS
PALEDRY
PHAEDRA
POSEURS
REHEARD
REHEARS
RELEARN
RETEARS
REVELRY
SIDEARM
THREERS
TINEARS
TONEARM
UNHEARD
UNLEARN
VENEERS

•••E••R
ACCEDER
ALIENOR
ALLEGER
ALTERER
AMMETER
BLEEPER
BREEDER
BRIEFER
CAREFOR
CATERER
CHEEVER
CREEPER
CRUELER
DEMETER
DONEFOR
EAGERER
EMPEROR
FAKEFUR
FLEETER
FOREVER
FREEZER
GREENER
GREETER
GRIEVER
HOVERER
HOWEVER
INGEMAR
INTEGER
JEWELER
KNEELER
LABELER
LEVELER
LIBELER
MADEFOR
MADEPAR
MAKEFOR
MAKEPAR
MODELER
OFFERER
OFTENER
ORDERER
PACECAR
PAPERER
PINEFOR
PINETAR
POLECAR
PRAETOR
PREENER
QUEERER
QUIETER
RACECAR
RENEGER
RENEWER
REVELER
RIVETER
SCHEMER
SECEDER
SERENER
SEVERER
SHEERER
SIDEBAR
SIDECAR
SKEETER
SLEEKER
SLEEPER
SNEERER
SNEEZER
SOBERER
SPEEDER
SPIELER
STEELER
STEEPER
STEERER
STPETER
STREWER
SWEEPER
SWEETER
TIREDER
TUTELAR
TWEETER
UTTERER
VINEGAR
VOTEFOR
WAGERER
WAKENER
WATERER
WAVERER
WHEELER
WHEEZER
WHOEVER
WINEBAR
YODELER

••••ER•
ABUSERS
ADORERS
AETHERS
ALFIERI
ALGIERS
ALLHERE
AMBLERS
ANGLERS
ANSWERS
ANTHERS
ANTLERS
ANTWERP
ARCHERS
ARCHERY
ARGUERS
ARRIERE
AUSTERE
AVOWERS
BACKERS
BADGERS
BAGGERS
BAILERS
BANKERS
BANNERS
BANTERS
BARBERS
BARKERS
BARTERS
BASTERS
BATHERS
BATTERS
BATTERY
BAWLERS
BEAKERS
BEANERY
BEARERS
BEATERS
BEAVERS
BEEPERS
BENDERS
BERBERS
BERGERE
BERSERK
BETTERS
BEZIERS
BICKERS
BIDDERS
BIGGERS
BINDERS
BINDERY
BIRDERS
BITTERN
BITTERS
BLADERS
BLAZERS
BLOWERS
BOATERS
BOBBERS
BOILERS
BOMBERS
BONKERS
BOOMERS
BOPPERS
BORDERS
BOTHERS
BOVVERS
BOWLERS
BOWYERS
BRACERO
BRACERS
BRAVERY
BRAYERS
BREWERS
BREWERY
BRIBERY
BROKERS
BUFFERS
BUGLERS
BUMMERS
BUMPERS
BUNKERS
BURGERS
BURNERS
BUSTERS
BUTLERS
BUTTERS
BUTTERY
BUZZERS
CABLERS
CADGERS
CAHIERS
CALDERA
CALLERS
CALVERT
CAMBERS
CAMPERS
CANKERS
CANNERS
CANNERY
CANTERS
CAPPERS
CARDERS
CAREERS
CARNERA
CARPERS
CARTERS
CARVERS
CASTERS
CATBERT
CENSERS
CENTERS
CHASERS
CHEWERS
CHIDERS
CHIMERA
CHOKERS
CINDERS
CINDERY
CIPHERS
CISTERN
CLAWERS
CLOVERS
COALERS
COAXERS
COCHERE
COCKERS
CODGERS
COFFERS
COINERS
COLBERT
COMBERS
COMPERE
CONCERN
CONCERT
CONFERS
CONGERS
CONKERS
CONNERY
CONVERT
COOKERS
COOKERY
COOLERS
COOPERS
COPIERS
COPPERS
COPPERY
COPTERS
CORDERO
CORKERS
CORNERS
COTTERS
COWHERD
CRATERS
CRAVERS
CROWERS
CULLERS
CULVERS
CULVERT
CURLERS
CUTLERS
CUTLERY
CUTTERS
CYCLERS
CYPHERS
DAGGERS
DAMPERS
DANCERS
DANDERS
DANGERS
DARNERS
DARTERS
DASHERS
DAUBERS
DEALERS
DEANERY
DEBEERS
DEICERS
DEKLERK
DELVERS
DENIERS
DESSERT
DEUTERO
DIALERS
DIAPERS
DICKERS
DIETERS
DIFFERS
DIGGERS
DILBERT
DIMMERS
DINNERS
DIPPERS
DISCERN
DITHERS
DITHERY
DOCKERS
DODDERS
DODGERS
DOGBERT
DORMERS
DOSSERS
DOWNERS
DOWSERS
DRAPERS
DRAPERY
DRAWERS
DRIVERS
DRONERS
DROVERS
DUBBERS
DUELERS
DUFFERS
DUNKERS
DUSTERS
EARNERS
EASTERN
EASTERS
ELATERS
ELOPERS
EMOTERS
ENVIERS
ERASERS
ESOTERY
ETAGERE
ETCHERS
EVADERS
EVOKERS
EXUPERY
FABLERS
FALTERS
FARMERS
FARMERY
FATHERS
FAWNERS
FEARERS
FEEDERS
FEELERS
FELLERS
FENCERS
FENDERS
FESTERS
FETTERS
FIBBERS
FILBERT
FILLERS
FILTERS
FINDERS
FINGERS
FISHERS
FISHERY
FITTERS
FLAKERS
FLOWERS
FLOWERY
FODDERS
FOGGERS
FOLDERS
FOLGERS
FOOLERY
FOOTERS
FOPPERY
FORCERS
FORGERS
FORGERY
FORKERS
FOSTERS
FOWLERS
FUELERS
GABBERS
GADDERS
GAFFERS
GAINERS
GAITERS
GALLERY
GAMMERS
GANDERS
GANGERS
GAOLERS
GARNERS
GARTERS
GASPERS
GASSERS
GATHERS
GAUGERS
GAWKERS
GEEZERS
GENDERS
GEYSERS
GIBBERS
GILBERT
GILDERS
GINGERS
GINGERY
GIRDERS
GLAZERS
GLIDERS
GLOWERS
GNAWERS
GOLFERS
GOMPERS
GOOBERS
GOPHERS
GOUGERS
GRADERS
GRATERS
GRAVERS
GRAZERS
GRIPERS
GROCERS
GROCERY
GROWERS
GRUYERE
GUNNERS
GUNNERY
GUSHERS
GUTTERS
GYPPERS
HACKERS
HALTERS
HAMMERS
HAMPERS
HANGERS
HANKERS
HARPERS
HATTERS
HAUBERK
HAULERS
HAWKERS
HAWSERS
HEADERS
HEALERS
HEARERS
HEATERS
HEAVERS
HEDGERS
HEELERS
HEIFERS
HELLERS
HELPERS
HEMMERS
HENNERY
HERBERT
HERDERS
HINDERS
HISSERS
HITHERE
HITTERS
HOAXERS
HOLDERS
HOLLERS
HONKERS
HOOFERS
HOOTERS
HOOVERS
HOPPERS
HOSIERS
HOSIERY
HOWLERS
HUGGERS
HULLERS
HUMMERS
HUNGERS
HUNKERS
HUNTERS
HURLERS
HUSKERS
ICEBERG
IMAGERS
IMAGERY
IRONERS
ISOMERS
ISSUERS
JABBERS
JAEGERS
JAILERS
JAMMERS
JASPERS
JEERERS
JEFFERS
JESTERS
JIGGERS
JIGGERY
JITTERS
JITTERY
JOBBERS
JOBBERY
JOGGERS
JOINERS
JOINERY
JOSSERS
JUDDERS
JUICERS
JUMPERS
JUNKERS
KAISERS
KEENERS
KEEPERS
KEGLERS
KICKERS
KIDDERS
KILLERS
KIPPERS
KISSERS
KNAVERY
KOSHERS
KRATERS
LAAGERS
LADDERS
LADLERS
LAGGERS
LAMBERT
LANCERS
LANDERS
LANTERN
LARDERS
LASHERS
LATHERS
LATHERY
LAWYERS
LEADERS
LEAKERS
LEANERS
LEAPERS
LEASERS
LECTERN
LEDGERS
LEERERS
LENDERS
LETTERS
LEVIERS
LIBBERS
LIFTERS
LIMBERS
LIMNERS
LINGERS
LINKERS
LITTERS
LOADERS
LOAFERS
LOANERS
LOBBERS
LOCKERS
LODGERS
LOGGERS
LOITERS
LOOKERS
LOOPERS
LOOTERS
LOPPERS
LOTTERY
LOUVERS
LUBBERS
LUGGERS
LUMBERS
LUMIERE
LUMPERS
LUNKERS
LUSTERS
MADDERS
MAILERS
MANGERS
MANNERS
MAPPERS
MARKERS
MASHERS
MASKERS
MASTERS
MASTERY
MATHERS
MATTERS
MEMBERS

MENDERS
MERCERS
MERCERY
MERGERS
METIERS
MEWLERS
MIDTERM
MILKERS
MILLERS
MINCERS
MINDERS
MINTERS
MISTERS
MOANERS
MOCKERS
MOCKERY
MOILERS
MOLDERS
MOLIERE
MOLTERS
MONGERS
MONTERO
MOPPERS
MOSHERS
MOTHERS
MOUSERS
MUDDERS
MUGGERS
MULLERS
MUMMERS
MUMMERY
MURDERS
MUSHERS
MUSTERS
MUTTERS
MYSTERY
NABBERS
NAILERS
NAPPERS
NATTERS
NECKERS
NESTERS
NEWBERY
NICKERS
NIPPERS
NODDERS
NONZERO
NORBERT
NOSHERS
NOWHERE
NUDGERS
NUMBERS
NUNNERY
NURSERS
NURSERY
NUTTERS
OAKFERN
ONAGERS
OPENERS
OPINERS
OSTLERS
OUSTERS
OYSTERS
PACKERS
PADDERS
PALTERS
PAMPERS
PANDERS
PANNERS
PANZERS
PARSERS
PASSERS
PASTERN
PATTERN

PATTERS
PAUPERS
PAWNERS
PEEKERS
PEELERS
PEEPERS
PELTERS
PENNERS
PEPPERS
PEPPERY
PESTERS
PETTERS
PHASERS
PICKERS
PIECERS
PIGGERY
PILFERS
PINCERS
PINNERS
PITIERS
PITTERS
PLACERS
PLANERS
PLATERS
PLAYERS
PLOVERS
PLOWERS
POLDERS
POLLERS
PONDERS
POPPERS
PORKERS
PORTERS
POSTERN
POSTERS
POTHERB
POTHERS
POTTERS
POTTERY
POURERS
POUTERS
POWDERS
POWDERY
PRATERS
PRAYERS
PREFERS
PRICERS
PRIMERS
PROBERS
PROSERS
PROVERB
PROVERS
PRUDERY
PRUNERS
PUCKERS
PUFFERS
PUFFERY
PUMPERS
PUNKERS
PUNTERS
PURRERS
PURSERS
PUTTERS
QUAKERS
QUAVERS
QUAVERY
QUEUERS
QUIVERS
QUIVERY
QUOTERS
RAFTERS
RAIDERS
RAILERS
RAISERS

RANGERS
RANKERS
RANTERS
RAPIERS
RAPPERS
RASHERS
RASPERS
RASTERS
RATBERT
RATTERS
READERS
REAMERS
REAPERS
REARERS
REEFERS
RENDERS
RENTERS
RESTERS
REUTERS
RHYMERS
RIFLERS
RIFLERY
RIGGERS
RINGERS
RIOTERS
RIPPERS
RISKERS
RIVIERA
RIVIERE
ROAMERS
ROARERS
ROBBERS
ROBBERY
ROCKERS
ROCKERY
RODGERS
ROGUERY
ROLLERS
ROMPERS
ROOFERS
ROOKERY
ROOMERS
ROOTERS
ROSTERS
ROTTERS
ROUSERS
ROUTERS
ROZZERS
RUBBERS
RUBBERY
RUDDERS
RUINERS
RUNNERS
RUSHERS
RUTGERS
SACKERS
SALIERI
SALTERS
SALVERS
SANDERS
SAPPERS
SASSERS
SAUCERS
SAWYERS
SCALERS
SCARERS
SCENERY
SCORERS
SCOTERS
SEALERS
SEATERS
SEEDERS
SEEHERE
SEEKERS

SEINERS
SEIZERS
SELLERS
SENDERS
SERVERS
SERVERY
SETTERS
SHAKERS
SHAPERS
SHARERS
SHAVERS
SHINERS
SHIVERS
SHIVERY
SHOVERS
SHOWERS
SHOWERY
SHUBERT
SIFTERS
SIGHERS
SIGNERS
SILVERS
SILVERY
SIMMERS
SIMPERS
SINCERE
SINGERS
SINKERS
SINNERS
SIPPERS
SISTERS
SITTERS
SKATERS
SKEWERS
SKIVERS
SLAVERS
SLAVERY
SLAYERS
SLICERS
SLIDERS
SLIVERS
SMILERS
SMOKERS
SNIPERS
SNORERS
SOAKERS
SOAPERS
SOARERS
SOBBERS
SOLDERS
SOLVERS
SOONERS
SORCERY
SORTERS
SOTHERE
SOTHERN
SPACERS
SPADERS
SPICERY
SPIDERS
SPIDERY
SPIKERS
STAGERS
STARERS
STEWERS
STOKERS
STONERS
STORERS
STUMERS
STYLERS
SUBVERT
SUBZERO
SUCKERS
SUFFERS

SULKERS
SUMMERS
SUMMERY
SUNDERS
SUPPERS
SURFERS
SURGERY
SUTLERS
SUTTERS
SWAYERS
SWIPERS
TACKERS
TALKERS
TAMPERS
TANGERE
TANKERS
TANNERS
TANNERY
TAPPERS
TASTERS
TATTERS
TEASERS
TEDDERS
TEENERS
TEETERS
TELLERS
TEMPERA
TEMPERS
TENDERS
TENNERS
TENTERS
TESSERA
TESTERS
TETHERS
THALERS
THREERS
TICKERS
TILLERS
TILTERS
TIMBERS
TINDERS
TINKERS
TINNERS
TINTERN
TINTERS
TIPPERS
TITFERS
TITHERS
TITTERS
TOGGERY
TOILERS
TOOTERS
TOPPERS
TOSSERS
TOTTERS
TOTTERY
TOURERS
TOUTERS
TOWNERS
TRABERT
TRACERS
TRACERY
TRADERS
TRAVERS
TROWERS
TUCKERS
TUGGERS
TURNERS
TURNERY
TUSKERS
TWOFERS
ULSTERS
UNITERS
USURERS

VAMPERS
VAQUERO
VENEERS
VENTERS
VERGERS
VESPERS
VETOERS
VIEWERS
VISCERA
VIZIERS
WAGGERY
WAILERS
WAITERS
WAIVERS
WALKERS
WALTERS
WANDERS
WARDERS
WASHERS
WASTERS
WEARERS
WEAVERS
WEEDERS
WEEPERS
WELDERS
WELTERS
WENDERS
WESTERN
WETHERS
WHALERS
WHERERE
WHINERS
WICKERS
WIENERS
WINCERS
WINDERS
WINGERS
WINKERS
WINNERS
WINTERS
WINTERY
WISHERS
WITHERS
WONDERS
WOOFERS
WOOMERA
WORKERS
WOWSERS
WRITERS
YABBERS
YAKKERS
YAMMERS
YAPPERS
YAWNERS
YAWPERS
YELLERS
YELPERS
YONKERS
YOWLERS
ZAFFERS
ZANDERS
ZAPPERS
ZINGERS
ZIPPERS
ZITHERS
ZONKERS

••••E•R

AMATEUR
ANTBEAR
BESMEAR
BUGBEAR
COMPEER
DANSEUR
FLANEUR
FORBEAR
HAUTEUR
ICEBEER
LIQUEUR
LOWGEAR
MANYEAR
MASSEUR
MIDYEAR
MISHEAR
MYNHEER
NEWYEAR
NUCLEAR
OFFYEAR
ONATEAR
OUTWEAR
PASTEUR
PIONEER
REDDEER
ROEDEER
SCHMEER
SKIWEAR
UNCLEAR
VERMEER
YESDEAR

•••••ER

ABRADER
ACCEDER
ACCUSER
ADAPTER
ADMIRER
ADOPTER
ADORNER
ADVISER
ALARMER
ALERTER
ALIGNER
ALLAYER
ALLEGER
ALLOVER
ALTERER
ALUNSER
AMASSER
AMMETER
ANDOVER
ANGRIER
ANOTHER
ANTSIER
AQUIFER
AQUIVER
ARBITER
ARMORER
ARRIVER
ARTSIER
ASPIRER
ASSAYER
ASUNDER
ATELIER
AVENGER
AWARDER
BAFFLER
BAGGIER
BAINTER
BALKIER
BALMIER
BARKIER
BARMIER
BARRIER
BATTIER
BATTLER
BAWDIER
BEADIER
BEAMIER

BEECHER
BEEFIER
BEERIER
BENDIER
BILGIER
BITSIER
BITTIER
BLABBER
BLACKER
BLADDER
BLANDER
BLANKER
BLASTER
BLATHER
BLEAKER
BLEEPER
BLENDER
BLINDER
BLINKER
BLISTER
BLITHER
BLOCKER
BLONDER
BLOOMER
BLOOPER
BLOTTER
BLOWIER
BLUBBER
BLUFFER
BLUNDER
BLUNTER
BLUSHER
BLUSTER
BOARDER
BOASTER
BOGGIER
BOGGLER
BOLSTER
BONNIER
BOOMIER
BOOSLER
BOOSTER
BOSKIER
BOSSIER
BOTTLER
BOULDER
BOUNCER
BOUNDER
BOWDLER
BRAGGER
BRAIDER
BRANDER
BRASHER
BRAWLER
BRAZIER
BREAKER
BREEDER
BRENNER
BRIEFER
BRINGER
BRINIER
BRISKER
BROADER
BROILER
BROODER
BROTHER
BROWNER
BROWSER
BRUISER
BRYNNER
BUCKLER
BUGGIER
BUILDER
BULGIER

BULKIER
BUMBLER
BUMPIER
BUNGLER
BURGHER
BURLIER
BUSHIER
BUTCHER
CACKLER
CAJOLER
CALIBER
CALIPER
CAMPIER
CANNIER
CAROLER
CARRIER
CARTIER
CASHIER
CATCHER
CATERER
CATTIER
CAULKER
CAVILER
CCRIDER
CHAMBER
CHAMFER
CHANCER
CHANGER
CHANTER
CHAPTER
CHARGER
CHARIER
CHARMER
CHARTER
CHASTER
CHATTER
CHAUCER
CHEAPER
CHEATER
CHECKER
CHEEVER
CHENIER
CHEQUER
CHESTER
CHEWIER
CHIGGER
CHILLER
CHIPPER
CHITTER
CHOICER
CHOKIER
CHOOSER
CHOPPER
CHOWDER
CHUKKER
CHUNTER
CLABBER
CLAIMER
CLAMBER
CLAMMER
CLAPPER
CLATTER
CLAVIER
CLAYIER
CLEANER
CLEARER
CLEAVER
CLIMBER
CLINKER
CLIPPER
CLOBBER
CLOCKER
CLOWDER
CLUNKER

CLUSTER
CLUTTER
CNTOWER
COARSER
COASTER
COBBLER
COCKIER
CODDLER
COERCER
COLLIER
COLLYER
COMFIER
COMPEER
CONIFER
CONQUER
CORKIER
CORNIER
COSTNER
COULTER
COUNTER
COURIER
COURSER
CRABBER
CRACKER
CRAFTER
CRAMMER
CRASSER
CRAWLER
CRAZIER
CREAMER
CREEPER
CRIMPER
CRISPER
CRITTER
CROFTER
CROONER
CROPPER
CROSIER
CROSSER
CRUELER
CRUISER
CRULLER
CRUSHER
CURDIER
CURLIER
CURRIER
CURVIER
CUSHIER
CUSSLER
DABBLER
DAFFIER
DAIMLER
DALLIER
DANDIER
DANGLER
DAUMIER
DAWDLER
DAZZLER
DEBATER
DECODER
DECRIER
DEFILER
DELAYER
DELIVER
DEMETER
DEMURER
DEPOSER
DERNIER
DIDOVER
DILUTER
DINGIER
DINKIER
DIOPTER
DIPPIER

DIRTIER
DISHIER
DITSIER
DITZIER
DIVIDER
DIVINER
DIZZIER
DODGIER
DOGGIER
DOODLER
DOPPLER
DOSSIER
DOTTIER
DOUBTER
DOWAGER
DOWDIER
DOWNIER
DRABBER
DRAGGER
DRAINER
DREAMER
DREDGER
DREISER
DRESSER
DRIFTER
DRILLER
DRINKER
DROLLER
DROOLER
DROPPER
DRUCKER
DRUMMER
DUCKIER
DUMPIER
DUSKIER
DUSTIER
DWELLER
EAGERER
EARLIER
EDASNER
EMENDER
EMITTER
EMPOWER
EMPTIER
ENCODER
ENDUSER
ENTICER
ERECTER
EVANDER
EVILLER
EXACTER
FAINTER
FANCIER
FARRIER
FARTHER
FATTIER
FEATHER
FEEBLER
FEIFFER
FENNIER
FERNIER
FICKLER
FIDDLER
FIEDLER
FIELDER
FIERCER
FIERIER
FIGHTER
FIGURER
FILCHER
FILMIER
FINNIER
FIRRIER
FISCHER

FISHIER
FIZZIER
FLAKIER
FLAMIER
FLANKER
FLAPPER
FLASHER
FLATTER
FLAXIER
FLEETER
FLEXNER
FLICKER
FLIPPER
FLITTER
FLIVVER
FLOATER
FLUBBER
FLUKIER
FLUSTER
FLUTIER
FLUTTER
FLYOVER
FNUMBER
FOAMIER
FOGGIER
FOLKIER
FORAGER
FOREVER
FORKIER
FORSTER
FOUNDER
FOURIER
FRAILER
FRANKER
FRASIER
FRAZIER
FREEZER
FRESHER
FRITTER
FROWNER
FUBSIER
FUMBLER
FUNKIER
FUNNIER
FURRIER
FURTHER
FUSSIER
FUSTIER
FUZZIER
GABBIER
GAGSTER
GAMBLER
GAMMIER
GARDNER
GASSIER
GAUCHER
GAUDIER
GAUNTER
GAUZIER
GAWKIER
GEEKIER
GEMMIER
GENTLER
GERMIER
GETOVER
GIDDIER
GIGGLER
GLACIER
GLADDER
GLAZIER
GLEANER
GLIBBER
GLIMMER
GLITTER

GLUMMER
GOAFTER
GOBBLER
GODLIER
GOOFIER
GOONIER
GOOPIER
GOOSIER
GORSIER
GOTOVER
GOUNDER
GOUTIER
GRABBER
GRAMMER
GRANDER
GRANGER
GRAPIER
GREASER
GREATER
GREENER
GREETER
GRIDDER
GRIEVER
GRIFTER
GRIMIER
GRIMMER
GRINDER
GRINNER
GRIPPER
GROANER
GRODIER
GROLIER
GROOMER
GROSSER
GROUPER
GROUSER
GROWLER
GRUFFER
GUESSER
GUILDER
GULPIER
GUMMIER
GUNKIER
GUNTHER
GUSHIER
GUSTIER
GUTSIER
GUTTIER
GUZZLER
HAGGLER
HAIRIER
HAMMIER
HAMSTER
HANDIER
HANDLER
HANOVER
HAPPIER
HARDIER
HARRIER
HARSHER
HASTIER
HATCHER
HEADIER
HEATHER
HEATTER
HEAVIER
HECKLER
HEDGIER
HEFTIER
HERBIER
HILLIER
HIPPIER
HIPSTER
HITCHER

HOARDER
HOARIER
HOARSER
HOLSTER
HONORER
HOOSIER
HOPOVER
HORSIER
HOSTLER
HOVERER
HOWEVER
HUFFIER
HUMBLER
HUMPIER
HUNKIER
HURDLER
HUSKIER
HUSTLER
ICEBEER
IGNITER
IGNORER
IMPURER
INAPTER
INCITER
INDUCER
INHALER
INPOWER
INSIDER
INSURER
INTEGER
INTONER
INVADER
INVOKER
IONIZER
ITCHIER
JAGGIER
JAMMIER
JANVIER
JAZZIER
JERKIER
JEWELER
JOINDER
JOLLIER
JOLTIER
JOSTLER
JOUSTER
JOWLIER
JUGGLER
JUICIER
JUMPIER
JUNIPER
JUNKIER
JUPITER
KAYAKER
KEEBLER
KICKIER
KINKIER
KNACKER
KNEADER
KNEELER
KNITTER
KNOCKER
KOOKIER
LABELER
LABORER
LACQUER
LALAKER
LANKIER
LARDIER
LARDNER
LASSOER
LAUGHER
LAUNDER
LAYOVER

LEADIER
LEAFIER
LEAKIER
LEANDER
LEARIER
LEARNER
LEATHER
LEDGIER
LEERIER
LEGGIER
LEISTER
LEVELER
LIBELER
LIEOVER
LIGHTER
LINTIER
LIPPIER
LITTLER
LOAMIER
LOBBYER
LOBSTER
LOCATER
LOESSER
LOFTIER
LOONIER
LOOPIER
LOPPIER
LOUNGER
LOUSIER
LOWLIER
LUCIFER
LUCKIER
LUMPIER
LUSTIER
MALTIER
MANAGER
MANGIER
MANLIER
MARCHER
MARINER
MASSIER
MATURER
MAUNDER
MAXBAER
MEALIER
MEANDER
MEATIER
MEDDLER
MEISTER
MERRIER
MESHIER
MESSIER
METOOER
MIFFIER
MILKIER
MINGIER
MINGLER
MINIVER
MINTIER
MIRKIER
MISTIER
MOBSTER
MODELER
MOISTER
MOLDIER
MONIKER
MONOMER
MONSTER
MOOCHER
MOODIER
MOONIER
MOORIER
MOSSIER
MOTHIER

MOULDER
MOUSIER
MUCKIER
MUDDIER
MUDDLER
MUFFLER
MUGGIER
MUMBLER
MUNCHER
MURKIER
MUSHIER
MUSKIER
MUSSIER
MUSTIER
MUZZIER
MYNHEER
NAGGIER
NASTIER
NATTIER
NEEDIER
NEGATER
NEITHER
NERDIER
NERVIER
NESTLER
NEWAGER
NEWSIER
NIBBLER
NIFTIER
NIMBLER
NIPPIER
NITTIER
NOBBIER
NOBBLER
NOISIER
NONUSER
NORTHER
NUBBIER
NUTSIER
NUTTIER
NUZZLER
OBTUSER
OCTOBER
OFFERER
OFFICER
OFTENER
OLDSTER
OLIVIER
OMITTER
ONORDER
OPPOSER
ORBITER
ORDERER
PADDLER
PAINTER
PALAVER
PALLIER
PALMIER
PANNIER
PANTHER
PAPERER
PARDNER
PARRIER
PARTIER
PARTNER
PASTIER
PAWKIER
PEATIER
PECKIER
PEDDLER
PEPPIER
PERKIER
PERRIER
PERUSER

PESKIER
PETTIER
PHILTER
PHONIER
PIASTER
PICKIER
PIGGIER
PILSNER
PINCHER
PIONEER
PITCHER
PITHIER
PLAINER
PLANNER
PLANTER
PLASTER
PLATIER
PLATTER
PLEADER
PLEASER
PLEDGER
PLODDER
PLOTTER
PLUGGER
PLUMBER
PLUMIER
PLUMMER
PLUMPER
PLUNDER
PLUNGER
PLUSHER
POACHER
PODGIER
POINTER
POITIER
POLITER
POLYMER
POPOVER
PORKIER
POTSIER
POTTIER
POUNCER
POUNDER
POUTIER
PRAISER
PRANCER
PREENER
PREMIER
PRESSER
PRICIER
PRIMMER
PRINTER
PRIVIER
PRODDER
PROFFER
PROOFER
PROPTER
PROSIER
PROSPER
PROUDER
PROWLER
PSALTER
PUDGIER
PUFFIER
PULPIER
PUNCHER
PUNKIER
PUNNIER
PUNSTER
PURSIER
PURSUER
PUSHIER
PUTOVER
PUZZLER

QUAFFER
QUAKIER
QUARTER
QUEERER
QUERIER
QUICKER
QUIETER
QUILLER
QUILTER
QUIPPER
QUITTER
RAFFLER
RAINIER
RALLIER
RAMBLER
RANCHER
RANDIER
RANGIER
RANOVER
RAPIDER
RASPIER
RATTIER
RATTLER
RAVAGER
READIER
RECITER
RECOVER
REDDEER
REDUCER
REEDIER
REENTER
REFINER
REFUSER
REFUTER
REMOTER
REMOVER
RENEGER
RENEWER
REORDER
REPAPER
RESCUER
REUTHER
REVELER
REVISER
RICHTER
RIDDLER
RIDGIER
RIGHTER
RISKIER
RITZIER
RIVETER
ROASTER
ROCKIER
ROEDEER
ROILIER
ROISTER
ROOKIER
ROOMIER
ROOSTER
ROOTIER
ROTIFER
ROUGHER
ROUNDER
ROWDIER
RUDDIER
RUMMIER
RUNNIER
RUNOVER
RUNTIER
RUSHIER
RUSTIER
RUSTLER
RUTTIER
SADDLER

SAGGIER
SALTIER
SAMPLER
SANDIER
SAPPIER
SARKIER
SASSIER
SAUCIER
SAUNTER
SAVAGER
SAVVIER
SCALIER
SCALPER
SCAMPER
SCANNER
SCANTER
SCARCER
SCARIER
SCARPER
SCATTER
SCEPTER
SCHEMER
SCHMEER
SCOFFER
SCOLDER
SCOOPER
SCOOTER
SCORNER
SCOURER
SCOUTER
SCOWLER
SCRAPER
SCULLER
SCUPPER
SEAMIER
SECEDER
SECURER
SEDATER
SEDGIER
SEDUCER
SEEDIER
SEEPIER
SELTZER
SERENER
SETTLER
SEVERER
SHADIER
SHAFFER
SHAKIER
SHARPER
SHATNER
SHATTER
SHEARER
SHEERER
SHELLER
SHELTER
SHIMMER
SHINIER
SHIPPER
SHIRKER
SHOCKER
SHOOTER
SHOPPER
SHORTER
SHOUTER
SHOWIER
SHRINER
SHRIVER
SHUCKER
SHUDDER
SHUTTER
SHYSTER
SILKIER
SILLIER

SILTIER
SIMPLER
SKANKER
SKEETER
SKELTER
SKIDDER
SKIMMER
SKINNER
SKIPPER
SKITTER
SKULKER
SLACKER
SLAMMER
SLANDER
SLASHER
SLATHER
SLATIER
SLEDDER
SLEEKER
SLEEPER
SLENDER
SLICKER
SLIMIER
SLIMMER
SLINGER
SLIPPER
SLITHER
SLOBBER
SLUGGER
SLUMBER
SMACKER
SMALLER
SMARTER
SMASHER
SMATTER
SMELTER
SMOKIER
SMOLDER
SMOTHER
SMUGGER
SNACKER
SNAKIER
SNAPPER
SNEAKER
SNEERER
SNEEZER
SNICKER
SNIFFER
SNIFTER
SNIGGER
SNOOKER
SNOOPER
SNORTER
SNOWIER
SNUFFER
SNUGGER
SOAPIER
SOBERER
SODDIER
SOGGIER
SOLDIER
SOLIDER
SOOTHER
SOOTIER
SOPPIER
SORRIER
SOUNDER
SOUPIER
SPACIER
SPAMMER
SPANKER
SPANNER
SPARSER
SPATTER

SPEAKER
SPECTER
SPEEDER
SPELLER
SPENCER
SPENDER
SPENSER
SPICIER
SPIELER
SPIKIER
SPINIER
SPINNER
SPIRIER
SPLICER
SPOILER
SPONGER
SPOOFER
SPOONER
SPOTTER
SPOUTER
SPRAYER
SPRUCER
SPUMIER
SPURNER
SPUTTER
SQUARER
STABLER
STAFFER
STAGGER
STAGIER
STAIDER
STAINER
STALKER
STAMMER
STAPLER
STARKER
STARTER
STEAMER
STEELER
STEEPER
STEERER
STEIGER
STEINER
STEPPER
STERNER
STICKER
STIFFER
STILLER
STINGER
STINKER
STIRRER
STOLLER
STONIER
STOPPER
STOUTER
STPETER
STREWER
STRIDER
STRIKER
STRIPER
STRIVER
STUFFER
STUMPER
STUNNER
SUBDUER
SUBTLER
SUDSIER
SULKIER
SUNNIER
SUPPLER
SURFIER
SURLIER
SVELTER
SWAGGER

SWANKER
SWAPPER
SWATTER
SWEARER
SWEATER
SWEEPER
SWEETER
SWELTER
SWIFTER
SWIMMER
SWINGER
SWITZER
TACKIER
TACKLER
TALKIER
TALLIER
TANAGER
TANGIER
TAPSTER
TARDIER
TARRIER
TARSIER
TASTIER
TATTIER
TATTLER
TAWNIER
TEACHER
TEARIER
TECHIER
TEENIER
TEETHER
TEICHER
TEMPTER
TERRIER
TESTIER
THEATER
THEWIER
THICKER
THINKER
THINNER
THITHER
THROWER
THUMPER
THUNDER
THURBER
TICKLER
TIGHTER
TIMIDER
TINNIER
TIPPIER
TIPPLER
TIPSIER
TIPSTER
TIREDER
TOASTER
TODDLER
TOFFLER
TOORDER
TOUGHER
TRACKER
TRAILER
TRAINER
TRAPPER
TRAWLER
TREADER
TREKKER
TRICKER
TRIFLER
TRIGGER
TRIMMER
TRIPPER
TROOPER
TROTTER
TROUPER

TROUSER
TRUCKER
TRUDGER
TRYSTER
TUBBIER
TUFTIER
TUMBLER
TURFIER
TWEETER
TWIRLER
TWISTER
TWITTER
UNCOVER
UNIFIER
UNWISER
UPRIVER
URBANER
USURPER
UTTERER
VASTIER
VAULTER
VAUNTER
VEALIER
VEINIER
VERMEER
VERNIER
VIEWIER
VINTNER
VIVIDER
VOUCHER
VOYAGER
WACKIER
WADDLER
WAFFLER
WAGERER
WAGONER
WAKENER
WALTZER
WANGLER
WARBLER
WARTIER
WASHIER
WASPIER
WATCHER
WATERER
WAVERER
WEARIER
WEATHER
WEBBIER
WEBSTER
WEDGIER
WEEDIER
WEENIER
WEEPIER
WEIRDER
WERNHER
WERTHER
WHEELER
WHEEZER
WHETHER
WHIMPER
WHINIER
WHISKER
WHISPER
WHITHER
WHITIER
WHIZZER
WHOEVER
WHOPPER
WIDOWER
WIGGIER
WIGGLER
WIMPIER
WINDIER

WINKLER
WISPIER
WITHIER
WITTIER
WONKIER
WOODIER
WOOLIER
WOOSTER
WOOZIER
WORDIER
WORMIER
WORRIER
WRAPPER
WRECKER
WRINGER
WRONGER
YEARNER
YODELER
YOUNGER
YUCKIER
YUMMIER
ZAPPIER
ZESTIER
ZINGIER
ZIPPIER
ZOELLER

ES•••••

ESCAPED
ESCAPEE
ESCAPES
ESCARPS
ESCHEAT
ESCHEWS
ESCORTS
ESCROWS
ESCUDOS
ESKIMOS
ESOTERY
ESPANOL
ESPARTO
ESPIALS
ESPOSAS
ESPOSOS
ESPOUSE
ESPYING
ESQUIRE
ESSAYED
ESSENCE
ESSENES
ESTATES
ESTEEMS
ESTELLE
ESTEVEZ
ESTHETE
ESTIVAL
ESTONIA
ESTORIL
ESTRADA
ESTRAYS
ESTUARY

E•S•••••

EASEDIN
EASEDUP
EASEFUL
EASEOFF
EASEOUT
EASESIN
EASESUP
EASIEST
EASTEND
EASTERN
EASTERS

EASTMAN
EASYOFF
ECSTASY
ENSIGNS
ENSILED
ENSILES
ENSKIED
ENSKIES
ENSLAVE
ENSNARE
ENSNARL
ENSOULS
ENSUING
ENSUITE
ENSURED
ENSURES
EPSILON
EPSTEIN
ERSKINE
ESSAYED
ESSENCE
ESSENES
EXSERTS

E••S•••

EARSHOT
EATSOUT
EDASNER
EELSKIN
EGESTED
EKESOUT
ELASTIC
ELISION
ELUSIVE
ELUSORY
ELYSEES
ELYSIAN
ELYSIUM
ENISLED
ENISLES
EPISODE
EPISTLE
ERASERS
ERASING
ERASMUS
ERASURE
ERISTIC
EROSELY
EROSION
EROSIVE
ETESIAN
EVASION
EVASIVE
EXISTED
EYESHOT
EYESORE

E•••S••

EASESIN
EASESUP
ECDYSES
ECDYSIS
EDGESIN
EFFUSED
EFFUSES
EGOISTS
ELAPSED
ELAPSES
ELEISON
ELLISON
ELMISTI
EMBASSY
EMERSED
EMERSON

ENCASED
ENCASES
ENDUSER
ENDUSES
ENLISTS
ENMASSE
ERICSON
ERNESTO
ESPOSAS
ESPOSOS
EURASIA
EVENSUP
EVULSED
EVULSES
EXCISED
EXCISES
EXCUSED
EXCUSES
EXPOSED
EXPOSES

E••••S•

EARLESS
EARNEST
EASIEST
ECLIPSE
ECSTASY
EDGIEST
EELIEST
EERIEST
EGGCASE
EGGIEST
EGGLESS
EGOTISM
EGOTIST
ELEGIST
ELITISM
ELITIST
ELLIPSE
EMBASSY
EMPRESS
ENCLOSE
ENCRUST
ENDLESS
ENDMOST
ENDORSE
ENDWISE
ENGLISH
ENGROSS
ENMASSE
ENTHUSE
ENTRUST
EPEEIST
ESPOUSE
EVANISH
EVENEST
EVEREST
EVILEST
EXHAUST
EXPANSE
EXPENSE
EXPRESS
EYELASH
EYELESS
EYEWASH

E•••••S

EAGLETS
EARFULS
EARLESS
EARNERS
EARWIGS
EASTERS
EBONIES

ECDYSES
ECDYSIS
ECHINUS
ECLAIRS
ECTYPES
EDGINGS
EDIBLES
EDIFIES
EDITORS
EDWARDS
EFFACES
EFFECTS
EFFORTS
EFFUSES
EGGCUPS
EGGLESS
EGGNOGS
EGOISTS
EIGHTHS
ELAPIDS
ELAPSES
ELATERS
ELEGIES
ELEVENS
ELICITS
ELIXIRS
ELOIGNS
ELOPERS
ELYSEES
EMBANKS
EMBARKS
EMBLEMS
EMBRYOS
EMERGES
EMIGRES
EMOTERS
EMPIRES
EMPLOYS
EMPRESS
EMPTIES
ENABLES
ENAMELS
ENAMORS
ENCAGES
ENCAMPS
ENCASES
ENCINAS
ENCODES
ENCORES
ENDEARS
ENDINGS
ENDIVES
ENDLESS
ENDRUNS
ENDURES
ENDUROS
ENDUSES
ENDWAYS
ENEMIES
ENFOLDS
ENGAGES
ENGINES
ENGIRDS
ENGRAMS
ENGROSS
ENGULFS
ENIGMAS
ENISLES
ENJOINS
ENLACES
ENLISTS
ENNEADS
ENRAGES
ENROBES

ENROLLS
ENROOTS
ENSIGNS
ENSILES
ENSKIES
ENSOULS
ENSURES
ENTAILS
ENTICES
ENTRAPS
ENTREES
ENTRIES
ENVIERS
ENVIOUS
ENWRAPS
ENZYMES
EOLITHS
EPARCHS
EPILOGS
EPONYMS
EPOPEES
EPOXIES
EQUATES
EQUINES
ERASERS
ERASMUS
ERGATES
ERMINES
ERRANDS
ESCAPES
ESCARPS
ESCHEWS
ESCORTS
ESCROWS
ESCUDOS
ESKIMOS
ESPIALS
ESPOSAS
ESPOSOS
ESSENES
ESTATES
ESTEEMS
ESTRAYS
ETCHERS
ETHNICS
ETOILES
EUCHRES
EVADERS
EVENKIS
EVINCES
EVOKERS
EVOLVES
EVULSES
EVZONES
EXACTAS
EXARCHS
EXCEEDS
EXCEPTS
EXCISES
EXCITES
EXCUSES
EXEMPTS
EXHALES
EXHORTS
EXOTICS
EXPANDS
EXPECTS
EXPENDS
EXPERTS
EXPIRES
EXPORTS
EXPOSES
EXPRESS
EXSERTS

EXTENDS
EXTENTS
EXTERNS
EXTORTS
EXWIVES
EXWORKS
EYECUPS
EYEFULS
EYELESS
EYELETS
EYELIDS

•ES••••

BESEECH
BESEEMS
BESIDES
BESIEGE
BESMEAR
BESPEAK
BESPOKE
BESTBOY
BESTIAL
BESTING
BESTIRS
BESTMAN
BESTMEN
BESTOWS
BESTREW
CESSING
CESSION
DESALTS
DESCANT
DESCEND
DESCENT
DESERTS
DESERVE
DESIGNS
DESIRED
DESIREE
DESIRES
DESISTS
DESKSET
DESKTOP
DESMOND
DESOTOS
DESPAIR
DESPISE
DESPITE
DESPOIL
DESPOTS
DESSERT
DESTINE
DESTINY
DESTROY
FESCUES
FESSING
FESTERS
FESTIVA
FESTIVE
FESTOON
GESSOES
GESTALT
GESTATE
GESTURE
HESHVAN
HESSIAN
JESSICA
JESTERS
JESTING
JESUITS
KESTREL
LESOTHO
LESPAUL
LESSEES
LESSENS
LESSING
LESSONS
LESSORS
MESCALS
MESHIER
MESHING
MESSAGE
MESSALA
MESSIAH
MESSIER
MESSILY
MESSINA
MESSING
MESSKIT
MESTIZA
MESTIZO
NESCAFE
NESMITH
NESTEGG
NESTERS
NESTING
NESTLED
NESTLER
NESTLES
PESAWAS
PESETAS
PESKIER
PESKILY
PESTERS
PESTLED
PESTLES
RESALES
RESALTS
RESANDS
RESAWED
RESCALE
RESCIND
RESCUED
RESCUER
RESCUES
RESEALS
RESEATS
RESECTS
RESEEDS
RESELLS
RESENDS
RESENTS
RESERVE
RESHIPS
RESHOES
RESHOOT
RESIDED
RESIDES
RESIDUE
RESIGNS
RESILED
RESILES
RESINGS
RESISTS
RESOLED
RESOLES
RESOLVE
RESORBS
RESORTS
RESOUND
RESPECT
RESPINS
RESPIRE
RESPITE
RESPOND
RESTAGE
RESTAIN
RESTAMP
RESTART
RESTATE
RESTERS
RESTFUL
RESTING
RESTIVE
RESTOCK
RESTORE
RESTSUP
RESTYLE
RESULTS
RESUMED
RESUMES
RESURGE
SESAMES
SESSILE
SESSION
SESTETS
SESTINA
TESSERA
TESTBAN
TESTEES
TESTERS
TESTFLY
TESTIER
TESTIFY
TESTILY
TESTING
TESTOUT
TESTUDO
VESPERS
VESPIDS
VESSELS
VESTEES
VESTIGE
VESTING
VESTURE
WESKITS
WESTEND
WESTERN
YESDEAR
YESHIVA
YESMAAM
YESSING
ZESTFUL
ZESTIER

•E•S•••

BEASTIE
BEASTLY
BEDSIDE
BEESWAX
BEGSOFF
BERSERK
CEASING
CELSIUS
CENSERS
CENSING
CENSORS
CENSURE
CESSING
CESSION
DENSELY
DENSEST
DENSITY
DESSERT
EELSKIN
FEASTED
FESSING
GEISHAS
GEMSBOK
GESSOES
GETSOFF
GETSOUT
GETSSET
GEYSERS
HEISMAN
HEISTED
HEMSLEY
HERSELF
HERSHEY
HESSIAN
HEXSIGN
JERSEYS
JESSICA
JETSKIS
JETSONS
KEESHAN
LEASERS
LEASHED
LEASHES
LEASING
LEISTER
LEISURE
LESSEES
LESSENS
LESSING
LESSONS
LESSORS
LETSFLY
LETSLIP
LETSOFF
LETSOUT
LETSSEE
MEASLES
MEASURE
MEISSEN
MEISTER
MESSAGE
MESSALA
MESSIAH
MESSIER
MESSILY
MESSINA
MESSING
MESSKIT
NELSONS
NETSUKE
NETSURF
NEWSBOY
NEWSDAY
NEWSIER
NEWSIES
NEWSMAN
NEWSMEN
PEASANT
PEASOUP
PENSEES
PENSION
PENSIVE
PEPSINS
PERSEID
PERSEUS
PERSIAN
PERSIST
PERSIUS
PERSONA
PERSONS
REASONS
REDSPOT
REDSTAR
REISSUE
RETSINA
SEASALT
SEASICK
SEASIDE
SEASLUG
SEASONS
SEASTAR
SEESAWS
SEESFIT
SEESOFF
SEESOUT
SEESRED
SEISMIC
SENSATE
SENSING
SENSORS
SENSORY
SENSUAL
SESSILE
SESSION
SETSAIL
SETSOFF
SETSOUT
TEASELS
TEASERS
TEASETS
TEASHOP
TEASING
TEESOFF
TELSTAR
TENSELY
TENSEST
TENSEUP
TENSILE
TENSING
TENSION
TENSIVE
TENSORS
TENSPOT
TERSELY
TERSEST
TESSERA
VERSIFY
VERSION
VESSELS
WEASELS
WEBSITE
WEBSTER
WETSUIT
YESSING
ZEMSTVO

•E••S••

AEROSOL
BEADSUP
BEAMSUP
BEARSON
BEARSUP
BEATSIT
BEATSME
BEATSUP
BEEFSUP
BEHESTS
BELASCO
BELUSHI
BEMUSED
BEMUSES
BENISON
BENTSEN
BERGSON
BERNSEN
BETISES
CELESTA
CELESTE
DEADSEA
DEADSET
DEALSIN
DEARSIR
DEBASED
DEBASES
DEBUSSY
DEEPSEA
DEEPSET
DEEPSIX
DEFUSED
DEFUSES
DEGUSTS
DEHISCE
DELISTS
DEMESNE
DEMISED
DEMISES
DEMPSEY
DEPOSAL
DEPOSED
DEPOSER
DEPOSES
DEPOSIT
DESISTS
DESKSET
DETESTS
DEVISED
DEVISES
FEEDSON
GEARSTO
GEARSUP
GENESEE
GENESES
GENESIS
GETSSET
HEADSET
HEADSIN
HEADSUP
HEARSAY
HEARSOF
HEATSUP
JEERSAT
JEWISON
KEEPSAT
KEEPSIN
KEEPSON
KEEPSTO
KEEPSUP
KENOSHA
LEADSIN
LEADSON
LEADSTO
LEADSUP
LEANSON
LEERSAT
LEGISTS
LETSSEE
MEDUSAE
MEDUSAS
MEIOSES
MEIOSIS
MEISSEN
MELISSA
MENISCI
NEMESES
NEMESIS
NEXUSES
PEARSON
PECKSAT
PEEKSAT
PEERSAT
PEERSIN
PEGASUS
PELISSE
PERKSUP
PERUSAL
PERUSED
PERUSER
PERUSES
READSIN
REARSUP
REBASTE
REBUSES
RECASTS
RECUSED
RECUSES
REELSIN
REFUSAL
REFUSED
REFUSER
REFUSES
REINSIN
REISSUE
RELISTS
REPASTE
REPASTS
REPOSED
REPOSES
RESISTS
RESTSUP
RETESTS
REVISED
REVISER
REVISES
REVISIT
SEALSUP
SEEPSIN
SENDSIN
SENDSUP
SEXISTS
TEAMSUP
TEARSAT
TEARSUP
TELLSOF
TELLSON
TENDSTO
VENISON
VERISMO
WELLSET
WELLSUP
YELLSAT
YELTSIN
ZEROSUM

•E•••S•

AERIEST
BEAMISH
BEARISH
BEAUISH
BECAUSE
BEDLESS
BEDPOST
BEDREST
BELFAST
BEQUEST
BERNESE
CELLIST
DEAFEST
DEAREST
DEBUSSY
DECLASS
DEEPEST
DEFENSE
DEFROST
DEFTEST
DEGAUSS
DELUISE
DENSEST
DENTIST
DEPRESS
DERVISH
DESPISE
DEWLESS
EELIEST
EERIEST
FEELESS
GEMLESS
GENOESE
GEODESY
GETLOST
HEIRESS
HELLISH
HELOISE
HENNISH
HEPPEST
HEROISM
JETWASH
KEENEST
KENTISH
KEYLESS
KEYWEST
LEANEST
LEFTIST
LEGLESS
LETTISH
LEWDEST
MEANEST
MEEKEST
MELISSA
MELROSE
NEAREST
NEATEST
NEBBISH
NEWNESS
PEAKISH
PECKISH
PEERESS
PEEVISH
PEGLESS
PELISSE
PELTISH
PERKISH
PERSIST
PERTEST
PETTISH
REALISE
REALISM
REALIST
REAMASS
RECHOSE
RECLUSE
RECROSS
REDDEST
REDDISH
REDNESS
REDRESS
REDROSE
REFRESH
REGRESS
RELAPSE
RELEASE
REMORSE
REPRESS
REPRISE
REPULSE
REQUEST
RERAISE
RERINSE
REVERSE
SEABASS
SEAMOSS
SEERESS
SELFISH
SEXIEST
TEALESS
TEAROSE
TEMPEST
TENSEST
TERSEST
VERBOSE
WEAKEST
WEAKISH
WEBLESS
WENDISH
WETNESS
WETTEST
WETTISH
YERKISH

•E••••S

AEDILES
AERATES
AERIALS
AEROBES
AETHERS
BEACHES
BEACONS
BEADLES
BEAGLES
BEAKERS
BEANIES
BEARERS
BEATERS
BEATLES
BEAVERS
BECALMS
BECKONS
BECOMES
BEDAUBS
BEDBUGS
BEDECKS
BEDLESS
BEECHES
BEEGEES
BEEGUMS
BEEPERS
BEETLES
BEFALLS
BEFOULS
BEGGARS
BEHAVES
BEHEADS
BEHESTS
BEHOLDS
BEHOVES
BELCHES
BELDAMS
BELIEFS
BELLIES
BELLOWS
BELONGS
BEMIRES
BEMOANS
BEMUSES
BENCHES
BENDERS
BENGALS
BENUMBS
BERATES
BERBERS
BERRIES
BESEEMS
BESIDES
BESTIRS
BESTOWS
BETAKES
BETHELS
BETIDES
BETIMES
BETISES
BETRAYS
BETTERS
BETTORS
BEWAILS
BEZIERS
CELEBES
CELLARS
CELSIUS
CELTICS
CEMENTS
CENSERS
CENSORS
CENTERS
CENTRES
CEPHEUS
CEREALS
CERIPHS
CERVIDS
CETERIS
DEACONS
DEADENS
DEAFENS
DEALERS
DEARIES
DEARTHS
DEBARKS
DEBASES
DEBATES
DEBEERS
DEBONES
DEBTORS
DEBUNKS
DECADES
DECAMPS
DECANTS
DECEITS
DECIDES
DECKLES
DECLASS
DECOCTS
DECODES
DECREES
DECRIES
DEDALUS
DEDUCES
DEDUCTS
DEEJAYS
DEEPENS
DEFACES
DEFAMES
DEFEATS
DEFECTS
DEFENDS
DEFILES
DEFINES
DEFORMS
DEFRAYS
DEFUSES
DEGAUSS
DEGREES
DEGUSTS
DEHORNS
DEICERS
DEIFIES
DEITIES
DEJECTS
DELETES
DELIBES
DELICTS
DELISTS
DELUDES
DELUGES
DELVERS
DEMANDS
DEMEANS
DEMISES
DEMOTES
DENIALS
DENIERS
DENOTES
DENUDES
DEODARS
DEPARTS
DEPENDS
DEPICTS
DEPLOYS
DEPONES
DEPORTS
DEPOSES
DEPRESS
DEPUTES
DERAILS
DERBIES
DERIDES
DERIVES
DESALTS
DESERTS
DESIGNS
DESIRES
DESISTS
DESOTOS
DESPOTS
DETAILS
DETAINS
DETECTS
DETESTS
DETOURS
DEVEINS
DEVICES
DEVIOUS
DEVISES
DEVOTES
DEVOURS
DEVRIES
DEWLAPS
DEWLESS
FEARERS
FEDORAS
FEEDERS
FEELERS
FEELESS
FELINES
FELLAHS
FELLERS
FELLIES
FELLOWS
FEMALES
FENCERS
FENDERS
FENIANS
FERRETS
FERRIES
FERROUS
FERULES
FERVORS
FESCUES
FESTERS
FETCHES
FETTERS
FETTLES
GECKOES
GEEGAWS
GEEZERS
GEISHAS
GELADAS
GELATIS
GEMLESS
GEMOTES
GENDERS
GENERIS
GENESES
GENESIS
GENGHIS
GENOMES
GENTLES
GEORGES
GERBILS
GERENTS
GERMANS
GERUNDS
GESSOES
GEWGAWS
GEYSERS
HEADERS
HEALERS
HEARERS
HEARTHS
HEATERS
HEAVENS
HEAVERS
HEAVIES
HEBREWS
HECKLES
HECTORS
HEDDLES
HEDGERS
HEEHAWS
HEELERS
HEGIRAS
HEIFERS
HEIGHTS
HEINOUS
HEIRESS
HELICES
HELIXES
HELLERS
HELMETS
HELPERS
HEMMERS
HENBITS
HEPCATS
HEPTADS
HERALDS
HERBALS
HERDERS
HERMITS
HEROICS
HETMANS
HEXNUTS
HEYDAYS
JEALOUS
JEEBIES
JEERERS
JEFFERS
JELLIES
JEMMIES
JENNETS
JENNIES
JERBOAS
JERKINS
JERSEYS
JESTERS
JESUITS
JETGUNS
JETSKIS
JETSONS
JETTIES
JETWAYS
KEENERS
KEEPERS
KEGLERS
KELPIES
KENNELS
KENYANS
KERNELS
KETCHES
KETONES
KETTLES
KEWPIES
KEYLESS
KEYPADS
LEACHES
LEADERS
LEADINS
LEAGUES
LEAKERS
LEANERS
LEANTOS
LEAPERS
LEASERS
LEASHES
LEAVENS
LECTORS
LEDGERS
LEECHES
LEERERS
LEFTIES
LEGATES
LEGATOS
LEGENDS
LEGIONS
LEGISTS
LEGLESS
LEGUMES
LEKVARS
LENDERS
LENGTHS
LENTILS
LEONIDS
LEPPIES
LEPTONS
LESSEES
LESSENS
LESSONS
LESSORS
LETTERS
LETTRES
LEVANTS
LEVIERS
LEVITES
LEXEMES
MEADOWS
MEALIES
MEANIES
MEASLES
MEDDLES
MEDIANS
MEDICOS
MEDIUMS
MEDLEYS
MEDUSAS
MEGOHMS
MEGRIMS
MEINIES
MEIOSES
MEIOSIS
MELLOWS
MEMBERS
MEMOIRS
MEMPHIS
MENACES
MENAGES
MENDERS
MENHIRS
MENIALS
MENTORS
MENZIES
MERCERS
MERCIES
MERGERS
MERINOS
MERLOTS
MESCALS
METATES
METEORS
METHODS
METIERS
METRICS
METTLES
MEWLERS
NEATENS
NEBULAS
NECKERS
NECTARS
NEDDIES
NEEDLES
NEGATES
NELSONS
NEMESES
NEMESIS
NEPALIS
NEPHEWS
NEREIDS
NERVOUS
NESTERS
NESTLES
NETTLES
NEURONS
NEWNESS
NEWSIES
NEWTONS
NEXUSES
OEDIPUS
OEUVRES
PEACHES
PEAHENS
PEANUTS
PEAPODS
PEAVEYS
PEBBLES
PECTINS
PEDANTS
PEDDLES
PEDLARS
PEDWAYS
PEEKERS
PEELERS
PEEPERS
PEEPLES
PEERESS
PEEWEES
PEGASUS
PEGLESS
PEGTOPS
PELAGES
PELLETS
PELOTAS
PELTERS
PENATES
PENCILS
PENNERS
PENNIES
PENNONS
PENPALS
PENSEES
PENTADS
PENULTS
PEONIES
PEOPLES
PEPLUMS
PEPPERS

PEPSINS
PEQUOTS
PERCHES
PERHAPS
PERIODS
PERKINS
PERMITS
PERSEUS
PERSIUS
PERSONS
PERUKES
PERUSES
PESAWAS
PESETAS
PESTERS
PESTLES
PETARDS
PETITES
PETRELS
PETROLS
PETROUS
PETTERS
REACHES
READERS
READIES
REAMASS
REAMERS
REAPERS
REARERS
REASONS
REBATES
REBENDS
REBINDS
REBOILS
REBOLTS
REBOOTS
REBOZOS
REBUFFS
REBUKES
REBUSES
RECALLS
RECANES
RECANTS
RECASTS
RECEDES
RECIPES
RECITES
RECKONS
RECOATS
RECODES
RECOILS
RECORDS
RECORKS
RECOUPS
RECROSS
RECTORS
RECUSES
REDACTS
REDANTS
REDATES
REDBUDS
REDCAPS
REDDENS
REDDOGS
REDEALS
REDEEMS
REDEYES
REDFINS
REDFIRS
REDGUMS
REDHATS
REDHOTS
REDIALS
REDNESS
REDOAKS
REDRAWS
REDRESS
REDTOPS
REDUCES
REEDITS
REEFERS
REFACES
REFILES
REFILLS
REFILMS
REFINES
REFIRES
REFLAGS
REFOCUS
REFORMS
REFRIES
REFUELS
REFUGES
REFUNDS
REFUSES
REFUTES
REGAINS
REGALES
REGARDS
REGENTS
REGIMES
REGIONS
REGLETS
REGLUES
REGRESS
REGRETS
REGULUS
REHANGS
REHEALS
REHEARS
REHEATS
REHEELS
REHIRES
REHOOKS
REIFIES
REJECTS
REJOINS
RELACES
RELATES
RELAXES
RELENTS
RELICTS
RELIEFS
RELINES
RELISTS
RELIVES
RELOADS
RELOCKS
RELUCTS
RELUMES
REMAILS
REMAINS
REMAKES
REMANDS
REMARKS
REMELTS
REMENDS
REMIGES
REMINDS
REMIXES
REMOLDS
REMORAS
REMOTES
REMOVES
REMUDAS
RENAILS
RENAMES
RENARDS
RENDERS
RENEGES
RENNINS
RENOTES
RENTALS
RENTERS
REOPENS
REPAIRS
REPASTS
REPAVES
REPEALS
REPEATS
REPENTS
REPINES
REPLANS
REPLAYS
REPLIES
REPLOWS
REPOLLS
REPORTS
REPOSES
REPRESS
REPUGNS
REPUTES
RERATES
REREADS
REREDOS
RERENTS
RESALES
RESALTS
RESANDS
RESCUES
RESEALS
RESEATS
RESECTS
RESEEDS
RESELLS
RESENDS
RESENTS
RESHIPS
RESHOES
RESIDES
RESIGNS
RESILES
RESINGS
RESISTS
RESOLES
RESORBS
RESORTS
RESPINS
RESTERS
RESULTS
RESUMES
RETAILS
RETAINS
RETAKES
RETAPES
RETARDS
RETAXES
RETEARS
RETELLS
RETESTS
RETILES
RETIMES
RETINAS
RETIRES
RETOOLS
RETORTS
RETOURS
RETRIES
RETRIMS
RETUNES
RETURNS
RETYPES
REUBENS
REUTERS
REVAMPS
REVEALS
REVERBS
REVERES
REVERTS
REVIEWS
REVILES
REVISES
REVIVES
REVOKES
REVOLTS
REWARDS
REWARMS
REWAXES
REWELDS
REWINDS
REWIRES
REWORDS
REWORKS
REWRAPS
REXCATS
REZONES
SEABAGS
SEABASS
SEABEDS
SEABEES
SEACOWS
SEADOGS
SEAFANS
SEALABS
SEALEGS
SEALERS
SEAMOSS
SEANCES
SEASONS
SEATERS
SEAWAYS
SECANTS
SECEDES
SECKELS
SECONDS
SECRETS
SECTORS
SECURES
SEDATES
SEDUCES
SEEDERS
SEEKERS
SEERESS
SEESAWS
SEETHES
SEICHES
SEIDELS
SEINERS
SEIZERS
SELECTS
SELLERS
SEMITES
SENATES
SENDERS
SENDUPS
SENECAS
SENIORS
SENORAS
SENORES
SENSORS
SENUFOS
SEPTETS
SEQUELS
SEQUINS
SERAPES
SERAPHS
SERAPIS
SERIALS
SERIOUS
SERMONS
SERVALS
SERVERS
SESAMES
SESTETS
SETTEES
SETTERS
SETTLES
SEXISTS
SEXTANS
SEXTETS
SEXTONS
TEABAGS
TEACHES
TEACUPS
TEALESS
TEAPOTS
TEAPOYS
TEARGAS
TEASELS
TEASERS
TEASETS
TECHIES
TEDDERS
TEDDIES
TEDIOUS
TEDIUMS
TEENERS
TEEPEES
TEETERS
TEETHES
TELEXES
TELLERS
TELLIES
TEMPEHS
TEMPERS
TEMPLES
TENACES
TENANTS
TENDERS
TENDONS
TENNERS
TENPINS
TENRECS
TENSORS
TENTERS
TENUOUS
TENURES
TERAPHS
TERCELS
TERCETS
TEREDOS
TERRETS
TERRIES
TERRORS
TESTEES
TESTERS
TETANUS
TETHERS
TETRADS
TEUTONS
VECTORS
VEEJAYS
VEERIES
VEGGIES
VEIGHTS
VELLUMS
VELOURS
VELVETS
VENDORS
VENEERS
VENTERS
VERBALS
VERGERS
VERITAS
VERVETS
VESPERS
VESPIDS
VESSELS
VESTEES
VETCHES
VETOERS
WEAKENS
WEAPONS
WEARERS
WEARIES
WEASELS
WEAVERS
WEBLESS
WEDGIES
WEEDERS
WEENIES
WEEPERS
WEEPIES
WEEVILS
WEIGHTS
WEIRDOS
WELCHES
WELDERS
WELKINS
WELTERS
WENCHES
WENDERS
WESKITS
WETBARS
WETHERS
WETMOPS
WETNESS
YELLERS
YELLOWS
YELPERS
YEMENIS
ZEALOTS
ZEALOUS
ZEDBARS
ZENANAS
ZENITHS
ZEPHYRS
ZEUGMAS

••ES•••

ACESOUT
AGESAGO
AWESOME
BEESWAX
BLESSED
BLESSES
BRESLIN
CAESARS
CAESIUM
CAESURA
CHESTER
CRESSES
CRESTED
DIESELS
DIESOFF
DIESOUT
DOESKIN
DRESDEN
DRESSED
DRESSER
DRESSES
DRESSUP
EGESTED
EKESOUT
ETESIAN
EYESHOT
EYESORE
FIESTAS
FLESHED
FLESHES
FLESHLY
FRESCOS
FRESHEN
FRESHER
FRESHET
FRESHLY
GOESAPE
GOESBAD
GOESFOR
GOESOFF
GOESOUT
GUESSED
GUESSER
GUESSES
GUESTED
ICESHOW
ICESOUT
KEESHAN
KMESONS
KNESSET
LIESLOW
LOESSER
LOESSES
MAESTRI
MAESTRO
OLESTRA
ONESELF
ONESHOT
ONESTAR
ONESTEP
ORESTES
PRESAGE
PRESALE
PRESELL
PRESENT
PRESETS
PRESIDE
PRESLEY
PRESOAK
PRESORT
PRESSED
PRESSER
PRESSES
PRESSON
PRESSUP
PRESTON
PRESTOS
PRESUME
QUESTED
SEESAWS
SEESFIT
SEESOFF
SEESOUT
SEESRED
SIESTAS
TEESOFF
THESEUS
THESPIS
TOESHOE
TRESSES
TRESTLE
TUESDAY
WRESTED
WRESTLE

••E•S••

AGEISTS
ASEPSIS
BEEFSUP
BLESSED
BLESSES
BREASTS
CHEESES
CHELSEA
CHEWSUP
CLEMSON
CREASED
CREASES
CREOSOL
CRESSES
DEEPSEA
DEEPSET
DEEPSIX
DREISER
DRESSED
DRESSER
DRESSES
DRESSUP
ELEISON
EMERSED
EMERSON
EVENSUP
FEEDSON
FLENSED
FLENSES
FREESIA
FRETSAW
GLEASON
GREASED
GREASER
GREASES
GUESSED
GUESSER
GUESSES
JEERSAT
KEEPSAT
KEEPSIN
KEEPSON
KEEPSTO
KEEPSUP
KNEESUP
KNESSET
LEERSAT
LOESSER
LOESSES
NIELSEN
OPENSEA
OPENSUP
OVERSAW
OVERSEA
OVERSEE
PEEKSAT
PEERSAT
PEERSIN
PLEASED
PLEASER
PLEASES
PRESSED
PRESSER
PRESSES
PRESSON
PRESSUP
PREYSON
REELSIN
SEEPSIN
SPENSER
STEPSIN
STEPSON
STEPSUP
STETSON
THEISTS
TREASON
TRESSES
TSETSES
UTENSIL
WOEISME

••E••S•

ACEROSE
AGELESS
AWELESS
BLEMISH
CHEMISE
CHEMIST
CHERISH
CLEANSE
CLERISY
COEXIST
DEEPEST
DUELIST
ELEGIST
EPEEIST
EVENEST
EVEREST
EYELASH
EYELESS
EYEWASH
FEELESS
FLEMISH
GREYEST
GREYISH
HUELESS
ICELESS
IRELESS
ITEMISE
KEENEST
MAEWEST
MEEKEST
OBELISK
OLEMISS
ONENESS
OPEROSE
OVERUSE
PEERESS
PEEVISH
PIETISM
PIETIST
PRECAST
PRECISE
PREMISE
PREMISS
PRETEST
PREWASH
QUERIST
RHENISH
SEERESS
SWEDISH
THERESA
TIELESS
TOELESS
USELESS
WHEYISH

••E•••S

AGEISTS
AGELESS
AGENDAS
AMERCES
APERCUS
APERIES
AREOLAS
ASEPSIS
AVENGES
AVENUES
AWELESS
AYEAYES
BEECHES
BEEGEES
BEEGUMS
BEEPERS
BEETLES
BLESSES
BREASTS
BREATHS
BREEZES
BRETONS
BREVETS
BREWERS
CAESARS
CHEESES
CHEETOS
CHEQUES
CHERUBS
CHEVIES
CHEVRES
CHEWERS
CLEAVES
CLEMENS
CLERICS
COEDITS
COEPTIS
COERCES
COEVALS
CREASES
CREATES
CRECHES
CREDITS
CRENELS
CREOLES
CRESSES
CRETANS
CRETINS
CREWELS
DEEJAYS
DEEPENS
DIESELS
DIETERS
DREDGES
DRESSES
DREYFUS
DUELERS
DUENNAS
ELEGIES
ELEVENS
EMERGES
ENEMIES
EVENKIS
EXEMPTS
EYECUPS
EYEFULS
EYELESS
EYELETS
EYELIDS
FAERIES
FEEDERS
FEELERS
FEELESS
FIENNES
FIESTAS
FLECHES
FLEDGES
FLEECES
FLENSES
FLESHES
FLEXORS
FREEZES
FRESCOS
FUELERS
GEEGAWS
GEEZERS
GHETTOS
GREASES
GREAVES
GUELPHS
GUESSES
HEEHAWS
HEELERS
HUELESS
ICEAGES
ICEAXES
ICEBAGS
ICECAPS
ICEFOGS
ICELESS
IDEATES
IRELESS
JAEGERS
JEEBIES
JEERERS
KEENERS
KEEPERS
KMESONS
LAERTES
LEECHES
LEERERS
LIENEES
LIERNES
LOESSES
MAENADS
NEEDLES
NOETICS
OCEANUS
OCELLUS
OCELOTS
OLEATES
OLEFINS
OLEMISS
OMELETS
ONEIDAS
ONENESS
ONEROUS
OPENERS
ORESTES
PEEKERS
PEELERS
PEEPERS
PEEPLES
PEERESS
PEEWEES
PHENOLS
PHENOMS
PIECERS
PIEPANS
PIERCES
PIETIES
PIETINS
PLEASES
PLEDGES
PLENUMS
PLEXORS
POETICS
PREAMPS
PREFABS
PREFERS
PRELIMS
PREMEDS
PREMISS
PRENUPS
PREPAYS
PRESETS
PRESSES
PRESTOS
PREXIES
PUEBLOS
PYEDOGS
QUERIES
QUEUERS
REEDITS
REEFERS
RHEBOKS
RHETORS
SEEDERS
SEEKERS
SEERESS
SEESAWS
SEETHES
SHEATHS
SHEAVES
SHEIKHS
SHEILAS
SHEKELS
SHELVES
SHERPAS
SIENNAS
SIERRAS
SIESTAS
SKEWERS
SLEDGES
SLEEVES
SLEIGHS
SLEUTHS
SNEEZES
SPECIES
SPEEDOS
STEPINS
STEPPES
STEPUPS
STEREOS
STEROLS
STEVENS
STEWERS
SWERVES
TEENERS
TEEPEES
TEETERS
TEETHES
THECARS
THEISTS
THENARS
THEPITS
THERMOS
THESEUS
THESPIS
TIEDYES
TIELESS
TIEPINS
TIERODS
TOECAPS
TOELESS
TOETAPS
TREBLES
TRELLIS
TREMORS
TREPANS
TRESSES
TSETSES
TWEEZES
TWELVES
USELESS
USERIDS
VEEJAYS
VEERIES
VIEWERS
WEEDERS
WEENIES
WEEPERS
WEEPIES
WEEVILS
WHEEZES
WHEREAS
WIENERS
WIENIES
WREATHS

•••ES••

ACHESON
AMNESIA
AMNESTY
ANTESUP
APHESES
ARRESTS
ATTESTS
BEHESTS
BLUESKY
BONESET
BONESUP
BOXESIN
BOXESUP
CAVESIN
CELESTA
CELESTE
CHEESES
CLUESIN
COMESAT
COMESBY
COMESIN
COMESON
COMESTO
COMESUP
CROESUS
DARESAY
DARESTO
DEMESNE
DETESTS
DIGESTS
DINESEN
DINESIN
DINESON
DIVESIN
DIVESTS
DOTESON
DRIESUP
EASESIN
EASESUP
EDGESIN
ERNESTO
FADESIN
FINESSE
FIRESUP
FIXESUP
FLIESAT
FLIESIN
FORESAW
FORESEE
FORESTS
FREESIA
GENESEE
GENESES
GENESIS
GIVESIN
GIVESTO
GIVESUP
GLUESON
HIKESUP
HIRESON
HOLESUP
HONESTY
HYPESUP
ILIESCU
INFESTS
INGESTS
INVESTS
IONESCO
IQTESTS
JAMESON
JONESES
KNEESUP
LACESUP
LINESUP
LIVESIN
LIVESON
LOSESIT
MAJESTE
MAJESTY
MAKESDO
MAKESIT
MAKESUP
MIMESIS
MIXESIN
MIXESUP
MODESTO
MODESTY
MOLESTS
MORESBY
MOVESIN
MOVESON
MOVESUP
MUMESON
NEMESES
NEMESIS
PILESIN
PILESON
PILESUP
PIMESON
PINESAP
PIPESUP
POKESAT
PRIESTS
RAKESIN
RAKESUP
RAMESES
RETESTS
RILESUP
ROBESON
ROPESIN
RULESON
SAVESUP
SILESIA
SIZESUP
SPIESON
TAKESIN
TAKESON
TAKESTO
TAKESUP
TIMESUP
TONESUP
TRIESON
TRIESTE
TUNESIN
TUNESUP
TYPESET
TYPESUP
VANESSA
VOTESIN
WADESIN
WAKESUP
WAVESIN
WINESAP
WIPESUP
WISESUP

•••E•S•

ABREAST
ADVERSE
AMHERST
APPEASE

ASPERSE
ATHEISM
ATHEIST
ATLEAST
BLUEISH
BONEASH
DEFENSE
DISEASE
DIVERSE
DRSEUSS
EPEEIST
EXPENSE
FAREAST
FINESSE
IMMENSE
IMMERSE
INCENSE
INTENSE
INTERSE
INVERSE
LICENSE
MIDEAST
OBVERSE
OFFENSE
OGREISH
RELEASE
REVERSE
UNLEASH
VANESSA

•••E••S

ABSENTS
ACCEDES
ACCENTS
ACCEPTS
ACHENES
ADDENDS
ADHERES
ADVENTS
ADVERBS
ADVERTS
AFFECTS
AFREETS
ALBEDOS
ALKENES
ALLEARS
ALLEGES
ALLELES
ALLEYES
AMOEBAS
AMPERES
ANDEANS
ANGELES
ANGELUS
ANNEALS
ANNEXES
APHESES
APPEALS
APPEARS
APPENDS
AQUEOUS
ARPENTS
ARREARS
ARRESTS
ARTEMIS
ARTEMUS
ASCENDS
ASCENTS
ASPECTS
ASSENTS
ASSERTS
ATTENDS
ATTESTS
AUGENDS
AUTEURS
AXSEEDS
BADEGGS
BALEENS
BARENTS
BEDECKS
BEHEADS
BEHESTS
BESEEMS
BIGEYES
BIREMES
BISECTS
BODEGAS
BOLEROS
BREEZES
BUREAUS
CALENDS
CAMERAS
CAREENS
CAREERS
CASERNS
CAVEATS
CAVEINS
CAVERNS
CELEBES
CEMENTS
CEREALS
CETERIS
CHEESES
CHEETOS
CINEMAS
CLIENTS
COHEIRS
COHERES
COMEONS
CROESUS
CSLEWIS
DALETHS
DEBEERS
DECEITS
DEFEATS
DEFECTS
DEFENDS
DEJECTS
DELETES
DEMEANS
DEPENDS
DESERTS
DETECTS
DETESTS
DEVEINS
DIGESTS
DIRECTS
DIVERTS
DIVESTS
DOCENTS
DOGEARS
DRSEUSS
DUTEOUS
EFFECTS
ENDEARS
ENNEADS
ESSENES
ESTEEMS
EXCEEDS
EXCEPTS
EXPECTS
EXPENDS
EXPERTS
EXSERTS
EXTENDS
EXTENTS
EXTERNS
FADEINS
FAGENDS
FIDELIS
FILENES
FLEECES
FOMENTS
FORESTS
FREEZES
FRIENDS
FRIEZES
GAMETES
GASEOUS
GAZEBOS
GENERIS
GENESES
GENESIS
GERENTS
GIDEONS
GIVEUPS
GOVERNS
GRIEVES
GYRENES
HGWELLS
HIDEOUS
HOWELLS
HUMERUS
IGNEOUS
IMPEDES
IMPENDS
IMPETUS
INCEPTS
INDENTS
INDEXES
INFECTS
INFESTS
INGESTS
INHERES
INJECTS
INSEAMS
INSECTS
INSERTS
INTEARS
INTENDS
INTENTS
INTERNS
INVENTS
INVERTS
INVESTS
IQTESTS
JONESES
KINEMAS
KOPECKS
KOREANS
LAMEDHS
LAMENTS
LATEENS
LATENTS
LATEXES
LEGENDS
LEXEMES
LINEUPS
LOVEINS
LYCEUMS
MAKEUPS
MANEGES
METEORS
MIMESIS
MODELAS
MODELTS
MODERNS
MOLESTS
MOMENTS
MRDEEDS
MUDEELS
MULETAS
MUSEUMS
NEMESES
NEMESIS
NEREIDS
NOVENAS
OBJECTS
OBVERTS
OFFENDS
ORDEALS
ORGEATS
ORIENTS
ORLEANS
OSSEOUS
OUTEATS
PARENTS
PATENTS
PESETAS
PHOEBES
PHOEBUS
PIGEONS
PILEUPS
PITEOUS
POMELOS
POSEURS
PRIESTS
RACEMES
RAMESES
RAREGAS
RAVEUPS
RAWEGGS
REBENDS
RECEDES
REDEALS
REDEEMS
REDEYES
REGENTS
REHEALS
REHEARS
REHEATS
REHEELS
REJECTS
RELENTS
REMELTS
REMENDS
RENEGES
REPEALS
REPEATS
REPENTS
REREADS
REREDOS
RERENTS
RESEALS
RESEATS
RESECTS
RESEEDS
RESELLS
RESENDS
RESENTS
RETEARS
RETELLS
RETESTS
REVEALS
REVERBS
REVERES
REVERTS
REWELDS
RIBEYES
ROBERTS
RODENTS
SAMECHS
SATEENS
SCHEMAS
SCHEMES
SCLERAS
SCREAKS
SCREAMS
SCREEDS
SCREENS
SECEDES
SELECTS
SENECAS
SHIELDS
SILENTS
SLEEVES
SNEEZES
SPEEDOS
SPHERES
SPLEENS
SPREADS
SQUEAKS
SQUEALS
STDENIS
STREAKS
STREAMS
STREETS
TAGENDS
TALENTS
TAVERNS
TELEXES
TEREDOS
THIEVES
THREADS
THREATS
THREERS
TINEARS
TOREROS
TUNEUPS
TUPELOS
TUREENS
TUXEDOS
TWEEZES
UNBENDS
UNREELS
UNSEALS
UNSEATS
UNVEILS
UPBEATS
URTEXTS
VENEERS
VOTECHS
WHEEZES
WYVERNS
YEMENIS
ZAREBAS
ZYDECOS

••••ES•

ACHIEST
ACTRESS
ADDRESS
AERIEST
AGELESS
AGGRESS
AIDLESS
AIMLESS
AIRIEST
AIRLESS
AMPLEST
ANAPEST
ANDRESS
APTNESS
ARIDEST
ARMLESS
ARMREST
ARTIEST
ARTLESS
ASHIEST
ASHLESS
AWELESS
AWNLESS
BADDEST
BADNESS
BALDEST
BARLESS
BEDLESS
BEDREST
BEQUEST
BERNESE
BIBLESS
BIGGEST
BIGNESS
BITLESS
BOLDEST
BONIEST
BOWLESS
BOXIEST
BRALESS
BRAVEST
BUDLESS
BURGESS
BURMESE
BUSIEST
CAGIEST
CAKIEST
CALMEST
CANIEST
CAPLESS
CARLESS
CHINESE
CLOSEST
COKIEST
COLDEST
CONFESS
CONGEST
CONTEST
COOLEST
COSIEST
COYNESS
COZIEST
CRUDEST
CURTEST
CYPRESS
DAFTEST
DAMPEST
DANKEST
DARKEST
DEAFEST
DEAREST
DEEPEST
DEFTEST
DENSEST
DEPRESS
DEWLESS
DICIEST
DIGRESS
DIMMEST
DIMNESS
DIOCESE
DOGLESS
DOPIEST
DOUREST
DOZIEST
DRYNESS
DUCHESS
DULLEST
DUMBEST
EARLESS
EARNEST
EASIEST
EDGIEST
EELIEST
EERIEST
EGGIEST
EGGLESS
EMPRESS
ENDLESS
EVENEST
EVEREST
EVILEST
EXPRESS
EYELESS
FAIREST
FALSEST
FARWEST
FASTEST
FATLESS
FATNESS
FATTEST
FEELESS
FIRMEST
FITNESS
FITTEST
FLYLESS
FOGLESS
FONDEST
FORREST
FOULEST
FOXIEST
FULLEST
FUMIEST
FUNFEST
FURLESS
GABFEST
GAMIEST
GAPLESS
GASLESS
GEMLESS
GENOESE
GEODESY
GLUIEST
GODDESS
GODLESS
GOOIEST
GORIEST
GRAVEST
GRAYEST
GREYEST
GUMLESS
GUNLESS
GUTLESS
HAPLESS
HARDEST
HARNESS
HARVEST
HATLESS
HAZIEST
HEIRESS
HEPPEST
HIGHEST
HIPLESS
HIPNESS
HIPPEST
HITLESS
HOKIEST
HOLIEST
HOMIEST
HOSTESS
HOTNESS
HOTTEST
HUELESS
ICELESS
ICINESS
ICKIEST
IFFIEST
ILLNESS
IMPRESS
INAMESS
INANEST
INGRESS
INKIEST
INKLESS
INNLESS
INQUEST
IPCRESS
IRATEST
IRELESS
JAGLESS
JARLESS
JAWLESS
JIVIEST
JOBLESS
JOKIEST
JOYLESS
KEENEST
KEYLESS
KEYWEST
KINDEST
KINLESS
LACIEST
LAKIEST
LANKEST
LARGESS
LARGEST
LAWLESS
LAXNESS
LAZIEST
LEANEST
LEGLESS
LEWDEST
LIDLESS
LIMIEST
LIMPEST
LINIEST
LIONESS
LIPLESS
LITHEST
LOGIEST
LONGEST
LOOSEST
LOUDEST
LOWNESS
LUSHEST
MADDEST
MADNESS
MAEWEST
MALTESE
MANLESS
MATLESS
MAZIEST
MEANEST
MEEKEST
MIDWEST
MILDEST
MIRIEST
MOPIEST
NAPLESS
NEAREST
NEATEST
NEWNESS
NIGHEST
NOBLEST
NOSIEST
NUMBEST
OARLESS
ODDNESS
OILIEST
OILLESS
OLDNESS
OLDWEST
ONENESS
OOZIEST
OPPRESS
ORBLESS
PALIEST
PATNESS
PEERESS
PEGLESS
PERTEST
PINIEST
PINKEST
PINLESS
PIPIEST
POKIEST
POOREST
POSHEST
POSSESS
PRETEST
PROCESS
PROFESS
PROTEST
PROWESS
PUNIEST
PUNLESS
RACIEST
RANKEST
RASHEST
RAWNESS
REDDEST
REDNESS
REDRESS
REFRESH
REGRESS
REPRESS
REQUEST
RIBLESS
RICHEST
RIMIEST
RIMLESS
RODLESS
ROPIEST
ROSIEST
RUMLESS
SADDEST
SADNESS
SAPLESS
SEERESS
SEXIEST
SHYNESS
SIAMESE
SICKEST
SINLESS
SKYLESS
SLOWEST
SLYNESS
SNIDEST
SODLESS
SOFTEST
SONLESS
SOONEST
SOUREST
SPAREST
SPRIEST
SPRYEST
STALEST
SUAVEST
SUCCESS
SUGGEST
SUMLESS
SUNLESS
TALLEST
TANNEST
TARTEST
TAUTEST
TAXLESS
TEALESS
TEMPEST
TENSEST
TERSEST
THERESA
TIDIEST
TIELESS
TIGRESS
TINIEST
TIPLESS
TOELESS
TONIEST
TOYLESS
TRITEST
TUGLESS
TYPIEST
UGLIEST
UNBLEST
UNDRESS
USELESS
VAGUEST
VAINEST
VASTEST
VINIEST
VOWLESS
WANIEST
WANNESS
WANNEST
WARIEST
WARLESS
WARMEST
WAVIEST
WAXIEST
WAYLESS
WEAKEST
WEBLESS
WETNESS
WETTEST
WHITEST
WIGLESS
WILDEST
WILIEST
WINIEST
WIRIEST
WITLESS
WITNESS
WRYNESS
ZANIEST

••••E•S

ABUSERS
ACTRESS
ACUMENS
ADDRESS
ADORERS
AETHERS
AFREETS
AGELESS
AGGRESS
AIDLESS
AIGRETS
AIMLESS
AIRLESS
ALGIERS
AMADEUS
AMBLERS
AMULETS
ANADEMS
ANDREAS
ANDRESS
ANDREWS
ANGLERS
ANKLETS
ANSWERS
ANTAEUS
ANTHEMS
ANTHERS
ANTLERS
APOGEES
APPLETS
APTNESS
ARCHERS
ARGUERS
ARMLESS
ARMLETS
ARTLESS
ASHLESS
AUKLETS
AVOCETS
AVOWERS
AWAKENS
AWELESS
AWNLESS
AXSEEDS
AZALEAS
BACKERS
BADGERS
BADNESS
BAGGERS
BAILEES
BAILERS
BAILEYS
BALEENS
BALLETS
BANKERS
BANNERS
BANTERS
BARBELS
BARBERS
BARKERS
BARLESS
BARLEYS
BARNEYS
BARRELS
BARRENS
BARTERS
BASKETS
BASSETS
BASTERS
BATHERS
BATTELS
BATTENS
BATTERS
BAWLERS
BEAKERS
BEARERS
BEATERS
BEAVERS
BEDLESS
BEEGEES
BEEPERS
BELIEFS
BENDERS
BERBERS
BESEEMS
BETHELS
BETTERS
BEZIERS
BIBLESS
BICKERS
BIDDERS
BIGGERS
BIGNESS
BILLETS
BINDERS
BIRDERS
BITLESS
BITTERS
BLADERS
BLAZERS
BLOWERS
BOATELS
BOATERS
BOBBERS
BOILERS
BOMBERS
BONKERS
BONNETS
BOOMERS
BOOTEES
BOPPERS
BORDERS
BOSKETS
BOTHERS
BOVVERS
BOWLERS
BOWLESS
BOWYERS
BRACERS
BRALESS
BRAYERS
BREVETS
BREWERS
BROKERS
BRUNETS
BUCKETS
BUDGETS
BUDLESS
BUFFERS
BUFFETS
BUGLERS
BULLETS
BUMMERS
BUMPERS
BUNGEES
BUNKERS
BURDENS
BURGEES
BURGERS
BURGESS
BURNERS
BUSHELS
BUSTERS
BUTLERS
BUTTERS
BUZZERS
CABLERS
CACHETS
CADGERS
CAHIERS
CALLERS
CAMBERS
CAMPERS
CANCELS
CANKERS
CANNERS
CANTERS
CAPLESS
CAPLETS
CAPPERS
CARDERS
CAREENS
CAREERS
CARLESS
CARNETS
CARPELS
CARPERS
CARPETS
CARRELS
CARTELS
CARTERS
CARVERS
CASHEWS
CASTERS
CENSERS
CENTERS
CEPHEUS
CHALETS
CHAPELS
CHASERS
CHEWERS
CHIDERS
CHISELS
CHOKERS
CINDERS
CIPHERS
CLARETS
CLAWERS
CLEMENS
CLORETS
CLOSETS
CLOVERS
COALERS
COAXERS
COBWEBS
COCKERS
CODGERS
COFFEES
COFFERS
COINERS
COLLETS
COMBERS
COMPELS
CONFERS
CONFESS
CONGERS
CONKERS
CONVEYS
COOKERS
COOLERS
COOPERS
COPIERS
COPPERS
COPTERS
CORBELS
CORKERS
CORNEAS
CORNERS
CORNETS
CORSETS
COSSETS
COTTERS
COULEES
COWPEAS
COYNESS
COZZENS
CRATERS
CRAVENS
CRAVERS
CRENELS
CREWELS
CROWERS
CUDGELS
CULLERS
CULVERS
CURFEWS
CURLERS
CURLEWS
CURVETS
CUTLERS
CUTLETS
CUTTERS
CYCLERS
CYGNETS
CYPHERS
CYPRESS
DAGGERS
DAMPENS
DAMPERS
DAMSELS
DANCERS
DANDERS
DANGERS
DANIELS
DARKENS
DARNERS
DARTERS
DASHERS
DAUBERS
DAYBEDS
DEADENS
DEAFENS
DEALERS
DEBEERS
DECREES
DEEPENS
DEGREES
DEICERS
DELVERS
DENIERS
DEPRESS
DEWLESS
DIADEMS
DIALERS
DIAPERS
DICKENS
DICKERS
DICKEYS
DIESELS
DIETERS
DIFFERS
DIGGERS
DIGRESS
DIMMERS
DIMNESS
DINNERS
DIPPERS
DISPELS
DITHERS
DOCKERS
DOCKETS
DODDERS
DODGERS
DOGLEGS
DOGLESS
DOLMENS
DONKEYS
DORMERS
DOSSERS
DOWNERS
DOWSERS
DRAPERS
DRAWERS
DRIVELS
DRIVERS
DRONERS
DROVERS
DRYNESS
DUBBERS
DUCHESS
DUELERS
DUFFELS
DUFFERS
DUNKERS
DUSTERS
EAGLETS
EARLESS
EARNERS
EASTERS
EGGLESS

ELATERS
ELEVENS
ELOPERS
ELYSEES
EMBLEMS
EMOTERS
EMPRESS
ENAMELS
ENDLESS
ENTREES
ENVIERS
EPOPEES
ERASERS
ESCHEWS
ESTEEMS
ETCHERS
EVADERS
EVOKERS
EXCEEDS
EXPRESS
EYELESS
EYELETS
FABLERS
FALTERS
FANJETS
FARMERS
FASTENS
FATHERS
FATLESS
FATNESS
FATTENS
FAUCETS
FAWNERS
FEARERS
FEEDERS
FEELERS
FEELESS
FELLERS
FENCERS
FENDERS
FERRETS
FESTERS
FETTERS
FIBBERS
FIDGETS
FILLERS
FILLETS
FILTERS
FINDERS
FINGERS
FISHERS
FITNESS
FITTERS
FLAKERS
FLORETS
FLOWERS
FLYLESS
FLYNETS
FODDERS
FOGGERS
FOGLESS
FOLDERS
FOLGERS
FOOTERS
FORCEPS
FORCERS
FORGERS
FORGETS
FORKERS
FOSTERS
FOWLERS
FUELERS
FUNNELS
FURLESS

GABBERS
GADDERS
GADGETS
GAFFERS
GAINERS
GAITERS
GALLEYS
GAMMERS
GANDERS
GANGERS
GANNETS
GAOLERS
GAPLESS
GARDENS
GARNERS
GARNETS
GARRETS
GARTERS
GASJETS
GASKETS
GASLESS
GASPERS
GASSERS
GATHERS
GAUGERS
GAWKERS
GEEZERS
GEMLESS
GENDERS
GEYSERS
GIBBERS
GIBBETS
GIBLETS
GILDERS
GIMLETS
GINGERS
GIRDERS
GLAZERS
GLIDERS
GLOWERS
GNAWERS
GOATEES
GOBLETS
GODDESS
GODLESS
GOLFERS
GOMPERS
GOOBERS
GOPHERS
GORGETS
GOSPELS
GOUGERS
GRADERS
GRATERS
GRAVELS
GRAVERS
GRAZERS
GRIPERS
GRIVETS
GROCERS
GROVELS
GROWERS
GUINEAS
GULLETS
GUMLESS
GUNLESS
GUNNELS
GUNNERS
GURNEYS
GUSHERS
GUSSETS
GUTLESS
GUTTERS
GYPPERS

HACKERS
HALTERS
HAMLETS
HAMMERS
HAMPERS
HANGERS
HANKERS
HAPLESS
HAPPENS
HARDENS
HARKENS
HARNESS
HARPERS
HASTENS
HATLESS
HATTERS
HAULERS
HAWKERS
HAWSERS
HEADERS
HEALERS
HEARERS
HEATERS
HEAVENS
HEAVERS
HEBREWS
HEDGERS
HEELERS
HEIFERS
HEIRESS
HELLERS
HELMETS
HELPERS
HEMMERS
HERDERS
HINDERS
HIPLESS
HIPNESS
HISSERS
HITLESS
HITTERS
HOAXERS
HOGGETS
HOLDERS
HOLLERS
HONKERS
HOOFERS
HOOTERS
HOOVERS
HOPPERS
HORNETS
HOSIERS
HOSTELS
HOSTESS
HOTBEDS
HOTNESS
HOWLERS
HOYDENS
HUELESS
HUGGERS
HULLERS
HUMMERS
HUMVEES
HUNGERS
HUNKERS
HUNTERS
HURLERS
HURLEYS
HUSKERS
HUYGENS
HYPHENS
ICELESS
ICINESS
ILLNESS

IMAGERS
IMARETS
IMPRESS
INAMESS
INGRESS
INKLESS
INNLESS
INSTEPS
IPCRESS
IRELESS
IRONERS
ISOHELS
ISOMERS
ISSUERS
JABBERS
JACKETS
JACKEYS
JAEGERS
JAGLESS
JAILERS
JAMMERS
JARLESS
JASPERS
JAWLESS
JAYCEES
JAYVEES
JEERERS
JEFFERS
JENNETS
JERSEYS
JESTERS
JIGGERS
JITNEYS
JITTERS
JOBBERS
JOBLESS
JOCKEYS
JOGGERS
JOINERS
JOSSERS
JOYLESS
JUDDERS
JUICERS
JUMPERS
JUNKERS
JUNKETS
KAISERS
KEENERS
KEEPERS
KEGLERS
KENNELS
KERNELS
KEYLESS
KICKERS
KIDDERS
KIDNEYS
KILLERS
KINLESS
KIPPERS
KISSERS
KITTENS
KOSHERS
KRATERS
KUCHENS
LAAGERS
LABRETS
LACKEYS
LADDERS
LADLERS
LAGGERS
LANCERS
LANCETS
LANDERS
LAPPETS

LARDERS
LARGESS
LASHERS
LATEENS
LATHERS
LATTENS
LAURELS
LAWLESS
LAWYERS
LAXNESS
LEADERS
LEAKERS
LEANERS
LEAPERS
LEASERS
LEAVENS
LEDGERS
LEERERS
LEGLESS
LENDERS
LESSEES
LESSENS
LETTERS
LEVIERS
LIBBERS
LICHENS
LIDLESS
LIENEES
LIFTERS
LIMBERS
LIMNERS
LIMPETS
LINDENS
LINGERS
LINKERS
LINNETS
LINTELS
LIONESS
LIONETS
LIPLESS
LISTEES
LISTELS
LISTENS
LITTERS
LOADERS
LOAFERS
LOANERS
LOBBERS
LOCKERS
LOCKETS
LODGERS
LOGGERS
LOITERS
LOOKERS
LOONEYS
LOOPERS
LOOSENS
LOOTERS
LOPPERS
LOUVERS
LOWNESS
LUBBERS
LUGGERS
LUMBERS
LUMPERS
LUNKERS
LUSTERS
MADDENS
MADDERS
MADNESS
MAGNETS
MAGUEYS
MAIDENS
MAILERS

MALLETS
MALTEDS
MANGERS
MANLESS
MANNERS
MANTELS
MAPPERS
MARCELS
MARKERS
MARKETS
MARTENS
MARVELS
MASHERS
MASKERS
MASTERS
MATHERS
MATHEWS
MATLESS
MATTERS
MAYHEMS
MEDLEYS
MEMBERS
MENDERS
MERCERS
MERGERS
METIERS
MEWLERS
MICKEYS
MIDDENS
MIDGETS
MILDEWS
MILIEUS
MILKERS
MILLERS
MILLETS
MINCERS
MINDERS
MINTERS
MINUETS
MISTERS
MITTENS
MIZZENS
MOANERS
MOCKERS
MOILERS
MOLDERS
MOLTERS
MONGERS
MONKEES
MONKEYS
MOPPERS
MOPPETS
MORSELS
MOSHERS
MOSLEMS
MOTHERS
MOUSERS
MRDEEDS
MUDDERS
MUDEELS
MUDHENS
MUGGERS
MULLERS
MULLETS
MUMMERS
MUPPETS
MURDERS
MUSHERS
MUSKEGS
MUSKETS
MUSSELS
MUSTERS
MUTTERS
NABBERS

NAILERS
NAPLESS
NAPPERS
NATTERS
NEATENS
NECKERS
NEPHEWS
NESTERS
NEWNESS
NICKELS
NICKERS
NIPPERS
NODDERS
NOSHERS
NUCLEUS
NUDGERS
NUGGETS
NUMBERS
NURSERS
NUTLETS
NUTMEGS
NUTTERS
OARLESS
ODDNESS
OFFSETS
OILLESS
OLDNESS
OLDNEWS
OMELETS
ONAGERS
ONENESS
OPENERS
OPINERS
OPPRESS
ORBLESS
ORPHEUS
OSPREYS
OSTLERS
OUSTERS
OUTLETS
OUTSETS
OYSTERS
PACKERS
PACKETS
PADDERS
PALLETS
PALTERS
PAMPERS
PANDERS
PANNERS
PANZERS
PARCELS
PARGETS
PARLEYS
PARSECS
PARSEES
PARSERS
PASSELS
PASSERS
PASTELS
PATNESS
PATTENS
PATTERS
PAUPERS
PAWNEES
PAWNERS
PEAHENS
PEAVEYS
PEEKERS
PEELERS
PEEPERS
PEERESS
PEEWEES
PEGLESS

PELLETS
PELTERS
PENNERS
PENSEES
PEPPERS
PERSEUS
PESTERS
PETRELS
PETTERS
PHASERS
PHINEAS
PHONEYS
PICKENS
PICKERS
PICKETS
PIECERS
PIGLETS
PIGPENS
PILFERS
PINCERS
PINLESS
PINNERS
PIOLETS
PIRAEUS
PITIERS
PITTERS
PLACERS
PLANERS
PLANETS
PLATENS
PLATERS
PLAYERS
PLOVERS
PLOWERS
POCKETS
POLDERS
POLLENS
POLLERS
POMMELS
PONDERS
PONGEES
POPPERS
POPPETS
PORKERS
PORTERS
POSSESS
POSSETS
POSTERS
POTHERS
POTTERS
POURERS
POUTERS
POWDERS
PRATERS
PRAYERS
PREFERS
PREMEDS
PRESETS
PRICERS
PRIMERS
PRIVETS
PROBERS
PROCESS
PROFESS
PROPELS
PROSERS
PROTEUS
PROVERS
PROWESS
PRUNERS
PUCKERS
PUFFERS
PUGREES
PULLETS

PULLEYS
PUMMELS
PUMPERS
PUNKERS
PUNLESS
PUNNETS
PUNTERS
PUPPETS
PURRERS
PURSERS
PURVEYS
PUTTEES
PUTTERS
QUAKERS
QUAVERS
QUEUERS
QUIVERS
QUOTERS
RABBETS
RACKETS
RAFTERS
RAIDERS
RAILERS
RAISERS
RAMJETS
RANGERS
RANKERS
RANTERS
RAPIERS
RAPPELS
RAPPERS
RASHERS
RASPERS
RASTERS
RATTERS
RAWNESS
READERS
REAMERS
REAPERS
REARERS
REDDENS
REDEEMS
REDNESS
REDRESS
REEFERS
REFUELS
REGLETS
REGRESS
REGRETS
REHEELS
RELIEFS
RENDERS
RENTERS
REOPENS
REPRESS
RESEEDS
RESTERS
REUBENS
REUTERS
REVIEWS
RHYMERS
RIBLESS
RICKEYS
RIFLERS
RIGGERS
RILLETS
RIMLESS
RINGERS
RIOTERS
RIPPERS
RISKERS
ROAMERS
ROARERS
ROBBERS

ROCHETS
ROCKERS
ROCKETS
RODGERS
RODLESS
ROLLERS
ROMNEYS
ROMPERS
RONDELS
ROOFERS
ROOMERS
ROOTERS
ROSTERS
ROTTERS
ROUSERS
ROUTERS
ROZZERS
RUBBERS
RUDDERS
RUINERS
RUMLESS
RUNLETS
RUNNELS
RUNNERS
RUSHEES
RUSHERS
RUSSETS
RUTGERS
SACHEMS
SACHETS
SACKERS
SADDENS
SADNESS
SALLETS
SALTERS
SALVERS
SAMLETS
SANDERS
SAPIENS
SAPLESS
SAPPERS
SASSERS
SATEENS
SAUCERS
SAWYERS
SCALERS
SCARERS
SCHLEPS
SCORERS
SCOTERS
SCREEDS
SCREENS
SEABEDS
SEABEES
SEALEGS
SEALERS
SEATERS
SECKELS
SECRETS
SEEDERS
SEEKERS
SEERESS
SEIDELS
SEINERS
SEIZERS
SELLERS
SENDERS
SEPTETS
SEQUELS
SERVERS
SESTETS
SETTEES
SETTERS
SEXTETS

SHAKERS
SHAPERS
SHARERS
SHAVERS
SHEKELS
SHINERS
SHIVERS
SHOVELS
SHOVERS
SHOWERS
SHRIEKS
SHYNESS
SICKENS
SIFTERS
SIGHERS
SIGNEES
SIGNERS
SIGNETS
SILVERS
SIMMERS
SIMPERS
SINGERS
SINKERS
SINLESS
SINNERS
SIPPERS
SIPPETS
SISTERS
SITTERS
SKATERS
SKEWERS
SKIVERS
SKYLESS
SLAVERS
SLAVEYS
SLAYERS
SLICERS
SLIDERS
SLIVERS
SLOVENS
SLYNESS
SMILERS
SMOKERS
SNIPERS
SNIVELS
SNORERS
SOAKERS
SOAPERS
SOARERS
SOBBERS
SOCKETS
SODLESS
SOFTENS
SOIREES
SOLDERS
SOLVERS
SONLESS
SONNETS
SOONERS
SORBETS
SORRELS
SORTERS
SOVIETS
SPACERS
SPADERS
SPIDERS
SPIKERS
SPINELS
SPINETS
SPIREAS
SPLEENS
STAGERS
STAMENS
STARERS

STARETS
STEREOS
STEVENS
STEWERS
STOKERS
STONERS
STORERS
STOREYS
STREETS
STUMERS
STYLERS
STYLETS
SUBDEBS
SUBLETS
SUBSETS
SUCCESS
SUCKERS
SUFFERS
SULKERS
SUMLESS
SUMMERS
SUNDERS
SUNDEWS
SUNLESS
SUNSETS
SUPPERS
SURFERS
SURREYS
SURVEYS
SUTLERS
SUTTERS
SWAYERS
SWIPERS
SWIVELS
SWIVETS
SYSTEMS
TABLETS
TACKERS
TALKERS
TAMPERS
TANDEMS
TANKERS
TANNERS
TAPPERS
TAPPETS
TARGETS
TASSELS
TASTERS
TATTERS
TAUTENS
TAXLESS
TEALESS
TEASELS
TEASERS
TEASETS
TEDDERS
TEENERS
TEEPEES
TEETERS
TELLERS
TEMPEHS
TEMPERS
TENDERS
TENNERS
TENRECS
TENTERS
TERCELS
TERCETS
TERRETS
TESTEES
TESTERS
TETHERS
THALERS
THESEUS

THREERS
TICKERS
TICKETS
TIELESS
TIGRESS
TILLERS
TILTERS
TIMBERS
TINDERS
TINKERS
TINNERS
TINSELS
TINTERS
TIPLESS
TIPPERS
TIPPETS
TITFERS
TITHERS
TITTERS
TOELESS
TOFFEES
TOILERS
TOILETS
TOLTECS
TOOTERS
TOPPERS
TORRENS
TOSSERS
TOTTERS
TOUPEES
TOURERS
TOUTERS
TOWHEES
TOWNERS
TOYLESS
TRACERS
TRADERS
TRAVELS
TRAVERS
TRICEPS
TRIJETS
TRIVETS
TROWELS
TROWERS
TUAREGS
TUCKERS
TUFFETS
TUGGERS
TUGLESS
TUNNELS
TUREENS
TURKEYS
TURNERS
TURRETS
TUSKERS
TWOFERS
ULSTERS
UNDRESS
UNITERS
UNREELS
USELESS
USOPENS
USURERS
VALLEYS
VAMPERS
VARLETS
VELVETS
VENEERS
VENTERS
VERGERS
VERVETS
VESPERS
VESSELS
VESTEES

VETOERS
VIEWERS
VIOLETS
VIZIERS
VOLLEYS
VOWLESS
WAILERS
WAITERS
WAIVERS
WALKERS
WALLETS
WALTERS
WANDERS
WANNESS
WARDENS
WARDERS
WARLESS
WARRENS
WASHERS
WASTERS
WAYLESS
WEAKENS
WEARERS
WEASELS
WEAVERS
WEBLESS
WEEDERS
WEEPERS
WELDERS
WELTERS
WENDERS
WETHERS
WETNESS
WHALERS
WHEREAS
WHINERS
WHITENS
WICKERS
WICKETS
WIDGETS
WIENERS
WIGLESS
WIGLETS
WILLETS
WINCERS
WINDERS
WINGERS
WINKERS
WINNERS
WINTERS
WISHERS
WITHERS
WITLESS
WITNESS
WONDERS
WOOFERS
WOOLENS
WORKERS
WORSENS
WOWSERS
WRITERS
WRYNESS
WURLEYS
YABBERS
YAKKERS
YAMMERS
YANKEES
YAPPERS
YAWNERS
YAWPERS
YELLERS
YELPERS
YONKERS
YOWLERS

ZAFFERS
ZANDERS
ZAPPERS
ZINGERS
ZIPPERS
ZITHERS
ZONKERS

•••••ES

ABASHES
ABJURES
ABLATES
ABRADES
ABYSSES
ACCEDES
ACCRUES
ACCUSES
ACHATES
ACHENES
ACTIVES
ADDUCES
ADHERES
ADJURES
ADMIRES
ADMIXES
ADVISES
AEDILES
AERATES
AEROBES
AFFINES
AFFIXES
AFRAMES
AGNATES
AITCHES
ALCOVES
ALIASES
ALKENES
ALLEGES
ALLELES
ALLEYES
ALLUDES
ALLURES
AMASSES
AMBRIES
AMERCES
AMPERES
AMPULES
ANGELES
ANNEXES
ANOMIES
ANTARES
ANTIBES
ANYONES
APACHES
APERIES
APHESES
APOGEES
APPLIES
APPOSES
APSIDES
ARCADES
ARGIVES
ARGYLES
ARMURES
AROUSES
ARRASES
ARRISES
ARRIVES
ASPIRES
ASSIZES
ASSUMES
ASSURES
ATHOMES
ATLASES
ATOMIES
ATONIES
ATTIMES
ATTIRES
ATTUNES
AUBADES
AUDILES
AUNTIES
AUSSIES
AVENGES
AVENUES
AVIATES
AVULSES
AYEAYES
AZODYES
BABBLES
BADDIES
BAFFLES
BAGGIES
BAILEES
BANDIES
BANGLES
BANJOES
BASQUES
BATCHES
BATTLES
BATTUES
BAUBLES
BEACHES
BEADLES
BEAGLES
BEANIES
BEATLES
BECOMES
BEECHES
BEEGEES
BEETLES
BEHAVES
BEHOVES
BELCHES
BELLIES
BEMIRES
BEMUSES
BENCHES
BERATES
BERRIES
BESIDES
BETAKES
BETIDES
BETIMES
BETISES
BIALIES
BIDDIES
BIGEYES
BIGGIES
BIGLIES
BIGOSES
BIGTOES
BILBIES
BILBOES
BILLIES
BINGOES
BIRCHES
BIRDIES
BIREMES
BISQUES
BLESSES
BLITZES
BLONDES
BLOUSES
BLUSHES
BMOVIES
BOBBIES
BOBBLES
BODICES
BOGGLES
BOLIDES
BOLUSES
BONGOES
BONUSES
BOOBIES
BOODLES
BOOGIES
BOOKIES
BOONIES
BOOTEES
BOOTIES
BORATES
BOTCHES
BOTTLES
BOULLES
BOUNCES
BOURSES
BOVINES
BOWTIES
BRAISES
BRASSES
BRAVOES
BREEZES
BRIDGES
BRIDLES
BROGUES
BRONZES
BROWSES
BRUISES
BRUSHES
BUBBLES
BUCKLES
BUCKOES
BUDDIES
BUDGIES
BUGGIES
BULLIES
BUMBLES
BUNCHES
BUNDLES
BUNGEES
BUNGLES
BUNNIES
BURBLES
BURGEES
BURGLES
BUSBIES
BUSTLES
BUTTIES
BYGONES
BYLINES
CABBIES
CACKLES
CADDIES
CAIQUES
CAJOLES
CALICES
CALYCES
CALYXES
CAMISES
CANAPES
CANDIES
CANDLES
CANINES
CANTLES
CARAFES
CARGOES
CARIBES
CARNIES
CARRIES
CASQUES
CASTLES
CATCHES
CAUDLES
CAYUSES
CELEBES
CENTRES
CHAISES
CHANCES
CHANGES
CHARGES
CHARLES
CHASSES
CHEESES
CHEQUES
CHEVIES
CHEVRES
CHIGOES
CHILIES
CHOICES
CHOOSES
CHROMES
CINCHES
CIRCLES
CIRQUES
CIVVIES
CLAQUES
CLASHES
CLASSES
CLAUSES
CLEAVES
CLICHES
CLIQUES
CLOCHES
CLOQUES
CLOTHES
COACHES
COBBLES
COCKLES
CODDLES
CODICES
COERCES
COFFEES
COHERES
COLLIES
COLONES
CONCHES
CONURES
COOKIES
COOTIES
COSINES
COUCHES
COULEES
COUPLES
COURSES
COWRIES
COYOTES
CRADLES
CRASHES
CRAZIES
CREASES
CREATES
CRECHES
CREOLES
CRESSES
CRINGES
CRONIES
CROSSES
CRUISES
CRUSHES
CUBBIES
CUDDIES
CUDDLES
CULLIES
CURATES
CURDLES
CURRIES
DABBLES
DADDIES
DAILIES
DAIRIES
DAISIES
DALLIES
DAMAGES
DANDIES
DANDLES
DANGLES
DAPPLES
DARBIES
DAWDLES
DAZZLES
DEARIES
DEBASES
DEBATES
DEBONES
DECADES
DECIDES
DECKLES
DECODES
DECREES
DECRIES
DEDUCES
DEFACES
DEFAMES
DEFILES
DEFINES
DEFUSES
DEGREES
DEIFIES
DEITIES
DELETES
DELIBES
DELUDES
DELUGES
DEMISES
DEMOTES
DENOTES
DENUDES
DEPONES
DEPOSES
DEPUTES
DERBIES
DERIDES
DERIVES
DESIRES
DEVICES
DEVISES
DEVOTES
DEVRIES
DIARIES
DIBBLES
DICKIES
DIDDLES
DILATES
DILLIES
DILUTES
DIMPLES
DINGLES
DINGOES
DINKIES
DIPOLES
DIRTIES
DITCHES
DITTIES
DIVIDES
DIVINES
DIVVIES
DIZZIES
DOBBIES
DOGGIES
DOILIES
DOLLIES
DOLORES
DONATES
DONGLES
DOODLES
DOOZIES
DOSAGES
DOTTLES
DOUBLES
DOWRIES
DREDGES
DRESSES
DROWSES
DRUDGES
DUCHIES
DUMMIES
DWARVES
EBONIES
ECDYSES
ECTYPES
EDIBLES
EDIFIES
EFFACES
EFFUSES
ELAPSES
ELEGIES
ELYSEES
EMERGES
EMIGRES
EMPIRES
EMPTIES
ENABLES
ENCAGES
ENCASES
ENCODES
ENCORES
ENDIVES
ENDURES
ENDUSES
ENEMIES
ENGAGES
ENGINES
ENISLES
ENLACES
ENRAGES
ENROBES
ENSILES
ENSKIES
ENSURES
ENTICES
ENTREES
ENTRIES
ENZYMES
EPOPEES
EPOXIES
EQUATES
EQUINES
ERGATES
ERMINES
ESCAPES
ESSENES
ESTATES
ETOILES
EUCHRES
EVINCES
EVOLVES
EVULSES
EVZONES
EXCISES
EXCITES
EXCUSES
EXHALES
EXPIRES
EXPOSES
EXWIVES
FABARES
FACADES
FAERIES
FAIRIES
FAMINES
FANCIES
FELINES
FELLIES
FEMALES
FERRIES
FERULES
FESCUES
FETCHES
FETTLES
FIACRES
FIANCES
FICUSES
FIDDLES
FIENNES
FIFTIES
FIGURES
FILCHES
FILENES
FILLIES
FINALES
FINCHES
FIPPLES
FITCHES
FIXATES
FIZZLES
FLAMBES
FLANGES
FLASHES
FLECHES
FLEDGES
FLEECES
FLENSES
FLESHES
FLOSSES
FLUSHES
FOCSLES
FOCUSES
FOIBLES
FOLKIES
FOLLIES
FONDLES
FONDUES
FOODIES
FOOZLES
FORAGES
FORGOES
FORTIES
FRAISES
FRANCES
FRAPPES
FREEZES
FRIDGES
FRIEZES
FRINGES
FRIZZES
FUDDLES
FUMBLES
FUNGOES
FUNNIES
FURORES
FUTURES
GABBLES
GAGGLES
GAMBLES
GAMETES
GAMINES
GARAGES
GARBLES
GARGLES
GECKOES
GEMOTES
GENESES
GENOMES
GENTLES
GEORGES
GESSOES
GIBLUES
GIGGLES
GILLIES
GIPSIES
GIRDLES
GLANCES
GLASSES
GLITZES
GLORIES
GLOSSES
GNASHES
GOALIES
GOATEES
GOBBLES
GOGGLES
GOODIES
GOURDES
GRAMMES
GRANGES
GRASSES
GRAVIES
GREASES
GREAVES
GRIEVES
GRILLES
GROOVES
GROSSES
GROUSES
GRUDGES
GRUNGES
GUESSES
GUIMPES
GULCHES
GULLIES
GUNNIES
GUPPIES
GURGLES
GUSSIES
GUSTOES
GUZZLES
GYPSIES
GYRATES
GYRENES
HACKIES
HACKLES
HAGGLES
HALIDES
HALITES
HAMITES
HANDLES
HANKIES
HARPIES
HARRIES
HASSLES
HATCHES
HEAVIES
HECKLES
HEDDLES
HELICES
HELIXES
HIGGLES
HINNIES
HIPPIES
HITCHES
HOAGIES
HOBBIES
HOBBLES
HOGTIES
HOLLIES
HOMBRES
HOOPOES
HOPPLES
HUBBIES
HUDDLES
HUMBLES
HUMVEES
HUNCHES
HURDLES
HURLIES
HURRIES
HURTLES
HUSKIES
HUSSIES
HUSTLES
HUTCHES
HYRACES
HYRAXES
ICEAGES
ICEAXES
ICICLES
IDEATES
IGNITES
IGNORES
ILLUDES
ILLUMES
ILLUSES
IMAGOES
IMBIBES
IMBRUES
IMMIXES
IMMURES
IMPALES
IMPEDES
IMPLIES
IMPOSES
IMPUTES
INBOXES
INCASES
INCISES
INCITES
INCOMES
INCUDES
INDEXES
INDICES
INDITES
INDUCES
INFUSES
INHALES
INHERES
INJOKES
INJURES
INMATES
INSIDES
INSOLES
INSURES
INTAKES
INTONES
INVADES
INVITES
INVOKES
IODATES
IODIDES
IODISES
IODIZES
IONISES
IONIZES
IRONIES
IVORIES
JACKIES
JACQUES
JAGGIES
JANGLES
JAYCEES
JAYVEES
JEEBIES
JELLIES
JEMMIES
JENNIES
JETTIES
JIFFIES
JIGGLES
JIMMIES
JINGLES
JINGOES
JOGGLES
JOLLIES
JONESES
JOSTLES
JOUNCES
JUGGLES
JUJUBES
JUMBLES
JUNCOES
JUNGLES
JUNKIES
JUTTIES
KELPIES
KETCHES
KETONES
KETTLES
KEWPIES
KIBBLES
KIDDIES
KILTIES
KINDLES
KIRTLES
KISHKES
KITTIES
KLUDGES
KLUTZES
KNISHES
KYLIKES
LADDIES
LAERTES
LARCHES
LASSIES
LASSOES
LATCHES
LATEXES
LATICES
LEACHES
LEAGUES
LEASHES
LEECHES
LEFTIES
LEGATES
LEGUMES
LEPPIES
LESSEES
LETTRES
LEVITES
LEXEMES
LIAISES
LIENEES
LIERNES
LIGATES
LIMOGES
LINAGES
LINDIES
LINGOES
LIPIDES
LISTEES
LITOTES
LOACHES
LOATHES
LOBBIES
LOBULES
LOCALES
LOCATES
LOESSES
LOLLIES
LONGIES
LONGUES
LOOBIES
LOONIES
LORISES
LORRIES
LOTUSES
LOUNGES
LOURDES
LOUVRES
LUNCHES
LUPINES
LURCHES
LUSTRES
LUXATES
MAGPIES
MANAGES
MANEGES
MANGLES
MANGOES
MANTLES
MARBLES
MARCHES
MARINES
MARQUES
MARRIES
MARSHES
MASHIES
MASQUES
MATCHES
MATURES
MEALIES
MEANIES
MEASLES
MEDDLES
MEINIES
MEIOSES
MENACES
MENAGES
MENZIES
MERCIES
METATES
METTLES
MIDDIES
MIDDLES
MIGGLES
MINGLES
MINUSES
MINUTES
MIRAGES
MISCUES
MISDOES
MISSIES
MISUSES
MITOSES
MIZZLES
MOBILES
MODULES
MOGGIES
MOMMIES
MONKEES
MOOCHES
MORALES
MOSQUES
MOTIVES
MOTTLES
MOTTOES
MOUSSES
MRBONES
MUDDIES
MUDDLES
MUDPIES
MUFFLES
MULCHES
MUMBLES
MUMMIES
MUNCHES
MUSCLES
MUSKIES
MUTATES
MUZZLES
MYRTLES
NAIADES
NANNIES
NAPPIES
NATIVES
NATURES
NAVVIES
NEDDIES
NEEDLES
NEGATES
NEMESES
NESTLES
NETTLES
NEWSIES
NEXUSES
NIBBLES
NIGGLES
NINNIES
NOBBLES
NODULES
NOGALES
NONAGES
NOODLES
NOTATES
NOTCHES
NOTICES
NOVICES
NOZZLES
NUANCES
NUBBLES
NUTATES
NUZZLES
OBLATES
OBLIGES
OCTANES
OCTAVES
OEUVRES
OFFICES
OLEATES
ONSIDES
OOCYTES
OOLITES
OPAQUES
OPHITES
OPIATES
OPPOSES
ORACLES
ORANGES
ORDINES
ORESTES
ORGATES
ORIOLES
ORPINES
OSCINES
OSMOSES
OUTAGES
OUTDOES
OUTGOES
PADDIES
PADDLES
PAIUTES
PALACES
PALATES
PANSIES
PARADES
PARCHES
PAROLES
PARRIES
PARSEES
PARTIES
PARURES
PATCHES
PATSIES
PATTIES
PAVANES
PAWNEES
PDJAMES
PEACHES
PEBBLES
PEDDLES
PEEPLES
PEEWEES
PELAGES
PENATES
PENNIES
PENSEES
PEONIES
PEOPLES
PERCHES
PERUKES
PERUSES
PESTLES
PETITES
PHLOXES
PHOEBES
PHONIES
PHRASES
PICKLES
PIERCES
PIETIES
PIFFLES
PIGGIES
PINCHES
PINKIES
PINONES
PIRATES
PITCHES
PLAGUES
PLAICES
PLAQUES
PLASHES
PLEASES
PLEDGES
PLUNGES
PLUSHES
PLUSSES
POACHES
POBOXES
POLICES
POMADES
PONGEES
POOCHES
POODLES
POPPIES
POPPLES
PORCHES
PORGIES
POTAGES
POTPIES
POTTLES
POUCHES
POUNCES
PRAISES
PRANCES
PRESSES
PREXIES
PRINCES
PRIVIES
PROXIES
PSYCHES
PUDDLES
PUGREES
PULQUES
PUMICES
PUNCHES
PUNKIES
PUNTIES
PUPPIES
PURFLES
PURPLES
PURSUES
PUTTEES
PUTTIES
PUZZLES
PYGMIES
PYRITES
PYXIDES
QUASHES
QUERIES
QUICHES
QUINCES
QUIZZES
RABBLES
RACEMES
RADDLES
RADICES
RADIXES
RADOMES
RAFFLES
RALLIES
RAMBLES
RAMESES
RANCHES
RANKLES
RAPINES
RASSLES
RATITES
RATTLES
RAVAGES
RAVINES
REACHES
READIES
REBATES
REBUKES
REBUSES
RECANES
RECEDES
RECIPES
RECITES
RECODES
RECUSES
REDATES
REDEYES
REDUCES
REFACES
REFILES
REFINES
REFIRES
REFRIES
REFUGES
REFUSES
REFUTES
REGALES
REGIMES
REGLUES
REHIRES
REIFIES

RELACES
RELATES
RELAXES
RELINES
RELIVES
RELUMES
REMAKES
REMIGES
REMIXES
REMOTES
REMOVES
RENAMES
RENEGES
RENOTES
REPAVES
REPINES
REPLIES
REPOSES
REPUTES
RERATES
RESALES
RESCUES
RESHOES
RESIDES
RESILES
RESOLES
RESUMES
RETAKES
RETAPES
RETAXES
RETILES
RETIMES
RETIRES
RETRIES
RETUNES
RETYPES
REVERES
REVILES
REVISES
REVIVES
REVOKES
REWAXES
REWIRES
REZONES
RIBBIES
RIBEYES
RICKLES
RIDDLES
RIFFLES
RIMPLES
RIPPLES
ROACHES
ROADIES
ROCKIES
ROOKIES
ROOMIES
ROTATES
ROUBLES
ROWDIES
RUBBLES
RUFFLES
RUMBLES
RUMPLES
RUNDLES
RUSHEES
RUSTLES
SABINES
SACQUES
SADDLES
SALLIES
SALUTES
SALVOES
SAMITES
SAMPLES

SASSIES
SATIRES
SAVAGES
SCARVES
SCATHES
SCHEMES
SCHMOES
SCONCES
SCOUSES
SCRAPES
SCRIBES
SCURVES
SCYTHES
SEABEES
SEANCES
SECEDES
SECURES
SEDATES
SEDUCES
SEETHES
SEICHES
SEMITES
SENATES
SENORES
SERAPES
SESAMES
SETTEES
SETTLES
SHAKOES
SHEAVES
SHELVES
SHIITES
SHOPPES
SHRIKES
SHRINES
SHRIVES
SHUSHES
SICKLES
SIGNEES
SILLIES
SIMILES
SINGLES
SINUSES
SISSIES
SIXTIES
SIZZLES
SKOSHES
SLASHES
SLEDGES
SLEEVES
SLOSHES
SLUDGES
SLUICES
SLUSHES
SMASHES
SMOKIES
SMUDGES
SNEEZES
SNOOZES
SODDIES
SOFTIES
SOIREES
SOLACES
SOLUTES
SOOTHES
SORITES
SORTIES
SOURCES
SPARGES
SPECIES
SPHERES
SPITZES
SPLICES
SPLINES

SPONGES
SPOUSES
SPRITES
SPRUCES
SQUARES
SQUIRES
STABLES
STANCES
STAPLES
STARVES
STASHES
STATUES
STEPPES
STICHES
STIFLES
STOGIES
STOOGES
STORIES
STRAFES
STRIDES
STRIKES
STRIPES
STRIVES
STROBES
STROKES
STUDIES
STURGES
STYMIES
SUBDUES
SULKIES
SULLIES
SUNDAES
SUTURES
SWATHES
SWERVES
SWISHES
SYNCHES
TABBIES
TACKLES
TAFFIES
TAILLES
TALKIES
TALLIES
TALUSES
TAMALES
TANGLES
TANSIES
TARRIES
TATTLES
TEACHES
TECHIES
TEDDIES
TEEPEES
TEETHES
TELEXES
TELLIES
TEMPLES
TENACES
TENURES
TERRIES
TESTEES
THIEVES
THRIVES
THRONES
TICKLES
TIEDYES
TIMBRES
TINGLES
TINKLES
TIPPLES
TIPTOES
TIRADES
TISANES
TISSUES

TITTLES
TIZZIES
TOADIES
TODDIES
TODDLES
TOFFEES
TOGGLES
TOLLIES
TONGUES
TOONIES
TOOTLES
TOPAZES
TOPPLES
TORCHES
TORQUES
TOUCHES
TOUPEES
TOUSLES
TOWHEES
TOWNIES
TRANCES
TRASHES
TREBLES
TRESSES
TRIFLES
TRIODES
TRIPLES
TRIUNES
TROCHES
TROUPES
TRUDGES
TRUSSES
TSETSES
TUMBLES
TUMMIES
TUNNIES
TURTLES
TUSSLES
TWEEZES
TWELVES
TWINGES
ULYSSES
UMPIRES
UNBOXES
UNCAGES
UNCASES
UNIFIES
UNITIES
UNLACES
UNLADES
UNMAKES
UNPILES
UNROBES
UNTUNES
UNYOKES
UPDATES
UPRISES
UPTAKES
USURIES
VACATES
VALISES
VEERIES
VEGGIES
VESTEES
VETCHES
VIRTUES
VIRUSES
VISAGES
VITTLES
VOLUMES
VOUCHES
VOYAGES
WADDIES
WADDLES

WAFFLES
WAGGLES
WAHINES
WALTZES
WAMBLES
WANGLES
WARBLES
WATCHES
WATTLES
WEARIES
WEDGIES
WEENIES
WEEPIES
WELCHES
WENCHES
WHARVES
WHEEZES
WHISHES
WHIZZES
WIENIES
WIGGLES
WILLIES
WIMBLES
WIMPLES
WINCHES
WINKLES
WITCHES
WITHIES
WOBBLES
WOODIES
WOOKIES
WOOLIES
WORRIES
WRITHES
YANKEES
YORKIES
YUPPIES
ZILCHES
ZOMBIES
ZOUAVES
ZYGOTES

ET•••••

ETAGERE
ETAMINE
ETCHANT
ETCHERS
ETCHING
ETERNAL
ETESIAN
ETHANOL
ETHICAL
ETHNICS
ETIENNE
ETOILES
ETONIAN
ETRURIA

E•T••••

EATABLE
EATAWAY
EATCROW
EATENAT
EATENUP
EATSOUT
ECTYPES
ENTAILS
ENTEBBE
ENTENTE
ENTERED
ENTERON
ENTHRAL
ENTHUSE
ENTICED

ENTICER
ENTICES
ENTITLE
ENTRAIN
ENTRANT
ENTRAPS
ENTREAT
ENTREES
ENTRIES
ENTROPY
ENTRUST
ENTWINE
ESTATES
ESTEEMS
ESTELLE
ESTEVEZ
ESTHETE
ESTIVAL
ESTONIA
ESTORIL
ESTRADA
ESTRAYS
ESTUARY
EUTERPE
EXTENDS
EXTENTS
EXTERNS
EXTINCT
EXTORTS
EXTRACT
EXTREME
EXTRUDE

E••T•••

EARTHEN
EARTHLY
EASTEND
EASTERN
EASTERS
EASTMAN
EBBTIDE
ECSTASY
EDITING
EDITION
EDITORS
EDITOUT
EGOTISM
EGOTIST
EGOTRIP
ELATERS
ELATING
ELATION
ELITISM
ELITIST
ELMTREE
ELUTING
ELUTION
EMITTED
EMITTER
EMOTERS
EMOTING
EMOTION
EMOTIVE
EMPTIED
EMPTIER
EMPTIES
EMPTILY
EPITHET
EPITOME
EPSTEIN
ERITREA
EROTICA
ESOTERY
EXITING

EXOTICA
EXOTICS

E•••T••

EGESTED
EIGHTAM
EIGHTHS
EIGHTPM
EJECTED
ELASTIC
ELECTED
ELECTEE
ELECTOR
ELECTRA
ELECTRO
ELEKTRA
EMITTED
EMITTER
EMPATHY
ENACTED
ENACTOR
ENTITLE
EOLITHS
EPISTLE
EQUATED
EQUATES
EQUATOR
ERECTED
ERECTER
ERECTLY
ERECTOR
ERGATES
ERISTIC
ERRATIC
ERRATUM
ERUCTED
ERUPTED
ESTATES
EVERTED
EVICTED
EXACTAS
EXACTED
EXACTER
EXACTLY
EXACTOR
EXALTED
EXCITED
EXCITES
EXERTED
EXISTED
EXULTED

E••••T•

EAGLETS
EBONITE
EBWHITE
EDACITY
EDUCATE
EFFECTS
EFFORTS
EGALITE
EGOISTS
ELEVATE
ELICITS
ELLIOTT
ELMISTI
EMANATE
EMERITA
EMERITI
EMIRATE
EMULATE
ENLISTS
ENROOTS
ENROUTE

ENSUITE
ENTENTE
EREMITE
ERNESTO
ERUDITE
ESCORTS
ESPARTO
ESTHETE
EVERETT
EXCEPTS
EXCRETE
EXECUTE
EXEMPTS
EXFACTO
EXHORTS
EXPARTE
EXPECTS
EXPERTS
EXPIATE
EXPORTS
EXSERTS
EXTENTS
EXTORTS
EYELETS

E•••••T

EARHART
EARNEST
EARSHOT
EASEOUT
EASIEST
EATENAT
EATSOUT
ECKHART
EDGEOUT
EDGIEST
EDITOUT
EELIEST
EERIEST
EGGIEST
EGOTIST
EKEDOUT
EKESOUT
ELEGANT
ELEGIST
ELEMENT
ELITIST
ELKHART
ELLIOTT
EMANANT
EMINENT
ENCHANT
ENCRUST
ENCRYPT
ENDMOST
ENGRAFT
ENTRANT
ENTREAT
ENTRUST
EPAULET
EPEEIST
EPITHET
ERODENT
ESCHEAT
ETCHANT
EVENEST
EVENOUT
EVEREST
EVERETT
EVIDENT
EVILEST
EXCERPT
EXHAUST
EXHIBIT

EXIGENT
EXPLOIT
EXTINCT
EXTRACT
EYEBOLT
EYESHOT

•ET••••

AETHERS
BETAKEN
BETAKES
BETAMAX
BETARAY
BETHANY
BETHELS
BETHINK
BETIDED
BETIDES
BETIMES
BETISES
BETOKEN
BETRAYS
BETROTH
BETTERS
BETTING
BETTORS
BETWEEN
BETWIXT
CETERIS
DETAILS
DETAINS
DETECTS
DETENTE
DETESTS
DETOURS
DETRACT
DETRAIN
DETROIT
FETCHED
FETCHES
FETIDLY
FETLOCK
FETTERS
FETTLES
GETAWAY
GETBACK
GETDOWN
GETEVEN
GETINTO
GETITON
GETLOST
GETOVER
GETREAL
GETSOFF
GETSOUT
GETSSET
GETTING
GETWELL
HETMANS
JETBOAT
JETGUNS
JETPORT
JETSKIS
JETSONS
JETTIES
JETTING
JETWASH
JETWAYS
KETCHAM
KETCHES
KETCHUP
KETONES
KETTLES
LETDOWN

LETINON
LETITBE
LETITIA
LETSFLY
LETSLIP
LETSOFF
LETSOUT
LETSSEE
LETTERS
LETTING
LETTISH
LETTRES
LETTUCE
LETUPON
METATES
METEORS
METEOUT
METERED
METHANE
METHODS
METIERS
METOOER
METRICS
METTLES
NETIZEN
NETLIKE
NETSUKE
NETSURF
NETTING
NETTLED
NETTLES
NETWORK
PETALED
PETARDS
PETCOCK
PETERED
PETIOLE
PETITES
PETNAME
PETRELS
PETRIFY
PETROCK
PETROLS
PETROUS
PETTERS
PETTIER
PETTILY
PETTING
PETTISH
PETUNIA
RETAILS
RETAINS
RETAKEN
RETAKES
RETAPED
RETAPES
RETARDS
RETAXED
RETAXES
RETEACH
RETEARS
RETELLS
RETESTS
RETHINK
RETIARY
RETICLE
RETILED
RETILES
RETIMED
RETIMES
RETINAE
RETINAL
RETINAS
RETINUE

RETIRED
RETIREE
RETIRES
RETITLE
RETOOLS
RETORTS
RETOUCH
RETOURS
RETOWED
RETRACE
RETRACK
RETRACT
RETRADE
RETRAIN
RETREAD
RETREAT
RETRIAL
RETRIED
RETRIES
RETRIMS
RETSINA
RETUNED
RETUNES
RETURNS
RETYPED
RETYPES
SETBACK
SETDOWN
SETINTO
SETLINE
SETSAIL
SETSOFF
SETSOUT
SETTEES
SETTERS
SETTING
SETTLED
SETTLER
SETTLES
SETUPON
TETANUS
TETCHED
TETHERS
TETRADS
VETCHES
VETERAN
VETOERS
VETOING
VETTING
WETBARS
WETCELL
WETHERS
WETLAND
WETMOPS
WETNESS
WETSUIT
WETTEST
WETTING
WETTISH

•E•T•••

BEATERS
BEATIFY
BEATING
BEATLES
BEATNIK
BEATOUT
BEATRIX
BEATSIT
BEATSME
BEATSUP
BEATTIE
BEDTIME
BEETLES

BELTANE
BELTBAG
BELTING
BELTWAY
BENTHAM
BENTLEY
BENTSEN
BERTHED
BERTOLT
BESTBOY
BESTIAL
BESTING
BESTIRS
BESTMAN
BESTMEN
BESTOWS
BESTREW
BETTERS
BETTING
BETTORS
CELTICS
CENTAUR
CENTAVO
CENTERS
CENTIME
CENTIMO
CENTRAL
CENTRED
CENTRES
CENTRIC
CENTURY
CERTAIN
CERTIFY
DEBTORS
DEFTEST
DEITIES
DELTAIC
DELTOID
DENTATE
DENTINE
DENTING
DENTIST
DENTURE
DESTINE
DESTINY
DESTROY
DEUTERO
DEXTRIN
FEATHER
FEATURE
FELTFOR
FELTOUT
FERTILE
FESTERS
FESTIVA
FESTIVE
FESTOON
FETTERS
FETTLES
GENTEEL
GENTIAN
GENTILE
GENTLED
GENTLER
GENTLES
GESTALT
GESTATE
GESTURE
GETTING
HEATERS
HEATFUL
HEATHEN
HEATHER
HEATING

HEATSUP
HEATTER
HECTARE
HECTORS
HEFTIER
HEFTILY
HEFTING
HENTING
HEPTADS
JESTERS
JESTING
JETTIES
JETTING
KENTISH
KEPTOFF
KEPTOUT
KESTREL
KETTLES
LEATHER
LECTERN
LECTORS
LECTURE
LEETIDE
LEFTIES
LEFTIST
LEFTOFF
LEFTOUT
LENTIGO
LENTILS
LEOTARD
LEPTONS
LETTERS
LETTING
LETTISH
LETTRES
LETTUCE
MEATIER
MEATILY
MEETING
MELTING
MENTHOL
MENTION
MENTORS
MESTIZA
MESTIZO
METTLES
NEATENS
NEATEST
NECTARS
NEITHER
NEPTUNE
NESTEGG
NESTERS
NESTING
NESTLED
NESTLER
NESTLES
NETTING
NETTLED
NETTLES
NEUTRAL
NEUTRON
NEWTONS
NEWTOWN
PEATBOG
PEATIER
PECTINS
PEGTOPS
PELTATE
PELTERS
PELTING
PELTISH
PENTADS
PENTIUM

PEPTALK
PEPTIDE
PERTAIN
PERTEST
PERTURB
PESTERS
PESTLED
PESTLES
PETTERS
PETTIER
PETTILY
PETTING
PETTISH
RECTIFY
RECTORS
RECTORY
REDTAPE
REDTOPS
REITMAN
RENTALS
RENTERS
RENTING
REPTILE
RESTAGE
RESTAIN
RESTAMP
RESTART
RESTATE
RESTERS
RESTFUL
RESTING
RESTIVE
RESTOCK
RESTORE
RESTSUP
RESTYLE
REUTERS
REUTHER
SEATERS
SEATING
SEATTLE
SECTION
SECTORS
SEETHED
SEETHES
SEETOIT
SELTZER
SENTFOR
SENTOFF
SENTOUT
SEPTETS
SESTETS
SESTINA
SETTEES
SETTERS
SETTING
SETTLED
SETTLER
SETTLES
SEXTANS
SEXTANT
SEXTETS
SEXTONS
TEATIME
TEATRAY
TEATREE
TEETERS
TEETHED
TEETHER
TEETHES
TEETIME
TEKTITE
TENTERS
TENTHLY

TENTING
TERTIAL
TESTBAN
TESTEES
TESTERS
TESTFLY
TESTIER
TESTIFY
TESTILY
TESTING
TESTOUT
TESTUDO
TEUTONS
TEXTILE
TEXTUAL
TEXTURE
VECTORS
VENTERS
VENTING
VENTRAL
VENTURA
VENTURE
VERTIGO
VESTEES
VESTIGE
VESTING
VESTURE
VETTING
WEATHER
WEBTOED
WELTERS
WELTING
WENTAPE
WENTBAD
WENTFOR
WENTOFF
WENTOUT
WERTHER
WESTEND
WESTERN
WETTEST
WETTING
WETTISH
YEATEAM
YELTSIN
ZEITUNG
ZESTFUL
ZESTIER

•E••T••

AERATED
AERATES
AERATOR
BEASTIE
BEASTLY
BEATTIE
BEEFTEA
BELATED
BENATAR
BERATED
BERATES
BERETTA
BEWITCH
DEALTIN
DEARTHS
DEBATED
DEBATER
DEBATES
DEBITED
DEBUTED
DECATUR
DELETED
DELETES
DEMETER
DEMOTED
DEMOTES
DENOTED
DENOTES
DEPUTED
DEPUTES
DESKTOP
DESOTOS
DEVOTED
DEVOTEE
DEVOTES
FEASTED
FEINTED
GELATIN
GELATIS
GEMOTES
GENETIC
GERITOL
GETITON
HEALTHY
HEARTED
HEARTEN
HEARTHS
HEATTER
HEELTAP
HEISTED
HELOTRY
HEPATIC
HERBTEA
HERETIC
KERATIN
LEANTOS
LEGATEE
LEGATES
LEGATOS
LEISTER
LENGTHS
LENGTHY
LESOTHO
LETITBE
LETITIA
LEVITES
MEIOTIC
MEISTER
MENOTTI
MERITED
METATES
NECKTIE
NEGATED
NEGATER
NEGATES
NEGATOR
PELOTAS
PENATES
PESETAS
PETITES
REACTED
REACTOR
REACTTO
REALTOR
REBATED
REBATES
RECITAL
RECITED
RECITER
RECITES
REDATED
REDATES
REDSTAR
REENTER
REENTRY
REFUTED
REFUTER
REFUTES
REGATTA
RELATED
RELATES
REMOTER
REMOTES
RENOTED
RENOTES
REPUTED
REPUTES
RERATED
RERATES
RETITLE
SEASTAR
SEATTLE
SEDATED
SEDATER
SEDATES
SEMITES
SEMITIC
SENATES
SENATOR
TELSTAR
TEMPTED
TEMPTER
VEGETAL
VERITAS
WEALTHY
WEBSTER
ZEMSTVO
ZENITHS

•E•••T•

BECKETT
BEHESTS
BENEATH
BENNETT
BERETTA
BERLITZ
BETROTH
CELESTA
CELESTE
CEMENTS
DECANTS
DECEITS
DECOCTS
DEDUCTS
DEFACTO
DEFEATS
DEFECTS
DEFLATE
DEGUSTS
DEJECTS
DELICTI
DELICTS
DELISTS
DENSITY
DENTATE
DEPARTS
DEPICTS
DEPLETE
DEPORTS
DESALTS
DESERTS
DESISTS
DESPITE
DESPOTS
DETECTS
DETENTE
DETESTS
DEVIATE
FERRATE
FERRETS
FERRITE
GEARSTO
GEFILTE
GERENTS
GESTATE
GETINTO
HEAVETO
HEIFETZ
HEIGHTS
HELMETS
HENBITS
HEPCATS
HERMITS
HEWLETT
HEXNUTS
JENNETS
JESUITS
KEEPSTO
KENNETH
KEYNOTE
LEADSTO
LEDUPTO
LEGISTS
LEPANTO
LEVANTS
MEDIATE
MEMENTO
MENOTTI
MERLOTS
NEOLITH
NEONATE
NESMITH
NEWGATE
NEWMATH
PEANUTS
PEDANTS
PELLETS
PELTATE
PENALTY
PENNATE
PENULTS
PEQUOTS
PERLITE
PERMITS
REACTTO
REALITY
REBASTE
REBIRTH
REBOLTS
REBOOTS
RECANTS
RECASTS
RECOATS
REDACTS
REDANTS
REDHATS
REDHOTS
REEDITS
REFERTO
REGATTA
REGENTS
REGLETS
REGRETS
REHEATS
REJECTS
RELENTS
RELICTS
RELISTS
RELUCTS
REMELTS
REPASTE
REPASTS
REPEATS
REPENTS
REPLATE
REPLETE
REPORTS
REQUITE
RERENTS
REROUTE
RESALTS
RESEATS
RESECTS
RESENTS
RESISTS
RESORTS
RESPITE
RESTATE
RESULTS
RETESTS
RETORTS
REUNITE
REVERTS
REVOLTS
REWRITE
REWROTE
REXCATS
SEADUTY
SEAGATE
SECANTS
SECRETE
SECRETS
SELECTS
SENNETT
SENSATE
SEPTETS
SERIATE
SERRATE
SESTETS
SETINTO
SEVENTH
SEVENTY
SEXISTS
SEXTETS
TEAPOTS
TEASETS
TEKTITE
TENANTS
TENDSTO
TENUITY
TERCETS
TERMITE
TERNATE
TERRETS
VEDANTA
VEIGHTS
VELVETS
VELVETY
VERVETS
WEBSITE
WEIGHTS
WEIGHTY
WESKITS
ZEALOTS
ZERMATT

•E••••T

AERIEST
AEROBAT
BEARCAT
BEAROUT
BEATOUT
BEATSIT
BECKETT
BEDPOST
BEDREST
BELFAST
BELMONT
BENEFIT
BENNETT
BEQUEST
BERTOLT
BETWIXT
CELLIST
DEADSET
DEAFEST
DEALOUT
DEAREST
DECKOUT
DECRYPT
DEEPEST
DEEPFAT
DEEPSET
DEFAULT
DEFIANT
DEFICIT
DEFLECT
DEFROST
DEFTEST
DEFUNCT
DELIGHT
DELIMIT
DEMERIT
DENSEST
DENTIST
DEPOSIT
DESCANT
DESCENT
DESKSET
DESSERT
DETRACT
DETROIT
DEVIANT
EELIEST
EERIEST
FEEDLOT
FEELOUT
FELLOUT
FELTOUT
FERMENT
FERVENT
GERAINT
GESTALT
GETLOST
GETSOUT
GETSSET
HEADOUT
HEADSET
HEAROUT
HELDOUT
HELLCAT
HELPOUT
HEPPEST
HERBERT
HERRIOT
HEWLETT
JEERSAT
JETBOAT
JETPORT
KEENEST
KEEPSAT
KEPTOUT
KEYWEST
LEADOUT
LEAFLET
LEANEST
LEARJET
LEERSAT
LEFTIST
LEFTOUT
LENFANT
LENIENT
LETSOUT
LEVERET
LEWDEST
MEANEST
MEDIANT
MEEKEST
MEGAHIT
MESSKIT
METEOUT
NEAREST
NEATEST
NEGLECT
NEWHART
NEWLEFT
NEWPORT
PEACOAT
PEASANT
PECCANT
PECKSAT
PEEKOUT
PEEKSAT
PEEROUT
PEERSAT
PENDANT
PENDENT
PENNANT
PERCENT
PERFECT
PERIDOT
PERSIST
PERTEST
PEUGEOT
READMIT
READOUT
REAGENT
REALIST
REBUILT
RECEIPT
RECOUNT
RECRUIT
REDCENT
REDCOAT
REDDEST
REDEALT
REDHEAT
REDMEAT
REDOUBT
REDSPOT
REELECT
REENACT
REFLECT
REFRACT
REGNANT
RELIANT
RELIGHT
REMNANT
REMOUNT
RENAULT
REPAINT
REPLANT
REPRINT
REQUEST
RESHOOT
RESPECT
RESTART
RETRACT
RETREAT
REVISIT
SEAGIRT
SEALANT
SEAPORT
SEASALT
SEEKOUT
SEENFIT
SEENOUT
SEESFIT
SEESOUT
SEETOIT
SEGMENT
SELLOUT
SENDOUT
SENNETT
SENTOUT
SERPENT
SERVANT
SETSOUT
SEXIEST
SEXTANT
TEACART
TEAROUT
TEARSAT
TEMPEST
TENCENT
TENSEST
TENSPOT
TERSEST
TESTOUT
VERDANT
VERDICT
VERMONT
WEAKEST
WEAROUT
WEBFEET
WEBFOOT
WEEDOUT
WELLSET
WENTOUT
WETSUIT
WETTEST
YELLSAT
ZERMATT

••ET•••

ABETTED
ABETTOR
ACETATE
ACETONE
ARETINO
BEETLES
BRETONS
CHETRUM
CRETANS
CRETINS
DIETARY
DIETERS
DIETING
FRETFUL
FRETSAW
FRETTED
GHETTOS
GRETZKY
LEETIDE
MEETING
NOETICS
ONETIME
PIETIES
PIETINS
PIETISM
PIETIST
POETICS
PRETAPE
PRETEEN
PRETEND
PRETEST
PRETEXT
PRETZEL
QUETZAL
RHETORS
SEETHED
SEETHES
SEETOIT
SKETCHY
SMETANA
STETSON
STETTED
TEETERS
TEETHED
TEETHER
TEETHES
TEETIME
TIETACK
TOETAPS
TSETSES
VIETNAM
WHETHER
WHETTED

••E•T••

ABETTED
ABETTOR
ABEXTRA
ADEPTLY
ALERTED
ALERTER
ALERTLY
ASEPTIC
AVERTED
BEEFTEA
BIENTOT
BLEATED
BREATHE
BREATHS
BREATHY
CHEATED
CHEATER
CHEATIN
CHEETAH
CHEETOS
CHESTER
CHEWTOY
COEPTIS
CREATED
CREATES
CREATOR
CRESTED
EGESTED
EJECTED
ELECTED
ELECTEE
ELECTOR
ELECTRA
ELECTRO
ELEKTRA
ERECTED
ERECTER
ERECTLY
ERECTOR
EVERTED
EXERTED
FIESTAS
FLEETER
FLEETLY
FRETTED
GHETTOS
GREATER
GREATLY
GREETED
GREETER
GUESTED
HEELTAP
ICEDTEA
IDEATED
IDEATES
IDENTIC
INEPTLY
INERTIA
INERTLY
LAERTES
MAESTRI
MAESTRO
OLEATES
OLESTRA
OMENTUM
ONESTAR
ONESTEP
OPENTOE
ORESTES
OVERTAX
OVERTLY
PLEATED
PLECTRA
PRESTON
PRESTOS
QUENTIN
QUESTED
REENTER
REENTRY
SCENTED
SCEPTER
SCEPTIC
SCEPTRE
SHEATHE
SHEATHS
SHEETED
SHELTER
SHELTIE
SHELTON
SIESTAS
SKEETER
SKELTER
SKELTON
SKEPTIC
SLEETED
SLEPTIN
SLEPTON
SLEUTHS
SMELTED
SMELTER
SPECTER
SPECTOR
SPECTRA
SPECTRE
STENTOR
STETTED
SVELTER
SWEATED
SWEATER
SWEETEN
SWEETER
SWEETIE
SWEETLY
SWEETON
SWELTER
SWELTRY
SWEPTUP
THEATER
THEATRE
TREATED
TREETOP
TRENTON
TRESTLE
TWEETED
TWEETER
UNEATEN
WHEATON
WHETTED
WREATHE
WREATHS
WRESTED
WRESTLE

••E••T•

ACETATE
AGEISTS
AMENITY
BREADTH
BREASTS
BREVETS
BREVITY
COEDITS
CREDITS
DUEDATE
ELEVATE
EMERITA
EMERITI
EREMITE
EVERETT
EXECUTE
EXEMPTS
EYELETS
HAEMATO
ITERATE
KEEPSTO
OCELOTS
OMELETS
ONENOTE
OPERATE
OVERATE
PREDATE
PRELATE
PRESETS
REEDITS
STEALTH
SWEARTO
THEISTS
THEPITS
THERETO
TIEINTO
TWELFTH
UNEARTH
WHERETO

••E•••T

ABEYANT
ACEDOUT
ACESOUT
BIENTOT
BLERIOT
BLEWOUT
CHEMIST
CHEROOT
CHEVIOT
CHEWOUT
CLEMENT
COEXIST
CREWCUT
DEEPEST
DEEPFAT
DEEPSET
DIEDOUT
DIESOUT
DREWOUT
DUELIST
EKEDOUT
EKESOUT
ELEGANT
ELEGIST
ELEMENT
EPEEIST
EVENEST
EVENOUT
EVEREST
EVERETT
EYEBOLT
EYESHOT
FEEDLOT
FEELOUT
FLEAPIT
FREIGHT
FREMONT
FRESHET
GOESOUT
GREYEST
ICEBOAT
ICEDOUT
ICESOUT
INEXACT
ITERANT
JEERSAT
KEENEST
KEEPSAT
KNESSET
LEERSAT
MAEWEST
MEEKEST
ONESHOT
OPENPIT
OVERACT
OVEREAT
PEEKOUT
PEEKSAT
PEEROUT
PEERSAT
PIERROT
PIETIST
PRECAST
PRECEPT
PREDICT
PREEMPT
PREFECT
PREHEAT
PRESENT
PRESORT
PRETEST
PRETEXT
PREVENT
QUERIST
REELECT
REENACT
SEEKOUT
SEENFIT
SEENOUT
SEESFIT
SEESOUT
SEETOIT
SHERBET
SLEIGHT
SNEERAT
STEPOUT
STEWART
SWEARAT
THEREAT
TREERAT
TSELIOT
WEEDOUT
WHEREAT
XHEIGHT

•••ET••

AMMETER
ANNETTE
ARIETTA
ASCETIC
BABETTE
BARETTA
BERETTA
BIRETTA
BURETTE
CADETTE
CAVETTO
CHEETAH
CHEETOS
COLETTE
CORETTA
COVETED
DALETHS
DELETED
DELETES
DEMETER
DINETTE
FACETED
FLEETER
FLEETLY
GAMETES
GAZETTE
GENETIC
GORETEX
GREETED
GREETER
HERETIC
IMPETUS
INPETTO
KINETIC
LAYETTE
LORETTA
MIMETIC
MULETAS
MUSETTE
NAMETAG
NANETTE
ORNETTE
PALETTE
PESETAS
PHAETON
PINETAR
PINETUM
PIPETTE
PRAETOR
QUIETED
QUIETEN
QUIETER
QUIETLY
RIVETED
RIVETER
ROPETOW
ROSETTA
ROSETTE
SHEETED
SKEETER
SLEETED
STPETER
STRETCH
STRETTO
SUZETTE
SWEETEN
SWEETER
SWEETIE
SWEETLY
SWEETON
TAKETEN
TIBETAN
TREETOP
TWEETED
TWEETER
VEGETAL
WIRETAP
WYNETTE

•••E•T•

ABSENTS
ACCENTS
ACCEPTS
ADDEDTO
ADVENTS
ADVERTS
AFFECTS
AFREETS
AGREETO
AIMEDTO
ALBERTA
ALBERTO
ALDENTE
AMNESTY
ANNETTE
APLENTY
ARIETTA
ARPENTS
ARRESTS
ASCENTS
ASPECTS
ASSENTS
ASSERTS
ATTESTS
AUREATE
BABETTE
BARENTS
BARETTA
BEHESTS
BENEATH
BERETTA
BIRETTA
BISECTS
BURETTE
CADETTE
CATERTO
CAVEATS
CAVETTO
CELESTA
CELESTE
CEMENTS
CLIENTS
COLETTE
COMESTO
CORETTA
CRUELTY
DARESTO
DECEITS
DEFEATS
DEFECTS
DEJECTS
DESERTS
DETECTS
DETENTE
DETESTS
DIGESTS
DINETTE
DIRECTS
DIVERTS
DIVESTS
DOCENTS
DOZENTH
EFFECTS
ENTENTE
ERNESTO
EXCEPTS
EXPECTS
EXPERTS
EXSERTS
EXTENTS
FOMENTS
FORESTS
GAZETTE
GERENTS
GIVENTO

GIVESTO
HONESTY
INCEPTS
INDENTS
INDEPTH
INFECTS
INFESTS
INGESTS
INJECTS
INPETTO
INSECTS
INSERTS
INTENTS
INVENTS
INVERTS
INVESTS
IQTESTS
JADEITE
LAMENTS
LATENTS
LAYETTE
LIBERTY
LINEATE
LISENTE
LORETTA
MAGENTA
MAJESTE
MAJESTY
MALEATE
MEMENTO
MODELTS
MODESTO
MODESTY
MOLESTS
MOMENTS
MUSETTE
NANETTE
NOVELTY
OBJECTS
OBVERTS
ORGEATS
ORIENTE
ORIENTS
ORNETTE
OUTEATS
PALETTE
PAPEETE
PARENTS
PATENTS
PIMENTO
PIPETTE
POLENTA
POVERTY
PRIESTS
PUBERTY
REFERTO
REGENTS
REHEATS
REJECTS
RELENTS
REMELTS
REPEATS
REPENTS
RERENTS
RESEATS
RESECTS
RESENTS
RETESTS
REVERTS
ROBERTA
ROBERTO
ROBERTS
RODENTS
ROSEATE
ROSETTA
ROSETTE
SELECTS
SEVENTH
SEVENTY
SILENTS
STREETS
STRETTO
SUZETTE
TAKESTO
TALENTS
THREATS
TRIESTE
UMBERTO
UNSEATS
UPBEATS
URTEXTS
WYNETTE

•••E•T

ABREAST
AIMEDAT
AMHERST
ATHEART
ATHEIST
ATLEAST
ATTEMPT
BASEHIT
BENEFIT
BIBELOT
BONESET
BOREOUT
BYHEART
CAMELOT
CAMEOUT
CAPELET
COMEOUT
COMESAT
DEMERIT
DIDEROT
DOLEOUT
DOPEOUT
DOVECOT
EASEOUT
EATENAT
EDGEOUT
EPEEIST
EXCERPT
FADEOUT
FAREAST
FINEART
FIREANT
FIRELIT
FLIESAT
GAVEOUT
GIVEOUT
HAVENOT
HIDEOUT
HOLEOUT
INHERIT
LEVERET
LIFENET
LIVEOUT
LOSEOUT
LOSESIT
MADEOUT
MAKEOUT
MAKESIT
MATELOT
METEOUT
MIDEAST
MOVEOUT
NOSEOUT
PAGEANT
PAWEDAT
PINENUT
POKEDAT
POKESAT
POLECAT
PREEMPT
RAREBIT
RECEIPT
REDEALT
RICERAT
RIDEOUT
RODEOUT
RULEOUT
SIDEBET
SNEERAT
TAKEOUT
TIMEOUT
TIREOUT
TOREOUT
TREERAT
TUNEOUT
TYPESET
UNKEMPT
UTRECHT
VOTEOUT
WAVELET
WIPEOUT
WOREOUT

••••ET•

ACCRETE
AFREETS
AGREETO
AIGRETS
AMULETS
ANKLETS
ANXIETY
APPLETS
ARMLETS
ATHLETE
AUKLETS
AVOCETS
BALLETS
BARRETT
BASKETS
BASSETS
BECKETT
BENNETT
BILLETS
BONNETS
BOSKETS
BREVETS
BRUNETS
BUCKETS
BUDGETS
BUFFETS
BUFFETT
BULLETS
BURNETT
CABLETV
CACHETS
CAPLETS
CARNETS
CARPETS
CHALETS
CLARETS
CLORETS
CLOSETS
COLLETS
COMPETE
CORBETT
CORNETS
CORSETS
COSSETS
CURVETS
CUTLETS
CYGNETS
DEPLETE
DOCKETS
DORSETT
DUBIETY
EAGLETS
ESTHETE
EVERETT
EXCRETE
EYELETS
FANJETS
FAUCETS
FAWCETT
FERRETS
FIDGETS
FIDGETY
FILLETS
FLORETS
FLYNETS
FOLLETT
FORGETS
GADGETS
GADGETY
GANNETS
GANNETT
GARNETS
GARRETS
GARRETT
GASJETS
GASKETS
GIBBETS
GIBLETS
GIMLETS
GOBLETS
GORGETS
GOSSETT
GRIVETS
GULLETS
GUSSETS
GWYNETH
HACKETT
HAMLETS
HAMMETT
HEAVETO
HEIFETZ
HELMETS
HEWLETT
HOGGETS
HORNETS
IMARETS
IMPIETY
JACKETS
JAPHETH
JENNETS
JUNKETS
KENNETH
LABRETS
LANCETS
LAPPETS
LIMPETS
LINNETS
LIONETS
LOCKETS
MACBETH
MACHETE
MAGNETO
MAGNETS
MALLETS
MARKETS
MIDGETS
MILLETS
MILLETT
MINUETS
MOPPETS
MULLETS
MUPPETS
MUSKETS
NAIVETE
NAIVETY
NCWYETH
NIMIETY
NUGGETS
NUTLETS
OFFSETS
OMELETS
OUTLETS
OUTSETS
PACKETS
PALLETS
PAPEETE
PARGETS
PELLETS
PICKETS
PICKETT
PIGLETS
PIOLETS
PLANETS
POCKETS
POPPETS
POSSETS
PRESETS
PRIVETS
PUCKETT
PULLETS
PUNNETS
PUPPETS
RABBETS
RACKETS
RAMJETS
REGLETS
REGRETS
REPLETE
RICKETY
RILLETS
ROCHETS
ROCKETS
RUNLETS
RUSSETS
RUSSETY
SACHETS
SALLETS
SAMLETS
SATIETY
SECRETE
SECRETS
SENNETT
SEPTETS
SESTETS
SEXTETS
SIGNETS
SIPPETS
SOCIETY
SOCKETS
SONNETS
SORBETS
SOVIETS
SPINETS
STARETS
STREETS
STYLETS
SUBLETS
SUBSETS
SUNSETS
SWIVETS
TABLETS
TAFFETA
TAPPETS
TARGETS
TEASETS
TERCETS
TERRETS
THERETO
TICKETS
TICKETY
TIPPETS
TOILETS
TRIJETS
TRIVETS
TUFFETS
TURRETS
VARIETY
VARLETS
VELVETS
VELVETY
VERVETS
VIOLETS
WALLETS
WHERETO
WICKETS
WIDGETS
WIGLETS
WILLETS
WRITETO
WROTETO

••••E•T

ACHIEST
AERIEST
AILMENT
AIRIEST
ALIMENT
AMBIENT
AMPLEST
ANAPEST
ANCIENT
ARIDEST
ARMREST
ARTIEST
ASHIEST
AUGMENT
BADDEST
BALDEST
BARRETT
BECKETT
BEDREST
BENNETT
BEQUEST
BIGFEET
BIGGEST
BOLDEST
BONIEST
BOXIEST
BOXSEAT
BRAVEST
BUFFETT
BURNETT
BUSIEST
CAGIEST
CAKIEST
CALMEST
CALVERT
CANIEST
CARSEAT
CATBERT
CLEMENT
CLOSEST
COKIEST
COLBERT
COLDEST
COLLECT
COMMENT
CONCEIT
CONCEPT
CONCERT
CONGEST
CONNECT
CONSENT
CONTENT
CONTEST
CONTEXT
CONVENT
CONVERT
COOLEST
CORBETT
CORRECT
COSIEST
COZIEST
CRUDEST
CULVERT
CURRENT
CURTEST
DAFTEST
DAMPEST
DANKEST
DARKEST
DEAFEST
DEAREST
DEEPEST
DEFLECT
DEFTEST
DENSEST
DESCENT
DESSERT
DIALECT
DICIEST
DILBERT
DIMMEST
DISSECT
DISSENT
DOGBERT
DOPIEST
DORSETT
DOUREST
DOZIEST
DRIVEAT
DULLEST
DUMBEST
EARNEST
EASIEST
EDGIEST
EELIEST
EERIEST
EGGIEST
ELEMENT
EMINENT
ENTREAT
ERODENT
ESCHEAT
EVENEST
EVEREST
EVERETT
EVIDENT
EVILEST
EXIGENT
FAIREST
FALSEST
FANBELT
FARLEFT
FARWEST
FASTEST
FATTEST
FAWCETT
FERMENT
FERVENT
FIGMENT
FILBERT
FIRMEST
FITTEST
FOLLETT
FONDEST
FORFEIT
FORRENT
FORREST
FORWENT
FOULEST
FOXIEST
FULGENT
FULLEST
FUMIEST
FUNFEST
GABFEST
GAMIEST
GANNETT
GARMENT
GARRETT
GILBERT
GLUIEST
GOOIEST
GORIEST
GOSSETT
GRAVEST
GRAYEST
GREYEST
HACKETT
HAMMETT
HARDEST
HARVEST
HAZIEST
HEPPEST
HERBERT
HEWLETT
HIGHEST
HIPPEST
HOKIEST
HOLIEST
HOMIEST
HOTSEAT
HOTTEST
HOWBEIT
ICKIEST
IFFIEST
INANEST
INFLECT
INKIEST
INQUEST
INSPECT
IRATEST
JIVIEST
JOKIEST
KEENEST
KEYWEST
KINDEST
LACIEST
LAKIEST
LAMBENT
LAMBERT
LANKEST
LAPBELT
LARGEST
LAURENT
LAZIEST
LEANEST
LENIENT
LEWDEST
LIMIEST
LIMPEST
LINIEST
LITHEST
LOGIEST
LONGEST
LOOSEST
LOUDEST
LUNGEAT
LUSHEST
MADDEST
MAEWEST
MAZIEST
MEANEST
MEEKEST
MIDWEST
MILDEST
MILLETT
MIRIEST
MOPIEST
MORDENT
NASCENT
NEAREST
NEATEST
NEGLECT
NEWLEFT
NIGHEST
NOBLEST
NORBERT
NOSIEST
NOSWEAT
NUMBEST
NUTMEAT
ODDMENT
OFFBEAT
OILIEST
OLDWEST
ONTHEQT
OOZIEST
OPULENT
OVEREAT
PALIEST
PANDECT
PATIENT
PAYMENT
PENDENT
PERCENT
PERFECT
PERTEST
PEUGEOT
PICKETT
PIGMENT
PINIEST
PINKEST
PIPIEST
POKIEST
POOREST
PORTENT
POSHEST
PRECEPT
PREFECT
PREHEAT
PRESENT
PRETEST
PRETEXT
PREVENT
PROJECT
PROTECT
PROTEST
PRUDENT
PUCKETT
PUNGENT
PUNIEST
PUPTENT
RACIEST
RAIMENT
RANKEST
RASHEST
RATBERT
REAGENT
REDCENT
REDDEST
REDHEAT
REDMEAT
REELECT
REFLECT
REQUEST
RESPECT
RETREAT
RICHEST
RIMIEST
ROPIEST
ROSIEST
SADDEST
SALIENT
SAPIENT
SARGENT
SEGMENT
SENNETT
SERPENT
SEXIEST
SHUBERT
SICKEST
SLOWEST
SNIDEST
SNIPEAT
SOFTEST
SOLVENT
SOONEST
SOUREST
SPAREST
SPRIEST
SPRYEST
STALEST
STAREAT
STUDENT
SUAVEST
SUBJECT
SUBTEXT
SUBVERT
SUGGEST
SUNBELT
SURFEIT
SUSPECT
SWOREAT
TALLEST
TANGENT
TANNEST
TARTEST
TAUTEST
TEMPEST
TENCENT
TENSEST
TERSEST
THEREAT
TIDIEST
TINIEST
TONIEST
TORMENT
TORRENT
TRABERT
TRIDENT
TRISECT
TRITEST
TYPIEST
UGLIEST
UNBLEST
UNGUENT
UNSPENT
UNSWEPT
UPSWEPT
VAGUEST
VAINEST
VASTEST
VINCENT
VINIEST
VIOLENT
WANIEST
WANNEST
WARIEST
WARMEST
WAVIEST
WAXIEST
WEAKEST
WEBFEET
WETTEST
WHEREAT
WHITEST
WILDEST
WILIEST
WINIEST
WIRIEST
ZANIEST

•••••ET

BANQUET
BARONET
BAYONET
BIGFEET
BLANKET
BONESET
BOOKLET
BOUQUET
BRACKET
BRIDGET
BRIQUET
BRISKET
BULBLET
CABARET
CABINET
CALUMET
CAPELET
CAPULET
CHAPLET
CIRCLET
CORONET
COUPLET
CRICKET
CROCHET
CROQUET
CRUMPET
DATASET
DEADSET
DEEPSET
DESKSET
DOUBLET
DRAGNET
DRIBLET
DROPLET
EPAULET
EPITHET
FISHNET
FLATLET
FRESHET
FRIPPET
GANTLET
GETSSET
GILLNET
GOURMET
GRILLET
GROMMET
HAIRNET
HANDSET
HARDSET
HARRIET
HATCHET
HEADSET
JACONET
JOLLIET
KNESSET
LEAFLET
LEARJET
LEVERET
LIFENET
MAIGRET
MARGRET
MINARET
MINDSET
MOONSET
NAILSET
ONADIET
PARAPET
PARQUET
PLACKET
PLAYLET
PLUMMET
PROPHET
PROPJET
QUARTET
QUINTET
QUONSET
RACQUET
RATCHET
RINGLET
RIVULET
ROOTLET
SATINET
SCARLET
SHERBET
SIDEBET
SKILLET
SNIGLET
SNIPPET
STARLET
SWALLET
TABORET
THICKET
TRINKET
TRIPLET
TRIPPET
TRUMPET
TYPESET
WAVELET
WEBFEET
WELLSET
WHIPPET

EU•••••

EUCHRED
EUCHRES
EUGENIE
EUPHONY
EURASIA
EUTERPE

E•U••••

ECUADOR
EDUCATE
EDUCING
ELUDING
ELUSIVE
ELUSORY
ELUTING
ELUTION
ELUVIUM
EMULATE
ENURING
EQUABLE
EQUABLY
EQUALED
EQUALLY
EQUATED
EQUATES
EQUATOR
EQUERRY
EQUINES
EQUINOX
ERUCTED
ERUDITE
ERUPTED
EVULSED
EVULSES
EXUDING
EXULTED
EXUPERY
EXURBAN
EXURBIA

E••U•••

EDOUARD
EFFUSED
EFFUSES
ENDUING
ENDURED
ENDURES
ENDUROS
ENDUSER
ENDUSES
ENGULFS
ENOUNCE
ENQUIRE
ENQUIRY
ENSUING
ENSUITE
ENSURED
ENSURES
EPAULET
ESCUDOS
ESQUIRE
ESTUARY
ETRURIA
EXCUSED
EXCUSES
EXPUNGE

E•••U••

EARFULS
EARMUFF
EGGCUPS
EMANUEL
ENCRUST
ENDRUNS
ENGLUND
ENROUTE
ENSOULS
ENTHUSE
ENTRUST
EPICURE
ERASURE
ESPOUSE
EVACUEE
EXCLUDE
EXECUTE
EXHAUST
EXPOUND
EXTRUDE
EYECUPS
EYEFULS

E••••U•

EARDRUM
EARPLUG
EASEDUP
EASEFUL
EASEOUT
EASESUP
EATENUP
EATSOUT
ECHINUS
ECLOGUE
EDGEOUT
EDITOUT
EKEDOUT
EKESOUT
ELAAIUN
ELUVIUM
ELYSIUM
ENAMOUR
ENDEDUP
ENVIOUS
ERASMUS
ERRATUM
EVENOUT
EVENSUP

E•••••U

EMMYLOU

•EU••••

DEUTERO
FEUDING
LEUCINE
NEURONE
NEURONS
NEUTRAL
NEUTRON
OEUVRES
PEUGEOT
REUBENS
REUNIFY
REUNION
REUNITE
REUPPED
REUTERS
REUTHER
TEUTONS
ZEUGMAS

•E•U•••

BEAUISH
BEGUILE
BEGUINE
BELUSHI
BEMUSED
BEMUSES
BENUMBS
BEQUEST
CEBUANO
CERUMEN
DEBUNKS
DEBUSSY
DEBUTED
DEDUCED
DEDUCES
DEDUCTS
DEFUNCT
DEFUSED
DEFUSES
DEGUSTS
DELUDED
DELUDES
DELUGED
DELUGES
DELUISE
DEMURER
DENUDED
DENUDES
DEPUTED

DEPUTES
FELUCCA
FERULES
GENUINE
GERUNDS
JEJUNUM
JESUITS
LEDUPTO
LEGUMES
LETUPON
MEDULLA
MEDUSAE
MEDUSAS
MENUHIN
NEBULAE
NEBULAR
NEBULAS
NEXUSES
PENUCHE
PENULTS
PEQUOTS
PERUKES
PERUSAL
PERUSED
PERUSER
PERUSES
PETUNIA
REBUFFS
REBUILD
REBUILT
REBUKED
REBUKES
REBUSES
RECUSED
RECUSES
REDUCED
REDUCER
REDUCES
REFUELS
REFUGEE
REFUGES
REFUNDS
REFUSAL
REFUSED
REFUSER
REFUSES
REFUTED
REFUTER
REFUTES
REGULAR
REGULUS
RELUCTS
RELUMED
RELUMES
REMUDAS
REPUGNS
REPULSE
REPUTED
REPUTES
REQUEST
REQUIEM
REQUIRE
REQUITE
RESULTS
RESUMED
RESUMES
RESURGE
RETUNED
RETUNES
RETURNS
SECULAR
SECURED
SECURER
SECURES
SEDUCED
SEDUCER
SEDUCES
SENUFOS
SEQUELS
SEQUINS
SEQUOIA
SETUPON
TENUITY
TENUOUS
TENURED
TENURES
TEQUILA
ZEBULON

•E••U••

BECAUSE
BEDAUBS
BEDBUGS
BEDOUIN
BEEGUMS
BEFOULS
BEOWULF
BERMUDA
CENSURE
CENTURY
DEBAUCH
DEBOUCH
DEFAULT
DEGAUSS
DENEUVE
DENTURE
DETOURS
DEVOURS
FEATURE
FERRULE
FESCUES
GESTURE
HEPBURN
HERCULE
HEXNUTS
HEYJUDE
JETGUNS
KEROUAC
LEAGUES
LECTURE
LEGPULL
LEISURE
LETTUCE
MEASURE
MEDIUMS
MERCURY
NEPTUNE
NETSUKE
NETSURF
PEANUTS
PENGUIN
PEPLUMS
PERFUME
PERJURE
PERJURY
PERTURB
REBOUND
RECLUSE
RECOUNT
RECOUPS
RECRUIT
REDBUDS
REDGUMS
REDOUBT
REDOUND
REGLUED
REGLUES
REMOUNT
RENAULT
REROUTE
RESCUED
RESCUER
RESCUES
RESOUND
RETOUCH
RETOURS
REWOUND
SEADUTY
SEAGULL
SECLUDE
SENDUPS
SENSUAL
TEACUPS
TEDIUMS
TEMPURA
TERHUNE
TESTUDO
TEXTUAL
TEXTURE
VELLUMS
VELOURS
VENTURA
VENTURE
VERDUGO
VERDURE
VESTURE
WETSUIT
ZEITUNG

•E•••U•

BEADSUP
BEAMSUP
BEARCUB
BEARHUG
BEAROUT
BEARSUP
BEATOUT
BEATSUP
BECLOUD
BEEFSUP
BELAKUN
BELGIUM
BELLYUP
BENELUX
BEZIQUE
CELSIUS
CENTAUR
CEPHEUS
DEALOUT
DECATUR
DECKOUT
DECORUM
DEDALUS
DEFRAUD
DEVALUE
DEVIOUS
FEARFUL
FEELOUT
FELLOUT
FELTOUT
FERMIUM
FERROUS
FERVOUR
GEARSUP
GETSOUT
HEADOUT
HEADSUP
HEAROUT
HEATFUL
HEATSUP
HEEDFUL
HEINOUS
HELDOUT
HELPFUL
HELPOUT
JEALOUS
JEANLUC
JEJUNUM
KEEPSUP
KEPTOUT
KETCHUP
KEYCLUB
KEYEDUP
LEADOUT
LEADSUP
LEFTOUT
LEMIEUX
LESPAUL
LETSOUT
METEOUT
NEEDFUL
NERVOUS
OEDIPUS
PEASOUP
PEEKOUT
PEEROUT
PEGASUS
PENTIUM
PERKSUP
PERSEUS
PERSIUS
PETROUS
READOUT
REARGUE
REARSUP
REFOCUS
REGROUP
REGULUS
REISSUE
RENEGUE
REOCCUR
RESIDUE
RESTFUL
RESTSUP
RETINUE
REVALUE
REVENUE
SEABLUE
SEALSUP
SEASLUG
SEEKOUT
SEENOUT
SEESOUT
SELLOUT
SENDOUT
SENDSUP
SENTOUT
SERIOUS
SERVEUP
SETSOUT
SEVENUP
SEWEDUP
SEYMOUR
TEAMSUP
TEARFUL
TEAROUT
TEARSUP
TEDIOUS
TENFOUR
TENSEUP
TENUOUS
TERBIUM
TESTOUT
TETANUS
VERDOUX
WEAROUT
WEEDOUT
WELLRUN
WELLSUP
WENTOUT
ZEALOUS
ZEROSUM
ZESTFUL

•E••••U

NEARYOU

••EU•••

QUEUERS
QUEUEUP
QUEUING
SLEUTHS
STEUBEN
THEURGY

••E•U••

AVENUES
BEEGUMS
CAESURA
CHEQUER
CHEQUES
CHERUBS
COEQUAL
EXECUTE
EYECUPS
EYEFULS
ICECUBE
NIEBUHR
OVERUSE
PLENUMS
PRELUDE
PRENUPS
PREQUEL
PRESUME
ROEBUCK
SPELUNK
STEPUPS
UNEQUAL

••E••U•

ACEDOUT
ACESOUT
APERCUS
AREARUG
BEEFSUP
BLEWOUT
BREAKUP
CAESIUM
CHECKUP
CHEERUP
CHETRUM
CHEWOUT
CHEWSUP
CLEANUP
CLEARUP
CREEPUP
CREWCUT
DIEDOUT
DIESOUT
DREAMUP
DRESSUP
DREWOUT
DREYFUS
EKEDOUT
EKESOUT
EVENOUT
EVENSUP
FEELOUT
FRETFUL
GIELGUD
GLEEFUL
GOESOUT
HEEDFUL
ICEBLUE
ICEDOUT
ICESOUT
KEEPSUP
KNEESUP
NEEDFUL
OCEANUS
OCELLUS
OMENTUM
ONEROUS
OPENSUP
OVERBUY
OVERDUB
OVERDUE
OVERRUN
PEEKOUT
PEEROUT
PREMIUM
PRESSUP
QUECHUA
QUEUEUP
RHENIUM
SEEKOUT
SEENOUT
SEESOUT
SPEAKUP
SPEEDUP
STEPOUT
STEPSUP
STERNUM
SWEEPUP
SWELLUP
SWEPTUP
THEROUX
THESEUS
WEEDOUT

••E•••U

FRENEAU

•••EU••

AUTEURS
DENEUVE
DRSEUSS
GIVEUPS
LINEUPS
LYCEUMS
MAJEURE
MAKEUPS
MUSEUMS
PILEUPS
POSEURS
RAVEUPS
TUNEUPS

•••E•U•

ACTEDUP
ADDEDUP
ANGELUS
ANTEDUP
ANTESUP
AQUEOUS
ARTEMUS
BALEFUL
BANEFUL
BATEAUX
BENELUX
BLUEGUM
BONEDUP
BONESUP
BOREOUT
BOXEDUP
BOXESUP
BUREAUS
CAMEDUE
CAMEOUT
CAREFUL
CHEERUP
COMEDUE
COMEOUT
COMESUP
COVERUP
CREEPUP
CROESUS
DAREFUL
DIREFUL
DOLEFUL
DOLEOUT
DOPEOUT
DRIEDUP
DRIESUP
DUDEDUP
DUTEOUS
EASEDUP
EASEFUL
EASEOUT
EASESUP
EATENUP
EDGEOUT
ENDEDUP
FADEOUT
FAKEFUR
FATEFUL
FIREBUG
FIREDUP
FIRESUP
FIXEDUP
FIXESUP
FORERUN
GASEOUS
GATEAUX
GAVEOUT
GIVENUP
GIVEOUT
GIVESUP
GLEEFUL
HATEFUL
HIDEOUS
HIDEOUT
HIKEDUP
HIKESUP
HOLEDUP
HOLEOUT
HOLESUP
HOMERUN
HOPEFUL
HUMERUS
HYPEDUP
HYPESUP
IGNEOUS
IMPETUS
INGENUE
JUNEBUG
KEYEDUP
KNEESUP
LACEDUP
LACESUP
LIFEFUL
LINEDUP
LINESUP
LIVEOUT
LOSEOUT
LOVEBUG
MADEOUT
MAKEOUT
MAKESUP
METEOUT
MIXEDUP
MIXESUP
MOVEDUP
MOVEOUT
MOVESUP
MUSEFUL
NOSEEUM
NOSEOUT
OSSEOUS
OWNEDUP
PAGEFUL
PHOEBUS
PILEDUP
PILESUP
PINENUT
PINETUM
PIPEDUP
PIPEFUL
PIPESUP
PITEOUS
POKEFUN
RAGEFUL
RAKEDUP
RAKESUP
RENEGUE
REVENUE
RIDEOUT
RILESUP
RODEOUT
ROSEBUD
RULEOUT
SAVEDUP
SAVESUP
SCREWUP
SEVENUP
SEWEDUP
SIZEDUP
SIZESUP
SPEEDUP
SWEEPUP
TAKEOUT
TAKESUP
TIMEOUT
TIMESUP
TIREOUT
TONEDUP
TONESUP
TOREOUT
TUNEDUP
TUNEFUL
TUNEOUT
TUNESUP
TYPEDUP
TYPESUP
VOTEOUT
WAKEFUL
WAKESUP
WIPEDUP
WIPEOUT
WIPESUP
WISEDUP
WISEGUY
WISESUP
WOKENUP
WOREOUT

•••E••U

ANGELOU
ILIESCU

••••EU•

AMADEUS
AMATEUR
ANTAEUS
BORNEUP
BRACEUP
BROKEUP
CEPHEUS
CHOKEUP
CLOSEUP
DANSEUR
DRIVEUP
FLANEUR
FLAREUP
FRAMEUP
HAUTEUR
IGIVEUP
JUICEUP
LEMIEUX
LIQUEUR
LOUSEUP
MASSEUR
MILIEUS
MILIEUX
MIMIEUX
NOSEEUM
NUCLEUS
ORPHEUS
PASSEUL
PASTEUP
PASTEUR
PERSEUS
PIRAEUS
PROTEUS
QUEUEUP
RAISEUP
SCAREUP
SERVEUP
SHAKEUP
SHAPEUP
SPICEUP
SPOKEUP
STOREUP
TENSEUP
THESEUS
TRADEUP
WRITEUP
WROTEUP

••••E•U

CHAPEAU
CHATEAU
COCTEAU
FRENEAU
LAMBEAU
MARCEAU
NOUVEAU
PARVENU
PLATEAU
RAMBEAU
RONDEAU
TABLEAU
THOREAU
TONNEAU
TRUDEAU
WATTEAU

•••••EU

DOUBLEU
PURLIEU

EV•••••

EVACUEE
EVADERS
EVADING
EVANDER
EVANGEL
EVANISH
EVASION
EVASIVE
EVENEST
EVENING
EVENKIS
EVENOUT
EVENSUP
EVEREST
EVERETT
EVERTED
EVICTED
EVIDENT
EVILEST
EVILEYE
EVILLER
EVINCED
EVINCES
EVOKERS
EVOKING
EVOLVED
EVOLVES
EVULSED
EVULSES
EVZONES

E•V••••

ENVELOP
ENVIERS
ENVIOUS
ENVYING

E••V•••

ELEVATE
ELEVENS
ELUVIUM

E•••V••

ENDIVES
ENLIVEN
ESTEVEZ
ESTIVAL
EVOLVED
EVOLVES
EXWIVES

E••••V•

ELUSIVE
EMOTIVE
ENCLAVE
ENGRAVE
ENSLAVE
EROSIVE
EVASIVE

•EV••••

BEVELED
BEVERLY
DEVALUE
DEVEINS
DEVELOP
DEVIANT
DEVIATE
DEVICES
DEVILED
DEVILLE
DEVILRY
DEVIOUS
DEVISED
DEVISES
DEVOLVE
DEVOTED
DEVOTEE
DEVOTES
DEVOURS
DEVRIES
LEVANTS
LEVELED
LEVELER
LEVELLY
LEVERED
LEVERET
LEVIERS
LEVITES
LEVYING
NEVADAN
NEVILLE
REVALUE
REVAMPS
REVEALS
REVELED
REVELER
REVELRY
REVENGE
REVENUE
REVERBS
REVERED
REVERES
REVERIE
REVERSE
REVERTS
REVIEWS
REVILED
REVILES
REVISED
REVISER
REVISES
REVISIT
REVIVAL
REVIVED
REVIVES
REVOICE
REVOKED
REVOKES
REVOLTS
REVOLVE
REVVING
SEVENAM
SEVENPM
SEVENTH
SEVENTY
SEVENUP
SEVERAL
SEVERED
SEVERER
SEVIGNE
SEVILLE
YEVGENY

•E•V•••

BEAVERS
CERVIDS
DELVERS
DELVING
DERVISH
FERVENT
FERVORS
FERVOUR
HEAVEHO
HEAVENS
HEAVERS
HEAVETO
HEAVIER
HEAVIES
HEAVILY
HEAVING
LEAVEIN
LEAVENS
LEAVING
LEKVARS
NERVIER
NERVILY
NERVOUS
OEUVRES
PEAVEYS
PEEVING
PEEVISH
PERVADE
REAVAIL
REVVING
SELVAGE
SERVALS
SERVANT
SERVERS
SERVERY
SERVEUP
SERVICE
SERVILE
SERVING
VELVETS
VELVETY
VERVETS
WEAVERS
WEAVING
WEEVILS

•E••V••

BEDEVIL
BEHAVED
BEHAVES
BEHOVED
BEHOVES
BELOVED
DELIVER
DERIVED
DERIVES
GETEVEN
GETOVER
HESHVAN
LEHAVRE
MEDEVAC
RECOVER
RELIVED
RELIVES
REMOVAL
REMOVED
REMOVER
REMOVES
REPAVED
REPAVES
REVIVAL
REVIVED
REVIVES
REWOVEN
SEGOVIA
TELAVIV
YEREVAN

•E•••V•

BEEHIVE
BEHOOVE
BELIEVE
BEREAVE
CENTAVO
DECEIVE
DENEUVE
DEPRAVE
DEPRIVE
DESERVE
DEVOLVE
FESTIVA
FESTIVE
KEDROVA
NEWWAVE
PENSIVE
RECEIVE
RELIEVE
RELIEVO
REPROVE
RESERVE
RESOLVE
RESTIVE
REVOLVE
REWEAVE
TENSIVE
YESHIVA
ZEMSTVO

•E••••V

HENRYIV
NEMEROV
TELAVIV

••EV•••

BREVETS
BREVITY
CHEVIED
CHEVIES
CHEVIOT
CHEVRES
CHEVRON
COEVALS
CREVICE
ELEVATE
ELEVENS
GUEVARA
PEEVING
PEEVISH
PREVAIL
PREVENT
PREVIEW
STEVENS
TREVINO
WEEVILS

••E•V••

CHEEVER
CHERVIL
CLEAVED
CLEAVER
CLEAVES
CLEAVON
GREAVES
LIEOVER
SHEAVED
SHEAVES
SHELVED
SHELVES
SLEEVES
SWERVED
SWERVES
TWELVES

••E••V•

BEEHIVE
WHEREVE

••E•••V

CHEKHOV

•••EV••

BEDEVIL
BILEVEL
CHEEVER
ESTEVEZ
FOREVER
GETEVEN
GOTEVEN
GRIEVED
GRIEVER
GRIEVES
HOWEVER
KNIEVEL
MEDEVAC
NINEVEH
SLEEVES
THIEVED
THIEVES
WHOEVER
YEREVAN

•••E•V•

BEREAVE
DECEIVE
DENEUVE
DESERVE
MINERVA
OBSERVE
ONLEAVE
ONSERVE
RECEIVE
RESERVE
REWEAVE
UNNERVE
UNWEAVE

•••E••V

NEMEROV
NUREYEV

••••EV•

ACHIEVE
BELIEVE
RELIEVE
RELIEVO
WHEREVE

••••E•V

CABLETV

•••••EV

NUREYEV

E•W••••

EBWHITE
EDWARDS
ENWRAPS
EXWIVES
EXWORKS

E••W•••

EARWIGS
ENDWAYS
ENDWISE
ENTWINE
EREWHON
EYEWASH

E•••W••

EATAWAY
ELBOWED
EMPOWER
ENDOWED

E••••W•

ESCHEWS
ESCROWS

E•••••W
EATCROW
EYEBROW

•EW••••
BEWAILS
BEWITCH
DEWCLAW
DEWDROP
DEWLAPS
DEWLESS
DEWLINE
GEWGAWS
HEWLETT
JEWELED
JEWELER
JEWELRY
JEWISON
KEWPIES
LEWDEST
MEWLERS
MEWLING
NEWAGER
NEWBERY
NEWBORN
NEWDEAL
NEWGATE
NEWHART
NEWLEFT
NEWLOOK
NEWMATH
NEWMOON
NEWMOWN
NEWNESS
NEWPORT
NEWSBOY
NEWSDAY
NEWSIER
NEWSIES
NEWSMAN
NEWSMEN
NEWTONS
NEWTOWN
NEWWAVE
NEWYEAR
NEWYORK
REWARDS
REWARMS
REWAXED
REWAXES
REWEAVE
REWELDS
REWINDS
REWIRED
REWIRES
REWORDS
REWORKS
REWOUND
REWOVEN
REWRAPS
REWRITE
REWROTE
SEWEDON
SEWEDUP

•E•W•••
BEOWULF
BETWEEN
BETWIXT
GEEWHIZ
GETWELL
HEYWOOD
JETWASH
JETWAYS
KEYWEST
KEYWORD
LEEWARD
LEGWORK
MEOWING
NETWORK
NEWWAVE
PEDWAYS
PEEWEES
REDWINE
REDWING
REDWOLF
REDWOOD
SEAWALL
SEAWARD
SEAWAYS
SEAWEED
SEAWOLF

•E••W••
BEDEWED
BEESWAX
BELTWAY
GETAWAY
HEADWAY
PESAWAS
REMOWED
RENEWAL
RENEWED
RENEWER
RESAWED
RETOWED

•E•••W•
BEDDOWN
BELLOWS
BESTOWS
FELLOWS
GEEGAWS
GETDOWN
GEWGAWS
HEBREWS
HEEHAWS
LETDOWN
MEADOWS
MEADOWY
MELLOWS
NEPHEWS
NEWMOWN
NEWTOWN
PEAFOWL
REDRAWN
REDRAWS
REPLOWS
REVIEWS
SEACOWS
SEESAWS
SETDOWN
YELLOWS
YELLOWY

•E••••W
BEARPAW
BESTREW
DEWCLAW

••EW•••
ALEWIFE
BLEWOFF
BLEWOUT
BREWERS
BREWERY
BREWING
CHEWERS
CHEWIER
CHEWING
CHEWOUT
CHEWSUP
CHEWTOY
CREWCUT
CREWELS
CREWING
CREWMAN
CREWMEN
DREWOUT
EREWHON
EYEWASH
GEEWHIZ
JREWING
LEEWARD
MAEWEST
PEEWEES
PREWASH
SHEWOLF
SKEWERS
SKEWING
SPEWING
STEWARD
STEWART
STEWERS
STEWING
THEWIER
VIEWERS
VIEWIER
VIEWING

••E•W••
AREAWAY
BEESWAX
BOERWAR
FREEWAY
SHERWIN

••E••W•
DIEDOWN
GEEGAWS
HEEHAWS
HOEDOWN
LIEDOWN
OVERAWE
PREDAWN
SEESAWS
TIEDOWN

••E•••W
ATECROW
EYEBROW
FRETSAW
ICESHOW
JOEBLOW
LIESLOW
OVERSAW
PREVIEW
THECROW

•••EW••
BEDEWED
BIKEWAY
CSLEWIS
FREEWAY
GATEWAY
GAVEWAY
GIVEWAY
JANEWAY
MADEWAY
MAKEWAY
MATEWAN
RACEWAY
RENEWAL
RENEWED
RENEWER
SCREWED
SCREWUP
SOMEWAY
STREWED
STREWER
THREWIN
UNSEWED

•••E••W
BIGELOW
BLUELAW
CASELAW
DANELAW
FOREPAW
FORESAW
GAMELAW
LIKENEW
ROPETOW
SOMEHOW
TONEROW

••••EW•
ANDREWS
CASHEWS
CURFEWS
CURLEWS
ESCHEWS
HEBREWS
MATHEWS
MILDEWS
MILDEWY
NEPHEWS
OLDNEWS
REVIEWS
SUNDEWS

•••••EW
AIRCREW
BESTREW
INASTEW
LIKENEW
MATTHEW
OUTDREW
OUTGREW
PREVIEW
PURVIEW
UNSCREW

EX•••••
EXACTAS
EXACTED
EXACTER
EXACTLY
EXACTOR
EXALTED
EXAMINE
EXAMPLE
EXANIMO
EXARCHS
EXCEEDS
EXCEPTS
EXCERPT
EXCISED
EXCISES
EXCITED
EXCITES
EXCLAIM
EXCLUDE
EXCRETE
EXCUSED
EXCUSES
EXECUTE
EXEMPLI
EXEMPTS
EXERTED
EXFACTO
EXHALED
EXHALES
EXHAUST
EXHIBIT
EXHORTS
EXIGENT
EXILING
EXISTED
EXITING
EXOTICA
EXOTICS
EXPANDS
EXPANSE
EXPARTE
EXPECTS
EXPENDS
EXPENSE
EXPERTS
EXPIATE
EXPIRED
EXPIRES
EXPLAIN
EXPLODE
EXPLOIT
EXPLORE
EXPORTS
EXPOSED
EXPOSES
EXPOUND
EXPRESS
EXPUNGE
EXSERTS
EXTENDS
EXTENTS
EXTERNS
EXTINCT
EXTORTS
EXTRACT
EXTREME
EXTRUDE
EXUDING
EXULTED
EXUPERY
EXURBAN
EXURBIA
EXWIVES
EXWORKS

E••X•••
ELIXIRS
EPOXIES

E•••••X
EQUINOX

•EX••••
DEXTRIN
HEXAGON
HEXNUTS
HEXSIGN
LEXEMES
LEXICAL
LEXICON
MEXICAN
NEXUSES
REXCATS
SEXIEST
SEXISTS
SEXTANS
SEXTANT
SEXTETS
SEXTONS
TEXTILE
TEXTUAL
TEXTURE
VEXEDLY

•E••X••
HELIXES
RELAXED
RELAXES
REMIXED
REMIXES
RETAXED
RETAXES
REWAXED
REWAXES
TELEXED
TELEXES

•E•••X•
BETWIXT

•E••••X
BEATRIX
BEESWAX
BENELUX
BETAMAX
DEEPSIX
GEARBOX
HENDRIX
LEMIEUX
MEMOREX
PERPLEX
REAFFIX
VERDOUX

••EX•••
ABEXTRA
COEXIST
FLEXING
FLEXNER
FLEXORS
INEXACT
PLEXORS
PREXIES

••E•X••
ICEAXES

••E••X•
PRETEXT

••E•••X
BEESWAX
BRERFOX
DEEPSIX
KLEENEX
OVERTAX
SKEEZIX
THEROUX

•••EX••
ANNEXED
ANNEXES
INDEXED
INDEXES
LATEXES
TELEXED
TELEXES
URTEXTS

•••E•X•
POLEAXE

•••E••X
BATEAUX
BENELUX
BLUEFOX
CAKEMIX
CINEMAX
FIREBOX
GATEAUX
GORETEX
JUKEBOX
KLEENEX
PHOENIX
SHOEBOX
SKEEZIX

••••EX•
CONTEXT
PRETEXT
SUBTEXT

••••E•X
LEMIEUX
MILIEUX
MIMIEUX

•••••EX
COMPLEX
GORETEX
KLEENEX
MADAMEX
MEMOREX
NARTHEX
PERPLEX
ROLODEX
SIMPLEX
SPANDEX
TRIPLEX

EY•••••
EYEBALL
EYEBANK
EYEBOLT
EYEBROW
EYECUPS
EYEFULS
EYEHOLE
EYELASH
EYELESS
EYELETS
EYELIDS
EYELIKE
EYESHOT
EYESORE
EYEWASH

E•Y••••
ELYSEES
ELYSIAN
ELYSIUM

E••Y•••
EASYOFF
ECDYSES
ECDYSIS
ECTYPES
EDDYING
EMMYLOU
ENVYING
ENZYMES
ESPYING

E•••Y••
EARLYON
EMBAYED
EMBRYOS
ENCRYPT
ENJOYED
EPONYMS
EPONYMY
ESSAYED

E••••Y•
EMPLOYE
EMPLOYS
ENDWAYS
ESTRAYS
EVILEYE

E•••••Y
EAGERLY
EARTHLY
EATAWAY
ECOLOGY
ECONOMY
ECSTASY
EDACITY
ELDERLY
ELUSORY
EMBASSY
EMPATHY
EMPTILY
ENDPLAY
ENQUIRY
ENTROPY
EPARCHY
EPONYMY
EQUABLY
EQUALLY
EQUERRY
ERECTLY
EROSELY
ERRANCY
ESOTERY
ESTUARY
EUPHONY
EXACTLY
EXUPERY

•EY••••
FEYNMAN
GEYSERS
HEYDAYS
HEYJUDE
HEYWOOD
KEYCARD
KEYCLUB
KEYEDIN
KEYEDUP
KEYGRIP
KEYHOLE
KEYLESS
KEYLIME
KEYNOTE
KEYPADS
KEYRING
KEYWEST
KEYWORD
REYNARD
SEYMOUR

•E•Y•••
BELYING
DEFYING
DENYING
KENYANS
LEVYING
NEWYEAR
NEWYORK
RECYCLE
RELYING
RETYPED
RETYPES

•E••Y••
BELAYED
BELLYUP
DECAYED
DECOYED
DECRYPT
DELAYED
DELAYER
HENRYIV
MEGRYAN
NEARYOU
REDEYED
REDEYES
REKEYED
RELAYED
RESTYLE
ZEPHYRS

•E•••Y•
BETRAYS
DEADEYE
DEEJAYS
DEFRAYS
DEPLOYS
HEYDAYS
JERSEYS
JETWAYS
MEDLEYS
PEAVEYS
PEDWAYS
REPLAYS
SEAWAYS
TEAPOYS
VEEJAYS

•E••••Y
BEANERY
BEASTLY
BEATIFY
BELLAMY
BELLBOY
BELTWAY
BENTLEY
BESTBOY
BETARAY
BETHANY
BEVERLY
CENTURY
CERTIFY
DEANERY
DEBAKEY
DEBUSSY
DECENCY
DEEPFRY
DEERFLY
DELANEY
DEMPSEY
DENNEHY
DENSELY
DENSITY
DESTINY
DESTROY
DEVILRY
FETIDLY
GELIDLY
GEODESY
GEOLOGY
GERMANY
GETAWAY
HEADILY
HEADWAY
HEALTHY
HEARSAY
HEAVILY
HEFTILY
HELOTRY
HEMSLEY
HENNERY
HERSHEY
JEEPNEY
JEFFREY
JERKILY
JEWELRY
KEARNEY
KENNEDY
LEERILY
LEGALLY
LEGIBLY
LENGTHY
LETSFLY
LEVELLY
MEADOWY
MEATILY
MERCERY
MERCURY
MERRILY
MESSILY
NEEDILY
NERVILY
NEWBERY
NEWSBOY
NEWSDAY
PEABODY
PECCARY
PENALTY
PEPPERY
PEPPILY
PERFIDY
PERJURY
PERKILY
PESKILY
PETRIFY
PETTILY
READILY
REALITY
RECENCY
RECTIFY
RECTORY
REENTRY
REGALLY
REGENCY
REMARRY
RETIARY
REUNIFY
REVELRY
SEADUTY
SEALILY
SECRECY
SEEDILY
SENSORY
SERVERY
SEVENTY
TEARILY
TEATRAY
TENABLY
TENANCY
TENSELY
TENTHLY
TENUITY
TEPIDLY
TERNARY
TERRIFY
TERSELY
TESTFLY
TESTIFY
TESTILY
VELVETY
VENALLY
VERSIFY
VEXEDLY
WEALTHY
WEARILY
WEEDILY
WEEKDAY
WEIGHTY
WEIRDLY
YELLOWY
YEVGENY

••EY•••
ABEYANT
DREYFUS
FLEYING
GREYEST
GREYHEN
GREYING
GREYISH
OBEYING
PREYSON
WHEYISH

••E•Y••
AYEAYES
ONEEYED
TIEDYED
TIEDYES

••E••Y•
DEEJAYS
PREPAYS
VEEJAYS

••E•••Y
ADEPTLY
ALERTLY
AMENITY
AREAWAY
BLEAKLY
BREATHY
BREVITY
BREWERY
CHEAPLY
CHEWTOY
CLEANLY
CLEARLY
CLERISY
DEEPFRY
DEERFLY
DIETARY
ERECTLY
FIERILY
FLEETLY
FLESHLY
FRECKLY
FREEWAY
FRESHLY
GREATLY
GREELEY
GREGORY
GRETZKY
IDEALLY
INEPTLY
INERTLY
JEEPNEY
LEERILY
NEEDILY
OVERBUY
OVERFLY
OVERJOY
OVERLAY
OVERTLY
PLENARY
PREACHY
PRESLEY
QUEENLY
QUEERLY
REENTRY
SCENERY
SEEDILY
SHEERLY
SHELLEY
SKETCHY
SLEEKLY
SPECIFY
STEEPLY
STERNLY
SWEARBY
SWEENEY
SWEETLY
SWELTRY
THERAPY
THEREBY
THEURGY
TIERNEY
TREACLY
TREMBLY
TRENARY
TUESDAY
WEEDILY
WEEKDAY
WHEREBY

•••EY••
ALLEYES
BIGEYES
BOGEYED
BUGEYED
DRYEYED
HONEYED
MONEYED
MOSEYED
NUREYEV
ONEEYED
POPEYED
REDEYED
REDEYES
REKEYED
RIBEYES
VANEYCK

•••E••Y
ALLENBY
ALLERGY
ALREADY
AMNESTY
APLENTY
ARDENCY
BASEPAY
BEVERLY
BIKEWAY
BLUEBOY
BLUEJAY
BLUESKY
BONEDRY
BRIEFLY
CADENCY
CHIEFLY
COGENCY
COMESBY
CRUELLY
CRUELTY
DARESAY
DATEDLY
DAZEDLY
DECENCY
EAGERLY
ELDERLY
EQUERRY
FIREFLY
FIXEDLY
FLEETLY
FLUENCY
FREEWAY
GATEWAY
GAVEWAY
GIVEWAY
GREELEY
HAPENNY
HOMEBOY
HONESTY
JADEDLY
JANEWAY
JEWELRY
LATENCY
LEVELLY
LIBERTY
LOVERLY
LUCENCY
MADEHAY
MADEWAY
MAJESTY
MAKEHAY
MAKEWAY
MCHENRY
MISERLY
MODESTY
MORESBY
NAKEDLY
NAMEDAY
NOSEGAY
NOTEDLY
NOVELTY
ORDERLY
PAGEBOY
PALEDRY
POTENCY
POVERTY
PUBERTY
PUDENCY
QUEENLY
QUEERLY
QUIETLY
RACEWAY
RECENCY
REGENCY
REVELRY
ROSEBAY
SAMEDAY
SAVELOY
SEVENTY
SHEERLY
SLEEKLY
SOBERLY
SOMEDAY
SOMEWAY
SQUEAKY
STEEPLY
STREAKY
SWEENEY
SWEETLY
SYNERGY
THREADY
TIREDLY
UNREADY
URGENCY
UTTERLY
VALENCY
VEXEDLY
VICEROY
WISEGUY

••••EY•
BAILEYS
BARLEYS
BARNEYS
BUCKEYE
CATSEYE
CONVEYS
DEADEYE
DICKEYS
DONKEYS
EVILEYE
FISHEYE
FONTEYN
GALLEYS
GLADEYE
GURNEYS
HAWKEYE
HURLEYS
JACKEYS
JERSEYS
JITNEYS
JOCKEYS
KIDNEYS
LACKEYS
LOONEYS
MAGUEYS
MEDLEYS
MICKEYS
MONKEYS
OSPREYS
PARLEYS
PEAVEYS
PHONEYS
PULLEYS
PURVEYS
RICKEYS
ROMNEYS
SHUTEYE
SLAVEYS
SOCKEYE
STOREYS
SURREYS
SURVEYS
TURKEYS
VALLEYS
VOLLEYS
WALLEYE
WURLEYS

••••E•Y
ABIDEBY
ACADEMY
ACUTELY
AGILELY
ALCHEMY
ANXIETY
ARCHERY
BATTERY
BEANERY
BINDERY
BIOGENY
BRAVELY
BRAVERY
BREWERY
BRIBERY

BRUTELY
BUTTERY
BYTHEBY
CANNERY
CINDERY
CLOSEBY
CLOSELY
CONNERY
COOKERY
COPPERY
CRUDELY
CUTLERY
DEANERY
DENNEHY
DENSELY
DITHERY
DRAPERY
DUBIETY
EROSELY
ESOTERY
EXUPERY
FALSELY
FARMERY
FIDGETY
FISHERY
FLOWERY
FOOLERY
FOPPERY
FORGERY
GADGETY
GALLERY
GEODESY
GINGERY
GRAVELY
GROCERY
GUNNERY
HENNERY
HOSIERY
IMAGERY
IMPIETY
INANELY
IRATELY
JIGGERY
JITTERY
JOBBERY
JOINERY
KENNEDY
KNAVERY
LARCENY
LARGELY
LATHERY
LIQUEFY
LITHELY
LOOSELY
LOTTERY
MASTERY
MERCERY
MILDEWY
MOCKERY
MUMMERY
MYSTERY
NAIVELY
NAIVETY
NEWBERY
NIMIETY
NUNNERY
NURSERY
OROGENY
PEPPERY
PIGGERY
POTTERY
POWDERY
PROGENY
PRONELY
PRUDERY
PTOLEMY
PUFFERY
QUAVERY
QUIVERY
RAGGEDY
RICKETY
RIFLERY
ROBBERY
ROCKERY
ROGUERY
ROOKERY
RUBBERY
RUSSETY
SATIETY
SCENERY
SECRECY
SERVERY
SHAPELY
SHIVERY
SHOWERY
SILVERY
SLAVERY
SNIDELY
SOCIETY
SORCERY
SPARELY
SPICERY
SPIDERY
STALELY
STATELY
STOKELY
STUPEFY
SUAVELY
SUMMERY
SURGERY
SWOREBY
TANNERY
TENSELY
TERSELY
THEREBY
TICKETY
TOGGERY
TOTTERY
TRACERY
TRAGEDY
TRITELY
TURNERY
VAGUELY
VARIETY
VELVETY
WAGGERY
WHEREBY
WINTERY
YEVGENY

•••••EY
BALONEY
BARKLEY
BENTLEY
BLARNEY
BRADLEY
BRIMLEY
BUCKLEY
CHANTEY
CHARLEY
CHIMNEY
CHUTNEY
CLIQUEY
CLOONEY
COCKNEY
COMFREY
CURTSEY
DAHOMEY
DALTREY
DARNLEY
DEBAKEY
DELANEY
DEMPSEY
DIDDLEY
DISOBEY
FRAWLEY
GODFREY
GREELEY
GRIFFEY
HACKNEY
HEMSLEY
HERSHEY
HUNTLEY
JEEPNEY
JEFFREY
JOFFREY
JOURNEY
KEARNEY
LAMPREY
LANGLEY
LINDSEY
MAHONEY
MALMSEY
ODYSSEY
ORANGEY
ORPHREY
PAISLEY
PALFREY
PALJOEY
PARSLEY
PASSKEY
PRESLEY
QUIGLEY
SHANTEY
SHAPLEY
SHARKEY
SHELLEY
SHIRLEY
SOUTHEY
SPINNEY
STANLEY
STOOKEY
SURTSEY
SWEENEY
TIERNEY
TOURNEY
TROLLEY
TURNKEY
WHISKEY
WHITNEY
WINFREY
WOOLLEY
WOOLSEY
WRIGLEY

EZ•••••
EZEKIEL

E•Z••••
ENZYMES
EVZONES

E••Z•••
ENDZONE

E•••••Z
ESTEVEZ

•EZ••••
BEZIERS
BEZIQUE
CEZANNE
JEZEBEL
REZONED
REZONES

•E•Z•••
BENZENE
GEEZERS
MENZIES
SEIZERS
SEIZING
TENZING

•E••Z••
BEDIZEN
BENAZIR
DENIZEN
LEIPZIG
NETIZEN
REBOZOS
SELTZER

•E•••Z•
MENDOZA
MESTIZA
MESTIZO
REALIZE

•E••••Z
BERLIOZ
BERLITZ
GEEWHIZ
HEIFETZ
LEIBNIZ

••EZ•••
GEEZERS
MUEZZIN

••E•Z••
BREEZED
BREEZES
DWEEZIL
FREEZER
FREEZES
GRETZKY
MUEZZIN
PRETZEL
QUETZAL
SKEEZIX
SNEEZED
SNEEZER
SNEEZES
TWEEZED
TWEEZES
WHEEZED
WHEEZER
WHEEZES

••E••Z•
ITEMIZE

••E•••Z
GEEWHIZ
THEFONZ

•••EZ••
BREEZED
BREEZES
DWEEZIL
FREEZER
FREEZES
FRIEZES
SKEEZIX
SNEEZED
SNEEZER
SNEEZES
TWEEZED
TWEEZES
WHEEZED
WHEEZER
WHEEZES

•••E•Z•
CADENZA
FIRENZE
LORENZO
SCHERZI
SCHERZO
SQUEEZE

•••E••Z
ALBENIZ
ESTEVEZ
JIMENEZ

••••EZ•
SQUEEZE
TRAPEZE
ZAMBEZI

••••E•Z
HEIFETZ
KOBLENZ

•••••EZ
ALVAREZ
ESTEVEZ
JIMENEZ
LAISSEZ
MARQUEZ
NATCHEZ

FA•••••
FABARES
FABERGE
FABLERS
FABRICS
FACADES
FACEOFF
FACETED
FACIALS
FACINGS
FACTFUL
FACTION
FACTOID
FACTORS
FACTORY
FACTUAL
FACULAE
FACULTY
FADDISH
FADDISM
FADDIST
FADEDIN
FADEINS
FADEOUT
FADESIN
FADIMAN
FADLIKE
FAERIES
FAGENDS
FAGGING
FAGOTED
FAIENCE
FAILING
FAILURE
FAINTED
FAINTER
FAINTLY
FAIREST
FAIRIES
FAIRING
FAIRISH
FAIROFF
FAIRSUP
FAIRWAY
FAJITAS
FAKEFUR
FALAFEL
FALCONS
FALLACY
FALLFOR
FALLGUY
FALLING
FALLOFF
FALLOUT
FALLOWS
FALLSIN
FALLSON
FALLSTO
FALSELY
FALSEST
FALSIFY
FALSITY
FALTERS
FALWELL
FAMINES
FAMULUS
FANATIC
FANBELT
FANCIED
FANCIER
FANCIES
FANCIFY
FANCILY
FANCLUB
FANFARE
FANIONS
FANJETS
FANLIKE
FANMAIL
FANNING
FANOUTS
FANSOUT
FANTAIL
FANTASY
FANZINE
FARADAY
FARAWAY
FARCING
FAREAST
FARGONE
FARLEFT
FARMERS
FARMERY
FARMING
FARMOUT
FARRAGO
FARRIER
FARROWS
FARTHER
FARWEST
FASCIAS
FASHION
FASTENS
FASTEST
FASTING
FASTONE
FATBACK
FATCATS
FATCITY
FATEFUL
FATHEAD
FATHERS
FATHOMS
FATIGUE
FATLESS
FATLIKE
FATNESS
FATTENS
FATTEST
FATTIER
FATTILY
FATTISH
FATUITY
FATUOUS
FAUCETS
FAULTED
FAUSTUS
FAUVISM
FAUVIST
FAUXPAS
FAVORED
FAVOURS
FAWCETT
FAWNERS
FAWNING
FAYWRAY

F•A••••
FEARERS
FEARFUL
FEARING
FEASTED
FEATHER
FEATURE
FIACRES
FIANCEE
FIANCES
FIASCOS
FIATLUX
FLACCID
FLACONS
FLAGDAY
FLAGGED
FLAGMAN
FLAGMEN
FLAGONS
FLAILED
FLAKERS
FLAKIER
FLAKILY
FLAKING
FLAMBED
FLAMBES
FLAMIER
FLAMING
FLANEUR
FLANGES
FLANKED
FLANKER
FLANNEL
FLAPPED
FLAPPER
FLAREUP
FLARING
FLASHED
FLASHER
FLASHES
FLATBED
FLATCAR
FLATLET
FLATOUT
FLATTAX
FLATTED
FLATTEN
FLATTER
FLATTOP
FLAUNTS
FLAUNTY
FLAVORS
FLAVOUR
FLAWING
FLAXIER
FLAYING
FOALING
FOAMIER
FOAMILY
FOAMING
FRACTAL
FRAGILE
FRAILER
FRAILLY
FRAILTY
FRAISES
FRAMEUP
FRAMING
FRANCES
FRANCIS
FRANKED
FRANKEN
FRANKER
FRANKIE
FRANKLY
FRANKOZ
FRANTIC
FRAPPES
FRASIER
FRAUGHT
FRAWLEY
FRAYING
FRAZIER
FRAZZLE

F••A•••
FABARES
FACADES
FALAFEL
FANATIC
FARADAY
FARAWAY
FEMALES
FINAGLE
FINALES
FINALLY
FINANCE
FIXABLE
FIXATED
FIXATES
FLEABAG
FLEAPIT
FLOATED
FLOATER
FLYAWAY
FMRADIO
FORAGED
FORAGER
FORAGES
FREAKED
FRIABLE

F•••A••
FACIALS
FALLACY
FANFARE
FANMAIL
FANTAIL
FANTASY
FAREAST
FARRAGO
FATBACK
FATCATS
FELLAHS
FENIANS
FERRARI
FERRARO
FERRATE
FIJIANS
FINEART
FINIALS
FINLAND
FIREANT
FIREARM
FLYBALL
FLYCAST
FLYPAST
FLYWAYS
FOGBANK
FOLIAGE
FOLIATE
FOLKART
FONDANT
FOOTAGE
FORBADE
FOREARM
FORGAVE
FORMALS
FORMATS
FORSAKE
FORSALE
FORWARD
FOULARD
FOXTAIL
FRIDAYS
FRIGATE
FROMAGE
FROWARD
FRYPANS
FUNFAIR
FURBALL
FURNACE

F••••A•
FACTUAL
FACULAE
FADIMAN
FAIRWAY
FAJITAS
FARADAY
FARAWAY
FASCIAS
FATHEAD
FAUXPAS
FAYWRAY
FEDERAL
FEDORAS
FEEDBAG
FELDMAN
FEMORAL
FERNBAR
FEYNMAN
FIBULAE
FIBULAS
FIESTAS
FIGLEAF
FIREMAN
FLAGDAY
FLAGMAN
FLATCAR
FLATTAX
FLEABAG
FLIESAT
FLOTSAM
FLOWNAT
FLUVIAL
FLYAWAY
FLYLEAF
FLYTRAP
FOLKWAY
FOOTMAN
FOOTPAD
FOOTWAY
FORBEAR
FORDHAM
FOREMAN
FOREPAW
FORERAN
FORESAW
FORREAL
FORTRAN
FOURWAY
FRACTAL
FREEMAN
FREEWAY
FRENEAU
FRETSAW
FRIEDAN
FRISIAN
FROGMAN
FRONTAL
FROWNAT
FUNCHAL
FURSEAL
FUSTIAN

F•••••A
FELICIA
FELUCCA
FESTIVA
FLORIDA
FONTINA
FORMICA
FORMOSA
FORMULA
FORTUNA
FREESIA
FUCHSIA

•FA••••
OFASORT

•F•A•••
AFFABLE
AFFABLY
AFFAIRE
AFFAIRS
AFRAMES
EFFACED
EFFACES

•F••A••
AFFRAYS
AFGHANI
AFGHANS
OFFBASE
OFFHAND
OFFRAMP
SFUMATO

•F•••A•
AFRICAN
OFFBEAT
OFFLOAD
OFFPEAK
OFFROAD
OFFYEAR

••FA•••
AFFABLE
AFFABLY
AFFAIRE
AFFAIRS
ALFALFA
ASFARAS
ATFAULT
BEFALLS
DEFACED
DEFACES
DEFACTO
DEFALLA
DEFAMED
DEFAMES
DEFARGE
DEFAULT
EFFACED
EFFACES
EXFACTO
INFANCY
INFANTA
INFANTS
INFAVOR
LAFARGE
NOFAULT
REFACED
REFACES
SAFARIS
SOFABED
UNFAZED

••F•A••
AFFRAYS
BUFFALO
CAFTANS
DEFEATS
DEFIANT
DEFLATE
DEFRAUD
DEFRAYS
GUFFAWS
INFLAME
INFLATE
KAFTANS
OFFBASE
OFFHAND
OFFRAMP
REFLAGS
REFRACT
REFRAIN
REFRAME
TIFFANY

••F••A•
ASFARAS
BIFOCAL
HOFBRAU
HOFFMAN
OFFBEAT
OFFLOAD
OFFPEAK
OFFROAD
OFFYEAR
REFUSAL
RUFFIAN
RUFIYAA

••F•••A
ALFALFA
ALFORJA
DEFALLA
INFANTA
RUFIYAA
TAFFETA

•••FA••
AIRFARE
ANTFARM
BEEFALO
BELFAST
BIDFAIR
BUFFALO
BUSFARE
CARFARE
CONFABS
DOGFACE
FANFARE
FUNFAIR
GUFFAWS
LEAFAGE
LENFANT
LOOFAHS
MAYFAIR
OUTFACE
PARFAIT
PITFALL
PREFABS
PREFACE
PROFANE
SEAFANS
SHOFARS
SULFATE
SURFACE
TIFFANY
WARFARE
WELFARE

•••F•A•
EARFLAP
HALFDAN
HALFWAY
HOFFMAN
KAUFMAN
REDFLAG
RUFFIAN
SNIFFAT
TURFWAR
WOLFGAL
WOLFMAN
WOLFRAM

•••F••A
ARAFURA
BEEFTEA
TAFFETA

••••FA•
BODYFAT
DEEPFAT
HALIFAX
INSOFAR
LATIFAH
SNIFFAT
THUSFAR

••••F•A
RATAFIA

•••••FA
ALFALFA
MUSTAFA

F•B••••
FABARES
FABERGE
FABLERS
FABRICS
FEBRILE
FIBBERS
FIBBING
FIBRILS
FIBRINS
FIBROUS
FIBULAE
FIBULAS
FOBBING
FOBSOFF
FUBBING
FUBSIER

F••B•••
FANBELT
FATBACK
FEEBLER
FIBBERS
FIBBING
FILBERT
FLUBBED
FLUBBER
FLYBALL
FLYBOYS
FOBBING
FOGBANK
FOGBOWS
FOIBLES
FORBADE
FORBEAR
FORBIDS
FORBORE
FUBBING
FUMBLED
FUMBLER
FUMBLES
FURBALL
FURBISH

F•••B••
FEEDBAG
FERNBAR
FIREBOX
FIREBUG
FIXABLE
FLAMBED
FLAMBES
FLATBED
FLEABAG
FLUBBED
FLUBBER
FNUMBER
FREEBEE
FREEBIE
FRIABLE
FRISBEE

F•••••B
FANCLUB
FOODWEB

•F•B•••
OFFBASE
OFFBEAT

•F••B••
AFFABLE
AFFABLY

••FB•••
HOFBRAU
OFFBASE
OFFBEAT

••F•B••
AFFABLE
AFFABLY
SOFABED

•••F•B•
CONFABS
PREFABS

F•C••••
FACADES
FACEOFF
FACETED
FACIALS
FACINGS
FACTFUL
FACTION
FACTOID
FACTORS
FACTORY
FACTUAL
FACULAE
FACULTY
FICKLER
FICTION
FICTIVE
FICUSES
FOCSLES
FOCUSED
FOCUSES
FUCHSIA

F••C•••
FALCONS
FANCIED
FANCIER
FANCIES
FANCIFY
FANCILY
FANCLUB
FARCING
FASCIAS
FATCATS
FATCITY
FAUCETS
FAWCETT
FENCERS
FENCING
FESCUES
FETCHED
FETCHES
FIACRES
FILCHED
FILCHER
FILCHES
FINCHES
FISCHER
FITCHES
FLACCID
FLACONS
FLECHES
FLECKED
FLICKED
FLICKER
FLOCKED
FLOCKTO
FLYCAST
FORCEPS
FORCERS
FORCING
FRACTAL
FRECKLE
FRECKLY
FRICKIE

FROCKED
FRYCOOK
FULCRUM
FUNCHAL

F•••C••
FELICIA
FELUCCA
FIANCEE
FIANCES
FIASCOS
FIERCER
FINICKY
FLACCID
FLATCAR
FLEECED
FLEECES
FRANCES
FRANCIS
FRESCOS

F••••C•
FABRICS
FAIENCE
FALLACY
FATBACK
FELUCCA
FETLOCK
FINANCE
FLOUNCE
FLOUNCY
FLUENCY
FORMICA
FOSDICK
FROLICS
FURNACE
FUSTICS

F•••••C
FANATIC
FRANTIC
FREDRIC

•F••C••
AFFECTS
AFRICAN
EFFACED
EFFACES
EFFECTS
OFFICER
OFFICES

•F•••C•
AFFLICT
OFFENCE

••F•C••
AFFECTS
BIFOCAL
DEFACED
DEFACES
DEFACTO
DEFECTS
DEFICIT
EFFACED
EFFACES
EFFECTS
EXFACTO
INFECTS
INFOCUS
OFFICER
OFFICES
REFACED
REFACES
REFOCUS

••F••C•
AFFLICT
BYFORCE
DEFENCE
DEFLECT
DEFROCK
DEFUNCT
ENFORCE
INFANCY
INFLECT
INFLICT
INFORCE
MAFFICK
OFFENCE
REFLECT
REFRACT
SUFFICE
UNFROCK

•••F•C•
DOGFACE
EDIFICE
MAFFICK
ORIFICE
OUTFACE
PERFECT
PREFACE
PREFECT
SUFFICE
SURFACE

•••F••C
AELFRIC
TRAFFIC

••••F•C
MALEFIC
OSSIFIC
PACIFIC
TRAFFIC

F•D••••
FADDISH
FADDISM
FADDIST
FADEDIN
FADEINS
FADEOUT
FADESIN
FADIMAN
FADLIKE
FEDERAL
FEDORAS
FIDDLED
FIDDLER
FIDDLES
FIDELIO
FIDELIS
FIDGETS
FIDGETY
FODDERS
FUDDLED
FUDDLES
FUDGING

F••D•••
FADDISH
FADDISM
FADDIST
FEEDBAG
FEEDERS
FEEDING
FEEDLOT
FEEDSON
FELDMAN
FENDERS
FENDING
FEUDING
FIDDLED
FIDDLER
FIDDLES
FIEDLER
FINDERS
FINDING
FINDOUT
FLEDGED
FLEDGES
FODDERS
FOLDERS
FOLDING
FOLDOUT
FOLDSUP
FOLDUPS
FONDANT
FONDEST
FONDLED
FONDLES
FONDUES
FOODIES
FOODWEB
FORDHAM
FORDING
FOSDICK
FREDDIE
FREDRIC
FRIDAYS
FRIDGES
FUDDLED
FUDDLES
FUNDING

F•••D••
FACADES
FADEDIN
FARADAY
FETIDLY
FIEFDOM
FIELDED
FIELDER
FIREDOG
FIREDUP
FIXEDLY
FIXEDUP
FLAGDAY
FLOODED
FLUIDLY
FMRADIO
FOUNDED
FOUNDER
FOUNDRY
FREDDIE
FREEDOM
FRIEDAN

F••••D•
FAGENDS
FLORIDA
FLYRODS
FORBADE
FORBIDS
FRIENDS

F•••••D
FACETED
FACTOID
FAGOTED
FAINTED
FANCIED
FATHEAD
FAULTED
FAVORED
FEASTED
FEIGNED
FEINTED
FERRIED
FETCHED
FIDDLED
FIELDED
FIGURED
FILCHED
FINLAND
FIXATED
FIZZLED
FLACCID
FLAGGED
FLAILED
FLAMBED
FLANKED
FLAPPED
FLASHED
FLATBED
FLATTED
FLECKED
FLEDGED
FLEECED
FLENSED
FLESHED
FLICKED
FLIPPED
FLIRTED
FLITTED
FLOATED
FLOCKED
FLOGGED
FLOODED
FLOORED
FLOPPED
FLOSSED
FLOURED
FLOUTED
FLUBBED
FLUFFED
FLUNKED
FLUSHED
FOCUSED
FOISTED
FONDLED
FOOTPAD
FOOZLED
FORAGED
FORFEND
FORGOOD
FORWARD
FOULARD
FOUNDED
FRANKED
FREAKED
FRETTED
FRILLED
FRINGED
FRISKED
FRITTED
FRIZZED
FROCKED
FRONTED
FROSTED
FROTHED
FROWARD
FROWNED
FRUITED
FUDDLED
FUELLED
FUELROD
FUMBLED

•F•D•••
OFFDUTY

•F•••D•
AFFORDS
EFFENDI
OFFENDS
OFFSIDE

•F••••D
AFFIXED
EFFACED
EFFUSED
OFFERED
OFFHAND
OFFLOAD
OFFROAD

••FD•••
OFFDUTY

••F•D••
INFIDEL

••F••D•
AFFORDS
ALFREDO
DEFENDS
EFFENDI
ENFOLDS
OFFENDS
OFFSIDE
OXFORDS
REFUNDS
UNFOLDS

••F•••D
AFFIXED
BAFFLED
DEFACED
DEFAMED
DEFILED
DEFINED
DEFRAUD
DEFUSED
EFFACED
EFFUSED
GIFFORD
INFIELD
INFUSED
MUFFLED
OFFERED
OFFHAND
OFFLOAD
OFFROAD
PIFFLED
RAFFLED
REFACED
REFILED
REFINED
REFRIED
REFUSED
REFUTED
RIFFLED
RUFFLED
SOFABED
UNFAZED
UNFIXED
WAFFLED

•••FD••
FIEFDOM
HALFDAN
SERFDOM

•••F•D•
CONFIDE
PERFIDY
SULFIDE

•••F••D
ASHFORD
BAFFLED
BLUFFED
CATFOOD
CRAFTED
DEIFIED
DOGFOOD
DRAFTED
DRIFTED
EDIFIED
FLUFFED
FORFEND
GIFFORD
GRAFTED
LANFORD
LAWFORD
MANFRED
MITFORD
MUFFLED
MUMFORD
PIFFLED
PURFLED
QUAFFED
RAFFLED
REDFORD
REIFIED
RIFFLED
RUFFLED
SANFORD
SCOFFED
SCUFFED
SEAFOOD
SHAFTED
SHIFTED
SIXFOLD
SNAFUED
SNIFFED
SNUFFED
STAFFED
STIFFED
STIFLED
STUFFED
TENFOLD
TRIFLED
TWOFOLD
UNIFIED
WAFFLED
WHIFFED
WILFORD
WILFRID

••••F•D
BLUFFED
BRIEFED
CORNFED
DWARFED
FLUFFED
HANDFED
PROOFED
QUAFFED
SCARFED
SCOFFED
SCUFFED
SNIFFED
SNUFFED
SPOOFED
STAFFED
STIFFED
STRAFED
STUFFED
WELLFED
WHARFED
WHIFFED

FE•••••
FEARERS
FEARFUL
FEARING
FEASTED
FEATHER
FEATURE
FEBRILE
FEDERAL
FEDORAS
FEEBLER
FEEDBAG
FEEDERS
FEEDING
FEEDLOT
FEEDSON
FEELERS
FEELESS
FEELFOR
FEELING
FEELOUT
FEIFFER
FEIGNED
FEINTED
FELDMAN
FELICIA
FELINES
FELLAHS
FELLERS
FELLFOR
FELLIES
FELLING
FELLINI
FELLOFF
FELLOUT
FELLOWS
FELTFOR
FELTOUT
FELUCCA
FEMALES
FEMORAL
FENCERS
FENCING
FENDERS
FENDING
FENIANS
FENNIER
FERMENT
FERMIUM
FERNBAR
FERNIER
FERRARI
FERRARO
FERRATE
FERRETS
FERRIED
FERRIES
FERRITE
FERROUS
FERRULE
FERTILE
FERULES
FERVENT
FERVORS
FERVOUR
FESCUES
FESSING
FESTERS
FESTIVA
FESTIVE
FESTOON
FETCHED
FETCHES
FETIDLY
FETLOCK
FETTERS
FETTLES
FEUDING
FEYNMAN

F•E••••
FAERIES
FEEBLER
FEEDBAG
FEEDERS
FEEDING
FEEDLOT
FEEDSON
FEELERS
FEELESS
FEELFOR
FEELING
FEELOUT
FIEDLER
FIEFDOM
FIELDED
FIELDER
FIENNES
FIERCER
FIERIER
FIERILY
FIESTAS
FLEABAG
FLEAPIT
FLECHES
FLECKED
FLEDGED
FLEDGES
FLEECED
FLEECES
FLEEING
FLEETER
FLEETLY
FLEMING
FLEMISH
FLENSED
FLENSES
FLESHED
FLESHES
FLESHLY
FLEXING
FLEXNER
FLEXORS
FLEYING
FREAKED
FRECKLE
FRECKLY
FREDDIE
FREDRIC
FREEBEE
FREEBIE
FREEDOM
FREEING
FREEMAN
FREEMEN
FREESIA
FREEWAY
FREEZER
FREEZES
FREIGHT
FREMONT
FRENEAU
FRESCOS
FRESHEN
FRESHER
FRESHET
FRESHLY
FRETFUL
FRETSAW
FRETTED
FUELERS
FUELING
FUELLED
FUELOIL
FUELROD

F••E•••
FABERGE
FACEOFF
FACETED
FADEDIN
FADEINS
FADEOUT
FADESIN
FAGENDS
FAIENCE
FAKEFUR
FAREAST
FATEFUL
FEDERAL
FIDELIO
FIDELIS
FILENES
FINEART
FINESSE
FIREANT
FIREARM
FIREBOX
FIREBUG
FIREDOG
FIREDUP
FIREFLY
FIRELIT
FIREMAN
FIREMEN
FIRENZE
FIREOFF
FIRESUP
FIXEDLY
FIXEDUP
FIXESUP
FLEECED
FLEECES
FLEEING
FLEETER
FLEETLY
FLIESAT
FLIESIN
FLUENCY
FOMENTS
FOREARM
FOREIGN
FORELEG
FOREMAN
FOREMEN
FOREPAW
FORERAN
FORERUN
FORESAW
FORESEE
FORESTS
FOREVER
FREEBEE
FREEBIE
FREEDOM
FREEING
FREEMAN
FREEMEN
FREESIA
FREEWAY
FREEZER
FREEZES
FRIEDAN
FRIENDS
FRIEZES

F•••E••
FABLERS
FAIREST
FALSELY
FALSEST
FALTERS
FALWELL
FANBELT
FANJETS
FARLEFT
FARMERS
FARMERY
FARWEST
FASTENS
FASTEST
FATHEAD
FATHERS
FATLESS
FATNESS
FATTENS
FATTEST
FAUCETS
FAWCETT
FAWNERS
FEARERS
FEEDERS
FEELERS
FEELESS
FELLERS
FENCERS
FENDERS
FERMENT
FERRETS
FERVENT
FESTERS
FETTERS
FIBBERS
FIDGETS
FIDGETY
FIFTEEN
FIGLEAF
FIGMENT
FILBERT
FILLERS
FILLETS
FILTERS
FINDERS
FINGERS
FIRMEST
FISHERS
FISHERY
FISHEYE
FITNESS
FITTERS
FITTEST
FLAKERS
FLANEUR
FLAREUP
FLORETS
FLOWERS
FLOWERY
FLYLEAF
FLYLESS
FLYNETS
FODDERS
FOGGERS
FOGLESS
FOLDERS
FOLGERS
FOLLETT
FONDEST
FONTEYN
FOOLERY
FOOTERS
FOPPERY
FORBEAR
FORCEPS
FORCERS
FORFEIT
FORFEND
FORGERS
FORGERY
FORGETS
FORKERS
FORREAL
FORRENT
FORREST
FORWENT
FOSTERS
FOULEST
FOWLERS
FOXIEST
FRAMEUP
FRENEAU
FUELERS
FULGENT
FULLEST
FUMIEST
FUNFEST
FUNNELS
FURLESS
FURSEAL

F••••E•
FABARES
FACADES
FACETED
FAERIES
FAGOTED
FAINTED
FAINTER
FAIRIES
FALAFEL
FAMINES
FANCIED
FANCIER
FANCIES
FARRIER
FARTHER
FATTIER
FAULTED
FAVORED
FEASTED
FEATHER
FEEBLER
FEIFFER
FEIGNED
FEINTED
FELINES
FELLIES
FEMALES
FENNIER
FERNIER
FERRIED
FERRIES
FERULES
FESCUES
FETCHED
FETCHES
FETTLES
FIACRES
FIANCEE
FIANCES
FICKLER
FICUSES
FIDDLED
FIDDLER
FIDDLES
FIEDLER
FIELDED
FIELDER
FIENNES
FIERCER
FIERIER
FIFTEEN
FIFTIES
FIGHTER
FIGURED
FIGURER
FIGURES
FILCHED
FILCHER
FILCHES
FILENES
FILLIES
FILMIER
FINALES
FINCHES
FINNIER
FIPPLES
FIREMEN
FIRRIER
FISCHER
FISHIER
FISHNET
FITCHES
FIXATED
FIXATES
FIZZIER
FIZZLED
FIZZLES
FLAGGED
FLAGMEN
FLAILED
FLAKIER
FLAMBED
FLAMBES
FLAMIER
FLANGES
FLANKED
FLANKER
FLANNEL
FLAPPED
FLAPPER
FLASHED
FLASHER
FLASHES
FLATBED
FLATLET
FLATTED
FLATTEN
FLATTER
FLAXIER
FLECHES
FLECKED
FLEDGED
FLEDGES
FLEECED
FLEECES
FLEETER
FLENSED
FLENSES
FLESHED
FLESHES
FLEXNER
FLICKED
FLICKER
FLIPPED
FLIPPER
FLIRTED
FLITTED
FLITTER
FLIVVER
FLOATED
FLOATER
FLOCKED
FLOGGED
FLOODED
FLOORED
FLOPPED
FLOSSED
FLOSSES
FLOURED
FLOUTED
FLUBBED
FLUBBER
FLUFFED
FLUKIER
FLUNKED
FLUSHED
FLUSHES
FLUSTER
FLUTIER
FLUTTER
FLYOVER
FNUMBER
FOAMIER
FOCSLES
FOCUSED
FOCUSES
FOGGIER
FOIBLES
FOISTED
FOLKIER
FOLKIES
FOLLIES
FONDLED
FONDLES
FONDUES
FOODIES
FOODWEB
FOOTMEN
FOOZLED
FOOZLES
FORAGED
FORAGER
FORAGES
FORELEG
FOREMEN
FORESEE
FOREVER
FORFREE
FORGOES
FORKIER
FORSTER
FORTIES
FOUNDED
FOUNDER
FOURIER
FRAILER
FRAISES
FRANCES
FRANKED
FRANKEN
FRANKER
FRAPPES
FRASIER
FRAWLEY
FRAZIER
FREAKED
FREEBEE
FREEMEN
FREEZER
FREEZES
FRESHEN
FRESHER
FRESHET
FRETTED
FRIDGES
FRIEZES
FRILLED
FRINGED
FRINGES
FRIPPET
FRISBEE
FRISKED
FRITTED
FRITTER
FRIZZED
FRIZZES
FROCKED
FROGMEN
FRONTED
FROSTED
FROTHED
FROWNED
FROWNER
FRUITED
FUBSIER
FUDDLED
FUDDLES
FUELLED
FUMBLED
FUMBLER
FUMBLES
FUNGOES
FUNKIER
FUNNIER
FUNNIES
FURORES
FURRIER
FURTHER
FUSSIER
FUSTIER
FUTURES
FUZZIER

F•••••E
FABERGE
FACULAE
FADLIKE
FAIENCE
FAILURE
FANFARE
FANLIKE
FANZINE
FARGONE
FASTONE
FATIGUE
FATLIKE
FEATURE
FEBRILE
FERRATE
FERRITE
FERRULE

FERTILE FESTIVE FIANCEE FIBULAE FICTIVE FINAGLE FINANCE FINESSE FINLIKE FIRENZE FISHEYE FISSILE FISSURE FIXABLE FIXTURE FLOUNCE FOLIAGE FOLIATE FOOTAGE FOOTSIE FORBADE FORBORE FORESEE FORFREE FORGAVE FORGIVE FORGONE FORLIFE FORSAKE FORSALE FORSURE FORTUNE FOXFIRE FOXHOLE FOXLIKE FRAGILE FRANKIE FRAZZLE FRECKLE FREDDIE FREEBEE FREEBIE FRIABLE FRICKIE FRIGATE FRISBEE FRIZZLE FROMAGE FULSOME FURNACE FURTIVE

•FE••••

PFENNIG

•F•E•••

AFFECTS AFREETS EFFECTS EFFENDI OFFENCE OFFENDS OFFENSE OFFERED OFFERER OFTENER

•F••E••

AFREETS IFFIEST OFFBEAT OFFPEAK OFFSETS OFFYEAR

•F•••E•

AFFINES AFFIXED AFFIXES AFRAMES EFFACED EFFACES EFFUSED EFFUSES OFFERED OFFERER OFFICER OFFICES OFTENER

•F••••E

AFFABLE AFFAIRE IFSTONE OFFBASE OFFENCE OFFENSE OFFLINE OFFSIDE OFFSITE

••FE•••

AFFECTS DEFEATS DEFECTS DEFENCE DEFENDS DEFENSE EFFECTS EFFENDI INFECTS INFERNO INFESTS LIFEFUL LIFENET OFFENCE OFFENDS OFFENSE OFFERED OFFERER REFEREE REFERTO

••F•E••

ALFIERI ALFREDO BUFFERS BUFFETS BUFFETT COFFEES COFFERS DAFTEST DEFLECT DEFTEST DIFFERS DUFFELS DUFFERS FIFTEEN GAFFERS IFFIEST INFIELD INFLECT JEFFERS LIFTERS OFFBEAT OFFPEAK OFFSETS OFFYEAR PUFFERS PUFFERY RAFTERS REFLECT REFRESH REFUELS RIFLERS RIFLERY SIFTERS SOFTENS SOFTEST SUFFERS TAFFETA TOFFEES TUFFETS ZAFFERS

••F••E•

ADFINEM AFFINES AFFIXED AFFIXES BAFFLED BAFFLER BAFFLES COFFEES DAFFIER DEFACED DEFACES DEFAMED DEFAMES DEFILED DEFILER DEFILES DEFINED DEFINES DEFUSED DEFUSES EFFACED EFFACES EFFUSED EFFUSES FIFTEEN FIFTIES HEFTIER HUFFIER INFIDEL INFUSED INFUSES JEFFREY JIFFIES JOFFREY LEFTIES LIFENET LOFTIER MIFFIER MUFFLED MUFFLER MUFFLES NIFTIER OFFERED OFFERER OFFICER OFFICES PIFFLED PIFFLES PUFFIER RAFFLED RAFFLER RAFFLES REFACED REFACES REFEREE REFILED REFILES REFINED REFINER REFINES REFIRES REFRIED REFRIES REFUGEE REFUGES REFUSED REFUSER REFUSES REFUTED REFUTER REFUTES RIFFLED RIFFLES RUFFLED RUFFLES SOFABED SOFTIES TAFFIES TOFFEES TOFFLER TUFTIER UNFAZED UNFIXED WAFFLED WAFFLER WAFFLES

••F•••E

AFFABLE AFFAIRE BYFORCE DEFARGE DEFENCE DEFENSE DEFLATE DIFFUSE ELFLIKE ENFORCE GEFILTE INFLAME INFLATE INFORCE LAFARGE LAFITTE OFFBASE OFFENCE OFFENSE OFFLINE OFFSIDE OFFSITE REFEREE REFRAME REFUGEE SUFFICE SUFFUSE

•••FE••

BIGFEET BUFFERS BUFFETS BUFFETT COFFEES COFFERS CONFERS CONFESS CURFEWS DEAFENS DEAFEST DIFFERS DUFFELS DUFFERS FORFEIT FORFEND FUNFEST GABFEST GAFFERS GOLFERS HEIFERS HEIFETZ HOOFERS JEFFERS LOAFERS OAKFERN PERFECT PILFERS PREFECT PREFERS PROFESS PUFFERS PUFFERY REEFERS ROOFERS SOLFEGE SUFFERS SURFEIT SURFERS TAFFETA TITFERS TOFFEES TUFFETS TWOFERS WEBFEET WOOFERS ZAFFERS

•••F•E•

BAFFLED BAFFLER BAFFLES BEEFIER BEEFTEA BIGFEET BLUFFED BLUFFER BUGFREE COFFEES COMFIER COMFREY CRAFTED CRAFTER CROFTER DAFFIER DEIFIED DEIFIES DRAFTED DRAFTEE DRIFTED DRIFTER EDIFIED EDIFIES FEIFFER FLUFFED FORFREE GOAFTER GODFREY GOLFTEE GOOFIER GRAFTED GRIFFEY GRIFTER GRUFFER HUFFIER ICEFREE JEFFREY JIFFIES JOFFREY LEAFIER LEAFLET MANFRED MIFFIER MUFFLED MUFFLER MUFFLES PALFREY PIFFLED PIFFLES PROFFER PUFFIER PURFLED PURFLES QUAFFED QUAFFER RAFFLED RAFFLER RAFFLES REIFIED REIFIES RIFFLED RIFFLES RUFFLED RUFFLES SCOFFED SCOFFER SCUFFED SHAFFER SHAFTED SHIFTED SNAFUED SNIFFED SNIFFER SNIFTER SNUFFED SNUFFER STAFFED STAFFER STIFFED STIFFEN STIFFER STIFLED STIFLES STUFFED STUFFER SURFIER SWIFTER SYNFUEL TAFFIES TAXFREE TOFFEES TOFFLER TRIFLED TRIFLER TRIFLES TURFIER UNIFIED UNIFIER UNIFIES WAFFLED WAFFLER WAFFLES WEBFEET WHIFFED WINFREY WOLFMEN

•••F••E

ACTFIVE AIRFARE BONFIRE BUGFREE BUSFARE CARFARE CONFIDE CONFINE CONFUSE CONFUTE DIFFUSE DOGFACE DRAFTEE EDIFICE FANFARE FORFREE FOXFIRE GOLFTEE GUNFIRE ICEFLOE ICEFREE LEAFAGE MISFILE MISFIRE ORIFICE OUTFACE PERFUME PREFACE PROFANE PROFILE PROFUSE SCUFFLE SEAFIRE SHUFFLE SNAFFLE SNIFFLE SNUFFLE SOLFEGE SOUFFLE SUFFICE SUFFUSE SULFATE SULFIDE SULFITE SURFACE TAXFREE TRUFFLE WARFARE WELFARE

••••FE•

AQUIFER BLUFFED BLUFFER BRIEFED BRIEFER CARAFES CHAMFER CONIFER CORNFED DWARFED FALAFEL FEIFFER FLUFFED GRIFFEY GRUFFER HANDFED LUCIFER PROFFER PROOFED PROOFER QUAFFED QUAFFER ROTIFER SCARFED SCOFFED SCOFFER SCUFFED SHAFFER SNIFFED SNIFFER SNUFFED SNUFFER SPOOFED SPOOFER STAFFED STAFFER STIFFED STIFFEN STIFFER STRAFED STRAFES STUFFED STUFFER WELLFED WHARFED WHIFFED

••••F•E

AGRAFFE ALLOFME GIRAFFE OKEEFFE SCUFFLE SHUFFLE SNAFFLE SNIFFLE SNUFFLE SOUFFLE TRUFFLE

•••••FE

AGRAFFE ALEWIFE FORLIFE GIRAFFE LOWLIFE MIDLIFE MIDWIFE NESCAFE OKEEFFE SANTAFE

F•F••••

FIFTEEN FIFTHLY FIFTIES

F••F•••

FANFARE FEIFFER FIEFDOM FLUFFED FLYFISH FORFEIT FORFEND FORFREE FOXFIRE FULFILL FULFILS FUNFAIR FUNFEST

F•••F••

FACTFUL FAKEFUR FALAFEL FALLFOR FATEFUL FEARFUL FEELFOR FEIFFER FELLFOR FELTFOR FIREFLY FISHFRY FISTFUL FLUFFED FORKFUL FORMFUL FRETFUL

F••••F•

FACEOFF FAIROFF FALLOFF FALSIFY FANCIFY FARLEFT FELLOFF FIREOFF FOBSOFF FORLIFE FORTIFY

F•••••F

FACEOFF FAIROFF FALLOFF FELLOFF FIGLEAF FIREOFF FLYLEAF FOBSOFF

•FF••••

AFFABLE AFFABLY AFFAIRE AFFAIRS AFFECTS AFFINES AFFIRMS AFFIXED AFFIXES AFFLICT AFFORDS AFFRAYS AFFRONT EFFACED EFFACES EFFECTS EFFENDI EFFORTS EFFUSED EFFUSES IFFIEST OFFBASE OFFBEAT OFFDUTY OFFENCE OFFENDS OFFENSE OFFERED OFFERER OFFHAND OFFHOUR OFFICER OFFICES OFFLINE OFFLOAD OFFPEAK OFFRAMP OFFROAD OFFSETS OFFSIDE OFFSITE OFFYEAR

••FF•••

BAFFLED BAFFLER BAFFLES BOFFINS BUFFALO BUFFERS BUFFETS BUFFETT BUFFING BUFFOON COFFEES COFFERS CUFFING DAFFIER DAFFILY DAFFING DIFFERS DIFFUSE DOFFING DUFFELS DUFFERS GAFFERS GAFFING GIFFORD GUFFAWS HOFFMAN HUFFIER HUFFILY HUFFING HUFFISH JEFFERS JEFFREY JIFFIES JOFFREY KAFFIRS LUFFING MAFFICK MIFFIER MIFFING MUFFING MUFFINS MUFFLED MUFFLER MUFFLES PIFFLED PIFFLES PUFFERS PUFFERY PUFFIER PUFFILY PUFFING PUFFINS RAFFISH RAFFLED RAFFLER RAFFLES REFFING RIFFING RIFFLED RIFFLES RUFFIAN RUFFLED RUFFLES SAFFRON SOFFITS SUFFERS SUFFICE SUFFOLK SUFFUSE TAFFETA TAFFIES TIFFANY TIFFING TIFFINS TOFFEES TOFFLER TUFFETS WAFFLED WAFFLER WAFFLES ZAFFERS

••F•F••

LIFEFUL

••F••F•

ALFALFA LEFTOFF LIFTOFF

••F•••F

LEFTOFF LIFTOFF

•••FF••

BLUFFED BLUFFER BLUFFLY CHIFFON FEIFFER FLUFFED GRIFFEY GRIFFIN GRIFFON GRUFFER GRUFFLY PROFFER QUAFFED QUAFFER REAFFIX SCOFFED SCOFFER SCUFFED SCUFFLE SHAFFER SHUFFLE SNAFFLE SNIFFAT SNIFFED SNIFFER SNIFFLE SNIFFLY SNUFFED SNUFFER SNUFFLE SNUFFLY SOUFFLE STAFFED STAFFER STIFFED STIFFEN STIFFER STIFFLY STUFFED STUFFER TRAFFIC TRUFFLE WHIFFED

•••F•F•

GOOFOFF

•••F••F

GOOFOFF

••••FF•

AGRAFFE CUTOFFS GIRAFFE LAYOFFS OKEEFFE PAYOFFS POPOFFS REBUFFS RIPOFFS RUNOFFS SCRUFFS SCRUFFY TARIFFS TIPOFFS

•••••FF

BACKOFF BAILIFF BAKEOFF BEAROFF BEGSOFF BITEOFF BLEWOFF BLOWOFF BUGSOFF BUYSOFF BUZZOFF CALLOFF CAMEOFF CASTOFF COMEOFF CONNIFF COOKOFF CUTSOFF DASHOFF DIEDOFF DIESOFF DISTAFF DOZEOFF DROPOFF DUSTOFF EARMUFF EASEOFF EASYOFF FACEOFF FAIROFF FALLOFF FELLOFF FIREOFF FOBSOFF GAVEOFF GETSOFF GIVEOFF GOESOFF GOOFOFF HANDOFF HANGOFF HAULOFF HEADOFF HELDOFF HOLDOFF HOPSOFF JUMPOFF KARLOFF KEEPOFF KEPTOFF KICKOFF KISSOFF LAIDOFF LAYSOFF LEADOFF LEFTOFF LETSOFF LIFTOFF LOGSOFF MACDUFF MADEOFF MAKEOFF MARKOFF MASTIFF MIDRIFF NODSOFF PAIDOFF PAIROFF PALMOFF PASSOFF PAWNOFF PAYSOFF PEELOFF PICKOFF PLAYOFF PONTIFF POPSOFF PULLOFF PUSHOFF PUTSOFF RAKEOFF RANGOFF REELOFF RIDEOFF RINGOFF RIPSOFF RODEOFF RUBSOFF RUNGOFF RUNSOFF RUSHOFF SEALOFF SEENOFF SEESOFF SELLOFF SENDOFF SENTOFF SETSOFF SHERIFF SHOWOFF SHUTOFF SIGNOFF SOLDOFF SPINOFF SPUNOFF STOPOFF TAILOFF TAKEOFF TAPSOFF TEAROFF TEEDOFF TEESOFF TELLOFF TICKOFF TIMEOFF TIPSOFF TOLDOFF TOOKOFF TOPSOFF TOREOFF TORNOFF TOSSOFF TURNOFF WARDOFF WASHOFF WAVEOFF WEAROFF WELLOFF WENTOFF WOREOFF WORKOFF WORNOFF

F•G••••

FAGENDS FAGGING FAGOTED FIGHTER FIGLEAF FIGMENT FIGURED FIGURER FIGURES FOGBANK FOGBOWS FOGGERS FOGGIER FOGGILY FOGGING FOGHORN FOGLESS FOGYISH FOGYISM

F••G•••

FAGGING FARGONE FEIGNED FIDGETS FIDGETY FINGERS FIZGIGS FLAGDAY FLAGGED FLAGMAN FLAGMEN FLAGONS FLIGHTS FLIGHTY FLOGGED FOGGERS FOGGIER FOGGILY FOGGING FOLGERS FORGAVE FORGERS FORGERY FORGETS FORGING FORGIVE FORGOES FORGONE FORGOOD FRAGILE FRIGATE FRIGHTS FROGMAN FROGMEN FUDGING FULGENT FULGHUM FUNGOES

F•••G••

FALLGUY FATIGUE FINAGLE FLAGGED FLANGES FLEDGED FLEDGES FLOGGED FORAGED FORAGER

FORAGES
FRAUGHT
FREIGHT
FRIDGES
FRINGED
FRINGES

F••••G•
FABERGE
FACINGS
FARRAGO
FILINGS
FIRINGS
FIXINGS
FIZGIGS
FLYHIGH
FOLIAGE
FOOTAGE
FOREIGN
FROMAGE

F•••••G
FAGGING
FAILING
FAIRING
FALLING
FANNING
FARCING
FARMING
FASTING
FAWNING
FEARING
FEEDBAG
FEEDING
FEELING
FELLING
FENCING
FENDING
FESSING
FEUDING
FIBBING
FILLING
FILMING
FINDING
FINKING
FIREBUG
FIREDOG
FIRMING
FISHING
FITTING
FIZZING
FLAKING
FLAMING
FLARING
FLAWING
FLAYING
FLEABAG
FLEEING
FLEMING
FLEXING
FLEYING
FLOWING
FLUTING
FLUXING
FOALING
FOAMING
FOBBING
FOGGING
FOILING
FOINING
FOLDING
FOOLING
FOOTING
FORCING
FORDING
FORELEG
FORGING
FORKING
FORMING
FOULING
FOWLING
FRAMING
FRAYING
FREEING
FUBBING
FUDGING
FUELING
FUNDING
FUNKING
FUNNING
FURLING
FURLONG
FURRING
FUSSING
FUTZING
FUZZING

•FG••••
AFGHANI
AFGHANS

•F••••G
PFENNIG

••F•G••
REFUGEE
REFUGES

••F••G•
DEFARGE
LAFARGE
REFLAGS

••F•••G
BUFFING
CUFFING
DAFFING
DEFYING
DOFFING
GAFFING
HAFTING
HEFTING
HUFFING
LIFTING
LOFTING
LUFFING
MIFFING
MUFFING
PUFFING
RAFTING
REFFING
RIFFING
RIFLING
RIFTING
SIFTING
TIFFING
TUFTING
WAFTING

•••FG••
WOLFGAL

•••F•G•
ICEFOGS
LEAFAGE
OLDFOGY
SOLFEGE

•••F••G
BEEFING
BUFFING
CHAFING
COIFING
CUFFING
DAFFING
DOFFING
GAFFING
GOLFING
GOOFING
GULFING
HOOFING
HUFFING
KNIFING
LEAFING
LOAFING
LUFFING
MIFFING
MUFFING
PUFFING
REDFLAG
REEFING
REFFING
RIFFING
ROOFING
SURFING
TIFFING
WOLFING
WOOFING

••••F•G
ANTIFOG

F••H•••
FASHION
FATHEAD
FATHERS
FATHOMS
FIGHTER
FISHERS
FISHERY
FISHEYE
FISHFRY
FISHIER
FISHILY
FISHING
FISHNET
FISHOUT
FLYHIGH
FOGHORN
FOXHOLE
FUCHSIA

F•••H••
FARTHER
FEATHER
FETCHED
FETCHES
FIFTHLY
FILCHED
FILCHER
FILCHES
FINCHES
FISCHER
FITCHES
FLASHED
FLASHER
FLASHES
FLECHES
FLESHED
FLESHES
FLESHLY
FLIGHTS
FLIGHTY
FLUSHED
FLUSHES
FORDHAM
FRESHEN
FRESHER
FRESHET
FRESHLY
FRIGHTS
FROTHED
FULGHUM
FUNCHAL
FURTHER

F••••H•
FELLAHS
FOURTHS
FRAUGHT
FREIGHT

F•••••H
FADDISH
FAIRISH
FATTISH
FINNISH
FLEMISH
FLYFISH
FLYHIGH
FOGYISH
FOLKISH
FOOLISH
FOPPISH
FORSYTH
FURBISH
FURNISH

•F•H•••
AFGHANI
AFGHANS
OFFHAND
OFFHOUR

••FH•••
OFFHAND
OFFHOUR

••F•H••
FIFTHLY

••F•••H
HUFFISH
RAFFISH
REFRESH
SOFTISH

•••F•H•
LOOFAHS

•••F••H
CATFISH
CODFISH
DOGFISH
FLYFISH
HUFFISH
PANFISH
RAFFISH
SAWFISH
SELFISH
SUNFISH
WOLFISH

••••F•H
LATIFAH
TWELFTH

FI•••••
FIACRES
FIANCEE
FIANCES
FIASCOS
FIATLUX
FIBBERS
FIBBING
FIBRILS
FIBRINS
FIBROUS
FIBULAE
FIBULAS
FICKLER
FICTION
FICTIVE
FICUSES
FIDDLED
FIDDLER
FIDDLES
FIDELIO
FIDELIS
FIDGETS
FIDGETY
FIEDLER
FIEFDOM
FIELDED
FIELDER
FIENNES
FIERCER
FIERIER
FIERILY
FIESTAS
FIFTEEN
FIFTHLY
FIFTIES
FIGHTER
FIGLEAF
FIGMENT
FIGURED
FIGURER
FIGURES
FIJIANS
FILBERT
FILCHED
FILCHER
FILCHES
FILENES
FILINGS
FILLERS
FILLETS
FILLIES
FILLING
FILLINS
FILLIPS
FILLOUT
FILLSIN
FILLSUP
FILLUPS
FILMIER
FILMING
FILTERS
FINAGLE
FINALES
FINALLY
FINANCE
FINCHES
FINDERS
FINDING
FINDOUT
FINEART
FINESSE
FINGERS
FINIALS
FINICKY
FINKING
FINLAND
FINLIKE
FINNIER
FINNISH
FIPPLES
FIREANT
FIREARM
FIREBOX
FIREBUG
FIREDOG
FIREDUP
FIREFLY
FIRELIT
FIREMAN
FIREMEN
FIRENZE
FIREOFF
FIRESUP
FIRINGS
FIRKINS
FIRMEST
FIRMING
FIRMSUP
FIRRIER
FIRSTLY
FISCHER
FISHERS
FISHERY
FISHEYE
FISHFRY
FISHIER
FISHILY
FISHING
FISHNET
FISHOUT
FISSILE
FISSION
FISSURE
FISTFUL
FITCHES
FITNESS
FITTERS
FITTEST
FITTING
FIXABLE
FIXATED
FIXATES
FIXEDLY
FIXEDUP
FIXESUP
FIXINGS
FIXTURE
FIZGIGS
FIZZIER
FIZZING
FIZZLED
FIZZLES

F•I••••
FAIENCE
FAILING
FAILURE
FAINTED
FAINTER
FAINTLY
FAIREST
FAIRIES
FAIRING
FAIRISH
FAIROFF
FAIRSUP
FAIRWAY
FEIFFER
FEIGNED
FEINTED
FLICKED
FLICKER
FLIESAT
FLIESIN
FLIGHTS
FLIGHTY
FLIPOUT
FLIPPED
FLIPPER
FLIPUPS
FLIRTED
FLITTED
FLITTER
FLIVVER
FOIBLES
FOILING
FOINING
FOISTED
FRIABLE
FRICKIE
FRIDAYS
FRIDGES
FRIEDAN
FRIENDS
FRIEZES
FRIGATE
FRIGHTS
FRILLED
FRINGED
FRINGES
FRIPPET
FRISBEE
FRISIAN
FRISKED
FRISSON
FRITTED
FRITTER
FRIZZED
FRIZZES
FRIZZLE
FRIZZLY

F••I•••
FACIALS
FACINGS
FADIMAN
FAJITAS
FAMINES
FANIONS
FATIGUE
FELICIA
FELINES
FENIANS
FETIDLY
FIJIANS
FILINGS
FINIALS
FINICKY
FIRINGS
FIXINGS
FLAILED
FLUIDLY
FOLIAGE
FOLIATE
FORINTS
FOXIEST
FRAILER
FRAILLY
FRAILTY
FRAISES
FREIGHT
FRUITED
FUJITSU
FUMIEST
FURIOUS

F•••I••
FABRICS
FACTION
FADDISH
FADDISM
FADDIST
FADEINS
FADLIKE
FAERIES
FAGGING
FAILING
FAIRIES
FAIRING
FAIRISH
FALLING
FALSIFY
FALSITY
FANCIED
FANCIER
FANCIES
FANCIFY
FANCILY
FANLIKE
FANNING
FANZINE
FARCING
FARMING
FARRIER
FASCIAS
FASHION
FASTING
FATCITY
FATLIKE
FATTIER
FATTILY
FATTISH
FATUITY
FAUVISM
FAUVIST
FAWNING
FEARING
FEBRILE
FEEDING
FEELING
FELLIES
FELLING
FELLINI
FENCING
FENDING
FENNIER
FERMIUM
FERNIER
FERRIED
FERRIES
FERRITE
FERTILE
FESSING
FESTIVA
FESTIVE
FEUDING
FIBBING
FIBRILS
FIBRINS
FICTION
FICTIVE
FIERIER
FIERILY
FIFTIES
FILLIES
FILLING
FILLINS
FILLIPS
FILMIER
FILMING
FINDING
FINKING
FINLIKE
FINNIER
FINNISH
FIRKINS
FIRMING
FIRRIER
FISHIER
FISHILY
FISHING
FISSILE
FISSION
FITTING
FIZGIGS
FIZZIER
FIZZING
FLAKIER
FLAKILY
FLAKING
FLAMIER
FLAMING
FLARING
FLAWING
FLAXIER
FLAYING
FLEEING
FLEMING
FLEMISH
FLEXING
FLEYING
FLORIDA
FLORINS
FLORIST
FLOWING
FLUKIER
FLUTIER
FLUTING
FLUTIST
FLUVIAL
FLUXING
FLYFISH
FLYHIGH
FOALING
FOAMIER
FOAMILY
FOAMING
FOBBING
FOGGIER
FOGGILY
FOGGING
FOGYISH
FOGYISM
FOILING
FOINING
FOLDING
FOLKIER
FOLKIES
FOLKISH
FOLLIES
FONTINA
FOODIES
FOOLING
FOOLISH
FOOTING
FOPPISH
FORBIDS
FORCING
FORDING
FOREIGN
FORGING
FORGIVE
FORKIER
FORKING
FORLIFE
FORMICA
FORMING
FORTIES
FORTIFY
FORTIUS
FOSDICK
FOSSILS
FOULING
FOURIER
FOWLING
FOXFIRE
FOXLIKE
FRAGILE
FRAMING
FRASIER
FRAYING
FRAZIER
FREEING
FRISIAN
FROLICS
FUBBING
FUBSIER
FUDGING
FUELING
FULFILL
FULFILS
FUNDING
FUNKIER
FUNKILY
FUNKING
FUNNIER
FUNNIES
FUNNILY
FUNNING
FURBISH
FURLING
FURNISH
FURRIER
FURRING
FURTIVE
FUSSIER
FUSSILY
FUSSING
FUSTIAN
FUSTICS
FUSTIER
FUSTILY
FUTZING
FUZZIER
FUZZILY
FUZZING

F••••I•
FACTOID
FADEDIN
FADESIN
FALLSIN
FANATIC
FANMAIL
FANTAIL
FELICIA
FIDELIO
FIDELIS
FILLSIN
FIRELIT
FLACCID
FLEAPIT
FLIESIN
FLORUIT
FLOWNIN
FMRADIO
FOOTSIE
FORFEIT
FOULTIP
FOXTAIL
FRANCIS
FRANKIE
FRANTIC
FREDDIE
FREDRIC
FREEBIE
FREESIA
FRICKIE
FUCHSIA
FUELOIL
FUNFAIR

F•••••I
FELLINI
FERRARI

•F•I•••
AFFINES
AFFIRMS
AFFIXED
AFFIXES
AFRICAN
IFFIEST
OFFICER
OFFICES

•F••I••
AFFAIRE
AFFAIRS
AFFLICT
OFFLINE
OFFSIDE
OFFSITE

•F•••I•
PFENNIG

•F••••I
AFGHANI
EFFENDI

••FI•••
ADFINEM
AFFINES
AFFIRMS
AFFIXED
AFFIXES
ALFIERI
DEFIANT
DEFICIT
DEFILED
DEFILER
DEFILES
DEFINED
DEFINES
GEFILTE
IFFIEST
INFIDEL
INFIELD
LAFITTE
MRFIXIT
OFFICER
OFFICES
REFILED
REFILES
REFILLS
REFILMS
REFINED
REFINER
REFINES
REFIRES
RUFIYAA
UNFIXED

••F•I••
AFFAIRE
AFFAIRS
AFFLICT
BOFFINS
BUFFING
CUFFING
DAFFIER
DAFFILY
DAFFING
DEFYING
DOFFING
ELFLIKE
FIFTIES
GAFFING
HAFNIUM
HAFTING
HEFTIER
HEFTILY
HEFTING
HUFFIER
HUFFILY
HUFFING
HUFFISH
INFLICT
JIFFIES
KAFFIRS
LEFTIES
LEFTIST
LIFTING
LOFTIER
LOFTILY
LOFTING
LUFFING
MAFFICK
MIFFIER
MIFFING
MUFFING
MUFFINS
NIFTIER
NIFTILY
OFFLINE
OFFSIDE
OFFSITE
PUFFIER
PUFFILY
PUFFING
PUFFINS
RAFFISH
RAFTING
REFFING
REFRIED
REFRIES
RIFFING
RIFLING
RIFTING
RUFFIAN
SIFTING
SOFFITS
SOFTIES
SOFTISH
SUFFICE
TAFFIES
TIFFING
TIFFINS
TUFTIER
TUFTING
WAFTING

••F••I•
DEFICIT
GOFORIT
MRFIXIT
REFRAIN
SAFARIS

••F•••I
ALFIERI
EFFENDI

•••FI••
ACTFIVE
ARTFILM
BEEFIER
BEEFING
BOFFINS
BONFIRE
BOWFINS
BUFFING
CATFISH
CHAFING
CODFISH
COIFING
COMFIER
COMFITS
CONFIDE
CONFINE
CONFIRM
CUFFING
DAFFIER
DAFFILY
DAFFING
DEIFIED
DEIFIES
DOFFING
DOGFISH
EDIFICE
EDIFIED
EDIFIES
FLYFISH
FOXFIRE
FULFILL
FULFILS
GAFFING
GINFIZZ
GOLFING
GOOFIER
GOOFILY
GOOFING
GULFING
GUNFIRE
HOOFING
HUFFIER
HUFFILY
HUFFING
HUFFISH
JIFFIES
KAFFIRS
KNIFING
LEAFIER
LEAFING
LOAFING
LUFFING
MAFFICK
MIFFIER
MIFFING
MISFILE
MISFIRE
MISFITS
MUFFING
MUFFINS
OLEFINS
ORIFICE
OUTFITS
PANFISH
PERFIDY
PROFILE
PROFITS
PUFFIER
PUFFILY
PUFFING
PUFFINS
RAFFISH
RATFINK
REDFINS
REDFIRS
REEFING
REFFING
REIFIED
REIFIES
RIFFING
ROOFING
RUFFIAN
SAWFISH
SEAFIRE
SELFISH
SOFFITS
SUFFICE
SULFIDE
SULFITE
SUNFISH
SURFIER
SURFING
TAFFIES
THEFIRM
TIFFING
TIFFINS
TURFIER
UNIFIED
UNIFIER
UNIFIES
WOLFING
WOLFISH
WOOFING

•••F•I•
AELFRIC
AIRFOIL
BIDFAIR
FORFEIT
FUNFAIR
GRIFFIN
HALFWIT
HOOFSIT
MAYFAIR
PARFAIT
REAFFIX
SURFEIT
TINFOIL
TRAFFIC
TREFOIL
WILFRID

••••FI•
BENEFIT
BLUEFIN
GRIFFIN
MALEFIC
OSSIFIC
OUTOFIT
PACIFIC
RATAFIA
REAFFIX
SEENFIT
SEESFIT

TAILFIN
TRAFFIC

F•J••••
FAJITAS
FIJIANS
FUJITSU

F••J•••
FANJETS

••F••J•
ALFORJA

F•K••••
FAKEFUR

F••K•••
FICKLER
FINKING
FIRKINS
FLAKERS
FLAKIER
FLAKILY
FLAKING
FLUKIER
FOLKART
FOLKIER
FOLKIES
FOLKISH
FOLKWAY
FORKERS
FORKFUL
FORKIER
FORKING
FUNKIER
FUNKILY
FUNKING

F•••K••
FLANKED
FLANKER
FLECKED
FLICKED
FLICKER
FLOCKED
FLOCKTO
FLUNKED
FRANKED
FRANKEN
FRANKER
FRANKIE
FRANKLY
FRANKOZ
FREAKED
FRECKLE
FRECKLY
FRICKIE
FRISKED
FROCKED

F••••K•
FADLIKE
FANLIKE
FATLIKE
FINICKY
FINLIKE
FORSAKE
FOXLIKE

F•••••K
FATBACK
FETLOCK
FOGBANK
FORSOOK
FOSDICK
FRYCOOK

•F••••K
OFFPEAK

••F••K•
ELFLIKE

••F•••K
DEFROCK
MAFFICK
OFFPEAK
SUFFOLK
UNFROCK

•••F••K
HAYFORK
KINFOLK
MAFFICK
MENFOLK
NORFOLK
RATFINK
SUFFOLK

FL•••••
FLACCID
FLACONS
FLAGDAY
FLAGGED
FLAGMAN
FLAGMEN
FLAGONS
FLAILED
FLAKERS
FLAKIER
FLAKILY
FLAKING
FLAMBED
FLAMBES
FLAMIER
FLAMING
FLANEUR
FLANGES
FLANKED
FLANKER
FLANNEL
FLAPPED
FLAPPER
FLAREUP
FLARING
FLASHED
FLASHER
FLASHES
FLATBED
FLATCAR
FLATLET
FLATOUT
FLATTAX
FLATTED
FLATTEN
FLATTER
FLATTOP
FLAUNTS
FLAUNTY
FLAVORS
FLAVOUR
FLAWING
FLAXIER
FLAYING
FLEABAG
FLEAPIT
FLECHES
FLECKED
FLEDGED
FLEDGES
FLEECED
FLEECES
FLEEING
FLEETER
FLEETLY
FLEMING
FLEMISH
FLENSED
FLENSES
FLESHED
FLESHES
FLESHLY
FLEXING
FLEXNER
FLEXORS
FLEYING
FLICKED
FLICKER
FLIESAT
FLIESIN
FLIGHTS
FLIGHTY
FLIPOUT
FLIPPED
FLIPPER
FLIPUPS
FLIRTED
FLITTED
FLITTER
FLIVVER
FLOATED
FLOATER
FLOCKED
FLOCKTO
FLOGGED
FLOODED
FLOORED
FLOPPED
FLORETS
FLORIDA
FLORINS
FLORIST
FLORUIT
FLOSSED
FLOSSES
FLOTSAM
FLOUNCE
FLOUNCY
FLOURED
FLOUTED
FLOWERS
FLOWERY
FLOWING
FLOWNAT
FLOWNIN
FLUBBED
FLUBBER
FLUENCY
FLUFFED
FLUIDLY
FLUKIER
FLUMMOX
FLUNKED
FLUSHED
FLUSHES
FLUSTER
FLUTIER
FLUTING
FLUTIST
FLUTTER
FLUVIAL
FLUXING
FLYAWAY
FLYBALL
FLYBOYS
FLYCAST
FLYFISH
FLYHIGH
FLYLEAF
FLYLESS
FLYNETS
FLYOVER
FLYPAST
FLYRODS
FLYTRAP
FLYWAYS

F•L••••
FALAFEL
FALCONS
FALLACY
FALLFOR
FALLGUY
FALLING
FALLOFF
FALLOUT
FALLOWS
FALLSIN
FALLSON
FALLSTO
FALSELY
FALSEST
FALSIFY
FALSITY
FALTERS
FALWELL
FELDMAN
FELICIA
FELINES
FELLAHS
FELLERS
FELLFOR
FELLIES
FELLING
FELLINI
FELLOFF
FELLOUT
FELLOWS
FELTFOR
FELTOUT
FELUCCA
FILBERT
FILCHED
FILCHER
FILCHES
FILENES
FILINGS
FILLERS
FILLETS
FILLIES
FILLING
FILLINS
FILLIPS
FILLOUT
FILLSIN
FILLSUP
FILLUPS
FILMIER
FILMING
FILTERS
FOLDERS
FOLDING
FOLDOUT
FOLDSUP
FOLDUPS
FOLGERS
FOLIAGE
FOLIATE
FOLKART
FOLKIER
FOLKIES
FOLKISH
FOLKWAY
FOLLETT
FOLLIES
FOLLOWS
FULCRUM
FULFILL
FULFILS
FULGENT
FULGHUM
FULLEST
FULSOME

F••L•••
FABLERS
FADLIKE
FAILING
FAILURE
FALLACY
FALLFOR
FALLGUY
FALLING
FALLOFF
FALLOUT
FALLOWS
FALLSIN
FALLSON
FALLSTO
FANLIKE
FARLEFT
FATLESS
FATLIKE
FAULTED
FEELERS
FEELESS
FEELFOR
FEELING
FEELOUT
FELLAHS
FELLERS
FELLFOR
FELLIES
FELLING
FELLINI
FELLOFF
FELLOUT
FELLOWS
FETLOCK
FIELDED
FIELDER
FIGLEAF
FILLERS
FILLETS
FILLIES
FILLING
FILLINS
FILLIPS
FILLOUT
FILLSIN
FILLSUP
FILLUPS
FINLAND
FINLIKE
FLYLEAF
FLYLESS
FOALING
FOGLESS
FOILING
FOLLETT
FOLLIES
FOLLOWS
FOOLERY
FOOLING
FOOLISH
FORLIFE
FORLORN
FOULARD
FOULEST
FOULING
FOULOUT
FOULSUP
FOULTIP
FOULUPS
FOWLERS
FOWLING
FOXLIKE
FRILLED
FROLICS
FUELERS
FUELING
FUELLED
FUELOIL
FUELROD
FULLEST
FURLESS
FURLING
FURLONG

F•••L••
FACULAE
FACULTY
FAMULUS
FANCLUB
FEEBLER
FEEDLOT
FEMALES
FERULES
FETTLES
FIATLUX
FIBULAE
FIBULAS
FICKLER
FIDDLED
FIDDLER
FIDDLES
FIDELIO
FIDELIS
FIEDLER
FINALES
FINALLY
FIPPLES
FIRELIT
FIZZLED
FIZZLES
FLAILED
FLATLET
FOCSLES
FOIBLES
FONDLED
FONDLES
FOOZLED
FOOZLES
FORELEG
FRAILER
FRAILLY
FRAILTY
FRAWLEY
FRILLED
FUDDLED
FUDDLES
FUELLED
FUMBLED
FUMBLER
FUMBLES

F••••L•
FACIALS
FAINTLY
FALSELY
FALWELL
FANBELT
FANCILY
FATTILY
FEBRILE
FERRULE
FERTILE
FETIDLY
FIBRILS
FIERILY
FIFTHLY
FINAGLE
FINALLY
FINIALS
FIREFLY
FIRSTLY
FISHILY
FISSILE
FIXABLE
FIXEDLY
FLAKILY
FLEETLY
FLESHLY
FLUIDLY
FLYBALL
FOAMILY
FOGGILY
FORMALS
FORMULA
FORSALE
FOSSILS
FOXHOLE
FRAGILE
FRAILLY
FRANKLY
FRAZZLE
FRECKLE
FRECKLY
FRESHLY
FRIABLE
FRIZZLE
FRIZZLY
FULFILL
FULFILS
FUNKILY
FUNNELS
FUNNILY
FURBALL
FUSSILY
FUSTILY
FUZZILY

F•••••L
FACTFUL
FACTUAL
FALAFEL
FALWELL
FANMAIL
FANTAIL
FATEFUL
FEARFUL
FEDERAL
FEMORAL
FISTFUL
FLANNEL
FLUVIAL
FLYBALL
FORKFUL
FORMFUL
FORREAL
FOXTAIL
FRACTAL
FRETFUL
FRONTAL
FUELOIL
FULFILL
FUNCHAL
FURBALL
FURSEAL

•F•L•••
AFFLICT
OFFLINE
OFFLOAD

•F•••L•
AFFABLE
AFFABLY

••FL•••
AFFLICT
DEFLATE
DEFLECT
ELFLIKE
INFLAME
INFLATE
INFLECT
INFLICT
INFLOWS
OFFLINE
OFFLOAD
REFLAGS
REFLECT
RIFLERS
RIFLERY
RIFLING

••F•L••
ALFALFA
AWFULLY
BAFFLED
BAFFLER
BAFFLES
BEFALLS
DEFALLA
DEFILED
DEFILER
DEFILES
ENFOLDS
GEFILTE
MUFFLED
MUFFLER
MUFFLES
PIFFLED
PIFFLES
RAFFLED
RAFFLER
RAFFLES
REFILED
REFILES
REFILLS
REFILMS
RIFFLED
RIFFLES
RUFFLED
RUFFLES
TOFFLER
UNFOLDS
WAFFLED
WAFFLER
WAFFLES

••F••L•
AFFABLE
AFFABLY
ATFAULT
AWFULLY
BEFALLS
BEFOULS
BUFFALO
DAFFILY
DEFALLA
DEFAULT
DUFFELS
FIFTHLY
HEFTILY
HUFFILY
INFIELD
LOFTILY
NIFTILY
NOFAULT
PUFFILY
REFILLS
REFUELS
SUFFOLK
UNFURLS

••F•••L
BIFOCAL
INFIDEL
LIFEFUL
REFUSAL

•••FL••
AIRFLOW
BAFFLED
BAFFLER
BAFFLES
EARFLAP
ICEFLOE
LEAFLET
MOUFLON
MUFFLED
MUFFLER
MUFFLES
OUTFLOW
PIFFLED
PIFFLES
PURFLED
PURFLES
RAFFLED
RAFFLER
RAFFLES
REDFLAG
RIFFLED
RIFFLES
RUFFLED
RUFFLES
STIFLED
STIFLES
TOFFLER
TRIFLED
TRIFLER
TRIFLES
WAFFLED
WAFFLER
WAFFLES

•••F•L•
ARMFULS
ARTFILM
BAGFULS
BEEFALO
BLUFFLY
BOXFULS
BUFFALO
CANFULS
CAPFULS
CARFULS
CUPFULS
DAFFILY
DUFFELS
EARFULS
EYEFULS
FULFILL
FULFILS
GOOFILY
GRUFFLY
HUFFILY
JARFULS
JUGFULS
KINFOLK
LAPFULS
MENFOLK
MISFILE
NORFOLK
PANFULS
PITFALL
POTFULS
PROFILE
PUFFILY
SCUFFLE
SHUFFLE
SIXFOLD
SNAFFLE
SNIFFLE
SNIFFLY
SNUFFLE
SNUFFLY
SOUFFLE
STIFFLY
SUFFOLK
SWIFTLY
TENFOLD
TRUFFLE
TWOFOLD
VATFULS

•••F••L
AIRFOIL
FULFILL
PEAFOWL
PITFALL
SYNFUEL
TINFOIL
TOMFOOL
TREFOIL
WOLFGAL

••••FL•
ALOOFLY
BLOWFLY
BLUFFLY
BRIEFLY
CHIEFLY
DEERFLY
FIREFLY
GRUFFLY
LETSFLY
OVERFLY
SANDFLY
SCUFFLE
SHOOFLY
SHUFFLE
SNAFFLE
SNIFFLE
SNIFFLY
SNUFFLE
SNUFFLY
SOUFFLE
STIFFLY
TESTFLY
TRUFFLE

••••F•L
BALEFUL
BANEFUL
BASHFUL
BOWLFUL
BRIMFUL
CAREFUL
DAREFUL
DIREFUL
DISHFUL
DOLEFUL
DOOMFUL
DUTIFUL
EASEFUL
FACTFUL
FALAFEL
FATEFUL
FEARFUL
FISTFUL
FORKFUL
FORMFUL
FRETFUL
GAINFUL
GLEEFUL
HANDFUL
HARMFUL
HATEFUL
HEATFUL
HEEDFUL
HELPFUL
HOPEFUL
HURTFUL
HUSHFUL
LIFEFUL
LUSTFUL
MINDFUL
MOANFUL
MUSEFUL
NEEDFUL
ODORFUL
PAGEFUL
PAILFUL
PAINFUL
PIPEFUL
PITIFUL
PLAYFUL
PLOTFUL
POUTFUL
PUSHFUL
RAGEFUL
RESTFUL
ROOMFUL
RUTHFUL
SACKFUL
SHOPFUL
SIGHFUL
SKILFUL
SKINFUL
SONGFUL
SOULFUL
TACTFUL
TANKFUL
TEARFUL
TOILFUL
TRAYFUL
TUNEFUL
UNAWFUL
WAILFUL
WAKEFUL
WILLFUL
WISHFUL
WISTFUL
YAWNFUL
ZESTFUL

FM•••••
FMRADIO

F•M••••
FAMINES
FAMULUS
FEMALES
FEMORAL
FOMENTS
FUMBLED
FUMBLER
FUMBLES
FUMIEST

F••M•••
FANMAIL
FARMERS
FARMERY
FARMING
FARMOUT
FERMENT
FERMIUM
FIGMENT
FILMIER
FILMING
FIRMEST
FIRMING
FIRMSUP
FLAMBED
FLAMBES
FLAMIER
FLAMING
FLEMING
FLEMISH
FLUMMOX
FNUMBER
FOAMIER
FOAMILY
FOAMING
FORMALS
FORMATS
FORMFUL
FORMICA
FORMING
FORMOSA
FORMULA
FRAMEUP
FRAMING
FREMONT
FROMAGE

F•••M••
FADIMAN
FELDMAN
FEYNMAN
FIREMAN
FIREMEN
FLAGMAN
FLAGMEN
FLUMMOX
FOOTMAN
FOOTMEN
FOREMAN
FOREMEN
FREEMAN
FREEMEN
FROGMAN
FROGMEN

F••••M•
FATHOMS
FULSOME

F•••••M
FADDISM
FAUVISM
FERMIUM
FIEFDOM
FIREARM
FLOTSAM
FOGYISM
FORDHAM
FOREARM
FREEDOM
FULCRUM
FULGHUM

•F•M•••
SFUMATO

•F••M••
AFRAMES

•F•••M•
AFFIRMS
OFFRAMP

••F•M••
DEFAMED
DEFAMES
HOFFMAN

••F••M•
AFFIRMS
DEFORMS
INFLAME
INFORMS
OFFRAMP
REFILMS
REFORMS
REFRAME

••F•••M
ADFINEM
HAFNIUM

•••FM••
HOFFMAN
KAUFMAN
WOLFMAN
WOLFMEN

•••F•M•
PERFUME

•••F••M
ANTFARM
ARTFILM
ARTFORM
CONFIRM
CONFORM
FIEFDOM
PERFORM
SERFDOM
THEFIRM
UNIFORM
WOLFRAM

••••FM•
ALLOFME

FN•••••
FNUMBER

F•N••••
FANATIC
FANBELT
FANCIED
FANCIER
FANCIES
FANCIFY
FANCILY
FANCLUB
FANFARE
FANIONS
FANJETS
FANLIKE
FANMAIL
FANNING
FANOUTS
FANSOUT
FANTAIL
FANTASY
FANZINE
FENCERS
FENCING
FENDERS
FENDING
FENIANS
FENNIER
FINAGLE
FINALES
FINALLY
FINANCE
FINCHES
FINDERS
FINDING
FINDOUT
FINEART
FINESSE
FINGERS
FINIALS
FINICKY
FINKING
FINLAND
FINLIKE
FINNIER
FINNISH
FONDANT
FONDEST
FONDLED
FONDLES
FONDUES
FONTEYN
FONTINA
FUNCHAL
FUNDING
FUNFAIR
FUNFEST
FUNGOES
FUNKIER
FUNKILY
FUNKING
FUNNELS
FUNNIER
FUNNIES
FUNNILY
FUNNING

F••N•••
FAINTED
FAINTER
FAINTLY
FANNING
FATNESS
FAWNERS
FAWNING
FEINTED

FENNIER
FERNBAR
FERNIER
FEYNMAN
FIANCEE
FIANCES
FIENNES
FINNIER
FINNISH
FITNESS
FLANEUR
FLANGES
FLANKED
FLANKER
FLANNEL
FLENSED
FLENSES
FLUNKED
FLYNETS
FOINING
FOUNDED
FOUNDER
FOUNDRY
FRANCES
FRANCIS
FRANKED
FRANKEN
FRANKER
FRANKIE
FRANKLY
FRANKOZ
FRANTIC
FRENEAU
FRINGED
FRINGES
FRONTAL
FRONTED
FRONTON
FUNNELS
FUNNIER
FUNNIES
FUNNILY
FUNNING
FURNACE
FURNISH

F•••N••

FACINGS
FAGENDS
FAIENCE
FAMINES
FEIGNED
FELINES
FIENNES
FILENES
FILINGS
FINANCE
FIRENZE
FIRINGS
FISHNET
FIXINGS
FLANNEL
FLAUNTS
FLAUNTY
FLEXNER
FLOUNCE
FLOUNCY
FLOWNAT
FLOWNIN
FLUENCY
FOMENTS
FORINTS
FRIENDS
FROWNAT
FROWNED
FROWNER

F••••N•

FADEINS
FAGGING
FAILING
FAIRING
FALCONS
FALLING
FANIONS
FANNING
FANZINE
FARCING
FARGONE
FARMING
FASTENS
FASTING
FASTONE
FATTENS
FAWNING
FEARING
FEEDING
FEELING
FELLING
FELLINI
FENCING
FENDING
FENIANS
FERMENT
FERVENT
FESSING
FEUDING
FIBBING
FIBRINS
FIGMENT
FIJIANS
FILLING
FILLINS
FILMING
FINDING
FINKING
FINLAND
FIREANT
FIRKINS
FIRMING
FISHING
FITTING
FIZZING
FLACONS
FLAGONS
FLAKING
FLAMING
FLARING
FLAWING
FLAYING
FLEEING
FLEMING
FLEXING
FLEYING
FLORINS
FLOWING
FLUTING
FLUXING
FOALING
FOAMING
FOBBING
FOGBANK
FOGGING
FOILING
FOINING
FOLDING
FONDANT
FONTINA
FOOLING
FOOTING
FORCING
FORDING
FORFEND
FORGING
FORGONE
FORKING
FORMING
FORRENT
FORTUNA
FORTUNE
FORWENT
FOULING
FOWLING
FRAMING
FRAYING
FREEING
FREMONT
FRYPANS
FUBBING
FUDGING
FUELING
FULGENT
FUNDING
FUNKING
FUNNING
FURLING
FURLONG
FURRING
FUSSING
FUTZING
FUZZING

F•••••N

FACTION
FADEDIN
FADESIN
FADIMAN
FALLSIN
FALLSON
FASHION
FEEDSON
FELDMAN
FESTOON
FEYNMAN
FICTION
FIFTEEN
FILLSIN
FIREMAN
FIREMEN
FISSION
FLAGMAN
FLAGMEN
FLATTEN
FLIESIN
FLOWNIN
FOGHORN
FONTEYN
FOOTMAN
FOOTMEN
FOREIGN
FOREMAN
FOREMEN
FORERAN
FORERUN
FORLORN
FORTRAN
FRANKEN
FREEMAN
FREEMEN
FRESHEN
FRIEDAN
FRISIAN
FRISSON
FROGMAN
FROGMEN
FRONTON
FUSTIAN

•F•N•••

PFENNIG

•F••N••

AFFINES
EFFENDI
OFFENCE
OFFENDS
OFFENSE
OFTENER
PFENNIG

•F•••N•

AFFRONT
AFGHANI
AFGHANS
IFSTONE
OFFHAND
OFFLINE

•F••••N

AFRICAN

••FN•••

HAFNIUM

••F•N••

ADFINEM
AFFINES
ALFONSO
DEFENCE
DEFENDS
DEFENSE
DEFINED
DEFINES
DEFUNCT
EFFENDI
INFANCY
INFANTA
INFANTS
LIFENET
OFFENCE
OFFENDS
OFFENSE
REFINED
REFINER
REFINES
REFUNDS

••F••N•

AFFRONT
BOFFINS
BUFFING
CAFTANS
CUFFING
DAFFING
DEFIANT
DEFYING
DOFFING
GAFFING
HAFTING
HEFTING
HUFFING
INFERNO
INFRONT
KAFTANS
LIFTING
LOFTING
LUFFING
MIFFING
MUFFING
MUFFINS
OFFHAND
OFFLINE
PUFFING
PUFFINS
RAFTING
REFFING
RIFFING
RIFLING
RIFTING
SIFTING
SOFTENS
TIFFANY
TIFFING
TIFFINS
TUFTING
UPFRONT
WAFTING

••F•••N

BUFFOON
FIFTEEN
HOFFMAN
REFRAIN
RUFFIAN
SAFFRON

•••FN••

ASOFNOW

•••F•N•

BEEFING
BOFFINS
BOWFINS
BUFFING
CHAFING
COIFING
CONFINE
CUFFING
DAFFING
DEAFENS
DOFFING
FORFEND
GAFFING
GOLFING
GOOFING
GULFING
HOOFING
HUFFING
KNIFING
LEAFING
LENFANT
LOAFING
LUFFING
MIFFING
MUFFING
MUFFINS
OLEFINS
PROFANE
PUFFING
PUFFINS
RATFINK
REDFINS
REEFING
REFFING
RIFFING
ROOFING
SEAFANS
SURFING
THEFONZ
TIFFANY
TIFFING
TIFFINS
WOLFING
WOOFING

•••F••N

BUFFOON
CHIFFON
CLIFTON
GRAFTON
GRIFFIN
GRIFFON
HALFDAN
HOFFMAN
KAUFMAN
MOUFLON
OAKFERN
RUFFIAN
SAFFRON
STIFFEN
WOLFMAN
WOLFMEN

••••F•N

BLUEFIN
CHIFFON
GRIFFIN
GRIFFON
POKEFUN
STIFFEN
TAILFIN

FO•••••

FOALING
FOAMIER
FOAMILY
FOAMING
FOBBING
FOBSOFF
FOCSLES
FOCUSED
FOCUSES
FODDERS
FOGBANK
FOGBOWS
FOGGERS
FOGGIER
FOGGILY
FOGGING
FOGHORN
FOGLESS
FOGYISH
FOGYISM
FOIBLES
FOILING
FOINING
FOISTED
FOLDERS
FOLDING
FOLDOUT
FOLDSUP
FOLDUPS
FOLGERS
FOLIAGE
FOLIATE
FOLKART
FOLKIER
FOLKIES
FOLKISH
FOLKWAY
FOLLETT
FOLLIES
FOLLOWS
FOMENTS
FONDANT
FONDEST
FONDLED
FONDLES
FONDUES
FONTEYN
FONTINA
FOODIES
FOODWEB
FOOLERY
FOOLING
FOOLISH
FOOTAGE
FOOTERS
FOOTING
FOOTMAN
FOOTMEN
FOOTPAD
FOOTSIE
FOOTWAY
FOOZLED
FOOZLES
FOPPERY
FOPPISH
FORAGED
FORAGER
FORAGES
FORBADE
FORBEAR
FORBIDS
FORBORE
FORCEPS
FORCERS
FORCING
FORDHAM
FORDING
FOREARM
FOREIGN
FORELEG
FOREMAN
FOREMEN
FOREPAW
FORERAN
FORERUN
FORESAW
FORESEE
FORESTS
FOREVER
FORFEIT
FORFEND
FORFREE
FORGAVE
FORGERS
FORGERY
FORGETS
FORGING
FORGIVE
FORGOES
FORGONE
FORGOOD
FORINTS
FORKERS
FORKFUL
FORKIER
FORKING
FORLIFE
FORLORN
FORMALS
FORMATS
FORMFUL
FORMICA
FORMING
FORMOSA
FORMULA
FORREAL
FORRENT
FORREST
FORSAKE
FORSALE
FORSOOK
FORSTER
FORSURE
FORSYTH
FORTIES
FORTIFY
FORTIUS
FORTRAN
FORTUNA
FORTUNE
FORWARD
FORWENT
FOSDICK
FOSSILS
FOSTERS
FOULARD
FOULEST
FOULING
FOULOUT
FOULSUP
FOULTIP
FOULUPS
FOUNDED
FOUNDER
FOUNDRY
FOURIER
FOURTHS
FOURWAY
FOWLERS
FOWLING
FOXFIRE
FOXHOLE
FOXIEST
FOXLIKE
FOXTAIL
FOXTROT

F•O••••

FLOATED
FLOATER
FLOCKED
FLOCKTO
FLOGGED
FLOODED
FLOORED
FLOPPED
FLORETS
FLORIDA
FLORINS
FLORIST
FLORUIT
FLOSSED
FLOSSES
FLOTSAM
FLOUNCE
FLOUNCY
FLOURED
FLOUTED
FLOWERS
FLOWERY
FLOWING
FLOWNAT
FLOWNIN
FOODIES
FOODWEB
FOOLERY
FOOLING
FOOLISH
FOOTAGE
FOOTERS
FOOTING
FOOTMAN
FOOTMEN
FOOTPAD
FOOTSIE
FOOTWAY
FOOZLED
FOOZLES
FROCKED
FROGMAN
FROGMEN
FROLICS
FROMAGE
FRONTAL
FRONTED
FRONTON
FROSTED
FROTHED
FROWARD
FROWNAT
FROWNED
FROWNER
FROWSTY

F••O•••

FAGOTED
FANOUTS
FAVORED
FAVOURS
FEDORAS
FEMORAL
FLOODED
FLOORED
FLYOVER
FURORES

F•••O••

FACEOFF
FACTOID
FACTORS
FACTORY
FADEOUT
FAIROFF
FALCONS
FALLOFF
FALLOUT
FALLOWS
FANIONS
FANSOUT
FARGONE
FARMOUT
FARROWS
FASTONE
FATHOMS
FATUOUS
FEELOUT
FELLOFF
FELLOUT
FELLOWS
FELTOUT
FERROUS
FERVORS
FERVOUR
FESTOON
FETLOCK
FIBROUS
FILLOUT
FINDOUT
FIREOFF
FISHOUT
FLACONS
FLAGONS
FLATOUT
FLAVORS
FLAVOUR
FLEXORS
FLIPOUT
FLYBOYS
FLYRODS
FOBSOFF
FOGBOWS
FOGHORN
FOLDOUT
FOLLOWS
FORBORE
FORGOES
FORGONE
FORGOOD
FORLORN
FORMOSA
FORSOOK
FOULOUT
FOXHOLE
FREMONT
FRYCOOK
FUELOIL
FULSOME
FUNGOES
FURIOUS
FURLONG
FURROWS

F••••O•

FACTION
FALLFOR
FALLSON
FASHION
FEEDLOT
FEEDSON
FEELFOR
FELLFOR
FELTFOR
FESTOON
FIASCOS
FICTION
FIEFDOM
FIREBOX
FIREDOG
FISSION
FLATTOP
FLUMMOX
FORGOOD
FORSOOK
FOXTROT
FRANKOZ
FREEDOM
FRESCOS
FRISSON
FRONTON
FRYCOOK
FUELROD
FUSSPOT

F•••••O

FALLSTO
FARRAGO
FERRARO
FIDELIO
FLOCKTO
FMRADIO

•F•O•••

AFFORDS
EFFORTS
OFSORTS

•F••O••

AFFRONT
IFSTONE
OFASORT
OFFHOUR
OFFLOAD
OFFROAD

•F••••O

SFUMATO

••FO•••

AFFORDS
ALFONSO
ALFORJA
BEFOULS
BIFOCAL
BYFORCE
DEFORMS
EFFORTS
ENFOLDS
ENFORCE
GOFORIT
INFOCUS
INFORCE
INFORMS
OXFORDS
REFOCUS
REFORMS
UNFOLDS

••F•O••

AFFRONT
BUFFOON
DEFROCK
DEFROST
GIFFORD
INFLOWS
INFRONT
LEFTOFF
LEFTOUT
LIFTOFF
OFFHOUR
OFFLOAD
OFFROAD
SUFFOLK
UNFROCK
UPFRONT

••F••O•

BUFFOON
INFAVOR
SAFFRON
SOFTTOP

••F•••O

ALFONSO
ALFREDO
BUFFALO
DEFACTO
EXFACTO
INFERNO
REFERTO

•••FO••

ACTFOUR
AIRFOIL
ARTFORM
ASHFORD
BALFOUR
BIGFOOT
BUFFOON
CATFOOD
COMFORT
CONFORM
DOGFOOD
GIFFORD
GOOFOFF
HAYFORK
HOTFOOT
ICEFOGS
KINFOLK
LANFORD
LAWFORD
MENFOLK
MITFORD
MUMFORD
NORFOLK
OLDFOGY
PEAFOWL
PERFORM
REDFORD
SANFORD
SEAFOOD
SIXFOLD
SUFFOLK
TENFOLD
TENFOUR
THEFONZ
TINFOIL
TOMFOOL
TREFOIL
TWOFOLD
UNIFORM
WEBFOOT
WILFORD

•••F•O•

AIRFLOW
ASOFNOW
BIGFOOT
BUFFOON
CATFOOD
CHIFFON
CLIFTON
DOGFOOD
FIEFDOM
GRAFTON
GRIFFON
HOTFOOT
ICEFLOE
MOUFLON
OUTFLOW
ROOFTOP
SAFFRON
SEAFOOD
SERFDOM
TOMFOOL
WEBFOOT

•••F••O

BEEFALO
BUFFALO
GOLFPRO

••••FO•

AIMSFOR
ANTIFOG
ASKSFOR
BLUEFOX
BRERFOX
CALLFOR
CAREFOR
CHIFFON
DONEFOR
FALLFOR
FEELFOR
FELLFOR
FELTFOR
GOESFOR
GOINFOR
GRIFFON
GUNSFOR
LAIDFOR
LAYSFOR
LOOKFOR
MADEFOR
MAKEFOR
OPTSFOR
PAIDFOR
PASSFOR
PAYSFOR
PINEFOR
PRAYFOR
PULLFOR
ROOTFOR
RUNSFOR
SELLFOR
SENDFOR
SENTFOR
SENUFOS
SHOTFOR
VOTEFOR
WAITFOR
WENTFOR
WHATFOR
WORKFOR

•••••FO

RODOLFO

F•P••••

FIPPLES
FOPPERY
FOPPISH

F••P•••

FIPPLES
FLAPPED
FLAPPER
FLIPOUT
FLIPPED
FLIPPER
FLIPUPS
FLOPPED
FLYPAST
FOPPERY
FOPPISH
FRAPPES
FRIPPET
FRYPANS

F•••P••

FAUXPAS
FLAPPED
FLAPPER
FLEAPIT
FLIPPED
FLIPPER
FLOPPED
FOOTPAD
FOREPAW
FRAPPES
FRIPPET
FUSSPOT

F••••P•

FILLIPS
FILLUPS
FLIPUPS
FOLDUPS
FORCEPS
FOULUPS

F•••••P

FAIRSUP
FILLSUP
FIREDUP
FIRESUP
FIRMSUP
FIXEDUP
FIXESUP
FLAREUP
FLATTOP
FLYTRAP
FOLDSUP
FOULSUP
FOULTIP
FRAMEUP

•F•P•••

OFFPEAK

•F••••P

OFFRAMP

••FP•••

OFFPEAK

••F•••P

LIFTSUP
OFFRAMP
SOFTTOP

•••FP••

GOLFPRO

•••F•P•

GOOFUPS

•••F••P

BEEFSUP
EARFLAP
GOOFSUP
ROOFTOP

FR•••••

FRACTAL
FRAGILE
FRAILER
FRAILLY
FRAILTY
FRAISES
FRAMEUP
FRAMING
FRANCES
FRANCIS
FRANKED
FRANKEN
FRANKER
FRANKIE
FRANKLY
FRANKOZ
FRANTIC
FRAPPES
FRASIER
FRAUGHT
FRAWLEY
FRAYING
FRAZIER
FRAZZLE
FREAKED
FRECKLE
FRECKLY
FREDDIE
FREDRIC

FREEBEE
FREEBIE
FREEDOM
FREEING
FREEMAN
FREEMEN
FREESIA
FREEWAY
FREEZER
FREEZES
FREIGHT
FREMONT
FRENEAU
FRESCOS
FRESHEN
FRESHER
FRESHET
FRESHLY
FRETFUL
FRETSAW
FRETTED
FRIABLE
FRICKIE
FRIDAYS
FRIDGES
FRIEDAN
FRIENDS
FRIEZES
FRIGATE
FRIGHTS
FRILLED
FRINGED
FRINGES
FRIPPET
FRISBEE
FRISIAN
FRISKED
FRISSON
FRITTED
FRITTER
FRIZZED
FRIZZES
FRIZZLE
FRIZZLY
FROCKED
FROGMAN
FROGMEN
FROLICS
FROMAGE
FRONTAL
FRONTED
FRONTON
FROSTED
FROTHED
FROWARD
FROWNAT
FROWNED
FROWNER
FROWSTY
FRUITED
FRYCOOK
FRYPANS

F•R••••

FARADAY
FARAWAY
FARCING
FAREAST
FARGONE
FARLEFT
FARMERS
FARMERY
FARMING
FARMOUT
FARRAGO
FARRIER
FARROWS
FARTHER
FARWEST
FERMENT
FERMIUM
FERNBAR
FERNIER
FERRARI
FERRARO
FERRATE
FERRETS
FERRIED
FERRIES
FERRITE
FERROUS
FERRULE
FERTILE
FERULES
FERVENT
FERVORS
FERVOUR
FIREANT
FIREARM
FIREBOX
FIREBUG
FIREDOG
FIREDUP
FIREFLY
FIRELIT
FIREMAN
FIREMEN
FIRENZE
FIREOFF
FIRESUP
FIRINGS
FIRKINS
FIRMEST
FIRMING
FIRMSUP
FIRRIER
FIRSTLY
FMRADIO
FORAGED
FORAGER
FORAGES
FORBADE
FORBEAR
FORBIDS
FORBORE
FORCEPS
FORCERS
FORCING
FORDHAM
FORDING
FOREARM
FOREIGN
FORELEG
FOREMAN
FOREMEN
FOREPAW
FORERAN
FORERUN
FORESAW
FORESEE
FORESTS
FOREVER
FORFEIT
FORFEND
FORFREE
FORGAVE
FORGERS
FORGERY
FORGETS
FORGING
FORGIVE
FORGOES
FORGONE
FORGOOD
FORINTS
FORKERS
FORKFUL
FORKIER
FORKING
FORLIFE
FORLORN
FORMALS
FORMATS
FORMFUL
FORMICA
FORMING
FORMOSA
FORMULA
FORREAL
FORRENT
FORREST
FORSAKE
FORSALE
FORSOOK
FORSTER
FORSURE
FORSYTH
FORTIES
FORTIFY
FORTIUS
FORTRAN
FORTUNA
FORTUNE
FORWARD
FORWENT
FURBALL
FURBISH
FURIOUS
FURLESS
FURLING
FURLONG
FURNACE
FURNISH
FURORES
FURRIER
FURRING
FURROWS
FURSEAL
FURTHER
FURTIVE

F••R•••

FABRICS
FAERIES
FAIREST
FAIRIES
FAIRING
FAIRISH
FAIROFF
FAIRSUP
FAIRWAY
FARRAGO
FARRIER
FARROWS
FEARERS
FEARFUL
FEARING
FEBRILE
FERRARI
FERRARO
FERRATE
FERRETS
FERRIED
FERRIES
FERRITE
FERROUS
FERRULE
FIBRILS
FIBRINS
FIBROUS
FIERCER
FIERIER
FIERILY
FIRRIER
FLAREUP
FLARING
FLIRTED
FLORETS
FLORIDA
FLORINS
FLORIST
FLORUIT
FLYRODS
FORREAL
FORRENT
FORREST
FOURIER
FOURTHS
FOURWAY
FURRIER
FURRING
FURROWS

F•••R••

FABARES
FABERGE
FAVORED
FAYWRAY
FEDERAL
FEDORAS
FEMORAL
FIACRES
FIGURED
FIGURER
FIGURES
FLOORED
FLOURED
FLYTRAP
FORERAN
FORERUN
FORFREE
FORTRAN
FOXTROT
FREDRIC
FUELROD
FULCRUM
FURORES
FUTURES

F••••R•

FABLERS
FACTORS
FACTORY
FAILURE
FALTERS
FANFARE
FARMERS
FARMERY
FATHERS
FAVOURS
FAWNERS
FEARERS
FEATURE
FEEDERS
FEELERS
FELLERS
FENCERS
FENDERS
FERRARI
FERRARO
FERVORS
FESTERS
FETTERS
FIBBERS
FILBERT
FILLERS
FILTERS
FINDERS
FINEART
FINGERS
FIREARM
FISHERS
FISHERY
FISHFRY
FISSURE
FITTERS
FIXTURE
FLAKERS
FLAVORS
FLEXORS
FLOWERS
FLOWERY
FODDERS
FOGGERS
FOGHORN
FOLDERS
FOLGERS
FOLKART
FOOLERY
FOOTERS
FOPPERY
FORBORE
FORCERS
FOREARM
FORGERS
FORGERY
FORKERS
FORLORN
FORSURE
FORWARD
FOSTERS
FOULARD
FOUNDRY
FOWLERS
FOXFIRE
FROWARD
FUELERS

F•••••R

FAINTER
FAKEFUR
FALLFOR
FANCIER
FARRIER
FARTHER
FATTIER
FEATHER
FEEBLER
FEELFOR
FEIFFER
FELLFOR
FELTFOR
FENNIER
FERNBAR
FERNIER
FERVOUR
FICKLER
FIDDLER
FIEDLER
FIELDER
FIERCER
FIERIER
FIGHTER
FIGURER
FILCHER
FILMIER
FINNIER
FIRRIER
FISCHER
FISHIER
FIZZIER
FLAKIER
FLAMIER
FLANEUR
FLANKER
FLAPPER
FLASHER
FLATCAR
FLATTER
FLAVOUR
FLAXIER
FLEETER
FLEXNER
FLICKER
FLIPPER
FLITTER
FLIVVER
FLOATER
FLUBBER
FLUKIER
FLUSTER
FLUTIER
FLUTTER
FLYOVER
FNUMBER
FOAMIER
FOGGIER
FOLKIER
FORAGER
FORBEAR
FOREVER
FORKIER
FORSTER
FOUNDER
FOURIER
FRAILER
FRANKER
FRASIER
FRAZIER
FREEZER
FRESHER
FRITTER
FROWNER
FUBSIER
FUMBLER
FUNFAIR
FUNKIER
FUNNIER
FURRIER
FURTHER
FUSSIER
FUSTIER
FUZZIER

•FR••••

AFRAMES
AFREETS
AFRICAN

•F•R•••

AFFRAYS
AFFRONT
OFFRAMP
OFFROAD

•F••R••

AFFIRMS
AFFORDS
EFFORTS
OFFERED
OFFERER
OFSORTS

•F•••R•

AFFAIRE
AFFAIRS
OFASORT

•F••••R

OFFERER
OFFHOUR
OFFICER
OFFYEAR
OFTENER

••FR•••

AFFRAYS
AFFRONT
ALFREDO
DEFRAUD
DEFRAYS
DEFROCK
DEFROST
INFRONT
OFFRAMP
OFFROAD
REFRACT
REFRAIN
REFRAME
REFRESH
REFRIED
REFRIES
UNFROCK
UPFRONT

••F•R••

AFFIRMS
AFFORDS
ALFORJA
ASFARAS
BYFORCE
DEFARGE
DEFORMS
EFFORTS
ENFORCE
GOFORIT
HOFBRAU
INFERNO
INFORCE
INFORMS
JEFFREY
JOFFREY
LAFARGE
OFFERED
OFFERER
OXFORDS
REFEREE
REFERTO
REFIRES
REFORMS
SAFARIS
SAFFRON
UNFURLS

••F••R•

AFFAIRE
AFFAIRS
ALFIERI
BUFFERS
COFFERS
DIFFERS
DUFFERS
GAFFERS
GIFFORD
JEFFERS
KAFFIRS
LIFTERS
PUFFERS
PUFFERY
RAFTERS
RIFLERS
RIFLERY
SIFTERS
SUFFERS
ZAFFERS

••F•••R

BAFFLER
DAFFIER
DEFILER
HEFTIER
HUFFIER
INFAVOR
LOFTIER
MIFFIER
MUFFLER
NIFTIER
OFFERER
OFFHOUR
OFFICER
OFFYEAR
PUFFIER
RAFFLER
REFINER
REFUSER
REFUTER
TOFFLER
TUFTIER
WAFFLER

•••FR••

AELFRIC
BUGFREE
COMFREY
FORFREE
GODFREY
ICEFREE
JEFFREY
JOFFREY
MANFRED
PALFREY
SAFFRON
TAXFREE
WILFRID
WINFREY
WOLFRAM

•••F•R•

AIRFARE
ANTFARM
ARAFURA
ARTFORM
ASHFORD
BONFIRE
BUFFERS
BUSFARE
CARFARE
COFFERS
COMFORT
CONFERS
CONFIRM
CONFORM
DIFFERS
DUFFERS
FANFARE
FOXFIRE
GAFFERS
GIFFORD
GOLFERS
GOLFPRO
GUNFIRE
HAYFORK
HEIFERS
HOOFERS
JEFFERS
KAFFIRS
LANFORD
LAWFORD
LOAFERS
MISFIRE
MITFORD
MUMFORD
OAKFERN
PERFORM
PILFERS
PREFERS
PUFFERS
PUFFERY
REDFIRS
REDFORD
REEFERS
ROOFERS
SANFORD
SEAFIRE
SHOFARS
SUFFERS
SURFERS
THEFIRM
TITFERS
TWOFERS
UNIFORM
WARFARE
WELFARE
WILFORD
WOOFERS
ZAFFERS

•••F••R

ACTFOUR
BAFFLER
BALFOUR
BEEFIER
BIDFAIR
BLUFFER
COMFIER
CRAFTER
CROFTER
DAFFIER
DRIFTER
FEIFFER
FUNFAIR
GOAFTER
GOOFIER
GRIFTER
GRUFFER
HUFFIER
LEAFIER
MAYFAIR
MIFFIER
MUFFLER
PROFFER
PUFFIER
QUAFFER
RAFFLER
SCOFFER
SHAFFER
SNIFFER
SNIFTER
SNUFFER
STAFFER
STIFFER
STUFFER
SURFIER
SWIFTER
TENFOUR
TOFFLER
TRIFLER
TURFIER
TURFWAR
UNIFIER
WAFFLER

••••FR•

DEEPFRY
FISHFRY
STIRFRY

••••F•R

AIMSFOR
AQUIFER
ASKSFOR
BLUFFER
BRIEFER
CALLFOR
CAREFOR
CHAMFER
CONIFER
DONEFOR
FAKEFUR
FALLFOR
FEELFOR
FEIFFER
FELLFOR
FELTFOR
GOESFOR
GOINFOR
GRUFFER
GUNSFOR
INSOFAR
LAIDFOR
LAYSFOR
LOOKFOR
LUCIFER
MADEFOR
MAKEFOR
OPTSFOR
PAIDFOR
PASSFOR
PAYSFOR
PINEFOR
PRAYFOR
PROFFER
PROOFER
PULLFOR
QUAFFER
ROOTFOR
ROTIFER
RUNSFOR
SCOFFER
SELLFOR
SENDFOR
SENTFOR
SHAFFER
SHOTFOR
SNIFFER
SNUFFER
SPOOFER
STAFFER
STIFFER
STUFFER
THUSFAR
VOTEFOR
WAITFOR
WENTFOR
WHATFOR
WORKFOR

F•S••••

FASCIAS
FASHION
FASTENS
FASTEST
FASTING
FASTONE
FESCUES
FESSING
FESTERS
FESTIVA
FESTIVE
FESTOON
FISCHER
FISHERS
FISHERY
FISHEYE
FISHFRY
FISHIER
FISHILY
FISHING
FISHNET
FISHOUT
FISSILE
FISSION
FISSURE
FISTFUL
FOSDICK
FOSSILS
FOSTERS
FUSSIER
FUSSILY
FUSSING
FUSSPOT
FUSTIAN
FUSTICS
FUSTIER
FUSTILY

F••S•••

FALSELY
FALSEST
FALSIFY
FALSITY
FANSOUT
FAUSTUS
FEASTED
FESSING
FIASCOS
FIESTAS
FIRSTLY
FISSILE
FISSION
FISSURE
FLASHED
FLASHER
FLASHES
FLESHED
FLESHES
FLESHLY
FLOSSED
FLOSSES
FLUSHED
FLUSHES
FLUSTER
FOBSOFF
FOCSLES
FOISTED
FORSAKE
FORSALE
FORSOOK
FORSTER
FORSURE
FORSYTH
FOSSILS
FRASIER
FRESCOS
FRESHEN
FRESHER
FRESHET
FRESHLY
FRISBEE
FRISIAN
FRISKED
FRISSON
FROSTED
FUBSIER
FULSOME
FURSEAL
FUSSIER
FUSSILY
FUSSING
FUSSPOT

F•••S••

FADESIN
FAIRSUP
FALLSIN
FALLSON
FALLSTO
FEEDSON
FICUSES
FILLSIN
FILLSUP
FINESSE
FIRESUP
FIRMSUP
FIXESUP
FLENSED
FLENSES
FLIESAT
FLIESIN
FLOSSED
FLOSSES
FLOTSAM
FOCUSED
FOCUSES
FOLDSUP
FOOTSIE
FORESAW
FORESEE
FORESTS
FOULSUP
FRAISES
FREESIA
FRETSAW
FRISSON
FROWSTY
FUCHSIA

F••••S•

FADDISH
FADDISM
FADDIST
FAIREST
FAIRISH
FALSEST
FANTASY
FAREAST
FARWEST
FASTEST
FATLESS
FATNESS
FATTEST
FATTISH
FAUVISM
FAUVIST
FEELESS
FINESSE
FINNISH
FIRMEST
FITNESS
FITTEST
FLEMISH
FLORIST
FLUTIST
FLYCAST
FLYFISH
FLYLESS
FLYPAST
FOGLESS
FOGYISH
FOGYISM
FOLKISH
FONDEST
FOOLISH
FOPPISH
FORMOSA
FORREST
FOULEST
FOXIEST
FUJITSU
FULLEST
FUMIEST
FUNFEST
FURBISH
FURLESS
FURNISH

F•••••S

FABARES
FABLERS
FABRICS
FACADES
FACIALS
FACINGS
FACTORS
FADEINS
FAERIES
FAGENDS
FAIRIES
FAJITAS
FALCONS
FALLOWS
FALTERS
FAMINES
FAMULUS
FANCIES
FANIONS
FANJETS
FANOUTS
FARMERS
FARROWS
FASCIAS
FASTENS
FATCATS
FATHERS
FATHOMS
FATLESS
FATNESS
FATTENS
FATUOUS
FAUCETS
FAUSTUS
FAUXPAS
FAVOURS
FAWNERS
FEARERS
FEDORAS
FEEDERS
FEELERS
FEELESS
FELINES
FELLAHS
FELLERS
FELLIES
FELLOWS
FEMALES
FENCERS
FENDERS
FENIANS
FERRETS
FERRIES
FERROUS
FERULES
FERVORS
FESCUES
FESTERS
FETCHES
FETTERS
FETTLES
FIACRES
FIANCES
FIASCOS
FIBBERS
FIBRILS
FIBRINS
FIBROUS
FIBULAS
FICUSES
FIDDLES
FIDELIS
FIDGETS
FIENNES
FIESTAS
FIFTIES
FIGURES
FIJIANS
FILCHES
FILENES
FILINGS
FILLERS
FILLETS
FILLIES
FILLINS
FILLIPS
FILLUPS
FILTERS
FINALES
FINCHES
FINDERS
FINGERS
FINIALS
FIPPLES
FIRINGS
FIRKINS
FISHERS
FITCHES
FITNESS
FITTERS
FIXATES
FIXINGS
FIZGIGS
FIZZLES
FLACONS
FLAGONS
FLAKERS
FLAMBES
FLANGES
FLASHES

FLAUNTS
FLAVORS
FLECHES
FLEDGES
FLEECES
FLENSES
FLESHES
FLEXORS
FLIGHTS
FLIPUPS
FLORETS
FLORINS
FLOSSES
FLOWERS
FLUSHES
FLYBOYS
FLYLESS
FLYNETS
FLYRODS
FLYWAYS
FOCSLES
FOCUSES
FODDERS
FOGBOWS
FOGGERS
FOGLESS
FOIBLES
FOLDERS
FOLDUPS
FOLGERS
FOLKIES
FOLLIES
FOLLOWS
FOMENTS
FONDLES
FONDUES
FOODIES
FOOTERS
FOOZLES
FORAGES
FORBIDS
FORCEPS
FORCERS
FORESTS
FORGERS
FORGETS
FORGOES
FORINTS
FORKERS
FORMALS
FORMATS
FORTIES
FORTIUS
FOSSILS
FOSTERS
FOULUPS
FOURTHS
FOWLERS
FRAISES
FRANCES
FRANCIS
FRAPPES
FREEZES
FRESCOS
FRIDAYS
FRIDGES
FRIENDS
FRIEZES
FRIGHTS
FRINGES
FRIZZES
FROLICS
FRYPANS
FUDDLES
FUELERS
FULFILS
FUMBLES
FUNGOES
FUNNELS
FUNNIES
FURIOUS
FURLESS
FURORES
FURROWS
FUSTICS
FUTURES

•FS••••
IFSTONE
OFSORTS

•F•S•••
OFASORT
OFFSETS
OFFSIDE
OFFSITE

•F••S••
EFFUSED
EFFUSES

•F•••S•
IFFIEST
OFFBASE
OFFENSE

•F••••S
AFFAIRS
AFFECTS
AFFINES
AFFIRMS
AFFIXES
AFFORDS
AFFRAYS
AFGHANS
AFRAMES
AFREETS
EFFACES
EFFECTS
EFFORTS
EFFUSES
OFFENDS
OFFICES
OFFSETS
OFSORTS

••FS•••
OFFSETS
OFFSIDE
OFFSITE

••F•S••
DEFUSED
DEFUSES
EFFUSED
EFFUSES
INFESTS
INFUSED
INFUSES
LIFTSUP
REFUSAL
REFUSED
REFUSER
REFUSES

••F••S•
ALFONSO
DAFTEST
DEFENSE
DEFROST
DEFTEST
DIFFUSE
HUFFISH
IFFIEST
LEFTIST
OFFBASE
OFFENSE
RAFFISH
REFRESH
SOFTEST
SOFTISH
SUFFUSE

••F•••S
AFFAIRS
AFFECTS
AFFINES
AFFIRMS
AFFIXES
AFFORDS
AFFRAYS
ASFARAS
BAFFLES
BEFALLS
BEFOULS
BOFFINS
BUFFERS
BUFFETS
CAFTANS
COFFEES
COFFERS
DEFACES
DEFAMES
DEFEATS
DEFECTS
DEFENDS
DEFILES
DEFINES
DEFORMS
DEFRAYS
DEFUSES
DIFFERS
DUFFELS
DUFFERS
EFFACES
EFFECTS
EFFORTS
EFFUSES
ENFOLDS
FIFTIES
GAFFERS
GUFFAWS
INFANTS
INFECTS
INFESTS
INFLOWS
INFOCUS
INFORMS
INFUSES
JEFFERS
JIFFIES
KAFFIRS
KAFTANS
LEFTIES
LIFTERS
MUFFINS
MUFFLES
OFFENDS
OFFICES
OFFSETS
OXFORDS
PIFFLES
PUFFERS
PUFFINS
RAFFLES
RAFTERS
REFACES
REFILES
REFILLS
REFILMS
REFINES
REFIRES
REFLAGS
REFOCUS
REFORMS
REFRIES
REFUELS
REFUGES
REFUNDS
REFUSES
REFUTES
RIFFLES
RIFLERS
RUFFLES
SAFARIS
SIFTERS
SOFFITS
SOFTENS
SOFTIES
SUFFERS
TAFFIES
TIFFINS
TOFFEES
TUFFETS
UNFOLDS
UNFURLS
WAFFLES
ZAFFERS

•••FS••
BEEFSUP
GOOFSUP
HOOFSIT

•••F•S•
BELFAST
CATFISH
CODFISH
CONFESS
CONFUSE
CRAFTSY
DEAFEST
DIFFUSE
DOGFISH
FLYFISH
FUNFEST
GABFEST
HUFFISH
PANFISH
PROFESS
PROFUSE
RAFFISH
SAWFISH
SELFISH
SUFFUSE
SUNFISH
WOLFISH

•••F••S
ARMFULS
BAFFLES
BAGFULS
BOFFINS
BOWFINS
BOXFULS
BUFFERS
BUFFETS
CANFULS
CAPFULS
CARFULS
COFFEES
COFFERS
COMFITS
CONFABS
CONFERS
CONFESS
CUPFULS
CURFEWS
DEAFENS
DEIFIES
DIFFERS
DUFFELS
DUFFERS
EARFULS
EDIFIES
EYEFULS
FULFILS
GAFFERS
GOLFERS
GOOFUPS
GUFFAWS
HEIFERS
HOOFERS
ICEFOGS
JARFULS
JEFFERS
JIFFIES
JUGFULS
KAFFIRS
LAPFULS
LOAFERS
LOOFAHS
MISFITS
MUFFINS
MUFFLES
OLEFINS
OUTFITS
PANFULS
PIFFLES
PILFERS
POTFULS
PREFABS
PREFERS
PROFESS
PROFITS
PUFFERS
PUFFINS
PURFLES
RAFFLES
REDFINS
REDFIRS
REEFERS
REIFIES
RIFFLES
ROOFERS
RUFFLES
SEAFANS
SHOFARS
SOFFITS
STIFLES
SUFFERS
SURFERS
TAFFIES
TIFFINS
TITFERS
TOFFEES
TRIFLES
TUFFETS
TWOFERS
UNIFIES
VATFULS
WAFFLES
WOOFERS
ZAFFERS

••••F•S
CARAFES
CUTOFFS
DREYFUS
LAYOFFS
PAYOFFS
POPOFFS
REBUFFS
RIPOFFS
RUNOFFS
SCRUFFS
SENUFOS
SHRIFTS
STRAFES
TARIFFS
THRIFTS
TIPOFFS
UPLIFTS

•••••FS
BELIEFS
CUTOFFS
ENGULFS
LAYOFFS
MASSIFS
PAYOFFS
POPOFFS
REBUFFS
RELIEFS
RIPOFFS
RUNOFFS
SCRUFFS
TARIFFS
TIPOFFS

F•T••••
FATBACK
FATCATS
FATCITY
FATEFUL
FATHEAD
FATHERS
FATHOMS
FATIGUE
FATLESS
FATLIKE
FATNESS
FATTENS
FATTEST
FATTIER
FATTILY
FATTISH
FATUITY
FATUOUS
FETCHED
FETCHES
FETIDLY
FETLOCK
FETTERS
FETTLES
FITCHES
FITNESS
FITTERS
FITTEST
FITTING
FUTURES
FUTZING

F••T•••
FACTFUL
FACTION
FACTOID
FACTORS
FACTORY
FACTUAL
FALTERS
FANTAIL
FANTASY
FARTHER
FASTENS
FASTEST
FASTING
FASTONE
FATTENS
FATTEST
FATTIER
FATTILY
FATTISH
FEATHER
FEATURE
FELTFOR
FELTOUT
FERTILE
FESTERS
FESTIVA
FESTIVE
FESTOON
FETTERS
FETTLES
FIATLUX
FICTION
FICTIVE
FIFTEEN
FIFTHLY
FIFTIES
FILTERS
FISTFUL
FITTERS
FITTEST
FITTING
FIXTURE
FLATBED
FLATCAR
FLATLET
FLATOUT
FLATTAX
FLATTED
FLATTEN
FLATTER
FLATTOP
FLITTED
FLITTER
FLOTSAM
FLUTIER
FLUTING
FLUTIST
FLUTTER
FLYTRAP
FONTEYN
FONTINA
FOOTAGE
FOOTERS
FOOTING
FOOTMAN
FOOTMEN
FOOTPAD
FOOTSIE
FOOTWAY
FORTIES
FORTIFY
FORTIUS
FORTRAN
FORTUNA
FORTUNE
FOSTERS
FOXTAIL
FOXTROT
FRETFUL
FRETSAW
FRETTED
FRITTED
FRITTER
FROTHED
FURTHER
FURTIVE
FUSTIAN
FUSTICS
FUSTIER
FUSTILY

F•••T••
FACETED
FAGOTED
FAINTED
FAINTER
FAINTLY
FAJITAS
FANATIC
FAULTED
FAUSTUS
FEASTED
FEINTED
FIESTAS
FIGHTER
FIRSTLY
FIXATED
FIXATES
FLATTAX
FLATTED
FLATTEN
FLATTER
FLATTOP
FLEETER
FLEETLY
FLIRTED
FLITTED
FLITTER
FLOATED
FLOATER
FLOUTED
FLUSTER
FLUTTER
FOISTED
FORSTER
FOULTIP
FOURTHS
FRACTAL
FRANTIC
FRETTED
FRITTED
FRITTER
FRONTAL
FRONTED
FRONTON
FROSTED
FRUITED
FUJITSU

F••••T•
FACULTY
FALLSTO
FALSITY
FANJETS
FANOUTS
FATCATS
FATCITY
FATUITY
FAUCETS
FAWCETT
FERRATE
FERRETS
FERRITE
FIDGETS
FIDGETY
FILLETS
FLAUNTS
FLAUNTY
FLIGHTS
FLIGHTY
FLOCKTO
FLORETS
FLYNETS
FOLIATE
FOLLETT
FOMENTS
FORESTS
FORGETS
FORINTS
FORMATS
FORSYTH
FRAILTY
FRIGATE
FRIGHTS
FROWSTY

F•••••T
FADDIST
FADEOUT
FAIREST
FALLOUT
FALSEST
FANBELT
FANSOUT
FAREAST
FARLEFT
FARMOUT
FARWEST
FASTEST
FATTEST
FAUVIST
FAWCETT
FEEDLOT
FEELOUT
FELLOUT
FELTOUT
FERMENT
FERVENT
FIGMENT
FILBERT
FILLOUT
FINDOUT
FINEART
FIREANT
FIRELIT
FIRMEST
FISHNET
FISHOUT
FITTEST
FLATLET
FLATOUT
FLEAPIT
FLIESAT
FLIPOUT
FLORIST
FLORUIT
FLOWNAT
FLUTIST
FLYCAST
FLYPAST
FOLDOUT
FOLKART
FOLLETT
FONDANT
FONDEST
FORFEIT
FORRENT
FORREST
FORWENT
FOULEST
FOULOUT
FOXIEST
FOXTROT
FRAUGHT
FREIGHT
FREMONT
FRESHET
FRIPPET
FROWNAT
FULGENT
FULLEST
FUMIEST
FUNFEST
FUSSPOT

•FT••••
OFTENER

•F•T•••
IFSTONE

•F•••T•
AFFECTS
AFREETS
EFFECTS
EFFORTS
OFFDUTY
OFFSETS
OFFSITE
OFSORTS
SFUMATO

•F••••T
AFFLICT
AFFRONT
IFFIEST
OFASORT
OFFBEAT

••FT•••
CAFTANS
DAFTEST
DEFTEST
FIFTEEN
FIFTHLY
FIFTIES
HAFTING
HEFTIER
HEFTILY
HEFTING
KAFTANS
LEFTIES
LEFTIST
LEFTOFF
LEFTOUT
LIFTERS
LIFTING
LIFTOFF
LIFTSUP
LOFTIER
LOFTILY
LOFTING
NIFTIER
NIFTILY
RAFTERS
RAFTING
RIFTING
SIFTERS
SIFTING
SOFTENS
SOFTEST
SOFTIES
SOFTISH
SOFTTOP
TUFTIER
TUFTING
WAFTING

••F•T••
LAFITTE
REFUTED
REFUTER
REFUTES
SOFTTOP

••F••T•
AFFECTS
BUFFETS
BUFFETT
DEFACTO
DEFEATS
DEFECTS
DEFLATE
EFFECTS
EFFORTS
EXFACTO
GEFILTE
INFANTA
INFANTS
INFECTS
INFESTS
INFLATE
LAFITTE
OFFDUTY
OFFSETS
OFFSITE
REFERTO
SOFFITS
TAFFETA
TUFFETS

••F•••T
AFFLICT
AFFRONT
ATFAULT
BUFFETT
DAFTEST
DEFAULT
DEFIANT
DEFICIT
DEFLECT
DEFROST
DEFTEST
DEFUNCT
GOFORIT
IFFIEST
INFLECT
INFLICT
INFRONT
LEFTIST
LEFTOUT
LIFENET
MRFIXIT
NOFAULT
OFFBEAT
REFLECT
REFRACT
SOFTEST
UPFRONT

•••FT••
BEEFTEA
CLIFTON
CRAFTED
CRAFTER
CRAFTSY
CROFTER
DRAFTED
DRAFTEE
DRIFTED
DRIFTER
GOAFTER
GOLFTEE
GRAFTED
GRAFTON
GRIFTER
ROOFTOP
SHAFTED
SHIFTED
SNIFTER
SWIFTER
SWIFTLY

•••F•T•
BUFFETS
BUFFETT
COMFITS
CONFUTE
HEIFETZ
MISFITS
OUTFITS
PROFITS
SOFFITS
SULFATE
SULFITE
TAFFETA
TUFFETS

•••F••T
BELFAST
BIGFEET
BIGFOOT
BUFFETT
COMFORT
DEAFEST
FORFEIT
FUNFEST
GABFEST
HALFWIT
HOOFSIT
HOTFOOT
LEAFLET
LENFANT
PARFAIT
PERFECT
PREFECT
SNIFFAT
SURFEIT
WEBFEET
WEBFOOT

••••FT•
SHRIFTS
THRIFTS
THRIFTY
TWELFTH
UPLIFTS

••••F•T
BENEFIT
BODYFAT
DEEPFAT
OUTOFIT
SEENFIT
SEESFIT
SNIFFAT

•••••FT
AIRLIFT
ENGRAFT
FARLEFT
HAYLOFT
NEWLEFT
SKILIFT
UPDRAFT

FU•••••
FUBBING
FUBSIER
FUCHSIA
FUDDLED
FUDDLES
FUDGING
FUELERS
FUELING
FUELLED
FUELOIL
FUELROD
FUJITSU
FULCRUM
FULFILL
FULFILS
FULGENT
FULGHUM
FULLEST
FULSOME
FUMBLED
FUMBLER
FUMBLES
FUMIEST
FUNCHAL
FUNDING
FUNFAIR
FUNFEST
FUNGOES
FUNKIER
FUNKILY
FUNKING
FUNNELS
FUNNIER
FUNNIES
FUNNILY
FUNNING
FURBALL
FURBISH
FURIOUS
FURLESS
FURLING
FURLONG
FURNACE
FURNISH
FURORES
FURRIER
FURRING
FURROWS
FURSEAL
FURTHER
FURTIVE
FUSSIER
FUSSILY
FUSSING
FUSSPOT
FUSTIAN
FUSTICS
FUSTIER
FUSTILY
FUTURES
FUTZING
FUZZIER
FUZZILY
FUZZING

F•U••••
FAUCETS
FAULTED
FAUSTUS
FAUVISM
FAUVIST
FAUXPAS
FEUDING
FLUBBED
FLUBBER
FLUENCY
FLUFFED
FLUIDLY
FLUKIER
FLUMMOX
FLUNKED
FLUSHED
FLUSHES
FLUSTER
FLUTIER
FLUTING
FLUTIST
FLUTTER
FLUVIAL
FLUXING
FNUMBER
FOULARD
FOULEST
FOULING
FOULOUT
FOULSUP
FOULTIP
FOULUPS
FOUNDED
FOUNDER
FOUNDRY
FOURIER
FOURTHS
FOURWAY
FRUITED

F••U•••
FACULAE
FACULTY
FAMULUS
FATUITY
FATUOUS
FELUCCA
FERULES
FIBULAE
FIBULAS
FICUSES
FIGURED
FIGURER
FIGURES
FLAUNTS
FLAUNTY
FLOUNCE
FLOUNCY
FLOURED
FLOUTED
FOCUSED
FOCUSES
FRAUGHT
FUTURES

F•••U••
FACTUAL
FAILURE
FANOUTS

FAVOURS
FEATURE
FERRULE
FESCUES
FILLUPS
FISSURE
FIXTURE
FLIPUPS
FLORUIT
FOLDUPS
FONDUES
FORMULA
FORSURE
FORTUNA
FORTUNE
FOULUPS

F••••U•
FACTFUL
FADEOUT
FAIRSUP
FAKEFUR
FALLGUY
FALLOUT
FAMULUS
FANCLUB
FANSOUT
FARMOUT
FATEFUL
FATIGUE
FATUOUS
FAUSTUS
FEARFUL
FEELOUT
FELLOUT
FELTOUT
FERMIUM
FERROUS
FERVOUR
FIATLUX
FIBROUS
FILLOUT
FILLSUP
FINDOUT
FIREBUG
FIREDUP
FIRESUP
FIRMSUP
FISHOUT
FISTFUL
FIXEDUP
FIXESUP
FLANEUR
FLAREUP
FLATOUT
FLAVOUR
FLIPOUT
FOLDOUT
FOLDSUP
FORERUN
FORKFUL
FORMFUL
FORTIUS
FOULOUT
FOULSUP
FRAMEUP
FRETFUL
FULCRUM
FULGHUM
FURIOUS

F•••••U
FRENEAU
FUJITSU

•FU••••
SFUMATO

•F•U•••
EFFUSED
EFFUSES

•F••U••
OFFDUTY

•F•••U•
OFFHOUR

••FU•••
AWFULLY
DEFUNCT
DEFUSED
DEFUSES
EFFUSED
EFFUSES
INFUSED
INFUSES
REFUELS
REFUGEE
REFUGES
REFUNDS
REFUSAL
REFUSED
REFUSER
REFUSES
REFUTED
REFUTER
REFUTES
UNFURLS

••F•U••
ATFAULT
BEFOULS
DEFAULT
DIFFUSE
NOFAULT
OFFDUTY
SUFFUSE

••F••U•
DEFRAUD
HAFNIUM
INFOCUS
LEFTOUT
LIFEFUL
LIFTSUP
OFFHOUR
REFOCUS

••F•••U
HOFBRAU

•••FU••
ARAFURA
ARMFULS
BAGFULS
BOXFULS
CANFULS
CAPFULS
CARFULS
CONFUSE
CONFUTE
CUPFULS
DIFFUSE
EARFULS
EYEFULS
GOOFUPS
JARFULS
JUGFULS
LAPFULS
PANFULS
PERFUME
POTFULS
PROFUSE
SNAFUED
SUFFUSE
SYNFUEL
VATFULS

•••F•U•
ACTFOUR
BALFOUR
BEEFSUP
GOOFSUP
TENFOUR

••••FU•
BALEFUL
BANEFUL
BASHFUL
BOWLFUL
BRIMFUL
CAREFUL
DAREFUL
DIREFUL
DISHFUL
DOLEFUL
DOOMFUL
DREYFUS
DUTIFUL
EASEFUL
FACTFUL
FAKEFUR
FATEFUL
FEARFUL
FISTFUL
FORKFUL
FORMFUL
FRETFUL
GAINFUL
GLEEFUL
HANDFUL
HARMFUL
HATEFUL
HEATFUL
HEEDFUL
HELPFUL
HOPEFUL
HURTFUL
HUSHFUL
LIFEFUL
LUSTFUL
MINDFUL
MOANFUL
MUSEFUL
NEEDFUL
ODORFUL
PAGEFUL
PAILFUL
PAINFUL
PIPEFUL
PITIFUL
PLAYFUL
PLOTFUL
POKEFUN
POUTFUL
PUSHFUL
RAGEFUL
RESTFUL
ROOMFUL
RUTHFUL
SACKFUL
SHOPFUL
SIGHFUL
SKILFUL
SKINFUL
SONGFUL
SOULFUL
TACTFUL
TANKFUL
TEARFUL
TOILFUL
TRAYFUL
TUNEFUL
UNAWFUL
WAILFUL
WAKEFUL
WILLFUL
WISHFUL
WISTFUL
YAWNFUL
ZESTFUL

F•V••••
FAVORED
FAVOURS

F••V•••
FAUVISM
FAUVIST
FERVENT
FERVORS
FERVOUR
FLAVORS
FLAVOUR
FLIVVER
FLUVIAL

F•••V••
FLIVVER
FLYOVER
FOREVER

F••••V•
FESTIVA
FESTIVE
FICTIVE
FORGAVE
FORGIVE
FURTIVE

••F•V••
INFAVOR

•••F•V•
ACTFIVE

F•W••••
FAWCETT
FAWNERS
FAWNING
FOWLERS
FOWLING

F••W•••
FALWELL
FARWEST
FAYWRAY
FLAWING
FLOWERS
FLOWERY
FLOWING
FLOWNAT
FLOWNIN
FLYWAYS
FORWARD
FORWENT
FRAWLEY
FROWARD
FROWNAT
FROWNED
FROWNER
FROWSTY

F•••W••
FAIRWAY
FARAWAY
FLYAWAY
FOLKWAY
FOODWEB
FOOTWAY
FOURWAY
FREEWAY

F••••W•
FALLOWS
FARROWS
FELLOWS
FOGBOWS
FOLLOWS
FURROWS

F•••••W
FOREPAW
FORESAW
FRETSAW

••F••W•
GUFFAWS
INFLOWS

•••FW••
HALFWAY
HALFWIT
TURFWAR

•••F•W•
CURFEWS
GUFFAWS
PEAFOWL

•••F••W
AIRFLOW
ASOFNOW
OUTFLOW

F•X••••
FIXABLE
FIXATED
FIXATES
FIXEDLY
FIXEDUP
FIXESUP
FIXINGS
FIXTURE
FOXFIRE
FOXHOLE
FOXIEST
FOXLIKE
FOXTAIL
FOXTROT

F••X•••
FAUXPAS
FLAXIER
FLEXING
FLEXNER
FLEXORS
FLUXING

F•••••X
FIATLUX
FIREBOX
FLATTAX
FLUMMOX

•F••X••
AFFIXED
AFFIXES

••F•X••
AFFIXED
AFFIXES
MRFIXIT
UNFIXED

•••F••X
REAFFIX

••••F•X
BLUEFOX
BRERFOX
HALIFAX
REAFFIX

F•Y••••
FAYWRAY
FEYNMAN
FLYAWAY
FLYBALL
FLYBOYS
FLYCAST
FLYFISH
FLYHIGH
FLYLEAF
FLYLESS
FLYNETS
FLYOVER
FLYPAST
FLYRODS
FLYTRAP
FLYWAYS
FRYCOOK
FRYPANS

F••Y•••
FLAYING
FLEYING
FOGYISH
FOGYISM
FRAYING

F•••Y••
FORSYTH

F••••Y•
FISHEYE
FLYBOYS
FLYWAYS
FONTEYN
FRIDAYS

F•••••Y
FACTORY
FACULTY
FAINTLY
FAIRWAY
FALLACY
FALLGUY
FALSELY
FALSIFY
FALSITY
FANCIFY
FANCILY
FANTASY
FARADAY
FARAWAY
FARMERY
FATCITY
FATTILY
FATUITY
FAYWRAY
FETIDLY
FIDGETY
FIERILY
FIFTHLY
FINALLY
FINICKY
FIREFLY
FIRSTLY
FISHERY
FISHFRY
FISHILY
FIXEDLY
FLAGDAY
FLAKILY
FLAUNTY
FLEETLY
FLESHLY
FLIGHTY
FLOUNCY
FLOWERY
FLUENCY
FLUIDLY
FLYAWAY
FOAMILY
FOGGILY
FOLKWAY
FOOLERY
FOOTWAY
FOPPERY
FORGERY
FORTIFY
FOUNDRY
FOURWAY
FRAILLY
FRAILTY
FRANKLY
FRAWLEY
FRECKLY
FREEWAY
FRESHLY
FRIZZLY
FROWSTY
FUNKILY
FUNNILY
FUSSILY
FUSTILY
FUZZILY

•F•Y•••
OFFYEAR

•F•••Y•
AFFRAYS

•F••••Y
AFFABLY
OFFDUTY

••FY•••
DEFYING
OFFYEAR

••F•Y••
RUFIYAA

••F••Y•
AFFRAYS
DEFRAYS

••F•••Y
AFFABLY
AWFULLY
DAFFILY
FIFTHLY
HEFTILY
HUFFILY
INFANCY
JEFFREY
JOFFREY
LOFTILY
NIFTILY
OFFDUTY
PUFFERY
PUFFILY
RIFLERY
TIFFANY

•••F••Y
BLUFFLY
COMFREY
CRAFTSY
DAFFILY
GODFREY
GOOFILY
GRIFFEY
GRUFFLY
HALFWAY
HUFFILY
JEFFREY
JOFFREY
OLDFOGY
PALFREY
PERFIDY
PUFFERY
PUFFILY
SNIFFLY
SNUFFLY
STIFFLY
SWIFTLY
TIFFANY
WINFREY

••••F•Y
ALOOFLY
BLOWFLY
BLUFFLY
BRIEFLY
CHIEFLY
DEEPFRY
DEERFLY
FIREFLY
FISHFRY
GRIFFEY
GRUFFLY
LETSFLY
OVERFLY
SANDFLY
SCRUFFY
SHOOFLY
SNIFFLY
SNUFFLY
STIFFLY
STIRFRY
TESTFLY
THRIFTY

•••••FY
ACIDIFY
AMPLIFY
BEATIFY
CALCIFY
CERTIFY
CLARIFY
CRUCIFY
DANDIFY
DIGNIFY
DULCIFY
FALSIFY
FANCIFY
FORTIFY
GLORIFY
GRATIFY
HORRIFY
JOLLIFY
JUSTIFY
LIQUEFY
MAGNIFY
MOLLIFY
MORTIFY
MYSTIFY
NULLIFY
PETRIFY
QUALIFY
RECTIFY
REUNIFY
SALSIFY
SATISFY
SCARIFY
SCRUFFY
SIGNIFY
SPECIFY
STUPEFY
TERRIFY
TESTIFY
VERSIFY
VITRIFY
ZOMBIFY

F•Z••••
FIZGIGS
FIZZIER
FIZZING
FIZZLED
FIZZLES
FUZZIER
FUZZILY
FUZZING

F••Z•••
FANZINE
FIZZIER
FIZZING
FIZZLED
FIZZLES
FOOZLED
FOOZLES
FRAZIER
FRAZZLE
FRIZZED
FRIZZES
FRIZZLE
FRIZZLY
FUTZING
FUZZIER
FUZZILY
FUZZING

F•••Z••
FRAZZLE
FREEZER
FREEZES
FRIEZES
FRIZZED
FRIZZES
FRIZZLE
FRIZZLY

F••••Z•
FIRENZE

F•••••Z
FRANKOZ

••F•Z••
UNFAZED

•••F•Z•
GINFIZZ

•••F••Z
GINFIZZ
HEIFETZ
THEFONZ

GA•••••
GABBERS
GABBIER
GABBING
GABBLED
GABBLES
GABBROS
GABFEST
GABRIEL
GADDERS
GADDING
GADGETS
GADGETY
GADSDEN
GAFFERS
GAFFING
GAGARIN
GAGGING
GAGGLES
GAGLAWS
GAGLINE
GAGRULE
GAGSTER
GAINERS
GAINFUL
GAINING
GAINSAY
GAINSON
GAITERS
GAITING
GALAGOS
GALAHAD
GALATEA
GALATIA
GALILEE
GALILEI
GALILEO
GALLANT
GALLEON
GALLERY
GALLEYS
GALLING
GALLIUM
GALLONS
GALLOPS
GALOOTS
GALPALS
GALUMPH
GALVANI
GAMBADO
GAMBIAN
GAMBITS
GAMBLED
GAMBLER
GAMBLES
GAMBOLS
GAMBREL
GAMELAW
GAMETES
GAMIEST
GAMINES
GAMMERS
GAMMIER
GAMMING
GAMMONS
GANDERS
GANGERS
GANGING
GANGLED
GANGLIA
GANGSAW
GANGSTA
GANGSUP
GANGTOK
GANGWAY
GANNETS
GANNETT
GANTLET
GAOLERS
GAOLING
GAPLESS
GAPPING
GARAGED
GARAGES
GARBAGE
GARBING
GARBLED
GARBLES
GARCONS
GARDENS
GARDNER
GARGLED
GARGLES
GARLAND
GARMENT
GARNERS
GARNETS
GARNISH
GARONNE
GARRETS
GARRETT
GARRICK
GARTERS
GASBAGS
GASCAPS
GASCONS
GASCONY
GASEOUS
GASHING
GASJETS
GASKETS
GASKINS
GASLESS
GASLOGS
GASMAIN
GASOHOL
GASPERS
GASPING
GASPUMP
GASSERS
GASSIER
GASTRIC
GATEAUX
GATELEG
GATEMAN
GATEMEN
GATEWAY
GATHERS
GATLING
GAUCHER
GAUCHOS
GAUDIER
GAUDILY
GAUGERS
GAUGING
GAUGUIN
GAULISH
GAUMING
GAUNTER
GAUNTLY
GAUTAMA
GAUZIER
GAUZILY
GAVELED
GAVEOFF
GAVEOUT
GAVEWAY
GAVIALS
GAVOTTE
GAWKERS
GAWKIER
GAWKILY
GAWKING
GAWKISH
GAWPING
GAZEBOS
GAZELLE
GAZETTE
GAZUMPS

G•A••••
GEARBOX
GEARING
GEARSTO
GEARSUP
GHANIAN
GHASTLY
GIACOMO
GLACEED
GLACIAL
GLACIER
GLADDEN
GLADDER
GLADEYE
GLAIRED
GLAMOUR
GLANCED
GLANCES
GLARING
GLASGOW
GLASSED
GLASSES
GLAZERS
GLAZIER
GLAZING
GNARLED
GNARRED
GNASHED
GNASHES
GNAWERS
GNAWING
GOABOUT
GOADING
GOAFTER
GOAHEAD
GOALIES
GOALONG
GOATEED
GOATEES
GOATISH
GRABBAG
GRABBED
GRABBER
GRABSAT
GRACIAS
GRACILE
GRACING
GRACKLE
GRADERS
GRADING
GRADUAL
GRAFTED
GRAFTON
GRAHAME
GRAHAMS
GRAINED
GRAMMAR
GRAMMER
GRAMMES
GRAMMYS
GRAMPAS
GRAMPUS
GRANADA
GRANARY
GRANDAM
GRANDEE
GRANDER
GRANDLY
GRANDMA
GRANDPA
GRANGER
GRANGES
GRANITE
GRANOLA
GRANTED
GRANTEE
GRANTOR
GRANULE
GRAPHED
GRAPHIC
GRAPIER
GRAPNEL
GRAPPAS
GRAPPLE
GRASPED
GRASSED
GRASSES
GRATERS
GRATIAS
GRATIFY
GRATING
GRAVELS
GRAVELY
GRAVERS
GRAVEST
GRAVIES
GRAVING
GRAVITY
GRAVURE
GRAYEST
GRAYING
GRAYISH
GRAYJAY
GRAYLAG
GRAYSON
GRAZERS
GRAZING
GUANACO
GUANINE
GUARANI
GUARDED
GUARDEE
GUARGUM

G••A•••
GAGARIN
GALAGOS
GALAHAD
GALATEA
GALATIA
GARAGED
GARAGES
GELADAS
GELATIN
GELATIS
GERAINT
GERALDO
GETAWAY
GIRAFFE
GIRASOL
GLEAMED
GLEANED
GLEANER
GLEASON
GLOATED
GOCARTS
GOKARTS
GOTAWAY
GOUACHE
GREASED
GREASER
GREASES
GREATER
GREATLY
GREAVES
GROANED
GROANER
GYRATED
GYRATES
GYRATOR

G•••A••
GAGLAWS
GALLANT
GALPALS
GALVANI
GAMBADO
GARBAGE
GARLAND
GASBAGS
GASCAPS
GASMAIN
GATEAUX
GAUTAMA
GAVIALS
GEEGAWS
GENNARO
GERMANE
GERMANS
GERMANY
GESTALT
GESTATE
GETBACK
GEWGAWS
GIMBALS
GIZZARD
GODDARD
GOESAPE
GOLIATH
GOODALL
GOSHAWK
GOTBACK
GOTLAND
GOULASH
GOURAMI
GRAHAME
GRAHAMS
GRANADA

GRANARY
GRENADA
GRENADE
GRIMACE
GUANACO
GUARANI
GUEVARA
GUFFAWS
GUITARS
GULLAHS
GUMBALL
GUNWALE
GYMBAGS
GYMNAST

G••••A•
GAINSAY
GALAHAD
GAMBIAN
GAMELAW
GANGSAW
GANGWAY
GATEMAN
GATEWAY
GAVEWAY
GEISHAS
GELADAS
GENERAL
GENTIAN
GETAWAY
GETREAL
GHANIAN
GIDDYAP
GILBLAS
GILLIAN
GINGHAM
GIVEWAY
GLACIAL
GLORIAM
GLORIAS
GLOSSAE
GLOTTAL
GOAHEAD
GODTHAB
GOESBAD
GOINGAT
GOODBAR
GOODMAN
GORDIAN
GOTAWAY
GOTCHAS
GRABBAG
GRABSAT
GRACIAS
GRADUAL
GRAMMAR
GRAMPAS
GRANDAM
GRAPPAS
GRATIAS
GRAYJAY
GRAYLAG
GRECIAN
GRISHAM
GUINEAS
GUNBOAT
GUNPLAY
GURKHAS

G•••••A
GALATEA
GALATIA
GANGLIA
GANGSTA
GAUTAMA
GEORGIA
GINGIVA
GONDOLA
GORILLA
GRANADA
GRANDMA
GRANDPA
GRANOLA
GRENADA
GUEVARA

•GA••••
AGAINST
AGAKHAN
AGARICS
AGASSIZ
EGALITE
UGANDAN

•G•A•••
AGNATES
AGRAFFE
IGUANAS
OGLALAS

•G••A••
AGESAGO
AGITATE
AGITATO
EGGCASE
OGDOADS

•G•••A•
AGAKHAN
AGENDAS
EGGHEAD
IGUANAS
OGLALAS
UGANDAN

•G••••A
AGRIPPA

••GA•••
BUGABOO
BUGALOO
DEGAUSS
ENGAGED
ENGAGES
ENGARDE
ERGATES
GAGARIN
HOGARTH
INGALLS
LEGALLY
LEGATEE
LEGATES
LEGATOS
LIGANDS
LIGATED
LIGATES
MCGAVIN
MEGAHIT
MOGAMBO
NEGATED
NEGATER
NEGATES
NEGATOR
NOGALES
ORGANDY
ORGANIC
ORGANON
ORGANUM
ORGANZA
ORGATES
PEGASUS
REGAINS
REGALED
REGALES
REGALIA
REGALLY
REGARDS
REGATTA
ROGAINE
SUGARED
TAGALOG

••G•A••
AFGHANI
AFGHANS
BAGGAGE
BEGGARS
BIGBAND
BIGBANG
BIGGAME
BIGNAME
BIGTALK
COGNACS
COGNATE
DEGRADE
DIGRAMS
DIGRAPH
DOGBANE
DOGCART
DOGDAYS
DOGEARS
DOGFACE
DOGMATA
DOGTAGS
EGGCASE
ENGLAND
ENGRAFT
ENGRAMS
ENGRAVE
FOGBANK
GAGLAWS
HAGGARD
HOGBACK
HOGWASH
INGRAIN
INGRATE
JAGUARS
JIGSAWS
JUGBAND
LAGGARD
LEGRAND
LOGJAMS
LUGGAGE
MAGNANI
MAGNATE
MAGYARS
MIGRANT
MIGRATE
NIGGARD
ONGUARD
ORGEATS
PAGEANT
PIGTAIL
RAGBAGS
RAGLANS
REGNANT
REGRADE
SAGUARO
SIGNALS
TAGGANT
TAGSALE
UPGRADE
USGRANT
VAGRANT
WAGTAIL
WIGWAGS
WIGWAMS
ZIGZAGS

••G••A•
ANGOLAN
ANGORAS
ANGULAR
AUGURAL
BAGHDAD
BIGDEAL
BIGHEAD
BUGBEAR
DIGITAL
DOGSTAR
EGGHEAD
EIGHTAM
FIGLEAF
HEGIRAS
HIGHDAY
HIGHHAT
HIGHWAY
INGEMAR
JUGHEAD
JUGULAR
LAGUNAS
LOGGIAS
LOGICAL
MAGICAL
MEGRYAN
PAGODAS
REGULAR
SAGINAW
TAGTEAM
TUGBOAT
VEGETAL

••G•••A
ALGEBRA
ALGERIA
AUGUSTA
BEGONIA
BEGORRA
DOGMATA
HIGHTEA
HYGIEIA
MAGENTA
NIGERIA
ORGANZA
REGALIA
REGATTA
RIGVEDA
SEGOVIA

•••GA••
ABIGAIL
BAGGAGE
BARGAIN
BEGGARS
BENGALI
BENGALS
BIGGAME
BRIGADE
BRIGAND
BROGANS
BULGARS
CALGARY
CHAGALL
COLGATE
CONGAED
CONGAME
COUGARS
ELEGANT
ENDGAME
FORGAVE
FRIGATE
GEEGAWS
GEWGAWS
HAGGARD
HANGARS
HUNGARY
LAGGARD
LONGAGO
LONGARM
LUGGAGE
MARGATE
MARGAUX
MARGAYS
MORGANA
MORGANS
NEWGATE
NIAGARA
NIGGARD
NOUGATS
OREGANO
ORIGAMI
OURGANG
SEAGATE
SLOGANS
TAGGANT
TONGANS
VULGATE
WARGAME

•••G•A•
ANAGRAM
BELGIAN
BERGMAN
BINGHAM
BRIGHAM
BURGLAR
CONGEAL
DIAGRAM
DINGBAT
DOUGLAS
ELEGIAC
ENIGMAS
EPIGRAM
FLAGDAY
FLAGMAN
FROGMAN
GANGSAW
GANGWAY
GINGHAM
HANGMAN
KINGMAN
KINGRAT
KLUGMAN
LAUGHAT
LINGUAL
LOGGIAS
LOWGEAR
LUNGEAT
MACGRAW
MAUGHAM
PROGRAM
QINGDAO
QUAGGAS
RIDGWAY
SEAGRAM
STIGMAS
STYGIAN
SYNGMAN
TANGRAM
TRIGRAM
URUGUAY
VAUGHAN
VIRGOAN
ZEUGMAS

•••G••A
ARUGULA
GANGLIA
GANGSTA
GINGIVA
MORGANA
NIAGARA
PERGOLA
SANGRIA

••••GA•
AMALGAM
ASSEGAI
BODEGAS
CAYUGAS
COALGAS
DONEGAL
GOINGAT
ILLEGAL
JOHNGAY
MADIGAN
MEDIGAP
NOSEGAY
NYUNGAR
PAANGAS
QUAGGAS
RAREGAS
SENEGAL
STOPGAP
TEARGAS
VINEGAR
WOLFGAL

••••G•A
ANTIGUA
BOLOGNA
GEORGIA
INTEGRA
LASAGNA
MANAGUA

•••••GA
NORIEGA
REDALGA
SYRINGA

G•B••••
GABBERS
GABBIER
GABBING
GABBLED
GABBLES
GABBROS
GABFEST
GABRIEL
GIBBERS
GIBBETS
GIBBING
GIBBONS
GIBBOUS
GIBLETS
GIBLUES
GOBBLED
GOBBLER
GOBBLES
GOBLETS
GOBLINS
GOBROKE

G••B•••
GABBERS
GABBIER
GABBING
GABBLED
GABBLES
GABBROS
GAMBADO
GAMBIAN
GAMBITS
GAMBLED
GAMBLER
GAMBLES
GAMBOLS
GAMBREL
GARBAGE
GARBING
GARBLED
GARBLES
GASBAGS
GERBILS
GETBACK
GIBBERS
GIBBETS
GIBBING
GIBBONS
GIBBOUS
GILBERT
GILBLAS
GIMBALS
GLIBBER
GLOBING
GLOBULE
GOABOUT
GOBBLED
GOBBLER
GOBBLES
GOOBERS
GOTBACK
GRABBAG
GRABBED
GRABBER
GRABSAT
GRUBBED
GUMBALL
GUNBOAT
GYMBAGS

G•••B••
GAZEBOS
GEARBOX
GEMSBOK
GLIBBER
GOESBAD
GOLDBUG
GOODBAR
GOODBYE
GOODBYS
GRABBAG
GRABBED
GRABBER
GRUBBED
GRUMBLE
GRUMBLY

G••••B•
GOINGBY

G•••••B
GODTHAB
GOODJOB

•G••B••
IGNOBLE
IGNOBLY

••GB•••
BIGBAND
BIGBANG
BIGBEND
BIGBIRD
BIGBOYS
BUGBEAR
COGBURN
DOGBANE
DOGBERT
FOGBANK
FOGBOWS
HOGBACK
JUGBAND
LOGBOOK
RAGBAGS
TUGBOAT

••G•B••
ALGEBRA
BUGABOO
HIGHBOY
LEGIBLE
LEGIBLY
PAGEBOY

••G••B•
MOGAMBO

•••GB••
DINGBAT
LONGBOW

••••GB•
GOINGBY
SWINGBY

G•C••••
GECKOES
GOCARTS

G••C•••
GARCONS
GASCAPS
GASCONS
GASCONY
GAUCHER
GAUCHOS
GIACOMO
GLACEED
GLACIAL
GLACIER
GLUCOSE
GNOCCHI
GOTCHAS
GRACIAS
GRACILE
GRACING
GRACKLE
GRECIAN
GROCERS
GROCERY
GULCHES

G•••C••
GLANCED
GLANCES
GNOCCHI
GOUACHE
GROUCHO
GROUCHY

G••••C•
GARRICK
GETBACK
GIMMICK
GODUTCH
GOTBACK
GOTHICS
GRIMACE
GUANACO
GUNLOCK

G•••••C
GASTRIC
GENERIC
GENETIC
GNOSTIC
GRAPHIC

•G•C•••
EGGCASE
EGGCUPS

•G•••C•
AGARICS

••GC•••
DOGCART
DOGCHOW
EGGCASE
EGGCUPS

••G•C••
LOGICAL
MAGICAL
NOGUCHI

••G••C•
COGENCY
COGNACS
DOGFACE
ELGRECO
HOGBACK
NEGLECT
REGENCY
URGENCY

••G•••C
ANGELIC
ORGANIC

•••G••C
ELEGIAC

••••G•C
ILLOGIC
PELAGIC
YOUNGMC

G•D••••
GADDERS
GADDING
GADGETS
GADGETY
GADSDEN
GIDDIER
GIDDILY
GIDDYAP
GIDDYUP
GIDEONS
GODDARD
GODDESS
GODFREY
GODLESS
GODLIER
GODLIKE
GODSEND
GODSONS
GODTHAB
GODUNOV
GODUTCH
GODWITS

G••D•••
GADDERS
GADDING
GANDERS
GARDENS
GARDNER
GAUDIER
GAUDILY
GELDING
GENDERS
GEODESY
GETDOWN
GIDDIER
GIDDILY
GIDDYAP
GIDDYUP
GILDERS
GILDING
GIRDERS
GIRDING
GIRDLED
GIRDLES
GLADDEN
GLADDER
GLADEYE
GLIDERS
GLIDING
GOADING
GODDARD
GODDESS
GOLDBUG
GOLDING
GOLDWYN
GONDOLA
GOODALL
GOODBAR
GOODBYE
GOODBYS
GOODEGG
GOODIES
GOODING
GOODISH
GOODJOB
GOODJOE
GOODMAN
GOODMEN
GOODONE
GOODSON
GOODWIN
GORDIAN
GOTDOWN
GRADERS
GRADING
GRADUAL
GRIDDED
GRIDDER
GRIDDLE
GRODIER
GRUDGED
GRUDGES
GUIDING
GUIDONS
GUMDROP
GUNDOGS

G•••D••
GADSDEN
GELADAS
GELIDLY
GEORDIE
GLADDEN
GLADDER
GLUEDON
GOUNDER
GOURDES
GRANDAM
GRANDEE
GRANDER
GRANDLY
GRANDMA
GRANDPA
GRENDEL
GRIDDED
GRIDDER
GRIDDLE
GRINDER
GUARDED
GUARDEE
GUILDER

G••••D•
GAMBADO
GERALDO
GERUNDS
GIRONDE
GRANADA
GRENADA
GRENADE
GROUNDS

G•••••D
GABBLED
GALAHAD
GAMBLED
GANGLED
GARAGED
GARBLED
GARGLED
GARLAND
GAVELED
GENTLED
GHOSTED
GIELGUD
GIFFORD
GIGGLED
GIRDLED
GIZZARD
GLACEED
GLAIRED
GLANCED
GLASSED
GLEAMED
GLEANED
GLINTED
GLITZED
GLOATED
GLOMMED
GLOOMED
GLORIED
GLOSSED
GLUGGED
GLUTTED
GNARLED
GNARRED
GNASHED
GOAHEAD
GOATEED
GOBBLED
GODDARD
GODSEND
GOESBAD
GOGGLED
GOROUND
GOTLAND
GRABBED
GRAFTED
GRAINED
GRANTED
GRAPHED
GRASPED
GRASSED
GREASED
GREENED
GREETED
GRIDDED
GRIEVED
GRILLED
GRINNED
GRIPPED
GRITTED
GROANED
GROOMED
GROOVED
GROSSED
GROUPED
GROUSED
GROUTED
GROWLED
GRUBBED
GRUDGED
GRUMPED
GRUNTED
GUARDED
GUESSED
GUESTED
GURGLED
GUSSIED
GUZZLED
GYRATED

•GD••••
OGDOADS

•G•D•••
AGENDAS
EGGEDON
UGANDAN

•G•••D•
OGDOADS

•G••••D
AGROUND
EGESTED
EGGHEAD
IGNITED
IGNORED

••GD•••
BIGDEAL
BOGDOWN
DOGDAYS
HAGDONS
RAGDOLL

••G•D••
BAGHDAD
EDGEDIN
EGGEDON
HIGHDAY
MEGIDDO
PAGODAS
RIGIDLY
UNGODLY

••G••D•
AUGENDS
DEGRADE
ENGARDE
ENGIRDS
FAGENDS
LEGENDS
LIGANDS
MEGIDDO
ORGANDY
RAGGEDY
REGARDS
REGRADE
RIGVEDA
TAGENDS
TVGUIDE
UNGIRDS
UPGRADE

••G•••D
ANGERED
AUGURED
BAGHDAD
BAGNOLD
BIGBAND
BIGBEND
BIGBIRD
BIGHEAD
BIGOTED
BOGEYED
BOGGLED
BUGEYED
DAGWOOD
DOGFOOD
DOGSLED
DOGWOOD
EGGHEAD
ENGAGED
ENGLAND
ENGLUND
FAGOTED
FIGURED
GIGGLED
GOGGLED
HAGGARD
HAGGLED
HIGGLED
HIGHEND
HOGTIED
HOGWILD
JIGGLED
JOGGLED
JUGBAND
JUGGLED
JUGHEAD
LAGGARD
LEGRAND
LIGATED
LIGHTED
NEGATED
NIGGARD
NIGGLED
ONGUARD
RAGWEED
REGALED
REGLUED
RIGHTED
SIGHTED
SIGMUND
SUGARED
TOGGLED
UNGLUED
WAGERED
WAGGLED
WIGGLED

•••GD••
FLAGDAY
HANGDOG
KINGDOM
LANGDON
QINGDAO

•••G•D•
BRIGADE
PONGIDS
RAGGEDY
SUNGODS
TRAGEDY
WARGODS

•••G••D
ALIGNED
BOGGLED
BOOGIED
BRAGGED
BRIGAND
BUNGLED
BURGLED
CHUGGED
CLOGGED
CONGAED
COUGHED
DANGLED
DEIGNED
DIDGOOD
DRAGGED
DRUGGED
FEIGNED
FLAGGED
FLOGGED
FORGOOD
GANGLED
GARGLED
GIGGLED
GLUGGED
GOGGLED
GURGLED
HAGGARD
HAGGLED
HIGGLED
HOUGHED
JANGLED
JIGGLED
JINGLED
JOGGLED
JUGGLED
LAGGARD
LANGUID
LAUGHED
MANGLED
MINGLED
NEIGHED
NIGGARD
NIGGLED
OLDGOLD
PLAGUED
PLUGGED
PROGGED
REIGNED
ROUGHED
SHAGGED
SINGLED
SLOGGED
SLUGGED
SNAGGED

SNOGGED
SOUGHED
STAGGED
SWIGGED
TANGLED
TANGOED
TINGLED
TOGGLED
TONGUED
TRIGGED
WAGGLED
WANGLED
WEIGHED
WIGGLED

••••G•D

ALLEGED
AVENGED
BRAGGED
BRIDGED
CHANGED
CHARGED
CHUGGED
CLANGED
CLOGGED
CRINGED
DAMAGED
DELUGED
DEMIGOD
DRAGGED
DREDGED
DRUDGED
DRUGGED
EMERGED
ENCAGED
ENGAGED
ENRAGED
FLAGGED
FLEDGED
FLOGGED
FORAGED
FRINGED
GARAGED
GIELGUD
GLUGGED
GRUDGED
LOUNGED
MANAGED
OBLIGED
PLEDGED
PLUGGED
PLUNGED
PRANGED
PROGGED
PRONGED
RAVAGED
RENEGED
SAVAGED
SHAGGED
SLOGGED
SLUGGED
SMUDGED
SNAGGED
SNOGGED
SPARGED
SPONGED
STAGGED
SWIGGED
TRIGGED
TRUDGED
TWANGED
TWINGED
UNCAGED
VOYAGED
WHANGED
WRONGED

GE•••••

GEARBOX
GEARING
GEARSTO
GEARSUP
GECKOES
GEEGAWS
GEEKIER
GEEWHIZ
GEEZERS
GEFILTE
GEISHAS
GELADAS
GELATIN
GELATIS
GELDING
GELIDLY
GELLING
GEMLESS
GEMLIKE
GEMMIER
GEMOTES
GEMSBOK
GENDERS
GENERAL
GENERIC
GENERIS
GENESEE
GENESES
GENESIS
GENETIC
GENGHIS
GENNARO
GENOESE
GENOMES
GENTEEL
GENTIAN
GENTILE
GENTLED
GENTLER
GENTLES
GENUINE
GEODESY
GEOLOGY
GEORDIE
GEORGES
GEORGIA
GERAINT
GERALDO
GERBILS
GERENTS
GERITOL
GERMANE
GERMANS
GERMANY
GERMIER
GERUNDS
GESSOES
GESTALT
GESTATE
GESTURE
GETAWAY
GETBACK
GETDOWN
GETEVEN
GETINTO
GETITON
GETLOST
GETOVER
GETREAL
GETSOFF
GETSOUT
GETSSET
GETTING
GETWELL
GEWGAWS
GEYSERS

G•E••••

GEEGAWS
GEEKIER
GEEWHIZ
GEEZERS
GHERKIN
GHETTOS
GIELGUD
GLEAMED
GLEANED
GLEANER
GLEASON
GLEEFUL
GOESAPE
GOESBAD
GOESFOR
GOESOFF
GOESOUT
GREASED
GREASER
GREASES
GREATER
GREATLY
GREAVES
GRECIAN
GREELEY
GREENED
GREENER
GREETED
GREETER
GREGORY
GREMLIN
GRENADA
GRENADE
GRENDEL
GRETZKY
GREYEST
GREYHEN
GREYING
GREYISH
GUELPHS
GUESSED
GUESSER
GUESSES
GUESTED
GUEVARA

G••E•••

GAMELAW
GAMETES
GASEOUS
GATEAUX
GATELEG
GATEMAN
GATEMEN
GATEWAY
GAVELED
GAVEOFF
GAVEOUT
GAVEWAY
GAZEBOS
GAZELLE
GAZETTE
GENERAL
GENERIC
GENERIS
GENESEE
GENESES
GENESIS
GENETIC
GERENTS
GETEVEN
GIDEONS
GISELLE
GIVENIN
GIVENTO
GIVENUP
GIVEOFF
GIVEOUT
GIVESIN
GIVESTO
GIVESUP
GIVEUPS
GIVEWAY
GLEEFUL
GLUEDON
GLUESON
GONERIL
GORETEX
GOTEVEN
GOVERNS
GREELEY
GREENED
GREENER
GREETED
GREETER
GRIEVED
GRIEVER
GRIEVES
GYRENES

G•••E••

GABBERS
GABFEST
GADDERS
GADGETS
GADGETY
GAFFERS
GAINERS
GAITERS
GALLEON
GALLERY
GALLEYS
GAMIEST
GAMMERS
GANDERS
GANGERS
GANNETS
GANNETT
GAOLERS
GAPLESS
GARDENS
GARMENT
GARNERS
GARNETS
GARRETS
GARRETT
GARTERS
GASJETS
GASKETS
GASLESS
GASPERS
GASSERS
GATHERS
GAUGERS
GAWKERS
GEEZERS
GEMLESS
GENDERS
GENOESE
GENTEEL
GEODESY
GETREAL
GETWELL
GEYSERS
GIBBERS
GIBBETS
GIBLETS
GILBERT
GILDERS
GIMLETS
GINGERS
GINGERY
GINSENG
GIRDERS
GLACEED
GLADEYE
GLAZERS
GLIDERS
GLOWERS
GLUIEST
GNAWERS
GOAHEAD
GOATEED
GOATEES
GOBLETS
GODDESS
GODLESS
GODSEND
GOLFERS
GOMPERS
GOOBERS
GOODEGG
GOOIEST
GOPHERS
GORGETS
GORIEST
GOSPELS
GOSSETT
GOTWELL
GOUGERS
GRADERS
GRATERS
GRAVELS
GRAVELY
GRAVERS
GRAVEST
GRAYEST
GRAZERS
GREYEST
GRIPERS
GRIVETS
GROCERS
GROCERY
GROVELS
GROWERS
GRUYERE
GUINEAS
GULLETS
GUMLESS
GUNLESS
GUNNELS
GUNNERS
GUNNERY
GURNEYS
GUSHERS
GUSSETS
GUTLESS
GUTTERS
GWYNETH
GYPPERS

G••••E•

GABBIER
GABBLED
GABBLES
GABRIEL
GADSDEN
GAGGLES
GAGSTER
GALATEA
GALILEE
GALILEI
GALILEO
GAMBLED
GAMBLER
GAMBLES
GAMBREL
GAMETES
GAMINES
GAMMIER
GANGLED
GANTLET
GARAGED
GARAGES
GARBLED
GARBLES
GARDNER
GARGLED
GARGLES
GASSIER
GATELEG
GATEMEN
GAUCHER
GAUDIER
GAUNTER
GAUZIER
GAVELED
GAWKIER
GECKOES
GEEKIER
GEMMIER
GEMOTES
GENESEE
GENESES
GENOMES
GENTEEL
GENTLED
GENTLER
GENTLES
GEORGES
GERMIER
GESSOES
GETEVEN
GETOVER
GETSSET
GHOSTED
GIBLUES
GIDDIER
GIGGLED
GIGGLER
GIGGLES
GILLIES
GILLNET
GIPSIES
GIRDLED
GIRDLES
GLACEED
GLACIER
GLADDEN
GLADDER
GLAIRED
GLANCED
GLANCES
GLASSED
GLASSES
GLAZIER
GLEAMED
GLEANED
GLEANER
GLIBBER
GLIMMER
GLINTED
GLISTEN
GLITTER
GLITZED
GLITZES
GLOATED
GLOMMED
GLOOMED
GLORIED
GLORIES
GLOSSED
GLOSSES
GLUGGED
GLUMMER
GLUTTED
GNARLED
GNARRED
GNASHED
GNASHES
GOAFTER
GOALIES
GOATEED
GOATEES
GOBBLED
GOBBLER
GOBBLES
GODFREY
GODLIER
GOGGLED
GOGGLES
GOLFTEE
GOODIES
GOODMEN
GOOFIER
GOONIER
GOOPIER
GOOSIER
GORETEX
GORSIER
GOTEVEN
GOTOVER
GOUNDER
GOURDES
GOURMET
GOUTIER
GRABBED
GRABBER
GRAFTED
GRAINED
GRAMMER
GRAMMES
GRANDEE
GRANDER
GRANGER
GRANGES
GRANTED
GRANTEE
GRAPHED
GRAPIER
GRAPNEL
GRASPED
GRASSED
GRASSES
GRAVIES
GREASED
GREASER
GREASES
GREATER
GREAVES
GREELEY
GREENED
GREENER
GREETED
GREETER
GRENDEL
GREYHEN
GRIDDED
GRIDDER
GRIEVED
GRIEVER
GRIEVES
GRIFFEY
GRIFTER
GRILLED
GRILLES
GRILLET
GRIMIER
GRIMMER
GRINDER
GRINNED
GRINNER
GRIPPED
GRIPPER
GRITTED
GROANED
GROANER
GRODIER
GROLIER
GROMMET
GROOMED
GROOMER
GROOVED
GROOVES
GROSSED
GROSSER
GROSSES
GROUPED
GROUPER
GROUSED
GROUSER
GROUSES
GROUTED
GROWLED
GROWLER
GRUBBED
GRUDGED
GRUDGES
GRUFFER
GRUMPED
GRUNGES
GRUNTED
GUARDED
GUARDEE
GUESSED
GUESSER
GUESSES
GUESTED
GUILDER
GUIMPES
GULCHES
GULLIES
GULPIER
GUMMIER
GUMTREE
GUNKIER
GUNNIES
GUNTHER
GUPPIES
GURGLED
GURGLES
GUSHIER
GUSSIED
GUSSIES
GUSTIER
GUSTOES
GUTSIER
GUTTIER
GUZZLED
GUZZLER
GUZZLES
GYPSIES
GYRATED
GYRATES
GYRENES

G•••••E

GAGLINE
GAGRULE
GALILEE
GARBAGE
GARONNE
GAVOTTE
GAZELLE
GAZETTE
GEFILTE
GEMLIKE
GENESEE
GENOESE
GENTILE
GENUINE
GEORDIE
GERMANE
GESTATE
GESTURE
GIRAFFE
GIRONDE
GISELLE
GLADEYE
GLIMPSE
GLOBULE
GLOSSAE
GLUCOSE
GOBROKE
GODLIKE
GOESAPE
GOLFTEE
GOODBYE
GOODJOE
GOODONE
GOUACHE
GRACILE
GRACKLE
GRAHAME
GRANDEE
GRANITE
GRANTEE
GRANULE
GRAPPLE
GRAVURE
GRENADE
GRIDDLE
GRIMACE
GRISTLE
GRIZZLE
GROUPIE
GRUMBLE
GRUYERE
GUANINE
GUARDEE
GUMLIKE
GUMSHOE
GUMTREE
GUNFIRE
GUNWALE
GUTHRIE
GYMSHOE

•GE••••

AGEISTS
AGELESS
AGENDAS
AGESAGO
EGESTED

•G•E•••

AGREETO
EGGEDON
HGWELLS
IGNEOUS
OGREISH

•G••E••

AGELESS
AGGRESS
AGILELY
AGREETO
EGGHEAD
EGGIEST
EGGLESS
IGIVEUP
UGLIEST

•G•••E•

AGNATES
AGNOMEN
EGESTED
IGNITED
IGNITER
IGNITES
IGNORED
IGNORER
IGNORES

•G••••E

AGITATE
AGONISE
AGONIZE
AGRAFFE
EGALITE
EGGCASE
IGNOBLE

••GE•••

ALGEBRA
ALGERIA
ANGELES
ANGELIC
ANGELOU
ANGELUS
ANGERED
AUGENDS
BIGELOW
BIGEYES
BOGEYED
BUGEYED
COGENCY
DIGESTS
DOGEARS
EAGERER
EAGERLY
EDGEDIN
EDGEOUT
EDGESIN
EGGEDON
EUGENIE
FAGENDS
INGEMAR
INGENUE
INGESTS
LEGENDS
MAGENTA
NIGERIA
ORGEATS
PAGEANT
PAGEBOY
PAGEFUL
PIGEONS
RAGEFUL
REGENCY
REGENTS
SAGEHEN
TAGENDS
URGENCY
VEGETAL
WAGERED
WAGERER

••G•E••

AGGRESS
AIGRETS
ALGIERS
ANGLERS
ARGUERS
AUGMENT
BAGGERS
BIGBEND
BIGDEAL
BIGFEET
BIGGERS
BIGGEST
BIGHEAD
BIGNESS
BUGBEAR
BUGLERS
CAGIEST
CYGNETS
DAGGERS
DEGREES
DIGGERS
DIGRESS
DOGBERT
DOGLEGS
DOGLESS
EAGLETS
EDGIEST
EGGHEAD
EGGIEST
EGGLESS
ELGRECO
FIGLEAF
FIGMENT
FOGGERS
FOGLESS
HIGHEND
HIGHEST
HOGGETS
HUGGERS
HYGIEIA
HYGIENE
INGRESS
JAGLESS
JIGGERS
JIGGERY
JOGGERS
JUGHEAD
KEGLERS
LAGGERS
LEGLESS
LOGGERS
LOGIEST
LUGGERS
MAGNETO
MAGNETS
MAGUEYS
MUGGERS
NEGLECT
NIGHEST
NUGGETS
PEGLESS
PIGGERY
PIGLETS
PIGMENT
PIGPENS
PUGREES
RAGGEDY
RAGWEED
REGLETS
REGRESS
REGRETS
RIGGERS
RIGVEDA
ROGUERY
SEGMENT
SIGHERS
SIGNEES
SIGNERS
SIGNETS
SUGGEST
TAGTEAM
TIGRESS
TOGGERY
TUGGERS
TUGLESS
UNGUENT
VAGUELY
VAGUEST
WAGGERY
WIGLESS
WIGLETS

••G••E•

ANGELES
ANGERED
ANGRIER
ARGIVES
ARGYLES
AUGURED
BAGGIER
BAGGIES
BIGEYES
BIGFEET
BIGGIES
BIGLIES
BIGOSES
BIGOTED
BIGTOES
BOGEYED
BOGGIER
BOGGLED
BOGGLER
BOGGLES
BUGEYED
BUGFREE
BUGGIER
BUGGIES
BYGONES
DEGREES
DOGGIER
DOGGIES
DOGSLED
EAGERER
ENGAGED
ENGAGES
ENGINES
ERGATES
FAGOTED
FIGHTER
FIGURED
FIGURER
FIGURES
FOGGIER
GAGGLES
GAGSTER
GIGGLED
GIGGLER
GIGGLES
GOGGLED
GOGGLES
HAGGLED
HAGGLER
HAGGLES
HIGGLED
HIGGLES
HIGHTEA
HOGTIED
HOGTIES
JAGGIER
JAGGIES
JIGGLED
JIGGLES
JOGGLED
JOGGLES
JUGGLED
JUGGLER
JUGGLES
LEGATEE
LEGATES
LEGGIER
LEGUMES
LIGATED
LIGATES
LIGHTED
LIGHTEN
LIGHTER
MAGPIES
MIGGLES
MOGGIES
MUGGIER
NAGGIER
NEGATED
NEGATER
NEGATES
NIGGLED
NIGGLES
NOGALES
ORGATES
PIGGIER
PIGGIES
PUGREES
PYGMIES
RAGWEED
REGALED
REGALES
REGIMEN
REGIMES
REGLUED
REGLUES
RIGHTED
RIGHTER
SAGEHEN
SAGGIER
SIGHTED
SIGNEES
SOGGIER
SUGARED
TIGHTEN
TIGHTER
TOGGLED
TOGGLES
UNGLUED
VEGGIES
WAGERED
WAGERER
WAGGLED
WAGGLES
WAGONER
WIGGIER
WIGGLED
WIGGLER
WIGGLES
ZYGOTES

••G•••E

ARGONNE
AUGUSTE
BAGGAGE
BAGLIKE
BAGPIPE
BEGRIME
BEGUILE
BEGUINE
BIGGAME
BIGNAME
BIGTIME
BOGHOLE
BUGFREE
COGNATE
DEGRADE
DOGBANE
DOGFACE
DOGGONE
DOGLIKE
EGGCASE
ENGARDE
ENGORGE
ENGRAVE
EUGENIE
GAGLINE
GAGRULE
HAGLIKE
HOGLIKE
HYGIENE
INGENUE
INGRATE
JIGLIKE
JUGWINE
LEGATEE
LEGIBLE
LEGLIKE
LIGNITE
LUGGAGE
MAGNATE
MAGUIRE
MCGUIRE
MIGRATE
NIGHTIE
PEGLIKE
PIGLIKE
PUGNOSE
RAGTIME
REGRADE
ROGAINE
RUGLIKE
TAGLIKE
TAGLINE
TAGSALE
TVGUIDE
UPGRADE
WIGLIKE

•••GE••

APOGEES
BADGERS
BAGGERS
BARGEIN
BEEGEES
BERGERE
BIGGERS
BIGGEST

BIOGENY
BUDGETS
BUNGEES
BURGEES
BURGEON
BURGERS
BURGESS
CADGERS
CODGERS
CONGEAL
CONGERS
CONGEST
CUDGELS
DAGGERS
DANGERS
DIGGERS
DODGERS
DUDGEON
DUNGEON
EPIGENE
ETAGERE
EXIGENT
FIDGETS
FIDGETY
FINGERS
FOGGERS
FOLGERS
FORGERS
FORGERY
FORGETS
FULGENT
GADGETS
GADGETY
GANGERS
GAUGERS
GINGERS
GINGERY
GORGETS
GOUGERS
HANGERS
HEDGERS
HOGGETS
HUGGERS
HUNGERS
HUYGENS
IMAGERS
IMAGERY
IMOGENE
JAEGERS
JIGGERS
JIGGERY
JOGGERS
LAAGERS
LAGGERS
LARGELY
LARGESS
LARGEST
LEDGERS
LINGERS
LODGERS
LOGGERS
LONGEST
LOWGEAR
LUGGERS
LUNGEAT
MANGERS
MERGERS
MIDGETS
MONGERS
MUGGERS
NUDGERS
NUGGETS
ONAGERS
OROGENY
PARGETS
PEUGEOT
PIDGEON
PIGGERY
PONGEES
PROGENY
PUNGENT
RAGGEDY
RANGERS
REAGENT
RIGGERS
RINGERS
RODGERS
RUTGERS
SARGENT
SINGERS
STAGERS
SUGGEST
SURGEON
SURGERY
TANGELO
TANGENT
TANGERE
TARGETS
TOGGERY
TRAGEDY
TUGGERS
VERGERS
WAGGERY
WIDGEON
WIDGETS
WINGERS
YEVGENY
ZINGERS

•••G•E•

ALIGNED
ALIGNER
APOGEES
BAGGIER
BAGGIES
BANGLES
BEAGLES
BEEGEES
BIGGIES
BILGIER
BINGOES
BOGGIER
BOGGLED
BOGGLER
BOGGLES
BONGOES
BOOGIED
BOOGIES
BRAGGED
BRAGGER
BROGUES
BUDGIES
BUGGIER
BUGGIES
BULGIER
BUNGEES
BUNGLED
BUNGLER
BUNGLES
BURGEES
BURGHER
BURGLED
BURGLES
CARGOES
CHIGGER
CHIGOES
CHUGGED
CLOGGED
CONGAED
COUGHED
DANGLED
DANGLER
DANGLES
DEIGNED
DINGIER
DINGLES
DINGOES
DODGIER
DOGGIER
DOGGIES
DONGLES
DRAGGED
DRAGGER
DRAGNET
DRUGGED
ELEGIES
EMIGRES
FEIGNED
FLAGGED
FLAGMEN
FLOGGED
FOGGIER
FORGOES
FROGMEN
FUNGOES
GAGGLES
GANGLED
GARGLED
GARGLES
GIGGLED
GIGGLER
GIGGLES
GLUGGED
GOGGLED
GOGGLES
GURGLED
GURGLES
HAGGLED
HAGGLER
HAGGLES
HANGMEN
HANGTEN
HEDGIER
HIGGLED
HIGGLES
HOAGIES
HOUGHED
IMAGOES
JAGGIER
JAGGIES
JANGLED
JANGLES
JIGGLED
JIGGLES
JINGLED
JINGLES
JINGOES
JOGGLED
JOGGLES
JUGGLED
JUGGLER
JUGGLES
JUNGLES
LANGLEY
LAUGHED
LAUGHER
LEAGUES
LEDGIER
LEGGIER
LINGOES
LONGIES
LONGUES
MAIGRET
MANGIER
MANGLED
MANGLES
MANGOES
MARGRET
MIGGLES
MINGIER
MINGLED
MINGLER
MINGLES
MOGGIES
MONGREL
MUGGIER
NAGGIER
NEIGHED
NIGGLED
NIGGLES
OUTGOES
OUTGREW
PIGGIER
PIGGIES
PLAGUED
PLAGUES
PLUGGED
PLUGGER
PODGIER
PONGEES
PORGIES
PROGGED
PUDGIER
QUIGLEY
RANGIER
REIGNED
RIDGIER
RINGLET
ROUGHED
ROUGHEN
ROUGHER
SAGGIER
SEDGIER
SHAGGED
SINGLED
SINGLES
SLOGGED
SLUGGED
SLUGGER
SMUGGER
SNAGGED
SNIGGER
SNIGLET
SNOGGED
SNUGGER
SOGGIER
SOIGNEE
SOUGHED
STAGGED
STAGGER
STAGIER
STOGIES
SWAGGER
SWIGGED
TANGIER
TANGLED
TANGLES
TANGOED
TINGLED
TINGLES
TOGGLED
TOGGLES
TONGUED
TONGUES
TOUGHEN
TOUGHER
TRIGGED
TRIGGER
VEGGIES
WAGGLED
WAGGLES
WANGLED
WANGLER
WANGLES
WEDGIER
WEDGIES
WEIGHED
WIGGIER
WIGGLED
WIGGLER
WIGGLES
WRIGLEY
ZINGIER

•••G••E

ALLGONE
BAGGAGE
BERGERE
BIGGAME
BRIGADE
COLGATE
CONGAME
DOGGONE
ENDGAME
EPIGENE
EPIGONE
ETAGERE
FARGONE
FORGAVE
FORGIVE
FORGONE
FRAGILE
FRIGATE
IMAGINE
IMOGENE
LUGGAGE
MARGATE
NEWGATE
SEAGATE
SMUGGLE
SNIGGLE
SNUGGLE
SOIGNEE
TANGERE
TOUGHIE
VIRGULE
VULGATE
WARGAME
WRIGGLE
YANGTZE

••••GE•

ALLEGED
ALLEGER
ALLEGES
ANTIGEN
AVENGED
AVENGER
AVENGES
BRAGGED
BRAGGER
BRIDGED
BRIDGES
BRIDGET
BRINGER
BRUEGEL
CHANGED
CHANGER
CHANGES
CHARGED
CHARGER
CHARGES
CHIGGER
CHUGGED
CLANGED
CLOGGED
CRINGED
CRINGES
CRYOGEN
DAMAGED
DAMAGES
DELUGED
DELUGES
DOSAGES
DOWAGER
DRAGGED
DRAGGER
DREDGED
DREDGER
DREDGES
DRUDGED
DRUDGES
DRUGGED
EMERGED
EMERGES
ENCAGED
ENCAGES
ENGAGED
ENGAGES
ENRAGED
ENRAGES
EVANGEL
FLAGGED
FLANGES
FLEDGED
FLEDGES
FLOGGED
FORAGED
FORAGER
FORAGES
FRIDGES
FRINGED
FRINGES
GARAGED
GARAGES
GEORGES
GLUGGED
GRANGER
GRANGES
GRUDGED
GRUDGES
GRUNGES
HALOGEN
ICEAGES
INTEGER
KLUDGES
LIMOGES
LINAGES
LOUNGED
LOUNGER
LOUNGES
MANAGED
MANAGER
MANAGES
MANEGES
MENAGES
MIRAGES
MUTAGEN
NEWAGER
NONAGES
OBLIGED
OBLIGES
ORANGES
ORANGEY
OUTAGES
PELAGES
PERIGEE
PLEDGED
PLEDGEE
PLEDGER
PLEDGES
PLUGGED
PLUGGER
PLUNGED
PLUNGER
PLUNGES
POTAGES
PRANGED
PROGGED
PRONGED
RAVAGED
RAVAGER
RAVAGES
REFUGEE
REFUGES
REMIGES
RENEGED
RENEGER
RENEGES
RONTGEN
SAVAGED
SAVAGER
SAVAGES
SHAGGED
SLEDGES
SLINGER
SLOGGED
SLUDGES
SLUGGED
SLUGGER
SMIDGEN
SMUDGED
SMUDGES
SMUGGER
SNAGGED
SNIGGER
SNOGGED
SNUGGER
SPARGED
SPARGES
SPIEGEL
SPONGED
SPONGER
SPONGES
STAGGED
STAGGER
STEIGER
STENGEL
STIEGEL
STINGER
STOOGES
STURGES
SWAGGER
SWIGGED
SWINGER
TANAGER
TRIGGED
TRIGGER
TRUDGED
TRUDGER
TRUDGES
TWANGED
TWINGED
TWINGES
UNCAGED
UNCAGES
VISAGES
VOYAGED
VOYAGER
VOYAGES
WHANGED
WRINGER
WRONGED
WRONGER
YOUNGER

••••G•E

ATINGLE
COLOGNE
ECLOGUE
EPERGNE
FATIGUE
FINAGLE
INVOGUE
KRINGLE
LASAGNE
PERIGEE
PIROGUE
PLEDGEE
REARGUE
REFUGEE
RENEGUE
SEVIGNE
SHINGLE
SMUGGLE
SNIGGLE
SNUGGLE
SPANGLE
WRANGLE
WRIGGLE

•••••GE

ABRIDGE
ACREAGE
ADJUDGE
ARLEDGE
ARRANGE
ASSUAGE
ATLARGE
AVERAGE
BABBAGE
BAGGAGE
BANDAGE
BARRAGE
BESIEGE
BONDAGE
CABBAGE
CARTAGE
COINAGE
COLLAGE
COLLEGE
CORDAGE
CORKAGE
CORSAGE
CORTEGE
COTTAGE
COURAGE
DEBARGE
DEFARGE
DIVERGE
DIVULGE
DOCKAGE
DRAYAGE
ENGORGE
ENLARGE
EXPUNGE
FABERGE
FOLIAGE
FOOTAGE
FROMAGE
GARBAGE
HAULAGE
HERBAGE
HOSTAGE
IMPINGE
INDULGE
IRONAGE
JAZZAGE
LAFARGE
LEAFAGE
LEAKAGE
LINEAGE
LINKAGE
LOZENGE
LUGGAGE
MASSAGE
MELANGE
MESSAGE
MILEAGE
MONTAGE
MOORAGE
MOULAGE
ONSTAGE
OUTRAGE
OVERAGE
PACKAGE
PANURGE
PASSAGE
PEERAGE
PEONAGE
PILLAGE
PLUMAGE
PORTAGE
POSTAGE
POTTAGE
PRESAGE
PROTEGE
RAMPAGE
RESTAGE
RESURGE
REVENGE
RIBCAGE
RUMMAGE
SALVAGE
SAUSAGE
SCOURGE
SCROOGE
SELVAGE
SINKAGE
SOLFEGE
SPLURGE
STORAGE
STRANGE
SYRINGE
TEENAGE
TILLAGE
TONNAGE
UMBRAGE
UPSTAGE
UPSURGE
VANTAGE
VESTIGE
VILLAGE
VINTAGE
VOLTAGE
WASTAGE
WATTAGE
WEBPAGE
YARDAGE

G•F••••

GAFFERS
GAFFING
GEFILTE
GIFFORD
GOFORIT
GUFFAWS

G••F•••

GABFEST
GAFFERS
GAFFING
GIFFORD
GINFIZZ
GOAFTER
GODFREY
GOLFERS
GOLFING
GOLFPRO
GOLFTEE
GOOFIER
GOOFILY
GOOFING
GOOFOFF
GOOFSUP
GOOFUPS
GRAFTED
GRAFTON
GRIFFEY
GRIFFIN
GRIFFON
GRIFTER
GRUFFER
GRUFFLY
GUFFAWS
GULFING
GUNFIRE

G•••F••

GAINFUL
GIRAFFE
GLEEFUL
GOESFOR
GOINFOR
GRIFFEY
GRIFFIN
GRIFFON
GRUFFER
GRUFFLY
GUNSFOR

G••••F•

GAVEOFF
GETSOFF
GIRAFFE
GIVEOFF
GLORIFY
GOESOFF
GOOFOFF
GRATIFY

G•••••F

GAVEOFF
GETSOFF
GIVEOFF
GOESOFF
GOOFOFF

•G••F••

AGRAFFE

•G•••F•

AGRAFFE

••GF•••

BAGFULS
BIGFEET
BIGFOOT
BUGFREE
DOGFACE
DOGFISH
DOGFOOD
JUGFULS

••G•F••

PAGEFUL
RAGEFUL
SIGHFUL

••G••F•

BEGSOFF
BUGSOFF
DIGNIFY
ENGRAFT
ENGULFS
LOGSOFF
MAGNIFY
SIGNIFY
SIGNOFF

••G•••F

BEGSOFF
BUGSOFF
FIGLEAF
LOGSOFF
SIGNOFF

•••GF••

SONGFUL

•••G•F•

HANGOFF
RANGOFF
RINGOFF
RUNGOFF

•••G••F

HANGOFF
RANGOFF
RINGOFF
RUNGOFF

G•G••••

GAGARIN
GAGGING
GAGGLES
GAGLAWS
GAGLINE
GAGRULE
GAGSTER
GIGGLED
GIGGLER
GIGGLES
GIGOLOS
GOGGLED
GOGGLES

G••G•••

GADGETS
GADGETY
GAGGING
GAGGLES
GANGERS
GANGING
GANGLED
GANGLIA
GANGSAW
GANGSTA
GANGSUP
GANGTOK
GANGWAY
GARGLED
GARGLES
GAUGERS
GAUGING
GAUGUIN
GEEGAWS
GENGHIS
GEWGAWS
GIGGLED
GIGGLER
GIGGLES
GILGUYS
GINGERS
GINGERY
GINGHAM
GINGIVA
GLUGGED
GOGGLED
GOGGLES
GONGING
GOOGOLS
GORGETS
GORGING
GORGONS
GOUGERS
GOUGING
GREGORY
GRIGRIS
GURGLED
GURGLES

G•••G••

GALAGOS
GARAGED
GARAGES
GEORGES
GEORGIA
GIELGUD
GIORGIO
GLASGOW
GLUGGED
GOINGAT
GOINGBY
GOINGIN
GOINGON
GOINGUP
GRANGER
GRANGES
GRUDGED
GRUDGES
GRUNGES
GUARGUM

G••••G•

GARBAGE
GASBAGS
GASLOGS
GEOLOGY
GOODEGG
GUNDOGS
GYMBAGS

G•••••G

GABBING
GADDING
GAFFING
GAGGING
GAINING
GAITING
GALLING
GAMMING
GANGING
GAOLING
GAPPING
GARBING
GASHING
GASPING
GATELEG
GATLING
GAUGING
GAUMING
GAWKING
GAWPING
GEARING
GELDING
GELLING
GETTING
GIBBING
GILDING
GILLING
GINNING
GINSENG
GIPPING
GIRDING
GIRNING
GLARING
GLAZING
GLIDING
GLOBING
GLOWING
GLOZING
GNAWING
GOADING
GOALONG
GOLDBUG
GOLDING
GOLFING
GONGING
GOODEGG
GOODING
GOOFING
GOOSING
GORGING
GOSLING
GOUGING
GOWRONG
GRABBAG
GRACING
GRADING
GRATING
GRAVING
GRAYING
GRAYLAG
GRAZING
GREYING
GRIMING
GRIPING
GROPING
GROWING
GUIDING
GULFING
GULLING
GULPING
GUMMING
GUNNING
GUSHING
GUSTING
GUTTING
GYPPING

•GG••••

AGGRESS
EGGCASE
EGGCUPS
EGGEDON
EGGHEAD
EGGIEST
EGGLESS
EGGNOGS
EGGROLL

•G•••G•

AGESAGO
EGGNOGS

••GG•••

BAGGAGE
BAGGERS
BAGGIER
BAGGIES
BAGGILY
BAGGING
BEGGARS
BEGGING
BIGGAME
BIGGERS
BIGGEST
BIGGIES
BIGGISH
BIGGUNS
BOGGIER
BOGGING
BOGGISH
BOGGLED
BOGGLER
BOGGLES
BUGGIER
BUGGIES
BUGGING
DAGGERS
DIGGERS
DIGGING
DOGGIER
DOGGIES
DOGGING
DOGGISH
DOGGONE
FAGGING
FOGGERS
FOGGIER
FOGGILY
FOGGING
GAGGING
GAGGLES
GIGGLED
GIGGLER
GIGGLES
GOGGLED
GOGGLES
HAGGARD
HAGGISH
HAGGLED
HAGGLER
HAGGLES
HIGGINS
HIGGLED
HIGGLES
HOGGETS
HOGGING
HOGGISH
HUGGERS
HUGGING
HUGGINS
JAGGIER
JAGGIES
JAGGING
JIGGERS
JIGGERY
JIGGING
JIGGISH
JIGGLED
JIGGLES
JOGGERS
JOGGING
JOGGLED

JOGGLES
JUGGING
JUGGINS
JUGGLED
JUGGLER
JUGGLES
LAGGARD
LAGGERS
LAGGING
LEGGIER
LEGGING
LOGGERS
LOGGIAS
LOGGING
LOGGINS
LOGGISH
LUGGAGE
LUGGERS
LUGGING
MIGGLES
MOGGIES
MUGGERS
MUGGIER
MUGGING
NAGGIER
NAGGING
NAGGISH
NIGGARD
NIGGLED
NIGGLES
NOGGINS
NUGGETS
PEGGING
PIGGERY
PIGGIER
PIGGIES
PIGGING
PIGGISH
PUGGISH
RAGGEDY
RAGGING
RIGGERS
RIGGING
SAGGIER
SAGGING
SOGGIER
SOGGILY
SUGGEST
TAGGANT
TAGGING
TOGGERY
TOGGING
TOGGLED
TOGGLES
TUGGERS
TUGGING
VEGGIES
VEGGING
WAGGERY
WAGGING
WAGGISH
WAGGLED
WAGGLES
WAGGONS
WIGGIER
WIGGLED
WIGGLER
WIGGLES
ZAGGING
ZIGGING

••G•G••
ENGAGED
ENGAGES

••G••G•
BAGGAGE
BIGWIGS
DOGLEGS
DOGTAGS
DUGONGS
EDGINGS
EGGNOGS
ENGORGE
LUGGAGE
RAGBAGS
RAGRUGS
WIGWAGS
ZIGZAGS

••G•••G
ANGLING
ARGUING
BAGGING
BEGGING
BIGBANG
BOGGING
BUGGING
BUGLING
DIGGING
DOGGING
EAGLING
FAGGING
FOGGING
GAGGING
HOGGING
HUGGING
JAGGING
JIGGING
JOGGING
JUGGING
LAGGING
LEGGING
LOGGING
LUGGING
MUGGING
NAGGING
ONGOING
PEGGING
PIGGING
RAGGING
RIGGING
SAGGING
SIGHING
SIGNING
TAGALOG
TAGGING
TOGGING
TUGGING
VEGGING
WAGGING
ZAGGING
ZIGGING

•••GG••
BRAGGED
BRAGGER
CHIGGER
CHUGGED
CLOGGED
DRAGGED
DRAGGER
DRUGGED
FLAGGED
FLOGGED
GLUGGED
PLUGGED
PLUGGER
PROGGED
QUAGGAS
SHAGGED
SLOGGED
SLUGGED
SLUGGER
SMUGGER
SMUGGLE
SNAGGED
SNIGGER
SNIGGLE
SNOGGED
SNUGGER
SNUGGLE
STAGGED
STAGGER
SWAGGER
SWIGGED
TRIGGED
TRIGGER
WRIGGLE
WRIGGLY

•••G•G•
BAGGAGE
FIZGIGS
LONGAGO
LUGGAGE
VANGOGH

•••G••G
BAGGING
BANGING
BARGING
BEGGING
BINGING
BOGGING
BONGING
BUDGING
BUGGING
BULGING
BUNGING
CADGING
DIGGING
DINGING
DODGING
DOGGING
FAGGING
FOGGING
FORGING
FUDGING
GAGGING
GANGING
GAUGING
GONGING
GORGING
GOUGING
HANGDOG
HANGING
HEDGING
HINGING
HOGGING
HUGGING
IMAGING
JAGGING
JIGGING
JOGGING
JUDGING
JUGGING
KINGING
LAGGING
LEGGING
LODGING
LOGGING
LONGING
LUGGING
LUNGING
MERGING
MUGGING
NAGGING
NUDGING
OURGANG
PEGGING
PIGGING
PINGING
PONGING
PURGING
RAGGING
RANGING
RIDGING
RIGGING
RINGING
ROUGING
SAGGING
SINGING
STAGING
SURGING
TAGGING
TINGING
TOGGING
TUGGING
VEGGING
VERGING
WAGGING
WEDGING
WINGING
ZAGGING
ZIGGING
ZINGING

••••GG•
BADEGGS
RAWEGGS
SCRAGGY

•••••GG
GOODEGG
KELLOGG
NESTEGG

GH•••••
GHANIAN
GHASTLY
GHERKIN
GHETTOS
GHOSTED
GHOSTLY

G••H•••
GASHING
GATHERS
GOAHEAD
GOPHERS
GOSHAWK
GOTHICS
GRAHAME
GRAHAMS
GUSHERS
GUSHIER
GUSHILY
GUSHING
GUTHRIE

G•••H••
GALAHAD
GASOHOL
GAUCHER
GAUCHOS
GEEWHIZ
GEISHAS
GENGHIS
GINGHAM
GNASHED
GNASHES
GODTHAB
GOTCHAS
GRAPHED
GRAPHIC
GREYHEN
GRISHAM
GRYPHON
GULCHES
GUMSHOE
GUNSHOT
GUNTHER
GURKHAS
GYMSHOE

G••••H•
GNOCCHI
GOUACHE
GROUCHO
GROUCHY
GROWTHS
GUELPHS
GULLAHS

G•••••H
GALUMPH
GARNISH
GAULISH
GAWKISH
GIRLISH
GNOMISH
GOATISH
GODUTCH
GOLIATH
GOODISH
GOULASH
GOUTISH
GRAYISH
GREYISH
GWYNETH

•G•H•••
EGGHEAD

•G••H••
AGAKHAN

•G••••H
OGREISH

••GH•••
AFGHANI
AFGHANS
BAGHDAD
BIGHEAD
BIGHORN
BOGHOLE
EGGHEAD
EIGHTAM
EIGHTHS
EIGHTPM
FIGHTER
FOGHORN
HIGHBOY
HIGHDAY
HIGHEND
HIGHEST
HIGHHAT
HIGHLOW
HIGHTEA
HIGHTOP
HIGHWAY
JUGHEAD
LEGHORN
LIGHTED
LIGHTEN
LIGHTER
LIGHTLY
LIGHTUP
MIGHTNT
NIGHEST
NIGHTIE
NIGHTLY
OUGHTNT
RIGHTED
RIGHTER
RIGHTLY
RIGHTON
SIGHERS
SIGHFUL
SIGHING
SIGHTED
SIGHTLY
TIGHTEN
TIGHTER
TIGHTLY
YOGHURT

••G•H••
BIGSHOT
DOGCHOW
DOGSHOW
HIGHHAT
MEGAHIT
MEGOHMS
MUGSHOT
SAGEHEN

••G••H•
BIGJOHN
EIGHTHS
NOGUCHI

••G•••H
BIGGISH
BOGGISH
DIGRAPH
DOGFISH
DOGGISH
ENGLISH
FOGYISH
HAGGISH
HOGARTH
HOGGISH
HOGWASH
JIGGISH
LOGGISH
NAGGISH
PIGGISH
PUGGISH
ROGUISH
TIGRISH
VOGUISH
WAGGISH

•••GH••
ALIGHTS
BINGHAM
BLIGHTS
BLIGHTY
BRIGHAM
BULGHUR
BURGHER
COUGHED
COUGHUP
DOUGHTY
FLIGHTS
FLIGHTY
FRIGHTS
FULGHUM
GENGHIS
GINGHAM
HAUGHTY
HEIGHHO
HEIGHTS
HOUGHED
KNIGHTS
LAUGHAT
LAUGHED
LAUGHER
LAUGHIN
MAUGHAM
NAUGHTS
NAUGHTY
NEIGHED
NOUGHTS
PLIGHTS
ROUGHED
ROUGHEN
ROUGHER
ROUGHIT
ROUGHLY
ROUGHUP
SLIGHTS
SORGHUM
SOUGHED
TOUGHEN
TOUGHER
TOUGHIE
TOUGHLY
VAUGHAN
VEIGHTS
WEIGHED
WEIGHIN
WEIGHTS
WEIGHTY
WRIGHTS

•••G•H•
HEIGHHO
LENGTHS
LENGTHY

•••G••H
BIGGISH
BOGGISH
DOGGISH
HAGGISH
HOGGISH
JIGGISH
LARGISH
LOGGISH
LONGISH
NAGGISH
OMIGOSH
PIGGISH
PUGGISH
VANGOGH
WAGGISH

••••GH•
ABOUGHT
ALRIGHT
BROUGHT
DELIGHT
DRAUGHT
DROUGHT
FRAUGHT
FREIGHT
INSIGHT
MRRIGHT
ONSIGHT
PLOUGHS
RELIGHT
SLEIGHS
SLEIGHT
SLOUGHS
THOUGHT
TONIGHT
TROUGHS
UPRIGHT
UPTIGHT
WROUGHT
XHEIGHT

•••••GH
BOROUGH
BRANAGH
FLYHIGH
INVEIGH
RALEIGH
SKYHIGH
THROUGH
VANGOGH

GI•••••
GIACOMO
GIBBERS
GIBBETS
GIBBING
GIBBONS
GIBBOUS
GIBLETS
GIBLUES
GIDDIER
GIDDILY
GIDDYAP
GIDDYUP
GIDEONS
GIELGUD
GIFFORD
GIGGLED
GIGGLER
GIGGLES
GIGOLOS
GILBERT
GILBLAS
GILDERS
GILDING
GILGUYS
GILLIAN
GILLIES
GILLING
GILLNET
GIMBALS
GIMLETS
GIMMICK
GINFIZZ
GINGERS
GINGERY
GINGHAM
GINGIVA
GINMILL
GINNING
GINSENG
GIORGIO
GIPPING
GIPSIES
GIRAFFE
GIRASOL
GIRDERS
GIRDING
GIRDLED
GIRDLES
GIRLISH
GIRNING
GIRONDE
GISELLE
GIVENIN
GIVENTO
GIVENUP
GIVEOFF
GIVEOUT
GIVESIN
GIVESTO
GIVESUP
GIVEUPS
GIVEWAY
GIZZARD

G•I••••
GAINERS
GAINFUL
GAINING
GAINSAY
GAINSON
GAITERS
GAITING
GEISHAS
GLIBBER
GLIDERS
GLIDING
GLIMMER
GLIMPSE
GLINTED
GLISTEN
GLITTER
GLITZED
GLITZES
GOINFOR
GOINGAT
GOINGBY
GOINGIN
GOINGON
GOINGUP
GRIDDED
GRIDDER
GRIDDLE
GRIEVED
GRIEVER
GRIEVES
GRIFFEY
GRIFFIN
GRIFFON
GRIFTER
GRIGRIS
GRILLED
GRILLES
GRILLET
GRIMACE
GRIMIER
GRIMILY
GRIMING
GRIMMER
GRINDER
GRINNED
GRINNER
GRIPERS
GRIPING
GRIPPED
GRIPPER
GRISHAM
GRISKIN
GRISSOM
GRISTLE
GRISTLY
GRITTED
GRIVETS
GRIZZLE
GRIZZLY
GUIDING
GUIDONS
GUILDER
GUIMPES
GUINEAS
GUITARS

G••I•••
GALILEE
GALILEI
GALILEO
GAMIEST
GAMINES
GAVIALS
GEFILTE
GELIDLY
GERITOL
GETINTO
GETITON
GLAIRED
GLUIEST
GOLIATH
GOOIEST
GORIEST
GORILLA
GOTINTO
GOTITON
GRAINED

G•••I••
GABBIER
GABBING
GABRIEL
GADDING
GAFFING
GAGGING
GAGLINE
GAINING
GAITING
GALLING
GALLIUM
GAMBIAN
GAMBITS
GAMMIER
GAMMING
GANGING
GAOLING
GAPPING
GARBING
GARNISH
GARRICK
GASHING
GASKINS
GASPING
GASSIER
GATLING
GAUDIER
GAUDILY
GAUGING
GAULISH
GAUMING
GAUZIER
GAUZILY
GAWKIER
GAWKILY
GAWKING
GAWKISH
GAWPING
GEARING
GEEKIER
GELDING
GELLING
GEMLIKE
GEMMIER
GENTIAN
GENTILE
GENUINE
GERAINT
GERBILS
GERMIER
GETTING
GHANIAN
GIBBING
GIDDIER
GIDDILY
GILDING
GILLIAN
GILLIES
GILLING
GIMMICK
GINFIZZ
GINGIVA
GINMILL
GINNING
GIPPING
GIPSIES
GIRDING
GIRLISH
GIRNING
GLACIAL
GLACIER
GLARING
GLAZIER
GLAZING
GLIDING
GLOBING
GLORIAM
GLORIAS
GLORIED
GLORIES
GLORIFY
GLOWING
GLOZING
GNAWING
GNOMISH
GOADING
GOALIES
GOATISH
GOBLINS
GODLIER
GODLIKE
GODWITS
GOLDING
GOLFING
GONGING
GOODIES
GOODING
GOODISH
GOOFIER
GOOFILY
GOOFING
GOONIER
GOONILY
GOOPIER
GOOSIER
GOOSING
GORDIAN
GORGING
GORSIER
GOSLING
GOSSIPS
GOSSIPY
GOTHICS
GOUGING
GOUTIER
GOUTILY
GOUTISH
GRACIAS
GRACILE
GRACING
GRADING
GRANITE
GRAPIER
GRATIAS
GRATIFY
GRATING
GRAVIES
GRAVING
GRAVITY
GRAYING
GRAYISH
GRAZING
GRECIAN
GREYING
GREYISH
GRIMIER
GRIMILY
GRIMING
GRIPING
GRODIER
GROLIER
GROPING
GROPIUS
GROWING
GRUNION
GUANINE
GUIDING
GULFING
GULLIES
GULLING
GULPIER
GULPING
GUMLIKE
GUMMIER
GUMMING
GUNFIRE
GUNKIER
GUNNIES
GUNNING
GUPPIES
GUSHIER
GUSHILY
GUSHING
GUSSIED
GUSSIES
GUSTIER
GUSTILY
GUSTING
GUTSIER
GUTSILY
GUTTIER
GUTTING
GYPPING
GYPSIES

G••••I•
GAGARIN
GALATIA
GANGLIA
GASMAIN
GASTRIC
GAUGUIN
GEEWHIZ
GELATIN
GELATIS
GENERIC
GENERIS
GENESIS
GENETIC
GENGHIS
GEORDIE
GEORGIA
GHERKIN
GIORGIO
GIVENIN
GIVESIN
GLOTTIS
GNOSTIC
GOFORIT
GOINGIN
GONERIL
GOODWIN
GRAPHIC
GREMLIN
GRIFFIN
GRIGRIS
GRISKIN
GROUPIE
GUTHRIE

G•••••I
GALILEI
GALVANI
GNOCCHI
GOURAMI
GUARANI

•GI••••
AGILELY
AGILITY
AGITATE
AGITATO
IGIVEUP

•G•I•••
AGAINST
AGEISTS
AGRIPPA
EGGIEST
EGOISTS
IGNITED
IGNITER
IGNITES
UGLIEST

•G••I••
AGARICS
AGILITY
AGONISE
AGONIST
AGONIZE
EGALITE
EGOTISM
EGOTIST
OGREISH

•G•••I•
AGASSIZ
AGOUTIS
EGOTRIP

••GI•••
ALGIERS
ARGIVES
CAGIEST
DIGITAL
EDGIEST
EDGINGS
EGGIEST
ENGINES
ENGIRDS
HEGIRAS
HYGIEIA
HYGIENE
LEGIBLE
LEGIBLY
LEGIONS
LEGISTS
LOGICAL
LOGIEST
MAGICAL
MAGINOT
MEGIDDO
PIGIRON
REGIMEN
REGIMES
REGIONS
RIGIDLY
SAGINAW
UNGIRDS

••G•I••
ANGLING
ANGRIER
ANGRILY
ARGUING
BAGGIER
BAGGIES
BAGGILY
BAGGING
BAGLIKE
BAGPIPE
BEGGING
BEGRIME
BEGUILE
BEGUINE
BIGBIRD
BIGGIES
BIGGISH
BIGLIES
BIGTIME
BIGWIGS
BOGGIER
BOGGING
BOGGISH
BUGGIER
BUGGIES
BUGGING
BUGLING
DIGGING
DIGNIFY
DIGNITY
DOGFISH
DOGGIER
DOGGIES
DOGGING
DOGGISH
DOGLIKE
DOGSITS
EAGLING
ENGLISH
FAGGING
FOGGIER
FOGGILY
FOGGING
FOGYISH
FOGYISM
GAGGING
GAGLINE
HAGGISH
HAGLIKE
HIGGINS
HOGGING
HOGGISH
HOGLIKE
HOGTIED

HOGTIES
HOGWILD
HUGGING
HUGGINS
JAGGIER
JAGGIES
JAGGING
JIGGING
JIGGISH
JIGLIKE
JOGGING
JUGGING
JUGGINS
JUGWINE
LAGGING
LEGGIER
LEGGING
LEGLIKE
LIGNITE
LOGGIAS
LOGGING
LOGGINS
LOGGISH
LUGGING
MAGNIFY
MAGPIES
MAGUIRE
MCGUIRE
MEGRIMS
MOGGIES
MUGGIER
MUGGING
NAGGIER
NAGGING
NAGGISH
NOGGINS
ONGOING
PEGGING
PEGLIKE
PIGGIER
PIGGIES
PIGGING
PIGGISH
PIGLIKE
PUGGISH
PYGMIES
RAGGING
RAGTIME
REGAINS
RIGGING
ROGAINE
ROGUISH
RUGLIKE
SAGGIER
SAGGING
SIGHING
SIGNIFY
SIGNING
SOGGIER
SOGGILY
TAGGING
TAGLIKE
TAGLINE
TIGRISH
TOGGING
TUGGING
TUGRIKS
TVGUIDE
VEGGIES
VEGGING
VOGUISH
WAGGING
WAGGISH
WIGGIER
WIGLIKE
ZAGGING
ZIGGING

••G••I•

ALGERIA
ANGELIC
BEGONIA
EDGEDIN
EDGESIN
EUGENIE
GAGARIN
HYGIEIA
INGRAIN
MCGAVIN
MEGAHIT
NIGERIA
NIGHTIE
ORGANIC
PIGSKIN
PIGTAIL
REGALIA
SEGOVIA
SIGNSIN
WAGTAIL

••G•••I

AFGHANI
MAGNANI
NOGUCHI

•••GI••

ADAGIOS
BAGGIER
BAGGIES
BAGGILY
BAGGING
BANGING
BARGING
BATGIRL
BEGGING
BELGIAN
BELGIUM
BIGGIES
BIGGISH
BILGIER
BINGING
BOGGIER
BOGGING
BOGGISH
BONGING
BOOGIED
BOOGIES
BUDGIES
BUDGING
BUGGIER
BUGGIES
BUGGING
BULGIER
BULGING
BUNGING
BUSGIRL
CADGING
COWGIRL
DIGGING
DINGIER
DINGILY
DINGING
DODGIER
DODGING
DOGGIER
DOGGIES
DOGGING
DOGGISH
ELEGIAC
ELEGIES
ELEGIST
FAGGING
FIZGIGS
FOGGIER
FOGGILY
FOGGING
FORGING
FORGIVE
FRAGILE
FUDGING
GAGGING
GANGING
GAUGING
GINGIVA
GONGING
GORGING
GOUGING
HAGGISH
HANGING
HEDGIER
HEDGING
HIGGINS
HINGING
HOAGIES
HOGGING
HOGGISH
HUGGING
HUGGINS
IMAGINE
IMAGING
JAGGIER
JAGGIES
JAGGING
JIGGING
JIGGISH
JOGGING
JUDGING
JUGGING
JUGGINS
KINGING
LAGGING
LARGISH
LEDGIER
LEGGIER
LEGGING
LODGING
LOGGIAS
LOGGING
LOGGINS
LOGGISH
LONGIES
LONGING
LONGISH
LUGGING
LUNGING
MANGIER
MARGINS
MERGING
MINGIER
MOGGIES
MUGGIER
MUGGING
NAGGIER
NAGGING
NAGGISH
NOGGINS
NUDGING
ORIGINS
PEGGING
PIDGINS
PIGGIER
PIGGIES
PIGGING
PIGGISH
PINGING
PLUGINS
PODGIER
PODGILY
PONGIDS
PONGING
PORGIES
PUDGIER
PUDGILY
PUGGISH
PURGING
RAGGING
RANGIER
RANGING
RIDGIER
RIDGING
RIGGING
RINGING
ROUGING
SAGGIER
SAGGING
SEAGIRT
SEDGIER
SINGING
SOGGIER
SOGGILY
STAGIER
STAGILY
STAGING
STOGIES
STYGIAN
SURGING
TAGGING
TANGIER
TINGING
TOGGING
TUGGING
VEGGIES
VEGGING
VERGING
VIRGINS
WAGGING
WAGGISH
WEDGIER
WEDGIES
WEDGING
WIGGIER
WINGING
ZAGGING
ZIGGING
ZINGIER
ZINGING

•••G•I•

ABIGAIL
BARGAIN
BARGEIN
CHAGRIN
DRAGSIN
GANGLIA
GAUGUIN
GENGHIS
GRIGRIS
HANGSIN
KEYGRIP
KINGPIN
LANGUID
LAUGHIN
PENGUIN
PILGRIM
PLUGSIN
ROUGHIT
SANGRIA
TOUGHIE
TUNGOIL
WEIGHIN
WINGSIT
WINGTIP

•••G••I

BENGALI
ORIGAMI

••••GI•

BRINGIN
DOINGIN
GEORGIA
GIORGIO
GOINGIN
ICINGIN
ILLOGIC
KOSYGIN
PELAGIC
SLOEGIN
TLINGIT
TYINGIN

••••G•I

ASSEGAI
SHANGRI
ZWINGLI

G••J•••

GASJETS

G•••J••

GOODJOB
GOODJOE
GRAYJAY

••GJ•••

BIGJOHN
LOGJAMS

G•K••••

GOKARTS

G••K•••

GASKETS
GASKINS
GAWKERS
GAWKIER
GAWKILY
GAWKING
GAWKISH
GECKOES
GEEKIER
GUNKIER
GURKHAS

G•••K••

GHERKIN
GRACKLE
GRISKIN

G••••K•

GEMLIKE
GOBROKE
GODLIKE
GRETZKY
GROMYKO
GUMLIKE

G•••••K

GANGTOK
GARRICK
GEMSBOK
GETBACK
GIMMICK
GOSHAWK
GOTBACK
GUNLOCK

•G•K•••

AGAKHAN

••G•K••

PIGSKIN

••G••K•

BAGLIKE
DOGLIKE
HAGLIKE
HOGLIKE
JIGLIKE
LEGLIKE
PEGLIKE
PIGLIKE
RUGLIKE
TAGLIKE
TUGRIKS
WIGLIKE

••G•••K

BIGTALK
FOGBANK
HOGBACK
LEGWORK
LOGBOOK

•••GK••

BANGKOK

•••G••K

BANGKOK
GANGTOK

GL•••••

GLACEED
GLACIAL
GLACIER
GLADDEN
GLADDER
GLADEYE
GLAIRED
GLAMOUR
GLANCED
GLANCES
GLARING
GLASGOW
GLASSED
GLASSES
GLAZERS
GLAZIER
GLAZING
GLEAMED
GLEANED
GLEANER
GLEASON
GLEEFUL
GLIBBER
GLIDERS
GLIDING
GLIMMER
GLIMPSE
GLINTED
GLISTEN
GLITTER
GLITZED
GLITZES
GLOATED
GLOBING
GLOBULE
GLOMMED
GLOOMED
GLORIAM
GLORIAS
GLORIED
GLORIES
GLORIFY
GLOSSAE
GLOSSED
GLOSSES
GLOTTAL
GLOTTIS
GLOWERS
GLOWING
GLOZING
GLUCOSE
GLUEDON
GLUESON
GLUGGED
GLUIEST
GLUMMER
GLUTTED
GLUTTON

G•L••••

GALAGOS
GALAHAD
GALATEA
GALATIA
GALILEE
GALILEI
GALILEO
GALLANT
GALLEON
GALLERY
GALLEYS
GALLING
GALLIUM
GALLONS
GALLOPS
GALOOTS
GALPALS
GALUMPH
GALVANI
GELADAS
GELATIN
GELATIS
GELDING
GELIDLY
GELLING
GILBERT
GILBLAS
GILDERS
GILDING
GILGUYS
GILLIAN
GILLIES
GILLING
GILLNET
GOLDBUG
GOLDING
GOLDWYN
GOLFERS
GOLFING
GOLFPRO
GOLFTEE
GOLIATH
GULCHES
GULFING
GULLAHS
GULLETS
GULLIES
GULLING
GULPIER
GULPING

G••L•••

GAGLAWS
GAGLINE
GALLANT
GALLEON
GALLERY
GALLEYS
GALLING
GALLIUM
GALLONS
GALLOPS
GAOLERS
GAOLING
GAPLESS
GARLAND
GASLESS
GASLOGS
GATLING
GAULISH
GELLING
GEMLESS
GEMLIKE
GEOLOGY
GETLOST
GIBLETS
GIBLUES
GIELGUD
GILLIAN
GILLIES
GILLING
GILLNET
GIMLETS
GIRLISH
GOALIES
GOALONG
GOBLETS
GOBLINS
GODLESS
GODLIER
GODLIKE
GOSLING
GOSLOWS
GOTLAND
GOTLOST
GOULASH
GRILLED
GRILLES
GRILLET
GROLIER
GUELPHS
GUILDER
GULLAHS
GULLETS
GULLIES
GULLING
GUMLESS
GUMLIKE
GUNLESS
GUNLOCK
GUTLESS

G•••L••

GABBLED
GABBLES
GAGGLES
GALILEE
GALILEI
GALILEO
GAMBLED
GAMBLER
GAMBLES
GAMELAW
GANGLED
GANGLIA
GANTLET
GARBLED
GARBLES
GARGLED
GARGLES
GATELEG
GAVELED
GAZELLE
GEFILTE
GENTLED
GENTLER
GENTLES
GERALDO
GIGGLED
GIGGLER
GIGGLES
GIGOLOS
GILBLAS
GIRDLED
GIRDLES
GISELLE
GNARLED
GOBBLED
GOBBLER
GOBBLES
GOGGLED
GOGGLES
GORILLA
GRAYLAG
GREELEY
GREMLIN
GRILLED
GRILLES
GRILLET
GROWLED
GROWLER
GUNPLAY
GURGLED
GURGLES
GUZZLED
GUZZLER
GUZZLES

G••••L•

GAGRULE
GALPALS
GAMBOLS
GAUDILY
GAUNTLY
GAUZILY
GAVIALS
GAWKILY
GAZELLE
GELIDLY
GENTILE
GERBILS
GESTALT
GETWELL
GHASTLY
GHOSTLY
GIDDILY
GIMBALS
GINMILL
GISELLE
GLOBULE
GONDOLA
GOODALL
GOOFILY
GOOGOLS
GOONILY
GORILLA
GOSPELS
GOTWELL
GOUTILY
GRACILE
GRACKLE
GRANDLY
GRANOLA
GRANULE
GRAPPLE
GRAVELS
GRAVELY
GREATLY
GRIDDLE
GRIMILY
GRISTLE
GRISTLY
GRIZZLE
GRIZZLY
GROSSLY
GROVELS
GRUFFLY
GRUMBLE
GRUMBLY
GUMBALL
GUNMOLL
GUNNELS
GUNWALE
GUSHILY
GUSTILY
GUTSILY

G•••••L

GABRIEL
GAINFUL
GAMBREL
GASOHOL
GENERAL
GENTEEL
GERITOL
GETREAL
GETWELL
GINMILL
GIRASOL
GLACIAL
GLEEFUL
GLOTTAL
GONERIL
GOODALL
GOTWELL
GRADUAL
GRAPNEL
GRENDEL
GUMBALL
GUNMOLL

•GL••••

OGLALAS
UGLIEST

•G•L•••

AGELESS
AGILELY
AGILITY
EGALITE
EGGLESS

•G••L••

HGWELLS
OGLALAS

•G•••L•

AGILELY
EGGROLL
HGWELLS
IGNOBLE
IGNOBLY

•G••••L

EGGROLL

••GL•••

ANGLERS
ANGLING
BAGLIKE
BIGLIES
BUGLERS
BUGLING
DOGLEGS
DOGLESS
DOGLIKE
EAGLETS
EAGLING
EGGLESS
ENGLAND
ENGLISH
ENGLUND
FIGLEAF
FOGLESS
GAGLAWS
GAGLINE
HAGLIKE
HOGLIKE
JAGLESS
JIGLIKE
KEGLERS
LEGLESS
LEGLIKE
NEGLECT
PEGLESS
PEGLIKE
PIGLETS
PIGLIKE
RAGLANS
REGLETS
REGLUED
REGLUES
RUGLIKE
TAGLIKE
TAGLINE
TIGLONS
TUGLESS
UNGLUED
WIGLESS
WIGLETS
WIGLIKE

••G•L••

ANGELES
ANGELIC
ANGELOU
ANGELUS
ANGOLAN
ANGULAR
ARGYLES
BIGELOW
BOGGLED
BOGGLER
BOGGLES
BUGALOO
BYGOLLY
DOGSLED
ENGULFS
GAGGLES
GIGGLED
GIGGLER
GIGGLES
GIGOLOS
GOGGLED
GOGGLES
HAGGLED
HAGGLER
HAGGLES
HIGGLED
HIGGLES
HIGHLOW
INGALLS
JIGGLED
JIGGLES
JOGGLED
JOGGLES
JUGGLED
JUGGLER
JUGGLES
JUGULAR
LEGALLY
MIGGLES
NIGGLED
NIGGLES
NOGALES
REGALED
REGALES
REGALIA
REGALLY
REGULAR
REGULUS
TAGALOG
TOGGLED
TOGGLES
WAGGLED
WAGGLES
WIGGLED
WIGGLER
WIGGLES

••G••L•

ANGRILY
BAGFULS
BAGGILY
BAGNOLD
BEGUILE
BIGTALK
BOGHOLE
BYGOLLY
EAGERLY
EGGROLL
FOGGILY
GAGRULE
HOGWILD
INGALLS
JUGFULS
LEGALLY
LEGIBLE
LEGIBLY
LEGPULL
LIGHTLY
LOGROLL
NIGHTLY
RAGDOLL
REGALLY
RIGHTLY
RIGIDLY
SIGHTLY
SIGNALS
SOGGILY
TAGSALE
TIGHTLY
UNGODLY
VAGUELY

••G•••L

AUGURAL
BIGDEAL
DIGITAL
EGGROLL
LEGPULL
LOGICAL
LOGROLL
MAGICAL
PAGEFUL
PIGTAIL
RAGDOLL
RAGEFUL
SIGHFUL
VEGETAL
WAGTAIL

•••GL••

BANGLES
BEAGLES
BOGGLED
BOGGLER
BOGGLES
BUNGLED
BUNGLER
BUNGLES
BURGLAR
BURGLED
BURGLES
DANGLED
DANGLER
DANGLES
DINGLES
DONGLES
DOUGLAS
GAGGLES
GANGLED
GANGLIA
GARGLED
GARGLES
GIGGLED
GIGGLER
GIGGLES
GOGGLED
GOGGLES
GURGLED
GURGLES
HAGGLED
HAGGLER
HAGGLES
HIGGLED
HIGGLES
JANGLED
JANGLES
JIGGLED
JIGGLES
JINGLED
JINGLES
JOGGLED
JOGGLES
JUGGLED
JUGGLER
JUGGLES
JUNGLES
LANGLEY
MANGLED
MANGLES
MIGGLES
MINGLED
MINGLER
MINGLES
NIGGLED
NIGGLES
QUIGLEY
RINGLET
SINGLED
SINGLES
SNIGLET
TANGLED
TANGLES
TINGLED
TINGLES
TOGGLED
TOGGLES
WAGGLED
WAGGLES
WANGLED
WANGLER
WANGLES
WIGGLED
WIGGLER
WIGGLES
WRIGLEY

•••G•L•

ARUGULA
BAGGILY
BENGALI
BENGALS
CHAGALL
CUDGELS
DINGILY
FOGGILY
FRAGILE
GOOGOLS
LARGELY
MONGOLS
OLDGOLD
PERGOLA
PODGILY
PUDGILY
ROUGHLY
SEAGULL
SMUGGLE
SNIGGLE
SNUGGLE
SOGGILY
STAGILY
TANGELO
TOUGHLY
VIRGULE
WRIGGLE
WRIGGLY

•••G••L

ABIGAIL
BATGIRL
BUSGIRL
CHAGALL
CONGEAL
COWGIRL
LINGUAL
MONGREL
SEAGULL
SONGFUL
TUNGOIL

••••GL•

ATINGLE
FINAGLE
KRINGLE
SHINGLE
SMUGGLE
SNIGGLE
SNUGGLE
SPANGLE
SPANGLY
WRANGLE

WRIGGLE
WRIGGLY
WRONGLY
ZWINGLI

••••G•L

BRUEGEL
DONEGAL
EVANGEL
ILLEGAL
SENEGAL
SPIEGEL
STENGEL
STIEGEL
WOLFGAL

G•M••••

GAMBADO
GAMBIAN
GAMBITS
GAMBLED
GAMBLER
GAMBLES
GAMBOLS
GAMBREL
GAMELAW
GAMETES
GAMIEST
GAMINES
GAMMERS
GAMMIER
GAMMING
GAMMONS
GEMLESS
GEMLIKE
GEMMIER
GEMOTES
GEMSBOK
GIMBALS
GIMLETS
GIMMICK
GOMPERS
GUMBALL
GUMDROP
GUMLESS
GUMLIKE
GUMMIER
GUMMING
GUMSHOE
GUMTREE
GYMBAGS
GYMNAST
GYMSHOE

G••M•••

GAMMERS
GAMMIER
GAMMING
GAMMONS
GARMENT
GASMAIN
GAUMING
GEMMIER
GERMANE
GERMANS
GERMANY
GERMIER
GIMMICK
GINMILL
GLAMOUR
GLIMMER
GLIMPSE
GLOMMED
GLUMMER
GNOMISH
GNOMONS
GRAMMAR
GRAMMER
GRAMMES
GRAMMYS
GRAMPAS
GRAMPUS
GREMLIN
GRIMACE
GRIMIER
GRIMILY
GRIMING
GRIMMER
GROMMET
GROMYKO
GRUMBLE
GRUMBLY
GRUMPED
GUIMPES
GUMMIER
GUMMING
GUNMOLL

G•••M••

GALUMPH
GATEMAN
GATEMEN
GAZUMPS
GENOMES
GLEAMED
GLIMMER
GLOMMED
GLOOMED
GLUMMER
GOODMAN
GOODMEN
GOURMET
GRAMMAR
GRAMMER
GRAMMES
GRAMMYS
GRIMMER
GROMMET
GROOMED
GROOMER

G••••M•

GASPUMP
GAUTAMA
GIACOMO
GOURAMI
GRAHAME
GRAHAMS
GRANDMA

G•••••M

GALLIUM
GINGHAM
GLORIAM
GRANDAM
GRISHAM
GRISSOM
GUARGUM
GYPROOM

•G••M••

AGNOMEN

•G••••M

EGOTISM

••GM•••

AUGMENT
DOGMATA
FIGMENT
PIGMENT
PYGMIES
RAGMOPS
SEGMENT
SIGMUND

••G•M••

INGEMAR
LEGUMES
MOGAMBO
REGIMEN
REGIMES

••G••M•

BEGRIME
BIGGAME
BIGNAME
BIGTIME
DIGRAMS
ENGRAMS
LOGJAMS
MAGNUMS
MEGOHMS
MEGRIMS
MUGWUMP
RAGTIME
WIGWAMS

••G•••M

EIGHTAM
EIGHTPM
FOGYISM
LEGROOM
ORGANUM
TAGTEAM

•••GM••

BERGMAN
ENIGMAS
FLAGMAN
FLAGMEN
FROGMAN
FROGMEN
HANGMAN
HANGMEN
KINGMAN
KLUGMAN
STIGMAS
SYNGMAN
ZEUGMAS

•••G•M•

BEEGUMS
BIGGAME
CONGAME
ENDGAME
ORIGAMI
REDGUMS
WARGAME

•••G••M

ANAGRAM
BELGIUM
BINGHAM
BRIGHAM
DIAGRAM
EPIGRAM
FULGHUM
GINGHAM
KINGDOM
LONGARM
MAUGHAM
PILGRIM
PROGRAM
SEAGRAM
SORGHUM
TANGRAM
TRIGRAM

••••GM•

YOUNGMC

••••G•M

AMALGAM
BLUEGUM
GUARGUM

GN•••••

GNARLED
GNARRED
GNASHED
GNASHES
GNAWERS
GNAWING
GNOCCHI
GNOMISH
GNOMONS
GNOSTIC

G•N••••

GANDERS
GANGERS
GANGING
GANGLED
GANGLIA
GANGSAW
GANGSTA
GANGSUP
GANGTOK
GANGWAY
GANNETS
GANNETT
GANTLET
GENDERS
GENERAL
GENERIC
GENERIS
GENESEE
GENESES
GENESIS
GENETIC
GENGHIS
GENNARO
GENOESE
GENOMES
GENTEEL
GENTIAN
GENTILE
GENTLED
GENTLER
GENTLES
GENUINE
GINFIZZ
GINGERS
GINGERY
GINGHAM
GINGIVA
GINMILL
GINNING
GINSENG
GONDOLA
GONERIL
GONGING
GUNBOAT
GUNDOGS
GUNFIRE
GUNKIER
GUNLESS
GUNLOCK
GUNMOLL
GUNNELS
GUNNERS
GUNNERY
GUNNIES
GUNNING
GUNPLAY
GUNSFOR
GUNSHOT
GUNTHER
GUNWALE

G••N•••

GAINERS
GAINFUL
GAINING
GAINSAY
GAINSON
GANNETS
GANNETT
GARNERS
GARNETS
GARNISH
GAUNTER
GAUNTLY
GENNARO
GHANIAN
GINNING
GIRNING
GLANCED
GLANCES
GLINTED
GOINFOR
GOINGAT
GOINGBY
GOINGIN
GOINGON
GOINGUP
GOONIER
GOONILY
GOUNDER
GRANADA
GRANARY
GRANDAM
GRANDEE
GRANDER
GRANDLY
GRANDMA
GRANDPA
GRANGER
GRANGES
GRANITE
GRANOLA
GRANTED
GRANTEE
GRANTOR
GRANULE
GRENADA
GRENADE
GRENDEL
GRINDER
GRINNED
GRINNER
GRUNGES
GRUNION
GRUNTED
GUANACO
GUANINE
GUINEAS
GUNNELS
GUNNERS
GUNNERY
GUNNIES
GUNNING
GURNEYS
GWYNETH
GYMNAST

G•••N••

GAMINES
GARDNER
GARONNE
GERENTS
GERUNDS
GETINTO
GILLNET
GIRONDE
GIVENIN
GIVENTO
GIVENUP
GLEANED
GLEANER
GODUNOV
GOTINTO
GRAINED
GRAPNEL
GREENED
GREENER
GRINNED
GRINNER
GROANED
GROANER
GROUNDS
GROWNUP
GYRENES

G••••N•

GABBING
GADDING
GAFFING
GAGGING
GAGLINE
GAINING
GAITING
GALLANT
GALLING
GALLONS
GALVANI
GAMMING
GAMMONS
GANGING
GAOLING
GAPPING
GARBING
GARCONS
GARDENS
GARLAND
GARMENT
GARONNE
GASCONS
GASCONY
GASHING
GASKINS
GASPING
GATLING
GAUGING
GAUMING
GAWKING
GAWPING
GEARING
GELDING
GELLING
GENUINE
GERAINT
GERMANE
GERMANS
GERMANY
GETTING
GIBBING
GIBBONS
GIDEONS
GILDING
GILLING
GINNING
GINSENG
GIPPING
GIRDING
GIRNING
GLARING
GLAZING
GLIDING
GLOBING
GLOWING
GLOZING
GNAWING
GNOMONS
GOADING
GOALONG
GOBLINS
GODSEND
GODSONS
GOLDING
GOLFING
GONGING
GOODING
GOODONE
GOOFING
GOOSING
GORGING
GORGONS
GOROUND
GOSLING
GOTLAND
GOUGING
GOVERNS
GOWRONG
GRACING
GRADING
GRATING
GRAVING
GRAYING
GRAZING
GREYING
GRIMING
GRIPING
GROPING
GROWING
GUANINE
GUARANI
GUIDING
GUIDONS
GULFING
GULLING
GULPING
GUMMING
GUNNING
GUSHING
GUSTING
GUTTING
GYPPING

G•••••N

GADSDEN
GAGARIN
GAINSON
GALLEON
GAMBIAN
GASMAIN
GATEMAN
GATEMEN
GAUGUIN
GELATIN
GENTIAN
GETDOWN
GETEVEN
GETITON
GHANIAN
GHERKIN
GILLIAN
GIVENIN
GIVESIN
GLADDEN
GLEASON
GLISTEN
GLUEDON
GLUESON
GLUTTON
GOINGIN
GOINGON
GOLDWYN
GOODMAN
GOODMEN
GOODSON
GOODWIN
GORDIAN
GOTDOWN
GOTEVEN
GOTITON
GRAFTON
GRAYSON
GRECIAN
GREMLIN
GREYHEN
GRIFFIN
GRIFFON
GRISKIN
GROWSON
GRUNION
GRYPHON

•GN••••

AGNATES
AGNOMEN
IGNEOUS
IGNITED
IGNITER
IGNITES
IGNOBLE
IGNOBLY
IGNORED
IGNORER
IGNORES

•G•N•••

AGENDAS
AGONISE
AGONIST
AGONIZE
EGGNOGS
UGANDAN

•G••N••

AGAINST
IGUANAS

•G•••N•

AGROUND

•G••••N

AGAKHAN
AGNOMEN
EGGEDON
UGANDAN

••GN•••

BAGNOLD
BIGNAME
BIGNESS
COGNACS
COGNATE
CYGNETS
DIGNIFY
DIGNITY
EGGNOGS
LIGNITE
LUGNUTS
MAGNANI
MAGNATE
MAGNETO
MAGNETS
MAGNIFY
MAGNUMS
PIGNUTS
PUGNOSE
REGNANT
SIGNALS
SIGNEES
SIGNERS
SIGNETS
SIGNIFY
SIGNING
SIGNOFF
SIGNOUT
SIGNSIN
SIGNSON
SIGNSUP

••G•N••

ARGONNE
AUGENDS
BEGONIA
BYGONES
COGENCY
DUGONGS
EDGINGS
ENGINES
EUGENIE
FAGENDS
INGENUE
LAGUNAS
LEGENDS
LIGANDS
MAGENTA
MAGINOT
ORGANDY
ORGANIC
ORGANON
ORGANUM
ORGANZA
REGENCY
REGENTS
SAGINAW
TAGENDS
URGENCY
WAGONER

••G••N•

AFGHANI
AFGHANS
ANGLING
ARGONNE
ARGUING
AUGMENT
BAGGING
BEGGING
BEGUINE
BIGBAND
BIGBANG
BIGBEND
BIGGUNS
BOGGING
BUGGING
BUGLING
DIGGING
DOGBANE
DOGGING
DOGGONE
EAGLING
ENGLAND
ENGLUND
FAGGING
FIGMENT
FOGBANK
FOGGING
GAGGING
GAGLINE
HAGDONS
HIGGINS
HIGHEND
HOGGING
HUGGING
HUGGINS
HYGIENE
JAGGING
JIGGING
JOGGING
JUGBAND
JUGGING
JUGGINS
JUGWINE
LAGGING
LAGOONS
LEGGING
LEGIONS
LEGRAND
LOGGING
LOGGINS
LUGGING
MAGNANI
MIGHTNT
MIGRANT
MUGGING
NAGGING
NOGGINS
ONGOING
OUGHTNT
PAGEANT
PEGGING
PIGEONS
PIGGING
PIGMENT
PIGPENS
RAGGING
RAGLANS
REGAINS
REGIONS
REGNANT
RIGGING
ROGAINE
SAGGING
SEGMENT
SIGHING
SIGMUND
SIGNING
TAGGANT
TAGGING
TAGLINE
TIGLONS
TOGGING
TUGGING
UNGUENT
USGRANT
VAGRANT
VEGGING
WAGGING
WAGGONS
ZAGGING
ZIGGING

••G•••N

ANGOLAN
BIGHORN
BIGJOHN
BOGDOWN
COGBURN
EDGEDIN
EDGESIN
EGGEDON
FOGHORN
GAGARIN
INGRAIN
INGROWN
LEGHORN
LIGHTEN
MCGAVIN
MEGRYAN
ORGANON
PIGIRON
PIGSKIN
REGIMEN
RIGHTON
SAGEHEN
SIGNSIN
SIGNSON
TIGHTEN

•••GN••

ALIGNED
ALIGNER
AVIGNON
CHIGNON
DEIGNED
DRAGNET
FEIGNED
REIGNED
SOIGNEE
WINGNUT

•••G•N•

AIRGUNS
ALLGONE
BAGGING
BANGING
BARGING
BEGGING
BIGGUNS
BINGING
BIOGENY
BOGGING
BONGING
BRIGAND
BROGANS
BUDGING
BUGGING
BULGING
BUNGING
CADGING
CAPGUNS
DIGGING
DINGING
DODGING
DOGGING
DOGGONE
DRAGONS
ELEGANT
EPIGENE
EPIGONE
EXIGENT
FAGGING
FARGONE
FLAGONS
FOGGING
FORGING
FORGONE
FUDGING
FULGENT
GAGGING
GANGING
GAUGING
GONGING
GORGING
GORGONS
GOUGING
HANGING
HEDGING
HIGGINS
HINGING
HOGGING
HUGGING
HUGGINS
HUYGENS
IMAGINE
IMAGING
IMOGENE
ISOGONS
JAGGING
JARGONS
JARGONY
JETGUNS
JIGGING
JOGGING
JUDGING
JUGGING
JUGGINS
KINGING
LAGGING
LEGGING
LODGING
LOGGING
LOGGINS
LONGING
LUGGING
LUNGING
MARGINS
MERGING
MORGANA
MORGANS
MUGGING
NAGGING
NOGGINS
NUDGING
OREGANO
ORIGINS
OROGENY
OURGANG
OUTGUNS
PEGGING
PIDGINS
PIGGING
PINGING
PLUGINS
PONGING
POPGUNS
PROGENY
PUNGENT
PURGING
RAGGING
RANGING
RAYGUNS
REAGENT
RIDGING
RIGGING
RINGING
ROUGING
SAGGING
SARGENT
SHOGUNS
SINGING
SIXGUNS
SLOGANS
STAGING
SURGING
TAGGANT
TAGGING
TANGENT
TINGING
TOGGING
TONGANS
TOPGUNS
TRIGONS
TROGONS
TUGGING
VEGGING
VERGING
VIRGINS
WAGGING
WAGGONS
WEDGING
WINGING
YEVGENY
ZAGGING
ZIGGING
ZINGING

•••G••N

AVIGNON
BARGAIN
BARGEIN
BELGIAN
BERGMAN
BERGSON
BURGEON
CHAGRIN
CHIGNON
DODGSON
DRAGOON
DRAGSIN
DRAGSON
DUDGEON
DUNGEON
FLAGMAN
FLAGMEN
FROGMAN
FROGMEN
GAUGUIN
HANGMAN
HANGMEN
HANGSIN
HANGSON
HANGTEN
KINGMAN
KINGPIN
KLUGMAN
LANGDON
LAUGHIN
LONGRUN
LONGTON
PENGUIN
PIDGEON
PLUGSIN
RANGOON
ROUGHEN
STYGIAN
SURGEON
SYNGMAN
TOUGHEN
VAUGHAN
VIRGOAN
WEIGHIN
WIDGEON

••••GN•

ASSIGNS
BOLOGNA
COLOGNE
COSIGNS
DESIGNS
ELOIGNS
ENSIGNS
EPERGNE
IMPUGNS
LASAGNA
LASAGNE
MALIGNS
OPPUGNS
REPUGNS
RESIGNS
SEVIGNE

••••G•N

ANTIGEN
BLOWGUN
BRINGIN
BRINGON
BURPGUN
CRYOGEN
DECAGON
DOINGIN
GOINGIN
GOINGON
HALOGEN
HANDGUN
HEXAGON
ICINGIN
KLINGON
KOSYGIN
MADIGAN
MUTAGEN
NONAGON
OCTAGON
PARAGON
POLYGON
RONTGEN
SHOTGUN
SLOEGIN
SMIDGEN
STUNGUN
TYINGIN
WOBEGON
YOUNGUN

•••••GN

ARRAIGN
CONDIGN
CONSIGN
FOREIGN
HEXSIGN

GO•••••

GOABOUT
GOADING
GOAFTER
GOAHEAD
GOALIES
GOALONG
GOATEED
GOATEES
GOATISH

GOBBLED
GOBBLER
GOBBLES
GOBLETS
GOBLINS
GOBROKE
GOCARTS
GODDARD
GODDESS
GODFREY
GODLESS
GODLIER
GODLIKE
GODSEND
GODSONS
GODTHAB
GODUNOV
GODUTCH
GODWITS
GOESAPE
GOESBAD
GOESFOR
GOESOFF
GOESOUT
GOFORIT
GOGGLED
GOGGLES
GOINFOR
GOINGAT
GOINGBY
GOINGIN
GOINGON
GOINGUP
GOKARTS
GOLDBUG
GOLDING
GOLDWYN
GOLFERS
GOLFING
GOLFPRO
GOLFTEE
GOLIATH
GOMPERS
GONDOLA
GONERIL
GONGING
GOOBERS
GOODALL
GOODBAR
GOODBYE
GOODBYS
GOODEGG
GOODIES
GOODING
GOODISH
GOODJOB
GOODJOE
GOODMAN
GOODMEN
GOODONE
GOODSON
GOODWIN
GOOFIER
GOOFILY
GOOFING
GOOFOFF
GOOFSUP
GOOFUPS
GOOGOLS
GOOIEST
GOONIER
GOONILY
GOOPIER
GOOSIER
GOOSING
GOPHERS
GORDIAN
GORETEX
GORGETS
GORGING
GORGONS
GORIEST
GORILLA
GOROUND
GORSIER
GOSHAWK
GOSLING
GOSLOWS
GOSPELS
GOSSETT
GOSSIPS
GOSSIPY
GOTAWAY
GOTBACK
GOTCHAS
GOTDOWN
GOTEVEN
GOTHICS
GOTINTO
GOTITON
GOTLAND
GOTLOST
GOTOPOT
GOTOVER
GOTWELL
GOUACHE
GOUGERS
GOUGING
GOULASH
GOUNDER
GOURAMI
GOURDES
GOURMET
GOUTIER
GOUTILY
GOUTISH
GOVERNS
GOWRONG

G•O••••

GAOLERS
GAOLING
GEODESY
GEOLOGY
GEORDIE
GEORGES
GEORGIA
GHOSTED
GHOSTLY
GIORGIO
GLOATED
GLOBING
GLOBULE
GLOMMED
GLOOMED
GLORIAM
GLORIAS
GLORIED
GLORIES
GLORIFY
GLOSSAE
GLOSSED
GLOSSES
GLOTTAL
GLOTTIS
GLOWERS
GLOWING
GLOZING
GNOCCHI
GNOMISH
GNOMONS
GNOSTIC
GOOBERS
GOODALL
GOODBAR
GOODBYE
GOODBYS
GOODEGG
GOODIES
GOODING
GOODISH
GOODJOB
GOODJOE
GOODMAN
GOODMEN
GOODONE
GOODSON
GOODWIN
GOOFIER
GOOFILY
GOOFING
GOOFOFF
GOOFSUP
GOOFUPS
GOOGOLS
GOOIEST
GOONIER
GOONILY
GOOPIER
GOOSIER
GOOSING
GROANED
GROANER
GROCERS
GROCERY
GRODIER
GROLIER
GROMMET
GROMYKO
GROOMED
GROOMER
GROOVED
GROOVES
GROPING
GROPIUS
GROSSED
GROSSER
GROSSES
GROSSLY
GROTTOS
GROUCHO
GROUCHY
GROUNDS
GROUPED
GROUPER
GROUPIE
GROUSED
GROUSER
GROUSES
GROUTED
GROVELS
GROWERS
GROWING
GROWLED
GROWLER
GROWNUP
GROWSON
GROWSUP
GROWTHS

G••O•••

GALOOTS
GARONNE
GASOHOL
GAVOTTE
GEMOTES
GENOESE
GENOMES
GETOVER
GIGOLOS
GIRONDE
GLOOMED
GOFORIT
GOROUND
GOTOPOT
GOTOVER
GROOMED
GROOMER
GROOVED
GROOVES

G•••O••

GALLONS
GALLOPS
GALOOTS
GAMBOLS
GAMMONS
GARCONS
GASCONS
GASCONY
GASEOUS
GASLOGS
GAVEOFF
GAVEOUT
GECKOES
GEOLOGY
GESSOES
GETDOWN
GETLOST
GETSOFF
GETSOUT
GIACOMO
GIBBONS
GIBBOUS
GIDEONS
GIFFORD
GIVEOFF
GIVEOUT
GLAMOUR
GLUCOSE
GNOMONS
GOABOUT
GOALONG
GOBROKE
GODSONS
GOESOFF
GOESOUT
GONDOLA
GOODONE
GOOFOFF
GOOGOLS
GORGONS
GOSLOWS
GOTDOWN
GOTLOST
GOWRONG
GRANOLA
GREGORY
GUIDONS
GUNBOAT
GUNDOGS
GUNLOCK
GUNMOLL
GUSTOES
GYPROOM

G••••O•

GABBROS
GAINSON
GALAGOS
GALLEON
GANGTOK
GASOHOL
GAUCHOS
GAZEBOS
GEARBOX
GEMSBOK
GERITOL
GETITON
GHETTOS
GIGOLOS
GIRASOL
GLASGOW
GLEASON
GLUEDON
GLUESON
GLUTTON
GODUNOV
GOESFOR
GOINFOR
GOINGON
GOODJOB
GOODJOE
GOODSON
GOTITON
GOTOPOT
GRAFTON
GRANTOR
GRAYSON
GRIFFON
GRISSOM
GROTTOS
GROWSON
GRUNION
GRYPHON
GUMDROP
GUMSHOE
GUNSFOR
GUNSHOT
GYMSHOE
GYPROOM
GYRATOR

G•••••O

GALILEO
GAMBADO
GEARSTO
GENNARO
GERALDO
GETINTO
GIACOMO
GIORGIO
GIVENTO
GIVESTO
GOLFPRO
GOTINTO
GROMYKO
GROUCHO
GUANACO

•GO••••

AGONISE
AGONIST
AGONIZE
AGOUTIS
EGOISTS
EGOTISM
EGOTIST
EGOTRIP

•G•O•••

AGNOMEN
AGROUND
IGNOBLE
IGNOBLY
IGNORED
IGNORER
IGNORES
OGDOADS

•G••O••

EGGNOGS
EGGROLL
IGNEOUS

•G•••O•

EGGEDON

•G••••O

AGESAGO
AGITATO
AGREETO

••GO•••

ANGOLAN
ANGORAS
ARGONNE
BEGONIA
BEGORRA
BIGOSES
BIGOTED
BIGOTRY
BYGOLLY
BYGONES
DUGONGS
DUGOUTS
ENGORGE
FAGOTED
GIGOLOS
LAGOONS
MEGOHMS
ONGOING
PAGODAS
RAGOUTS
RIGOURS
SEGOVIA
UNGODLY
VIGOURS
WAGONER
ZYGOTES

••G•O••

BAGNOLD
BEGSOFF
BIGBOYS
BIGFOOT
BIGHORN
BIGJOHN
BIGTOES
BIGTOPS
BOGDOWN
BOGHOLE
BUGSOFF
BUGSOUT
DAGWOOD
DIGSOUT
DOGFOOD
DOGGONE
DOGWOOD
EDGEOUT
EGGNOGS
EGGROLL
ENGROSS
FOGBOWS
FOGHORN
HAGDONS
INGROUP
INGROWN
LAGOONS
LEGHORN
LEGIONS
LEGROOM
LEGWORK
LOGBOOK
LOGROLL
LOGSOFF
LOGSOUT
PEGTOPS
PIGEONS
PIGSOUT
PUGNOSE
RAGDOLL
RAGMOPS
RAGTOPS
REGIONS
REGROUP
SIGNOFF
SIGNOUT
TAGSOUT
TIGLONS
TUGBOAT
WAGGONS
WIGSOUT

••G••O•

ANGELOU
BIGELOW
BIGFOOT
BIGSHOT
BUGABOO
BUGALOO
DAGWOOD
DOGCHOW
DOGFOOD
DOGSHOW
DOGTROT
DOGWOOD
EGGEDON
GIGOLOS
HIGHBOY
HIGHLOW
HIGHTOP
LEGATOS
LEGROOM
LOGBOOK
MAGINOT
MUGSHOT
NEGATOR
ORGANON
PAGEBOY
PIGIRON
RIGHTON
SIGNSON
TAGALOG

••G•••O

BUGABOO
BUGALOO
ELGRECO
MAGNETO
MEGIDDO
MOGAMBO
SAGUARO

•••GO••

ALLGONE
BINGOES
BONGOES
BURGOOS
CARGOES
CHIGOES
DIDGOOD
DINGOES
DOGGONE
DRAGONS
DRAGOON
DRAGOUT
EPIGONE
FARGONE
FLAGONS
FORGOES
FORGONE
FORGOOD
FUNGOES
GOOGOLS
GORGONS
GREGORY
HANGOFF
HANGOUT
HUNGOUT
IMAGOES
ISOGONS
JARGONS
JARGONY
JINGOES
LINGOES
MANGOES
MONGOLS
OLDGOLD
OMIGOSH
OUTGOES
PERGOLA
RANGOFF
RANGOON
RANGOUT
RINGOFF
RINGOUT
RUNGOFF
RUNGOUT
SANGOUT
SINGOUT
SPIGOTS
SUNGODS
TANGOED
TRIGONS
TROGONS
TUNGOIL
VANGOGH
VIRGOAN
WAGGONS
WARGODS
XINGOUT

•••G•O•

ADAGIOS
AVIGNON
BANGKOK
BERGSON
BURGEON
BURGOOS
CHIGNON
DIDGOOD
DODGSON
DRAGOON
DRAGSON
DUDGEON
DUNGEON
FORGOOD
GANGTOK
HANGDOG
HANGSON
KINGDOM
LANGDON
LANGUOR
LONGBOW
LONGTON
OUTGROW
PEUGEOT
PIDGEON
RANGOON
SURGEON
WIDGEON

•••G••O

HEIGHHO
LONGAGO
OREGANO
QINGDAO
SINGSTO
TANGELO

••••GO•

BRINGON
CLANGOR
DECAGON
DEMIGOD
GALAGOS
GLASGOW
GOINGON
HEXAGON
INDIGOS
KLINGON
LITHGOW
MRMAGOO
NONAGON
OCTAGON
PAPAGOS
PARAGON
POLYGON
QUANGOS
STINGOS
VIRAGOS
WOBEGON

••••G•O

ALLEGRO
BRINGTO
GIORGIO
LYINGTO
MRMAGOO
OWINGTO

•••••GO

AGESAGO
AMERIGO
BENDIGO
CHICAGO
DOMINGO
DURANGO
EMBARGO
FARRAGO
HIDALGO
LENTIGO
LONGAGO
LUMBAGO
MARENGO
MONTEGO
ONTHEGO
SAPSAGO
UNDERGO
VERDUGO
VERTIGO
ZHIVAGO

G•P••••

GAPLESS
GAPPING
GIPPING
GIPSIES
GOPHERS
GUPPIES
GYPPERS
GYPPING
GYPROOM
GYPSIES

G••P•••

GALPALS
GAPPING
GASPERS
GASPING
GASPUMP
GAWPING
GIPPING
GOMPERS
GOOPIER
GOSPELS
GRAPHED
GRAPHIC
GRAPIER
GRAPNEL
GRAPPAS
GRAPPLE
GRIPERS
GRIPING
GRIPPED
GRIPPER
GROPING
GROPIUS
GRYPHON
GULPIER
GULPING
GUNPLAY
GUPPIES
GYPPERS
GYPPING

G•••P••

GLIMPSE
GOLFPRO
GOTOPOT
GRAMPAS
GRAMPUS
GRAPPAS
GRAPPLE
GRASPED
GRIPPED
GRIPPER
GROUPED
GROUPER
GROUPIE
GRUMPED
GUELPHS
GUIMPES

G••••P•

GALLOPS
GALUMPH
GASCAPS
GAZUMPS
GIVEUPS
GOESAPE
GOOFUPS
GOSSIPS
GOSSIPY
GRANDPA

G•••••P

GANGSUP
GASPUMP
GEARSUP
GIDDYAP
GIDDYUP
GIVENUP
GIVESUP
GOINGUP
GOOFSUP
GROWNUP
GROWSUP
GUMDROP
GUSSYUP

•G••P••

AGRIPPA

•G•••P•

AGRIPPA
EGGCUPS

•G••••P

EGOTRIP
IGIVEUP

••GP•••

BAGPIPE
LEGPULL
MAGPIES
PIGPENS

••G•P••

BAGPIPE
BIGTOPS
DIGRAPH
EGGCUPS
EIGHTPM
PEGTOPS
RAGMOPS
RAGTOPS

••G•••P

HIGHTOP
INGROUP
LIGHTUP
MUGWUMP
REGROUP
SIGNSUP

•••GP••

KINGPIN

•••G•P•

HANGUPS

•••G••P

BANGSUP
CLOGSUP
COUGHUP
GANGSUP
HANGSUP
KEYGRIP
RINGSUP
ROUGHUP
WINGTIP

••••G•P

BRINGUP
DOINGUP
GOINGUP
ICINGUP
MEDIGAP
STOPGAP
TYINGUP
USINGUP

GR•••••

GRABBAG
GRABBED
GRABBER
GRABSAT
GRACIAS
GRACILE
GRACING
GRACKLE
GRADERS
GRADING
GRADUAL
GRAFTED
GRAFTON
GRAHAME
GRAHAMS
GRAINED
GRAMMAR
GRAMMER
GRAMMES
GRAMMYS
GRAMPAS
GRAMPUS
GRANADA
GRANARY
GRANDAM
GRANDEE
GRANDER
GRANDLY
GRANDMA
GRANDPA
GRANGER
GRANGES
GRANITE
GRANOLA
GRANTED
GRANTEE
GRANTOR
GRANULE
GRAPHED
GRAPHIC
GRAPIER
GRAPNEL
GRAPPAS
GRAPPLE
GRASPED
GRASSED
GRASSES
GRATERS
GRATIAS
GRATIFY
GRATING
GRAVELS
GRAVELY
GRAVERS
GRAVEST
GRAVIES
GRAVING
GRAVITY
GRAVURE
GRAYEST
GRAYING
GRAYISH
GRAYJAY
GRAYLAG
GRAYSON
GRAZERS
GRAZING
GREASED
GREASER
GREASES
GREATER
GREATLY
GREAVES
GRECIAN
GREELEY
GREENED
GREENER
GREETED
GREETER
GREGORY
GREMLIN
GRENADA
GRENADE
GRENDEL
GRETZKY
GREYEST
GREYHEN
GREYING
GREYISH
GRIDDED
GRIDDER
GRIDDLE
GRIEVED
GRIEVER
GRIEVES
GRIFFEY
GRIFFIN
GRIFFON
GRIFTER
GRIGRIS
GRILLED
GRILLES
GRILLET
GRIMACE
GRIMIER
GRIMILY
GRIMING
GRIMMER
GRINDER
GRINNED
GRINNER
GRIPERS
GRIPING
GRIPPED
GRIPPER
GRISHAM
GRISKIN
GRISSOM
GRISTLE
GRISTLY
GRITTED
GRIVETS
GRIZZLE
GRIZZLY
GROANED
GROANER
GROCERS
GROCERY
GRODIER
GROLIER
GROMMET
GROMYKO
GROOMED
GROOMER
GROOVED
GROOVES
GROPING
GROPIUS
GROSSED
GROSSER
GROSSES
GROSSLY
GROTTOS
GROUCHO
GROUCHY
GROUNDS
GROUPED
GROUPER
GROUPIE
GROUSED
GROUSER
GROUSES
GROUTED
GROVELS
GROWERS
GROWING
GROWLED
GROWLER
GROWNUP
GROWSON
GROWSUP
GROWTHS
GRUBBED
GRUDGED
GRUDGES
GRUFFER
GRUFFLY
GRUMBLE
GRUMBLY
GRUMPED
GRUNGES
GRUNION
GRUNTED
GRUYERE
GRYPHON

G•R••••

GARAGED
GARAGES
GARBAGE
GARBING
GARBLED
GARBLES
GARCONS
GARDENS
GARDNER
GARGLED
GARGLES
GARLAND
GARMENT
GARNERS
GARNETS
GARNISH
GARONNE
GARRETS
GARRETT
GARRICK
GARTERS
GERAINT
GERALDO
GERBILS
GERENTS
GERITOL
GERMANE
GERMANS
GERMANY
GERMIER
GERUNDS
GIRAFFE
GIRASOL
GIRDERS
GIRDING
GIRDLED
GIRDLES
GIRLISH
GIRNING
GIRONDE
GORDIAN
GORETEX
GORGETS
GORGING

GORGONS
GORIEST
GORILLA
GOROUND
GORSIER
GURGLED
GURGLES
GURKHAS
GURNEYS
GYRATED
GYRATES
GYRATOR
GYRENES

G••R•••

GABRIEL
GAGRULE
GARRETS
GARRETT
GARRICK
GEARBOX
GEARING
GEARSTO
GEARSUP
GEORDIE
GEORGES
GEORGIA
GETREAL
GHERKIN
GIORGIO
GLARING
GLORIAM
GLORIAS
GLORIED
GLORIES
GLORIFY
GNARLED
GNARRED
GOBROKE
GOURAMI
GOURDES
GOURMET
GOWRONG
GUARANI
GUARDED
GUARDEE
GUARGUM
GYPROOM

G•••R••

GABBROS
GAGARIN
GAMBREL
GASTRIC
GENERAL
GENERIC
GENERIS
GLAIRED
GNARRED
GOCARTS
GODFREY
GOFORIT
GOKARTS
GONERIL
GOVERNS
GRIGRIS
GUMDROP
GUMTREE
GUTHRIE

G••••R•

GABBERS
GADDERS
GAFFERS
GAINERS
GAITERS
GALLERY
GAMMERS
GANDERS
GANGERS
GAOLERS
GARNERS
GARTERS
GASPERS
GASSERS
GATHERS
GAUGERS
GAWKERS
GEEZERS
GENDERS
GENNARO
GESTURE
GEYSERS
GIBBERS
GIFFORD
GILBERT
GILDERS
GINGERS
GINGERY
GIRDERS
GIZZARD
GLAZERS
GLIDERS
GLOWERS
GNAWERS
GODDARD
GOLFERS
GOLFPRO
GOMPERS
GOOBERS
GOPHERS
GOUGERS
GRADERS
GRANARY
GRATERS
GRAVERS
GRAVURE
GRAZERS
GREGORY
GRIPERS
GROCERS
GROCERY
GROWERS
GRUYERE
GUEVARA
GUITARS
GUNFIRE
GUNNERS
GUNNERY
GUSHERS
GUTTERS
GYPPERS

G•••••R

GABBIER
GAGSTER
GAMBLER
GAMMIER
GARDNER
GASSIER
GAUCHER
GAUDIER
GAUNTER
GAUZIER
GAWKIER
GEEKIER
GEMMIER
GENTLER
GERMIER
GETOVER
GIDDIER
GIGGLER
GLACIER
GLADDER
GLAMOUR
GLAZIER
GLEANER
GLIBBER
GLIMMER
GLITTER
GLUMMER
GOAFTER
GOBBLER
GODLIER
GOESFOR
GOINFOR
GOODBAR
GOOFIER
GOONIER
GOOPIER
GOOSIER
GORSIER
GOTOVER
GOUNDER
GOUTIER
GRABBER
GRAMMAR
GRAMMER
GRANDER
GRANGER
GRANTOR
GRAPIER
GREASER
GREATER
GREENER
GREETER
GRIDDER
GRIEVER
GRIFTER
GRIMIER
GRIMMER
GRINDER
GRINNER
GRIPPER
GROANER
GRODIER
GROLIER
GROOMER
GROSSER
GROUPER
GROUSER
GROWLER
GRUFFER
GUESSER
GUILDER
GULPIER
GUMMIER
GUNKIER
GUNSFOR
GUNTHER
GUSHIER
GUSTIER
GUTSIER
GUTTIER
GUZZLER
GYRATOR

•GR••••

AGRAFFE
AGREETO
AGRIPPA
AGROUND
OGREISH

•G•R•••

AGARICS
AGGRESS
EGGROLL

•G••R••

EGOTRIP
IGNORED
IGNORER
IGNORES

•G••••R

IGNITER
IGNORER

••GR•••

AGGRESS
AIGRETS
ANGRIER
ANGRILY
BEGRIME
DEGRADE
DEGREES
DIGRAMS
DIGRAPH
DIGRESS
EGGROLL
ELGRECO
ENGRAFT
ENGRAMS
ENGRAVE
ENGROSS
GAGRULE
INGRAIN
INGRATE
INGRESS
INGROUP
INGROWN
LEGRAND
LEGROOM
LOGROLL
MEGRIMS
MEGRYAN
MIGRANT
MIGRATE
PUGREES
RAGRUGS
REGRADE
REGRESS
REGRETS
REGROUP
TIGRESS
TIGRISH
TUGRIKS
UPGRADE
USGRANT
VAGRANT

••G•R••

ALGERIA
ANGERED
ANGORAS
AUGURAL
AUGURED
BEGORRA
BUGFREE
DOGTROT
EAGERER
EAGERLY
ENGARDE
ENGIRDS
ENGORGE
FIGURED
FIGURER
FIGURES
GAGARIN
HEGIRAS
HOGARTH
NIGERIA
PIGIRON
REGARDS
SUGARED
UNGIRDS
WAGERED
WAGERER
YOGURTS

••G••R•

ALGEBRA
ALGIERS
ANGLERS
ARGUERS
BAGGERS
BEGGARS
BEGORRA
BIGBIRD
BIGGERS
BIGHORN
BIGOTRY
BUGLERS
COGBURN
DAGGERS
DIGGERS
DOGBERT
DOGCART
DOGEARS
FOGGERS
FOGHORN
HAGGARD
HUGGERS
JAGUARS
JIGGERS
JIGGERY
JOGGERS
KEGLERS
LAGGARD
LAGGERS
LEGHORN
LEGWORK
LOGGERS
LUGGERS
MAGUIRE
MAGYARS
MCGUIRE
MUGGERS
NIGGARD
ONGUARD
PIGGERY
RIGGERS
RIGOURS
ROGUERY
SAGUARO
SIGHERS
SIGNERS
TOGGERY
TUGGERS
VIGOURS
WAGGERY
YOGHURT

••G•••R

ANGRIER
ANGULAR
BAGGIER
BOGGIER
BOGGLER
BUGBEAR
BUGGIER
DOGGIER
DOGSTAR
EAGERER
FIGHTER
FIGURER
FOGGIER
GAGSTER
GIGGLER
HAGGLER
INGEMAR
JAGGIER
JUGGLER
JUGULAR
LEGGIER
LIGHTER
MUGGIER
NAGGIER
NEGATER
NEGATOR
PIGGIER
REGULAR
RIGHTER
SAGGIER
SOGGIER
TIGHTER
WAGERER
WAGONER
WIGGIER
WIGGLER

•••GR••

ANAGRAM
CHAGRIN
DIAGRAM
EMIGRES
EPIGRAM
GRIGRIS
KEYGRIP
KINGRAT
LONGRUN
MACGRAW
MAIGRET
MARGRET
MONGREL
OUTGREW
OUTGROW
PILGRIM
PROGRAM
SANGRIA
SEAGRAM
TANGRAM
TRIGRAM

•••G•R•

BADGERS
BAGGERS
BATGIRL
BEGGARS
BERGERE
BIGGERS
BULGARS
BURGERS
BUSGIRL
CADGERS
CALGARY
CODGERS
CONGERS
COUGARS
COWGIRL
DAGGERS
DANGERS
DIGGERS
DODGERS
ETAGERE
FINGERS
FOGGERS
FOLGERS
FORGERS
FORGERY
GANGERS
GAUGERS
GINGERS
GINGERY
GOUGERS
GREGORY
HAGGARD
HANGARS
HANGERS
HEDGERS
HUGGERS
HUNGARY
HUNGERS
IMAGERS
IMAGERY
JAEGERS
JIGGERS
JIGGERY
JOGGERS
LAAGERS
LAGGARD
LAGGERS
LANGTRY
LANGURS
LEDGERS
LINGERS
LODGERS
LOGGERS
LONGARM
LUGGERS
MANGERS
MERGERS
MONGERS
MUGGERS
NIAGARA
NIGGARD
NUDGERS
ONAGERS
PIGGERY
RANGERS
RIGGERS
RINGERS
RODGERS
RUTGERS
SEAGIRT
SINGERS
STAGERS
SURGERY
TANGERE
TOGGERY
TUGGERS
VERGERS
WAGGERY
WINGERS
ZINGERS

•••G••R

ALIGNER
BAGGIER
BILGIER
BOGGIER
BOGGLER
BRAGGER
BUGGIER
BULGHUR
BULGIER
BUNGLER
BURGHER
BURGLAR
CHIGGER
DANGLER
DINGIER
DODGIER
DOGGIER
DRAGGER
FOGGIER
GIGGLER
HAGGLER
HEDGIER
JAGGIER
JUGGLER
LANGUOR
LAUGHER
LEDGIER
LEGGIER
LOWGEAR
MANGIER
MINGIER
MINGLER
MUGGIER
NAGGIER
PIGGIER
PLUGGER
PODGIER
PUDGIER
RANGIER
RIDGIER
ROUGHER
SAGGIER
SEDGIER
SLUGGER
SMUGGER
SNIGGER
SNUGGER
SOGGIER
STAGGER
STAGIER
SWAGGER
TANGIER
TOUGHER
TRIGGER
WANGLER
WEDGIER
WIGGIER
WIGGLER
ZINGIER

••••GR•

ALLEGRO
INTEGRA
SHANGRI

••••G•R

ALLEGER
AVENGER
BRAGGER
BRINGER
CHANGER
CHARGER
CHIGGER
CLANGOR
DOWAGER
DRAGGER
DREDGER
FORAGER
GRANGER
INTEGER
LOUNGER
MANAGER
NEWAGER
NYUNGAR
PLEDGER
PLUGGER
PLUNGER
RAVAGER
RENEGER
SAVAGER
SLINGER
SLUGGER
SMUGGER
SNIGGER
SNUGGER
SPONGER
STAGGER
STEIGER
STINGER
SWAGGER
SWINGER
TANAGER
TRIGGER
TRUDGER
VINEGAR
VOYAGER
WRINGER
WRONGER
YOUNGER

G•S••••

GASBAGS
GASCAPS
GASCONS
GASCONY
GASEOUS
GASHING
GASJETS
GASKETS
GASKINS
GASLESS
GASLOGS
GASMAIN
GASOHOL
GASPERS
GASPING
GASPUMP
GASSERS
GASSIER
GASTRIC
GESSOES
GESTALT
GESTATE
GESTURE
GISELLE
GOSHAWK
GOSLING
GOSLOWS
GOSPELS
GOSSETT
GOSSIPS
GOSSIPY
GUSHERS
GUSHIER
GUSHILY
GUSHING
GUSSETS
GUSSIED
GUSSIES
GUSSYUP
GUSTIER
GUSTILY
GUSTING
GUSTOES

G••S•••

GADSDEN
GAGSTER
GASSERS
GASSIER
GEISHAS
GEMSBOK
GESSOES
GETSOFF
GETSOUT
GETSSET
GEYSERS
GHASTLY
GHOSTED
GHOSTLY
GINSENG
GIPSIES
GLASGOW
GLASSED
GLASSES
GLISTEN
GLOSSAE
GLOSSED
GLOSSES
GNASHED
GNASHES
GNOSTIC
GODSEND
GODSONS
GOESAPE
GOESBAD
GOESFOR
GOESOFF
GOESOUT
GOOSIER
GOOSING
GORSIER
GOSSETT
GOSSIPS
GOSSIPY
GRASPED
GRASSED
GRASSES
GRISHAM
GRISKIN
GRISSOM
GRISTLE
GRISTLY
GROSSED
GROSSER
GROSSES
GROSSLY
GUESSED
GUESSER
GUESSES
GUESTED
GUMSHOE
GUNSFOR
GUNSHOT
GUSSETS
GUSSIED
GUSSIES
GUSSYUP
GUTSIER
GUTSILY
GYMSHOE
GYPSIES

G•••S••

GAINSAY
GAINSON
GANGSAW
GANGSTA
GANGSUP
GEARSTO
GEARSUP
GENESEE
GENESES
GENESIS
GETSSET
GIRASOL
GIVESIN
GIVESTO
GIVESUP
GLASSED
GLASSES
GLEASON
GLOSSAE
GLOSSED
GLOSSES
GLUESON
GOODSON
GOOFSUP
GRABSAT
GRASSED
GRASSES
GRAYSON
GREASED
GREASER
GREASES
GRISSOM
GROSSED
GROSSER
GROSSES
GROSSLY
GROUSED
GROUSER
GROUSES
GROWSON
GROWSUP
GUESSED
GUESSER
GUESSES

G••••S•

GABFEST
GAMIEST
GAPLESS
GARNISH
GASLESS
GAULISH
GAWKISH
GEMLESS
GENOESE
GEODESY
GETLOST
GIRLISH
GLIMPSE
GLUCOSE
GLUIEST
GNOMISH
GOATISH
GODDESS
GODLESS
GOODISH
GOOIEST
GORIEST
GOTLOST
GOULASH
GOUTISH
GRAVEST
GRAYEST
GRAYISH
GREYEST
GREYISH
GUMLESS
GUNLESS
GUTLESS
GYMNAST

G•••••S

GABBERS
GABBLES
GABBROS
GADDERS
GADGETS
GAFFERS
GAGGLES
GAGLAWS
GAINERS
GAITERS
GALAGOS
GALLEYS
GALLONS
GALLOPS
GALOOTS
GALPALS
GAMBITS
GAMBLES
GAMBOLS
GAMETES
GAMINES
GAMMERS
GAMMONS
GANDERS
GANGERS
GANNETS
GAOLERS
GAPLESS
GARAGES
GARBLES
GARCONS
GARDENS
GARGLES
GARNERS
GARNETS
GARRETS
GARTERS
GASBAGS
GASCAPS
GASCONS
GASEOUS
GASJETS
GASKETS
GASKINS
GASLESS
GASLOGS
GASPERS
GASSERS
GATHERS
GAUCHOS
GAUGERS
GAVIALS
GAWKERS
GAZEBOS
GAZUMPS
GECKOES
GEEGAWS
GEEZERS
GEISHAS
GELADAS
GELATIS
GEMLESS
GEMOTES
GENDERS
GENERIS
GENESES
GENESIS
GENGHIS
GENOMES
GENTLES
GEORGES
GERBILS
GERENTS
GERMANS
GERUNDS
GESSOES
GEWGAWS
GEYSERS
GHETTOS
GIBBERS
GIBBETS
GIBBONS
GIBBOUS
GIBLETS
GIBLUES
GIDEONS
GIGGLES
GIGOLOS
GILBLAS
GILDERS
GILGUYS
GILLIES
GIMBALS
GIMLETS
GINGERS
GIPSIES
GIRDERS
GIRDLES
GIVEUPS
GLANCES
GLASSES
GLAZERS
GLIDERS
GLITZES
GLORIAS
GLORIES
GLOSSES
GLOTTIS
GLOWERS
GNASHES
GNAWERS
GNOMONS
GOALIES
GOATEES
GOBBLES
GOBLETS
GOBLINS
GOCARTS
GODDESS
GODLESS
GODSONS
GODWITS
GOGGLES
GOKARTS
GOLFERS
GOMPERS
GOOBERS
GOODBYS
GOODIES
GOOFUPS
GOOGOLS
GOPHERS
GORGETS
GORGONS
GOSLOWS
GOSPELS
GOSSIPS
GOTCHAS
GOTHICS
GOUGERS
GOURDES
GOVERNS
GRACIAS
GRADERS
GRAHAMS
GRAMMES
GRAMMYS
GRAMPAS
GRAMPUS
GRANGES
GRAPPAS
GRASSES
GRATERS
GRATIAS
GRAVELS
GRAVERS
GRAVIES
GRAZERS
GREASES
GREAVES
GRIEVES
GRIGRIS
GRILLES
GRIPERS
GRIVETS
GROCERS
GROOVES
GROPIUS
GROSSES
GROTTOS
GROUNDS
GROUSES
GROVELS
GROWERS
GROWTHS
GRUDGES
GRUNGES
GUELPHS
GUESSES
GUFFAWS
GUIDONS
GUIMPES
GUINEAS
GUITARS
GULCHES
GULLAHS
GULLETS
GULLIES
GUMLESS
GUNDOGS
GUNLESS
GUNNELS
GUNNERS
GUNNIES
GUPPIES
GURGLES
GURKHAS
GURNEYS
GUSHERS
GUSSETS
GUSSIES
GUSTOES
GUTLESS
GUTTERS
GUZZLES
GYMBAGS
GYPPERS
GYPSIES
GYRATES
GYRENES

•G•S•••

AGASSIZ
AGESAGO
EGESTED

•G••S••

AGASSIZ
AGEISTS
EGOISTS

•G•••S•
AGAINST
AGELESS
AGGRESS
AGONISE
AGONIST
EGGCASE
EGGIEST
EGGLESS
EGOTISM
EGOTIST
OGREISH
UGLIEST

•G••••S
AGARICS
AGEISTS
AGELESS
AGENDAS
AGGRESS
AGNATES
AGOUTIS
EGGCUPS
EGGLESS
EGGNOGS
EGOISTS
HGWELLS
IGNEOUS
IGNITES
IGNORES
IGUANAS
OGDOADS
OGLALAS

••GS•••
BEGSOFF
BIGSHOT
BUGSOFF
BUGSOUT
DIGSOUT
DOGSHOW
DOGSITS
DOGSLED
DOGSTAR
GAGSTER
JIGSAWS
LOGSOFF
LOGSOUT
MUGSHOT
PIGSKIN
PIGSOUT
TAGSALE
TAGSOUT
WIGSOUT

••G•S••
AUGUSTA
AUGUSTE
BIGOSES
DEGUSTS
DIGESTS
EDGESIN
INGESTS
LEGISTS
PEGASUS
SIGNSIN
SIGNSON
SIGNSUP

••G••S•
AGGRESS
BIGGEST
BIGGISH
BIGNESS
BOGGISH
CAGIEST
DEGAUSS
DIGRESS
DOGFISH
DOGGISH
DOGLESS
EDGIEST
EGGCASE
EGGIEST
EGGLESS
ENGLISH
ENGROSS
FOGLESS
FOGYISH
FOGYISM
HAGGISH
HIGHEST
HOGGISH
HOGWASH
INGRESS
JAGLESS
JIGGISH
LEGLESS
LOGGISH
LOGIEST
NAGGISH
NIGHEST
PEGLESS
PIGGISH
PUGGISH
PUGNOSE
REGRESS
ROGUISH
SUGGEST
TIGRESS
TIGRISH
TUGLESS
VAGUEST
VOGUISH
WAGGISH
WIGLESS

••G•••S
AFGHANS
AGGRESS
AIGRETS
ALGIERS
ANGELES
ANGELUS
ANGLERS
ANGORAS
ARGIVES
ARGUERS
ARGYLES
AUGENDS
BAGFULS
BAGGERS
BAGGIES
BEGGARS
BIGBOYS
BIGEYES
BIGGERS
BIGGIES
BIGGUNS
BIGLIES
BIGNESS
BIGOSES
BIGTOES
BIGTOPS
BIGWIGS
BOGGLES
BUGGIES
BUGLERS
BYGONES
COGNACS
CYGNETS
DAGGERS
DEGAUSS
DEGREES
DEGUSTS
DIGESTS
DIGGERS
DIGRAMS
DIGRESS
DOGDAYS
DOGEARS
DOGGIES
DOGLEGS
DOGLESS
DOGSITS
DOGTAGS
DUGONGS
DUGOUTS
EAGLETS
EDGINGS
EGGCUPS
EGGLESS
EGGNOGS
EIGHTHS
ENGAGES
ENGINES
ENGIRDS
ENGRAMS
ENGROSS
ENGULFS
ERGATES
FAGENDS
FIGURES
FOGBOWS
FOGGERS
FOGLESS
GAGGLES
GAGLAWS
GIGGLES
GIGOLOS
GOGGLES
HAGDONS
HAGGLES
HEGIRAS
HIGGINS
HIGGLES
HOGGETS
HOGTIES
HUGGERS
HUGGINS
INGALLS
INGESTS
INGRESS
JAGGIES
JAGLESS
JAGUARS
JIGGERS
JIGGLES
JIGSAWS
JOGGERS
JOGGLES
JUGFULS
JUGGINS
JUGGLES
KEGLERS
LAGGERS
LAGOONS
LAGUNAS
LEGATES
LEGATOS
LEGENDS
LEGIONS
LEGISTS
LEGLESS
LEGUMES
LIGANDS
LIGATES
LOGGERS
LOGGIAS
LOGGINS
LOGJAMS
LUGGERS
LUGNUTS
MAGNETS
MAGNUMS
MAGPIES
MAGUEYS
MAGYARS
MEGOHMS
MEGRIMS
MIGGLES
MOGGIES
MUGGERS
NEGATES
NIGGLES
NOGALES
NOGGINS
NUGGETS
ORGATES
ORGEATS
PAGODAS
PEGASUS
PEGLESS
PEGTOPS
PIGEONS
PIGGIES
PIGLETS
PIGNUTS
PIGPENS
PUGREES
PYGMIES
RAGBAGS
RAGLANS
RAGMOPS
RAGOUTS
RAGRUGS
RAGTOPS
REGAINS
REGALES
REGARDS
REGENTS
REGIMES
REGIONS
REGLETS
REGLUES
REGRESS
REGRETS
REGULUS
RIGGERS
RIGOURS
SIGHERS
SIGNALS
SIGNEES
SIGNERS
SIGNETS
TAGENDS
TIGLONS
TIGRESS
TOGGLES
TUGGERS
TUGLESS
TUGRIKS
UNGIRDS
VEGGIES
VIGOURS
WAGGLES
WAGGONS
WIGGLES
WIGLESS
WIGLETS
WIGWAGS
WIGWAMS
YOGURTS
ZIGZAGS
ZYGOTES

•••GS••
BANGSUP
BERGSON
CLOGSUP
DODGSON
DRAGSIN
DRAGSON
GANGSAW
GANGSTA
GANGSUP
HANGSIN
HANGSON
HANGSUP
PLUGSIN
RINGSUP
SINGSTO
WINGSIT

•••G•S•
BIGGEST
BIGGISH
BOGGISH
BURGESS
CONGEST
DISGUST
DOGGISH
ELEGIST
HAGGISH
HOGGISH
JIGGISH
LARGESS
LARGEST
LARGISH
LOGGISH
LONGEST
LONGISH
NAGGISH
OMIGOSH
PIGGISH
PUGGISH
SUGGEST
WAGGISH

•••G••S
ADAGIOS
AIRGUNS
ALIGHTS
APOGEES
BADGERS
BADGUYS
BAGGERS
BAGGIES
BANGLES
BEAGLES
BEEGEES
BEEGUMS
BEGGARS
BENGALS
BIGGERS
BIGGIES
BIGGUNS
BINGOES
BLIGHTS
BOGGLES
BONGOES
BOOGIES
BROGANS
BROGUES
BUDGETS
BUDGIES
BUGGIES
BULGARS
BUNGEES
BUNGLES
BURGEES
BURGERS
BURGESS
BURGLES
BURGOOS
CADGERS
CAPGUNS
CARGOES
CHIGOES
CODGERS
CONGERS
COUGARS
CUDGELS
DAGGERS
DANGERS
DANGLES
DIGGERS
DINGLES
DINGOES
DODGERS
DOGGIES
DONGLES
DOUGLAS
DRAGONS
ELEGIES
EMIGRES
ENIGMAS
FIDGETS
FINGERS
FIZGIGS
FLAGONS
FLIGHTS
FOGGERS
FOLGERS
FORGERS
FORGETS
FORGOES
FRIGHTS
FUNGOES
GADGETS
GAGGLES
GANGERS
GARGLES
GAUGERS
GEEGAWS
GENGHIS
GEWGAWS
GIGGLES
GILGUYS
GINGERS
GOGGLES
GOOGOLS
GORGETS
GORGONS
GOUGERS
GRIGRIS
GURGLES
HAGGLES
HANGARS
HANGERS
HANGUPS
HEDGERS
HEIGHTS
HIGGINS
HIGGLES
HOAGIES
HOGGETS
HUGGERS
HUGGINS
HUNGERS
HUYGENS
IMAGERS
IMAGOES
ISOGONS
JAEGERS
JAGGIES
JANGLES
JARGONS
JETGUNS
JIGGERS
JIGGLES
JINGLES
JINGOES
JOGGERS
JOGGLES
JUGGINS
JUGGLES
JUNGLES
KNIGHTS
LAAGERS
LAGGERS
LANGURS
LARGESS
LEAGUES
LEDGERS
LENGTHS
LINGERS
LINGOES
LODGERS
LOGGERS
LOGGIAS
LOGGINS
LONGIES
LONGUES
LUGGERS
MANGERS
MANGLES
MANGOES
MARGAYS
MARGINS
MERGERS
MIDGETS
MIGGLES
MINGLES
MOGGIES
MONGERS
MONGOLS
MORGANS
MUGGERS
NAUGHTS
NIGGLES
NOGGINS
NOUGATS
NOUGHTS
NUDGERS
NUGGETS
ONAGERS
ORIGINS
OUTGOES
OUTGUNS
PARGETS
PIDGINS
PIGGIES
PLAGUES
PLIGHTS
PLUGINS
PONGEES
PONGIDS
POPGUNS
PORGIES
QUAGGAS
RANGERS
RAYGUNS
REDGUMS
RIGGERS
RINGERS
RODGERS
RUTGERS
SHOGUNS
SINGERS
SINGLES
SIXGUNS
SLIGHTS
SLOGANS
SPIGOTS
STAGERS
STIGMAS
STOGIES
SUNGODS
TANGLES
TARGETS
TINGLES
TOGGLES
TONGANS
TONGUES
TOPGUNS
TRIGONS
TROGONS
TUGGERS
VEGGIES
VEIGHTS
VERGERS
VIRGINS
WAGGLES
WAGGONS
WANGLES
WARGODS
WEDGIES
WEIGHTS
WIDGETS
WIGGLES
WINGERS
WRIGHTS
ZEUGMAS
ZINGERS

••••GS•
AMONGST

••••G•S
ALLEGES
ASSIGNS
AVENGES
BADEGGS
BODEGAS
BRIDGES
CAYUGAS
CHANGES
CHARGES
COALGAS
COSIGNS
CRINGES
DAMAGES
DELUGES
DESIGNS
DOSAGES
DREDGES
DRUDGES
ELOIGNS
EMERGES
ENCAGES
ENGAGES
ENRAGES
ENSIGNS
FLANGES
FLEDGES
FORAGES
FRIDGES
FRINGES
GALAGOS
GARAGES
GEORGES
GRANGES
GRUDGES
GRUNGES
ICEAGES
IMPUGNS
INDIGOS
KLUDGES
LIMOGES
LINAGES
LOUNGES
MALIGNS
MANAGES
MANEGES
MENAGES
MIRAGES
NONAGES
OBLIGES
OPPUGNS
ORANGES
OUTAGES
PAANGAS
PAPAGOS
PELAGES
PLEDGES
PLOUGHS
PLUNGES
POTAGES
QUAGGAS
QUANGOS
RAREGAS
RAVAGES
RAWEGGS
REFUGES
REMIGES
RENEGES
REPUGNS
RESIGNS
SAVAGES
SLEDGES
SLEIGHS
SLOUGHS
SLUDGES
SMUDGES
SPARGES
SPONGES
STINGOS
STOOGES
STURGES
TEARGAS
TROUGHS
TRUDGES
TWINGES
UNCAGES
VIRAGOS
VISAGES
VOYAGES

•••••GS
AIRBAGS
AIRINGS
ANALOGS
AWNINGS
BADEGGS
BARONGS
BEDBUGS
BELONGS
BIGWIGS
CASINGS
COMINGS
CYBORGS
DIALOGS
DOGLEGS
DOGTAGS
DUGONGS
EARWIGS
EDGINGS
EGGNOGS
ENDINGS
EPILOGS
FACINGS
FILINGS
FIRINGS
FIXINGS
FIZGIGS
GASBAGS
GASLOGS
GUNDOGS
GYMBAGS
HAZINGS
HIDINGS
HOTDOGS
HUMBUGS
ICEBAGS
ICEFOGS
INNINGS
KITBAGS
LACINGS
LAPDOGS
LININGS
LIVINGS
MAKINGS
MUSKEGS
NUTMEGS
OBLONGS
OILRIGS
OUTINGS
PARINGS
PHOTOGS
PILINGS
PIPINGS
PROLOGS
PYEDOGS
QUAHOGS
RAGBAGS
RAGRUGS
RATINGS
RAVINGS
RAWEGGS
REDDOGS
REFLAGS
REHANGS
RESINGS
RISINGS
RULINGS
SARONGS
SAVINGS
SAWLOGS
SAYINGS
SEABAGS
SEADOGS
SEALEGS
SIDINGS
SIZINGS
SOWBUGS
SPRINGS
STALAGS
STRINGS
SUNDOGS
TAPINGS
TEABAGS
THRONGS
TIDINGS
TILINGS
TIMINGS
TOPDOGS
TOYDOGS
TUAREGS
UNCLOGS
UNPLUGS
UNSNAGS
VIKINGS
WIGWAGS
ZIGZAGS

G•T••••
GATEAUX
GATELEG
GATEMAN
GATEMEN
GATEWAY
GATHERS
GATLING
GETAWAY
GETBACK
GETDOWN
GETEVEN
GETINTO
GETITON
GETLOST
GETOVER
GETREAL
GETSOFF
GETSOUT
GETSSET
GETTING
GETWELL
GOTAWAY
GOTBACK
GOTCHAS
GOTDOWN
GOTEVEN
GOTHICS
GOTINTO
GOTITON
GOTLAND
GOTLOST
GOTOPOT
GOTOVER
GOTWELL
GUTHRIE
GUTLESS
GUTSIER
GUTSILY
GUTTERS
GUTTIER
GUTTING

G••T•••
GAITERS
GAITING
GANTLET
GARTERS
GASTRIC
GAUTAMA
GENTEEL
GENTIAN
GENTILE
GENTLED
GENTLER
GENTLES
GESTALT
GESTATE
GESTURE
GETTING
GHETTOS
GLITTER
GLITZED
GLITZES
GLOTTAL
GLOTTIS
GLUTTED
GLUTTON
GOATEED
GOATEES
GOATISH
GODTHAB
GOUTIER
GOUTILY
GOUTISH
GRATERS
GRATIAS
GRATIFY
GRATING
GRETZKY
GRITTED
GROTTOS
GUITARS
GUMTREE
GUNTHER
GUSTIER
GUSTILY
GUSTING
GUSTOES
GUTTERS
GUTTIER
GUTTING

G•••T••
GAGSTER
GALATEA
GALATIA
GAMETES
GANGTOK
GAUNTER
GAUNTLY
GAVOTTE
GAZETTE
GELATIN
GELATIS
GEMOTES
GENETIC
GERITOL
GETITON
GHASTLY
GHETTOS
GHOSTED
GHOSTLY
GLINTED
GLISTEN
GLITTER
GLOATED
GLOTTAL
GLOTTIS
GLUTTED
GLUTTON
GNOSTIC
GOAFTER
GODUTCH
GOLFTEE
GORETEX
GOTITON
GRAFTED
GRAFTON
GRANTED
GRANTEE
GRANTOR
GREATER
GREATLY
GREETED
GREETER
GRIFTER
GRISTLE
GRISTLY
GRITTED
GROTTOS
GROUTED
GROWTHS
GRUNTED
GUESTED
GYRATED
GYRATES
GYRATOR

G••••T•
GADGETS
GADGETY
GALOOTS
GAMBITS
GANGSTA
GANNETS
GANNETT
GARNETS
GARRETS
GARRETT
GASJETS
GASKETS
GAVOTTE
GAZETTE
GEARSTO
GEFILTE
GERENTS
GESTATE
GETINTO
GIBBETS
GIBLETS
GIMLETS
GIVENTO
GIVESTO
GOBLETS
GOCARTS
GODWITS
GOKARTS
GOLIATH
GORGETS
GOSSETT
GOTINTO
GRANITE
GRAVITY
GRIVETS
GULLETS
GUSSETS
GWYNETH

G•••••T
GABFEST
GALLANT
GAMIEST
GANNETT
GANTLET
GARMENT
GARRETT
GAVEOUT
GERAINT
GESTALT
GETLOST
GETSOUT
GETSSET
GILBERT
GILLNET
GIVEOUT
GLUIEST
GOABOUT
GOESOUT
GOFORIT
GOINGAT
GOOIEST
GORIEST
GOSSETT
GOTLOST
GOTOPOT
GOURMET
GRABSAT
GRAVEST
GRAYEST
GREYEST
GRILLET
GROMMET
GUNBOAT
GUNSHOT
GYMNAST

•G•T•••
AGITATE
AGITATO
EGOTISM
EGOTIST
EGOTRIP

•G••T••
AGNATES
AGOUTIS
EGESTED
IGNITED
IGNITER
IGNITES

•G•••T•
AGEISTS
AGILITY
AGITATE
AGITATO
AGREETO
EGALITE
EGOISTS

•G••••T
AGAINST
AGONIST
EGGIEST
EGOTIST
UGLIEST

••GT•••
BIGTALK
BIGTIME
BIGTOES
BIGTOPS
DOGTAGS
DOGTROT
HOGTIED
HOGTIES
PEGTOPS
PIGTAIL
RAGTIME
RAGTOPS
TAGTEAM
WAGTAIL

••G•T••
BIGOTED
BIGOTRY
DIGITAL
DOGSTAR
EIGHTAM

EIGHTHS
EIGHTPM
ERGATES
FAGOTED
FIGHTER
GAGSTER
HIGHTEA
HIGHTOP
LEGATEE
LEGATES
LEGATOS
LIGATED
LIGATES
LIGHTED
LIGHTEN
LIGHTER
LIGHTLY
LIGHTUP
MIGHTNT
NEGATED
NEGATER
NEGATES
NEGATOR
NIGHTIE
NIGHTLY
ORGATES
OUGHTNT
REGATTA
RIGHTED
RIGHTER
RIGHTLY
RIGHTON
SIGHTED
SIGHTLY
TIGHTEN
TIGHTER
TIGHTLY
VEGETAL
ZYGOTES

••G••T•
AIGRETS
AUGUSTA
AUGUSTE
COGNATE
CYGNETS
DEGUSTS
DIGESTS
DIGNITY
DOGMATA
DOGSITS
DUGOUTS
EAGLETS
HOGARTH
HOGGETS
INGESTS
INGRATE
LEGISTS
LIGNITE
LUGNUTS
MAGENTA
MAGNATE
MAGNETO
MAGNETS
MIGRATE
NUGGETS
ORGEATS
PIGLETS
PIGNUTS
RAGOUTS
REGATTA
REGENTS
REGLETS
REGRETS
SIGNETS
WIGLETS
YOGURTS

••G•••T
AUGMENT
BIGFEET
BIGFOOT
BIGGEST
BIGSHOT
BUGSOUT
CAGIEST
DIGSOUT
DOGBERT
DOGCART
DOGTROT
EDGEOUT
EDGIEST
EGGIEST
ENGRAFT
FIGMENT
HIGHEST
HIGHHAT
LOGIEST
LOGSOUT
MAGINOT
MEGAHIT
MIGHTNT
MIGRANT
MUGSHOT
NEGLECT
NIGHEST
OUGHTNT
PAGEANT
PIGMENT
PIGSOUT
REGNANT
SEGMENT
SIGNOUT
SUGGEST
TAGGANT
TAGSOUT
TUGBOAT
UNGUENT
USGRANT
VAGRANT
VAGUEST
WIGSOUT
YOGHURT

•••GT••
GANGTOK
HANGTEN
KINGTUT
LANGTRY
LENGTHS
LENGTHY
LONGTON
WINGTIP
YANGTZE

•••G•T•
ALIGHTS
BLIGHTS
BLIGHTY
BUDGETS
COLGATE
DOUGHTY
FIDGETS
FIDGETY
FLIGHTS
FLIGHTY
FORGETS
FRIGATE
FRIGHTS
GADGETS
GADGETY
GANGSTA
GORGETS
HAUGHTY
HEIGHTS
HOGGETS
KNIGHTS
MARGATE
MIDGETS
NAUGHTS
NAUGHTY
NEWGATE
NOUGATS
NOUGHTS
NUGGETS
PARGETS
PLIGHTS
SEAGATE
SINGSTO
SLIGHTS
SPIGOTS
TARGETS
VEIGHTS
VULGATE
WEIGHTS
WEIGHTY
WIDGETS
WRIGHTS

•••G••T
BIGGEST
CONGEST
DINGBAT
DISGUST
DRAGNET
DRAGOUT
ELEGANT
ELEGIST
EXIGENT
FULGENT
HANGOUT
HUNGOUT
KINGRAT
KINGTUT
LARGEST
LAUGHAT
LONGEST
LUNGEAT
MAIGRET
MARGRET
PEUGEOT
PUNGENT
RANGOUT
REAGENT
RINGLET
RINGOUT
ROUGHIT
RUNGOUT
SANGOUT
SARGENT
SEAGIRT
SINGOUT
SNIGLET
SUGGEST
TAGGANT
TANGENT
WINGNUT
WINGSIT
XINGOUT

••••GT•
BRINGTO
LYINGTO
OWINGTO

••••G•T
ABOUGHT
ALRIGHT
AMONGST
BRIDGET
BROUGHT
DELIGHT
DRAUGHT
DROUGHT
FRAUGHT
FREIGHT
GOINGAT
INSIGHT
MRRIGHT
ONSIGHT
RELIGHT
SLEIGHT
THOUGHT
TLINGIT
TONIGHT
UPRIGHT
UPTIGHT
WROUGHT
XHEIGHT

GU•••••
GUANACO
GUANINE
GUARANI
GUARDED
GUARDEE
GUARGUM
GUELPHS
GUESSED
GUESSER
GUESSES
GUESTED
GUEVARA
GUFFAWS
GUIDING
GUIDONS
GUILDER
GUIMPES
GUINEAS
GUITARS
GULCHES
GULFING
GULLAHS
GULLETS
GULLIES
GULLING
GULPIER
GULPING
GUMBALL
GUMDROP
GUMLESS
GUMLIKE
GUMMIER
GUMMING
GUMSHOE
GUMTREE
GUNBOAT
GUNDOGS
GUNFIRE
GUNKIER
GUNLESS
GUNLOCK
GUNMOLL
GUNNELS
GUNNERS
GUNNERY
GUNNIES
GUNNING
GUNPLAY
GUNSFOR
GUNSHOT
GUNTHER
GUNWALE
GUPPIES
GURGLED
GURGLES
GURKHAS
GURNEYS
GUSHERS
GUSHIER
GUSHILY
GUSHING
GUSSETS
GUSSIED
GUSSIES
GUSSYUP
GUSTIER
GUSTILY
GUSTING
GUSTOES
GUTHRIE
GUTLESS
GUTSIER
GUTSILY
GUTTERS
GUTTIER
GUTTING
GUZZLED
GUZZLER
GUZZLES

G•U••••
GAUCHER
GAUCHOS
GAUDIER
GAUDILY
GAUGERS
GAUGING
GAUGUIN
GAULISH
GAUMING
GAUNTER
GAUNTLY
GAUTAMA
GAUZIER
GAUZILY
GLUCOSE
GLUEDON
GLUESON
GLUGGED
GLUIEST
GLUMMER
GLUTTED
GLUTTON
GOUACHE
GOUGERS
GOUGING
GOULASH
GOUNDER
GOURAMI
GOURDES
GOURMET
GOUTIER
GOUTILY
GOUTISH
GRUBBED
GRUDGED
GRUDGES
GRUFFER
GRUFFLY
GRUMBLE
GRUMBLY
GRUMPED
GRUNGES
GRUNION
GRUNTED
GRUYERE

G••U•••
GALUMPH
GAZUMPS
GENUINE
GERUNDS
GODUNOV
GODUTCH
GROUCHO
GROUCHY
GROUNDS
GROUPED
GROUPER
GROUPIE
GROUSED
GROUSER
GROUSES
GROUTED

G•••U••
GAGRULE
GASPUMP
GAUGUIN
GESTURE
GIBLUES
GILGUYS
GIVEUPS
GLOBULE
GOOFUPS
GOROUND
GRADUAL
GRANULE
GRAVURE

G••••U•
GAINFUL
GALLIUM
GANGSUP
GASEOUS
GATEAUX
GAVEOUT
GEARSUP
GETSOUT
GIBBOUS
GIDDYUP
GIELGUD
GIVENUP
GIVEOUT
GIVESUP
GLAMOUR
GLEEFUL
GOABOUT
GOESOUT
GOINGUP
GOLDBUG
GOOFSUP
GRAMPUS
GROPIUS
GROWNUP
GROWSUP
GUARGUM
GUSSYUP

•GU••••
IGUANAS

•G•U•••
AGOUTIS

•G••U••
AGROUND
EGGCUPS

•G•••U•
IGIVEUP
IGNEOUS

••GU•••
ANGULAR
ARGUERS
ARGUING
AUGURAL
AUGURED
AUGUSTA
AUGUSTE
BEGUILE
BEGUINE
DEGUSTS
ENGULFS
FIGURED
FIGURER
FIGURES
JAGUARS
JUGULAR
LAGUNAS
LEGUMES
MAGUEYS
MAGUIRE
MCGUIRE
NOGUCHI
ONGUARD
REGULAR
REGULUS
ROGUERY
ROGUISH
SAGUARO
TVGUIDE
UNGUENT
VAGUELY
VAGUEST
VOGUISH
YOGURTS

••G•U••
BAGFULS
BIGGUNS
COGBURN
DEGAUSS
DUGOUTS
EGGCUPS
ENGLUND
GAGRULE
JUGFULS
LEGPULL
LUGNUTS
MAGNUMS
MUGWUMP
PIGNUTS
RAGOUTS
RAGRUGS
REGLUED
REGLUES
RIGOURS
SIGMUND
UNGLUED
VIGOURS
YOGHURT

••G••U•
ANGELUS
BUGSOUT
DIGSOUT
EDGEOUT
INGENUE
INGROUP
LIGHTUP
LOGSOUT
ORGANUM
PAGEFUL
PEGASUS
PIGSOUT
RAGEFUL
REGROUP
REGULUS
SIGHFUL
SIGNOUT
SIGNSUP
TAGSOUT
WIGSOUT

••G•••U
ANGELOU

•••GU••
AIRGUNS
ARUGULA
BADGUYS
BEEGUMS
BIGGUNS
BROGUES
CAPGUNS
DISGUST
GAUGUIN
GILGUYS
HANGUPS
JETGUNS
LANGUID
LANGUOR
LANGURS
LEAGUES
LINGUAL
LONGUES
OUTGUNS
PENGUIN
PLAGUED
PLAGUES
POPGUNS
RAYGUNS
REDGUMS
SEAGULL
SHOGUNS
SIXGUNS
TONGUED
TONGUES
TOPGUNS
URUGUAY
VIRGULE

•••G•U•
BANGSUP
BELGIUM
BULGHUR
CLOGSUP
COUGHUP
DRAGOUT
FULGHUM
GANGSUP
HANGOUT
HANGSUP
HUNGOUT
KINGTUT
LONGRUN
MARGAUX
RANGOUT
RINGOUT
RINGSUP
ROUGHUP
RUNGOUT
SANGOUT
SINGOUT
SONGFUL
SORGHUM
WINGNUT
XINGOUT

••••GU•
ANTIGUA
BLOWGUN
BLUEGUM
BRINGUP
BURPGUN
DOINGUP
ECLOGUE
FALLGUY
FATIGUE
GIELGUD
GOINGUP
GUARGUM
HANDGUN
ICINGUP
INVOGUE
MANAGUA
PIROGUE
REARGUE
RENEGUE
SHOTGUN
STUNGUN
TYINGUP
USINGUP
WISEGUY
YOUNGUN

G•V••••
GAVELED
GAVEOFF
GAVEOUT
GAVEWAY
GAVIALS
GAVOTTE
GIVENIN
GIVENTO
GIVENUP
GIVEOFF
GIVEOUT
GIVESIN
GIVESTO
GIVESUP
GIVEUPS
GIVEWAY
GOVERNS

G••V•••
GALVANI
GRAVELS
GRAVELY
GRAVERS
GRAVEST
GRAVIES
GRAVING
GRAVITY
GRAVURE
GRIVETS
GROVELS
GUEVARA

G•••V••
GETEVEN
GETOVER
GOTEVEN
GOTOVER
GREAVES
GRIEVED
GRIEVER
GRIEVES
GROOVED
GROOVES

G••••V•
GINGIVA

G•••••V
GODUNOV

•G•V•••
IGIVEUP

••GV•••
RIGVEDA

••G•V••
ARGIVES
MCGAVIN
SEGOVIA

••G••V•
ENGRAVE

•••G•V•
FORGAVE
FORGIVE
GINGIVA

GW•••••
GWYNETH

G•W••••
GAWKERS
GAWKIER
GAWKILY
GAWKING
GAWKISH
GAWPING
GEWGAWS
GOWRONG

G••W•••
GEEWHIZ
GETWELL
GLOWERS
GLOWING
GNAWERS
GNAWING
GODWITS
GOTWELL
GROWERS
GROWING
GROWLED
GROWLER
GROWNUP
GROWSON
GROWSUP
GROWTHS
GUNWALE

G•••W••
GANGWAY
GATEWAY
GAVEWAY
GETAWAY
GIVEWAY
GOLDWYN
GOODWIN
GOTAWAY

G••••W•
GAGLAWS
GEEGAWS
GETDOWN
GEWGAWS
GOSHAWK
GOSLOWS
GOTDOWN
GUFFAWS

G•••••W
GAMELAW
GANGSAW
GLASGOW

•GW••••
HGWELLS

••GW•••
BIGWIGS
DAGWOOD
DOGWOOD
HOGWASH
HOGWILD
JUGWINE
LEGWORK
MUGWUMP
RAGWEED
WIGWAGS
WIGWAMS

••G•W••
HIGHWAY

••G••W•
BOGDOWN
FOGBOWS
GAGLAWS
INGROWN
JIGSAWS

••G•••W
BIGELOW
DOGCHOW
DOGSHOW
HIGHLOW
SAGINAW

•••GW••
GANGWAY
RIDGWAY

•••G•W•
GEEGAWS
GEWGAWS

•••G••W
GANGSAW
LONGBOW
MACGRAW
OUTGREW
OUTGROW

••••G•W
GLASGOW
LITHGOW

G•••••X
GATEAUX
GEARBOX
GORETEX

•••G••X
MARGAUX

GY•••••
GYMBAGS
GYMNAST
GYMSHOE
GYPPERS
GYPPING
GYPROOM
GYPSIES
GYRATED
GYRATES
GYRATOR
GYRENES

G•Y••••
GEYSERS
GRYPHON
GWYNETH

G••Y•••
GRAYEST
GRAYING
GRAYISH
GRAYJAY
GRAYLAG
GRAYSON
GREYEST
GREYHEN
GREYING
GREYISH
GRUYERE

G•••Y••
GIDDYAP
GIDDYUP
GROMYKO
GUSSYUP

G••••Y•
GALLEYS
GILGUYS
GLADEYE
GOLDWYN
GOODBYE
GOODBYS
GRAMMYS
GURNEYS

G•••••Y
GADGETY
GAINSAY
GALLERY
GANGWAY
GASCONY
GATEWAY
GAUDILY
GAUNTLY
GAUZILY
GAVEWAY
GAWKILY
GELIDLY
GEODESY
GEOLOGY
GERMANY
GETAWAY
GHASTLY
GHOSTLY
GIDDILY
GINGERY
GIVEWAY
GLORIFY
GODFREY
GOINGBY
GOOFILY
GOONILY
GOSSIPY
GOTAWAY
GOUTILY
GRANARY
GRANDLY
GRATIFY
GRAVELY
GRAVITY
GRAYJAY
GREATLY
GREELEY
GREGORY
GRETZKY
GRIFFEY
GRIMILY
GRISTLY
GRIZZLY
GROCERY
GROSSLY
GROUCHY
GRUFFLY
GRUMBLY
GUNNERY
GUNPLAY
GUSHILY
GUSTILY
GUTSILY

•G••••Y
AGILELY
AGILITY
IGNOBLY

••GY•••
ARGYLES
FOGYISH
FOGYISM
MAGYARS

••G•Y••
BIGEYES
BOGEYED
BUGEYED
MEGRYAN

••G••Y•
BIGBOYS
DOGDAYS
MAGUEYS

••G•••Y
ANGRILY
BAGGILY
BIGOTRY
BYGOLLY
COGENCY
DIGNIFY
DIGNITY
EAGERLY
FOGGILY
HIGHBOY
HIGHDAY
HIGHWAY
JIGGERY
LEGALLY
LEGIBLY
LIGHTLY
MAGNIFY
NIGHTLY
ORGANDY
PAGEBOY
PIGGERY
RAGGEDY
REGALLY
REGENCY
RIGHTLY
RIGIDLY
ROGUERY
SIGHTLY
SIGNIFY
SOGGILY
TIGHTLY
TOGGERY
UNGODLY
URGENCY
VAGUELY
WAGGERY

•••G•Y•
BADGUYS
GILGUYS
MARGAYS

•••G••Y
BAGGILY
BIOGENY
BLIGHTY
CALGARY
DINGILY
DOUGHTY
FIDGETY
FLAGDAY
FLIGHTY
FOGGILY
FORGERY
GADGETY
GANGWAY
GINGERY
GREGORY
HAUGHTY
HUNGARY
IMAGERY
JARGONY
JIGGERY
LANGLEY
LANGTRY
LARGELY
LENGTHY
NAUGHTY
OROGENY
PIGGERY
PODGILY
PROGENY
PUDGILY
QUIGLEY
RAGGEDY
RIDGWAY
ROUGHLY
SOGGILY
STAGILY
SURGERY
TOGGERY
TOUGHLY
TRAGEDY
URUGUAY
WAGGERY
WEIGHTY
WRIGGLY
WRIGLEY
YEVGENY

••••G•Y
FALLGUY
GOINGBY
JOHNGAY

NOSEGAY
ORANGEY
SCRAGGY
SPANGLY
SWINGBY
WISEGUY
WRIGGLY
WRONGLY

•••••GY
ALLERGY
ANALOGY
APOLOGY
BIOLOGY
ECOLOGY
GEOLOGY
LITURGY
OLDFOGY
PRODIGY
SCRAGGY
SPRINGY
STRINGY
SYNERGY
THEURGY
TRILOGY
ZOOLOGY
ZYMURGY

G•Z••••
GAZEBOS
GAZELLE
GAZETTE
GAZUMPS
GIZZARD
GUZZLED
GUZZLER
GUZZLES

G••Z•••
GAUZIER
GAUZILY
GEEZERS
GIZZARD
GLAZERS
GLAZIER
GLAZING
GLOZING
GRAZERS
GRAZING
GRIZZLE
GRIZZLY
GUZZLED
GUZZLER
GUZZLES

G•••Z••
GLITZED
GLITZES
GRETZKY
GRIZZLE
GRIZZLY

G••••Z•
GINFIZZ

G•••••Z
GEEWHIZ
GINFIZZ

•G•••Z•
AGONIZE

•G••••Z
AGASSIZ

••GZ•••
ZIGZAGS

••G••Z•
ORGANZA

•••G•Z•
YANGTZE

HA•••••
HAARLEM
HABITAT
HABITED
HABITUE
HACKERS
HACKETT
HACKIES
HACKING
HACKLED
HACKLES
HACKMAN
HACKNEY
HACKSAW
HADDOCK
HADRIAN
HAEMATO
HAFNIUM
HAFTING
HAGDONS
HAGGARD
HAGGISH
HAGGLED
HAGGLER
HAGGLES
HAGLIKE
HAHNIUM
HAILING
HAIRCUT
HAIRDOS
HAIRDYE
HAIRIER
HAIRNET
HAIRPIN
HAITIAN
HALCYON
HALFDAN
HALFWAY
HALFWIT
HALIBUT
HALIDES
HALIFAX
HALITES
HALLOWS
HALLWAY
HALOGEN
HALOING
HALSTON
HALTERS
HALTING
HALVAHS
HALVING
HALYARD
HAMBURG
HAMELIN
HAMHOCK
HAMITES
HAMITIC
HAMITUP
HAMLETS
HAMMERS
HAMMETT
HAMMIER
HAMMILY
HAMMING
HAMMOCK
HAMMOND
HAMPERS
HAMPTON
HAMSTER
HANCOCK
HANDBAG
HANDCAR
HANDFED
HANDFUL
HANDGUN
HANDIER
HANDILY
HANDING
HANDLED
HANDLER
HANDLES
HANDOFF
HANDOUT
HANDSAW
HANDSET
HANDSIN
HANDSON
HANDSUP
HANGARS
HANGDOG
HANGERS
HANGING
HANGMAN
HANGMEN
HANGOFF
HANGOUT
HANGSIN
HANGSON
HANGSUP
HANGTEN
HANGUPS
HANKERS
HANKIES
HANOVER
HANSARP
HANSOLO
HANSOMS
HANUKAH
HAPENNY
HAPLESS
HAPPENS
HAPPIER
HAPPILY
HAPPING
HARBORS
HARBOUR
HARBURG
HARDENS
HARDEST
HARDHAT
HARDHIT
HARDIER
HARDILY
HARDING
HARDPAN
HARDPUT
HARDSET
HARDTOP
HARDWON
HARICOT
HARKENS
HARKING
HARMFUL
HARMING
HARMONY
HARNESS
HARPERS
HARPIES
HARPING
HARPIST
HARPOON
HARPSON
HARRIED
HARRIER
HARRIES
HARRIET
HARROWS
HARSHEN
HARSHER
HARSHLY
HARTMAN
HARVARD
HARVEST
HASBEEN
HASHING
HASIDIC
HASIDIM
HASPING
HASSLED
HASSLES
HASSOCK
HASTENS
HASTIER
HASTILY
HASTING
HATBAND
HATCHED
HATCHER
HATCHES
HATCHET
HATEFUL
HATLESS
HATLIKE
HATPINS
HATRACK
HATTERS
HATTING
HAUBERK
HAUGHTY
HAULAGE
HAULERS
HAULING
HAULOFF
HAULSUP
HAUNTED
HAUTBOY
HAUTEUR
HAVARTI
HAVENOT
HAVERED
HAWHAWS
HAWKERS
HAWKEYE
HAWKING
HAWKINS
HAWKISH
HAWSERS
HAYFORK
HAYLOFT
HAYMOWS
HAYRACK
HAYRIDE
HAYSEED
HAYWARD
HAYWIRE
HAZARDS
HAZIEST
HAZINGS

H•A••••
HAARLEM
HEADERS
HEADIER
HEADILY
HEADING
HEADMAN
HEADMEN
HEADOFF
HEADOUT
HEADPIN
HEADSET
HEADSIN
HEADSUP
HEADWAY
HEALALL
HEALERS
HEALING
HEALTHY
HEAPING
HEARDOF
HEARERS
HEARING
HEARKEN
HEAROUT
HEARSAY
HEARSOF
HEARTED
HEARTEN
HEARTHS
HEATERS
HEATFUL
HEATHEN
HEATHER
HEATING
HEATSUP
HEATTER
HEAVEHO
HEAVENS
HEAVERS
HEAVETO
HEAVIER
HEAVIES
HEAVILY
HEAVING
HIALEAH
HOAGIES
HOARDED
HOARDER
HOARIER
HOARILY
HOARSEN
HOARSER
HOAXERS
HOAXING
HYALINE

H••A•••
HAVARTI
HAZARDS
HEPARIN
HEPATIC
HERALDS
HEXAGON
HIBACHI
HIDALGO
HIJACKS
HILAIRE
HIRABLE
HITACHI
HOGARTH
HORATIO
HOSANNA
HOWARDS
HUMANLY
HUMANUM
HYRACES
HYRAXES

H•••A••
HAEMATO
HAGGARD
HALVAHS
HALYARD
HANGARS
HANSARP
HARVARD
HATBAND
HATRACK
HAULAGE
HAWHAWS
HAYRACK
HAYWARD
HEALALL
HEBRAIC
HECTARE
HEEHAWS
HENBANE
HENNAED
HEPCATS
HEPTADS
HERBAGE
HERBALS
HERMANN
HETMANS
HEYDAYS
HILLARY
HISPANO
HOBNAIL
HOECAKE
HOGBACK
HOGWASH
HOLLAND
HOLYARK
HONIARA
HOOHAHS
HOOKAHS
HOSTAGE
HOTCAKE
HOTCAPS
HOTCARS
HOTWARS
HOVLANE
HOWDAHS
HUBBARD
HUBCAPS
HUNGARY
HUNYADY
HURRAHS
HUSBAND
HUSHABY
HUSSARS
HUZZAHS
HYDRANT
HYDRATE
HYMNALS

H••••A•
HABITAT
HACKMAN
HACKSAW
HADRIAN
HAITIAN
HALFDAN
HALFWAY
HALIFAX
HALLWAY
HANDBAG
HANDCAR
HANDSAW
HANGMAN
HANUKAH
HARDHAT
HARDPAN
HARTMAN
HEADMAN
HEADWAY
HEARSAY
HEELTAP
HEGIRAS
HEISMAN
HELICAL
HELIPAD
HELLCAT
HELLMAN
HESHVAN
HESSIAN
HIALEAH
HICKMAN
HIGHDAY
HIGHHAT
HIGHWAY
HINTSAT
HOFBRAU
HOFFMAN
HOLIDAY
HOLMOAK
HOLYDAY
HOLYWAR
HOOPLAS
HOOTSAT
HOTHEAD
HOTSEAT
HOUSMAN
HULLOAS
HUMERAL
HYUNDAI

H•••••A
HERBTEA
HIGHTEA
HONIARA
HOSANNA
HYGIEIA

•HA••••
CHABLIS
CHACHAS
CHAFING
CHAGALL
CHAGRIN
CHAINED
CHAIRED
CHAISES
CHALETS
CHALICE
CHALKED
CHALKUP
CHALONS
CHAMBER
CHAMFER
CHAMOIS
CHAMPED
CHANCED
CHANCEL
CHANCER
CHANCES
CHANGED
CHANGER
CHANGES
CHANNEL
CHANSON
CHANTED
CHANTER
CHANTEY
CHAOTIC
CHAPATI
CHAPEAU
CHAPELS
CHAPLET
CHAPLIN
CHAPMAN
CHAPMEN
CHAPPED
CHAPPIE
CHAPTER
CHARADE
CHARGED
CHARGER
CHARGES
CHARIER
CHARILY
CHARIOT
CHARITY
CHARLES
CHARLEY
CHARLIE
CHARMED
CHARMER
CHARMIN
CHARRED
CHARTED
CHARTER
CHASERS
CHASING
CHASSES
CHASSIS
CHASTEN
CHASTER
CHATEAU
CHATHAM
CHATSUP
CHATTED
CHATTEL
CHATTER
CHAUCER
GHANIAN
GHASTLY
KHAYYAM
PHAEDRA
PHAETON
PHALANX
PHANTOM
PHARAOH
PHARLAP
PHARYNX
PHASEIN
PHASERS
PHASING
SHACKLE
SHADIER
SHADILY
SHADING
SHADOOF
SHADOWS
SHADOWY
SHAFFER
SHAFTED
SHAGGED
SHAHDOM
SHAKERS
SHAKEUP
SHAKIER
SHAKILY
SHAKING
SHAKOES
SHALALA
SHALLOT
SHALLOW
SHALOMS
SHAMANS
SHAMBLE
SHAMING
SHAMMED
SHAMPOO
SHANANA
SHANGRI
SHANKAR
SHANKED
SHANNON
SHANTEY
SHAPELY
SHAPERS
SHAPEUP
SHAPING
SHAPIRO
SHAPLEY
SHAREIN
SHARERS
SHARING
SHARKEY
SHARPED
SHARPEI
SHARPEN
SHARPER
SHARPLY
SHASTRI
SHATNER
SHATTER
SHAVERS
SHAVING
SHAWNEE
SHAWWAL
THALERS
THANKED
THATCHY
THATSIT
THAWING
WHACKED
WHALERS
WHALING
WHAMMED
WHANGED
WHARFED
WHARTON
WHARVES
WHATFOR
WHATNOT
WHAUDEN

•H•A•••
AHEADOF
CHEAPEN
CHEAPER
CHEAPIE
CHEAPLY
CHEATED
CHEATER
CHEATIN
CHIANTI
PHRASAL
PHRASED
PHRASES
SHEARED
SHEARER
SHEATHE
SHEATHS
SHEAVED
SHEAVES
SHIATSU
THEATER
THEATRE
THRALLS
THWACKS
THWARTS
WHEATON

•H••A••
CHAGALL
CHAPATI
CHARADE
CHICAGO
CHICANA
CHICANO
CHORALE
CHORALS
OHIOANS
PHALANX
PHARAOH
RHUBARB
SHALALA
SHAMANS
SHANANA
SHEBANG
SHEPARD
SHIKARI
SHOFARS
THEBABE
THECARS
THENARS
THERAPY
THINAIR
THREADS
THREADY
THREATS
THROATS
THROATY
WHYDAHS
ZHIVAGO

•H•••A•
CHACHAS
CHAPEAU
CHAPMAN
CHATEAU
CHATHAM
CHEDDAR
CHEETAH
CHEMLAB
CHILEAN
CHLORAL
CHOCTAW
CHOLLAS
CHUKKAS
GHANIAN
KHAYYAM
PHARLAP
PHIDIAS
PHINEAS
PHOBIAS
PHRASAL
RHUMBAS
SHANKAR
SHAWWAL
SHEILAS
SHELLAC
SHERMAN
SHERPAS
SHIPMAN
SHOOTAT
SHOWMAN
THEREAT
THERMAL
THOREAU
THREEAM
THRUWAY
THURMAN
THUSFAR
WHEREAS
WHEREAT
WHIPSAW
WHITMAN

•H••••A
CHELSEA
CHICANA
CHIMERA
PHAEDRA
SHALALA
SHANANA
SHOULDA
THERESA

••HA•••
ACHATES
AMHARIC
ASHAMED
ASHANTI
BAHAMAS
BEHAVED
BEHAVES
COHABIT
ENHANCE
ETHANOL
EXHALED
EXHALES
EXHAUST
ICHABOD
INHABIT
INHALED
INHALER
INHALES
INHASTE
INHAULS
ITHACAN
JOHANNA
LEHAVRE
MAHALIA
MAHARIS
MAHATMA
MOHAIRS
MOHAWKS
REHANGS
SAHARAN
SCHATZI
SUHARTO
UNHANDS
UNHANDY
UNHAPPY
WCHANDY

••H•A••
ASHCANS
ASHLAND
ASHLARS
ASHRAMS
ATHEART
ATHWART
BAHRAIN
BEHEADS
BYHEART
ISHMAEL
NAHUATL
OOHLALA
PAHLAVI
REHEALS
REHEARD
REHEARS
REHEATS
SCHNAPS
UNHEARD

••H••A•
ASHTRAY
BAHAMAS
DAHLIAS
ETHICAL
INHUMAN
ITHACAN
JOHNGAY
JOHNJAY
KAHUNAS
MOHICAN
SAHARAN
SCHEMAS
SCHOLAR
TEHERAN

••H•••A
APHELIA
BOHEMIA
ECHIDNA
JOHANNA
MAHALIA
MAHATMA
OOHLALA
OPHELIA
SCHIRRA

•••HA••
AFGHANI
AFGHANS
ALLHAIL
ALOHAOE
ARCHAIC
ASPHALT
BAUHAUS
BETHANY
BOKHARA
CATHAIR
COCHAIR
COWHAND
CUSHAWS
DABHAND
DIEHARD
EARHART
ECKHART
ELKHART
ENCHAIN
ENCHANT
ETCHANT
GOSHAWK
GRAHAME
GRAHAMS
HAWHAWS
HEEHAWS
HOOHAHS
HUSHABY
INPHASE
INSHAPE
METHANE
MICHAEL
MIKHAIL
MILHAUD
MISHAPS
NEWHART
OFFHAND
OLDHAND
OMPHALI
ORCHARD
ORPHANS
PERHAPS
RAPHAEL
RECHALK
REDHAIR
REDHATS
RICHARD
SASHAYS
TINHATS
TOPHATS
UNCHAIN
UTAHANS
ZACHARY

•••H•A•
AIRHEAD
ALLHEAL
ANAHUAC
ARCHWAY
BAGHDAD
BATHMAT
BIGHEAD
BRAHMAN
BRAHMAS
BUSHMAN
CASHBAR
CATHEAD
COCHRAN
DISHPAN
DISHRAG
EGGHEAD
EIGHTAM
ENTHRAL
ESCHEAT
FATHEAD
GOAHEAD
HESHVAN
HIGHDAY
HIGHHAT
HIGHWAY
HOTHEAD
IDAHOAN
INAHEAP
JUGHEAD
LACHLAN
MATHIAS
MISHEAR
MITHRAS
ORPHEAN
PATHWAY
PINHEAD
POOHBAH
PREHEAT
PYTHIAN
PYTHIAS
REDHEAD
REDHEAT
RICHMAN
SASHBAR
SICHUAN
SUBHEAD
TASHMAN
TOWHEAD
TUCHMAN
WASHRAG
YASHMAK

•••H••A
AMPHORA
BOKHARA
BOTHNIA
COCHLEA
FUCHSIA
HIGHTEA
KACHINA
MACHINA
NAPHTHA
TOSHIBA
WICHITA
YESHIVA

••••HA•
ABRAHAM
AGAKHAN
ALYKHAN
BALIHAI
BEECHAM
BENTHAM
BINGHAM
BRIGHAM
BUDDHAS
CAPSHAW
CHACHAS
CHATHAM
EPOCHAL
FORDHAM
FUNCHAL
GALAHAD
GEISHAS
GINGHAM
GODTHAB
GOTCHAS
GRISHAM
GURKHAS
HARDHAT
HIGHHAT
KEESHAN
KETCHAM
KWACHAS
LAUGHAT
MADEHAY
MAKEHAY
MARKHAM
MARSHAL
MATTHAU
MAUGHAM
MCLUHAN
NARWHAL
NEEDHAM
OLDCHAP
PANCHAX
PASCHAL
PINCHAS
RAINHAT
SILKHAT
SIOBHAN
TRISHAW
VAUGHAN
XANTHAN
YITZHAK

••••H•A
BOOTHIA
CYNTHIA
DRACHMA
KRISHNA
QUECHUA
TRACHEA

•••••HA
ALYOSHA
KENOSHA
NAPHTHA
NATASHA
PIRANHA
RICKSHA
TABITHA

H•B••••
HABITAT
HABITED
HABITUE
HEBRAIC
HEBREWS
HIBACHI

HOBBIES
HOBBITS
HOBBLED
HOBBLES
HOBNAIL
HOBNOBS
HOBOING
HOBOKEN
HUBBARD
HUBBELL
HUBBIES
HUBBUBS
HUBCAPS
HYBRIDS

H••B•••
HAMBURG
HARBORS
HARBOUR
HARBURG
HASBEEN
HATBAND
HAUBERK
HENBANE
HENBITS
HEPBURN
HERBAGE
HERBALS
HERBERT
HERBIER
HERBTEA
HIPBONE
HIPBOOT
HOBBIES
HOBBITS
HOBBLED
HOBBLES
HOFBRAU
HOGBACK
HOLBEIN
HOMBRES
HOMBURG
HOTBEDS
HOWBEIT
HUBBARD
HUBBELL
HUBBIES
HUBBUBS
HUMBLED
HUMBLER
HUMBLES
HUMBUGS
HUSBAND

H•••B••
HALIBUT
HANDBAG
HAUTBOY
HIGHBOY
HIRABLE
HOMEBOY

H••••B•
HOBNOBS
HORNSBY
HOTTUBS
HUBBUBS
HUSHABY

H•••••B
HOTCOMB

•H•B•••
CHABLIS
PHOBIAS
PHOBICS
RHEBOKS
RHUBARB
SHEBANG
SHUBERT
THEBABE
THEBLOB

•H••B••
CHAMBER
PHILBIN
PHOEBES
PHOEBUS
RHOMBUS
RHUMBAS
SHAMBLE
SHERBET
SHOEBOX
SHOWBIZ
SHRUBBY
THIMBLE
THUMBED
THURBER

•H•••B•
CHERUBS
SHRUBBY
THEBABE
THEREBY
WHEREBY

•H••••B
CHEMLAB
RHUBARB
THEBLOB

••HB•••
ASHBURY

••H•B••
COHABIT
EXHIBIT
ICHABOD
INHABIT
INHIBIT

•••HB••
CASHBAR
CASHBOX
HIGHBOY
POOHBAH
SASHBAR

•••H•B•
BYTHEBY
HUSHABY
TOSHIBA

•••H••B
BATHTUB
POTHERB
WASHTUB

••••H•B
GODTHAB

H•C••••
HACKERS
HACKETT
HACKIES
HACKING
HACKLED
HACKLES
HACKMAN
HACKNEY
HACKSAW
HECKLED
HECKLER
HECKLES
HECTARE
HECTORS
HICCUPS
HICKMAN
HICKORY
HOCKING

H••C•••
HALCYON
HANCOCK
HATCHED
HATCHER
HATCHES
HATCHET
HENCOOP
HEPCATS
HERCULE
HICCUPS
HITCHED
HITCHER
HITCHES
HOECAKE
HONCHOS
HOTCAKE
HOTCAPS
HOTCARS
HOTCOMB
HOWCOME
HUBCAPS
HUNCHED
HUNCHES
HUTCHES

H•••C••
HAIRCUT
HANDCAR
HARICOT
HELICAL
HELICES
HELICON
HELLCAT
HIBACHI
HIJACKS
HITACHI
HOLYCOW
HYRACES

H••••C•
HADDOCK
HAMHOCK
HAMMOCK
HANCOCK
HASSOCK
HATRACK
HAYRACK
HEMLOCK
HENPECK
HEROICS
HILLOCK
HOGBACK
HOSPICE
HUMMOCK

H•••••C
HAMITIC
HASIDIC
HEBRAIC
HEPATIC
HERETIC
HOMERIC

•H•C•••
CHACHAS
CHECHEN
CHECKED
CHECKER
CHECKIN
CHECKUP
CHICAGO
CHICANA
CHICANO
CHICHEN
CHICKEN
CHICORY
CHOCTAW
CHUCKED
CHUCKLE
SHACKLE
SHOCKED
SHOCKER
SHUCKED
SHUCKER
THECARS
THECROW
THICKEN
THICKER
THICKET
THICKLY
WHACKED

•H••C••
CHANCED
CHANCEL
CHANCER
CHANCES
CHAUCER
CHOICER
CHOICES
SHTICKS
THATCHY
THWACKS

•H•••C•
CHALICE
CHIRICO
EHRLICH
PHOBICS
PHONICS
PHOTICS
PHYSICS
SHYLOCK
THINICE

•H••••C
CHAOTIC
CHRONIC
PHRENIC
SHELLAC

••HC•••
ASHCANS

••H•C••
ETHICAL
ITHACAN
MOHICAN
VEHICLE

••H••C•
DEHISCE
ENHANCE
ETHNICS
SCHLOCK
UNHITCH

••H•••C
AMHARIC

•••HC••
CASHCOW

•••H•C•
GOTHICS
HAMHOCK
RECHECK

•••H••C
ANAHUAC
ARCHAIC

••••H•C
DELPHIC
EDAPHIC
GRAPHIC
PSYCHIC
PYRRHIC
TROPHIC
XANTHIC

H•D••••
HADDOCK
HADRIAN
HEDDLES
HEDGERS
HEDGIER
HEDGING
HIDALGO
HIDEOUS
HIDEOUT
HIDINGS
HUDDLED
HUDDLES
HYDRANT
HYDRATE
HYDROUS

H••D•••
HADDOCK
HAGDONS
HANDBAG
HANDCAR
HANDFED
HANDFUL
HANDGUN
HANDIER
HANDILY
HANDING
HANDLED
HANDLER
HANDLES
HANDOFF
HANDOUT
HANDSAW
HANDSET
HANDSIN
HANDSON
HANDSUP
HARDENS
HARDEST
HARDHAT
HARDHIT
HARDIER
HARDILY
HARDING
HARDPAN
HARDPUT
HARDSET
HARDTOP
HARDWON
HEADERS
HEADIER
HEADILY
HEADING
HEADMAN
HEADMEN
HEADOFF
HEADOUT
HEADPIN
HEADSET
HEADSIN
HEADSUP
HEADWAY
HEDDLES
HEEDFUL
HEEDING
HELDOFF
HELDOUT
HENDRIX
HERDERS
HERDING
HEYDAYS
HINDERS
HOEDOWN
HOLDERS
HOLDING
HOLDOFF
HOLDOUT
HOLDSIN
HOLDSON
HOLDSTO
HOLDSUP
HOLDUPS
HOODLUM
HOODOOS
HOTDOGS
HOUDINI
HOWDAHS
HOYDENS
HUDDLED
HUDDLES
HUMDRUM
HUNDRED
HURDLED
HURDLER
HURDLES

H•••D••
HAIRDOS
HAIRDYE
HALFDAN
HALIDES
HANGDOG
HASIDIC
HASIDIM
HEARDOF
HIGHDAY
HIKEDUP
HOARDED
HOARDER
HOLEDUP
HOLIDAY
HOLYDAY
HOUNDED
HUMIDLY
HUMIDOR
HYPEDUP
HYUNDAI

H••••D•
HAYRIDE
HAZARDS
HEPTADS
HERALDS
HEYJUDE
HOTBEDS
HOTRODS
HOWARDS
HUNYADY
HYBRIDS
HYMNODY

H•••••D
HABITED
HACKLED
HAGGARD
HAGGLED
HALYARD
HAMMOND
HANDFED
HANDLED
HARRIED
HARVARD
HASSLED
HATBAND
HATCHED
HAUNTED
HAVERED
HAYSEED
HAYWARD
HEARTED
HECKLED
HEISTED
HELIPAD
HENNAED
HEYWOOD
HIGGLED
HIGHEND
HITCHED
HOARDED
HOBBLED
HOGTIED
HOGWILD
HOISTED
HOLLAND
HOMERED
HOMINID
HONEYED
HONORED
HOPPLED
HOTHEAD
HOUGHED
HOUNDED
HOVERED
HUBBARD
HUDDLED
HULLOED
HUMBLED
HUMORED
HUNCHED
HUNDRED
HURDLED
HURRIED
HURTLED
HUSBAND
HUSTLED

•H•D•••
CHEDDAR
CHIDERS
CHIDING
PHIDIAS
RHODIUM
SHADIER
SHADILY
SHADING
SHADOOF
SHADOWS
SHADOWY
SHODDEN
SHUDDER
THEDEEP
THUDDED
WHYDAHS

•H••D••
AHEADOF
CHEDDAR
CHOWDER
PHAEDRA
SHAHDOM
SHELDON
SHINDIG
SHODDEN
SHOWDOG
SHUDDER
THIRDLY
THUDDED
THUNDER
WHAUDEN
WHEEDLE

•H•••D•
CHARADE
SHIELDS
SHOULDA
SHROUDS
THREADS
THREADY

•H••••D
CHAINED
CHAIRED
CHALKED
CHAMPED
CHANCED
CHANGED
CHANTED
CHAPPED
CHARGED
CHARMED
CHARRED
CHARTED
CHATTED
CHEATED
CHECKED
CHEEPED
CHEERED
CHEVIED
CHILLED
CHINKED
CHINNED
CHIPPED
CHIRPED
CHOMPED
CHOPPED
CHUCKED
CHUGGED
CHUMMED
CHURNED
GHOSTED
PHOTOED
PHRASED
SHAFTED
SHAGGED
SHAMMED
SHANKED
SHARPED
SHEARED
SHEAVED
SHEERED
SHEETED
SHELLED
SHELVED
SHEPARD
SHIFTED
SHILLED
SHINNED
SHIPPED
SHIRKED
SHIRRED
SHOCKED
SHOPPED
SHORTED
SHOUTED
SHUCKED
SHUNNED
SHUNTED
SHUSHED
THANKED
THIEVED
THINNED
THRIVED
THUDDED
THUMBED
THUMPED
WHACKED
WHAMMED
WHANGED
WHARFED
WHEELED
WHEEZED
WHELMED
WHELPED
WHETTED
WHIFFED
WHIPPED
WHIRLED
WHIRRED
WHISHED
WHISKED
WHIZKID
WHIZZED
WHOMPED
WHOOPED
WHOPPED
WHORLED
WHUPPED

••H•D••
ECHIDNA
JOHNDOE

••H••D•
BEHEADS
BEHOLDS
SCHMIDT
UNHANDS
UNHANDY
UPHOLDS
WCHANDY

••H•••D
ADHERED
ASHAMED
ASHFORD
ASHLAND
BEHAVED
BEHOVED
COHERED
EXHALED
ICHABOD
INHALED
INHERED
REHEARD
REHIRED
SCHEMED
UNHEARD
USHERED

•••HD••
BAGHDAD
HIGHDAY
RUSHDIE
SHAHDOM

•••H•D•
BUSHIDO
CATHODE
COWHIDE
METHODS
ORCHIDS
RAWHIDE

•••H••D
AIRHEAD
BAGHDAD
BIGHEAD
BOYHOOD
CATHEAD
COWHAND
COWHERD
DABHAND
DIEHARD
EGGHEAD
EUCHRED
FATHEAD
GOAHEAD
HIGHEND
HOTHEAD
JUGHEAD
LIGHTED
MANHOOD
MILHAUD
OFFHAND
OLDHAND
ORCHARD
PINHEAD
REDHEAD
RICHARD
RIGHTED
SIGHTED
SUBHEAD
TOEHOLD
TOWHEAD
YACHTED

••••H•D
ABASHED
BATCHED
BEACHED
BELCHED
BENCHED
BERTHED
BIRCHED
BIRTHED
BLUSHED
BOTCHED
BRUSHED
BUNCHED
CINCHED
CLASHED
CLOTHED
COACHED
COUCHED
COUGHED
CRASHED
CRUSHED
DITCHED
FETCHED
FILCHED
FLASHED
FLESHED
FLUSHED
FROTHED
GALAHAD
GNASHED
GRAPHED
HATCHED
HITCHED
HOUGHED
HUNCHED
LATCHED
LAUGHED
LEACHED
LEASHED
LEECHED
LOATHED
LUNCHED
LURCHED
MARCHED
MATCHED
MOOCHED
MORPHED
MOUTHED
MULCHED
MUNCHED
NEIGHED
NOTCHED
PARCHED
PATCHED
PEACHED
PERCHED
PINCHED
PITCHED
PLASHED
POACHED
POUCHED
PSYCHED
PUNCHED
QUASHED
RANCHED
REACHED
ROACHED
ROUGHED
SCATHED
SCYTHED
SEETHED
SHUSHED
SLASHED
SLOSHED
SMASHED
SOOTHED
SOUGHED
STASHED
SWATHED
SWISHED
SYNCHED
TEETHED
TETCHED
TOOTHED
TORCHED
TOUCHED
TRASHED
TROTHED
VOUCHED
WATCHED
WEIGHED
WELCHED
WHISHED
WINCHED
WRITHED

HE•••••
HEADERS
HEADIER
HEADILY
HEADING
HEADMAN
HEADMEN
HEADOFF
HEADOUT
HEADPIN
HEADSET
HEADSIN
HEADSUP
HEADWAY
HEALALL
HEALERS
HEALING
HEALTHY
HEAPING
HEARDOF
HEARERS
HEARING
HEARKEN
HEAROUT
HEARSAY
HEARSOF
HEARTED
HEARTEN
HEARTHS
HEATERS
HEATFUL
HEATHEN
HEATHER
HEATING
HEATSUP
HEATTER
HEAVEHO
HEAVENS
HEAVERS
HEAVETO
HEAVIER
HEAVIES
HEAVILY
HEAVING
HEBRAIC
HEBREWS
HECKLED
HECKLER
HECKLES
HECTARE
HECTORS
HEDDLES
HEDGERS
HEDGIER
HEDGING
HEEDFUL
HEEDING
HEEHAWS
HEELERS
HEELING
HEELTAP
HEFTIER
HEFTILY
HEFTING
HEGIRAS
HEIFERS
HEIFETZ
HEIGHHO
HEIGHTS
HEINOUS
HEIRESS
HEISMAN
HEISTED
HELDOFF
HELDOUT
HELICAL
HELICES
HELICON
HELIPAD
HELIXES
HELLCAT
HELLENE
HELLERS
HELLION
HELLISH
HELLMAN
HELMETS
HELMING
HELOISE
HELOTRY
HELPERS
HELPFUL
HELPING
HELPOUT
HEMLINE
HEMLOCK
HEMMERS
HEMMING
HEMSLEY
HENBANE
HENBITS
HENCOOP
HENDRIX
HENLIKE
HENNAED
HENNERY
HENNISH
HENPECK
HENRYIV
HENTING
HEPARIN
HEPATIC
HEPBURN
HEPCATS
HEPPEST
HEPTADS
HERALDS
HERBAGE
HERBALS
HERBERT
HERBIER
HERBTEA
HERCULE
HERDERS
HERDING
HERETIC
HERMANN
HERMITS
HEROICS
HEROINE
HEROISM
HERRING
HERRIOT
HERSELF
HERSHEY
HESHVAN
HESSIAN
HETMANS
HEWLETT
HEXAGON
HEXNUTS
HEXSIGN
HEYDAYS
HEYJUDE
HEYWOOD

H•E••••
HAEMATO
HEEDFUL
HEEDING
HEEHAWS
HEELERS
HEELING
HEELTAP
HOECAKE
HOEDOWN
HUELESS

H••E•••
HAMELIN
HAPENNY
HATEFUL
HAVENOT
HAVERED
HERETIC
HGWELLS
HIDEOUS
HIDEOUT
HIKEDUP
HIKESUP
HIRESON
HOLEDUP
HOLEOUT
HOLESUP
HOMEBOY
HOMERED
HOMERIC
HOMERUN
HONESTY
HONEYED
HOPEFUL
HOVERED
HOVERER
HOWELLS
HOWEVER
HUMERAL
HUMERUS
HYPEDUP
HYPESUP

H•••E••
HACKERS
HACKETT
HALTERS
HAMLETS
HAMMERS
HAMMETT
HAMPERS
HANGERS
HANKERS
HAPLESS
HAPPENS
HARDENS
HARDEST
HARKENS
HARNESS
HARPERS
HARVEST
HASBEEN
HASTENS
HATLESS
HATTERS
HAUBERK
HAULERS
HAUTEUR
HAWKERS
HAWKEYE
HAWSERS
HAYSEED
HAZIEST

HEADERS
HEALERS
HEARERS
HEATERS
HEAVEHO
HEAVENS
HEAVERS
HEAVETO
HEBREWS
HEDGERS
HEELERS
HEIFERS
HEIFETZ
HEIRESS
HELLENE
HELLERS
HELMETS
HELPERS
HEMMERS
HENNERY
HENPECK
HEPPEST
HERBERT
HERDERS
HERSELF
HEWLETT
HIALEAH
HIGHEND
HIGHEST
HIMSELF
HINDERS
HIPLESS
HIPNESS
HIPPEST
HISSERS
HITHERE
HITLESS
HITTERS
HOAXERS
HOGGETS
HOKIEST
HOLBEIN
HOLDERS
HOLIEST
HOLLERS
HOMIEST
HONKERS
HOOFERS
HOOTERS
HOOVERS
HOPPERS
HORNETS
HOSIERS
HOSIERY
HOSTELS
HOSTESS
HOTBEDS
HOTHEAD
HOTNESS
HOTSEAT
HOTTEST
HOWBEIT
HOWLERS
HOYDENS
HUBBELL
HUELESS
HUGGERS
HULLERS
HUMMERS
HUMVEES
HUNGERS
HUNKERS
HUNTERS
HURLERS
HURLEYS
HUSKERS
HUSSEIN
HUYGENS
HYGIEIA
HYGIENE
HYPHENS

H••••E•

HAARLEM
HABITED
HACKIES
HACKLED
HACKLES
HACKNEY
HAGGLED
HAGGLER
HAGGLES
HAIRIER
HAIRNET
HALIDES
HALITES
HALOGEN
HAMITES
HAMMIER
HAMSTER
HANDFED
HANDIER
HANDLED
HANDLER
HANDLES
HANDSET
HANGMEN
HANGTEN
HANKIES
HANOVER
HAPPIER
HARDIER
HARDSET
HARPIES
HARRIED
HARRIER
HARRIES
HARRIET
HARSHEN
HARSHER
HASBEEN
HASSLED
HASSLES
HASTIER
HATCHED
HATCHER
HATCHES
HATCHET
HAUNTED
HAVERED
HAYSEED
HEADIER
HEADMEN
HEADSET
HEARKEN
HEARTED
HEARTEN
HEATHEN
HEATHER
HEATTER
HEAVIER
HEAVIES
HECKLED
HECKLER
HECKLES
HEDDLES
HEDGIER
HEFTIER
HEISTED
HELICES
HELIXES
HEMSLEY
HENNAED
HERBIER
HERBTEA
HERSHEY
HIGGLED
HIGGLES
HIGHTEA
HILLIER
HINNIES
HIPPIER
HIPPIES
HIPSTER
HITCHED
HITCHER
HITCHES
HOAGIES
HOARDED
HOARDER
HOARIER
HOARSEN
HOARSER
HOBBIES
HOBBLED
HOBBLES
HOBOKEN
HOGTIED
HOGTIES
HOISTED
HOLLIES
HOLSTER
HOLYSEE
HOMBRES
HOMERED
HONEYED
HONORED
HONOREE
HONORER
HOOPOES
HOOSIER
HOPOVER
HOPPLED
HOPPLES
HORSIER
HOSTLER
HOUGHED
HOUNDED
HOVERED
HOVERER
HOWEVER
HUBBIES
HUDDLED
HUDDLES
HUFFIER
HULLOED
HUMBLED
HUMBLER
HUMBLES
HUMORED
HUMPIER
HUMVEES
HUNCHED
HUNCHES
HUNDRED
HUNKIER
HUNTLEY
HURDLED
HURDLER
HURDLES
HURLIES
HURRIED
HURRIES
HURTLED
HURTLES
HUSKIER
HUSKIES
HUSSIES
HUSTLED
HUSTLER
HUSTLES
HUTCHES
HYRACES
HYRAXES

H•••••E

HABITUE
HAGLIKE
HAIRDYE
HATLIKE
HAULAGE
HAWKEYE
HAYRIDE
HAYWIRE
HECTARE
HELLENE
HELOISE
HEMLINE
HENBANE
HENLIKE
HERBAGE
HERCULE
HEROINE
HEYJUDE
HILAIRE
HIPBONE
HIPLIKE
HIRABLE
HIRSUTE
HITHERE
HITTITE
HOECAKE
HOGLIKE
HOLYOKE
HOLYSEE
HONOREE
HOPLIKE
HORMONE
HOSPICE
HOSTAGE
HOSTILE
HOTCAKE
HOTLINE
HOTWIRE
HOVLANE
HOWCOME
HUNLIKE
HUTLIKE
HYALINE
HYDRATE
HYGIENE

•HE••••

AHEADOF
CHEAPEN
CHEAPER
CHEAPIE
CHEAPLY
CHEATED
CHEATER
CHEATIN
CHECHEN
CHECKED
CHECKER
CHECKIN
CHECKUP
CHEDDAR
CHEEPED
CHEERED
CHEERIO
CHEERUP
CHEESES
CHEETAH
CHEETOS
CHEEVER
CHEKHOV
CHELSEA
CHEMISE
CHEMIST
CHEMLAB
CHENIER
CHEQUER
CHEQUES
CHERISH
CHEROOT
CHERUBS
CHERVIL
CHESTER
CHETRUM
CHEVIED
CHEVIES
CHEVIOT
CHEVRES
CHEVRON
CHEWERS
CHEWIER
CHEWING
CHEWOUT
CHEWSUP
CHEWTOY
GHERKIN
GHETTOS
PHENOLS
PHENOMS
RHEBOKS
RHENISH
RHENIUM
RHETORS
SHEARED
SHEARER
SHEATHE
SHEATHS
SHEAVED
SHEAVES
SHEBANG
SHEERED
SHEERER
SHEERLY
SHEETED
SHEIKHS
SHEILAS
SHEKELS
SHELDON
SHELLAC
SHELLED
SHELLER
SHELLEY
SHELTER
SHELTIE
SHELTON
SHELVED
SHELVES
SHEPARD
SHERBET
SHERIFF
SHERMAN
SHERPAS
SHERWIN
SHEWOLF
THEATER
THEATRE
THEBABE
THEBLOB
THECARS
THECROW
THEDEEP
THEFIRM
THEFONZ
THEISTS
THENARS
THEOMEN
THEOREM
THEPITS
THERAPY
THEREAT
THEREBY
THEREIN
THERELL
THEREOF
THEREON
THERESA
THERETO
THERMAL
THERMOS
THEROUX
THESEUS
THESPIS
THEURGY
THEWIER
WHEATON
WHEEDLE
WHEELED
WHEELER
WHEELIE
WHEEZED
WHEEZER
WHEEZES
WHELMED
WHELPED
WHEREAS
WHEREAT
WHEREBY
WHEREIN
WHERELL
WHEREOF
WHERERE
WHERETO
WHEREVE
WHETHER
WHETTED
WHEYISH
XHEIGHT

•H•E•••

CHEEPED
CHEERED
CHEERIO
CHEERUP
CHEESES
CHEETAH
CHEETOS
CHEEVER
CHIEFLY
PHAEDRA
PHAETON
PHOEBES
PHOEBUS
PHOENIX
PHRENIC
SHEERED
SHEERER
SHEERLY
SHEETED
SHIELDS
SHOEBOX
SHOEING
THIEVED
THIEVES
THREADS
THREADY
THREATS
THREEAM
THREEPM
THREERS
THREWIN
WHEEDLE
WHEELED
WHEELER
WHEELIE
WHEEZED
WHEEZER
WHEEZES
WHOEVER

•H••E••

CHALETS
CHAPEAU
CHAPELS
CHASERS
CHATEAU
CHEWERS
CHIDERS
CHILEAN
CHIMERA
CHINESE
CHISELS
CHOKERS
CHOKEUP
PHASEIN
PHASERS
PHINEAS
PHONEME
PHONEYS
RHYMERS
SHAKERS
SHAKEUP
SHAPELY
SHAPERS
SHAPEUP
SHAREIN
SHARERS
SHAVERS
SHEKELS
SHINERS
SHIVERS
SHIVERY
SHOVELS
SHOVERS
SHOWERS
SHOWERY
SHRIEKS
SHUBERT
SHUTEYE
SHYNESS
THALERS
THEDEEP
THEREAT
THEREBY
THEREIN
THERELL
THEREOF
THEREON
THERESA
THERETO
THESEUS
THOREAU
THREEAM
THREEPM
THREERS
THYSELF
WHALERS
WHEREAS
WHEREAT
WHEREBY
WHEREIN
WHERELL
WHEREOF
WHERERE
WHERETO
WHEREVE
WHINERS
WHITENS
WHITEST

•H•••E•

CHAINED
CHAIRED
CHAISES
CHALKED
CHAMBER
CHAMFER
CHAMPED
CHANCED
CHANCEL
CHANCER
CHANCES
CHANGED
CHANGER
CHANGES
CHANNEL
CHANTED
CHANTER
CHANTEY
CHAPLET
CHAPMEN
CHAPPED
CHAPTER
CHARGED
CHARGER
CHARGES
CHARIER
CHARLES
CHARLEY
CHARMED
CHARMER
CHARRED
CHARTED
CHARTER
CHASSES
CHASTEN
CHASTER
CHATTED
CHATTEL
CHATTER
CHAUCER
CHEAPEN
CHEAPER
CHEATED
CHEATER
CHECHEN
CHECKED
CHECKER
CHEEPED
CHEERED
CHEESES
CHEEVER
CHELSEA
CHENIER
CHEQUER
CHEQUES
CHESTER
CHEVIED
CHEVIES
CHEVRES
CHEWIER
CHICHEN
CHICKEN
CHIGGER
CHIGOES
CHILIES
CHILLED
CHILLER
CHIMNEY
CHINKED
CHINNED
CHIPPED
CHIPPER
CHIRPED
CHITTER
CHOICER
CHOICES
CHOKIER
CHOMPED
CHOOSER
CHOOSES
CHOPPED
CHOPPER
CHOWDER
CHROMES
CHUCKED
CHUGGED
CHUKKER
CHUMMED
CHUNNEL
CHUNTER
CHURNED
CHUTNEY
GHOSTED
PHILTER
PHLOXES
PHOEBES
PHONIER
PHONIES
PHOTOED
PHRASED
PHRASES
SHADIER
SHAFFER
SHAFTED
SHAGGED
SHAKIER
SHAKOES
SHAMMED
SHANKED
SHANTEY
SHAPLEY
SHARKEY
SHARPED
SHARPEI
SHARPEN
SHARPER
SHATNER
SHATTER
SHAWNEE
SHEARED
SHEARER
SHEAVED
SHEAVES
SHEERED
SHEERER
SHEETED
SHELLED
SHELLER
SHELLEY
SHELTER
SHELVED
SHELVES
SHERBET
SHIFTED
SHIITES
SHILLED
SHIMMER
SHINIER
SHINNED
SHIPMEN
SHIPPED
SHIPPER
SHIRKED
SHIRKER
SHIRLEY
SHIRRED
SHOCKED
SHOCKER
SHODDEN
SHOOTER
SHOPPED
SHOPPER
SHOPPES
SHORTED
SHORTEN
SHORTER
SHOUTED
SHOUTER
SHOWIER
SHOWMEN
SHRIKES
SHRINER
SHRINES
SHRIVEL
SHRIVER
SHRIVES
SHUCKED
SHUCKER
SHUDDER
SHUNNED
SHUNTED
SHUSHED
SHUSHES
SHUTTER
SHYSTER
THANKED
THEATER
THEDEEP
THEOMEN
THEOREM
THEWIER
THICKEN
THICKER
THICKET
THIEVED
THIEVES
THINKER
THINNED
THINNER
THITHER
THRIVED
THRIVES
THRONES
THROWER
THUDDED
THUMBED
THUMPED
THUMPER
THUNDER
THURBER
WHACKED
WHAMMED
WHANGED
WHARFED
WHARVES
WHAUDEN
WHEELED
WHEELER
WHEEZED
WHEEZER
WHEEZES
WHELMED
WHELPED
WHETHER
WHETTED
WHIFFED
WHIMPER
WHINIER
WHIPPED
WHIPPET
WHIRLED
WHIRRED
WHISHED
WHISHES
WHISKED
WHISKER
WHISKEY
WHISPER
WHITHER
WHITIER
WHITNEY
WHIZZED
WHIZZER
WHIZZES
WHOEVER
WHOMPED
WHOOPED
WHOOPEE
WHOPPED
WHOPPER
WHORLED
WHUPPED

•H••••E

CHALICE
CHAPPIE
CHARADE
CHARLIE
CHEAPIE
CHEMISE
CHINESE
CHOLINE
CHORALE
CHORINE
CHORTLE
CHUCKLE
DHURRIE
PHILTRE
PHONEME
RHIZOME
SHACKLE
SHAMBLE
SHAWNEE
SHEATHE
SHELTIE
SHINGLE
SHUFFLE
SHUTEYE
SHUTTLE
THEATRE
THEBABE
THIMBLE
THINICE
THISTLE
THYMINE
WHEEDLE
WHEELIE
WHERERE
WHEREVE
WHISTLE
WHITTLE
WHOOPEE

••HE•••

ACHENES
ACHERON
ACHESON
ADHERED
ADHERES
AMHERST
APHELIA
APHESES
ATHEART
ATHEISM
ATHEIST
BEHEADS
BEHESTS
BOHEMIA
BYHEART
COHEIRS
COHERED
COHERES
ECHELON
INHERED
INHERES
INHERIT
MCHENRY
OPHELIA
OTHELLO
REHEALS
REHEARD
REHEARS
REHEATS
REHEELS
SCHEMAS
SCHEMED
SCHEMER
SCHEMES
SCHERZI
SCHERZO
SPHERES
TEHERAN
UNHEARD
USHERED

••H•E••

ACHIEST
ACHIEVE
ASHIEST
ASHLESS
ATHLETE
CAHIERS
REHEELS
SCHLEPP
SCHLEPS
SCHMEER

••H••E•

ACHATES
ACHENES
ADHERED
ADHERES
APHESES
ASHAMED
ATHOMES
BEHAVED
BEHAVES
BEHOVED
BEHOVES
COHERED
COHERES
DAHOMEY
EXHALED
EXHALES
INHALED
INHALER
INHALES
INHERED
INHERES
ISHMAEL
MAHONEY
OPHITES
REHIRED
REHIRES
SCHEMED
SCHEMER
SCHEMES
SCHMEER
SCHMOES
SPHERES
USHERED
WAHINES
YAHTZEE

••H•••E

ACHIEVE
ATHLETE
BEHOOVE
DEHISCE
ENHANCE
INHASTE
INHOUSE
JOHNDOE
JOHNNIE
LEHAVRE
UNHORSE
VEHICLE
YAHTZEE

•••HE••

AETHERS
AIRHEAD
ALCHEMY
ALLHEAL
ALLHERE
ANAHEIM
ANTHEMS
ANTHERS
ARCHERS
ARCHERY
BATHERS
BETHELS
BIGHEAD
BOTHERS
BUSHELS
BYTHEBY
CACHETS
CASHEWS
CATHEAD
CEPHEUS
CIPHERS
COCHERE
COWHERD
CYPHERS
DASHERS
DITHERS
DITHERY
DUCHESS
EGGHEAD
ESCHEAT
ESCHEWS
ESTHETE
ETCHERS
FATHEAD
FATHERS
FISHERS
FISHERY
FISHEYE
GATHERS
GOAHEAD
GOPHERS
GUSHERS
HIGHEND
HIGHEST
HITHERE
HOTHEAD
HYPHENS
INAHEAP
ISOHELS
JAPHETH
JUGHEAD
KOSHERS
KUCHENS
LASHERS
LATHERS
LATHERY
LICHENS
LITHELY
LITHEST
LOWHEEL
LUSHEST
MACHETE
MASHERS
MATHERS
MATHEWS
MAYHEMS
MICHELE
MISHEAR
MOSHERS
MOTHERS
MUDHENS
MUSHERS
MYNHEER
NEPHEWS
NIGHEST
NOSHERS
NOWHERE
ONTHEGO
ONTHEQT
ORPHEAN
ORPHEUS
PEAHENS
PINHEAD
POSHEST
POTHERB
POTHERS
PREHEAT
RASHERS
RASHEST
RECHECK
REDHEAD
REDHEAT
RICHEST
ROCHETS
RUSHEES
RUSHERS
SACHEMS
SACHETS
SEEHERE
SIGHERS
SOTHERE
SOTHERN
SUBHEAD
TARHEEL
TETHERS
TITHERS
TOWHEAD
TOWHEES
WASHERS
WETHERS
WILHELM

WISHERS
WITHERS
WYCHELM
ZITHERS

•••H•E•
BUSHIER
BUSHMEN
CASHIER
COCHLEA
CUSHIER
DISHIER
DUCHIES
EUCHRED
EUCHRES
FIGHTER
FISHIER
FISHNET
GUSHIER
HIGHTEA
ITCHIER
KISHKES
LIGHTED
LIGHTEN
LIGHTER
LOWHEEL
MASHIES
MESHIER
MICHAEL
MOTHIER
MUSHIER
MYNHEER
ORPHREY
PITHIER
PUSHIER
RAPHAEL
RESHOES
RICHTER
RIGHTED
RIGHTER
RUSHEES
RUSHIER
SIGHTED
TARHEEL
TECHIER
TECHIES
TIGHTEN
TIGHTER
TOWHEES
WASHIER
WITHIER
WITHIES
YACHTED

•••H••E
AIRHOLE
ALLHERE
ALOHAOE
ARCHIVE
ARMHOLE
BEEHIVE
BOBHOPE
BOGHOLE
CATHODE
COCHERE
COCHISE
COWHIDE
DRYHOLE
EBWHITE
ENTHUSE
ESTHETE
EYEHOLE
FISHEYE
FOXHOLE
GRAHAME
GUTHRIE
HITHERE
INPHASE
INSHAPE
KEYHOLE
MACHETE
MACHINE
MANHOLE
METHANE
MICHELE
NIGHTIE
NOWHERE
ONSHORE
PINHOLE
POTHOLE
RATHOLE
RAWHIDE
RECHOSE
RUNHOME
RUSHDIE
SEEHERE
SOTHERE
TERHUNE
TOPHOLE

••••HE•
ABASHED
ABASHES
AITCHES
ANOTHER
APACHES
APOTHEM
BANSHEE
BATCHED
BATCHES
BEACHED
BEACHES
BEECHER
BEECHES
BELCHED
BELCHES
BENCHED
BENCHES
BERTHED
BIRCHED
BIRCHES
BIRTHED
BLATHER
BLITHER
BLUSHED
BLUSHER
BLUSHES
BOTCHED
BOTCHES
BRASHER
BROTHER
BRUSHED
BRUSHES
BUNCHED
BUNCHES
BURGHER
BUTCHER
CATCHER
CATCHES
CHECHEN
CHICHEN
CINCHED
CINCHES
CLASHED
CLASHES
CLICHES
CLOCHES
CLOTHED
CLOTHES
COACHED
COACHES
CONCHES
COUCHED
COUCHES
COUGHED
CRASHED
CRASHES
CRECHES
CROCHET
CRUSHED
CRUSHER
CRUSHES
DITCHED
DITCHES
EARTHEN
EPITHET
FARTHER
FEATHER
FETCHED
FETCHES
FILCHED
FILCHER
FILCHES
FINCHES
FISCHER
FITCHES
FLASHED
FLASHER
FLASHES
FLECHES
FLESHED
FLESHES
FLUSHED
FLUSHES
FRESHEN
FRESHER
FRESHET
FROTHED
FURTHER
GAUCHER
GNASHED
GNASHES
GRAPHED
GREYHEN
GULCHES
GUNTHER
HARSHEN
HARSHER
HATCHED
HATCHER
HATCHES
HATCHET
HEATHEN
HEATHER
HERSHEY
HITCHED
HITCHER
HITCHES
HOUGHED
HUNCHED
HUNCHES
HUTCHES
JIMCHEE
KAISHEK
KETCHES
KIMCHEE
KITCHEN
KNISHES
LARCHES
LATCHED
LATCHES
LAUGHED
LAUGHER
LEACHED
LEACHES
LEASHED
LEASHES
LEATHER
LEECHED
LEECHES
LOACHES
LOATHED
LOATHES
LUNCHED
LUNCHES
LURCHED
LURCHES
MADCHEN
MARCHED
MARCHER
MARCHES
MARSHES
MATCHED
MATCHES
MATTHEW
MOOCHED
MOOCHER
MOOCHES
MOORHEN
MORPHED
MOUTHED
MULCHED
MULCHES
MUNCHED
MUNCHER
MUNCHES
NARTHEX
NATCHEZ
NEIGHED
NEITHER
NORTHER
NOTCHED
NOTCHES
PANTHER
PARCHED
PARCHES
PATCHED
PATCHES
PEACHED
PEACHES
PERCHED
PERCHES
PINCHED
PINCHER
PINCHES
PITCHED
PITCHER
PITCHES
PLASHED
PLASHES
PLUSHER
PLUSHES
POACHED
POACHER
POACHES
POOCHES
PORCHES
POUCHED
POUCHES
PRITHEE
PROPHET
PSYCHED
PSYCHES
PUNCHED
PUNCHER
PUNCHES
QUASHED
QUASHES
QUICHES
RANCHED
RANCHER
RANCHES
RATCHET
REACHED
REACHES
REUTHER
ROACHED
ROACHES
ROUGHED
ROUGHEN
ROUGHER
SAGEHEN
SATCHEL
SAYWHEN
SCATHED
SCATHES
SCYTHED
SCYTHES
SEETHED
SEETHES
SEICHES
SHUSHED
SHUSHES
SKOSHES
SLASHED
SLASHER
SLASHES
SLATHER
SLITHER
SLOSHED
SLOSHES
SLUSHES
SMASHED
SMASHER
SMASHES
SMOTHER
SOOTHED
SOOTHER
SOOTHES
SOUGHED
SOUTHEY
STASHED
STASHES
STEPHEN
STICHES
SWATHED
SWATHES
SWISHED
SWISHES
SYNCHED
SYNCHES
TEACHER
TEACHES
TEETHED
TEETHER
TEETHES
TEICHER
TETCHED
THITHER
TOOTHED
TORCHED
TORCHES
TOUCHED
TOUCHES
TOUGHEN
TOUGHER
TRACHEA
TRASHED
TRASHES
TROCHEE
TROCHES
TROTHED
VETCHES
VOUCHED
VOUCHER
VOUCHES
WATCHED
WATCHER
WATCHES
WEATHER
WEIGHED
WELCHED
WELCHES
WENCHES
WERNHER
WERTHER
WHETHER
WHISHED
WHISHES
WHITHER
WINCHED
WINCHES
WITCHES
WRITHED
WRITHES
ZILCHES

••••H•E
ARACHNE
BACKHOE
BANSHEE
DONAHUE
GUMSHOE
GYMSHOE
IVANHOE
JIMCHEE
KIMCHEE
PRITHEE
PRUDHOE
TOESHOE
TOUGHIE
TROCHEE

•••••HE
ADOLPHE
ATTACHE
BINOCHE
BLANCHE
BREATHE
BRIOCHE
EARACHE
GOUACHE
PANACHE
PENUCHE
PORSCHE
SHEATHE
STROPHE
WREATHE

H•F••••
HAFNIUM
HAFTING
HEFTIER
HEFTILY
HEFTING
HOFBRAU
HOFFMAN
HUFFIER
HUFFILY
HUFFING
HUFFISH

H••F•••
HALFDAN
HALFWAY
HALFWIT
HAYFORK
HEIFERS
HEIFETZ
HOFFMAN
HOOFERS
HOOFING
HOOFSIT
HOTFOOT
HUFFIER
HUFFILY
HUFFING
HUFFISH

H•••F••
HALIFAX
HANDFED
HANDFUL
HARMFUL
HATEFUL
HEATFUL
HEEDFUL
HELPFUL
HOPEFUL
HURTFUL
HUSHFUL

H••••F•
HANDOFF
HANGOFF
HAULOFF
HAYLOFT
HEADOFF
HELDOFF
HOLDOFF
HOPSOFF
HORRIFY

H•••••F
HANDOFF
HANGOFF
HAULOFF
HEADOFF
HEARDOF
HEARSOF
HELDOFF
HERSELF
HIMSELF
HIPROOF
HOLDOFF
HOPSOFF

•H•F•••
CHAFING
CHIFFON
SHAFFER
SHAFTED
SHIFTED
SHOFARS
SHUFFLE
THEFIRM
THEFONZ
WHIFFED

•H••F••
CHAMFER
CHIEFLY
CHIFFON
SHAFFER
SHOOFLY
SHOPFUL
SHOTFOR
SHRIFTS
SHUFFLE
THRIFTS
THRIFTY
THUSFAR
WHARFED
WHATFOR
WHIFFED

•H•••F•
SHERIFF
SHOWOFF
SHUTOFF

•H••••F
AHEADOF
SHADOOF
SHERIFF
SHEWOLF
SHORTOF
SHOWOFF
SHUTOFF
THEREOF
THINKOF
THYSELF
WHEREOF

••HF•••
ASHFORD

•••HF••
BASHFUL
DISHFUL
FISHFRY
HUSHFUL
PUSHFUL
RUTHFUL
SIGHFUL
WISHFUL

•••H•F•
DASHOFF
PUSHOFF
RUSHOFF
WASHOFF

•••H••F
DASHOFF
PUSHOFF
RUSHOFF
WASHOFF

HG•••••
HGWELLS

H•G••••
HAGDONS
HAGGARD
HAGGISH
HAGGLED
HAGGLER
HAGGLES
HAGLIKE
HEGIRAS
HIGGINS
HIGGLED
HIGGLES
HIGHBOY
HIGHDAY
HIGHEND
HIGHEST
HIGHHAT
HIGHLOW
HIGHTEA
HIGHTOP
HIGHWAY
HOGARTH
HOGBACK
HOGGETS
HOGGING
HOGGISH
HOGLIKE
HOGTIED
HOGTIES
HOGWASH
HOGWILD
HUGGERS
HUGGING
HUGGINS
HYGIEIA
HYGIENE

H••G•••
HAGGARD
HAGGISH
HAGGLED
HAGGLER
HAGGLES
HANGARS
HANGDOG
HANGERS
HANGING
HANGMAN
HANGMEN
HANGOFF
HANGOUT
HANGSIN
HANGSON
HANGSUP
HANGTEN
HANGUPS
HAUGHTY
HEDGERS
HEDGIER
HEDGING
HEIGHHO
HEIGHTS
HIGGINS
HIGGLED
HIGGLES
HINGING
HOAGIES
HOGGETS
HOGGING
HOGGISH
HOUGHED
HUGGERS
HUGGING
HUGGINS
HUNGARY
HUNGERS
HUNGOUT
HUYGENS

H•••G••
HALOGEN
HANDGUN
HEXAGON

H••••G•
HAULAGE
HAZINGS
HERBAGE
HEXSIGN
HIDALGO
HIDINGS
HOSTAGE
HOTDOGS
HUMBUGS

H•••••G
HACKING
HAFTING
HAILING
HALOING
HALTING
HALVING
HAMBURG
HAMMING
HANDBAG
HANDING
HANGDOG
HANGING
HAPPING
HARBURG
HARDING
HARKING
HARMING
HARPING
HASHING
HASPING
HASTING
HATTING
HAULING
HAWKING
HEADING
HEALING
HEAPING
HEARING
HEATING
HEAVING
HEDGING
HEEDING
HEELING
HEFTING
HELMING
HELPING
HEMMING
HENTING
HERDING
HERRING
HILLING
HINGING
HINTING
HISSING
HITTING
HOAXING
HOBOING
HOCKING
HOGGING
HOLDING
HOMBURG
HONKING
HOOFING
HOOKING
HOOPING
HOOTING
HOPPING
HORNING
HORSING
HOSTING
HOUSING
HOWLING
HUFFING
HUGGING
HULKING
HULLING
HUMMING
HUNTING
HURLING
HURTING
HUSHING
HUSKING
HYPOING

•H•G•••
CHAGALL
CHAGRIN
CHIGGER
CHIGNON
CHIGOES
CHUGGED
SHAGGED
SHOGUNS

•H••G••
CHANGED
CHANGER
CHANGES
CHARGED
CHARGER
CHARGES
CHIGGER
CHUGGED
SHAGGED
SHANGRI
SHINGLE
SHOTGUN
THOUGHT
WHANGED
XHEIGHT

•H•••G•
CHICAGO
PHOTOGS
THEURGY
THRONGS
THROUGH
ZHIVAGO

•H••••G
CHAFING
CHASING
CHEWING
CHIDING
CHIMING
PHASING
PHONING
RHYMING
SHADING
SHAKING
SHAMING
SHAPING
SHARING
SHAVING
SHEBANG
SHINDIG
SHINING
SHOEING
SHOOING
SHORING
SHOVING
SHOWDOG
SHOWING
THAWING
WHALING
WHILING
WHINING
WHITING

••H•G••
JOHNGAY

••H••G•
REHANGS

••H•••G
ACHTUNG
ECHOING

•••HG••
LITHGOW

•••H•G•
FLYHIGH
ONTHEGO
QUAHOGS
SKYHIGH

•••H••G
ARCHING
BACHING
BASHING
BATHING
BUSHHOG
BUSHING
BUSHPIG
CACHING
CASHING
COSHING
CUSHING
DASHING
DISHING
DISHRAG
ETCHING
FISHING
GASHING
GUSHING
HASHING
HUSHING
INCHING
ITCHING
JOSHING
LASHING
LATHING
MASHING
MESHING
MOSHING
MUSHING
NOSHING
NOTHING
PITHING
PUSHING
RUCHING
RUSHING
SIGHING
TITHING
WASHING
WASHRAG
WISHING

••••H•G
BEARHUG
BUSHHOG
ROADHOG
SANDHOG
WARTHOG

HH•••••
HHMUNRO

H•H••••
HAHNIUM

H••H•••
HAMHOCK
HASHING
HAWHAWS
HEEHAWS
HESHVAN
HIGHBOY
HIGHDAY
HIGHEND
HIGHEST
HIGHHAT
HIGHLOW
HIGHTEA
HIGHTOP
HIGHWAY
HITHERE
HOOHAHS
HOTHEAD
HUSHABY
HUSHFUL
HUSHING
HYPHENS

H•••H••
HARDHAT
HARDHIT
HARSHEN
HARSHER
HARSHLY
HATCHED
HATCHER
HATCHES
HATCHET
HAUGHTY
HEATHEN
HEATHER
HEIGHHO
HEIGHTS
HERSHEY
HIGHHAT
HITCHED
HITCHER
HITCHES
HONCHOS
HOTSHOT
HOUGHED
HUNCHED
HUNCHES
HUTCHES

H••••H•
HALVAHS
HEALTHY
HEARTHS
HEAVEHO
HEIGHHO
HIBACHI
HITACHI
HOOHAHS
HOOKAHS
HOWDAHS
HURRAHS
HUZZAHS

H•••••H
HAGGISH
HANUKAH
HAWKISH
HELLISH
HENNISH
HIALEAH
HOGARTH
HOGGISH
HOGWASH
HORNISH
HUFFISH
HUNNISH

•H•H•••
SHAHDOM
SHIHTZU

•H••H••
CHACHAS
CHATHAM
CHECHEN
CHEKHOV
CHICHEN
RHYTHMS
SHUSHED
SHUSHES
THITHER
WHETHER
WHISHED
WHISHES
WHITHER

•H•••H•
SHEATHE
SHEATHS
SHEIKHS
THATCHY
THIMPHU
THOUGHT
WHOSWHO
WHYDAHS
XHEIGHT

•H••••H
CHEETAH
CHERISH
EHRLICH
PHARAOH
RHENISH
THROUGH
WHEYISH
WHITISH

••H•••H
OSHKOSH
UNHITCH

•••HH••
BUSHHOG
HIGHHAT

•••H•H•
EIGHTHS
HOOHAHS
NAPHTHA

•••H••H
FLYHIGH
JAPHETH
POOHBAH
SKYHIGH

••••HH•
HEIGHHO

HI•••••
HIALEAH
HIBACHI
HICCUPS
HICKMAN
HICKORY
HIDALGO
HIDEOUS
HIDEOUT
HIDINGS
HIGGINS
HIGGLED
HIGGLES
HIGHBOY
HIGHDAY
HIGHEND
HIGHEST
HIGHHAT

HIGHLOW HIGHTEA HIGHTOP HIGHWAY HIJACKS HIJINKS HIKEDUP HIKESUP HILAIRE HILLARY HILLIER HILLING HILLOCK HILLTOP HIMSELF HINDERS HINGING HINNIES HINTING HINTSAT HIPBONE HIPBOOT HIPLESS HIPLIKE HIPNESS HIPPEST HIPPIER HIPPIES HIPROOF HIPSTER HIRABLE HIRESON HIRSUTE HISPANO HISSERS HISSING HISTORY HITACHI HITCHED HITCHER HITCHES HITHERE HITLESS HITLIST HITSOUT HITTERS HITTING HITTITE

H•I••••

HAILING HAIRCUT HAIRDOS HAIRDYE HAIRIER HAIRNET HAIRPIN HAITIAN HEIFERS HEIFETZ HEIGHHO HEIGHTS HEINOUS HEIRESS HEISMAN HEISTED HOISTED

H••I•••

HABITAT HABITED HABITUE HALIBUT HALIDES HALIFAX HALITES HAMITES HAMITIC HAMITUP HARICOT HASIDIC HASIDIM HAZIEST HAZINGS HEGIRAS HELICAL HELICES HELICON HELIPAD HELIXES HIDINGS HIJINKS HOKIEST HOLIDAY HOLIEST HOLISTS HOMIEST HOMINID HONIARA HORIZON HOSIERS HOSIERY HUMIDLY HUMIDOR HYGIEIA HYGIENE

H•••I••

HACKIES HACKING HADRIAN HAFNIUM HAFTING HAGGISH HAGLIKE HAHNIUM HAILING HAIRIER HAITIAN HALOING HALTING HALVING HAMMIER HAMMILY HAMMING HANDIER HANDILY HANDING HANGING HANKIES HAPPIER HAPPILY HAPPING HARDIER HARDILY HARDING HARKING HARMING HARPIES HARPING HARPIST HARRIED HARRIER HARRIES HARRIET HASHING HASPING HASTIER HASTILY HASTING HATLIKE HATPINS HATTING HAULING HAWKING HAWKINS HAWKISH HAYRIDE HAYWIRE HEADIER HEADILY HEADING HEALING HEAPING HEARING HEATING HEAVIER HEAVIES HEAVILY HEAVING HEDGIER HEDGING HEEDING HEELING HEFTIER HEFTILY HEFTING HELLION HELLISH HELMING HELOISE HELPING HEMLINE HEMMING HENBITS HENLIKE HENNISH HENTING HERBIER HERDING HERMITS HEROICS HEROINE HEROISM HERRING HERRIOT HESSIAN HEXSIGN HIGGINS HILAIRE HILLIER HILLING HINGING HINNIES HINTING HIPLIKE HIPPIER HIPPIES HISSING HITLIST HITTING HITTITE HOAGIES HOARIER HOARILY HOAXING HOBBIES HOBBITS HOBOING HOCKING HOGGING HOGGISH HOGLIKE HOGTIED HOGTIES HOGWILD HOLDING HOLLIES HOLMIUM HONKING HOOFING HOOKING HOOPING HOOSIER HOOTING HOPKINS HOPLIKE HOPPING HORNING HORNISH HORNIST HORRIFY HORSIER HORSING HOSKINS HOSPICE HOSTILE HOSTING HOTLINE HOTLINK HOTLIPS HOTTIPS HOTWIRE HOUDINI HOUSING HOWLING HUBBIES HUFFIER HUFFILY HUFFING HUFFISH HUGGING HUGGINS HULKING HULLING HUMMING HUMPIER HUNKIER HUNLIKE HUNNISH HUNTING HURLIES HURLING HURRIED HURRIES HURTING HUSHING HUSKIER HUSKIES HUSKILY HUSKING HUSSIES HUTLIKE HYALINE HYBRIDS HYPOING

H••••I•

HAIRPIN HALFWIT HAMELIN HAMITIC HANDSIN HANGSIN HARDHIT HASIDIC HASIDIM HEADPIN HEADSIN HEBRAIC HENDRIX HENRYIV HEPARIN HEPATIC HERETIC HOBNAIL HOLBEIN HOLDSIN HOMERIC HOMINID HONORIS HOOFSIT HOPTOIT HORATIO HORNSIN HOWBEIT HUSSEIN HYGIEIA

H•••••I

HAVARTI HIBACHI HITACHI HOUDINI HYUNDAI

•HI••••

CHIANTI CHICAGO CHICANA CHICANO CHICHEN CHICKEN CHICORY CHIDERS CHIDING CHIEFLY CHIFFON CHIGGER CHIGNON CHIGOES CHILEAN CHILIES CHILLED CHILLER CHIMERA CHIMING CHIMNEY CHINESE CHINKED CHINNED CHINOOK CHINTZY CHINUPS CHIPPED CHIPPER CHIPSIN CHIRICO CHIRPED CHISELS CHITTER OHIOANS PHIDIAS PHILBIN PHILLIP PHILTER PHILTRE PHINEAS RHIZOME SHIATSU SHIELDS SHIFTED SHIHTZU SHIITES SHIKARI SHIKOKU SHILLED SHIMMER SHINDIG SHINERS SHINGLE SHINIER SHINILY SHINING SHINNED SHIPMAN SHIPMEN SHIPOUT SHIPPED SHIPPER SHIRKED SHIRKER SHIRLEY SHIRRED SHIVERS SHIVERY THICKEN THICKER THICKET THICKLY THIEVED THIEVES THIMBLE THIMPHU THINAIR THINICE THINKER THINKOF THINKUP THINNED THINNER THIRDLY THIRSTS THIRSTY THISTLE THISTLY THITHER WHIFFED WHILING WHIMPER WHINERS WHINIER WHINING WHIPPED WHIPPET WHIPSAW WHIPSUP WHIRLED WHIRRED WHISHED WHISHES WHISKED WHISKER WHISKEY WHISPER WHISTLE WHITENS WHITEST WHITHER WHITIER WHITING WHITISH WHITMAN WHITNEY WHITTLE WHIZKID WHIZZED WHIZZER WHIZZES ZHIVAGO

•H•I•••

CHAINED CHAIRED CHAISES CHOICER CHOICES CHRISMS CHRISTI CHRISTO CHRISTY SHEIKHS SHEILAS SHIITES SHRIEKS SHRIFTS SHRIKES SHRILLS SHRILLY SHRIMPS SHRINER SHRINES SHRINKS SHRIVEL SHRIVER SHRIVES SHTICKS THEISTS THRIFTS THRIFTY THRILLS THRIVED THRIVES XHEIGHT

•H••I••

CHAFING CHALICE CHARIER CHARILY CHARIOT CHARITY CHASING CHEMISE CHEMIST CHENIER CHERISH CHEVIED CHEVIES CHEVIOT CHEWIER CHEWING CHIDING CHILIES CHIMING CHIRICO CHOKIER CHOLINE CHORINE CHORIZO EHRLICH GHANIAN PHASING PHIDIAS PHOBIAS PHOBICS PHONICS PHONIER PHONIES PHONILY PHONING PHOTICS PHYSICS RHENISH RHENIUM RHODIUM RHYMING SHADIER SHADILY SHADING SHAKIER SHAKILY SHAKING SHAMING SHAPING SHAPIRO SHARING SHAVING SHERIFF SHINIER SHINILY SHINING SHOEING SHOOING SHOOINS SHORING SHOVING SHOWIER SHOWILY SHOWING SHUTINS THAWING THEFIRM THEPITS THEWIER THINICE THORIUM THULIUM THYMINE WHALING WHEYISH WHILING WHINIER WHITIER WHITING WHITISH

•H•••I•

CHABLIS CHAGRIN CHAMOIS CHAOTIC CHAPLIN CHAPPIE CHARLIE CHARMIN CHASSIS CHEAPIE CHEATIN CHECKIN CHEERIO CHERVIL CHIPSIN CHRONIC DHURRIE GHERKIN PHASEIN PHILBIN PHILLIP PHOENIX PHRENIC PHYLLIS SHAREIN SHELTIE SHERWIN SHINDIG SHOWBIZ SHOWNIN SHOWSIN SHUTSIN THATSIT THEREIN THESPIS THINAIR THREWIN THROWIN WHEELIE WHEREIN WHIZKID

•H••••I

CHAPATI CHIANTI CHRISTI SHANGRI SHARPEI SHASTRI SHIKARI

••HI•••

ACHIEST ACHIEVE ASHIEST ATHIRST CAHIERS DEHISCE ECHIDNA ECHINUS ETHICAL EXHIBIT INHIBIT MOHICAN OPHITES REHIRED REHIRES SCHIRRA SCHISMS TSHIRTS UNHITCH VEHICLE WAHINES

••H•I••

ATHEISM ATHEIST COHEIRS DAHLIAS ECHOING ETHNICS HAHNIUM MOHAIRS SCHMIDT SCHWINN

••H••I•

AMHARIC APHELIA BAHRAIN BOHEMIA COHABIT EXHIBIT INHABIT INHERIT INHIBIT JOHNNIE MAHALIA MAHARIS OPHELIA

••H•••I

ASHANTI PAHLAVI SCHATZI SCHERZI

•••HI••

AKIHITO ANTHILL ARCHING ARCHIVE BACHING BASHING BATHING BEEHIVE BETHINK BUSHIDO BUSHIER BUSHILY BUSHING CACHING CASHIER CASHING COCHISE COSHING COWHIDE CUSHIER CUSHING CUSHION DASHIKI DASHING DISHIER DISHING DUCHIES EBWHITE ETCHING FASHION FISHIER FISHILY FISHING FLYHIGH GASHING GOTHICS GUSHIER GUSHILY GUSHING HASHING HUSHING INCHING ITCHIER ITCHING JOEHILL JOSHING KACHINA LASHING LATHING LITHIUM MACHINA MACHINE MASHIES MASHING MATHIAS MENHIRS MESHIER MESHING MISHITS MOSHING MOTHIER MRCHIPS MUSHIER MUSHILY MUSHING MUZHIKS NOBHILL NOSHING NOTHING ORCHIDS OUTHITS PACHISI PITHIER PITHILY PITHING PUSHIER PUSHILY PUSHING PYTHIAN PYTHIAS RAWHIDE RESHIPS RETHINK RUCHING RUSHIER RUSHING SAMHILL SASHIMI SIGHING SIKHISM SKYHIGH SOPHISM SOPHIST SWAHILI TECHIER TECHIES TITHING TOSHIBA URCHINS WASHIER WASHING WICHITA WISHING WITHIER WITHIES YESHIVA

•••H•I•

ALLHAIL ANAHEIM ARCHAIC BATHOIL BOTHNIA BRAHMIN BUSHPIG CATHAIR COCHAIR DAPHNIS ENCHAIN FUCHSIA GUTHRIE KASHMIR MIKHAIL MOSHPIT NIGHTIE PUSHKIN PUSHPIN REDHAIR RUSHDIE TASHLIN UNCHAIN

•••H••I

AFGHANI DASHIKI OMPHALI PACHISI SASHIMI SWAHILI

••••HI•

AIRSHIP BASEHIT BIOCHIP BOOTHIA CYNTHIA DAUPHIN DELPHIC DOLPHIN EDAPHIC GEEWHIZ GENGHIS GRAPHIC HARDHIT JOACHIM KINCHIN KINSHIP KUTCHIN LAUGHIN LITCHIS MEGAHIT MEMPHIS MENUHIN PITCHIN PSYCHIC PUNCHIN PYRRHIC ROUGHIT TEACHIN TOUGHIE TROPHIC WARSHIP WATCHIT WEIGHIN WORSHIP XANTHIC

••••H•I

BALIHAI BOLSHOI LAKSHMI

•••••HI

ACANTHI BELUSHI BRONCHI GNOCCHI HIBACHI HITACHI KARACHI MALACHI NOGUCHI

H•J••••

HIJACKS HIJINKS

H••J•••

HEYJUDE

••H•J••

JOHNJAY

H•K••••

HIKEDUP HIKESUP HOKIEST

H••K•••

HACKERS HACKETT HACKIES HACKING HACKLED HACKLES HACKMAN HACKNEY HACKSAW HANKERS HANKIES HARKENS HARKING HAWKERS HAWKEYE HAWKING HAWKINS HAWKISH HECKLED HECKLER HECKLES HICKMAN HICKORY HOCKING HONKERS HONKING HOOKAHS HOOKING HOOKSUP HOOKUPS HOPKINS HOSKINS HULKING HUNKERS HUNKIER HUSKERS HUSKIER HUSKIES HUSKILY HUSKING

H•••K••

HANUKAH HEARKEN HOBOKEN

H••••K•

HAGLIKE HATLIKE HENLIKE HIJACKS HIJINKS HIPLIKE HOECAKE HOGLIKE HOLYOKE HOPLIKE HOTCAKE HUNLIKE HUTLIKE

H•••••K

HADDOCK HAMHOCK HAMMOCK HANCOCK HASSOCK HATRACK HAUBERK HAYFORK HAYRACK HEMLOCK HENPECK HILLOCK HOGBACK HOLMOAK HOLYARK HOTLINK HUMMOCK

•H•K•••

CHEKHOV CHOKERS CHOKEUP CHOKIER CHUKKAS CHUKKER SHAKERS SHAKEUP SHAKIER SHAKILY SHAKING SHAKOES SHEKELS SHIKARI SHIKOKU

•H••K••

CHALKED CHALKUP CHECKED CHECKER CHECKIN CHECKUP CHICKEN CHINKED CHUCKED CHUCKLE CHUKKAS CHUKKER GHERKIN SHACKLE SHANKAR SHANKED SHARKEY SHEIKHS SHIRKED SHIRKER SHOCKED SHOCKER SHOOKUP SHRIKES SHUCKED SHUCKER THANKED THICKEN THICKER THICKET THICKLY THINKER THINKOF THINKUP WHACKED WHISKED WHISKER WHISKEY WHIZKID

•H•••K•

CHOMSKY RHEBOKS SHIKOKU SHRIEKS SHRINKS SHTICKS THWACKS

•H••••K

CHINOOK SHYLOCK

••HK•••
OSHKOSH

••H••K•
MOHAWKS
REHOOKS
UNHOOKS

••H•••K
OKHOTSK
SCHLOCK

•••HK••
KISHKES
PUSHKIN

•••H•K•
DASHIKI
MUZHIKS

•••H••K
BETHINK
GOSHAWK
HAMHOCK
POTHOOK
RECHALK
RECHECK
RETHINK
SKYHOOK
YASHMAK

••••HK•
DROSHKY

••••H•K
KAISHEK
YITZHAK

H•L••••
HALCYON
HALFDAN
HALFWAY
HALFWIT
HALIBUT
HALIDES
HALIFAX
HALITES
HALLOWS
HALLWAY
HALOGEN
HALOING
HALSTON
HALTERS
HALTING
HALVAHS
HALVING
HALYARD
HELDOFF
HELDOUT
HELICAL
HELICES
HELICON
HELIPAD
HELIXES
HELLCAT
HELLENE
HELLERS
HELLION
HELLISH
HELLMAN
HELMETS
HELMING
HELOISE
HELOTRY
HELPERS
HELPFUL
HELPING
HELPOUT
HILAIRE
HILLARY
HILLIER
HILLING
HILLOCK
HILLTOP
HOLBEIN
HOLDERS
HOLDING
HOLDOFF
HOLDOUT
HOLDSIN
HOLDSON
HOLDSTO
HOLDSUP
HOLDUPS
HOLEDUP
HOLEOUT
HOLESUP
HOLIDAY
HOLIEST
HOLISTS
HOLLAND
HOLLERS
HOLLIES
HOLLOWS
HOLMIUM
HOLMOAK
HOLSTER
HOLYARK
HOLYCOW
HOLYDAY
HOLYOKE
HOLYSEE
HOLYWAR
HULKING
HULLERS
HULLING
HULLOAS
HULLOED

H••L•••
HAGLIKE
HAILING
HALLOWS
HALLWAY
HAMLETS
HAPLESS
HATLESS
HATLIKE
HAULAGE
HAULERS
HAULING
HAULOFF
HAULSUP
HAYLOFT
HEALALL
HEALERS
HEALING
HEALTHY
HEELERS
HEELING
HEELTAP
HELLCAT
HELLENE
HELLERS
HELLION
HELLISH
HELLMAN
HEMLINE
HEMLOCK
HENLIKE
HEWLETT
HIALEAH
HILLARY
HILLIER
HILLING
HILLOCK
HILLTOP
HIPLESS
HIPLIKE
HITLESS
HITLIST
HOGLIKE
HOLLAND
HOLLERS
HOLLIES
HOLLOWS
HOPLIKE
HOTLINE
HOTLINK
HOTLIPS
HOVLANE
HOWLERS
HOWLING
HUELESS
HULLERS
HULLING
HULLOAS
HULLOED
HUNLIKE
HURLERS
HURLEYS
HURLIES
HURLING
HUTLIKE
HYALINE

H•••L••
HAARLEM
HACKLED
HACKLES
HAGGLED
HAGGLER
HAGGLES
HAMELIN
HANDLED
HANDLER
HANDLES
HASSLED
HASSLES
HECKLED
HECKLER
HECKLES
HEDDLES
HEMSLEY
HERALDS
HGWELLS
HIDALGO
HIGGLED
HIGGLES
HIGHLOW
HOBBLED
HOBBLES
HOODLUM
HOOPLAS
HOPPLED
HOPPLES
HOSTLER
HOWELLS
HUDDLED
HUDDLES
HUMBLED
HUMBLER
HUMBLES
HUNTLEY
HURDLED
HURDLER
HURDLES
HURTLED
HURTLES
HUSTLED
HUSTLER
HUSTLES

H••••L•
HAMMILY
HANDILY
HANSOLO
HAPPILY
HARDILY
HARSHLY
HASTILY
HEADILY
HEALALL
HEAVILY
HEFTILY
HERBALS
HERCULE
HERSELF
HGWELLS
HIMSELF
HIRABLE
HOARILY
HOGWILD
HOSTELS
HOSTILE
HOWELLS
HUBBELL
HUFFILY
HUMANLY
HUMIDLY
HUSKILY
HYMNALS

H•••••L
HANDFUL
HARMFUL
HATEFUL
HEALALL
HEATFUL
HEEDFUL
HELICAL
HELPFUL
HOBNAIL
HOOTOWL
HOPEFUL
HUBBELL
HUMERAL
HURTFUL
HUSHFUL

•HL••••
CHLORAL
PHLOXES

•H•L•••
CHALETS
CHALICE
CHALKED
CHALKUP
CHALONS
CHELSEA
CHILEAN
CHILIES
CHILLED
CHILLER
CHOLINE
CHOLLAS
EHRLICH
PHALANX
PHILBIN
PHILLIP
PHILTER
PHILTRE
PHYLLIS
SHALALA
SHALLOT
SHALLOW
SHALOMS
SHELDON
SHELLAC
SHELLED
SHELLER
SHELLEY
SHELTER
SHELTIE
SHELTON
SHELVED
SHELVES
SHILLED
SHYLOCK
THALERS
THULIUM
WHALERS
WHALING
WHELMED
WHELPED
WHILING

•H••L••
CHABLIS
CHAPLET
CHAPLIN
CHARLES
CHARLEY
CHARLIE
CHEMLAB
CHILLED
CHILLER
CHOLLAS
PHARLAP
PHILLIP
PHYLLIS
SHALLOT
SHALLOW
SHAPLEY
SHEILAS
SHELLAC
SHELLED
SHELLER
SHELLEY
SHIELDS
SHILLED
SHIRLEY
SHOULDA
SHRILLS
SHRILLY
THEBLOB
THRALLS
THRILLS
WHEELED
WHEELER
WHEELIE
WHIRLED
WHORLED

•H•••L•
CHAGALL
CHAPELS
CHARILY
CHEAPLY
CHIEFLY
CHISELS
CHORALE
CHORALS
CHORTLE
CHUCKLE
GHASTLY
GHOSTLY
PHENOLS
PHONILY
SHACKLE
SHADILY
SHAKILY
SHALALA
SHAMBLE
SHAPELY
SHARPLY
SHEERLY
SHEKELS
SHEWOLF
SHINGLE
SHINILY
SHOOFLY
SHORTLY
SHOVELS
SHOWILY
SHRILLS
SHRILLY
SHUFFLE
SHUTTLE
THERELL
THICKLY
THIMBLE
THIRDLY
THISTLE
THISTLY
THRALLS
THRILLS
THYSELF
WHEEDLE
WHERELL
WHISTLE
WHITTLE

•H••••L
CHAGALL
CHANCEL
CHANNEL
CHATTEL
CHERVIL
CHLORAL
CHUNNEL
PHRASAL
SHAWWAL
SHOPFUL
SHRIVEL
THERELL
THERMAL
WHERELL

••HL•••
ASHLAND
ASHLARS
ASHLESS
ATHLETE
DAHLIAS
OOHLALA
PAHLAVI
SCHLEPP
SCHLEPS
SCHLOCK

••H•L••
APHELIA
BEHOLDS
ECHELON
EXHALED
EXHALES
INHALED
INHALER
INHALES
MAHALIA
OPHELIA
OTHELLO
SCHOLAR
SCHULTZ
UPHOLDS

••H••L•
INHAULS
OOHLALA
OTHELLO
REHEALS
REHEELS
SCHOOLS
VEHICLE

••H•••L
ETHANOL
ETHICAL
ISHMAEL
NAHUATL

•••HL••
COCHLEA
HIGHLOW
LACHLAN
TASHLIN

•••H•L•
AIRHOLE
ANTHILL
ARMHOLE
ASPHALT
BETHELS
BOGHOLE
BUSHELS
BUSHILY
DRYHOLE
EYEHOLE
FISHILY
FOXHOLE
GUSHILY
ISOHELS
JOEHILL
KEYHOLE
LIGHTLY
LITHELY
MANHOLE
MICHELE
MUSHILY
NICHOLS
NIGHTLY
NOBHILL
OMPHALI
PINHOLE
PITHILY
POTHOLE
PUSHILY
RATHOLE
RECHALK
RIGHTLY
SAMHILL
SIGHTLY
SWAHILI
TIGHTLY
TOEHOLD
TOPHOLE
WILHELM
WYCHELM

•••H••L
ALLHAIL
ALLHEAL
ANTHILL
BASHFUL
BATHOIL
BSCHOOL
DISHFUL
ENTHRAL
HUSHFUL
JOEHILL
LOWHEEL
MICHAEL
MIKHAIL
NOBHILL
PUSHFUL
RAPHAEL
RUTHFUL
SAMHILL
SIGHFUL
TARHEEL
WISHFUL

••••HL•
APISHLY
BRASHLY
EARTHLY
FIFTHLY
FLESHLY
FRESHLY
HARSHLY
MONTHLY
NINTHLY
PLUSHLY
ROUGHLY
SIXTHLY
TENTHLY
TOUGHLY

••••H•L
ALCOHOL
EPOCHAL
FUNCHAL
GASOHOL
MARSHAL
MENTHOL
NARWHAL
PASCHAL
SATCHEL

H•M••••
HAMBURG
HAMELIN
HAMHOCK
HAMITES
HAMITIC
HAMITUP
HAMLETS
HAMMERS
HAMMETT
HAMMIER
HAMMILY
HAMMING
HAMMOCK
HAMMOND
HAMPERS
HAMPTON
HAMSTER
HEMLINE
HEMLOCK
HEMMERS
HEMMING
HEMSLEY
HHMUNRO
HIMSELF
HOMBRES
HOMBURG
HOMEBOY
HOMERED
HOMERIC
HOMERUN
HOMIEST
HOMINID
HOMONYM
HUMANLY
HUMANUM
HUMBLED
HUMBLER
HUMBLES
HUMBUGS
HUMDRUM
HUMERAL
HUMERUS
HUMIDLY
HUMIDOR
HUMMERS
HUMMING
HUMMOCK
HUMORED
HUMOURS
HUMPIER
HUMVEES
HYMNALS
HYMNODY

H••M•••
HAEMATO
HAMMERS
HAMMETT
HAMMIER
HAMMILY
HAMMING
HAMMOCK
HAMMOND
HARMFUL
HARMING
HARMONY
HAYMOWS
HELMETS
HELMING
HEMMERS
HEMMING
HERMANN
HERMITS
HETMANS
HOLMIUM
HOLMOAK
HORMONE
HUMMERS
HUMMING
HUMMOCK

H•••M••
HACKMAN
HANGMAN
HANGMEN
HARTMAN
HEADMAN
HEADMEN
HEISMAN
HELLMAN
HICKMAN
HOFFMAN
HOUSMAN

H••••M•
HANSOMS
HOTCOMB
HOWCOME

H•••••M
HAARLEM
HAFNIUM
HAHNIUM
HASIDIM
HEROISM
HOLMIUM
HOMONYM
HOODLUM
HUMANUM
HUMDRUM
HYPONYM

•HM••••
HHMUNRO

•H•M•••
CHAMBER
CHAMFER
CHAMOIS
CHAMPED
CHEMISE
CHEMIST
CHEMLAB
CHIMERA
CHIMING
CHIMNEY
CHOMPED
CHOMSKY
CHUMMED
RHOMBUS
RHUMBAS
RHYMERS
RHYMING
SHAMANS
SHAMBLE
SHAMING
SHAMMED
SHAMPOO
SHIMMER
THIMBLE
THIMPHU
THOMSON
THUMBED
THUMPED
THUMPER
THYMINE
WHAMMED
WHIMPER
WHOMPED

•H••M••
CHAPMAN
CHAPMEN
CHARMED
CHARMER
CHARMIN
CHROMES
CHUMMED
SHAMMED
SHERMAN
SHIMMER
SHIPMAN
SHIPMEN
SHOWMAN
SHOWMEN
SHRIMPS
THEOMEN
THERMAL
THERMOS
THURMAN
WHAMMED
WHELMED
WHITMAN

•H•••M•
CHRISMS
PHENOMS
PHONEME
RHIZOME
RHYTHMS
SHALOMS

•H••••M
CHATHAM
CHETRUM
KHAYYAM
PHANTOM
RHENIUM
RHODIUM
SHAHDOM
THEFIRM
THEOREM
THORIUM
THREEAM
THREEPM
THULIUM

••HM•••
ISHMAEL
SCHMEER
SCHMIDT
SCHMOES
SCHMOOS

••H•M••
ASHAMED
ATHOMES
BAHAMAS
BOHEMIA
DAHOMEY
INHUMAN
SCHEMAS
SCHEMED
SCHEMER
SCHEMES

••H••M•
ASHRAMS
MAHATMA
SCHISMS

••H•••M
ATHEISM
HAHNIUM

•••HM••
BATHMAT
BRAHMAN
BRAHMAS
BRAHMIN
BUSHMAN
BUSHMEN
ISTHMUS
KASHMIR
RICHMAN
TASHMAN
TUCHMAN
YASHMAK

•••H•M•
ALCHEMY
ANTHEMS
FATHOMS
GRAHAME
GRAHAMS
MAYHEMS
RUNHOME
SACHEMS
SASHIMI

•••H••M
ANAHEIM
EIGHTAM
EIGHTPM
LITHIUM
SHAHDOM
SIKHISM
SOPHISM
WILHELM
WYCHELM

••••HM•
DRACHMA
DRACHMS
LAKSHMI
MEGOHMS
RHYTHMS
SATCHMO

••••H•M
ABRAHAM
APOTHEM
BEECHAM
BENTHAM
BINGHAM
BRIGHAM
CHATHAM
FORDHAM
FULGHUM
GINGHAM
GRISHAM
JOACHIM
KETCHAM
MARKHAM
MAUGHAM
MITCHUM
NEEDHAM
SORGHUM

H•N••••
HANCOCK
HANDBAG
HANDCAR
HANDFED
HANDFUL
HANDGUN
HANDIER
HANDILY
HANDING
HANDLED
HANDLER
HANDLES
HANDOFF
HANDOUT
HANDSAW
HANDSET
HANDSIN
HANDSON
HANDSUP
HANGARS
HANGDOG
HANGERS
HANGING
HANGMAN
HANGMEN
HANGOFF
HANGOUT
HANGSIN
HANGSON
HANGSUP
HANGTEN
HANGUPS
HANKERS
HANKIES
HANOVER
HANSARP
HANSOLO
HANSOMS
HANUKAH
HENBANE
HENBITS
HENCOOP
HENDRIX
HENLIKE
HENNAED
HENNERY
HENNISH
HENPECK
HENRYIV
HENTING
HINDERS
HINGING
HINNIES
HINTING
HINTSAT
HONCHOS
HONESTY
HONEYED
HONIARA
HONKERS
HONKING
HONORED
HONOREE
HONORER
HONORIS
HONOURS
HUNCHED
HUNCHES
HUNDRED
HUNGARY
HUNGERS
HUNGOUT
HUNKERS
HUNKIER
HUNLIKE
HUNNISH
HUNTERS
HUNTING
HUNTLEY
HUNYADY

H••N•••
HAFNIUM
HAHNIUM
HARNESS
HAUNTED
HEINOUS
HENNAED
HENNERY
HENNISH
HEXNUTS
HINNIES
HIPNESS
HOBNAIL
HOBNOBS
HORNETS
HORNING
HORNISH
HORNIST
HORNSBY
HORNSIN
HOTNESS
HOUNDED
HUNNISH
HYMNALS
HYMNODY
HYUNDAI

H•••N••
HACKNEY
HAIRNET
HAPENNY
HAVENOT
HAZINGS
HHMUNRO
HIDINGS
HIJINKS
HOMINID
HOMONYM
HOSANNA
HUMANLY
HUMANUM
HYPONYM

H••••N•
HACKING
HAFTING
HAGDONS
HAILING
HALOING
HALTING
HALVING
HAMMING
HAMMOND
HANDING
HANGING
HAPENNY
HAPPENS
HAPPING
HARDENS
HARDING
HARKENS
HARKING
HARMING
HARMONY
HARPING
HASHING
HASPING
HASTENS
HASTING
HATBAND
HATPINS
HATTING
HAULING
HAWKING
HAWKINS
HEADING
HEALING
HEAPING
HEARING
HEATING
HEAVENS
HEAVING
HEDGING
HEEDING
HEELING
HEFTING
HELLENE
HELMING
HELPING
HEMLINE
HEMMING
HENBANE
HENTING

HERDING HERMANN HEROINE HERRING HETMANS HIGGINS HIGHEND HILLING HINGING HINTING HIPBONE HISPANO HISSING HITTING HOAXING HOBOING HOCKING HOGGING HOLDING HOLLAND HONKING HOOFING HOOKING HOOPING HOOTING HOPKINS HOPPING HORMONE HORNING HORSING HOSANNA HOSKINS HOSTING HOTLINE HOTLINK HOUDINI HOUSING HOVLANE HOWLING HOYDENS HUFFING HUGGING HUGGINS HULKING HULLING HUMMING HUNTING HURLING HURTING HUSBAND HUSHING HUSKING HUYGENS HYALINE HYDRANT HYGIENE HYPHENS HYPOING

H•••••N

HACKMAN HADRIAN HAIRPIN HAITIAN HALCYON HALFDAN HALOGEN HALSTON HAMELIN HAMPTON HANDGUN HANDSIN HANDSON HANGMAN HANGMEN HANGSIN HANGSON HANGTEN HARDPAN HARDWON HARPOON HARPSON HARSHEN HARTMAN HASBEEN HEADMAN HEADMEN HEADPIN HEADSIN HEARKEN HEARTEN HEATHEN HEISMAN HELICON HELLION HELLMAN HEPARIN HEPBURN HERMANN HESHVAN HESSIAN HEXAGON HEXSIGN HICKMAN HIRESON HOARSEN HOBOKEN HOEDOWN HOFFMAN HOLBEIN HOLDSIN HOLDSON HOMERUN HORIZON HORNSIN HOUSMAN HOUSTON HUSSEIN

•H•N•••

CHANCED CHANCEL CHANCER CHANCES CHANGED CHANGER CHANGES CHANNEL CHANSON CHANTED CHANTER CHANTEY CHENIER CHINESE CHINKED CHINNED CHINOOK CHINTZY CHINUPS CHUNNEL CHUNTER GHANIAN PHANTOM PHENOLS PHENOMS PHINEAS PHONEME PHONEYS PHONICS PHONIER PHONIES PHONILY PHONING RHENISH RHENIUM SHANANA SHANGRI SHANKAR SHANKED SHANNON SHANTEY SHINDIG SHINERS SHINGLE SHINIER SHINILY SHINING SHINNED SHUNNED SHUNTED SHYNESS THANKED THENARS THINAIR THINICE THINKER THINKOF THINKUP THINNED THINNER THUNDER WHANGED WHINERS WHINIER WHINING

•H••N••

CHAINED CHANNEL CHIANTI CHIGNON CHIMNEY CHINNED CHRONIC CHUNNEL CHURNED CHUTNEY HHMUNRO PHOENIX PHRENIC SHANNON SHATNER SHAWNEE SHINNED SHOWNIN SHRINER SHRINES SHRINKS SHUNNED THINNED THINNER THRONES THRONGS WHATNOT WHITNEY

•H•••N•

CHAFING CHALONS CHASING CHEWING CHICANA CHICANO CHIDING CHIMING CHOLINE CHORINE OHIOANS PHALANX PHARYNX PHASING PHONING PHOTONS RHYMING SHADING SHAKING SHAMANS SHAMING SHANANA SHAPING SHARING SHAVING SHEBANG SHINING SHOEING SHOGUNS SHOOING SHOOINS SHORING SHOVING SHOWING SHUTINS THAWING THEFONZ THYMINE WHALING WHILING WHINING WHITENS WHITING

•H••••N

CHAGRIN CHANSON CHAPLIN CHAPMAN CHAPMEN CHARMIN CHASTEN CHEAPEN CHEATIN CHECHEN CHECKIN CHEVRON CHICHEN CHICKEN CHIFFON CHIGNON CHILEAN CHIPSIN GHANIAN GHERKIN PHAETON PHASEIN PHILBIN SHANNON SHAREIN SHARPEN SHELDON SHELTON SHERMAN SHERWIN SHIPMAN SHIPMEN SHODDEN SHORTEN SHOTGUN SHOWMAN SHOWMEN SHOWNIN SHOWSIN SHUTSIN THEOMEN THEREIN THEREON THICKEN THOMSON THREWIN THROWIN THURMAN WHARTON WHAUDEN WHEATON WHEREIN WHITMAN

••HN•••

ETHNICS HAHNIUM JOHNDOE JOHNGAY JOHNJAY JOHNNIE JOHNSON SCHNAPS

••H•N••

ACHENES ASHANTI ECHINUS ENHANCE ETHANOL JOHANNA JOHNNIE KAHUNAS MAHONEY MCHENRY REHANGS UNHANDS UNHANDY WAHINES WCHANDY

••H••N•

ACHTUNG ASHCANS ASHLAND DEHORNS ECHIDNA ECHOING JOHANNA SCHWINN

••H•••N

ACHERON ACHESON BAHRAIN ECHELON INHUMAN ITHACAN JOHNSON MOHICAN SAHARAN SCHWINN TEHERAN

•••HN••

BOTHNIA DAPHNIS FISHNET

•••H•N•

AFGHANI AFGHANS ANTHONY ARCHING ARCHONS BACHING BASHING BATHING BETHANY BETHINK BUSHING CACHING CASHING COSHING COWHAND CUSHING DABHAND DASHING DISHING ENCHANT ETCHANT ETCHING EUPHONY FISHING GASHING GUSHING HASHING HIGHEND HUSHING HYPHENS INCHING ITCHING JOBHUNT JOSHING KACHINA KUCHENS LASHING LATHING LICHENS MACHINA MACHINE MANHUNT MASHING MESHING METHANE MIGHTNT MOSHING MUDHENS MUSHING NOSHING NOTHING OFFHAND OLDHAND ORPHANS OUGHTNT PEAHENS PITHING PUSHING PYTHONS RETHINK RUCHING RUSHING SIGHING SIPHONS SYPHONS TERHUNE TITHING URCHINS UTAHANS WASHING WISHING

•••H••N

BIGHORN BRAHMAN BRAHMIN BUSHMAN BUSHMEN CALHOUN COCHRAN CUSHION DISHPAN ENCHAIN FASHION FOGHORN HESHVAN IDAHOAN INKHORN KATHRYN LACHLAN LEGHORN LIGHTEN ORPHEAN PUSHKIN PUSHPIN PYTHIAN RICHMAN RIGHTON SAXHORN SICHUAN SOTHERN TASHLIN TASHMAN TIGHTEN TINHORN TUCHMAN TYPHOON UNCHAIN UNSHORN

••••HN•

ARACHNE KRISHNA STJOHNS

••••H•N

AGAKHAN ALYKHAN BLUSHON CATCHON CHECHEN CHICHEN DAUPHIN DOLPHIN EARTHEN EREWHON FRESHEN GREYHEN GRYPHON HARSHEN HEATHEN KEESHAN KINCHIN KITCHEN KUTCHIN LAUGHIN MADCHEN MARCHON MCLUHAN MCMAHON MENUHIN MOORHEN PITCHIN PUNCHIN PYNCHON ROUGHEN SAGEHEN SAYWHEN SIOBHAN STEPHEN TEACHIN TOUCHON TOUGHEN VAUGHAN WEIGHIN XANTHAN

•••••HN

BIGJOHN

HO•••••

HOAGIES HOARDED HOARDER HOARIER HOARILY HOARSEN HOARSER HOAXERS HOAXING HOBBIES HOBBITS HOBBLED HOBBLES HOBNAIL HOBNOBS HOBOING HOBOKEN HOCKING HOECAKE HOEDOWN HOFBRAU HOFFMAN HOGARTH HOGBACK HOGGETS HOGGING HOGGISH HOGLIKE HOGTIED HOGTIES HOGWASH HOGWILD HOISTED HOKIEST HOLBEIN HOLDERS HOLDING HOLDOFF HOLDOUT HOLDSIN HOLDSON HOLDSTO HOLDSUP HOLDUPS HOLEDUP HOLEOUT HOLESUP HOLIDAY HOLIEST HOLISTS HOLLAND HOLLERS HOLLIES HOLLOWS HOLMIUM HOLMOAK HOLSTER HOLYARK HOLYCOW HOLYDAY HOLYOKE HOLYSEE HOLYWAR HOMBRES HOMBURG HOMEBOY HOMERED HOMERIC HOMERUN HOMIEST HOMINID HOMONYM HONCHOS HONESTY HONEYED HONIARA HONKERS HONKING HONORED HONOREE HONORER HONORIS HONOURS HOODLUM HOODOOS HOOFERS HOOFING HOOFSIT HOOHAHS HOOKAHS HOOKING HOOKSUP HOOKUPS HOOPING HOOPLAS HOOPOES HOOSIER HOOTERS HOOTING HOOTOWL HOOTSAT HOOVERS HOPEFUL HOPKINS HOPLIKE HOPOVER HOPPERS HOPPING HOPPLED HOPPLES HOPSOFF HOPTOIT HORATIO HORIZON HORMONE HORNETS HORNING HORNISH HORNIST HORNSBY HORNSIN HORRIFY HORRORS HORSIER HORSING HOSANNA HOSIERS HOSIERY HOSKINS HOSPICE HOSTAGE HOSTELS HOSTESS HOSTILE HOSTING HOSTLER HOTBEDS HOTCAKE HOTCAPS HOTCARS HOTCOMB HOTDOGS HOTFOOT HOTHEAD HOTLINE HOTLINK HOTLIPS HOTNESS HOTPOTS HOTRODS HOTSEAT HOTSHOT HOTSPOT HOTSPUR HOTTEST HOTTIPS HOTTUBS HOTWARS HOTWIRE HOUDINI HOUGHED HOUNDED HOUSING HOUSMAN HOUSTON HOVERED HOVERER HOVLANE HOWARDS HOWBEIT HOWCOME HOWDAHS HOWELLS HOWEVER HOWLERS HOWLING HOYDENS

H•O••••

HOODLUM HOODOOS HOOFERS HOOFING HOOFSIT HOOHAHS HOOKAHS HOOKING HOOKSUP HOOKUPS HOOPING HOOPLAS HOOPOES HOOSIER HOOTERS HOOTING HOOTOWL HOOTSAT HOOVERS

H••O•••

HALOGEN HALOING HANOVER HELOISE HELOTRY HEROICS HEROINE HEROISM HOBOING HOBOKEN HOMONYM HONORED HONOREE HONORER HONORIS HONOURS HOPOVER HUMORED HUMOURS HYPOING HYPONYM

H•••O••

HADDOCK HAGDONS HALLOWS HAMHOCK HAMMOCK HAMMOND HANCOCK HANDOFF HANDOUT HANGOFF HANGOUT HANSOLO HANSOMS HARBORS HARBOUR HARMONY HARPOON HARROWS HASSOCK HAULOFF HAYFORK HAYLOFT HAYMOWS HEADOFF HEADOUT HEAROUT HECTORS HEINOUS HELDOFF HELDOUT HELPOUT HEMLOCK HENCOOP HEYWOOD HICKORY HIDEOUS HIDEOUT HILLOCK HIPBONE HIPBOOT HIPROOF HISTORY HITSOUT HOBNOBS HOEDOWN HOLDOFF HOLDOUT HOLEOUT HOLLOWS HOLMOAK HOLYOKE HOODOOS HOOPOES HOOTOWL HOPSOFF HOPTOIT HORMONE HORRORS HOTCOMB HOTDOGS HOTFOOT HOTPOTS HOTRODS HOWCOME HULLOAS HULLOED HUMMOCK HUNGOUT HYDROUS HYMNODY HYSSOPS

H••••O•

HAIRDOS HALCYON HALSTON HAMPTON HANDSON HANGDOG HANGSON HARDTOP HARDWON HARICOT HARPOON HARPSON HAUTBOY HAVENOT HEARDOF HEARSOF HELICON HELLION HENCOOP HERRIOT HEXAGON HEYWOOD HIGHBOY HIGHLOW HIGHTOP HILLTOP HIPBOOT HIPROOF HIRESON HOLDSON HOLYCOW HOMEBOY HONCHOS HOODOOS HORIZON HOTFOOT HOTSHOT HOTSPOT HOUSTON HUMIDOR

H•••••O

HAEMATO HANSOLO HEAVEHO HEAVETO HEIGHHO HHMUNRO HIDALGO HISPANO HOLDSTO HORATIO

•HO••••

CHOCTAW CHOICER CHOICES CHOKERS CHOKEUP CHOKIER CHOLINE CHOLLAS CHOMPED CHOMSKY CHOOSER CHOOSES CHOPPED CHOPPER CHORALE CHORALS CHORINE CHORIZO CHORTLE CHOWDER GHOSTED GHOSTLY PHOBIAS PHOBICS PHOEBES PHOEBUS PHOENIX PHONEME PHONEYS PHONICS PHONIER PHONIES PHONILY PHONING PHOTICS PHOTOED PHOTOGS PHOTONS PHOTOOP RHODIUM RHOMBUS SHOCKED SHOCKER SHODDEN SHOEBOX SHOEING SHOFARS SHOGUNS SHOOFLY SHOOING SHOOINS SHOOKUP SHOOTAT SHOOTER SHOOTUP SHOPFUL SHOPPED SHOPPER SHOPPES SHORING SHORTED SHORTEN SHORTER SHORTLY SHORTOF SHOTFOR SHOTGUN SHOTOUT SHOTPUT SHOULDA SHOUTED SHOUTER SHOVELS SHOVERS SHOVING SHOWBIZ SHOWDOG SHOWERS SHOWERY SHOWIER SHOWILY SHOWING SHOWMAN SHOWMEN SHOWNIN SHOWOFF SHOWOUT SHOWSIN SHOWSUP THOMSON THOREAU THORIUM THOUGHT WHOEVER WHOMPED WHOOPED WHOOPEE WHOPPED WHOPPER WHORLED WHOSWHO

•H•O•••

CHAOTIC CHLORAL CHOOSER CHOOSES CHROMES CHRONIC OHIOANS PHLOXES SHOOFLY SHOOING SHOOINS SHOOKUP SHOOTAT SHOOTER SHOOTUP SHROUDS THEOMEN THEOREM THROATS THROATY THRONES THRONGS THROUGH THROWER THROWIN WHOOPED WHOOPEE

•H••O••

CHALONS CHAMOIS CHEROOT CHEWOUT CHICORY CHIGOES CHINOOK PHENOLS PHENOMS PHOTOED PHOTOGS PHOTONS PHOTOOP RHEBOKS RHETORS RHIZOME SHADOOF SHADOWS SHADOWY SHAKOES SHALOMS

SHEWOLF
SHIKOKU
SHIPOUT
SHOTOUT
SHOWOFF
SHOWOUT
SHUTOFF
SHUTOUT
SHYLOCK
THEFONZ
THEROUX

•H•••O•
AHEADOF
CHANSON
CHARIOT
CHEETOS
CHEKHOV
CHEROOT
CHEVIOT
CHEVRON
CHEWTOY
CHIFFON
CHIGNON
CHINOOK
GHETTOS
PHAETON
PHANTOM
PHARAOH
PHOTOOP
SHADOOF
SHAHDOM
SHALLOT
SHALLOW
SHAMPOO
SHANNON
SHELDON
SHELTON
SHOEBOX
SHORTOF
SHOTFOR
SHOWDOG
THEBLOB
THECROW
THEREOF
THEREON
THERMOS
THINKOF
THOMSON
WHARTON
WHATFOR
WHATNOT
WHEATON
WHEREOF

•H••••O
CHEERIO
CHICAGO
CHICANO
CHIRICO
CHORIZO
CHRISTO
HHMUNRO
SHAMPOO
SHAPIRO
THERETO
WHERETO
WHOSWHO
ZHIVAGO

••HO•••
ATHOMES
BEHOLDS
BEHOOVE
BEHOVED
BEHOVES
CAHOOTS
COHORTS
COHOSTS
DAHOMEY
DEHORNS
ECHOING
EXHORTS
INHOUSE
MAHONEY
MAHOUTS
OKHOTSK
REHOOKS
SCHOLAR
SCHOOLS
UNHOOKS
UNHORSE
UPHOLDS

••H•O••
ASHFORD
BEHOOVE
CAHOOTS
OSHKOSH
REHOOKS
SCHLOCK
SCHMOES
SCHMOOS
SCHOOLS
UNHOOKS

••H••O•
ACHERON
ACHESON
ECHELON
ETHANOL
ICHABOD
JOHNDOE
JOHNSON
SCHMOOS

••H•••O
OTHELLO
SCHERZO
SUHARTO

•••HO••
AIRHOLE
AMPHORA
ANCHORS
ANCHOVY
ANTHONY
ARCHONS
ARMHOLE
AUTHORS
BARHOPS
BATHOIL
BIGHORN
BISHOPS
BOBHOPE
BOGHOLE
BOOHOOS
BOYHOOD
BSCHOOL
CACHOUS
CALHOUN
CARHOPS
CASHOUT
CATHODE
DASHOFF
DISHOUT
DRYHOLE
EUPHONY
EYEHOLE
FATHOMS
FISHOUT
FOGHORN
FOXHOLE
HAMHOCK
IDAHOAN
INKHORN
INSHORT
JOBHOPS
KEYHOLE
LEGHORN
MANHOLE
MANHOOD
MANHOUR
METHODS
NICHOLS
NOSHOWS
OFFHOUR
ONSHORE
PINHOLE
POTHOLE
POTHOOK
PUSHOFF
PYTHONS
QUAHOGS
RATHOLE
RECHOSE
REDHOTS
RESHOES
RESHOOT
RUNHOME
RUSHOFF
SAXHORN
SIPHONS
SKYHOOK
SYPHONS
TINHORN
TOEHOLD
TOPHOLE
TVSHOWS
TYPHOON
UNSHORN
UPSHOTS
WASHOFF
WASHOUT
WITHOUT

•••H•O•
ALOHAOE
BOOHOOS
BOYHOOD
BSCHOOL
BUSHHOG
CASHBOX
CASHCOW
CUSHION
FASHION
HIGHBOY
HIGHLOW
HIGHTOP
LITHGOW
MANHOOD
POTHOOK
RESHOOT
RIGHTON
SHAHDOM
SKYHOOK
TYPHOON

•••H••O
AKIHITO
BUSHIDO
ONTHEGO

••••HO•
AIRSHOW
ALCOHOL
BACKHOE
BELLHOP
BIGSHOT
BLUSHON
BOKCHOY
BOLSHOI
BUSHHOG
CAMPHOR
CATCHON
CATSHOW
CHEKHOV
DOGCHOW
DOGSHOW
EARSHOT
EREWHON
EYESHOT
GASOHOL
GAUCHOS
GRYPHON
GUMSHOE
GUNSHOT
GYMSHOE
HONCHOS
HOTSHOT
ICESHOW
IVANHOE
KERCHOO
KNOWHOW
MARCHON
MARKHOR
MCMAHON
MENTHOL
MUGSHOT
NAVAHOS
ONESHOT
PONCHOS
PORTHOS
POTSHOT
PROSHOP
PRUDHOE
PYNCHON
RANCHOS
RIMSHOT
ROADHOG
SALCHOW
SANDHOG
SOMEHOW
TEASHOP
TOESHOE
TOUCHON
TOYSHOP
USOSHOW
WARTHOG

••••H•O
HEIGHHO
KERCHOO
SATCHMO

•••••HO
ARAPAHO
GROUCHO
HEAVEHO
HEIGHHO
JERICHO
LESOTHO
ORNITHO
TALLYHO
WHOSWHO

H•P••••
HAPENNY
HAPLESS
HAPPENS
HAPPIER
HAPPILY
HAPPING
HEPARIN
HEPATIC
HEPBURN
HEPCATS
HEPPEST
HEPTADS
HIPBONE
HIPBOOT
HIPLESS
HIPLIKE
HIPNESS
HIPPEST
HIPPIER
HIPPIES
HIPROOF
HIPSTER
HOPEFUL
HOPKINS
HOPLIKE
HOPOVER
HOPPERS
HOPPING
HOPPLED
HOPPLES
HOPSOFF
HOPTOIT
HYPEDUP
HYPESUP
HYPHENS
HYPOING
HYPONYM

H••P•••
HAMPERS
HAMPTON
HAPPENS
HAPPIER
HAPPILY
HAPPING
HARPERS
HARPIES
HARPING
HARPIST
HARPOON
HARPSON
HASPING
HATPINS
HEAPING
HELPERS
HELPFUL
HELPING
HELPOUT
HENPECK
HEPPEST
HIPPEST
HIPPIER
HIPPIES
HISPANO
HOOPING
HOOPLAS
HOOPOES
HOPPERS
HOPPING
HOPPLED
HOPPLES
HOSPICE
HOTPOTS
HUMPIER

H•••P••
HAIRPIN
HARDPAN
HARDPUT
HEADPIN
HELIPAD
HOTSPOT
HOTSPUR

H••••P•
HANGUPS
HICCUPS
HOLDUPS
HOOKUPS
HOTCAPS
HOTLIPS
HOTTIPS
HUBCAPS
HYSSOPS

H•••••P
HAMITUP
HANDSUP
HANGSUP
HANSARP
HARDTOP
HAULSUP
HEADSUP
HEATSUP
HEELTAP
HENCOOP
HIGHTOP
HIKEDUP
HIKESUP
HILLTOP
HOLDSUP
HOLEDUP
HOLESUP
HOOKSUP
HURRYUP
HYPEDUP
HYPESUP

•H•P•••
CHAPATI
CHAPEAU
CHAPELS
CHAPLET
CHAPLIN
CHAPMAN
CHAPMEN
CHAPPED
CHAPPIE
CHAPTER
CHIPPED
CHIPPER
CHIPSIN
CHOPPED
CHOPPER
SHAPELY
SHAPERS
SHAPEUP
SHAPING
SHAPIRO
SHAPLEY
SHEPARD
SHIPMAN
SHIPMEN
SHIPOUT
SHIPPED
SHIPPER
SHOPFUL
SHOPPED
SHOPPER
SHOPPES
THEPITS
WHIPPED
WHIPPET
WHIPSAW
WHIPSUP
WHOPPED
WHOPPER
WHUPPED

•H••P••
CHAMPED
CHAPPED
CHAPPIE
CHEAPEN
CHEAPER
CHEAPIE
CHEAPLY
CHEEPED
CHIPPED
CHIPPER
CHIRPED
CHOMPED
CHOPPED
CHOPPER
SHAMPOO
SHARPED
SHARPEI
SHARPEN
SHARPER
SHARPLY
SHERPAS
SHIPPED
SHIPPER
SHOPPED
SHOPPER
SHOPPES
SHOTPUT
THESPIS
THIMPHU
THUMPED
THUMPER
WHELPED
WHIMPER
WHIPPED
WHIPPET
WHISPER
WHOMPED
WHOOPED
WHOOPEE
WHOPPED
WHOPPER
WHUPPED

•H•••P•
CHINUPS
SHRIMPS
THERAPY
THREEPM

•H••••P
CHALKUP
CHATSUP
CHECKUP
CHEERUP
CHEWSUP
CHOKEUP
PHARLAP
PHILLIP
PHOTOOP
SHAKEUP
SHAPEUP
SHOOKUP
SHOOTUP
SHOWSUP
SHUTSUP
THEDEEP
THINKUP
WHIPSUP

••H•P••
UNHAPPY

••H••P•
SCHLEPP
SCHLEPS
SCHNAPS
UNHAPPY

••H•••P
SCHLEPP

•••HP••
BUSHPIG
DISHPAN
MOSHPIT
PUSHPIN

•••H•P•
BARHOPS
BISHOPS
BOBHOPE
CARHOPS
EIGHTPM
INSHAPE
JOBHOPS
LASHUPS
MISHAPS
MRCHIPS
PERHAPS
PUSHUPS
RESHIPS
WASHUPS

•••H••P
HIGHTOP
INAHEAP
LIGHTUP

••••H•P
AIRSHIP
BELLHOP
BIOCHIP
BOTCHUP
BRUSHUP
CATCHUP
COUGHUP
KETCHUP
KINSHIP
MATCHUP
OLDCHAP
PATCHUP
PROSHOP
PSYCHUP
PUNCHUP
ROUGHUP
SMASHUP
TEASHOP
TOUCHUP
TOYSHOP
WARSHIP
WORSHIP

•H•Q•••
CHEQUER
CHEQUES

•••H•Q•
ONTHEQT

H•R••••
HARBORS
HARBOUR
HARBURG
HARDENS
HARDEST
HARDHAT
HARDHIT
HARDIER
HARDILY
HARDING
HARDPAN
HARDPUT
HARDSET
HARDTOP
HARDWON
HARICOT
HARKENS
HARKING
HARMFUL
HARMING
HARMONY
HARNESS
HARPERS
HARPIES
HARPING
HARPIST
HARPOON
HARPSON
HARRIED
HARRIER
HARRIES
HARRIET
HARROWS
HARSHEN
HARSHER
HARSHLY
HARTMAN
HARVARD
HARVEST
HERALDS
HERBAGE
HERBALS
HERBERT
HERBIER
HERBTEA
HERCULE
HERDERS
HERDING
HERETIC
HERMANN
HERMITS
HEROICS
HEROINE
HEROISM
HERRING
HERRIOT
HERSELF
HERSHEY
HIRABLE
HIRESON
HIRSUTE
HORATIO
HORIZON
HORMONE
HORNETS
HORNING
HORNISH
HORNIST
HORNSBY
HORNSIN
HORRIFY
HORRORS
HORSIER
HORSING
HURDLED
HURDLER
HURDLES
HURLERS
HURLEYS
HURLIES
HURLING
HURRAHS
HURRIED
HURRIES
HURRYUP
HURTFUL
HURTING
HURTLED
HURTLES
HYRACES
HYRAXES

H••R•••
HAARLEM
HADRIAN
HAIRCUT
HAIRDOS
HAIRDYE
HAIRIER
HAIRNET
HAIRPIN
HARRIED
HARRIER
HARRIES
HARRIET
HARROWS
HATRACK
HAYRACK
HAYRIDE
HEARDOF
HEARERS
HEARING
HEARKEN
HEAROUT
HEARSAY
HEARSOF
HEARTED
HEARTEN
HEARTHS
HEBRAIC
HEBREWS
HEIRESS
HENRYIV
HERRING
HERRIOT
HIPROOF
HOARDED
HOARDER
HOARIER
HOARILY
HOARSEN
HOARSER
HORRIFY
HORRORS
HOTRODS
HURRAHS
HURRIED
HURRIES
HURRYUP
HYBRIDS
HYDRANT
HYDRATE
HYDROUS

H•••R••
HAVARTI
HAVERED
HAZARDS
HEGIRAS
HENDRIX
HEPARIN
HOFBRAU
HOGARTH
HOMBRES
HOMERED
HOMERIC
HOMERUN
HONORED
HONOREE
HONORER
HONORIS
HOVERED
HOVERER
HOWARDS
HUMDRUM
HUMERAL
HUMERUS
HUMORED
HUNDRED

H••••R•
HACKERS
HAGGARD
HALTERS
HALYARD
HAMBURG
HAMMERS
HAMPERS
HANGARS
HANGERS
HANKERS
HANSARP
HARBORS
HARBURG
HARPERS
HARVARD
HATTERS
HAUBERK
HAULERS
HAWKERS
HAWSERS
HAYFORK
HAYWARD
HAYWIRE
HEADERS
HEALERS
HEARERS
HEATERS
HEAVERS
HECTARE
HECTORS
HEDGERS
HEELERS
HEIFERS
HELLERS
HELOTRY
HELPERS
HEMMERS
HENNERY
HEPBURN
HERBERT
HERDERS
HHMUNRO
HICKORY
HILAIRE
HILLARY
HINDERS
HISSERS
HISTORY
HITHERE
HITTERS
HOAXERS
HOLDERS
HOLLERS
HOLYARK
HOMBURG
HONIARA
HONKERS
HONOURS
HOOFERS
HOOTERS
HOOVERS
HOPPERS
HORRORS
HOSIERS
HOSIERY
HOTCARS
HOTWARS
HOTWIRE
HOWLERS
HUBBARD
HUGGERS
HULLERS
HUMMERS
HUMOURS
HUNGARY
HUNGERS
HUNKERS
HUNTERS
HURLERS
HUSKERS
HUSSARS

H•••••R
HAGGLER
HAIRIER
HAMMIER
HAMSTER
HANDCAR
HANDIER
HANDLER
HANOVER
HAPPIER
HARBOUR
HARDIER
HARRIER
HARSHER
HASTIER
HATCHER
HAUTEUR
HEADIER
HEATHER
HEATTER
HEAVIER
HECKLER
HEDGIER
HEFTIER
HERBIER
HILLIER
HIPPIER
HIPSTER
HITCHER
HOARDER
HOARIER
HOARSER
HOLSTER
HOLYWAR
HONORER
HOOSIER
HOPOVER
HORSIER
HOSTLER
HOTSPUR
HOVERER
HOWEVER
HUFFIER
HUMBLER
HUMIDOR
HUMPIER
HUNKIER
HURDLER
HUSKIER
HUSTLER

•HR••••
CHRISMS
CHRISTI
CHRISTO
CHRISTY
CHROMES
CHRONIC
EHRLICH
PHRASAL
PHRASED
PHRASES
PHRENIC
SHRIEKS
SHRIFTS
SHRIKES
SHRILLS
SHRILLY
SHRIMPS
SHRINER
SHRINES
SHRINKS
SHRIVEL
SHRIVER
SHRIVES
SHROUDS
SHRUBBY
THRALLS
THREADS
THREADY
THREATS
THREEAM
THREEPM
THREERS
THREWIN
THRIFTS
THRIFTY
THRILLS
THRIVED
THRIVES
THROATS
THROATY
THRONES
THRONGS
THROUGH
THROWER
THROWIN
THRUSTS
THRUWAY

•H•R•••
CHARADE
CHARGED
CHARGER
CHARGES
CHARIER
CHARILY
CHARIOT
CHARITY
CHARLES
CHARLEY
CHARLIE
CHARMED
CHARMER
CHARMIN
CHARRED
CHARTED
CHARTER
CHERISH
CHEROOT
CHERUBS
CHERVIL
CHIRICO
CHIRPED
CHORALE
CHORALS
CHORINE
CHORIZO
CHORTLE
CHURNED
DHURRIE
GHERKIN
PHARAOH
PHARLAP
PHARYNX
SHAREIN
SHARERS
SHARING
SHARKEY
SHARPED
SHARPEI
SHARPEN
SHARPER
SHARPLY
SHERBET
SHERIFF
SHERMAN
SHERPAS
SHERWIN
SHIRKED
SHIRKER
SHIRLEY
SHIRRED
SHORING
SHORTED
SHORTEN
SHORTER
SHORTLY
SHORTOF
THERAPY
THEREAT
THEREBY
THEREIN
THERELL
THEREOF
THEREON
THERESA
THERETO
THERMAL
THERMOS
THEROUX
THIRDLY
THIRSTS
THIRSTY
THOREAU
THORIUM
THURBER
THURMAN
WHARFED
WHARTON
WHARVES
WHEREAS
WHEREAT
WHEREBY
WHEREIN
WHERELL
WHEREOF

WHERERE
WHERETO
WHEREVE
WHIRLED
WHIRRED
WHORLED

•H••R••
CHAGRIN
CHAIRED
CHARRED
CHEERED
CHEERIO
CHEERUP
CHETRUM
CHEVRES
CHEVRON
CHLORAL
DHURRIE
SHEARED
SHEARER
SHEERED
SHEERER
SHEERLY
SHIRRED
THECROW
THEOREM
THEURGY
THWARTS
WHIRRED

•H•••R•
CHASERS
CHEWERS
CHICORY
CHIDERS
CHIMERA
CHOKERS
HHMUNRO
PHAEDRA
PHASERS
PHILTRE
RHETORS
RHUBARB
RHYMERS
SHAKERS
SHANGRI
SHAPERS
SHAPIRO
SHARERS
SHASTRI
SHAVERS
SHEPARD
SHIKARI
SHINERS
SHIVERS
SHIVERY
SHOFARS
SHOVERS
SHOWERS
SHOWERY
SHUBERT
THALERS
THEATRE
THECARS
THEFIRM
THENARS
THREERS
WHALERS
WHERERE
WHINERS

•H••••R
CHAMBER
CHAMFER
CHANCER
CHANGER
CHANTER
CHAPTER
CHARGER
CHARIER
CHARMER
CHARTER
CHASTER
CHATTER
CHAUCER
CHEAPER
CHEATER
CHECKER
CHEDDAR
CHEEVER
CHENIER
CHEQUER
CHESTER
CHEWIER
CHIGGER
CHILLER
CHIPPER
CHITTER
CHOICER
CHOKIER
CHOOSER
CHOPPER
CHOWDER
CHUKKER
CHUNTER
PHILTER
PHONIER
SHADIER
SHAFFER
SHAKIER
SHANKAR
SHARPER
SHATNER
SHATTER
SHEARER
SHEERER
SHELLER
SHELTER
SHIMMER
SHINIER
SHIPPER
SHIRKER
SHOCKER
SHOOTER
SHOPPER
SHORTER
SHOTFOR
SHOUTER
SHOWIER
SHRINER
SHRIVER
SHUCKER
SHUDDER
SHUTTER
SHYSTER
THEATER
THEWIER
THICKER
THINAIR
THINKER
THINNER
THITHER
THROWER
THUMPER
THUNDER
THURBER
THUSFAR
WHATFOR
WHEELER
WHEEZER
WHETHER
WHIMPER
WHINIER
WHISKER
WHISPER
WHITHER
WHITIER
WHIZZER
WHOEVER
WHOPPER

••HR•••
ASHRAMS
BAHRAIN

••H•R••
ACHERON
ADHERED
ADHERES
AMHARIC
AMHERST
ASHTRAY
ATHIRST
COHERED
COHERES
COHORTS
DEHORNS
EXHORTS
INHERED
INHERES
INHERIT
MAHARIS
REHIRED
REHIRES
SAHARAN
SCHERZI
SCHERZO
SCHIRRA
SPHERES
SUHARTO
TEHERAN
TSHIRTS
UNHORSE
USHERED

••H••R•
ASHBURY
ASHFORD
ASHLARS
ATHEART
ATHWART
BYHEART
CAHIERS
COHEIRS
LEHAVRE
MCHENRY
MOHAIRS
REHEARD
REHEARS
SCHIRRA
UNHEARD

••H•••R
INHALER
SCHEMER
SCHMEER
SCHOLAR

•••HR••
COCHRAN
DISHRAG
ENTHRAL
EUCHRED
EUCHRES
GUTHRIE
KATHRYN
MITHRAS
ORPHREY
WASHRAG

•••H•R•
AETHERS
ALLHERE
AMPHORA
ANCHORS
ANTHERS
ARCHERS
ARCHERY
AUTHORS
BATHERS
BIGHORN
BOKHARA
BOTHERS
CIPHERS
COCHERE
COWHERD
CYPHERS
DASHERS
DIEHARD
DITHERS
DITHERY
EARHART
ECKHART
ELKHART
ETCHERS
FATHERS
FISHERS
FISHERY
FISHFRY
FOGHORN
GATHERS
GOPHERS
GUSHERS
HITHERE
INKHORN
INSHORT
KOSHERS
LASHERS
LATHERS
LATHERY
LEGHORN
MASHERS
MATHERS
MENHIRS
MOSHERS
MOTHERS
MUSHERS
NEWHART
NOSHERS
NOWHERE
ONSHORE
ORCHARD
POTHERB
POTHERS
RASHERS
RICHARD
RUSHERS
SAXHORN
SEEHERE
SIGHERS
SOTHERE
SOTHERN
TETHERS
TINHORN
TITHERS
UNSHORN
WASHERS
WETHERS
WISHERS
WITHERS
YOGHURT
ZACHARY
ZEPHYRS
ZITHERS

•••H••R
BUSHIER
CASHBAR
CASHIER
CATHAIR
COCHAIR
CUSHIER
DISHIER
FIGHTER
FISHIER
GUSHIER
ITCHIER
KASHMIR
LIGHTER
MANHOUR
MESHIER
MISHEAR
MOTHIER
MUSHIER
MYNHEER
OFFHOUR
PITHIER
PUSHIER
REDHAIR
RICHTER
RIGHTER
RUSHIER
SASHBAR
TECHIER
TIGHTER
WASHIER
WITHIER

••••H•R
ANOTHER
BEECHER
BLATHER
BLITHER
BLUSHER
BRASHER
BROTHER
BULGHUR
BURGHER
BUTCHER
CAMPHOR
CATCHER
CRUSHER
FARTHER
FEATHER
FILCHER
FISCHER
FLASHER
FRESHER
FURTHER
GAUCHER
GUNTHER
HARSHER
HATCHER
HEATHER
HITCHER
LAUGHER
LEATHER
MARCHER
MARKHOR
MOOCHER
MUNCHER
NEITHER
NORTHER
PANTHER
PINCHER
PITCHER
PLUSHER
POACHER
PUNCHER
RANCHER
REUTHER
ROUGHER
SLASHER
SLATHER
SLITHER
SMASHER
SMOTHER
SOOTHER
SULPHUR
TEACHER
TEETHER
TEICHER
THITHER
TOUGHER
VOUCHER
WATCHER
WEATHER
WERNHER
WERTHER
WHETHER
WHITHER

•••••HR
NIEBUHR

H•S••••
HASBEEN
HASHING
HASIDIC
HASIDIM
HASPING
HASSLED
HASSLES
HASSOCK
HASTENS
HASTIER
HASTILY
HASTING
HESHVAN
HESSIAN
HISPANO
HISSERS
HISSING
HISTORY
HOSANNA
HOSIERS
HOSIERY
HOSKINS
HOSPICE
HOSTAGE
HOSTELS
HOSTESS
HOSTILE
HOSTING
HOSTLER
HUSBAND
HUSHABY
HUSHFUL
HUSHING
HUSKERS
HUSKIER
HUSKIES
HUSKILY
HUSKING
HUSSARS
HUSSEIN
HUSSIES
HUSTLED
HUSTLER
HUSTLES
HYSSOPS

H••S•••
HALSTON
HAMSTER
HANSARP
HANSOLO
HANSOMS
HARSHEN
HARSHER
HARSHLY
HASSLED
HASSLES
HASSOCK
HAWSERS
HAYSEED
HEISMAN
HEISTED
HEMSLEY
HERSELF
HERSHEY
HESSIAN
HEXSIGN
HIMSELF
HIPSTER
HIRSUTE
HISSERS
HISSING
HITSOUT
HOISTED
HOLSTER
HOOSIER
HOPSOFF
HORSIER
HORSING
HOTSEAT
HOTSHOT
HOTSPOT
HOTSPUR
HOUSING
HOUSMAN
HOUSTON
HUSSARS
HUSSEIN
HUSSIES
HYSSOPS

H•••S••
HACKSAW
HANDSAW
HANDSET
HANDSIN
HANDSON
HANDSUP
HANGSIN
HANGSON
HANGSUP
HARDSET
HARPSON
HAULSUP
HEADSET
HEADSIN
HEADSUP
HEARSAY
HEARSOF
HEATSUP
HIKESUP
HINTSAT
HIRESON
HOARSEN
HOARSER
HOLDSIN
HOLDSON
HOLDSTO
HOLDSUP
HOLESUP
HOLISTS
HOLYSEE
HONESTY
HOOFSIT
HOOKSUP
HOOTSAT
HORNSBY
HORNSIN
HYPESUP

H••••S•
HAGGISH
HAPLESS
HARDEST
HARNESS
HARPIST
HARVEST
HATLESS
HAWKISH
HAZIEST
HEIRESS
HELLISH
HELOISE
HENNISH
HEPPEST
HEROISM
HIGHEST
HIPLESS
HIPNESS
HIPPEST
HITLESS
HITLIST
HOGGISH
HOGWASH
HOKIEST
HOLIEST
HOMIEST
HORNISH
HORNIST
HOSTESS
HOTNESS
HOTTEST
HUELESS
HUFFISH
HUNNISH

H•••••S
HACKERS
HACKIES
HACKLES
HAGDONS
HAGGLES
HAIRDOS
HALIDES
HALITES
HALLOWS
HALTERS
HALVAHS
HAMITES
HAMLETS
HAMMERS
HAMPERS
HANDLES
HANGARS
HANGERS
HANGUPS
HANKERS
HANKIES
HANSOMS
HAPLESS
HAPPENS
HARBORS
HARDENS
HARKENS
HARNESS
HARPERS
HARPIES
HARRIES
HARROWS
HASSLES
HASTENS
HATCHES
HATLESS
HATPINS
HATTERS
HAULERS
HAWHAWS
HAWKERS
HAWKINS
HAWSERS
HAYMOWS
HAZARDS
HAZINGS
HEADERS
HEALERS
HEARERS
HEARTHS
HEATERS
HEAVENS
HEAVERS
HEAVIES
HEBREWS
HECKLES
HECTORS
HEDDLES
HEDGERS
HEEHAWS
HEELERS
HEGIRAS
HEIFERS
HEIGHTS
HEINOUS
HEIRESS
HELICES
HELIXES
HELLERS
HELMETS
HELPERS
HEMMERS
HENBITS
HEPCATS
HEPTADS
HERALDS
HERBALS
HERDERS
HERMITS
HEROICS
HETMANS
HEXNUTS
HEYDAYS
HGWELLS
HICCUPS
HIDEOUS
HIDINGS
HIGGINS
HIGGLES
HIJACKS
HIJINKS
HINDERS
HINNIES
HIPLESS
HIPNESS
HIPPIES
HISSERS
HITCHES
HITLESS
HITTERS
HOAGIES
HOAXERS
HOBBIES
HOBBITS
HOBBLES
HOBNOBS
HOGGETS
HOGTIES
HOLDERS
HOLDUPS
HOLISTS
HOLLERS
HOLLIES
HOLLOWS
HOMBRES
HONCHOS
HONKERS
HONORIS
HONOURS
HOODOOS
HOOFERS
HOOHAHS
HOOKAHS
HOOKUPS
HOOPLAS
HOOPOES
HOOTERS
HOOVERS
HOPKINS
HOPPERS
HOPPLES
HORNETS
HORRORS
HOSIERS
HOSKINS
HOSTELS
HOSTESS
HOTBEDS
HOTCAPS
HOTCARS
HOTDOGS
HOTLIPS
HOTNESS
HOTPOTS
HOTRODS
HOTTIPS
HOTTUBS
HOTWARS
HOWARDS
HOWDAHS
HOWELLS
HOWLERS
HOYDENS
HUBBIES
HUBBUBS
HUBCAPS
HUDDLES
HUELESS
HUGGERS
HUGGINS
HULLERS
HULLOAS
HUMBLES
HUMBUGS
HUMERUS
HUMMERS
HUMOURS
HUMVEES
HUNCHES
HUNGERS
HUNKERS
HUNTERS
HURDLES
HURLERS
HURLEYS
HURLIES
HURRAHS
HURRIES
HURTLES
HUSKERS
HUSKIES
HUSSARS
HUSSIES
HUSTLES
HUTCHES
HUYGENS
HUZZAHS
HYBRIDS
HYDROUS
HYMNALS
HYPHENS
HYRACES
HYRAXES
HYSSOPS

•H•S•••
CHASERS
CHASING
CHASSES
CHASSIS
CHASTEN
CHASTER
CHESTER
CHISELS
GHASTLY
GHOSTED
GHOSTLY
PHASEIN
PHASERS
PHASING
PHYSICS
SHASTRI
SHUSHED
SHUSHES
SHYSTER
THESEUS
THESPIS
THISTLE
THISTLY
THUSFAR
THYSELF
WHISHED
WHISHES
WHISKED
WHISKER
WHISKEY
WHISPER
WHISTLE
WHOSWHO

•H••S••
CHAISES
CHANSON
CHASSES
CHASSIS
CHATSUP
CHEESES
CHELSEA
CHEWSUP
CHIPSIN
CHOMSKY
CHOOSER
CHOOSES
CHRISMS
CHRISTI
CHRISTO
CHRISTY
PHRASAL
PHRASED
PHRASES
SHOWSIN
SHOWSUP
SHUTSIN
SHUTSUP
THATSIT
THEISTS
THIRSTS
THIRSTY
THOMSON
THRUSTS
WHIPSAW
WHIPSUP

•H•••S•
CHEMISE
CHEMIST
CHERISH
CHINESE
RHENISH
SHIATSU
SHYNESS
THERESA
WHEYISH
WHITEST
WHITISH

•H••••S
CHABLIS
CHACHAS
CHAISES
CHALETS
CHALONS
CHAMOIS
CHANCES
CHANGES
CHAPELS
CHARGES
CHARLES
CHASERS
CHASSES
CHASSIS
CHEESES
CHEETOS
CHEQUES
CHERUBS
CHEVIES
CHEVRES
CHEWERS
CHIDERS
CHIGOES
CHILIES
CHINUPS
CHISELS
CHOICES
CHOKERS
CHOLLAS
CHOOSES
CHORALS
CHRISMS
CHROMES
CHUKKAS
GHETTOS
OHIOANS
PHASERS
PHENOLS
PHENOMS
PHIDIAS
PHINEAS
PHLOXES
PHOBIAS
PHOBICS
PHOEBES
PHOEBUS
PHONEYS
PHONICS
PHONIES
PHOTICS
PHOTOGS
PHOTONS
PHRASES
PHYLLIS
PHYSICS
RHEBOKS
RHETORS
RHOMBUS
RHUMBAS
RHYMERS
RHYTHMS
SHADOWS
SHAKERS
SHAKOES
SHALOMS
SHAMANS
SHAPERS
SHARERS
SHAVERS
SHEATHS
SHEAVES
SHEIKHS
SHEILAS
SHEKELS
SHELVES
SHERPAS
SHIELDS
SHIITES
SHINERS
SHIVERS
SHOFARS
SHOGUNS
SHOOINS
SHOPPES
SHOVELS
SHOVERS
SHOWERS
SHRIEKS
SHRIFTS
SHRIKES
SHRILLS
SHRIMPS
SHRINES
SHRINKS
SHRIVES
SHROUDS
SHTICKS
SHUSHES
SHUTINS
SHYNESS
THALERS
THECARS
THEISTS
THENARS
THEPITS
THERMOS
THESEUS
THESPIS
THIEVES
THIRSTS
THRALLS
THREADS
THREATS
THREERS
THRIFTS
THRILLS
THRIVES
THROATS
THRONES
THRONGS
THRUSTS
THWACKS
THWARTS
WHALERS
WHARVES
WHEEZES
WHEREAS
WHINERS
WHISHES
WHITENS
WHIZZES
WHYDAHS

••H•S••
ACHESON
APHESES
BEHESTS
COHOSTS
DEHISCE
INHASTE
JOHNSON
SCHISMS

••H••S•
ACHIEST
AMHERST
ASHIEST
ASHLESS
ATHEISM
ATHEIST
ATHIRST
EXHAUST
INHOUSE
OKHOTSK
OSHKOSH
UNHORSE

••H•••S
ACHATES
ACHENES
ADHERES
APHESES
ASHCANS
ASHLARS
ASHLESS
ASHRAMS
ATHOMES
BAHAMAS
BEHAVES
BEHEADS
BEHESTS
BEHOLDS
BEHOVES
CAHIERS
CAHOOTS
COHEIRS
COHERES
COHORTS
COHOSTS
DAHLIAS
DEHORNS
ECHINUS
ETHNICS
EXHALES
EXHORTS

INHALES
INHAULS
INHERES
KAHUNAS
MAHARIS
MAHOUTS
MOHAIRS
MOHAWKS
OPHITES
REHANGS
REHEALS
REHEARS
REHEATS
REHEELS
REHIRES
REHOOKS
SCHEMAS
SCHEMES
SCHISMS
SCHLEPS
SCHMOES
SCHMOOS
SCHNAPS
SCHOOLS
SPHERES
TSHIRTS
UNHANDS
UNHOOKS
UPHOLDS
WAHINES

•••HS••

FUCHSIA

•••H•S•

COCHISE
DUCHESS
ENTHUSE
HIGHEST
INPHASE
LITHEST
LUSHEST
NIGHEST
PACHISI
POSHEST
RASHEST
RECHOSE
RICHEST
SIKHISM
SOPHISM
SOPHIST

•••H••S

AETHERS
AFGHANS
ANCHORS
ANTHEMS
ANTHERS
ARCHERS
ARCHONS
AUTHORS
BARHOPS
BATHERS
BAUHAUS
BETHELS
BISHOPS
BOOHOOS
BOTHERS
BRAHMAS
BUSHELS
CACHETS
CACHOUS
CARHOPS
CASHEWS
CEPHEUS
CIPHERS
CUSHAWS
CYPHERS
DAPHNIS
DASHERS
DITHERS
DUCHESS
DUCHIES
EIGHTHS
ESCHEWS
ETCHERS
EUCHRES
FATHERS
FATHOMS
FISHERS
GATHERS
GOPHERS
GOTHICS
GRAHAMS
GUSHERS
HAWHAWS
HEEHAWS
HOOHAHS
HYPHENS
ISOHELS
ISTHMUS
JOBHOPS
KISHKES
KOSHERS
KUCHENS
LASHERS
LASHUPS
LATHERS
LICHENS
MASHERS
MASHIES
MATHERS
MATHEWS
MATHIAS
MAYHEMS
MENHIRS
METHODS
MISHAPS
MISHITS
MITHRAS
MOSHERS
MOTHERS
MRCHIPS
MUDHENS
MUSHERS
MUZHIKS
NEPHEWS
NICHOLS
NOSHERS
NOSHOWS
ORCHIDS
ORPHANS
ORPHEUS
OUTHITS
PEAHENS
PERHAPS
POTHERS
PUSHUPS
PYTHIAS
PYTHONS
QUAHOGS
RASHERS
REDHATS
REDHOTS
RESHIPS
RESHOES
ROCHETS
RUSHEES
RUSHERS
SACHEMS
SACHETS
SASHAYS
SIGHERS
SIPHONS
SYPHONS
TECHIES
TETHERS
TINHATS
TITHERS
TOPHATS
TOWHEES
TVSHOWS
UPSHOTS
URCHINS
UTAHANS
WASHERS
WASHUPS
WETHERS
WISHERS
WITHERS
WITHIES
ZEPHYRS
ZITHERS

••••H•S

ABASHES
AITCHES
ALIGHTS
APACHES
BACCHUS
BATCHES
BEACHES
BEECHES
BELCHES
BENCHES
BIRCHES
BLIGHTS
BLUSHES
BOTCHES
BRUSHES
BUDDHAS
BUNCHES
CATCHES
CHACHAS
CINCHES
CLASHES
CLICHES
CLOCHES
CLOTHES
COACHES
CONCHES
COUCHES
CRASHES
CRECHES
CRUSHES
DITCHES
DRACHMS
FETCHES
FILCHES
FINCHES
FITCHES
FLASHES
FLECHES
FLESHES
FLIGHTS
FLUSHES
FRIGHTS
GAUCHOS
GEISHAS
GENGHIS
GNASHES
GOTCHAS
GULCHES
GURKHAS
HATCHES
HEIGHTS
HITCHES
HONCHOS
HUNCHES
HUTCHES
KETCHES
KNIGHTS
KNISHES
KWACHAS
LARCHES
LATCHES
LEACHES
LEASHES
LEECHES
LITCHIS
LOACHES
LOATHES
LUNCHES
LURCHES
MALTHUS
MARCHES
MARSHES
MATCHES
MEGOHMS
MEMPHIS
MOOCHES
MULCHES
MUNCHES
NAUGHTS
NAVAHOS
NOTCHES
NOUGHTS
PARCHES
PATCHES
PEACHES
PERCHES
PINCHAS
PINCHES
PITCHES
PLASHES
PLIGHTS
PLUSHES
POACHES
PONCHOS
POOCHES
PORCHES
PORTHOS
POUCHES
PSYCHES
PUNCHES
PYRRHUS
QUASHES
QUICHES
RANCHES
RANCHOS
REACHES
RHYTHMS
ROACHES
SCATHES
SCYTHES
SEETHES
SEICHES
SHUSHES
SKOSHES
SLASHES
SLIGHTS
SLOSHES
SLUSHES
SMASHES
SOOTHES
STASHES
STICHES
STJOHNS
SWATHES
SWISHES
SYNCHES
TEACHES
TEETHES
TORCHES
TOUCHES
TRASHES
TROCHES
VEIGHTS
VETCHES
VOUCHES
WATCHES
WEIGHTS
WELCHES
WENCHES
WHISHES
WINCHES
WITCHES
WRIGHTS
WRITHES
ZILCHES

•••••HS

AUROCHS
BREATHS
BYPATHS
CALIPHS
CERIPHS
DALETHS
DEARTHS
DOODAHS
EIGHTHS
EOLITHS
EPARCHS
EXARCHS
FELLAHS
FOURTHS
GROWTHS
GUELPHS
GULLAHS
HALVAHS
HEARTHS
HOOHAHS
HOOKAHS
HOWDAHS
HURRAHS
HUZZAHS
IOMOTHS
KAZAKHS
LAMEDHS
LENGTHS
LOOFAHS
MATZOHS
MOLOCHS
MULLAHS
NULLAHS
OOLITHS
OOMPAHS
PARAPHS
PARIAHS
PLINTHS
PLOUGHS
PUNKAHS
PURDAHS
RUPIAHS
SAMECHS
SERAPHS
SHEATHS
SHEIKHS
SLEIGHS
SLEUTHS
SLOUGHS
SMOOTHS
TEMPEHS
TERAPHS
TROUGHS
VOTECHS
WHYDAHS
WRAITHS
WREATHS
ZENITHS

H•T••••

HATBAND
HATCHED
HATCHER
HATCHES
HATCHET
HATEFUL
HATLESS
HATLIKE
HATPINS
HATRACK
HATTERS
HATTING
HETMANS
HITACHI
HITCHED
HITCHER
HITCHES
HITHERE
HITLESS
HITLIST
HITSOUT
HITTERS
HITTING
HITTITE
HOTBEDS
HOTCAKE
HOTCAPS
HOTCARS
HOTCOMB
HOTDOGS
HOTFOOT
HOTHEAD
HOTLINE
HOTLINK
HOTLIPS
HOTNESS
HOTPOTS
HOTRODS
HOTSEAT
HOTSHOT
HOTSPOT
HOTSPUR
HOTTEST
HOTTIPS
HOTTUBS
HOTWARS
HOTWIRE
HUTCHES
HUTLIKE

H••T•••

HAFTING
HAITIAN
HALTERS
HALTING
HARTMAN
HASTENS
HASTIER
HASTILY
HASTING
HATTERS
HATTING
HAUTBOY
HAUTEUR
HEATERS
HEATFUL
HEATHEN
HEATHER
HEATING
HEATSUP
HEATTER
HECTARE
HECTORS
HEFTIER
HEFTILY
HEFTING
HENTING
HEPTADS
HINTING
HINTSAT
HISTORY
HITTERS
HITTING
HITTITE
HOGTIED
HOGTIES
HOOTERS
HOOTING
HOOTOWL
HOOTSAT
HOPTOIT
HOSTAGE
HOSTELS
HOSTESS
HOSTILE
HOSTING
HOSTLER
HOTTEST
HOTTIPS
HOTTUBS
HUNTERS
HUNTING
HUNTLEY
HURTFUL
HURTING
HURTLED
HURTLES
HUSTLED
HUSTLER
HUSTLES

H•••T••

HABITAT
HABITED
HABITUE
HALITES
HALSTON
HAMITES
HAMITIC
HAMITUP
HAMPTON
HAMSTER
HANGTEN
HARDTOP
HAUNTED
HEALTHY
HEARTED
HEARTEN
HEARTHS
HEATTER
HEELTAP
HEISTED
HELOTRY
HEPATIC
HERBTEA
HERETIC
HIGHTEA
HIGHTOP
HILLTOP
HIPSTER
HOISTED
HOLSTER
HORATIO
HOUSTON

H••••T•

HACKETT
HAEMATO
HAMLETS
HAMMETT
HAUGHTY
HAVARTI
HEAVETO
HEIFETZ
HEIGHTS
HELMETS
HENBITS
HEPCATS
HERMITS
HEWLETT
HEXNUTS
HIRSUTE
HITTITE
HOBBITS
HOGARTH
HOGGETS
HOLDSTO
HOLISTS
HONESTY
HORNETS
HOTPOTS
HYDRATE

H•••••T

HABITAT
HACKETT
HAIRCUT
HAIRNET
HALFWIT
HALIBUT
HAMMETT
HANDOUT
HANDSET
HANGOUT
HARDEST
HARDHAT
HARDHIT
HARDPUT
HARDSET
HARICOT
HARPIST
HARRIET
HARVEST
HATCHET
HAVENOT
HAYLOFT
HAZIEST
HEADOUT
HEADSET
HEAROUT
HELDOUT
HELLCAT
HELPOUT
HEPPEST
HERBERT
HERRIOT
HEWLETT
HIDEOUT
HIGHEST
HIGHHAT
HINTSAT
HIPBOOT
HIPPEST
HITLIST
HITSOUT
HOKIEST
HOLDOUT
HOLEOUT
HOLIEST
HOMIEST
HOOFSIT
HOOTSAT
HOPTOIT
HORNIST
HOTFOOT
HOTSEAT
HOTSHOT
HOTSPOT
HOTTEST
HOWBEIT
HUNGOUT
HYDRANT

•HT••••

SHTICKS

•H•T•••

CHATEAU
CHATHAM
CHATSUP
CHATTED
CHATTEL
CHATTER
CHETRUM
CHITTER
CHUTNEY
GHETTOS
PHOTICS
PHOTOED
PHOTOGS
PHOTONS
PHOTOOP
RHETORS
RHYTHMS
SHATNER
SHATTER
SHOTFOR
SHOTGUN
SHOTOUT
SHOTPUT
SHUTEYE
SHUTINS
SHUTOFF
SHUTOUT
SHUTSIN
SHUTSUP
SHUTTER
SHUTTLE
THATCHY
THATSIT
THITHER
WHATFOR
WHATNOT
WHETHER
WHETTED
WHITENS
WHITEST
WHITHER
WHITIER
WHITING
WHITISH
WHITMAN
WHITNEY
WHITTLE

•H••T••

CHANTED
CHANTER
CHANTEY
CHAOTIC
CHAPTER
CHARTED
CHARTER
CHASTEN
CHASTER
CHATTED
CHATTEL
CHATTER
CHEATED
CHEATER
CHEATIN
CHEETAH
CHEETOS
CHESTER
CHEWTOY
CHINTZY
CHITTER
CHOCTAW
CHORTLE
CHUNTER
GHASTLY
GHETTOS
GHOSTED
GHOSTLY
PHAETON
PHANTOM
PHILTER
PHILTRE
SHAFTED
SHANTEY
SHASTRI
SHATTER
SHEATHE
SHEATHS
SHEETED
SHELTER
SHELTIE
SHELTON
SHIATSU
SHIFTED
SHIHTZU
SHIITES
SHOOTAT
SHOOTER
SHOOTUP
SHORTED
SHORTEN
SHORTER
SHORTLY
SHORTOF
SHOUTED
SHOUTER
SHUNTED
SHUTTER
SHUTTLE
SHYSTER
THEATER
THEATRE
THISTLE
THISTLY
WHARTON
WHEATON
WHETTED
WHISTLE
WHITTLE

•H•••T•

CHALETS
CHAPATI
CHARITY
CHIANTI
CHRISTI
CHRISTO
CHRISTY
SHRIFTS
THEISTS
THEPITS
THERETO
THIRSTS
THIRSTY
THREATS
THRIFTS
THRIFTY
THROATS
THROATY
THRUSTS
THWARTS
WHERETO

•H••••T

CHAPLET
CHARIOT
CHEMIST
CHEROOT
CHEVIOT
CHEWOUT
SHALLOT
SHERBET
SHIPOUT
SHOOTAT
SHOTOUT
SHOTPUT
SHOWOUT
SHUBERT
SHUTOUT
THATSIT
THEREAT
THICKET
THOUGHT
WHATNOT
WHEREAT
WHIPPET
WHITEST
XHEIGHT

••HT•••

ACHTUNG
ASHTRAY
YAHTZEE

••H•T••

ACHATES
MAHATMA
OKHOTSK
OPHITES
SCHATZI
UNHITCH

••H••T•

ASHANTI
ATHLETE
BEHESTS
CAHOOTS
COHORTS
COHOSTS
EXHORTS
INHASTE
MAHOUTS
NAHUATL
REHEATS
SCHULTZ
SUHARTO
TSHIRTS

••H•••T

ACHIEST
AMHERST
ASHIEST
ATHEART
ATHEIST
ATHIRST
ATHWART
BYHEART
COHABIT
EXHAUST
EXHIBIT
INHABIT
INHERIT
INHIBIT
SCHMIDT

•••HT••

BATHTUB
EIGHTAM
EIGHTHS
EIGHTPM
FIGHTER
HIGHTEA
HIGHTOP
LIGHTED
LIGHTEN
LIGHTER
LIGHTLY
LIGHTUP
MIGHTNT
NAPHTHA
NIGHTIE
NIGHTLY
OUGHTNT
RICHTER
RIGHTED
RIGHTER
RIGHTLY
RIGHTON
SHIHTZU
SIGHTED
SIGHTLY
TIGHTEN
TIGHTER
TIGHTLY
WASHTUB
YACHTED

•••H•T•

AKIHITO
CACHETS
EBWHITE
ESTHETE
JAPHETH
MACHETE
MISHITS
OUTHITS
REDHATS
REDHOTS
ROCHETS
SACHETS
TINHATS
TOPHATS
UPSHOTS
WICHITA

•••H••T

ASPHALT
BATHMAT
CASHOUT
DISHOUT
EARHART
ECKHART
ELKHART
ENCHANT
ESCHEAT
ETCHANT
FISHNET
FISHOUT
HIGHEST
HIGHHAT
INSHORT
JOBHUNT
LITHEST
LUSHEST
MANHUNT
MIGHTNT
MOSHPIT
NEWHART
NIGHEST
ONTHEQT
OUGHTNT
POSHEST
PREHEAT
RASHEST
REDHEAT
RESHOOT
RICHEST
SOPHIST
WASHOUT
WITHOUT
YOGHURT

••••HT•

ALIGHTS
BLIGHTS
BLIGHTY
DOUGHTY
FLIGHTS
FLIGHTY
FRIGHTS
HAUGHTY
HEIGHTS
KNIGHTS
NAUGHTS
NAUGHTY
NOUGHTS
PLIGHTS
SLIGHTS
VEIGHTS
WEIGHTS
WEIGHTY
WRIGHTS

••••H•T

BASEHIT
BIGSHOT
CROCHET
EARSHOT
EPITHET
EYESHOT
FRESHET
GUNSHOT
HARDHAT
HARDHIT
HATCHET
HIGHHAT
HOTSHOT
LAUGHAT
MEGAHIT
MUGSHOT
ONESHOT
POTSHOT
PROPHET
RAINHAT
RATCHET
RIMSHOT
ROUGHIT
SILKHAT
WATCHIT

•••••HT

ABOUGHT
ALRIGHT
BORSCHT
BROUGHT
DELIGHT
DRAUGHT
DROUGHT
FRAUGHT
FREIGHT
INSIGHT
MRRIGHT
ONSIGHT
RELIGHT
SLEIGHT
THOUGHT
TONIGHT
UPRIGHT
UPTIGHT
UTRECHT
WROUGHT
XHEIGHT

HU•••••

HUBBARD
HUBBELL
HUBBIES
HUBBUBS
HUBCAPS
HUDDLED
HUDDLES
HUELESS
HUFFIER
HUFFILY
HUFFING
HUFFISH
HUGGERS
HUGGING
HUGGINS
HULKING
HULLERS
HULLING
HULLOAS
HULLOED
HUMANLY
HUMANUM
HUMBLED
HUMBLER
HUMBLES
HUMBUGS
HUMDRUM
HUMERAL
HUMERUS
HUMIDLY
HUMIDOR
HUMMERS
HUMMING
HUMMOCK
HUMORED
HUMOURS
HUMPIER
HUMVEES
HUNCHED
HUNCHES
HUNDRED
HUNGARY
HUNGERS
HUNGOUT
HUNKERS
HUNKIER

HUNLIKE
HUNNISH
HUNTERS
HUNTING
HUNTLEY
HUNYADY
HURDLED
HURDLER
HURDLES
HURLERS
HURLEYS
HURLIES
HURLING
HURRAHS
HURRIED
HURRIES
HURRYUP
HURTFUL
HURTING
HURTLED
HURTLES
HUSBAND
HUSHABY
HUSHFUL
HUSHING
HUSKERS
HUSKIER
HUSKIES
HUSKILY
HUSKING
HUSSARS
HUSSEIN
HUSSIES
HUSTLED
HUSTLER
HUSTLES
HUTCHES
HUTLIKE
HUYGENS
HUZZAHS

H•U••••

HAUBERK
HAUGHTY
HAULAGE
HAULERS
HAULING
HAULOFF
HAULSUP
HAUNTED
HAUTBOY
HAUTEUR
HOUDINI
HOUGHED
HOUNDED
HOUSING
HOUSMAN
HOUSTON
HYUNDAI

H••U•••

HANUKAH
HHMUNRO

H•••U••

HAMBURG
HANGUPS
HARBURG
HEPBURN
HERCULE
HEXNUTS
HEYJUDE
HICCUPS
HIRSUTE
HOLDUPS
HOMBURG
HONOURS
HOOKUPS
HOTTUBS
HUBBUBS
HUMBUGS
HUMOURS

H••••U•

HABITUE
HAFNIUM
HAHNIUM
HAIRCUT
HALIBUT
HAMITUP
HANDFUL
HANDGUN
HANDOUT
HANDSUP
HANGOUT
HANGSUP
HARBOUR
HARDPUT
HARMFUL
HATEFUL
HAULSUP
HAUTEUR
HEADOUT
HEADSUP
HEAROUT
HEATFUL
HEATSUP
HEEDFUL
HEINOUS
HELDOUT
HELPFUL
HELPOUT
HIDEOUS
HIDEOUT
HIKEDUP
HIKESUP
HITSOUT
HOLDOUT
HOLDSUP
HOLEDUP
HOLEOUT
HOLESUP
HOLMIUM
HOMERUN
HOODLUM
HOOKSUP
HOPEFUL
HOTSPUR
HUMANUM
HUMDRUM
HUMERUS
HUNGOUT
HURRYUP
HURTFUL
HUSHFUL
HYDROUS
HYPEDUP
HYPESUP

H•••••U

HOFBRAU

•HU••••

CHUCKED
CHUCKLE
CHUGGED
CHUKKAS
CHUKKER
CHUMMED
CHUNNEL
CHUNTER
CHURNED
CHUTNEY
DHURRIE
RHUBARB
RHUMBAS
SHUBERT
SHUCKED
SHUCKER
SHUDDER
SHUFFLE
SHUNNED
SHUNTED
SHUSHED
SHUSHES
SHUTEYE
SHUTINS
SHUTOFF
SHUTOUT
SHUTSIN
SHUTSUP
SHUTTER
SHUTTLE
THUDDED
THULIUM
THUMBED
THUMPED
THUMPER
THUNDER
THURBER
THURMAN
THUSFAR
WHUPPED

•H•U•••

CHAUCER
HHMUNRO
SHOULDA
SHOUTED
SHOUTER
SHRUBBY
THEURGY
THOUGHT
THRUSTS
THRUWAY
WHAUDEN

•H••U••

CHEQUER
CHEQUES
CHERUBS
CHINUPS
SHOGUNS
SHROUDS
THROUGH

•H•••U•

CHALKUP
CHATSUP
CHECKUP
CHEERUP
CHETRUM
CHEWOUT
CHEWSUP
CHOKEUP
PHOEBUS
RHENIUM
RHODIUM
RHOMBUS
SHAKEUP
SHAPEUP
SHIPOUT
SHOOKUP
SHOOTUP
SHOPFUL
SHOTGUN
SHOTOUT
SHOTPUT
SHOWOUT
SHOWSUP
SHUTOUT
SHUTSUP
THEROUX
THESEUS
THINKUP
THORIUM
THULIUM
WHIPSUP

•H••••U

CHAPEAU
CHATEAU
SHIATSU
SHIHTZU
SHIKOKU
THIMPHU
THOREAU

••HU•••

INHUMAN
KAHUNAS
NAHUATL
SCHULTZ

••H•U••

ACHTUNG
ASHBURY
EXHAUST
INHAULS
INHOUSE
MAHOUTS

••H••U•

ECHINUS
HAHNIUM

•••HU••

ANAHUAC
ENTHUSE
JOBHUNT
LASHUPS
MANHUNT
PUSHUPS
SICHUAN
TERHUNE
WASHUPS
YOGHURT

•••H•U•

BASHFUL
BATHTUB
BAUHAUS
CACHOUS
CALHOUN
CASHOUT
CEPHEUS
DISHFUL
DISHOUT
FISHOUT
HUSHFUL
ISTHMUS
LIGHTUP
LITHIUM
MANHOUR
MILHAUD
OFFHOUR
ORPHEUS
PUSHFUL
RUTHFUL
SIGHFUL
WASHOUT
WASHTUB
WISHFUL
WITHOUT

•••H••U

SHIHTZU

••••HU•

BACCHUS
BEARHUG
BOTCHUP
BRUSHUP
BULGHUR
CATCHUP
COUGHUP
DONAHUE
FULGHUM
KETCHUP
MALTHUS
MATCHUP
MITCHUM
PATCHUP
PSYCHUP
PUNCHUP
PYRRHUS
QUECHUA
ROUGHUP
SMASHUP
SORGHUM
SULPHUR
TOUCHUP

••••H•U

MATTHAU

•••••HU

THIMPHU

H•V••••

HAVARTI
HAVENOT
HAVERED
HOVERED
HOVERER
HOVLANE

H••V•••

HALVAHS
HALVING
HARVARD
HARVEST
HEAVEHO
HEAVENS
HEAVERS
HEAVETO
HEAVIER
HEAVIES
HEAVILY
HEAVING
HOOVERS
HUMVEES

H•••V••

HANOVER
HESHVAN
HOPOVER
HOWEVER

H•••••V

HENRYIV

•H•V•••

CHEVIED
CHEVIES
CHEVIOT
CHEVRES
CHEVRON
SHAVERS
SHAVING
SHIVERS
SHIVERY
SHOVELS
SHOVERS
SHOVING
ZHIVAGO

•H••V••

CHEEVER
CHERVIL
SHEAVED
SHEAVES
SHELVED
SHELVES
SHRIVEL
SHRIVER
SHRIVES
THIEVED
THIEVES
THRIVED
THRIVES
WHARVES
WHOEVER

•H•••V•

WHEREVE

•H••••V

CHEKHOV

••H•V••

BEHAVED
BEHAVES
BEHOVED
BEHOVES
LEHAVRE

••H••V•

ACHIEVE
BEHOOVE
PAHLAVI

•••HV••

HESHVAN

•••H•V•

ANCHOVY
ARCHIVE
BEEHIVE
YESHIVA

••••H•V

CHEKHOV

H•W••••

HAWHAWS
HAWKERS
HAWKEYE
HAWKING
HAWKINS
HAWKISH
HAWSERS
HEWLETT
HGWELLS
HOWARDS
HOWBEIT
HOWCOME
HOWDAHS
HOWELLS
HOWEVER
HOWLERS
HOWLING

H••W•••

HAYWARD
HAYWIRE
HEYWOOD
HOGWASH
HOGWILD
HOTWARS
HOTWIRE

H•••W••

HALFWAY
HALFWIT
HALLWAY
HARDWON
HEADWAY
HIGHWAY
HOLYWAR

H••••W•

HALLOWS
HARROWS
HAWHAWS
HAYMOWS
HEBREWS
HEEHAWS
HOEDOWN
HOLLOWS
HOOTOWL

H•••••W

HACKSAW
HANDSAW
HIGHLOW
HOLYCOW

•HW••••

THWACKS
THWARTS

•H•W•••

CHEWERS
CHEWIER
CHEWING
CHEWOUT
CHEWSUP
CHEWTOY
CHOWDER
SHAWNEE
SHAWWAL
SHEWOLF
SHOWBIZ
SHOWDOG
SHOWERS
SHOWERY
SHOWIER
SHOWILY
SHOWING
SHOWMAN
SHOWMEN
SHOWNIN
SHOWOFF
SHOWOUT
SHOWSIN
SHOWSUP
THAWING
THEWIER

•H••W••

SHAWWAL
SHERWIN
THREWIN
THROWER
THROWIN
THRUWAY
WHOSWHO

•H•••W•

SHADOWS
SHADOWY

•H••••W

CHOCTAW
SHALLOW
THECROW
WHIPSAW

••HW•••

ATHWART
SCHWINN

••H•W••

MOHAWKS

•••HW••

ARCHWAY
HIGHWAY
PATHWAY

•••H•W•

CASHEWS
CUSHAWS
ESCHEWS
GOSHAWK
HAWHAWS
HEEHAWS
MATHEWS
NEPHEWS
NOSHOWS
TVSHOWS

•••H••W

CASHCOW
HIGHLOW
LITHGOW

••••H•W

AIRSHOW
CAPSHAW
CATSHOW
DOGCHOW
DOGSHOW
ICESHOW
KNOWHOW
MATTHEW
SALCHOW
SOMEHOW
TRISHAW
USOSHOW

H•X••••

HEXAGON
HEXNUTS
HEXSIGN

H••X•••

HOAXERS
HOAXING

H•••X••

HELIXES
HYRAXES

H•••••X

HALIFAX
HENDRIX

•H••X••

PHLOXES

•H••••X

PHALANX
PHARYNX
PHOENIX
SHOEBOX
THEROUX

•••H••X

CASHBOX

••••H•X

NARTHEX
PANCHAX

HY•••••

HYALINE
HYBRIDS
HYDRANT
HYDRATE
HYDROUS
HYGIEIA
HYGIENE
HYMNALS
HYMNODY
HYPEDUP
HYPESUP
HYPHENS
HYPOING
HYPONYM
HYRACES
HYRAXES
HYSSOPS
HYUNDAI

H•Y••••

HAYFORK
HAYLOFT
HAYMOWS
HAYRACK
HAYRIDE
HAYSEED
HAYWARD
HAYWIRE
HEYDAYS
HEYJUDE
HEYWOOD
HOYDENS
HUYGENS

H••Y•••

HALYARD
HOLYARK
HOLYCOW
HOLYDAY
HOLYOKE
HOLYSEE
HOLYWAR
HUNYADY

H•••Y••

HALCYON
HENRYIV
HONEYED
HURRYUP

H••••Y•

HAIRDYE
HAWKEYE
HEYDAYS
HOMONYM
HURLEYS
HYPONYM

H•••••Y

HACKNEY
HALFWAY
HALLWAY
HAMMILY
HANDILY
HAPENNY
HAPPILY
HARDILY
HARMONY
HARSHLY
HASTILY
HAUGHTY
HAUTBOY
HEADILY
HEADWAY
HEALTHY
HEARSAY
HEAVILY
HEFTILY
HELOTRY
HEMSLEY
HENNERY
HERSHEY
HICKORY
HIGHBOY
HIGHDAY
HIGHWAY
HILLARY
HISTORY
HOARILY
HOLIDAY
HOLYDAY
HOMEBOY
HONESTY
HORNSBY
HORRIFY
HOSIERY
HUFFILY
HUMANLY
HUMIDLY
HUNGARY
HUNTLEY
HUNYADY
HUSHABY
HUSKILY
HYMNODY

•HY••••

PHYLLIS
PHYSICS
RHYMERS
RHYMING
RHYTHMS
SHYLOCK
SHYNESS
SHYSTER
THYMINE
THYSELF
WHYDAHS

•H•Y•••

KHAYYAM
WHEYISH

•H••Y••

KHAYYAM
PHARYNX

•H•••Y•

PHONEYS
SHUTEYE

•H••••Y

CHANTEY
CHARILY
CHARITY
CHARLEY
CHEAPLY
CHEWTOY
CHICORY
CHIEFLY
CHIMNEY
CHINTZY
CHOMSKY
CHRISTY
CHUTNEY
GHASTLY
GHOSTLY
PHONILY
SHADILY
SHADOWY
SHAKILY
SHANTEY
SHAPELY
SHAPLEY
SHARKEY
SHARPLY
SHEERLY
SHELLEY
SHINILY
SHIRLEY
SHIVERY
SHOOFLY
SHORTLY
SHOWERY
SHOWILY
SHRILLY
SHRUBBY
THATCHY
THERAPY
THEREBY
THEURGY
THICKLY
THIRDLY
THIRSTY
THISTLY
THREADY
THRIFTY
THROATY
THRUWAY
WHEREBY
WHISKEY
WHITNEY

••H•••Y

ASHBURY
ASHTRAY
DAHOMEY
JOHNGAY
JOHNJAY
MAHONEY
MCHENRY
UNHANDY
UNHAPPY
WCHANDY

•••HY••

ZEPHYRS

•••H•Y•

FISHEYE
KATHRYN
SASHAYS

•••H••Y

ALCHEMY
ANCHOVY
ANTHONY
ARCHERY
ARCHWAY
BETHANY
BUSHILY
BYTHEBY
DITHERY
EUPHONY
FISHERY
FISHFRY
FISHILY
GUSHILY
HIGHBOY
HIGHDAY
HIGHWAY
HUSHABY
LATHERY
LIGHTLY
LITHELY
MUSHILY
NIGHTLY
ORPHREY
PATHWAY
PITHILY
PUSHILY
RIGHTLY
SIGHTLY
TIGHTLY
ZACHARY

••••H•Y

APISHLY
BLIGHTY
BOKCHOY
BRASHLY
DOUGHTY
DROSHKY
EARTHLY
FIFTHLY
FLESHLY
FLIGHTY
FRESHLY
HARSHLY
HAUGHTY
HERSHEY
MADEHAY
MAKEHAY
MONTHLY
NAUGHTY
NINTHLY
PLUSHLY
ROUGHLY
SIXTHLY
SOUTHEY
TENTHLY
TOUGHLY
WEIGHTY

•••••HY

ANARCHY
ATROPHY
BLOTCHY
BREATHY
COCKSHY
CRUNCHY
DENNEHY
DOROTHY
EMPATHY
EPARCHY
GROUCHY
HEALTHY
KITSCHY
LENGTHY
PAUNCHY
PREACHY
SKETCHY
SLOUCHY
SMOOTHY
SNITCHY
SPLASHY
SQUISHY
STARCHY
SWARTHY
THATCHY
TIMOTHY
TWITCHY
WEALTHY

H•Z••••

HAZARDS
HAZIEST
HAZINGS
HUZZAHS

H••Z•••

HUZZAHS

H•••Z••

HORIZON

H•••••Z

HEIFETZ

•H•Z•••

RHIZOME
WHIZKID
WHIZZED
WHIZZER
WHIZZES

•H••Z••

WHEEZED
WHEEZER
WHEEZES
WHIZZED
WHIZZER
WHIZZES

•H•••Z•

CHINTZY
CHORIZO
SHIHTZU

•H••••Z

SHOWBIZ
THEFONZ

••H•Z••

YAHTZEE

••H••Z•

SCHATZI
SCHERZI
SCHERZO

••H•••Z

SCHULTZ

•••H•Z•

SHIHTZU

••••H•Z

GEEWHIZ
NATCHEZ

IA•••••

IACOCCA

I•A••••

IDAHOAN
IMAGERS
IMAGERY
IMAGINE
IMAGING
IMAGOES
IMAMATE
IMARETS
INADAZE
INAHEAP
INAMESS
INANELY
INANEST
INANITY
INAPTER
INAPTLY
INARUSH
INASNIT
INASPIN
INASPOT
INASTEW
INAWEOF
INAWORD
IPANEMA
IRANIAN
IRATELY
IRATEST
ISADORA
ITALIAN
ITALICS
IVANHOE
IVANOVO

I••A•••

ICEAGES
ICEAXES
ICHABOD
IDCARDS
IDEALLY
IDEAMAN
IDEAMEN
IDEATED
IDEATES
IDIAMIN
IGUANAS
IMPACTS
IMPAIRS
IMPALAS
IMPALED
IMPALES
IMPANEL
IMPARTS
IMPASSE
IMPASTO
INCANTS
INCASED
INCASES
INFANCY
INFANTA
INFANTS
INFAVOR
INGALLS
INHABIT
INHALED
INHALER
INHALES

INHASTE
INHAULS
INMATES
INNARDS
INTAKES
INVACUO
INVADED
INVADER
INVADES
INVALID
INWARDS
IODATES
ISLAMIC
ISLANDS
ISRAELI
ITHACAN
IZZARDS

I • • • A • •

IBNSAUD
ICEBAGS
ICECAPS
ICELAND
ICEPACK
IKEBANA
ILOCANO
IMAMATE
IMITATE
IMPEACH
IMPLANT
INADAZE
INBOARD
INDIANA
INDIANS
INEXACT
INFLAME
INFLATE
INGRAIN
INGRATE
INPEACE
INPHASE
INPLACE
INROADS
INSCAPE
INSEAMS
INSHAPE
INSPANS
INSTALL
INSTALS
INSTANT
INSTARS
INSTATE
INTEARS
IRELAND
IRONAGE
ISHMAEL
ISOBARS
ISOLATE
ITERANT
ITERATE

I • • • • A •

IBERIAN
ICEBOAT
IDAHOAN
IDEAMAN
IGUANAS
ILLEGAL
IMMORAL
IMPALAS
INAHEAP
INGEMAR
INHUMAN
INITIAL
INKYCAP
INNOWAY
INSOFAR
INSTEAD
INSULAR
IRANIAN
IRONMAN
ITALIAN
ITHACAN

I • • • • • A

IACOCCA
ICEDTEA
IKEBANA
INDIANA
INDICIA
INERTIA
INFANTA
INOCULA
INTEGRA
IPANEMA
ISADORA
IWOJIMA

• I A • • • •

BIALIES
BIASING
BIASSED
DIABOLI
DIADEMS
DIAGRAM
DIALECT
DIALERS
DIALING
DIALOGS
DIAMOND
DIAPERS
DIARIES
DIATOMS
FIACRES
FIANCEE
FIANCES
FIASCOS
FIATLUX
GIACOMO
HIALEAH
LIAISED
LIAISES
LIAISON
MIAMIAN
MIAMIAS
MIAOYAO
MIASMAS
MIASMIC
NIAGARA
PIANISM
PIANIST
PIASTER
PIASTRE
PIAZZAS
RIANTLY
SIAMESE
TIANJIN
VIADUCT

• I • A • • •

BIVALVE
BIZARRE
CICADAE
CICADAS
CITABLE
CITADEL
DIDACTS
DILATED
DILATES
DISABLE
DISARMS
DISAVOW
FINAGLE
FINALES
FINALLY
FINANCE
FIXABLE
FIXATED
FIXATES
GIRAFFE
GIRASOL
HIBACHI
HIDALGO
HIJACKS
HILAIRE
HIRABLE
HITACHI
JICAMAS
KILAUEA
KIWANIS
LIEABED
LIGANDS
LIGATED
LIGATES
LIKABLE
LINAGES
LIVABLE
LIZARDS
MIKADOS
MINABLE
MINARET
MIRACLE
MIRADOR
MIRAGES
MIRAMAR
MIRAMAX
MIRANDA
MISALLY
MIXABLE
PICADOR
PICANTE
PICARDY
PICAROS
PICASSO
PINATAS
PIRAEUS
PIRANHA
PIRATED
PIRATES
PIRATIC
PITAPAT
PIZARRO
RIBANDS
RICARDO
RIVALED
RIVALRY
SINATRA
SIZABLE
SIZABLY
TIRADES
TISANES
TITANIA
TITANIC
VIDALIA
VIRAGOS
VISAGES
VISAING
VISALIA
VISAVIS
VITALLY
VITAMIN
VIVALDI
WIZARDS

• I • • A • •

AIRBAGS
AIRBALL
AIRBASE
AIRDAMS
AIRDATE
AIRFARE
AIRLANE
AIRMADA
AIRMAIL
AIRMASS
AIRRAID
AIRSACS
AIRTAXI
AIRWAVE
AIRWAYS
BIDFAIR
BIGBAND
BIGBANG
BIGGAME
BIGNAME
BIGTALK
BIOMASS
BIPLANE
BITMAPS
BITPART
CILIATE
CINZANO
CITRATE
DICTATE
DIEHARD
DIETARY
DIGRAMS
DIGRAPH
DIKTATS
DILLARD
DIORAMA
DISBAND
DISBARS
DISCARD
DISDAIN
DISEASE
DISMAYS
DISTAFF
DISTANT
DITTANY
FIJIANS
FINEART
FINIALS
FINLAND
FIREANT
FIREARM
GIMBALS
GIZZARD
HILLARY
HISPANO
JIGSAWS
JIMJAMS
KIDNAPS
KILDARE
KIMBALL
KIRMANS
KITBAGS
LIBRARY
LIBYANS
LIMEADE
LINEAGE
LINEATE
LINKAGE
LIPBALM
MICHAEL
MICMACS
MIDDAYS
MIDEAST
MIDLAND
MIDWAYS
MIGRANT
MIGRATE
MIKHAIL
MILEAGE
MILHAUD
MILLAND
MILLARD
MINOANS
MINYANS
MISCALL
MISCAST
MISDATE
MISHAPS
MISLAID
MISLAYS
MISMATE
MISNAME
MISSAID
MISSALS
MISSAYS
MISTAKE
NIAGARA
NIGGARD
NIRVANA
NITRATE
NITTANY
OILCAKE
OILCANS
OILLAMP
OILPANS
PICCARD
PICKAXE
PIEBALD
PIEPANS
PIGTAIL
PILLAGE
PILLARS
PINBALL
PINNACE
PINNATE
PINOAKS
PINTAIL
PINWALE
PIQUANT
PITFALL
PITSAWS
PIZZAZZ
QINTARS
RIBCAGE
RICHARD
RIMBAUD
RIOTACT
RIPRAPS
RIPSAWS
RITUALS
SIDEARM
SIGNALS
SIMIANS
SINKAGE
SIOUANS
SITUATE
SIXPACK
TICTACS
TIERACK
TIETACK
TIFFANY
TIJUANA
TILLAGE
TIMBALE
TIMBALS
TINCANS
TINEARS
TINHATS
TINTACK
TINWARE
TITRATE
VIBRANT
VIBRATE
VIBRATO
VILLAGE
VILLAIN
VINTAGE
VIOLATE
VISUALS
VITIATE
WIDMARK
WIGWAGS
WIGWAMS
WILLARD
ZIGZAGS

• I • • • A •

AIMEDAT
AIRBOAT
AIRHEAD
AIRPLAY
BIFOCAL
BIGDEAL
BIGHEAD
BIKEWAY
BIMODAL
BINGHAM
BIPEDAL
BIPOLAR
BIRDMAN
BIVOUAC
CICADAE
CICADAS
CINEMAS
CINEMAX
DIAGRAM
DIGITAL
DINGBAT
DIPOLAR
DISHPAN
DISHRAG
DISPLAY
DIURNAL
EIGHTAM
FIBULAE
FIBULAS
FIESTAS
FIGLEAF
FIREMAN
GIDDYAP
GILBLAS
GILLIAN
GINGHAM
GIVEWAY
HIALEAH
HICKMAN
HIGHDAY
HIGHHAT
HIGHWAY
HINTSAT
JICAMAS
JILLIAN
KINEMAS
KINGMAN
KINGRAT
KINSMAN
LIBERAL
LIKEMAD
LILLIAN
LILYPAD
LINBIAO
LINDSAY
LINEMAN
LINGUAL
LINPIAO
LIPREAD
LITERAL
LIVEOAK
MIAMIAN
MIAMIAS
MIAOYAO
MIASMAS
MIDYEAR
MILKMAN
MILLDAM
MIMOSAS
MINERAL
MINICAB
MINICAM
MINIMAL
MINIVAN
MIRAMAR
MIRAMAX
MISDEAL
MISDIAL
MISHEAR
MISLEAD
MISPLAY
MISREAD
MISTRAL
MITHRAS
MITZVAH
NICOLAS
NIKOLAI
PIAZZAS
PICKSAT
PIKEMAN
PINATAS
PINCHAS
PINESAP
PINETAR
PINHEAD
PITAPAT
PITTMAN
PIVOTAL
QINGDAO
RICERAT
RICHMAN
RICKMAN
RIDGWAY
SICHUAN
SICKBAY
SICKDAY
SICKPAY
SIDEBAR
SIDECAR
SIDEMAN
SIENNAS
SIERRAS
SIESTAS
SILICAS
SILKHAT
SIMILAR
SIOBHAN
TIBETAN
TIMELAG
TINSTAR
TITULAR
VICTUAL
VICUNAS
VIETNAM
VINEGAR
VIRGOAN
VIRTUAL
VIZSLAS
WILDCAT
WILLIAM
WINDBAG
WINEBAR
WINESAP
WINKSAT
WIRETAP
WISEMAN
YITZHAK
ZINNIAS

• I • • • • A

AIRMADA
BIRETTA
CIBORIA
DILEMMA
DIORAMA
DIPLOMA
GINGIVA
HIGHTEA
KILAUEA
LIBERIA
MILITIA
MINERVA
MINOLTA
MINORCA
MINUTIA
MIRANDA
NIAGARA
NICOSIA
NIGERIA
NIRVANA
PIPEMMA
PIRANHA
RICKSHA
RICOTTA
RIGVEDA
RIORITA
RIVIERA
SIBERIA
SILESIA
SINATRA
TIJUANA
TITANIA
VIDALIA
VISALIA
VISCERA
VISTULA
WICHITA

• • I A • • •

ALIASES
AMIABLE
AMIABLY
ARIADNE
ASIATIC
AVIANCA
AVIATED
AVIATES
AVIATOR
AXIALLY
BOIARDO
BRIARDS
CHIANTI
FRIABLE
IDIAMIN
JAIALAI
NAIADES
OPIATES
PLIABLE
PLIABLY
PLIANCY
SHIATSU

• • I • A • •

ABIGAIL
AGITATE
AGITATO
ALIBABA
ALIDADE
ANIMALS
ANIMATE
ANIMATO
ARIKARA
BOITANO
BRIDALS
BRIGADE
BRIGAND
BRITAIN
CAIMANS
CHICAGO
CHICANA
CHICANO
CLIMATE
CLIPART
COINAGE
CUIRASS
EMIRATE
FRIDAYS
FRIGATE
GRIMACE
GUITARS
IMITATE
MAITAIS
OHIOANS
OKINAWA
ORIGAMI
OVIPARA
OVISACS
OXIDANT
OXIDASE
PAISANO
PRIMACY
PRIMARY
PRIMATE
PRIVACY
PRIVATE
QUINARY
SHIKARI
SKIMASK
SKIRACK
SPINACH
SPIRALS
SPIRANT
TAIPANS
THINAIR
UNITARY
ZHIVAGO

• • I • • A •

AMISTAD
ARISTAE
ARISTAS
AXILLAE
BLINKAT
BRIGHAM
CHILEAN
CRIMEAN
DRIPPAN
DRISTAN
DRIVEAT
ENIGMAS
EPIGRAM
FAIRWAY
FLIESAT
FRIEDAN
FRISIAN
GAINSAY
GEISHAS
GOINGAT
GRISHAM
GUINEAS
HAITIAN
HEISMAN
INITIAL
JAIALAI
MAILBAG
MAILCAR
OJIBWAS
OJIBWAY
PHIDIAS
PHINEAS
QUINOAS
RAILSAT
RAILWAY
RAINHAT
RAINMAN
REITMAN
SHIPMAN
SKIWEAR
SNIFFAT
SNIPEAT
SPIREAS
STIGMAS
TRIGRAM
TRISHAW
TRISTAN
TRISTAR
TRIVIAL
WHIPSAW
WHITMAN
ZAIREAN
ZAIRIAN

• • I • • • A

ABINTRA
ALIBABA
ARIETTA
ARIKARA
ARIZONA
AVIANCA
CHICANA
CHIMERA
ERITREA
KRISHNA
OKINAWA
OVIPARA
SCIORRA
SPINOZA

• • • I A • •

AERIALS
ANTIART
CAVIARS
CILIATE
DEFIANT
DENIALS
DEVIANT
DEVIATE
ESPIALS
EXPIATE
FACIALS
FENIANS
FIJIANS
FINIALS
FOLIAGE
FOLIATE
GAVIALS
GOLIATH
HONIARA
INDIANA
INDIANS
JULIANA
KODIAKS
LABIALS
LABIATE
LARIATS
LUCIANO
MANIACS
MARIANA
MEDIANS
MEDIANT
MEDIATE
MENIALS
MYRIADS
NUBIANS
OBVIATE
PARIAHS
PONIARD
RADIALS
RADIANS
RADIANT
RADIATE
REDIALS
RELIANT
RETIARY
RUPIAHS
SATIATE
SERIALS
SERIATE
SIMIANS
SOCIALS
STRIATE
SYRIANS
TATIANA
TOPIARY
UNCIALS
VALIANT
VARIANT
VITIATE
ZODIACS

• • • I • A •

ADMIRAL
AFRICAN
ANTITAX
ANTIWAR
AQUINAS
ARNICAS
ARRIVAL
ARTISAN
BALIHAI
BKLIBAN
BOLIVAR
CALIBAN
CAPITAL
CAPITAN
CARINAS
COMICAL
CONICAL
CYNICAL
DECIMAL
DELILAH
DIGITAL
ENCINAS
ESTIVAL
ETHICAL
FADIMAN
FAJITAS
HABITAT
HALIFAX
HEGIRAS
HELICAL
HELIPAD
HOLIDAY
LAMINAE
LAMINAL
LAMINAR
LAMINAS
LATIFAH
LATINAS
LEXICAL
LOGICAL
LORICAE
LYRICAL
MADIGAN
MAGICAL
MARINAS
MARITAL
MAXIMAL
MEDICAL
MEDIGAP
MEXICAN
MINICAB
MINICAM
MINIMAL
MINIVAN
MOHICAN
MUSICAL
NOMINAL
OEDIPAL
ONEIDAS
OPTICAL
OPTIMAL
ORBITAL
ORDINAL
OVOIDAL
PATINAS
PEDICAB
PELICAN
PEMICAN
PURITAN
RADICAL
RARITAN
RECITAL
RETINAE
RETINAL
RETINAS
REVIVAL
RUFIYAA
SAGINAW
SALINAS
SEMINAL
SEMINAR
SHEILAS
SILICAS
SIMILAR
STOICAL
SURINAM
TAXICAB
TAXIMAN
TAXIWAY
TOPICAL
TROIKAS
TYPICAL
ULTIMAS
VATICAN
VERITAS
YAKIMAS

• • • I • • A

AGRIPPA
ANTIGUA
BATISTA
BELINDA
BOLIVIA
CARIOCA
CECILIA
CEDILLA
DELIRIA
ECHIDNA
FELICIA
GORILLA
HONIARA
HYGIEIA
INDIANA
INDICIA
JULIANA
LAVINIA
LETITIA
MARIANA
MARIMBA
MATILDA
MAXILLA
MELINDA
MELISSA
MILITIA
NAMIBIA
NORIEGA
PAPILLA
RIVIERA
RUFIYAA
SCHIRRA
SOYINKA
SYRINGA
TABITHA
TAPIOCA
TATIANA
TUNISIA
VANILLA

• • • • I A •

ACACIAS
ACADIAN
AEOLIAN
ANANIAS
ARABIAN
ASOCIAL
BELGIAN
BESTIAL
CARDIAC
CASPIAN
CASSIAS
COAXIAL
CORDIAL
CRANIAL
CRUCIAL
DAHLIAS
ELEGIAC
ELYSIAN
ETESIAN
ETONIAN
FASCIAS
FLUVIAL
FRISIAN
FUSTIAN
GAMBIAN
GENTIAN
GHANIAN
GILLIAN
GLACIAL
GLORIAM
GLORIAS
GORDIAN
GRACIAS
GRATIAS
GRECIAN
HADRIAN
HAITIAN
HESSIAN
IBERIAN
INITIAL
IRANIAN
ITALIAN
JILLIAN
LAOTIAN
LATVIAN
LILLIAN
LINBIAO
LINPIAO
LOGGIAS
MARTIAL
MARTIAN
MATHIAS
MESSIAH
MIAMIAN
MIAMIAS
MISDIAL
NUPTIAL
NUTRIAS
OBADIAH
ONTRIAL
OXONIAN
PARTIAL
PATRIAL
PERSIAN
PHIDIAS
PHOBIAS
PLUVIAL
PONTIAC
PYTHIAN
PYTHIAS
RETRIAL
RUFFIAN
RUSSIAN
SALVIAS
SAURIAN
SERBIAN
SPATIAL
SPECIAL
STYGIAN
STYRIAN
SUNDIAL
TERTIAL
TRIVIAL
TRUCIAL
UMBRIAN
UTOPIAN
UTOPIAS
UXORIAL
WILLIAM
WOZNIAK
ZAIRIAN
ZAMBIAN
ZINNIAS
ZOYSIAS

• • • • I • A

AMERICA
AMERIKA
BOBVILA
BURKINA
CANDIDA
CANTINA
CONDITA
CORRIDA
CORSICA
CZARINA
EMERITA
EROTICA
EXOTICA
FESTIVA
FLORIDA
FONTINA
FORMICA
GINGIVA

IWOJIMA
JAMAICA
JESSICA
KACHINA
LEMPIRA
MACHINA
MADEIRA
MARTINA
MESSINA
MESTIZA
OCARINA
PAPRIKA
PARTITA
PASTINA
PAULINA
PODRIDA
REPLICA
RETSINA
RIORITA
SABRINA
SESTINA
STAMINA
TEQUILA
TOSHIBA
TSARINA
TZARINA
VAMPIRA
WICHITA
YESHIVA

•••••IA

ALBANIA
ALGERIA
ALLUVIA
ALSATIA
AMMONIA
AMNESIA
ANAEMIA
ANOSMIA
ANTONIA
APHELIA
AQUARIA
ARCADIA
ARMENIA
ASSYRIA
ASTORIA
AUSTRIA
BAVARIA
BEDELIA
BEGONIA
BOHEMIA
BOLIVIA
BOOTHIA
BOTHNIA
CAMELIA
CARAMIA
CECILIA
CIBORIA
CLAUDIA
CROATIA
CYNTHIA
DELIRIA
EMPORIA
ENCOMIA
ESTONIA
ETRURIA
EURASIA
EXURBIA
FELICIA
FREESIA
FUCHSIA
GALATIA
GANGLIA
GEORGIA
HYGIEIA
INDICIA
INERTIA
LAVINIA
LETITIA
LIBERIA
MAHALIA
MILITIA
MINUTIA
MORAVIA
NAMIBIA
NATALIA
NICOSIA
NIGERIA
OCEANIA
OCTAVIA
OLYMPIA
OPHELIA
PETUNIA
POMPEIA
PRUSSIA
RATAFIA
REGALIA
ROMANIA
SAMARIA
SANGRIA
SEDALIA
SEGOVIA
SEQUOIA
SIBERIA
SILESIA
SOLARIA
SOMALIA
STLUCIA
TALARIA
TITANIA
TUNISIA
VIDALIA
VISALIA
ZENOBIA

IB•••••

IBERIAN
IBNSAUD

I•B••••

IMBIBED
IMBIBES
IMBRUED
IMBRUES
IMBUING
INBLOOM
INBOARD
INBOUND
INBOXES
INBREED
INBRIEF

I••B•••

ICEBAGS
ICEBEER
ICEBERG
ICEBLUE
ICEBOAT
IKEBANA
ILLBRED
INKBLOT
ISOBARS

I•••B••

ICHABOD
IGNOBLE
IGNOBLY
IMBIBED
IMBIBES
INHABIT
INHIBIT
INORBIT

I••••B•

ICECUBE
INDOUBT

•IB••••

BIBELOT
BIBLESS
BIBLIKE
CIBORIA
DIBBLED
DIBBLES
FIBBERS
FIBBING
FIBRILS
FIBRINS
FIBROUS
FIBULAE
FIBULAS
GIBBERS
GIBBETS
GIBBING
GIBBONS
GIBBOUS
GIBLETS
GIBLUES
HIBACHI
JIBBING
JIBBOOM
KIBBLED
KIBBLES
KIBBUTZ
LIBBERS
LIBBING
LIBELED
LIBELER
LIBERAL
LIBERIA
LIBERTY
LIBIDOS
LIBRARY
LIBYANS
NIBBLED
NIBBLER
NIBBLES
NIBLICK
NIBLIKE
RIBANDS
RIBBIES
RIBBING
RIBBONS
RIBCAGE
RIBEYES
RIBLESS
RIBLIKE
SIBERIA
SIBLING
TIBETAN
VIBRANT
VIBRATE
VIBRATO

•I•B•••

AIRBAGS
AIRBALL
AIRBASE
AIRBOAT
BIGBAND
BIGBANG
BIGBEND
BIGBIRD
BIGBOYS
BILBIES
BILBOES
DIABOLI
DIBBLED
DIBBLES
DILBERT
DIMBULB
DISBAND
DISBARS
FIBBERS
FIBBING
FILBERT
GIBBERS
GIBBETS
GIBBING
GIBBONS
GIBBOUS
GILBERT
GILBLAS
GIMBALS
HIPBONE
HIPBOOT
JIBBING
JIBBOOM
KIBBLED
KIBBLES
KIBBUTZ
KIMBALL
KITBAGS
LIBBERS
LIBBING
LIMBERS
LIMBING
LINBIAO
LIPBALM
NIBBLED
NIBBLER
NIBBLES
NIEBUHR
NIMBLER
NIOBIUM
PIEBALD
PINBALL
PITBOSS
PITBULL
RIBBIES
RIBBING
RIBBONS
RIMBAUD
SIOBHAN
TIDBITS
TIMBALE
TIMBALS
TIMBERS
TIMBRES
TITBITS
WIMBLED
WIMBLES

•I••B••

CITABLE
DINGBAT
DISABLE
DISOBEY
FIREBOX
FIREBUG
FIXABLE
HIGHBOY
HIRABLE
LIEABED
LIKABLE
LIVABLE
MINABLE
MINIBUS
MIXABLE
PILLBOX
PILLBUG
RISIBLE
RISIBLY
SICKBAY
SIDEBAR
SIDEBET
SIZABLE
SIZABLY
VIRIBUS
VISIBLE
VISIBLY
WINDBAG
WINEBAR

•I•••B•

DISROBE
MICROBE
MIDRIBS
RIOLOBO

•I••••B

DIMBULB
DISTURB
LIONCUB
MINICAB

••IB•••

ALIBABA
AMIBLUE
BRIBERY
BRIBING
CLIBURN
CRIBBED
CUIBONO
DRIBBLE
DRIBLET
EDIBLES
FOIBLES
GLIBBER
LEIBNIZ
OJIBWAS
OJIBWAY
QUIBBLE
SKIBOBS
SKIBOOT
TRIBUNE
TRIBUTE

••I•B••

AMIABLE
AMIABLY
CLIMBED
CLIMBER
CRIBBED
DRIBBLE
FRIABLE
FRISBEE
GLIBBER
MAILBAG
MAILBOX
PHILBIN
PLIABLE
PLIABLY
QUIBBLE
RAINBOW
THIMBLE
TWINBED

••I••B•

ABIDEBY
ABITIBI
ALIBABA
GOINGBY
NAIROBI
SKIBOBS
SWINGBY

•••IB••

ADDIBLE
ANTIBES
AUDIBLE
AUDIBLY
BKLIBAN
CALIBAN
CALIBER
CALIBRE
CARIBES
CARIBOU
DECIBEL
DELIBES
EXHIBIT
HALIBUT
IMBIBED
IMBIBES
INHIBIT
LEGIBLE
LEGIBLY
MINIBUS
NAMIBIA
OMNIBUS
RISIBLE
RISIBLY
SANIBEL
SCRIBES
VIRIBUS
VISIBLE
VISIBLY

•••I•B•

LETITBE
MARIMBA

•••I••B

MINICAB
PEDICAB
TAXICAB

••••IB•

ABITIBI
ARECIBO
ASCRIBE
MADLIBS
MIDRIBS
TOSHIBA

IC•••••

ICEAGES
ICEAXES
ICEBAGS
ICEBEER
ICEBERG
ICEBLUE
ICEBOAT
ICECAPS
ICECOLD
ICECUBE
ICEDOUT
ICEDTEA
ICEFLOE
ICEFOGS
ICEFREE
ICELAND
ICELESS
ICELIKE
ICEMILK
ICEPACK
ICEPICK
ICERINK
ICESHOW
ICESOUT
ICHABOD
ICICLES
ICINESS
ICINGIN
ICINGUP
ICKIEST

I•C••••

IACOCCA
IDCARDS
INCANTS
INCASED
INCASES
INCENSE
INCEPTS
INCHING
INCIPIT
INCISED
INCISES
INCISOR
INCITED
INCITER
INCITES
INCIVIL
INCLINE
INCLOSE
INCLUDE
INCOMES
INCUDES
IPCRESS
ITCHIER
ITCHING

I••C•••

ICECAPS
ICECOLD
ICECUBE
ICICLES
ILOCANO
INOCULA
INSCAPE
IRECKON

I•••C••

IACOCCA
ILLICIT
IMPACTS
INDICES
INDICIA
INDICTS
INDUCED
INDUCER
INDUCES
INDUCTS
INFECTS
INFOCUS
INJECTS
INKYCAP
INSECTS
INVACUO
ITHACAN

I••••C•

IACOCCA
ICEPACK
ICEPICK
ILIESCU
IMPEACH
INDUTCH
INEXACT
INFANCY
INFLECT
INFLICT
INFORCE
INPEACE
INPLACE
INSPECT
INSTOCK
INVOICE
IONESCO
IPSWICH
ITALICS

I•••••C

IDENTIC
IDIOTIC
IDYLLIC
ILLOGIC
ISLAMIC

•IC••••

BICKERS
BICOLOR
BICYCLE
CICADAE
CICADAS
DICIEST
DICKENS
DICKERS
DICKEYS
DICKIES
DICTATE
DICTION
DICTUMS
FICKLER
FICTION
FICTIVE
FICUSES
HICCUPS
HICKMAN
HICKORY
JICAMAS
KICKERS
KICKIER
KICKING
KICKOFF
KICKOUT
KICKSIN
KICKSUP
KICKUPS
LICENCE
LICENSE
LICHENS
LICITLY
LICKING
LICTORS
MICHAEL
MICHELE
MICKEYS
MICMACS
MICROBE
MICRONS
NICCOLO
NICHOLS
NICKELS
NICKERS
NICKING
NICOLAS
NICOSIA
PICADOR
PICANTE
PICARDY
PICAROS
PICASSO
PICCARD
PICCOLO
PICKAXE
PICKENS
PICKERS
PICKETS
PICKETT
PICKIER
PICKING
PICKLED
PICKLES
PICKOFF
PICKOUT
PICKSAT
PICKSON
PICKSUP
PICKUPS
PICNICS
PICTISH
PICTURE
RICARDO
RICERAT
RICHARD
RICHEST
RICHMAN
RICHTER
RICKETY
RICKEYS
RICKLES
RICKMAN
RICKSHA
RICOTTA
SICCING
SICHUAN
SICKBAY
SICKDAY
SICKENS
SICKEST
SICKISH
SICKLES
SICKOUT
SICKPAY
TICKERS
TICKETS
TICKETY
TICKING
TICKLED
TICKLER
TICKLES
TICKOFF
TICTACS
VICEROY
VICIOUS
VICTIMS
VICTORS
VICTORY
VICTUAL
VICUNAS
WICHITA
WICKERS
WICKETS
WICKIUP

•I•C•••

AIRCOOL
AIRCREW
AITCHES
BIOCHIP
BIRCHED
BIRCHES
BISCUIT
CINCHED
CINCHES
CIRCLED
CIRCLES
CIRCLET
CIRCUIT
CIRCUSY
DIOCESE
DISCARD
DISCERN
DISCOED
DISCORD
DISCUSS
DITCHED
DITCHES
FIACRES
FILCHED
FILCHER
FILCHES
FINCHES
FISCHER
FITCHES
GIACOMO
HICCUPS
HITCHED
HITCHER
HITCHES
JIMCHEE
KIMCHEE
KINCHIN
KITCHEN
LINCOLN
LITCHIS
LITCRIT
MINCERS
MINCING
MIOCENE
MISCALL
MISCAST
MISCUED
MISCUES
MITCHUM
NICCOLO
OILCAKE
OILCANS
PICCARD
PICCOLO
PIECERS
PIECING
PINCERS
PINCHAS
PINCHED
PINCHER
PINCHES
PINCURL
PISCINE
PISCOPO
PITCHED
PITCHER
PITCHES
PITCHIN
RIBCAGE
RIPCORD
SICCING
SINCERE
SITCOMS
TIECLIP
TINCANS
VINCENT
VISCERA
VISCOUS
WINCERS
WINCHED
WINCHES
WINCING
WITCHES
ZILCHES
ZIPCODE
ZIRCONS

•I••C••

BICYCLE
BIFOCAL
BINOCHE
BISECTS
DIDACTS
DIRECTS
FIANCEE
FIANCES
FIASCOS
FIERCER
FINICKY
HIBACHI
HIJACKS
HITACHI
KITSCHY
LIONCUB
MILKCOW
MIMICRY
MINICAB
MINICAM
MIRACLE
PIERCED
PIERCES
PINOCLE
SIDECAR
SILICAS
SILICON
SIROCCO
TIMECOP
WILDCAT

•I•••C•

AIRLOCK
AIRSACS
AIRSOCK
BIONICS
DIALECT
DIPTYCH
DISSECT
DIVORCE
FINANCE
GIMMICK
HILLOCK
LICENCE
MICMACS
MINORCA
NIBLICK
NITPICK
PICNICS
PIMLICO
PINNACE
RIDDICK
RIOTACT
SILENCE
SIROCCO
SIXPACK
TICTACS
TIERACK
TIETACK
TINTACK
TITMICE
VIADUCT

•I••••C

BIVOUAC
KINETIC
LIPSYNC
MIASMIC
MIDDLEC
MIMETIC
MITOTIC
PIRATIC
TITANIC

••IC•••

BRICKED
CHICAGO
CHICANA
CHICANO
CHICHEN
CHICKEN
CHICORY
CLICHES
CLICKED
CRICKED
CRICKET
DEICERS
DEICING
ELICITS
EPICENE
EPICURE
ERICSON
EVICTED
FLICKED
FLICKER
FRICKIE
ICICLES
JUICERS
JUICEUP
JUICIER
JUICILY
JUICING
OMICRON
PRICERS
PRICIER
PRICING
PRICKED
PRICKLE
PRICKLY
QUICHES
QUICKEN
QUICKER
QUICKIE
QUICKLY
SEICHES
SLICERS
SLICING
SLICKED
SLICKER
SLICKLY
SNICKER
SPICERY
SPICEUP
SPICIER
SPICILY
SPICING
STICHES
STICKER
STICKTO
STICKUP
TEICHER
THICKEN
THICKER
THICKET
THICKLY
TRICEPS
TRICKED
TRICKER
TRICKLE
TRICORN
TRICOTS
UNICORN
VOICING

••I•C••

BRIOCHE
EVINCED
EVINCES
HAIRCUT
MAILCAR
PRINCES
QUINCES
SNITCHY
TWITCHY

••I••C•

AVIANCA
CHIRICO
CLINICS
CRITICS
EDIFICE
FAIENCE
GRIMACE
ILIESCU
ORIFICE
ORINOCO
OVISACS
PLIANCY
PRIMACY
PRIVACY
SCIENCE
SKIRACK
SPINACH
THINICE
TRISECT

••I•••C

ASIATIC
ERISTIC
IDIOTIC
MEIOTIC
SEISMIC

•••IC••

AFRICAN
APRICOT
ARNICAS
ARTICLE
ATTICUS
AURICLE
BODICES
CALICES
CALICOS
CHOICER
CHOICES
CODICES
CODICIL
COMICAL
CONICAL
CUBICLE
CUTICLE
CYNICAL
DEFICIT
DELICTI
DELICTS
DEPICTS
DEVICES
ENTICED
ENTICER
ENTICES
ETHICAL
FELICIA
FINICKY
HARICOT
HELICAL
HELICES
HELICON
ILLICIT
INDICES
INDICIA
INDICTS
JERICHO
LATICES
LEXICAL
LEXICON
LOGICAL
LORICAE
LYRICAL
MAGICAL
MEDICAL
MEDICOS
MEXICAN
MIMICRY
MINICAB
MINICAM
MODICUM
MOHICAN
MUSICAL
NOTICED
NOTICES
NOVICES
OFFICER
OFFICES
OPTICAL
OSSICLE
PANICKY
PANICLE
PEDICAB
PEDICEL
PEDICLE
PELICAN
PEMICAN
PLAICES
POLICED
POLICES
PUMICES
RADICAL
RADICES
RADICLE
RELICTS
RETICLE
RUBICON
SHTICKS
SILICAS
SILICON
SLUICED
SLUICES
SOLICIT
SPLICED
SPLICER
SPLICES
STOICAL
TAXICAB
TOPICAL
TUNICLE
TYPICAL
UPTICKS
VATICAN
VEHICLE

•••I•C•

ANTIOCH
BEWITCH
CARIOCA
DAVINCI
DEHISCE
EXTINCT
JALISCO
MANIACS
MANIOCS

MENISCI
NABISCO
SQUINCH
TAPIOCA
UNHITCH
ZODIACS

•••I••C
ACTINIC
HAMITIC
HASIDIC
JURIDIC
OSSIFIC
PACIFIC
POLITIC
SATIRIC
SEMITIC

••••IC•
AFFLICT
AGARICS
ALDRICH
AMERICA
AUSPICE
AVARICE
BERNICE
BIONICS
CANDICE
CAPRICE
CARRICK
CELTICS
CHALICE
CHIRICO
CLARICE
CLERICS
CLINICS
CONNICK
CONVICT
COPPICE
CORNICE
CORSICA
COWLICK
CREVICE
CRITICS
DERRICK
DNOTICE
DORMICE
EDIFICE
EHRLICH
EROTICA
ETHNICS
EXOTICA
EXOTICS
FABRICS
FORMICA
FOSDICK
FROLICS
FUSTICS
GARRICK
GIMMICK
GOTHICS
HEROICS
HOSPICE
ICEPICK
INFLICT
INVOICE
IPSWICH
ITALICS
JAMAICA
JESSICA
JONNICK
JUSTICE
KUBRICK
LATTICE
MAFFICK
MASTICS
MAURICE
METRICS
MOSAICS
MYSTICS
NIBLICK
NITPICK
NOETICS
NORDICS
OLDNICK
ORIFICE
OSTRICH
PACKICE
PATRICE
PATRICK
PHOBICS
PHONICS
PHOTICS
PHYSICS
PICNICS
PIMLICO
POETICS
PORTICO
PREDICT
PUBLICS
REJOICE
REPLICA
REPRICE
REVOICE
RIDDICK
ROLLICK
RUBRICS
RUSTICS
SEASICK
SERPICO
SERVICE
STATICE
STATICS
SUFFICE
TACTICS
TAMPICO
THINICE
TITMICE
TOPKICK
TROPICS
UNSTICK
VERDICT
WARWICK

••••I•C
CARDIAC
ELEGIAC
PONTIAC

•••••IC
ACERBIC
ACRYLIC
ACTINIC
AELFRIC
AEROBIC
ALEMBIC
AMHARIC
AMOEBIC
ANAEMIC
ANGELIC
ANOSMIC
AQUATIC
ARAMAIC
ARCHAIC
ARSENIC
ASCETIC
ASEPTIC
ASIATIC
BALDRIC
BORACIC
BUCOLIC
CALORIC
CAMBRIC
CANONIC
CAUSTIC
CENTRIC
CERAMIC
CHAOTIC
CHRONIC
CLASSIC
COMEDIC
CRYPTIC
DELPHIC
DELTAIC
DEMONIC
DRASTIC
DYNAMIC
EDAPHIC
ELASTIC
ENDEMIC
ERISTIC
ERRATIC
FANATIC
FRANTIC
FREDRIC
GASTRIC
GENERIC
GENETIC
GNOSTIC
GRAPHIC
HAMITIC
HASIDIC
HEBRAIC
HEPATIC
HERETIC
HOMERIC
IDENTIC
IDIOTIC
IDYLLIC
ILLOGIC
ISLAMIC
JURIDIC
KINETIC
LACONIC
LUNATIC
MALEFIC
MANTRIC
MASONIC
MEIOTIC
MELODIC
MIASMIC
MIMETIC
MITOTIC
MONODIC
NOMADIC
NUCLEIC
NUMERIC
OCEANIC
OLYMPIC
ORGANIC
OSMOTIC
OSSIFIC
PACIFIC
PELAGIC
PHRENIC
PIRATIC
PLASTIC
POLEMIC
POLITIC
PROSAIC
PSYCHIC
PYRRHIC
ROBOTIC
SATIRIC
SCEPTIC
SEISMIC
SELENIC
SEMITIC
SKEPTIC
SOMATIC
STANNIC
STYPTIC
SYNODIC
TITANIC
TOTEMIC
TRAFFIC
TROPHIC
VOCALIC
VOLTAIC
XANTHIC

ID•••••
IDAHOAN
IDCARDS
IDEALLY
IDEAMAN
IDEAMEN
IDEATED
IDEATES
IDENTIC
IDIAMIN
IDIOTIC
IDOLISE
IDOLIZE
IDYLLIC

I•D••••
INDENTS
INDEPTH
INDEXED
INDEXES
INDIANA
INDIANS
INDICES
INDICIA
INDICTS
INDIGOS
INDITED
INDITES
INDOORS
INDORSE
INDOUBT
INDUCED
INDUCER
INDUCES
INDUCTS
INDULGE
INDUTCH
INDWELL
IODATES
IODIDES
IODISED
IODISES
IODIZED
IODIZES

I••D•••
ICEDOUT
ICEDTEA
INADAZE
IRIDIUM
ISADORA

I•••D••
ILLUDED
ILLUDES
IMPEDED
IMPEDES
INCUDES
INFIDEL
INSIDER
INSIDES
INVADED
INVADER
INVADES
IODIDES

I••••D•
IDCARDS
IMPENDS
IMPLODE
INCLUDE
INNARDS
INROADS
INTENDS
INTRUDE
INWARDS
ISLANDS
ISOPODS
IZZARDS

I•••••D
IBNSAUD
ICECOLD
ICELAND
ICHABOD
IDEATED
IGNITED
IGNORED
ILLBRED
ILLUDED
ILLUMED
ILLUSED
ILLWIND
IMBIBED
IMBRUED
IMMIXED
IMMURED
IMPALED
IMPEDED
IMPLIED
IMPOSED
IMPOUND
IMPUTED
INAWORD
INBOARD
INBOUND
INBREED
INCASED
INCISED
INCITED
INDEXED
INDITED
INDUCED
INFIELD
INFUSED
INHALED
INHERED
INJURED
INSIPID
INSTEAD
INSURED
INTONED
INVADED
INVALID
INVITED
INVOKED
IODISED
IODIZED
IONISED
IONIZED
IRELAND

•ID••••
AIDLESS
BIDDERS
BIDDIES
BIDDING
BIDFAIR
DIDACTS
DIDDLED
DIDDLES
DIDDLEY
DIDEROT
DIDGOOD
DIDOVER
FIDDLED
FIDDLER
FIDDLES
FIDELIO
FIDELIS
FIDGETS
FIDGETY
GIDDIER
GIDDILY
GIDDYAP
GIDDYUP
GIDEONS
HIDALGO
HIDEOUS
HIDEOUT
HIDINGS
KIDDERS
KIDDIES
KIDDING
KIDDISH
KIDLIKE
KIDNAPS
KIDNEYS
KIDSKIN
LIDLESS
MIDDAYS
MIDDENS
MIDDIES
MIDDLEC
MIDDLES
MIDEAST
MIDGETS
MIDLAND
MIDLIFE
MIDLINE
MIDMOST
MIDRIBS
MIDRIFF
MIDRISE
MIDSIZE
MIDTERM
MIDTOWN
MIDWAYS
MIDWEEK
MIDWEST
MIDWIFE
MIDYEAR
PIDGEON
PIDGINS
RIDDICK
RIDDING
RIDDLED
RIDDLER
RIDDLES
RIDEOFF
RIDEOUT
RIDGIER
RIDGING
RIDGWAY
RIDOTTO
SIDEARM
SIDEBAR
SIDEBET
SIDECAR
SIDEMAN
SIDEMEN
SIDINGS
SIDLING
TIDBITS
TIDIEST
TIDINGS
TIDYING
VIDALIA
WIDENED
WIDGEON
WIDGETS
WIDMARK
WIDOWED
WIDOWER
YIDDISH

•I•D•••
AIRDAMS
AIRDATE
AIRDROP
BIDDERS
BIDDIES
BIDDING
BIGDEAL
BINDERS
BINDERY
BINDING
BINDSUP
BIRDDOG
BIRDERS
BIRDIED
BIRDIES
BIRDING
BIRDMAN
BIRDMEN
CINDERS
CINDERY
DIADEMS
DIDDLED
DIDDLES
DIDDLEY
DIEDOFF
DIEDOUT
DIEDOWN
DIKDIKS
DISDAIN
FIDDLED
FIDDLER
FIDDLES
FIEDLER
FINDERS
FINDING
FINDOUT
GIDDIER
GIDDILY
GIDDYAP
GIDDYUP
GILDERS
GILDING
GIRDERS
GIRDING
GIRDLED
GIRDLES
HINDERS
KIDDERS
KIDDIES
KIDDING
KIDDISH
KILDARE
KINDEST
KINDLED
KINDLES
KINDRED
LIEDOWN
LINDENS
LINDIED
LINDIES
LINDSAY
LINDSEY
MIDDAYS
MIDDENS
MIDDIES
MIDDLEC
MIDDLES
MILDEST
MILDEWS
MILDEWY
MILDRED
MINDERS
MINDFUL
MINDING
MINDSET
MISDATE
MISDEAL
MISDEED
MISDIAL
MISDOES
MISDONE
PINDOWN
RIDDICK
RIDDING
RIDDLED
RIDDLER
RIDDLES
SITDOWN
TIEDOWN
TIEDYED
TIEDYES
TINDERS
VIADUCT
WILDCAT
WILDEST
WILDING
WILDISH
WILDONE
WINDBAG
WINDERS
WINDIER
WINDILY
WINDING
WINDOWS
WINDROW
WINDSOR
WINDSUP
WINDUPS
YIDDISH

•I••D••
AIMEDAT
AIMEDTO
BIMODAL
BIPEDAL
BIRDDOG
CICADAE
CICADAS
CITADEL
DINEDIN
DINEDON
DIRNDLS
DIVIDED
DIVIDER
DIVIDES
FIEFDOM
FIELDED
FIELDER
FIREDOG
FIREDUP
FIXEDLY
FIXEDUP
HIGHDAY
HIKEDUP
KINGDOM
LIBIDOS
LINEDUP
LIPIDES
LIVEDIN
LIVEDON
LIVIDLY
MIKADOS
MILLDAM
MIRADOR
MIXEDIN
MIXEDUP
PICADOR
PILEDIN
PILEDON
PILEDUP
PIPEDUP
QINGDAO
RIGIDLY
SICKDAY
SINEDIE
SIZEDUP
TIMIDER
TIMIDLY
TIRADES
TIREDER
TIREDLY
TIREDOF
VIVIDER
VIVIDLY
WIELDED
WIPEDUP
WISEDUP
YIELDED

•I•••D•
AIRMADA
DIOMEDE
DIOXIDE
GIRONDE
LIGANDS
LIMEADE
LIQUIDS
LIZARDS
MILORDS
MIRANDA
NIMRODS
NITRIDE
PICARDY
RIBANDS
RICARDO
RIGVEDA
RIPTIDE
TIERODS
VIVALDI
VIVENDI
WIZARDS
ZIPCODE

•I••••D
AIRHEAD
AIRRAID
BIASSED
BIGBAND
BIGBEND
BIGBIRD
BIGHEAD
BIGOTED
BIRCHED
BIRDIED
BIRTHED
CINCHED
CIRCLED
DIAMOND
DIBBLED
DIDDLED
DIDGOOD
DIEHARD
DILATED
DILLARD
DILUTED
DIMPLED
DIPLOID
DIRTIED
DISBAND
DISCARD
DISCOED
DISCORD
DISTEND
DISUSED
DITCHED
DITTOED
DIVIDED
DIVINED
DIVVIED
DIZENED
DIZZIED
FIDDLED
FIELDED
FIGURED
FILCHED
FINLAND
FIXATED
FIZZLED
GIELGUD
GIFFORD
GIGGLED
GIRDLED
GIZZARD
HIGGLED
HIGHEND
HITCHED
JIGGLED
JIMMIED
JINGLED
KIBBLED
KINDLED
KINDRED
LIAISED
LIBELED
LIEABED
LIGATED
LIGHTED
LIKEMAD
LIKENED
LILYPAD
LIMITED
LINDIED
LINSEED
LIPREAD
LIVENED
MIDLAND
MILDRED
MILHAUD
MILLAND
MILLARD
MILLEND
MINGLED
MINORED
MINUEND
MISCUED
MISDEED
MISLAID
MISLEAD
MISREAD
MISSAID
MISUSED
MISWORD
MITERED
MITFORD
MIZZLED
NIBBLED
NIGGARD
NIGGLED
PICCARD
PICKLED
PIEBALD
PIERCED
PIFFLED
PILOTED
PINCHED
PINHEAD
PIRATED
PITCHED
PIVOTED
RICHARD
RIDDLED
RIFFLED
RIGHTED
RIMBAUD
RIMPLED
RIPCORD
RIPENED
RIPPLED
RIVALED
RIVETED
SIGHTED
SIGMUND
SINGLED
SIXFOLD
SIZZLED
TICKLED
TIEDYED
TINGLED
TINKLED
TIPPLED
TIPTOED
VISITED
WIDENED
WIDOWED
WIELDED
WIGGLED
WILFORD
WILFRID
WILLARD
WIMBLED
WIMPLED
WINCHED
WINERED
WINKLED
WIZENED
YIELDED

••ID•••
ABIDEBY
ABIDING
ACIDIFY
ACIDITY
ALIDADE
ARIDEST
ARIDITY
AVIDITY
BRIDALS
BRIDGED
BRIDGES
BRIDGET
BRIDLED
BRIDLES
CHIDERS
CHIDING
ELIDING
EVIDENT
FRIDAYS
FRIDGES
GLIDERS
GLIDING
GRIDDED
GRIDDER
GRIDDLE
GUIDING
GUIDONS
IRIDIUM
LAIDFOR
LAIDLOW
LAIDOFF
LAIDOUT
MAIDENS
MAIDISH
OXIDANT
OXIDASE
OXIDISE
OXIDIZE
PAIDFOR
PAIDOFF
PAIDOUT
PHIDIAS
PRIDING
RAIDERS
RAIDING
SEIDELS
SKIDDED
SKIDDER
SKIDDOO
SKIDROW
SLIDEIN
SLIDERS
SLIDING
SMIDGEN
SNIDELY
SNIDEST
SPIDERS
SPIDERY
TRIDENT
TWIDDLE
VOIDING

••I•D••
ARIADNE
BLINDED
BLINDER
BLINDLY
BRINDLE
BUILDER
BUILDIN
BUILDUP
DRIEDUP
DRIPDRY
DWINDLE
FRIEDAN
GRIDDED
GRIDDER
GRIDDLE
GRINDER
GUILDER
HAIRDOS
HAIRDYE
JOINDER
NAIADES
SHINDIG
SKIDDED
SKIDDER
SKIDDOO
SPIEDON
SPINDLE
SPINDLY
SPINDRY
SWINDLE
THIRDLY
TRIEDON
TRIODES
TWIDDLE
WEIRDER
WEIRDLY
WEIRDOS

••I••D•
ALIDADE
BOIARDO
BRIARDS
BRIGADE
EPISODE
FRIENDS
SHIELDS
TRIPODS
UNIPODS

••I•••D
ALIGNED
AMISTAD
ANISEED
AVIATED
BLINDED
BLINKED
BLIPPED
BLITZED
BRICKED
BRIDGED
BRIDLED
BRIEFED
BRIGAND
BRIMMED
CHILLED
CHINKED
CHINNED
CHIPPED
CHIRPED
CLICKED
CLIMBED
CLINKED
CLIPPED
CRIBBED
CRICKED
CRIMPED
CRINGED
CRINOID
CRISPED
DEIFIED
DEIGNED
DRIFTED
DRILLED
DRIPPED
EDIFIED
EMITTED
ENISLED
EVICTED
EVINCED
EXISTED
FAINTED
FEIGNED
FEINTED
FLICKED
FLIPPED
FLIRTED
FLITTED
FOISTED
FRILLED
FRINGED
FRISKED
FRITTED
FRIZZED
GLINTED
GLITZED
GRIDDED
GRIEVED
GRILLED
GRINNED
GRIPPED
GRITTED
HEISTED
HOISTED
JOINTED
JOISTED
KNITTED
MAITRED
NEIGHED
OMITTED
OSIERED
PAINTED
PLINKED
POINTED
PRICKED
PRIMPED
PRINKED
PRINTED
QUIETED
QUILLED
QUILTED
QUIPPED
QUIZZED
REIFIED
REIGNED
REINKED
SAINTED
SHIFTED
SHILLED
SHINNED
SHIPPED
SHIRKED
SHIRRED
SKIDDED
SKILLED
SKIMMED
SKIMPED
SKINNED
SKIPPED
SKIRLED
SKIRRED
SKIRTED
SLICKED
SLIMMED
SLINKED
SLIPPED
SMIRKED
SNIFFED
SNIPPED
SPIELED
SPILLED
STIFFED
STIFLED
STILLED
STILTED
STINTED
STIPEND
STIRRED

SWIGGED
SWILLED
SWIRLED
SWISHED
TAILEND
TAINTED
THIEVED
THINNED
TRICKED
TRIFLED
TRIGGED
TRILLED
TRIMMED
TRIPLED
TRIPPED
TWILLED
TWINBED
TWINGED
TWINNED
TWIRLED
TWISTED
TWITTED
UNIFIED
WEIGHED
WHIFFED
WHIPPED
WHIRLED
WHIRRED
WHISHED
WHISKED
WHIZKID
WHIZZED
WRITHED

•••ID••

ABRIDGE
ACRIDLY
APSIDES
AVOIDED
BERIDOF
BESIDES
BETIDED
BETIDES
BOLIDES
BRAIDED
BRAIDER
CCRIDER
DECIDED
DECIDES
DERIDED
DERIDES
DIVIDED
DIVIDER
DIVIDES
DOSIDOS
DREIDEL
ECHIDNA
FETIDLY
FLUIDLY
GELIDLY
HALIDES
HASIDIC
HASIDIM
HOLIDAY
HUMIDLY
HUMIDOR
INFIDEL
INSIDER
INSIDES
IODIDES
JURIDIC
LIBIDOS
LIPIDES
LIVIDLY
LUCIDLY
LURIDLY
MEGIDDO
ONEIDAS
ONSIDES
OVOIDAL
PERIDOT
PYXIDES
RABIDLY
RAPIDER
RAPIDLY
RESIDED
RESIDES
RESIDUE
RIGIDLY
SOLIDER
SOLIDLY
STAIDER
STAIDLY
STRIDER
STRIDES
TEPIDLY
TIMIDER
TIMIDLY
TOTIDEM
UNAIDED
VALIDLY
VAPIDLY
VIVIDER
VIVIDLY

•••I•D•

BELINDA
ENGIRDS
MATILDA
MEGIDDO
MELINDA
MYRIADS
PERIODS
REBINDS
REMINDS
REWINDS
UNBINDS
UNGIRDS
UNWINDS

•••I••D

ADMIRED
ADMIXED
ADVISED
AFFIXED
ARRIVED
ASPIRED
ATTIRED
AUDITED
AVAILED
AVOIDED
AWAITED
BATIKED
BEMIRED
BETIDED
BRAIDED
BRAINED
BRAISED
BROILED
BRUISED
BRUITED
BYLINED
CAVILED
CHAINED
CHAIRED
CLAIMED
CRUISED
DEBITED
DECIDED
DEFILED
DEFINED
DEMIGOD
DEMISED
DERIDED
DERIVED
DESIRED
DEVILED
DEVISED
DIVIDED
DIVINED
DRAINED
EMAILED
ENSILED
ENTICED
EXCISED
EXCITED
EXPIRED
FLAILED
FRUITED
GLAIRED
GRAINED
HABITED
HELIPAD
HOMINID
IGNITED
IMBIBED
IMMIXED
INCISED
INCITED
INDITED
INFIELD
INSIPID
INVITED
IODISED
IODIZED
IONISED
IONIZED
LIAISED
LIMITED
MERITED
NOTICED
OBLIGED
ORBITED
PLAITED
POLICED
PONIARD
POSITED
PRAISED
QUAILED
RADIOED
REAIMED
REAIRED
RECITED
REFILED
REFINED
REHIRED
RELINED
RELIVED
REMIXED
REOILED
REPINED
RESIDED
RESILED
RETILED
RETIMED
RETIRED
REVILED
REVISED
REVIVED
REWIRED
SLUICED
SPLICED
SPOILED
SQUIRED
STAINED
STRIPED
STRIVED
THRIVED
TRAILED
TRAINED
UMPIRED
UNAIDED
UNAIMED
UNAIRED
UNFIXED
UNLIKED
UNLINED
UNOILED
UNPILED
VISITED

••••ID•

ACARIDS
ASTRIDE
BEDSIDE
BROMIDE
BUSHIDO
CANDIDA
CANDIDE
CANDIDS
CAPSIDS
CARBIDE
CASSIDY
CERVIDS
COLLIDE
CONFIDE
CONOIDS
CORRIDA
COWHIDE
CUSPIDS
DIOXIDE
EBBTIDE
ELAPIDS
EYELIDS
FLORIDA
FORBIDS
HAYRIDE
HYBRIDS
JOYRIDE
LEETIDE
LEONIDS
LIQUIDS
LOWTIDE
NEREIDS
NITRIDE
NUCLIDE
OFFSIDE
ORCHIDS
OUTBIDS
OUTSIDE
PEPTIDE
PERFIDY
PLACIDO
PODRIDA
PONGIDS
PRESIDE
PROVIDE
RAWHIDE
RIPTIDE
ROLAIDS
SAYYIDS
SCHMIDT
SEASIDE
SUBSIDE
SUBSIDY
SULFIDE
TOPSIDE
TOROIDS
TVGUIDE
USERIDS
VESPIDS
WAYSIDE

••••I•D

AMERIND
APPLIED
BANDIED
BELLIED
BERRIED
BIGBIRD
BIRDIED
BOOGIED
BULLIED
CADDIED
CANDIED
CARRIED
CATBIRD
CHEVIED
CONRIED
COWBIRD
CULLIED
CURRIED
DALLIED
DECRIED
DEIFIED
DIRTIED
DIVVIED
DIZZIED
DOLLIED
DUMMIED
EDIFIED
EMPTIED
ENSKIED
FANCIED
FERRIED
GLORIED
GUSSIED
HARRIED
HOGTIED
HOGWILD
HURRIED
ILLWIND
IMPLIED
JAYBIRD
JELLIED
JEMMIED
JIMMIED
JOLLIED
JUTTIED
LINDIED
LOBBIED
MANKIND
MARRIED
MUDDIED
PARRIED
PARTIED
PUTTIED
QUERIED
RALLIED
READIED
REBUILD
REDBIRD
REFRIED
REIFIED
REPLIED
RESCIND
RETRIED
SALLIED
SEABIRD
SERRIED
SORTIED
STORIED
STUDIED
STYMIED
SULLIED
TALLIED
TARRIED
TOADIED
UNIFIED
UNTRIED
WEARIED
WORRIED

•••••ID

AIRRAID
ANDROID
ANEROID
ANNELID
ANTACID
BANDAID
BARMAID
CAROTID
COLLOID
CRINOID
DELTOID
DIPLOID
FACTOID
FLACCID
HOMINID
INSIPID
INVALID
KATYDID
KOOLAID
LANGUID
LOWPAID
MASTOID
MERMAID
MISLAID
MISSAID
NAYSAID
NONSKID
OCEANID
OLDMAID
OSTEOID
OUTLAID
OVERDID
PERSEID
PREPAID
PYRAMID
SQUALID
STEROID
SUNMAID
TABLOID
UPBRAID
WAYLAID
WHIZKID
WILFRID

I•E••••

IBERIAN
ICEAGES
ICEAXES
ICEBAGS
ICEBEER
ICEBERG
ICEBLUE
ICEBOAT
ICECAPS
ICECOLD
ICECUBE
ICEDOUT
ICEDTEA
ICEFLOE
ICEFOGS
ICEFREE
ICELAND
ICELESS
ICELIKE
ICEMILK
ICEPACK
ICEPICK
ICERINK
ICESHOW
ICESOUT
IDEALLY
IDEAMAN
IDEAMEN
IDEATED
IDEATES
IDENTIC
IKEBANA
INEPTLY
INERROR
INERTIA
INERTLY
INEXACT
IRECKON
IRELAND
IRELESS
ITEMISE
ITEMIZE
ITERANT
ITERATE

I••E•••

IGNEOUS
ILIESCU
ILLEGAL
IMMENSE
IMMERSE
IMPEACH
IMPEDED
IMPEDES
IMPENDS
IMPERIL
IMPETUS
INCENSE
INCEPTS
INDENTS
INDEPTH
INDEXED
INDEXES
INFECTS
INFERNO
INFESTS
INGEMAR
INGENUE
INGESTS
INHERED
INHERES
INHERIT
INJECTS
INPEACE
INPETTO
INSEAMS
INSECTS
INSERTS
INTEARS
INTEGER
INTEGRA
INTENDS
INTENSE
INTENTS
INTERIM
INTERNS
INTERSE
INVEIGH
INVENTS
INVERSE
INVERTS
INVESTS
IONESCO
IQTESTS

I•••E••

ICEBEER
ICEBERG
ICELESS
ICINESS
ICKIEST
IFFIEST
IGIVEUP
ILLNESS
IMAGERS
IMAGERY
IMARETS
IMOGENE
IMPIETY
IMPRESS
INAHEAP
INAMESS
INANELY
INANEST
INAWEOF
INBREED
INDWELL
INFIELD
INFLECT
INGRESS
INKIEST
INKLESS
INKWELL
INNLESS
INQUEST
INSPECT
INSTEAD
INSTEPS
IPANEMA
IPCRESS
IRATELY
IRATEST
IRELESS
IRONERS
ISOHELS
ISOMERS
ISRAELI
ISSUERS

I••••E•

ICEAGES
ICEAXES
ICEBEER
ICEDTEA
ICEFREE
ICICLES
IDEAMEN
IDEATED
IDEATES
IGNITED
IGNITER
IGNITES
IGNORED
IGNORER
IGNORES
ILLBRED
ILLUDED
ILLUDES
ILLUMED
ILLUMES
ILLUSED
ILLUSES
IMAGOES
IMBIBED
IMBIBES
IMBRUED
IMBRUES
IMMIXED
IMMIXES
IMMURED
IMMURES
IMPALED
IMPALES
IMPANEL
IMPEDED
IMPEDES
IMPLIED
IMPLIES
IMPOSED
IMPOSES
IMPURER
IMPUTED
IMPUTES
INAPTER
INASTEW
INBOXES
INBREED
INBRIEF
INCASED
INCASES
INCISED
INCISES
INCITED
INCITER
INCITES
INCOMES
INCUDES
INDEXED
INDEXES
INDICES
INDITED
INDITES
INDUCED
INDUCER
INDUCES
INFIDEL
INFUSED
INFUSES
INHALED
INHALER
INHALES
INHERED
INHERES
INJOKES
INJURED
INJURES
INMATES
INPOWER
INSIDER
INSIDES
INSOLES
INSURED
INSURER
INSURES
INTAKES
INTEGER
INTONED
INTONER
INTONES
INVADED
INVADER
INVADES
INVITED
INVITES
INVOKED
INVOKER
INVOKES
IODATES
IODIDES
IODISED
IODISES
IODIZED
IODIZES
IONISED
IONISES
IONIZED
IONIZER
IONIZES
IRONIES
IRONMEN
ISHMAEL
ITCHIER
IVORIES

I•••••E

ICEBLUE
ICECUBE
ICEFLOE
ICEFREE
ICELIKE
IDOLISE
IDOLIZE
IFSTONE
IGNOBLE
IMAGINE
IMAMATE
IMITATE
IMMENSE
IMMERSE
IMOGENE
IMPASSE
IMPINGE
IMPLODE
IMPLORE
IMPROVE
IMPULSE
INADAZE
INCENSE
INCLINE
INCLOSE
INCLUDE
INDORSE
INDULGE
INFLAME
INFLATE
INFORCE
INGENUE
INGRATE
INHASTE
INHOUSE
INKLIKE
INPEACE
INPHASE
INPLACE
INQUIRE
INSCAPE
INSHAPE
INSPIRE
INSTATE
INSTORE
INSTYLE
INTENSE
INTERSE
INTRUDE
INUTILE
INVERSE
INVOGUE
INVOICE
INVOLVE
IRKSOME
IRONAGE
IRONORE
ISOLATE
ISOTOPE
ITEMISE
ITEMIZE
ITERATE
IVANHOE
IVYLIKE

•IE••••

BIENTOT
DIEDOFF
DIEDOUT
DIEDOWN
DIEHARD
DIESELS
DIESOFF
DIESOUT
DIETARY
DIETERS
DIETING
FIEDLER
FIEFDOM
FIELDED
FIELDER
FIENNES
FIERCER
FIERIER
FIERILY
FIESTAS
GIELGUD
LIEABED
LIEDOWN
LIENEES
LIEOVER
LIERNES
LIESLOW
NIEBUHR
NIELSEN
PIEBALD
PIECERS
PIECING
PIELIKE
PIEPANS
PIERCED
PIERCES
PIERROT
PIETIES
PIETINS
PIETISM
PIETIST
SIENNAS
SIERRAS
SIESTAS
TIECLIP
TIEDOWN
TIEDYED
TIEDYES
TIEINTO
TIELESS
TIELINE
TIEPINS
TIEPOLO
TIERACK
TIERING
TIERNEY
TIERODS
TIETACK
VIETNAM
VIEWERS
VIEWIER
VIEWING
WIELDED
WIENERS
WIENIES
YIELDED

•I•E•••

AILERON
AIMEDAT
AIMEDTO
BIBELOT
BIGELOW
BIGEYES
BIKEWAY
BILEVEL
BIPEDAL
BIREMES
BIRETTA
BISECTS
BITEOFF
CINEMAS
CINEMAX
DIDEROT
DIGESTS
DILEMMA
DINEDIN
DINEDON
DINESEN
DINESIN
DINESON
DINETTE
DIRECTS
DIREFUL
DISEASE
DIVERGE
DIVERSE
DIVERTS
DIVESIN
DIVESTS
DIZENED
FIDELIO
FIDELIS
FILENES
FINEART
FINESSE
FIREANT
FIREARM
FIREBOX
FIREBUG
FIREDOG
FIREDUP
FIREFLY
FIRELIT
FIREMAN
FIREMEN
FIRENZE
FIREOFF
FIRESUP
FIXEDLY
FIXEDUP
FIXESUP
GIDEONS
GISELLE
GIVENIN
GIVENTO
GIVENUP
GIVEOFF
GIVEOUT
GIVESIN
GIVESTO
GIVESUP
GIVEUPS
GIVEWAY
HIDEOUS
HIDEOUT
HIKEDUP
HIKESUP
HIRESON
JIMENEZ
KINEMAS
KINETIC
LIBELED
LIBELER
LIBERAL
LIBERIA
LIBERTY
LICENCE
LICENSE
LIFEFUL
LIFENET
LIKEMAD
LIKENED
LIKENEW
LIMEADE
LINEAGE
LINEATE
LINEDUP
LINEMAN
LINEMEN
LINESUP
LINEUPS
LISENTE
LITERAL
LIVEDIN
LIVEDON
LIVENED
LIVEOAK
LIVEONE
LIVEOUT
LIVESIN
LIVESON
MIDEAST
MILEAGE
MIMESIS
MIMETIC
MINERAL
MINERVA
MISERLY
MITERED
MIXEDIN
MIXEDUP
MIXESIN
MIXESUP
NIGERIA
NINEPIN
NINEVEH
PIGEONS
PIKEMAN
PIKEMEN
PILEDIN
PILEDON
PILEDUP
PILESIN
PILESON
PILESUP
PILEUPS
PIMENTO
PIMESON
PINEFOR
PINENUT
PINESAP
PINETAR
PINETUM
PIPEDUP
PIPEFUL
PIPEMMA
PIPESUP
PIPETTE
PITEOUS
RIBEYES
RICERAT
RIDEOFF
RIDEOUT
RILESUP
RIPENED
RIVETED
RIVETER
SIBERIA
SIDEARM
SIDEBAR
SIDEBET
SIDECAR
SIDEMAN
SIDEMEN
SILENCE
SILENTS
SILESIA
SIMENON
SINEDIE
SIZEDUP
SIZESUP
TIBETAN
TIMECOP
TIMELAG
TIMEOFF
TIMEOUT
TIMESUP
TINEARS
TIREDER
TIREDLY
TIREDOF
TIREOUT
VICEROY
VINEGAR
VIVENDI
WIDENED
WINEBAR
WINERED
WINESAP
WIPEDUP
WIPEOUT
WIPESUP
WIRETAP
WISEDUP
WISEGUY
WISEMAN
WISEMEN
WISESUP
WIZENED

•I••E••

AIDLESS
AIGRETS
AILMENT
AIMLESS
AIRHEAD
AIRIEST
AIRLESS
BIBLESS
BICKERS
BIDDERS
BIGBEND
BIGDEAL
BIGFEET
BIGGERS
BIGGEST
BIGHEAD
BIGNESS
BILLETS
BINDERS
BINDERY
BIOGENY
BIRDERS
BITLESS
BITTERN

BITTERS
CINDERS
CINDERY
CIPHERS
CISTERN
DIADEMS
DIALECT
DIALERS
DIAPERS
DICIEST
DICKENS
DICKERS
DICKEYS
DIESELS
DIETERS
DIFFERS
DIGGERS
DIGRESS
DILBERT
DIMMERS
DIMMEST
DIMNESS
DINNERS
DIOCESE
DIOMEDE
DIPPERS
DISCERN
DISPELS
DISSECT
DISSENT
DISTEND
DITHERS
DITHERY
FIBBERS
FIDGETS
FIDGETY
FIFTEEN
FIGLEAF
FIGMENT
FILBERT
FILLERS
FILLETS
FILTERS
FINDERS
FINGERS
FIRMEST
FISHERS
FISHERY
FISHEYE
FITNESS
FITTERS
FITTEST
GIBBERS
GIBBETS
GIBLETS
GILBERT
GILDERS
GIMLETS
GINGERS
GINGERY
GINSENG
GIRDERS
HIALEAH
HIGHEND
HIGHEST
HIMSELF
HINDERS
HIPLESS
HIPNESS
HIPPEST
HISSERS
HITHERE
HITLESS
HITTERS
JIGGERS
JIGGERY
JITNEYS
JITTERS
JITTERY
JIVIEST
KICKERS
KIDDERS
KIDNEYS
KILLERS
KINDEST
KINLESS
KIPPERS
KISSERS
KITTENS
LIBBERS
LICHENS
LIDLESS
LIENEES
LIFTERS
LIMBERS
LIMIEST
LIMNERS
LIMPEST
LIMPETS
LINDENS
LINGERS
LINIEST
LINKERS
LINNETS
LINSEED
LINTELS
LIONESS
LIONETS
LIPLESS
LIPREAD
LIQUEFY
LIQUEUR
LISTEES
LISTELS
LISTENS
LITHELY
LITHEST
LITTERS
MICHELE
MICKEYS
MIDDENS
MIDGETS
MIDTERM
MIDWEEK
MIDWEST
MIDYEAR
MILDEST
MILDEWS
MILDEWY
MILIEUS
MILIEUX
MILKERS
MILLEND
MILLERS
MILLETS
MILLETT
MIMIEUX
MINCERS
MINDERS
MINTERS
MINUEND
MINUETS
MIOCENE
MIRIEST
MISDEAL
MISDEED
MISHEAR
MISLEAD
MISREAD
MISTERS
MITTENS
MIZZENS
NICKELS
NICKERS
NIGHEST
NIMIETY
NIPPERS
OILIEST
OILLESS
OILWELL
PICKENS
PICKERS
PICKETS
PICKETT
PIDGEON
PIECERS
PIGGERY
PIGLETS
PIGMENT
PIGPENS
PILFERS
PINCERS
PINHEAD
PINIEST
PINKEST
PINLESS
PINNERS
PIOLETS
PIONEER
PIPIEST
PIRAEUS
PITIERS
PITTERS
RIBLESS
RICHEST
RICKETY
RICKEYS
RIFLERS
RIFLERY
RIGGERS
RIGVEDA
RILLETS
RIMIEST
RIMLESS
RINGERS
RIOTERS
RIPIENO
RIPPERS
RISKERS
RIVIERA
RIVIERE
SIAMESE
SICKENS
SICKEST
SIFTERS
SIGHERS
SIGNEES
SIGNERS
SIGNETS
SILVERS
SILVERY
SIMMERS
SIMPERS
SINCERE
SINGERS
SINKERS
SINLESS
SINNERS
SIPPERS
SIPPETS
SISTERS
SITTERS
SITWELL
SIXTEEN
TICKERS
TICKETS
TICKETY
TIDIEST
TIELESS
TIGRESS
TILLERS
TILTERS
TIMBERS
TINDERS
TINIEST
TINKERS
TINNERS
TINSELS
TINTERN
TINTERS
TIPLESS
TIPPERS
TIPPETS
TITFERS
TITHERS
TITTERS
VIEWERS
VILLEIN
VINCENT
VINIEST
VIOLENT
VIOLETS
VISCERA
VIZIERS
WICKERS
WICKETS
WIDGEON
WIDGETS
WIENERS
WIGLESS
WIGLETS
WILDEST
WILHELM
WILIEST
WILLETS
WINCERS
WINDERS
WINGERS
WINIEST
WINKERS
WINNERS
WINTERS
WINTERY
WIRIEST
WISHERS
WITHERS
WITLESS
WITNESS
ZINGERS
ZIPPERS
ZITHERS

•I•••E•

AIRCREW
AITCHES
BIALIES
BIASSED
BIDDIES
BIGEYES
BIGFEET
BIGGIES
BIGLIES
BIGOSES
BIGOTED
BIGTOES
BILBIES
BILBOES
BILEVEL
BILGIER
BILLIES
BINGOES
BIRCHED
BIRCHES
BIRDIED
BIRDIES
BIRDMEN
BIREMES
BIRTHED
BISQUES
BITSIER
BITTIER
BITUMEN
CINCHED
CINCHES
CIRCLED
CIRCLES
CIRCLET
CIRQUES
CITADEL
CITIZEN
CITROEN
CIVVIES
DIARIES
DIBBLED
DIBBLES
DICKIES
DIDDLED
DIDDLES
DIDDLEY
DIDOVER
DILATED
DILATES
DILLIES
DILUTED
DILUTER
DILUTES
DIMPLED
DIMPLES
DINESEN
DINGIER
DINGLES
DINGOES
DINKIER
DINKIES
DIOPTER
DIPOLES
DIPPIER
DIRTIED
DIRTIER
DIRTIES
DISCOED
DISHIER
DISOBEY
DISUSED
DITCHED
DITCHES
DITSIER
DITTIES
DITTOED
DITZIER
DIVIDED
DIVIDER
DIVIDES
DIVINED
DIVINER
DIVINES
DIVVIED
DIVVIES
DIZENED
DIZZIED
DIZZIER
DIZZIES
FIACRES
FIANCEE
FIANCES
FICKLER
FICUSES
FIDDLED
FIDDLER
FIDDLES
FIEDLER
FIELDED
FIELDER
FIENNES
FIERCER
FIERIER
FIFTEEN
FIFTIES
FIGHTER
FIGURED
FIGURER
FIGURES
FILCHED
FILCHER
FILCHES
FILENES
FILLIES
FILMIER
FINALES
FINCHES
FINNIER
FIPPLES
FIREMEN
FIRRIER
FISCHER
FISHIER
FISHNET
FITCHES
FIXATED
FIXATES
FIZZIER
FIZZLED
FIZZLES
GIBLUES
GIDDIER
GIGGLED
GIGGLER
GIGGLES
GILLIES
GILLNET
GIPSIES
GIRDLED
GIRDLES
HIGGLED
HIGGLES
HIGHTEA
HILLIER
HINNIES
HIPPIER
HIPPIES
HIPSTER
HITCHED
HITCHER
HITCHES
JIFFIES
JIGGLED
JIGGLES
JIMCHEE
JIMENEZ
JIMMIED
JIMMIES
JINGLED
JINGLES
JINGOES
KIBBLED
KIBBLES
KICKIER
KIDDIES
KILAUEA
KILTIES
KIMCHEE
KINDLED
KINDLES
KINDRED
KINKIER
KINSMEN
KIRTLES
KISHKES
KITCHEN
KITTIES
LIAISED
LIAISES
LIBELED
LIBELER
LIEABED
LIENEES
LIEOVER
LIERNES
LIFENET
LIGATED
LIGATES
LIGHTED
LIGHTEN
LIGHTER
LIKENED
LIKENEW
LIMITED
LIMOGES
LINAGES
LINDIED
LINDIES
LINDSEY
LINEMEN
LINGOES
LINSEED
LINTIER
LIPIDES
LIPPIER
LISTEES
LITOTES
LITTLER
LIVENED
MICHAEL
MIDDIES
MIDDLEC
MIDDLES
MIDWEEK
MIFFIER
MIGGLES
MILDRED
MILKIER
MILKMEN
MINARET
MINDSET
MINGIER
MINGLED
MINGLER
MINGLES
MINIVER
MINORED
MINTIER
MINUSES
MINUTES
MIRAGES
MIRKIER
MISCUED
MISCUES
MISDEED
MISDOES
MISSIES
MISSTEP
MISTIER
MISUSED
MISUSES
MITERED
MITOSES
MIZZLED
MIZZLES
NIBBLED
NIBBLER
NIBBLES
NIELSEN
NIFTIER
NIGGLED
NIGGLES
NIMBLER
NINEVEH
NINNIES
NIPPIER
NITTIER
PIASTER
PICKIER
PICKLED
PICKLES
PIERCED
PIERCES
PIETIES
PIFFLED
PIFFLES
PIGGIER
PIGGIES
PIKEMEN
PILOTED
PILSNER
PINCHED
PINCHER
PINCHES
PINKIES
PINONES
PIONEER
PIRATED
PIRATES
PITCHED
PITCHER
PITCHES
PITHIER
PIVOTED
RIBBIES
RIBEYES
RICHTER
RICKLES
RIDDLED
RIDDLER
RIDDLES
RIDGIER
RIFFLED
RIFFLES
RIGHTED
RIGHTER
RIMPLED
RIMPLES
RINGLET
RIPENED
RIPPLED
RIPPLES
RISKIER
RITZIER
RIVALED
RIVETED
RIVETER
RIVULET
SICKLES
SIDEBET
SIDEMEN
SIGHTED
SIGNEES
SILKIER
SILLIER
SILLIES
SILTIER
SIMILES
SIMPLER
SIMPLEX
SINGLED
SINGLES
SINUSES
SISSIES
SIXTEEN
SIXTIES
SIZZLED
SIZZLES
TICKLED
TICKLER
TICKLES
TIEDYED
TIEDYES
TIERNEY
TIGHTEN
TIGHTER
TIMBRES
TIMIDER
TINGLED
TINGLES
TINKLED
TINKLES
TINNIER
TIPPIER
TIPPLED
TIPPLER
TIPPLES
TIPSIER
TIPSTER
TIPTOED
TIPTOES
TIRADES
TIREDER
TISANES
TISSUES
TITTLES
TIZZIES
VIEWIER
VINTNER
VIRTUES
VIRUSES
VISAGES
VISITED
VITTLES
VIVIDER
WIDENED
WIDOWED
WIDOWER
WIELDED
WIENIES
WIGGIER
WIGGLED
WIGGLER
WIGGLES
WILLIES
WIMBLED
WIMBLES
WIMPIER
WIMPLED
WIMPLES
WINCHED
WINCHES
WINDIER
WINERED
WINFREY
WINKLED
WINKLER
WINKLES
WISEMEN
WISPIER
WITCHES
WITHIER
WITHIES
WITTIER
WIZENED
YIELDED
ZILCHES
ZINGIER
ZIPPIER

•I••••E

AIRBASE
AIRDATE
AIRFARE
AIRHOLE
AIRLANE
AIRLIKE
AIRLINE
AIRMILE
AIRTIME
AIRWAVE
BIBLIKE
BICYCLE
BIGGAME
BIGNAME
BIGTIME
BINOCHE
BIPLANE
BIVALVE
BIZARRE
CICADAE
CILIATE
CITABLE
CITRATE
CITRINE
DICTATE
DIFFUSE
DINETTE
DIOCESE
DIOMEDE
DIOXIDE
DISABLE
DISEASE
DISLIKE
DISPOSE
DISPUTE
DISROBE
DIVERGE
DIVERSE
DIVORCE
DIVULGE
FIANCEE
FIBULAE
FICTIVE
FINAGLE
FINANCE
FINESSE
FINLIKE
FIRENZE
FISHEYE
FISSILE
FISSURE
FIXABLE
FIXTURE
GIRAFFE
GIRONDE
GISELLE
HILAIRE
HIPBONE
HIPLIKE
HIRABLE
HIRSUTE
HITHERE
HITTITE
JIGLIKE
JIMCHEE
KIDLIKE
KILDARE
KIMCHEE
KIRSTIE
LICENCE
LICENSE
LIGNITE
LIKABLE
LIMEADE
LINEAGE
LINEATE
LINKAGE
LIONISE
LIONIZE
LIPLIKE
LISENTE
LISSOME
LIVABLE
LIVEONE
MICHELE
MICROBE
MIDLIFE
MIDLINE
MIDRISE
MIDSIZE
MIDWIFE
MIGRATE
MILEAGE
MINABLE
MIOCENE
MIRACLE
MISDATE
MISDONE
MISFILE
MISFIRE
MISLIKE
MISMATE
MISNAME
MISRULE
MISSILE
MISSIVE
MISTAKE
MISTYPE
MIXABLE
MIXTURE
NIBLIKE
NIGHTIE
NITRATE
NITRIDE
NITRITE
OILCAKE
OILLIKE
PIASTRE
PICANTE
PICKAXE
PICTURE
PIELIKE
PIGLIKE
PILLAGE
PINHOLE
PINNACE
PINNATE
PINOCLE
PINWALE
PIPETTE
PIROGUE
PISCINE
PISMIRE
PISTOLE
RIBCAGE
RIBLIKE
RIPOSTE
RIPTIDE
RISIBLE
RISSOLE
RIVIERE
SIAMESE
SILENCE
SINCERE
SINEDIE
SINKAGE
SINLIKE
SISTINE
SITUATE
SIZABLE
TIELINE
TILLAGE
TIMBALE
TINLIKE
TINTYPE
TINWARE
TITMICE
TITRATE
VIBRATE
VILLAGE
VINTAGE
VIOLATE
VIRGULE
VIRTUTE
VISIBLE
VITIATE
WIGLIKE
WILDONE
WILLKIE
WIMPOLE
WINSOME
ZIPCODE

••IE•••

ALIENEE
ALIENOR
ARIETTA
BRIEFED
BRIEFER
BRIEFLY
CHIEFLY
CLIENTS
DRIEDUP
DRIESUP
ETIENNE
FAIENCE
FLIESAT
FLIESIN
FRIEDAN
FRIENDS
FRIEZES
GRIEVED
GRIEVER
GRIEVES
ILIESCU
KNIEVEL
ORIENTE
ORIENTS
OSIERED
PRIESTS
QUIETED
QUIETEN
QUIETER
QUIETLY
SCIENCE
SHIELDS
SPIEDON
SPIEGEL
SPIELED
SPIELER
SPIESON
STIEGEL
THIEVED
THIEVES
TRIEDON
TRIESON
TRIESTE

••I•E••

ABIDEBY
ABILENE
AGILELY
ALIMENT
ANISEED
ARIDEST
BAILEES
BAILERS
BAILEYS
BOILERS
BRIBERY
CHIDERS
CHILEAN
CHIMERA
CHINESE
CHISELS
COINERS
CRIMEAN
DEICERS
DRIVEAT
DRIVEIN
DRIVELS
DRIVERS
DRIVEUP
EMINENT
EPICENE
EPIGENE
EVIDENT
EVILEST
EVILEYE
EXIGENT
FAIREST
GAINERS
GAITERS
GLIDERS
GRIPERS
GRIVETS
GUINEAS
HEIFERS
HEIFETZ
HEIRESS
ICINESS
IGIVEUP
JAILERS
JOINERS
JOINERY
JUICERS
JUICEUP
KAISERS
LOITERS
MAIDENS
MAILERS
MOILERS
NAILERS
NAIVELY
NAIVETE
NAIVETY
OPINERS
PHINEAS
PRICERS
PRIMERS
PRIVETS
QUIVERS
QUIVERY
RAIDERS
RAILERS
RAIMENT
RAISERS
RAISEUP
RUINERS
SEIDELS
SEINERS
SEIZERS
SHINERS
SHIVERS
SHIVERY
SKIVERS
SKIWEAR
SLICERS
SLIDEIN
SLIDERS
SLIVERS
SMILERS
SNIDELY
SNIDEST
SNIPEAT
SNIPERS
SNIVELS
SOIREES
SPICERY
SPICEUP
SPIDERS
SPIDERY
SPIKERS
SPINELS
SPINETS
SPIREAS
STIPEND
SWIPERS
SWIVELS
SWIVETS
TAILEND
TOILERS
TOILETS
TRICEPS
TRIDENT
TRIJETS
TRIREME
TRISECT
TRITELY
TRITEST
TRIVETS
UNITERS
VAINEST
WAILERS
WAITERS
WAIVERS
WHINERS
WHITENS
WHITEST
WRITEIN
WRITERS
WRITETO
WRITEUP
ZAIREAN

••I••E•

ALIASES
ALIENEE
ALIGNED
ALIGNER
ANISEED
AVIATED

AVIATES
BAILEES
BAINTER
BLINDED
BLINDER
BLINKED
BLINKER
BLIPPED
BLISTER
BLITHER
BLITZED
BLITZEN
BLITZES
BRICKED
BRIDGED
BRIDGES
BRIDGET
BRIDLED
BRIDLES
BRIEFED
BRIEFER
BRIMLEY
BRIMMED
BRINGER
BRINIER
BRIQUET
BRISKER
BRISKET
BRITTEN
BUILDER
CAIQUES
CHICHEN
CHICKEN
CHIGGER
CHIGOES
CHILIES
CHILLED
CHILLER
CHIMNEY
CHINKED
CHINNED
CHIPPED
CHIPPER
CHIRPED
CHITTER
CLICHES
CLICKED
CLIMBED
CLIMBER
CLINKED
CLINKER
CLIPPED
CLIPPER
CLIQUES
CLIQUEY
CRIBBED
CRICKED
CRICKET
CRIMPED
CRIMPER
CRINGED
CRINGES
CRISPED
CRISPER
CRITTER
DAILIES
DAIMLER
DAIRIES
DAISIES
DEIFIED
DEIFIES
DEIGNED
DEITIES
DOILIES
DRIBLET
DRIFTED
DRIFTER
DRILLED
DRILLER
DRINKER
DRIPPED
EDIBLES
EDIFIED
EDIFIES
EMIGRES
EMITTED
EMITTER
ENISLED
ENISLES
EPITHET
ERITREA
EVICTED
EVILLER
EVINCED
EVINCES
EXISTED
FAINTED
FAINTER
FAIRIES
FEIFFER
FEIGNED
FEINTED
FLICKED
FLICKER
FLIPPED
FLIPPER
FLIRTED
FLITTED
FLITTER
FLIVVER
FOIBLES
FOISTED
FRIDGES
FRIEZES
FRILLED
FRINGED
FRINGES
FRIPPET
FRISBEE
FRISKED
FRITTED
FRITTER
FRIZZED
FRIZZES
GLIBBER
GLIMMER
GLINTED
GLISTEN
GLITTER
GLITZED
GLITZES
GRIDDED
GRIDDER
GRIEVED
GRIEVER
GRIEVES
GRIFFEY
GRIFTER
GRILLED
GRILLES
GRILLET
GRIMIER
GRIMMER
GRINDER
GRINNED
GRINNER
GRIPPED
GRIPPER
GRITTED
GUILDER
GUIMPES
HAIRIER
HAIRNET
HEISTED
HOISTED
ICICLES
JOINDER
JOINTED
JOISTED
JUICIER
KAISHEK
KNIEVEL
KNISHES
KNITTED
KNITTER
LAISSEZ
LEISTER
MAIGRET
MAITRED
MEINIES
MEIOSES
MEISSEN
MEISTER
MOISTEN
MOISTER
NAIADES
NAILSET
NEIGHED
NEITHER
NOISIER
OLIVIER
OMITTED
OMITTER
OPIATES
ORIOLES
OSIERED
PAINTED
PAINTER
PAISLEY
PAIUTES
PHILTER
PLINKED
POINTED
POINTER
POITIER
PRICIER
PRICKED
PRIMMER
PRIMPED
PRINCES
PRINKED
PRINTED
PRINTER
PRITHEE
PRIVIER
PRIVIES
QUICHES
QUICKEN
QUICKER
QUIETED
QUIETEN
QUIETER
QUIGLEY
QUILLED
QUILLER
QUILTED
QUILTER
QUINCES
QUINTET
QUIPPED
QUIPPER
QUITTER
QUIZZED
QUIZZES
RAINIER
REIFIED
REIFIES
REIGNED
REINKED
ROILIER
ROISTER
SAINTED
SEICHES
SHIFTED
SHIITES
SHILLED
SHIMMER
SHINIER
SHINNED
SHIPMEN
SHIPPED
SHIPPER
SHIRKED
SHIRKER
SHIRLEY
SHIRRED
SKIDDED
SKIDDER
SKILLED
SKILLET
SKIMMED
SKIMMER
SKIMPED
SKINNED
SKINNER
SKIPPED
SKIPPER
SKIRLED
SKIRRED
SKIRTED
SKITTER
SLICKED
SLICKER
SLIMIER
SLIMMED
SLIMMER
SLINGER
SLINKED
SLIPPED
SLIPPER
SLITHER
SMIDGEN
SMIRKED
SMITTEN
SNICKER
SNIFFED
SNIFFER
SNIFTER
SNIGGER
SNIGLET
SNIPPED
SNIPPET
SOIGNEE
SOIREES
SPICIER
SPIEGEL
SPIELED
SPIELER
SPIKIER
SPILLED
SPINIER
SPINNER
SPINNEY
SPIRIER
SPITZES
STICHES
STICKER
STIEGEL
STIFFED
STIFFEN
STIFFER
STIFLED
STIFLES
STILLED
STILLER
STILTED
STINGER
STINKER
STINTED
STIRRED
STIRRER
SWIFTER
SWIGGED
SWILLED
SWIMMER
SWINGER
SWIRLED
SWISHED
SWISHES
SWITZER
TAILLES
TAINTED
TEICHER
THICKEN
THICKER
THICKET
THIEVED
THIEVES
THINKER
THINNED
THINNER
THITHER
TRICKED
TRICKER
TRIFLED
TRIFLER
TRIFLES
TRIGGED
TRIGGER
TRILLED
TRIMMED
TRIMMER
TRINKET
TRIODES
TRIPLED
TRIPLES
TRIPLET
TRIPLEX
TRIPPED
TRIPPER
TRIPPET
TRIUNES
TWILLED
TWINBED
TWINGED
TWINGES
TWINNED
TWIRLED
TWIRLER
TWISTED
TWISTER
TWITTED
TWITTER
UNIFIED
UNIFIER
UNIFIES
UNITIES
VEINIER
WEIGHED
WEIRDER
WHIFFED
WHIMPER
WHINIER
WHIPPED
WHIPPET
WHIRLED
WHIRRED
WHISHED
WHISHES
WHISKED
WHISKER
WHISKEY
WHISPER
WHITHER
WHITIER
WHITNEY
WHIZZED
WHIZZER
WHIZZES
WRIGLEY
WRINGER
WRITHED
WRITHES
WRITTEN

••I•••E

ABILENE
ADIPOSE
AGITATE
ALIDADE
ALIENEE
AMIABLE
AMIBLUE
ANILINE
ANIMATE
ARIADNE
ARISTAE
ASININE
ATINGLE
ATISSUE
AXILLAE
BRIGADE
BRINDLE
BRIOCHE
BRISTLE
BRITTLE
CHINESE
CLIMATE
COINAGE
CRINKLE
CUISINE
DRIBBLE
DRIZZLE
DWINDLE
EDIFICE
EMIRATE
EPICENE
EPICURE
EPIGENE
EPIGONE
EPISODE
EPISTLE
EPITOME
ETIENNE
EVILEYE
FAIENCE
FAILURE
FRIABLE
FRICKIE
FRIGATE
FRISBEE
FRIZZLE
GLIMPSE
GRIDDLE
GRIMACE
GRISTLE
GRIZZLE
HAIRDYE
IMITATE
KRINGLE
LEISURE
NAIVETE
NOISOME
OLIVINE
ORIENTE
ORIFICE
OXIDASE
OXIDISE
OXIDIZE
PHILTRE
PLIABLE
PRICKLE
PRIMATE
PRITHEE
PRIVATE
QUIBBLE
QUICKIE
QUININE
QUINQUE
QUIXOTE
REISSUE
RHIZOME
SCIENCE
SHINGLE
SKIPOLE
SKITTLE
SNIFFLE
SNIGGLE
SOIGNEE
SPINDLE
STIPPLE
SWINDLE
SWIZZLE
THIMBLE
THINICE
THISTLE
TRIBUNE
TRIBUTE
TRICKLE
TRIESTE
TRIREME
TRITONE
TWIDDLE
TWINKLE
UNITIVE
UTILISE
UTILIZE
WHISTLE
WHITTLE
WRIGGLE
WRINKLE

•••IE••

ACHIEST
ACHIEVE
AERIEST
AIRIEST
ALFIERI
ALGIERS
AMBIENT
ANCIENT
ANXIETY
ARRIERE
ARTIEST
ASHIEST
BELIEFS
BELIEVE
BESIEGE
BEZIERS
BONIEST
BOXIEST
BUSIEST
CAGIEST
CAHIERS
CAKIEST
CANIEST
COKIEST
COPIERS
COSIEST
COZIEST
DANIELS
DENIERS
DICIEST
DOPIEST
DOZIEST
DUBIETY
EASIEST
EDGIEST
EELIEST
EERIEST
EGGIEST
ENVIERS
FOXIEST
FUMIEST
GAMIEST
GLUIEST
GOOIEST
GORIEST
HAZIEST
HOKIEST
HOLIEST
HOMIEST
HOSIERS
HOSIERY
HYGIEIA
HYGIENE
ICKIEST
IFFIEST
IMPIETY
INFIELD
INKIEST
JIVIEST
JOKIEST
LACIEST
LAKIEST
LAZIEST
LEMIEUX
LENIENT
LEVIERS
LIMIEST
LINIEST
LOGIEST
LUMIERE
MAZIEST
METIERS
MILIEUS
MILIEUX
MIMIEUX
MIRIEST
MOLIERE
MOPIEST
NIMIETY
NORIEGA
NOSIEST
OILIEST
OOZIEST
PALIEST
PATIENT
PINIEST
PIPIEST
PITIERS
POKIEST
PUNIEST
RACIEST
RAPIERS
RELIEFS
RELIEVE
RELIEVO
REVIEWS
RIMIEST
RIPIENO
RIVIERA
RIVIERE
ROPIEST
ROSIEST
SALIENT
SALIERI
SAPIENS
SAPIENT
SATIETY
SEXIEST
SHRIEKS
SOCIETY
SOVIETS
SPRIEST
TIDIEST
TINIEST
TONIEST
TYPIEST
UGLIEST
VARIETY
VINIEST
VIZIERS
WANIEST
WARIEST
WAVIEST
WAXIEST
WILIEST
WINIEST
WIRIEST
ZANIEST

•••I•E•

ACTIVES
ADFINEM
ADMIRED
ADMIRER
ADMIRES
ADMIXED
ADMIXES
ADVISED
ADVISER
ADVISES
AEDILES
AFFINES
AFFIXED
AFFIXES
ANTIBES
ANTIGEN
APSIDES
AQUIFER
AQUIVER
ARBITER
ARGIVES
ARRISES
ARRIVED
ARRIVER
ARRIVES
ASPIRED
ASPIRER
ASPIRES
ASSIZES
ATTIMES
ATTIRED
ATTIRES
AUDILES
AUDITED
AVAILED
AVOIDED
AWAITED
BATIKED
BEDIZEN
BEMIRED
BEMIRES
BESIDES
BETIDED
BETIDES
BETIMES
BETISES
BODICES
BOLIDES
BOVINES
BRAIDED
BRAIDER
BRAINED
BRAISED
BRAISES
BROILED
BROILER
BRUISED
BRUISER
BRUISES
BRUITED
BYLINED
BYLINES
CABINET
CALIBER
CALICES
CALIPER
CAMISES
CANINES
CARIBES
CAVILED
CAVILER
CCRIDER
CHAINED
CHAIRED
CHAISES
CHOICER
CHOICES
CITIZEN
CLAIMED
CLAIMER
CODICES
CONIFER
COSINES
CRUISED
CRUISER
CRUISES
DEBITED
DECIBEL
DECIDED
DECIDES
DEFILED
DEFILER
DEFILES
DEFINED
DEFINES
DELIBES
DELIVER
DEMISED
DEMISES
DENIZEN
DERIDED
DERIDES
DERIVED
DERIVES
DESIRED
DESIREE
DESIRES
DEVICES
DEVILED
DEVISED
DEVISES
DIVIDED
DIVIDER
DIVIDES
DIVINED
DIVINER
DIVINES
DRAINED
DRAINER
DREIDEL
DREISER
EMAILED
EMPIRES
ENDIVES
ENGINES
ENLIVEN
ENSILED
ENSILES
ENTICED
ENTICER
ENTICES
EQUINES
ERMINES
ETOILES
EXCISED
EXCISES
EXCITED
EXCITES
EXPIRED
EXPIRES
EXWIVES
FAMINES
FELINES
FLAILED
FRAILER
FRAISES
FRUITED
GALILEE
GALILEI
GALILEO
GAMINES
GLAIRED
GRAINED
HABITED
HALIDES
HALITES
HAMITES
HELICES
HELIXES
IGNITED
IGNITER
IGNITES
IMBIBED
IMBIBES
IMMIXED
IMMIXES
INCISED
INCISES
INCITED
INCITER
INCITES
INDICES
INDITED
INDITES
INFIDEL
INSIDER
INSIDES
INVITED
INVITES
IODIDES
IODISED
IODISES
IODIZED
IODIZES
IONISED
IONISES
IONIZED
IONIZER
IONIZES
JUBILEE
JUNIPER
JUPITER
KYLIKES
LATICES
LEVITES
LIAISED
LIAISES
LIMITED
LIPIDES
LORISES
LUCIFER
LUPINES
MARINER
MARINES
MATINEE
MERIMEE
MERITED
MINIVER
MOBILES
MONIKER
MOTIVES
NATIVES
NETIZEN
NOMINEE
NOTICED
NOTICES
NOVICES
OBLIGED
OBLIGES
OFFICER
OFFICES
ONSIDES
OOLITES
OPHITES
ORBITED
ORBITER
ORDINES
ORPINES
OSCINES
PEDICEL
PERIGEE
PETITES
PLAICES
PLAINER
PLAITED
POLICED
POLICES
POLITER
POSITED
PRAISED
PRAISER
PRAISES
PUMICES
PYRITES
PYXIDES
QUAILED
RADICES
RADIOED
RADIXES
RAPIDER
RAPINES
RATITES
RAVINES
REAIMED
REAIRED
RECIPES
RECITED
RECITER
RECITES
REFILED
REFILES
REFINED
REFINER
REFINES
REFIRES
REGIMEN
REGIMES
REHIRED
REHIRES
RELINED
RELINES
RELIVED
RELIVES
REMIGES
REMIXED
REMIXES
REOILED
REPINED
REPINES
RESIDED
RESIDES
RESILED
RESILES
RETILED
RETILES
RETIMED
RETIMES
RETIRED
RETIREE
RETIRES
REVILED
REVILES
REVISED
REVISER
REVISES
REVIVED
REVIVES
REWIRED
REWIRES
ROTIFER
SABINES
SAMISEN
SAMITES
SANIBEL
SATINET
SATIRES
SCRIBES
SCRIVEN
SEMITES
SHIITES
SHRIKES
SHRINER
SHRINES
SHRIVEL
SHRIVER
SHRIVES
SIMILES
SLUICED
SLUICES
SOLIDER
SORITES
SPLICED
SPLICER
SPLICES
SPLINES
SPOILED
SPOILER
SPRITES
SQUIRED
SQUIRES
STAIDER
STAINED
STAINER
STEIGER
STEINEM
STEINER
STRIDER
STRIDES
STRIKER
STRIKES
STRIPED
STRIPER
STRIPES
STRIVED
STRIVEN
STRIVER
STRIVES
TAXIMEN
THRIVED
THRIVES
TIMIDER
TOTIDEM
TRAILED
TRAILER
TRAINED
TRAINEE
TRAINER
UMPIRED
UMPIRES
UNAIDED
UNAIMED
UNAIRED
UNFIXED
UNLIKED
UNLINED
UNOILED
UNPILED
UNPILES
UNWISER
UPRISEN
UPRISES
UPRIVER
VALISES
VISITED
VIVIDER
WAHINES

•••I••E

AAMILNE
ABRIDGE
ACHIEVE
ADDIBLE
ANTIQUE
ARRIERE
ARTICLE
ARTISTE
AUDIBLE
AURICLE
BATISTE
BELIEVE
BESIEGE
BEZIQUE
BRAILLE
CALIBRE
CAMILLE
CILIATE
COMIQUE
CUBICLE
CUTICLE
DEHISCE
DEMILLE
DESIREE
DEVIATE

DEVILLE
ECLIPSE
ELLIPSE
ENTITLE
EXPIATE
FATIGUE
FOLIAGE
FOLIATE
GALILEE
GEFILTE
HABITUE
HYGIENE
IMPINGE
JUBILEE
LABIATE
LAFITTE
LALIQUE
LAMINAE
LEGIBLE
LETITBE
LORICAE
LUCILLE
LUMIERE
MANIPLE
MATINEE
MATISSE
MEDIATE
MERIMEE
MODISTE
MOLIERE
MONIQUE
NEVILLE
NOMINEE
OBLIQUE
OBVIATE
ORVILLE
OSSICLE
PANICLE
PEDICLE
PELISSE
PERIGEE
PETIOLE
PRAIRIE
RADIATE
RADICLE
RELIEVE
RERINSE
RESIDUE
RETICLE
RETINAE
RETINUE
RETIREE
RETITLE
RISIBLE
RIVIERE
SATIATE
SERIATE
SEVIGNE
SEVILLE
STRIATE
SYRINGE
TRAINEE
TRAIPSE
TUNICLE
VEHICLE
VISIBLE
VITIATE
WOEISME

••••IE•

AMBRIES
ANGRIER
ANOMIES
ANTSIER
APERIES
APPLIED
APPLIES
ARTSIER
ATELIER
ATOMIES
ATONIES
AUNTIES
AUSSIES
BADDIES
BAGGIER
BAGGIES
BALKIER
BALMIER
BANDIED
BANDIES
BARKIER
BARMIER
BARRIER
BATTIER
BAWDIER
BEADIER
BEAMIER
BEANIES
BEEFIER
BEERIER
BELLIED
BELLIES
BENDIER
BERRIED
BERRIES
BIALIES
BIDDIES
BIGGIES
BIGLIES
BILBIES
BILGIER
BILLIES
BIRDIED
BIRDIES
BITSIER
BITTIER
BLOWIER
BMOVIES
BOBBIES
BOGGIER
BONNIER
BOOBIES
BOOGIED
BOOGIES
BOOKIES
BOOMIER
BOONIES
BOOTIES
BOSKIER
BOSSIER
BOWTIES
BRAZIER
BRINIER
BUDDIES
BUDGIES
BUGGIER
BUGGIES
BULGIER
BULKIER
BULLIED
BULLIES
BUMPIER
BUNNIES
BURLIER
BUSBIES
BUSHIER
BUTTIES
CABBIES
CADDIED
CADDIES
CAMPIER
CANDIED
CANDIES
CANNIER
CARNIES
CARRIED
CARRIER
CARRIES
CARTIER
CASHIER
CATTIER
CHARIER
CHENIER
CHEVIED
CHEVIES
CHEWIER
CHILIES
CHOKIER
CIVVIES
CLAVIER
CLAYIER
COCKIER
COLLIER
COLLIES
COMFIER
CONRIED
COOKIES
COOTIES
CORKIER
CORNIER
COURIER
COWRIES
CRAZIER
CRAZIES
CRONIES
CROSIER
CUBBIES
CUDDIES
CULLIED
CULLIES
CURDIER
CURLIER
CURRIED
CURRIER
CURRIES
CURVIER
CUSHIER
DADDIES
DAFFIER
DAILIES
DAIRIES
DAISIES
DALLIED
DALLIER
DALLIES
DANDIER
DANDIES
DARBIES
DAUMIER
DEARIES
DEBRIEF
DECRIED
DECRIER
DECRIES
DEIFIED
DEIFIES
DEITIES
DERBIES
DERNIER
DEVRIES
DIARIES
DICKIES
DILLIES
DINGIER
DINKIER
DINKIES
DIPPIER
DIRTIED
DIRTIER
DIRTIES
DISHIER
DITSIER
DITTIES
DITZIER
DIVVIED
DIVVIES
DIZZIED
DIZZIER
DIZZIES
DOBBIES
DODGIER
DOGGIER
DOGGIES
DOILIES
DOLLIED
DOLLIES
DOOZIES
DOSSIER
DOTTIER
DOWDIER
DOWNIER
DOWRIES
DUCHIES
DUCKIER
DUMMIED
DUMMIES
DUMPIER
DUSKIER
DUSTIER
EARLIER
EBONIES
EDIFIED
EDIFIES
ELEGIES
EMPTIED
EMPTIER
EMPTIES
ENEMIES
ENSKIED
ENSKIES
ENTRIES
EPOXIES
EZEKIEL
FAERIES
FAIRIES
FANCIED
FANCIER
FANCIES
FARRIER
FATTIER
FELLIES
FENNIER
FERNIER
FERRIED
FERRIES
FIERIER
FIFTIES
FILLIES
FILMIER
FINNIER
FIRRIER
FISHIER
FIZZIER
FLAKIER
FLAMIER
FLAXIER
FLUKIER
FLUTIER
FOAMIER
FOGGIER
FOLKIER
FOLKIES
FOLLIES
FOODIES
FORKIER
FORTIES
FOURIER
FRASIER
FRAZIER
FUBSIER
FUNKIER
FUNNIER
FUNNIES
FURRIER
FUSSIER
FUSTIER
FUZZIER
GABBIER
GABRIEL
GAMMIER
GASSIER
GAUDIER
GAUZIER
GAWKIER
GEEKIER
GEMMIER
GERMIER
GIDDIER
GILLIES
GIPSIES
GLACIER
GLAZIER
GLORIED
GLORIES
GOALIES
GODLIER
GOODIES
GOOFIER
GOONIER
GOOPIER
GOOSIER
GORSIER
GOUTIER
GRAPIER
GRAVIES
GRIMIER
GRODIER
GROLIER
GULLIES
GULPIER
GUMMIER
GUNKIER
GUNNIES
GUPPIES
GUSHIER
GUSSIED
GUSSIES
GUSTIER
GUTSIER
GUTTIER
GYPSIES
HACKIES
HAIRIER
HAMMIER
HANDIER
HANKIES
HAPPIER
HARDIER
HARPIES
HARRIED
HARRIER
HARRIES
HARRIET
HASTIER
HEADIER
HEAVIER
HEAVIES
HEDGIER
HEFTIER
HERBIER
HILLIER
HINNIES
HIPPIER
HIPPIES
HOAGIES
HOARIER
HOBBIES
HOGTIED
HOGTIES
HOLLIES
HOOSIER
HORSIER
HUBBIES
HUFFIER
HUMPIER
HUNKIER
HURLIES
HURRIED
HURRIES
HUSKIER
HUSKIES
HUSSIES
IMPLIED
IMPLIES
INBRIEF
IRONIES
ITCHIER
IVORIES
JACKIES
JAGGIER
JAGGIES
JAMMIER
JANVIER
JAZZIER
JEEBIES
JELLIED
JELLIES
JEMMIED
JEMMIES
JENNIES
JERKIER
JETTIES
JIFFIES
JIMMIED
JIMMIES
JOLLIED
JOLLIER
JOLLIES
JOLLIET
JOLTIER
JOWLIER
JUICIER
JUMPIER
JUNKIER
JUNKIES
JUTTIED
JUTTIES
KELPIES
KEWPIES
KICKIER
KIDDIES
KILTIES
KINKIER
KITTIES
KOOKIER
LADDIES
LANKIER
LARDIER
LASSIES
LEADIER
LEAFIER
LEAKIER
LEARIER
LEDGIER
LEERIER
LEFTIES
LEGGIER
LEPPIES
LINDIED
LINDIES
LINTIER
LIPPIER
LOAMIER
LOBBIED
LOBBIES
LOFTIER
LOLLIES
LONGIES
LOOBIES
LOONIER
LOONIES
LOOPIER
LOPPIER
LORRIES
LOUSIER
LOWLIER
LUCKIER
LUMPIER
LUSTIER
MAGPIES
MALTIER
MANGIER
MANLIER
MARRIED
MARRIES
MASHIES
MASSIER
MEALIER
MEALIES
MEANIES
MEATIER
MEINIES
MENZIES
MERCIES
MERRIER
MESHIER
MESSIER
MIDDIES
MIFFIER
MILKIER
MINGIER
MINTIER
MIRKIER
MISSIES
MISTIER
MOGGIES
MOLDIER
MOMMIES
MOODIER
MOONIER
MOORIER
MOSSIER
MOTHIER
MOUSIER
MUCKIER
MUDDIED
MUDDIER
MUDDIES
MUDPIES
MUGGIER
MUMMIES
MURKIER
MUSHIER
MUSKIER
MUSKIES
MUSSIER
MUSTIER
MUZZIER
NAGGIER
NANNIES
NAPPIES
NASTIER
NATTIER
NAVVIES
NEDDIES
NEEDIER
NERDIER
NERVIER
NEWSIER
NEWSIES
NIFTIER
NINNIES
NIPPIER
NITTIER
NOBBIER
NOISIER
NUBBIER
NUTSIER
NUTTIER
OLIVIER
ONADIET
PADDIES
PALLIER
PALMIER
PANNIER
PANSIES
PARRIED
PARRIER
PARRIES
PARTIED
PARTIER
PARTIES
PASTIER
PATSIES
PATTIES
PAWKIER
PEATIER
PECKIER
PENNIES
PEONIES
PEPPIER
PERDIEM
PERKIER
PERRIER
PESKIER
PETTIER
PHONIER
PHONIES
PICKIER
PIETIES
PIGGIER
PIGGIES
PINKIES
PITHIER
PLATIER
PLUMIER
PODGIER
POITIER
POPPIES
PORGIES
PORKIER
POTPIES
POTSIER
POTTIER
POUTIER
PREMIER
PREVIEW
PREXIES
PRICIER
PRIVIER
PRIVIES
PROSIER
PROXIES
PUDGIER
PUFFIER
PULPIER
PUNKIER
PUNKIES
PUNNIER
PUNTIES
PUPPIES
PURLIEU
PURSIER
PURVIEW
PUSHIER
PUTTIED
PUTTIES
PYGMIES
QUAKIER
QUERIED
QUERIER
QUERIES
RAINIER
RALLIED
RALLIER
RALLIES
RANDIER
RANGIER
RASPIER
RATTIER
READIED
READIER
READIES
REEDIER
REFRIED
REFRIES
REIFIED
REIFIES
REPLIED
REPLIES
REQUIEM
RETRIED
RETRIES
RIBBIES
RIDGIER
RISKIER
RITZIER
ROADIES
ROCKIER
ROCKIES
ROILIER
ROOKIER
ROOKIES
ROOMIER
ROOMIES
ROOTIER
ROWDIER
ROWDIES
RUDDIER
RUMMIER
RUNNIER
RUNTIER
RUSHIER
RUSTIER
RUTTIER
SAGGIER
SALLIED
SALLIES
SALTIER
SANDIER
SAPPIER
SARKIER
SASSIER
SASSIES
SAUCIER
SAVVIER
SCALIER
SCARIER
SEAMIER
SEDGIER
SEEDIER
SEEPIER
SERRIED
SHADIER
SHAKIER
SHINIER
SHOWIER
SILKIER
SILLIER
SILLIES
SILTIER
SISSIES
SIXTIES
SLATIER
SLIMIER
SMOKIER
SMOKIES
SNAKIER
SNOWIER
SOAPIER
SODDIER
SODDIES
SOFTIES
SOGGIER
SOLDIER
SOOTIER
SOPPIER
SORRIER
SORTIED
SORTIES
SOUPIER
SPACIER
SPANIEL
SPECIES
SPICIER
SPIKIER
SPINIER
SPIRIER
SPUMIER
STAGIER
STOGIES
STONIER
STORIED
STORIES
STUDIED
STUDIES
STYMIED
STYMIES
SUDSIER
SULKIER
SULKIES
SULLIED
SULLIES
SUNNIER
SURFIER
SURLIER
TABBIES
TACKIER
TAFFIES
TALKIER
TALKIES
TALLIED
TALLIER
TALLIES
TANGIER
TANSIES
TARDIER
TARRIED
TARRIER
TARRIES
TARSIER
TASTIER
TATTIER
TAWNIER
TEARIER
TECHIER
TECHIES
TEDDIES
TEENIER
TELLIES
TENNIEL
TERRIER
TERRIES
TESTIER
THEWIER
TINNIER
TIPPIER
TIPSIER
TIZZIES
TOADIED
TOADIES
TODDIES
TOLKIEN
TOLLIES
TOONIES
TOWNIES
TUBBIER
TUFTIER
TUMMIES
TUNNIES
TURFIER
UNIFIED
UNIFIER
UNIFIES
UNITIES
UNTRIED
USURIES
VASTIER
VEALIER
VEERIES
VEGGIES
VEINIER
VERNIER
VIEWIER
WACKIER
WADDIES
WARTIER
WASHIER
WASPIER
WEARIED
WEARIER
WEARIES
WEBBIER
WEDGIER
WEDGIES
WEEDIER
WEENIER
WEENIES
WEEPIER
WEEPIES
WHINIER
WHITIER
WIENIES
WIGGIER
WILLIES
WIMPIER
WINDIER
WISPIER
WITHIER
WITHIES
WITTIER
WONKIER
WOODIER
WOODIES
WOOKIES
WOOLIER
WOOLIES
WOOZIER
WORDIER
WORMIER
WORRIED
WORRIER
WORRIES
YORKIES
YUCKIER
YUMMIER
YUPPIES
ZAPPIER
ZESTIER
ZINGIER
ZIPPIER
ZOMBIES

••••I•E

ABUSIVE
ACONITE
ACQUIRE
ACTFIVE
ADAMITE
ADELINE
ADENINE
AFFAIRE
AGONISE
AGONIZE
AIRLIKE
AIRLINE
AIRMILE
AIRTIME
ALEWIFE
ALLTIME
AMATIVE
ANILINE
ANODISE
ANODIZE
ANTLIKE
ANTOINE
ANYTIME
APATITE
APELIKE
APPRISE
APPRIZE
ARCHIVE
ARCSINE
ARMLIKE
ARMOIRE
ASCRIBE
ASININE
ASSLIKE
ASTAIRE
ASTRIDE
ATOMISE
ATOMIZE
ATTRITE
AUSPICE
AVARICE
AZURITE
BAGLIKE
BAGPIPE
BAPTISE
BAPTIZE
BATLIKE
BAUXITE
BEDLIKE
BEDSIDE
BEDTIME
BEEHIVE
BEELIKE
BEELINE
BEGRIME
BEGUILE
BEGUINE
BERNICE
BIBLIKE
BIGTIME
BONFIRE
BOWLIKE
BOWLINE
BOXKITE
BOXLIKE
BROMIDE
BROMINE
BUDLIKE
BUSLINE
BUYTIME
CALCITE
CANDICE
CANDIDE
CAPRICE
CAPSIZE
CAPTIVE
CARBIDE
CARBINE
CARMINE
CASTILE
CATLIKE
CENTIME
CHALICE
CHEMISE
CHOLINE
CHORINE
CITRINE
CLARICE
COCHISE
CODEINE
COLLIDE
COMBINE
COMPILE
CONCISE
CONFIDE
CONFINE
CONNIVE
COPPICE
CORDITE
CORNICE
COWHIDE
COWLIKE
CREVICE
CUISINE
CUPLIKE
CURLIKE
CURSIVE
CUTTIME
DAYTIME
DECEIVE
DECLINE
DELUISE
DENTINE
DEPRIVE
DESPISE
DESPITE
DESTINE
DEWLINE
DIOXIDE
DISLIKE
DNOTICE
DOGLIKE
DORMICE
DOTLIKE
DUCTILE
EARLIKE
EBBTIDE
EBONITE
EBWHITE
EDIFICE
EELLIKE
EGALITE
ELFLIKE
ELUSIVE
EMOTIVE
ENDWISE
ENQUIRE
ENSUITE
ENTWINE
EREMITE
EROSIVE
ERSKINE
ERUDITE
ESQUIRE
ETAMINE
EVASIVE
EXAMINE
EYELIKE
FADLIKE
FANLIKE
FANZINE
FATLIKE
FEBRILE
FERRITE
FERTILE
FESTIVE
FICTIVE
FINLIKE
FISSILE
FORGIVE
FORLIFE
FOXFIRE
FOXLIKE
FRAGILE
FURTIVE
GAGLINE
GEMLIKE
GENTILE
GENUINE
GODLIKE
GRACILE
GRANITE
GUANINE
GUMLIKE
GUNFIRE
HAGLIKE
HATLIKE
HAYRIDE
HAYWIRE
HELOISE
HEMLINE
HENLIKE
HEROINE
HILAIRE
HIPLIKE
HITTITE
HOGLIKE
HOPLIKE
HOSPICE
HOSTILE
HOTLINE
HOTWIRE

HUNLIKE
HUTLIKE
HYALINE
ICELIKE
IDOLISE
IDOLIZE
IMAGINE
INCLINE
INKLIKE
INQUIRE
INSPIRE
INUTILE
INVOICE
ITEMISE
ITEMIZE
IVYLIKE
JADEITE
JAMLIKE
JASMINE
JAWLIKE
JAWLINE
JIGLIKE
JOYRIDE
JUGWINE
JUSTICE
JUSTINE
KEYLIME
KIDLIKE
LARAINE
LATTICE
LAWLIKE
LEETIDE
LEGLIKE
LEONINE
LEUCINE
LIGNITE
LIONISE
LIONIZE
LIPLIKE
LOWLIFE
LOWRISE
LOWTIDE
LUDDITE
MACHINE
MAGUIRE
MALAISE
MANLIKE
MASSIVE
MAURICE
MAYTIME
MAYWINE
MCGUIRE
MCSWINE
MEMOIRE
MIDLIFE
MIDLINE
MIDRISE
MIDSIZE
MIDWIFE
MISFILE
MISFIRE
MISLIKE
MISSILE
MISSIVE
MORAINE
MORTISE
NAPTIME
NETLIKE
NIBLIKE
NITRIDE
NITRITE
NUCLIDE
NUNLIKE
NUTLIKE
OAKLIKE
OARLIKE
OATLIKE
OFFLINE
OFFSIDE
OFFSITE
OILLIKE
OLDLINE
OLDTIME
OLIVINE
ONETIME
OPALINE
ORBLIKE
ORIFICE
OUTLINE
OUTLIVE
OUTSIDE
OUTSIZE
OWLLIKE
OXIDISE
OXIDIZE
PACKICE
PANPIPE
PAPLIKE
PARTITE
PASSIVE
PASTIME
PATRICE
PAULINE
PEALIKE
PEGLIKE
PENLIKE
PENSIVE
PEPTIDE
PERLITE
PIELIKE
PIGLIKE
PISCINE
PISMIRE
PLOSIVE
PODLIKE
PONTINE
PORCINE
PRALINE
PRECISE
PREMISE
PRESIDE
PROFILE
PROMISE
PROVIDE
PUERILE
QUININE
RAGTIME
RAMLIKE
RATLIKE
RATLINE
RAWHIDE
RAYLIKE
REALISE
REALIZE
RECEIVE
RECLINE
REDLINE
REDPINE
REDWINE
REJOICE
REPRICE
REPRISE
REPTILE
REQUIRE
REQUITE
RERAISE
RESPIRE
RESPITE
RESTIVE
REUNITE
REVOICE
REWRITE
RIBLIKE
RIPTIDE
RODLIKE
ROGAINE
ROMAINE
ROUTINE
RUGLIKE
SACLIKE
SALTINE
SARDINE
SAWLIKE
SEAFIRE
SEASIDE
SERVICE
SERVILE
SESSILE
SETLINE
SINLIKE
SISTINE
SKYDIVE
SKYLIKE
SKYLINE
SONLIKE
SOWLIKE
STABILE
STATICE
STERILE
STYLISE
STYLIZE
SUBLIME
SUBSIDE
SUFFICE
SULFIDE
SULFITE
SUNLIKE
SUNRISE
SURMISE
SURVIVE
TACTILE
TAGLIKE
TAGLINE
TANLINE
TAURINE
TEATIME
TEETIME
TEKTITE
TENSILE
TENSIVE
TERMITE
TEXTILE
THINICE
THYMINE
TIELINE
TINLIKE
TITMICE
TOELIKE
TONTINE
TOPSIDE
TOYLIKE
TUBLIKE
TURBINE
TVGUIDE
TWOTIME
UKRAINE
UNALIKE
UNITIVE
UPRAISE
URANITE
URNLIKE
UTILISE
UTILIZE
VACCINE
VAMPIRE
VANDINE
VESTIGE
VULPINE
WARLIKE
WARTIME
WAXLIKE
WAYSIDE
WEBLIKE
WEBSITE
WIGLIKE

•••••IE

BEASTIE
BEATTIE
BLACKIE
BLONDIE
BOLOTIE
BRASSIE
BROWNIE
CALORIE
CAPAPIE
CHAPPIE
CHARLIE
CHEAPIE
COTERIE
CRAPPIE
DHURRIE
DOORDIE
EUGENIE
FOOTSIE
FRANKIE
FREDDIE
FREEBIE
FRICKIE
GEORDIE
GROUPIE
GUTHRIE
JEANNIE
JOHNNIE
KIRSTIE
LARAMIE
MELANIE
MOUNTIE
NATALIE
NECKTIE
NIGHTIE
OVERLIE
PORKPIE
PRAIRIE
PREEMIE
PREPPIE
QUICKIE
REVERIE
ROSALIE
RUSHDIE
SCOTTIE
SHELTIE
SINEDIE
STEELIE
STOOLIE
SWEETIE
SWOOSIE
TOOTSIE
TOUGHIE
TREKKIE
TWOONIE
VALERIE
WHEELIE
WILLKIE

IF•••••

IFFIEST
IFSTONE

I•F••••

IFFIEST
INFANCY
INFANTA
INFANTS
INFAVOR
INFECTS
INFERNO
INFESTS
INFIDEL
INFIELD
INFLAME
INFLATE
INFLECT
INFLICT
INFLOWS
INFOCUS
INFORCE
INFORMS
INFRONT
INFUSED
INFUSES

I••F•••

ICEFLOE
ICEFOGS
ICEFREE

I•••F••

INSOFAR

I•••••F

INAWEOF
INBRIEF

•IF••••

BIFOCAL
DIFFERS
DIFFUSE
FIFTEEN
FIFTHLY
FIFTIES
GIFFORD
JIFFIES
LIFEFUL
LIFENET
LIFTERS
LIFTING
LIFTOFF
LIFTSUP
MIFFIER
MIFFING
NIFTIER
NIFTILY
PIFFLED
PIFFLES
RIFFING
RIFFLED
RIFFLES
RIFLERS
RIFLERY
RIFLING
RIFTING
SIFTERS
SIFTING
TIFFANY
TIFFING
TIFFINS

•I•F•••

AIRFARE
AIRFLOW
AIRFOIL
BIDFAIR
BIGFEET
BIGFOOT
DIFFERS
DIFFUSE
FIEFDOM
GIFFORD
GINFIZZ
JIFFIES
KINFOLK
MIFFIER
MIFFING
MISFILE
MISFIRE
MISFITS
MITFORD
PIFFLED
PIFFLES
PILFERS
PITFALL
RIFFING
RIFFLED
RIFFLES
SIXFOLD
TIFFANY
TIFFING
TIFFINS
TINFOIL
TITFERS
WILFORD
WILFRID
WINFREY

•I••F••

AIMSFOR
DIREFUL
DISHFUL
FIREFLY
FISHFRY
FISTFUL
GIRAFFE
LIFEFUL
MINDFUL
PINEFOR
PIPEFUL
PITIFUL
RIPOFFS
SIGHFUL
TIPOFFS
WILLFUL
WISHFUL
WISTFUL

•I•••F•

AIRLIFT
BITEOFF
DIEDOFF
DIESOFF
DIGNIFY
DISTAFF
FIREOFF
GIRAFFE
GIVEOFF
KICKOFF
KISSOFF
LIFTOFF
LIQUEFY
MIDLIFE
MIDRIFF
MIDWIFE
PICKOFF
RIDEOFF
RINGOFF
RIPOFFS
RIPSOFF
SIGNIFY
SIGNOFF
TICKOFF
TIMEOFF
TIPOFFS
TIPSOFF
VITRIFY

•I••••F

AIRWOLF
BITEOFF
DIEDOFF
DIESOFF
DISTAFF
FIGLEAF
FIREOFF
GIVEOFF
HIMSELF
HIPROOF
KICKOFF
KISSOFF
LIFTOFF
MIDRIFF
PICKOFF
RIDEOFF
RINGOFF
RIPSOFF
SIGNOFF
TICKOFF
TIMEOFF
TIPSOFF
TIREDOF

••IF•••

CHIFFON
CLIFTON
COIFING
DEIFIED
DEIFIES
DRIFTED
DRIFTER
EDIFICE
EDIFIED
EDIFIES
FEIFFER
GRIFFEY
GRIFFIN
GRIFFON
GRIFTER
HEIFERS
HEIFETZ
KNIFING
ORIFICE
REIFIED
REIFIES
SHIFTED
SNIFFAT
SNIFFED
SNIFFER
SNIFFLE
SNIFFLY
SNIFTER
STIFFED
STIFFEN
STIFFER
STIFFLY
STIFLED
STIFLES
SWIFTER
SWIFTLY
TRIFLED
TRIFLER
TRIFLES
UNIFIED
UNIFIER
UNIFIES
UNIFORM
WHIFFED

••I•F••

BRIEFED
BRIEFER
BRIEFLY
BRIMFUL
CHIEFLY
CHIFFON
FEIFFER
GAINFUL
GOINFOR
GRIFFEY
GRIFFIN
GRIFFON
LAIDFOR
PAIDFOR
PAILFUL
PAINFUL
SKILFUL
SKINFUL
SNIFFAT
SNIFFED
SNIFFER
SNIFFLE
SNIFFLY
STIFFED
STIFFEN
STIFFER
STIFFLY
STIRFRY
TAILFIN
TOILFUL
WAILFUL
WAITFOR
WHIFFED

••I••F•

ACIDIFY
BAILIFF
FAIROFF
LAIDOFF
PAIDOFF
PAIROFF
SKILIFT
SPINOFF
TAILOFF

••I•••F

BAILIFF
FAIROFF
LAIDOFF
PAIDOFF
PAIROFF
SPINOFF
TAILOFF
THINKOF

•••IF••

ANTIFOG
AQUIFER
CONIFER
DUTIFUL
HALIFAX
LATIFAH
LUCIFER
OSSIFIC
PACIFIC
PITIFUL
ROTIFER
SHRIFTS
TARIFFS
THRIFTS
THRIFTY
UPLIFTS

•••I•F•

BELIEFS
RELIEFS
SATISFY
TARIFFS

•••I••F

BERIDOF

••••IF•

ACIDIFY
AIRLIFT
ALEWIFE
AMPLIFY
BAILIFF
BEATIFY
CALCIFY
CERTIFY
CLARIFY
CONNIFF
CRUCIFY
DANDIFY
DIGNIFY
DULCIFY
FALSIFY
FANCIFY
FORLIFE
FORTIFY
GLORIFY
GRATIFY
HORRIFY
JOLLIFY
JUSTIFY
LOWLIFE
MAGNIFY
MASSIFS
MASTIFF
MIDLIFE
MIDRIFF
MIDWIFE
MOLLIFY
MORTIFY
MYSTIFY
NULLIFY
PETRIFY
PONTIFF
QUALIFY
RECTIFY
REUNIFY
SALSIFY
SCARIFY
SHERIFF
SIGNIFY
SKILIFT
SPECIFY
TERRIFY
TESTIFY
VERSIFY
VITRIFY
ZOMBIFY

••••I•F

BAILIFF
CONNIFF
DEBRIEF
INBRIEF
MASTIFF
MIDRIFF
PONTIFF
SHERIFF

IG•••••

IGIVEUP
IGNEOUS
IGNITED
IGNITER
IGNITES
IGNOBLE
IGNOBLY
IGNORED
IGNORER
IGNORES
IGUANAS

I•G••••

INGALLS
INGEMAR
INGENUE
INGESTS
INGRAIN
INGRATE
INGRESS
INGROUP
INGROWN

I••G•••

IMAGERS
IMAGERY
IMAGINE
IMAGING
IMAGOES
IMOGENE
ISOGONS

I•••G••

ICEAGES
ICINGIN
ICINGUP
ILLEGAL
ILLOGIC
IMPUGNS
INDIGOS
INSIGHT
INTEGER
INTEGRA
INVOGUE

I••••G•

ICEBAGS
ICEFOGS
IMPINGE
INDULGE
INNINGS
INVEIGH
IRONAGE

I•••••G

ICEBERG
IMAGING
IMBUING
INCHING
INKLING
INURING
IRONING
ISSUING
ITCHING

•IG••••

AIGRETS
BIGBAND
BIGBANG
BIGBEND
BIGBIRD
BIGBOYS
BIGDEAL
BIGELOW
BIGEYES
BIGFEET
BIGFOOT
BIGGAME
BIGGERS
BIGGEST
BIGGIES
BIGGISH
BIGGUNS
BIGHEAD
BIGHORN
BIGJOHN
BIGLIES
BIGNAME
BIGNESS
BIGOSES
BIGOTED
BIGOTRY
BIGSHOT
BIGTALK
BIGTIME
BIGTOES
BIGTOPS
BIGWIGS
DIGESTS
DIGGERS
DIGGING
DIGITAL
DIGNIFY
DIGNITY
DIGRAMS
DIGRAPH
DIGRESS
DIGSOUT
EIGHTAM
EIGHTHS
EIGHTPM
FIGHTER
FIGLEAF
FIGMENT
FIGURED
FIGURER
FIGURES
GIGGLED
GIGGLER
GIGGLES
GIGOLOS
HIGGINS
HIGGLED
HIGGLES
HIGHBOY
HIGHDAY
HIGHEND
HIGHEST
HIGHHAT
HIGHLOW
HIGHTEA
HIGHTOP
HIGHWAY
JIGGERS
JIGGERY
JIGGING
JIGGISH
JIGGLED
JIGGLES
JIGLIKE
JIGSAWS
LIGANDS
LIGATED
LIGATES
LIGHTED
LIGHTEN
LIGHTER
LIGHTLY
LIGHTUP
LIGNITE
MIGGLES
MIGHTNT
MIGRANT
MIGRATE
NIGERIA
NIGGARD
NIGGLED
NIGGLES
NIGHEST
NIGHTIE
NIGHTLY
PIGEONS
PIGGERY
PIGGIER
PIGGIES
PIGGING
PIGGISH
PIGIRON
PIGLETS
PIGLIKE
PIGMENT
PIGNUTS
PIGPENS
PIGSKIN
PIGSOUT
PIGTAIL
RIGGERS
RIGGING
RIGHTED
RIGHTER
RIGHTLY
RIGHTON
RIGIDLY
RIGOURS
RIGVEDA
SIGHERS
SIGHFUL
SIGHING
SIGHTED
SIGHTLY
SIGMUND
SIGNALS
SIGNEES
SIGNERS
SIGNETS
SIGNIFY
SIGNING
SIGNOFF
SIGNOUT
SIGNSIN
SIGNSON
SIGNSUP
TIGHTEN
TIGHTER
TIGHTLY
TIGLONS
TIGRESS
TIGRISH
VIGOURS
WIGGIER
WIGGLED
WIGGLER
WIGGLES
WIGLESS
WIGLETS
WIGLIKE
WIGSOUT
WIGWAGS
WIGWAMS
ZIGGING
ZIGZAGS

•I•G•••

AIRGUNS
BIGGAME
BIGGERS
BIGGEST
BIGGIES
BIGGISH
BIGGUNS
BILGIER
BINGHAM
BINGING
BINGOES
BIOGENY
DIAGRAM
DIDGOOD
DIGGERS
DIGGING
DINGBAT
DINGIER
DINGILY
DINGING
DINGLES
DINGOES
DISGUST
FIDGETS
FIDGETY
FINGERS
FIZGIGS
GIGGLED
GIGGLER
GIGGLES
GILGUYS
GINGERS
GINGERY
GINGHAM
GINGIVA
HIGGINS
HIGGLED
HIGGLES
HINGING
JIGGERS
JIGGERY
JIGGING
JIGGISH
JIGGLED
JIGGLES
JINGLED
JINGLES
JINGOES
KINGDOM
KINGING
KINGMAN
KINGPIN
KINGRAT
KINGTUT
LINGERS
LINGOES
LINGUAL
MIDGETS
MIGGLES
MINGIER
MINGLED
MINGLER
MINGLES
NIAGARA
NIGGARD
NIGGLED
NIGGLES
PIDGEON
PIDGINS
PIGGERY
PIGGIER
PIGGIES
PIGGING
PIGGISH
PILGRIM
PINGING
QINGDAO
RIDGIER
RIDGING
RIDGWAY
RIGGERS
RIGGING
RINGERS
RINGING
RINGLET
RINGOFF
RINGOUT
RINGSUP
SINGERS
SINGING
SINGLED
SINGLES
SINGOUT
SINGSTO
SIXGUNS
TINGING
TINGLED
TINGLES
VIRGINS
VIRGOAN
VIRGULE
WIDGEON
WIDGETS
WIGGIER
WIGGLED
WIGGLER
WIGGLES
WINGERS
WINGING
WINGNUT
WINGSIT
WINGTIP
XINGOUT
ZIGGING
ZINGERS
ZINGIER
ZINGING

•I••G••

FINAGLE
GIELGUD
GIORGIO
LIMOGES
LINAGES
LITHGOW
MIRAGES
PIROGUE
VINEGAR
VIRAGOS
VISAGES
WISEGUY

•I•••G•

AIRBAGS
AIRINGS
BIGWIGS
BIOLOGY
DIALOGS

DIVERGE
DIVULGE
FILINGS
FIRINGS
FIXINGS
FIZGIGS
HIDALGO
HIDINGS
KITBAGS
LINEAGE
LININGS
LINKAGE
LITURGY
LIVINGS
MILEAGE
OILRIGS
PILINGS
PILLAGE
PIPINGS
RIBCAGE
RISINGS
SIDINGS
SINKAGE
SIZINGS
TIDINGS
TILINGS
TILLAGE
TIMINGS
VIKINGS
VILLAGE
VINTAGE
WIGWAGS
ZIGZAGS

•I••••G

BIASING
BIDDING
BIGBANG
BILKING
BILLING
BINDING
BINGING
BINNING
BIRDDOG
BIRDING
BIRLING
BITTING
DIALING
DIETING
DIGGING
DIMMING
DINGING
DIPPING
DISHING
DISHRAG
DISSING
FIBBING
FILLING
FILMING
FINDING
FINKING
FIREBUG
FIREDOG
FIRMING
FISHING
FITTING
FIZZING
GIBBING
GILDING
GILLING
GINNING
GINSENG
GIPPING
GIRDING
GIRNING
HILLING
HINGING
HINTING
HISSING
HITTING
JIBBING
JIGGING
JILTING
JINKING
JINXING
KICKING
KIDDING
KILLING
KILTING
KINGING
KINKING
KIPLING
KISSING
LIBBING
LICKING
LIFTING
LILTING
LIMBING
LIMNING
LIMPING
LINKING
LIPPING
LISPING
LISTING
MIFFING
MILKING
MILLING
MINCING
MINDING
MINTING
MISSING
MISTING
MITRING
NICKING
NIPPING
OINKING
PICKING
PIECING
PIGGING
PILLBUG
PILLING
PINGING
PINKING
PINNING
PIQUING
PITHING
PITTING
PITYING
RIBBING
RIDDING
RIDGING
RIFFING
RIFLING
RIFTING
RIGGING
RIMMING
RINGING
RINSING
RIOTING
RIPPING
RISKING
SIBLING
SICCING
SIDLING
SIFTING
SIGHING
SIGNING
SILOING
SILTING
SINGING
SINKING
SIPPING
SITTING
TICKING
TIDYING
TIERING
TIFFING
TILLING
TILTING
TIMELAG
TINGING
TINTING
TIPPING
TITHING
TITLING
TITRING
VIEWING
VISAING
WILDING
WILLING
WILTING
WINCING
WINDBAG
WINDING
WINGING
WINKING
WINNING
WISHING
WISPING
WITTING
YIPPING
ZIGGING
ZINGING
ZIPPING

••IG•••

ABIGAIL
ALIGHTS
ALIGNED
ALIGNER
AVIGNON
BLIGHTS
BLIGHTY
BRIGADE
BRIGAND
BRIGHAM
CHIGGER
CHIGNON
CHIGOES
DEIGNED
EMIGRES
ENIGMAS
EPIGENE
EPIGONE
EPIGRAM
EXIGENT
FEIGNED
FLIGHTS
FLIGHTY
FRIGATE
FRIGHTS
GRIGRIS
HEIGHHO
HEIGHTS
KNIGHTS
MAIGRET
NEIGHED
OMIGOSH
ORIGAMI
ORIGINS
PLIGHTS
QUIGLEY
REIGNED
SLIGHTS
SNIGGER
SNIGGLE
SNIGLET
SOIGNEE
SPIGOTS
STIGMAS
SWIGGED
TRIGGED
TRIGGER
TRIGONS
TRIGRAM
VEIGHTS
WEIGHED
WEIGHIN
WEIGHTS
WEIGHTY
WRIGGLE
WRIGGLY
WRIGHTS
WRIGLEY

••I•G••

ATINGLE
BRIDGED
BRIDGES
BRIDGET
BRINGER
BRINGIN
BRINGON
BRINGTO
BRINGUP
CHIGGER
CRINGED
CRINGES
DOINGIN
DOINGUP
FRIDGES
FRINGED
FRINGES
GOINGAT
GOINGBY
GOINGIN
GOINGON
GOINGUP
ICINGIN
ICINGUP
KLINGON
KRINGLE
LYINGTO
OWINGTO
SHINGLE
SLINGER
SMIDGEN
SNIGGER
SNIGGLE
SPIEGEL
STIEGEL
STINGER
STINGOS
SWIGGED
SWINGBY
SWINGER
TLINGIT
TRIGGED
TRIGGER
TWINGED
TWINGES
TYINGIN
TYINGUP
USINGUP
WRIGGLE
WRIGGLY
WRINGER
ZWINGLI

••I••G•

CHICAGO
COINAGE
EPILOGS
TRILOGY
ZHIVAGO

••I•••G

ABIDING
ALINING
ARISING
BAILING
BAITING
BEIJING
BOILING
BRIBING
BRINING
CEILING
CHIDING
CHIMING
COIFING
COILING
COINING
DEICING
DRIVING
EDITING
ELIDING
EXILING
EXITING
FAILING
FAIRING
FOILING
FOINING
GAINING
GAITING
GLIDING
GRIMING
GRIPING
GUIDING
HAILING
JAILING
JOINING
JUICING
KNIFING
LEIPZIG
MAILBAG
MAILING
MOILING
NAILING
NOISING
OPINING
PAIRING
POISING
PRICING
PRIDING
PRIMING
PRIZING
RAIDING
RAILING
RAINING
RAISING
REINING
ROILING
RUINING
SAILING
SEINING
SEIZING
SHINDIG
SHINING
SLICING
SLIDING
SMILING
SMITING
SNIPING
SOILING
SPICING
SPIKING
SPITING
SUITING
SWIPING
TAILING
TOILING
TWINING
UNITING
VEILING
VEINING
VOICING
VOIDING
WAILING
WAITING
WAIVING
WHILING
WHINING
WHITING
WRITING
ZEITUNG

•••IG••

ALRIGHT
ANTIGEN
ANTIGUA
ASSIGNS
COSIGNS
DELIGHT
DEMIGOD
DESIGNS
ELOIGNS
ENSIGNS
FATIGUE
FREIGHT
INDIGOS
INSIGHT
MADIGAN
MALIGNS
MEDIGAP
MRRIGHT
OBLIGED
OBLIGES
ONSIGHT
PERIGEE
RELIGHT
REMIGES
RESIGNS
SEVIGNE
SLEIGHS
SLEIGHT
STEIGER
TONIGHT
UPRIGHT
UPTIGHT
XHEIGHT

•••I•G•

ABRIDGE
AIRINGS
AWNINGS
BESIEGE
CASINGS
COMINGS
DOMINGO
EDGINGS
ENDINGS
FACINGS
FILINGS
FIRINGS
FIXINGS
FOLIAGE
HAZINGS
HIDINGS
IMPINGE
INNINGS
LACINGS
LININGS
LIVINGS
MAKINGS
NORIEGA
OUTINGS
PARINGS
PILINGS
PIPINGS
RATINGS
RAVINGS
RESINGS
RISINGS
RULINGS
SAVINGS
SAYINGS
SIDINGS
SIZINGS
SPRINGS
SPRINGY
STRINGS
STRINGY
SYRINGA
SYRINGE
TAPINGS
TIDINGS
TILINGS
TIMINGS
VIKINGS

•••I••G

ANTIFOG
ANTILOG
SEMILOG
TAXIING
WYSIWYG

••••IG•

AMERIGO
ARRAIGN
BENDIGO
BIGWIGS
CONDIGN
CONSIGN
EARWIGS
FIZGIGS
FLYHIGH
FOREIGN
HEXSIGN
INVEIGH
LENTIGO
OILRIGS
PRODIGY
RALEIGH
SKYHIGH
VERTIGO
VESTIGE

••••I•G

ABASING
ABATING
ABIDING
ABUSING
ADDLING
ADORING
ALAKING
ALINING
ALLYING
AMAZING
AMBLING
AMUSING
ANELING
ANGLING
ANTEING
ARCHING
ARGUING
ARISING
ATONING
AVOWING
AWAKING
BABYING
BACHING
BACKING
BAGGING
BAILING
BAITING
BALDING
BALKING
BANDING
BANGING
BANKING
BANNING
BARBING
BARGING
BARKING
BARRING
BASHING
BASKING
BASTING
BATHING
BATTING
BATWING
BAWLING
BEADING
BEAMING
BEANING
BEARING
BEATING
BEDDING
BEEFING
BEEPING
BEGGING
BEIJING
BELLING
BELTING
BELYING
BENDING
BESTING
BETTING
BIASING
BIDDING
BILKING
BILLING
BINDING
BINGING
BINNING
BIRDING
BIRLING
BITTING
BLADING
BLAMING
BLARING
BLAZING
BLOWING
BLUEING
BOATING
BOBBING
BOGGING
BOILING
BOLTING
BOMBING
BONDING
BONGING
BOOKING
BOOMING
BOOTING
BOPPING
BOSSING
BOUSING
BOWLING
BRACING
BRAKING
BRAVING
BRAYING
BRAZING
BREWING
BRIBING
BRINING
BRUXING
BUCKING
BUDDING
BUDGING
BUFFING
BUGGING
BUGLING
BULGING
BULKING
BULLING
BUMMING
BUMPING
BUNGING
BUNKING
BUNTING
BUOYING
BURLING
BURNING
BURPING
BURYING
BUSHING
BUSKING
BUSSING
BUSTING
BUSYING
BUTTING
BUZZING
CABLING
CACHING
CADGING
CALKING
CALLING
CALMING
CALVING
CAMPING
CANNING
CANTING
CAPPING
CARDING
CARKING
CARPING
CARTING
CARVING
CASHING
CASTING
CATTING
CAUSING
CEASING
CEILING
CENSING
CESSING
CHAFING
CHASING
CHEWING
CHIDING
CHIMING
CLAWING
CLONING
CLOSING
CLOYING
CLUEING
COATING
COAXING
COCKING
COIFING
COILING
COINING
COMBING
CONKING
CONNING
COOKING
COOLING
COOPING
COPPING
COPYING
CORDING
CORKING
CORNING
COSHING
COSTING
COWLING
COZYING
CRANING
CRATING
CRAVING
CRAZING
CREWING
CROWING
CUFFING
CULLING
CUNNING
CUPPING
CURBING
CURDING
CURLING
CURSING
CURVING
CUSHING
CUSSING
CUTTING
CYCLING
DABBING
DAFFING
DAMMING
DAMNING
DAMPING
DANCING
DAPPING
DARLING
DARNING
DARTING
DASHING
DAUBING
DAWNING
DEALING
DECKING
DEEDING
DEEMING
DEFYING
DEICING
DELEING
DELVING
DENTING
DENYING
DERRING
DIALING
DIETING
DIGGING
DIMMING
DINGING
DIPPING
DISHING
DISSING
DOCKING
DODGING
DOFFING
DOGGING
DOLLING
DONKING
DONNING
DOOMING
DOTTING
DOUSING
DOWNING
DOWSING
DRAPING
DRAWING
DRAYING
DRIVING
DRONING
DUBBING
DUCKING
DUCTING
DUELING
DULLING
DUMBING
DUMPING
DUNKING
DUNNING
DURNING
DUSTING
EAGLING
EARNING
EARRING
ECHOING
EDDYING
EDITING
EDUCING
ELATING
ELIDING
ELOPING
ELUDING
ELUTING
EMOTING
ENDUING
ENSUING
ENURING
ENVYING
ERASING
ERODING
ESPYING
ETCHING
EVADING
EVENING
EVOKING
EXILING
EXITING
EXUDING
FAGGING
FAILING
FAIRING
FALLING
FANNING
FARCING
FARMING
FASTING
FAWNING
FEARING
FEEDING
FEELING
FELLING
FENCING
FENDING
FESSING
FEUDING
FIBBING
FILLING
FILMING
FINDING
FINKING
FIRMING
FISHING
FITTING
FIZZING
FLAKING
FLAMING
FLARING
FLAWING
FLAYING
FLEEING
FLEMING
FLEXING
FLEYING
FLOWING
FLUTING
FLUXING
FOALING
FOAMING
FOBBING
FOGGING
FOILING
FOINING
FOLDING
FOOLING
FOOTING
FORCING
FORDING
FORGING
FORKING
FORMING
FOULING
FOWLING
FRAMING
FRAYING
FREEING
FUBBING
FUDGING
FUELING
FUNDING
FUNKING
FUNNING
FURLING
FURRING
FUSSING
FUTZING
FUZZING
GABBING
GADDING
GAFFING
GAGGING
GAINING
GAITING
GALLING
GAMMING
GANGING
GAOLING
GAPPING
GARBING
GASHING
GASPING
GATLING
GAUGING
GAUMING
GAWKING
GAWPING
GEARING
GELDING
GELLING
GETTING
GIBBING
GILDING
GILLING
GINNING
GIPPING
GIRDING
GIRNING
GLARING
GLAZING
GLIDING
GLOBING
GLOWING
GLOZING
GNAWING
GOADING
GOLDING
GOLFING
GONGING
GOODING
GOOFING
GOOSING
GORGING
GOSLING
GOUGING
GRACING
GRADING
GRATING
GRAVING
GRAYING
GRAZING
GREYING
GRIMING
GRIPING
GROPING
GROWING
GUIDING
GULFING
GULLING
GULPING
GUMMING
GUNNING
GUSHING
GUSTING
GUTTING
GYPPING
HACKING
HAFTING
HAILING
HALOING
HALTING
HALVING
HAMMING
HANDING
HANGING
HAPPING
HARDING
HARKING
HARMING
HARPING
HASHING
HASPING
HASTING
HATTING
HAULING
HAWKING
HEADING
HEALING
HEAPING
HEARING
HEATING
HEAVING
HEDGING
HEEDING
HEELING
HEFTING
HELMING
HELPING
HEMMING
HENTING
HERDING
HERRING
HILLING
HINGING
HINTING
HISSING
HITTING
HOAXING
HOBOING
HOCKING
HOGGING
HOLDING
HONKING
HOOFING
HOOKING
HOOPING
HOOTING
HOPPING
HORNING
HORSING
HOSTING
HOUSING
HOWLING
HUFFING
HUGGING
HULKING
HULLING
HUMMING
HUNTING
HURLING
HURTING
HUSHING
HUSKING
HYPOING
IMAGING
IMBUING
INCHING
INKLING
INURING
IRONING
ISSUING
ITCHING
JABBING
JACKING
JAGGING
JAILING
JAMMING
JARRING
JAZZING
JEERING
JELLING
JERKING
JESTING
JETTING
JIBBING
JIGGING
JILTING
JINKING
JINXING
JOBBING
JOGGING
JOINING
JOLTING
JOSHING
JOTTING
JREWING
JUDGING
JUGGING
JUICING
JUMPING

JUNKING
JURYING
JUTTING
KAYOING
KEELING
KEENING
KEEPING
KERNING
KEYRING
KICKING
KIDDING
KILLING
KILTING
KINGING
KINKING
KIPLING
KISSING
KNEEING
KNIFING
KNOWING
LACKING
LADLING
LAGGING
LAMMING
LANDING
LANSING
LAPPING
LAPSING
LAPWING
LARDING
LASHING
LASTING
LATHING
LAUDING
LEADING
LEAFING
LEAKING
LEANING
LEAPING
LEASING
LEAVING
LEERING
LEGGING
LEMMING
LENDING
LESSING
LETTING
LEVYING
LIBBING
LICKING
LIFTING
LILTING
LIMBING
LIMNING
LIMPING
LINKING
LIPPING
LISPING
LISTING
LOADING
LOAFING
LOAMING
LOANING
LOBBING
LOCKING
LODGING
LOFTING
LOGGING
LOLLING
LONGING
LOOKING
LOOMING
LOOPING
LOOSING
LOOTING
LOPPING
LORDING
LOTTING
LOUSING
LUCKING
LUFFING
LUGGING
LULLING
LUMPING
LUNGING
LURKING
LUSTING
MADDING
MAILING
MALTING
MANNING
MAPPING
MARKING
MARRING
MASHING
MASKING
MASSING
MATTING
MAULING
MEANING
MEETING
MELDING
MELTING
MENDING
MEOWING
MERGING
MESHING
MESSING
MEWLING
MIFFING
MILKING
MILLING
MINCING
MINDING
MINTING
MISSING
MISTING
MITRING
MOANING
MOBBING
MOCKING
MOILING
MOLDING
MOLTING
MOONING
MOORING
MOPPING
MORNING
MOSHING
MOSSING
MOUSING
MUCKING
MUFFING
MUGGING
MULLING
MUMMING
MUMPING
MUSHING
MUSSING
MUZZING
NABBING
NAGGING
NAILING
NAPPING
NEARING
NECKING
NEEDING
NESTING
NETTING
NICKING
NIPPING
NODDING
NOISING
NOOSING
NOSHING
NOTHING
NUDGING
NULLING
NUMBING
NURSING
NUTTING
OBEYING
OINKING
OKAYING
ONGOING
OPENING
OPINING
ORATING
OUSTING
PACKING
PADDING
PAIRING
PALLING
PALMING
PANNING
PANTING
PARKING
PARRING
PARSING
PARTING
PASSING
PASTING
PATTING
PAULING
PAUSING
PAWNING
PEAKING
PEALING
PECKING
PEEKING
PEELING
PEEPING
PEERING
PEEVING
PEGGING
PELTING
PENDING
PENNING
PEPPING
PERKING
PERMING
PETTING
PHASING
PHONING
PICKING
PIECING
PIGGING
PILLING
PINGING
PINKING
PINNING
PIQUING
PITHING
PITTING
PITYING
PLACING
PLANING
PLATING
PLAYING
PLOWING
PLUMING
POISING
POLLING
PONGING
PONYING
POOLING
POOPING
POPPING
POSTING
POTTING
POURING
POUTING
PRATING
PRAYING
PRICING
PRIDING
PRIMING
PRIZING
PROBING
PROSING
PROVING
PRUNING
PUDDING
PUFFING
PULLING
PULSING
PUMPING
PUNNING
PUNTING
PURGING
PURLING
PURRING
PURSING
PUSHING
PUTTING
QUAKING
QUEUING
QUOTING
RACKING
RAFTING
RAGGING
RAIDING
RAILING
RAINING
RAISING
RAMMING
RANGING
RANKING
RANTING
RAPPING
RASPING
RATTING
RAZZING
RDLAING
READING
REAMING
REAPING
REARING
REDDING
REDOING
REDWING
REEDING
REEFING
REEKING
REELING
REFFING
REINING
RELYING
RENDING
RENTING
RESTING
REVVING
RHYMING
RIBBING
RIDDING
RIDGING
RIFFING
RIFLING
RIFTING
RIGGING
RIMMING
RINGING
RINSING
RIOTING
RIPPING
RISKING
ROAMING
ROARING
ROBBING
ROCKING
RODDING
ROILING
ROLLING
ROMPING
ROOFING
ROOKING
ROOMING
ROOTING
ROTTING
ROUGING
ROUSING
ROUTING
RUBBING
RUCHING
RUCKING
RUINING
RUNNING
RUSHING
RUSTING
SACKING
SAGGING
SAILING
SALTING
SALVING
SANDING
SAPLING
SAPPING
SASSING
SCALING
SCARING
SCOPING
SCORING
SEALING
SEAMING
SEARING
SEATING
SEEDING
SEEKING
SEEMING
SEEPING
SEINING
SEIZING
SELLING
SENDING
SENSING
SERLING
SERVING
SETTING
SHADING
SHAKING
SHAMING
SHAPING
SHARING
SHAVING
SHINING
SHOEING
SHOOING
SHORING
SHOVING
SHOWING
SIBLING
SICCING
SIDLING
SIFTING
SIGHING
SIGNING
SILOING
SILTING
SINGING
SINKING
SIPPING
SITTING
SKATING
SKEWING
SLAKING
SLATING
SLAVING
SLICING
SLIDING
SLOPING
SLOWING
SMILING
SMITING
SMOKING
SNAKING
SNARING
SNIPING
SNORING
SNOWING
SOAKING
SOAPING
SOARING
SOBBING
SOCKING
SODDING
SOILING
SOLOING
SOLVING
SOPPING
SORTING
SOURING
SPACING
SPADING
SPARING
SPAYING
SPECING
SPEWING
SPICING
SPIKING
SPITING
SPOKING
SPUMING
STAGING
STAKING
STARING
STATING
STAVING
STAYING
STEWING
STOKING
STONING
STORING
STOWING
STYLING
SUBBING
SUCKING
SUDSING
SUITING
SULKING
SUMMING
SUNNING
SUPPING
SURFING
SURGING
SUSSING
SWAYING
SWIPING
SYNCING
TABBING
TABLING
TACKING
TAGGING
TAILING
TALKING
TAMPING
TANKING
TANNING
TAPPING
TARRING
TASKING
TASTING
TATTING
TAXIING
TEAMING
TEARING
TEASING
TEDDING
TEEMING
TELLING
TENDING
TENSING
TENTING
TENZING
TERMING
TESTING
THAWING
TICKING
TIDYING
TIERING
TIFFING
TILLING
TILTING
TINGING
TINTING
TIPPING
TITHING
TITLING
TITRING
TOGGING
TOILING
TOLLING
TOOLING
TOOTING
TOPPING
TOSSING
TOTTING
TOURING
TOUTING
TRACING
TRADING
TREEING
TRUEING
TUCKING
TUFTING
TUGGING
TUMMING
TURNING
TWINING
UNDOING
UNDYING
UNITING
UNTYING
UPSWING
VALUING
VAMPING
VARYING
VATTING
VEERING
VEGGING
VEILING
VEINING
VENDING
VENTING
VERGING
VESTING
VETOING
VETTING
VIEWING
VISAING
VOICING
VOIDING
WADDING
WAFTING
WAGGING
WAILING
WAITING
WAIVING
WALKING
WALLING
WANTING
WARDING
WARMING
WARNING
WARPING
WARRING
WASHING
WASTING
WAXWING
WEANING
WEARING
WEAVING
WEBBING
WEDDING
WEDGING
WEEDING
WEEPING
WELDING
WELLING
WELTING
WENDING
WETTING
WHALING
WHILING
WHINING
WHITING
WILDING
WILLING
WILTING
WINCING
WINDING
WINGING
WINKING
WINNING
WISHING
WISPING
WITTING
WOLFING
WOOFING
WORDING
WORKING
WRITING
WYOMING
XRATING
XRAYING
YACKING
YAKKING
YANKING
YAPPING
YARNING
YAWNING
YAWPING
YEANING
YELLING
YELPING
YERKING
YESSING
YIPPING
YOWLING
YOYOING
ZAGGING
ZAPPING
ZEROING
ZIGGING
ZINGING
ZIPPING
ZONKING
ZOOMING

•••••IG

BUSHPIG
JURYRIG
LEIPZIG
OVERBIG
PFENNIG
SHINDIG
TALKBIG

I•H••••

ICHABOD
INHABIT
INHALED
INHALER
INHALES
INHASTE
INHAULS
INHERED
INHERES
INHERIT
INHIBIT
INHOUSE
INHUMAN
ISHMAEL
ITHACAN

I••H•••

IDAHOAN
INAHEAP
INCHING
INKHORN
INPHASE
INSHAPE
INSHORT
ISOHELS
ISTHMUS
ITCHIER
ITCHING

I•••H••

ICESHOW
IVANHOE

I••••H•

INSIGHT
IOMOTHS

I•••••H

IMPEACH
INARUSH
INDEPTH
INDUTCH
INTRUTH
INVEIGH
IPSWICH

•I•H•••

AIRHEAD
AIRHOLE
BIGHEAD
BIGHORN
BISHOPS
CIPHERS
DIEHARD
DISHFUL
DISHIER
DISHING
DISHOUT
DISHPAN
DISHRAG
DITHERS
DITHERY
EIGHTAM
EIGHTHS
EIGHTPM
FIGHTER
FISHERS
FISHERY
FISHEYE
FISHFRY
FISHIER
FISHILY
FISHING
FISHNET
FISHOUT
HIGHBOY
HIGHDAY
HIGHEND
HIGHEST
HIGHHAT
HIGHLOW
HIGHTEA
HIGHTOP
HIGHWAY
HITHERE
KISHKES
LICHENS
LIGHTED
LIGHTEN
LIGHTER
LIGHTLY
LIGHTUP
LITHELY
LITHEST
LITHGOW
LITHIUM
MICHAEL
MICHELE
MIGHTNT
MIKHAIL
MILHAUD
MISHAPS
MISHEAR
MISHITS
MITHRAS
NICHOLS
NIGHEST
NIGHTIE
NIGHTLY
PINHEAD
PINHOLE
PITHIER
PITHILY
PITHING
RICHARD
RICHEST
RICHMAN
RICHTER
RIGHTED
RIGHTER
RIGHTLY
RIGHTON
SICHUAN
SIGHERS
SIGHFUL
SIGHING
SIGHTED
SIGHTLY
SIKHISM
SIPHONS
TIGHTEN
TIGHTER
TIGHTLY
TINHATS
TINHORN
TITHERS
TITHING
WICHITA
WILHELM
WISHERS
WISHFUL
WISHING
WITHERS
WITHIER
WITHIES
WITHOUT
ZITHERS

•I••H••

AIRSHIP
AIRSHOW
AITCHES
BIGSHOT
BINGHAM
BIOCHIP
BIRCHED
BIRCHES
BIRTHED
CINCHED
CINCHES
DITCHED
DITCHES
FIFTHLY
FILCHED
FILCHER
FILCHES
FINCHES
FISCHER
FITCHES
GINGHAM
HIGHHAT
HITCHED
HITCHER
HITCHES
JIMCHEE
KIMCHEE
KINCHIN
KINSHIP
KITCHEN
LITCHIS
MITCHUM
NINTHLY
PINCHAS
PINCHED
PINCHER
PINCHES
PITCHED
PITCHER
PITCHES
PITCHIN
RIMSHOT
SILKHAT
SIOBHAN
SIXTHLY
WINCHED
WINCHES
WITCHES
YITZHAK
ZILCHES

•I•••H•

BIGJOHN
BINOCHE
EIGHTHS
HIBACHI
HITACHI
KITSCHY
NIEBUHR
PIRANHA
RICKSHA
TIMOTHY

•I••••H

BIGGISH
BISMUTH
DIGRAPH
DIPTYCH
FINNISH
GIRLISH
HIALEAH
JIGGISH
KIDDISH
MINXISH
MISSISH
MITZVAH
NINEVEH
PICTISH
PIGGISH
PINKISH
PIXYISH
SICKISH
TIGRISH
WILDISH
WIMPISH
YIDDISH

••IH•••

AKIHITO
SHIHTZU

••I•H••

ALIGHTS
APISHLY
BLIGHTS
BLIGHTY
BLITHER
BRIGHAM
CHICHEN
CLICHES
EPITHET
FLIGHTS
FLIGHTY
FRIGHTS
GEISHAS
GRISHAM
HEIGHHO
HEIGHTS
KAISHEK
KNIGHTS
KNISHES
KRISHNA
NEIGHED
NEITHER
PLIGHTS
PRITHEE
QUICHES
RAINHAT
SEICHES
SLIGHTS
SLITHER
STICHES
SWISHED
SWISHES
TEICHER
THITHER
TRISHAW
VEIGHTS
WEIGHED
WEIGHIN
WEIGHTS
WEIGHTY
WHISHED
WHISHES
WHITHER
WRIGHTS
WRITHED
WRITHES

••I••H•

BRIOCHE
HEIGHHO
PLINTHS
SNITCHY
THIMPHU
TWITCHY

••I•••H

AZIMUTH
BRINISH
BRITISH
FAIRISH
MAIDISH
OMIGOSH
SPINACH
SWINISH
TRIUMPH
WHITISH

•••IH••

BALIHAI

•••I•H•

ALRIGHT
CALIPHS
CERIPHS
DELIGHT
EOLITHS
FREIGHT
INSIGHT
JERICHO
MRRIGHT
ONSIGHT
OOLITHS
ORNITHO
PARIAHS
RELIGHT
RUPIAHS
SHEIKHS
SLEIGHS
SLEIGHT
SQUISHY
TABITHA
TONIGHT
UPRIGHT
UPTIGHT
WRAITHS
XHEIGHT
ZENITHS

•••I••H

ANTIOCH
BEWITCH
CORINTH
DELILAH
GOLIATH
JACINTH
LATIFAH
REBIRTH
SQUINCH
UNHITCH

••••I•H

ABOLISH
ALDRICH
ANOUILH
BABYISH
BADDISH
BALDISH
BARDISH
BEAMISH
BEARISH
BEAUISH
BIGGISH
BLEMISH
BLUEISH
BOARISH
BOGGISH
BOOKISH
BOORISH
BRINISH
BRITISH
BRUTISH
BULLISH
BURNISH
CADDISH
CATFISH
CATTISH
CHERISH
CLAYISH
COCKISH
CODFISH
COLDISH
COLTISH
COOLISH
CORNISH
CRONISH
CUBBISH
CULTISH
CURRISH
DAMPISH
DARKISH
DAWKISH
DERVISH
DOGFISH
DOGGISH
DOLLISH
DOLTISH
DONNISH
DRONISH
DULLISH
DUMPISH
DUNCISH
DUSKISH
EHRLICH
ENGLISH
EVANISH
FADDISH
FAIRISH
FATTISH
FINNISH
FLEMISH
FLYFISH
FLYHIGH
FOGYISH
FOLKISH
FOOLISH
FOPPISH
FURBISH

FURNISH
GARNISH
GAULISH
GAWKISH
GIRLISH
GNOMISH
GOATISH
GOODISH
GOUTISH
GRAYISH
GREYISH
HAGGISH
HAWKISH
HELLISH
HENNISH
HOGGISH
HORNISH
HUFFISH
HUNNISH
INVEIGH
IPSWICH
JIGGISH
KADDISH
KENTISH
KIDDISH
KNAVISH
KURDISH
LADDISH
LADYISH
LAPPISH
LARGISH
LARKISH
LAZYISH
LETTISH
LOGGISH
LONGISH
LOUDISH
LOUTISH
LUMPISH
MADDISH
MAIDISH
MANNISH
MAWKISH
MESSIAH
MINXISH
MISSISH
MOBBISH
MONKISH
MOONISH
MOORISH
NAGGISH
NEBBISH
NEOLITH
NESMITH
NOURISH
OBADIAH
OGREISH
OSTRICH
PANFISH
PARRISH
PEAKISH
PECKISH
PEEVISH
PELTISH
PERKISH
PETTISH
PICTISH
PIGGISH
PINKISH
PIXYISH
PLANISH
POORISH
PORKISH
PRUDISH
PUBLISH
PUCKISH
PUGGISH
RAFFISH
RALEIGH
RAMMISH
RANKISH
RASPISH
RATTISH
REDDISH
RHENISH
ROGUISH
ROMPISH
RUBBISH
RUNTISH
RUNWITH
RUTTISH
SALTISH
SAWFISH
SELFISH
SICKISH
SKYHIGH
SLAVISH
SOFTISH
SOPWITH
SOTTISH
SOURISH
SPANISH
STYLISH
SUNFISH
SWEDISH
SWINISH
TALLISH
TANNISH
TARNISH
TARTISH
TIGRISH
TOADISH
TONNISH
TORYISH
TOWNISH
TURKISH
VAMPISH
VARNISH
VOGUISH
WAGGISH
WANNISH
WARMISH
WASPISH
WEAKISH
WENDISH
WETTISH
WHEYISH
WHITISH
WILDISH
WIMPISH
WOLFISH
WORMISH
YERKISH
YIDDISH
ZANYISH

I•I••••

ICICLES
ICINESS
ICINGIN
ICINGUP
IDIAMIN
IDIOTIC
IGIVEUP
ILIESCU
IMITATE
INITIAL
IRIDIUM
IRISOUT

I••I•••

ICKIEST
IFFIEST
IGNITED
IGNITER
IGNITES
ILLICIT
IMBIBED
IMBIBES
IMMIXED
IMMIXES
IMPIETY
IMPINGE
IMPIOUS
INCIPIT
INCISED
INCISES
INCISOR
INCITED
INCITER
INCITES
INCIVIL
INDIANA
INDIANS
INDICES
INDICIA
INDICTS
INDIGOS
INDITED
INDITES
INFIDEL
INFIELD
INHIBIT
INKIEST
INNINGS
INSIDER
INSIDES
INSIGHT
INSIPID
INSISTS
INVITED
INVITES
INVITRO
IODIDES
IODISED
IODISES
IODIZED
IODIZES
IONISED
IONISES
IONIZED
IONIZER
IONIZES

I•••I••

IBERIAN
ICELIKE
ICEMILK
ICEPICK
ICERINK
IDOLISE
IDOLIZE
ILLWILL
ILLWIND
IMAGINE
IMAGING
IMBUING
IMPAIRS
IMPLIED
IMPLIES
IMPRINT
INANITY
INBRIEF
INCHING
INCLINE
INFLICT
INITIAL
INKLIKE
INKLING
INPRINT
INQUIRE
INQUIRY
INSPIRE
INSTILL
INSTILS
INTUITS
INURING
INUTILE
INVEIGH
INVOICE
IPSWICH
IRANIAN
IRIDIUM
IRONIES
IRONING
ISSUING
ITALIAN
ITALICS
ITCHIER
ITCHING
ITEMISE
ITEMIZE
IVORIES
IVYLIKE
IWOJIMA

I•••••I•

ICINGIN
IDENTIC
IDIAMIN
IDIOTIC
IDYLLIC
ILLICIT
ILLOGIC
IMPERIL
INASNIT
INASPIN
INCIPIT
INCIVIL
INDICIA
INERTIA
INGRAIN
INHABIT
INHERIT
INHIBIT
INORBIT
INSIPID
INSULIN
INTERIM
INTROIT
INVALID
ISLAMIC

I•••••I

ISRAELI

•I•I•••

AIRIEST
AIRINGS
BIKINIS
BILIOUS
CILIATE
CITIZEN
CIVILLY
DICIEST
DIGITAL
DIMITRI
DIVIDED
DIVIDER
DIVIDES
DIVINED
DIVINER
DIVINES
DIVINUM
DIVISOR
FIJIANS
FILINGS
FINIALS
FINICKY
FIRINGS
FIXINGS
HIDINGS
HIJINKS
JIVIEST
LIAISED
LIAISES
LIAISON
LIBIDOS
LICITLY
LIMIEST
LIMITED
LINIEST
LININGS
LIPIDES
LITINTO
LIVIDLY
LIVINGS
MILIEUS
MILIEUX
MILITIA
MIMICRY
MIMIEUX
MINIBUS
MINICAB
MINICAM
MINIMAL
MINIMUM
MINIONS
MINIVAN
MINIVER
MIRIEST
MIXITUP
NIMIETY
OILIEST
PIGIRON
PILINGS
PINIEST
PINIONS
PIPIEST
PIPINGS
PITIERS
PITIFUL
QIVIUTS
RIGIDLY
RIMIEST
RIPIENO
RIPINTO
RISIBLE
RISIBLY
RISINGS
RIVIERA
RIVIERE
SIDINGS
SILICAS
SILICON
SIMIANS
SIMILAR
SIMILES
SIXIRON
SIZINGS
TIDIEST
TIDINGS
TIEINTO
TILINGS
TIMIDER
TIMIDLY
TIMINGS
TINIEST
VICIOUS
VIKINGS
VINIEST
VIRIBUS
VISIBLE
VISIBLY
VISIONS
VISITED
VISITOR
VITIATE
VIVIDER
VIVIDLY
VIZIERS
WILIEST
WINIEST
WIRIEST

•I••I••

AIRKISS
AIRLIFT
AIRLIKE
AIRLINE
AIRMILE
AIRTIME
BIALIES
BIASING
BIBLIKE
BIDDIES
BIDDING
BIGBIRD
BIGGIES
BIGGISH
BIGLIES
BIGTIME
BIGWIGS
BILBIES
BILGIER
BILKING
BILLIES
BILLING
BILLION
BINDING
BINGING
BINNING
BIONICS
BIRDIED
BIRDIES
BIRDING
BIRLING
BITSIER
BITTIER
BITTING
CITRINE
CIVVIES
DIALING
DIARIES
DICKIES
DICTION
DIETING
DIGGING
DIGNIFY
DIGNITY
DIKDIKS
DILLIES
DIMMING
DIMWITS
DINGIER
DINGILY
DINGING
DINKIER
DINKIES
DIOXIDE
DIPPIER
DIPPING
DIRTIED
DIRTIER
DIRTIES
DIRTILY
DISHIER
DISHING
DISLIKE
DISMISS
DISSING
DISTILL
DISTILS
DITSIER
DITTIES
DITZIER
DIVVIED
DIVVIES
DIZZIED
DIZZIER
DIZZIES
DIZZILY
FIBBING
FIBRILS
FIBRINS
FICTION
FICTIVE
FIERIER
FIERILY
FIFTIES
FILLIES
FILLING
FILLINS
FILLIPS
FILMIER
FILMING
FINDING
FINKING
FINLIKE
FINNIER
FINNISH
FIRKINS
FIRMING
FIRRIER
FISHIER
FISHILY
FISHING
FISSILE
FISSION
FITTING
FIZGIGS
FIZZIER
FIZZING
GIBBING
GIDDIER
GIDDILY
GILDING
GILLIAN
GILLIES
GILLING
GIMMICK
GINFIZZ
GINGIVA
GINMILL
GINNING
GIPPING
GIPSIES
GIRDING
GIRLISH
GIRNING
HIGGINS
HILAIRE
HILLIER
HILLING
HINGING
HINNIES
HINTING
HIPLIKE
HIPPIER
HIPPIES
HISSING
HITLIST
HITTING
HITTITE
JIBBING
JIFFIES
JIGGING
JIGGISH
JIGLIKE
JILLIAN
JILLION
JILTING
JIMMIED
JIMMIES
JINKING
JINXING
KICKIER
KICKING
KIDDIES
KIDDING
KIDDISH
KIDLIKE
KILLING
KILTIES
KILTING
KINGING
KINKIER
KINKILY
KINKING
KIPLING
KISSING
KITTIES
LIBBING
LICKING
LIFTING
LIGNITE
LILLIAN
LILTING
LIMBING
LIMNING
LIMPING
LINBIAO
LINDIED
LINDIES
LINKING
LINPIAO
LINTIER
LIONISE
LIONIZE
LIPLIKE
LIPPIER
LIPPING
LIQUIDS
LISPING
LISTING
LITHIUM
MIAMIAN
MIAMIAS
MIDDIES
MIDLIFE
MIDLINE
MIDRIBS
MIDRIFF
MIDRISE
MIDSIZE
MIDWIFE
MIFFIER
MIFFING
MILKIER
MILKING
MILLING
MILLION
MINCING
MINDING
MINGIER
MINTIER
MINTING
MINXISH
MIRKIER
MISDIAL
MISFILE
MISFIRE
MISFITS
MISHITS
MISLIKE
MISSIES
MISSILE
MISSING
MISSION
MISSISH
MISSIVE
MISTIER
MISTILY
MISTING
MITRING
NIBLICK
NIBLIKE
NICKING
NIFTIER
NIFTILY
NINNIES
NIOBIUM
NIPPIER
NIPPING
NITPICK
NITRIDE
NITRITE
NITTIER
NITWITS
OILLIKE
OILRIGS
OINKING
PIANISM
PIANIST
PICKIER
PICKING
PICNICS
PICTISH
PIDGINS
PIECING
PIELIKE
PIETIES
PIETINS
PIETISM
PIETIST
PIGGIER
PIGGIES
PIGGING
PIGGISH
PIGLIKE
PILLING
PILLION
PIMLICO
PINGING
PINKIES
PINKING
PINKISH
PINNING
PIPKINS
PIPPINS
PIQUING
PISCINE
PISMIRE
PISTILS
PITHIER
PITHILY
PITHING
PITTING
PITYING
PIXYISH
RIBBIES
RIBBING
RIBLIKE
RIDDICK
RIDDING
RIDGIER
RIDGING
RIFFING
RIFLING
RIFTING
RIGGING
RIMMING
RINGING
RINSING
RIORITA
RIOTING
RIPPING
RIPTIDE
RISKIER
RISKILY
RISKING
RITZIER
RITZILY
SIBLING
SICCING
SICKISH
SIDLING
SIFTING
SIGHING
SIGNIFY
SIGNING
SIKHISM
SILKIER
SILKILY
SILLIER
SILLIES
SILOING
SILTIER
SILTING
SINGING
SINKING
SINLIKE
SIPPING
SISKINS
SISSIES
SISTINE
SITTING
SIXTIES
TICKING
TIDBITS
TIDYING
TIELINE
TIEPINS
TIERING
TIFFING
TIFFINS
TIGRISH
TILLING
TILTING
TIMMINS
TINGING
TINLIKE
TINNIER
TINNILY
TINTING
TIPPIER
TIPPING
TIPSIER
TIPSILY
TITBITS
TITHING
TITLING
TITLIST
TITMICE
TITRING
TIZZIES
VICTIMS
VIEWIER
VIEWING
VILNIUS
VIOLINS
VIOLIST
VIRGINS
VISAING
VITRIFY
VITRIOL
WICHITA
WICKIUP
WIENIES
WIGGIER
WIGLIKE
WILDING
WILDISH
WILLIAM
WILLIES
WILLING
WILTING
WIMPIER
WIMPISH
WINCING
WINDIER
WINDILY
WINDING
WINGING
WINKING
WINNING
WISHING
WISPIER
WISPILY
WISPING
WITHIER
WITHIES
WITTIER
WITTILY
WITTING
YIDDISH
YIPPING
ZIGGING
ZILLION
ZINGIER
ZINGING
ZINNIAS
ZIPPIER
ZIPPING

•I•••I•

AIRFOIL
AIRMAIL
AIRRAID
AIRSHIP
BIDFAIR
BIKINIS
BIOCHIP
BISCUIT
CIBORIA
CIRCUIT
DINEDIN
DINESIN
DIPLOID
DISDAIN
DISJOIN
DIVESIN
FIDELIO
FIDELIS
FILLSIN
FIRELIT
GIORGIO
GIVENIN
GIVESIN
KICKSIN
KIDSKIN
KINCHIN
KINETIC
KINGPIN
KINSHIP
KIRSTIE
KIWANIS
LIBERIA
LITCHIS
LITCRIT
LIVEDIN
LIVESIN
MIASMIC
MIKHAIL
MILITIA
MIMESIS
MIMETIC
MINUTIA
MISLAID
MISSAID
MITOSIS
MITOTIC
MIXEDIN
MIXESIN
NICOSIA
NIGERIA
NIGHTIE
NINEPIN
OILSKIN
PIGSKIN
PIGTAIL
PILEDIN
PILESIN
PILGRIM
PINTAIL
PIRATIC
PITCHIN
SIBERIA
SIGNSIN
SILESIA
SINEDIE
SINKSIN
SIRLOIN
TIANJIN
TIECLIP
TINFOIL
TINYTIM
TIOMKIN
TITANIA
TITANIC
VIDALIA
VILLAIN
VILLEIN
VISALIA
VISAVIS
VITAMIN
WILFRID
WILLKIE
WINGSIT
WINGTIP

•I••••I

AIRTAXI
DIABOLI
DIMITRI
HIBACHI
HITACHI
NIKOLAI
VIVALDI
VIVENDI

••II•••

SHIITES

••I•I••

ABIDING
ABILITY
ABITIBI
ACIDIFY
ACIDITY
AGILITY
AKIHITO
ALINING
ANILINE
ANIMISM
ANIMIST
ARIDITY
ARISING
ASININE
AVIDITY
BAILIFF
BAILING
BAITING
BEIJING
BOILING
BRIBING
BRINIER
BRINING
BRINISH
BRITISH
CEILING
CHIDING
CHILIES
CHIMING
CHIRICO
CLINICS
COIFING
COILING
COINING
CRITICS
CUISINE
DAILIES
DAIRIES
DAISIES
DEICING
DEIFIED
DEIFIES
DEITIES
DOILIES
DRIVING
EDIFICE
EDIFIED
EDIFIES
EDITING
EDITION
ELICITS
ELIDING
ELISION
ELITISM
ELITIST
ELIXIRS
EXILING
EXITING
FAILING
FAIRIES
FAIRING
FAIRISH
FOILING
FOINING
FRISIAN
GAINING
GAITING
GLIDING
GRIMIER
GRIMILY
GRIMING
GRIPING
GUIDING
HAILING
HAIRIER
HAITIAN
INITIAL
IRIDIUM
JAILING
JOINING
JUICIER
JUICILY
JUICING
KNIFING
MAIDISH
MAILING
MEINIES
MOILING
NAILING
NOISIER
NOISILY
NOISING
OLIVIER
OLIVINE
OPINING
OPINION
ORIFICE
ORIGINS
OXIDISE
OXIDIZE
PAIRING
PHIDIAS
POISING
POITIER
PRICIER
PRICING
PRIDING
PRIMING
PRIVIER
PRIVIES
PRIVILY
PRIVITY
PRIZING
QUININE
RAIDING
RAILING
RAINIER
RAINILY
RAINING
RAISING
RAISINS
REIFIED
REIFIES
REINING
ROILIER
ROILING
RUINING
SAILING
SEINING
SEIZING
SHINIER

SHINILY
SHINING
SKILIFT
SLICING
SLIDING
SLIMIER
SLIMILY
SMILING
SMITING
SNIPING
SOILING
SPICIER
SPICILY
SPICING
SPIKIER
SPIKILY
SPIKING
SPINIER
SPIRIER
SPIRITO
SPIRITS
SPITING
SUITING
SWINISH
SWIPING
TAILING
TBILISI
THINICE
TOILING
TRINITY
TRITIUM
TRIVIAL
TUITION
TWINING
UNIFIED
UNIFIER
UNIFIES
UNITIES
UNITING
UNITIVE
UTILISE
UTILITY
UTILIZE
VEILING
VEINIER
VEINING
VOICING
VOIDING
WAIKIKI
WAILING
WAITING
WAIVING
WHILING
WHINIER
WHINING
WHITIER
WHITING
WHITISH
WRITING
ZAIRIAN

••I••I•
ABIGAIL
ASIATIC
BRINGIN
BRITAIN
BUILDIN
BUILTIN
CHIPSIN
CRINOID
CRISPIN
DOINGIN
DRIVEIN
ERISTIC
FLIESIN
FRICKIE
GOINGIN
GRIFFIN
GRIGRIS
GRISKIN
HAIRPIN
ICINGIN
IDIAMIN
IDIOTIC
JOINSIN
LEIBNIZ
LEIPZIG
MAILSIN
MAITAIS
MEIOSIS
MEIOTIC
NAILSIN
PHILBIN
PHILLIP
QUICKIE
REINSIN
SEISMIC
SHINDIG
SKISUIT
SLIDEIN
SLIMJIM
SLIPSIN
STIRSIN
TAILFIN
THINAIR
TLINGIT
TRILLIN
TYINGIN
WEIGHIN
WHIZKID
WRITEIN

••I•••I
ABITIBI
CHIANTI
JAIALAI
NAIROBI
ORIGAMI
SHIKARI
STIMULI
TBILISI
TRIPOLI
WAIKIKI
ZWINGLI

•••II••
TAXIING

•••I•I•
ACTINIC
ASPIRIN
BIKINIS
BOLIVIA
CECILIA
CODICIL
DEFICIT
DELIMIT
DELIRIA
EXHIBIT
FELICIA
HAMITIC
HASIDIC
HASIDIM
HOMINID
HYGIEIA
ILLICIT
INCIPIT
INCIVIL
INDICIA
INHIBIT
INSIPID
JURIDIC
LAVINIA
LETITIA
MILITIA
MRFIXIT
NAMIBIA
OSSIFIC
PACIFIC
POLITIC
PRAIRIE
REVISIT
RUBITIN
SATIRIC
SEMITIC
SOLICIT
TUNISIA
UNCIVIL
WAPITIS

•••I••I
ALFIERI
APRIORI
BACILLI
BALIHAI
CHRISTI
DAVINCI
DELICTI
DIMITRI
ELMISTI
GALILEI
MENISCI
RAVIOLI
SALIERI
VANILLI

••••I•I
ABITIBI
BELLINI
CABRINI
CASSINI
CELLINI
DASHIKI
EMERITI
FELLINI
HOUDINI
KONTIKI
KUWAITI
MANCINI
MARTINI
PACHISI
PUCCINI
ROSSINI
SANTINI
SASHIMI
SORDINI
SWAHILI
TBILISI
TERMINI
WAIKIKI

•••••II
DENARII
POMPEII
ROCKYII

I•J••••
INJECTS
INJOKES
INJURED
INJURES

I••J•••
IWOJIMA

•IJ••••
FIJIANS
HIJACKS
HIJINKS
TIJUANA

•I•J•••
BIGJOHN
DISJOIN
JIMJAMS

•I••J••
KILLJOY
TIANJIN

••IJ•••
BEIJING
SKIJUMP
TRIJETS

••I•J••
SLIMJIM

IK•••••
IKEBANA

I•K••••
ICKIEST
INKBLOT
INKHORN
INKIEST
INKLESS
INKLIKE
INKLING
INKSPOT
INKWELL
INKYCAP
IRKSOME

I•••K••
INJOKES
INTAKES
INVOKED
INVOKER
INVOKES
IRECKON

I••••K•
ICELIKE
INKLIKE
IVYLIKE

I•••••K
ICEMILK
ICEPACK
ICEPICK
ICERINK
INSTOCK

•IK••••
BIKEWAY
BIKINIS
DIKDIKS
DIKTATS
HIKEDUP
HIKESUP
KIKUYUS
LIKABLE
LIKEMAD
LIKENED
LIKENEW
MIKADOS
MIKHAIL
NIKOLAI
PIKEMAN
PIKEMEN
SIKHISM
VIKINGS

•I•K•••
AIRKISS
BICKERS
BILKING
DICKENS
DICKERS
DICKEYS
DICKIES
DINKIER
DINKIES
FICKLER
FINKING
FIRKINS
HICKMAN
HICKORY
JINKING
KICKERS
KICKIER
KICKING
KICKOFF
KICKOUT
KICKSIN
KICKSUP
KICKUPS
KINKIER
KINKILY
KINKING
LICKING
LINKAGE
LINKERS
LINKING
LINKUPS
MICKEYS
MILKCOW
MILKERS
MILKIER
MILKING
MILKMAN
MILKMEN
MILKRUN
MILKSOP
MIRKIER
NICKELS
NICKERS
NICKING
OINKING
PICKAXE
PICKENS
PICKERS
PICKETS
PICKETT
PICKIER
PICKING
PICKLED
PICKLES
PICKOFF
PICKOUT
PICKSAT
PICKSON
PICKSUP
PICKUPS
PINKEST
PINKIES
PINKING
PINKISH
PIPKINS
RICKETY
RICKEYS
RICKLES
RICKMAN
RICKSHA
RISKERS
RISKIER
RISKILY
RISKING
SICKBAY
SICKDAY
SICKENS
SICKEST
SICKISH
SICKLES
SICKOUT
SICKPAY
SILKHAT
SILKIER
SILKILY
SINKAGE
SINKERS
SINKING
SINKSIN
SISKINS
TICKERS
TICKETS
TICKETY
TICKING
TICKLED
TICKLER
TICKLES
TICKOFF
TINKERS
TINKLED
TINKLES
WICKERS
WICKETS
WICKIUP
WINKERS
WINKING
WINKLED
WINKLER
WINKLES
WINKOUT
WINKSAT

•I••K••
KIDSKIN
KISHKES
OILSKIN
PIGSKIN
TIOMKIN
WILLKIE

•I•••K•
AIRLIKE
BIBLIKE
DIKDIKS
DISLIKE
FINICKY
FINLIKE
HIJACKS
HIJINKS
HIPLIKE
JIGLIKE
KIDLIKE
LIPLIKE
MISLIKE
MISTAKE
NIBLIKE
OILCAKE
OILLIKE
PIELIKE
PIGLIKE
PINOAKS
RIBLIKE
SINLIKE
TINLIKE
WIGLIKE

•I••••K
AIRLOCK
AIRSOCK
BIGTALK
GIMMICK
HILLOCK
KINFOLK
LIVEOAK
MIDWEEK
MISTOOK
NIBLICK
NITPICK
RIDDICK
SIXPACK
TIERACK
TIETACK
TINTACK
TINWORK
WIDMARK
YITZHAK

••IK•••
ARIKARA
SHIKARI
SHIKOKU
SPIKERS
SPIKIER
SPIKILY
SPIKING
WAIKIKI

••I•K••
BLINKAT
BLINKED
BLINKER
BRICKED
BRISKER
BRISKET
BRISKLY
CHICKEN
CHINKED
CLICKED
CLINKED
CLINKER
CRICKED
CRICKET
CRINKLE
CRINKLY
DRINKER
FLICKED
FLICKER
FRICKIE
FRISKED
GRISKIN
PLINKED
PRICKED
PRICKLE
PRICKLY
PRINKED
QUICKEN
QUICKER
QUICKIE
QUICKLY
REINKED
SHIRKED
SHIRKER
SLICKED
SLICKER
SLICKLY
SLINKED
SMIRKED
SNICKER
STICKER
STICKTO
STICKUP
STINKER
THICKEN
THICKER
THICKET
THICKLY
THINKER
THINKOF
THINKUP
TRICKED
TRICKER
TRICKLE
TRINKET
TWINKLE
TWINKLY
WHISKED
WHISKER
WHISKEY
WHIZKID
WRINKLE
WRINKLY

••I••K•
SHIKOKU
WAIKIKI

••I•••K
CHINOOK
KAISHEK
SKIMASK
SKIRACK

•••IK••
BATIKED
KYLIKES
MONIKER
SHEIKHS
SHRIKES
STRIKER
STRIKES
TROIKAS
UNLIKED

•••I•K•
FINICKY
HIJINKS
KODIAKS
PANICKY
SHRIEKS
SHRINKS
SHTICKS
SOYINKA
UNKINKS
UNLINKS
UPLINKS
UPTICKS

••••IK•
AIRLIKE
AMERIKA
ANTLIKE
APELIKE
ARMLIKE
ASSLIKE
BAGLIKE
BATLIKE
BEDLIKE
BEELIKE
BIBLIKE
BOWLIKE
BOXLIKE
BUDLIKE
CATLIKE
COWLIKE
CUPLIKE
CURLIKE
DASHIKI
DIKDIKS
DISLIKE
DOGLIKE
DOTLIKE
EARLIKE
EELLIKE
ELFLIKE
EYELIKE
FADLIKE
FANLIKE
FATLIKE
FINLIKE
FOXLIKE
GEMLIKE
GODLIKE
GUMLIKE
HAGLIKE
HATLIKE
HENLIKE
HIPLIKE
HOGLIKE
HOPLIKE
HUNLIKE
HUTLIKE
ICELIKE
INKLIKE
IVYLIKE
JAMLIKE
JAWLIKE
JIGLIKE
KIDLIKE
KONTIKI
LAWLIKE
LEGLIKE
LIPLIKE
MANLIKE
MISLIKE
MUZHIKS
NETLIKE
NIBLIKE
NUDNIKS
NUNLIKE
NUTLIKE
OAKLIKE
OARLIKE
OATLIKE
OILLIKE
ORBLIKE
OWLLIKE
PAPLIKE
PAPRIKA
PEALIKE
PEGLIKE
PENLIKE
PIELIKE
PIGLIKE
PODLIKE
RAMLIKE
RATLIKE
RAYLIKE
RIBLIKE
RODLIKE
RUGLIKE
SACLIKE
SAWLIKE
SINLIKE
SKYLIKE
SONLIKE
SOWLIKE
SUNLIKE
SUSLIKS
TAGLIKE
TINLIKE
TOELIKE
TOYLIKE
TUBLIKE
TUGRIKS
UNALIKE
URNLIKE
WAIKIKI
WARLIKE
WAXLIKE
WEBLIKE
WIGLIKE

••••I•K
BETHINK
CARRICK
CONNICK
COWLICK
DERRICK
DUNKIRK
FOSDICK
GARRICK
GIMMICK
HOTLINK
ICEMILK
ICEPICK
ICERINK
JONNICK
KUBRICK
MAFFICK
NIBLICK
NITPICK
OBELISK
OLDNICK
PATRICK
RATFINK
RAWSILK
RETHINK
RIDDICK
ROLLICK
SEASICK
SELKIRK
TOPKICK
UNSTICK
WARWICK
WOZNIAK

•••••IK
BEATNIK
SPUTNIK

IL•••••
ILIESCU
ILLBRED
ILLEGAL
ILLICIT
ILLNESS
ILLOGIC
ILLUDED
ILLUDES
ILLUMED
ILLUMES
ILLUSED
ILLUSES
ILLWILL
ILLWIND
ILOCANO

I•L••••
ILLBRED
ILLEGAL
ILLICIT
ILLNESS
ILLOGIC
ILLUDED
ILLUDES
ILLUMED
ILLUMES
ILLUSED
ILLUSES
ILLWILL
ILLWIND
ISLAMIC
ISLANDS

I••L•••
ICELAND
ICELESS
ICELIKE
IDOLISE
IDOLIZE
IDYLLIC
IMPLANT
IMPLIED
IMPLIES
IMPLODE
IMPLORE
INBLOOM
INCLINE
INCLOSE
INCLUDE
INFLAME
INFLATE
INFLECT
INFLICT
INFLOWS
INKLESS
INKLIKE
INKLING
INNLESS
INPLACE
IRELAND
IRELESS
ISOLATE
ITALIAN
ITALICS
IVYLIKE

I•••L••
ICEBLUE
ICEFLOE
ICICLES
IDEALLY
IDYLLIC
IMPALAS
IMPALED
IMPALES
IMPULSE
INDULGE
INGALLS
INHALED
INHALER
INHALES
INKBLOT
INSOLES
INSULAR
INSULIN
INSULTS
INVALID
INVOLVE

I••••L•
ICECOLD
ICEMILK
IDEALLY
IGNOBLE
IGNOBLY
ILLWILL
INANELY
INAPTLY
INDWELL
INEPTLY
INERTLY
INFIELD
INGALLS
INHAULS
INKWELL
INOCULA
INSTALL
INSTALS
INSTILL
INSTILS
INSTYLE
INUTILE
IRATELY
ISOHELS
ISRAELI

I•••••L
ILLEGAL
ILLWILL
IMMORAL
IMPANEL
IMPERIL
INCIVIL
INDWELL
INFIDEL
INITIAL
INKWELL
INSTALL
INSTILL
ISHMAEL

•IL••••
AILERON
AILMENT
BILBIES
BILBOES
BILEVEL
BILGIER
BILIOUS
BILKING
BILLETS
BILLIES
BILLING
BILLION
BILLOWS
BILLOWY
CILIATE
DILATED
DILATES
DILBERT
DILEMMA
DILLARD
DILLIES
DILUTED
DILUTER
DILUTES
FILBERT
FILCHED
FILCHER
FILCHES
FILENES
FILINGS
FILLERS
FILLETS
FILLIES
FILLING
FILLINS
FILLIPS
FILLOUT
FILLSIN
FILLSUP
FILLUPS
FILMIER
FILMING
FILTERS
GILBERT
GILBLAS
GILDERS
GILDING
GILGUYS
GILLIAN
GILLIES
GILLING
GILLNET
HILAIRE
HILLARY
HILLIER
HILLING
HILLOCK
HILLTOP
JILLIAN
JILLION
JILTING
KILAUEA
KILDARE
KILLERS
KILLING
KILLJOY
KILOTON
KILTIES
KILTING
LILLIAN
LILTING
LILYPAD
MILDEST
MILDEWS
MILDEWY
MILDRED
MILEAGE
MILHAUD
MILIEUS
MILIEUX
MILITIA
MILKCOW
MILKERS
MILKIER
MILKING
MILKMAN
MILKMEN
MILKRUN
MILKSOP
MILLAND
MILLARD
MILLDAM
MILLEND
MILLERS
MILLETS
MILLETT
MILLING
MILLION
MILLRUN
MILORDS
NILSSON
OILCAKE
OILCANS
OILIEST
OILLAMP
OILLESS
OILLIKE
OILPANS
OILRIGS
OILSKIN
OILWELL
PILEDIN
PILEDON
PILEDUP
PILESIN
PILESON
PILESUP
PILEUPS
PILFERS
PILGRIM
PILINGS
PILLAGE
PILLARS
PILLBOX
PILLBUG
PILLING
PILLION
PILLORY
PILLOWS
PILLOWY
PILOTED
PILSNER
RILESUP
RILLETS
SILENCE
SILENTS
SILESIA
SILICAS
SILICON
SILKHAT
SILKIER
SILKILY
SILLIER
SILLIES
SILOING
SILTIER
SILTING
SILVERS
SILVERY
TILINGS
TILLAGE
TILLERS
TILLING
TILTERS
TILTING
VILLAGE
VILLAIN
VILLEIN
VILNIUS
WILDCAT
WILDEST
WILDING
WILDISH
WILDONE
WILFORD
WILFRID
WILHELM
WILIEST
WILLARD
WILLETS
WILLFUL
WILLIAM
WILLIES
WILLING
WILLKIE
WILLOWS
WILLOWY
WILLSON
WILTING

ZILCHES
ZILLION

•I•L•••

AIDLESS
AIMLESS
AIRLANE
AIRLESS
AIRLIFT
AIRLIKE
AIRLINE
AIRLOCK
BIALIES
BIBLESS
BIBLIKE
BIGLIES
BILLETS
BILLIES
BILLING
BILLION
BILLOWS
BILLOWY
BIOLOGY
BIPLANE
BIRLING
BITLESS
DIALECT
DIALERS
DIALING
DIALOGS
DILLARD
DILLIES
DIPLOID
DIPLOMA
DISLIKE
FIELDED
FIELDER
FIGLEAF
FILLERS
FILLETS
FILLIES
FILLING
FILLINS
FILLIPS
FILLOUT
FILLSIN
FILLSUP
FILLUPS
FINLAND
FINLIKE
GIBLETS
GIBLUES
GIELGUD
GILLIAN
GILLIES
GILLING
GILLNET
GIMLETS
GIRLISH
HIALEAH
HILLARY
HILLIER
HILLING
HILLOCK
HILLTOP
HIPLESS
HIPLIKE
HITLESS
HITLIST
JIGLIKE
JILLIAN
JILLION
KIDLIKE
KILLERS
KILLING
KILLJOY
KINLESS
KIPLING
LIDLESS
LILLIAN
LIPLESS
LIPLIKE
MIDLAND
MIDLIFE
MIDLINE
MILLAND
MILLARD
MILLDAM
MILLEND
MILLERS
MILLETS
MILLETT
MILLING
MILLION
MILLRUN
MISLAID
MISLAYS
MISLEAD
MISLIKE
NIBLICK
NIBLIKE
NIELSEN
OILLAMP
OILLESS
OILLIKE
PIELIKE
PIGLETS
PIGLIKE
PILLAGE
PILLARS
PILLBOX
PILLBUG
PILLING
PILLION
PILLORY
PILLOWS
PILLOWY
PIMLICO
PINLESS
PIOLETS
RIBLESS
RIBLIKE
RIFLERS
RIFLERY
RIFLING
RILLETS
RIMLESS
RIOLOBO
SIBLING
SIDLING
SILLIER
SILLIES
SINLESS
SINLIKE
SIRLOIN
TIELESS
TIELINE
TIGLONS
TILLAGE
TILLERS
TILLING
TINLIKE
TIPLESS
TITLING
TITLIST
VILLAGE
VILLAIN
VILLEIN
VIOLATE
VIOLENT
VIOLETS
VIOLINS
VIOLIST
WIELDED
WIGLESS
WIGLETS
WIGLIKE
WILLARD
WILLETS
WILLFUL
WILLIAM
WILLIES
WILLING
WILLKIE
WILLOWS
WILLOWY
WILLSON
WITLESS
YIELDED
ZILLION

•I••L••

AIRFLOW
AIRPLAY
BIBELOT
BICOLOR
BIGELOW
BIPOLAR
BIVALVE
CIRCLED
CIRCLES
CIRCLET
CIVILLY
DIBBLED
DIBBLES
DIDDLED
DIDDLES
DIDDLEY
DIMPLED
DIMPLES
DINGLES
DIPOLAR
DIPOLES
DISPLAY
DIVULGE
FIATLUX
FIBULAE
FIBULAS
FICKLER
FIDDLED
FIDDLER
FIDDLES
FIDELIO
FIDELIS
FIEDLER
FINALES
FINALLY
FIPPLES
FIRELIT
FIZZLED
FIZZLES
GIGGLED
GIGGLER
GIGGLES
GIGOLOS
GILBLAS
GIRDLED
GIRDLES
GISELLE
HIDALGO
HIGGLED
HIGGLES
HIGHLOW
JIGGLED
JIGGLES
JINGLED
JINGLES
KIBBLED
KIBBLES
KINDLED
KINDLES
KIRTLES
LIBELED
LIBELER
LIESLOW
LITTLER
MIDDLEC
MIDDLES
MIGGLES
MINGLED
MINGLER
MINGLES
MINOLTA
MISALLY
MISPLAY
MIZZLED
MIZZLES
NIBBLED
NIBBLER
NIBBLES
NICOLAS
NIGGLED
NIGGLES
NIKOLAI
NIMBLER
PICKLED
PICKLES
PIFFLED
PIFFLES
RICKLES
RIDDLED
RIDDLER
RIDDLES
RIFFLED
RIFFLES
RIMPLED
RIMPLES
RINGLET
RIPPLED
RIPPLES
RIVALED
RIVALRY
RIVULET
SICKLES
SIMILAR
SIMILES
SIMPLER
SIMPLEX
SINGLED
SINGLES
SIZZLED
SIZZLES
TICKLED
TICKLER
TICKLES
TIECLIP
TIMELAG
TINGLED
TINGLES
TINKLED
TINKLES
TIPPLED
TIPPLER
TIPPLES
TITTLES
TITULAR
VIDALIA
VISALIA
VITALLY
VITTLES
VIVALDI
VIZSLAS
WIGGLED
WIGGLER
WIGGLES
WIMBLED
WIMBLES
WIMPLED
WIMPLES
WINKLED
WINKLER
WINKLES
WINSLOW

•I•••L•

AIRBALL
AIRHOLE
AIRMILE
AIRWOLF
BICYCLE
BIGTALK
CITABLE
CIVILLY
DIABOLI
DIESELS
DIMBULB
DINGILY
DIRNDLS
DIRTILY
DISABLE
DISPELS
DISTILL
DISTILS
DIZZILY
FIBRILS
FIERILY
FIFTHLY
FINAGLE
FINALLY
FINIALS
FIREFLY
FIRSTLY
FISHILY
FISSILE
FIXABLE
FIXEDLY
GIDDILY
GIMBALS
GINMILL
GISELLE
HIMSELF
HIRABLE
KIMBALL
KINFOLK
KINKILY
LICITLY
LIGHTLY
LIKABLE
LINCOLN
LINTELS
LIPBALM
LISTELS
LITHELY
LIVABLE
LIVIDLY
MICHELE
MINABLE
MIRACLE
MISALLY
MISCALL
MISERLY
MISFILE
MISRULE
MISSALS
MISSILE
MISTILY
MIXABLE
NICCOLO
NICHOLS
NICKELS
NIFTILY
NIGHTLY
NINTHLY
OILWELL
PICCOLO
PIEBALD
PINBALL
PINHOLE
PINOCLE
PINWALE
PIOUSLY
PISTILS
PISTOLE
PISTOLS
PITBULL
PITFALL
PITHILY
RIANTLY
RIGHTLY
RIGIDLY
RISIBLE
RISIBLY
RISKILY
RISSOLE
RITUALS
RITZILY
SIGHTLY
SIGNALS
SILKILY
SITWELL
SIXFOLD
SIXTHLY
SIZABLE
SIZABLY
TIEPOLO
TIGHTLY
TIMBALE
TIMBALS
TIMIDLY
TINNILY
TINSELS
TIPSILY
TIREDLY
VIRGULE
VISIBLE
VISIBLY
VISTULA
VISUALS
VITALLY
VIVIDLY
WILHELM
WIMPOLE
WINDILY
WISPILY
WITTILY

•I••••L

AIRBALL
AIRCOOL
AIRFOIL
AIRMAIL
BIFOCAL
BIGDEAL
BILEVEL
BIMODAL
BIPEDAL
CITADEL
DIGITAL
DIREFUL
DISHFUL
DISTILL
DIURNAL
FISTFUL
GINMILL
GIRASOL
KIMBALL
LIBERAL
LIFEFUL
LINGUAL
LITERAL
MICHAEL
MIKHAIL
MINDFUL
MINERAL
MINIMAL
MISCALL
MISDEAL
MISDIAL
MISTRAL
OILWELL
PIGTAIL
PINBALL
PINCURL
PINTAIL
PIPEFUL
PITBULL
PITFALL
PITIFUL
PIVOTAL
SIGHFUL
SITWELL
TINFOIL
VICTUAL
VIRTUAL
VITRIOL
WILLFUL
WISHFUL
WISTFUL

••IL•••

ABILENE
ABILITY
AGILELY
AGILITY
ANILINE
AXILLAE
BAILEES
BAILERS
BAILEYS
BAILIFF
BAILING
BAILORS
BAILOUT
BOILERS
BOILING
BUILDER
BUILDIN
BUILDUP
BUILTIN
BUILTUP
CEILING
CHILEAN
CHILIES
CHILLED
CHILLER
COILING
COILSUP
DAILIES
DOILIES
DRILLED
DRILLER
EPILOGS
EVILEST
EVILEYE
EVILLER
EXILING
FAILING
FAILURE
FOILING
FRILLED
GRILLED
GRILLES
GRILLET
GUILDER
HAILING
JAILERS
JAILING
KEILLOR
MAILBAG
MAILBOX
MAILCAR
MAILERS
MAILING
MAILLOT
MAILOUT
MAILSIN
MOILERS
MOILING
NAILERS
NAILING
NAILSET
NAILSIN
PAILFUL
PAILOUS
PHILBIN
PHILLIP
PHILTER
PHILTRE
QUILLED
QUILLER
QUILTED
QUILTER
RAILERS
RAILING
RAILSAT
RAILWAY
ROILIER
ROILING
SAILING
SAILORS
SHILLED
SKILFUL
SKILIFT
SKILLED
SKILLET
SMILERS
SMILING
SOILING
SPILLED
STILLED
STILLER
STILTED
STILTON
SWILLED
TAILEND
TAILFIN
TAILING
TAILLES
TAILOFF
TAILORS
TBILISI
TOILERS
TOILETS
TOILFUL
TOILING
TRILLED
TRILLIN
TRILOGY
TWILLED
UTILISE
UTILITY
UTILIZE
VEILING
WAILERS
WAILFUL
WAILING
WHILING

••I•L••

AMIBLUE
AXIALLY
AXILLAE
BRIDLED
BRIDLES
BRIMLEY
CHILLED
CHILLER
CRIOLLO
DAIMLER
DRIBLET
DRILLED
DRILLER
EDIBLES
ENISLED
ENISLES
EVILLER
FOIBLES
FRILLED
GRILLED
GRILLES
GRILLET
ICICLES
JAIALAI
KEILLOR
LAIDLOW
MAILLOT
ORIOLES
PAISLEY
PHILLIP
QUIGLEY
QUILLED
QUILLER
SHIELDS
SHILLED
SHIRLEY
SKILLED
SKILLET
SKIRLED
SNIGLET
SPIELED
SPIELER
SPILLED
STIFLED
STIFLES
STILLED
STILLER
SWILLED
SWIRLED
TAILLES
TRIFLED
TRIFLER
TRIFLES
TRILLED
TRILLIN
TRIPLED
TRIPLES
TRIPLET
TRIPLEX
TWILLED
TWIRLED
TWIRLER
WHIRLED
WRIGLEY

••I••L•

AGILELY
AMIABLE
AMIABLY
ANIMALS
APISHLY
ATINGLE
AXIALLY
BLINDLY
BRIDALS
BRIEFLY
BRINDLE
BRISKLY
BRISTLE
BRISTLY
BRITTLE
CHIEFLY
CHISELS
CRINKLE
CRINKLY
CRIOLLO
CRISPLY
DRIBBLE
DRIVELS
DRIZZLE
DRIZZLY
DWINDLE
EPISTLE
FAINTLY
FRIABLE
FRIZZLE
FRIZZLY
GRIDDLE
GRIMILY
GRISTLE
GRISTLY
GRIZZLE
GRIZZLY
JOINTLY
JUICILY
KRINGLE
MOISTLY
NAIVELY
NOISILY
PLIABLE
PLIABLY
PRICKLE
PRICKLY
PRIVILY
QUIBBLE
QUICKLY
QUIETLY
RAINILY
SAINTLY
SEIDELS
SHINGLE
SHINILY
SKIPOLE
SKITTLE
SLICKLY
SLIMILY
SNIDELY
SNIFFLE
SNIFFLY
SNIGGLE
SNIVELS
SPICILY
SPIKILY
SPINDLE
SPINDLY
SPINELS
SPIRALS
STIFFLY
STIMULI
STIPPLE
SWIFTLY
SWINDLE
SWIVELS
SWIZZLE
THICKLY
THIMBLE
THIRDLY
THISTLE
THISTLY
TRICKLE
TRIPOLI
TRITELY
TWIDDLE
TWINKLE
TWINKLY
WEIRDLY
WHISTLE
WHITTLE
WRIGGLE
WRIGGLY
WRINKLE
WRINKLY
ZWINGLI

••I•••L

ABIGAIL
BRIMFUL
BRISTOL
GAINFUL
INITIAL
KNIEVEL
PAILFUL
PAINFUL
SKILFUL
SKINFUL
SPIEGEL
STIEGEL
TOILFUL
TRIVIAL
WAILFUL

•••IL••

AAMILNE
AEDILES
ANTILOG
AUDILES
AVAILED
BACILLI
BRAILLE
BROILED
BROILER
CAMILLE
CAVILED
CAVILER
CECILIA
CEDILLA
CIVILLY
COPILOT
DEFILED
DEFILER
DEFILES
DELILAH
DEMILLE
DEVILED
DEVILLE
DEVILRY
EMAILED
ENSILED
ENSILES
EPSILON
ETOILES
FLAILED
FRAILER
FRAILLY
FRAILTY
GALILEE
GALILEI
GALILEO
GEFILTE
GORILLA
JUBILEE
LUCILLE
MANILOW
MARILYN
MATILDA
MAXILLA
MOBILES
MURILLO
NEVILLE
ORVILLE
PAPILLA
QUAILED
REFILED
REFILES
REFILLS
REFILMS
REOILED
RESILED
RESILES
RETILED
RETILES
REVILED
REVILES
SEMILOG
SEVILLE
SHEILAS
SHRILLS
SHRILLY
SIMILAR
SIMILES
SPOILED
SPOILER
SQUILLS
THRILLS
TRAILED
TRAILER
TROILUS
UNOILED
UNPILED
UNPILES
UPSILON
UTRILLO
VANILLA
VANILLI

•••I•L•

ACRIDLY
ADDIBLE
AERIALS
ARTICLE
AUDIBLE
AUDIBLY
AURICLE
BACILLI
BRAILLE
CAMILLE
CEDILLA
CIVILLY
CUBICLE
CUTICLE
DANIELS
DEMILLE
DENIALS
DEVILLE
ENTITLE
ESPIALS
FACIALS
FETIDLY
FINIALS
FLUIDLY
FRAILLY
GAVIALS
GELIDLY
GORILLA
HUMIDLY
INFIELD
LABIALS
LEGIBLE
LEGIBLY
LICITLY
LIVIDLY
LUCIDLY
LUCILLE
LURIDLY
MANIPLE
MAXILLA
MENIALS
MURILLO
NEVILLE
ORVILLE
OSSICLE
PANICLE
PAPILLA
PEDICLE
PETIOLE
PLAINLY
RABIDLY
RADIALS
RADICLE
RAPIDLY
RAVIOLI
REDIALS
REFILLS
RETICLE
RETITLE
RIGIDLY
RISIBLE
RISIBLY
SERIALS
SEVILLE
SHRILLS
SHRILLY
SOCIALS
SOLIDLY
SQUILLS
STAIDLY
TACITLY
TEPIDLY
THRILLS
TIMIDLY
TUNICLE
UNCIALS
UTRILLO
VALIDLY
VANILLA
VANILLI
VAPIDLY
VEHICLE
VISIBLE
VISIBLY
VIVIDLY

•••I••L

ADMIRAL
ARRIVAL
CAPITAL
CAPITOL
CLAIROL
CODICIL
COMICAL
CONICAL
CYNICAL
DECIBEL
DECIMAL
DIGITAL
DREIDEL
DUTIFUL
ESTIVAL
ETHICAL
GERITOL
HELICAL
INCIVIL
INFIDEL
LAMINAL
LEXICAL
LOGICAL
LYRICAL
MAGICAL
MARITAL
MAXIMAL
MEDICAL
MINIMAL
MUSICAL
NOMINAL
OEDIPAL
OPTICAL
OPTIMAL
ORBITAL
ORDINAL
OVOIDAL
PEDICEL
PITIFUL
RADICAL
RECITAL
RETINAL
REVIVAL
SANIBEL
SEMINAL
SHRIVEL
STOICAL
TOPICAL
TYPICAL
UNCIVIL

••••IL•

AIRMILE
ANGRILY
ANOUILH
ANTHILL
ARTFILM
ASSAILS
BAGGILY
BALKILY
BALMILY
BAWDILY
BEGUILE
BEWAILS
BOBVILA
BONNILY
BOSSILY
BUMPILY
BUSHILY
CAMPILY
CANNILY
CANTILY
CASTILE

CATTILY
CHARILY
COCKILY
COMPILE
CORNILY
CRAZILY
DAFFILY
DAYLILY
DERAILS
DETAILS
DINGILY
DIRTILY
DISTILL
DISTILS
DIZZILY
DOTTILY
DOWDILY
DUCTILE
DUSKILY
DUSTILY
EMPTILY
ENTAILS
FANCILY
FATTILY
FEBRILE
FERTILE
FIBRILS
FIERILY
FISHILY
FISSILE
FLAKILY
FOAMILY
FOGGILY
FOSSILS
FRAGILE
FULFILL
FULFILS
FUNKILY
FUNNILY
FUSSILY
FUSTILY
FUZZILY
GAUDILY
GAUZILY
GAWKILY
GENTILE
GERBILS
GIDDILY
GINMILL
GOOFILY
GOONILY
GOUTILY
GRACILE
GRIMILY
GUSHILY
GUSTILY
GUTSILY
HAMMILY
HANDILY
HAPPILY
HARDILY
HASTILY
HEADILY
HEAVILY
HEFTILY
HOARILY
HOGWILD
HOSTILE
HUFFILY
HUSKILY
ICEMILK
ILLWILL
INSTILL
INSTILS
INUTILE
JAZZILY
JERKILY
JOEHILL
JOLLILY
JUICILY
JUMPILY
KINKILY
LANKILY
LEERILY
LENTILS
LOFTILY
LOUSILY
LUCKILY
LUMPILY
LUSTILY
MEATILY
MERRILL
MERRILY
MESSILY
MISFILE
MISSILE
MISTILY
MOODILY
MOONILY
MUCKILY
MUDDILY
MURKILY
MUSHILY
MUSSILY
MUSTILY
MUZZILY
NASTILY
NATTILY
NEEDILY
NERVILY
NIFTILY
NOBHILL
NOISILY
NUTTILY
PENCILS
PEPPILY
PERKILY
PESKILY
PETTILY
PHONILY
PISTILS
PITHILY
PODGILY
PRIVILY
PROFILE
PROSILY
PUDGILY
PUERILE
PUFFILY
PUNNILY
PUSHILY
QUAKILY
RAINILY
RAWSILK
READILY
REBOILS
REBUILD
REBUILT
RECOILS
REMAILS
RENAILS
REPTILE
RETAILS
RISKILY
RITZILY
ROOMILY
ROWDILY
RUDDILY
RUSTILY
SALTILY
SAMHILL
SAPPILY
SASSILY
SAUCILY
SAVVILY
SAWMILL
SCARILY
SEALILY
SEEDILY
SERVILE
SESSILE
SHADILY
SHAKILY
SHINILY
SHOWILY
SILKILY
SLIMILY
SMOKILY
SNAKILY
SNOWILY
SOAPILY
SOGGILY
SOOTILY
SORRILY
SPICILY
SPIKILY
STABILE
STAGILY
STERILE
STONILY
SULKILY
SUNNILY
SURLILY
SWAHILI
TACKILY
TACTILE
TARDILY
TASTILY
TATTILY
TAWNILY
TEARILY
TENSILE
TEQUILA
TESTILY
TEXTILE
TINNILY
TIPSILY
TONSILS
UNCOILS
UNVEILS
WACKILY
WASPILY
WAYBILL
WEARILY
WEEDILY
WEEVILS
WINDILY
WISPILY
WITTILY
WOOZILY
WORDILY

••••I•L
ANTHILL
ASOCIAL
BATGIRL
BESTIAL
BUSGIRL
COAXIAL
CORDIAL
COWGIRL
CRANIAL
CRUCIAL
DISTILL
EZEKIEL
FLUVIAL
FULFILL
GABRIEL
GINMILL
GLACIAL
ILLWILL
INITIAL
INSTILL
JOEHILL
MARTIAL
MERRILL
MISDIAL
NOBHILL
NUPTIAL
ONTRIAL
PARTIAL
PATRIAL
PLUVIAL
RETRIAL
SAMHILL
SAWMILL
SPANIEL
SPATIAL
SPECIAL
SUNDIAL
TENNIEL
TERTIAL
TRIVIAL
TRUCIAL
UXORIAL
VITRIOL
WAYBILL

•••••IL
ABIGAIL
AIRFOIL
AIRMAIL
ALLHAIL
BATHOIL
BEDEVIL
BOBTAIL
CATTAIL
CHERVIL
COALOIL
CODICIL
CORNOIL
COUNCIL
CURTAIL
DESPOIL
DWEEZIL
EMBROIL
ESTORIL
FANMAIL
FANTAIL
FOXTAIL
FUELOIL
GONERIL
HOBNAIL
IMPERIL
INCIVIL
JONQUIL
LAMPOIL
MIKHAIL
NOSTRIL
PALMOIL
PARBOIL
PIGTAIL
PINTAIL
PREVAIL
RATTAIL
REAVAIL
ROSEOIL
SETSAIL
STENCIL
SUBSOIL
TENDRIL
TINFOIL
TOENAIL
TOPSAIL
TOPSOIL
TRAVAIL
TREFOIL
TUNGOIL
TURMOIL
UNCIVIL
UTENSIL
VERMEIL
WAGTAIL
WASSAIL

IM•••••
IMAGERS
IMAGERY
IMAGINE
IMAGING
IMAGOES
IMAMATE
IMARETS
IMBIBED
IMBIBES
IMBRUED
IMBRUES
IMBUING
IMITATE
IMMENSE
IMMERSE
IMMIXED
IMMIXES
IMMORAL
IMMURED
IMMURES
IMOGENE
IMPACTS
IMPAIRS
IMPALAS
IMPALED
IMPALES
IMPANEL
IMPARTS
IMPASSE
IMPASTO
IMPEACH
IMPEDED
IMPEDES
IMPENDS
IMPERIL
IMPETUS
IMPIETY
IMPINGE
IMPIOUS
IMPLANT
IMPLIED
IMPLIES
IMPLODE
IMPLORE
IMPORTS
IMPOSED
IMPOSES
IMPOSTS
IMPOUND
IMPRESS
IMPRINT
IMPROVE
IMPUGNS
IMPULSE
IMPURER
IMPUTED
IMPUTES
IMSORRY

I•M••••
IMMENSE
IMMERSE
IMMIXED
IMMIXES
IMMORAL
IMMURED
IMMURES
INMATES
IOMOTHS

I••M•••
ICEMILK
IMAMATE
INAMESS
ISHMAEL
ISOMERS
ITEMISE
ITEMIZE

I•••M••
IDEAMAN
IDEAMEN
IDIAMIN
ILLUMED
ILLUMES
INCOMES
INGEMAR
INHUMAN
IRONMAN
IRONMEN
ISLAMIC
ISTHMUS

I••••M•
INFLAME
INFORMS
INSEAMS
IPANEMA
IRKSOME
ISONOMY
IWOJIMA

I•••••M
INBLOOM
INTERIM
IRIDIUM

•IM••••
AIMEDAT
AIMEDTO
AIMLESS
AIMSFOR
BIMODAL
DIMBULB
DIMITRI
DIMMERS
DIMMEST
DIMMING
DIMNESS
DIMOUTS
DIMPLED
DIMPLES
DIMWITS
GIMBALS
GIMLETS
GIMMICK
HIMSELF
JIMCHEE
JIMENEZ
JIMJAMS
JIMMIED
JIMMIES
KIMBALL
KIMCHEE
KIMONOS
LIMBERS
LIMBING
LIMEADE
LIMIEST
LIMITED
LIMNERS
LIMNING
LIMOGES
LIMPEST
LIMPETS
LIMPING
LIMPOPO
MIMESIS
MIMETIC
MIMICRY
MIMIEUX
MIMOSAS
NIMBLER
NIMIETY
NIMRODS
PIMENTO
PIMESON
PIMLICO
RIMBAUD
RIMIEST
RIMLESS
RIMMING
RIMPLED
RIMPLES
RIMSHOT
SIMENON
SIMIANS
SIMILAR
SIMILES
SIMMERS
SIMMONS
SIMPERS
SIMPLER
SIMPLEX
SIMPSON
TIMBALE
TIMBALS
TIMBERS
TIMBRES
TIMECOP
TIMELAG
TIMEOFF
TIMEOUT
TIMESUP
TIMIDER
TIMIDLY
TIMINGS
TIMMINS
TIMOTHY
WIMBLED
WIMBLES
WIMPIER
WIMPISH
WIMPLED
WIMPLES
WIMPOLE

•I•M•••
AILMENT
AIRMADA
AIRMAIL
AIRMASS
AIRMILE
BIOMASS
BISMUTH
BITMAPS
DIAMOND
DIMMERS
DIMMEST
DIMMING
DINMONT
DIOMEDE
DISMAYS
DISMISS
FIGMENT
FILMIER
FILMING
FIRMEST
FIRMING
FIRMSUP
GIMMICK
GINMILL
JIMMIED
JIMMIES
KIRMANS
MIAMIAN
MIAMIAS
MICMACS
MIDMOST
MISMATE
PIGMENT
PISMIRE
RIMMING
SIAMESE
SIGMUND
SIMMERS
SIMMONS
TIMMINS
TIOMKIN
TITMICE
WIDMARK

•I••M••
BIRDMAN
BIRDMEN
BIREMES
BITUMEN
CINEMAS
CINEMAX
DILEMMA
FIREMAN
FIREMEN
HICKMAN
JICAMAS
KINEMAS
KINGMAN
KINSMAN
KINSMEN
LIKEMAD
LINEMAN
LINEMEN
MIASMAS
MIASMIC
MILKMAN
MILKMEN
MINIMAL
MINIMUM
MIRAMAR
MIRAMAX
PIKEMAN
PIKEMEN
PIPEMMA
PITTMAN
RICHMAN
RICKMAN
SIDEMAN
SIDEMEN
VITAMIN
WISEMAN
WISEMEN

•I•••M•
AIRDAMS
AIRPUMP
AIRTIME
BIGGAME
BIGNAME
BIGTIME
DIADEMS
DIATOMS
DICTUMS
DIGRAMS
DILEMMA
DIORAMA
DIPLOMA
DISARMS
GIACOMO
JIMJAMS
LISSOME
MISNAME
OILLAMP
PIPEMMA
SITCOMS
VICTIMS
WIGWAMS
WINSOME

•I••••M
BINGHAM
DIAGRAM
DIVINUM
EIGHTAM
EIGHTPM
FIEFDOM
FIREARM
GINGHAM
JIBBOOM
KINGDOM
LIPBALM
LITHIUM
MIDTERM
MILLDAM
MINICAM
MINIMUM
MITCHUM
NIOBIUM
PIANISM
PIETISM
PILGRIM
PINETUM
SIDEARM
SIKHISM
SISTRUM
TINYTIM
VIETNAM
WILHELM
WILLIAM

••IM•••
ALIMENT
ALIMONY
ANIMALS
ANIMATE
ANIMATO
ANIMISM
ANIMIST
AZIMUTH
BRIMFUL
BRIMLEY
BRIMMED
CAIMANS
CHIMERA
CHIMING
CHIMNEY
CLIMATE
CLIMBED
CLIMBER
CRIMEAN
CRIMPED
CRIMPER
CRIMSON
DAIMLER
DAIMONS
GLIMMER
GLIMPSE
GRIMACE
GRIMIER
GRIMILY
GRIMING
GRIMMER
GUIMPES
PRIMACY
PRIMARY
PRIMATE
PRIMERS
PRIMING
PRIMMER
PRIMPED
RAIMENT
SHIMMER
SKIMASK
SKIMMED
SKIMMER
SKIMPED
SLIMIER
SLIMILY
SLIMJIM
SLIMMED
SLIMMER
STIMULI
SWIMMER
THIMBLE
THIMPHU
TRIMMED
TRIMMER
WHIMPER

••I•M••
BRIMMED
ENIGMAS
GLIMMER
GRIMMER
HEISMAN
IDIAMIN
PRIMMER
RAINMAN
REITMAN
SEISMIC
SHIMMER
SHIPMAN
SHIPMEN
SKIMMED
SKIMMER
SLIMMED
SLIMMER
STIGMAS
SWIMMER
TRIMMED
TRIMMER
TRIUMPH
WHITMAN

••I••M•
EPITOME
NOISOME
ORIGAMI
RHIZOME
SKIJUMP
TRIREME

••I•••M
ANIMISM
BRIGHAM
ELITISM
EPIGRAM
GRISHAM
GRISSOM
IRIDIUM
SLIMJIM
TRIGRAM
TRITIUM
UNIFORM

•••IM••
ATTIMES
BETIMES
CLAIMED
CLAIMER
DECIMAL
DELIMIT
DONIMUS
ESKIMOS
FADIMAN
MARIMBA
MAXIMAL
MAXIMUM
MAXIMUS
MERIMEE
MINIMAL
MINIMUM
OPTIMAL
OPTIMUM
REAIMED
REGIMEN
REGIMES
RETIMED
RETIMES
SCRIMPS
SCRIMPY
SHRIMPS
TAXIMAN
TAXIMEN
ULTIMAS
UNAIMED
YAKIMAS

•••I•M•
AFFIRMS
ATRIUMS
CHRISMS
MEDIUMS
PODIUMS
REFILMS
SCHISMS
SQUIRMS
SQUIRMY
TEDIUMS
TRUISMS
VERISMO
WOEISME

•••I••M
ADFINEM
DIVINUM
HASIDIM
MAXIMUM
MINICAM
MINIMUM
MODICUM
OPTIMUM
STEINEM
SURINAM
TOTIDEM

••••IM•
AIRTIME
ALLTIME
ANYTIME
BEDTIME
BEGRIME
BIGTIME
BUYTIME
CENTIME
CENTIMO
CUTTIME
DAYTIME
EXANIMO
IWOJIMA
KEYLIME
MAYTIME
MEGRIMS
MUSLIMS
NANAIMO
NAPTIME
OLDTIME
ONETIME
PASTIME
PRELIMS
PROXIMO
RAGTIME
RETRIMS
SASHIMI
SUBLIME
TEATIME
TEETIME
TWOTIME
VICTIMS
WARTIME

••••I•M
ANIMISM
ARTFILM
ATAVISM
ATHEISM
BAPTISM
BELGIUM
CADMIUM
CAESIUM
CALCIUM
CAMBIUM
CONFIRM
CRANIUM
CULTISM
CZARISM
DADAISM
EGOTISM
ELITISM
ELUVIUM
ELYSIUM
FADDISM
FAUVISM
FERMIUM
FOGYISM
GALLIUM
GLORIAM
HAFNIUM
HAHNIUM
HEROISM
HOLMIUM
IRIDIUM
JUDAISM
LAMAISM
LITHIUM
MARXISM
NATRIUM
NIOBIUM
PALLIUM
PENTIUM
PERDIEM
PIANISM
PIETISM
PREMIUM
REALISM
REQUIEM
RHENIUM
RHODIUM
SIKHISM
SOPHISM
STADIUM
TERBIUM
THEFIRM
THORIUM
THULIUM
TORYISM
TOURISM
TRITIUM
TROPISM
URANIUM
WILLIAM
YTTRIUM

•••••IM
ACCLAIM
ANAHEIM
DECLAIM
EXCLAIM
HASIDIM
INTERIM
JOACHIM
LORDJIM
PILGRIM
RECLAIM
SLIMJIM
TAKEAIM
TINYTIM

IN•••••
INADAZE
INAHEAP
INAMESS
INANELY
INANEST
INANITY
INAPTER
INAPTLY
INARUSH
INASNIT
INASPIN
INASPOT
INASTEW
INAWEOF
INAWORD
INBLOOM
INBOARD
INBOUND
INBOXES
INBREED
INBRIEF
INCANTS
INCASED
INCASES
INCENSE
INCEPTS
INCHING
INCIPIT
INCISED
INCISES
INCISOR
INCITED
INCITER
INCITES
INCIVIL
INCLINE
INCLOSE
INCLUDE
INCOMES
INCUDES
INDENTS
INDEPTH
INDEXED
INDEXES
INDIANA
INDIANS
INDICES
INDICIA
INDICTS
INDIGOS
INDITED
INDITES
INDOORS
INDORSE
INDOUBT
INDUCED
INDUCER
INDUCES
INDUCTS
INDULGE
INDUTCH
INDWELL
INEPTLY
INERROR
INERTIA
INERTLY
INEXACT
INFANCY
INFANTA
INFANTS
INFAVOR
INFECTS
INFERNO
INFESTS
INFIDEL
INFIELD
INFLAME
INFLATE
INFLECT
INFLICT
INFLOWS
INFOCUS
INFORCE
INFORMS
INFRONT
INFUSED
INFUSES
INGALLS
INGEMAR
INGENUE
INGESTS
INGRAIN
INGRATE
INGRESS
INGROUP
INGROWN
INHABIT
INHALED
INHALER
INHALES
INHASTE
INHAULS
INHERED

INHERES
INHERIT
INHIBIT
INHOUSE
INHUMAN
INITIAL
INJECTS
INJOKES
INJURED
INJURES
INKBLOT
INKHORN
INKIEST
INKLESS
INKLIKE
INKLING
INKSPOT
INKWELL
INKYCAP
INMATES
INNARDS
INNINGS
INNLESS
INNOWAY
INOCULA
INORBIT
INPEACE
INPETTO
INPHASE
INPLACE
INPOWER
INPRINT
INQUEST
INQUIRE
INQUIRY
INROADS
INSCAPE
INSEAMS
INSECTS
INSERTS
INSHAPE
INSHORT
INSIDER
INSIDES
INSIGHT
INSIPID
INSISTS
INSOFAR
INSOLES
INSPANS
INSPECT
INSPIRE
INSPOTS
INSTALL
INSTALS
INSTANT
INSTARS
INSTATE
INSTEAD
INSTEPS
INSTILL
INSTILS
INSTOCK
INSTORE
INSTYLE
INSULAR
INSULIN
INSULTS
INSURED
INSURER
INSURES
INTAKES
INTEARS
INTEGER
INTEGRA
INTENDS
INTENSE
INTENTS
INTERIM
INTERNS
INTERSE
INTONED
INTONER
INTONES
INTROIT
INTRUDE
INTRUST
INTRUTH
INTUITS
INURING
INUTILE
INVACUO
INVADED
INVADER
INVADES
INVALID
INVEIGH
INVENTS
INVERSE
INVERTS
INVESTS
INVITED
INVITES
INVITRO
INVOGUE
INVOICE
INVOKED
INVOKER
INVOKES
INVOLVE
INWARDS

I•N••••

IBNSAUD
IGNEOUS
IGNITED
IGNITER
IGNITES
IGNOBLE
IGNOBLY
IGNORED
IGNORER
IGNORES
INNARDS
INNINGS
INNLESS
INNOWAY
IONESCO
IONISED
IONISES
IONIZED
IONIZER
IONIZES

I••N•••

ICINESS
ICINGIN
ICINGUP
IDENTIC
ILLNESS
INANELY
INANEST
INANITY
IPANEMA
IRANIAN
IRONAGE
IRONERS
IRONIES
IRONING
IRONMAN
IRONMEN
IRONONS
IRONORE
IRONOUT
ISONOMY
IVANHOE
IVANOVO

I•••N••

IGUANAS
IMMENSE
IMPANEL
IMPENDS
IMPINGE
INASNIT
INCANTS
INCENSE
INDENTS
INFANCY
INFANTA
INFANTS
INGENUE
INNINGS
INTENDS
INTENSE
INTENTS
INTONED
INTONER
INTONES
INVENTS
ISLANDS

I••••N•

ICELAND
ICERINK
IFSTONE
IKEBANA
ILLWIND
ILOCANO
IMAGINE
IMAGING
IMBUING
IMOGENE
IMPLANT
IMPOUND
IMPRINT
IMPUGNS
INBOUND
INCHING
INCLINE
INDIANA
INDIANS
INFERNO
INFRONT
INKLING
INPRINT
INSPANS
INSTANT
INTERNS
INURING
IRELAND
IRONING
IRONONS
ISOGONS
ISSUING
ITCHING
ITERANT

I•••••N

IBERIAN
ICINGIN
IDAHOAN
IDEAMAN
IDEAMEN
IDIAMIN
INASPIN
INGRAIN
INGROWN
INHUMAN
INKHORN
INSULIN
IRANIAN
IRECKON
IRONMAN
IRONMEN
ITALIAN
ITHACAN

•IN••••

BINDERS
BINDERY
BINDING
BINDSUP
BINGHAM
BINGING
BINGOES
BINNING
BINOCHE
CINCHED
CINCHES
CINDERS
CINDERY
CINEMAS
CINEMAX
CINZANO
DINEDIN
DINEDON
DINESEN
DINESIN
DINESON
DINETTE
DINGBAT
DINGIER
DINGILY
DINGING
DINGLES
DINGOES
DINKIER
DINKIES
DINMONT
DINNERS
FINAGLE
FINALES
FINALLY
FINANCE
FINCHES
FINDERS
FINDING
FINDOUT
FINEART
FINESSE
FINGERS
FINIALS
FINICKY
FINKING
FINLAND
FINLIKE
FINNIER
FINNISH
GINFIZZ
GINGERS
GINGERY
GINGHAM
GINGIVA
GINMILL
GINNING
GINSENG
HINDERS
HINGING
HINNIES
HINTING
HINTSAT
JINGLED
JINGLES
JINGOES
JINKING
JINXING
KINCHIN
KINDEST
KINDLED
KINDLES
KINDRED
KINEMAS
KINETIC
KINFOLK
KINGDOM
KINGING
KINGMAN
KINGPIN
KINGRAT
KINGTUT
KINKIER
KINKILY
KINKING
KINLESS
KINSHIP
KINSMAN
KINSMEN
LINAGES
LINBIAO
LINCOLN
LINDENS
LINDIED
LINDIES
LINDSAY
LINDSEY
LINEAGE
LINEATE
LINEDUP
LINEMAN
LINEMEN
LINESUP
LINEUPS
LINGERS
LINGOES
LINGUAL
LINIEST
LININGS
LINKAGE
LINKERS
LINKING
LINKUPS
LINNETS
LINPIAO
LINSEED
LINTELS
LINTIER
MINABLE
MINARET
MINCERS
MINCING
MINDERS
MINDFUL
MINDING
MINDSET
MINERAL
MINERVA
MINGIER
MINGLED
MINGLER
MINGLES
MINIBUS
MINICAB
MINICAM
MINIMAL
MINIMUM
MINIONS
MINIVAN
MINIVER
MINNOWS
MINOANS
MINOLTA
MINORCA
MINORED
MINTERS
MINTIER
MINTING
MINUEND
MINUETS
MINUSES
MINUTES
MINUTIA
MINXISH
MINYANS
NINEPIN
NINEVEH
NINNIES
NINTHLY
OINKING
PINATAS
PINBALL
PINCERS
PINCHAS
PINCHED
PINCHER
PINCHES
PINCURL
PINDOWN
PINEFOR
PINENUT
PINESAP
PINETAR
PINETUM
PINGING
PINHEAD
PINHOLE
PINIEST
PINIONS
PINKEST
PINKIES
PINKING
PINKISH
PINLESS
PINNACE
PINNATE
PINNERS
PINNING
PINOAKS
PINOCLE
PINONES
PINTAIL
PINWALE
QINGDAO
QINTARS
RINGERS
RINGING
RINGLET
RINGOFF
RINGOUT
RINGSUP
RINSING
SINATRA
SINCERE
SINEDIE
SINGERS
SINGING
SINGLED
SINGLES
SINGOUT
SINGSTO
SINKAGE
SINKERS
SINKING
SINKSIN
SINLESS
SINLIKE
SINNERS
SINUOUS
SINUSES
TINCANS
TINDERS
TINEARS
TINFOIL
TINGING
TINGLED
TINGLES
TINHATS
TINHORN
TINIEST
TINKERS
TINKLED
TINKLES
TINLIKE
TINNERS
TINNIER
TINNILY
TINSELS
TINSTAR
TINTACK
TINTERN
TINTERS
TINTING
TINTYPE
TINWARE
TINWORK
TINYTIM
VINCENT
VINEGAR
VINIEST
VINTAGE
VINTNER
WINCERS
WINCHED
WINCHES
WINCING
WINDBAG
WINDERS
WINDIER
WINDILY
WINDING
WINDOWS
WINDROW
WINDSOR
WINDSUP
WINDUPS
WINEBAR
WINERED
WINESAP
WINFREY
WINGERS
WINGING
WINGNUT
WINGSIT
WINGTIP
WINIEST
WINKERS
WINKING
WINKLED
WINKLER
WINKLES
WINKOUT
WINKSAT
WINNERS
WINNING
WINNOWS
WINSLOW
WINSOME
WINSOUT
WINSTON
WINTERS
WINTERY
XINGOUT
ZINGERS
ZINGIER
ZINGING
ZINNIAS

•I•N•••

BIENTOT
BIGNAME
BIGNESS
BINNING
BIONICS
DIGNIFY
DIGNITY
DIMNESS
DINNERS
DIRNDLS
FIANCEE
FIANCES
FIENNES
FINNIER
FINNISH
FITNESS
GINNING
GIRNING
HINNIES
HIPNESS
JITNEYS
KIDNAPS
KIDNEYS
LIENEES
LIGNITE
LIMNERS
LIMNING
LINNETS
LIONCUB
LIONESS
LIONETS
LIONISE
LIONIZE
MINNOWS
MISNAME
NINNIES
PIANISM
PIANIST
PICNICS
PIGNUTS
PINNACE
PINNATE
PINNERS
PINNING
PIONEER
RIANTLY
SIENNAS
SIGNALS
SIGNEES
SIGNERS
SIGNETS
SIGNIFY
SIGNING
SIGNOFF
SIGNOUT
SIGNSIN
SIGNSON
SIGNSUP
SINNERS
TIANJIN
TINNERS
TINNIER
TINNILY
VILNIUS
WIENERS
WIENIES
WINNERS
WINNING
WINNOWS
WITNESS
ZINNIAS

•I••N••

AIRINGS
BIKINIS
DIURNAL
DIVINED
DIVINER
DIVINES
DIVINUM
DIZENED
FIENNES
FILENES
FILINGS
FINANCE
FIRENZE
FIRINGS
FISHNET
FIXINGS
GILLNET
GIRONDE
GIVENIN
GIVENTO
GIVENUP
HIDINGS
HIJINKS
JIMENEZ
KIMONOS
KIWANIS
LICENCE
LICENSE
LIERNES
LIFENET
LIGANDS
LIKENED
LIKENEW
LININGS
LISENTE
LITINTO
LIVENED
LIVINGS
MIRANDA
PICANTE
PILINGS
PILSNER
PIMENTO
PINENUT
PINONES
PIPINGS
PIRANHA
RIBANDS
RIPENED
RIPINTO
RISINGS
SIDINGS
SIENNAS
SILENCE
SILENTS
SIMENON
SIZINGS
TIDINGS
TIEINTO
TIERNEY
TILINGS
TIMINGS
TISANES
TITANIA
TITANIC
VICUNAS
VIETNAM
VIKINGS
VINTNER
VIVENDI
WIDENED
WINGNUT
WIZENED

•I•••N•

AILMENT
AIRGUNS
AIRLANE
AIRLINE
BIASING
BIDDING
BIGBAND
BIGBANG
BIGBEND
BIGGUNS
BILKING
BILLING
BINDING
BINGING
BINNING
BIOGENY
BIPLANE
BIRDING
BIRLING
BITTING
CINZANO
CITRINE
CITRONS
DIALING
DIAMOND
DICKENS
DIETING
DIGGING
DIMMING
DINGING
DINMONT
DIPPING
DISBAND
DISHING
DISOWNS
DISSENT
DISSING
DISTANT
DISTEND
DITTANY
FIBBING
FIBRINS
FIGMENT
FIJIANS
FILLING
FILLINS
FILMING
FINDING
FINKING
FINLAND
FIREANT
FIRKINS
FIRMING
FISHING
FITTING
FIZZING
GIBBING
GIBBONS
GIDEONS
GILDING
GILLING
GINNING
GINSENG
GIPPING
GIRDING
GIRNING
HIGGINS
HIGHEND
HILLING
HINGING
HINTING
HIPBONE
HISPANO
HISSING
HITTING
JIBBING
JIGGING
JILTING
JINKING
JINXING
KICKING
KIDDING
KILLING
KILTING
KINGING
KINKING
KIPLING
KIRMANS
KISSING
KITTENS
LIBBING
LIBYANS
LICHENS
LICKING
LIFTING
LILTING
LIMBING
LIMNING
LIMPING
LINDENS
LINKING
LIPPING
LIPSYNC
LISPING
LISTENS
LISTING
LIVEONE
LIVORNO
MICRONS
MIDDENS
MIDLAND
MIDLINE
MIFFING
MIGHTNT
MIGRANT
MILKING
MILLAND
MILLEND
MILLING
MINCING
MINDING
MINIONS
MINOANS
MINTING
MINUEND
MINYANS
MIOCENE
MISDONE
MISSING
MISTING
MITRING
MITTENS
MIZZENS
NICKING
NIPPING
NIRVANA
NITTANY
OILCANS
OILPANS
OINKING
PICKENS
PICKING
PIDGINS
PIECING
PIEPANS
PIETINS
PIGEONS
PIGGING
PIGMENT
PIGPENS
PILLING
PINGING
PINIONS
PINKING
PINNING
PIPKINS
PIPPINS
PIQUANT
PIQUING
PISCINE
PISTONS
PITHING
PITTING
PITYING
RIBBING
RIBBONS
RIDDING
RIDGING
RIFFING
RIFLING
RIFTING
RIGGING
RIMMING
RINGING
RINSING
RIOTING
RIPIENO
RIPPING
RISKING
SIBLING
SICCING
SICKENS
SIDLING
SIFTING
SIGHING
SIGMUND
SIGNING
SILOING
SILTING
SIMIANS
SIMMONS
SINGING
SINKING
SIOUANS
SIPHONS
SIPPING
SISKINS
SISTINE
SITTING
SIXGUNS
TICKING
TIDYING
TIELINE
TIEPINS
TIERING
TIFFANY
TIFFING
TIFFINS
TIGLONS
TIJUANA
TILLING
TILTING
TIMMINS
TINCANS
TINGING
TINTING
TIPPING
TITHING
TITLING
TITRING
VIBRANT
VIEWING
VINCENT
VIOLENT
VIOLINS
VIRGINS
VISAING
VISIONS
WILDING
WILDONE
WILLING
WILTING
WINCING
WINDING
WINGING
WINKING
WINNING
WISHING
WISPING
WITTING
YIPPING
ZIGGING
ZINGING
ZIPPING
ZIRCONS

•I••••N

AILERON
BIGHORN
BIGJOHN
BILLION
BIRDMAN
BIRDMEN
BITTERN
BITUMEN
CISTERN
CITIZEN
CITROEN
DICTION
DIEDOWN
DINEDIN
DINEDON
DINESEN
DINESIN
DINESON
DISCERN
DISDAIN
DISHPAN
DISJOIN
DIVESIN
FICTION
FIFTEEN
FILLSIN
FIREMAN
FIREMEN
FISSION
GILLIAN
GIVENIN
GIVESIN
HICKMAN
HIRESON
JILLIAN
JILLION
KICKSIN
KIDSKIN
KILOTON
KINCHIN
KINGMAN
KINGPIN
KINSMAN
KINSMEN
KITCHEN
LIAISON
LIEDOWN
LIGHTEN
LILLIAN
LINCOLN
LINEMAN
LINEMEN
LIVEDIN
LIVEDON
LIVESIN
LIVESON
MIAMIAN
MIDTOWN
MILKMAN
MILKMEN
MILKRUN
MILLION
MILLRUN
MINIVAN
MISSION
MIXEDIN
MIXESIN
NIELSEN
NILSSON
NINEPIN
OILSKIN
PICKSON
PIDGEON
PIGIRON
PIGSKIN
PIKEMAN
PIKEMEN
PILEDIN
PILEDON
PILESIN
PILESON
PILLION
PIMESON
PINDOWN
PITCHIN
PITTMAN
RICHMAN
RICKMAN
RIGHTON
RIPTORN
SICHUAN
SIDEMAN
SIDEMEN
SIGNSIN
SIGNSON
SILICON
SIMENON
SIMPSON
SINKSIN
SIOBHAN
SIRLOIN
SITDOWN
SIXIRON

SIXTEEN
TIANJIN
TIBETAN
TIEDOWN
TIGHTEN
TINHORN
TINTERN
TIOMKIN
VILLAIN
VILLEIN
VIRGOAN
VITAMIN
WIDGEON
WILLSON
WINSTON
WISEMAN
WISEMEN
ZILLION

••IN•••

ABINTRA
ALINING
ASININE
ATINGLE
BAINTER
BLINDED
BLINDER
BLINDLY
BLINKAT
BLINKED
BLINKER
BRINDLE
BRINGER
BRINGIN
BRINGON
BRINGTO
BRINGUP
BRINIER
BRINING
BRINISH
CHINESE
CHINKED
CHINNED
CHINOOK
CHINTZY
CHINUPS
CLINICS
CLINKED
CLINKER
CLINTON
COINAGE
COINERS
COINING
CRINGED
CRINGES
CRINKLE
CRINKLY
CRINOID
DOINGIN
DOINGUP
DRINKER
DWINDLE
EMINENT
EVINCED
EVINCES
FAINTED
FAINTER
FAINTLY
FEINTED
FOINING
FRINGED
FRINGES
GAINERS
GAINFUL
GAINING
GAINSAY
GAINSON
GLINTED
GOINFOR
GOINGAT
GOINGBY
GOINGIN
GOINGON
GOINGUP
GRINDER
GRINNED
GRINNER
GUINEAS
HEINOUS
ICINESS
ICINGIN
ICINGUP
JOINDER
JOINERS
JOINERY
JOINING
JOINSIN
JOINSUP
JOINTED
JOINTLY
KLINGON
KRINGLE
LYINGTO
MAINTOP
MEINIES
OKINAWA
OMINOUS
OPINERS
OPINING
OPINION
ORINOCO
OWINGTO
PAINFUL
PAINTED
PAINTER
PHINEAS
PLINKED
PLINTHS
POINTED
POINTER
POINTTO
PRINCES
PRINKED
PRINTED
PRINTER
QUINARY
QUINCES
QUININE
QUINOAS
QUINQUE
QUINTET
RAINBOW
RAINHAT
RAINIER
RAINILY
RAINING
RAINMAN
RAINOUT
REINING
REINKED
REINSIN
RUINERS
RUINING
RUINOUS
SAINTED
SAINTLY
SEINERS
SEINING
SHINDIG
SHINERS
SHINGLE
SHINIER
SHINILY
SHINING
SHINNED
SKINFUL
SKINNED
SKINNER
SLINGER
SLINKED
SPINACH
SPINDLE
SPINDLY
SPINDRY
SPINELS
SPINETS
SPINIER
SPINNER
SPINNEY
SPINOFF
SPINOUT
SPINOZA
STINGER
STINGOS
STINKER
STINTED
SWINDLE
SWINGBY
SWINGER
SWINISH
TAINTED
THINAIR
THINICE
THINKER
THINKOF
THINKUP
THINNED
THINNER
TLINGIT
TRINITY
TRINKET
TWINBED
TWINGED
TWINGES
TWINING
TWINKLE
TWINKLY
TWINNED
TYINGIN
TYINGUP
USINGUP
VAINEST
VEINIER
VEINING
WHINERS
WHINIER
WHINING
WRINGER
WRINKLE
WRINKLY
ZWINGLI

••I•N••

ALIENEE
ALIENOR
ALIGNED
ALIGNER
AVIANCA
AVIGNON
CHIANTI
CHIGNON
CHIMNEY
CHINNED
CLIENTS
DEIGNED
ETIENNE
FAIENCE
FEIGNED
FRIENDS
GRINNED
GRINNER
HAIRNET
LEIBNIZ
ORIENTE
ORIENTS
PLIANCY
REIGNED
SCIENCE
SHINNED
SKINNED
SKINNER
SOIGNEE
SPINNER
SPINNEY
THINNED
THINNER
TRIUNES
TWINNED
WHITNEY

••I••N•

ABIDING
ABILENE
ALIMENT
ALIMONY
ALINING
ANILINE
ARIADNE
ARISING
ARIZONA
ASININE
BAILING
BAITING
BEIJING
BOILING
BOITANO
BRIBING
BRIGAND
BRINING
BRITONS
CAIMANS
CEILING
CHICANA
CHICANO
CHIDING
CHIMING
CLIPONS
COIFING
COILING
COINING
CUIBONO
CUISINE
DAIMONS
DEICING
DRIVING
EDITING
ELIDING
EMINENT
EPICENE
EPIGENE
EPIGONE
ETIENNE
EVIDENT
EXIGENT
EXILING
EXITING
FAILING
FAIRING
FOILING
FOINING
GAINING
GAITING
GLIDING
GRIMING
GRIPING
GUIDING
GUIDONS
HAILING
JAILING
JOINING
JUICING
KNIFING
KRISHNA
MAIDENS
MAILING
MOILING
NAILING
NOISING
OHIOANS
OLIVINE
OPINING
ORIGINS
ORISONS
OXIDANT
PAIRING
PAISANO
POISING
POISONS
PRICING
PRIDING
PRIMING
PRISONS
PRIZING
QUININE
RAIDING
RAILING
RAIMENT
RAINING
RAISING
RAISINS
REINING
ROILING
RUINING
SAILING
SEINING
SEIZING
SHINING
SKIRUNS
SLICING
SLIDING
SLIPONS
SMILING
SMITING
SNIPING
SOILING
SPICING
SPIKING
SPIRANT
SPITING
STIPEND
SUITING
SWIPING
TAILEND
TAILING
TAIPANS
TOILING
TRIBUNE
TRIDENT
TRIGONS
TRITONE
TRITONS
TWINING
UNISONS
UNITING
VEILING
VEINING
VOICING
VOIDING
WAILING
WAITING
WAIVING
WHILING
WHINING
WHITENS
WHITING
WRITING
ZEITUNG

••I•••N

ANISTON
AVIGNON
BLITZEN
BRINGIN
BRINGON
BRITAIN
BRITTEN
BRITTON
BUILDIN
BUILTIN
CAISSON
CHICHEN
CHICKEN
CHIFFON
CHIGNON
CHILEAN
CHIPSIN
CLIBURN
CLIFTON
CLINTON
CRIMEAN
CRIMSON
CRISPIN
DOINGIN
DRIPPAN
DRISTAN
DRIVEIN
EDITION
ELISION
ERICSON
FLIESIN
FRIEDAN
FRISIAN
FRISSON
GAINSON
GLISTEN
GOINGIN
GOINGON
GRIFFIN
GRIFFON
GRISKIN
HAIRPIN
HAITIAN
HEISMAN
ICINGIN
IDIAMIN
JOINSIN
KLINGON
MAILSIN
MEISSEN
MOISTEN
NAILSIN
OMICRON
OPINION
PHILBIN
POISSON
QUICKEN
QUIETEN
RAINMAN
REINSIN
REITMAN
SHIPMAN
SHIPMEN
SLIDEIN
SLIPSIN
SLIPSON
SMIDGEN
SMITTEN
SPIEDON
SPIESON
STIFFEN
STILTON
STIRSIN
TAILFIN
THICKEN
TRICORN
TRIEDON
TRIESON
TRILLIN
TRISTAN
TUITION
TYINGIN
UNICORN
WAITRON
WAITSON
WEIGHIN
WHITMAN
WRITEIN
WRITTEN
ZAIREAN
ZAIRIAN

•••IN••

ACTINIC
ADFINEM
AFFINES
AGAINST
AIRINGS
ALBINOS
ANOINTS
AQUINAS
AWNINGS
BELINDA
BIKINIS
BOVINES
BRAINED
BYLINED
BYLINES
CABINET
CANINES
CARINAS
CASINGS
CASINOS
CHAINED
COMINGS
CORINTH
COSINES
CUTINTO
DAVINCI
DEFINED
DEFINES
DIVINED
DIVINER
DIVINES
DIVINUM
DOMINGO
DOMINOS
DOMINUS
DRAINED
DRAINER
ECHINUS
EDGINGS
ENCINAS
ENDINGS
ENGINES
EQUINES
EQUINOX
ERMINES
EXTINCT
FACINGS
FAMINES
FELINES
FILINGS
FIRINGS
FIXINGS
FORINTS
GAMINES
GETINTO
GOTINTO
GRAINED
HAZINGS
HIDINGS
HIJINKS
HOMINID
IMPINGE
INNINGS
JACINTH
LACINGS
LADINOS
LAMINAE
LAMINAL
LAMINAR
LAMINAS
LATINAS
LATINOS
LAVINIA
LAYINTO
LETINON
LININGS
LITINTO
LIVINGS
LUPINES
MAGINOT
MAKINGS
MARINAS
MARINER
MARINES
MATINEE
MELINDA
MERINOS
NOMINAL
NOMINEE
ORDINAL
ORDINES
ORPINES
OSCINES
OUTINGS
PARINGS
PATINAS
PILINGS
PIPINGS
PLAINER
PLAINLY
PLAINTS
PRYINTO
RAMINTO
RANINTO
RAPINES
RATINGS
RAVINES
RAVINGS
REBINDS
REFINED
REFINER
REFINES
RELINED
RELINES
REMINDS
REPINED
REPINES
RERINSE
RESINGS
RETINAE
RETINAL
RETINAS
RETINUE
REWINDS
RIPINTO
RISINGS
RULINGS
RUNINTO
SABINES
SAGINAW
SALINAS
SATINET
SAVINGS
SAYINGS
SEMINAL
SEMINAR
SETINTO
SHRINER
SHRINES
SHRINKS
SIDINGS
SIZINGS
SOYINKA
SPLINES
SPLINTS
SPRINGS
SPRINGY
SPRINTS
SQUINCH
SQUINTS
SQUINTY
STAINED
STAINER
STEINEM
STEINER
STRINGS
STRINGY
SURINAM
SYRINGA
SYRINGE
TAPINGS
TAPINTO
TIDINGS
TIEINTO
TILINGS
TIMINGS
TRAINED
TRAINEE
TRAINER
UNBINDS
UNKINKS
UNLINED
UNLINKS
UNWINDS
UPLINKS
USTINOV
VIKINGS
WAHINES

•••I•N•

AAMILNE
ACTIONS
AMBIENT
AMNIONS
ANCIENT
ASSIGNS
BUNIONS
CATIONS
COSIGNS
DEFIANT
DESIGNS
DEVIANT
ECHIDNA
ELOIGNS
ENSIGNS
FANIONS
FENIANS
FIJIANS
HYGIENE
INDIANA
INDIANS
JULIANA
LEGIONS
LENIENT
LOTIONS
LUCIANO
MALIGNS
MARIANA
MEDIANS
MEDIANT
MINIONS
MOTIONS
NATIONS
NOTIONS
NUBIANS
OPTIONS
PATIENT
PINIONS
POTIONS
RADIANS
RADIANT
RATIONS
REGIONS
RELIANT
RESIGNS
RIPIENO
SALIENT
SAPIENS
SAPIENT
SEVIGNE
SIMIANS
SYRIANS
TATIANA
TAXIING
VALIANT
VARIANT
VISIONS

•••I••N

ADDISON
AFRICAN
ALLISON
ANDIRON
ANTIGEN
ARTISAN
ASPIRIN
BEDIZEN
BENISON
BKLIBAN
CALIBAN
CAPITAN
CITIZEN
DENIZEN
ELEISON
ELLISON
ENLIVEN
EPSILON
FADIMAN
GETITON
GOTITON
HELICON
HORIZON
JEWISON
LAYITON
LETINON
LEXICON
LIAISON
MADIGAN
MADISON
MARILYN
MEXICAN
MINIVAN
MOHICAN
NETIZEN
NONIRON
ONEIRON
ORBISON
PELICAN
PEMICAN
PIGIRON
PURITAN
RARITAN
REGIMEN
RUBICON
RUBITIN
SAMISEN
SCRIVEN
SILICON
SIXIRON
STRIVEN
TAXIMAN
TAXIMEN
TWOIRON
UPRISEN
UPSILON
VATICAN
VENISON

••••IN•

ABASING
ABATING
ABIDING
ABUSING
ADDLING
ADELINE
ADENINE
ADJOINS
ADORING
AIRLINE
ALAKING
ALINING
ALLYING
AMAZING
AMBLING
AMERIND
AMUSING
ANELING
ANGLING
ANILINE
ANTEING
ANTOINE
APPOINT
ARCHING
ARCSINE
ARETINO
ARGUING
ARISING
ASININE
ATONING
ATTAINS
AVOWING
AWAKING
BABYING
BACHING
BACKING
BAGGING
BAILING
BAITING
BALDING
BALKING
BAMBINO
BANDING
BANGING
BANKING
BANNING
BARBING
BARGING
BARKING
BARRING
BASHING
BASKING
BASTING
BATHING
BATTING
BATWING
BAWLING
BEADING
BEAMING
BEANING
BEARING
BEATING
BEDDING
BEEFING
BEELINE
BEEPING
BEGGING
BEGUINE
BEIJING
BELLING
BELLINI
BELTING
BELYING
BENDING
BESTING
BETHINK
BETTING
BIASING
BIDDING
BILKING
BILLING
BINDING
BINGING
BINNING
BIRDING
BIRLING
BITTING
BLADING
BLAMING
BLARING
BLAZING
BLOWING
BLUEING
BOATING
BOBBING
BOBBINS
BODKINS
BOFFINS
BOGGING
BOILING
BOLTING
BOMBING
BONDING
BONGING
BOOKING
BOOMING
BOOTING
BOPPING
BOSSING
BOUSING
BOWFINS
BOWLINE
BOWLING
BRACING
BRAKING
BRAVING
BRAYING
BRAZING
BREWING
BRIBING
BRINING
BROMINE
BRUXING
BUCKING
BUDDING
BUDGING
BUFFING
BUGGING
BUGLING
BULGING
BULKING
BULLING
BUMMING
BUMPING
BUNGING
BUNKING
BUNTING
BUOYING
BURKINA
BURLING
BURNING
BURPING
BURYING
BUSHING
BUSKING
BUSKINS
BUSLINE
BUSSING
BUSTING
BUSYING
BUTTING
BUZZING
CABLING
CABRINI
CACHING
CADGING
CALKING
CALKINS
CALLING
CALLINS
CALMING
CALVING
CAMPING
CANNING
CANTINA
CANTING
CAPPING
CARBINE
CARDING
CARKING
CARMINE
CARPING
CARTING
CARVING
CASHING
CASSINI
CASSINO
CASTING
CATKINS
CATTING
CAUSING
CAVEINS
CEASING
CEILING
CELLINI
CENSING
CESSING
CHAFING
CHASING
CHEWING
CHIDING
CHIMING
CHOLINE
CHORINE
CITRINE
CLAWING
CLONING
CLOSING
CLOYING
CLUEING
COATING
COAXING
COCKING
CODEINE
COIFING
COILING
COINING
COLLINS
COMBINE
COMBING
CONFINE
CONKING
CONNING
COOKING
COOLING
COOPING
COPPING
COPYING
CORDING
CORKING
CORNING
COSHING
COSTING
COUSINS
COWLING
COZYING
CRANING
CRATING
CRAVING
CRAZING
CRETINS
CREWING
CROWING
CUFFING
CUISINE
CULLING
CUNNING
CUPPING
CURBING
CURDING
CURLING
CURSING
CURVING
CUSHING
CUSSING
CUTTING
CYCLING
CZARINA
DABBING
DAFFING
DAMMING
DAMNING
DAMPING
DANCING
DAPPING

DARLING
DARNING
DARTING
DASHING
DAUBING
DAWNING
DAYSINN
DEALING
DECKING
DECLINE
DEEDING
DEEMING
DEFYING
DEICING
DELEING
DELVING
DENTINE
DENTING
DENYING
DERRING
DESTINE
DESTINY
DETAINS
DEVEINS
DEWLINE
DIALING
DIETING
DIGGING
DIMMING
DINGING
DIPPING
DISHING
DISSING
DOBBINS
DOCKING
DODGING
DOFFING
DOGGING
DOLLING
DOMAINS
DONKING
DONNING
DOOMING
DOTTING
DOUSING
DOWNING
DOWSING
DRAPING
DRAWING
DRAYING
DRIVING
DRONING
DROPINS
DUBBING
DUCKING
DUCTING
DUELING
DULLING
DUMBING
DUMPING
DUNKING
DUNLINS
DUNNING
DURNING
DUSTING
EAGLING
EARNING
EARRING
ECHOING
EDDYING
EDITING
EDUCING
ELATING
ELIDING

ELOPING
ELUDING
ELUTING
EMOTING
ENDUING
ENJOINS
ENSUING
ENTWINE
ENURING
ENVYING
ERASING
ERODING
ERSKINE
ESPYING
ETAMINE
ETCHING
EVADING
EVENING
EVOKING
EXAMINE
EXILING
EXITING
EXUDING
FADEINS
FAGGING
FAILING
FAIRING
FALLING
FANNING
FANZINE
FARCING
FARMING
FASTING
FAWNING
FEARING
FEEDING
FEELING
FELLING
FELLINI
FENCING
FENDING
FESSING
FEUDING
FIBBING
FIBRINS
FILLING
FILLINS
FILMING
FINDING
FINKING
FIRKINS
FIRMING
FISHING
FITTING
FIZZING
FLAKING
FLAMING
FLARING
FLAWING
FLAYING
FLEEING
FLEMING
FLEXING
FLEYING
FLORINS
FLOWING
FLUTING
FLUXING
FOALING
FOAMING
FOBBING
FOGGING
FOILING
FOINING

FOLDING
FONTINA
FOOLING
FOOTING
FORCING
FORDING
FORGING
FORKING
FORMING
FOULING
FOWLING
FRAMING
FRAYING
FREEING
FUBBING
FUDGING
FUELING
FUNDING
FUNKING
FUNNING
FURLING
FURRING
FUSSING
FUTZING
FUZZING
GABBING
GADDING
GAFFING
GAGGING
GAGLINE
GAINING
GAITING
GALLING
GAMMING
GANGING
GAOLING
GAPPING
GARBING
GASHING
GASKINS
GASPING
GATLING
GAUGING
GAUMING
GAWKING
GAWPING
GEARING
GELDING
GELLING
GENUINE
GERAINT
GETTING
GIBBING
GILDING
GILLING
GINNING
GIPPING
GIRDING
GIRNING
GLARING
GLAZING
GLIDING
GLOBING
GLOWING
GLOZING
GNAWING
GOADING
GOBLINS
GOLDING
GOLFING
GONGING
GOODING
GOOFING
GOOSING

GORGING
GOSLING
GOUGING
GRACING
GRADING
GRATING
GRAVING
GRAYING
GRAZING
GREYING
GRIMING
GRIPING
GROPING
GROWING
GUANINE
GUIDING
GULFING
GULLING
GULPING
GUMMING
GUNNING
GUSHING
GUSTING
GUTTING
GYPPING
HACKING
HAFTING
HAILING
HALOING
HALTING
HALVING
HAMMING
HANDING
HANGING
HAPPING
HARDING
HARKING
HARMING
HARPING
HASHING
HASPING
HASTING
HATPINS
HATTING
HAULING
HAWKING
HAWKINS
HEADING
HEALING
HEAPING
HEARING
HEATING
HEAVING
HEDGING
HEEDING
HEELING
HEFTING
HELMING
HELPING
HEMLINE
HEMMING
HENTING
HERDING
HEROINE
HERRING
HIGGINS
HILLING
HINGING
HINTING
HISSING
HITTING
HOAXING
HOBOING
HOCKING

HOGGING
HOLDING
HONKING
HOOFING
HOOKING
HOOPING
HOOTING
HOPKINS
HOPPING
HORNING
HORSING
HOSKINS
HOSTING
HOTLINE
HOTLINK
HOUDINI
HOUSING
HOWLING
HUFFING
HUGGING
HUGGINS
HULKING
HULLING
HUMMING
HUNTING
HURLING
HURTING
HUSHING
HUSKING
HYALINE
HYPOING
ICERINK
ILLWIND
IMAGINE
IMAGING
IMBUING
IMPRINT
INCHING
INCLINE
INKLING
INPRINT
INURING
IRONING
ISSUING
ITCHING
JABBING
JACKING
JAGGING
JAILING
JAMMING
JARRING
JASMINE
JAWLINE
JAZZING
JEERING
JELLING
JERKING
JERKINS
JESTING
JETTING
JIBBING
JIGGING
JILTING
JINKING
JINXING
JOBBING
JOGGING
JOINING
JOLTING
JOSHING
JOSKINS
JOTTING
JREWING
JUDGING

JUGGING
JUGGINS
JUGWINE
JUICING
JUMPING
JUNKING
JURYING
JUSTINE
JUTTING
KACHINA
KAYOING
KEELING
KEENING
KEEPING
KERNING
KEYRING
KICKING
KIDDING
KILLING
KILTING
KINGING
KINKING
KIPLING
KISSING
KNEEING
KNIFING
KNOWING
LACKING
LADLING
LAGGING
LAMMING
LANDING
LANSING
LAPPING
LAPSING
LAPWING
LARAINE
LARDING
LASHING
LASTING
LATHING
LAUDING
LEADING
LEADINS
LEAFING
LEAKING
LEANING
LEAPING
LEASING
LEAVING
LEERING
LEGGING
LEMMING
LENDING
LEONINE
LESSING
LETTING
LEUCINE
LEVYING
LIBBING
LICKING
LIFTING
LILTING
LIMBING
LIMNING
LIMPING
LINKING
LIPPING
LISPING
LISTING
LOADING
LOAFING
LOAMING
LOANING

LOBBING
LOCKING
LOCKINS
LODGING
LOFTING
LOGGING
LOGGINS
LOLLING
LONGING
LOOKING
LOOMING
LOOPING
LOOSING
LOOTING
LOPPING
LORDING
LOTTING
LOUSING
LOVEINS
LUCKING
LUFFING
LUGGING
LULLING
LUMPING
LUNGING
LURKING
LUSTING
MACHINA
MACHINE
MADDING
MAILING
MALKINS
MALTING
MANCINI
MANKIND
MANNING
MAPPING
MARGINS
MARKING
MARLINS
MARRING
MARTINA
MARTINI
MARTINO
MARTINS
MASHING
MASKING
MASSING
MATTING
MAULING
MAYWINE
MCSWINE
MEANING
MEETING
MELDING
MELTING
MENDING
MEOWING
MERGING
MESHING
MESSINA
MESSING
MEWLING
MIDLINE
MIFFING
MILKING
MILLING
MINCING
MINDING
MINTING
MISSING
MISTING
MITRING
MOANING

MOBBING
MOCKING
MOILING
MOLDING
MOLTING
MOONING
MOORING
MOPPING
MORAINE
MORNING
MOSHING
MOSSING
MOUSING
MUCKING
MUFFING
MUFFINS
MUGGING
MULLING
MUMMING
MUMPING
MUNTINS
MUSHING
MUSLINS
MUSSING
MUZZING
NABBING
NAGGING
NAILING
NAPKINS
NAPPING
NEARING
NECKING
NEEDING
NESTING
NETTING
NICKING
NIPPING
NODDING
NOGGINS
NOISING
NOOSING
NOSHING
NOTHING
NUBBINS
NUDGING
NULLING
NUMBING
NURSING
NUTTING
OBEYING
OBTAINS
OCARINA
OFFLINE
OINKING
OKAYING
OLDLINE
OLEFINS
OLIVINE
ONGOING
OPALINE
OPENING
OPINING
ORATING
ORDAINS
ORIGINS
OUSTING
OUTLINE
PACKING
PADDING
PAIRING
PALLING
PALMING
PANNING
PANTING

PARKING
PARRING
PARSING
PARTING
PASSING
PASTINA
PASTING
PATTING
PAULINA
PAULINE
PAULING
PAUSING
PAWNING
PEAKING
PEALING
PECKING
PECTINS
PEEKING
PEELING
PEEPING
PEERING
PEEVING
PEGGING
PELTING
PENDING
PENNING
PEPPING
PEPSINS
PERKING
PERKINS
PERMING
PETTING
PHASING
PHONING
PICKING
PIDGINS
PIECING
PIETINS
PIGGING
PILLING
PINGING
PINKING
PINNING
PIPKINS
PIPPINS
PIQUING
PISCINE
PITHING
PITTING
PITYING
PLACING
PLANING
PLATING
PLAYING
PLOWING
PLUGINS
PLUMING
POISING
POLLING
PONGING
PONTINE
PONYING
POOLING
POOPING
POPLINS
POPPING
POPPINS
PORCINE
POSTING
POTTING
POURING
POUTING
PRALINE
PRATING

PRAYING
PRICING
PRIDING
PRIMING
PRIZING
PROBING
PROSING
PROVING
PRUNING
PUCCINI
PUDDING
PUFFING
PUFFINS
PULLING
PULLINS
PULSING
PUMPING
PUNNING
PUNTING
PURGING
PURLING
PURLINS
PURRING
PURSING
PUSHING
PUTTING
QUAKING
QUEUING
QUININE
QUOTING
RACKING
RAFTING
RAGGING
RAIDING
RAILING
RAINING
RAISING
RAISINS
RAMMING
RANGING
RANKING
RANTING
RAPPING
RASPING
RATFINK
RATLINE
RATTING
RAZZING
RDLAING
READING
REAMING
REAPING
REARING
RECLINE
REDDING
REDFINS
REDLINE
REDOING
REDPINE
REDWINE
REDWING
REEDING
REEFING
REEKING
REELING
REFFING
REGAINS
REINING
REJOINS
RELYING
REMAINS
RENDING
RENNINS
RENTING

REPAINT
REPRINT
RESCIND
RESPINS
RESTING
RETAINS
RETHINK
RETSINA
REVVING
RHYMING
RIBBING
RIDDING
RIDGING
RIFFING
RIFLING
RIFTING
RIGGING
RIMMING
RINGING
RINSING
RIOTING
RIPPING
RISKING
ROAMING
ROARING
ROBBING
ROBBINS
ROCKING
RODDING
ROGAINE
ROILING
ROLLING
ROLLINS
ROMAINE
ROMPING
ROOFING
ROOKING
ROOMING
ROOTING
ROSSINI
ROTTING
ROUGING
ROUSING
ROUTINE
ROUTING
RUBBING
RUCHING
RUCKING
RUINING
RUNNING
RUSHING
RUSTING
SABRINA
SACKING
SAGGING
SAILING
SALTINE
SALTING
SALVING
SANDING
SANTINI
SAPLING
SAPPING
SARDINE
SASSING
SCALING
SCARING
SCHWINN
SCOPING
SCORING
SEALING
SEAMING
SEARING
SEATING

SEEDING
SEEKING
SEEMING
SEEPING
SEINING
SEIZING
SELLING
SENDING
SENSING
SEQUINS
SERLING
SERVING
SESTINA
SETLINE
SETTING
SHADING
SHAKING
SHAMING
SHAPING
SHARING
SHAVING
SHINING
SHOEING
SHOOING
SHOOINS
SHORING
SHOVING
SHOWING
SHUTINS
SIBLING
SICCING
SIDLING
SIFTING
SIGHING
SIGNING
SILOING
SILTING
SINGING
SINKING
SIPPING
SISKINS
SISTINE
SITTING
SKATING
SKEWING
SKYLINE
SLAKING
SLATING
SLAVING
SLICING
SLIDING
SLOPING
SLOWING
SMILING
SMITING
SMOKING
SNAKING
SNARING
SNIPING
SNORING
SNOWING
SOAKING
SOAPING
SOARING
SOBBING
SOCKING
SODDING
SOILING
SOLOING
SOLVING
SOPPING
SORDINI
SORDINO
SORTING

SORVINO
SOURING
SPACING
SPADING
SPARING
SPAVINS
SPAYING
SPECING
SPEWING
SPICING
SPIKING
SPITING
SPOKING
SPRAINS
SPUMING
STAGING
STAKING
STAMINA
STARING
STATING
STAVING
STAYING
STEPINS
STEWING
STOKING
STONING
STORING
STOWING
STRAINS
STYLING
SUBBING
SUCKING
SUDSING
SUITING
SULKING
SUMMING
SUNNING
SUPPING
SURFING
SURGING
SUSSING
SWAYING
SWIPING
SYNCING
TABBING
TABLING
TACKING
TAGGING
TAGLINE
TAILING
TALKING
TALLINN
TAMPING
TANKING
TANLINE
TANNING
TANNINS
TAPPING
TARRING
TASKING
TASTING
TATTING
TAURINE
TAXIING
TEAMING
TEARING
TEASING
TEDDING
TEEMING
TELLING
TENDING
TENPINS
TENSING
TENTING

TENZING
TERMING
TERMINI
TESTING
THAWING
THYMINE
TICKING
TIDYING
TIELINE
TIEPINS
TIERING
TIFFING
TIFFINS
TILLING
TILTING
TIMMINS
TINGING
TINTING
TIPPING
TITHING
TITLING
TITRING
TOCSINS
TOGGING
TOILING
TOLLING
TONTINE
TOOLING
TOOTING
TOPPING
TOSSING
TOTTING
TOURING
TOUTING
TRACING
TRADING
TREEING
TREVINO
TRUEING
TSARINA
TUCKING
TUFTING
TUGGING
TUMMING
TURBINE
TURNING
TWINING
TZARINA
UKRAINE
UNDOING
UNDYING
UNITING
UNTYING
UPSWING
URCHINS
VACCINE
VALUING
VAMPING
VANDINE
VARMINT
VARYING
VATTING
VEERING
VEGGING
VEILING
VEINING
VENDING
VENTING
VERGING
VESTING
VETOING
VETTING
VIEWING
VIOLINS

VIRGINS
VISAING
VOICING
VOIDING
VULPINE
WADDING
WAFTING
WAGGING
WAILING
WAITING
WAIVING
WALKING
WALKINS
WALLING
WANTING
WARDING
WARMING
WARNING
WARPING
WARRING
WASHING
WASTING
WAXWING
WEANING
WEARING
WEAVING
WEBBING
WEDDING
WEDGING
WEEDING
WEEPING
WELDING
WELKINS
WELLING
WELTING
WENDING
WETTING
WHALING
WHILING
WHINING
WHITING
WILDING
WILLING
WILTING
WINCING
WINDING
WINGING
WINKING
WINNING
WISHING
WISPING
WITTING
WOLFING
WOOFING
WORDING
WORKING
WRITING
WYOMING
XRATING
XRAYING
YACKING
YAKKING
YANKING
YAPPING
YARNING
YAWNING
YAWPING
YEANING
YELLING
YELPING
YERKING
YESSING
YIPPING
YOWLING
YOYOING
ZAGGING
ZAPPING
ZEROING
ZIGGING
ZINGING
ZIPPING
ZONKING
ZOOMING

••••I•N

ACADIAN
AEOLIAN
ANTLION
ARABIAN
ARRAIGN
AUCTION
BASTION
BELGIAN
BILLION
BULLION
CAMPION
CAPTION
CARRION
CASPIAN
CAUTION
CESSION
CLARION
CONDIGN
CONSIGN
CUSHION
DAYSINN
DICTION
EDITION
ELAAIUN
ELATION
ELISION
ELUTION
ELYSIAN
EMOTION
EROSION
ETESIAN
ETONIAN
EVASION
FACTION
FASHION
FICTION
FISSION
FOREIGN
FRISIAN
FUSTIAN
GAMBIAN
GENTIAN
GHANIAN
GILLIAN
GORDIAN
GRECIAN
GRUNION
HADRIAN
HAITIAN
HELLION
HESSIAN
HEXSIGN
IBERIAN
IRANIAN
ITALIAN
JILLIAN
JILLION
KRATION
LAOTIAN
LATVIAN
LILLIAN
MANSION
MARMION
MARTIAN
MENTION
MIAMIAN
MILLION
MISSION
MULLION
OPINION
ORATION
OVATION
OXONIAN
PASSION
PENSION
PERSIAN
PILLION
PLOSION
PORTION
PYTHIAN
REUNION
RUCTION
RUFFIAN
RUSSIAN
SAURIAN
SCHWINN
SEALION
SECTION
SERBIAN
SESSION
STATION
STYGIAN
STYRIAN
SUASION
SUCTION
TALLINN
TENSION
TOLKIEN
TORSION
TUITION
UMBRIAN
UNCTION
UTOPIAN
VERSION
ZAIRIAN
ZAMBIAN
ZILLION

•••••IN

ABSTAIN
ADDEDIN
ALADDIN
ALAMEIN
ALBUMIN
ANTONIN
ASKEDIN
ASPIRIN
BACKSIN
BAHRAIN
BALDWIN
BARGAIN
BARGEIN
BEDOUIN
BLOWSIN
BLUEFIN
BORODIN
BOXEDIN
BOXESIN
BRAHMIN
BREAKIN
BRESLIN
BRINGIN
BRITAIN
BROKEIN
BUILDIN
BUILTIN
BUMPKIN
BUTTSIN
CALLSIN
CAPTAIN
CAVEDIN
CAVESIN
CERTAIN
CHAGRIN
CHAPLIN
CHARMIN
CHEATIN
CHECKIN
CHIPSIN
CLOCKIN
CLOSEIN
CLUEDIN
CLUESIN
COALBIN
COMESIN
CONJOIN
CONTAIN
COSTAIN
CRISPIN
CURTAIN
DAUPHIN
DEALSIN
DEALTIN
DETRAIN
DEXTRIN
DINEDIN
DINESIN
DISDAIN
DISJOIN
DIVESIN
DOESKIN
DOINGIN
DOLPHIN
DRAGSIN
DRAWNIN
DRAWSIN
DRIVEIN
DROPSIN
DRUMLIN
DUCKPIN
DUSTBIN
EASEDIN
EASESIN
EDGEDIN
EDGESIN
EELSKIN
ENCHAIN
ENTRAIN
EPSTEIN
EXPLAIN
FADEDIN
FADESIN
FALLSIN
FILLSIN
FLIESIN
FLOWNIN
GAGARIN
GASMAIN
GAUGUIN
GELATIN
GHERKIN
GIVENIN
GIVESIN
GOINGIN
GOODWIN
GREMLIN
GRIFFIN
GRISKIN
HAIRPIN
HAMELIN
HANDSIN
HANGSIN
HEADPIN
HEADSIN
HEPARIN
HOLBEIN
HOLDSIN
HORNSIN
HUSSEIN
ICINGIN
IDIAMIN
INASPIN
INGRAIN
INSULIN
JACOBIN
JAVELIN
JOAQUIN
JOINSIN
JUMPSIN
KEEPSIN
KERATIN
KEYEDIN
KICKSIN
KIDSKIN
KINCHIN
KINGPIN
KOSYGIN
KREMLIN
KTOSLIN
KUTCHIN
LANOLIN
LAUGHIN
LEADSIN
LEAVEIN
LIVEDIN
LIVESIN
LOOKSIN
MAILSIN
MAUDLIN
MAULDIN
MAYALIN
MCGAVIN
MELANIN
MENUHIN
MIXEDIN
MIXESIN
MOVEDIN
MOVESIN
MUEZZIN
MULLEIN
NAILSIN
NINEPIN
OBERLIN
OILSKIN
PALADIN
PEERSIN
PENGUIN
PERTAIN
PHASEIN
PHILBIN
PIGSKIN
PILEDIN
PILESIN
PITCHIN
PLUGSIN
POURSIN
PROTEIN
PULLSIN
PUMPKIN
PUNCHIN
PURLOIN
PUSHKIN
PUSHPIN
QUENTIN
RAKEDIN
RAKESIN
RAMEKIN
READSIN
REELSIN
REFRAIN
REINSIN
RESTAIN
RETRAIN
ROLLSIN
ROPEDIN
ROPESIN
RUBITIN
SALADIN
SAVARIN
SEEPSIN
SENDSIN
SHAREIN
SHERWIN
SHOWNIN
SHOWSIN
SHUTSIN
SIGNSIN
SINKSIN
SIRLOIN
SLEEPIN
SLEPTIN
SLIDEIN
SLIPSIN
SLOEGIN
SNEAKIN
SNOWSIN
SOCKSIN
STANDIN
STEPSIN
STIRSIN
STOODIN
STOPSIN
SUBJOIN
SUCKSIN
SUSTAIN
SWEARIN
SWOREIN
TAILFIN
TAKENIN
TAKESIN
TAMARIN
TASHLIN
TEACHIN
TERRAIN
THEREIN
THREWIN
THROWIN
TIANJIN
TIOMKIN
TRADEIN
TREMAIN
TRILLIN
TUCKSIN
TUNEDIN
TUNESIN
TURNSIN
TYINGIN
UNCHAIN
VILLAIN
VILLEIN
VITAMIN
VOTEDIN
VOTESIN
WADEDIN
WADESIN
WANTSIN
WAVEDIN
WAVESIN
WEIGHIN
WHEREIN
WORKSIN
WRITEIN
WROTEIN
YELTSIN
ZOOMSIN

IO•••••

IODATES
IODIDES
IODISED
IODISES
IODIZED
IODIZES
IOMOTHS
IONESCO
IONISED
IONISES
IONIZED
IONIZER
IONIZES

I•O••••

IDOLISE
IDOLIZE
ILOCANO
IMOGENE
INOCULA
INORBIT
IRONAGE
IRONERS
IRONIES
IRONING
IRONMAN
IRONMEN
IRONONS
IRONORE
IRONOUT
ISOBARS
ISOGONS
ISOHELS
ISOLATE
ISOMERS
ISONOMY
ISOPODS
ISOTOPE
IVORIES
IWOJIMA

I••O•••

IACOCCA
IDIOTIC
IGNOBLE
IGNOBLY
IGNORED
IGNORER
IGNORES
ILLOGIC
IMMORAL
IMPORTS
IMPOSED
IMPOSES
IMPOSTS
IMPOUND
IMSORRY
INBOARD
INBOUND
INBOXES
INCOMES
INDOORS
INDORSE
INDOUBT
INFOCUS
INFORCE
INFORMS
INHOUSE
INJOKES
INNOWAY
INPOWER
INROADS
INSOFAR
INSOLES
INTONED
INTONER
INTONES
INVOGUE
INVOICE
INVOKED
INVOKER
INVOKES
INVOLVE
IOMOTHS

I•••O••

ICEBOAT
ICECOLD
ICEDOUT
ICEFOGS
ICESOUT
IDAHOAN
IFSTONE
IGNEOUS
IMAGOES
IMPIOUS
IMPLODE
IMPLORE
IMPROVE
INAWORD
INBLOOM
INCLOSE
INDOORS
INFLOWS
INFRONT
INGROUP
INGROWN
INKHORN
INSHORT
INSPOTS
INSTOCK
INSTORE
INTROIT
IRISOUT
IRKSOME
IRONONS
IRONORE
IRONOUT
ISADORA
ISOGONS
ISONOMY
ISOPODS
ISOTOPE
IVANOVO

I••••O•

ICEFLOE
ICESHOW
ICHABOD
INASPOT
INAWEOF
INBLOOM
INCISOR
INDIGOS
INERROR
INFAVOR
INKBLOT
INKSPOT
IRECKON
IVANHOE

I•••••O

ILOCANO
IMPASTO
INFERNO
INPETTO
INVACUO
INVITRO
IONESCO
IVANOVO

•IO••••

BIOCHIP
BIOGENY
BIOLOGY
BIOMASS
BIONICS
DIOCESE
DIOMEDE
DIOPTER
DIORAMA
DIOXIDE
GIORGIO
LIONCUB
LIONESS
LIONETS
LIONISE
LIONIZE
MIOCENE
NIOBIUM
PIOLETS
PIONEER
PIOUSLY
RIOLOBO
RIORITA
RIOTACT
RIOTERS
RIOTING
RIOTOUS
SIOBHAN
SIOUANS
TIOMKIN
VIOLATE
VIOLENT
VIOLETS
VIOLINS
VIOLIST

•I•O•••

BICOLOR
BIFOCAL
BIGOSES
BIGOTED
BIGOTRY
BIMODAL
BINOCHE
BIPOLAR
BIVOUAC
CIBORIA
DIDOVER
DIMOUTS
DIPOLAR
DIPOLES
DISOBEY
DISOWNS
DIVORCE
GIGOLOS
GIRONDE
KILOTON
KIMONOS
LIEOVER
LIMOGES
LITOTES
LIVORNO
MIAOYAO
MILORDS
MIMOSAS
MINOANS
MINOLTA
MINORCA
MINORED
MITOSES
MITOSIS
MITOTIC
NICOLAS
NICOSIA
NIKOLAI
PILOTED
PINOAKS
PINOCLE
PINONES
PIROGUE
PIVOTAL
PIVOTED
RICOTTA
RIDOTTO
RIGOURS
RIPOFFS
RIPOSTE
RISOTTO
SILOING
SIROCCO
TIMOTHY
TIPOFFS
VIGOURS
WIDOWED
WIDOWER

•I••O••

AIRBOAT
AIRCOOL
AIRFOIL
AIRHOLE
AIRLOCK
AIRPORT
AIRSOCK
AIRSOUT
AIRWOLF
BIGBOYS
BIGFOOT
BIGHORN
BIGJOHN
BIGTOES
BIGTOPS
BILBOES
BILIOUS
BILLOWS
BILLOWY
BINGOES
BIOLOGY
BISHOPS
BITEOFF
CITROEN
CITRONS
CITROUS
DIABOLI
DIALOGS
DIAMOND
DIATOMS
DIDGOOD
DIEDOFF
DIEDOUT
DIEDOWN
DIESOFF
DIESOUT
DIGSOUT
DINGOES
DINMONT
DIPLOID
DIPLOMA
DISCOED
DISCORD
DISHOUT
DISJOIN
DISPORT
DISPOSE
DISROBE
DISTORT
DITTOED
FIBROUS
FILLOUT
FINDOUT
FIREOFF
FISHOUT
GIACOMO
GIBBONS
GIBBOUS
GIDEONS
GIFFORD
GIVEOFF
GIVEOUT
HICKORY
HIDEOUS
HIDEOUT
HILLOCK
HIPBONE
HIPBOOT
HIPROOF
HISTORY
HITSOUT
JIBBOOM
JINGOES
KICKOFF
KICKOUT
KINFOLK
KISSOFF
LICTORS
LIEDOWN
LIFTOFF
LIMPOPO
LINCOLN
LINGOES
LIQUORS
LISSOME
LIVEOAK
LIVEONE
LIVEOUT
MICROBE
MICRONS
MIDMOST
MIDTOWN
MINIONS
MINNOWS
MIRRORS
MISDOES
MISDONE
MISSOUT
MISTOOK
MISWORD
MITFORD
NICCOLO
NICHOLS
NIMRODS
NITROUS
PICCOLO
PICKOFF
PICKOUT
PIGEONS
PIGSOUT
PILLORY
PILLOWS
PILLOWY
PINDOWN
PINHOLE
PINIONS
PISCOPO
PISTOLE
PISTOLS
PISTONS
PITBOSS
PITEOUS
RIBBONS
RIDEOFF
RIDEOUT
RINGOFF
RINGOUT
RIOLOBO
RIOTOUS
RIPCORD
RIPSOFF
RIPSOUT
RIPTORN
RISSOLE
SICKOUT
SIGNOFF
SIGNOUT
SIMMONS
SINGOUT
SINUOUS
SIPHONS
SIRLOIN
SITCOMS
SITDOWN
SITSOUT
SIXFOLD
TICKOFF
TIEDOWN
TIEPOLO
TIERODS
TIGLONS
TIMEOFF
TIMEOUT
TINFOIL
TINHORN
TINWORK
TIPSOFF
TIPTOED
TIPTOES
TIPTOPS
TIREOUT
VICIOUS
VICTORS
VICTORY
VIRGOAN
VISCOUS
VISIONS
WIGSOUT
WILDONE
WILFORD
WILLOWS
WILLOWY
WIMPOLE
WINDOWS
WINKOUT
WINNOWS
WINSOME
WINSOUT
WIPEOUT
WITHOUT
XINGOUT
ZIPCODE
ZIRCONS

•I•••O•

AILERON
AIMSFOR
AIRCOOL
AIRDROP
AIRFLOW
AIRSHOW
BIBELOT
BICOLOR
BIENTOT
BIGELOW
BIGFOOT
BIGSHOT
BILLION
BIRDDOG
BISTROS
DICTION
DIDEROT
DIDGOOD
DINEDON
DINESON
DISAVOW
DIVISOR
FIASCOS
FICTION
FIEFDOM
FIREBOX
FIREDOG
FISSION
GIGOLOS
GIRASOL
HIGHBOY
HIGHLOW
HIGHTOP
HILLTOP
HIPBOOT
HIPROOF
HIRESON
JIBBOOM
JILLION
KILLJOY
KILOTON
KIMONOS
KINGDOM
LIAISON
LIBIDOS
LIESLOW
LITHGOW
LIVEDON
LIVESON
MIKADOS
MILKCOW
MILKSOP
MILLION
MIRADOR
MISSION
MISTOOK
NILSSON
PICADOR
PICAROS
PICKSON
PIDGEON
PIERROT
PIGIRON
PILEDON
PILESON
PILLBOX
PILLION
PIMESON
PINEFOR
PITSTOP
RIGHTON
RIMSHOT
SIGNSON
SILICON
SIMENON
SIMPSON
SIXIRON
TIMECOP
TIREDOF
VICEROY
VIRAGOS
VISITOR
VITRIOL
WIDGEON
WILLSON
WINDROW
WINDSOR
WINSLOW
WINSTON
ZILLION

•I••••O

AIMEDTO
CINZANO
FIDELIO
GIACOMO
GIORGIO
GIVENTO
GIVESTO
HIDALGO
HISPANO
LIMPOPO
LINBIAO
LINPIAO
LITINTO
LIVORNO
MIAOYAO
NICCOLO
PICASSO
PICCOLO
PIMENTO
PIMLICO
PISCOPO
PIZARRO
QINGDAO
RICARDO
RIDOTTO
RIOLOBO
RIPIENO
RIPINTO
RISOTTO
SINGSTO
SIROCCO
TIEINTO
TIEPOLO
VIBRATO

••IO•••

ARIOSOS
ARIOSTO
BRIOCHE
CRIOLLO
IDIOTIC
MEIOSES
MEIOSIS
MEIOTIC
OHIOANS
ORIOLES
PRIORTO
SCIORRA
TRIODES

••I•O••

ADIPOSE
ALIMONY
ARIZONA
BAILORS
BAILOUT
BRITONS
CHICORY
CHIGOES

CHINOOK
CLIPONS
CRINOID
CUIBONO
DAIMONS
EDITORS
EDITOUT
EPIGONE
EPILOGS
EPISODE
EPITOME
FAIROFF
FLIPOUT
GUIDONS
HEINOUS
IRISOUT
LAIDOFF
LAIDOUT
MAILOUT
NAIROBI
NOISOME
OMIGOSH
OMINOUS
ORINOCO
ORISONS
PAIDOFF
PAIDOUT
PAILOUS
PAIROFF
POISONS
PRISONS
QUINOAS
QUIXOTE
RAINOUT
RHIZOME
RUINOUS
SAILORS
SHIKOKU
SHIPOUT
SKIBOBS
SKIBOOT
SKIPOLE
SKIPOUT
SKITOWS
SLIPONS
SLIPOUT
SPIGOTS
SPINOFF
SPINOUT
SPINOZA
SUITORS
TAILOFF
TAILORS
TRICORN
TRICOTS
TRIGONS
TRILOGY
TRIPODS
TRIPOLI
TRITONE
TRITONS
UNICORN
UNIFORM
UNIPODS
UNISONS
WAITOUT

••I••O•
ALIENOR
ANISTON
ARIOSOS
ARISTOS
AVIATOR
AVIGNON

BRINGON
BRISTOL
BRITTON
CAISSON
CHIFFON
CHIGNON
CHINOOK
CLIFTON
CLINTON
CRIMSON
EDITION
ELISION
ERICSON
FRISSON
GAINSON
GOINFOR
GOINGON
GRIFFON
GRISSOM
HAIRDOS
KEILLOR
KLINGON
LAIDFOR
LAIDLOW
MAILBOX
MAILLOT
MAINTOP
OMICRON
OPINION
PAIDFOR
POISSON
RAINBOW
SCISSOR
SKIBOOT
SKIDDOO
SKIDROW
SLIPSON
SPIEDON
SPIESON
STILTON
STINGOS
THINKOF
TRIEDON
TRIESON
TUITION
WAITFOR
WAITRON
WAITSON
WEIRDOS

••I•••O
AGITATO
AKIHITO
ANIMATO
ARIOSTO
BOIARDO
BOITANO
BRINGTO
CHICAGO
CHICANO
CHIRICO
CRIOLLO
CUIBONO
HEIGHHO
LYINGTO
ORINOCO
OWINGTO
PAISANO
POINTTO
PRIORTO
SKIDDOO
SPIRITO
STICKTO
WRITETO

ZHIVAGO

•••IO••
ACTIONS
AMNIONS
ANTIOCH
ANXIOUS
APRIORI
BILIOUS
BUNIONS
CARIOCA
CATIONS
COPIOUS
CURIOUS
DEVIOUS
DUBIOUS
ELLIOTT
ENVIOUS
FANIONS
FURIOUS
IMPIOUS
JUNIORS
LEGIONS
LOTIONS
MANIOCS
MINIONS
MOTIONS
NATIONS
NOTIONS
NOXIOUS
OBVIOUS
OPTIONS
PAVIOUR
PERIODS
PETIOLE
PINIONS
POTIONS
RADIOED
RATIONS
RAVIOLI
REGIONS
SAVIORS
SAVIOUR
SENIORS
SERIOUS
TAPIOCA
TEDIOUS
VARIOUS
VICIOUS
VISIONS

•••I•O•
ADDISON
ADVISOR
ALBINOS
ALLISON
ANDIRON
ANTIFOG
ANTILOG
APRICOT
AUDITOR
BENISON
BERIDOF
BONITOS
CALICOS
CAPITOL
CARIBOU
CASINOS
CLAIROL
COPILOT
DEMIGOD
DIVISOR
DOMINOS
DORITOS

DOSIDOS
ELEISON
ELLISON
EPSILON
EQUINOX
ESKIMOS
GERITOL
GETITON
GOTITON
HARICOT
HELICON
HORIZON
HUMIDOR
INCISOR
INDIGOS
JANITOR
JEWISON
LADINOS
LATINOS
LAYITON
LETINON
LEXICON
LIAISON
LIBIDOS
MADISON
MAGINOT
MANILOW
MANITOU
MEDICOS
MERINOS
MONITOR
NONIRON
ONEIRON
ORBISON
PERIDOT
PIGIRON
RUBICON
SEMILOG
SILICON
SIXIRON
TRAITOR
TWOIRON
UPSILON
USTINOV
VENISON
VISITOR

•••I••O
ADMITTO
CHRISTO
CUTINTO
DOMINGO
GALILEO
GETINTO
GOTINTO
INVITRO
JALISCO
JERICHO
LAYINTO
LITINTO
LUCIANO
MEGIDDO
MURILLO
NABISCO
ORNITHO
PRYINTO
PUTITTO
RAMINTO
RANINTO
RELIEVO
RIPIENO
RIPINTO
RUNINTO
SEMIPRO

SETINTO
TAPINTO
TIEINTO
UTRILLO
VERISMO

••••IO•
ADAGIOS
ANTLION
AUCTION
BARRIOS
BASTION
BERLIOZ
BILLION
BLERIOT
BULLION
CAMPION
CAPTION
CARRION
CAUTION
CESSION
CHARIOT
CHEVIOT
CLARION
CUSHION
CYPRIOT
DICTION
EDITION
ELATION
ELISION
ELUTION
EMOTION
EROSION
EVASION
FACTION
FASHION
FICTION
FISSION
GRUNION
HELLION
HERRIOT
JILLION
KRATION
MANSION
MARMION
MENTION
MILLION
MISSION
MULLION
NUNCIOS
OPINION
ORATION
OVATION
PASSION
PATRIOT
PENSION
PILLION
PLOSION
PORTION
RANRIOT
REUNION
RUCTION
RUNRIOT
SEALION
SECTION
SESSION
STATION
STUDIOS
SUASION
SUCTION
TENSION
TORSION
TSELIOT
TUITION

UNCTION
VERSION
VITRIOL
WARRIOR
ZILLION

••••I•O
AKIHITO
AMERIGO
ARECIBO
ARETINO
BAMBINO
BANDITO
BENDIGO
BURRITO
BUSHIDO
CASSINO
CENTIMO
CHIRICO
CHORIZO
EXANIMO
LENTIGO
LINBIAO
LINPIAO
MARTINO
MESTIZO
NANAIMO
PIMLICO
PLACIDO
PORTICO
PROVISO
PROXIMO
SERPICO
SHAPIRO
SORDINO
SORVINO
SPIRITO
TAMPICO
TREVINO
VERTIGO

•••••IO
AJACCIO
AMRADIO
ANTONIO
ARSENIO
CBRADIO
CHEERIO
CLAUDIO
CONBRIO
FIDELIO
FMRADIO
GIORGIO
HORATIO
ONTARIO
PROPRIO
ROSARIO
SCORPIO

IP•••••
IPANEMA
IPCRESS
IPSWICH

I•P••••
IMPACTS
IMPAIRS
IMPALAS
IMPALED
IMPALES
IMPANEL
IMPARTS
IMPASSE
IMPASTO
IMPEACH
IMPEDED
IMPEDES
IMPENDS
IMPERIL
IMPETUS
IMPIETY
IMPINGE
IMPIOUS
IMPLANT
IMPLIED
IMPLIES
IMPLODE
IMPLORE
IMPORTS
IMPOSED
IMPOSES
IMPOSTS
IMPOUND
IMPRESS
IMPRINT
IMPROVE
IMPUGNS
IMPULSE
IMPURER
IMPUTED
IMPUTES
INPEACE
INPETTO
INPHASE
INPLACE
INPOWER
INPRINT

I••P•••
ICEPACK
ICEPICK
INAPTER
INAPTLY
INEPTLY
INSPANS
INSPECT
INSPIRE
INSPOTS
ISOPODS

I•••P••
INASPIN
INASPOT
INCEPTS
INCIPIT
INDEPTH
INKSPOT
INSIPID
IRRUPTS

I••••P•
ICECAPS
INSCAPE
INSHAPE
INSTEPS
ISOTOPE

I•••••P
ICINGUP
IGIVEUP
INAHEAP
INGROUP
INKYCAP

•IP••••
BIPEDAL
BIPLANE
BIPOLAR
CIPHERS
DIPLOID
DIPLOMA
DIPOLAR
DIPOLES
DIPPERS
DIPPIER
DIPPING
DIPTYCH
FIPPLES
GIPPING
GIPSIES
HIPBONE
HIPBOOT
HIPLESS
HIPLIKE
HIPNESS
HIPPEST
HIPPIER
HIPPIES
HIPROOF
HIPSTER
KIPLING
KIPPERS
LIPBALM
LIPIDES
LIPLESS
LIPLIKE
LIPPIER
LIPPING
LIPREAD
LIPSYNC
NIPPERS
NIPPIER
NIPPING
PIPEDUP
PIPEFUL
PIPEMMA
PIPESUP
PIPETTE
PIPIEST
PIPINGS
PIPKINS
PIPPINS
RIPCORD
RIPENED
RIPIENO
RIPINTO
RIPOFFS
RIPOSTE
RIPPERS
RIPPING
RIPPLED
RIPPLES
RIPRAPS
RIPSAWS
RIPSOFF
RIPSOUT
RIPTIDE
RIPTORN
SIPHONS
SIPPERS
SIPPETS
SIPPING
TIPLESS
TIPOFFS
TIPPERS
TIPPETS
TIPPIER
TIPPING
TIPPLED
TIPPLER
TIPPLES
TIPSIER
TIPSILY
TIPSOFF
TIPSTER
TIPTOED
TIPTOES
TIPTOPS
WIPEDUP
WIPEOUT
WIPESUP
YIPPING
ZIPCODE
ZIPPERS
ZIPPIER
ZIPPING

•I•P•••
AIRPLAY
AIRPORT
AIRPUMP
BITPART
DIAPERS
DIMPLED
DIMPLES
DIOPTER
DIPPERS
DIPPIER
DIPPING
DISPELS
DISPLAY
DISPORT
DISPOSE
DISPUTE
FIPPLES
GIPPING
HIPPEST
HIPPIER
HIPPIES
HISPANO
KIPPERS
LIMPEST
LIMPETS
LIMPING
LIMPOPO
LINPIAO
LIPPIER
LIPPING
LISPING
MISPLAY
NIPPERS
NIPPIER
NIPPING
NITPICK
OILPANS
PIEPANS
PIGPENS
PIPPINS
RIMPLED
RIMPLES
RIPPERS
RIPPING
RIPPLED
RIPPLES
SIMPERS
SIMPLER
SIMPLEX
SIMPSON
SIPPERS
SIPPETS
SIPPING
SIXPACK
TIEPINS
TIEPOLO
TIPPERS
TIPPETS
TIPPIER
TIPPING
TIPPLED
TIPPLER
TIPPLES
WIMPIER
WIMPISH
WIMPLED
WIMPLES
WIMPOLE
WISPIER
WISPILY
WISPING
YIPPING
ZIPPERS
ZIPPIER
ZIPPING

•I••P••
DISHPAN
KINGPIN
LILYPAD
NINEPIN
PITAPAT
SICKPAY

•I•••P•
BIGTOPS
BISHOPS
BITMAPS
DIGRAPH
DISRUPT
EIGHTPM
FILLIPS
FILLUPS
GIVEUPS
HICCUPS
KICKUPS
KIDNAPS
LIMPOPO
LINEUPS
LINKUPS
MISHAPS
MISTYPE
PICKUPS
PILEUPS
PISCOPO
RIPRAPS
TINTYPE
TIPTOPS
TITTUPS
WINDUPS

•I••••P
AIRDROP
AIRPUMP
AIRSHIP
BINDSUP
BIOCHIP
FILLSUP
FIREDUP
FIRESUP
FIRMSUP
FIXEDUP
FIXESUP
GIDDYAP
GIDDYUP
GIVENUP
GIVESUP
HIGHTOP
HIKEDUP
HIKESUP
HILLTOP
KICKSUP
KINSHIP
LIFTSUP
LIGHTUP
LINEDUP
LINESUP
MILKSOP
MISSTEP
MIXEDUP
MIXESUP
MIXITUP
OILLAMP
PICKSUP
PILEDUP
PILESUP
PINESAP
PIPEDUP
PIPESUP
PITSTOP
RILESUP
RINGSUP
SIGNSUP
SIZEDUP
SIZESUP
TIECLIP
TIMECOP
TIMESUP
WICKIUP
WINDSUP
WINESAP
WINGTIP
WIPEDUP
WIPESUP
WIRETAP
WISEDUP
WISESUP

••IP•••
ADIPOSE
BLIPPED
CHIPPED
CHIPPER
CHIPSIN
CLIPART
CLIPONS
CLIPPED
CLIPPER
DRIPDRY
DRIPPAN
DRIPPED
FLIPOUT
FLIPPED
FLIPPER
FLIPUPS
FRIPPET
GRIPERS
GRIPING
GRIPPED
GRIPPER
LEIPZIG
OVIPARA
QUIPPED
QUIPPER
SHIPMAN
SHIPMEN
SHIPOUT
SHIPPED
SHIPPER
SKIPOLE
SKIPOUT
SKIPPED
SKIPPER
SLIPONS
SLIPOUT
SLIPPED
SLIPPER
SLIPSIN
SLIPSON
SLIPSUP
SLIPUPS
SNIPEAT
SNIPERS
SNIPING
SNIPPED
SNIPPET
STIPEND
STIPPLE
SWIPERS
SWIPING
TAIPANS
TRIPLED
TRIPLES
TRIPLET
TRIPLEX
TRIPODS
TRIPOLI
TRIPPED
TRIPPER
TRIPPET
TRIPSUP
UNIPODS
WHIPPED
WHIPPET
WHIPSAW
WHIPSUP

••I•P••
BLIPPED
CHIPPED
CHIPPER
CHIRPED
CLIPPED
CLIPPER
CRIMPED
CRIMPER
CRISPED
CRISPER
CRISPIN
CRISPLY
CRISPUS
DRIPPAN
DRIPPED
FLIPPED
FLIPPER
FRIPPET
GLIMPSE
GRIPPED
GRIPPER
GUIMPES
HAIRPIN
PRIMPED
QUIPPED
QUIPPER
SHIPPED
SHIPPER
SKIMPED
SKIPPED
SKIPPER
SLIPPED
SLIPPER
SNIPPED
SNIPPET
STIPPLE
THIMPHU
TRIPPED
TRIPPER
TRIPPET
WHIMPER
WHIPPED
WHIPPET
WHISPER

••I••P•
CHINUPS
FLIPUPS
SLIPUPS
TRICEPS
TRIUMPH

••I•••P
BRINGUP
BUILDUP
BUILTUP
COILSUP
DOINGUP
DRIEDUP
DRIESUP
DRIVEUP
FAIRSUP
GOINGUP
ICINGUP
IGIVEUP
JOINSUP
JUICEUP
MAINTOP
PAIRSUP
PHILLIP
RAISEUP
SKIJUMP
SLIPSUP
SPICEUP
STICKUP
STIRRUP
STIRSUP
SUITSUP
THINKUP
TRIPSUP
TYINGUP
USINGUP
WAITSUP
WHIPSUP
WRITEUP

•••IP••
AGRIPPA
CALIPER
CALIPHS
CERIPHS
ECLIPSE
ELLIPSE
HELIPAD
INCIPIT
INSIPID
JUNIPER
MANIPLE
OCCIPUT
OEDIPAL
OEDIPUS
RECIPES
SCRIPPS
SCRIPTS
SEMIPRO
STRIPED
STRIPER
STRIPES
TRAIPSE

•••I•P•
AGRIPPA
SCRIMPS
SCRIMPY
SCRIPPS
SHRIMPS

•••I••P
HAMITUP
MEDIGAP
MIXITUP
SPLITUP

••••IP•
BAGPIPE
BUNYIPS
CATNIPS
FILLIPS
GOSSIPS
GOSSIPY
HOTLIPS
HOTTIPS
MRCHIPS
PANPIPE
RECEIPT
RESHIPS
TURNIPS

••••I•P
WICKIUP

•••••IP
AIRSHIP
BIOCHIP
CANTRIP
COWSLIP
DAYTRIP
EGOTRIP
FOULTIP
KEYGRIP
KINSHIP
LETSLIP
NONSLIP
PARSNIP
PHILLIP
TIECLIP
WARSHIP
WINGTIP
WORSHIP

IQ•••••
IQTESTS

I•Q••••
INQUEST
INQUIRE
INQUIRY

•IQ••••
LIQUEFY
LIQUEUR
LIQUIDS
LIQUORS
PIQUANT
PIQUING

•I•Q•••
BISQUES
CIRQUES

••IQ•••
BRIQUET
CAIQUES
CLIQUES
CLIQUEY

••I•Q••
QUINQUE

•••IQ••
ANTIQUE

BEZIQUE
COMIQUE
LALIQUE
MONIQUE
OBLIQUE

IR•••••
IRANIAN
IRATELY
IRATEST
IRECKON
IRELAND
IRELESS
IRIDIUM
IRISOUT
IRKSOME
IRONAGE
IRONERS
IRONIES
IRONING
IRONMAN
IRONMEN
IRONONS
IRONORE
IRONOUT
IRRUPTS

I•R••••
INROADS
IRRUPTS
ISRAELI

I••R•••
IBERIAN
ICERINK
IMARETS
IMBRUED
IMBRUES
IMPRESS
IMPRINT
IMPROVE
INARUSH
INBREED
INBRIEF
INERROR
INERTIA
INERTLY
INFRONT
INGRAIN
INGRATE
INGRESS
INGROUP
INGROWN
INORBIT
INPRINT
INTROIT
INTRUDE
INTRUST
INTRUTH
INURING
IPCRESS
ITERANT
ITERATE
IVORIES

I•••R••
ICEFREE
IDCARDS
IGNORED
IGNORER
IGNORES
ILLBRED
IMMERSE
IMMORAL
IMMURED
IMMURES
IMPARTS
IMPERIL
IMPORTS
IMPURER
IMSORRY
INDORSE
INERROR
INFERNO
INFORCE
INFORMS
INHERED
INHERES
INHERIT
INJURED
INJURES
INNARDS
INSERTS
INSURED
INSURER
INSURES
INTERIM
INTERNS
INTERSE
INVERSE
INVERTS
INWARDS
IZZARDS

I••••R•
ICEBERG
IMAGERS
IMAGERY
IMPAIRS
IMPLORE
IMSORRY
INAWORD
INBOARD
INDOORS
INKHORN
INQUIRE
INQUIRY
INSHORT
INSPIRE
INSTARS
INSTORE
INTEARS
INTEGRA
INVITRO
IRONERS
IRONORE
ISADORA
ISOBARS
ISOMERS
ISSUERS

I•••••R
ICEBEER
IGNITER
IGNORER
IMPURER
INAPTER
INCISOR
INCITER
INDUCER
INERROR
INFAVOR
INGEMAR
INHALER
INPOWER
INSIDER
INSOFAR
INSULAR
INSURER
INTEGER
INTONER
INVADER
INVOKER
IONIZER
ITCHIER

•IR••••
AIRBAGS
AIRBALL
AIRBASE
AIRBOAT
AIRCOOL
AIRCREW
AIRDAMS
AIRDATE
AIRDROP
AIRFARE
AIRFLOW
AIRFOIL
AIRGUNS
AIRHEAD
AIRHOLE
AIRIEST
AIRINGS
AIRKISS
AIRLANE
AIRLESS
AIRLIFT
AIRLIKE
AIRLINE
AIRLOCK
AIRMADA
AIRMAIL
AIRMASS
AIRMILE
AIRPLAY
AIRPORT
AIRPUMP
AIRRAID
AIRSACS
AIRSHIP
AIRSHOW
AIRSOCK
AIRSOUT
AIRTAXI
AIRTIME
AIRWAVE
AIRWAYS
AIRWOLF
BIRCHED
BIRCHES
BIRDDOG
BIRDERS
BIRDIED
BIRDIES
BIRDING
BIRDMAN
BIRDMEN
BIREMES
BIRETTA
BIRLING
BIRTHED
CIRCLED
CIRCLES
CIRCLET
CIRCUIT
CIRCUSY
CIRQUES
DIRECTS
DIREFUL
DIRNDLS
DIRTIED
DIRTIER
DIRTIES
DIRTILY
FIREANT
FIREARM
FIREBOX
FIREBUG
FIREDOG
FIREDUP
FIREFLY
FIRELIT
FIREMAN
FIREMEN
FIRENZE
FIREOFF
FIRESUP
FIRINGS
FIRKINS
FIRMEST
FIRMING
FIRMSUP
FIRRIER
FIRSTLY
GIRAFFE
GIRASOL
GIRDERS
GIRDING
GIRDLED
GIRDLES
GIRLISH
GIRNING
GIRONDE
HIRABLE
HIRESON
HIRSUTE
KIRMANS
KIRSTIE
KIRTLES
MIRACLE
MIRADOR
MIRAGES
MIRAMAR
MIRAMAX
MIRANDA
MIRIEST
MIRKIER
MIRRORS
NIRVANA
PIRAEUS
PIRANHA
PIRATED
PIRATES
PIRATIC
PIROGUE
SIRLOIN
SIROCCO
TIRADES
TIREDER
TIREDLY
TIREDOF
TIREOUT
VIRAGOS
VIRGINS
VIRGOAN
VIRGULE
VIRIBUS
VIRTUAL
VIRTUES
VIRTUTE
VIRUSES
WIRETAP
WIRIEST
ZIRCONS

•I•R•••
AIGRETS
AIRRAID
CITRATE
CITRINE
CITROEN
CITRONS
CITROUS
DIARIES
DIGRAMS
DIGRAPH
DIGRESS
DIORAMA
DISROBE
DISRUPT
DIURNAL
FIBRILS
FIBRINS
FIBROUS
FIERCER
FIERIER
FIERILY
FIRRIER
GIORGIO
HIPROOF
LIBRARY
LIERNES
LIPREAD
MICROBE
MICRONS
MIDRIBS
MIDRIFF
MIDRISE
MIGRANT
MIGRATE
MIRRORS
MISREAD
MISRULE
MITRING
NIMRODS
NITRATE
NITRIDE
NITRITE
NITROUS
OILRIGS
PIERCED
PIERCES
PIERROT
RIORITA
RIPRAPS
SIERRAS
TIERACK
TIERING
TIERNEY
TIERODS
TIGRESS
TIGRISH
TITRATE
TITRING
VIBRANT
VIBRATE
VIBRATO
VITRIFY
VITRIOL

•I••R••
AILERON
AIRCREW
AIRDROP
BISTROS
BIZARRE
CIBORIA
DIAGRAM
DIDEROT
DISARMS
DISHRAG
DIVERGE
DIVERSE
DIVERTS
DIVORCE
FIACRES
FIGURED
FIGURER
FIGURES
KINDRED
KINGRAT
LIBERAL
LIBERIA
LIBERTY
LITCRIT
LITERAL
LITURGY
LIVORNO
LIZARDS
MILDRED
MILKRUN
MILLRUN
MILORDS
MINARET
MINERAL
MINERVA
MINORCA
MINORED
MISERLY
MISTRAL
MITERED
MITHRAS
NIGERIA
PICARDY
PICAROS
PIERROT
PIGIRON
PILGRIM
PIZARRO
RICARDO
RICERAT
SIBERIA
SIERRAS
SISTRUM
SIXIRON
TIMBRES
VICEROY
WILFRID
WINDROW
WINERED
WINFREY
WIZARDS

•I•••R•
AIRFARE
AIRPORT
BICKERS
BIDDERS
BIGBIRD
BIGGERS
BIGHORN
BIGOTRY
BINDERS
BINDERY
BIRDERS
BITPART
BITTERN
BITTERS
BIZARRE
CINDERS
CINDERY
CIPHERS
CISTERN
DIALERS
DIAPERS
DICKERS
DIEHARD
DIETARY
DIETERS
DIFFERS
DIGGERS
DILBERT
DILLARD
DIMITRI
DIMMERS
DINNERS
DIPPERS
DISBARS
DISCARD
DISCERN
DISCORD
DISPORT
DISTORT
DISTURB
DITHERS
DITHERY
FIBBERS
FILBERT
FILLERS
FILTERS
FINDERS
FINEART
FINGERS
FIREARM
FISHERS
FISHERY
FISHFRY
FISSURE
FITTERS
FIXTURE
GIBBERS
GIFFORD
GILBERT
GILDERS
GINGERS
GINGERY
GIRDERS
GIZZARD
HICKORY
HILAIRE
HILLARY
HINDERS
HISSERS
HISTORY
HITHERE
HITTERS
JIGGERS
JIGGERY
JITTERS
JITTERY
KICKERS
KIDDERS
KILDARE
KILLERS
KIPPERS
KISSERS
LIBBERS
LIBRARY
LICTORS
LIFTERS
LIMBERS
LIMNERS
LINGERS
LINKERS
LIQUORS
LITTERS
MIDTERM
MILKERS
MILLARD
MILLERS
MIMICRY
MINCERS
MINDERS
MINTERS
MIRRORS
MISFIRE
MISTERS
MISWORD
MITFORD
MIXTURE
NIAGARA
NICKERS
NIGGARD
NIPPERS
PIASTRE
PICCARD
PICKERS
PICTURE
PIECERS
PIGGERY
PILFERS
PILLARS
PILLORY
PINCERS
PINCURL
PINNERS
PISMIRE
PITIERS
PITTERS
PIZARRO
QINTARS
RICHARD
RIFLERS
RIFLERY
RIGGERS
RIGOURS
RINGERS
RIOTERS
RIPCORD
RIPPERS
RIPTORN
RISKERS
RIVALRY
RIVIERA
RIVIERE
SIDEARM
SIFTERS
SIGHERS
SIGNERS
SILVERS
SILVERY
SIMMERS
SIMPERS
SINATRA
SINCERE
SINGERS
SINKERS
SINNERS
SIPPERS
SISTERS
SITTERS
TICKERS
TILLERS
TILTERS
TIMBERS
TINDERS
TINEARS
TINHORN
TINKERS
TINNERS
TINTERN
TINTERS
TINWARE
TINWORK
TIPPERS
TITFERS
TITHERS
TITTERS
VICTORS
VICTORY
VIEWERS
VIGOURS
VISCERA
VIZIERS
WICKERS
WIDMARK
WIENERS
WILFORD
WILLARD
WINCERS
WINDERS
WINGERS
WINKERS
WINNERS
WINTERS
WINTERY
WISHERS
WITHERS
ZINGERS
ZIPPERS
ZITHERS

•I••••R
AIMSFOR
BICOLOR
BIDFAIR
BILGIER
BIPOLAR
BITSIER
BITTIER
DIDOVER
DILUTER
DINGIER
DINKIER
DIOPTER
DIPOLAR
DIPPIER
DIRTIER
DISHIER
DITSIER
DITZIER
DIVIDER
DIVINER
DIVISOR
DIZZIER
FICKLER
FIDDLER
FIEDLER
FIELDER
FIERCER
FIERIER
FIGHTER
FIGURER
FILCHER
FILMIER
FINNIER
FIRRIER
FISCHER
FISHIER
FIZZIER
GIDDIER
GIGGLER
HILLIER
HIPPIER
HIPSTER
HITCHER
KICKIER
KINKIER
LIBELER
LIEOVER
LIGHTER
LINTIER
LIPPIER
LIQUEUR
LITTLER
MIDYEAR
MIFFIER
MILKIER
MINGIER
MINGLER
MINIVER
MINTIER
MIRADOR
MIRAMAR
MIRKIER
MISHEAR
MISTIER
NIBBLER
NIEBUHR
NIFTIER
NIMBLER
NIPPIER
NITTIER
PIASTER
PICADOR
PICKIER
PIGGIER
PILSNER
PINCHER
PINEFOR
PINETAR
PIONEER
PITCHER
PITHIER
RICHTER
RIDDLER
RIDGIER
RIGHTER
RISKIER
RITZIER
RIVETER
SIDEBAR
SIDECAR
SILKIER
SILLIER
SILTIER
SIMILAR
SIMPLER
TICKLER
TIGHTER
TIMIDER
TINNIER
TINSTAR
TIPPIER
TIPPLER
TIPSIER
TIPSTER
TIREDER
TITULAR
VIEWIER
VINEGAR
VINTNER
VISITOR
VIVIDER
WIDOWER
WIGGIER
WIGGLER
WIMPIER
WINDIER
WINDSOR
WINEBAR
WINKLER
WISPIER
WITHIER
WITTIER
ZINGIER
ZIPPIER

••IR•••
CHIRICO
CHIRPED
CUIRASS
DAIRIES
EMIRATE
FAIREST
FAIRIES
FAIRING
FAIRISH
FAIROFF
FAIRSUP
FAIRWAY
FLIRTED
HAIRCUT
HAIRDOS
HAIRDYE
HAIRIER
HAIRNET
HAIRPIN
HEIRESS
NAIROBI
PAIRING
PAIROFF
PAIRSUP
SHIRKED
SHIRKER
SHIRLEY
SHIRRED
SKIRACK
SKIRLED
SKIRRED
SKIRTED
SKIRUNS
SMIRKED
SOIREES
SPIRALS
SPIRANT
SPIREAS
SPIRIER
SPIRITO
SPIRITS
STIRFRY
STIRRED
STIRRER
STIRRUP
STIRSIN
STIRSUP
SWIRLED
THIRDLY
THIRSTS
THIRSTY
TRIREME
TWIRLED
TWIRLER
WEIRDER
WEIRDLY
WEIRDOS
WHIRLED
WHIRRED
ZAIREAN
ZAIRIAN

••I•R••
BOIARDO
BRIARDS
EMIGRES
EPIGRAM
ERITREA
GRIGRIS
MAIGRET
MAITRED
OMICRON
OSIERED
PRIORTO
SCIORRA
SHIRRED
SKIDROW
SKIRRED
STIRRED
STIRRER
STIRRUP
TRIGRAM
WAITRON
WHIRRED

••I••R•
ABINTRA
ARIKARA
BAILERS
BAILORS
BOILERS
BRIBERY
CHICORY
CHIDERS
CHIMERA
CLIBURN
CLIPART
COINERS
DEICERS
DRIPDRY
DRIVERS
EDITORS
ELIXIRS
EPICURE
FAILURE
GAINERS
GAITERS
GLIDERS
GRIPERS
GUITARS
HEIFERS
JAILERS
JOINERS
JOINERY
JUICERS
KAISERS
LEISURE
LOITERS
MAILERS
MOILERS
NAILERS
OPINERS
OVIPARA
PHILTRE
PRICERS
PRIMARY
PRIMERS
QUINARY
QUIVERS
QUIVERY
RAIDERS
RAILERS
RAISERS
RUINERS
SAILORS
SCIORRA
SEINERS
SEIZERS
SHIKARI
SHINERS
SHIVERS
SHIVERY
SKIVERS
SLICERS
SLIDERS
SLIVERS
SMILERS
SNIPERS
SPICERY
SPIDERS
SPIDERY
SPIKERS
SPINDRY
STIRFRY
SUITORS
SWIPERS
TAILORS
TOILERS
TRICORN
UNICORN
UNIFORM
UNITARY
UNITERS
WAILERS
WAITERS
WAIVERS
WHINERS
WRITERS

••I•••R
ALIENOR
ALIGNER
AVIATOR
BAINTER
BLINDER
BLINKER
BLISTER
BLITHER
BRIEFER
BRINGER
BRINIER
BRISKER
BUILDER
CHIGGER
CHILLER
CHIPPER
CHITTER
CLIMBER
CLINKER
CLIPPER
CRIMPER
CRISPER
CRITTER
DAIMLER
DRIFTER
DRILLER
DRINKER
EMITTER
EVILLER
FAINTER
FEIFFER
FLICKER
FLIPPER
FLITTER
FLIVVER
FRITTER
GLIBBER
GLIMMER
GLITTER
GOINFOR
GRIDDER
GRIEVER
GRIFTER
GRIMIER
GRIMMER
GRINDER
GRINNER
GRIPPER
GUILDER
HAIRIER
JOINDER
JUICIER
KEILLOR
KNITTER
LAIDFOR
LEISTER
MAILCAR
MEISTER
MOISTER
NEITHER
NOISIER
OLIVIER
OMITTER
PAIDFOR
PAINTER
PHILTER
POINTER
POITIER
PRICIER
PRIMMER
PRINTER
PRIVIER
QUICKER
QUIETER
QUILLER
QUILTER
QUIPPER
QUITTER
RAINIER
ROILIER
ROISTER
SCISSOR
SHIMMER
SHINIER
SHIPPER
SHIRKER
SKIDDER
SKIMMER
SKINNER
SKIPPER
SKITTER
SKIWEAR
SLICKER
SLIMIER
SLIMMER
SLINGER
SLIPPER
SLITHER
SNICKER
SNIFFER
SNIFTER
SNIGGER
SPICIER
SPIELER
SPIKIER
SPINIER
SPINNER
SPIRIER
STICKER
STIFFER
STILLER
STINGER
STINKER
STIRRER
SWIFTER
SWIMMER

SWINGER
SWITZER
TEICHER
THICKER
THINAIR
THINKER
THINNER
THITHER
TRICKER
TRIFLER
TRIGGER
TRIMMER
TRIPPER
TRISTAR
TWIRLER
TWISTER
TWITTER
UNIFIER
VEINIER
WAITFOR
WEIRDER
WHIMPER
WHINIER
WHISKER
WHISPER
WHITHER
WHITIER
WHIZZER
WRINGER

•••IR••

ADMIRAL
ADMIRED
ADMIRER
ADMIRES
AFFIRMS
ANDIRON
ASPIRED
ASPIRER
ASPIRES
ASPIRIN
ATHIRST
ATTIRED
ATTIRES
BEMIRED
BEMIRES
CHAIRED
CLAIROL
DELIRIA
DESIRED
DESIREE
DESIRES
EMPIRES
ENGIRDS
EXPIRED
EXPIRES
GLAIRED
HEGIRAS
JABIRUS
NONIRON
ONEIRON
PIGIRON
PRAIRIE
REAIRED
REBIRTH
REFIRES
REHIRED
REHIRES
RETIRED
RETIREE
RETIRES
REWIRED
REWIRES
SATIRES
SATIRIC
SCHIRRA
SIXIRON
SQUIRED
SQUIRES
SQUIRMS
SQUIRMY
SQUIRTS
TSHIRTS
TWOIRON
UMPIRED
UMPIRES
UNAIRED
UNGIRDS

•••I•R•

ALFIERI
ALGIERS
ANTIART
APRIORI
ARRIERE
BEZIERS
CAHIERS
CALIBRE
CAVIARS
COPIERS
DENIERS
DEVILRY
DIMITRI
ENVIERS
HONIARA
HOSIERS
HOSIERY
INVITRO
JUNIORS
LEVIERS
LUMIERE
METIERS
MIMICRY
MOLIERE
PITIERS
PONIARD
RAPIERS
RETIARY
RIVIERA
RIVIERE
SALIERI
SAVIORS
SCHIRRA
SEMIPRO
SENIORS
TOPIARY
VIZIERS

•••I••R

ADMIRER
ADVISER
ADVISOR
ANTIWAR
AQUIFER
AQUIVER
ARBITER
ARRIVER
ASPIRER
AUDITOR
BOLIVAR
BRAIDER
BROILER
BRUISER
CALIBER
CALIPER
CAVILER
CCRIDER
CHOICER
CLAIMER
CONIFER
CRUISER
DEFILER
DELIVER
DIVIDER
DIVINER
DIVISOR
DRAINER
DREISER
ENTICER
FRAILER
HUMIDOR
IGNITER
INCISOR
INCITER
INSIDER
IONIZER
JANITOR
JUNIPER
JUPITER
LAMINAR
LUCIFER
MARINER
MINIVER
MONIKER
MONITOR
OFFICER
ORBITER
PAVIOUR
PLAINER
POLITER
PRAISER
RAPIDER
RECITER
REFINER
REVISER
ROTIFER
SAVIOUR
SEMINAR
SHRINER
SHRIVER
SIMILAR
SOLIDER
SPLICER
SPOILER
STAIDER
STAINER
STEIGER
STEINER
STRIDER
STRIKER
STRIPER
STRIVER
TIMIDER
TRAILER
TRAINER
TRAITOR
UNWISER
UPRIVER
VISITOR
VIVIDER

••••IR•

ACQUIRE
AFFAIRE
AFFAIRS
ARMOIRE
ASTAIRE
AUPAIRS
BATGIRL
BESTIRS
BIGBIRD
BONFIRE
BUSGIRL
CATBIRD
COHEIRS
CONFIRM
COWBIRD
COWGIRL
DUNKIRK
ECLAIRS
ELIXIRS
ENQUIRE
ENQUIRY
ESQUIRE
FOXFIRE
GUNFIRE
HAYWIRE
HILAIRE
HOTWIRE
IMPAIRS
INQUIRE
INQUIRY
INSPIRE
JAYBIRD
KAFFIRS
LEMPIRA
MADEIRA
MAGUIRE
MCGUIRE
MEMOIRE
MEMOIRS
MENHIRS
MISFIRE
MOHAIRS
PAYDIRT
PISMIRE
REDBIRD
REDFIRS
REPAIRS
REQUIRE
RESPIRE
SANTIRS
SEABIRD
SEAFIRE
SEAGIRT
SELKIRK
SHAPIRO
THEFIRM
VAMPIRA
VAMPIRE

••••I•R

ANGRIER
ANTSIER
ARTSIER
ATELIER
BAGGIER
BALKIER
BALMIER
BARKIER
BARMIER
BARRIER
BATTIER
BAWDIER
BEADIER
BEAMIER
BEEFIER
BEERIER
BENDIER
BILGIER
BITSIER
BITTIER
BLOWIER
BOGGIER
BONNIER
BOOMIER
BOSKIER
BOSSIER
BRAZIER
BRINIER
BUGGIER
BULGIER
BULKIER
BUMPIER
BURLIER
BUSHIER
CAMPIER
CANNIER
CARRIER
CARTIER
CASHIER
CATTIER
CHARIER
CHENIER
CHEWIER
CHOKIER
CLAVIER
CLAYIER
COCKIER
COLLIER
COMFIER
CORKIER
CORNIER
COURIER
CRAZIER
CROSIER
CURDIER
CURLIER
CURRIER
CURVIER
CUSHIER
DAFFIER
DALLIER
DANDIER
DAUMIER
DECRIER
DERNIER
DINGIER
DINKIER
DIPPIER
DIRTIER
DISHIER
DITSIER
DITZIER
DIZZIER
DODGIER
DOGGIER
DOSSIER
DOTTIER
DOWDIER
DOWNIER
DUCKIER
DUMPIER
DUSKIER
DUSTIER
EARLIER
EMPTIER
FANCIER
FARRIER
FATTIER
FENNIER
FERNIER
FIERIER
FILMIER
FINNIER
FIRRIER
FISHIER
FIZZIER
FLAKIER
FLAMIER
FLAXIER
FLUKIER
FLUTIER
FOAMIER
FOGGIER
FOLKIER
FORKIER
FOURIER
FRASIER
FRAZIER
FUBSIER
FUNKIER
FUNNIER
FURRIER
FUSSIER
FUSTIER
FUZZIER
GABBIER
GAMMIER
GASSIER
GAUDIER
GAUZIER
GAWKIER
GEEKIER
GEMMIER
GERMIER
GIDDIER
GLACIER
GLAZIER
GODLIER
GOOFIER
GOONIER
GOOPIER
GOOSIER
GORSIER
GOUTIER
GRAPIER
GRIMIER
GRODIER
GROLIER
GULPIER
GUMMIER
GUNKIER
GUSHIER
GUSTIER
GUTSIER
GUTTIER
HAIRIER
HAMMIER
HANDIER
HAPPIER
HARDIER
HARRIER
HASTIER
HEADIER
HEAVIER
HEDGIER
HEFTIER
HERBIER
HILLIER
HIPPIER
HOARIER
HOOSIER
HORSIER
HUFFIER
HUMPIER
HUNKIER
HUSKIER
ITCHIER
JAGGIER
JAMMIER
JANVIER
JAZZIER
JERKIER
JOLLIER
JOLTIER
JOWLIER
JUICIER
JUMPIER
JUNKIER
KICKIER
KINKIER
KOOKIER
LANKIER
LARDIER
LEADIER
LEAFIER
LEAKIER
LEARIER
LEDGIER
LEERIER
LEGGIER
LINTIER
LIPPIER
LOAMIER
LOFTIER
LOONIER
LOOPIER
LOPPIER
LOUSIER
LOWLIER
LUCKIER
LUMPIER
LUSTIER
MALTIER
MANGIER
MANLIER
MASSIER
MEALIER
MEATIER
MERRIER
MESHIER
MESSIER
MIFFIER
MILKIER
MINGIER
MINTIER
MIRKIER
MISTIER
MOLDIER
MOODIER
MOONIER
MOORIER
MOSSIER
MOTHIER
MOUSIER
MUCKIER
MUDDIER
MUGGIER
MURKIER
MUSHIER
MUSKIER
MUSSIER
MUSTIER
MUZZIER
NAGGIER
NASTIER
NATTIER
NEEDIER
NERDIER
NERVIER
NEWSIER
NIFTIER
NIPPIER
NITTIER
NOBBIER
NOISIER
NUBBIER
NUTSIER
NUTTIER
OLIVIER
PALLIER
PALMIER
PANNIER
PARRIER
PARTIER
PASTIER
PAWKIER
PEATIER
PECKIER
PEPPIER
PERKIER
PERRIER
PESKIER
PETTIER
PHONIER
PICKIER
PIGGIER
PITHIER
PLATIER
PLUMIER
PODGIER
POITIER
PORKIER
POTSIER
POTTIER
POUTIER
PREMIER
PRICIER
PRIVIER
PROSIER
PUDGIER
PUFFIER
PULPIER
PUNKIER
PUNNIER
PURSIER
PUSHIER
QUAKIER
QUERIER
RAINIER
RALLIER
RANDIER
RANGIER
RASPIER
RATTIER
READIER
REEDIER
RIDGIER
RISKIER
RITZIER
ROCKIER
ROILIER
ROOKIER
ROOMIER
ROOTIER
ROWDIER
RUDDIER
RUMMIER
RUNNIER
RUNTIER
RUSHIER
RUSTIER
RUTTIER
SAGGIER
SALTIER
SANDIER
SAPPIER
SARKIER
SASSIER
SAUCIER
SAVVIER
SCALIER
SCARIER
SEAMIER
SEDGIER
SEEDIER
SEEPIER
SHADIER
SHAKIER
SHINIER
SHOWIER
SILKIER
SILLIER
SILTIER
SLATIER
SLIMIER
SMOKIER
SNAKIER
SNOWIER
SOAPIER
SODDIER
SOGGIER
SOLDIER
SOOTIER
SOPPIER
SORRIER
SOUPIER
SPACIER
SPICIER
SPIKIER
SPINIER
SPIRIER
SPUMIER
STAGIER
STONIER
SUDSIER
SULKIER
SUNNIER
SURFIER
SURLIER
TACKIER
TALKIER
TALLIER
TANGIER
TARDIER
TARRIER
TARSIER
TASTIER
TATTIER
TAWNIER
TEARIER
TECHIER
TEENIER
TERRIER
TESTIER
THEWIER
TINNIER
TIPPIER
TIPSIER
TUBBIER
TUFTIER
TURFIER
UNIFIER
VASTIER
VEALIER
VEINIER
VERNIER
VIEWIER
WACKIER
WARRIOR
WARTIER
WASHIER
WASPIER
WEARIER
WEBBIER
WEDGIER
WEEDIER
WEENIER
WEEPIER
WHINIER
WHITIER
WIGGIER
WIMPIER
WINDIER
WISPIER
WITHIER
WITTIER
WONKIER
WOODIER
WOOLIER
WOOZIER
WORDIER
WORMIER
WORRIER
YUCKIER
YUMMIER
ZAPPIER
ZESTIER
ZINGIER
ZIPPIER

•••••IR

BENAZIR
BIDFAIR
BONSOIR
BOUDOIR
CATHAIR
COCHAIR
CORSAIR
DEADAIR
DEARSIR
DESPAIR
FUNFAIR
KASHMIR
MAYFAIR
OPENAIR
REDHAIR
THINAIR

IS•••••

ISADORA
ISHMAEL
ISLAMIC
ISLANDS
ISOBARS
ISOGONS
ISOHELS
ISOLATE
ISOMERS
ISONOMY
ISOPODS
ISOTOPE
ISRAELI
ISSUERS
ISSUING
ISTHMUS

I•S••••

IFSTONE
IMSORRY
INSCAPE
INSEAMS
INSECTS
INSERTS
INSHAPE
INSHORT
INSIDER
INSIDES
INSIGHT
INSIPID
INSISTS
INSOFAR
INSOLES
INSPANS
INSPECT
INSPIRE
INSPOTS
INSTALL
INSTALS
INSTANT
INSTARS
INSTATE
INSTEAD
INSTEPS
INSTILL
INSTILS
INSTOCK
INSTORE
INSTYLE
INSULAR
INSULIN
INSULTS
INSURED
INSURER
INSURES
IPSWICH
ISSUERS
ISSUING

I••S•••

IBNSAUD
ICESHOW
ICESOUT
INASNIT
INASPIN
INASPOT
INASTEW
INKSPOT
IRISOUT
IRKSOME

I•••S••

ILIESCU
ILLUSED
ILLUSES
IMPASSE
IMPASTO
IMPOSED
IMPOSES
IMPOSTS
INCASED
INCASES
INCISED
INCISES
INCISOR
INFESTS
INFUSED
INFUSES
INGESTS
INHASTE
INSISTS
INVESTS
IODISED
IODISES
IONESCO
IONISED
IONISES
IQTESTS

I••••S•

ICELESS
ICINESS
ICKIEST
IDOLISE
IFFIEST
ILLNESS
IMMENSE
IMMERSE
IMPASSE
IMPRESS
IMPULSE
INAMESS
INANEST
INARUSH
INCENSE
INCLOSE
INDORSE
INGRESS
INHOUSE
INKIEST
INKLESS
INNLESS
INPHASE
INQUEST
INTENSE
INTERSE
INTRUST
INVERSE
IPCRESS
IRATEST
IRELESS
ITEMISE

I•••••S

ICEAGES
ICEAXES
ICEBAGS
ICECAPS
ICEFOGS
ICELESS
ICICLES
ICINESS
IDCARDS
IDEATES
IGNEOUS
IGNITES
IGNORES
IGUANAS
ILLNESS
ILLUDES
ILLUMES
ILLUSES
IMAGERS
IMAGOES
IMARETS
IMBIBES
IMBRUES
IMMIXES
IMMURES
IMPACTS
IMPAIRS
IMPALAS
IMPALES
IMPARTS
IMPEDES
IMPENDS
IMPETUS
IMPIOUS
IMPLIES
IMPORTS
IMPOSES
IMPOSTS
IMPRESS
IMPUGNS
IMPUTES
INAMESS
INBOXES
INCANTS
INCASES
INCEPTS
INCISES
INCITES
INCOMES
INCUDES
INDENTS
INDEXES
INDIANS
INDICES
INDICTS
INDIGOS
INDITES
INDOORS
INDUCES
INDUCTS
INFANTS
INFECTS
INFESTS
INFLOWS
INFOCUS
INFORMS
INFUSES
INGALLS
INGESTS
INGRESS
INHALES
INHAULS
INHERES
INJECTS
INJOKES
INJURES
INKLESS
INMATES
INNARDS
INNINGS
INNLESS
INROADS
INSEAMS
INSECTS
INSERTS
INSIDES
INSISTS
INSOLES
INSPANS
INSPOTS
INSTALS
INSTARS
INSTEPS
INSTILS
INSULTS
INSURES
INTAKES
INTEARS
INTENDS
INTENTS
INTERNS
INTONES
INTUITS
INVADES
INVENTS
INVERTS
INVESTS
INVITES
INVOKES
INWARDS
IODATES
IODIDES
IODISES
IODIZES
IOMOTHS
IONISES
IONIZES
IPCRESS
IQTESTS
IRELESS
IRONERS
IRONIES
IRONONS
IRRUPTS
ISLANDS
ISOBARS
ISOGONS
ISOHELS
ISOMERS
ISOPODS
ISSUERS
ISTHMUS
ITALICS
IVORIES
IZZARDS

•IS••••

BISCUIT
BISECTS
BISHOPS
BISMUTH
BISQUES
BISTROS
CISTERN
DISABLE
DISARMS
DISAVOW
DISBAND
DISBARS
DISCARD
DISCERN
DISCOED
DISCORD
DISCUSS
DISDAIN
DISEASE
DISGUST
DISHFUL
DISHIER
DISHING
DISHOUT
DISHPAN
DISHRAG
DISJOIN
DISLIKE
DISMAYS
DISMISS
DISOBEY
DISOWNS
DISPELS
DISPLAY
DISPORT
DISPOSE
DISPUTE
DISROBE
DISRUPT
DISSECT
DISSENT
DISSING
DISTAFF
DISTANT
DISTEND
DISTILL
DISTILS
DISTORT
DISTURB
DISUSED
FISCHER
FISHERS
FISHERY
FISHEYE

FISHFRY
FISHIER
FISHILY
FISHING
FISHNET
FISHOUT
FISSILE
FISSION
FISSURE
FISTFUL
GISELLE
HISPANO
HISSERS
HISSING
HISTORY
KISHKES
KISSERS
KISSING
KISSOFF
LISENTE
LISPING
LISSOME
LISTEES
LISTELS
LISTENS
LISTING
MISALLY
MISCALL
MISCAST
MISCUED
MISCUES
MISDATE
MISDEAL
MISDEED
MISDIAL
MISDOES
MISDONE
MISERLY
MISFILE
MISFIRE
MISFITS
MISHAPS
MISHEAR
MISHITS
MISLAID
MISLAYS
MISLEAD
MISLIKE
MISMATE
MISNAME
MISPLAY
MISREAD
MISRULE
MISSAID
MISSALS
MISSAYS
MISSIES
MISSILE
MISSING
MISSION
MISSISH
MISSIVE
MISSOUT
MISSTEP
MISTAKE
MISTERS
MISTIER
MISTILY
MISTING
MISTOOK
MISTRAL
MISTYPE
MISUSED
MISUSES
MISWORD
PISCINE
PISCOPO
PISMIRE
PISTILS
PISTOLE
PISTOLS
PISTONS
RISIBLE
RISIBLY
RISINGS
RISKERS
RISKIER
RISKILY
RISKING
RISOTTO
RISSOLE
SISKINS
SISSIES
SISTERS
SISTINE
SISTRUM
TISANES
TISSUES
VISAGES
VISAING
VISALIA
VISAVIS
VISCERA
VISCOUS
VISIBLE
VISIBLY
VISIONS
VISITED
VISITOR
VISTULA
VISUALS
WISEDUP
WISEGUY
WISEMAN
WISEMEN
WISESUP
WISHERS
WISHFUL
WISHING
WISPIER
WISPILY
WISPING
WISTFUL

•I•S•••

AIMSFOR
AIRSACS
AIRSHIP
AIRSHOW
AIRSOCK
AIRSOUT
BIASING
BIASSED
BIGSHOT
BITSIER
DIESELS
DIESOFF
DIESOUT
DIGSOUT
DISSECT
DISSENT
DISSING
DITSIER
FIASCOS
FIESTAS
FIRSTLY
FISSILE
FISSION
FISSURE
GINSENG
GIPSIES
HIMSELF
HIPSTER
HIRSUTE
HISSERS
HISSING
HITSOUT
JIGSAWS
KIDSKIN
KINSHIP
KINSMAN
KINSMEN
KIRSTIE
KISSERS
KISSING
KISSOFF
KITSCHY
LIESLOW
LINSEED
LIPSYNC
LISSOME
MIASMAS
MIASMIC
MIDSIZE
MISSAID
MISSALS
MISSAYS
MISSIES
MISSILE
MISSING
MISSION
MISSISH
MISSIVE
MISSOUT
MISSTEP
NILSSON
OILSKIN
PIASTER
PIASTRE
PIGSKIN
PIGSOUT
PILSNER
PITSAWS
PITSTOP
RIMSHOT
RINSING
RIPSAWS
RIPSOFF
RIPSOUT
RISSOLE
SIESTAS
SISSIES
SITSOUT
TINSELS
TINSTAR
TIPSIER
TIPSILY
TIPSOFF
TIPSTER
TISSUES
VIZSLAS
WIGSOUT
WINSLOW
WINSOME
WINSOUT
WINSTON

•I••S••

BIASSED
BIGOSES
BINDSUP
DIGESTS
DINESEN
DINESIN
DINESON
DISUSED
DIVESIN
DIVESTS
DIVISOR
FICUSES
FILLSIN
FILLSUP
FINESSE
FIRESUP
FIRMSUP
FIXESUP
GIRASOL
GIVESIN
GIVESTO
GIVESUP
HIKESUP
HINTSAT
HIRESON
KICKSIN
KICKSUP
LIAISED
LIAISES
LIAISON
LIFTSUP
LINDSAY
LINDSEY
LINESUP
LIVESIN
LIVESON
MILKSOP
MIMESIS
MIMOSAS
MINDSET
MINUSES
MISUSED
MISUSES
MITOSES
MITOSIS
MIXESIN
MIXESUP
NICOSIA
NIELSEN
NILSSON
PICASSO
PICKSAT
PICKSON
PICKSUP
PILESIN
PILESON
PILESUP
PIMESON
PINESAP
PIOUSLY
PIPESUP
RICKSHA
RILESUP
RINGSUP
RIPOSTE
SIGNSIN
SIGNSON
SIGNSUP
SILESIA
SIMPSON
SINGSTO
SINKSIN
SINUSES
SIZESUP
TIMESUP
VIRUSES
WILLSON
WINDSOR
WINDSUP
WINESAP
WINGSIT
WINKSAT
WIPESUP
WISESUP

•I•••S•

AIDLESS
AIMLESS
AIRBASE
AIRIEST
AIRKISS
AIRLESS
AIRMASS
BIBLESS
BIGGEST
BIGGISH
BIGNESS
BIOMASS
BITLESS
CIRCUSY
DICIEST
DIFFUSE
DIGRESS
DIMMEST
DIMNESS
DIOCESE
DISCUSS
DISEASE
DISGUST
DISMISS
DISPOSE
DIVERSE
FINESSE
FINNISH
FIRMEST
FITNESS
FITTEST
GIRLISH
HIGHEST
HIPLESS
HIPNESS
HIPPEST
HITLESS
HITLIST
JIGGISH
JIVIEST
KIDDISH
KINDEST
KINLESS
LICENSE
LIDLESS
LIMIEST
LIMPEST
LINIEST
LIONESS
LIONISE
LIPLESS
LITHEST
MIDEAST
MIDMOST
MIDRISE
MIDWEST
MILDEST
MINXISH
MIRIEST
MISCAST
MISSISH
NIGHEST
OILIEST
OILLESS
PIANISM
PIANIST
PICASSO
PICTISH
PIETISM
PIETIST
PIGGISH
PINIEST
PINKEST
PINKISH
PINLESS
PIPIEST
PITBOSS
PIXYISH
RIBLESS
RICHEST
RIMIEST
RIMLESS
SIAMESE
SICKEST
SICKISH
SIKHISM
SINLESS
TIDIEST
TIELESS
TIGRESS
TIGRISH
TINIEST
TIPLESS
TITLIST
VINIEST
VIOLIST
WIGLESS
WILDEST
WILDISH
WILIEST
WIMPISH
WINIEST
WIRIEST
WITLESS
WITNESS
YIDDISH

•I••••S

AIDLESS
AIGRETS
AIMLESS
AIRBAGS
AIRDAMS
AIRGUNS
AIRINGS
AIRKISS
AIRLESS
AIRMASS
AIRSACS
AIRWAYS
AITCHES
BIALIES
BIBLESS
BICKERS
BIDDERS
BIDDIES
BIGBOYS
BIGEYES
BIGGERS
BIGGIES
BIGGUNS
BIGLIES
BIGNESS
BIGOSES
BIGTOES
BIGTOPS
BIGWIGS
BIKINIS
BILBIES
BILBOES
BILIOUS
BILLETS
BILLIES
BILLOWS
BINDERS
BINGOES
BIOMASS
BIONICS
BIRCHES
BIRDERS
BIRDIES
BIREMES
BISECTS
BISHOPS
BISQUES
BISTROS
BITLESS
BITMAPS
BITTERS
CICADAS
CINCHES
CINDERS
CINEMAS
CIPHERS
CIRCLES
CIRQUES
CITRONS
CITROUS
CIVVIES
DIADEMS
DIALERS
DIALOGS
DIAPERS
DIARIES
DIATOMS
DIBBLES
DICKENS
DICKERS
DICKEYS
DICKIES
DICTUMS
DIDACTS
DIDDLES
DIESELS
DIETERS
DIFFERS
DIGESTS
DIGGERS
DIGRAMS
DIGRESS
DIKDIKS
DIKTATS
DILATES
DILLIES
DILUTES
DIMMERS
DIMNESS
DIMOUTS
DIMPLES
DIMWITS
DINGLES
DINGOES
DINKIES
DINNERS
DIPOLES
DIPPERS
DIRECTS
DIRNDLS
DIRTIES
DISARMS
DISBARS
DISCUSS
DISMAYS
DISMISS
DISOWNS
DISPELS
DISTILS
DITCHES
DITHERS
DITTIES
DIVERTS
DIVESTS
DIVIDES
DIVINES
DIVVIES
DIZZIES
EIGHTHS
FIACRES
FIANCES
FIASCOS
FIBBERS
FIBRILS
FIBRINS
FIBROUS
FIBULAS
FICUSES
FIDDLES
FIDELIS
FIDGETS
FIENNES
FIESTAS
FIFTIES
FIGURES
FIJIANS
FILCHES
FILENES
FILINGS
FILLERS
FILLETS
FILLIES
FILLINS
FILLIPS
FILLUPS
FILTERS
FINALES
FINCHES
FINDERS
FINGERS
FINIALS
FIPPLES
FIRINGS
FIRKINS
FISHERS
FITCHES
FITNESS
FITTERS
FIXATES
FIXINGS
FIZGIGS
FIZZLES
GIBBERS
GIBBETS
GIBBONS
GIBBOUS
GIBLETS
GIBLUES
GIDEONS
GIGGLES
GIGOLOS
GILBLAS
GILDERS
GILGUYS
GILLIES
GIMBALS
GIMLETS
GINGERS
GIPSIES
GIRDERS
GIRDLES
GIVEUPS
HICCUPS
HIDEOUS
HIDINGS
HIGGINS
HIGGLES
HIJACKS
HIJINKS
HINDERS
HINNIES
HIPLESS
HIPNESS
HIPPIES
HISSERS
HITCHES
HITLESS
HITTERS
JICAMAS
JIFFIES
JIGGERS
JIGGLES
JIGSAWS
JIMJAMS
JIMMIES
JINGLES
JINGOES
JITNEYS
JITTERS
KIBBLES
KICKERS
KICKUPS
KIDDERS
KIDDIES
KIDNAPS
KIDNEYS
KIKUYUS
KILLERS
KILTIES
KIMONOS
KINDLES
KINEMAS
KINLESS
KIPPERS
KIRMANS
KIRTLES
KISHKES
KISSERS
KITBAGS
KITTENS
KITTIES
KIWANIS
LIAISES
LIBBERS
LIBIDOS
LIBYANS
LICHENS
LICTORS
LIDLESS
LIENEES
LIERNES
LIFTERS
LIGANDS
LIGATES
LIMBERS
LIMNERS
LIMOGES
LIMPETS
LINAGES
LINDENS
LINDIES
LINEUPS
LINGERS
LINGOES
LININGS
LINKERS
LINKUPS
LINNETS
LINTELS
LIONESS
LIONETS
LIPIDES
LIPLESS
LIQUIDS
LIQUORS
LISTEES
LISTELS
LISTENS
LITCHIS
LITOTES
LITTERS
LIVINGS
LIZARDS
MIAMIAS
MIASMAS
MICKEYS
MICMACS
MICRONS
MIDDAYS
MIDDENS
MIDDIES
MIDDLES
MIDGETS
MIDRIBS
MIDWAYS
MIGGLES
MIKADOS
MILDEWS
MILIEUS
MILKERS
MILLERS
MILLETS
MILORDS
MIMESIS
MIMOSAS
MINCERS
MINDERS
MINGLES
MINIBUS
MINIONS
MINNOWS
MINOANS
MINTERS
MINUETS
MINUSES
MINUTES
MINYANS
MIRAGES
MIRRORS
MISCUES
MISDOES
MISFITS
MISHAPS
MISHITS
MISLAYS
MISSALS
MISSAYS
MISSIES
MISTERS
MISUSES
MITHRAS
MITOSES
MITOSIS
MITTENS
MIZZENS
MIZZLES
NIBBLES
NICHOLS
NICKELS
NICKERS
NICOLAS
NIGGLES
NIMRODS
NINNIES
NIPPERS
NITROUS
NITWITS
OILCANS
OILLESS
OILPANS
OILRIGS
PIAZZAS
PICAROS
PICKENS
PICKERS
PICKETS
PICKLES
PICKUPS
PICNICS
PIDGINS
PIECERS
PIEPANS
PIERCES
PIETIES
PIETINS
PIFFLES
PIGEONS
PIGGIES
PIGLETS
PIGNUTS
PIGPENS
PILEUPS
PILFERS
PILINGS
PILLARS
PILLOWS
PINATAS
PINCERS
PINCHAS
PINCHES
PINIONS
PINKIES
PINLESS
PINNERS
PINOAKS
PINONES
PIOLETS
PIPINGS
PIPKINS
PIPPINS
PIRAEUS
PIRATES
PISTILS
PISTOLS
PISTONS
PITBOSS
PITCHES
PITEOUS
PITIERS
PITSAWS
PITTERS
QINTARS
QIVIUTS
RIBANDS
RIBBIES
RIBBONS
RIBEYES
RIBLESS
RICKEYS
RICKLES
RIDDLES
RIFFLES
RIFLERS
RIGGERS
RIGOURS
RILLETS
RIMLESS
RIMPLES
RINGERS
RIOTERS
RIOTOUS
RIPOFFS
RIPPERS
RIPPLES
RIPRAPS
RIPSAWS
RISINGS
RISKERS
RITUALS
SICKENS
SICKLES
SIDINGS
SIENNAS
SIERRAS
SIESTAS
SIFTERS
SIGHERS
SIGNALS
SIGNEES
SIGNERS
SIGNETS
SILENTS
SILICAS
SILLIES
SILVERS
SIMIANS
SIMILES
SIMMERS
SIMMONS
SIMPERS
SINGERS
SINGLES
SINKERS
SINLESS
SINNERS
SINUOUS
SINUSES
SIOUANS
SIPHONS
SIPPERS
SIPPETS
SISKINS
SISSIES
SISTERS
SITCOMS
SITTERS
SIXGUNS
SIXTIES
SIZINGS
SIZZLES
TICKERS
TICKETS
TICKLES
TICTACS
TIDBITS
TIDINGS
TIEDYES
TIELESS
TIEPINS
TIERODS
TIFFINS
TIGLONS
TIGRESS
TILINGS
TILLERS
TILTERS
TIMBALS
TIMBERS
TIMBRES
TIMINGS
TIMMINS
TINCANS
TINDERS
TINEARS
TINGLES
TINHATS
TINKERS
TINKLES
TINNERS
TINSELS
TINTERS
TIPLESS
TIPOFFS
TIPPERS
TIPPETS
TIPPLES
TIPTOES
TIPTOPS
TIRADES
TISANES
TISSUES
TITBITS
TITFERS
TITHERS
TITTERS
TITTLES
TITTUPS
TIZZIES
VICIOUS
VICTIMS
VICTORS
VICUNAS
VIEWERS
VIGOURS
VIKINGS
VILNIUS
VIOLETS
VIOLINS
VIRAGOS
VIRGINS
VIRIBUS
VIRTUES
VIRUSES
VISAGES
VISAVIS
VISCOUS
VISIONS
VISUALS
VITTLES
VIZIERS
VIZSLAS
WICKERS
WICKETS
WIDGETS
WIENERS
WIENIES
WIGGLES
WIGLESS
WIGLETS
WIGWAGS
WIGWAMS
WILLETS
WILLIES
WILLOWS
WIMBLES
WIMPLES
WINCERS
WINCHES
WINDERS
WINDOWS
WINDUPS
WINGERS
WINKERS
WINKLES
WINNERS
WINNOWS
WINTERS
WISHERS
WITCHES
WITHERS
WITHIES
WITLESS
WITNESS
WIZARDS
ZIGZAGS
ZILCHES
ZINGERS
ZINNIAS
ZIPPERS
ZIRCONS
ZITHERS

••IS•••

AMISTAD
ANISEED
ANISTON
APISHLY
ARISING
ARISTAE
ARISTAS
ARISTOS
ATISSUE
BLISTER
BRISKER
BRISKET
BRISKLY
BRISTLE
BRISTLY
BRISTOL
CAISSON
CHISELS
CRISPED
CRISPER
CRISPIN
CRISPLY
CRISPUS
CUISINE
DAISIES
DRISTAN
ELISION
ENISLED
ENISLES
EPISODE
EPISTLE
ERISTIC
EXISTED
FOISTED
FRISBEE
FRISIAN
FRISKED
FRISSON
GEISHAS
GLISTEN
GRISHAM
GRISKIN
GRISSOM
GRISTLE
GRISTLY
HEISMAN
HEISTED
HOISTED
IRISOUT
JOISTED
KAISERS

KAISHEK
KNISHES
KRISHNA
LAISSEZ
LEISTER
LEISURE
MEISSEN
MEISTER
MOISTEN
MOISTER
MOISTLY
NOISIER
NOISILY
NOISING
NOISOME
ORISONS
OVISACS
PAISANO
PAISLEY
POISING
POISONS
POISSON
PRISONS
RAISERS
RAISEUP
RAISING
RAISINS
REISSUE
ROISTER
SCISSOR
SEISMIC
SKISUIT
SWISHED
SWISHES
THISTLE
THISTLY
TRISECT
TRISHAW
TRISTAN
TRISTAR
TWISTED
TWISTER
UNISONS
WHISHED
WHISHES
WHISKED
WHISKER
WHISKEY
WHISPER
WHISTLE
MEIOSES
MEIOSIS
MEISSEN
NAILSET
NAILSIN
PAIRSUP
POISSON
PRIESTS
RAILSAT
REINSIN
REISSUE
SCISSOR
SLIPSIN
SLIPSON
SLIPSUP
SPIESON
STIRSIN
STIRSUP
SUITSUP
THIRSTS
THIRSTY
TRIESON
TRIESTE
TRIPSUP
WAITSON
WAITSUP
WHIPSAW
WHIPSUP
BLITZES
BOILERS
BRIARDS
BRIDALS
BRIDGES
BRIDLES
BRITONS
CAIMANS
CAIQUES
CHIDERS
CHIGOES
CHILIES
CHINUPS
CHISELS
CLICHES
CLIENTS
CLINICS
CLIPONS
CLIQUES
COINERS
CRINGES
CRISPUS
CRITICS
CUIRASS
DAILIES
DAIMONS
DAIRIES
DAISIES
DEICERS
DEIFIES
DEITIES
DOILIES
DRIVELS
DRIVERS
EDIBLES
EDIFIES
EDITORS
ELICITS
ELIXIRS
EMIGRES
ENIGMAS
ENISLES
EPILOGS
EVINCES
FAIRIES
FLIGHTS
FLIPUPS
FOIBLES
FRIDAYS
FRIDGES
FRIENDS
FRIEZES
FRIGHTS
FRINGES
FRIZZES
GAINERS
GAITERS
GEISHAS
GLIDERS
GLITZES
GRIEVES
GRIGRIS
GRILLES
GRIPERS
GRIVETS
GUIDONS
GUIMPES
GUINEAS
GUITARS
HAIRDOS
HEIFERS
HEIGHTS
HEINOUS
HEIRESS
ICICLES
ICINESS
JAILERS
JOINERS
JUICERS
KAISERS
KNIGHTS
KNISHES
LOITERS
MAIDENS
MAILERS
MAITAIS
MEINIES
MEIOSES
MEIOSIS
MOILERS
NAIADES
NAILERS
OHIOANS
OJIBWAS
OMINOUS
OPIATES
OPINERS
ORIENTS
ORIGINS
ORIOLES
ORISONS
OVISACS
PAILOUS
PAIUTES
PHIDIAS
PHINEAS
PLIGHTS
PLINTHS
POISONS
PRICERS
PRIESTS
PRIMERS
PRINCES
PRISONS
PRIVETS
PRIVIES
QUICHES
QUINCES
QUINOAS
QUIVERS
QUIZZES
RAIDERS
RAILERS
RAISERS
RAISINS
REIFIES
RUINERS
RUINOUS
SAILORS
SEICHES
SEIDELS
SEINERS
SEIZERS
SHIELDS
SHIITES
SHINERS
SHIVERS
SKIBOBS
SKIRUNS
SKITOWS
SKIVERS
SLICERS
SLIDERS
SLIGHTS
SLIPONS
SLIPUPS
SLIVERS
SMILERS
SNIPERS
SNIVELS
SOIREES
SPIDERS
SPIGOTS
SPIKERS
SPINELS
SPINETS
SPIRALS
SPIREAS
SPIRITS
SPITZES
STICHES
STIFLES
STIGMAS
STINGOS
SUITORS
SWIPERS
SWISHES
SWIVELS
SWIVETS
TAILLES
TAILORS
TAIPANS
THIEVES
THIRSTS
TOILERS
TOILETS
TRICEPS
TRICOTS
TRIFLES
TRIGONS
TRIJETS
TRIODES
TRIPLES
TRIPODS
TRITONS
TRIUNES
TRIVETS
TWINGES
UNIFIES
UNIPODS
UNISONS
UNITERS
UNITIES
VEIGHTS
WAILERS
WAITERS
WAIVERS
WEIGHTS
WEIRDOS
WHINERS
WHISHES
WHITENS
WHIZZES
WRIGHTS
WRITERS
WRITHES

••I•S••

ALIASES
ARIOSOS
ARIOSTO
ATISSUE
CAISSON
CHIPSIN
COILSUP
CRIMSON
DRIESUP
ERICSON
FAIRSUP
FLIESAT
FLIESIN
FRISSON
GAINSAY
GAINSON
GRISSOM
ILIESCU
JOINSIN
JOINSUP
LAISSEZ
MAILSIN

••I••S•

ADIPOSE
ANIMISM
ANIMIST
ARIDEST
BRINISH
BRITISH
CHINESE
CUIRASS
ELITISM
ELITIST
EVILEST
FAIREST
FAIRISH
GLIMPSE
HEIRESS
ICINESS
MAIDISH
OMIGOSH
OXIDASE
OXIDISE
SHIATSU
SKIMASK
SNIDEST
SWINISH
TBILISI
TRITEST
UTILISE
VAINEST
WHITEST
WHITISH

••I•••S

ALIASES
ALIGHTS
ANIMALS
ARIOSOS
ARISTAS
ARISTOS
AVIATES
BAILEES
BAILERS
BAILEYS
BAILORS
BLIGHTS

•••IS••

ADDISON
ADVISED
ADVISER
ADVISES
ADVISOR
AGEISTS
ALLISON
AORISTS
ARRISES
ARTISAN
ARTISTE
ARTISTS
ASSISTS
BATISTA
BATISTE
BENISON
BETISES
BRAISED
BRAISES
BRUISED
BRUISER
BRUISES
CAMISES
CHAISES
CHRISMS
CHRISTI
CHRISTO
CHRISTY
CRUISED
CRUISER
CRUISES
CUBISTS
DEHISCE
DELISTS
DEMISED
DEMISES
DESISTS
DEVISED
DEVISES
DIVISOR
DREISER
EGOISTS
ELEISON
ELLISON
ELMISTI
ENLISTS
EXCISED
EXCISES
FRAISES
HOLISTS
INCISED
INCISES
INCISOR
INSISTS
IODISED
IODISES
IONISED
IONISES
JALISCO
JEWISON
JURISTS
LEGISTS
LIAISED
LIAISES
LIAISON
LORISES
LUTISTS
LYRISTS
MADISON
MAOISTS
MATISSE
MELISSA
MENISCI
MODISTE
NABISCO
NUDISTS
OBOISTS
ORBISON
PELISSE
PRAISED
PRAISER
PRAISES
PURISTS
RELISTS
RESISTS
REVISED
REVISER
REVISES
REVISIT
SAMISEN
SATISFY
SCHISMS
SEXISTS
SQUISHY
TAOISTS
THEISTS
TRUISMS
TUBISTS
TUNISIA
TYPISTS
UNWISER
UPRISEN
UPRISES
VALISES
VENISON
VERISMO
WOEISME

•••I•S•

ACHIEST
AERIEST
AGAINST
AIRIEST
ARTIEST
ASHIEST
ATHIRST
BONIEST
BOXIEST
BUSIEST
CAGIEST
CAKIEST
CANIEST
COKIEST
COSIEST
COZIEST
DICIEST
DOPIEST
DOZIEST
EASIEST
ECLIPSE
EDGIEST
EELIEST
EERIEST
EGGIEST
ELLIPSE
FOXIEST
FUJITSU
FUMIEST
GAMIEST
GLUIEST
GOOIEST
GORIEST
HAZIEST
HOKIEST
HOLIEST
HOMIEST
ICKIEST
IFFIEST
INKIEST
JIVIEST
JOKIEST
JUJITSU
LACIEST
LAKIEST
LAZIEST
LIMIEST
LINIEST
LOGIEST
MATISSE
MAZIEST
MELISSA
MIRIEST
MOPIEST
NOSIEST
OILIEST
OOZIEST
PALIEST
PELISSE
PINIEST
PIPIEST
POKIEST
PUNIEST
RACIEST
RERINSE
RIMIEST
ROPIEST
ROSIEST
SEXIEST
SPRIEST
TIDIEST
TINIEST
TONIEST
TRAIPSE
TYPIEST
UGLIEST
VINIEST
WANIEST
WARIEST
WAVIEST
WAXIEST
WILIEST
WINIEST
WIRIEST
ZANIEST

•••I••S

ACTIONS
ACTIVES
ADMIRES
ADMIXES
ADVISES
AEDILES
AERIALS
AFFINES
AFFIRMS
AFFIXES
AGEISTS
AIRINGS
ALBINOS
ALGIERS
AMNIONS
ANOINTS
ANTIBES
ANXIOUS
AORISTS
APSIDES
AQUINAS
ARGIVES
ARNICAS
ARRISES
ARRIVES
ARTISTS
ASPIRES
ASSIGNS
ASSISTS
ASSIZES
ATRIUMS
ATTICUS
ATTIMES
ATTIRES
AUDILES
AWNINGS
BELIEFS
BEMIRES
BESIDES
BETIDES
BETIMES
BETISES
BEZIERS
BIKINIS
BILIOUS
BODICES
BOLIDES
BONITOS
BOVINES
BRAISES
BRUISES
BUNIONS
BYLINES
CAHIERS
CALICES
CALICOS
CALIPHS
CAMISES
CANINES
CARIBES
CARINAS
CASINGS
CASINOS
CATIONS
CAVIARS
CERIPHS
CHAISES
CHOICES
CHRISMS
CODICES
COMINGS
COPIERS
COPIOUS
COSIGNS
COSINES
CRUISES
CUBISTS
CURIOUS
DANIELS
DECIDES
DEFILES
DEFINES
DELIBES
DELICTS
DELISTS
DEMISES
DENIALS
DENIERS
DEPICTS
DERIDES
DERIVES
DESIGNS
DESIRES
DESISTS
DEVICES
DEVIOUS
DEVISES
DIVIDES
DIVINES
DOMINOS
DOMINUS
DONIMUS
DORITOS
DOSIDOS
DUBIOUS
ECHINUS
EDGINGS
EGOISTS
ELOIGNS
EMPIRES
ENCINAS
ENDINGS
ENDIVES
ENGINES
ENGIRDS
ENLISTS
ENSIGNS
ENSILES
ENTICES
ENVIERS
ENVIOUS
EOLITHS
EQUINES
ERMINES
ESKIMOS
ESPIALS
ETOILES
EXCISES
EXCITES
EXPIRES
EXWIVES
FACIALS
FACINGS
FAJITAS
FAMINES
FANIONS
FELINES
FENIANS
FIJIANS
FILINGS
FINIALS
FIRINGS
FIXINGS
FORINTS
FRAISES
FURIOUS
GAMINES
GAVIALS
HALIDES
HALITES
HAMITES
HAZINGS
HEGIRAS
HELICES
HELIXES
HIDINGS
HIJINKS
HOLISTS
HOSIERS
IGNITES
IMBIBES
IMMIXES
IMPIOUS
INCISES
INCITES
INDIANS
INDICES
INDICTS
INDIGOS
INDITES
INNINGS
INSIDES
INSISTS
INVITES
IODIDES
IODISES
IODIZES
IONISES
IONIZES
JABIRUS
JUNIORS
JURISTS
KODIAKS
KYLIKES
LABIALS
LACINGS
LADINOS
LAMINAS
LARIATS
LATICES
LATINAS
LATINOS
LEGIONS
LEGISTS
LEVIERS
LEVITES
LIAISES
LIBIDOS
LININGS
LIPIDES
LIVINGS
LORISES
LOTIONS
LUPINES
LUTISTS
LYRISTS
MAKINGS
MALIGNS
MANIACS
MANIOCS
MAOISTS
MARINAS
MARINES
MAXIMUS
MEDIANS
MEDICOS
MEDIUMS
MENIALS
MERINOS
METIERS
MILIEUS
MINIBUS
MINIONS
MOBILES
MOTIONS
MOTIVES
MYRIADS
NATIONS
NATIVES
NOTICES
NOTIONS
NOVICES
NOXIOUS
NUBIANS
NUDISTS
OBLIGES
OBOISTS
OBVIOUS
OEDIPUS
OFFICES
OMNIBUS
ONEIDAS
ONSIDES
OOLITES
OOLITHS
OPHITES
OPTIONS
ORDINES
ORPINES
OSCINES
OUTINGS
PARIAHS
PARINGS
PATINAS
PERIODS
PETITES
PILINGS
PINIONS
PIPINGS
PITIERS
PLAICES
PLAINTS
PODIUMS
POLICES
POTIONS
PRAISES
PUMICES
PURISTS
PYRITES
PYXIDES
QIVIUTS
RADIALS
RADIANS
RADICES
RADIXES
RAPIERS
RAPINES
RATINGS
RATIONS
RATITES
RAVINES
RAVINGS
REBINDS
RECIPES
RECITES
REDIALS
REFILES
REFILLS
REFILMS
REFINES
REFIRES
REGIMES
REGIONS
REHIRES
RELICTS
RELIEFS
RELINES
RELISTS
RELIVES
REMIGES
REMINDS
REMIXES
REPINES
RESIDES
RESIGNS
RESILES
RESINGS
RESISTS
RETILES
RETIMES
RETINAS
RETIRES
REVIEWS
REVILES
REVISES
REVIVES
REWINDS
REWIRES
RISINGS
RULINGS
RUPIAHS
SABINES
SALINAS
SAMITES
SAPIENS
SATIRES
SAVINGS
SAVIORS
SAYINGS
SCHISMS
SCRIBES
SCRIMPS
SCRIPPS
SCRIPTS
SEMITES
SENIORS
SERIALS
SERIOUS
SEXISTS
SHEIKHS
SHEILAS
SHIITES
SHRIEKS
SHRIFTS
SHRIKES
SHRILLS
SHRIMPS
SHRINES
SHRINKS
SHRIVES
SHTICKS
SIDINGS
SILICAS
SIMIANS
SIMILES
SIZINGS
SLEIGHS
SLUICES
SOCIALS
SORITES
SOVIETS
SPLICES
SPLINES
SPLINTS
SPRINGS
SPRINTS
SPRITES
SQUILLS
SQUINTS
SQUIRES
SQUIRMS
SQUIRTS
STKITTS
STRIDES
STRIKES
STRINGS
STRIPES
STRIVES
SYRIANS
TACITUS
TAOISTS
TAPINGS
TARIFFS
TEDIOUS
TEDIUMS
THEISTS
THRIFTS
THRILLS
THRIVES
TIDINGS
TILINGS
TIMINGS
TROIKAS
TROILUS
TRUISMS
TSHIRTS
TUBISTS
TYPISTS
ULTIMAS
UMPIRES
UNBINDS
UNCIALS
UNGIRDS
UNKINKS
UNLINKS
UNPILES
UNWINDS
UPLIFTS
UPLINKS
UPRISES
UPTICKS
VALISES
VARIOUS
VERITAS
VICIOUS
VIKINGS
VIRIBUS
VISIONS
VIZIERS
WAHINES
WAPITIS
WRAITHS
YAKIMAS
ZENITHS
ZODIACS

••••IS•

ABOLISH
AGONISE
AGONIST
AIRKISS
ANIMISM
ANIMIST
ANODISE
APPRISE
ATAVISM
ATAVIST
ATHEISM
ATHEIST
ATOMISE
BABYISH
BADDISH
BALDISH
BAPTISE
BAPTISM
BAPTIST
BARDISH
BASSIST
BEAMISH
BEARISH
BEAUISH
BIGGISH
BLEMISH
BLUEISH
BOARISH
BOGGISH
BOOKISH
BOORISH
BRINISH
BRITISH
BRUTISH
BULLISH
BURNISH
CADDISH
CATFISH
CATTISH
CELLIST
CHEMISE
CHEMIST
CHERISH
CLAYISH
CLERISY
COCHISE
COCKISH
CODFISH
COEXIST
COLDISH
COLTISH
CONCISE
CONSIST
COOLISH
COPYIST
CORNISH
CRONISH

CUBBISH
CULTISH
CULTISM
CULTIST
CURRISH
CURTISS
CYCLIST
CZARISM
CZARIST
DADAISM
DADAIST
DAMPISH
DARKISH
DAWKISH
DELUISE
DENTIST
DERVISH
DESPISE
DISMISS
DOGFISH
DOGGISH
DOLLISH
DOLTISH
DONNISH
DRONISH
DUELIST
DULLISH
DUMPISH
DUNCISH
DUSKISH
EGOTISM
EGOTIST
ELEGIST
ELITISM
ELITIST
ENDWISE
ENGLISH
EPEEIST
EVANISH
FADDISH
FADDISM
FADDIST
FAIRISH
FATTISH
FAUVISM
FAUVIST
FINNISH
FLEMISH
FLORIST
FLUTIST
FLYFISH
FOGYISH
FOGYISM
FOLKISH
FOOLISH
FOPPISH
FURBISH
FURNISH
GARNISH
GAULISH
GAWKISH
GIRLISH
GNOMISH
GOATISH
GOODISH
GOUTISH
GRAYISH
GREYISH
HAGGISH
HARPIST
HAWKISH
HELLISH
HELOISE
HENNISH

HEROISM
HITLIST
HOGGISH
HORNISH
HORNIST
HUFFISH
HUNNISH
IDOLISE
ITEMISE
JIGGISH
JUDAISM
JUDOIST
KADDISH
KENTISH
KIDDISH
KNAVISH
KURDISH
LADDISH
LADYISH
LAMAISM
LAMAIST
LAPPISH
LARGISH
LARKISH
LAZYISH
LEFTIST
LETTISH
LIONISE
LOGGISH
LONGISH
LOUDISH
LOUTISH
LOWRISE
LUMPISH
MADDISH
MAIDISH
MALAISE
MANNISH
MARXISM
MARXIST
MAWKISH
MIDRISE
MINXISH
MISSISH
MOBBISH
MONKISH
MOONISH
MOORISH
MORTISE
NAGGISH
NEBBISH
NOURISH
OBELISK
OCULIST
OGREISH
OLEMISS
OXIDISE
PACHISI
PALMIST
PANFISH
PARRISH
PAULIST
PEAKISH
PECKISH
PEEVISH
PELTISH
PERKISH
PERSIST
PETTISH
PIANISM
PIANIST
PICTISH
PIETISM
PIETIST

PIGGISH
PINKISH
PIXYISH
PLANISH
POLOIST
POORISH
PORKISH
PRECISE
PREMISE
PREMISS
PROMISE
PROTIST
PROVISO
PRUDISH
PUBLISH
PUCKISH
PUGGISH
QUERIST
RAFFISH
RAMMISH
RANKISH
RASPISH
RATTISH
REALISE
REALISM
REALIST
REDDISH
REPRISE
RERAISE
RHENISH
ROGUISH
ROMPISH
RUBBISH
RUNTISH
RUTTISH
SALTISH
SAWFISH
SELFISH
SICKISH
SIKHISM
SLAVISH
SOFTISH
SOLOIST
SOPHISM
SOPHIST
SOTTISH
SOURISH
SPANISH
STATIST
STYLISE
STYLISH
STYLIST
SUBSIST
SUNFISH
SUNKIST
SUNRISE
SURMISE
SWEDISH
SWINISH
TALLISH
TANNISH
TARNISH
TARTISH
TBILISI
TIGRISH
TITLIST
TOADISH
TONNISH
TORYISH
TORYISM
TOURISM
TOURIST
TOWNISH
TROPISM

TSARIST
TUBAIST
TURKISH
UNTWIST
UPRAISE
UTILISE
VAMPISH
VARNISH
VIOLIST
VOGUISH
WAGGISH
WANNISH
WARMISH
WASPISH
WEAKISH
WENDISH
WETTISH
WHEYISH
WHITISH
WILDISH
WIMPISH
WOLFISH
WORMISH
YERKISH
YIDDISH
YORKIST
ZANYISH

••••I•S

ACACIAS
ACARIDS
ACQUITS
ADAGIOS
ADJOINS
AFFAIRS
AGARICS
AIRKISS
AMBRIES
ANANIAS
ANOMIES
APERIES
APPLIES
ARMPITS
ASSAILS
ATOMIES
ATONIES
ATTAINS
ATTRITS
AUNTIES
AUPAIRS
AUSSIES
BADDIES
BAGGIES
BANDIES
BANDITS
BARRIOS
BEANIES
BELLIES
BERRIES
BESTIRS
BEWAILS
BIALIES
BIDDIES
BIGGIES
BIGLIES
BIGWIGS
BILBIES
BILLIES
BIONICS
BIRDIES
BMOVIES
BOBBIES
BOBBINS
BODKINS

BOFFINS
BOOBIES
BOOGIES
BOOKIES
BOONIES
BOOTIES
BOWFINS
BOWTIES
BUDDIES
BUDGIES
BUGGIES
BULLIES
BUNNIES
BUNYIPS
BUSBIES
BUSKINS
BUTTIES
CABBIES
CADDIES
CALKINS
CALLINS
CANDIDS
CANDIES
CAPSIDS
CARNIES
CARRIES
CASSIAS
CASSIUS
CATKINS
CATNIPS
CAVEINS
CELSIUS
CELTICS
CERVIDS
CHEVIES
CHILIES
CIVVIES
CLERICS
CLINICS
COEDITS
COHEIRS
COLLIES
COLLINS
COMFITS
COMMITS
CONOIDS
COOKIES
COOTIES
COUSINS
COWRIES
CRAZIES
CREDITS
CRETINS
CRITICS
CRONIES
CUBBIES
CUDDIES
CULLIES
CURRIES
CURTISS
CUSPIDS
DADDIES
DAHLIAS
DAILIES
DAIRIES
DAISIES
DALLIES
DANDIES
DARBIES
DEARIES
DECEITS
DECRIES
DEIFIES
DEITIES

DERAILS
DERBIES
DETAILS
DETAINS
DEVEINS
DEVRIES
DIARIES
DICKIES
DIKDIKS
DILLIES
DIMWITS
DINKIES
DIRTIES
DISMISS
DISTILS
DITTIES
DIVVIES
DIZZIES
DOBBIES
DOBBINS
DOGGIES
DOGSITS
DOILIES
DOLLIES
DOMAINS
DOOZIES
DOWRIES
DROPINS
DUCHIES
DUMMIES
DUNLINS
EARWIGS
EBONIES
ECLAIRS
EDIFIES
ELAPIDS
ELEGIES
ELICITS
ELIXIRS
EMPTIES
ENEMIES
ENJOINS
ENSKIES
ENTAILS
ENTRIES
EPOXIES
ETHNICS
EXOTICS
EYELIDS
FABRICS
FADEINS
FAERIES
FAIRIES
FANCIES
FASCIAS
FELLIES
FERRIES
FIBRILS
FIBRINS
FIFTIES
FILLIES
FILLINS
FILLIPS
FIRKINS
FIZGIGS
FLORINS
FOLKIES
FOLLIES
FOODIES
FORBIDS
FORTIES
FORTIUS
FOSSILS
FROLICS

FULFILS
FUNNIES
FUSTICS
GAMBITS
GASKINS
GERBILS
GILLIES
GIPSIES
GLORIAS
GLORIES
GOALIES
GOBLINS
GODWITS
GOODIES
GOSSIPS
GOTHICS
GRACIAS
GRATIAS
GRAVIES
GROPIUS
GULLIES
GUNNIES
GUPPIES
GUSSIES
GYPSIES
HACKIES
HANKIES
HARPIES
HARRIES
HATPINS
HAWKINS
HEAVIES
HENBITS
HERMITS
HEROICS
HIGGINS
HINNIES
HIPPIES
HOAGIES
HOBBIES
HOBBITS
HOGTIES
HOLLIES
HOPKINS
HOSKINS
HOTLIPS
HOTTIPS
HUBBIES
HUGGINS
HURLIES
HURRIES
HUSKIES
HUSSIES
HYBRIDS
IMPAIRS
IMPLIES
INSTILS
INTUITS
IRONIES
ITALICS
IVORIES
JACKIES
JAGGIES
JEEBIES
JELLIES
JEMMIES
JENNIES
JERKINS
JESUITS
JETTIES
JIFFIES
JIMMIES
JOLLIES
JOSKINS

JUGGINS
JUNKIES
JUTTIES
KAFFIRS
KELPIES
KEWPIES
KIDDIES
KILTIES
KITTIES
LADDIES
LASSIES
LEADINS
LEFTIES
LENTILS
LEONIDS
LEPPIES
LINDIES
LIQUIDS
LOBBIES
LOCKINS
LOGGIAS
LOGGINS
LOLLIES
LONGIES
LOOBIES
LOONIES
LORRIES
LOVEINS
MADLIBS
MAGPIES
MALKINS
MARGINS
MARLINS
MARRIES
MARTINS
MASHIES
MASSIFS
MASTICS
MATHIAS
MEALIES
MEANIES
MEGRIMS
MEINIES
MEMOIRS
MENHIRS
MENZIES
MERCIES
METRICS
MIAMIAS
MIDDIES
MIDRIBS
MISFITS
MISHITS
MISSIES
MOGGIES
MOHAIRS
MOMMIES
MOSAICS
MRCHIPS
MUDDIES
MUDPIES
MUFFINS
MUMMIES
MUNTINS
MUSKIES
MUSLIMS
MUSLINS
MUZHIKS
MYSTICS
NANNIES
NAPKINS
NAPPIES
NAVVIES
NEDDIES

NEREIDS
NEWSIES
NINNIES
NITWITS
NOETICS
NOGGINS
NORDICS
NUBBINS
NUDNIKS
NUNCIOS
NUTRIAS
OBTAINS
OILRIGS
OLEFINS
OLEMISS
ORCHIDS
ORDAINS
ORIGINS
OUTBIDS
OUTFITS
OUTHITS
OUTWITS
PADDIES
PANDITS
PANSIES
PARRIES
PARTIES
PATSIES
PATTIES
PECTINS
PENCILS
PENNIES
PEONIES
PEPSINS
PERKINS
PERMITS
PERSIUS
PHIDIAS
PHOBIAS
PHOBICS
PHONICS
PHONIES
PHOTICS
PHYSICS
PICNICS
PIDGINS
PIETIES
PIETINS
PIGGIES
PINKIES
PIPKINS
PIPPINS
PISTILS
PLUGINS
POETICS
PONGIDS
PONTIUS
POPLINS
POPPIES
POPPINS
PORGIES
POSTITS
POTPIES
PRELIMS
PREMISS
PREXIES
PRIVIES
PROFITS
PROXIES
PUBLICS
PUFFINS
PULLINS
PULPITS
PUNDITS

PUNKIES
PUNTIES
PUPPIES
PURLINS
PUTTIES
PYGMIES
PYTHIAS
QUERIES
RABBITS
RAISINS
RALLIES
READIES
REBOILS
RECOILS
REDFINS
REDFIRS
REEDITS
REFRIES
REGAINS
REIFIES
REJOINS
REMAILS
REMAINS
RENAILS
RENNINS
REPAIRS
REPLIES
RESHIPS
RESPINS
RETAILS
RETAINS
RETRIES
RETRIMS
RIBBIES
ROADIES
ROBBINS
ROCKIES
ROLAIDS
ROLLINS
ROOKIES
ROOMIES
ROWDIES
RUBRICS
RUSTICS
SALLIES
SALVIAS
SANTIRS
SASSIES
SAYYIDS
SEQUINS
SHOOINS
SHUTINS
SILLIES
SISKINS
SISSIES
SIXTIES
SMOKIES
SODDIES
SOFFITS
SOFTIES
SORTIES
SPAVINS
SPECIES
SPIRITS
SPRAINS
STATICS
STEPINS
STOGIES
STORIES
STRAINS
STRAITS
STUDIES
STUDIOS
STYMIES

SUBMITS
SULKIES
SULLIES
SUMMITS
SUSLIKS
TABBIES
TACTICS
TAFFIES
TALKIES
TALLIES
TANNINS
TANSIES
TARPITS
TARRIES
TECHIES
TEDDIES
TELLIES
TENPINS
TERRIES
THEPITS
TIDBITS
TIEPINS
TIFFINS
TIMMINS
TITBITS
TIZZIES
TOADIES
TOCSINS
TODDIES
TOLLIES
TOMTITS
TONSILS
TOONIES
TOROIDS
TOWNIES
TROPICS
TUGRIKS
TUMMIES
TUNNIES
TURBITS
TURNIPS
TWOBITS
UNCOILS
UNIFIES
UNITIES
UNKNITS
UNVEILS
URCHINS
USERIDS
USURIES
UTOPIAS
VEERIES
VEGGIES
VESPIDS
VICTIMS
VILNIUS
VIOLINS
VIRGINS
WADDIES
WALKINS
WEARIES
WEDGIES
WEENIES
WEEPIES
WEEVILS
WELKINS
WESKITS
WIENIES
WILLIES
WITHIES
WOODIES
WOOKIES
WOOLIES
WORRIES

YORKIES
YUPPIES
ZINNIAS
ZOMBIES
ZOYSIAS

•••••IS

ABNAKIS
ADONAIS
AGOUTIS
ALKALIS
ARTEMIS
ASEPSIS
BIKINIS
BORZOIS
CETERIS
CHABLIS
CHAMOIS
CHASSIS
COEPTIS
CSLEWIS
DAPHNIS
DUKAKIS
ECDYSIS
EVENKIS
FIDELIS
FRANCIS
GELATIS
GENERIS
GENESIS
GENGHIS
GLOTTIS
GRIGRIS
HONORIS
JETSKIS
KABUKIS
KIWANIS
LITCHIS
MAHARIS
MAITAIS
MARQUIS
MAUROIS
MEIOSIS
MEMPHIS
MIMESIS
MITOSIS
MORANIS
NEMESIS
NEPALIS
NOKOMIS
OCTROIS
ONASSIS
OSMOSIS
PHYLLIS
POLARIS
QATARIS
SAFARIS
SALAMIS
SALUKIS
SANLUIS
SERAPIS
SOMALIS
STDENIS
STLOUIS
TATAMIS
THESPIS
TRAVOIS
TRELLIS
TSOURIS
VISAVIS
WAPITIS
YANQUIS
YEMENIS

IT•••••

ITALIAN
ITALICS
ITCHIER
ITCHING
ITEMISE
ITEMIZE
ITERANT
ITERATE
ITHACAN

I•T••••

INTAKES
INTEARS
INTEGER
INTEGRA
INTENDS
INTENSE
INTENTS
INTERIM
INTERNS
INTERSE
INTONED
INTONER
INTONES
INTROIT
INTRUDE
INTRUST
INTRUTH
INTUITS
IQTESTS
ISTHMUS

I••T•••

IFSTONE
IMITATE
INITIAL
INSTALL
INSTALS
INSTANT
INSTARS
INSTATE
INSTEAD
INSTEPS
INSTILL
INSTILS
INSTOCK
INSTORE
INSTYLE
INUTILE
IRATELY
IRATEST
ISOTOPE

I•••T••

ICEDTEA
IDEATED
IDEATES
IDENTIC
IDIOTIC
IGNITED
IGNITER
IGNITES
IMPETUS
IMPUTED
IMPUTES
INAPTER
INAPTLY
INASTEW
INCITED
INCITER
INCITES
INDITED
INDITES

INDUTCH
INEPTLY
INERTIA
INERTLY
INMATES
INPETTO
INVITED
INVITES
INVITRO
IODATES
IOMOTHS

I••••T•

IMAMATE
IMARETS
IMITATE
IMPACTS
IMPARTS
IMPASTO
IMPIETY
IMPORTS
IMPOSTS
INANITY
INCANTS
INCEPTS
INDENTS
INDEPTH
INDICTS
INDUCTS
INFANTA
INFANTS
INFECTS
INFESTS
INFLATE
INGESTS
INGRATE
INHASTE
INJECTS
INPETTO
INSECTS
INSERTS
INSISTS
INSPOTS
INSTATE
INSULTS
INTENTS
INTRUTH
INTUITS
INVENTS
INVERTS
INVESTS
IQTESTS
IRRUPTS
ISOLATE
ITERATE

I•••••T

ICEBOAT
ICEDOUT
ICESOUT
ICKIEST
IFFIEST
ILLICIT
IMPLANT
IMPRINT
INANEST
INASNIT
INASPOT
INCIPIT
INDOUBT
INEXACT
INFLECT
INFLICT
INFRONT

INHABIT
INHERIT
INHIBIT
INKBLOT
INKIEST
INKSPOT
INORBIT
INPRINT
INQUEST
INSHORT
INSIGHT
INSPECT
INSTANT
INTROIT
INTRUST
IRATEST
IRISOUT
IRONOUT
ITERANT

•IT••••

AITCHES
BITEOFF
BITLESS
BITMAPS
BITPART
BITSIER
BITTERN
BITTERS
BITTIER
BITTING
BITUMEN
CITABLE
CITADEL
CITIZEN
CITRATE
CITRINE
CITROEN
CITRONS
CITROUS
DITCHED
DITCHES
DITHERS
DITHERY
DITSIER
DITTANY
DITTIES
DITTOED
DITZIER
FITCHES
FITNESS
FITTERS
FITTEST
FITTING
HITACHI
HITCHED
HITCHER
HITCHES
HITHERE
HITLESS
HITLIST
HITSOUT
HITTERS
HITTING
HITTITE
JITNEYS
JITTERS
JITTERY
KITBAGS
KITCHEN
KITSCHY
KITTENS
KITTIES
LITCHIS
LITCRIT
LITERAL
LITHELY
LITHEST
LITHGOW
LITHIUM
LITINTO
LITOTES
LITTERS
LITTLER
LITURGY
MITCHUM
MITERED
MITFORD
MITHRAS
MITOSES
MITOSIS
MITOTIC
MITRING
MITTENS
MITZVAH
NITPICK
NITRATE
NITRIDE
NITRITE
NITROUS
NITTANY
NITTIER
NITWITS
PITAPAT
PITBOSS
PITBULL
PITCHED
PITCHER
PITCHES
PITCHIN
PITEOUS
PITFALL
PITHIER
PITHILY
PITHING
PITIERS
PITIFUL
PITSAWS
PITSTOP
PITTERS
PITTING
PITTMAN
PITYING
RITUALS
RITZIER
RITZILY
SITCOMS
SITDOWN
SITSOUT
SITTERS
SITTING
SITUATE
SITWELL
TITANIA
TITANIC
TITBITS
TITFERS
TITHERS
TITHING
TITLING
TITLIST
TITMICE
TITRATE
TITRING
TITTERS
TITTLES
TITTUPS
TITULAR
VITALLY
VITAMIN
VITIATE
VITRIFY
VITRIOL
VITTLES
WITCHES
WITHERS
WITHIER
WITHIES
WITHOUT
WITLESS
WITNESS
WITTIER
WITTILY
WITTING
YITZHAK
ZITHERS

•I•T•••

AIRTAXI
AIRTIME
BIGTALK
BIGTIME
BIGTOES
BIGTOPS
BIRTHED
BISTROS
BITTERN
BITTERS
BITTIER
BITTING
CISTERN
DIATOMS
DICTATE
DICTION
DICTUMS
DIETARY
DIETERS
DIETING
DIKTATS
DIPTYCH
DIRTIED
DIRTIER
DIRTIES
DIRTILY
DISTAFF
DISTANT
DISTEND
DISTILL
DISTILS
DISTORT
DISTURB
DITTANY
DITTIES
DITTOED
FIATLUX
FICTION
FICTIVE
FIFTEEN
FIFTHLY
FIFTIES
FILTERS
FISTFUL
FITTERS
FITTEST
FITTING
FIXTURE
HINTING
HINTSAT
HISTORY
HITTERS
HITTING
HITTITE
JILTING
JITTERS
JITTERY
KILTIES
KILTING
KIRTLES
KITTENS
KITTIES
LICTORS
LIFTERS
LIFTING
LIFTOFF
LIFTSUP
LILTING
LINTELS
LINTIER
LISTEES
LISTELS
LISTENS
LISTING
LITTERS
LITTLER
MIDTERM
MIDTOWN
MINTERS
MINTIER
MINTING
MISTAKE
MISTERS
MISTIER
MISTILY
MISTING
MISTOOK
MISTRAL
MISTYPE
MITTENS
MIXTURE
NIFTIER
NIFTILY
NINTHLY
NITTANY
NITTIER
PICTISH
PICTURE
PIETIES
PIETINS
PIETISM
PIETIST
PIGTAIL
PINTAIL
PISTILS
PISTOLE
PISTOLS
PISTONS
PITTERS
PITTING
PITTMAN
QINTARS
RIFTING
RIOTACT
RIOTERS
RIOTING
RIOTOUS
RIPTIDE
RIPTORN
SIFTERS
SIFTING
SILTIER
SILTING
SISTERS
SISTINE
SISTRUM
SITTERS
SITTING
SIXTEEN
SIXTHLY
SIXTIES
TICTACS
TIETACK
TILTERS
TILTING
TINTACK
TINTERN
TINTERS
TINTING
TINTYPE
TIPTOED
TIPTOES
TIPTOPS
TITTERS
TITTLES
TITTUPS
VICTIMS
VICTORS
VICTORY
VICTUAL
VIETNAM
VINTAGE
VINTNER
VIRTUAL
VIRTUES
VIRTUTE
VISTULA
VITTLES
WILTING
WINTERS
WINTERY
WISTFUL
WITTIER
WITTILY
WITTING

•I••T••

BIENTOT
BIGOTED
BIGOTRY
BIRETTA
DIGITAL
DILATED
DILATES
DILUTED
DILUTER
DILUTES
DIMITRI
DINETTE
DIOPTER
EIGHTAM
EIGHTHS
EIGHTPM
FIESTAS
FIGHTER
FIRSTLY
FIXATED
FIXATES
HIGHTEA
HIGHTOP
HILLTOP
HIPSTER
KILOTON
KINETIC
KINGTUT
KIRSTIE
LICITLY
LIGATED
LIGATES
LIGHTED
LIGHTEN
LIGHTER
LIGHTLY
LIGHTUP
LIMITED
LITOTES
MIGHTNT
MILITIA
MIMETIC
MINUTES
MINUTIA
MISSTEP
MITOTIC
MIXITUP
NIGHTIE
NIGHTLY
PIASTER
PIASTRE
PILOTED
PINATAS
PINETAR
PINETUM
PIPETTE
PIRATED
PIRATES
PIRATIC
PITSTOP
PIVOTAL
PIVOTED
RIANTLY
RICHTER
RICOTTA
RIDOTTO
RIGHTED
RIGHTER
RIGHTLY
RIGHTON
RISOTTO
RIVETED
RIVETER
SIESTAS
SIGHTED
SIGHTLY
SINATRA
TIBETAN
TIGHTEN
TIGHTER
TIGHTLY
TIMOTHY
TINSTAR
TINYTIM
TIPSTER
VISITED
VISITOR
WINGTIP
WINSTON
WIRETAP

•I•••T•

AIGRETS
AIMEDTO
AIRDATE
BILLETS
BIRETTA
BISECTS
BISMUTH
CILIATE
CITRATE
DICTATE
DIDACTS
DIGESTS
DIGNITY
DIKTATS
DIMOUTS
DIMWITS
DINETTE
DIRECTS
DISPUTE
DIVERTS
DIVESTS
FIDGETS
FIDGETY
FILLETS
GIBBETS
GIBLETS
GIMLETS
GIVENTO
GIVESTO
HIRSUTE
HITTITE
KIBBUTZ
LIBERTY
LIGNITE
LIMPETS
LINEATE
LINNETS
LIONETS
LISENTE
LITINTO
MIDGETS
MIGRATE
MILLETS
MILLETT
MINOLTA
MINUETS
MISDATE
MISFITS
MISHITS
MISMATE
NIMIETY
NITRATE
NITRITE
NITWITS
PICANTE
PICKETS
PICKETT
PIGLETS
PIGNUTS
PIMENTO
PINNATE
PIOLETS
PIPETTE
QIVIUTS
RICKETY
RICOTTA
RIDOTTO
RILLETS
RIORITA
RIPINTO
RIPOSTE
RISOTTO
SIGNETS
SILENTS
SINGSTO
SIPPETS
SITUATE
TICKETS
TICKETY
TIDBITS
TIEINTO
TINHATS
TIPPETS
TITBITS
TITRATE
VIBRATE
VIBRATO
VIOLATE
VIOLETS
VIRTUTE
VITIATE
WICHITA
WICKETS
WIDGETS
WIGLETS
WILLETS

•I••••T

AILMENT
AIMEDAT
AIRBOAT
AIRIEST
AIRLIFT
AIRPORT
AIRSOUT
BIBELOT
BIENTOT
BIGFEET
BIGFOOT
BIGGEST
BIGSHOT
BISCUIT
BITPART
CIRCLET
CIRCUIT
DIALECT
DICIEST
DIDEROT
DIEDOUT
DIESOUT
DIGSOUT
DILBERT
DIMMEST
DINGBAT
DINMONT
DISGUST
DISHOUT
DISPORT
DISRUPT
DISSECT
DISSENT
DISTANT
DISTORT
FIGMENT
FILBERT
FILLOUT
FINDOUT
FINEART
FIREANT
FIRELIT
FIRMEST
FISHNET
FISHOUT
FITTEST
GILBERT
GILLNET
GIVEOUT
HIDEOUT
HIGHEST
HIGHHAT
HINTSAT
HIPBOOT
HIPPEST
HITLIST
HITSOUT
JIVIEST
KICKOUT
KINDEST
KINGRAT
KINGTUT
LIFENET
LIMIEST
LIMPEST
LINIEST
LITCRIT
LITHEST
LIVEOUT
MIDEAST
MIDMOST
MIDWEST
MIGHTNT
MIGRANT
MILDEST
MILLETT
MINARET
MINDSET
MIRIEST
MISCAST
MISSOUT
NIGHEST
OILIEST
PIANIST
PICKETT
PICKOUT
PICKSAT
PIERROT
PIETIST
PIGMENT
PIGSOUT
PINENUT
PINIEST
PINKEST
PIPIEST
PIQUANT
PITAPAT
RICERAT
RICHEST
RIDEOUT
RIMIEST
RIMSHOT
RINGLET
RINGOUT
RIOTACT
RIPSOUT
RIVULET
SICKEST
SICKOUT
SIDEBET
SIGNOUT
SILKHAT
SINGOUT
SITSOUT
TIDIEST
TIMEOUT
TINIEST
TIREOUT
TITLIST
VIADUCT
VIBRANT
VINCENT
VINIEST
VIOLENT
VIOLIST
WIGSOUT
WILDCAT
WILDEST
WILIEST
WINGNUT
WINGSIT
WINIEST
WINKOUT
WINKSAT
WINSOUT
WIPEOUT
WIRIEST
WITHOUT
XINGOUT

••IT•••

ABITIBI
AGITATE
AGITATO
BAITING
BLITHER
BLITZED
BLITZEN
BLITZES
BOITANO
BRITAIN
BRITISH
BRITONS
BRITTEN
BRITTLE
BRITTON
CHITTER
CRITICS
CRITTER
DEITIES
EDITING
EDITION
EDITORS
EDITOUT
ELITISM
ELITIST
EMITTED
EMITTER
EPITHET
EPITOME
ERITREA
EXITING
FLITTED
FLITTER
FRITTED
FRITTER
GAITERS
GAITING
GLITTER
GLITZED
GLITZES
GRITTED
GUITARS
HAITIAN
IMITATE
INITIAL
KNITTED
KNITTER
LOITERS
MAITAIS
MAITRED
NEITHER
OMITTED
OMITTER
POITIER
PRITHEE
QUITTER
REITMAN
SKITOWS
SKITTER
SKITTLE
SLITHER
SMITING
SMITTEN
SNITCHY
SPITING
SPITZES
SUITING
SUITORS
SUITSUP
SWITZER
THITHER
TRITELY
TRITEST
TRITIUM
TRITONE
TRITONS
TUITION
TWITCHY
TWITTED
TWITTER
UNITARY
UNITERS
UNITIES
UNITING
UNITIVE
WAITERS
WAITFOR
WAITING
WAITOUT
WAITRON
WAITSON
WAITSUP
WHITENS
WHITEST
WHITHER
WHITIER
WHITING
WHITISH
WHITMAN
WHITNEY
WHITTLE
WRITEIN
WRITERS
WRITETO
WRITEUP
WRITHED
WRITHES
WRITING
WRITTEN
ZEITUNG

••I•T••

ABINTRA
AMISTAD
ANISTON
ARIETTA
ARISTAE
ARISTAS
ARISTOS
ASIATIC
AVIATED
AVIATES
AVIATOR
BAINTER
BLISTER
BRISTLE
BRISTLY
BRISTOL
BRITTEN
BRITTLE
BRITTON
BUILTIN
BUILTUP
CHINTZY
CHITTER
CLIFTON
CLINTON
CRITTER
DRIFTED
DRIFTER
DRISTAN
EMITTED
EMITTER
EPISTLE
ERISTIC
EVICTED
EXISTED
FAINTED
FAINTER
FAINTLY
FEINTED
FLIRTED
FLITTED
FLITTER
FOISTED
FRITTED
FRITTER
GLINTED
GLISTEN
GLITTER
GRIFTER
GRISTLE
GRISTLY
GRITTED
HEISTED
HOISTED
IDIOTIC
JOINTED
JOINTLY
JOISTED
KNITTED
KNITTER
LEISTER
MAINTOP
MEIOTIC
MEISTER
MOISTEN
MOISTER
MOISTLY
OMITTED
OMITTER
OPIATES
PAINTED
PAINTER
PAIUTES
PHILTER
PHILTRE
PLINTHS
POINTED
POINTER
POINTTO
PRINTED
PRINTER
QUIETED
QUIETEN
QUIETER
QUIETLY
QUILTED
QUILTER
QUINTET
QUITTER
ROISTER
SAINTED
SAINTLY
SHIATSU
SHIFTED
SHIHTZU
SHIITES
SKIRTED
SKITTER
SKITTLE
SMITTEN
SNIFTER
STILTED
STILTON
STINTED
SWIFTER
SWIFTLY
TAINTED
THISTLE
THISTLY
TRISTAN
TRISTAR
TWISTED
TWISTER
TWITTED
TWITTER
WHISTLE
WHITTLE
WRITTEN

••I••T•

ABILITY
ACIDITY
AGILITY
AGITATE
AGITATO
AKIHITO
ALIGHTS
ANIMATE
ANIMATO
ARIDITY
ARIETTA
ARIOSTO
AVIDITY
AZIMUTH
BLIGHTS
BLIGHTY
BRINGTO
CHIANTI
CLIENTS
CLIMATE
ELICITS
EMIRATE
FLIGHTS
FLIGHTY
FRIGATE
FRIGHTS
GRIVETS
HEIFETZ
HEIGHTS
IMITATE
KNIGHTS
LYINGTO
NAIVETE
NAIVETY
ORIENTE
ORIENTS
OWINGTO
PLIGHTS
POINTTO
PRIESTS
PRIMATE
PRIORTO
PRIVATE
PRIVETS
PRIVITY
QUIXOTE
SLIGHTS
SPIGOTS
SPINETS
SPIRITO
SPIRITS
STICKTO
SWIVETS
THIRSTS
THIRSTY
TOILETS
TRIBUTE
TRICOTS
TRIESTE
TRIJETS
TRINITY
TRIVETS
UTILITY
VEIGHTS
WEIGHTS
WEIGHTY
WRIGHTS
WRITETO

••I•••T

ALIMENT
ANIMIST
ARIDEST
BAILOUT
BLINKAT
BRIDGET
BRIQUET
BRISKET
CLIPART
CRICKET
DRIBLET
DRIVEAT
EDITOUT
ELITIST
EMINENT
EPITHET
EVIDENT
EVILEST
EXIGENT
FAIREST
FLIESAT
FLIPOUT
FRIPPET
GOINGAT
GRILLET
HAIRCUT
HAIRNET
IRISOUT
LAIDOUT
MAIGRET
MAILLOT
MAILOUT
NAILSET
OXIDANT
PAIDOUT
QUINTET
RAILSAT
RAIMENT
RAINHAT
RAINOUT
SHIPOUT
SKIBOOT
SKILIFT
SKILLET
SKIPOUT
SKISUIT
SLIPOUT
SNIDEST
SNIFFAT
SNIGLET
SNIPEAT
SNIPPET
SPINOUT
SPIRANT
THICKET
TLINGIT
TRIDENT
TRINKET
TRIPLET
TRIPPET
TRISECT
TRITEST
VAINEST
WAITOUT
WHIPPET
WHITEST

•••IT••

ADMITTO
ANTITAX
ARBITER
AUDITED
AUDITOR
AWAITED
BEWITCH
BONITOS
BRUITED
CAPITAL
CAPITAN
CAPITOL
DEBITED
DIGITAL
DIMITRI
DORITOS
ENTITLE
EOLITHS
EXCITED
EXCITES
FAJITAS
FRUITED
FUJITSU
GERITOL
GETITON
GOTITON
HABITAT
HABITED
HABITUE
HALITES
HAMITES
HAMITIC
HAMITUP
IGNITED
IGNITER
IGNITES
INCITED
INCITER
INCITES
INDITED
INDITES
INVITED
INVITES
INVITRO
JANITOR
JUJITSU
JUPITER
LAFITTE
LAYITON
LETITBE
LETITIA
LEVITES
LICITLY
LIMITED
MANITOU
MARITAL
MERITED
MILITIA
MIXITUP
MONITOR
OOLITES
OOLITHS
OPHITES
ORBITAL
ORBITED
ORBITER
ORNITHO
PETITES
PLAITED
POLITER
POLITIC
POSITED
PURITAN
PUTITTO
PYRITES
RARITAN
RATITES
RECITAL
RECITED
RECITER
RECITES
RETITLE
RUBITIN
SAMITES
SEMITES
SEMITIC
SHIITES
SORITES
SPLITUP
SPRITES
STKITTS
TABITHA
TACITLY
TACITUS
TRAITOR
UNHITCH
VERITAS
VISITED
VISITOR
WAPITIS
WRAITHS
ZENITHS

•••I•T•

ADMITTO
AGEISTS
ANOINTS
ANXIETY
AORISTS
ARTISTE
ARTISTS
ASSISTS
BATISTA
BATISTE
CHRISTI
CHRISTO
CHRISTY
CILIATE
CORINTH
CUBISTS
CUTINTO
DELICTI
DELICTS
DELISTS
DEPICTS
DESISTS
DEVIATE
DUBIETY
EGOISTS
ELLIOTT
ELMISTI
ENLISTS
EXPIATE
FOLIATE
FORINTS
FRAILTY
GEFILTE
GETINTO
GOLIATH
GOTINTO
HOLISTS
IMPIETY
INDICTS
INSISTS
JACINTH
JURISTS
LABIATE
LAFITTE
LARIATS
LAYINTO
LEGISTS
LITINTO
LUTISTS
LYRISTS
MAOISTS
MEDIATE
MODISTE
NIMIETY
NUDISTS
OBOISTS
OBVIATE
PLAINTS
PRYINTO
PURISTS
PUTITTO
QIVIUTS
RADIATE
RAMINTO
RANINTO
REBIRTH
RELICTS
RELISTS
RESISTS
RIPINTO
RUNINTO
SATIATE
SATIETY
SCRIPTS
SERIATE
SETINTO
SEXISTS
SHRIFTS
SOCIETY
SOVIETS
SPLINTS
SPRINTS
SQUINTS
SQUINTY
SQUIRTS
STKITTS
STRIATE
TAOISTS
TAPINTO
THEISTS
THRIFTS
THRIFTY
TIEINTO
TSHIRTS
TUBISTS
TYPISTS
UPLIFTS
VARIETY
VITIATE

•••I••T

ACHIEST
AERIEST
AGAINST
AIRIEST
ALRIGHT
AMBIENT
ANCIENT
ANTIART
APRICOT
ARTIEST
ASHIEST
ATHIRST
BONIEST
BOXIEST
BUSIEST
CABINET
CAGIEST
CAKIEST
CANIEST
COKIEST
COPILOT
COSIEST
COZIEST
DEFIANT
DEFICIT
DELIGHT
DELIMIT
DEVIANT
DICIEST
DOPIEST
DOZIEST
EASIEST
EDGIEST
EELIEST
EERIEST
EGGIEST
ELLIOTT
EXHIBIT
EXTINCT
FOXIEST
FREIGHT
FUMIEST
GAMIEST
GLUIEST
GOOIEST
GORIEST
HABITAT
HALIBUT
HARICOT
HAZIEST
HOKIEST
HOLIEST
HOMIEST
ICKIEST
IFFIEST
ILLICIT
INCIPIT
INHIBIT
INKIEST
INSIGHT
JIVIEST
JOKIEST
LACIEST
LAKIEST
LAZIEST
LENIENT
LIMIEST
LINIEST
LOGIEST
MAGINOT
MAZIEST
MEDIANT
MIRIEST
MOPIEST
MRFIXIT
MRRIGHT
NOSIEST
OCCIPUT
OILIEST
ONSIGHT
OOZIEST
PALIEST
PATIENT
PERIDOT
PINIEST
PIPIEST
POKIEST
PUNIEST
RACIEST
RADIANT
RELIANT
RELIGHT
REVISIT
RIMIEST
ROPIEST
ROSIEST
SALIENT
SAPIENT
SATINET
SEXIEST
SLEIGHT
SOLICIT
SPRIEST
TIDIEST
TINIEST
TONIEST
TONIGHT
TYPIEST
UGLIEST
UPRIGHT
UPTIGHT
VALIANT
VARIANT
VINIEST
WANIEST
WARIEST
WAVIEST
WAXIEST
WILIEST
WINIEST
WIRIEST
XHEIGHT
ZANIEST

••••IT•

ABILITY
ACIDITY
ACONITE
ACQUITS
ADAMITE
AGILITY
AKIHITO
AMENITY
ANNUITY
APATITE
ARIDITY
ARMPITS
ATTRITE
ATTRITS
AVIDITY
AZURITE
BABBITT
BANDITO
BANDITS
BAUXITE
BAYCITY
BERLITZ
BOXKITE
BREVITY
BULLITT
BURRITO
CALCITE
CHARITY
CLARITY
COEDITS
COMFITS
COMMITS
CONDITA
CORDITE
CREDITS
CRUDITY
DECEITS
DENSITY
DESPITE
DIGNITY
DIMWITS
DOGSITS
DUALITY
EBONITE
EBWHITE
EDACITY
EGALITE
ELICITS
EMERITA
EMERITI
ENSUITE
EREMITE
ERUDITE
FALSITY
FATCITY
FATUITY
FERRITE
GAMBITS
GODWITS
GRANITE
GRAVITY
HENBITS
HERMITS
HITTITE
HOBBITS
INANITY
INTUITS
JADEITE
JESUITS
JOLLITY
KUWAITI
LIGNITE
LUDDITE
MISFITS
MISHITS
NEOLITH
NESMITH
NITRITE
NITWITS
NULLITY
OFFSITE
OPACITY
OUTFITS
OUTHITS
OUTWITS
PANDITS
PARTITA
PARTITE
PAUCITY
PERLITE
PERMITS
POSTITS
PRIVITY
PROBITY
PROFITS
PULPITS
PUNDITS
QUALITY
RABBITS
RABBITT
REALITY
REEDITS
REQUITE
RESPITE
REUNITE
REWRITE
RIORITA
RUNWITH
SOFFITS
SOPWITH
SPIRITO
SPIRITS
STRAITS
SUAVITY
SUBMITS
SULFITE
SUMMITS
SUNCITY
TARPITS
TEKTITE
TENUITY
TERMITE
THEPITS
TIDBITS
TITBITS
TOMTITS
TRINITY
TURBITS
TWOBITS
UNKNITS
URANITE
UTILITY
VACUITY
VARSITY
WEBSITE
WESKITS
WICHITA

••••I•T

AFFLICT
AGONIST
AIRLIFT
ANIMIST
APPOINT
ATAVIST
ATHEIST
BABBITT
BAPTIST
BASSIST
BETWIXT
BLERIOT
BULLITT
CELLIST
CHARIOT
CHEMIST
CHEVIOT
COEXIST
CONSIST
CONVICT
COPYIST
CULTIST
CYCLIST
CYPRIOT
CZARIST
DADAIST
DENTIST
DUELIST
EGOTIST
ELEGIST
ELITIST
EPEEIST
FADDIST
FAUVIST
FLORIST
FLUTIST
GERAINT
HARPIST
HARRIET
HERRIOT
HITLIST
HORNIST
IMPRINT
INFLICT
INPRINT
JOLLIET
JUDOIST
LAMAIST
LEFTIST
MARXIST
OCULIST
ONADIET
PALMIST
PATRIOT
PAULIST
PAYDIRT
PERSIST
PIANIST
PIETIST
POLOIST
PREDICT
PROTIST
QUERIST
RABBITT
RANRIOT
REALIST
REBUILT
RECEIPT
REPAINT
REPRINT
RUNRIOT
SCHMIDT
SEAGIRT
SKILIFT
SOLOIST
SOPHIST
STATIST
STYLIST
SUBSIST
SUNKIST
TITLIST
TOURIST
TSARIST
TSELIOT
TUBAIST
UNTWIST
VARMINT
VERDICT
VIOLIST
YORKIST

•••••IT

AQUAVIT
BABYSIT
BACKBIT
BACKLIT
BASEHIT
BEATSIT
BENEFIT
BISCUIT
BLOWSIT
CATSUIT
CIRCUIT
COCKPIT
COHABIT
CONCEIT
CONDUIT
COOLSIT
CULPRIT
DEFICIT
DELIMIT
DEMERIT
DEPOSIT
DETROIT
DRYSUIT
EXHIBIT
EXPLOIT
FIRELIT
FLEAPIT
FLORUIT
FORFEIT
GOFORIT
HALFWIT
HARDHIT
HOOFSIT
HOPTOIT
HOWBEIT
ILLICIT
INASNIT
INCIPIT
INHABIT
INHERIT
INHIBIT
INORBIT
INTROIT
LAWSUIT
LITCRIT
LOSESIT
MAKESIT
MANUMIT
MEGAHIT
MESSKIT
MOONLIT
MOSHPIT
MRFIXIT
NOTABIT
OPENPIT
OUTOFIT
PARFAIT
PLAUDIT
PURSUIT
RAREBIT
READMIT
RECRUIT
REVISIT
ROUGHIT
SEENFIT
SEESFIT
SEETOIT
SKISUIT
SOLICIT
SPOTLIT
STARLIT
SUBUNIT
SUNSUIT
SURFEIT
THATSIT
TLINGIT
TRANSIT
WATCHIT
WETSUIT
WINGSIT

I•U••••

IGUANAS
INURING
INUTILE

I••U•••

ILLUDED
ILLUDES
ILLUMED
ILLUMES
ILLUSED
ILLUSES
IMBUING
IMMURED
IMMURES
IMPUGNS
IMPULSE
IMPURER
IMPUTED
IMPUTES
INCUDES
INDUCED
INDUCER
INDUCES
INDUCTS
INDULGE
INDUTCH
INFUSED
INFUSES
INHUMAN
INJURED
INJURES
INQUEST
INQUIRE
INQUIRY
INSULAR
INSULIN
INSULTS
INSURED
INSURER
INSURES
INTUITS
IRRUPTS
ISSUERS
ISSUING

I•••U••

ICECUBE
IMBRUED
IMBRUES
IMPOUND
INARUSH
INBOUND
INCLUDE
INDOUBT
INHAULS
INHOUSE
INOCULA
INTRUDE
INTRUST
INTRUTH

I••••U•

IBNSAUD
ICEBLUE
ICEDOUT
ICESOUT
ICINGUP
IGIVEUP
IGNEOUS
IMPETUS
IMPIOUS
INFOCUS
INGENUE
INGROUP
INVACUO
INVOGUE
IRIDIUM
IRISOUT
IRONOUT
ISTHMUS

I•••••U

ILIESCU

•IU••••

DIURNAL

•I•U•••

BITUMEN
DILUTED
DILUTER
DILUTES
DISUSED
DIVULGE
FIBULAE
FIBULAS
FICUSES
FIGURED
FIGURER
FIGURES
KIKUYUS
LIQUEFY
LIQUEUR
LIQUIDS
LIQUORS
LITURGY
MINUEND
MINUETS
MINUSES
MINUTES
MINUTIA
MISUSED
MISUSES
PIOUSLY
PIQUANT
PIQUING
RITUALS
RIVULET
SINUOUS
SINUSES
SIOUANS
SITUATE
TIJUANA
TITULAR
VICUNAS
VIRUSES
VISUALS

•I••U••

AIRGUNS
AIRPUMP
BIGGUNS
BISCUIT
BISMUTH
BISQUES
BIVOUAC
CIRCUIT
CIRCUSY
CIRQUES
DICTUMS
DIFFUSE
DIMBULB
DIMOUTS
DISCUSS
DISGUST
DISPUTE
DISRUPT
DISTURB
FILLUPS
FISSURE
FIXTURE
GIBLUES
GILGUYS
GIVEUPS
HICCUPS
HIRSUTE
KIBBUTZ
KICKUPS
KILAUEA
LINEUPS
LINGUAL
LINKUPS
MISCUED
MISCUES
MISRULE
MIXTURE
NIEBUHR
PICKUPS
PICTURE
PIGNUTS
PILEUPS
PINCURL
PITBULL
QIVIUTS
RIGOURS
SICHUAN
SIGMUND
SIXGUNS
TISSUES
TITTUPS
VIADUCT
VICTUAL
VIGOURS
VIRGULE
VIRTUAL
VIRTUES
VIRTUTE
VISTULA
WINDUPS

•I•••U•

AIRSOUT
BILIOUS
BINDSUP
CITROUS
DIEDOUT
DIESOUT
DIGSOUT
DIREFUL
DISHFUL
DISHOUT
DIVINUM
FIATLUX
FIBROUS
FILLOUT
FILLSUP
FINDOUT
FIREBUG
FIREDUP
FIRESUP
FIRMSUP
FISHOUT
FISTFUL
FIXEDUP
FIXESUP
GIBBOUS
GIDDYUP
GIELGUD
GIVENUP
GIVEOUT
GIVESUP
HIDEOUS
HIDEOUT
HIKEDUP
HIKESUP
HITSOUT
KICKOUT
KICKSUP
KIKUYUS
KINGTUT
LIFEFUL
LIFTSUP
LIGHTUP
LINEDUP
LINESUP
LIONCUB
LIQUEUR
LITHIUM
LIVEOUT
MILHAUD
MILIEUS
MILIEUX
MILKRUN
MILLRUN
MIMIEUX
MINDFUL
MINIBUS
MINIMUM
MISSOUT
MITCHUM
MIXEDUP
MIXESUP
MIXITUP
NIOBIUM
NITROUS
PICKOUT
PICKSUP
PIGSOUT
PILEDUP
PILESUP
PILLBUG
PINENUT
PINETUM
PIPEDUP
PIPEFUL
PIPESUP
PIRAEUS
PIROGUE
PITEOUS
PITIFUL
RIDEOUT
RILESUP
RIMBAUD
RINGOUT
RINGSUP
RIOTOUS
RIPSOUT
SICKOUT
SIGHFUL
SIGNOUT
SIGNSUP
SINGOUT
SINUOUS
SISTRUM
SITSOUT
SIZEDUP
SIZESUP
TIMEOUT
TIMESUP
TIREOUT
VICIOUS
VILNIUS
VIRIBUS
VISCOUS
WICKIUP
WIGSOUT
WILLFUL
WINDSUP
WINGNUT
WINKOUT
WINSOUT
WIPEDUP
WIPEOUT
WIPESUP
WISEDUP
WISEGUY
WISESUP
WISHFUL
WISTFUL
WITHOUT
XINGOUT

••IU•••

PAIUTES
TRIUMPH
TRIUNES

••I•U••

AZIMUTH
BRIQUET
CAIQUES
CHINUPS
CLIBURN
CLIQUES
CLIQUEY
EPICURE
FAILURE
FLIPUPS
LEISURE
SKIJUMP
SKIRUNS
SKISUIT
SLIPUPS
STIMULI
TRIBUNE
TRIBUTE
ZEITUNG

••I••U•

AMIBLUE
ATISSUE
BAILOUT
BRIMFUL
BRINGUP
BUILDUP
BUILTUP
COILSUP
CRISPUS
DOINGUP
DRIEDUP
DRIESUP
DRIVEUP
EDITOUT
FAIRSUP
FLIPOUT
GAINFUL
GOINGUP
HAIRCUT
HEINOUS
ICINGUP
IGIVEUP
IRIDIUM
IRISOUT
JOINSUP
JUICEUP
LAIDOUT
MAILOUT
OMINOUS
PAIDOUT
PAILFUL
PAILOUS
PAINFUL
PAIRSUP
QUINQUE
RAINOUT
RAISEUP
REISSUE
RUINOUS
SHIPOUT
SKILFUL
SKINFUL
SKIPOUT
SLIPOUT
SLIPSUP
SPICEUP
SPINOUT
STICKUP
STIRRUP
STIRSUP
SUITSUP
THINKUP

TOILFUL
TRIPSUP
TRITIUM
TYINGUP
USINGUP
WAILFUL
WAITOUT
WAITSUP
WHIPSUP
WRITEUP

••I•••U
ILIESCU
SHIATSU
SHIHTZU
SHIKOKU
THIMPHU

•••IU••
ATRIUMS
MEDIUMS
PODIUMS
QIVIUTS
TEDIUMS

•••I•U•
ANTIGUA
ANTIQUE
ANXIOUS
ATTICUS
BEZIQUE
BILIOUS
COMIQUE
COPIOUS
CURIOUS
DEVIOUS
DIVINUM
DOMINUS
DONIMUS
DUBIOUS
DUTIFUL
ECHINUS
ENVIOUS
FATIGUE
FURIOUS
HABITUE
HALIBUT
HAMITUP
IMPIOUS
JABIRUS
LALIQUE
LEMIEUX
MAXIMUM
MAXIMUS
MILIEUS
MILIEUX
MIMIEUX
MINIBUS
MINIMUM
MIXITUP
MODICUM
MONIQUE
NOXIOUS
OBLIQUE
OBVIOUS
OCCIPUT
OEDIPUS
OMNIBUS
OPTIMUM
PAVIOUR
PITIFUL
RESIDUE
RETINUE
SAVIOUR
SERIOUS
SPLITUP
TACITUS
TEDIOUS
TROILUS
VARIOUS
VICIOUS
VIRIBUS

•••I••U
CARIBOU
FUJITSU
JUJITSU
MANITOU

••••IU•
BELGIUM
CADMIUM
CAESIUM
CALCIUM
CAMBIUM
CASSIUS
CELSIUS
CRANIUM
ELAAIUN
ELUVIUM
ELYSIUM
FERMIUM
FORTIUS
GALLIUM
GROPIUS
HAFNIUM
HAHNIUM
HOLMIUM
IRIDIUM
LITHIUM
NATRIUM
NIOBIUM
PALLIUM
PENTIUM
PERSIUS
PONTIUS
PREMIUM
RHENIUM
RHODIUM
STADIUM
TERBIUM
THORIUM
THULIUM
TRITIUM
URANIUM
VILNIUS
WICKIUP
YTTRIUM

••••I•U
PURLIEU

IV•••••
IVANHOE
IVANOVO
IVORIES
IVYLIKE

I•V••••
INVACUO
INVADED
INVADER
INVADES
INVALID
INVEIGH
INVENTS
INVERSE
INVERTS
INVESTS
INVITED
INVITES
INVITRO
INVOGUE
INVOICE
INVOKED
INVOKER
INVOKES
INVOLVE

I••V•••
IGIVEUP

I•••V••
INCIVIL
INFAVOR

I••••V•
IMPROVE
INVOLVE
IVANOVO

•IV••••
BIVALVE
BIVOUAC
CIVILLY
CIVVIES
DIVERGE
DIVERSE
DIVERTS
DIVESIN
DIVESTS
DIVIDED
DIVIDER
DIVIDES
DIVINED
DIVINER
DIVINES
DIVINUM
DIVISOR
DIVORCE
DIVULGE
DIVVIED
DIVVIES
GIVENIN
GIVENTO
GIVENUP
GIVEOFF
GIVEOUT
GIVESIN
GIVESTO
GIVESUP
GIVEUPS
GIVEWAY
JIVIEST
LIVABLE
LIVEDIN
LIVEDON
LIVENED
LIVEOAK
LIVEONE
LIVEOUT
LIVESIN
LIVESON
LIVIDLY
LIVINGS
LIVORNO
PIVOTAL
PIVOTED
QIVIUTS
RIVALED
RIVALRY
RIVETED
RIVETER
RIVIERA
RIVIERE
RIVULET
VIVALDI
VIVENDI
VIVIDER
VIVIDLY

•I•V•••
CIVVIES
DIVVIED
DIVVIES
NIRVANA
RIGVEDA
SILVERS
SILVERY

•I••V••
BILEVEL
DIDOVER
DISAVOW
LIEOVER
MINIVAN
MINIVER
MITZVAH
NINEVEH
VISAVIS

•I•••V•
AIRWAVE
BIVALVE
FICTIVE
GINGIVA
MINERVA
MISSIVE

••IV•••
DRIVEAT
DRIVEIN
DRIVELS
DRIVERS
DRIVEUP
DRIVING
FLIVVER
GRIVETS
IGIVEUP
NAIVELY
NAIVETE
NAIVETY
OLIVIER
OLIVINE
PRIVACY
PRIVATE
PRIVETS
PRIVIER
PRIVIES
PRIVILY
PRIVITY
QUIVERS
QUIVERY
SHIVERS
SHIVERY
SKIVERS
SLIVERS
SNIVELS
SWIVELS
SWIVETS
TRIVETS
TRIVIAL
WAIVERS
WAIVING
ZHIVAGO

••I•V••
FLIVVER
GRIEVED
GRIEVER
GRIEVES
KNIEVEL
THIEVED
THIEVES

••I••V•
UNITIVE

•••IV••
ACTIVES
AQUIVER
ARGIVES
ARRIVAL
ARRIVED
ARRIVER
ARRIVES
BOLIVAR
BOLIVIA
DELIVER
DERIVED
DERIVES
ENDIVES
ENLIVEN
ESTIVAL
EXWIVES
INCIVIL
MINIVAN
MINIVER
MOTIVES
NATIVES
RELIVED
RELIVES
REVIVAL
REVIVED
REVIVES
SCRIVEN
SHRIVEL
SHRIVER
SHRIVES
STRIVED
STRIVEN
STRIVER
STRIVES
THRIVED
THRIVES
UNCIVIL
UPRIVER

•••I•V•
ACHIEVE
BELIEVE
RELIEVE
RELIEVO

•••I••V
USTINOV

••••IV•
ABUSIVE
ACTFIVE
AMATIVE
ARCHIVE
BEEHIVE
CAPTIVE
CONNIVE
CURSIVE
DECEIVE
DEPRIVE
ELUSIVE
EMOTIVE
EROSIVE
EVASIVE
FESTIVA
FESTIVE
FICTIVE
FORGIVE
FURTIVE
GINGIVA
MASSIVE
MISSIVE
OUTLIVE
PASSIVE
PENSIVE
PLOSIVE
RECEIVE
RESTIVE
SKYDIVE
SURVIVE
TANTIVY
TENSIVE
UNITIVE
YESHIVA

•••••IV
HENRYIV
ROCKYIV
TELAVIV

IW•••••
IWOJIMA

I•W••••
INWARDS

I••W•••
ILLWILL
ILLWIND
INAWEOF
INAWORD
INDWELL
INKWELL
IPSWICH

I•••W••
INNOWAY
INPOWER

I••••W•
INFLOWS
INGROWN

I•••••W
ICESHOW
INASTEW

•IW••••
KIWANIS

•I•W•••
AIRWAVE
AIRWAYS
AIRWOLF
BIGWIGS
DIMWITS
MIDWAYS
MIDWEEK
MIDWEST
MIDWIFE
MISWORD
NITWITS
OILWELL
PINWALE
SITWELL
TINWARE
TINWORK
VIEWERS
VIEWIER
VIEWING
WIGWAGS
WIGWAMS

•I••W••
BIKEWAY
DISOWNS
GIVEWAY
HIGHWAY
RIDGWAY
WIDOWED
WIDOWER

•I•••W•
BILLOWS
BILLOWY
DIEDOWN
JIGSAWS
LIEDOWN
MIDTOWN
MILDEWS
MILDEWY
MINNOWS
PILLOWS
PILLOWY
PINDOWN
PITSAWS
RIPSAWS
SITDOWN
TIEDOWN
WILLOWS
WILLOWY
WINDOWS
WINNOWS

•I••••W
AIRCREW
AIRFLOW
AIRSHOW
BIGELOW
DISAVOW
HIGHLOW
LIESLOW
LIKENEW
LITHGOW
MILKCOW
WINDROW
WINSLOW

••IW•••
SKIWEAR

••I•W••
FAIRWAY
OJIBWAS
OJIBWAY
RAILWAY

••I••W•
OKINAWA
SKITOWS

••I•••W
LAIDLOW
RAINBOW
SKIDROW
TRISHAW
WHIPSAW

•••IW••
ANTIWAR
TAXIWAY
WYSIWYG

•••I•W•
REVIEWS

•••I••W
MANILOW
SAGINAW

••••I•W
PREVIEW
PURVIEW

I••X•••
INEXACT

I•••X••
ICEAXES
IMMIXED
IMMIXES
INBOXES
INDEXED
INDEXES

•IX••••
FIXABLE
FIXATED
FIXATES
FIXEDLY
FIXEDUP
FIXESUP
FIXINGS
FIXTURE
MIXABLE
MIXEDIN
MIXEDUP
MIXESIN
MIXESUP
MIXITUP
MIXTURE
PIXYISH
SIXFOLD
SIXGUNS
SIXIRON
SIXPACK
SIXTEEN
SIXTHLY
SIXTIES

•I•X•••
DIOXIDE
JINXING
MINXISH

•I•••X•
AIRTAXI
PICKAXE

•I••••X
CINEMAX
FIATLUX
FIREBOX
MILIEUX
MIMIEUX
MIRAMAX
PILLBOX
SIMPLEX

••IX•••
ELIXIRS
QUIXOTE

••I•••X
MAILBOX
TRIPLEX

•••IX••
ADMIXED
ADMIXES
AFFIXED
AFFIXES
HELIXES
IMMIXED
IMMIXES
MRFIXIT
RADIXES
REMIXED
REMIXES
UNFIXED

•••I••X
ANTITAX
EQUINOX
HALIFAX
LEMIEUX
MILIEUX
MIMIEUX

••••IX•
BETWIXT

•••••IX
BEATRIX
CAKEMIX
DEEPSIX
HENDRIX
PHOENIX
REAFFIX
SKEEZIX
STCROIX

I•Y••••
IDYLLIC
IVYLIKE

I••Y•••
INKYCAP

I•••Y••
INSTYLE

I•••••Y
IDEALLY
IGNOBLY
IMAGERY
IMPIETY
IMSORRY
INANELY
INANITY
INAPTLY
INEPTLY
INERTLY
INFANCY
INNOWAY
INQUIRY
IRATELY
ISONOMY

•I•Y•••
BICYCLE
LIBYANS
LILYPAD
MIDYEAR
MINYANS
PITYING
PIXYISH
TIDYING
TINYTIM

•I••Y••
BIGEYES
DIPTYCH
GIDDYAP
GIDDYUP
KIKUYUS
LIPSYNC
MIAOYAO
MISTYPE
RIBEYES
TIEDYED
TIEDYES
TINTYPE

•I•••Y•
AIRWAYS
BIGBOYS
DICKEYS
DISMAYS
FISHEYE
GILGUYS
JITNEYS
KIDNEYS
MICKEYS
MIDDAYS
MIDWAYS
MISLAYS
MISSAYS
RICKEYS

•I••••Y
AIRPLAY
BIGOTRY
BIKEWAY
BILLOWY
BINDERY
BIOGENY
BIOLOGY
CINDERY
CIRCUSY
CIVILLY
DIDDLEY
DIETARY
DIGNIFY
DIGNITY
DINGILY
DIRTILY
DISOBEY
DISPLAY
DITHERY
DITTANY
DIZZILY
FIDGETY
FIERILY
FIFTHLY
FINALLY
FINICKY
FIREFLY
FIRSTLY
FISHERY
FISHFRY
FISHILY
FIXEDLY
GIDDILY
GINGERY
GIVEWAY
HICKORY
HIGHBOY
HIGHDAY
HIGHWAY
HILLARY
HISTORY
JIGGERY
JITTERY
KILLJOY
KINKILY
KITSCHY
LIBERTY
LIBRARY
LICITLY
LIGHTLY
LINDSAY
LINDSEY
LIQUEFY
LITHELY
LITURGY
LIVIDLY
MILDEWY
MIMICRY
MISALLY
MISERLY
MISPLAY
MISTILY
NIFTILY
NIGHTLY
NIMIETY
NINTHLY
NITTANY
PICARDY
PIGGERY
PILLORY
PILLOWY
PIOUSLY
PITHILY
RIANTLY
RICKETY
RIDGWAY
RIFLERY
RIGHTLY
RIGIDLY
RISIBLY
RISKILY
RITZILY
RIVALRY
SICKBAY
SICKDAY
SICKPAY
SIGHTLY
SIGNIFY
SILKILY
SILVERY
SIXTHLY
SIZABLY
TICKETY
TIERNEY
TIFFANY
TIGHTLY
TIMIDLY
TIMOTHY
TINNILY
TIPSILY
TIREDLY
VICEROY
VICTORY
VISIBLY
VITALLY
VITRIFY
VIVIDLY
WILLOWY
WINDILY
WINFREY
WINTERY
WISEGUY
WISPILY
WITTILY

••I••Y•
BAILEYS
EVILEYE
FRIDAYS
HAIRDYE

••I•••Y
ABIDEBY
ABILITY
ACIDIFY
ACIDITY
AGILELY
AGILITY
ALIMONY
AMIABLY
APISHLY
ARIDITY
AVIDITY
AXIALLY
BLIGHTY
BLINDLY
BRIBERY
BRIEFLY
BRIMLEY
BRISKLY
BRISTLY
CHICORY
CHIEFLY
CHIMNEY
CHINTZY
CLIQUEY
CRINKLY
CRISPLY
DRIPDRY
DRIZZLY
FAINTLY
FAIRWAY
FLIGHTY
FRIZZLY
GAINSAY
GOINGBY
GRIFFEY
GRIMILY
GRISTLY
GRIZZLY
JOINERY
JOINTLY
JUICILY
MOISTLY
NAIVELY
NAIVETY
NOISILY
OJIBWAY
PAISLEY
PLIABLY
PLIANCY
PRICKLY
PRIMACY
PRIMARY
PRIVACY
PRIVILY
PRIVITY
QUICKLY
QUIETLY
QUIGLEY
QUINARY
QUIVERY
RAILWAY
RAINILY
SAINTLY
SHINILY
SHIRLEY
SHIVERY
SLICKLY
SLIMILY
SNIDELY
SNIFFLY
SNITCHY
SPICERY
SPICILY
SPIDERY
SPIKILY
SPINDLY
SPINDRY
SPINNEY
STIFFLY
STIRFRY
SWIFTLY
SWINGBY
THICKLY
THIRDLY
THIRSTY
THISTLY
TRILOGY
TRINITY
TRITELY
TWINKLY
TWITCHY
UNITARY
UTILITY
WEIGHTY
WEIRDLY
WHISKEY
WHITNEY
WRIGGLY
WRIGLEY
WRINKLY

•••IY••
RUFIYAA

•••I•Y•
MARILYN
WYSIWYG

•••I••Y
ACRIDLY
ANXIETY
AUDIBLY
CHRISTY
CIVILLY
DEVILRY
DUBIETY
FETIDLY
FINICKY
FLUIDLY
FRAILLY
FRAILTY
GELIDLY
HOLIDAY
HOSIERY
HUMIDLY
IMPIETY
LEGIBLY
LICITLY
LIVIDLY
LUCIDLY
LURIDLY
MIMICRY
NIMIETY
PANICKY
PLAINLY
RABIDLY
RAPIDLY
RETIARY
RIGIDLY
RISIBLY
SATIETY
SATISFY
SCRIMPY
SHRILLY
SOCIETY
SOLIDLY
SPRINGY
SQUINTY
SQUIRMY
SQUISHY
STAIDLY
STRINGY
TACITLY
TAXIWAY
TEPIDLY
THRIFTY
TIMIDLY
TOPIARY
VALIDLY
VAPIDLY
VARIETY
VISIBLY
VIVIDLY

••••I•Y
ABILITY
ACIDIFY
ACIDITY
AGILITY
AMENITY
AMPLIFY
ANGRILY
ANNUITY
ARIDITY
AVIDITY
BAGGILY
BALKILY
BALMILY
BAWDILY
BAYCITY
BEATIFY
BONNILY
BOSSILY
BREVITY
BUMPILY
BUSHILY
CALCIFY
CAMPILY
CANNILY
CANTILY
CASSIDY
CATTILY
CERTIFY
CHARILY
CHARITY
CLARIFY
CLARITY
CLERISY
COCKILY
CORNILY
CRAZILY
CRUCIFY
CRUDITY
DAFFILY
DANDIFY
DAYLILY
DENSITY
DESTINY
DIGNIFY
DIGNITY
DINGILY
DIRTILY
DIZZILY
DOTTILY
DOWDILY

DUALITY
DULCIFY
DUSKILY
DUSTILY
EDACITY
EMPTILY
ENQUIRY
FALSIFY
FALSITY
FANCIFY
FANCILY
FATCITY
FATTILY
FATUITY
FIERILY
FISHILY
FLAKILY
FOAMILY
FOGGILY
FORTIFY
FUNKILY
FUNNILY
FUSSILY
FUSTILY
FUZZILY
GAUDILY
GAUZILY
GAWKILY
GIDDILY
GLORIFY
GOOFILY
GOONILY
GOSSIPY
GOUTILY
GRATIFY
GRAVITY
GRIMILY
GUSHILY
GUSTILY
GUTSILY
HAMMILY
HANDILY
HAPPILY
HARDILY
HASTILY
HEADILY
HEAVILY
HEFTILY
HOARILY
HORRIFY
HUFFILY
HUSKILY
INANITY
INQUIRY
JAZZILY
JERKILY
JOLLIFY
JOLLILY
JOLLITY
JUICILY
JUMPILY
JUSTIFY
KINKILY
LANKILY
LEERILY
LOFTILY
LOUSILY
LUCKILY
LUMPILY
LUSTILY
MAGNIFY
MEATILY
MERRILY
MESSILY
MISTILY
MOLLIFY
MOODILY
MOONILY
MORTIFY
MUCKILY
MUDDILY
MURKILY
MUSHILY
MUSSILY
MUSTILY
MUZZILY
MYSTIFY
NASTILY
NATTILY
NEEDILY
NERVILY
NIFTILY
NOISILY
NULLIFY
NULLITY
NUTTILY
OPACITY
PAUCITY
PEPPILY
PERFIDY
PERKILY
PESKILY
PETRIFY
PETTILY
PHONILY
PITHILY
PODGILY
PRIVILY
PRIVITY
PROBITY
PRODIGY
PROSILY
PUDGILY
PUFFILY
PUNNILY
PUSHILY
QUAKILY
QUALIFY
QUALITY
RAINILY
READILY
REALITY
RECTIFY
REUNIFY
RISKILY
RITZILY
ROOMILY
ROWDILY
RUDDILY
RUSTILY
SALSIFY
SALTILY
SAPPILY
SASSILY
SAUCILY
SAVVILY
SCARIFY
SCARILY
SEALILY
SEEDILY
SHADILY
SHAKILY
SHINILY
SHOWILY
SIGNIFY
SILKILY
SLIMILY
SMOKILY
SNAKILY
SNOWILY
SOAPILY
SOGGILY
SOOTILY
SORRILY
SPECIFY
SPICILY
SPIKILY
STAGILY
STONILY
SUAVITY
SUBSIDY
SULKILY
SUNCITY
SUNNILY
SURLILY
TACKILY
TANTIVY
TARDILY
TASTILY
TATTILY
TAWNILY
TEARILY
TENUITY
TERRIFY
TESTIFY
TESTILY
TINNILY
TIPSILY
TRINITY
UTILITY
VACUITY
VARSITY
VERSIFY
VITRIFY
WACKILY
WASPILY
WEARILY
WEEDILY
WINDILY
WISPILY
WITTILY
WOOZILY
WORDILY
ZOMBIFY

IZ•••••
IZZARDS

I•Z••••
IZZARDS

I•••Z••
IODIZED
IODIZES
IONIZED
IONIZER
IONIZES

I••••Z•
IDOLIZE
INADAZE
ITEMIZE

•IZ••••
BIZARRE
DIZENED
DIZZIED
DIZZIER
DIZZIES
DIZZILY
FIZGIGS
FIZZIER
FIZZING
FIZZLED
FIZZLES
GIZZARD
LIZARDS
MIZZENS
MIZZLED
MIZZLES
PIZARRO
PIZZAZZ
SIZABLE
SIZABLY
SIZEDUP
SIZESUP
SIZINGS
SIZZLED
SIZZLES
TIZZIES
VIZIERS
VIZSLAS
WIZARDS
WIZENED

•I•Z•••
CINZANO
DITZIER
DIZZIED
DIZZIER
DIZZIES
DIZZILY
FIZZIER
FIZZING
FIZZLED
FIZZLES
GIZZARD
MITZVAH
MIZZENS
MIZZLED
MIZZLES
PIAZZAS
PIZZAZZ
RITZIER
RITZILY
SIZZLED
SIZZLES
TIZZIES
YITZHAK
ZIGZAGS

•I••Z••
CITIZEN
PIAZZAS

•I•••Z•
FIRENZE
GINFIZZ
LIONIZE
MIDSIZE
PIZZAZZ

•I••••Z
GINFIZZ
JIMENEZ
KIBBUTZ
PIZZAZZ

••IZ•••
ARIZONA
DRIZZLE
DRIZZLY
FRIZZED
FRIZZES
FRIZZLE
FRIZZLY
GRIZZLE
GRIZZLY
PRIZING
QUIZZED
QUIZZES
RHIZOME
SEIZERS
SEIZING
SWIZZLE
WHIZKID
WHIZZED
WHIZZER
WHIZZES

••I•Z••
BLITZED
BLITZEN
BLITZES
DRIZZLE
DRIZZLY
FRIEZES
FRIZZED
FRIZZES
FRIZZLE
FRIZZLY
GLITZED
GLITZES
GRIZZLE
GRIZZLY
LEIPZIG
QUIZZED
QUIZZES
SPITZES
SWITZER
SWIZZLE
WHIZZED
WHIZZER
WHIZZES

••I••Z•
CHINTZY
OXIDIZE
SHIHTZU
SPINOZA
UTILIZE

••I•••Z
HEIFETZ
LAISSEZ
LEIBNIZ

•••IZ••
ASSIZES
BEDIZEN
CITIZEN
DENIZEN
HORIZON
IODIZED
IODIZES
IONIZED
IONIZER
IONIZES
NETIZEN

••••IZ•
AGONIZE
ANODIZE
APPRIZE
ATOMIZE
BAPTIZE
CAPSIZE
CHORIZO
GINFIZZ
IDOLIZE
ITEMIZE
LIONIZE
MESTIZA
MESTIZO
MIDSIZE
OUTSIZE
OXIDIZE
REALIZE
STYLIZE
UTILIZE

••••I•Z
BERLIOZ
BERLITZ
GINFIZZ

•••••IZ
AGASSIZ
ALBENIZ
GEEWHIZ
LEIBNIZ
SHOWBIZ

JA•••••
JABBERS
JABBING
JABIRUS
JACANAS
JACCUSE
JACINTH
JACKALS
JACKASS
JACKDAW
JACKETS
JACKEYS
JACKIES
JACKING
JACKPOT
JACKSON
JACKSUP
JACKTAR
JACOBIN
JACONET
JACQUES
JACUZZI
JADEDLY
JADEITE
JAEGERS
JAGGIER
JAGGIES
JAGGING
JAGLESS
JAGUARS
JAIALAI
JAILERS
JAILING
JAKARTA
JALISCO
JAMAICA
JAMESON
JAMLIKE
JAMMERS
JAMMIER
JAMMING
JAMPACK
JANACEK
JANEDOE
JANEWAY
JANGLED
JANGLES
JANITOR
JANNOCK
JANSSEN
JANUARY
JANVIER
JAPHETH
JARFULS
JARGONS
JARGONY
JARLESS
JARRING
JASMINE
JASPERS
JAUNTED
JAVAMAN
JAVELIN
JAWBONE
JAWLESS
JAWLIKE
JAWLINE
JAYBIRD
JAYCEES
JAYLENO
JAYVEES
JAYWALK
JAZZAGE
JAZZIER
JAZZILY
JAZZING
JAZZMAN
JAZZMEN

J•A••••
JEALOUS
JEANARP
JEANLUC
JEANNIE
JOACHIM
JOAQUIN

J••A•••
JACANAS
JAIALAI
JAKARTA
JAMAICA
JANACEK
JAVAMAN
JICAMAS
JOCASTA
JOHANNA
JUDAISM
JUMANJI

J•••A••
JACKALS
JACKASS
JAGUARS
JAMPACK
JANUARY
JAYWALK
JAZZAGE
JEANARP
JETWASH
JETWAYS
JIGSAWS
JIMJAMS
JOBBANK
JUGBAND
JULIANA
JUNKART
JUTLAND

J••••A•
JACANAS
JACKDAW
JACKTAR
JAIALAI
JANEWAY
JAVAMAN
JAZZMAN
JEERSAT
JERBOAS
JETBOAT
JICAMAS
JILLIAN
JOCULAR
JOHNGAY
JOHNJAY
JOURDAN
JOURNAL
JUGHEAD
JUGULAR
JUMPSAT
JUNKMAN
JUVENAL

J•••••A
JAKARTA
JAMAICA
JESSICA
JOCASTA
JOHANNA
JULIANA
JUNKDNA

•JA••••
AJACCIO

•J•••A•
OJIBWAS
OJIBWAY

••JA•••
HIJACKS
PAJAMAS
PDJAMES
PYJAMAS

••J•A••
FIJIANS
TIJUANA

••J••A•
FAJITAS
PAJAMAS
PYJAMAS

••J•••A
LAJOLLA
MAJORCA
TIJUANA

•••JA••
DEEJAYS
JIMJAMS
LOGJAMS
PUNJABI
SKYJACK
TROJANS
VEEJAYS

•••J•A•
DONJUAN
SANJUAN
VALJEAN

•••J••A
IWOJIMA

••••JA•
BELLJAR
BLUEJAY
CULTJAM
GRAYJAY
JOHNJAY
KARAJAN

•••••JA
ALFORJA

J•B••••
JABBERS
JABBING
JABIRUS
JIBBING
JIBBOOM
JOBBANK
JOBBERS
JOBBERY
JOBBING
JOBHOPS
JOBHUNT
JOBLESS
JOBLOTS
JUBILEE

J••B•••
JABBERS
JABBING
JAWBONE
JAYBIRD
JEEBIES
JERBOAS
JETBOAT
JIBBING
JIBBOOM
JOBBANK
JOBBERS
JOBBERY
JOBBING
JOEBLOW
JUGBAND
JUMBLED
JUMBLES

J•••B••
JACOBIN
JEZEBEL
JUJUBES
JUKEBOX
JUNEBUG

•J•B•••
OJIBWAS
OJIBWAY

••J•B••
JUJUBES

•••J•B•
CONJOBS
DAYJOBS
ODDJOBS
PUNJABI

••••J•B
GOODJOB
LUBEJOB
NOSEJOB
SNOWJOB

J•C••••
JACANAS
JACCUSE
JACINTH
JACKALS
JACKASS
JACKDAW
JACKETS
JACKEYS
JACKIES
JACKING
JACKPOT
JACKSON
JACKSUP
JACKTAR
JACOBIN
JACONET
JACQUES
JACUZZI
JICAMAS
JOCASTA
JOCKEYS
JOCULAR

J••C•••
JACCUSE
JAYCEES
JIMCHEE
JOACHIM
JUICERS
JUICEUP
JUICIER
JUICILY
JUICING
JUNCOES

J•••C••
JANACEK
JERICHO
JOUNCED
JOUNCES
JUMPCUT

J••••C•
JALISCO
JAMAICA
JAMPACK
JANNOCK
JESSICA
JONNICK
JUSTICE

J•••••C
JEANLUC
JURIDIC

•J•C•••
AJACCIO
EJECTED

•J••C••
AJACCIO

••J•C••
DEJECTS
HIJACKS
INJECTS
OBJECTS
REJECTS

••J••C•
ADJUNCT
MAJORCA
REJOICE

•••J•C•
PROJECT
SKYJACK
SUBJECT

J•D••••
JADEDLY
JADEITE
JUDAISM
JUDDERS
JUDGING
JUDOIST

J••D•••
JUDDERS

J•••D••
JACKDAW
JADEDLY
JANEDOE
JOHNDOE
JOINDER
JOURDAN
JUNKDNA
JURIDIC

J••••D•
JOYRIDE

J•••••D
JANGLED
JAUNTED
JAYBIRD
JELLIED
JEMMIED
JEWELED
JIGGLED
JIMMIED
JINGLED
JOGGLED
JOINTED
JOISTED
JOLLIED
JOSTLED
JOUNCED
JOUSTED
JUGBAND
JUGGLED
JUGHEAD
JUMBLED
JUTLAND
JUTTIED

•J••••D
EJECTED

••J•D••
ADJUDGE

••J•••D
ABJURED
ADJURED
CAJOLED
ENJOYED
INJURED
MAJORED

•••J•D•
HEYJUDE

JE•••••
JEALOUS
JEANARP
JEANLUC
JEANNIE
JEEBIES
JEEPNEY
JEERERS
JEERING
JEERSAT
JEFFERS
JEFFREY
JEJUNUM
JELLIED
JELLIES
JELLING
JEMMIED
JEMMIES
JENNETS
JENNIES
JERBOAS
JERICHO
JERKIER
JERKILY
JERKING
JERKINS
JERSEYS
JESSICA
JESTERS
JESTING
JESUITS
JETBOAT
JETGUNS
JETPORT
JETSKIS
JETSONS
JETTIES
JETTING
JETWASH
JETWAYS
JEWELED
JEWELER
JEWELRY
JEWISON
JEZEBEL

J•E••••
JAEGERS
JEEBIES
JEEPNEY
JEERERS
JEERING
JEERSAT
JOEBLOW
JOEHILL
JREWING

J••E•••
JADEDLY
JADEITE
JAMESON
JANEDOE
JANEWAY
JAVELIN
JEWELED
JEWELER
JEWELRY
JEZEBEL
JIMENEZ
JONESES
JUKEBOX
JUNEBUG
JUVENAL

J•••E••
JABBERS
JACKETS
JACKEYS
JAEGERS
JAGLESS
JAILERS
JAMMERS
JAPHETH
JARLESS
JASPERS
JAWLESS
JAYCEES
JAYLENO
JAYVEES
JEERERS
JEFFERS
JENNETS
JERSEYS
JESTERS
JIGGERS
JIGGERY
JITNEYS
JITTERS
JITTERY
JIVIEST
JOBBERS
JOBBERY
JOBLESS
JOCKEYS
JOGGERS
JOINERS
JOINERY
JOKIEST
JOSSERS
JOYLESS
JUDDERS
JUGHEAD
JUICERS
JUICEUP
JUMPERS
JUNKERS
JUNKETS

J••••E•
JACKIES
JACONET
JACQUES
JAGGIER
JAGGIES
JAMMIER
JANACEK
JANGLED
JANGLES
JANSSEN
JANVIER
JAUNTED
JAYCEES
JAYVEES
JAZZIER
JAZZMEN
JEEBIES
JEEPNEY
JEFFREY
JELLIED
JELLIES
JEMMIED
JEMMIES
JENNIES
JERKIER
JETTIES
JEWELED
JEWELER
JEZEBEL
JIFFIES
JIGGLED
JIGGLES
JIMCHEE
JIMENEZ
JIMMIED
JIMMIES
JINGLED
JINGLES
JINGOES
JOFFREY
JOGGLED
JOGGLES
JOINDER
JOINTED
JOISTED
JOLLIED
JOLLIER
JOLLIES
JOLLIET
JOLTIER
JONESES
JOSTLED
JOSTLER
JOSTLES
JOUNCED
JOUNCES
JOURNEY
JOUSTED
JOUSTER
JOWLIER
JUBILEE
JUGGLED
JUGGLER
JUGGLES
JUICIER
JUJUBES
JUMBLED
JUMBLES
JUMPIER
JUNCOES
JUNGLES
JUNIPER
JUNKIER
JUNKIES
JUPITER
JUTTIED
JUTTIES

J•••••E
JACCUSE
JADEITE
JAMLIKE
JANEDOE
JASMINE
JAWBONE
JAWLIKE
JAWLINE
JAZZAGE
JEANNIE
JIGLIKE
JIMCHEE
JOHNDOE
JOHNNIE
JOYRIDE
JUBILEE
JUGWINE
JUSTICE
JUSTINE

•JE••••
EJECTED

•J•••E•
EJECTED

••JE•••
DEJECTS
INJECTS
MAJESTE
MAJESTY
MAJEURE
OBJECTS

REJECTS

••J••E•
ABJURED
ABJURES
ADJURED
ADJURES
CAJOLED
CAJOLER
CAJOLES
ENJOYED
INJOKES
INJURED
INJURES
JUJUBES
MAJORED
PDJAMES

••J•••E
ADJUDGE
MAJESTE
MAJEURE
REJOICE

•••JE••
FANJETS
GASJETS
PROJECT
RAMJETS
SUBJECT
TRIJETS
VALJEAN

•••J•E•
BANJOES
PALJOEY

•••J••E
CONJURE
DONJOSE
HEYJUDE
PERJURE
SANJOSE
SUOJURE

••••JE•
LEARJET
PROPJET

••••J•E
GOODJOE

J•F••••
JEFFERS
JEFFREY
JIFFIES
JOFFREY

J••F•••
JARFULS
JEFFERS
JEFFREY
JIFFIES
JOFFREY
JUGFULS

J••••F•
JOLLIFY
JUMPOFF
JUSTIFY

J•••••F
JUMPOFF

J•G••••
JAGGIER
JAGGIES
JAGGING
JAGLESS
JAGUARS
JIGGERS
JIGGERY
JIGGING
JIGGISH
JIGGLED
JIGGLES
JIGLIKE
JIGSAWS
JOGGERS
JOGGING
JOGGLED
JOGGLES
JUGBAND
JUGFULS
JUGGING
JUGGINS
JUGGLED
JUGGLER
JUGGLES
JUGHEAD
JUGULAR
JUGWINE

J••G•••
JAEGERS
JAGGIER
JAGGIES
JAGGING
JANGLED
JANGLES
JARGONS
JARGONY
JETGUNS
JIGGERS
JIGGERY
JIGGING
JIGGISH
JIGGLED
JIGGLES
JINGLED
JINGLES
JINGOES
JOGGERS
JOGGING
JOGGLED
JOGGLES
JUDGING
JUGGING
JUGGINS
JUGGLED
JUGGLER
JUGGLES
JUNGLES

J•••G••
JOHNGAY

J••••G•
JAZZAGE

J•••••G
JABBING
JACKING
JAGGING
JAILING
JAMMING
JARRING
JAZZING
JEERING
JELLING
JERKING
JESTING
JETTING
JIBBING
JIGGING
JILTING
JINKING
JINXING
JOBBING
JOGGING
JOINING
JOLTING
JOSHING
JOTTING
JREWING
JUDGING
JUGGING
JUICING
JUMPING
JUNEBUG
JUNKING
JURYING
JURYRIG
JUTTING

••J••G•
ADJUDGE

•••J••G
BEIJING

J•H••••
JOHANNA
JOHNDOE
JOHNGAY
JOHNJAY
JOHNNIE
JOHNSON

J••H•••
JAPHETH
JOBHOPS
JOBHUNT
JOEHILL
JOSHING
JUGHEAD

J•••H••
JIMCHEE
JOACHIM

J••••H•
JERICHO

J•••••H
JACINTH
JAPHETH
JETWASH
JIGGISH

••J•H••
STJOHNS

•••J•H•
BIGJOHN

JI•••••
JIBBING
JIBBOOM
JICAMAS
JIFFIES
JIGGERS
JIGGERY
JIGGING
JIGGISH
JIGGLED
JIGGLES
JIGLIKE
JIGSAWS
JILLIAN
JILLION
JILTING
JIMCHEE
JIMENEZ
JIMJAMS
JIMMIED
JIMMIES
JINGLED
JINGLES
JINGOES
JINKING
JINXING
JITNEYS
JITTERS
JITTERY
JIVIEST

J•I••••
JAIALAI
JAILERS
JAILING
JOINDER
JOINERS
JOINERY
JOINING
JOINSIN
JOINSUP
JOINTED
JOINTLY
JOISTED
JUICERS
JUICEUP
JUICIER
JUICILY
JUICING

J••I•••
JABIRUS
JACINTH
JALISCO
JANITOR
JERICHO
JEWISON
JIVIEST
JOKIEST
JUBILEE
JUJITSU
JULIANA
JUNIORS
JUNIPER
JUPITER
JURIDIC
JURISTS

J•••I••
JABBING
JACKIES
JACKING
JADEITE
JAGGIER
JAGGIES
JAGGING
JAILING
JAMAICA
JAMLIKE
JAMMIER
JAMMING
JANVIER
JARRING
JASMINE
JAWLIKE
JAWLINE
JAYBIRD
JAZZIER
JAZZILY
JAZZING
JEEBIES
JEERING
JELLIED
JELLIES
JELLING
JEMMIED
JEMMIES
JENNIES
JERKIER
JERKILY
JERKING
JERKINS
JESSICA
JESTING
JESUITS
JETTIES
JETTING
JIBBING
JIFFIES
JIGGING
JIGGISH
JIGLIKE
JILLIAN
JILLION
JILTING
JIMMIED
JIMMIES
JINKING
JINXING
JOBBING
JOEHILL
JOGGING
JOINING
JOLLIED
JOLLIER
JOLLIES
JOLLIET
JOLLIFY
JOLLILY
JOLLITY
JOLTIER
JOLTING
JONNICK
JOSHING
JOSKINS
JOTTING
JOWLIER
JOYRIDE
JREWING
JUDAISM
JUDGING
JUDOIST
JUGGING
JUGGINS
JUGWINE
JUICIER
JUICILY
JUICING
JUMPIER
JUMPILY
JUMPING
JUNKIER
JUNKIES
JUNKING
JURYING
JUSTICE
JUSTIFY
JUSTINE
JUTTIED
JUTTIES
JUTTING

J••••I•
JACOBIN
JAVELIN
JEANNIE
JETSKIS
JOACHIM
JOAQUIN
JOHNNIE
JOINSIN
JONQUIL
JUMPSIN
JURIDIC
JURYRIG

J•••••I
JACUZZI
JAIALAI
JUMANJI

•JI••••
OJIBWAS
OJIBWAY

•J•••I•
AJACCIO

••JI•••
FAJITAS
FIJIANS
FUJITSU
HIJINKS
JUJITSU

••J•I••
ADJOINS
ENJOINS
REJOICE
REJOINS

•••JI••
BEIJING
IWOJIMA

•••J•I•
CONJOIN
DISJOIN
SUBJOIN

•••J••I
BONJOVI
PUNJABI

••••JI•
LORDJIM
SLIMJIM
TIANJIN

•••••JI
BASENJI
JUMANJI

J•J••••
JEJUNUM
JUJITSU
JUJUBES

J••J•••
JIMJAMS

J•••J••
JOHNJAY

J••••J•
JUMANJI

J•K••••
JAKARTA
JOKIEST
JUKEBOX

J••K•••
JACKALS
JACKASS
JACKDAW
JACKETS
JACKEYS
JACKIES
JACKING
JACKPOT
JACKSON
JACKSUP
JACKTAR
JERKIER
JERKILY
JERKING
JERKINS
JINKING
JOCKEYS
JOSKINS
JUNKART
JUNKDNA
JUNKERS
JUNKETS
JUNKIER
JUNKIES
JUNKING
JUNKMAN

J•••K••
JETSKIS

J••••K•
JAMLIKE
JAWLIKE
JIGLIKE

J•••••K
JAMPACK
JANACEK
JANNOCK
JAYWALK
JOBBANK
JONNICK

••J•K••
INJOKES

••J••K•
HIJACKS
HIJINKS

•••J••K
SKYJACK

J•L••••
JALISCO
JELLIED
JELLIES
JELLING
JILLIAN
JILLION
JILTING
JOLLIED
JOLLIER
JOLLIES
JOLLIET
JOLLIFY
JOLLILY
JOLLITY
JOLTIER
JOLTING
JULIANA

J••L•••
JAGLESS
JAILERS
JAILING
JAMLIKE
JARLESS
JAWLESS
JAWLIKE
JAWLINE
JAYLENO
JEALOUS
JELLIED
JELLIES
JELLING
JIGLIKE
JILLIAN
JILLION
JOBLESS
JOBLOTS
JOLLIED
JOLLIER
JOLLIES
JOLLIET
JOLLIFY
JOLLILY
JOLLITY
JOWLIER
JOYLESS
JUTLAND

J•••L••
JAIALAI
JANGLED
JANGLES
JAVELIN
JEANLUC
JEWELED
JEWELER
JEWELRY
JIGGLED
JIGGLES
JINGLED
JINGLES
JOCULAR
JOEBLOW
JOGGLED
JOGGLES
JOSTLED
JOSTLER
JOSTLES
JUBILEE
JUGGLED
JUGGLER
JUGGLES
JUGULAR
JUMBLED
JUMBLES
JUNGLES

J••••L•
JACKALS
JADEDLY
JARFULS
JAYWALK
JAZZILY
JERKILY
JOEHILL
JOINTLY
JOLLILY
JUGFULS
JUICILY
JUMPILY

J•••••L
JEZEBEL
JOEHILL
JONQUIL
JOURNAL
JUVENAL

••J•L••
CAJOLED
CAJOLER
CAJOLES
LAJOLLA

••J••L•
LAJOLLA

J•M••••
JAMAICA
JAMESON
JAMLIKE
JAMMERS
JAMMIER
JAMMING
JAMPACK
JEMMIED
JEMMIES
JIMCHEE
JIMENEZ
JIMJAMS
JIMMIED
JIMMIES
JUMANJI
JUMBLED
JUMBLES
JUMPCUT
JUMPERS
JUMPIER
JUMPILY
JUMPING
JUMPOFF
JUMPSAT
JUMPSIN
JUMPSON
JUMPSUP

J••M•••
JAMMERS
JAMMIER
JAMMING
JASMINE
JEMMIED
JEMMIES
JIMMIED
JIMMIES

J•••M••
JAVAMAN
JAZZMAN
JAZZMEN
JICAMAS
JUNKMAN

J••••M•
JIMJAMS

J•••••M
JEJUNUM
JIBBOOM
JOACHIM
JUDAISM

••J•M••
PAJAMAS
PDJAMES
PYJAMAS

••J•••M
JEJUNUM

•••J•M•
IWOJIMA
JIMJAMS
LOGJAMS
OUTJUMP
SKIJUMP

••••J•M
CULTJAM
LORDJIM
SLIMJIM

J•N••••
JANACEK
JANEDOE
JANEWAY
JANGLED
JANGLES
JANITOR
JANNOCK
JANSSEN
JANUARY
JANVIER
JENNETS
JENNIES
JINGLED
JINGLES
JINGOES
JINKING
JINXING
JONESES
JONNICK
JONQUIL
JUNCOES
JUNEBUG
JUNGLES
JUNIORS
JUNIPER
JUNKART
JUNKDNA
JUNKERS
JUNKETS
JUNKIER
JUNKIES
JUNKING
JUNKMAN

J••N•••
JANNOCK
JAUNTED
JEANARP
JEANLUC
JEANNIE
JENNETS
JENNIES
JITNEYS
JOHNDOE
JOHNGAY
JOHNJAY
JOHNNIE
JOHNSON
JOINDER
JOINERS
JOINERY
JOINING
JOINSIN
JOINSUP
JOINTED
JOINTLY
JONNICK
JOUNCED
JOUNCES

J•••N••
JACANAS
JACINTH
JACONET
JEANNIE
JEEPNEY
JEJUNUM
JIMENEZ
JOHANNA
JOHNNIE
JOURNAL
JOURNEY
JOURNOS
JUMANJI
JUSTNOW
JUVENAL

J••••N•
JABBING
JACKING
JAGGING
JAILING
JAMMING
JARGONS
JARGONY
JARRING
JASMINE
JAWBONE
JAWLINE
JAYLENO
JAZZING
JEERING
JELLING
JERKING
JERKINS
JESTING
JETGUNS
JETSONS
JETTING
JIBBING
JIGGING
JILTING
JINKING
JINXING
JOBBANK
JOBBING
JOBHUNT
JOGGING
JOHANNA
JOINING
JOLTING
JOSHING
JOSKINS
JOTTING
JREWING
JUDGING
JUGBAND
JUGGING
JUGGINS
JUGWINE
JUICING
JULIANA
JUMPING
JUNKDNA
JUNKING
JURYING
JUSTINE
JUTLAND
JUTTING

J•••••N
JACKSON
JACOBIN
JAMESON
JANSSEN
JAVAMAN
JAVELIN
JAZZMAN
JAZZMEN
JEWISON
JILLIAN
JILLION
JOAQUIN
JOHNSON
JOINSIN
JOURDAN
JUMPSIN
JUMPSON
JUNKMAN

••J•N••
ADJUNCT
HIJINKS
JEJUNUM

••J••N•
ADJOINS
ENJOINS
FIJIANS
REJOINS
STJOHNS
TIJUANA

••J•••N
ADJOURN
SOJOURN

•••J•N•
BEIJING
DONJONS
TROJANS

•••J••N
BIGJOHN
CONJOIN
DISJOIN
DONJUAN
SANJUAN
SUBJOIN
VALJEAN

••••J•N
KARAJAN
TIANJIN

JO•••••
JOACHIM
JOAQUIN
JOBBANK
JOBBERS
JOBBERY
JOBBING
JOBHOPS
JOBHUNT
JOBLESS
JOBLOTS
JOCASTA
JOCKEYS
JOCULAR
JOEBLOW
JOEHILL
JOFFREY
JOGGERS
JOGGING
JOGGLED
JOGGLES
JOHANNA
JOHNDOE
JOHNGAY
JOHNJAY
JOHNNIE
JOHNSON
JOINDER
JOINERS
JOINERY
JOINING
JOINSIN
JOINSUP
JOINTED
JOINTLY
JOISTED
JOKIEST
JOLLIED
JOLLIER
JOLLIES
JOLLIET
JOLLIFY
JOLLILY
JOLLITY
JOLTIER
JOLTING
JONESES
JONNICK
JONQUIL
JOSHING
JOSKINS
JOSSERS
JOSTLED
JOSTLER
JOSTLES
JOTTING
JOUNCED
JOUNCES
JOURDAN
JOURNAL
JOURNEY
JOURNOS
JOUSTED
JOUSTER
JOWLIER
JOYLESS
JOYRIDE

J•O••••
JACOBIN
JACONET
JUDOIST

J•••O••
JANNOCK
JARGONS
JARGONY
JAWBONE
JEALOUS
JERBOAS
JETBOAT
JETPORT
JETSONS
JIBBOOM
JINGOES
JOBHOPS
JOBLOTS
JUMPOFF
JUNCOES
JUNIORS

J••••O•
JACKPOT
JACKSON
JAMESON
JANEDOE
JANITOR
JEWISON
JIBBOOM
JILLION
JOEBLOW
JOHNDOE
JOHNSON
JOURNOS
JUKEBOX
JUMPSON
JUSTNOW

J•••••O
JALISCO
JAYLENO
JERICHO

•J••••O
AJACCIO

••JO•••
ADJOINS
ADJOURN
CAJOLED
CAJOLER
CAJOLES
ENJOINS
ENJOYED
INJOKES
LAJOLLA
MAJORCA
MAJORED
REJOICE
REJOINS
SOJOURN
STJOHNS

•••JO••
BANJOES
BIGJOHN
BONJOUR
BONJOVI
CONJOBS
CONJOIN
DAYJOBS
DISJOIN
DONJONS
DONJOSE
ODDJOBS
PALJOEY
SANJOSE
SUBJOIN

••••JO•
GOODJOB
GOODJOE
KILLJOY
LUBEJOB
NAVAJOS

NOSEJOB
OVERJOY
SNOWJOB

•••••JO
BERMEJO
VALLEJO

J•P••••
JAPHETH
JUPITER

J••P•••
JAMPACK
JASPERS
JEEPNEY
JETPORT
JUMPCUT
JUMPERS
JUMPIER
JUMPILY
JUMPING
JUMPOFF
JUMPSAT
JUMPSIN
JUMPSON
JUMPSUP

J•••P••
JACKPOT
JUNIPER

J••••P•
JOBHOPS

J•••••P
JACKSUP
JEANARP
JOINSUP
JUICEUP
JUMPSUP

••JP•••
RAJPUTS

•••J••P
OUTJUMP
SKIJUMP

J••Q•••
JACQUES
JOAQUIN
JONQUIL

JR•••••
JREWING

J•R••••
JARFULS
JARGONS
JARGONY
JARLESS
JARRING
JERBOAS
JERICHO
JERKIER
JERKILY
JERKING
JERKINS
JERSEYS
JURIDIC
JURISTS
JURYING
JURYRIG

J••R•••
JARRING
JEERERS
JEERING
JEERSAT
JOURDAN
JOURNAL
JOURNEY
JOURNOS
JOYRIDE

J•••R••
JABIRUS
JAKARTA
JEFFREY
JOFFREY
JURYRIG

J••••R•
JABBERS
JAEGERS
JAGUARS
JAILERS
JAMMERS
JANUARY
JASPERS
JAYBIRD
JEANARP
JEERERS
JEFFERS
JESTERS
JETPORT
JEWELRY
JIGGERS
JIGGERY
JITTERS
JITTERY
JOBBERS
JOBBERY
JOGGERS
JOINERS
JOINERY
JOSSERS
JUDDERS
JUICERS
JUMPERS
JUNIORS
JUNKART
JUNKERS

J•••••R
JACKTAR
JAGGIER
JAMMIER
JANITOR
JANVIER
JAZZIER
JERKIER
JEWELER
JOCULAR
JOINDER
JOLLIER
JOLTIER
JOSTLER
JOUSTER
JOWLIER
JUGGLER
JUGULAR
JUICIER
JUMPIER
JUNIPER
JUNKIER
JUPITER

••J•R••
ABJURED
ABJURES
ADJURED
ADJURES
INJURED
INJURES
MAJORCA
MAJORED

••J••R•
ADJOURN
MAJEURE
SOJOURN

••J•••R
CAJOLER

•••J•R•
CONJURE
PERJURE
PERJURY
SUOJURE

•••J••R
BONJOUR

••••J•R
BELLJAR

J•S••••
JASMINE
JASPERS
JESSICA
JESTERS
JESTING
JESUITS
JOSHING
JOSKINS
JOSSERS
JOSTLED
JOSTLER
JOSTLES
JUSTICE
JUSTIFY
JUSTINE
JUSTNOW

J••S•••
JANSSEN
JERSEYS
JESSICA
JETSKIS
JETSONS
JIGSAWS
JOISTED
JOSSERS
JOUSTED
JOUSTER

J•••S••
JACKSON
JACKSUP
JALISCO
JAMESON
JANSSEN
JEERSAT
JEWISON
JOCASTA
JOHNSON
JOINSIN
JOINSUP
JONESES
JUMPSAT
JUMPSIN
JUMPSON
JUMPSUP
JURISTS

J••••S•
JACCUSE
JACKASS
JAGLESS
JARLESS
JAWLESS
JETWASH
JIGGISH
JIVIEST
JOBLESS
JOKIEST
JOYLESS
JUDAISM
JUDOIST
JUJITSU

J•••••S
JABBERS
JABIRUS
JACANAS
JACKALS
JACKASS
JACKETS
JACKEYS
JACKIES
JACQUES
JAEGERS
JAGGIES
JAGLESS
JAGUARS
JAILERS
JAMMERS
JANGLES
JARFULS
JARGONS
JARLESS
JASPERS
JAWLESS
JAYCEES
JAYVEES
JEALOUS
JEEBIES
JEERERS
JEFFERS
JELLIES
JEMMIES
JENNETS
JENNIES
JERBOAS
JERKINS
JERSEYS
JESTERS
JESUITS
JETGUNS
JETSKIS
JETSONS
JETTIES
JETWAYS
JICAMAS
JIFFIES
JIGGERS
JIGGLES
JIGSAWS
JIMJAMS
JIMMIES
JINGLES
JINGOES
JITNEYS
JITTERS
JOBBERS
JOBHOPS
JOBLESS
JOBLOTS
JOCKEYS
JOGGERS
JOGGLES
JOINERS
JOLLIES
JONESES
JOSKINS
JOSSERS
JOSTLES
JOUNCES
JOURNOS
JOYLESS
JUDDERS
JUGFULS
JUGGINS
JUGGLES
JUICERS
JUJUBES
JUMBLES
JUMPERS
JUNCOES
JUNGLES
JUNIORS
JUNKERS
JUNKETS
JUNKIES
JURISTS
JUTTIES

•J••••S
OJIBWAS

••J•S••
ADJUSTS
MAJESTE
MAJESTY

••J••S•
FUJITSU
JUJITSU

••J•••S
ABJURES
ADJOINS
ADJURES
ADJUSTS
CAJOLES
DEJECTS
ENJOINS
FAJITAS
FIJIANS
HIJACKS
HIJINKS
INJECTS
INJOKES
INJURES
JUJUBES
OBJECTS
PAJAMAS
PDJAMES
PYJAMAS
RAJPUTS
REJECTS
REJOINS
STJOHNS

•••J•S•
DONJOSE
SANJOSE

•••J••S
BANJOES
CONJOBS
DAYJOBS
DEEJAYS
DONJONS
FANJETS
GASJETS
JIMJAMS
LOGJAMS
ODDJOBS
RAMJETS
TRIJETS
TROJANS
VEEJAYS

••••J•S
NAVAJOS

J•T••••
JETBOAT
JETGUNS
JETPORT
JETSKIS
JETSONS
JETTIES
JETTING
JETWASH
JETWAYS
JITNEYS
JITTERS
JITTERY
JOTTING
JUTLAND
JUTTIED
JUTTIES
JUTTING

J••T•••
JESTERS
JESTING
JETTIES
JETTING
JILTING
JITTERS
JITTERY
JOLTIER
JOLTING
JOSTLED
JOSTLER
JOSTLES
JOTTING
JUSTICE
JUSTIFY
JUSTINE
JUSTNOW
JUTTIED
JUTTIES
JUTTING

J•••T••
JACKTAR
JANITOR
JAUNTED
JOINTED
JOINTLY
JOISTED
JOUSTED
JOUSTER
JUJITSU
JUPITER

J••••T•
JACINTH
JACKETS
JADEITE
JAKARTA
JAPHETH
JENNETS
JESUITS
JOBLOTS
JOCASTA
JOLLITY
JUNKETS
JURISTS

J•••••T
JACKPOT
JACONET
JEERSAT
JETBOAT
JETPORT
JIVIEST
JOBHUNT
JOKIEST
JOLLIET
JUDOIST
JUMPCUT
JUMPSAT
JUNKART

•J••T••
EJECTED

••J•T••
FAJITAS
FUJITSU
JUJITSU

••J••T•
ADJUSTS
DEJECTS
INJECTS
MAJESTE
MAJESTY
OBJECTS
RAJPUTS
REJECTS

••J•••T
ADJUNCT

•••J•T•
FANJETS
GASJETS
RAMJETS
TRIJETS

•••J••T
PROJECT
SUBJECT

••••J•T
LEARJET
PROPJET

JU•••••
JUBILEE
JUDAISM
JUDDERS
JUDGING
JUDOIST
JUGBAND
JUGFULS
JUGGING
JUGGINS
JUGGLED
JUGGLER
JUGGLES
JUGHEAD
JUGULAR
JUGWINE
JUICERS
JUICEUP
JUICIER
JUICILY
JUICING
JUJITSU
JUJUBES
JUKEBOX
JULIANA
JUMANJI
JUMBLED
JUMBLES
JUMPCUT
JUMPERS
JUMPIER
JUMPILY
JUMPING
JUMPOFF
JUMPSAT
JUMPSIN
JUMPSON
JUMPSUP
JUNCOES
JUNEBUG
JUNGLES
JUNIORS
JUNIPER
JUNKART
JUNKDNA
JUNKERS
JUNKETS
JUNKIER
JUNKIES
JUNKING
JUNKMAN
JUPITER
JURIDIC
JURISTS
JURYING
JURYRIG
JUSTICE
JUSTIFY
JUSTINE
JUSTNOW
JUTLAND
JUTTIED
JUTTIES
JUTTING
JUVENAL

J•U••••
JAUNTED
JOUNCED
JOUNCES
JOURDAN
JOURNAL
JOURNEY
JOURNOS
JOUSTED
JOUSTER

J••U•••
JACUZZI
JAGUARS
JANUARY
JEJUNUM
JESUITS
JOCULAR
JUGULAR
JUJUBES

J•••U••
JACCUSE
JACQUES
JARFULS
JETGUNS
JOAQUIN
JOBHUNT
JONQUIL
JUGFULS

J••••U•
JABIRUS
JACKSUP
JEALOUS
JEANLUC
JEJUNUM
JOINSUP
JUICEUP
JUMPCUT
JUMPSUP
JUNEBUG

J•••••U
JUJITSU

••JU•••
ABJURED
ABJURES
ADJUDGE
ADJUNCT
ADJURED
ADJURES
ADJUSTS
INJURED
INJURES
JEJUNUM
JUJUBES
TIJUANA

••J•U••
ADJOURN
MAJEURE
RAJPUTS
SOJOURN

••J••U•
JEJUNUM

••J•••U
FUJITSU
JUJITSU

•••JU••
CONJURE
DONJUAN
HEYJUDE
OUTJUMP
PERJURE
PERJURY
SANJUAN
SKIJUMP
SUOJURE

•••J•U•
BONJOUR

J•V••••
JAVAMAN
JAVELIN
JIVIEST
JUVENAL

J••V•••
JANVIER
JAYVEES

•••J•V•
BONJOVI

J•W••••
JAWBONE
JAWLESS
JAWLIKE
JAWLINE
JEWELED
JEWELER
JEWELRY
JEWISON
JOWLIER

J••W•••
JAYWALK
JETWASH
JETWAYS
JREWING
JUGWINE

J•••W••
JANEWAY

J••••W•
JIGSAWS

J•••••W
JACKDAW
JOEBLOW
JUSTNOW

•J••W••
OJIBWAS
OJIBWAY

J••X•••
JINXING

J•••••X
JUKEBOX

J•Y••••
JAYBIRD
JAYCEES
JAYLENO
JAYVEES
JAYWALK
JOYLESS
JOYRIDE

J••Y•••
JURYING
JURYRIG

J••••Y•
JACKEYS
JERSEYS
JETWAYS
JITNEYS
JOCKEYS

J•••••Y
JADEDLY
JANEWAY
JANUARY
JARGONY
JAZZILY
JEEPNEY
JEFFREY
JERKILY
JEWELRY
JIGGERY
JITTERY
JOBBERY
JOFFREY
JOHNGAY
JOHNJAY
JOINERY
JOINTLY
JOLLIFY
JOLLILY
JOLLITY
JOURNEY
JUICILY
JUMPILY
JUSTIFY

•J••••Y
OJIBWAY

••J•Y••
ENJOYED

••J•••Y
MAJESTY

•••J•Y•
DEEJAYS
VEEJAYS

•••J••Y
PALJOEY
PERJURY

••••J•Y
BLUEJAY
GRAYJAY
JOHNJAY
KILLJOY
OVERJOY

J•Z••••
JAZZAGE
JAZZIER
JAZZILY
JAZZING
JAZZMAN
JAZZMEN
JEZEBEL

J••Z•••
JAZZAGE
JAZZIER
JAZZILY
JAZZING
JAZZMAN
JAZZMEN

J•••Z••
JACUZZI

J••••Z•
JACUZZI

J•••••Z
JIMENEZ

KA•••••
KABUKIS
KACHINA
KADDISH
KAFFIRS
KAFTANS
KAHUNAS
KAISERS
KAISHEK
KAMPALA
KANAKAS
KANSANS
KARACHI
KARAJAN
KARAKUL
KARAKUM
KARAOKE
KARASEA
KARLOFF
KAROLYI
KASHMIR
KATHRYN
KATYDID
KAUFMAN
KAYAKED
KAYAKER
KAYOING
KAZAKHS

K•A••••
KEARNEY
KHAYYAM
KLAMATH
KLATSCH
KLAXONS
KNACKER
KNAVERY
KNAVISH
KRATERS
KRATION
KWACHAS
KWANZAS

K••A•••
KANAKAS
KARACHI
KARAJAN
KARAKUL
KARAKUM
KARAOKE
KARASEA
KAYAKED
KAYAKER
KAZAKHS
KERATIN
KILAUEA
KIWANIS
KNEADED
KNEADER
KOLACKY
KOMATSU
KUWAITI

K•••A••
KAFTANS
KAMPALA
KANSANS
KENDALL
KENYANS
KEYCARD
KEYPADS
KIDNAPS
KILDARE
KIMBALL
KIRMANS
KITBAGS
KKKKATY
KLAMATH
KODIAKS
KOOLAID
KOREANS

K••••A•
KAHUNAS
KANAKAS
KARAJAN
KAUFMAN
KEEPSAT
KEESHAN
KEROUAC
KETCHAM
KHAYYAM
KINEMAS
KINGMAN
KINGRAT
KINSMAN
KLUGMAN
KNEECAP
KNEEPAD
KORUNAS
KUMQUAT
KUTENAI
KWACHAS
KWANZAS

K•••••A
KACHINA
KAMPALA
KARASEA
KEDROVA
KENOSHA
KILAUEA
KRISHNA

•KA••••
OKAYING
SKANKED
SKANKER
SKATERS
SKATING

•K•A•••
UKRAINE

•K••A••
IKEBANA
KKKKATY
OKINAWA
SKIMASK
SKIRACK
SKYCAPS
SKYJACK
SKYLARK
SKYWARD
SKYWAYS

•K•••A•
BKLIBAN
SKIWEAR

•K••••A
IKEBANA
OKINAWA

••KA•••
ACKACKS
ALKALIS
ASKANCE
DUKAKIS
GOKARTS
JAKARTA
LIKABLE
MIKADOS
SUKARNO

••K•A••
AWKWARD
BAKLAVA
BOKHARA
DIKTATS
ECKHART
ELKHART
KKKKATY
LEKVARS
MIKHAIL
OAKLAND
OAKLAWN
TAKEAIM

••K••A•
BIKEWAY
DAKOTAN
DAKOTAS
INKYCAP
LAKOTAS
LIKEMAD
MAKEHAY
MAKEPAR
MAKEWAY
NIKOLAI
OAKLEAF
PIKEMAN
POKEDAT
POKESAT
YAKIMAS
YAKUZAS

••K•••A
BAKLAVA
BOKHARA
DYKSTRA
JAKARTA

•••KA••
ARIKARA
BALKANS
COCKADE
CORKAGE
DOCKAGE
FOLKART
HOOKAHS
JACKALS
JACKASS
JUNKART
KKKKATY
LEAKAGE
LINKAGE
PACKAGE
PACKARD
PARKADE
PICKAXE
POLKAED
PUNKAHS
SHIKARI
SINKAGE
SPOKANE
TANKARD
TOPKAPI

•••K•A•
AGAKHAN
ALYKHAN
BACKBAY
BARKSAT
BUCKRAM
BUCKSAW
CHUKKAS
DARKMAN
FOLKWAY

GURKHAS
HACKMAN
HACKSAW
HICKMAN
JACKDAW
JACKTAR
JUNKMAN
LOOKSAT
MARKHAM
MARKKAA
MILKMAN
MUSKRAT
PACKRAT
PARKWAY
PECKSAT
PEEKSAT
PICKSAT
QUOKKAS
RICKMAN
SICKBAY
SICKDAY
SICKPAY
SILKHAT
TALKSAT
WALKMAN
WALKWAY
WEEKDAY
WINKSAT
WORKDAY
WORKMAN

•••K••A
ARIKARA
BURKINA
ELEKTRA
JUNKDNA
MARKKAA
MARKOVA
RICKSHA

••••KA•
ALASKAN
BLINKAT
CHUKKAS
HANUKAH
KANAKAS
MARKKAA
MARYKAY
MOLOKAI
QUOKKAS
REBEKAH
SHANKAR
TROIKAS

••••K•A
MARKKAA

•••••KA
AMERIKA
BAZOOKA
MAZURKA
PALOOKA
PAPRIKA
SOYINKA

K•B••••
KABUKIS
KIBBLED
KIBBLES
KIBBUTZ
KOBLENZ
KOBOLDS
KUBRICK

K••B•••
KEEBLER
KIBBLED
KIBBLES
KIBBUTZ
KIMBALL
KITBAGS
KNOBBED

K•••B••
KNOBBED

K•••••B
KEYCLUB

•K•B•••
IKEBANA
SKIBOBS
SKIBOOT
SKYBLUE

•K••B••
BKLIBAN

•K•••B•
SKIBOBS

••KB•••
INKBLOT

••K•B••
JUKEBOX
LIKABLE

•••KB••
BACKBAY
BACKBIT
BUNKBED
LOCKBOX
SICKBAY
TALKBIG

•••K••B
BACKRUB

K•C••••
KACHINA
KICKERS
KICKIER
KICKING
KICKOFF
KICKOUT
KICKSIN
KICKSUP
KICKUPS
KUCHENS

K••C•••
KERCHOO
KETCHAM
KETCHES
KETCHUP
KEYCARD
KEYCLUB
KIMCHEE
KINCHIN
KITCHEN
KNACKER
KNOCKED
KNOCKER
KNUCKLE
KUTCHIN
KWACHAS

K•••C••
KARACHI
KITSCHY
KNEECAP
KOLACKY
KOPECKS

K••••C•
KLATSCH
KUBRICK

K•••••C
KEROUAC
KINETIC

•K•C•••
SKYCAPS

•K••C••
SKETCHY

•K•••C•
SKIRACK
SKYJACK

•K••••C
SKEPTIC

••KC•••
BOKCHOY

••K•C••
ACKACKS
INKYCAP

••K••C•
ASKANCE

•••KC••
MILKCOW

•••K•C•
PACKICE
TOPKICK

•••K••C
RAYKROC

K•D••••
KADDISH
KEDROVA
KIDDERS
KIDDIES
KIDDING
KIDDISH
KIDLIKE
KIDNAPS
KIDNEYS
KIDSKIN
KODIAKS

K••D•••
KADDISH
KENDALL
KIDDERS
KIDDIES
KIDDING
KIDDISH
KILDARE
KINDEST
KINDLED
KINDLES
KINDRED
KLUDGES
KURDISH

K•••D••
KATYDID
KEYEDIN
KEYEDUP
KINGDOM
KNEADED
KNEADER

K••••D•
KENNEDY
KEYPADS
KOBOLDS

K•••••D
KATYDID
KAYAKED
KEYCARD
KEYWORD
KIBBLED
KINDLED
KINDRED
KNEADED
KNEELED
KNEEPAD
KNELLED
KNITTED
KNOBBED
KNOCKED
KNOTTED
KNOUTED
KNURLED
KOOLAID

•K•D•••
EKEDOUT
SKIDDED
SKIDDER
SKIDDOO
SKIDROW
SKYDIVE

•K••D••
SKIDDED
SKIDDER
SKIDDOO

•K••••D
SKANKED
SKIDDED
SKILLED
SKIMMED
SKIMPED
SKINNED
SKIPPED
SKIRLED
SKIRRED
SKIRTED
SKULKED
SKUNKED
SKYWARD

••KD•••
DIKDIKS

••K•D••
ASKEDIN
DUKEDOM
HIKEDUP
MIKADOS
NAKEDLY
POKEDAT
RAKEDIN
RAKEDUP

••K••D•
MAKESDO

••K•••D
AWKWARD
AYKROYD
LIKEMAD
LIKENED
OAKLAND
REKEYED
TOKENED
WAKENED

•••KD••
JACKDAW
JUNKDNA
SICKDAY
WEEKDAY
WORKDAY

•••K•D•
COCKADE
PARKADE

•••K••D
BACKEND
BOOKEND
BUCKLED
BUNKBED
BUNKOED
CACKLED
ENSKIED
HACKLED
HECKLED
MANKIND
PACKARD
PICKLED
POLKAED
RANKLED
TACKLED
TANKARD
TICKLED
TINKLED
TREKKED
WEEKEND
WINKLED

••••K•D
BATIKED
BAULKED
BLACKED
BLANKED
BLINKED
BLOCKED
BRICKED
BROOKED
CAULKED
CHALKED
CHECKED
CHINKED
CHUCKED
CLACKED
CLANKED
CLERKED
CLICKED
CLINKED
CLOAKED
CLOCKED
CLUCKED
CLUNKED
CRACKED
CRANKED
CREAKED
CRICKED
CROAKED
CROOKED
FLANKED
FLECKED
FLICKED
FLOCKED
FLUNKED
FRANKED
FREAKED
FRISKED
FROCKED
INVOKED
KAYAKED
KNOCKED
NONSKID
PLANKED
PLINKED
PLUCKED
PLUNKED
PRANKED
PRICKED
PRINKED
QUACKED
REBUKED
REINKED
REVOKED
SHANKED
SHIRKED
SHOCKED
SHUCKED
SKANKED
SKULKED
SKUNKED
SLACKED
SLEEKED
SLICKED
SLINKED
SMACKED
SMIRKED
SNACKED
SNEAKED
SPANKED
SPARKED
SPECKED
SPOOKED
STACKED
STALKED
STOCKED
STOOKED
STROKED
SWANKED
THANKED
TRACKED
TREKKED
TRICKED
TRUCKED
TWEAKED
UNASKED
UNBAKED
UNLIKED
UNYOKED
WHACKED
WHISKED
WHIZKID
WRACKED
WREAKED
WRECKED

KE•••••
KEARNEY
KEDROVA
KEEBLER
KEELING
KEENERS
KEENEST
KEENING
KEEPERS
KEEPING
KEEPOFF
KEEPSAT
KEEPSIN
KEEPSON
KEEPSTO
KEEPSUP
KEESHAN
KEGLERS
KEILLOR
KELLOGG
KELPIES
KENDALL
KENNEDY
KENNELS
KENNETH
KENOSHA
KENTISH
KENYANS
KEPTOFF
KEPTOUT
KERATIN
KERCHOO
KERNELS
KERNING
KEROUAC
KERPLOP
KESTREL
KETCHAM
KETCHES
KETCHUP
KETONES
KETTLES
KEWPIES
KEYCARD
KEYCLUB
KEYEDIN
KEYEDUP
KEYGRIP
KEYHOLE
KEYLESS
KEYLIME
KEYNOTE
KEYPADS
KEYRING
KEYWEST
KEYWORD

K•E••••
KEEBLER
KEELING
KEENERS
KEENEST
KEENING
KEEPERS
KEEPING
KEEPOFF
KEEPSAT
KEEPSIN
KEEPSON
KEEPSTO
KEEPSUP
KEESHAN
KLEENEX
KMESONS
KNEADED
KNEADER
KNEECAP
KNEEING
KNEELED
KNEELER
KNEEPAD
KNEESUP
KNELLED
KNESSET
KREMLIN

K••E•••
KEYEDIN
KEYEDUP
KINEMAS
KINETIC
KLEENEX
KNEECAP
KNEEING
KNEELED
KNEELER
KNEEPAD
KNEESUP
KNIEVEL
KOPECKS
KOREANS
KUTENAI

K•••E••
KAISERS
KEENERS
KEENEST
KEEPERS
KEGLERS
KENNEDY
KENNELS
KENNETH
KERNELS
KEYLESS
KEYWEST
KICKERS
KIDDERS
KIDNEYS
KILLERS
KINDEST
KINLESS
KIPPERS
KISSERS
KITTENS
KNAVERY
KOBLENZ
KOSHERS
KRATERS
KUCHENS

K••••E•
KAISHEK
KARASEA
KAYAKED
KAYAKER
KEARNEY
KEEBLER
KELPIES
KESTREL
KETCHES
KETONES
KETTLES
KEWPIES
KIBBLED
KIBBLES
KICKIER
KIDDIES
KILAUEA
KILTIES
KIMCHEE
KINDLED
KINDLES
KINDRED
KINKIER
KINSMEN
KIRTLES
KISHKES
KITCHEN
KITTIES
KLEENEX
KLUDGES
KLUTZES
KNACKER
KNEADED
KNEADER
KNEELED
KNEELER
KNELLED
KNESSET
KNIEVEL
KNISHES
KNITTED
KNITTER
KNOBBED
KNOCKED
KNOCKER
KNOTTED
KNOUTED
KNURLED
KOOKIER
KYLIKES

K•••••E
KARAOKE
KEYHOLE
KEYLIME
KEYNOTE
KIDLIKE
KILDARE
KIMCHEE
KIRSTIE
KNUCKLE
KRINGLE

•KE••••
EKEDOUT
EKESOUT
IKEBANA
OKEEFFE
SKEETER
SKEEZIX
SKELTER
SKELTON
SKEPTIC
SKETCHY
SKEWERS
SKEWING

•K•E•••
OKEEFFE
SKEETER
SKEEZIX

•K••E••
SKATERS
SKEWERS
SKIVERS
SKIWEAR
SKYLESS
UKULELE

•K•••E•
SKANKED
SKANKER
SKEETER
SKELTER
SKIDDED
SKIDDER
SKILLED
SKILLET
SKIMMED
SKIMMER
SKIMPED
SKINNED
SKINNER
SKIPPED
SKIPPER
SKIRLED
SKIRRED
SKIRTED
SKITTER
SKOSHES
SKULKED
SKULKER
SKUNKED

•K••••E
OKEEFFE
SKIPOLE
SKITTLE
SKYBLUE
SKYDIVE
SKYLIKE
SKYLINE
UKRAINE
UKULELE

••KE•••
ALKENES
ASKEDIN
BAKEOFF
BIKEWAY
CAKEMIX
DUKEDOM
FAKEFUR
HIKEDUP
HIKESUP
JUKEBOX
LIKEMAD
LIKENED
LIKENEW
MAKEFOR
MAKEHAY
MAKEOFF
MAKEOUT
MAKEPAR
MAKESDO
MAKESIT
MAKESUP
MAKEUPS
MAKEWAY
NAKEDLY
PIKEMAN
PIKEMEN
POKEDAT
POKEFUN
POKESAT
RAKEDIN
RAKEDUP
RAKEOFF
RAKESIN
RAKESUP
REKEYED
TAKEAIM
TAKENIN
TAKENON
TAKEOFF
TAKEONE
TAKEOUT
TAKESIN
TAKESON
TAKESTO
TAKESUP
TAKETEN
TOKENED
UNKEMPT
WAKEFUL
WAKENED
WAKENER
WAKESUP
WOKENUP

••K•E••
ANKLETS
AUKLETS
CAKIEST
COKIEST
DEKLERK
HOKIEST
ICKIEST
INKIEST
INKLESS
INKWELL
JOKIEST
LAKIEST
OAKFERN
OAKLEAF
POKIEST
YAKKERS

••K••E•
ALKENES
LIKENED
LIKENEW
OAKTREE
PIKEMEN
REKEYED
TAKETEN
TOKENED
WAKENED
WAKENER

••K•••E
ASKANCE
INKLIKE
IRKSOME
LIKABLE
OAKLIKE
OAKTREE
TAKEONE
TEKTITE

•••KE••
AWAKENS
BACKEND
BACKERS
BANKERS
BARKEEP
BARKERS
BASKETS
BEAKERS
BECKETT
BICKERS
BONKERS
BOOKEND
BOSKETS
BROKEIN
BROKERS
BROKEUP
BUCKETS
BUCKEYE
BUNKERS
CANKERS
CHOKERS
CHOKEUP
COCKERS
CONKERS
COOKERS
COOKERY
CORKERS
DANKEST
DARKENS
DARKEST
DICKENS
DICKERS
DICKEYS
DOCKERS
DOCKETS
DONKEYS
DUNKERS
EVOKERS
FLAKERS
FORKERS
GASKETS
GAWKERS
HACKERS
HACKETT
HANKERS
HARKENS
HAWKERS
HAWKEYE
HONKERS
HUNKERS
HUSKERS
JACKETS
JACKEYS
JOCKEYS
JUNKERS
JUNKETS
KICKERS
LACKEYS
LANKEST
LEAKERS
LINKERS
LOCKERS
LOCKETS
LOOKERS
LUNKERS
MARKERS
MARKETS
MASKERS
MEEKEST
MICKEYS
MILKERS
MOCKERS
MOCKERY
MONKEES
MONKEYS
MUSKEGS
MUSKETS
NANKEEN
NECKERS
NICKELS
NICKERS
PACKERS
PACKETS
PEEKERS
PICKENS
PICKERS
PICKETS
PICKETT
PINKEST
POCKETS
PORKERS
PUCKERS
PUCKETT
PUNKERS
QUAKERS
RACKETS
RANKERS
RANKEST
RICKETY
RICKEYS
RISKERS
ROCKERS
ROCKERY
ROCKETS
ROOKERY
SACKERS
SECKELS
SEEKERS
SHAKERS
SHAKEUP
SHEKELS
SICKENS
SICKEST
SINKERS
SMOKERS
SOAKERS
SOCKETS
SOCKEYE
SPIKERS
SPOKEOF
SPOKEUP
STOKELY
STOKERS
SUCKERS
SULKERS
TACKERS
TALKERS
TANKERS
TICKERS
TICKETS
TICKETY
TINKERS
TUCKERS
TURKEYS
TUSKERS
WALKERS
WEAKENS
WEAKEST
WEEKEND
WICKERS
WICKETS
WINKERS
WORKERS
YAKKERS
YANKEES
YONKERS
ZONKERS

•••K•E•
BALKIER
BARKEEP
BARKIER
BARKLEY
BOOKIES
BOOKLET
BOSKIER
BUCKLED
BUCKLER
BUCKLES
BUCKLEY
BUCKOES
BULKIER
BUNKBED
BUNKOED
CACKLED
CACKLER
CACKLES
CHOKIER
CHUKKER
COCKIER
COCKLES
COCKNEY
COOKIES
CORKIER
DECKLES
DESKSET
DICKIES
DINKIER
DINKIES
DUCKIER
DUSKIER
ENSKIED
ENSKIES
EZEKIEL
FICKLER
FLAKIER
FLUKIER
FOLKIER
FOLKIES
FORKIER
FUNKIER
GAWKIER
GECKOES
GEEKIER
GUNKIER
HACKIES
HACKLED
HACKLES
HACKNEY
HANKIES
HECKLED
HECKLER
HECKLES
HUNKIER
HUSKIER
HUSKIES
JACKIES
JERKIER
JUNKIER
JUNKIES
KICKIER
KINKIER
KOOKIER
LANKIER
LEAKIER
LOOKSEE
LUCKIER
MILKIER
MILKMEN
MIRKIER
MONKEES
MUCKIER
MURKIER
MUSKIER
MUSKIES
NANKEEN
PAWKIER
PECKIER
PERKIER
PESKIER
PICKIER
PICKLED
PICKLES
PINKIES
POLKAED
PORKIER
PUNKIER
PUNKIES
QUAKIER
RANKLED
RANKLES
RICKLES
RISKIER

ROCKIER
ROCKIES
ROOKIER
ROOKIES
SARKIER
SHAKIER
SHAKOES
SICKLES
SILKIER
SMOKIER
SMOKIES
SNAKIER
SPIKIER
SULKIER
SULKIES
TACKIER
TACKLED
TACKLER
TACKLES
TALKIER
TALKIES
TICKLED
TICKLER
TICKLES
TINKLED
TINKLES
TOLKIEN
TOOKTEN
TREKKED
TREKKER
WACKIER
WINKLED
WINKLER
WINKLES
WONKIER
WOOKIES
WORKMEN
YANKEES
YORKIES
YUCKIER

•••K••E
BACKHOE
BOXKITE
BUCKEYE
COCKADE
CORKAGE
DOCKAGE
ERSKINE
HAWKEYE
LEAKAGE
LINKAGE
LOOKSEE
NECKTIE
PACKAGE
PACKICE
PARKADE
PICKAXE
PORKPIE
SINKAGE
SOCKEYE
SPOKANE
TREKKIE

••••KE•
BATIKED
BAULKED
BETAKEN
BETAKES
BETOKEN
BLACKED
BLACKEN
BLACKER
BLANKED
BLANKER
BLANKET
BLEAKER
BLINKED
BLINKER
BLOCKED
BLOCKER
BRACKEN
BRACKET
BREAKER
BRICKED
BRISKER
BRISKET
BROOKED
CAULKED
CAULKER
CHALKED
CHECKED
CHECKER
CHICKEN
CHINKED
CHUCKED
CHUKKER
CLACKED
CLANKED
CLERKED
CLICKED
CLINKED
CLINKER
CLOAKED
CLOCKED
CLOCKER
CLUCKED
CLUNKED
CLUNKER
CRACKED
CRACKER
CRANKED
CREAKED
CRICKED
CRICKET
CROAKED
CROOKED
DEBAKEY
DRINKER
DRUCKER
FLANKED
FLANKER
FLECKED
FLICKED
FLICKER
FLOCKED
FLUNKED
FRANKED
FRANKEN
FRANKER
FREAKED
FRISKED
FROCKED
HEARKEN
HOBOKEN
INJOKES
INTAKES
INVOKED
INVOKER
INVOKES
KAYAKED
KAYAKER
KISHKES
KNACKER
KNOCKED
KNOCKER
KYLIKES
LALAKER
MENCKEN
MONIKER
PASSKEY
PERUKES
PLACKET
PLANKED
PLINKED
PLUCKED
PLUNKED
PRANKED
PRICKED
PRINKED
QUACKED
QUICKEN
QUICKER
REBUKED
REBUKES
REINKED
REMAKES
RETAKEN
RETAKES
REVOKED
REVOKES
SHANKED
SHARKEY
SHIRKED
SHIRKER
SHOCKED
SHOCKER
SHRIKES
SHUCKED
SHUCKER
SKANKED
SKANKER
SKULKED
SKULKER
SKUNKED
SLACKED
SLACKEN
SLACKER
SLEEKED
SLEEKEN
SLEEKER
SLICKED
SLICKER
SLINKED
SMACKED
SMACKER
SMIRKED
SNACKED
SNACKER
SNEAKED
SNEAKER
SNICKER
SNOOKER
SNORKEL
SPANKED
SPANKER
SPARKED
SPEAKER
SPECKED
SPOOKED
STACKED
STALKED
STALKER
STARKER
STICKER
STINKER
STOCKED
STOOKED
STOOKEY
STRIKER
STRIKES
STROKED
STROKES
SWANKED
SWANKER
SWONKEN
THANKED
THICKEN
THICKER
THICKET
THINKER
TRACKED
TRACKER
TREKKED
TREKKER
TRICKED
TRICKER
TRINKET
TRUCKED
TRUCKEE
TRUCKER
TURNKEY
TWEAKED
UNASKED
UNBAKED
UNLIKED
UNMAKES
UNYOKED
UNYOKES
UPTAKES
WHACKED
WHISKED
WHISKER
WHISKEY
WRACKED
WREAKED
WRECKED
WRECKER

••••K•E
BLACKIE
CHUCKLE
CRACKLE
CRINKLE
FRANKIE
FRECKLE
FRICKIE
GRACKLE
KNUCKLE
PRICKLE
QUICKIE
SHACKLE
SPACKLE
SPARKLE
SPECKLE
TREKKIE
TRICKLE
TRUCKEE
TRUCKLE
TWINKLE
WILLKIE
WRINKLE

•••••KE
AIRLIKE
ANTLIKE
APELIKE
ARMLIKE
ASSLIKE
ATSTAKE
BAGLIKE
BATLIKE
BEDLIKE
BEELIKE
BESPOKE
BIBLIKE
BOWLIKE
BOXLIKE
BUDLIKE
CATLIKE
CONVOKE
COWLIKE
COWPOKE
CUPCAKE
CUPLIKE
CURLIKE
DISLIKE
DOGLIKE
DOTLIKE
EARLIKE
EELLIKE
ELFLIKE
EYELIKE
FADLIKE
FANLIKE
FATLIKE
FINLIKE
FORSAKE
FOXLIKE
GEMLIKE
GOBROKE
GODLIKE
GUMLIKE
HAGLIKE
HATLIKE
HENLIKE
HIPLIKE
HOECAKE
HOGLIKE
HOLYOKE
HOPLIKE
HOTCAKE
HUNLIKE
HUTLIKE
ICELIKE
INKLIKE
IVYLIKE
JAMLIKE
JAWLIKE
JIGLIKE
KARAOKE
KIDLIKE
LAWLIKE
LEGLIKE
LIPLIKE
MANLIKE
MISLIKE
MISTAKE
NETLIKE
NETSUKE
NIBLIKE
NUNLIKE
NUTLIKE
OAKLIKE
OARLIKE
OATLIKE
OILCAKE
OILLIKE
ORBLIKE
OROURKE
OUTTAKE
OWLLIKE
PANCAKE
PAPLIKE
PARTAKE
PEALIKE
PEGLIKE
PENLIKE
PIELIKE
PIGLIKE
PODLIKE
PROVOKE
RAMLIKE
RATLIKE
RAYLIKE
RIBLIKE
ROANOKE
RODLIKE
RUGLIKE
SACLIKE
SAWLIKE
SINLIKE
SKYLIKE
SONLIKE
SOWLIKE
SUNLIKE
TAGLIKE
TEACAKE
TINLIKE
TOELIKE
TOYLIKE
TUBLIKE
UNALIKE
URNLIKE
VANDYKE
WARLIKE
WAXLIKE
WEBLIKE
WIGLIKE

K•F••••
KAFFIRS
KAFTANS

K••F•••
KAFFIRS
KAUFMAN
KINFOLK
KNIFING

K••••F•
KARLOFF
KEEPOFF
KEPTOFF
KICKOFF
KISSOFF

K•••••F
KARLOFF
KEEPOFF
KEPTOFF
KICKOFF
KISSOFF

•K••F••
OKEEFFE
SKILFUL
SKINFUL

•K•••F•
OKEEFFE
SKILIFT

••KF•••
OAKFERN

••K•F••
ASKSFOR
FAKEFUR
MAKEFOR
POKEFUN
WAKEFUL

••K••F•
BAKEOFF
MAKEOFF
RAKEOFF
TAKEOFF

••K•••F
BAKEOFF
MAKEOFF
OAKLEAF
RAKEOFF
TAKEOFF

•••KF••
FORKFUL
LOOKFOR
SACKFUL
TANKFUL
WORKFOR

•••K•F•
BACKOFF
COOKOFF
KICKOFF
MARKOFF
PICKOFF
TICKOFF
TOOKOFF
WORKOFF

•••K••F
BACKOFF
COOKOFF
KICKOFF
MARKOFF
PICKOFF
SPOKEOF
TICKOFF
TOOKOFF
WORKOFF

••••K•F
SPEAKOF
THINKOF

K•G••••
KEGLERS

K••G•••
KEYGRIP
KINGDOM
KINGING
KINGMAN
KINGPIN
KINGRAT
KINGTUT
KLUGMAN
KNIGHTS

K•••G••
KLINGON
KLUDGES
KOSYGIN
KRINGLE

K••••G•
KELLOGG
KITBAGS

K•••••G
KAYOING
KEELING
KEENING
KEEPING
KELLOGG
KERNING
KEYRING
KICKING
KIDDING
KILLING
KILTING
KINGING
KINKING
KIPLING
KISSING
KNEEING
KNIFING
KNOWING

•K•••G•
SKYHIGH

•K••••G
OKAYING
SKATING
SKEWING

••K••G•
MAKINGS
VIKINGS

••K•••G
INKLING
YAKKING

•••K•G•
CORKAGE
DOCKAGE
LEAKAGE
LINKAGE
MUSKEGS
PACKAGE
SINKAGE

•••K••G
ALAKING
AWAKING
BACKING
BACKLOG
BALKING
BANKING
BARKING
BASKING
BILKING
BOOKING
BRAKING
BUCKING
BULKING
BUNKING
BUSKING
CALKING
CARKING
COCKING
CONKING
COOKING
CORKING
DECKING
DOCKING
DONKING
DUCKING
DUNKING
EVOKING
FINKING
FLAKING
FORKING
FUNKING
GAWKING
HACKING
HARKING
HAWKING
HOCKING
HONKING
HOOKING
HULKING
HUSKING
JACKING
JERKING
JINKING
JUNKING
KICKING
KINKING
LACKING
LEAKING
LICKING
LINKING
LOCKING
LOOKING
LUCKING
LURKING
MARKING
MASKING
MILKING
MOCKING
MUCKING
NECKING
NICKING
OINKING
PACKING
PARKING
PEAKING
PECKING
PEEKING
PERKING
PICKING
PINKING
QUAKING
RACKING
RANKING
REEKING
RISKING
ROCKING
ROOKING
RUCKING
SACKING
SEEKING
SHAKING
SINKING
SLAKING
SMOKING
SNAKING
SOAKING
SOCKING
SPIKING
SPOKING
STAKING
STOKING
SUCKING
SULKING
TACKING
TALKBIG
TALKING
TANKING
TASKING
TICKING
TUCKING
WALKING
WINKING
WORKING
YACKING
YAKKING
YANKING
YERKING
ZONKING

KH•••••
KHAYYAM

K•H••••
KAHUNAS

K••H•••
KACHINA
KASHMIR
KATHRYN
KEYHOLE
KISHKES
KOSHERS
KUCHENS

K•••H••
KAISHEK
KEESHAN
KERCHOO
KETCHAM
KETCHES
KETCHUP
KIMCHEE
KINCHIN
KINSHIP
KITCHEN
KNIGHTS
KNISHES
KNOWHOW
KRISHNA
KUTCHIN
KWACHAS

K••••H•
KARACHI
KAZAKHS
KENOSHA
KITSCHY

K•••••H
KADDISH
KENNETH
KENTISH
KIDDISH
KLAMATH
KLATSCH
KNAVISH
KURDISH

•KH••••
OKHOTSK

•K•H•••
AKIHITO
SKYHIGH
SKYHOOK

•K••H••
SKOSHES

•K•••H•
SKETCHY

•K••••H
SKYHIGH

••KH•••
BOKHARA
ECKHART
ELKHART
INKHORN
MIKHAIL
SIKHISM

••K•H••
BOKCHOY
LAKSHMI
MAKEHAY

•••KH••
AGAKHAN
ALYKHAN
BACKHOE
CHEKHOV
GURKHAS
MARKHAM
MARKHOR
SILKHAT

•••K•H•
COCKSHY
HOOKAHS
PUNKAHS
RICKSHA

•••K••H
BOOKISH
COCKISH
DARKISH
DAWKISH
DUSKISH
FOLKISH
GAWKISH
HAWKISH
LARKISH
MAWKISH
MONKISH
OSHKOSH
PEAKISH
PECKISH
PERKISH
PINKISH
PORKISH
PUCKISH
RANKISH
SICKISH
TURKISH
WEAKISH
YERKISH

••••KH•
KAZAKHS
SHEIKHS

••••K•H
HANUKAH
REBEKAH

KI•••••
KIBBLED
KIBBLES
KIBBUTZ
KICKERS
KICKIER
KICKING
KICKOFF
KICKOUT
KICKSIN
KICKSUP
KICKUPS
KIDDERS
KIDDIES
KIDDING
KIDDISH
KIDLIKE
KIDNAPS
KIDNEYS
KIDSKIN
KIKUYUS
KILAUEA
KILDARE
KILLERS
KILLING
KILLJOY
KILOTON
KILTIES
KILTING
KIMBALL
KIMCHEE
KIMONOS
KINCHIN
KINDEST
KINDLED
KINDLES
KINDRED
KINEMAS
KINETIC
KINFOLK
KINGDOM
KINGING
KINGMAN
KINGPIN
KINGRAT
KINGTUT
KINKIER
KINKILY
KINKING
KINLESS
KINSHIP
KINSMAN
KINSMEN
KIPLING
KIPPERS
KIRMANS
KIRSTIE
KIRTLES
KISHKES
KISSERS
KISSING
KISSOFF
KITBAGS
KITCHEN
KITSCHY
KITTENS
KITTIES
KIWANIS

K•I••••
KAISERS
KAISHEK
KEILLOR
KLINGON
KNIEVEL
KNIFING
KNIGHTS
KNISHES
KNITTED
KNITTER
KRINGLE
KRISHNA

K••I•••
KODIAKS
KYLIKES

K•••I••
KACHINA
KADDISH
KAFFIRS
KAYOING
KEELING
KEENING
KEEPING
KELPIES
KENTISH
KERNING
KEWPIES
KEYLIME
KEYRING
KICKIER
KICKING
KIDDIES
KIDDING
KIDDISH
KIDLIKE
KILLING
KILTIES
KILTING
KINGING
KINKIER
KINKILY
KINKING
KIPLING
KISSING
KITTIES
KNAVISH
KNEEING
KNIFING
KNOWING
KONTIKI
KOOKIER
KRATION
KUBRICK
KURDISH
KUWAITI

K••••I•
KABUKIS
KASHMIR
KATYDID
KEEPSIN
KERATIN
KEYEDIN
KEYGRIP
KICKSIN
KIDSKIN
KINCHIN
KINETIC
KINGPIN
KINSHIP
KIRSTIE
KIWANIS
KOOLAID
KOSYGIN
KREMLIN
KTOSLIN
KUTCHIN

K•••••I
KARACHI
KAROLYI
KONTIKI
KUTENAI
KUWAITI

•KI••••
AKIHITO
OKINAWA
SKIBOBS
SKIBOOT
SKIDDED
SKIDDER
SKIDDOO
SKIDROW
SKIJUMP
SKILFUL
SKILIFT
SKILLED
SKILLET
SKIMASK
SKIMMED
SKIMMER
SKIMPED
SKINFUL
SKINNED
SKINNER
SKIPOLE
SKIPOUT
SKIPPED
SKIPPER
SKIRACK
SKIRLED
SKIRRED
SKIRTED
SKIRUNS
SKISUIT
SKITOWS
SKITTER
SKITTLE
SKIVERS
SKIWEAR

•K•I•••
BKLIBAN

•K••I••
AKIHITO
OKAYING
SKATING
SKEWING
SKILIFT
SKYDIVE
SKYHIGH
SKYLIKE
SKYLINE
UKRAINE

•K•••I•
SKEEZIX
SKEPTIC
SKISUIT

••KI•••
BIKINIS
CAKIEST
COKIEST
ESKIMOS
HOKIEST
ICKIEST
INKIEST
JOKIEST
LAKIEST
MAKINGS
POKIEST
STKITTS
UNKINKS
VIKINGS
YAKIMAS

••K•I••
DIKDIKS
INKLIKE
INKLING
OAKLIKE
SIKHISM
TEKTITE
UNKNITS
YAKKING

••K••I•
ALKALIS
ASKEDIN
BIKINIS
CAKEMIX
DUKAKIS
MAKESIT
MIKHAIL
NOKOMIS
RAKEDIN
RAKESIN
TAKEAIM
TAKENIN
TAKESIN

••K•••I
LAKSHMI
NIKOLAI

•••KI••
AIRKISS
ALAKING
AWAKING
BACKING
BALKIER
BALKILY
BALKING
BANKING
BARKIER
BARKING
BASKING
BILKING
BODKINS
BOOKIES
BOOKING
BOOKISH
BOSKIER
BOXKITE
BRAKING
BUCKING
BULKIER
BULKING
BUNKING
BURKINA
BUSKING
BUSKINS
CALKING
CALKINS
CARKING
CATKINS
CHOKIER
COCKIER
COCKILY
COCKING
COCKISH
CONKING
COOKIES
COOKING
CORKIER
CORKING
DARKISH
DAWKISH
DECKING
DICKIES
DINKIER
DINKIES
DOCKING
DONKING
DUCKIER
DUCKING
DUNKING
DUNKIRK
DUSKIER
DUSKILY
DUSKISH
ENSKIED
ENSKIES
ERSKINE
EVOKING
EZEKIEL
FINKING
FIRKINS
FLAKIER
FLAKILY
FLAKING
FLUKIER
FOLKIER
FOLKIES
FOLKISH
FORKIER
FORKING
FUNKIER
FUNKILY
FUNKING
GASKINS
GAWKIER
GAWKILY
GAWKING
GAWKISH
GEEKIER
GUNKIER
HACKIES
HACKING
HANKIES
HARKING
HAWKING
HAWKINS
HAWKISH
HOCKING
HONKING
HOOKING
HOPKINS
HOSKINS
HULKING
HUNKIER
HUSKIER
HUSKIES
HUSKILY
HUSKING
JACKIES
JACKING
JERKIER
JERKILY
JERKING
JERKINS
JINKING
JOSKINS
JUNKIER
JUNKIES
JUNKING
KICKIER
KICKING
KINKIER
KINKILY
KINKING
KOOKIER
LACKING
LANKIER
LANKILY
LARKISH
LEAKIER
LEAKING
LICKING
LINKING
LOCKING
LOCKINS
LOOKING
LUCKIER
LUCKILY
LUCKING
LURKING
MALKINS
MANKIND
MARKING
MASKING
MAWKISH
MILKIER
MILKING
MIRKIER
MOCKING
MONKISH
MUCKIER
MUCKILY
MUCKING
MURKIER
MURKILY
MUSKIER
MUSKIES
NAPKINS
NECKING
NICKING
OINKING
PACKICE
PACKING
PARKING
PAWKIER
PEAKING
PEAKISH
PECKIER
PECKING
PECKISH
PEEKING
PERKIER
PERKILY
PERKING
PERKINS
PERKISH
PESKIER
PESKILY
PICKIER
PICKING
PINKIES
PINKING
PINKISH
PIPKINS
PORKIER
PORKISH
PUCKISH
PUNKIER
PUNKIES
QUAKIER
QUAKILY
QUAKING
RACKING
RANKING
RANKISH
REEKING
RISKIER
RISKILY
RISKING
ROCKIER
ROCKIES
ROCKING
ROOKIER
ROOKIES
ROOKING
RUCKING
SACKING
SARKIER
SEEKING
SELKIRK
SHAKIER
SHAKILY
SHAKING
SICKISH
SILKIER
SILKILY
SINKING
SISKINS
SLAKING
SMOKIER
SMOKIES
SMOKILY
SMOKING
SNAKIER
SNAKILY
SNAKING
SOAKING
SOCKING
SPIKIER
SPIKILY
SPIKING
SPOKING
STAKING
STOKING
SUCKING
SULKIER
SULKIES
SULKILY
SULKING
SUNKIST
TACKIER
TACKILY
TACKING
TALKIER
TALKIES
TALKING
TANKING
TASKING
TICKING
TOLKIEN
TOPKICK
TUCKING
TURKISH
WACKIER
WACKILY
WAIKIKI
WALKING
WALKINS
WEAKISH
WELKINS
WESKITS
WICKIUP
WINKING
WONKIER
WOOKIES
WORKING
YACKING
YAKKING
YANKING
YERKING
YERKISH
YORKIES
YORKIST
YUCKIER
ZONKING

•••K•I•
BACKBIT
BACKLIT
BACKSIN
BROKEIN
COCKPIT
DUCKPIN
KICKSIN
LOOKSIN
NECKTIE
PORKPIE
ROCKYII
ROCKYIV
SINKSIN
SOCKSIN
SUCKSIN
TALKBIG
TREKKIE
TUCKSIN
WORKSIN

•••K••I
ROCKYII
SHIKARI
TOPKAPI
WAIKIKI

••••KI•
ABNAKIS
BLACKIE
BREAKIN
BUMPKIN
CHECKIN
CLOCKIN
DOESKIN
DUKAKIS
EELSKIN
EVENKIS
FRANKIE
FRICKIE
GHERKIN
GRISKIN
JETSKIS
KABUKIS
KIDSKIN
MESSKIT
NONSKID
OILSKIN
PIGSKIN
PUMPKIN
PUSHKIN
QUICKIE
RAMEKIN
SALUKIS
SNEAKIN
TIOMKIN
TREKKIE
WHIZKID
WILLKIE

••••K•I
MOLOKAI

•••••KI
ABENAKI
DASHIKI
KONTIKI
PULASKI
WAIKIKI

K•••J••
KARAJAN
KILLJOY

•K•J•••
SKIJUMP
SKYJACK

KK•••••
KKKKATY

K•K••••
KIKUYUS
KKKKATY

K••K•••
KICKERS
KICKIER
KICKING
KICKOFF
KICKOUT
KICKSIN
KICKSUP
KICKUPS
KINKIER
KINKILY
KINKING
KKKKATY
KOOKIER

K•••K••
KABUKIS
KANAKAS
KARAKUL
KARAKUM
KAYAKED
KAYAKER
KAZAKHS
KIDSKIN
KISHKES
KNACKER
KNOCKED
KNOCKER
KNUCKLE
KYLIKES

K••••K•
KARAOKE
KIDLIKE
KODIAKS
KOLACKY
KONTIKI
KOPECKS
KUSPUKS

K•••••K
KAISHEK
KINFOLK
KUBRICK

•KK••••
KKKKATY

•K•K•••
KKKKATY

•K••K••
SKANKED
SKANKER
SKOOKUM
SKULKED
SKULKER
SKUNKED

•K•••K•
SKYLIKE

•K••••K
OKHOTSK
SKIMASK
SKIRACK
SKYHOOK
SKYJACK
SKYLARK

••KK•••
KKKKATY
YAKKERS
YAKKING

••K•K••
DUKAKIS

••K••K•
ACKACKS
DIKDIKS
INKLIKE
MUKLUKS
OAKLIKE
UNKINKS

••K•••K
DEKLERK
YAKUTSK

•••KK••
CHUKKAS
CHUKKER
MARKKAA
QUOKKAS
TREKKED
TREKKER
TREKKIE

•••K•K•
SHIKOKU
WAIKIKI

•••K••K
DUNKIRK
SELKIRK
TOPKICK

••••K•K
BANGKOK

KL•••••
KLAMATH
KLATSCH
KLAXONS
KLEENEX
KLINGON
KLUDGES
KLUGMAN
KLUTZES

K•L••••
KELLOGG
KELPIES
KILAUEA
KILDARE
KILLERS
KILLING
KILLJOY
KILOTON
KILTIES
KILTING
KOLACKY
KYLIKES

K••L•••
KARLOFF
KEELING
KEGLERS
KEILLOR
KELLOGG
KEYLESS
KEYLIME
KIDLIKE
KILLERS
KILLING
KILLJOY
KINLESS
KIPLING
KNELLED
KOBLENZ
KOOLAID
KOWLOON

K•••L••
KAROLYI
KEEBLER
KEILLOR
KERPLOP
KETTLES
KEYCLUB
KIBBLED
KIBBLES
KINDLED
KINDLES
KIRTLES
KNEELED
KNEELER
KNELLED
KNURLED
KOBOLDS
KREMLIN
KTOSLIN

K••••L•
KAMPALA
KENDALL
KENNELS
KERNELS
KEYHOLE
KIMBALL
KINFOLK
KINKILY
KNUCKLE
KRINGLE

K•••••L
KARAKUL
KENDALL
KESTREL
KIMBALL
KNIEVEL

•KL••••
BKLIBAN

•K•L•••
SKELTER
SKELTON
SKILFUL
SKILIFT
SKILLED
SKILLET
SKULKED
SKULKER
SKYLARK
SKYLESS
SKYLIKE
SKYLINE
UKULELE

•K••L••
SKILLED
SKILLET
SKIRLED
SKYBLUE

•K•••L•
SKIPOLE
SKITTLE
UKULELE

•K••••L
SKILFUL
SKINFUL

••KL•••
ANKLETS
AUKLETS
BAKLAVA
DEKLERK
INKLESS
INKLIKE
INKLING
MUKLUKS
OAKLAND
OAKLAWN
OAKLEAF
OAKLIKE

••K•L••
ALKALIS
INKBLOT
NIKOLAI

••K••L•
INKWELL
LIKABLE
NAKEDLY

••K•••L
INKWELL
MIKHAIL
WAKEFUL

•••KL••
BACKLIT
BACKLOG
BARKLEY
BOOKLET
BUCKLED
BUCKLER
BUCKLES
BUCKLEY
CACKLED
CACKLER
CACKLES
COCKLES
DECKLES
FICKLER
HACKLED
HACKLES
HECKLED
HECKLER
HECKLES
PICKLED
PICKLES
RANKLED
RANKLES
RICKLES
SICKLES
TACKLED
TACKLER
TACKLES
TICKLED
TICKLER
TICKLES
TINKLED
TINKLES
WINKLED
WINKLER
WINKLES

•••K•L•
BALKILY
COCKILY
DUSKILY
FLAKILY
FUNKILY
GAWKILY
HUSKILY
JACKALS
JERKILY
KINKILY
LANKILY
LUCKILY
MUCKILY
MURKILY
NICKELS
PERKILY
PESKILY
QUAKILY
RISKILY
SECKELS
SHAKILY
SHEKELS
SILKILY
SMOKILY
SNAKILY
SPIKILY
STOKELY
SULKILY
TACKILY
WACKILY

•••K••L
EZEKIEL
FORKFUL
SACKFUL
TANKFUL

••••KL•
BLACKLY
BLANKLY
BLEAKLY
BRISKLY
CHUCKLE
CRACKLE
CRACKLY
CRINKLE
CRINKLY
FRANKLY
FRECKLE
FRECKLY
GRACKLE
KNUCKLE
PRICKLE
PRICKLY
QUICKLY
SHACKLE
SLACKLY
SLEEKLY
SLICKLY
SPACKLE
SPARKLE
SPECKLE
STARKLY
THICKLY
TRICKLE
TRUCKLE
TWINKLE
TWINKLY
WRINKLE
WRINKLY

••••K•L
KARAKUL
SNORKEL

KM•••••
KMESONS

K•M••••
KAMPALA
KIMBALL
KIMCHEE
KIMONOS
KOMATSU
KUMQUAT

K••M•••
KIRMANS
KLAMATH
KREMLIN

K•••M••
KASHMIR
KAUFMAN
KINEMAS
KINGMAN
KINSMAN
KINSMEN
KLUGMAN

K••••M•
KEYLIME

K•••••M
KARAKUM
KETCHAM
KHAYYAM
KINGDOM

•K•M•••
SKIMASK
SKIMMED
SKIMMER
SKIMPED

•K••M••
SKIMMED
SKIMMER

•K•••M•
SKIJUMP

•K••••M
SKOOKUM

••KM•••
OAKMOSS

••K•M••
CAKEMIX
ESKIMOS
LIKEMAD
NOKOMIS
PIKEMAN
PIKEMEN
UNKEMPT
YAKIMAS

••K••M•
IRKSOME
LAKSHMI

••K•••M
DUKEDOM
SIKHISM
TAKEAIM

•••KM••
DARKMAN
HACKMAN
HICKMAN
JUNKMAN
MILKMAN
MILKMEN
RICKMAN
WALKMAN
WORKMAN
WORKMEN

•••K••M
BUCKRAM
MARKHAM

••••K•M
KARAKUM
SKOOKUM

KN•••••
KNACKER
KNAVERY
KNAVISH
KNEADED
KNEADER
KNEECAP
KNEEING
KNEELED
KNEELER
KNEEPAD
KNEESUP
KNELLED
KNESSET
KNIEVEL
KNIFING
KNIGHTS
KNISHES
KNITTED
KNITTER
KNOBBED
KNOCKED
KNOCKER
KNOSSOS
KNOTTED
KNOUTED
KNOWHOW
KNOWING
KNUCKLE
KNURLED

K•N••••
KANAKAS
KANSANS
KENDALL
KENNEDY
KENNELS
KENNETH
KENOSHA
KENTISH
KENYANS
KINCHIN
KINDEST
KINDLED
KINDLES
KINDRED
KINEMAS
KINETIC
KINFOLK
KINGDOM
KINGING
KINGMAN
KINGPIN
KINGRAT
KINGTUT
KINKIER
KINKILY
KINKING
KINLESS
KINSHIP
KINSMAN
KINSMEN
KONTIKI

K••N•••
KEENERS
KEENEST
KEENING
KENNEDY
KENNELS
KENNETH
KERNELS
KERNING
KEYNOTE
KIDNAPS
KIDNEYS
KLINGON
KRINGLE
KWANZAS

K•••N••
KAHUNAS
KEARNEY
KETONES
KIMONOS
KIWANIS
KLEENEX
KORUNAS
KUTENAI

K••••N•
KACHINA
KAFTANS
KANSANS
KAYOING
KEELING
KEENING
KEEPING
KENYANS
KERNING
KEYRING
KICKING
KIDDING
KILLING
KILTING
KINGING
KINKING
KIPLING
KIRMANS
KISSING
KITTENS
KLAXONS
KMESONS
KNEEING
KNIFING
KNOWING
KOBLENZ
KOREANS
KRISHNA
KUCHENS

K•••••N
KARAJAN
KATHRYN
KAUFMAN
KEEPSIN
KEEPSON
KEESHAN
KERATIN
KEYEDIN
KICKSIN
KIDSKIN
KILOTON
KINCHIN
KINGMAN
KINGPIN
KINSMAN
KINSMEN
KITCHEN
KLINGON
KLUGMAN
KOSYGIN
KOWLOON
KRATION
KREMLIN
KRYPTON
KTOSLIN
KUTCHIN

•K•N•••
OKINAWA
SKANKED
SKANKER
SKINFUL
SKINNED
SKINNER
SKUNKED

•K••N••
SKINNED
SKINNER

•K•••N•
IKEBANA
OKAYING
SKATING
SKEWING
SKIRUNS
SKYLINE
UKRAINE

•K••••N
BKLIBAN
SKELTON

••KN•••
UNKNITS
UNKNOTS
UNKNOWN

••K•N••
ALKENES
ASKANCE
BIKINIS
LIKENED
LIKENEW
MAKINGS
TAKENIN
TAKENON
TOKENED
UNKINKS
VIKINGS
WAKENED
WAKENER
WOKENUP

••K••N•
INKLING
OAKLAND
SUKARNO
TAKEONE
YAKKING

YOKOONO

••K•••N
ASKEDIN
DAKOTAN
INKHORN
OAKFERN
OAKLAWN
PIKEMAN
PIKEMEN
POKEFUN
RAKEDIN
RAKESIN
TAKENIN
TAKENON
TAKESIN
TAKESON
TAKETEN
UNKNOWN

•••KN••
BOWKNOT
COCKNEY
HACKNEY
LOCKNUT
TOPKNOT
YOUKNOW

•••K•N•
ALAKING
AWAKENS
AWAKING
BACKEND
BACKING
BALKANS
BALKING
BANKING
BARKING
BASKING
BECKONS
BILKING
BODKINS
BOOKEND
BOOKING
BRAKING
BUCKING
BULKING
BUNKING
BURKINA
BUSKING
BUSKINS
CALKING
CALKINS
CARKING
CATKINS
COCKING
CONKING
COOKING
CORKING
DARKENS
DECKING
DICKENS
DOCKING
DONKING
DUCKING
DUNKING
ERSKINE
EVOKING
FINKING
FIRKINS
FLAKING
FORKING
FUNKING
GASKINS
GAWKING
HACKING
HARKENS
HARKING
HAWKING
HAWKINS
HOCKING
HONKING
HOOKING
HOPKINS
HOSKINS
HULKING
HUSKING
JACKING
JERKING
JERKINS
JINKING
JOSKINS
JUNKDNA
JUNKING
KICKING
KINKING
LACKING
LEAKING
LICKING
LINKING
LOCKING
LOCKINS
LOOKING
LUCKING
LURKING
MALKINS
MANKIND
MARKING
MASKING
MILKING
MOCKING
MUCKING
NAPKINS
NECKING
NICKING
OINKING
PACKING
PARKING
PEAKING
PECKING
PEEKING
PERKING
PERKINS
PICKENS
PICKING
PINKING
PIPKINS
QUAKING
RACKING
RANKING
RECKONS
REEKING
RISKING
ROCKING
ROOKING
RUCKING
SACKING
SEEKING
SHAKING
SICKENS
SINKING
SISKINS
SLAKING
SMOKING
SNAKING
SOAKING
SOCKING
SPIKING
SPOKANE
SPOKING
STAKING
STOKING
SUCKING
SULKING
TACKING
TALKING
TANKING
TASKING
TICKING
TUCKING
WALKING
WALKINS
WALKONS
WEAKENS
WEEKEND
WELKINS
WINKING
WORKING
YACKING
YAKKING
YANKING
YERKING
ZONKING

•••K••N
AGAKHAN
ALYKHAN
BACKSIN
BANKSON
BROKEIN
DARKMAN
DUCKPIN
HACKMAN
HICKMAN
JACKSON
JUNKMAN
KICKSIN
LOCKSON
LOOKSIN
LOOKSON
MILKMAN
MILKMEN
MILKRUN
NANKEEN
PICKSON
RICKMAN
SINKSIN
SOCKSIN
SUCKSIN
TACKSON
TOLKIEN
TOOKTEN
TUCKSIN
WALKMAN
WALKSON
WORKMAN
WORKMEN
WORKSIN
WORKSON
YANKTON

••••K•N
ALASKAN
BELAKUN
BETAKEN
BETOKEN
BLACKEN
BRACKEN
BREAKIN
BUMPKIN
CHECKIN
CHICKEN
CLOCKIN
DOESKIN
EELSKIN
FRANKEN
GHERKIN
GRISKIN
HEARKEN
HOBOKEN
IRECKON
KIDSKIN
MENCKEN
OILSKIN
PIGSKIN
PUMPKIN
PUSHKIN
QUICKEN
RAMEKIN
RETAKEN
SLACKEN
SLEEKEN
SNEAKIN
SWONKEN
THICKEN
TIOMKIN

KO•••••
KOBLENZ
KOBOLDS
KODIAKS
KOLACKY
KOMATSU
KONTIKI
KOOKIER
KOOLAID
KOPECKS
KOREANS
KORUNAS
KOSHERS
KOSYGIN
KOWLOON
KOWTOWS

K•O••••
KNOBBED
KNOCKED
KNOCKER
KNOSSOS
KNOTTED
KNOUTED
KNOWHOW
KNOWING
KOOKIER
KOOLAID
KTOSLIN

K••O•••
KAROLYI
KAYOING
KENOSHA
KEROUAC
KETONES
KILOTON
KIMONOS
KOBOLDS

K•••O••
KARAOKE
KARLOFF
KEDROVA
KEEPOFF
KELLOGG
KEPTOFF
KEPTOUT
KEYHOLE
KEYNOTE
KEYWORD
KICKOFF
KICKOUT
KINFOLK
KISSOFF
KLAXONS
KMESONS
KOWLOON
KOWTOWS

K••••O•
KEEPSON
KEILLOR
KERCHOO
KERPLOP
KILLJOY
KILOTON
KIMONOS
KINGDOM
KLINGON
KNOSSOS
KNOWHOW
KOWLOON
KRATION
KRYPTON

K•••••O
KEEPSTO
KERCHOO

•KO••••
SKOOKUM
SKOSHES

•K•O•••
OKHOTSK
SKOOKUM

•K••O••
EKEDOUT
EKESOUT
SKIBOBS
SKIBOOT
SKIPOLE
SKIPOUT
SKITOWS
SKYHOOK

•K•••O•
SKELTON
SKIBOOT
SKIDDOO
SKIDROW
SKYHOOK

•K••••O
AKIHITO
SKIDDOO

••KO•••
DAKOTAN
DAKOTAS
LAKOTAS
NIKOLAI
NOKOMIS
YOKOONO

••K•O••
ASKSOUT
AYKROYD
BAKEOFF
INKHORN
IRKSOME
MAKEOFF
MAKEOUT
OAKMOSS
RAKEOFF
TAKEOFF
TAKEONE
TAKEOUT
UNKNOTS
UNKNOWN
YOKOONO

••K••O•
ASKSFOR
BOKCHOY
DUKEDOM
ESKIMOS
INKBLOT
INKSPOT
JUKEBOX
MAKEFOR
MIKADOS
TAKENON
TAKESON

••K•••O
MAKESDO
SUKARNO
TAKESTO
YOKOONO

•••KO••
BACKOFF
BACKOUT
BECKONS
BUCKOES
BUNKOED
CONKOUT
COOKOFF
COOKOUT
CUCKOOS
DECKOUT
GECKOES
HICKORY
KICKOFF
KICKOUT
LOCKOUT
LOOKOUT
LUCKOUT
MARKOFF
MARKOVA
OSHKOSH
PEEKOUT
PICKOFF
PICKOUT
RECKONS
SACKOUT
SEEKOUT
SHAKOES
SHIKOKU
SICKOUT
SOUKOUS
TALKOUT
TICKOFF
TOOKOFF
TOOKOUT
WALKONS
WALKOUT
WINKOUT
WORKOFF
WORKOUT
ZONKOUT

•••K•O•
BACKHOE
BACKLOG
BANKSON
BOWKNOT
CHEKHOV
COOKTOP
CUCKOOS
DESKTOP
JACKPOT
JACKSON
LOCKBOX
LOCKSON
LOOKFOR
LOOKSON
MARKHOR
MILKCOW
MILKSOP
PICKSON
RAYKROC
SPOKEOF
TACKSON
TANKTOP
TOPKNOT
WALKSON
WORKFOR
WORKSON
YANKTON
YOUKNOW

•••K••O
LOOKSTO
TALKSTO

••••KO•
BANGKOK
FRANKOZ
IRECKON
NABOKOV
SPEAKOF
THINKOF

••••K•O
FLOCKTO
STICKTO
STUCKTO

•••••KO
GROMYKO
LYSENKO

K•P••••
KEPTOFF
KEPTOUT
KIPLING
KIPPERS
KOPECKS

K••P•••
KAMPALA
KEEPERS
KEEPING
KEEPOFF
KEEPSAT
KEEPSIN
KEEPSON
KEEPSTO
KEEPSUP
KELPIES
KERPLOP
KEWPIES
KEYPADS
KIPPERS
KRYPTON
KUSPUKS

K•••P••
KINGPIN
KNEEPAD

K••••P•
KICKUPS
KIDNAPS

K•••••P
KEEPSUP
KERPLOP
KETCHUP
KEYEDUP
KEYGRIP
KICKSUP
KINSHIP
KNEECAP
KNEESUP

•K•P•••
SKEPTIC
SKIPOLE
SKIPOUT
SKIPPED
SKIPPER

•K••P••
SKIMPED
SKIPPED
SKIPPER

•K•••P•
SKYCAPS

•K••••P
SKIJUMP

••K•P••
INKSPOT
MAKEPAR

••K••P•
MAKEUPS
UNKEMPT

••K•••P
HIKEDUP
HIKESUP
INKYCAP
MAKESUP
RAKEDUP
RAKESUP
TAKESUP
WAKESUP
WOKENUP

•••KP••
COCKPIT
DUCKPIN
JACKPOT
PORKPIE
SICKPAY

•••K•P•
BACKUPS
HOOKUPS
KICKUPS
LINKUPS
LOCKUPS
LOOKUPS
MARKUPS
MOCKUPS
PICKUPS
TOPKAPI
WALKUPS
WORKUPS

•••K••P
BACKSUP
BARKEEP
BROKEUP
BUCKSUP
CHOKEUP
COOKSUP
COOKTOP
DESKTOP
HOOKSUP
JACKSUP
KICKSUP
LOCKSUP
LOOKSUP
MARKSUP
MILKSOP
MUCKSUP
PACKSUP
PERKSUP
PICKSUP
RACKSUP
SHAKEUP
SOAKSUP
SPOKEUP
TALKSUP
TANKSUP
TANKTOP
WICKIUP
WORKSUP

••••K•P
BREAKUP
CHALKUP
CHECKUP
CRACKUP
CRANKUP
SHOOKUP
SPEAKUP
STACKUP
STICKUP
STOCKUP
STUCKUP
THINKUP

K••Q•••
KUMQUAT

KR•••••
KRATERS
KRATION
KREMLIN
KRINGLE
KRISHNA
KRYPTON

K•R••••
KARACHI
KARAJAN
KARAKUL
KARAKUM
KARAOKE
KARASEA
KARLOFF
KAROLYI
KERATIN
KERCHOO
KERNELS
KERNING
KEROUAC
KERPLOP
KIRMANS
KIRSTIE
KIRTLES
KOREANS
KORUNAS
KURDISH

K••R•••
KEARNEY
KEDROVA
KEYRING
KNURLED
KUBRICK

K•••R••
KATHRYN
KESTREL
KEYGRIP
KINDRED
KINGRAT

K••••R•
KAFFIRS
KAISERS
KEENERS
KEEPERS
KEGLERS
KEYCARD
KEYWORD
KICKERS
KIDDERS
KILDARE
KILLERS
KIPPERS
KISSERS
KNAVERY
KOSHERS
KRATERS

K•••••R
KASHMIR
KAYAKER
KEEBLER
KEILLOR
KICKIER
KINKIER
KNACKER
KNEADER
KNEELER
KNITTER
KNOCKER
KOOKIER

•KR••••
UKRAINE

•K•R•••
SKIRACK
SKIRLED
SKIRRED
SKIRTED
SKIRUNS

•K••R••
SKIDROW
SKIRRED

•K•••R•
SKATERS
SKEWERS
SKIVERS
SKYLARK
SKYWARD

•K••••R
SKANKER
SKEETER
SKELTER
SKIDDER
SKIMMER
SKINNER
SKIPPER
SKITTER
SKIWEAR
SKULKER

••KR•••
AYKROYD

••K•R••
GOKARTS
JAKARTA
OAKTREE
SUKARNO

••K••R•
AWKWARD
BOKHARA
DEKLERK
DYKSTRA
ECKHART
ELKHART
INKHORN
LEKVARS
OAKFERN
YAKKERS

••K•••R
ASKSFOR
FAKEFUR
MAKEFOR
MAKEPAR
WAKENER

•••KR••
BACKRUB
BUCKRAM
MILKRUN
MUSKRAT
PACKRAT
RAYKROC

•••K•R•
ARIKARA
BACKERS
BANKERS
BARKERS
BEAKERS
BICKERS
BONKERS
BROKERS
BUNKERS
CANKERS
CHOKERS
COCKERS
CONKERS
COOKERS
COOKERY
CORKERS
DICKERS
DOCKERS
DUNKERS
DUNKIRK
ELEKTRA
EVOKERS
FLAKERS
FOLKART
FORKERS
GAWKERS
HACKERS
HANKERS
HAWKERS
HICKORY
HONKERS
HUNKERS
HUSKERS
JUNKART
JUNKERS
KICKERS
LEAKERS
LINKERS
LOCKERS
LOOKERS
LUNKERS
MARKERS
MASKERS
MILKERS
MOCKERS
MOCKERY
NECKERS
NICKERS
PACKARD
PACKERS
PEEKERS
PICKERS
PORKERS
PUCKERS
PUNKERS
QUAKERS
RANKERS
RISKERS
ROCKERS
ROCKERY
ROOKERY
SACKERS
SEEKERS
SELKIRK
SHAKERS
SHIKARI
SINKERS
SMOKERS
SOAKERS
SPIKERS
STOKERS
SUCKERS
SULKERS
TACKERS
TALKERS
TANKARD
TANKERS
TICKERS
TINKERS
TUCKERS
TUSKERS
WALKERS
WICKERS
WINKERS
WORKERS
YAKKERS
YONKERS
ZONKERS

•••K••R
BALKIER
BARKIER
BOSKIER
BUCKLER
BULKIER
CACKLER
CHOKIER
CHUKKER
COCKIER
CORKIER
DINKIER
DUCKIER
DUSKIER
FICKLER
FLAKIER
FLUKIER
FOLKIER
FORKIER
FUNKIER
GAWKIER
GEEKIER
GUNKIER
HECKLER
HUNKIER
HUSKIER
JACKTAR
JERKIER
JUNKIER
KICKIER
KINKIER
KOOKIER
LANKIER
LEAKIER
LOOKFOR
LUCKIER
MARKHOR
MILKIER
MIRKIER
MUCKIER
MURKIER
MUSKIER
PAWKIER
PECKIER
PERKIER
PESKIER
PICKIER
PORKIER
PUNKIER
QUAKIER
RISKIER
ROCKIER
ROOKIER
SARKIER
SHAKIER
SILKIER
SMOKIER
SNAKIER
SPIKIER
SULKIER
TACKIER
TACKLER
TALKIER
TICKLER
TREKKER
WACKIER
WINKLER
WONKIER
WORKFOR
YUCKIER

••••KR•
CONAKRY

••••K•R
BLACKER
BLANKER
BLEAKER
BLINKER
BLOCKER
BREAKER
BRISKER
CAULKER
CHECKER
CHUKKER
CLINKER
CLOCKER
CLUNKER
CRACKER
DRINKER
DRUCKER
FLANKER
FLICKER
FRANKER
INVOKER
KAYAKER
KNACKER
KNOCKER
LALAKER
MONIKER
QUICKER
SHANKAR
SHIRKER
SHOCKER
SHUCKER
SKANKER
SKULKER
SLACKER
SLEEKER
SLICKER
SMACKER
SNACKER
SNEAKER
SNICKER
SNOOKER
SPANKER
SPEAKER
STALKER
STARKER
STICKER
STINKER
STRIKER
SWANKER
THICKER
THINKER
TRACKER
TREKKER
TRICKER
TRUCKER
WHISKER
WRECKER

•••••KR
ABUBAKR

K•S••••
KASHMIR
KESTREL
KISHKES
KISSERS
KISSING
KISSOFF
KOSHERS
KOSYGIN
KUSPUKS

K••S•••
KAISERS
KAISHEK
KANSANS
KEESHAN
KIDSKIN
KINSHIP
KINSMAN
KINSMEN
KIRSTIE
KISSERS
KISSING

KISSOFF
KITSCHY
KMESONS
KNESSET
KNISHES
KNOSSOS
KRISHNA
KTOSLIN

K•••S••
KARASEA
KEEPSAT
KEEPSIN
KEEPSON
KEEPSTO
KEEPSUP
KENOSHA
KICKSIN
KICKSUP
KLATSCH
KNEESUP
KNESSET
KNOSSOS

K••••S•
KADDISH
KEENEST
KENTISH
KEYLESS
KEYWEST
KIDDISH
KINDEST
KINLESS
KNAVISH
KOMATSU
KURDISH

K•••••S
KABUKIS
KAFFIRS
KAFTANS
KAHUNAS
KAISERS
KANAKAS
KANSANS
KAZAKHS
KEENERS
KEEPERS
KEGLERS
KELPIES
KENNELS
KENYANS
KERNELS
KETCHES
KETONES
KETTLES
KEWPIES
KEYLESS
KEYPADS
KIBBLES
KICKERS
KICKUPS
KIDDERS
KIDDIES
KIDNAPS
KIDNEYS
KIKUYUS
KILLERS
KILTIES
KIMONOS
KINDLES
KINEMAS
KINLESS
KIPPERS
KIRMANS
KIRTLES
KISHKES
KISSERS
KITBAGS
KITTENS
KITTIES
KIWANIS
KLAXONS
KLUDGES
KLUTZES
KMESONS
KNIGHTS
KNISHES
KNOSSOS
KOBOLDS
KODIAKS
KOPECKS
KOREANS
KORUNAS
KOSHERS
KOWTOWS
KRATERS
KUCHENS
KUSPUKS
KWACHAS
KWANZAS
KYLIKES

•K•S•••
EKESOUT
SKISUIT
SKOSHES

•K•••S•
OKHOTSK
SKIMASK
SKYLESS

•K••••S
SKATERS
SKEWERS
SKIBOBS
SKIRUNS
SKITOWS
SKIVERS
SKOSHES
SKYCAPS
SKYLESS
SKYWAYS

••KS•••
ASKSFOR
ASKSOUT
DYKSTRA
INKSPOT
IRKSOME
LAKSHMI

••K•S••
HIKESUP
MAKESDO
MAKESIT
MAKESUP
POKESAT
RAKESIN
RAKESUP
TAKESIN
TAKESON
TAKESTO
TAKESUP
WAKESUP

••K••S•
CAKIEST
COKIEST
HOKIEST
ICKIEST
INKIEST
INKLESS
JOKIEST
LAKIEST
OAKMOSS
POKIEST
SIKHISM
YAKUTSK

••K•••S
ACKACKS
ALKALIS
ALKENES
ANKLETS
AUKLETS
BIKINIS
DAKOTAS
DIKDIKS
DIKTATS
DUKAKIS
ESKIMOS
GOKARTS
INKLESS
KIKUYUS
LAKOTAS
LEKVARS
MAKEUPS
MAKINGS
MIKADOS
MUKLUKS
NOKOMIS
OAKMOSS
STKITTS
UNKINKS
UNKNITS
UNKNOTS
VIKINGS
YAKIMAS
YAKKERS
YAKUZAS

•••KS••
BACKSIN
BACKSUP
BANKSON
BARKSAT
BUCKSAW
BUCKSUP
COCKSHY
COOKSUP
DESKSET
HACKSAW
HOOKSUP
JACKSON
JACKSUP
KICKSIN
KICKSUP
LOCKSON
LOCKSUP
LOOKSAT
LOOKSEE
LOOKSIN
LOOKSON
LOOKSTO
LOOKSUP
MARKSUP
MILKSOP
MUCKSUP
PACKSUP
PECKSAT
PEEKSAT
PERKSUP
PICKSAT
PICKSON
PICKSUP
RACKSUP
RICKSHA
SINKSIN
SOAKSUP
SOCKSIN
SUCKSIN
TACKSON
TALKSAT
TALKSTO
TALKSUP
TANKSUP
TUCKSIN
WALKSON
WINKSAT
WORKSIN
WORKSON
WORKSUP

•••K•S•
AIRKISS
BOOKISH
COCKISH
DANKEST
DARKEST
DARKISH
DAWKISH
DUSKISH
FOLKISH
GAWKISH
HAWKISH
JACKASS
LANKEST
LARKISH
MAWKISH
MEEKEST
MONKISH
OSHKOSH
PEAKISH
PECKISH
PERKISH
PINKEST
PINKISH
PORKISH
PUCKISH
RANKEST
RANKISH
SICKEST
SICKISH
SUNKIST
TURKISH
WEAKEST
WEAKISH
YERKISH
YORKIST

•••K••S
AIRKISS
AWAKENS
BACKERS
BACKUPS
BALKANS
BANKERS
BARKERS
BASKETS
BEAKERS
BECKONS
BICKERS
BODKINS
BONKERS
BOOKIES
BOSKETS
BROKERS
BUCKETS
BUCKLES
BUCKOES
BUNKERS
BUSKINS
CACKLES
CALKINS
CANKERS
CATKINS
CHOKERS
CHUKKAS
COCKERS
COCKLES
CONKERS
COOKERS
COOKIES
CORKERS
CUCKOOS
DARKENS
DECKLES
DICKENS
DICKERS
DICKEYS
DICKIES
DINKIES
DOCKERS
DOCKETS
DONKEYS
DUNKERS
ENSKIES
EVOKERS
FIRKINS
FLAKERS
FOLKIES
FORKERS
GASKETS
GASKINS
GAWKERS
GECKOES
GURKHAS
HACKERS
HACKIES
HACKLES
HANKERS
HANKIES
HARKENS
HAWKERS
HAWKINS
HECKLES
HONKERS
HOOKAHS
HOOKUPS
HOPKINS
HOSKINS
HUNKERS
HUSKERS
HUSKIES
JACKALS
JACKASS
JACKETS
JACKEYS
JACKIES
JERKINS
JOCKEYS
JOSKINS
JUNKERS
JUNKETS
JUNKIES
KICKERS
KICKUPS
LACKEYS
LEAKERS
LINKERS
LINKUPS
LOCKERS
LOCKETS
LOCKINS
LOCKUPS
LOOKERS
LOOKUPS
LUNKERS
MALKINS
MARKERS
MARKETS
MARKUPS
MASKERS
MICKEYS
MILKERS
MOCKERS
MOCKUPS
MONKEES
MONKEYS
MUSKEGS
MUSKETS
MUSKIES
NAPKINS
NECKERS
NICKELS
NICKERS
PACKERS
PACKETS
PEEKERS
PERKINS
PICKENS
PICKERS
PICKETS
PICKLES
PICKUPS
PINKIES
PIPKINS
POCKETS
PORKERS
PUCKERS
PUNKAHS
PUNKERS
PUNKIES
QUAKERS
QUOKKAS
RACKETS
RANKERS
RANKLES
RECKONS
RICKEYS
RICKLES
RISKERS
ROCKERS
ROCKETS
ROCKIES
ROOKIES
SACKERS
SECKELS
SEEKERS
SHAKERS
SHAKOES
SHEKELS
SICKENS
SICKLES
SINKERS
SISKINS
SMOKERS
SMOKIES
SOAKERS
SOCKETS
SOUKOUS
SPIKERS
STOKERS
SUCKERS
SULKERS
SULKIES
TACKERS
TACKLES
TALKERS
TALKIES
TANKERS
TICKERS
TICKETS
TICKLES
TINKERS
TINKLES
TUCKERS
TURKEYS
TUSKERS
WALKERS
WALKINS
WALKONS
WALKUPS
WEAKENS
WELKINS
WESKITS
WICKERS
WICKETS
WINKERS
WINKLES
WOOKIES
WORKERS
WORKUPS
YAKKERS
YANKEES
YONKERS
YORKIES
ZONKERS

••••K•S
ABNAKIS
BETAKES
CHUKKAS
DUKAKIS
EVENKIS
INJOKES
INTAKES
INVOKES
JETSKIS
KABUKIS
KANAKAS
KAZAKHS
KISHKES
KYLIKES
PERUKES
QUOKKAS
REBUKES
REMAKES
RETAKES
REVOKES
SALUKIS
SHEIKHS
SHRIKES
STRIKES
STROKES
TROIKAS
UNMAKES
UNYOKES
UPTAKES

•••••KS
ACKACKS
ANORAKS
ARAWAKS
ATTACKS
ATTUCKS
BEDECKS
BUROAKS
DAMASKS
DEBARKS
DEBUNKS
DIKDIKS
DYBBUKS
EMBANKS
EMBARKS
EXWORKS
HIJACKS
HIJINKS
KODIAKS
KOPECKS
KUSPUKS
MOHAWKS
MUKLUKS
MUZHIKS
NUDNIKS
PINOAKS
RECORKS
REDOAKS
REHOOKS
RELOCKS
REMARKS
REWORKS
RHEBOKS
SCREAKS
SHRIEKS
SHRINKS
SHTICKS
SLOVAKS
SQUAWKS
SQUEAKS
STREAKS
SUSLIKS
TANOAKS
THWACKS
TUGRIKS
UNCORKS
UNHOOKS
UNKINKS
UNLINKS
UNLOCKS
UNMASKS
UNPACKS
UNTACKS
UPLINKS
UPTICKS

KT•••••
KTOSLIN

K•T••••
KATHRYN
KATYDID
KETCHAM
KETCHES
KETCHUP
KETONES
KETTLES
KITBAGS
KITCHEN
KITSCHY
KITTENS
KITTIES
KUTCHIN
KUTENAI

K••T•••
KAFTANS
KENTISH
KEPTOFF
KEPTOUT
KESTREL
KETTLES
KILTIES
KILTING
KIRTLES
KITTENS
KITTIES
KLATSCH
KLUTZES
KNITTED
KNITTER
KNOTTED
KONTIKI
KOWTOWS
KRATERS
KRATION

K•••T••
KERATIN
KILOTON
KINETIC
KINGTUT
KIRSTIE
KNITTED
KNITTER
KNOTTED
KNOUTED
KOMATSU
KRYPTON

K••••T•
KEEPSTO
KENNETH
KEYNOTE
KIBBUTZ
KKKKATY
KLAMATH
KNIGHTS
KUWAITI

K•••••T
KEENEST
KEEPSAT
KEPTOUT
KEYWEST
KICKOUT
KINDEST
KINGRAT
KINGTUT
KNESSET
KUMQUAT

•K•T•••
SKATERS
SKATING
SKETCHY
SKITOWS
SKITTER
SKITTLE

•K••T••
OKHOTSK
SKEETER
SKELTER
SKELTON
SKEPTIC
SKIRTED
SKITTER
SKITTLE

•K•••T•
AKIHITO
KKKKATY

•K••••T
EKEDOUT
EKESOUT
SKIBOOT
SKILIFT
SKILLET
SKIPOUT
SKISUIT

••KT•••
DIKTATS
OAKTREE
TEKTITE

••K•T••
DAKOTAN
DAKOTAS
DYKSTRA
LAKOTAS
STKITTS
TAKETEN
YAKUTSK

••K••T•
ANKLETS
AUKLETS
DIKTATS
GOKARTS
JAKARTA
KKKKATY
STKITTS
TAKESTO
TEKTITE
UNKNITS
UNKNOTS

••K•••T
ASKSOUT
CAKIEST
COKIEST
ECKHART
ELKHART
HOKIEST
ICKIEST
INKBLOT
INKIEST
INKSPOT
JOKIEST
LAKIEST
MAKEOUT
MAKESIT
POKEDAT
POKESAT
POKIEST
TAKEOUT
UNKEMPT

•••KT••
COOKTOP
DESKTOP
ELEKTRA
JACKTAR
NECKTIE
TANKTOP
TOOKTEN
YANKTON

•••K•T•
BASKETS
BECKETT
BOSKETS
BOXKITE
BUCKETS
DOCKETS
GASKETS
HACKETT
JACKETS
JUNKETS
KKKKATY
LOCKETS
LOOKSTO
MARKETS
MUSKETS
PACKETS
PICKETS
PICKETT
POCKETS
PUCKETT
RACKETS
RICKETY
ROCKETS
SOCKETS
TALKSTO
TICKETS
TICKETY
WESKITS
WICKETS

•••K••T
BACKBIT
BACKLIT
BACKOUT
BARKSAT
BECKETT
BOOKLET
BOWKNOT
COCKPIT
CONKOUT
COOKOUT
DANKEST
DARKEST
DECKOUT
DESKSET
FOLKART
HACKETT
JACKPOT
JUNKART
KICKOUT
LANKEST
LOCKNUT
LOCKOUT
LOOKOUT
LOOKSAT
LUCKOUT
MEEKEST
MUSKRAT
PACKRAT
PECKSAT
PEEKOUT
PEEKSAT
PICKETT
PICKOUT
PICKSAT
PINKEST
PUCKETT
RANKEST
SACKOUT
SEEKOUT
SICKEST
SICKOUT
SILKHAT
SUNKIST
TALKOUT
TALKSAT
TOOKOUT
TOPKNOT
WALKOUT
WEAKEST
WINKOUT
WINKSAT
WORKOUT
YORKIST
ZONKOUT

••••KT•
FLOCKTO
STICKTO
STUCKTO

••••K•T
BLANKET
BLINKAT
BRACKET
BRISKET
CRICKET
MESSKIT
PLACKET
THICKET
TRINKET

KU•••••
KUBRICK
KUCHENS
KUMQUAT
KURDISH
KUSPUKS
KUTCHIN
KUTENAI
KUWAITI

K•U••••
KAUFMAN
KLUDGES
KLUGMAN
KLUTZES
KNUCKLE
KNURLED

K••U•••
KABUKIS
KAHUNAS
KIKUYUS
KNOUTED
KORUNAS

K•••U••
KEROUAC
KIBBUTZ
KICKUPS
KILAUEA
KUMQUAT
KUSPUKS

K••••U•
KARAKUL
KARAKUM
KEEPSUP
KEPTOUT
KETCHUP
KEYCLUB
KEYEDUP
KICKOUT
KICKSUP
KIKUYUS
KINGTUT
KNEESUP

K•••••U
KOMATSU

•KU••••
SKULKED
SKULKER
SKUNKED
UKULELE

•K••U••
SKIJUMP
SKIRUNS
SKISUIT

•K•••U•
EKEDOUT
EKESOUT
SKILFUL
SKINFUL
SKIPOUT
SKOOKUM
SKYBLUE

••KU•••
KIKUYUS
YAKUTSK
YAKUZAS

••K•U••
MAKEUPS
MUKLUKS

••K••U•
ASKSOUT
FAKEFUR
HIKEDUP
HIKESUP
KIKUYUS
MAKEOUT
MAKESUP
POKEFUN
RAKEDUP
RAKESUP
TAKEOUT
TAKESUP
WAKEFUL
WAKESUP
WOKENUP

•••KU••
BACKUPS
HOOKUPS
KICKUPS
LINKUPS
LOCKUPS
LOOKUPS
MARKUPS
MOCKUPS
PICKUPS
WALKUPS
WORKUPS

•••K•U•
BACKOUT
BACKRUB
BACKSUP
BROKEUP
BUCKSUP
CHOKEUP
CONKOUT
COOKOUT
COOKSUP
DECKOUT
FORKFUL
HOOKSUP
JACKSUP
KICKOUT
KICKSUP
LOCKNUT
LOCKOUT
LOCKSUP
LOOKOUT
LOOKSUP
LUCKOUT
MARKSUP
MILKRUN
MUCKSUP
PACKSUP
PEEKOUT
PERKSUP
PICKOUT
PICKSUP
RACKSUP
SACKFUL
SACKOUT
SEEKOUT
SHAKEUP
SICKOUT
SOAKSUP
SOUKOUS
SPOKEUP
TALKOUT
TALKSUP
TANKFUL
TANKSUP
TOOKOUT
WALKOUT
WICKIUP
WINKOUT
WORKOUT
WORKSUP
ZONKOUT

••••K•U
SHIKOKU

••••KU•
BELAKUN
BREAKUP
CHALKUP
CHECKUP
CRACKUP
CRANKUP
KARAKUL
KARAKUM
SHOOKUP
SKOOKUM
SPEAKUP
STACKUP
STICKUP
STOCKUP
STUCKUP
THINKUP

•••••KU
SHIKOKU

K••V•••
KNAVERY
KNAVISH

K•••V••
KNIEVEL

K••••V•
KEDROVA

•K•V•••
SKIVERS

•K•••V•
SKYDIVE

••KV•••
LEKVARS

••K••V•
BAKLAVA

•••K•V•
MARKOVA

•••K••V
CHEKHOV
ROCKYIV

••••K•V
NABOKOV

KW•••••
KWACHAS
KWANZAS

K•W••••
KEWPIES
KIWANIS
KOWLOON
KOWTOWS
KUWAITI

K••W•••
KEYWEST
KEYWORD
KNOWHOW
KNOWING

K••••W•
KOWTOWS

K•••••W
KNOWHOW

•K•W•••
SKEWERS
SKEWING
SKIWEAR
SKYWARD
SKYWAYS

•K•••W•
OKINAWA
SKITOWS

•K••••W
SKIDROW

••KW•••
AWKWARD
INKWELL

••K•W••
BIKEWAY
MAKEWAY

••K••W•
OAKLAWN
UNKNOWN

••K•••W
LIKENEW

•••KW••
FOLKWAY
PARKWAY
WALKWAY

•••K••W
BUCKSAW
HACKSAW
JACKDAW
MILKCOW
YOUKNOW

K••X•••
KLAXONS

K•••••X
KLEENEX

•K••••X
SKEEZIX

••K•••X
CAKEMIX
JUKEBOX

•••K•X•
PICKAXE

•••K••X
LOCKBOX

KY•••••
KYLIKES

K•Y••••
KAYAKED
KAYAKER
KAYOING
KEYCARD
KEYCLUB
KEYEDIN
KEYEDUP
KEYGRIP
KEYHOLE
KEYLESS
KEYLIME
KEYNOTE
KEYPADS
KEYRING
KEYWEST
KEYWORD
KRYPTON

K••Y•••
KATYDID
KENYANS
KHAYYAM
KOSYGIN

K•••Y••
KHAYYAM
KIKUYUS

K••••Y•
KAROLYI
KATHRYN
KIDNEYS

K•••••Y
KEARNEY
KENNEDY
KILLJOY
KINKILY
KITSCHY
KKKKATY
KNAVERY
KOLACKY

•KY••••
SKYBLUE
SKYCAPS
SKYDIVE
SKYHIGH
SKYHOOK
SKYJACK
SKYLARK
SKYLESS
SKYLIKE
SKYLINE
SKYWARD
SKYWAYS

•K•Y•••
OKAYING

•K•••Y•
SKYWAYS

•K••••Y
KKKKATY
SKETCHY

••KY•••
INKYCAP

••K•Y••
KIKUYUS
REKEYED

••K••Y•
AYKROYD

••K•••Y
BIKEWAY
BOKCHOY
KKKKATY
MAKEHAY
MAKEWAY
NAKEDLY

•••KY••
ROCKYII
ROCKYIV

•••K•Y•
BUCKEYE
DICKEYS
DONKEYS
HAWKEYE
JACKEYS
JOCKEYS
LACKEYS
MICKEYS
MONKEYS
RICKEYS
SOCKEYE
TURKEYS

•••K••Y
BACKBAY
BALKILY
BARKLEY
BUCKLEY
COCKILY
COCKNEY
COCKSHY
COOKERY
DUSKILY
FLAKILY
FOLKWAY
FUNKILY
GAWKILY
HACKNEY
HICKORY
HUSKILY
JERKILY
KINKILY
KKKKATY
LANKILY
LUCKILY
MOCKERY
MUCKILY
MURKILY
PARKWAY
PERKILY
PESKILY
QUAKILY
RICKETY
RISKILY
ROCKERY
ROOKERY
SHAKILY
SICKBAY
SICKDAY
SICKPAY
SILKILY
SMOKILY
SNAKILY
SPIKILY
STOKELY
SULKILY
TACKILY
TICKETY
WACKILY
WALKWAY
WEEKDAY
WORKDAY

••••K•Y
BLACKLY
BLANKLY
BLEAKLY
BRISKLY
CONAKRY
CRACKLY
CRINKLY
DEBAKEY
FRANKLY
FRECKLY
MARYKAY
PASSKEY
PRICKLY
QUICKLY
SHARKEY
SLACKLY
SLEEKLY
SLICKLY
STARKLY
STOOKEY
THICKLY
TURNKEY
TWINKLY
WHISKEY
WRINKLY

•••••KY
AUTARKY
BLUESKY
CHOMSKY
DROSHKY
FINICKY
GRETZKY
KOLACKY
PANICKY
SPASSKY
SQUAWKY
SQUEAKY
STREAKY
TROTSKY
UNLUCKY
VRONSKY

K•Z••••
KAZAKHS

K•••Z••
KLUTZES
KWANZAS

K•••••Z
KIBBUTZ
KOBLENZ

•K••Z••
SKEEZIX

••K•Z••
YAKUZAS

••••K•Z
FRANKOZ

LA•••••
LAAGERS
LABAMBA
LABCOAT
LABELED
LABELER
LABELLE
LABIALS
LABIATE
LABORED
LABORER
LABOURS
LABRETS
LACEDUP
LACESUP
LACHLAN
LACIEST
LACINGS
LACKEYS
LACKING
LACONIC
LACOSTE
LACQUER
LACTASE
LACTATE
LACTEAL
LACTOSE
LACUNAE
LACUNAL
LACUNAS
LADDERS
LADDIES
LADDISH
LADINOS
LADLERS
LADLING
LADYBUG
LADYDAY
LADYISH
LAENNEC
LAERTES
LAFARGE
LAFITTE
LAGGARD
LAGGERS
LAGGING
LAGOONS
LAGUNAS
LAIDFOR
LAIDLOW
LAIDOFF
LAIDOUT
LAISSEZ
LAJOLLA
LAKIEST
LAKOTAS
LAKSHMI
LALAKER
LALANNE
LALIQUE
LAMAISM
LAMAIST
LAMARCK
LAMBADA
LAMBDAS
LAMBEAU
LAMBENT
LAMBERT
LAMEDHS
LAMENTS
LAMINAE
LAMINAL
LAMINAR
LAMINAS
LAMMING
LAMOTTA
LAMPOIL
LAMPOON
LAMPREY
LANCERS
LANCETS
LANDAUS
LANDERS
LANDING
LANDSAT
LANFORD
LANGDON
LANGLEY
LANGTRY
LANGUID
LANGUOR
LANGURS
LANKEST
LANKIER
LANKILY
LANOLIN
LANSING
LANTANA
LANTERN
LANYARD
LAOCOON
LAOTIAN
LAPALMA
LAPBELT
LAPDOGS
LAPELED
LAPFULS
LAPLACE
LAPLAND
LAPLATA
LAPORTE
LAPPETS
LAPPING
LAPPISH
LAPROBE
LAPSING
LAPTOPS
LAPWING
LARAINE
LARAMIE
LARCENY
LARCHES
LARDERS
LARDIER
LARDING
LARDNER
LARDONS
LARGELY
LARGESS
LARGEST
LARGISH
LARIATS
LARKISH
LARRUPS
LASAGNA
LASAGNE
LASALLE
LASCALA
LASCAUX
LASHERS
LASHING
LASHUPS
LASORDA
LASSIES
LASSOED
LASSOER
LASSOES
LASTING
LASTORY
LATCHED
LATCHES
LATEENS
LATENCY
LATENTS
LATERAL
LATERAN
LATERON
LATEXES
LATHERS
LATHERY
LATHING
LATICES
LATIFAH
LATINAS
LATINOS
LATOSCA
LATTENS
LATTICE
LATVIAN
LAUDING
LAUGHAT
LAUGHED
LAUGHER
LAUGHIN
LAUNDER
LAUNDRY
LAURELS
LAURENT
LAUTREC
LAVALSE
LAVERNE
LAVINIA
LAWFORD
LAWLESS
LAWLIKE
LAWSUIT
LAWYERS
LAXNESS
LAYAWAY
LAYBACK
LAYDOWN
LAYERED
LAYETTE
LAYINTO
LAYITON
LAYOFFS
LAYOPEN
LAYOUTS
LAYOVER
LAYSFOR
LAYSLOW
LAYSOFF
LAYSOUT
LAZARUS
LAZIEST
LAZYISH

L•A••••
LAAGERS
LEACHED
LEACHES
LEACOCK
LEADERS
LEADIER
LEADING
LEADINS
LEADOFF
LEADOUT
LEADSIN
LEADSON
LEADSTO
LEADSUP
LEAFAGE
LEAFIER
LEAFING
LEAFLET
LEAGUES
LEAKAGE
LEAKERS
LEAKIER
LEAKING
LEANDER
LEANERS
LEANEST
LEANING
LEANSON
LEANTOS
LEAPERS
LEAPING
LEARIER
LEARJET
LEARNED
LEARNER
LEASERS
LEASHED
LEASHES
LEASING
LEATHER
LEAVEIN
LEAVENS
LEAVING
LIAISED
LIAISES
LIAISON
LOACHES
LOADERS
LOADING
LOAFERS
LOAFING
LOAMIER
LOAMING
LOANERS
LOANING
LOATHED
LOATHES

L••A•••
LABAMBA
LAFARGE
LALAKER
LALANNE
LAMAISM
LAMAIST
LAMARCK
LAPALMA
LARAINE
LARAMIE
LASAGNA
LASAGNE
LASALLE
LAVALSE
LAYAWAY
LAZARUS
LEBANON
LEBARON
LECARRE
LEGALLY
LEGATEE
LEGATES
LEGATOS
LEHAVRE
LEPANTO
LEVANTS
LIEABED
LIGANDS
LIGATED
LIGATES
LIKABLE
LINAGES
LIVABLE
LIZARDS
LOCALES
LOCALLY
LOCARNO
LOCATED
LOCATER
LOCATES
LOCATOR
LOVABLE
LOVABLY
LOYALLY
LOYALTY
LUNATIC
LUXATED
LUXATES

L•••A••
LABIALS
LABIATE
LACTASE
LACTATE
LAGGARD
LAMBADA
LANDAUS
LANTANA
LANYARD
LAPLACE
LAPLAND
LAPLATA
LARIATS
LASCALA
LASCAUX
LAYBACK
LEAFAGE
LEAKAGE
LEEWARD
LEGRAND
LEKVARS
LENFANT
LEONARD
LEOPARD
LEOTARD
LESPAUL
LIBRARY
LIBYANS
LIMEADE
LINEAGE
LINEATE
LINKAGE
LIPBALM
LOGJAMS
LOLLARD
LOMBARD
LONGAGO
LONGARM
LOOFAHS
LOQUATS
LOWBALL
LOWLAND
LOWPAID
LUCIANO
LUGGAGE
LULLABY
LUMBAGO
LUMBARS

L••••A•
LABCOAT
LACHLAN
LACTEAL
LACUNAE
LACUNAL
LACUNAS
LADYDAY
LAGUNAS
LAKOTAS
LAMBDAS
LAMBEAU
LAMINAE
LAMINAL
LAMINAR
LAMINAS
LANDSAT
LAOTIAN
LATERAL
LATERAN
LATIFAH
LATINAS
LATVIAN
LAUGHAT
LAYAWAY
LEERSAT
LEXICAL
LIBERAL
LIKEMAD
LILLIAN
LILYPAD
LINBIAO
LINDSAY
LINEMAN
LINGUAL
LINPIAO
LIPREAD
LITERAL
LIVEOAK
LOCOMAN
LOGGIAS
LOGICAL
LOOKSAT
LORICAE
LOWBEAM
LOWGEAR
LOWROAD
LUNGEAT
LYRICAL

L•••••A
LABAMBA
LAJOLLA
LAMBADA
LAMOTTA
LANTANA
LAPALMA
LAPLATA
LASAGNA
LASCALA
LASORDA
LATOSCA
LAVINIA
LEMPIRA
LEONORA
LETITIA
LIBERIA
LORETTA
LOUELLA

•LA••••
ALABAMA
ALADDIN
ALAKING
ALAMEDA
ALAMEIN
ALAMODE
ALARCON
ALARMED
ALARMER
ALARUMS
ALASKAN
BLABBED
BLABBER
BLACKED
BLACKEN
BLACKER
BLACKIE
BLACKLY
BLACULA
BLADDER
BLADERS
BLADING
BLAMING
BLANCHE
BLANDER
BLANDLY
BLANKED
BLANKER
BLANKET
BLANKLY
BLARING
BLARNEY
BLASTED
BLASTER
BLATANT
BLATHER
BLATTED
BLAZERS
BLAZING
BLAZONS
CLABBER
CLACKED
CLAIMED
CLAIMER
CLAIROL
CLAMBER
CLAMMED
CLAMMER
CLAMORS
CLAMOUR
CLAMPED
CLAMSUP
CLANGED
CLANGOR
CLANKED
CLAPPED
CLAPPER
CLAPTON
CLAQUES
CLARETS
CLARICE
CLARIFY
CLARION
CLARITY
CLASHED
CLASHES
CLASPED
CLASSED
CLASSES
CLASSIC
CLATTER
CLAUDIA
CLAUDIO
CLAUSES
CLAVELL
CLAVIER
CLAWERS
CLAWING
CLAYIER
CLAYISH
CLAYTON
ELAAIUN
ELAPIDS
ELAPSED
ELAPSES
ELASTIC
ELATERS
ELATING
ELATION
FLACCID
FLACONS
FLAGDAY
FLAGGED
FLAGMAN
FLAGMEN
FLAGONS
FLAILED
FLAKERS
FLAKIER
FLAKILY
FLAKING
FLAMBED
FLAMBES
FLAMIER
FLAMING
FLANEUR
FLANGES
FLANKED
FLANKER
FLANNEL
FLAPPED
FLAPPER
FLAREUP
FLARING
FLASHED
FLASHER
FLASHES
FLATBED
FLATCAR
FLATLET
FLATOUT
FLATTAX
FLATTED
FLATTEN
FLATTER
FLATTOP
FLAUNTS
FLAUNTY
FLAVORS
FLAVOUR
FLAWING
FLAXIER
FLAYING
GLACEED
GLACIAL
GLACIER
GLADDEN
GLADDER
GLADEYE
GLAIRED
GLAMOUR
GLANCED
GLANCES
GLARING
GLASGOW
GLASSED
GLASSES
GLAZERS
GLAZIER
GLAZING
KLAMATH
KLATSCH
KLAXONS
PLACARD
PLACATE
PLACEBO
PLACERS
PLACIDO
PLACING
PLACKET
PLAGUED
PLAGUES
PLAICES
PLAINER
PLAINLY
PLAINTS
PLAITED
PLANERS
PLANETS
PLANING
PLANISH
PLANKED
PLANNED
PLANNER
PLANOUT
PLANSON
PLANTAR
PLANTED
PLANTER
PLAQUES
PLASHED
PLASHES
PLASMAS
PLASTER
PLASTIC
PLATEAU
PLATENS
PLATERS
PLATIER
PLATING
PLATOON
PLATTER
PLATYPI
PLAUDIT
PLAUTUS
PLAYACT
PLAYBOY
PLAYDOH
PLAYERS
PLAYFUL
PLAYING
PLAYLET
PLAYOFF
PLAYOUT
PLAYPEN
PLAYSAT
PLAYSON
PLAYSUP
SLABBED
SLACKED
SLACKEN
SLACKER
SLACKLY
SLAKING
SLALOMS
SLAMMED
SLAMMER
SLANDER
SLANTED
SLAPPED
SLASHED
SLASHER
SLASHES
SLATHER
SLATIER
SLATING
SLATTED
SLAVERS
SLAVERY
SLAVEYS
SLAVING
SLAVISH
SLAYERS
SLAYTON
ULALUME
ULANOVA

•L•A•••
ALBANIA
ALCAZAR
ALFALFA
ALIASES
ALKALIS
ALLAYED
ALLAYER
ALMAATA
ALMADEN
ALMANAC
ALPACAS
ALSATIA
ALVAREZ
BLEAKER
BLEAKLY
BLEARED
BLEATED
BLOATED
CLEANED
CLEANER
CLEANLY
CLEANSE
CLEANUP
CLEARED
CLEARER
CLEARLY
CLEARUP
CLEAVED
CLEAVER
CLEAVES
CLEAVON
CLOACAE
CLOACAS
CLOAKED
ELAAIUN
ELEANOR
FLEABAG
FLEAPIT
FLOATED

FLOATER
FLYAWAY
GLEAMED
GLEANED
GLEANER
GLEASON
GLOATED
OLEATES
PLEADED
PLEADER
PLEASED
PLEASER
PLEASES
PLEATED
PLIABLE
PLIABLY
PLIANCY
ULYANOV

•L•••A••

ALABAMA
ALIBABA
ALIDADE
ALLEARS
ALLHAIL
ALMAATA
ALOHAOE
ALREADY
BLATANT
CLIMATE
CLIPART
ELEGANT
ELEVATE
ELKHART
FLYBALL
FLYCAST
FLYPAST
FLYWAYS
ILOCANO
KLAMATH
OLDDAYS
OLDHAND
OLDMAID
OLDSAWS
PLACARD
PLACATE
PLAYACT
PLENARY
PLUMAGE
PLURALS
SLOGANS
SLOVAKS
ULLMANN
ULULANT
ULULATE

•L•••A•

ALASKAN
ALCAZAR
ALLHEAL
ALLOWAY
ALLSTAR
ALMANAC
ALPACAS
ALSORAN
ALTOSAX
ALUMNAE
ALUMNAL
ALYKHAN
BLINKAT
BLUEJAY
BLUELAW
CLOACAE
CLOACAS
CLUBCAR
ELEGIAC
ELYSIAN
FLAGDAY
FLAGMAN
FLATCAR
FLATTAX
FLEABAG
FLIESAT
FLOTSAM
FLOWNAT
FLUVIAL
FLYAWAY
FLYLEAF
FLYTRAP
GLACIAL
GLORIAM
GLORIAS
GLOSSAE
GLOTTAL
ILLEGAL
KLUGMAN
OLDCHAP
OLDUVAI
PLANTAR
PLASMAS
PLATEAU
PLAYSAT
PLOWMAN
PLUVIAL
SLOTCAR
ULTIMAS

•L••••A

ALABAMA
ALAMEDA
ALBANIA
ALBERTA
ALFALFA
ALFORJA
ALGEBRA
ALGERIA
ALIBABA
ALLUVIA
ALMAATA
ALSATIA
ALTOONA
ALYOSHA
BLACULA
CLAUDIA
ELECTRA
ELEKTRA
FLORIDA
OLESTRA
OLYMPIA
PLECTRA
ULANOVA

••LA•••

ABLATED
ABLATES
ABLAUTS
ALLAYED
ALLAYER
ATLANTA
ATLARGE
ATLASES
ATLATLS
BALANCE
BALATON
BELABOR
BELAKUN
BELASCO
BELATED
BELAYED
CCLAMPS
CELADON
DELANEY
DELAYED
DELAYER
DILATED
DILATES
ECLAIRS
ENLACED
ENLACES
ENLARGE
FALAFEL
GALAGOS
GALAHAD
GALATEA
GALATIA
GELADAS
GELATIN
GELATIS
HILAIRE
ISLAMIC
ISLANDS
KILAUEA
KOLACKY
LALAKER
LALANNE
MALABAR
MALACCA
MALACHI
MALAISE
MALAMUD
MALAYAN
MELANGE
MELANIE
MELANIN
OBLASTS
OBLATES
OGLALAS
ORLANDO
PALACES
PALADIN
PALANCE
PALATAL
PALATES
PALAVER
PALAZZI
PALAZZO
PELAGES
PELAGIC
POLARIS
PULASKI
RDLAING
RELACED
RELACES
RELAPSE
RELATED
RELATES
RELAXED
RELAXES
RELAYED
ROLAIDS
SALAAMS
SALABLE
SALADIN
SALAMIS
SALAZAR
SOLACES
SOLARIA
SPLASHY
SPLAYED
TALARIA
TELAVIV
UMLAUTS
UNLACED
UNLACES
UNLADES
UNLATCH
UPLANDS
VALANCE

••L•A••

ALLEARS
ALLHAIL
ATLEAST
BALKANS
BALLADE
BALLADS
BALLARD
BALLAST
BALSAMS
BELDAME
BELDAMS
BELFAST
BELLAMY
BELTANE
BULGARS
BULWARK
CALGARY
CALPACS
CALVARY
CELLARS
CILIATE
COLGATE
COLLAGE
COLLARD
COLLARS
COLLATE
DELTAIC
DILLARD
DOLLARS
DOLMANS
DULLARD
FALLACY
FELLAHS
FOLIAGE
FOLIATE
FOLKART
GALLANT
GALPALS
GALVANI
GOLIATH
GULLAHS
HALVAHS
HALYARD
HILLARY
HOLLAND
HOLYARK
JULIANA
KILDARE
LOLLARD
LULLABY
MALEATE
MALLARD
MALRAUX
MILEAGE
MILHAUD
MILLAND
MILLARD
MULLAHS
NULLAHS
OILCAKE
OILCANS
OILLAMP
OILPANS
ONLEAVE
ORLEANS
PALMARY
PALMATE
PELTATE
PILLAGE
PILLARS
POLEAXE
POLKAED
POLLACK
PULSARS
PULSATE
RELEARN
RELEASE
RELIANT
RELOADS
ROLVAAG
SALAAMS
SALVAGE
SELVAGE
SULFATE
SULTANA
SULTANS
SYLLABI
SYLVANS
TELLALL
TILLAGE
TULSANS
ULLMANN
UNLEARN
UNLEASH
UNLOADS
UPLOADS
VALIANT
VALUATE
VALVATE
VILLAGE
VILLAIN
VOLCANO
VOLTAGE
VOLTAIC
VULCANS
VULGATE
WALLABY
WALLACE
WALLACH
WALMART
WELFARE
WELLAND
WILLARD

••L••A•

ALLHEAL
ALLOWAY
ALLSTAR
BALBOAS
BALIHAI
BELGIAN
BELLJAR
BELLMAN
BELTBAG
BELTWAY
BKLIBAN
BOLIVAR
CALIBAN
CHLORAL
COLDWAR
COLEMAN
CULTJAM
DELILAH
FELDMAN
FOLKWAY
GALAHAD
GELADAS
GILBLAS
GILLIAN
HALFDAN
HALFWAY
HALIFAX
HALLWAY
HELICAL
HELIPAD
HELLCAT
HELLMAN
HOLIDAY
HOLMOAK
HOLYDAY
HOLYWAR
HULLOAS
ILLEGAL
JILLIAN
LILLIAN
LILYPAD
MALABAR
MALAYAN
MALLRAT
MCLUHAN
MILKMAN
MILLDAM
MOLOKAI
MULETAS
OGLALAS
PALATAL
PALOMAR
PELICAN
PELOTAS
POLECAR
POLECAT
POLLTAX
PULLMAN
PULLTAB
ROLLBAR
ROLVAAG
SALAZAR
SALINAS
SALVIAS
SCLERAS
SILICAS
SILKHAT
SOLEDAD
TALKSAT
TELERAN
TELSTAR
TOLLWAY
VALJEAN
WALKMAN
WALKWAY
WELLMAN
WILDCAT
WILLIAM
WOLFGAL
WOLFMAN
WOLFRAM
YELLSAT

••L•••A

ALLUVIA
ATLANTA
BELINDA
BOLIVIA
BOLOGNA
CALDERA
CELESTA
CULEBRA
DELIRIA
DILEMMA
FELICIA
FELUCCA
GALATEA
GALATIA
JULIANA
KILAUEA
MALACCA
MELINDA
MELISSA
MILITIA
MOLDOVA
PALOOKA
POLENTA
SALSODA
SILESIA
SOLARIA
STLUCIA
SULTANA
SULUSEA
TALARIA

•••LA••

ABELARD
ACCLAIM
ADULATE
AIRLANE
AMYLASE
APPLAUD
ARCLAMP
ASHLAND
ASHLARS
BAKLAVA
BALLADE
BALLADS
BALLARD
BALLAST
BEDLAMP
BELLAMY
BIPLANE
BURLAPS
BYPLAYS
CELLARS
COLLAGE
COLLARD
COLLARS
COLLATE
COOLANT
COPLAND
CUTLASS
DECLAIM
DECLARE
DECLASS
DEFLATE
DEPLANE
DEWLAPS
DILLARD
DOLLARS
DULLARD
EMULATE
ENCLAVE
ENGLAND
ENPLANE
ENSLAVE
EXCLAIM
EXPLAIN
EYELASH
FALLACY
FELLAHS
FINLAND
FOULARD
GAGLAWS
GALLANT
GARLAND
GOTLAND
GOULASH
GULLAHS
HAULAGE
HEALALL
HILLARY
HOLLAND
HOVLANE
ICELAND
IMPLANT
INFLAME
INFLATE
INPLACE
IRELAND
ISOLATE
JUTLAND
KOOLAID
LAPLACE
LAPLAND
LAPLATA
LOLLARD
LOWLAND
LULLABY
MALLARD
MIDLAND
MILLAND
MILLARD
MISLAID
MISLAYS
MOULAGE
MULLAHS
NULLAHS
OAKLAND
OAKLAWN
OILLAMP
ONELANE
OOHLALA
OUTLAID
OUTLAND
OUTLAST
OUTLAWS
OUTLAYS
PAHLAVI
PARLAYS
PEDLARS
PHALANX
PILLAGE
PILLARS
POLLACK
POPLARS
PRELATE
RAGLANS
RANLATE
RECLAIM
RECLAME
REFLAGS
REPLACE
REPLANS
REPLANT
REPLATE
REPLAYS
ROULADE
RUNLATE
SCALARS
SEALABS
SEALANE
SEALANT
SHALALA
SKYLARK
STALAGS
SUNLAMP
SYLLABI
TELLALL
TILLAGE
TOYLAND
TRALALA
TWOLANE
ULULANT
ULULATE
UNCLASP
VILLAGE
VILLAIN
VIOLATE
WALLABY
WALLACE
WALLACH
WAYLAID
WAYLAYS
WELLAND
WETLAND
WILLARD
ZEALAND

•••L•A•

AEOLIAN
AMALGAM
ARMLOAD
AXILLAE
AZALEAS
BAYLEAF
BELLJAR
BELLMAN
BOOLEAN
CARLOAD
CHILEAN
CHOLLAS
COALCAR
COALGAS
COALTAR
DAHLIAS
FIGLEAF
FLYLEAF
GILLIAN
HALLWAY
HEELTAP
HELLCAT
HELLMAN
HIALEAH
HULLOAS
ITALIAN
JILLIAN
LILLIAN
MAILBAG
MAILCAR
MALLRAT
MILLDAM
MISLEAD
MRCLEAN
NUCLEAR
OAKLEAF
OFFLOAD
PAYLOAD
PERLMAN
POLLTAX
PRELOAD
PULLMAN
PULLTAB
RAILSAT
RAILWAY
RECLEAN
ROLLBAR
SHELLAC
STELLAR
TABLEAU
TEALEAF
TOLLWAY
UNCLEAN
UNCLEAR
UNCLOAK
WELLMAN
WILLIAM
YELLSAT

•••L••A

ARALSEA
BAKLAVA
CHELSEA
DIPLOMA
LAPLATA
OOHLALA
PAULINA
PAVLOVA
REPLICA
SHALALA
TRALALA

••••LA•

AIRPLAY
ANGOLAN
ANGULAR
ANNULAR
AREOLAE
AREOLAR
AREOLAS
ASTOLAT
AXILLAE
BACALAO
BIPOLAR
BLUELAW
BURGLAR
CABALAS
CASELAW
CATALAN
CHEMLAB
CHOLLAS
COPULAE
COPULAS
CUPOLAS
DANELAW
DELILAH
DEWCLAW
DIPOLAR
DISPLAY
DOUGLAS
EARFLAP
ENDPLAY
FACULAE
FIBULAE
FIBULAS
GAMELAW
GILBLAS
GRAYLAG
GUNPLAY
HOOPLAS
IMPALAS
INSULAR
JAIALAI
JOCULAR
JUGULAR
LACHLAN
MACULAE
MISPLAY
MODELAS
MODULAR
NEBULAE
NEBULAR
NEBULAS
NICOLAS
NIKOLAI
NODULAR
OGLALAS
ORTOLAN
OUTPLAY
OVERLAP
OVERLAY
PAYOLAS
PHARLAP
POPULAR
RADULAE
REDFLAG
REGULAR
ROMULAN
SAVALAS
SCHOLAR
SECULAR
SHEILAS
SHELLAC
SIMILAR
STELLAR
TABULAR
TEMPLAR
TIMELAG
TITULAR
TUBULAR
TUTELAR
VIZSLAS

••••L•A

ALFALFA
APHELIA
AVONLEA
BEDELIA
CAMELIA
CAPELLA
CATALPA
CECILIA
CEDILLA
COCHLEA
COROLLA
DEFALLA
DEPALMA
GANGLIA
GORILLA
LAJOLLA
LAPALMA
LOUELLA
MAHALIA
MATILDA
MAXILLA
MEDULLA
MINOLTA
NATALIA
NOVELLA
OPHELIA
PAPILLA
PATELLA
REDALGA
REGALIA
SEDALIA
SHOULDA
SOMALIA
VANILLA
VIDALIA
VISALIA

•••••LA

ACEROLA
AMAPOLA
ARUGULA
AUREOLA
BLACULA
BOBVILA
CANDELA
CAPELLA
CEDILLA
COPPOLA
COROLLA
CRAYOLA
DEFALLA
DRACULA
FORMULA
GONDOLA
GORILLA
GRANOLA
INOCULA
KAMPALA
LAJOLLA
LASCALA
LOUELLA
MANDALA
MANDELA
MARSALA
MAXILLA
MEDULLA
MESSALA
NOVELLA
OOHLALA
OSCEOLA
PAPILLA
PATELLA
PERGOLA
SCAPULA
SHALALA
SPATULA
TAMBALA
TEQUILA
TOMBOLA
TRALALA
UPPSALA
VANILLA
VISTULA

L•B••••

LABAMBA
LABCOAT
LABELED
LABELER
LABELLE
LABIALS
LABIATE
LABORED
LABORER
LABOURS
LABRETS
LEBANON
LEBARON
LIBBERS
LIBBING
LIBELED
LIBELER
LIBERAL
LIBERIA
LIBERTY
LIBIDOS
LIBRARY
LIBYANS
LOBBERS
LOBBIED
LOBBIES
LOBBING
LOBBYER
LOBSTER
LOBULES
LUBBERS
LUBBOCK
LUBEJOB

L••B•••

LAMBADA
LAMBDAS
LAMBEAU
LAMBENT
LAMBERT
LAPBELT
LAYBACK
LEIBNIZ
LIBBERS
LIBBING
LIMBERS
LIMBING
LINBIAO
LIPBALM
LOBBERS
LOBBIED
LOBBIES
LOBBING
LOBBYER
LOGBOOK
LOMBARD
LOOBIES
LOWBALL
LOWBEAM
LOWBLOW
LOWBORN
LOWBOYS
LOWBRED
LOWBROW
LUBBERS
LUBBOCK
LUMBAGO
LUMBARS
LUMBERS

L•••B••

LADYBUG
LEGIBLE
LEGIBLY
LIEABED
LIKABLE
LIVABLE
LOCKBOX
LONGBOW
LOVABLE
LOVABLY
LOVEBUG

L••••B•

LABAMBA
LAPROBE
LETITBE
LULLABY

L•••••B

LIONCUB
LUBEJOB

•LB••••

ALBANIA
ALBEDOS
ALBENIZ
ALBERTA
ALBERTO
ALBINOS
ALBUMEN
ALBUMIN
ALBUNDY
ELBOWED

•L•B•••

ALABAMA
ALIBABA
BLABBED
BLABBER
BLUBBER
CLABBER
CLIBURN
CLOBBER
CLUBBED
CLUBCAR
FLUBBED
FLUBBER
FLYBALL
FLYBOYS
GLIBBER
GLOBING
GLOBULE
ILLBRED
SLABBED
SLOBBER

•L••B••

ALEMBIC
ALGEBRA
BLABBED
BLABBER
BLUBBER
BLUEBOY
CLABBER
CLAMBER
CLIMBED
CLIMBER
CLOBBER
CLUBBED
FLAMBED
FLAMBES
FLATBED
FLEABAG
FLUBBED
FLUBBER
GLIBBER
PLAYBOY
PLIABLE
PLIABLY
PLOWBOY
PLUMBED
PLUMBER
SLABBED
SLOBBER
SLUMBER

•L•••B•

ALIBABA
ALLENBY
CLOSEBY
PLACEBO

••LB•••

BALBOAS
BILBIES
BILBOES
BULBLET
BULBOUS
BULBULS
COLBERT
DILBERT
FILBERT
GILBERT
GILBLAS
HOLBEIN
ILLBRED

••L•B••

BALLBOY
BELABOR
BELLBOY
BELTBAG
BKLIBAN
CALIBAN
CALIBER
CALIBRE
CALLBOX
CELEBES
CELEBRE

COLOBUS
CULEBRA
DELIBES
GOLDBUG
HALIBUT
MALABAR
PILLBOX
PILLBUG
ROLLBAR
SALABLE
SALTBOX
SOLUBLE
TALKBIG
VOLUBLE
VOLUBLY

••L••B•

ALLENBY
COLUMBO
LULLABY
SYLLABI
WALLABY

••L•••B

PULLTAB

•••LB••

BALLBOY
BELLBOY
CALLBOX
COALBIN
MAILBAG
MAILBOX
PHILBIN
PILLBOX
PILLBUG
ROLLBAR
TOOLBOX

•••L•B•

EARLOBE
LULLABY
MADLIBS
RIOLOBO
SEALABS
SYLLABI
WALLABY
WOULDBE

•••L••B

COULOMB
PULLTAB

••••L•B

CHEMLAB
FANCLUB
KEYCLUB
THEBLOB

•••••LB

DIMBULB

L•C••••

LACEDUP
LACESUP
LACHLAN
LACIEST
LACINGS
LACKEYS
LACKING
LACONIC
LACOSTE
LACQUER
LACTASE
LACTATE
LACTEAL
LACTOSE
LACUNAE
LACUNAL
LACUNAS
LECARRE
LECTERN
LECTORS
LECTURE
LICENCE
LICENSE
LICHENS
LICITLY
LICKING
LICTORS
LLCOOLJ
LOCALES
LOCALLY
LOCARNO
LOCATED
LOCATER
LOCATES
LOCATOR
LOCKBOX
LOCKERS
LOCKETS
LOCKING
LOCKINS
LOCKNUT
LOCKOUT
LOCKSON
LOCKSUP
LOCKUPS
LOCOMAN
LOCOMEN
LOCUSTS
LUCENCY
LUCERNE
LUCIANO
LUCIDLY
LUCIFER
LUCILLE
LUCKIER
LUCKILY
LUCKING
LUCKOUT
LYCEUMS

L••C•••

LABCOAT
LANCERS
LANCETS
LAOCOON
LARCENY
LARCHES
LASCALA
LASCAUX
LATCHED
LATCHES
LEACHED
LEACHES
LEACOCK
LEECHED
LEECHES
LEUCINE
LINCOLN
LITCHIS
LITCRIT
LOACHES
LOWCOST
LUNCHED
LUNCHES
LURCHED
LURCHES

L•••C••

LATICES
LEXICAL
LEXICON
LIONCUB
LOGICAL
LORICAE
LYRICAL

L••••C•

LAMARCK
LAPLACE
LATENCY
LATOSCA
LATTICE
LAYBACK
LEACOCK
LETTUCE
LICENCE
LOWNECK
LOWTECH
LUBBOCK
LUCENCY

L•••••C

LACONIC
LAENNEC
LAUTREC
LIPSYNC
LUNATIC

•LC••••

ALCAZAR
ALCHEMY
ALCOHOL
ALCOVES
LLCOOLJ

•L•C•••

BLACKED
BLACKEN
BLACKER
BLACKIE
BLACKLY
BLACULA
BLOCKED
BLOCKER
CLACKED
CLICHES
CLICKED
CLOCHES
CLOCKED
CLOCKER
CLOCKIN
CLUCKED
ELECTED
ELECTEE
ELECTOR
ELECTRA
ELECTRO
ELICITS
FLACCID
FLACONS
FLECHES
FLECKED
FLICKED
FLICKER
FLOCKED
FLOCKTO
FLYCAST
GLACEED
GLACIAL
GLACIER
GLUCOSE
ILOCANO
OLDCHAP
PLACARD
PLACATE
PLACEBO
PLACERS
PLACIDO
PLACING
PLACKET
PLECTRA
PLUCKED
SLACKED
SLACKEN
SLACKER
SLACKLY
SLICERS
SLICING
SLICKED
SLICKER
SLICKLY

•L••C••

ALARCON
ALENCON
ALPACAS
BLANCHE
BLOTCHY
CLOACAE
CLOACAS
CLUBCAR
FLACCID
FLATCAR
FLEECED
FLEECES
GLANCED
GLANCES
ILLICIT
PLAICES
SLOTCAR
SLOUCHY
SLUICED
SLUICES

•L•••C•

ALDRICH
CLARICE
CLERICS
CLINICS
ELGRECO
FLOUNCE
FLOUNCY
FLUENCY
ILIESCU
KLATSCH
OLDNICK
PLAYACT
PLIANCY

•L••••C

ALEMBIC
ALMANAC
CLASSIC
ELASTIC
ELEGIAC
ILLOGIC
OLYMPIC
PLASTIC

••LC•••

BALCONY
BELCHED
BELCHES
CALCIFY
CALCITE
CALCIUM
DULCIFY
FALCONS
FILCHED
FILCHER
FILCHES
FULCRUM
GULCHES
HALCYON
MALCOLM
MULCHED
MULCHES
MULCTED
OILCAKE
OILCANS
SALCHOW
TALCUMS
VOLCANO
VULCANS
WALCOTT
WELCHED
WELCHES
WELCOME
ZILCHES

••L•C••

CALICES
CALICOS
CALYCES
COLDCUT
DELICTI
DELICTS
ENLACED
ENLACES
FELICIA
FELUCCA
HELICAL
HELICES
HELICON
HELLCAT
HOLYCOW
ILLICIT
KOLACKY
MALACCA
MALACHI
MILKCOW
MOLOCHS
PALACES
PELICAN
POLECAR
POLECAT
POLICED
POLICES
RELACED
RELACES
RELICTS
RELOCKS
RELUCTS
SELECTS
SILICAS
SILICON
SOLACES
SOLICIT
SPLICED
SPLICER
SPLICES
STLUCIA
UNLACED
UNLACES
UNLOCKS
UNLUCKY
WILDCAT

••L••C•

BALANCE
BELASCO
BULLOCK
CALPACS
CALTECH
CELTICS
COLLECT
FALLACY
FELUCCA
HILLOCK
JALISCO
MALACCA
PALANCE
POLLACK
POLLOCK
ROLLICK
SELLECK
SILENCE
SPLOTCH
TOLTECS
UNLATCH
VALANCE
VALENCE
VALENCY
WALLACE
WALLACH

••L•••C

AELFRIC
BALDRIC
CALORIC
DELPHIC
DELTAIC
ILLOGIC
ISLAMIC
MALEFIC
MELODIC
MOLLUSC
PELAGIC
POLEMIC
POLITIC
SELENIC
VOLTAIC

•••LC••

COALCAR
HELLCAT
MAILCAR

•••L•C•

AFFLICT
AIRLOCK
ARMLOCK
BULLOCK
CHALICE
COLLECT
COWLICK
DEFLECT
DIALECT
EARLOCK
EHRLICH
FALLACY
FETLOCK
FROLICS
GUNLOCK
HEMLOCK
HILLOCK
INFLECT
INFLICT
INPLACE
ITALICS
LAPLACE
MATLOCK
NEGLECT
NIBLICK
OARLOCK
PADLOCK
PIMLICO
POLLACK
POLLOCK
POTLUCK
PUBLICS
REELECT
REFLECT
REPLACE
REPLICA
ROLLICK
SCHLOCK
SELLECK
SHYLOCK
SUOLOCO
UNBLOCK
WALLACE
WALLACH
WARLOCK
WEDLOCK

•••L••C

IDYLLIC
MOLLUSC
NUCLEIC
POULENC
SHELLAC

••••LC•

NORELCO
SQUELCH

••••L•C

ACRYLIC
ANGELIC
BUCOLIC
IDYLLIC
JEANLUC
MIDDLEC
SHELLAC
TONELOC
VOCALIC

L•D••••

LADDERS
LADDIES
LADDISH
LADINOS
LADLERS
LADLING
LADYBUG
LADYDAY
LADYISH
LEDGERS
LEDGIER
LEDUPTO
LIDLESS
LODGERS
LODGING
LUDDITE

L••D•••

LADDERS
LADDIES
LADDISH
LAIDFOR
LAIDLOW
LAIDOFF
LAIDOUT
LANDAUS
LANDERS
LANDING
LANDSAT
LAPDOGS
LARDERS
LARDIER
LARDING
LARDNER
LARDONS
LAUDING
LAYDOWN
LEADERS
LEADIER
LEADING
LEADINS
LEADOFF
LEADOUT
LEADSIN
LEADSON
LEADSTO
LEADSUP
LENDERS
LENDING
LETDOWN
LEWDEST
LIEDOWN
LINDENS
LINDIED
LINDIES
LINDSAY
LINDSEY
LOADERS
LOADING
LORDING
LORDJIM
LOUDEST
LOUDISH
LOWDOWN
LUDDITE

L•••D••

LACEDUP
LADYDAY
LAMBDAS
LAMEDHS
LANGDON
LAUNDER
LAUNDRY
LEANDER
LIBIDOS
LINEDUP
LIPIDES
LIVEDIN
LIVEDON
LIVIDLY
LOURDES
LUCIDLY
LURIDLY

L••••D•

LAMBADA
LASORDA
LEETIDE
LEGENDS
LEMONDE
LEONIDS
LIGANDS
LIMEADE
LIQUIDS
LIZARDS
LOWTIDE

L•••••D

LABELED
LABORED
LAGGARD
LANFORD
LANGUID
LANYARD
LAPELED
LAPLAND
LASSOED
LATCHED
LAUGHED
LAWFORD
LAYERED
LEACHED
LEARNED
LEASHED
LEECHED
LEEWARD
LEGRAND
LEONARD
LEOPARD
LEOPOLD
LEOTARD
LEVELED
LEVERED
LIAISED
LIBELED
LIEABED
LIGATED
LIGHTED
LIKEMAD
LIKENED
LILYPAD
LIMITED
LINDIED
LINSEED
LIPREAD
LIVENED
LOATHED
LOBBIED
LOCATED
LOLLARD
LOMBARD
LOUNGED
LOUVRED
LOWBRED
LOWERED
LOWLAND
LOWPAID
LOWROAD
LUNCHED
LURCHED
LUSTRED
LUXATED

•LD••••

ALDENTE
ALDRICH
ELDERLY
OLDCHAP
OLDDAYS
OLDFOGY
OLDGOLD
OLDHAND
OLDLINE
OLDMAID
OLDMOON
OLDNESS
OLDNEWS
OLDNICK
OLDPROS
OLDROSE
OLDSAWS
OLDSTER
OLDTIME
OLDUVAI
OLDWEST

•L•D•••

ALADDIN
ALIDADE
BLADDER
BLADERS
BLADING
ELIDING
ELUDING
FLEDGED
FLEDGES
GLADDEN
GLADDER
GLADEYE
GLIDERS
GLIDING
KLUDGES
OLDDAYS
PLEDGED
PLEDGEE
PLEDGER
PLEDGES
PLODDED
PLODDER
SLEDDED
SLEDDER
SLEDDOG
SLEDGES
SLIDEIN
SLIDERS
SLIDING
SLUDGES

•L••D••

ALADDIN
ALBEDOS
ALLUDED
ALLUDES
ALMADEN
BLADDER
BLANDER
BLANDLY
BLENDED
BLENDER
BLINDED
BLINDER
BLINDLY
BLONDER
BLONDES
BLONDIE
BLOODED
BLOWDRY
BLUNDER
CLAUDIA
CLAUDIO
CLOUDED
CLOWDER
CLUEDIN
FLAGDAY
FLOODED
FLUIDLY
GLADDEN
GLADDER
GLUEDON
ILLUDED
ILLUDES
PLAUDIT
PLAYDOH
PLEADED
PLEADER
PLODDED
PLODDER
PLUNDER
SLANDER
SLEDDED
SLEDDER
SLEDDOG
SLENDER

•L•••D•

ALAMEDA
ALAMODE
ALBUNDY
ALFREDO
ALIDADE
ALLENDE
ALMONDS
ALREADY
ELAPIDS
FLORIDA
FLYRODS
PLACIDO

•L••••D

ALARMED
ALERTED
ALIGNED
ALLAYED
ALLEGED
ALLOWED
ALLOYED
ALLTOLD
ALLUDED
ALLURED
ALTERED
BLABBED
BLACKED
BLANKED
BLASTED
BLATTED
BLEARED
BLEATED
BLEEPED
BLENDED
BLESSED
BLINDED
BLINKED
BLIPPED
BLITZED
BLOATED
BLOCKED
BLOODED
BLOOMED
BLOOPED
BLOTTED
BLOUSED
BLUFFED
BLUNTED
BLURRED
BLURTED
BLUSHED
CLACKED
CLAIMED
CLAMMED
CLAMPED
CLANGED
CLANKED
CLAPPED
CLASHED
CLASPED
CLASSED
CLEANED
CLEARED
CLEAVED
CLERKED
CLICKED
CLIMBED
CLINKED
CLIPPED
CLOAKED
CLOCKED
CLOGGED
CLOMPED
CLOPPED
CLOTHED
CLOTTED
CLOUDED
CLOUTED
CLOWNED
CLUBBED
CLUCKED
CLUMPED
CLUNKED
ELAPSED
ELBOWED
ELECTED
FLACCID
FLAGGED
FLAILED
FLAMBED
FLANKED
FLAPPED
FLASHED
FLATBED
FLATTED
FLECKED
FLEDGED
FLEECED
FLENSED
FLESHED
FLICKED
FLIPPED
FLIRTED
FLITTED
FLOATED
FLOCKED
FLOGGED
FLOODED
FLOORED
FLOPPED
FLOSSED
FLOURED
FLOUTED
FLUBBED
FLUFFED
FLUNKED
FLUSHED
GLACEED
GLAIRED
GLANCED
GLASSED
GLEAMED
GLEANED
GLINTED
GLITZED
GLOATED
GLOMMED
GLOOMED
GLORIED
GLOSSED
GLUGGED
GLUTTED
ILLBRED
ILLUDED
ILLUMED
ILLUSED
ILLWIND
OLDGOLD
OLDHAND
OLDMAID
PLACARD
PLAGUED
PLAITED
PLANKED
PLANNED
PLANTED
PLASHED
PLEADED
PLEASED
PLEATED
PLEDGED
PLINKED
PLODDED
PLOPPED
PLOTTED
PLUCKED
PLUGGED
PLUMBED
PLUMPED
PLUNGED
PLUNKED
PLYWOOD
SLABBED
SLACKED
SLAMMED
SLANTED
SLAPPED
SLASHED
SLATTED
SLEDDED
SLEEKED
SLEETED
SLICKED
SLIMMED
SLINKED
SLIPPED
SLOGGED
SLOPPED
SLOSHED
SLOTTED
SLUGGED
SLUICED
SLUMMED
SLUMPED
SLURPED
SLURRED

••LD•••

BALDEST
BALDING
BALDISH
BALDRIC
BALDWIN
BELDAME
BELDAMS
BOLDEST
CALDERA
CALDRON
COLDCUT
COLDEST
COLDISH
COLDWAR
FELDMAN
FOLDERS
FOLDING
FOLDOUT
FOLDSUP
FOLDUPS
GELDING
GILDERS
GILDING
GOLDBUG
GOLDING
GOLDWYN
HELDOFF
HELDOUT
HOLDERS
HOLDING
HOLDOFF
HOLDOUT
HOLDSIN
HOLDSON
HOLDSTO
HOLDSUP
HOLDUPS
KILDARE
MELDING
MILDEST
MILDEWS
MILDEWY
MILDRED
MOLDERS
MOLDIER
MOLDING
MOLDOVA
POLDERS
SOLDERS
SOLDIER
SOLDOFF
SOLDOUT
TOLDOFF
WALDORF
WELDERS
WELDING
WILDCAT
WILDEST
WILDING
WILDISH
WILDONE

••L•D••

ALLUDED
ALLUDES
ARLEDGE
BOLIDES
BULLDOG
CELADON
DELUDED
DELUDES
GELADAS
GELIDLY
HALFDAN
HALIDES
HOLEDUP
HOLIDAY
HOLYDAY
ILLUDED
ILLUDES
MALODOR
MELODIC
MILLDAM
PALADIN
PALEDRY
PILEDIN
PILEDON
PILEDUP
ROLODEX
SALADIN
SOLEDAD
SOLIDER
SOLIDLY
UNLADES
VALIDLY

••L••D•

ALLENDE
BALLADE
BALLADS
BELINDA

CALENDS
COLLIDE
COLLODI
COLLUDE
ISLANDS
MALTEDS
MELINDA
MILORDS
ORLANDO
RELOADS
ROLAIDS
SALSODA
SULFIDE
UNLOADS
UPLANDS
UPLOADS

••L•••D

ABLATED
ALLAYED
ALLEGED
ALLOWED
ALLOYED
ALLTOLD
ALLUDED
ALLURED
BALLARD
BELATED
BELAYED
BELCHED
BELLIED
BELOVED
BULLIED
BYLINED
COLLARD
COLLOID
COLORED
CULLIED
DALLIED
DELAYED
DELETED
DELTOID
DELUDED
DELUGED
DILATED
DILLARD
DILUTED
DOLLIED
DULLARD
ENLACED
FILCHED
GALAHAD
HALYARD
HELIPAD
HOLLAND
HULLOED
ILLBRED
ILLUDED
ILLUMED
ILLUSED
ILLWIND
JELLIED
JOLLIED
LILYPAD
LOLLARD
MALAMUD
MALLARD
MILDRED
MILHAUD
MILLAND
MILLARD
MILLEND
MULCHED
MULCTED
OBLIGED
PILOTED
POLICED
POLKAED
RALLIED
RELACED
RELATED
RELAXED
RELAYED
RELINED
RELIVED
RELUMED
SALLIED
SALUTED
SOLEDAD
SPLAYED
SPLICED
SULLIED
TALLIED
TALONED
TELEXED
UNLACED
UNLIKED
UNLINED
UNLOVED
WALTZED
WELCHED
WELLAND
WELLFED
WILFORD
WILFRID
WILLARD

•••LD••

BOULDER
BUILDER
BUILDIN
BUILDUP
BULLDOG
COULDNT
EARLDOM
FIELDED
FIELDER
GUILDER
MAULDIN
MILLDAM
MOULDED
MOULDER
SCALDED
SCOLDED
SCOLDER
SHELDON
SMOLDER
WIELDED
WORLDLY
WOULDBE
WOULDNT
YIELDED

•••L•D•

BALLADE
BALLADS
COLLIDE
COLLODI
COLLUDE
EXCLUDE
EXPLODE
EYELIDS
IMPLODE
INCLUDE
NUCLIDE
OCCLUDE
PRELUDE
ROULADE
SECLUDE

•••L••D

ABELARD
APPLAUD
APPLIED
ARMLOAD
ASHLAND
AVULSED
BALLARD
BAULKED
BECLOUD
BELLIED
BULLIED
CARLOAD
CAULKED
CHALKED
CHILLED
COLLARD
COLLOID
COPLAND
CULLIED
DALLIED
DILLARD
DIPLOID
DOLLIED
DRILLED
DULLARD
DWELLED
ENGLAND
ENGLUND
EVOLVED
EVULSED
EXALTED
EXULTED
FAULTED
FIELDED
FINLAND
FOULARD
FRILLED
FUELLED
FUELROD
GARLAND
GIELGUD
GOTLAND
GRILLED
HOLLAND
HULLOED
ICELAND
IMPLIED
IRELAND
JELLIED
JOLLIED
JUTLAND
KNELLED
KOOLAID
LAPLAND
LOLLARD
LOWLAND
MALLARD
MCCLOUD
MIDLAND
MILLAND
MILLARD
MILLEND
MISLAID
MISLEAD
MOULDED
MOULTED
OAKLAND
OFFLOAD
OUTLAID
OUTLAND
OUTLOUD
OXBLOOD
PAYLOAD
PRELOAD
PSALMED
QUELLED
QUILLED
QUILTED
RALLIED
REGLUED
REPLIED
SALLIED
SCALDED
SCALPED
SCOLDED
SCULLED
SHELLED
SHELVED
SHILLED
SKILLED
SKULKED
SMELLED
SMELTED
SPALLED
SPELLED
SPILLED
STALKED
STALLED
STILLED
STILTED
SULLIED
SWELLED
SWILLED
TABLOID
TAILEND
TALLIED
TOYLAND
TRILLED
TROLLED
TWILLED
UNGLUED
VAULTED
WARLORD
WAYLAID
WELLAND
WELLFED
WETLAND
WHELMED
WHELPED
WIELDED
WILLARD
YIELDED
ZEALAND

••••LD•

BEHOLDS
ENFOLDS
GERALDO
HERALDS
KOBOLDS
MATILDA
REMOLDS
REWELDS
SHIELDS
SHOULDA
UNFOLDS
UPHOLDS
VIVALDI

••••L•D

ANNELID
AVAILED
BABBLED
BAFFLED
BATTLED
BEVELED
BOBBLED
BOBSLED
BOGGLED
BOTTLED
BRAWLED
BRIDLED
BROILED
BUBBLED
BUCKLED
BUMBLED
BUNDLED
BUNGLED
BURBLED
BURGLED
BUSTLED
CACKLED
CAJOLED
CAROLED
CASTLED
CAVILED
CHILLED
CIRCLED
COBBLED
CODDLED
COUPLED
CRADLED
CRAWLED
CUDDLED
CURDLED
DABBLED
DANDLED
DANGLED
DAPPLED
DAWDLED
DAZZLED
DEFILED
DEVILED
DIBBLED
DIDDLED
DIMPLED
DOGSLED
DOODLED
DOUBLED
DRAWLED
DRILLED
DROOLED
DWELLED
EMAILED
ENABLED
ENISLED
ENSILED
EQUALED
EXHALED
FIDDLED
FIZZLED
FLAILED
FONDLED
FOOZLED
FRILLED
FUDDLED
FUELLED
FUMBLED
GABBLED
GAMBLED
GANGLED
GARBLED
GARGLED
GAVELED
GENTLED
GIGGLED
GIRDLED
GNARLED
GOBBLED
GOGGLED
GRILLED
GROWLED
GURGLED
GUZZLED
HACKLED
HAGGLED
HANDLED
HASSLED
HECKLED
HIGGLED
HOBBLED
HOPPLED
HUDDLED
HUMBLED
HURDLED
HURTLED
HUSTLED
IMPALED
INHALED
INVALID
JANGLED
JEWELED
JIGGLED
JINGLED
JOGGLED
JOSTLED
JUGGLED
JUMBLED
KIBBLED
KINDLED
KNEELED
KNELLED
KNURLED
LABELED
LAPELED
LEVELED
LIBELED
MANGLED
MANTLED
MARBLED
MEDALED
MEDDLED
MINGLED
MIZZLED
MODELED
MOTTLED
MUDDLED
MUFFLED
MUMBLED
MUSCLED
MUZZLED
NEEDLED
NESTLED
NETTLED
NIBBLED
NIGGLED
NOBBLED
NUZZLED
PADDLED
PANELED
PAROLED
PEARLED
PEBBLED
PEDALED
PEDDLED
PEOPLED
PESTLED
PETALED
PICKLED
PIFFLED
POPPLED
PROWLED
PUDDLED
PURFLED
PURPLED
PUZZLED
QUAILED
QUELLED
QUILLED
RADDLED
RAFFLED
RAMBLED
RANKLED
RASSLED
RATTLED
RAVELED
REFILED
REGALED
REOILED
RESILED
RESOLED
RETILED
REVELED
REVILED
RIDDLED
RIFFLED
RIMPLED
RIPPLED
RIVALED
RUFFLED
RUMBLED
RUMPLED
RUSTLED
SADDLED
SAMPLED
SCOWLED
SCULLED
SETTLED
SHELLED
SHILLED
SINGLED
SIZZLED
SKILLED
SKIRLED
SMELLED
SNARLED
SPALLED
SPELLED
SPIELED
SPILLED
SPOILED
SPOOLED
SQUALID
STABLED
STALLED
STAPLED
STEELED
STIFLED
STILLED
SWELLED
SWILLED
SWIRLED
TACKLED
TANGLED
TATTLED
TICKLED
TINGLED
TINKLED
TIPPLED
TODDLED
TOGGLED
TOOTLED
TOPPLED
TOTALED
TOUSLED
TOWELED
TRAILED
TRAWLED
TREBLED
TRIFLED
TRILLED
TRIPLED
TROLLED
TUMBLED
TURTLED
TUSSLED
TWILLED
TWIRLED
UNOILED
UNPILED
WADDLED
WAFFLED
WAGGLED
WAMBLED
WANGLED
WARBLED
WHEELED
WHIRLED
WHORLED
WIGGLED
WIMBLED
WIMPLED
WINKLED
WOBBLED
YODELED

•••••LD

ALLTOLD
BAGNOLD
EMERALD
HOGWILD
ICECOLD
INFIELD
LEOPOLD
OLDGOLD
OUTSOLD
PIEBALD
REBUILD
SIXFOLD
TENFOLD
TOEHOLD
TWOFOLD

LE•••••

LEACHED
LEACHES
LEACOCK
LEADERS
LEADIER
LEADING
LEADINS
LEADOFF
LEADOUT
LEADSIN
LEADSON
LEADSTO
LEADSUP
LEAFAGE
LEAFIER
LEAFING
LEAFLET
LEAGUES
LEAKAGE
LEAKERS
LEAKIER
LEAKING
LEANDER
LEANERS
LEANEST
LEANING
LEANSON
LEANTOS
LEAPERS
LEAPING
LEARIER
LEARJET
LEARNED
LEARNER
LEASERS
LEASHED
LEASHES
LEASING
LEATHER
LEAVEIN
LEAVENS
LEAVING
LEBANON
LEBARON
LECARRE
LECTERN
LECTORS
LECTURE
LEDGERS
LEDGIER
LEDUPTO
LEECHED
LEECHES
LEERERS
LEERIER
LEERILY
LEERING
LEERSAT
LEETIDE
LEEWARD
LEFTIES
LEFTIST
LEFTOFF
LEFTOUT
LEGALLY
LEGATEE
LEGATES
LEGATOS
LEGENDS
LEGGIER
LEGGING
LEGHORN
LEGIBLE
LEGIBLY
LEGIONS
LEGISTS
LEGLESS
LEGLIKE
LEGPULL
LEGRAND
LEGROOM
LEGUMES
LEGWORK
LEHAVRE
LEIBNIZ
LEIPZIG
LEISTER
LEISURE
LEKVARS
LEMIEUX
LEMMING
LEMONDE
LEMPIRA
LENDERS
LENDING
LENFANT
LENGTHS
LENGTHY
LENIENT
LENTIGO
LENTILS
LEONARD
LEONIDS
LEONINE
LEONORA
LEOPARD
LEOPOLD
LEOTARD
LEPANTO
LEPPIES
LEPTONS
LESOTHO
LESPAUL
LESSEES
LESSENS
LESSING
LESSONS
LESSORS
LETDOWN
LETINON
LETITBE
LETITIA
LETSFLY
LETSLIP
LETSOFF
LETSOUT
LETSSEE
LETTERS
LETTING
LETTISH
LETTRES
LETTUCE
LETUPON
LEUCINE
LEVANTS
LEVELED
LEVELER
LEVELLY
LEVERED
LEVERET
LEVIERS
LEVITES
LEVYING
LEWDEST
LEXEMES
LEXICAL
LEXICON

L•E••••

LAENNEC
LAERTES
LEECHED
LEECHES
LEERERS
LEERIER
LEERILY
LEERING
LEERSAT
LEETIDE
LEEWARD
LIEABED
LIEDOWN
LIENEES
LIEOVER
LIERNES
LIESLOW
LOESSER
LOESSES

L••E•••

LABELED
LABELER
LABELLE
LACEDUP
LACESUP
LAMEDHS
LAMENTS
LAPELED
LATEENS
LATENCY
LATENTS
LATERAL
LATERAN
LATERON
LATEXES
LAVERNE
LAYERED
LAYETTE
LEGENDS
LEVELED
LEVELER
LEVELLY
LEVERED
LEVERET
LEXEMES
LIBELED
LIBELER
LIBERAL
LIBERIA
LIBERTY
LICENCE
LICENSE
LIFEFUL
LIFENET
LIKEMAD
LIKENED
LIKENEW
LIMEADE
LINEAGE
LINEATE
LINEDUP
LINEMAN
LINEMEN
LINESUP
LINEUPS
LISENTE
LITERAL
LIVEDIN
LIVEDON
LIVENED
LIVEOAK
LIVEONE
LIVEOUT
LIVESIN
LIVESON
LORELEI
LORENZO
LORETTA
LOSEOUT
LOSESIT
LOUELLA
LOVEBUG
LOVEINS
LOVERLY
LOWERED
LOZENGE
LUBEJOB
LUCENCY
LUCERNE
LYCEUMS
LYSENKO

L•••E••

LAAGERS
LABRETS
LACIEST
LACKEYS
LACTEAL
LADDERS
LADLERS
LAGGERS
LAKIEST
LAMBEAU
LAMBENT
LAMBERT
LANCERS
LANCETS
LANDERS
LANKEST
LANTERN
LAPBELT
LAPPETS
LARCENY
LARDERS
LARGELY
LARGESS
LARGEST
LASHERS
LATEENS
LATHERS
LATHERY
LATTENS
LAURELS
LAURENT
LAWLESS
LAWYERS
LAXNESS
LAZIEST
LEADERS
LEAKERS
LEANERS
LEANEST
LEAPERS
LEASERS
LEAVEIN
LEAVENS
LECTERN
LEDGERS
LEERERS
LEGLESS
LEMIEUX
LENDERS
LENIENT
LESSEES
LESSENS
LETTERS
LEVIERS
LEWDEST
LIBBERS
LICHENS
LIDLESS
LIENEES
LIFTERS
LIMBERS
LIMIEST
LIMNERS
LIMPEST
LIMPETS
LINDENS
LINGERS
LINIEST
LINKERS
LINNETS
LINSEED
LINTELS
LIONESS
LIONETS
LIPLESS
LIPREAD
LIQUEFY
LIQUEUR
LISTEES
LISTELS
LISTENS
LITHELY
LITHEST
LITTERS
LOADERS
LOAFERS
LOANERS
LOBBERS
LOCKERS
LOCKETS
LODGERS
LOGGERS
LOGIEST
LOITERS
LONGEST
LOOKERS
LOONEYS
LOOPERS
LOOSELY
LOOSENS
LOOSEST
LOOTERS
LOPPERS
LOTTERY
LOUDEST
LOUSEUP
LOUVERS
LOWBEAM
LOWGEAR
LOWHEEL
LOWNECK
LOWNESS
LOWTECH
LUBBERS
LUGGERS
LUMBERS
LUMIERE
LUMPERS
LUNGEAT
LUNKERS
LUSHEST
LUSTERS

L••••E•

LABELED
LABELER
LABORED
LABORER
LACQUER
LADDIES
LAENNEC
LAERTES
LAISSEZ
LALAKER
LAMPREY
LANGLEY
LANKIER
LAPELED
LARCHES
LARDIER
LARDNER
LASSIES
LASSOED
LASSOER
LASSOES
LATCHED
LATCHES
LATEXES
LATICES
LAUGHED
LAUGHER
LAUNDER
LAUTREC
LAYERED
LAYOPEN
LAYOVER
LEACHED
LEACHES
LEADIER
LEAFIER
LEAFLET
LEAGUES
LEAKIER
LEANDER
LEARIER
LEARJET
LEARNED
LEARNER
LEASHED
LEASHES
LEATHER
LEDGIER
LEECHED
LEECHES
LEERIER
LEFTIES
LEGATEE
LEGATES
LEGGIER
LEGUMES
LEISTER
LEPPIES
LESSEES
LETSSEE
LETTRES
LEVELED
LEVELER
LEVERED
LEVERET
LEVITES
LEXEMES
LIAISED
LIAISES
LIBELED
LIBELER
LIEABED
LIENEES
LIEOVER
LIERNES
LIFENET
LIGATED
LIGATES
LIGHTED
LIGHTEN
LIGHTER
LIKENED
LIKENEW
LIMITED
LIMOGES
LINAGES
LINDIED
LINDIES
LINDSEY
LINEMEN
LINGOES
LINSEED
LINTIER
LIPIDES
LIPPIER
LISTEES
LITOTES
LITTLER
LIVENED
LOACHES
LOAMIER
LOATHED
LOATHES
LOBBIED

LOBBIES
LOBBYER
LOBSTER
LOBULES
LOCALES
LOCATED
LOCATER
LOCATES
LOCOMEN
LOESSER
LOESSES
LOFTIER
LOLLIES
LONGIES
LONGUES
LOOBIES
LOOKSEE
LOONIER
LOONIES
LOOPIER
LOPPIER
LORELEI
LORISES
LORRIES
LOTUSES
LOUNGED
LOUNGER
LOUNGES
LOURDES
LOUSIER
LOUVRED
LOUVRES
LOWBRED
LOWERED
LOWHEEL
LOWLIER
LUCIFER
LUCKIER
LUMPIER
LUNCHED
LUNCHES
LUPINES
LURCHED
LURCHES
LUSTIER
LUSTRED
LUSTRES
LUXATED
LUXATES

L•••••E

LABELLE
LABIATE
LACOSTE
LACTASE
LACTATE
LACTOSE
LACUNAE
LAFARGE
LAFITTE
LALANNE
LALIQUE
LAMINAE
LAPLACE
LAPORTE
LAPROBE
LARAINE
LARAMIE
LASAGNE
LASALLE
LATTICE
LAVALSE
LAVERNE
LAWLIKE
LAYETTE
LEAFAGE
LEAKAGE
LECARRE
LECTURE
LEETIDE
LEGATEE
LEGIBLE
LEGLIKE
LEHAVRE
LEISURE
LEMONDE
LEONINE
LETITBE
LETSSEE
LETTUCE
LEUCINE
LICENCE
LICENSE
LIGNITE
LIKABLE
LIMEADE
LINEAGE
LINEATE
LINKAGE
LIONISE
LIONIZE
LIPLIKE
LISENTE
LISSOME
LIVABLE
LIVEONE
LOOKSEE
LORICAE
LOVABLE
LOWLIFE
LOWRISE
LOWTIDE
LOZENGE
LUCERNE
LUCILLE
LUDDITE
LUGGAGE
LUMIERE

•LE••••

ALEMBIC
ALENCON
ALERTED
ALERTER
ALERTLY
ALEWIFE
BLEAKER
BLEAKLY
BLEARED
BLEATED
BLEEPED
BLEEPER
BLEMISH
BLENDED
BLENDER
BLERIOT
BLESSED
BLESSES
BLEWOFF
BLEWOUT
CLEANED
CLEANER
CLEANLY
CLEANSE
CLEANUP
CLEARED
CLEARER
CLEARLY
CLEARUP
CLEAVED
CLEAVER
CLEAVES
CLEAVON
CLEMENS
CLEMENT
CLEMSON
CLERICS
CLERISY
CLERKED
ELEANOR
ELECTED
ELECTEE
ELECTOR
ELECTRA
ELECTRO
ELEGANT
ELEGIAC
ELEGIES
ELEGIST
ELEISON
ELEKTRA
ELEMENT
ELEVATE
ELEVENS
FLEABAG
FLEAPIT
FLECHES
FLECKED
FLEDGED
FLEDGES
FLEECED
FLEECES
FLEEING
FLEETER
FLEETLY
FLEMING
FLEMISH
FLENSED
FLENSES
FLESHED
FLESHES
FLESHLY
FLEXING
FLEXNER
FLEXORS
FLEYING
GLEAMED
GLEANED
GLEANER
GLEASON
GLEEFUL
KLEENEX
OLEATES
OLEFINS
OLEMISS
OLESTRA
PLEADED
PLEADER
PLEASED
PLEASER
PLEASES
PLEATED
PLECTRA
PLEDGED
PLEDGEE
PLEDGER
PLEDGES
PLENARY
PLENUMS
PLEXORS
SLEDDED
SLEDDER
SLEDDOG
SLEDGES
SLEEKED
SLEEKEN
SLEEKER
SLEEKLY
SLEEPER
SLEEPIN
SLEEPON
SLEETED
SLEEVES
SLEIGHS
SLEIGHT
SLENDER
SLEPTIN
SLEPTON
SLEUTHS

•L•E•••

ALBEDOS
ALBENIZ
ALBERTA
ALBERTO
ALDENTE
ALGEBRA
ALGERIA
ALIENEE
ALIENOR
ALKENES
ALLEARS
ALLEGED
ALLEGER
ALLEGES
ALLEGRO
ALLELES
ALLENBY
ALLENDE
ALLERGY
ALLEYES
ALREADY
ALTERED
ALTERER
ALVEOLI
BLEEPED
BLEEPER
BLUEBOY
BLUEFIN
BLUEFOX
BLUEGUM
BLUEING
BLUEISH
BLUEJAY
BLUELAW
BLUESKY
CLIENTS
CLUEDIN
CLUEING
CLUESIN
ELDERLY
FLEECED
FLEECES
FLEEING
FLEETER
FLEETLY
FLIESAT
FLIESIN
FLUENCY
GLEEFUL
GLUEDON
GLUESON
ILIESCU
ILLEGAL
KLEENEX
SLEEKED
SLEEKEN
SLEEKER
SLEEKLY
SLEEPER
SLEEPIN
SLEEPON
SLEETED
SLEEVES
SLOEGIN

•L••E••

ALAMEDA
ALAMEIN
ALCHEMY
ALFIERI
ALFREDO
ALGIERS
ALIMENT
ALLHEAL
ALLHERE
BLADERS
BLAZERS
BLOWERS
CLARETS
CLAVELL
CLAWERS
CLEMENS
CLEMENT
CLORETS
CLOSEBY
CLOSEIN
CLOSELY
CLOSEST
CLOSETS
CLOSEUP
CLOVERS
ELATERS
ELEMENT
ELEVENS
ELGRECO
ELOPERS
ELYSEES
FLAKERS
FLANEUR
FLAREUP
FLORETS
FLOWERS
FLOWERY
FLYLEAF
FLYLESS
FLYNETS
GLACEED
GLADEYE
GLAZERS
GLIDERS
GLOWERS
GLUIEST
ILLNESS
OLDNESS
OLDNEWS
OLDWEST
PLACEBO
PLACERS
PLANERS
PLANETS
PLATEAU
PLATENS
PLATERS
PLAYERS
PLOVERS
PLOWERS
SLAVERS
SLAVERY
SLAVEYS
SLAYERS
SLICERS
SLIDEIN
SLIDERS
SLIVERS
SLOVENE
SLOVENS
SLOWEST
SLYNESS
ULSTERS

•L•••E•

ALARMED
ALARMER
ALBUMEN
ALCOVES
ALERTED
ALERTER
ALIASES
ALIENEE
ALIGNED
ALIGNER
ALKENES
ALLAYED
ALLAYER
ALLEGED
ALLEGER
ALLEGES
ALLELES
ALLEYES
ALLOVER
ALLOWED
ALLOYED
ALLUDED
ALLUDES
ALLURED
ALLURES
ALMADEN
ALTERED
ALTERER
ALUNSER
ALVAREZ
BLABBED
BLABBER
BLACKED
BLACKEN
BLACKER
BLADDER
BLANDER
BLANKED
BLANKER
BLANKET
BLARNEY
BLASTED
BLASTER
BLATHER
BLATTED
BLEAKER
BLEARED
BLEATED
BLEEPED
BLEEPER
BLENDED
BLENDER
BLESSED
BLESSES
BLINDED
BLINDER
BLINKED
BLINKER
BLIPPED
BLISTER
BLITHER
BLITZED
BLITZEN
BLITZES
BLOATED
BLOCKED
BLOCKER
BLONDER
BLONDES
BLOODED
BLOOMED
BLOOMER
BLOOPED
BLOOPER
BLOTTED
BLOTTER
BLOUSED
BLOUSES
BLOWIER
BLUBBER
BLUFFED
BLUFFER
BLUNDER
BLUNTED
BLUNTER
BLURRED
BLURTED
BLUSHED
BLUSHER
BLUSHES
BLUSTER
CLABBER
CLACKED
CLAIMED
CLAIMER
CLAMBER
CLAMMED
CLAMMER
CLAMPED
CLANGED
CLANKED
CLAPPED
CLAPPER
CLAQUES
CLASHED
CLASHES
CLASPED
CLASSED
CLASSES
CLATTER
CLAUSES
CLAVIER
CLAYIER
CLEANED
CLEANER
CLEARED
CLEARER
CLEAVED
CLEAVER
CLEAVES
CLERKED
CLICHES
CLICKED
CLIMBED
CLIMBER
CLINKED
CLINKER
CLIPPED
CLIPPER
CLIQUES
CLIQUEY
CLOAKED
CLOBBER
CLOCHES
CLOCKED
CLOCKER
CLOGGED
CLOMPED
CLOONEY
CLOPPED
CLOQUES
CLOTHED
CLOTHES
CLOTTED
CLOUDED
CLOUTED
CLOWDER
CLOWNED
CLUBBED
CLUCKED
CLUMPED
CLUNKED
CLUNKER
CLUSTER
CLUTTER
ELAPSED
ELAPSES
ELBOWED
ELECTED
ELECTEE
ELEGIES
ELMTREE
ELYSEES
FLAGGED
FLAGMEN
FLAILED
FLAKIER
FLAMBED
FLAMBES
FLAMIER
FLANGES
FLANKED
FLANKER
FLANNEL
FLAPPED
FLAPPER
FLASHED
FLASHER
FLASHES
FLATBED
FLATLET
FLATTED
FLATTEN
FLATTER
FLAXIER
FLECHES
FLECKED
FLEDGED
FLEDGES
FLEECED
FLEECES
FLEETER
FLENSED
FLENSES
FLESHED
FLESHES
FLEXNER
FLICKED
FLICKER
FLIPPED
FLIPPER
FLIRTED
FLITTED
FLITTER
FLIVVER
FLOATED
FLOATER
FLOCKED
FLOGGED
FLOODED
FLOORED
FLOPPED
FLOSSED
FLOSSES
FLOURED
FLOUTED
FLUBBED
FLUBBER
FLUFFED
FLUKIER
FLUNKED
FLUSHED
FLUSHES
FLUSTER
FLUTIER
FLUTTER
FLYOVER
GLACEED
GLACIER
GLADDEN
GLADDER
GLAIRED
GLANCED
GLANCES
GLASSED
GLASSES
GLAZIER
GLEAMED
GLEANED
GLEANER
GLIBBER
GLIMMER
GLINTED
GLISTEN
GLITTER
GLITZED
GLITZES
GLOATED
GLOMMED
GLOOMED
GLORIED
GLORIES
GLOSSED
GLOSSES
GLUGGED
GLUMMER
GLUTTED
ILLBRED
ILLUDED
ILLUDES
ILLUMED
ILLUMES
ILLUSED
ILLUSES
KLEENEX
KLUDGES
KLUTZES
OLDSTER
OLEATES
OLIVIER
PLACKET
PLAGUED
PLAGUES
PLAICES
PLAINER
PLAITED
PLANKED
PLANNED
PLANNER
PLANTED
PLANTER
PLAQUES
PLASHED
PLASHES
PLASTER
PLATIER
PLATTER
PLAYLET
PLAYPEN
PLEADED
PLEADER
PLEASED
PLEASER
PLEASES
PLEATED
PLEDGED
PLEDGEE
PLEDGER
PLEDGES
PLINKED
PLODDED
PLODDER
PLOPPED
PLOTTED
PLOTTER
PLOWMEN
PLUCKED
PLUGGED
PLUGGER
PLUMBED
PLUMBER
PLUMIER
PLUMMER
PLUMMET
PLUMPED
PLUMPER
PLUNDER
PLUNGED
PLUNGER
PLUNGES
PLUNKED
PLUSHER
PLUSHES
PLUSSES
SLABBED
SLACKED
SLACKEN
SLACKER
SLAMMED
SLAMMER
SLANDER
SLANTED
SLAPPED
SLASHED
SLASHER
SLASHES
SLATHER
SLATIER
SLATTED
SLEDDED
SLEDDER
SLEDGES
SLEEKED
SLEEKEN
SLEEKER
SLEEPER
SLEETED
SLEEVES
SLENDER
SLICKED
SLICKER
SLIMIER
SLIMMED
SLIMMER
SLINGER
SLINKED
SLIPPED
SLIPPER
SLITHER
SLOBBER
SLOGGED
SLOPPED
SLOSHED
SLOSHES
SLOTTED
SLUDGES
SLUGGED
SLUGGER
SLUICED
SLUICES
SLUMBER
SLUMMED
SLUMPED
SLURPED
SLURRED
SLUSHES
ULYSSES

•L••••E

ALAMODE
ALDENTE
ALEWIFE
ALIDADE
ALIENEE
ALLENDE
ALLGONE
ALLHERE
ALLOFME
ALLTIME
ALOHAOE
ALUMNAE
BLACKIE
BLANCHE
BLONDIE
CLARICE
CLEANSE
CLIMATE
CLOACAE
CLOSURE
CLOTURE
ELECTEE
ELEVATE
ELFLIKE
ELLIPSE
ELMTREE
ELUSIVE
FLOUNCE
GLADEYE
GLIMPSE
GLOBULE
GLOSSAE
GLUCOSE
OLDLINE
OLDROSE
OLDTIME
OLIVINE
PLACATE
PLEDGEE
PLIABLE
PLOSIVE
PLUMAGE
SLOVENE
ULALUME
ULULATE

••LE•••

AILERON
ALLEARS
ALLEGED
ALLEGER
ALLEGES
ALLEGRO
ALLELES
ALLENBY
ALLENDE
ALLERGY
ALLEYES
APLENTY
ARLEDGE
ATLEAST
BALEENS
BALEFUL
BILEVEL
BOLEROS
CALENDS
CELEBES
CELEBRE
CELESTA
CELESTE
COLEMAN
COLETTE
CSLEWIS
CULEBRA
DALETHS
DELEING
DELETED
DELETES
DILEMMA
DOLEFUL
DOLEOUT
FILENES
HOLEDUP
HOLEOUT
HOLESUP
ILLEGAL
MALEATE
MALEFIC
MILEAGE
MOLESTS
MULETAS
ONLEAVE
ORLEANS
PALEDRY
PALERMO
PALETTE
PILEDIN
PILEDON
PILEDUP
PILESIN
PILESON
PILESUP
PILEUPS
POLEAXE
POLECAR
POLECAT
POLEMIC
POLENTA
RALEIGH
RELEARN
RELEASE
RELENTS
RILESUP
RULEOUT
RULESON
SALERNO
SCLERAS
SELECTS
SELENIC
SILENCE
SILENTS
SILESIA
SOLEDAD
SPLEENS
TALENTS
TELERAN
TELEXED
TELEXES
TYLENOL
UNLEARN
UNLEASH
VALENCE
VALENCY
VALERIE
YULELOG

••L•E••

AILMENT
ALLHEAL
ALLHERE
BALDEST
BALEENS
BALLETS
BELIEFS
BELIEVE
BELLEEK
BILLETS
BOLDEST
BULLETS
CALDERA
CALLERS
CALMEST
CALTECH
CALVERT
COLBERT
COLDEST
COLLECT
COLLEEN
COLLEGE
COLLETS
CULLERS
CULVERS
CULVERT
DELVERS
DILBERT
DOLMENS
DULLEST
EELIEST
FALSELY
FALSEST
FALTERS
FALWELL
FELLERS
FILBERT
FILLERS
FILLETS
FILTERS
FOLDERS
FOLGERS
FOLLETT
FULGENT
FULLEST
GALLEON
GALLERY
GALLEYS
GILBERT
GILDERS
GOLFERS
GULLETS
HALTERS
HELLENE
HELLERS
HELMETS
HELPERS
HOLBEIN
HOLDERS
HOLIEST
HOLLERS
HULLERS
ILLNESS
KILLERS
MALLETS
MALTEDS
MALTESE
MILDEST
MILDEWS
MILDEWY
MILIEUS
MILIEUX
MILKERS
MILLEND
MILLERS
MILLETS
MILLETT
MOLDERS
MOLIERE
MOLTERS
MULLEIN
MULLERS
MULLETS
OILIEST
OILLESS
OILWELL
PALIEST
PALLETS
PALTERS
PELLETS
PELTERS
PILFERS
POLDERS
POLLENS
POLLERS
PULLETS
PULLEYS
RELIEFS
RELIEVE
RELIEVO
RELLENO
RILLETS
ROLLERS
SALIENT
SALIERI
SALLETS
SALTERS
SALVERS
SELLECK
SELLERS
SILVERS
SILVERY
SOLDERS
SOLFEGE
SOLVENT
SOLVERS
SPLEENS
SULKERS
TALKERS
TALLEST
TELLERS
TILLERS
TILTERS
TOLTECS
TOLUENE
UGLIEST
VALJEAN
VALLEJO
VALLEYS
VELVETS
VELVETY
VILLEIN
VOLLEYS
WALKERS
WALLETS
WALLEYE
WALTERS
WELDERS

WELTERS WILDEST WILHELM WILIEST WILLETS YELLERS YELPERS

••L••E•

ABLATED ABLATES ALLAYED ALLAYER ALLEGED ALLEGER ALLEGES ALLELES ALLEYES ALLOVER ALLOWED ALLOYED ALLUDED ALLUDES ALLURED ALLURES ATLASES BALKIER BALMIER BALONEY BELATED BELAYED BELCHED BELCHES BELLEEK BELLIED BELLIES BELLMEN BELOVED BILBIES BILBOES BILEVEL BILGIER BILLIES BOLIDES BOLSTER BOLUSES BULBLET BULGIER BULKIER BULLIED BULLIES BULLPEN BYLINED BYLINES CALIBER CALICES CALIPER CALOMEL CALUMET CALYCES CALYXES CELEBES COLLEEN COLLIER COLLIES COLLYER COLONEL COLONES COLORED CULLIED CULLIES DALLIED DALLIER DALLIES

DALTREY DELANEY DELAYED DELAYER DELETED DELETES DELIBES DELIVER DELUDED DELUDES DELUGED DELUGES DILATED DILATES DILLIES DILUTED DILUTER DILUTES DOLLIED DOLLIES DOLORES ENLACED ENLACES ENLIVEN FALAFEL FELINES FELLIES FILCHED FILCHER FILCHES FILENES FILLIES FILMIER FOLKIER FOLKIES FOLLIES GALATEA GALILEE GALILEI GALILEO GILLIES GILLNET GOLFTEE GULCHES GULLIES GULPIER HALIDES HALITES HALOGEN HELICES HELIXES HILLIER HOLLIES HOLSTER HOLYSEE HULLOED ILLBRED ILLUDED ILLUDES ILLUMED ILLUMES ILLUSED ILLUSES JELLIED JELLIES JOLLIED JOLLIER JOLLIES JOLLIET JOLTIER KELPIES KILAUEA KILTIES KYLIKES

LALAKER LOLLIES MALMSEY MALTIER MILDRED MILKIER MILKMEN MOLDIER MULCHED MULCHES MULCTED OBLATES OBLIGED OBLIGES OOLITES PALACES PALATES PALAVER PALFREY PALJOEY PALLIER PALMIER PELAGES PHLOXES PILOTED PILSNER POLICED POLICES POLITER POLKAED POLYMER PULPIER PULQUES RALLIED RALLIER RALLIES RELACED RELACES RELATED RELATES RELAXED RELAXES RELAYED RELINED RELINES RELIVED RELIVES RELUMED RELUMES ROLODEX SALLIED SALLIES SALTIER SALUTED SALUTES SALVOES SELTZER SILKIER SILLIER SILLIES SILTIER SOLACES SOLDIER SOLIDER SOLUTES SPLAYED SPLICED SPLICER SPLICES SPLINES SULKIER SULKIES SULLIED SULLIES

SULUSEA TALKIER TALKIES TALLIED TALLIER TALLIES TALONED TALUSES TELEXED TELEXES TELLIES TOLKIEN TOLLIES UNLACED UNLACES UNLADES UNLIKED UNLINED UNLOVED VALISES VOLUMES WALTZED WALTZER WALTZES WELCHED WELCHES WELLFED WELLSET WILLIES WOLFMEN ZILCHES

••L•••E

ALLENDE ALLGONE ALLHERE ALLOFME ALLTIME ARLEDGE ATLARGE BALANCE BALLADE BELDAME BELIEVE BELTANE BOLOTIE CALCITE CALIBRE CALORIE CALZONE CELEBRE CELESTE CILIATE COLETTE COLGATE COLLAGE COLLATE COLLEGE COLLIDE COLLUDE COLOGNE CULOTTE CULTURE DELUISE ECLIPSE ECLOGUE EELLIKE ELLIPSE ENLARGE FOLIAGE FOLIATE FULSOME GALILEE GOLFTEE

HELLENE HELOISE HILAIRE HOLYOKE HOLYSEE KILDARE LALANNE LALIQUE MALAISE MALEATE MALTESE MALTOSE MELANGE MELANIE MELROSE MILEAGE MOLIERE OBLIQUE OILCAKE OILLIKE ONLEAVE OWLLIKE PALANCE PALETTE PALMATE PELISSE PELTATE PILLAGE POLEAXE POLLUTE PULSATE RELAPSE RELEASE RELIEVE SALABLE SALTINE SALVAGE SELVAGE SILENCE SOLFEGE SOLUBLE SPLURGE SULFATE SULFIDE SULFITE TILLAGE TOLUENE UNLOOSE VALANCE VALENCE VALERIE VALUATE VALVATE VILLAGE VOLPONE VOLTAGE VOLUBLE VULGATE VULPINE VULTURE WALLACE WALLEYE WALPOLE WELCOME WELFARE WILDONE WILLKIE

•••LE••

ABILENE AGELESS AGILELY AIDLESS AIMLESS

AIRLESS AMBLERS AMPLEST AMULETS ANGLERS ANKLETS ANTLERS APPLETS ARMLESS ARMLETS ARTLESS ASHLESS ATHLETE AUKLETS AWELESS AWNLESS AZALEAS BAILEES BAILERS BAILEYS BALLETS BARLESS BARLEYS BAWLERS BAYLEAF BEDLESS BELLEEK BIBLESS BILLETS BITLESS BOILERS BOOLEAN BOWLERS BOWLESS BRALESS BUDLESS BUGLERS BULLETS BUTLERS CABLERS CABLETV CALLERS CAPLESS CAPLETS CARLESS CHALETS CHILEAN COALERS COLLECT COLLEEN COLLEGE COLLETS COOLERS COOLEST COULEES CULLERS CURLERS CURLEWS CUTLERS CUTLERY CUTLETS CYCLERS DARLENE DEALERS DEFLECT DEKLERK DEPLETE DEWLESS DIALECT DIALERS DOGLEGS DOGLESS DUELERS DULLEST

EAGLETS EARLESS EGGLESS EMBLEMS ENDLESS EVILEST EVILEYE EYELESS EYELETS FABLERS FARLEFT FATLESS FEELERS FEELESS FELLERS FIGLEAF FILLERS FILLETS FLYLEAF FLYLESS FOGLESS FOLLETT FOOLERY FOULEST FOWLERS FUELERS FULLEST FURLESS GALLEON GALLERY GALLEYS GAOLERS GAPLESS GASLESS GEMLESS GIBLETS GIMLETS GOBLETS GODLESS GULLETS GUMLESS GUNLESS GUTLESS HAMLETS HAPLESS HATLESS HAULERS HEALERS HEELERS HELLENE HELLERS HEWLETT HIALEAH HIPLESS HITLESS HOLLERS HOWLERS HUELESS HULLERS HURLERS HURLEYS ICELESS INFLECT INKLESS INNLESS IRELESS JAGLESS JAILERS JARLESS JAWLESS JAYLENO JOBLESS JOYLESS KEGLERS

KEYLESS KILLERS KINLESS KOBLENZ LADLERS LAWLESS LEGLESS LIDLESS LIPLESS MAILERS MALLETS MANLESS MARLENE MATLESS MEDLEYS MEWLERS MILLEND MILLERS MILLETS MILLETT MISLEAD MOILERS MOSLEMS MRCLEAN MULLEIN MULLERS MULLETS NAILERS NAPLESS NEGLECT NEWLEFT NOBLEST NUCLEAR NUCLEIC NUCLEON NUCLEUS NUTLETS OAKLEAF OARLESS OILLESS OMELETS OPULENT ORBLESS OSTLERS OUTLETS PALLETS PARLEYS PEELERS PEGLESS PELLETS PIGLETS PINLESS PIOLETS POLLENS POLLERS POULENC PTOLEMY PULLETS PULLEYS PUNLESS RAILERS RECLEAN REELECT REFLECT REGLETS RELLENO REPLETE RIBLESS RIFLERS RIFLERY RILLETS RIMLESS RODLESS ROLLERS

RUMLESS RUNLETS SALLETS SAMLETS SAPLESS SCALENE SCALERS SCHLEPP SCHLEPS SEALEGS SEALERS SELLECK SELLERS SINLESS SKYLESS SMILERS SODLESS SONLESS STALELY STALEST STYLERS STYLETS SUBLETS SUMLESS SUNLESS SUTLERS TABLEAU TABLETS TAILEND TALLEST TAXLESS TEALEAF TEALESS TELLERS THALERS TIELESS TILLERS TIPLESS TOELESS TOILERS TOILETS TOYLESS TUGLESS UKULELE UNBLEST UNCLEAN UNCLEAR USELESS VALLEJO VALLEYS VARLETS VILLEIN VIOLENT VIOLETS VOLLEYS VOWLESS WAILERS WALLETS WALLEYE WARLESS WAYLESS WEBLESS WHALERS WIGLESS WIGLETS WILLETS WITLESS WOOLENS WURLEYS YELLERS YOWLERS

•••L•E•

APPLIED

APPLIES ARALSEA ATELIER AVULSED AVULSES BAILEES BAULKED BELLEEK BELLIED BELLIES BELLMEN BIALIES BIGLIES BILLIES BOULDER BOULLES BUILDER BULLIED BULLIES BULLPEN BURLIER CAULKED CAULKER CHALKED CHELSEA CHILIES CHILLED CHILLER COLLEEN COLLIER COLLIES COLLYER COULEES COULTER CRULLER CULLIED CULLIES CURLIER DAILIES DALLIED DALLIER DALLIES DILLIES DOILIES DOLLIED DOLLIES DRILLED DRILLER DROLLER DWELLED DWELLER EARLIER EVILLER EVOLVED EVOLVES EVULSED EVULSES EXALTED EXULTED FAULTED FELLIES FIELDED FIELDER FILLIES FOLLIES FRILLED FUELLED GIBLUES GILLIES GILLNET GOALIES GODLIER GRILLED GRILLES

GRILLET GROLIER GUILDER GULLIES HILLIER HOLLIES HULLOED HURLIES IMPLIED IMPLIES JELLIED JELLIES JOLLIED JOLLIER JOLLIES JOLLIET JOWLIER KNELLED LOLLIES LOWLIER MANLIER MEALIER MEALIES MOULDED MOULDER MOULTED NAILSET NIELSEN PALLIER PAULSEN PHILTER PSALMED PSALTER PURLIEU QUELLED QUILLED QUILLER QUILTED QUILTER RALLIED RALLIER RALLIES REGLUED REGLUES REPLIED REPLIES ROILIER SALLIED SALLIES SCALDED SCALIER SCALPED SCALPEL SCALPER SCOLDED SCOLDER SCULLED SCULLER SHELLED SHELLER SHELLEY SHELTER SHELVED SHELVES SHILLED SILLIER SILLIES SKELTER SKILLED SKILLET SKULKED SKULKER SMALLER SMELLED

SMELTED SMELTER SMOLDER SNELLEN SPALLED SPELLED SPELLER SPILLED STALKED STALKER STALLED STILLED STILLER STILTED STOLLEN STOLLER SULLIED SULLIES SURLIER SVELTER SWALLET SWELLED SWELTER SWILLED SWOLLEN TAILLES TALLIED TALLIER TALLIES TELLIES TOLLIES TRILLED TROLLED TROLLEY TWELVES TWILLED UNGLUED VAULTED VAULTER VEALIER WELLFED WELLSET WHELMED WHELPED WIELDED WILLIES WOOLIER WOOLIES WOOLLEN WOOLLEY WOOLSEY YIELDED ZOELLER

•••L••E

ABALONE ABILENE ACOLYTE ADELINE ADOLPHE ADULATE AIRLANE AIRLIKE AIRLINE AMYLASE ANALYSE ANALYZE ANILINE ANTLIKE APELIKE ARMLIKE ASSLIKE ATHLETE AXILLAE

BAGLIKE BALLADE BATLIKE BEDLIKE BEELIKE BEELINE BIBLIKE BIPLANE BOWLIKE BOWLINE BOXLIKE BUDLIKE BUSLINE CARLYLE CATLIKE CHALICE CHOLINE COLLAGE COLLATE COLLEGE COLLIDE COLLUDE COWLIKE CUPLIKE CURLIKE CYCLONE DARLENE DECLARE DECLINE DEFLATE DEPLANE DEPLETE DEPLORE DEWLINE DISLIKE DOGLIKE DOTLIKE EARLIKE EARLOBE EELLIKE EGALITE ELFLIKE EMPLOYE EMULATE ENCLAVE ENCLOSE ENPLANE ENSLAVE EVILEYE EXCLUDE EXPLODE EXPLORE EYELIKE FADLIKE FAILURE FANLIKE FATLIKE FINLIKE FORLIFE FOXLIKE GAGLINE GEMLIKE GODLIKE GUMLIKE HAGLIKE HATLIKE HAULAGE HELLENE HEMLINE HENLIKE HIPLIKE HOGLIKE HOPLIKE HOTLINE

HOVLANE HUNLIKE HUTLIKE HYALINE ICELIKE IDOLISE IDOLIZE IMPLODE IMPLORE INCLINE INCLOSE INCLUDE INFLAME INFLATE INKLIKE INPLACE ISOLATE IVYLIKE JAMLIKE JAWLIKE JAWLINE JIGLIKE KEYLIME KIDLIKE LAPLACE LAWLIKE LEGLIKE LIPLIKE LOWLIFE MANLIKE MARLENE MARLOWE MCCLURE MIDLIFE MIDLINE MISLIKE MOULAGE NETLIKE NIBLIKE NUCLIDE NUNLIKE NUTLIKE OAKLIKE OARLIKE OATLIKE OCCLUDE OFFLINE OILLIKE OLDLINE ONELANE OPALINE ORBLIKE OUTLINE OUTLIVE OWLLIKE PAPLIKE PAULINE PEALIKE PEGLIKE PENLIKE PERLITE PHILTRE PIELIKE PIGLIKE PILLAGE PODLIKE POLLUTE PRALINE PRELATE PRELUDE RAMLIKE RANLATE RATLIKE RATLINE

RAYLIKE
REALISE
REALIZE
RECLAME
RECLINE
RECLUSE
REDLINE
REPLACE
REPLATE
REPLETE
RIBLIKE
ROBLOWE
RODLIKE
ROULADE
RUGLIKE
RUNLATE
SACLIKE
SAWLIKE
SCALENE
SEALANE
SECLUDE
SETLINE
SHELTIE
SINLIKE
SKYLIKE
SKYLINE
SONLIKE
SOWLIKE
STYLISE
STYLIZE
SUBLIME
SUNLIKE
TAGLIKE
TAGLINE
TANLINE
TIELINE
TILLAGE
TINLIKE
TOELIKE
TOYLIKE
TUBLIKE
TWOLANE
UKULELE
ULALUME
ULULATE
UNALIKE
UNCLOSE
UPCLOSE
URNLIKE
UTILISE
UTILIZE
VILLAGE
VIOLATE
WALLACE
WALLEYE
WARLIKE
WAXLIKE
WEBLIKE
WIGLIKE
WILLKIE
WOULDBE

••••LE•

AEDILES
ALLELES
AMPULES
ANGELES
ANNALEE
ARGYLES
AUDILES
AURALEE
AVAILED
AVONLEA
BABBLED
BABBLES
BAFFLED
BAFFLER
BAFFLES
BANGLES
BARKLEY
BATTLED
BATTLER
BATTLES
BAUBLES
BEADLES
BEAGLES
BEATLES
BEETLES
BENTLEY
BEVELED
BOBBLED
BOBBLES
BOBSLED
BOGGLED
BOGGLER
BOGGLES
BOODLES
BOOKLET
BOOSLER
BOOTLEG
BOTTLED
BOTTLER
BOTTLES
BOULLES
BOWDLER
BRADLEE
BRADLEY
BRAWLED
BRAWLER
BRIDLED
BRIDLES
BRIMLEY
BROILED
BROILER
BUBBLED
BUBBLES
BUCKLED
BUCKLER
BUCKLES
BUCKLEY
BULBLET
BUMBLED
BUMBLER
BUMBLES
BUNDLED
BUNDLES
BUNGLED
BUNGLER
BUNGLES
BURBLED
BURBLES
BURGLED
BURGLES
BUSTLED
BUSTLES
CACKLED
CACKLER
CACKLES
CAJOLED
CAJOLER
CAJOLES
CANDLES
CANTLES
CAPELET
CAPULET
CAROLED
CAROLER
CASTLED
CASTLES
CAUDLES
CAVILED
CAVILER
CHAPLET
CHARLES
CHARLEY
CHILLED
CHILLER
CIRCLED
CIRCLES
CIRCLET
COBBLED
COBBLER
COBBLES
COCHLEA
COCKLES
CODDLED
CODDLER
CODDLES
COMPLEX
COUPLED
COUPLES
COUPLET
CRADLED
CRADLES
CRAWLED
CRAWLER
CREOLES
CRUELER
CRULLER
CUDDLED
CUDDLES
CURDLED
CURDLES
CUSSLER
DABBLED
DABBLER
DABBLES
DAIMLER
DANDLED
DANDLES
DANGLED
DANGLER
DANGLES
DAPPLED
DAPPLES
DARNLEY
DAWDLED
DAWDLER
DAWDLES
DAZZLED
DAZZLER
DAZZLES
DECKLES
DEFILED
DEFILER
DEFILES
DEVILED
DIBBLED
DIBBLES
DIDDLED
DIDDLES
DIDDLEY
DIMPLED
DIMPLES
DINGLES
DIPOLES
DOGSLED
DONGLES
DOODLED
DOODLER
DOODLES
DOPPLER
DOTTLES
DOUBLED
DOUBLES
DOUBLET
DOUBLEU
DRAWLED
DRIBLET
DRILLED
DRILLER
DROLLER
DROOLED
DROOLER
DROPLET
DWELLED
DWELLER
EDIBLES
EMAILED
ENABLED
ENABLES
ENISLED
ENISLES
ENSILED
ENSILES
EPAULET
EQUALED
ETOILES
EVILLER
EXHALED
EXHALES
FEEBLER
FEMALES
FERULES
FETTLES
FICKLER
FIDDLED
FIDDLER
FIDDLES
FIEDLER
FINALES
FIPPLES
FIZZLED
FIZZLES
FLAILED
FLATLET
FOCSLES
FOIBLES
FONDLED
FONDLES
FOOZLED
FOOZLES
FORELEG
FRAILER
FRAWLEY
FRILLED
FUDDLED
FUDDLES
FUELLED
FUMBLED
FUMBLER
FUMBLES
GABBLED
GABBLES
GAGGLES
GALILEE
GALILEI
GALILEO
GAMBLED
GAMBLER
GAMBLES
GANGLED
GANTLET
GARBLED
GARBLES
GARGLED
GARGLES
GATELEG
GAVELED
GENTLED
GENTLER
GENTLES
GIGGLED
GIGGLER
GIGGLES
GIRDLED
GIRDLES
GNARLED
GOBBLED
GOBBLER
GOBBLES
GOGGLED
GOGGLES
GREELEY
GRILLED
GRILLES
GRILLET
GROWLED
GROWLER
GURGLED
GURGLES
GUZZLED
GUZZLER
GUZZLES
HAARLEM
HACKLED
HACKLES
HAGGLED
HAGGLER
HAGGLES
HANDLED
HANDLER
HANDLES
HASSLED
HASSLES
HECKLED
HECKLER
HECKLES
HEDDLES
HEMSLEY
HIGGLED
HIGGLES
HOBBLED
HOBBLES
HOPPLED
HOPPLES
HOSTLER
HUDDLED
HUDDLES
HUMBLED
HUMBLER
HUMBLES
HUNTLEY
HURDLED
HURDLER
HURDLES
HURTLED
HURTLES
HUSTLED
HUSTLER
HUSTLES
ICICLES
IMPALED
IMPALES
INHALED
INHALER
INHALES
INSOLES
JANGLED
JANGLES
JEWELED
JEWELER
JIGGLED
JIGGLES
JINGLED
JINGLES
JOGGLED
JOGGLES
JOSTLED
JOSTLER
JOSTLES
JUBILEE
JUGGLED
JUGGLER
JUGGLES
JUMBLED
JUMBLES
JUNGLES
KEEBLER
KETTLES
KIBBLED
KIBBLES
KINDLED
KINDLES
KIRTLES
KNEELED
KNEELER
KNELLED
KNURLED
LABELED
LABELER
LANGLEY
LAPELED
LEAFLET
LEVELED
LEVELER
LIBELED
LIBELER
LITTLER
LOBULES
LOCALES
LORELEI
MANGLED
MANGLES
MANTLED
MANTLES
MARBLED
MARBLES
MEASLES
MEDALED
MEDDLED
MEDDLER
MEDDLES
METTLES
MIDDLEC
MIDDLES
MIGGLES
MINGLED
MINGLER
MINGLES
MIZZLED
MIZZLES
MOBILES
MODELED
MODELER
MODULES
MORALES
MOTTLED
MOTTLES
MUDDLED
MUDDLER
MUDDLES
MUFFLED
MUFFLER
MUFFLES
MUMBLED
MUMBLER
MUMBLES
MUSCLED
MUSCLES
MUZZLED
MUZZLES
MYRTLES
NEEDLED
NEEDLES
NESTLED
NESTLER
NESTLES
NETTLED
NETTLES
NIBBLED
NIBBLER
NIBBLES
NIGGLED
NIGGLES
NIMBLER
NOBBLED
NOBBLER
NOBBLES
NODULES
NOGALES
NOODLES
NOZZLES
NUBBLES
NUZZLED
NUZZLER
NUZZLES
ORACLES
ORIOLES
PADDLED
PADDLER
PADDLES
PAISLEY
PANELED
PAROLED
PAROLEE
PAROLES
PARSLEY
PEARLED
PEBBLED
PEBBLES
PEDALED
PEDDLED
PEDDLER
PEDDLES
PEEPLES
PEOPLED
PEOPLES
PERPLEX
PESTLED
PESTLES
PETALED
PICKLED
PICKLES
PIFFLED
PIFFLES
PLAYLET
POODLES
POPPLED
POPPLES
POTTLES
PRESLEY
PROBLEM
PROWLED
PROWLER
PUDDLED
PUDDLES
PURFLED
PURFLES
PURPLED
PURPLES
PUZZLED
PUZZLER
PUZZLES
QUAILED
QUELLED
QUIGLEY
QUILLED
QUILLER
RABBLES
RADDLED
RADDLES
RAFFLED
RAFFLER
RAFFLES
RAMBLED
RAMBLER
RAMBLES
RANKLED
RANKLES
RASSLED
RASSLES
RATTLED
RATTLER
RATTLES
RAVELED
REFILED
REFILES
REGALED
REGALES
REOILED
RESALES
RESILED
RESILES
RESOLED
RESOLES
RETILED
RETILES
REVELED
REVELER
REVILED
REVILES
RICKLES
RIDDLED
RIDDLER
RIDDLES
RIFFLED
RIFFLES
RIMPLED
RIMPLES
RINGLET
RIPPLED
RIPPLES
RIVALED
RIVULET
ROOTLET
ROUBLES
RUBBLES
RUFFLED
RUFFLES
RUMBLED
RUMBLES
RUMPLED
RUMPLES
RUNDLES
RUSTLED
RUSTLER
RUSTLES
SADDLED
SADDLER
SADDLES
SAMPLED
SAMPLER
SAMPLES
SARALEE
SCARLET
SCOWLED
SCOWLER
SCULLED
SCULLER
SETTLED
SETTLER
SETTLES
SHAPLEY
SHELLED
SHELLER
SHELLEY
SHILLED
SHIRLEY
SICKLES
SIMILES
SIMPLER
SIMPLEX
SINGLED
SINGLES
SIZZLED
SIZZLES
SKILLED
SKILLET
SKIRLED
SMALLER
SMELLED
SNARLED
SNELLEN
SNIGLET
SPALLED
SPELLED
SPELLER
SPIELED
SPIELER
SPILLED
SPOILED
SPOILER
SPOOLED
STABLED
STABLER
STABLES
STALLED
STANLEE
STANLEY
STAPLED
STAPLER
STAPLES
STARLET
STEELED
STEELER
STIFLED
STIFLES
STILLED
STILLER
STOLLEN
STOLLER
SUBTLER
SUPPLER
SWALLET
SWELLED
SWILLED
SWIRLED
SWOLLEN
TACKLED
TACKLER
TACKLES
TAILLES
TAMALES
TANGLED
TANGLES
TATTLED
TATTLER
TATTLES
TEMPLES
TICKLED
TICKLER
TICKLES
TINGLED
TINGLES
TINKLED
TINKLES
TIPPLED
TIPPLER
TIPPLES
TITTLES
TODDLED
TODDLER
TODDLES
TOFFLER
TOGGLED
TOGGLES
TOOTLED
TOOTLES
TOPPLED
TOPPLES
TOTALED
TOUSLED
TOUSLES
TOWELED
TRAILED
TRAILER
TRAWLED
TRAWLER
TREBLED
TREBLES
TRIFLED
TRIFLER
TRIFLES
TRILLED
TRIPLED
TRIPLES
TRIPLET
TRIPLEX
TROLLED
TROLLEY
TUMBLED
TUMBLER
TUMBLES
TURTLED
TURTLES
TUSSLED
TUSSLES
TWILLED
TWIRLED
TWIRLER
UNOILED
UNPILED
UNPILES
VITTLES
WADDLED
WADDLER
WADDLES
WAFFLED
WAFFLER
WAFFLES
WAGGLED
WAGGLES
WAMBLED
WAMBLES
WANGLED
WANGLER
WANGLES
WARBLED
WARBLER
WARBLES
WATTLES
WAVELET
WHEELED
WHEELER
WHIRLED
WHORLED
WIGGLED
WIGGLER
WIGGLES
WIMBLED
WIMBLES
WIMPLED
WIMPLES
WINKLED
WINKLER
WINKLES
WOBBLED
WOBBLES
WOOLLEN
WOOLLEY
WRIGLEY
YODELED
YODELER
ZOELLER

••••L•E

AAMILNE
ABSOLVE
AMIBLUE
ANNALEE
AREOLAE
AURALEE
AXILLAE
BIVALVE
BRADLEE
BRAILLE
CAMILLE
CHARLIE
COPULAE
DEMILLE
DEVALUE
DEVILLE
DEVOLVE
DIVULGE
ESTELLE
FACULAE
FIBULAE
GALILEE
GAZELLE
GEFILTE
GISELLE
ICEBLUE
ICEFLOE
IMPULSE
INDULGE
INVOLVE
JUBILEE
LABELLE
LASALLE
LAVALSE
LUCILLE
MACULAE
MOSELLE
NACELLE
NATALIE
NEBULAE
NEVILLE
NOVELLE
ORVILLE
OVERLIE
PAROLEE
RADULAE
REPULSE
RESOLVE
REVALUE
REVOLVE
ROSALIE
ROSELLE
ROYALWE
ROZELLE
SARALEE
SEABLUE
SEVILLE
SKYBLUE
STANLEE
STEELIE
STOOLIE
WHEELIE

•••••LE

ACTABLE
ADDABLE
ADDIBLE
AFFABLE
AIRHOLE
AIRMILE
AMIABLE
AMPOULE
ANATOLE
APOSTLE
ARMHOLE
ARTICLE
ASARULE
ATINGLE
AUDIBLE
AUREOLE
AURICLE
BEGUILE
BICYCLE
BOBDOLE
BOGHOLE
BRAILLE
BRAMBLE
BRINDLE
BRISTLE
BRITTLE
BUYABLE
CAMILLE
CAPABLE
CAPSULE
CARLYLE
CASTILE
CHORALE
CHORTLE
CHUCKLE
CITABLE
COMPILE
CONDOLE
CONSOLE
CRACKLE
CRINKLE
CRUMBLE
CRUMPLE
CUBICLE
CUTICLE
DEBACLE
DEMILLE
DEVILLE
DISABLE
DRIBBLE
DRIZZLE
DRYHOLE
DUCTILE
DURABLE
DWINDLE
EATABLE
ENNOBLE
ENTITLE
EPISTLE
EQUABLE
ESTELLE
EXAMPLE
EYEHOLE
FEBRILE
FERRULE
FERTILE
FINAGLE
FISSILE
FIXABLE
FORSALE
FOXHOLE
FRAGILE
FRAZZLE
FRECKLE
FRIABLE
FRIZZLE
GAGRULE
GAZELLE
GENTILE
GISELLE
GLOBULE
GRACILE
GRACKLE
GRANULE
GRAPPLE
GRIDDLE
GRISTLE
GRIZZLE
GRUMBLE
GUNWALE
HERCULE
HIRABLE
HOSTILE
IGNOBLE
INSTYLE
INUTILE
KEYHOLE
KNUCKLE
KRINGLE
LABELLE
LASALLE
LEGIBLE
LIKABLE
LIVABLE
LOVABLE
LUCILLE
MANACLE
MANHOLE
MANIPLE
MAYPOLE
MICHELE
MINABLE
MIRACLE
MISFILE
MISRULE
MISSILE
MIXABLE
MONDALE
MONOCLE
MOSELLE
MOVABLE
MUTABLE
NACELLE
NEVILLE
NOTABLE
NOVELLE
OCTUPLE
ORVILLE
OSSICLE
PANICLE
PARABLE
PAYABLE
PEDICLE
PERCALE
PETIOLE
PINHOLE
PINOCLE
PINWALE
PISTOLE
PLIABLE
POTABLE
POTHOLE
PRATTLE
PRESALE
PRICKLE
PROFILE
PUERILE
QUIBBLE
RADICLE
RATABLE
RATHOLE
RECYCLE
REPTILE
RESCALE
RESTYLE
RETICLE
RETITLE
RISIBLE
RISSOLE
ROSELLE
ROZELLE
RUMPOLE
SALABLE
SAVABLE
SCRUPLE
SCUFFLE
SCUTTLE
SEATTLE
SEEABLE
SERVILE
SESSILE
SEVILLE
SHACKLE
SHAMBLE
SHINGLE
SHUFFLE
SHUTTLE
SIZABLE
SKIPOLE
SKITTLE
SMUGGLE
SNAFFLE
SNAPPLE
SNIFFLE
SNIGGLE
SNUFFLE
SNUGGLE
SOLUBLE
SOUFFLE
SPACKLE
SPANGLE
SPARKLE
SPECKLE
SPINDLE
STABILE
STARTLE
STEEPLE
STERILE
STIPPLE
STUBBLE
STUMBLE
SWADDLE
SWINDLE
SWIZZLE
SYSTOLE

TACTILE
TADPOLE
TAGSALE
TAMABLE
TAXABLE
TENABLE
TENSILE
TEXTILE
THIMBLE
THISTLE
TIMBALE
TOPHOLE
TOSCALE
TRAMPLE
TREACLE
TREADLE
TREMBLE
TRESTLE
TRICKLE
TROUBLE
TRUCKLE
TRUFFLE
TRUNDLE
TUNICLE
TWADDLE
TWIDDLE
TWINKLE
UKULELE
UPSCALE
USEABLE
VACUOLE
VEHICLE
VIRGULE
VISIBLE
VOLUBLE
WALPOLE
WHEEDLE
WHISTLE
WHITTLE
WIMPOLE
WRANGLE
WRESTLE
WRIGGLE
WRINKLE

L•F••••

LAFARGE
LAFITTE
LEFTIES
LEFTIST
LEFTOFF
LEFTOUT
LIFEFUL
LIFENET
LIFTERS
LIFTING
LIFTOFF
LIFTSUP
LOFTIER
LOFTILY
LOFTING
LUFFING

L••F•••

LANFORD
LAPFULS
LAWFORD
LEAFAGE
LEAFIER
LEAFING
LEAFLET
LENFANT
LOAFERS
LOAFING
LOOFAHS
LUFFING

L•••F••

LAIDFOR
LATIFAH
LAYOFFS
LAYSFOR
LETSFLY
LIFEFUL
LOOKFOR
LUCIFER
LUSTFUL

L••••F•

LAIDOFF
LAYOFFS
LAYSOFF
LEADOFF
LEFTOFF
LETSOFF
LIFTOFF
LIQUEFY
LOGSOFF
LOWLIFE

L•••••F

LAIDOFF
LAYSOFF
LEADOFF
LEFTOFF
LETSOFF
LIFTOFF
LOGSOFF

•LF••••

ALFALFA
ALFIERI
ALFONSO
ALFORJA
ALFREDO
ELFLIKE

•L•F•••

BLUFFED
BLUFFER
BLUFFLY
CLIFTON
FLUFFED
FLYFISH
OLDFOGY
OLEFINS

•L••F••

ALLOFME
ALOOFLY
BLOWFLY
BLUEFIN
BLUEFOX
BLUFFED
BLUFFER
BLUFFLY
FLUFFED
GLEEFUL
PLAYFUL
PLOTFUL

•L•••F•

ALEWIFE
ALFALFA
BLEWOFF
BLOWOFF
CLARIFY
GLORIFY
PLAYOFF

•L••••F

BLEWOFF
BLOWOFF
FLYLEAF
PLAYOFF

••LF•••

AELFRIC
BALFOUR
BELFAST
FULFILL
FULFILS
GOLFERS
GOLFING
GOLFPRO
GOLFTEE
GULFING
HALFDAN
HALFWAY
HALFWIT
PALFREY
PILFERS
SELFISH
SOLFEGE
SULFATE
SULFIDE
SULFITE
WELFARE
WILFORD
WILFRID
WOLFGAL
WOLFING
WOLFISH
WOLFMAN
WOLFMEN
WOLFRAM

••L•F••

ALLOFME
BALEFUL
CALLFOR
DOLEFUL
FALAFEL
FALLFOR
FELLFOR
FELTFOR
HALIFAX
HELPFUL
MALEFIC
PULLFOR
SELLFOR
UPLIFTS
WELLFED
WILLFUL

••L••F•

BELIEFS
CALCIFY
CALLOFF
DULCIFY
FALLOFF
FALSIFY
FELLOFF
HELDOFF
HOLDOFF
JOLLIFY
MOLLIFY
NULLIFY
PALMOFF
PULLOFF
RELIEFS
SALSIFY
SELLOFF
SOLDOFF
TELLOFF
TOLDOFF
WELLOFF

••L•••F

CALLOFF
FALLOFF
FELLOFF
HELDOFF
HOLDOFF
PALMOFF
PULLOFF
SELLOFF
SOLDOFF
TELLOFF
TELLSOF
TOLDOFF
WALDORF
WELLOFF

•••LF••

BOWLFUL
CALLFOR
FALLFOR
FEELFOR
FELLFOR
PAILFUL
PULLFOR
SELLFOR
SKILFUL
SOULFUL
TAILFIN
TOILFUL
TWELFTH
WAILFUL
WELLFED
WILLFUL

•••L•F•

AIRLIFT
AMPLIFY
BAILIFF
CALLOFF
FALLOFF
FARLEFT
FELLOFF
FORLIFE
HAULOFF
HAYLOFT
JOLLIFY
KARLOFF
LOWLIFE
MIDLIFE
MOLLIFY
NEWLEFT
NULLIFY
PEELOFF
PULLOFF
QUALIFY
REELOFF
SEALOFF
SELLOFF
SKILIFT
TAILOFF
TELLOFF
WELLOFF

•••L••F

BAILIFF
BAYLEAF
CALLOFF
FALLOFF
FELLOFF
FIGLEAF
FLYLEAF
HAULOFF
KARLOFF
OAKLEAF
PEELOFF
PULLOFF
REELOFF
SEALOFF
SELLOFF
TAILOFF
TEALEAF
TELLOFF
TELLSOF
WELLOFF

••••LF•

ALFALFA
ENGULFS
RODOLFO

•••••LF

AIRWOLF
BEOWULF
CRYWOLF
HERSELF
HIMSELF
NONSELF
ONESELF
OURSELF
REDWOLF
SEAWOLF
SHEWOLF
THYSELF

L•G••••

LAGGARD
LAGGERS
LAGGING
LAGOONS
LAGUNAS
LEGALLY
LEGATEE
LEGATES
LEGATOS
LEGENDS
LEGGIER
LEGGING
LEGHORN
LEGIBLE
LEGIBLY
LEGIONS
LEGISTS
LEGLESS
LEGLIKE
LEGPULL
LEGRAND
LEGROOM
LEGUMES
LEGWORK
LIGANDS
LIGATED
LIGATES
LIGHTED
LIGHTEN
LIGHTER
LIGHTLY
LIGHTUP
LIGNITE
LOGBOOK
LOGGERS
LOGGIAS
LOGGING
LOGGINS
LOGGISH
LOGICAL
LOGIEST
LOGJAMS
LOGROLL
LOGSOFF
LOGSOUT
LUGGAGE
LUGGERS
LUGGING
LUGNUTS

L••G•••

LAAGERS
LAGGARD
LAGGERS
LAGGING
LANGDON
LANGLEY
LANGTRY
LANGUID
LANGUOR
LANGURS
LARGELY
LARGESS
LARGEST
LARGISH
LAUGHAT
LAUGHED
LAUGHER
LAUGHIN
LEAGUES
LEDGERS
LEDGIER
LEGGIER
LEGGING
LENGTHS
LENGTHY
LINGERS
LINGOES
LINGUAL
LODGERS
LODGING
LOGGERS
LOGGIAS
LOGGING
LOGGINS
LOGGISH
LONGAGO
LONGARM
LONGBOW
LONGEST
LONGIES
LONGING
LONGISH
LONGRUN
LONGTON
LONGUES
LOWGEAR
LUGGAGE
LUGGERS
LUGGING
LUNGEAT
LUNGING

L•••G••

LASAGNA
LASAGNE
LIMOGES
LINAGES
LITHGOW
LOUNGED
LOUNGER
LOUNGES
LYINGTO

L••••G•

LACINGS
LAFARGE
LAPDOGS
LEAFAGE
LEAKAGE
LENTIGO
LINEAGE
LININGS
LINKAGE
LITURGY
LIVINGS
LONGAGO
LOZENGE
LUGGAGE
LUMBAGO

L•••••G

LACKING
LADLING
LADYBUG
LAGGING
LAMMING
LANDING
LANSING
LAPPING
LAPSING
LAPWING
LARDING
LASHING
LASTING
LATHING
LAUDING
LEADING
LEAFING
LEAKING
LEANING
LEAPING
LEASING
LEAVING
LEERING
LEGGING
LEIPZIG
LEMMING
LENDING
LESSING
LETTING
LEVYING
LIBBING
LICKING
LIFTING
LILTING
LIMBING
LIMNING
LIMPING
LINKING
LIPPING
LISPING
LISTING
LOADING
LOAFING
LOAMING
LOANING
LOBBING
LOCKING
LODGING
LOFTING
LOGGING
LOLLING
LONGING
LOOKING
LOOMING
LOOPING
LOOSING
LOOTING
LOPPING
LORDING
LOTTING
LOUSING
LOVEBUG
LUCKING
LUFFING
LUGGING
LULLING
LUMPING
LUNGING
LURKING
LUSTING

•LG••••

ALGEBRA
ALGERIA
ALGIERS
ELGRECO

•L•G•••

ALIGHTS
ALIGNED
ALIGNER
ALLGONE
BLIGHTS
BLIGHTY
CLOGGED
CLOGSUP
ELEGANT
ELEGIAC
ELEGIES
ELEGIST
FLAGDAY
FLAGGED
FLAGMAN
FLAGMEN
FLAGONS
FLIGHTS
FLIGHTY
FLOGGED
GLUGGED
KLUGMAN
OLDGOLD
PLAGUED
PLAGUES
PLIGHTS
PLUGGED
PLUGGER
PLUGINS
PLUGSIN
SLIGHTS
SLOGANS
SLOGGED
SLUGGED
SLUGGER

•L••G••

ALLEGED
ALLEGER
ALLEGES
ALLEGRO
ALRIGHT
BLOWGUN
BLUEGUM
CLANGED
CLANGOR
CLOGGED
ELOIGNS
FLAGGED
FLANGES
FLEDGED
FLEDGES
FLOGGED
GLASGOW
GLUGGED
ILLEGAL
ILLOGIC
KLINGON
KLUDGES
PLEDGED
PLEDGEE
PLEDGER
PLEDGES
PLOUGHS
PLUGGED
PLUGGER
PLUNGED
PLUNGER
PLUNGES
SLEDGES
SLEIGHS
SLEIGHT
SLINGER
SLOEGIN
SLOGGED
SLOUGHS
SLUDGES
SLUGGED
SLUGGER
TLINGIT

•L•••G•

ALLERGY
FLYHIGH
OLDFOGY
PLUMAGE

•L••••G

ALAKING
ALINING
ALLYING
BLADING
BLAMING
BLARING
BLAZING
BLOWING
BLUEING
CLAWING
CLONING
CLOSING
CLOYING
CLUEING
ELATING
ELIDING
ELOPING
ELUDING
ELUTING
FLAKING
FLAMING
FLARING
FLAWING
FLAYING
FLEABAG
FLEEING
FLEMING
FLEXING
FLEYING
FLOWING
FLUTING
FLUXING
GLARING
GLAZING
GLIDING
GLOBING
GLOWING
GLOZING
PLACING
PLANING
PLATING
PLAYING
PLOWING
PLUMING
SLAKING
SLATING
SLAVING
SLEDDOG
SLICING
SLIDING
SLOPING
SLOWING

••LG•••

ALLGONE
BELGIAN
BELGIUM
BILGIER
BULGARS
BULGHUR
BULGIER
BULGING
CALGARY
COLGATE
FOLGERS
FULGENT
FULGHUM
GILGUYS
PILGRIM
VULGATE

••L•G••

ALLEGED
ALLEGER
ALLEGES
ALLEGRO
BOLOGNA
COLOGNE
DELIGHT
DELUGED
DELUGES
ECLOGUE
FALLGUY
GALAGOS
HALOGEN
ILLEGAL
ILLOGIC
MALIGNS
OBLIGED
OBLIGES
PELAGES
PELAGIC
POLYGON
RELIGHT
WOLFGAL

••L••G•

ALLERGY
ARLEDGE
ATLARGE
BELONGS
COLLAGE
COLLEGE
ENLARGE
FILINGS
FOLIAGE
KELLOGG
MELANGE
MILEAGE
OBLONGS
OILRIGS
PILINGS
PILLAGE
RALEIGH
RULINGS
SALVAGE
SELVAGE
SOLFEGE
SPLURGE
TILINGS
TILLAGE
VILLAGE
VOLTAGE

••L•••G

ALLYING
BALDING
BALKING
BELLING
BELTBAG
BELTING
BELYING
BILKING
BILLING
BOLTING
BULGING
BULKING
BULLDOG
BULLING
CALKING
CALLING
CALMING
CALVING
CULLING
DELEING
DELVING
DOLLING
DULLING
FALLING
FELLING
FILLING
FILMING
FOLDING
GALLING
GELDING
GELLING
GILDING
GILLING
GOLDBUG
GOLDING
GOLFING
GULFING
GULLING
GULPING
HALOING
HALTING
HALVING
HELMING
HELPING
HILLING
HOLDING
HULKING
HULLING
JELLING
JILTING
JOLTING
KELLOGG
KILLING
KILTING
LILTING
LOLLING
LULLING
MALTING
MELDING
MELTING
MILKING
MILLING
MOLDING
MOLTING
MULLING
NULLING
PALLING
PALMING
PELTING
PILLBUG
PILLING
POLLING
PULLING
PULSING
RDLAING
RELYING
ROLLING
ROLVAAG
SALTING
SALVING
SELLING
SILOING
SILTING
SOLOING
SOLVING
SULKING
TALKBIG
TALKING
TELLING
TILLING
TILTING
TOLLING
VALUING
WALKING
WALLING
WELDING
WELLING
WELTING
WILDING
WILLING
WILTING
WOLFING
YELLING
YELPING
YULELOG

•••LG••

AMALGAM
COALGAS
FALLGUY
GIELGUD

•••L•G•

ANALOGS
ANALOGY
APOLOGY
BIOLOGY
COLLAGE
COLLEGE
DIALOGS
DOGLEGS
ECOLOGY
EPILOGS
GASLOGS
GEOLOGY
HAULAGE
KELLOGG
MOULAGE
PILLAGE
PROLOGS
REFLAGS
SAWLOGS
SEALEGS
STALAGS
TILLAGE
TRILOGY
UNCLOGS
UNPLUGS
VILLAGE
ZOOLOGY

•••L••G

ADDLING
AMBLING
ANELING
ANGLING
BAILING
BAWLING
BELLING
BILLING
BIRLING
BOILING
BOWLING
BUGLING
BULLDOG
BULLING
BURLING
CABLING
CALLING
CEILING
COILING
COOLING
COWLING
CULLING
CURLING
CYCLING
DARLING
DAYLONG
DEALING
DIALING
DOLLING
DUELING
DULLING
EAGLING
ERELONG
EXILING
FAILING
FALLING
FEELING
FELLING
FILLING
FOALING
FOILING
FOOLING
FOULING
FOWLING
FUELING
FURLING
FURLONG
GALLING
GAOLING
GATLING
GELLING
GILLING
GOALONG
GOSLING
GULLING
HAILING
HAULING
HEALING
HEELING
HILLING
HOWLING
HULLING
HURLING
INKLING
JAILING
JELLING
KEELING
KELLOGG
KILLING
KIPLING
LADLING
LOLLING
LULLING
MAILBAG
MAILING
MAULING
MEWLING
MILLING
MOILING
MULLING
NAILING
NULLING
PALLING
PAULING
PEALING
PEELING
PILLBUG
PILLING
POLLING
POOLING
PROLONG
PULLING
PURLING
RAILING
REELING
RIFLING
ROILING
ROLLING
SAILING
SAPLING
SCALING
SEALING
SELLING
SERLING
SIBLING
SIDLING
SMILING
SOILING
STYLING
TABLING
TAILING
TELLING
TILLING
TITLING
TOILING
TOLLING
TOOLING
VEILING
WAILING
WALLING
WELLING
WHALING
WHILING
WILLING
YELLING
YOWLING

••••LG•

DIVULGE
HIDALGO
INDULGE
REDALGA

••••L•G

ANTILOG
BACKLOG
BOOTLEG
CATALOG

DECALOG
EARPLUG
FORELEG
GATELEG
GRAYLAG
MONOLOG
REDFLAG
SEASLUG
SEMILOG
TAGALOG
TIMELAG
YULELOG

L•H••••

LEHAVRE

L••H•••

LACHLAN
LASHERS
LASHING
LASHUPS
LATHERS
LATHERY
LATHING
LEGHORN
LICHENS
LIGHTED
LIGHTEN
LIGHTER
LIGHTLY
LIGHTUP
LITHELY
LITHEST
LITHGOW
LITHIUM
LOWHEEL
LUSHEST

L•••H••

LAKSHMI
LARCHES
LATCHED
LATCHES
LAUGHAT
LAUGHED
LAUGHER
LAUGHIN
LEACHED
LEACHES
LEASHED
LEASHES
LEATHER
LEECHED
LEECHES
LITCHIS
LOACHES
LOATHED
LOATHES
LUNCHED
LUNCHES
LURCHED
LURCHES

L••••H•

LAMEDHS
LENGTHS
LENGTHY
LESOTHO
LOOFAHS

L•••••H

LADDISH
LADYISH
LAPPISH
LARGISH
LARKISH
LATIFAH
LAZYISH
LETTISH
LOGGISH
LONGISH
LOUDISH
LOUTISH
LOWTECH
LUMPISH

•L•H•••

ALCHEMY
ALLHAIL
ALLHEAL
ALLHERE
ALOHAOE
ELKHART
FLYHIGH
OLDHAND

•L••H••

ALCOHOL
ALIGHTS
ALYKHAN
BLATHER
BLIGHTS
BLIGHTY
BLITHER
BLUSHED
BLUSHER
BLUSHES
BLUSHON
CLASHED
CLASHES
CLICHES
CLOCHES
CLOTHED
CLOTHES
FLASHED
FLASHER
FLASHES
FLECHES
FLESHED
FLESHES
FLESHLY
FLIGHTS
FLIGHTY
FLUSHED
FLUSHES
OLDCHAP
PLASHED
PLASHES
PLIGHTS
PLUSHER
PLUSHES
PLUSHLY
SLASHED
SLASHER
SLASHES
SLATHER
SLIGHTS
SLITHER
SLOSHED
SLOSHES
SLUSHES

•L•••H•

ALRIGHT
ALYOSHA
BLANCHE
BLOTCHY
PLINTHS
PLOUGHS
SLEIGHS
SLEIGHT
SLEUTHS
SLOUCHY
SLOUGHS

•L••••H

ALDRICH
ALWORTH
BLEMISH
BLUEISH
CLAYISH
FLEMISH
FLYFISH
FLYHIGH
KLAMATH
KLATSCH
PLANISH
PLAYDOH
SLAVISH

••LH•••

ALLHAIL
ALLHEAL
ALLHERE
CALHOUN
MILHAUD
WILHELM

••L•H••

BALIHAI
BELCHED
BELCHES
BELLHOP
BOLSHOI
BULGHUR
DELPHIC
DOLPHIN
FILCHED
FILCHER
FILCHES
FULGHUM
GALAHAD
GULCHES
MALTHUS
MCLUHAN
MULCHED
MULCHES
SALCHOW
SILKHAT
SULPHUR
WELCHED
WELCHES
ZILCHES

••L••H•

BELUSHI
CALIPHS
DALETHS
DELIGHT
EOLITHS
FELLAHS
GULLAHS
HALVAHS
MALACHI
MOLOCHS
MULLAHS
NULLAHS
OOLITHS
RELIGHT
SPLASHY
TALLYHO

••L•••H

BALDISH
BULLISH
BULRUSH
CALTECH
COLDISH
COLTISH
CULTISH
DELILAH
DOLLISH
DOLTISH
DULLISH
FOLKISH
GALUMPH
GOLIATH
HELLISH
PELTISH
RALEIGH
SALTISH
SELFISH
SPLOTCH
TALLISH
UNLATCH
UNLEASH
WALLACH
WILDISH
WOLFISH

•••LH••

BELLHOP

•••L•H•

ADOLPHE
FELLAHS
GUELPHS
GULLAHS
HEALTHY
MULLAHS
NULLAHS
TALLYHO
WEALTHY

•••L••H

ABOLISH
BULLISH
COOLISH
DOLLISH
DULLISH
EHRLICH
ENGLISH
EYELASH
FOOLISH
GAULISH
GIRLISH
GOULASH
HELLISH
HIALEAH
NEOLITH
PUBLISH
STYLISH
TALLISH
TWELFTH
WALLACH

••••L•H

DELILAH
RUDOLPH
SQUELCH
STEALTH

•••••LH

ANOUILH

LI•••••

LIAISED
LIAISES
LIAISON
LIBBERS
LIBBING
LIBELED
LIBELER
LIBERAL
LIBERIA
LIBERTY
LIBIDOS
LIBRARY
LIBYANS
LICENCE
LICENSE
LICHENS
LICITLY
LICKING
LICTORS
LIDLESS
LIEABED
LIEDOWN
LIENEES
LIEOVER
LIERNES
LIESLOW
LIFEFUL
LIFENET
LIFTERS
LIFTING
LIFTOFF
LIFTSUP
LIGANDS
LIGATED
LIGATES
LIGHTED
LIGHTEN
LIGHTER
LIGHTLY
LIGHTUP
LIGNITE
LIKABLE
LIKEMAD
LIKENED
LIKENEW
LILLIAN
LILTING
LILYPAD
LIMBERS
LIMBING
LIMEADE
LIMIEST
LIMITED
LIMNERS
LIMNING
LIMOGES
LIMPEST
LIMPETS
LIMPING
LIMPOPO
LINAGES
LINBIAO
LINCOLN
LINDENS
LINDIED
LINDIES
LINDSAY
LINDSEY
LINEAGE
LINEATE
LINEDUP
LINEMAN
LINEMEN
LINESUP
LINEUPS
LINGERS
LINGOES
LINGUAL
LINIEST
LININGS
LINKAGE
LINKERS
LINKING
LINKUPS
LINNETS
LINPIAO
LINSEED
LINTELS
LINTIER
LIONCUB
LIONESS
LIONETS
LIONISE
LIONIZE
LIPBALM
LIPIDES
LIPLESS
LIPLIKE
LIPPIER
LIPPING
LIPREAD
LIPSYNC
LIQUEFY
LIQUEUR
LIQUIDS
LIQUORS
LISENTE
LISPING
LISSOME
LISTEES
LISTELS
LISTENS
LISTING
LITCHIS
LITCRIT
LITERAL
LITHELY
LITHEST
LITHGOW
LITHIUM
LITINTO
LITOTES
LITTERS
LITTLER
LITURGY
LIVABLE
LIVEDIN
LIVEDON
LIVENED
LIVEOAK
LIVEONE
LIVEOUT
LIVESIN
LIVESON
LIVIDLY
LIVINGS
LIVORNO
LIZARDS

L•I••••

LAIDFOR
LAIDLOW
LAIDOFF
LAIDOUT
LAISSEZ
LEIBNIZ
LEIPZIG
LEISTER
LEISURE
LOITERS
LYINGTO

L••I•••

LABIALS
LABIATE
LACIEST
LACINGS
LADINOS
LAFITTE
LAKIEST
LALIQUE
LAMINAE
LAMINAL
LAMINAR
LAMINAS
LARIATS
LATICES
LATIFAH
LATINAS
LATINOS
LAVINIA
LAYINTO
LAYITON
LAZIEST
LEGIBLE
LEGIBLY
LEGIONS
LEGISTS
LEMIEUX
LENIENT
LETINON
LETITBE
LETITIA
LEVIERS
LEVITES
LEXICAL
LEXICON
LIAISED
LIAISES
LIAISON
LIBIDOS
LICITLY
LIMIEST
LIMITED
LINIEST
LININGS
LIPIDES
LITINTO
LIVIDLY
LIVINGS
LOGICAL
LOGIEST
LORICAE
LORISES
LOTIONS
LUCIANO
LUCIDLY
LUCIFER
LUCILLE
LUMIERE
LUPINES
LURIDLY
LUTISTS
LYRICAL
LYRISTS

L•••I••

LACKING
LADDIES
LADDISH
LADLING
LADYISH
LAGGING
LAMAISM
LAMAIST
LAMMING
LANDING
LANKIER
LANKILY
LANSING
LAOTIAN
LAPPING
LAPPISH
LAPSING
LAPWING
LARAINE
LARDIER
LARDING
LARGISH
LARKISH
LASHING
LASSIES
LASTING
LATHING
LATTICE
LATVIAN
LAUDING
LAWLIKE
LAZYISH
LEADIER
LEADING
LEADINS
LEAFIER
LEAFING
LEAKIER
LEAKING
LEANING
LEAPING
LEARIER
LEASING
LEAVING
LEDGIER
LEERIER
LEERILY
LEERING
LEETIDE
LEFTIES
LEFTIST
LEGGIER
LEGGING
LEGLIKE
LEMMING
LEMPIRA
LENDING
LENTIGO
LENTILS
LEONIDS
LEONINE
LEPPIES
LESSING
LETTING
LETTISH
LEUCINE
LEVYING
LIBBING
LICKING
LIFTING
LIGNITE
LILLIAN
LILTING
LIMBING
LIMNING
LIMPING
LINBIAO
LINDIED
LINDIES
LINKING
LINPIAO
LINTIER
LIONISE
LIONIZE
LIPLIKE
LIPPIER
LIPPING
LIQUIDS
LISPING
LISTING
LITHIUM
LOADING
LOAFING
LOAMIER
LOAMING
LOANING
LOBBIED
LOBBIES
LOBBING
LOCKING
LOCKINS
LODGING
LOFTIER
LOFTILY
LOFTING
LOGGIAS
LOGGING
LOGGINS
LOGGISH
LOLLIES
LOLLING
LONGIES
LONGING
LONGISH
LOOBIES
LOOKING
LOOMING
LOONIER
LOONIES
LOOPIER
LOOPING
LOOSING
LOOTING
LOPPIER
LOPPING
LORDING
LORRIES
LOTTING
LOUDISH
LOUSIER
LOUSILY
LOUSING
LOUTISH
LOVEINS
LOWLIER
LOWLIFE
LOWRISE
LOWTIDE
LUCKIER
LUCKILY
LUCKING
LUDDITE
LUFFING
LUGGING
LULLING
LUMPIER
LUMPILY
LUMPING
LUMPISH
LUNGING
LURKING
LUSTIER
LUSTILY
LUSTING

L••••I•

LACONIC
LAMPOIL
LANGUID
LANOLIN
LARAMIE
LAUGHIN
LAVINIA
LAWSUIT
LEADSIN
LEAVEIN
LEIBNIZ
LEIPZIG
LETITIA
LETSLIP
LIBERIA
LITCHIS
LITCRIT
LIVEDIN
LIVESIN
LOOKSIN
LORDJIM
LOSESIT
LOWPAID
LUNATIC

L•••••I

LAKSHMI
LORELEI

•LI••••

ALIASES
ALIBABA
ALIDADE
ALIENEE
ALIENOR
ALIGHTS
ALIGNED
ALIGNER
ALIMENT
ALIMONY
ALINING
BLIGHTS
BLIGHTY
BLINDED
BLINDER
BLINDLY
BLINKAT
BLINKED
BLINKER
BLIPPED
BLISTER
BLITHER
BLITZED
BLITZEN
BLITZES
CLIBURN
CLICHES
CLICKED
CLIENTS
CLIFTON
CLIMATE
CLIMBED
CLIMBER
CLINICS
CLINKED
CLINKER
CLINTON
CLIPART
CLIPONS
CLIPPED
CLIPPER
CLIQUES
CLIQUEY
ELICITS
ELIDING
ELISION
ELITISM
ELITIST
ELIXIRS
FLICKED
FLICKER
FLIESAT
FLIESIN
FLIGHTS
FLIGHTY
FLIPOUT
FLIPPED
FLIPPER
FLIPUPS
FLIRTED
FLITTED
FLITTER
FLIVVER
GLIBBER
GLIDERS
GLIDING
GLIMMER
GLIMPSE
GLINTED
GLISTEN
GLITTER
GLITZED
GLITZES
ILIESCU
KLINGON
OLIVIER
OLIVINE
PLIABLE
PLIABLY
PLIANCY
PLIGHTS
PLINKED
PLINTHS
SLICERS
SLICING
SLICKED
SLICKER
SLICKLY
SLIDEIN
SLIDERS
SLIDING
SLIGHTS
SLIMIER
SLIMILY
SLIMJIM
SLIMMED
SLIMMER
SLINGER
SLINKED
SLIPONS
SLIPOUT
SLIPPED
SLIPPER
SLIPSIN
SLIPSON
SLIPSUP
SLIPUPS
SLITHER
SLIVERS
TLINGIT

•L•I•••

ALBINOS
ALFIERI
ALGIERS
ALLISON
ALRIGHT
CLAIMED
CLAIMER
CLAIROL
ELEISON
ELLIOTT
ELLIPSE
ELLISON
ELMISTI
ELOIGNS
FLAILED
FLUIDLY
GLAIRED
GLUIEST
ILLICIT
PLAICES
PLAINER
PLAINLY
PLAINTS
PLAITED
SLEIGHS
SLEIGHT
SLUICED
SLUICES
ULTIMAS

•L••I••

ALAKING
ALDRICH
ALEWIFE
ALINING
ALLTIME
ALLYING
BLADING
BLAMING
BLARING
BLAZING
BLEMISH
BLERIOT
BLOWIER
BLOWING
BLUEING
BLUEISH
CLARICE
CLARIFY
CLARION
CLARITY
CLAVIER
CLAWING
CLAYIER
CLAYISH
CLERICS
CLERISY
CLINICS
CLONING
CLOSING
CLOYING
CLUEING
ELAAIUN
ELAPIDS
ELATING
ELATION
ELEGIAC
ELEGIES
ELEGIST
ELFLIKE
ELICITS
ELIDING
ELISION
ELITISM
ELITIST
ELIXIRS
ELOPING
ELUDING
ELUSIVE
ELUTING
ELUTION
ELUVIUM
ELYSIAN
ELYSIUM
FLAKIER
FLAKILY
FLAKING
FLAMIER
FLAMING
FLARING
FLAWING
FLAXIER
FLAYING
FLEEING
FLEMING
FLEMISH
FLEXING
FLEYING
FLORIDA
FLORINS
FLORIST
FLOWING
FLUKIER
FLUTIER
FLUTING
FLUTIST
FLUVIAL
FLUXING
FLYFISH
FLYHIGH
GLACIAL
GLACIER
GLARING
GLAZIER
GLAZING
GLIDING
GLOBING
GLORIAM
GLORIAS
GLORIED
GLORIES
GLORIFY
GLOWING
GLOZING
ILLWILL
ILLWIND
OLDLINE
OLDNICK
OLDTIME
OLEFINS
OLEMISS
OLIVIER
OLIVINE
PLACIDO
PLACING
PLANING
PLANISH
PLATIER
PLATING
PLAYING
PLOSION
PLOSIVE
PLOWING
PLUGINS
PLUMIER
PLUMING
PLUVIAL
SLAKING
SLATIER
SLATING
SLAVING
SLAVISH
SLICING
SLIDING
SLIMIER
SLIMILY
SLOPING
SLOWING

•L•••I•

ALADDIN
ALAMEIN
ALBANIA
ALBENIZ
ALBUMIN
ALEMBIC
ALGERIA
ALKALIS
ALLHAIL
ALLUVIA
ALSATIA
BLACKIE
BLONDIE
BLOWSIN
BLOWSIT
BLUEFIN
CLASSIC
CLAUDIA
CLAUDIO
CLOCKIN
CLOSEIN
CLUEDIN
CLUESIN
ELASTIC
FLACCID
FLEAPIT
FLIESIN
FLORUIT
FLOWNIN
GLOTTIS
ILLICIT
ILLOGIC
OLDMAID
OLYMPIA
OLYMPIC
PLASTIC
PLAUDIT
PLUGSIN
SLEEPIN
SLEPTIN
SLIDEIN
SLIMJIM
SLIPSIN
SLOEGIN
TLINGIT

•L••••I

ALFIERI
ALVEOLI
ELMISTI
OLDUVAI
PLATYPI

••LI•••

ALLISON
BALIHAI
BELIEFS
BELIEVE
BELINDA
BILIOUS
BKLIBAN
BOLIDES
BOLIVAR
BOLIVIA

BYLINED
BYLINES
CALIBAN
CALIBER
CALIBRE
CALICES
CALICOS
CALIPER
CALIPHS
CILIATE
DELIBES
DELICTI
DELICTS
DELIGHT
DELILAH
DELIMIT
DELIRIA
DELISTS
DELIVER
ECLIPSE
EELIEST
ELLIOTT
ELLIPSE
ELLISON
ENLISTS
ENLIVEN
EOLITHS
FELICIA
FELINES
FILINGS
FOLIAGE
FOLIATE
GALILEE
GALILEI
GALILEO
GELIDLY
GOLIATH
HALIBUT
HALIDES
HALIFAX
HALITES
HELICAL
HELICES
HELICON
HELIPAD
HELIXES
HOLIDAY
HOLIEST
HOLISTS
ILLICIT
JALISCO
JULIANA
KYLIKES
LALIQUE
MALIGNS
MELINDA
MELISSA
MILIEUS
MILIEUX
MILITIA
MOLIERE
OBLIGED
OBLIGES
OBLIQUE
OILIEST
OOLITES
OOLITHS
PALIEST
PELICAN
PELISSE
PILINGS
POLICED
POLICES
POLITER
POLITIC
RELIANT
RELICTS
RELIEFS
RELIEVE
RELIEVO
RELIGHT
RELINED
RELINES
RELISTS
RELIVED
RELIVES
RULINGS
SALIENT
SALIERI
SALINAS
SILICAS
SILICON
SOLICIT
SOLIDER
SOLIDLY
SPLICED
SPLICER
SPLICES
SPLINES
SPLINTS
SPLITUP
TILINGS
UGLIEST
UNLIKED
UNLINED
UNLINKS
UPLIFTS
UPLINKS
VALIANT
VALIDLY
VALISES
WILIEST

••L•I••

ALLTIME
ALLYING
BALDING
BALDISH
BALKIER
BALKILY
BALKING
BALMIER
BALMILY
BELGIAN
BELGIUM
BELLIED
BELLIES
BELLING
BELLINI
BELTING
BELYING
BILBIES
BILGIER
BILKING
BILLIES
BILLING
BILLION
BOLTING
BULGIER
BULGING
BULKIER
BULKING
BULLIED
BULLIES
BULLING
BULLION
BULLISH
BULLITT
CALCIFY
CALCITE
CALCIUM
CALKING
CALKINS
CALLING
CALLINS
CALMING
CALVING
CELLINI
CELLIST
CELSIUS
CELTICS
COLDISH
COLLIDE
COLLIER
COLLIES
COLLINS
COLTISH
CULLIED
CULLIES
CULLING
CULTISH
CULTISM
CULTIST
DALLIED
DALLIER
DALLIES
DELEING
DELUISE
DELVING
DILLIES
DOLLIED
DOLLIES
DOLLING
DOLLISH
DOLTISH
DULCIFY
DULLING
DULLISH
ECLAIRS
EELLIKE
FALLING
FALSIFY
FALSITY
FELLIES
FELLING
FELLINI
FILLIES
FILLING
FILLINS
FILLIPS
FILMIER
FILMING
FOLDING
FOLKIER
FOLKIES
FOLKISH
FOLLIES
FULFILL
FULFILS
GALLING
GALLIUM
GELDING
GELLING
GILDING
GILLIAN
GILLIES
GILLING
GOLDING
GOLFING
GULFING
GULLIES
GULLING
GULPIER
GULPING
HALOING
HALTING
HALVING
HELLION
HELLISH
HELMING
HELOISE
HELPING
HILAIRE
HILLIER
HILLING
HOLDING
HOLLIES
HOLMIUM
HULKING
HULLING
ILLWILL
ILLWIND
JELLIED
JELLIES
JELLING
JILLIAN
JILLION
JILTING
JOLLIED
JOLLIER
JOLLIES
JOLLIET
JOLLIFY
JOLLILY
JOLLITY
JOLTIER
JOLTING
KELPIES
KILLING
KILTIES
KILTING
LILLIAN
LILTING
LOLLIES
LOLLING
LULLING
MALAISE
MALKINS
MALTIER
MALTING
MELDING
MELTING
MILKIER
MILKING
MILLING
MILLION
MOLDIER
MOLDING
MOLLIFY
MOLTING
MULLING
MULLION
NULLIFY
NULLING
NULLITY
OILLIKE
OILRIGS
OWLLIKE
PALLIER
PALLING
PALLIUM
PALMIER
PALMING
PALMIST
PELTING
PELTISH
PILLING
PILLION
POLLING
POLOIST
PULLING
PULLINS
PULPIER
PULPITS
PULSING
RALEIGH
RALLIED
RALLIER
RALLIES
RDLAING
RELYING
ROLAIDS
ROLLICK
ROLLING
ROLLINS
SALLIED
SALLIES
SALSIFY
SALTIER
SALTILY
SALTINE
SALTING
SALTISH
SALVIAS
SALVING
SELFISH
SELKIRK
SELLING
SILKIER
SILKILY
SILLIER
SILLIES
SILOING
SILTIER
SILTING
SOLDIER
SOLOING
SOLOIST
SOLVING
SULFIDE
SULFITE
SULKIER
SULKIES
SULKILY
SULKING
SULLIED
SULLIES
TALKIER
TALKIES
TALKING
TALLIED
TALLIER
TALLIES
TALLINN
TALLISH
TELLIES
TELLING
TILLING
TILTING
TOLKIEN
TOLLIES
TOLLING
VALUING
VILNIUS
VULPINE
WALKING
WALKINS
WALLING
WELDING
WELKINS
WELLING
WELTING
WILDING
WILDISH
WILLIAM
WILLIES
WILLING
WILTING
WOLFING
WOLFISH
YELLING
YELPING
ZILLION

••L••I•

AELFRIC
ALLHAIL
ALLUVIA
BALDRIC
BALDWIN
BOLIVIA
BOLOTIE
CALLSIN
CALORIC
CALORIE
COLLOID
CSLEWIS
CULPRIT
DELIMIT
DELIRIA
DELPHIC
DELTAIC
DELTOID
DOLPHIN
EELSKIN
FALLSIN
FELICIA
FILLSIN
GALATIA
GELATIN
GELATIS
HALFWIT
HOLBEIN
HOLDSIN
ILLICIT
ILLOGIC
ISLAMIC
MALEFIC
MELANIE
MELANIN
MELODIC
MILITIA
MULLEIN
OILSKIN
PALADIN
PALMOIL
PELAGIC
PILEDIN
PILESIN
PILGRIM
POLARIS
POLEMIC
POLITIC
PULLSIN
ROLLSIN
SALADIN
SALAMIS
SALUKIS
SELENIC
SILESIA
SOLARIA
SOLICIT
STLOUIS
STLUCIA
TALARIA
TALKBIG
TELAVIV
VALERIE
VILLAIN
VILLEIN
VOLTAIC
WILFRID
WILLKIE
YELTSIN

••L•••I

BALIHAI
BELLINI
BELUSHI
BOLSHOI
CELLINI
COLLODI
COLOSSI
DELICTI
FELLINI
GALILEI
GALVANI
MALACHI
MOLOKAI
PALAZZI
PULASKI
SALIERI
SYLLABI
TOLSTOI

•••LI••

ABILITY
ABOLISH
ADDLING
ADELINE
AEOLIAN
AFFLICT
AGILITY
AIRLIFT
AIRLIKE
AIRLINE
AMBLING
AMPLIFY
ANELING
ANGLING
ANILINE
ANTLIKE
ANTLION
APELIKE
APPLIED
APPLIES
ARMLIKE
ASSLIKE
ATELIER
BAGLIKE
BAILIFF
BAILING
BATLIKE
BAWLING
BEDLIKE
BEELIKE
BEELINE
BELLIED
BELLIES
BELLING
BELLINI
BERLIOZ
BERLITZ
BIALIES
BIBLIKE
BIGLIES
BILLIES
BILLING
BILLION
BIRLING
BOILING
BOWLIKE
BOWLINE
BOWLING
BOXLIKE
BUDLIKE
BUGLING
BULLIED
BULLIES
BULLING
BULLION
BULLISH
BULLITT
BURLIER
BURLING
BUSLINE
CABLING
CALLING
CALLINS
CATLIKE
CEILING
CELLINI
CELLIST
CHALICE
CHILIES
CHOLINE
COILING
COLLIDE
COLLIER
COLLIES
COLLINS
COOLING
COOLISH
COWLICK
COWLIKE
COWLING
CULLIED
CULLIES
CULLING
CUPLIKE
CURLIER
CURLIKE
CURLING
CYCLING
CYCLIST
DAHLIAS
DAILIES
DALLIED
DALLIER
DALLIES
DARLING
DAYLILY
DEALING
DECLINE
DEWLINE
DIALING
DILLIES
DISLIKE
DOGLIKE
DOILIES
DOLLIED
DOLLIES
DOLLING
DOLLISH
DOTLIKE
DUALITY
DUELING
DUELIST
DULLING
DULLISH
DUNLINS
EAGLING
EARLIER
EARLIKE
EELLIKE
EGALITE
EHRLICH
ELFLIKE
ENGLISH
EXILING
EYELIDS
EYELIKE
FADLIKE
FAILING
FALLING
FANLIKE
FATLIKE
FEELING
FELLIES
FELLING
FELLINI
FILLIES
FILLING
FILLINS
FILLIPS
FINLIKE
FOALING
FOILING
FOLLIES
FOOLING
FOOLISH
FORLIFE
FOULING
FOWLING
FOXLIKE
FROLICS
FUELING
FURLING
GAGLINE
GALLING
GALLIUM
GAOLING
GATLING
GAULISH
GELLING
GEMLIKE
GILLIAN
GILLIES
GILLING
GIRLISH
GOALIES
GOBLINS
GODLIER
GODLIKE
GOSLING
GROLIER
GULLIES
GULLING
GUMLIKE
HAGLIKE
HAILING
HATLIKE
HAULING
HEALING
HEELING
HELLION
HELLISH
HEMLINE
HENLIKE
HILLIER
HILLING
HIPLIKE
HITLIST
HOGLIKE
HOLLIES
HOPLIKE
HOTLINE
HOTLINK
HOTLIPS
HOWLING
HULLING
HUNLIKE
HURLIES
HURLING
HUTLIKE
HYALINE
ICELIKE
IDOLISE
IDOLIZE
IMPLIED
IMPLIES
INCLINE
INFLICT
INKLIKE
INKLING
ITALIAN
ITALICS
IVYLIKE
JAILING
JAMLIKE
JAWLIKE
JAWLINE
JELLIED
JELLIES
JELLING
JIGLIKE
JILLIAN
JILLION
JOLLIED
JOLLIER
JOLLIES
JOLLIET
JOLLIFY
JOLLILY
JOLLITY
JOWLIER
KEELING
KEYLIME
KIDLIKE
KILLING
KIPLING
LADLING
LAWLIKE
LEGLIKE
LILLIAN
LIPLIKE
LOLLIES
LOLLING
LOWLIER
LOWLIFE
LULLING
MADLIBS
MAILING
MANLIER
MANLIKE
MARLINS
MAULING
MEALIER
MEALIES
MEWLING
MIDLIFE
MIDLINE
MILLING
MILLION
MISLIKE
MOILING
MOLLIFY
MULLING
MULLION
MUSLIMS
MUSLINS
NAILING
NEOLITH
NETLIKE
NIBLICK
NIBLIKE
NUCLIDE
NULLIFY
NULLING
NULLITY
NUNLIKE
NUTLIKE
OAKLIKE
OARLIKE
OATLIKE
OBELISK
OCULIST
OFFLINE
OILLIKE
OLDLINE
OPALINE
ORBLIKE
OUTLINE
OUTLIVE
OWLLIKE
PALLIER
PALLING
PALLIUM
PAPLIKE
PAULINA
PAULINE
PAULING
PAULIST
PEALIKE
PEALING
PEELING
PEGLIKE
PENLIKE
PERLITE
PIELIKE
PIGLIKE
PILLING
PILLION
PIMLICO
PODLIKE
POLLING
POOLING
POPLINS
PRALINE
PRELIMS
PUBLICS
PUBLISH
PULLING
PULLINS
PURLIEU
PURLING
PURLINS
QUALIFY
QUALITY
RAILING
RALLIED
RALLIER
RALLIES
RAMLIKE
RATLIKE
RATLINE
RAYLIKE
REALISE
REALISM
REALIST
REALITY
REALIZE
RECLINE
REDLINE
REELING
REPLICA
REPLIED
REPLIES
RIBLIKE
RIFLING
RODLIKE
ROILIER
ROILING
ROLLICK
ROLLING
ROLLINS
RUGLIKE
SACLIKE
SAILING
SALLIED
SALLIES
SAPLING
SAWLIKE
SCALIER
SCALING
SEALILY
SEALING
SEALION
SELLING
SERLING
SETLINE
SIBLING
SIDLING
SILLIER
SILLIES
SINLIKE
SKILIFT
SKYLIKE
SKYLINE
SMILING
SOILING
SONLIKE
SOWLIKE
STYLING
STYLISE
STYLISH
STYLIST
STYLIZE
SUBLIME
SULLIED
SULLIES
SUNLIKE
SURLIER
SURLILY
SUSLIKS
TABLING
TAGLIKE
TAGLINE
TAILING
TALLIED
TALLIER
TALLIES
TALLINN
TALLISH
TANLINE
TBILISI
TELLIES
TELLING
THULIUM
TIELINE
TILLING
TINLIKE
TITLING
TITLIST
TOELIKE
TOILING
TOLLIES
TOLLING
TOOLING
TOYLIKE
TSELIOT
TUBLIKE
UNALIKE
URNLIKE
UTILISE
UTILITY
UTILIZE
VEALIER
VEILING
VIOLINS
VIOLIST
WAILING
WALLING
WARLIKE
WAXLIKE
WEBLIKE
WELLING
WHALING
WHILING
WIGLIKE
WILLIAM
WILLIES
WILLING
WOOLIER
WOOLIES
YELLING
YOWLING
ZILLION

•••L•I•

ACCLAIM
BUILDIN
BUILTIN
CALLSIN
COALBIN
COALOIL
COLLOID
COOLSIT
DEALSIN
DEALTIN
DECLAIM
DIPLOID
EXCLAIM
EXPLAIN
EXPLOIT
FALLSIN
FILLSIN
FOULTIP
FUELOIL
IDYLLIC
KOOLAID
MAILSIN
MAULDIN
MISLAID
MULLEIN
NAILSIN
NUCLEIC
OUTLAID
PHILBIN
PHILLIP
PHYLLIS
PULLSIN
PURLOIN
RECLAIM
REELSIN
ROLLSIN
SANLUIS
SHELTIE
SIRLOIN
TABLOID
TAILFIN
TRELLIS
TRILLIN
VILLAIN
VILLEIN
WAYLAID
WILLKIE

•••L••I

BELLINI
CELLINI
COLLODI
FELLINI
PAHLAVI
SYLLABI
TBILISI

••••LI•

ACRYLIC
ALKALIS
ANGELIC
ANNELID
APHELIA
BACKLIT
BEDELIA
BRESLIN
BUCOLIC
CAMELIA
CECILIA
CHABLIS
CHAPLIN
CHARLIE
COWSLIP
DRUMLIN
FIDELIO
FIDELIS
FIRELIT
GANGLIA
GREMLIN
HAMELIN
IDYLLIC
INSULIN
INVALID
JAVELIN
KREMLIN
KTOSLIN
LANOLIN
LETSLIP
MAHALIA
MAUDLIN
MAYALIN
MOONLIT
NATALIA
NATALIE
NEPALIS
NONSLIP
OBERLIN
OPHELIA
OVERLIE
PHILLIP
PHYLLIS
REGALIA
ROSALIE
SEDALIA
SOMALIA
SOMALIS
SPOTLIT
SQUALID
STARLIT
STEELIE
STOOLIE
TASHLIN
TIECLIP
TRELLIS
TRILLIN
VIDALIA

VISALIA
VOCALIC
WHEELIE

••••L•I
BACILLI
CORELLI
GALILEI
JAIALAI
KAROLYI
LORELEI
NIKOLAI
VANILLI
VIVALDI

•••••LI
ALVEOLI
BACILLI
BENGALI
CANNOLI
CORELLI
DIABOLI
EXEMPLI
ISRAELI
OMPHALI
RAVIOLI
STIMULI
SWAHILI
TRIPOLI
VANILLI
ZWINGLI

L•J••••
LAJOLLA

L••J•••
LOGJAMS

L•••J••
LEARJET
LORDJIM
LUBEJOB

L•••••J
LLCOOLJ

•L••J••
BLUEJAY
SLIMJIM

•L•••J•
ALFORJA

•L••••J
LLCOOLJ

••LJ•••
PALJOEY
VALJEAN

••L•J••
BELLJAR
CULTJAM
KILLJOY

••L••J•
VALLEJO

•••LJ••
BELLJAR
KILLJOY

•••L•J•
VALLEJO

•••••LJ
LLCOOLJ

L•K••••
LAKIEST
LAKOTAS
LAKSHMI
LEKVARS
LIKABLE
LIKEMAD
LIKENED
LIKENEW

L••K•••
LACKEYS
LACKING
LANKEST
LANKIER
LANKILY
LARKISH
LEAKAGE
LEAKERS
LEAKIER
LEAKING
LICKING
LINKAGE
LINKERS
LINKING
LINKUPS
LOCKBOX
LOCKERS
LOCKETS
LOCKING
LOCKINS
LOCKNUT
LOCKOUT
LOCKSON
LOCKSUP
LOCKUPS
LOOKERS
LOOKFOR
LOOKING
LOOKOUT
LOOKSAT
LOOKSEE
LOOKSIN
LOOKSON
LOOKSTO
LOOKSUP
LOOKUPS
LUCKIER
LUCKILY
LUCKING
LUCKOUT
LUNKERS
LURKING

L•••K••
LALAKER

L••••K•
LAWLIKE
LEGLIKE
LIPLIKE
LYSENKO

L•••••K
LAMARCK
LAYBACK
LEACOCK
LEGWORK
LIVEOAK
LOGBOOK
LOWNECK
LUBBOCK

•LK••••
ALKALIS
ALKENES
ELKHART

•L•K•••
ALAKING
ALYKHAN
ELEKTRA
FLAKERS
FLAKIER
FLAKILY
FLAKING
FLUKIER
SLAKING

•L••K••
ALASKAN
BLACKED
BLACKEN
BLACKER
BLACKIE
BLACKLY
BLANKED
BLANKER
BLANKET
BLANKLY
BLEAKER
BLEAKLY
BLINKAT
BLINKED
BLINKER
BLOCKED
BLOCKER
CLACKED
CLANKED
CLERKED
CLICKED
CLINKED
CLINKER
CLOAKED
CLOCKED
CLOCKER
CLOCKIN
CLUCKED
CLUNKED
CLUNKER
FLANKED
FLANKER
FLECKED
FLICKED
FLICKER
FLOCKED
FLOCKTO
FLUNKED
PLACKET
PLANKED
PLINKED
PLUCKED
PLUNKED
SLACKED
SLACKEN
SLACKER
SLACKLY
SLEEKED
SLEEKEN
SLEEKER
SLEEKLY
SLICKED
SLICKER
SLICKLY
SLINKED

•L•••K•
BLUESKY
ELFLIKE
SLOVAKS

•L••••K
OLDNICK

••LK•••
BALKANS
BALKIER
BALKILY
BALKING
BILKING
BULKIER
BULKING
CALKING
CALKINS
FOLKART
FOLKIER
FOLKIES
FOLKISH
FOLKWAY
HULKING
MALKINS
MILKCOW
MILKERS
MILKIER
MILKING
MILKMAN
MILKMEN
MILKRUN
MILKSOP
POLKAED
SELKIRK
SILKHAT
SILKIER
SILKILY
SULKERS
SULKIER
SULKIES
SULKILY
SULKING
TALKBIG
TALKERS
TALKIER
TALKIES
TALKING
TALKOUT
TALKSAT
TALKSTO
TALKSUP
TOLKIEN
WALKERS
WALKING
WALKINS
WALKMAN
WALKONS
WALKOUT
WALKSON
WALKUPS
WALKWAY
WELKINS

••L•K••
BELAKUN
EELSKIN
KYLIKES
LALAKER
MOLOKAI
OILSKIN
SALUKIS
UNLIKED
WILLKIE

••L••K•
EELLIKE
HOLYOKE
KOLACKY
OILCAKE
OILLIKE
OWLLIKE
PALOOKA
PULASKI
RELOCKS
UNLINKS
UNLOCKS
UNLUCKY
UPLINKS

••L•••K
BELLEEK
BULLOCK
BULWARK
HILLOCK
HOLMOAK
HOLYARK
MOLLUSK
POLLACK
POLLOCK
ROLLICK
SELKIRK
SELLECK

•••LK••
BAULKED
CAULKED
CAULKER
CHALKED
CHALKUP
SKULKED
SKULKER
STALKED
STALKER
WILLKIE

•••L•K•
AIRLIKE
ANTLIKE
APELIKE
ARMLIKE
ASSLIKE
BAGLIKE
BATLIKE
BEDLIKE
BEELIKE
BIBLIKE
BOWLIKE
BOXLIKE
BUDLIKE
CATLIKE
COWLIKE
CUPLIKE
CURLIKE
DISLIKE
DOGLIKE
DOTLIKE
EARLIKE
EELLIKE
ELFLIKE
EYELIKE
FADLIKE
FANLIKE
FATLIKE
FINLIKE
FOXLIKE
GEMLIKE
GODLIKE
GUMLIKE
HAGLIKE
HATLIKE
HENLIKE
HIPLIKE
HOGLIKE
HOPLIKE
HUNLIKE
HUTLIKE
ICELIKE
INKLIKE
IVYLIKE
JAMLIKE
JAWLIKE
JIGLIKE
KIDLIKE
LAWLIKE
LEGLIKE
LIPLIKE
MANLIKE
MISLIKE
MUKLUKS
NETLIKE
NIBLIKE
NUNLIKE
NUTLIKE
OAKLIKE
OARLIKE
OATLIKE
OILLIKE
ORBLIKE
OWLLIKE
PAPLIKE
PEALIKE
PEGLIKE
PENLIKE
PIELIKE
PIGLIKE
PODLIKE
RAMLIKE
RATLIKE
RAYLIKE
RIBLIKE
RODLIKE
RUGLIKE
SACLIKE
SAWLIKE
SINLIKE
SKYLIKE
SONLIKE
SOWLIKE
SUNLIKE
SUSLIKS
TAGLIKE
TINLIKE
TOELIKE
TOYLIKE
TUBLIKE
UNALIKE
URNLIKE
WARLIKE
WAXLIKE
WEBLIKE
WIGLIKE

•••L••K
AIRLOCK
ARMLOCK
BELLEEK
BULLOCK
COWLICK
DEKLERK
EARLOCK
FETLOCK
GUNLOCK
HEMLOCK
HILLOCK
HOTLINK
MATLOCK
MOLLUSK
NEWLOOK
NIBLICK
OARLOCK
OBELISK
OUTLOOK
PADLOCK
POLLACK
POLLOCK
POTLUCK
ROLLICK
SCHLOCK
SELLECK
SHYLOCK
SKYLARK
SPELUNK
UNBLOCK
UNCLOAK
WARLOCK
WEDLOCK

•••••LK
BIGTALK
CATWALK
ICEMILK
JAYWALK
KINFOLK
MENFOLK
NORFOLK
OUTTALK
PEPTALK
RAWSILK
RECHALK
SUFFOLK

LL•••••
LLCOOLJ

L•L••••
LALAKER
LALANNE
LALIQUE
LILLIAN
LILTING
LILYPAD
LOLLARD
LOLLIES
LOLLING
LOLLOPS
LULLABY
LULLING

L••L•••
LADLERS
LADLING
LAPLACE
LAPLAND
LAPLATA
LAWLESS
LAWLIKE
LEGLESS
LEGLIKE
LIDLESS
LILLIAN
LIPLESS
LIPLIKE
LOLLARD
LOLLIES
LOLLING
LOLLOPS
LOWLAND
LOWLIER
LOWLIFE
LULLABY
LULLING

L•••L••
LABELED
LABELER
LABELLE
LACHLAN
LAIDLOW
LAJOLLA
LANGLEY
LANOLIN
LAPALMA
LAPELED
LASALLE
LAVALSE
LAYSLOW
LEAFLET
LEGALLY
LETSLIP
LEVELED
LEVELER
LEVELLY
LIBELED
LIBELER
LIESLOW
LITTLER
LOBULES
LOCALES
LOCALLY
LORELEI
LOUELLA
LOWBLOW
LOYALLY
LOYALTY
LUCILLE

L••••L•
LABELLE
LABIALS
LAJOLLA
LANKILY
LAPBELT
LAPFULS
LARGELY
LASALLE
LASCALA
LAURELS
LEERILY
LEGALLY
LEGIBLE
LEGIBLY
LEGPULL
LENTILS
LEOPOLD
LETSFLY
LEVELLY
LICITLY
LIGHTLY
LIKABLE
LINCOLN
LINTELS
LIPBALM
LISTELS
LITHELY
LIVABLE
LIVIDLY
LLCOOLJ
LOCALLY
LOFTILY
LOGROLL
LOOSELY
LOUELLA
LOUSILY
LOVABLE
LOVABLY
LOVERLY
LOWBALL
LOYALLY
LUCIDLY
LUCILLE
LUCKILY
LUMPILY
LURIDLY
LUSTILY

L•••••L
LACTEAL
LACUNAL
LAMINAL
LAMPOIL
LATERAL
LEGPULL
LESPAUL
LEXICAL
LIBERAL
LIFEFUL
LINGUAL
LITERAL
LOGICAL
LOGROLL
LOWBALL
LOWHEEL
LUSTFUL
LYRICAL

•LL••••
ALLAYED
ALLAYER
ALLEARS
ALLEGED
ALLEGER
ALLEGES
ALLEGRO
ALLELES
ALLENBY
ALLENDE
ALLERGY
ALLEYES
ALLGONE
ALLHAIL
ALLHEAL
ALLHERE
ALLISON
ALLOFME
ALLOVER
ALLOWAY
ALLOWED
ALLOYED
ALLSTAR
ALLSTON
ALLTIME
ALLTOLD
ALLUDED
ALLUDES
ALLURED
ALLURES
ALLUVIA
ALLYING
ALLYSON
ELLIOTT
ELLIPSE
ELLISON
ILLBRED
ILLEGAL
ILLICIT
ILLNESS
ILLOGIC
ILLUDED
ILLUDES
ILLUMED
ILLUMES
ILLUSED
ILLUSES
ILLWILL
ILLWIND
ULLMANN

•L•L•••
ELFLIKE
FLYLEAF
FLYLESS
OLDLINE
SLALOMS
ULALUME
ULULANT
ULULATE

•L••L••
ALFALFA
ALKALIS
ALLELES
BLUELAW
FLAILED
FLATLET
PLAYLET

•L•••L•
ALERTLY
ALLTOLD
ALOOFLY
ALVEOLI
BLACKLY
BLACULA
BLANDLY
BLANKLY
BLEAKLY
BLINDLY
BLOWFLY
BLUFFLY
BLUNTLY
CLAVELL
CLEANLY
CLEARLY
CLOSELY
ELDERLY
FLAKILY
FLEETLY
FLESHLY
FLUIDLY
FLYBALL
GLOBULE
ILLWILL
LLCOOLJ
OLDGOLD
PLAINLY
PLIABLE
PLIABLY
PLUMPLY
PLURALS
PLUSHLY
SLACKLY
SLEEKLY
SLICKLY
SLIMILY

•L••••L
ALCOHOL
ALLHAIL
ALLHEAL
ALUMNAL
CLAIROL
CLAVELL
FLANNEL
FLUVIAL
FLYBALL
GLACIAL
GLEEFUL
GLOTTAL
ILLEGAL
ILLWILL
PLAYFUL
PLOTFUL
PLUVIAL

••LL•••
BALLADE
BALLADS
BALLARD
BALLAST
BALLBOY
BALLETS
BALLOON
BALLOTS
BALLSUP
BELLAMY
BELLBOY
BELLEEK
BELLHOP
BELLIED
BELLIES
BELLING
BELLINI
BELLJAR
BELLMAN
BELLMEN
BELLOWS
BELLYUP
BILLETS
BILLIES
BILLING
BILLION
BILLOWS
BILLOWY
BULLDOG
BULLETS
BULLIED
BULLIES
BULLING
BULLION
BULLISH
BULLITT
BULLOCK
BULLPEN
BULLRUN
CALLBOX
CALLERS
CALLFOR
CALLING
CALLINS
CALLOFF
CALLOUS
CALLOUT
CALLSIN
CALLSON
CALLSUP
CELLARS
CELLINI
CELLIST
COLLAGE
COLLARD
COLLARS
COLLATE
COLLECT
COLLEEN
COLLEGE
COLLETS
COLLIDE
COLLIER
COLLIES
COLLINS
COLLODI
COLLOID
COLLOPS
COLLUDE
COLLYER
CULLERS
CULLIED
CULLIES
CULLING
DALLIED
DALLIER
DALLIES
DILLARD
DILLIES
DOLLARS
DOLLIED
DOLLIES
DOLLING
DOLLISH
DOLLOPS
DOLLSUP
DULLARD
DULLEST
DULLING
DULLISH
EELLIKE
FALLACY
FALLFOR
FALLGUY
FALLING
FALLOFF
FALLOUT
FALLOWS
FALLSIN
FALLSON
FALLSTO
FELLAHS
FELLERS
FELLFOR
FELLIES
FELLING
FELLINI
FELLOFF
FELLOUT
FELLOWS
FILLERS
FILLETS
FILLIES
FILLING
FILLINS
FILLIPS
FILLOUT
FILLSIN
FILLSUP
FILLUPS
FOLLETT
FOLLIES
FOLLOWS
FULLEST
GALLANT
GALLEON
GALLERY
GALLEYS
GALLING
GALLIUM
GALLONS
GALLOPS
GELLING
GILLIAN
GILLIES
GILLING
GILLNET
GULLAHS
GULLETS
GULLIES
GULLING
HALLOWS
HALLWAY
HELLCAT
HELLENE
HELLERS
HELLION
HELLISH
HELLMAN
HILLARY
HILLIER
HILLING
HILLOCK
HILLTOP
HOLLAND
HOLLERS
HOLLIES
HOLLOWS
HULLERS
HULLING
HULLOAS
HULLOED
JELLIED
JELLIES
JELLING
JILLIAN
JILLION
JOLLIED
JOLLIER
JOLLIES
JOLLIET
JOLLIFY
JOLLILY
JOLLITY
KELLOGG
KILLERS
KILLING
KILLJOY
LILLIAN
LOLLARD
LOLLIES
LOLLING
LOLLOPS
LULLABY
LULLING
MALLARD
MALLETS
MALLOWS
MALLRAT
MELLOWS
MILLAND
MILLARD
MILLDAM
MILLEND
MILLERS
MILLETS
MILLETT
MILLING
MILLION
MILLRUN
MOLLIFY
MOLLUSC
MOLLUSK
MULLAHS
MULLEIN
MULLERS
MULLETS
MULLING
MULLION
NULLAHS
NULLIFY
NULLING
NULLITY
OILLAMP
OILLESS
OILLIKE
OWLLIKE
PALLETS
PALLIER
PALLING
PALLIUM
PALLORS
PELLETS
PILLAGE
PILLARS
PILLBOX
PILLBUG
PILLING
PILLION
PILLORY
PILLOWS
PILLOWY
POLLACK
POLLENS
POLLERS
POLLING
POLLOCK
POLLTAX
POLLUTE
PULLETS
PULLEYS
PULLFOR
PULLING
PULLINS
PULLMAN
PULLOFF
PULLONS
PULLOUT
PULLSIN
PULLSON
PULLSUP
PULLTAB
PULLUPS
RALLIED
RALLIER
RALLIES
RALLYTO
RELLENO
RILLETS
ROLLBAR
ROLLERS
ROLLICK
ROLLING
ROLLINS
ROLLOUT
ROLLSIN
ROLLSON
ROLLSUP
ROLLTOP
SALLETS
SALLIED
SALLIES
SALLOWS
SELLECK
SELLERS
SELLFOR
SELLING
SELLOFF
SELLOUT

SILLIER
SILLIES
SULLIED
SULLIES
SYLLABI
TALLEST
TALLIED
TALLIER
TALLIES
TALLINN
TALLISH
TALLOWS
TALLYHO
TALLYUP
TELLALL
TELLERS
TELLIES
TELLING
TELLOFF
TELLSOF
TELLSON
TILLAGE
TILLERS
TILLING
TOLLIES
TOLLING
TOLLWAY
VALLEJO
VALLEYS
VELLUMS
VILLAGE
VILLAIN
VILLEIN
VOLLEYS
WALLABY
WALLACE
WALLACH
WALLETS
WALLEYE
WALLING
WALLOON
WALLOPS
WALLOWS
WALLSUP
WELLAND
WELLFED
WELLING
WELLMAN
WELLOFF
WELLRUN
WELLSET
WELLSUP
WILLARD
WILLETS
WILLFUL
WILLIAM
WILLIES
WILLING
WILLKIE
WILLOWS
WILLOWY
WILLSON
YELLERS
YELLING
YELLOWS
YELLOWY
YELLSAT
ZILLION

••L•L••

ALLELES
BULBLET
DELILAH
GALILEE
GALILEI
GALILEO
GILBLAS
OGLALAS
YULELOG

••L••L•

ALLTOLD
ATLATLS
BALKILY
BALMILY
BULBULS
FALSELY
FALWELL
FULFILL
FULFILS
GALPALS
GELIDLY
ILLWILL
JOLLILY
MALCOLM
OILWELL
SALABLE
SALTILY
SILKILY
SOLIDLY
SOLUBLE
SULKILY
TELLALL
VALIDLY
VOLUBLE
VOLUBLY
WALPOLE
WILHELM

••L•••L

ALLHAIL
ALLHEAL
BALEFUL
BILEVEL
CALOMEL
CHLORAL
COLONEL
DOLEFUL
FALAFEL
FALWELL
FULFILL
HELICAL
HELPFUL
ILLEGAL
ILLWILL
OILWELL
PALATAL
PALMOIL
TELLALL
TYLENOL
WILLFUL
WOLFGAL

•••LL••

AXILLAE
BOULLES
CHILLED
CHILLER
CHOLLAS
CRULLER
DRILLED
DRILLER
DROLLER
DWELLED
DWELLER
EVILLER
FRILLED
FUELLED
GRILLED
GRILLES
GRILLET
IDYLLIC
KEILLOR
KNELLED
MAILLOT
OCELLUS
PHILLIP
PHYLLIS
QUELLED
QUILLED
QUILLER
SCALLOP
SCULLED
SCULLER
SHALLOT
SHALLOW
SHELLAC
SHELLED
SHELLER
SHELLEY
SHILLED
SKILLED
SKILLET
SMALLER
SMELLED
SNELLEN
SPALLED
SPELLED
SPELLER
SPILLED
STALLED
STELLAR
STILLED
STILLER
STOLLEN
STOLLER
SWALLET
SWALLOW
SWELLED
SWELLUP
SWILLED
SWOLLEN
TAILLES
TRELLIS
TRILLED
TRILLIN
TROLLED
TROLLEY
TWILLED
WOOLLEN
WOOLLEY
ZOELLER

•••L•L•

ADULTLY
AGILELY
CARLYLE
DAYLILY
HEALALL
JOLLILY
OOHLALA
SEALILY
SHALALA
STALELY
SURLILY
TELLALL
TRALALA
UKULELE
WORLDLY

•••L••L

AXOLOTL
BOWLFUL
COALOIL
FUELOIL
HEALALL
PAILFUL
SCALPEL
SKILFUL
SOULFUL
TELLALL
TOILFUL
WAILFUL
WILLFUL

••••LL•

APPALLS
AURALLY
AWFULLY
AXIALLY
BACILLI
BANALLY
BASALLY
BEFALLS
BRAILLE
BYGOLLY
CAMILLE
CAPELLA
CEDILLA
CIVILLY
CORELLI
COROLLA
CRIOLLO
CRUELLY
DEFALLA
DEMILLE
DEVILLE
ENROLLS
EQUALLY
ESTELLE
FINALLY
FRAILLY
GAZELLE
GISELLE
GORILLA
HGWELLS
HOWELLS
IDEALLY
INGALLS
LABELLE
LAJOLLA
LASALLE
LEGALLY
LEVELLY
LOCALLY
LOUELLA
LOYALLY
LUCILLE
MAXILLA
MCCALLS
MEDULLA
MISALLY
MORALLY
MORELLO
MOSELLE
MURILLO
NACELLE
NASALLY
NEVILLE
NOVELLA
NOVELLE
ORVILLE
OTHELLO
PAPILLA
PATELLA
RECALLS
REFILLS
REGALLY
REPOLLS
RESELLS
RETELLS
ROSELLE
ROYALLY
ROZELLE
RURALLY
SCROLLS
SEVILLE
SHRILLS
SHRILLY
SQUALLS
SQUILLS
STROLLS
THRALLS
THRILLS
TONALLY
TOTALLY
UCCELLO
UNROLLS
USUALLY
UTRILLO
VANILLA
VANILLI
VENALLY
VITALLY
VOCALLY
ZONALLY

•••••LL

AIRBALL
ANTHILL
BARBELL
BEDROLL
BOSWELL
CARROLL
CATCALL
CHAGALL
CLAVELL
CORDELL
CORNELL
COWBELL
CUEBALL
CUREALL
DISTILL
DRYCELL
DRYWALL
DRYWELL
DURRELL
EGGROLL
EYEBALL
FALWELL
FLYBALL
FULFILL
FURBALL
GETWELL
GINMILL
GOODALL
GOTWELL
GUMBALL
GUNMOLL
HEALALL
HUBBELL
ILLWILL
INDWELL
INKWELL
INSTALL
INSTILL
JOEHILL
KENDALL
KIMBALL
LEGPULL
LOGROLL
LOWBALL
MAXWELL
MERRILL
MISCALL
NOBHILL
NOTWELL
ODDBALL
OILWELL
ONAROLL
OUTPOLL
OUTSELL
OVERALL
PAYROLL
PINBALL
PITBULL
PITFALL
PRESELL
PURCELL
RAGDOLL
RANDALL
REDCELL
REDPOLL
ROSWELL
RUSSELL
SAMHILL
SAWMILL
SEAGULL
SEAWALL
SITWELL
TARBELL
TEABALL
TELLALL
THERELL
WAYBILL
WENDELL
WETCELL
WHERELL

L•M••••

LAMAISM
LAMAIST
LAMARCK
LAMBADA
LAMBDAS
LAMBEAU
LAMBENT
LAMBERT
LAMEDHS
LAMENTS
LAMINAE
LAMINAL
LAMINAR
LAMINAS
LAMMING
LAMOTTA
LAMPOIL
LAMPOON
LAMPREY
LEMIEUX
LEMMING
LEMONDE
LEMPIRA
LIMBERS
LIMBING
LIMEADE
LIMIEST
LIMITED
LIMNERS
LIMNING
LIMOGES
LIMPEST
LIMPETS
LIMPING
LIMPOPO
LOMBARD
LUMBAGO
LUMBARS
LUMBERS
LUMIERE
LUMPERS
LUMPIER
LUMPILY
LUMPING
LUMPISH
LUMPSUM

L••M•••

LAMMING
LEMMING
LOAMIER
LOAMING
LOOMING

L•••M••

LABAMBA
LARAMIE
LEGUMES
LEXEMES
LIKEMAD
LINEMAN
LINEMEN
LOCOMAN
LOCOMEN

L••••M•

LAKSHMI
LAPALMA
LISSOME
LOGJAMS
LYCEUMS

L•••••M

LAMAISM
LEGROOM
LIPBALM
LITHIUM
LONGARM
LORDJIM
LOWBEAM
LUMPSUM

•LM••••

ALMAATA
ALMADEN
ALMANAC
ALMONDS
ELMISTI
ELMTREE

•L•M•••

ALAMEDA
ALAMEIN
ALAMODE
ALEMBIC
ALIMENT
ALIMONY
ALUMNAE
ALUMNAL
ALUMNUS
BLAMING
BLEMISH
CLAMBER
CLAMMED
CLAMMER
CLAMORS
CLAMOUR
CLAMPED
CLAMSUP
CLEMENS
CLEMENT
CLEMSON
CLIMATE
CLIMBED
CLIMBER
CLOMPED
CLUMPED
ELEMENT
FLAMBED
FLAMBES
FLAMIER
FLAMING
FLEMING
FLEMISH
FLUMMOX
GLAMOUR
GLIMMER
GLIMPSE
GLOMMED
GLUMMER
KLAMATH
OLDMAID
OLDMOON
OLEMISS
OLYMPIA
OLYMPIC
OLYMPUS
PLUMAGE
PLUMBED
PLUMBER
PLUMIER
PLUMING
PLUMMER
PLUMMET
PLUMPED
PLUMPER
PLUMPLY
SLAMMED
SLAMMER
SLIMIER
SLIMILY
SLIMJIM
SLIMMED
SLIMMER
SLUMBER
SLUMMED
SLUMPED
ULLMANN

•L••M••

ALARMED
ALARMER
ALBUMEN
ALBUMIN
BLOOMED
BLOOMER
CLAIMED
CLAIMER
CLAMMED
CLAMMER
FLAGMAN
FLAGMEN
FLUMMOX
GLEAMED
GLIMMER
GLOMMED
GLOOMED
GLUMMER
ILLUMED
ILLUMES
KLUGMAN
PLASMAS
PLOWMAN
PLOWMEN
PLUMMER
PLUMMET
SLAMMED
SLAMMER
SLIMMED
SLIMMER
SLUMMED
ULTIMAS

•L•••M•

ALABAMA
ALARUMS
ALCHEMY
ALLOFME
ALLTIME
OLDTIME
PLENUMS
SLALOMS
ULALUME

•L••••M

ALYSSUM
BLOSSOM
BLUEGUM
ELITISM
ELUVIUM
ELYSIUM
FLOTSAM
GLORIAM
SLIMJIM

••LM•••

AILMENT
BALMIER
BALMILY
BELMONT
CALMEST
CALMING
DOLMANS
DOLMENS
FILMIER
FILMING
HELMETS
HELMING
HOLMIUM
HOLMOAK
MALMSEY
PALMARY
PALMATE
PALMIER
PALMING
PALMIST
PALMOFF
PALMOIL
PALMTOP
SALMONS
ULLMANN
WALMART

••L•M••

BELLMAN
BELLMEN
CALOMEL
CALUMET
CALUMNY
CCLAMPS
COLEMAN
COLUMBO
COLUMNS
DELIMIT
DILEMMA
FELDMAN
GALUMPH
HELLMAN
ILLUMED
ILLUMES
ISLAMIC
MALAMUD
MILKMAN
MILKMEN
PALOMAR
POLEMIC
POLYMER
PULLMAN
RELUMED
RELUMES
SALAMIS
SOLOMON
VOLUMES
WALKMAN
WELLMAN
WOLFMAN
WOLFMEN

••L••M•

ALLOFME
ALLTIME
BALSAMS
BELDAME
BELDAMS
BELLAMY
DILEMMA
FULSOME
OILLAMP
PALERMO
SALAAMS
TALCUMS
VELLUMS
WELCOME

••L•••M

BELGIUM
CALCIUM
CULTISM
CULTJAM
FULCRUM
FULGHUM
GALLIUM
HOLMIUM
MALCOLM
MILLDAM
PALLIUM
PILGRIM
WILHELM
WILLIAM
WOLFRAM

•••LM••

BELLMAN
BELLMEN
HELLMAN
PERLMAN
PSALMED
PULLMAN
WELLMAN
WHELMED

•••L•M•

ARCLAMP
ASYLUMS
BEDLAMP
BELLAMY
COULOMB
DIPLOMA
EMBLEMS
INFLAME
KEYLIME
MOSLEMS
MUSLIMS
OILLAMP
PABLUMS
PEPLUMS
PRELIMS
PTOLEMY
RECLAME
SHALOMS
SLALOMS
SUBLIME
SUNLAMP
ULALUME
VELLUMS

•••L••M

ACCLAIM
AMALGAM
DECLAIM
EARLDOM
EXCLAIM
GALLIUM
INBLOOM
MILLDAM
PALLIUM
REALISM
REBLOOM
RECLAIM
THULIUM
WILLIAM

••••LM•

BECALMS
DEPALMA
LAPALMA
REFILMS

••••L•M

ABSALOM
HAARLEM
HOODLUM
PABULUM
PROBLEM

•••••LM

ARTFILM
BEEBALM
LIPBALM
MALCOLM
WILHELM
WYCHELM

L•N••••

LANCERS
LANCETS
LANDAUS
LANDERS
LANDING
LANDSAT
LANFORD
LANGDON
LANGLEY
LANGTRY
LANGUID
LANGUOR
LANGURS
LANKEST
LANKIER
LANKILY
LANOLIN
LANSING
LANTANA
LANTERN
LANYARD
LENDERS
LENDING
LENFANT
LENGTHS
LENGTHY
LENIENT
LENTIGO
LENTILS
LINAGES
LINBIAO
LINCOLN
LINDENS
LINDIED
LINDIES
LINDSAY
LINDSEY
LINEAGE
LINEATE
LINEDUP
LINEMAN
LINEMEN
LINESUP
LINEUPS
LINGERS
LINGOES
LINGUAL
LINIEST
LININGS
LINKAGE
LINKERS
LINKING
LINKUPS
LINNETS
LINPIAO
LINSEED
LINTELS
LINTIER
LONGAGO
LONGARM
LONGBOW
LONGEST
LONGIES
LONGING
LONGISH
LONGRUN
LONGTON
LONGUES
LUNATIC
LUNCHED
LUNCHES
LUNGEAT
LUNGING
LUNKERS

L••N•••

LAENNEC
LAUNDER
LAUNDRY
LAXNESS
LEANDER
LEANERS
LEANEST
LEANING
LEANSON
LEANTOS
LEONARD
LEONIDS
LEONINE
LEONORA
LIENEES
LIGNITE
LIMNERS
LIMNING
LINNETS
LIONCUB
LIONESS
LIONETS
LIONISE
LIONIZE
LOANERS
LOANING
LOONEYS
LOONIER
LOONIES
LOUNGED
LOUNGER
LOUNGES
LOWNECK
LOWNESS
LUGNUTS
LYINGTO

L•••N••

LACINGS
LACONIC
LACUNAE
LACUNAL
LACUNAS
LADINOS
LAENNEC
LAGUNAS
LALANNE
LAMENTS
LAMINAE
LAMINAL
LAMINAR
LAMINAS
LARDNER
LATENCY
LATENTS
LATINAS
LATINOS
LAVINIA
LAYINTO
LEARNED
LEARNER
LEBANON
LEGENDS
LEIBNIZ
LEMONDE
LEPANTO
LETINON
LEVANTS
LICENCE
LICENSE
LIERNES
LIFENET
LIGANDS
LIKENED
LIKENEW
LININGS
LISENTE
LITINTO
LIVENED
LIVINGS
LOCKNUT
LORENZO
LOZENGE
LUCENCY
LUPINES
LYSENKO

L••••N•

LACKING
LADLING
LAGGING
LAGOONS
LALANNE
LAMBENT
LAMMING
LANDING
LANSING
LANTANA
LAPLAND
LAPPING
LAPSING
LAPWING
LARAINE
LARCENY
LARDING
LARDONS
LASAGNA
LASAGNE
LASHING
LASTING
LATEENS
LATHING
LATTENS
LAUDING
LAURENT
LAVERNE
LEADING
LEADINS
LEAFING
LEAKING
LEANING
LEAPING
LEASING
LEAVENS
LEAVING
LEERING
LEGGING
LEGIONS
LEGRAND
LEMMING
LENDING
LENFANT
LENIENT
LEONINE
LEPTONS
LESSENS
LESSING
LESSONS
LETTING
LEUCINE
LEVYING
LIBBING
LIBYANS
LICHENS
LICKING
LIFTING
LILTING
LIMBING
LIMNING
LIMPING
LINDENS
LINKING
LIPPING
LIPSYNC
LISPING
LISTENS
LISTING
LIVEONE
LIVORNO
LOADING
LOAFING
LOAMING
LOANING
LOBBING
LOCARNO
LOCKING

LOCKINS
LODGING
LOFTING
LOGGING
LOGGINS
LOLLING
LONGING
LOOKING
LOOMING
LOOPING
LOOSENS
LOOSING
LOOTING
LOPPING
LORDING
LOTIONS
LOTTING
LOUSING
LOVEINS
LOWLAND
LUCERNE
LUCIANO
LUCKING
LUFFING
LUGGING
LULLING
LUMPING
LUNGING
LURKING
LUSTING

L•••••N

LACHLAN
LAMPOON
LANGDON
LANOLIN
LANTERN
LAOCOON
LAOTIAN
LATERAN
LATERON
LATVIAN
LAUGHIN
LAYDOWN
LAYITON
LAYOPEN
LEADSIN
LEADSON
LEANSON
LEAVEIN
LEBANON
LEBARON
LECTERN
LEGHORN
LETDOWN
LETINON
LETUPON
LEXICON
LIAISON
LIEDOWN
LIGHTEN
LILLIAN
LINCOLN
LINEMAN
LINEMEN
LIVEDIN
LIVEDON
LIVESIN
LIVESON
LOCKSON
LOCOMAN
LOCOMEN
LONGRUN
LONGTON
LOOKSIN
LOOKSON
LOWBORN
LOWDOWN

•L•N•••

ALENCON
ALINING
ALUNSER
BLANCHE
BLANDER
BLANDLY
BLANKED
BLANKER
BLANKET
BLANKLY
BLENDED
BLENDER
BLINDED
BLINDER
BLINDLY
BLINKAT
BLINKED
BLINKER
BLONDER
BLONDES
BLONDIE
BLUNDER
BLUNTED
BLUNTER
BLUNTLY
CLANGED
CLANGOR
CLANKED
CLINICS
CLINKED
CLINKER
CLINTON
CLONING
CLUNKED
CLUNKER
FLANEUR
FLANGES
FLANKED
FLANKER
FLANNEL
FLENSED
FLENSES
FLUNKED
FLYNETS
GLANCED
GLANCES
GLINTED
ILLNESS
KLINGON
OLDNESS
OLDNEWS
OLDNICK
PLANERS
PLANETS
PLANING
PLANISH
PLANKED
PLANNED
PLANNER
PLANOUT
PLANSON
PLANTAR
PLANTED
PLANTER
PLENARY
PLENUMS
PLINKED
PLINTHS
PLUNDER
PLUNGED
PLUNGER
PLUNGES
PLUNKED
SLANDER
SLANTED
SLENDER
SLINGER
SLINKED
SLYNESS
TLINGIT
ULANOVA

•L••N••

ALBANIA
ALBENIZ
ALBINOS
ALBUNDY
ALDENTE
ALFONSO
ALIENEE
ALIENOR
ALIGNED
ALIGNER
ALKENES
ALLENBY
ALLENDE
ALMANAC
ALMONDS
ALUMNAE
ALUMNAL
ALUMNUS
BLARNEY
BLOWNUP
CLEANED
CLEANER
CLEANLY
CLEANSE
CLEANUP
CLIENTS
CLOONEY
CLOWNED
ELEANOR
FLANNEL
FLAUNTS
FLAUNTY
FLEXNER
FLOUNCE
FLOUNCY
FLOWNAT
FLOWNIN
FLUENCY
GLEANED
GLEANER
KLEENEX
PLAINER
PLAINLY
PLAINTS
PLANNED
PLANNER
PLIANCY
ULYANOV

•L•••N•

ALAKING
ALIMENT
ALIMONY
ALINING
ALLGONE
ALLYING
ALTOONA
BLADING
BLAMING
BLARING
BLATANT
BLAZING
BLAZONS
BLOWING
BLUEING
CLAWING
CLEMENS
CLEMENT
CLIPONS
CLONING
CLOSING
CLOYING
CLUEING
ELATING
ELEGANT
ELEMENT
ELEVENS
ELIDING
ELOIGNS
ELOPING
ELUDING
ELUTING
FLACONS
FLAGONS
FLAKING
FLAMING
FLARING
FLAWING
FLAYING
FLEEING
FLEMING
FLEXING
FLEYING
FLORINS
FLOWING
FLUTING
FLUXING
GLARING
GLAZING
GLIDING
GLOBING
GLOWING
GLOZING
ILLWIND
ILOCANO
KLAXONS
OLDHAND
OLDLINE
OLEFINS
OLIVINE
PLACING
PLANING
PLATENS
PLATING
PLAYING
PLOWING
PLUGINS
PLUMING
SLAKING
SLATING
SLAVING
SLICING
SLIDING
SLIPONS
SLOGANS
SLOPING
SLOVENE
SLOVENS
SLOWING
ULLMANN
ULULANT

•L••••N

ALADDIN
ALAMEIN
ALARCON
ALASKAN
ALBUMEN
ALBUMIN
ALENCON
ALLISON
ALLSTON
ALLYSON
ALMADEN
ALSORAN
ALYKHAN
BLACKEN
BLITZEN
BLOUSON
BLOWGUN
BLOWSIN
BLUEFIN
BLUSHON
CLAPTON
CLARION
CLAYTON
CLEAVON
CLEMSON
CLIBURN
CLIFTON
CLINTON
CLOCKIN
CLOSEIN
CLUEDIN
CLUESIN
ELAAIUN
ELATION
ELEISON
ELISION
ELLISON
ELUTION
ELYSIAN
FLAGMAN
FLAGMEN
FLATTEN
FLIESIN
FLOWNIN
GLADDEN
GLEASON
GLISTEN
GLUEDON
GLUESON
GLUTTON
KLINGON
KLUGMAN
OLDMOON
PLANSON
PLATOON
PLAYPEN
PLAYSON
PLOSION
PLOWMAN
PLOWMEN
PLUGSIN
SLACKEN
SLAYTON
SLEEKEN
SLEEPIN
SLEEPON
SLEPTIN
SLEPTON
SLIDEIN
SLIPSIN
SLIPSON
SLOEGIN
ULLMANN

••LN•••

ILLNESS
VILNIUS
WALNUTS

••L•N••

ALLENBY
ALLENDE
APLENTY
ATLANTA
BALANCE
BALONEY
BELINDA
BELONGS
BYLINED
BYLINES
CALENDS
COLONEL
COLONES
DELANEY
FELINES
FILENES
FILINGS
GILLNET
ISLANDS
LALANNE
MELANGE
MELANIE
MELANIN
MELINDA
OBLONGS
ORLANDO
PALANCE
PILINGS
PILSNER
POLENTA
RELENTS
RELINED
RELINES
RULINGS
SALINAS
SELENIC
SILENCE
SILENTS
SPLINES
SPLINTS
TALENTS
TALONED
TILINGS
TYLENOL
UNLINED
UNLINKS
UPLANDS
UPLINKS
VALANCE
VALENCE
VALENCY

••L••N•

AILMENT
ALLGONE
ALLYING
BALCONY
BALDING
BALEENS
BALKANS
BALKING
BELLING
BELLINI
BELMONT
BELTANE
BELTING
BELYING
BILKING
BILLING
BOLOGNA
BOLTING
BULGING
BULKING
BULLING
CALKING
CALKINS
CALLING
CALLINS
CALMING
CALUMNY
CALVING
CALZONE
CELLINI
COLLINS
COLOGNE
COLUMNS
CULLING
DELEING
DELVING
DOLLING
DOLMANS
DOLMENS
DULLING
FALCONS
FALLING
FELLING
FELLINI
FILLING
FILLINS
FILMING
FOLDING
FULGENT
GALLANT
GALLING
GALLONS
GALVANI
GELDING
GELLING
GILDING
GILLING
GOLDING
GOLFING
GULFING
GULLING
GULPING
HALOING
HALTING
HALVING
HELLENE
HELMING
HELPING
HILLING
HOLDING
HOLLAND
HULKING
HULLING
ILLWIND
JELLING
JILTING
JOLTING
JULIANA
KILLING
KILTING
LALANNE
LILTING
LOLLING
LULLING
MALIGNS
MALKINS
MALTING
MELDING
MELTING
MILKING
MILLAND
MILLEND
MILLING
MOLDING
MOLTING
MULLING
NELSONS
NULLING
OILCANS
OILPANS
ORLEANS
PALLING
PALMING
PELTING
PILLING
POLLENS
POLLING
PULLING
PULLINS
PULLONS
PULSING
RDLAING
RELIANT
RELLENO
RELYING
ROLLING
ROLLINS
SALERNO
SALIENT
SALMONS
SALOONS
SALTINE
SALTING
SALVING
SELLING
SILOING
SILTING
SOLOING
SOLVENT
SOLVING
SPLEENS
SULKING
SULTANA
SULTANS
SYLVANS
TALKING
TALLINN
TELLING
TILLING
TILTING
TOLLING
TOLUENE
TULSANS
ULLMANN
VALIANT
VALUING
VOLCANO
VOLPONE
VULCANS
VULPINE
WALKING
WALKINS
WALKONS
WALLING
WELDING
WELKINS
WELLAND
WELLING
WELTING
WILDING
WILDONE
WILLING
WILTING
WOLFING
YELLING
YELPING

••L•••N

AILERON
ALLISON
ALLSTON
ALLYSON
BALATON
BALDWIN
BALLOON
BELAKUN
BELGIAN
BELLMAN
BELLMEN
BILLION
BKLIBAN
BULLION
BULLPEN
BULLRUN
CALDRON
CALHOUN
CALIBAN
CALLSIN
CALLSON
CELADON
COLEMAN
COLLEEN
DOLPHIN
EELSKIN
ELLISON
ENLIVEN
FALLSIN
FALLSON
FELDMAN
FILLSIN
GALLEON
GELATIN
GILLIAN
GOLDWYN
HALCYON
HALFDAN
HALOGEN
HALSTON
HELICON
HELLION
HELLMAN
HOLBEIN
HOLDSIN
HOLDSON
JILLIAN
JILLION
KILOTON
LILLIAN
MALAYAN
MCLUHAN
MELANIN
MILKMAN
MILKMEN
MILKRUN
MILLION
MILLRUN
MULLEIN
MULLION
NILSSON
OILSKIN
PALADIN
PELICAN
PILEDIN
PILEDON
PILESIN
PILESON
PILLION
POLYGON
PULLMAN
PULLSIN
PULLSON
RALSTON
RELEARN
ROLLSIN
ROLLSON
RULESON
SALADIN
SILICON
SOLOMON
TALLINN
TELERAN
TELLSON
TOLKIEN
ULLMANN
UNLEARN
VALJEAN
VILLAIN
VILLEIN
WALKMAN
WALKSON
WALLOON
WALSTON
WELLMAN
WELLRUN
WILLSON
WOLFMAN
WOLFMEN
YELTSIN
ZILLION

•••LN••

GILLNET

•••L•N•

ABALONE
ABILENE
ADDLING
ADELINE
AIRLANE
AIRLINE
AMBLING
ANELING
ANGLING
ANILINE
ASHLAND
BAILING
BAWLING
BEELINE
BELLING
BELLINI
BILLING
BIPLANE
BIRLING
BOILING
BOWLINE
BOWLING
BUGLING
BULLING
BURLING
BUSLINE
CABLING
CALLING
CALLINS
CEILING
CELLINI
CHALONS
CHOLINE
COILING
COLLINS
COOLANT
COOLING
COPLAND
COULDNT
COWLING
CULLING
CURLING
CYCLING
CYCLONE
DARLENE
DARLING
DAYLONG
DEALING
DECLINE
DEPLANE
DEWLINE
DIALING
DOLLING
DUELING
DULLING
DUNLINS
EAGLING
ENGLAND
ENGLUND
ENPLANE
ERELONG
EXILING
FAILING
FALLING
FEELING
FELLING
FELLINI
FILLING
FILLINS
FINLAND
FOALING
FOILING
FOOLING
FOULING
FOWLING
FUELING
FURLING
FURLONG
GAGLINE
GALLANT
GALLING
GALLONS
GAOLING
GARLAND
GATLING
GELLING
GILLING
GOALONG
GOBLINS
GOSLING
GOTLAND
GULLING
HAILING
HAULING
HEALING
HEELING
HELLENE
HEMLINE
HILLING
HOLLAND
HOTLINE
HOTLINK
HOVLANE
HOWLING
HULLING
HURLING
HYALINE
ICELAND
IMPLANT
INCLINE
INKLING
IRELAND
JAILING
JAWLINE
JAYLENO
JELLING
JUTLAND
KEELING
KILLING
KIPLING
KOBLENZ
LADLING
LAPLAND
LOLLING
LOWLAND
LULLING
MAILING
MARLENE
MARLINS
MAULING
MEWLING
MIDLAND
MIDLINE
MILLAND
MILLEND
MILLING
MOILING
MULLING
MUSLINS
NAILING
NULLING
OAKLAND
OFFLINE
OLDLINE
ONELANE
OPALINE
OPULENT
OUTLAND
OUTLINE
PALLING
PAULINA
PAULINE
PAULING
PEALING
PEELING
PHALANX
PILLING
POLLENS
POLLING
POOLING
POPLINS
POULENC
PRALINE
PROLONG
PULLING
PULLINS
PULLONS
PURLING
PURLINS
RAGLANS
RAILING
RATLINE
RECLINE
REDLINE
REELING
RELLENO
REPLANS
REPLANT
RIFLING
ROILING
ROLLING
ROLLINS
SAILING
SAPLING
SCALENE
SCALING
SEALANE
SEALANT
SEALING
SELLING
SERLING
SETLINE
SIBLING
SIDLING
SKYLINE
SMILING
SOILING
SPELUNK
STOLONS
STYLING
TABLING
TAGLINE
TAILEND
TAILING
TALLINN
TANLINE
TELLING
TIELINE
TIGLONS
TILLING
TITLING
TOILING
TOLLING
TOOLING
TOYLAND
TWOLANE
ULULANT
VEILING
VIOLENT
VIOLINS
WAILING
WALLING
WELLAND
WELLING
WETLAND
WHALING
WHILING
WILLING
WOOLENS
WOULDNT
YELLING
YOWLING
ZEALAND

•••L••N

AEOLIAN
ANTLION
BALLOON
BELLMAN
BELLMEN
BILLION
BOOLEAN
BUILDIN
BUILTIN
BULLION
BULLPEN
BULLRUN
CALLSIN
CALLSON
CARLSON
CARLTON
CHILEAN
COALBIN
COLLEEN
DEALSIN
DEALTIN
EARLYON
EXPLAIN
FALLSIN
FALLSON
FILLSIN
FORLORN
GALLEON
GILLIAN
HELLION
HELLMAN
ITALIAN
JILLIAN
JILLION
KOWLOON
LILLIAN
MAILSIN
MAULDIN
MILLION
MILLRUN
MRCLEAN
MULLEIN
MULLION
NAILSIN
NIELSEN
NUCLEON
OAKLAWN
PAULSEN
PERLMAN
PHILBIN
PILLION
PULLMAN
PULLSIN
PULLSON
PURLOIN
RECLEAN
REELSIN
ROLLSIN
ROLLSON
SEALION
SHELDON
SHELTON
SIRLOIN
SKELTON
SNELLEN
STILTON
STOLLEN
SWOLLEN
TAILFIN
TALLINN
TELLSON
TRILLIN
UNCLEAN
VILLAIN
VILLEIN
WALLOON
WELLMAN
WELLRUN
WILLSON
WOOLLEN
ZILLION

••••LN•

AAMILNE

••••L•N

ANGOLAN
BABYLON
BRESLIN
CAROLYN
CATALAN
CHAPLIN
DRUMLIN
ECHELON
EPSILON
GREMLIN
HAMELIN
INSULIN

JAVELIN
KREMLIN
KTOSLIN
LACHLAN
LANOLIN
MARILYN
MAUDLIN
MAYALIN
MOUFLON
OBERLIN
ORTOLAN
ROMULAN
SNELLEN
STOLLEN
SWOLLEN
TASHLIN
TRILLIN
UPSILON
WOOLLEN
ZEBULON

•••••LN

LINCOLN

LO•••••

LOACHES
LOADERS
LOADING
LOAFERS
LOAFING
LOAMIER
LOAMING
LOANERS
LOANING
LOATHED
LOATHES
LOBBERS
LOBBIED
LOBBIES
LOBBING
LOBBYER
LOBSTER
LOBULES
LOCALES
LOCALLY
LOCARNO
LOCATED
LOCATER
LOCATES
LOCATOR
LOCKBOX
LOCKERS
LOCKETS
LOCKING
LOCKINS
LOCKNUT
LOCKOUT
LOCKSON
LOCKSUP
LOCKUPS
LOCOMAN
LOCOMEN
LOCUSTS
LODGERS
LODGING
LOESSER
LOESSES
LOFTIER
LOFTILY
LOFTING
LOGBOOK
LOGGERS
LOGGIAS
LOGGING
LOGGINS
LOGGISH
LOGICAL
LOGIEST
LOGJAMS
LOGROLL
LOGSOFF
LOGSOUT
LOITERS
LOLLARD
LOLLIES
LOLLING
LOLLOPS
LOMBARD
LONGAGO
LONGARM
LONGBOW
LONGEST
LONGIES
LONGING
LONGISH
LONGRUN
LONGTON
LONGUES
LOOBIES
LOOFAHS
LOOKERS
LOOKFOR
LOOKING
LOOKOUT
LOOKSAT
LOOKSEE
LOOKSIN
LOOKSON
LOOKSTO
LOOKSUP
LOOKUPS
LOOMING
LOONEYS
LOONIER
LOONIES
LOOPERS
LOOPIER
LOOPING
LOOSELY
LOOSENS
LOOSEST
LOOSING
LOOTERS
LOOTING
LOPPERS
LOPPIER
LOPPING
LOQUATS
LORDING
LORDJIM
LORELEI
LORENZO
LORETTA
LORICAE
LORISES
LORRIES
LOSEOUT
LOSESIT
LOSTOUT
LOTIONS
LOTTERY
LOTTING
LOTUSES
LOUDEST
LOUDISH
LOUELLA
LOUNGED
LOUNGER
LOUNGES
LOURDES
LOUSEUP
LOUSIER
LOUSILY
LOUSING
LOUTISH
LOUVERS
LOUVRED
LOUVRES
LOVABLE
LOVABLY
LOVEBUG
LOVEINS
LOVERLY
LOWBALL
LOWBEAM
LOWBLOW
LOWBORN
LOWBOYS
LOWBRED
LOWBROW
LOWCOST
LOWDOWN
LOWERED
LOWGEAR
LOWHEEL
LOWLAND
LOWLIER
LOWLIFE
LOWNECK
LOWNESS
LOWPAID
LOWRISE
LOWROAD
LOWTECH
LOWTIDE
LOYALLY
LOYALTY
LOZENGE

L•O••••

LAOCOON
LAOTIAN
LEONARD
LEONIDS
LEONINE
LEONORA
LEOPARD
LEOPOLD
LEOTARD
LIONCUB
LIONESS
LIONETS
LIONISE
LIONIZE
LOOBIES
LOOFAHS
LOOKERS
LOOKFOR
LOOKING
LOOKOUT
LOOKSAT
LOOKSEE
LOOKSIN
LOOKSON
LOOKSTO
LOOKSUP
LOOKUPS
LOOMING
LOONEYS
LOONIER
LOONIES
LOOPERS
LOOPIER
LOOPING
LOOSELY
LOOSENS
LOOSEST
LOOSING
LOOTERS
LOOTING

L••O•••

LABORED
LABORER
LABOURS
LACONIC
LACOSTE
LAGOONS
LAJOLLA
LAKOTAS
LAMOTTA
LANOLIN
LAPORTE
LASORDA
LATOSCA
LAYOFFS
LAYOPEN
LAYOUTS
LAYOVER
LEMONDE
LESOTHO
LIEOVER
LIMOGES
LITOTES
LIVORNO
LLCOOLJ
LOCOMAN
LOCOMEN

L•••O••

LABCOAT
LACTOSE
LAGOONS
LAIDOFF
LAIDOUT
LAMPOIL
LAMPOON
LANFORD
LAOCOON
LAPDOGS
LAPROBE
LAPTOPS
LARDONS
LASSOED
LASSOER
LASSOES
LASTORY
LAWFORD
LAYDOWN
LAYSOFF
LAYSOUT
LEACOCK
LEADOFF
LEADOUT
LECTORS
LEFTOFF
LEFTOUT
LEGHORN
LEGIONS
LEGROOM
LEGWORK
LEONORA
LEOPOLD
LEPTONS
LESSONS
LESSORS
LETDOWN
LETSOFF
LETSOUT
LICTORS
LIEDOWN
LIFTOFF
LIMPOPO
LINCOLN
LINGOES
LIQUORS
LISSOME
LIVEOAK
LIVEONE
LIVEOUT
LLCOOLJ
LOCKOUT
LOGBOOK
LOGROLL
LOGSOFF
LOGSOUT
LOLLOPS
LOOKOUT
LOSEOUT
LOSTOUT
LOTIONS
LOWBORN
LOWBOYS
LOWCOST
LOWDOWN
LOWROAD
LUBBOCK
LUCKOUT

L••••O•

LADINOS
LAIDFOR
LAIDLOW
LAMPOON
LANGDON
LANGUOR
LAOCOON
LATERON
LATINOS
LAYITON
LAYSFOR
LAYSLOW
LEADSON
LEANSON
LEANTOS
LEBANON
LEBARON
LEGATOS
LEGROOM
LETINON
LETUPON
LEXICON
LIAISON
LIBIDOS
LIESLOW
LITHGOW
LIVEDON
LIVESON
LOCATOR
LOCKBOX
LOCKSON
LOGBOOK
LONGBOW
LONGTON
LOOKFOR
LOOKSON
LOWBLOW
LOWBROW
LUBEJOB

L•••••O

LAYINTO
LEADSTO
LEDUPTO
LENTIGO
LEPANTO
LESOTHO
LIMPOPO
LINBIAO
LINPIAO
LITINTO
LIVORNO
LOCARNO
LONGAGO
LOOKSTO
LORENZO
LUCIANO
LUMBAGO
LYINGTO
LYSENKO

•LO••••

ALOHAOE
ALOOFLY
BLOATED
BLOCKED
BLOCKER
BLONDER
BLONDES
BLONDIE
BLOODED
BLOOMED
BLOOMER
BLOOPED
BLOOPER
BLOSSOM
BLOTCHY
BLOTOUT
BLOTTED
BLOTTER
BLOUSED
BLOUSES
BLOUSON
BLOWDRY
BLOWERS
BLOWFLY
BLOWGUN
BLOWIER
BLOWING
BLOWNUP
BLOWOFF
BLOWOUT
BLOWSIN
BLOWSIT
BLOWSUP
BLOWUPS
CLOACAE
CLOACAS
CLOAKED
CLOBBER
CLOCHES
CLOCKED
CLOCKER
CLOCKIN
CLOGGED
CLOGSUP
CLOMPED
CLONING
CLOONEY
CLOPPED
CLOQUES
CLORETS
CLOSEBY
CLOSEIN
CLOSELY
CLOSEST
CLOSETS
CLOSEUP
CLOSING
CLOSURE
CLOTHED
CLOTHES
CLOTTED
CLOTURE
CLOUDED
CLOUTED
CLOVERS
CLOWDER
CLOWNED
CLOYING
ELOIGNS
ELOPERS
ELOPING
FLOATED
FLOATER
FLOCKED
FLOCKTO
FLOGGED
FLOODED
FLOORED
FLOPPED
FLORETS
FLORIDA
FLORINS
FLORIST
FLORUIT
FLOSSED
FLOSSES
FLOTSAM
FLOUNCE
FLOUNCY
FLOURED
FLOUTED
FLOWERS
FLOWERY
FLOWING
FLOWNAT
FLOWNIN
GLOATED
GLOBING
GLOBULE
GLOMMED
GLOOMED
GLORIAM
GLORIAS
GLORIED
GLORIES
GLORIFY
GLOSSAE
GLOSSED
GLOSSES
GLOTTAL
GLOTTIS
GLOWERS
GLOWING
GLOZING
ILOCANO
OLOROSO
PLODDED
PLODDER
PLOPPED
PLOSION
PLOSIVE
PLOTFUL
PLOTTED
PLOTTER
PLOUGHS
PLOVERS
PLOWBOY
PLOWERS
PLOWING
PLOWMAN
PLOWMEN
SLOBBER
SLOEGIN
SLOGANS
SLOGGED
SLOPING
SLOPPED
SLOSHED
SLOSHES
SLOTCAR
SLOTTED
SLOUCHY
SLOUGHS
SLOVAKS
SLOVENE
SLOVENS
SLOWEST
SLOWING
SLOWSUP
SLOWUPS

•L•O•••

ALCOHOL
ALCOVES
ALFONSO
ALFORJA
ALLOFME
ALLOVER
ALLOWAY
ALLOWED
ALLOYED
ALMONDS
ALOOFLY
ALSORAN
ALTOONA
ALTOSAX
ALWORTH
ALYOSHA
BLOODED
BLOOMED
BLOOMER
BLOOPED
BLOOPER
CLOONEY
ELBOWED
FLOODED
FLOORED
FLYOVER
GLOOMED
ILLOGIC
LLCOOLJ

•L••O••

ALAMODE
ALIMONY
ALLGONE
ALLTOLD
ALTOONA
ALVEOLI
BLAZONS
BLEWOFF
BLEWOUT
BLOTOUT
BLOWOFF
BLOWOUT
CLAMORS
CLAMOUR
CLIPONS
ELLIOTT
ELUSORY
FLACONS
FLAGONS
FLATOUT
FLAVORS
FLAVOUR
FLEXORS
FLIPOUT
FLYBOYS
FLYRODS
GLAMOUR
GLUCOSE
KLAXONS
LLCOOLJ
OLDFOGY
OLDGOLD
OLDMOON
OLDROSE
OLOROSO
PLANOUT
PLATOON
PLAYOFF
PLAYOUT
PLEXORS
PLYWOOD
SLALOMS
SLIPONS
SLIPOUT
ULANOVA

•L•••O•

ALARCON
ALBEDOS
ALBINOS
ALCOHOL
ALENCON
ALIENOR
ALLISON
ALLSTON
ALLYSON
ALOHAOE
BLERIOT
BLOSSOM
BLOUSON
BLUEBOY
BLUEFOX
BLUSHON
CLAIROL
CLANGOR
CLAPTON
CLARION
CLAYTON
CLEAVON
CLEMSON
CLIFTON
CLINTON
ELATION
ELEANOR
ELECTOR
ELEISON
ELISION
ELLISON
ELUTION
FLATTOP
FLUMMOX
GLASGOW
GLEASON
GLUEDON
GLUESON
GLUTTON
KLINGON
OLDMOON
OLDPROS
PLANSON
PLATOON
PLAYBOY
PLAYDOH
PLAYSON
PLOSION
PLOWBOY
PLYWOOD
SLAYTON
SLEDDOG
SLEEPON
SLEPTON
SLIPSON
ULYANOV

•L••••O

ALBERTO
ALFONSO
ALFREDO
ALLEGRO
CLAUDIO
ELECTRO
ELGRECO
FLOCKTO
ILOCANO
OLOROSO
PLACEBO
PLACIDO

••LO•••

ALLOFME
ALLOVER
ALLOWAY
ALLOWED
ALLOYED
BALONEY
BELONGS
BELOVED
BOLOGNA
BOLOTIE
CALOMEL
CALORIC
CALORIE
CHLORAL
COLOBUS
COLOGNE
COLONEL
COLONES
COLORED
COLOSSI
COLOURS
CULOTTE
DOLORES
DOLOURS
ECLOGUE
GALOOTS
HALOGEN
HALOING
HELOISE
HELOTRY
ILLOGIC
KILOTON
MALODOR
MELODIC
MILORDS
MOLOCHS
MOLOKAI
MOLOTOV
OBLONGS
OBLOQUY
PALOMAR
PALOOKA
PELOTAS
PHLOXES
PILOTED
POLOIST
RELOADS
RELOCKS
ROLODEX
SALOONS
SILOING
SOLOING
SOLOIST
SOLOMON
SPLOTCH
STLOUIS
TALONED
UNLOADS
UNLOCKS
UNLOOSE
UNLOVED
UPLOADS
VALOURS
VELOURS

••L•O••

ALLGONE
ALLTOLD
BALBOAS
BALCONY
BALFOUR
BALLOON
BALLOTS
BELLOWS
BELMONT
BILBOES
BILIOUS
BILLOWS
BILLOWY
BULBOUS
BULLOCK
CALHOUN
CALLOFF
CALLOUS
CALLOUT
CALZONE
COLLODI
COLLOID
COLLOPS
DELTOID
DOLEOUT
DOLLOPS
ELLIOTT
FALCONS
FALLOFF
FALLOUT
FALLOWS
FELLOFF
FELLOUT
FELLOWS
FELTOUT
FILLOUT
FOLDOUT
FOLLOWS
FULSOME
GALLONS
GALLOPS
GALOOTS
HALLOWS
HELDOFF
HELDOUT
HELPOUT
HILLOCK
HOLDOFF
HOLDOUT
HOLEOUT
HOLLOWS
HOLMOAK
HOLYOKE
HULLOAS
HULLOED
KELLOGG
LOLLOPS
MALCOLM
MALLOWS
MALTOSE
MELLOWS
MELROSE
MOLDOVA
NELSONS
PALJOEY
PALLORS
PALMOFF
PALMOIL
PALOOKA
PILLORY
PILLOWS
PILLOWY
POLLOCK
PULLOFF
PULLONS
PULLOUT
ROLLOUT
RULEOUT
SALLOWS
SALMONS
SALOONS
SALSODA
SALVOES
SALVORS
SELLOFF
SELLOUT
SOLDOFF
SOLDOUT
TALKOUT
TALLOWS
TELLOFF
TOLDOFF
UNLOOSE
VOLPONE
WALCOTT
WALDORF
WALKONS
WALKOUT
WALLOON
WALLOPS
WALLOWS
WALPOLE
WELCOME
WELLOFF
WILDONE
WILFORD
WILLOWS
WILLOWY
YELLOWS
YELLOWY

••L••O•

AILERON
ALLISON
ALLSTON
ALLYSON
BALATON
BALLBOY
BALLOON
BELABOR
BELLBOY
BELLHOP
BILLION
BOLEROS
BOLSHOI
BULLDOG
BULLION
CALDRON
CALICOS
CALLBOX
CALLFOR
CALLSON
CELADON
ELLISON
FALLFOR
FALLSON
FELLFOR
FELTFOR
GALAGOS
GALLEON
HALCYON
HALSTON
HELICON
HELLION
HILLTOP
HOLDSON
HOLYCOW
JILLION
KILLJOY
KILOTON
MALODOR
MILKCOW
MILKSOP
MILLION
MOLOTOV
MULLION
NILSSON
ONLYTOO
ONLYYOU
PALMTOP
PALTROW
PILEDON
PILESON
PILLBOX
PILLION
POLYGON
PULLFOR
PULLSON
RALSTON
ROLLSON
ROLLTOP
RULESON
SALCHOW
SALTBOX
SELLFOR
SILICON
SOLOMON
TELLSOF
TELLSON
TOLSTOI
TOLSTOY
TYLENOL
WALKSON
WALLOON
WALSTON
WILLSON
YULELOG
ZILLION

••L•••O

ALLEGRO
BELASCO
CALYPSO
COLUMBO
FALLSTO
GALILEO
GOLFPRO
HOLDSTO
JALISCO
ONLYTOO
ORLANDO
PALAZZO
PALERMO
RALLYTO
RELIEVO
RELLENO
SALERNO
TALKSTO
TALLYHO
VALLEJO
VOLCANO

•••LO••

ABALONE
AIRLOCK
ANALOGS
ANALOGY
APOLOGY
ARMLOAD
ARMLOCK
ATALOSS
AXOLOTL
BAILORS
BAILOUT
BALLOON
BALLOTS
BAWLOUT
BECLOUD
BELLOWS
BILLOWS
BILLOWY
BIOLOGY
BULLOCK
CALLOFF
CALLOUS
CALLOUT
CARLOAD
CHALONS
COALOIL
COLLODI
COLLOID
COLLOPS
COULOMB
CYCLONE
CYCLOPS
DAYLONG
DEALOUT
DEPLORE
DEPLOYS
DIALOGS
DIPLOID
DIPLOMA
DOLLOPS
EARLOBE
EARLOCK
ECOLOGY
EMPLOYE
EMPLOYS
ENCLOSE
EPILOGS
ERELONG
EXPLODE
EXPLOIT
EXPLORE
FALLOFF
FALLOUT
FALLOWS
FEELOUT
FELLOFF
FELLOUT
FELLOWS
FETLOCK
FILLOUT
FOLLOWS
FORLORN
FOULOUT

FUELOIL
FURLONG
GALLONS
GALLOPS
GASLOGS
GEOLOGY
GETLOST
GOALONG
GOSLOWS
GOTLOST
GUNLOCK
HALLOWS
HAULOFF
HAYLOFT
HEMLOCK
HILLOCK
HOLLOWS
HULLOAS
HULLOED
IMPLODE
IMPLORE
INBLOOM
INCLOSE
INFLOWS
JEALOUS
JOBLOTS
KARLOFF
KELLOGG
KOWLOON
LOLLOPS
MAILOUT
MALLOWS
MARLOWE
MATLOCK
MCCLOUD
MELLOWS
MERLOTS
NEWLOOK
OARLOCK
OCELOTS
ODDLOTS
OFFLOAD
OUTLOOK
OUTLOUD
OXBLOOD
PADLOCK
PAILOUS
PALLORS
PARLORS
PARLOUR
PARLOUS
PAVLOVA
PAYLOAD
PEELOFF
PILLORY
PILLOWS
PILLOWY
POLLOCK
PRELOAD
PROLOGS
PROLONG
PULLOFF
PULLONS
PULLOUT
PURLOIN
REBLOOM
REELOFF
REPLOWS
RIOLOBO
ROBLOWE
ROLLOUT
SAILORS
SALLOWS
SAWLOGS
SCHLOCK
SEALOFF
SELLOFF
SELLOUT
SHALOMS
SHYLOCK
SIRLOIN
SLALOMS
STOLONS
SUOLOCO
TABLOID
TAILOFF
TAILORS
TALLOWS
TELLOFF
TIGLONS
TOELOOP
TRILOGY
UNBLOCK
UNCLOAK
UNCLOGS
UNCLOSE
UPCLOSE
WALLOON
WALLOPS
WALLOWS
WARLOCK
WARLORD
WEDLOCK
WELLOFF
WILLOWS
WILLOWY
YELLOWS
YELLOWY
ZEALOTS
ZEALOUS
ZOOLOGY

•••L•O•
ANTLION
BALLBOY
BALLOON
BELLBOY
BELLHOP
BERLIOZ
BILLION
BULLDOG
BULLION
CALLBOX
CALLFOR
CALLSON
CARLSON
CARLTON
EARLDOM
EARLYON
FALLFOR
FALLSON
FEELFOR
FELLFOR
FUELROD
GALLEON
HELLION
HILLTOP
INBLOOM
JILLION
KEILLOR
KILLJOY
KOWLOON
MAILBOX
MAILLOT
MILLION
MULLION
NEWLOOK
NUCLEON
OUTLOOK
OXBLOOD
PILLBOX
PILLION
PULLFOR
PULLSON
REALTOR
REBLOOM
ROLLSON
ROLLTOP
SCALLOP
SEALION
SELLFOR
SHALLOT
SHALLOW
SHELDON
SHELTON
SKELTON
SMALTOS
STILTON
SWALLOW
TELLSOF
TELLSON
TOELOOP
TOOLBOX
TSELIOT
WALLOON
WILLSON
ZILLION

•••L••O
FALLSTO
JAYLENO
PIMLICO
RALLYTO
RELLENO
RIOLOBO
SUOLOCO
TALLYHO
VALLEJO

••••LO•
ABSALOM
AIRFLOW
ANGELOU
ANTILOG
BABALOO
BABYLON
BACKLOG
BIBELOT
BICOLOR
BIGELOW
BUGALOO
CAMELOT
CATALOG
COPILOT
DECALOG
DEVELOP
ECHELON
EMMYLOU
ENVELOP
EPSILON
FEEDLOT
GIGOLOS
HIGHLOW
ICEFLOE
INKBLOT
JOEBLOW
KEILLOR
KERPLOP
LAIDLOW
LAYSLOW
LIESLOW
LOWBLOW
MAILLOT
MANILOW
MARYLOU
MATELOT
MONOLOG
MOUFLON
OUTFLOW
POMELOS
PUEBLOS
RECOLOR
SANDLOT
SAVELOY
SCALLOP
SEMILOG
SHALLOT
SHALLOW
SQUALOR
SUBPLOT
SWALLOW
TAGALOG
TEMBLOR
THEBLOB
TONELOC
TUPELOS
UPSILON
WINSLOW
WOODLOT
YULELOG
ZEBULON

••••L•O
BABALOO
BACALAO
BUGALOO
CRIOLLO
FIDELIO
GALILEO
GERALDO
HIDALGO
MORELLO
MURILLO
NORELCO
OTHELLO
RODOLFO
UCCELLO
UTRILLO

•••••LO
BEEFALO
BUFFALO
CEMBALO
CRIOLLO
DECARLO
HANSOLO
MORELLO
MURILLO
NICCOLO
OTHELLO
PICCOLO
TANGELO
TIEPOLO
TREMOLO
UCCELLO
UTRILLO

L•P••••
LAPALMA
LAPBELT
LAPDOGS
LAPELED
LAPFULS
LAPLACE
LAPLAND
LAPLATA
LAPORTE
LAPPETS
LAPPING
LAPPISH
LAPROBE
LAPSING
LAPTOPS
LAPWING
LEPANTO
LEPPIES
LEPTONS
LIPBALM
LIPIDES
LIPLESS
LIPLIKE
LIPPIER
LIPPING
LIPREAD
LIPSYNC
LOPPERS
LOPPIER
LOPPING
LUPINES

L••P•••
LAMPOIL
LAMPOON
LAMPREY
LAPPETS
LAPPING
LAPPISH
LEAPERS
LEAPING
LEGPULL
LEIPZIG
LEMPIRA
LEOPARD
LEOPOLD
LEPPIES
LESPAUL
LIMPEST
LIMPETS
LIMPING
LIMPOPO
LINPIAO
LIPPIER
LIPPING
LISPING
LOOPERS
LOOPIER
LOOPING
LOPPERS
LOPPIER
LOPPING
LOWPAID
LUMPERS
LUMPIER
LUMPILY
LUMPING
LUMPISH
LUMPSUM

L•••P••
LAYOPEN
LEDUPTO
LETUPON
LILYPAD

L••••P•
LAPTOPS
LARRUPS
LASHUPS
LIMPOPO
LINEUPS
LINKUPS
LOCKUPS
LOLLOPS
LOOKUPS

L•••••P
LACEDUP
LACESUP
LEADSUP
LETSLIP
LIFTSUP
LIGHTUP
LINEDUP
LINESUP
LOCKSUP
LOOKSUP
LOUSEUP

•LP••••
ALPACAS

•L•P•••
BLIPPED
CLAPPED
CLAPPER
CLAPTON
CLIPART
CLIPONS
CLIPPED
CLIPPER
CLOPPED
ELAPIDS
ELAPSED
ELAPSES
ELOPERS
ELOPING
FLAPPED
FLAPPER
FLIPOUT
FLIPPED
FLIPPER
FLIPUPS
FLOPPED
FLYPAST
OLDPROS
PLOPPED
SLAPPED
SLEPTIN
SLEPTON
SLIPONS
SLIPOUT
SLIPPED
SLIPPER
SLIPSIN
SLIPSON
SLIPSUP
SLIPUPS
SLOPING
SLOPPED

•L••P••
BLEEPED
BLEEPER
BLIPPED
BLOOPED
BLOOPER
CLAMPED
CLAPPED
CLAPPER
CLASPED
CLIPPED
CLIPPER
CLOMPED
CLOPPED
CLUMPED
ELLIPSE
FLAPPED
FLAPPER
FLEAPIT
FLIPPED
FLIPPER
FLOPPED
GLIMPSE
OLYMPIA
OLYMPIC
OLYMPUS
PLAYPEN
PLOPPED
PLUMPED
PLUMPER
PLUMPLY
SLAPPED
SLEEPER
SLEEPIN
SLEEPON
SLIPPED
SLIPPER
SLOPPED
SLUMPED
SLURPED

•L•••P•
BLOWUPS
FLIPUPS
PLATYPI
SLIPUPS
SLOWUPS

•L••••P
BLOWNUP
BLOWSUP
CLAMSUP
CLEANUP
CLEARUP
CLOGSUP
CLOSEUP
FLAREUP
FLATTOP
FLYTRAP
OLDCHAP
PLAYSUP
SLIPSUP
SLOWSUP

••LP•••
CALPACS
CULPRIT
DELPHIC
DOLPHIN
GALPALS
GULPIER
GULPING
HELPERS
HELPFUL
HELPING
HELPOUT
KELPIES
OILPANS
PULPIER
PULPITS
SULPHUR
VOLPONE
VULPINE
WALPOLE
YELPERS
YELPING

••L•P••
BULLPEN
CALIPER
CALIPHS
CALYPSO
ECLIPSE
ELLIPSE
GOLFPRO
HELIPAD
LILYPAD
RELAPSE

••L••P•
CCLAMPS
COLLOPS
DOLLOPS
FILLIPS
FILLUPS
FOLDUPS
GALLOPS
GALUMPH
HOLDUPS
LOLLOPS
PILEUPS
PULLUPS
WALKUPS
WALLOPS

••L•••P
BALLSUP
BELLHOP
BELLYUP
CALLSUP
DOLLSUP
FILLSUP
FOLDSUP
HILLTOP
HOLDSUP
HOLEDUP
HOLESUP
MILKSOP
OILLAMP
PALMTOP
PILEDUP
PILESUP
PULLSUP
RILESUP
ROLLSUP
ROLLTOP
SPLITUP
TALKSUP
TALLYUP
WALLSUP
WELLSUP

•••LP••
ADOLPHE
BULLPEN
GUELPHS
SCALPED
SCALPEL
SCALPER
SCULPTS
WHELPED

•••L•P•
BURLAPS
COLLOPS
CYCLOPS
DEWLAPS
DOLLOPS
FILLIPS
FILLUPS
FOULUPS
GALLOPS
HOTLIPS
LOLLOPS
PULLUPS
SCHLEPP
SCHLEPS
WALLOPS

•••L••P
ARCLAMP
BALLSUP
BEDLAMP
BELLHOP
BELLYUP
BUILDUP
BUILTUP
CALLSUP
CHALKUP
COILSUP
CURLSUP
DOLLSUP
FILLSUP
FOULSUP
FOULTIP
HAULSUP
HEELTAP
HILLTOP
OILLAMP
PHILLIP
PULLSUP
ROLLSUP
ROLLTOP
SCALLOP
SCHLEPP
SEALSUP
SUNLAMP
SWELLUP
TALLYUP
TOELOOP
TOOLSUP
UNCLASP
WALLSUP
WELLSUP

••••LP•
CATALPA
RUDOLPH

••••L•P
COWSLIP
DEVELOP
EARFLAP
ENVELOP
KERPLOP
LETSLIP
NONSLIP
OVERLAP
PHARLAP
PHILLIP
SCALLOP
SWELLUP
TIECLIP

L•Q••••
LIQUEFY
LIQUEUR
LIQUIDS
LIQUORS
LOQUATS

L••Q•••
LACQUER

L•••Q••
LALIQUE

•L•Q•••
CLAQUES
CLIQUES
CLIQUEY
CLOQUES
PLAQUES

••LQ•••
PULQUES

••L•Q••
LALIQUE
OBLIQUE
OBLOQUY

••••LQ•
POSSLQS

L•R••••
LARAINE
LARAMIE
LARCENY
LARCHES
LARDERS
LARDIER
LARDING
LARDNER
LARDONS
LARGELY
LARGESS
LARGEST
LARGISH
LARIATS
LARKISH
LARRUPS
LORDING
LORDJIM
LORELEI
LORENZO
LORETTA
LORICAE
LORISES
LORRIES
LURCHED
LURCHES
LURIDLY
LURKING
LYRICAL
LYRISTS

L••R•••
LABRETS
LAERTES
LAPROBE
LARRUPS
LAURELS
LAURENT
LEARIER
LEARJET
LEARNED
LEARNER
LEERERS
LEERIER
LEERILY
LEERING
LEERSAT
LEGRAND
LEGROOM
LIBRARY
LIERNES
LIPREAD
LOGROLL
LORRIES
LOURDES
LOWRISE
LOWROAD

L•••R••
LABORED
LABORER
LAFARGE
LAMARCK
LAMPREY
LAPORTE
LASORDA
LATERAL
LATERAN
LATERON
LAUTREC
LAVERNE
LAYERED
LAZARUS
LEBARON
LECARRE
LETTRES
LEVERED
LEVERET
LIBERAL
LIBERIA
LIBERTY
LITCRIT
LITERAL
LITURGY
LIVORNO
LIZARDS
LOCARNO
LONGRUN
LOUVRED
LOUVRES
LOVERLY
LOWBRED
LOWBROW
LOWERED
LUCERNE
LUSTRED
LUSTRES

L••••R•
LAAGERS
LABOURS
LADDERS
LADLERS
LAGGARD
LAGGERS
LAMBERT
LANCERS
LANDERS
LANFORD
LANGTRY
LANGURS
LANTERN
LANYARD
LARDERS
LASHERS
LASTORY
LATHERS
LATHERY
LAUNDRY
LAWFORD
LAWYERS
LEADERS
LEAKERS
LEANERS
LEAPERS
LEASERS
LECARRE
LECTERN
LECTORS
LECTURE
LEDGERS
LEERERS
LEEWARD
LEGHORN
LEGWORK
LEHAVRE
LEISURE
LEKVARS
LEMPIRA
LENDERS
LEONARD
LEONORA
LEOPARD
LEOTARD
LESSORS
LETTERS
LEVIERS
LIBBERS
LIBRARY
LICTORS
LIFTERS
LIMBERS
LIMNERS
LINGERS
LINKERS
LIQUORS
LITTERS
LOADERS
LOAFERS
LOANERS
LOBBERS
LOCKERS
LODGERS
LOGGERS
LOITERS
LOLLARD
LOMBARD
LONGARM
LOOKERS
LOOPERS
LOOTERS
LOPPERS
LOTTERY
LOUVERS
LOWBORN
LUBBERS
LUGGERS
LUMBARS
LUMBERS
LUMIERE
LUMPERS
LUNKERS
LUSTERS

L•••••R
LABELER
LABORER
LACQUER
LAIDFOR
LALAKER
LAMINAR
LANGUOR
LANKIER
LARDIER
LARDNER
LASSOER
LAUGHER
LAUNDER
LAYOVER
LAYSFOR
LEADIER
LEAFIER
LEAKIER
LEANDER
LEARIER
LEARNER
LEATHER
LEDGIER
LEERIER
LEGGIER
LEISTER
LEVELER
LIBELER
LIEOVER
LIGHTER
LINTIER
LIPPIER
LIQUEUR
LITTLER
LOAMIER
LOBBYER
LOBSTER
LOCATER
LOCATOR
LOESSER
LOFTIER
LOOKFOR
LOONIER
LOOPIER
LOPPIER
LOUNGER
LOUSIER
LOWGEAR
LOWLIER
LUCIFER
LUCKIER
LUMPIER
LUSTIER

•LR••••
ALREADY
ALRIGHT

•L•R•••
ALARCON
ALARMED
ALARMER
ALARUMS
ALDRICH
ALERTED
ALERTER
ALERTLY
ALFREDO
BLARING
BLARNEY
BLERIOT
BLURRED
BLURTED
CLARETS
CLARICE
CLARIFY
CLARION
CLARITY
CLERICS
CLERISY
CLERKED
CLORETS
ELGRECO
FLAREUP
FLARING
FLIRTED
FLORETS
FLORIDA
FLORINS
FLORIST
FLORUIT
FLYRODS
GLARING
GLORIAM
GLORIAS
GLORIED
GLORIES
GLORIFY
OLDROSE
OLOROSO
PLURALS
SLURPED
SLURRED

•L••R••
ALBERTA
ALBERTO
ALFORJA
ALGERIA
ALLERGY
ALLURED
ALLURES
ALSORAN
ALTERED
ALTERER
ALVAREZ
ALWORTH
BLEARED
BLURRED
CLAIROL
CLEARED
CLEARER
CLEARLY
CLEARUP
ELDERLY
ELMTREE
FLOORED
FLOURED
FLYTRAP
GLAIRED
ILLBRED
OLDPROS
SLURRED

•L•••R•
ALFIERI
ALGEBRA
ALGIERS
ALLEARS
ALLEGRO
ALLHERE
BLADERS
BLAZERS
BLOWDRY
BLOWERS
CLAMORS
CLAWERS
CLIBURN
CLIPART
CLOSURE
CLOTURE
CLOVERS
ELATERS
ELECTRA
ELECTRO
ELEKTRA
ELIXIRS
ELKHART
ELOPERS
ELUSORY
FLAKERS
FLAVORS
FLEXORS

FLOWERS
FLOWERY
GLAZERS
GLIDERS
GLOWERS
OLESTRA
PLACARD
PLACERS
PLANERS
PLATERS
PLAYERS
PLECTRA
PLENARY
PLEXORS
PLOVERS
PLOWERS
SLAVERS
SLAVERY
SLAYERS
SLICERS
SLIDERS
SLIVERS
ULSTERS

•L••••R

ALARMER
ALCAZAR
ALERTER
ALIENOR
ALIGNER
ALLAYER
ALLEGER
ALLOVER
ALLSTAR
ALTERER
ALUNSER
BLABBER
BLACKER
BLADDER
BLANDER
BLANKER
BLASTER
BLATHER
BLEAKER
BLEEPER
BLENDER
BLINDER
BLINKER
BLISTER
BLITHER
BLOCKER
BLONDER
BLOOMER
BLOOPER
BLOTTER
BLOWIER
BLUBBER
BLUFFER
BLUNDER
BLUNTER
BLUSHER
BLUSTER
CLABBER
CLAIMER
CLAMBER
CLAMMER
CLAMOUR
CLANGOR
CLAPPER
CLATTER
CLAVIER
CLAYIER
CLEANER
CLEARER
CLEAVER
CLIMBER
CLINKER
CLIPPER
CLOBBER
CLOCKER
CLOWDER
CLUBCAR
CLUNKER
CLUSTER
CLUTTER
ELEANOR
ELECTOR
FLAKIER
FLAMIER
FLANEUR
FLANKER
FLAPPER
FLASHER
FLATCAR
FLATTER
FLAVOUR
FLAXIER
FLEETER
FLEXNER
FLICKER
FLIPPER
FLITTER
FLIVVER
FLOATER
FLUBBER
FLUKIER
FLUSTER
FLUTIER
FLUTTER
FLYOVER
GLACIER
GLADDER
GLAMOUR
GLAZIER
GLEANER
GLIBBER
GLIMMER
GLITTER
GLUMMER
OLDSTER
OLIVIER
PLAINER
PLANNER
PLANTAR
PLANTER
PLASTER
PLATIER
PLATTER
PLEADER
PLEASER
PLEDGER
PLODDER
PLOTTER
PLUGGER
PLUMBER
PLUMIER
PLUMMER
PLUMPER
PLUNDER
PLUNGER
PLUSHER
SLACKER
SLAMMER
SLANDER
SLASHER
SLATHER
SLATIER
SLEDDER
SLEEKER
SLEEPER
SLENDER
SLICKER
SLIMIER
SLIMMER
SLINGER
SLIPPER
SLITHER
SLOBBER
SLOTCAR
SLUGGER
SLUMBER

••LR•••

BULRUSH
MALRAUX
MELROSE
OILRIGS

••L•R••

AELFRIC
AILERON
ALLERGY
ALLURED
ALLURES
ATLARGE
BALDRIC
BOLEROS
BULLRUN
CALDRON
CALORIC
CALORIE
CHLORAL
COLORED
CULPRIT
DALTREY
DELIRIA
DOLORES
ENLARGE
FULCRUM
ILLBRED
MALLRAT
MILDRED
MILKRUN
MILLRUN
MILORDS
PALERMO
PALFREY
PALTROW
PILGRIM
POLARIS
SALERNO
SCLERAS
SOLARIA
SPLURGE
TALARIA
TELERAN
VALERIE
WELLRUN
WILFRID
WOLFRAM

••L••R•

ALLEARS
ALLEGRO
ALLHERE
BALLARD
BULGARS
BULWARK
CALDERA
CALGARY
CALIBRE
CALLERS
CALVARY
CALVERT
CELEBRE
CELLARS
COLBERT
COLLARD
COLLARS
COLOURS
CULEBRA
CULLERS
CULTURE
CULVERS
CULVERT
DELVERS
DILBERT
DILLARD
DOLLARS
DOLOURS
DULLARD
ECLAIRS
FALTERS
FELLERS
FILBERT
FILLERS
FILTERS
FOLDERS
FOLGERS
FOLKART
GALLERY
GILBERT
GILDERS
GOLFERS
GOLFPRO
HALTERS
HALYARD
HELLERS
HELOTRY
HELPERS
HILAIRE
HILLARY
HOLDERS
HOLLERS
HOLYARK
HULLERS
KILDARE
KILLERS
LOLLARD
MALLARD
MILKERS
MILLARD
MILLERS
MOLDERS
MOLIERE
MOLTERS
MULLERS
PALEDRY
PALLORS
PALMARY
PALTERS
PELTERS
PILFERS
PILLARS
PILLORY
POLDERS
POLLERS
PULSARS
RELEARN
ROLLERS
SALIERI
SALTERS
SALVERS
SALVORS
SELKIRK
SELLERS
SILVERS
SILVERY
SOLDERS
SOLVERS
SULKERS
TALKERS
TELLERS
TILLERS
TILTERS
UNLEARN
VALOURS
VELOURS
VULTURE
WALDORF
WALKERS
WALMART
WALTERS
WELDERS
WELFARE
WELTERS
WILFORD
WILLARD
YELLERS
YELPERS

••L•••R

ALLAYER
ALLEGER
ALLOVER
ALLSTAR
BALFOUR
BALKIER
BALMIER
BELABOR
BELLJAR
BILGIER
BOLIVAR
BOLSTER
BULGHUR
BULGIER
BULKIER
CALIBER
CALIPER
CALLFOR
COLDWAR
COLLIER
COLLYER
DALLIER
DELAYER
DELIVER
DILUTER
FALLFOR
FELLFOR
FELTFOR
FILCHER
FILMIER
FOLKIER
GULPIER
HILLIER
HOLSTER
HOLYWAR
JOLLIER
JOLTIER
LALAKER
MALABAR
MALODOR
MALTIER
MILKIER
MOLDIER
PALAVER
PALLIER
PALMIER
PALOMAR
PILSNER
POLECAR
POLITER
POLYMER
PULLFOR
PULPIER
RALLIER
ROLLBAR
SALAZAR
SALTIER
SELLFOR
SELTZER
SILKIER
SILLIER
SILTIER
SOLDIER
SOLIDER
SPLICER
SULKIER
SULPHUR
TALKIER
TALLIER
TELSTAR
WALTZER

•••LR••

BULLRUN
FUELROD
MALLRAT
MILLRUN
WELLRUN

•••L•R•

ABELARD
AMBLERS
ANGLERS
ANTLERS
ASHLARS
BAILERS
BAILORS
BALLARD
BAWLERS
BOILERS
BOWLERS
BUGLERS
BUTLERS
CABLERS
CALLERS
CELLARS
COALERS
COLLARD
COLLARS
COOLERS
CULLERS
CURLERS
CUTLERS
CUTLERY
CYCLERS
DEALERS
DECLARE
DEKLERK
DEPLORE
DIALERS
DILLARD
DOLLARS
DUELERS
DULLARD
EXPLORE
FABLERS
FAILURE
FEELERS
FELLERS
FILLERS
FOOLERY
FORLORN
FOULARD
FOWLERS
FUELERS
GALLERY
GAOLERS
HAULERS
HEALERS
HEELERS
HELLERS
HILLARY
HOLLERS
HOWLERS
HULLERS
HURLERS
IMPLORE
JAILERS
KEGLERS
KILLERS
LADLERS
LOLLARD
MAILERS
MALLARD
MCCLURE
MEWLERS
MILLARD
MILLERS
MOILERS
MULLERS
NAILERS
OSTLERS
PALLORS
PARLORS
PEDLARS
PEELERS
PHILTRE
PILLARS
PILLORY
POLLERS
POPLARS
POULTRY
RAILERS
RIFLERS
RIFLERY
ROLLERS
SAILORS
SCALARS
SCALERS
SEALERS
SELLERS
SKYLARK
SMILERS
STYLERS
SUTLERS
SWELTRY
TAILORS
TELLERS
THALERS
TILLERS
TOILERS
WAILERS
WARLORD
WHALERS
WILLARD
YELLERS
YOWLERS

•••L••R

ATELIER
BELLJAR
BOULDER
BUILDER
BURLIER
CALLFOR
CAULKER
CHILLER
COALCAR
COALTAR
COLLIER
COLLYER
COULTER
CRULLER
CURLIER
DALLIER
DRILLER
DROLLER
DWELLER
EARLIER
EVILLER
FALLFOR
FEELFOR
FELLFOR
FIELDER
GODLIER
GROLIER
GUILDER
HILLIER
JOLLIER
JOWLIER
KEILLOR
LOWLIER
MAILCAR
MANLIER
MEALIER
MOULDER
NUCLEAR
PALLIER
PARLOUR
PHILTER
PSALTER
PULLFOR
QUILLER
QUILTER
RALLIER
REALTOR
ROILIER
ROLLBAR
SCALIER
SCALPER
SCOLDER
SCULLER
SELLFOR
SHELLER
SHELTER
SILLIER
SKELTER
SKULKER
SMALLER
SMELTER
SMOLDER
SPELLER
STALKER
STELLAR
STILLER
STOLLER
SURLIER
SVELTER
SWELTER
TALLIER
UNCLEAR
VAULTER
VEALIER
WOOLIER
ZOELLER

••••LR•

CAVALRY
DEVILRY
JEWELRY
REVELRY
RIVALRY

••••L•R

ANGULAR
ANNULAR
AREOLAR
BAFFLER
BATTLER
BICOLOR
BIPOLAR
BOGGLER
BOOSLER
BOTTLER
BOWDLER
BRAWLER
BROILER
BUCKLER
BUMBLER
BUNGLER
BURGLAR
CACKLER
CAJOLER
CAROLER
CAVILER
CHILLER
COBBLER
CODDLER
CRAWLER
CRUELER
CRULLER
CUSSLER
DABBLER
DAIMLER
DANGLER
DAWDLER
DAZZLER
DEFILER
DIPOLAR
DOODLER
DOPPLER
DRILLER
DROLLER
DROOLER
DWELLER
EVILLER
FEEBLER
FICKLER
FIDDLER
FIEDLER
FRAILER
FUMBLER
GAMBLER
GENTLER
GIGGLER
GOBBLER
GROWLER
GUZZLER
HAGGLER
HANDLER
HECKLER
HOSTLER
HUMBLER
HURDLER
HUSTLER
INHALER
INSULAR
JEWELER
JOCULAR
JOSTLER
JUGGLER
JUGULAR
KEEBLER
KEILLOR
KNEELER
LABELER
LEVELER
LIBELER
LITTLER
MEDDLER
MINGLER
MODELER
MODULAR
MUDDLER
MUFFLER
MUMBLER
NEBULAR
NESTLER
NIBBLER
NIMBLER
NOBBLER
NODULAR
NUZZLER
PADDLER
PEDDLER
POPULAR
PROWLER
PUZZLER
QUILLER
RAFFLER
RAMBLER
RATTLER
RECOLOR
REGULAR
REVELER
RIDDLER
RUSTLER
SADDLER
SAMPLER
SCHOLAR
SCOWLER
SCULLER
SECULAR
SETTLER
SHELLER
SIMILAR
SIMPLER
SMALLER
SPELLER
SPIELER
SPOILER
SQUALOR
STABLER
STAPLER
STEELER
STELLAR
STILLER
STOLLER
SUBTLER
SUPPLER
TABULAR
TACKLER
TATTLER
TEMBLOR
TEMPLAR
TICKLER
TIPPLER
TITULAR
TODDLER
TOFFLER
TRAILER
TRAWLER
TRIFLER
TUBULAR
TUMBLER
TUTELAR
TWIRLER
WADDLER
WAFFLER
WANGLER
WARBLER
WHEELER
WIGGLER
WINKLER
YODELER
ZOELLER

L•S••••

LASAGNA
LASAGNE
LASALLE
LASCALA
LASCAUX
LASHERS
LASHING
LASHUPS
LASORDA
LASSIES
LASSOED
LASSOER
LASSOES
LASTING
LASTORY
LESOTHO
LESPAUL
LESSEES
LESSENS
LESSING
LESSONS
LESSORS
LISENTE
LISPING
LISSOME
LISTEES
LISTELS
LISTENS
LISTING
LOSEOUT
LOSESIT
LOSTOUT
LUSHEST
LUSTERS
LUSTFUL
LUSTIER
LUSTILY
LUSTING
LUSTRED
LUSTRES
LYSENKO

L••S•••

LAISSEZ
LAKSHMI
LANSING
LAPSING
LASSIES
LASSOED
LASSOER
LASSOES
LAWSUIT
LAYSFOR
LAYSLOW
LAYSOFF
LAYSOUT
LEASERS
LEASHED
LEASHES
LEASING
LEISTER
LEISURE
LESSEES
LESSENS
LESSING
LESSONS
LESSORS
LETSFLY
LETSLIP
LETSOFF
LETSOUT
LETSSEE
LIESLOW
LINSEED
LIPSYNC
LISSOME
LOBSTER
LOESSER
LOESSES
LOGSOFF
LOGSOUT
LOOSELY
LOOSENS
LOOSEST
LOOSING
LOUSEUP
LOUSIER
LOUSILY
LOUSING

L•••S••

LACESUP
LACOSTE
LAISSEZ
LANDSAT
LATOSCA
LEADSIN
LEADSON
LEADSTO
LEADSUP
LEANSON
LEERSAT
LEGISTS
LETSSEE
LIAISED
LIAISES
LIAISON
LIFTSUP
LINDSAY
LINDSEY
LINESUP
LIVESIN
LIVESON
LOCKSON
LOCKSUP
LOCUSTS
LOESSER
LOESSES
LOOKSAT
LOOKSEE
LOOKSIN
LOOKSON
LOOKSTO
LOOKSUP
LORISES
LOSESIT
LOTUSES
LUMPSUM
LUTISTS
LYRISTS

L••••S•

LACIEST
LACTASE
LACTOSE
LADDISH
LADYISH
LAKIEST
LAMAISM
LAMAIST
LANKEST
LAPPISH
LARGESS
LARGEST
LARGISH
LARKISH
LAVALSE
LAWLESS
LAXNESS
LAZIEST
LAZYISH
LEANEST
LEFTIST
LEGLESS
LETTISH
LEWDEST
LICENSE
LIDLESS
LIMIEST
LIMPEST
LINIEST
LIONESS
LIONISE
LIPLESS
LITHEST
LOGGISH
LOGIEST
LONGEST
LONGISH
LOOSEST
LOUDEST
LOUDISH
LOUTISH
LOWCOST
LOWNESS
LOWRISE
LUMPISH
LUSHEST

L•••••S

LAAGERS
LABIALS
LABOURS
LABRETS
LACINGS
LACKEYS
LACUNAS
LADDERS
LADDIES
LADINOS
LADLERS
LAERTES
LAGGERS
LAGOONS
LAGUNAS
LAKOTAS
LAMBDAS
LAMEDHS
LAMENTS
LAMINAS
LANCERS
LANCETS
LANDAUS
LANDERS
LANGURS
LAPDOGS
LAPFULS
LAPPETS
LAPTOPS
LARCHES
LARDERS
LARDONS
LARGESS
LARIATS
LARRUPS
LASHERS
LASHUPS
LASSIES
LASSOES
LATCHES
LATEENS
LATENTS
LATEXES
LATHERS
LATICES
LATINAS
LATINOS
LATTENS
LAURELS
LAWLESS
LAWYERS
LAXNESS
LAYOFFS
LAYOUTS
LAZARUS
LEACHES
LEADERS
LEADINS
LEAGUES
LEAKERS
LEANERS
LEANTOS
LEAPERS
LEASERS
LEASHES
LEAVENS
LECTORS
LEDGERS
LEECHES
LEERERS
LEFTIES
LEGATES
LEGATOS
LEGENDS
LEGIONS
LEGISTS
LEGLESS
LEGUMES
LEKVARS
LENDERS
LENGTHS
LENTILS
LEONIDS
LEPPIES
LEPTONS
LESSEES
LESSENS
LESSONS
LESSORS
LETTERS
LETTRES
LEVANTS
LEVIERS
LEVITES
LEXEMES
LIAISES
LIBBERS
LIBIDOS
LIBYANS
LICHENS
LICTORS
LIDLESS
LIENEES
LIERNES
LIFTERS
LIGANDS

LIGATES
LIMBERS
LIMNERS
LIMOGES
LIMPETS
LINAGES
LINDENS
LINDIES
LINEUPS
LINGERS
LINGOES
LININGS
LINKERS
LINKUPS
LINNETS
LINTELS
LIONESS
LIONETS
LIPIDES
LIPLESS
LIQUIDS
LIQUORS
LISTEES
LISTELS
LISTENS
LITCHIS
LITOTES
LITTERS
LIVINGS
LIZARDS
LOACHES
LOADERS
LOAFERS
LOANERS
LOATHES
LOBBERS
LOBBIES
LOBULES
LOCALES
LOCATES
LOCKERS
LOCKETS
LOCKINS
LOCKUPS
LOCUSTS
LODGERS
LOESSES
LOGGERS
LOGGIAS
LOGGINS
LOGJAMS
LOITERS
LOLLIES
LOLLOPS
LONGIES
LONGUES
LOOBIES
LOOFAHS
LOOKERS
LOOKUPS
LOONEYS
LOONIES
LOOPERS
LOOSENS
LOOTERS
LOPPERS
LOQUATS
LORISES
LORRIES
LOTIONS
LOTUSES
LOUNGES
LOURDES
LOUVERS
LOUVRES
LOVEINS
LOWBOYS
LOWNESS
LUBBERS
LUGGERS
LUGNUTS
LUMBARS
LUMBERS
LUMPERS
LUNCHES
LUNKERS
LUPINES
LURCHES
LUSTERS
LUSTRES
LUTISTS
LUXATES
LYCEUMS
LYRISTS

•LS••••
ALSATIA
ALSORAN
ULSTERS

•L•S•••
ALASKAN
ALLSTAR
ALLSTON
ALYSSUM
BLASTED
BLASTER
BLESSED
BLESSES
BLISTER
BLOSSOM
BLUSHED
BLUSHER
BLUSHES
BLUSHON
BLUSTER
CLASHED
CLASHES
CLASPED
CLASSED
CLASSES
CLASSIC
CLOSEBY
CLOSEIN
CLOSELY
CLOSEST
CLOSETS
CLOSEUP
CLOSING
CLOSURE
CLUSTER
ELASTIC
ELISION
ELUSIVE
ELUSORY
ELYSEES
ELYSIAN
ELYSIUM
FLASHED
FLASHER
FLASHES
FLESHED
FLESHES
FLESHLY
FLOSSED
FLOSSES
FLUSHED
FLUSHES
FLUSTER
GLASGOW
GLASSED
GLASSES
GLISTEN
GLOSSAE
GLOSSED
GLOSSES
OLDSAWS
OLDSTER
OLESTRA
PLASHED
PLASHES
PLASMAS
PLASTER
PLASTIC
PLOSION
PLOSIVE
PLUSHER
PLUSHES
PLUSHLY
PLUSSES
SLASHED
SLASHER
SLASHES
SLOSHED
SLOSHES
SLUSHES
ULYSSES

•L••S••
ALIASES
ALLISON
ALLYSON
ALTOSAX
ALUNSER
ALYOSHA
ALYSSUM
BLESSED
BLESSES
BLOSSOM
BLOUSED
BLOUSES
BLOUSON
BLOWSIN
BLOWSIT
BLOWSUP
BLUESKY
CLAMSUP
CLASSED
CLASSES
CLASSIC
CLAUSES
CLEMSON
CLOGSUP
CLUESIN
ELAPSED
ELAPSES
ELEISON
ELLISON
ELMISTI
FLENSED
FLENSES
FLIESAT
FLIESIN
FLOSSED
FLOSSES
FLOTSAM
GLASSED
GLASSES
GLEASON
GLOSSAE
GLOSSED
GLOSSES
GLUESON
ILIESCU
ILLUSED
ILLUSES
KLATSCH
PLANSON
PLAYSAT
PLAYSON
PLAYSUP
PLEASED
PLEASER
PLEASES
PLUGSIN
PLUSSES
SLIPSIN
SLIPSON
SLIPSUP
SLOWSUP
ULYSSES

•L•••S•
ALFONSO
BLEMISH
BLUEISH
CLAYISH
CLEANSE
CLERISY
CLOSEST
ELEGIST
ELITISM
ELITIST
ELLIPSE
FLEMISH
FLORIST
FLUTIST
FLYCAST
FLYFISH
FLYLESS
FLYPAST
GLIMPSE
GLUCOSE
GLUIEST
ILLNESS
OLDNESS
OLDROSE
OLDWEST
OLEMISS
OLOROSO
PLANISH
SLAVISH
SLOWEST
SLYNESS

•L••••S
ALARUMS
ALBEDOS
ALBINOS
ALCOVES
ALGIERS
ALIASES
ALIGHTS
ALKALIS
ALKENES
ALLEARS
ALLEGES
ALLELES
ALLEYES
ALLUDES
ALLURES
ALMONDS
ALPACAS
ALUMNUS
BLADERS
BLAZERS
BLAZONS
BLESSES
BLIGHTS
BLITZES
BLONDES
BLOUSES
BLOWERS
BLOWUPS
BLUSHES
CLAMORS
CLAQUES
CLARETS
CLASHES
CLASSES
CLAUSES
CLAWERS
CLEAVES
CLEMENS
CLERICS
CLICHES
CLIENTS
CLINICS
CLIPONS
CLIQUES
CLOACAS
CLOCHES
CLOQUES
CLORETS
CLOSETS
CLOTHES
CLOVERS
ELAPIDS
ELAPSES
ELATERS
ELEGIES
ELEVENS
ELICITS
ELIXIRS
ELOIGNS
ELOPERS
ELYSEES
FLACONS
FLAGONS
FLAKERS
FLAMBES
FLANGES
FLASHES
FLAUNTS
FLAVORS
FLECHES
FLEDGES
FLEECES
FLENSES
FLESHES
FLEXORS
FLIGHTS
FLIPUPS
FLORETS
FLORINS
FLOSSES
FLOWERS
FLUSHES
FLYBOYS
FLYLESS
FLYNETS
FLYRODS
FLYWAYS
GLANCES
GLASSES
GLAZERS
GLIDERS
GLITZES
GLORIAS
GLORIES
GLOSSES
GLOTTIS
GLOWERS
ILLNESS
ILLUDES
ILLUMES
ILLUSES
KLAXONS
KLUDGES
KLUTZES
OLDDAYS
OLDNESS
OLDNEWS
OLDPROS
OLDSAWS
OLEATES
OLEFINS
OLEMISS
OLYMPUS
PLACERS
PLAGUES
PLAICES
PLAINTS
PLANERS
PLANETS
PLAQUES
PLASHES
PLASMAS
PLATENS
PLATERS
PLAUTUS
PLAYERS
PLEASES
PLEDGES
PLENUMS
PLEXORS
PLIGHTS
PLINTHS
PLOUGHS
PLOVERS
PLOWERS
PLUGINS
PLUNGES
PLURALS
PLUSHES
PLUSSES
SLALOMS
SLASHES
SLAVERS
SLAVEYS
SLAYERS
SLEDGES
SLEEVES
SLEIGHS
SLEUTHS
SLICERS
SLIDERS
SLIGHTS
SLIPONS
SLIPUPS
SLIVERS
SLOGANS
SLOSHES
SLOUGHS
SLOVAKS
SLOVENS
SLOWUPS
SLUDGES
SLUICES
SLUSHES
SLYNESS
ULSTERS
ULTIMAS
ULYSSES

••LS•••
ALLSTAR
ALLSTON
BALSAMS
BOLSHOI
BOLSTER
CELSIUS
EELSKIN
FALSELY
FALSEST
FALSIFY
FALSITY
FULSOME
HALSTON
HOLSTER
NELSONS
NILSSON
OILSKIN
PILSNER
PULSARS
PULSATE
PULSING
RALSTON
SALSIFY
SALSODA
TELSTAR
TOLSTOI
TOLSTOY
TULSANS
WALSTON

••L•S••
ALLISON
ALLYSON
ATLASES
BALLSUP
BELASCO
BELUSHI
BOLUSES
CALLSIN
CALLSON
CALLSUP
CELESTA
CELESTE
COLOSSI
DELISTS
DOLLSUP
ELLISON
ENLISTS
FALLSIN
FALLSON
FALLSTO
FILLSIN
FILLSUP
FOLDSUP
HOLDSIN
HOLDSON
HOLDSTO
HOLDSUP
HOLESUP
HOLISTS
HOLYSEE
ILLUSED
ILLUSES
JALISCO
MALMSEY
MELISSA
MILKSOP
MOLESTS
NILSSON
OBLASTS
PELISSE
PILESIN
PILESON
PILESUP
PULASKI
PULLSIN
PULLSON
PULLSUP
RELISTS
RILESUP
ROLLSIN
ROLLSON
ROLLSUP
RULESON
SILESIA
SPLASHY
SULUSEA
TALKSAT
TALKSTO
TALKSUP
TALUSES
TELLSOF
TELLSON
VALISES
WALKSON
WALLSUP
WELLSET
WELLSUP
WILLSON
YELLSAT
YELTSIN

••L••S•
ATLEAST
BALDEST
BALDISH
BALLAST
BELFAST
BOLDEST
BULLISH
BULRUSH
CALMEST
CALYPSO
CELLIST
COLDEST
COLDISH
COLOSSI
COLTISH
CULTISH
CULTISM
CULTIST
DELUISE
DOLLISH
DOLTISH
DULLEST
DULLISH
ECLIPSE
EELIEST
ELLIPSE
FALSEST
FOLKISH
FULLEST
HELLISH
HELOISE
HOLIEST
ILLNESS
MALAISE
MALTESE
MALTOSE
MELISSA
MELROSE
MILDEST
MOLLUSC
MOLLUSK
OILIEST
OILLESS
PALIEST
PALMIST
PELISSE
PELTISH
POLOIST
RELAPSE
RELEASE
SALTISH
SELFISH
SOLOIST
TALLEST
TALLISH
UGLIEST
UNLEASH
UNLOOSE
WILDEST
WILDISH
WILIEST
WOLFISH

••L•••S
ABLATES
ABLAUTS
ALLEARS
ALLEGES
ALLELES
ALLEYES
ALLUDES
ALLURES
ATLASES
ATLATLS
BALBOAS
BALEENS
BALKANS
BALLADS
BALLETS
BALLOTS
BALSAMS
BELCHES
BELDAMS
BELIEFS
BELLIES
BELLOWS
BELONGS
BILBIES
BILBOES
BILIOUS
BILLETS
BILLIES
BILLOWS
BOLEROS
BOLIDES
BOLUSES
BULBOUS
BULBULS
BULGARS
BULLETS
BULLIES
BYLINES
CALENDS
CALICES
CALICOS
CALIPHS
CALKINS
CALLERS
CALLINS
CALLOUS
CALPACS
CALYCES
CALYXES
CCLAMPS
CELEBES
CELLARS
CELSIUS
CELTICS
COLLARS
COLLETS
COLLIES
COLLINS
COLLOPS
COLOBUS
COLONES
COLOURS
COLUMNS
CSLEWIS
CULLERS
CULLIES
CULVERS
DALETHS
DALLIES
DELETES
DELIBES
DELICTS
DELISTS
DELUDES
DELUGES
DELVERS
DILATES
DILLIES
DILUTES
DOLLARS
DOLLIES
DOLLOPS
DOLMANS
DOLMENS
DOLORES
DOLOURS
ECLAIRS
ENLACES
ENLISTS
EOLITHS
FALCONS
FALLOWS
FALTERS
FELINES
FELLAHS
FELLERS
FELLIES
FELLOWS
FILCHES
FILENES
FILINGS
FILLERS
FILLETS
FILLIES
FILLINS
FILLIPS
FILLUPS
FILTERS
FOLDERS
FOLDUPS
FOLGERS
FOLKIES
FOLLIES
FOLLOWS
FULFILS
GALAGOS
GALLEYS
GALLONS
GALLOPS
GALOOTS
GALPALS
GELADAS
GELATIS
GILBLAS
GILDERS
GILGUYS
GILLIES
GOLFERS
GULCHES
GULLAHS
GULLETS
GULLIES
HALIDES
HALITES
HALLOWS
HALTERS
HALVAHS
HELICES
HELIXES
HELLERS
HELMETS
HELPERS
HOLDERS
HOLDUPS
HOLISTS
HOLLERS
HOLLIES
HOLLOWS
HULLERS
HULLOAS
ILLNESS
ILLUDES
ILLUMES
ILLUSES
ISLANDS
JELLIES
JOLLIES
KELPIES
KILLERS
KILTIES
KYLIKES
LOLLIES
LOLLOPS
MALIGNS
MALKINS
MALLETS
MALLOWS
MALTEDS
MALTHUS
MELLOWS
MILDEWS
MILIEUS
MILKERS
MILLERS
MILLETS
MILORDS
MOLDERS
MOLESTS
MOLOCHS
MOLTERS
MULCHES
MULETAS
MULLAHS
MULLERS
MULLETS
NELSONS
NULLAHS
OBLASTS
OBLATES
OBLIGES
OBLONGS
OGLALAS
OILCANS
OILLESS
OILPANS
OILRIGS
OOLITES
OOLITHS
ORLEANS
PALACES
PALATES
PALLETS
PALLORS
PALTERS
PELAGES
PELLETS
PELOTAS
PELTERS
PHLOXES
PILEUPS
PILFERS
PILINGS
PILLARS
PILLOWS
POLARIS
POLDERS
POLICES
POLLENS
POLLERS
PULLETS
PULLEYS
PULLINS
PULLONS
PULLUPS
PULPITS
PULQUES
PULSARS
RALLIES
RELACES
RELATES
RELAXES
RELENTS
RELICTS
RELIEFS
RELINES
RELISTS
RELIVES
RELOADS
RELOCKS
RELUCTS
RELUMES
RILLETS
ROLAIDS
ROLLERS
ROLLINS
RULINGS
SALAAMS
SALAMIS
SALINAS
SALLETS
SALLIES
SALLOWS
SALMONS
SALOONS
SALTERS
SALUKIS
SALUTES
SALVERS
SALVIAS
SALVOES
SALVORS
SCLERAS
SELECTS
SELLERS
SILENTS
SILICAS
SILLIES
SILVERS
SOLACES
SOLDERS
SOLUTES
SOLVERS
SPLEENS
SPLICES
SPLINES
SPLINTS
STLOUIS
SULKERS
SULKIES
SULLIES
SULTANS
SYLVANS
TALCUMS
TALENTS
TALKERS
TALKIES
TALLIES
TALLOWS
TALUSES
TELEXES
TELLERS
TELLIES
TILINGS
TILLERS
TILTERS
TOLLIES
TOLTECS
TULSANS
UMLAUTS
UNLACES
UNLADES
UNLINKS
UNLOADS
UNLOCKS
UPLANDS
UPLIFTS
UPLINKS
UPLOADS
VALISES
VALLEYS
VALOURS
VELLUMS
VELOURS
VELVETS
VILNIUS
VOLLEYS
VOLUMES
VULCANS
WALKERS
WALKINS
WALKONS
WALKUPS
WALLETS
WALLOPS
WALLOWS
WALNUTS
WALTERS
WALTZES
WELCHES
WELDERS
WELKINS
WELTERS
WILLETS
WILLIES
WILLOWS
YELLERS
YELLOWS
YELPERS
ZILCHES

•••LS••
ARALSEA
AVULSED
AVULSES
BALLSUP
CALLSIN
CALLSON
CALLSUP
CARLSON
CHELSEA
COILSUP
COOLSIT
CURLSUP
DEALSIN
DOLLSUP
EVULSED
EVULSES
FALLSIN
FALLSON
FALLSTO
FILLSIN
FILLSUP
FOULSUP
HAULSUP
MAILSIN
NAILSET
NAILSIN
NIELSEN
PAULSEN
PULLSIN
PULLSON
PULLSUP
RAILSAT
REELSIN
ROLLSIN
ROLLSON
ROLLSUP
SEALSUP
TELLSOF
TELLSON
TOOLSUP
WALLSUP
WELLSET
WELLSUP
WILLSON
WOOLSEY
YELLSAT

•••L•S•
ABOLISH
AGELESS
AIDLESS
AIMLESS
AIRLESS
AMPLEST
AMYLASE
ANALYSE
ANALYST
ARMLESS
ARTLESS
ASHLESS
ATALOSS
AWELESS
AWNLESS
BALLAST
BARLESS
BEDLESS
BIBLESS
BITLESS
BOWLESS
BRALESS
BUDLESS
BULLISH
CAPLESS
CARLESS
CELLIST
COOLEST
COOLISH
CUTLASS
CYCLIST
DECLASS
DEWLESS
DOGLESS
DOLLISH

DUELIST
DULLEST
DULLISH
EARLESS
EGGLESS
ENCLOSE
ENDLESS
ENGLISH
EVILEST
EYELASH
EYELESS
FATLESS
FEELESS
FLYLESS
FOGLESS
FOOLISH
FOULEST
FULLEST
FURLESS
GAPLESS
GASLESS
GAULISH
GEMLESS
GETLOST
GIRLISH
GODLESS
GOTLOST
GOULASH
GUMLESS
GUNLESS
GUTLESS
HAPLESS
HATLESS
HELLISH
HIPLESS
HITLESS
HITLIST
HUELESS
ICELESS
IDOLISE
INCLOSE
INKLESS
INNLESS
IRELESS
JAGLESS
JARLESS
JAWLESS
JOBLESS
JOYLESS
KEYLESS
KINLESS
LAWLESS
LEGLESS
LIDLESS
LIPLESS
MANLESS
MATLESS
MOLLUSC
MOLLUSK
NAPLESS
NOBLEST
OARLESS
OBELISK
OCULIST
OILLESS
ORBLESS
OUTLAST
PAULIST
PEGLESS
PINLESS
PUBLISH
PUNLESS
REALISE
REALISM
REALIST
RECLUSE
RIBLESS
RIMLESS
RODLESS
RUMLESS
SAPLESS
SINLESS
SKYLESS
SODLESS
SONLESS
STALEST
STYLISE
STYLISH
STYLIST
SUMLESS
SUNLESS
TALLEST
TALLISH
TAXLESS
TBILISI
TEALESS
TIELESS
TIPLESS
TITLIST
TOELESS
TOYLESS
TUGLESS
UNBLEST
UNCLASP
UNCLOSE
UPCLOSE
USELESS
UTILISE
VIOLIST
VOWLESS
WARLESS
WAYLESS
WEBLESS
WIGLESS
WITLESS

•••L••S

AGELESS
AIDLESS
AIMLESS
AIRLESS
AMBLERS
AMULETS
ANALOGS
ANGLERS
ANKLETS
ANTLERS
APPLETS
APPLIES
ARMLESS
ARMLETS
ARTLESS
ASHLARS
ASHLESS
ASYLUMS
ATALOSS
AUKLETS
AVULSES
AWELESS
AWNLESS
AZALEAS
BAILEES
BAILERS
BAILEYS
BAILORS
BALLADS
BALLETS
BALLOTS
BARLESS
BARLEYS
BAWLERS
BEDLESS
BELLIES
BELLOWS
BIALIES
BIBLESS
BIGLIES
BILLETS
BILLIES
BILLOWS
BITLESS
BOILERS
BOULLES
BOWLERS
BOWLESS
BRALESS
BUDLESS
BUGLERS
BULLETS
BULLIES
BURLAPS
BUTLERS
BYPLAYS
CABLERS
CALLERS
CALLINS
CALLOUS
CAPLESS
CAPLETS
CARLESS
CELLARS
CHALETS
CHALONS
CHILIES
CHOLLAS
COALERS
COALGAS
COLLARS
COLLETS
COLLIES
COLLINS
COLLOPS
COOLERS
COULEES
CULLERS
CULLIES
CURLERS
CURLEWS
CUTLASS
CUTLERS
CUTLETS
CYCLERS
CYCLOPS
DAHLIAS
DAILIES
DALLIES
DEALERS
DECLASS
DEPLOYS
DEWLAPS
DEWLESS
DIALERS
DIALOGS
DILLIES
DOGLEGS
DOGLESS
DOILIES
DOLLARS
DOLLIES
DOLLOPS
DUELERS
DUNLINS
EAGLETS
EARLESS
EGGLESS
EMBLEMS
EMPLOYS
ENDLESS
EPILOGS
EVOLVES
EVULSES
EYELESS
EYELETS
EYELIDS
FABLERS
FALLOWS
FATLESS
FEELERS
FEELESS
FELLAHS
FELLERS
FELLIES
FELLOWS
FILLERS
FILLETS
FILLIES
FILLINS
FILLIPS
FILLUPS
FLYLESS
FOGLESS
FOLLIES
FOLLOWS
FOULUPS
FOWLERS
FROLICS
FUELERS
FURLESS
GAGLAWS
GALLEYS
GALLONS
GALLOPS
GAOLERS
GAPLESS
GASLESS
GASLOGS
GEMLESS
GIBLETS
GIBLUES
GILLIES
GIMLETS
GOALIES
GOBLETS
GOBLINS
GODLESS
GOSLOWS
GRILLES
GUELPHS
GULLAHS
GULLETS
GULLIES
GUMLESS
GUNLESS
GUTLESS
HALLOWS
HAMLETS
HAPLESS
HATLESS
HAULERS
HEALERS
HEELERS
HELLERS
HIPLESS
HITLESS
HOLLERS
HOLLIES
HOLLOWS
HOTLIPS
HOWLERS
HUELESS
HULLERS
HULLOAS
HURLERS
HURLEYS
HURLIES
ICELESS
IMPLIES
INFLOWS
INKLESS
INNLESS
IRELESS
ITALICS
JAGLESS
JAILERS
JARLESS
JAWLESS
JEALOUS
JELLIES
JOBLESS
JOBLOTS
JOLLIES
JOYLESS
KEGLERS
KEYLESS
KILLERS
KINLESS
LADLERS
LAWLESS
LEGLESS
LIDLESS
LIPLESS
LOLLIES
LOLLOPS
MADLIBS
MAILERS
MALLETS
MALLOWS
MANLESS
MARLINS
MATLESS
MEALIES
MEDLEYS
MELLOWS
MERLOTS
MEWLERS
MILLERS
MILLETS
MISLAYS
MOILERS
MOSLEMS
MUKLUKS
MULLAHS
MULLERS
MULLETS
MUSLIMS
MUSLINS
NAILERS
NAPLESS
NUCLEUS
NULLAHS
NUTLETS
OARLESS
OCELLUS
OCELOTS
ODDLOTS
OILLESS
OMELETS
ORBLESS
OSTLERS
OUTLAWS
OUTLAYS
OUTLETS
PABLUMS
PAILOUS
PALLETS
PALLORS
PARLAYS
PARLEYS
PARLORS
PARLOUS
PEDLARS
PEELERS
PEGLESS
PELLETS
PEPLUMS
PHYLLIS
PIGLETS
PILLARS
PILLOWS
PINLESS
PIOLETS
POLLENS
POLLERS
POPLARS
POPLINS
PRELIMS
PROLOGS
PUBLICS
PULLETS
PULLEYS
PULLINS
PULLONS
PULLUPS
PUNLESS
PURLINS
RAGLANS
RAILERS
RALLIES
REFLAGS
REGLETS
REGLUES
REPLANS
REPLAYS
REPLIES
REPLOWS
RIBLESS
RIFLERS
RILLETS
RIMLESS
RODLESS
ROLLERS
ROLLINS
RUMLESS
RUNLETS
SAILORS
SALLETS
SALLIES
SALLOWS
SAMLETS
SANLUIS
SAPLESS
SAWLOGS
SCALARS
SCALERS
SCHLEPS
SCULPTS
SEALABS
SEALEGS
SEALERS
SELLERS
SHALOMS
SHELVES
SILLIES
SINLESS
SKYLESS
SLALOMS
SMALTOS
SMILERS
SODLESS
SONLESS
STALAGS
STOLONS
STYLERS
STYLETS
SUBLETS
SULLIES
SUMLESS
SUNLESS
SUSLIKS
SUTLERS
TABLETS
TAILLES
TAILORS
TALLIES
TALLOWS
TAXLESS
TEALESS
TELLERS
TELLIES
THALERS
TIELESS
TIGLONS
TILLERS
TIPLESS
TOELESS
TOILERS
TOILETS
TOLLIES
TOYLESS
TRELLIS
TUGLESS
TWELVES
UNCLOGS
UNPLUGS
USELESS
VALLEYS
VARLETS
VELLUMS
VIOLETS
VIOLINS
VOLLEYS
VOWLESS
WAILERS
WALLETS
WALLOPS
WALLOWS
WARLESS
WAYLAYS
WAYLESS
WEBLESS
WHALERS
WIGLESS
WIGLETS
WILLETS
WILLIES
WILLOWS
WITLESS
WOOLENS
WOOLIES
WURLEYS
YELLERS
YELLOWS
YOWLERS
ZEALOTS
ZEALOUS

••••LS•

IMPULSE
LAVALSE
REPULSE

••••L•S

AEDILES
ALKALIS
ALLELES
AMPULES
ANGELES
ANGELUS
ANNULUS
APPALLS
AREOLAS
ARGYLES
AUDILES
BABBLES
BAFFLES
BANGLES
BASALTS
BATTLES
BAUBLES
BEADLES
BEAGLES
BEATLES
BECALMS
BEETLES
BEFALLS
BEHOLDS
BOBBLES
BOGGLES
BOODLES
BOTTLES
BOULLES
BRIDLES
BUBBLES
BUCKLES
BUMBLES
BUNDLES
BUNGLES
BURBLES
BURGLES
BUSTLES
CABALAS
CACKLES
CAJOLES
CANDLES
CANTLES
CAROLUS
CASTLES
CAUDLES
CHABLIS
CHARLES
CHOLLAS
CIRCLES
COBBLES
COCKLES
CODDLES
COPULAS
COUPLES
CRADLES
CREOLES
CUDDLES
CUMULUS
CUPOLAS
CURDLES
DABBLES
DANDLES
DANGLES
DAPPLES
DAWDLES
DAZZLES
DECKLES
DEDALUS
DEFILES
DESALTS
DIBBLES
DIDDLES
DIMPLES
DINGLES
DIPOLES
DONGLES
DOODLES
DOTTLES
DOUBLES
DOUGLAS
EDIBLES
ENABLES
ENFOLDS
ENGULFS
ENISLES
ENROLLS
ENSILES
ETOILES
EXHALES
FAMULUS
FEMALES
FERULES
FETTLES
FIBULAS
FIDDLES
FIDELIS
FINALES
FIPPLES
FIZZLES
FOCSLES
FOIBLES
FONDLES
FOOZLES
FUDDLES
FUMBLES
GABBLES
GAGGLES
GAMBLES
GARBLES
GARGLES
GENTLES
GIGGLES
GIGOLOS
GILBLAS
GIRDLES
GOBBLES
GOGGLES
GRILLES
GURGLES
GUZZLES
HACKLES
HAGGLES
HANDLES
HASSLES
HECKLES
HEDDLES
HERALDS
HGWELLS
HIGGLES
HOBBLES
HOOPLAS
HOPPLES
HOWELLS
HUDDLES
HUMBLES
HURDLES
HURTLES
HUSTLES
ICICLES
IMPALAS
IMPALES
INGALLS
INHALES
INSOLES
INSULTS
JANGLES
JIGGLES
JINGLES
JOGGLES
JOSTLES
JUGGLES
JUMBLES
JUNGLES
KETTLES
KIBBLES
KINDLES
KIRTLES
KOBOLDS
LOBULES
LOCALES
MANGLES
MANTLES
MARBLES
MCCALLS
MEASLES
MEDDLES
METTLES
MIDDLES
MIGGLES
MINGLES
MIZZLES
MOBILES
MODELAS
MODELTS
MODULES
MORALES
MOTTLES
MUDDLES
MUFFLES
MUMBLES
MUSCLES
MUZZLES
MYRTLES
NEBULAS
NEEDLES
NEPALIS
NESTLES
NETTLES
NIBBLES
NICOLAS
NIGGLES
NOBBLES
NODULES
NOGALES
NONPLUS
NOODLES
NOZZLES
NUBBLES
NUZZLES
OCCULTS
OCELLUS
OGLALAS
ORACLES
ORIOLES
ORMOLUS
PADDLES
PAROLES
PAYOLAS
PEBBLES
PEDDLES
PEEPLES
PENULTS
PEOPLES
PESTLES
PHYLLIS
PICKLES
PIFFLES
POMELOS
POODLES
POPPLES
POPULUS
POSSLQS
POTTLES
PUDDLES
PUEBLOS
PURFLES
PURPLES
PUZZLES
RABBLES
RADDLES
RAFFLES
RAMBLES
RANKLES
RASSLES
RATTLES
REBOLTS
RECALLS
REFILES
REFILLS
REFILMS
REGALES
REGULUS
REMELTS
REMOLDS
REPOLLS
RESALES
RESALTS
RESELLS
RESILES
RESOLES
RESULTS
RETELLS
RETILES
REVILES
REVOLTS
REWELDS
RICKLES
RIDDLES
RIFFLES
RIMPLES
RIPPLES
ROMULUS
ROUBLES
RUBBLES
RUFFLES
RUMBLES
RUMPLES
RUNDLES
RUSTLES
SADDLES
SAMPLES
SAVALAS
SCROLLS
SETTLES
SHEILAS
SHIELDS
SHRILLS
SICKLES
SIMILES
SINGLES
SIZZLES
SOMALIS
SQUALLS
SQUILLS
STABLES
STAPLES
STIFLES
STROLLS
SURPLUS
TACKLES
TAILLES
TAMALES
TANGLES
TATTLES
TEMPLES
THRALLS
THRILLS
TICKLES
TINGLES
TINKLES
TIPPLES
TITTLES
TODDLES
TOGGLES
TOOTLES
TOPPLES
TOUSLES
TREBLES
TRELLIS
TRIFLES
TRIPLES
TROILUS
TUMBLES
TUMULTS
TUMULUS
TUPELOS
TURTLES
TUSSLES
UNBOLTS
UNFOLDS
UNPILES
UNROLLS
UPHOLDS
VITTLES
VIZSLAS
WADDLES
WAFFLES
WAGGLES
WAMBLES
WANGLES
WARBLES
WATTLES
WIGGLES
WIMBLES
WIMPLES
WINKLES
WOBBLES

•••••LS

AERIALS
ANIMALS
ANNEALS
ANNUALS
APPALLS
APPEALS
ARMFULS
ASSAILS
ATLATLS
AVOWALS
BAGFULS
BARBELS
BARRELS
BATTELS
BEFALLS
BEFOULS
BENGALS
BETHELS
BEWAILS
BOATELS
BOXFULS
BRIDALS
BULBULS
BUSHELS
CANCELS
CANFULS
CAPFULS
CARFULS
CARPALS
CARPELS
CARRELS
CARTELS
CASUALS
CEREALS
CHAPELS
CHISELS
CHORALS
COEVALS
COMPELS
CONSULS
CORBELS
CORRALS
CRENELS
CREWELS
CUDGELS
CUPFULS
CYMBALS
DACTYLS
DAMSELS
DANIELS
DENIALS
DERAILS
DETAILS
DIESELS
DIRNDLS
DISPELS
DISTILS
DORSALS
DOSSALS
DRIVELS
DUFFELS
EARFULS
ENAMELS
ENROLLS
ENSOULS
ENTAILS
ESPIALS
EYEFULS
FACIALS
FIBRILS
FINIALS
FORMALS
FOSSILS
FULFILS
FUNNELS
GALPALS
GAMBOLS
GAVIALS
GERBILS
GIMBALS
GOOGOLS
GOSPELS
GRAVELS
GROVELS
GUNNELS
HERBALS
HGWELLS
HOSTELS
HOWELLS
HYMNALS
INGALLS
INHAULS
INSTALS
INSTILS
ISOHELS
JACKALS
JARFULS
JUGFULS
KENNELS
KERNELS
LABIALS
LAPFULS
LAURELS
LENTILS
LINTELS
LISTELS
MAMMALS
MANTELS
MANUALS
MARCELS
MARVELS
MCCALLS
MENIALS
MESCALS
MISSALS
MONGOLS
MORSELS
MORTALS
MUDEELS
MUSSELS
MUTUALS
NARWALS
NICHOLS
NICKELS
NORMALS
ORDEALS
PANFULS
PARCELS
PASSELS
PASTELS
PATROLS
PENCILS
PENPALS
PETRELS
PETROLS
PHENOLS
PISTILS
PISTOLS
PLURALS
POMMELS
PORTALS
POTFULS
PROPELS
PUMMELS
RADIALS
RAPPELS
RASCALS
REBOILS
RECALLS
RECOILS
REDEALS
REDIALS
REFILLS
REFUELS
REHEALS
REHEELS
REMAILS
RENAILS
RENTALS
REPEALS
REPOLLS
RESEALS
RESELLS
RETAILS
RETELLS
RETOOLS
REVEALS
RITUALS
RONDELS
RUNNELS
SAMBALS
SANDALS
SCHOOLS
SCRAWLS

SCROLLS
SECKELS
SEIDELS
SEQUELS
SERIALS
SERVALS
SHEKELS
SHOVELS
SHRILLS
SIGNALS
SNIVELS
SOCIALS
SORRELS
SPINELS
SPIRALS
SPRAWLS
SQUALLS
SQUEALS
SQUILLS
STEROLS
STROLLS
SWIVELS
SYMBOLS
TARSALS
TASSELS
TEASELS
TERCELS
THRALLS
THRILLS
TIMBALS
TINSELS
TONSILS
TRAVELS
TROWELS
TUNNELS
UNCIALS
UNCOILS
UNCURLS
UNFURLS
UNREELS
UNROLLS
UNSEALS
UNVEILS
VANDALS
VASSALS
VATFULS
VERBALS
VESSELS
VISUALS
WEASELS
WEEVILS

L•T••••

LATCHED
LATCHES
LATEENS
LATENCY
LATENTS
LATERAL
LATERAN
LATERON
LATEXES
LATHERS
LATHERY
LATHING
LATICES
LATIFAH
LATINAS
LATINOS
LATOSCA
LATTENS
LATTICE
LATVIAN
LETDOWN
LETINON
LETITBE
LETITIA
LETSFLY
LETSLIP
LETSOFF
LETSOUT
LETSSEE
LETTERS
LETTING
LETTISH
LETTRES
LETTUCE
LETUPON
LITCHIS
LITCRIT
LITERAL
LITHELY
LITHEST
LITHGOW
LITHIUM
LITINTO
LITOTES
LITTERS
LITTLER
LITURGY
LOTIONS
LOTTERY
LOTTING
LOTUSES
LUTISTS

L••T•••

LACTASE
LACTATE
LACTEAL
LACTOSE
LANTANA
LANTERN
LAOTIAN
LAPTOPS
LASTING
LASTORY
LATTENS
LATTICE
LAUTREC
LEATHER
LECTERN
LECTORS
LECTURE
LEETIDE
LEFTIES
LEFTIST
LEFTOFF
LEFTOUT
LENTIGO
LENTILS
LEOTARD
LEPTONS
LETTERS
LETTING
LETTISH
LETTRES
LETTUCE
LICTORS
LIFTERS
LIFTING
LIFTOFF
LIFTSUP
LILTING
LINTELS
LINTIER
LISTEES
LISTELS
LISTENS
LISTING
LITTERS
LITTLER
LOATHED
LOATHES
LOFTIER
LOFTILY
LOFTING
LOITERS
LOOTERS
LOOTING
LOSTOUT
LOTTERY
LOTTING
LOUTISH
LOWTECH
LOWTIDE
LUSTERS
LUSTFUL
LUSTIER
LUSTILY
LUSTING
LUSTRED
LUSTRES

L•••T••

LAERTES
LAFITTE
LAKOTAS
LAMOTTA
LANGTRY
LAYETTE
LAYITON
LEANTOS
LEGATEE
LEGATES
LEGATOS
LEISTER
LENGTHS
LENGTHY
LESOTHO
LETITBE
LETITIA
LEVITES
LICITLY
LIGATED
LIGATES
LIGHTED
LIGHTEN
LIGHTER
LIGHTLY
LIGHTUP
LIMITED
LITOTES
LOBSTER
LOCATED
LOCATER
LOCATES
LOCATOR
LONGTON
LORETTA
LUNATIC
LUXATED
LUXATES

L••••T•

LABIATE
LABRETS
LACOSTE
LACTATE
LAFITTE
LAMENTS
LAMOTTA
LANCETS
LAPLATA
LAPORTE
LAPPETS
LARIATS
LATENTS
LAYETTE
LAYINTO
LAYOUTS
LEADSTO
LEDUPTO
LEGISTS
LEPANTO
LEVANTS
LIBERTY
LIGNITE
LIMPETS
LINEATE
LINNETS
LIONETS
LISENTE
LITINTO
LOCKETS
LOCUSTS
LOOKSTO
LOQUATS
LORETTA
LOYALTY
LUDDITE
LUGNUTS
LUTISTS
LYINGTO
LYRISTS

L•••••T

LABCOAT
LACIEST
LAIDOUT
LAKIEST
LAMAIST
LAMBENT
LAMBERT
LANDSAT
LANKEST
LAPBELT
LARGEST
LAUGHAT
LAURENT
LAWSUIT
LAYSOUT
LAZIEST
LEADOUT
LEAFLET
LEANEST
LEARJET
LEERSAT
LEFTIST
LEFTOUT
LENFANT
LENIENT
LETSOUT
LEVERET
LEWDEST
LIFENET
LIMIEST
LIMPEST
LINIEST
LITCRIT
LITHEST
LIVEOUT
LOCKNUT
LOCKOUT
LOGIEST
LOGSOUT
LONGEST
LOOKOUT
LOOKSAT
LOOSEST
LOSEOUT
LOSESIT
LOSTOUT
LOUDEST
LOWCOST
LUCKOUT
LUNGEAT
LUSHEST

•LT••••

ALTERED
ALTERER
ALTOONA
ALTOSAX
ULTIMAS

•L•T•••

ALLTIME
ALLTOLD
BLATANT
BLATHER
BLATTED
BLITHER
BLITZED
BLITZEN
BLITZES
BLOTCHY
BLOTOUT
BLOTTED
BLOTTER
CLATTER
CLOTHED
CLOTHES
CLOTTED
CLOTURE
CLUTTER
ELATERS
ELATING
ELATION
ELITISM
ELITIST
ELMTREE
ELUTING
ELUTION
FLATBED
FLATCAR
FLATLET
FLATOUT
FLATTAX
FLATTED
FLATTEN
FLATTER
FLATTOP
FLITTED
FLITTER
FLOTSAM
FLUTIER
FLUTING
FLUTIST
FLUTTER
FLYTRAP
GLITTER
GLITZED
GLITZES
GLOTTAL
GLOTTIS
GLUTTED
GLUTTON
KLATSCH
KLUTZES
OLDTIME
PLATEAU
PLATENS
PLATERS
PLATIER
PLATING
PLATOON
PLATTER
PLATYPI
PLOTFUL
PLOTTED
PLOTTER
SLATHER
SLATIER
SLATING
SLATTED
SLITHER
SLOTCAR
SLOTTED
ULSTERS

•L••T••

ALERTED
ALERTER
ALERTLY
ALLSTAR
ALLSTON
ALSATIA
BLASTED
BLASTER
BLATTED
BLEATED
BLISTER
BLOATED
BLOTTED
BLOTTER
BLUNTED
BLUNTER
BLUNTLY
BLURTED
BLUSTER
CLAPTON
CLATTER
CLAYTON
CLIFTON
CLINTON
CLOTTED
CLOUTED
CLUSTER
CLUTTER
ELASTIC
ELECTED
ELECTEE
ELECTOR
ELECTRA
ELECTRO
ELEKTRA
FLATTAX
FLATTED
FLATTEN
FLATTER
FLATTOP
FLEETER
FLEETLY
FLIRTED
FLITTED
FLITTER
FLOATED
FLOATER
FLOUTED
FLUSTER
FLUTTER
GLINTED
GLISTEN
GLITTER
GLOATED
GLOTTAL
GLOTTIS
GLUTTED
GLUTTON
OLDSTER
OLEATES
OLESTRA
PLAITED
PLANTAR
PLANTED
PLANTER
PLASTER
PLASTIC
PLATTER
PLAUTUS
PLEATED
PLECTRA
PLINTHS
PLOTTED
PLOTTER
SLANTED
SLATTED
SLAYTON
SLEETED
SLEPTIN
SLEPTON
SLEUTHS
SLOTTED

•L•••T•

ALBERTA
ALBERTO
ALDENTE
ALIGHTS
ALMAATA
ALWORTH
BLIGHTS
BLIGHTY
CLARETS
CLARITY
CLIENTS
CLIMATE
CLORETS
CLOSETS
ELEVATE
ELICITS
ELLIOTT
ELMISTI
FLAUNTS
FLAUNTY
FLIGHTS
FLIGHTY
FLOCKTO
FLORETS
FLYNETS
KLAMATH
PLACATE
PLAINTS
PLANETS
PLIGHTS
SLIGHTS
ULULATE

•L••••T

ALIMENT
ALRIGHT
BLANKET
BLATANT
BLERIOT
BLEWOUT
BLINKAT
BLOTOUT
BLOWOUT
BLOWSIT
CLEMENT
CLIPART
CLOSEST
ELEGANT
ELEGIST
ELEMENT
ELITIST
ELKHART
ELLIOTT
FLATLET
FLATOUT
FLEAPIT
FLIESAT
FLIPOUT
FLORIST
FLORUIT
FLOWNAT
FLUTIST
FLYCAST
FLYPAST
GLUIEST
ILLICIT
OLDWEST
PLACKET
PLANOUT
PLAUDIT
PLAYACT
PLAYLET
PLAYOUT
PLAYSAT
PLUMMET
SLEIGHT
SLIPOUT
SLOWEST
TLINGIT
ULULANT

••LT•••

ALLTIME
ALLTOLD
BELTANE
BELTBAG
BELTING
BELTWAY
BOLTING
CALTECH
CELTICS
COLTISH
CULTISH
CULTISM
CULTIST
CULTJAM
CULTURE
DALTREY
DELTAIC
DELTOID
DOLTISH
FALTERS
FELTFOR
FELTOUT
FILTERS
HALTERS
HALTING
JILTING
JOLTIER
JOLTING
KILTIES
KILTING
LILTING
MALTEDS
MALTESE
MALTHUS
MALTIER
MALTING
MALTOSE
MELTING
MOLTERS
MOLTING
PALTERS
PALTROW
PELTATE
PELTERS
PELTING
PELTISH
SALTBOX
SALTERS
SALTIER
SALTILY
SALTINE
SALTING
SALTISH
SELTZER
SILTIER
SILTING
SULTANA
SULTANS
TILTERS
TILTING
TOLTECS
VOLTAGE
VOLTAIC
VULTURE
WALTERS
WALTZED
WALTZER
WALTZES
WELTERS
WELTING
WILTING
YELTSIN

••L•T••

ABLATED
ABLATES
ALLSTAR
ALLSTON
ATLATLS
BALATON
BELATED
BOLOTIE
BOLSTER
COLETTE
CULOTTE
DALETHS
DELETED
DELETES
DILATED
DILATES
DILUTED
DILUTER
DILUTES
EOLITHS
GALATEA
GALATIA
GELATIN
GELATIS
GOLFTEE
HALITES
HALSTON
HELOTRY
HILLTOP
HOLSTER
KILOTON
MILITIA
MOLOTOV
MULCTED
MULETAS
OBLATES
ONLYTOO
OOLITES
OOLITHS
PALATAL
PALATES
PALETTE
PALMTOP
PELOTAS
PILOTED
POLITER
POLITIC
POLLTAX
PULLTAB
RALSTON
RELATED
RELATES
ROLLTOP
SALUTED
SALUTES
SOLUTES
SPLITUP
SPLOTCH
TELSTAR
TOLSTOI
TOLSTOY
UNLATCH
WALSTON

••L••T•

ABLAUTS
APLENTY
ATLANTA
BALLETS
BALLOTS
BILLETS
BULLETS
BULLITT
CALCITE
CELESTA
CELESTE
CILIATE
COLETTE
COLGATE
COLLATE
COLLETS
CULOTTE
DELICTI
DELICTS
DELISTS
ELLIOTT
ENLISTS
FALLSTO
FALSITY
FILLETS
FOLIATE
FOLLETT
GALOOTS
GOLIATH
GULLETS
HELMETS
HOLDSTO
HOLISTS
JOLLITY
MALEATE
MALLETS
MILLETS
MILLETT
MOLESTS
MULLETS
NULLITY
OBLASTS
PALETTE
PALLETS
PALMATE
PELLETS
PELTATE
POLENTA
POLLUTE
PULLETS
PULPITS
PULSATE
RALLYTO
RELENTS
RELICTS
RELISTS
RELUCTS
RILLETS
SALLETS
SELECTS
SILENTS
SPLINTS
SULFATE
SULFITE
TALENTS
TALKSTO
UMLAUTS
UPLIFTS
VALUATE
VALVATE
VELVETS
VELVETY
VULGATE
WALCOTT
WALLETS
WALNUTS
WILLETS

••L•••T

AILMENT
ATLEAST
BALDEST
BALLAST
BELFAST
BELMONT
BOLDEST
BULBLET
BULLITT
CALLOUT
CALMEST
CALUMET
CALVERT
CELLIST
COLBERT
COLDCUT
COLDEST
COLLECT
CULPRIT
CULTIST
CULVERT
DELIGHT
DELIMIT
DILBERT
DOLEOUT
DULLEST
EELIEST
ELLIOTT
FALLOUT
FALSEST
FELLOUT
FELTOUT
FILBERT
FILLOUT
FOLDOUT
FOLKART
FOLLETT
FULGENT
FULLEST
GALLANT
GILBERT
GILLNET
HALFWIT
HALIBUT
HELDOUT
HELLCAT
HELPOUT
HOLDOUT
HOLEOUT
HOLIEST
ILLICIT
JOLLIET
MALLRAT
MILDEST
MILLETT
OILIEST
PALIEST
PALMIST
POLECAT
POLOIST
PULLOUT
RELIANT
RELIGHT
ROLLOUT
RULEOUT
SALIENT
SELLOUT
SILKHAT
SOLDOUT
SOLICIT
SOLOIST
SOLVENT
TALKOUT
TALKSAT
TALLEST
UGLIEST
VALIANT
WALCOTT
WALKOUT
WALMART
WELLSET
WILDCAT
WILDEST
WILIEST
YELLSAT

•••LT••

ADULTLY
BUILTIN
BUILTUP
CARLTON
COALTAR
COULTER
DEALTIN
EXALTED
EXULTED
FAULTED
FOULTIP
HEALTHY
HEELTAP
HILLTOP
MOULTED
PHILTER
PHILTRE
POLLTAX
POULTRY
PSALTER
PULLTAB
QUILTED
QUILTER
REALTOR
ROLLTOP
SHELTER
SHELTIE
SHELTON
SKELTER
SKELTON
SMALTOS
SMELTED
SMELTER
STILTED
STILTON
SVELTER
SWELTER
SWELTRY
VAULTED
VAULTER
WEALTHY

•••L•T•

ABILITY
ACOLYTE
ADULATE
AGILITY
AMULETS
ANKLETS
APPLETS
ARMLETS
ATHLETE
AUKLETS
AXOLOTL
BALLETS
BALLOTS
BERLITZ
BILLETS
BULLETS
BULLITT
CABLETV
CAPLETS
CHALETS
COLLATE
COLLETS
CUTLETS
DEFLATE
DEPLETE
DUALITY
EAGLETS
EGALITE
EMULATE
EYELETS
FALLSTO
FILLETS
FOLLETT
GIBLETS
GIMLETS
GOBLETS
GULLETS
HAMLETS
HEWLETT
INFLATE
ISOLATE
JOBLOTS
JOLLITY
LAPLATA
MALLETS
MERLOTS
MILLETS
MILLETT
MULLETS
NEOLITH
NULLITY
NUTLETS
OCELOTS
ODDLOTS
OMELETS
OUTLETS
PALLETS
PELLETS
PERLITE
PIGLETS
PIOLETS
POLLUTE
PRELATE
PULLETS
QUALITY
RALLYTO
RANLATE
REALITY
REGLETS
REPLATE
REPLETE
RILLETS
RUNLATE
RUNLETS
SALLETS
SAMLETS
SCULPTS
STYLETS
SUBLETS
TABLETS
TOILETS
TWELFTH
ULULATE
UTILITY
VARLETS
VIOLATE
VIOLETS
WALLETS
WIGLETS
WILLETS
ZEALOTS

•••L••T

AFFLICT
AIRLIFT
AMPLEST
ANALYST
BAILOUT
BALLAST
BAWLOUT
BULLITT
CALLOUT
CELLIST
COLLECT
COOLANT
COOLEST
COOLSIT
COULDNT
CYCLIST
DEALOUT
DEFLECT
DIALECT
DUELIST
DULLEST
EVILEST
EXPLOIT
FALLOUT
FARLEFT
FEELOUT
FELLOUT
FILLOUT
FOLLETT
FOULEST
FOULOUT
FULLEST
GALLANT
GETLOST
GILLNET
GOTLOST
GRILLET

HAYLOFT
HELLCAT
HEWLETT
HITLIST
IMPLANT
INFLECT
INFLICT
JOLLIET
MAILLOT
MAILOUT
MALLRAT
MILLETT
NAILSET
NEGLECT
NEWLEFT
NOBLEST
OCULIST
OPULENT
OUTLAST
PAULIST
PULLOUT
RAILSAT
REALIST
REELECT
REFLECT
REPLANT
ROLLOUT
SEALANT
SELLOUT
SHALLOT
SKILIFT
SKILLET
STALEST
STYLIST
SWALLET
TALLEST
TITLIST
TSELIOT
ULULANT
UNBLEST
VIOLENT
VIOLIST
WELLSET
WOULDNT
YELLSAT

••••LT•

BASALTS
CRUELTY
DESALTS
FACULTY
FRAILTY
GEFILTE
INSULTS
LOYALTY
MINOLTA
MODELTS
NOVELTY
OCCULTS
PENALTY
PENULTS
REBOLTS
REMELTS
RESALTS
RESULTS
REVOLTS
ROYALTY
SCHULTZ
STEALTH
TUMULTS
UNBOLTS

••••L•T

ABSOLUT
ASTOLAT
BACKLIT
BIBELOT
BOOKLET
BULBLET
CAMELOT
CAPELET
CAPULET
CHAPLET
CIRCLET
COPILOT
COUPLET
DOUBLET
DRIBLET
DROPLET
EPAULET
FEEDLOT
FIRELIT
FLATLET
GANTLET
GRILLET
INKBLOT
LEAFLET
MAILLOT
MATELOT
MOONLIT
PLAYLET
RINGLET
RIVULET
ROOTLET
SANDLOT
SCARLET
SHALLOT
SKILLET
SNIGLET
SPOTLIT
STARLET
STARLIT
SUBPLOT
SWALLET
TRIPLET
WAVELET
WOODLOT

•••••LT

ASPHALT
ASSAULT
ATFAULT
BERTOLT
CONSULT
DEFAULT
EYEBOLT
FANBELT
GESTALT
LAPBELT
NOFAULT
REBUILT
REDEALT
RENAULT
SEASALT
SUNBELT

LU•••••

LUBBERS
LUBBOCK
LUBEJOB
LUCENCY
LUCERNE
LUCIANO
LUCIDLY
LUCIFER
LUCILLE
LUCKIER
LUCKILY
LUCKING
LUCKOUT
LUDDITE
LUFFING
LUGGAGE
LUGGERS
LUGGING
LUGNUTS
LULLABY
LULLING
LUMBAGO
LUMBARS
LUMBERS
LUMIERE
LUMPERS
LUMPIER
LUMPILY
LUMPING
LUMPISH
LUMPSUM
LUNATIC
LUNCHED
LUNCHES
LUNGEAT
LUNGING
LUNKERS
LUPINES
LURCHED
LURCHES
LURIDLY
LURKING
LUSHEST
LUSTERS
LUSTFUL
LUSTIER
LUSTILY
LUSTING
LUSTRED
LUSTRES
LUTISTS
LUXATED
LUXATES

L•U••••

LAUDING
LAUGHAT
LAUGHED
LAUGHER
LAUGHIN
LAUNDER
LAUNDRY
LAURELS
LAURENT
LAUTREC
LEUCINE
LOUDEST
LOUDISH
LOUELLA
LOUNGED
LOUNGER
LOUNGES
LOURDES
LOUSEUP
LOUSIER
LOUSILY
LOUSING
LOUTISH
LOUVERS
LOUVRED
LOUVRES

L••U•••

LACUNAE
LACUNAL
LACUNAS
LAGUNAS
LEDUPTO
LEGUMES
LETUPON
LIQUEFY
LIQUEUR
LIQUIDS
LIQUORS
LITURGY
LOBULES
LOCUSTS
LOQUATS
LOTUSES

L•••U••

LABOURS
LACQUER
LANGUID
LANGUOR
LANGURS
LAPFULS
LARRUPS
LASHUPS
LAWSUIT
LAYOUTS
LEAGUES
LECTURE
LEGPULL
LEISURE
LETTUCE
LINEUPS
LINGUAL
LINKUPS
LOCKUPS
LONGUES
LOOKUPS
LUGNUTS
LYCEUMS

L••••U•

LACEDUP
LACESUP
LADYBUG
LAIDOUT
LALIQUE
LANDAUS
LASCAUX
LAYSOUT
LAZARUS
LEADOUT
LEADSUP
LEFTOUT
LEMIEUX
LESPAUL
LETSOUT
LIFEFUL
LIFTSUP
LIGHTUP
LINEDUP
LINESUP
LIONCUB
LIQUEUR
LITHIUM
LIVEOUT
LOCKNUT
LOCKOUT
LOCKSUP
LOGSOUT
LONGRUN
LOOKOUT
LOOKSUP
LOSEOUT
LOSTOUT
LOUSEUP
LOVEBUG
LUCKOUT
LUMPSUM
LUSTFUL

L•••••U

LAMBEAU

•LU••••

ALUMNAE
ALUMNAL
ALUMNUS
ALUNSER
BLUBBER
BLUEBOY
BLUEFIN
BLUEFOX
BLUEGUM
BLUEING
BLUEISH
BLUEJAY
BLUELAW
BLUESKY
BLUFFED
BLUFFER
BLUFFLY
BLUNDER
BLUNTED
BLUNTER
BLUNTLY
BLURRED
BLURTED
BLUSHED
BLUSHER
BLUSHES
BLUSHON
BLUSTER
CLUBBED
CLUBCAR
CLUCKED
CLUEDIN
CLUEING
CLUESIN
CLUMPED
CLUNKED
CLUNKER
CLUSTER
CLUTTER
ELUDING
ELUSIVE
ELUSORY
ELUTING
ELUTION
ELUVIUM
FLUBBED
FLUBBER
FLUENCY
FLUFFED
FLUIDLY
FLUKIER
FLUMMOX
FLUNKED
FLUSHED
FLUSHES
FLUSTER
FLUTIER
FLUTING
FLUTIST
FLUTTER
FLUVIAL
FLUXING
GLUCOSE
GLUEDON
GLUESON
GLUGGED
GLUIEST
GLUMMER
GLUTTED
GLUTTON
KLUDGES
KLUGMAN
KLUTZES
PLUCKED
PLUGGED
PLUGGER
PLUGINS
PLUGSIN
PLUMAGE
PLUMBED
PLUMBER
PLUMIER
PLUMING
PLUMMER
PLUMMET
PLUMPED
PLUMPER
PLUMPLY
PLUNDER
PLUNGED
PLUNGER
PLUNGES
PLUNKED
PLURALS
PLUSHER
PLUSHES
PLUSHLY
PLUSSES
PLUVIAL
SLUDGES
SLUGGED
SLUGGER
SLUICED
SLUICES
SLUMBER
SLUMMED
SLUMPED
SLURPED
SLURRED
SLUSHES
ULULANT
ULULATE

•L•U•••

ALBUMEN
ALBUMIN
ALBUNDY
ALLUDED
ALLUDES
ALLURED
ALLURES
ALLUVIA
BLOUSED
BLOUSES
BLOUSON
CLAUDIA
CLAUDIO
CLAUSES
CLOUDED
CLOUTED
FLAUNTS
FLAUNTY
FLOUNCE
FLOUNCY
FLOURED
FLOUTED
ILLUDED
ILLUDES
ILLUMED
ILLUMES
ILLUSED
ILLUSES
OLDUVAI
PLAUDIT
PLAUTUS
PLOUGHS
SLEUTHS
SLOUCHY
SLOUGHS

•L••U••

ALARUMS
BLACULA
BLOWUPS
CLAQUES
CLIBURN
CLIQUES
CLIQUEY
CLOQUES
CLOSURE
CLOTURE
FLIPUPS
FLORUIT
GLOBULE
PLAGUED
PLAGUES
PLAQUES
PLENUMS
SLIPUPS
SLOWUPS
ULALUME

•L•••U•

ALUMNUS
ALYSSUM
BLEWOUT
BLOTOUT
BLOWGUN
BLOWNUP
BLOWOUT
BLOWSUP
BLUEGUM
CLAMOUR
CLAMSUP
CLEANUP
CLEARUP
CLOGSUP
CLOSEUP
ELAAIUN
ELUVIUM
ELYSIUM
FLANEUR
FLAREUP
FLATOUT
FLAVOUR
FLIPOUT
GLAMOUR
GLEEFUL
OLYMPUS
PLANOUT
PLAUTUS
PLAYFUL
PLAYOUT
PLAYSUP
PLOTFUL
SLIPOUT
SLIPSUP
SLOWSUP

•L••••U

ILIESCU
PLATEAU

••LU•••

ALLUDED
ALLUDES
ALLURED
ALLURES
ALLUVIA
BELUSHI
BOLUSES
CALUMET
CALUMNY
COLUMBO
COLUMNS
DELUDED
DELUDES
DELUGED
DELUGES
DELUISE
DILUTED
DILUTER
DILUTES
FELUCCA
GALUMPH
ILLUDED
ILLUDES
ILLUMED
ILLUMES
ILLUSED
ILLUSES
MCLUHAN
RELUCTS
RELUMED
RELUMES
SALUKIS
SALUTED
SALUTES
SOLUBLE
SOLUTES
SPLURGE
STLUCIA
SULUSEA
TALUSES
TOLUENE
UNLUCKY
VALUATE
VALUING
VOLUBLE
VOLUBLY
VOLUMES

••L•U••

ABLAUTS
BULBULS
BULRUSH
COLLUDE
COLOURS
CULTURE
DOLOURS
FILLUPS
FOLDUPS
GILGUYS
HOLDUPS
KILAUEA
MOLLUSC
MOLLUSK
PILEUPS
POLLUTE
PULLUPS
PULQUES
STLOUIS
TALCUMS
UMLAUTS
VALOURS
VELLUMS
VELOURS
VULTURE
WALKUPS
WALNUTS

••L••U•

BALEFUL
BALFOUR
BALLSUP
BELAKUN
BELGIUM
BELLYUP
BILIOUS
BULBOUS
BULGHUR
BULLRUN
CALCIUM
CALHOUN
CALLOUS
CALLOUT
CALLSUP
CELSIUS
COLDCUT
COLOBUS
DOLEFUL
DOLEOUT
DOLLSUP
ECLOGUE
FALLGUY
FALLOUT
FELLOUT
FELTOUT
FILLOUT
FILLSUP
FOLDOUT
FOLDSUP
FULCRUM
FULGHUM
GALLIUM
GOLDBUG
HALIBUT
HELDOUT
HELPFUL
HELPOUT
HOLDOUT
HOLDSUP
HOLEDUP
HOLEOUT
HOLESUP
HOLMIUM
LALIQUE
MALAMUD
MALRAUX
MALTHUS
MILHAUD
MILIEUS
MILIEUX
MILKRUN
MILLRUN
OBLIQUE
OBLOQUY
PALLIUM
PILEDUP
PILESUP
PILLBUG
PULLOUT
PULLSUP
RILESUP
ROLLOUT
ROLLSUP
RULEOUT
SELLOUT
SOLDOUT
SPLITUP
SULPHUR
TALKOUT
TALKSUP
TALLYUP
VILNIUS
WALKOUT
WALLSUP
WELLRUN
WELLSUP
WILLFUL

••L•••U

ONLYYOU

•••LU••

ASYLUMS
COLLUDE
ENGLUND
EXCLUDE
FAILURE
FILLUPS
FOULUPS
GIBLUES
INCLUDE
MCCLURE
MOLLUSC
MOLLUSK
MUKLUKS
OCCLUDE
PABLUMS
PEPLUMS
POLLUTE
POTLUCK
PRELUDE
PULLUPS
RECLUSE
REGLUED
REGLUES
SANLUIS
SECLUDE
SPELUNK
ULALUME
UNGLUED
UNPLUGS
VELLUMS

•••L•U•

APPLAUD
BAILOUT
BALLSUP
BAWLOUT
BECLOUD
BELLYUP
BOWLFUL
BUILDUP
BUILTUP
BULLRUN
CALLOUS
CALLOUT
CALLSUP
CHALKUP
COILSUP
CURLSUP
DEALOUT
DOLLSUP
FALLGUY
FALLOUT
FEELOUT
FELLOUT
FILLOUT
FILLSUP
FOULOUT
FOULSUP
GALLIUM
GIELGUD
HAULSUP
JEALOUS
MAILOUT
MCCLOUD
MILLRUN
NUCLEUS
OCELLUS
OUTLOUD
PAILFUL
PAILOUS
PALLIUM
PARLOUR
PARLOUS
PILLBUG
PULLOUT
PULLSUP
ROLLOUT
ROLLSUP
SEALSUP
SELLOUT
SKILFUL
SOULFUL
SWELLUP
TALLYUP
THULIUM
TOILFUL
TOOLSUP
WAILFUL
WALLSUP
WELLRUN
WELLSUP
WILLFUL
ZEALOUS

•••L••U

PURLIEU
TABLEAU

••••LU•

ABSOLUT
AMIBLUE
ANGELUS
ANNULUS
BENELUX
CAROLUS
CUMULUS
DEDALUS
DEVALUE
EARPLUG
FAMULUS
FANCLUB
FIATLUX
HOODLUM
ICEBLUE
JEANLUC
KEYCLUB
NONPLUS
OCELLUS
ORMOLUS
PABULUM
POPULUS
REGULUS
REVALUE
ROMULUS
SEABLUE
SEASLUG
SKYBLUE
SURPLUS
SWELLUP
TROILUS
TUMULUS

••••L•U

ANGELOU
DOUBLEU
EMMYLOU
MARYLOU

L•V••••

LAVALSE
LAVERNE
LAVINIA
LEVANTS
LEVELED
LEVELER
LEVELLY
LEVERED
LEVERET
LEVIERS
LEVITES
LEVYING
LIVABLE
LIVEDIN
LIVEDON
LIVENED
LIVEOAK
LIVEONE
LIVEOUT
LIVESIN
LIVESON
LIVIDLY
LIVINGS
LIVORNO
LOVABLE
LOVABLY
LOVEBUG
LOVEINS
LOVERLY

L••V•••

LATVIAN
LEAVEIN
LEAVENS
LEAVING
LEKVARS
LOUVERS
LOUVRED
LOUVRES

L•••V••

LAYOVER
LEHAVRE
LIEOVER

•LV••••

ALVAREZ
ALVEOLI

•L•V•••

CLAVELL
CLAVIER
CLOVERS
ELEVATE
ELEVENS
ELUVIUM
FLAVORS
FLAVOUR
FLIVVER
FLUVIAL
OLIVIER
OLIVINE
PLOVERS
PLUVIAL
SLAVERS
SLAVERY
SLAVEYS
SLAVING
SLAVISH
SLIVERS
SLOVAKS
SLOVENE
SLOVENS

•L••V••

ALCOVES
ALLOVER
ALLUVIA
CLEAVED
CLEAVER
CLEAVES
CLEAVON
FLIVVER
FLYOVER
OLDUVAI
SLEEVES

•L•••V•

ELUSIVE
PLOSIVE
ULANOVA

•L••••V

ULYANOV

••LV•••

CALVARY
CALVERT
CALVING
CULVERS
CULVERT
DELVERS
DELVING
GALVANI
HALVAHS
HALVING
ROLVAAG
SALVAGE
SALVERS
SALVIAS
SALVING
SALVOES
SALVORS
SELVAGE
SILVERS
SILVERY
SOLVENT
SOLVERS
SOLVING
SYLVANS
VALVATE
VELVETS
VELVETY

••L•V••

ALLOVER
ALLUVIA
BELOVED
BILEVEL
BOLIVAR
BOLIVIA
DELIVER
ENLIVEN
PALAVER
RELIVED
RELIVES
TELAVIV
UNLOVED

••L••V•

BELIEVE
MOLDOVA
ONLEAVE
RELIEVE
RELIEVO

••L•••V

MOLOTOV
TELAVIV

•••LV••

EVOLVED
EVOLVES
SHELVED
SHELVES
TWELVES

•••L•V•

BAKLAVA
ENCLAVE
ENSLAVE
OUTLIVE
PAHLAVI
PAVLOVA

•••L••V

CABLETV

••••LV•

ABSOLVE
BIVALVE
DEVOLVE
INVOLVE
RESOLVE
REVOLVE

L•W••••

LAWFORD
LAWLESS
LAWLIKE
LAWSUIT
LAWYERS
LEWDEST
LOWBALL
LOWBEAM
LOWBLOW
LOWBORN
LOWBOYS
LOWBRED
LOWBROW
LOWCOST
LOWDOWN
LOWERED
LOWGEAR
LOWHEEL
LOWLAND
LOWLIER
LOWLIFE
LOWNECK
LOWNESS
LOWPAID
LOWRISE
LOWROAD
LOWTECH
LOWTIDE

L••W•••

LAPWING
LEEWARD
LEGWORK

L•••W••

LAYAWAY

L••••W•

LAYDOWN
LETDOWN

LIEDOWN
LOWDOWN

L•••••W
LAIDLOW
LAYSLOW
LIESLOW
LIKENEW
LITHGOW
LONGBOW
LOWBLOW
LOWBROW

•LW••••
ALWORTH

•L•W•••
ALEWIFE
BLEWOFF
BLEWOUT
BLOWDRY
BLOWERS
BLOWFLY
BLOWGUN
BLOWIER
BLOWING
BLOWNUP
BLOWOFF
BLOWOUT
BLOWSIN
BLOWSIT
BLOWSUP
BLOWUPS
CLAWERS
CLAWING
CLOWDER
CLOWNED
FLAWING
FLOWERS
FLOWERY
FLOWING
FLOWNAT
FLOWNIN
FLYWAYS
GLOWERS
GLOWING
ILLWILL
ILLWIND
OLDWEST
PLOWBOY
PLOWERS
PLOWING
PLOWMAN
PLOWMEN
PLYWOOD
SLOWEST
SLOWING
SLOWSUP
SLOWUPS

•L••W••
ALLOWAY
ALLOWED
ELBOWED
FLYAWAY

•L•••W•
OLDNEWS
OLDSAWS

•L••••W
BLUELAW
GLASGOW

••LW•••
BULWARK
FALWELL
ILLWILL
ILLWIND
OILWELL

••L•W••
ALLOWAY
ALLOWED
BALDWIN
BELTWAY
COLDWAR
CSLEWIS
FOLKWAY
GOLDWYN
HALFWAY
HALFWIT
HALLWAY
HOLYWAR
TOLLWAY
WALKWAY

••L••W•
BELLOWS
BILLOWS
BILLOWY
FALLOWS
FELLOWS
FOLLOWS
HALLOWS
HOLLOWS
MALLOWS
MELLOWS
MILDEWS
MILDEWY
PILLOWS
PILLOWY
SALLOWS
TALLOWS
WALLOWS
WILLOWS
WILLOWY
YELLOWS
YELLOWY

••L•••W
HOLYCOW
MILKCOW
PALTROW
SALCHOW

•••LW••
HALLWAY
RAILWAY
TOLLWAY

•••L•W•
BELLOWS
BILLOWS
BILLOWY
CURLEWS
FALLOWS
FELLOWS
FOLLOWS
GAGLAWS
GOSLOWS
HALLOWS
HOLLOWS
INFLOWS
MALLOWS
MARLOWE
MELLOWS
OAKLAWN
OUTLAWS
PILLOWS
PILLOWY
REPLOWS
ROBLOWE
SALLOWS
TALLOWS
WALLOWS
WILLOWS
WILLOWY
YELLOWS
YELLOWY

•••L••W
SHALLOW
SWALLOW

••••LW•
ROYALWE

••••L•W
AIRFLOW
BIGELOW
BLUELAW
CASELAW
DANELAW
DEWCLAW
GAMELAW
HIGHLOW
JOEBLOW
LAIDLOW
LAYSLOW
LIESLOW
LOWBLOW
MANILOW
OUTFLOW
SHALLOW
SWALLOW
WINSLOW

L•X••••
LAXNESS
LEXEMES
LEXICAL
LEXICON
LUXATED
LUXATES

L•••X••
LATEXES

L•••••X
LASCAUX
LEMIEUX
LOCKBOX

•L•X•••
ELIXIRS
FLAXIER
FLEXING
FLEXNER
FLEXORS
FLUXING
KLAXONS
PLEXORS

•L••••X
ALTOSAX
BLUEFOX
FLATTAX
FLUMMOX
KLEENEX

••L•X••
CALYXES
HELIXES
PHLOXES
RELAXED
RELAXES
TELEXED
TELEXES

••L••X•
POLEAXE

••L•••X
CALLBOX
HALIFAX
MALRAUX
MILIEUX
PILLBOX
POLLTAX
ROLODEX
SALTBOX

•••L••X
CALLBOX
MAILBOX
PHALANX
PILLBOX
POLLTAX
TOOLBOX

••••L•X
BENELUX
COMPLEX
FIATLUX
PERPLEX
SIMPLEX
TRIPLEX

LY•••••
LYCEUMS
LYINGTO
LYRICAL
LYRISTS
LYSENKO

L•Y••••
LAYAWAY
LAYBACK
LAYDOWN
LAYERED
LAYETTE
LAYINTO
LAYITON
LAYOFFS
LAYOPEN
LAYOUTS
LAYOVER
LAYSFOR
LAYSLOW
LAYSOFF
LAYSOUT
LOYALLY
LOYALTY

L••Y•••
LADYBUG
LADYDAY
LADYISH
LANYARD
LAWYERS
LAZYISH
LEVYING
LIBYANS
LILYPAD

L•••Y••
LIPSYNC
LOBBYER

L••••Y•
LACKEYS
LOONEYS
LOWBOYS

L•••••Y
LADYDAY
LAMPREY
LANGLEY
LANGTRY
LANKILY
LARCENY
LARGELY
LASTORY
LATENCY
LATHERY
LAUNDRY
LAYAWAY
LEERILY
LEGALLY
LEGIBLY
LENGTHY
LETSFLY
LEVELLY
LIBERTY
LIBRARY
LICITLY
LIGHTLY
LINDSAY
LINDSEY
LIQUEFY
LITHELY
LITURGY
LIVIDLY
LOCALLY
LOFTILY
LOOSELY
LOTTERY
LOUSILY
LOVABLY
LOVERLY
LOYALLY
LOYALTY
LUCENCY
LUCIDLY
LUCKILY
LULLABY
LUMPILY
LURIDLY
LUSTILY

•LY••••
ALYKHAN
ALYOSHA
ALYSSUM
ELYSEES
ELYSIAN
ELYSIUM
FLYAWAY
FLYBALL
FLYBOYS
FLYCAST
FLYFISH
FLYHIGH
FLYLEAF
FLYLESS
FLYNETS
FLYOVER
FLYPAST
FLYRODS
FLYTRAP
FLYWAYS
OLYMPIA
OLYMPIC
OLYMPUS
PLYWOOD
SLYNESS
ULYANOV
ULYSSES

•L•Y•••
ALLYING
ALLYSON
CLAYIER
CLAYISH
CLAYTON
CLOYING
FLAYING
FLEYING
PLAYACT
PLAYBOY
PLAYDOH
PLAYERS
PLAYFUL
PLAYING
PLAYLET
PLAYOFF
PLAYOUT
PLAYPEN
PLAYSAT
PLAYSON
PLAYSUP
SLAYERS
SLAYTON

•L••Y••
ALLAYED
ALLAYER
ALLEYES
ALLOYED
PLATYPI

•L•••Y•
FLYBOYS
FLYWAYS
GLADEYE
OLDDAYS
SLAVEYS

•L••••Y
ALBUNDY
ALCHEMY
ALERTLY
ALIMONY
ALLENBY
ALLERGY
ALLOWAY
ALOOFLY
ALREADY
BLACKLY
BLANDLY
BLANKLY
BLARNEY
BLEAKLY
BLIGHTY
BLINDLY
BLOTCHY
BLOWDRY
BLOWFLY
BLUEBOY
BLUEJAY
BLUESKY
BLUFFLY
BLUNTLY
CLARIFY
CLARITY
CLEANLY
CLEARLY
CLERISY
CLIQUEY
CLOONEY
CLOSEBY
CLOSELY
ELDERLY
ELUSORY
FLAGDAY
FLAKILY
FLAUNTY
FLEETLY
FLESHLY
FLIGHTY
FLOUNCY
FLOWERY
FLUENCY
FLUIDLY
FLYAWAY
GLORIFY
OLDFOGY
PLAINLY
PLAYBOY
PLENARY
PLIABLY
PLIANCY
PLOWBOY
PLUMPLY
PLUSHLY
SLACKLY
SLAVERY
SLEEKLY
SLICKLY
SLIMILY
SLOUCHY

••LY•••
ALLYING
ALLYSON
BELYING
CALYCES
CALYPSO
CALYXES
HALYARD
HOLYARK
HOLYCOW
HOLYDAY
HOLYOKE
HOLYSEE
HOLYWAR
LILYPAD
ONLYTOO
ONLYYOU
POLYGON
POLYMER
RELYING

••L•Y••
ALLAYED
ALLAYER
ALLEYES
ALLOYED
BELAYED
BELLYUP
COLLYER
DELAYED
DELAYER
HALCYON
MALAYAN
ONLYYOU
RALLYTO
RELAYED
SPLAYED
TALLYHO
TALLYUP

••L••Y•
GALLEYS
GILGUYS
GOLDWYN
PULLEYS
VALLEYS
VOLLEYS
WALLEYE

••L•••Y
ALLENBY
ALLERGY
ALLOWAY
APLENTY
BALCONY
BALKILY
BALLBOY
BALMILY
BALONEY
BELLAMY
BELLBOY
BELTWAY
BILLOWY
CALCIFY
CALGARY
CALUMNY
CALVARY
DALTREY
DELANEY
DULCIFY
FALLACY
FALLGUY
FALSELY
FALSIFY
FALSITY
FOLKWAY
GALLERY
GELIDLY
HALFWAY
HALLWAY
HELOTRY
HILLARY
HOLIDAY
HOLYDAY
JOLLIFY
JOLLILY
JOLLITY
KILLJOY
KOLACKY
LULLABY
MALMSEY
MILDEWY
MOLLIFY
NULLIFY
NULLITY
OBLOQUY
PALEDRY
PALFREY
PALJOEY
PALMARY
PILLORY
PILLOWY
SALSIFY
SALTILY
SILKILY
SILVERY
SOLIDLY
SPLASHY
SULKILY
TOLLWAY
TOLSTOY
UNLUCKY
VALENCY
VALIDLY
VELVETY
VOLUBLY
WALKWAY
WALLABY
WILLOWY
YELLOWY

•••LY••
ACOLYTE
ANALYSE
ANALYST
ANALYZE
BELLYUP
CARLYLE
COLLYER
EARLYON
RALLYTO
TALLYHO
TALLYUP

•••L•Y•
BAILEYS
BARLEYS
BYPLAYS
DEPLOYS
EMPLOYE
EMPLOYS
EVILEYE
GALLEYS
HURLEYS
MEDLEYS
MISLAYS
OUTLAYS
PARLAYS
PARLEYS
PULLEYS
REPLAYS
VALLEYS
VOLLEYS
WALLEYE
WAYLAYS
WURLEYS

•••L••Y
ABILITY
ADULTLY
AGILELY
AGILITY
AMPLIFY
ANALOGY
APOLOGY
BALLBOY
BELLAMY
BELLBOY
BILLOWY
BIOLOGY
CUTLERY
DAYLILY
DUALITY
ECOLOGY
FALLACY
FALLGUY
FOOLERY
GALLERY
GEOLOGY
HALLWAY
HEALTHY
HILLARY
JOLLIFY
JOLLILY
JOLLITY
KILLJOY
LULLABY
MOLLIFY
NULLIFY
NULLITY
PILLORY
PILLOWY
POULTRY
PTOLEMY
QUALIFY
QUALITY
RAILWAY
REALITY
RIFLERY
SEALILY
SHELLEY
STALELY
SURLILY
SWELTRY
TOLLWAY
TRILOGY
TROLLEY
UTILITY
WALLABY
WEALTHY
WILLOWY
WOOLLEY
WOOLSEY
WORLDLY
YELLOWY
ZOOLOGY

••••LY•
CAROLYN
KAROLYI
MARILYN

••••L•Y
AIRPLAY
AURALLY
AWFULLY
AXIALLY
BANALLY
BARKLEY
BASALLY
BENTLEY
BRADLEY
BRIMLEY
BUCKLEY
BYGOLLY
CAVALRY
CHARLEY
CIVILLY
CRUELLY
CRUELTY
DARNLEY
DEVILRY
DIDDLEY
DISPLAY
ENDPLAY
EQUALLY
FACULTY
FINALLY
FRAILLY
FRAILTY
FRAWLEY
GREELEY
GUNPLAY
HEMSLEY
HUNTLEY
IDEALLY
JEWELRY
LANGLEY
LEGALLY
LEVELLY
LOCALLY
LOYALLY
LOYALTY
MISALLY
MISPLAY
MORALLY
NASALLY
NOVELTY
OUTPLAY
OVERLAY
PAISLEY
PARSLEY
PENALTY
PRESLEY
QUIGLEY
REGALLY
REVELRY
RIVALRY
ROYALLY
ROYALTY
RURALLY
SAVELOY
SHAPLEY
SHELLEY
SHIRLEY
SHRILLY
STANLEY
TONALLY
TOTALLY
TROLLEY
USUALLY
VENALLY
VITALLY
VOCALLY
WOOLLEY
WRIGLEY
ZONALLY

•••••LY
ACRIDLY
ACUTELY
ADEPTLY
ADULTLY
AFFABLY
AGILELY
ALERTLY
ALOOFLY
AMIABLY
ANGRILY
ANOMALY
APISHLY
AUDIBLY
AURALLY
AWFULLY
AXIALLY
BAGGILY
BALKILY
BALMILY
BANALLY
BASALLY
BAWDILY
BEASTLY
BEVERLY
BLACKLY
BLANDLY
BLANKLY
BLEAKLY
BLINDLY
BLOWFLY
BLUFFLY
BLUNTLY
BONNILY
BOSSILY
BRAMBLY
BRASHLY
BRAVELY
BRIEFLY
BRISKLY
BRISTLY
BROADLY
BRUTELY
BUMPILY
BUSHILY
BYGOLLY
CAMPILY
CANNILY
CANTILY
CAPABLY
CATTILY
CHARILY
CHEAPLY
CHIEFLY
CIVILLY
CLEANLY
CLEARLY
CLOSELY
COCKILY
CORNILY
COURTLY
CRACKLY
CRASSLY
CRAZILY
CRINKLY
CRISPLY
CROSSLY
CRUDELY
CRUELLY
CRUMBLY
CRUMPLY
DAFFILY
DATEDLY
DAYLILY
DAZEDLY
DEERFLY
DENSELY
DINGILY
DIRTILY
DIZZILY
DOTTILY
DOWDILY
DRIZZLY
DURABLY
DUSKILY
DUSTILY
EAGERLY
EARTHLY
ELDERLY
EMPTILY
EQUABLY
EQUALLY
ERECTLY
EROSELY
EXACTLY
FAINTLY
FALSELY
FANCILY
FATTILY
FETIDLY
FIERILY
FIFTHLY
FINALLY
FIREFLY
FIRSTLY
FISHILY
FIXEDLY
FLAKILY
FLEETLY
FLESHLY
FLUIDLY
FOAMILY
FOGGILY
FRAILLY
FRANKLY
FRECKLY
FRESHLY
FRIZZLY
FUNKILY
FUNNILY
FUSSILY
FUSTILY
FUZZILY
GAUDILY
GAUNTLY
GAUZILY
GAWKILY
GELIDLY
GHASTLY
GHOSTLY
GIDDILY
GOOFILY
GOONILY
GOUTILY
GRANDLY
GRAVELY
GREATLY
GRIMILY
GRISTLY
GRIZZLY
GROSSLY
GRUFFLY
GRUMBLY
GUSHILY
GUSTILY
GUTSILY
HAMMILY
HANDILY
HAPPILY
HARDILY
HARSHLY
HASTILY
HEADILY
HEAVILY
HEFTILY
HOARILY
HUFFILY
HUMANLY
HUMIDLY
HUSKILY
IDEALLY
IGNOBLY
INANELY
INAPTLY
INEPTLY
INERTLY
IRATELY
JADEDLY
JAZZILY
JERKILY
JOINTLY
JOLLILY
JUICILY
JUMPILY
KINKILY
LANKILY
LARGELY
LEERILY
LEGALLY
LEGIBLY
LETSFLY
LEVELLY
LICITLY
LIGHTLY
LITHELY
LIVIDLY
LOCALLY
LOFTILY
LOOSELY
LOUSILY
LOVABLY
LOVERLY
LOYALLY
LUCIDLY
LUCKILY
LUMPILY
LURIDLY
LUSTILY
MEATILY
MERRILY
MESSILY
MISALLY
MISERLY
MISTILY
MOISTLY
MONTHLY
MOODILY
MOONILY
MORALLY
MOVABLY
MUCKILY
MUDDILY
MURKILY
MUSHILY
MUSSILY
MUSTILY
MUTABLY
MUZZILY
NAIVELY
NAKEDLY
NASALLY
NASTILY
NATTILY
NEEDILY
NERVILY
NIFTILY
NIGHTLY
NINTHLY
NOISILY
NOTABLY
NOTEDLY
NUTTILY
ORDERLY
OVERFLY
OVERTLY
PANOPLY
PEPPILY
PERKILY
PESKILY
PETTILY
PHONILY
PIOUSLY
PITHILY
PLAINLY
PLIABLY
PLUMPLY
PLUSHLY
PODGILY
PRICKLY
PRIVILY
PRONELY
PROSILY
PROUDLY
PUDGILY
PUFFILY

PUNNILY
PUSHILY
QUAKILY
QUEENLY
QUEERLY
QUICKLY
QUIETLY
RABIDLY
RAINILY
RAPIDLY
READILY
REGALLY
RIANTLY
RIGHTLY
RIGIDLY
RISIBLY
RISKILY
RITZILY
ROOMILY
ROUGHLY
ROUNDLY
ROWDILY
ROYALLY
RUDDILY
RURALLY
RUSTILY
SAINTLY
SALTILY
SANDFLY
SAPPILY
SASSILY
SAUCILY
SAVVILY
SCANTLY
SCARILY
SCRAWLY
SEALILY
SEEDILY
SHADILY
SHAKILY
SHAPELY
SHARPLY
SHEERLY
SHINILY
SHOOFLY
SHORTLY
SHOWILY
SHRILLY
SIGHTLY
SILKILY
SIXTHLY
SIZABLY
SLACKLY
SLEEKLY
SLICKLY
SLIMILY
SMARTLY
SMOKILY
SNAKILY
SNIDELY
SNIFFLY
SNOWILY
SNUFFLY
SOAPILY
SOBERLY
SOGGILY
SOLIDLY
SOOTILY
SORRILY
SOUNDLY
SPANGLY
SPARELY
SPICILY
SPIKILY

SPINDLY
SQUATLY
STAGILY
STAIDLY
STALELY
STARKLY
STATELY
STEEPLY
STERNLY
STIFFLY
STOKELY
STONILY
STOUTLY
STUBBLY
SUAVELY
SULKILY
SUNNILY
SURLILY
SWEETLY
SWIFTLY
TACITLY
TACKILY
TARDILY
TASTILY
TATTILY
TAWNILY
TEARILY
TENABLY
TENSELY
TENTHLY
TEPIDLY
TERSELY
TESTFLY
TESTILY
THICKLY
THIRDLY
THISTLY
TIGHTLY
TIMIDLY
TINNILY
TIPSILY
TIREDLY
TONALLY
TOTALLY
TOUGHLY
TREACLY
TREMBLY
TRITELY
TWINKLY
UNAPTLY
UNGODLY
USUALLY
UTTERLY
VAGUELY
VALIDLY
VAPIDLY
VENALLY
VEXEDLY
VISIBLY
VITALLY
VIVIDLY
VOCALLY
VOLUBLY
WACKILY
WASPILY
WEARILY
WEEDILY
WEIRDLY
WINDILY
WISPILY
WITTILY
WOMANLY
WOOZILY
WORDILY

WORLDLY
WRIGGLY
WRINKLY
WRONGLY
ZONALLY

L•Z••••
LAZARUS
LAZIEST
LAZYISH
LIZARDS
LOZENGE

L•••Z••
LEIPZIG

L••••Z•
LIONIZE
LORENZO

L•••••Z
LAISSEZ
LEIBNIZ

•L•Z•••
BLAZERS
BLAZING
BLAZONS
GLAZERS
GLAZIER
GLAZING
GLOZING

•L••Z••
ALCAZAR
BLITZED
BLITZEN
BLITZES
GLITZED
GLITZES
KLUTZES

•L••••Z
ALBENIZ
ALVAREZ

••LZ•••
CALZONE

••L•Z••
PALAZZI
PALAZZO
SALAZAR
SELTZER
WALTZED
WALTZER
WALTZES

••L••Z•
PALAZZI
PALAZZO

•••L•Z•
ANALYZE
IDOLIZE
REALIZE
STYLIZE
UTILIZE

•••L••Z
BERLIOZ
BERLITZ
KOBLENZ

••••L•Z
SCHULTZ

MA•••••
MACABRE
MACADAM
MACAQUE
MACBETH
MACDUFF
MACGRAW
MACHETE
MACHINA
MACHINE
MACRAME
MACRONS
MACULAE
MADAMEX
MADCAPS
MADCHEN
MADDENS
MADDERS
MADDEST
MADDING
MADDISH
MADEFOR
MADEHAY
MADEIRA
MADEOFF
MADEOUT
MADEPAR
MADEWAY
MADIGAN
MADISON
MADLIBS
MADNESS
MADONNA
MAENADS
MAESTRI
MAESTRO
MAEWEST
MAFFICK
MAGENTA
MAGICAL
MAGINOT
MAGNANI
MAGNATE
MAGNETO
MAGNETS
MAGNIFY
MAGNUMS
MAGPIES
MAGUEYS
MAGUIRE
MAGYARS
MAHALIA
MAHARIS
MAHATMA
MAHONEY
MAHOUTS
MAIDENS
MAIDISH
MAIGRET
MAILBAG
MAILBOX
MAILCAR
MAILERS
MAILING
MAILLOT
MAILOUT
MAILSIN
MAINTOP
MAITAIS
MAITRED
MAJESTE

MAJESTY
MAJEURE
MAJORCA
MAJORED
MAKEFOR
MAKEHAY
MAKEOFF
MAKEOUT
MAKEPAR
MAKESDO
MAKESIT
MAKESUP
MAKEUPS
MAKEWAY
MAKINGS
MALABAR
MALACCA
MALACHI
MALAISE
MALAMUD
MALAYAN
MALCOLM
MALEATE
MALEFIC
MALIGNS
MALKINS
MALLARD
MALLETS
MALLOWS
MALLRAT
MALMSEY
MALODOR
MALRAUX
MALTEDS
MALTESE
MALTHUS
MALTIER
MALTING
MALTOSE
MAMBOED
MAMMALS
MAMMOTH
MANACLE
MANAGED
MANAGER
MANAGES
MANAGUA
MANANAS
MANATEE
MANCINI
MANDALA
MANDANS
MANDATE
MANDAYS
MANDELA
MANEGES
MANFRED
MANGERS
MANGIER
MANGLED
MANGLES
MANGOES
MANHOLE
MANHOOD
MANHOUR
MANHUNT
MANIACS
MANILOW
MANIOCS
MANIPLE
MANITOU
MANKIND
MANLESS
MANLIER

MANLIKE
MANMADE
MANNERS
MANNING
MANNISH
MANOWAR
MANSARD
MANSION
MANTELS
MANTLED
MANTLES
MANTRAP
MANTRAS
MANTRIC
MANUALS
MANUMIT
MANXCAT
MANXMAN
MANXMEN
MANYEAR
MAOISTS
MAPPERS
MAPPING
MARABOU
MARACAS
MARAUDS
MARBLED
MARBLES
MARCATO
MARCEAU
MARCELS
MARCHED
MARCHER
MARCHES
MARCHON
MARCONI
MARENGO
MARGATE
MARGAUX
MARGAYS
MARGINS
MARGRET
MARIANA
MARILYN
MARIMBA
MARINAS
MARINER
MARINES
MARITAL
MARKERS
MARKETS
MARKHAM
MARKHOR
MARKING
MARKKAA
MARKOFF
MARKOVA
MARKSUP
MARKUPS
MARLENE
MARLINS
MARLOWE
MARMARA
MARMION
MARMOTS
MAROONS
MARQUEE
MARQUES
MARQUEZ
MARQUIS
MARRIED
MARRIES
MARRING
MARROWS

MARRYME
MARSALA
MARSHAL
MARSHES
MARTENS
MARTIAL
MARTIAN
MARTINA
MARTINI
MARTINO
MARTINS
MARTYRS
MARVELS
MARXISM
MARXIST
MARYANN
MARYKAY
MARYLOU
MASARYK
MASCARA
MASCOTS
MASHERS
MASHIES
MASHING
MASKERS
MASKING
MASONIC
MASONRY
MASQUES
MASSAGE
MASSEUR
MASSIER
MASSIFS
MASSING
MASSIVE
MASTABA
MASTERS
MASTERY
MASTICS
MASTIFF
MASTOID
MATADOR
MATCHED
MATCHES
MATCHUP
MATELOT
MATEWAN
MATHERS
MATHEWS
MATHIAS
MATILDA
MATINEE
MATISSE
MATLESS
MATLOCK
MATRONS
MATTERS
MATTHAU
MATTHEW
MATTING
MATTOCK
MATURED
MATURER
MATURES
MATZOHS
MAUDLIN
MAUGHAM
MAULDIN
MAULING
MAUMAUS
MAUNDER
MAUREEN
MAURICE
MAUROIS

MAWKISH
MAXBAER
MAXBORN
MAXILLA
MAXIMAL
MAXIMUM
MAXIMUS
MAXWELL
MAYALIN
MAYDAYS
MAYFAIR
MAYHEMS
MAYNARD
MAYORAL
MAYPOLE
MAYTIME
MAYTREE
MAYWINE
MAZIEST
MAZURKA

M•A••••
MBABANE
MEADOWS
MEADOWY
MEALIER
MEALIES
MEANDER
MEANEST
MEANIES
MEANING
MEASLES
MEASURE
MEATIER
MEATILY
MIAMIAN
MIAMIAS
MIAOYAO
MIASMAS
MIASMIC
MOANERS
MOANFUL
MOANING
MUAMMAR
MYANMAR

M••A•••
MACABRE
MACADAM
MACAQUE
MADAMEX
MAHALIA
MAHARIS
MAHATMA
MALABAR
MALACCA
MALACHI
MALAISE
MALAMUD
MALAYAN
MANACLE
MANAGED
MANAGER
MANAGES
MANAGUA
MANANAS
MANATEE
MARABOU
MARACAS
MARAUDS
MASARYK
MATADOR
MAYALIN
MCCALLS

MCGAVIN
MCMAHON
MEDALED
MEGAHIT
MELANGE
MELANIE
MELANIN
MENACED
MENACES
MENAGES
METATES
MIKADOS
MINABLE
MINARET
MIRACLE
MIRADOR
MIRAGES
MIRAMAR
MIRAMAX
MIRANDA
MISALLY
MIXABLE
MOGAMBO
MOHAIRS
MOHAWKS
MONARCH
MORAINE
MORALES
MORALLY
MORANIS
MORAVIA
MOSAICS
MOVABLE
MOVABLY
MRMAGOO
MUBARAK
MUTABLE
MUTABLY
MUTAGEN
MUTANTS
MUTATED
MUTATES
MYMAMMY

M•••A••
MACRAME
MADCAPS
MAENADS
MAGNANI
MAGNATE
MAGYARS
MAITAIS
MALEATE
MALLARD
MALRAUX
MAMMALS
MANDALA
MANDANS
MANDATE
MANDAYS
MANIACS
MANMADE
MANSARD
MANUALS
MARCATO
MARGATE
MARGAUX
MARGAYS
MARIANA
MARMARA
MARSALA
MARYANN
MASCARA
MASSAGE

MASTABA
MAUMAUS
MAXBAER
MAYDAYS
MAYFAIR
MAYNARD
MBABANE
MEDIANS
MEDIANT
MEDIATE
MENIALS
MERMAID
MESCALS
MESSAGE
MESSALA
METHANE
MICHAEL
MICMACS
MIDDAYS
MIDEAST
MIDLAND
MIDWAYS
MIGRANT
MIGRATE
MIKHAIL
MILEAGE
MILHAUD
MILLAND
MILLARD
MINOANS
MINYANS
MISCALL
MISCAST
MISDATE
MISHAPS
MISLAID
MISLAYS
MISMATE
MISNAME
MISSAID
MISSALS
MISSAYS
MISTAKE
MOBCAPS
MOMBASA
MONDALE
MONDAYS
MONTAGE
MONTANA
MONTAND
MONTANE
MONTANI
MOORAGE
MORDANT
MORGANA
MORGANS
MORTALS
MORTARS
MOULAGE
MUDCATS
MUDPACK
MULLAHS
MUNDANE
MUSCATS
MUSTAFA
MUSTANG
MUSTARD
MUTUALS
MYRIADS

M••••A•
MACADAM
MACGRAW
MACULAE

MADEHAY
MADEPAR
MADEWAY
MADIGAN
MAGICAL
MAILBAG
MAILCAR
MAKEHAY
MAKEPAR
MAKEWAY
MALABAR
MALAYAN
MALLRAT
MANANAS
MANOWAR
MANTRAP
MANTRAS
MANXCAT
MANXMAN
MANYEAR
MARACAS
MARCEAU
MARINAS
MARITAL
MARKHAM
MARKKAA
MARSHAL
MARTIAL
MARTIAN
MARYKAY
MATEWAN
MATHIAS
MATTHAU
MAUGHAM
MAXIMAL
MAYORAL
MCLUHAN
MEDEVAC
MEDICAL
MEDIGAP
MEDUSAE
MEDUSAS
MEGRYAN
MENORAH
MESSIAH
MEXICAN
MIAMIAN
MIAMIAS
MIAOYAO
MIASMAS
MIDYEAR
MILKMAN
MILLDAM
MIMOSAS
MINERAL
MINICAB
MINICAM
MINIMAL
MINIVAN
MIRAMAR
MIRAMAX
MISDEAL
MISDIAL
MISHEAR
MISLEAD
MISPLAY
MISREAD
MISTRAL
MITHRAS
MITZVAH
MODELAS
MODULAR
MOHICAN
MOLOKAI

MRCLEAN
MUAMMAR
MUBARAK
MULETAS
MUSICAL
MUSKRAT
MYANMAR

M•••••A
MACHINA
MADEIRA
MADONNA
MAGENTA
MAHALIA
MAHATMA
MAJORCA
MALACCA
MANAGUA
MANDALA
MANDELA
MARIANA
MARIMBA
MARKKAA
MARKOVA
MARMARA
MARSALA
MARTINA
MASCARA
MASTABA
MATILDA
MAXILLA
MAZURKA
MEDULLA
MELINDA
MELISSA
MENDOZA
MESSALA
MESSINA
MESTIZA
MILITIA
MINERVA
MINOLTA
MINORCA
MINUTIA
MIRANDA
MOLDOVA
MOMBASA
MONTANA
MONTOYA
MORAVIA
MORGANA
MUSTAFA

•MA••••
AMADEUS
AMALGAM
AMAPOLA
AMASSED
AMASSER
AMASSES
AMATEUR
AMATIVE
AMATORY
AMAZING
AMAZONS
EMAILED
EMANANT
EMANATE
EMANUEL
IMAGERS
IMAGERY
IMAGINE
IMAGING
IMAGOES

IMAMATE
IMARETS
SMACKED
SMACKER
SMALLER
SMALTOS
SMARTED
SMARTEN
SMARTER
SMARTLY
SMASHED
SMASHER
SMASHES
SMASHUP
SMATTER

•M•A•••
AMHARIC
AMIABLE
AMIABLY
AMRADIO
EMBANKS
EMBARGO
EMBARKS
EMBASSY
EMBAYED
EMPANEL
EMPATHY
FMRADIO
IMPACTS
IMPAIRS
IMPALAS
IMPALED
IMPALES
IMPANEL
IMPARTS
IMPASSE
IMPASTO
SMEARED
UMLAUTS

•M••A••
AMYLASE
EMANANT
EMANATE
EMBRACE
EMERALD
EMIRATE
EMULATE
IMAMATE
IMITATE
IMPEACH
IMPLANT
OMPHALI
SMETANA
UMBRAGE

•M•••A•
AMALGAM
AMISTAD
AMOEBAE
AMOEBAS
AMSCRAY
IMMORAL
IMPALAS
UMBRIAN

•M••••A
AMAPOLA
AMERICA
AMERIKA
AMMONIA
AMNESIA
AMPHORA

EMERITA
EMPORIA
SMETANA

••MA•••
ALMAATA
ALMADEN
ALMANAC
ARMADAS
DAMAGED
DAMAGES
DAMASKS
DEMANDS
DOMAINS
ENMASSE
FEMALES
HUMANLY
HUMANUM
INMATES
JAMAICA
JUMANJI
KOMATSU
LAMAISM
LAMAIST
LAMARCK
MCMAHON
MRMAGOO
MYMAMMY
NOMADIC
ORMANDY
POMADED
POMADES
RAMADAN
RAMADAS
REMAILS
REMAINS
REMAKES
REMANDS
REMARKS
REMARRY
ROMAINE
ROMANCE
ROMANIA
ROMANOV
ROMANSH
SAMARIA
SOMALIA
SOMALIS
SOMATIC
SUMATRA
TAMABLE
TAMALES
TAMARIN
UNMAKES
UNMASKS
WOMANLY

••M•A••
ALMAATA
ARMBAND
ARMYANT
BEMOANS
BOMBARD
BOMBAST
BUMRAPS
CAMPARI
CEMBALO
COMBATS
COMMAND
COMPACT
COMPANY
COMPARE
COMPASS
COMRADE

CYMBALS
DAMMARS
DEMEANS
GAMBADO
GIMBALS
GUMBALL
GYMBAGS
GYMNAST
HYMNALS
JAMPACK
JIMJAMS
KAMPALA
KIMBALL
LAMBADA
LIMEADE
LOMBARD
LUMBAGO
LUMBARS
MAMMALS
MOMBASA
NUMBATS
OOMPAHS
POMPANO
RAMPAGE
RAMPANT
RAMPART
REMNANT
RIMBAUD
RUMBAED
RUMMAGE
SAMBAED
SAMBALS
SAMBARS
SAMOANS
SAMPANS
SAMSARA
SIMIANS
SUMMARY
TAMBALA
TAMMANY
TAMTAMS
TIMBALE
TIMBALS
TOMCATS
TYMPANA
TYMPANI
WOMBATS

••M••A•
ADMIRAL
AIMEDAT
ALMANAC
ARMADAS
ARMLOAD
BIMODAL
CAMERAS
COMESAT
COMICAL
FEMORAL
GAMBIAN
GAMELAW
HUMERAL
IMMORAL
JUMPSAT
KUMQUAT
LAMBDAS
LAMBEAU
LAMINAE
LAMINAL
LAMINAR
LAMINAS
MIMOSAS
NAMEDAY
NAMETAG
NOMINAL
NUMERAL
PEMICAN
RAMADAN
RAMADAS
RAMBEAU
REMORAS
REMOVAL
REMUDAS
ROMULAN
SAMEDAY
SAMOVAR
SAMPRAS
SAMURAI
SEMINAL
SEMINAR
SIMILAR
SOMEDAY
SOMEWAY
TEMPLAR
TIMELAG
ZAMBIAN

••M•••A
ALMAATA
AMMONIA
ARMENIA
CAMELIA
JAMAICA
KAMPALA
LAMBADA
LAMOTTA
LEMPIRA
MOMBASA
NAMIBIA
POMPEIA
ROMANIA
SAMARIA
SAMSARA
SOMALIA
SUMATRA
TAMBALA
TEMPERA
TEMPURA
TOMBOLA
TYMPANA
VAMPIRA

•••MA••
ADAMANT
AIRMADA
AIRMAIL
AIRMASS
ANIMALS
ANIMATE
ANIMATO
ANOMALY
ARAMAIC
ATAMANS
BARMAID
BIOMASS
BITMAPS
BROMATE
BURMANS
CAIMANS
CAYMANS
CLIMATE
COMMAND
DAMMARS
DAYMARE
DENMARK
DISMAYS
DOGMATA
DOLMANS
DORMANT
EARMARK
FANMAIL
FORMALS
FORMATS
FROMAGE
GASMAIN
GERMANE
GERMANS
GERMANY
GRIMACE
HAEMATO
HERMANN
HETMANS
IMAMATE
ISHMAEL
KIRMANS
KLAMATH
MAMMALS
MANMADE
MARMARA
MAUMAUS
MERMAID
MICMACS
MISMATE
NEWMATH
NORMALS
NORMAND
NORMANS
OLDMAID
PALMARY
PALMATE
PLUMAGE
PRIMACY
PRIMARY
PRIMATE
REAMASS
RUMMAGE
SFUMATO
SHAMANS
SKIMASK
STOMACH
STOMATA
SUMMARY
SUNMAID
TAMMANY
TARMACS
TEDMACK
TOPMAST
TREMAIN
ULLMANN
WALMART
WIDMARK
YESMAAM
YOUMANS
ZERMATT

•••M•A•
ALUMNAE
ALUMNAL
ARAMEAN
BESMEAR
CHEMLAB
CRIMEAN
GRAMMAR
GRAMPAS
HOLMOAK
MIAMIAN
MIAMIAS
MUAMMAR
NUTMEAT
OATMEAL
REDMEAT
RHUMBAS
TRAMCAR
TRAMPAS
YESMAAM

•••M••A
AIRMADA
ALAMEDA
BERMUDA
CHIMERA
CREMONA
DOGMATA
FORMICA
FORMOSA
FORMULA
MARMARA
OLYMPIA
OXYMORA
STAMINA
STOMATA
WOOMERA

••••MA•
ABYSMAL
AUTOMAT
BAHAMAS
BASEMAN
BATEMAN
BATHMAT
BATSMAN
BELLMAN
BERGMAN
BESTMAN
BETAMAX
BIRDMAN
BOATMAN
BONDMAN
BRAHMAN
BRAHMAS
BUSHMAN
BYREMAN
CAVEMAN
CHAPMAN
CINEMAS
CINEMAX
COLEMAN
CREWMAN
DARKMAN
DECIMAL
DOORMAN
DOORMAT
DUSTMAN
EASTMAN
ENIGMAS
FADIMAN
FELDMAN
FEYNMAN
FIREMAN
FLAGMAN
FOOTMAN
FOREMAN
FREEMAN
FROGMAN
GATEMAN
GOODMAN
GRAMMAR
HACKMAN
HANGMAN
HARTMAN
HEADMAN
HEISMAN
HELLMAN
HICKMAN
HOFFMAN
HOUSMAN
IDEAMAN
INGEMAR
INHUMAN
IRONMAN
JAVAMAN
JAZZMAN
JICAMAS
JUNKMAN
KAUFMAN
KINEMAS
KINGMAN
KINSMAN
KLUGMAN
LIKEMAD
LINEMAN
LOCOMAN
MANXMAN
MAXIMAL
MIASMAS
MILKMAN
MINIMAL
MIRAMAR
MIRAMAX
MUAMMAR
MYANMAR
NEWSMAN
OPTIMAL
OTTOMAN
PAJAMAS
PALOMAR
PANAMAS
PERLMAN
PIKEMAN
PITTMAN
PLASMAS
PLOWMAN
PORTMAN
POSTMAN
POTOMAC
PROPMAN
PULLMAN
PYJAMAS
RAINMAN
REITMAN
REPOMAN
RICHMAN
RICKMAN
ROADMAP
SANDMAN
SCHEMAS
SHERMAN
SHIPMAN
SHOWMAN
SIDEMAN
SNOWMAN
STARMAN
STARMAP
STIGMAS
SYNGMAN
TAPEMAN
TASHMAN
TAXIMAN
THERMAL
THURMAN
TRAUMAS
TUCHMAN
ULTIMAS
WALKMAN
WELLMAN
WHITMAN
WISEMAN
WOLFMAN
WORKMAN
YAKIMAS
YARDMAN
YASHMAK
ZEUGMAS

••••M•A
ANAEMIA
ANOSMIA
BOHEMIA
CARAMBA
CARAMIA
DILEMMA
ENCOMIA
LABAMBA
MARIMBA
PIPEMMA

•••••MA
ALABAMA
ATACAMA
DEPALMA
DILEMMA
DIORAMA
DIPLOMA
DRACHMA
GAUTAMA
GRANDMA
IPANEMA
IWOJIMA
LAPALMA
MAHATMA
NOXZEMA
PIPEMMA
SATSUMA

MB•••••
MBABANE

M•B••••
MOBBING
MOBBISH
MOBCAPS
MOBILES
MOBSTER
MRBONES
MUBARAK

M••B•••
MACBETH
MAMBOED
MARBLED
MARBLES
MAXBAER
MAXBORN
MBABANE
MEMBERS
MOBBING
MOBBISH
MOMBASA
MUMBLED
MUMBLER
MUMBLES

M•••B••
MACABRE
MAILBAG
MAILBOX
MALABAR
MARABOU
MINABLE
MINIBUS
MIXABLE
MOVABLE
MOVABLY
MUTABLE
MUTABLY

M••••B•
MADLIBS
MARIMBA
MASTABA
MICROBE
MIDRIBS
MOGAMBO
MORESBY

M•••••B
MINICAB

•MB••••
AMBIENT
AMBLERS
AMBLING
AMBRIES
AMBROSE
EMBANKS
EMBARGO
EMBARKS
EMBASSY
EMBAYED
EMBLEMS
EMBRACE
EMBROIL
EMBRYOS
IMBIBED
IMBIBES
IMBRUED
IMBRUES
IMBUING
UMBERTO
UMBRAGE
UMBRIAN

•M•B•••
AMIBLUE

•M••B••
AMIABLE
AMIABLY
AMOEBAE
AMOEBAS
AMOEBIC
IMBIBED
IMBIBES
OMNIBUS

••MB•••
ARMBAND
BAMBINO
BAMBOOS
BOMBARD
BOMBAST
BOMBECK
BOMBERS
BOMBING
BUMBLED
BUMBLER
BUMBLES
CAMBERS
CAMBIUM
CAMBRIC
CEMBALO
COMBATS
COMBERS
COMBINE
COMBING
COMBUST
CYMBALS
DIMBULB
DUMBEST
DUMBING
FUMBLED
FUMBLER
FUMBLES
GAMBADO
GAMBIAN
GAMBITS
GAMBLED
GAMBLER
GAMBLES
GAMBOLS
GAMBREL
GIMBALS
GUMBALL
GYMBAGS
HAMBURG
HOMBRES
HOMBURG
HUMBLED
HUMBLER
HUMBLES
HUMBUGS
JUMBLED
JUMBLES
KIMBALL
LAMBADA
LAMBDAS
LAMBEAU
LAMBENT
LAMBERT
LIMBERS
LIMBING
LOMBARD
LUMBAGO
LUMBARS
LUMBERS
MAMBOED
MEMBERS
MOMBASA
MUMBLED
MUMBLER
MUMBLES
NIMBLER
NUMBATS
NUMBERS
NUMBEST
NUMBING
RAMBEAU
RAMBLED
RAMBLER
RAMBLES
RIMBAUD
RUMBAED
RUMBLED
RUMBLES
SAMBAED
SAMBALS
SAMBARS
SYMBOLS
TAMBALA
TAMBOUR
TEMBLOR
TIMBALE
TIMBALS
TIMBERS
TIMBRES
TOMBOLA
TOMBOYS
TUMBLED
TUMBLER
TUMBLES
TUMBREL
WAMBLED
WAMBLES
WIMBLED
WIMBLES
WOMBATS
ZAMBEZI
ZAMBIAN
ZAMBONI
ZOMBIES
ZOMBIFY

••M•B••
GEMSBOK
HOMEBOY
NAMIBIA
TAMABLE

••M••B•
COMESBY

••M•••B
DIMBULB

•••MB••
ALEMBIC
BOOMBOX
BRAMBLE
BRAMBLY
CHAMBER
CLAMBER
CLIMBED
CLIMBER
CRUMBLE
CRUMBLY
FLAMBED
FLAMBES
FNUMBER
GRUMBLE
GRUMBLY
PLUMBED
PLUMBER
RHOMBUS
RHUMBAS
SHAMBLE
SLUMBER
STUMBLE
THIMBLE
THUMBED
TREMBLE
TREMBLY

•••M••B
CHEMLAB

••••MB•
BENUMBS
CARAMBA
COLUMBO
LABAMBA
MARIMBA
MOGAMBO

•••••MB
COULOMB
COXCOMB
HOTCOMB
SUCCUMB

MC•••••
MCCALLS
MCCLOUD
MCCLURE
MCENROE
MCGAVIN
MCGUIRE
MCHENRY
MCLUHAN
MCMAHON
MCQUEEN
MCSWINE

M•C••••
MACABRE
MACADAM
MACAQUE
MACBETH
MACDUFF
MACGRAW
MACHETE
MACHINA
MACHINE
MACRAME
MACRONS
MACULAE
MCCALLS
MCCLOUD
MCCLURE
MICHAEL
MICHELE
MICKEYS
MICMACS
MICROBE
MICRONS
MOCKERS
MOCKERY
MOCKING
MOCKUPS
MRCHIPS
MRCLEAN
MUCKIER
MUCKILY
MUCKING
MUCKSUP

M••C•••
MADCAPS
MADCHEN
MALCOLM
MANCINI
MARCATO
MARCEAU
MARCELS
MARCHED
MARCHER
MARCHES
MARCHON
MARCONI
MASCARA
MASCOTS
MATCHED
MATCHES
MATCHUP
MENCKEN
MERCERS
MERCERY
MERCIES
MERCURY
MESCALS
MINCERS
MINCING
MIOCENE
MISCALL
MISCAST
MISCUED
MISCUES
MITCHUM
MOBCAPS
MOOCHED
MOOCHER
MOOCHES
MUDCATS
MULCHED
MULCHES
MULCTED
MUNCHED
MUNCHER
MUNCHES
MUSCATS
MUSCLED
MUSCLES
MUSCOVY

M•••C••
MAGICAL
MAILCAR
MALACCA
MALACHI
MANACLE
MANXCAT
MARACAS
MEDICAL
MEDICOS
MENACED
MENACES
MEXICAN
MILKCOW
MIMICRY
MINICAB
MINICAM
MIRACLE
MODICUM
MOHICAN
MOLOCHS
MONOCLE
MONOCOT
MOROCCO
MUSICAL

M••••C•
MAFFICK
MAJORCA
MALACCA
MANIACS
MANIOCS
MASTICS
MATLOCK
MATTOCK
MAURICE
MENISCI
METRICS
MICMACS
MINORCA
MONARCH
MOROCCO
MOSAICS
MRSPOCK
MUDPACK
MURDOCH
MYSTICS

M•••••C
MALEFIC
MANTRIC
MASONIC
MEDEVAC
MEIOTIC
MELODIC
MIASMIC
MIDDLEC
MIMETIC
MITOTIC
MOLLUSC
MONODIC

•M•C•••
AMSCRAY
OMICRON
SMACKED
SMACKER

•M••C••
AMERCED
AMERCES
IMPACTS

•M•••C•
AMERICA
EMBRACE
IMPEACH

•M••••C
AMHARIC
AMOEBIC

••MC•••
JIMCHEE
KIMCHEE
TOMCATS

••M•C••
COMICAL
JUMPCUT
MIMICRY
PEMICAN
PUMICES
SAMECHS
TIMECOP

••M••C•
ARMLOCK
BOMBECK
COMPACT
GIMMICK
HAMHOCK
HAMMOCK
HEMLOCK
HUMMOCK
JAMAICA
JAMPACK
LAMARCK
PIMLICO
ROMANCE
TAMPICO

••M•••C
ALMANAC
CAMBRIC
COMEDIC
DEMONIC
HAMITIC
HOMERIC
MIMETIC
NOMADIC
NUMERIC
OSMOTIC
SEMITIC
SOMATIC

•••MC••
TRAMCAR

•••M•C•
DORMICE
FORMICA
GIMMICK
GRIMACE
HAMMOCK
HUMMOCK
MICMACS
PRIMACY
STOMACH
TARMACS
TEDMACK
TITMICE

•••M••C
ALEMBIC
ARAMAIC
OLYMPIC

••••M•C
ANAEMIC
ANOSMIC
CERAMIC
DYNAMIC
ENDEMIC
ISLAMIC
MIASMIC
POLEMIC
POTOMAC
SEISMIC
TOTEMIC

•••••MC
YOUNGMC

M•D••••
MADAMEX
MADCAPS
MADCHEN
MADDENS
MADDERS
MADDEST
MADDING
MADDISH
MADEFOR
MADEHAY
MADEIRA
MADEOFF
MADEOUT
MADEPAR
MADEWAY
MADIGAN
MADISON
MADLIBS
MADNESS
MADONNA
MEDALED
MEDDLED
MEDDLER
MEDDLES
MEDEVAC
MEDIANS
MEDIANT
MEDIATE
MEDICAL
MEDICOS
MEDIGAP
MEDIUMS
MEDLEYS
MEDULLA
MEDUSAE
MEDUSAS
MIDDAYS
MIDDENS
MIDDIES
MIDDLEC
MIDDLES
MIDEAST
MIDGETS
MIDLAND
MIDLIFE
MIDLINE
MIDMOST
MIDRIBS
MIDRIFF
MIDRISE
MIDSIZE
MIDTERM
MIDTOWN
MIDWAYS
MIDWEEK
MIDWEST
MIDWIFE
MIDYEAR
MODELAS
MODELED
MODELER
MODELTS
MODERNS
MODESTO
MODESTY
MODICUM
MODISTE
MODULAR
MODULES
MRDEEDS
MUDCATS
MUDDERS
MUDDIED
MUDDIER
MUDDIES
MUDDILY
MUDDLED
MUDDLER
MUDDLES
MUDEELS
MUDHENS
MUDPACK
MUDPIES

M••D•••
MACDUFF
MADDENS
MADDERS
MADDEST
MADDING
MADDISH
MAIDENS
MAIDISH
MANDALA
MANDANS
MANDATE
MANDAYS
MANDELA
MAUDLIN
MAYDAYS
MEADOWS
MEADOWY
MEDDLED
MEDDLER
MEDDLES
MELDING
MENDERS
MENDING
MENDOZA
MIDDAYS
MIDDENS
MIDDIES
MIDDLEC
MIDDLES
MILDEST
MILDEWS
MILDEWY
MILDRED
MINDERS

MINDFUL
MINDING
MINDSET
MISDATE
MISDEAL
MISDEED
MISDIAL
MISDOES
MISDONE
MOLDERS
MOLDIER
MOLDING
MOLDOVA
MONDALE
MONDAYS
MOODIER
MOODILY
MORDANT
MORDENT
MORDRED
MOWDOWN
MUDDERS
MUDDIED
MUDDIER
MUDDIES
MUDDILY
MUDDLED
MUDDLER
MUDDLES
MUNDANE
MURDERS
MURDOCH

M•••D••

MACADAM
MALODOR
MATADOR
MAULDIN
MAUNDER
MEANDER
MEGIDDO
MELODIC
MIKADOS
MILLDAM
MIRADOR
MIXEDIN
MIXEDUP
MONODIC
MOONDOG
MOULDED
MOULDER
MOUNDED
MOVEDIN
MOVEDON
MOVEDUP

M••••D•

MAENADS
MAKESDO
MALTEDS
MANMADE
MARAUDS
MATILDA
MEGIDDO
MELINDA
METHODS
MILORDS
MIRANDA
MRDEEDS
MYRIADS

M•••••D

MAITRED
MAJORED
MALAMUD
MALLARD
MAMBOED
MANAGED
MANFRED
MANGLED
MANHOOD
MANKIND
MANSARD
MANTLED
MARBLED
MARCHED
MARRIED
MASTOID
MATCHED
MATURED
MAYNARD
MCCLOUD
MEDALED
MEDDLED
MENACED
MERITED
MERMAID
METERED
MIDLAND
MILDRED
MILHAUD
MILLAND
MILLARD
MILLEND
MINGLED
MINORED
MINUEND
MISCUED
MISDEED
MISLAID
MISLEAD
MISREAD
MISSAID
MISUSED
MISWORD
MITERED
MITFORD
MIZZLED
MODELED
MONEYED
MONTAND
MOOCHED
MORDRED
MORPHED
MOSEYED
MOTORED
MOTTLED
MOULDED
MOULTED
MOUNDED
MOUNTED
MOURNED
MOUSSED
MOUTHED
MUDDIED
MUDDLED
MUFFLED
MULCHED
MULCTED
MUMBLED
MUMFORD
MUNCHED
MUSCLED
MUSTARD
MUTATED
MUZZLED

•M•D•••

AMADEUS
SMIDGEN
SMUDGED
SMUDGES

•M••D••

AMENDED
AMRADIO
EMENDED
EMENDER
FMRADIO
IMPEDED
IMPEDES
SMOLDER

•M•••D•

IMPENDS
IMPLODE

•M••••D

AMASSED
AMENDED
AMERCED
AMERIND
AMISTAD
EMAILED
EMBAYED
EMENDED
EMERALD
EMERGED
EMERSED
EMITTED
EMPTIED
IMBIBED
IMBRUED
IMMIXED
IMMURED
IMPALED
IMPEDED
IMPLIED
IMPOSED
IMPOUND
IMPUTED
OMITTED
SMACKED
SMARTED
SMASHED
SMEARED
SMELLED
SMELTED
SMIRKED
SMUDGED
UMPIRED

••MD•••

DUMDUMS
GUMDROP
HUMDRUM

••M•D••

AIMEDAT
AIMEDTO
ALMADEN
ARMADAS
BIMODAL
CAMEDUE
COMEDIC
COMEDUE
HUMIDLY
HUMIDOR
LAMBDAS
LAMEDHS
NAMEDAY
NOMADIC
POMADED
POMADES
RAMADAN
RAMADAS
REMODEL
REMUDAS
SAMEDAY
SOMEDAY
TIMIDER
TIMIDLY

••M••D•

ALMONDS
COMMODE
COMRADE
DEMANDS
GAMBADO
HYMNODY
LAMBADA
LEMONDE
LIMEADE
NIMRODS
ORMANDY
RAMRODS
REMANDS
REMENDS
REMINDS
REMOLDS

••M•••D

ADMIRED
ADMIXED
ARMBAND
ARMLOAD
ARMORED
BEMIRED
BEMUSED
BOMBARD
BUMBLED
CAMEOED
COMMAND
COMMEND
DAMAGED
DEMIGOD
DEMISED
DEMOTED
DIMPLED
DUMMIED
FUMBLED
GAMBLED
HAMMOND
HOMERED
HOMINID
HUMBLED
HUMORED
IMMIXED
IMMURED
JEMMIED
JIMMIED
JUMBLED
LIMITED
LOMBARD
MAMBOED
MUMBLED
MUMFORD
OSMOSED
POMADED
RAMBLED
REMIXED
REMOVED
REMOWED
RIMBAUD
RIMPLED
RUMBAED
RUMBLED
RUMORED
RUMPLED
SAMBAED
SAMOYED
SAMPLED
TEMPTED
TUMBLED
UNMOVED
WAMBLED
WIMBLED
WIMPLED

•••M•D•

AIRMADA
ALAMEDA
ALAMODE
BERMUDA
BROMIDE
COMMODE
DIOMEDE
MANMADE
PREMEDS
SCHMIDT

•••M••D

BARMAID
BRIMMED
CHAMPED
CHOMPED
CHUMMED
CLAMMED
CLAMPED
CLIMBED
CLOMPED
CLUMPED
COMMAND
COMMEND
CRAMMED
CRAMPED
CRIMPED
DESMOND
DIAMOND
DRUMMED
DUMMIED
FLAMBED
GLOMMED
GRUMPED
HAMMOND
JEMMIED
JIMMIED
MERMAID
NORMAND
OLDMAID
PLUMBED
PLUMPED
PRIMPED
RAYMOND
SCAMMED
SCAMPED
SHAMMED
SIGMUND
SKIMMED
SKIMPED
SLAMMED
SLIMMED
SLUMMED
SLUMPED
SPAMMED
STAMPED
STEMMED
STOMPED
STUMPED
STYMIED
SUNMAID
SWAMPED
THUMBED
THUMPED
TRAMPED
TRIMMED
TRUMPED
WHAMMED
WHOMPED

••••M•D

ALARMED
ASHAMED
ASSUMED
BLOOMED
BRIMMED
CAROMED
CHARMED
CHUMMED
CLAIMED
CLAMMED
CRAMMED
CREAMED
DEFAMED
DREAMED
DRUMMED
GLEAMED
GLOMMED
GLOOMED
GROOMED
ILLUMED
LIKEMAD
MALAMUD
PSALMED
PYRAMID
REAIMED
REARMED
RELUMED
RENAMED
RESUMED
RETIMED
SCAMMED
SCHEMED
SHAMMED
SKIMMED
SLAMMED
SLIMMED
SLUMMED
SPAMMED
STEAMED
STEMMED
STORMED
SWARMED
TRIMMED
UNAIMED
UNARMED
UNNAMED
UNTAMED
WHAMMED
WHELMED

ME•••••

MEADOWS
MEADOWY
MEALIER
MEALIES
MEANDER
MEANEST
MEANIES
MEANING
MEASLES
MEASURE
MEATIER
MEATILY
MEDALED
MEDDLED
MEDDLER
MEDDLES
MEDEVAC
MEDIANS
MEDIANT
MEDIATE
MEDICAL
MEDICOS
MEDIGAP
MEDIUMS
MEDLEYS
MEDULLA
MEDUSAE
MEDUSAS
MEEKEST
MEETING
MEGAHIT
MEGIDDO
MEGOHMS
MEGRIMS
MEGRYAN
MEINIES
MEIOSES
MEIOSIS
MEIOTIC
MEISSEN
MEISTER
MELANGE
MELANIE
MELANIN
MELDING
MELINDA
MELISSA
MELLOWS
MELODIC
MELROSE
MELTING
MEMBERS
MEMENTO
MEMOIRE
MEMOIRS
MEMOREX
MEMPHIS
MENACED
MENACES
MENAGES
MENCKEN
MENDERS
MENDING
MENDOZA
MENFOLK
MENHIRS
MENIALS
MENISCI
MENORAH
MENOTTI
MENTHOL
MENTION
MENTORS
MENUHIN
MENZIES
MEOWING
MERCERS
MERCERY
MERCIES
MERCURY
MERGERS
MERGING
MERIMEE
MERINOS
MERITED
MERLOTS
MERMAID
MERRIER
MERRILL
MERRILY
MESCALS
MESHIER
MESHING
MESSAGE
MESSALA
MESSIAH
MESSIER
MESSILY
MESSINA
MESSING
MESSKIT
MESTIZA
MESTIZO
METATES
METEORS
METEOUT
METERED
METHANE
METHODS
METIERS
METOOER
METRICS
METTLES
MEWLERS
MEWLING
MEXICAN

M•E••••

MAENADS
MAESTRI
MAESTRO
MAEWEST
MCENROE
MEEKEST
MEETING
MUEZZIN

M••E•••

MADEFOR
MADEHAY
MADEIRA
MADEOFF
MADEOUT
MADEPAR
MADEWAY
MAGENTA
MAJESTE
MAJESTY
MAJEURE
MAKEFOR
MAKEHAY
MAKEOFF
MAKEOUT
MAKEPAR
MAKESDO
MAKESIT
MAKESUP
MAKEUPS
MAKEWAY
MALEATE
MALEFIC
MANEGES
MARENGO
MATELOT
MATEWAN
MCHENRY
MEDEVAC
MEMENTO
METEORS
METEOUT
METERED
MIDEAST
MILEAGE
MIMESIS
MIMETIC
MINERAL
MINERVA
MISERLY
MITERED
MIXEDIN
MIXEDUP
MIXESIN
MIXESUP
MODELAS
MODELED
MODELER
MODELTS
MODERNS
MODESTO
MODESTY
MOLESTS
MOMENTS
MONEYED
MORELLO
MORESBY
MOSELLE
MOSEYED
MOVEDIN
MOVEDON
MOVEDUP
MOVEOUT
MOVESIN
MOVESON
MOVESUP
MRDEEDS
MUDEELS
MULETAS
MUMESON
MUSEFUL
MUSETTE
MUSEUMS

M•••E••

MACBETH
MACHETE
MADDENS
MADDERS
MADDEST
MADNESS
MAEWEST
MAGNETO
MAGNETS
MAGUEYS
MAIDENS
MAILERS
MALLETS
MALTEDS
MALTESE
MANDELA
MANGERS
MANLESS
MANNERS
MANTELS
MANYEAR
MAPPERS
MARCEAU
MARCELS
MARKERS
MARKETS
MARLENE
MARTENS
MARVELS
MASHERS
MASKERS
MASSEUR
MASTERS
MASTERY
MATHERS
MATHEWS
MATLESS
MATTERS
MAUREEN
MAXWELL
MAYHEMS
MAZIEST
MCQUEEN
MEANEST
MEDLEYS
MEEKEST
MEMBERS
MENDERS
MERCERS
MERCERY
MERGERS
METIERS
MEWLERS
MICHELE
MICKEYS
MIDDENS
MIDGETS
MIDTERM
MIDWEEK
MIDWEST
MIDYEAR
MILDEST
MILDEWS
MILDEWY
MILIEUS
MILIEUX
MILKERS
MILLEND
MILLERS
MILLETS
MILLETT
MIMIEUX
MINCERS
MINDERS
MINTERS
MINUEND
MINUETS
MIOCENE
MIRIEST
MISDEAL
MISDEED
MISHEAR
MISLEAD
MISREAD
MISTERS
MITTENS
MIZZENS
MOANERS
MOCKERS
MOCKERY
MOILERS
MOLDERS
MOLIERE
MOLTERS
MONGERS
MONKEES
MONKEYS
MONTEGO
MONTERO
MOPIEST
MOPPERS
MOPPETS
MORDENT
MORSELS
MOSHERS
MOSLEMS
MOTHERS
MOUSERS
MRCLEAN
MRDEEDS
MUDDERS
MUDEELS
MUDHENS
MUGGERS
MULLEIN
MULLERS
MULLETS
MUMMERS
MUMMERY
MUPPETS
MURDERS
MUSHERS
MUSKEGS
MUSKETS
MUSSELS
MUSTERS
MUTTERS
MYNHEER
MYSTERY

M••••E•

MADAMEX
MADCHEN
MAGPIES
MAHONEY
MAIGRET
MAITRED
MAJORED
MALMSEY
MALTIER
MAMBOED
MANAGED
MANAGER
MANAGES
MANATEE
MANEGES
MANFRED
MANGIER
MANGLED
MANGLES
MANGOES
MANLIER
MANTLED
MANTLES
MANXMEN
MARBLED
MARBLES
MARCHED
MARCHER
MARCHES
MARGRET
MARINER
MARINES
MARQUEE
MARQUES
MARQUEZ
MARRIED
MARRIES
MARSHES
MASHIES
MASQUES
MASSIER
MATCHED
MATCHES
MATINEE
MATTHEW
MATURED
MATURER
MATURES
MAUNDER
MAUREEN
MAXBAER
MAYTREE
MCQUEEN
MEALIER
MEALIES
MEANDER
MEANIES
MEASLES
MEATIER
MEDALED
MEDDLED
MEDDLER
MEDDLES
MEINIES
MEIOSES
MEISSEN
MEISTER
MEMOREX
MENACED
MENACES
MENAGES
MENCKEN
MENZIES
MERCIES
MERIMEE
MERITED
MERRIER
MESHIER
MESSIER
METATES
METERED
METOOER
METTLES
MICHAEL
MIDDIES
MIDDLEC
MIDDLES
MIDWEEK
MIFFIER
MIGGLES
MILDRED
MILKIER
MILKMEN
MINARET
MINDSET
MINGIER
MINGLED
MINGLER
MINGLES
MINIVER
MINORED
MINTIER
MINUSES
MINUTES
MIRAGES
MIRKIER
MISCUED
MISCUES
MISDEED
MISDOES
MISSIES
MISSTEP
MISTIER
MISUSED
MISUSES
MITERED
MITOSES
MIZZLED
MIZZLES
MOBILES
MOBSTER
MODELED
MODELER
MODULES
MOGGIES
MOISTEN
MOISTER
MOLDIER
MOMMIES
MONEYED
MONGREL
MONIKER
MONKEES
MONOMER
MONSTER
MOOCHED
MOOCHER
MOOCHES
MOODIER
MOONIER
MOONSET
MOORHEN
MOORIER
MORALES
MORDRED
MORPHED
MOSEYED
MOSQUES
MOSSIER
MOTHIER
MOTIVES
MOTORED
MOTTLED
MOTTLES
MOTTOES
MOULDED
MOULDER
MOULTED
MOUNDED
MOUNTED
MOURNED
MOUSIER
MOUSSED
MOUSSES
MOUTHED
MRBONES
MUCKIER
MUDDIED
MUDDIER
MUDDIES
MUDDLED
MUDDLER
MUDDLES
MUDPIES
MUFFLED
MUFFLER
MUFFLES
MUGGIER
MULCHED
MULCHES
MULCTED
MUMBLED
MUMBLER
MUMBLES
MUMMIES
MUNCHED
MUNCHER
MUNCHES
MURKIER
MUSCLED
MUSCLES
MUSHIER
MUSKIER
MUSKIES
MUSSIER
MUSTIER
MUSTSEE
MUTAGEN
MUTATED
MUTATES
MUZZIER
MUZZLED
MUZZLES
MYNHEER
MYRTLES

M•••••E

MACABRE
MACAQUE
MACHETE
MACHINE
MACRAME
MACULAE
MAGNATE
MAGUIRE
MAJESTE
MAJEURE
MALAISE
MALEATE
MALTESE
MALTOSE
MANACLE
MANATEE
MANDATE
MANHOLE
MANIPLE
MANLIKE
MANMADE
MARGATE
MARLENE
MARLOWE
MARQUEE
MARRYME
MASSAGE
MASSIVE
MATINEE
MATISSE
MAURICE
MAYPOLE
MAYTIME
MAYTREE
MAYWINE
MBABANE
MCCLURE
MCENROE
MCGUIRE
MCSWINE
MEASURE
MEDIATE
MEDUSAE
MELANGE
MELANIE
MELROSE
MEMOIRE
MERIMEE
MESSAGE
METHANE
MICHELE
MICROBE
MIDLIFE
MIDLINE
MIDRISE
MIDSIZE
MIDWIFE
MIGRATE
MILEAGE
MINABLE
MIOCENE
MIRACLE

MISDATE
MISDONE
MISFILE
MISFIRE
MISLIKE
MISMATE
MISNAME
MISRULE
MISSILE
MISSIVE
MISTAKE
MISTYPE
MIXABLE
MIXTURE
MODISTE
MOLIERE
MONDALE
MONIQUE
MONOCLE
MONTAGE
MONTANE
MOORAGE
MORAINE
MORTISE
MOSELLE
MOULAGE
MOUNTIE
MOVABLE
MUNDANE
MUSETTE
MUSTSEE
MUTABLE

•ME••••

AMENDED
AMENITY
AMERCED
AMERCES
AMERICA
AMERIGO
AMERIKA
AMERIND
EMENDED
EMENDER
EMERALD
EMERGED
EMERGES
EMERITA
EMERITI
EMERSED
EMERSON
KMESONS
OMELETS
OMENTUM
SMEARED
SMELLED
SMELTED
SMELTER
SMETANA

•M•E•••

AMHERST
AMMETER
AMNESIA
AMNESTY
AMOEBAE
AMOEBAS
AMOEBIC
AMPERES
EMPEROR
IMMENSE
IMMERSE
IMPEACH
IMPEDED
IMPEDES
IMPENDS
IMPERIL
IMPETUS
UMBERTO

•M••E••

AMADEUS
AMATEUR
AMBIENT
AMBLERS
AMPLEST
AMULETS
EMBLEMS
EMINENT
EMOTERS
EMPRESS
IMAGERS
IMAGERY
IMARETS
IMOGENE
IMPIETY
IMPRESS
OMELETS
SMILERS
SMOKERS
UMPTEEN

•M•••E•

AMASSED
AMASSER
AMASSES
AMBRIES
AMENDED
AMERCED
AMERCES
AMMETER
AMPERES
AMPULES
BMOVIES
EMAILED
EMANUEL
EMBAYED
EMENDED
EMENDER
EMERGED
EMERGES
EMERSED
EMIGRES
EMITTED
EMITTER
EMPANEL
EMPIRES
EMPOWER
EMPTIED
EMPTIER
EMPTIES
IMAGOES
IMBIBED
IMBIBES
IMBRUED
IMBRUES
IMMIXED
IMMIXES
IMMURED
IMMURES
IMPALED
IMPALES
IMPANEL
IMPEDED
IMPEDES
IMPLIED
IMPLIES
IMPOSED
IMPOSES
IMPURER
IMPUTED
IMPUTES
OMITTED
OMITTER
SMACKED
SMACKER
SMALLER
SMARTED
SMARTEN
SMARTER
SMASHED
SMASHER
SMASHES
SMATTER
SMEARED
SMELLED
SMELTED
SMELTER
SMIDGEN
SMIRKED
SMITTEN
SMOKIER
SMOKIES
SMOLDER
SMOTHER
SMUDGED
SMUDGES
SMUGGER
UMPIRED
UMPIRES
UMPTEEN

•M••••E

AMATIVE
AMBROSE
AMIABLE
AMIBLUE
AMOEBAE
AMPOULE
AMYLASE
EMANATE
EMBRACE
EMIRATE
EMOTIVE
EMPLOYE
EMULATE
IMAGINE
IMAMATE
IMITATE
IMMENSE
IMMERSE
IMOGENE
IMPASSE
IMPINGE
IMPLODE
IMPLORE
IMPROVE
IMPULSE
SMUGGLE
UMBRAGE

••ME•••

AIMEDAT
AIMEDTO
AMMETER
ARMENIA
CAMEDUE
CAMELIA
CAMELOT
CAMEOED
CAMEOFF
CAMEOUT
CAMERAS
CAMERON
CEMENTS
COMEDIC
COMEDUE
COMEOFF
COMEONS
COMEOUT
COMESAT
COMESBY
COMESIN
COMESON
COMESTO
COMESUP
DEMEANS
DEMERIT
DEMEROL
DEMESNE
DEMETER
FOMENTS
GAMELAW
GAMETES
HAMELIN
HOMEBOY
HOMERED
HOMERIC
HOMERUN
HUMERAL
HUMERUS
IMMENSE
IMMERSE
JAMESON
JIMENEZ
LAMEDHS
LAMENTS
LIMEADE
MEMENTO
MIMESIS
MIMETIC
MOMENTS
MUMESON
NAMEDAY
NAMETAG
NEMEROV
NEMESES
NEMESIS
NUMERAL
NUMERIC
PIMENTO
PIMESON
POMELOS
RAMEKIN
RAMESES
REMELTS
REMENDS
SAMECHS
SAMEDAY
SIMENON
SOMEDAY
SOMEHOW
SOMEONE
SOMEWAY
TIMECOP
TIMELAG
TIMEOFF
TIMEOUT
TIMESUP
YEMENIS

••M•E••

AIMLESS
ARMLESS
ARMLETS
ARMREST
BOMBECK
BOMBERS
BUMMERS
BUMPERS
CAMBERS
CAMPERS
COMBERS
COMMEND
COMMENT
COMPEER
COMPELS
COMPERE
COMPETE
DAMPENS
DAMPERS
DAMPEST
DAMSELS
DIMMERS
DIMMEST
DIMNESS
DUMBEST
FUMIEST
GAMIEST
GAMMERS
GEMLESS
GIMLETS
GOMPERS
GUMLESS
HAMLETS
HAMMERS
HAMMETT
HAMPERS
HEMMERS
HIMSELF
HOMIEST
HUMMERS
HUMVEES
JAMMERS
JUMPERS
LAMBEAU
LAMBENT
LAMBERT
LEMIEUX
LIMBERS
LIMIEST
LIMNERS
LIMPEST
LIMPETS
LUMBERS
LUMIERE
LUMPERS
MEMBERS
MIMIEUX
MUMMERS
MUMMERY
NIMIETY
NUMBERS
NUMBEST
PAMPERS
POMMELS
POMPEIA
POMPEII
PUMMELS
PUMPERS
RAMBEAU
RAMJETS
RIMIEST
RIMLESS
ROMNEYS
ROMPERS
RUMLESS
SAMLETS
SIMMERS
SIMPERS
SUMLESS
SUMMERS
SUMMERY
TAMPERS
TEMPEHS
TEMPERA
TEMPERS
TEMPEST
TIMBERS
VAMPERS
YAMMERS
ZAMBEZI

••M••E•

ADMIRED
ADMIRER
ADMIRES
ADMIXED
ADMIXES
ALMADEN
AMMETER
ARMORED
ARMORER
ARMURES
BEMIRED
BEMIRES
BEMUSED
BEMUSES
BUMBLED
BUMBLER
BUMBLES
BUMPIER
CAMEOED
CAMISES
CAMPIER
COMFIER
COMFREY
COMPEER
COMPLEX
DAMAGED
DAMAGES
DEMETER
DEMISED
DEMISES
DEMOTED
DEMOTES
DEMPSEY
DEMURER
DIMPLED
DIMPLES
DUMMIED
DUMMIES
DUMPIER
ELMTREE
ERMINES
FAMINES
FEMALES
FUMBLED
FUMBLER
FUMBLES
GAMBLED
GAMBLER
GAMBLES
GAMBREL
GAMETES
GAMINES
GAMMIER
GEMMIER
GEMOTES
GUMMIER
GUMTREE
HAMITES
HAMMIER
HAMSTER
HEMSLEY
HOMBRES
HOMERED
HUMBLED
HUMBLER
HUMBLES
HUMORED
HUMPIER
HUMVEES
IMMIXED
IMMIXES
IMMURED
IMMURES
INMATES
JAMMIER
JEMMIED
JEMMIES
JIMCHEE
JIMENEZ
JIMMIED
JIMMIES
JUMBLED
JUMBLES
JUMPIER
KIMCHEE
LAMPREY
LIMITED
LIMOGES
LUMPIER
MAMBOED
MEMOREX
MOMMIES
MUMBLED
MUMBLER
MUMBLES
MUMMIES
NEMESES
NIMBLER
NOMINEE
OSMOSED
OSMOSES
POMADED
POMADES
PUMICES
RAMBLED
RAMBLER
RAMBLES
RAMESES
REMAKES
REMIGES
REMIXED
REMIXES
REMODEL
REMOTER
REMOTES
REMOVED
REMOVER
REMOVES
REMOWED
RIMPLED
RIMPLES
RUMBAED
RUMBLED
RUMBLES
RUMMIER
RUMORED
RUMPLED
RUMPLES
SAMBAED
SAMISEN
SAMITES
SAMOYED
SAMPLED
SAMPLER
SAMPLES
SEMITES
SIMILES
SIMPLER
SIMPLEX
TAMALES
TEMPLES
TEMPTED
TEMPTER
TIMBRES
TIMIDER
TUMBLED
TUMBLER
TUMBLES
TUMBREL
TUMMIES
UNMAKES
UNMOVED
WAMBLED
WAMBLES
WIMBLED
WIMBLES
WIMPIER
WIMPLED
WIMPLES
YUMMIER
ZOMBIES

••M•••E

AAMILNE
ARMHOLE
ARMLIKE
ARMOIRE
CAMEDUE
CAMILLE
COMBINE
COMEDUE
COMIQUE
COMMODE
COMMOVE
COMMUNE
COMMUTE
COMPARE
COMPERE
COMPETE
COMPILE
COMPOSE
COMPOTE
COMPUTE
COMRADE
DEMESNE
DEMILLE
ELMTREE
ENMASSE
GEMLIKE
GUMLIKE
GUMSHOE
GUMTREE
GYMSHOE
HEMLINE
IMMENSE
IMMERSE
JAMLIKE
JIMCHEE
KIMCHEE
LAMINAE
LEMONDE
LIMEADE
LUMIERE
MEMOIRE
NOMINEE
RAMLIKE
RAMPAGE
REMORSE
ROMAINE
ROMANCE
RUMMAGE
RUMPOLE
SOMEONE
TAMABLE
TIMBALE
VAMOOSE
VAMPIRE
WIMPOLE

•••ME••

ACUMENS
AILMENT
ALAMEDA
ALAMEIN
ALIMENT
ARAMEAN
AUGMENT
BERMEJO
BESMEAR
BOOMERS
BUMMERS
BURMESE
CALMEST
CHIMERA
CLEMENS
CLEMENT
COMMEND
COMMENT
CRIMEAN
DIMMERS
DIMMEST
DIOMEDE
DOLMENS
DORMERS
ELEMENT
ENAMELS
FARMERS
FARMERY
FERMENT
FIGMENT
FIRMEST
FRAMEUP
GAMMERS
GARMENT
HAMMERS
HAMMETT
HELMETS
HEMMERS
HUMMERS
INAMESS
ISOMERS
JAMMERS
MUMMERS
MUMMERY
NUTMEAT
NUTMEGS
OATMEAL
ODDMENT
PAYMENT
PIGMENT
POMMELS
PREMEDS
PRIMERS
PUMMELS
RAIMENT
REAMERS
REDMEAT
RHYMERS
ROAMERS
ROOMERS
SCHMEER
SEGMENT
SIAMESE
SIMMERS
STAMENS
STUMERS
SUMMERS
SUMMERY
TORMENT
VERMEER
VERMEIL
WARMEST
WOOMERA
YAMMERS

•••M•E•

ANOMIES
ATOMIES
BALMIER
BARMIER
BEAMIER
BOOMIER
BRIMLEY
BRIMMED
BRUMMEL
CHAMBER
CHAMFER
CHAMPED
CHIMNEY
CHOMPED
CHUMMED
CLAMBER
CLAMMED
CLAMMER
CLAMPED
CLIMBED
CLIMBER
CLOMPED
CLUMPED
CRAMMED
CRAMMER
CRAMPED
CRIMPED
CRIMPER
CRUMPET
DAIMLER
DAUMIER
DRUMMED
DRUMMER
DUMMIED
DUMMIES
ENEMIES
FILMIER
FLAMBED
FLAMBES
FLAMIER
FNUMBER
FOAMIER
GAMMIER
GEMMIER
GERMIER
GLIMMER
GLOMMED
GLUMMER
GRAMMER
GRAMMES
GRIMIER
GRIMMER
GROMMET
GRUMPED
GUIMPES
GUMMIER
HAMMIER
ISHMAEL
JAMMIER
JEMMIED
JEMMIES
JIMMIED
JIMMIES
LOAMIER
MALMSEY
MOMMIES
MUMMIES
PALMIER
PLUMBED
PLUMBER
PLUMIER
PLUMMER
PLUMMET
PLUMPED
PLUMPER
PREMIER
PRIMMER
PRIMPED
PYGMIES
ROOMIER
ROOMIES
RUMMIER
SCAMMED
SCAMPED
SCAMPER
SCHMEER
SCHMOES
SEAMIER
SHAMMED
SHIMMER
SKIMMED
SKIMMER
SKIMPED
SLAMMED
SLAMMER
SLIMIER
SLIMMED
SLIMMER
SLUMBER
SLUMMED
SLUMPED
SPAMMED
SPAMMER
SPUMIER
STAMMER
STAMPED
STEMMED
STOMPED
STUMPED
STUMPER
STYMIED
STYMIES
SWAMPED
SWIMMER
THUMBED
THUMPED
THUMPER
TRAMMEL
TRAMPED
TRIMMED
TRIMMER
TRUMPED
TRUMPET
TUMMIES
VERMEER
WHAMMED
WHIMPER
WHOMPED
WORMIER
YUMMIER

•••M••E

ADAMITE
AIRMILE
ALAMODE
ALUMNAE
ANEMONE
ANIMATE
ANYMORE
ARDMORE
ATOMISE
ATOMIZE
BRAMBLE
BROMATE
BROMIDE
BROMINE
BURMESE
CARMINE
CHEMISE
CLIMATE
COMMODE
COMMOVE
COMMUNE
COMMUTE
CRUMBLE
CRUMPLE
DAYMARE
DIOMEDE
DORMICE
EREMITE
ETAMINE
EXAMINE
EXAMPLE
FROMAGE
GERMANE
GLIMPSE
GRIMACE
GRUMBLE
HORMONE
IMAMATE
ITEMISE
ITEMIZE
JASMINE
MANMADE
MISMATE
PALMATE
PISMIRE
PLUMAGE
PREMISE
PRIMATE
PROMISE
PROMOTE
RUMMAGE
SHAMBLE
SIAMESE
SPUMONE
STUMBLE
SURMISE
TERMITE
THIMBLE
THYMINE
TITMICE
TRAMPLE
TREMBLE

••••ME•

ABDOMEN
AFRAMES
AGNOMEN
ALARMED
ALARMER
ALBUMEN
ASHAMED
ASSUMED
ASSUMES
ATHOMES
ATTIMES
BASEMEN
BATSMEN
BECOMES
BELLMEN
BESTMEN
BETIMES
BIRDMEN
BIREMES
BITUMEN
BLOOMED
BLOOMER
BOATMEN
BONDMEN
BRIMMED
BRUMMEL
BUSHMEN
BYREMEN
CALOMEL
CALUMET
CARAMEL
CAROMED
CAVEMEN
CERUMEN
CHAPMEN
CHARMED
CHARMER
CHROMES
CHUMMED
CLAIMED
CLAIMER
CLAMMED
CLAMMER
COZUMEL
CRAMMED
CRAMMER
CREAMED
CREAMER
CREWMEN
DAHOMEY
DEFAMED
DEFAMES
DOORMEN
DREAMED
DREAMER
DRUMMED
DRUMMER
DUSTMEN
ENZYMES
FIREMEN
FLAGMEN
FOOTMEN
FOREMEN
FREEMEN
FROGMEN
GATEMEN
GENOMES
GLEAMED
GLIMMER
GLOMMED
GLOOMED
GLUMMER
GOODMEN
GOURMET
GRAMMER
GRAMMES
GRIMMER
GROMMET
GROOMED
GROOMER
HANGMEN
HEADMEN
IDEAMEN
ILLUMED
ILLUMES
INCOMES
IRONMEN
JAZZMEN
KINSMEN
LEGUMES
LEXEMES
LINEMEN
LOCOMEN
MADAMEX
MANXMEN
MERIMEE
MILKMEN
MONOMER
NEWSMEN
PDJAMES
PIKEMEN
PLOWMEN
PLUMMER
PLUMMET
POLYMER
POSTMEN
PRIMMER
PROPMEN
PSALMED
PUTAMEN
RACEMES
RADOMES
REAIMED
REARMED
REGIMEN
REGIMES
RELUMED
RELUMES
RENAMED
RENAMES
RESUMED
RESUMES
RETIMED
RETIMES
SANDMEN
SCAMMED
SCHEMED
SCHEMER
SCHEMES
SESAMES
SHAMMED
SHIMMER
SHIPMEN
SHOWMEN
SIDEMEN
SKIMMED
SKIMMER
SLAMMED
SLAMMER
SLIMMED
SLIMMER
SLUMMED
SNOWMEN
SPAMMED
SPAMMER
STAMMER
STEAMED
STEAMER
STEMMED
STORMED
SWARMED
SWIMMER
TAPEMEN
TAXIMEN
THEOMEN
TRAMMEL
TRIMMED
TRIMMER
UNAIMED
UNARMED

UNNAMED
UNTAMED
VOLUMES
WHAMMED
WHELMED
WISEMEN
WOLFMEN
WORKMEN
YARDMEN

••••M•E
LARAMIE
MERIMEE
PREEMIE

•••••ME
ACADEME
AIRTIME
ALLOFME
ALLTIME
ANYTIME
AWESOME
BEATSME
BEDTIME
BEGRIME
BELDAME
BIGGAME
BIGNAME
BIGTIME
BUYTIME
CENTIME
CONGAME
CONSUME
COSTUME
CUTTIME
DAYTIME
ENDGAME
EPITOME
EXTREME
FULSOME
GRAHAME
HOWCOME
INFLAME
IRKSOME
KEYLIME
LISSOME
MACRAME
MARRYME
MAYTIME
MISNAME
NAPTIME
NOISOME
OLDTIME
ONETIME
OUTCOME
PASTIME
PENNAME
PERFUME
PETNAME
PHONEME
PRESUME
RAGTIME
RECLAME
REFRAME
RHIZOME
RUNHOME
SAOTOME
SOSUEME
SUBLIME
SUBSUME
SUPREME
SURNAME
TEATIME
TEETIME
TRIREME
TWOSOME
TWOTIME
ULALUME
WARGAME
WARTIME
WELCOME
WINSOME
WOEISME

M•F••••
MAFFICK
MIFFIER
MIFFING
MRFIXIT
MUFFING
MUFFINS
MUFFLED
MUFFLER
MUFFLES

M••F•••
MAFFICK
MANFRED
MAYFAIR
MENFOLK
MIFFIER
MIFFING
MISFILE
MISFIRE
MISFITS
MITFORD
MOUFLON
MUFFING
MUFFINS
MUFFLED
MUFFLER
MUFFLES
MUMFORD

M•••F••
MADEFOR
MAKEFOR
MALEFIC
MINDFUL
MOANFUL
MUSEFUL

M••••F•
MACDUFF
MADEOFF
MAGNIFY
MAKEOFF
MARKOFF
MASSIFS
MASTIFF
MIDLIFE
MIDRIFF
MIDWIFE
MOLLIFY
MORTIFY
MUSTAFA
MYSTIFY

M•••••F
MACDUFF
MADEOFF
MAKEOFF
MARKOFF
MASTIFF
MIDRIFF

•M•••F•
AMPLIFY

••MF•••
ARMFULS
COMFIER
COMFITS
COMFORT
COMFREY
MUMFORD
TOMFOOL

••M•F••
AIMSFOR

••M••F•
CAMEOFF
COMEOFF
JUMPOFF
TIMEOFF
ZOMBIFY

••M•••F
CAMEOFF
COMEOFF
HIMSELF
JUMPOFF
TIMEOFF

•••MF••
BRIMFUL
CHAMFER
DOOMFUL
FORMFUL
HARMFUL
ROOMFUL

•••M•F•
EARMUFF
PALMOFF

•••M••F
EARMUFF
PALMOFF

M•G••••
MAGENTA
MAGICAL
MAGINOT
MAGNANI
MAGNATE
MAGNETO
MAGNETS
MAGNIFY
MAGNUMS
MAGPIES
MAGUEYS
MAGUIRE
MAGYARS
MCGAVIN
MCGUIRE
MEGAHIT
MEGIDDO
MEGOHMS
MEGRIMS
MEGRYAN
MIGGLES
MIGHTNT
MIGRANT
MIGRATE
MOGAMBO
MOGGIES
MUGGERS
MUGGIER
MUGGING
MUGSHOT
MUGWUMP

M••G•••
MACGRAW
MAIGRET
MANGERS
MANGIER
MANGLED
MANGLES
MANGOES
MARGATE
MARGAUX
MARGAYS
MARGINS
MARGRET
MAUGHAM
MERGERS
MERGING
MIDGETS
MIGGLES
MINGIER
MINGLED
MINGLER
MINGLES
MOGGIES
MONGERS
MONGOLS
MONGREL
MORGANA
MORGANS
MUGGERS
MUGGIER
MUGGING

M•••G••
MADIGAN
MALIGNS
MANAGED
MANAGER
MANAGES
MANAGUA
MANEGES
MEDIGAP
MENAGES
MIRAGES
MRMAGOO
MRRIGHT
MUTAGEN

M••••G•
MAKINGS
MARENGO
MASSAGE
MELANGE
MESSAGE
MILEAGE
MONTAGE
MONTEGO
MOORAGE
MOULAGE
MUSKEGS

M•••••G
MADDING
MAILBAG
MAILING
MALTING
MANNING
MAPPING
MARKING
MARRING
MASHING
MASKING
MASSING
MATTING
MAULING
MEANING
MEETING
MELDING
MELTING
MENDING
MEOWING
MERGING
MESHING
MESSING
MEWLING
MIFFING
MILKING
MILLING
MINCING
MINDING
MINTING
MISSING
MISTING
MITRING
MOANING
MOBBING
MOCKING
MOILING
MOLDING
MOLTING
MONOLOG
MOONDOG
MOONING
MOORING
MOPPING
MORNING
MOSHING
MOSSING
MOUSING
MUCKING
MUFFING
MUGGING
MULLING
MUMMING
MUMPING
MUSHING
MUSSING
MUSTANG
MUZZING

•M•G•••
EMIGRES
IMAGERS
IMAGERY
IMAGINE
IMAGING
IMAGOES
IMOGENE
OMIGOSH
SMUGGER
SMUGGLE

•M••G••
AMALGAM
AMONGST
EMERGED
EMERGES
IMPUGNS
SMIDGEN
SMUDGED
SMUDGES
SMUGGER
SMUGGLE

•M•••G•
AMERIGO
EMBARGO
IMPINGE
UMBRAGE

•M••••G
AMAZING
AMBLING
AMUSING
EMOTING
IMAGING
IMBUING
SMILING
SMITING
SMOKING

••M•G••
DAMAGED
DAMAGES
DEMIGOD
LIMOGES
MRMAGOO
REMIGES

••M••G•
COMINGS
DOMINGO
GYMBAGS
HUMBUGS
LUMBAGO
RAMPAGE
RUMMAGE
TIMINGS
ZYMURGY

••M•••G
BOMBING
BUMMING
BUMPING
CAMPING
COMBING
DAMMING
DAMNING
DAMPING
DIMMING
DUMBING
DUMPING
GAMMING
GUMMING
HAMBURG
HAMMING
HEMMING
HOMBURG
HUMMING
JAMMING
JUMPING
LAMMING
LEMMING
LIMBING
LIMNING
LIMPING
LUMPING
MUMMING
MUMPING
NAMETAG
NUMBING
PUMPING
RAMMING
RIMMING
ROMPING
SAMSUNG
SEMILOG
SUMMING
TAMPING
TIMELAG
TUMMING
VAMPING

•••M•G•
FROMAGE
NUTMEGS
PLUMAGE
RUMMAGE

•••M••G
BEAMING
BLAMING
BOOMING
BUMMING
CALMING
CHIMING
DAMMING
DEEMING
DIMMING
DOOMING
FARMING
FILMING
FIRMING
FLAMING
FLEMING
FOAMING
FORMING
FRAMING
GAMMING
GAUMING
GRIMING
GUMMING
HAMMING
HARMING
HELMING
HEMMING
HUMMING
JAMMING
LAMMING
LEMMING
LOAMING
LOOMING
MUMMING
PALMING
PERMING
PLUMING
PRIMING
RAMMING
REAMING
RHYMING
RIMMING
ROAMING
ROOMING
SEAMING
SEEMING
SHAMING
SPUMING
SUMMING
TEAMING
TEEMING
TERMING
TUMMING
WARMING
WYOMING
ZOOMING

M•H••••
MAHALIA
MAHARIS
MAHATMA
MAHONEY
MAHOUTS
MCHENRY
MOHAIRS
MOHAWKS
MOHICAN

M••H•••
MACHETE
MACHINA
MACHINE
MANHOLE
MANHOOD
MANHOUR
MANHUNT
MASHERS
MASHIES
MASHING
MATHERS
MATHEWS
MATHIAS
MAYHEMS
MENHIRS
MESHIER
MESHING
METHANE
METHODS
MICHAEL
MICHELE
MIGHTNT
MIKHAIL
MILHAUD
MISHAPS
MISHEAR
MISHITS
MITHRAS
MOSHERS
MOSHING
MOSHPIT
MOTHERS
MOTHIER
MRCHIPS
MUDHENS
MUSHERS
MUSHIER
MUSHILY
MUSHING
MUZHIKS
MYNHEER

M•••H••
MADCHEN
MADEHAY
MAKEHAY
MALTHUS
MARCHED
MARCHER
MARCHES
MARCHON
MARKHAM
MARKHOR
MARSHAL
MARSHES
MATCHED
MATCHES
MATCHUP
MATTHAU
MATTHEW
MAUGHAM
MCLUHAN
MCMAHON
MEGAHIT
MEGOHMS
MEMPHIS
MENTHOL
MENUHIN
MITCHUM
MONTHLY
MOOCHED
MOOCHER
MOOCHES
MOORHEN
MORPHED
MOUTHED
MUGSHOT
MULCHED
MULCHES
MUNCHED
MUNCHER
MUNCHES

M••••H•
MALACHI
MATZOHS
MOLOCHS
MRRIGHT
MULLAHS

M•••••H
MACBETH
MADDISH
MAIDISH
MAMMOTH
MANNISH
MAWKISH
MENORAH
MESSIAH
MINXISH
MISSISH
MITZVAH
MOBBISH
MONARCH
MONKISH
MOONISH
MOORISH
MURDOCH

•MH••••
AMHARIC
AMHERST

•M•H•••
AMPHORA
OMPHALI

•M••H••
SMASHED
SMASHER
SMASHES
SMASHUP
SMOTHER

•M•••H•
EMPATHY
SMOOTHS
SMOOTHY

•M••••H
IMPEACH
OMIGOSH

••MH•••
ARMHOLE
HAMHOCK
SAMHILL

••M•H••
CAMPHOR
GUMSHOE
GYMSHOE
JIMCHEE
KIMCHEE
MCMAHON
MEMPHIS
RIMSHOT
SOMEHOW

••M••H•
IOMOTHS
LAMEDHS
OOMPAHS
SAMECHS
TEMPEHS
TIMOTHY

••M•••H
BUMRUSH
DAMPISH
DUMPISH
LUMPISH
MAMMOTH
RAMMISH
ROMANSH
ROMPISH
VAMPISH
WIMPISH

•••M•H•
THIMPHU

•••M••H
AZIMUTH
BEAMISH
BISMUTH
BLEMISH
FLEMISH
GNOMISH
KLAMATH
MAMMOTH
NESMITH
NEWMATH
RAMMISH
STOMACH
WARMISH
WORMISH

••••M•H
GALUMPH
TRIUMPH

MI•••••
MIAMIAN
MIAMIAS
MIAOYAO
MIASMAS
MIASMIC
MICHAEL
MICHELE
MICKEYS
MICMACS
MICROBE
MICRONS
MIDDAYS
MIDDENS
MIDDIES
MIDDLEC
MIDDLES
MIDEAST
MIDGETS
MIDLAND
MIDLIFE
MIDLINE
MIDMOST
MIDRIBS
MIDRIFF
MIDRISE
MIDSIZE
MIDTERM
MIDTOWN
MIDWAYS
MIDWEEK
MIDWEST
MIDWIFE
MIDYEAR
MIFFIER
MIFFING
MIGGLES
MIGHTNT
MIGRANT
MIGRATE
MIKADOS
MIKHAIL
MILDEST
MILDEWS
MILDEWY
MILDRED
MILEAGE
MILHAUD
MILIEUS
MILIEUX
MILITIA
MILKCOW
MILKERS
MILKIER
MILKING
MILKMAN
MILKMEN
MILKRUN
MILKSOP
MILLAND
MILLARD
MILLDAM
MILLEND
MILLERS
MILLETS
MILLETT
MILLING
MILLION
MILLRUN
MILORDS
MIMESIS
MIMETIC
MIMICRY
MIMIEUX
MIMOSAS
MINABLE
MINARET
MINCERS
MINCING
MINDERS
MINDFUL
MINDING
MINDSET
MINERAL
MINERVA
MINGIER
MINGLED
MINGLER
MINGLES
MINIBUS
MINICAB
MINICAM
MINIMAL
MINIMUM
MINIONS
MINIVAN
MINIVER
MINNOWS
MINOANS
MINOLTA
MINORCA
MINORED
MINTERS
MINTIER
MINTING
MINUEND
MINUETS
MINUSES
MINUTES
MINUTIA
MINXISH
MINYANS
MIOCENE
MIRACLE
MIRADOR
MIRAGES
MIRAMAR
MIRAMAX
MIRANDA
MIRIEST
MIRKIER
MIRRORS
MISALLY
MISCALL
MISCAST
MISCUED
MISCUES
MISDATE
MISDEAL
MISDEED
MISDIAL
MISDOES
MISDONE
MISERLY
MISFILE
MISFIRE
MISFITS
MISHAPS
MISHEAR
MISHITS
MISLAID
MISLAYS
MISLEAD
MISLIKE
MISMATE
MISNAME
MISPLAY
MISREAD
MISRULE
MISSAID
MISSALS
MISSAYS
MISSIES
MISSILE
MISSING
MISSION
MISSISH
MISSIVE
MISSOUT
MISSTEP
MISTAKE
MISTERS
MISTIER
MISTILY
MISTING
MISTOOK
MISTRAL
MISTYPE
MISUSED
MISUSES
MISWORD
MITCHUM
MITERED
MITFORD
MITHRAS
MITOSES
MITOSIS
MITOTIC
MITRING
MITTENS
MITZVAH
MIXABLE
MIXEDIN
MIXEDUP
MIXESIN
MIXESUP
MIXITUP
MIXTURE
MIZZENS
MIZZLED
MIZZLES

M•I••••
MAIDENS
MAIDISH
MAIGRET
MAILBAG
MAILBOX
MAILCAR
MAILERS
MAILING
MAILLOT
MAILOUT
MAILSIN
MAINTOP
MAITAIS
MAITRED
MEINIES
MEIOSES
MEIOSIS
MEIOTIC
MEISSEN
MEISTER
MOILERS
MOILING
MOISTEN
MOISTER
MOISTLY

M••I•••
MADIGAN
MADISON
MAGICAL
MAGINOT
MAKINGS
MALIGNS
MANIACS
MANILOW
MANIOCS
MANIPLE
MANITOU
MAOISTS
MARIANA
MARILYN
MARIMBA
MARINAS
MARINER
MARINES
MARITAL
MATILDA
MATINEE
MATISSE
MAXILLA
MAXIMAL
MAXIMUM
MAXIMUS
MAZIEST
MEDIANS
MEDIANT
MEDIATE
MEDICAL
MEDICOS
MEDIGAP
MEDIUMS
MEGIDDO
MELINDA
MELISSA
MENIALS
MENISCI
MERIMEE
MERINOS
MERITED
METIERS
MEXICAN
MILIEUS
MILIEUX
MILITIA
MIMICRY
MIMIEUX
MINIBUS
MINICAB
MINICAM
MINIMAL
MINIMUM
MINIONS
MINIVAN
MINIVER
MIRIEST
MIXITUP
MOBILES
MODICUM
MODISTE
MOHICAN
MOLIERE
MONIKER
MONIQUE
MONITOR
MOPIEST
MOTIONS
MOTIVES
MRFIXIT
MRRIGHT
MURILLO
MUSICAL
MYRIADS

M•••I••
MACHINA
MACHINE
MADDING
MADDISH
MADEIRA
MADLIBS
MAFFICK
MAGNIFY
MAGPIES
MAGUIRE
MAIDISH
MAILING
MALAISE
MALKINS
MALTIER
MALTING
MANCINI
MANGIER
MANKIND
MANLIER
MANLIKE
MANNING
MANNISH
MANSION
MAPPING
MARGINS
MARKING
MARLINS

MARMION
MARRIED
MARRIES
MARRING
MARTIAL
MARTIAN
MARTINA
MARTINI
MARTINO
MARTINS
MARXISM
MARXIST
MASHIES
MASHING
MASKING
MASSIER
MASSIFS
MASSING
MASSIVE
MASTICS
MASTIFF
MATHIAS
MATTING
MAULING
MAURICE
MAWKISH
MAYTIME
MAYWINE
MCGUIRE
MCSWINE
MEALIER
MEALIES
MEANIES
MEANING
MEATIER
MEATILY
MEETING
MEGRIMS
MEINIES
MELDING
MELTING
MEMOIRE
MEMOIRS
MENDING
MENHIRS
MENTION
MENZIES
MEOWING
MERCIES
MERGING
MERRIER
MERRILL
MERRILY
MESHIER
MESHING
MESSIAH
MESSIER
MESSILY
MESSINA
MESSING
MESTIZA
MESTIZO
METRICS
MEWLING
MIAMIAN
MIAMIAS
MIDDIES
MIDLIFE
MIDLINE
MIDRIBS
MIDRIFF
MIDRISE
MIDSIZE
MIDWIFE

MIFFIER
MIFFING
MILKIER
MILKING
MILLING
MILLION
MINCING
MINDING
MINGIER
MINTIER
MINTING
MINXISH
MIRKIER
MISDIAL
MISFILE
MISFIRE
MISFITS
MISHITS
MISLIKE
MISSIES
MISSILE
MISSING
MISSION
MISSISH
MISSIVE
MISTIER
MISTILY
MISTING
MITRING
MOANING
MOBBING
MOBBISH
MOCKING
MOGGIES
MOHAIRS
MOILING
MOLDIER
MOLDING
MOLLIFY
MOLTING
MOMMIES
MONKISH
MOODIER
MOODILY
MOONIER
MOONILY
MOONING
MOONISH
MOORIER
MOORING
MOORISH
MOPPING
MORAINE
MORNING
MORTIFY
MORTISE
MOSAICS
MOSHING
MOSSIER
MOSSING
MOTHIER
MOUSIER
MOUSING
MRCHIPS
MUCKIER
MUCKILY
MUCKING
MUDDIED
MUDDIER
MUDDIES
MUDDILY
MUDPIES
MUFFING
MUFFINS

MUGGIER
MUGGING
MULLING
MULLION
MUMMIES
MUMMING
MUMPING
MUNTINS
MURKIER
MURKILY
MUSHIER
MUSHILY
MUSHING
MUSKIER
MUSKIES
MUSLIMS
MUSLINS
MUSSIER
MUSSILY
MUSSING
MUSTIER
MUSTILY
MUZHIKS
MUZZIER
MUZZILY
MUZZING
MYSTICS
MYSTIFY

M••••I•

MAHALIA
MAHARIS
MAILSIN
MAITAIS
MAKESIT
MALEFIC
MANTRIC
MANUMIT
MARQUIS
MASONIC
MASTOID
MAUDLIN
MAULDIN
MAUROIS
MAYALIN
MAYFAIR
MCGAVIN
MEGAHIT
MEIOSIS
MEIOTIC
MELANIE
MELANIN
MELODIC
MEMPHIS
MENUHIN
MERMAID
MESSKIT
MIASMIC
MIKHAIL
MILITIA
MIMESIS
MIMETIC
MINUTIA
MISLAID
MISSAID
MITOSIS
MITOTIC
MIXEDIN
MIXESIN
MONODIC
MOONLIT
MORANIS
MORAVIA
MOSHPIT

MOUNTIE
MOVEDIN
MOVESIN
MRFIXIT
MUEZZIN
MULLEIN

M•••••I

MAESTRI
MAGNANI
MALACHI
MANCINI
MARCONI
MARTINI
MENISCI
MENOTTI
MOLOKAI
MONTANI

•MI••••

AMIABLE
AMIABLY
AMIBLUE
AMISTAD
EMIGRES
EMINENT
EMIRATE
EMITTED
EMITTER
IMITATE
OMICRON
OMIGOSH
OMINOUS
OMITTED
OMITTER
SMIDGEN
SMILERS
SMILING
SMIRKED
SMITING
SMITTEN

•M•I•••

AMBIENT
AMNIONS
EMAILED
EMPIRES
IMBIBED
IMBIBES
IMMIXED
IMMIXES
IMPIETY
IMPINGE
IMPIOUS
OMNIBUS
UMPIRED
UMPIRES

•M••I••

AMATIVE
AMAZING
AMBLING
AMBRIES
AMENITY
AMERICA
AMERIGO
AMERIKA
AMERIND
AMPLIFY
AMUSING
BMOVIES
EMERITA
EMERITI
EMOTING

EMOTION
EMOTIVE
EMPTIED
EMPTIER
EMPTIES
EMPTILY
IMAGINE
IMAGING
IMBUING
IMPAIRS
IMPLIED
IMPLIES
IMPRINT
SMILING
SMITING
SMOKIER
SMOKIES
SMOKILY
SMOKING
UMBRIAN

•M•••I•

AMHARIC
AMMONIA
AMNESIA
AMOEBIC
AMRADIO
EMBROIL
EMPORIA
FMRADIO
IMPERIL

•M••••I

EMERITI
OMPHALI

••MI•••

AAMILNE
ADMIRAL
ADMIRED
ADMIRER
ADMIRES
ADMITTO
ADMIXED
ADMIXES
BEMIRED
BEMIRES
CAMILLE
CAMISES
COMICAL
COMINGS
COMIQUE
DEMIGOD
DEMILLE
DEMISED
DEMISES
DIMITRI
DOMINGO
DOMINOS
DOMINUS
ELMISTI
ERMINES
FAMINES
FUMIEST
GAMIEST
GAMINES
HAMITES
HAMITIC
HAMITUP
HOMIEST
HOMINID
HUMIDLY
HUMIDOR
IMMIXED

IMMIXES
LAMINAE
LAMINAL
LAMINAR
LAMINAS
LEMIEUX
LIMIEST
LIMITED
LUMIERE
MIMICRY
MIMIEUX
NAMIBIA
NIMIETY
NOMINAL
NOMINEE
PEMICAN
PUMICES
RAMINTO
REMIGES
REMINDS
REMIXED
REMIXES
RIMIEST
SAMISEN
SAMITES
SEMILOG
SEMINAL
SEMINAR
SEMIPRO
SEMITES
SEMITIC
SIMIANS
SIMILAR
SIMILES
TIMIDER
TIMIDLY
TIMINGS

••M•I••

ARMLIKE
ARMOIRE
ARMPITS
BAMBINO
BOMBING
BUMMING
BUMPIER
BUMPILY
BUMPING
CAMBIUM
CAMPIER
CAMPILY
CAMPING
CAMPION
COMBINE
COMBING
COMFIER
COMFITS
COMMITS
COMPILE
DAMMING
DAMNING
DAMPING
DAMPISH
DIMMING
DIMWITS
DOMAINS
DUMBING
DUMMIED
DUMMIES
DUMPIER
DUMPING
DUMPISH
GAMBIAN
GAMBITS

GAMMIER
GAMMING
GEMLIKE
GEMMIER
GIMMICK
GUMLIKE
GUMMIER
GUMMING
HAMMIER
HAMMILY
HAMMING
HEMLINE
HEMMING
HUMMING
HUMPIER
JAMAICA
JAMLIKE
JAMMIER
JAMMING
JEMMIED
JEMMIES
JIMMIED
JIMMIES
JUMPIER
JUMPILY
JUMPING
LAMAISM
LAMAIST
LAMMING
LEMMING
LEMPIRA
LIMBING
LIMNING
LIMPING
LUMPIER
LUMPILY
LUMPING
LUMPISH
MEMOIRE
MEMOIRS
MOMMIES
MUMMIES
MUMMING
MUMPING
NUMBING
PIMLICO
PUMPING
RAMLIKE
RAMMING
RAMMISH
REMAILS
REMAINS
RIMMING
ROMAINE
ROMPING
ROMPISH
RUMMIER
SAMHILL
SUMMING
SUMMITS
TAMPICO
TAMPING
TIMMINS
TOMTITS
TUMMIES
TUMMING
VAMPING
VAMPIRA
VAMPIRE
VAMPISH
WIMPIER
WIMPISH
YUMMIER
ZAMBIAN

ZOMBIES
ZOMBIFY

••M••I•

AMMONIA
ARMENIA
BUMPKIN
CAMBRIC
CAMELIA
COMEDIC
COMESIN
DEMERIT
DEMONIC
HAMELIN
HAMITIC
HOMERIC
HOMINID
JUMPSIN
LAMPOIL
MEMPHIS
MIMESIS
MIMETIC
NAMIBIA
NEMESIS
NOMADIC
NUMERIC
OSMOSIS
OSMOTIC
POMPEIA
POMPEII
PUMPKIN
RAMEKIN
ROMANIA
SAMARIA
SEMITIC
SOMALIA
SOMALIS
SOMATIC
TAMARIN
YEMENIS

••M•••I

CAMPARI
DIMITRI
ELMISTI
JUMANJI
POMPEII
SAMURAI
TYMPANI
ZAMBEZI
ZAMBONI

•••MI••

ADAMITE
AIRMILE
ANIMISM
ANIMIST
ANOMIES
ATOMIES
ATOMISE
ATOMIZE
BALMIER
BALMILY
BARMIER
BEAMIER
BEAMING
BEAMISH
BLAMING
BLEMISH
BOOMIER
BOOMING
BROMIDE
BROMINE
BUMMING

CADMIUM
CALMING
CARMINE
CHEMISE
CHEMIST
CHIMING
COMMITS
DAMMING
DAUMIER
DEEMING
DIMMING
DISMISS
DOOMING
DORMICE
DUMMIED
DUMMIES
ENEMIES
EREMITE
ETAMINE
EXAMINE
FARMING
FERMIUM
FILMIER
FILMING
FIRMING
FLAMIER
FLAMING
FLEMING
FLEMISH
FOAMIER
FOAMILY
FOAMING
FORMICA
FORMING
FRAMING
GAMMIER
GAMMING
GAUMING
GEMMIER
GERMIER
GIMMICK
GINMILL
GNOMISH
GRIMIER
GRIMILY
GRIMING
GUMMIER
GUMMING
HAMMIER
HAMMILY
HAMMING
HARMING
HELMING
HEMMING
HERMITS
HOLMIUM
HUMMING
ICEMILK
ITEMISE
ITEMIZE
JAMMIER
JAMMING
JASMINE
JEMMIED
JEMMIES
JIMMIED
JIMMIES
LAMMING
LEMMING
LOAMIER
LOAMING
LOOMING
MARMION
MIAMIAN

MIAMIAS
MOMMIES
MUMMIES
MUMMING
NESMITH
OLEMISS
PALMIER
PALMING
PALMIST
PERMING
PERMITS
PISMIRE
PLUMIER
PLUMING
PREMIER
PREMISE
PREMISS
PREMIUM
PRIMING
PROMISE
PYGMIES
RAMMING
RAMMISH
REAMING
RHYMING
RIMMING
ROAMING
ROOMIER
ROOMIES
ROOMILY
ROOMING
RUMMIER
SAWMILL
SCHMIDT
SEAMIER
SEAMING
SEEMING
SHAMING
SLIMIER
SLIMILY
SPUMIER
SPUMING
STAMINA
STYMIED
STYMIES
SUBMITS
SUMMING
SUMMITS
SURMISE
TEAMING
TEEMING
TERMING
TERMINI
TERMITE
THYMINE
TIMMINS
TITMICE
TUMMIES
TUMMING
VARMINT
WARMING
WARMISH
WORMIER
WORMISH
WYOMING
YUMMIER
ZOOMING

•••M•I•

AIRMAIL
ALAMEIN
ALEMBIC
ARAMAIC
BARMAID

CHAMOIS
DRUMLIN
FANMAIL
GASMAIN
GREMLIN
KREMLIN
MERMAID
OLDMAID
OLYMPIA
OLYMPIC
PALMOIL
SLIMJIM
SUNMAID
TIOMKIN
TREMAIN
TURMOIL
VERMEIL
ZOOMSIN

•••M••I

EXEMPLI
SPUMONI
STIMULI
TERMINI

••••MI•

ALBUMIN
ANAEMIA
ANAEMIC
ANOSMIA
ANOSMIC
ARTEMIS
BOHEMIA
BRAHMIN
CAKEMIX
CARAMIA
CERAMIC
CHARMIN
DELIMIT
DYNAMIC
ENCOMIA
ENDEMIC
IDIAMIN
ISLAMIC
KASHMIR
LARAMIE
MANUMIT
MIASMIC
NOKOMIS
POLEMIC
PREEMIE
PYRAMID
READMIT
SALAMIS
SEISMIC
TATAMIS
TOTEMIC
VITAMIN

•••••MI

GOURAMI
LAKSHMI
ORIGAMI
SASHIMI
TSUNAMI

M•J••••

MAJESTE
MAJESTY
MAJEURE
MAJORCA
MAJORED

••MJ•••

JIMJAMS
RAMJETS

••M••J•

JUMANJI

•••MJ••

SLIMJIM

•••M•J•

BERMEJO

M•K••••

MAKEFOR
MAKEHAY
MAKEOFF
MAKEOUT
MAKEPAR
MAKESDO
MAKESIT
MAKESUP
MAKEUPS
MAKEWAY
MAKINGS
MIKADOS
MIKHAIL
MUKLUKS

M••K•••

MALKINS
MANKIND
MARKERS
MARKETS
MARKHAM
MARKHOR
MARKING
MARKKAA
MARKOFF
MARKOVA
MARKSUP
MARKUPS
MASKERS
MASKING
MAWKISH
MEEKEST
MICKEYS
MILKCOW
MILKERS
MILKIER
MILKING
MILKMAN
MILKMEN
MILKRUN
MILKSOP
MIRKIER
MOCKERS
MOCKERY
MOCKING
MOCKUPS
MONKEES
MONKEYS
MONKISH
MUCKIER
MUCKILY
MUCKING
MUCKSUP
MURKIER
MURKILY
MUSKEGS
MUSKETS
MUSKIER
MUSKIES
MUSKRAT

M•••K••

MARKKAA
MARYKAY
MENCKEN
MESSKIT
MOLOKAI
MONIKER

M••••K•

MANLIKE
MAZURKA
MISLIKE
MISTAKE
MOHAWKS
MUKLUKS
MUZHIKS

M•••••K

MAFFICK
MASARYK
MATLOCK
MATTOCK
MENFOLK
MIDWEEK
MISTOOK
MOLLUSK
MRSPOCK
MUBARAK
MUDPACK

•M•K•••

SMOKERS
SMOKIER
SMOKIES
SMOKILY
SMOKING

•M••K••

SMACKED
SMACKER
SMIRKED

•M•••K•

AMERIKA
EMBANKS
EMBARKS

•M••••K

DMYTRYK

••M•K••

BUMPKIN
PUMPKIN
RAMEKIN
REMAKES
UNMAKES

••M••K•

ARMLIKE
DAMASKS
GEMLIKE
GUMLIKE
JAMLIKE
RAMLIKE
REMARKS
UNMASKS

••M•••K

ARMLOCK
BOMBECK
GEMSBOK
GIMMICK
HAMHOCK
HAMMOCK

HEMLOCK
HUMMOCK
JAMPACK
LAMARCK

•••MK••

TIOMKIN

•••M•K•

CHOMSKY
GROMYKO

•••M••K

DENMARK
EARMARK
GIMMICK
HAMMOCK
HOLMOAK
HUMMOCK
ICEMILK
SKIMASK
TEDMACK
WIDMARK

••••M•K

RUNAMOK
YASHMAK

M•L••••

MALABAR
MALACCA
MALACHI
MALAISE
MALAMUD
MALAYAN
MALCOLM
MALEATE
MALEFIC
MALIGNS
MALKINS
MALLARD
MALLETS
MALLOWS
MALLRAT
MALMSEY
MALODOR
MALRAUX
MALTEDS
MALTESE
MALTHUS
MALTIER
MALTING
MALTOSE
MCLUHAN
MELANGE
MELANIE
MELANIN
MELDING
MELINDA
MELISSA
MELLOWS
MELODIC
MELROSE
MELTING
MILDEST
MILDEWS
MILDEWY
MILDRED
MILEAGE
MILHAUD
MILIEUS
MILIEUX
MILITIA
MILKCOW

MILKERS
MILKIER
MILKING
MILKMAN
MILKMEN
MILKRUN
MILKSOP
MILLAND
MILLARD
MILLDAM
MILLEND
MILLERS
MILLETS
MILLETT
MILLING
MILLION
MILLRUN
MILORDS
MOLDERS
MOLDIER
MOLDING
MOLDOVA
MOLESTS
MOLIERE
MOLLIFY
MOLLUSC
MOLLUSK
MOLOCHS
MOLOKAI
MOLOTOV
MOLTERS
MOLTING
MULCHED
MULCHES
MULCTED
MULETAS
MULLAHS
MULLEIN
MULLERS
MULLETS
MULLING
MULLION

M••L•••

MADLIBS
MAILBAG
MAILBOX
MAILCAR
MAILERS
MAILING
MAILLOT
MAILOUT
MAILSIN
MALLARD
MALLETS
MALLOWS
MALLRAT
MANLESS
MANLIER
MANLIKE
MARLENE
MARLINS
MARLOWE
MATLESS
MATLOCK
MAULDIN
MAULING
MCCLOUD
MCCLURE
MEALIER
MEALIES
MEDLEYS
MELLOWS
MERLOTS
MEWLERS
MEWLING
MIDLAND
MIDLIFE
MIDLINE
MILLAND
MILLARD
MILLDAM
MILLEND
MILLERS
MILLETS
MILLETT
MILLING
MILLION
MILLRUN
MISLAID
MISLAYS
MISLEAD
MISLIKE
MOILERS
MOILING
MOLLIFY
MOLLUSC
MOLLUSK
MOSLEMS
MOULAGE
MOULDED
MOULDER
MOULTED
MRCLEAN
MUKLUKS
MULLAHS
MULLEIN
MULLERS
MULLETS
MULLING
MULLION
MUSLIMS
MUSLINS

M•••L••

MACULAE
MAHALIA
MAILLOT
MANGLED
MANGLES
MANILOW
MANTLED
MANTLES
MARBLED
MARBLES
MARILYN
MARYLOU
MATELOT
MATILDA
MAUDLIN
MAXILLA
MAYALIN
MCCALLS
MEASLES
MEDALED
MEDDLED
MEDDLER
MEDDLES
MEDULLA
METTLES
MIDDLEC
MIDDLES
MIGGLES
MINGLED
MINGLER
MINGLES
MINOLTA
MISALLY
MISPLAY
MIZZLED
MIZZLES
MOBILES
MODELAS
MODELED
MODELER
MODELTS
MODULAR
MODULES
MONOLOG
MOONLIT
MORALES
MORALLY
MORELLO
MOSELLE
MOTTLED
MOTTLES
MOUFLON
MUDDLED
MUDDLER
MUDDLES
MUFFLED
MUFFLER
MUFFLES
MUMBLED
MUMBLER
MUMBLES
MURILLO
MUSCLED
MUSCLES
MUZZLED
MUZZLES
MYRTLES

M••••L•

MALCOLM
MAMMALS
MANACLE
MANDALA
MANDELA
MANHOLE
MANIPLE
MANTELS
MANUALS
MARCELS
MARSALA
MARVELS
MAXILLA
MAXWELL
MAYPOLE
MCCALLS
MEATILY
MEDULLA
MENFOLK
MENIALS
MERRILL
MERRILY
MESCALS
MESSALA
MESSILY
MICHELE
MINABLE
MIRACLE
MISALLY
MISCALL
MISERLY
MISFILE
MISRULE
MISSALS
MISSILE
MISTILY
MIXABLE
MOISTLY
MONDALE
MONGOLS
MONOCLE
MONTHLY
MOODILY
MOONILY
MORALLY
MORELLO
MORSELS
MORTALS
MOSELLE
MOVABLE
MOVABLY
MUCKILY
MUDDILY
MUDEELS
MURILLO
MURKILY
MUSHILY
MUSSELS
MUSSILY
MUSTILY
MUTABLE
MUTABLY
MUTUALS
MUZZILY

M•••••L

MAGICAL
MARITAL
MARSHAL
MARTIAL
MAXIMAL
MAXWELL
MAYORAL
MEDICAL
MENTHOL
MERRILL
MICHAEL
MIKHAIL
MINDFUL
MINERAL
MINIMAL
MISCALL
MISDEAL
MISDIAL
MISTRAL
MOANFUL
MONGREL
MUSEFUL
MUSICAL

•ML••••

UMLAUTS

•M•L•••

AMALGAM
AMBLERS
AMBLING
AMPLEST
AMPLIFY
AMULETS
AMYLASE
EMBLEMS
EMPLOYE
EMPLOYS
EMULATE
IMPLANT
IMPLIED
IMPLIES
IMPLODE
IMPLORE
OMELETS
SMALLER
SMALTOS
SMELLED
SMELTED
SMELTER
SMILERS
SMILING
SMOLDER

•M••L••

AMIBLUE
AMPULES
EMAILED
EMMYLOU
IMPALAS
IMPALED
IMPALES
IMPULSE
SMALLER
SMELLED

•M•••L•

AMAPOLA
AMIABLE
AMIABLY
AMPOULE
EMERALD
EMPTILY
OMPHALI
SMARTLY
SMOKILY
SMUGGLE

•M••••L

EMANUEL
EMBROIL
EMPANEL
IMMORAL
IMPANEL
IMPERIL

••ML•••

AIMLESS
ARMLESS
ARMLETS
ARMLIKE
ARMLOAD
ARMLOCK
GEMLESS
GEMLIKE
GIMLETS
GUMLESS
GUMLIKE
HAMLETS
HEMLINE
HEMLOCK
JAMLIKE
PIMLICO
RAMLIKE
RIMLESS
RUMLESS
SAMLETS
SUMLESS

••M•L••

AAMILNE
BUMBLED
BUMBLER
BUMBLES
CAMELIA
CAMELOT
CAMILLE
COMPLEX
CUMULUS
DEMILLE
DIMPLED
DIMPLES
EMMYLOU
FAMULUS
FEMALES
FUMBLED
FUMBLER
FUMBLES
GAMBLED
GAMBLER
GAMBLES
GAMELAW
HAMELIN
HEMSLEY
HUMBLED
HUMBLER
HUMBLES
JUMBLED
JUMBLES
MUMBLED
MUMBLER
MUMBLES
NIMBLER
ORMOLUS
POMELOS
RAMBLED
RAMBLER
RAMBLES
REMELTS
REMOLDS
RIMPLED
RIMPLES
ROMULAN
ROMULUS
RUMBLED
RUMBLES
RUMPLED
RUMPLES
SAMPLED
SAMPLER
SAMPLES
SEMILOG
SIMILAR
SIMILES
SIMPLER
SIMPLEX
SOMALIA
SOMALIS
TAMALES
TEMBLOR
TEMPLAR
TEMPLES
TIMELAG
TUMBLED
TUMBLER
TUMBLES
TUMULTS
TUMULUS
WAMBLED
WAMBLES
WIMBLED
WIMBLES
WIMPLED
WIMPLES

••M••L•

ARMFULS
ARMHOLE
BUMPILY
CAMILLE
CAMPILY
CEMBALO
COMPELS
COMPILE
CYMBALS
DAMSELS
DEMILLE
DIMBULB
GAMBOLS
GIMBALS
GUMBALL
HAMMILY
HIMSELF
HUMANLY
HUMIDLY
HYMNALS
JUMPILY
KAMPALA
KIMBALL
LUMPILY
MAMMALS
POMMELS
PUMMELS
REMAILS
RUMPOLE
SAMBALS
SAMHILL
SYMBOLS
TAMABLE
TAMBALA
TIMBALE
TIMBALS
TIMIDLY
TOMBOLA
WIMPOLE
WOMANLY

••M•••L

ADMIRAL
BIMODAL
COMICAL
DEMEROL
FEMORAL
GAMBREL
GUMBALL
HUMERAL
IMMORAL
KIMBALL
LAMINAL
LAMPOIL
NOMINAL
NUMERAL
REMODEL
REMOVAL
SAMHILL
SEMINAL
TOMFOOL
TUMBREL

•••ML••

BRIMLEY
CHEMLAB
DAIMLER
DRUMLIN
GREMLIN
KREMLIN

•••M•L•

AIRMILE
ANIMALS
ANOMALY
BALMILY
BRAMBLE
BRAMBLY
CRUMBLE
CRUMBLY
CRUMPLE
CRUMPLY
ENAMELS
EXAMPLE
EXEMPLI
FOAMILY
FORMALS
FORMULA
GINMILL
GRIMILY
GRUMBLE
GRUMBLY
GUNMOLL
HAMMILY
ICEMILK
MAMMALS
NORMALS
PLUMPLY
POMMELS
PUMMELS
ROOMILY
SAWMILL
SHAMBLE
SLIMILY
STIMULI
STUMBLE
THIMBLE
TRAMPLE
TREMBLE
TREMBLY
TREMOLO

•••M••L

AIRMAIL
ALUMNAL
BRIMFUL
BRUMMEL
DOOMFUL
FANMAIL
FORMFUL
GINMILL
GUNMOLL
HARMFUL
ISHMAEL
OATMEAL
PALMOIL
ROOMFUL
SAWMILL
TRAMMEL
TURMOIL
VERMEIL

••••M•L

ABYSMAL
BRUMMEL
CALOMEL
CARAMEL
COZUMEL
DECIMAL
MAXIMAL
MINIMAL
OPTIMAL
THERMAL
TRAMMEL

M•M••••

MAMBOED
MAMMALS
MAMMOTH
MCMAHON
MEMBERS
MEMENTO
MEMOIRE
MEMOIRS
MEMOREX
MEMPHIS
MIMESIS
MIMETIC
MIMICRY
MIMIEUX
MIMOSAS
MOMBASA
MOMENTS
MOMMIES
MRMAGOO
MUMBLED
MUMBLER
MUMBLES
MUMESON
MUMFORD
MUMMERS
MUMMERY
MUMMIES
MUMMING
MUMPING
MYMAMMY

M••M•••

MALMSEY
MAMMALS
MAMMOTH
MANMADE
MARMARA
MARMION
MARMOTS
MAUMAUS
MERMAID
MIAMIAN
MIAMIAS
MICMACS
MIDMOST
MISMATE
MOMMIES
MORMONS
MUAMMAR
MUMMERS
MUMMERY
MUMMIES
MUMMING
MURMURS
MUUMUUS

M•••M••

MADAMEX
MALAMUD
MANUMIT
MANXMAN
MANXMEN
MARIMBA
MAXIMAL
MAXIMUM
MAXIMUS
MERIMEE
MIASMAS
MIASMIC
MILKMAN
MILKMEN
MINIMAL
MINIMUM
MIRAMAR
MIRAMAX
MOGAMBO
MONOMER
MUAMMAR
MYANMAR
MYMAMMY

M••••M•

MACRAME
MAGNUMS
MAHATMA
MARRYME
MAYHEMS
MAYTIME
MEDIUMS
MEGOHMS
MEGRIMS
MISNAME
MOSLEMS
MUGWUMP
MUSEUMS
MUSLIMS
MYMAMMY

M•••••M

MACADAM
MALCOLM
MARKHAM
MARXISM
MAUGHAM
MAXIMUM
MIDTERM
MILLDAM
MINICAM
MINIMUM
MITCHUM
MODICUM

•MM••••

AMMETER
AMMONIA
EMMYLOU
IMMENSE
IMMERSE
IMMIXED
IMMIXES
IMMORAL
IMMURED
IMMURES

•M•M•••

IMAMATE

•M•••M•

EMBLEMS

•M••••M

AMALGAM
OMENTUM

••MM•••

BUMMERS
BUMMING
COMMAND
COMMEND
COMMENT
COMMITS
COMMODE
COMMONS
COMMOVE
COMMUNE
COMMUTE
DAMMARS
DAMMING
DIMMERS
DIMMEST
DIMMING
DUMMIED
DUMMIES
DUMMYUP
GAMMERS
GAMMIER
GAMMING
GAMMONS
GEMMIER
GIMMICK
GUMMIER
GUMMING
HAMMERS
HAMMETT
HAMMIER
HAMMILY
HAMMING
HAMMOCK
HAMMOND
HEMMERS
HEMMING
HUMMERS
HUMMING
HUMMOCK
JAMMERS
JAMMIER
JAMMING
JEMMIED
JEMMIES
JIMMIED
JIMMIES
LAMMING
LEMMING
MAMMALS
MAMMOTH
MOMMIES
MUMMERS
MUMMERY
MUMMIES
MUMMING
POMMELS
PUMMELS
RAMMING
RAMMISH
RIMMING
RUMMAGE
RUMMIER
SIMMERS
SIMMONS
SUMMARY
SUMMERS
SUMMERY
SUMMING
SUMMITS
SUMMONS
TAMMANY
TIMMINS
TUMMIES
TUMMING
YAMMERS
YUMMIER

••M•M••

MYMAMMY

••M••M•

DUMDUMS
JIMJAMS
MYMAMMY
POMPOMS
TAMTAMS
TOMTOMS

••M•••M

CAMBIUM
HOMONYM
HUMANUM
HUMDRUM
LAMAISM
LUMPSUM
SYMPTOM

•••MM••

BRIMMED
BRUMMEL
CHUMMED
CLAMMED
CLAMMER
CRAMMED
CRAMMER
DRUMMED
DRUMMER
FLUMMOX
GLIMMER
GLOMMED
GLUMMER
GRAMMAR
GRAMMER
GRAMMES
GRAMMYS
GRIMMER
GROMMET
MUAMMAR
PLUMMER
PLUMMET
PRIMMER
SCAMMED
SHAMMED
SHIMMER
SKIMMED
SKIMMER
SLAMMED
SLAMMER
SLIMMED
SLIMMER
SLUMMED
SPAMMED
SPAMMER
STAMMER
STEMMED
SWIMMER
TRAMMEL
TRIMMED
TRIMMER
WHAMMED

•••M••M

ANIMISM
CADMIUM
FERMIUM
HOLMIUM
PREMIUM
SLIMJIM
YESMAAM

••••MM•

DILEMMA
MYMAMMY
PIPEMMA
SCRUMMY

••••M•M

MAXIMUM
MINIMUM
OPTIMUM

M•N••••

MANACLE
MANAGED
MANAGER
MANAGES
MANAGUA
MANANAS
MANATEE
MANCINI
MANDALA
MANDANS
MANDATE
MANDAYS
MANDELA
MANEGES
MANFRED
MANGERS
MANGIER
MANGLED
MANGLES
MANGOES
MANHOLE
MANHOOD
MANHOUR
MANHUNT
MANIACS
MANILOW
MANIOCS
MANIPLE
MANITOU
MANKIND
MANLESS
MANLIER
MANLIKE
MANMADE
MANNERS
MANNING
MANNISH
MANOWAR
MANSARD
MANSION
MANTELS
MANTLED
MANTLES
MANTRAP
MANTRAS
MANTRIC
MANUALS
MANUMIT
MANXCAT
MANXMAN
MANXMEN
MANYEAR
MENACED
MENACES
MENAGES
MENCKEN
MENDERS
MENDING
MENDOZA
MENFOLK
MENHIRS
MENIALS
MENISCI
MENORAH
MENOTTI
MENTHOL
MENTION
MENTORS
MENUHIN
MENZIES
MINABLE
MINARET
MINCERS
MINCING
MINDERS
MINDFUL
MINDING
MINDSET
MINERAL
MINERVA
MINGIER
MINGLED
MINGLER
MINGLES
MINIBUS
MINICAB
MINICAM
MINIMAL
MINIMUM
MINIONS
MINIVAN
MINIVER
MINNOWS
MINOANS
MINOLTA
MINORCA
MINORED
MINTERS
MINTIER
MINTING
MINUEND
MINUETS
MINUSES
MINUTES
MINUTIA
MINXISH
MINYANS
MONARCH
MONDALE
MONDAYS
MONEYED
MONGERS
MONGOLS
MONGREL
MONIKER
MONIQUE
MONITOR
MONKEES
MONKEYS
MONKISH
MONOCLE
MONOCOT
MONODIC
MONOLOG
MONOMER
MONSOON
MONSTER
MONTAGE
MONTANA
MONTAND
MONTANE
MONTANI
MONTEGO
MONTERO
MONTHLY
MONTOYA
MUNCHED
MUNCHER
MUNCHES
MUNDANE
MUNTINS
MYNHEER

M••N•••

MADNESS
MAENADS
MAGNANI
MAGNATE
MAGNETO
MAGNETS
MAGNIFY
MAGNUMS
MAINTOP
MANNERS
MANNING
MANNISH
MAUNDER

MAYNARD
MCENROE
MEANDER
MEANEST
MEANIES
MEANING
MEINIES
MINNOWS
MISNAME
MOANERS
MOANFUL
MOANING
MOONDOG
MOONIER
MOONILY
MOONING
MOONISH
MOONLIT
MOONSET
MORNING
MOUNDED
MOUNTED
MOUNTIE
MYANMAR

M•••N••

MADONNA
MAGENTA
MAGINOT
MAHONEY
MAKINGS
MANANAS
MARENGO
MARINAS
MARINER
MARINES
MASONIC
MASONRY
MATINEE
MCHENRY
MELANGE
MELANIE
MELANIN
MELINDA
MEMENTO
MERINOS
MIRANDA
MOMENTS
MORANIS
MOURNED
MRBONES
MUTANTS

M••••N•

MACHINA
MACHINE
MACRONS
MADDENS
MADDING
MADONNA
MAGNANI
MAIDENS
MAILING
MALIGNS
MALKINS
MALTING
MANCINI
MANDANS
MANHUNT
MANKIND
MANNING
MAPPING
MARCONI
MARGINS
MARIANA
MARKING
MARLENE
MARLINS
MAROONS
MARRING
MARTENS
MARTINA
MARTINI
MARTINO
MARTINS
MARYANN
MASHING
MASKING
MASSING
MATRONS
MATTING
MAULING
MAYWINE
MBABANE
MCSWINE
MEANING
MEDIANS
MEDIANT
MEETING
MELDING
MELTING
MENDING
MEOWING
MERGING
MESHING
MESSINA
MESSING
METHANE
MEWLING
MICRONS
MIDDENS
MIDLAND
MIDLINE
MIFFING
MIGHTNT
MIGRANT
MILKING
MILLAND
MILLEND
MILLING
MINCING
MINDING
MINIONS
MINOANS
MINTING
MINUEND
MINYANS
MIOCENE
MISDONE
MISSING
MISTING
MITRING
MITTENS
MIZZENS
MOANING
MOBBING
MOCKING
MODERNS
MOILING
MOLDING
MOLTING
MONTANA
MONTAND
MONTANE
MONTANI
MOONING
MOORING
MOPPING
MORAINE
MORDANT
MORDENT
MORGANA
MORGANS
MORMONS
MORNING
MOSHING
MOSSING
MOTIONS
MOUSING
MOUTONS
MUCKING
MUDHENS
MUFFING
MUFFINS
MUGGING
MULLING
MUMMING
MUMPING
MUNDANE
MUNTINS
MUSHING
MUSLINS
MUSSING
MUSTANG
MUTTONS
MUZZING

M•••••N

MADCHEN
MADIGAN
MADISON
MAILSIN
MALAYAN
MANSION
MANXMAN
MANXMEN
MARCHON
MARILYN
MARMION
MARTIAN
MARYANN
MATEWAN
MAUDLIN
MAULDIN
MAUREEN
MAXBORN
MAYALIN
MCGAVIN
MCLUHAN
MCMAHON
MCQUEEN
MEGRYAN
MEISSEN
MELANIN
MENCKEN
MENTION
MENUHIN
MEXICAN
MIAMIAN
MIDTOWN
MILKMAN
MILKMEN
MILKRUN
MILLION
MILLRUN
MINIVAN
MISSION
MIXEDIN
MIXESIN
MOHICAN
MOISTEN
MONSOON
MOORHEN
MOUFLON
MOVEDIN
MOVEDON
MOVESIN
MOVESON
MOWDOWN
MRCLEAN
MUEZZIN
MULLEIN
MULLION
MUMESON
MUTAGEN

•MN••••

AMNESIA
AMNESTY
AMNIONS
OMNIBUS

•M•N•••

AMENDED
AMENITY
AMONGST
EMANANT
EMANATE
EMANUEL
EMENDED
EMENDER
EMINENT
OMENTUM
OMINOUS

•M••N••

AMMONIA
AMOUNTS
EMBANKS
EMPANEL
IMMENSE
IMPANEL
IMPENDS
IMPINGE

•M•••N•

AMAZING
AMAZONS
AMBIENT
AMBLING
AMERIND
AMNIONS
AMUSING
EMANANT
EMINENT
EMOTING
IMAGINE
IMAGING
IMBUING
IMOGENE
IMPLANT
IMPOUND
IMPRINT
IMPUGNS
KMESONS
SMETANA
SMILING
SMITING
SMOKING

•M••••N

EMERSON
EMOTION
OMICRON
SMARTEN
SMIDGEN
SMITTEN
UMBRIAN
UMPTEEN

••MN•••

DAMNING
DIMNESS
GYMNAST
HYMNALS
HYMNODY
LIMNERS
LIMNING
REMNANT
ROMNEYS

••M•N••

ALMANAC
ALMONDS
AMMONIA
ARMENIA
CEMENTS
COMINGS
DEMANDS
DEMONIC
DOMINGO
DOMINOS
DOMINUS
ERMINES
FAMINES
FOMENTS
GAMINES
HHMUNRO
HOMINID
HOMONYM
HUMANLY
HUMANUM
IMMENSE
JIMENEZ
JUMANJI
KIMONOS
LAMENTS
LAMINAE
LAMINAL
LAMINAR
LAMINAS
LEMONDE
MEMENTO
MOMENTS
NOMINAL
NOMINEE
ORMANDY
PIMENTO
RAMINTO
REMANDS
REMENDS
REMINDS
ROMANCE
ROMANIA
ROMANOV
ROMANSH
SEMINAL
SEMINAR
SIMENON
TIMINGS
WOMANLY
YEMENIS

••M••N•

AAMILNE
ARMBAND
ARMYANT
BAMBINO
BEMOANS
BOMBING
BUMMING
BUMPING
CAMPING
COMBINE
COMBING
COMEONS
COMMAND
COMMEND
COMMENT
COMMONS
COMMUNE
COMPANY
DAMMING
DAMNING
DAMPENS
DAMPING
DAMSONS
DEMEANS
DEMESNE
DIMMING
DOMAINS
DUMBING
DUMPING
GAMMING
GAMMONS
GUMMING
HAMMING
HAMMOND
HEMLINE
HEMMING
HUMMING
JAMMING
JUMPING
LAMBENT
LAMMING
LEMMING
LIMBING
LIMNING
LIMPING
LUMPING
MUMMING
MUMPING
NUMBING
POMPANO
POMPONS
PUMPING
RAMMING
RAMPANT
REMAINS
REMNANT
REMOUNT
RIMMING
ROMAINE
ROMPING
SAMOANS
SAMPANS
SAMSUNG
SIMIANS
SIMMONS
SOMEONE
SUMMING
SUMMONS
TAMMANY
TAMPING
TIMMINS
TUMMING
TYMPANA
TYMPANI
VAMPING
ZAMBONI

••M•••N

ALMADEN
BUMPKIN
CAMERON
CAMPION
COMESIN
COMESON
GAMBIAN
HAMELIN
HAMPTON
HOMERUN
JAMESON
JUMPSIN
JUMPSON
LAMPOON
MCMAHON
MUMESON
PEMICAN
PIMESON
PUMPKIN
RAMADAN
RAMEKIN
ROMULAN
SAMISEN
SAMPSON
SIMENON
SIMPSON
TAMARIN
ZAMBIAN

•••MN••

ALUMNAE
ALUMNAL
ALUMNUS
CHIMNEY

•••M•N•

ACUMENS
ADAMANT
AILMENT
ALIMENT
ALIMONY
ANEMONE
ATAMANS
AUGMENT
BEAMING
BELMONT
BLAMING
BOOMING
BROMINE
BUMMING
BURMANS
CAIMANS
CALMING
CARMINE
CAYMANS
CHIMING
CLEMENS
CLEMENT
COMMAND
COMMEND
COMMENT
COMMONS
COMMUNE
CREMONA
DAIMONS
DAMMING
DEEMING
DESMOND
DIAMOND
DIMMING
DINMONT
DOLMANS
DOLMENS
DOOMING
DORMANT
ELEMENT
ETAMINE
EXAMINE
FARMING
FERMENT
FIGMENT
FILMING
FIRMING
FLAMING
FLEMING
FOAMING
FORMING
FRAMING
FREMONT
GAMMING
GAMMONS
GARMENT
GAUMING
GERMANE
GERMANS
GERMANY
GNOMONS
GRIMING
GUMMING
HAMMING
HAMMOND
HARMING
HARMONY
HELMING
HEMMING
HERMANN
HETMANS
HORMONE
HUMMING
JAMMING
JASMINE
KIRMANS
LAMMING
LEMMING
LOAMING
LOOMING
MORMONS
MUMMING
NORMAND
NORMANS
ODDMENT
PALMING
PAYMENT
PERMING
PIGMENT
PLUMING
PRIMING
RAIMENT
RAMMING
RAYMOND
REAMING
RHYMING
RIMMING
ROAMING
ROOMING
SALMONS
SEAMING
SEEMING
SEGMENT
SERMONS
SHAMANS
SHAMING
SIGMUND
SIMMONS
SPUMING
SPUMONE
SPUMONI
STAMENS
STAMINA
SUMMING
SUMMONS
TAMMANY
TEAMING
TEEMING
TERMING
TERMINI
THYMINE
TIMMINS
TORMENT
TUMMING
ULLMANN
UNAMUNO
VARMINT
VERMONT
WARMING
WYOMING
YOUMANS
ZOOMING

•••M••N

ADAMSON
ALAMEIN
ARAMEAN
CLEMSON
CRAMPON
CRIMEAN
CRIMSON
DRUMLIN
GASMAIN
GREMLIN
HERMANN
KREMLIN
MARMION
MIAMIAN
NEWMOON
NEWMOWN
OLDMOON
THOMSON
TIOMKIN
TREMAIN
ULLMANN
ZOOMSIN

••••MN•

AUTUMNS
CALUMNY
COLUMNS

••••M•N

ABDOMEN
AGNOMEN
ALBUMEN
ALBUMIN
BASEMAN
BASEMEN
BATEMAN
BATSMAN
BATSMEN
BELLMAN
BELLMEN
BERGMAN
BESTMAN
BESTMEN
BIRDMAN
BIRDMEN
BITUMEN
BOATMAN
BOATMEN
BONDMAN
BONDMEN
BRAHMAN
BRAHMIN
BUSHMAN
BUSHMEN
BYREMAN
BYREMEN
CAVEMAN
CAVEMEN
CERUMEN
CHAPMAN
CHAPMEN
CHARMIN
COLEMAN
CREWMAN
CREWMEN
DARKMAN
DOORMAN
DOORMEN
DREAMON
DUSTMAN
DUSTMEN
EASTMAN
FADIMAN
FELDMAN
FEYNMAN
FIREMAN
FIREMEN
FLAGMAN
FLAGMEN
FOOTMAN
FOOTMEN
FOREMAN
FOREMEN
FREEMAN
FREEMEN
FROGMAN
FROGMEN
GATEMAN
GATEMEN
GOODMAN
GOODMEN
HACKMAN
HANGMAN
HANGMEN
HARTMAN
HEADMAN
HEADMEN
HEISMAN
HELLMAN
HICKMAN
HOFFMAN
HOUSMAN
IDEAMAN
IDEAMEN
IDIAMIN
INHUMAN
IRONMAN
IRONMEN
JAVAMAN
JAZZMAN
JAZZMEN
JUNKMAN
KAUFMAN
KINGMAN
KINSMAN
KINSMEN
KLUGMAN
LINEMAN
LINEMEN
LOCOMAN
LOCOMEN
MANXMAN
MANXMEN
MILKMAN
MILKMEN
NEWSMAN
NEWSMEN
OTTOMAN
PERLMAN
PIKEMAN
PIKEMEN
PITTMAN
PLOWMAN
PLOWMEN
PORTMAN
POSTMAN
POSTMEN
PROPMAN
PROPMEN
PULLMAN
PUTAMEN
RAINMAN
REGIMEN
REITMAN
REPOMAN
RICHMAN
RICKMAN
SANDMAN
SANDMEN
SHERMAN
SHIPMAN
SHIPMEN
SHOWMAN
SHOWMEN
SIDEMAN
SIDEMEN
SNOWMAN
SNOWMEN
SOLOMON
STARMAN
SYNGMAN
TAPEMAN
TAPEMEN
TASHMAN
TAXIMAN
TAXIMEN
THEOMEN
THURMAN
TUCHMAN
VITAMIN
WALKMAN
WELLMAN
WHITMAN
WISEMAN
WISEMEN
WOLFMAN
WOLFMEN
WORKMAN
WORKMEN
YARDMAN
YARDMEN

•••••MN

CONDEMN
CONTEMN

MO•••••

MOANERS
MOANFUL
MOANING
MOBBING
MOBBISH
MOBCAPS
MOBILES
MOBSTER
MOCKERS
MOCKERY
MOCKING
MOCKUPS
MODELAS
MODELED
MODELER
MODELTS
MODERNS
MODESTO
MODESTY
MODICUM
MODISTE
MODULAR
MODULES
MOGAMBO
MOGGIES
MOHAIRS
MOHAWKS
MOHICAN
MOILERS
MOILING
MOISTEN
MOISTER
MOISTLY
MOLDERS
MOLDIER
MOLDING
MOLDOVA
MOLESTS
MOLIERE
MOLLIFY
MOLLUSC
MOLLUSK
MOLOCHS
MOLOKAI
MOLOTOV
MOLTERS
MOLTING
MOMBASA
MOMENTS
MOMMIES
MONARCH
MONDALE
MONDAYS
MONEYED
MONGERS
MONGOLS
MONGREL
MONIKER
MONIQUE
MONITOR
MONKEES
MONKEYS
MONKISH
MONOCLE
MONOCOT
MONODIC
MONOLOG
MONOMER
MONSOON
MONSTER
MONTAGE
MONTANA
MONTAND
MONTANE
MONTANI
MONTEGO
MONTERO
MONTHLY
MONTOYA
MOOCHED
MOOCHER
MOOCHES
MOODIER
MOODILY
MOONDOG
MOONIER
MOONILY
MOONING
MOONISH
MOONLIT
MOONSET
MOORAGE
MOORHEN
MOORIER
MOORING
MOORISH
MOPIEST
MOPPERS
MOPPETS
MOPPING
MOPTOPS
MORAINE
MORALES
MORALLY
MORANIS
MORAVIA
MORDANT
MORDENT
MORDRED
MORELLO
MORESBY
MORGANA
MORGANS
MORMONS
MORNING
MOROCCO
MORPHED
MORROWS
MORSELS
MORTALS
MORTARS
MORTIFY
MORTISE
MOSAICS
MOSELLE
MOSEYED
MOSHERS
MOSHING
MOSHPIT
MOSLEMS
MOSQUES
MOSSIER
MOSSING
MOTHERS
MOTHIER
MOTIONS
MOTIVES
MOTORED
MOTTLED
MOTTLES
MOTTOES
MOUFLON
MOULAGE
MOULDED
MOULDER
MOULTED
MOUNDED
MOUNTED
MOUNTIE
MOURNED
MOUSERS
MOUSIER
MOUSING
MOUSSED
MOUSSES
MOUTHED
MOUTONS
MOVABLE
MOVABLY
MOVEDIN
MOVEDON
MOVEDUP
MOVEOUT
MOVESIN
MOVESON
MOVESUP
MOWDOWN

M•O••••

MAOISTS
MEOWING
MIOCENE
MOOCHED
MOOCHER
MOOCHES
MOODIER
MOODILY
MOONDOG
MOONIER
MOONILY
MOONING
MOONISH
MOONLIT
MOONSET
MOORAGE
MOORHEN
MOORIER
MOORING
MOORISH

M••O•••

MADONNA
MAHONEY
MAHOUTS
MAJORCA
MAJORED
MALODOR
MANOWAR
MAROONS
MASONIC
MASONRY
MAYORAL
MEGOHMS
MEIOSES
MEIOSIS
MEIOTIC
MELODIC
MEMOIRE
MEMOIRS
MEMOREX
MENORAH
MENOTTI
METOOER
MIAOYAO
MILORDS
MIMOSAS
MINOANS
MINOLTA
MINORCA
MINORED
MITOSES
MITOSIS
MITOTIC
MOLOCHS
MOLOKAI
MOLOTOV
MONOCLE
MONOCOT
MONODIC
MONOLOG
MONOMER
MOROCCO
MOTORED
MRBONES

M•••O••

MACRONS

MADEOFF
MADEOUT
MAILOUT
MAKEOFF
MAKEOUT
MALCOLM
MALLOWS
MALTOSE
MAMBOED
MAMMOTH
MANGOES
MANHOLE
MANHOOD
MANHOUR
MANIOCS
MARCONI
MARKOFF
MARKOVA
MARLOWE
MARMOTS
MAROONS
MARROWS
MASCOTS
MASTOID
MATLOCK
MATRONS
MATTOCK
MATZOHS
MAUROIS
MAXBORN
MAYPOLE
MCCLOUD
MEADOWS
MEADOWY
MELLOWS
MELROSE
MENDOZA
MENFOLK
MENTORS
MERLOTS
METEORS
METEOUT
METHODS
METOOER
MICROBE
MICRONS
MIDMOST
MIDTOWN
MINIONS
MINNOWS
MIRRORS
MISDOES
MISDONE
MISSOUT
MISTOOK
MISWORD
MITFORD
MOLDOVA
MONGOLS
MONSOON
MONTOYA
MOPTOPS
MORMONS
MORROWS
MOTIONS
MOTTOES
MOUTONS
MOVEOUT
MOWDOWN
MRSPOCK
MUMFORD
MURDOCH
MUSCOVY
MUTTONS

M••••O•

MADEFOR
MADISON
MAGINOT
MAILBOX
MAILLOT
MAINTOP
MAKEFOR
MALODOR
MANHOOD
MANILOW
MANITOU
MANSION
MARABOU
MARCHON
MARKHOR
MARMION
MARYLOU
MATADOR
MATELOT
MCENROE
MCMAHON
MEDICOS
MENTHOL
MENTION
MERINOS
MIKADOS
MILKCOW
MILKSOP
MILLION
MIRADOR
MISSION
MISTOOK
MOLOTOV
MONITOR
MONOCOT
MONOLOG
MONSOON
MOONDOG
MOUFLON
MOVEDON
MOVESON
MRMAGOO
MUGSHOT
MULLION
MUMESON

M•••••O

MAESTRO
MAGNETO
MAKESDO
MARCATO
MARENGO
MARTINO
MEGIDDO
MEMENTO
MESTIZO
MIAOYAO
MODESTO
MOGAMBO
MONTEGO
MONTERO
MORELLO
MOROCCO
MRMAGOO
MURILLO

•MO••••

AMOEBAE
AMOEBAS
AMOEBIC
AMONGST
AMOROUS
AMOUNTS
BMOVIES
EMOTERS
EMOTING
EMOTION
EMOTIVE
IMOGENE
SMOKERS
SMOKIER
SMOKIES
SMOKILY
SMOKING
SMOLDER
SMOOTHS
SMOOTHY
SMOTHER

•M•O•••

AMMONIA
AMPOULE
EMPORIA
EMPOWER
IMMORAL
IMPORTS
IMPOSED
IMPOSES
IMPOSTS
IMPOUND
IMSORRY
SMOOTHS
SMOOTHY

•M••O••

AMAPOLA
AMATORY
AMAZONS
AMBROSE
AMNIONS
AMOROUS
AMPHORA
EMBROIL
EMPLOYE
EMPLOYS
IMAGOES
IMPIOUS
IMPLODE
IMPLORE
IMPROVE
KMESONS
OMIGOSH
OMINOUS

•M•••O•

EMBRYOS
EMERSON
EMMYLOU
EMOTION
EMPEROR
OMICRON
SMALTOS

•M••••O

AMERIGO
AMRADIO
EMBARGO
FMRADIO
IMPASTO
UMBERTO

••MO•••

ALMONDS
AMMONIA
ARMOIRE
ARMORED
ARMORER
ARMOURS
ARMOURY
BEMOANS
BIMODAL
COMOROS
DEMONIC
DEMOTED
DEMOTES
DIMOUTS
FEMORAL
GEMOTES
HOMONYM
HUMORED
HUMOURS
IMMORAL
IOMOTHS
KIMONOS
LAMOTTA
LEMONDE
LIMOGES
MEMOIRE
MEMOIRS
MEMOREX
MIMOSAS
ORMOLUS
OSMOSED
OSMOSES
OSMOSIS
OSMOTIC
REMODEL
REMOLDS
REMORAS
REMORSE
REMOTER
REMOTES
REMOUNT
REMOVAL
REMOVED
REMOVER
REMOVES
REMOWED
RUMORED
RUMOURS
SAMOANS
SAMOVAR
SAMOYED
TIMOTHY
UNMOVED
VAMOOSE

••M•O••

ARMHOLE
ARMLOAD
ARMLOCK
BAMBOOS
BUMSOUT
CAMEOED
CAMEOFF
CAMEOUT
CAMPOUT
COMEOFF
COMEONS
COMEOUT
COMFORT
COMMODE
COMMONS
COMMOVE
COMPORT
COMPOSE
COMPOST
COMPOTE
DAMSONS
GAMBOLS
GAMMONS
HAMHOCK
HAMMOCK
HAMMOND
HEMLOCK
HUMMOCK
HYMNODY
JUMPOFF
LAMPOIL
LAMPOON
LIMPOPO
MAMBOED
MAMMOTH
MUMFORD
NIMRODS
POMPOMS
POMPONS
POMPOUS
RAMRODS
RUMPOLE
SIMMONS
SOMEONE
SUMMONS
SYMBOLS
TAMBOUR
TIMEOFF
TIMEOUT
TOMBOLA
TOMBOYS
TOMFOOL
TOMTOMS
VAMOOSE
WIMPOLE
YOMTOVS
ZAMBONI

••M••O•

AIMSFOR
BAMBOOS
CAMELOT
CAMERON
CAMPHOR
CAMPION
COMESON
COMOROS
DEMEROL
DEMIGOD
DOMINOS
EMMYLOU
GEMSBOK
GUMDROP
GUMSHOE
GYMSHOE
HAMPTON
HOMEBOY
HUMIDOR
JAMESON
JUMPSON
KIMONOS
LAMPOON
MCMAHON
MRMAGOO
MUMESON
NEMEROV
PIMESON
POMELOS
RIMSHOT
ROMANOV
SAMPSON
SEMILOG
SIMENON
SIMPSON
SOMEHOW
SYMPTOM
TEMBLOR
TIMECOP
TOMFOOL

••M•••O

ADMITTO
AIMEDTO
BAMBINO
CEMBALO
COMESTO
DOMINGO
GAMBADO
HHMUNRO
LIMPOPO
LUMBAGO
MEMENTO
MRMAGOO
PIMENTO
PIMLICO
POMPANO
RAMINTO
SEMIPRO
TAMPICO
ZEMSTVO

•••MO••

ALAMODE
ALIMONY
ANEMONE
ANYMORE
ARDMORE
BELMONT
BONMOTS
CHAMOIS
CLAMORS
CLAMOUR
COMMODE
COMMONS
COMMOVE
CONMOTO
CREMONA
DAIMONS
DESMOND
DIAMOND
DINMONT
ENAMORS
ENAMOUR
ENDMOST
FARMOUT
FORMOSA
FREMONT
GAMMONS
GLAMOUR
GNOMONS
GUNMOLL
HAMMOCK
HAMMOND
HARMONY
HAYMOWS
HOLMOAK
HORMONE
HUMMOCK
MAMMOTH
MARMOTS
MIDMOST
MORMONS
NEWMOON
NEWMOWN
OAKMOSS
OLDMOON
OXYMORA
PALMOFF
PALMOIL
PROMOTE
RAGMOPS
RAYMOND
SALMONS
SCHMOES
SCHMOOS
SEAMOSS
SERMONS
SEYMOUR
SIMMONS
SPUMONE
SPUMONI
SPUMOUS
SUMMONS
TOPMOST
TREMOLO
TREMORS
TURMOIL
VERMONT
WETMOPS

•••M•O•

ADAMSON
BOOMBOX
CLEMSON
CRAMPON
CRIMSON
FLUMMOX
MARMION
NEWMOON
OLDMOON
PALMTOP
SCHMOOS
SHAMPOO
THOMSON

•••M••O

ANIMATO
BERMEJO
CONMOTO
GROMYKO
HAEMATO
SFUMATO
SHAMPOO
TREMOLO
UNAMUNO

••••MO•

DREAMON
DUSTMOP
DYNAMOS
ESKIMOS
FLUMMOX
RUNAMOK
SOLOMON
THERMOS

••••M•O

COLUMBO
MOGAMBO
UPTEMPO

•••••MO

CENTIMO
EXANIMO
GIACOMO
NANAIMO
PALERMO
PROXIMO
SANREMO
SATCHMO
SUPREMO
VERISMO

M•P••••

MAPPERS
MAPPING
MOPIEST
MOPPERS
MOPPETS
MOPPING
MOPTOPS
MUPPETS

M••P•••

MAGPIES
MAPPERS
MAPPING
MAYPOLE
MEMPHIS
MISPLAY
MOPPERS
MOPPETS
MOPPING
MORPHED
MRSPOCK
MUDPACK
MUDPIES
MUMPING
MUPPETS

M•••P••

MADEPAR
MAKEPAR
MANIPLE
MOSHPIT

M••••P•

MADCAPS
MAKEUPS
MARKUPS
MISHAPS
MISTYPE
MOBCAPS
MOCKUPS
MOPTOPS
MRCHIPS

M•••••P

MAINTOP
MAKESUP
MANTRAP
MARKSUP
MATCHUP
MEDIGAP
MILKSOP
MISSTEP
MIXEDUP
MIXESUP
MIXITUP
MOVEDUP
MOVESUP
MUCKSUP
MUGWUMP

•MP••••

AMPERES
AMPHORA
AMPLEST
AMPLIFY
AMPOULE
AMPULES
EMPANEL
EMPATHY
EMPEROR
EMPIRES
EMPLOYE
EMPLOYS
EMPORIA
EMPOWER
EMPRESS
EMPTIED
EMPTIER
EMPTIES
EMPTILY
IMPACTS
IMPAIRS
IMPALAS
IMPALED
IMPALES
IMPANEL
IMPARTS
IMPASSE
IMPASTO
IMPEACH
IMPEDED
IMPEDES
IMPENDS
IMPERIL
IMPETUS
IMPIETY
IMPINGE
IMPIOUS
IMPLANT
IMPLIED
IMPLIES
IMPLODE
IMPLORE
IMPORTS
IMPOSED
IMPOSES
IMPOSTS
IMPOUND
IMPRESS
IMPRINT
IMPROVE
IMPUGNS
IMPULSE
IMPURER
IMPUTED
IMPUTES
OMPHALI
UMPIRED
UMPIRES
UMPTEEN

•M•P•••

AMAPOLA

•M••••P

SMASHUP

••MP•••

ARMPITS
BUMPERS
BUMPIER
BUMPILY
BUMPING
BUMPKIN
BUMPSUP
CAMPARI
CAMPERS
CAMPHOR
CAMPIER
CAMPILY
CAMPING
CAMPION
CAMPOUT
COMPACT
COMPANY
COMPARE
COMPASS
COMPEER
COMPELS
COMPERE
COMPETE
COMPILE
COMPLEX
COMPORT
COMPOSE
COMPOST
COMPOTE
COMPUTE
DAMPENS
DAMPERS
DAMPEST
DAMPING
DAMPISH
DEMPSEY
DIMPLED
DIMPLES
DUMPIER
DUMPING
DUMPISH
GOMPERS
HAMPERS
HAMPTON
HUMPIER
JAMPACK
JUMPCUT
JUMPERS
JUMPIER
JUMPILY
JUMPING
JUMPOFF
JUMPSAT
JUMPSIN
JUMPSON
JUMPSUP
KAMPALA
LAMPOIL
LAMPOON
LAMPREY
LEMPIRA
LIMPEST
LIMPETS
LIMPING
LIMPOPO
LUMPERS
LUMPIER
LUMPILY
LUMPING
LUMPISH
LUMPSUM
MEMPHIS
MUMPING
OOMPAHS
PAMPERS
POMPANO
POMPEIA
POMPEII
POMPOMS
POMPONS
POMPOUS
PUMPERS
PUMPING
PUMPKIN
PUMPSUP
RAMPAGE
RAMPANT
RAMPART
RIMPLED
RIMPLES
ROMPERS
ROMPING
ROMPISH
RUMPLED
RUMPLES
RUMPOLE
SAMPANS
SAMPLED
SAMPLER
SAMPLES
SAMPRAS
SAMPSON
SIMPERS
SIMPLER
SIMPLEX
SIMPSON
SYMPTOM
TAMPERS
TAMPICO
TAMPING
TEMPEHS
TEMPERA
TEMPERS
TEMPEST
TEMPLAR
TEMPLES
TEMPTED
TEMPTER
TEMPURA
TYMPANA
TYMPANI
VAMPERS
VAMPING
VAMPIRA
VAMPIRE
VAMPISH
WIMPIER
WIMPISH
WIMPLED
WIMPLES
WIMPOLE

••M•P••

SEMIPRO

••M••P•

BUMRAPS
LIMPOPO

••M•••P

BUMPSUP
COMESUP
DUMMYUP
GUMDROP
HAMITUP
JUMPSUP
PUMPSUP
TIMECOP
TIMESUP

•••MP••

CHAMPED
CHOMPED
CLAMPED
CLOMPED
CLUMPED
CRAMPED
CRAMPON
CRIMPED
CRIMPER
CRUMPET
CRUMPLE
CRUMPLY
EXAMPLE
EXEMPLI
EXEMPTS
GLIMPSE
GRAMPAS
GRAMPUS
GRUMPED
GUIMPES
OLYMPIA
OLYMPIC
OLYMPUS
PLUMPED
PLUMPER
PLUMPLY
PRIMPED
PROMPTS
SCAMPED
SCAMPER
SHAMPOO
SKIMPED
SLUMPED
STAMPED
STOMPED
STUMPED
STUMPER
SWAMPED
THIMPHU
THUMPED
THUMPER
TRAMPAS
TRAMPED
TRAMPLE
TRUMPED
TRUMPET
TRUMPUP
WHIMPER
WHOMPED

•••M•P•

BITMAPS
RAGMOPS
WARMUPS
WETMOPS

•••M••P

BEAMSUP
CLAMSUP
DRUMSUP
DUMMYUP
FIRMSUP
FRAMEUP
PALMTOP
TEAMSUP
TRUMPUP
WARMSUP

••••MP•

ATTEMPT
CCLAMPS
DECAMPS
ENCAMPS
GALUMPH
GAZUMPS
PREAMPS
PREEMPT
REVAMPS
SCRIMPS
SCRIMPY
SHRIMPS
TRIUMPH
UNKEMPT
UPTEMPO

••••M•P

DREAMUP
DUSTMOP
ROADMAP
STARMAP

•••••MP

AIRPUMP
ARCLAMP
BEDLAMP
DAYCAMP
GASPUMP
MUGWUMP
NOTRUMP
OFFRAMP
OILLAMP
OUTJUMP
RESTAMP
SKIJUMP
SUNLAMP

M•Q••••

MCQUEEN

M••Q•••

MARQUEE
MARQUES
MARQUEZ
MARQUIS
MASQUES
MOSQUES

M•••Q••

MACAQUE
MONIQUE

••MQ•••

KUMQUAT

••M•Q••

COMIQUE

MR•••••

MRBONES
MRCHIPS
MRCLEAN
MRDEEDS
MRFIXIT
MRMAGOO
MRRIGHT
MRSPOCK

M•R••••

MARABOU
MARACAS
MARAUDS
MARBLED
MARBLES
MARCATO
MARCEAU
MARCELS
MARCHED
MARCHER
MARCHES
MARCHON
MARCONI
MARENGO
MARGATE
MARGAUX
MARGAYS
MARGINS
MARGRET
MARIANA
MARILYN
MARIMBA
MARINAS
MARINER
MARINES
MARITAL
MARKERS
MARKETS
MARKHAM
MARKHOR
MARKING
MARKKAA
MARKOFF
MARKOVA
MARKSUP
MARKUPS
MARLENE
MARLINS
MARLOWE
MARMARA
MARMION
MARMOTS
MAROONS
MARQUEE
MARQUES
MARQUEZ
MARQUIS
MARRIED
MARRIES
MARRING
MARROWS
MARRYME
MARSALA
MARSHAL
MARSHES
MARTENS
MARTIAL
MARTIAN
MARTINA
MARTINI
MARTINO
MARTINS
MARTYRS
MARVELS
MARXISM
MARXIST
MARYANN
MARYKAY
MARYLOU
MERCERS
MERCERY
MERCIES
MERCURY
MERGERS
MERGING
MERIMEE
MERINOS
MERITED
MERLOTS
MERMAID
MERRIER
MERRILL
MERRILY
MIRACLE
MIRADOR
MIRAGES
MIRAMAR
MIRAMAX
MIRANDA
MIRIEST
MIRKIER
MIRRORS
MORAINE
MORALES
MORALLY
MORANIS
MORAVIA
MORDANT
MORDENT
MORDRED
MORELLO

MORESBY
MORGANA
MORGANS
MORMONS
MORNING
MOROCCO
MORPHED
MORROWS
MORSELS
MORTALS
MORTARS
MORTIFY
MORTISE
MRRIGHT
MURDERS
MURDOCH
MURILLO
MURKIER
MURKILY
MURMURS
MYRIADS
MYRTLES

M••R•••

MACRAME
MACRONS
MALRAUX
MARRIED
MARRIES
MARRING
MARROWS
MARRYME
MATRONS
MAUREEN
MAURICE
MAUROIS
MEGRIMS
MEGRYAN
MELROSE
MERRIER
MERRILL
MERRILY
METRICS
MICROBE
MICRONS
MIDRIBS
MIDRIFF
MIDRISE
MIGRANT
MIGRATE
MIRRORS
MISREAD
MISRULE
MITRING
MOORAGE
MOORHEN
MOORIER
MOORING
MOORISH
MORROWS
MOURNED

M•••R••

MACGRAW
MAHARIS
MAIGRET
MAITRED
MAJORCA
MAJORED
MALLRAT
MANFRED
MANTRAP
MANTRAS
MANTRIC
MARGRET
MASARYK
MATURED
MATURER
MATURES
MAYORAL
MAYTREE
MAZURKA
MCENROE
MEMOREX
MENORAH
METERED
MILDRED
MILKRUN
MILLRUN
MILORDS
MINARET
MINERAL
MINERVA
MINORCA
MINORED
MISERLY
MISTRAL
MITERED
MITHRAS
MODERNS
MONARCH
MONGREL
MORDRED
MOTORED
MUBARAK
MUSKRAT

M••••R•

MACABRE
MADDERS
MADEIRA
MAESTRI
MAESTRO
MAGUIRE
MAGYARS
MAILERS
MAJEURE
MALLARD
MANGERS
MANNERS
MANSARD
MAPPERS
MARKERS
MARMARA
MARTYRS
MASCARA
MASHERS
MASKERS
MASONRY
MASTERS
MASTERY
MATHERS
MATTERS
MAXBORN
MAYNARD
MCCLURE
MCGUIRE
MCHENRY
MEASURE
MEMBERS
MEMOIRE
MEMOIRS
MENDERS
MENHIRS
MENTORS
MERCERS
MERCERY
MERCURY
MERGERS
METEORS
METIERS
MEWLERS
MIDTERM
MILKERS
MILLARD
MILLERS
MIMICRY
MINCERS
MINDERS
MINTERS
MIRRORS
MISFIRE
MISTERS
MISWORD
MITFORD
MIXTURE
MOANERS
MOCKERS
MOCKERY
MOHAIRS
MOILERS
MOLDERS
MOLIERE
MOLTERS
MONGERS
MONTERO
MOPPERS
MORTARS
MOSHERS
MOTHERS
MOUSERS
MUDDERS
MUGGERS
MULLERS
MUMFORD
MUMMERS
MUMMERY
MURDERS
MURMURS
MUSHERS
MUSTARD
MUSTERS
MUTTERS
MYSTERY

M•••••R

MADEFOR
MADEPAR
MAILCAR
MAKEFOR
MAKEPAR
MALABAR
MALODOR
MALTIER
MANAGER
MANGIER
MANHOUR
MANLIER
MANOWAR
MANYEAR
MARCHER
MARINER
MARKHOR
MASSEUR
MASSIER
MATADOR
MATURER
MAUNDER
MAXBAER
MAYFAIR
MEALIER
MEANDER
MEATIER
MEDDLER
MEISTER
MERRIER
MESHIER
MESSIER
METOOER
MIDYEAR
MIFFIER
MILKIER
MINGIER
MINGLER
MINIVER
MINTIER
MIRADOR
MIRAMAR
MIRKIER
MISHEAR
MISTIER
MOBSTER
MODELER
MODULAR
MOISTER
MOLDIER
MONIKER
MONITOR
MONOMER
MONSTER
MOOCHER
MOODIER
MOONIER
MOORIER
MOSSIER
MOTHIER
MOULDER
MOUSIER
MUAMMAR
MUCKIER
MUDDIER
MUDDLER
MUFFLER
MUGGIER
MUMBLER
MUNCHER
MURKIER
MUSHIER
MUSKIER
MUSSIER
MUSTIER
MUZZIER
MYANMAR
MYNHEER

•MR••••

AMRADIO
FMRADIO

•M•R•••

AMBRIES
AMBROSE
AMERCED
AMERCES
AMERICA
AMERIGO
AMERIKA
AMERIND
AMOROUS
EMBRACE
EMBROIL
EMBRYOS
EMERALD
EMERGED
EMERGES
EMERITA
EMERITI
EMERSED
EMERSON
EMIRATE
EMPRESS
IMARETS
IMBRUED
IMBRUES
IMPRESS
IMPRINT
IMPROVE
SMARTED
SMARTEN
SMARTER
SMARTLY
SMIRKED
UMBRAGE
UMBRIAN

•M••R••

AMHARIC
AMHERST
AMPERES
AMSCRAY
DMYTRYK
EMBARGO
EMBARKS
EMIGRES
EMPEROR
EMPIRES
EMPORIA
IMMERSE
IMMORAL
IMMURED
IMMURES
IMPARTS
IMPERIL
IMPORTS
IMPURER
IMSORRY
OMICRON
SMEARED
UMBERTO
UMPIRED
UMPIRES

•M•••R•

AMATORY
AMBLERS
AMPHORA
EMOTERS
IMAGERS
IMAGERY
IMPAIRS
IMPLORE
IMSORRY
SMILERS
SMOKERS

•M••••R

AMASSER
AMATEUR
AMMETER
EMENDER
EMITTER
EMPEROR
EMPOWER
EMPTIER
IMPURER
OMITTER
SMACKER
SMALLER
SMARTER
SMASHER
SMATTER
SMELTER
SMOKIER
SMOLDER
SMOTHER
SMUGGER

••MR•••

ARMREST
BUMRAPS
BUMRUSH
COMRADE
NIMRODS
RAMRODS

••M•R••

ADMIRAL
ADMIRED
ADMIRER
ADMIRES
ARMORED
ARMORER
ARMURES
BEMIRED
BEMIRES
CAMBRIC
CAMERAS
CAMERON
COMFREY
COMOROS
DEMERIT
DEMEROL
DEMURER
ELMTREE
FEMORAL
GAMBREL
GUMDROP
GUMTREE
HOMBRES
HOMERED
HOMERIC
HOMERUN
HUMDRUM
HUMERAL
HUMERUS
HUMORED
IMMERSE
IMMORAL
IMMURED
IMMURES
LAMARCK
LAMPREY
MEMOREX
NEMEROV
NUMERAL
NUMERIC
REMARKS
REMARRY
REMORAS
REMORSE
RUMORED
SAMARIA
SAMPRAS
SAMURAI
TAMARIN
TIMBRES
TUMBREL
ZYMURGY

••M••R•

ARMOIRE
ARMOURS
ARMOURY
BOMBARD
BOMBERS
BUMMERS
BUMPERS
CAMBERS
CAMPARI
CAMPERS
COMBERS
COMFORT
COMPARE
COMPERE
COMPORT
DAMMARS
DAMPERS
DIMITRI
DIMMERS
GAMMERS
GOMPERS
HAMBURG
HAMMERS
HAMPERS
HEMMERS
HHMUNRO
HOMBURG
HUMMERS
HUMOURS
JAMMERS
JUMPERS
LAMBERT
LEMPIRA
LIMBERS
LIMNERS
LOMBARD
LUMBARS
LUMBERS
LUMIERE
LUMPERS
MEMBERS
MEMOIRE
MEMOIRS
MIMICRY
MUMFORD
MUMMERS
MUMMERY
NUMBERS
PAMPERS
PUMPERS
RAMPART
REMARRY
ROMPERS
RUMOURS
SAMBARS
SAMSARA
SEMIPRO
SIMMERS
SIMPERS
SUMATRA
SUMMARY
SUMMERS
SUMMERY
TAMPERS
TEMPERA
TEMPERS
TEMPURA
TIMBERS
VAMPERS
VAMPIRA
VAMPIRE
YAMMERS

••M•••R

ADMIRER
AIMSFOR
AMMETER
ARMORER
BUMBLER
BUMPIER
CAMPHOR
CAMPIER
COMFIER
COMPEER
DEMETER
DEMURER
DUMPIER
FUMBLER
GAMBLER
GAMMIER
GEMMIER
GUMMIER
HAMMIER
HAMSTER
HUMBLER
HUMIDOR
HUMPIER
JAMMIER
JUMPIER
LAMINAR
LUMPIER
MUMBLER
NIMBLER
RAMBLER
REMOTER
REMOVER
RUMMIER
SAMOVAR
SAMPLER
SEMINAR
SIMILAR
SIMPLER
TAMBOUR
TEMBLOR
TEMPLAR
TEMPTER
TIMIDER
TUMBLER
WIMPIER
YUMMIER

•••M•R•

ANYMORE
ARDMORE
BOOMERS
BUMMERS
CHIMERA
CLAMORS
DAMMARS
DAYMARE
DENMARK
DIMMERS
DORMERS
EARMARK
ENAMORS
FARMERS
FARMERY
GAMMERS
HAMMERS
HEMMERS
HUMMERS
ISOMERS
JAMMERS
MARMARA
MUMMERS
MUMMERY
MURMURS
OXYMORA
PALMARY
PISMIRE
PRIMARY
PRIMERS
REAMERS
RHYMERS
ROAMERS
ROOMERS
SIMMERS
STUMERS
SUMMARY
SUMMERS
SUMMERY
TREMORS
WALMART
WIDMARK
WOOMERA
YAMMERS

•••M••R

BALMIER
BARMIER
BEAMIER
BESMEAR
BOOMIER
CHAMBER
CHAMFER
CLAMBER
CLAMMER
CLAMOUR
CLIMBER
CRAMMER
CRIMPER
DAIMLER
DAUMIER
DRUMMER
ENAMOUR
FILMIER
FLAMIER
FNUMBER
FOAMIER
GAMMIER
GEMMIER
GERMIER
GLAMOUR
GLIMMER
GLUMMER
GRAMMAR
GRAMMER
GRIMIER
GRIMMER
GUMMIER
HAMMIER
JAMMIER
LOAMIER
MUAMMAR
PALMIER
PLUMBER
PLUMIER
PLUMMER
PLUMPER
PREMIER
PRIMMER
ROOMIER
RUMMIER
SCAMPER
SCHMEER
SEAMIER
SEYMOUR
SHIMMER
SKIMMER
SLAMMER
SLIMIER
SLIMMER
SLUMBER
SPAMMER
SPUMIER
STAMMER
STUMPER
SWIMMER
THUMPER
TRAMCAR
TRIMMER
VERMEER
WHIMPER
WORMIER
YUMMIER

••••M•R

ALARMER
BLOOMER
CHARMER
CLAIMER
CLAMMER
CRAMMER
CREAMER
DREAMER
DRUMMER
GLIMMER
GLUMMER
GRAMMAR
GRAMMER
GRIMMER
GROOMER
INGEMAR
KASHMIR
MIRAMAR
MONOMER
MUAMMAR
MYANMAR
PALOMAR
PLUMMER
POLYMER
PRIMMER
SCHEMER
SHIMMER
SKIMMER
SLAMMER
SLIMMER
SPAMMER
STAMMER
STEAMER
SWIMMER
TRIMMER

M•S••••

MASARYK
MASCARA
MASCOTS
MASHERS
MASHIES
MASHING
MASKERS
MASKING
MASONIC
MASONRY
MASQUES
MASSAGE
MASSEUR
MASSIER
MASSIFS
MASSING
MASSIVE
MASTABA
MASTERS
MASTERY
MASTICS
MASTIFF
MASTOID
MCSWINE
MESCALS
MESHIER
MESHING
MESSAGE
MESSALA
MESSIAH
MESSIER
MESSILY
MESSINA
MESSING
MESSKIT
MESTIZA
MESTIZO
MISALLY
MISCALL
MISCAST
MISCUED
MISCUES
MISDATE
MISDEAL
MISDEED
MISDIAL
MISDOES
MISDONE
MISERLY
MISFILE
MISFIRE
MISFITS
MISHAPS
MISHEAR
MISHITS
MISLAID
MISLAYS
MISLEAD
MISLIKE
MISMATE
MISNAME
MISPLAY
MISREAD
MISRULE
MISSAID
MISSALS
MISSAYS
MISSIES
MISSILE
MISSING
MISSION
MISSISH
MISSIVE
MISSOUT
MISSTEP
MISTAKE
MISTERS
MISTIER
MISTILY
MISTING
MISTOOK
MISTRAL
MISTYPE
MISUSED
MISUSES
MISWORD
MOSAICS
MOSELLE
MOSEYED
MOSHERS
MOSHING
MOSHPIT
MOSLEMS
MOSQUES
MOSSIER
MOSSING
MRSPOCK
MUSCATS
MUSCLED
MUSCLES
MUSCOVY
MUSEFUL
MUSETTE
MUSEUMS
MUSHERS
MUSHIER
MUSHILY
MUSHING
MUSICAL
MUSKEGS
MUSKETS
MUSKIER
MUSKIES
MUSKRAT
MUSLIMS
MUSLINS
MUSSELS
MUSSIER
MUSSILY
MUSSING
MUSTAFA
MUSTANG
MUSTARD
MUSTERS
MUSTIER
MUSTILY
MUSTSEE
MYSTERY
MYSTICS
MYSTIFY

M••S•••

MAESTRI
MAESTRO
MANSARD
MANSION
MARSALA
MARSHAL
MARSHES
MASSAGE
MASSEUR
MASSIER
MASSIFS
MASSING
MASSIVE
MEASLES
MEASURE
MEISSEN
MEISTER
MESSAGE
MESSALA
MESSIAH
MESSIER
MESSILY
MESSINA
MESSING
MESSKIT
MIASMAS
MIASMIC
MIDSIZE
MISSAID
MISSALS
MISSAYS
MISSIES
MISSILE
MISSING
MISSION
MISSISH
MISSIVE
MISSOUT
MISSTEP
MOBSTER
MOISTEN
MOISTER
MOISTLY
MONSOON
MONSTER
MORSELS
MOSSIER
MOSSING
MOUSERS
MOUSIER
MOUSING
MOUSSED
MOUSSES
MUGSHOT
MUSSELS
MUSSIER
MUSSILY
MUSSING

M•••S••

MADISON
MAILSIN
MAJESTE
MAJESTY
MAKESDO
MAKESIT
MAKESUP
MALMSEY
MAOISTS
MARKSUP
MATISSE
MEDUSAE
MEDUSAS
MEIOSES
MEIOSIS
MEISSEN
MELISSA
MENISCI
MILKSOP
MIMESIS
MIMOSAS
MINDSET
MINUSES
MISUSED
MISUSES
MITOSES
MITOSIS
MIXESIN
MIXESUP
MODESTO
MODESTY
MODISTE
MOLESTS
MOONSET
MORESBY
MOUSSED
MOUSSES
MOVESIN
MOVESON
MOVESUP
MUCKSUP
MUMESON
MUSTSEE

M••••S•

MADDEST
MADDISH
MADNESS
MAEWEST
MAIDISH
MALAISE
MALTESE
MALTOSE
MANLESS
MANNISH
MARXISM
MARXIST
MATISSE
MATLESS
MAWKISH
MAZIEST
MEANEST
MEEKEST
MELISSA
MELROSE
MIDEAST
MIDMOST
MIDRISE
MIDWEST
MILDEST
MINXISH
MIRIEST
MISCAST
MISSISH
MOBBISH
MOLLUSC
MOLLUSK
MOMBASA
MONKISH
MOONISH
MOORISH
MOPIEST
MORTISE

M•••••S

MACRONS
MADCAPS
MADDENS
MADDERS
MADLIBS
MADNESS
MAENADS
MAGNETS
MAGNUMS
MAGPIES
MAGUEYS
MAGYARS
MAHARIS
MAHOUTS
MAIDENS
MAILERS
MAITAIS
MAKEUPS
MAKINGS
MALIGNS
MALKINS
MALLETS
MALLOWS
MALTEDS
MALTHUS
MAMMALS
MANAGES
MANANAS
MANDANS
MANDAYS
MANEGES
MANGERS
MANGLES
MANGOES
MANIACS
MANIOCS
MANLESS
MANNERS
MANTELS
MANTLES
MANTRAS
MANUALS
MAOISTS
MAPPERS
MARACAS

MARAUDS
MARBLES
MARCELS
MARCHES
MARGAYS
MARGINS
MARINAS
MARINES
MARKERS
MARKETS
MARKUPS
MARLINS
MARMOTS
MAROONS
MARQUES
MARQUIS
MARRIES
MARROWS
MARSHES
MARTENS
MARTINS
MARTYRS
MARVELS
MASCOTS
MASHERS
MASHIES
MASKERS
MASQUES
MASSIFS
MASTERS
MASTICS
MATCHES
MATHERS
MATHEWS
MATHIAS
MATLESS
MATRONS
MATTERS
MATURES
MATZOHS
MAUMAUS
MAUROIS
MAXIMUS
MAYDAYS
MAYHEMS
MCCALLS
MEADOWS
MEALIES
MEANIES
MEASLES
MEDDLES
MEDIANS
MEDICOS
MEDIUMS
MEDLEYS
MEDUSAS
MEGOHMS
MEGRIMS
MEINIES
MEIOSES
MEIOSIS
MELLOWS
MEMBERS
MEMOIRS
MEMPHIS
MENACES
MENAGES
MENDERS
MENHIRS
MENIALS
MENTORS
MENZIES
MERCERS
MERCIES
MERGERS
MERINOS
MERLOTS
MESCALS
METATES
METEORS
METHODS
METIERS
METRICS
METTLES
MEWLERS
MIAMIAS
MIASMAS
MICKEYS
MICMACS
MICRONS
MIDDAYS
MIDDENS
MIDDIES
MIDDLES
MIDGETS
MIDRIBS
MIDWAYS
MIGGLES
MIKADOS
MILDEWS
MILIEUS
MILKERS
MILLERS
MILLETS
MILORDS
MIMESIS
MIMOSAS
MINCERS
MINDERS
MINGLES
MINIBUS
MINIONS
MINNOWS
MINOANS
MINTERS
MINUETS
MINUSES
MINUTES
MINYANS
MIRAGES
MIRRORS
MISCUES
MISDOES
MISFITS
MISHAPS
MISHITS
MISLAYS
MISSALS
MISSAYS
MISSIES
MISTERS
MISUSES
MITHRAS
MITOSES
MITOSIS
MITTENS
MIZZENS
MIZZLES
MOANERS
MOBCAPS
MOBILES
MOCKERS
MOCKUPS
MODELAS
MODELTS
MODERNS
MODULES
MOGGIES
MOHAIRS
MOHAWKS
MOILERS
MOLDERS
MOLESTS
MOLOCHS
MOLTERS
MOMENTS
MOMMIES
MONDAYS
MONGERS
MONGOLS
MONKEES
MONKEYS
MOOCHES
MOPPERS
MOPPETS
MOPTOPS
MORALES
MORANIS
MORGANS
MORMONS
MORROWS
MORSELS
MORTALS
MORTARS
MOSAICS
MOSHERS
MOSLEMS
MOSQUES
MOTHERS
MOTIONS
MOTIVES
MOTTLES
MOTTOES
MOUSERS
MOUSSES
MOUTONS
MRBONES
MRCHIPS
MRDEEDS
MUDCATS
MUDDERS
MUDDIES
MUDDLES
MUDEELS
MUDHENS
MUDPIES
MUFFINS
MUFFLES
MUGGERS
MUKLUKS
MULCHES
MULETAS
MULLAHS
MULLERS
MULLETS
MUMBLES
MUMMERS
MUMMIES
MUNCHES
MUNTINS
MUPPETS
MURDERS
MURMURS
MUSCATS
MUSCLES
MUSEUMS
MUSHERS
MUSKEGS
MUSKETS
MUSKIES
MUSLIMS
MUSLINS
MUSSELS
MUSTERS
MUTANTS
MUTATES
MUTTERS
MUTTONS
MUTUALS
MUUMUUS
MUZHIKS
MUZZLES
MYRIADS
MYRTLES
MYSTICS

•MS••••

AMSCRAY
IMSORRY

•M•S•••

AMASSED
AMASSER
AMASSES
AMISTAD
AMUSING
KMESONS
SMASHED
SMASHER
SMASHES
SMASHUP

•M••S••

AMASSED
AMASSER
AMASSES
AMNESIA
AMNESTY
EMBASSY
EMERSED
EMERSON
IMPASSE
IMPASTO
IMPOSED
IMPOSES
IMPOSTS

•M•••S•

AMBROSE
AMHERST
AMONGST
AMPLEST
AMYLASE
EMBASSY
EMPRESS
IMMENSE
IMMERSE
IMPASSE
IMPRESS
IMPULSE
OMIGOSH

•M••••S

AMADEUS
AMASSES
AMAZONS
AMBLERS
AMBRIES
AMERCES
AMNIONS
AMOEBAS
AMOROUS
AMOUNTS
AMPERES
AMPULES
AMULETS
BMOVIES
EMBANKS
EMBARKS
EMBLEMS
EMBRYOS
EMERGES
EMIGRES
EMOTERS
EMPIRES
EMPLOYS
EMPRESS
EMPTIES
IMAGERS
IMAGOES
IMARETS
IMBIBES
IMBRUES
IMMIXES
IMMURES
IMPACTS
IMPAIRS
IMPALAS
IMPALES
IMPARTS
IMPEDES
IMPENDS
IMPETUS
IMPIOUS
IMPLIES
IMPORTS
IMPOSES
IMPOSTS
IMPRESS
IMPUGNS
IMPUTES
KMESONS
OMELETS
OMINOUS
OMNIBUS
SMALTOS
SMASHES
SMILERS
SMOKERS
SMOKIES
SMOOTHS
SMUDGES
UMLAUTS
UMPIRES

••MS•••

AIMSFOR
BUMSOUT
DAMSELS
DAMSONS
GEMSBOK
GUMSHOE
GYMSHOE
HAMSTER
HEMSLEY
HIMSELF
RIMSHOT
SAMSARA
SAMSUNG
ZEMSTVO

••M•S••

BEMUSED
BEMUSES
BUMPSUP
CAMISES
COMESAT
COMESBY
COMESIN
COMESON
COMESTO
COMESUP
DAMASKS
DEMESNE
DEMISED
DEMISES
DEMPSEY
ELMISTI
ENMASSE
JAMESON
JUMPSAT
JUMPSIN
JUMPSON
JUMPSUP
LUMPSUM
MIMESIS
MIMOSAS
MUMESON
NEMESES
NEMESIS
OSMOSED
OSMOSES
OSMOSIS
PIMESON
PUMPSUP
RAMESES
SAMISEN
SAMPSON
SIMPSON
TIMESUP
UNMASKS

••M••S•

AIMLESS
ARMLESS
ARMREST
BOMBAST
BUMRUSH
COMBUST
COMPASS
COMPOSE
COMPOST
DAMPEST
DAMPISH
DIMMEST
DIMNESS
DUMBEST
DUMPISH
ENMASSE
FUMIEST
GAMIEST
GEMLESS
GUMLESS
GYMNAST
HOMIEST
IMMENSE
IMMERSE
KOMATSU
LAMAISM
LAMAIST
LIMIEST
LIMPEST
LUMPISH
MOMBASA
NUMBEST
RAMMISH
REMORSE
RIMIEST
RIMLESS
ROMANSH
ROMPISH
RUMLESS
SUMLESS
TEMPEST
VAMOOSE
VAMPISH
WIMPISH

••M•••S

ADMIRES
ADMIXES
AIMLESS
ALMONDS
ARMADAS
ARMFULS
ARMLESS
ARMLETS
ARMOURS
ARMPITS
ARMURES
BAMBOOS
BEMIRES
BEMOANS
BEMUSES
BOMBERS
BUMBLES
BUMMERS
BUMPERS
BUMRAPS
CAMBERS
CAMERAS
CAMISES
CAMPERS
CEMENTS
COMBATS
COMBERS
COMEONS
COMFITS
COMINGS
COMMITS
COMMONS
COMOROS
COMPASS
COMPELS
CUMULUS
CYMBALS
DAMAGES
DAMASKS
DAMMARS
DAMPENS
DAMPERS
DAMSELS
DAMSONS
DEMANDS
DEMEANS
DEMISES
DEMOTES
DIMMERS
DIMNESS
DIMOUTS
DIMPLES
DIMWITS
DOMAINS
DOMINOS
DOMINUS
DUMDUMS
DUMMIES
ERMINES
FAMINES
FAMULUS
FEMALES
FOMENTS
FUMBLES
GAMBITS
GAMBLES
GAMBOLS
GAMETES
GAMINES
GAMMERS
GAMMONS
GEMLESS
GEMOTES
GIMBALS
GIMLETS
GOMPERS
GUMLESS
GYMBAGS
HAMITES
HAMLETS
HAMMERS
HAMPERS
HEMMERS
HOMBRES
HUMBLES
HUMBUGS
HUMERUS
HUMMERS
HUMOURS
HUMVEES
HYMNALS
IMMIXES
IMMURES
INMATES
IOMOTHS
JAMMERS
JEMMIES
JIMJAMS
JIMMIES
JUMBLES
JUMPERS
KIMONOS
LAMBDAS
LAMEDHS
LAMENTS
LAMINAS
LIMBERS
LIMNERS
LIMOGES
LIMPETS
LUMBARS
LUMBERS
LUMPERS
MAMMALS
MEMBERS
MEMOIRS
MEMPHIS
MIMESIS
MIMOSAS
MOMENTS
MOMMIES
MUMBLES
MUMMERS
MUMMIES
NEMESES
NEMESIS
NIMRODS
NUMBATS
NUMBERS
OOMPAHS
ORMOLUS
OSMOSES
OSMOSIS
PAMPERS
POMADES
POMELOS
POMMELS
POMPOMS
POMPONS
POMPOUS
PUMICES
PUMMELS
PUMPERS
RAMADAS
RAMBLES
RAMESES
RAMJETS
RAMRODS
REMAILS
REMAINS
REMAKES
REMANDS
REMARKS
REMELTS
REMENDS
REMIGES
REMINDS
REMIXES
REMOLDS
REMORAS
REMOTES
REMOVES
REMUDAS
RIMLESS
RIMPLES
ROMNEYS
ROMPERS
ROMULUS
RUMBLES
RUMLESS
RUMOURS
RUMPLES
SAMBALS
SAMBARS
SAMECHS
SAMITES
SAMLETS
SAMOANS
SAMPANS
SAMPLES
SAMPRAS
SEMITES
SIMIANS
SIMILES
SIMMERS
SIMMONS
SIMPERS
SOMALIS
SUMLESS
SUMMERS
SUMMITS
SUMMONS
SYMBOLS
TAMALES
TAMPERS
TAMTAMS
TEMPEHS
TEMPERS
TEMPLES
TIMBALS
TIMBERS
TIMBRES
TIMINGS
TIMMINS
TOMBOYS
TOMCATS
TOMTITS
TOMTOMS
TUMBLES
TUMMIES
TUMULTS
TUMULUS
UNMAKES
UNMASKS
VAMPERS
WAMBLES
WIMBLES
WIMPLES
WOMBATS
YAMMERS
YEMENIS
YOMTOVS
ZOMBIES

•••MS••

ADAMSON
BEAMSUP
CHOMSKY
CLAMSUP
CLEMSON
CRIMSON
DRUMSUP
FIRMSUP
MALMSEY
TEAMSUP
THOMSON
WARMSUP
ZOOMSIN

•••M•S•

AIRMASS
ANIMISM
ANIMIST
ATOMISE
BEAMISH
BIOMASS
BLEMISH
BURMESE
CALMEST
CHEMISE
CHEMIST
DIMMEST
DISMISS
ENDMOST
FIRMEST
FLEMISH
FORMOSA
GLIMPSE
GNOMISH
INAMESS
ITEMISE
MIDMOST
OAKMOSS
OLEMISS
PALMIST
PREMISE
PREMISS
PROMISE
RAMMISH
REAMASS
SEAMOSS
SIAMESE
SKIMASK
SURMISE
TOPMAST
TOPMOST
WARMEST
WARMISH
WORMISH

•••M••S

ACUMENS
AIRMASS
ALUMNUS
ANIMALS
ANOMIES
ATAMANS
ATOMIES
BIOMASS
BITMAPS
BONMOTS
BOOMERS
BUMMERS
BURMANS
CAIMANS
CAYMANS
CHAMOIS
CLAMORS
CLEMENS
COMMITS
COMMONS
DAIMONS
DAMMARS
DIMMERS
DISMAYS
DISMISS
DOLMANS
DOLMENS
DORMERS
DUMMIES
ENAMELS
ENAMORS
ENEMIES
EXEMPTS
FARMERS
FLAMBES
FORMALS
FORMATS
GAMMERS
GAMMONS
GERMANS
GNOMONS
GRAMMES
GRAMMYS
GRAMPAS
GRAMPUS
GUIMPES
HAMMERS
HAYMOWS
HELMETS
HEMMERS
HERMITS
HETMANS
HUMMERS
INAMESS
ISOMERS
JAMMERS
JEMMIES
JIMMIES
KIRMANS
MAMMALS
MARMOTS
MAUMAUS
MIAMIAS
MICMACS
MOMMIES
MORMONS
MUMMERS
MUMMIES
MURMURS
MUUMUUS
NORMALS
NORMANS
NUTMEGS
OAKMOSS
OLEMISS
OLYMPUS
PERMITS
POMMELS
PREMEDS
PREMISS
PRIMERS
PROMPTS
PUMMELS
PYGMIES
RAGMOPS
REAMASS
REAMERS
RHOMBUS
RHUMBAS
RHYMERS
ROAMERS
ROOMERS
ROOMIES
SALMONS
SCHMOES
SCHMOOS
SEAMOSS
SERMONS
SHAMANS
SIMMERS
SIMMONS
SPUMOUS
STAMENS
STUMERS
STYMIES
SUBMITS
SUMMERS
SUMMITS
SUMMONS
TARMACS
TIMMINS
TRAMPAS
TREMORS
TUMMIES
WARMUPS
WETMOPS
YAMMERS
YOUMANS

••••M•S

AFRAMES
ARTEMIS
ARTEMUS
ASSUMES
ATHOMES
ATTIMES
AUTUMNS
BAHAMAS
BECOMES
BENUMBS
BETIMES
BIREMES
BRAHMAS
CCLAMPS
CHROMES
CINEMAS
COLUMNS
DECAMPS
DEFAMES
DONIMUS
DYNAMOS
ENCAMPS
ENIGMAS
ENZYMES
ERASMUS
ESKIMOS
GAZUMPS
GENOMES
GRAMMES
GRAMMYS
ILLUMES
INCOMES
ISTHMUS
JICAMAS
KINEMAS
LEGUMES
LEXEMES
MAXIMUS
MIASMAS
NOKOMIS
PAJAMAS
PANAMAS
PDJAMES
PLASMAS
PREAMPS
PYJAMAS
PYRAMUS
RACEMES
RADOMES
REGIMES
RELUMES
RENAMES
RESUMES
RETIMES
REVAMPS
SALAMIS
SCHEMAS
SCHEMES
SCRIMPS
SESAMES
SHRIMPS
STIGMAS
TATAMIS
THERMOS
TRAUMAS
ULTIMAS
VOLUMES
YAKIMAS
ZEUGMAS

•••••MS

AFFIRMS
AIRDAMS
ALARUMS
ANADEMS
ANONYMS
ANTHEMS
ASHRAMS
ASYLUMS
ATRIUMS
BALSAMS
BANTAMS
BECALMS
BEEGUMS
BELDAMS
BESEEMS
BOTTOMS
CHRISMS
CUSTOMS
DEFORMS
DIADEMS
DIATOMS
DICTUMS
DIGRAMS
DISARMS
DRACHMS
DUMDUMS
EMBLEMS
ENGRAMS
EPONYMS
ESTEEMS
FATHOMS
GRAHAMS
HANSOMS
INFORMS
INSEAMS
JIMJAMS
LOGJAMS
LYCEUMS
MAGNUMS
MAYHEMS
MEDIUMS
MEGOHMS
MEGRIMS
MOSLEMS
MUSEUMS
MUSLIMS
NONCOMS
PABLUMS
PEPLUMS
PHENOMS
PLENUMS
PODIUMS
POMPOMS
POSSUMS
PRELIMS
QUORUMS
RANSOMS
REDEEMS
REDGUMS
REFILMS
REFORMS
RETRIMS
REWARMS
RHYTHMS
SACHEMS
SALAAMS
SCHISMS
SCREAMS
SHALOMS
SITCOMS
SLALOMS
SQUIRMS
STREAMS
SYSTEMS
TALCUMS
TAMTAMS
TANDEMS
TEDIUMS
TOMTOMS
TRUISMS
VACUUMS
VELLUMS
VICTIMS
WIGWAMS

M•T••••

MATADOR
MATCHED
MATCHES
MATCHUP
MATELOT
MATEWAN
MATHERS
MATHEWS
MATHIAS
MATILDA
MATINEE
MATISSE
MATLESS
MATLOCK
MATRONS
MATTERS
MATTHAU
MATTHEW
MATTING
MATTOCK
MATURED
MATURER
MATURES
MATZOHS
METATES
METEORS
METEOUT
METERED
METHANE

METHODS
METIERS
METOOER
METRICS
METTLES
MITCHUM
MITERED
MITFORD
MITHRAS
MITOSES
MITOSIS
MITOTIC
MITRING
MITTENS
MITZVAH
MOTHERS
MOTHIER
MOTIONS
MOTIVES
MOTORED
MOTTLED
MOTTLES
MOTTOES
MUTABLE
MUTABLY
MUTAGEN
MUTANTS
MUTATED
MUTATES
MUTTERS
MUTTONS
MUTUALS

M••T•••
MAITAIS
MAITRED
MALTEDS
MALTESE
MALTHUS
MALTIER
MALTING
MALTOSE
MANTELS
MANTLED
MANTLES
MANTRAP
MANTRAS
MANTRIC
MARTENS
MARTIAL
MARTIAN
MARTINA
MARTINI
MARTINO
MARTINS
MARTYRS
MASTABA
MASTERS
MASTERY
MASTICS
MASTIFF
MASTOID
MATTERS
MATTHAU
MATTHEW
MATTING
MATTOCK
MAYTIME
MAYTREE
MEATIER
MEATILY
MEETING
MELTING
MENTHOL
MENTION
MENTORS
MESTIZA
MESTIZO
METTLES
MIDTERM
MIDTOWN
MINTERS
MINTIER
MINTING
MISTAKE
MISTERS
MISTIER
MISTILY
MISTING
MISTOOK
MISTRAL
MISTYPE
MITTENS
MIXTURE
MOLTERS
MOLTING
MONTAGE
MONTANA
MONTAND
MONTANE
MONTANI
MONTEGO
MONTERO
MONTHLY
MONTOYA
MOPTOPS
MORTALS
MORTARS
MORTIFY
MORTISE
MOTTLED
MOTTLES
MOTTOES
MOUTHED
MOUTONS
MUNTINS
MUSTAFA
MUSTANG
MUSTARD
MUSTERS
MUSTIER
MUSTILY
MUSTSEE
MUTTERS
MUTTONS
MYRTLES
MYSTERY
MYSTICS
MYSTIFY

M•••T••
MAESTRI
MAESTRO
MAHATMA
MAINTOP
MANATEE
MANITOU
MARITAL
MEIOTIC
MEISTER
MENOTTI
MERITED
METATES
MIGHTNT
MILITIA
MIMETIC
MINUTES
MINUTIA
MISSTEP
MITOTIC
MIXITUP
MOBSTER
MOISTEN
MOISTER
MOISTLY
MOLOTOV
MONITOR
MONSTER
MOULTED
MOUNTED
MOUNTIE
MULCTED
MULETAS
MUSETTE
MUTATED
MUTATES

M••••T•
MACBETH
MACHETE
MAGENTA
MAGNATE
MAGNETO
MAGNETS
MAHOUTS
MAJESTE
MAJESTY
MALEATE
MALLETS
MAMMOTH
MANDATE
MAOISTS
MARCATO
MARGATE
MARKETS
MARMOTS
MASCOTS
MEDIATE
MEMENTO
MENOTTI
MERLOTS
MIDGETS
MIGRATE
MILLETS
MILLETT
MINOLTA
MINUETS
MISDATE
MISFITS
MISHITS
MISMATE
MODELTS
MODESTO
MODESTY
MODISTE
MOLESTS
MOMENTS
MOPPETS
MUDCATS
MULLETS
MUPPETS
MUSCATS
MUSETTE
MUSKETS
MUTANTS

M•••••T
MADDEST
MADEOUT
MAEWEST
MAGINOT
MAIGRET
MAILLOT
MAILOUT
MAKEOUT
MAKESIT
MALLRAT
MANHUNT
MANUMIT
MANXCAT
MARGRET
MARXIST
MATELOT
MAZIEST
MEANEST
MEDIANT
MEEKEST
MEGAHIT
MESSKIT
METEOUT
MIDEAST
MIDMOST
MIDWEST
MIGHTNT
MIGRANT
MILDEST
MILLETT
MINARET
MINDSET
MIRIEST
MISCAST
MISSOUT
MONOCOT
MOONLIT
MOONSET
MOPIEST
MORDANT
MORDENT
MOSHPIT
MOVEOUT
MRFIXIT
MRRIGHT
MUGSHOT
MUSKRAT

•M•T•••
AMATEUR
AMATIVE
AMATORY
DMYTRYK
EMITTED
EMITTER
EMOTERS
EMOTING
EMOTION
EMOTIVE
EMPTIED
EMPTIER
EMPTIES
EMPTILY
IMITATE
OMITTED
OMITTER
SMATTER
SMETANA
SMITING
SMITTEN
SMOTHER
UMPTEEN

•M••T••
AMISTAD
AMMETER
EMITTED
EMITTER
EMPATHY
IMPETUS
IMPUTED
IMPUTES
OMENTUM
OMITTED
OMITTER
SMALTOS
SMARTED
SMARTEN
SMARTER
SMARTLY
SMATTER
SMELTED
SMELTER
SMITTEN
SMOOTHS
SMOOTHY

•M•••T•
AMENITY
AMNESTY
AMOUNTS
AMULETS
EMANATE
EMERITA
EMERITI
EMIRATE
EMULATE
IMAMATE
IMARETS
IMITATE
IMPACTS
IMPARTS
IMPASTO
IMPIETY
IMPORTS
IMPOSTS
OMELETS
UMBERTO
UMLAUTS

•M••••T
AMBIENT
AMHERST
AMONGST
AMPLEST
EMANANT
EMINENT
IMPLANT
IMPRINT

••MT•••
ELMTREE
GUMTREE
TAMTAMS
TOMTITS
TOMTOMS
YOMTOVS

••M•T••
ADMITTO
AMMETER
DEMETER
DEMOTED
DEMOTES
DIMITRI
GAMETES
GEMOTES
HAMITES
HAMITIC
HAMITUP
HAMPTON
HAMSTER
INMATES
IOMOTHS
KOMATSU
LAMOTTA
LIMITED
MIMETIC
NAMETAG
OSMOTIC
REMOTER
REMOTES
SAMITES
SEMITES
SEMITIC
SOMATIC
SUMATRA
SYMPTOM
TEMPTED
TEMPTER
TIMOTHY
ZEMSTVO

••M••T•
ADMITTO
AIMEDTO
ALMAATA
ARMLETS
ARMPITS
CEMENTS
COMBATS
COMESTO
COMFITS
COMMITS
COMMUTE
COMPETE
COMPOTE
COMPUTE
DIMOUTS
DIMWITS
ELMISTI
FOMENTS
GAMBITS
GIMLETS
HAMLETS
HAMMETT
LAMENTS
LAMOTTA
LIMPETS
MAMMOTH
MEMENTO
MOMENTS
NIMIETY
NUMBATS
PIMENTO
RAMINTO
RAMJETS
REMELTS
SAMLETS
SUMMITS
TOMCATS
TOMTITS
TUMULTS
WOMBATS

••M•••T
AIMEDAT
ARMREST
ARMYANT
BOMBAST
BUMSOUT
CAMELOT
CAMEOUT
CAMPOUT
COMBUST
COMEOUT
COMESAT
COMFORT
COMMENT
COMPACT
COMPORT
COMPOST
DAMPEST
DEMERIT
DIMMEST
DUMBEST
FUMIEST
GAMIEST
GYMNAST
HAMMETT
HOMIEST
JUMPCUT
JUMPSAT
KUMQUAT
LAMAIST
LAMBENT
LAMBERT
LIMIEST
LIMPEST
NUMBEST
RAMPANT
RAMPART
REMNANT
REMOUNT
RIMIEST
RIMSHOT
TEMPEST
TIMEOUT

•••MT••
PALMTOP

•••M•T•
ADAMITE
ANIMATE
ANIMATO
AZIMUTH
BISMUTH
BONMOTS
BROMATE
CLIMATE
COMMITS
COMMUTE
CONMOTO
DOGMATA
EREMITE
EXEMPTS
FORMATS
HAEMATO
HAMMETT
HELMETS
HERMITS
IMAMATE
KLAMATH
MAMMOTH
MARMOTS
MISMATE
NESMITH
NEWMATH
PALMATE
PERMITS
PRIMATE
PROMOTE
PROMPTS
SFUMATO
STOMATA
SUBMITS
SUMMITS
TERMITE
ZERMATT

•••M••T
ADAMANT
AILMENT
ALIMENT
ANIMIST
AUGMENT
BELMONT
CALMEST
CHEMIST
CLEMENT
COMMENT
CRUMPET
DIMMEST
DINMONT
DORMANT
ELEMENT
ENDMOST
FARMOUT
FERMENT
FIGMENT
FIRMEST
FREMONT
GARMENT
GROMMET
HAMMETT
MIDMOST
NUTMEAT
ODDMENT
PALMIST
PAYMENT
PIGMENT
PLUMMET
RAIMENT
REDMEAT
SCHMIDT
SEGMENT
TOPMAST
TOPMOST
TORMENT
TRUMPET
VARMINT
VERMONT
WALMART
WARMEST
ZERMATT

••••M•T
ATTEMPT
AUTOMAT
BATHMAT
CALUMET
DELIMIT
DOORMAT
GOURMET
GROMMET
MANUMIT
PLUMMET
PREEMPT
READMIT
UNKEMPT

MU•••••
MUAMMAR
MUBARAK
MUCKIER
MUCKILY
MUCKING
MUCKSUP
MUDCATS
MUDDERS
MUDDIED
MUDDIER
MUDDIES
MUDDILY
MUDDLED
MUDDLER
MUDDLES
MUDEELS
MUDHENS
MUDPACK
MUDPIES
MUEZZIN
MUFFING
MUFFINS
MUFFLED
MUFFLER
MUFFLES
MUGGERS
MUGGIER
MUGGING
MUGSHOT
MUGWUMP
MUKLUKS
MULCHED
MULCHES
MULCTED
MULETAS
MULLAHS
MULLEIN
MULLERS
MULLETS
MULLING
MULLION
MUMBLED
MUMBLER
MUMBLES
MUMESON
MUMFORD
MUMMERS
MUMMERY
MUMMIES
MUMMING
MUMPING
MUNCHED
MUNCHER
MUNCHES
MUNDANE
MUNTINS
MUPPETS
MURDERS
MURDOCH
MURILLO
MURKIER
MURKILY
MURMURS
MUSCATS
MUSCLED
MUSCLES
MUSCOVY
MUSEFUL
MUSETTE
MUSEUMS
MUSHERS
MUSHIER
MUSHILY
MUSHING
MUSICAL
MUSKEGS
MUSKETS
MUSKIER
MUSKIES
MUSKRAT
MUSLIMS
MUSLINS
MUSSELS
MUSSIER
MUSSILY
MUSSING
MUSTAFA
MUSTANG
MUSTARD
MUSTERS
MUSTIER
MUSTILY
MUSTSEE
MUTABLE
MUTABLY
MUTAGEN
MUTANTS
MUTATED
MUTATES
MUTTERS
MUTTONS
MUTUALS
MUUMUUS
MUZHIKS
MUZZIER
MUZZILY
MUZZING
MUZZLED
MUZZLES

M•U••••
MAUDLIN
MAUGHAM
MAULDIN
MAULING
MAUMAUS
MAUNDER
MAUREEN
MAURICE
MAUROIS
MOUFLON
MOULAGE
MOULDED
MOULDER
MOULTED
MOUNDED
MOUNTED
MOUNTIE
MOURNED
MOUSERS
MOUSIER
MOUSING
MOUSSED
MOUSSES
MOUTHED
MOUTONS
MUUMUUS

M••U•••
MACULAE
MAGUEYS
MAGUIRE
MANUALS
MANUMIT
MATURED
MATURER
MATURES
MAZURKA
MCGUIRE
MCLUHAN
MCQUEEN
MEDULLA
MEDUSAE
MEDUSAS
MENUHIN
MINUEND
MINUETS
MINUSES
MINUTES
MINUTIA
MISUSED
MISUSES
MODULAR
MODULES
MUTUALS

M•••U••
MACDUFF
MAGNUMS
MAHOUTS
MAJEURE
MAKEUPS
MANHUNT
MARAUDS
MARKUPS
MARQUEE
MARQUES
MARQUEZ
MARQUIS
MASQUES
MCCLURE
MEASURE
MEDIUMS
MERCURY
MISCUED
MISCUES
MISRULE
MIXTURE
MOCKUPS
MOLLUSC
MOLLUSK
MOSQUES
MUGWUMP
MUKLUKS
MURMURS
MUSEUMS
MUUMUUS

M••••U•
MACAQUE
MADEOUT
MAILOUT
MAKEOUT
MAKESUP
MALAMUD
MALRAUX
MALTHUS
MANAGUA
MANHOUR
MARGAUX
MARKSUP
MASSEUR
MATCHUP
MAUMAUS
MAXIMUM
MAXIMUS
MCCLOUD
METEOUT
MILHAUD
MILIEUS
MILIEUX
MILKRUN
MILLRUN
MIMIEUX
MINDFUL
MINIBUS
MINIMUM
MISSOUT
MITCHUM
MIXEDUP
MIXESUP
MIXITUP
MOANFUL
MODICUM
MONIQUE
MOVEDUP
MOVEOUT
MOVESUP
MUCKSUP
MUSEFUL
MUUMUUS

M•••••U
MANITOU
MARABOU
MARCEAU
MARYLOU
MATTHAU

•MU••••
AMULETS
AMUSING
EMULATE
SMUDGED
SMUDGES
SMUGGER
SMUGGLE

•M•U•••
AMOUNTS
AMPULES
IMBUING
IMMURED
IMMURES
IMPUGNS
IMPULSE
IMPURER
IMPUTED
IMPUTES

•M••U••
AMPOULE
EMANUEL
IMBRUED
IMBRUES
IMPOUND
UMLAUTS

•M•••U•
AMADEUS
AMATEUR
AMIBLUE
AMOROUS
IMPETUS
IMPIOUS
OMENTUM
OMINOUS
OMNIBUS
SMASHUP

•M••••U
EMMYLOU

••MU•••
ARMURES
BEMUSED
BEMUSES
CUMULUS
DEMURER
FAMULUS
HHMUNRO
IMMURED
IMMURES
REMUDAS
ROMULAN
ROMULUS
SAMURAI
TUMULTS
TUMULUS
ZYMURGY

••M•U••
ARMFULS
ARMOURS
ARMOURY
BUMRUSH
COMBUST
COMMUNE
COMMUTE
COMPUTE
DIMBULB
DIMOUTS
DUMDUMS
HAMBURG
HOMBURG
HUMBUGS
HUMOURS
KUMQUAT
REMOUNT
RUMOURS
SAMSUNG
TEMPURA

••M••U•
BUMPSUP
BUMSOUT
CAMBIUM
CAMEDUE
CAMEOUT
CAMPOUT
COMEDUE
COMEOUT
COMESUP
COMIQUE
CUMULUS
DOMINUS
DUMMYUP
FAMULUS
HAMITUP
HOMERUN
HUMANUM
HUMDRUM
HUMERUS
JUMPCUT
JUMPSUP
LEMIEUX
LUMPSUM
MIMIEUX
ORMOLUS
POMPOUS
PUMPSUP
RIMBAUD
ROMULUS
TAMBOUR
TIMEOUT
TIMESUP
TUMULUS

••M•••U
EMMYLOU
KOMATSU
LAMBEAU
RAMBEAU

•••MU••
AZIMUTH
BERMUDA
BISMUTH
COMMUNE
COMMUTE
EARMUFF
FORMULA
MURMURS
MUUMUUS
SIGMUND
STIMULI
UNAMUNO
WARMUPS

•••M•U•
ALUMNUS
BEAMSUP
BRIMFUL
CADMIUM
CLAMOUR
CLAMSUP
DOOMFUL
DRUMSUP
DUMMYUP
ENAMOUR
FARMOUT
FERMIUM
FIRMSUP
FORMFUL
FRAMEUP
GLAMOUR
GRAMPUS
HARMFUL
HOLMIUM
MAUMAUS
MUUMUUS
OLYMPUS
PREMIUM
RHOMBUS
ROOMFUL
SEYMOUR
SPUMOUS
TEAMSUP
TRUMPUP
WARMSUP

•••M••U
THIMPHU

••••MU•
ARTEMUS
DONIMUS
DREAMUP
ERASMUS
ISTHMUS
MALAMUD
MAXIMUM
MAXIMUS
MINIMUM
OPTIMUM
PYRAMUS

M•V••••
MOVABLE
MOVABLY
MOVEDIN
MOVEDON
MOVEDUP
MOVEOUT
MOVESIN
MOVESON
MOVESUP

M••V•••
MARVELS

M•••V••
MCGAVIN
MEDEVAC
MINIVAN
MINIVER

MITZVAH
MORAVIA
MOTIVES

M••••V•
MARKOVA
MASSIVE
MINERVA
MISSIVE
MOLDOVA
MUSCOVY

M•••••V
MOLOTOV

•M•V•••
BMOVIES

•M•••V•
AMATIVE
EMOTIVE
IMPROVE

••MV•••
HUMVEES

••M•V••
REMOVAL
REMOVED
REMOVER
REMOVES
SAMOVAR
UNMOVED

••M••V•
COMMOVE
YOMTOVS
ZEMSTVO

••M•••V
NEMEROV
ROMANOV

•••M•V•
COMMOVE

M•W••••
MAWKISH
MEWLERS
MEWLING
MOWDOWN

M••W•••
MAEWEST
MAXWELL
MAYWINE
MCSWINE
MEOWING
MIDWAYS
MIDWEEK
MIDWEST
MIDWIFE
MISWORD
MUGWUMP

M•••W••
MADEWAY
MAKEWAY
MANOWAR
MATEWAN
MOHAWKS

M••••W•
MALLOWS
MARLOWE
MARROWS
MATHEWS
MEADOWS
MEADOWY
MELLOWS
MIDTOWN
MILDEWS
MILDEWY
MINNOWS
MORROWS
MOWDOWN

M•••••W
MACGRAW
MANILOW
MATTHEW
MILKCOW

•M•W•••
EMPOWER

••MW•••
DIMWITS

••M•W••
REMOWED
SOMEWAY

••M•••W
GAMELAW
SOMEHOW

•••M•W•
HAYMOWS
NEWMOWN

M•X••••
MAXBAER
MAXBORN
MAXILLA
MAXIMAL
MAXIMUM
MAXIMUS
MAXWELL
MEXICAN
MIXABLE
MIXEDIN
MIXEDUP
MIXESIN
MIXESUP
MIXITUP
MIXTURE

M••X•••
MANXCAT
MANXMAN
MANXMEN
MARXISM
MARXIST
MINXISH

M•••X••
MRFIXIT

M•••••X
MADAMEX
MAILBOX
MALRAUX
MARGAUX
MEMOREX
MILIEUX
MIMIEUX
MIRAMAX

•M••X••
IMMIXED
IMMIXES

••M•X••
ADMIXED
ADMIXES
IMMIXED
IMMIXES
REMIXED
REMIXES

••M•••X
COMPLEX
LEMIEUX
MEMOREX
MIMIEUX
SIMPLEX

•••M••X
BOOMBOX
FLUMMOX

••••M•X
BETAMAX
CAKEMIX
CINEMAX
FLUMMOX
MADAMEX
MIRAMAX

MY•••••
MYANMAR
MYMAMMY
MYNHEER
MYRIADS
MYRTLES
MYSTERY
MYSTICS
MYSTIFY

M•Y••••
MAYALIN
MAYDAYS
MAYFAIR
MAYHEMS
MAYNARD
MAYORAL
MAYPOLE
MAYTIME
MAYTREE
MAYWINE

M••Y•••
MAGYARS
MANYEAR
MARYANN
MARYKAY
MARYLOU
MIDYEAR
MINYANS

M•••Y••
MALAYAN
MARRYME
MARTYRS
MEGRYAN
MIAOYAO
MISTYPE
MONEYED
MOSEYED

M••••Y•
MAGUEYS
MANDAYS
MARGAYS
MARILYN
MASARYK
MAYDAYS
MEDLEYS
MICKEYS
MIDDAYS
MIDWAYS
MISLAYS
MISSAYS
MONDAYS
MONKEYS
MONTOYA

M•••••Y
MADEHAY
MADEWAY
MAGNIFY
MAHONEY
MAJESTY
MAKEHAY
MAKEWAY
MALMSEY
MARYKAY
MASONRY
MASTERY
MCHENRY
MEADOWY
MEATILY
MERCERY
MERCURY
MERRILY
MESSILY
MILDEWY
MIMICRY
MISALLY
MISERLY
MISPLAY
MISTILY
MOCKERY
MODESTY
MOISTLY
MOLLIFY
MONTHLY
MOODILY
MOONILY
MORALLY
MORESBY
MORTIFY
MOVABLY
MUCKILY
MUDDILY
MUMMERY
MURKILY
MUSCOVY
MUSHILY
MUSSILY
MUSTILY
MUTABLY
MUZZILY
MYMAMMY
MYSTERY
MYSTIFY

•MY••••
AMYLASE
DMYTRYK

•M•Y•••
EMMYLOU

•M••Y••
EMBAYED
EMBRYOS

•M•••Y•
DMYTRYK
EMPLOYE
EMPLOYS

•M••••Y
AMATORY
AMENITY
AMIABLY
AMNESTY
AMPLIFY
AMSCRAY
EMBASSY
EMPATHY
EMPTILY
IMAGERY
IMPIETY
IMSORRY
SMARTLY
SMOKILY
SMOOTHY

••MY•••
ARMYANT
EMMYLOU

••M•Y••
DUMMYUP
SAMOYED

••M••Y•
HOMONYM
ROMNEYS
TOMBOYS

••M•••Y
ARMOURY
BUMPILY
CAMPILY
COMESBY
COMFREY
COMPANY
DEMPSEY
HAMMILY
HEMSLEY
HOMEBOY
HUMANLY
HUMIDLY
HYMNODY
JUMPILY
LAMPREY
LUMPILY
MIMICRY
MUMMERY
MYMAMMY
NAMEDAY
NIMIETY
ORMANDY
REMARRY
SAMEDAY
SOMEDAY
SOMEWAY
SUMMARY
SUMMERY
TAMMANY
TIMIDLY
TIMOTHY
WOMANLY
ZOMBIFY
ZYMURGY

•••MY••
DUMMYUP
GROMYKO

•••M•Y•
DISMAYS
GRAMMYS

•••M••Y
ALIMONY
ANOMALY
BALMILY
BRAMBLY
BRIMLEY
CHIMNEY
CHOMSKY
CRUMBLY
CRUMPLY
FARMERY
FOAMILY
GERMANY
GRIMILY
GRUMBLY
HAMMILY
HARMONY
MALMSEY
MUMMERY
PALMARY
PLUMPLY
PRIMACY
PRIMARY
ROOMILY
SLIMILY
SUMMARY
SUMMERY
TAMMANY
TREMBLY

••••MY•
GRAMMYS

••••M•Y
CALUMNY
DAHOMEY
MYMAMMY
SCRIMPY
SCRUMMY

•••••MY
ACADEMY
ALCHEMY
ANATOMY
BELLAMY
ECONOMY
EPONYMY
ISONOMY
MIMICRY
MUMMERY
MYMAMMY
PTOLEMY
SCRUMMY
SQUIRMY

M•Z••••
MAZIEST
MAZURKA
MIZZENS
MIZZLED
MIZZLES
MUZHIKS
MUZZIER
MUZZILY
MUZZING
MUZZLED
MUZZLES

M••Z•••
MATZOHS
MENZIES
MITZVAH
MIZZENS
MIZZLED
MIZZLES
MUEZZIN
MUZZIER
MUZZILY
MUZZING
MUZZLED
MUZZLES

M•••Z••
MUEZZIN

M••••Z•
MENDOZA
MESTIZA
MESTIZO
MIDSIZE

M•••••Z
MARQUEZ

•M•Z•••
AMAZING
AMAZONS

••M••Z•
ZAMBEZI

••M•••Z
JIMENEZ

•••M•Z•
ATOMIZE
ITEMIZE

NA•••••
NABBERS
NABBING
NABISCO
NABOKOV
NACELLE
NAGGIER
NAGGING
NAGGISH
NAHUATL
NAIADES
NAILERS
NAILING
NAILSET
NAILSIN
NAIROBI
NAIVELY
NAIVETE
NAIVETY
NAKEDLY
NAMEDAY
NAMETAG
NAMIBIA
NANAIMO
NANETTE
NANKEEN
NANNIES
NAPHTHA
NAPKINS
NAPLESS
NAPPERS
NAPPIES
NAPPING
NAPTIME
NARRATE
NARROWS
NARTHEX
NARWALS
NARWHAL
NASALLY
NASCENT
NASTASE
NASTIER
NASTILY
NATALIA
NATALIE
NATASHA
NATCHEZ
NATIONS
NATIVES
NATRIUM
NATTERS
NATTIER
NATTILY
NATURAL
NATURED
NATURES
NAUGHTS
NAUGHTY
NAVAHOS
NAVAJOS
NAVARRE
NAVVIES
NAYSAID
NAYSAYS

N•A••••
NEAREST
NEARING
NEARYOU
NEATENS
NEATEST
NIAGARA
NUANCED
NUANCES

N••A•••
NAIADES
NANAIMO
NASALLY
NATALIA
NATALIE
NATASHA
NAVAHOS
NAVAJOS
NAVARRE
NEGATED
NEGATER
NEGATES
NEGATOR
NEPALIS
NEVADAN
NEWAGER
NOCANDO
NOFAULT
NOGALES
NOMADIC
NONAGES
NONAGON
NOTABIT
NOTABLE
NOTABLY
NOTATED
NOTATES
NOVARRO
NUTATED
NUTATES

N•••A••
NAHUATL
NARRATE
NARWALS
NASTASE
NAYSAID
NAYSAYS
NECTARS
NEONATE
NESCAFE
NEWGATE
NEWHART
NEWMATH
NEWWAVE
NIAGARA
NIGGARD
NIRVANA
NITRATE
NITTANY
NORMALS
NORMAND
NORMANS
NOUGATS
NUBIANS
NULLAHS
NUMBATS

N••••A•
NAMEDAY
NAMETAG
NARWHAL
NATURAL
NEBULAE
NEBULAR
NEBULAS
NEEDHAM
NEUTRAL
NEVADAN
NEWDEAL
NEWSDAY
NEWSMAN
NEWYEAR
NICOLAS
NIKOLAI
NODULAR
NOMINAL
NOONDAY
NOSEBAG
NOSEGAY
NOSWEAT
NOTEPAD
NOUVEAU
NOVENAS
NUCLEAR
NUMERAL
NUPTIAL
NUTMEAT
NUTRIAS
NYUNGAR

N•••••A
NAMIBIA
NAPHTHA
NATALIA
NATASHA
NIAGARA
NICOSIA
NIGERIA
NIRVANA
NORIEGA
NOVELLA
NOXZEMA

•NA••••
ANADEMS
ANAEMIA
ANAEMIC
ANAGRAM
ANAHEIM
ANAHUAC
ANALOGS
ANALOGY
ANALYSE
ANALYST
ANALYZE
ANANIAS
ANAPEST
ANARCHY
ANASAZI
ANATOLE
ANATOMY
ENABLED
ENABLES
ENACTED
ENACTOR
ENAMELS
ENAMORS
ENAMOUR
GNARLED
GNARRED
GNASHED
GNASHES
GNAWERS
GNAWING
INADAZE
INAHEAP
INAMESS
INANELY
INANEST
INANITY
INAPTER
INAPTLY
INARUSH
INASNIT
INASPIN
INASPOT
INASTEW
INAWEOF
INAWORD
KNACKER
KNAVERY
KNAVISH
ONADARE
ONADATE
ONADIET
ONAGERS
ONANDON
ONAROLL
ONASSIS
ONATEAR
SNACKED
SNACKER
SNAFFLE
SNAFUED
SNAGGED
SNAKIER
SNAKILY
SNAKING
SNAPONS
SNAPPED
SNAPPER
SNAPPLE
SNAPSAT
SNAPSTO
SNAPSUP
SNARING
SNARLED
UNAIDED
UNAIMED
UNAIRED
UNALIKE
UNAMUNO
UNAPTLY
UNARMED
UNASKED
UNAVOCE
UNAWARE
UNAWFUL

•N•A•••
ANDANTE
ANNABEL
ANNALEE
ANNATTO
ANTACID
ANTAEUS
ANTARES
ENCAGED
ENCAGES
ENCAMPS
ENCASED
ENCASES
ENGAGED
ENGAGES
ENGARDE
ENHANCE
ENLACED
ENLACES
ENLARGE
ENMASSE
ENRAGED
ENRAGES
ENTAILS
INCANTS
INCASED
INCASES
INFANCY
INFANTA
INFANTS
INFAVOR
INGALLS
INHABIT
INHALED
INHALER
INHALES
INHASTE
INHAULS
INMATES
INNARDS
INTAKES
INVACUO
INVADED
INVADER
INVADES
INVALID
INWARDS
KNEADED
KNEADER
ONTARIO
ONWARDS
SNEAKED
SNEAKER
SNEAKIN
UNBAKED
UNCAGED
UNCAGES
UNCANNY
UNCASED
UNCASES
UNDATED
UNEARTH
UNEATEN
UNFAZED
UNHANDS
UNHANDY
UNHAPPY
UNLACED
UNLACES
UNLADES
UNLATCH
UNMAKES
UNMASKS
UNNAMED
UNPACKS
UNPAVED
UNRATED
UNRAVEL
UNSATED
UNTACKS
UNTAMED
UNTAPED

•N••A••
ANASAZI
ANDEANS
ANIMALS
ANIMATE
ANIMATO
ANNEALS
ANNUALS
ANOMALY
ANORAKS
ANTFARM
ANTIART
ENCHAIN
ENCHANT
ENCLAVE
ENDEARS
ENDGAME
ENDWAYS
ENGLAND
ENGRAFT
ENGRAMS
ENGRAVE
ENNEADS
ENPLANE
ENSLAVE
ENSNARE
ENSNARL
ENTRAIN
ENTRANT
ENTRAPS
ENWRAPS
INADAZE
INBOARD
INDIANA
INDIANS
INEXACT
INFLAME
INFLATE
INGRAIN
INGRATE
INPEACE
INPHASE
INPLACE
INROADS
INSCAPE
INSEAMS
INSHAPE
INSPANS
INSTALL
INSTALS
INSTANT
INSTARS
INSTATE
INTEARS
ONADARE
ONADATE
ONBOARD
ONELANE
ONGUARD
ONLEAVE
ONSTAGE
ONTRACK
SNOCATS
UNAWARE
UNCHAIN
UNCIALS
UNCLASP
UNCRATE
UNDRAPE
UNDRAWN
UNHEARD
UNITARY
UNLEARN
UNLEASH
UNLOADS
UNREADY
UNSEALS
UNSEATS
UNSNAGS
UNSNAPS
UNSNARL
UNSTACK
UNTRAPS
UNWEAVE
UNWRAPS

•N•••A•
ANAGRAM
ANAHUAC
ANANIAS
ANDREAS
ANGOLAN
ANGORAS
ANGULAR
ANNULAR
ANTBEAR
ANTITAX
ANTIWAR
ANYROAD
ENCINAS
ENDPLAY
ENIGMAS
ENTHRAL
ENTREAT
INAHEAP
INGEMAR
INHUMAN
INITIAL
INKYCAP
INNOWAY
INSOFAR
INSTEAD
INSULAR
KNEECAP
KNEEPAD
ONATEAR
ONEIDAS
ONESTAR
ONTRIAL
SNAPSAT
SNEERAT
SNIFFAT
SNIPEAT
SNOWCAP
SNOWCAT
SNOWDAY
SNOWMAN
UNCLEAN
UNCLEAR
UNCLOAK
UNEQUAL
UNSTRAP
UNUSUAL

•N••••A
ANAEMIA
ANDORRA
ANOSMIA
ANTENNA
ANTIGUA
ANTONIA
ENCOMIA
INDIANA
INDICIA
INERTIA
INFANTA
INOCULA
INTEGRA
SNOWPEA

••NA•••
ABNAKIS
AGNATES
ANNABEL
ANNALEE
ANNATTO
BANALLY
BANANAS
BENATAR
BENAZIR
BONANZA
CANAPES
CANARDS
CANASTA
CONAKRY
DENARII
DONAHUE
DONATED
DONATES
DONATOR
DUNAWAY
DYNAMIC
DYNAMOS
DYNASTS
DYNASTY
FANATIC
FINAGLE
FINALES
FINALLY
FINANCE
INNARDS
JANACEK
KANAKAS
LINAGES
LUNATIC
MANACLE
MANAGED
MANAGER
MANAGES
MANAGUA
MANANAS
MANATEE
MENACED
MENACES
MENAGES
MINABLE
MINARET
MONARCH
NANAIMO
NONAGES
NONAGON

PANACEA
PANACHE
PANADAS
PANAMAS
PANARAB
PENALTY
PENANCE
PENATES
PINATAS
RANAWAY
RENAILS
RENAMED
RENAMES
RENARDS
RENAULT
RUNAMOK
RUNAWAY
SENATES
SENATOR
SINATRA
SONATAS
SYNAPSE
TANAGER
TENABLE
TENABLY
TENACES
TENANCY
TENANTS
TONALLY
UNNAMED
VENALLY
ZENANAS
ZONALLY

••N•A••

ANNEALS
ANNUALS
AYNRAND
BANDAGE
BANDAID
BANDANA
BANTAMS
BANYANS
BENEATH
BENGALI
BENGALS
BONDAGE
BONEASH
CANCANS
CANTATA
CANVASS
CENTAUR
CENTAVO
CINZANO
CONCAVE
CONFABS
CONGAED
CONGAME
CONTACT
CONTAIN
DENIALS
DENMARK
DENTATE
ENNEADS
FANFARE
FANMAIL
FANTAIL
FANTASY
FENIANS
FINEART
FINIALS
FINLAND
FONDANT
FUNFAIR
GENNARO
GUNWALE
HANGARS
HANSARP
HENBANE
HENNAED
HONIARA
HUNGARY
HUNYADY
IBNSAUD
JANUARY
JUNKART
KANSANS
KENDALL
KENYANS
LANDAUS
LANTANA
LANYARD
LENFANT
LINEAGE
LINEATE
LINKAGE
LONGAGO
LONGARM
MANDALA
MANDANS
MANDATE
MANDAYS
MANIACS
MANMADE
MANSARD
MANUALS
MENIALS
MINOANS
MINYANS
MONDALE
MONDAYS
MONTAGE
MONTANA
MONTAND
MONTANE
MONTANI
MUNDANE
PANCAKE
PENDANT
PENNAME
PENNANT
PENNATE
PENPALS
PENTADS
PINBALL
PINNACE
PINNATE
PINOAKS
PINTAIL
PINWALE
PONIARD
PUNJABI
PUNKAHS
QINTARS
RANDALL
RANLATE
RANSACK
RENTALS
RUNBACK
RUNLATE
RUNWAYS
SANDALS
SANTAFE
SANTANA
SENSATE
SINKAGE
SUNBATH
SUNDAES
SUNDAYS
SUNLAMP
SUNMAID
SUNRAYS
SUNTANS
TANKARD
TANOAKS
TANTARA
TINCANS
TINEARS
TINHATS
TINTACK
TINWARE
TONEARM
TONGANS
TONNAGE
VANDALS
VANTAGE
VANUATU
VINTAGE
WANNABE
WANTADS
WENTAPE

••N••A•

ANNULAR
ARNICAS
BANANAS
BANDSAW
BENATAR
BENTHAM
BINGHAM
BONDMAN
CENTRAL
CINEMAS
CINEMAX
CONCEAL
CONGEAL
CONICAL
CONTRAS
CYNICAL
DANELAW
DINGBAT
DONEGAL
DONJUAN
DONOVAN
DUNAWAY
FUNCHAL
GANGSAW
GANGWAY
GENERAL
GENTIAN
GINGHAM
GUNBOAT
GUNPLAY
HANDBAG
HANDCAR
HANDSAW
HANGMAN
HANUKAH
HINTSAT
INNOWAY
JANEWAY
JUNKMAN
KANAKAS
KINEMAS
KINGMAN
KINGRAT
KINSMAN
LANDSAT
LINBIAO
LINDSAY
LINEMAN
LINGUAL
LINPIAO
LUNGEAT
MANANAS
MANOWAR
MANTRAP
MANTRAS
MANXCAT
MANXMAN
MANYEAR
MENORAH
MINERAL
MINICAB
MINICAM
MINIMAL
MINIVAN
PANADAS
PANAMAS
PANARAB
PANCHAX
PINATAS
PINCHAS
PINESAP
PINETAR
PINHEAD
PONTIAC
QINGDAO
RANAWAY
RENEWAL
RONDEAU
RUNAWAY
SANDBAG
SANDBAR
SANDMAN
SANJUAN
SENECAS
SENEGAL
SENORAS
SENSUAL
SONATAS
SUNBEAM
SUNDIAL
SYNGMAN
SYNODAL
TANGRAM
TINSTAR
TONNEAU
TUNDRAS
VENTRAL
VINEGAR
WENTBAD
WINDBAG
WINEBAR
WINESAP
WINKSAT
XANTHAN
ZENANAS
ZINNIAS

••N•••A

AMNESIA
BANDANA
BONANZA
CANASTA
CANDELA
CANDIDA
CANTATA
CANTINA
CONDITA
CYNTHIA
FONTINA
GANGLIA
GANGSTA
GINGIVA
GONDOLA
HONIARA
JUNKDNA
KENOSHA
LANTANA
MANAGUA
MANDALA
MANDELA
MENDOZA
MINERVA
MINOLTA
MINORCA
MINUTIA
MONTANA
MONTOYA
PANACEA
PANDORA
SANGRIA
SANTANA
SINATRA
TANTARA
TUNISIA
VANESSA
VANILLA
VENTURA
WYNONNA
ZENOBIA

•••NA••

ABENAKI
ADONAIS
BARNABY
BARNARD
BERNARD
BIGNAME
BRANAGH
CATNAPS
COGNACS
COGNATE
COINAGE
EMANANT
EMANATE
ENSNARE
ENSNARL
FURNACE
GENNARO
GRANADA
GRANARY
GRENADA
GRENADE
GUANACO
GYMNAST
HENNAED
HOBNAIL
HYMNALS
IRONAGE
JEANARP
KIDNAPS
LEONARD
MAENADS
MAGNANI
MAGNATE
MAYNARD
MISNAME
NEONATE
OCANADA
OKINAWA
OPENAIR
PENNAME
PENNANT
PENNATE
PEONAGE
PETNAME
PINNACE
PINNATE
PLENARY
QUINARY
REENACT
REGNANT
REMNANT
REYNARD
SCHNAPS
SHANANA
SIGNALS
SPINACH
SURNAME
TEENAGE
TERNARY
TERNATE
THENARS
THINAIR
TOENAIL
TONNAGE
TORNADO
TRENARY
TSUNAMI
UNSNAGS
UNSNAPS
UNSNARL
WANNABE

•••N•A•

AGENDAS
ANANIAS
BEANBAG
BLINKAT
BRENDAN
BRENNAN
COONCAT
CORNEAL
CORNEAS
CRANIAL
DOWNPAT
DUENNAS
ETONIAN
FERNBAR
FEYNMAN
FRENEAU
FRONTAL
GAINSAY
GHANIAN
GOINGAT
GRANDAM
GUINEAS
HYUNDAI
IRANIAN
IRONMAN
JOHNGAY
JOHNJAY
KWANZAS
MYANMAR
NOONDAY
NYUNGAR
OPENBAR
OXONIAN
PAANGAS
PHINEAS
PLANTAR
QUINOAS
RAINHAT
RAINMAN
RUANDAN
RWANDAN
SCANDAL
SHANKAR
SIENNAS
STANZAS
TONNEAU
UGANDAN
WOZNIAK
ZINNIAS

•••N••A

ABINTRA
AVONLEA
CARNERA
GRANADA
GRANDMA
GRANDPA
GRANOLA
GRENADA
IPANEMA
LEONORA
OCANADA
OKINAWA
OPENSEA
SHANANA
SPINOZA
SWANSEA
ULANOVA

••••NA•

ADRENAL
ALMANAC
ALUMNAE
ALUMNAL
AQUINAS
ARSENAL
BANANAS
BRENNAN
BROSNAN
CABANAS
CARINAS
CATENAE
CORONAE
CORONAS
DIURNAL
DUENNAS
EATENAT
ENCINAS
ETERNAL
FLOWNAT
FROWNAT
IGUANAS
JACANAS
JOURNAL
JUVENAL
KAHUNAS
KORUNAS
KUTENAI
LACUNAE
LACUNAL
LACUNAS
LAGUNAS
LAMINAE
LAMINAL
LAMINAR
LAMINAS
LATINAS
MANANAS
MARINAS
NOMINAL
NOVENAS
ORDINAL
PATINAS
RETINAE
RETINAL
RETINAS
SAGINAW
SALINAS
SARANAC
SEMINAL
SEMINAR
SEVENAM
SIENNAS
STERNAL
SURINAM
VICUNAS
VIETNAM
ZENANAS

••••N•A

ADDENDA
ALBANIA
AMMONIA
ANTENNA
ANTONIA
ARMENIA
ATLANTA
AVIANCA
BEGONIA
BELINDA
BONANZA
BOTHNIA
CADENZA
ESTONIA
HOSANNA
INFANTA
JOHANNA
LAVINIA
MADONNA
MAGENTA
MELINDA
MIRANDA
OCEANIA
ORGANZA
PETUNIA
PIRANHA
POLENTA
RAVENNA
ROMANIA
ROSANNA
ROTUNDA
SAVANNA
SOYINKA
SUSANNA
SYRINGA
TITANIA
VEDANTA
VERANDA
WYNONNA

•••••NA

ALTOONA
ANTENNA
ARIZONA
BANDANA
BOLOGNA
BURKINA
CANTINA
CHICANA
CREMONA
CZARINA
DAYTONA
DUODENA
ECHIDNA
FONTINA
FORTUNA
HOSANNA
IKEBANA
INDIANA
JOHANNA
JULIANA
JUNKDNA
KACHINA
KRISHNA
LANTANA
LASAGNA
MACHINA
MADONNA
MARIANA
MARTINA
MESSINA
MONTANA
MORGANA
NIRVANA
OCARINA
PASTINA
PAULINA
PERSONA
PORSENA
RAVENNA
RETSINA
ROSANNA
SABRINA
SANTANA
SAVANNA
SESTINA
SHANANA
SMETANA
STAMINA
SULTANA
SUSANNA
TARZANA
TATIANA
TIJUANA
TSARINA
TYMPANA
TZARINA
VERBENA
WYNONNA

N•B••••

NABBERS
NABBING
NABISCO
NABOKOV
NEBBISH
NEBULAE
NEBULAR
NEBULAS
NIBBLED
NIBBLER
NIBBLES
NIBLICK
NIBLIKE
NOBBIER
NOBBLED
NOBBLER
NOBBLES
NOBHILL
NOBLEST
NOBODYS
NUBBIER
NUBBINS
NUBBLES
NUBIANS

N••B•••

NABBERS
NABBING
NEBBISH
NEWBERY
NEWBORN
NIBBLED
NIBBLER
NIBBLES
NIEBUHR
NIMBLER
NIOBIUM
NOBBIER
NOBBLED
NOBBLER
NOBBLES
NORBERT
NUBBIER
NUBBINS
NUBBLES
NUMBATS
NUMBERS
NUMBEST
NUMBING

N•••B••

NAMIBIA
NEWSBOY
NOSEBAG
NOTABIT
NOTABLE
NOTABLY

N••••B•

NAIROBI
NODOUBT

N•••••B

NOSEJOB

•NB••••

INBLOOM
INBOARD
INBOUND
INBOXES
INBREED
INBRIEF
ONBOARD
UNBAKED
UNBENDS
UNBINDS
UNBLEST
UNBLOCK
UNBOLTS
UNBOUND
UNBOWED
UNBOXED
UNBOXES

•N•B•••

ANTBEAR
ANYBODY
ENABLED
ENABLES
INKBLOT
KNOBBED
SNUBBED

•N••B••

ANNABEL
ANTIBES
ENNOBLE
ENROBED
ENROBES
ENTEBBE
FNUMBER
INHABIT
INHIBIT
INORBIT
KNOBBED
SNUBBED
UNROBED
UNROBES

•N•••B•

ENTEBBE
INDOUBT

•N••••B

SNOWJOB

••NB•••

BONBONS
CONBRIO
DANBURY
FANBELT
GUNBOAT
HENBANE
HENBITS
LINBIAO
PINBALL
RUNBACK
SUNBATH
SUNBEAM
SUNBELT
SUNBOWL
SUNBURN

••N•B••

ANNABEL
BANDBOX
BUNKBED
DINGBAT
ENNOBLE
HANDBAG
IGNOBLE
IGNOBLY
JUNEBUG
LONGBOW
MINABLE
MINIBUS
OMNIBUS
SANDBAG
SANDBAR
SANDBOX
SANIBEL
TENABLE
TENABLY
WENTBAD
WINDBAG
WINEBAR
ZENOBIA

••N••B•

BENUMBS
CONFABS
CONJOBS
PUNJABI
WANNABE

••N•••B

FANCLUB
MINICAB
PANARAB

•••NB••

BEANBAG
DOWNBOW
FERNBAR
OPENBAR
RAINBOW
TOYNBEE
TWINBED

•••N•B•

BARNABY
BYANDBY
GOINGBY
HOBNOBS
HORNSBY
STANDBY
SWINGBY
WANNABE

•••N••B

CORNCOB
LIONCUB

••••NB•

ALLENBY

NC•••••

NCWYETH

N•C••••

NACELLE
NECKERS
NECKING
NECKTIE
NECTARS
NICCOLO
NICHOLS
NICKELS
NICKERS
NICKING
NICOLAS
NICOSIA
NOCANDO
NOCTURN
NOCUOUS
NUCLEAR
NUCLEIC
NUCLEON
NUCLEUS
NUCLIDE

N••C•••

NASCENT
NATCHEZ
NESCAFE
NICCOLO
NONCOMS
NOTCHED
NOTCHES
NUNCIOS

N•••C••

NOGUCHI
NOTICED
NOTICES
NOVICES
NUANCED
NUANCES

N••••C•

NABISCO
NEGLECT
NIBLICK
NITPICK
NOETICS
NORDICS
NORELCO

N•••••C

NOMADIC
NUCLEIC
NUMERIC

•NC••••

ANCHORS
ANCHOVY
ANCIENT
ENCAGED
ENCAGES
ENCAMPS
ENCASED
ENCASES
ENCHAIN
ENCHANT
ENCINAS
ENCLAVE
ENCLOSE
ENCODED
ENCODER
ENCODES
ENCOMIA
ENCORES
ENCRUST
ENCRYPT
INCANTS
INCASED
INCASES
INCENSE
INCEPTS
INCHING
INCIPIT
INCISED
INCISES
INCISOR
INCITED
INCITER
INCITES
INCIVIL
INCLINE
INCLOSE
INCLUDE
INCOMES
INCUDES
UNCAGED
UNCAGES
UNCANNY
UNCASED
UNCASES
UNCHAIN
UNCIALS
UNCIVIL
UNCLASP
UNCLEAN
UNCLEAR
UNCLOAK
UNCLOGS
UNCLOSE
UNCOILS
UNCORKS
UNCOUTH
UNCOVER
UNCRATE
UNCTION
UNCURLS

•N•C•••

ANTCOWS
ENACTED
ENACTOR
GNOCCHI
INOCULA
INSCAPE
KNACKER
KNOCKED
KNOCKER
KNUCKLE
SNACKED
SNACKER
SNICKER
SNOCATS
SNOCONE
UNICORN
UNSCREW

•N••C••

ANARCHY
ANTACID
ENLACED
ENLACES
ENTICED
ENTICER
ENTICES
GNOCCHI
INDICES
INDICIA
INDICTS
INDUCED
INDUCER
INDUCES
INDUCTS
INFECTS
INFOCUS
INJECTS
INKYCAP
INSECTS
INVACUO
KNEECAP
SNITCHY
SNOWCAP
SNOWCAT
UNLACED
UNLACES
UNLOCKS
UNLUCKY
UNPACKS
UNTACKS

•N•••C•

ANTIOCH
DNOTICE
ENFORCE
ENHANCE
ENOUNCE
INDUTCH
INEXACT
INFANCY
INFLECT
INFLICT
INFORCE
INPEACE
INPLACE
INSPECT
INSTOCK
INVOICE
ONTRACK
UNAVOCE
UNBLOCK
UNFROCK
UNHITCH
UNLATCH
UNSTACK
UNSTICK
UNSTUCK

•N••••C

ANAEMIC
ANAHUAC
ANGELIC
ANOSMIC
ENDEMIC
GNOSTIC

••NC•••

BENCHED
BENCHES
BUNCHED
BUNCHES
BUNCOED

CANCANS
CANCELS
CINCHED
CINCHES
CONCAVE
CONCEAL
CONCEDE
CONCEIT
CONCEPT
CONCERN
CONCERT
CONCHES
CONCISE
CONCOCT
CONCORD
CONCURS
DANCERS
DANCING
DUNCISH
FANCIED
FANCIER
FANCIES
FANCIFY
FANCILY
FANCLUB
FENCERS
FENCING
FINCHES
FUNCHAL
HANCOCK
HENCOOP
HONCHOS
HUNCHED
HUNCHES
JUNCOES
KINCHIN
LANCERS
LANCETS
LINCOLN
LUNCHED
LUNCHES
MANCINI
MENCKEN
MINCERS
MINCING
MUNCHED
MUNCHER
MUNCHES
NONCOMS
NUNCIOS
PANCAKE
PANCHAX
PENCILS
PINCERS
PINCHAS
PINCHED
PINCHER
PINCHES
PINCURL
PONCHOS
PUNCHED
PUNCHER
PUNCHES
PUNCHIN
PUNCHUP
PYNCHON
RANCHED
RANCHER
RANCHES
RANCHOS
RANCOUR
SANCTUM
SINCERE
SUNCITY
SYNCHED
SYNCHES
SYNCING
TENCENT
TINCANS
VINCENT
WENCHES
WINCERS
WINCHED
WINCHES
WINCING

••N•C••

ARNICAS
BINOCHE
CONICAL
CYNICAL
FINICKY
HANDCAR
JANACEK
MANACLE
MANXCAT
MENACED
MENACES
MINICAB
MINICAM
MONOCLE
MONOCOT
PANACEA
PANACHE
PANICKY
PANICLE
PENUCHE
PINOCLE
SENECAS
TENACES
TUNICLE

••N••C•

BANNOCK
CANDICE
CANSECO
CONCOCT
CONDUCE
CONDUCT
CONNECT
CONNICK
CONTACT
CONVICT
DUNNOCK
FINANCE
GUNLOCK
HANCOCK
HENPECK
IONESCO
JANNOCK
JONNICK
MANIACS
MANIOCS
MENISCI
MINORCA
MONARCH
PANDECT
PENANCE
PINNACE
RANSACK
RUNBACK
SUNDECK
TENANCY
TENRECS
TINTACK
VANDYCK
VANEYCK

••N•••C

CANONIC
CENTRIC
DYNAMIC
FANATIC
GENERIC
GENETIC
KINETIC
LUNATIC
MANTRIC
MONODIC
PONTIAC
SYNODIC
TONELOC
XANTHIC

•••NC••

ALENCON
BLANCHE
BOUNCED
BOUNCER
BOUNCES
BRONCHI
BRONCOS
CHANCED
CHANCEL
CHANCER
CHANCES
COONCAT
CORNCOB
COUNCIL
CRUNCHY
EVINCED
EVINCES
FIANCEE
FIANCES
FRANCES
FRANCIS
GLANCED
GLANCES
JOUNCED
JOUNCES
LIONCUB
NUANCED
NUANCES
PAUNCHY
POUNCED
POUNCER
POUNCES
PRANCED
PRANCER
PRANCES
PRINCES
QUINCES
SCONCES
SEANCES
SPENCER
STANCES
STENCIL
TRANCES

•••N•C•

BANNOCK
BERNICE
BIONICS
CLINICS
COGNACS
CONNECT
CONNICK
CORNICE
DUNNOCK
ETHNICS
FURNACE
GUANACO
JANNOCK
JONNICK
LOWNECK
OLDNICK
ORINOCO
PHONICS
PICNICS
PINNACE
REENACT
SPINACH
THINICE
VEENECK

•••N••C

FRANTIC
IDENTIC
JEANLUC
LAENNEC
STANNIC
YOUNGMC

••••NC•

ABSENCE
ADJUNCT
ADVANCE
ARDENCY
ASKANCE
AVIANCA
BALANCE
CADENCE
CADENCY
COGENCY
DAVINCI
DECENCY
DEFENCE
DEFUNCT
DURANCE
ENHANCE
ENOUNCE
ERRANCY
ESSENCE
EXTINCT
FAIENCE
FINANCE
FLOUNCE
FLOUNCY
FLUENCY
INFANCY
LATENCY
LICENCE
LUCENCY
OFFENCE
PALANCE
PENANCE
PLIANCY
POTENCY
PUDENCY
RECENCY
REGENCY
ROMANCE
SCIENCE
SCRUNCH
SILENCE
SQUINCH
STAUNCH
TENANCY
TERENCE
TROUNCE
TRUANCY
URGENCY
VACANCY
VALANCE
VALENCE
VALENCY

••••N•C

ACTINIC
ALMANAC
ARSENIC
CANONIC
CHRONIC
DEMONIC
LACONIC
LAENNEC
MASONIC
OCEANIC
ORGANIC
PHRENIC
SARANAC
SELENIC
STANNIC
TITANIC

•••••NC

LIPSYNC
POULENC

N•D••••

NEDDIES
NODDERS
NODDING
NODOUBT
NODSOFF
NODULAR
NODULES
NUDGERS
NUDGING
NUDISTS
NUDNIKS

N••D•••

NEDDIES
NEEDFUL
NEEDHAM
NEEDIER
NEEDILY
NEEDING
NEEDLED
NEEDLES
NERDIER
NEWDEAL
NODDERS
NODDING
NOODLES
NORDICS

N•••D••

NAIADES
NAKEDLY
NAMEDAY
NEVADAN
NEWSDAY
NOBODYS
NOMADIC
NOONDAY
NOTEDLY

N••••D•

NEREIDS
NIMRODS
NITRIDE
NOCANDO
NUCLIDE

N•••••D

NATURED
NAYSAID
NEEDLED
NEGATED
NEIGHED
NESTLED
NETTLED
NIBBLED
NIGGARD
NIGGLED
NOBBLED
NONSKID
NORMAND
NOTATED
NOTCHED
NOTEPAD
NOTICED
NUANCED
NUTATED
NUZZLED

•ND••••

ANDANTE
ANDEANS
ANDIRON
ANDORRA
ANDOVER
ANDREAS
ANDRESS
ANDREWS
ANDROID
ANDSOON
ENDEARS
ENDEDUP
ENDEMIC
ENDGAME
ENDINGS
ENDIVES
ENDLESS
ENDMOST
ENDORSE
ENDOWED
ENDPLAY
ENDRUNS
ENDUING
ENDURED
ENDURES
ENDUROS
ENDUSER
ENDUSES
ENDWAYS
ENDWISE
ENDZONE
INDENTS
INDEPTH
INDEXED
INDEXES
INDIANA
INDIANS
INDICES
INDICIA
INDICTS
INDIGOS
INDITED
INDITES
INDOORS
INDORSE
INDOUBT
INDUCED
INDUCER
INDUCES
INDUCTS
INDULGE
INDUTCH
INDWELL
UNDATED
UNDERDO
UNDERGO
UNDOING
UNDRAPE
UNDRAWN
UNDRESS
UNDYING

•N•D•••

ANADEMS
ANODISE
ANODIZE
ANODYNE
INADAZE
ONADARE
ONADATE
ONADIET
SNIDELY
SNIDEST

•N••D••

ANTEDUP
ENCODED
ENCODER
ENCODES
ENDEDUP
INCUDES
INFIDEL
INSIDER
INSIDES
INVADED
INVADER
INVADES
KNEADED
KNEADER
ONANDON
ONEIDAS
ONORDER
ONSIDES
SNOWDAY
SNOWDON
UNAIDED
UNENDED
UNGODLY
UNLADES

•N•••D•

ANYBODY
ENFOLDS
ENGARDE
ENGIRDS
ENNEADS
INCLUDE
INNARDS
INROADS
INTENDS
INTRUDE
INWARDS
ONWARDS
UNBENDS
UNBINDS
UNDERDO
UNFOLDS
UNGIRDS
UNHANDS
UNHANDY
UNIPODS
UNLOADS
UNREADY
UNWINDS

•N••••D

ANDROID
ANEROID
ANGERED
ANISEED
ANNELID
ANNEXED
ANNOYED
ANTACID
ANYROAD
ENABLED
ENACTED
ENCAGED
ENCASED
ENCODED
ENDOWED
ENDURED
ENGAGED
ENGLAND
ENGLUND
ENISLED
ENJOYED
ENLACED
ENRAGED
ENROBED
ENSILED
ENSKIED
ENSURED
ENTERED
ENTICED
GNARLED
GNARRED
GNASHED
INAWORD
INBOARD
INBOUND
INBREED
INCASED
INCISED
INCITED
INDEXED
INDITED
INDUCED
INFIELD
INFUSED
INHALED
INHERED
INJURED
INSIPID
INSTEAD
INSURED
INTONED
INVADED
INVALID
INVITED
INVOKED
KNEADED
KNEELED
KNEEPAD
KNELLED
KNITTED
KNOBBED
KNOCKED
KNOTTED
KNOUTED
KNURLED
ONBOARD
ONEEYED
ONGUARD
SNACKED
SNAFUED
SNAGGED
SNAPPED
SNARLED
SNEAKED
SNEERED
SNEEZED
SNIFFED
SNIPPED
SNOGGED
SNOOPED
SNOOTED
SNOOZED
SNORTED
SNUBBED
SNUFFED
UNAIDED
UNAIMED
UNAIRED
UNARMED
UNASKED
UNBAKED
UNBOUND
UNBOWED
UNBOXED
UNCAGED
UNCASED
UNDATED
UNENDED
UNFAZED
UNFIXED
UNGLUED
UNHEARD
UNIFIED
UNLACED
UNLIKED
UNLINED
UNLOVED
UNMOVED
UNNAMED
UNOILED
UNPAVED
UNPILED
UNRATED
UNROBED
UNSATED
UNSEWED
UNSOUND
UNTAMED
UNTAPED
UNTRIED
UNTUNED
UNWOUND
UNYOKED
UNZONED

••ND•••

BANDAGE
BANDAID
BANDANA
BANDBOX
BANDIED
BANDIES
BANDING
BANDITO
BANDITS
BANDSAW
BENDERS
BENDIER
BENDIGO
BENDING
BINDERS
BINDERY
BINDING
BINDSUP
BONDAGE
BONDING
BONDMAN
BONDMEN
BUNDLED
BUNDLES
CANDELA
CANDICE
CANDIDA
CANDIDE
CANDIDS
CANDIED
CANDIES
CANDLES
CANDOUR
CINDERS
CINDERY
CONDEMN
CONDIGN
CONDITA
CONDOLE
CONDONE
CONDORS
CONDUCE
CONDUCT
CONDUIT
DANDERS
DANDIER
DANDIES
DANDIFY
DANDLED
DANDLES
DENDRON
FENDERS
FENDING
FINDERS
FINDING
FINDOUT
FONDANT
FONDEST
FONDLED
FONDLES
FONDUES
FUNDING
GANDERS
GENDERS
GONDOLA
GUNDOGS
HANDBAG
HANDCAR
HANDFED
HANDFUL
HANDGUN
HANDIER
HANDILY
HANDING
HANDLED
HANDLER
HANDLES
HANDOFF
HANDOUT
HANDSAW
HANDSET
HANDSIN
HANDSON
HANDSUP
HENDRIX
HINDERS
HUNDRED
KENDALL
KINDEST
KINDLED
KINDLES
KINDRED
LANDAUS
LANDERS
LANDING
LANDSAT
LENDERS
LENDING
LINDENS
LINDIED
LINDIES
LINDSAY
LINDSEY
MANDALA
MANDANS
MANDATE
MANDAYS
MANDELA
MENDERS
MENDING
MENDOZA
MINDERS
MINDFUL
MINDING
MINDSET
MONDALE
MONDAYS
MUNDANE
PANDECT
PANDERS
PANDITS
PANDORA
PENDANT
PENDENT
PENDING
PINDOWN
PONDERS
PUNDITS
RANDALL
RANDIER
RANDOWN
RENDERS
RENDING
RONDEAU
RONDELS
RUNDEEP
RUNDLES
RUNDOWN
SANDALS
SANDBAG
SANDBAR
SANDBOX
SANDERS
SANDFLY
SANDHOG
SANDIER
SANDING
SANDLOT
SANDMAN
SANDMEN
SENDERS
SENDFOR
SENDING
SENDOFF
SENDOUT
SENDSIN
SENDSUP
SENDUPS
SUNDAES
SUNDAYS
SUNDECK
SUNDERS
SUNDEWS
SUNDIAL
SUNDOGS
SUNDOWN
TANDEMS
TENDERS
TENDING
TENDONS
TENDRIL
TENDSTO
TINDERS
TUNDRAS
VANDALS
VANDINE
VANDYCK
VANDYKE
VENDING
VENDORS
WANDERS
WENDELL
WENDERS
WENDING
WENDISH
WINDBAG
WINDERS
WINDIER
WINDILY
WINDING
WINDOWS
WINDROW
WINDSOR
WINDSUP
WINDUPS
WONDERS
ZANDERS

••N•D••

BONEDRY
BONEDUP
DENUDED
DENUDES
DINEDIN
DINEDON
HANGDOG
JANEDOE
JUNKDNA
KINGDOM
LANGDON
LINEDUP
MONODIC
OWNEDUP
PANADAS
QINGDAO
RUNSDRY
SINEDIE
SYNODAL
SYNODIC
TONEDUP
TUNEDIN
TUNEDUP

••N••D•

CANARDS
CANDIDA
CANDIDE
CANDIDS
CONCEDE
CONFIDE
CONOIDS
ENNEADS
HUNYADY
INNARDS
KENNEDY
MANMADE
PENTADS
PONGIDS
RENARDS
SUNGODS
WANTADS

••N•••D

ANNELID
ANNEXED
ANNOYED
AYNRAND
BANDAID
BANDIED
BENCHED
BUNCHED
BUNCOED
BUNDLED
BUNGLED
BUNKBED
BUNKOED
CANDIED
CENTRED
CINCHED
CONCORD
CONGAED
CONRIED
CONTEND
DANDLED
DANGLED
DENOTED
DENUDED
DONATED
FANCIED
FINLAND
FONDLED
GANGLED
GENTLED
HANDFED
HANDLED
HENNAED
HONEYED
HONORED
HUNCHED
HUNDRED
IBNSAUD
IGNITED
IGNORED
IONISED
IONIZED
JANGLED
JINGLED
KINDLED
KINDRED
LANFORD
LANGUID
LANYARD
LINDIED
LINSEED
LUNCHED
MANAGED
MANFRED
MANGLED
MANHOOD
MANKIND
MANSARD
MANTLED
MENACED
MINGLED
MINORED
MINUEND
MONEYED
MONTAND
MUNCHED
NONSKID
PANELED
PINCHED
PINHEAD
PONIARD
PUNCHED
RANCHED
RANKLED
RENAMED
RENEGED
RENEWED
RENOTED
SANFORD
SINGLED
SUNMAID
SYNCHED
TANGLED
TANGOED
TANKARD
TENFOLD
TENONED
TENURED
TINGLED
TINKLED
TONGUED
UNNAMED
WANGLED
WENTBAD
WINCHED
WINERED
WINKLED

•••ND••

ABANDON
AGENDAS
AMENDED
ASUNDER
BLANDER
BLANDLY
BLENDED
BLENDER
BLINDED
BLINDER
BLINDLY
BLONDER
BLONDES
BLONDIE
BLUNDER
BOUNDED
BOUNDER
BOUNDUP
BRANDED
BRANDER
BRANDON
BRENDAN
BRINDLE
BYANDBY
CORNDOG
DIRNDLS
DWINDLE
EMENDED
EMENDER
EVANDER
FOUNDED
FOUNDER
FOUNDRY
GOUNDER
GRANDAM
GRANDEE
GRANDER
GRANDLY
GRANDMA
GRANDPA
GRENDEL
GRINDER
HOUNDED
HYUNDAI
JOHNDOE
JOINDER
LAUNDER
LAUNDRY
LEANDER
MAUNDER
MEANDER
MOONDOG
MOUNDED
NOONDAY

ONANDON
PLUNDER
POUNDED
POUNDER
PSANDQS
ROUNDED
ROUNDER
ROUNDLY
ROUNDON
ROUNDUP
RUANDAN
RWANDAN
SCANDAL
SCENDED
SHINDIG
SLANDER
SLENDER
SOANDSO
SOUNDED
SOUNDER
SOUNDLY
SPANDEX
SPENDER
SPINDLE
SPINDLY
SPINDRY
SPONDEE
STANDBY
STANDEE
STANDIN
STANDON
STANDUP
SWINDLE
THUNDER
TRENDED
TRUNDLE
UGANDAN
UNENDED
UPENDED
WOUNDED
WOUNDUP
WYANDOT

•••N•D•

GRANADA
GRENADA
GRENADE
HYMNODY
KENNEDY
LEONIDS
MAENADS
OCANADA
TORNADO

•••N••D

AMENDED
AVENGED
BAGNOLD
BARNARD
BERNARD
BLANKED
BLENDED
BLINDED
BLINKED
BLUNTED
BOUNCED
BOUNDED
BRANDED
BRONZED
CHANCED
CHANGED
CHANTED
CHINKED
CHINNED
CLANGED
CLANKED
CLINKED
CLUNKED
CORNFED
COUNTED
CRANKED
CRINGED
CRINOID
DAUNTED
EMENDED
EVINCED
FAINTED
FEINTED
FLANKED
FLENSED
FLUNKED
FOUNDED
FRANKED
FRINGED
FRONTED
GLANCED
GLINTED
GRANTED
GRINNED
GRUNTED
HAUNTED
HENNAED
HOUNDED
JAUNTED
JOINTED
JOUNCED
LEONARD
LOUNGED
MAYNARD
MOUNDED
MOUNTED
NUANCED
OPENEND
PAINTED
PLANKED
PLANNED
PLANTED
PLINKED
PLUNGED
PLUNKED
POINTED
POUNCED
POUNDED
PRANCED
PRANGED
PRANKED
PRINKED
PRINTED
PRONGED
REINKED
REYNARD
ROUNDED
SAINTED
SCANNED
SCANTED
SCENDED
SCENTED
SHANKED
SHINNED
SHUNNED
SHUNTED
SKANKED
SKINNED
SKUNKED
SLANTED
SLINKED
SOUNDED
SPANKED
SPANNED
SPONGED
STINTED
STUNNED
STUNTED
SWANKED
TAINTED
TAUNTED
THANKED
THINNED
TRENDED
TWANGED
TWINBED
TWINGED
TWINNED
UNENDED
UPENDED
VAUNTED
WHANGED
WOUNDED
WRONGED

••••ND•

ABOUNDS
ADDENDA
ADDENDS
ALBUNDY
ALLENDE
ALMONDS
APPENDS
ASCENDS
ATTENDS
AUGENDS
BELINDA
CALENDS
DEFENDS
DEMANDS
DEPENDS
EFFENDI
ERRANDS
EXPANDS
EXPENDS
EXTENDS
FAGENDS
FRIENDS
GERUNDS
GIRONDE
GROUNDS
IMPENDS
INTENDS
ISLANDS
LEGENDS
LEMONDE
LIGANDS
MELINDA
MIRANDA
NOCANDO
OBTUNDS
OFFENDS
ORGANDY
ORLANDO
ORMANDY
REBENDS
REBINDS
REFUNDS
REMANDS
REMENDS
REMINDS
RESANDS
RESENDS
REWINDS
RIBANDS
ROTUNDA
SECONDS
STRANDS
TAGENDS
UNBENDS
UNBINDS
UNHANDS
UNHANDY
UNWINDS
UPLANDS
VERANDA
VIVENDI
WCHANDY
YAOUNDE

••••N•D

ADORNED
ALIGNED
APRONED
ATTUNED
BRAINED
BROWNED
BYLINED
CHAINED
CHINNED
CHURNED
CLEANED
CLOWNED
COZENED
CROONED
CROWNED
DEBONED
DEFINED
DEIGNED
DEPONED
DIVINED
DIZENED
DRAINED
DROWNED
FEIGNED
FROWNED
GLEANED
GRAINED
GREENED
GRINNED
GROANED
HOMINID
INTONED
LEARNED
LIKENED
LIVENED
MOURNED
OCEANID
PLANNED
PREENED
RAVENED
RECANED
REFINED
REIGNED
RELINED
REPINED
RETUNED
REZONED
RIPENED
SCANNED
SCORNED
SHINNED
SHUNNED
SKINNED
SPANNED
SPAWNED
SPOONED
SPURNED
STAINED
STUNNED
SWOONED
TALONED
TENONED
THINNED
TOKENED
TRAINED
TWINNED
UNLINED
UNTUNED
UNZONED
WAKENED
WIDENED
WIZENED
YEARNED

•••••ND

ABSCOND
AGROUND
AMERIND
ARMBAND
ASHLAND
ASTOUND
AYNRAND
BACKEND
BARTEND
BIGBAND
BIGBEND
BOOKEND
BRIGAND
COMMAND
COMMEND
CONTEND
COPLAND
COWHAND
DABHAND
DEADEND
DEEPEND
DESCEND
DESMOND
DIAMOND
DISBAND
DISTEND
EASTEND
ENGLAND
ENGLUND
EXPOUND
FINLAND
FORFEND
GARLAND
GODSEND
GOROUND
GOTLAND
HAMMOND
HATBAND
HIGHEND
HOLLAND
HUSBAND
ICELAND
ILLWIND
IMPOUND
INBOUND
IRELAND
JUGBAND
JUTLAND
LAPLAND
LEGRAND
LOWLAND
MANKIND
MIDLAND
MILLAND
MILLEND
MINUEND
MONTAND
NORMAND
OAKLAND
OFFHAND
OLDHAND
OPENEND
OPERAND
OROTUND
OUTLAND
PORTEND
PREBEND
PRETEND
RAYMOND
REAREND
REBOUND
REDOUND
RESCIND
RESOUND
RESPOND
REWOUND
ROSTAND
SIGMUND
STIPEND
SUBTEND
SUSPEND
TAILEND
TOYLAND
UNBOUND
UNSOUND
UNWOUND
WEEKEND
WELLAND
WESTEND
WETLAND
YEAREND
ZEALAND

NE•••••

NEAREST
NEARING
NEARYOU
NEATENS
NEATEST
NEBBISH
NEBULAE
NEBULAR
NEBULAS
NECKERS
NECKING
NECKTIE
NECTARS
NEDDIES
NEEDFUL
NEEDHAM
NEEDIER
NEEDILY
NEEDING
NEEDLED
NEEDLES
NEGATED
NEGATER
NEGATES
NEGATOR
NEGLECT
NEIGHED
NEITHER
NELSONS
NEMEROV
NEMESES
NEMESIS
NEOLITH
NEONATE
NEPALIS
NEPHEWS
NEPTUNE
NERDIER
NEREIDS
NERVIER
NERVILY
NERVOUS
NESCAFE
NESMITH
NESTEGG
NESTERS
NESTING
NESTLED
NESTLER
NESTLES
NETIZEN
NETLIKE
NETSUKE
NETSURF
NETTING
NETTLED
NETTLES
NETWORK
NEURONE
NEURONS
NEUTRAL
NEUTRON
NEVADAN
NEVILLE
NEWAGER
NEWBERY
NEWBORN
NEWDEAL
NEWGATE
NEWHART
NEWLEFT
NEWLOOK
NEWMATH
NEWMOON
NEWMOWN
NEWNESS
NEWPORT
NEWSBOY
NEWSDAY
NEWSIER
NEWSIES
NEWSMAN
NEWSMEN
NEWTONS
NEWTOWN
NEWWAVE
NEWYEAR
NEWYORK
NEXUSES

N•E••••

NEEDFUL
NEEDHAM
NEEDIER
NEEDILY
NEEDING
NEEDLED
NEEDLES
NIEBUHR
NIELSEN
NOETICS

N••E•••

NACELLE
NAKEDLY
NAMEDAY
NAMETAG
NANETTE
NEMEROV
NEMESES
NEMESIS
NEREIDS
NIGERIA
NINEPIN
NINEVEH
NORELCO
NOSEBAG
NOSEEUM
NOSEGAY
NOSEJOB
NOSEOUT
NOTEDLY
NOTEPAD
NOVELLA
NOVELLE
NOVELTY
NOVENAS
NUMERAL
NUMERIC
NUREYEV

N•••E••

NABBERS
NAILERS
NAIVELY
NAIVETE
NAIVETY
NANKEEN
NAPLESS
NAPPERS
NASCENT
NATTERS
NCWYETH
NEAREST
NEATENS
NEATEST
NECKERS
NEGLECT
NEPHEWS
NESTEGG
NESTERS
NEWBERY
NEWDEAL
NEWLEFT
NEWNESS
NEWYEAR
NICKELS
NICKERS
NIGHEST
NIMIETY
NIPPERS
NOBLEST
NODDERS
NONSELF
NONZERO
NORBERT
NORIEGA
NOSEEUM
NOSHERS
NOSIEST
NOSWEAT
NOTWELL
NOUVEAU
NOWHERE
NOXZEMA
NUCLEAR
NUCLEIC
NUCLEON
NUCLEUS
NUDGERS
NUGGETS
NUMBERS
NUMBEST
NUNNERY
NURSERS
NURSERY
NUTLETS
NUTMEAT
NUTMEGS
NUTTERS

N••••E•

NAGGIER
NAIADES
NAILSET
NANKEEN
NANNIES
NAPPIES
NARTHEX
NASTIER
NATCHEZ
NATIVES
NATTIER
NATURED
NATURES
NAVVIES
NEDDIES
NEEDIER
NEEDLED
NEEDLES
NEGATED
NEGATER
NEGATES
NEIGHED
NEITHER
NEMESES
NERDIER
NERVIER
NESTLED
NESTLER
NESTLES
NETIZEN
NETTLED
NETTLES
NEWAGER
NEWSIER
NEWSIES
NEWSMEN
NEXUSES
NIBBLED
NIBBLER
NIBBLES
NIELSEN
NIFTIER
NIGGLED
NIGGLES
NIMBLER
NINEVEH
NINNIES
NIPPIER
NITTIER
NOBBIER
NOBBLED
NOBBLER
NOBBLES
NODULES
NOGALES
NOISIER
NOMINEE
NONAGES
NONUSER
NOODLES
NORTHER
NOTATED
NOTATES
NOTCHED
NOTCHES
NOTICED
NOTICES
NOVICES
NOZZLES
NUANCED
NUANCES
NUBBIER
NUBBLES
NUREYEV
NUTATED
NUTATES
NUTSIER
NUTTIER
NUZZLED
NUZZLER
NUZZLES

N•••••E

NACELLE
NAIVETE
NANETTE
NAPTIME
NARRATE
NASTASE
NATALIE
NAVARRE
NEBULAE
NECKTIE
NEONATE
NEPTUNE
NESCAFE
NETLIKE
NETSUKE
NEURONE
NEVILLE
NEWGATE
NEWWAVE
NIBLIKE
NIGHTIE
NITRATE
NITRIDE
NITRITE
NOISOME
NOMINEE
NOTABLE
NOTSURE
NOTTRUE
NOVELLE
NOWHERE
NUCLIDE
NUNLIKE
NURTURE
NUTLIKE

•NE••••

ANELING
ANEMONE
ANEROID
ENEMIES
INEPTLY
INERROR
INERTIA
INERTLY
INEXACT
KNEADED
KNEADER
KNEECAP
KNEEING
KNEELED
KNEELER
KNEEPAD
KNEESUP
KNELLED
KNESSET
ONEEYED
ONEIDAS
ONEIRON
ONELANE
ONENESS
ONENOTE
ONEROUS
ONESELF
ONESHOT
ONESTAR
ONESTEP
ONETIME
SNEAKED
SNEAKER
SNEAKIN
SNEERAT
SNEERED
SNEERER
SNEEZED
SNEEZER
SNEEZES
SNELLEN
UNEARTH
UNEATEN
UNENDED
UNEQUAL

•N•E•••

ANAEMIA
ANAEMIC
ANDEANS
ANGELES
ANGELIC
ANGELOU
ANGELUS
ANGERED
ANNEALS
ANNELID
ANNETTE
ANNEXED
ANNEXES
ANTEDUP
ANTEING
ANTENNA
ANTESUP
ENDEARS
ENDEDUP
ENDEMIC
ENNEADS
ENTEBBE
ENTENTE
ENTERED
ENTERON
ENVELOP
INCENSE
INCEPTS
INDENTS
INDEPTH
INDEXED
INDEXES
INFECTS
INFERNO
INFESTS
INGEMAR
INGENUE
INGESTS
INHERED
INHERES
INHERIT
INJECTS
INPEACE
INPETTO
INSEAMS
INSECTS
INSERTS
INTEARS
INTEGER
INTEGRA
INTENDS
INTENSE
INTENTS
INTERIM
INTERNS
INTERSE
INVEIGH
INVENTS
INVERSE
INVERTS
INVESTS
KNEECAP
KNEEING
KNEELED
KNEELER
KNEEPAD
KNEESUP
KNIEVEL
ONEEYED
ONLEAVE
ONSERVE
SNEERAT
SNEERED
SNEERER
SNEEZED
SNEEZER
SNEEZES
UNBENDS
UNDERDO
UNDERGO
UNHEARD
UNKEMPT
UNLEARN
UNLEASH
UNNERVE
UNREADY
UNREELS
UNSEALS
UNSEATS
UNSEWED
UNVEILS
UNWEAVE

•N••E••

ANADEMS
ANAHEIM
ANAPEST
ANCIENT
ANDREAS
ANDRESS
ANDREWS
ANGLERS
ANISEED
ANKLETS
ANSWERS
ANTAEUS
ANTBEAR
ANTHEMS
ANTHERS
ANTLERS
ANTWERP
ANXIETY
ENAMELS
ENDLESS
ENTREAT
ENTREES
ENVIERS
GNAWERS
INAHEAP
INAMESS
INANELY
INANEST
INAWEOF
INBREED
INDWELL
INFIELD
INFLECT
INGRESS
INKIEST
INKLESS
INKWELL
INNLESS
INQUEST
INSPECT
INSTEAD
INSTEPS
KNAVERY
ONAGERS
ONATEAR
ONENESS
ONESELF
ONTHEGO
ONTHEQT
SNIDELY
SNIDEST
SNIPEAT
SNIPERS
SNIVELS
SNORERS
UNBLEST
UNCLEAN
UNCLEAR
UNDRESS
UNGUENT
UNITERS
UNREELS
UNSPENT
UNSWEPT

•N•••E•

ANDOVER
ANGELES
ANGERED
ANGRIER
ANISEED
ANNABEL
ANNALEE
ANNEXED
ANNEXES
ANNOYED
ANOMIES
ANOTHER
ANTARES
ANTIBES
ANTIGEN
ANTSIER
ANYONES
CNTOWER
ENABLED
ENABLES
ENACTED
ENCAGED
ENCAGES
ENCASED
ENCASES
ENCODED
ENCODER
ENCODES
ENCORES
ENDIVES
ENDOWED
ENDURED
ENDURES
ENDUSER
ENDUSES
ENEMIES
ENGAGED
ENGAGES
ENGINES
ENISLED
ENISLES
ENJOYED
ENLACED
ENLACES
ENLIVEN
ENRAGED
ENRAGES
ENROBED
ENROBES
ENSILED
ENSILES
ENSKIED
ENSKIES
ENSURED
ENSURES
ENTERED
ENTICED
ENTICER
ENTICES
ENTREES
ENTRIES
ENZYMES
FNUMBER
GNARLED
GNARRED
GNASHED
GNASHES
INAPTER
INASTEW
INBOXES
INBREED
INBRIEF
INCASED
INCASES
INCISED
INCISES
INCITED
INCITER
INCITES
INCOMES
INCUDES
INDEXED
INDEXES
INDICES
INDITED
INDITES
INDUCED
INDUCER
INDUCES
INFIDEL
INFUSED
INFUSES
INHALED
INHALER
INHALES
INHERED
INHERES
INJOKES
INJURED
INJURES
INMATES
INPOWER
INSIDER
INSIDES
INSOLES
INSURED
INSURER
INSURES
INTAKES
INTEGER
INTONED
INTONER

INTONES
INVADED
INVADER
INVADES
INVITED
INVITES
INVOKED
INVOKER
INVOKES
KNACKER
KNEADED
KNEADER
KNEELED
KNEELER
KNELLED
KNESSET
KNIEVEL
KNISHES
KNITTED
KNITTER
KNOBBED
KNOCKED
KNOCKER
KNOTTED
KNOUTED
KNURLED
ONADIET
ONEEYED
ONESTEP
ONORDER
ONSIDES
SNACKED
SNACKER
SNAFUED
SNAGGED
SNAKIER
SNAPPED
SNAPPER
SNARLED
SNEAKED
SNEAKER
SNEERED
SNEERER
SNEEZED
SNEEZER
SNEEZES
SNELLEN
SNICKER
SNIFFED
SNIFFER
SNIFTER
SNIGGER
SNIGLET
SNIPPED
SNIPPET
SNOGGED
SNOOKER
SNOOPED
SNOOPER
SNOOTED
SNOOZED
SNOOZES
SNORKEL
SNORTED
SNORTER
SNOWIER
SNOWMEN
SNOWPEA
SNUBBED
SNUFFED
SNUFFER
SNUGGER
UNAIDED
UNAIMED
UNAIRED
UNARMED
UNASKED
UNBAKED
UNBOWED
UNBOXED
UNBOXES
UNCAGED
UNCAGES
UNCASED
UNCASES
UNCOVER
UNDATED
UNEATEN
UNENDED
UNFAZED
UNFIXED
UNGLUED
UNIFIED
UNIFIER
UNIFIES
UNITIES
UNLACED
UNLACES
UNLADES
UNLIKED
UNLINED
UNLOVED
UNMAKES
UNMOVED
UNNAMED
UNOILED
UNPAVED
UNPILED
UNPILES
UNRATED
UNRAVEL
UNROBED
UNROBES
UNSATED
UNSCREW
UNSEWED
UNTAMED
UNTAPED
UNTRIED
UNTUNED
UNTUNES
UNWISER
UNWOVEN
UNYOKED
UNYOKES
UNZONED

•N••••E

ANALYSE
ANALYZE
ANATOLE
ANDANTE
ANEMONE
ANILINE
ANIMATE
ANNALEE
ANNETTE
ANODISE
ANODIZE
ANODYNE
ANTIQUE
ANTLIKE
ANTOINE
ANYMORE
ANYTIME
DNOTICE
ENCLAVE
ENCLOSE
ENDGAME
ENDORSE
ENDWISE
ENDZONE
ENFORCE
ENGARDE
ENGORGE
ENGRAVE
ENHANCE
ENLARGE
ENMASSE
ENNOBLE
ENOUNCE
ENPLANE
ENQUIRE
ENROUTE
ENSLAVE
ENSNARE
ENSUITE
ENTEBBE
ENTENTE
ENTHUSE
ENTITLE
ENTWINE
INADAZE
INCENSE
INCLINE
INCLOSE
INCLUDE
INDORSE
INDULGE
INFLAME
INFLATE
INFORCE
INGENUE
INGRATE
INHASTE
INHOUSE
INKLIKE
INPEACE
INPHASE
INPLACE
INQUIRE
INSCAPE
INSHAPE
INSPIRE
INSTATE
INSTORE
INSTYLE
INTENSE
INTERSE
INTRUDE
INUTILE
INVERSE
INVOGUE
INVOICE
INVOLVE
KNUCKLE
ONADARE
ONADATE
ONELANE
ONENOTE
ONETIME
ONLEAVE
ONSERVE
ONSHORE
ONSTAGE
SNAFFLE
SNAPPLE
SNIFFLE
SNIGGLE
SNOCONE
SNUFFLE
SNUGGLE
UNALIKE
UNAVOCE
UNAWARE
UNCLOSE
UNCRATE
UNDRAPE
UNHORSE
UNITIVE
UNLOOSE
UNNERVE
UNQUOTE
UNWEAVE

••NE•••

AMNESIA
AMNESTY
ANNEALS
ANNELID
ANNETTE
ANNEXED
ANNEXES
BANEFUL
BENEATH
BENEFIT
BENELUX
BONEASH
BONEDRY
BONEDUP
BONESET
BONESUP
CINEMAS
CINEMAX
DANELAW
DENEUVE
DINEDIN
DINEDON
DINESEN
DINESIN
DINESON
DINETTE
DONEFOR
DONEGAL
ENNEADS
ERNESTO
FINEART
FINESSE
GENERAL
GENERIC
GENERIS
GENESEE
GENESES
GENESIS
GENETIC
GONERIL
HONESTY
HONEYED
IGNEOUS
IONESCO
JANEDOE
JANEWAY
JONESES
JUNEBUG
KINEMAS
KINETIC
LINEAGE
LINEATE
LINEDUP
LINEMAN
LINEMEN
LINESUP
LINEUPS
MANEGES
MINERAL
MINERVA
MONEYED
NANETTE
NINEPIN
NINEVEH
ORNETTE
OWNEDUP
PANELED
PINEFOR
PINENUT
PINESAP
PINETAR
PINETUM
RENEGED
RENEGER
RENEGES
RENEGUE
RENEWAL
RENEWED
RENEWER
SENECAS
SENEGAL
SINEDIE
SYNERGY
TINEARS
TONEARM
TONEDUP
TONELOC
TONEROW
TONESUP
TUNEDIN
TUNEDUP
TUNEFUL
TUNEOUT
TUNESIN
TUNESUP
TUNEUPS
UNNERVE
VANESSA
VANEYCK
VENEERS
VINEGAR
WINEBAR
WINERED
WINESAP
WYNETTE

••N•E••

AWNLESS
BANKERS
BANNERS
BANTERS
BENDERS
BENNETT
BENZENE
BINDERS
BINDERY
BONIEST
BONKERS
BONNETS
BUNGEES
BUNKERS
CANCELS
CANDELA
CANIEST
CANKERS
CANNERS
CANNERY
CANSECO
CANTEEN
CANTERS
CENSERS
CENTERS
CINDERS
CINDERY
CONCEAL
CONCEDE
CONCEIT
CONCEPT
CONCERN
CONCERT
CONDEMN
CONFERS
CONFESS
CONGEAL
CONGERS
CONGEST
CONKERS
CONNECT
CONNERY
CONSENT
CONTEMN
CONTEND
CONTENT
CONTEST
CONTEXT
CONVENE
CONVENT
CONVERT
CONVEYS
DANCERS
DANDERS
DANGERS
DANIELS
DANKEST
DANSEUR
DENIERS
DENNEHY
DENSELY
DENSEST
DINNERS
DONKEYS
DUNGEON
DUNKERS
FANBELT
FANJETS
FENCERS
FENDERS
FINDERS
FINGERS
FONDEST
FONTEYN
FUNFEST
FUNNELS
GANDERS
GANGERS
GANNETS
GANNETT
GENDERS
GENOESE
GENTEEL
GINGERS
GINGERY
GINSENG
GUNLESS
GUNNELS
GUNNERS
GUNNERY
HANGERS
HANKERS
HENNERY
HENPECK
HINDERS
HONKERS
HUNGERS
HUNKERS
HUNTERS
INNLESS
JENNETS
JUNKERS
JUNKETS
KENNEDY
KENNELS
KENNETH
KINDEST
KINLESS
LANCERS
LANCETS
LANDERS
LANKEST
LANTERN
LENDERS
LENIENT
LINDENS
LINGERS
LINIEST
LINKERS
LINNETS
LINSEED
LINTELS
LONGEST
LUNGEAT
LUNKERS
MANDELA
MANGERS
MANLESS
MANNERS
MANTELS
MANYEAR
MENDERS
MINCERS
MINDERS
MINTERS
MINUEND
MINUETS
MONGERS
MONKEES
MONKEYS
MONTEGO
MONTERO
MYNHEER
NANKEEN
NONSELF
NONZERO
NUNNERY
PANDECT
PANDERS
PANNERS
PANZERS
PENDENT
PENNERS
PENSEES
PINCERS
PINHEAD
PINIEST
PINKEST
PINLESS
PINNERS
PONDERS
PONGEES
PUNGENT
PUNIEST
PUNKERS
PUNLESS
PUNNETS
PUNTERS
RANGERS
RANKERS
RANKEST
RANTERS
RENDERS
RENTERS
RINGERS
RONDEAU
RONDELS
RUNDEEP
RUNLETS
RUNNELS
RUNNERS
SANDERS
SANREMO
SENDERS
SENNETT
SINCERE
SINGERS
SINKERS
SINLESS
SINNERS
SONLESS
SONNETS
SUNBEAM
SUNBELT
SUNDECK
SUNDERS
SUNDEWS
SUNLESS
SUNSETS
TANDEMS
TANGELO
TANGENT
TANGERE
TANKERS
TANNERS
TANNERY
TANNEST
TENCENT
TENDERS
TENNERS
TENRECS
TENSELY
TENSEST
TENSEUP
TENTERS
TINDERS
TINIEST
TINKERS
TINNERS
TINSELS
TINTERN
TINTERS
TONIEST
TONNEAU
TUNNELS
VENEERS
VENTERS
VINCENT
VINIEST
WANDERS
WANIEST
WANNESS
WANNEST
WENDELL
WENDERS
WINCERS
WINDERS
WINGERS
WINIEST
WINKERS
WINNERS
WINTERS
WINTERY
WONDERS
YANKEES
YONKERS
ZANDERS
ZANIEST
ZINGERS
ZONKERS

••N••E•

AGNATES
AGNOMEN
ANNABEL
ANNALEE
ANNEXED
ANNEXES
ANNOYED
AUNTIES
BANDIED
BANDIES
BANGLES
BANJOES
BANQUET
BANSHEE
BENCHED
BENCHES
BENDIER
BENTLEY
BENTSEN
BINGOES
BONDMEN
BONESET
BONGOES
BONNIER
BONUSES
BUNCHED
BUNCHES
BUNCOED
BUNDLED
BUNDLES
BUNGEES
BUNGLED
BUNGLER
BUNGLES
BUNKBED
BUNKOED
BUNNIES
CANAPES
CANDIED
CANDIES
CANDLES
CANINES
CANNIER
CANTEEN
CANTLES
CENTRED
CENTRES
CINCHED
CINCHES
CONCHES
CONGAED
CONIFER
CONQUER
CONRIED
CONURES
DANDIER
DANDIES
DANDLED
DANDLES
DANGLED
DANGLER
DANGLES
DENIZEN
DENOTED
DENOTES
DENUDED
DENUDES
DINESEN
DINGIER
DINGLES
DINGOES
DINKIER
DINKIES
DONATED
DONATES
DONGLES
FANCIED
FANCIER
FANCIES
FENNIER
FINALES
FINCHES
FINNIER
FONDLED
FONDLES
FONDUES
FUNGOES
FUNKIER
FUNNIER
FUNNIES
GANGLED
GANTLET
GENESEE
GENESES
GENOMES
GENTEEL
GENTLED
GENTLER
GENTLES
GUNKIER
GUNNIES
GUNTHER
HANDFED
HANDIER
HANDLED
HANDLER
HANDLES
HANDSET
HANGMEN
HANGTEN
HANKIES
HANOVER
HENNAED
HINNIES
HONEYED
HONORED
HONOREE
HONORER
HUNCHED
HUNCHES
HUNDRED
HUNKIER
HUNTLEY
IGNITED
IGNITER
IGNITES
IGNORED
IGNORER
IGNORES
IONISED
IONISES
IONIZED
IONIZER
IONIZES
JANACEK
JANGLED
JANGLES
JANSSEN
JANVIER
JENNIES
JINGLED
JINGLES
JINGOES
JONESES
JUNCOES
JUNGLES
JUNIPER
JUNKIER
JUNKIES
KINDLED
KINDLES
KINDRED
KINKIER
KINSMEN
LANGLEY
LANKIER
LINAGES
LINDIED
LINDIES
LINDSEY
LINEMEN
LINGOES
LINSEED
LINTIER
LONGIES
LONGUES
LUNCHED
LUNCHES
MANAGED
MANAGER
MANAGES
MANATEE
MANEGES
MANFRED
MANGIER
MANGLED
MANGLES
MANGOES
MANLIER
MANTLED
MANTLES
MANXMEN
MENACED
MENACES
MENAGES
MENCKEN
MENZIES
MINARET
MINDSET
MINGIER
MINGLED
MINGLER
MINGLES
MINIVER
MINORED
MINTIER
MINUSES
MINUTES
MONEYED
MONGREL
MONIKER
MONKEES
MONOMER
MONSTER
MUNCHED
MUNCHER
MUNCHES
MYNHEER
NANKEEN
NANNIES
NINEVEH
NINNIES
NONAGES
NONUSER
PANACEA
PANELED
PANNIER
PANSIES
PANTHER
PENATES
PENNIES
PENSEES
PINCHED
PINCHER
PINCHES
PINKIES
PINONES
PONGEES
PUNCHED
PUNCHER
PUNCHES
PUNKIER
PUNKIES
PUNNIER
PUNSTER
PUNTIES
RANCHED
RANCHER
RANCHES
RANDIER
RANGIER
RANKLED
RANKLES
RANOVER
RENAMED
RENAMES
RENEGED
RENEGER
RENEGES
RENEWED
RENEWER
RENOTED
RENOTES
RINGLET
RONTGEN
RUNDEEP
RUNDLES
RUNNIER
RUNOVER
RUNTIER
SANDIER
SANDMEN
SANIBEL
SENATES
SENORES
SINGLED
SINGLES
SINUSES
SUNDAES
SUNNIER
SYNCHED
SYNCHES
SYNFUEL
TANAGER
TANGIER
TANGLED
TANGLES
TANGOED
TANSIES
TENACES
TENNIEL
TENONED
TENURED
TENURES
TINGLED
TINGLES
TINKLED
TINKLES
TINNIER
TONGUED
TONGUES
TUNNIES
UNNAMED
VINTNER
WANGLED
WANGLER
WANGLES
WENCHES
WINCHED
WINCHES
WINDIER
WINERED
WINFREY
WINKLED
WINKLER
WINKLES
WONKIER
YANKEES
ZINGIER

••N•••E

ANNALEE
ANNETTE
BANDAGE
BANSHEE
BENZENE
BINOCHE
BONDAGE
BONFIRE
CANDICE
CANDIDE
CANZONE
CENSURE
CENTIME
CONCAVE
CONCEDE
CONCISE
CONDOLE
CONDONE
CONDUCE
CONFIDE
CONFINE
CONFUSE
CONFUTE
CONGAME
CONJURE
CONNIVE
CONNOTE
CONSOLE
CONSUME
CONTUSE
CONVENE
CONVOKE
DENEUVE
DENTATE
DENTINE
DENTURE
DINETTE
DONAHUE
DONJOSE
ENNOBLE
FANFARE
FANLIKE
FANZINE
FINAGLE
FINANCE
FINESSE
FINLIKE
GENESEE
GENOESE
GENTILE
GENUINE
GUNFIRE
GUNWALE
HENBANE
HENLIKE
HONOREE
HUNLIKE
IGNOBLE
JANEDOE
LINEAGE
LINEATE
LINKAGE
MANACLE
MANATEE
MANDATE
MANHOLE
MANIPLE
MANLIKE
MANMADE
MINABLE
MONDALE
MONIQUE
MONOCLE
MONTAGE
MONTANE
MUNDANE
NANETTE
NUNLIKE
ORNETTE
PANACHE
PANCAKE
PANICLE
PANPIPE
PANURGE
PENANCE
PENLIKE
PENNAME
PENNATE
PENSIVE
PENUCHE
PINHOLE
PINNACE
PINNATE
PINOCLE
PINWALE
PONTINE
RANLATE
RENEGUE
RUNHOME
RUNLATE
SANJOSE
SANTAFE
SENSATE
SINCERE
SINEDIE
SINKAGE
SINLIKE
SONLIKE
SUNLIKE
SUNRISE
SYNAPSE
TANGERE
TANLINE
TENABLE
TENSILE
TENSIVE
TINLIKE
TINTYPE
TINWARE
TONNAGE
TONSURE
TONTINE
TUNICLE
UNNERVE
URNLIKE
VANDINE
VANDYKE
VANTAGE
VENTURE
VINTAGE

WANNABE
WENTAPE
WINSOME
WYNETTE
YANGTZE

•••NE••

APTNESS
BADNESS
BANNERS
BARNEYS
BEANERY
BENNETT
BERNESE
BIGNESS
BONNETS
BORNEUP
BRUNETS
BURNERS
BURNETT
CANNERS
CANNERY
CARNERA
CARNETS
CHINESE
COINERS
CONNECT
CONNERY
CORNEAL
CORNEAS
CORNELL
CORNERS
CORNETS
COYNESS
CRENELS
CYGNETS
DARNERS
DEANERY
DENNEHY
DIMNESS
DINNERS
DOWNERS
DRONERS
DRYNESS
EARNERS
EARNEST
EMINENT
EVENEST
FATNESS
FAWNERS
FITNESS
FLANEUR
FLYNETS
FRENEAU
FUNNELS
GAINERS
GANNETS
GANNETT
GARNERS
GARNETS
GUINEAS
GUNNELS
GUNNERS
GUNNERY
GURNEYS
GWYNETH
HARNESS
HENNERY
HIPNESS
HORNETS
HOTNESS
ICINESS
ILLNESS
INANELY
INANEST
IPANEMA
IRONERS
JENNETS
JITNEYS
JOINERS
JOINERY
KEENERS
KEENEST
KENNEDY
KENNELS
KENNETH
KERNELS
KIDNEYS
LAXNESS
LEANERS
LEANEST
LIENEES
LIMNERS
LINNETS
LIONESS
LIONETS
LOANERS
LOONEYS
LOWNECK
LOWNESS
MADNESS
MAGNETO
MAGNETS
MANNERS
MEANEST
MOANERS
NEWNESS
NUNNERY
ODDNESS
OLDNESS
OLDNEWS
ONENESS
OPENEND
OPENERS
OPINERS
PANNERS
PATNESS
PAWNEES
PAWNERS
PENNERS
PHINEAS
PHONEME
PHONEYS
PINNERS
PIONEER
PLANERS
PLANETS
PRONELY
PRUNERS
PUNNETS
RAWNESS
REDNESS
ROMNEYS
RUINERS
RUNNELS
RUNNERS
SADNESS
SCENERY
SEINERS
SENNETT
SHINERS
SHYNESS
SIGNEES
SIGNERS
SIGNETS
SINNERS
SLYNESS
SONNETS
SOONERS
SOONEST
SPINELS
SPINETS
STONERS
TANNERS
TANNERY
TANNEST
TEENERS
TENNERS
TINNERS
TONNEAU
TOWNERS
TUNNELS
TURNERS
TURNERY
VAINEST
VEENECK
WANNESS
WANNEST
WETNESS
WHINERS
WIENERS
WINNERS
WITNESS
WRYNESS
YAWNERS

•••N•E•

ALUNSER
AMENDED
ASUNDER
ATONIES
AVENGED
AVENGER
AVENGES
AVENUES
AVONLEA
BAINTER
BEANIES
BERNSEN
BLANDER
BLANKED
BLANKER
BLANKET
BLENDED
BLENDER
BLINDED
BLINDER
BLINKED
BLINKER
BLONDER
BLONDES
BLUNDER
BLUNTED
BLUNTER
BONNIER
BOONIES
BOUNCED
BOUNCER
BOUNCES
BOUNDED
BOUNDER
BRANDED
BRANDER
BRENNER
BRINGER
BRINIER
BRONZED
BRONZES
BRYNNER
BUNNIES
CANNIER
CARNIES
CHANCED
CHANCEL
CHANCER
CHANCES
CHANGED
CHANGER
CHANGES
CHANNEL
CHANTED
CHANTER
CHANTEY
CHENIER
CHINKED
CHINNED
CHUNNEL
CHUNTER
CLANGED
CLANKED
CLINKED
CLINKER
CLUNKED
CLUNKER
CORNFED
CORNIER
COUNSEL
COUNTED
COUNTER
CRANKED
CRINGED
CRINGES
CRONIES
DARNLEY
DAUNTED
DERNIER
DOWNIER
DRINKER
EBONIES
EMANUEL
EMENDED
EMENDER
EVANDER
EVANGEL
EVINCED
EVINCES
FAINTED
FAINTER
FEINTED
FENNIER
FERNIER
FIANCEE
FIANCES
FIENNES
FINNIER
FLANGES
FLANKED
FLANKER
FLANNEL
FLENSED
FLENSES
FLUNKED
FOUNDED
FOUNDER
FRANCES
FRANKED
FRANKEN
FRANKER
FRINGED
FRINGES
FRONTED
FUNNIER
FUNNIES
GAUNTER
GLANCED
GLANCES
GLINTED
GOONIER
GOUNDER
GRANDEE
GRANDER
GRANGER
GRANGES
GRANTED
GRANTEE
GRENDEL
GRINDER
GRINNED
GRINNER
GRUNGES
GRUNTED
GUNNIES
HAUNTED
HENNAED
HINNIES
HOUNDED
IRONIES
IRONMEN
JAUNTED
JENNIES
JOINDER
JOINTED
JOUNCED
JOUNCES
LAENNEC
LAUNDER
LEANDER
LIENEES
LOONIER
LOONIES
LOUNGED
LOUNGER
LOUNGES
MAUNDER
MEANDER
MEANIES
MEINIES
MOONIER
MOONSET
MOUNDED
MOUNTED
NANNIES
NINNIES
NUANCED
NUANCES
OPENSEA
ORANGES
ORANGEY
PAINTED
PAINTER
PANNIER
PAWNEES
PENNIES
PEONIES
PHONIER
PHONIES
PIONEER
PLANKED
PLANNED
PLANNER
PLANTED
PLANTER
PLINKED
PLUNDER
PLUNGED
PLUNGER
PLUNGES
PLUNKED
POINTED
POINTER
POUNCED
POUNCER
POUNCES
POUNDED
POUNDER
PRANCED
PRANCER
PRANCES
PRANGED
PRANKED
PRINCES
PRINKED
PRINTED
PRINTER
PRONGED
PUNNIER
QUINCES
QUINTET
QUONSET
RAINIER
REENTER
REINKED
ROUNDED
ROUNDER
RUNNIER
SAINTED
SAUNTER
SCANNED
SCANNER
SCANTED
SCANTER
SCENDED
SCENTED
SCONCES
SEANCES
SHANKED
SHANTEY
SHINIER
SHINNED
SHUNNED
SHUNTED
SIGNEES
SKANKED
SKANKER
SKINNED
SKINNER
SKUNKED
SLANDER
SLANTED
SLENDER
SLINGER
SLINKED
SOUNDED
SOUNDER
SPANDEX
SPANIEL
SPANKED
SPANKER
SPANNED
SPANNER
SPENCER
SPENDER
SPENSER
SPINIER
SPINNER
SPINNEY
SPONDEE
SPONGED
SPONGER
SPONGES
STANCES
STANDEE
STANLEE
STANLEY
STENGEL
STINGER
STINKER
STINTED
STONIER
STUNNED
STUNNER
STUNTED
SUNNIER
SWANKED
SWANKER
SWANSEA
SWINGER
SWONKEN
TAINTED
TAUNTED
TAWNIER
TEENIER
TENNIEL
THANKED
THINKER
THINNED
THINNER
THUNDER
TINNIER
TOONIES
TOWNIES
TOYNBEE
TRANCES
TRENDED
TRINKET
TUNNIES
TURNKEY
TWANGED
TWINBED
TWINGED
TWINGES
TWINNED
UNENDED
UPENDED
VAUNTED
VAUNTER
VEINIER
VERNIER
WEENIER
WEENIES
WERNHER
WHANGED
WHINIER
WIENIES
WOUNDED
WRINGER
WRONGED
WRONGER
YOUNGER

•••N••E

ACONITE
ADENINE
AGONISE
AGONIZE
ASININE
ATINGLE
BARNONE
BERNESE
BERNICE
BIGNAME
BLANCHE
BLONDIE
BRINDLE
BYANOSE
CHINESE
COGNATE
COINAGE
CONNIVE
CONNOTE
CORNICE
CRINKLE
DWINDLE
EBONITE
EMANATE
ENSNARE
FIANCEE
FRANKIE
FURNACE
GRANDEE
GRANITE
GRANTEE
GRANULE
GRENADE
GUANINE
IRONAGE
IRONORE
IVANHOE
JEANNIE
JOHNDOE
JOHNNIE
KEYNOTE
KRINGLE
LEONINE
LIGNITE
LIONISE
LIONIZE
MAGNATE
MCENROE
MISNAME
MOUNTIE
NEONATE
ONENOTE
OPENTOE
PENNAME
PENNATE
PEONAGE
PETNAME
PHONEME
PINNACE
PINNATE
PUGNOSE
QUININE
QUINQUE
REUNITE
ROANOKE
SHINGLE
SPANGLE
SPINDLE
SPONDEE
STANDEE
STANLEE
SURNAME
SWINDLE
TEENAGE
TERNATE
THINICE
TONNAGE
TOYNBEE
TRUNDLE
TWINKLE
URANITE
WANNABE
WRANGLE
WRINKLE

••••NE•

ACHENES
ADFINEM
ADORNED
ADORNER
AFFINES
ALIENEE
ALIGNED
ALIGNER
ALKENES
ANYONES
APRONED
ATTUNED
ATTUNES
BALONEY
BARONET
BAYONET
BLARNEY
BOVINES
BRAINED
BRENNER
BROWNED
BROWNER
BRYNNER
BYGONES
BYLINED
BYLINES
CABINET
CANINES
CHAINED
CHANNEL
CHIMNEY
CHINNED
CHUNNEL
CHURNED
CHUTNEY
CLEANED
CLEANER
CLOONEY
CLOWNED
COCKNEY
COLONEL
COLONES
CORONET
COSINES
COSTNER
COZENED
CROONED
CROONER
CROWNED
DEBONED
DEBONES
DEFINED
DEFINES
DEIGNED
DELANEY
DEPONED
DEPONES
DIVINED
DIVINER
DIVINES
DIZENED
DRAGNET
DRAINED
DRAINER
DROWNED
EDASNER
EMPANEL
ENGINES
EQUINES
ERMINES
ESSENES
EVZONES
FAMINES
FEIGNED
FELINES
FIENNES
FILENES
FISHNET
FLANNEL
FLEXNER
FROWNED
FROWNER
GAMINES
GARDNER
GILLNET
GLEANED
GLEANER
GRAINED
GRAPNEL
GREENED
GREENER
GRINNED
GRINNER
GROANED
GROANER
GYRENES
HACKNEY
HAIRNET
IMPANEL
INTONED
INTONER
INTONES
JACONET
JEEPNEY
JIMENEZ
JOURNEY
KEARNEY
KETONES
KLEENEX
LAENNEC
LARDNER
LEARNED
LEARNER
LIERNES
LIFENET
LIKENED
LIKENEW
LIVENED
LUPINES
MAHONEY
MARINER
MARINES
MATINEE
MOURNED
MRBONES
NOMINEE
OCTANES
OFTENER
ORDINES
ORPINES
OSCINES
PARDNER
PARTNER
PAVANES
PILSNER
PINONES
PLAINER
PLANNED
PLANNER
PREENED
PREENER
RAPINES
RAVENED
RAVINES
RECANED
RECANES
REFINED
REFINER
REFINES
REIGNED
RELINED
RELINES
REPINED
REPINES
RETUNED
RETUNES
REZONED
REZONES
RIPENED
SABINES
SATINET
SCANNED
SCANNER
SCORNED
SCORNER
SERENER
SHATNER
SHAWNEE
SHINNED
SHRINER
SHRINES
SHUNNED
SKINNED
SKINNER
SOIGNEE
SPANNED
SPANNER
SPAWNED
SPINNER
SPINNEY
SPLINES
SPOONED
SPOONER
SPURNED
SPURNER
STAINED
STAINER
STEINEM
STEINER
STERNER
STUNNED
STUNNER
SWEENEY
SWOONED
TALONED
TENONED
THINNED
THINNER
THRONES
TIERNEY
TISANES
TOKENED
TOURNEY
TRAINED
TRAINEE
TRAINER
TRIUNES
TWINNED
UNLINED
UNTUNED
UNTUNES
UNZONED
URBANER
VINTNER
WAGONER
WAHINES
WAKENED
WAKENER
WHITNEY
WIDENED
WIZENED
YEARNED
YEARNER

••••N•E

ABSENCE
ADVANCE
ALDENTE
ALIENEE
ALLENDE
ALUMNAE
ANDANTE
ARGONNE
ARRANGE
ASKANCE
BALANCE
BROWNIE
CADENCE
CATENAE
CAYENNE
CEZANNE
CLEANSE
CORONAE
DEFENCE
DEFENSE
DETENTE
DOYENNE
DURANCE
DURANTE
ENHANCE
ENOUNCE
ENTENTE
ESSENCE
ETIENNE
EUGENIE
EXPANSE
EXPENSE
EXPUNGE
FAIENCE
FINANCE
FIRENZE
FLOUNCE
GARONNE
GIRONDE
IMMENSE
IMPINGE
INCENSE
INGENUE
INTENSE
JEANNIE
JOHNNIE
LACUNAE
LALANNE
LAMINAE
LEMONDE
LICENCE
LICENSE
LISENTE
LOZENGE
MATINEE
MELANGE
MELANIE
NOMINEE
OFFENCE
OFFENSE
ORIENTE
PALANCE
PENANCE
PICANTE
RERINSE
RETINAE
RETINUE
REVENGE
REVENUE
ROMANCE
ROSANNE
ROXANNE
SCIENCE
SHAWNEE
SILENCE
SOIGNEE
STRANGE
SUSANNE
SUZANNE
SYRINGE
TERENCE
TRAINEE
TROUNCE
TWOONIE
VALANCE
VALENCE
YAOUNDE

•••••NE

AAMILNE
ABALONE
ABILENE
ACETONE
ADELINE
ADENINE
AIRLANE
AIRLINE
ALLGONE
ANEMONE
ANILINE
ANODYNE
ANTOINE
ARACHNE
ARCSINE
ARGONNE
ARIADNE
ASININE
BARNONE
BEELINE
BEGUINE
BELTANE
BENZENE
BIPLANE
BOWLINE
BROMINE
BUSLINE
CALZONE
CANZONE
CARBINE
CARMINE
CASERNE
CAYENNE
CEZANNE
CHOLINE
CHORINE
CITRINE
CODEINE
COLOGNE
COMBINE
COMMUNE
CONDONE
CONFINE
CONVENE
CUISINE
CYCLONE
DARLENE
DECLINE
DEMESNE
DENTINE
DEPLANE
DESTINE
DEWLINE
DOGBANE
DOGGONE
DOYENNE
ENDZONE
ENPLANE
ENTWINE
EPERGNE
EPICENE
EPIGENE
EPIGONE
ERSKINE
ETAMINE
ETIENNE
EXAMINE
FANZINE
FARGONE
FASTONE
FORGONE
FORTUNE
GAGLINE
GARONNE
GENUINE
GERMANE
GOODONE
GUANINE
HELLENE
HEMLINE
HENBANE
HEROINE
HIPBONE
HORMONE
HOTLINE
HOVLANE
HYALINE
HYGIENE
IFSTONE
IMAGINE
IMOGENE
INCLINE
JASMINE
JAWBONE
JAWLINE
JUGWINE
JUSTINE
LALANNE
LARAINE
LASAGNE
LAVERNE
LEONINE
LEUCINE
LIVEONE
LUCERNE
MACHINE
MARLENE
MAYWINE
MBABANE
MCSWINE
METHANE
MIDLINE
MIOCENE
MISDONE
MONTANE
MORAINE
MUNDANE
NEPTUNE
NEURONE
OBSCENE
OFFLINE
OLDLINE
OLIVINE
ONELANE
OPALINE
OSBORNE
OUTDONE
OUTLINE
PADRONE
PAULINE
PISCINE
PONTINE
PORCINE
PRALINE
PROFANE

PROPANE QUININE RATLINE RECLINE REDLINE REDPINE REDWINE ROGAINE ROMAINE ROSANNE ROUTINE ROXANNE SALTINE SARDINE SCALENE SEALANE SETLINE SEVIGNE SISTINE SKYLINE SLOVENE SNOCONE SOMEONE SOUTANE SPOKANE SPUMONE STYRENE SUSANNE SUZANNE TAGLINE TAKEONE TANLINE TAURINE TERHUNE TERRENE THYMINE TIELINE TOLUENE TONTINE TRIBUNE TRITONE TURBINE TWOLANE TWOTONE UKRAINE UPBORNE VACCINE VANDINE VOLPONE VULPINE WARZONE WILDONE WORDONE

N•F••••

NIFTIER NIFTILY NOFAULT

N••F•••

NORFOLK

N•••F••

NEEDFUL

N••••F•

NESCAFE NEWLEFT NODSOFF NULLIFY

N•••••F

NETSURF NODSOFF NONSELF

•NF••••

ENFOLDS ENFORCE INFANCY INFANTA INFANTS INFAVOR INFECTS INFERNO INFESTS INFIDEL INFIELD INFLAME INFLATE INFLECT INFLICT INFLOWS INFOCUS INFORCE INFORMS INFRONT INFUSED INFUSES UNFAZED UNFIXED UNFOLDS UNFROCK UNFURLS

•N•F•••

ANTFARM KNIFING SNAFFLE SNAFUED SNIFFAT SNIFFED SNIFFER SNIFFLE SNIFFLY SNIFTER SNUFFED SNUFFER SNUFFLE SNUFFLY UNIFIED UNIFIER UNIFIES UNIFORM

•N••F••

ANTIFOG INSOFAR SNAFFLE SNIFFAT SNIFFED SNIFFER SNIFFLE SNIFFLY SNUFFED SNUFFER SNUFFLE SNUFFLY UNAWFUL

•N•••F•

ENGRAFT ENGULFS

•N••••F

INAWEOF INBRIEF ONESELF ONTOPOF

••NF•••

BONFIRE CANFULS CONFABS CONFERS CONFESS CONFIDE CONFINE CONFIRM CONFORM CONFUSE CONFUTE FANFARE FUNFAIR FUNFEST GINFIZZ GUNFIRE KINFOLK LANFORD LENFANT MANFRED MENFOLK PANFISH PANFULS SANFORD SUNFISH SYNFUEL TENFOLD TENFOUR TINFOIL WINFREY

••N•F••

BANEFUL BENEFIT CONIFER DONEFOR GUNSFOR HANDFED HANDFUL MINDFUL PINEFOR RUNOFFS RUNSFOR SANDFLY SENDFOR SENTFOR SENUFOS SONGFUL TANKFUL TUNEFUL WENTFOR

••N••F•

CONNIFF DANDIFY FANCIFY HANDOFF HANGOFF PONTIFF RANGOFF RINGOFF RUNGOFF RUNOFFS RUNSOFF SANTAFE SENDOFF SENTOFF WENTOFF

••N•••F

CONNIFF HANDOFF HANGOFF NONSELF PONTIFF RANGOFF RINGOFF RUNGOFF RUNSOFF SENDOFF SENTOFF SUNROOF WENTOFF

•••NF••

CORNFED GAINFUL GOINFOR MOANFUL PAINFUL SEENFIT SKINFUL YAWNFUL

•••N•F•

CONNIFF DIGNIFY MAGNIFY PAWNOFF REUNIFY SEENOFF SIGNIFY SIGNOFF SPINOFF SPUNOFF TORNOFF TURNOFF WORNOFF

•••N••F

CONNIFF PAWNOFF SEENOFF SIGNOFF SPINOFF SPUNOFF THINKOF TORNOFF TURNOFF WORNOFF

••••N•F

BARANOF

N•G••••

NAGGIER NAGGING NAGGISH NEGATED NEGATER NEGATES NEGATOR NEGLECT NIGERIA NIGGARD NIGGLED NIGGLES NIGHEST NIGHTIE NIGHTLY NOGALES NOGGINS NOGUCHI NUGGETS

N••G•••

NAGGIER NAGGING NAGGISH NAUGHTS NAUGHTY NEIGHED NEWGATE NIAGARA NIGGARD NIGGLED NIGGLES NOGGINS NOUGATS NOUGHTS NUDGERS NUDGING NUGGETS

N•••G••

NEWAGER NONAGES NONAGON NOSEGAY NYUNGAR

N••••G•

NESTEGG NORIEGA NUTMEGS

N•••••G

NABBING NAGGING NAILING NAMETAG NAPPING NEARING NECKING NEEDING NESTEGG NESTING NETTING NICKING NIPPING NODDING NOISING NOOSING NOSEBAG NOSHING NOTHING NUDGING NULLING NUMBING NURSING NUTTING

•NG••••

ANGELES ANGELIC ANGELOU ANGELUS ANGERED ANGLERS ANGLING ANGOLAN ANGORAS ANGRIER ANGRILY ANGULAR ENGAGED ENGAGES ENGARDE ENGINES ENGIRDS ENGLAND ENGLISH ENGLUND ENGORGE ENGRAFT ENGRAMS ENGRAVE ENGROSS ENGULFS INGALLS INGEMAR INGENUE INGESTS INGRAIN INGRATE INGRESS INGROUP INGROWN ONGOING ONGUARD UNGIRDS UNGLUED UNGODLY UNGUENT

•N•G•••

ANAGRAM ENDGAME ENIGMAS KNIGHTS ONAGERS SNAGGED SNIGGER SNIGGLE SNIGLET SNOGGED SNUGGER SNUGGLE

•N••G••

ANTIGEN ANTIGUA ENCAGED ENCAGES ENGAGED ENGAGES ENRAGED ENRAGES ENSIGNS INDIGOS INSIGHT INTEGER INTEGRA INVOGUE ONSIGHT SNAGGED SNIGGER SNIGGLE SNOGGED SNUGGER SNUGGLE UNCAGED UNCAGES

•N•••G•

ANALOGS ANALOGY ENDINGS ENGORGE ENLARGE INDULGE INNINGS INVEIGH ONSTAGE ONTHEGO UNCLOGS UNDERGO UNPLUGS UNSNAGS

•N••••G

ANELING ANGLING ANTEING ANTIFOG ANTILOG ENDUING ENSUING ENURING ENVYING GNAWING INCHING INKLING INURING KNEEING KNIFING KNOWING ONGOING SNAKING SNARING SNIPING SNORING SNOWING UNDOING UNDYING UNITING UNTYING

••NG•••

BANGING BANGKOK BANGLES BANGSUP BENGALI BENGALS BINGHAM BINGING BINGOES BONGING BONGOES BUNGEES BUNGING BUNGLED BUNGLER BUNGLES CONGAED CONGAME CONGEAL CONGERS CONGEST DANGERS DANGLED DANGLER DANGLES DINGBAT DINGIER DINGILY DINGING DINGLES DINGOES DONGLES DUNGEON FINGERS FUNGOES GANGERS GANGING GANGLED GANGLIA GANGSAW GANGSTA GANGSUP GANGTOK GANGWAY GENGHIS GINGERS GINGERY GINGHAM GINGIVA GONGING HANGARS HANGDOG HANGERS HANGING HANGMAN HANGMEN HANGOFF HANGOUT HANGSIN HANGSON HANGSUP HANGTEN HANGUPS HINGING HUNGARY HUNGERS HUNGOUT JANGLED JANGLES JINGLED JINGLES JINGOES JUNGLES KINGDOM KINGING KINGMAN KINGPIN KINGRAT KINGTUT LANGDON LANGLEY LANGTRY LANGUID LANGUOR LANGURS LENGTHS LENGTHY LINGERS LINGOES LINGUAL LONGAGO LONGARM LONGBOW LONGEST LONGIES LONGING LONGISH LONGRUN LONGTON LONGUES LUNGEAT LUNGING MANGERS MANGIER MANGLED MANGLES MANGOES MINGIER MINGLED MINGLER MINGLES MONGERS MONGOLS MONGREL PENGUIN PINGING PONGEES PONGIDS PONGING PUNGENT QINGDAO RANGERS RANGIER RANGING RANGOFF RANGOON RANGOUT RINGERS RINGING RINGLET RINGOFF RINGOUT RINGSUP RUNGOFF RUNGOUT SANGOUT SANGRIA SINGERS SINGING SINGLED SINGLES SINGOUT SINGSTO SONGFUL SUNGODS SYNGMAN TANGELO TANGENT TANGERE TANGIER TANGLED TANGLES TANGOED TANGRAM TINGING TINGLED TINGLES TONGANS TONGUED TONGUES TUNGOIL VANGOGH WANGLED WANGLER WANGLES WINGERS WINGING WINGNUT WINGSIT WINGTIP XINGOUT YANGTZE ZINGERS ZINGIER ZINGING

••N•G••

DONEGAL FINAGLE HANDGUN LINAGES MANAGED MANAGER MANAGES MANAGUA MANEGES MENAGES NONAGES NONAGON RENEGED RENEGER RENEGES RENEGUE RONTGEN SENEGAL TANAGER TONIGHT VINEGAR

••N••G•

AWNINGS BANDAGE BENDIGO BONDAGE CONDIGN CONSIGN GUNDOGS INNINGS LENTIGO LINEAGE LININGS LINKAGE LONGAGO MONTAGE MONTEGO PANURGE SINKAGE SUNDOGS SYNERGY TONNAGE VANGOGH VANTAGE VINTAGE

••N•••G

BANDING BANGING BANKING BANNING BENDING BINDING BINGING BINNING BONDING BONGING BUNGING BUNKING BUNTING CANNING CANTING CENSING CONKING CONNING CUNNING DANCING DENTING DENYING DINGING DONKING DONNING DUNKING DUNNING FANNING FENCING FENDING FINDING FINKING FUNDING FUNKING FUNNING GANGING GINNING GINSENG GONGING GUNNING HANDBAG HANDING HANGDOG HANGING HENTING HINGING HINTING HONKING HUNTING JINKING JINXING JUNEBUG JUNKING KINGING KINKING LANDING LANSING LENDING LINKING LONGING LUNGING MANNING MENDING MINCING MINDING MINTING MONOLOG OINKING PANNING PANTING PENDING PENNING PINGING PINKING PINNING PONGING PONYING PUNNING PUNTING RANGING RANKING RANTING RENDING RENTING RINGING RINSING RUNNING SANDBAG SANDHOG SANDING SENDING SENSING SINGING SINKING SUNNING SYNCING TANKING TANNING TENDING TENSING TENTING TENZING TINGING TINTING VENDING VENTING WANTING WENDING WINCING WINDBAG WINDING WINGING WINKING WINNING YANKING ZINGING ZONKING

•••NG••

AMONGST ATINGLE AVENGED AVENGER AVENGES BRINGER BRINGIN BRINGON BRINGTO BRINGUP CHANGED CHANGER CHANGES CLANGED CLANGOR CRINGED CRINGES DOINGIN DOINGUP EVANGEL FLANGES FRINGED FRINGES GOINGAT GOINGBY GOINGIN GOINGON GOINGUP GRANGER GRANGES GRUNGES ICINGIN ICINGUP JOHNGAY KLINGON KRINGLE LOUNGED LOUNGER LOUNGES LYINGTO NYUNGAR ORANGES ORANGEY OWINGTO PAANGAS PLUNGED PLUNGER PLUNGES PRANGED PRONGED QUANGOS SHANGRI SHINGLE SLINGER SPANGLE SPANGLY SPONGED SPONGER SPONGES STENGEL STINGER STINGOS STUNGUN SWINGBY SWINGER TLINGIT TWANGED TWINGED TWINGES TYINGIN TYINGUP USINGUP WHANGED WRANGLE WRINGER WRONGED WRONGER WRONGLY YOUNGER YOUNGMC YOUNGUN ZWINGLI

•••N•G•

BRANAGH COINAGE EGGNOGS IRONAGE PEONAGE TEENAGE TONNAGE UNSNAGS

•••N••G

ALINING ATONING BANNING BEANBAG BEANING BINNING BRINING BURNING CANNING CLONING COINING CONNING CORNDOG CORNING CRANING CUNNING DAMNING DARNING DAWNING DONNING DOWNING DRONING DUNNING DURNING EARNING EVENING FANNING FAWNING FOINING FUNNING GAINING GINNING GIRNING GUNNING HORNING IRONING JOINING KEENING KERNING LEANING LIMNING LOANING MANNING MEANING MOANING MOONDOG MOONING MORNING OPENING OPINING PANNING PAWNING PENNING PFENNIG PHONING PINNING PLANING PRUNING PUNNING RAINING REINING RUINING RUNNING SEINING SHINDIG SHINING SIGNING STONING SUNNING TANNING TURNING TWINING VEINING WARNING WEANING WHINING WINNING YARNING YAWNING YEANING

••••NG•

AIRINGS ARRANGE AWNINGS BARONGS BELONGS CASINGS COMINGS DOMINGO DUGONGS DURANGO EDGINGS ENDINGS EXPUNGE FACINGS FILINGS FIRINGS FIXINGS HAZINGS HIDINGS IMPINGE INNINGS LACINGS LININGS LIVINGS LOZENGE MAKINGS MARENGO MELANGE OBLONGS OUTINGS PARINGS PILINGS PIPINGS RATINGS RAVINGS REHANGS

RESINGS
REVENGE
RISINGS
RULINGS
SARONGS
SAVINGS
SAYINGS
SIDINGS
SIZINGS
SPRINGS
SPRINGY
STRANGE
STRINGS
STRINGY
SYRINGA
SYRINGE
TAPINGS
THRONGS
TIDINGS
TILINGS
TIMINGS
VIKINGS

••••N•G

PFENNIG

•••••NG

ABASING
ABATING
ABIDING
ABUSING
ACHTUNG
ADDLING
ADORING
ALAKING
ALINING
ALLYING
AMAZING
AMBLING
AMUSING
ANELING
ANGLING
ANTEING
ARCHING
ARGUING
ARISING
ARTSONG
ATONING
AVOWING
AWAKING
BABYING
BACHING
BACKING
BAGGING
BAILING
BAITING
BALDING
BALKING
BANDING
BANGING
BANKING
BANNING
BARBING
BARGING
BARKING
BARRING
BASHING
BASKING
BASTING
BATHING
BATTING
BATWING
BAWLING
BEADING

BEAMING
BEANING
BEARING
BEATING
BEDDING
BEEFING
BEEPING
BEGGING
BEIJING
BELLING
BELTING
BELYING
BENDING
BESTING
BETTING
BIASING
BIDDING
BIGBANG
BILKING
BILLING
BINDING
BINGING
BINNING
BIRDING
BIRLING
BITTING
BLADING
BLAMING
BLARING
BLAZING
BLOWING
BLUEING
BOATING
BOBBING
BOGGING
BOILING
BOLTING
BOMBING
BONDING
BONGING
BOOKING
BOOMING
BOOTING
BOPPING
BOSSING
BOUSING
BOWLING
BRACING
BRAKING
BRAVING
BRAYING
BRAZING
BREWING
BRIBING
BRINING
BRUXING
BUCKING
BUDDING
BUDGING
BUFFING
BUGGING
BUGLING
BULGING
BULKING
BULLING
BUMMING
BUMPING
BUNGING
BUNKING
BUNTING
BUOYING
BURLING
BURNING
BURPING

BURYING
BUSHING
BUSKING
BUSSING
BUSTING
BUSYING
BUTTING
BUZZING
CABLING
CACHING
CADGING
CALKING
CALLING
CALMING
CALVING
CAMPING
CANNING
CANTING
CAPPING
CARDING
CARKING
CARPING
CARTING
CARVING
CASHING
CASTING
CATTING
CAUSING
CEASING
CEILING
CENSING
CESSING
CHAFING
CHASING
CHEWING
CHIDING
CHIMING
CLAWING
CLONING
CLOSING
CLOYING
CLUEING
COATING
COAXING
COCKING
COIFING
COILING
COINING
COMBING
CONKING
CONNING
COOKING
COOLING
COOPING
COPPING
COPYING
CORDING
CORKING
CORNING
COSHING
COSTING
COWLING
COZYING
CRANING
CRATING
CRAVING
CRAZING
CREWING
CROWING
CUFFING
CULLING
CUNNING
CUPPING
CURBING

CURDING
CURLING
CURSING
CURVING
CUSHING
CUSSING
CUTTING
CYCLING
CYYOUNG
DABBING
DAFFING
DAMMING
DAMNING
DAMPING
DANCING
DAPPING
DARLING
DARNING
DARTING
DASHING
DAUBING
DAWNING
DAYLONG
DEALING
DECKING
DEEDING
DEEMING
DEFYING
DEICING
DELEING
DELVING
DENTING
DENYING
DERRING
DIALING
DIETING
DIGGING
DIMMING
DINGING
DIPPING
DISHING
DISSING
DOCKING
DODGING
DOFFING
DOGGING
DOLLING
DONKING
DONNING
DOOMING
DOTTING
DOUSING
DOWNING
DOWSING
DRAPING
DRAWING
DRAYING
DRIVING
DRONING
DUBBING
DUCKING
DUCTING
DUELING
DULLING
DUMBING
DUMPING
DUNKING
DUNNING
DURNING
DUSTING
EAGLING
EARNING
EARRING
ECHOING

EDDYING
EDITING
EDUCING
ELATING
ELIDING
ELOPING
ELUDING
ELUTING
EMOTING
ENDUING
ENSUING
ENURING
ENVYING
ERASING
ERELONG
ERODING
ESPYING
ETCHING
EVADING
EVENING
EVOKING
EXILING
EXITING
EXUDING
FAGGING
FAILING
FAIRING
FALLING
FANNING
FARCING
FARMING
FASTING
FAWNING
FEARING
FEEDING
FEELING
FELLING
FENCING
FENDING
FESSING
FEUDING
FIBBING
FILLING
FILMING
FINDING
FINKING
FIRMING
FISHING
FITTING
FIZZING
FLAKING
FLAMING
FLARING
FLAWING
FLAYING
FLEEING
FLEMING
FLEXING
FLEYING
FLOWING
FLUTING
FLUXING
FOALING
FOAMING
FOBBING
FOGGING
FOILING
FOINING
FOLDING
FOOLING
FOOTING
FORCING
FORDING
FORGING

FORKING
FORMING
FOULING
FOWLING
FRAMING
FRAYING
FREEING
FUBBING
FUDGING
FUELING
FUNDING
FUNKING
FUNNING
FURLING
FURLONG
FURRING
FUSSING
FUTZING
FUZZING
GABBING
GADDING
GAFFING
GAGGING
GAINING
GAITING
GALLING
GAMMING
GANGING
GAOLING
GAPPING
GARBING
GASHING
GASPING
GATLING
GAUGING
GAUMING
GAWKING
GAWPING
GEARING
GELDING
GELLING
GETTING
GIBBING
GILDING
GILLING
GINNING
GINSENG
GIPPING
GIRDING
GIRNING
GLARING
GLAZING
GLIDING
GLOBING
GLOWING
GLOZING
GNAWING
GOADING
GOALONG
GOLDING
GOLFING
GONGING
GOODING
GOOFING
GOOSING
GORGING
GOSLING
GOUGING
GOWRONG
GRACING
GRADING
GRATING
GRAVING
GRAYING

GRAZING
GREYING
GRIMING
GRIPING
GROPING
GROWING
GUIDING
GULFING
GULLING
GULPING
GUMMING
GUNNING
GUSHING
GUSTING
GUTTING
GYPPING
HACKING
HAFTING
HAILING
HALOING
HALTING
HALVING
HAMMING
HANDING
HANGING
HAPPING
HARDING
HARKING
HARMING
HARPING
HASHING
HASPING
HASTING
HATTING
HAULING
HAWKING
HEADING
HEALING
HEAPING
HEARING
HEATING
HEAVING
HEDGING
HEEDING
HEELING
HEFTING
HELMING
HELPING
HEMMING
HENTING
HERDING
HERRING
HILLING
HINGING
HINTING
HISSING
HITTING
HOAXING
HOBOING
HOCKING
HOGGING
HOLDING
HONKING
HOOFING
HOOKING
HOOPING
HOOTING
HOPPING
HORNING
HORSING
HOSTING
HOUSING
HOWLING
HUFFING

HUGGING
HULKING
HULLING
HUMMING
HUNTING
HURLING
HURTING
HUSHING
HUSKING
HYPOING
IMAGING
IMBUING
INCHING
INKLING
INURING
IRONING
ISSUING
ITCHING
JABBING
JACKING
JAGGING
JAILING
JAMMING
JARRING
JAZZING
JEERING
JELLING
JERKING
JESTING
JETTING
JIBBING
JIGGING
JILTING
JINKING
JINXING
JOBBING
JOGGING
JOINING
JOLTING
JOSHING
JOTTING
JREWING
JUDGING
JUGGING
JUICING
JUMPING
JUNKING
JURYING
JUTTING
KAYOING
KEELING
KEENING
KEEPING
KERNING
KEYRING
KICKING
KIDDING
KILLING
KILTING
KINGING
KINKING
KIPLING
KISSING
KNEEING
KNIFING
KNOWING
LACKING
LADLING
LAGGING
LAMMING
LANDING
LANSING
LAPPING
LAPSING

LAPWING
LARDING
LASHING
LASTING
LATHING
LAUDING
LEADING
LEAFING
LEAKING
LEANING
LEAPING
LEASING
LEAVING
LEERING
LEGGING
LEMMING
LENDING
LESSING
LETTING
LEVYING
LIBBING
LICKING
LIFTING
LILTING
LIMBING
LIMNING
LIMPING
LINKING
LIPPING
LISPING
LISTING
LOADING
LOAFING
LOAMING
LOANING
LOBBING
LOCKING
LODGING
LOFTING
LOGGING
LOLLING
LONGING
LOOKING
LOOMING
LOOPING
LOOSING
LOOTING
LOPPING
LORDING
LOTTING
LOUSING
LUCKING
LUFFING
LUGGING
LULLING
LUMPING
LUNGING
LURKING
LUSTING
MADDING
MAILING
MALTING
MANNING
MAPPING
MARKING
MARRING
MASHING
MASKING
MASSING
MATTING
MAULING
MEANING
MEETING
MELDING

MELTING
MENDING
MEOWING
MERGING
MESHING
MESSING
MEWLING
MIFFING
MILKING
MILLING
MINCING
MINDING
MINTING
MISSING
MISTING
MITRING
MOANING
MOBBING
MOCKING
MOILING
MOLDING
MOLTING
MOONING
MOORING
MOPPING
MORNING
MOSHING
MOSSING
MOUSING
MUCKING
MUFFING
MUGGING
MULLING
MUMMING
MUMPING
MUSHING
MUSSING
MUSTANG
MUZZING
NABBING
NAGGING
NAILING
NAPPING
NEARING
NECKING
NEEDING
NESTING
NETTING
NICKING
NIPPING
NODDING
NOISING
NOOSING
NOSHING
NOTHING
NUDGING
NULLING
NUMBING
NURSING
NUTTING
OBEYING
OINKING
OKAYING
ONGOING
OPENING
OPINING
ORATING
OURGANG
OUSTING
PACKING
PADDING
PAIRING
PALLING
PALMING

PANNING
PANTING
PARKING
PARRING
PARSING
PARTING
PASSING
PASTING
PATTING
PAULING
PAUSING
PAWNING
PEAKING
PEALING
PECKING
PEEKING
PEELING
PEEPING
PEERING
PEEVING
PEGGING
PELTING
PENDING
PENNING
PEPPING
PERKING
PERMING
PETTING
PHASING
PHONING
PICKING
PIECING
PIGGING
PILLING
PINGING
PINKING
PINNING
PIQUING
PITHING
PITTING
PITYING
PLACING
PLANING
PLATING
PLAYING
PLOWING
PLUMING
POISING
POLLING
PONGING
PONYING
POOLING
POOPING
POPPING
POSTING
POTTING
POURING
POUTING
PRATING
PRAYING
PRICING
PRIDING
PRIMING
PRIZING
PROBING
PROLONG
PROSING
PROVING
PRUNING
PUDDING
PUFFING
PULLING
PULSING
PUMPING

PUNNING
PUNTING
PURGING
PURLING
PURRING
PURSING
PUSHING
PUTTING
QUAKING
QUEUING
QUOTING
RACKING
RAFTING
RAGGING
RAIDING
RAILING
RAINING
RAISING
RAMMING
RANGING
RANKING
RANTING
RAPPING
RASPING
RATTING
RAZZING
RDLAING
READING
REAMING
REAPING
REARING
REDDING
REDOING
REDWING
REEDING
REEFING
REEKING
REELING
REFFING
REINING
RELYING
RENDING
RENTING
RESTING
REVVING
RHYMING
RIBBING
RIDDING
RIDGING
RIFFING
RIFLING
RIFTING
RIGGING
RIMMING
RINGING
RINSING
RIOTING
RIPPING
RISKING
ROAMING
ROARING
ROBBING
ROCKING
RODDING
ROILING
ROLLING
ROMPING
ROOFING
ROOKING
ROOMING
ROOTING
ROTTING
ROUGING
ROUSING

ROUTING
RUBBING
RUCHING
RUCKING
RUINING
RUNNING
RUSHING
RUSTING
SACKING
SAGGING
SAILING
SALTING
SALVING
SAMSUNG
SANDING
SAPLING
SAPPING
SASSING
SCALING
SCARING
SCOPING
SCORING
SEALING
SEAMING
SEARING
SEATING
SEEDING
SEEKING
SEEMING
SEEPING
SEINING
SEIZING
SELLING
SENDING
SENSING
SERLING
SERVING
SETTING
SHADING
SHAKING
SHAMING
SHAPING
SHARING
SHAVING
SHEBANG
SHINING
SHOEING
SHOOING
SHORING
SHOVING
SHOWING
SIBLING
SICCING
SIDLING
SIFTING
SIGHING
SIGNING
SILOING
SILTING
SINGING
SINKING
SIPPING
SITTING
SKATING
SKEWING
SLAKING
SLATING
SLAVING
SLICING
SLIDING
SLOPING
SLOWING
SMILING
SMITING

SMOKING
SNAKING
SNARING
SNIPING
SNORING
SNOWING
SOAKING
SOAPING
SOARING
SOBBING
SOCKING
SODDING
SOILING
SOLOING
SOLVING
SOPPING
SORTING
SOURING
SPACING
SPADING
SPARING
SPAYING
SPECING
SPEWING
SPICING
SPIKING
SPITING
SPOKING
SPUMING
STAGING
STAKING
STARING
STATING
STAVING
STAYING
STEWING
STOKING
STONING
STORING
STOWING
STYLING
SUBBING
SUCKING
SUDSING
SUITING
SULKING
SUMMING
SUNNING
SUPPING
SURFING
SURGING
SUSSING
SWAYING
SWIPING
SYNCING
TABBING
TABLING
TACKING
TAGGING
TAILING
TALKING
TAMPING
TANKING
TANNING
TAPPING
TARRING
TASKING
TASTING
TATTING
TAXIING
TEAMING
TEARING
TEASING
TEDDING

TEEMING
TELLING
TENDING
TENSING
TENTING
TENZING
TERMING
TESTING
THAWING
TICKING
TIDYING
TIERING
TIFFING
TILLING
TILTING
TINGING
TINTING
TIPPING
TITHING
TITLING
TITRING
TOGGING
TOILING
TOLLING
TOOLING
TOOTING
TOPPING
TOSSING
TOTTING
TOURING
TOUTING
TRACING
TRADING
TREEING
TRUEING
TUCKING
TUFTING
TUGGING
TUMMING
TURNING
TWINING
UNDOING
UNDYING
UNITING
UNTYING
UPSWING
VALUING
VAMPING
VARYING
VATTING
VEERING
VEGGING
VEILING
VEINING
VENDING
VENTING
VERGING
VESTING
VETOING
VETTING
VIEWING
VISAING
VOICING
VOIDING
WADDING
WAFTING
WAGGING
WAILING
WAITING
WAIVING
WALKING
WALLING
WANTING
WARDING
WARMING
WARNING
WARPING
WARRING
WASHING
WASTING
WAXWING
WEANING
WEARING
WEAVING
WEBBING
WEDDING
WEDGING
WEEDING
WEEPING
WELDING
WELLING
WELTING
WENDING
WETTING
WHALING
WHILING
WHINING
WHITING
WILDING
WILLING
WILTING
WINCING
WINDING
WINGING
WINKING
WINNING
WISHING
WISPING
WITTING
WOLFING
WOOFING
WORDING
WORKING
WRITING
WYOMING
XRATING
XRAYING
YACKING
YAKKING
YANKING
YAPPING
YARNING
YAWNING
YAWPING
YEANING
YELLING
YELPING
YERKING
YESSING
YIPPING
YOWLING
YOYOING
ZAGGING
ZAPPING
ZEITUNG
ZEROING
ZIGGING
ZINGING
ZIPPING
ZONKING
ZOOMING

N•H••••
NAHUATL

N••H•••
NAPHTHA
NEPHEWS
NEWHART
NICHOLS
NIGHEST
NIGHTIE
NIGHTLY
NOBHILL
NOSHERS
NOSHING
NOSHOWS
NOTHING
NOWHERE

N•••H••
NARTHEX
NARWHAL
NATCHEZ
NAUGHTS
NAUGHTY
NAVAHOS
NEEDHAM
NEIGHED
NEITHER
NINTHLY
NORTHER
NOTCHED
NOTCHES
NOUGHTS

N••••H•
NAPHTHA
NATASHA
NIEBUHR
NOGUCHI
NULLAHS

N•••••H
NAGGISH
NCWYETH
NEBBISH
NEOLITH
NESMITH
NEWMATH
NINEVEH
NOURISH

•NH••••
ENHANCE
INHABIT
INHALED
INHALER
INHALES
INHASTE
INHAULS
INHERED
INHERES
INHERIT
INHIBIT
INHOUSE
INHUMAN
UNHANDS
UNHANDY
UNHAPPY
UNHEARD
UNHITCH
UNHOOKS
UNHORSE

•N•H•••
ANAHEIM
ANAHUAC
ANCHORS
ANCHOVY
ANTHEMS
ANTHERS
ANTHILL
ANTHONY
ENCHAIN
ENCHANT
ENTHRAL
ENTHUSE
INAHEAP
INCHING
INKHORN
INPHASE
INSHAPE
INSHORT
ONSHORE
ONTHEGO
ONTHEQT
UNCHAIN
UNSHORN

•N••H••
ANOTHER
GNASHED
GNASHES
KNIGHTS
KNISHES
KNOWHOW
ONESHOT

•N•••H•
ANARCHY
GNOCCHI
INSIGHT
ONSIGHT
SNITCHY

•N••••H
ANOUILH
ANTIOCH
ENGLISH
GNOMISH
INARUSH
INDEPTH
INDUTCH
INTRUTH
INVEIGH
KNAVISH
UNCOUTH
UNEARTH
UNHITCH
UNLATCH
UNLEASH
UNTRUTH

••NH•••
MANHOLE
MANHOOD
MANHOUR
MANHUNT
MENHIRS
MYNHEER
PINHEAD
PINHOLE
RUNHOME
TINHATS
TINHORN

••N•H••
BANSHEE
BENCHED
BENCHES
BENTHAM
BINGHAM
BUNCHED
BUNCHES
CINCHED
CINCHES
CONCHES
CYNTHIA
DONAHUE
FINCHES
FUNCHAL
GENGHIS
GINGHAM
GUNSHOT
GUNTHER
HONCHOS
HUNCHED
HUNCHES
KINCHIN
KINSHIP
LUNCHED
LUNCHES
MENTHOL
MENUHIN
MONTHLY
MUNCHED
MUNCHER
MUNCHES
NINTHLY
PANCHAX
PANTHER
PINCHAS
PINCHED
PINCHER
PINCHES
PONCHOS
PUNCHED
PUNCHER
PUNCHES
PUNCHIN
PUNCHUP
PYNCHON
RANCHED
RANCHER
RANCHES
RANCHOS
SANDHOG
SYNCHED
SYNCHES
TENTHLY
WENCHES
WINCHED
WINCHES
XANTHAN
XANTHIC

••N••H•
BINOCHE
DENNEHY
KENOSHA
LENGTHS
LENGTHY
ORNITHO
PANACHE
PENUCHE
PUNKAHS
TONIGHT
ZENITHS

••N•••H
BENEATH
BONEASH
DONNISH
DUNCISH
FINNISH
HANUKAH
HENNISH
HUNNISH
KENNETH
KENTISH
LONGISH
MANNISH
MENORAH
MINXISH
MONARCH
MONKISH
NINEVEH
PANFISH
PINKISH
RANKISH
RUNTISH
RUNWITH
SUNBATH
SUNFISH
TANNISH
TONNISH
VANGOGH
WANNISH
WENDISH
ZANYISH

•••NH••
IVANHOE
RAINHAT
WERNHER

•••N•H•
ACANTHI
BLANCHE
BRONCHI
CRUNCHY
DENNEHY
PAUNCHY
PLINTHS

•••N••H
BRANAGH
BRINISH
BURNISH
CORNISH
CRONISH
DONNISH
DRONISH
EVANISH
FINNISH
FURNISH
GARNISH
GWYNETH
HENNISH
HORNISH
HUNNISH
KENNETH
MANNISH
MOONISH
PLANISH
RHENISH
SPANISH
SPINACH
SWINISH
TANNISH
TARNISH
TONNISH
TOWNISH
VARNISH
WANNISH

••••NH•
PIRANHA

••••N•H
CORINTH
DOZENTH
JACINTH
ROMANSH
SCRUNCH
SEVENTH
SQUINCH
STAUNCH

NI•••••
NIAGARA
NIBBLED
NIBBLER
NIBBLES
NIBLICK
NIBLIKE
NICCOLO
NICHOLS
NICKELS
NICKERS
NICKING
NICOLAS
NICOSIA
NIEBUHR
NIELSEN
NIFTIER
NIFTILY
NIGERIA
NIGGARD
NIGGLED
NIGGLES
NIGHEST
NIGHTIE
NIGHTLY
NIKOLAI
NILSSON
NIMBLER
NIMIETY
NIMRODS
NINEPIN
NINEVEH
NINNIES
NINTHLY
NIOBIUM
NIPPERS
NIPPIER
NIPPING
NIRVANA
NITPICK
NITRATE
NITRIDE
NITRITE
NITROUS
NITTANY
NITTIER
NITWITS

N•I••••
NAIADES
NAILERS
NAILING
NAILSET
NAILSIN
NAIROBI
NAIVELY
NAIVETE
NAIVETY
NEIGHED
NEITHER
NOISIER
NOISILY
NOISING
NOISOME

N••I•••
NABISCO
NAMIBIA
NATIONS
NATIVES
NETIZEN
NEVILLE
NIMIETY
NOMINAL
NOMINEE
NONIRON
NORIEGA
NOSIEST
NOTICED
NOTICES
NOTIONS
NOVICES
NOXIOUS
NUBIANS
NUDISTS

N•••I••
NABBING
NAGGIER
NAGGING
NAGGISH
NAILING
NANAIMO
NANNIES
NAPKINS
NAPPIES
NAPPING
NAPTIME
NASTIER
NASTILY
NATRIUM
NATTIER
NATTILY
NAVVIES
NEARING
NEBBISH
NECKING
NEDDIES
NEEDIER
NEEDILY
NEEDING
NEOLITH
NERDIER
NEREIDS
NERVIER
NERVILY
NESMITH
NESTING
NETLIKE
NETTING
NEWSIER
NEWSIES
NIBLICK
NIBLIKE
NICKING
NIFTIER
NIFTILY
NINNIES
NIOBIUM
NIPPIER
NIPPING
NITPICK
NITRIDE
NITRITE
NITTIER
NITWITS
NOBBIER
NOBHILL
NODDING
NOETICS
NOGGINS
NOISIER
NOISILY
NOISING
NOOSING
NORDICS
NOSHING
NOTHING
NOURISH
NUBBIER
NUBBINS
NUCLIDE
NUDGING
NUDNIKS
NULLIFY
NULLING
NULLITY
NUMBING
NUNCIOS
NUNLIKE
NUPTIAL
NURSING
NUTLIKE
NUTRIAS
NUTSIER
NUTTIER
NUTTILY
NUTTING

N••••I•
NAILSIN
NAMIBIA
NATALIA
NATALIE
NAYSAID
NECKTIE
NEMESIS
NEPALIS
NICOSIA
NIGERIA
NIGHTIE
NINEPIN
NOKOMIS
NOMADIC
NONSKID
NONSLIP
NOSTRIL
NOTABIT
NUCLEIC
NUMERIC

N•••••I
NAIROBI
NIKOLAI
NOGUCHI

•NI••••
ANILINE
ANIMALS
ANIMATE
ANIMATO
ANIMISM
ANIMIST
ANISEED
ANISTON
ENIGMAS
ENISLED
ENISLES
INITIAL
KNIEVEL
KNIFING
KNIGHTS
KNISHES
KNITTED
KNITTER
SNICKER
SNIDELY
SNIDEST
SNIFFAT
SNIFFED
SNIFFER
SNIFFLE
SNIFFLY
SNIFTER
SNIGGER
SNIGGLE
SNIGLET
SNIPEAT
SNIPERS
SNIPING
SNIPPED
SNIPPET
SNITCHY
SNIVELS
UNICORN
UNIFIED
UNIFIER
UNIFIES
UNIFORM
UNIPODS
UNISONS
UNITARY
UNITERS
UNITIES
UNITING
UNITIVE

•N•I•••
ANCIENT
ANDIRON
ANOINTS
ANTIART
ANTIBES
ANTIFOG
ANTIGEN
ANTIGUA
ANTILOG
ANTIOCH
ANTIQUE
ANTITAX
ANTIWAR
ANXIETY
ANXIOUS
ENCINAS
ENDINGS
ENDIVES
ENGINES
ENGIRDS
ENLISTS
ENLIVEN
ENSIGNS
ENSILED
ENSILES
ENTICED
ENTICER
ENTICES
ENTITLE
ENVIERS
ENVIOUS
INCIPIT
INCISED
INCISES
INCISOR
INCITED
INCITER
INCITES
INCIVIL
INDIANA
INDIANS
INDICES
INDICIA
INDICTS
INDIGOS
INDITED
INDITES
INFIDEL
INFIELD
INHIBIT
INKIEST
INNINGS
INSIDER
INSIDES
INSIGHT
INSIPID
INSISTS
INVITED
INVITES
INVITRO
ONEIDAS
ONEIRON
ONSIDES
ONSIGHT
UNAIDED
UNAIMED
UNAIRED
UNBINDS
UNCIALS
UNCIVIL
UNFIXED
UNGIRDS
UNHITCH
UNKINKS
UNLIKED
UNLINED
UNLINKS
UNOILED
UNPILED
UNPILES
UNWINDS
UNWISER

•N••I••
ANANIAS
ANELING
ANGLING
ANGRIER
ANGRILY
ANILINE
ANIMISM
ANIMIST
ANNUITY
ANODISE
ANODIZE
ANOMIES
ANOUILH
ANTEING
ANTHILL
ANTLIKE
ANTLION
ANTOINE
ANTSIER
ANYTIME
DNOTICE
ENDUING
ENDWISE
ENEMIES
ENGLISH
ENJOINS
ENQUIRE
ENQUIRY
ENSKIED
ENSKIES
ENSUING
ENSUITE
ENTAILS
ENTRIES
ENTWINE
ENURING
ENVYING
GNAWING
GNOMISH
INANITY
INBRIEF
INCHING
INCLINE
INFLICT
INITIAL
INKLIKE
INKLING
INPRINT
INQUIRE
INQUIRY
INSPIRE
INSTILL
INSTILS
INTUITS
INURING
INUTILE
INVEIGH
INVOICE
KNAVISH
KNEEING
KNIFING
KNOWING
ONADIET
ONETIME
ONGOING
ONTRIAL
SNAKIER
SNAKILY
SNAKING
SNARING
SNIPING
SNORING
SNOWIER
SNOWILY
SNOWING
UNALIKE
UNCOILS
UNCTION
UNDOING
UNDYING
UNIFIED
UNIFIER
UNIFIES
UNITIES
UNITING
UNITIVE
UNKNITS
UNSTICK
UNTRIED
UNTWIST
UNTYING
UNVEILS

•N•••I•
ANAEMIA
ANAEMIC
ANAHEIM
ANDROID
ANEROID
ANGELIC
ANNELID
ANOSMIA
ANOSMIC
ANTACID
ANTONIA
ANTONIN
ANTONIO
ENCHAIN
ENCOMIA
ENDEMIC
ENTRAIN
GNOSTIC
INASNIT
INASPIN
INCIPIT
INCIVIL
INDICIA
INERTIA
INGRAIN
INHABIT
INHERIT
INHIBIT
INORBIT
INSIPID
INSULIN
INTERIM
INTROIT
INVALID
ONASSIS
ONTARIO
SNEAKIN
SNOWSIN
UNCHAIN
UNCIVIL

•N••••I
ANASAZI
GNOCCHI

••NI•••
AMNIONS
ARNICAS
AWNINGS
BENISON
BONIEST
BONITOS
BUNIONS
CANIEST
CANINES
CONICAL
CONIFER
CYNICAL
DANIELS
DENIALS
DENIERS
DENIZEN
DONIMUS
FANIONS
FENIANS
FINIALS
FINICKY
HONIARA
IGNITED
IGNITER
IGNITES
INNINGS
IONISED
IONISES
IONIZED
IONIZER
IONIZES
JANITOR
JUNIORS
JUNIPER
LENIENT
LINIEST
LININGS
MANIACS
MANILOW
MANIOCS
MANIPLE
MANITOU
MENIALS
MENISCI
MINIBUS
MINICAB
MINICAM
MINIMAL
MINIMUM
MINIONS
MINIVAN
MINIVER
MONIKER
MONIQUE
MONITOR
NONIRON
OMNIBUS
ORNITHO
PANICKY
PANICLE
PINIEST
PINIONS
PONIARD
PUNIEST
RANINTO
RUNINTO
SANIBEL
SENIORS
TINIEST
TONIEST
TONIGHT
TUNICLE
TUNISIA
VANILLA
VANILLI
VENISON
VINIEST
WANIEST
WINIEST
ZANIEST
ZENITHS

••N•I••
ANNUITY
AUNTIES
BANDIED
BANDIES
BANDING
BANDITO
BANDITS
BANGING
BANKING
BANNING
BENDIER
BENDIGO
BENDING
BINDING
BINGING
BINNING
BONDING
BONFIRE
BONGING
BONNIER
BONNILY
BUNGING
BUNKING
BUNNIES
BUNTING
BUNYIPS
CANDICE
CANDIDA
CANDIDE
CANDIDS
CANDIED

CANDIES
CANNIER
CANNILY
CANNING
CANTILY
CANTINA
CANTING
CENSING
CENTIME
CENTIMO
CONCISE
CONDIGN
CONDITA
CONFIDE
CONFINE
CONFIRM
CONKING
CONNICK
CONNIFF
CONNING
CONNIVE
CONOIDS
CONRIED
CONSIGN
CONSIST
CONVICT
CUNNING
DANCING
DANDIER
DANDIES
DANDIFY
DENSITY
DENTINE
DENTING
DENTIST
DENYING
DINGIER
DINGILY
DINGING
DINKIER
DINKIES
DONKING
DONNING
DONNISH
DUNCISH
DUNKING
DUNKIRK
DUNLINS
DUNNING
FANCIED
FANCIER
FANCIES
FANCIFY
FANCILY
FANLIKE
FANNING
FANZINE
FENCING
FENDING
FENNIER
FINDING
FINKING
FINLIKE
FINNIER
FINNISH
FONTINA
FUNDING
FUNKIER
FUNKILY
FUNKING
FUNNIER
FUNNIES
FUNNILY
FUNNING

GANGING
GENTIAN
GENTILE
GENUINE
GINFIZZ
GINGIVA
GINMILL
GINNING
GONGING
GUNFIRE
GUNKIER
GUNNIES
GUNNING
HANDIER
HANDILY
HANDING
HANGING
HANKIES
HENBITS
HENLIKE
HENNISH
HENTING
HINGING
HINNIES
HINTING
HONKING
HUNKIER
HUNLIKE
HUNNISH
HUNTING
JANVIER
JENNIES
JINKING
JINXING
JONNICK
JUNKIER
JUNKIES
JUNKING
KENTISH
KINGING
KINKIER
KINKILY
KINKING
KONTIKI
LANDING
LANKIER
LANKILY
LANSING
LENDING
LENTIGO
LENTILS
LINBIAO
LINDIED
LINDIES
LINKING
LINPIAO
LINTIER
LONGIES
LONGING
LONGISH
LUNGING
MANCINI
MANGIER
MANKIND
MANLIER
MANLIKE
MANNING
MANNISH
MANSION
MENDING
MENHIRS
MENTION
MENZIES
MINCING

MINDING
MINGIER
MINTIER
MINTING
MINXISH
MONKISH
MUNTINS
NANAIMO
NANNIES
NINNIES
NUNCIOS
NUNLIKE
OINKING
PANDITS
PANFISH
PANNIER
PANNING
PANPIPE
PANSIES
PANTING
PENCILS
PENDING
PENLIKE
PENNIES
PENNING
PENSION
PENSIVE
PENTIUM
PINGING
PINKIES
PINKING
PINKISH
PINNING
PONGIDS
PONGING
PONTIAC
PONTIFF
PONTINE
PONTIUS
PONYING
PUNDITS
PUNKIER
PUNKIES
PUNNIER
PUNNILY
PUNNING
PUNTIES
PUNTING
RANDIER
RANGIER
RANGING
RANKING
RANKISH
RANRIOT
RANTING
RENAILS
RENDING
RENNINS
RENTING
RINGING
RINSING
RUNNIER
RUNNING
RUNRIOT
RUNTIER
RUNTISH
RUNWITH
SANDIER
SANDING
SANTINI
SANTIRS
SENDING
SENSING
SINGING

SINKING
SINLIKE
SONLIKE
SUNCITY
SUNDIAL
SUNFISH
SUNKIST
SUNLIKE
SUNNIER
SUNNILY
SUNNING
SUNRISE
SYNCING
TANGIER
TANKING
TANLINE
TANNING
TANNINS
TANNISH
TANSIES
TANTIVY
TENDING
TENNIEL
TENPINS
TENSILE
TENSING
TENSION
TENSIVE
TENTING
TENUITY
TENZING
TINGING
TINLIKE
TINNIER
TINNILY
TINTING
TONNISH
TONSILS
TONTINE
TUNNIES
URNLIKE
VANDINE
VENDING
VENTING
WANNISH
WANTING
WENDING
WENDISH
WINCING
WINDIER
WINDILY
WINDING
WINGING
WINKING
WINNING
WONKIER
YANKING
ZANYISH
ZINGIER
ZINGING
ZINNIAS
ZONKING

••N••I•

ABNAKIS
AMNESIA
ANNELID
BANDAID
BENAZIR
BENEFIT
BONSOIR
CANONIC
CANTRIP
CENTRIC

CONBRIO
CONCEIT
CONDUIT
CONJOIN
CONTAIN
CYNTHIA
DENARII
DINEDIN
DINESIN
DYNAMIC
FANATIC
FANMAIL
FANTAIL
FUNFAIR
GANGLIA
GENERIC
GENERIS
GENESIS
GENETIC
GENGHIS
GONERIL
HANDSIN
HANGSIN
HENDRIX
HENRYIV
HONORIS
JONQUIL
KINCHIN
KINETIC
KINGPIN
KINSHIP
LANGUID
LANOLIN
LUNATIC
MANTRIC
MANUMIT
MENUHIN
MINUTIA
MONODIC
NINEPIN
NONSKID
NONSLIP
PENGUIN
PINTAIL
PUNCHIN
SANGRIA
SANLUIS
SENDSIN
SINEDIE
SINKSIN
SUNMAID
SUNSUIT
SYNODIC
TENDRIL
TINFOIL
TINYTIM
TUNEDIN
TUNESIN
TUNGOIL
TUNISIA
WANTSIN
WINGSIT
WINGTIP
XANTHIC
YANQUIS
ZENOBIA

••N•••I

BENGALI
BONJOVI
CANNOLI
DENARII
KONTIKI
MANCINI

MENISCI
MENOTTI
MONTANI
PUNJABI
SANTINI
VANILLI

•••NI••

ACONITE
ADENINE
AGONISE
AGONIST
AGONIZE
ALINING
AMENITY
ANANIAS
ASININE
ATONIES
ATONING
BANNING
BEANIES
BEANING
BERNICE
BINNING
BIONICS
BONNIER
BONNILY
BOONIES
BRINIER
BRINING
BRINISH
BUNNIES
BURNING
BURNISH
CANNIER
CANNILY
CANNING
CARNIES
CATNIPS
CHENIER
CLINICS
CLONING
COINING
CONNICK
CONNIFF
CONNING
CONNIVE
CORNICE
CORNIER
CORNILY
CORNING
CORNISH
CRANIAL
CRANING
CRANIUM
CRONIES
CRONISH
CUNNING
DAMNING
DARNING
DAWNING
DERNIER
DIGNIFY
DIGNITY
DONNING
DONNISH
DOWNIER
DOWNING
DRONING
DRONISH
DUNNING
DURNING
EARNING
EBONIES

EBONITE
ETHNICS
ETONIAN
EVANISH
EVENING
EXANIMO
FANNING
FAWNING
FENNIER
FERNIER
FINNIER
FINNISH
FOINING
FUNNIER
FUNNIES
FUNNILY
FUNNING
FURNISH
GAINING
GARNISH
GHANIAN
GINNING
GIRNING
GOONIER
GOONILY
GRANITE
GRUNION
GUANINE
GUNNIES
GUNNING
HAFNIUM
HAHNIUM
HENNISH
HINNIES
HORNING
HORNISH
HORNIST
HUNNISH
INANITY
IRANIAN
IRONIES
IRONING
JENNIES
JOINING
JONNICK
KEENING
KERNING
LEANING
LEONIDS
LEONINE
LIGNITE
LIMNING
LIONISE
LIONIZE
LOANING
LOONIER
LOONIES
MAGNIFY
MANNING
MANNISH
MEANIES
MEANING
MEINIES
MOANING
MOONIER
MOONILY
MOONING
MOONISH
MORNING
NANNIES
NINNIES
NUDNIKS
OLDNICK
OPENING

OPINING
OPINION
OXONIAN
PANNIER
PANNING
PAWNING
PENNIES
PENNING
PEONIES
PHONICS
PHONIER
PHONIES
PHONILY
PHONING
PIANISM
PIANIST
PICNICS
PINNING
PLANING
PLANISH
PRUNING
PUNNIER
PUNNILY
PUNNING
QUININE
RAINIER
RAINILY
RAINING
REINING
RENNINS
REUNIFY
REUNION
REUNITE
RHENISH
RHENIUM
RUINING
RUNNIER
RUNNING
SEINING
SHINIER
SHINILY
SHINING
SIGNIFY
SIGNING
SPANIEL
SPANISH
SPINIER
STONIER
STONILY
STONING
SUNNIER
SUNNILY
SUNNING
SWINISH
TANNING
TANNINS
TANNISH
TARNISH
TAWNIER
TAWNILY
TEENIER
TENNIEL
THINICE
TINNIER
TINNILY
TONNISH
TOONIES
TOWNIES
TOWNISH
TRINITY
TUNNIES
TURNING
TURNIPS
TWINING

UNKNITS
URANITE
URANIUM
VARNISH
VEINIER
VEINING
VERNIER
VILNIUS
WANNISH
WARNING
WEANING
WEENIER
WEENIES
WHINIER
WHINING
WIENIES
WINNING
WOZNIAK
YARNING
YAWNING
YEANING
ZINNIAS

•••N•I•

ADONAIS
BLONDIE
BRINGIN
CORNOIL
COUNCIL
CRINOID
DOINGIN
EVENKIS
FRANCIS
FRANKIE
FRANTIC
GOINGIN
HOBNAIL
HORNSIN
ICINGIN
IDENTIC
JEANNIE
JOHNNIE
JOINSIN
MOONLIT
MOUNTIE
OPENAIR
OPENPIT
PFENNIG
QUENTIN
REINSIN
SEENFIT
SHINDIG
SIGNSIN
STANDIN
STANNIC
STENCIL
THINAIR
TIANJIN
TLINGIT
TOENAIL
TRANSIT
TURNSIN
TYINGIN
UTENSIL

•••N••I

ABENAKI
ACANTHI
BRONCHI
CANNOLI
HYUNDAI
MAGNANI
SHANGRI
TSUNAMI

ZWINGLI

••••NI•

ACTINIC
ALBANIA
ALBENIZ
AMMONIA
ANTONIA
ANTONIN
ANTONIO
ARMENIA
ARSENIC
ARSENIO
BEATNIK
BEGONIA
BIKINIS
BOTHNIA
BROWNIE
CANONIC
CHRONIC
DAPHNIS
DEMONIC
DRAWNIN
ESTONIA
EUGENIE
FLOWNIN
GIVENIN
HOMINID
INASNIT
JEANNIE
JOHNNIE
KIWANIS
LACONIC
LAVINIA
LEIBNIZ
MASONIC
MELANIE
MELANIN
MORANIS
OCEANIA
OCEANIC
OCEANID
ORGANIC
PARSNIP
PETUNIA
PFENNIG
PHOENIX
PHRENIC
ROMANIA
SELENIC
SHOWNIN
SPUTNIK
STANNIC
STDENIS
SUBUNIT
TAKENIN
TITANIA
TITANIC
TWOONIE
YEMENIS

••••N•I

ASHANTI
BASENJI
CHIANTI
DAVINCI
EFFENDI
JUMANJI
KUTENAI
RAPANUI
VIVENDI

•••••NI

AFGHANI
BELLINI
CABRINI
CASSINI
CELLINI
FELLINI
GALVANI
GUARANI
HOUDINI
MAGNANI
MANCINI
MARCONI
MARTINI
MONTANI
PADRONI
PUCCINI
ROSSINI
SANTINI
SORDINI
SPUMONI
TERMINI
TORTONI
TYMPANI
ZAMBONI

N•••J••

NAVAJOS
NOSEJOB

•NJ••••

ENJOINS
ENJOYED
INJECTS
INJOKES
INJURED
INJURES

•N••J••

SNOWJOB

••NJ•••

BANJOES
BONJOUR
BONJOVI
CONJOBS
CONJOIN
CONJURE
DONJONS
DONJOSE
DONJUAN
FANJETS
PUNJABI
SANJOSE
SANJUAN

•••NJ••

JOHNJAY
TIANJIN

••••NJ•

BASENJI
JUMANJI

N•K••••

NAKEDLY
NIKOLAI
NOKOMIS

N••K•••

NANKEEN
NAPKINS
NECKERS
NECKING
NECKTIE
NICKELS
NICKERS
NICKING

N•••K••

NABOKOV
NONSKID

N••••K•

NETLIKE
NETSUKE
NIBLIKE
NUDNIKS
NUNLIKE
NUTLIKE

N•••••K

NETWORK
NEWLOOK
NEWYORK
NIBLICK
NITPICK
NORFOLK

•NK••••

ANKLETS
INKBLOT
INKHORN
INKIEST
INKLESS
INKLIKE
INKLING
INKSPOT
INKWELL
INKYCAP
UNKEMPT
UNKINKS
UNKNITS
UNKNOTS
UNKNOWN

•N•K•••

ENSKIED
ENSKIES
SNAKIER
SNAKILY
SNAKING

•N••K••

INJOKES
INTAKES
INVOKED
INVOKER
INVOKES
KNACKER
KNOCKED
KNOCKER
KNUCKLE
SNACKED
SNACKER
SNEAKED
SNEAKER
SNEAKIN
SNICKER
SNOOKER
SNORKEL
UNASKED
UNBAKED
UNLIKED
UNMAKES
UNYOKED
UNYOKES

•N•••K•

ANORAKS
ANTLIKE
INKLIKE
UNALIKE
UNCORKS
UNHOOKS
UNKINKS
UNLINKS
UNLOCKS
UNLUCKY
UNMASKS
UNPACKS
UNTACKS

•N••••K

INSTOCK
ONTRACK
UNBLOCK
UNCLOAK
UNFROCK
UNSTACK
UNSTICK
UNSTUCK

••NK•••

BANKERS
BANKING
BANKSON
BONKERS
BUNKBED
BUNKERS
BUNKING
BUNKOED
CANKERS
CONKERS
CONKING
CONKOUT
DANKEST
DINKIER
DINKIES
DONKEYS
DONKING
DUNKERS
DUNKING
DUNKIRK
FINKING
FUNKIER
FUNKILY
FUNKING
GUNKIER
HANKERS
HANKIES
HONKERS
HONKING
HUNKERS
HUNKIER
JINKING
JUNKART
JUNKDNA
JUNKERS
JUNKETS
JUNKIER
JUNKIES
JUNKING
JUNKMAN
KINKIER
KINKILY
KINKING
LANKEST
LANKIER
LANKILY
LINKAGE
LINKERS
LINKING
LINKUPS
LUNKERS
MANKIND
MONKEES
MONKEYS
MONKISH
NANKEEN
OINKING
PINKEST
PINKIES
PINKING
PINKISH
PUNKAHS
PUNKERS
PUNKIER
PUNKIES
RANKERS
RANKEST
RANKING
RANKISH
RANKLED
RANKLES
SINKAGE
SINKERS
SINKING
SINKSIN
SUNKIST
TANKARD
TANKERS
TANKFUL
TANKING
TANKSUP
TANKTOP
TINKERS
TINKLED
TINKLES
WINKERS
WINKING
WINKLED
WINKLER
WINKLES
WINKOUT
WINKSAT
WONKIER
YANKEES
YANKING
YANKTON
YONKERS
ZONKERS
ZONKING
ZONKOUT

••N•K••

ABNAKIS
BANGKOK
CONAKRY
HANUKAH
KANAKAS
MENCKEN
MONIKER
NONSKID

••N••K•

CONVOKE
FANLIKE
FINICKY
FINLIKE
HENLIKE
HUNLIKE
KONTIKI
MANLIKE
NUNLIKE
PANCAKE
PANICKY
PENLIKE

PINOAKS
SINLIKE
SONLIKE
SUNLIKE
TANOAKS
TINLIKE
URNLIKE
VANDYKE

••N•••K

BANGKOK
BANNOCK
CONNICK
DENMARK
DUNKIRK
DUNNOCK
GANGTOK
GUNLOCK
HANCOCK
HENPECK
JANACEK
JANNOCK
JONNICK
KINFOLK
MENFOLK
RANSACK
RUNAMOK
RUNBACK
SUNDECK
TINTACK
TINWORK
VANDYCK
VANEYCK

•••NK••

BLANKED
BLANKER
BLANKET
BLANKLY
BLINKAT
BLINKED
BLINKER
CHINKED
CLANKED
CLINKED
CLINKER
CLUNKED
CLUNKER
CRANKED
CRANKUP
CRINKLE
CRINKLY
DRINKER
EVENKIS
FLANKED
FLANKER
FLUNKED
FRANKED
FRANKEN
FRANKER
FRANKIE
FRANKLY
FRANKOZ
PLANKED
PLINKED
PLUNKED
PRANKED
PRINKED
REINKED
SHANKAR
SHANKED
SKANKED
SKANKER
SKUNKED
SLINKED
SPANKED
SPANKER
STINKER
SWANKED
SWANKER
SWONKEN
THANKED
THINKER
THINKOF
THINKUP
TRINKET
TURNKEY
TWINKLE
TWINKLY
WRINKLE
WRINKLY

•••N•K•

ABENAKI
NUDNIKS
ROANOKE
VRONSKY

•••N••K

BANNOCK
CHINOOK
CONNICK
DUNNOCK
JANNOCK
JONNICK
LOWNECK
OLDNICK
VEENECK
WOZNIAK

••••NK•

DEBUNKS
EMBANKS
HIJINKS
LYSENKO
SHRINKS
SOYINKA
UNKINKS
UNLINKS
UPLINKS

••••N•K

BEATNIK
SPUTNIK

•••••NK

BETHINK
BURBANK
EYEBANK
FOGBANK
HOTLINK
ICERINK
JOBBANK
OUTRANK
RATFINK
RETHINK
SPELUNK

N•L••••

NELSONS
NILSSON
NULLAHS
NULLIFY
NULLING
NULLITY

N••L•••

NAILERS
NAILING
NAILSET
NAILSIN
NAPLESS
NEGLECT
NEOLITH
NETLIKE
NEWLEFT
NEWLOOK
NIBLICK
NIBLIKE
NIELSEN
NOBLEST
NUCLEAR
NUCLEIC
NUCLEON
NUCLEUS
NUCLIDE
NULLAHS
NULLIFY
NULLING
NULLITY
NUNLIKE
NUTLETS
NUTLIKE

N•••L••

NACELLE
NASALLY
NATALIA
NATALIE
NEBULAE
NEBULAR
NEBULAS
NEEDLED
NEEDLES
NEPALIS
NESTLED
NESTLER
NESTLES
NETTLED
NETTLES
NEVILLE
NIBBLED
NIBBLER
NIBBLES
NICOLAS
NIGGLED
NIGGLES
NIKOLAI
NIMBLER
NOBBLED
NOBBLER
NOBBLES
NODULAR
NODULES
NOGALES
NONPLUS
NONSLIP
NOODLES
NORELCO
NOVELLA
NOVELLE
NOVELTY
NOZZLES
NUBBLES
NUZZLED
NUZZLER
NUZZLES

N••••L•

NACELLE
NAIVELY
NAKEDLY
NARWALS
NASALLY
NASTILY
NATTILY
NEEDILY
NERVILY
NEVILLE
NICCOLO
NICHOLS
NICKELS
NIFTILY
NIGHTLY
NINTHLY
NOBHILL
NOFAULT
NOISILY
NONSELF
NORFOLK
NORMALS
NOTABLE
NOTABLY
NOTEDLY
NOTWELL
NOVELLA
NOVELLE
NUTTILY

N•••••L

NAHUATL
NARWHAL
NATURAL
NEEDFUL
NEUTRAL
NEWDEAL
NOBHILL
NOMINAL
NOSTRIL
NOTWELL
NUMERAL
NUPTIAL

•NL••••

ENLACED
ENLACES
ENLARGE
ENLISTS
ENLIVEN
ONLEAVE
ONLYTOO
ONLYYOU
UNLACED
UNLACES
UNLADES
UNLATCH
UNLEARN
UNLEASH
UNLIKED
UNLINED
UNLINKS
UNLOADS
UNLOCKS
UNLOOSE
UNLOVED
UNLUCKY

•N•L•••

ANALOGS
ANALOGY
ANALYSE
ANALYST
ANALYZE
ANELING
ANGLERS
ANGLING
ANILINE
ANKLETS
ANTLERS
ANTLIKE
ANTLION
ENCLAVE
ENCLOSE
ENDLESS
ENGLAND
ENGLISH
ENGLUND
ENPLANE
ENSLAVE
INBLOOM
INCLINE
INCLOSE
INCLUDE
INFLAME
INFLATE
INFLECT
INFLICT
INFLOWS
INKLESS
INKLIKE
INKLING
INNLESS
INPLACE
KNELLED
ONELANE
SNELLEN
UNALIKE
UNBLEST
UNBLOCK
UNCLASP
UNCLEAN
UNCLEAR
UNCLOAK
UNCLOGS
UNCLOSE
UNGLUED
UNPLUGS

•N••L••

ANGELES
ANGELIC
ANGELOU
ANGELUS
ANGOLAN
ANGULAR
ANNALEE
ANNELID
ANNULAR
ANNULUS
ANTILOG
ENABLED
ENABLES
ENDPLAY
ENFOLDS
ENGULFS
ENISLED
ENISLES
ENROLLS
ENSILED
ENSILES
ENVELOP
GNARLED
INDULGE
INGALLS
INHALED
INHALER
INHALES
INKBLOT
INSOLES
INSULAR
INSULIN
INSULTS
INVALID
INVOLVE
KNEELED
KNEELER
KNELLED
KNURLED
SNARLED
SNELLEN
SNIGLET
UNBOLTS
UNFOLDS
UNOILED
UNPILED
UNPILES
UNROLLS

•N•••L•

ANATOLE
ANGRILY
ANIMALS
ANNEALS
ANNUALS
ANOMALY
ANOUILH
ANTHILL
ENAMELS
ENNOBLE
ENROLLS
ENSOULS
ENTAILS
ENTITLE
INANELY
INAPTLY
INDWELL
INEPTLY
INERTLY
INFIELD
INGALLS
INHAULS
INKWELL
INOCULA
INSTALL
INSTALS
INSTILL
INSTILS
INSTYLE
INUTILE
KNUCKLE
ONAROLL
ONESELF
SNAFFLE
SNAKILY
SNAPPLE
SNIDELY
SNIFFLE
SNIFFLY
SNIGGLE
SNIVELS
SNOWILY
SNUFFLE
SNUFFLY
SNUGGLE
UNAPTLY
UNCIALS
UNCOILS
UNCURLS
UNFURLS
UNGODLY
UNREELS
UNROLLS
UNSEALS
UNVEILS

•N••••L

ANNABEL
ANTHILL
ENSNARL
ENTHRAL
INCIVIL
INDWELL
INFIDEL
INITIAL
INKWELL
INSTALL
INSTILL
KNIEVEL
ONAROLL
ONTRIAL
SNORKEL
UNAWFUL
UNCIVIL
UNEQUAL
UNRAVEL
UNSNARL
UNUSUAL

••NL•••

AWNLESS
DUNLINS
FANLIKE
FINLAND
FINLIKE
GUNLESS
GUNLOCK
HENLIKE
HUNLIKE
INNLESS
KINLESS
MANLESS
MANLIER
MANLIKE
NUNLIKE
PENLIKE
PINLESS
PUNLESS
RANLATE
RUNLATE
RUNLETS
SANLUIS
SINLESS
SINLIKE
SONLESS
SONLIKE
SUNLAMP
SUNLESS
SUNLIKE
TANLINE
TINLIKE
URNLIKE

••N•L••

ANNALEE
ANNELID
ANNULAR
ANNULUS
BANALLY
BANGLES
BENELUX
BENTLEY
BUNDLED
BUNDLES
BUNGLED
BUNGLER
BUNGLES
CANDLES
CANTLES
DANDLED
DANDLES
DANELAW
DANGLED
DANGLER
DANGLES
DINGLES
DONGLES
FANCLUB
FINALES
FINALLY
FONDLED
FONDLES
GANGLED
GANGLIA
GANTLET
GENTLED
GENTLER
GENTLES
GUNPLAY
HANDLED
HANDLER
HANDLES
HUNTLEY
JANGLED
JANGLES
JINGLED
JINGLES
JUNGLES
KINDLED
KINDLES
LANGLEY
LANOLIN
MANGLED
MANGLES
MANILOW
MANTLED
MANTLES
MINGLED
MINGLER
MINGLES
MINOLTA
MONOLOG
NONPLUS
NONSLIP
PANELED
PENALTY
PENULTS
RANKLED
RANKLES
RINGLET
RUNDLES
SANDLOT
SINGLED
SINGLES
TANGLED
TANGLES
TINGLED
TINGLES
TINKLED
TINKLES
TONALLY
TONELOC
VANILLA
VANILLI
VENALLY
WANGLED
WANGLER
WANGLES
WINKLED
WINKLER
WINKLES
WINSLOW
ZONALLY

••N••L•

ANNEALS
ANNUALS
BANALLY
BENGALI
BENGALS
BONNILY
CANCELS
CANDELA
CANFULS
CANNILY
CANNOLI
CANTILY
CONDOLE
CONSOLE
CONSULS
CONSULT
DANIELS
DENIALS
DENSELY
DINGILY
ENNOBLE
FANBELT
FANCILY
FINAGLE
FINALLY
FINIALS
FUNKILY
FUNNELS
FUNNILY
GENTILE
GINMILL
GONDOLA
GUNMOLL
GUNNELS
GUNWALE
HANDILY
HANSOLO
IGNOBLE
IGNOBLY
KENDALL
KENNELS
KINFOLK
KINKILY
LANKILY
LENTILS
LINCOLN
LINTELS
MANACLE
MANDALA
MANDELA
MANHOLE
MANIPLE
MANTELS
MANUALS
MENFOLK
MENIALS
MINABLE
MONDALE
MONGOLS
MONOCLE
MONTHLY
NINTHLY
NONSELF
PANFULS
PANICLE
PANOPLY
PENCILS
PENPALS
PINBALL
PINHOLE
PINOCLE
PINWALE
PUNNILY
RANDALL
RENAILS
RENAULT
RENTALS
RONDELS
RUNNELS
SANDALS
SANDFLY
SUNBELT
SUNNILY
TANGELO
TENABLE
TENABLY
TENFOLD
TENSELY
TENSILE
TENTHLY
TINNILY
TINSELS
TONALLY
TONSILS
TUNICLE
TUNNELS
VANDALS
VANILLA
VANILLI
VENALLY
WENDELL
WINDILY
ZONALLY

••N•••L

ANNABEL
BANEFUL
CENTRAL
CONCEAL
CONGEAL
CONICAL
CONTROL
CYNICAL
DONEGAL
FANMAIL
FANTAIL
FUNCHAL
GENERAL
GENTEEL
GINMILL
GONERIL
GUNMOLL
HANDFUL
JONQUIL
KENDALL
LINGUAL
MENTHOL
MINDFUL
MINERAL
MINIMAL
MONGREL
PINBALL
PINCURL
PINTAIL
RANDALL
RENEWAL
SANIBEL
SENEGAL
SENSUAL
SONGFUL
SUNBOWL
SUNDIAL
SYNFUEL
SYNODAL
TANKFUL
TENDRIL
TENNIEL
TINFOIL
TUNEFUL
TUNGOIL
VANPOOL
VENTRAL
WENDELL

•••NL••

AVONLEA
DARNLEY
JEANLUC
MOONLIT
STANLEE
STANLEY

•••N•L•

ATINGLE
BAGNOLD
BLANDLY
BLANKLY
BLINDLY
BLUNTLY
BONNILY
BRINDLE
CANNILY
CANNOLI
CORNELL
CORNILY
CRENELS
CRINKLE
CRINKLY
DIRNDLS
DWINDLE
FAINTLY
FRANKLY
FUNNELS
FUNNILY
GAUNTLY
GOONILY
GRANDLY
GRANOLA
GRANULE
GUNNELS
HYMNALS
INANELY
JOINTLY
KENNELS
KERNELS
KRINGLE
MOONILY
PHENOLS
PHONILY
PRONELY
PUNNILY
RAINILY
RIANTLY
ROUNDLY
RUNNELS
SAINTLY
SCANTLY
SHINGLE
SHINILY
SIGNALS
SOUNDLY
SPANGLE
SPANGLY
SPINDLE
SPINDLY
SPINELS
STONILY
SUNNILY
SWINDLE
TAWNILY
TINNILY
TRUNDLE
TUNNELS
TWINKLE
TWINKLY
WRANGLE
WRINKLE
WRINKLY
WRONGLY
ZWINGLI

•••N••L

BARNOWL
CHANCEL
CHANNEL
CHUNNEL
CORNEAL
CORNELL
CORNOIL
COUNCIL
COUNSEL
CRANIAL
EMANUEL
ENSNARL
EVANGEL
FLANNEL
FRONTAL
GAINFUL
GRENDEL
HOBNAIL
MOANFUL
PAINFUL
SCANDAL
SKINFUL
SPANIEL
STENCIL
STENGEL
TENNIEL
TOENAIL
UNSNARL
UTENSIL
YAWNFUL

••••NL•

CLEANLY
HUMANLY
PLAINLY
QUEENLY
STERNLY
WOMANLY

••••N•L

ADRENAL
ALUMNAL
ARSENAL
BUTANOL
CHANNEL
CHUNNEL
COLONEL
DIURNAL
EMPANEL
ESPANOL
ETERNAL
ETHANOL
FLANNEL
GRAPNEL
IMPANEL
JOURNAL
JUVENAL
LACUNAL
LAMINAL
NOMINAL
ORDINAL
RETINAL
SEMINAL
STERNAL
TYLENOL

N•M••••

NAMEDAY
NAMETAG
NAMIBIA
NEMEROV
NEMESES
NEMESIS
NIMBLER
NIMIETY
NIMRODS
NOMADIC
NOMINAL
NOMINEE
NUMBATS
NUMBERS
NUMBEST
NUMBING
NUMERAL
NUMERIC

N••M•••

NESMITH
NEWMATH
NEWMOON
NEWMOWN
NORMALS
NORMAND
NORMANS
NUTMEAT
NUTMEGS

N•••M••

NEWSMAN
NEWSMEN
NOKOMIS

N••••M•

NANAIMO
NAPTIME
NOISOME
NONCOMS
NOTRUMP
NOXZEMA

N•••••M

NATRIUM
NEEDHAM
NIOBIUM
NOSEEUM
NOSTRUM

•NM••••

ENMASSE
INMATES
UNMAKES
UNMASKS
UNMOVED

•N•M•••

ANEMONE
ANIMALS
ANIMATE
ANIMATO
ANIMISM
ANIMIST
ANOMALY
ANOMIES
ANYMORE
ENAMELS
ENAMORS
ENAMOUR
ENDMOST
ENEMIES
FNUMBER
GNOMISH
GNOMONS
INAMESS
UNAMUNO

•N••M••

ANAEMIA
ANAEMIC
ANOSMIA
ANOSMIC
ENCAMPS
ENCOMIA
ENDEMIC
ENIGMAS
ENZYMES
INCOMES
INGEMAR
INHUMAN
SNOWMAN
SNOWMEN
UNAIMED
UNARMED
UNKEMPT
UNNAMED
UNTAMED

•N•••M•

ANADEMS
ANATOMY
ANONYMS
ANTHEMS
ANYTIME
ENDGAME
ENGRAMS
INFLAME
INFORMS
INSEAMS
ONETIME

•N••••M

ANAGRAM
ANAHEIM
ANIMISM
ANTFARM
ANTONYM
INBLOOM
INTERIM
UNIFORM

••NM•••

BONMOTS
CONMOTO
DENMARK
DINMONT
FANMAIL
GINMILL
GUNMOLL
MANMADE
SUNMAID

••N•M••

AGNOMEN
BENUMBS
BONDMAN
BONDMEN
CINEMAS
CINEMAX
DONIMUS
DYNAMIC
DYNAMOS
GENOMES

HANGMAN
HANGMEN
JUNKMAN
KINEMAS
KINGMAN
KINSMAN
KINSMEN
LINEMAN
LINEMEN
MANUMIT
MANXMAN
MANXMEN
MINIMAL
MINIMUM
MONOMER
PANAMAS
RENAMED
RENAMES
RUNAMOK
SANDMAN
SANDMEN
SYNGMAN
UNNAMED

••N••M•

BANTAMS
CENTIME
CENTIMO
CONDEMN
CONGAME
CONSUME
CONTEMN
HANSOMS
NANAIMO
NONCOMS
PENNAME
RANSOMS
RUNHOME
SANREMO
SUNLAMP
TANDEMS
WINSOME

••N•••M

BENTHAM
BINGHAM
CONFIRM
CONFORM
GINGHAM
KINGDOM
LONGARM
MINICAM
MINIMUM
PENTIUM
PINETUM
SANCTUM
SUNBEAM
SUNROOM
SYNONYM
TANGRAM
TANTRUM
TINYTIM
TONEARM

•••NM••

FEYNMAN
IRONMAN
IRONMEN
MYANMAR
RAINMAN

•••N•M•

ANONYMS
BIGNAME
ECONOMY
EPONYMS
EPONYMY
EXANIMO
GRANDMA
IPANEMA
ISONOMY
MAGNUMS
MISNAME
PENNAME
PETNAME
PHENOMS
PHONEME
PLENUMS
SURNAME
TSUNAMI
YOUNGMC

•••N••M

CRANIUM
GRANDAM
HAFNIUM
HAHNIUM
OMENTUM
PHANTOM
PIANISM
QUANTUM
RHENIUM
TRANSOM
URANIUM

••••N•M

ACRONYM
ADFINEM
ANTONYM
ARCANUM
DIVINUM
HOMONYM
HUMANUM
HYPONYM
JEJUNUM
ORGANUM
SEVENAM
SEVENPM
STEINEM
STERNUM
SURINAM
SYNONYM
VIETNAM

N•N••••

NANAIMO
NANETTE
NANKEEN
NANNIES
NINEPIN
NINEVEH
NINNIES
NINTHLY
NONAGES
NONAGON
NONCOMS
NONIRON
NONPLUS
NONSELF
NONSKID
NONSLIP
NONSTOP
NONUSER
NONZERO
NUNCIOS
NUNLIKE
NUNNERY

N••N•••

NANNIES
NEONATE
NEWNESS
NINNIES
NOONDAY
NUANCED
NUANCES
NUDNIKS
NUNNERY
NYUNGAR

N•••N••

NOCANDO
NOMINAL
NOMINEE
NOVENAS

N••••N•

NABBING
NAGGING
NAILING
NAPKINS
NAPPING
NASCENT
NATIONS
NEARING
NEATENS
NECKING
NEEDING
NELSONS
NEPTUNE
NESTING
NETTING
NEURONE
NEURONS
NEWTONS
NICKING
NIPPING
NIRVANA
NITTANY
NODDING
NOGGINS
NOISING
NOOSING
NORMAND
NORMANS
NOSHING
NOTHING
NOTIONS
NUBBINS
NUBIANS
NUDGING
NULLING
NUMBING
NURSING
NUTTING

N•••••N

NAILSIN
NANKEEN
NETIZEN
NEUTRON
NEVADAN
NEWBORN
NEWMOON
NEWMOWN
NEWSMAN
NEWSMEN
NEWTOWN
NIELSEN
NILSSON
NINEPIN
NOCTURN
NONAGON
NONIRON
NUCLEON

•NN••••

ANNABEL
ANNALEE
ANNATTO
ANNEALS
ANNELID
ANNETTE
ANNEXED
ANNEXES
ANNOYED
ANNUALS
ANNUITY
ANNULAR
ANNULUS
ENNEADS
ENNOBLE
INNARDS
INNINGS
INNLESS
INNOWAY
UNNAMED
UNNERVE

•N•N•••

ANANIAS
ANONYMS
ENSNARE
ENSNARL
INANELY
INANEST
INANITY
ONANDON
ONENESS
ONENOTE
UNENDED
UNKNITS
UNKNOTS
UNKNOWN
UNSNAGS
UNSNAPS
UNSNARL

•N••N••

ANDANTE
ANOINTS
ANTENNA
ANTONIA
ANTONIN
ANTONIO
ANTONYM
ANYONES
ENCINAS
ENDINGS
ENGINES
ENHANCE
ENOUNCE
ENTENTE
INASNIT
INCANTS
INCENSE
INDENTS
INFANCY
INFANTA
INFANTS
INGENUE
INNINGS
INTENDS
INTENSE
INTENTS
INTONED
INTONER
INTONES
INVENTS
UNBENDS
UNBINDS
UNCANNY
UNHANDS
UNHANDY
UNKINKS
UNLINED
UNLINKS
UNTUNED
UNTUNES
UNWINDS
UNZONED

•N•••N•

ANCIENT
ANDEANS
ANELING
ANEMONE
ANGLING
ANILINE
ANODYNE
ANTEING
ANTENNA
ANTHONY
ANTOINE
ENCHANT
ENDRUNS
ENDUING
ENDZONE
ENGLAND
ENGLUND
ENJOINS
ENPLANE
ENSIGNS
ENSUING
ENTRANT
ENTWINE
ENURING
ENVYING
GNAWING
GNOMONS
INBOUND
INCHING
INCLINE
INDIANA
INDIANS
INFERNO
INFRONT
INKLING
INPRINT
INSPANS
INSTANT
INTERNS
INURING
KNEEING
KNIFING
KNOWING
ONELANE
ONGOING
SNAKING
SNAPONS
SNARING
SNIPING
SNOCONE
SNORING
SNOWING
UNAMUNO
UNBOUND
UNCANNY
UNDOING
UNDYING
UNGUENT
UNISONS
UNITING
UNSOUND
UNSPENT
UNTYING
UNWOUND

•N••••N

ANDIRON
ANDSOON
ANGOLAN
ANISTON
ANTIGEN
ANTLION
ANTONIN
ENCHAIN
ENLIVEN
ENTERON
ENTRAIN
INASPIN
INGRAIN
INGROWN
INHUMAN
INKHORN
INSULIN
ONANDON
ONEIRON
SNEAKIN
SNELLEN
SNOWDON
SNOWMAN
SNOWMEN
SNOWSIN
UNCHAIN
UNCLEAN
UNCTION
UNDRAWN
UNEATEN
UNICORN
UNKNOWN
UNLEARN
UNSHORN
UNWOVEN

••NN•••

BANNERS
BANNING
BANNOCK
BENNETT
BINNING
BONNETS
BONNIER
BONNILY
BUNNIES
CANNERS
CANNERY
CANNIER
CANNILY
CANNING
CANNOLI
CANNONS
CONNECT
CONNERY
CONNICK
CONNIFF
CONNING
CONNIVE
CONNORS
CONNOTE
CUNNING
DENNEHY
DINNERS
DONNING
DONNISH
DUNNING
DUNNOCK
FANNING
FENNIER
FINNIER
FINNISH
FUNNELS
FUNNIER
FUNNIES
FUNNILY
FUNNING
GANNETS
GANNETT
GENNARO
GINNING
GUNNELS
GUNNERS
GUNNERY
GUNNIES
GUNNING
HENNAED
HENNERY
HENNISH
HINNIES
HUNNISH
JANNOCK
JENNETS
JENNIES
JONNICK
KENNEDY
KENNELS
KENNETH
LINNETS
MANNERS
MANNING
MANNISH
MINNOWS
NANNIES
NINNIES
NUNNERY
PANNERS
PANNIER
PANNING
PENNAME
PENNANT
PENNATE
PENNERS
PENNIES
PENNING
PENNONS
PINNACE
PINNATE
PINNERS
PINNING
PUNNETS
PUNNIER
PUNNILY
PUNNING
RENNINS
RUNNELS
RUNNERS
RUNNIER
RUNNING
SENNETT
SINNERS
SONNETS
SUNNIER
SUNNILY
SUNNING
TANNERS
TANNERY
TANNEST
TANNING
TANNINS
TANNISH
TENNERS
TENNIEL
TINNERS
TINNIER
TINNILY
TONNAGE
TONNEAU
TONNISH
TUNNELS
TUNNIES
WANNABE
WANNESS
WANNEST
WANNISH
WINNERS
WINNING
WINNOWS
ZINNIAS

••N•N••

AWNINGS
BANANAS
BONANZA
CANINES
CANONIC
FINANCE
INNINGS
LININGS
MANANAS
PENANCE
PINENUT
PINONES
RANINTO
RUNINTO
SYNONYM
TENANCY
TENANTS
TENONED
VINTNER
WINGNUT
WYNONNA
ZENANAS

••N••N•

AMNIONS
AYNRAND
BANDANA
BANDING
BANGING
BANKING
BANNING
BANYANS
BENDING
BENZENE
BINDING
BINGING
BINNING
BONBONS
BONDING
BONGING
BUNGING
BUNIONS
BUNKING
BUNTING
CANCANS
CANNING
CANNONS
CANTINA
CANTING
CANTONS
CANYONS
CANZONE
CENSING
CINZANO
CONDONE
CONFINE
CONKING
CONNING
CONSENT
CONTEND
CONTENT
CONVENE
CONVENT
CUNNING
DANCING
DENTINE
DENTING
DENYING
DINGING
DINMONT
DONJONS
DONKING
DONNING
DUNKING
DUNLINS
DUNNING
FANIONS
FANNING
FANZINE
FENCING
FENDING
FENIANS
FINDING
FINKING
FINLAND
FONDANT
FONTINA
FUNDING
FUNKING
FUNNING
GANGING
GENUINE
GINNING
GINSENG
GONGING
GUNNING
HANDING
HANGING
HENBANE
HENTING
HINGING
HINTING
HONKING
HUNTING
JINKING
JINXING
JUNKDNA
JUNKING
KANSANS
KENYANS
KINGING
KINKING
LANDING
LANSING
LANTANA
LENDING
LENFANT
LENIENT
LINDENS
LINKING
LONGING
LUNGING
MANCINI
MANDANS
MANHUNT
MANKIND
MANNING
MENDING
MINCING
MINDING
MINIONS
MINOANS
MINTING
MINUEND
MINYANS
MONTANA
MONTAND
MONTANE
MONTANI
MUNDANE
MUNTINS
OINKING
PANNING
PANTING
PENDANT
PENDENT
PENDING
PENNANT
PENNING
PENNONS
PINGING
PINIONS
PINKING
PINNING
PONGING
PONTINE
PONYING
PUNGENT
PUNNING
PUNTING
RANGING
RANKING
RANTING
RENDING
RENNINS
RENTING
RINGING
RINSING
RUNNING
SANDING
SANTANA
SANTINI
SENDING
SENSING
SINGING
SINKING
SUNNING
SUNTANS
SYNCING
TANGENT
TANKING
TANLINE
TANNING
TANNINS
TENCENT
TENDING
TENDONS
TENPINS
TENSING
TENTING
TENZING
TINCANS
TINGING
TINTING
TONGANS
TONTINE
VANDINE
VENDING
VENTING
VINCENT
WANTING
WENDING
WINCING
WINDING
WINGING
WINKING
WINNING
WONTONS
WYNONNA
YANKING
ZINGING
ZONKING

••N•••N

AGNOMEN
BANKSON
BENISON
BENTSEN
BONDMAN
BONDMEN
CANTEEN
CONCERN
CONDEMN
CONDIGN
CONJOIN
CONSIGN
CONTAIN
CONTEMN
DENDRON
DENIZEN
DINEDIN
DINEDON
DINESEN
DINESIN
DINESON
DONJUAN
DONOVAN
DUNGEON
FONTEYN
GENTIAN
HANDGUN
HANDSIN
HANDSON
HANGMAN
HANGMEN
HANGSIN
HANGSON
HANGTEN
JANSSEN
JUNKMAN
KINCHIN
KINGMAN
KINGPIN
KINSMAN
KINSMEN
LANGDON
LANOLIN
LANTERN
LINCOLN
LINEMAN
LINEMEN
LONGRUN
LONGTON
MANSION
MANXMAN
MANXMEN
MENCKEN
MENTION
MENUHIN
MINIVAN
MONSOON
NANKEEN
NINEPIN
NONAGON
NONIRON
PENGUIN
PENSION
PINDOWN
PONTOON
PUNCHIN
PYNCHON
RANDOWN
RANGOON
RONTGEN
RUNDOWN
SANDMAN
SANDMEN
SANJUAN
SENDSIN
SINKSIN
SUNBURN
SUNDOWN
SYNGMAN
TENSION
TINHORN
TINTERN
TUNEDIN
TUNESIN
VENISON
WANTSIN
WINSTON
XANTHAN
YANKTON

•••NN••

BRENNAN
BRENNER
BRYNNER
CHANNEL
CHINNED
CHUNNEL
DUENNAS
FIENNES
FLANNEL
GRINNED
GRINNER
JEANNIE
JOHNNIE
LAENNEC
OCONNOR
PFENNIG
PLANNED
PLANNER
SCANNED
SCANNER
SHANNON
SHINNED
SHUNNED
SIENNAS
SKINNED
SKINNER
SPANNED
SPANNER
SPINNER
SPINNEY
STANNIC
STUNNED
STUNNER
THINNED
THINNER
TWINNED

•••N•N•

ADENINE
ALINING
ASININE
ATONING
BANNING
BARNONE
BEANING
BINNING
BRINING
BURNING
CANNING
CANNONS
CLONING
COINING
CONNING
CORNING
CRANING
CUNNING
DAMNING
DARNING
DAWNING
DONNING
DOWNING
DRONING
DUNNING
DURNING
EARNING
EMANANT
EMINENT
EVENING
FANNING
FAWNING
FOINING
FUNNING
GAINING
GINNING
GIRNING
GUANINE
GUNNING
HORNING
IRONING
IRONONS
JOINING
KEENING
KERNING
LEANING
LEONINE
LIMNING
LOANING
MAGNANI
MANNING
MEANING
MOANING
MOONING
MORNING
OPENEND
OPENING
OPINING
PANNING
PAWNING
PENNANT
PENNING
PENNONS
PHONING
PINNING
PLANING
PRUNING
PUNNING
QUININE
RAINING
REGNANT
REINING
REMNANT
RENNINS
RUINING
RUNNING
SEINING
SHANANA
SHINING
SIGNING
STONING
SUNNING
TANNING
TANNINS
TURNING
TWINING
VEINING
WARNING
WEANING
WHINING
WINNING
YARNING
YAWNING
YEANING

•••N••N

ABANDON
ALENCON
BERNSEN
BRANDON
BRANSON
BRENDAN
BRENNAN
BRINGIN
BRINGON
BRONSON
CHANSON
CLINTON
COUNTON
DAWNSON
DOINGIN
ETONIAN
FEYNMAN
FRANKEN
FRONTON
GAINSON
GHANIAN
GOINGIN
GOINGON
GRUNION
HORNSIN
ICINGIN
IRANIAN
IRONMAN
IRONMEN
JOHNSON
JOINSIN
KLINGON
LEANSON
ONANDON
OPINION
OXONIAN
PLANSON
PRONOUN
QUENTIN
RAINMAN
REINSIN
REUNION
ROUNDON
RUANDAN
RWANDAN
SHANNON
SIGNSIN
SIGNSON
STANDIN
STANDON
STANTON
STUNGUN
SWANSON
SWONKEN
TIANJIN
TRENTON
TURNSIN

TURNSON TYINGIN UGANDAN UNKNOWN YOUNGUN

••••NN•

ANTENNA ARGONNE CACANNY CAYENNE CEZANNE DOYENNE ETIENNE GARONNE HAPENNY HOSANNA JOHANNA LALANNE MADONNA RAVENNA ROSANNA ROSANNE ROXANNE SAVANNA SUSANNA SUSANNE SUZANNE TYRANNY UNCANNY WYNONNA

••••N•N

ANTONIN AVIGNON BRENNAN BROSNAN CHIGNON DRAWNIN DRAWNON FLOWNIN GIVENIN LEBANON LETINON MELANIN ORGANON SHANNON SHOWNIN SIMENON TAKENIN TAKENON

•••••NN

CAPEANN DAYSINN HERMANN MARYANN SCHWINN TALLINN ULLMANN

NO•••••

NOBBIER NOBBLED NOBBLER NOBBLES NOBHILL NOBLEST NOBODYS NOCANDO NOCTURN NOCUOUS NODDERS NODDING NODOUBT NODSOFF NODULAR NODULES NOETICS NOFAULT NOGALES NOGGINS NOGUCHI NOISIER NOISILY NOISING NOISOME NOKOMIS NOMADIC NOMINAL NOMINEE NONAGES NONAGON NONCOMS NONIRON NONPLUS NONSELF NONSKID NONSLIP NONSTOP NONUSER NONZERO NOODLES NOONDAY NOOSING NORBERT NORDICS NORELCO NORFOLK NORIEGA NORMALS NORMAND NORMANS NORTHER NOSEBAG NOSEEUM NOSEGAY NOSEJOB NOSEOUT NOSHERS NOSHING NOSHOWS NOSIEST NOSTRIL NOSTRUM NOSWEAT NOTABIT NOTABLE NOTABLY NOTATED NOTATES NOTCHED NOTCHES NOTEDLY NOTEPAD NOTHING NOTICED NOTICES NOTIONS NOTRUMP NOTSURE NOTTRUE NOTWELL NOUGATS NOUGHTS NOURISH NOUVEAU NOVARRO NOVELLA NOVELLE NOVELTY NOVENAS NOVICES NOWHERE NOXIOUS NOXZEMA NOZZLES

N•O••••

NEOLITH NEONATE NIOBIUM NOODLES NOONDAY NOOSING

N••O•••

NABOKOV NICOLAS NICOSIA NIKOLAI NOBODYS NODOUBT NOKOMIS

N•••O••

NAIROBI NARROWS NATIONS NELSONS NERVOUS NETWORK NEURONE NEURONS NEWBORN NEWLOOK NEWMOON NEWMOWN NEWPORT NEWTONS NEWTOWN NEWYORK NICCOLO NICHOLS NIMRODS NITROUS NOCUOUS NODSOFF NOISOME NONCOMS NORFOLK NOSEOUT NOSHOWS NOTIONS NOXIOUS

N••••O•

NABOKOV NAVAHOS NAVAJOS NEARYOU NEGATOR NEMEROV NEUTRON NEWLOOK NEWMOON NEWSBOY NILSSON NONAGON NONIRON NONSTOP NOSEJOB NUCLEON NUNCIOS

N•••••O

NABISCO NANAIMO NICCOLO NOCANDO NONZERO NORELCO NOVARRO

•NO••••

ANODISE ANODIZE ANODYNE ANOINTS ANOMALY ANOMIES ANONYMS ANORAKS ANOSMIA ANOSMIC ANOTHER ANOUILH DNOTICE ENOUNCE GNOCCHI GNOMISH GNOMONS GNOSTIC INOCULA INORBIT KNOBBED KNOCKED KNOCKER KNOSSOS KNOTTED KNOUTED KNOWHOW KNOWING ONORDER SNOCATS SNOCONE SNOGGED SNOOKER SNOOPED SNOOPER SNOOTED SNOOZED SNOOZES SNORERS SNORING SNORKEL SNORTED SNORTER SNOWCAP SNOWCAT SNOWDAY SNOWDON SNOWIER SNOWILY SNOWING SNOWJOB SNOWMAN SNOWMEN SNOWPEA SNOWSIN UNOILED

•N•O•••

ANDORRA ANDOVER ANGOLAN ANGORAS ANNOYED ANTOINE ANTONIA ANTONIN ANTONIO ANTONYM ANYONES CNTOWER ENCODED ENCODER ENCODES ENCOMIA ENCORES ENDORSE ENDOWED ENFOLDS ENFORCE ENGORGE ENJOINS ENJOYED ENNOBLE ENROBED ENROBES ENROLLS ENROOTS ENROUTE ENSOULS INBOARD INBOUND INBOXES INCOMES INDOORS INDORSE INDOUBT INFOCUS INFORCE INFORMS INHOUSE INJOKES INNOWAY INPOWER INROADS INSOFAR INSOLES INTONED INTONER INTONES INVOGUE INVOICE INVOKED INVOKER INVOKES INVOLVE ONBOARD ONGOING ONTOPOF SNOOKER SNOOPED SNOOPER SNOOTED SNOOZED SNOOZES UNBOLTS UNBOUND UNBOWED UNBOXED UNBOXES UNCOILS UNCORKS UNCOUTH UNCOVER UNDOING UNFOLDS UNGODLY UNHOOKS UNHORSE UNLOADS UNLOCKS UNLOOSE UNLOVED UNMOVED UNROBED UNROBES UNROLLS UNSOUND UNWOUND UNWOVEN UNYOKED UNYOKES UNZONED

•N••O••

ANALOGS ANALOGY ANATOLE ANATOMY ANCHORS ANCHOVY ANDROID ANDSOON ANEMONE ANEROID ANTCOWS ANTHONY ANTIOCH ANXIOUS ANYBODY ANYMORE ANYROAD ENAMORS ENAMOUR ENCLOSE ENDMOST ENDZONE ENGROSS ENROOTS ENTROPY ENVIOUS GNOMONS INAWORD INBLOOM INCLOSE INDOORS INFLOWS INFRONT INGROUP INGROWN INKHORN INSHORT INSPOTS INSTOCK INSTORE INTROIT ONAROLL ONENOTE ONEROUS ONSHORE SNAPONS SNOCONE UNAVOCE UNBLOCK UNCLOAK UNCLOGS UNCLOSE UNFROCK UNHOOKS UNICORN UNIFORM UNIPODS UNISONS UNKNOTS UNKNOWN UNLOOSE UNQUOTE UNSHORN UNSTOPS

•N•••O•

ANDIRON ANDSOON ANGELOU ANISTON ANTIFOG ANTILOG ANTLION ENACTOR ENDUROS ENTERON ENVELOP INASPOT INAWEOF INBLOOM INCISOR INDIGOS INERROR INFAVOR INKBLOT INKSPOT KNOSSOS KNOWHOW ONANDON ONEIRON ONESHOT ONLYTOO ONLYYOU ONTOPOF SNOWDON SNOWJOB UNCTION

•N••••O

ANIMATO ANNATTO ANTONIO INFERNO INPETTO INVACUO INVITRO ONLYTOO ONTARIO ONTHEGO SNAPSTO UNAMUNO UNDERDO UNDERGO

••NO•••

AGNOMEN ANNOYED BINOCHE CANONIC CANOPUS CONOIDS DENOTED DENOTES DONOVAN ENNOBLE FANOUTS GENOESE GENOMES HANOVER HONORED HONOREE HONORER HONORIS HONOURS IGNOBLE IGNOBLY IGNORED IGNORER IGNORES INNOWAY KENOSHA LANOLIN MANOWAR MENORAH MENOTTI MINOANS MINOLTA MINORCA MINORED MONOCLE MONOCOT MONODIC MONOLOG MONOMER PANOPLY PINOAKS PINOCLE PINONES RANOVER RENOTED RENOTES RUNOFFS RUNOUTS RUNOVER SENORAS SENORES SYNODAL SYNODIC SYNONYM TANOAKS TENONED WYNONNA ZENOBIA

••N•O••

AMNIONS BANJOES BANNOCK BINGOES BONBONS BONGOES BONJOUR BONJOVI BONMOTS BONSOIR BUNCOED BUNIONS BUNKOED CANDOUR CANNOLI CANNONS CANTONS CANTORS CANYONS CANZONE CENSORS CONCOCT CONCORD CONDOLE CONDONE CONDORS CONFORM CONJOBS CONJOIN CONKOUT CONMOTO CONNORS CONNOTE CONSOLE CONSORT CONTORT CONTOUR CONVOKE CONVOYS DINGOES DINMONT DONJONS DONJOSE DUNNOCK FANIONS FANSOUT FINDOUT FUNGOES GONDOLA GUNBOAT GUNDOGS GUNLOCK GUNMOLL HANCOCK HANDOFF HANDOUT HANGOFF HANGOUT HANSOLO HANSOMS HENCOOP HUNGOUT IGNEOUS JANNOCK JINGOES JUNCOES JUNIORS KINFOLK LANFORD LINCOLN LINGOES MANGOES MANHOLE MANHOOD MANHOUR MANIOCS MENDOZA MENFOLK MENTORS MINIONS MINNOWS MONGOLS MONSOON MONTOYA NONCOMS PANDORA PANSOUT PENNONS PINDOWN PINHOLE PINIONS PONTOON RANCOUR RANDOWN RANGOFF RANGOON RANGOUT RANSOMS RINGOFF RINGOUT RUNDOWN RUNGOFF RUNGOUT RUNHOME RUNSOFF RUNSOUT SANFORD SANGOUT SANJOSE SENDOFF SENDOUT SENIORS SENSORS SENSORY SENTOFF SENTOUT SINGOUT SINUOUS SUNBOWL SUNDOGS SUNDOWN SUNGODS SUNROOF SUNROOM TANGOED TENDONS TENFOLD TENFOUR TENSORS TENUOUS TINFOIL TINHORN TINWORK TUNEOUT TUNGOIL VANGOGH VANPOOL VENDORS WANTOUT WENTOFF WENTOUT WINDOWS WINKOUT WINNOWS WINSOME WINSOUT WONTONS XINGOUT ZONKOUT

••N••O•

BANDBOX BANGKOK BANKSON BENISON BONITOS CONTROL DENDRON DINEDON DINESON DONATOR DONEFOR DUNGEON DYNAMOS GANGTOK GUNSFOR GUNSHOT HANDSON HANGDOG HANGSON HENCOOP HONCHOS JANEDOE JANITOR KINGDOM LANGDON LANGUOR LONGBOW LONGTON MANHOOD MANILOW MANITOU MANSION MENTHOL MENTION MONITOR MONOCOT MONOLOG MONSOON NONAGON NONIRON NONSTOP NUNCIOS PENSION PINEFOR PONCHOS PONTOON PYNCHON RANCHOS RANGOON RANRIOT RUNAMOK RUNRIOT RUNSFOR SANDBOX SANDHOG SANDLOT SENATOR SENDFOR SENTFOR SENUFOS SUNROOF SUNROOM SUNSPOT TANKTOP TENSION TENSPOT TONELOC TONEROW VANPOOL VENISON WENTFOR WINDROW WINDSOR WINSLOW WINSTON YANKTON

••N•••O

ANNATTO BANDITO BENDIGO CANSECO CENTAVO CENTIMO CINZANO CONBRIO CONMOTO ERNESTO GENNARO HANSOLO IONESCO LENTIGO LINBIAO LINPIAO LONGAGO MONTEGO MONTERO NANAIMO NONZERO ORNITHO QINGDAO RANINTO RUNINTO SANREMO SINGSTO TANGELO TENDSTO WANTSTO

•••NO••

BAGNOLD BANNOCK BARNONE BARNOWL BURNOUT BYANOSE CANNOLI CANNONS CHINOOK CONNORS CONNOTE CORNOIL CRINOID DUNNOCK ECONOMY EGGNOGS EVENOUT GRANOLA HEINOUS HOBNOBS HYMNODY IRONONS IRONORE IRONOUT ISONOMY IVANOVO JANNOCK KEYNOTE LEONORA MINNOWS OMINOUS ONENOTE ORINOCO OZONOUS PAWNOFF PENNONS PHENOLS PHENOMS PLANOUT PRONOUN PUGNOSE QUINOAS RAINOUT ROANOKE RUINOUS SEENOFF SEENOUT SIGNOFF SIGNOUT SPINOFF SPINOUT SPINOZA SPUNOFF SPUNOUT TORNOFF TORNOUT TURNOFF TURNOUT ULANOVA UNKNOTS UNKNOWN WINNOWS WORNOFF WORNOUT

•••N•O•

ABANDON ALENCON BIENTOT BRANDON BRANSON BRINGON BRONCOS BRONSON CHANSON CHINOOK CLANGOR CLINTON CORNCOB CORNDOG CORNROW COUNTON DAWNSON DOWNBOW FRANKOZ FRONTON GAINSON GOINFOR GOINGON GRANTOR GRUNION IVANHOE JOHNDOE JOHNSON KLINGON LEANSON LEANTOS MAINTOP MCENROE MOONDOG OCONNOR ONANDON OPENTOE OPINION PHANTOM PLANSON QUANGOS RAINBOW REUNION ROUNDON SHANNON SIGNSON SPONSOR STANDON STANTON STENTOR STINGOS SWANSON THINKOF TRANSOM TRENTON TURNSON WYANDOT

•••N••O

BRINGTO EXANIMO GENNARO GUANACO IVANOVO LYINGTO MAGNETO ORINOCO OWINGTO POINTTO SOANDSO TORNADO TURNSTO

••••NO•

ALBINOS ALIENOR ASOFNOW AVIGNON BARANOF BOWKNOT BUTANOL CASINOS CHIGNON DOMINOS DRAWNON ELEANOR EQUINOX ESPANOL ETHANOL GODUNOV HAVENOT JOURNOS JUSTNOW KIMONOS LADINOS LATINOS LEBANON LETINON MAGINOT MERINOS OCONNOR ORGANON POCONOS ROMANOV SHANNON SIMENON TAKENON TOPKNOT TYLENOL ULYANOV UPTONOW USTINOV WHATNOT YOUKNOW

••••N•O

ADDONTO ALFONSO ANTONIO ARSENIO CUTINTO DOMINGO DURANGO GETINTO GIVENTO GOTINTO HHMUNRO LAYINTO LEPANTO LITINTO LORENZO LYSENKO MARENGO MEMENTO NOCANDO ORLANDO OTRANTO PIMENTO PRYINTO RAMINTO RANINTO RIPINTO RUNINTO SETINTO SQUANTO

TAPINTO
TARANTO
TIEINTO
TORONTO

•••••NO
ARETINO
BAMBINO
BOITANO
CASSINO
CEBUANO
CHICANO
CINZANO
CUIBONO
HISPANO
ILOCANO
INFERNO
JAYLENO
LIVORNO
LOCARNO
LUCIANO
MARTINO
OREGANO
PAISANO
PATERNO
POMPANO
PROBONO
RELLENO
RIPIENO
SALERNO
SOPRANO
SORDINO
SORVINO
SUKARNO
TREVINO
UNAMUNO
VOLCANO
YOKOONO

N•P••••
NAPHTHA
NAPKINS
NAPLESS
NAPPERS
NAPPIES
NAPPING
NAPTIME
NEPALIS
NEPHEWS
NEPTUNE
NIPPERS
NIPPIER
NIPPING
NUPTIAL

N••P•••
NAPPERS
NAPPIES
NAPPING
NEWPORT
NIPPERS
NIPPIER
NIPPING
NITPICK
NONPLUS

N•••P••
NINEPIN
NOTEPAD

N•••••P
NONSLIP
NONSTOP
NOTRUMP

•NP••••
ENPLANE
INPEACE
INPETTO
INPHASE
INPLACE
INPOWER
INPRINT
UNPACKS
UNPAVED
UNPILED
UNPILES
UNPLUGS

•N•P•••
ANAPEST
ENDPLAY
INAPTER
INAPTLY
INEPTLY
INSPANS
INSPECT
INSPIRE
INSPOTS
SNAPONS
SNAPPED
SNAPPER
SNAPPLE
SNAPSAT
SNAPSTO
SNAPSUP
SNIPEAT
SNIPERS
SNIPING
SNIPPED
SNIPPET
UNAPTLY
UNIPODS
UNSPENT

•N••P••
INASPIN
INASPOT
INCEPTS
INCIPIT
INDEPTH
INKSPOT
INSIPID
KNEEPAD
ONTOPOF
SNAPPED
SNAPPER
SNAPPLE
SNIPPED
SNIPPET
SNOOPED
SNOOPER
SNOWPEA
UNHAPPY
UNTAPED

•N•••P•
ENCAMPS
ENCRYPT
ENTRAPS
ENTROPY
ENWRAPS
INSCAPE
INSHAPE
INSTEPS
UNDRAPE
UNHAPPY
UNKEMPT
UNSNAPS
UNSTOPS
UNSWEPT
UNTRAPS
UNWRAPS

•N••••P
ANTEDUP
ANTESUP
ANTWERP
ENDEDUP
ENVELOP
INAHEAP
INGROUP
INKYCAP
KNEECAP
KNEESUP
ONESTEP
SNAPSUP
SNOWCAP
UNCLASP
UNSTRAP

••NP•••
GUNPLAY
HENPECK
LINPIAO
NONPLUS
PANPIPE
PENPALS
TENPINS
VANPOOL

••N•P••
CANAPES
CANOPUS
JUNIPER
KINGPIN
MANIPLE
NINEPIN
PANOPLY
SUNSPOT
SYNAPSE
TENSPOT

••N••P•
BUNYIPS
CONCEPT
HANGUPS
LINEUPS
LINKUPS
PANPIPE
SENDUPS
TINTYPE
TUNEUPS
WENTAPE
WINDUPS

••N•••P
BANGSUP
BINDSUP
BONEDUP
BONESUP
CANTRIP
GANGSUP
HANDSUP
HANGSUP
HANSARP
HENCOOP
KINSHIP
LINEDUP
LINESUP
MANTRAP
NONSLIP
NONSTOP
OWNEDUP
PINESAP
PUNCHUP
RINGSUP
RUNDEEP
SENDSUP
SUNLAMP
TANKSUP
TANKTOP
TENSEUP
TONEDUP
TONESUP
TUNEDUP
TUNESUP
WINDSUP
WINESAP
WINGTIP

•••NP••
DOWNPAT
OPENPIT

•••N•P•
CATNAPS
CATNIPS
CHINUPS
GRANDPA
KIDNAPS
PRENUPS
SCHNAPS
TURNIPS
UNSNAPS

•••N••P
BORNEUP
BOUNDUP
BRINGUP
BURNSUP
BURNTUP
CRANKUP
DOINGUP
EVENSUP
GOINGUP
ICINGUP
JEANARP
JOINSUP
MAINTOP
OPENSUP
ROUNDUP
SIGNSUP
STANDUP
THINKUP
TURNSUP
TYINGUP
USINGUP
WOUNDUP

••••NP•
SEVENPM

••••N•P
BLOWNUP
CLEANUP
DRAWNUP
EATENUP
GIVENUP
GROWNUP
PARSNIP
SEVENUP
WOKENUP

•NQ••••
ENQUIRE
ENQUIRY
INQUEST
INQUIRE
INQUIRY
UNQUOTE

•N•Q•••
UNEQUAL

•N••Q••
ANTIQUE

•N•••Q•
ONTHEQT

••NQ•••
BANQUET
CONQUER
JONQUIL
YANQUIS

••N•Q••
MONIQUE

•••NQ••
QUINQUE

•••N•Q•
PSANDQS

N•R••••
NARRATE
NARROWS
NARTHEX
NARWALS
NARWHAL
NERDIER
NEREIDS
NERVIER
NERVILY
NERVOUS
NIRVANA
NORBERT
NORBERT
NORDICS
NORELCO
NORFOLK
NORIEGA
NORMALS
NORMAND
NORMANS
NORTHER
NUREYEV
NURSERS
NURSERY
NURSING
NURTURE

N••R•••
NAIROBI
NARRATE
NARROWS
NATRIUM
NEAREST
NEARING
NEARYOU
NEURONE
NEURONS
NIMRODS
NITRATE
NITRIDE
NITRITE
NITROUS
NOTRUMP
NOURISH
NUTRIAS

N•••R••
NATURAL
NATURED
NATURES
NAVARRE
NEMEROV
NEUTRAL
NEUTRON
NIGERIA
NONIRON
NOSTRIL
NOSTRUM
NOTTRUE
NOVARRO
NUMERAL
NUMERIC

N••••R•
NABBERS
NAILERS
NAPPERS
NATTERS
NAVARRE
NECKERS
NECTARS
NESTERS
NETSURF
NETWORK
NEWBERY
NEWBORN
NEWHART
NEWPORT
NEWYORK
NIAGARA
NICKERS
NIGGARD
NIPPERS
NOCTURN
NODDERS
NONZERO
NORBERT
NOSHERS
NOTSURE
NOVARRO
NOWHERE
NUDGERS
NUMBERS
NUNNERY
NURSERS
NURSERY
NURTURE
NUTTERS

N•••••R
NAGGIER
NASTIER
NATTIER
NEBULAR
NEEDIER
NEGATER
NEGATOR
NEITHER
NERDIER
NERVIER
NESTLER
NEWAGER
NEWSIER
NEWYEAR
NIBBLER
NIEBUHR
NIFTIER
NIMBLER
NIPPIER
NITTIER
NOBBIER
NOBBLER
NODULAR
NOISIER
NONUSER
NORTHER
NUBBIER
NUCLEAR
NUTSIER
NUTTIER
NUZZLER
NYUNGAR

•NR••••
ENRAGED
ENRAGES
ENROBED
ENROBES
ENROLLS
ENROOTS
ENROUTE
INROADS
UNRATED
UNRAVEL
UNREADY
UNREELS
UNROBED
UNROBES
UNROLLS

•N•R•••
ANARCHY
ANDREAS
ANDRESS
ANDREWS
ANDROID
ANEROID
ANGRIER
ANGRILY
ANORAKS
ANYROAD
ENCRUST
ENCRYPT
ENDRUNS
ENGRAFT
ENGRAMS
ENGRAVE
ENGROSS
ENTRAIN
ENTRANT
ENTRAPS
ENTREAT
ENTREES
ENTRIES
ENTROPY
ENTRUST
ENURING
ENWRAPS
GNARLED
GNARRED
INARUSH
INBREED
INBRIEF
INERROR
INERTIA
INERTLY
INFRONT
INGRAIN
INGRATE
INGRESS
INGROUP
INGROWN
INORBIT
INPRINT
INTROIT
INTRUDE
INTRUST
INTRUTH
INURING
KNURLED
ONAROLL
ONEROUS
ONORDER
ONTRACK
ONTRIAL
SNARING
SNARLED
SNORERS
SNORING
SNORKEL
SNORTED
SNORTER
UNARMED
UNCRATE
UNDRAPE
UNDRAWN
UNDRESS
UNFROCK
UNTRAPS
UNTRIED
UNTRUTH
UNWRAPS

•N••R••
ANAGRAM
ANDIRON
ANDORRA
ANGERED
ANGORAS
ANTARES
ENCORES
ENDORSE
ENDURED
ENDURES
ENDUROS
ENFORCE
ENGARDE
ENGIRDS
ENGORGE
ENLARGE
ENSURED
ENSURES
ENTERED
ENTERON
ENTHRAL
GNARRED
INDORSE
INERROR
INFERNO
INFORCE
INFORMS
INHERED
INHERES
INHERIT
INJURED
INJURES
INNARDS
INSERTS
INSURED
INSURER
INSURES
INTERIM
INTERNS
INTERSE
INVERSE
INVERTS
INWARDS
ONEIRON
ONSERVE
ONTARIO
ONWARDS
SNEERAT
SNEERED
SNEERER
UNAIRED
UNCORKS
UNCURLS
UNDERDO
UNDERGO
UNEARTH
UNFURLS
UNGIRDS
UNHORSE
UNNERVE
UNSCREW
UNSTRAP

•N•••R•
ANCHORS
ANDORRA
ANGLERS
ANSWERS
ANTFARM
ANTHERS
ANTIART
ANTLERS
ANTWERP
ANYMORE
ENAMORS
ENDEARS
ENQUIRE
ENQUIRY
ENSNARE
ENSNARL
ENVIERS
GNAWERS
INAWORD
INBOARD
INDOORS
INKHORN
INQUIRE
INQUIRY
INSHORT
INSPIRE
INSTARS
INSTORE
INTEARS
INTEGRA
INVITRO
KNAVERY
ONADARE
ONAGERS
ONBOARD
ONGUARD
ONSHORE
SNIPERS
SNORERS
UNAWARE
UNHEARD
UNICORN
UNIFORM
UNITARY
UNITERS
UNLEARN
UNSHORN
UNSNARL

•N••••R
ANDOVER
ANGRIER
ANGULAR
ANNULAR
ANOTHER
ANTBEAR
ANTIWAR
ANTSIER
CNTOWER
ENACTOR
ENAMOUR
ENCODER
ENDUSER
ENTICER
FNUMBER
INAPTER
INCISOR
INCITER
INDUCER
INERROR
INFAVOR
INGEMAR
INHALER
INPOWER
INSIDER
INSOFAR
INSULAR
INSURER
INTEGER
INTONER
INVADER
INVOKER
KNACKER
KNEADER
KNEELER
KNITTER
KNOCKER
ONATEAR
ONESTAR
ONORDER
SNACKER
SNAKIER
SNAPPER
SNEAKER
SNEERER
SNEEZER
SNICKER
SNIFFER
SNIFTER
SNIGGER
SNOOKER
SNOOPER
SNORTER
SNOWIER
SNUFFER
SNUGGER
UNCLEAR
UNCOVER
UNIFIER
UNWISER

••NR•••
AYNRAND
CONRIED
HENRYIV
RANRIOT
RUNRIOT
SANREMO
SUNRAYS
SUNRISE
SUNROOF
SUNROOM
TENRECS

••N•R••
CANARDS
CANTRIP
CENTRAL
CENTRED
CENTRES
CENTRIC
CONBRIO
CONTRAS
CONTROL
CONURES
DENARII
DENDRON
GENERAL
GENERIC
GENERIS
GONERIL
HENDRIX
HONORED
HONOREE
HONORER
HONORIS
HUNDRED
IGNORED
IGNORER
IGNORES
INNARDS
KINDRED
KINGRAT
LONGRUN
MANFRED
MANTRAP
MANTRAS
MANTRIC
MENORAH
MINARET
MINERAL
MINERVA
MINORCA
MINORED
MONARCH
MONGREL
NONIRON
PANARAB
PANURGE
RENARDS
SANGRIA
SENORAS
SENORES
SYNERGY
TANGRAM
TANTRUM
TENDRIL
TENURED
TENURES
TONEROW
TUNDRAS
UNNERVE
VENTRAL
WINDROW
WINERED
WINFREY

••N••R•
BANKERS
BANNERS
BANTERS
BENDERS
BINDERS
BINDERY
BONEDRY
BONFIRE
BONKERS
BUNKERS
CANKERS
CANNERS
CANNERY
CANTERS
CANTORS
CENSERS
CENSORS
CENSURE
CENTERS
CENTURY
CINDERS
CINDERY
CONAKRY
CONCERN
CONCERT
CONCORD
CONCURS
CONDORS
CONFERS
CONFIRM
CONFORM
CONGERS
CONJURE
CONKERS
CONNERY
CONNORS
CONSORT
CONTORT
CONVERT
DANBURY
DANCERS
DANDERS
DANGERS
DENIERS
DENMARK
DENTURE
DINNERS
DUNKERS
DUNKIRK
FANFARE
FENCERS
FENDERS
FINDERS
FINEART
FINGERS
GANDERS
GANGERS
GENDERS
GENNARO
GINGERS
GINGERY
GUNFIRE
GUNNERS
GUNNERY
HANGARS
HANGERS
HANKERS
HANSARP
HENNERY
HINDERS
HONIARA
HONKERS
HONOURS
HUNGARY
HUNGERS
HUNKERS
HUNTERS
JANUARY
JUNIORS
JUNKART
JUNKERS
LANCERS
LANDERS
LANFORD
LANGTRY
LANGURS
LANTERN
LANYARD
LENDERS
LINGERS
LINKERS
LONGARM
LUNKERS
MANGERS
MANNERS
MANSARD
MENDERS
MENHIRS
MENTORS
MINCERS
MINDERS
MINTERS
MONGERS
MONTERO
NONZERO
NUNNERY
PANDERS
PANDORA
PANNERS
PANZERS
PENNERS
PINCERS
PINCURL
PINNERS
PONDERS
PONIARD
PUNKERS
PUNTERS
QINTARS
RANGERS
RANKERS
RANTERS
RENDERS
RENTERS
RINGERS
RUNNERS
RUNSDRY
SANDERS
SANFORD
SANTIRS
SENDERS
SENIORS
SENSORS
SENSORY
SINATRA
SINCERE
SINGERS
SINKERS
SINNERS
SUNBURN
SUNDERS
TANGERE
TANKARD
TANKERS
TANNERS
TANNERY
TANTARA
TENDERS
TENNERS
TENSORS
TENTERS
TINDERS
TINEARS
TINHORN
TINKERS
TINNERS
TINTERN
TINTERS
TINWARE
TINWORK
TONEARM
TONSURE
VENDORS
VENEERS
VENTERS
VENTURA
VENTURE
WANDERS
WENDERS
WINCERS
WINDERS
WINGERS
WINKERS
WINNERS
WINTERS
WINTERY
WONDERS
YONKERS
ZANDERS
ZINGERS
ZONKERS

••N•••R
ANNULAR
BENATAR
BENAZIR
BENDIER
BONJOUR
BONNIER
BONSOIR
BUNGLER
CANDOUR
CANNIER
CENTAUR
CONIFER
CONQUER
CONTOUR
DANDIER
DANGLER
DANSEUR
DINGIER
DINKIER
DONATOR
DONEFOR
FANCIER
FENNIER
FINNIER
FUNFAIR
FUNKIER
FUNNIER
GENTLER
GUNKIER
GUNSFOR
GUNTHER
HANDCAR
HANDIER
HANDLER
HANOVER
HONORER
HUNKIER
IGNITER
IGNORER
IONIZER
JANITOR
JANVIER
JUNIPER
JUNKIER
KINKIER
LANGUOR
LANKIER
LINTIER
MANAGER
MANGIER
MANHOUR
MANLIER
MANOWAR

MANYEAR
MINGIER
MINGLER
MINIVER
MINTIER
MONIKER
MONITOR
MONOMER
MONSTER
MUNCHER
MYNHEER
NONUSER
PANNIER
PANTHER
PINCHER
PINEFOR
PINETAR
PUNCHER
PUNKIER
PUNNIER
PUNSTER
RANCHER
RANCOUR
RANDIER
RANGIER
RANOVER
RENEGER
RENEWER
RUNNIER
RUNOVER
RUNSFOR
RUNTIER
SANDBAR
SANDIER
SENATOR
SENDFOR
SENTFOR
SUNNIER
TANAGER
TANGIER
TENFOUR
TINNIER
TINSTAR
VINEGAR
VINTNER
WANGLER
WENTFOR
WINDIER
WINDSOR
WINEBAR
WINKLER
WONKIER
ZINGIER

•••NR••

CORNROW
MCENROE

•••N•R•

ABINTRA
BANNERS
BARNARD
BEANERY
BERNARD
BURNERS
CANNERS
CANNERY
CARNERA
COINERS
CONNERY
CONNORS
CORNERS
COUNTRY
DARNERS
DEANERY
DINNERS
DOWNERS
DRONERS
EARNERS
ENSNARE
ENSNARL
FAWNERS
FOUNDRY
GAINERS
GARNERS
GENNARO
GRANARY
GUNNERS
GUNNERY
HENNERY
IRONERS
IRONORE
JEANARP
JOINERS
JOINERY
KEENERS
LAUNDRY
LEANERS
LEONARD
LEONORA
LIMNERS
LOANERS
MANNERS
MAYNARD
MOANERS
NUNNERY
OPENERS
OPINERS
PANNERS
PAWNERS
PENNERS
PINNERS
PLANERS
PLENARY
PRUNERS
QUINARY
REENTRY
REYNARD
RUINERS
RUNNERS
SCENERY
SEINERS
SHANGRI
SHINERS
SIGNERS
SINNERS
SOONERS
SPINDRY
STONERS
TANNERS
TANNERY
TEENERS
TENNERS
TERNARY
THENARS
TINNERS
TOWNERS
TRENARY
TURNERS
TURNERY
UNSNARL
WHINERS
WIENERS
WINNERS
YAWNERS

•••N••R

ALUNSER
ASUNDER
AVENGER
BAINTER
BLANDER
BLANKER
BLENDER
BLINDER
BLINKER
BLONDER
BLUNDER
BLUNTER
BONNIER
BOUNCER
BOUNDER
BRANDER
BRENNER
BRINGER
BRINIER
BRYNNER
CANNIER
CHANCER
CHANGER
CHANTER
CHENIER
CHUNTER
CLANGOR
CLINKER
CLUNKER
CORNIER
COUNTER
DERNIER
DOWNIER
DRINKER
EMENDER
EVANDER
FAINTER
FENNIER
FERNBAR
FERNIER
FINNIER
FLANEUR
FLANKER
FOUNDER
FRANKER
FUNNIER
GAUNTER
GOINFOR
GOONIER
GOUNDER
GRANDER
GRANGER
GRANTOR
GRINDER
GRINNER
JOINDER
LAUNDER
LEANDER
LOONIER
LOUNGER
MAUNDER
MEANDER
MOONIER
MYANMAR
NYUNGAR
OCONNOR
OPENAIR
OPENBAR
PAINTER
PANNIER
PHONIER
PIONEER
PLANNER
PLANTAR
PLANTER
PLUNDER
PLUNGER
POINTER
POUNCER
POUNDER
PRANCER
PRINTER
PUNNIER
RAINIER
REENTER
ROUNDER
RUNNIER
SAUNTER
SCANNER
SCANTER
SHANKAR
SHINIER
SKANKER
SKINNER
SLANDER
SLENDER
SLINGER
SOUNDER
SPANKER
SPANNER
SPENCER
SPENDER
SPENSER
SPINIER
SPINNER
SPONGER
SPONSOR
STENTOR
STINGER
STINKER
STONIER
STUNNER
SUNNIER
SWANKER
SWINGER
TAWNIER
TEENIER
THINAIR
THINKER
THINNER
THUNDER
TINNIER
VAUNTER
VEINIER
VERNIER
WEENIER
WERNHER
WHINIER
WRINGER
WRONGER
YOUNGER

••••NR•

HHMUNRO
MASONRY
MCHENRY

••••N•R

ADORNER
ALIENOR
ALIGNER
BRENNER
BROWNER
BRYNNER
CLEANER
COSTNER
CROONER
DIVINER
DRAINER
EDASNER
ELEANOR
FLEXNER
FROWNER
GARDNER
GLEANER
GREENER
GRINNER
GROANER
INTONER
LAMINAR
LARDNER
LEARNER
MARINER
OCONNOR
OFTENER
PARDNER
PARTNER
PILSNER
PLAINER
PLANNER
PREENER
REFINER
SCANNER
SCORNER
SEMINAR
SERENER
SHATNER
SHRINER
SKINNER
SPANNER
SPINNER
SPOONER
SPURNER
STAINER
STEINER
STERNER
STUNNER
THINNER
TRAINER
URBANER
VINTNER
WAGONER
WAKENER
YEARNER

N•S••••

NASALLY
NASCENT
NASTASE
NASTIER
NASTILY
NESCAFE
NESMITH
NESTEGG
NESTERS
NESTING
NESTLED
NESTLER
NESTLES
NOSEBAG
NOSEEUM
NOSEGAY
NOSEJOB
NOSEOUT
NOSHERS
NOSHING
NOSHOWS
NOSIEST
NOSTRIL
NOSTRUM
NOSWEAT

N••S•••

NAYSAID
NAYSAYS
NELSONS
NETSUKE
NETSURF
NEWSBOY
NEWSDAY
NEWSIER
NEWSIES
NEWSMAN
NEWSMEN
NILSSON
NODSOFF
NOISIER
NOISILY
NOISING
NOISOME
NONSELF
NONSKID
NONSLIP
NONSTOP
NOOSING
NOTSURE
NURSERS
NURSERY
NURSING
NUTSIER

N•••S••

NABISCO
NAILSET
NAILSIN
NATASHA
NEMESES
NEMESIS
NEXUSES
NICOSIA
NIELSEN
NILSSON
NONUSER
NUDISTS

N••••S•

NAGGISH
NAPLESS
NASTASE
NEAREST
NEATEST
NEBBISH
NEWNESS
NIGHEST
NOBLEST
NOSIEST
NOURISH
NUMBEST

N•••••S

NABBERS
NAIADES
NAILERS
NANNIES
NAPKINS
NAPLESS
NAPPERS
NAPPIES
NARROWS
NARWALS
NATIONS
NATIVES
NATTERS
NATURES
NAUGHTS
NAVAHOS
NAVAJOS
NAVVIES
NAYSAYS
NEATENS
NEBULAS
NECKERS
NECTARS
NEDDIES
NEEDLES
NEGATES
NELSONS
NEMESES
NEMESIS
NEPALIS
NEPHEWS
NEREIDS
NERVOUS
NESTERS
NESTLES
NETTLES
NEURONS
NEWNESS
NEWSIES
NEWTONS
NEXUSES
NIBBLES
NICHOLS
NICKELS
NICKERS
NICOLAS
NIGGLES
NIMRODS
NINNIES
NIPPERS
NITROUS
NITWITS
NOBBLES
NOBODYS
NOCUOUS
NODDERS
NODULES
NOETICS
NOGALES
NOGGINS
NOKOMIS
NONAGES
NONCOMS
NONPLUS
NOODLES
NORDICS
NORMALS
NORMANS
NOSHERS
NOSHOWS
NOTATES
NOTCHES
NOTICES
NOTIONS
NOUGATS
NOUGHTS
NOVENAS
NOVICES
NOXIOUS
NOZZLES
NUANCES
NUBBINS
NUBBLES
NUBIANS
NUCLEUS
NUDGERS
NUDISTS
NUDNIKS
NUGGETS
NULLAHS
NUMBATS
NUMBERS
NUNCIOS
NURSERS
NUTATES
NUTLETS
NUTMEGS
NUTRIAS
NUTTERS
NUZZLES

•NS••••

ANSWERS
ENSIGNS
ENSILED
ENSILES
ENSKIED
ENSKIES
ENSLAVE
ENSNARE
ENSNARL
ENSOULS
ENSUING
ENSUITE
ENSURED
ENSURES
INSCAPE
INSEAMS
INSECTS
INSERTS
INSHAPE
INSHORT
INSIDER
INSIDES
INSIGHT
INSIPID
INSISTS
INSOFAR
INSOLES
INSPANS
INSPECT
INSPIRE
INSPOTS
INSTALL
INSTALS
INSTANT
INSTARS
INSTATE
INSTEAD
INSTEPS
INSTILL
INSTILS
INSTOCK
INSTORE
INSTYLE
INSULAR
INSULIN
INSULTS
INSURED
INSURER
INSURES
ONSERVE
ONSHORE
ONSIDES
ONSIGHT
ONSTAGE
UNSATED
UNSCREW
UNSEALS
UNSEATS
UNSEWED
UNSHORN
UNSNAGS
UNSNAPS
UNSNARL
UNSOUND
UNSPENT
UNSTACK
UNSTICK
UNSTOPS
UNSTRAP
UNSTUCK
UNSWEPT

•N•S•••

ANASAZI
ANDSOON
ANISEED
ANISTON
ANOSMIA
ANOSMIC
ANTSIER
ENISLED
ENISLES
GNASHED
GNASHES
GNOSTIC
INASNIT
INASPIN
INASPOT
INASTEW
INKSPOT
KNESSET
KNISHES
KNOSSOS
ONASSIS
ONESELF
ONESHOT
ONESTAR
ONESTEP
UNASKED
UNISONS
UNUSUAL

•N••S••

ANTESUP
ENCASED
ENCASES
ENDUSER
ENDUSES
ENLISTS
ENMASSE
INCASED
INCASES
INCISED
INCISES
INCISOR
INFESTS
INFUSED
INFUSES
INGESTS
INHASTE
INSISTS
INVESTS
KNEESUP
KNESSET
KNOSSOS
ONASSIS
SNAPSAT
SNAPSTO
SNAPSUP
SNOWSIN
UNCASED
UNCASES
UNMASKS
UNWISER

•N•••S•

ANALYSE
ANALYST
ANAPEST
ANDRESS
ANIMISM
ANIMIST
ANODISE
ENCLOSE
ENCRUST
ENDLESS
ENDMOST
ENDORSE
ENDWISE
ENGLISH
ENGROSS
ENMASSE
ENTHUSE
ENTRUST
GNOMISH
INAMESS
INANEST
INARUSH
INCENSE
INCLOSE
INDORSE
INGRESS
INHOUSE
INKIEST
INKLESS
INNLESS
INPHASE
INQUEST
INTENSE
INTERSE
INTRUST
INVERSE
KNAVISH
ONENESS
SNIDEST
UNBLEST
UNCLASP
UNCLOSE
UNDRESS
UNHORSE
UNLEASH
UNLOOSE
UNTWIST

•N••••S

ANADEMS
ANALOGS
ANANIAS
ANCHORS
ANDEANS
ANDREAS
ANDRESS
ANDREWS
ANGELES
ANGELUS
ANGLERS
ANGORAS
ANIMALS
ANKLETS
ANNEALS
ANNEXES
ANNUALS
ANNULUS
ANOINTS
ANOMIES
ANONYMS
ANORAKS
ANSWERS
ANTAEUS
ANTARES
ANTCOWS
ANTHEMS
ANTHERS
ANTIBES
ANTLERS
ANXIOUS
ANYONES
ENABLES
ENAMELS
ENAMORS
ENCAGES
ENCAMPS
ENCASES
ENCINAS
ENCODES
ENCORES
ENDEARS
ENDINGS
ENDIVES
ENDLESS
ENDRUNS
ENDURES
ENDUROS
ENDUSES
ENDWAYS
ENEMIES
ENFOLDS
ENGAGES
ENGINES
ENGIRDS
ENGRAMS
ENGROSS
ENGULFS
ENIGMAS
ENISLES
ENJOINS
ENLACES
ENLISTS
ENNEADS
ENRAGES
ENROBES
ENROLLS
ENROOTS
ENSIGNS
ENSILES
ENSKIES
ENSOULS
ENSURES
ENTAILS
ENTICES
ENTRAPS
ENTREES
ENTRIES
ENVIERS
ENVIOUS
ENWRAPS
ENZYMES
GNASHES
GNAWERS
GNOMONS
INAMESS
INBOXES
INCANTS
INCASES
INCEPTS
INCISES
INCITES
INCOMES
INCUDES
INDENTS
INDEXES
INDIANS
INDICES
INDICTS
INDIGOS
INDITES
INDOORS
INDUCES
INDUCTS
INFANTS
INFECTS
INFESTS
INFLOWS
INFOCUS
INFORMS
INFUSES
INGALLS
INGESTS
INGRESS
INHALES
INHAULS
INHERES
INJECTS
INJOKES
INJURES
INKLESS
INMATES
INNARDS
INNINGS
INNLESS
INROADS
INSEAMS
INSECTS
INSERTS
INSIDES
INSISTS
INSOLES
INSPANS
INSPOTS
INSTALS
INSTARS
INSTEPS
INSTILS
INSULTS
INSURES
INTAKES
INTEARS
INTENDS
INTENTS
INTERNS
INTONES
INTUITS
INVADES
INVENTS
INVERTS
INVESTS
INVITES
INVOKES
INWARDS
KNIGHTS
KNISHES
KNOSSOS
ONAGERS
ONASSIS
ONEIDAS
ONENESS
ONEROUS
ONSIDES
ONWARDS
SNAPONS
SNEEZES
SNIPERS
SNIVELS
SNOCATS
SNOOZES
SNORERS
UNBENDS
UNBINDS
UNBOLTS
UNBOXES
UNCAGES
UNCASES
UNCIALS
UNCLOGS
UNCOILS
UNCORKS
UNCURLS
UNDRESS
UNFOLDS
UNFURLS
UNGIRDS
UNHANDS
UNHOOKS
UNIFIES
UNIPODS
UNISONS
UNITERS
UNITIES
UNKINKS
UNKNITS
UNKNOTS
UNLACES
UNLADES
UNLINKS
UNLOADS
UNLOCKS
UNMAKES
UNMASKS
UNPACKS
UNPILES
UNPLUGS
UNREELS
UNROBES
UNROLLS
UNSEALS
UNSEATS
UNSNAGS
UNSNAPS
UNSTOPS
UNTACKS
UNTRAPS
UNTUNES
UNVEILS
UNWINDS
UNWRAPS
UNYOKES

••NS•••

BANSHEE
BONSOIR
CANSECO
CENSERS
CENSING
CENSORS
CENSURE
CONSENT
CONSIGN
CONSIST
CONSOLE
CONSORT
CONSULS
CONSULT
CONSUME
DANSEUR
DENSELY
DENSEST
DENSITY
FANSOUT
GINSENG
GUNSFOR
GUNSHOT
HANSARP
HANSOLO
HANSOMS
IBNSAUD
JANSSEN
KANSANS
KINSHIP
KINSMAN
KINSMEN
LANSING
LINSEED
MANSARD
MANSION
MONSOON
MONSTER
NONSELF
NONSKID
NONSLIP
NONSTOP
PANSIES
PANSOUT
PENSEES
PENSION
PENSIVE
PUNSTER
RANSACK
RANSOMS
RINSING
RUNSDRY
RUNSFOR
RUNSOFF
RUNSOUT
SENSATE
SENSING
SENSORS
SENSORY
SENSUAL
SUNSETS
SUNSPOT
SUNSUIT
TANSIES
TENSELY
TENSEST
TENSEUP
TENSILE
TENSING
TENSION
TENSIVE
TENSORS
TENSPOT
TINSELS
TINSTAR
TONSILS
TONSURE
WINSLOW
WINSOME
WINSOUT
WINSTON

••N•S••

AMNESIA
AMNESTY
BANDSAW
BANGSUP
BANKSON
BENISON
BENTSEN
BINDSUP
BONESET
BONESUP
BONUSES
CANASTA
DINESEN
DINESIN

DINESON
DYNASTS
DYNASTY
ERNESTO
FINESSE
GANGSAW
GANGSTA
GANGSUP
GENESEE
GENESES
GENESIS
HANDSAW
HANDSET
HANDSIN
HANDSON
HANDSUP
HANGSIN
HANGSON
HANGSUP
HINTSAT
HONESTY
IONESCO
IONISED
IONISES
JANSSEN
JONESES
KENOSHA
LANDSAT
LINDSAY
LINDSEY
LINESUP
MENISCI
MINDSET
MINUSES
NONUSER
PINESAP
RINGSUP
SENDSIN
SENDSUP
SINGSTO
SINKSIN
SINUSES
TANKSUP
TENDSTO
TONESUP
TUNESIN
TUNESUP
TUNISIA
VANESSA
VENISON
WANTSIN
WANTSTO
WINDSOR
WINDSUP
WINESAP
WINGSIT
WINKSAT

••N••S•

AWNLESS
BONEASH
BONIEST
CANIEST
CANVASS
CONCISE
CONFESS
CONFUSE
CONGEST
CONSIST
CONTEST
CONTUSE
DANKEST
DENSEST
DENTIST
DONJOSE
DONNISH
DUNCISH
FANTASY
FINESSE
FINNISH
FONDEST
FUNFEST
GENOESE
GUNLESS
HENNISH
HUNNISH
INNLESS
KENTISH
KINDEST
KINLESS
LANKEST
LINIEST
LONGEST
LONGISH
MANLESS
MANNISH
MINXISH
MONKISH
PANFISH
PINIEST
PINKEST
PINKISH
PINLESS
PUNIEST
PUNLESS
RANKEST
RANKISH
RUNTISH
SANJOSE
SINLESS
SONLESS
SUNFISH
SUNKIST
SUNLESS
SUNRISE
SYNAPSE
TANNEST
TANNISH
TENSEST
TINIEST
TONIEST
TONNISH
VANESSA
VINIEST
WANIEST
WANNESS
WANNEST
WANNISH
WENDISH
WINIEST
ZANIEST
ZANYISH

••N•••S

ABNAKIS
AGNATES
AMNIONS
ANNEALS
ANNEXES
ANNUALS
ANNULUS
ARNICAS
AUNTIES
AWNINGS
AWNLESS
BANANAS
BANDIES
BANDITS
BANGLES
BANJOES
BANKERS
BANNERS
BANTAMS
BANTERS
BANYANS
BENCHES
BENDERS
BENGALS
BENUMBS
BINDERS
BINGOES
BONBONS
BONGOES
BONITOS
BONKERS
BONMOTS
BONNETS
BONUSES
BUNCHES
BUNDLES
BUNGEES
BUNGLES
BUNIONS
BUNKERS
BUNNIES
BUNYIPS
CANAPES
CANARDS
CANCANS
CANCELS
CANDIDS
CANDIES
CANDLES
CANFULS
CANINES
CANKERS
CANNERS
CANNONS
CANOPUS
CANTERS
CANTLES
CANTONS
CANTORS
CANVASS
CANYONS
CENSERS
CENSORS
CENTERS
CENTRES
CINCHES
CINDERS
CINEMAS
CONCHES
CONCURS
CONDORS
CONFABS
CONFERS
CONFESS
CONGERS
CONJOBS
CONKERS
CONNORS
CONOIDS
CONSULS
CONTRAS
CONURES
CONVEYS
CONVOYS
DANCERS
DANDERS
DANDIES
DANDLES
DANGERS
DANGLES
DANIELS
DENIALS
DENIERS
DENOTES
DENUDES
DINGLES
DINGOES
DINKIES
DINNERS
DONATES
DONGLES
DONIMUS
DONJONS
DONKEYS
DUNKERS
DUNLINS
DYNAMOS
DYNASTS
ENNEADS
FANCIES
FANIONS
FANJETS
FANOUTS
FENCERS
FENDERS
FENIANS
FINALES
FINCHES
FINDERS
FINGERS
FINIALS
FONDLES
FONDUES
FUNGOES
FUNNELS
FUNNIES
GANDERS
GANGERS
GANNETS
GENDERS
GENERIS
GENESES
GENESIS
GENGHIS
GENOMES
GENTLES
GINGERS
GUNDOGS
GUNLESS
GUNNELS
GUNNERS
GUNNIES
HANDLES
HANGARS
HANGERS
HANGUPS
HANKERS
HANKIES
HANSOMS
HENBITS
HINDERS
HINNIES
HONCHOS
HONKERS
HONORIS
HONOURS
HUNCHES
HUNGERS
HUNKERS
HUNTERS
IGNEOUS
IGNITES
IGNORES
INNARDS
INNINGS
INNLESS
IONISES
IONIZES
JANGLES
JENNETS
JENNIES
JINGLES
JINGOES
JONESES
JUNCOES
JUNGLES
JUNIORS
JUNKERS
JUNKETS
JUNKIES
KANAKAS
KANSANS
KENNELS
KENYANS
KINDLES
KINEMAS
KINLESS
LANCERS
LANCETS
LANDAUS
LANDERS
LANGURS
LENDERS
LENGTHS
LENTILS
LINAGES
LINDENS
LINDIES
LINEUPS
LINGERS
LINGOES
LININGS
LINKERS
LINKUPS
LINNETS
LINTELS
LONGIES
LONGUES
LUNCHES
LUNKERS
MANAGES
MANANAS
MANDANS
MANDAYS
MANEGES
MANGERS
MANGLES
MANGOES
MANIACS
MANIOCS
MANLESS
MANNERS
MANTELS
MANTLES
MANTRAS
MANUALS
MENACES
MENAGES
MENDERS
MENHIRS
MENIALS
MENTORS
MENZIES
MINCERS
MINDERS
MINGLES
MINIBUS
MINIONS
MINNOWS
MINOANS
MINTERS
MINUETS
MINUSES
MINUTES
MINYANS
MONDAYS
MONGERS
MONGOLS
MONKEES
MONKEYS
MUNCHES
MUNTINS
NANNIES
NINNIES
NONAGES
NONCOMS
NONPLUS
NUNCIOS
OMNIBUS
PANADAS
PANAMAS
PANDERS
PANDITS
PANFULS
PANNERS
PANSIES
PANZERS
PENATES
PENCILS
PENNERS
PENNIES
PENNONS
PENPALS
PENSEES
PENTADS
PENULTS
PINATAS
PINCERS
PINCHAS
PINCHES
PINIONS
PINKIES
PINLESS
PINNERS
PINOAKS
PINONES
PONCHOS
PONDERS
PONGEES
PONGIDS
PONTIUS
PUNCHES
PUNDITS
PUNKAHS
PUNKERS
PUNKIES
PUNLESS
PUNNETS
PUNTERS
PUNTIES
QINTARS
RANCHES
RANCHOS
RANGERS
RANKERS
RANKLES
RANSOMS
RANTERS
RENAILS
RENAMES
RENARDS
RENDERS
RENEGES
RENNINS
RENOTES
RENTALS
RENTERS
RINGERS
RONDELS
RUNDLES
RUNLETS
RUNNELS
RUNNERS
RUNOFFS
RUNOUTS
RUNWAYS
SANDALS
SANDERS
SANLUIS
SANTIRS
SENATES
SENDERS
SENDUPS
SENECAS
SENIORS
SENORAS
SENORES
SENSORS
SENUFOS
SINGERS
SINGLES
SINKERS
SINLESS
SINNERS
SINUOUS
SINUSES
SONATAS
SONLESS
SONNETS
SUNDAES
SUNDAYS
SUNDERS
SUNDEWS
SUNDOGS
SUNGODS
SUNLESS
SUNRAYS
SUNSETS
SUNTANS
SYNCHES
TANDEMS
TANGLES
TANKERS
TANNERS
TANNINS
TANOAKS
TANSIES
TENACES
TENANTS
TENDERS
TENDONS
TENNERS
TENPINS
TENRECS
TENSORS
TENTERS
TENUOUS
TENURES
TINCANS
TINDERS
TINEARS
TINGLES
TINHATS
TINKERS
TINKLES
TINNERS
TINSELS
TINTERS
TONGANS
TONGUES
TONSILS
TUNDRAS
TUNEUPS
TUNNELS
TUNNIES
VANDALS
VENDORS
VENEERS
VENTERS
WANDERS
WANGLES
WANNESS
WANTADS
WENCHES
WENDERS
WINCERS
WINCHES
WINDERS
WINDOWS
WINDUPS
WINGERS
WINKERS
WINKLES
WINNERS
WINNOWS
WINTERS
WONDERS
WONTONS
YANKEES
YANQUIS
YONKERS
ZANDERS
ZENANAS
ZENITHS
ZINGERS
ZINNIAS
ZONKERS

•••NS••

ALUNSER
BERNSEN
BRANSON
BRONSON
BURNSUP
CHANSON
COUNSEL
DAWNSON
EVENSUP
FLENSED
FLENSES
GAINSAY
GAINSON
HORNSBY
HORNSIN
JOHNSON
JOINSIN
JOINSUP
LEANSON
MOONSET
OPENSEA
OPENSUP
PLANSON
QUONSET
REINSIN
SIGNSIN
SIGNSON
SIGNSUP
SPENSER
SPONSOR
SWANSEA
SWANSON
TRANSIT
TRANSOM
TURNSIN
TURNSON
TURNSTO
TURNSUP
UTENSIL
VRONSKY

•••N•S•

AGONISE
AGONIST
AMONGST
APTNESS
BADNESS
BERNESE
BIGNESS
BRINISH
BURNISH
BYANOSE
CHINESE
CORNISH
COYNESS
CRONISH
DIMNESS
DONNISH
DRONISH
DRYNESS
EARNEST
EVANISH
EVENEST
FATNESS
FINNISH
FITNESS
FURNISH
GARNISH
GYMNAST
HARNESS
HENNISH
HIPNESS
HORNISH
HORNIST
HOTNESS
HUNNISH
ICINESS
ILLNESS
INANEST
KEENEST
LAXNESS
LEANEST
LIONESS
LIONISE
LOWNESS
MADNESS
MANNISH
MEANEST
MOONISH
NEWNESS
ODDNESS
OLDNESS
ONENESS
PATNESS
PIANISM
PIANIST
PLANISH
PUGNOSE
RAWNESS
REDNESS
RHENISH
SADNESS
SHYNESS
SLYNESS
SOANDSO
SOONEST
SPANISH
SWINISH
TANNEST
TANNISH
TARNISH
TONNISH
TOWNISH
VAINEST
VARNISH
WANNESS
WANNEST
WANNISH
WETNESS
WITNESS
WRYNESS

•••N••S

ADONAIS
AGENDAS
ANANIAS
ANONYMS
APTNESS
ATONIES
AVENGES
AVENUES
BADNESS
BANNERS
BARNEYS
BEANIES
BIGNESS
BIONICS
BLONDES
BONNETS
BOONIES
BOUNCES
BRONCOS
BRONZES
BRUNETS
BUNNIES
BURNERS
CANNERS
CANNONS
CAPNUTS
CARNETS
CARNIES
CATNAPS
CATNIPS
CHANCES
CHANGES
CHINUPS
CLINICS
COGNACS
COINERS
CONNORS
CORNEAS
CORNERS
CORNETS
COYNESS
CRENELS
CRINGES
CRONIES
CYGNETS
DARNERS
DIMNESS
DINNERS
DIRNDLS
DOWNERS
DRONERS
DRYNESS
DUENNAS
EARNERS
EBONIES
EGGNOGS
EPONYMS
ETHNICS
EVENKIS
EVINCES
FATNESS
FAWNERS
FIANCES
FIENNES
FITNESS
FLANGES
FLENSES
FLYNETS
FRANCES
FRANCIS
FRINGES
FUNNELS
FUNNIES
GAINERS
GANNETS
GARNERS
GARNETS
GLANCES
GRANGES
GRUNGES
GUINEAS
GUNNELS
GUNNERS
GUNNIES
GURNEYS
HARNESS
HEINOUS
HEXNUTS
HINNIES
HIPNESS
HOBNOBS
HORNETS
HOTNESS
HYMNALS
ICINESS
ILLNESS
IRONERS
IRONIES
IRONONS
JENNETS
JENNIES
JITNEYS
JOINERS
JOUNCES
KEENERS
KENNELS
KERNELS
KIDNAPS
KIDNEYS
KWANZAS
LAXNESS
LEANERS
LEANTOS
LEONIDS
LIENEES
LIMNERS
LINNETS
LIONESS
LIONETS
LOANERS
LOONEYS
LOONIES
LOUNGES
LOWNESS
LUGNUTS
MADNESS
MAENADS
MAGNETS
MAGNUMS
MANNERS
MEANIES
MEINIES
MINNOWS
MOANERS
NANNIES
NEWNESS
NINNIES
NUANCES
NUDNIKS
ODDNESS
OLDNESS
OLDNEWS
OMINOUS
ONENESS
OPENERS
OPINERS
ORANGES
OZONOUS
PAANGAS
PANNERS
PATNESS
PAWNEES
PAWNERS
PEANUTS
PENNERS
PENNIES
PENNONS
PEONIES
PHENOLS
PHENOMS
PHINEAS
PHONEYS
PHONICS
PHONIES
PICNICS
PIGNUTS
PINNERS
PLANERS
PLANETS
PLENUMS
PLINTHS
PLUNGES
POUNCES
PRANCES
PRENUPS
PRINCES
PRUNERS
PSANDQS
PUNNETS
QUANGOS
QUINCES
QUINOAS
RAWNESS
REDNESS
RENNINS
ROMNEYS
RUINERS
RUINOUS
RUNNELS
RUNNERS
SADNESS
SCHNAPS
SCONCES
SEANCES
SEINERS
SHINERS
SHYNESS
SIENNAS
SIGNALS
SIGNEES
SIGNERS
SIGNETS
SINNERS
SLYNESS
SONNETS
SOONERS
SPINELS
SPINETS
SPONGES
STANCES
STANZAS
STINGOS
STONERS
TANNERS
TANNINS
TEENERS
TENNERS
THENARS
TINNERS
TOONIES
TOWNERS
TOWNIES
TRANCES
TUNNELS
TUNNIES
TURNERS
TURNIPS
TWINGES
UNKNITS
UNKNOTS
UNSNAGS
UNSNAPS
VILNIUS
WALNUTS
WANNESS
WEENIES
WETNESS
WHINERS
WIENERS
WIENIES
WINNERS
WINNOWS
WITNESS
WRYNESS
YAWNERS
ZINNIAS

••••NS•

AGAINST
ALFONSO
CLEANSE
DEFENSE
EXPANSE
EXPENSE
IMMENSE
INCENSE
INTENSE
LICENSE
OFFENSE
RERINSE
ROMANSH

••••N•S

ABOUNDS
ABSENTS
ACCENTS
ACHENES
ADDENDS
ADVENTS
AFFINES
AIRINGS
ALBINOS
ALKENES
ALMONDS
ALUMNUS
AMOUNTS
ANOINTS
ANYONES
APPENDS
AQUINAS
ARPENTS
ASCENDS
ASCENTS
ASSENTS
ATTENDS
ATTUNES
AUGENDS
AWNINGS
BANANAS
BARENTS
BARONGS
BELONGS
BIKINIS
BOVINES
BYGONES
BYLINES
CABANAS
CALENDS
CANINES
CARINAS
CASINGS
CASINOS
CEMENTS
CLIENTS
COLONES
COMINGS
CORONAS
COSINES
DAPHNIS
DEBONES
DEBUNKS
DECANTS
DEFENDS
DEFINES
DEMANDS
DEPENDS
DEPONES
DIVINES
DOCENTS
DOMINOS
DOMINUS
DOPANTS
DUENNAS
DUGONGS
ECHINUS
EDGINGS
EMBANKS
ENCINAS
ENDINGS
ENGINES
EQUINES
ERMINES
ERRANDS
ESSENES
EVZONES
EXPANDS
EXPENDS
EXTENDS
EXTENTS
FACINGS
FAGENDS
FAMINES
FELINES
FIENNES
FILENES
FILINGS
FIRINGS
FIXINGS
FLAUNTS
FOMENTS

FORINTS
FRIENDS
GAMINES
GERENTS
GERUNDS
GROUNDS
GYRENES
HAZINGS
HIDINGS
HIJINKS
IGUANAS
IMPENDS
INCANTS
INDENTS
INFANTS
INNINGS
INTENDS
INTENTS
INTONES
INVENTS
ISLANDS
JACANAS
JOURNOS
KAHUNAS
KETONES
KIMONOS
KIWANIS
KORUNAS
LACINGS
LACUNAS
LADINOS
LAGUNAS
LAMENTS
LAMINAS
LATENTS
LATINAS
LATINOS
LEGENDS
LEVANTS
LIERNES
LIGANDS
LININGS
LIVINGS
LUPINES
MAKINGS
MANANAS
MARINAS
MARINES
MERINOS
MOMENTS
MORANIS
MRBONES
MUTANTS
NOVENAS
OBLONGS
OBTUNDS
OCEANUS
OCTANES
OCTANTS
OFFENDS
ORDINES
ORIENTS
ORPINES
OSCINES
OUTINGS
PARENTS
PARINGS
PATENTS
PATINAS
PAVANES
PEDANTS
PILINGS
PINONES
PIPINGS
PLAINTS
POCONOS
RAPINES
RATINGS
RAVINES
RAVINGS
REBENDS
REBINDS
RECANES
RECANTS
REDANTS
REFINES
REFUNDS
REGENTS
REHANGS
RELENTS
RELINES
REMANDS
REMENDS
REMINDS
REPENTS
REPINES
RERENTS
RESANDS
RESENDS
RESENTS
RESINGS
RETINAS
RETUNES
REWINDS
REZONES
RIBANDS
RISINGS
RODENTS
RULINGS
SABINES
SALINAS
SARONGS
SAVANTS
SAVINGS
SAYINGS
SECANTS
SECONDS
SHRINES
SHRINKS
SIDINGS
SIENNAS
SILENTS
SIZINGS
SPLINES
SPLINTS
SPRINGS
SPRINTS
SQUINTS
STDENIS
STRANDS
STRINGS
TAGENDS
TALENTS
TAPINGS
TENANTS
TETANUS
THRONES
THRONGS
TIDINGS
TILINGS
TIMINGS
TISANES
TRIUNES
TRUANTS
TYRANTS
UNBENDS
UNBINDS
UNHANDS
UNKINKS
UNLINKS
UNTUNES
UNWINDS
UPLANDS
UPLINKS
VICUNAS
VIKINGS
WAHINES
YEMENIS
ZENANAS

•••••NS

ACTIONS
ACUMENS
ADJOINS
AFGHANS
AIRGUNS
AMAZONS
AMNIONS
ANDEANS
ARCHONS
ASHCANS
ASSIGNS
ATAMANS
ATTAINS
AUBURNS
AUTUMNS
AWAKENS
BABOONS
BALEENS
BALKANS
BANYANS
BARRENS
BARYONS
BATTENS
BEACONS
BECKONS
BEMOANS
BIGGUNS
BLAZONS
BOBBINS
BODKINS
BOFFINS
BONBONS
BOWFINS
BRETONS
BRITONS
BROGANS
BUNIONS
BURDENS
BURMANS
BUSKINS
BUTTONS
BYTURNS
CAFTANS
CAIMANS
CALKINS
CALLINS
CANCANS
CANNONS
CANTONS
CANYONS
CAPGUNS
CARBONS
CAREENS
CARTONS
CASERNS
CATIONS
CATKINS
CAVEINS
CAVERNS
CAYMANS
CHALONS
CITRONS
CLEMENS
CLIPONS
COCOONS
COLLINS
COLUMNS
COMEONS
COMMONS
CORDONS
COSIGNS
COTTONS
COUPONS
COUSINS
COZZENS
CRAVENS
CRAYONS
CRETANS
CRETINS
DAIMONS
DAMPENS
DAMSONS
DARKENS
DEACONS
DEADENS
DEAFENS
DEEPENS
DEHORNS
DEMEANS
DESIGNS
DETAINS
DEVEINS
DICKENS
DISOWNS
DOBBINS
DOLMANS
DOLMENS
DOMAINS
DONJONS
DRAGONS
DROPINS
DRYRUNS
DUNLINS
ELEVENS
ELOIGNS
ENDRUNS
ENJOINS
ENSIGNS
EXTERNS
FADEINS
FALCONS
FANIONS
FASTENS
FATTENS
FENIANS
FIBRINS
FIJIANS
FILLINS
FIRKINS
FLACONS
FLAGONS
FLORINS
FRYPANS
GALLONS
GAMMONS
GARCONS
GARDENS
GASCONS
GASKINS
GERMANS
GIBBONS
GIDEONS
GNOMONS
GOBLINS
GODSONS
GORGONS
GOVERNS
GUIDONS
HAGDONS
HAPPENS
HARDENS
HARKENS
HASTENS
HATPINS
HAWKINS
HEAVENS
HETMANS
HIGGINS
HOPKINS
HOSKINS
HOYDENS
HUGGINS
HUYGENS
HYPHENS
IMPUGNS
INDIANS
INSPANS
INTERNS
IRONONS
ISOGONS
JARGONS
JERKINS
JETGUNS
JETSONS
JOSKINS
JUGGINS
KAFTANS
KANSANS
KENYANS
KIRMANS
KITTENS
KLAXONS
KMESONS
KOREANS
KUCHENS
LAGOONS
LARDONS
LATEENS
LATTENS
LEADINS
LEAVENS
LEGIONS
LEPTONS
LESSENS
LESSONS
LIBYANS
LICHENS
LINDENS
LISTENS
LOCKINS
LOGGINS
LOOSENS
LOTIONS
LOVEINS
MACRONS
MADDENS
MAIDENS
MALIGNS
MALKINS
MANDANS
MARGINS
MARLINS
MAROONS
MARTENS
MARTINS
MATRONS
MEDIANS
MICRONS
MIDDENS
MINIONS
MINOANS
MINYANS
MITTENS
MIZZENS
MODERNS
MORGANS
MORMONS
MOTIONS
MOUTONS
MUDHENS
MUFFINS
MUNTINS
MUSLINS
MUTTONS
NAPKINS
NATIONS
NEATENS
NELSONS
NEURONS
NEWTONS
NOGGINS
NORMANS
NOTIONS
NUBBINS
NUBIANS
OBTAINS
OHIOANS
OILCANS
OILPANS
OLEFINS
OPPUGNS
OPTIONS
ORDAINS
ORIGINS
ORISONS
ORLEANS
ORPHANS
OUTGUNS
OUTRUNS
PADUANS
PAPUANS
PARDONS
PARSONS
PATRONS
PATTENS
PEAHENS
PECTINS
PENNONS
PEPSINS
PERKINS
PERSONS
PHOTONS
PICKENS
PIDGINS
PIEPANS
PIETINS
PIGEONS
PIGPENS
PINIONS
PIPKINS
PIPPINS
PISTONS
PLATENS
PLUGINS
POISONS
POLLENS
POMPONS
POPGUNS
POPLINS
POPPINS
POTIONS
PRISONS
PROTONS
PUFFINS
PULLINS
PULLONS
PURLINS
PYTHONS
RADIANS
RAGLANS
RAISINS
RATIONS
RATTANS
RAYGUNS
REASONS
RECKONS
REDDENS
REDFINS
REGAINS
REGIONS
REJOINS
REMAINS
RENNINS
REOPENS
REPLANS
REPUGNS
RESIGNS
RESPINS
RETAINS
RETURNS
REUBENS
RIBBONS
ROBBINS
ROLLINS
SADDENS
SALMONS
SALOONS
SAMOANS
SAMPANS
SAPIENS
SATEENS
SCREENS
SEAFANS
SEASONS
SEQUINS
SERMONS
SEXTANS
SEXTONS
SHAMANS
SHOGUNS
SHOOINS
SHUTINS
SICKENS
SIMIANS
SIMMONS
SIOUANS
SIPHONS
SISKINS
SIXGUNS
SKIRUNS
SLIPONS
SLOGANS
SLOVENS
SNAPONS
SOFTENS
SPAVINS
SPLEENS
SPRAINS
STAMENS
STEPINS
STEVENS
STJOHNS
STOLONS
STRAINS
SUBORNS
SULTANS
SUMMONS
SUNTANS
SYLVANS
SYPHONS
SYRIANS
TAIPANS
TANNINS
TARPONS
TARTANS
TAUTENS
TAVERNS
TENDONS
TENPINS
TEUTONS
TIEPINS
TIFFINS
TIGLONS
TIMMINS
TINCANS
TOCSINS
TONGANS
TOPGUNS
TORRENS
TOUCANS
TREPANS
TRIGONS
TRITONS
TROGONS
TROJANS
TULSANS
TURBANS
TUREENS
TYCOONS
UNISONS
UPTURNS
URCHINS
USOPENS
UTAHANS
VIOLINS
VIRGINS
VISIONS
VULCANS
WAGGONS
WALKINS
WALKONS
WARDENS
WARRENS
WEAKENS
WEAPONS
WELKINS
WHITENS
WONTONS
WOOLENS
WORSENS
WYVERNS
YAUPONS
YOUMANS
ZIRCONS

N•T••••

NATALIA
NATALIE
NATASHA
NATCHEZ
NATIONS
NATIVES
NATRIUM
NATTERS
NATTIER
NATTILY
NATURAL
NATURED
NATURES
NETIZEN
NETLIKE
NETSUKE
NETSURF
NETTING
NETTLED
NETTLES
NETWORK
NITPICK
NITRATE
NITRIDE
NITRITE
NITROUS
NITTANY
NITTIER
NITWITS
NOTABIT
NOTABLE
NOTABLY
NOTATED
NOTATES
NOTCHED
NOTCHES
NOTEDLY
NOTEPAD
NOTHING
NOTICED
NOTICES
NOTIONS
NOTRUMP
NOTSURE
NOTTRUE
NOTWELL
NUTATED
NUTATES
NUTLETS
NUTLIKE
NUTMEAT
NUTMEGS
NUTRIAS
NUTSIER
NUTTERS
NUTTIER
NUTTILY
NUTTING

N••T•••

NAPTIME
NARTHEX
NASTASE
NASTIER
NASTILY
NATTERS
NATTIER
NATTILY
NEATENS
NEATEST
NECTARS
NEITHER
NEPTUNE
NESTEGG
NESTERS
NESTING
NESTLED
NESTLER
NESTLES
NETTING
NETTLED
NETTLES
NEUTRAL
NEUTRON
NEWTONS
NEWTOWN
NIFTIER
NIFTILY
NINTHLY
NITTANY
NITTIER
NOCTURN
NOETICS
NORTHER
NOSTRIL
NOSTRUM
NOTTRUE
NUPTIAL
NURTURE
NUTTERS
NUTTIER
NUTTILY
NUTTING

N•••T••

NAMETAG
NANETTE
NAPHTHA
NECKTIE
NEGATED
NEGATER
NEGATES
NEGATOR
NIGHTIE
NIGHTLY
NONSTOP
NOTATED
NOTATES
NUTATED
NUTATES

N••••T•

NAHUATL
NAIVETE
NAIVETY
NANETTE
NARRATE
NAUGHTS
NAUGHTY
NCWYETH
NEOLITH
NEONATE
NESMITH
NEWGATE
NEWMATH
NIMIETY
NITRATE
NITRITE
NITWITS
NOUGATS
NOUGHTS
NOVELTY
NUDISTS
NUGGETS
NULLITY
NUMBATS
NUTLETS

N•••••T

NAILSET
NASCENT
NEAREST
NEATEST
NEGLECT
NEWHART
NEWLEFT
NEWPORT
NIGHEST
NOBLEST
NODOUBT
NOFAULT
NORBERT
NOSEOUT
NOSIEST
NOSWEAT
NOTABIT
NUMBEST
NUTMEAT

•NT••••

ANTACID
ANTAEUS
ANTARES
ANTBEAR
ANTCOWS
ANTEDUP
ANTEING
ANTENNA
ANTESUP
ANTFARM
ANTHEMS
ANTHERS
ANTHILL
ANTHONY
ANTIART
ANTIBES
ANTIFOG
ANTIGEN
ANTIGUA
ANTILOG
ANTIOCH
ANTIQUE
ANTITAX
ANTIWAR
ANTLERS
ANTLIKE
ANTLION
ANTOINE
ANTONIA
ANTONIN
ANTONIO
ANTONYM
ANTSIER
ANTWERP
CNTOWER
ENTAILS
ENTEBBE
ENTENTE
ENTERED
ENTERON
ENTHRAL
ENTHUSE
ENTICED
ENTICER
ENTICES
ENTITLE
ENTRAIN
ENTRANT
ENTRAPS
ENTREAT
ENTREES
ENTRIES
ENTROPY
ENTRUST
ENTWINE
INTAKES
INTEARS
INTEGER
INTEGRA
INTENDS
INTENSE
INTENTS
INTERIM
INTERNS
INTERSE
INTONED
INTONER
INTONES
INTROIT
INTRUDE
INTRUST
INTRUTH
INTUITS
ONTARIO
ONTHEGO
ONTHEQT
ONTOPOF
ONTRACK
ONTRIAL
UNTACKS
UNTAMED
UNTAPED
UNTRAPS
UNTRIED
UNTRUTH
UNTUNED
UNTUNES
UNTWIST
UNTYING

•N•T•••

ANATOLE
ANATOMY
ANOTHER
ANYTIME
DNOTICE
INITIAL
INSTALL
INSTALS
INSTANT
INSTARS
INSTATE
INSTEAD
INSTEPS
INSTILL
INSTILS
INSTOCK
INSTORE
INSTYLE
INUTILE
KNITTED
KNITTER
KNOTTED
ONATEAR
ONETIME
ONSTAGE
SNITCHY
UNCTION
UNITARY
UNITERS
UNITIES
UNITING
UNITIVE
UNSTACK
UNSTICK
UNSTOPS
UNSTRAP
UNSTUCK

•N••T••

ANISTON
ANNATTO
ANNETTE
ANTITAX
ENACTED
ENACTOR
ENTITLE
GNOSTIC
INAPTER
INAPTLY
INASTEW
INCITED
INCITER
INCITES
INDITED
INDITES
INDUTCH
INEPTLY
INERTIA
INERTLY
INMATES
INPETTO
INVITED
INVITES
INVITRO
KNITTED
KNITTER
KNOTTED
KNOUTED
ONESTAR
ONESTEP
ONLYTOO
SNIFTER
SNOOTED
SNORTED
SNORTER
UNAPTLY
UNDATED
UNEATEN
UNHITCH
UNLATCH
UNRATED
UNSATED

•N•••T•

ANDANTE
ANIMATE
ANIMATO
ANKLETS
ANNATTO
ANNETTE
ANNUITY
ANOINTS
ANXIETY
ENLISTS
ENROOTS
ENROUTE
ENSUITE
ENTENTE
INANITY
INCANTS
INCEPTS
INDENTS
INDEPTH
INDICTS
INDUCTS
INFANTA
INFANTS
INFECTS
INFESTS
INFLATE
INGESTS
INGRATE
INHASTE
INJECTS
INPETTO
INSECTS
INSERTS
INSISTS
INSPOTS
INSTATE
INSULTS
INTENTS
INTRUTH
INTUITS
INVENTS
INVERTS
INVESTS
KNIGHTS
ONADATE
ONENOTE
SNAPSTO
SNOCATS
UNBOLTS
UNCOUTH
UNCRATE
UNEARTH
UNKNITS
UNKNOTS
UNQUOTE
UNSEATS
UNTRUTH

•N••••T

ANALYST
ANAPEST
ANCIENT
ANIMIST
ANTIART
ENCHANT
ENCRUST
ENCRYPT
ENDMOST
ENGRAFT
ENTRANT
ENTREAT
ENTRUST
INANEST
INASNIT
INASPOT
INCIPIT
INDOUBT
INEXACT
INFLECT
INFLICT
INFRONT
INHABIT
INHERIT
INHIBIT
INKBLOT
INKIEST
INKSPOT
INORBIT
INPRINT
INQUEST
INSHORT
INSIGHT
INSPECT
INSTANT
INTROIT
INTRUST
KNESSET
ONADIET
ONESHOT
ONSIGHT
ONTHEQT
SNAPSAT
SNEERAT
SNIDEST
SNIFFAT
SNIGLET
SNIPEAT
SNIPPET
SNOWCAT
UNBLEST
UNGUENT
UNKEMPT
UNSPENT
UNSWEPT

UNTWIST

••NT•••
AUNTIES
BANTAMS
BANTERS
BENTHAM
BENTLEY
BENTSEN
BUNTING
CANTATA
CANTEEN
CANTERS
CANTILY
CANTINA
CANTING
CANTLES
CANTONS
CANTORS
CANTRIP
CENTAUR
CENTAVO
CENTERS
CENTIME
CENTIMO
CENTRAL
CENTRED
CENTRES
CENTRIC
CENTURY
CONTACT
CONTAIN
CONTEMN
CONTEND
CONTENT
CONTEST
CONTEXT
CONTORT
CONTOUR
CONTRAS
CONTROL
CONTUSE
CYNTHIA
DENTATE
DENTINE
DENTING
DENTIST
DENTURE
FANTAIL
FANTASY
FONTEYN
FONTINA
GANTLET
GENTEEL
GENTIAN
GENTILE
GENTLED
GENTLER
GENTLES
GUNTHER
HENTING
HINTING
HINTSAT
HUNTERS
HUNTING
HUNTLEY
KENTISH
KONTIKI
LANTANA
LANTERN
LENTIGO
LENTILS
LINTELS
LINTIER
MANTELS
MANTLED
MANTLES
MANTRAP
MANTRAS
MANTRIC
MENTHOL
MENTION
MENTORS
MINTERS
MINTIER
MINTING
MONTAGE
MONTANA
MONTAND
MONTANE
MONTANI
MONTEGO
MONTERO
MONTHLY
MONTOYA
MUNTINS
NINTHLY
PANTHER
PANTING
PENTADS
PENTIUM
PINTAIL
PONTIAC
PONTIFF
PONTINE
PONTIUS
PONTOON
PUNTERS
PUNTIES
PUNTING
QINTARS
RANTERS
RANTING
RENTALS
RENTERS
RENTING
RONTGEN
RUNTIER
RUNTISH
SANTAFE
SANTANA
SANTINI
SANTIRS
SENTFOR
SENTOFF
SENTOUT
SUNTANS
TANTARA
TANTIVY
TANTRUM
TENTERS
TENTHLY
TENTING
TINTACK
TINTERN
TINTERS
TINTING
TINTYPE
TONTINE
VANTAGE
VENTERS
VENTING
VENTRAL
VENTURA
VENTURE
VINTAGE
VINTNER
WANTADS
WANTING
WANTOUT
WANTSIN
WANTSTO
WENTAPE
WENTBAD
WENTFOR
WENTOFF
WENTOUT
WINTERS
WINTERY
WONTONS
XANTHAN
XANTHIC

••N•T••
AGNATES
ANNATTO
ANNETTE
BENATAR
BONITOS
DENOTED
DENOTES
DINETTE
DONATED
DONATES
DONATOR
FANATIC
GANGTOK
GENETIC
HANGTEN
IGNITED
IGNITER
IGNITES
JANITOR
KINETIC
KINGTUT
LANGTRY
LENGTHS
LENGTHY
LONGTON
LUNATIC
MANATEE
MANITOU
MENOTTI
MINUTES
MINUTIA
MONITOR
MONSTER
NANETTE
NONSTOP
ORNETTE
ORNITHO
PENATES
PINATAS
PINETAR
PINETUM
PUNSTER
RENOTED
RENOTES
SANCTUM
SENATES
SENATOR
SINATRA
SONATAS
TANKTOP
TINSTAR
TINYTIM
WINGTIP
WINSTON
WYNETTE
YANGTZE
YANKTON
ZENITHS

••N••T•
AMNESTY
ANNATTO
ANNETTE
ANNUITY
BANDITO
BANDITS
BENEATH
BENNETT
BONMOTS
BONNETS
CANASTA
CANTATA
CONDITA
CONFUTE
CONMOTO
CONNOTE
DENSITY
DENTATE
DINETTE
DYNASTS
DYNASTY
ERNESTO
FANJETS
FANOUTS
GANGSTA
GANNETS
GANNETT
HENBITS
HONESTY
JENNETS
JUNKETS
KENNETH
LANCETS
LINEATE
LINNETS
MANDATE
MENOTTI
MINOLTA
MINUETS
NANETTE
ORNETTE
PANDITS
PENALTY
PENNATE
PENULTS
PINNATE
PUNDITS
PUNNETS
RANINTO
RANLATE
RUNINTO
RUNLATE
RUNLETS
RUNOUTS
RUNWITH
SENNETT
SENSATE
SINGSTO
SONNETS
SUNBATH
SUNCITY
SUNSETS
TENANTS
TENDSTO
TENUITY
TINHATS
VANUATU
WANTSTO
WYNETTE

••N•••T
BANQUET
BENEFIT
BENNETT
BONESET
BONIEST
CANIEST
CONCEIT
CONCEPT
CONCERT
CONCOCT
CONDUCT
CONDUIT
CONGEST
CONKOUT
CONNECT
CONSENT
CONSIST
CONSORT
CONSULT
CONTACT
CONTENT
CONTEST
CONTEXT
CONTORT
CONVENT
CONVERT
CONVICT
DANKEST
DENSEST
DENTIST
DINGBAT
DINMONT
FANBELT
FANSOUT
FINDOUT
FINEART
FONDANT
FONDEST
FUNFEST
GANNETT
GANTLET
GUNBOAT
GUNSHOT
HANDOUT
HANDSET
HANGOUT
HINTSAT
HUNGOUT
JUNKART
KINDEST
KINGRAT
KINGTUT
LANDSAT
LANKEST
LENFANT
LENIENT
LINIEST
LONGEST
LUNGEAT
MANHUNT
MANUMIT
MANXCAT
MINARET
MINDSET
MONOCOT
PANDECT
PANSOUT
PENDANT
PENDENT
PENNANT
PINENUT
PINIEST
PINKEST
PUNGENT
PUNIEST
RANGOUT
RANKEST
RANRIOT
RENAULT
RINGLET
RINGOUT
RUNGOUT
RUNRIOT
RUNSOUT
SANDLOT
SANGOUT
SENDOUT
SENNETT
SENTOUT
SINGOUT
SUNBELT
SUNKIST
SUNSPOT
SUNSUIT
TANGENT
TANNEST
TENCENT
TENSEST
TENSPOT
TINIEST
TONIEST
TONIGHT
TUNEOUT
VINCENT
VINIEST
WANIEST
WANNEST
WANTOUT
WENTOUT
WINGNUT
WINGSIT
WINIEST
WINKOUT
WINKSAT
WINSOUT
XINGOUT
ZANIEST
ZONKOUT

•••NT••
ABINTRA
ACANTHI
BAINTER
BIENTOT
BLUNTED
BLUNTER
BLUNTLY
BURNTUP
CHANTED
CHANTER
CHANTEY
CHINTZY
CHUNTER
CLINTON
COUNTED
COUNTER
COUNTON
COUNTRY
DAUNTED
FAINTED
FAINTER
FAINTLY
FEINTED
FRANTIC
FRONTAL
FRONTED
FRONTON
GAUNTER
GAUNTLY
GLINTED
GRANTED
GRANTEE
GRANTOR
GRUNTED
HAUNTED
IDENTIC
JAUNTED
JOINTED
JOINTLY
LEANTOS
MAINTOP
MOUNTED
MOUNTIE
OMENTUM
OPENTOE
PAINTED
PAINTER
PHANTOM
PLANTAR
PLANTED
PLANTER
PLINTHS
POINTED
POINTER
POINTTO
PRINTED
PRINTER
QUANTUM
QUENTIN
QUINTET
REENTER
REENTRY
RIANTLY
SAINTED
SAINTLY
SAUNTER
SCANTED
SCANTER
SCANTLY
SCENTED
SHANTEY
SHUNTED
SLANTED
STANTON
STENTOR
STINTED
STUNTED
TAINTED
TAUNTED
TRENTON
VAUNTED
VAUNTER

•••N•T•
ACONITE
AMENITY
BENNETT
BONNETS
BRINGTO
BRUNETS
BURNETT
CAPNUTS
CARNETS
COGNATE
CONNOTE
CORNETS
CYGNETS
DIGNITY
EBONITE
EMANATE
FLYNETS
GANNETS
GANNETT
GARNETS
GRANITE
GWYNETH
HEXNUTS
HORNETS
INANITY
JENNETS
KENNETH
KEYNOTE
LIGNITE
LINNETS
LIONETS
LUGNUTS
LYINGTO
MAGNATE
MAGNETO
MAGNETS
NEONATE
ONENOTE
OWINGTO
PEANUTS
PENNATE
PIGNUTS
PINNATE
PLANETS
POINTTO
PUNNETS
REUNITE
SENNETT
SIGNETS
SONNETS
SPINETS
TERNATE
TRINITY
TURNSTO
UNKNITS
UNKNOTS
URANITE
WALNUTS

•••N••T
AGONIST
AMONGST
BENNETT
BIENTOT
BLANKET
BLINKAT
BURNETT
BURNOUT
CONNECT
COONCAT
DOWNPAT
EARNEST
EMANANT
EMINENT
EVENEST
EVENOUT
GANNETT
GOINGAT
GYMNAST
HORNIST
INANEST
IRONOUT
KEENEST
LEANEST
MEANEST
MOONLIT
MOONSET
OPENPIT
PENNANT
PIANIST
PLANOUT
QUINTET
QUONSET
RAINHAT
RAINOUT
REENACT
REGNANT
REMNANT
SEENFIT
SEENOUT
SENNETT
SIGNOUT
SOONEST
SPINOUT
SPUNOUT
TANNEST
TLINGIT
TORNOUT
TRANSIT
TRINKET
TURNOUT
VAINEST
WANNEST
WORNOUT
WYANDOT

••••NT•
ABSENTS
ACCENTS
ADDONTO
ADVENTS
ALDENTE
AMOUNTS
ANDANTE
ANOINTS
APLENTY
ARPENTS
ASCENTS
ASHANTI
ASSENTS
ATLANTA
BARENTS
CEMENTS
CHIANTI
CLIENTS
CORINTH
CUTINTO
DECANTS
DETENTE
DOCENTS
DOPANTS
DOZENTH
DURANTE
ENTENTE
EXTENTS
FLAUNTS
FLAUNTY
FOMENTS
FORINTS
GERENTS
GETINTO
GIVENTO
GOTINTO
INCANTS
INDENTS
INFANTA
INFANTS
INTENTS
INVENTS
JACINTH
LAMENTS
LATENTS
LAYINTO
LEPANTO
LEVANTS
LISENTE
LITINTO
MAGENTA
MEMENTO
MOMENTS
MUTANTS
OCTANTS
ORIENTE
ORIENTS
OTRANTO
PARENTS
PATENTS
PEDANTS
PICANTE
PIMENTO
PLAINTS
POLENTA
PRYINTO
RAMINTO
RANINTO
RECANTS
REDANTS
REGENTS
RELENTS
REPENTS
RERENTS
RESENTS
RIPINTO
RODENTS
RUNINTO
SAVANTS
SECANTS
SETINTO
SEVENTH
SEVENTY
SILENTS
SPLINTS
SPRINTS
SQUANTO
SQUINTS
SQUINTY
TALENTS
TAPINTO
TARANTO
TENANTS
TIEINTO
TORONTO
TRUANTS
TYRANTS
VEDANTA

••••N•T
ADJUNCT
AGAINST
BARONET
BAYONET
BOWKNOT
CABINET
COCONUT
CORONET
DEFUNCT
DRAGNET
EATENAT
EXTINCT
FISHNET
FLOWNAT
FROWNAT
GILLNET
HAIRNET
HAVENOT
INASNIT
JACONET
LIFENET
LOCKNUT
MAGINOT
PINENUT
SATINET
SUBUNIT
TOPKNOT
WHATNOT
WINGNUT

•••••NT
ABEYANT
ACCOUNT
ADAMANT
AFFRONT
AILMENT
ALIMENT
AMBIENT
ANCIENT
APPOINT
ARMYANT
AUGMENT
BELMONT
BLATANT
BUOYANT
CLEMENT
COMMENT
CONSENT
CONTENT
CONVENT
COOLANT
COULDNT
COURANT
CURRANT
CURRENT
DEFIANT
DESCANT
DESCENT
DEVIANT
DINMONT
DISSENT
DISTANT
DORMANT
ELEGANT
ELEMENT
EMANANT
EMINENT
ENCHANT
ENTRANT
ERODENT
ETCHANT
EVIDENT
EXIGENT
FERMENT
FERVENT
FIGMENT
FIREANT
FONDANT
FORRENT
FORWENT
FREMONT
FULGENT
GALLANT
GARMENT
GERAINT
HYDRANT
IMPLANT
IMPRINT
INFRONT
INPRINT
INSTANT
ITERANT
JOBHUNT
LAMBENT
LAURENT
LENFANT
LENIENT
MANHUNT
MEDIANT
MIGHTNT
MIGRANT
MORDANT
MORDENT
NASCENT
ODDMENT
OPULENT
OUGHTNT
OXIDANT
PAGEANT
PATIENT
PAYMENT
PEASANT
PECCANT
PENDANT
PENDENT
PENNANT
PERCENT
PIGMENT
PIQUANT
PORTENT
PRESENT
PREVENT
PRUDENT
PUNGENT
PUPTENT
RADIANT
RAIMENT
RAMPANT
REAGENT
RECOUNT
REDCENT
REGNANT
RELIANT
REMNANT
REMOUNT
REPAINT
REPLANT
REPRINT
SALIENT
SAPIENT
SARGENT
SEALANT
SEGMENT
SERPENT
SERVANT
SEXTANT
SOLVENT
SPIRANT
STUDENT
TAGGANT
TANGENT
TENCENT
TORMENT
TORRENT
TRIDENT
ULULANT
UNGUENT
UNSPENT
UPFRONT
USGRANT
VAGRANT
VALIANT
VARIANT
VARMINT
VERDANT
VERMONT
VIBRANT
VINCENT
VIOLENT
WARRANT
WOULDNT

NU•••••
NUANCED
NUANCES
NUBBIER
NUBBINS
NUBBLES
NUBIANS
NUCLEAR
NUCLEIC
NUCLEON
NUCLEUS
NUCLIDE
NUDGERS
NUDGING
NUDISTS
NUDNIKS
NUGGETS
NULLAHS
NULLIFY
NULLING
NULLITY
NUMBATS
NUMBERS
NUMBEST
NUMBING
NUMERAL
NUMERIC
NUNCIOS
NUNLIKE
NUNNERY
NUPTIAL
NUREYEV
NURSERS
NURSERY
NURSING
NURTURE
NUTATED
NUTATES
NUTLETS
NUTLIKE
NUTMEAT
NUTMEGS
NUTRIAS
NUTSIER
NUTTERS
NUTTIER
NUTTILY
NUTTING
NUZZLED
NUZZLER
NUZZLES

N•U••••
NAUGHTS
NAUGHTY
NEURONE
NEURONS
NEUTRAL
NEUTRON
NOUGATS
NOUGHTS
NOURISH
NOUVEAU
NYUNGAR

N••U•••
NAHUATL
NATURAL
NATURED
NATURES
NEBULAE
NEBULAR
NEBULAS
NEXUSES
NOCUOUS
NODULAR
NODULES
NOGUCHI
NONUSER

N•••U••
NEPTUNE
NETSUKE
NETSURF
NIEBUHR
NOCTURN
NODOUBT
NOFAULT
NOTRUMP
NOTSURE
NURTURE

N••••U•
NATRIUM
NEEDFUL
NERVOUS
NIOBIUM
NITROUS
NOCUOUS
NONPLUS
NOSEEUM
NOSEOUT
NOSTRUM
NOTTRUE
NOXIOUS
NUCLEUS

N•••••U
NEARYOU
NOUVEAU

•NU••••
ENURING
FNUMBER
INURING
INUTILE
KNUCKLE
KNURLED
SNUBBED
SNUFFED
SNUFFER
SNUFFLE
SNUFFLY
SNUGGER
SNUGGLE
UNUSUAL

•N•U•••
ANGULAR
ANNUALS
ANNUITY
ANNULAR
ANNULUS
ANOUILH
ENDUING
ENDURED
ENDURES
ENDUROS
ENDUSER
ENDUSES
ENGULFS
ENOUNCE
ENQUIRE
ENQUIRY
ENSUING
ENSUITE
ENSURED
ENSURES

INCUDES
INDUCED
INDUCER
INDUCES
INDUCTS
INDULGE
INDUTCH
INFUSED
INFUSES
INHUMAN
INJURED
INJURES
INQUEST
INQUIRE
INQUIRY
INSULAR
INSULIN
INSULTS
INSURED
INSURER
INSURES
INTUITS
KNOUTED
ONGUARD
UNCURLS
UNFURLS
UNGUENT
UNLUCKY
UNQUOTE
UNTUNED
UNTUNES

•N••U••
ANAHUAC
ENCRUST
ENDRUNS
ENGLUND
ENROUTE
ENSOULS
ENTHUSE
ENTRUST
INARUSH
INBOUND
INCLUDE
INDOUBT
INHAULS
INHOUSE
INOCULA
INTRUDE
INTRUST
INTRUTH
SNAFUED
UNAMUNO
UNBOUND
UNCOUTH
UNEQUAL
UNGLUED
UNPLUGS
UNSOUND
UNSTUCK
UNTRUTH
UNUSUAL
UNWOUND

•N•••U•
ANGELUS
ANNULUS
ANTAEUS
ANTEDUP
ANTESUP
ANTIGUA
ANTIQUE
ANXIOUS
ENAMOUR
ENDEDUP
ENVIOUS
INFOCUS
INGENUE
INGROUP
INVACUO
INVOGUE
KNEESUP
ONEROUS
SNAPSUP
UNAWFUL

•N••••U
ANGELOU
ONLYYOU

••NU•••
ANNUALS
ANNUITY
ANNULAR
ANNULUS
BENUMBS
BONUSES
CONURES
DENUDED
DENUDES
GENUINE
HANUKAH
JANUARY
MANUALS
MANUMIT
MENUHIN
MINUEND
MINUETS
MINUSES
MINUTES
MINUTIA
NONUSER
PANURGE
PENUCHE
PENULTS
SENUFOS
SINUOUS
SINUSES
TENUITY
TENUOUS
TENURED
TENURES
VANUATU

••N•U••
BANQUET
CANFULS
CENSURE
CENTURY
CONCURS
CONDUCE
CONDUCT
CONDUIT
CONFUSE
CONFUTE
CONJURE
CONQUER
CONSULS
CONSULT
CONSUME
CONTUSE
DANBURY
DENEUVE
DENTURE
DONJUAN
FANOUTS
FONDUES
HANGUPS
HONOURS
JONQUIL
LANGUID
LANGUOR
LANGURS
LINEUPS
LINGUAL
LINKUPS
LONGUES
MANHUNT
PANFULS
PENGUIN
PINCURL
RENAULT
RUNOUTS
SANJUAN
SANLUIS
SENDUPS
SENSUAL
SUNBURN
SUNSUIT
SYNFUEL
TONGUED
TONGUES
TONSURE
TUNEUPS
VENTURA
VENTURE
WINDUPS
YANQUIS

••N••U•
ANNULUS
BANEFUL
BANGSUP
BENELUX
BINDSUP
BONEDUP
BONESUP
BONJOUR
CANDOUR
CANOPUS
CENTAUR
CONKOUT
CONTOUR
DANSEUR
DONAHUE
DONIMUS
FANCLUB
FANSOUT
FINDOUT
GANGSUP
HANDFUL
HANDGUN
HANDOUT
HANDSUP
HANGOUT
HANGSUP
HUNGOUT
IBNSAUD
IGNEOUS
JUNEBUG
KINGTUT
LANDAUS
LINEDUP
LINESUP
LONGRUN
MANAGUA
MANHOUR
MINDFUL
MINIBUS
MINIMUM
MONIQUE
NONPLUS
OMNIBUS
OWNEDUP
PANSOUT
PENTIUM
PINENUT
PINETUM
PONTIUS
PUNCHUP
RANCOUR
RANGOUT
RENEGUE
RINGOUT
RINGSUP
RUNGOUT
RUNSOUT
SANCTUM
SANGOUT
SENDOUT
SENDSUP
SENTOUT
SINGOUT
SINUOUS
SONGFUL
TANKFUL
TANKSUP
TANTRUM
TENFOUR
TENSEUP
TENUOUS
TONEDUP
TONESUP
TUNEDUP
TUNEFUL
TUNEOUT
TUNESUP
WANTOUT
WENTOUT
WINDSUP
WINGNUT
WINKOUT
WINSOUT
XINGOUT
ZONKOUT

••N•••U
MANITOU
RONDEAU
TONNEAU
VANUATU

•••NU••
AVENUES
CAPNUTS
CHINUPS
EMANUEL
GRANULE
HEXNUTS
LUGNUTS
MAGNUMS
PEANUTS
PIGNUTS
PLENUMS
PRENUPS
WALNUTS

•••N•U•
BORNEUP
BOUNDUP
BRINGUP
BURNOUT
BURNSUP
BURNTUP
CRANIUM
CRANKUP
DOINGUP
EVENOUT
EVENSUP
FLANEUR
GAINFUL
GOINGUP
HAFNIUM
HAHNIUM
HEINOUS
ICINGUP
IRONOUT
JEANLUC
JOINSUP
LIONCUB
MOANFUL
OMENTUM
OMINOUS
OPENSUP
OZONOUS
PAINFUL
PLANOUT
PRONOUN
QUANTUM
QUINQUE
RAINOUT
RHENIUM
ROUNDUP
RUINOUS
SEENOUT
SIGNOUT
SIGNSUP
SKINFUL
SPINOUT
SPUNOUT
STANDUP
STUNGUN
THINKUP
TORNOUT
TURNOUT
TURNSUP
TYINGUP
URANIUM
USINGUP
VILNIUS
WORNOUT
WOUNDUP
YAWNFUL
YOUNGUN

•••N••U
FRENEAU
TONNEAU

••••NU•
ALUMNUS
ARCANUM
BLOWNUP
CLEANUP
COCONUT
DIVINUM
DOMINUS
DRAWNUP
EATENUP
ECHINUS
GIVENUP
GROWNUP
HUMANUM
INGENUE
JEJUNUM
LOCKNUT
OCEANUS
ORGANUM
PINENUT
RAPANUI
RETINUE
REVENUE
SEVENUP
STERNUM
TETANUS
WINGNUT
WOKENUP

•••••NU
PARVENU

N•V••••
NAVAHOS
NAVAJOS
NAVARRE
NAVVIES
NEVADAN
NEVILLE
NOVARRO
NOVELLA
NOVELLE
NOVELTY
NOVENAS
NOVICES

N••V•••
NAIVELY
NAIVETE
NAIVETY
NAVVIES
NERVIER
NERVILY
NERVOUS
NIRVANA
NOUVEAU

N•••V••
NATIVES
NINEVEH

N••••V•
NEWWAVE

N•••••V
NABOKOV
NEMEROV
NUREYEV

•NV••••
ENVELOP
ENVIERS
ENVIOUS
ENVYING
INVACUO
INVADED
INVADER
INVADES
INVALID
INVEIGH
INVENTS
INVERSE
INVERTS
INVESTS
INVITED
INVITES
INVITRO
INVOGUE
INVOICE
INVOKED
INVOKER
INVOKES
INVOLVE
UNVEILS

•N•V•••
KNAVERY
KNAVISH
SNIVELS
UNAVOCE

•N••V••
ANDOVER
ENDIVES
ENLIVEN
INCIVIL
INFAVOR
KNIEVEL
UNCIVIL
UNCOVER
UNLOVED
UNMOVED
UNPAVED
UNRAVEL
UNWOVEN

•N•••V•
ANCHOVY
ENCLAVE
ENGRAVE
ENSLAVE
INVOLVE
ONLEAVE
ONSERVE
UNITIVE
UNNERVE
UNWEAVE

••NV•••
CANVASS
CONVENE
CONVENT
CONVERT
CONVEYS
CONVICT
CONVOKE
CONVOYS
JANVIER

••N•V••
DONOVAN
HANOVER
MINIVAN
MINIVER
NINEVEH
RANOVER
RUNOVER

••N••V•
BONJOVI
CENTAVO
CONCAVE
CONNIVE
DENEUVE
GINGIVA
MINERVA
PENSIVE
TANTIVY
TENSIVE
UNNERVE

••N•••V
HENRYIV

•••N•V•
CONNIVE
IVANOVO
ULANOVA

••••N•V
GODUNOV
ROMANOV
ULYANOV
USTINOV

N•W••••
NCWYETH
NEWAGER
NEWBERY
NEWBORN
NEWDEAL
NEWGATE
NEWHART
NEWLEFT
NEWLOOK
NEWMATH
NEWMOON
NEWMOWN
NEWNESS
NEWPORT
NEWSBOY
NEWSDAY
NEWSIER
NEWSIES
NEWSMAN
NEWSMEN
NEWTONS
NEWTOWN
NEWWAVE
NEWYEAR
NEWYORK
NOWHERE

N••W•••
NARWALS
NARWHAL
NETWORK
NEWWAVE
NITWITS
NOSWEAT
NOTWELL

N••••W•
NARROWS
NEPHEWS
NEWMOWN
NEWTOWN
NOSHOWS

•NW••••
ENWRAPS
INWARDS
ONWARDS
UNWEAVE
UNWINDS
UNWISER
UNWOUND
UNWOVEN
UNWRAPS

•N•W•••
ANSWERS
ANTWERP
ENDWAYS
ENDWISE
ENTWINE
GNAWERS
GNAWING
INAWEOF
INAWORD
INDWELL
INKWELL
KNOWHOW
KNOWING
SNOWCAP
SNOWCAT
SNOWDAY
SNOWDON
SNOWIER
SNOWILY
SNOWING
SNOWJOB
SNOWMAN
SNOWMEN
SNOWPEA
SNOWSIN
UNAWARE
UNAWFUL
UNSWEPT
UNTWIST

•N••W••
ANTIWAR
CNTOWER
ENDOWED
INNOWAY
INPOWER
UNBOWED
UNSEWED

•N•••W•
ANDREWS
ANTCOWS
INFLOWS
INGROWN
UNDRAWN
UNKNOWN

•N••••W
INASTEW
KNOWHOW
UNSCREW

••NW•••
GUNWALE
PINWALE
RUNWAYS
RUNWITH
TINWARE
TINWORK

••N•W••
DUNAWAY
GANGWAY
INNOWAY
JANEWAY
MANOWAR
RANAWAY
RENEWAL
RENEWED
RENEWER
RUNAWAY

••N••W•
MINNOWS
PINDOWN
RANDOWN
RUNDOWN
SUNBOWL
SUNDEWS
SUNDOWN
WINDOWS
WINNOWS

••N•••W
BANDSAW
DANELAW
GANGSAW
HANDSAW
LONGBOW
MANILOW
TONEROW
WINDROW
WINSLOW

•••N•W•
BARNOWL
MINNOWS
OKINAWA
OLDNEWS
UNKNOWN
WINNOWS

•••N••W
CORNROW
DOWNBOW
RAINBOW

••••N•W
ASOFNOW
JUSTNOW
LIKENEW
SAGINAW
UPTONOW
YOUKNOW

N•X••••
NEXUSES
NOXIOUS
NOXZEMA

N•••••X
NARTHEX

•NX••••
ANXIETY
ANXIOUS

•N•X•••
INEXACT

•N••X••
ANNEXED
ANNEXES
INBOXES
INDEXED
INDEXES
UNBOXED
UNBOXES
UNFIXED

•N••••X
ANTITAX

••NX•••
JINXING
MANXCAT
MANXMAN
MANXMEN
MINXISH

••N•X••
ANNEXED
ANNEXES

••N••X•
CONTEXT

••N•••X
BANDBOX
BENELUX
CINEMAX
HENDRIX
PANCHAX
SANDBOX

•••N••X
SPANDEX

••••N•X
EQUINOX
KLEENEX
PHOENIX

•••••NX
PHALANX
PHARYNX

NY•••••
NYUNGAR

N•Y••••
NAYSAID
NAYSAYS

N••Y•••
NCWYETH
NEWYEAR
NEWYORK

N•••Y••
NEARYOU
NUREYEV

N••••Y•
NAYSAYS
NOBODYS

N•••••Y
NAIVELY
NAIVETY
NAKEDLY
NAMEDAY
NASALLY
NASTILY
NATTILY
NAUGHTY
NEEDILY
NERVILY
NEWBERY
NEWSBOY
NEWSDAY
NIFTILY
NIGHTLY
NIMIETY
NINTHLY
NITTANY
NOISILY
NOONDAY
NOSEGAY
NOTABLY
NOTEDLY
NOVELTY
NULLIFY
NULLITY
NUNNERY
NURSERY
NUTTILY

•NY••••
ANYBODY
ANYMORE
ANYONES
ANYROAD
ANYTIME
UNYOKED
UNYOKES

•N•Y•••
ENVYING
ENZYMES
INKYCAP
ONLYTOO
ONLYYOU
UNDYING
UNTYING

•N••Y••
ANALYSE
ANALYST
ANALYZE
ANNOYED
ANODYNE
ANONYMS
ENCRYPT
ENJOYED
INSTYLE
ONEEYED
ONLYYOU

•N•••Y•
ANTONYM
ENDWAYS

•N••••Y
ANALOGY
ANARCHY
ANATOMY
ANCHOVY
ANGRILY
ANNUITY
ANOMALY
ANTHONY
ANXIETY
ANYBODY
ENDPLAY
ENQUIRY
ENTROPY
INANELY
INANITY
INAPTLY
INEPTLY
INERTLY
INFANCY
INNOWAY
INQUIRY
KNAVERY
SNAKILY
SNIDELY
SNIFFLY
SNITCHY
SNOWDAY
SNOWILY
SNUFFLY
UNAPTLY
UNCANNY
UNGODLY
UNHANDY
UNHAPPY
UNITARY
UNLUCKY
UNREADY

••NY•••
BANYANS
BUNYIPS
CANYONS
DENYING
HUNYADY
KENYANS
LANYARD
MANYEAR
MINYANS
PONYING
TINYTIM
ZANYISH

••N•Y••
ANNOYED
HENRYIV
HONEYED
MONEYED
TINTYPE
VANDYCK
VANDYKE
VANEYCK

••N••Y•
CONVEYS
CONVOYS
DONKEYS
FONTEYN
MANDAYS
MONDAYS
MONKEYS
MONTOYA
RUNWAYS
SUNDAYS
SUNRAYS
SYNONYM

••N•••Y
AMNESTY
ANNUITY
BANALLY
BENTLEY
BINDERY
BONEDRY
BONNILY
CANNERY
CANNILY
CANTILY
CENTURY
CINDERY
CONAKRY
CONNERY
DANBURY
DANDIFY
DENNEHY
DENSELY
DENSITY
DINGILY
DUNAWAY
DYNASTY
FANCIFY
FANCILY
FANTASY
FINALLY
FINICKY
FUNKILY
FUNNILY
GANGWAY
GINGERY
GUNNERY
GUNPLAY
HANDILY
HENNERY
HONESTY
HUNGARY
HUNTLEY
HUNYADY
IGNOBLY
INNOWAY
JANEWAY
JANUARY
KENNEDY
KINKILY
LANGLEY
LANGTRY
LANKILY
LENGTHY
LINDSAY
LINDSEY
MONTHLY
NINTHLY
NUNNERY
PANICKY
PANOPLY
PENALTY
PUNNILY
RANAWAY
RUNAWAY
RUNSDRY
SANDFLY
SENSORY
SUNCITY
SUNNILY
SYNERGY
TANNERY
TANTIVY
TENABLY
TENANCY
TENSELY
TENTHLY
TENUITY
TINNILY
TONALLY
VENALLY
WINDILY
WINFREY
WINTERY
ZONALLY

•••NY••
ANONYMS
EPONYMS
EPONYMY

•••N•Y•
BARNEYS
GURNEYS
JITNEYS
KIDNEYS
LOONEYS
PHONEYS
ROMNEYS

•••N••Y
AMENITY
BARNABY
BEANERY
BLANDLY
BLANKLY
BLINDLY
BLUNTLY
BONNILY
BYANDBY
CANNERY
CANNILY
CHANTEY
CHINTZY
CONNERY
CORNILY
COUNTRY
CRINKLY
CRUNCHY
DARNLEY

DEANERY
DENNEHY
DIGNIFY
DIGNITY
ECONOMY
EPONYMY
FAINTLY
FOUNDRY
FRANKLY
FUNNILY
GAINSAY
GAUNTLY
GOINGBY
GOONILY
GRANARY
GRANDLY
GUNNERY
HENNERY
HORNSBY
HYMNODY
INANELY
INANITY
ISONOMY
JOHNGAY
JOHNJAY
JOINERY
JOINTLY
KENNEDY
LAUNDRY
MAGNIFY
MOONILY
NOONDAY
NUNNERY
ORANGEY
PAUNCHY
PHONILY
PLENARY
PRONELY
PUNNILY
QUINARY
RAINILY
REENTRY
REUNIFY
RIANTLY
ROUNDLY
SAINTLY
SCANTLY
SCENERY
SHANTEY
SHINILY
SIGNIFY
SOUNDLY
SPANGLY
SPINDLY
SPINDRY
SPINNEY
STANDBY
STANLEY
STONILY
SUNNILY
SWINGBY
TANNERY
TAWNILY
TERNARY
TINNILY
TRENARY
TRINITY
TURNERY
TURNKEY
TWINKLY
VRONSKY
WRINKLY
WRONGLY

••••NY•

ACRONYM
ANTONYM
HOMONYM
HYPONYM
SYNONYM

••••N•Y

ALBUNDY
ALLENBY
APLENTY
ARDENCY
BALONEY
BLARNEY
CACANNY
CADENCY
CHIMNEY
CHUTNEY
CLEANLY
CLOONEY
COCKNEY
COGENCY
DECENCY
DELANEY
ERRANCY
FLAUNTY
FLOUNCY
FLUENCY
HACKNEY
HAPENNY
HUMANLY
INFANCY
JEEPNEY
JOURNEY
KEARNEY
LATENCY
LUCENCY
MAHONEY
MASONRY
MCHENRY
ORGANDY
ORMANDY
PLAINLY
PLIANCY
POTENCY
PUDENCY
QUEENLY
RECENCY
REGENCY
SEVENTY
SPINNEY
SPRINGY
SQUINTY
STERNLY
STRINGY
SWEENEY
TENANCY
TIERNEY
TOURNEY
TRUANCY
TYRANNY
UNCANNY
UNHANDY
URGENCY
VACANCY
VALENCY
WCHANDY
WHITNEY
WOMANLY

•••••NY

ALIMONY
ANTHONY
BALCONY
BETHANY
BIOGENY
CACANNY
CALUMNY
COMPANY
COTTONY
COWPONY
DESTINY
DITTANY
EUPHONY
GASCONY
GERMANY
HAPENNY
HARMONY
JARGONY
LARCENY
NITTANY
OROGENY
PROGENY
SCRAWNY
TAMMANY
TIFFANY
TUSCANY
TYRANNY
UNCANNY
YEVGENY

N•Z••••

NOZZLES
NUZZLED
NUZZLER
NUZZLES

N••Z•••

NONZERO
NOXZEMA
NOZZLES
NUZZLED
NUZZLER
NUZZLES

N•••Z••

NETIZEN

N•••••Z

NATCHEZ

•NZ••••

ENZYMES
UNZONED

•N•Z•••

ENDZONE

•N••Z••

SNEEZED
SNEEZER
SNEEZES
SNOOZED
SNOOZES
UNFAZED

•N•••Z•

ANALYZE
ANASAZI
ANODIZE
INADAZE

••NZ•••

BENZENE
CANZONE
CINZANO
FANZINE
MENZIES
NONZERO
PANZERS
TENZING

••N•Z••

BENAZIR
DENIZEN
IONIZED
IONIZER
IONIZES

••N••Z•

BONANZA
GINFIZZ
MENDOZA
YANGTZE

••N•••Z

GINFIZZ

•••NZ••

BRONZED
BRONZES
KWANZAS
STANZAS

•••N•Z•

AGONIZE
CHINTZY
LIONIZE
SPINOZA

•••N••Z

FRANKOZ

••••NZ•

BONANZA
CADENZA
FIRENZE
LORENZO
ORGANZA

••••N•Z

ALBENIZ
JIMENEZ
LEIBNIZ

•••••NZ

KOBLENZ
THEFONZ

OA•••••

OAKFERN
OAKLAND
OAKLAWN
OAKLEAF
OAKLIKE
OAKMOSS
OAKTREE
OARLESS
OARLIKE
OARLOCK
OATLIKE
OATMEAL

O•A••••

OBADIAH
OCANADA
OCARINA
OFASORT
OKAYING
ONADARE
ONADATE
ONADIET
ONAGERS
ONANDON
ONAROLL
ONASSIS
ONATEAR
OPACITY
OPALINE
OPAQUES
ORACLES
ORANGES
ORANGEY
ORATING
ORATION
ORATORS
ORATORY
OVATION

O••A•••

OBLASTS
OBLATES
OBTAINS
OCEANIA
OCEANIC
OCEANID
OCEANUS
OCTAGON
OCTANES
OCTANTS
OCTAVES
OCTAVIA
OCTAVOS
OGLALAS
OLEATES
ONTARIO
ONWARDS
OPIATES
ORDAINS
ORGANDY
ORGANIC
ORGANON
ORGANUM
ORGANZA
ORGATES
ORLANDO
ORMANDY
OTRANTO
OTTAWAS
OUTACTS
OUTAGES
OXCARTS

O•••A••

OAKLAND
OAKLAWN
OBVIATE
OCANADA
ODDBALL
OFFBASE
OFFHAND
OFFRAMP
OGDOADS
OHIOANS
OILCAKE
OILCANS
OILLAMP
OILPANS
OKINAWA
OLDDAYS
OLDHAND
OLDMAID
OLDSAWS
OMPHALI
ONADARE
ONADATE
ONBOARD
ONELANE
ONGUARD
ONLEAVE
ONSTAGE
ONTRACK
OOHLALA
OOMPAHS
OPENAIR
OPERAND
OPERATE
ORCHARD
ORDEALS
OREGANO
ORGEATS
ORIGAMI
ORLEANS
ORPHANS
OURGANG
OUTBACK
OUTCAST
OUTEATS
OUTFACE
OUTLAID
OUTLAND
OUTLAST
OUTLAWS
OUTLAYS
OUTPACE
OUTRACE
OUTRAGE
OUTRANK
OUTTAKE
OUTTALK
OUTWARD
OVERACT
OVERAGE
OVERALL
OVERATE
OVERAWE
OVIPARA
OVISACS
OXIDANT
OXIDASE

O••••A•

OAKLEAF
OATMEAL
OBADIAH
OEDIPAL
OFFBEAT
OFFLOAD
OFFPEAK
OFFROAD
OFFYEAR
OGLALAS
OJIBWAS
OJIBWAY
OLDCHAP
OLDUVAI
ONATEAR
ONEIDAS
ONESTAR
ONTRIAL
OPENBAR
OPTICAL
OPTIMAL
ORBITAL
ORDINAL
ORPHEAN
ORTOLAN
OTTAWAS
OTTOMAN
OUTDRAW
OUTPLAY
OUTWEAR
OVEREAT
OVERLAP
OVERLAY
OVERRAN
OVERSAW
OVERTAX
OVOIDAL
OXONIAN

O•••••A

OCANADA
OCARINA
OCEANIA
OCTAVIA
OKINAWA
OLESTRA
OLYMPIA
OOHLALA
OPENSEA
OPHELIA
ORGANZA
OSCEOLA
OVERSEA
OVIPARA
OXYMORA

•OA••••

BOARDED
BOARDER
BOARISH
BOASTED
BOASTER
BOATELS
BOATERS
BOATING
BOATMAN
BOATMEN
COACHED
COACHES
COALBIN
COALCAR
COALERS
COALGAS
COALOIL
COALTAR
COARSEN
COARSER
COASTAL
COASTED
COASTER
COATING
COAXERS
COAXIAL
COAXING
FOALING
FOAMIER
FOAMILY
FOAMING
GOABOUT
GOADING
GOAFTER
GOAHEAD
GOALIES
GOALONG
GOATEED
GOATEES
GOATISH
HOAGIES
HOARDED
HOARDER
HOARIER
HOARILY
HOARSEN
HOARSER
HOAXERS
HOAXING
JOACHIM
JOAQUIN
LOACHES
LOADERS
LOADING
LOAFERS
LOAFING
LOAMIER
LOAMING
LOANERS
LOANING
LOATHED
LOATHES
MOANERS
MOANFUL
MOANING
POACHED
POACHER
POACHES
ROACHED
ROACHES
ROADBED
ROADHOG
ROADIES
ROADMAP
ROADWAY
ROAMERS
ROAMING
ROANOKE
ROARERS
ROARING
ROASTED
ROASTER
SOAKERS
SOAKING
SOAKSUP
SOANDSO
SOAPBOX
SOAPERS
SOAPIER
SOAPILY
SOAPING
SOARERS
SOARING
TOADIED
TOADIES
TOADISH
TOASTED
TOASTER

•O•A•••

BOIARDO
BONANZA
BORACIC
BORATES
COHABIT
CONAKRY
CORAZON
COWARDS
DOMAINS
DONAHUE
DONATED
DONATES
DONATOR
DOPANTS
DOSAGES
DOTARDS
DOWAGER
FORAGED
FORAGER
FORAGES
GOCARTS
GOKARTS
GOTAWAY
GOUACHE
HOGARTH
HORATIO
HOSANNA
HOWARDS
IODATES
JOCASTA
JOHANNA
KOLACKY
KOMATSU
LOCALES
LOCALLY
LOCARNO
LOCATED
LOCATER
LOCATES
LOCATOR
LOVABLE
LOVABLY
LOYALLY
LOYALTY
MOGAMBO
MOHAIRS
MOHAWKS
MONARCH
MORAINE
MORALES
MORALLY
MORANIS
MORAVIA
MOSAICS
MOVABLE
MOVABLY
NOCANDO
NOFAULT
NOGALES
NOMADIC
NONAGES
NONAGON
NOTABIT
NOTABLE
NOTABLY
NOTATED
NOTATES
NOVARRO
POLARIS
POMADED
POMADES
POSADAS
POTABLE
POTAGES
ROBARDS
ROGAINE
ROLAIDS
ROMAINE
ROMANCE
ROMANIA
ROMANOV
ROMANSH
ROSALIE
ROSANNA
ROSANNE
ROSARIO
ROTATED
ROTATES
ROTATOR
ROXANNE
ROYALLY
ROYALTY
ROYALWE
SODAPOP
SOFABED
SOLACES
SOLARIA
SOMALIA
SOMALIS
SOMATIC
SONATAS
TOBACCO
TONALLY
TOPAZES
TOTALED
TOTALLY
TOWARDS
TOWAWAY
VOCALIC
VOCALLY
VOYAGED
VOYAGER
VOYAGES
WOMANLY
ZONALLY
ZOUAVES

•O••A••

AOUDADS
BOBCATS
BOBTAIL
BOITANO
BOKHARA
BOMBARD
BOMBAST
BONDAGE
BONEASH
BOWSAWS
BOXCARS
COCHAIR
COCKADE
COEVALS
COGNACS
COGNATE
COINAGE
COLGATE
COLLAGE
COLLARD
COLLARS
COLLATE
COMBATS
COMMAND
COMPACT
COMPANY
COMPARE
COMPASS
COMRADE
CONCAVE
CONFABS
CONGAED
CONGAME
CONTACT
CONTAIN
COOLANT
COPLAND
CORDAGE
CORDATE
CORKAGE
CORRALS
CORSAGE
CORSAIR
COSSACK
COSTAIN
COSTARS
COTTAGE
COUGARS
COURAGE
COURANT
COWHAND
DOCKAGE
DOGBANE
DOGCART
DOGDAYS
DOGEARS
DOGFACE
DOGMATA
DOGTAGS
DOLLARS
DOLMANS
DOODADS
DOODAHS
DORMANT
DORSALS
DOSSALS
FOGBANK
FOLIAGE
FOLIATE
FOLKART
FONDANT
FOOTAGE
FORBADE
FOREARM
FORGAVE
FORMALS
FORMATS
FORSAKE
FORSALE
FORWARD
FOULARD
FOXTAIL
GODDARD
GOESAPE
GOLIATH
GOODALL
GOSHAWK
GOTBACK
GOTLAND
GOULASH
GOURAMI
HOBNAIL
HOECAKE
HOGBACK
HOGWASH
HOLLAND
HOLYARK
HONIARA
HOOHAHS
HOOKAHS
HOSTAGE
HOTCAKE
HOTCAPS
HOTCARS
HOTWARS
HOVLANE
HOWDAHS
JOBBANK
KODIAKS
KOOLAID
KOREANS
LOGJAMS
LOLLARD
LOMBARD
LONGAGO
LONGARM
LOOFAHS
LOQUATS
LOWBALL
LOWLAND
LOWPAID
MOBCAPS
MOMBASA
MONDALE
MONDAYS
MONTAGE
MONTANA
MONTAND
MONTANE
MONTANI
MOORAGE
MORDANT
MORGANA
MORGANS
MORTALS
MORTARS
MOULAGE
NORMALS
NORMAND
NORMANS
NOUGATS
OOHLALA
OOMPAHS
POLEAXE
POLKAED
POLLACK
POMPANO
PONIARD
POPLARS
POPTART
PORTAGE
PORTALS
POSTAGE
POTTAGE
ROLVAAG
ROSEATE
ROSTAND
ROULADE
SOCIALS
SOPRANO
SORBATE
SOUTANE
TOCCATA
TOECAPS
TOENAIL
TOETAPS
TOMCATS
TONEARM
TONGANS
TONNAGE
TOPHATS
TOPIARY
TOPKAPI
TOPMAST
TOPSAIL
TORNADO
TOSCALE
TOSPARE
TOSTADA
TOUCANS
TOURACO
TOWCARS
TOWPATH
TOYLAND
VOLCANO
VOLTAGE
VOLTAIC
WOMBATS
WOODARD
YOUMANS
ZODIACS

•O•••A•

BOATMAN
BODEGAS
BODYFAT
BOERWAR
BOLIVAR
BONDMAN
BOOLEAN
BOXSEAT
COALCAR
COALGAS
COALTAR
COASTAL
COAXIAL
COCHRAN
COCTEAU
COEQUAL
COLDWAR
COLEMAN
COMESAT
COMICAL
CONCEAL
CONGEAL
CONICAL
CONTRAS
COONCAT
COPULAE
COPULAS
COPYCAT
CORDIAL
CORNEAL
CORNEAS
CORONAE
CORONAS
COWPEAS
DOGSTAR
DONEGAL
DONJUAN
DONOVAN
DOORMAN
DOORMAT
DOORWAY
DOUGLAS
DOWNPAT
FOLKWAY
FOOTMAN
FOOTPAD
FOOTWAY
FORBEAR
FORDHAM
FOREMAN
FOREPAW
FORERAN
FORESAW
FORREAL
FORTRAN
FOURWAY
GOAHEAD
GODTHAB
GOESBAD
GOINGAT
GOODBAR
GOODMAN
GORDIAN
GOTAWAY
GOTCHAS
HOFBRAU
HOFFMAN
HOLIDAY
HOLMOAK
HOLYDAY
HOLYWAR
HOOPLAS
HOOTSAT
HOTHEAD
HOTSEAT
HOUSMAN
JOCULAR
JOHNGAY
JOHNJAY
JOURDAN
JOURNAL
KORUNAS
LOCOMAN
LOGGIAS
LOGICAL
LOOKSAT
LORICAE
LOWBEAM
LOWGEAR
LOWROAD
MODELAS
MODULAR
MOHICAN
MOLOKAI
NODULAR
NOMINAL
NOONDAY
NOSEBAG
NOSEGAY
NOSWEAT
NOTEPAD
NOUVEAU
NOVENAS
POKEDAT
POKESAT
POLECAR
POLECAT
POLLTAX
PONTIAC
POOHBAH
POPULAR
PORTMAN
PORTRAY
POSADAS
POSTBAG
POSTMAN
POSTWAR
POTOMAC
POTSDAM
ROADMAP
ROADWAY
ROLLBAR
ROLVAAG
ROMULAN
RONDEAU
RORQUAL
ROSEBAY
ROWBOAT
SOLEDAD
SOMEDAY
SOMEWAY
SONATAS
SORORAL
SOYBEAN
TOLLWAY
TONNEAU
TOPCOAT
TOPICAL
TOTEBAG
TOWAWAY
TOWHEAD
WOLFGAL
WOLFMAN
WOLFRAM
WORKDAY
WORKMAN
WOZNIAK
ZOYSIAS

•O••••A

BOBVILA
BOHEMIA

BOKHARA
BOLIVIA
BOLOGNA
BONANZA
BOOTHIA
BOTHNIA
COCHLEA
CONDITA
COPPOLA
CORDOBA
CORETTA
COROLLA
CORRIDA
CORSICA
DOGMATA
FONTINA
FORMICA
FORMOSA
FORMULA
FORTUNA
GONDOLA
GORILLA
HONIARA
HOSANNA
JOCASTA
JOHANNA
LORETTA
LOUELLA
MOLDOVA
MOMBASA
MONTANA
MONTOYA
MORAVIA
MORGANA
NORIEGA
NOVELLA
NOXZEMA
OOHLALA
PODRIDA
POLENTA
POMPEIA
PORSENA
ROBERTA
ROBUSTA
ROMANIA
ROSANNA
ROSETTA
ROSSSEA
ROTUNDA
SOLARIA
SOMALIA
SOYINKA
TOCCATA
TOMBOLA
TOSHIBA
TOSTADA
WOOMERA

••OA•••
BLOATED
BROADAX
BROADEN
BROADER
BROADLY
CLOACAE
CLOACAS
CLOAKED
CROAKED
CROATIA
FLOATED
FLOATER
GLOATED
GROANED
GROANER

••O•A••
ADONAIS
ALOHAOE
ANOMALY
ANORAKS
AVOCADO
AVOWALS
BAOBABS
BIOMASS
BROCADE
BROGANS
BROMATE
BUOYANT
CHORALE
CHORALS
COOLANT
DEODARS
DIORAMA
DOODADS
DOODAHS
EDOUARD
FOOTAGE
FROMAGE
FROWARD
GOODALL
HOOHAHS
HOOKAHS
ILOCANO
IRONAGE
ISOBARS
ISOLATE
KOOLAID
LEONARD
LEOPARD
LEOTARD
LOOFAHS
MOORAGE
NEONATE
PEONAGE
PROBATE
PROFANE
PROPANE
PRORATA
PRORATE
PROSAIC
RIOTACT
SHOFARS
SIOUANS
SLOGANS
SLOVAKS
SNOCATS
SPOKANE
STOMACH
STOMATA
STORAGE
TROCARS
TROJANS
TWOBASE
TWOLANE
VIOLATE
WOODARD

••O••A•
AEOLIAN
AMOEBAE
AMOEBAS
AROUSAL
ASOCIAL
BOOLEAN
BROADAX
BROSNAN
CHOCTAW
CHOLLAS
CLOACAE
CLOACAS
COONCAT
CROWBAR
DOORMAN
DOORMAT
DOORWAY
EPOCHAL
ETONIAN
FLOTSAM
FLOWNAT
FOOTMAN
FOOTPAD
FOOTWAY
FROGMAN
FRONTAL
FROWNAT
GLORIAM
GLORIAS
GLOSSAE
GLOTTAL
GOODBAR
GOODMAN
HOOPLAS
HOOTSAT
IRONMAN
LAOTIAN
LOOKSAT
NOONDAY
OVOIDAL
OXONIAN
PHOBIAS
PLOWMAN
POOHBAH
PROGRAM
PROPMAN
PROTEAN
QUOKKAS
SHOOTAT
SHOWMAN
SIOBHAN
SLOTCAR
SNOWCAP
SNOWCAT
SNOWDAY
SNOWMAN
SPORRAN
SPOUSAL
STOICAL
STOPGAP
SWOREAT
THOREAU
TROIKAS
TWOSTAR
UTOPIAN
UTOPIAS
UXORIAL

••O•••A
ANOSMIA
AVONLEA
BOOTHIA
CROATIA
DIORAMA
DUODENA
EROTICA
EXOTICA
FLORIDA
GEORGIA
INOCULA
IWOJIMA
LEONORA
PRORATA
RIORITA
SHOULDA
SNOWPEA
STOMATA
WOOMERA

•••OA••
BEMOANS
BUROAKS
BYROADS
INBOARD
INROADS
MINOANS
OGDOADS
OHIOANS
ONBOARD
PINOAKS
PTBOATS
RECOATS
REDOAKS
RELOADS
SAMOANS
TANOAKS
THROATS
THROATY
UNLOADS
UPLOADS
UPROARS

•••O•A•
ACROBAT
AEROBAT
ALLOWAY
ALSORAN
ALTOSAX
ANGOLAN
ANGORAS
AREOLAE
AREOLAR
AREOLAS
ARROBAS
ASTOLAT
AURORAE
AURORAL
AURORAS
AUTOMAT
BIFOCAL
BIMODAL
BIPOLAR
BIVOUAC
CHLORAL
CORONAE
CORONAS
CUPOLAS
DAKOTAN
DAKOTAS
DEBORAH
DEPOSAL
DIPOLAR
DONOVAN
ESPOSAS
FEDORAS
FEMORAL
IMMORAL
INNOWAY
INSOFAR
KEROUAC
LAKOTAS
LOCOMAN
MANOWAR
MAYORAL
MENORAH
MIAOYAO
MIMOSAS
MOLOKAI
NICOLAS
NIKOLAI
ORTOLAN
OTTOMAN
PAGODAS
PALOMAR
PAYOLAS
PELOTAS
PIVOTAL
POTOMAC
RAYOVAC
REMORAS
REMOVAL
REPOMAN
SAMOVAR
SAROYAN
SCHOLAR
SENORAS
SHOOTAT
SORORAL
SYNODAL
UPTOPAR

•••O••A
ALFORJA
ALTOONA
ALYOSHA
AMMONIA
ANDORRA
ANTONIA
ASTORIA
BAZOOKA
BEGONIA
BEGORRA
BOLOGNA
CIBORIA
COROLLA
EMPORIA
ENCOMIA
ESTONIA
IACOCCA
KENOSHA
LAJOLLA
LAMOTTA
LASORDA
LATOSCA
MADONNA
MAJORCA
MINOLTA
MINORCA
NICOSIA
PALOOKA
RICOTTA
SCIORRA
SEGOVIA
WYNONNA
ZENOBIA

••••OA•
AIRBOAT
ANYROAD
ARMLOAD
BALBOAS
BARSOAP
CADDOAN
CARCOAT
CARLOAD
CATBOAT
GUNBOAT
HOLMOAK
HULLOAS
ICEBOAT
IDAHOAN
JERBOAS
JETBOAT
LABCOAT
LIVEOAK
LOWROAD
OFFLOAD
OFFROAD
PAYLOAD
PEACOAT
PRELOAD
PRESOAK
QUINOAS
REDCOAT
ROWBOAT
SURCOAT
TOPCOAT
TUGBOAT
UNCLOAK
VIRGOAN

••••O•A
ACEROLA
ALTOONA
AMAPOLA
AMPHORA
ARIZONA
AUREOLA
BAZOOKA
CARIOCA
COPPOLA
CORDOBA
CRAYOLA
CREMONA
DAYTONA
DIPLOMA
FORMOSA
GONDOLA
GRANOLA
ISADORA
KEDROVA
LEONORA
MARKOVA
MENDOZA
MOLDOVA
MONTOYA
OSCEOLA
OXYMORA
PALOOKA
PANDORA
PAVLOVA
PERGOLA
PERSONA
SALSODA
SEQUOIA
SPINOZA
SUBROSA
TAPIOCA
TOMBOLA
ULANOVA

OB•••••
OBADIAH
OBELISK
OBERLIN
OBEYING
OBJECTS
OBLASTS
OBLATES
OBLIGED
OBLIGES
OBLIQUE
OBLONGS
OBLOQUY
OBOISTS
OBSCENE
OBSCURE
OBSERVE
OBTAINS
OBTRUDE
OBTUNDS
OBTUSER
OBVERSE
OBVERTS
OBVIATE
OBVIOUS

O•B••••
ONBOARD
ORBISON
ORBITAL
ORBITED
ORBITER
ORBLESS
ORBLIKE
OSBORNE
OXBLOOD

O••B•••
ODDBALL
OFFBASE
OFFBEAT
OJIBWAS
OJIBWAY
OUTBACK
OUTBIDS

O•••B••
OCTOBER
OMNIBUS
OPENBAR
OVERBIG
OVERBUY

O••••B•
ODDJOBS

O•••••B
OVERDUB

•OB••••
BOBBERS
BOBBIES
BOBBING
BOBBINS
BOBBLED
BOBBLES
BOBCATS
BOBDOLE
BOBHOPE
BOBSLED
BOBTAIL
BOBVILA
COBBLED
COBBLER
COBBLES
COBWEBS
DOBBIES
DOBBINS
FOBBING
FOBSOFF
GOBBLED
GOBBLER
GOBBLES
GOBLETS
GOBLINS
GOBROKE
HOBBIES
HOBBITS
HOBBLED
HOBBLES
HOBNAIL
HOBNOBS
HOBOING
HOBOKEN
JOBBANK
JOBBERS
JOBBERY
JOBBING
JOBHOPS
JOBHUNT
JOBLESS
JOBLOTS
KOBLENZ
KOBOLDS
LOBBERS
LOBBIED
LOBBIES
LOBBING
LOBBYER
LOBSTER
LOBULES
MOBBING
MOBBISH
MOBCAPS
MOBILES
MOBSTER
NOBBIER
NOBBLED
NOBBLER
NOBBLES
NOBHILL
NOBLEST
NOBODYS
POBOXES
ROBARDS
ROBBERS
ROBBERY
ROBBING
ROBBINS
ROBERTA
ROBERTO
ROBERTS
ROBESON
ROBLOWE
ROBOCOP
ROBOTIC
ROBROYS
ROBUSTA
SOBBERS
SOBBING
SOBERED
SOBERER
SOBERLY
TOBACCO
WOBBLED
WOBBLES
WOBEGON

•O•B•••
BOBBERS
BOBBIES
BOBBING
BOBBINS
BOBBLED
BOBBLES
BOMBARD
BOMBAST
BOMBECK
BOMBERS
BOMBING
BONBONS
BOOBIES
BOOBOOS
COBBLED
COBBLER
COBBLES
COGBURN
COLBERT
COMBATS
COMBERS
COMBINE
COMBING
COMBUST
CONBRIO
CORBELS
CORBETT
COWBELL
COWBIRD
COWBOYS
DOBBIES
DOBBINS
DOGBANE
DOGBERT
DOUBLED
DOUBLES
DOUBLET
DOUBLEU
DOUBTED
DOUBTER
FOBBING
FOGBANK
FOGBOWS
FOIBLES
FORBADE
FORBEAR
FORBIDS
FORBORE
GOABOUT
GOBBLED
GOBBLER
GOBBLES
GOOBERS
GOTBACK
HOBBIES
HOBBITS
HOBBLED
HOBBLES
HOFBRAU
HOGBACK
HOLBEIN
HOMBRES
HOMBURG
HOTBEDS
HOWBEIT
JOBBANK
JOBBERS
JOBBERY
JOBBING
JOEBLOW
LOBBERS
LOBBIED
LOBBIES
LOBBING
LOBBYER
LOGBOOK
LOMBARD
LOOBIES
LOWBALL
LOWBEAM
LOWBLOW
LOWBORN
LOWBOYS
LOWBRED
LOWBROW
MOBBING
MOBBISH
MOMBASA
NOBBIER
NOBBLED
NOBBLER
NOBBLES
NORBERT
ROBBERS
ROBBERY
ROBBING
ROBBINS
ROEBUCK
ROUBLES
ROWBOAT
SOBBERS
SOBBING
SORBATE
SORBETS
SOWBUGS
SOYBEAN
TOMBOLA
TOMBOYS
WOBBLED
WOBBLES
WOMBATS
ZOMBIES
ZOMBIFY

•O••B••
BOOMBOX
BOURBON
COALBIN
COHABIT
COLOBUS
COPYBOY
DOWNBOW
GOESBAD
GOLDBUG
GOODBAR
GOODBYE
GOODBYS
HOMEBOY
LOCKBOX
LONGBOW
LOVABLE
LOVABLY
LOVEBUG
MOVABLE
MOVABLY
NOSEBAG
NOTABIT
NOTABLE
NOTABLY
POOHBAH
POORBOX
POORBOY
POSTBAG
POSTBOX
POTABLE
ROADBED
ROLLBAR
ROSEBAY
ROSEBUD
SOAPBOX
SOFABED
SOLUBLE
TOOLBOX
TOTEBAG
TOYNBEE
VOLUBLE
VOLUBLY

•O•••B•
COBWEBS
COLUMBO
COMESBY
CONFABS
CONJOBS
CORDOBA
GOINGBY
HOBNOBS
HORNSBY
HOTTUBS
MOGAMBO
MORESBY
NODOUBT
TOSHIBA
WOULDBE

•O••••B
CORNCOB
COULOMB
COXCOMB
FOODWEB
GODTHAB
GOODJOB
HOTCOMB
NOSEJOB
POTHERB

••OB•••
BAOBABS
BOOBIES
BOOBOOS
CLOBBER
GLOBING
GLOBULE
GOOBERS
ISOBARS
KNOBBED
LOOBIES
NIOBIUM
PHOBIAS
PHOBICS
PROBATE
PROBERS
PROBING
PROBITY
PROBLEM
PROBONO
SIOBHAN
SLOBBER
SWOBBED
TWOBASE
TWOBITS

••O•B••
AMOEBAE
AMOEBAS
AMOEBIC
BOOMBOX
CLOBBER
CROWBAR
GOODBAR
GOODBYE
GOODBYS
INORBIT
KNOBBED
PHOEBES
PHOEBUS
PLOWBOY
POOHBAH
POORBOX
POORBOY
RHOMBUS
SHOEBOX
SHOWBIZ
SLOBBER
SWOBBED
TOOLBOX
TROUBLE

••O••B•
BAOBABS
CLOSEBY
DROPSBY
RIOLOBO
STOODBY
SWOREBY

••O•••B
FOODWEB
GOODJOB
LIONCUB
PROVERB
SNOWJOB

•••OB••
ACROBAT
AEROBAT
AEROBES
AEROBIC
ARROBAS
COLOBUS
DISOBEY
ENNOBLE
ENROBED
ENROBES
IGNOBLE
IGNOBLY
JACOBIN
OCTOBER
STROBES
UNROBED
UNROBES
ZENOBIA

•••O•B•
ABSORBS
ADSORBS
INDOUBT
NODOUBT
REDOUBT
RESORBS
STOODBY

••••OB•
CONJOBS
CORDOBA
DAYJOBS
DISROBE
EARLOBE
HOBNOBS
LAPROBE
MICROBE
NAIROBI
ODDJOBS
RIOLOBO
SKIBOBS

••••O•B
COULOMB
COXCOMB
HOTCOMB

•••••OB
CORNCOB
GOODJOB
LUBEJOB
NOSEJOB
SNOWJOB
THEBLOB

OC•••••
OCANADA
OCARINA
OCCIPUT
OCCLUDE
OCCULTS
OCEANIA
OCEANIC
OCEANID
OCEANUS
OCELLUS
OCELOTS
OCONNOR
OCTAGON
OCTANES
OCTANTS
OCTAVES
OCTAVIA
OCTAVOS
OCTOBER
OCTOPOD
OCTOPUS
OCTROIS
OCTUPLE
OCULIST

O•C••••
OCCIPUT
OCCLUDE
OCCULTS
OOCYTES
ORCHARD
ORCHIDS
OSCEOLA
OSCINES
OXCARTS

O••C•••
OBSCENE
OBSCURE
OILCAKE
OILCANS
OLDCHAP
OMICRON
OPACITY
ORACLES
OUTCAST
OUTCOME
OUTCROP

O•••C••
OBJECTS
OFFICER
OFFICES
OPTICAL
OSSICLE
OUTACTS

O••••C•
OARLOCK
OFFENCE
OLDNICK
ONTRACK
ORIFICE
ORINOCO
OSTRICH
OUTBACK
OUTFACE
OUTPACE
OUTRACE
OVERACT
OVISACS

O•••••C
OCEANIC
OLYMPIC
ORGANIC
OSMOTIC
OSSIFIC

•OC••••
COCHAIR
COCHERE
COCHISE
COCHLEA
COCHRAN
COCKADE
COCKERS
COCKIER
COCKILY
COCKING
COCKISH
COCKLES
COCKNEY
COCKPIT
COCKSHY
COCONUT
COCOONS
COCTEAU
DOCENTS
DOCKAGE
DOCKERS
DOCKETS
DOCKING
DOCTORS
FOCSLES
FOCUSED
FOCUSES
GOCARTS
HOCKING
JOCASTA
JOCKEYS
JOCULAR
LOCALES
LOCALLY
LOCARNO
LOCATED
LOCATER
LOCATES
LOCATOR
LOCKBOX
LOCKERS
LOCKETS
LOCKING
LOCKINS
LOCKNUT
LOCKOUT
LOCKSON
LOCKSUP
LOCKUPS
LOCOMAN
LOCOMEN
LOCUSTS
MOCKERS
MOCKERY
MOCKING
MOCKUPS
NOCANDO
NOCTURN
NOCUOUS
OOCYTES
POCKETS
POCONOS
ROCHETS
ROCKERS
ROCKERY
ROCKETS
ROCKIER
ROCKIES
ROCKING
ROCKYII

ROCKYIV
SOCIALS
SOCIETY
SOCKETS
SOCKEYE
SOCKING
SOCKSIN
TOCCATA
TOCSINS
VOCALIC
VOCALLY

•O•C•••
BOBCATS
BOKCHOY
BOTCHED
BOTCHES
BOTCHUP
BOXCARS
BOYCOTT
COACHED
COACHES
CONCAVE
CONCEAL
CONCEDE
CONCEIT
CONCEPT
CONCERN
CONCERT
CONCHES
CONCISE
CONCOCT
CONCORD
CONCURS
COUCHED
COUCHES
COXCOMB
DOGCART
DOGCHOW
FORCEPS
FORCERS
FORCING
GOTCHAS
HOECAKE
HONCHOS
HOTCAKE
HOTCAPS
HOTCARS
HOTCOMB
HOWCOME
JOACHIM
LOACHES
LOWCOST
MOBCAPS
MOOCHED
MOOCHER
MOOCHES
NONCOMS
NOTCHED
NOTCHES
POACHED
POACHER
POACHES
PONCHOS
POOCHES
POPCORN
PORCHES
PORCINE
POUCHED
POUCHES
ROACHED
ROACHES
SORCERY
TOCCATA
TOECAPS
TOMCATS
TOPCOAT
TORCHED
TORCHES
TOSCALE
TOUCANS
TOUCHED
TOUCHES
TOUCHON
TOUCHUP
TOWCARS
VOICING
VOLCANO
VOUCHED
VOUCHER
VOUCHES

•O••C••
BODICES
BORACIC
BORSCHT
BOUNCED
BOUNCER
BOUNCES
COALCAR
CODICES
CODICIL
COERCED
COERCER
COERCES
COLDCUT
COMICAL
CONICAL
COONCAT
COPYCAT
CORNCOB
COUNCIL
DOVECOT
GOUACHE
HOLYCOW
JOUNCED
JOUNCES
KOLACKY
KOPECKS
LOGICAL
LORICAE
MODICUM
MOHICAN
MOLOCHS
MONOCLE
MONOCOT
MOROCCO
NOGUCHI
NOTICED
NOTICES
NOVICES
POLECAR
POLECAT
POLICED
POLICES
PORSCHE
POUNCED
POUNCER
POUNCES
ROBOCOP
SOLACES
SOLICIT
SOUPCON
SOURCED
SOURCES
TOBACCO
TOPICAL
VOTECHS
WOODCUT

•O•••C•
BOMBECK
COGENCY
COGNACS
COLLECT
COMPACT
CONCOCT
CONDUCE
CONDUCT
CONNECT
CONNICK
CONTACT
CONVICT
COPPICE
CORNICE
CORRECT
CORSICA
COSSACK
COWLICK
DOGFACE
DORMICE
FORMICA
FOSDICK
GODUTCH
GOTBACK
GOTHICS
HOGBACK
HOSPICE
IONESCO
JONNICK
LOWNECK
LOWTECH
MONARCH
MOROCCO
MOSAICS
NOETICS
NORDICS
NORELCO
POETICS
POLLACK
POLLOCK
PORTICO
POTENCY
POTLUCK
ROEBUCK
ROLLICK
ROMANCE
TOBACCO
TOLTECS
TOPKICK
TOURACO
WOZZECK
ZODIACS

•O••••C
BORACIC
COMEDIC
HOMERIC
MOLLUSC
MONODIC
NOMADIC
POLEMIC
POLITIC
PONTIAC
POTOMAC
POULENC
ROBOTIC
SOMATIC
TONELOC
TOTEMIC
VOCALIC
VOLTAIC
YOUNGMC

••OC•••
APOCOPE
ASOCIAL
AVOCADO
AVOCETS
BIOCHIP
BLOCKED
BLOCKER
BROCADE
CHOCTAW
CLOCHES
CLOCKED
CLOCKER
CLOCKIN
CROCHET
DIOCESE
EPOCHAL
FLOCKED
FLOCKTO
FROCKED
GNOCCHI
GROCERS
GROCERY
ILOCANO
INOCULA
KNOCKED
KNOCKER
LAOCOON
MIOCENE
MOOCHED
MOOCHER
MOOCHES
POOCHES
PROCEED
PROCESS
PROCTOR
PROCURE
PROCYON
REOCCUR
SHOCKED
SHOCKER
SNOCATS
SNOCONE
STOCKED
STOCKUP
TROCARS
TROCHEE
TROCHES

••O•C••
BLOTCHY
BRONCHI
BRONCOS
CHOICER
CHOICES
CLOACAE
CLOACAS
COONCAT
GNOCCHI
GROUCHO
GROUCHY
LIONCUB
REOCCUR
SCONCES
SLOTCAR
SLOUCHY
SNOWCAP
SNOWCAT
STOICAL
WOODCUT

••O••C•
BIONICS
DNOTICE
ENOUNCE
EROTICA
EXOTICA
EXOTICS
FLOUNCE
FLOUNCY
FROLICS
PHOBICS
PHONICS
PHOTICS
PRODUCE
PRODUCT
PROJECT
PROTECT
RIOTACT
STOMACH
SUOLOCO
TROPICS
TROUNCE

••O•••C
AMOEBIC
ANOSMIC
GNOSTIC
PROSAIC
TROPHIC

•••OC••
AUROCHS
BIFOCAL
BINOCHE
BRIOCHE
DECOCTS
IACOCCA
INFOCUS
MOLOCHS
MONOCLE
MONOCOT
MOROCCO
PINOCLE
REFOCUS
RELOCKS
ROBOCOP
SIROCCO
UNLOCKS

•••O•C•
ABBOTCY
BYFORCE
DEBOUCH
DIVORCE
ENFORCE
HEROICS
IACOCCA
INFORCE
INVOICE
LATOSCA
MAJORCA
MINORCA
MOROCCO
REJOICE
RETOUCH
REVOICE
SIROCCO
SPLOTCH

•••O••C
AEROBIC
BIVOUAC
BUCOLIC
CALORIC
CANONIC
CHAOTIC
CHRONIC
DEMONIC
IDIOTIC
ILLOGIC
KEROUAC
LACONIC
MASONIC
MEIOTIC
MELODIC
MITOTIC
MONODIC
OSMOTIC
POTOMAC
RAYOVAC
ROBOTIC
SYNODIC
ZAPOTEC

••••OC•
AIRLOCK
AIRSOCK
ANTIOCH
ARMLOCK
BANNOCK
BEDROCK
BULLOCK
BURDOCK
CARIOCA
CASSOCK
CONCOCT
DEFROCK
DRSPOCK
DRYDOCK
DUNNOCK
EARLOCK
FETLOCK
GUNLOCK
HADDOCK
HAMHOCK
HAMMOCK
HANCOCK
HASSOCK
HEMLOCK
HILLOCK
HUMMOCK
INSTOCK
JANNOCK
LEACOCK
LUBBOCK
MANIOCS
MATLOCK
MATTOCK
MRSPOCK
MURDOCH
OARLOCK
ORINOCO
PADDOCK
PADLOCK
PEACOCK
PETCOCK
PETROCK
POLLOCK
RESTOCK
SCHLOCK
SHYLOCK
SUBVOCE
SUOLOCO
TAPIOCA
TUSSOCK
UNAVOCE
UNBLOCK
UNFROCK
WARLOCK
WEDLOCK

•••••OC
PAPADOC
RAYKROC
TONELOC

OD•••••
ODDBALL
ODDJOBS
ODDLOTS
ODDMENT
ODDNESS
ODORFUL
ODOROUS
ODYSSEY

O•D••••
ODDBALL
ODDJOBS
ODDLOTS
ODDMENT
ODDNESS
OEDIPAL
OEDIPUS
OGDOADS
OLDCHAP
OLDDAYS
OLDFOGY
OLDGOLD
OLDHAND
OLDLINE
OLDMAID
OLDMOON
OLDNESS
OLDNEWS
OLDNICK
OLDPROS
OLDROSE
OLDSAWS
OLDSTER
OLDTIME
OLDUVAI
OLDWEST
ORDAINS
ORDEALS
ORDERED
ORDERER
ORDERLY
ORDINAL
ORDINES

O••D•••
OBADIAH
OFFDUTY
OLDDAYS
ONADARE
ONADATE
ONADIET
OUTDOES
OUTDONE
OUTDOOR
OUTDRAW
OUTDREW
OXIDANT
OXIDASE
OXIDISE
OXIDIZE

O•••D••
ONANDON
ONEIDAS
ONORDER
ONSIDES
OVERDID
OVERDUB
OVERDUE
OVOIDAL
OWNEDUP

O••••D•
OBTRUDE
OBTUNDS
OCANADA
OCCLUDE
OFFENDS
OFFSIDE
OGDOADS
ONWARDS
ORCHIDS
ORGANDY
ORLANDO
ORMANDY
OUTBIDS
OUTSIDE
OXFORDS

O•••••D
OAKLAND
OBLIGED
OCEANID
OCTOPOD
OFFERED
OFFHAND
OFFLOAD
OFFROAD
OLDGOLD
OLDHAND
OLDMAID
OMITTED
ONBOARD
ONEEYED
ONGUARD
OPENEND
OPERAND
OPPOSED
ORBITED
ORCHARD
ORDERED
OROTUND
OSIERED
OSMOSED
OSTEOID
OUTLAID
OUTLAND
OUTLOUD
OUTSOLD
OUTWARD
OVERDID
OXBLOOD

•OD••••
BODEGAS
BODEREK
BODICES
BODKINS
BODYFAT
CODDLED
CODDLER
CODDLES
CODEINE
CODFISH
CODGERS
CODICES
CODICIL
DODDERS
DODGERS
DODGIER
DODGING
DODGSON
FODDERS
GODDARD
GODDESS
GODFREY
GODLESS
GODLIER
GODLIKE
GODSEND
GODSONS
GODTHAB
GODUNOV
GODUTCH
GODWITS
IODATES
IODIDES
IODISED
IODISES
IODIZED
IODIZES
KODIAKS
LODGERS
LODGING
MODELAS
MODELED
MODELER
MODELTS
MODERNS
MODESTO
MODESTY
MODICUM
MODISTE
MODULAR
MODULES
NODDERS
NODDING
NODOUBT
NODSOFF
NODULAR
NODULES
PODGIER
PODGILY
PODIUMS
PODLIKE
PODRIDA
RODDING
RODENTS
RODEOFF
RODEOUT
RODGERS
RODLESS
RODLIKE
RODOLFO
SODAPOP
SODDIER
SODDIES
SODDING
SODLESS
TODDIES
TODDLED
TODDLER
TODDLES
YODELED
YODELER
ZODIACS

•O•D•••
AOUDADS
BOBDOLE
BOGDOWN
BOLDEST
BONDAGE
BONDING
BONDMAN
BONDMEN
BOODLES
BORDERS
BOUDOIR
BOWDLER
CODDLED
CODDLER
CODDLES
COEDITS
COLDCUT
COLDEST
COLDISH
COLDWAR
CONDEMN
CONDIGN
CONDITA
CONDOLE
CONDONE
CONDORS
CONDUCE
CONDUCT
CONDUIT
CORDAGE
CORDATE
CORDELL
CORDERO
CORDIAL
CORDING
CORDITE
CORDOBA
CORDONS
DODDERS
DOGDAYS
DOODADS
DOODAHS
DOODLED
DOODLER
DOODLES
DOWDIER
DOWDILY
FODDERS
FOLDERS
FOLDING
FOLDOUT
FOLDSUP
FOLDUPS
FONDANT
FONDEST
FONDLED
FONDLES
FONDUES
FOODIES
FOODWEB
FORDHAM
FORDING
FOSDICK
GOADING
GODDARD
GODDESS
GOLDBUG
GOLDING
GOLDWYN
GONDOLA
GOODALL
GOODBAR
GOODBYE
GOODBYS
GOODEGG
GOODIES
GOODING
GOODISH
GOODJOB
GOODJOE
GOODMAN
GOODMEN
GOODONE
GOODSON
GOODWIN
GORDIAN
GOTDOWN
HOEDOWN
HOLDERS
HOLDING
HOLDOFF
HOLDOUT
HOLDSIN
HOLDSON
HOLDSTO
HOLDSUP
HOLDUPS
HOODLUM
HOODOOS
HOTDOGS
HOUDINI
HOWDAHS
HOYDENS
LOADERS
LOADING
LORDING
LORDJIM
LOUDEST
LOUDISH
LOWDOWN
MOLDERS
MOLDIER
MOLDING
MOLDOVA
MONDALE
MONDAYS
MOODIER
MOODILY
MORDANT
MORDENT
MORDRED
MOWDOWN
NODDERS
NODDING
NOODLES
NORDICS
POLDERS
PONDERS
POODLES
POWDERS
POWDERY
ROADBED
ROADHOG
ROADIES
ROADMAP
ROADWAY
RODDING
ROEDEER
RONDEAU
RONDELS
ROWDIER
ROWDIES
ROWDILY
SODDIER
SODDIES
SODDING
SOLDERS
SOLDIER
SOLDOFF
SOLDOUT
SORDINI
SORDINO
TOADIED
TOADIES
TOADISH
TODDIES
TODDLED
TODDLER
TODDLES
TOLDOFF
TOPDOGS
TOPDOWN
TOYDOGS
VOIDING
VOODOOS
WONDERS
WOODARD
WOODCUT
WOODIER
WOODIES
WOODLOT
WOODROW
WORDIER
WORDILY
WORDING
WORDONE

•O••D••
BOARDED
BOARDER
BOLIDES
BONEDRY
BONEDUP
BOREDOM
BORODIN
BOULDER
BOUNDED
BOUNDER
BOUNDUP
BOXEDIN
BOXEDUP
COMEDIC
COMEDUE
CORNDOG
COULDNT
DOORDIE
DOSIDOS
DOTEDON
FOUNDED
FOUNDER
FOUNDRY
GOUNDER
GOURDES
HOARDED
HOARDER
HOLEDUP
HOLIDAY
HOLYDAY
HOUNDED
IODIDES
JOHNDOE
JOINDER
JOURDAN
LOURDES
MONODIC
MOONDOG
MOULDED
MOULDER
MOUNDED
MOVEDIN
MOVEDON
MOVEDUP
NOBODYS
NOMADIC
NOONDAY
NOTEDLY
POKEDAT
POMADED
POMADES
POSADAS
POTSDAM
POUNDED
POUNDER
ROLODEX
ROPEDIN
ROUNDED
ROUNDER
ROUNDLY
ROUNDON
ROUNDUP
SOANDSO
SOLEDAD
SOLIDER
SOLIDLY
SOMEDAY
SOUNDED
SOUNDER
SOUNDLY
TONEDUP
TOORDER
TOTIDEM
VOTEDIN
WORKDAY
WORLDLY
WOULDBE
WOULDNT
WOUNDED
WOUNDUP

•O•••D•
AOUDADS
BOIARDO
COCKADE
COLLIDE
COLLODI
COLLUDE
COMMODE
COMRADE
CONCEDE
CONFIDE
CONOIDS
CORRIDA
CORRODE
COWARDS
COWHIDE
DOODADS
DOTARDS
FORBADE
FORBIDS
HOTBEDS
HOTRODS
HOWARDS
JOYRIDE
KOBOLDS
LOWTIDE
NOCANDO
PODRIDA
PONGIDS
ROBARDS
ROLAIDS
ROTUNDA
ROULADE
TOPSIDE
TORNADO
TOROIDS
TORPEDO
TOSTADA
TOWARDS

•O••••D
BOARDED
BOASTED
BOBBLED
BOBSLED
BOGEYED
BOGGLED
BOMBARD
BOOGIED
BOOKEND
BOOSTED
BOTCHED
BOTTLED
BOUNCED
BOUNDED
BOWERED
BOXWOOD
BOYHOOD
COACHED
COASTED
COBBLED
CODDLED
COERCED
COHERED
COLLARD
COLLOID
COLORED
COMMAND
COMMEND
CONCORD
CONGAED
CONRIED
CONTEND
COOPTED
COPLAND
CORNFED
COUCHED
COUGHED
COUNTED
COUPLED
COURSED
COURTED
COVERED
COVETED
COWBIRD
COWERED
COWHAND
COWHERD
COZENED
DOGFOOD
DOGSLED
DOGWOOD
DOLLIED
DONATED
DOODLED
DOUBLED
DOUBTED
DOWERED
FOCUSED
FOISTED
FONDLED
FOOTPAD
FOOZLED
FORAGED
FORFEND
FORGOOD
FORWARD
FOULARD
FOUNDED
GOAHEAD
GOATEED
GOBBLED
GODDARD
GODSEND
GOESBAD
GOGGLED

GOROUND
GOTLAND
HOARDED
HOBBLED
HOGTIED
HOGWILD
HOISTED
HOLLAND
HOMERED
HOMINID
HONEYED
HONORED
HOPPLED
HOTHEAD
HOUGHED
HOUNDED
HOVERED
IODISED
IODIZED
IONISED
IONIZED
JOGGLED
JOINTED
JOISTED
JOLLIED
JOSTLED
JOUNCED
JOUSTED
KOOLAID
LOATHED
LOBBIED
LOCATED
LOLLARD
LOMBARD
LOUNGED
LOUVRED
LOWBRED
LOWERED
LOWLAND
LOWPAID
LOWROAD
MODELED
MONEYED
MONTAND
MOOCHED
MORDRED
MORPHED
MOSEYED
MOTORED
MOTTLED
MOULDED
MOULTED
MOUNDED
MOUNTED
MOURNED
MOUSSED
MOUTHED
NOBBLED
NONSKID
NORMAND
NOTATED
NOTCHED
NOTEPAD
NOTICED
POACHED
POINTED
POLICED
POLKAED
POMADED
PONIARD
POPEYED
POPPLED
PORTEND
POSITED
POUCHED
POUNCED
POUNDED
POWERED
ROACHED
ROADBED
ROASTED
ROOSTED
ROSEBUD
ROSERED
ROSTAND
ROTATED
ROUGHED
ROUNDED
ROUSTED
SOBERED
SOFABED
SOLEDAD
SOOTHED
SORTIED
SOUGHED
SOUNDED
SOURCED
TOADIED
TOASTED
TODDLED
TOEHOLD
TOGGLED
TOKENED
TONGUED
TOOTHED
TOOTLED
TOPPLED
TORCHED
TOTALED
TOUCHED
TOUSLED
TOWELED
TOWERED
TOWHEAD
TOYLAND
VOUCHED
VOYAGED
WOBBLED
WOODARD
WORRIED
WORSTED
WOUNDED
YODELED

••OD•••

ANODISE
ANODIZE
ANODYNE
AZODYES
BOODLES
DEODARS
DOODADS
DOODAHS
DOODLED
DOODLER
DOODLES
DUODENA
ERODENT
ERODING
FOODIES
FOODWEB
GEODESY
GOODALL
GOODBAR
GOODBYE
GOODBYS
GOODEGG
GOODIES
GOODING
GOODISH
GOODJOB
GOODJOE
GOODMAN
GOODMEN
GOODONE
GOODSON
GOODWIN
GRODIER
HOODLUM
HOODOOS
MOODIER
MOODILY
NOODLES
PLODDED
PLODDER
POODLES
PRODDED
PRODDER
PRODIGY
PRODUCE
PRODUCT
RHODIUM
SHODDEN
TRODDEN
VOODOOS
WOODARD
WOODCUT
WOODIER
WOODIES
WOODLOT
WOODROW

••O•D••

AVOIDED
BLONDER
BLONDES
BLONDIE
BLOODED
BLOWDRY
BROADAX
BROADEN
BROADER
BROADLY
BROODED
BROODER
CHOWDER
CLOUDED
CLOWDER
CROWDED
DOORDIE
FLOODED
GEORDIE
MOONDOG
NOONDAY
ONORDER
OVOIDAL
PLODDED
PLODDER
PRODDED
PRODDER
PROUDER
PROUDLY
REORDER
SCOLDED
SCOLDER
SHODDEN
SHOWDOG
SMOLDER
SNOWDAY
SNOWDON
SPONDEE
STOODBY
STOODIN
STOODUP
TOORDER
TRODDEN

••O••D•

ABOUNDS
AVOCADO
BROCADE
BROMIDE
DIOMEDE
DIOXIDE
DOODADS
FLORIDA
GROUNDS
ISOPODS
LEONIDS
PROSODY
PROVIDE
SHOULDA
YAOUNDE

••O•••D

ABORTED
ADOPTED
ADORNED
AROUSED
AVOIDED
BLOATED
BLOCKED
BLOODED
BLOOMED
BLOOPED
BLOTTED
BLOUSED
BOOGIED
BOOKEND
BOOSTED
BROILED
BRONZED
BROODED
BROOKED
BROWNED
BROWSED
CHOMPED
CHOPPED
CLOAKED
CLOCKED
CLOGGED
CLOMPED
CLOPPED
CLOTHED
CLOTTED
CLOUDED
CLOUTED
CLOWNED
COOPTED
CROAKED
CROOKED
CROONED
CROPPED
CROSSED
CROWDED
CROWNED
DOODLED
DROOLED
DROOPED
DROPPED
DROWNED
DROWSED
EDOUARD
EVOLVED
FLOATED
FLOCKED
FLOGGED
FLOODED
FLOORED
FLOPPED
FLOSSED
FLOURED
FLOUTED
FOOTPAD
FOOZLED
FROCKED
FRONTED
FROSTED
FROTHED
FROWARD
FROWNED
GHOSTED
GLOATED
GLOMMED
GLOOMED
GLORIED
GLOSSED
GROANED
GROOMED
GROOVED
GROSSED
GROUPED
GROUSED
GROUTED
GROWLED
KNOBBED
KNOCKED
KNOTTED
KNOUTED
KOOLAID
LEONARD
LEOPARD
LEOPOLD
LEOTARD
MOOCHED
OROTUND
PEOPLED
PHOTOED
PLODDED
PLOPPED
PLOTTED
PROCEED
PRODDED
PROGGED
PRONGED
PROOFED
PROPPED
PROWLED
REOILED
ROOSTED
SCOFFED
SCOLDED
SCOOPED
SCOOTED
SCORNED
SCOURED
SCOUTED
SCOWLED
SHOCKED
SHOPPED
SHORTED
SHOUTED
SLOGGED
SLOPPED
SLOSHED
SLOTTED
SNOGGED
SNOOPED
SNOOTED
SNOOZED
SNORTED
SOOTHED
SPOILED
SPONGED
SPOOFED
SPOOKED
SPOOLED
SPOONED
SPORTED
SPOTTED
SPOUTED
STOCKED
STOMPED
STOOKED
STOOPED
STOPPED
STORIED
STORMED
SWOBBED
SWOONED
SWOOPED
SWOPPED
TOOTHED
TOOTLED
TROLLED
TROOPED
TROTHED
TROTTED
TWOFOLD
UNOILED
WHOMPED
WHOOPED
WHOPPED
WHORLED
WOODARD
WRONGED

•••OD••

BIMODAL
BLOODED
BORODIN
BROODED
BROODER
DECODED
DECODER
DECODES
ENCODED
ENCODER
ENCODES
FLOODED
MALODOR
MELODIC
MONODIC
NOBODYS
PAGODAS
RECODED
RECODES
REMODEL
ROLODEX
STOODBY
STOODIN
STOODUP
SYNODAL
SYNODIC
TRIODES
UNGODLY

•••O•D•

ACCORDS
AFFORDS
ALMONDS
BEHOLDS
BYROADS
BYWORDS
CONOIDS
ENFOLDS
GIRONDE
INROADS
KOBOLDS
LASORDA
LEMONDE
MILORDS
OGDOADS
OXFORDS
RECORDS
RELOADS
REMOLDS
REWORDS
SECONDS
SHROUDS
TOROIDS
UNFOLDS
UNLOADS
UPHOLDS
UPLOADS

•••O••D

AGROUND
ALLOWED
ALLOYED
ANNOYED
APPOSED
APRONED
ARBORED
ARMORED
ASTOUND
BEHOVED
BELOVED
BIGOTED
BLOODED
BLOOMED
BLOOPED
BROODED
BROOKED
CAJOLED
CAROLED
CAROMED
CAROTID
COLORED
CROOKED
CROONED
DEBONED
DECODED
DECOYED
DEMOTED
DENOTED
DEPONED
DEPOSED
DEVOTED
DROOLED
DROOPED
ELBOWED
ENCODED
ENDOWED
ENJOYED
ENROBED
EXPOSED
EXPOUND
FAGOTED
FAVORED
FLOODED
FLOORED
GLOOMED
GOROUND
GROOMED
GROOVED
HONORED
HUMORED
IGNORED
IMPOSED
IMPOUND
INBOARD
INBOUND
INTONED
INVOKED
LABORED
MAJORED
MINORED
MOTORED
OCTOPOD
ONBOARD
OPPOSED
OSMOSED
PAROLED
PILOTED
PIVOTED
PROOFED
RAZORED
REBOUND
RECODED
REDOUND
REMOVED
REMOWED
RENOTED
REPOSED
RESOLED
RESOUND
RETOWED
REVOKED
REWOUND
REZONED
RUMORED
SAMOYED
SAVORED
SCOOPED
SCOOTED
SNOOPED
SNOOTED
SNOOZED
SPOOFED
SPOOKED
SPOOLED
SPOONED
STOOKED
STOOPED
STROKED
SWOONED
SWOOPED
TALONED
TENONED
TROOPED
TUTORED
UNBOUND
UNBOWED
UNBOXED
UNLOVED
UNMOVED
UNROBED
UNSOUND
UNWOUND
UNYOKED
UNZONED
WHOOPED
WIDOWED

••••OD•

ALAMODE
ANYBODY
BARCODE
CATHODE
COLLODI
COMMODE
CORRODE
CUSTODY
EPISODE
EXPLODE
FLYRODS
HOTRODS
HYMNODY
IMPLODE
ISOPODS
METHODS
NIMRODS
PEABODY
PEAPODS
PERIODS
PROSODY
RAMRODS
SALSODA
SUNGODS
TIERODS
TRIPODS
UNIPODS
WARGODS
ZIPCODE

••••O•D

ABSCOND
ALLTOLD
ANDROID
ANEROID
ANYROAD
ARMLOAD
ASHFORD
AYKROYD
BAGNOLD
BECLOUD
BOXWOOD
BOYHOOD
BUNCOED
BUNKOED
CAMEOED
CARLOAD
CATFOOD
COLLOID
CONCORD
CRINOID
DAGWOOD
DELTOID
DESMOND
DIAMOND
DIDGOOD
DIPLOID
DISCOED
DISCORD
DITTOED
DOGFOOD
DOGWOOD
FACTOID
FORGOOD
GIFFORD
HAMMOND
HEYWOOD
HULLOED
ICECOLD
INAWORD
KEYWORD
LANFORD
LASSOED
LAWFORD
LEOPOLD
LOWROAD
MAMBOED
MANHOOD
MASTOID
MCCLOUD
MISWORD
MITFORD
MUMFORD
OFFLOAD
OFFROAD
OLDGOLD
OSTEOID
OUTLOUD
OUTSOLD
OXBLOOD
PAYLOAD
PHOTOED
PLYWOOD
PRELOAD
RADIOED
RAYMOND
REDFORD
REDWOOD
RESPOND
RIPCORD
SANFORD
SAWWOOD
SEAFOOD
SIXFOLD
STEROID
TABLOID
TANGOED
TENFOLD
TIPTOED
TOEHOLD
TWOFOLD
WARLORD
WEBTOED
WILFORD

•••••OD

BOXWOOD
BOYHOOD
CAPECOD
CATFOOD
DAGWOOD
DECAPOD
DEMIGOD
DIDGOOD
DOGFOOD
DOGWOOD
FORGOOD
FUELROD
HEYWOOD
ICHABOD
MANHOOD
OCTOPOD
OXBLOOD
PLYWOOD
REDWOOD
SAWWOOD
SEAFOOD
SEEDPOD

OE•••••

OEDIPAL
OEDIPUS
OEUVRES

O•E••••

OBELISK
OBERLIN
OBEYING
OCEANIA
OCEANIC
OCEANID
OCEANUS
OCELLUS
OCELOTS
OKEEFFE
OLEATES
OLEFINS
OLEMISS
OLESTRA
OMELETS
OMENTUM
ONEEYED
ONEIDAS
ONEIRON
ONELANE
ONENESS
ONENOTE
ONEROUS
ONESELF
ONESHOT
ONESTAR
ONESTEP
ONETIME
OPENAIR
OPENBAR
OPENEND
OPENERS
OPENING
OPENPIT
OPENSEA
OPENSUP
OPENTOE
OPERAND
OPERATE
OPEROSE
OREGANO
ORESTES
OVERACT
OVERAGE
OVERALL
OVERATE
OVERAWE
OVERBIG
OVERBUY
OVERDID
OVERDUB
OVERDUE
OVEREAT
OVERFLY
OVERJOY
OVERLAP
OVERLAY
OVERLIE
OVERRAN
OVERRUN
OVERSAW
OVERSEA
OVERSEE
OVERTAX
OVERTLY
OVERUSE

O••E•••

OBJECTS
OBSERVE
OBVERSE
OBVERTS
OFFENCE
OFFENDS
OFFENSE
OFFERED
OFFERER
OFTENER
OGREISH
OKEEFFE
ONEEYED
ONLEAVE
ONSERVE
OPHELIA
ORDEALS
ORDERED
ORDERER
ORDERLY
ORGEATS
ORIENTE
ORIENTS
ORLEANS
ORNETTE
OSCEOLA
OSIERED
OSSEOUS
OSTEOID
OTHELLO
OUTEATS
OWNEDUP

O•••E••

OAKFERN
OAKLEAF
OARLESS
OATMEAL
OBSCENE
ODDMENT
ODDNESS
OFFBEAT
OFFPEAK
OFFSETS
OFFYEAR
OILIEST
OILLESS
OILWELL
OLDNESS
OLDNEWS
OLDWEST
OMELETS
ONAGERS
ONATEAR
ONENESS
ONESELF
ONTHEGO
ONTHEQT
OOZIEST
OPENEND
OPENERS
OPINERS
OPPRESS
OPULENT
ORBLESS
OROGENY
ORPHEAN
ORPHEUS
OSPREYS
OSTLERS
OURSELF
OUSTERS
OUTLETS
OUTSELL
OUTSETS
OUTWEAR
OVEREAT
OYSTERS

O••••E•

OAKTREE
OBLATES
OBLIGED
OBLIGES
OBTUSER
OCTANES
OCTAVES
OCTOBER
ODYSSEY
OEUVRES
OFFERED
OFFERER
OFFICER
OFFICES
OFTENER
OLDSTER
OLEATES
OLIVIER
OMITTED
OMITTER
ONADIET
ONEEYED
ONESTEP
ONORDER
ONSIDES
OOCYTES
OOLITES
OPAQUES
OPENSEA
OPHITES
OPIATES
OPPOSED
OPPOSER
OPPOSES
ORACLES
ORANGES
ORANGEY
ORBITED
ORBITER
ORDERED
ORDERER
ORDINES
ORESTES
ORGATES
ORIOLES
ORPHREY
ORPINES
OSCINES
OSIERED
OSMOSED
OSMOSES
OUTAGES
OUTDOES
OUTDREW
OUTGOES
OUTGREW
OUTSTEP
OVERSEA
OVERSEE

O•••••E

OAKLIKE
OAKTREE
OARLIKE
OATLIKE
OBLIQUE
OBSCENE
OBSCURE
OBSERVE
OBTRUDE
OBVERSE
OBVIATE
OCCLUDE
OCTUPLE
OFFBASE
OFFENCE
OFFENSE
OFFLINE
OFFSIDE
OFFSITE
OILCAKE
OILLIKE
OKEEFFE
OLDLINE
OLDROSE
OLDTIME
OLIVINE
ONADARE
ONADATE
ONELANE
ONENOTE
ONETIME
ONLEAVE
ONSERVE
ONSHORE
ONSTAGE
OPALINE
OPENTOE
OPERATE
OPEROSE
ORBLIKE
ORIENTE
ORIFICE
ORNETTE
OROURKE
ORVILLE
OSBORNE
OSSICLE
OUTCOME
OUTDONE
OUTFACE
OUTLINE
OUTLIVE
OUTPACE
OUTRACE
OUTRAGE
OUTSIDE
OUTSIZE
OUTTAKE
OUTVOTE
OUTWORE
OVERAGE
OVERATE
OVERAWE
OVERDUE
OVERLIE
OVERSEE
OVERUSE
OWLLIKE
OXIDASE
OXIDISE
OXIDIZE

•OE••••

BOERWAR
COEDITS
COEPTIS
COEQUAL
COERCED
COERCER
COERCES
COEVALS
COEXIST
DOESKIN
GOESAPE
GOESBAD
GOESFOR
GOESOFF
GOESOUT
HOECAKE
HOEDOWN
JOEBLOW
JOEHILL
LOESSER
LOESSES
NOETICS
POETICS

ROEBUCK
ROEDEER
TOECAPS
TOEHOLD
TOELESS
TOELIKE
TOELOOP
TOENAIL
TOESHOE
TOETAPS
WOEISME
ZOELLER

•O•E•••

BODEGAS
BODEREK
BOGEYED
BOHEMIA
BOLEROS
BONEASH
BONEDRY
BONEDUP
BONESET
BONESUP
BOREDOM
BOREOUT
BOWERED
BOXEDIN
BOXEDUP
BOXESIN
BOXESUP
CODEINE
COGENCY
COHEIRS
COHERED
COHERES
COLEMAN
COLETTE
COMEDIC
COMEDUE
COMEOFF
COMEONS
COMEOUT
COMESAT
COMESBY
COMESIN
COMESON
COMESTO
COMESUP
CORELLI
CORETTA
COTERIE
COVERED
COVERUP
COVETED
COWERED
COZENED
DOCENTS
DOGEARS
DOLEFUL
DOLEOUT
DONEFOR
DONEGAL
DOPEOUT
DOTEDON
DOTESON
DOVECOT
DOWERED
DOYENNE
DOZENTH
DOZEOFF
FOMENTS
FOREARM
FOREIGN
FORELEG
FOREMAN
FOREMEN
FOREPAW
FORERAN
FORERUN
FORESAW
FORESEE
FORESTS
FOREVER
GONERIL
GORETEX
GOTEVEN
GOVERNS
HOLEDUP
HOLEOUT
HOLESUP
HOMEBOY
HOMERED
HOMERIC
HOMERUN
HONESTY
HONEYED
HOPEFUL
HOVERED
HOVERER
HOWELLS
HOWEVER
IONESCO
JONESES
KOPECKS
KOREANS
LORELEI
LORENZO
LORETTA
LOSEOUT
LOSESIT
LOUELLA
LOVEBUG
LOVEINS
LOVERLY
LOWERED
LOZENGE
MODELAS
MODELED
MODELER
MODELTS
MODERNS
MODESTO
MODESTY
MOLESTS
MOMENTS
MONEYED
MORELLO
MORESBY
MOSELLE
MOSEYED
MOVEDIN
MOVEDON
MOVEDUP
MOVEOUT
MOVESIN
MOVESON
MOVESUP
NORELCO
NOSEBAG
NOSEEUM
NOSEGAY
NOSEJOB
NOSEOUT
NOTEDLY
NOTEPAD
NOVELLA
NOVELLE
NOVELTY
NOVENAS
POKEDAT
POKEFUN
POKESAT
POLEAXE
POLECAR
POLECAT
POLEMIC
POLENTA
POMELOS
POPEYED
POSEURS
POTENCY
POVERTY
POWERED
ROBERTA
ROBERTO
ROBERTS
ROBESON
RODENTS
RODEOFF
RODEOUT
ROPEDIN
ROPESIN
ROPETOW
ROSEATE
ROSEBAY
ROSEBUD
ROSELLE
ROSEOIL
ROSERED
ROSETTA
ROSETTE
ROZELLE
SOBERED
SOBERER
SOBERLY
SOLEDAD
SOMEDAY
SOMEHOW
SOMEONE
SOMEWAY
TOKENED
TONEARM
TONEDUP
TONELOC
TONEROW
TONESUP
TOREOFF
TOREOUT
TOREROS
TOTEBAG
TOTEMIC
TOWELED
TOWERED
VOTECHS
VOTEDIN
VOTEFOR
VOTEOUT
VOTESIN
WOBEGON
WOKENUP
WOREOFF
WOREOUT
YODELED
YODELER

•O••E••

BOATELS
BOATERS
BOBBERS
BOILERS
BOLDEST
BOMBECK
BOMBERS
BONIEST
BONKERS
BONNETS
BOOKEND
BOOLEAN
BOOMERS
BOOTEES
BOPPERS
BORDERS
BORNEUP
BOSKETS
BOSWELL
BOTHERS
BOVVERS
BOWLERS
BOWLESS
BOWYERS
BOXIEST
BOXSEAT
COALERS
COAXERS
COBWEBS
COCHERE
COCKERS
COCTEAU
CODGERS
COFFEES
COFFERS
COINERS
COKIEST
COLBERT
COLDEST
COLLECT
COLLEEN
COLLEGE
COLLETS
COMBERS
COMMEND
COMMENT
COMPEER
COMPELS
COMPERE
COMPETE
CONCEAL
CONCEDE
CONCEIT
CONCEPT
CONCERN
CONCERT
CONDEMN
CONFERS
CONFESS
CONGEAL
CONGERS
CONGEST
CONKERS
CONNECT
CONNERY
CONSENT
CONTEMN
CONTEND
CONTENT
CONTEST
CONTEXT
CONVENE
CONVENT
CONVERT
CONVEYS
COOKERS
COOKERY
COOLERS
COOLEST
COOPERS
COPIERS
COPPERS
COPPERY
COPTERS
CORBELS
CORBETT
CORDELL
CORDERO
CORKERS
CORNEAL
CORNEAS
CORNELL
CORNERS
CORNETS
CORRECT
CORSETS
CORTEGE
COSIEST
COSSETS
COTTERS
COULEES
COWBELL
COWHERD
COWPEAS
COYNESS
COZIEST
COZZENS
DOCKERS
DOCKETS
DODDERS
DODGERS
DOGBERT
DOGLEGS
DOGLESS
DOLMENS
DONKEYS
DOPIEST
DORMERS
DORSETT
DOSSERS
DOUREST
DOWNERS
DOWSERS
DOZIEST
FODDERS
FOGGERS
FOGLESS
FOLDERS
FOLGERS
FOLLETT
FONDEST
FONTEYN
FOOLERY
FOOTERS
FOPPERY
FORBEAR
FORCEPS
FORCERS
FORFEIT
FORFEND
FORGERS
FORGERY
FORGETS
FORKERS
FORREAL
FORRENT
FORREST
FORWENT
FOSTERS
FOULEST
FOWLERS
FOXIEST
GOAHEAD
GOATEED
GOATEES
GOBLETS
GODDESS
GODLESS
GODSEND
GOLFERS
GOMPERS
GOOBERS
GOODEGG
GOOIEST
GOPHERS
GORGETS
GORIEST
GOSPELS
GOSSETT
GOTWELL
GOUGERS
HOAXERS
HOGGETS
HOKIEST
HOLBEIN
HOLDERS
HOLIEST
HOLLERS
HOMIEST
HONKERS
HOOFERS
HOOTERS
HOOVERS
HOPPERS
HORNETS
HOSIERS
HOSIERY
HOSTELS
HOSTESS
HOTBEDS
HOTHEAD
HOTNESS
HOTSEAT
HOTTEST
HOWBEIT
HOWLERS
HOYDENS
JOBBERS
JOBBERY
JOBLESS
JOCKEYS
JOGGERS
JOINERS
JOINERY
JOKIEST
JOSSERS
JOYLESS
KOBLENZ
KOSHERS
LOADERS
LOAFERS
LOANERS
LOBBERS
LOCKERS
LOCKETS
LODGERS
LOGGERS
LOGIEST
LOITERS
LONGEST
LOOKERS
LOONEYS
LOOPERS
LOOSELY
LOOSENS
LOOSEST
LOOTERS
LOPPERS
LOTTERY
LOUDEST
LOUSEUP
LOUVERS
LOWBEAM
LOWGEAR
LOWHEEL
LOWNECK
LOWNESS
LOWTECH
MOANERS
MOCKERS
MOCKERY
MOILERS
MOLDERS
MOLIERE
MOLTERS
MONGERS
MONKEES
MONKEYS
MONTEGO
MONTERO
MOPIEST
MOPPERS
MOPPETS
MORDENT
MORSELS
MOSHERS
MOSLEMS
MOTHERS
MOUSERS
NOBLEST
NODDERS
NONSELF
NONZERO
NORBERT
NORIEGA
NOSEEUM
NOSHERS
NOSIEST
NOSWEAT
NOTWELL
NOUVEAU
NOWHERE
NOXZEMA
OOZIEST
POCKETS
POKIEST
POLDERS
POLLENS
POLLERS
POMMELS
POMPEIA
POMPEII
PONDERS
PONGEES
POOREST
POPPERS
POPPETS
PORKERS
PORSENA
PORTEND
PORTENT
PORTERS
POSHEST
POSSESS
POSSETS
POSTERN
POSTERS
POTHERB
POTHERS
POTTERS
POTTERY
POULENC
POURERS
POUTERS
POWDERS
POWDERY
ROAMERS
ROARERS
ROBBERS
ROBBERY
ROCHETS
ROCKERS
ROCKERY
ROCKETS
RODGERS
RODLESS
ROEDEER
ROGUERY
ROLLERS
ROMNEYS
ROMPERS
RONDEAU
RONDELS
ROOFERS
ROOKERY
ROOMERS
ROOTERS
ROPIEST
ROSIEST
ROSTERS
ROSWELL
ROTTERS
ROUSERS
ROUTERS
ROZZERS
SOAKERS
SOAPERS
SOARERS
SOBBERS
SOCIETY
SOCKETS
SOCKEYE
SODLESS
SOFTENS
SOFTEST
SOIREES
SOLDERS
SOLFEGE
SOLVENT
SOLVERS
SONLESS
SONNETS
SOONERS
SOONEST
SORBETS
SORCERY
SORRELS
SORTERS
SOSUEME
SOTHERE
SOTHERN
SOUREST
SOVIETS
SOYBEAN
TOELESS
TOFFEES
TOGGERY
TOILERS
TOILETS
TOLTECS
TOLUENE
TONIEST
TONNEAU
TOOTERS
TOPPERS
TORMENT
TORPEDO
TORRENS
TORRENT
TOSSERS
TOTTERS
TOTTERY
TOUPEES
TOURERS
TOUTERS
TOWHEAD
TOWHEES
TOWNERS
TOYLESS
VOLLEYS
VOWLESS
WONDERS
WOOFERS
WOOLENS
WOOMERA
WORKERS
WORSENS
WOWSERS
WOZZECK
YONKERS
YOWLERS
ZONKERS

•O•••E•

BOARDED
BOARDER
BOASTED
BOASTER
BOATMEN
BOBBIES
BOBBLED
BOBBLES
BOBSLED
BODEREK
BODICES
BOGEYED
BOGGIER
BOGGLED
BOGGLER
BOGGLES
BOLIDES
BOLSTER
BOLUSES
BONDMEN
BONESET
BONGOES
BONNIER
BONUSES
BOOBIES
BOODLES
BOOGIED
BOOGIES
BOOKIES
BOOKLET
BOOMIER
BOONIES
BOOSLER
BOOSTED
BOOSTER
BOOTEES
BOOTIES
BOOTLEG
BORATES
BOSKIER
BOSSIER
BOTCHED
BOTCHES
BOTTLED
BOTTLER
BOTTLES
BOULDER
BOULLES
BOUNCED
BOUNCER
BOUNCES
BOUNDED
BOUNDER
BOUQUET
BOURREE
BOURSES
BOVINES
BOWDLER
BOWERED
BOWTIES
BOXSTEP
COACHED
COACHES
COARSEN
COARSER
COASTED
COASTER
COBBLED
COBBLER
COBBLES
COCHLEA
COCKIER
COCKLES
COCKNEY
CODDLED
CODDLER
CODDLES
CODICES
COERCED
COERCER
COERCES
COFFEES
COHERED
COHERES
COLLEEN
COLLIER
COLLIES
COLLYER
COLONEL
COLONES
COLORED
COMFIER
COMFREY
COMPEER
COMPLEX
CONCHES
CONGAED
CONIFER
CONQUER
CONRIED
CONURES
COOKIES
COOPTED
COOTIES
CORKIER
CORNFED
CORNIER
CORONET
COSINES
COSTNER
COUCHED
COUCHES
COUGHED
COULEES
COULTER
COUNSEL
COUNTED
COUNTER
COUPLED
COUPLES
COUPLET
COURIER
COURSED
COURSER
COURSES
COURTED
COVERED
COVETED
COWERED
COWRIES
COYOTES
COZENED
COZUMEL
DOBBIES
DODGIER
DOGGIER
DOGGIES
DOGSLED
DOILIES
DOLLIED
DOLLIES
DOLORES
DONATED
DONATES
DONGLES
DOODLED
DOODLER
DOODLES
DOORMEN
DOOZIES
DOPPLER
DOSAGES
DOSSIER
DOTTIER
DOTTLES
DOUBLED
DOUBLES
DOUBLET
DOUBLEU
DOUBTED
DOUBTER
DOWAGER
DOWDIER
DOWERED
DOWNIER
DOWRIES
FOAMIER
FOCSLES
FOCUSED
FOCUSES
FOGGIER
FOIBLES
FOISTED
FOLKIER
FOLKIES
FOLLIES
FONDLED
FONDLES
FONDUES
FOODIES
FOODWEB
FOOTMEN
FOOZLED
FOOZLES
FORAGED
FORAGER
FORAGES
FORELEG
FOREMEN
FORESEE
FOREVER
FORFREE
FORGOES
FORKIER
FORSTER
FORTIES
FOUNDED
FOUNDER
FOURIER
GOAFTER
GOALIES
GOATEED
GOATEES
GOBBLED
GOBBLER
GOBBLES
GODFREY
GODLIER
GOGGLED
GOGGLES
GOLFTEE
GOODIES
GOODMEN
GOOFIER
GOONIER
GOOPIER
GOOSIER
GORETEX
GORSIER
GOTEVEN
GOTOVER
GOUNDER
GOURDES
GOURMET
GOUTIER
HOAGIES
HOARDED
HOARDER
HOARIER
HOARSEN
HOARSER
HOBBIES
HOBBLED
HOBBLES
HOBOKEN
HOGTIED
HOGTIES
HOISTED
HOLLIES
HOLSTER
HOLYSEE
HOMBRES
HOMERED
HONEYED
HONORED
HONOREE
HONORER
HOOPOES
HOOSIER
HOPOVER
HOPPLED
HOPPLES
HORSIER
HOSTLER
HOUGHED
HOUNDED
HOVERED
HOVERER
HOWEVER
IODATES
IODIDES
IODISED
IODISES
IODIZED
IODIZES
IONISED
IONISES
IONIZED
IONIZER
IONIZES
JOFFREY
JOGGLED
JOGGLES
JOINDER
JOINTED
JOISTED
JOLLIED
JOLLIER
JOLLIES
JOLLIET
JOLTIER
JONESES
JOSTLED
JOSTLER
JOSTLES
JOUNCED
JOUNCES
JOURNEY
JOUSTED
JOUSTER
JOWLIER
KOOKIER
LOACHES
LOAMIER
LOATHED
LOATHES
LOBBIED
LOBBIES
LOBBYER
LOBSTER
LOBULES
LOCALES
LOCATED
LOCATER
LOCATES
LOCOMEN
LOESSER
LOESSES
LOFTIER
LOLLIES
LONGIES
LONGUES
LOOBIES
LOOKSEE
LOONIER
LOONIES
LOOPIER
LOPPIER
LORELEI
LORISES
LORRIES
LOTUSES
LOUNGED
LOUNGER
LOUNGES
LOURDES
LOUSIER
LOUVRED
LOUVRES
LOWBRED
LOWERED
LOWHEEL
LOWLIER
MOBILES
MOBSTER
MODELED
MODELER
MODULES
MOGGIES
MOISTEN
MOISTER
MOLDIER
MOMMIES
MONEYED
MONGREL
MONIKER
MONKEES
MONOMER
MONSTER
MOOCHED
MOOCHER
MOOCHES
MOODIER
MOONIER
MOONSET
MOORHEN
MOORIER
MORALES
MORDRED
MORPHED
MOSEYED
MOSQUES
MOSSIER
MOTHIER
MOTIVES
MOTORED
MOTTLED
MOTTLES
MOTTOES
MOULDED
MOULDER
MOULTED
MOUNDED
MOUNTED
MOURNED
MOUSIER
MOUSSED
MOUSSES
MOUTHED
NOBBIER
NOBBLED
NOBBLER
NOBBLES
NODULES
NOGALES
NOISIER
NOMINEE
NONAGES
NONUSER
NOODLES
NORTHER
NOTATED
NOTATES
NOTCHED
NOTCHES
NOTICED
NOTICES
NOVICES
NOZZLES
OOCYTES
OOLITES
POACHED
POACHER
POACHES
POBOXES
PODGIER
POINTED
POINTER
POITIER
POLICED
POLICES
POLITER
POLKAED
POLYMER
POMADED

POMADES
PONGEES
POOCHES
POODLES
POPEYED
POPOVER
POPPIES
POPPLED
POPPLES
PORCHES
PORGIES
PORKIER
POSITED
POSTMEN
POTAGES
POTPIES
POTSIER
POTTIER
POTTLES
POUCHED
POUCHES
POUNCED
POUNCER
POUNCES
POUNDED
POUNDER
POUTIER
POWERED
ROACHED
ROACHES
ROADBED
ROADIES
ROASTED
ROASTER
ROCKIER
ROCKIES
ROEDEER
ROILIER
ROISTER
ROLODEX
RONTGEN
ROOKIER
ROOKIES
ROOMIER
ROOMIES
ROOSTED
ROOSTER
ROOTIER
ROOTLET
ROSERED
ROSSSEA
ROTATED
ROTATES
ROTIFER
ROUBLES
ROUGHED
ROUGHEN
ROUGHER
ROUNDED
ROUNDER
ROUSTED
ROWDIER
ROWDIES
SOAPIER
SOBERED
SOBERER
SODDIER
SODDIES
SOFABED
SOFTIES
SOGGIER
SOIGNEE
SOIREES
SOLACES
SOLDIER
SOLIDER
SOLUTES
SOOTHED
SOOTHER
SOOTHES
SOOTIER
SOPPIER
SORITES
SORRIER
SORTIED
SORTIES
SOUGHED
SOUNDED
SOUNDER
SOUPIER
SOURCED
SOURCES
SOUTHEY
TOADIED
TOADIES
TOASTED
TOASTER
TODDIES
TODDLED
TODDLER
TODDLES
TOFFEES
TOFFLER
TOGGLED
TOGGLES
TOKENED
TOLKIEN
TOLLIES
TONGUED
TONGUES
TOOKTEN
TOONIES
TOORDER
TOOTHED
TOOTLED
TOOTLES
TOPAZES
TOPPLED
TOPPLES
TORCHED
TORCHES
TORQUES
TOTALED
TOTIDEM
TOUCHED
TOUCHES
TOUGHEN
TOUGHER
TOUPEES
TOURNEY
TOUSLED
TOUSLES
TOWELED
TOWERED
TOWHEES
TOWNIES
TOYNBEE
VOLUMES
VOUCHED
VOUCHER
VOUCHES
VOYAGED
VOYAGER
VOYAGES
WOBBLED
WOBBLES
WOLFMEN
WONKIER
WOODIER
WOODIES
WOOKIES
WOOLIER
WOOLIES
WOOLLEN
WOOLLEY
WOOLSEY
WOOSTER
WOOZIER
WORDIER
WORKMEN
WORMIER
WORRIED
WORRIER
WORRIES
WORSTED
WOUNDED
YODELED
YODELER
YORKIES
YOUNGER
ZOELLER
ZOMBIES
ZOUAVES

•O••••E

BOBDOLE
BOBHOPE
BOGHOLE
BOLOTIE
BONDAGE
BONFIRE
BOURREE
BOWLIKE
BOWLINE
BOXKITE
BOXLIKE
COCHERE
COCHISE
COCKADE
CODEINE
COGNATE
COINAGE
COLETTE
COLGATE
COLLAGE
COLLATE
COLLEGE
COLLIDE
COLLUDE
COLOGNE
COMBINE
COMEDUE
COMIQUE
COMMODE
COMMOVE
COMMUNE
COMMUTE
COMPARE
COMPERE
COMPETE
COMPILE
COMPOSE
COMPOTE
COMPUTE
COMRADE
CONCAVE
CONCEDE
CONCISE
CONDOLE
CONDONE
CONDUCE
CONFIDE
CONFINE
CONFUSE
CONFUTE
CONGAME
CONJURE
CONNIVE
CONNOTE
CONSOLE
CONSUME
CONTUSE
CONVENE
CONVOKE
COPPICE
COPULAE
CORDAGE
CORDATE
CORDITE
CORKAGE
CORNICE
CORONAE
CORRODE
CORSAGE
CORTEGE
COSTUME
COTERIE
COTTAGE
COURAGE
COUTURE
COWHIDE
COWLIKE
COWPOKE
DOCKAGE
DOGBANE
DOGFACE
DOGGONE
DOGLIKE
DONAHUE
DONJOSE
DOORDIE
DORMICE
DOTLIKE
DOYENNE
FOLIAGE
FOLIATE
FOOTAGE
FOOTSIE
FORBADE
FORBORE
FORESEE
FORFREE
FORGAVE
FORGIVE
FORGONE
FORLIFE
FORSAKE
FORSALE
FORSURE
FORTUNE
FOXFIRE
FOXHOLE
FOXLIKE
GOBROKE
GODLIKE
GOESAPE
GOLFTEE
GOODBYE
GOODJOE
GOODONE
GOUACHE
HOECAKE
HOGLIKE
HOLYOKE
HOLYSEE
HONOREE
HOPLIKE
HORMONE
HOSPICE
HOSTAGE
HOSTILE
HOTCAKE
HOTLINE
HOTWIRE
HOVLANE
HOWCOME
JOHNDOE
JOHNNIE
JOYRIDE
LOOKSEE
LORICAE
LOVABLE
LOWLIFE
LOWRISE
LOWTIDE
LOZENGE
MODISTE
MOLIERE
MONDALE
MONIQUE
MONOCLE
MONTAGE
MONTANE
MOORAGE
MORAINE
MORTISE
MOSELLE
MOULAGE
MOUNTIE
MOVABLE
NOISOME
NOMINEE
NOTABLE
NOTSURE
NOTTRUE
NOVELLE
NOWHERE
PODLIKE
POLEAXE
POLLUTE
PONTINE
PORCINE
PORKPIE
PORSCHE
PORTAGE
POSTAGE
POSTURE
POTABLE
POTHOLE
POTTAGE
ROANOKE
ROBLOWE
RODLIKE
ROGAINE
ROMAINE
ROMANCE
ROSALIE
ROSANNE
ROSEATE
ROSELLE
ROSETTE
ROULADE
ROUTINE
ROXANNE
ROYALWE
ROZELLE
SOCKEYE
SOIGNEE
SOLFEGE
SOLUBLE
SOMEONE
SONLIKE
SORBATE
SOSUEME
SOTHERE
SOUFFLE
SOUTANE
SOWLIKE
TOELIKE
TOESHOE
TOLUENE
TONNAGE
TONSURE
TONTINE
TOOTSIE
TOPHOLE
TOPSIDE
TOSCALE
TOSPARE
TOUGHIE
TOWROPE
TOYLIKE
TOYNBEE
VOLPONE
VOLTAGE
VOLUBLE
WOEISME
WORDONE
WOULDBE

••OE•••

AMOEBAE
AMOEBAS
AMOEBIC
CROESUS
PHOEBES
PHOEBUS
PHOENIX
SHOEBOX
SHOEING
SLOEGIN
WHOEVER

••O•E••

ADORERS
APOGEES
AVOCETS
AVOWERS
BIOGENY
BLOWERS
BOOKEND
BOOLEAN
BOOMERS
BOOTEES
BROKEIN
BROKERS
BROKEUP
CHOKERS
CHOKEUP
CLORETS
CLOSEBY
CLOSEIN
CLOSELY
CLOSEST
CLOSETS
CLOSEUP
CLOVERS
COOKERS
COOKERY
COOLERS
COOLEST
COOPERS
CROWERS
DIOCESE
DIOMEDE
DRONERS
DROVERS
DUODENA
ELOPERS
EMOTERS
EPOPEES
ERODENT
EROSELY
ESOTERY
EVOKERS
FLORETS
FLOWERS
FLOWERY
FOOLERY
FOOTERS
GAOLERS
GEODESY
GLOWERS
GOOBERS
GOODEGG
GOOIEST
GROCERS
GROCERY
GROVELS
GROWERS
HOOFERS
HOOTERS
HOOVERS
IMOGENE
IRONERS
ISOHELS
ISOMERS
LIONESS
LIONETS
LOOKERS
LOONEYS
LOOPERS
LOOSELY
LOOSENS
LOOSEST
LOOTERS
MIOCENE
OROGENY
PHONEME
PHONEYS
PIOLETS
PIONEER
PLOVERS
PLOWERS
POOREST
PROBERS
PROCEED
PROCESS
PROFESS
PROGENY
PROJECT
PRONELY
PROPELS
PROSERS
PROTEAN
PROTECT
PROTEGE
PROTEIN
PROTEST
PROTEUS
PROVERB
PROVERS
PROWESS
PTOLEMY
QUOTERS
REOPENS
RIOTERS
ROOFERS
ROOKERY
ROOMERS
ROOTERS
SCORERS
SCOTERS
SHOVELS
SHOVERS
SHOWERS
SHOWERY
SLOVENE
SLOVENS
SLOWEST
SMOKERS
SNORERS
SOONERS
SOONEST
SPOKEOF
SPOKEUP
STOKELY
STOKERS
STONERS
STORERS
STOREUP
STOREYS
SWOREAT
SWOREBY
SWOREIN
THOREAU
TOOTERS
TROWELS
TROWERS
TWOFERS
USOPENS
VIOLENT
VIOLETS
WOOFERS
WOOLENS
WOOMERA
WROTEIN
WROTETO
WROTEUP

••O••E•

ABORTED
ADOPTED
ADOPTEE
ADOPTER
ADORNED
ADORNER
ANOMIES
ANOTHER
APOGEES
APOTHEM
AROUSED
AROUSES
ATOMIES
ATONIES
AVOIDED
AVONLEA
AZODYES
BLOATED
BLOCKED
BLOCKER
BLONDER
BLONDES
BLOODED
BLOOMED
BLOOMER
BLOOPED
BLOOPER
BLOTTED
BLOTTER
BLOUSED
BLOUSES
BLOWIER
BMOVIES
BOOBIES
BOODLES
BOOGIED
BOOGIES
BOOKIES
BOOKLET
BOOMIER
BOONIES
BOOSLER
BOOSTED
BOOSTER
BOOTEES
BOOTIES
BOOTLEG
BROADEN
BROADER
BROGUES
BROILED
BROILER
BRONZED
BRONZES
BROODED
BROODER
BROOKED
BROTHER
BROWNED
BROWNER
BROWSED
BROWSER
BROWSES
CHOICER
CHOICES
CHOKIER
CHOMPED
CHOOSER
CHOOSES
CHOPPED
CHOPPER
CHOWDER
CLOAKED
CLOBBER
CLOCHES
CLOCKED
CLOCKER
CLOGGED
CLOMPED
CLOONEY
CLOPPED
CLOQUES
CLOTHED
CLOTHES
CLOTTED
CLOUDED
CLOUTED
CLOWDER
CLOWNED
COOKIES
COOPTED
COOTIES
CROAKED
CROCHET
CROFTER
CRONIES
CROOKED
CROONED
CROONER
CROPPED
CROPPER
CROQUET
CROSIER
CROSSED
CROSSER
CROSSES
CROWDED
CROWNED
DIOPTER
DOODLED
DOODLER
DOODLES
DOORMEN
DOOZIES
DROLLER
DROOLED
DROOLER
DROOPED
DROPLET
DROPPED
DROPPER
DROWNED
DROWSED
DROWSES
EBONIES
EPOPEES
EPOXIES
ETOILES
EVOLVED
EVOLVES
FLOATED
FLOATER
FLOCKED
FLOGGED
FLOODED
FLOORED
FLOPPED
FLOSSED
FLOSSES
FLOURED
FLOUTED
FOODIES
FOODWEB
FOOTMEN
FOOZLED
FOOZLES
FROCKED
FROGMEN
FRONTED
FROSTED
FROTHED
FROWNED
FROWNER
GEORGES
GHOSTED
GLOATED
GLOMMED
GLOOMED
GLORIED
GLORIES
GLOSSED
GLOSSES
GOODIES
GOODMEN
GOOFIER
GOONIER
GOOPIER
GOOSIER
GROANED
GROANER
GRODIER
GROLIER
GROMMET
GROOMED
GROOMER
GROOVED
GROOVES
GROSSED
GROSSER
GROSSES
GROUPED
GROUPER
GROUSED
GROUSER
GROUSES
GROUTED
GROWLED
GROWLER
HOOPOES
HOOSIER
IRONIES
IRONMEN
IVORIES
KNOBBED
KNOCKED
KNOCKER
KNOTTED
KNOUTED
KOOKIER
LOOBIES
LOOKSEE
LOONIER
LOONIES
LOOPIER
MOOCHED
MOOCHER
MOOCHES
MOODIER
MOONIER
MOONSET
MOORHEN
MOORIER
NOODLES
ONORDER
PEONIES
PEOPLED
PEOPLES
PHOEBES
PHONIER
PHONIES
PHOTOED
PIONEER
PLODDED
PLODDER
PLOPPED
PLOTTED
PLOTTER
PLOWMEN
POOCHES
POODLES
PROBLEM
PROCEED
PRODDED
PRODDER
PROFFER
PROGGED
PRONGED
PROOFED
PROOFER
PROPHET
PROPJET
PROPMEN
PROPPED
PROPTER
PROSIER
PROSPER
PROUDER
PROWLED
PROWLER
PROXIES
QUONSET
REOILED
REORDER
ROOKIER
ROOKIES
ROOMIER
ROOMIES
ROOSTED
ROOSTER
ROOTIER
ROOTLET
SCOFFED
SCOFFER
SCOLDED
SCOLDER
SCONCES
SCOOPED
SCOOPER
SCOOTED
SCOOTER
SCORNED
SCORNER
SCOURED
SCOURER
SCOUSES
SCOUTED
SCOUTER
SCOWLED
SCOWLER
SHOCKED
SHOCKER
SHODDEN
SHOOTER
SHOPPED
SHOPPER
SHOPPES
SHORTED
SHORTEN
SHORTER
SHOUTED
SHOUTER
SHOWIER
SHOWMEN
SKOSHES
SLOBBER
SLOGGED
SLOPPED
SLOSHED
SLOSHES
SLOTTED
SMOKIER
SMOKIES
SMOLDER
SMOTHER
SNOGGED
SNOOKER
SNOOPED
SNOOPER
SNOOTED
SNOOZED
SNOOZES
SNORKEL
SNORTED
SNORTER
SNOWIER
SNOWMEN
SNOWPEA
SOOTHED
SOOTHER
SOOTHES
SOOTIER
SPOILED
SPOILER
SPONDEE
SPONGED
SPONGER
SPONGES
SPOOFED
SPOOFER
SPOOKED
SPOOLED
SPOONED
SPOONER
SPORTED
SPOTTED
SPOTTER
SPOUSES
SPOUTED
SPOUTER
STOCKED
STOGIES
STOLLEN
STOLLER
STOMPED
STONIER
STOOGES
STOOKED
STOOKEY
STOOPED
STOPPED
STOPPER
STORIED
STORIES
STORMED
STOUTEN
STOUTER
SWOBBED
SWOLLEN
SWONKEN
SWOONED
SWOOPED
SWOPPED
TOOKTEN
TOONIES
TOORDER
TOOTHED
TOOTLED
TOOTLES
TROCHEE
TROCHES
TRODDEN
TROLLED
TROLLEY
TROOPED
TROOPER
TROTHED
TROTTED
TROTTER
TROUPER
TROUPES
TROUSER
TWOSTEP
UNOILED
WHOEVER
WHOMPED
WHOOPED
WHOOPEE
WHOPPED
WHOPPER
WHORLED
WOODIER
WOODIES
WOOKIES
WOOLIER
WOOLIES
WOOLLEN
WOOLLEY
WOOLSEY
WOOSTER
WOOZIER
WRONGED
WRONGER

••O•••E

ACOLYTE
ACONITE
ADOLPHE
ADOPTEE
AGONISE
AGONIZE
ALOHAOE
AMOEBAE
ANODISE
ANODIZE
ANODYNE
APOCOPE
APOSTLE
ATOMISE
ATOMIZE
BLONDIE
BROCADE
BROMATE
BROMIDE
BROMINE
BROWNIE
CHOLINE
CHORALE
CHORINE
CHORTLE
CLOACAE
CLOSURE
CLOTURE
DIOCESE
DIOMEDE
DIOXIDE
DNOTICE
DOORDIE
EBONITE
EMOTIVE
ENOUNCE
EROSIVE
FLOUNCE
FOOTAGE
FOOTSIE
FROMAGE
GEORDIE
GLOBULE
GLOSSAE
GOODBYE
GOODJOE
GOODONE
GROUPIE
IDOLISE
IDOLIZE
IMOGENE
IRONAGE
IRONORE
ISOLATE
ISOTOPE
LEONINE
LIONISE
LIONIZE
LOOKSEE
MIOCENE
MOORAGE
NEONATE
OROURKE
PEONAGE
PHONEME
PLOSIVE
PROBATE
PROCURE
PRODUCE
PROFANE
PROFILE

PROFUSE
PROMISE
PROMOTE
PROPANE
PROPOSE
PRORATE
PROTEGE
PROVIDE
PROVOKE
SAOTOME
SCOTTIE
SCOURGE
SLOVENE
SNOCONE
SPOKANE
SPONDEE
STOOLIE
STORAGE
SUOJURE
SWOOSIE
TOOTSIE
TROCHEE
TROUBLE
TROUNCE
TWOBASE
TWOLANE
TWOONIE
TWOSOME
TWOTIME
TWOTONE
VIOLATE
WHOOPEE
YAOUNDE

•••OE••

GENOESE
VETOERS

•••O•E•

ABDOMEN
AEROBES
AGNOMEN
ALCOVES
ALLOVER
ALLOWED
ALLOYED
ANDOVER
ANNOYED
ANYONES
APPOSED
APPOSES
APRONED
ARBORED
ARMORED
ARMORER
ATHOMES
BALONEY
BARONET
BAYONET
BECOMES
BEHOVED
BEHOVES
BELOVED
BETOKEN
BIGOSES
BIGOTED
BLOODED
BLOOMED
BLOOMER
BLOOPED
BLOOPER
BROODED
BROODER
BROOKED
BYGONES
CAJOLED
CAJOLER
CAJOLES
CALOMEL
CAROLED
CAROLER
CAROMED
CHOOSER
CHOOSES
CHROMES
CLOONEY
CNTOWER
COLONEL
COLONES
COLORED
CORONET
COYOTES
CREOLES
CROOKED
CROONED
CROONER
CRYOGEN
DAHOMEY
DEBONED
DEBONES
DECODED
DECODER
DECODES
DECOYED
DEMOTED
DEMOTES
DENOTED
DENOTES
DEPONED
DEPONES
DEPOSED
DEPOSER
DEPOSES
DEVOTED
DEVOTEE
DEVOTES
DIDOVER
DIPOLES
DISOBEY
DOLORES
DROOLED
DROOLER
DROOPED
ELBOWED
EMPOWER
ENCODED
ENCODER
ENCODES
ENCORES
ENDOWED
ENJOYED
ENROBED
ENROBES
EVZONES
EXPOSED
EXPOSES
FAGOTED
FAVORED
FLOODED
FLOORED
FLYOVER
FURORES
GEMOTES
GENOMES
GETOVER
GLOOMED
GOTOVER
GROOMED
GROOMER
GROOVED
GROOVES
HALOGEN
HANOVER
HOBOKEN
HONORED
HONOREE
HONORER
HOPOVER
HUMORED
IGNORED
IGNORER
IGNORES
IMPOSED
IMPOSES
INBOXES
INCOMES
INJOKES
INPOWER
INSOLES
INTONED
INTONER
INTONES
INVOKED
INVOKER
INVOKES
JACONET
KETONES
LABORED
LABORER
LAYOPEN
LAYOVER
LIEOVER
LIMOGES
LITOTES
LOCOMEN
MAHONEY
MAJORED
MEIOSES
MEMOREX
METOOER
MINORED
MITOSES
MONOMER
MOTORED
MRBONES
OCTOBER
OPPOSED
OPPOSER
OPPOSES
ORIOLES
OSMOSED
OSMOSES
PAROLED
PAROLEE
PAROLES
PHLOXES
PILOTED
PINONES
PIVOTED
POBOXES
POPOVER
PROOFED
PROOFER
PUTOVER
RADOMES
RANOVER
RAZORED
RECODED
RECODES
RECOVER
REMODEL
REMOTER
REMOTES
REMOVED
REMOVER
REMOVES
REMOWED
RENOTED
RENOTES
REPOSED
REPOSES
RESOLED
RESOLES
RETOWED
REVOKED
REVOKES
REWOVEN
REZONED
REZONES
ROLODEX
RUMORED
RUNOVER
SAMOYED
SAVORED
SCOOPED
SCOOPER
SCOOTED
SCOOTER
SENORES
SHOOTER
SNOOKER
SNOOPED
SNOOPER
SNOOTED
SNOOZED
SNOOZES
SPOOFED
SPOOFER
SPOOKED
SPOOLED
SPOONED
SPOONER
STOOGES
STOOKED
STOOKEY
STOOPED
STROBES
STROKED
STROKES
SWOONED
SWOOPED
TABORET
TALONED
TENONED
THEOMEN
THEOREM
THRONES
THROWER
TRIODES
TROOPED
TROOPER
TUTORED
UNBOWED
UNBOXED
UNBOXES
UNCOVER
UNLOVED
UNMOVED
UNROBED
UNROBES
UNWOVEN
UNYOKED
UNYOKES
UNZONED
WAGONER
WHOOPED
WHOOPEE
WIDOWED
WIDOWER
ZAPOTEC
ZATOPEK
ZYGOTES

•••O••E

ABSOLVE
ALLOFME
AMPOULE
ANTOINE
AREOLAE
ARGONNE
ARMOIRE
AURORAE
BAROQUE
BEHOOVE
BINOCHE
BOLOTIE
BRIOCHE
BYFORCE
CABOOSE
CALORIE
CAROUSE
COLOGNE
CORONAE
CULOTTE
DEVOLVE
DEVOTEE
DIVORCE
ECLOGUE
ENDORSE
ENFORCE
ENGORGE
ENNOBLE
ENROUTE
ESPOUSE
GARONNE
GAVOTTE
GENOESE
GIRONDE
HELOISE
HEROINE
HONOREE
IGNOBLE
INDORSE
INFORCE
INHOUSE
INVOGUE
INVOICE
INVOLVE
LACOSTE
LAPORTE
LEMONDE
MEMOIRE
MONOCLE
OSBORNE
PAPOOSE
PAROLEE
PINOCLE
PIROGUE
REJOICE
REMORSE
REROUTE
RESOLVE
REVOICE
REVOLVE
RIPOSTE
SCROOGE
STOOLIE
STROPHE
SWOOSIE
TWOONIE
UNHORSE
UNLOOSE
UPBORNE
VAMOOSE
WHOOPEE

••••OE•

BANJOES
BIGTOES
BILBOES
BINGOES
BONGOES
BRAVOES
BUCKOES
BUNCOED
BUNKOED
CAMEOED
CARGOES
CHIGOES
CITROEN
DINGOES
DISCOED
DITTOED
FORGOES
FUNGOES
GECKOES
GESSOES
GUSTOES
HOOPOES
HULLOED
IMAGOES
JINGOES
JUNCOES
LASSOED
LASSOER
LASSOES
LINGOES
MAMBOED
MANGOES
METOOER
MISDOES
MOTTOES
OUTDOES
OUTGOES
PALJOEY
PHOTOED
RADIOED
RESHOES
SALVOES
SCHMOES
SHAKOES
TANGOED
TIPTOED
TIPTOES
WEBTOED

••••O•E

ABALONE
ACEROSE
ACETONE
ADIPOSE
AIRHOLE
ALAMODE
ALLGONE
AMBROSE
ANATOLE
ANEMONE
ANYMORE
APOCOPE
APPROVE
ARDMORE
ARMHOLE
AUREOLE
AWESOME
BARCODE
BARNONE
BEHOOVE
BESPOKE
BOBDOLE
BOBHOPE
BOGHOLE
BYANOSE
CABOOSE
CALZONE
CANZONE
CATHODE
COMMODE
COMMOVE
COMPOSE
COMPOTE
CONDOLE
CONDONE
CONNOTE
CONSOLE
CONVOKE
CORRODE
COWPOKE
CYCLONE
DEPLORE
DISPOSE
DISROBE
DOGGONE
DONJOSE
DRYHOLE
EARLOBE
EMPLOYE
ENCLOSE
ENDZONE
EPIGONE
EPISODE
EPITOME
EXPLODE
EXPLORE
EYEHOLE
EYESORE
FARGONE
FASTONE
FORBORE
FORGONE
FOXHOLE
FULSOME
GLUCOSE
GOBROKE
GOODONE
HIPBONE
HOLYOKE
HORMONE
HOWCOME
IFSTONE
IMPLODE
IMPLORE
IMPROVE
INCLOSE
INSTORE
IRKSOME
IRONORE
ISOTOPE
JAWBONE
KARAOKE
KEYHOLE
KEYNOTE
LACTOSE
LAPROBE
LISSOME
LIVEONE
MALTOSE
MANHOLE
MARLOWE
MAYPOLE
MELROSE
MICROBE
MISDONE
NEURONE
NOISOME
OLDROSE
ONENOTE
ONSHORE
OPEROSE
OUTCOME
OUTDONE
OUTVOTE
OUTWORE
PADRONE
PAPOOSE
PETIOLE
PINHOLE
PISTOLE
POTHOLE
PROMOTE
PROPOSE
PROVOKE
PUGNOSE
PURPOSE
QUIXOTE
RATHOLE
RECHOSE
REDROSE
REPROVE
RESTORE
REWROTE
RHIZOME
RISSOLE
ROANOKE
ROBLOWE
RUMPOLE
RUNHOME
SANJOSE
SAOTOME
SCROOGE
SKIPOLE
SNOCONE
SOMEONE
SPUMONE
SUBVOCE
SUCROSE
SUPPOSE
SYSTOLE
TADPOLE
TAKEONE
TEAROSE
TOPHOLE
TOWROPE
TRITONE
TWOSOME
TWOTONE
UNAVOCE
UNCLOSE
UNLOOSE
UNQUOTE
UPCLOSE
VACUOLE
VAMOOSE
VERBOSE
VOLPONE
WALPOLE
WARZONE
WELCOME
WILDONE
WIMPOLE
WINSOME
WORDONE
ZIPCODE

•••••OE

ALOHAOE
BACKHOE
GOODJOE
GUMSHOE
GYMSHOE
ICEFLOE
IVANHOE
JANEDOE
JOHNDOE
MCENROE
OPENTOE
PRUDHOE
TOESHOE

OF•••••

OFASORT
OFFBASE
OFFBEAT
OFFDUTY
OFFENCE
OFFENDS
OFFENSE
OFFERED
OFFERER
OFFHAND
OFFHOUR
OFFICER
OFFICES
OFFLINE
OFFLOAD
OFFPEAK
OFFRAMP
OFFROAD
OFFSETS
OFFSIDE
OFFSITE
OFFYEAR
OFSORTS
OFTENER

O•F••••

OFFBASE
OFFBEAT
OFFDUTY
OFFENCE
OFFENDS
OFFENSE
OFFERED
OFFERER
OFFHAND
OFFHOUR
OFFICER
OFFICES
OFFLINE
OFFLOAD
OFFPEAK
OFFRAMP
OFFROAD
OFFSETS
OFFSIDE
OFFSITE
OFFYEAR
OXFORDS

O••F•••

OAKFERN
OLDFOGY
OLEFINS
ORIFICE
OUTFACE
OUTFITS
OUTFLOW

O•••F••

ODORFUL
OKEEFFE
OPTSFOR
OSSIFIC
OUTOFIT
OVERFLY

O••••F•

OKEEFFE

O•••••F

OAKLEAF
ONESELF
ONTOPOF
OURSELF

•OF••••

BOFFINS
COFFEES
COFFERS
DOFFING
GOFORIT
HOFBRAU
HOFFMAN
JOFFREY
LOFTIER
LOFTILY
LOFTING
NOFAULT
SOFABED
SOFFITS
SOFTENS
SOFTEST
SOFTIES
SOFTISH
SOFTTOP
TOFFEES
TOFFLER

•O•F•••

BOFFINS
BONFIRE
BOWFINS
BOXFULS
CODFISH
COFFEES
COFFERS
COIFING
COMFIER
COMFITS
COMFORT
COMFREY
CONFABS
CONFERS
CONFESS
CONFIDE
CONFINE
CONFIRM
CONFORM
CONFUSE
CONFUTE
DOFFING
DOGFACE
DOGFISH
DOGFOOD
FORFEIT
FORFEND
FORFREE
FOXFIRE
GOAFTER
GODFREY
GOLFERS
GOLFING
GOLFPRO
GOLFTEE
GOOFIER
GOOFILY
GOOFING
GOOFOFF
GOOFSUP
GOOFUPS
HOFFMAN
HOOFERS
HOOFING
HOOFSIT
HOTFOOT
JOFFREY
LOAFERS
LOAFING
LOOFAHS
MOUFLON
NORFOLK
POTFULS
ROOFERS
ROOFING
ROOFTOP
SOFFITS
SOLFEGE
SOUFFLE
TOFFEES
TOFFLER
TOMFOOL
WOLFGAL
WOLFING
WOLFISH
WOLFMAN
WOLFMEN
WOLFRAM
WOOFERS
WOOFING

•O••F••

BODYFAT
BOWLFUL
CONIFER
CORNFED
DOLEFUL
DONEFOR
DOOMFUL
FORKFUL
FORMFUL
GOESFOR
GOINFOR
HOPEFUL
LOOKFOR
MOANFUL
POKEFUN
POPOFFS
POUTFUL
ROOMFUL
ROOTFOR
ROTIFER
SONGFUL
SOUFFLE
SOULFUL
TOILFUL
VOTEFOR
WORKFOR

•O•••F•

COMEOFF
CONNIFF
COOKOFF
DOZEOFF
FOBSOFF
FORLIFE
FORTIFY
GOESOFF
GOOFOFF
HOLDOFF
HOPSOFF
HORRIFY
JOLLIFY
LOGSOFF
LOWLIFE
MOLLIFY
MORTIFY
NODSOFF
PONTIFF
POPOFFS
POPSOFF
RODEOFF
RODOLFO
SOLDOFF
TOLDOFF
TOOKOFF
TOPSOFF
TOREOFF
TORNOFF
TOSSOFF
WOREOFF
WORKOFF
WORNOFF
ZOMBIFY

•O••••F

COMEOFF
CONNIFF
COOKOFF
DOZEOFF
FOBSOFF
GOESOFF
GOOFOFF
HOLDOFF
HOPSOFF
LOGSOFF
NODSOFF
NONSELF
PONTIFF
POPSOFF
RODEOFF
SOLDOFF
TOLDOFF
TOOKOFF
TOPSOFF
TOREOFF
TORNOFF
TOSSOFF
WOREOFF
WORKOFF
WORNOFF

••OF•••

ASOFNOW
CROFTER
GOOFIER
GOOFILY
GOOFING
GOOFOFF
GOOFSUP
GOOFUPS
HOOFERS
HOOFING
HOOFSIT
LOOFAHS
PROFANE
PROFESS
PROFFER
PROFILE
PROFITS
PROFUSE
ROOFERS
ROOFING
ROOFTOP
SCOFFED
SCOFFER
SHOFARS
TWOFERS
TWOFOLD
WOOFERS
WOOFING

••O•F••

ALOOFLY
BLOWFLY
DOOMFUL
LOOKFOR
ODORFUL
PLOTFUL
PROFFER
PROOFED
PROOFER
ROOMFUL
ROOTFOR
SCOFFED
SCOFFER
SHOOFLY
SHOPFUL
SHOTFOR
SPOOFED
SPOOFER

••O••F•

BLOWOFF
COOKOFF
DROPOFF
GLORIFY
GOOFOFF
SHOWOFF
STOPOFF
TOOKOFF

••O•••F

BEOWULF
BLOWOFF
COOKOFF
DROPOFF
GOOFOFF
SHORTOF
SHOWOFF
SPOKEOF
STOPOFF
TOOKOFF

•••OF••

ALLOFME
ALOOFLY
CUTOFFS
INSOFAR
LAYOFFS
OUTOFIT
PAYOFFS
POPOFFS
PROOFED
PROOFER
RIPOFFS
RUNOFFS
SHOOFLY
SPOOFED
SPOOFER
TIPOFFS

•••O•F•

CUTOFFS
LAYOFFS
PAYOFFS
POPOFFS
RIPOFFS
RODOLFO
RUNOFFS
TIPOFFS

•••O••F

ONTOPOF

••••OF•

BACKOFF
BAKEOFF
BEAROFF
BEGSOFF
BITEOFF
BLEWOFF
BLOWOFF
BUGSOFF
BUYSOFF
BUZZOFF
CALLOFF
CAMEOFF
CASTOFF
COMEOFF
COOKOFF
CUTSOFF
DASHOFF
DIEDOFF
DIESOFF
DOZEOFF
DROPOFF
DUSTOFF
EASEOFF
EASYOFF
FACEOFF
FAIROFF
FALLOFF
FELLOFF
FIREOFF
FOBSOFF
GAVEOFF
GETSOFF
GIVEOFF
GOESOFF
GOOFOFF
HANDOFF
HANGOFF
HAULOFF
HAYLOFT
HEADOFF
HELDOFF
HOLDOFF
HOPSOFF
JUMPOFF
KARLOFF
KEEPOFF
KEPTOFF
KICKOFF
KISSOFF
LAIDOFF
LAYSOFF
LEADOFF
LEFTOFF
LETSOFF
LIFTOFF
LOGSOFF
MADEOFF
MAKEOFF
MARKOFF
NODSOFF
PAIDOFF
PAIROFF
PALMOFF

PASSOFF
PAWNOFF
PAYSOFF
PEELOFF
PICKOFF
PLAYOFF
POPSOFF
PULLOFF
PUSHOFF
PUTSOFF
RAKEOFF
RANGOFF
REELOFF
RIDEOFF
RINGOFF
RIPSOFF
RODEOFF
RUBSOFF
RUNGOFF
RUNSOFF
RUSHOFF
SEALOFF
SEENOFF
SEESOFF
SELLOFF
SENDOFF
SENTOFF
SETSOFF
SHOWOFF
SHUTOFF
SIGNOFF
SOLDOFF
SPINOFF
SPUNOFF
STOPOFF
TAILOFF
TAKEOFF
TAPSOFF
TEAROFF
TEEDOFF
TEESOFF
TELLOFF
TICKOFF
TIMEOFF
TIPSOFF
TOLDOFF
TOOKOFF
TOPSOFF
TOREOFF
TORNOFF
TOSSOFF
TURNOFF
WARDOFF
WASHOFF
WAVEOFF
WEAROFF
WELLOFF
WENTOFF
WOREOFF
WORKOFF
WORNOFF

••••O•F

AIRWOLF
BACKOFF
BAKEOFF
BEAROFF
BEGSOFF
BITEOFF
BLEWOFF
BLOWOFF
BUGSOFF
BUYSOFF
BUZZOFF
CALLOFF
CAMEOFF
CASTOFF
COMEOFF
COOKOFF
CRYWOLF
CUTSOFF
DASHOFF
DIEDOFF
DIESOFF
DOZEOFF
DROPOFF
DUSTOFF
EASEOFF
EASYOFF
FACEOFF
FAIROFF
FALLOFF
FELLOFF
FIREOFF
FOBSOFF
GAVEOFF
GETSOFF
GIVEOFF
GOESOFF
GOOFOFF
HANDOFF
HANGOFF
HAULOFF
HEADOFF
HELDOFF
HIPROOF
HOLDOFF
HOPSOFF
JUMPOFF
KARLOFF
KEEPOFF
KEPTOFF
KICKOFF
KISSOFF
LAIDOFF
LAYSOFF
LEADOFF
LEFTOFF
LETSOFF
LIFTOFF
LOGSOFF
MADEOFF
MAKEOFF
MARKOFF
NODSOFF
PAIDOFF
PAIROFF
PALMOFF
PASSOFF
PAWNOFF
PAYSOFF
PEELOFF
PICKOFF
PLAYOFF
POPSOFF
PULLOFF
PUSHOFF
PUTSOFF
RAKEOFF
RANGOFF
REDWOLF
REELOFF
REPROOF
RIDEOFF
RINGOFF
RIPSOFF
RODEOFF
RUBSOFF
RUNGOFF
RUNSOFF
RUSHOFF
SEALOFF
SEAWOLF
SEENOFF
SEESOFF
SELLOFF
SENDOFF
SENTOFF
SETSOFF
SHADOOF
SHEWOLF
SHOWOFF
SHUTOFF
SIGNOFF
SOLDOFF
SPINOFF
SPUNOFF
STOPOFF
SUNROOF
TAILOFF
TAKEOFF
TAPSOFF
TEAROFF
TEEDOFF
TEESOFF
TELLOFF
TICKOFF
TIMEOFF
TIPSOFF
TOLDOFF
TOOKOFF
TOPSOFF
TOREOFF
TORNOFF
TOSSOFF
TURNOFF
WALDORF
WARDOFF
WASHOFF
WAVEOFF
WEAROFF
WELLOFF
WENTOFF
WOREOFF
WORKOFF
WORNOFF

•••••OF

AHEADOF
AWAREOF
BARANOF
BERIDOF
BYWAYOF
HEARDOF
HEARSOF
HIPROOF
INAWEOF
ONTOPOF
REPROOF
SHADOOF
SHORTOF
SPEAKOF
SPOKEOF
SUNROOF
TELLSOF
THEREOF
THINKOF
TIREDOF
WHEREOF

OG•••••

OGDOADS
OGLALAS
OGREISH

O•G••••

ONGOING
ONGUARD
ORGANDY
ORGANIC
ORGANON
ORGANUM
ORGANZA
ORGATES
ORGEATS
OUGHTNT

O••G•••

OLDGOLD
OMIGOSH
ONAGERS
OREGANO
ORIGAMI
ORIGINS
OROGENY
OURGANG
OUTGOES
OUTGREW
OUTGROW
OUTGUNS

O•••G••

OBLIGED
OBLIGES
OCTAGON
ONSIGHT
OPPUGNS
ORANGES
ORANGEY
OUTAGES
OWINGTO

O••••G•

OBLONGS
OILRIGS
OLDFOGY
ONSTAGE
ONTHEGO
OUTINGS
OUTRAGE
OVERAGE

O•••••G

OBEYING
OINKING
OKAYING
ONGOING
OPENING
OPINING
ORATING
OURGANG
OUSTING
OVERBIG

•OG••••

BOGDOWN
BOGEYED
BOGGIER
BOGGING
BOGGISH
BOGGLED
BOGGLER
BOGGLES
BOGHOLE
COGBURN
COGENCY
COGNACS
COGNATE
DOGBANE
DOGBERT
DOGCART
DOGCHOW
DOGDAYS
DOGEARS
DOGFACE
DOGFISH
DOGFOOD
DOGGIER
DOGGIES
DOGGING
DOGGISH
DOGGONE
DOGLEGS
DOGLESS
DOGLIKE
DOGMATA
DOGSHOW
DOGSITS
DOGSLED
DOGSTAR
DOGTAGS
DOGTROT
DOGWOOD
FOGBANK
FOGBOWS
FOGGERS
FOGGIER
FOGGILY
FOGGING
FOGHORN
FOGLESS
FOGYISH
FOGYISM
GOGGLED
GOGGLES
HOGARTH
HOGBACK
HOGGETS
HOGGING
HOGGISH
HOGLIKE
HOGTIED
HOGTIES
HOGWASH
HOGWILD
JOGGERS
JOGGING
JOGGLED
JOGGLES
LOGBOOK
LOGGERS
LOGGIAS
LOGGING
LOGGINS
LOGGISH
LOGICAL
LOGIEST
LOGJAMS
LOGROLL
LOGSOFF
LOGSOUT
MOGAMBO
MOGGIES
NOGALES
NOGGINS
NOGUCHI
ROGAINE
ROGUERY
ROGUISH
SOGGIER
SOGGILY
TOGGERY
TOGGING
TOGGLED
TOGGLES
VOGUISH
YOGHURT
YOGURTS

•O•G•••

BOGGIER
BOGGING
BOGGISH
BOGGLED
BOGGLER
BOGGLES
BONGING
BONGOES
BOOGIED
BOOGIES
CODGERS
COLGATE
CONGAED
CONGAME
CONGEAL
CONGERS
CONGEST
COUGARS
COUGHED
COUGHUP
COWGIRL
DODGERS
DODGIER
DODGING
DODGSON
DOGGIER
DOGGIES
DOGGING
DOGGISH
DOGGONE
DONGLES
DOUGHTY
DOUGLAS
FOGGERS
FOGGIER
FOGGILY
FOGGING
FOLGERS
FORGAVE
FORGERS
FORGERY
FORGETS
FORGING
FORGIVE
FORGOES
FORGONE
FORGOOD
GOGGLED
GOGGLES
GONGING
GOOGOLS
GORGETS
GORGING
GORGONS
GOUGERS
GOUGING
HOAGIES
HOGGETS
HOGGING
HOGGISH
HOUGHED
JOGGERS
JOGGING
JOGGLED
JOGGLES
LODGERS
LODGING
LOGGERS
LOGGIAS
LOGGING
LOGGINS
LOGGISH
LONGAGO
LONGARM
LONGBOW
LONGEST
LONGIES
LONGING
LONGISH
LONGRUN
LONGTON
LONGUES
LOWGEAR
MOGGIES
MONGERS
MONGOLS
MONGREL
MORGANA
MORGANS
NOGGINS
NOUGATS
NOUGHTS
PODGIER
PODGILY
PONGEES
PONGIDS
PONGING
POPGUNS
PORGIES
RODGERS
ROUGHED
ROUGHEN
ROUGHER
ROUGHIT
ROUGHLY
ROUGHUP
ROUGING
SOGGIER
SOGGILY
SOIGNEE
SONGFUL
SORGHUM
SOUGHED
TOGGERY
TOGGING
TOGGLED
TOGGLES
TONGANS
TONGUED
TONGUES
TOPGUNS
TOUGHEN
TOUGHER
TOUGHIE
TOUGHLY

•O••G••

BODEGAS
BOLOGNA
COALGAS
COLOGNE
COSIGNS
DOINGIN
DOINGUP
DONEGAL
DOSAGES
DOWAGER
FORAGED
FORAGER
FORAGES
GOINGAT
GOINGBY
GOINGIN
GOINGON
GOINGUP
JOHNGAY
KOSYGIN
LOUNGED
LOUNGER
LOUNGES
NONAGES
NONAGON
NOSEGAY
POLYGON
POTAGES
RONTGEN
TONIGHT
VOYAGED
VOYAGER
VOYAGES
WOBEGON
WOLFGAL
YOUNGER
YOUNGMC
YOUNGUN

•O•••G•

BONDAGE
BOROUGH
COINAGE
COLLAGE
COLLEGE
COMINGS
CONDIGN
CONSIGN
CORDAGE
CORKAGE
CORSAGE
CORTEGE
COTTAGE
COURAGE
DOCKAGE
DOGLEGS
DOGTAGS
DOMINGO
FOLIAGE
FOOTAGE
FOREIGN
GOODEGG
HOSTAGE
HOTDOGS
LONGAGO
LOZENGE
MONTAGE
MONTEGO
MOORAGE
MOULAGE
NORIEGA
PORTAGE
POSTAGE
POTTAGE
SOLFEGE
SOWBUGS
TONNAGE
TOPDOGS
TOYDOGS
VOLTAGE
ZOOLOGY

•O••••G

BOATING
BOBBING
BOGGING
BOILING
BOLTING
BOMBING
BONDING
BONGING
BOOKING
BOOMING
BOOTING
BOOTLEG
BOPPING
BOSSING
BOUSING
BOWLING
COATING
COAXING
COCKING
COIFING
COILING
COINING
COMBING
CONKING
CONNING
COOKING
COOLING
COOPING
COPPING
COPYING
CORDING
CORKING
CORNDOG
CORNING
COSHING
COSTING
COWLING
COZYING
DOCKING
DODGING
DOFFING
DOGGING
DOLLING
DONKING
DONNING
DOOMING
DOTTING
DOUSING
DOWNING
DOWSING
FOALING
FOAMING
FOBBING
FOGGING
FOILING
FOINING
FOLDING
FOOLING
FOOTING
FORCING
FORDING
FORELEG
FORGING
FORKING
FORMING
FOULING
FOWLING
GOADING
GOALONG
GOLDBUG
GOLDING
GOLFING
GONGING
GOODEGG
GOODING
GOOFING
GOOSING
GORGING
GOSLING
GOUGING
GOWRONG
HOAXING
HOBOING
HOCKING
HOGGING
HOLDING
HOMBURG
HONKING
HOOFING
HOOKING
HOOPING
HOOTING
HOPPING
HORNING
HORSING
HOSTING
HOUSING
HOWLING
JOBBING
JOGGING
JOINING
JOLTING
JOSHING
JOTTING
LOADING
LOAFING
LOAMING
LOANING
LOBBING
LOCKING
LODGING
LOFTING
LOGGING
LOLLING
LONGING
LOOKING
LOOMING
LOOPING
LOOSING
LOOTING
LOPPING
LORDING
LOTTING
LOUSING
LOVEBUG
MOANING
MOBBING
MOCKING
MOILING
MOLDING
MOLTING
MONOLOG
MOONDOG
MOONING
MOORING
MOPPING
MORNING
MOSHING
MOSSING
MOUSING
NODDING
NOISING
NOOSING
NOSEBAG
NOSHING
NOTHING
POISING
POLLING
PONGING
PONYING
POOLING
POOPING
POPPING
POSTBAG
POSTING
POTTING
POURING
POUTING
ROADHOG
ROAMING
ROARING
ROBBING
ROCKING
RODDING
ROILING
ROLLING
ROLVAAG
ROMPING
ROOFING
ROOKING
ROOMING
ROOTING
ROTTING
ROUGING
ROUSING
ROUTING
SOAKING
SOAPING
SOARING
SOBBING
SOCKING
SODDING
SOILING
SOLOING
SOLVING
SOPPING
SORTING
SOURING
TOGGING
TOILING
TOLLING
TOOLING
TOOTING
TOPPING
TOSSING
TOTEBAG
TOTTING
TOURING
TOUTING
VOICING
VOIDING
WOLFING
WOOFING
WORDING
WORKING
YOWLING
YOYOING
ZONKING
ZOOMING

••OG•••

APOGEES
BIOGENY
BOOGIED
BOOGIES
BROGANS
BROGUES
CLOGGED
CLOGSUP
FLOGGED
FROGMAN
FROGMEN
GOOGOLS
IMOGENE
ISOGONS
OROGENY
PROGENY
PROGGED
PROGRAM
SHOGUNS
SLOGANS
SLOGGED
SNOGGED
STOGIES
TROGONS

••O•G••

ABOUGHT
AMONGST
BLOWGUN
BROUGHT
CLOGGED
DROUGHT
ELOIGNS
FLOGGED
GEORGES
GEORGIA
GIORGIO
PLOUGHS
PROGGED
PRONGED
SHOTGUN
SLOEGIN
SLOGGED
SLOUGHS
SNOGGED
SPONGED
SPONGER
SPONGES
STOOGES
STOPGAP
THOUGHT
TROUGHS
WRONGED
WRONGER
WRONGLY
WROUGHT

••O••G•

APOLOGY
BIOLOGY
ECOLOGY
FOOTAGE
FROMAGE
GEOLOGY
GOODEGG
IRONAGE
MOORAGE
PEONAGE
PHOTOGS
PRODIGY
PROLOGS
PROTEGE
SCOURGE
STORAGE
ZOOLOGY

••O•••G

ADORING
ATONING
AVOWING
BLOWING
BOOKING
BOOMING
BOOTING
BOOTLEG
BUOYING
CLONING
CLOSING
CLOYING
COOKING
COOLING
COOPING
CROWING
DOOMING
DRONING
ELOPING
EMOTING
ERODING
EVOKING
FLOWING
FOOLING
FOOTING
GAOLING
GLOBING
GLOWING
GLOZING
GOODEGG
GOODING
GOOFING
GOOSING
GROPING
GROWING
HOOFING
HOOKING
HOOPING
HOOTING
IRONING
KNOWING
LOOKING
LOOMING
LOOPING
LOOSING
LOOTING
MEOWING
MOONDOG
MOONING
MOORING
NOOSING
PHONING
PLOWING
POOLING
POOPING
PROBING
PROLONG
PROSING
PROVING
QUOTING
RIOTING
ROOFING
ROOKING
ROOMING
ROOTING
SCOPING
SCORING
SHOEING
SHOOING
SHORING
SHOVING
SHOWDOG
SHOWING
SLOPING
SLOWING
SMOKING
SNORING
SNOWING
SPOKING
STOKING
STONING
STORING
STOWING
TOOLING
TOOTING
WOOFING
WYOMING
ZOOMING

•••OG••

BOLOGNA
COLOGNE
CRYOGEN
ECLOGUE
HALOGEN
ILLOGIC
INVOGUE
LIMOGES
PIROGUE
STOOGES

•••O•G•

BARONGS
BELONGS
BOROUGH
CYBORGS
DUGONGS
ENGORGE
OBLONGS
SARONGS
SCROOGE
THRONGS
THROUGH

•••O••G

CYYOUNG
ECHOING
HALOING
HOBOING
HYPOING
KAYOING
MONOLOG
ONGOING
REDOING
SHOOING
SILOING
SOLOING
UNDOING
VETOING
YOYOING
ZEROING

••••OG•

ANALOGS
ANALOGY
APOLOGY
BIOLOGY
DIALOGS
ECOLOGY
EGGNOGS
EPILOGS
GASLOGS
GEOLOGY
GUNDOGS
HOTDOGS
ICEFOGS
KELLOGG
LAPDOGS
OLDFOGY
PHOTOGS
PROLOGS
PYEDOGS
QUAHOGS
REDDOGS
SAWLOGS
SCROOGE
SEADOGS
SUNDOGS

TOPDOGS
TOYDOGS
TRILOGY
UNCLOGS
VANGOGH
ZOOLOGY

••••O•G
ARTSONG
DAYLONG
ERELONG
FURLONG
GOALONG
GOWRONG
KELLOGG
PROLONG
SEABORG

•••••OG
ANTIFOG
ANTILOG
BACKLOG
BIRDDOG
BULLDOG
BUSHHOG
CATALOG
CORNDOG
DECALOG
FIREDOG
HANGDOG
MONOLOG
MOONDOG
PEATBOG
ROADHOG
SANDHOG
SEMILOG
SHOWDOG
SLEDDOG
TAGALOG
WARTHOG
YULELOG

OH•••••
OHIOANS

O•H••••
OKHOTSK
OOHLALA
OPHELIA
OPHITES
OSHKOSH
OTHELLO

O••H•••
OFFHAND
OFFHOUR
OLDHAND
OMPHALI
ONSHORE
ONTHEGO
ONTHEQT
ORCHARD
ORCHIDS
ORPHANS
ORPHEAN
ORPHEUS
ORPHREY
OUGHTNT
OUTHITS

O•••H••
OLDCHAP
ONESHOT

O••••H•
ONSIGHT
OOLITHS
OOMPAHS
ORNITHO

O•••••H
OBADIAH
OGREISH
OMIGOSH
OSHKOSH
OSTRICH

•OH••••
BOHEMIA
COHABIT
COHEIRS
COHERED
COHERES
COHORTS
COHOSTS
JOHANNA
JOHNDOE
JOHNGAY
JOHNJAY
JOHNNIE
JOHNSON
MOHAIRS
MOHAWKS
MOHICAN
OOHLALA

•O•H•••
BOBHOPE
BOGHOLE
BOKHARA
BOOHOOS
BOTHERS
BOTHNIA
BOYHOOD
COCHAIR
COCHERE
COCHISE
COCHLEA
COCHRAN
COSHING
COWHAND
COWHERD
COWHIDE
FOGHORN
FOXHOLE
GOAHEAD
GOPHERS
GOSHAWK
GOTHICS
HOOHAHS
HOTHEAD
JOBHOPS
JOBHUNT
JOEHILL
JOSHING
KOSHERS
LOWHEEL
MOSHERS
MOSHING
MOSHPIT
MOTHERS
MOTHIER
NOBHILL
NOSHERS
NOSHING
NOSHOWS
NOTHING
NOWHERE
POOHBAH
POSHEST
POTHERB
POTHERS
POTHOLE
POTHOOK
ROCHETS
SOPHISM
SOPHIST
SOTHERE
SOTHERN
TOEHOLD
TOPHATS
TOPHOLE
TOSHIBA
TOWHEAD
TOWHEES
YOGHURT

•O••H••
BOKCHOY
BOLSHOI
BOOTHIA
BOTCHED
BOTCHES
BOTCHUP
COACHED
COACHES
CONCHES
COUCHED
COUCHES
COUGHED
COUGHUP
DOGCHOW
DOGSHOW
DOLPHIN
DONAHUE
DOUGHTY
FORDHAM
GODTHAB
GOTCHAS
HONCHOS
HOTSHOT
HOUGHED
JOACHIM
LOACHES
LOATHED
LOATHES
MONTHLY
MOOCHED
MOOCHER
MOOCHES
MOORHEN
MORPHED
MOUTHED
NORTHER
NOTCHED
NOTCHES
NOUGHTS
POACHED
POACHER
POACHES
PONCHOS
POOCHES
PORCHES
PORTHOS
POTSHOT
POUCHED
POUCHES
ROACHED
ROACHES
ROADHOG
ROUGHED
ROUGHEN
ROUGHER
ROUGHIT
ROUGHLY
ROUGHUP
SOMEHOW
SOOTHED
SOOTHER
SOOTHES
SORGHUM
SOUGHED
SOUTHEY
TOESHOE
TOOTHED
TORCHED
TORCHES
TOUCHED
TOUCHES
TOUCHON
TOUCHUP
TOUGHEN
TOUGHER
TOUGHIE
TOUGHLY
TOYSHOP
VOUCHED
VOUCHER
VOUCHES
WORSHIP

•O•••H•
BORSCHT
COCKSHY
DOODAHS
DOROTHY
EOLITHS
FOURTHS
GOUACHE
HOOHAHS
HOOKAHS
HOWDAHS
IOMOTHS
LOOFAHS
MOLOCHS
NOGUCHI
OOLITHS
OOMPAHS
PORSCHE
TONIGHT
VOTECHS

•O••••H
BOARISH
BOGGISH
BONEASH
BOOKISH
BOORISH
BOROUGH
COCKISH
CODFISH
COLDISH
COLTISH
COOLISH
CORINTH
CORNISH
DOGFISH
DOGGISH
DOLLISH
DOLTISH
DONNISH
DOZENTH
FOGYISH
FOLKISH
FOOLISH
FOPPISH
FORSYTH
GOATISH
GODUTCH
GOLIATH
GOODISH
GOULASH
GOUTISH
HOGARTH
HOGGISH
HOGWASH
HORNISH
LOGGISH
LONGISH
LOUDISH
LOUTISH
LOWTECH
MOBBISH
MONARCH
MONKISH
MOONISH
MOORISH
NOURISH
POOHBAH
POORISH
PORKISH
ROGUISH
ROMANSH
ROMPISH
SOFTISH
SOPWITH
SOTTISH
SOURISH
TOADISH
TONNISH
TORYISH
TOWNISH
TOWPATH
VOGUISH
WOLFISH
WORMISH

••OH•••
ALOHAOE
BOOHOOS
HOOHAHS
ISOHELS
POOHBAH

••O•H••
ANOTHER
APOTHEM
BIOCHIP
BOOTHIA
BROTHER
CLOCHES
CLOTHED
CLOTHES
CROCHET
DROSHKY
EPOCHAL
FROTHED
KNOWHOW
MOOCHED
MOOCHER
MOOCHES
MOORHEN
POOCHES
PROPHET
PROSHOP
SIOBHAN
SKOSHES
SLOSHED
SLOSHES
SMOTHER
SOOTHED
SOOTHER
SOOTHES
TOOTHED
TROCHEE
TROCHES
TROPHIC
TROTHED
USOSHOW

••O••H•
ABOUGHT
ADOLPHE
BLOTCHY
BRONCHI
BROUGHT
DOODAHS
DROUGHT
GNOCCHI
GROUCHO
GROUCHY
GROWTHS
HOOHAHS
HOOKAHS
LOOFAHS
PLOUGHS
SLOUCHY
SLOUGHS
SMOOTHS
SMOOTHY
THOUGHT
TROUGHS
WHOSWHO
WROUGHT

••O•••H
ABOLISH
ANOUILH
BOOKISH
BOORISH
COOLISH
CRONISH
DRONISH
FOOLISH
GNOMISH
GOODISH
MOONISH
MOORISH
NEOLITH
POOHBAH
POORISH
STOMACH

•••OH••
ALCOHOL
GASOHOL
MEGOHMS
STJOHNS

•••O•H•
ALYOSHA
ATROPHY
AUROCHS
BINOCHE
BRIOCHE
DOROTHY
IOMOTHS
KENOSHA
LESOTHO
MOLOCHS
SMOOTHS
SMOOTHY
STROPHE
TIMOTHY

•••O••H
ALWORTH
BOROUGH
DEBORAH
DEBOUCH
MENORAH
RETOUCH
RUDOLPH
SPLOTCH
THROUGH
UNCOUTH

••••OH•
BIGJOHN
MATZOHS

••••O•H
ANTIOCH
BETROTH
MAMMOTH
MURDOCH
OMIGOSH
OSHKOSH
VANGOGH

•••••OH
PHARAOH
PLAYDOH

OI•••••
OILCAKE
OILCANS
OILIEST
OILLAMP
OILLESS
OILLIKE
OILPANS
OILRIGS
OILSKIN
OILWELL
OINKING

O•I••••
OHIOANS
OJIBWAS
OJIBWAY
OKINAWA
OLIVIER
OLIVINE
OMICRON
OMIGOSH
OMINOUS
OMITTED
OMITTER
OPIATES
OPINERS
OPINING
OPINION
ORIENTE
ORIENTS
ORIFICE
ORIGAMI
ORIGINS
ORINOCO
ORIOLES
ORISONS
OSIERED
OVIPARA
OVISACS
OWINGTO
OXIDANT
OXIDASE
OXIDISE
OXIDIZE

O••I•••
OBLIGED
OBLIGES
OBLIQUE
OBOISTS
OBVIATE
OBVIOUS
OCCIPUT
OEDIPAL
OEDIPUS
OFFICER
OFFICES
OILIEST
OMNIBUS
ONEIDAS
ONEIRON
ONSIDES
ONSIGHT
OOLITES
OOLITHS
OOZIEST
OPHITES
OPTICAL
OPTIMAL
OPTIMUM
OPTIONS
ORBISON
ORBITAL
ORBITED
ORBITER
ORDINAL
ORDINES
ORNITHO
ORPINES
ORVILLE
OSCINES
OSSICLE
OSSIFIC
OUTINGS
OVOIDAL

O•••I••
OAKLIKE
OARLIKE
OATLIKE
OBADIAH
OBELISK
OBEYING
OBTAINS
OCARINA
OCULIST
OFFLINE
OFFSIDE
OFFSITE
OGREISH
OILLIKE
OILRIGS
OINKING
OKAYING
OLDLINE
OLDNICK
OLDTIME
OLEFINS
OLEMISS
OLIVIER
OLIVINE
ONADIET
ONETIME
ONGOING
ONTRIAL
OPACITY
OPALINE
OPENING
OPINING
OPINION
ORATING
ORATION
ORBLIKE
ORCHIDS
ORDAINS
ORIFICE
ORIGINS
OSTRICH
OUSTING
OUTBIDS
OUTFITS
OUTHITS
OUTLINE
OUTLIVE
OUTSIDE
OUTSIZE
OUTWITS
OVATION
OWLLIKE
OXIDISE
OXIDIZE
OXONIAN

O••••I•
OBERLIN
OCEANIA
OCEANIC
OCEANID
OCTAVIA
OCTROIS
OILSKIN
OLDMAID
OLYMPIA
OLYMPIC
ONASSIS
ONTARIO
OPENAIR
OPENPIT
OPHELIA
ORGANIC
OSMOSIS
OSMOTIC
OSSIFIC
OSTEOID
OUTLAID
OUTOFIT
OVERBIG
OVERDID
OVERLIE

O•••••I
OLDUVAI
OMPHALI
ORIGAMI

•OI••••
BOIARDO
BOILERS
BOILING
BOITANO
COIFING
COILING
COILSUP
COINAGE
COINERS
COINING
DOILIES
DOINGIN
DOINGUP
FOIBLES
FOILING
FOINING
FOISTED
GOINFOR
GOINGAT
GOINGBY
GOINGIN
GOINGON
GOINGUP
HOISTED
JOINDER
JOINERS
JOINERY
JOINING
JOINSIN
JOINSUP
JOINTED
JOINTLY
JOISTED
LOITERS
MOILERS
MOILING
MOISTEN
MOISTER
MOISTLY
NOISIER
NOISILY
NOISING
NOISOME
POINTED
POINTER
POINTTO
POISING
POISONS
POISSON
POITIER
ROILIER
ROILING
ROISTER
SOIGNEE
SOILING
SOIREES
TOILERS
TOILETS
TOILFUL
TOILING
VOICING
VOIDING

•O•I•••
AORISTS
BODICES
BOLIDES
BOLIVAR
BOLIVIA
BONIEST
BONITOS
BOVINES
BOXIEST
CODICES
CODICIL
COKIEST
COMICAL
COMINGS
COMIQUE
CONICAL
CONIFER
COPIERS
COPILOT
COPIOUS
CORINTH
COSIEST
COSIGNS
COSINES
COZIEST
DOMINGO
DOMINOS
DOMINUS
DONIMUS
DOPIEST
DORITOS
DOSIDOS
DOZIEST
EOLITHS
FOLIAGE
FOLIATE
FORINTS
FOXIEST
GOLIATH
GOOIEST
GORIEST
GORILLA
GOTINTO
GOTITON
HOKIEST
HOLIDAY
HOLIEST
HOLISTS
HOMIEST
HOMINID
HONIARA
HORIZON
HOSIERS
HOSIERY
IODIDES
IODISED
IODISES
IODIZED
IODIZES
IONISED
IONISES
IONIZED
IONIZER
IONIZES
JOKIEST
KODIAKS
LOGICAL
LOGIEST
LORICAE
LORISES
LOTIONS
MOBILES
MODICUM
MODISTE
MOHICAN
MOLIERE
MONIKER
MONIQUE
MONITOR
MOPIEST
MOTIONS
MOTIVES
NOMINAL
NOMINEE
NONIRON
NORIEGA
NOSIEST
NOTICED
NOTICES
NOTIONS
NOVICES
NOXIOUS
OOLITES
OOLITHS
OOZIEST
PODIUMS
POKIEST
POLICED
POLICES
POLITER
POLITIC
PONIARD
POSITED
POTIONS
ROPIEST
ROSIEST
ROTIFER
SOCIALS
SOCIETY
SOLICIT
SOLIDER
SOLIDLY
SORITES
SOVIETS
SOYINKA
TONIEST
TONIGHT
TOPIARY
TOPICAL
TOTIDEM
WOEISME
ZODIACS

•O••I••
BOARISH
BOATING
BOBBIES
BOBBING
BOBBINS
BOBVILA
BODKINS
BOFFINS
BOGGIER
BOGGING
BOGGISH
BOILING
BOLTING
BOMBING
BONDING
BONFIRE
BONGING
BONNIER
BONNILY
BOOBIES
BOOGIED
BOOGIES
BOOKIES
BOOKING
BOOKISH
BOOMIER
BOOMING
BOONIES
BOORISH
BOOTIES
BOOTING
BOPPING
BOSKIER
BOSSIER
BOSSILY
BOSSING
BOUSING
BOWFINS
BOWLIKE
BOWLINE
BOWLING
BOWTIES
BOXKITE
BOXLIKE
COATING
COAXIAL
COAXING
COCHISE
COCKIER
COCKILY
COCKING
COCKISH
CODEINE
CODFISH
COEDITS
COEXIST
COHEIRS
COIFING
COILING
COINING
COLDISH
COLLIDE
COLLIER
COLLIES
COLLINS
COLTISH
COMBINE
COMBING
COMFIER
COMFITS
COMMITS
COMPILE
CONCISE
CONDIGN
CONDITA
CONFIDE
CONFINE
CONFIRM
CONKING
CONNICK
CONNIFF
CONNING
CONNIVE
CONOIDS
CONRIED
CONSIGN
CONSIST
CONVICT
COOKIES
COOKING
COOLING
COOLISH
COOPING
COOTIES
COPPICE
COPPING
COPYING
COPYIST
CORDIAL
CORDING
CORDITE
CORKIER
CORKING
CORNICE
CORNIER
CORNILY
CORNING
CORNISH
CORRIDA
CORSICA
COSHING
COSTING
COURIER
COUSINS
COWBIRD
COWGIRL
COWHIDE
COWLICK
COWLIKE
COWLING
COWRIES
COZYING
DOBBIES
DOBBINS
DOCKING
DODGIER
DODGING
DOFFING
DOGFISH
DOGGIER
DOGGIES
DOGGING
DOGGISH
DOGLIKE
DOGSITS
DOILIES
DOLLIED
DOLLIES
DOLLING
DOLLISH
DOLTISH
DOMAINS
DONKING
DONNING
DONNISH
DOOMING
DOOZIES
DORMICE
DOSSIER
DOTLIKE
DOTTIER
DOTTILY
DOTTING
DOUSING
DOWDIER
DOWDILY
DOWNIER
DOWNING
DOWRIES
DOWSING
FOALING
FOAMIER
FOAMILY
FOAMING
FOBBING
FOGGIER
FOGGILY
FOGGING
FOGYISH
FOGYISM
FOILING
FOINING
FOLDING
FOLKIER
FOLKIES
FOLKISH
FOLLIES
FONTINA
FOODIES
FOOLING
FOOLISH
FOOTING
FOPPISH
FORBIDS
FORCING
FORDING
FOREIGN
FORGING
FORGIVE
FORKIER
FORKING
FORLIFE
FORMICA
FORMING
FORTIES
FORTIFY
FORTIUS
FOSDICK
FOSSILS

FOULING
FOURIER
FOWLING
FOXFIRE
FOXLIKE
GOADING
GOALIES
GOATISH
GOBLINS
GODLIER
GODLIKE
GODWITS
GOLDING
GOLFING
GONGING
GOODIES
GOODING
GOODISH
GOOFIER
GOOFILY
GOOFING
GOONIER
GOONILY
GOOPIER
GOOSIER
GOOSING
GORDIAN
GORGING
GORSIER
GOSLING
GOSSIPS
GOSSIPY
GOTHICS
GOUGING
GOUTIER
GOUTILY
GOUTISH
HOAGIES
HOARIER
HOARILY
HOAXING
HOBBIES
HOBBITS
HOBOING
HOCKING
HOGGING
HOGGISH
HOGLIKE
HOGTIED
HOGTIES
HOGWILD
HOLDING
HOLLIES
HOLMIUM
HONKING
HOOFING
HOOKING
HOOPING
HOOSIER
HOOTING
HOPKINS
HOPLIKE
HOPPING
HORNING
HORNISH
HORNIST
HORRIFY
HORSIER
HORSING
HOSKINS
HOSPICE
HOSTILE
HOSTING
HOTLINE
HOTLINK
HOTLIPS
HOTTIPS
HOTWIRE
HOUDINI
HOUSING
HOWLING
JOBBING
JOEHILL
JOGGING
JOINING
JOLLIED
JOLLIER
JOLLIES
JOLLIET
JOLLIFY
JOLLILY
JOLLITY
JOLTIER
JOLTING
JONNICK
JOSHING
JOSKINS
JOTTING
JOWLIER
JOYRIDE
KONTIKI
KOOKIER
LOADING
LOAFING
LOAMIER
LOAMING
LOANING
LOBBIED
LOBBIES
LOBBING
LOCKING
LOCKINS
LODGING
LOFTIER
LOFTILY
LOFTING
LOGGIAS
LOGGING
LOGGINS
LOGGISH
LOLLIES
LOLLING
LONGIES
LONGING
LONGISH
LOOBIES
LOOKING
LOOMING
LOONIER
LOONIES
LOOPIER
LOOPING
LOOSING
LOOTING
LOPPIER
LOPPING
LORDING
LORRIES
LOTTING
LOUDISH
LOUSIER
LOUSILY
LOUSING
LOUTISH
LOVEINS
LOWLIER
LOWLIFE
LOWRISE
LOWTIDE
MOANING
MOBBING
MOBBISH
MOCKING
MOGGIES
MOHAIRS
MOILING
MOLDIER
MOLDING
MOLLIFY
MOLTING
MOMMIES
MONKISH
MOODIER
MOODILY
MOONIER
MOONILY
MOONING
MOONISH
MOORIER
MOORING
MOORISH
MOPPING
MORAINE
MORNING
MORTIFY
MORTISE
MOSAICS
MOSHING
MOSSIER
MOSSING
MOTHIER
MOUSIER
MOUSING
NOBBIER
NOBHILL
NODDING
NOETICS
NOGGINS
NOISIER
NOISILY
NOISING
NOOSING
NORDICS
NOSHING
NOTHING
NOURISH
PODGIER
PODGILY
PODLIKE
PODRIDA
POETICS
POISING
POITIER
POLLING
POLOIST
PONGIDS
PONGING
PONTIAC
PONTIFF
PONTINE
PONTIUS
PONYING
POOLING
POOPING
POORISH
POPLINS
POPPIES
POPPING
POPPINS
PORCINE
PORGIES
PORKIER
PORKISH
PORTICO
PORTION
POSTING
POSTITS
POTPIES
POTSIER
POTTIER
POTTING
POURING
POUTIER
POUTING
ROADIES
ROAMING
ROARING
ROBBING
ROBBINS
ROCKIER
ROCKIES
ROCKING
RODDING
RODLIKE
ROGAINE
ROGUISH
ROILIER
ROILING
ROLAIDS
ROLLICK
ROLLING
ROLLINS
ROMAINE
ROMPING
ROMPISH
ROOFING
ROOKIER
ROOKIES
ROOKING
ROOMIER
ROOMIES
ROOMILY
ROOMING
ROOTIER
ROOTING
ROSSINI
ROTTING
ROUGING
ROUSING
ROUTINE
ROUTING
ROWDIER
ROWDIES
ROWDILY
SOAKING
SOAPIER
SOAPILY
SOAPING
SOARING
SOBBING
SOCKING
SODDIER
SODDIES
SODDING
SOFFITS
SOFTIES
SOFTISH
SOGGIER
SOGGILY
SOILING
SOLDIER
SOLOING
SOLOIST
SOLVING
SONLIKE
SOOTIER
SOOTILY
SOPHISM
SOPHIST
SOPPIER
SOPPING
SOPWITH
SORDINI
SORDINO
SORRIER
SORRILY
SORTIED
SORTIES
SORTING
SORVINO
SOTTISH
SOUPIER
SOURING
SOURISH
SOWLIKE
TOADIED
TOADIES
TOADISH
TOCSINS
TODDIES
TOELIKE
TOGGING
TOILING
TOLKIEN
TOLLIES
TOLLING
TOMTITS
TONNISH
TONSILS
TONTINE
TOOLING
TOONIES
TOOTING
TOPKICK
TOPPING
TOPSIDE
TOROIDS
TORSION
TORYISH
TORYISM
TOSHIBA
TOSSING
TOTTING
TOURING
TOURISM
TOURIST
TOUTING
TOWNIES
TOWNISH
TOYLIKE
VOGUISH
VOICING
VOIDING
WOLFING
WOLFISH
WONKIER
WOODIER
WOODIES
WOOFING
WOOKIES
WOOLIER
WOOLIES
WOOZIER
WOOZILY
WORDIER
WORDILY
WORDING
WORKING
WORMIER
WORMISH
WORRIED
WORRIER
WORRIES
WOZNIAK
YORKIES
YORKIST
YOWLING
YOYOING
ZOMBIES
ZOMBIFY
ZONKING
ZOOMING
ZOYSIAS

•O•••I•

BOBTAIL
BOHEMIA
BOLIVIA
BOLOTIE
BONSOIR
BOOTHIA
BORACIC
BORODIN
BORZOIS
BOTHNIA
BOUDOIR
BOXEDIN
BOXESIN
COALBIN
COALOIL
COCHAIR
COCKPIT
CODICIL
COEPTIS
COHABIT
COLLOID
COMEDIC
COMESIN
CONBRIO
CONCEIT
CONDUIT
CONJOIN
CONTAIN
COOLSIT
CORNOIL
CORSAIR
COSTAIN
COTERIE
COUNCIL
COWSLIP
DOESKIN
DOINGIN
DOLPHIN
DOORDIE
FOOTSIE
FORFEIT
FOULTIP
FOXTAIL
GOFORIT
GOINGIN
GONERIL
GOODWIN
HOBNAIL
HOLBEIN
HOLDSIN
HOMERIC
HOMINID
HONORIS
HOOFSIT
HOPTOIT
HORATIO
HORNSIN
HOWBEIT
JOACHIM
JOAQUIN
JOHNNIE
JOINSIN
JONQUIL
KOOLAID
KOSYGIN
LOOKSIN
LORDJIM
LOSESIT
LOWPAID
MONODIC
MOONLIT
MORANIS
MORAVIA
MOSHPIT
MOUNTIE
MOVEDIN
MOVESIN
NOKOMIS
NOMADIC
NONSKID
NONSLIP
NOSTRIL
NOTABIT
POLARIS
POLEMIC
POLITIC
POMPEIA
POMPEII
PORKPIE
POURSIN
ROBOTIC
ROCKYII
ROCKYIV
ROLLSIN
ROMANIA
ROPEDIN
ROPESIN
ROSALIE
ROSARIO
ROSEOIL
ROUGHIT
SOCKSIN
SOLARIA
SOLICIT
SOMALIA
SOMALIS
SOMATIC
TOENAIL
TOOTSIE
TOPSAIL
TOPSOIL
TOTEMIC
TOUGHIE
VOCALIC
VOLTAIC
VOTEDIN
VOTESIN
WORKSIN
WORSHIP
ZOOMSIN

•O••••I

BOLSHOI
BONJOVI
COLLODI
COLOSSI
CORELLI
GOURAMI
HOUDINI
KONTIKI
LORELEI
MOLOKAI
MONTANI
NOGUCHI
POMPEII
ROCKYII
ROSSINI
SORDINI
TOLSTOI
TOPKAPI
TORTONI

••OI•••

ANOINTS
AVOIDED
BROILED
BROILER
CHOICER
CHOICES
EGOISTS
ELOIGNS
ETOILES
GOOIEST
MAOISTS
OBOISTS
OVOIDAL
REOILED
SPOILED
SPOILER
STOICAL
TAOISTS
TROIKAS
TROILUS
TWOIRON
UNOILED

••O•I••

ABOLISH
ACONITE
ADORING
AEOLIAN
AGONISE
AGONIST
AGONIZE
ANODISE
ANODIZE
ANOMIES
ANOUILH
ASOCIAL
ATOMIES
ATOMISE
ATOMIZE
ATONIES
ATONING
AVOWING
BIONICS
BLOWIER
BLOWING
BMOVIES
BOOBIES
BOOGIED
BOOGIES
BOOKIES
BOOKING
BOOKISH
BOOMIER
BOOMING
BOONIES
BOORISH
BOOTIES
BOOTING
BROMIDE
BROMINE
BUOYING
CHOKIER
CHOLINE
CHORINE
CHORIZO
CLONING
CLOSING
CLOYING
COOKIES
COOKING
COOLING
COOLISH
COOPING
COOTIES
CRONIES
CRONISH
CROSIER
CROWING
DIOXIDE
DNOTICE
DOOMING
DOOZIES
DRONING
DRONISH
DROPINS
EBONIES
EBONITE
EGOTISM
EGOTIST
ELOPING
EMOTING
EMOTION
EMOTIVE
EPOXIES
ERODING
EROSION
EROSIVE
EROTICA
ETONIAN
EVOKING
EXOTICA
EXOTICS
FLORIDA
FLORINS
FLORIST
FLOWING
FOODIES
FOOLING
FOOLISH
FOOTING
FROLICS
GAOLING
GLOBING
GLORIAM
GLORIAS
GLORIED
GLORIES
GLORIFY
GLOWING
GLOZING
GNOMISH
GOODIES
GOODING
GOODISH
GOOFIER
GOOFILY
GOOFING
GOONIER
GOONILY
GOOPIER
GOOSIER
GOOSING
GRODIER
GROLIER
GROPING
GROPIUS
GROWING
HOOFING
HOOKING
HOOPING
HOOSIER
HOOTING
IDOLISE
IDOLIZE
IRONIES
IRONING
IVORIES
IWOJIMA
KNOWING
KOOKIER
LAOTIAN
LEONIDS
LEONINE
LIONISE
LIONIZE
LOOBIES
LOOKING
LOOMING
LOONIER
LOONIES
LOOPIER
LOOPING
LOOSING
LOOTING
MEOWING
MOODIER
MOODILY
MOONIER
MOONILY
MOONING
MOONISH
MOORIER
MOORING
MOORISH
NEOLITH
NIOBIUM
NOOSING
OXONIAN
PEONIES
PHOBIAS
PHOBICS
PHONICS
PHONIER
PHONIES
PHONILY
PHONING
PHOTICS
PLOSION
PLOSIVE
PLOWING
POOLING
POOPING
POORISH
PROBING
PROBITY
PRODIGY
PROFILE
PROFITS
PROMISE
PROSIER
PROSILY
PROSING
PROTIST
PROVIDE
PROVING
PROVISO
PROXIES
PROXIMO
QUOTING
RHODIUM
RIORITA
RIOTING
ROOFING
ROOKIER
ROOKIES
ROOKING
ROOMIER
ROOMIES
ROOMILY
ROOMING
ROOTIER
ROOTING
SCOPING
SCORING
SHOEING
SHOOING
SHOOINS
SHORING
SHOVING
SHOWIER
SHOWILY
SHOWING
SLOPING
SLOWING
SMOKIER
SMOKIES
SMOKILY
SMOKING
SNORING
SNOWIER
SNOWILY
SNOWING
SOOTIER
SOOTILY
SPOKING
STOGIES
STOKING
STONIER
STONILY
STONING
STORIED
STORIES
STORING
STOWING
THORIUM
TOOLING
TOONIES
TOOTING
TROPICS
TROPISM
TWOBITS
TWOTIME
UTOPIAN
UTOPIAS
UXORIAL
VIOLINS
VIOLIST
WOODIER
WOODIES
WOOFING
WOOKIES
WOOLIER
WOOLIES
WOOZIER
WOOZILY
WYOMING
ZOOMING

••O••I•

ADONAIS
AGOUTIS
AMOEBIC
ANOSMIA
ANOSMIC
BIOCHIP
BLONDIE
BLOWSIN
BLOWSIT
BOOTHIA
BROKEIN
BROWNIE
CLOCKIN
CLOSEIN
COOLSIT
CROATIA
DOORDIE
DROPSIN
EGOTRIP
FLORUIT
FLOWNIN
FOOTSIE
GEORDIE
GEORGIA
GIORGIO
GLOTTIS
GNOSTIC
GOODWIN
GROUPIE
HOOFSIT
INORBIT
KOOLAID
KTOSLIN
LOOKSIN
MOONLIT
PHOENIX
PROPRIO
PROSAIC
PROTEIN
SCORPIO
SCOTTIE
SHOWBIZ
SHOWNIN
SHOWSIN
SLOEGIN
SNOWSIN
SPOTLIT
STOODIN
STOOLIE
STOPSIN
SWOOSIE
SWOREIN
TIOMKIN
TOOTSIE
TROPHIC
TSOURIS
TWOONIE
WROTEIN
ZOOMSIN

••O•••I

BRONCHI
GNOCCHI

•••OI••

ADJOINS
ANTOINE
APPOINT
ARMOIRE
CONOIDS
ECHOING
ENJOINS
HALOING
HELOISE
HEROICS
HEROINE
HEROISM
HOBOING
HYPOING
INVOICE
JUDOIST
KAYOING
MEMOIRE
MEMOIRS
ONGOING
POLOIST
REBOILS
RECOILS
REDOING
REJOICE
REJOINS
REVOICE
SHOOING
SHOOINS
SILOING
SOLOING
SOLOIST
TOROIDS
UNCOILS
UNDOING
VETOING
YOYOING
ZEROING

•••O•I•

AEROBIC
AMMONIA
ANTONIA
ANTONIN
ANTONIO
ASTORIA
BEDOUIN
BEGONIA
BOLOTIE
BORODIN
BUCOLIC
CALORIC
CALORIE
CANONIC
CAROTID
CHAOTIC
CHRONIC
CIBORIA
DEMONIC
DEPOSIT
EMPORIA
ENCOMIA
ESTONIA
ESTORIL
GOFORIT
HONORIS
IDIOTIC
ILLOGIC
JACOBIN
LACONIC
LANOLIN
MASONIC
MEIOSIS
MEIOTIC
MELODIC
MITOSIS
MITOTIC
MONODIC
NICOSIA
NOKOMIS
OSMOSIS
OSMOTIC
OUTOFIT
ROBOTIC
SEGOVIA
STLOUIS
STOODIN
STOOLIE
SWOOSIE
SYNODIC
THROWIN
TWOONIE
ZENOBIA

•••O••I

COLOSSI
KAROLYI
MENOTTI
MOLOKAI
NIKOLAI

••••OI•

AIRFOIL
ANDROID
ANEROID
BATHOIL
BONSOIR
BORZOIS
BOUDOIR
CHAMOIS
COALOIL
COLLOID
CONJOIN
CORNOIL
CRINOID
DELTOID
DESPOIL
DETROIT
DIPLOID
DISJOIN
EMBROIL
EXPLOIT
FACTOID
FUELOIL
HOPTOIT
INTROIT
LAMPOIL
MASTOID
MAUROIS
OCTROIS
OSTEOID
PALMOIL
PARBOIL
PURLOIN
ROSEOIL
SEETOIT
SEQUOIA
SIRLOIN
STCROIX
STEROID
SUBJOIN
SUBSOIL
TABLOID
TINFOIL
TOPSOIL
TRAVOIS
TREFOIL
TUNGOIL
TURMOIL

••••O•I

ALVEOLI
APRIORI
BONJOVI
CANNOLI
COLLODI
DIABOLI
MARCONI
NAIROBI
PADRONI
RAVIOLI
SPUMONI
TORTONI
TRIPOLI

ZAMBONI

•••••OI
BOLSHOI
TOLSTOI

OJ•••••
OJIBWAS
OJIBWAY

O•J••••
OBJECTS

O••J•••
ODDJOBS
OUTJUMP

O•••J••
OVERJOY

•OJ••••
SOJOURN

•O•J•••
BONJOUR
BONJOVI
CONJOBS
CONJOIN
CONJURE
DONJONS
DONJOSE
DONJUAN
LOGJAMS

•O••J••
GOODJOB
GOODJOE
JOHNJAY
LORDJIM
NOSEJOB

••OJ•••
IWOJIMA
PROJECT
SUOJURE
TROJANS

••O•J••
GOODJOB
GOODJOE
PROPJET
SNOWJOB

•••O•J•
ALFORJA

•••O••J
LLCOOLJ

••••O•J
LLCOOLJ

OK•••••
OKAYING
OKEEFFE
OKHOTSK
OKINAWA

O•K••••
OAKFERN
OAKLAND
OAKLAWN
OAKLEAF
OAKLIKE
OAKMOSS
OAKTREE

O••K•••
OINKING
OSHKOSH

O•••K••
OILSKIN

O••••K•
OAKLIKE
OARLIKE
OATLIKE
OILCAKE
OILLIKE
ORBLIKE
OROURKE
OUTTAKE
OWLLIKE

O•••••K
OARLOCK
OBELISK
OFFPEAK
OKHOTSK
OLDNICK
ONTRACK
OUTBACK
OUTLOOK
OUTRANK
OUTTALK
OUTWORK

•OK••••
BOKCHOY
BOKHARA
COKIEST
GOKARTS
HOKIEST
JOKIEST
NOKOMIS
POKEDAT
POKEFUN
POKESAT
POKIEST
TOKENED
WOKENUP
YOKOONO

•O•K•••
BODKINS
BONKERS
BOOKEND
BOOKIES
BOOKING
BOOKISH
BOOKLET
BOSKETS
BOSKIER
BOWKNOT
BOXKITE
COCKADE
COCKERS
COCKIER
COCKILY
COCKING
COCKISH
COCKLES
COCKNEY
COCKPIT
COCKSHY
CONKERS
CONKING
CONKOUT
COOKERS
COOKERY
COOKIES
COOKING
COOKOFF
COOKOUT
COOKSUP
COOKTOP
CORKAGE
CORKERS
CORKIER
CORKING
DOCKAGE
DOCKERS
DOCKETS
DOCKING
DONKEYS
DONKING
FOLKART
FOLKIER
FOLKIES
FOLKISH
FOLKWAY
FORKERS
FORKFUL
FORKIER
FORKING
HOCKING
HONKERS
HONKING
HOOKAHS
HOOKING
HOOKSUP
HOOKUPS
HOPKINS
HOSKINS
JOCKEYS
JOSKINS
KOOKIER
LOCKBOX
LOCKERS
LOCKETS
LOCKING
LOCKINS
LOCKNUT
LOCKOUT
LOCKSON
LOCKSUP
LOCKUPS
LOOKERS
LOOKFOR
LOOKING
LOOKOUT
LOOKSAT
LOOKSEE
LOOKSIN
LOOKSON
LOOKSTO
LOOKSUP
LOOKUPS
MOCKERS
MOCKERY
MOCKING
MOCKUPS
MONKEES
MONKEYS
MONKISH
POCKETS
POLKAED
PORKERS
PORKIER
PORKISH
PORKPIE
ROCKERS
ROCKERY
ROCKETS
ROCKIER
ROCKIES
ROCKING
ROCKYII
ROCKYIV
ROOKERY
ROOKIER
ROOKIES
ROOKING
SOAKERS
SOAKING
SOAKSUP
SOCKETS
SOCKEYE
SOCKING
SOCKSIN
SOUKOUS
TOLKIEN
TOOKOFF
TOOKOUT
TOOKTEN
TOPKAPI
TOPKICK
TOPKNOT
WONKIER
WOOKIES
WORKDAY
WORKERS
WORKFOR
WORKING
WORKMAN
WORKMEN
WORKOFF
WORKOUT
WORKSIN
WORKSON
WORKSUP
WORKUPS
YONKERS
YORKIES
YORKIST
YOUKNOW
ZONKERS
ZONKING
ZONKOUT

•O••K••
CONAKRY
DOESKIN
HOBOKEN
MOLOKAI
MONIKER
NONSKID

•O•••K•
BOWLIKE
BOXLIKE
CONVOKE
COWLIKE
COWPOKE
DOGLIKE
DOTLIKE
FORSAKE
FOXLIKE
GOBROKE
GODLIKE
HOECAKE
HOGLIKE
HOLYOKE
HOPLIKE
HOTCAKE
KODIAKS
KOLACKY
KONTIKI
KOPECKS
MOHAWKS
PODLIKE
ROANOKE
RODLIKE
SONLIKE
SOWLIKE
SOYINKA
TOELIKE
TOYLIKE

•O••••K
BODEREK
BOMBECK
CONNICK
COSSACK
COWLICK
FOGBANK
FORSOOK
FOSDICK
GOSHAWK
GOTBACK
HOGBACK
HOLMOAK
HOLYARK
HOTLINK
JOBBANK
JONNICK
LOGBOOK
LOWNECK
MOLLUSK
NORFOLK
POLLACK
POLLOCK
POTHOOK
POTLUCK
ROEBUCK
ROLLICK
TOPKICK
WOZNIAK
WOZZECK

••OK•••
BOOKEND
BOOKIES
BOOKING
BOOKISH
BOOKLET
BROKEIN
BROKERS
BROKEUP
CHOKERS
CHOKEUP
CHOKIER
COOKERS
COOKERY
COOKIES
COOKING
COOKOFF
COOKOUT
COOKSUP
COOKTOP
EVOKERS
EVOKING
HOOKAHS
HOOKING
HOOKSUP
HOOKUPS
KOOKIER
LOOKERS
LOOKFOR
LOOKING
LOOKOUT
LOOKSAT
LOOKSEE
LOOKSIN
LOOKSON
LOOKSTO
LOOKSUP
LOOKUPS
QUOKKAS
ROOKERY
ROOKIER
ROOKIES
ROOKING
SMOKERS
SMOKIER
SMOKIES
SMOKILY
SMOKING
SPOKANE
SPOKEOF
SPOKEUP
SPOKING
STOKELY
STOKERS
STOKING
TOOKOFF
TOOKOUT
TOOKTEN
WOOKIES

••O•K••
BLOCKED
BLOCKER
BROOKED
CLOAKED
CLOCKED
CLOCKER
CLOCKIN
CROAKED
CROOKED
FLOCKED
FLOCKTO
FROCKED
KNOCKED
KNOCKER
QUOKKAS
SHOCKED
SHOCKER
SHOOKUP
SKOOKUM
SNOOKER
SNORKEL
SPOOKED
STOCKED
STOCKUP
STOOKED
STOOKEY
SWONKEN
TIOMKIN
TROIKAS

••O••K•
ANORAKS
CHOMSKY
DROSHKY
GROMYKO
OROURKE
PROVOKE
SLOVAKS
TROTSKY
VRONSKY

•••OK••
BETOKEN
BROOKED
CROOKED
HOBOKEN
INJOKES
INVOKED
INVOKER
INVOKES
MOLOKAI
NABOKOV
REVOKED
REVOKES
SHOOKUP
SKOOKUM
SNOOKER
SPOOKED
STOOKED
STOOKEY
STROKED
STROKES
UNYOKED
UNYOKES

•••O•K•
BAZOOKA
BUROAKS
EXWORKS
PALOOKA
PINOAKS
RECORKS
REDOAKS
REHOOKS
RELOCKS
REWORKS
TANOAKS
UNCORKS
UNHOOKS
UNLOCKS

•••O••K
OKHOTSK
ZATOPEK

••••OK•
BAZOOKA
BESPOKE
CONVOKE
COWPOKE
GOBROKE
HOLYOKE
KARAOKE
PALOOKA
PROVOKE
REHOOKS
RHEBOKS
ROANOKE
SHIKOKU
UNHOOKS

••••O•K
AIRLOCK
AIRSOCK
ARMLOCK
ARTWORK
BANNOCK
BEDROCK
BULLOCK
BURDOCK
CASSOCK
CHINOOK
DAYBOOK
DEFROCK
DRSPOCK
DRYDOCK
DUNNOCK
EARLOCK
FETLOCK
FORSOOK
FRYCOOK
GUNLOCK
HADDOCK
HAMHOCK
HAMMOCK
HANCOCK
HASSOCK
HAYFORK
HEMLOCK
HILLOCK
HOLMOAK
HUMMOCK
INSTOCK
JANNOCK
KINFOLK
LEACOCK
LEGWORK
LIVEOAK
LOGBOOK
LUBBOCK
MATLOCK
MATTOCK
MENFOLK
MISTOOK
MRSPOCK
NETWORK
NEWLOOK
NEWYORK
NORFOLK
OARLOCK
OUTLOOK
OUTWORK
PADDOCK
PADLOCK
PARTOOK
PEACOCK
PETCOCK
PETROCK
POLLOCK
POTHOOK
PRECOOK
PRESOAK
REDBOOK
RESTOCK
SCHLOCK
SHYLOCK
SKYHOOK
SUFFOLK
TINWORK
TUSSOCK
UNBLOCK
UNCLOAK
UNFROCK
WARLOCK
WAXWORK
WEDLOCK

•••••OK
BANGKOK
CHINOOK
DAYBOOK
FORSOOK
FRYCOOK
GANGTOK
GEMSBOK
LOGBOOK
MISTOOK
NEWLOOK
OUTLOOK
PARTOOK
POTHOOK
PRECOOK
REDBOOK
RUNAMOK
SKYHOOK

OL•••••
OLDCHAP
OLDDAYS
OLDFOGY
OLDGOLD
OLDHAND
OLDLINE
OLDMAID
OLDMOON
OLDNESS
OLDNEWS
OLDNICK
OLDPROS
OLDROSE
OLDSAWS
OLDSTER
OLDTIME
OLDUVAI
OLDWEST
OLEATES
OLEFINS
OLEMISS
OLESTRA
OLIVIER
OLIVINE
OLOROSO
OLYMPIA
OLYMPIC
OLYMPUS

O•L••••
OBLASTS
OBLATES
OBLIGED
OBLIGES
OBLIQUE
OBLONGS
OBLOQUY
OGLALAS
OILCAKE
OILCANS
OILIEST
OILLAMP
OILLESS
OILLIKE
OILPANS
OILRIGS
OILSKIN
OILWELL
ONLEAVE
ONLYTOO
ONLYYOU
OOLITES
OOLITHS
ORLANDO
ORLEANS
OWLLIKE

O••L•••
OAKLAND
OAKLAWN
OAKLEAF
OAKLIKE
OARLESS
OARLIKE
OARLOCK
OATLIKE
OBELISK
OCCLUDE
OCELLUS
OCELOTS
OCULIST
ODDLOTS
OFFLINE
OFFLOAD
OILLAMP
OILLESS
OILLIKE
OLDLINE
OMELETS
ONELANE
OOHLALA
OPALINE
OPULENT
ORBLESS
ORBLIKE
OSTLERS
OUTLAID
OUTLAND
OUTLAST
OUTLAWS
OUTLAYS
OUTLETS
OUTLINE
OUTLIVE
OUTLOOK
OUTLOUD
OWLLIKE
OXBLOOD

O•••L••
OBERLIN
OCCULTS
OCELLUS
OGLALAS
OPHELIA
ORACLES
ORIOLES
ORMOLUS
ORTOLAN
ORVILLE
OTHELLO
OUTFLOW
OUTPLAY
OVERLAP
OVERLAY
OVERLIE

O••••L•
OCTUPLE
ODDBALL
OILWELL
OLDGOLD
OMPHALI
ONAROLL
ONESELF
OOHLALA
ORDEALS
ORDERLY
ORVILLE
OSCEOLA
OSSICLE
OTHELLO
OURSELF
OUTPOLL
OUTSELL
OUTSOLD
OUTTALK
OVERALL
OVERFLY
OVERTLY

O•••••L
OATMEAL
ODDBALL
ODORFUL
OEDIPAL
OILWELL
ONAROLL
ONTRIAL
OPTICAL
OPTIMAL
ORBITAL
ORDINAL
OUTPOLL
OUTSELL
OVERALL
OVOIDAL

•OL••••
BOLDEST
BOLEROS
BOLIDES
BOLIVAR
BOLIVIA
BOLOGNA
BOLOTIE
BOLSHOI
BOLSTER
BOLTING
BOLUSES
COLBERT
COLDCUT
COLDEST
COLDISH
COLDWAR
COLEMAN
COLETTE
COLGATE
COLLAGE
COLLARD
COLLARS
COLLATE
COLLECT
COLLEEN
COLLEGE
COLLETS
COLLIDE
COLLIER
COLLIES
COLLINS
COLLODI
COLLOID
COLLOPS
COLLUDE
COLLYER
COLOBUS
COLOGNE
COLONEL
COLONES
COLORED
COLOSSI
COLOURS
COLTISH
COLUMBO
COLUMNS
DOLEFUL
DOLEOUT
DOLLARS
DOLLIED
DOLLIES
DOLLING
DOLLISH
DOLLOPS
DOLLSUP
DOLMANS
DOLMENS
DOLORES
DOLOURS
DOLPHIN
DOLTISH
EOLITHS
FOLDERS
FOLDING
FOLDOUT
FOLDSUP
FOLDUPS
FOLGERS
FOLIAGE
FOLIATE
FOLKART
FOLKIER
FOLKIES
FOLKISH
FOLKWAY
FOLLETT
FOLLIES
FOLLOWS
GOLDBUG
GOLDING
GOLDWYN
GOLFERS
GOLFING
GOLFPRO
GOLFTEE
GOLIATH
HOLBEIN
HOLDERS
HOLDING
HOLDOFF
HOLDOUT
HOLDSIN
HOLDSON
HOLDSTO
HOLDSUP
HOLDUPS
HOLEDUP
HOLEOUT
HOLESUP
HOLIDAY
HOLIEST
HOLISTS
HOLLAND
HOLLERS
HOLLIES
HOLLOWS
HOLMIUM
HOLMOAK
HOLSTER
HOLYARK
HOLYCOW
HOLYDAY
HOLYOKE
HOLYSEE
HOLYWAR
JOLLIED
JOLLIER
JOLLIES
JOLLIET
JOLLIFY
JOLLILY
JOLLITY
JOLTIER
JOLTING
KOLACKY
LOLLARD
LOLLIES
LOLLING
LOLLOPS
MOLDERS
MOLDIER
MOLDING
MOLDOVA
MOLESTS
MOLIERE
MOLLIFY
MOLLUSC
MOLLUSK
MOLOCHS
MOLOKAI
MOLOTOV
MOLTERS
MOLTING
OOLITES
OOLITHS
POLARIS
POLDERS
POLEAXE
POLECAR
POLECAT
POLEMIC
POLENTA
POLICED
POLICES
POLITER
POLITIC
POLKAED
POLLACK
POLLENS
POLLERS
POLLING
POLLOCK
POLLTAX
POLLUTE
POLOIST
POLYGON
POLYMER
ROLAIDS
ROLLBAR
ROLLERS
ROLLICK
ROLLING
ROLLINS
ROLLOUT
ROLLSIN
ROLLSON
ROLLSUP
ROLLTOP
ROLODEX
ROLVAAG
SOLACES
SOLARIA
SOLDERS
SOLDIER
SOLDOFF
SOLDOUT
SOLEDAD
SOLFEGE
SOLICIT
SOLIDER
SOLIDLY
SOLOING
SOLOIST
SOLOMON
SOLUBLE
SOLUTES
SOLVENT
SOLVERS
SOLVING
TOLDOFF
TOLKIEN
TOLLIES
TOLLING
TOLLWAY
TOLSTOI
TOLSTOY
TOLTECS
TOLUENE
VOLCANO
VOLLEYS
VOLPONE
VOLTAGE
VOLTAIC
VOLUBLE
VOLUBLY
VOLUMES
WOLFGAL
WOLFING
WOLFISH
WOLFMAN
WOLFMEN
WOLFRAM

•O•L•••
BOILERS
BOILING
BOOLEAN
BOULDER
BOULLES
BOWLERS
BOWLESS
BOWLFUL
BOWLIKE
BOWLINE
BOWLING
BOXLIKE
COALBIN
COALCAR
COALERS
COALGAS
COALOIL
COALTAR
COILING
COILSUP
COLLAGE
COLLARD
COLLARS
COLLATE
COLLECT
COLLEEN
COLLEGE
COLLETS
COLLIDE
COLLIER
COLLIES
COLLINS
COLLODI
COLLOID
COLLOPS
COLLUDE
COLLYER
COOLANT
COOLERS
COOLEST
COOLING
COOLISH
COOLSIT
COPLAND
COULDNT
COULEES
COULOMB
COULTER
COWLICK
COWLIKE
COWLING
DOGLEGS
DOGLESS
DOGLIKE

DOILIES
DOLLARS
DOLLIED
DOLLIES
DOLLING
DOLLISH
DOLLOPS
DOLLSUP
DOTLIKE
FOALING
FOGLESS
FOILING
FOLLETT
FOLLIES
FOLLOWS
FOOLERY
FOOLING
FOOLISH
FORLIFE
FORLORN
FOULARD
FOULEST
FOULING
FOULOUT
FOULSUP
FOULTIP
FOULUPS
FOWLERS
FOWLING
FOXLIKE
GOALIES
GOALONG
GOBLETS
GOBLINS
GODLESS
GODLIER
GODLIKE
GOSLING
GOSLOWS
GOTLAND
GOTLOST
GOULASH
HOGLIKE
HOLLAND
HOLLERS
HOLLIES
HOLLOWS
HOPLIKE
HOTLINE
HOTLINK
HOTLIPS
HOVLANE
HOWLERS
HOWLING
JOBLESS
JOBLOTS
JOLLIED
JOLLIER
JOLLIES
JOLLIET
JOLLIFY
JOLLILY
JOLLITY
JOWLIER
JOYLESS
KOBLENZ
KOOLAID
KOWLOON
LOLLARD
LOLLIES
LOLLING
LOLLOPS
LOWLAND
LOWLIER
LOWLIFE
MOILERS
MOILING
MOLLIFY
MOLLUSC
MOLLUSK
MOSLEMS
MOULAGE
MOULDED
MOULDER
MOULTED
NOBLEST
OOHLALA
PODLIKE
POLLACK
POLLENS
POLLERS
POLLING
POLLOCK
POLLTAX
POLLUTE
POOLING
POPLARS
POPLINS
POTLUCK
POULENC
POULTRY
ROBLOWE
RODLESS
RODLIKE
ROILIER
ROILING
ROLLBAR
ROLLERS
ROLLICK
ROLLING
ROLLINS
ROLLOUT
ROLLSIN
ROLLSON
ROLLSUP
ROLLTOP
ROULADE
SODLESS
SOILING
SONLESS
SONLIKE
SOULFUL
SOWLIKE
TOELESS
TOELIKE
TOELOOP
TOILERS
TOILETS
TOILFUL
TOILING
TOLLIES
TOLLING
TOLLWAY
TOOLBOX
TOOLING
TOOLSUP
TOYLAND
TOYLESS
TOYLIKE
VOLLEYS
VOWLESS
WOOLENS
WOOLIER
WOOLIES
WOOLLEN
WOOLLEY
WOOLSEY
WORLDLY
WOULDBE
WOULDNT
YOWLERS
YOWLING
ZOELLER
ZOOLOGY

•O••L••

BOBBLED
BOBBLES
BOBSLED
BOGGLED
BOGGLER
BOGGLES
BOODLES
BOOKLET
BOOSLER
BOOTLEG
BOTTLED
BOTTLER
BOTTLES
BOULLES
BOWDLER
COBBLED
COBBLER
COBBLES
COCHLEA
COCKLES
CODDLED
CODDLER
CODDLES
COMPLEX
COPILOT
COPULAE
COPULAS
CORELLI
COROLLA
COUPLED
COUPLES
COUPLET
COWSLIP
DOGSLED
DONGLES
DOODLED
DOODLER
DOODLES
DOPPLER
DOTTLES
DOUBLED
DOUBLES
DOUBLET
DOUBLEU
DOUGLAS
FOCSLES
FOIBLES
FONDLED
FONDLES
FOOZLED
FOOZLES
FORELEG
GOBBLED
GOBBLER
GOBBLES
GOGGLED
GOGGLES
GORILLA
HOBBLED
HOBBLES
HOODLUM
HOOPLAS
HOPPLED
HOPPLES
HOSTLER
HOWELLS
JOCULAR
JOEBLOW
JOGGLED
JOGGLES
JOSTLED
JOSTLER
JOSTLES
KOBOLDS
LOBULES
LOCALES
LOCALLY
LORELEI
LOUELLA
LOWBLOW
LOYALLY
LOYALTY
MOBILES
MODELAS
MODELED
MODELER
MODELTS
MODULAR
MODULES
MONOLOG
MOONLIT
MORALES
MORALLY
MORELLO
MOSELLE
MOTTLED
MOTTLES
MOUFLON
NOBBLED
NOBBLER
NOBBLES
NODULAR
NODULES
NOGALES
NONPLUS
NONSLIP
NOODLES
NORELCO
NOVELLA
NOVELLE
NOVELTY
NOZZLES
POMELOS
POODLES
POPPLED
POPPLES
POPULAR
POPULUS
POSSLQS
POTTLES
RODOLFO
ROMULAN
ROMULUS
ROOTLET
ROSALIE
ROSELLE
ROUBLES
ROYALLY
ROYALTY
ROYALWE
ROZELLE
SOMALIA
SOMALIS
TODDLED
TODDLER
TODDLES
TOFFLER
TOGGLED
TOGGLES
TONALLY
TONELOC
TOOTLED
TOOTLES
TOPPLED
TOPPLES
TOTALED
TOTALLY
TOUSLED
TOUSLES
TOWELED
VOCALIC
VOCALLY
WOBBLED
WOBBLES
WOODLOT
WOOLLEN
WOOLLEY
YODELED
YODELER
ZOELLER
ZONALLY

•O•••L•

BOATELS
BOBDOLE
BOBVILA
BOGHOLE
BONNILY
BOSSILY
BOSWELL
BOXFULS
COCKILY
COEVALS
COMPELS
COMPILE
CONDOLE
CONSOLE
CONSULS
CONSULT
COPPOLA
CORBELS
CORDELL
CORELLI
CORNELL
CORNILY
COROLLA
CORRALS
COURTLY
COWBELL
DORSALS
DOSSALS
DOTTILY
DOWDILY
FOAMILY
FOGGILY
FORMALS
FORMULA
FORSALE
FOSSILS
FOXHOLE
GONDOLA
GOODALL
GOOFILY
GOOGOLS
GOONILY
GORILLA
GOSPELS
GOTWELL
GOUTILY
HOARILY
HOGWILD
HOSTELS
HOSTILE
HOWELLS
JOEHILL
JOINTLY
JOLLILY
LOCALLY
LOFTILY
LOGROLL
LOOSELY
LOUELLA
LOUSILY
LOVABLE
LOVABLY
LOVERLY
LOWBALL
LOYALLY
MOISTLY
MONDALE
MONGOLS
MONOCLE
MONTHLY
MOODILY
MOONILY
MORALLY
MORELLO
MORSELS
MORTALS
MOSELLE
MOVABLE
MOVABLY
NOBHILL
NOFAULT
NOISILY
NONSELF
NORFOLK
NORMALS
NOTABLE
NOTABLY
NOTEDLY
NOTWELL
NOVELLA
NOVELLE
OOHLALA
PODGILY
POMMELS
PORTALS
POTABLE
POTFULS
POTHOLE
RONDELS
ROOMILY
ROSELLE
ROSWELL
ROUGHLY
ROUNDLY
ROWDILY
ROYALLY
ROZELLE
SOAPILY
SOBERLY
SOCIALS
SOGGILY
SOLIDLY
SOLUBLE
SOOTILY
SORRELS
SORRILY
SOUFFLE
SOUNDLY
TOEHOLD
TOMBOLA
TONALLY
TONSILS
TOPHOLE
TOSCALE
TOTALLY
TOUGHLY
VOCALLY
VOLUBLE
VOLUBLY
WOMANLY
WOOZILY
WORDILY
WORLDLY
ZONALLY

•O••••L

BOBTAIL
BOSWELL
BOWLFUL
COALOIL
COASTAL
COAXIAL
CODICIL
COEQUAL
COLONEL
COMICAL
CONCEAL
CONGEAL
CONICAL
CONTROL
CORDELL
CORDIAL
CORNEAL
CORNELL
CORNOIL
COUNCIL
COUNSEL
COWBELL
COWGIRL
COZUMEL
DOLEFUL
DONEGAL
DOOMFUL
FORKFUL
FORMFUL
FORREAL
FOXTAIL
GONERIL
GOODALL
GOTWELL
HOBNAIL
HOOTOWL
HOPEFUL
JOEHILL
JONQUIL
JOURNAL
LOGICAL
LOGROLL
LOWBALL
LOWHEEL
MOANFUL
MONGREL
NOBHILL
NOMINAL
NOSTRIL
NOTWELL
POUTFUL
ROOMFUL
RORQUAL
ROSEOIL
ROSWELL
SONGFUL
SORORAL
SOULFUL
TOENAIL
TOILFUL
TOMFOOL
TOPICAL
TOPSAIL
TOPSOIL
WOLFGAL

••OL•••

ABOLISH
ACOLYTE
ADOLPHE
AEOLIAN
APOLOGY
AXOLOTL
BIOLOGY
BOOLEAN
CHOLINE
CHOLLAS
COOLANT
COOLERS
COOLEST
COOLING
COOLISH
COOLSIT
DROLLER
ECOLOGY
EVOLVED
EVOLVES
FOOLERY
FOOLING
FOOLISH
FROLICS
GAOLERS
GAOLING
GEOLOGY
GROLIER
IDOLISE
IDOLIZE
ISOLATE
KOOLAID
NEOLITH
PIOLETS
POOLING
PROLOGS
PROLONG
PTOLEMY
RIOLOBO
SCOLDED
SCOLDER
SMOLDER
STOLLEN
STOLLER
STOLONS
SUOLOCO
SWOLLEN
TOOLBOX
TOOLING
TOOLSUP
TROLLED
TROLLEY
TWOLANE
VIOLATE
VIOLENT
VIOLETS
VIOLINS
VIOLIST
WOOLENS
WOOLIER
WOOLIES
WOOLLEN
WOOLLEY
WOOLSEY
ZOOLOGY

••O•L••

AVONLEA
BOODLES
BOOKLET
BOOSLER
BOOTLEG
BROILED
BROILER
CHOLLAS
DOODLED
DOODLER
DOODLES
DROLLER
DROOLED
DROOLER
DROPLET
ETOILES
FOOZLED
FOOZLES
GROWLED
GROWLER
HOODLUM
HOOPLAS
KTOSLIN
MOONLIT
NOODLES
PEOPLED
PEOPLES
POODLES
PROBLEM
PROWLED
PROWLER
REOILED
ROOTLET
SCOWLED
SCOWLER
SHOULDA
SPOILED
SPOILER
SPOOLED
SPOTLIT
STOLLEN
STOLLER
STOOLIE
SWOLLEN
TOOTLED
TOOTLES
TROILUS
TROLLED
TROLLEY
UNOILED
WHORLED
WOODLOT
WOOLLEN
WOOLLEY

••O••L•

ALOOFLY
ANOMALY
ANOUILH
APOSTLE
AVOWALS
BEOWULF
BLOWFLY
BROADLY
CHORALE
CHORALS
CHORTLE
CLOSELY
CROSSLY
EROSELY
GHOSTLY
GLOBULE
GOODALL
GOOFILY
GOOGOLS
GOONILY
GROSSLY
GROVELS
INOCULA
ISOHELS
LEOPOLD
LOOSELY
MOODILY
MOONILY
PHONILY
PIOUSLY
PROFILE
PRONELY
PROPELS
PROSILY
PROUDLY
ROOMILY
SHOOFLY
SHORTLY
SHOVELS
SHOWILY
SMOKILY
SNOWILY
SOOTILY
STOKELY
STONILY
STOUTLY
TROUBLE
TROWELS
TWOFOLD
WOOZILY
WRONGLY

••O•••L

AROUSAL
ASOCIAL
AXOLOTL
DOOMFUL
EPOCHAL
FRONTAL
GLOTTAL
GOODALL
HOOTOWL
ODORFUL
OVOIDAL
PLOTFUL
ROOMFUL
SHOPFUL
SNORKEL
SPOUSAL
STOICAL
UXORIAL

•••OL••

ABSOLUT
ABSOLVE
ANGOLAN
AREOLAE
AREOLAR
AREOLAS
ASTOLAT
BEHOLDS
BICOLOR
BIPOLAR
BUCOLIC
BYGOLLY
CAJOLED
CAJOLER
CAJOLES
CAROLED
CAROLER
CAROLUS
CAROLYN
COROLLA
CREOLES
CRIOLLO
CUPOLAS
DEVOLVE
DIPOLAR
DIPOLES
DROOLED
DROOLER
ENFOLDS
ENROLLS
GIGOLOS
INSOLES
INVOLVE
KAROLYI
KOBOLDS
LAJOLLA
LANOLIN
MINOLTA
MONOLOG
NICOLAS
NIKOLAI
ORIOLES
ORMOLUS
ORTOLAN
PAROLED
PAROLEE
PAROLES
PAYOLAS
REBOLTS
RECOLOR
REMOLDS
REPOLLS
RESOLED
RESOLES
RESOLVE
REVOLTS
REVOLVE
RODOLFO
RUDOLPH
SCHOLAR
SCROLLS
SPOOLED
STOOLIE
STROLLS
UNBOLTS
UNFOLDS
UNROLLS
UPHOLDS

•••O•L•

ALOOFLY
AMPOULE
BEFOULS
BYGOLLY
COROLLA
CRIOLLO
ENNOBLE
ENROLLS
ENSOULS
IGNOBLE
IGNOBLY
LAJOLLA
LLCOOLJ
MONOCLE
PANOPLY
PINOCLE
REBOILS
RECOILS
REPOLLS
RETOOLS
SCHOOLS
SCROLLS
SHOOFLY
STROLLS
UNCOILS
UNGODLY
UNROLLS

•••O••L

AEROSOL
ALCOHOL
AURORAL
BIFOCAL
BIMODAL
CALOMEL
CHLORAL
COLONEL
CREOSOL
DEPOSAL
ESTORIL
FEMORAL
GASOHOL
IMMORAL
MAYORAL
PIVOTAL
REMODEL
REMOVAL
SORORAL
SYNODAL

••••OL•

ACEROLA
AIRHOLE
AIRWOLF
ALLTOLD
ALVEOLI
AMAPOLA
ANATOLE
ARMHOLE
AUREOLA
AUREOLE
BAGNOLD
BEDROLL
BERTOLT
BOBDOLE
BOGHOLE
CANNOLI
CARROLL
CONDOLE
CONSOLE
COPPOLA
CRAYOLA
CRYWOLF
DIABOLI
DRYHOLE
EGGROLL
EYEBOLT
EYEHOLE
FOXHOLE
GAMBOLS
GONDOLA
GOOGOLS
GRANOLA
GUNMOLL
HANSOLO
ICECOLD
KEYHOLE
KINFOLK
LEOPOLD
LINCOLN
LLCOOLJ
LOGROLL
MALCOLM
MANHOLE
MAYPOLE
MENFOLK
MONGOLS
NICCOLO
NICHOLS
NORFOLK
OLDGOLD
ONAROLL
OSCEOLA
OUTPOLL
OUTSOLD
PATROLS
PAYROLL
PERGOLA
PETIOLE
PETROLS
PHENOLS
PICCOLO
PINHOLE
PISTOLE
PISTOLS
POTHOLE
RAGDOLL
RATHOLE
RAVIOLI
REDPOLL
REDWOLF
RETOOLS
RISSOLE
RUMPOLE
SCHOOLS
SEAWOLF
SHEWOLF
SIXFOLD
SKIPOLE
STEROLS
SUFFOLK
SYMBOLS
SYSTOLE
TADPOLE
TENFOLD
TIEPOLO
TOEHOLD
TOMBOLA
TOPHOLE
TREMOLO
TRIPOLI
TWOFOLD
VACUOLE
WALPOLE
WIMPOLE

••••O•L

AIRCOOL
AIRFOIL
AXOLOTL
BARNOWL
BATHOIL
BEDROLL
BSCHOOL
CARPOOL
CARROLL
COALOIL
CORNOIL
DESPOIL
EGGROLL
EMBROIL
FUELOIL
GUNMOLL
HOOTOWL
LAMPOIL
LOGROLL
ONAROLL
OUTPOLL
PALMOIL
PARBOIL
PAYROLL
PEAFOWL
PRECOOL
RAGDOLL
REDPOLL
ROSEOIL
SUBSOIL
SUNBOWL
TINFOIL
TOMFOOL
TOPSOIL
TREFOIL
TUNGOIL
TURMOIL
VANPOOL
WAYCOOL

•••••OL

AEROSOL
AIRCOOL
ALCOHOL
BRISTOL
BSCHOOL
BUTANOL
CAPITOL
CARPOOL
CLAIROL
CONTROL
CREOSOL
DEMEROL
ESPANOL
ETHANOL
GASOHOL
GERITOL
GIRASOL
MENTHOL
PARASOL
PRECOOL
TOMFOOL
TYLENOL
VANPOOL
VITRIOL
WAYCOOL

OM•••••

OMELETS
OMENTUM
OMICRON
OMIGOSH
OMINOUS
OMITTED
OMITTER
OMNIBUS
OMPHALI

O•M••••

OOMPAHS
ORMANDY
ORMOLUS
OSMOSED
OSMOSES
OSMOSIS
OSMOTIC

O••M•••

OAKMOSS
OATMEAL
ODDMENT
OLDMAID
OLDMOON
OLEMISS
OLYMPIA
OLYMPIC
OLYMPUS
OXYMORA

O•••M••

OPTIMAL

OPTIMUM
OTTOMAN

O••••M•
OFFRAMP
OILLAMP
OLDTIME
ONETIME
ORIGAMI
OUTCOME
OUTJUMP

O•••••M
OMENTUM
OPOSSUM
OPTIMUM
ORGANUM

•OM••••
BOMBARD
BOMBAST
BOMBECK
BOMBERS
BOMBING
COMBATS
COMBERS
COMBINE
COMBING
COMBUST
COMEDIC
COMEDUE
COMEOFF
COMEONS
COMEOUT
COMESAT
COMESBY
COMESIN
COMESON
COMESTO
COMESUP
COMFIER
COMFITS
COMFORT
COMFREY
COMICAL
COMINGS
COMIQUE
COMMAND
COMMEND
COMMENT
COMMITS
COMMODE
COMMONS
COMMOVE
COMMUNE
COMMUTE
COMOROS
COMPACT
COMPANY
COMPARE
COMPASS
COMPEER
COMPELS
COMPERE
COMPETE
COMPILE
COMPLEX
COMPORT
COMPOSE
COMPOST
COMPOTE
COMPUTE
COMRADE
DOMAINS
DOMINGO
DOMINOS
DOMINUS
FOMENTS
GOMPERS
HOMBRES
HOMBURG
HOMEBOY
HOMERED
HOMERIC
HOMERUN
HOMIEST
HOMINID
HOMONYM
IOMOTHS
KOMATSU
LOMBARD
MOMBASA
MOMENTS
MOMMIES
NOMADIC
NOMINAL
NOMINEE
OOMPAHS
POMADED
POMADES
POMELOS
POMMELS
POMPANO
POMPEIA
POMPEII
POMPOMS
POMPONS
POMPOUS
ROMAINE
ROMANCE
ROMANIA
ROMANOV
ROMANSH
ROMNEYS
ROMPERS
ROMPING
ROMPISH
ROMULAN
ROMULUS
SOMALIA
SOMALIS
SOMATIC
SOMEDAY
SOMEHOW
SOMEONE
SOMEWAY
TOMBOLA
TOMBOYS
TOMCATS
TOMFOOL
TOMTITS
TOMTOMS
WOMANLY
WOMBATS
YOMTOVS
ZOMBIES
ZOMBIFY

•O•M•••
BONMOTS
BOOMBOX
BOOMERS
BOOMIER
BOOMING
COMMAND
COMMEND
COMMENT
COMMITS
COMMODE
COMMONS
COMMOVE
COMMUNE
COMMUTE
CONMOTO
DOGMATA
DOLMANS
DOLMENS
DOOMFUL
DOOMING
DORMANT
DORMERS
DORMICE
FOAMIER
FOAMILY
FOAMING
FORMALS
FORMATS
FORMFUL
FORMICA
FORMING
FORMOSA
FORMULA
HOLMIUM
HOLMOAK
HORMONE
LOAMIER
LOAMING
LOOMING
MOMMIES
MORMONS
NORMALS
NORMAND
NORMANS
POMMELS
ROAMERS
ROAMING
ROOMERS
ROOMFUL
ROOMIER
ROOMIES
ROOMILY
ROOMING
TOPMAST
TOPMOST
TORMENT
WOOMERA
WORMIER
WORMISH
YOUMANS
ZOOMING
ZOOMSIN

•O••M••
BOATMAN
BOATMEN
BOHEMIA
BONDMAN
BONDMEN
COLEMAN
COLUMBO
COLUMNS
COZUMEL
DONIMUS
DOORMAN
DOORMAT
DOORMEN
FOOTMAN
FOOTMEN
FOREMAN
FOREMEN
GOODMAN
GOODMEN
GOURMET
HOFFMAN
HOUSMAN
LOCOMAN
LOCOMEN
MOGAMBO
MONOMER
NOKOMIS
POLEMIC
POLYMER
PORTMAN
POSTMAN
POSTMEN
POTOMAC
ROADMAP
SOLOMON
TOTEMIC
VOLUMES
WOLFMAN
WOLFMEN
WORKMAN
WORKMEN

•O•••M•
BOTTOMS
CONDEMN
CONGAME
CONSUME
CONTEMN
COSTUME
COULOMB
COXCOMB
GOURAMI
HOTCOMB
HOWCOME
LOGJAMS
MOSLEMS
NOISOME
NONCOMS
NOTRUMP
NOXZEMA
PODIUMS
POMPOMS
POSSUMS
SOSUEME
TOMTOMS
WOEISME
YOUNGMC

•O••••M
BOREDOM
BOXROOM
CONFIRM
CONFORM
FOGYISM
FORDHAM
FOREARM
HOLMIUM
HOMONYM
HOODLUM
JOACHIM
LONGARM
LORDJIM
LOWBEAM
MODICUM
NOSEEUM
NOSTRUM
POTSDAM
ROSTRUM
SOPHISM
SORGHUM
TONEARM
TORYISM
TOTIDEM
TOURISM
WOLFRAM

••OM•••
ANOMALY
ANOMIES
ATOMIES
ATOMISE
ATOMIZE
BIOMASS
BOOMBOX
BOOMERS
BOOMIER
BOOMING
BROMATE
BROMIDE
BROMINE
CHOMPED
CHOMSKY
CLOMPED
DIOMEDE
DOOMFUL
DOOMING
FROMAGE
GLOMMED
GNOMISH
GNOMONS
GROMMET
GROMYKO
ISOMERS
LOOMING
PROMISE
PROMOTE
PROMPTS
RHOMBUS
ROOMERS
ROOMFUL
ROOMIER
ROOMIES
ROOMILY
ROOMING
STOMACH
STOMATA
STOMPED
THOMSON
TIOMKIN
WHOMPED
WOOMERA
WYOMING
ZOOMING
ZOOMSIN

••O•M••
ANOSMIA
ANOSMIC
BLOOMED
BLOOMER
DOORMAN
DOORMAT
DOORMEN
FOOTMAN
FOOTMEN
FROGMAN
FROGMEN
GLOMMED
GLOOMED
GOODMAN
GOODMEN
GROMMET
GROOMED
GROOMER
IRONMAN
IRONMEN
PLOWMAN
PLOWMEN
PROPMAN
PROPMEN
SHOWMAN
SHOWMEN
SNOWMAN
SNOWMEN
STORMED

••O••M•
ANONYMS
DIORAMA
ECONOMY
EPONYMS
EPONYMY
ISONOMY
IWOJIMA
PHONEME
PROXIMO
PTOLEMY
QUORUMS
SAOTOME
TWOSOME
TWOTIME

••O•••M
APOTHEM
BLOSSOM
EGOTISM
FLOTSAM
GLORIAM
HOODLUM
NIOBIUM
OPOSSUM
PROBLEM
PROGRAM
RHODIUM
SKOOKUM
THORIUM
TROPISM

•••OM••
ABDOMEN
AGNOMEN
ATHOMES
AUTOMAT
BECOMES
BLOOMED
BLOOMER
CALOMEL
CAROMED
CHROMES
DAHOMEY
ENCOMIA
GENOMES
GLOOMED
GROOMED
GROOMER
INCOMES
LOCOMAN
LOCOMEN
MONOMER
NOKOMIS
OTTOMAN
PALOMAR
POTOMAC
RADOMES
REPOMAN
SOLOMON
THEOMEN

•••O•M•
ALLOFME
DEFORMS
INFORMS
MEGOHMS
REFORMS

•••O••M
ACRONYM
ANTONYM
DECORUM
HEROISM
HOMONYM
HYPONYM
SKOOKUM
SYNONYM
THEOREM
ZEROSUM

••••OM•
ANATOMY
AWESOME
BOTTOMS
COULOMB
COXCOMB
CUSTOMS
DIATOMS
DIPLOMA
ECONOMY
EPITOME
FATHOMS
FULSOME
GIACOMO
HANSOMS
HOTCOMB
HOWCOME
IRKSOME
ISONOMY
LISSOME
NOISOME
NONCOMS
OUTCOME
PHENOMS
POMPOMS
RANSOMS
RHIZOME
RUNHOME
SAOTOME
SHALOMS
SITCOMS
SLALOMS
TOMTOMS
TWOSOME
WELCOME
WINSOME

••••O•M
ARTFORM
BARROOM
BEDROOM
BOXROOM
CONFORM
DAYROOM
GYPROOM
INBLOOM
JIBBOOM
LEGROOM
MALCOLM
PERFORM
REBLOOM
RECROOM
SUNROOM
TAPROOM
TEAROOM
UNIFORM

•••••OM
ABSALOM
BARROOM
BEDROOM
BLOSSOM
BOREDOM
BOXROOM
CZARDOM
DAYROOM
DUKEDOM
EARLDOM
FIEFDOM
FREEDOM
GRISSOM
GYPROOM
INBLOOM
JIBBOOM
KINGDOM
LEGROOM
PHANTOM
REBLOOM
RECROOM
SERFDOM
SHAHDOM
STARDOM
SUNROOM
SYMPTOM
TAPROOM
TEAROOM
TRANSOM

ON•••••
ONADARE
ONADATE
ONADIET
ONAGERS
ONANDON
ONAROLL
ONASSIS
ONATEAR
ONBOARD
ONEEYED
ONEIDAS
ONEIRON
ONELANE
ONENESS
ONENOTE
ONEROUS
ONESELF
ONESHOT
ONESTAR
ONESTEP
ONETIME
ONGOING
ONGUARD
ONLEAVE
ONLYTOO
ONLYYOU
ONORDER
ONSERVE
ONSHORE
ONSIDES
ONSIGHT
ONSTAGE
ONTARIO
ONTHEGO
ONTHEQT
ONTOPOF
ONTRACK
ONTRIAL
ONWARDS

O•N••••
OINKING
OMNIBUS
ORNETTE
ORNITHO
OWNEDUP

O••N•••
OCANADA
OCONNOR
ODDNESS
OKINAWA
OLDNESS
OLDNEWS
OLDNICK
OMENTUM
OMINOUS
ONANDON
ONENESS
ONENOTE
OPENAIR
OPENBAR
OPENEND
OPENERS
OPENING
OPENPIT
OPENSEA
OPENSUP
OPENTOE
OPINERS
OPINING
OPINION
ORANGES
ORANGEY
ORINOCO
OWINGTO
OXONIAN
OZONOUS

O•••N••
OBLONGS
OBTUNDS
OCEANIA
OCEANIC
OCEANID
OCEANUS
OCONNOR
OCTANES
OCTANTS
OFFENCE
OFFENDS
OFFENSE
OFTENER
ORDINAL
ORDINES
ORGANDY
ORGANIC
ORGANON
ORGANUM
ORGANZA
ORIENTE
ORIENTS
ORLANDO
ORMANDY
ORPINES
OSCINES
OTRANTO
OUTINGS

O••••N•
OAKLAND
OBEYING
OBSCENE
OBTAINS
OCARINA
ODDMENT
OFFHAND
OFFLINE
OHIOANS
OILCANS
OILPANS
OINKING
OKAYING
OLDHAND
OLDLINE
OLEFINS
OLIVINE
ONELANE
ONGOING
OPALINE
OPENEND
OPENING
OPERAND
OPINING
OPPUGNS
OPTIONS
OPULENT
ORATING
ORDAINS
OREGANO
ORIGINS
ORISONS
ORLEANS
OROGENY
OROTUND
ORPHANS
OSBORNE
OUGHTNT
OURGANG
OUSTING
OUTDONE
OUTGUNS
OUTLAND
OUTLINE
OUTRANK
OUTRUNS
OXIDANT

O•••••N
OAKFERN
OAKLAWN
OBERLIN
OCTAGON
OILSKIN
OLDMOON
OMICRON
ONANDON
ONEIRON
OPINION
ORATION
ORBISON
ORGANON
ORPHEAN
ORTOLAN
OTTOMAN
OURTOWN
OUTWORN
OVATION
OVERRAN
OVERRUN
OXONIAN

•ON••••
BONANZA
BONBONS
BONDAGE
BONDING
BONDMAN
BONDMEN
BONEASH
BONEDRY
BONEDUP
BONESET
BONESUP
BONFIRE
BONGING
BONGOES
BONIEST
BONITOS
BONJOUR
BONJOVI
BONKERS
BONMOTS
BONNETS
BONNIER
BONNILY
BONSOIR
BONUSES
CONAKRY
CONBRIO
CONCAVE
CONCEAL
CONCEDE
CONCEIT
CONCEPT
CONCERN
CONCERT
CONCHES
CONCISE
CONCOCT
CONCORD
CONCURS
CONDEMN
CONDIGN
CONDITA
CONDOLE
CONDONE
CONDORS
CONDUCE
CONDUCT
CONDUIT
CONFABS
CONFERS
CONFESS
CONFIDE
CONFINE
CONFIRM
CONFORM
CONFUSE
CONFUTE
CONGAED
CONGAME
CONGEAL
CONGERS
CONGEST
CONICAL
CONIFER
CONJOBS
CONJOIN
CONJURE
CONKERS
CONKING
CONKOUT
CONMOTO
CONNECT
CONNERY
CONNICK
CONNIFF
CONNING
CONNIVE
CONNORS
CONNOTE
CONOIDS
CONQUER
CONRIED
CONSENT
CONSIGN
CONSIST
CONSOLE
CONSORT
CONSULS
CONSULT
CONSUME
CONTACT
CONTAIN
CONTEMN
CONTEND
CONTENT
CONTEST
CONTEXT
CONTORT
CONTOUR
CONTRAS
CONTROL
CONTUSE
CONURES
CONVENE
CONVENT
CONVERT
CONVEYS
CONVICT
CONVOKE
CONVOYS
DONAHUE
DONATED
DONATES
DONATOR
DONEFOR
DONEGAL
DONGLES
DONIMUS
DONJONS
DONJOSE
DONJUAN
DONKEYS
DONKING
DONNING
DONNISH
DONOVAN
FONDANT
FONDEST
FONDLED
FONDLES
FONDUES
FONTEYN
FONTINA
GONDOLA
GONERIL
GONGING
HONCHOS
HONESTY
HONEYED
HONIARA
HONKERS
HONKING
HONORED
HONOREE
HONORER
HONORIS
HONOURS
IONESCO
IONISED
IONISES
IONIZED
IONIZER
IONIZES
JONESES
JONNICK
JONQUIL
KONTIKI
LONGAGO
LONGARM
LONGBOW
LONGEST
LONGIES
LONGING
LONGISH
LONGRUN
LONGTON
LONGUES
MONARCH
MONDALE
MONDAYS
MONEYED
MONGERS
MONGOLS
MONGREL
MONIKER
MONIQUE
MONITOR
MONKEES
MONKEYS
MONKISH
MONOCLE
MONOCOT
MONODIC
MONOLOG
MONOMER
MONSOON
MONSTER
MONTAGE
MONTANA
MONTAND
MONTANE
MONTANI
MONTEGO
MONTERO
MONTHLY
MONTOYA
NONAGES
NONAGON
NONCOMS
NONIRON
NONPLUS
NONSELF
NONSKID
NONSLIP
NONSTOP
NONUSER
NONZERO
PONCHOS
PONDERS
PONGEES
PONGIDS
PONGING
PONIARD
PONTIAC
PONTIFF
PONTINE
PONTIUS
PONTOON
PONYING
RONDEAU
RONDELS
RONTGEN
SONATAS
SONGFUL
SONLESS
SONLIKE
SONNETS
TONALLY
TONEARM
TONEDUP
TONELOC
TONEROW
TONESUP
TONGANS
TONGUED
TONGUES
TONIEST
TONIGHT
TONNAGE
TONNEAU
TONNISH
TONSILS
TONSURE
TONTINE
WONDERS
WONKIER
WONTONS
YONKERS
ZONALLY
ZONKERS
ZONKING
ZONKOUT

•O•N•••
BONNETS
BONNIER
BONNILY
BOONIES
BORNEUP
BOUNCED
BOUNCER
BOUNCES
BOUNDED
BOUNDER
BOUNDUP
COGNACS
COGNATE
COINAGE
COINERS
COINING
CONNECT
CONNERY
CONNICK
CONNIFF
CONNING
CONNIVE
CONNORS
CONNOTE
COONCAT
CORNCOB
CORNDOG
CORNEAL
CORNEAS
CORNELL
CORNERS
CORNETS
CORNFED
CORNICE
CORNIER
CORNILY
CORNING
CORNISH
CORNOIL
CORNROW
COUNCIL
COUNSEL
COUNTED
COUNTER
COUNTON
COUNTRY
COYNESS
DOINGIN
DOINGUP

DONNING
DONNISH
DOWNBOW
DOWNERS
DOWNIER
DOWNING
DOWNPAT
FOINING
FOUNDED
FOUNDER
FOUNDRY
GOINFOR
GOINGAT
GOINGBY
GOINGIN
GOINGON
GOINGUP
GOONIER
GOONILY
GOUNDER
HOBNAIL
HOBNOBS
HORNETS
HORNING
HORNISH
HORNIST
HORNSBY
HORNSIN
HOTNESS
HOUNDED
JOHNDOE
JOHNGAY
JOHNJAY
JOHNNIE
JOHNSON
JOINDER
JOINERS
JOINERY
JOINING
JOINSIN
JOINSUP
JOINTED
JOINTLY
JONNICK
JOUNCED
JOUNCES
LOANERS
LOANING
LOONEYS
LOONIER
LOONIES
LOUNGED
LOUNGER
LOUNGES
LOWNECK
LOWNESS
MOANERS
MOANFUL
MOANING
MOONDOG
MOONIER
MOONILY
MOONING
MOONISH
MOONLIT
MOONSET
MORNING
MOUNDED
MOUNTED
MOUNTIE
NOONDAY
POINTED
POINTER
POINTTO

POUNCED
POUNCER
POUNCES
POUNDED
POUNDER
ROANOKE
ROMNEYS
ROUNDED
ROUNDER
ROUNDLY
ROUNDON
ROUNDUP
SOANDSO
SONNETS
SOONERS
SOONEST
SOUNDED
SOUNDER
SOUNDLY
TOENAIL
TONNAGE
TONNEAU
TONNISH
TOONIES
TORNADO
TORNOFF
TORNOUT
TOWNERS
TOWNIES
TOWNISH
TOYNBEE
WORNOFF
WORNOUT
WOUNDED
WOUNDUP
WOZNIAK
YOUNGER
YOUNGMC
YOUNGUN

•O••N••

BONANZA
BOTHNIA
BOVINES
BOWKNOT
COCKNEY
COCONUT
COGENCY
COLONEL
COLONES
COMINGS
CORINTH
CORONAE
CORONAS
CORONET
COSINES
COSTNER
COZENED
DOCENTS
DOMINGO
DOMINOS
DOMINUS
DOPANTS
DOYENNE
DOZENTH
FOMENTS
FORINTS
GODUNOV
GOTINTO
HOMINID
HOMONYM
HOSANNA
JOHANNA
JOHNNIE

JOURNAL
JOURNEY
JOURNOS
KORUNAS
LOCKNUT
LORENZO
LOZENGE
MOMENTS
MORANIS
MOURNED
NOCANDO
NOMINAL
NOMINEE
NOVENAS
POCONOS
POLENTA
POTENCY
RODENTS
ROMANCE
ROMANIA
ROMANOV
ROMANSH
ROSANNA
ROSANNE
ROTUNDA
ROXANNE
SOIGNEE
SOYINKA
TOKENED
TOPKNOT
TORONTO
TOURNEY
WOKENUP
WOMANLY
YOUKNOW

•O•••N•

BOATING
BOBBING
BOBBINS
BODKINS
BOFFINS
BOGGING
BOILING
BOITANO
BOLOGNA
BOLTING
BOMBING
BONBONS
BONDING
BONGING
BOOKEND
BOOKING
BOOMING
BOOTING
BOPPING
BOSSING
BOUSING
BOWFINS
BOWLINE
BOWLING
COATING
COAXING
COCKING
COCOONS
CODEINE
COIFING
COILING
COINING
COLLINS
COLOGNE
COLUMNS
COMBINE
COMBING

COMEONS
COMMAND
COMMEND
COMMENT
COMMONS
COMMUNE
COMPANY
CONDONE
CONFINE
CONKING
CONNING
CONSENT
CONTEND
CONTENT
CONVENE
CONVENT
COOKING
COOLANT
COOLING
COOPING
COPLAND
COPPING
COPYING
CORDING
CORDONS
CORKING
CORNING
COSHING
COSIGNS
COSTING
COTTONS
COTTONY
COULDNT
COUPONS
COURANT
COUSINS
COWHAND
COWLING
COWPONY
COZYING
COZZENS
DOBBINS
DOCKING
DODGING
DOFFING
DOGBANE
DOGGING
DOGGONE
DOLLING
DOLMANS
DOLMENS
DOMAINS
DONJONS
DONKING
DONNING
DOOMING
DORMANT
DOTTING
DOUSING
DOWNING
DOWSING
DOYENNE
FOALING
FOAMING
FOBBING
FOGBANK
FOGGING
FOILING
FOINING
FOLDING
FONDANT
FONTINA
FOOLING
FOOTING

FORCING
FORDING
FORFEND
FORGING
FORGONE
FORKING
FORMING
FORRENT
FORTUNA
FORTUNE
FORWENT
FOULING
FOWLING
GOADING
GOALONG
GOBLINS
GODSEND
GODSONS
GOLDING
GOLFING
GONGING
GOODING
GOODONE
GOOFING
GOOSING
GORGING
GORGONS
GOROUND
GOSLING
GOTLAND
GOUGING
GOVERNS
GOWRONG
HOAXING
HOBOING
HOCKING
HOGGING
HOLDING
HOLLAND
HONKING
HOOFING
HOOKING
HOOPING
HOOTING
HOPKINS
HOPPING
HORMONE
HORNING
HORSING
HOSANNA
HOSKINS
HOSTING
HOTLINE
HOTLINK
HOUDINI
HOUSING
HOVLANE
HOWLING
HOYDENS
JOBBANK
JOBBING
JOBHUNT
JOGGING
JOHANNA
JOINING
JOLTING
JOSHING
JOSKINS
JOTTING
KOBLENZ
KOREANS
LOADING
LOAFING
LOAMING

LOANING
LOBBING
LOCARNO
LOCKING
LOCKINS
LODGING
LOFTING
LOGGING
LOGGINS
LOLLING
LONGING
LOOKING
LOOMING
LOOPING
LOOSENS
LOOSING
LOOTING
LOPPING
LORDING
LOTIONS
LOTTING
LOUSING
LOVEINS
LOWLAND
MOANING
MOBBING
MOCKING
MODERNS
MOILING
MOLDING
MOLTING
MONTANA
MONTAND
MONTANE
MONTANI
MOONING
MOORING
MOPPING
MORAINE
MORDANT
MORDENT
MORGANA
MORGANS
MORMONS
MORNING
MOSHING
MOSSING
MOTIONS
MOUSING
MOUTONS
NODDING
NOGGINS
NOISING
NOOSING
NORMAND
NORMANS
NOSHING
NOTHING
NOTIONS
POISING
POISONS
POLLENS
POLLING
POMPANO
POMPONS
PONGING
PONTINE
PONYING
POOLING
POOPING
POPGUNS
POPLINS
POPPING
POPPINS

PORCINE
PORSENA
PORTEND
PORTENT
POSTING
POTIONS
POTTING
POULENC
POURING
POUTING
ROAMING
ROARING
ROBBING
ROBBINS
ROCKING
RODDING
ROGAINE
ROILING
ROLLING
ROLLINS
ROMAINE
ROMPING
ROOFING
ROOKING
ROOMING
ROOTING
ROSANNA
ROSANNE
ROSSINI
ROSTAND
ROTTING
ROUGING
ROUSING
ROUTINE
ROUTING
ROXANNE
SOAKING
SOAPING
SOARING
SOBBING
SOCKING
SODDING
SOFTENS
SOILING
SOLOING
SOLVENT
SOLVING
SOMEONE
SOPPING
SOPRANO
SORDINI
SORDINO
SORTING
SORVINO
SOURING
SOUTANE
TOCSINS
TOGGING
TOILING
TOLLING
TOLUENE
TONGANS
TONTINE
TOOLING
TOOTING
TOPGUNS
TOPPING
TORMENT
TORRENS
TORRENT
TORTONI
TOSSING
TOTTING
TOUCANS

TOURING
TOUTING
TOYLAND
VOICING
VOIDING
VOLCANO
VOLPONE
WOLFING
WONTONS
WOOFING
WOOLENS
WORDING
WORDONE
WORKING
WORSENS
WOULDNT
YOKOONO
YOUMANS
YOWLING
YOYOING
ZONKING
ZOOMING

•O••••N

BOATMAN
BOATMEN
BOGDOWN
BONDMAN
BONDMEN
BOOLEAN
BORODIN
BOURBON
BOXEDIN
BOXESIN
COALBIN
COARSEN
COCHRAN
COGBURN
COLEMAN
COLLEEN
COMESIN
COMESON
CONCERN
CONDEMN
CONDIGN
CONJOIN
CONSIGN
CONTAIN
CONTEMN
CORAZON
COSTAIN
COUNTON
COWTOWN
DODGSON
DOESKIN
DOINGIN
DOLPHIN
DONJUAN
DONOVAN
DOORMAN
DOORMEN
DOTEDON
DOTESON
FOGHORN
FONTEYN
FOOTMAN
FOOTMEN
FOREIGN
FOREMAN
FOREMEN
FORERAN
FORERUN
FORLORN
FORTRAN

GOINGIN
GOINGON
GOLDWYN
GOODMAN
GOODMEN
GOODSON
GOODWIN
GORDIAN
GOTDOWN
GOTEVEN
GOTITON
HOARSEN
HOBOKEN
HOEDOWN
HOFFMAN
HOLBEIN
HOLDSIN
HOLDSON
HOMERUN
HORIZON
HORNSIN
HOUSMAN
HOUSTON
JOAQUIN
JOHNSON
JOINSIN
JOURDAN
KOSYGIN
KOWLOON
LOCKSON
LOCOMAN
LOCOMEN
LONGRUN
LONGTON
LOOKSIN
LOOKSON
LOWBORN
LOWDOWN
MOHICAN
MOISTEN
MONSOON
MOORHEN
MOUFLON
MOVEDIN
MOVEDON
MOVESIN
MOVESON
MOWDOWN
NOCTURN
NONAGON
NONIRON
POISSON
POKEFUN
POLYGON
PONTOON
POPCORN
PORTION
PORTMAN
POSTERN
POSTMAN
POSTMEN
POURSIN
ROBESON
ROLLSIN
ROLLSON
ROMULAN
RONTGEN
ROPEDIN
ROPESIN
ROUGHEN
ROUNDON
SOCKSIN
SOJOURN
SOLOMON

SOTHERN
SOUPCON
SOYBEAN
TOLKIEN
TOOKTEN
TOPDOWN
TORSION
TOUCHON
TOUGHEN
VOTEDIN
VOTESIN
WOBEGON
WOLFMAN
WOLFMEN
WOOLLEN
WORKMAN
WORKMEN
WORKSIN
WORKSON
YOUNGUN
ZOOMSIN

••ON•••

ACONITE
ADONAIS
AGONISE
AGONIST
AGONIZE
AMONGST
ANONYMS
ATONIES
ATONING
AVONLEA
BIONICS
BLONDER
BLONDES
BLONDIE
BOONIES
BRONCHI
BRONCOS
BRONSON
BRONZED
BRONZES
CLONING
COONCAT
CRONIES
CRONISH
DRONERS
DRONING
DRONISH
EBONIES
EBONITE
ECONOMY
EPONYMS
EPONYMY
ETONIAN
FRONTAL
FRONTED
FRONTON
GOONIER
GOONILY
IRONAGE
IRONERS
IRONIES
IRONING
IRONMAN
IRONMEN
IRONONS
IRONORE
IRONOUT
ISONOMY
LEONARD
LEONIDS
LEONINE

LEONORA
LIONCUB
LIONESS
LIONETS
LIONISE
LIONIZE
LOONEYS
LOONIER
LOONIES
MOONDOG
MOONIER
MOONILY
MOONING
MOONISH
MOONLIT
MOONSET
NEONATE
NOONDAY
OCONNOR
OXONIAN
OZONOUS
PEONAGE
PEONIES
PHONEME
PHONEYS
PHONICS
PHONIER
PHONIES
PHONILY
PHONING
PIONEER
PRONELY
PRONGED
PRONOUN
QUONSET
SCONCES
SOONERS
SOONEST
SPONDEE
SPONGED
SPONGER
SPONGES
SPONSOR
STONERS
STONIER
STONILY
STONING
SWONKEN
TOONIES
VRONSKY
WRONGED
WRONGER
WRONGLY

••O•N••

ABOUNDS
ADORNED
ADORNER
AMOUNTS
ANOINTS
ASOFNOW
BLOWNUP
BROSNAN
BROWNED
BROWNER
BROWNIE
CLOONEY
CLOWNED
CROONED
CROONER
CROWNED
DROWNED
ENOUNCE
FLOUNCE

FLOUNCY
FLOWNAT
FLOWNIN
FROWNAT
FROWNED
FROWNER
GROANED
GROANER
GROUNDS
GROWNUP
OCONNOR
PHOENIX
SCORNED
SCORNER
SHOWNIN
SPOONED
SPOONER
SWOONED
TROUNCE
TWOONIE
YAOUNDE

••O••N•

ADORING
ANODYNE
ATONING
AVOWING
BIOGENY
BLOWING
BOOKEND
BOOKING
BOOMING
BOOTING
BROGANS
BROMINE
BUOYANT
BUOYING
CHOLINE
CHORINE
CLONING
CLOSING
CLOYING
COOKING
COOLANT
COOLING
COOPING
CROWING
DOOMING
DRONING
DROPINS
DUODENA
ELOIGNS
ELOPING
EMOTING
ERODENT
ERODING
EVOKING
FLORINS
FLOWING
FOOLING
FOOTING
GAOLING
GLOBING
GLOWING
GLOZING
GNOMONS
GOODING
GOODONE
GOOFING
GOOSING
GROPING
GROWING
HOOFING
HOOKING

HOOPING
HOOTING
ILOCANO
IMOGENE
IRONING
IRONONS
ISOGONS
KNOWING
LEONINE
LOOKING
LOOMING
LOOPING
LOOSENS
LOOSING
LOOTING
MEOWING
MIOCENE
MOONING
MOORING
NOOSING
OROGENY
OROTUND
PHONING
PHOTONS
PLOWING
POOLING
POOPING
PROBING
PROBONO
PROFANE
PROGENY
PROLONG
PROPANE
PROSING
PROTONS
PROVING
QUOTING
REOPENS
RIOTING
ROOFING
ROOKING
ROOMING
ROOTING
SCOPING
SCORING
SHOEING
SHOGUNS
SHOOING
SHOOINS
SHORING
SHOVING
SHOWING
SIOUANS
SLOGANS
SLOPING
SLOVENE
SLOVENS
SLOWING
SMOKING
SNOCONE
SNORING
SNOWING
SPOKANE
SPOKING
STOKING
STOLONS
STONING
STORING
STOWING
TOOLING
TOOTING
TROGONS
TROJANS
TWOLANE

TWOTONE
USOPENS
VIOLENT
VIOLINS
WOOFING
WOOLENS
WYOMING
ZOOMING

••O•••N

AEOLIAN
BLOUSON
BLOWGUN
BLOWSIN
BOOLEAN
BROADEN
BROKEIN
BRONSON
BROSNAN
CLOCKIN
CLOSEIN
CROUTON
DOORMAN
DOORMEN
DROPSIN
EMOTION
EROSION
ETONIAN
FLOWNIN
FOOTMAN
FOOTMEN
FROGMAN
FROGMEN
FRONTON
GOODMAN
GOODMEN
GOODSON
GOODWIN
GROWSON
IRONMAN
IRONMEN
KTOSLIN
LAOCOON
LAOTIAN
LOOKSIN
LOOKSON
MOORHEN
OXONIAN
PLOSION
PLOWMAN
PLOWMEN
PROCYON
PRONOUN
PROPMAN
PROPMEN
PROTEAN
PROTEIN
SHODDEN
SHORTEN
SHOTGUN
SHOWMAN
SHOWMEN
SHOWNIN
SHOWSIN
SIOBHAN
SLOEGIN
SNOWDON
SNOWMAN
SNOWMEN
SNOWSIN
SPORRAN
STOLLEN
STOODIN
STOPSIN

STOUTEN
SWOLLEN
SWONKEN
SWOREIN
THOMSON
TIOMKIN
TOOKTEN
TRODDEN
TWOIRON
UTOPIAN
WOOLLEN
WROTEIN
ZOOMSIN

•••ON••

ACRONYM
ADDONTO
ALFONSO
ALMONDS
AMMONIA
ANTONIA
ANTONIN
ANTONIO
ANTONYM
ANYONES
APRONED
ARGONNE
BALONEY
BARONET
BARONGS
BAYONET
BEGONIA
BELONGS
BYGONES
CANONIC
CHRONIC
CLOONEY
COCONUT
COLONEL
COLONES
CORONAE
CORONAS
CORONET
CROONED
CROONER
DEBONED
DEBONES
DEMONIC
DEPONED
DEPONES
DUGONGS
ESTONIA
EVZONES
GARONNE
GIRONDE
HOMONYM
HYPONYM
INTONED
INTONER
INTONES
JACONET
KETONES
KIMONOS
LACONIC
LEMONDE
MADONNA
MAHONEY
MASONIC
MASONRY
MRBONES
OBLONGS
PINONES
POCONOS
REZONED
REZONES
SARONGS
SECONDS
SPOONED
SPOONER
SWOONED
SYNONYM
TALONED
TENONED
THRONES
THRONGS
TORONTO
TWOONIE
UNZONED
UPTONOW
WAGONER
WYNONNA

•••O•N•

ACCOUNT
ADJOINS
AGROUND
ALTOONA
ANTOINE
APPOINT
ARGONNE
ASTOUND
BABOONS
BEMOANS
BOLOGNA
COCOONS
COLOGNE
CYYOUNG
DEHORNS
DISOWNS
ECHOING
ENJOINS
EXPOUND
GARONNE
GOROUND
HALOING
HEROINE
HOBOING
HYPOING
IMPOUND
INBOUND
KAYOING
LAGOONS
LIVORNO
MADONNA
MAROONS
MINOANS
OHIOANS
ONGOING
OSBORNE
REBOUND
RECOUNT
REDOING
REDOUND
REJOINS
REMOUNT
RESOUND
REWOUND
SALOONS
SAMOANS
SHOOING
SHOOINS
SILOING
SOLOING
STJOHNS
SUBORNS
TYCOONS
UNBOUND
UNDOING
UNSOUND
UNWOUND
UPBORNE
VETOING
WYNONNA
YOKOONO
YOYOING
ZEROING

•••O••N

ABDOMEN
ADJOURN
AGNOMEN
ALSORAN
ANGOLAN
ANTONIN
BEDOUIN
BETOKEN
BORODIN
CAROLYN
CRYOGEN
DAKOTAN
DONOVAN
HALOGEN
HOBOKEN
JACOBIN
KILOTON
LANOLIN
LAYOPEN
LOCOMAN
LOCOMEN
ORTOLAN
OTTOMAN
REPOMAN
REWOVEN
SAROYAN
SOJOURN
SOLOMON
STOODIN
THEOMEN
THROWIN
UNWOVEN

••••ON•

ABALONE
ABSCOND
ACETONE
ACTIONS
AFFRONT
ALIMONY
ALLGONE
ALTOONA
AMAZONS
AMNIONS
ANEMONE
ANTHONY
ARCHONS
ARIZONA
ARTSONG
BABOONS
BALCONY
BARNONE
BARYONS
BEACONS
BECKONS
BELMONT
BLAZONS
BONBONS
BRETONS
BRITONS
BUNIONS
BUTTONS
CALZONE
CANNONS
CANTONS
CANYONS
CANZONE
CARBONS
CARTONS
CATIONS
CHALONS
CITRONS
CLIPONS
COCOONS
COMEONS
COMMONS
CONDONE
CORDONS
COTTONS
COTTONY
COUPONS
COWPONY
CRAYONS
CREMONA
CUIBONO
CYCLONE
DAIMONS
DAMSONS
DAYLONG
DAYTONA
DEACONS
DESMOND
DIAMOND
DINMONT
DOGGONE
DONJONS
DRAGONS
ENDZONE
EPIGONE
ERELONG
EUPHONY
FALCONS
FANIONS
FARGONE
FASTONE
FLACONS
FLAGONS
FORGONE
FREMONT
FURLONG
GALLONS
GAMMONS
GARCONS
GASCONS
GASCONY
GIBBONS
GIDEONS
GNOMONS
GOALONG
GODSONS
GOODONE
GORGONS
GOWRONG
GUIDONS
HAGDONS
HAMMOND
HARMONY
HIPBONE
HORMONE
IFSTONE
INFRONT
IRONONS
ISOGONS
JARGONS
JARGONY
JAWBONE
JETSONS
KLAXONS
KMESONS
LAGOONS
LARDONS
LEGIONS
LEPTONS
LESSONS
LIVEONE
LOTIONS
MACRONS
MARCONI
MAROONS
MATRONS
MICRONS
MINIONS
MISDONE
MORMONS
MOTIONS
MOUTONS
MUTTONS
NATIONS
NELSONS
NEURONE
NEURONS
NEWTONS
NOTIONS
OPTIONS
ORISONS
OUTDONE
PADRONE
PADRONI
PARDONS
PARSONS
PATRONS
PENNONS
PERSONA
PERSONS
PHOTONS
PIGEONS
PINIONS
PISTONS
POISONS
POMPONS
POTIONS
PRISONS
PROBONO
PROLONG
PROTONS
PULLONS
PYTHONS
RATIONS
RAYMOND
REASONS
RECKONS
REGIONS
RESPOND
RIBBONS
SALMONS
SALOONS
SEASONS
SERMONS
SEXTONS
SIMMONS
SIPHONS
SLIPONS
SNAPONS
SNOCONE
SOMEONE
SPUMONE
SPUMONI
STOLONS
SUMMONS
SYPHONS
TAKEONE
TARPONS
TENDONS
TEUTONS
THEFONZ
TIGLONS
TORTONI
TRIGONS
TRITONE
TRITONS
TROGONS
TWOTONE
TYCOONS
UNISONS
UPFRONT
VERMONT
VISIONS
VOLPONE
WAGGONS
WALKONS
WARZONE
WEAPONS
WILDONE
WONTONS
WORDONE
YAUPONS
YOKOONO
ZAMBONI
ZIRCONS

••••O•N

ANDSOON
BALLOON
BASSOON
BEDDOWN
BIGHORN
BIGJOHN
BOGDOWN
BUFFOON
CADDOAN
CALHOUN
CARTOON
CITROEN
CONJOIN
COWTOWN
CUTDOWN
DIEDOWN
DISJOIN
DRAGOON
FESTOON
FOGHORN
FORLORN
GETDOWN
GOTDOWN
HARPOON
HOEDOWN
IDAHOAN
INGROWN
INKHORN
KOWLOON
LAMPOON
LAOCOON
LAYDOWN
LEGHORN
LETDOWN
LIEDOWN
LINCOLN
LOWBORN
LOWDOWN
MAXBORN
MIDTOWN
MONSOON
MOWDOWN
NEWBORN
NEWMOON
NEWMOWN
NEWTOWN
OLDMOON
OURTOWN
OUTWORN
PATROON
PINDOWN
PLATOON
PONTOON
POPCORN
PRONOUN
PURLOIN
PUTDOWN
RACCOON
RANDOWN
RANGOON
RIPTORN
RUBDOWN
RUNDOWN
SASSOON
SATDOWN
SAXHORN
SETDOWN
SIRLOIN
SITDOWN
SUBJOIN
SUNDOWN
TIEDOWN
TINHORN
TOPDOWN
TRICORN
TYPHOON
UNICORN
UNKNOWN
UNSHORN
VIRGOAN
WALLOON
WAYWORN

•••••ON

ABANDON
ACHERON
ACHESON
ACTAEON
ACTEDON
ACTUPON
ADAMSON
ADDEDON
ADDISON
AILERON
ALARCON
ALENCON
ALLISON
ALLSTON
ALLYSON
ANDIRON
ANDSOON
ANISTON
ANTLION
AUCTION
AUDUBON
AVIGNON
BABYLON
BALATON
BALLOON
BANKSON
BASSOON
BASTION
BEARSON
BENISON
BERGSON
BILLION
BLOUSON
BLUSHON
BOURBON
BRANDON
BRANSON
BRAXTON
BRINGON
BRITTON
BRONSON
BUFFOON
BULLION
BURGEON
CAISSON
CALDRON
CALLSON
CAMERON
CAMPION
CAPTION
CARLSON
CARLTON
CARRION
CARRYON
CARTOON
CATCHON
CAUTION
CELADON
CESSION
CHANSON
CHEVRON
CHIFFON
CHIGNON
CLAPTON
CLARION
CLAYTON
CLEAVON
CLEMSON
CLIFTON
CLINTON
COMESON
CORAZON
COUNTON
CRAMPON
CRIMSON
CROUTON
CUSHION
DAWNSON
DECAGON
DENDRON
DICTION
DINEDON
DINESON
DODGSON
DOTEDON
DOTESON
DRAGOON
DRAGSON
DRAWNON
DRAWSON
DREAMON
DUDGEON
DUNGEON
EARLYON
ECHELON
EDITION
EGGEDON
ELATION
ELEISON
ELISION
ELLISON
ELUTION
EMERSON
EMOTION
ENTERON
EPSILON
EREWHON
ERICSON
EROSION
EVASION
FACTION
FALLSON
FASHION
FEEDSON
FESTOON
FICTION
FISSION
FRISSON
FRONTON
GAINSON
GALLEON
GETITON
GLEASON
GLUEDON
GLUESON
GLUTTON
GOINGON
GOODSON
GOTITON
GRAFTON
GRAYSON
GRIFFON
GROWSON
GRUNION
GRYPHON
HALCYON
HALSTON
HAMPTON
HANDSON
HANGSON
HARDWON
HARPOON
HARPSON
HELICON
HELLION
HEXAGON
HIRESON
HOLDSON
HORIZON
HOUSTON
IRECKON
JACKSON
JAMESON
JEWISON
JILLION
JOHNSON
JUMPSON
KEEPSON
KILOTON
KLINGON
KOWLOON
KRATION
KRYPTON
LAMPOON
LANGDON
LAOCOON
LATERON
LAYITON
LEADSON
LEANSON
LEBANON
LEBARON
LETINON
LETUPON
LEXICON
LIAISON
LIVEDON
LIVESON
LOCKSON
LONGTON
LOOKSON
MADISON
MANSION
MARCHON
MARMION
MCMAHON
MENTION
MILLION
MISSION
MONSOON
MOUFLON
MOVEDON
MOVESON
MULLION
MUMESON
NEUTRON
NEWMOON
NILSSON
NONAGON
NONIRON
NUCLEON
OCTAGON
OLDMOON
OMICRON
ONANDON
ONEIRON
OPINION
ORATION
ORBISON
ORGANON
OVATION
PARAGON
PASSION
PATROON
PEARSON
PENSION
PHAETON
PICKSON
PIDGEON
PIGIRON
PILEDON
PILESON
PILLION
PIMESON
PLANSON
PLATOON
PLAYSON
PLOSION
POISSON
POLYGON
PONTOON
PORTION
PRESSON
PRESTON
PREYSON
PROCYON
PULLSON
PUTUPON
PYNCHON
RACCOON
RALSTON
RANGOON
REUNION
RIGHTON
ROBESON
ROLLSON
ROUNDON
RUBICON
RUCTION
RULESON
SAFFRON
SAMPSON
SASSOON
SEALION
SECTION
SESSION
SETUPON
SEWEDON
SHANNON
SHELDON
SHELTON
SIGNSON
SILICON
SIMENON
SIMPSON
SIXIRON
SKELTON
SLAYTON
SLEEPON
SLEPTON
SLIPSON
SNOWDON
SOLOMON
SOUPCON
SPIEDON
SPIESON
SPURSON
STANDON
STANTON
STATION
STEPSON
STETSON
STILTON
SUASION
SUCTION
SURGEON
SWANSON
SWEETON
TACKSON
TAKENON
TAKESON
TELLSON
TENSION
THEREON
THOMSON
TORSION
TOUCHON
TRADEON
TREASON
TRENTON
TRIEDON
TRIESON
TUITION
TURNSON
TWOIRON
TYPHOON
UNCTION
UPSILON
VENISON
VERSION
WAITRON
WAITSON
WALKSON
WALLOON
WALSTON
WHARTON
WHEATON
WIDGEON
WILLSON
WINSTON
WOBEGON
WORKSON
YANKTON
ZEBULON
ZILLION

OO•••••

OOCYTES
OOHLALA
OOLITES
OOLITHS
OOMPAHS
OOZIEST

O•O••••

OBOISTS
OCONNOR
ODORFUL
ODOROUS
OLOROSO
ONORDER
OPOSSUM
OROGENY
OROTUND
OROURKE
OVOIDAL
OXONIAN
OZONOUS

O••O•••

OBLONGS
OBLOQUY
OCTOBER
OCTOPOD
OCTOPUS
OFSORTS
OGDOADS
OHIOANS
OKHOTSK
ONBOARD
ONGOING
ONTOPOF
OPPOSED
OPPOSER
OPPOSES
ORIOLES
ORMOLUS
ORTOLAN
OSBORNE
OSMOSED
OSMOSES
OSMOSIS
OSMOTIC
OTTOMAN
OUTOFIT
OXFORDS

O•••O••

OAKMOSS
OARLOCK
OBVIOUS
OCELOTS
OCTROIS
ODDJOBS
ODDLOTS
ODOROUS
OFASORT
OFFHOUR
OFFLOAD
OFFROAD
OLDFOGY
OLDGOLD
OLDMOON
OLDROSE
OLOROSO
OMIGOSH
OMINOUS
ONAROLL
ONENOTE
ONEROUS
ONSHORE
OPEROSE
OPTIONS
OPTSOUT
ORATORS
ORATORY
ORINOCO
ORISONS
OSCEOLA
OSHKOSH
OSSEOUS
OSTEOID
OURTOWN
OUTCOME
OUTDOES
OUTDONE
OUTDOOR
OUTGOES
OUTLOOK
OUTLOUD
OUTPOLL
OUTPOST
OUTSOLD
OUTVOTE
OUTWORE
OUTWORK
OUTWORN
OXBLOOD
OXYMORA
OZONOUS

O••••O•

OCONNOR
OCTAGON
OCTAVOS
OCTOPOD
OLDMOON
OLDPROS
OMICRON
ONANDON
ONEIRON
ONESHOT
ONLYTOO
ONLYYOU
ONTOPOF
OPENTOE
OPINION
OPTSFOR
ORATION
ORBISON
ORGANON
OUTCROP
OUTDOOR
OUTFLOW
OUTGROW
OUTLOOK
OVATION
OVERJOY
OXBLOOD

O•••••O

OLOROSO
ONLYTOO
ONTARIO
ONTHEGO
OREGANO
ORINOCO
ORLANDO
ORNITHO
OTHELLO
OTRANTO
OWINGTO

•OO••••

BOOBIES
BOOBOOS
BOODLES
BOOGIED
BOOGIES
BOOHOOS
BOOKEND
BOOKIES
BOOKING
BOOKISH
BOOKLET
BOOLEAN
BOOMBOX
BOOMERS
BOOMIER
BOOMING
BOONIES
BOORISH
BOOSLER
BOOSTED
BOOSTER
BOOSTUP
BOOTEES
BOOTHIA
BOOTIES
BOOTING
BOOTLEG
BOOTOUT
BOOTSUP
COOKERS
COOKERY
COOKIES
COOKING
COOKOFF
COOKOUT
COOKSUP
COOKTOP
COOLANT
COOLERS
COOLEST
COOLING
COOLISH
COOLSIT
COONCAT
COOPERS
COOPING
COOPSUP
COOPTED
COOTIES
DOODADS
DOODAHS
DOODLED
DOODLER
DOODLES
DOOMFUL
DOOMING
DOORDIE
DOORMAN
DOORMAT
DOORMEN
DOORWAY
DOOZIES
FOODIES
FOODWEB
FOOLERY
FOOLING
FOOLISH
FOOTAGE
FOOTERS
FOOTING
FOOTMAN
FOOTMEN
FOOTPAD
FOOTSIE
FOOTWAY
FOOZLED
FOOZLES
GOOBERS
GOODALL

GOODBAR
GOODBYE
GOODBYS
GOODEGG
GOODIES
GOODING
GOODISH
GOODJOB
GOODJOE
GOODMAN
GOODMEN
GOODONE
GOODSON
GOODWIN
GOOFIER
GOOFILY
GOOFING
GOOFOFF
GOOFSUP
GOOFUPS
GOOGOLS
GOOIEST
GOONIER
GOONILY
GOOPIER
GOOSIER
GOOSING
HOODLUM
HOODOOS
HOOFERS
HOOFING
HOOFSIT
HOOHAHS
HOOKAHS
HOOKING
HOOKSUP
HOOKUPS
HOOPING
HOOPLAS
HOOPOES
HOOSIER
HOOTERS
HOOTING
HOOTOWL
HOOTSAT
HOOVERS
KOOKIER
KOOLAID
LOOBIES
LOOFAHS
LOOKERS
LOOKFOR
LOOKING
LOOKOUT
LOOKSAT
LOOKSEE
LOOKSIN
LOOKSON
LOOKSTO
LOOKSUP
LOOKUPS
LOOMING
LOONEYS
LOONIER
LOONIES
LOOPERS
LOOPIER
LOOPING
LOOSELY
LOOSENS
LOOSEST
LOOSING
LOOTERS
LOOTING
MOOCHED
MOOCHER
MOOCHES
MOODIER
MOODILY
MOONDOG
MOONIER
MOONILY
MOONING
MOONISH
MOONLIT
MOONSET
MOORAGE
MOORHEN
MOORIER
MOORING
MOORISH
NOODLES
NOONDAY
NOOSING
POOCHES
POODLES
POOHBAH
POOLING
POOPING
POOPOUT
POORBOX
POORBOY
POOREST
POORISH
ROOFERS
ROOFING
ROOFTOP
ROOKERY
ROOKIER
ROOKIES
ROOKING
ROOMERS
ROOMFUL
ROOMIER
ROOMIES
ROOMILY
ROOMING
ROOSTED
ROOSTER
ROOTERS
ROOTFOR
ROOTIER
ROOTING
ROOTLET
ROOTOUT
SOONERS
SOONEST
SOOTHED
SOOTHER
SOOTHES
SOOTIER
SOOTILY
TOOKOFF
TOOKOUT
TOOKTEN
TOOLBOX
TOOLING
TOOLSUP
TOONIES
TOORDER
TOOTERS
TOOTHED
TOOTING
TOOTLED
TOOTLES
TOOTSIE
VOODOOS
WOODARD
WOODCUT
WOODIER
WOODIES
WOODLOT
WOODROW
WOOFERS
WOOFING
WOOKIES
WOOLENS
WOOLIER
WOOLIES
WOOLLEN
WOOLLEY
WOOLSEY
WOOMERA
WOOSTER
WOOZIER
WOOZILY
ZOOLOGY
ZOOMING
ZOOMSIN

•0•0•••

BOLOGNA
BOLOTIE
BORODIN
BOROUGH
COCONUT
COCOONS
COHORTS
COHOSTS
COLOBUS
COLOGNE
COLONEL
COLONES
COLORED
COLOSSI
COLOURS
COMOROS
CONOIDS
COPOUTS
COROLLA
CORONAE
CORONAS
CORONET
COYOTES
DOLORES
DOLOURS
DONOVAN
DOROTHY
GOFORIT
GOROUND
GOTOPOT
GOTOVER
HOBOING
HOBOKEN
HOMONYM
HONORED
HONOREE
HONORER
HONORIS
HONOURS
HOPOVER
IOMOTHS
KOBOLDS
LOCOMAN
LOCOMEN
MOLOCHS
MOLOKAI
MOLOTOV
MONOCLE
MONOCOT
MONODIC
MONOLOG
MONOMER
MOROCCO
MOTORED
NOBODYS
NODOUBT
NOKOMIS
POBOXES
POCONOS
POLOIST
POPOFFS
POPOVER
POTOMAC
POTOROO
ROBOCOP
ROBOTIC
RODOLFO
ROLODEX
SOJOURN
SOLOING
SOLOIST
SOLOMON
SORORAL
TOROIDS
TORONTO
YOKOONO
YOYOING

•0••0••

BOBDOLE
BOBHOPE
BOGDOWN
BOGHOLE
BONBONS
BONGOES
BONJOUR
BONJOVI
BONMOTS
BONSOIR
BOOBOOS
BOOHOOS
BOOTOUT
BOREOUT
BORROWS
BORZOIS
BOTTOMS
BOUDOIR
BOWSOUT
BOWWOWS
BOXROOM
BOXTOPS
BOXWOOD
BOYCOTT
BOYHOOD
COALOIL
COCOONS
COLLODI
COLLOID
COLLOPS
COMEOFF
COMEONS
COMEOUT
COMFORT
COMMODE
COMMONS
COMMOVE
COMPORT
COMPOSE
COMPOST
COMPOTE
CONCOCT
CONCORD
CONDOLE
CONDONE
CONDORS
CONFORM
CONJOBS
CONJOIN
CONKOUT
CONMOTO
CONNORS
CONNOTE
CONSOLE
CONSORT
CONTORT
CONTOUR
CONVOKE
CONVOYS
COOKOFF
COOKOUT
COPIOUS
COPPOLA
COPSOUT
CORDOBA
CORDONS
CORNOIL
CORRODE
COTTONS
COTTONY
COULOMB
COUPONS
COWBOYS
COWPOKE
COWPONY
COWTOWN
COXCOMB
DOCTORS
DOGFOOD
DOGGONE
DOGWOOD
DOLEOUT
DOLLOPS
DONJONS
DONJOSE
DOPEOUT
DOZEOFF
FOBSOFF
FOGBOWS
FOGHORN
FOLDOUT
FOLLOWS
FORBORE
FORGOES
FORGONE
FORGOOD
FORLORN
FORMOSA
FORSOOK
FOULOUT
FOXHOLE
GOABOUT
GOALONG
GOBROKE
GODSONS
GOESOFF
GOESOUT
GONDOLA
GOODONE
GOOFOFF
GOOGOLS
GORGONS
GOSLOWS
GOTDOWN
GOTLOST
GOWRONG
HOBNOBS
HOEDOWN
HOLDOFF
HOLDOUT
HOLEOUT
HOLLOWS
HOLMOAK
HOLYOKE
HOODOOS
HOOPOES
HOOTOWL
HOPSOFF
HOPTOIT
HORMONE
HORRORS
HOTCOMB
HOTDOGS
HOTFOOT
HOTPOTS
HOTRODS
HOWCOME
JOBHOPS
JOBLOTS
KOWLOON
KOWTOWS
LOCKOUT
LOGBOOK
LOGROLL
LOGSOFF
LOGSOUT
LOLLOPS
LOOKOUT
LOSEOUT
LOSTOUT
LOTIONS
LOWBORN
LOWBOYS
LOWCOST
LOWDOWN
LOWROAD
MOLDOVA
MONGOLS
MONSOON
MONTOYA
MOPTOPS
MORMONS
MORROWS
MOTIONS
MOTTOES
MOUTONS
MOVEOUT
MOWDOWN
NOCUOUS
NODSOFF
NOISOME
NONCOMS
NORFOLK
NOSEOUT
NOSHOWS
NOTIONS
NOXIOUS
POISONS
POLLOCK
POMPOMS
POMPONS
POMPOUS
PONTOON
POOPOUT
POPCORN
POPSOFF
POPSOUT
POPTOPS
POTHOLE
POTHOOK
POTIONS
POUROUT
POWWOWS
ROANOKE
ROBLOWE
ROBROYS
RODEOFF
RODEOUT
ROLLOUT
ROOTOUT
ROSEOIL
ROWBOAT
SOLDOFF
SOLDOUT
SOMEONE
SORROWS
SORTOUT
SOUKOUS
TOEHOLD
TOELOOP
TOLDOFF
TOMBOLA
TOMBOYS
TOMFOOL
TOMTOMS
TOOKOFF
TOOKOUT
TOPCOAT
TOPDOGS
TOPDOWN
TOPHOLE
TOPMOST
TOPSOFF
TOPSOIL
TOPSOUT
TOREOFF
TOREOUT
TORNOFF
TORNOUT
TORTONI
TOSSOFF
TOSSOUT
TOWROPE
TOYDOGS
VOLPONE
VOODOOS
VOTEOUT
WONTONS
WORDONE
WOREOFF
WOREOUT
WORKOFF
WORKOUT
WORNOFF
WORNOUT
YOKOONO
YOMTOVS
ZONKOUT
ZOOLOGY

•0•••0•

BOKCHOY
BOLEROS
BOLSHOI
BONITOS
BOOBOOS
BOOHOOS
BOOMBOX
BOREDOM
BOURBON
BOUTROS
BOWKNOT
BOXROOM
BOXWOOD
BOYHOOD
COMESON
COMOROS
CONTROL
COOKTOP
COPILOT
COPYBOY
CORAZON
CORNCOB
CORNDOG
CORNROW
COUNTON
DODGSON
DOGCHOW
DOGFOOD
DOGSHOW
DOGTROT
DOGWOOD
DOMINOS
DONATOR
DONEFOR
DORITOS
DOSIDOS
DOTEDON
DOTESON
DOVECOT
DOWNBOW
FORGOOD
FORSOOK
FOXTROT
GODUNOV
GOESFOR
GOINFOR
GOINGON
GOODJOB
GOODJOE
GOODSON
GOTITON
GOTOPOT
HOLDSON
HOLYCOW
HOMEBOY
HONCHOS
HOODOOS
HORIZON
HOTFOOT
HOTSHOT
HOTSPOT
HOUSTON
JOEBLOW
JOHNDOE
JOHNSON
JOURNOS
KOWLOON
LOCATOR
LOCKBOX
LOCKSON
LOGBOOK
LONGBOW
LONGTON
LOOKFOR
LOOKSON
LOWBLOW
LOWBROW
MOLOTOV
MONITOR
MONOCOT
MONOLOG
MONSOON
MOONDOG
MOUFLON
MOVEDON
MOVESON
NONAGON
NONIRON
NONSTOP
NOSEJOB
POCONOS
POISSON
POLYGON
POMELOS
PONCHOS
PONTOON
POORBOX
POORBOY
PORTHOS
PORTION
POSTBOX
POTHOOK
POTOROO
POTSHOT
ROADHOG
ROBESON
ROBOCOP
ROLLSON
ROLLTOP
ROMANOV
ROOFTOP
ROOTFOR
ROPETOW
ROTATOR
ROUNDON
SOAPBOX
SODAPOP
SOFTTOP
SOLOMON
SOMEHOW
SOUPCON
TOELOOP
TOESHOE
TOLSTOI
TOLSTOY
TOMFOOL
TONELOC
TONEROW
TOOLBOX
TOPKNOT
TOREROS
TORSION
TOUCHON
TOYSHOP
VOODOOS
VOTEFOR
WOBEGON
WOODLOT
WOODROW
WORKFOR
WORKSON
YOUKNOW

•0••••0

BOIARDO
BOITANO
COLUMBO
COMESTO
CONBRIO
CONMOTO
CORDERO
DOMINGO
GOLFPRO
GOTINTO
HOLDSTO
HORATIO
IONESCO
LOCARNO
LONGAGO
LOOKSTO
LORENZO
MODESTO
MOGAMBO
MONTEGO
MONTERO
MORELLO
MOROCCO
NOCANDO
NONZERO
NORELCO
NOVARRO
POINTTO
POMPANO
PORTICO
POTOROO
ROBERTO
RODOLFO
ROSARIO
SOANDSO
SOPRANO
SORDINO
SORVINO
TOBACCO
TORNADO
TORONTO
TORPEDO
TOURACO
VOLCANO
YOKOONO

••00•••

ALOOFLY
BLOODED
BLOOMED
BLOOMER
BLOOPED
BLOOPER
BROODED
BROODER
BROOKED
CHOOSER
CHOOSES
CLOONEY
CROOKED
CROONED
CROONER
DROOLED
DROOLER
DROOPED
FLOODED
FLOORED
GLOOMED
GROOMED
GROOMER
GROOVED
GROOVES
PROOFED
PROOFER
SCOOPED
SCOOPER
SCOOTED
SCOOTER
SHOOFLY
SHOOING
SHOOINS
SHOOKUP
SHOOTAT
SHOOTER
SHOOTUP
SKOOKUM
SMOOTHS
SMOOTHY
SNOOKER
SNOOPED
SNOOPER
SNOOTED
SNOOZED
SNOOZES
SPOOFED
SPOOFER
SPOOKED
SPOOLED
SPOONED
SPOONER
STOODBY
STOODIN
STOODUP
STOOGES
STOOKED
STOOKEY
STOOLIE
STOOPED
SWOONED
SWOOPED
SWOOSIE
TROOPED
TROOPER
TWOONIE
WHOOPED
WHOOPEE

••0•0••

AMOROUS
APOCOPE
APOLOGY
AXOLOTL
BIOLOGY
BLOTOUT
BLOWOFF
BLOWOUT
BOOBOOS
BOOHOOS
BOOTOUT
COOKOFF
COOKOUT
DROPOFF
DROPOUT
ECOLOGY
ECONOMY
GEOLOGY
GNOMONS
GOODONE
GOOFOFF
GOOGOLS
HOODOOS
HOOPOES
HOOTOWL
IRONONS
IRONORE
IRONOUT
ISOGONS
ISONOMY
ISOPODS
ISOTOPE
LAOCOON
LEONORA
LEOPOLD
LOOKOUT
ODOROUS
OLOROSO
OZONOUS
PHOTOED
PHOTOGS
PHOTONS
PHOTOOP
POOPOUT
PROBONO
PROLOGS
PROLONG
PROMOTE
PRONOUN
PROPOSE
PROSODY
PROTONS
PROVOKE
PROVOST
RIOLOBO
RIOTOUS
ROOTOUT
SAOTOME
SHOTOUT
SHOWOFF
SHOWOUT
SNOCONE
STOLONS
STOPOFF
SUOLOCO
TOOKOFF
TOOKOUT
TROGONS
TROTOUT
TWOFOLD
TWOSOME
TWOTONE
VOODOOS
ZOOLOGY

••0••0•

ALOHAOE
ASOFNOW
BLOSSOM
BLOUSON
BOOBOOS
BOOHOOS
BOOMBOX
BRONCOS
BRONSON
COOKTOP
CROUTON
EMOTION
EROSION
FRONTON
GOODJOB
GOODJOE
GOODSON
GROTTOS
GROWSON
HOODOOS
KNOSSOS
KNOWHOW
LAOCOON
LOOKFOR
LOOKSON
MOONDOG
OCONNOR
PHOTOOP
PLOSION
PLOWBOY
POORBOX
POORBOY
PROCTOR
PROCYON
PROSHOP
ROOFTOP
ROOTFOR
SHOEBOX
SHORTOF
SHOTFOR
SHOWDOG
SNOWDON
SNOWJOB
SPOKEOF
SPONSOR
THOMSON
TOOLBOX
TWOIRON
USOSHOW
VOODOOS
WOODLOT
WOODROW

••0•••0

AVOCADO
CHORIZO
FLOCKTO
GIORGIO
GROMYKO
GROUCHO
ILOCANO
LOOKSTO
OLOROSO
PROBONO
PROPRIO
PROVISO
PROXIMO
RIOLOBO
SCORPIO
SUOLOCO
WHOSWHO
WROTETO

•••00••

ALTOONA
BABOONS
BAZOOKA
BEHOOVE
CABOOSE
CAHOOTS
COCOONS
ENROOTS
GALOOTS
INDOORS
LAGOONS
LLCOOLJ
MAROONS
METOOER
PALOOKA
PAPOOSE
REBOOTS
REHOOKS
RETOOLS
SALOONS
SCHOOLS
SCROOGE
TYCOONS
UNHOOKS
UNLOOSE
UPROOTS
VAMOOSE
YOKOONO

•••0•0•

AEROSOL
ALCOHOL
APROPOS
ARIOSOS
ARROYOS
BICOLOR
COMOROS
CREOSOL
DESOTOS
ESPOSOS
GASOHOL
GIGOLOS
GOTOPOT
KILOTON
KIMONOS
MALODOR
MOLOTOV
MONOCOT
MONOLOG
NABOKOV
OCTOPOD
ONTOPOF
POCONOS
POTOROO
REBOZOS
RECOLOR
ROBOCOP
SOLOMON
UPTONOW

•••0••0

ADDONTO
ALFONSO
ANTONIO
ARIOSTO
CRIOLLO
LESOTHO
LIVORNO
MIAOYAO
MOROCCO
POTOROO
PRIORTO
RIDOTTO
RISOTTO
RODOLFO
SIROCCO
TORONTO
YOKOONO

••••00•

AIRCOOL
ANDSOON
BALLOON
BAMBOOS
BARROOM
BASSOON
BEDROOM
BIGFOOT
BOOBOOS
BOOHOOS
BOXROOM
BOXWOOD
BOYHOOD
BSCHOOL
BUFFOON
BURGOOS
CARPOOL
CARTOON
CATFOOD
CHEROOT
CHINOOK
CUCKOOS
DAGWOOD
DASBOOT
DAYBOOK
DAYROOM
DIDGOOD
DOGFOOD
DOGWOOD
DRAGOON
FESTOON
FORGOOD
FORSOOK
FRYCOOK
GYPROOM
HARPOON
HENCOOP
HEYWOOD
HIPBOOT
HIPROOF
HOODOOS
HOTFOOT
INBLOOM

JIBBOOM
KOWLOON
LAMPOON
LAOCOON
LEGROOM
LOGBOOK
MANHOOD
MISTOOK
MONSOON
NEWLOOK
NEWMOON
OLDMOON
OUTDOOR
OUTLOOK
OXBLOOD
PARTOOK
PATROON
PHOTOOP
PLATOON
PLYWOOD
PONTOON
POTHOOK
PRECOOK
PRECOOL
RACCOON
RANGOON
REBLOOM
RECROOM
REDBOOK
REDWOOD
REPROOF
RESHOOT
SASSOON
SAWWOOD
SCHMOOS
SEAFOOD
SHADOOF
SKIBOOT
SKYHOOK
SUNROOF
SUNROOM
TAPROOM
TAPROOT
TATTOOS
TEAROOM
TOELOOP
TOMFOOL
TYPHOON
VANPOOL
VOODOOS
WALLOON
WAYCOOL
WEBFOOT

••••O•O
CARDOZO
CONMOTO
CUIBONO
GIACOMO
HANSOLO
IVANOVO
LIMPOPO
NICCOLO
OLOROSO
ORINOCO
PICCOLO
PISCOPO
PROBONO
RIOLOBO
SAPPORO
SUOLOCO
TIEPOLO
TREMOLO
YOKOONO

•••••OO
BABALOO
BUGABOO
BUGALOO
KERCHOO
MRMAGOO
ONLYTOO
POTOROO
SHAMPOO
SKIDDOO

OP•••••
OPACITY
OPALINE
OPAQUES
OPENAIR
OPENBAR
OPENEND
OPENERS
OPENING
OPENPIT
OPENSEA
OPENSUP
OPENTOE
OPERAND
OPERATE
OPEROSE
OPHELIA
OPHITES
OPIATES
OPINERS
OPINING
OPINION
OPOSSUM
OPPOSED
OPPOSER
OPPOSES
OPPRESS
OPPUGNS
OPTICAL
OPTIMAL
OPTIMUM
OPTIONS
OPTSFOR
OPTSOUT
OPULENT

O•P••••
OMPHALI
OPPOSED
OPPOSER
OPPOSES
OPPRESS
OPPUGNS
ORPHANS
ORPHEAN
ORPHEUS
ORPHREY
ORPINES
OSPREYS

O••P•••
OFFPEAK
OILPANS
OLDPROS
OOMPAHS
OUTPACE
OUTPLAY
OUTPOLL
OUTPOST
OUTPUTS
OVIPARA

O•••P••
OCCIPUT
OCTOPOD
OCTOPUS
OCTUPLE
OEDIPAL
OEDIPUS
OLYMPIA
OLYMPIC
OLYMPUS
ONTOPOF
OPENPIT

O•••••P
OFFRAMP
OILLAMP
OLDCHAP
ONESTEP
OPENSUP
OUTCROP
OUTJUMP
OUTSTEP
OVERLAP
OWNEDUP

•OP••••
BOPPERS
BOPPING
COPIERS
COPILOT
COPIOUS
COPLAND
COPOUTS
COPPERS
COPPERY
COPPICE
COPPING
COPPOLA
COPSOUT
COPTERS
COPULAE
COPULAS
COPYBOY
COPYCAT
COPYING
COPYIST
DOPANTS
DOPEOUT
DOPIEST
DOPPLER
FOPPERY
FOPPISH
GOPHERS
HOPEFUL
HOPKINS
HOPLIKE
HOPOVER
HOPPERS
HOPPING
HOPPLED
HOPPLES
HOPSOFF
HOPTOIT
KOPECKS
LOPPERS
LOPPIER
LOPPING
MOPIEST
MOPPERS
MOPPETS
MOPPING
MOPTOPS
POPCORN
POPEYED
POPGUNS
POPLARS
POPLINS
POPOFFS
POPOVER
POPPERS
POPPETS
POPPIES
POPPING
POPPINS
POPPLED
POPPLES
POPSOFF
POPSOUT
POPTART
POPTOPS
POPULAR
POPULUS
ROPEDIN
ROPESIN
ROPETOW
ROPIEST
SOPHISM
SOPHIST
SOPPIER
SOPPING
SOPRANO
SOPWITH
TOPAZES
TOPCOAT
TOPDOGS
TOPDOWN
TOPGUNS
TOPHATS
TOPHOLE
TOPIARY
TOPICAL
TOPKAPI
TOPKICK
TOPKNOT
TOPMAST
TOPMOST
TOPPERS
TOPPING
TOPPLED
TOPPLES
TOPSAIL
TOPSIDE
TOPSOFF
TOPSOIL
TOPSOUT

•O•P•••
BOPPERS
BOPPING
COEPTIS
COMPACT
COMPANY
COMPARE
COMPASS
COMPEER
COMPELS
COMPERE
COMPETE
COMPILE
COMPLEX
COMPORT
COMPOSE
COMPOST
COMPOTE
COMPUTE
COOPERS
COOPING
COOPSUP
COOPTED
COPPERS
COPPERY
COPPICE
COPPING
COPPOLA
COUPLED
COUPLES
COUPLET
COUPONS
COWPEAS
COWPOKE
COWPONY
DOLPHIN
DOPPLER
FOPPERY
FOPPISH
GOMPERS
GOOPIER
GOSPELS
HOOPING
HOOPLAS
HOOPOES
HOPPERS
HOPPING
HOPPLED
HOPPLES
HOSPICE
HOTPOTS
LOOPERS
LOOPIER
LOOPING
LOPPERS
LOPPIER
LOPPING
LOWPAID
MOPPERS
MOPPETS
MOPPING
MORPHED
NONPLUS
OOMPAHS
POMPANO
POMPEIA
POMPEII
POMPOMS
POMPONS
POMPOUS
POOPING
POOPOUT
POPPERS
POPPETS
POPPIES
POPPING
POPPINS
POPPLED
POPPLES
POTPIES
ROMPERS
ROMPING
ROMPISH
SOAPBOX
SOAPERS
SOAPIER
SOAPILY
SOAPING
SOPPIER
SOPPING
SOUPCON
SOUPIER
SOUPSUP
TOPPERS
TOPPING
TOPPLED
TOPPLES
TORPEDO
TOSPARE
TOUPEES
TOWPATH
VOLPONE

•O••P••
COCKPIT
DOWNPAT
FOOTPAD
FOREPAW
GOLFPRO
GOTOPOT
HOTSPOT
HOTSPUR
MOSHPIT
NOTEPAD
PORKPIE
SODAPOP

•O•••P•
BOBHOPE
BOXTOPS
COLLOPS
CONCEPT
CORRUPT
DOLLOPS
FOLDUPS
FORCEPS
FOULUPS
GOESAPE
GOOFUPS
GOSSIPS
GOSSIPY
HOLDUPS
HOOKUPS
HOTCAPS
HOTLIPS
HOTTIPS
JOBHOPS
LOCKUPS
LOLLOPS
LOOKUPS
MOBCAPS
MOCKUPS
MOPTOPS
POPTOPS
TOECAPS
TOETAPS
TOPKAPI
TOSSUPS
TOWROPE
WORKUPS

•O••••P
BONEDUP
BONESUP
BOOSTUP
BOOTSUP
BORNEUP
BOTCHUP
BOUNDUP
BOXEDUP
BOXESUP
BOXSTEP
COILSUP
COMESUP
COOKSUP
COOKTOP
COOPSUP
COUGHUP
COVERUP
COWSLIP
DOINGUP
DOLLSUP
FOLDSUP
FOULSUP
FOULTIP
GOINGUP
GOOFSUP
HOLDSUP
HOLEDUP
HOLESUP
HOOKSUP
JOINSUP
LOCKSUP
LOOKSUP
LOUSEUP
MOVEDUP
MOVESUP
NONSLIP
NONSTOP
NOTRUMP
ROADMAP
ROBOCOP
ROLLSUP
ROLLTOP
ROOFTOP
ROUGHUP
ROUNDUP
SOAKSUP
SODAPOP
SOFTTOP
SOUPSUP
TOELOOP
TONEDUP
TONESUP
TOOLSUP
TOUCHUP
TOYSHOP
WOKENUP
WORKSUP
WORSHIP
WOUNDUP

••OP•••
ADOPTED
ADOPTEE
ADOPTER
CHOPPED
CHOPPER
CLOPPED
COOPERS
COOPING
COOPSUP
COOPTED
CROPPED
CROPPER
CROPSUP
DIOPTER
DROPINS
DROPLET
DROPOFF
DROPOUT
DROPPED
DROPPER
DROPSBY
DROPSIN
ELOPERS
ELOPING
EPOPEES
FLOPPED
GOOPIER
GROPING
GROPIUS
HOOPING
HOOPLAS
HOOPOES
ISOPODS
LEOPARD
LEOPOLD
LOOPERS
LOOPIER
LOOPING
PEOPLED
PEOPLES
PLOPPED
POOPING
POOPOUT
PROPANE
PROPELS
PROPHET
PROPJET
PROPMAN
PROPMEN
PROPOSE
PROPPED
PROPRIO
PROPSUP
PROPTER
REOPENS
SCOPING
SHOPFUL
SHOPPED
SHOPPER
SHOPPES
SLOPING
SLOPPED
STOPGAP
STOPOFF
STOPPED
STOPPER
STOPSIN
STOPSUP
SWOPPED
TROPHIC
TROPICS
TROPISM
USOPENS
UTOPIAN
UTOPIAS
WHOPPED
WHOPPER

••O•P••
ADOLPHE
BLOOPED
BLOOPER
CHOMPED
CHOPPED
CHOPPER
CLOMPED
CLOPPED
CROPPED
CROPPER
DROOPED
DROPPED
DROPPER
FLOPPED
FOOTPAD
GROUPED
GROUPER
GROUPIE
PLOPPED
PROMPTS
PROPPED
PROSPER
SCOOPED
SCOOPER
SCORPIO
SHOPPED
SHOPPER
SHOPPES
SHOTPUT
SLOPPED
SNOOPED
SNOOPER
SNOWPEA
STOMPED
STOOPED
STOPPED
STOPPER
SWOOPED
SWOPPED
TROOPED
TROOPER
TROUPER
TROUPES
WHOMPED
WHOOPED
WHOOPEE
WHOPPED
WHOPPER

••O••P•
APOCOPE
BLOWUPS
GOOFUPS
HOOKUPS
ISOTOPE
LOOKUPS
SLOWUPS

••O•••P
BIOCHIP
BLOWNUP
BLOWSUP
BOOSTUP
BOOTSUP
BROKEUP
BUOYSUP
CHOKEUP
CLOGSUP
CLOSEUP
COOKSUP
COOKTOP
COOPSUP
CROPSUP
CROSSUP
EGOTRIP
GOOFSUP
GROWNUP
GROWSUP
HOOKSUP
LOOKSUP
PHOTOOP
PROPSUP
PROSHOP
ROOFTOP
SHOOKUP
SHOOTUP
SHOWSUP
SLOWSUP
SNOWCAP
SPOKEUP
STOCKUP
STOODUP
STOPGAP
STOPSUP
STOREUP
TOOLSUP
TWOSTEP
WROTEUP

•••OP••
APROPOS
ATROPHY
BLOOPED
BLOOPER
CANOPUS
DROOPED
GOTOPOT
LAYOPEN
OCTOPOD
OCTOPUS
ONTOPOF
PANOPLY
SCOOPED
SCOOPER
SNOOPED
SNOOPER
STOOPED
STROPHE
STROPPY
SWOOPED
TROOPED
TROOPER
UPTOPAR
WHOOPED
WHOOPEE
ZATOPEK

•••O•P•
RECOUPS
RUDOLPH
STROPPY

•••O••P
ROBOCOP
SHOOKUP
SHOOTUP
STOODUP

••••OP•
APOCOPE
BARHOPS
BIGTOPS
BISHOPS
BOBHOPE
BOXTOPS
CARHOPS
COLLOPS
CYCLOPS
DOLLOPS
ENTROPY
GALLOPS
HYSSOPS
ISOTOPE
JOBHOPS
LAPTOPS
LIMPOPO
LOLLOPS
MOPTOPS
PEGTOPS
PISCOPO
POPTOPS
RAGMOPS
RAGTOPS
REDTOPS
TIPTOPS
TOWROPE
UNSTOPS
WALLOPS
WETMOPS

••••O•P
BARSOAP
HENCOOP
INGROUP
PEASOUP
PHOTOOP
REGROUP
TOELOOP

•••••OP
AIRDROP
BELLHOP
BUSSTOP
COOKTOP
DESKTOP
DEVELOP
DEWDROP
DUSTMOP
EARDROP
ENVELOP
FLATTOP
GUMDROP
HARDTOP
HENCOOP
HIGHTOP
HILLTOP
KERPLOP
MAINTOP
MILKSOP
NONSTOP
OUTCROP
PALMTOP
PHOTOOP
PITSTOP
PROSHOP
ROBOCOP
ROLLTOP
ROOFTOP
SCALLOP
SODAPOP
SOFTTOP
TANKTOP
TEASHOP
TIMECOP
TOELOOP
TOYSHOP
TREETOP

O••Q•••
OPAQUES

O•••Q••
OBLIQUE
OBLOQUY

O••••Q•
ONTHEQT

•OQ••••
LOQUATS

•O•Q•••
BOUQUET
COEQUAL
CONQUER
JOAQUIN
JONQUIL
MOSQUES
RORQUAL
TORQUES

•O••Q••
COMIQUE
MONIQUE

•O•••Q•
POSSLQS

••OQ•••
CLOQUES
CROQUET

•••OQ••
BAROQUE
OBLOQUY

OR•••••
ORACLES
ORANGES
ORANGEY
ORATING
ORATION
ORATORS
ORATORY
ORBISON
ORBITAL
ORBITED
ORBITER
ORBLESS
ORBLIKE
ORCHARD
ORCHIDS
ORDAINS
ORDEALS
ORDERED
ORDERER
ORDERLY
ORDINAL
ORDINES
OREGANO
ORESTES
ORGANDY
ORGANIC
ORGANON
ORGANUM
ORGANZA
ORGATES
ORGEATS
ORIENTE
ORIENTS
ORIFICE
ORIGAMI
ORIGINS
ORINOCO
ORIOLES
ORISONS
ORLANDO
ORLEANS
ORMANDY
ORMOLUS
ORNETTE
ORNITHO
OROGENY
OROTUND
OROURKE
ORPHANS
ORPHEAN
ORPHEUS
ORPHREY
ORPINES
ORTOLAN
ORVILLE

O•R••••
OARLESS
OARLIKE
OARLOCK
OGREISH
OTRANTO
OURGANG
OURSELF
OURTOWN

O••R•••
OBERLIN
OBTRUDE
OCARINA
OCTROIS
ODORFUL
ODOROUS
OFFRAMP
OFFROAD
OILRIGS
OLDROSE
OLOROSO
ONAROLL
ONEROUS
ONORDER
ONTRACK
ONTRIAL
OPERAND
OPERATE
OPEROSE
OPPRESS
OSPREYS
OSTRICH
OUTRACE
OUTRAGE
OUTRANK
OUTRUNS
OVERACT
OVERAGE
OVERALL
OVERATE
OVERAWE
OVERBIG
OVERBUY
OVERDID
OVERDUB
OVERDUE
OVEREAT
OVERFLY
OVERJOY
OVERLAP
OVERLAY
OVERLIE
OVERRAN
OVERRUN
OVERSAW
OVERSEA
OVERSEE
OVERTAX
OVERTLY
OVERUSE

O•••R••
OAKTREE
OBSERVE
OBVERSE
OBVERTS
OEUVRES
OFFERED
OFFERER
OFSORTS
OLDPROS
OMICRON
ONEIRON
ONSERVE
ONTARIO
ONWARDS
ORDERED
ORDERER
ORDERLY
OROURKE
ORPHREY
OSBORNE
OSIERED
OUTCROP
OUTDRAW
OUTDREW
OUTGREW
OUTGROW
OVERRAN
OVERRUN
OXCARTS
OXFORDS

O••••R•
OAKFERN
OBSCURE
OFASORT
OLESTRA
ONADARE
ONAGERS
ONBOARD
ONGUARD
ONSHORE
OPENERS
OPINERS
ORATORS
ORATORY
ORCHARD
OSTLERS
OUSTERS
OUTWARD
OUTWORE
OUTWORK
OUTWORN
OVIPARA
OXYMORA
OYSTERS

O•••••R
OBTUSER
OCONNOR
OCTOBER
OFFERER
OFFHOUR
OFFICER
OFFYEAR
OFTENER
OLDSTER
OLIVIER
OMITTER
ONATEAR
ONESTAR
ONORDER
OPENAIR
OPENBAR
OPPOSER
OPTSFOR
ORBITER
ORDERER
OUTDOOR
OUTWEAR

•OR••••
AORISTS
BORACIC
BORATES
BORDERS
BOREDOM
BOREOUT
BORNEUP
BORODIN
BOROUGH
BORROWS
BORSCHT
BORZOIS
CORAZON
CORBELS

CORBETT
CORDAGE
CORDATE
CORDELL
CORDERO
CORDIAL
CORDING
CORDITE
CORDOBA
CORDONS
CORELLI
CORETTA
CORINTH
CORKAGE
CORKERS
CORKIER
CORKING
CORNCOB
CORNDOG
CORNEAL
CORNEAS
CORNELL
CORNERS
CORNETS
CORNFED
CORNICE
CORNIER
CORNILY
CORNING
CORNISH
CORNOIL
CORNROW
COROLLA
CORONAE
CORONAS
CORONET
CORRALS
CORRECT
CORRIDA
CORRODE
CORRUPT
CORSAGE
CORSAIR
CORSETS
CORSICA
CORTEGE
DORITOS
DORMANT
DORMERS
DORMICE
DOROTHY
DORSALS
DORSETT
FORAGED
FORAGER
FORAGES
FORBADE
FORBEAR
FORBIDS
FORBORE
FORCEPS
FORCERS
FORCING
FORDHAM
FORDING
FOREARM
FOREIGN
FORELEG
FOREMAN
FOREMEN
FOREPAW
FORERAN
FORERUN
FORESAW
FORESEE
FORESTS
FOREVER
FORFEIT
FORFEND
FORFREE
FORGAVE
FORGERS
FORGERY
FORGETS
FORGING
FORGIVE
FORGOES
FORGONE
FORGOOD
FORINTS
FORKERS
FORKFUL
FORKIER
FORKING
FORLIFE
FORLORN
FORMALS
FORMATS
FORMFUL
FORMICA
FORMING
FORMOSA
FORMULA
FORREAL
FORRENT
FORREST
FORSAKE
FORSALE
FORSOOK
FORSTER
FORSURE
FORSYTH
FORTIES
FORTIFY
FORTIUS
FORTRAN
FORTUNA
FORTUNE
FORWARD
FORWENT
GORDIAN
GORETEX
GORGETS
GORGING
GORGONS
GORIEST
GORILLA
GOROUND
GORSIER
HORATIO
HORIZON
HORMONE
HORNETS
HORNING
HORNISH
HORNIST
HORNSBY
HORNSIN
HORRIFY
HORRORS
HORSIER
HORSING
KOREANS
KORUNAS
LORDING
LORDJIM
LORELEI
LORENZO
LORETTA
LORICAE
LORISES
LORRIES
MORAINE
MORALES
MORALLY
MORANIS
MORAVIA
MORDANT
MORDENT
MORDRED
MORELLO
MORESBY
MORGANA
MORGANS
MORMONS
MORNING
MOROCCO
MORPHED
MORROWS
MORSELS
MORTALS
MORTARS
MORTIFY
MORTISE
NORBERT
NORDICS
NORELCO
NORFOLK
NORIEGA
NORMALS
NORMAND
NORMANS
NORTHER
PORCHES
PORCINE
PORGIES
PORKERS
PORKIER
PORKISH
PORKPIE
PORSCHE
PORSENA
PORTAGE
PORTALS
PORTEND
PORTENT
PORTERS
PORTHOS
PORTICO
PORTION
PORTMAN
PORTRAY
RORQUAL
SORBATE
SORBETS
SORCERY
SORDINI
SORDINO
SORGHUM
SORITES
SORORAL
SORRELS
SORRIER
SORRILY
SORROWS
SORTERS
SORTIED
SORTIES
SORTING
SORTOUT
SORVINO
TORCHED
TORCHES
TOREOFF
TOREOUT
TOREROS
TORMENT
TORNADO
TORNOFF
TORNOUT
TOROIDS
TORONTO
TORPEDO
TORQUES
TORRENS
TORRENT
TORSION
TORTONI
TORYISH
TORYISM
WORDIER
WORDILY
WORDING
WORDONE
WOREOFF
WOREOUT
WORKDAY
WORKERS
WORKFOR
WORKING
WORKMAN
WORKMEN
WORKOFF
WORKOUT
WORKSIN
WORKSON
WORKSUP
WORKUPS
WORLDLY
WORMIER
WORMISH
WORNOFF
WORNOUT
WORRIED
WORRIER
WORRIES
WORSENS
WORSHIP
WORSTED
YORKIES
YORKIST

•O•R•••

BOARDED
BOARDER
BOARISH
BOERWAR
BOORISH
BORROWS
BOURBON
BOURREE
BOURSES
BOXROOM
COARSEN
COARSER
COERCED
COERCER
COERCES
COMRADE
CONRIED
CORRALS
CORRECT
CORRIDA
CORRODE
CORRUPT
COURAGE
COURANT
COURIER
COURSED
COURSER
COURSES
COURTED
COURTLY
COWRIES
DOORDIE
DOORMAN
DOORMAT
DOORMEN
DOORWAY
DOUREST
DOWRIES
FORREAL
FORRENT
FORREST
FOURIER
FOURTHS
FOURWAY
GOBROKE
GOURAMI
GOURDES
GOURMET
GOWRONG
HOARDED
HOARDER
HOARIER
HOARILY
HOARSEN
HOARSER
HORRIFY
HORRORS
HOTRODS
JOURDAN
JOURNAL
JOURNEY
JOURNOS
JOYRIDE
LOGROLL
LORRIES
LOURDES
LOWRISE
LOWROAD
MOORAGE
MOORHEN
MOORIER
MOORING
MOORISH
MORROWS
MOURNED
NOTRUMP
NOURISH
PODRIDA
POORBOX
POORBOY
POOREST
POORISH
POURERS
POURING
POUROUT
POURSIN
ROARERS
ROARING
ROBROYS
SOARERS
SOARING
SOIREES
SOPRANO
SORRELS
SORRIER
SORRILY
SORROWS
SOURCED
SOURCES
SOUREST
SOURING
SOURISH
TOORDER
TORRENS
TORRENT
TOURACO
TOURERS
TOURING
TOURISM
TOURIST
TOURNEY
TOWROPE
WORRIED
WORRIER
WORRIES

•O••R••

BODEREK
BOIARDO
BOLEROS
BOURREE
BOUTROS
BOWERED
COCHRAN
COHERED
COHERES
COHORTS
COLORED
COMFREY
COMOROS
CONBRIO
CONTRAS
CONTROL
CONURES
CORNROW
COTERIE
COVERED
COVERUP
COWARDS
COWERED
DOGTROT
DOLORES
DOTARDS
DOWERED
FORERAN
FORERUN
FORFREE
FORTRAN
FOXTROT
GOCARTS
GODFREY
GOFORIT
GOKARTS
GONERIL
GOVERNS
HOFBRAU
HOGARTH
HOMBRES
HOMERED
HOMERIC
HOMERUN
HONORED
HONOREE
HONORER
HONORIS
HOVERED
HOVERER
HOWARDS
JOFFREY
LOCARNO
LONGRUN
LOUVRED
LOUVRES
LOVERLY
LOWBRED
LOWBROW
LOWERED
MODERNS
MONARCH
MONGREL
MORDRED
MOTORED
NONIRON
NOSTRIL
NOSTRUM
NOTTRUE
NOVARRO
POLARIS
PORTRAY
POTOROO
POVERTY
POWERED
ROBARDS
ROBERTA
ROBERTO
ROBERTS
ROSARIO
ROSERED
ROSTRUM
SOBERED
SOBERER
SOBERLY
SOLARIA
SORORAL
TONEROW
TOREROS
TOWARDS
TOWERED
TOYSRUS
WOLFRAM
WOODROW
YOGURTS

•O•••R•

BOATERS
BOBBERS
BOILERS
BOKHARA
BOMBARD
BOMBERS
BONEDRY
BONFIRE
BONKERS
BOOMERS
BOPPERS
BORDERS
BOTHERS
BOVVERS
BOWLERS
BOWYERS
BOXCARS
COALERS
COAXERS
COCHERE
COCKERS
CODGERS
COFFERS
COGBURN
COHEIRS
COINERS
COLBERT
COLLARD
COLLARS
COLOURS
COMBERS
COMFORT
COMPARE
COMPERE
COMPORT
CONAKRY
CONCERN
CONCERT
CONCORD
CONCURS
CONDORS
CONFERS
CONFIRM
CONFORM
CONGERS
CONJURE
CONKERS
CONNERY
CONNORS
CONSORT
CONTORT
CONVERT
COOKERS
COOKERY
COOLERS
COOPERS
COPIERS
COPPERS
COPPERY
COPTERS
CORDERO
CORKERS
CORNERS
COSTARS
COTTERS
COUGARS
COUNTRY
COUTURE
COWBIRD
COWGIRL
COWHERD
DOCKERS
DOCTORS
DODDERS
DODGERS
DOGBERT
DOGCART
DOGEARS
DOLLARS
DOLOURS
DORMERS
DOSSERS
DOWNERS
DOWSERS
FODDERS
FOGGERS
FOGHORN
FOLDERS
FOLGERS
FOLKART
FOOLERY
FOOTERS
FOPPERY
FORBORE
FORCERS
FOREARM
FORGERS
FORGERY
FORKERS
FORLORN
FORSURE
FORWARD
FOSTERS
FOULARD
FOUNDRY
FOWLERS
FOXFIRE
GODDARD
GOLFERS
GOLFPRO
GOMPERS
GOOBERS
GOPHERS
GOUGERS
HOAXERS
HOLDERS
HOLLERS
HOLYARK
HOMBURG
HONIARA
HONKERS
HONOURS
HOOFERS
HOOTERS
HOOVERS
HOPPERS
HORRORS
HOSIERS
HOSIERY
HOTCARS
HOTWARS
HOTWIRE
HOWLERS
JOBBERS
JOBBERY
JOGGERS
JOINERS
JOINERY
JOSSERS
KOSHERS
LOADERS
LOAFERS
LOANERS
LOBBERS
LOCKERS
LODGERS
LOGGERS
LOITERS
LOLLARD
LOMBARD
LONGARM
LOOKERS
LOOPERS
LOOTERS
LOPPERS
LOTTERY
LOUVERS
LOWBORN
MOANERS
MOCKERS
MOCKERY
MOHAIRS
MOILERS
MOLDERS
MOLIERE
MOLTERS
MONGERS
MONTERO
MOPPERS
MORTARS
MOSHERS
MOTHERS
MOUSERS
NOCTURN
NODDERS
NONZERO
NORBERT
NOSHERS
NOTSURE
NOVARRO
NOWHERE
POLDERS
POLLERS
PONDERS
PONIARD
POPCORN
POPLARS
POPPERS
POPTART
PORKERS
PORTERS
POSEURS
POSTERN
POSTERS
POSTURE
POTHERB
POTHERS
POTTERS
POTTERY
POULTRY
POURERS
POUTERS
POWDERS
POWDERY
ROAMERS
ROARERS
ROBBERS
ROBBERY
ROCKERS
ROCKERY
RODGERS
ROGUERY
ROLLERS
ROMPERS
ROOFERS
ROOKERY
ROOMERS
ROOTERS
ROSTERS
ROTTERS
ROUSERS
ROUTERS
ROZZERS
SOAKERS
SOAPERS
SOARERS
SOBBERS
SOJOURN
SOLDERS
SOLVERS
SOONERS
SORCERY
SORTERS
SOTHERE
SOTHERN
TOGGERY
TOILERS
TONEARM
TONSURE
TOOTERS
TOPIARY
TOPPERS
TOSPARE
TOSSERS
TOTTERS
TOTTERY
TOURERS
TOUTERS
TOWCARS
TOWNERS
WONDERS
WOODARD
WOOFERS
WOOMERA
WORKERS
WOWSERS
YOGHURT
YONKERS
YOWLERS
ZONKERS

•O••••R

BOARDER
BOASTER
BOERWAR
BOGGIER
BOGGLER
BOLIVAR
BOLSTER
BONJOUR
BONNIER
BONSOIR
BOOMIER
BOOSLER
BOOSTER
BOSKIER
BOSSIER
BOTTLER
BOUDOIR
BOULDER
BOUNCER
BOUNDER
BOWDLER
COALCAR
COALTAR
COARSER
COASTER
COBBLER
COCHAIR
COCKIER
CODDLER
COERCER
COLDWAR
COLLIER
COLLYER
COMFIER
COMPEER
CONIFER
CONQUER
CONTOUR
CORKIER
CORNIER
CORSAIR
COSTNER
COULTER
COUNTER
COURIER
COURSER
DODGIER
DOGGIER
DOGSTAR
DONATOR
DONEFOR
DOODLER
DOPPLER
DOSSIER
DOTTIER
DOUBTER
DOWAGER
DOWDIER
DOWNIER
FOAMIER
FOGGIER
FOLKIER
FORAGER
FORBEAR
FOREVER
FORKIER
FORSTER
FOUNDER
FOURIER
GOAFTER
GOBBLER
GODLIER
GOESFOR
GOINFOR
GOODBAR
GOOFIER
GOONIER
GOOPIER
GOOSIER
GORSIER
GOTOVER
GOUNDER
GOUTIER
HOARDER
HOARIER
HOARSER
HOLSTER
HOLYWAR
HONORER
HOOSIER
HOPOVER
HORSIER
HOSTLER
HOTSPUR
HOVERER
HOWEVER
IONIZER
JOCULAR
JOINDER
JOLLIER
JOLTIER
JOSTLER
JOUSTER
JOWLIER
KOOKIER
LOAMIER
LOBBYER
LOBSTER
LOCATER
LOCATOR
LOESSER
LOFTIER
LOOKFOR
LOONIER
LOOPIER
LOPPIER
LOUNGER
LOUSIER
LOWGEAR
LOWLIER
MOBSTER
MODELER
MODULAR
MOISTER
MOLDIER
MONIKER
MONITOR
MONOMER
MONSTER
MOOCHER
MOODIER
MOONIER
MOORIER
MOSSIER
MOTHIER
MOULDER
MOUSIER
NOBBIER
NOBBLER
NODULAR
NOISIER
NONUSER
NORTHER
POACHER
PODGIER
POINTER
POITIER
POLECAR
POLITER
POLYMER
POPOVER
POPULAR
PORKIER
POSTWAR
POTSIER
POTTIER
POUNCER
POUNDER
POUTIER
ROASTER
ROCKIER
ROEDEER
ROILIER
ROISTER
ROLLBAR
ROOKIER
ROOMIER
ROOSTER
ROOTFOR
ROOTIER
ROTATOR
ROTIFER
ROUGHER
ROUNDER
ROWDIER
SOAPIER
SOBERER
SODDIER
SOGGIER
SOLDIER
SOLIDER
SOOTHER
SOOTIER
SOPPIER
SORRIER
SOUNDER
SOUPIER
TOASTER
TODDLER
TOFFLER
TOORDER
TOUGHER
VOTEFOR
VOUCHER
VOYAGER
WONKIER
WOODIER
WOOLIER
WOOSTER
WOOZIER
WORDIER
WORKFOR
WORMIER
WORRIER
YODELER
YOUNGER
ZOELLER

••OR•••

ABORTED
ADORERS
ADORING
ADORNED
ADORNER
AMOROUS
ANORAKS
BOORISH
CHORALE
CHORALS
CHORINE
CHORIZO
CHORTLE
CLORETS
DIORAMA
DOORDIE
DOORMAN
DOORMAT
DOORMEN
DOORWAY
FLORETS
FLORIDA
FLORINS
FLORIST
FLORUIT
GEORDIE
GEORGES
GEORGIA
GIORGIO
GLORIAM
GLORIAS
GLORIED
GLORIES
GLORIFY
INORBIT
IVORIES
MOORAGE
MOORHEN
MOORIER
MOORING
MOORISH
ODORFUL
ODOROUS
OLOROSO
ONORDER
POORBOX
POORBOY
POOREST
POORISH
PRORATA
PRORATE
QUORUMS
REORDER
RIORITA
SCORERS
SCORING
SCORNED
SCORNER
SCORPIO
SHORING
SHORTED
SHORTEN
SHORTER
SHORTLY
SHORTOF
SNORERS
SNORING
SNORKEL
SNORTED
SNORTER
SPORRAN
SPORTED
STORAGE
STORERS
STOREUP
STOREYS
STORIED
STORIES

STORING
STORMED
SWOREAT
SWOREBY
SWOREIN
THOREAU
THORIUM
TOORDER
UXORIAL
WHORLED

••O•R••

EGOTRIP
FLOORED
FLOURED
OROURKE
PROGRAM
PROPRIO
SCOURED
SCOURER
SCOURGE
SPORRAN
TSOURIS
TWOIRON
WOODROW

••O••R•

ADORERS
AVOWERS
BLOWDRY
BLOWERS
BOOMERS
BROKERS
CHOKERS
CLOSURE
CLOTURE
CLOVERS
COOKERS
COOKERY
COOLERS
COOPERS
CROWERS
DEODARS
DRONERS
DROVERS
EDOUARD
ELOPERS
EMOTERS
ESOTERY
EVOKERS
FLOWERS
FLOWERY
FOOLERY
FOOTERS
FROWARD
GAOLERS
GLOWERS
GOOBERS
GROCERS
GROCERY
GROWERS
HOOFERS
HOOTERS
HOOVERS
IRONERS
IRONORE
ISOBARS
ISOMERS
LEONARD
LEONORA
LEOPARD
LEOTARD
LOOKERS
LOOPERS
LOOTERS
PLOVERS
PLOWERS
PROBERS
PROCURE
PROSERS
PROVERB
PROVERS
QUOTERS
RIOTERS
ROOFERS
ROOKERY
ROOMERS
ROOTERS
SCORERS
SCOTERS
SHOFARS
SHOVERS
SHOWERS
SHOWERY
SMOKERS
SNORERS
SOONERS
STOKERS
STONERS
STORERS
SUOJURE
TOOTERS
TROCARS
TROWERS
TWOFERS
WOODARD
WOOFERS
WOOMERA

••O•••R

ADOPTER
ADORNER
ANOTHER
BLOCKER
BLONDER
BLOOMER
BLOOPER
BLOTTER
BLOWIER
BOOMIER
BOOSLER
BOOSTER
BROADER
BROILER
BROODER
BROTHER
BROWNER
BROWSER
CHOICER
CHOKIER
CHOOSER
CHOPPER
CHOWDER
CLOBBER
CLOCKER
CLOWDER
CROFTER
CROONER
CROPPER
CROSIER
CROSSER
CROWBAR
DIOPTER
DOODLER
DROLLER
DROOLER
DROPPER
FLOATER
FROWNER
GOODBAR
GOOFIER
GOONIER
GOOPIER
GOOSIER
GROANER
GRODIER
GROLIER
GROOMER
GROSSER
GROUPER
GROUSER
GROWLER
HOOSIER
KNOCKER
KOOKIER
LOOKFOR
LOONIER
LOOPIER
MOOCHER
MOODIER
MOONIER
MOORIER
OCONNOR
ONORDER
PHONIER
PIONEER
PLODDER
PLOTTER
PROCTOR
PRODDER
PROFFER
PROOFER
PROPTER
PROSIER
PROSPER
PROUDER
PROWLER
REOCCUR
REORDER
ROOKIER
ROOMIER
ROOSTER
ROOTFOR
ROOTIER
SCOFFER
SCOLDER
SCOOPER
SCOOTER
SCORNER
SCOURER
SCOUTER
SCOWLER
SHOCKER
SHOOTER
SHOPPER
SHORTER
SHOTFOR
SHOUTER
SHOWIER
SLOBBER
SLOTCAR
SMOKIER
SMOLDER
SMOTHER
SNOOKER
SNOOPER
SNORTER
SNOWIER
SOOTHER
SOOTIER
SPOILER
SPONGER
SPONSOR
SPOOFER
SPOONER
SPOTTER
SPOUTER
STOLLER
STONIER
STOPPER
STOUTER
TOORDER
TROOPER
TROTTER
TROUPER
TROUSER
TWOSTAR
WHOEVER
WHOPPER
WOODIER
WOOLIER
WOOSTER
WOOZIER
WRONGER

•••OR••

ABSORBS
ACCORDS
ADSORBS
AFFORDS
ALFORJA
ALSORAN
ALWORTH
ANDORRA
ANGORAS
ARBORED
ARMORED
ARMORER
ASSORTS
ASTORIA
ATWORST
AURORAE
AURORAL
AURORAS
BEGORRA
BYFORCE
BYWORDS
CALORIC
CALORIE
CAVORTS
CHLORAL
CIBORIA
COHORTS
COLORED
COMOROS
CYBORGS
DEBORAH
DECORUM
DEFORMS
DEHORNS
DEPORTS
DIVORCE
DOLORES
EFFORTS
EMPORIA
ENCORES
ENDORSE
ENFORCE
ENGORGE
ESCORTS
ESTORIL
EXHORTS
EXPORTS
EXTORTS
EXWORKS
FAVORED
FEDORAS
FEMORAL
FLOORED
FURORES
GOFORIT
HONORED
HONOREE
HONORER
HONORIS
HUMORED
IGNORED
IGNORER
IGNORES
IMMORAL
IMPORTS
IMSORRY
INDORSE
INFORCE
INFORMS
LABORED
LABORER
LAPORTE
LASORDA
LIVORNO
MAJORCA
MAJORED
MAYORAL
MEMOREX
MENORAH
MILORDS
MINORCA
MINORED
MOTORED
OFSORTS
OSBORNE
OXFORDS
POTOROO
PRIORTO
RAZORED
RECORDS
RECORKS
REFORMS
REMORAS
REMORSE
REPORTS
RESORBS
RESORTS
RETORTS
REWORDS
REWORKS
RUMORED
SAVORED
SCIORRA
SENORAS
SENORES
SORORAL
SUBORNS
TABORET
THEOREM
TUTORED
UNCORKS
UNHORSE
UPBORNE

•••O•R•

ADJOURN
ANDORRA
ARBOURS
ARDOURS
ARMOIRE
ARMOURS
ARMOURY
BEGORRA
BIGOTRY
COLOURS
DETOURS
DEVOURS
DOLOURS
FAVOURS
HELOTRY
HONOURS
HUMOURS
IMSORRY
INBOARD
INDOORS
LABOURS
MASONRY
MEMOIRE
MEMOIRS
ONBOARD
RETOURS
RIGOURS
RUMOURS
SAVOURS
SAVOURY
SCIORRA
SOJOURN
UPROARS
VALOURS
VAPOURS
VELOURS
VETOERS
VIGOURS

•••O••R

ALLOVER
ANDOVER
AREOLAR
ARMORER
BICOLOR
BIPOLAR
BLOOMER
BLOOPER
BROODER
CAJOLER
CAROLER
CHOOSER
CNTOWER
CROONER
DECODER
DEPOSER
DIDOVER
DIPOLAR
DROOLER
EMPOWER
ENCODER
FLYOVER
GETOVER
GOTOVER
GROOMER
HANOVER
HONORER
HOPOVER
IGNORER
INPOWER
INSOFAR
INTONER
INVOKER
LABORER
LAYOVER
LIEOVER
MALODOR
MANOWAR
METOOER
MONOMER
OCTOBER
OPPOSER
PALOMAR
POPOVER
PROOFER
PUTOVER
RANOVER
RECOLOR
RECOVER
REMOTER
REMOVER
RUNOVER
SAMOVAR
SCHOLAR
SCOOPER
SCOOTER
SHOOTER
SNOOKER
SNOOPER
SPOOFER
SPOONER
THROWER
TROOPER
UNCOVER
UPTOPAR
WAGONER
WIDOWER

••••OR•

AIRPORT
AMATORY
AMPHORA
ANCHORS
ANYMORE
APRIORI
ARDMORE
ARTFORM
ARTWORK
ASHFORD
AUTHORS
BAILORS
BETTORS
BIGHORN
CANTORS
CAPTORS
CARPORT
CENSORS
CHICORY
CLAMORS
COMFORT
COMPORT
CONCORD
CONDORS
CONFORM
CONNORS
CONSORT
CONTORT
CURSORS
CURSORY
DEBTORS
DEPLORE
DISCORD
DISPORT
DISTORT
DOCTORS
EDITORS
ELUSORY
ENAMORS
EXPLORE
EYESORE
FACTORS
FACTORY
FERVORS
FLAVORS
FLEXORS
FOGHORN
FORBORE
FORLORN
GIFFORD
GREGORY
HARBORS
HAYFORK
HECTORS
HICKORY
HISTORY
HORRORS
IMPLORE
INAWORD
INDOORS
INKHORN
INSHORT
INSTORE
IRONORE
ISADORA
JETPORT
JUNIORS
KEYWORD
LANFORD
LASTORY
LAWFORD
LECTORS
LEGHORN
LEGWORK
LEONORA
LESSORS
LICTORS
LIQUORS
LOWBORN
MAXBORN
MENTORS
METEORS
MIRRORS
MISWORD
MITFORD
MUMFORD
NETWORK
NEWBORN
NEWPORT
NEWYORK
OFASORT
ONSHORE
ORATORS
ORATORY
OUTWORE
OUTWORK
OUTWORN
OXYMORA
PALLORS
PANDORA
PARLORS
PASTORS
PERFORM
PILLORY
PLEXORS
POPCORN
PRESORT
PURPORT
RAPPORT
RAPTORS
RECTORS
RECTORY
REDFORD
RESTORE
RHETORS
RIPCORD
RIPTORN
SAILORS
SALVORS
SANFORD
SAPPORO
SAVIORS
SAXHORN
SEABORG
SEAPORT
SECTORS
SENIORS
SENSORS
SENSORY
STATORS
STUPORS
SUCCORS
SUITORS
SUPPORT
TAILORS
TENSORS
TERRORS
TINHORN
TINWORK
TREMORS
TRICORN
UNICORN
UNIFORM
UNSHORN
VECTORS
VENDORS
VICTORS
VICTORY
WALDORF
WARLORD
WAXWORK
WAYWORN
WILFORD

••••O•R

ACTFOUR
BALFOUR
BONJOUR
BONSOIR
BOUDOIR
CANDOUR
CLAMOUR
CONTOUR
ENAMOUR
FERVOUR
FLAVOUR
GLAMOUR
HARBOUR
LASSOER
MANHOUR
METOOER
OFFHOUR
OUTDOOR
PARLOUR
PAVIOUR
RANCOUR
SAVIOUR
SEYMOUR
SUCCOUR
TAMBOUR
TENFOUR

•••••OR

ABETTOR
ADAPTOR
ADVISOR
AERATOR
AIMSFOR
ALIENOR
ASKSFOR
AUDITOR
AVIATOR
BELABOR
BICOLOR
CALLFOR
CAMPHOR
CAREFOR
CLANGOR
CREATOR
CURATOR
DIVISOR
DONATOR
DONEFOR
ECUADOR
ELEANOR
ELECTOR
EMPEROR
ENACTOR
EQUATOR
ERECTOR
EXACTOR
FALLFOR
FEELFOR
FELLFOR
FELTFOR
GOESFOR
GOINFOR
GRANTOR
GUNSFOR
GYRATOR
HUMIDOR
INCISOR
INERROR
INFAVOR
JANITOR
KEILLOR
LAIDFOR
LANGUOR
LAYSFOR
LOCATOR
LOOKFOR
MADEFOR
MAKEFOR
MALODOR
MARKHOR
MATADOR
MIRADOR
MONITOR
NEGATOR
OCONNOR
OPTSFOR
OUTDOOR
PAIDFOR
PASSFOR
PAYSFOR
PICADOR
PINEFOR
PRAETOR
PRAYFOR
PROCTOR
PULLFOR
REACTOR
REALTOR
RECOLOR
ROOTFOR
ROTATOR
RUNSFOR
SCISSOR
SELLFOR
SENATOR
SENDFOR
SENTFOR
SHOTFOR
SPECTOR
SPONSOR
SQUALOR
STENTOR
TEMBLOR
TRACTOR
TRAITOR
VISITOR
VOTEFOR
WAITFOR
WARRIOR
WENTFOR
WHATFOR
WINDSOR
WORKFOR

OS•••••

OSBORNE
OSCEOLA
OSCINES
OSHKOSH
OSIERED
OSMOSED
OSMOSES
OSMOSIS
OSMOTIC
OSPREYS
OSSEOUS
OSSICLE
OSSIFIC
OSTEOID
OSTLERS
OSTRICH

O•S••••

OBSCENE
OBSCURE
OBSERVE
OFSORTS
ONSERVE
ONSHORE
ONSIDES
ONSIGHT
ONSTAGE
OSSEOUS
OSSICLE
OSSIFIC
OUSTERS
OUSTING
OYSTERS

O••S•••

ODYSSEY
OFASORT
OFFSETS
OFFSIDE
OFFSITE
OILSKIN
OLDSAWS
OLDSTER
OLESTRA
ONASSIS
ONESELF
ONESHOT
ONESTAR
ONESTEP
OPOSSUM
OPTSFOR
OPTSOUT
ORESTES
ORISONS
OURSELF
OUTSELL
OUTSETS
OUTSIDE
OUTSIZE
OUTSOLD
OUTSTEP
OVISACS

O•••S••

OBLASTS
OBOISTS
OBTUSER
ODYSSEY
ONASSIS
OPENSEA
OPENSUP
OPOSSUM
OPPOSED
OPPOSER
OPPOSES
ORBISON
OSMOSED
OSMOSES
OSMOSIS
OVERSAW
OVERSEA
OVERSEE

O••••S•

OAKMOSS
OARLESS
OBELISK
OBVERSE
OCULIST
ODDNESS
OFFBASE
OFFENSE
OGREISH
OILIEST
OILLESS
OKHOTSK
OLDNESS
OLDROSE
OLDWEST
OLEMISS
OLOROSO
OMIGOSH
ONENESS
OOZIEST
OPEROSE
OPPRESS
ORBLESS
OSHKOSH
OUTCAST
OUTLAST
OUTPOST
OVERUSE
OXIDASE
OXIDISE

O•••••S

OAKMOSS
OARLESS
OBJECTS
OBLASTS
OBLATES
OBLIGES
OBLONGS
OBOISTS
OBTAINS
OBTUNDS
OBVERTS
OBVIOUS
OCCULTS
OCEANUS
OCELLUS
OCELOTS
OCTANES
OCTANTS
OCTAVES
OCTAVOS
OCTOPUS
OCTROIS
ODDJOBS
ODDLOTS
ODDNESS
ODOROUS
OEDIPUS
OEUVRES
OFFENDS
OFFICES
OFFSETS
OFSORTS
OGDOADS
OGLALAS
OHIOANS
OILCANS
OILLESS
OILPANS
OILRIGS
OJIBWAS
OLDDAYS
OLDNESS
OLDNEWS
OLDPROS
OLDSAWS
OLEATES
OLEFINS
OLEMISS
OLYMPUS
OMELETS
OMINOUS
OMNIBUS
ONAGERS
ONASSIS
ONEIDAS
ONENESS
ONEROUS
ONSIDES
ONWARDS
OOCYTES
OOLITES
OOLITHS
OOMPAHS
OPAQUES
OPENERS
OPHITES
OPIATES
OPINERS
OPPOSES
OPPRESS
OPPUGNS
OPTIONS
ORACLES
ORANGES
ORATORS
ORBLESS
ORCHIDS
ORDAINS
ORDEALS
ORDINES
ORESTES
ORGATES
ORGEATS
ORIENTS
ORIGINS
ORIOLES
ORISONS
ORLEANS
ORMOLUS
ORPHANS
ORPHEUS
ORPINES
OSCINES
OSMOSES
OSMOSIS
OSPREYS
OSSEOUS
OSTLERS
OTTAWAS
OUSTERS
OUTACTS
OUTAGES
OUTBIDS
OUTDOES
OUTEATS
OUTFITS
OUTGOES
OUTGUNS
OUTHITS
OUTINGS
OUTLAWS
OUTLAYS
OUTLETS
OUTPUTS
OUTRUNS
OUTSETS
OUTWITS
OVISACS
OXCARTS
OXFORDS
OYSTERS
OZONOUS

•OS••••

BOSKETS
BOSKIER
BOSSIER
BOSSILY
BOSSING
BOSWELL
COSHING
COSIEST
COSIGNS
COSINES
COSSACK
COSSETS
COSTAIN
COSTARS
COSTING
COSTNER
COSTUME
DOSAGES
DOSIDOS
DOSSALS
DOSSERS
DOSSIER
FOSDICK
FOSSILS
FOSTERS
GOSHAWK
GOSLING
GOSLOWS
GOSPELS
GOSSETT
GOSSIPS
GOSSIPY
HOSANNA
HOSIERS
HOSIERY
HOSKINS
HOSPICE
HOSTAGE
HOSTELS
HOSTESS
HOSTILE
HOSTING
HOSTLER
JOSHING
JOSKINS

JOSSERS
JOSTLED
JOSTLER
JOSTLES
KOSHERS
KOSYGIN
LOSEOUT
LOSESIT
LOSTOUT
MOSAICS
MOSELLE
MOSEYED
MOSHERS
MOSHING
MOSHPIT
MOSLEMS
MOSQUES
MOSSIER
MOSSING
NOSEBAG
NOSEEUM
NOSEGAY
NOSEJOB
NOSEOUT
NOSHERS
NOSHING
NOSHOWS
NOSIEST
NOSTRIL
NOSTRUM
NOSWEAT
POSADAS
POSEURS
POSHEST
POSITED
POSSESS
POSSETS
POSSLQS
POSSUMS
POSTAGE
POSTBAG
POSTBOX
POSTERN
POSTERS
POSTING
POSTITS
POSTMAN
POSTMEN
POSTURE
POSTWAR
ROSALIE
ROSANNA
ROSANNE
ROSARIO
ROSEATE
ROSEBAY
ROSEBUD
ROSELLE
ROSEOIL
ROSERED
ROSETTA
ROSETTE
ROSIEST
ROSSINI
ROSSSEA
ROSTAND
ROSTERS
ROSTRUM
ROSWELL
SOSUEME
TOSCALE
TOSHIBA
TOSPARE
TOSSERS
TOSSING
TOSSOFF
TOSSOUT
TOSSUPS
TOSTADA

•O•S•••

BOASTED
BOASTER
BOBSLED
BOLSHOI
BOLSTER
BONSOIR
BOOSLER
BOOSTED
BOOSTER
BOOSTUP
BORSCHT
BOSSIER
BOSSILY
BOSSING
BOUSING
BOWSAWS
BOWSOUT
BOXSEAT
BOXSTEP
COASTAL
COASTED
COASTER
CONSENT
CONSIGN
CONSIST
CONSOLE
CONSORT
CONSULS
CONSULT
CONSUME
COPSOUT
CORSAGE
CORSAIR
CORSETS
CORSICA
COSSACK
COSSETS
COUSINS
COWSLIP
DOESKIN
DOGSHOW
DOGSITS
DOGSLED
DOGSTAR
DORSALS
DORSETT
DOSSALS
DOSSERS
DOSSIER
DOUSING
DOWSERS
DOWSING
FOBSOFF
FOCSLES
FOISTED
FORSAKE
FORSALE
FORSOOK
FORSTER
FORSURE
FORSYTH
FOSSILS
GODSEND
GODSONS
GOESAPE
GOESBAD
GOESFOR
GOESOFF
GOESOUT
GOOSIER
GOOSING
GORSIER
GOSSETT
GOSSIPS
GOSSIPY
HOISTED
HOLSTER
HOOSIER
HOPSOFF
HORSIER
HORSING
HOTSEAT
HOTSHOT
HOTSPOT
HOTSPUR
HOUSING
HOUSMAN
HOUSTON
JOISTED
JOSSERS
JOUSTED
JOUSTER
LOBSTER
LOESSER
LOESSES
LOGSOFF
LOGSOUT
LOOSELY
LOOSENS
LOOSEST
LOOSING
LOUSEUP
LOUSIER
LOUSILY
LOUSING
MOBSTER
MOISTEN
MOISTER
MOISTLY
MONSOON
MONSTER
MORSELS
MOSSIER
MOSSING
MOUSERS
MOUSIER
MOUSING
MOUSSED
MOUSSES
NODSOFF
NOISIER
NOISILY
NOISING
NOISOME
NONSELF
NONSKID
NONSLIP
NONSTOP
NOOSING
NOTSURE
POISING
POISONS
POISSON
POPSOFF
POPSOUT
PORSCHE
PORSENA
POSSESS
POSSETS
POSSLQS
POSSUMS
POTSDAM
POTSHOT
POTSIER
ROASTED
ROASTER
ROISTER
ROOSTED
ROOSTER
ROSSINI
ROSSSEA
ROUSERS
ROUSING
ROUSTED
TOASTED
TOASTER
TOCSINS
TOESHOE
TOLSTOI
TOLSTOY
TONSILS
TONSURE
TOPSAIL
TOPSIDE
TOPSOFF
TOPSOIL
TOPSOUT
TORSION
TOSSERS
TOSSING
TOSSOFF
TOSSOUT
TOSSUPS
TOUSLED
TOUSLES
TOYSHOP
TOYSRUS
WOOSTER
WORSENS
WORSHIP
WORSTED
WOWSERS
ZOYSIAS

•O••S••

AORISTS
BOLUSES
BONESET
BONESUP
BONUSES
BOOTSUP
BOURSES
BOXESIN
BOXESUP
COARSEN
COARSER
COCKSHY
COHOSTS
COILSUP
COLOSSI
COMESAT
COMESBY
COMESIN
COMESON
COMESTO
COMESUP
COOKSUP
COOLSIT
COOPSUP
COUNSEL
COURSED
COURSER
COURSES
DODGSON
DOLLSUP
DOTESON
FOCUSED
FOCUSES
FOLDSUP
FOOTSIE
FORESAW
FORESEE
FORESTS
FOULSUP
GOODSON
GOOFSUP
HOARSEN
HOARSER
HOLDSIN
HOLDSON
HOLDSTO
HOLDSUP
HOLESUP
HOLISTS
HOLYSEE
HONESTY
HOOFSIT
HOOKSUP
HOOTSAT
HORNSBY
HORNSIN
IODISED
IODISES
IONESCO
IONISED
IONISES
JOCASTA
JOHNSON
JOINSIN
JOINSUP
JONESES
LOCKSON
LOCKSUP
LOCUSTS
LOESSER
LOESSES
LOOKSAT
LOOKSEE
LOOKSIN
LOOKSON
LOOKSTO
LOOKSUP
LORISES
LOSESIT
LOTUSES
MODESTO
MODESTY
MODISTE
MOLESTS
MOONSET
MORESBY
MOUSSED
MOUSSES
MOVESIN
MOVESON
MOVESUP
NONUSER
POISSON
POKESAT
POURSIN
ROBESON
ROBUSTA
ROLLSIN
ROLLSON
ROLLSUP
ROPESIN
ROSSSEA
SOAKSUP
SOCKSIN
SOUPSUP
TONESUP
TOOLSUP
TOOTSIE
VOTESIN
WOEISME
WOOLSEY
WORKSIN
WORKSON
WORKSUP
ZOOMSIN

•O•••S•

BOARISH
BOGGISH
BOLDEST
BOMBAST
BONEASH
BONIEST
BOOKISH
BOORISH
BOWLESS
BOXIEST
COCHISE
COCKISH
CODFISH
COEXIST
COKIEST
COLDEST
COLDISH
COLOSSI
COLTISH
COMBUST
COMPASS
COMPOSE
COMPOST
CONCISE
CONFESS
CONFUSE
CONGEST
CONSIST
CONTEST
CONTUSE
COOLEST
COOLISH
COPYIST
CORNISH
COSIEST
COYNESS
COZIEST
DOGFISH
DOGGISH
DOGLESS
DOLLISH
DOLTISH
DONJOSE
DONNISH
DOPIEST
DOUREST
DOZIEST
FOGLESS
FOGYISH
FOGYISM
FOLKISH
FONDEST
FOOLISH
FOPPISH
FORMOSA
FORREST
FOULEST
FOXIEST
GOATISH
GODDESS
GODLESS
GOODISH
GOOIEST
GORIEST
GOTLOST
GOULASH
GOUTISH
HOGGISH
HOGWASH
HOKIEST
HOLIEST
HOMIEST
HORNISH
HORNIST
HOSTESS
HOTNESS
HOTTEST
JOBLESS
JOKIEST
JOYLESS
KOMATSU
LOGGISH
LOGIEST
LONGEST
LONGISH
LOOSEST
LOUDEST
LOUDISH
LOUTISH
LOWCOST
LOWNESS
LOWRISE
MOBBISH
MOLLUSC
MOLLUSK
MOMBASA
MONKISH
MOONISH
MOORISH
MOPIEST
MORTISE
NOBLEST
NOSIEST
NOURISH
OOZIEST
POKIEST
POLOIST
POOREST
POORISH
PORKISH
POSHEST
POSSESS
RODLESS
ROGUISH
ROMANSH
ROMPISH
ROPIEST
ROSIEST
SOANDSO
SODLESS
SOFTEST
SOFTISH
SOLOIST
SONLESS
SOONEST
SOPHISM
SOPHIST
SOTTISH
SOUREST
SOURISH
TOADISH
TOELESS
TONIEST
TONNISH
TOPMAST
TOPMOST
TORYISH
TORYISM
TOURISM
TOURIST
TOWNISH
TOYLESS
VOGUISH
VOWLESS
WOLFISH
WORMISH
YORKIST

•O••••S

AORISTS
AOUDADS
BOATELS
BOATERS
BOBBERS
BOBBIES
BOBBINS
BOBBLES
BOBCATS
BODEGAS
BODICES
BODKINS
BOFFINS
BOGGLES
BOILERS
BOLEROS
BOLIDES
BOLUSES
BOMBERS
BONBONS
BONGOES
BONITOS
BONKERS
BONMOTS
BONNETS
BONUSES
BOOBIES
BOOBOOS
BOODLES
BOOGIES
BOOHOOS
BOOKIES
BOOMERS
BOONIES
BOOTEES
BOOTIES
BOPPERS
BORATES
BORDERS
BORROWS
BORZOIS
BOSKETS
BOTCHES
BOTHERS
BOTTLES
BOTTOMS
BOULLES
BOUNCES
BOURSES
BOUTROS
BOVINES
BOVVERS
BOWFINS
BOWLERS
BOWLESS
BOWSAWS
BOWTIES
BOWWOWS
BOWYERS
BOXCARS
BOXFULS
BOXTOPS
COACHES
COALERS
COALGAS
COAXERS
COBBLES
COBWEBS
COCKERS
COCKLES
COCOONS
CODDLES
CODGERS
CODICES
COEDITS
COEPTIS
COERCES
COEVALS
COFFEES
COFFERS
COGNACS
COHEIRS
COHERES
COHORTS
COHOSTS
COINERS
COLLARS
COLLETS
COLLIES
COLLINS
COLLOPS
COLOBUS
COLONES
COLOURS
COLUMNS
COMBATS
COMBERS
COMEONS
COMFITS
COMINGS
COMMITS
COMMONS
COMOROS
COMPASS
COMPELS
CONCHES
CONCURS
CONDORS
CONFABS
CONFERS
CONFESS
CONGERS
CONJOBS
CONKERS
CONNORS
CONOIDS
CONSULS
CONTRAS
CONURES
CONVEYS
CONVOYS
COOKERS
COOKIES
COOLERS
COOPERS
COOTIES
COPIERS
COPIOUS
COPOUTS
COPPERS
COPTERS
COPULAS
CORBELS
CORDONS
CORKERS
CORNEAS
CORNERS
CORNETS
CORONAS
CORRALS
CORSETS
COSIGNS
COSINES
COSSETS
COSTARS
COTTERS
COTTONS
COUCHES
COUGARS
COULEES
COUPLES
COUPONS
COURSES
COUSINS
COWARDS
COWBOYS
COWPEAS
COWRIES
COYNESS
COYOTES
COZZENS
DOBBIES
DOBBINS
DOCENTS
DOCKERS
DOCKETS
DOCTORS
DODDERS
DODGERS
DOGDAYS
DOGEARS
DOGGIES
DOGLEGS
DOGLESS
DOGSITS
DOGTAGS
DOILIES
DOLLARS
DOLLIES
DOLLOPS
DOLMANS
DOLMENS
DOLORES
DOLOURS
DOMAINS
DOMINOS
DOMINUS
DONATES
DONGLES
DONIMUS
DONJONS
DONKEYS
DOODADS
DOODAHS
DOODLES
DOOZIES
DOPANTS
DORITOS
DORMERS
DORSALS
DOSAGES
DOSIDOS
DOSSALS
DOSSERS
DOTARDS
DOTTLES
DOUBLES
DOUGLAS
DOWNERS
DOWRIES
DOWSERS
EOLITHS
FOCSLES
FOCUSES
FODDERS
FOGBOWS
FOGGERS
FOGLESS
FOIBLES
FOLDERS
FOLDUPS
FOLGERS
FOLKIES
FOLLIES
FOLLOWS
FOMENTS
FONDLES
FONDUES
FOODIES
FOOTERS
FOOZLES
FORAGES
FORBIDS
FORCEPS
FORCERS
FORESTS
FORGERS
FORGETS
FORGOES
FORINTS
FORKERS
FORMALS
FORMATS
FORTIES
FORTIUS
FOSSILS
FOSTERS
FOULUPS
FOURTHS
FOWLERS
GOALIES
GOATEES
GOBBLES
GOBLETS
GOBLINS
GOCARTS
GODDESS
GODLESS
GODSONS
GODWITS
GOGGLES
GOKARTS
GOLFERS
GOMPERS
GOOBERS
GOODBYS
GOODIES
GOOFUPS
GOOGOLS
GOPHERS
GORGETS
GORGONS
GOSLOWS
GOSPELS
GOSSIPS
GOTCHAS
GOTHICS
GOUGERS
GOURDES
GOVERNS
HOAGIES
HOAXERS
HOBBIES
HOBBITS
HOBBLES
HOBNOBS
HOGGETS
HOGTIES
HOLDERS
HOLDUPS
HOLISTS
HOLLERS
HOLLIES
HOLLOWS
HOMBRES
HONCHOS
HONKERS
HONORIS
HONOURS
HOODOOS
HOOFERS
HOOHAHS
HOOKAHS
HOOKUPS
HOOPLAS
HOOPOES
HOOTERS
HOOVERS
HOPKINS
HOPPERS
HOPPLES
HORNETS
HORRORS
HOSIERS
HOSKINS
HOSTELS
HOSTESS
HOTBEDS
HOTCAPS
HOTCARS
HOTDOGS
HOTLIPS
HOTNESS
HOTPOTS
HOTRODS
HOTTIPS
HOTTUBS
HOTWARS
HOWARDS
HOWDAHS
HOWELLS
HOWLERS
HOYDENS
IODATES
IODIDES
IODISES
IODIZES
IOMOTHS
IONISES
IONIZES
JOBBERS
JOBHOPS
JOBLESS
JOBLOTS
JOCKEYS
JOGGERS
JOGGLES
JOINERS
JOLLIES
JONESES
JOSKINS
JOSSERS
JOSTLES
JOUNCES
JOURNOS
JOYLESS
KOBOLDS
KODIAKS
KOPECKS
KOREANS
KORUNAS
KOSHERS
KOWTOWS
LOACHES
LOADERS
LOAFERS
LOANERS
LOATHES
LOBBERS
LOBBIES
LOBULES
LOCALES
LOCATES
LOCKERS
LOCKETS
LOCKINS
LOCKUPS
LOCUSTS
LODGERS
LOESSES
LOGGERS
LOGGIAS
LOGGINS
LOGJAMS
LOITERS
LOLLIES
LOLLOPS
LONGIES
LONGUES
LOOBIES
LOOFAHS
LOOKERS
LOOKUPS
LOONEYS
LOONIES
LOOPERS
LOOSENS
LOOTERS
LOPPERS
LOQUATS
LORISES
LORRIES
LOTIONS
LOTUSES
LOUNGES
LOURDES
LOUVERS
LOUVRES
LOVEINS
LOWBOYS
LOWNESS
MOANERS
MOBCAPS
MOBILES
MOCKERS
MOCKUPS
MODELAS
MODELTS
MODERNS
MODULES
MOGGIES
MOHAIRS
MOHAWKS
MOILERS
MOLDERS
MOLESTS
MOLOCHS
MOLTERS
MOMENTS
MOMMIES
MONDAYS
MONGERS
MONGOLS
MONKEES
MONKEYS
MOOCHES
MOPPERS
MOPPETS
MOPTOPS
MORALES
MORANIS
MORGANS
MORMONS
MORROWS
MORSELS
MORTALS
MORTARS
MOSAICS
MOSHERS
MOSLEMS
MOSQUES
MOTHERS
MOTIONS
MOTIVES
MOTTLES
MOTTOES
MOUSERS
MOUSSES
MOUTONS
NOBBLES
NOBODYS
NOCUOUS
NODDERS
NODULES
NOETICS
NOGALES
NOGGINS
NOKOMIS
NONAGES
NONCOMS
NONPLUS
NOODLES
NORDICS
NORMALS
NORMANS
NOSHERS
NOSHOWS
NOTATES
NOTCHES
NOTICES
NOTIONS
NOUGATS
NOUGHTS
NOVENAS
NOVICES
NOXIOUS
NOZZLES
OOCYTES
OOLITES
OOLITHS
OOMPAHS
POACHES
POBOXES
POCKETS
POCONOS
PODIUMS
POETICS
POISONS
POLARIS
POLDERS
POLICES
POLLENS
POLLERS
POMADES

POMELOS
POMMELS
POMPOMS
POMPONS
POMPOUS
PONCHOS
PONDERS
PONGEES
PONGIDS
PONTIUS
POOCHES
POODLES
POPGUNS
POPLARS
POPLINS
POPOFFS
POPPERS
POPPETS
POPPIES
POPPINS
POPPLES
POPTOPS
POPULUS
PORCHES
PORGIES
PORKERS
PORTALS
PORTERS
PORTHOS
POSADAS
POSEURS
POSSESS
POSSETS
POSSLQS
POSSUMS
POSTERS
POSTITS
POTAGES
POTFULS
POTHERS
POTIONS
POTPIES
POTTERS
POTTLES
POUCHES
POUNCES
POURERS
POUTERS
POWDERS
POWWOWS
ROACHES
ROADIES
ROAMERS
ROARERS
ROBARDS
ROBBERS
ROBBINS
ROBERTS
ROBROYS
ROCHETS
ROCKERS
ROCKETS
ROCKIES
RODENTS
RODGERS
RODLESS
ROLAIDS
ROLLERS
ROLLINS
ROMNEYS
ROMPERS
ROMULUS
RONDELS
ROOFERS

ROOKIES
ROOMERS
ROOMIES
ROOTERS
ROSTERS
ROTATES
ROTTERS
ROUBLES
ROUSERS
ROUTERS
ROWDIES
ROZZERS
SOAKERS
SOAPERS
SOARERS
SOBBERS
SOCIALS
SOCKETS
SODDIES
SODLESS
SOFFITS
SOFTENS
SOFTIES
SOIREES
SOLACES
SOLDERS
SOLUTES
SOLVERS
SOMALIS
SONATAS
SONLESS
SONNETS
SOONERS
SOOTHES
SORBETS
SORITES
SORRELS
SORROWS
SORTERS
SORTIES
SOUKOUS
SOURCES
SOVIETS
SOWBUGS
TOADIES
TOCSINS
TODDIES
TODDLES
TOECAPS
TOELESS
TOETAPS
TOFFEES
TOGGLES
TOILERS
TOILETS
TOLLIES
TOLTECS
TOMBOYS
TOMCATS
TOMTITS
TOMTOMS
TONGANS
TONGUES
TONSILS
TOONIES
TOOTERS
TOOTLES
TOPAZES
TOPDOGS
TOPGUNS
TOPHATS
TOPPERS
TOPPLES
TORCHES

TOREROS
TOROIDS
TORQUES
TORRENS
TOSSERS
TOSSUPS
TOTTERS
TOUCANS
TOUCHES
TOUPEES
TOURERS
TOUSLES
TOUTERS
TOWARDS
TOWCARS
TOWHEES
TOWNERS
TOWNIES
TOYDOGS
TOYLESS
TOYSRUS
VOLLEYS
VOLUMES
VOODOOS
VOTECHS
VOUCHES
VOWLESS
VOYAGES
WOBBLES
WOMBATS
WONDERS
WONTONS
WOODIES
WOOFERS
WOOKIES
WOOLENS
WOOLIES
WORKERS
WORKUPS
WORRIES
WORSENS
WOWSERS
YOGURTS
YOMTOVS
YONKERS
YORKIES
YOUMANS
YOWLERS
ZODIACS
ZOMBIES
ZONKERS
ZOUAVES
ZOYSIAS

••OS•••

ANOSMIA
ANOSMIC
APOSTLE
BLOSSOM
BOOSLER
BOOSTED
BOOSTER
BOOSTUP
BROSNAN
CLOSEBY
CLOSEIN
CLOSELY
CLOSEST
CLOSETS
CLOSEUP
CLOSING
CLOSURE
CROSIER
CROSSED
CROSSER
CROSSES
CROSSLY
CROSSUP
DROSHKY
EROSELY
EROSION
EROSIVE
FLOSSED
FLOSSES
FROSTED
GHOSTED
GHOSTLY
GLOSSAE
GLOSSED
GLOSSES
GNOSTIC
GOOSIER
GOOSING
GROSSED
GROSSER
GROSSES
GROSSLY
HOOSIER
KNOSSOS
KTOSLIN
LOOSELY
LOOSENS
LOOSEST
LOOSING
NOOSING
OPOSSUM
PLOSION
PLOSIVE
PROSAIC
PROSERS
PROSHOP
PROSIER
PROSILY
PROSING
PROSODY
PROSPER
ROOSTED
ROOSTER
SKOSHES
SLOSHED
SLOSHES
TWOSOME
TWOSTAR
TWOSTEP
USOSHOW
WHOSWHO
WOOSTER

••O•S••

AROUSAL
AROUSED
AROUSES
BLOSSOM
BLOUSED
BLOUSES
BLOUSON
BLOWSIN
BLOWSIT
BLOWSUP
BOOTSUP
BRONSON
BROWSED
BROWSER
BROWSES
BUOYSUP
CHOMSKY
CHOOSER
CHOOSES
CLOGSUP
COOKSUP
COOLSIT
COOPSUP
CROESUS
CROPSUP
CROSSED
CROSSER
CROSSES
CROSSLY
CROSSUP
DROPSBY
DROPSIN
DROWSED
DROWSES
EGOISTS
FLOSSED
FLOSSES
FLOTSAM
FOOTSIE
FROWSTY
GLOSSAE
GLOSSED
GLOSSES
GOODSON
GOOFSUP
GROSSED
GROSSER
GROSSES
GROSSLY
GROUSED
GROUSER
GROUSES
GROWSON
GROWSUP
HOOFSIT
HOOKSUP
HOOTSAT
KNOSSOS
LOOKSAT
LOOKSEE
LOOKSIN
LOOKSON
LOOKSTO
LOOKSUP
MAOISTS
MOONSET
OBOISTS
OPOSSUM
PIOUSLY
PROPSUP
QUONSET
SCOUSES
SHOWSIN
SHOWSUP
SLOWSUP
SNOWSIN
SPONSOR
SPOUSAL
SPOUSES
STOPSIN
STOPSUP
SWOOSIE
TAOISTS
THOMSON
TOOLSUP
TOOTSIE
TROTSKY
TROUSER
VRONSKY
WOOLSEY
ZOOMSIN

••O••S•

ABOLISH
AGONISE
AGONIST
AMONGST
ANODISE
ATOMISE
BIOMASS
BOOKISH
BOORISH
CLOSEST
COOLEST
COOLISH
CRONISH
DIOCESE
DRONISH
EGOTISM
EGOTIST
FLORIST
FOOLISH
GEODESY
GNOMISH
GOODISH
GOOIEST
IDOLISE
LIONESS
LIONISE
LOOSEST
MOONISH
MOORISH
OLOROSO
POOREST
POORISH
PROCESS
PROFESS
PROFUSE
PROMISE
PROPOSE
PROTEST
PROTIST
PROVISO
PROVOST
PROWESS
SLOWEST
SOONEST
TROPISM
TWOBASE
VIOLIST

••O•••S

ABOUNDS
ADONAIS
ADORERS
AGOUTIS
AMOEBAS
AMOROUS
AMOUNTS
ANOINTS
ANOMIES
ANONYMS
ANORAKS
APOGEES
AROUSES
ATOMIES
ATONIES
AVOCETS
AVOWALS
AVOWERS
AZODYES
BAOBABS
BIOMASS
BIONICS
BLONDES
BLOUSES
BLOWERS
BLOWUPS
BMOVIES
BOOBIES
BOOBOOS
BOODLES
BOOGIES
BOOHOOS
BOOKIES
BOOMERS
BOONIES
BOOTEES
BOOTIES
BROGANS
BROGUES
BROKERS
BRONCOS
BRONZES
BROWSES
CHOICES
CHOKERS
CHOLLAS
CHOOSES
CHORALS
CLOACAS
CLOCHES
CLOQUES
CLORETS
CLOSETS
CLOTHES
CLOVERS
COOKERS
COOKIES
COOLERS
COOPERS
COOTIES
CROESUS
CRONIES
CROSSES
CROWERS
DEODARS
DOODADS
DOODAHS
DOODLES
DOOZIES
DRONERS
DROPINS
DROVERS
DROWSES
EBONIES
EGOISTS
ELOIGNS
ELOPERS
EMOTERS
EPONYMS
EPOPEES
EPOXIES
ETOILES
EVOKERS
EVOLVES
EXOTICS
FLORETS
FLORINS
FLOSSES
FLOWERS
FOODIES
FOOTERS
FOOZLES
FROLICS
GAOLERS
GEORGES
GLORIAS
GLORIES
GLOSSES
GLOTTIS
GLOWERS
GNOMONS
GOOBERS
GOODBYS
GOODIES
GOOFUPS
GOOGOLS
GROCERS
GROOVES
GROPIUS
GROSSES
GROTTOS
GROUNDS
GROUSES
GROVELS
GROWERS
GROWTHS
HOODOOS
HOOFERS
HOOHAHS
HOOKAHS
HOOKUPS
HOOPLAS
HOOPOES
HOOTERS
HOOVERS
IRONERS
IRONIES
IRONONS
ISOBARS
ISOGONS
ISOHELS
ISOMERS
ISOPODS
IVORIES
KNOSSOS
LEONIDS
LIONESS
LIONETS
LOOBIES
LOOFAHS
LOOKERS
LOOKUPS
LOONEYS
LOONIES
LOOPERS
LOOSENS
LOOTERS
MAOISTS
MOOCHES
NOODLES
OBOISTS
ODOROUS
OZONOUS
PEONIES
PEOPLES
PHOBIAS
PHOBICS
PHOEBES
PHOEBUS
PHONEYS
PHONICS
PHONIES
PHOTICS
PHOTOGS
PHOTONS
PIOLETS
PLOUGHS
PLOVERS
PLOWERS
POOCHES
POODLES
PROBERS
PROCESS
PROFESS
PROFITS
PROLOGS
PROMPTS
PROPELS
PROSERS
PROTEUS
PROTONS
PROVERS
PROWESS
PROXIES
QUOKKAS
QUORUMS
QUOTERS
REOPENS
RHOMBUS
RIOTERS
RIOTOUS
ROOFERS
ROOKIES
ROOMERS
ROOMIES
ROOTERS
SCONCES
SCORERS
SCOTERS
SCOUSES
SHOFARS
SHOGUNS
SHOOINS
SHOPPES
SHOVELS
SHOVERS
SHOWERS
SIOUANS
SKOSHES
SLOGANS
SLOSHES
SLOUGHS
SLOVAKS
SLOVENS
SLOWUPS
SMOKERS
SMOKIES
SMOOTHS
SNOCATS
SNOOZES
SNORERS
SOONERS
SOOTHES
SPONGES
SPOUSES
STOGIES
STOKERS
STOLONS
STONERS
STOOGES
STORERS
STOREYS
STORIES
TAOISTS
TOONIES
TOOTERS
TOOTLES
TROCARS
TROCHES
TROGONS
TROIKAS
TROILUS
TROJANS
TROPICS
TROUGHS
TROUPES
TROWELS
TROWERS
TSOURIS
TWOBITS
TWOFERS
USOPENS
UTOPIAS
VIOLETS
VIOLINS
VOODOOS
WOODIES
WOOFERS
WOOKIES
WOOLENS
WOOLIES

•••OS••

ACCOSTS
AEROSOL
ALTOSAX
ALYOSHA
APPOSED
APPOSES
ARIOSOS
ARIOSTO
BIGOSES
CHOOSER
CHOOSES
COHOSTS
COLOSSI
CREOSOL
DEPOSAL
DEPOSED
DEPOSER
DEPOSES
DEPOSIT
ESPOSAS
ESPOSOS
EXPOSED
EXPOSES
IMPOSED
IMPOSES
IMPOSTS
KENOSHA
LACOSTE
LATOSCA
MEIOSES
MEIOSIS
MIMOSAS
MITOSES
MITOSIS
NICOSIA
OPPOSED
OPPOSER
OPPOSES
OSMOSED
OSMOSES
OSMOSIS
REPOSED
REPOSES
RIPOSTE
SWOOSIE
ZEROSUM

•••O•S•

ALFONSO
ATWORST
CABOOSE
CAROUSE
COLOSSI
ENDORSE
ESPOUSE
GENOESE
HELOISE
HEROISM
INDORSE
INHOUSE
JUDOIST
OKHOTSK
PAPOOSE
POLOIST
REMORSE
SOLOIST
UNHORSE
UNLOOSE
VAMOOSE

•••O••S

ABSORBS
ACCORDS
ACCOSTS
ADJOINS
ADSORBS
AEROBES
AFFORDS
ALCOVES
ALMONDS
ANGORAS
ANYONES
APPOSES
APROPOS
ARBOURS
ARDOURS
AREOLAS
ARIOSOS
ARMOURS
ARROBAS
ARROYOS
ASSORTS
ATHOMES
AUROCHS
AURORAS
BABOONS
BARONGS
BECOMES
BEFOULS
BEHOLDS
BEHOVES
BELONGS
BEMOANS
BIGOSES
BUROAKS
BUYOUTS
BYGONES
BYROADS
BYWORDS
CAHOOTS
CAJOLES
CANOPUS
CAROLUS
CAVORTS
CHOOSES
CHROMES
COCOONS
COHORTS
COHOSTS
COLOBUS
COLONES
COLOURS
COMOROS
CONOIDS
COPOUTS
CORONAS
COYOTES
CREOLES
CUPOLAS
CUTOFFS
CUTOUTS
CYBORGS
DAKOTAS
DEBONES
DECOCTS
DECODES
DEFORMS
DEHORNS
DEMOTES
DENOTES
DEPONES
DEPORTS
DEPOSES
DESOTOS
DETOURS
DEVOTES
DEVOURS
DIMOUTS
DIPOLES
DISOWNS
DOLORES
DOLOURS
DUGONGS
DUGOUTS
EFFORTS
ENCODES
ENCORES
ENFOLDS
ENJOINS
ENROBES
ENROLLS
ENROOTS
ENSOULS
ESCORTS
ESPOSAS
ESPOSOS
EVZONES
EXHORTS
EXPORTS
EXPOSES
EXTORTS
EXWORKS
FANOUTS
FAVOURS
FEDORAS
FURORES
GALOOTS
GEMOTES
GENOMES
GIGOLOS
GROOVES
HEROICS
HONORIS
HONOURS
HUMOURS
IGNORES
IMPORTS
IMPOSES
IMPOSTS
INBOXES
INCOMES
INDOORS
INFOCUS
INFORMS
INJOKES
INROADS
INSOLES
INTONES
INVOKES
IOMOTHS
KETONES
KIMONOS
KOBOLDS
LABOURS
LAGOONS
LAKOTAS
LAYOFFS
LAYOUTS
LIMOGES
LITOTES
MAHOUTS
MAROONS
MEGOHMS
MEIOSES
MEIOSIS
MEMOIRS
MILORDS
MIMOSAS
MINOANS
MITOSES
MITOSIS
MOLOCHS
MRBONES
NICOLAS
NOBODYS
NOKOMIS
OBLONGS
OCTOPUS
OFSORTS
OGDOADS
OHIOANS
OPPOSES
ORIOLES
ORMOLUS
OSMOSES
OSMOSIS
OXFORDS
PAGODAS
PAROLES
PAYOFFS
PAYOLAS
PAYOUTS
PELOTAS
PHLOXES
PINOAKS
PINONES
POBOXES
POCONOS
POPOFFS
PTBOATS
PUTOUTS
RADOMES
RAGOUTS
REBOILS
REBOLTS
REBOOTS
REBOZOS
RECOATS
RECODES
RECOILS
RECORDS
RECORKS
RECOUPS
REDOAKS
REFOCUS
REFORMS
REHOOKS
REJOINS
RELOADS
RELOCKS
REMOLDS
REMORAS
REMOTES
REMOVES
RENOTES
REPOLLS
REPORTS
REPOSES
RESOLES
RESORBS
RESORTS
RETOOLS
RETORTS
RETOURS
REVOKES
REVOLTS
REWORDS
REWORKS
REZONES
RIGOURS
RIPOFFS
RUMOURS
RUNOFFS
RUNOUTS
SALOONS
SAMOANS
SARONGS
SAVOURS
SCHOOLS
SCROLLS
SECONDS
SENORAS
SENORES
SHOOINS
SHROUDS
SMOOTHS
SNOOZES
SPROUTS
STJOHNS
STLOUIS
STOOGES
STROBES
STROKES
STROLLS
SUBORNS
TANOAKS
THROATS
THRONES
THRONGS
TIPOFFS
TOROIDS
TRIODES
TRYOUTS
TYCOONS
UNBOLTS
UNBOXES
UNCOILS
UNCORKS
UNFOLDS
UNHOOKS
UNLOADS
UNLOCKS
UNROBES
UNROLLS
UNYOKES
UPHOLDS
UPLOADS
UPROARS
UPROOTS
VALOURS
VAPOURS
VELOURS
VETOERS
VIGOURS
ZYGOTES

••••OS•

ACEROSE
ADIPOSE
AMBROSE
ATALOSS
BEDPOST
BYANOSE

CABOOSE
COMPOSE
COMPOST
DEFROST
DISPOSE
DONJOSE
ENCLOSE
ENDMOST
ENGROSS
FORMOSA
GETLOST
GLUCOSE
GOTLOST
INCLOSE
LACTOSE
LOWCOST
MALTOSE
MELROSE
MIDMOST
OAKMOSS
OLDROSE
OLOROSO
OMIGOSH
OPEROSE
OSHKOSH
OUTPOST
PAPOOSE
PITBOSS
PROPOSE
PROVOST
PUGNOSE
PURPOSE
RECHOSE
RECROSS
REDROSE
SANJOSE
SEAMOSS
SUBROSA
SUCROSE
SUPPOSE
TEAROSE
TOPMOST
UNCLOSE
UNLOOSE
UPCLOSE
VAMOOSE
VERBOSE

••••O•S

ACTIONS
AMAZONS
AMNIONS
AMOROUS
ANALOGS
ANCHORS
ANTCOWS
ANXIOUS
AQUEOUS
ARCHONS
ARDUOUS
ATALOSS
AUTHORS
BABOONS
BADBOYS
BAILORS
BALBOAS
BALLOTS
BAMBOOS
BANJOES
BARHOPS
BARROWS
BARYONS
BATBOYS
BEACONS
BECKONS
BELLOWS
BESTOWS
BETTORS
BIGBOYS
BIGTOES
BIGTOPS
BILBOES
BILIOUS
BILLOWS
BINGOES
BISHOPS
BLAZONS
BONBONS
BONGOES
BONMOTS
BOOBOOS
BOOHOOS
BORROWS
BORZOIS
BOTTOMS
BOWWOWS
BOXTOPS
BRAVOES
BRETONS
BRITONS
BUCKOES
BULBOUS
BUNIONS
BURBOTS
BURGOOS
BURROWS
BUSBOYS
BUTTONS
CACHOUS
CAHOOTS
CALLOUS
CANNONS
CANTONS
CANTORS
CANYONS
CAPTORS
CARBONS
CARBOYS
CARGOES
CARHOPS
CARROTS
CARTONS
CATIONS
CENSORS
CHALONS
CHAMOIS
CHIGOES
CITRONS
CITROUS
CLAMORS
CLIPONS
COCOONS
COLLOPS
COMEONS
COMMONS
CONDORS
CONJOBS
CONNORS
CONVOYS
COPIOUS
CORDONS
COTTONS
COUPONS
COWBOYS
CRAYONS
CUCKOOS
CURIOUS
CURSORS
CUSTOMS
CYCLOPS
DAIMONS
DAMSONS
DAYBOYS
DAYJOBS
DEACONS
DEBTORS
DEPLOYS
DESPOTS
DEVIOUS
DIALOGS
DIATOMS
DINGOES
DOCTORS
DOLLOPS
DONJONS
DRAGONS
DRYROTS
DUBIOUS
DUTEOUS
EDITORS
EGGNOGS
EMPLOYS
ENAMORS
ENGROSS
ENROOTS
ENVIOUS
EPILOGS
ESCROWS
FACTORS
FALCONS
FALLOWS
FANIONS
FARROWS
FATHOMS
FATUOUS
FELLOWS
FERROUS
FERVORS
FIBROUS
FLACONS
FLAGONS
FLAVORS
FLEXORS
FLYBOYS
FLYRODS
FOGBOWS
FOLLOWS
FORGOES
FUNGOES
FURIOUS
FURROWS
GALLONS
GALLOPS
GALOOTS
GAMBOLS
GAMMONS
GARCONS
GASCONS
GASEOUS
GASLOGS
GECKOES
GESSOES
GIBBONS
GIBBOUS
GIDEONS
GNOMONS
GODSONS
GOOGOLS
GORGONS
GOSLOWS
GUIDONS
GUNDOGS
GUSTOES
HAGDONS
HALLOWS
HANSOMS
HARBORS
HARROWS
HAYMOWS
HECTORS
HEINOUS
HIDEOUS
HOBNOBS
HOLLOWS
HOODOOS
HOOPOES
HORRORS
HOTDOGS
HOTPOTS
HOTRODS
HULLOAS
HYDROUS
HYSSOPS
ICEFOGS
IGNEOUS
IMAGOES
IMPIOUS
INDOORS
INFLOWS
INSPOTS
IRONONS
ISOGONS
ISOPODS
JARGONS
JEALOUS
JERBOAS
JETSONS
JINGOES
JOBHOPS
JOBLOTS
JUNCOES
JUNIORS
KLAXONS
KMESONS
KOWTOWS
LAGOONS
LAPDOGS
LAPTOPS
LARDONS
LASSOES
LECTORS
LEGIONS
LEPTONS
LESSONS
LESSORS
LICTORS
LINGOES
LIQUORS
LOLLOPS
LOTIONS
LOWBOYS
MACRONS
MALLOWS
MANGOES
MANIOCS
MARMOTS
MAROONS
MARROWS
MASCOTS
MATRONS
MATZOHS
MAUROIS
MEADOWS
MELLOWS
MENTORS
MERLOTS
METEORS
METHODS
MICRONS
MINIONS
MINNOWS
MIRRORS
MISDOES
MONGOLS
MOPTOPS
MORMONS
MORROWS
MOTIONS
MOTTOES
MOUTONS
MUTTONS
NARROWS
NATIONS
NELSONS
NERVOUS
NEURONS
NEWTONS
NICHOLS
NIMRODS
NITROUS
NOCUOUS
NONCOMS
NOSHOWS
NOTIONS
NOXIOUS
OAKMOSS
OBVIOUS
OCELOTS
OCTROIS
ODDJOBS
ODDLOTS
ODOROUS
OMINOUS
ONEROUS
OPTIONS
ORATORS
ORISONS
OSSEOUS
OUTDOES
OUTGOES
OZONOUS
PAILOUS
PALLORS
PARDONS
PARLORS
PARLOUS
PARROTS
PARSONS
PASTORS
PATROLS
PATRONS
PEAPODS
PEGTOPS
PENNONS
PEQUOTS
PERIODS
PERSONS
PETROLS
PETROUS
PHENOLS
PHENOMS
PHOTOGS
PHOTONS
PIGEONS
PILLOWS
PINIONS
PISTOLS
PISTONS
PITBOSS
PITEOUS
PLEXORS
POISONS
POMPOMS
POMPONS
POMPOUS
POPTOPS
POTIONS
POWWOWS
PRISONS
PROLOGS
PROTONS
PULLONS
PYEDOGS
PYTHONS
QUAHOGS
QUINOAS
RAGMOPS
RAGTOPS
RAMRODS
RANSOMS
RAPTORS
RATIONS
RAUCOUS
REASONS
REBOOTS
RECKONS
RECROSS
RECTORS
REDDOGS
REDHOTS
REDTOPS
REGIONS
REHOOKS
REPLOWS
RESHOES
RETOOLS
RHEBOKS
RHETORS
RIBBONS
RIOTOUS
ROBROYS
RUINOUS
SAILORS
SALLOWS
SALMONS
SALOONS
SALVOES
SALVORS
SAVIORS
SAWLOGS
SCHMOES
SCHMOOS
SCHOOLS
SEACOWS
SEADOGS
SEAMOSS
SEASONS
SECTORS
SENIORS
SENSORS
SERIOUS
SERMONS
SEXTONS
SHADOWS
SHAKOES
SHALOMS
SIMMONS
SINUOUS
SIPHONS
SITCOMS
SKIBOBS
SKITOWS
SLALOMS
SLIPONS
SNAPONS
SORROWS
SOUKOUS
SPIGOTS
SPUMOUS
STATORS
STEROLS
STOLONS
STUPORS
SUCCORS
SUITORS
SUMMONS
SUNDOGS
SUNGODS
SYMBOLS
SYPHONS
TAILORS
TALLOWS
TARPONS
TATTOOS
TEAPOTS
TEAPOYS
TEDIOUS
TENDONS
TENSORS
TENUOUS
TERRORS
TEUTONS
TIERODS
TIGLONS
TIPTOES
TIPTOPS
TOMBOYS
TOMTOMS
TOPDOGS
TOYDOGS
TRAVOIS
TREMORS
TRICOTS
TRIGONS
TRIPODS
TRITONS
TROGONS
TURBOTS
TVSHOWS
TYCOONS
UNCLOGS
UNHOOKS
UNIPODS
UNISONS
UNKNOTS
UNSTOPS
UPROOTS
UPSHOTS
VACUOUS
VARIOUS
VECTORS
VENDORS
VICIOUS
VICTORS
VISCOUS
VISIONS
VOODOOS
WAGGONS
WALKONS
WALLOPS
WALLOWS
WARGODS
WEAPONS
WETMOPS
WILLOWS
WINDOWS
WINNOWS
WONTONS
YARROWS
YAUPONS
YELLOWS
YOMTOVS
ZEALOTS
ZEALOUS
ZIRCONS

•••••OS

ADAGIOS
ALBEDOS
ALBINOS
APROPOS
ARIOSOS
ARISTOS
ARROYOS
BAMBOOS
BARRIOS
BISTROS
BOLEROS
BONITOS
BOOBOOS
BOOHOOS
BOUTROS
BRONCOS
BURGOOS
CALICOS
CASINOS
CHEETOS
COMOROS
CRYPTOS
CUCKOOS
DESOTOS
DOMINOS
DORITOS
DOSIDOS
DYNAMOS
EMBRYOS
ENDUROS
ESCUDOS
ESKIMOS
ESPOSOS
FIASCOS
FRESCOS
GABBROS
GALAGOS
GAUCHOS
GAZEBOS
GHETTOS
GIGOLOS
GROTTOS
HAIRDOS
HONCHOS
HOODOOS
INDIGOS
JOURNOS
KIMONOS
KNOSSOS
LADINOS
LATINOS
LEANTOS
LEGATOS
LIBIDOS
MEDICOS
MERINOS
MIKADOS
NAVAHOS
NAVAJOS
NUNCIOS
OCTAVOS
OLDPROS
PAPAGOS
PICAROS
POCONOS
POMELOS
PONCHOS
PORTHOS
PRESTOS
PUEBLOS
QUANGOS
QUARTOS
RANCHOS
REBOZOS
REREDOS
RUBATOS
SCHMOOS
SENUFOS
SMALTOS
SPEEDOS
STEREOS
STINGOS
STUCCOS
STUDIOS
TATTOOS
TEREDOS
THERMOS
TOREROS
TUPELOS
TUXEDOS
VIRAGOS
VOODOOS
WEIRDOS
ZYDECOS

OT•••••

OTHELLO
OTRANTO
OTTAWAS
OTTOMAN

O•T••••

OATLIKE
OATMEAL
OBTAINS
OBTRUDE
OBTUNDS
OBTUSER
OCTAGON
OCTANES
OCTANTS
OCTAVES
OCTAVIA
OCTAVOS
OCTOBER
OCTOPOD
OCTOPUS
OCTROIS
OCTUPLE
OFTENER
ONTARIO
ONTHEGO
ONTHEQT
ONTOPOF
ONTRACK
ONTRIAL
OPTICAL
OPTIMAL
OPTIMUM
OPTIONS
OPTSFOR
OPTSOUT
ORTOLAN
OSTEOID
OSTLERS
OSTRICH
OTTAWAS
OTTOMAN
OUTACTS
OUTAGES
OUTBACK
OUTBIDS
OUTCAST
OUTCOME
OUTCROP
OUTDOES
OUTDONE
OUTDOOR
OUTDRAW
OUTDREW
OUTEATS
OUTFACE
OUTFITS
OUTFLOW
OUTGOES
OUTGREW
OUTGROW
OUTGUNS
OUTHITS
OUTINGS
OUTJUMP
OUTLAID
OUTLAND
OUTLAST
OUTLAWS
OUTLAYS
OUTLETS
OUTLINE
OUTLIVE
OUTLOOK
OUTLOUD
OUTOFIT
OUTPACE
OUTPLAY
OUTPOLL
OUTPOST
OUTPUTS
OUTRACE
OUTRAGE
OUTRANK
OUTRUNS
OUTSELL
OUTSETS
OUTSIDE
OUTSIZE
OUTSOLD
OUTSTEP
OUTTAKE
OUTTALK
OUTVOTE
OUTWARD
OUTWEAR
OUTWITS
OUTWORE
OUTWORK
OUTWORN

O••T•••

OAKTREE
OLDTIME
OMITTED
OMITTER
ONATEAR
ONETIME
ONSTAGE
ORATING
ORATION
ORATORS
ORATORY
OROTUND
OURTOWN
OUSTERS
OUSTING
OUTTAKE
OUTTALK
OVATION
OYSTERS

O•••T••

OBLATES
OKHOTSK
OLDSTER
OLEATES
OLESTRA
OMENTUM
OMITTED
OMITTER
ONESTAR
ONESTEP
ONLYTOO
OOCYTES
OOLITES
OOLITHS
OPENTOE
OPHITES
OPIATES
ORBITAL
ORBITED
ORBITER
ORESTES
ORGATES
ORNETTE
ORNITHO
OSMOTIC
OUGHTNT
OUTSTEP
OVERTAX
OVERTLY

O••••T•

OBJECTS
OBLASTS
OBOISTS
OBVERTS
OBVIATE
OCCULTS
OCELOTS
OCTANTS
ODDLOTS
OFFDUTY
OFFSETS
OFFSITE
OFSORTS
OMELETS
ONADATE
ONENOTE
OPACITY
OPERATE
ORGEATS
ORIENTE
ORIENTS
ORNETTE
OTRANTO
OUTACTS
OUTEATS
OUTFITS
OUTHITS
OUTLETS
OUTPUTS
OUTSETS
OUTVOTE
OUTWITS
OVERATE
OWINGTO
OXCARTS

O•••••T

OCCIPUT
OCULIST
ODDMENT
OFASORT
OFFBEAT
OILIEST
OLDWEST
ONADIET
ONESHOT
ONSIGHT
ONTHEQT
OOZIEST
OPENPIT
OPTSOUT
OPULENT
OUGHTNT
OUTCAST
OUTLAST
OUTOFIT
OUTPOST
OVERACT
OVEREAT
OXIDANT

•OT••••

BOTCHED
BOTCHES
BOTCHUP
BOTHERS
BOTHNIA
BOTTLED
BOTTLER
BOTTLES
BOTTOMS
COTERIE
COTTAGE
COTTERS
COTTONS
COTTONY
DOTARDS
DOTEDON
DOTESON
DOTLIKE
DOTTIER
DOTTILY
DOTTING
DOTTLES
GOTAWAY
GOTBACK
GOTCHAS
GOTDOWN
GOTEVEN
GOTHICS
GOTINTO
GOTITON
GOTLAND
GOTLOST
GOTOPOT
GOTOVER
GOTWELL
HOTBEDS
HOTCAKE
HOTCAPS
HOTCARS
HOTCOMB
HOTDOGS
HOTFOOT
HOTHEAD
HOTLINE
HOTLINK
HOTLIPS
HOTNESS
HOTPOTS
HOTRODS
HOTSEAT
HOTSHOT
HOTSPOT
HOTSPUR
HOTTEST
HOTTIPS
HOTTUBS
HOTWARS
HOTWIRE
JOTTING
LOTIONS
LOTTERY
LOTTING
LOTUSES
MOTHERS
MOTHIER
MOTIONS
MOTIVES
MOTORED
MOTTLED
MOTTLES
MOTTOES
NOTABIT
NOTABLE
NOTABLY
NOTATED
NOTATES
NOTCHED
NOTCHES
NOTEDLY
NOTEPAD
NOTHING
NOTICED
NOTICES
NOTIONS
NOTRUMP
NOTSURE
NOTTRUE
NOTWELL
POTABLE
POTAGES
POTENCY
POTFULS
POTHERB
POTHERS
POTHOLE
POTHOOK
POTIONS
POTLUCK
POTOMAC
POTOROO
POTPIES
POTSDAM
POTSHOT
POTSIER
POTTAGE
POTTERS
POTTERY
POTTIER
POTTING
POTTLES
ROTATED
ROTATES
ROTATOR
ROTIFER
ROTTERS
ROTTING
ROTUNDA
SOTHERE
SOTHERN
SOTTISH
TOTALED
TOTALLY
TOTEBAG
TOTEMIC
TOTIDEM
TOTTERS
TOTTERY
TOTTING
VOTECHS
VOTEDIN
VOTEFOR
VOTEOUT
VOTESIN

•O•T•••

BOATELS
BOATERS
BOATING
BOATMAN
BOATMEN
BOBTAIL
BOITANO
BOLTING
BOOTEES
BOOTHIA
BOOTIES
BOOTING
BOOTLEG
BOOTOUT
BOOTSUP
BOTTLED
BOTTLER
BOTTLES
BOTTOMS
BOUTROS
BOWTIES
BOXTOPS
COATING
COCTEAU
COLTISH
CONTACT
CONTAIN
CONTEMN
CONTEND
CONTENT
CONTEST
CONTEXT
CONTORT
CONTOUR
CONTRAS
CONTROL
CONTUSE
COOTIES
COPTERS
CORTEGE
COSTAIN
COSTARS
COSTING
COSTNER
COSTUME
COTTAGE
COTTERS
COTTONS
COTTONY
COUTURE
COWTOWN
DOCTORS
DOGTAGS
DOGTROT
DOLTISH
DOTTIER
DOTTILY
DOTTING
DOTTLES
FONTEYN
FONTINA

FOOTAGE
FOOTERS
FOOTING
FOOTMAN
FOOTMEN
FOOTPAD
FOOTSIE
FOOTWAY
FORTIES
FORTIFY
FORTIUS
FORTRAN
FORTUNA
FORTUNE
FOSTERS
FOXTAIL
FOXTROT
GOATEED
GOATEES
GOATISH
GODTHAB
GOUTIER
GOUTILY
GOUTISH
HOGTIED
HOGTIES
HOOTERS
HOOTING
HOOTOWL
HOOTSAT
HOPTOIT
HOSTAGE
HOSTELS
HOSTESS
HOSTILE
HOSTING
HOSTLER
HOTTEST
HOTTIPS
HOTTUBS
JOLTIER
JOLTING
JOSTLED
JOSTLER
JOSTLES
JOTTING
KONTIKI
KOWTOWS
LOATHED
LOATHES
LOFTIER
LOFTILY
LOFTING
LOITERS
LOOTERS
LOOTING
LOSTOUT
LOTTERY
LOTTING
LOUTISH
LOWTECH
LOWTIDE
MOLTERS
MOLTING
MONTAGE
MONTANA
MONTAND
MONTANE
MONTANI
MONTEGO
MONTERO
MONTHLY
MONTOYA
MOPTOPS
MORTALS
MORTARS
MORTIFY
MORTISE
MOTTLED
MOTTLES
MOTTOES
MOUTHED
MOUTONS
NOCTURN
NOETICS
NORTHER
NOSTRIL
NOSTRUM
NOTTRUE
POETICS
POITIER
PONTIAC
PONTIFF
PONTINE
PONTIUS
PONTOON
POPTART
POPTOPS
PORTAGE
PORTALS
PORTEND
PORTENT
PORTERS
PORTHOS
PORTICO
PORTION
PORTMAN
PORTRAY
POSTAGE
POSTBAG
POSTBOX
POSTERN
POSTERS
POSTING
POSTITS
POSTMAN
POSTMEN
POSTURE
POSTWAR
POTTAGE
POTTERS
POTTERY
POTTIER
POTTING
POTTLES
POUTERS
POUTFUL
POUTIER
POUTING
RONTGEN
ROOTERS
ROOTFOR
ROOTIER
ROOTING
ROOTLET
ROOTOUT
ROSTAND
ROSTERS
ROSTRUM
ROTTERS
ROTTING
ROUTERS
ROUTINE
ROUTING
SOFTENS
SOFTEST
SOFTIES
SOFTISH
SOFTTOP
SOOTHED
SOOTHER
SOOTHES
SOOTIER
SOOTILY
SORTERS
SORTIED
SORTIES
SORTING
SORTOUT
SOTTISH
SOUTANE
SOUTHEY
TOETAPS
TOLTECS
TOMTITS
TOMTOMS
TONTINE
TOOTERS
TOOTHED
TOOTING
TOOTLED
TOOTLES
TOOTSIE
TORTONI
TOSTADA
TOTTERS
TOTTERY
TOTTING
TOUTERS
TOUTING
VOLTAGE
VOLTAIC
WONTONS
YOMTOVS

•O••T••

BOASTED
BOASTER
BOLOTIE
BOLSTER
BONITOS
BOOSTED
BOOSTER
BOOSTUP
BORATES
BOXSTEP
COALTAR
COASTAL
COASTED
COASTER
COEPTIS
COLETTE
COOKTOP
COOPTED
CORETTA
COULTER
COUNTED
COUNTER
COUNTON
COUNTRY
COURTED
COURTLY
COVETED
COYOTES
DOGSTAR
DONATED
DONATES
DONATOR
DORITOS
DOROTHY
DOUBTED
DOUBTER
EOLITHS
FOISTED
FORSTER
FOULTIP
FOURTHS
GOAFTER
GODUTCH
GOLFTEE
GORETEX
GOTITON
HOISTED
HOLSTER
HORATIO
HOUSTON
IODATES
IOMOTHS
JOINTED
JOINTLY
JOISTED
JOUSTED
JOUSTER
KOMATSU
LOBSTER
LOCATED
LOCATER
LOCATES
LOCATOR
LONGTON
LORETTA
MOBSTER
MOISTEN
MOISTER
MOISTLY
MOLOTOV
MONITOR
MONSTER
MOULTED
MOUNTED
MOUNTIE
NONSTOP
NOTATED
NOTATES
OOCYTES
OOLITES
OOLITHS
POINTED
POINTER
POINTTO
POLITER
POLITIC
POLLTAX
POSITED
POULTRY
ROASTED
ROASTER
ROBOTIC
ROISTER
ROLLTOP
ROOFTOP
ROOSTED
ROOSTER
ROPETOW
ROSETTA
ROSETTE
ROTATED
ROTATES
ROTATOR
ROUSTED
SOFTTOP
SOLUTES
SOMATIC
SONATAS
SORITES
TOASTED
TOASTER
TOLSTOI
TOLSTOY
TOOKTEN
WOOSTER
WORSTED

•O•••T•

AORISTS
BOBCATS
BONMOTS
BONNETS
BOSKETS
BOXKITE
BOYCOTT
COEDITS
COGNATE
COHORTS
COHOSTS
COLETTE
COLGATE
COLLATE
COLLETS
COMBATS
COMESTO
COMFITS
COMMITS
COMMUTE
COMPETE
COMPOTE
COMPUTE
CONDITA
CONFUTE
CONMOTO
CONNOTE
COPOUTS
CORBETT
CORDATE
CORDITE
CORETTA
CORINTH
CORNETS
CORSETS
COSSETS
DOCENTS
DOCKETS
DOGMATA
DOGSITS
DOPANTS
DORSETT
DOUGHTY
DOZENTH
FOLIATE
FOLLETT
FOMENTS
FORESTS
FORGETS
FORINTS
FORMATS
FORSYTH
GOBLETS
GOCARTS
GODWITS
GOKARTS
GOLIATH
GORGETS
GOSSETT
GOTINTO
HOBBITS
HOGARTH
HOGGETS
HOLDSTO
HOLISTS
HONESTY
HORNETS
HOTPOTS
JOBLOTS
JOCASTA
JOLLITY
LOCKETS
LOCUSTS
LOOKSTO
LOQUATS
LORETTA
LOYALTY
MODELTS
MODESTO
MODESTY
MODISTE
MOLESTS
MOMENTS
MOPPETS
NOUGATS
NOUGHTS
NOVELTY
POCKETS
POINTTO
POLENTA
POLLUTE
POPPETS
POSSETS
POSTITS
POVERTY
ROBERTA
ROBERTO
ROBERTS
ROBUSTA
ROCHETS
ROCKETS
RODENTS
ROSEATE
ROSETTA
ROSETTE
ROYALTY
SOCIETY
SOCKETS
SOFFITS
SONNETS
SOPWITH
SORBATE
SORBETS
SOVIETS
TOCCATA
TOILETS
TOMCATS
TOMTITS
TOPHATS
TORONTO
TOWPATH
WOMBATS
YOGURTS

•O••••T

BODYFAT
BOLDEST
BOMBAST
BONESET
BONIEST
BOOKLET
BOOTOUT
BOREOUT
BORSCHT
BOUQUET
BOWKNOT
BOWSOUT
BOXIEST
BOXSEAT
BOYCOTT
COCKPIT
COCONUT
COEXIST
COHABIT
COKIEST
COLBERT
COLDCUT
COLDEST
COLLECT
COMBUST
COMEOUT
COMESAT
COMFORT
COMMENT
COMPACT
COMPORT
COMPOST
CONCEIT
CONCEPT
CONCERT
CONCOCT
CONDUCT
CONDUIT
CONGEST
CONKOUT
CONNECT
CONSENT
CONSIST
CONSORT
CONSULT
CONTACT
CONTENT
CONTEST
CONTEXT
CONTORT
CONVENT
CONVERT
CONVICT
COOKOUT
COOLANT
COOLEST
COOLSIT
COONCAT
COPILOT
COPSOUT
COPYCAT
COPYIST
CORBETT
CORONET
CORRECT
CORRUPT
COSIEST
COULDNT
COUPLET
COURANT
COZIEST
DOGBERT
DOGCART
DOGTROT
DOLEOUT
DOORMAT
DOPEOUT
DOPIEST
DORMANT
DORSETT
DOUBLET
DOUREST
DOVECOT
DOWNPAT
DOZIEST
FOLDOUT
FOLKART
FOLLETT
FONDANT
FONDEST
FORFEIT
FORRENT
FORREST
FORWENT
FOULEST
FOULOUT
FOXIEST
FOXTROT
GOABOUT
GOESOUT
GOFORIT
GOINGAT
GOOIEST
GORIEST
GOSSETT
GOTLOST
GOTOPOT
GOURMET
HOKIEST
HOLDOUT
HOLEOUT
HOLIEST
HOMIEST
HOOFSIT
HOOTSAT
HOPTOIT
HORNIST
HOTFOOT
HOTSEAT
HOTSHOT
HOTSPOT
HOTTEST
HOWBEIT
JOBHUNT
JOKIEST
JOLLIET
LOCKNUT
LOCKOUT
LOGIEST
LOGSOUT
LONGEST
LOOKOUT
LOOKSAT
LOOSEST
LOSEOUT
LOSESIT
LOSTOUT
LOUDEST
LOWCOST
MONOCOT
MOONLIT
MOONSET
MOPIEST
MORDANT
MORDENT
MOSHPIT
MOVEOUT
NOBLEST
NODOUBT
NOFAULT
NORBERT
NOSEOUT
NOSIEST
NOSWEAT
NOTABIT
OOZIEST
POKEDAT
POKESAT
POKIEST
POLECAT
POLOIST
POOPOUT
POOREST
POPSOUT
POPTART
PORTENT
POSHEST
POTSHOT
POUROUT
RODEOUT
ROLLOUT
ROOTLET
ROOTOUT
ROPIEST
ROSIEST
ROUGHIT
ROWBOAT
SOFTEST
SOLDOUT
SOLICIT
SOLOIST
SOLVENT
SOONEST
SOPHIST
SORTOUT
SOUREST
TONIEST
TONIGHT
TOOKOUT
TOPCOAT
TOPKNOT
TOPMAST
TOPMOST
TOPSOUT
TOREOUT
TORMENT
TORNOUT
TORRENT
TOSSOUT
TOURIST
VOTEOUT
WOODCUT
WOODLOT
WOREOUT
WORKOUT
WORNOUT
WOULDNT
YOGHURT
YORKIST
ZONKOUT

••OT•••

ANOTHER
APOTHEM
BLOTCHY
BLOTOUT
BLOTTED
BLOTTER
BOOTEES
BOOTHIA
BOOTIES
BOOTING
BOOTLEG
BOOTOUT
BOOTSUP
BROTHER
CLOTHED
CLOTHES
CLOTTED
CLOTURE
COOTIES
DNOTICE
EGOTISM
EGOTIST
EGOTRIP
EMOTERS
EMOTING
EMOTION
EMOTIVE
EROTICA
ESOTERY
EXOTICA
EXOTICS
FLOTSAM
FOOTAGE
FOOTERS
FOOTING
FOOTMAN
FOOTMEN
FOOTPAD
FOOTSIE
FOOTWAY
FROTHED
GLOTTAL
GLOTTIS
GROTTOS
HOOTERS
HOOTING
HOOTOWL
HOOTSAT
ISOTOPE
KNOTTED
LAOTIAN
LEOTARD
LOOTERS
LOOTING
OROTUND
PHOTICS
PHOTOED
PHOTOGS
PHOTONS
PHOTOOP
PLOTFUL
PLOTTED
PLOTTER
PROTEAN
PROTECT
PROTEGE
PROTEIN
PROTEST
PROTEUS
PROTIST
PROTONS
QUOTERS
QUOTING
RIOTACT
RIOTERS
RIOTING
RIOTOUS
ROOTERS
ROOTFOR
ROOTIER
ROOTING
ROOTLET
ROOTOUT
SAOTOME
SCOTERS
SCOTTIE
SHOTFOR
SHOTGUN
SHOTOUT
SHOTPUT
SLOTCAR
SLOTTED
SMOTHER
SOOTHED
SOOTHER
SOOTHES
SOOTIER
SOOTILY
SPOTLIT
SPOTTED
SPOTTER
TOOTERS
TOOTHED
TOOTING
TOOTLED
TOOTLES
TOOTSIE
TROTHED
TROTOUT
TROTSKY
TROTTED
TROTTER
TWOTIME
TWOTONE
WROTEIN
WROTETO
WROTEUP

••O•T••

ABORTED
ADOPTED
ADOPTEE
ADOPTER
AGOUTIS
APOSTLE
BLOATED
BLOTTED
BLOTTER
BOOSTED
BOOSTER
BOOSTUP
CHOCTAW
CHORTLE
CLOTTED
CLOUTED
COOKTOP
COOPTED
CROATIA
CROFTER
CROUTON
DIOPTER
FLOATED
FLOATER
FLOUTED
FRONTAL
FRONTED
FRONTON
FROSTED
GHOSTED
GHOSTLY
GLOATED
GLOTTAL
GLOTTIS
GNOSTIC
GROTTOS
GROUTED
GROWTHS
KNOTTED
KNOUTED
PLOTTED
PLOTTER
PROCTOR
PROPTER
ROOFTOP
ROOSTED
ROOSTER
SCOOTED
SCOOTER
SCOTTIE
SCOUTED
SCOUTER
SHOOTAT
SHOOTER
SHOOTUP
SHORTED
SHORTEN
SHORTER
SHORTLY
SHORTOF
SHOUTED
SHOUTER
SLOTTED
SMOOTHS
SMOOTHY
SNOOTED
SNORTED
SNORTER
SPORTED
SPOTTED
SPOTTER
SPOUTED
SPOUTER
STOUTEN
STOUTER
STOUTLY
TOOKTEN
TROTTED
TROTTER
TWOSTAR
TWOSTEP
WOOSTER

••O••T•

ACOLYTE
ACONITE
AMOUNTS
ANOINTS
AVOCETS
AXOLOTL
BROMATE
CLORETS
CLOSETS
EBONITE
EGOISTS
FLOCKTO
FLORETS
FROWSTY
ISOLATE
LIONETS
LOOKSTO
MAOISTS
NEOLITH
NEONATE
OBOISTS
PIOLETS
PROBATE
PROBITY
PROFITS
PROMOTE
PROMPTS
PRORATA
PRORATE
RIORITA
SNOCATS
STOMATA
TAOISTS
TWOBITS
VIOLATE
VIOLETS
WROTETO

••O•••T

ABOUGHT
AGONIST
AMONGST
BLOTOUT
BLOWOUT
BLOWSIT
BOOKLET
BOOTOUT
BROUGHT
BUOYANT
CLOSEST
COOKOUT
COOLANT
COOLEST
COOLSIT
COONCAT
CROCHET
CROQUET
DOORMAT
DROPLET
DROPOUT
DROUGHT
EGOTIST
ERODENT
FLORIST
FLORUIT
FLOWNAT
FROWNAT
GOOIEST
GROMMET
HOOFSIT
HOOTSAT
INORBIT
IRONOUT
LOOKOUT
LOOKSAT
LOOSEST
MOONLIT
MOONSET
POOPOUT
POOREST
PRODUCT
PROJECT
PROPHET
PROPJET
PROTECT
PROTEST
PROTIST
PROVOST
QUONSET
RIOTACT
ROOTLET
ROOTOUT
SHOOTAT
SHOTOUT
SHOTPUT
SHOWOUT
SLOWEST
SNOWCAT
SOONEST
SPOTLIT
SWOREAT
THOUGHT
TOOKOUT
TROTOUT
VIOLENT
VIOLIST
WOODCUT
WOODLOT
WROUGHT

•••OT••

ABBOTCY
BIGOTED
BIGOTRY
BOLOTIE
CAROTID
CHAOTIC
COYOTES
CULOTTE
DAKOTAN
DAKOTAS
DEMOTED
DEMOTES
DENOTED
DENOTES
DESOTOS
DEVOTED
DEVOTEE
DEVOTES
DOROTHY
FAGOTED
GAVOTTE
GEMOTES
HELOTRY
IDIOTIC
IOMOTHS
KILOTON
LAKOTAS
LAMOTTA
LESOTHO
LITOTES
MEIOTIC
MENOTTI
MITOTIC
MOLOTOV
OKHOTSK
OSMOTIC
PELOTAS
PILOTED
PIVOTAL
PIVOTED
REMOTER
REMOTES
RENOTED
RENOTES
RICOTTA
RIDOTTO
RISOTTO
ROBOTIC
SCOOTED
SCOOTER
SHOOTAT
SHOOTER
SHOOTUP
SMOOTHS
SMOOTHY
SNOOTED
SPLOTCH
TIMOTHY
ZAPOTEC
ZYGOTES

•••O•T•

ACCOSTS
ADDONTO
ALWORTH
ARIOSTO
ASSORTS
BUYOUTS
CAHOOTS
CAVORTS
COHORTS
COHOSTS
COPOUTS
CULOTTE
CUTOUTS
DECOCTS
DEPORTS
DIMOUTS
DUGOUTS
EFFORTS
ENROOTS

ENROUTE
ESCORTS
EXHORTS
EXPORTS
EXTORTS
FANOUTS
GALOOTS
GAVOTTE
IMPORTS
IMPOSTS
LACOSTE
LAMOTTA
LAPORTE
LAYOUTS
MAHOUTS
MENOTTI
MINOLTA
OFSORTS
PAYOUTS
PRIORTO
PTBOATS
PUTOUTS
RAGOUTS
REBOLTS
REBOOTS
RECOATS
REPORTS
REROUTE
RESORTS
RETORTS
REVOLTS
RICOTTA
RIDOTTO
RIPOSTE
RISOTTO
RUNOUTS
SPROUTS
THROATS
THROATY
TORONTO
TRYOUTS
UNBOLTS
UNCOUTH
UPROOTS

•••O••T

ABSOLUT
ACCOUNT
ACROBAT
AEROBAT
APPOINT
ASTOLAT
ATWORST
AUTOMAT
BARONET
BAYONET
COCONUT
CORONET
DEPOSIT
GOFORIT
GOTOPOT
INDOUBT
JACONET
JUDOIST
MONOCOT
NODOUBT
OUTOFIT
POLOIST
RECOUNT
REDOUBT
REMOUNT
SHOOTAT
SOLOIST
TABORET

••••OT•

AXOLOTL
BALLOTS
BETROTH
BONMOTS
BOYCOTT
BURBOTS
CAHOOTS
CARROTS
COMPOTE
CONMOTO
CONNOTE
DESPOTS
DRYROTS
ELLIOTT
ENROOTS
GALOOTS
HOTPOTS
INSPOTS
JOBLOTS
KEYNOTE
MAMMOTH
MARMOTS
MASCOTS
MERLOTS
OCELOTS
ODDLOTS
ONENOTE
OUTVOTE
PARROTS
PEQUOTS
PROMOTE
QUIXOTE
REBOOTS
REDHOTS
REWROTE
SPIGOTS
TEAPOTS
TRICOTS
TURBOTS
UNKNOTS
UNQUOTE
UPROOTS
UPSHOTS
WALCOTT
ZEALOTS

••••O•T

ACEDOUT
ACESOUT
ACTSOUT
AFFRONT
AIRBOAT
AIRPORT
AIRSOUT
ASKSOUT
BACKOUT
BAILOUT
BAWLOUT
BEAROUT
BEATOUT
BEDPOST
BELMONT
BERTOLT
BIGFOOT
BLEWOUT
BLOTOUT
BLOWOUT
BOOTOUT
BOREOUT
BOWSOUT
BOYCOTT
BUGSOUT
BUMSOUT
BURNOUT
BUSTOUT
BUTTOUT
BUYSOUT
CALLOUT
CAMEOUT
CAMPOUT
CARCOAT
CARPORT
CASHOUT
CASTOUT
CATBOAT
CHEROOT
CHEWOUT
COMEOUT
COMFORT
COMPORT
COMPOST
CONCOCT
CONKOUT
CONSORT
CONTORT
COOKOUT
COPSOUT
CUTSOUT
DASBOOT
DEALOUT
DECKOUT
DEFROST
DETROIT
DIEDOUT
DIESOUT
DIGSOUT
DINMONT
DISHOUT
DISPORT
DISTORT
DOLEOUT
DOPEOUT
DRAGOUT
DRAWOUT
DREWOUT
DROPOUT
EASEOUT
EATSOUT
EDGEOUT
EDITOUT
EKEDOUT
EKESOUT
ELLIOTT
ENDMOST
EVENOUT
EXPLOIT
EYEBOLT
FADEOUT
FALLOUT
FANSOUT
FARMOUT
FEELOUT
FELLOUT
FELTOUT
FILLOUT
FINDOUT
FISHOUT
FLATOUT
FLIPOUT
FOLDOUT
FOULOUT
FREMONT
GAVEOUT
GETLOST
GETSOUT
GIVEOUT
GOABOUT
GOESOUT
GOTLOST
GUNBOAT
HANDOUT
HANGOUT
HAYLOFT
HEADOUT
HEAROUT
HELDOUT
HELPOUT
HIDEOUT
HIPBOOT
HITSOUT
HOLDOUT
HOLEOUT
HOPTOIT
HOTFOOT
HUNGOUT
ICEBOAT
ICEDOUT
ICESOUT
INFRONT
INSHORT
INTROIT
IRISOUT
IRONOUT
JETBOAT
JETPORT
KEPTOUT
KICKOUT
LABCOAT
LAIDOUT
LAYSOUT
LEADOUT
LEFTOUT
LETSOUT
LIVEOUT
LOCKOUT
LOGSOUT
LOOKOUT
LOSEOUT
LOSTOUT
LOWCOST
LUCKOUT
MADEOUT
MAILOUT
MAKEOUT
METEOUT
MIDMOST
MISSOUT
MOVEOUT
NEWPORT
NOSEOUT
OFASORT
OPTSOUT
OUTPOST
PAIDOUT
PANSOUT
PARTOUT
PASSOUT
PAYSOUT
PEACOAT
PEEKOUT
PEEROUT
PICKOUT
PIGSOUT
PLANOUT
PLAYOUT
POOPOUT
POPSOUT
POUROUT
PRESORT
PROVOST
PULLOUT
PURPORT
PUTSOUT
RAINOUT
RANGOUT
RAPPORT
READOUT
REDCOAT
RESHOOT
RIDEOUT
RINGOUT
RIPSOUT
RODEOUT
ROLLOUT
ROOTOUT
ROWBOAT
RUBSOUT
RULEOUT
RUNGOUT
RUNSOUT
SACKOUT
SANGOUT
SEAPORT
SEEKOUT
SEENOUT
SEESOUT
SEETOIT
SELLOUT
SENDOUT
SENTOUT
SETSOUT
SHIPOUT
SHOTOUT
SHOWOUT
SHUTOUT
SICKOUT
SIGNOUT
SINGOUT
SITSOUT
SKIBOOT
SKIPOUT
SLIPOUT
SOLDOUT
SORTOUT
SPINOUT
SPUNOUT
STEPOUT
SUPPORT
SURCOAT
TAGSOUT
TAKEOUT
TALKOUT
TAPROOT
TAPSOUT
TEAROUT
TESTOUT
TIMEOUT
TIREOUT
TOOKOUT
TOPCOAT
TOPMOST
TOPSOUT
TOREOUT
TORNOUT
TOSSOUT
TROTOUT
TUGBOAT
TUNEOUT
TURNOUT
UPFRONT
VERMONT
VOTEOUT
WAITOUT
WALCOTT
WALKOUT
WANTOUT
WASHOUT
WEAROUT
WEBFOOT
WEEDOUT
WENTOUT
WIGSOUT
WINKOUT
WINSOUT
WIPEOUT
WITHOUT
WOREOUT
WORKOUT
WORNOUT
XINGOUT
ZONKOUT

•••••OT

APRICOT
BIBELOT
BIENTOT
BIGFOOT
BIGSHOT
BLERIOT
BOWKNOT
CAMELOT
CHARIOT
CHEROOT
CHEVIOT
COPILOT
CYPRIOT
DASBOOT
DIDEROT
DOGTROT
DOVECOT
EARSHOT
EYESHOT
FEEDLOT
FOXTROT
FUSSPOT
GOTOPOT
GUNSHOT
HARICOT
HAVENOT
HERRIOT
HIPBOOT
HOTFOOT
HOTSHOT
HOTSPOT
INASPOT
INKBLOT
INKSPOT
JACKPOT
MAGINOT
MAILLOT
MATELOT
MONOCOT
MUGSHOT
ONESHOT
PATRIOT
PERIDOT
PEUGEOT
PIERROT
POTSHOT
RANRIOT
REDSPOT
RESHOOT
RIMSHOT
RUNRIOT
SANDLOT
SHALLOT
SKIBOOT
SUBPLOT
SUNSPOT
TAPROOT
TENSPOT
TOPKNOT
TSELIOT
WEBFOOT
WHATNOT
WOODLOT
WYANDOT

OU•••••

OUGHTNT
OURGANG
OURSELF
OURTOWN
OUSTERS
OUSTING
OUTACTS
OUTAGES
OUTBACK
OUTBIDS
OUTCAST
OUTCOME
OUTCROP
OUTDOES
OUTDONE
OUTDOOR
OUTDRAW
OUTDREW
OUTEATS
OUTFACE
OUTFITS
OUTFLOW
OUTGOES
OUTGREW
OUTGROW
OUTGUNS
OUTHITS
OUTINGS
OUTJUMP
OUTLAID
OUTLAND
OUTLAST
OUTLAWS
OUTLAYS
OUTLETS
OUTLINE
OUTLIVE
OUTLOOK
OUTLOUD
OUTOFIT
OUTPACE
OUTPLAY
OUTPOLL
OUTPOST
OUTPUTS
OUTRACE
OUTRAGE
OUTRANK
OUTRUNS
OUTSELL
OUTSETS
OUTSIDE
OUTSIZE
OUTSOLD
OUTSTEP
OUTTAKE
OUTTALK
OUTVOTE
OUTWARD
OUTWEAR
OUTWITS
OUTWORE
OUTWORK
OUTWORN

O•U••••

OCULIST
OEUVRES
OPULENT

O••U•••

OBTUNDS
OBTUSER
OCCULTS
OCTUPLE
OLDUVAI
ONGUARD
OPPUGNS
OROURKE

O•••U••

OBSCURE
OBTRUDE
OCCLUDE
OFFDUTY
OPAQUES
OROTUND
OUTGUNS
OUTJUMP
OUTPUTS
OUTRUNS
OVERUSE

O••••U•

OBLIQUE
OBLOQUY
OBVIOUS
OCCIPUT
OCEANUS
OCELLUS
OCTOPUS
ODORFUL
ODOROUS
OEDIPUS
OFFHOUR
OLYMPUS
OMENTUM
OMINOUS
OMNIBUS
ONEROUS
OPENSUP
OPOSSUM
OPTIMUM
OPTSOUT
ORGANUM
ORMOLUS
ORPHEUS
OSSEOUS
OUTLOUD
OVERBUY
OVERDUB
OVERDUE
OVERRUN
OWNEDUP
OZONOUS

O•••••U

ONLYYOU

•OU••••

AOUDADS
BOUDOIR
BOULDER
BOULLES
BOUNCED
BOUNCER
BOUNCES
BOUNDED
BOUNDER
BOUNDUP
BOUQUET
BOURBON
BOURREE
BOURSES
BOUSING
BOUTROS
COUCHED
COUCHES
COUGARS
COUGHED
COUGHUP
COULDNT
COULEES
COULOMB
COULTER
COUNCIL
COUNSEL
COUNTED
COUNTER
COUNTON
COUNTRY
COUPLED
COUPLES
COUPLET
COUPONS
COURAGE
COURANT
COURIER
COURSED
COURSER
COURSES
COURTED
COURTLY
COUSINS
COUTURE
DOUBLED
DOUBLES
DOUBLET
DOUBLEU
DOUBTED
DOUBTER
DOUGHTY
DOUGLAS
DOUREST
DOUSING
FOULARD
FOULEST
FOULING
FOULOUT
FOULSUP
FOULTIP
FOULUPS
FOUNDED
FOUNDER
FOUNDRY
FOURIER
FOURTHS
FOURWAY
GOUACHE
GOUGERS
GOUGING
GOULASH
GOUNDER
GOURAMI
GOURDES
GOURMET
GOUTIER
GOUTILY
GOUTISH
HOUDINI
HOUGHED
HOUNDED
HOUSING
HOUSMAN
HOUSTON
JOUNCED
JOUNCES
JOURDAN
JOURNAL
JOURNEY
JOURNOS
JOUSTED
JOUSTER
LOUDEST
LOUDISH
LOUELLA
LOUNGED
LOUNGER
LOUNGES
LOURDES
LOUSEUP
LOUSIER
LOUSILY
LOUSING
LOUTISH
LOUVERS
LOUVRED
LOUVRES
MOUFLON
MOULAGE
MOULDED
MOULDER
MOULTED
MOUNDED
MOUNTED
MOUNTIE
MOURNED
MOUSERS
MOUSIER
MOUSING
MOUSSED
MOUSSES
MOUTHED
MOUTONS
NOUGATS
NOUGHTS
NOURISH
NOUVEAU
POUCHED
POUCHES
POULENC
POULTRY
POUNCED
POUNCER
POUNCES
POUNDED
POUNDER
POURERS
POURING
POUROUT
POURSIN
POUTERS
POUTFUL
POUTIER
POUTING
ROUBLES
ROUGHED
ROUGHEN
ROUGHER
ROUGHIT
ROUGHLY
ROUGHUP
ROUGING
ROULADE
ROUNDED
ROUNDER
ROUNDLY
ROUNDON
ROUNDUP
ROUSERS
ROUSING
ROUSTED
ROUTERS
ROUTINE
ROUTING
SOUFFLE
SOUGHED
SOUKOUS
SOULFUL
SOUNDED
SOUNDER
SOUNDLY
SOUPCON
SOUPIER
SOUPSUP
SOURCED
SOURCES
SOUREST
SOURING
SOURISH
SOUTANE
SOUTHEY
TOUCANS
TOUCHED
TOUCHES
TOUCHON
TOUCHUP
TOUGHEN
TOUGHER
TOUGHIE
TOUGHLY
TOUPEES
TOURACO
TOURERS
TOURING
TOURISM
TOURIST
TOURNEY
TOUSLED
TOUSLES
TOUTERS
TOUTING
VOUCHED
VOUCHER
VOUCHES
WOULDBE
WOULDNT
WOUNDED
WOUNDUP
YOUKNOW
YOUMANS
YOUNGER
YOUNGMC
YOUNGUN
ZOUAVES

•O•U•••

BOLUSES
BONUSES
COLUMBO
COLUMNS
CONURES
COPULAE
COPULAS
COZUMEL
FOCUSED
FOCUSES
GODUNOV
GODUTCH
JOCULAR
KORUNAS
LOBULES
LOCUSTS
LOQUATS
LOTUSES
MODULAR
MODULES
NOCUOUS
NODULAR
NODULES
NOGUCHI
NONUSER
POPULAR
POPULUS
ROBUSTA
ROGUERY
ROGUISH
ROMULAN
ROMULUS
ROTUNDA
SOLUBLE
SOLUTES
SOSUEME
TOLUENE
VOGUISH
VOLUBLE
VOLUBLY
VOLUMES
YOGURTS

•O••U••

BOROUGH
BOUQUET
BOXFULS
COEQUAL
COGBURN
COLLUDE
COLOURS
COMBUST
COMMUNE
COMMUTE
COMPUTE
CONCURS
CONDUCE
CONDUCT
CONDUIT
CONFUSE
CONFUTE
CONJURE
CONQUER
CONSULS
CONSULT
CONSUME
CONTUSE
COPOUTS
CORRUPT
COSTUME
COUTURE
DOLOURS
DONJUAN
FOLDUPS
FONDUES
FORMULA
FORSURE
FORTUNA
FORTUNE
FOULUPS
GOOFUPS
GOROUND
HOLDUPS
HOMBURG
HONOURS
HOOKUPS
HOTTUBS
JOAQUIN
JOBHUNT
JONQUIL
LOCKUPS
LONGUES
LOOKUPS
MOCKUPS
MOLLUSC
MOLLUSK
MOSQUES
NOCTURN
NODOUBT
NOFAULT
NOTRUMP
NOTSURE
PODIUMS
POLLUTE
POPGUNS
POSEURS
POSSUMS
POSTURE
POTFULS
POTLUCK
ROEBUCK
RORQUAL
SOJOURN
SOWBUGS
TONGUED
TONGUES
TONSURE
TOPGUNS
TORQUES
TOSSUPS
WORKUPS
YOGHURT

•O•••U•

BONEDUP
BONESUP
BONJOUR
BOOSTUP
BOOTOUT
BOOTSUP
BOREOUT
BORNEUP
BOTCHUP
BOUNDUP
BOWLFUL
BOWSOUT
BOXEDUP
BOXESUP
COCONUT
COILSUP
COLDCUT
COLOBUS
COMEDUE
COMEOUT
COMESUP
COMIQUE
CONKOUT
CONTOUR
COOKOUT
COOKSUP
COOPSUP
COPIOUS
COPSOUT
COUGHUP
COVERUP
DOINGUP
DOLEFUL
DOLEOUT
DOLLSUP
DOMINUS
DONAHUE
DONIMUS
DOOMFUL
DOPEOUT
FOLDOUT
FOLDSUP
FORERUN
FORKFUL
FORMFUL
FORTIUS
FOULOUT
FOULSUP
GOABOUT
GOESOUT
GOINGUP
GOLDBUG
GOOFSUP
HOLDOUT
HOLDSUP
HOLEDUP
HOLEOUT
HOLESUP
HOLMIUM
HOMERUN
HOODLUM
HOOKSUP
HOPEFUL
HOTSPUR
JOINSUP
LOCKNUT
LOCKOUT
LOCKSUP
LOGSOUT
LONGRUN
LOOKOUT
LOOKSUP
LOSEOUT
LOSTOUT
LOUSEUP
LOVEBUG
MOANFUL
MODICUM
MONIQUE
MOVEDUP
MOVEOUT
MOVESUP
NOCUOUS
NONPLUS
NOSEEUM
NOSEOUT
NOSTRUM
NOTTRUE
NOXIOUS
POKEFUN
POMPOUS
PONTIUS
POOPOUT
POPSOUT
POPULUS
POUROUT
POUTFUL
RODEOUT
ROLLOUT
ROLLSUP
ROMULUS
ROOMFUL
ROOTOUT
ROSEBUD
ROSTRUM
ROUGHUP
ROUNDUP
SOAKSUP
SOLDOUT
SONGFUL
SORGHUM
SORTOUT

SOUKOUS
SOULFUL
SOUPSUP
TOILFUL
TONEDUP
TONESUP
TOOKOUT
TOOLSUP
TOPSOUT
TOREOUT
TORNOUT
TOSSOUT
TOUCHUP
TOYSRUS
VOTEOUT
WOKENUP
WOODCUT
WOREOUT
WORKOUT
WORKSUP
WORNOUT
WOUNDUP
YOUNGUN
ZONKOUT

•O••••U

COCTEAU
DOUBLEU
HOFBRAU
KOMATSU
NOUVEAU
RONDEAU
TONNEAU

••OU•••

ABOUGHT
ABOUNDS
AGOUTIS
AMOUNTS
ANOUILH
AROUSAL
AROUSED
AROUSES
BLOUSED
BLOUSES
BLOUSON
BROUGHT
CLOUDED
CLOUTED
CROUTON
DROUGHT
EDOUARD
ENOUNCE
FLOUNCE
FLOUNCY
FLOURED
FLOUTED
GROUCHO
GROUCHY
GROUNDS
GROUPED
GROUPER
GROUPIE
GROUSED
GROUSER
GROUSES
GROUTED
KNOUTED
OROURKE
PIOUSLY
PLOUGHS
PROUDER
PROUDLY
SCOURED
SCOURER
SCOURGE
SCOUSES
SCOUTED
SCOUTER
SHOULDA
SHOUTED
SHOUTER
SIOUANS
SLOUCHY
SLOUGHS
SPOUSAL
SPOUSES
SPOUTED
SPOUTER
STOUTEN
STOUTER
STOUTLY
THOUGHT
TROUBLE
TROUGHS
TROUNCE
TROUPER
TROUPES
TROUSER
TSOURIS
WROUGHT
YAOUNDE

••O•U••

BEOWULF
BLOWUPS
BROGUES
CLOQUES
CLOSURE
CLOTURE
CROQUET
FLORUIT
GLOBULE
GOOFUPS
HOOKUPS
INOCULA
LOOKUPS
OROTUND
PROCURE
PRODUCE
PRODUCT
PROFUSE
QUORUMS
SHOGUNS
SLOWUPS
SUOJURE

••O••U•

AMOROUS
BLOTOUT
BLOWGUN
BLOWNUP
BLOWOUT
BLOWSUP
BOOSTUP
BOOTOUT
BOOTSUP
BROKEUP
BUOYSUP
CHOKEUP
CLOGSUP
CLOSEUP
COOKOUT
COOKSUP
COOPSUP
CROESUS
CROPSUP
CROSSUP
DOOMFUL
DROPOUT
GOOFSUP
GROPIUS
GROWNUP
GROWSUP
HOODLUM
HOOKSUP
IRONOUT
LIONCUB
LOOKOUT
LOOKSUP
NIOBIUM
ODORFUL
ODOROUS
OPOSSUM
OZONOUS
PHOEBUS
PLOTFUL
POOPOUT
PRONOUN
PROPSUP
PROTEUS
REOCCUR
RHODIUM
RHOMBUS
RIOTOUS
ROOMFUL
ROOTOUT
SHOOKUP
SHOOTUP
SHOPFUL
SHOTGUN
SHOTOUT
SHOTPUT
SHOWOUT
SHOWSUP
SKOOKUM
SLOWSUP
SPOKEUP
STOCKUP
STOODUP
STOPSUP
STOREUP
THORIUM
TOOKOUT
TOOLSUP
TROILUS
TROTOUT
WOODCUT
WROTEUP

••O•••U

THOREAU

•••OU••

ACCOUNT
ADJOURN
AGROUND
AMPOULE
ARBOURS
ARDOURS
ARMOURS
ARMOURY
ASTOUND
BEDOUIN
BEFOULS
BIVOUAC
BOROUGH
BUYOUTS
CAROUSE
COLOURS
COPOUTS
CUTOUTS
CYYOUNG
DEBOUCH
DETOURS
DEVOURS
DIMOUTS
DOLOURS
DUGOUTS
ENROUTE
ENSOULS
ESPOUSE
EXPOUND
FANOUTS
FAVOURS
GOROUND
HONOURS
HUMOURS
IMPOUND
INBOUND
INDOUBT
INHOUSE
KEROUAC
LABOURS
LAYOUTS
MAHOUTS
NODOUBT
PAYOUTS
PUTOUTS
RAGOUTS
REBOUND
RECOUNT
RECOUPS
REDOUBT
REDOUND
REMOUNT
REROUTE
RESOUND
RETOUCH
RETOURS
REWOUND
RIGOURS
RUMOURS
RUNOUTS
SAVOURS
SAVOURY
SHROUDS
SOJOURN
SPROUTS
STLOUIS
THROUGH
TRYOUTS
UNBOUND
UNCOUTH
UNSOUND
UNWOUND
VALOURS
VAPOURS
VELOURS
VIGOURS

•••O•U•

ABSOLUT
BAROQUE
CANOPUS
CAROLUS
COCONUT
COLOBUS
DECORUM
ECLOGUE
INFOCUS
INVOGUE
OBLOQUY
OCTOPUS
ORMOLUS
PIROGUE
REFOCUS
SHOOKUP
SHOOTUP
SKOOKUM
STOODUP
ZEROSUM

••••OU•

ACEDOUT
ACESOUT
ACTFOUR
ACTSOUT
AIRSOUT
AMOROUS
ANXIOUS
AQUEOUS
ARDUOUS
ASKSOUT
BACKOUT
BAILOUT
BALFOUR
BAWLOUT
BEAROUT
BEATOUT
BECLOUD
BILIOUS
BLEWOUT
BLOTOUT
BLOWOUT
BONJOUR
BOOTOUT
BOREOUT
BOWSOUT
BUGSOUT
BULBOUS
BUMSOUT
BURNOUT
BUSTOUT
BUTTOUT
BUYSOUT
CACHOUS
CALHOUN
CALLOUS
CALLOUT
CAMEOUT
CAMPOUT
CANDOUR
CASHOUT
CASTOUT
CHEWOUT
CITROUS
CLAMOUR
COMEOUT
CONKOUT
CONTOUR
COOKOUT
COPIOUS
COPSOUT
CURIOUS
CUTSOUT
DEALOUT
DECKOUT
DEVIOUS
DIEDOUT
DIESOUT
DIGSOUT
DISHOUT
DOLEOUT
DOPEOUT
DRAGOUT
DRAWOUT
DREWOUT
DROPOUT
DUBIOUS
DUTEOUS
EASEOUT
EATSOUT
EDGEOUT
EDITOUT
EKEDOUT
EKESOUT
ENAMOUR
ENVIOUS
EVENOUT
FADEOUT
FALLOUT
FANSOUT
FARMOUT
FATUOUS
FEELOUT
FELLOUT
FELTOUT
FERROUS
FERVOUR
FIBROUS
FILLOUT
FINDOUT
FISHOUT
FLATOUT
FLAVOUR
FLIPOUT
FOLDOUT
FOULOUT
FURIOUS
GASEOUS
GAVEOUT
GETSOUT
GIBBOUS
GIVEOUT
GLAMOUR
GOABOUT
GOESOUT
HANDOUT
HANGOUT
HARBOUR
HEADOUT
HEAROUT
HEINOUS
HELDOUT
HELPOUT
HIDEOUS
HIDEOUT
HITSOUT
HOLDOUT
HOLEOUT
HUNGOUT
HYDROUS
ICEDOUT
ICESOUT
IGNEOUS
IMPIOUS
INGROUP
IRISOUT
IRONOUT
JEALOUS
KEPTOUT
KICKOUT
LAIDOUT
LAYSOUT
LEADOUT
LEFTOUT
LETSOUT
LIVEOUT
LOCKOUT
LOGSOUT
LOOKOUT
LOSEOUT
LOSTOUT
LUCKOUT
MADEOUT
MAILOUT
MAKEOUT
MANHOUR
MCCLOUD
METEOUT
MISSOUT
MOVEOUT
NERVOUS
NITROUS
NOCUOUS
NOSEOUT
NOXIOUS
OBVIOUS
ODOROUS
OFFHOUR
OMINOUS
ONEROUS
OPTSOUT
OSSEOUS
OUTLOUD
OZONOUS
PAIDOUT
PAILOUS
PANSOUT
PARLOUR
PARLOUS
PARTOUT
PASSOUT
PAVIOUR
PAYSOUT
PEASOUP
PEEKOUT
PEEROUT
PETROUS
PICKOUT
PIGSOUT
PITEOUS
PLANOUT
PLAYOUT
POMPOUS
POOPOUT
POPSOUT
POUROUT
PRONOUN
PULLOUT
PUTSOUT
RAINOUT
RANCOUR
RANGOUT
RAUCOUS
READOUT
REGROUP
RIDEOUT
RINGOUT
RIOTOUS
RIPSOUT
RODEOUT
ROLLOUT
ROOTOUT
RUBSOUT
RUINOUS
RULEOUT
RUNGOUT
RUNSOUT
SACKOUT
SANGOUT
SAVIOUR
SEEKOUT
SEENOUT
SEESOUT
SELLOUT
SENDOUT
SENTOUT
SERIOUS
SETSOUT
SEYMOUR
SHIPOUT
SHOTOUT
SHOWOUT
SHUTOUT
SICKOUT
SIGNOUT
SINGOUT
SINUOUS
SITSOUT
SKIPOUT
SLIPOUT
SOLDOUT
SORTOUT
SOUKOUS
SPINOUT
SPUMOUS
SPUNOUT
STEPOUT
SUCCOUR
TAGSOUT
TAKEOUT
TALKOUT
TAMBOUR
TAPSOUT
TEAROUT
TEDIOUS
TENFOUR
TENUOUS
TESTOUT
THEROUX
TIMEOUT
TIREOUT
TOOKOUT
TOPSOUT
TOREOUT
TORNOUT
TOSSOUT
TROTOUT
TUNEOUT
TURNOUT
VACUOUS
VARIOUS
VERDOUX
VICIOUS
VISCOUS
VOTEOUT
WAITOUT
WALKOUT
WANTOUT
WASHOUT
WEAROUT
WEEDOUT
WENTOUT
WIGSOUT
WINKOUT
WINSOUT
WIPEOUT
WITHOUT
WOREOUT
WORKOUT
WORNOUT
XINGOUT
ZEALOUS
ZONKOUT

••••O•U

SHIKOKU

•••••OU

ANGELOU
CARIBOU
EMMYLOU
MANITOU
MARABOU
MARYLOU
NEARYOU
ONLYYOU

OV•••••

OVATION
OVERACT
OVERAGE
OVERALL
OVERATE
OVERAWE
OVERBIG
OVERBUY
OVERDID
OVERDUB
OVERDUE
OVEREAT
OVERFLY
OVERJOY
OVERLAP
OVERLAY
OVERLIE
OVERRAN
OVERRUN
OVERSAW
OVERSEA
OVERSEE
OVERTAX
OVERTLY
OVERUSE
OVIPARA
OVISACS
OVOIDAL

O•V••••

OBVERSE
OBVERTS
OBVIATE
OBVIOUS
ORVILLE

O••V•••

OEUVRES
OLIVIER
OLIVINE
OUTVOTE

O•••V••

OCTAVES
OCTAVIA
OCTAVOS
OLDUVAI

O••••V•

OBSERVE
ONLEAVE
ONSERVE
OUTLIVE

•OV••••

BOVINES
BOVVERS
COVERED
COVERUP
COVETED
DOVECOT
GOVERNS
HOVERED
HOVERER
HOVLANE
LOVABLE
LOVABLY
LOVEBUG
LOVEINS
LOVERLY
MOVABLE
MOVABLY
MOVEDIN
MOVEDON
MOVEDUP
MOVEOUT
MOVESIN
MOVESON
MOVESUP
NOVARRO
NOVELLA
NOVELLE
NOVELTY
NOVENAS
NOVICES
POVERTY
SOVIETS

•O•V•••

BOBVILA
BOVVERS
COEVALS
CONVENE
CONVENT
CONVERT
CONVEYS
CONVICT
CONVOKE
CONVOYS
HOOVERS
LOUVERS
LOUVRED
LOUVRES
NOUVEAU
ROLVAAG
SOLVENT
SOLVERS
SOLVING
SORVINO

•O••V••

BOLIVAR
BOLIVIA
DONOVAN
FOREVER
GOTEVEN
GOTOVER
HOPOVER
HOWEVER
MORAVIA
MOTIVES
POPOVER
ZOUAVES

•O•••V•

BONJOVI
COMMOVE
CONCAVE
CONNIVE
FORGAVE
FORGIVE
MOLDOVA
YOMTOVS

•O••••V

GODUNOV
MOLOTOV
ROCKYIV
ROMANOV

••OV•••

BMOVIES
CLOVERS
DROVERS
GROVELS
HOOVERS
PLOVERS
PROVERB
PROVERS
PROVIDE
PROVING
PROVISO
PROVOKE
PROVOST
SHOVELS
SHOVERS
SHOVING
SLOVAKS
SLOVENE
SLOVENS

••O•V••

EVOLVED
EVOLVES
GROOVED
GROOVES
WHOEVER

••O••V•

EMOTIVE
EROSIVE
PLOSIVE

•••OV••

ALCOVES
ALLOVER
ANDOVER
BEHOVED
BEHOVES
BELOVED
DIDOVER
DONOVAN
FLYOVER
GETOVER
GOTOVER
GROOVED
GROOVES
HANOVER
HOPOVER
LAYOVER
LIEOVER
POPOVER
PUTOVER
RANOVER
RAYOVAC
RECOVER
REMOVAL
REMOVED
REMOVER
REMOVES
REWOVEN
RUNOVER
SAMOVAR
SEGOVIA
UNCOVER
UNLOVED
UNMOVED
UNWOVEN

•••O•V•

ABSOLVE
BEHOOVE
DEVOLVE
INVOLVE
RESOLVE
REVOLVE

•••O••V

MOLOTOV
NABOKOV

••••OV•

ANCHOVY
APPROVE
BEHOOVE
BONJOVI
COMMOVE
IMPROVE
IVANOVO
KEDROVA
MARKOVA
MOLDOVA
MUSCOVY
PAVLOVA
REPROVE
ULANOVA
YOMTOVS

•••••OV

CHEKHOV
GODUNOV
MOLOTOV
NABOKOV
NEMEROV
ROMANOV
ULYANOV
USTINOV

OW•••••

OWINGTO
OWLLIKE
OWNEDUP

O•W••••

ONWARDS

O••W•••

OILWELL
OLDWEST
OUTWARD
OUTWEAR
OUTWITS
OUTWORE
OUTWORK
OUTWORN

O•••W••

OJIBWAS
OJIBWAY
OTTAWAS

O••••W•

OAKLAWN
OKINAWA
OLDNEWS
OLDSAWS
OURTOWN
OUTLAWS
OVERAWE

O•••••W

OUTDRAW
OUTDREW
OUTFLOW
OUTGREW
OUTGROW
OVERSAW

•OW••••

BOWDLER
BOWERED
BOWFINS
BOWKNOT
BOWLERS
BOWLESS
BOWLFUL
BOWLIKE
BOWLINE
BOWLING
BOWSAWS
BOWSOUT
BOWTIES
BOWWOWS
BOWYERS
COWARDS
COWBELL
COWBIRD
COWBOYS
COWERED
COWGIRL
COWHAND
COWHERD
COWHIDE
COWLICK
COWLIKE
COWLING
COWPEAS
COWPOKE
COWPONY
COWRIES
COWSLIP
COWTOWN
DOWAGER
DOWDIER
DOWDILY
DOWERED
DOWNBOW
DOWNERS
DOWNIER
DOWNING
DOWNPAT
DOWRIES
DOWSERS
DOWSING
FOWLERS
FOWLING
GOWRONG
HOWARDS
HOWBEIT
HOWCOME
HOWDAHS
HOWELLS
HOWEVER
HOWLERS
HOWLING
JOWLIER
KOWLOON
KOWTOWS
LOWBALL
LOWBEAM
LOWBLOW
LOWBORN
LOWBOYS
LOWBRED
LOWBROW
LOWCOST
LOWDOWN
LOWERED
LOWGEAR
LOWHEEL
LOWLAND
LOWLIER
LOWLIFE
LOWNECK
LOWNESS
LOWPAID
LOWRISE
LOWROAD
LOWTECH
LOWTIDE
MOWDOWN
NOWHERE
POWDERS
POWDERY
POWERED
POWWOWS
ROWBOAT
ROWDIER
ROWDIES
ROWDILY
SOWBUGS
SOWLIKE
TOWARDS
TOWAWAY
TOWCARS
TOWELED
TOWERED
TOWHEAD
TOWHEES
TOWNERS
TOWNIES
TOWNISH
TOWPATH
TOWROPE
VOWLESS
WOWSERS
YOWLERS
YOWLING

•O•W•••

BOSWELL
BOWWOWS
BOXWOOD
COBWEBS
DOGWOOD
FORWARD
FORWENT
GODWITS
GOTWELL
HOGWASH
HOGWILD
HOTWARS
HOTWIRE
NOSWEAT
NOTWELL
POWWOWS
ROSWELL
SOPWITH

•O••W••

BOERWAR
COLDWAR
DOORWAY
FOLKWAY
FOODWEB
FOOTWAY
FOURWAY
GOLDWYN
GOODWIN
GOTAWAY
HOLYWAR
MOHAWKS
POSTWAR
ROADWAY
SOMEWAY
TOLLWAY

TOWAWAY

•O•••W•

BOGDOWN
BORROWS
BOWSAWS
BOWWOWS
COWTOWN
FOGBOWS
FOLLOWS
GOSHAWK
GOSLOWS
GOTDOWN
HOEDOWN
HOLLOWS
HOOTOWL
KOWTOWS
LOWDOWN
MORROWS
MOWDOWN
NOSHOWS
POWWOWS
ROBLOWE
ROYALWE
SORROWS
TOPDOWN

•O••••W

CORNROW
DOGCHOW
DOGSHOW
DOWNBOW
FOREPAW
FORESAW
HOLYCOW
JOEBLOW
LONGBOW
LOWBLOW
LOWBROW
ROPETOW
SOMEHOW
TONEROW
WOODROW
YOUKNOW

••OW•••

AVOWALS
AVOWERS
AVOWING
BEOWULF
BLOWDRY
BLOWERS
BLOWFLY
BLOWGUN
BLOWIER
BLOWING
BLOWNUP
BLOWOFF
BLOWOUT
BLOWSIN
BLOWSIT
BLOWSUP
BLOWUPS
BROWNED
BROWNER
BROWNIE
BROWSED
BROWSER
BROWSES
CHOWDER
CLOWDER
CLOWNED
CROWBAR
CROWDED
CROWERS
CROWING
CROWNED
DROWNED
DROWSED
DROWSES
FLOWERS
FLOWERY
FLOWING
FLOWNAT
FLOWNIN
FROWARD
FROWNAT
FROWNED
FROWNER
FROWSTY
GLOWERS
GLOWING
GROWERS
GROWING
GROWLED
GROWLER
GROWNUP
GROWSON
GROWSUP
GROWTHS
KNOWHOW
KNOWING
MEOWING
PLOWBOY
PLOWERS
PLOWING
PLOWMAN
PLOWMEN
PROWESS
PROWLED
PROWLER
SCOWLED
SCOWLER
SHOWBIZ
SHOWDOG
SHOWERS
SHOWERY
SHOWIER
SHOWILY
SHOWING
SHOWMAN
SHOWMEN
SHOWNIN
SHOWOFF
SHOWOUT
SHOWSIN
SHOWSUP
SLOWEST
SLOWING
SLOWSUP
SLOWUPS
SNOWCAP
SNOWCAT
SNOWDAY
SNOWDON
SNOWIER
SNOWILY
SNOWING
SNOWJOB
SNOWMAN
SNOWMEN
SNOWPEA
SNOWSIN
STOWING
TROWELS
TROWERS

••O•W••

DOORWAY
FOODWEB
FOOTWAY
GOODWIN
WHOSWHO

••O••W•

HOOTOWL

••O•••W

ASOFNOW
CHOCTAW
KNOWHOW
USOSHOW
WOODROW

•••OW••

ALLOWAY
ALLOWED
CNTOWER
DISOWNS
ELBOWED
EMPOWER
ENDOWED
INNOWAY
INPOWER
MANOWAR
REMOWED
RETOWED
THROWER
THROWIN
UNBOWED
WIDOWED
WIDOWER

•••O••W

UPTONOW

••••OW•

ANTCOWS
BARNOWL
BARROWS
BEDDOWN
BELLOWS
BESTOWS
BILLOWS
BILLOWY
BOGDOWN
BORROWS
BOWWOWS
BURROWS
COWTOWN
CUTDOWN
DIEDOWN
ESCROWS
FALLOWS
FARROWS
FELLOWS
FOGBOWS
FOLLOWS
FURROWS
GETDOWN
GOSLOWS
GOTDOWN
HALLOWS
HARROWS
HAYMOWS
HOEDOWN
HOLLOWS
HOOTOWL
INFLOWS
INGROWN
KOWTOWS
LAYDOWN
LETDOWN
LIEDOWN
LOWDOWN
MALLOWS
MARLOWE
MARROWS
MEADOWS
MEADOWY
MELLOWS
MIDTOWN
MINNOWS
MORROWS
MOWDOWN
NARROWS
NEWMOWN
NEWTOWN
NOSHOWS
OURTOWN
PEAFOWL
PILLOWS
PILLOWY
PINDOWN
POWWOWS
PUTDOWN
RANDOWN
REPLOWS
ROBLOWE
RUBDOWN
RUNDOWN
SALLOWS
SATDOWN
SEACOWS
SETDOWN
SHADOWS
SHADOWY
SITDOWN
SKITOWS
SORROWS
SUNBOWL
SUNDOWN
TALLOWS
TIEDOWN
TOPDOWN
TVSHOWS
UNKNOWN
WALLOWS
WILLOWS
WILLOWY
WINDOWS
WINNOWS
YARROWS
YELLOWS
YELLOWY

•••••OW

AIRFLOW
AIRSHOW
ASOFNOW
ATECROW
BARSTOW
BIGELOW
CASHCOW
CATSHOW
CORNROW
DISAVOW
DOGCHOW
DOGSHOW
DOWNBOW
EATCROW
EYEBROW
GLASGOW
HIGHLOW
HOLYCOW
ICESHOW
JOEBLOW
JUSTNOW
KNOWHOW
LAIDLOW
LAYSLOW
LIESLOW
LITHGOW
LONGBOW
LOWBLOW
LOWBROW
MANILOW
MILKCOW
OUTFLOW
OUTGROW
PALTROW
RAINBOW
ROPETOW
SALCHOW
SHALLOW
SKIDROW
SOMEHOW
SPARROW
SWALLOW
THECROW
TONEROW
UPTONOW
USOSHOW
WINDROW
WINSLOW
WOODROW
YOUKNOW

OX•••••

OXBLOOD
OXCARTS
OXFORDS
OXIDANT
OXIDASE
OXIDISE
OXIDIZE
OXONIAN
OXYMORA

•OX••••

BOXCARS
BOXEDIN
BOXEDUP
BOXESIN
BOXESUP
BOXFULS
BOXIEST
BOXKITE
BOXLIKE
BOXROOM
BOXSEAT
BOXSTEP
BOXTOPS
BOXWOOD
COXCOMB
FOXFIRE
FOXHOLE
FOXIEST
FOXLIKE
FOXTAIL
FOXTROT
NOXIOUS
NOXZEMA
ROXANNE

•O•X•••

COAXERS
COAXIAL
COAXING
COEXIST
HOAXERS
HOAXING

•O••X••

POBOXES

•O•••X•

CONTEXT
POLEAXE

•O••••X

BOOMBOX
COMPLEX
GORETEX
LOCKBOX
POLLTAX
POORBOX
POSTBOX
ROLODEX
SOAPBOX
TOOLBOX

••OX•••

DIOXIDE
EPOXIES
PROXIES
PROXIMO

••O•••X

BOOMBOX
BROADAX
PHOENIX
POORBOX
SHOEBOX
TOOLBOX

•••OX••

INBOXES
PHLOXES
POBOXES
UNBOXED
UNBOXES

•••O••X

ALTOSAX
MEMOREX
ROLODEX

••••O•X

STCROIX
THEROUX
VERDOUX

•••••OX

BANDBOX
BLUEFOX
BOOMBOX
BRERFOX
CALLBOX
CASHBOX
EQUINOX
FIREBOX
FLUMMOX
GEARBOX
JUKEBOX
LOCKBOX
MAILBOX
PARADOX
PILLBOX
POORBOX
POSTBOX
SALTBOX
SANDBOX
SHOEBOX
SOAPBOX
TOOLBOX

OY•••••

OYSTERS

O•Y••••

ODYSSEY
OLYMPIA
OLYMPIC
OLYMPUS
OXYMORA

O••Y•••

OBEYING
OFFYEAR
OKAYING
ONLYTOO
ONLYYOU
OOCYTES

O•••Y••

ONEEYED
ONLYYOU

O••••Y•

OLDDAYS
OSPREYS
OUTLAYS

O•••••Y

OBLOQUY
ODYSSEY
OFFDUTY
OJIBWAY
OLDFOGY
OPACITY
ORANGEY
ORATORY
ORDERLY
ORGANDY
ORMANDY
OROGENY
ORPHREY
OUTPLAY
OVERBUY
OVERFLY
OVERJOY
OVERLAY
OVERTLY

•OY••••

BOYCOTT
BOYHOOD
COYNESS
COYOTES
DOYENNE
HOYDENS
JOYLESS
JOYRIDE
LOYALLY
LOYALTY
ROYALLY
ROYALTY
ROYALWE
SOYBEAN
SOYINKA
TOYDOGS
TOYLAND
TOYLESS
TOYLIKE
TOYNBEE
TOYSHOP
TOYSRUS
VOYAGED
VOYAGER
VOYAGES
YOYOING
ZOYSIAS

•O•Y•••

BODYFAT
BOWYERS
COPYBOY
COPYCAT
COPYING
COPYIST
COZYING
FOGYISH
FOGYISM
HOLYARK
HOLYCOW
HOLYDAY
HOLYOKE
HOLYSEE
HOLYWAR
KOSYGIN
OOCYTES
POLYGON
POLYMER
PONYING
TORYISH
TORYISM

•O••Y••

BOGEYED
COLLYER
FORSYTH
HONEYED
LOBBYER
MONEYED
MOSEYED
POPEYED
ROCKYII
ROCKYIV

•O•••Y•

CONVEYS
CONVOYS
COWBOYS
DOGDAYS
DONKEYS
FONTEYN
GOLDWYN
GOODBYE
GOODBYS
HOMONYM
JOCKEYS
LOONEYS
LOWBOYS
MONDAYS
MONKEYS
MONTOYA
NOBODYS
ROBROYS
ROMNEYS
SOCKEYE
TOMBOYS
VOLLEYS

•O••••Y

BOKCHOY
BONEDRY
BONNILY
BOSSILY
COCKILY
COCKNEY
COCKSHY
COGENCY
COMESBY
COMFREY
COMPANY
CONAKRY
CONNERY
COOKERY
COPPERY
COPYBOY
CORNILY
COTTONY
COUNTRY
COURTLY
COWPONY
DOORWAY
DOROTHY
DOTTILY
DOUGHTY
DOWDILY
FOAMILY
FOGGILY
FOLKWAY
FOOLERY
FOOTWAY
FOPPERY
FORGERY
FORTIFY
FOUNDRY
FOURWAY
GODFREY
GOINGBY
GOOFILY
GOONILY
GOSSIPY
GOTAWAY
GOUTILY
HOARILY
HOLIDAY
HOLYDAY
HOMEBOY
HONESTY
HORNSBY
HORRIFY
HOSIERY
JOBBERY
JOFFREY
JOHNGAY
JOHNJAY
JOINERY
JOINTLY
JOLLIFY
JOLLILY
JOLLITY
JOURNEY
KOLACKY
LOCALLY
LOFTILY
LOOSELY
LOTTERY
LOUSILY
LOVABLY
LOVERLY
LOYALLY
LOYALTY
MOCKERY
MODESTY
MOISTLY
MOLLIFY
MONTHLY
MOODILY
MOONILY
MORALLY
MORESBY
MORTIFY
MOVABLY
NOISILY
NOONDAY
NOSEGAY
NOTABLY
NOTEDLY
NOVELTY
PODGILY
POORBOY
PORTRAY
POTENCY
POTTERY
POULTRY
POVERTY
POWDERY
ROADWAY
ROBBERY
ROCKERY
ROGUERY
ROOKERY
ROOMILY
ROSEBAY
ROUGHLY
ROUNDLY
ROWDILY
ROYALLY
ROYALTY
SOAPILY
SOBERLY
SOCIETY
SOGGILY
SOLIDLY
SOMEDAY
SOMEWAY
SOOTILY
SORCERY
SORRILY
SOUNDLY
SOUTHEY
TOGGERY
TOLLWAY
TOLSTOY
TONALLY
TOPIARY
TOTALLY
TOTTERY
TOUGHLY
TOURNEY
TOWAWAY
VOCALLY
VOLUBLY
WOMANLY
WOOLLEY
WOOLSEY
WOOZILY
WORDILY
WORKDAY
WORLDLY
ZOMBIFY
ZONALLY
ZOOLOGY

••OY•••

BUOYANT
BUOYING
BUOYSUP
CLOYING

••O•Y••

ACOLYTE
ANODYNE
ANONYMS
AZODYES
EPONYMS
EPONYMY
GROMYKO
PROCYON

••O••Y•

GOODBYE
GOODBYS
LOONEYS
PHONEYS
STOREYS

••O•••Y

ALOOFLY
ANOMALY
APOLOGY
BIOGENY
BIOLOGY
BLOTCHY
BLOWDRY
BLOWFLY
BROADLY
CHOMSKY
CLOONEY
CLOSEBY
CLOSELY
COOKERY
CROSSLY
DOORWAY
DROPSBY
DROSHKY
ECOLOGY
ECONOMY
EPONYMY
EROSELY
ESOTERY
FLOUNCY
FLOWERY
FOOLERY
FOOTWAY
FROWSTY
GEODESY
GEOLOGY
GHOSTLY
GLORIFY
GOOFILY
GOONILY
GROCERY
GROSSLY
GROUCHY
ISONOMY
LOOSELY
MOODILY
MOONILY
NOONDAY
OROGENY
PHONILY
PIOUSLY
PLOWBOY
POORBOY
PROBITY
PRODIGY
PROGENY
PRONELY
PROSILY
PROSODY
PROUDLY
PTOLEMY
ROOKERY
ROOMILY
SHOOFLY
SHORTLY
SHOWERY
SHOWILY
SLOUCHY
SMOKILY
SMOOTHY
SNOWDAY
SNOWILY
SOOTILY
STOKELY
STONILY
STOODBY
STOOKEY
STOUTLY
SWOREBY
TROLLEY
TROTSKY
VRONSKY
WOOLLEY
WOOLSEY
WOOZILY
WRONGLY
ZOOLOGY

•••OY••

ALLOYED
ANNOYED
ARROYOS
DECOYED
ENJOYED
MIAOYAO
SAMOYED
SAROYAN

•••O•Y•

ACRONYM
ANTONYM
CAROLYN
HOMONYM
HYPONYM
KAROLYI
NOBODYS
SYNONYM

•••O••Y

ABBOTCY
ALLOWAY
ALOOFLY
ARMOURY
ATROPHY
BALONEY
BIGOTRY
BYGOLLY
CLOONEY
DAHOMEY
DISOBEY
DOROTHY
HELOTRY
IGNOBLY
IMSORRY
INNOWAY
MAHONEY
MASONRY
OBLOQUY
PANOPLY
SAVOURY
SHOOFLY
SMOOTHY
STOODBY
STOOKEY
STROPPY
THROATY
TIMOTHY
UNGODLY

••••OY•

AYKROYD
BADBOYS
BATBOYS
BIGBOYS
BUSBOYS
CARBOYS
CONVOYS
COWBOYS
DAYBOYS
DEPLOYS
EMPLOYE
EMPLOYS
FLYBOYS
LOWBOYS
MONTOYA
ROBROYS
TEAPOYS
TOMBOYS

••••O•Y

ALIMONY
AMATORY
ANALOGY
ANATOMY
ANCHOVY
ANTHONY
ANYBODY
APOLOGY
BALCONY
BILLOWY
BIOLOGY
CHICORY
COTTONY
COWPONY
CURSORY
CUSTODY
ECOLOGY
ECONOMY
ELUSORY
ENTROPY
EUPHONY
FACTORY
GASCONY
GEOLOGY
GREGORY
HARMONY
HICKORY
HISTORY
HYMNODY
ISONOMY
JARGONY
LASTORY
MEADOWY
MUSCOVY
OLDFOGY
ORATORY
PALJOEY
PEABODY
PILLORY
PILLOWY
PROSODY
RECTORY
SENSORY
SHADOWY
TRILOGY
VICTORY
WILLOWY
YELLOWY
ZOOLOGY

•••••OY

ATTABOY
BALLBOY
BELLBOY
BESTBOY
BLUEBOY
BOKCHOY
CHEWTOY
COPYBOY
DESTROY
HAUTBOY
HIGHBOY
HOMEBOY
KILLJOY
NEWSBOY
OVERJOY
PAGEBOY
PLAYBOY
PLOWBOY
POORBOY
SAVELOY
TOLSTOY
VICEROY

OZ•••••

OZONOUS

O•Z••••

OOZIEST

O••••Z•

ORGANZA
OUTSIZE
OXIDIZE

•OZ••••

COZENED
COZIEST
COZUMEL
COZYING
COZZENS
DOZENTH
DOZEOFF
DOZIEST
LOZENGE
NOZZLES
OOZIEST
ROZELLE
ROZZERS
WOZNIAK
WOZZECK

•O•Z•••

BORZOIS
COZZENS
DOOZIES
FOOZLED
FOOZLES
NONZERO
NOXZEMA
NOZZLES
ROZZERS
WOOZIER
WOOZILY
WOZZECK

•O••Z••

CORAZON
HORIZON
IODIZED
IODIZES
IONIZED
IONIZER
IONIZES

TOPAZES

•O••Z•
BONANZA
LORENZO

•O•••Z
KOBLENZ

••OZ•••
DOOZIES
FOOZLED
FOOZLES
GLOZING
WOOZIER
WOOZILY

••O•Z••
BRONZED
BRONZES
SNOOZED
SNOOZES

••O••Z•
AGONIZE
ANODIZE
ATOMIZE
CHORIZO
IDOLIZE
LIONIZE

••O•••Z
SHOWBIZ

•••OZ••
REBOZOS
SNOOZED
SNOOZES

••••OZ•
CARDOZO
MENDOZA
SPINOZA

••••O•Z
THEFONZ

•••••OZ
BERLIOZ
FRANKOZ

PA•••••
PAANGAS
PABLUMS
PABULUM
PACECAR
PACHISI
PACIFIC
PACKAGE
PACKARD
PACKERS
PACKETS
PACKICE
PACKING
PACKRAT
PACKSUP
PADDERS
PADDIES
PADDING
PADDLED
PADDLER
PADDLES
PADDOCK
PADLOCK
PADRONE
PADRONI
PADUANS
PADUCAH
PAGEANT
PAGEBOY
PAGEFUL
PAGODAS
PAHLAVI
PAIDFOR
PAIDOFF
PAIDOUT
PAILFUL
PAILOUS
PAINFUL
PAINTED
PAINTER
PAIRING
PAIROFF
PAIRSUP
PAISANO
PAISLEY
PAIUTES
PAJAMAS
PALACES
PALADIN
PALANCE
PALATAL
PALATES
PALAVER
PALAZZI
PALAZZO
PALEDRY
PALERMO
PALETTE
PALFREY
PALIEST
PALJOEY
PALLETS
PALLIER
PALLING
PALLIUM
PALLORS
PALMARY
PALMATE
PALMIER
PALMING
PALMIST
PALMOFF
PALMOIL
PALMTOP
PALOMAR
PALOOKA
PALTERS
PALTROW
PAMPERS
PANACEA
PANACHE
PANADAS
PANAMAS
PANARAB
PANCAKE
PANCHAX
PANDECT
PANDERS
PANDITS
PANDORA
PANELED
PANFISH
PANFULS
PANICKY
PANICLE
PANNERS
PANNIER
PANNING
PANOPLY
PANPIPE
PANSIES
PANSOUT
PANTHER
PANTING
PANURGE
PANZERS
PAPADOC
PAPAGOS
PAPAYAS
PAPEETE
PAPERED
PAPERER
PAPILLA
PAPLIKE
PAPOOSE
PAPRIKA
PAPUANS
PAPYRUS
PARABLE
PARADED
PARADES
PARADOX
PARAGON
PARAPET
PARAPHS
PARASOL
PARATUS
PARBOIL
PARCELS
PARCHED
PARCHES
PARDNER
PARDONS
PARENTS
PARFAIT
PARGETS
PARIAHS
PARINGS
PARKADE
PARKING
PARKWAY
PARLAYS
PARLEYS
PARLORS
PARLOUR
PARLOUS
PAROLED
PAROLEE
PAROLES
PARQUET
PARRIED
PARRIER
PARRIES
PARRING
PARRISH
PARROTS
PARSECS
PARSEES
PARSERS
PARSING
PARSLEY
PARSNIP
PARSONS
PARTAKE
PARTIAL
PARTIED
PARTIER
PARTIES
PARTING
PARTITA
PARTITE
PARTNER
PARTOOK
PARTOUT
PARTWAY
PARURES
PARVENU
PASCHAL
PASSADO
PASSAGE
PASSELS
PASSERS
PASSEUL
PASSFOR
PASSING
PASSION
PASSIVE
PASSKEY
PASSOFF
PASSOUT
PASTDUE
PASTELS
PASTERN
PASTEUP
PASTEUR
PASTIER
PASTIME
PASTINA
PASTING
PASTORS
PASTURE
PATACAS
PATCHED
PATCHES
PATCHUP
PATELLA
PATENTS
PATERNO
PATHWAY
PATIENT
PATINAS
PATNESS
PATRIAL
PATRICE
PATRICK
PATRIOT
PATROLS
PATRONS
PATROON
PATSIES
PATTENS
PATTERN
PATTERS
PATTIES
PATTING
PAUCITY
PAULINA
PAULINE
PAULING
PAULIST
PAULSEN
PAUNCHY
PAUPERS
PAUSING
PAVANES
PAVIOUR
PAVLOVA
PAWEDAT
PAWKIER
PAWNEES
PAWNERS
PAWNING
PAWNOFF
PAWPAWS
PAYABLE
PAYCASH
PAYDAYS
PAYDIRT
PAYLOAD
PAYMENT
PAYOFFS
PAYOLAS
PAYOUTS
PAYROLL
PAYSFOR
PAYSOFF
PAYSOUT

P•A••••
PAANGAS
PEABEAN
PEABODY
PEACHED
PEACHES
PEACOAT
PEACOCK
PEAFOWL
PEAHENS
PEAKING
PEAKISH
PEALIKE
PEALING
PEANUTS
PEAPODS
PEARLED
PEARSON
PEASANT
PEASOUP
PEATBOG
PEATIER
PEAVEYS
PHAEDRA
PHAETON
PHALANX
PHANTOM
PHARAOH
PHARLAP
PHARYNX
PHASEIN
PHASERS
PHASING
PIANISM
PIANIST
PIASTER
PIASTRE
PIAZZAS
PLACARD
PLACATE
PLACEBO
PLACERS
PLACIDO
PLACING
PLACKET
PLAGUED
PLAGUES
PLAICES
PLAINER
PLAINLY
PLAINTS
PLAITED
PLANERS
PLANETS
PLANING
PLANISH
PLANKED
PLANNED
PLANNER
PLANOUT
PLANSON
PLANTAR
PLANTED
PLANTER
PLAQUES
PLASHED
PLASHES
PLASMAS
PLASTER
PLASTIC
PLATEAU
PLATENS
PLATERS
PLATIER
PLATING
PLATOON
PLATTER
PLATYPI
PLAUDIT
PLAUTUS
PLAYACT
PLAYBOY
PLAYDOH
PLAYERS
PLAYFUL
PLAYING
PLAYLET
PLAYOFF
PLAYOUT
PLAYPEN
PLAYSAT
PLAYSON
PLAYSUP
POACHED
POACHER
POACHES
PRAETOR
PRAIRIE
PRAISED
PRAISER
PRAISES
PRALINE
PRANCED
PRANCER
PRANCES
PRANGED
PRANKED
PRATERS
PRATING
PRATTLE
PRAYERS
PRAYFOR
PRAYING
PRAYSTO
PSALMED
PSALTER
PSANDQS

P••A•••
PAJAMAS
PALACES
PALADIN
PALANCE
PALATAL
PALATES
PALAVER
PALAZZI
PALAZZO
PANACEA
PANACHE
PANADAS
PANAMAS
PANARAB
PAPADOC
PAPAGOS
PAPAYAS
PARABLE
PARADED
PARADES
PARADOX
PARAGON
PARAPET
PARAPHS
PARASOL
PARATUS
PATACAS
PAVANES
PAYABLE
PDJAMES
PEDALED
PEDANTS
PEGASUS
PELAGES
PELAGIC
PENALTY
PENANCE
PENATES
PESAWAS
PETALED
PETARDS
PHRASAL
PHRASED
PHRASES
PICADOR
PICANTE
PICARDY
PICAROS
PICASSO
PINATAS
PIRAEUS
PIRANHA
PIRATED
PIRATES
PIRATIC
PITAPAT
PIZARRO
PLEADED
PLEADER
PLEASED
PLEASER
PLEASES
PLEATED
PLIABLE
PLIABLY
PLIANCY
POLARIS
POMADED
POMADES
POSADAS
POTABLE
POTAGES
PREACHY
PREAMPS
PULASKI
PUTAMEN
PUTAWAY
PYJAMAS
PYRAMID
PYRAMUS

P•••A••
PACKAGE
PACKARD
PADUANS
PAGEANT
PAHLAVI
PAISANO
PALMARY
PALMATE
PANCAKE
PAPUANS
PARFAIT
PARIAHS
PARKADE
PARLAYS
PARTAKE
PASSADO
PASSAGE
PAWPAWS
PAYCASH
PAYDAYS
PEASANT
PECCANT
PECCARY
PEDLARS
PEDWAYS
PEERAGE
PELTATE
PENDANT
PENNAME
PENNANT
PENNATE
PENPALS
PENTADS
PEONAGE
PEPPARD
PEPTALK
PERCALE
PERHAPS
PERTAIN
PERVADE
PETNAME
PHALANX
PHARAOH
PICCARD
PICKAXE
PIEBALD
PIEPANS
PIGTAIL
PILLAGE
PILLARS
PINBALL
PINNACE
PINNATE
PINOAKS
PINTAIL
PINWALE
PIQUANT
PITFALL
PITSAWS
PIZZAZZ
PLACARD
PLACATE
PLAYACT
PLENARY
PLUMAGE
PLURALS
POLEAXE
POLKAED
POLLACK
POMPANO
PONIARD
POPLARS
POPTART
PORTAGE
PORTALS
POSTAGE
POTTAGE
PRECAST
PREDATE
PREDAWN
PREFABS
PREFACE
PRELATE
PREPAID
PREPARE
PREPAYS
PRESAGE
PRESALE
PRETAPE
PREVAIL
PREWASH
PRIMACY
PRIMARY
PRIMATE
PRIVACY
PRIVATE
PROBATE
PROFANE
PROPANE
PRORATA
PRORATE
PROSAIC
PTBOATS
PULSARS
PULSATE
PUNJABI
PUNKAHS
PURDAHS

P••••A•
PAANGAS
PACECAR
PACKRAT
PADUCAH
PAGODAS
PAJAMAS
PALATAL
PALOMAR
PANADAS
PANAMAS
PANARAB
PANCHAX
PAPAYAS
PARKWAY
PARTIAL
PARTWAY
PASCHAL
PATACAS
PATHWAY
PATINAS
PATRIAL
PAWEDAT
PAYLOAD
PAYOLAS
PEABEAN
PEACOAT
PECKSAT
PEDICAB
PEEKSAT
PEERSAT
PELICAN
PELOTAS
PEMICAN
PERLMAN
PERSIAN
PERUSAL
PESAWAS
PESETAS
PHARLAP
PHIDIAS
PHINEAS
PHOBIAS
PHRASAL
PIAZZAS
PICKSAT
PIKEMAN
PINATAS
PINCHAS
PINESAP
PINETAR
PINHEAD
PITAPAT
PITTMAN
PIVOTAL
PLANTAR
PLASMAS
PLATEAU
PLAYSAT
PLOWMAN
PLUVIAL
POKEDAT
POKESAT
POLECAR
POLECAT
POLLTAX
PONTIAC
POOHBAH
POPULAR
PORTMAN
PORTRAY
POSADAS
POSTBAG
POSTMAN
POSTWAR
POTOMAC
POTSDAM
PREHEAT
PRELOAD
PRESOAK
PROGRAM
PROPMAN
PROTEAN
PULLMAN
PULLTAB
PURITAN
PUTAWAY
PYJAMAS
PYTHIAN
PYTHIAS

P•••••A
PALOOKA
PANACEA
PANDORA
PAPILLA
PAPRIKA
PARTITA
PASTINA
PATELLA
PAULINA
PAVLOVA
PERGOLA
PERSONA
PETUNIA
PHAEDRA
PIPEMMA
PIRANHA
PLECTRA
PODRIDA
POLENTA
POMPEIA
PORSENA
PRORATA
PRUSSIA

•PA••••
APACHES
APATITE
EPARCHS
EPARCHY
EPAULET
IPANEMA
OPACITY
OPALINE
OPAQUES
SPACERS
SPACIER
SPACING
SPACKLE
SPADERS
SPADING
SPALLED
SPAMMED
SPAMMER
SPANDEX
SPANGLE
SPANGLY
SPANIEL
SPANISH
SPANKED
SPANKER
SPANNED
SPANNER
SPARELY
SPAREST
SPARGED
SPARGES
SPARING
SPARKED
SPARKLE
SPARRED
SPARROW
SPARSER
SPARTAN
SPASSKY
SPATIAL
SPATTED
SPATTER
SPATULA
SPAVINS
SPAWNED
SPAYING
UPATREE

•P•A•••
APPALLS
APPARAT
APPAREL
OPIATES
SPEAKER
SPEAKOF
SPEAKUP
SPEARED
SPLASHY
SPLAYED
SPRAINS
SPRAWLS
SPRAYED
SPRAYER
UPDATED
UPDATES
UPLANDS
UPRAISE
UPTAKES
UPWARDS

•P••A••
APPEALS
APPEARS
APPEASE
APPLAUD
OPENAIR
OPERAND
OPERATE
SPINACH
SPIRALS
SPIRANT
SPOKANE
SPREADS
UPBEATS
UPBRAID
UPDRAFT
UPGRADE
UPLOADS
UPPSALA
UPQUARK
UPROARS
UPSCALE
UPSTAGE
UPSTART
UPSTATE

•P•••A•
APPARAT
APTERAL
EPIGRAM
EPOCHAL
OPENBAR
OPTICAL
OPTIMAL
SPARTAN
SPATIAL
SPECIAL
SPIREAS
SPORRAN
SPOUSAL
UPTOPAR

•P••••A
APHELIA
IPANEMA
OPENSEA
OPHELIA
SPATULA
SPECTRA
SPINOZA
UPPSALA

••PA•••
ALPACAS
APPALLS
APPARAT
APPAREL
AUPAIRS
BYPATHS
CAPABLE
CAPABLY
CAPAPIE
DEPALMA
DEPARTS
DOPANTS
EMPANEL
EMPATHY
ESPANOL
ESPARTO
EXPANDS
EXPANSE
EXPARTE
HEPARIN
HEPATIC
IMPACTS
IMPAIRS
IMPALAS
IMPALED
IMPALES
IMPANEL
IMPARTS
IMPASSE
IMPASTO
LAPALMA
LEPANTO
NEPALIS
PAPADOC
PAPAGOS
PAPAYAS
RAPANUI
REPAINT
REPAIRS
REPAPER
REPASTE
REPASTS
REPAVED
REPAVES
TOPAZES
UNPACKS
UNPAVED
ZAPATEO

••P•A••
APPEALS
APPEARS
APPEASE
APPLAUD
ASPHALT
ATPEACE
BIPLANE
BYPLAYS
CAPEANN
CAPTAIN
COPLAND
CUPCAKE
DEPLANE
DEPRAVE
ENPLANE
ESPIALS
EXPIATE
EXPLAIN
HEPCATS
HEPTADS
IMPEACH
IMPLANT
INPEACE
INPHASE
INPLACE
LAPLACE
LAPLAND
LAPLATA
LIPBALM
OMPHALI
ORPHANS
PAPUANS
PEPPARD
PEPTALK
POPLARS
POPTART
RAPHAEL
REPEALS
REPEATS
REPLACE
REPLANS
REPLANT
REPLATE
REPLAYS
RIPRAPS
RIPSAWS
RUPIAHS
SAPSAGO
SOPRANO
TOPHATS
TOPIARY
TOPKAPI
TOPMAST
TOPSAIL
UPPSALA

••P••A•
ALPACAS
APPARAT
BIPEDAL
BIPOLAR
CAPITAL
CAPITAN
CAPSHAW
CAPSTAN
COPULAE
COPULAS
COPYCAT
CUPOLAS
DEPOSAL
DIPOLAR
ESPOSAS
IMPALAS
LIPREAD
NUPTIAL
ORPHEAN
PAPAYAS
POPULAR
REPOMAN
TAPEMAN
TOPCOAT
TOPICAL
TYPICAL

••P•••A
AMPHORA
CAPELLA
COPPOLA
DEPALMA
DIPLOMA
EMPORIA
LAPALMA
LAPLATA
NAPHTHA
PAPILLA
PAPRIKA
PIPEMMA
REPLICA
TAPIOCA
UPPSALA

•••PA••
ARAPAHO
BITPART
CALPACS
CAMPARI
CARPALS
CARPARK
CHAPATI
CLIPART
COMPACT
COMPANY
COMPARE
COMPASS
DESPAIR
FLYPAST
FRYPANS
GALPALS
HISPANO
ICEPACK
INSPANS
JAMPACK
KAMPALA
KEYPADS
LEOPARD
LESPAUL
LOWPAID

MUDPACK
OILPANS
OOMPAHS
OUTPACE
OVIPARA
PAWPAWS
PENPALS
PEPPARD
PIEPANS
POMPANO
PREPAID
PREPARE
PREPAYS
PROPANE
RAMPAGE
RAMPANT
RAMPART
RATPACK
SAMPANS
SHEPARD
SIXPACK
SURPASS
TAIPANS
TOSPARE
TOWPATH
TREPANS
TYMPANA
TYMPANI
WARPATH
WEBPAGE

•••P•A•
AIRPLAY
BESPEAK
CASPIAN
CHAPEAU
CHAPMAN
COWPEAS
DEEPFAT
DISPLAY
DRIPPAN
ENDPLAY
GRAPPAS
GUNPLAY
HOOPLAS
JUMPSAT
KEEPSAT
LINPIAO
MISPLAY
OFFPEAK
OUTPLAY
PROPMAN
SAMPRAS
SHIPMAN
SNAPSAT
SNIPEAT
STOPGAP
TEMPLAR
UTOPIAN
UTOPIAS
WHIPSAW

•••P••A
AMAPOLA
COPPOLA
DEEPSEA
KAMPALA
LEMPIRA
OVIPARA
POMPEIA
SCAPULA
TEMPERA
TEMPURA
TYMPANA
VAMPIRA

••••PA•
BASEPAY
BEARPAW
CATSPAW
DEADPAN
DISHPAN
DOWNPAT
DRIPPAN
DUSTPAN
FAUXPAS
FOOTPAD
FOREPAW
GRAMPAS
GRAPPAS
HARDPAN
HELIPAD
KNEEPAD
LILYPAD
MADEPAR
MAKEPAR
NOTEPAD
OEDIPAL
PITAPAT
SHERPAS
SICKPAY
TRAMPAS
UPTOPAR

••••P•A
AGRIPPA
OLYMPIA
SNOWPEA

•••••PA
AGRIPPA
CATALPA
GRANDPA

P•B••••
PABLUMS
PABULUM
PEBBLED
PEBBLES
POBOXES
PTBOATS
PUBERTY
PUBLICS
PUBLISH

P••B•••
PARBOIL
PEABEAN
PEABODY
PEBBLED
PEBBLES
PHOBIAS
PHOBICS
PIEBALD
PINBALL
PITBOSS
PITBULL
PREBEND
PROBATE
PROBERS
PROBING
PROBITY
PROBLEM
PROBONO
PUEBLOS

P•••B••
PAGEBOY
PARABLE
PAYABLE
PEATBOG
PHILBIN
PHOEBES
PHOEBUS
PILLBOX
PILLBUG
PLAYBOY
PLIABLE
PLIABLY
PLOWBOY
PLUMBED
PLUMBER
POOHBAH
POORBOX
POORBOY
POSTBAG
POSTBOX
POTABLE

P••••B•
PLACEBO
PREFABS
PUNJABI

P•••••B
PANARAB
PEDICAB
PERTURB
POTHERB
PROVERB
PULLTAB

•PB••••
UPBEATS
UPBORNE
UPBRAID

•P••B••
OPENBAR

••PB•••
HEPBURN
HIPBONE
HIPBOOT
LAPBELT
LIPBALM

••P•B••
CAPABLE
CAPABLY
COPYBOY

••P••B•
LAPROBE

•••PB••
SOAPBOX

•••P•B•
DROPSBY

P•C••••
PACECAR
PACHISI
PACIFIC
PACKAGE
PACKARD
PACKERS
PACKETS
PACKICE
PACKING
PACKRAT
PACKSUP
PECCANT
PECCARY
PECKIER
PECKING
PECKISH
PECKSAT
PECTINS
PICADOR
PICANTE
PICARDY
PICAROS
PICASSO
PICCARD
PICCOLO
PICKAXE
PICKENS
PICKERS
PICKETS
PICKETT
PICKIER
PICKING
PICKLED
PICKLES
PICKOFF
PICKOUT
PICKSAT
PICKSON
PICKSUP
PICKUPS
PICNICS
PICTISH
PICTURE
POCKETS
POCONOS
PUCCINI
PUCKERS
PUCKETT
PUCKISH

P••C•••
PANCAKE
PANCHAX
PARCELS
PARCHED
PARCHES
PASCHAL
PATCHED
PATCHES
PATCHUP
PAUCITY
PAYCASH
PEACHED
PEACHES
PEACOAT
PEACOCK
PECCANT
PECCARY
PENCILS
PERCALE
PERCENT
PERCHED
PERCHES
PETCOCK
PICCARD
PICCOLO
PIECERS
PIECING
PINCERS
PINCHAS
PINCHED
PINCHER
PINCHES
PINCURL
PISCINE
PISCOPO
PITCHED
PITCHER
PITCHES
PITCHIN
PLACARD
PLACATE
PLACEBO
PLACERS
PLACIDO
PLACING
PLACKET
PLECTRA
PLUCKED
POACHED
POACHER
POACHES
PONCHOS
POOCHES
POPCORN
PORCHES
PORCINE
POUCHED
POUCHES
PRECAST
PRECEDE
PRECEPT
PRECISE
PRECOOK
PRECOOL
PRICERS
PRICIER
PRICING
PRICKED
PRICKLE
PRICKLY
PROCEED
PROCESS
PROCTOR
PROCURE
PROCYON
PSYCHED
PSYCHES
PSYCHIC
PSYCHUP
PUCCINI
PUNCHED
PUNCHER
PUNCHES
PUNCHIN
PUNCHUP
PURCELL
PYNCHON

P•••C••
PACECAR
PADUCAH
PALACES
PANACEA
PANACHE
PANICKY
PANICLE
PATACAS
PAUNCHY
PEDICAB
PEDICEL
PEDICLE
PELICAN
PEMICAN
PENUCHE
PIERCED
PIERCES
PINOCLE
PLAICES
POLECAR
POLECAT
POLICED
POLICES
PORSCHE
POUNCED
POUNCER
POUNCES
PRANCED
PRANCER
PRANCES
PREACHY
PRINCES
PUMICES

P••••C•
PACKICE
PADDOCK
PADLOCK
PALANCE
PANDECT
PARSECS
PATRICE
PATRICK
PEACOCK
PENANCE
PERFECT
PETCOCK
PETROCK
PHOBICS
PHONICS
PHOTICS
PHYSICS
PICNICS
PIMLICO
PINNACE
PLAYACT
PLIANCY
POETICS
POLLACK
POLLOCK
PORTICO
POTENCY
POTLUCK
PREDICT
PREFACE
PREFECT
PRIMACY
PRIVACY
PRODUCE
PRODUCT
PROJECT
PROTECT
PUBLICS
PUDENCY

P•••••C
PACIFIC
PAPADOC
PELAGIC
PHRENIC
PIRATIC
PLASTIC
POLEMIC
POLITIC
PONTIAC
POTOMAC
POULENC
PROSAIC
PSYCHIC
PYRRHIC

•PC••••
IPCRESS
UPCLOSE

•P•C•••
APACHES
APOCOPE
EPICENE
EPICURE
EPOCHAL
OPACITY
SPACERS
SPACIER
SPACING
SPACKLE
SPECCED
SPECIAL
SPECIES
SPECIFY
SPECING
SPECKED
SPECKLE
SPECTER
SPECTOR
SPECTRA
SPECTRE
SPICERY
SPICEUP
SPICIER
SPICILY
SPICING
UPSCALE

•P••C••
APERCUS
APRICOT
EPARCHS
EPARCHY
OPTICAL
SPECCED
SPENCER
SPLICED
SPLICER
SPLICES
SPRUCED
SPRUCER
SPRUCES
UPTICKS

•P•••C•
IPSWICH
SPINACH
SPLOTCH

••PC•••
CUPCAKE
HEPCATS
POPCORN
RIPCORD
TOPCOAT
ZIPCODE

••P•C••
ALPACAS
ASPECTS
CAPECOD
COPYCAT
DEPICTS
EXPECTS
IMPACTS
KOPECKS
TOPICAL
TYPICAL
UNPACKS

••P••C•
ATPEACE
CAPRICE
COPPICE
DIPTYCH
IMPEACH
INPEACE
INPLACE
LAPLACE
REPLACE
REPLICA
REPRICE
TAPIOCA
TOPKICK

••P•••C
HEPATIC
LIPSYNC
PAPADOC
ZAPOTEC

•••PC••
JUMPCUT
SOUPCON

•••P•C•
AUSPICE
CALPACS
COMPACT
COPPICE
DRSPOCK
HENPECK
HOSPICE
ICEPACK
ICEPICK
INSPECT
JAMPACK
MRSPOCK
MUDPACK
NITPICK
OUTPACE
RATPACK
RESPECT
SERPICO
SIXPACK
SUSPECT
TAMPICO
TROPICS

•••P••C
ASEPTIC
CRYPTIC
DELPHIC
EDAPHIC
GRAPHIC
SCEPTIC
SKEPTIC
STYPTIC
TROPHIC

••••P•C
OLYMPIC

PD•••••
PDJAMES

P•D••••
PADDERS
PADDIES
PADDING
PADDLED
PADDLER
PADDLES
PADDOCK
PADLOCK
PADRONE
PADRONI
PADUANS
PADUCAH
PEDALED
PEDANTS
PEDDLED
PEDDLER
PEDDLES
PEDICAB
PEDICEL
PEDICLE
PEDLARS
PEDWAYS
PIDGEON
PIDGINS
PODGIER
PODGILY
PODIUMS
PODLIKE
PODRIDA
PUDDING
PUDDLED
PUDDLES
PUDENCY
PUDGIER
PUDGILY

P••D•••
PADDERS
PADDIES
PADDING
PADDLED
PADDLER
PADDLES
PADDOCK
PAIDFOR
PAIDOFF
PAIDOUT
PANDECT
PANDERS
PANDITS
PANDORA
PARDNER
PARDONS
PAYDAYS
PAYDIRT
PEDDLED
PEDDLER
PEDDLES
PENDANT
PENDENT
PENDING
PERDIEM
PHIDIAS
PINDOWN
PLEDGED
PLEDGEE
PLEDGER
PLEDGES
PLODDED
PLODDER
POLDERS
PONDERS
POODLES
POWDERS
POWDERY
PREDATE
PREDAWN
PREDICT
PRIDING
PRODDED
PRODDER
PRODIGY
PRODUCE
PRODUCT
PRUDENT
PRUDERY
PRUDHOE
PRUDISH
PUDDING
PUDDLED
PUDDLES
PUNDITS
PURDAHS
PUTDOWN
PYEDOGS

P•••D••
PAGODAS
PALADIN
PALEDRY
PANADAS
PAPADOC
PARADED
PARADES
PARADOX
PASTDUE
PAWEDAT
PERIDOT
PHAEDRA
PICADOR
PILEDIN
PILEDON
PILEDUP
PIPEDUP
PLAUDIT
PLAYDOH
PLEADED
PLEADER
PLODDED
PLODDER
PLUNDER
POKEDAT
POMADED
POMADES
POSADAS
POTSDAM
POUNDED
POUNDER
PRODDED
PRODDER
PROUDER
PROUDLY
PSANDQS
PYXIDES

P••••D•
PARKADE
PASSADO
PEABODY
PEAPODS
PENTADS
PEPTIDE
PERFIDY
PERIODS
PERVADE
PETARDS
PICARDY
PLACIDO
PODRIDA
PONGIDS
PRECEDE
PRELUDE
PREMEDS
PRESIDE
PROSODY
PROVIDE

P•••••D
PACKARD
PADDLED
PAINTED
PANELED
PAPERED
PARADED
PARCHED
PAROLED
PARRIED
PARTIED
PATCHED
PAYLOAD
PEACHED
PEARLED
PEBBLED
PEDALED
PEDDLED
PEOPLED
PEPPARD
PERCHED
PERSEID
PERUSED
PESTLED
PETALED
PETERED
PHOTOED
PHRASED
PICCARD
PICKLED
PIEBALD
PIERCED
PIFFLED
PILOTED
PINCHED
PINHEAD
PIRATED
PITCHED
PIVOTED
PLACARD
PLAGUED
PLAITED
PLANKED
PLANNED
PLANTED
PLASHED
PLEADED
PLEASED
PLEATED
PLEDGED
PLINKED
PLODDED
PLOPPED
PLOTTED
PLUCKED
PLUGGED
PLUMBED
PLUMPED
PLUNGED
PLUNKED
PLYWOOD
POACHED
POINTED
POLICED
POLKAED
POMADED
PONIARD
POPEYED
POPPLED
PORTEND
POSITED
POUCHED
POUNCED
POUNDED
POWERED
PRAISED
PRANCED
PRANGED
PRANKED
PREBEND
PREENED
PRELOAD
PREPAID
PRESSED
PRETEND
PRICKED
PRIMPED
PRINKED
PRINTED
PROCEED
PRODDED
PROGGED
PRONGED
PROOFED
PROPPED
PROWLED
PSALMED
PSYCHED
PUDDLED
PUNCHED
PURFLED
PURPLED
PURSUED
PUTTIED
PUZZLED
PYRAMID

•PD••••
UPDATED
UPDATES
UPDRAFT

•P•D•••
SPADERS
SPADING
SPIDERS
SPIDERY

•P••D••
APSIDES
SPANDEX
SPEEDED
SPEEDER
SPEEDOS
SPEEDUP
SPENDER
SPIEDON
SPINDLE
SPINDLY
SPINDRY
SPONDEE
UPENDED

•P•••D•
APPENDS
EPISODE
SPREADS
UPGRADE
UPHOLDS
UPLANDS
UPLOADS
UPWARDS

•P••••D
APPLAUD
APPLIED
APPOSED
APRONED
OPENEND
OPERAND
OPPOSED
SPALLED
SPAMMED
SPANKED
SPANNED
SPARGED
SPARKED
SPARRED
SPATTED
SPAWNED
SPEARED
SPECCED
SPECKED
SPEEDED
SPELLED
SPIELED
SPILLED
SPLAYED
SPLICED
SPOILED
SPONGED
SPOOFED
SPOOKED
SPOOLED
SPOONED
SPORTED
SPOTTED
SPOUTED
SPRAYED
SPRUCED
SPURNED
SPURRED
SPURTED
UPBRAID
UPDATED
UPENDED

••PD•••
LAPDOGS
TOPDOGS
TOPDOWN

••P•D••
BIPEDAL
HYPEDUP
IMPEDED
IMPEDES
LIPIDES
PAPADOC
PIPEDUP
RAPIDER
RAPIDLY
ROPEDIN
TEPIDLY
TYPEDUP
VAPIDLY
WIPEDUP

••P••D•
APPENDS
CAPSIDS
DEPENDS
EXPANDS
EXPENDS
EXPLODE
HEPTADS
IMPENDS
IMPLODE
PEPTIDE
RIPTIDE
TOPSIDE
ZIPCODE

••P•••D
APPLAUD
APPLIED
APPOSED
ASPIRED
CAPECOD
CAPERED
COPLAND
DAPPLED
DEPONED
DEPOSED
DEPUTED
DIPLOID
EMPTIED
EXPIRED
EXPOSED
EXPOUND
HOPPLED
IMPALED
IMPEDED
IMPLIED
IMPOSED
IMPOUND
IMPUTED
LAPELED
LAPLAND
LIPREAD
OPPOSED
PAPERED
PEPPARD
POPEYED
POPPLED
REPAVED
REPINED
REPLIED
REPOSED
REPUTED
RIPCORD
RIPENED
RIPPLED
TAPERED
TIPPLED
TIPTOED
TOPPLED
UMPIRED
UNPAVED
UNPILED

•••PD••
DRIPDRY

•••P•D•
CUSPIDS
ELAPIDS
ISOPODS
KEYPADS
PEAPODS
TORPEDO
TRIPODS
UNIPODS
VESPIDS

•••P••D
ADAPTED
ADOPTED
BLIPPED
CHAPPED
CHIPPED
CHOPPED
CLAPPED
CLIPPED

CLOPPED
COOPTED
COUPLED
CROPPED
DAPPLED
DEEPEND
DIMPLED
DRIPPED
DROPPED
ELAPSED
ERUPTED
FLAPPED
FLIPPED
FLOPPED
GRAPHED
GRIPPED
HOPPLED
LEOPARD
LEOPOLD
LOWPAID
MORPHED
PEOPLED
PEPPARD
PLOPPED
POPPLED
PREPAID
PROPPED
PURPLED
QUIPPED
RESPOND
REUPPED
RIMPLED
RIPPLED
RUMPLED
SAMPLED
SHEPARD
SHIPPED
SHOPPED
SKIPPED
SLAPPED
SLIPPED
SLOPPED
SNAPPED
SNIPPED
STAPLED
STEPPED
STIPEND
STOPPED
SUSPEND
SWAPPED
SWOPPED
TEMPTED
TIPPLED
TOPPLED
TRAPPED
TRIPLED
TRIPPED
WHIPPED
WHOPPED
WHUPPED
WIMPLED
WRAPPED

••••P•D

BLEEPED
BLIPPED
BLOOPED
CHAMPED
CHAPPED
CHEEPED
CHIPPED
CHIRPED
CHOMPED
CHOPPED
CLAMPED
CLAPPED
CLASPED
CLIPPED
CLOMPED
CLOPPED
CLUMPED
CRAMPED
CREEPED
CRIMPED
CRISPED
CROPPED
DECAPOD
DRIPPED
DROOPED
DROPPED
ESCAPED
FLAPPED
FLIPPED
FLOPPED
FOOTPAD
GRASPED
GRIPPED
GROUPED
GRUMPED
HELIPAD
INSIPID
KNEEPAD
LILYPAD
NOTEPAD
OCTOPOD
PLOPPED
PLUMPED
PRIMPED
PROPPED
QUIPPED
RETAPED
RETYPED
REUPPED
SCALPED
SCAMPED
SCARPED
SCOOPED
SCRAPED
SEEDPOD
SHARPED
SHIPPED
SHOPPED
SKIMPED
SKIPPED
SLAPPED
SLIPPED
SLOPPED
SLUMPED
SLURPED
SNAPPED
SNIPPED
SNOOPED
STAMPED
STEEPED
STEPPED
STOMPED
STOOPED
STOPPED
STRIPED
STUMPED
SWAMPED
SWAPPED
SWOOPED
SWOPPED
THUMPED
TRAMPED
TRAPPED
TRIPPED
TROOPED
TRUMPED
UNTAPED
USURPED
WHELPED
WHIPPED
WHOMPED
WHOOPED
WHOPPED
WHUPPED
WRAPPED

PE•••••

PEABEAN
PEABODY
PEACHED
PEACHES
PEACOAT
PEACOCK
PEAFOWL
PEAHENS
PEAKING
PEAKISH
PEALIKE
PEALING
PEANUTS
PEAPODS
PEARLED
PEARSON
PEASANT
PEASOUP
PEATBOG
PEATIER
PEAVEYS
PEBBLED
PEBBLES
PECCANT
PECCARY
PECKIER
PECKING
PECKISH
PECKSAT
PECTINS
PEDALED
PEDANTS
PEDDLED
PEDDLER
PEDDLES
PEDICAB
PEDICEL
PEDICLE
PEDLARS
PEDWAYS
PEEKERS
PEEKING
PEEKOUT
PEEKSAT
PEELERS
PEELING
PEELOFF
PEEPERS
PEEPING
PEEPLES
PEERAGE
PEERESS
PEERING
PEEROUT
PEERSAT
PEERSIN
PEEVING
PEEVISH
PEEWEES
PEGASUS
PEGGING
PEGLESS
PEGLIKE
PEGTOPS
PELAGES
PELAGIC
PELICAN
PELISSE
PELLETS
PELOTAS
PELTATE
PELTERS
PELTING
PELTISH
PEMICAN
PENALTY
PENANCE
PENATES
PENCILS
PENDANT
PENDENT
PENDING
PENGUIN
PENLIKE
PENNAME
PENNANT
PENNATE
PENNERS
PENNIES
PENNING
PENNONS
PENPALS
PENSEES
PENSION
PENSIVE
PENTADS
PENTIUM
PENUCHE
PENULTS
PEONAGE
PEONIES
PEOPLED
PEOPLES
PEPLUMS
PEPPARD
PEPPERS
PEPPERY
PEPPIER
PEPPILY
PEPPING
PEPSINS
PEPTALK
PEPTIDE
PEQUOTS
PERCALE
PERCENT
PERCHED
PERCHES
PERDIEM
PERFECT
PERFIDY
PERFORM
PERFUME
PERGOLA
PERHAPS
PERIDOT
PERIGEE
PERIODS
PERJURE
PERJURY
PERKIER
PERKILY
PERKING
PERKINS
PERKISH
PERKSUP
PERLITE
PERLMAN
PERMING
PERMITS
PERPLEX
PERRIER
PERSEID
PERSEUS
PERSIAN
PERSIST
PERSIUS
PERSONA
PERSONS
PERTAIN
PERTEST
PERTURB
PERUKES
PERUSAL
PERUSED
PERUSER
PERUSES
PERVADE
PESAWAS
PESETAS
PESKIER
PESKILY
PESTERS
PESTLED
PESTLES
PETALED
PETARDS
PETCOCK
PETERED
PETIOLE
PETITES
PETNAME
PETRELS
PETRIFY
PETROCK
PETROLS
PETROUS
PETTERS
PETTIER
PETTILY
PETTING
PETTISH
PETUNIA
PEUGEOT

P•E••••

PEEKERS
PEEKING
PEEKOUT
PEEKSAT
PEELERS
PEELING
PEELOFF
PEEPERS
PEEPING
PEEPLES
PEERAGE
PEERESS
PEERING
PEEROUT
PEERSAT
PEERSIN
PEEVING
PEEVISH
PEEWEES
PFENNIG
PHENOLS
PHENOMS
PIEBALD
PIECERS
PIECING
PIELIKE
PIEPANS
PIERCED
PIERCES
PIERROT
PIETIES
PIETINS
PIETISM
PIETIST
PLEADED
PLEADER
PLEASED
PLEASER
PLEASES
PLEATED
PLECTRA
PLEDGED
PLEDGEE
PLEDGER
PLEDGES
PLENARY
PLENUMS
PLEXORS
POETICS
PREACHY
PREAMPS
PREBEND
PRECAST
PRECEDE
PRECEPT
PRECISE
PRECOOK
PRECOOL
PREDATE
PREDAWN
PREDICT
PREEMIE
PREEMPT
PREENED
PREENER
PREFABS
PREFACE
PREFECT
PREFERS
PREHEAT
PRELATE
PRELIMS
PRELOAD
PRELUDE
PREMEDS
PREMIER
PREMISE
PREMISS
PREMIUM
PRENUPS
PREPAID
PREPARE
PREPAYS
PREPPIE
PREQUEL
PRESAGE
PRESALE
PRESELL
PRESENT
PRESETS
PRESIDE
PRESLEY
PRESOAK
PRESORT
PRESSED
PRESSER
PRESSES
PRESSON
PRESSUP
PRESTON
PRESTOS
PRESUME
PRETAPE
PRETEEN
PRETEND
PRETEST
PRETEXT
PRETZEL
PREVAIL
PREVENT
PREVIEW
PREWASH
PREXIES
PREYSON
PUEBLOS
PUERILE
PYEDOGS

P••E•••

PACECAR
PAGEANT
PAGEBOY
PAGEFUL
PALEDRY
PALERMO
PALETTE
PANELED
PAPEETE
PAPERED
PAPERER
PARENTS
PATELLA
PATENTS
PATERNO
PAWEDAT
PESETAS
PETERED
PHAEDRA
PHAETON
PHOEBES
PHOEBUS
PHOENIX
PHRENIC
PIGEONS
PIKEMAN
PIKEMEN
PILEDIN
PILEDON
PILEDUP
PILESIN
PILESON
PILESUP
PILEUPS
PIMENTO
PIMESON
PINEFOR
PINENUT
PINESAP
PINETAR
PINETUM
PIPEDUP
PIPEFUL
PIPEMMA
PIPESUP
PIPETTE
PITEOUS
POKEDAT
POKEFUN
POKESAT
POLEAXE
POLECAR
POLECAT
POLEMIC
POLENTA
POMELOS
POPEYED
POSEURS
POTENCY
POVERTY
POWERED
PRAETOR
PREEMIE
PREEMPT
PREENED
PREENER
PRIESTS
PUBERTY
PUDENCY

P•••E••

PACKERS
PACKETS
PADDERS
PALIEST
PALLETS
PALTERS
PAMPERS
PANDECT
PANDERS
PANNERS
PANZERS
PAPEETE
PARCELS
PARGETS
PARLEYS
PARSECS
PARSEES
PARSERS
PARVENU
PASSELS
PASSERS
PASSEUL
PASTELS
PASTERN
PASTEUP
PASTEUR
PATIENT
PATNESS
PATTENS
PATTERN
PATTERS
PAUPERS
PAWNEES
PAWNERS
PAYMENT
PEABEAN
PEAHENS
PEAVEYS
PEEKERS
PEELERS
PEEPERS
PEERESS
PEEWEES
PEGLESS
PELLETS
PELTERS
PENDENT
PENNERS
PENSEES
PEPPERS
PEPPERY
PERCENT
PERFECT
PERSEID
PERSEUS
PERTEST
PESTERS
PETRELS
PETTERS
PEUGEOT
PHASEIN
PHASERS
PHINEAS
PHONEME
PHONEYS
PICKENS
PICKERS
PICKETS
PICKETT
PIDGEON
PIECERS
PIGGERY
PIGLETS
PIGMENT
PIGPENS
PILFERS
PINCERS
PINHEAD
PINIEST
PINKEST
PINLESS
PINNERS
PIOLETS
PIONEER
PIPIEST
PIRAEUS
PITIERS
PITTERS
PLACEBO
PLACERS
PLANERS
PLANETS
PLATEAU
PLATENS
PLATERS
PLAYERS
PLOVERS
PLOWERS
POCKETS
POKIEST
POLDERS
POLLENS
POLLERS
POMMELS
POMPEIA
POMPEII
PONDERS
PONGEES
POOREST
POPPERS
POPPETS
PORKERS
PORSENA
PORTEND
PORTENT
PORTERS
POSHEST
POSSESS
POSSETS
POSTERN
POSTERS
POTHERB
POTHERS
POTTERS
POTTERY
POULENC
POURERS
POUTERS
POWDERS
POWDERY
PRATERS
PRAYERS
PREBEND
PRECEDE
PRECEPT
PREFECT
PREFERS
PREHEAT
PREMEDS
PRESELL
PRESENT
PRESETS
PRETEEN
PRETEND
PRETEST
PRETEXT
PREVENT
PRICERS
PRIMERS
PRIVETS
PROBERS
PROCEED
PROCESS
PROFESS
PROGENY
PROJECT
PRONELY
PROPELS
PROSERS
PROTEAN
PROTECT
PROTEGE
PROTEIN
PROTEST
PROTEUS
PROVERB
PROVERS
PROWESS
PRUDENT
PRUDERY
PRUNERS
PTOLEMY
PUCKERS
PUCKETT
PUFFERS
PUFFERY
PUGREES
PULLETS
PULLEYS
PUMMELS
PUMPERS
PUNGENT
PUNIEST
PUNKERS
PUNLESS
PUNNETS
PUNTERS
PUPPETS
PUPTENT
PURCELL
PURRERS
PURSERS
PURVEYS
PUTTEES
PUTTERS

P••••E•

PADDIES
PADDLED
PADDLER
PADDLES
PAINTED
PAINTER
PAISLEY
PAIUTES
PALACES
PALATES
PALAVER
PALFREY
PALJOEY
PALLIER
PALMIER
PANACEA
PANELED
PANNIER
PANSIES
PANTHER
PAPERED
PAPERER
PARADED
PARADES
PARAPET
PARCHED
PARCHES
PARDNER
PAROLED
PAROLEE
PAROLES
PARQUET
PARRIED
PARRIER
PARRIES
PARSEES
PARSLEY
PARTIED
PARTIER
PARTIES
PARTNER
PARURES
PASSKEY
PASTIER
PATCHED
PATCHES
PATSIES
PATTIES
PAULSEN
PAVANES
PAWKIER
PAWNEES
PDJAMES
PEACHED
PEACHES
PEARLED
PEATIER
PEBBLED
PEBBLES
PECKIER
PEDALED
PEDDLED
PEDDLER
PEDDLES
PEDICEL
PEEPLES
PEEWEES
PELAGES
PENATES
PENNIES
PENSEES
PEONIES
PEOPLED
PEOPLES
PEPPIER
PERCHED
PERCHES
PERDIEM
PERIGEE
PERKIER
PERPLEX
PERRIER
PERUKES
PERUSED
PERUSER
PERUSES
PESKIER
PESTLED
PESTLES
PETALED
PETERED
PETITES
PETTIER
PHILTER
PHLOXES
PHOEBES
PHONIER
PHONIES
PHOTOED
PHRASED
PHRASES
PIASTER
PICKIER
PICKLED
PICKLES
PIERCED
PIERCES
PIETIES
PIFFLED
PIFFLES
PIGGIER
PIGGIES
PIKEMEN
PILOTED
PILSNER
PINCHED
PINCHER
PINCHES
PINKIES
PINONES
PIONEER
PIRATED
PIRATES
PITCHED
PITCHER
PITCHES
PITHIER
PIVOTED
PLACKET
PLAGUED
PLAGUES
PLAICES
PLAINER
PLAITED
PLANKED
PLANNED
PLANNER
PLANTED
PLANTER
PLAQUES
PLASHED
PLASHES
PLASTER
PLATIER
PLATTER
PLAYLET
PLAYPEN
PLEADED
PLEADER
PLEASED
PLEASER
PLEASES
PLEATED
PLEDGED
PLEDGEE
PLEDGER
PLEDGES
PLINKED
PLODDED
PLODDER
PLOPPED
PLOTTED
PLOTTER
PLOWMEN
PLUCKED
PLUGGED
PLUGGER
PLUMBED
PLUMBER
PLUMIER
PLUMMER
PLUMMET
PLUMPED
PLUMPER
PLUNDER
PLUNGED
PLUNGER
PLUNGES
PLUNKED
PLUSHER
PLUSHES
PLUSSES
POACHED
POACHER
POACHES
POBOXES
PODGIER
POINTED
POINTER
POITIER
POLICED
POLICES
POLITER
POLKAED
POLYMER
POMADED
POMADES
PONGEES
POOCHES
POODLES
POPEYED
POPOVER
POPPIES
POPPLED
POPPLES
PORCHES
PORGIES
PORKIER
POSITED
POSTMEN
POTAGES
POTPIES
POTSIER
POTTIER
POTTLES
POUCHED
POUCHES
POUNCED
POUNCER
POUNCES
POUNDED
POUNDER
POUTIER
POWERED
PRAISED
PRAISER
PRAISES
PRANCED
PRANCER
PRANCES
PRANGED
PRANKED
PREENED
PREENER
PREMIER
PREQUEL
PRESLEY
PRESSED
PRESSER
PRESSES
PRETEEN
PRETZEL
PREVIEW
PREXIES
PRICIER
PRICKED
PRIMMER
PRIMPED
PRINCES
PRINKED
PRINTED
PRINTER
PRITHEE
PRIVIER
PRIVIES
PROBLEM
PROCEED
PRODDED
PRODDER
PROFFER
PROGGED
PRONGED
PROOFED
PROOFER
PROPHET
PROPJET
PROPMEN
PROPPED
PROPTER
PROSIER
PROSPER
PROUDER
PROWLED
PROWLER
PROXIES
PSALMED
PSALTER
PSYCHED
PSYCHES
PUDDLED
PUDDLES
PUDGIER
PUFFIER
PUGREES
PULPIER
PULQUES
PUMICES
PUNCHED
PUNCHER
PUNCHES
PUNKIER
PUNKIES
PUNNIER
PUNSTER
PUNTIES
PUPPIES
PURFLED
PURFLES
PURLIEU
PURPLED
PURPLES
PURSIER

PURSUED
PURSUER
PURSUES
PURVIEW
PUSHIER
PUTAMEN
PUTOVER
PUTTEES
PUTTIED
PUTTIES
PUZZLED
PUZZLER
PUZZLES
PYGMIES
PYRITES
PYXIDES

P•••••E

PACKAGE
PACKICE
PADRONE
PALANCE
PALETTE
PALMATE
PANACHE
PANCAKE
PANICLE
PANPIPE
PANURGE
PAPEETE
PAPLIKE
PAPOOSE
PARABLE
PARKADE
PAROLEE
PARTAKE
PARTITE
PASSAGE
PASSIVE
PASTDUE
PASTIME
PASTURE
PATRICE
PAULINE
PAYABLE
PEALIKE
PEDICLE
PEERAGE
PEGLIKE
PELISSE
PELTATE
PENANCE
PENLIKE
PENNAME
PENNATE
PENSIVE
PENUCHE
PEONAGE
PEPTIDE
PERCALE
PERFUME
PERIGEE
PERJURE
PERLITE
PERVADE
PETIOLE
PETNAME
PHILTRE
PHONEME
PIASTRE
PICANTE
PICKAXE
PICTURE
PIELIKE
PIGLIKE
PILLAGE
PINHOLE
PINNACE
PINNATE
PINOCLE
PINWALE
PIPETTE
PIROGUE
PISCINE
PISMIRE
PISTOLE
PLACATE
PLEDGEE
PLIABLE
PLOSIVE
PLUMAGE
PODLIKE
POLEAXE
POLLUTE
PONTINE
PORCINE
PORKPIE
PORSCHE
PORTAGE
POSTAGE
POSTURE
POTABLE
POTHOLE
POTTAGE
PRAIRIE
PRALINE
PRATTLE
PRECEDE
PRECISE
PREDATE
PREEMIE
PREFACE
PRELATE
PRELUDE
PREMISE
PREPARE
PREPPIE
PRESAGE
PRESALE
PRESIDE
PRESUME
PRETAPE
PRICKLE
PRIMATE
PRITHEE
PRIVATE
PROBATE
PROCURE
PRODUCE
PROFANE
PROFILE
PROFUSE
PROMISE
PROMOTE
PROPANE
PROPOSE
PRORATE
PROTEGE
PROVIDE
PROVOKE
PRUDHOE
PUERILE
PUGNOSE
PULSATE
PURPOSE

•PE••••

APELIKE
APERCUS
APERIES
EPEEIST
EPERGNE
OPENAIR
OPENBAR
OPENEND
OPENERS
OPENING
OPENPIT
OPENSEA
OPENSUP
OPENTOE
OPERAND
OPERATE
OPEROSE
SPEAKER
SPEAKOF
SPEAKUP
SPEARED
SPECCED
SPECIAL
SPECIES
SPECIFY
SPECING
SPECKED
SPECKLE
SPECTER
SPECTOR
SPECTRA
SPECTRE
SPEEDED
SPEEDER
SPEEDOS
SPEEDUP
SPELLED
SPELLER
SPELUNK
SPENCER
SPENDER
SPENSER
SPEWING
UPENDED

•P•E•••

APHELIA
APHESES
APLENTY
APPEALS
APPEARS
APPEASE
APPENDS
APTERAL
EPEEIST
OPHELIA
SPEEDED
SPEEDER
SPEEDOS
SPEEDUP
SPHERES
SPIEDON
SPIEGEL
SPIELED
SPIELER
SPIESON
SPLEENS
SPREADS
UPBEATS
UPTEMPO

•P••E••

APOGEES
APPLETS
APTNESS
EPICENE
EPIGENE
EPOPEES
EPSTEIN
IPANEMA
IPCRESS
OPENEND
OPENERS
OPINERS
OPPRESS
OPULENT
SPACERS
SPADERS
SPARELY
SPAREST
SPICERY
SPICEUP
SPIDERS
SPIDERY
SPIKERS
SPINELS
SPINETS
SPIREAS
SPLEENS
SPOKEOF
SPOKEUP
SPRIEST
SPRYEST
UPSWEEP
UPSWEPT

•P•••E•

APACHES
APERIES
APHESES
APOGEES
APOTHEM
APPAREL
APPLIED
APPLIES
APPOSED
APPOSES
APRONED
APSIDES
EPAULET
EPITHET
EPOPEES
EPOXIES
OPAQUES
OPENSEA
OPHITES
OPIATES
OPPOSED
OPPOSER
OPPOSES
SPACIER
SPALLED
SPAMMED
SPAMMER
SPANDEX
SPANIEL
SPANKED
SPANKER
SPANNED
SPANNER
SPARGED
SPARGES
SPARKED
SPARRED
SPARSER
SPATTED
SPATTER
SPAWNED
SPEAKER
SPEARED
SPECCED
SPECIES
SPECKED
SPECTER
SPEEDED
SPEEDER
SPELLED
SPELLER
SPENCER
SPENDER
SPENSER
SPHERES
SPICIER
SPIEGEL
SPIELED
SPIELER
SPIKIER
SPILLED
SPINIER
SPINNER
SPINNEY
SPIRIER
SPITZES
SPLAYED
SPLICED
SPLICER
SPLICES
SPLINES
SPOILED
SPOILER
SPONDEE
SPONGED
SPONGER
SPONGES
SPOOFED
SPOOFER
SPOOKED
SPOOLED
SPOONED
SPOONER
SPORTED
SPOTTED
SPOTTER
SPOUSES
SPOUTED
SPOUTER
SPRAYED
SPRAYER
SPRITES
SPRUCED
SPRUCER
SPRUCES
SPUMIER
SPURNED
SPURNER
SPURRED
SPURTED
SPUTTER
UPATREE
UPDATED
UPDATES
UPENDED
UPRISEN
UPRISES
UPRIVER
UPSWEEP
UPTAKES

•P••••E

APATITE
APELIKE
APOCOPE
APOSTLE
APPEASE
APPRISE
APPRIZE
APPROVE
EPERGNE
EPICENE
EPICURE
EPIGENE
EPIGONE
EPISODE
EPISTLE
EPITOME
OPALINE
OPENTOE
OPERATE
OPEROSE
SPACKLE
SPANGLE
SPARKLE
SPECKLE
SPECTRE
SPINDLE
SPLURGE
SPOKANE
SPONDEE
SPUMONE
UPATREE
UPBORNE
UPCLOSE
UPGRADE
UPRAISE
UPSCALE
UPSTAGE
UPSTATE
UPSURGE

••PE•••

AMPERES
APPEALS
APPEARS
APPEASE
APPENDS
ARPENTS
ASPECTS
ASPERSE
ATPEACE
BIPEDAL
CAPEANN
CAPECOD
CAPELET
CAPELLA
CAPERED
DEPENDS
DOPEOUT
EMPEROR
EXPECTS
EXPENDS
EXPENSE
EXPERTS
HAPENNY
HOPEFUL
HYPEDUP
HYPESUP
IMPEACH
IMPEDED
IMPEDES
IMPENDS
IMPERIL
IMPETUS
INPEACE
INPETTO
KOPECKS
LAPELED
PAPEETE
PAPERED
PAPERER
PIPEDUP
PIPEFUL
PIPEMMA
PIPESUP
PIPETTE
POPEYED
REPEALS
REPEATS
REPENTS
RIPENED
ROPEDIN
ROPESIN
ROPETOW
STPETER
TAPEMAN
TAPEMEN
TAPERED
TUPELOS
TYPEDUP
TYPESET
TYPESUP
WIPEDUP
WIPEOUT
WIPESUP

••P•E••

AMPLEST
APPLETS
BOPPERS
CAPLESS
CAPLETS
CAPPERS
CEPHEUS
CIPHERS
COPIERS
COPPERS
COPPERY
COPTERS
CYPHERS
CYPRESS
DEPLETE
DEPRESS
DIPPERS
DOPIEST
EMPRESS
EXPRESS
FOPPERY
GAPLESS
GOPHERS
GYPPERS
HAPLESS
HAPPENS
HEPPEST
HIPLESS
HIPNESS
HIPPEST
HOPPERS
HYPHENS
IMPIETY
IMPRESS
JAPHETH
KIPPERS
LAPBELT
LAPPETS
LIPLESS
LIPREAD
LOPPERS
MAPPERS
MOPIEST
MOPPERS
MOPPETS
MUPPETS
NAPLESS
NAPPERS
NEPHEWS
NIPPERS
OPPRESS
ORPHEAN
ORPHEUS
OSPREYS
PAPEETE
PEPPERS
PEPPERY
PIPIEST
POPPERS
POPPETS
PUPPETS
PUPTENT
RAPIERS
RAPPELS
RAPPERS
REPLETE
REPRESS
RIPIENO
RIPPERS
ROPIEST
SAPIENS
SAPIENT
SAPLESS
SAPPERS
SEPTETS
SIPPERS
SIPPETS
SUPPERS
SUPREME
SUPREMO
TAPPERS
TAPPETS
TIPLESS
TIPPERS
TIPPETS
TOPPERS
TYPIEST
UMPTEEN
YAPPERS
ZAPPERS
ZIPPERS

••P••E•

AMPERES
AMPULES
APPAREL
APPLIED
APPLIES
APPOSED
APPOSES
ASPIRED
ASPIRER
ASPIRES
CAPELET
CAPERED
CAPULET
DAPPLED
DAPPLES
DEPONED
DEPONES
DEPOSED
DEPOSER
DEPOSES
DEPUTED
DEPUTES
DIPOLES
DIPPIER
DOPPLER
EMPANEL
EMPIRES
EMPOWER
EMPTIED
EMPTIER
EMPTIES
EXPIRED
EXPIRES
EXPOSED
EXPOSES
FIPPLES
GIPSIES
GUPPIES
GYPSIES
HAPPIER
HIPPIER
HIPPIES
HIPSTER
HOPOVER
HOPPLED
HOPPLES
IMPALED
IMPALES
IMPANEL
IMPEDED
IMPEDES
IMPLIED
IMPLIES
IMPOSED
IMPOSES
IMPURER
IMPUTED
IMPUTES
INPOWER
JUPITER
LAPELED
LEPPIES
LIPIDES
LIPPIER
LOPPIER
LUPINES
NAPPIES
NIPPIER
OPPOSED
OPPOSER
OPPOSES
ORPHREY
ORPINES
PAPERED
PAPERER
PEPPIER
POPEYED
POPOVER
POPPIES
POPPLED
POPPLES
PUPPIES
RAPHAEL
RAPIDER
RAPINES
REPAPER
REPAVED
REPAVES
REPINED
REPINES
REPLIED
REPLIES
REPOSED
REPOSES
REPUTED
REPUTES
RIPENED
RIPPLED
RIPPLES
SAPPIER
SOPPIER
STPETER
SUPPLER
TAPEMEN
TAPERED
TAPSTER
TIPPIER
TIPPLED
TIPPLER
TIPPLES
TIPSIER
TIPSTER
TIPTOED
TIPTOES
TOPAZES
TOPPLED
TOPPLES
TYPESET
UMPIRED
UMPIRES
UMPTEEN
UNPAVED
UNPILED
UNPILES
YUPPIES
ZAPATEO
ZAPOTEC
ZAPPIER
ZIPPIER

••P•••E

AMPOULE
APPEASE
APPRISE
APPRIZE
APPROVE
ASPERSE
ATPEACE
BAPTISE
BAPTIZE
BIPLANE
CAPABLE
CAPAPIE
CAPRICE
CAPSIZE
CAPSULE
CAPTIVE
CAPTURE
COPPICE
COPULAE
CUPCAKE
CUPLIKE
DEPLANE
DEPLETE
DEPLORE
DEPRAVE
DEPRIVE
EMPLOYE
ENPLANE
ESPOUSE
EXPANSE
EXPARTE
EXPENSE
EXPIATE
EXPLODE
EXPLORE
EXPUNGE
HIPBONE
HIPLIKE
HOPLIKE
IMPASSE
IMPINGE
IMPLODE
IMPLORE
IMPROVE
IMPULSE
INPEACE
INPHASE
INPLACE
LAPLACE
LAPORTE
LAPROBE
LIPLIKE
NAPTIME
NEPTUNE
PAPEETE
PAPLIKE
PAPOOSE
PEPTIDE
PIPETTE
RAPTURE
REPASTE
REPLACE
REPLATE
REPLETE
REPRICE
REPRISE
REPROVE
REPTILE
REPULSE
RIPOSTE
RIPTIDE
RUPTURE
SUPPOSE
SUPREME
TOPHOLE
TOPSIDE
ZIPCODE

•••PE••

ANAPEST
BEEPERS
BESPEAK
BOPPERS
BUMPERS
CAMPERS
CAPPERS
CARPELS
CARPERS
CARPETS
CHAPEAU
CHAPELS
COMPEER
COMPELS
COMPERE
COMPETE
COOPERS
COPPERS
COPPERY
COWPEAS
DAMPENS
DAMPERS
DAMPEST
DEEPEND
DEEPENS
DEEPEST
DIAPERS
DIPPERS
DISPELS
DRAPERS
DRAPERY
ELOPERS
EPOPEES
EXUPERY
FOPPERY
GASPERS
GOMPERS
GOSPELS
GRIPERS
GYPPERS
HAMPERS
HAPPENS
HARPERS
HELPERS
HENPECK
HEPPEST
HIPPEST
HOPPERS
INSPECT
JASPERS
JUMPERS
KEEPERS
KIPPERS
LAPPETS
LEAPERS
LIMPEST
LIMPETS
LOOPERS
LOPPERS
LUMPERS
MAPPERS
MOPPERS
MOPPETS
MUPPETS
NAPPERS
NIPPERS
OFFPEAK
PAMPERS
PAUPERS
PEEPERS
PEPPERS
PEPPERY
PIGPENS
POMPEIA
POMPEII
POPPERS
POPPETS
PROPELS
PUMPERS
PUPPETS
RAPPELS
RAPPERS
RASPERS
REAPERS
REOPENS
RESPECT
RIPPERS
ROMPERS
SAPPERS
SERPENT
SHAPELY
SHAPERS
SHAPEUP
SIMPERS
SIPPERS
SIPPETS
SNIPEAT
SNIPERS
SOAPERS
STIPEND
STUPEFY
SUPPERS
SUSPECT
SUSPEND
SWIPERS
TAMPERS
TAPPERS
TAPPETS
TEEPEES
TEMPEHS
TEMPERA
TEMPERS
TEMPEST
TIPPERS
TIPPETS
TOPPERS
TORPEDO
TOUPEES
TRAPEZE
UNSPENT
USOPENS
VAMPERS
VESPERS
WEEPERS
YAPPERS
YAWPERS
YELPERS
ZAPPERS
ZIPPERS

•••P•E•

ADAPTED
ADAPTER
ADOPTED
ADOPTEE
ADOPTER
BLIPPED
BUMPIER
CAMPIER
CHAPLET
CHAPMEN
CHAPPED
CHAPTER
CHIPPED
CHIPPER
CHOPPED
CHOPPER
CLAPPED
CLAPPER
CLIPPED
CLIPPER
CLOPPED
COMPEER
COMPLEX
COOPTED
COUPLED
COUPLES
COUPLET
CROPPED
CROPPER
DAPPLED
DAPPLES
DEEPSEA
DEEPSET
DEMPSEY
DIMPLED
DIMPLES
DIOPTER
DIPPIER
DOPPLER
DRIPPED
DROPLET
DROPPED
DROPPER
DUMPIER
ELAPSED
ELAPSES
EPOPEES
ERUPTED
FIPPLES
FLAPPED
FLAPPER
FLIPPED
FLIPPER
FLOPPED
FRAPPES
FRIPPET
GOOPIER
GRAPHED
GRAPIER
GRAPNEL
GRIPPED
GRIPPER
GULPIER
GUPPIES
HAPPIER
HARPIES
HIPPIER
HIPPIES
HOOPOES
HOPPLED
HOPPLES
HUMPIER
INAPTER
JEEPNEY
JUMPIER
KELPIES
KEWPIES
LAMPREY
LEPPIES
LIPPIER
LOOPIER
LOPPIER
LUMPIER
MAGPIES
MORPHED
MUDPIES
NAPPIES
NIPPIER
PEEPLES
PEOPLED
PEOPLES
PEPPIER
PERPLEX
PLOPPED
POPPIES
POPPLED
POPPLES
POTPIES
PROPHET
PROPJET
PROPMEN
PROPPED
PROPTER
PULPIER
PUPPIES
PURPLED
PURPLES
QUIPPED
QUIPPER
RASPIER
REUPPED
RIMPLED
RIMPLES
RIPPLED
RIPPLES
RUMPLED
RUMPLES
SAMPLED
SAMPLER
SAMPLES
SAPPIER
SCEPTER
SCUPPER
SEEPIER
SHAPLEY
SHIPMEN
SHIPPED
SHIPPER
SHOPPED
SHOPPER

SHOPPES
SIMPLER
SIMPLEX
SKIPPED
SKIPPER
SLAPPED
SLIPPED
SLIPPER
SLOPPED
SNAPPED
SNAPPER
SNIPPED
SNIPPET
SOAPIER
SOPPIER
SOUPIER
STAPLED
STAPLER
STAPLES
STEPHEN
STEPPED
STEPPER
STEPPES
STOPPED
STOPPER
SUPPLER
SWAPPED
SWAPPER
SWOPPED
TEEPEES
TEMPLES
TEMPTED
TEMPTER
TIPPIER
TIPPLED
TIPPLER
TIPPLES
TOPPLED
TOPPLES
TOUPEES
TRAPPED
TRAPPER
TRIPLED
TRIPLES
TRIPLET
TRIPLEX
TRIPPED
TRIPPER
TRIPPET
WASPIER
WEEPIER
WEEPIES
WHIPPED
WHIPPET
WHOPPED
WHOPPER
WHUPPED
WIMPIER
WIMPLED
WIMPLES
WISPIER
WRAPPED
WRAPPER
YUPPIES
ZAPPIER
ZIPPIER

•••P••E
ADIPOSE
ADOPTEE
AUSPICE
BAGPIPE
BESPOKE
CHAPPIE
COMPARE
COMPERE
COMPETE
COMPILE
COMPOSE
COMPOTE
COMPUTE
COPPICE
COWPOKE
CRAPPIE
DESPISE
DESPITE
DISPOSE
DISPUTE
GRAPPLE
HOSPICE
INSPIRE
MAYPOLE
OUTPACE
PANPIPE
PREPARE
PREPPIE
PROPANE
PROPOSE
PURPOSE
RAMPAGE
REDPINE
RESPIRE
RESPITE
RUMPOLE
SCEPTRE
SKIPOLE
SNAPPLE
STIPPLE
SUPPOSE
TADPOLE
TOSPARE
TRAPEZE
VAMPIRE
VOLPONE
VULPINE
WALPOLE
WEBPAGE
WIMPOLE

••••PE•
BLEEPED
BLEEPER
BLIPPED
BLOOPED
BLOOPER
BULLPEN
CALIPER
CANAPES
CHAMPED
CHAPPED
CHEAPEN
CHEAPER
CHEEPED
CHIPPED
CHIPPER
CHIRPED
CHOMPED
CHOPPED
CHOPPER
CLAMPED
CLAPPED
CLAPPER
CLASPED
CLIPPED
CLIPPER
CLOMPED
CLOPPED
CLUMPED
CRAMPED
CREEPED
CREEPER
CRIMPED
CRIMPER
CRISPED
CRISPER
CROPPED
CROPPER
CRUMPET
DRIPPED
DROOPED
DROPPED
DROPPER
ECTYPES
ESCAPED
ESCAPEE
ESCAPES
FLAPPED
FLAPPER
FLIPPED
FLIPPER
FLOPPED
FRAPPES
FRIPPET
GRASPED
GRIPPED
GRIPPER
GROUPED
GROUPER
GRUMPED
GUIMPES
JUNIPER
LAYOPEN
PARAPET
PLAYPEN
PLOPPED
PLUMPED
PLUMPER
PRIMPED
PROPPED
PROSPER
QUIPPED
QUIPPER
RECIPES
REPAPER
RETAPED
RETAPES
RETYPED
RETYPES
REUPPED
SCALPED
SCALPEL
SCALPER
SCAMPED
SCAMPER
SCARPED
SCARPER
SCOOPED
SCOOPER
SCRAPED
SCRAPER
SCRAPES
SCUPPER
SERAPES
SHARPED
SHARPEI
SHARPEN
SHARPER
SHIPPED
SHIPPER
SHOPPED
SHOPPER
SHOPPES
SKIMPED
SKIPPED
SKIPPER
SLAPPED
SLEEPER
SLIPPED
SLIPPER
SLOPPED
SLUMPED
SLURPED
SNAPPED
SNAPPER
SNIPPED
SNIPPET
SNOOPED
SNOOPER
SNOWPEA
STAMPED
STEEPED
STEEPEN
STEEPER
STEPPED
STEPPER
STEPPES
STOMPED
STOOPED
STOPPED
STOPPER
STRIPED
STRIPER
STRIPES
STUMPED
STUMPER
SWAMPED
SWAPPED
SWAPPER
SWEEPER
SWOOPED
SWOPPED
THUMPED
THUMPER
TRAMPED
TRAPPED
TRAPPER
TRIPPED
TRIPPER
TRIPPET
TROOPED
TROOPER
TROUPER
TROUPES
TRUMPED
TRUMPET
UNTAPED
USURPED
USURPER
WHELPED
WHIMPER
WHIPPED
WHIPPET
WHISPER
WHOMPED
WHOOPED
WHOOPEE
WHOPPED
WHOPPER
WHUPPED
WRAPPED
WRAPPER
ZATOPEK

••••P•E
ADOLPHE
CAPAPIE
CHAPPIE
CHEAPIE
CRAPPIE
CRUMPLE
ECLIPSE
ELLIPSE
ESCAPEE
EXAMPLE
GLIMPSE
GRAPPLE
GROUPIE
MANIPLE
OCTUPLE
PORKPIE
PREPPIE
RELAPSE
SCRUPLE
SNAPPLE
STEEPLE
STIPPLE
STROPHE
SYNAPSE
TRAIPSE
TRAMPLE
WHOOPEE

•••••PE
APOCOPE
BAGPIPE
BOBHOPE
EUTERPE
GOESAPE
INSCAPE
INSHAPE
ISOTOPE
MISTYPE
PANPIPE
PRETAPE
REDTAPE
TINTYPE
TOWROPE
UNDRAPE
WENTAPE

PF•••••
PFENNIG

P•F••••
PIFFLED
PIFFLES
PUFFERS
PUFFERY
PUFFIER
PUFFILY
PUFFING
PUFFINS

P••F•••
PALFREY
PANFISH
PANFULS
PARFAIT
PEAFOWL
PERFECT
PERFIDY
PERFORM
PERFUME
PIFFLED
PIFFLES
PILFERS
PITFALL
POTFULS
PREFABS
PREFACE
PREFECT
PREFERS
PROFANE
PROFESS
PROFFER
PROFILE
PROFITS
PROFUSE
PUFFERS
PUFFERY
PUFFIER
PUFFILY
PUFFING
PUFFINS
PURFLED
PURFLES

P•••F••
PACIFIC
PAGEFUL
PAIDFOR
PAILFUL
PAINFUL
PASSFOR
PAYOFFS
PAYSFOR
PINEFOR
PIPEFUL
PITIFUL
PLAYFUL
PLOTFUL
POKEFUN
POPOFFS
POUTFUL
PRAYFOR
PROFFER
PROOFED
PROOFER
PULLFOR
PUSHFUL

P••••F•
PAIDOFF
PAIROFF
PALMOFF
PASSOFF
PAWNOFF
PAYOFFS
PAYSOFF
PEELOFF
PETRIFY
PICKOFF
PLAYOFF
PONTIFF
POPOFFS
POPSOFF
PULLOFF
PUSHOFF
PUTSOFF

P•••••F
PAIDOFF
PAIROFF
PALMOFF
PASSOFF
PAWNOFF
PAYSOFF
PEELOFF
PICKOFF
PLAYOFF
PONTIFF
POPSOFF
PULLOFF
PUSHOFF
PUTSOFF

•PF••••
UPFRONT

•P••F••
OPTSFOR
SPOOFED
SPOOFER
UPLIFTS

•P•••F•
SPECIFY
SPINOFF
SPUNOFF
UPDRAFT

•P••••F
SPEAKOF
SPINOFF
SPOKEOF
SPUNOFF

••PF•••
CAPFULS
CUPFULS
LAPFULS

••P•F••
HOPEFUL
PIPEFUL
POPOFFS
RIPOFFS
TIPOFFS

••P••F•
AMPLIFY
HOPSOFF
KEPTOFF
POPOFFS
POPSOFF
RIPOFFS
RIPSOFF
TAPSOFF
TIPOFFS
TIPSOFF
TOPSOFF

••P•••F
HIPROOF
HOPSOFF
KEPTOFF
POPSOFF
REPROOF
RIPSOFF
TAPSOFF
TIPSOFF
TOPSOFF

•••PF••
DEEPFAT
DEEPFRY
HELPFUL
SHOPFUL

•••P•F•
DROPOFF
JUMPOFF
KEEPOFF
STOPOFF
STUPEFY

•••P••F
DROPOFF
JUMPOFF
KEEPOFF
STOPOFF

••••P•F
ONTOPOF

P•G••••
PAGEANT
PAGEBOY
PAGEFUL
PAGODAS
PEGASUS
PEGGING
PEGLESS
PEGLIKE
PEGTOPS
PIGEONS
PIGGERY
PIGGIER
PIGGIES
PIGGING
PIGGISH
PIGIRON
PIGLETS
PIGLIKE
PIGMENT
PIGNUTS
PIGPENS
PIGSKIN
PIGSOUT
PIGTAIL
PUGGISH
PUGNOSE
PUGREES
PYGMIES

P••G•••
PARGETS
PEGGING
PENGUIN
PERGOLA
PEUGEOT
PIDGEON
PIDGINS
PIGGERY
PIGGIER
PIGGIES
PIGGING
PIGGISH
PILGRIM
PINGING
PLAGUED
PLAGUES
PLIGHTS
PLUGGED
PLUGGER
PLUGINS
PLUGSIN
PODGIER
PODGILY
PONGEES
PONGIDS
PONGING
POPGUNS
PORGIES
PROGENY
PROGGED
PROGRAM
PUDGIER
PUDGILY
PUGGISH
PUNGENT
PURGING

P•••G••
PAANGAS
PAPAGOS
PARAGON
PELAGES
PELAGIC
PERIGEE
PIROGUE
PLEDGED
PLEDGEE
PLEDGER
PLEDGES
PLOUGHS
PLUGGED
PLUGGER
PLUNGED
PLUNGER
PLUNGES
POLYGON
POTAGES
PRANGED
PROGGED
PRONGED

P••••G•
PACKAGE
PANURGE
PARINGS
PASSAGE
PEERAGE
PEONAGE
PHOTOGS
PILINGS
PILLAGE
PIPINGS
PLUMAGE
PORTAGE
POSTAGE
POTTAGE
PRESAGE
PRODIGY
PROLOGS
PROTEGE
PYEDOGS

P•••••G
PACKING
PADDING
PAIRING
PALLING
PALMING
PANNING
PANTING
PARKING
PARRING
PARSING
PARTING
PASSING
PASTING
PATTING
PAULING
PAUSING
PAWNING
PEAKING
PEALING
PEATBOG
PECKING
PEEKING
PEELING
PEEPING
PEERING
PEEVING
PEGGING
PELTING
PENDING
PENNING
PEPPING
PERKING
PERMING
PETTING
PFENNIG
PHASING
PHONING
PICKING
PIECING
PIGGING
PILLBUG
PILLING
PINGING
PINKING
PINNING
PIQUING
PITHING
PITTING
PITYING
PLACING
PLANING
PLATING
PLAYING
PLOWING
PLUMING
POISING
POLLING
PONGING
PONYING
POOLING
POOPING
POPPING
POSTBAG
POSTING
POTTING
POURING
POUTING
PRATING
PRAYING
PRICING
PRIDING
PRIMING
PRIZING
PROBING
PROLONG
PROSING
PROVING
PRUNING
PUDDING
PUFFING
PULLING
PULSING
PUMPING
PUNNING
PUNTING
PURGING
PURLING
PURRING
PURSING
PUSHING
PUTTING

•PG••••
UPGRADE

•P•G•••
APOGEES
EPIGENE
EPIGONE
EPIGRAM
SPIGOTS

•P••G••
EPERGNE
OPPUGNS
SPANGLE
SPANGLY
SPARGED
SPARGES
SPIEGEL
SPONGED
SPONGER
SPONGES
UPRIGHT
UPTIGHT

•P•••G•
APOLOGY
EPILOGS
SPLURGE
SPRINGS
SPRINGY
UPSTAGE
UPSURGE

•P••••G
OPENING
OPINING
SPACING
SPADING
SPARING
SPAYING
SPECING
SPEWING
SPICING
SPIKING
SPITING
SPOKING
SPUMING
UPSWING

••PG•••
CAPGUNS
POPGUNS
TOPGUNS

••P•G••
IMPUGNS
OPPUGNS
PAPAGOS
REPUGNS

••P••G•
EXPUNGE
IMPINGE
LAPDOGS
PIPINGS
SAPSAGO
TAPINGS
TOPDOGS
UNPLUGS

••P•••G
BOPPING
CAPPING
COPPING
COPYING
CUPPING
DAPPING
DIPPING
ESPYING
GAPPING
GIPPING
GYPPING
HAPPING
HOPPING
HYPOING
KIPLING
LAPPING
LAPSING
LAPWING
LIPPING
LOPPING
MAPPING
MOPPING
NAPPING
NIPPING
PEPPING
POPPING
RAPPING
RIPPING
SAPLING
SAPPING
SIPPING
SOPPING
SUPPING
TAPPING
TIPPING
TOPPING
YAPPING
YIPPING
ZAPPING
ZIPPING

•••PG••
BURPGUN
STOPGAP

•••P•G•
RAMPAGE
WEBPAGE

•••P••G
BEEPING
BOPPING
BUMPING
BURPING
CAMPING
CAPPING
CARPING
COOPING
COPPING
CUPPING
DAMPING
DAPPING
DIPPING
DRAPING
DUMPING
EARPLUG
ELOPING
GAPPING
GASPING
GAWPING
GIPPING
GRIPING
GROPING
GULPING
GYPPING
HAPPING
HARPING
HASPING
HEAPING
HELPING
HOOPING
HOPPING
JUMPING
KEEPING
LAPPING
LEAPING
LEIPZIG
LIMPING
LIPPING
LISPING
LOOPING
LOPPING
LUMPING
MAPPING
MOPPING
MUMPING
NAPPING
NIPPING
PEEPING
PEPPING
POOPING
POPPING
PUMPING
RAPPING
RASPING
REAPING
RIPPING
ROMPING
SAPPING
SCOPING
SEEPING
SHAPING
SIPPING
SLOPING
SNIPING
SOAPING
SOPPING
SUPPING
SWIPING
TAMPING
TAPPING
TIPPING
TOPPING
VAMPING
WARPING
WEEPING
WISPING
YAPPING
YAWPING
YELPING
YIPPING
ZAPPING
ZIPPING

••••P•G
BUSHPIG

PH•••••
PHAEDRA
PHAETON
PHALANX
PHANTOM
PHARAOH
PHARLAP
PHARYNX
PHASEIN
PHASERS
PHASING
PHENOLS
PHENOMS
PHIDIAS
PHILBIN
PHILLIP
PHILTER
PHILTRE
PHINEAS
PHLOXES
PHOBIAS
PHOBICS
PHOEBES
PHOEBUS
PHOENIX
PHONEME
PHONEYS
PHONICS
PHONIER
PHONIES
PHONILY
PHONING
PHOTICS
PHOTOED
PHOTOGS
PHOTONS
PHOTOOP
PHRASAL
PHRASED
PHRASES
PHRENIC
PHYLLIS
PHYSICS

P•H••••
PAHLAVI

P••H•••
PACHISI
PATHWAY
PEAHENS
PERHAPS
PINHEAD
PINHOLE
PITHIER
PITHILY
PITHING
POOHBAH
POSHEST
POTHERB
POTHERS
POTHOLE
POTHOOK
PREHEAT
PUSHFUL
PUSHIER
PUSHILY
PUSHING
PUSHKIN
PUSHOFF
PUSHPIN
PUSHUPS
PYTHIAN
PYTHIAS
PYTHONS

P•••H••
PANCHAX
PANTHER
PARCHED
PARCHES
PASCHAL
PATCHED
PATCHES
PATCHUP
PEACHED
PEACHES
PERCHED
PERCHES
PINCHAS
PINCHED
PINCHER
PINCHES
PITCHED
PITCHER
PITCHES
PITCHIN
PLASHED

PLASHES
PLIGHTS
PLUSHER
PLUSHES
PLUSHLY
POACHED
POACHER
POACHES
PONCHOS
POOCHES
PORCHES
PORTHOS
POTSHOT
POUCHED
POUCHES
PRITHEE
PROPHET
PROSHOP
PRUDHOE
PSYCHED
PSYCHES
PSYCHIC
PSYCHUP
PUNCHED
PUNCHER
PUNCHES
PUNCHIN
PUNCHUP
PYNCHON
PYRRHIC
PYRRHUS

P••••H•

PANACHE
PARAPHS
PARIAHS
PAUNCHY
PENUCHE
PIRANHA
PLINTHS
PLOUGHS
PORSCHE
PREACHY
PUNKAHS
PURDAHS

P•••••H

PADUCAH
PANFISH
PARRISH
PAYCASH
PEAKISH
PECKISH
PEEVISH
PELTISH
PERKISH
PETTISH
PHARAOH
PICTISH
PIGGISH
PINKISH
PIXYISH
PLANISH
PLAYDOH
POOHBAH
POORISH
PORKISH
PREWASH
PRUDISH
PUBLISH
PUCKISH
PUGGISH

•PH••••

APHELIA
APHESES
OPHELIA
OPHITES
SPHERES
UPHOLDS

•P•H•••

UPSHOTS

•P••H••

APACHES
APISHLY
APOTHEM
EPITHET
EPOCHAL

•P•••H•

EPARCHS
EPARCHY
SPLASHY
UPRIGHT
UPTIGHT

•P••••H

IPSWICH
SPANISH
SPINACH
SPLOTCH

••PH•••

AMPHORA
ASPHALT
CEPHEUS
CIPHERS
CYPHERS
DAPHNIS
EUPHONY
GOPHERS
HYPHENS
INPHASE
JAPHETH
NAPHTHA
NEPHEWS
OMPHALI
ORPHANS
ORPHEAN
ORPHEUS
ORPHREY
RAPHAEL
SIPHONS
SOPHISM
SOPHIST
SYPHONS
TOPHATS
TOPHOLE
TYPHOON
ZEPHYRS

••P•H••

CAPSHAW

••P••H•

BYPATHS
EMPATHY
NAPHTHA
RUPIAHS

••P•••H

DIPTYCH
FOPPISH
IMPEACH
JAPHETH
LAPPISH
SOPWITH

•••PH••

CAMPHOR
DAUPHIN
DELPHIC
DOLPHIN
EDAPHIC
GRAPHED
GRAPHIC
GRYPHON
MEMPHIS
MORPHED
PROPHET
STEPHEN
SULPHUR
TROPHIC

•••P•H•

ARAPAHO
OOMPAHS
TEMPEHS

•••P••H

DAMPISH
DUMPISH
FOPPISH
LAPPISH
LUMPISH
RASPISH
ROMPISH
TOWPATH
VAMPISH
WARPATH
WASPISH
WIMPISH

••••PH•

ADOLPHE
ATROPHY
CALIPHS
CERIPHS
GUELPHS
PARAPHS
SERAPHS
STROPHE
TERAPHS
THIMPHU

••••P•H

INDEPTH

•••••PH

DIGRAPH
GALUMPH
RUDOLPH
TRIUMPH

PI•••••

PIANISM
PIANIST
PIASTER
PIASTRE
PIAZZAS
PICADOR
PICANTE
PICARDY
PICAROS
PICASSO
PICCARD
PICCOLO
PICKAXE
PICKENS
PICKERS
PICKETS
PICKETT
PICKIER
PICKING
PICKLED
PICKLES
PICKOFF
PICKOUT
PICKSAT
PICKSON
PICKSUP
PICKUPS
PICNICS
PICTISH
PICTURE
PIDGEON
PIDGINS
PIEBALD
PIECERS
PIECING
PIELIKE
PIEPANS
PIERCED
PIERCES
PIERROT
PIETIES
PIETINS
PIETISM
PIETIST
PIFFLED
PIFFLES
PIGEONS
PIGGERY
PIGGIER
PIGGIES
PIGGING
PIGGISH
PIGIRON
PIGLETS
PIGLIKE
PIGMENT
PIGNUTS
PIGPENS
PIGSKIN
PIGSOUT
PIGTAIL
PIKEMAN
PIKEMEN
PILEDIN
PILEDON
PILEDUP
PILESIN
PILESON
PILESUP
PILEUPS
PILFERS
PILGRIM
PILINGS
PILLAGE
PILLARS
PILLBOX
PILLBUG
PILLING
PILLION
PILLORY
PILLOWS
PILLOWY
PILOTED
PILSNER
PIMENTO
PIMESON
PIMLICO
PINATAS
PINBALL
PINCERS
PINCHAS
PINCHED
PINCHER
PINCHES
PINCURL
PINDOWN
PINEFOR
PINENUT
PINESAP
PINETAR
PINETUM
PINGING
PINHEAD
PINHOLE
PINIEST
PINIONS
PINKEST
PINKIES
PINKING
PINKISH
PINLESS
PINNACE
PINNATE
PINNERS
PINNING
PINOAKS
PINOCLE
PINONES
PINTAIL
PINWALE
PIOLETS
PIONEER
PIOUSLY
PIPEDUP
PIPEFUL
PIPEMMA
PIPESUP
PIPETTE
PIPIEST
PIPINGS
PIPKINS
PIPPINS
PIQUANT
PIQUING
PIRAEUS
PIRANHA
PIRATED
PIRATES
PIRATIC
PIROGUE
PISCINE
PISCOPO
PISMIRE
PISTILS
PISTOLE
PISTOLS
PISTONS
PITAPAT
PITBOSS
PITBULL
PITCHED
PITCHER
PITCHES
PITCHIN
PITEOUS
PITFALL
PITHIER
PITHILY
PITHING
PITIERS
PITIFUL
PITSAWS
PITSTOP
PITTERS
PITTING
PITTMAN
PITYING
PIVOTAL
PIVOTED
PIXYISH
PIZARRO
PIZZAZZ

P•I••••

PAIDFOR
PAIDOFF
PAIDOUT
PAILFUL
PAILOUS
PAINFUL
PAINTED
PAINTER
PAIRING
PAIROFF
PAIRSUP
PAISANO
PAISLEY
PAIUTES
PHIDIAS
PHILBIN
PHILLIP
PHILTER
PHILTRE
PHINEAS
PLIABLE
PLIABLY
PLIANCY
PLIGHTS
PLINKED
PLINTHS
POINTED
POINTER
POINTTO
POISING
POISONS
POISSON
POITIER
PRICERS
PRICIER
PRICING
PRICKED
PRICKLE
PRICKLY
PRIDING
PRIESTS
PRIMACY
PRIMARY
PRIMATE
PRIMERS
PRIMING
PRIMMER
PRIMPED
PRINCES
PRINKED
PRINTED
PRINTER
PRIORTO
PRISONS
PRITHEE
PRIVACY
PRIVATE
PRIVETS
PRIVIER
PRIVIES
PRIVILY
PRIVITY
PRIZING

P••I•••

PACIFIC
PALIEST
PANICKY
PANICLE
PAPILLA
PARIAHS
PARINGS
PATIENT
PATINAS
PAVIOUR
PEDICAB
PEDICEL
PEDICLE
PELICAN
PELISSE
PEMICAN
PERIDOT
PERIGEE
PERIODS
PETIOLE
PETITES
PIGIRON
PILINGS
PINIEST
PINIONS
PIPIEST
PIPINGS
PITIERS
PITIFUL
PLAICES
PLAINER
PLAINLY
PLAINTS
PLAITED
PODIUMS
POKIEST
POLICED
POLICES
POLITER
POLITIC
PONIARD
POSITED
POTIONS
PRAIRIE
PRAISED
PRAISER
PRAISES
PRYINTO
PUMICES
PUNIEST
PURISTS
PURITAN
PUTITTO
PYRITES
PYXIDES

P•••I••

PACHISI
PACKICE
PACKING
PADDIES
PADDING
PAIRING
PALLIER
PALLING
PALLIUM
PALMIER
PALMING
PALMIST
PANDITS
PANFISH
PANNIER
PANNING
PANPIPE
PANSIES
PANTING
PAPLIKE
PAPRIKA
PARKING
PARRIED
PARRIER
PARRIES
PARRING
PARRISH
PARSING
PARTIAL
PARTIED
PARTIER
PARTIES
PARTING
PARTITA
PARTITE
PASSING
PASSION
PASSIVE
PASTIER
PASTIME
PASTINA
PASTING
PATRIAL
PATRICE
PATRICK
PATRIOT
PATSIES
PATTIES
PATTING
PAUCITY
PAULINA
PAULINE
PAULING
PAULIST
PAUSING
PAWKIER
PAWNING
PAYDIRT
PEAKING
PEAKISH
PEALIKE
PEALING
PEATIER
PECKIER
PECKING
PECKISH
PECTINS
PEEKING
PEELING
PEEPING
PEERING
PEEVING
PEEVISH
PEGGING
PEGLIKE
PELTING
PELTISH
PENCILS
PENDING
PENLIKE
PENNIES
PENNING
PENSION
PENSIVE
PENTIUM
PEONIES
PEPPIER
PEPPILY
PEPPING
PEPSINS
PEPTIDE
PERDIEM
PERFIDY
PERKIER
PERKILY
PERKING
PERKINS
PERKISH
PERLITE
PERMING
PERMITS
PERRIER
PERSIAN
PERSIST
PERSIUS
PESKIER
PESKILY
PETRIFY
PETTIER
PETTILY
PETTING
PETTISH
PHASING
PHIDIAS
PHOBIAS
PHOBICS
PHONICS
PHONIER
PHONIES
PHONILY
PHONING
PHOTICS
PHYSICS
PIANISM
PIANIST
PICKIER
PICKING
PICNICS
PICTISH
PIDGINS
PIECING
PIELIKE
PIETIES
PIETINS
PIETISM
PIETIST
PIGGIER
PIGGIES
PIGGING
PIGGISH
PIGLIKE
PILLING
PILLION
PIMLICO
PINGING
PINKIES
PINKING
PINKISH
PINNING
PIPKINS
PIPPINS
PIQUING
PISCINE
PISMIRE
PISTILS
PITHIER
PITHILY
PITHING
PITTING
PITYING
PIXYISH
PLACIDO
PLACING
PLANING
PLANISH
PLATIER
PLATING
PLAYING
PLOSION
PLOSIVE
PLOWING
PLUGINS
PLUMIER
PLUMING
PLUVIAL
PODGIER
PODGILY
PODLIKE
PODRIDA
POETICS
POISING
POITIER
POLLING
POLOIST
PONGIDS
PONGING
PONTIAC
PONTIFF
PONTINE
PONTIUS
PONYING
POOLING
POOPING
POORISH
POPLINS
POPPIES
POPPING
POPPINS
PORCINE
PORGIES
PORKIER
PORKISH
PORTICO
PORTION
POSTING
POSTITS
POTPIES
POTSIER
POTTIER
POTTING
POURING
POUTIER
POUTING
PRALINE
PRATING
PRAYING
PRECISE
PREDICT
PRELIMS
PREMIER
PREMISE
PREMISS
PREMIUM
PRESIDE
PREVIEW
PREXIES
PRICIER
PRICING
PRIDING
PRIMING
PRIVIER
PRIVIES
PRIVILY
PRIVITY
PRIZING
PROBING
PROBITY
PRODIGY
PROFILE
PROFITS
PROMISE
PROSIER
PROSILY
PROSING
PROTIST
PROVIDE
PROVING
PROVISO
PROXIES
PROXIMO
PRUDISH
PRUNING
PUBLICS
PUBLISH
PUCCINI
PUCKISH
PUDDING
PUDGIER
PUDGILY
PUERILE
PUFFIER
PUFFILY
PUFFING
PUFFINS
PUGGISH
PULLING
PULLINS
PULPIER
PULPITS
PULSING
PUMPING
PUNDITS
PUNKIER
PUNKIES
PUNNIER
PUNNILY
PUNNING
PUNTIES
PUNTING
PUPPIES
PURGING
PURLIEU
PURLING
PURLINS
PURRING
PURSIER
PURSING
PURVIEW
PUSHIER
PUSHILY
PUSHING
PUTTIED
PUTTIES
PUTTING
PYGMIES
PYTHIAN
PYTHIAS

P••••I•

PACIFIC
PALADIN
PALMOIL
PARBOIL
PARFAIT
PARSNIP
PEERSIN
PELAGIC
PENGUIN
PERSEID
PERTAIN
PETUNIA
PFENNIG
PHASEIN
PHILBIN
PHILLIP
PHOENIX
PHRENIC
PHYLLIS
PIGSKIN
PIGTAIL
PILEDIN
PILESIN
PILGRIM
PINTAIL
PIRATIC
PITCHIN
PLASTIC
PLAUDIT
PLUGSIN
POLARIS
POLEMIC
POLITIC
POMPEIA
POMPEII
PORKPIE
POURSIN
PRAIRIE
PREEMIE
PREPAID
PREPPIE
PREVAIL
PROPRIO
PROSAIC
PROTEIN
PRUSSIA
PSYCHIC
PULLSIN
PUMPKIN
PUNCHIN
PURLOIN
PURSUIT
PUSHKIN
PUSHPIN
PYRAMID
PYRRHIC

P•••••I

PACHISI
PADRONI
PAHLAVI
PALAZZI
PLATYPI
POMPEII
PUCCINI
PULASKI
PUNJABI

•PI••••

APISHLY
EPICENE
EPICURE
EPIGENE
EPIGONE
EPIGRAM
EPILOGS
EPISODE
EPISTLE
EPITHET
EPITOME
OPIATES
OPINERS
OPINING
OPINION
SPICERY
SPICEUP
SPICIER
SPICILY
SPICING
SPIDERS
SPIDERY
SPIEDON
SPIEGEL
SPIELED
SPIELER
SPIESON
SPIGOTS
SPIKERS
SPIKIER
SPIKILY
SPIKING
SPILLED
SPINACH
SPINDLE
SPINDLY
SPINDRY
SPINELS
SPINETS
SPINIER
SPINNER
SPINNEY
SPINOFF
SPINOUT
SPINOZA
SPIRALS
SPIRANT
SPIREAS
SPIRIER
SPIRITO
SPIRITS
SPITING
SPITZES

•P•I•••

APRICOT
APRIORI
APSIDES
EPSILON
OPHITES
OPTICAL
OPTIMAL
OPTIMUM
OPTIONS
SPLICED
SPLICER
SPLICES
SPLINES
SPLINTS
SPLITUP
SPOILED
SPOILER
SPRIEST
SPRINGS
SPRINGY
SPRINTS
SPRITES
UPLIFTS
UPLINKS
UPRIGHT
UPRISEN
UPRISES
UPRIVER
UPSILON
UPTICKS
UPTIGHT

•P••I••

APATITE
APELIKE
APERIES
APPLIED
APPLIES
APPOINT
APPRISE
APPRIZE
EPEEIST
EPOXIES
IPSWICH
OPACITY
OPALINE
OPENING
OPINING
OPINION
SPACIER
SPACING
SPADING
SPANIEL
SPANISH
SPARING
SPATIAL
SPAVINS
SPAYING
SPECIAL
SPECIES
SPECIFY
SPECING
SPEWING
SPICIER
SPICILY
SPICING
SPIKIER
SPIKILY
SPIKING
SPINIER
SPIRIER
SPIRITO
SPIRITS
SPITING
SPOKING
SPRAINS
SPUMIER
SPUMING
UPRAISE
UPSWING

•P•••I•

APHELIA
EPSTEIN
OPENAIR
OPENPIT
OPHELIA
SPOTLIT
SPUTNIK
UPBRAID

•P••••I

APRIORI
SPUMONI

••PI•••

ASPIRED
ASPIRER
ASPIRES
ASPIRIN
CAPITAL
CAPITAN
CAPITOL
COPIERS
COPILOT
COPIOUS
DEPICTS
DOPIEST
EMPIRES

ESPIALS
EXPIATE
EXPIRED
EXPIRES
IMPIETY
IMPINGE
IMPIOUS
JUPITER
LIPIDES
LUPINES
MOPIEST
ORPINES
PAPILLA
PIPIEST
PIPINGS
RAPIDER
RAPIDLY
RAPIERS
RAPINES
REPINED
REPINES
RIPIENO
RIPINTO
ROPIEST
RUPIAHS
SAPIENS
SAPIENT
TAPINGS
TAPINTO
TAPIOCA
TEPIDLY
TOPIARY
TOPICAL
TYPICAL
TYPIEST
TYPISTS
UMPIRED
UMPIRES
UNPILED
UNPILES
VAPIDLY
WAPITIS

••P•I••
AMPLIFY
APPLIED
APPLIES
APPOINT
APPRISE
APPRIZE
AUPAIRS
BAPTISE
BAPTISM
BAPTIST
BAPTIZE
BOPPING
CAPPING
CAPRICE
CAPSIDS
CAPSIZE
CAPTION
CAPTIVE
COPPICE
COPPING
COPYING
COPYIST
CUPLIKE
CUPPING
CYPRIOT
DAPPING
DEPRIVE
DIPPIER
DIPPING
EMPTIED
EMPTIER
EMPTIES
EMPTILY
ESPYING
FOPPISH
GAPPING
GIPPING
GIPSIES
GUPPIES
GYPPING
GYPSIES
HAPPIER
HAPPILY
HAPPING
HIPLIKE
HIPPIER
HIPPIES
HOPKINS
HOPLIKE
HOPPING
HYPOING
IMPAIRS
IMPLIED
IMPLIES
IMPRINT
INPRINT
KIPLING
LAPPING
LAPPISH
LAPSING
LAPWING
LEPPIES
LIPLIKE
LIPPIER
LIPPING
LOPPIER
LOPPING
MAPPING
MOPPING
NAPKINS
NAPPIES
NAPPING
NAPTIME
NIPPIER
NIPPING
NUPTIAL
PAPLIKE
PAPRIKA
PEPPIER
PEPPILY
PEPPING
PEPSINS
PEPTIDE
PIPKINS
PIPPINS
POPLINS
POPPIES
POPPING
POPPINS
PUPPIES
RAPPING
REPAINT
REPAIRS
REPLICA
REPLIED
REPLIES
REPRICE
REPRINT
REPRISE
REPTILE
RIPPING
RIPTIDE
SAPLING
SAPPIER
SAPPILY
SAPPING
SIPPING
SOPHISM
SOPHIST
SOPPIER
SOPPING
SOPWITH
SUPPING
TAPPING
TIPPIER
TIPPING
TIPSIER
TIPSILY
TOPKICK
TOPPING
TOPSIDE
YAPPING
YIPPING
YUPPIES
ZAPPIER
ZAPPING
ZIPPIER
ZIPPING

••P••I•
ASPIRIN
CAPAPIE
CAPTAIN
DAPHNIS
DEPOSIT
DIPLOID
EMPORIA
EXPLAIN
EXPLOIT
HEPARIN
HEPATIC
HOPTOIT
IMPERIL
NEPALIS
ROPEDIN
ROPESIN
TOPSAIL
TOPSOIL
WAPITIS

••P•••I
OMPHALI
RAPANUI
TOPKAPI

•••PI••
ARMPITS
AUSPICE
BAGPIPE
BEEPING
BOPPING
BUMPIER
BUMPILY
BUMPING
BURPING
CAMPIER
CAMPILY
CAMPING
CAMPION
CAPPING
CARPING
CASPIAN
COMPILE
COOPING
COPPICE
COPPING
CUPPING
CUSPIDS
DAMPING
DAMPISH
DAPPING
DESPISE
DESPITE
DIPPIER
DIPPING
DRAPING
DROPINS
DUMPIER
DUMPING
DUMPISH
ELAPIDS
ELOPING
FOPPISH
GAPPING
GASPING
GAWPING
GIPPING
GOOPIER
GRAPIER
GRIPING
GROPING
GROPIUS
GULPIER
GULPING
GUPPIES
GYPPING
HAPPIER
HAPPILY
HAPPING
HARPIES
HARPING
HARPIST
HASPING
HATPINS
HEAPING
HELPING
HIPPIER
HIPPIES
HOOPING
HOPPING
HOSPICE
HUMPIER
ICEPICK
INSPIRE
JUMPIER
JUMPILY
JUMPING
KEEPING
KELPIES
KEWPIES
LAPPING
LAPPISH
LEAPING
LEMPIRA
LEPPIES
LIMPING
LINPIAO
LIPPIER
LIPPING
LISPING
LOOPIER
LOOPING
LOPPIER
LOPPING
LUMPIER
LUMPILY
LUMPING
LUMPISH
MAGPIES
MAPPING
MOPPING
MUDPIES
MUMPING
NAPPIES
NAPPING
NIPPIER
NIPPING
NITPICK
PANPIPE
PEEPING
PEPPIER
PEPPILY
PEPPING
PIPPINS
POOPING
POPPIES
POPPING
POPPINS
POTPIES
PULPIER
PULPITS
PUMPING
PUPPIES
RAPPING
RASPIER
RASPING
RASPISH
REAPING
REDPINE
RESPINS
RESPIRE
RESPITE
RIPPING
ROMPING
ROMPISH
SAPPIER
SAPPILY
SAPPING
SCOPING
SEEPIER
SEEPING
SERPICO
SHAPING
SHAPIRO
SIPPING
SLOPING
SNIPING
SOAPIER
SOAPILY
SOAPING
SOPPIER
SOPPING
SOUPIER
STEPINS
SUPPING
SWIPING
TAMPICO
TAMPING
TAPPING
TARPITS
TENPINS
THEPITS
TIEPINS
TIPPIER
TIPPING
TOPPING
TROPICS
TROPISM
UTOPIAN
UTOPIAS
VAMPING
VAMPIRA
VAMPIRE
VAMPISH
VESPIDS
VULPINE
WARPING
WASPIER
WASPILY
WASPISH
WEEPIER
WEEPIES
WEEPING
WIMPIER
WIMPISH
WISPIER
WISPILY
WISPING
YAPPING
YAWPING
YELPING
YIPPING
YUPPIES
ZAPPIER
ZAPPING
ZIPPIER
ZIPPING

•••P•I•
ASEPSIS
ASEPTIC
BUMPKIN
CHAPLIN
CHAPPIE
CHIPSIN
COEPTIS
CRAPPIE
CRYPTIC
CULPRIT
DAUPHIN
DEEPSIX
DELPHIC
DESPAIR
DESPOIL
DOLPHIN
DROPSIN
EDAPHIC
GRAPHIC
JUMPSIN
KEEPSIN
LAMPOIL
LEIPZIG
LOWPAID
MEMPHIS
POMPEIA
POMPEII
PREPAID
PREPPIE
PROPRIO
PUMPKIN
SCEPTIC
SEEPSIN
SKEPTIC
SLEPTIN
SLIPSIN
STEPSIN
STOPSIN
STYPTIC
TROPHIC

•••P••I
CAMPARI
CHAPATI
POMPEII
TRIPOLI
TYMPANI

••••PI•
BUSHPIG
CAPAPIE
CHAPPIE
CHEAPIE
COCKPIT
CRAPPIE
CRISPIN
DUCKPIN
FLEAPIT
GROUPIE
HAIRPIN
HEADPIN
INASPIN
INCIPIT
INSIPID
KINGPIN
MOSHPIT
NINEPIN
OLYMPIA
OLYMPIC
OPENPIT
PORKPIE
PREPPIE
PUSHPIN
SCORPIO
SERAPIS
SLEEPIN
THESPIS

••••P•I
EXEMPLI
SHARPEI

•••••PI
PLATYPI
TOPKAPI

P•J••••
PAJAMAS
PDJAMES
PYJAMAS

P••J•••
PALJOEY
PERJURE
PERJURY
PROJECT
PUNJABI

P•••J••
PROPJET

•••PJ••
PROPJET

P•K••••
PIKEMAN
PIKEMEN
POKEDAT
POKEFUN
POKESAT
POKIEST

P••K•••
PACKAGE
PACKARD
PACKERS
PACKETS
PACKICE
PACKING
PACKRAT
PACKSUP
PARKADE
PARKING
PARKWAY
PAWKIER
PEAKING
PEAKISH
PECKIER
PECKING
PECKISH
PECKSAT
PEEKERS
PEEKING
PEEKOUT
PEEKSAT
PERKIER
PERKILY
PERKING
PERKINS
PERKISH
PERKSUP
PESKIER
PESKILY
PICKAXE
PICKENS
PICKERS
PICKETS
PICKETT
PICKIER
PICKING
PICKLED
PICKLES
PICKOFF
PICKOUT
PICKSAT
PICKSON
PICKSUP
PICKUPS
PINKEST
PINKIES
PINKING
PINKISH
PIPKINS
POCKETS
POLKAED
PORKERS
PORKIER
PORKISH
PORKPIE
PUCKERS
PUCKETT
PUCKISH
PUNKAHS
PUNKERS
PUNKIER
PUNKIES

P•••K••
PASSKEY
PERUKES
PIGSKIN
PLACKET
PLANKED
PLINKED
PLUCKED
PLUNKED
PRANKED
PRICKED
PRICKLE
PRICKLY
PRINKED
PUMPKIN
PUSHKIN

P••••K•
PALOOKA
PANCAKE
PANICKY
PAPLIKE
PAPRIKA
PARTAKE
PEALIKE
PEGLIKE
PENLIKE
PIELIKE
PIGLIKE
PINOAKS
PODLIKE
PROVOKE
PULASKI

P•••••K
PADDOCK
PADLOCK
PARTOOK
PATRICK
PEACOCK
PEPTALK
PETCOCK
PETROCK
POLLACK
POLLOCK
POTHOOK
POTLUCK
PRECOOK
PRESOAK

•P•K•••
SPIKERS
SPIKIER
SPIKILY
SPIKING
SPOKANE
SPOKEOF
SPOKEUP
SPOKING

•P••K••
SPACKLE
SPANKED
SPANKER
SPARKED
SPARKLE
SPEAKER
SPEAKOF
SPEAKUP
SPECKED
SPECKLE
SPOOKED
UPTAKES

•P•••K•
APELIKE
SPASSKY
UPLINKS
UPTICKS

•P••••K
SPELUNK
SPUTNIK
UPQUARK

••PK•••
HOPKINS
NAPKINS
PIPKINS
TOPKAPI
TOPKICK
TOPKNOT

••P••K•
CUPCAKE
CUPLIKE
HIPLIKE
HOPLIKE
KOPECKS
LIPLIKE
PAPLIKE
PAPRIKA
UNPACKS

••P•••K
PEPTALK
TOPKICK

•••PK••
BUMPKIN
PUMPKIN

•••P•K•
BESPOKE
COWPOKE
KUSPUKS

•••P••K
BESPEAK
CARPARK
DRSPOCK
HENPECK
ICEPACK
ICEPICK
JAMPACK
MRSPOCK
MUDPACK
NITPICK
OFFPEAK
RATPACK
SIXPACK

••••P•K
ZATOPEK

PL•••••
PLACARD
PLACATE
PLACEBO
PLACERS
PLACIDO
PLACING
PLACKET
PLAGUED
PLAGUES
PLAICES
PLAINER
PLAINLY
PLAINTS
PLAITED
PLANERS
PLANETS
PLANING
PLANISH
PLANKED
PLANNED
PLANNER
PLANOUT
PLANSON
PLANTAR
PLANTED
PLANTER
PLAQUES
PLASHED
PLASHES
PLASMAS
PLASTER
PLASTIC
PLATEAU
PLATENS
PLATERS
PLATIER
PLATING
PLATOON
PLATTER
PLATYPI
PLAUDIT
PLAUTUS
PLAYACT
PLAYBOY
PLAYDOH
PLAYERS
PLAYFUL
PLAYING
PLAYLET
PLAYOFF
PLAYOUT
PLAYPEN
PLAYSAT
PLAYSON
PLAYSUP
PLEADED
PLEADER
PLEASED
PLEASER
PLEASES
PLEATED
PLECTRA
PLEDGED
PLEDGEE
PLEDGER
PLEDGES
PLENARY
PLENUMS
PLEXORS
PLIABLE
PLIABLY
PLIANCY
PLIGHTS
PLINKED
PLINTHS
PLODDED
PLODDER
PLOPPED
PLOSION
PLOSIVE
PLOTFUL
PLOTTED
PLOTTER
PLOUGHS
PLOVERS
PLOWBOY
PLOWERS
PLOWING
PLOWMAN
PLOWMEN
PLUCKED
PLUGGED
PLUGGER
PLUGINS
PLUGSIN
PLUMAGE
PLUMBED
PLUMBER
PLUMIER
PLUMING
PLUMMER
PLUMMET
PLUMPED
PLUMPER
PLUMPLY
PLUNDER
PLUNGED
PLUNGER
PLUNGES
PLUNKED
PLURALS
PLUSHER
PLUSHES
PLUSHLY
PLUSSES
PLUVIAL
PLYWOOD

P•L••••
PALACES
PALADIN
PALANCE
PALATAL
PALATES
PALAVER
PALAZZI
PALAZZO
PALEDRY
PALERMO
PALETTE
PALFREY
PALIEST
PALJOEY
PALLETS
PALLIER
PALLING
PALLIUM
PALLORS
PALMARY
PALMATE
PALMIER
PALMING
PALMIST
PALMOFF
PALMOIL
PALMTOP
PALOMAR
PALOOKA
PALTERS
PALTROW
PELAGES
PELAGIC
PELICAN
PELISSE
PELLETS
PELOTAS
PELTATE
PELTERS
PELTING
PELTISH
PHLOXES
PILEDIN
PILEDON
PILEDUP
PILESIN
PILESON
PILESUP
PILEUPS
PILFERS
PILGRIM
PILINGS
PILLAGE
PILLARS
PILLBOX
PILLBUG
PILLING
PILLION
PILLORY
PILLOWS
PILLOWY
PILOTED
PILSNER
POLARIS
POLDERS
POLEAXE
POLECAR
POLECAT
POLEMIC
POLENTA
POLICED
POLICES
POLITER
POLITIC
POLKAED
POLLACK
POLLENS
POLLERS
POLLING
POLLOCK
POLLTAX
POLLUTE
POLOIST
POLYGON
POLYMER
PULASKI
PULLETS
PULLEYS
PULLFOR
PULLING
PULLINS
PULLMAN
PULLOFF
PULLONS
PULLOUT
PULLSIN
PULLSON
PULLSUP
PULLTAB
PULLUPS
PULPIER
PULPITS
PULQUES
PULSARS
PULSATE
PULSING

P••L•••
PABLUMS
PADLOCK
PAHLAVI
PAILFUL
PAILOUS
PALLETS
PALLIER
PALLING
PALLIUM
PALLORS
PAPLIKE
PARLAYS
PARLEYS
PARLORS
PARLOUR
PARLOUS
PAULINA
PAULINE
PAULING
PAULIST
PAULSEN
PAVLOVA
PAYLOAD
PEALIKE
PEALING
PEDLARS
PEELERS
PEELING
PEELOFF
PEGLESS
PEGLIKE
PELLETS
PENLIKE
PEPLUMS
PERLITE
PERLMAN
PHALANX
PHILBIN
PHILLIP
PHILTER
PHILTRE
PHYLLIS
PIELIKE
PIGLETS
PIGLIKE
PILLAGE
PILLARS
PILLBOX
PILLBUG
PILLING
PILLION
PILLORY
PILLOWS
PILLOWY
PIMLICO
PINLESS
PIOLETS
PODLIKE
POLLACK
POLLENS
POLLERS
POLLING
POLLOCK
POLLTAX
POLLUTE
POOLING
POPLARS
POPLINS
POTLUCK
POULENC
POULTRY
PRALINE
PRELATE
PRELIMS
PRELOAD
PRELUDE
PROLOGS
PROLONG
PSALMED
PSALTER
PTOLEMY
PUBLICS
PUBLISH
PULLETS
PULLEYS
PULLFOR
PULLING
PULLINS
PULLMAN
PULLOFF
PULLONS
PULLOUT
PULLSIN
PULLSON
PULLSUP
PULLTAB
PULLUPS
PUNLESS
PURLIEU
PURLING
PURLINS
PURLOIN

P•••L••
PABULUM
PADDLED
PADDLER
PADDLES
PAISLEY
PANELED
PAPILLA
PAROLED
PAROLEE
PAROLES
PARSLEY
PATELLA
PAYOLAS
PEARLED
PEBBLED
PEBBLES
PEDALED
PEDDLED
PEDDLER
PEDDLES
PEEPLES
PENALTY
PENULTS
PEOPLED
PEOPLES
PERPLEX
PESTLED
PESTLES
PETALED
PHARLAP
PHILLIP
PHYLLIS
PICKLED
PICKLES
PIFFLED
PIFFLES
PLAYLET
POMELOS
POODLES
POPPLED
POPPLES
POPULAR
POPULUS
POSSLQS
POTTLES
PRESLEY
PROBLEM
PROWLED
PROWLER
PUDDLED
PUDDLES
PUEBLOS
PURFLED
PURFLES
PURPLED
PURPLES
PUZZLED
PUZZLER
PUZZLES

P••••L•
PANFULS
PANICLE
PANOPLY
PAPILLA
PARABLE
PARCELS
PASSELS
PASTELS
PATELLA
PATROLS
PAYABLE
PAYROLL
PEDICLE
PENCILS
PENPALS
PEPPILY
PEPTALK
PERCALE
PERGOLA
PERKILY
PESKILY
PETIOLE
PETRELS
PETROLS
PETTILY
PHENOLS
PHONILY
PICCOLO
PIEBALD
PINBALL
PINHOLE
PINOCLE
PINWALE
PIOUSLY
PISTILS
PISTOLE
PISTOLS
PITBULL
PITFALL
PITHILY
PLAINLY
PLIABLE
PLIABLY
PLUMPLY
PLURALS
PLUSHLY
PODGILY
POMMELS
PORTALS
POTABLE
POTFULS
POTHOLE
PRATTLE
PRESALE
PRESELL
PRICKLE
PRICKLY
PRIVILY
PROFILE
PRONELY
PROPELS
PROSILY
PROUDLY
PUDGILY
PUERILE
PUFFILY
PUMMELS
PUNNILY
PURCELL
PUSHILY

P•••••L
PAGEFUL
PAILFUL
PAINFUL
PALATAL
PALMOIL
PARASOL
PARBOIL
PARTIAL
PASCHAL
PASSEUL
PATRIAL
PAYROLL
PEAFOWL
PEDICEL
PERUSAL
PHRASAL
PIGTAIL
PINBALL
PINCURL
PINTAIL
PIPEFUL
PITBULL
PITFALL
PITIFUL
PIVOTAL
PLAYFUL
PLOTFUL
PLUVIAL
POUTFUL
PRECOOL
PREQUEL
PRESELL
PRETZEL
PREVAIL
PURCELL
PUSHFUL

•PL••••
APLENTY
SPLASHY
SPLAYED
SPLEENS
SPLICED
SPLICER
SPLICES
SPLINES
SPLINTS
SPLITUP
SPLOTCH
SPLURGE
UPLANDS
UPLIFTS
UPLINKS
UPLOADS

•P•L•••
APELIKE
APOLOGY
APPLAUD
APPLETS
APPLIED
APPLIES
EPILOGS
OPALINE
OPULENT
SPALLED
SPELLED
SPELLER
SPELUNK
SPILLED
UPCLOSE

•P••L••
APHELIA
APPALLS
EPAULET
EPSILON
OPHELIA
SPALLED
SPELLED
SPELLER
SPIELED
SPIELER
SPILLED
SPOILED
SPOILER
SPOOLED
SPOTLIT
UPHOLDS
UPSILON

•P•••L•
APISHLY
APOSTLE
APPALLS
APPEALS
EPISTLE
SPACKLE
SPANGLE
SPANGLY
SPARELY
SPARKLE
SPATULA
SPECKLE
SPICILY
SPIKILY
SPINDLE
SPINDLY
SPINELS
SPIRALS
SPRAWLS
UPPSALA
UPSCALE

•P••••L
APPAREL
APTERAL
EPOCHAL
OPTICAL
OPTIMAL
SPANIEL
SPATIAL
SPECIAL
SPIEGEL
SPOUSAL

••PL•••
AMPLEST
AMPLIFY
APPLAUD
APPLETS
APPLIED
APPLIES
BIPLANE
BYPLAYS
CAPLESS
CAPLETS
COPLAND
CUPLIKE
DEPLANE
DEPLETE
DEPLORE
DEPLOYS
DIPLOID
DIPLOMA
EMPLOYE
EMPLOYS
ENPLANE
EXPLAIN
EXPLODE
EXPLOIT
EXPLORE
GAPLESS
HAPLESS
HIPLESS
HIPLIKE
HOPLIKE
IMPLANT
IMPLIED
IMPLIES
IMPLODE
IMPLORE
INPLACE
KIPLING
LAPLACE
LAPLAND
LAPLATA
LIPLESS
LIPLIKE
NAPLESS
PAPLIKE
PEPLUMS
POPLARS
POPLINS
REPLACE
REPLANS
REPLANT
REPLATE
REPLAYS
REPLETE
REPLICA
REPLIED
REPLIES
REPLOWS
SAPLESS
SAPLING
TIPLESS
UNPLUGS

••P•L••
AMPULES
APPALLS
BIPOLAR
CAPELET
CAPELLA
CAPULET
COPILOT
COPULAE
COPULAS
CUPOLAS
DAPPLED
DAPPLES
DEPALMA
DIPOLAR
DIPOLES
DOPPLER
FIPPLES
HOPPLED
HOPPLES
IMPALAS
IMPALED
IMPALES
IMPULSE
LAPALMA
LAPELED
NEPALIS
PAPILLA
POPPLED
POPPLES
POPULAR
POPULUS
REPOLLS
REPULSE
RIPPLED
RIPPLES
SUPPLER
TIPPLED
TIPPLER
TIPPLES
TOPPLED
TOPPLES
TUPELOS
UNPILED
UNPILES

••P••L•
AMPOULE
APPALLS
APPEALS
ASPHALT
CAPABLE
CAPABLY
CAPELLA
CAPFULS
CAPSULE
COPPOLA
CUPFULS
EMPTILY
ESPIALS
HAPPILY
LAPBELT
LAPFULS
LIPBALM
OMPHALI
PAPILLA
PEPPILY
PEPTALK
RAPIDLY
RAPPELS
REPEALS
REPOLLS
REPTILE
SAPPILY
TEPIDLY
TIPSILY
TOPHOLE
UPPSALA
VAPIDLY

••P•••L
APPAREL
BIPEDAL
CAPITAL
CAPITOL
DEPOSAL
EMPANEL
ESPANOL
HOPEFUL
IMPANEL
IMPERIL
NUPTIAL
PIPEFUL
RAPHAEL
TOPICAL
TOPSAIL
TOPSOIL
TYPICAL

•••PL••
AIRPLAY
CHAPLET
CHAPLIN
COMPLEX
COUPLED
COUPLES
COUPLET
DAPPLED
DAPPLES
DIMPLED
DIMPLES
DISPLAY
DOPPLER
DROPLET
EARPLUG
ENDPLAY
FIPPLES
GUNPLAY
HOOPLAS
HOPPLED
HOPPLES
KERPLOP
MISPLAY
NONPLUS
OUTPLAY
PEEPLES
PEOPLED
PEOPLES
PERPLEX
POPPLED
POPPLES
PURPLED
PURPLES
RIMPLED
RIMPLES
RIPPLED
RIPPLES
RUMPLED
RUMPLES
SAMPLED
SAMPLER
SAMPLES
SHAPLEY
SIMPLER
SIMPLEX
STAPLED
STAPLER
STAPLES
SUBPLOT
SUPPLER
SURPLUS
TEMPLAR
TEMPLES
TIPPLED
TIPPLER
TIPPLES
TOPPLED
TOPPLES
TRIPLED
TRIPLES
TRIPLET
TRIPLEX
WIMPLED
WIMPLES

•••P•L•
ADEPTLY
AMAPOLA
BUMPILY
CAMPILY
CARPALS
CARPELS
CHAPELS
COMPELS
COMPILE
COPPOLA
DISPELS
GALPALS
GOSPELS
GRAPPLE
HAPPILY
INAPTLY
INEPTLY
JUMPILY
KAMPALA
LEGPULL
LEOPOLD
LUMPILY
MAYPOLE
OUTPOLL
PENPALS
PEPPILY
PROPELS
RAPPELS
REDPOLL
RUMPOLE
SAPPILY
SCAPULA
SHAPELY
SKIPOLE
SNAPPLE
SOAPILY
STIPPLE
TADPOLE
TIEPOLO
TRIPOLI
UNAPTLY
WALPOLE
WASPILY
WIMPOLE
WISPILY

•••P••L
CARPOOL
DESPOIL
GRAPNEL
HELPFUL
LAMPOIL
LEGPULL
LESPAUL
OUTPOLL
REDPOLL
SHOPFUL
VANPOOL

••••PL•
CHEAPLY
CRISPLY
CRUMPLE
CRUMPLY
EXAMPLE
EXEMPLI
GRAPPLE
MANIPLE
OCTUPLE
PANOPLY
PLUMPLY
SCRUPLE
SHARPLY
SNAPPLE
STEEPLE
STEEPLY
STIPPLE
TRAMPLE

••••P•L
OEDIPAL
SCALPEL

P•M••••
PAMPERS
PEMICAN
PIMENTO
PIMESON
PIMLICO
POMADED
POMADES
POMELOS
POMMELS
POMPANO
POMPEIA
POMPEII
POMPOMS
POMPONS
POMPOUS
PUMICES
PUMMELS
PUMPERS
PUMPING
PUMPKIN
PUMPSUP

P••M•••
PALMARY
PALMATE
PALMIER
PALMING
PALMIST
PALMOFF
PALMOIL
PALMTOP
PAYMENT
PERMING
PERMITS
PIGMENT
PISMIRE
PLUMAGE
PLUMBED
PLUMBER
PLUMIER
PLUMING
PLUMMER
PLUMMET
PLUMPED
PLUMPER
PLUMPLY
POMMELS
PREMEDS
PREMIER
PREMISE
PREMISS
PREMIUM
PRIMACY
PRIMARY
PRIMATE
PRIMERS
PRIMING
PRIMMER
PRIMPED
PROMISE
PROMOTE
PROMPTS
PUMMELS
PYGMIES

P•••M••
PAJAMAS
PALOMAR
PANAMAS
PDJAMES
PERLMAN
PIKEMAN
PIKEMEN
PIPEMMA
PITTMAN
PLASMAS
PLOWMAN
PLOWMEN
PLUMMER
PLUMMET
POLEMIC
POLYMER
PORTMAN
POSTMAN
POSTMEN
POTOMAC
PREAMPS
PREEMIE
PREEMPT
PRIMMER
PROPMAN
PROPMEN
PSALMED
PULLMAN
PUTAMEN
PYJAMAS
PYRAMID
PYRAMUS

P••••M•
PABLUMS
PALERMO
PASTIME
PENNAME
PEPLUMS
PERFUME
PETNAME
PHENOMS
PHONEME
PIPEMMA
PLENUMS
PODIUMS
POMPOMS
POSSUMS
PRELIMS
PRESUME
PROXIMO
PTOLEMY

P•••••M
PABULUM
PALLIUM
PENTIUM
PERDIEM
PERFORM
PHANTOM
PIANISM
PIETISM
PILGRIM
PINETUM
POTSDAM
PREMIUM
PROBLEM
PROGRAM

•P•M•••
SPAMMED
SPAMMER
SPUMIER
SPUMING
SPUMONE
SPUMONI
SPUMOUS

•P••M••
OPTIMAL
OPTIMUM
SPAMMED
SPAMMER
UPTEMPO

•P•••M•
EPITOME
EPONYMS
EPONYMY
IPANEMA

•P••••M
APOTHEM
EPIGRAM
OPOSSUM
OPTIMUM

••PM•••
TOPMAST
TOPMOST

••P•M••
PIPEMMA
REPOMAN
TAPEMAN
TAPEMEN

••P••M•
DEPALMA
DIPLOMA
LAPALMA
NAPTIME
PEPLUMS
PIPEMMA
SUPREME
SUPREMO

••P•••M
BAPTISM
GYPROOM
HYPONYM
LIPBALM
SOPHISM
TAPROOM

•••PM••
CHAPMAN
CHAPMEN
PROPMAN
PROPMEN
SHIPMAN
SHIPMEN

•••P•M•
AIRPUMP
GASPUMP
POMPOMS

•••P••M
LUMPSUM
SYMPTOM
TROPISM

•••••PM
EIGHTPM
SEVENPM
THREEPM

P•N••••
PANACEA
PANACHE
PANADAS
PANAMAS
PANARAB
PANCAKE
PANCHAX
PANDECT
PANDERS
PANDITS
PANDORA
PANELED
PANFISH
PANFULS
PANICKY
PANICLE
PANNERS
PANNIER
PANNING
PANOPLY
PANPIPE
PANSIES
PANSOUT
PANTHER
PANTING
PANURGE
PANZERS
PENALTY
PENANCE
PENATES
PENCILS
PENDANT
PENDENT
PENDING
PENGUIN
PENLIKE
PENNAME
PENNANT
PENNATE
PENNERS
PENNIES
PENNING
PENNONS
PENPALS
PENSEES
PENSION
PENSIVE
PENTADS
PENTIUM
PENUCHE
PENULTS
PINATAS
PINBALL
PINCERS
PINCHAS
PINCHED
PINCHER
PINCHES
PINCURL
PINDOWN
PINEFOR
PINENUT
PINESAP
PINETAR
PINETUM
PINGING
PINHEAD
PINHOLE
PINIEST
PINIONS
PINKEST
PINKIES
PINKING
PINKISH
PINLESS
PINNACE
PINNATE
PINNERS
PINNING
PINOAKS
PINOCLE
PINONES
PINTAIL
PINWALE
PONCHOS
PONDERS
PONGEES
PONGIDS
PONGING
PONIARD
PONTIAC
PONTIFF
PONTINE
PONTIUS
PONTOON
PONYING
PUNCHED
PUNCHER
PUNCHES
PUNCHIN
PUNCHUP
PUNDITS
PUNGENT
PUNIEST
PUNJABI
PUNKAHS
PUNKERS
PUNKIER
PUNKIES
PUNLESS
PUNNETS
PUNNIER
PUNNILY
PUNNING
PUNSTER
PUNTERS
PUNTIES
PUNTING
PYNCHON

P••N•••
PAANGAS
PAINFUL
PAINTED
PAINTER
PANNERS
PANNIER
PANNING
PATNESS
PAUNCHY
PAWNEES
PAWNERS
PAWNING
PAWNOFF
PEANUTS
PENNAME
PENNANT
PENNATE
PENNERS
PENNIES
PENNING
PENNONS
PEONAGE
PEONIES
PETNAME
PFENNIG
PHANTOM
PHENOLS
PHENOMS
PHINEAS
PHONEME
PHONEYS
PHONICS
PHONIER
PHONIES
PHONILY
PHONING
PIANISM
PIANIST
PICNICS
PIGNUTS
PINNACE
PINNATE
PINNERS
PINNING
PIONEER
PLANERS
PLANETS
PLANING
PLANISH
PLANKED
PLANNED
PLANNER
PLANOUT
PLANSON
PLANTAR
PLANTED
PLANTER
PLENARY
PLENUMS
PLINKED
PLINTHS
PLUNDER
PLUNGED
PLUNGER
PLUNGES
PLUNKED
POINTED
POINTER
POINTTO
POUNCED
POUNCER
POUNCES
POUNDED
POUNDER
PRANCED
PRANCER
PRANCES
PRANGED
PRANKED
PRENUPS
PRINCES
PRINKED
PRINTED
PRINTER
PRONELY
PRONGED
PRONOUN
PRUNERS
PRUNING
PSANDQS
PUGNOSE
PUNNETS
PUNNIER
PUNNILY
PUNNING

P•••N••
PALANCE
PARDNER
PARENTS
PARINGS
PARSNIP
PARTNER
PATENTS
PATINAS
PAVANES
PEDANTS
PENANCE
PETUNIA
PFENNIG
PHOENIX
PHRENIC
PICANTE
PILINGS
PILSNER
PIMENTO
PINENUT
PINONES
PIPINGS
PIRANHA
PLAINER
PLAINLY
PLAINTS
PLANNED
PLANNER
PLIANCY
POCONOS

POLENTA
POTENCY
PREENED
PREENER
PRYINTO
PUDENCY

P••••N•

PACKING
PADDING
PADRONE
PADRONI
PADUANS
PAGEANT
PAIRING
PAISANO
PALLING
PALMING
PANNING
PANTING
PAPUANS
PARDONS
PARKING
PARRING
PARSING
PARSONS
PARTING
PARVENU
PASSING
PASTINA
PASTING
PATERNO
PATIENT
PATRONS
PATTENS
PATTING
PAULINA
PAULINE
PAULING
PAUSING
PAWNING
PAYMENT
PEAHENS
PEAKING
PEALING
PEASANT
PECCANT
PECKING
PECTINS
PEEKING
PEELING
PEEPING
PEERING
PEEVING
PEGGING
PELTING
PENDANT
PENDENT
PENDING
PENNANT
PENNING
PENNONS
PEPPING
PEPSINS
PERCENT
PERKING
PERKINS
PERMING
PERSONA
PERSONS
PETTING
PHALANX
PHARYNX
PHASING
PHONING
PHOTONS
PICKENS
PICKING
PIDGINS
PIECING
PIEPANS
PIETINS
PIGEONS
PIGGING
PIGMENT
PIGPENS
PILLING
PINGING
PINIONS
PINKING
PINNING
PIPKINS
PIPPINS
PIQUANT
PIQUING
PISCINE
PISTONS
PITHING
PITTING
PITYING
PLACING
PLANING
PLATENS
PLATING
PLAYING
PLOWING
PLUGINS
PLUMING
POISING
POISONS
POLLENS
POLLING
POMPANO
POMPONS
PONGING
PONTINE
PONYING
POOLING
POOPING
POPGUNS
POPLINS
POPPING
POPPINS
PORCINE
PORSENA
PORTEND
PORTENT
POSTING
POTIONS
POTTING
POULENC
POURING
POUTING
PRALINE
PRATING
PRAYING
PREBEND
PRESENT
PRETEND
PREVENT
PRICING
PRIDING
PRIMING
PRISONS
PRIZING
PROBING
PROBONO
PROFANE
PROGENY
PROLONG
PROPANE
PROSING
PROTONS
PROVING
PRUDENT
PRUNING
PUCCINI
PUDDING
PUFFING
PUFFINS
PULLING
PULLINS
PULLONS
PULSING
PUMPING
PUNGENT
PUNNING
PUNTING
PUPTENT
PURGING
PURLING
PURLINS
PURRING
PURSING
PUSHING
PUTTING
PYTHONS

P•••••N

PALADIN
PARAGON
PASSION
PASTERN
PATROON
PATTERN
PAULSEN
PEABEAN
PEARSON
PEERSIN
PELICAN
PEMICAN
PENGUIN
PENSION
PERLMAN
PERSIAN
PERTAIN
PHAETON
PHASEIN
PHILBIN
PICKSON
PIDGEON
PIGIRON
PIGSKIN
PIKEMAN
PIKEMEN
PILEDIN
PILEDON
PILESIN
PILESON
PILLION
PIMESON
PINDOWN
PITCHIN
PITTMAN
PLANSON
PLATOON
PLAYPEN
PLAYSON
PLOSION
PLOWMAN
PLOWMEN
PLUGSIN
POISSON
POKEFUN
POLYGON
PONTOON
POPCORN
PORTION
PORTMAN
POSTERN
POSTMAN
POSTMEN
POURSIN
PREDAWN
PRESSON
PRESTON
PRETEEN
PREYSON
PROCYON
PRONOUN
PROPMAN
PROPMEN
PROTEAN
PROTEIN
PULLMAN
PULLSIN
PULLSON
PUMPKIN
PUNCHIN
PURITAN
PURLOIN
PUSHKIN
PUSHPIN
PUTAMEN
PUTDOWN
PUTUPON
PYNCHON
PYTHIAN

•P•N•••

APTNESS
EPONYMS
EPONYMY
IPANEMA
OPENAIR
OPENBAR
OPENEND
OPENERS
OPENING
OPENPIT
OPENSEA
OPENSUP
OPENTOE
OPINERS
OPINING
OPINION
SPANDEX
SPANGLE
SPANGLY
SPANIEL
SPANISH
SPANKED
SPANKER
SPANNED
SPANNER
SPENCER
SPENDER
SPENSER
SPINACH
SPINDLE
SPINDLY
SPINDRY
SPINELS
SPINETS
SPINIER
SPINNER
SPINNEY
SPINOFF
SPINOUT
SPINOZA
SPONDEE
SPONGED
SPONGER
SPONGES
SPONSOR
SPUNOFF
SPUNOUT
UPENDED

•P••N••

APLENTY
APPENDS
APRONED
SPANNED
SPANNER
SPAWNED
SPINNER
SPINNEY
SPLINES
SPLINTS
SPOONED
SPOONER
SPRINGS
SPRINGY
SPRINTS
SPURNED
SPURNER
SPUTNIK
UPLANDS
UPLINKS
UPTONOW

•P•••N•

APPOINT
EPERGNE
EPICENE
EPIGENE
EPIGONE
OPALINE
OPENEND
OPENING
OPERAND
OPINING
OPPUGNS
OPTIONS
OPULENT
SPACING
SPADING
SPARING
SPAVINS
SPAYING
SPECING
SPELUNK
SPEWING
SPICING
SPIKING
SPIRANT
SPITING
SPLEENS
SPOKANE
SPOKING
SPRAINS
SPUMING
SPUMONE
SPUMONI
UPBORNE
UPFRONT
UPSWING
UPTURNS

•P••••N

EPSILON
EPSTEIN
OPINION
SPARTAN
SPIEDON
SPIESON
SPORRAN
SPURSON
UPRISEN
UPSILON

••PN•••

CAPNUTS
HIPNESS

••P•N••

APPENDS
ARPENTS
DAPHNIS
DEPENDS
DEPONED
DEPONES
DOPANTS
EMPANEL
ESPANOL
EXPANDS
EXPANSE
EXPENDS
EXPENSE
EXPUNGE
HAPENNY
HYPONYM
IMPANEL
IMPENDS
IMPINGE
LEPANTO
LUPINES
ORPINES
PIPINGS
RAPANUI
RAPINES
REPENTS
REPINED
REPINES
RIPENED
RIPINTO
TAPINGS
TAPINTO
TOPKNOT

••P••N•

APPOINT
BIPLANE
BOPPING
CAPEANN
CAPGUNS
CAPPING
COPLAND
COPPING
COPYING
CUPPING
DAPPING
DEPLANE
DIPPING
ENPLANE
ESPYING
EUPHONY
EXPOUND
GAPPING
GIPPING
GYPPING
HAPENNY
HAPPENS
HAPPING
HIPBONE
HOPKINS
HOPPING
HYPHENS
HYPOING
IMPLANT
IMPOUND
IMPRINT
IMPUGNS
INPRINT
KIPLING
LAPLAND
LAPPING
LAPSING
LAPWING
LEPTONS
LIPPING
LIPSYNC
LOPPING
MAPPING
MOPPING
NAPKINS
NAPPING
NEPTUNE
NIPPING
OPPUGNS
ORPHANS
PAPUANS
PEPPING
PEPSINS
PIPKINS
PIPPINS
POPGUNS
POPLINS
POPPING
POPPINS
PUPTENT
RAPPING
REPAINT
REPLANS
REPLANT
REPRINT
REPUGNS
RIPIENO
RIPPING
SAPIENS
SAPIENT
SAPLING
SAPPING
SIPHONS
SIPPING
SOPPING
SOPRANO
SUPPING
SYPHONS
TAPPING
TIPPING
TOPGUNS
TOPPING
YAPPING
YIPPING
ZAPPING
ZIPPING

••P•••N

ASPIRIN
CAPEANN
CAPITAN
CAPSTAN
CAPTAIN
CAPTION
EXPLAIN
HEPARIN
HEPBURN
ORPHEAN
POPCORN
REPOMAN
RIPTORN
ROPEDIN
ROPESIN
TAPEMAN
TAPEMEN
TOPDOWN
TYPHOON
UMPTEEN

•••PN••

GRAPNEL
JEEPNEY

•••P•N•

BEEPING
BOPPING
BUMPING
BURPING
CAMPING
CAPPING
CARPING
CLIPONS
COMPANY
COOPING
COPPING
COUPONS
COWPONY
CUPPING
DAMPENS
DAMPING
DAPPING
DEEPEND
DEEPENS
DIPPING
DRAPING
DROPINS
DUMPING
ELOPING
FRYPANS
GAPPING
GASPING
GAWPING
GIPPING
GRIPING
GROPING
GULPING
GYPPING
HAPPENS
HAPPING
HARPING
HASPING
HATPINS
HEAPING
HELPING
HISPANO
HOOPING
HOPPING
INSPANS
JUMPING
KEEPING
LAPPING
LEAPING
LIMPING
LIPPING
LISPING
LOOPING
LOPPING
LUMPING
MAPPING
MOPPING
MUMPING
NAPPING
NIPPING
OILPANS
PEEPING
PEPPING
PIEPANS
PIGPENS
PIPPINS
POMPANO
POMPONS
POOPING
POPPING
POPPINS
PROPANE
PUMPING
RAMPANT
RAPPING
RASPING
REAPING
REDPINE
REOPENS
RESPINS
RESPOND
RIPPING
ROMPING
SAMPANS
SAPPING
SCOPING
SEEPING
SERPENT
SHAPING
SIPPING
SLIPONS
SLOPING
SNAPONS
SNIPING
SOAPING
SOPPING
STEPINS
STIPEND
SUPPING
SUSPEND
SWIPING
TAIPANS
TAMPING
TAPPING
TARPONS
TENPINS
TIEPINS
TIPPING
TOPPING
TREPANS
TYMPANA
TYMPANI
UNSPENT
USOPENS
VAMPING
VOLPONE
VULPINE
WARPING
WEAPONS
WEEPING
WISPING
YAPPING
YAUPONS
YAWPING
YELPING
YIPPING
ZAPPING
ZIPPING

•••P••N

BUMPKIN
BURPGUN
CAMPION
CASPIAN
CHAPLIN
CHAPMAN
CHAPMEN
CHIPSIN
CLAPTON
DAUPHIN
DOLPHIN
DRIPPAN
DROPSIN
GRYPHON
HAMPTON
HARPOON
HARPSON
JUMPSIN
JUMPSON
KEEPSIN
KEEPSON
KRYPTON
LAMPOON
PROPMAN
PROPMEN
PUMPKIN
SAMPSON
SEEPSIN
SHIPMAN
SHIPMEN
SIMPSON
SLEPTIN
SLEPTON
SLIPSIN
SLIPSON
SOUPCON
STEPHEN
STEPSIN
STEPSON
STOPSIN
UTOPIAN

••••P•N

ACTUPON
BULLPEN
CHEAPEN
CRAMPON
CRISPIN
DEADPAN
DISHPAN
DRIPPAN
DUCKPIN
DUSTPAN
HAIRPIN
HARDPAN
HEADPIN
INASPIN
KINGPIN
LAYOPEN
LETUPON
NINEPIN
PLAYPEN
PUSHPIN
PUTUPON
SETUPON
SHARPEN
SLEEPIN
SLEEPON
STEEPEN

PO•••••

POACHED
POACHER
POACHES
POBOXES
POCKETS
POCONOS
PODGIER
PODGILY
PODIUMS
PODLIKE
PODRIDA
POETICS
POINTED
POINTER
POINTTO
POISING
POISONS
POISSON
POITIER
POKEDAT
POKEFUN
POKESAT
POKIEST
POLARIS
POLDERS
POLEAXE
POLECAR
POLECAT
POLEMIC
POLENTA
POLICED
POLICES
POLITER
POLITIC
POLKAED
POLLACK
POLLENS
POLLERS
POLLING
POLLOCK
POLLTAX
POLLUTE
POLOIST
POLYGON
POLYMER
POMADED
POMADES
POMELOS
POMMELS
POMPANO
POMPEIA
POMPEII
POMPOMS
POMPONS
POMPOUS
PONCHOS
PONDERS
PONGEES
PONGIDS
PONGING
PONIARD
PONTIAC
PONTIFF
PONTINE
PONTIUS
PONTOON
PONYING
POOCHES
POODLES
POOHBAH
POOLING
POOPING
POOPOUT
POORBOX
POORBOY
POOREST
POORISH
POPCORN
POPEYED
POPGUNS
POPLARS
POPLINS
POPOFFS
POPOVER
POPPERS
POPPETS
POPPIES
POPPING
POPPINS
POPPLED
POPPLES
POPSOFF
POPSOUT
POPTART
POPTOPS
POPULAR
POPULUS
PORCHES
PORCINE
PORGIES
PORKERS
PORKIER
PORKISH
PORKPIE
PORSCHE
PORSENA
PORTAGE
PORTALS
PORTEND
PORTENT
PORTERS
PORTHOS
PORTICO
PORTION
PORTMAN
PORTRAY
POSADAS
POSEURS
POSHEST
POSITED
POSSESS
POSSETS
POSSLQS
POSSUMS
POSTAGE
POSTBAG
POSTBOX
POSTERN
POSTERS
POSTING
POSTITS
POSTMAN
POSTMEN
POSTURE
POSTWAR
POTABLE
POTAGES
POTENCY
POTFULS
POTHERB
POTHERS
POTHOLE
POTHOOK
POTIONS
POTLUCK
POTOMAC
POTOROO
POTPIES
POTSDAM
POTSHOT
POTSIER
POTTAGE
POTTERS
POTTERY
POTTIER
POTTING
POTTLES
POUCHED
POUCHES
POULENC
POULTRY
POUNCED
POUNCER
POUNCES
POUNDED
POUNDER
POURERS
POURING
POUROUT
POURSIN
POUTERS
POUTFUL
POUTIER
POUTING
POVERTY
POWDERS
POWDERY
POWERED
POWWOWS

P•O••••

PEONAGE
PEONIES
PEOPLED
PEOPLES
PHOBIAS
PHOBICS
PHOEBES
PHOEBUS
PHOENIX
PHONEME
PHONEYS
PHONICS
PHONIER
PHONIES
PHONILY
PHONING
PHOTICS
PHOTOED
PHOTOGS
PHOTONS
PHOTOOP
PIOLETS
PIONEER
PIOUSLY
PLODDED
PLODDER
PLOPPED
PLOSION
PLOSIVE
PLOTFUL
PLOTTED
PLOTTER
PLOUGHS
PLOVERS
PLOWBOY
PLOWERS
PLOWING
PLOWMAN
PLOWMEN
POOCHES
POODLES
POOHBAH
POOLING
POOPING
POOPOUT
POORBOX
POORBOY
POOREST
POORISH
PROBATE
PROBERS
PROBING
PROBITY
PROBLEM
PROBONO
PROCEED
PROCESS
PROCTOR
PROCURE
PROCYON
PRODDED
PRODDER
PRODIGY
PRODUCE
PRODUCT
PROFANE
PROFESS
PROFFER
PROFILE
PROFITS
PROFUSE
PROGENY
PROGGED
PROGRAM
PROJECT
PROLOGS
PROLONG
PROMISE
PROMOTE
PROMPTS
PRONELY
PRONGED
PRONOUN
PROOFED
PROOFER
PROPANE
PROPELS
PROPHET
PROPJET
PROPMAN
PROPMEN
PROPOSE
PROPPED
PROPRIO
PROPSUP
PROPTER
PRORATA
PRORATE
PROSAIC
PROSERS
PROSHOP
PROSIER
PROSILY
PROSING
PROSODY
PROSPER
PROTEAN
PROTECT
PROTEGE
PROTEIN
PROTEST
PROTEUS
PROTIST
PROTONS
PROUDER
PROUDLY
PROVERB
PROVERS
PROVIDE

PROVING
PROVISO
PROVOKE
PROVOST
PROWESS
PROWLED
PROWLER
PROXIES
PROXIMO
PTOLEMY

P••O•••
PAGODAS
PALOMAR
PALOOKA
PANOPLY
PAPOOSE
PAROLED
PAROLEE
PAROLES
PAYOFFS
PAYOLAS
PAYOUTS
PELOTAS
PHLOXES
PILOTED
PINOAKS
PINOCLE
PINONES
PIROGUE
PIVOTAL
PIVOTED
POBOXES
POCONOS
POLOIST
POPOFFS
POPOVER
POTOMAC
POTOROO
PRIORTO
PROOFED
PROOFER
PTBOATS
PUTOUTS
PUTOVER

P•••O••
PADDOCK
PADLOCK
PADRONE
PADRONI
PAIDOFF
PAIDOUT
PAILOUS
PAIROFF
PALJOEY
PALLORS
PALMOFF
PALMOIL
PALOOKA
PANDORA
PANSOUT
PAPOOSE
PARBOIL
PARDONS
PARLORS
PARLOUR
PARLOUS
PARROTS
PARSONS
PARTOOK
PARTOUT
PASSOFF
PASSOUT
PASTORS
PATROLS
PATRONS
PATROON
PAVIOUR
PAVLOVA
PAWNOFF
PAYLOAD
PAYROLL
PAYSOFF
PAYSOUT
PEABODY
PEACOAT
PEACOCK
PEAFOWL
PEAPODS
PEASOUP
PEEKOUT
PEELOFF
PEEROUT
PEGTOPS
PENNONS
PEQUOTS
PERFORM
PERGOLA
PERIODS
PERSONA
PERSONS
PETCOCK
PETIOLE
PETROCK
PETROLS
PETROUS
PHENOLS
PHENOMS
PHOTOED
PHOTOGS
PHOTONS
PHOTOOP
PICCOLO
PICKOFF
PICKOUT
PIGEONS
PIGSOUT
PILLORY
PILLOWS
PILLOWY
PINDOWN
PINHOLE
PINIONS
PISCOPO
PISTOLE
PISTOLS
PISTONS
PITBOSS
PITEOUS
PLANOUT
PLATOON
PLAYOFF
PLAYOUT
PLEXORS
PLYWOOD
POISONS
POLLOCK
POMPOMS
POMPONS
POMPOUS
PONTOON
POOPOUT
POPCORN
POPSOFF
POPSOUT
POPTOPS
POTHOLE
POTHOOK
POTIONS
POUROUT
POWWOWS
PRECOOK
PRECOOL
PRELOAD
PRESOAK
PRESORT
PRISONS
PROBONO
PROLOGS
PROLONG
PROMOTE
PRONOUN
PROPOSE
PROSODY
PROTONS
PROVOKE
PROVOST
PUGNOSE
PULLOFF
PULLONS
PULLOUT
PURLOIN
PURPORT
PURPOSE
PUSHOFF
PUTDOWN
PUTSOFF
PUTSOUT
PYEDOGS
PYTHONS

P••••O•
PAGEBOY
PAIDFOR
PALMTOP
PALTROW
PAPADOC
PAPAGOS
PARADOX
PARAGON
PARASOL
PARTOOK
PASSFOR
PASSION
PATRIOT
PATROON
PAYSFOR
PEARSON
PEATBOG
PENSION
PERIDOT
PEUGEOT
PHAETON
PHANTOM
PHARAOH
PHOTOOP
PICADOR
PICAROS
PICKSON
PIDGEON
PIERROT
PIGIRON
PILEDON
PILESON
PILLBOX
PILLION
PIMESON
PINEFOR
PITSTOP
PLANSON
PLATOON
PLAYBOY
PLAYDOH
PLAYSON
PLOSION
PLOWBOY
PLYWOOD
POCONOS
POISSON
POLYGON
POMELOS
PONCHOS
PONTOON
POORBOX
POORBOY
PORTHOS
PORTION
POSTBOX
POTHOOK
POTOROO
POTSHOT
PRAETOR
PRAYFOR
PRECOOK
PRECOOL
PRESSON
PRESTON
PRESTOS
PREYSON
PROCTOR
PROCYON
PROSHOP
PRUDHOE
PUEBLOS
PULLFOR
PULLSON
PUTUPON
PYNCHON

P•••••O
PAISANO
PALAZZO
PALERMO
PASSADO
PATERNO
PICASSO
PICCOLO
PIMENTO
PIMLICO
PISCOPO
PIZARRO
PLACEBO
PLACIDO
POINTTO
POMPANO
PORTICO
POTOROO
PRAYSTO
PRIORTO
PROBONO
PROPRIO
PROVISO
PROXIMO
PRYINTO
PUTITTO

•PO••••
APOCOPE
APOGEES
APOLOGY
APOSTLE
APOTHEM
EPOCHAL
EPONYMS
EPONYMY
EPOPEES
EPOXIES
OPOSSUM
SPOILED
SPOILER
SPOKANE
SPOKEOF
SPOKEUP
SPOKING
SPONDEE
SPONGED
SPONGER
SPONGES
SPONSOR
SPOOFED
SPOOFER
SPOOKED
SPOOLED
SPOONED
SPOONER
SPORRAN
SPORTED
SPOTLIT
SPOTTED
SPOTTER
SPOUSAL
SPOUSES
SPOUTED
SPOUTER

•P•O•••
APPOINT
APPOSED
APPOSES
APRONED
APROPOS
OPPOSED
OPPOSER
OPPOSES
SPLOTCH
SPOOFED
SPOOFER
SPOOKED
SPOOLED
SPOONED
SPOONER
SPROUTS
UPBORNE
UPHOLDS
UPLOADS
UPROARS
UPROOTS
UPTONOW
UPTOPAR

•P••O••
APOCOPE
APOLOGY
APPROVE
APRIORI
EPIGONE
EPILOGS
EPISODE
EPITOME
OPEROSE
OPTIONS
OPTSOUT
SPIGOTS
SPINOFF
SPINOUT
SPINOZA
SPUMONE
SPUMONI
SPUMOUS
SPUNOFF
SPUNOUT
UPCLOSE
UPFRONT
UPROOTS
UPSHOTS

•P•••O•
APRICOT
APROPOS
EPSILON
OPENTOE
OPINION
OPTSFOR
SPARROW
SPEAKOF
SPECTOR
SPEEDOS
SPIEDON
SPIESON
SPOKEOF
SPONSOR
SPURSON
UPSILON
UPTONOW

•P••••O
SPIRITO
UPTEMPO

••PO•••
AMPOULE
APPOINT
APPOSED
APPOSES
BIPOLAR
COPOUTS
CUPOLAS
DEPONED
DEPONES
DEPORTS
DEPOSAL
DEPOSED
DEPOSER
DEPOSES
DEPOSIT
DIPOLAR
DIPOLES
EMPORIA
EMPOWER
ESPOSAS
ESPOSOS
ESPOUSE
EXPORTS
EXPOSED
EXPOSES
EXPOUND
HOPOVER
HYPOING
HYPONYM
IMPORTS
IMPOSED
IMPOSES
IMPOSTS
IMPOUND
INPOWER
LAPORTE
OPPOSED
OPPOSER
OPPOSES
PAPOOSE
POPOFFS
POPOVER
REPOLLS
REPOMAN
REPORTS
REPOSED
REPOSES
RIPOFFS
RIPOSTE
TIPOFFS
VAPOURS
ZAPOTEC

••P•O••
AMPHORA
APPROVE
CAPTORS
COPIOUS
COPPOLA
COPSOUT
DEPLORE
DEPLOYS
DIPLOID
DIPLOMA
DOPEOUT
EMPLOYE
EMPLOYS
EUPHONY
EXPLODE
EXPLOIT
EXPLORE
GYPROOM
HIPBONE
HIPBOOT
HIPROOF
HOPSOFF
HOPTOIT
IMPIOUS
IMPLODE
IMPLORE
IMPROVE
KEPTOFF
KEPTOUT
LAPDOGS
LAPROBE
LAPTOPS
LEPTONS
MOPTOPS
PAPOOSE
POPCORN
POPSOFF
POPSOUT
POPTOPS
RAPPORT
RAPTORS
REPLOWS
REPROOF
REPROVE
RIPCORD
RIPSOFF
RIPSOUT
RIPTORN
SAPPORO
SIPHONS
SUPPORT
SUPPOSE
SYPHONS
TAPIOCA
TAPROOM
TAPROOT
TAPSOFF
TAPSOUT
TIPSOFF
TIPTOED
TIPTOES
TIPTOPS
TOPCOAT
TOPDOGS
TOPDOWN
TOPHOLE
TOPMOST
TOPSOFF
TOPSOIL
TOPSOUT
TYPHOON
WIPEOUT
ZIPCODE

••P••O•
CAPECOD
CAPITOL
CAPTION
COPILOT
COPYBOY
CYPRIOT
EMPEROR
ESPANOL
ESPOSOS
GYPROOM
HIPBOOT
HIPROOF
PAPADOC
PAPAGOS
REPROOF
ROPETOW
TAPROOM
TAPROOT
TOPKNOT
TUPELOS
TYPHOON

••P•••O
ESPARTO
IMPASTO
INPETTO
LEPANTO
RIPIENO
RIPINTO
SAPPORO
SAPSAGO
SOPRANO
SUPREMO
TAPINTO
ZAPATEO

•••PO••
ADIPOSE
AIRPORT
AMAPOLA
BEDPOST
BESPOKE
CAMPOUT
CARPOOL
CARPORT
CLIPONS
COMPORT
COMPOSE
COMPOST
COMPOTE
COPPOLA
COUPONS
COWPOKE
COWPONY
DESPOIL
DESPOTS
DISPORT
DISPOSE
DROPOFF
DROPOUT
DRSPOCK
FLIPOUT
HARPOON
HELPOUT
HOOPOES
HOTPOTS
INSPOTS
ISOPODS
JETPORT
JUMPOFF
KEEPOFF
LAMPOIL
LAMPOON
LEOPOLD
LIMPOPO
MAYPOLE
MRSPOCK
NEWPORT
OUTPOLL
OUTPOST
PEAPODS
POMPOMS
POMPONS
POMPOUS
POOPOUT
PROPOSE
PURPORT
PURPOSE
RAPPORT
REDPOLL
RESPOND
RUMPOLE
SAPPORO
SEAPORT
SHIPOUT
SKIPOLE
SKIPOUT
SLIPONS
SLIPOUT
SNAPONS
STEPOUT
STOPOFF
STUPORS
SUPPORT
SUPPOSE
TADPOLE
TARPONS
TEAPOTS
TEAPOYS
TIEPOLO
TRIPODS
TRIPOLI
UNIPODS
VANPOOL
VOLPONE
WALPOLE
WEAPONS
WIMPOLE
YAUPONS

•••P•O•
ADAPTOR
CAMPHOR
CAMPION
CARPOOL
CLAPTON
CRYPTOS
GRYPHON
HAMPTON
HARPOON
HARPSON
JUMPSON
KEEPSON
KERPLOP
KRYPTON
LAMPOON
OLDPROS
SAMPSON
SIMPSON
SLEPTON
SLIPSON
SOAPBOX
SOUPCON
STEPSON
SUBPLOT
SYMPTOM
VANPOOL

•••P••O
ARAPAHO
HISPANO
KEEPSTO
LIMPOPO
LINPIAO
POMPANO
PROPRIO
SAPPORO
SERPICO
SHAPIRO
SNAPSTO
TAMPICO
TIEPOLO
TORPEDO

••••PO•
ACTUPON
APROPOS
CRAMPON
DECAPOD
FUSSPOT
GOTOPOT
HOTSPOT
INASPOT
INKSPOT
JACKPOT
LETUPON
OCTOPOD
ONTOPOF
PUTUPON
REDSPOT
SEEDPOD
SETUPON
SHAMPOO
SLEEPON
SODAPOP
SUNSPOT
TENSPOT

••••P•O
ADDUPTO
CALYPSO
GOLFPRO
LEDUPTO
SCORPIO
SEMIPRO
SHAMPOO

•••••PO
LIMPOPO
PISCOPO
UPTEMPO

P•P••••
PAPADOC
PAPAGOS
PAPAYAS
PAPEETE
PAPERED
PAPERER
PAPILLA
PAPLIKE
PAPOOSE
PAPRIKA
PAPUANS
PAPYRUS
PEPLUMS
PEPPARD
PEPPERS
PEPPERY
PEPPIER
PEPPILY
PEPPING
PEPSINS
PEPTALK
PEPTIDE
PIPEDUP
PIPEFUL
PIPEMMA
PIPESUP
PIPETTE
PIPIEST
PIPINGS
PIPKINS
PIPPINS
POPCORN
POPEYED
POPGUNS
POPLARS
POPLINS
POPOFFS
POPOVER
POPPERS
POPPETS
POPPIES
POPPING
POPPINS
POPPLED
POPPLES
POPSOFF
POPSOUT
POPTART
POPTOPS
POPULAR
POPULUS
PUPPETS
PUPPIES
PUPTENT

P••P•••
PAMPERS
PANPIPE
PAUPERS
PAWPAWS
PEAPODS
PEEPERS
PEEPING
PEEPLES
PENPALS
PEOPLED
PEOPLES
PEPPARD
PEPPERS
PEPPERY
PEPPIER
PEPPILY
PEPPING
PERPLEX
PIEPANS
PIGPENS
PIPPINS
PLOPPED
POMPANO
POMPEIA
POMPEII
POMPOMS
POMPONS
POMPOUS
POOPING
POOPOUT
POPPERS
POPPETS
POPPIES
POPPING
POPPINS
POPPLED
POPPLES
POTPIES
PREPAID
PREPARE
PREPAYS
PREPPIE
PROPANE
PROPELS
PROPHET
PROPJET
PROPMAN
PROPMEN
PROPOSE
PROPPED
PROPRIO
PROPSUP
PROPTER
PULPIER
PULPITS
PUMPERS
PUMPING
PUMPKIN
PUMPSUP
PUPPETS
PUPPIES
PURPLED
PURPLES
PURPORT
PURPOSE
PUTPUTS

P•••P••
PANOPLY
PARAPET
PARAPHS
PITAPAT
PLAYPEN
PLOPPED
PLUMPED
PLUMPER
PLUMPLY
PORKPIE
PREPPIE
PRIMPED
PROMPTS
PROPPED
PROSPER
PUSHPIN
PUTUPON

P••••P•
PANPIPE
PEGTOPS
PERHAPS
PICKUPS
PILEUPS
PISCOPO
PLATYPI
POPTOPS
PREAMPS
PRECEPT
PREEMPT
PRENUPS
PRETAPE
PULLUPS
PUSHUPS

P•••••P
PACKSUP
PAIRSUP
PALMTOP
PARSNIP
PASTEUP
PATCHUP
PEASOUP
PERKSUP
PHARLAP
PHILLIP
PHOTOOP
PICKSUP
PILEDUP
PILESUP
PINESAP
PIPEDUP
PIPESUP
PITSTOP
PLAYSUP
PRESSUP
PROPSUP
PROSHOP
PSYCHUP
PULLSUP
PUMPSUP
PUNCHUP

•PP••••
APPALLS
APPARAT
APPAREL
APPEALS
APPEARS
APPEASE
APPENDS
APPLAUD
APPLETS
APPLIED
APPLIES
APPOINT
APPOSED
APPOSES
APPRISE
APPRIZE
APPROVE
OPPOSED
OPPOSER
OPPOSES
OPPRESS
OPPUGNS
UPPSALA

•P•P•••
EPOPEES

•P••P••
APROPOS
OPENPIT
UPTOPAR

•P•••P•
APOCOPE
UPSWEPT
UPTEMPO

•P••••P
OPENSUP
SPEAKUP
SPEEDUP
SPICEUP
SPLITUP
SPOKEUP
UPSWEEP

••PP•••
BOPPERS
BOPPING
CAPPERS
CAPPING
COPPERS
COPPERY
COPPICE
COPPING
COPPOLA
CUPPING
DAPPING
DAPPLED
DAPPLES
DIPPERS
DIPPIER
DIPPING
DOPPLER
FIPPLES
FOPPERY
FOPPISH
GAPPING
GIPPING
GUPPIES
GYPPERS
GYPPING
HAPPENS
HAPPIER
HAPPILY
HAPPING
HEPPEST
HIPPEST
HIPPIER
HIPPIES
HOPPERS
HOPPING
HOPPLED
HOPPLES
KIPPERS
LAPPETS
LAPPING
LAPPISH
LEPPIES
LIPPIER
LIPPING
LOPPERS
LOPPIER
LOPPING
MAPPERS
MAPPING
MOPPERS
MOPPETS
MOPPING
MUPPETS
NAPPERS
NAPPIES
NAPPING
NIPPERS
NIPPIER
NIPPING
PEPPARD
PEPPERS
PEPPERY
PEPPIER
PEPPILY
PEPPING
PIPPINS
POPPERS
POPPETS

POPPIES
POPPING
POPPINS
POPPLED
POPPLES
PUPPETS
PUPPIES
RAPPELS
RAPPERS
RAPPING
RAPPORT
RIPPERS
RIPPING
RIPPLED
RIPPLES
SAPPERS
SAPPIER
SAPPILY
SAPPING
SAPPORO
SIPPERS
SIPPETS
SIPPING
SOPPIER
SOPPING
SUPPERS
SUPPING
SUPPLER
SUPPORT
SUPPOSE
TAPPERS
TAPPETS
TAPPING
TIPPERS
TIPPETS
TIPPIER
TIPPING
TIPPLED
TIPPLER
TIPPLES
TOPPERS
TOPPING
TOPPLED
TOPPLES
YAPPERS
YAPPING
YIPPING
YUPPIES
ZAPPERS
ZAPPIER
ZAPPING
ZIPPERS
ZIPPIER
ZIPPING

••P•P••

CAPAPIE
REPAPER

••P••P•

LAPTOPS
MOPTOPS
POPTOPS
RIPRAPS
TIPTOPS
TOPKAPI

••P•••P

HYPEDUP
HYPESUP
PIPEDUP
PIPESUP
TYPEDUP
TYPESUP
WIPEDUP
WIPESUP

•••PP••

BLIPPED
CHAPPED
CHAPPIE
CHIPPED
CHIPPER
CHOPPED
CHOPPER
CLAPPED
CLAPPER
CLIPPED
CLIPPER
CLOPPED
CRAPPIE
CROPPED
CROPPER
DRIPPAN
DRIPPED
DROPPED
DROPPER
FLAPPED
FLAPPER
FLIPPED
FLIPPER
FLOPPED
FRAPPES
FRIPPET
GRAPPAS
GRAPPLE
GRIPPED
GRIPPER
PLOPPED
PREPPIE
PROPPED
QUIPPED
QUIPPER
REUPPED
SCUPPER
SHIPPED
SHIPPER
SHOPPED
SHOPPER
SHOPPES
SKIPPED
SKIPPER
SLAPPED
SLIPPED
SLIPPER
SLOPPED
SNAPPED
SNAPPER
SNAPPLE
SNIPPED
SNIPPET
STEPPED
STEPPER
STEPPES
STIPPLE
STOPPED
STOPPER
SWAPPED
SWAPPER
SWOPPED
TRAPPED
TRAPPER
TRIPPED
TRIPPER
TRIPPET
WHIPPED
WHIPPET
WHOPPED
WHOPPER
WHUPPED
WRAPPED
WRAPPER

•••P•P•

BAGPIPE
FLIPUPS
LIMPOPO
PANPIPE
SLIPUPS
STEPUPS
WRAPUPS

•••P••P

AIRPUMP
BUMPSUP
COOPSUP
CROPSUP
GASPUMP
JUMPSUP
KEEPSUP
KERPLOP
PROPSUP
PUMPSUP
SHAPEUP
SLIPSUP
SNAPSUP
SOUPSUP
STEPSUP
STOPGAP
STOPSUP
SWEPTUP
TRIPSUP
WHIPSUP
WRAPSUP

••••PP•

AGRIPPA
SCRAPPY
SCRIPPS
STROPPY
UNHAPPY

••••P•P

CREEPUP
SODAPOP
SWEEPUP
TRUMPUP

•••••PP

SCHLEPP

P•Q••••

PEQUOTS
PIQUANT
PIQUING

P••Q•••

PARQUET
PLAQUES
PREQUEL
PULQUES

P••••Q•

POSSLQS
PSANDQS

•PQ••••

UPQUARK

•P•Q•••

OPAQUES

PR•••••

PRAETOR
PRAIRIE
PRAISED
PRAISER
PRAISES
PRALINE
PRANCED
PRANCER
PRANCES
PRANGED
PRANKED
PRATERS
PRATING
PRATTLE
PRAYERS
PRAYFOR
PRAYING
PRAYSTO
PREACHY
PREAMPS
PREBEND
PRECAST
PRECEDE
PRECEPT
PRECISE
PRECOOK
PRECOOL
PREDATE
PREDAWN
PREDICT
PREEMIE
PREEMPT
PREENED
PREENER
PREFABS
PREFACE
PREFECT
PREFERS
PREHEAT
PRELATE
PRELIMS
PRELOAD
PRELUDE
PREMEDS
PREMIER
PREMISE
PREMISS
PREMIUM
PRENUPS
PREPAID
PREPARE
PREPAYS
PREPPIE
PREQUEL
PRESAGE
PRESALE
PRESELL
PRESENT
PRESETS
PRESIDE
PRESLEY
PRESOAK
PRESORT
PRESSED
PRESSER
PRESSES
PRESSON
PRESSUP
PRESTON
PRESTOS
PRESUME
PRETAPE
PRETEEN
PRETEND
PRETEST
PRETEXT
PRETZEL
PREVAIL
PREVENT
PREVIEW
PREWASH
PREXIES
PREYSON
PRICERS
PRICIER
PRICING
PRICKED
PRICKLE
PRICKLY
PRIDING
PRIESTS
PRIMACY
PRIMARY
PRIMATE
PRIMERS
PRIMING
PRIMMER
PRIMPED
PRINCES
PRINKED
PRINTED
PRINTER
PRIORTO
PRISONS
PRITHEE
PRIVACY
PRIVATE
PRIVETS
PRIVIER
PRIVIES
PRIVILY
PRIVITY
PRIZING
PROBATE
PROBERS
PROBING
PROBITY
PROBLEM
PROBONO
PROCEED
PROCESS
PROCTOR
PROCURE
PROCYON
PRODDED
PRODDER
PRODIGY
PRODUCE
PRODUCT
PROFANE
PROFESS
PROFFER
PROFILE
PROFITS
PROFUSE
PROGENY
PROGGED
PROGRAM
PROJECT
PROLOGS
PROLONG
PROMISE
PROMOTE
PROMPTS
PRONELY
PRONGED
PRONOUN
PROOFED
PROOFER
PROPANE
PROPELS
PROPHET
PROPJET
PROPMAN
PROPMEN
PROPOSE
PROPPED
PROPRIO
PROPSUP
PROPTER
PRORATA
PRORATE
PROSAIC
PROSERS
PROSHOP
PROSIER
PROSILY
PROSING
PROSODY
PROSPER
PROTEAN
PROTECT
PROTEGE
PROTEIN
PROTEST
PROTEUS
PROTIST
PROTONS
PROUDER
PROUDLY
PROVERB
PROVERS
PROVIDE
PROVING
PROVISO
PROVOKE
PROVOST
PROWESS
PROWLED
PROWLER
PROXIES
PROXIMO
PRUDENT
PRUDERY
PRUDHOE
PRUDISH
PRUNERS
PRUNING
PRUSSIA
PRYINTO

P•R••••

PARABLE
PARADED
PARADES
PARADOX
PARAGON
PARAPET
PARAPHS
PARASOL
PARATUS
PARBOIL
PARCELS
PARCHED
PARCHES
PARDNER
PARDONS
PARENTS
PARFAIT
PARGETS
PARIAHS
PARINGS
PARKADE
PARKING
PARKWAY
PARLAYS
PARLEYS
PARLORS
PARLOUR
PARLOUS
PAROLED
PAROLEE
PAROLES
PARQUET
PARRIED
PARRIER
PARRIES
PARRING
PARRISH
PARROTS
PARSECS
PARSEES
PARSERS
PARSING
PARSLEY
PARSNIP
PARSONS
PARTAKE
PARTIAL
PARTIED
PARTIER
PARTIES
PARTING
PARTITA
PARTITE
PARTNER
PARTOOK
PARTOUT
PARTWAY
PARURES
PARVENU
PERCALE
PERCENT
PERCHED
PERCHES
PERDIEM
PERFECT
PERFIDY
PERFORM
PERFUME
PERGOLA
PERHAPS
PERIDOT
PERIGEE
PERIODS
PERJURE
PERJURY
PERKIER
PERKILY
PERKING
PERKINS
PERKISH
PERKSUP
PERLITE
PERLMAN
PERMING
PERMITS
PERPLEX
PERRIER
PERSEID
PERSEUS
PERSIAN
PERSIST
PERSIUS
PERSONA
PERSONS
PERTAIN
PERTEST
PERTURB
PERUKES
PERUSAL
PERUSED
PERUSER
PERUSES
PERVADE
PHRASAL
PHRASED
PHRASES
PHRENIC
PIRAEUS
PIRANHA
PIRATED
PIRATES
PIRATIC
PIROGUE
PORCHES
PORCINE
PORGIES
PORKERS
PORKIER
PORKISH
PORKPIE
PORSCHE
PORSENA
PORTAGE
PORTALS
PORTEND
PORTENT
PORTERS
PORTHOS
PORTICO
PORTION
PORTMAN
PORTRAY
PURCELL
PURDAHS
PURFLED
PURFLES
PURGING
PURISTS
PURITAN
PURLIEU
PURLING
PURLINS
PURLOIN
PURPLED
PURPLES
PURPORT
PURPOSE
PURRERS
PURRING
PURSERS
PURSIER
PURSING
PURSUED
PURSUER
PURSUES
PURSUIT
PURVEYS
PURVIEW
PYRAMID
PYRAMUS
PYRITES
PYRRHIC
PYRRHUS

P••R•••

PADRONE
PADRONI
PAIRING
PAIROFF
PAIRSUP
PAPRIKA
PARRIED
PARRIER
PARRIES
PARRING
PARRISH
PARROTS
PATRIAL
PATRICE
PATRICK
PATRIOT
PATROLS
PATRONS
PATROON
PAYROLL
PEARLED
PEARSON
PEERAGE
PEERESS
PEERING
PEEROUT
PEERSAT
PEERSIN
PERRIER
PETRELS
PETRIFY
PETROCK
PETROLS
PETROUS
PHARAOH
PHARLAP
PHARYNX
PIERCED
PIERCES
PIERROT
PLURALS
PODRIDA
POORBOX
POORBOY
POOREST
POORISH
POURERS
POURING
POUROUT
POURSIN
PRORATA
PRORATE
PUERILE
PUGREES
PURRERS
PURRING
PYRRHIC
PYRRHUS

P•••R••

PACKRAT
PALERMO
PALFREY
PALTROW
PANARAB
PANURGE
PAPERED
PAPERER
PAPYRUS
PARURES
PATERNO
PETARDS
PETERED
PICARDY
PICAROS
PIERROT
PIGIRON
PILGRIM
PIZARRO
POLARIS
PORTRAY
POTOROO
POVERTY
POWERED
PRAIRIE
PRIORTO
PROGRAM
PROPRIO
PUBERTY

P••••R•

PACKARD
PACKERS
PADDERS
PALEDRY
PALLORS
PALMARY
PALTERS
PAMPERS
PANDERS
PANDORA
PANNERS
PANZERS
PARLORS
PARSERS
PASSERS
PASTERN
PASTORS
PASTURE
PATTERN
PATTERS
PAUPERS
PAWNERS
PAYDIRT
PECCARY
PEDLARS
PEEKERS
PEELERS
PEEPERS
PELTERS
PENNERS
PEPPARD
PEPPERS
PEPPERY
PERFORM
PERJURE
PERJURY
PERTURB
PESTERS
PETTERS
PHAEDRA
PHASERS
PHILTRE
PIASTRE
PICCARD
PICKERS
PICTURE
PIECERS
PIGGERY
PILFERS
PILLARS
PILLORY
PINCERS
PINCURL
PINNERS
PISMIRE
PITIERS
PITTERS
PIZARRO
PLACARD
PLACERS
PLANERS
PLATERS
PLAYERS
PLECTRA
PLENARY
PLEXORS
PLOVERS
PLOWERS
POLDERS
POLLERS
PONDERS
PONIARD
POPCORN
POPLARS
POPPERS
POPTART
PORKERS
PORTERS
POSEURS
POSTERN
POSTERS
POSTURE
POTHERB
POTHERS
POTTERS
POTTERY
POULTRY
POURERS
POUTERS
POWDERS
POWDERY
PRATERS
PRAYERS
PREFERS
PREPARE
PRESORT
PRICERS
PRIMARY
PRIMERS
PROBERS
PROCURE
PROSERS
PROVERB
PROVERS
PRUDERY
PRUNERS
PUCKERS
PUFFERS
PUFFERY
PULSARS
PUMPERS
PUNKERS
PUNTERS
PURPORT
PURRERS
PURSERS
PUTTERS

P•••••R

PACECAR
PADDLER
PAIDFOR
PAINTER
PALAVER
PALLIER
PALMIER
PALOMAR
PANNIER
PANTHER
PAPERER
PARDNER
PARLOUR
PARRIER
PARTIER
PARTNER
PASSFOR
PASTEUR
PASTIER
PAVIOUR
PAWKIER
PAYSFOR
PEATIER
PECKIER
PEDDLER
PEPPIER
PERKIER
PERRIER
PERUSER
PESKIER
PETTIER
PHILTER
PHONIER
PIASTER
PICADOR
PICKIER
PIGGIER
PILSNER
PINCHER
PINEFOR
PINETAR
PIONEER
PITCHER
PITHIER
PLAINER
PLANNER
PLANTAR
PLANTER
PLASTER
PLATIER
PLATTER
PLEADER
PLEASER
PLEDGER
PLODDER
PLOTTER
PLUGGER
PLUMBER
PLUMIER
PLUMMER
PLUMPER
PLUNDER
PLUNGER
PLUSHER
POACHER
PODGIER
POINTER
POITIER
POLECAR
POLITER
POLYMER
POPOVER
POPULAR
PORKIER
POSTWAR
POTSIER
POTTIER
POUNCER
POUNDER
POUTIER
PRAETOR
PRAISER
PRANCER
PRAYFOR
PREENER
PREMIER
PRESSER
PRICIER
PRIMMER
PRINTER
PRIVIER
PROCTOR
PRODDER
PROFFER
PROOFER
PROPTER
PROSIER
PROSPER
PROUDER
PROWLER
PSALTER
PUDGIER
PUFFIER
PULLFOR
PULPIER
PUNCHER
PUNKIER
PUNNIER
PUNSTER
PURSIER
PURSUER
PUSHIER
PUTOVER
PUZZLER

•PR••••

APRICOT
APRIORI
APRONED
APROPOS
SPRAINS
SPRAWLS
SPRAYED
SPRAYER
SPREADS
SPRIEST
SPRINGS
SPRINGY
SPRINTS
SPRITES
SPROUTS
SPRUCED
SPRUCER
SPRUCES
SPRYEST
UPRAISE
UPRIGHT
UPRISEN
UPRISES
UPRIVER
UPROARS
UPROOTS

•P•R•••

APERCUS
APERIES
APPRISE
APPRIZE
APPROVE
EPARCHS
EPARCHY
EPERGNE
IPCRESS
OPERAND
OPERATE
OPEROSE
OPPRESS
SPARELY
SPAREST
SPARGED
SPARGES
SPARING
SPARKED
SPARKLE
SPARRED
SPARROW
SPARSER
SPARTAN
SPIRALS
SPIRANT
SPIREAS
SPIRIER
SPIRITO
SPIRITS
SPORRAN
SPORTED
SPURNED
SPURNER
SPURRED
SPURSON
SPURTED
UPBRAID
UPDRAFT
UPFRONT
UPGRADE

•P••R••

APPARAT
APPAREL
APTERAL
EPIGRAM
SPARRED
SPARROW
SPEARED
SPHERES
SPLURGE
SPORRAN
SPURRED
UPATREE
UPBORNE
UPSURGE
UPTURNS
UPWARDS

•P•••R•

APPEARS
APRIORI
EPICURE
OPENERS
OPINERS
SPACERS
SPADERS
SPECTRA
SPECTRE
SPICERY
SPIDERS
SPIDERY
SPIKERS
SPINDRY
UPQUARK
UPROARS
UPSTART

•P••••R

OPENAIR
OPENBAR
OPPOSER
OPTSFOR
SPACIER
SPAMMER
SPANKER
SPANNER
SPARSER
SPATTER
SPEAKER
SPECTER

SPECTOR
SPEEDER
SPELLER
SPENCER
SPENDER
SPENSER
SPICIER
SPIELER
SPIKIER
SPINIER
SPINNER
SPIRIER
SPLICER
SPOILER
SPONGER
SPONSOR
SPOOFER
SPOONER
SPOTTER
SPOUTER
SPRAYER
SPRUCER
SPUMIER
SPURNER
SPUTTER
UPRIVER
UPTOPAR

••PR•••

APPRISE
APPRIZE
APPROVE
CAPRICE
CYPRESS
CYPRIOT
DEPRAVE
DEPRESS
DEPRIVE
EMPRESS
EXPRESS
GYPROOM
HIPROOF
IMPRESS
IMPRINT
IMPROVE
INPRINT
LAPROBE
LIPREAD
OPPRESS
OSPREYS
PAPRIKA
REPRESS
REPRICE
REPRINT
REPRISE
REPROOF
REPROVE
RIPRAPS
SOPRANO
SUPREME
SUPREMO
TAPROOM
TAPROOT

••P•R••

AMPERES
APPARAT
APPAREL
ASPERSE
ASPIRED
ASPIRER
ASPIRES
ASPIRIN
CAPERED
DEPARTS
DEPORTS
EMPEROR
EMPIRES
EMPORIA
ESPARTO
EXPARTE
EXPERTS
EXPIRED
EXPIRES
EXPORTS
HEPARIN
IMPARTS
IMPERIL
IMPORTS
IMPURER
LAPORTE
ORPHREY
PAPERED
PAPERER
PAPYRUS
REPORTS
TAPERED
UMPIRED
UMPIRES

••P•R•

AMPHORA
APPEARS
AUPAIRS
BOPPERS
CAPPERS
CAPTORS
CAPTURE
CIPHERS
COPIERS
COPPERS
COPPERY
COPTERS
CYPHERS
DEPLORE
DIPPERS
EXPLORE
FOPPERY
GOPHERS
GYPPERS
HEPBURN
HOPPERS
IMPAIRS
IMPLORE
KIPPERS
LOPPERS
MAPPERS
MOPPERS
NAPPERS
NIPPERS
PEPPARD
PEPPERS
PEPPERY
POPCORN
POPLARS
POPPERS
POPTART
RAPIERS
RAPPERS
RAPPORT
RAPTORS
RAPTURE
REPAIRS
RIPCORD
RIPPERS
RIPTORN
RUPTURE
SAPPERS
SAPPORO
SIPPERS
SUPPERS
SUPPORT
TAPPERS
TIPPERS
TOPIARY
TOPPERS
VAPOURS
YAPPERS
ZAPPERS
ZEPHYRS
ZIPPERS

••P•••R

ASPIRER
BIPOLAR
DEPOSER
DIPOLAR
DIPPIER
DOPPLER
EMPEROR
EMPOWER
EMPTIER
HAPPIER
HIPPIER
HIPSTER
HOPOVER
IMPURER
INPOWER
JUPITER
LIPPIER
LOPPIER
NIPPIER
OPPOSER
PAPERER
PEPPIER
POPOVER
POPULAR
RAPIDER
REPAPER
SAPPIER
SOPPIER
STPETER
SUPPLER
TAPSTER
TIPPIER
TIPPLER
TIPSIER
TIPSTER
ZAPPIER
ZIPPIER

•••PR••

CULPRIT
LAMPREY
OLDPROS
PROPRIO
SAMPRAS

•••P•R•

AIRPORT
BEEPERS
BITPART
BOPPERS
BUMPERS
CAMPARI
CAMPERS
CAPPERS
CARPARK
CARPERS
CARPORT
CLIPART
COMPARE
COMPERE
COMPORT
COOPERS
COPPERS
COPPERY
DAMPERS
DEEPFRY
DIAPERS
DIPPERS
DISPORT
DRAPERS
DRAPERY
DRIPDRY
ELOPERS
EXUPERY
FOPPERY
GASPERS
GOMPERS
GRIPERS
GYPPERS
HAMPERS
HARPERS
HELPERS
HOPPERS
INSPIRE
JASPERS
JETPORT
JUMPERS
KEEPERS
KIPPERS
LEAPERS
LEMPIRA
LEOPARD
LOOPERS
LOPPERS
LUMPERS
MAPPERS
MOPPERS
NAPPERS
NEWPORT
NIPPERS
OVIPARA
PAMPERS
PAUPERS
PEEPERS
PEPPARD
PEPPERS
PEPPERY
POPPERS
PREPARE
PUMPERS
PURPORT
RAMPART
RAPPERS
RAPPORT
RASPERS
REAPERS
RESPIRE
RIPPERS
ROMPERS
SAPPERS
SAPPORO
SCEPTRE
SEAPORT
SHAPERS
SHAPIRO
SHEPARD
SIMPERS
SIPPERS
SNIPERS
SOAPERS
STUPORS
SUPPERS
SUPPORT
SWIPERS
TAMPERS
TAPPERS
TEMPERA
TEMPERS
TEMPURA
TIPPERS
TOPPERS
TOSPARE
VAMPERS
VAMPIRA
VAMPIRE
VESPERS
WEEPERS
YAPPERS
YAWPERS
YELPERS
ZAPPERS
ZIPPERS

•••P••R

ADAPTER
ADAPTOR
ADOPTER
BUMPIER
CAMPHOR
CAMPIER
CHAPTER
CHIPPER
CHOPPER
CLAPPER
CLIPPER
COMPEER
CROPPER
DESPAIR
DIOPTER
DIPPIER
DOPPLER
DROPPER
DUMPIER
FLAPPER
FLIPPER
GOOPIER
GRAPIER
GRIPPER
GULPIER
HAPPIER
HIPPIER
HUMPIER
INAPTER
JUMPIER
LIPPIER
LOOPIER
LOPPIER
LUMPIER
NIPPIER
PEPPIER
PROPTER
PULPIER
QUIPPER
RASPIER
SAMPLER
SAPPIER
SCEPTER
SCUPPER
SEEPIER
SHIPPER
SHOPPER
SIMPLER
SKIPPER
SLIPPER
SNAPPER
SOAPIER
SOPPIER
SOUPIER
STAPLER
STEPPER
STOPPER
SULPHUR
SUPPLER
SWAPPER
TEMPLAR
TEMPTER
TIPPIER
TIPPLER
TRAPPER
TRIPPER
WASPIER
WEEPIER
WHOPPER
WIMPIER
WISPIER
WRAPPER
ZAPPIER
ZIPPIER

••••PR•

GOLFPRO
SEMIPRO

••••P•R

BLEEPER
BLOOPER
CALIPER
CHEAPER
CHIPPER
CHOPPER
CLAPPER
CLIPPER
CREEPER
CRIMPER
CRISPER
CROPPER
DROPPER
FLAPPER
FLIPPER
GRIPPER
GROUPER
HOTSPUR
JUNIPER
MADEPAR
MAKEPAR
PLUMPER
PROSPER
QUIPPER
REPAPER
SCALPER
SCAMPER
SCARPER
SCOOPER
SCRAPER
SCUPPER
SHARPER
SHIPPER
SHOPPER
SKIPPER
SLEEPER
SLIPPER
SNAPPER
SNOOPER
STEEPER
STEPPER
STOPPER
STRIPER
STUMPER
SWAPPER
SWEEPER
THUMPER
TRAPPER
TRIPPER
TROOPER
TROUPER
UPTOPAR
USURPER
WHIMPER
WHISPER
WHOPPER
WRAPPER

PS•••••

PSALMED
PSALTER
PSANDQS
PSYCHED
PSYCHES
PSYCHIC
PSYCHUP

P•S••••

PASCHAL
PASSADO
PASSAGE
PASSELS
PASSERS
PASSEUL
PASSFOR
PASSING
PASSION
PASSIVE
PASSKEY
PASSOFF
PASSOUT
PASTDUE
PASTELS
PASTERN
PASTEUP
PASTEUR
PASTIER
PASTIME
PASTINA
PASTING
PASTORS
PASTURE
PESAWAS
PESETAS
PESKIER
PESKILY
PESTERS
PESTLED
PESTLES
PISCINE
PISCOPO
PISMIRE
PISTILS
PISTOLE
PISTOLS
PISTONS
POSADAS
POSEURS
POSHEST
POSITED
POSSESS
POSSETS
POSSLQS
POSSUMS
POSTAGE
POSTBAG
POSTBOX
POSTERN
POSTERS
POSTING
POSTITS
POSTMAN
POSTMEN
POSTURE
POSTWAR
PUSHFUL
PUSHIER
PUSHILY
PUSHING
PUSHKIN
PUSHOFF
PUSHPIN
PUSHUPS

P••S•••

PAISANO
PAISLEY
PANSIES
PANSOUT
PARSECS
PARSEES
PARSERS
PARSING
PARSLEY
PARSNIP
PARSONS
PASSADO
PASSAGE
PASSELS
PASSERS
PASSEUL
PASSFOR
PASSING
PASSION
PASSIVE
PASSKEY
PASSOFF
PASSOUT
PATSIES
PAUSING
PAYSFOR
PAYSOFF
PAYSOUT
PEASANT
PEASOUP
PENSEES
PENSION
PENSIVE
PEPSINS
PERSEID
PERSEUS
PERSIAN
PERSIST
PERSIUS
PERSONA
PERSONS
PHASEIN
PHASERS
PHASING
PHYSICS
PIASTER
PIASTRE
PIGSKIN
PIGSOUT
PILSNER
PITSAWS
PITSTOP
PLASHED
PLASHES
PLASMAS
PLASTER
PLASTIC
PLOSION
PLOSIVE
PLUSHER
PLUSHES
PLUSHLY
PLUSSES
POISING
POISONS
POISSON
POPSOFF
POPSOUT
PORSCHE
PORSENA
POSSESS
POSSETS
POSSLQS
POSSUMS
POTSDAM
POTSHOT
POTSIER
PRESAGE
PRESALE
PRESELL
PRESENT
PRESETS
PRESIDE
PRESLEY
PRESOAK
PRESORT
PRESSED
PRESSER
PRESSES
PRESSON
PRESSUP
PRESTON
PRESTOS
PRESUME
PRISONS
PROSAIC
PROSERS
PROSHOP
PROSIER
PROSILY
PROSING
PROSODY
PROSPER
PRUSSIA
PULSARS
PULSATE
PULSING
PUNSTER
PURSERS
PURSIER
PURSING
PURSUED
PURSUER
PURSUES
PURSUIT
PUTSOFF
PUTSOUT

P•••S••

PACKSUP
PAIRSUP
PARASOL
PAULSEN
PEARSON
PECKSAT
PEEKSAT
PEERSAT
PEERSIN
PEGASUS
PELISSE
PERKSUP
PERUSAL
PERUSED
PERUSER
PERUSES
PHRASAL
PHRASED
PHRASES
PICASSO
PICKSAT
PICKSON
PICKSUP
PILESIN
PILESON
PILESUP
PIMESON
PINESAP
PIOUSLY
PIPESUP
PLANSON
PLAYSAT
PLAYSON
PLAYSUP
PLEASED
PLEASER
PLEASES
PLUGSIN
PLUSSES
POISSON
POKESAT
POURSIN
PRAISED
PRAISER
PRAISES
PRAYSTO
PRESSED
PRESSER
PRESSES
PRESSON
PRESSUP
PREYSON
PRIESTS
PROPSUP
PRUSSIA
PULASKI
PULLSIN
PULLSON
PULLSUP
PUMPSUP
PURISTS

P••••S•

PACHISI
PALIEST
PALMIST
PANFISH
PAPOOSE
PARRISH
PATNESS
PAULIST
PAYCASH
PEAKISH
PECKISH
PEERESS
PEEVISH
PEGLESS
PELISSE
PELTISH
PERKISH
PERSIST
PERTEST
PETTISH
PIANISM
PIANIST
PICASSO
PICTISH
PIETISM
PIETIST
PIGGISH
PINIEST
PINKEST
PINKISH
PINLESS
PIPIEST
PITBOSS
PIXYISH
PLANISH
POKIEST
POLOIST
POOREST
POORISH
PORKISH
POSHEST
POSSESS
PRECAST
PRECISE
PREMISE
PREMISS
PRETEST
PREWASH
PROCESS
PROFESS
PROFUSE
PROMISE
PROPOSE
PROTEST
PROTIST
PROVISO
PROVOST
PROWESS
PRUDISH
PUBLISH
PUCKISH
PUGGISH
PUGNOSE
PUNIEST
PUNLESS
PURPOSE

P•••••S

PAANGAS
PABLUMS
PACKERS
PACKETS
PADDERS
PADDIES
PADDLES
PADUANS
PAGODAS
PAILOUS
PAIUTES
PAJAMAS
PALACES
PALATES
PALLETS
PALLORS
PALTERS
PAMPERS
PANADAS
PANAMAS
PANDERS
PANDITS
PANFULS
PANNERS
PANSIES
PANZERS
PAPAGOS
PAPAYAS
PAPUANS
PAPYRUS
PARADES
PARAPHS
PARATUS
PARCELS
PARCHES
PARDONS
PARENTS
PARGETS
PARIAHS
PARINGS
PARLAYS
PARLEYS
PARLORS
PARLOUS
PAROLES
PARRIES
PARROTS
PARSECS
PARSEES
PARSERS
PARSONS
PARTIES
PARURES
PASSELS
PASSERS
PASTELS
PASTORS
PATACAS
PATCHES
PATENTS
PATINAS
PATNESS
PATROLS
PATRONS
PATSIES
PATTENS
PATTERS
PATTIES
PAUPERS
PAVANES
PAWNEES
PAWNERS
PAWPAWS
PAYDAYS
PAYOFFS
PAYOLAS
PAYOUTS
PDJAMES
PEACHES
PEAHENS
PEANUTS
PEAPODS
PEAVEYS
PEBBLES
PECTINS
PEDANTS
PEDDLES
PEDLARS
PEDWAYS
PEEKERS
PEELERS
PEEPERS
PEEPLES
PEERESS
PEEWEES
PEGASUS
PEGLESS
PEGTOPS
PELAGES
PELLETS
PELOTAS
PELTERS
PENATES
PENCILS
PENNERS
PENNIES
PENNONS
PENPALS
PENSEES
PENTADS
PENULTS
PEONIES
PEOPLES
PEPLUMS
PEPPERS
PEPSINS
PEQUOTS
PERCHES
PERHAPS
PERIODS
PERKINS
PERMITS
PERSEUS
PERSIUS
PERSONS
PERUKES
PERUSES
PESAWAS
PESETAS
PESTERS
PESTLES
PETARDS
PETITES
PETRELS
PETROLS
PETROUS
PETTERS
PHASERS
PHENOLS
PHENOMS
PHIDIAS
PHINEAS
PHLOXES
PHOBIAS
PHOBICS
PHOEBES
PHOEBUS
PHONEYS
PHONICS
PHONIES
PHOTICS
PHOTOGS
PHOTONS
PHRASES
PHYLLIS
PHYSICS
PIAZZAS
PICAROS
PICKENS
PICKERS
PICKETS
PICKLES
PICKUPS
PICNICS
PIDGINS
PIECERS
PIEPANS
PIERCES
PIETIES
PIETINS
PIFFLES
PIGEONS
PIGGIES
PIGLETS
PIGNUTS
PIGPENS
PILEUPS
PILFERS
PILINGS
PILLARS
PILLOWS
PINATAS
PINCERS
PINCHAS
PINCHES
PINIONS
PINKIES
PINLESS
PINNERS
PINOAKS
PINONES
PIOLETS
PIPINGS
PIPKINS
PIPPINS
PIRAEUS
PIRATES
PISTILS
PISTOLS
PISTONS
PITBOSS
PITCHES
PITEOUS
PITIERS
PITSAWS
PITTERS
PLACERS
PLAGUES
PLAICES
PLAINTS
PLANERS
PLANETS
PLAQUES
PLASHES
PLASMAS
PLATENS
PLATERS
PLAUTUS
PLAYERS
PLEASES
PLEDGES
PLENUMS
PLEXORS
PLIGHTS
PLINTHS
PLOUGHS
PLOVERS
PLOWERS
PLUGINS
PLUNGES
PLURALS
PLUSHES
PLUSSES
POACHES
POBOXES
POCKETS
POCONOS
PODIUMS
POETICS
POISONS
POLARIS
POLDERS
POLICES
POLLENS
POLLERS
POMADES
POMELOS
POMMELS
POMPOMS
POMPONS
POMPOUS
PONCHOS
PONDERS
PONGEES

PONGIDS
PONTIUS
POOCHES
POODLES
POPGUNS
POPLARS
POPLINS
POPOFFS
POPPERS
POPPETS
POPPIES
POPPINS
POPPLES
POPTOPS
POPULUS
PORCHES
PORGIES
PORKERS
PORTALS
PORTERS
PORTHOS
POSADAS
POSEURS
POSSESS
POSSETS
POSSLQS
POSSUMS
POSTERS
POSTITS
POTAGES
POTFULS
POTHERS
POTIONS
POTPIES
POTTERS
POTTLES
POUCHES
POUNCES
POURERS
POUTERS
POWDERS
POWWOWS
PRAISES
PRANCES
PRATERS
PRAYERS
PREAMPS
PREFABS
PREFERS
PRELIMS
PREMEDS
PREMISS
PRENUPS
PREPAYS
PRESETS
PRESSES
PRESTOS
PREXIES
PRICERS
PRIESTS
PRIMERS
PRINCES
PRISONS
PRIVETS
PRIVIES
PROBERS
PROCESS
PROFESS
PROFITS
PROLOGS
PROMPTS
PROPELS
PROSERS
PROTEUS
PROTONS
PROVERS
PROWESS
PROXIES
PRUNERS
PSANDQS
PSYCHES
PTBOATS
PUBLICS
PUCKERS
PUDDLES
PUEBLOS
PUFFERS
PUFFINS
PUGREES
PULLETS
PULLEYS
PULLINS
PULLONS
PULLUPS
PULPITS
PULQUES
PULSARS
PUMICES
PUMMELS
PUMPERS
PUNCHES
PUNDITS
PUNKAHS
PUNKERS
PUNKIES
PUNLESS
PUNNETS
PUNTERS
PUNTIES
PUPPETS
PUPPIES
PURDAHS
PURFLES
PURISTS
PURLINS
PURPLES
PURRERS
PURSERS
PURSUES
PURVEYS
PUSHUPS
PUTOUTS
PUTPUTS
PUTTEES
PUTTERS
PUTTIES
PUZZLES
PYEDOGS
PYGMIES
PYJAMAS
PYRAMUS
PYRITES
PYRRHUS
PYTHIAS
PYTHONS
PYXIDES

•PS••••

APSIDES
EPSILON
EPSTEIN
IPSWICH
UPSCALE
UPSHOTS
UPSILON
UPSTAGE
UPSTART
UPSTATE
UPSURGE
UPSWEEP
UPSWEPT
UPSWING

•P•S•••

APISHLY
APOSTLE
EPISODE
EPISTLE
OPOSSUM
OPTSFOR
OPTSOUT
SPASSKY
UPPSALA

•P••S••

APHESES
APPOSED
APPOSES
OPENSEA
OPENSUP
OPOSSUM
OPPOSED
OPPOSER
OPPOSES
SPARSER
SPASSKY
SPENSER
SPIESON
SPLASHY
SPONSOR
SPOUSAL
SPOUSES
SPURSON
UPRISEN
UPRISES

•P•••S•

APPEASE
APPRISE
APTNESS
EPEEIST
IPCRESS
OPEROSE
OPPRESS
SPANISH
SPAREST
SPRIEST
SPRYEST
UPCLOSE
UPRAISE

•P••••S

APACHES
APERCUS
APERIES
APHESES
APOGEES
APPALLS
APPEALS
APPEARS
APPENDS
APPLETS
APPLIES
APPOSES
APROPOS
APSIDES
APTNESS
EPARCHS
EPILOGS
EPONYMS
EPOPEES
EPOXIES
IPCRESS
OPAQUES
OPENERS
OPHITES
OPIATES
OPINERS
OPPOSES
OPPRESS
OPPUGNS
OPTIONS
SPACERS
SPADERS
SPARGES
SPAVINS
SPECIES
SPEEDOS
SPHERES
SPIDERS
SPIGOTS
SPIKERS
SPINELS
SPINETS
SPIRALS
SPIREAS
SPIRITS
SPITZES
SPLEENS
SPLICES
SPLINES
SPLINTS
SPONGES
SPOUSES
SPRAINS
SPRAWLS
SPREADS
SPRINGS
SPRINTS
SPRITES
SPROUTS
SPRUCES
SPUMOUS
UPBEATS
UPDATES
UPHOLDS
UPLANDS
UPLIFTS
UPLINKS
UPLOADS
UPRISES
UPROARS
UPROOTS
UPSHOTS
UPTAKES
UPTICKS
UPTURNS
UPWARDS

••PS•••

CAPSHAW
CAPSIDS
CAPSIZE
CAPSTAN
CAPSULE
COPSOUT
GIPSIES
GYPSIES
HIPSTER
HOPSOFF
LAPSING
LIPSYNC
PEPSINS
POPSOFF
POPSOUT
RIPSAWS
RIPSOFF
RIPSOUT
SAPSAGO
TAPSOFF
TAPSOUT
TAPSTER
TIPSIER
TIPSILY
TIPSOFF
TIPSTER
TOPSAIL
TOPSIDE
TOPSOFF
TOPSOIL
TOPSOUT
UPPSALA

••P•S••

APPOSED
APPOSES
DEPOSAL
DEPOSED
DEPOSER
DEPOSES
DEPOSIT
ESPOSAS
ESPOSOS
EXPOSED
EXPOSES
HYPESUP
IMPASSE
IMPASTO
IMPOSED
IMPOSES
IMPOSTS
OPPOSED
OPPOSER
OPPOSES
PIPESUP
REPASTE
REPASTS
REPOSED
REPOSES
RIPOSTE
ROPESIN
TYPESET
TYPESUP
TYPISTS
WIPESUP

••P••S•

AMPLEST
APPEASE
APPRISE
ASPERSE
BAPTISE
BAPTISM
BAPTIST
CAPLESS
COPYIST
CYPRESS
DEPRESS
DOPIEST
EMPRESS
ESPOUSE
EXPANSE
EXPENSE
EXPRESS
FOPPISH
GAPLESS
HAPLESS
HEPPEST
HIPLESS
HIPNESS
HIPPEST
IMPASSE
IMPRESS
IMPULSE
INPHASE
LAPPISH
LIPLESS
MOPIEST
NAPLESS
OPPRESS
PAPOOSE
PIPIEST
REPRESS
REPRISE
REPULSE
ROPIEST
SAPLESS
SOPHISM
SOPHIST
SUPPOSE
TIPLESS
TOPMAST
TOPMOST
TYPIEST

••P•••S

ALPACAS
AMPERES
AMPULES
APPALLS
APPEALS
APPEARS
APPENDS
APPLETS
APPLIES
APPOSES
ARPENTS
ASPECTS
ASPIRES
AUPAIRS
BOPPERS
BYPATHS
BYPLAYS
CAPFULS
CAPGUNS
CAPLESS
CAPLETS
CAPNUTS
CAPPERS
CAPSIDS
CAPTORS
CEPHEUS
CIPHERS
COPIERS
COPIOUS
COPOUTS
COPPERS
COPTERS
COPULAS
CUPFULS
CUPOLAS
CYPHERS
CYPRESS
DAPHNIS
DAPPLES
DEPARTS
DEPENDS
DEPICTS
DEPLOYS
DEPONES
DEPORTS
DEPOSES
DEPRESS
DEPUTES
DIPOLES
DIPPERS
DOPANTS
EMPIRES
EMPLOYS
EMPRESS
EMPTIES
ESPIALS
ESPOSAS
ESPOSOS
EXPANDS
EXPECTS
EXPENDS
EXPERTS
EXPIRES
EXPORTS
EXPOSES
EXPRESS
FIPPLES
GAPLESS
GIPSIES
GOPHERS
GUPPIES
GYPPERS
GYPSIES
HAPLESS
HAPPENS
HEPCATS
HEPTADS
HIPLESS
HIPNESS
HIPPIES
HOPKINS
HOPPERS
HOPPLES
HYPHENS
IMPACTS
IMPAIRS
IMPALAS
IMPALES
IMPARTS
IMPEDES
IMPENDS
IMPETUS
IMPIOUS
IMPLIES
IMPORTS
IMPOSES
IMPOSTS
IMPRESS
IMPUGNS
IMPUTES
KIPPERS
KOPECKS
LAPDOGS
LAPFULS
LAPPETS
LAPTOPS
LEPPIES
LEPTONS
LIPIDES
LIPLESS
LOPPERS
LUPINES
MAPPERS
MOPPERS
MOPPETS
MOPTOPS
MUPPETS
NAPKINS
NAPLESS
NAPPERS
NAPPIES
NEPALIS
NEPHEWS
NIPPERS
OPPOSES
OPPRESS
OPPUGNS
ORPHANS
ORPHEUS
ORPINES
OSPREYS
PAPAGOS
PAPAYAS
PAPUANS
PAPYRUS
PEPLUMS
PEPPERS
PEPSINS
PIPINGS
PIPKINS
PIPPINS
POPGUNS
POPLARS
POPLINS
POPOFFS
POPPERS
POPPETS
POPPIES
POPPINS
POPPLES
POPTOPS
POPULUS
PUPPETS
PUPPIES
RAPIERS
RAPINES
RAPPELS
RAPPERS
RAPTORS
REPAIRS
REPASTS
REPAVES
REPEALS
REPEATS
REPENTS
REPINES
REPLANS
REPLAYS
REPLIES
REPLOWS
REPOLLS
REPORTS
REPOSES
REPRESS
REPUGNS
REPUTES
RIPOFFS
RIPPERS
RIPPLES
RIPRAPS
RIPSAWS
RUPIAHS
SAPIENS
SAPLESS
SAPPERS
SEPTETS
SIPHONS
SIPPERS
SIPPETS
SUPPERS
SYPHONS
TAPINGS
TAPPERS
TAPPETS
TIPLESS
TIPOFFS
TIPPERS
TIPPETS
TIPPLES
TIPTOES
TIPTOPS
TOPAZES
TOPDOGS
TOPGUNS
TOPHATS
TOPPERS
TOPPLES
TUPELOS
TYPISTS
UMPIRES
UNPACKS
UNPILES
UNPLUGS
VAPOURS
WAPITIS
YAPPERS
YUPPIES
ZAPPERS
ZEPHYRS
ZIPPERS

•••PS••

ASEPSIS
BUMPSUP
CHIPSIN
COOPSUP
CROPSUP
DEEPSEA
DEEPSET
DEEPSIX
DEMPSEY
DROPSBY
DROPSIN
ELAPSED
ELAPSES
HARPSON
JUMPSAT
JUMPSIN
JUMPSON
JUMPSUP
KEEPSAT
KEEPSIN
KEEPSON
KEEPSTO
KEEPSUP
LUMPSUM
PROPSUP
PUMPSUP
SAMPSON
SEEPSIN
SIMPSON
SLIPSIN
SLIPSON
SLIPSUP
SNAPSAT
SNAPSTO
SNAPSUP
SOUPSUP
STEPSIN
STEPSON
STEPSUP
STOPSIN
STOPSUP
TRIPSUP
WHIPSAW
WHIPSUP
WRAPSUP

•••P•S•

ADIPOSE
ANAPEST
BEDPOST
COMPASS
COMPOSE
COMPOST
DAMPEST
DAMPISH
DEEPEST
DESPISE
DISPOSE
DUMPISH
FLYPAST
FOPPISH
HARPIST
HEPPEST
HIPPEST
LAPPISH
LIMPEST
LUMPISH
OUTPOST
PROPOSE
PURPOSE
RASPISH
ROMPISH
SUPPOSE
SURPASS
TEMPEST
TROPISM
VAMPISH
WASPISH
WIMPISH

•••P••S

ARMPITS
ASEPSIS
BEEPERS
BOPPERS
BUMPERS
CALPACS
CAMPERS
CAPPERS
CARPALS
CARPELS
CARPERS
CARPETS
CHAPELS
CLIPONS
COEPTIS
COMPASS
COMPELS
COOPERS
COPPERS
COUPLES
COUPONS
COWPEAS
CRYPTOS
CUSPIDS
DAMPENS
DAMPERS
DAPPLES
DEEPENS
DESPOTS
DIAPERS
DIMPLES
DIPPERS
DISPELS
DRAPERS
DROPINS
ELAPIDS
ELAPSES
ELOPERS
EPOPEES
FIPPLES
FLIPUPS
FRAPPES
FRYPANS
GALPALS
GASPERS
GOMPERS
GOSPELS
GRAPPAS
GRIPERS
GROPIUS
GUPPIES
GYPPERS
HAMPERS
HAPPENS
HARPERS
HARPIES
HATPINS
HELPERS
HIPPIES
HOOPLAS
HOOPOES
HOPPERS
HOPPLES
HOTPOTS
INSPANS
INSPOTS
ISOPODS
JASPERS
JUMPERS
KEEPERS
KELPIES
KEWPIES
KEYPADS
KIPPERS
KUSPUKS
LAPPETS
LEAPERS
LEPPIES
LIMPETS
LOOPERS
LOPPERS
LUMPERS
MAGPIES
MAPPERS
MEMPHIS
MOPPERS
MOPPETS
MUDPIES
MUPPETS
NAPPERS
NAPPIES
NIPPERS
NONPLUS
OILPANS
OLDPROS
OOMPAHS
OUTPUTS
PAMPERS
PAUPERS
PAWPAWS
PEAPODS
PEEPERS
PEEPLES
PENPALS
PEOPLES
PEPPERS
PIEPANS
PIGPENS
PIPPINS
POMPOMS
POMPONS
POMPOUS
POPPERS
POPPETS
POPPIES
POPPINS
POPPLES
POTPIES
PREPAYS
PROPELS
PULPITS
PUMPERS
PUPPETS
PUPPIES
PURPLES
PUTPUTS
RAJPUTS
RAPPELS
RAPPERS
RASPERS
REAPERS
REOPENS
RESPINS
RIMPLES
RIPPERS
RIPPLES
ROMPERS
RUMPLES
SAMPANS
SAMPLES
SAMPRAS
SAPPERS
SHAPERS
SHOPPES
SIMPERS
SIPPERS
SIPPETS
SLIPONS
SLIPUPS
SNAPONS
SNIPERS
SOAPERS
STAPLES
STEPINS
STEPPES
STEPUPS
STUPORS
SUPPERS
SURPASS
SURPLUS
SWIPERS
TAIPANS
TAMPERS
TAPPERS
TAPPETS
TARPITS
TARPONS
TEAPOTS
TEAPOYS
TEEPEES
TEMPEHS
TEMPERS
TEMPLES
TENPINS
THEPITS
TIEPINS
TIPPERS
TIPPETS
TIPPLES
TOPPERS
TOPPLES
TOUPEES
TREPANS
TRIPLES
TRIPODS
TROPICS
UNIPODS
USOPENS
UTOPIAS
VAMPERS
VESPERS
VESPIDS
WEAPONS
WEEPERS
WEEPIES
WIMPLES
WRAPUPS
YAPPERS
YAUPONS
YAWPERS
YELPERS
YUPPIES
ZAPPERS
ZIPPERS

••••PS•

CALYPSO
ECLIPSE
ELLIPSE
GLIMPSE
RELAPSE
SYNAPSE
TRAIPSE

••••P•S

ACCEPTS
APROPOS
CALIPHS
CANAPES
CANOPUS
CERIPHS
CRISPUS
ECTYPES
ESCAPES
EXCEPTS
EXEMPTS
FAUXPAS
FRAPPES
GRAMPAS
GRAMPUS
GRAPPAS
GUELPHS
GUIMPES
INCEPTS
IRRUPTS
OCTOPUS
OEDIPUS
OLYMPUS
PARAPHS
PROMPTS
RECIPES
RETAPES
RETYPES
SCRAPES
SCRIPPS
SCRIPTS
SCULPTS
SERAPES
SERAPHS
SERAPIS
SHERPAS
SHOPPES
STEPPES
STRIPES
TERAPHS
THESPIS
TRAMPAS
TROUPES

•••••PS

BACKUPS
BARHOPS
BIGTOPS
BISHOPS
BITMAPS
BLOWUPS
BOXTOPS
BUMRAPS
BUNYIPS
BURLAPS
CARHOPS
CATNAPS
CATNIPS
CCLAMPS
CHINUPS
COLLOPS
CYCLOPS
DECAMPS
DEWLAPS
DOLLOPS
DUSTUPS
EGGCUPS
ENCAMPS
ENTRAPS
ENWRAPS
ESCARPS
EYECUPS
FILLIPS
FILLUPS
FLIPUPS
FOLDUPS
FORCEPS
FOULUPS
GALLOPS
GASCAPS
GAZUMPS
GIVEUPS
GOOFUPS
GOSSIPS
HANGUPS
HICCUPS
HOLDUPS
HOOKUPS
HOTCAPS
HOTLIPS
HOTTIPS
HUBCAPS
HYSSOPS
ICECAPS
INSTEPS
JOBHOPS
KICKUPS
KIDNAPS
LAPTOPS
LARRUPS
LASHUPS
LINEUPS
LINKUPS
LOCKUPS
LOLLOPS
LOOKUPS
MADCAPS
MAKEUPS
MARKUPS
MISHAPS
MOBCAPS
MOCKUPS
MOPTOPS
MRCHIPS
PEGTOPS
PERHAPS
PICKUPS
PILEUPS
POPTOPS
PREAMPS
PRENUPS
PULLUPS

PUSHUPS
RAGMOPS
RAGTOPS
RAVEUPS
RECOUPS
REDCAPS
REDTOPS
RESHIPS
REVAMPS
REWRAPS
RIPRAPS
SATRAPS
SCHLEPS
SCHNAPS
SCRIMPS
SCRIPPS
SENDUPS
SHRIMPS
SKYCAPS
SLIPUPS
SLOWUPS
STEPUPS
TEACUPS
TIPTOPS
TITTUPS
TOECAPS
TOETAPS
TOSSUPS
TRICEPS
TUNEUPS
TURNIPS
UNSNAPS
UNSTOPS
UNTRAPS
UNWRAPS
WALKUPS
WALLOPS
WARMUPS
WASHUPS
WETMOPS
WINDUPS
WORKUPS
WRAPUPS

PT•••••

PTBOATS
PTOLEMY

P•T••••

PATACAS
PATCHED
PATCHES
PATCHUP
PATELLA
PATENTS
PATERNO
PATHWAY
PATIENT
PATINAS
PATNESS
PATRIAL
PATRICE
PATRICK
PATRIOT
PATROLS
PATRONS
PATROON
PATSIES
PATTENS
PATTERN
PATTERS
PATTIES
PATTING
PETALED
PETARDS
PETCOCK
PETERED
PETIOLE
PETITES
PETNAME
PETRELS
PETRIFY
PETROCK
PETROLS
PETROUS
PETTERS
PETTIER
PETTILY
PETTING
PETTISH
PETUNIA
PITAPAT
PITBOSS
PITBULL
PITCHED
PITCHER
PITCHES
PITCHIN
PITEOUS
PITFALL
PITHIER
PITHILY
PITHING
PITIERS
PITIFUL
PITSAWS
PITSTOP
PITTERS
PITTING
PITTMAN
PITYING
POTABLE
POTAGES
POTENCY
POTFULS
POTHERB
POTHERS
POTHOLE
POTHOOK
POTIONS
POTLUCK
POTOMAC
POTOROO
POTPIES
POTSDAM
POTSHOT
POTSIER
POTTAGE
POTTERS
POTTERY
POTTIER
POTTING
POTTLES
PUTAMEN
PUTAWAY
PUTDOWN
PUTITTO
PUTOUTS
PUTOVER
PUTPUTS
PUTSOFF
PUTSOUT
PUTTEES
PUTTERS
PUTTIED
PUTTIES
PUTTING
PUTUPON
PYTHIAN
PYTHIAS
PYTHONS

P••T•••

PALTERS
PALTROW
PANTHER
PANTING
PARTAKE
PARTIAL
PARTIED
PARTIER
PARTIES
PARTING
PARTITA
PARTITE
PARTNER
PARTOOK
PARTOUT
PARTWAY
PASTDUE
PASTELS
PASTERN
PASTEUP
PASTEUR
PASTIER
PASTIME
PASTINA
PASTING
PASTORS
PASTURE
PATTENS
PATTERN
PATTERS
PATTIES
PATTING
PEATBOG
PEATIER
PECTINS
PEGTOPS
PELTATE
PELTERS
PELTING
PELTISH
PENTADS
PENTIUM
PEPTALK
PEPTIDE
PERTAIN
PERTEST
PERTURB
PESTERS
PESTLED
PESTLES
PETTERS
PETTIER
PETTILY
PETTING
PETTISH
PHOTICS
PHOTOED
PHOTOGS
PHOTONS
PHOTOOP
PICTISH
PICTURE
PIETIES
PIETINS
PIETISM
PIETIST
PIGTAIL
PINTAIL
PISTILS
PISTOLE
PISTOLS
PISTONS
PITTERS
PITTING
PITTMAN
PLATEAU
PLATENS
PLATERS
PLATIER
PLATING
PLATOON
PLATTER
PLATYPI
PLOTFUL
PLOTTED
PLOTTER
POETICS
POITIER
PONTIAC
PONTIFF
PONTINE
PONTIUS
PONTOON
POPTART
POPTOPS
PORTAGE
PORTALS
PORTEND
PORTENT
PORTERS
PORTHOS
PORTICO
PORTION
PORTMAN
PORTRAY
POSTAGE
POSTBAG
POSTBOX
POSTERN
POSTERS
POSTING
POSTITS
POSTMAN
POSTMEN
POSTURE
POSTWAR
POTTAGE
POTTERS
POTTERY
POTTIER
POTTING
POTTLES
POUTERS
POUTFUL
POUTIER
POUTING
PRATERS
PRATING
PRATTLE
PRETAPE
PRETEEN
PRETEND
PRETEST
PRETEXT
PRETZEL
PRITHEE
PROTEAN
PROTECT
PROTEGE
PROTEIN
PROTEST
PROTEUS
PROTIST
PROTONS
PUNTERS
PUNTIES
PUNTING
PUPTENT
PUTTEES
PUTTERS
PUTTIED
PUTTIES
PUTTING

P•••T••

PAINTED
PAINTER
PAIUTES
PALATAL
PALATES
PALETTE
PALMTOP
PARATUS
PELOTAS
PENATES
PESETAS
PETITES
PHAETON
PHANTOM
PHILTER
PHILTRE
PIASTER
PIASTRE
PILOTED
PINATAS
PINETAR
PINETUM
PIPETTE
PIRATED
PIRATES
PIRATIC
PITSTOP
PIVOTAL
PIVOTED
PLAITED
PLANTAR
PLANTED
PLANTER
PLASTER
PLASTIC
PLATTER
PLAUTUS
PLEATED
PLECTRA
PLINTHS
PLOTTED
PLOTTER
POINTED
POINTER
POINTTO
POLITER
POLITIC
POLLTAX
POSITED
POULTRY
PRAETOR
PRATTLE
PRESTON
PRESTOS
PRINTED
PRINTER
PROCTOR
PROPTER
PSALTER
PULLTAB
PUNSTER
PURITAN
PUTITTO
PYRITES

P••••T•

PACKETS
PALETTE
PALLETS
PALMATE
PANDITS
PAPEETE
PARENTS
PARGETS
PARROTS
PARTITA
PARTITE
PATENTS
PAUCITY
PAYOUTS
PEANUTS
PEDANTS
PELLETS
PELTATE
PENALTY
PENNATE
PENULTS
PEQUOTS
PERLITE
PERMITS
PICANTE
PICKETS
PICKETT
PIGLETS
PIGNUTS
PIMENTO
PINNATE
PIOLETS
PIPETTE
PLACATE
PLAINTS
PLANETS
PLIGHTS
POCKETS
POINTTO
POLENTA
POLLUTE
POPPETS
POSSETS
POSTITS
POVERTY
PRAYSTO
PREDATE
PRELATE
PRESETS
PRIESTS
PRIMATE
PRIORTO
PRIVATE
PRIVETS
PRIVITY
PROBATE
PROBITY
PROFITS
PROMOTE
PROMPTS
PRORATA
PRORATE
PRYINTO
PTBOATS
PUBERTY
PUCKETT
PULLETS
PULPITS
PULSATE
PUNDITS
PUNNETS
PUPPETS
PURISTS
PUTITTO
PUTOUTS
PUTPUTS

P•••••T

PACKRAT
PAGEANT
PAIDOUT
PALIEST
PALMIST
PANDECT
PANSOUT
PARAPET
PARFAIT
PARQUET
PARTOUT
PASSOUT
PATIENT
PATRIOT
PAULIST
PAWEDAT
PAYDIRT
PAYMENT
PAYSOUT
PEACOAT
PEASANT
PECCANT
PECKSAT
PEEKOUT
PEEKSAT
PEEROUT
PEERSAT
PENDANT
PENDENT
PENNANT
PERCENT
PERFECT
PERIDOT
PERSIST
PERTEST
PEUGEOT
PIANIST
PICKETT
PICKOUT
PICKSAT
PIERROT
PIETIST
PIGMENT
PIGSOUT
PINENUT
PINIEST
PINKEST
PIPIEST
PIQUANT
PITAPAT
PLACKET
PLANOUT
PLAUDIT
PLAYACT
PLAYLET
PLAYOUT
PLAYSAT
PLUMMET
POKEDAT
POKESAT
POKIEST
POLECAT
POLOIST
POOPOUT
POOREST
POPSOUT
POPTART
PORTENT
POSHEST
POTSHOT
POUROUT
PRECAST
PRECEPT
PREDICT
PREEMPT
PREFECT
PREHEAT
PRESENT
PRESORT
PRETEST
PRETEXT
PREVENT
PRODUCT
PROJECT
PROPHET
PROPJET
PROTECT
PROTEST
PROTIST
PROVOST
PRUDENT
PUCKETT
PULLOUT
PUNGENT
PUNIEST
PUPTENT
PURPORT
PURSUIT
PUTSOUT

•PT••••

APTERAL
APTNESS
OPTICAL
OPTIMAL
OPTIMUM
OPTIONS
OPTSFOR
OPTSOUT
UPTAKES
UPTEMPO
UPTICKS
UPTIGHT
UPTONOW
UPTOPAR
UPTURNS

•P•T•••

APATITE
APOTHEM
EPITHET
EPITOME
EPSTEIN
SPATIAL
SPATTED
SPATTER
SPATULA
SPITING
SPITZES
SPOTLIT
SPOTTED
SPOTTER
SPUTNIK
SPUTTER
UPATREE
UPSTAGE
UPSTART
UPSTATE

•P••T••

APOSTLE
EPISTLE
OPENTOE
OPHITES
OPIATES
SPARTAN
SPATTED
SPATTER
SPECTER
SPECTOR
SPECTRA
SPECTRE
SPLITUP
SPLOTCH
SPORTED
SPOTTED
SPOTTER
SPOUTED
SPOUTER
SPRITES
SPURTED
SPUTTER
UPDATED
UPDATES

•P•••T•

APATITE
APLENTY
APPLETS
OPACITY
OPERATE
SPIGOTS
SPINETS
SPIRITO
SPIRITS
SPLINTS
SPRINTS
SPROUTS
UPBEATS
UPLIFTS
UPROOTS
UPSHOTS
UPSTATE

•P••••T

APPARAT
APPOINT
APRICOT
EPAULET
EPEEIST
EPITHET
OPENPIT
OPTSOUT
OPULENT
SPAREST
SPINOUT
SPIRANT
SPOTLIT
SPRIEST
SPRYEST
SPUNOUT
UPDRAFT
UPFRONT
UPRIGHT
UPSTART
UPSWEPT
UPTIGHT

••PT•••

BAPTISE
BAPTISM
BAPTIST
BAPTIZE
CAPTAIN
CAPTION
CAPTIVE
CAPTORS
CAPTURE
COPTERS
DIPTYCH
EMPTIED
EMPTIER
EMPTIES
EMPTILY
HEPTADS
HOPTOIT
KEPTOFF
KEPTOUT
LAPTOPS
LEPTONS
MOPTOPS
NAPTIME
NEPTUNE
NUPTIAL
PEPTALK
PEPTIDE
POPTART
POPTOPS
PUPTENT
RAPTORS
RAPTURE
REPTILE
RIPTIDE
RIPTORN
RUPTURE
SEPTETS
TIPTOED
TIPTOES
TIPTOPS
UMPTEEN

••P•T••

BYPATHS
CAPITAL
CAPITAN
CAPITOL
CAPSTAN
DEPUTED
DEPUTES
EMPATHY
HEPATIC
HIPSTER
IMPETUS
IMPUTED
IMPUTES
INPETTO
JUPITER
NAPHTHA
PIPETTE
REPUTED
REPUTES
ROPETOW
STPETER
TAPSTER
TIPSTER
WAPITIS
ZAPATEO
ZAPOTEC

••P••T•

APPLETS
ARPENTS
ASPECTS
CAPLETS
CAPNUTS
COPOUTS
DEPARTS
DEPICTS
DEPLETE
DEPORTS
DOPANTS
ESPARTO
EXPARTE
EXPECTS
EXPERTS
EXPIATE
EXPORTS
HEPCATS
IMPACTS
IMPARTS
IMPASTO
IMPIETY
IMPORTS
IMPOSTS
INPETTO
JAPHETH
LAPLATA
LAPORTE
LAPPETS
LEPANTO
MOPPETS
MUPPETS
PAPEETE
PIPETTE
POPPETS
PUPPETS
REPASTE
REPASTS
REPEATS
REPENTS
REPLATE
REPLETE
REPORTS
RIPINTO
RIPOSTE
SEPTETS
SIPPETS
SOPWITH
TAPINTO
TAPPETS
TIPPETS
TOPHATS
TYPISTS

••P•••T

AMPLEST
APPARAT
APPOINT
ASPHALT
BAPTIST
CAPELET
CAPULET
COPILOT
COPSOUT
COPYCAT
COPYIST
CYPRIOT
DEPOSIT
DOPEOUT
DOPIEST
EXPLOIT
HEPPEST
HIPBOOT
HIPPEST
HOPTOIT
IMPLANT
IMPRINT
INPRINT
KEPTOUT
LAPBELT
MOPIEST
PIPIEST
POPSOUT
POPTART
PUPTENT
RAPPORT
REPAINT
REPLANT
REPRINT
RIPSOUT
ROPIEST
SAPIENT
SOPHIST
SUPPORT
TAPROOT
TAPSOUT
TOPCOAT
TOPKNOT
TOPMAST
TOPMOST
TOPSOUT
TYPESET
TYPIEST
WIPEOUT

•••PT••

ADAPTED
ADAPTER
ADAPTOR
ADEPTLY
ADOPTED
ADOPTEE
ADOPTER
ASEPTIC
CHAPTER
CLAPTON
COEPTIS
COOPTED
CRYPTIC
CRYPTOS
DIOPTER
ERUPTED
HAMPTON
INAPTER
INAPTLY
INEPTLY
KRYPTON
PROPTER
SCEPTER
SCEPTIC
SCEPTRE
SKEPTIC
SLEPTIN
SLEPTON
STYPTIC
SWEPTUP
SYMPTOM
TEMPTED
TEMPTER
UNAPTLY

•••P•T•

ARMPITS
CARPETS
CHAPATI
COMPETE
COMPOTE
COMPUTE
DESPITE
DESPOTS
DISPUTE
HOTPOTS
INSPOTS
KEEPSTO
LAPPETS
LIMPETS
MOPPETS
MUPPETS
OUTPUTS
POPPETS
PULPITS
PUPPETS
PUTPUTS
RAJPUTS
RESPITE
SIPPETS
SNAPSTO
TAPPETS
TARPITS
TEAPOTS
THEPITS
TIPPETS
TOWPATH
WARPATH

•••P••T

AIRPORT
ANAPEST
BEDPOST
BITPART
CAMPOUT
CARPORT
CHAPLET
CLIPART
COMPACT
COMPORT
COMPOST
COUPLET
CULPRIT
DAMPEST
DEEPEST
DEEPFAT
DEEPSET
DISPORT
DROPLET
DROPOUT
FLIPOUT
FLYPAST
FRIPPET
HARPIST
HELPOUT
HEPPEST
HIPPEST
INSPECT
JETPORT
JUMPCUT
JUMPSAT
KEEPSAT
LIMPEST
NEWPORT
OUTPOST
POOPOUT
PROPHET
PROPJET
PURPORT
RAMPANT
RAMPART
RAPPORT
RESPECT
SEAPORT
SERPENT
SHIPOUT
SKIPOUT
SLIPOUT
SNAPSAT
SNIPEAT
SNIPPET
STEPOUT
SUBPLOT
SUPPORT
SUSPECT
TEMPEST
TRIPLET
TRIPPET
UNSPENT
WHIPPET

••••PT•

ACCEPTS
ADDUPTO
EXCEPTS
EXEMPTS
INCEPTS
INDEPTH
IRRUPTS
LEDUPTO
PROMPTS
SCRIPTS
SCULPTS

••••P•T

COCKPIT
CRUMPET
DOWNPAT
FLEAPIT
FRIPPET
FUSSPOT
GOTOPOT
HARDPUT
HOTSPOT
INASPOT
INCIPIT
INKSPOT
JACKPOT
MOSHPIT
OCCIPUT
OPENPIT
PARAPET
PITAPAT
REDSPOT
SHOTPUT
SNIPPET
STAYPUT
SUNSPOT
TENSPOT
TRIPPET
TRUMPET
WHIPPET

•••••PT

ATTEMPT
CONCEPT
CORRUPT
DECRYPT
DISRUPT
ENCRYPT
EXCERPT
PRECEPT
PREEMPT
RECEIPT
UNKEMPT
UNSWEPT
UPSWEPT

PU•••••

PUBERTY
PUBLICS
PUBLISH
PUCCINI
PUCKERS
PUCKETT
PUCKISH
PUDDING

PUDDLED
PUDDLES
PUDENCY
PUDGIER
PUDGILY
PUEBLOS
PUERILE
PUFFERS
PUFFERY
PUFFIER
PUFFILY
PUFFING
PUFFINS
PUGGISH
PUGNOSE
PUGREES
PULASKI
PULLETS
PULLEYS
PULLFOR
PULLING
PULLINS
PULLMAN
PULLOFF
PULLONS
PULLOUT
PULLSIN
PULLSON
PULLSUP
PULLTAB
PULLUPS
PULPIER
PULPITS
PULQUES
PULSARS
PULSATE
PULSING
PUMICES
PUMMELS
PUMPERS
PUMPING
PUMPKIN
PUMPSUP
PUNCHED
PUNCHER
PUNCHES
PUNCHIN
PUNCHUP
PUNDITS
PUNGENT
PUNIEST
PUNJABI
PUNKAHS
PUNKERS
PUNKIER
PUNKIES
PUNLESS
PUNNETS
PUNNIER
PUNNILY
PUNNING
PUNSTER
PUNTERS
PUNTIES
PUNTING
PUPPETS
PUPPIES
PUPTENT
PURCELL
PURDAHS
PURFLED
PURFLES
PURGING
PURISTS
PURITAN
PURLIEU
PURLING
PURLINS
PURLOIN
PURPLED
PURPLES
PURPORT
PURPOSE
PURRERS
PURRING
PURSERS
PURSIER
PURSING
PURSUED
PURSUER
PURSUES
PURSUIT
PURVEYS
PURVIEW
PUSHFUL
PUSHIER
PUSHILY
PUSHING
PUSHKIN
PUSHOFF
PUSHPIN
PUSHUPS
PUTAMEN
PUTAWAY
PUTDOWN
PUTITTO
PUTOUTS
PUTOVER
PUTPUTS
PUTSOFF
PUTSOUT
PUTTEES
PUTTERS
PUTTIED
PUTTIES
PUTTING
PUTUPON
PUZZLED
PUZZLER
PUZZLES

P•U••••

PAUCITY
PAULINA
PAULINE
PAULING
PAULIST
PAULSEN
PAUNCHY
PAUPERS
PAUSING
PEUGEOT
PLUCKED
PLUGGED
PLUGGER
PLUGINS
PLUGSIN
PLUMAGE
PLUMBED
PLUMBER
PLUMIER
PLUMING
PLUMMER
PLUMMET
PLUMPED
PLUMPER
PLUMPLY
PLUNDER
PLUNGED
PLUNGER
PLUNGES
PLUNKED
PLURALS
PLUSHER
PLUSHES
PLUSHLY
PLUSSES
PLUVIAL
POUCHED
POUCHES
POULENC
POULTRY
POUNCED
POUNCER
POUNCES
POUNDED
POUNDER
POURERS
POURING
POUROUT
POURSIN
POUTERS
POUTFUL
POUTIER
POUTING
PRUDENT
PRUDERY
PRUDHOE
PRUDISH
PRUNERS
PRUNING
PRUSSIA

P••U•••

PABULUM
PADUANS
PADUCAH
PAIUTES
PANURGE
PAPUANS
PARURES
PENUCHE
PENULTS
PEQUOTS
PERUKES
PERUSAL
PERUSED
PERUSER
PERUSES
PETUNIA
PIOUSLY
PIQUANT
PIQUING
PLAUDIT
PLAUTUS
PLOUGHS
POPULAR
POPULUS
PROUDER
PROUDLY
PUTUPON

P•••U••

PABLUMS
PANFULS
PARQUET
PASTURE
PAYOUTS
PEANUTS
PENGUIN
PEPLUMS
PERFUME
PERJURE
PERJURY
PERTURB
PICKUPS
PICTURE
PIGNUTS
PILEUPS
PINCURL
PITBULL
PLAGUED
PLAGUES
PLAQUES
PLENUMS
PODIUMS
POLLUTE
POPGUNS
POSEURS
POSSUMS
POSTURE
POTFULS
POTLUCK
PRELUDE
PRENUPS
PREQUEL
PRESUME
PROCURE
PRODUCE
PRODUCT
PROFUSE
PULLUPS
PULQUES
PURSUED
PURSUER
PURSUES
PURSUIT
PUSHUPS
PUTOUTS
PUTPUTS

P••••U•

PABULUM
PACKSUP
PAGEFUL
PAIDOUT
PAILFUL
PAILOUS
PAINFUL
PAIRSUP
PALLIUM
PANSOUT
PAPYRUS
PARATUS
PARLOUR
PARLOUS
PARTOUT
PASSEUL
PASSOUT
PASTDUE
PASTEUP
PASTEUR
PATCHUP
PAVIOUR
PAYSOUT
PEASOUP
PEEKOUT
PEEROUT
PEGASUS
PENTIUM
PERKSUP
PERSEUS
PERSIUS
PETROUS
PHOEBUS
PICKOUT
PICKSUP
PIGSOUT
PILEDUP
PILESUP
PILLBUG
PINENUT
PINETUM
PIPEDUP
PIPEFUL
PIPESUP
PIRAEUS
PIROGUE
PITEOUS
PITIFUL
PLANOUT
PLAUTUS
PLAYFUL
PLAYOUT
PLAYSUP
PLOTFUL
POKEFUN
POMPOUS
PONTIUS
POOPOUT
POPSOUT
POPULUS
POUROUT
POUTFUL
PREMIUM
PRESSUP
PRONOUN
PROPSUP
PROTEUS
PSYCHUP
PULLOUT
PULLSUP
PUMPSUP
PUNCHUP
PUSHFUL
PUTSOUT
PYRAMUS
PYRRHUS

P•••••U

PARVENU
PLATEAU
PURLIEU

•PU••••

OPULENT
SPUMIER
SPUMING
SPUMONE
SPUMONI
SPUMOUS
SPUNOFF
SPUNOUT
SPURNED
SPURNER
SPURRED
SPURSON
SPURTED
SPUTNIK
SPUTTER

•P•U•••

EPAULET
OPPUGNS
SPLURGE
SPOUSAL
SPOUSES
SPOUTED
SPOUTER
SPRUCED
SPRUCER
SPRUCES
UPQUARK
UPSURGE
UPTURNS

•P••U••

EPICURE
OPAQUES
SPATULA
SPELUNK
SPROUTS

•P•••U•

APERCUS
APPLAUD
OPENSUP
OPOSSUM
OPTIMUM
OPTSOUT
SPEAKUP
SPEEDUP
SPICEUP
SPINOUT
SPLITUP
SPOKEUP
SPUMOUS
SPUNOUT

••PU•••

AMPULES
CAPULET
COPULAE
COPULAS
DEPUTED
DEPUTES
EXPUNGE
IMPUGNS
IMPULSE
IMPURER
IMPUTED
IMPUTES
OPPUGNS
PAPUANS
POPULAR
POPULUS
REPUGNS
REPULSE
REPUTED
REPUTES

••P•U••

AMPOULE
CAPFULS
CAPGUNS
CAPNUTS
CAPSULE
CAPTURE
COPOUTS
CUPFULS
ESPOUSE
EXPOUND
HEPBURN
IMPOUND
LAPFULS
NEPTUNE
PEPLUMS
POPGUNS
RAPTURE
RUPTURE
TOPGUNS
UNPLUGS
VAPOURS

••P••U•

APPLAUD
CEPHEUS
COPIOUS
COPSOUT
DOPEOUT
HOPEFUL
HYPEDUP
HYPESUP
IMPETUS
IMPIOUS
KEPTOUT
ORPHEUS
PAPYRUS
PIPEDUP
PIPEFUL
PIPESUP
POPSOUT
POPULUS
RAPANUI
RIPSOUT
TAPSOUT
TOPSOUT
TYPEDUP
TYPESUP
WIPEDUP
WIPEOUT
WIPESUP

•••PU••

AIRPUMP
COMPUTE
DISPUTE
FLIPUPS
GASPUMP
KUSPUKS
LEGPULL
OUTPUTS
PUTPUTS
RAJPUTS
SCAPULA
SLIPUPS
STEPUPS
TEMPURA
WRAPUPS

•••P•U•

BUMPSUP
BURPGUN
CAMPOUT
COOPSUP
CROPSUP
DROPOUT
EARPLUG
FLIPOUT
GROPIUS
HELPFUL
HELPOUT
JUMPCUT
JUMPSUP
KEEPSUP
LESPAUL
LUMPSUM
NONPLUS
POMPOUS
POOPOUT
PROPSUP
PUMPSUP
SHAPEUP
SHIPOUT
SHOPFUL
SKIPOUT
SLIPOUT
SLIPSUP
SNAPSUP
SOUPSUP
STEPOUT
STEPSUP
STOPSUP
SULPHUR
SURPLUS
SWEPTUP
TRIPSUP
WHIPSUP
WRAPSUP

•••P••U

CHAPEAU

••••PU•

CANOPUS
CREEPUP
CRISPUS
GRAMPUS
HARDPUT
HOTSPUR
OCCIPUT
OCTOPUS
OEDIPUS
OLYMPUS
SHOTPUT
STAYPUT
SWEEPUP
TRUMPUP

••••P•U

THIMPHU

P•V••••

PAVANES
PAVIOUR
PAVLOVA
PIVOTAL
PIVOTED
POVERTY

P••V•••

PARVENU
PEAVEYS
PEEVING
PEEVISH
PERVADE
PLOVERS
PLUVIAL
PREVAIL
PREVENT
PREVIEW
PRIVACY
PRIVATE
PRIVETS
PRIVIER
PRIVIES
PRIVILY
PRIVITY
PROVERB
PROVERS
PROVIDE
PROVING
PROVISO
PROVOKE
PROVOST
PURVEYS
PURVIEW

P•••V••

PALAVER
POPOVER
PUTOVER

P••••V•

PAHLAVI
PASSIVE
PAVLOVA
PENSIVE
PLOSIVE

•P•V•••

SPAVINS

•P••V••

UPRIVER

•P•••V•

APPROVE

••P•V••

HOPOVER
POPOVER
REPAVED
REPAVES
UNPAVED

••P••V•

APPROVE
CAPTIVE
DEPRAVE
DEPRIVE
IMPROVE
REPROVE

P•W••••

PAWEDAT
PAWKIER
PAWNEES
PAWNERS
PAWNING
PAWNOFF
PAWPAWS
POWDERS
POWDERY
POWERED
POWWOWS

P••W•••

PEDWAYS
PEEWEES
PINWALE
PLOWBOY
PLOWERS
PLOWING
PLOWMAN
PLOWMEN
PLYWOOD
POWWOWS
PREWASH
PROWESS
PROWLED
PROWLER

P•••W••

PARKWAY
PARTWAY
PATHWAY
PESAWAS
POSTWAR
PUTAWAY

P••••W•

PAWPAWS
PEAFOWL
PILLOWS
PILLOWY
PINDOWN
PITSAWS
POWWOWS
PREDAWN
PUTDOWN

P•••••W

PALTROW
PREVIEW
PURVIEW

•PW••••

UPWARDS

•P•W•••

IPSWICH
SPAWNED
SPEWING
UPSWEEP
UPSWEPT
UPSWING

•P••W••

SPRAWLS

•P••••W

SPARROW
UPTONOW

••PW•••

LAPWING
SOPWITH

••P•W••

EMPOWER
INPOWER

••P••W•

NEPHEWS
REPLOWS
RIPSAWS
TOPDOWN

••P•••W

CAPSHAW
ROPETOW

•••P•W•

PAWPAWS

•••P••W

WHIPSAW

••••P•W

BEARPAW
CATSPAW
FOREPAW

P•X••••

PIXYISH
PYXIDES

P••X•••

PLEXORS
PREXIES
PROXIES
PROXIMO

P•••X••

PHLOXES
POBOXES

P••••X•

PICKAXE
POLEAXE
PRETEXT

P•••••X

PANCHAX
PARADOX
PERPLEX
PHALANX
PHARYNX
PHOENIX
PILLBOX
POLLTAX
POORBOX
POSTBOX

•P•X•••

EPOXIES

•P••••X

SPANDEX

•••P••X

COMPLEX
DEEPSIX
PERPLEX
SIMPLEX
SOAPBOX
TRIPLEX

PY•••••

PYEDOGS
PYGMIES
PYJAMAS
PYNCHON
PYRAMID
PYRAMUS
PYRITES
PYRRHIC
PYRRHUS
PYTHIAN
PYTHIAS
PYTHONS
PYXIDES

P•Y••••

PAYABLE
PAYCASH
PAYDAYS
PAYDIRT
PAYLOAD
PAYMENT
PAYOFFS
PAYOLAS
PAYOUTS
PAYROLL
PAYSFOR
PAYSOFF
PAYSOUT
PHYLLIS
PHYSICS
PLYWOOD
PRYINTO
PSYCHED
PSYCHES
PSYCHIC
PSYCHUP

P••Y•••

PAPYRUS
PITYING
PIXYISH
PLAYACT
PLAYBOY
PLAYDOH
PLAYERS
PLAYFUL
PLAYING
PLAYLET
PLAYOFF
PLAYOUT
PLAYPEN
PLAYSAT
PLAYSON
PLAYSUP
POLYGON
POLYMER
PONYING
PRAYERS
PRAYFOR
PRAYING
PRAYSTO
PREYSON

P•••Y••

PAPAYAS
PHARYNX
PLATYPI
POPEYED
PROCYON

P••••Y•

PARLAYS
PARLEYS
PAYDAYS
PEAVEYS
PEDWAYS
PHONEYS
PREPAYS
PULLEYS
PURVEYS

P•••••Y

PAGEBOY
PAISLEY
PALEDRY
PALFREY
PALJOEY
PALMARY
PANICKY
PANOPLY
PARKWAY
PARSLEY
PARTWAY
PASSKEY
PATHWAY
PAUCITY
PAUNCHY
PEABODY
PECCARY
PENALTY
PEPPERY
PEPPILY
PERFIDY
PERJURY
PERKILY
PESKILY
PETRIFY
PETTILY
PHONILY
PICARDY
PIGGERY
PILLORY
PILLOWY
PIOUSLY
PITHILY
PLAINLY
PLAYBOY
PLENARY
PLIABLY
PLIANCY
PLOWBOY
PLUMPLY
PLUSHLY
PODGILY
POORBOY
PORTRAY
POTENCY
POTTERY
POULTRY
POVERTY
POWDERY
PREACHY
PRESLEY
PRICKLY
PRIMACY
PRIMARY
PRIVACY
PRIVILY
PRIVITY
PROBITY
PRODIGY
PROGENY
PRONELY
PROSILY
PROSODY
PROUDLY
PRUDERY
PTOLEMY
PUBERTY
PUDENCY
PUDGILY
PUFFERY
PUFFILY
PUNNILY
PUSHILY
PUTAWAY

•P•Y•••

SPAYING
SPRYEST

•P••Y••

EPONYMS
EPONYMY
SPLAYED
SPRAYED
SPRAYER

•P••••Y

APISHLY
APLENTY
APOLOGY
EPARCHY
EPONYMY
OPACITY
SPANGLY
SPARELY
SPASSKY
SPECIFY
SPICERY
SPICILY
SPIDERY
SPIKILY
SPINDLY
SPINDRY
SPINNEY
SPLASHY
SPRINGY

••PY•••

COPYBOY
COPYCAT
COPYING
COPYIST
ESPYING
PAPYRUS

••P•Y••

DIPTYCH
LIPSYNC
PAPAYAS
POPEYED
ZEPHYRS

••P••Y•

BYPLAYS
DEPLOYS
EMPLOYE
EMPLOYS
HYPONYM
OSPREYS
REPLAYS

••P•••Y

AMPLIFY
CAPABLY
COPPERY
COPYBOY
EMPATHY
EMPTILY
EUPHONY
FOPPERY
HAPENNY
HAPPILY
IMPIETY
ORPHREY
PEPPERY
PEPPILY
RAPIDLY
SAPPILY
TEPIDLY
TIPSILY
TOPIARY
VAPIDLY

•••P•Y•

PREPAYS
TEAPOYS

•••P••Y

ADEPTLY
AIRPLAY
BUMPILY
CAMPILY
COMPANY
COPPERY
COWPONY
DEEPFRY
DEMPSEY
DISPLAY
DRAPERY
DRIPDRY
DROPSBY
ENDPLAY
EXUPERY
FOPPERY
GUNPLAY
HAPPILY
INAPTLY
INEPTLY
JEEPNEY
JUMPILY
LAMPREY
LUMPILY
MISPLAY
OUTPLAY
PEPPERY

PEPPILY
SAPPILY
SHAPELY
SHAPLEY
SOAPILY
STUPEFY
UNAPTLY
WASPILY
WISPILY

••••P•Y
ATROPHY
BASEPAY
CHEAPLY
CRISPLY
CRUMPLY
PANOPLY
PLUMPLY
SCRAPPY
SHARPLY
SICKPAY
STEEPLY
STROPPY
UNHAPPY

•••••PY
ENTROPY
GOSSIPY
SCRAPPY
SCRIMPY
STROPPY
THERAPY
UNHAPPY

P•Z••••
PIZARRO
PIZZAZZ
PUZZLED
PUZZLER
PUZZLES

P••Z•••
PANZERS
PIAZZAS
PIZZAZZ
PRIZING
PUZZLED
PUZZLER
PUZZLES

P•••Z••
PALAZZI
PALAZZO
PIAZZAS
PRETZEL

P••••Z•
PALAZZI
PALAZZO
PIZZAZZ

P•••••Z
PIZZAZZ

•P••Z••
SPITZES

•P•••Z•
APPRIZE
SPINOZA

••P•Z••
TOPAZES

••P•Z•
APPRIZE
BAPTIZE
CAPSIZE

•••PZ••
LEIPZIG

•••P•Z•
TRAPEZE

QA•••••
QATARIS

Q•A••••
QUACKED
QUAFFED
QUAFFER
QUAGGAS
QUAHOGS
QUAILED
QUAKERS
QUAKIER
QUAKILY
QUAKING
QUALIFY
QUALITY
QUANGOS
QUANTUM
QUARREL
QUARTER
QUARTET
QUARTOS
QUASARS
QUASHED
QUASHES
QUAVERS
QUAVERY

Q••A•••
QATARIS

Q•••A••
QINTARS
QUASARS
QUINARY

Q••••A•
QINGDAO
QUAGGAS
QUETZAL
QUINOAS
QUOKKAS

Q•••••A
QUECHUA

•Q•A•••
AQUARIA
AQUATIC
AQUAVIT
EQUABLE
EQUABLY
EQUALED
EQUALLY
EQUATED
EQUATES
EQUATOR
SQUALID
SQUALLS
SQUALOR
SQUANTO
SQUARED
SQUARER
SQUARES
SQUATLY
SQUATTY
SQUAWKS
SQUAWKY

•Q••A••
SQUEAKS
SQUEAKY
SQUEALS

•Q•••A•
AQUINAS

•Q••••A
AQUARIA

••Q•A••
LOQUATS
PIQUANT
TSQUARE
UPQUARK

••Q•••A
SEQUOIA
TEQUILA

•••Q•A•
COEQUAL
KUMQUAT
RORQUAL
UNEQUAL

Q••B•••
QUIBBLE

Q•••B••
QUIBBLE

•Q••B••
EQUABLE
EQUABLY

Q••C•••
QUACKED
QUECHUA
QUICHES
QUICKEN
QUICKER
QUICKIE
QUICKLY

Q•••C••
QUINCES

•Q•••C•
SQUELCH
SQUINCH

•Q••••C
AQUATIC

Q•••D••
QINGDAO

Q•••••D
QUACKED
QUAFFED
QUAILED
QUASHED
QUEERED
QUELLED
QUERIED
QUESTED
QUIETED
QUILLED
QUILTED
QUIPPED
QUIZZED

•Q••••D
EQUALED
EQUATED
SQUALID
SQUARED
SQUIRED

••Q••D•
LIQUIDS

•••Q••D
CASQUED

Q•E••••
QUECHUA
QUEENLY
QUEERED
QUEERER
QUEERLY
QUELLED
QUENTIN
QUERIED
QUERIER
QUERIES
QUERIST
QUESTED
QUETZAL
QUEUERS
QUEUEUP
QUEUING

Q••E•••
QUEENLY
QUEERED
QUEERER
QUEERLY
QUIETED
QUIETEN
QUIETER
QUIETLY

Q•••E••
QUAKERS
QUAVERS
QUAVERY
QUEUERS
QUEUEUP
QUIVERS
QUIVERY
QUOTERS

Q••••E•
QUACKED
QUAFFED
QUAFFER
QUAILED
QUAKIER
QUARREL
QUARTER
QUARTET
QUASHED
QUASHES
QUEERED
QUEERER
QUELLED
QUERIED
QUERIER
QUERIES
QUESTED
QUICHES
QUICKEN
QUICKER
QUIETED
QUIETEN
QUIETER
QUIGLEY
QUILLED
QUILLER
QUILTED
QUILTER
QUINCES
QUINTET
QUIPPED
QUIPPER
QUITTER
QUIZZED
QUIZZES
QUONSET

Q•••••E
QUIBBLE
QUICKIE
QUININE
QUINQUE
QUIXOTE

•Q•E•••
AQUEOUS
EQUERRY
IQTESTS
SQUEAKS
SQUEAKY
SQUEALS
SQUEEZE
SQUELCH

•Q••E••
SQUEEZE

•Q•••E•
AQUIFER
AQUIVER
EQUALED
EQUATED
EQUATES
EQUINES
SQUARED
SQUARER
SQUARES
SQUIRED
SQUIRES

•Q••••E
EQUABLE
SQUEEZE

••Q•E••
BEQUEST
INQUEST
LIQUEFY
LIQUEUR
MCQUEEN
REQUEST
SEQUELS
VAQUERO

••Q••E•
MCQUEEN
REQUIEM

••Q•••E
ACQUIRE
ENQUIRE
ESQUIRE
INQUIRE
REQUIRE
REQUITE
TSQUARE
UNQUOTE

•••Q•E•
BANQUET
BASQUES
BISQUES
BOUQUET
BRIQUET
CAIQUES
CASQUED
CASQUES
CHEQUER
CHEQUES
CIRQUES
CLAQUES
CLIQUES
CLIQUEY
CLOQUES
CONQUER
CROQUET
JACQUES
LACQUER
MARQUEE
MARQUES
MARQUEZ
MASQUES
MOSQUES
OPAQUES
PARQUET
PLAQUES
PREQUEL
PULQUES
RACQUET
SACQUES
TORQUES

•••Q••E
MARQUEE

••••Q•E
ANTIQUE
BAROQUE
BEZIQUE
BRUSQUE
COMIQUE
DUBUQUE
LALIQUE
MACAQUE
MONIQUE
OBLIQUE
QUINQUE

Q••F•••
QUAFFED
QUAFFER

Q•••F••
QUAFFED
QUAFFER

Q••••F•
QUALIFY

•Q••F••
AQUIFER

••Q••F•
LIQUEFY

Q••G•••
QINGDAO
QUAGGAS
QUIGLEY

Q•••G••
QUAGGAS
QUANGOS

Q••••G•
QUAHOGS

Q•••••G
QUAKING
QUEUING
QUOTING

••Q•••G
PIQUING

Q••H•••
QUAHOGS

Q•••H••
QUASHED
QUASHES
QUECHUA
QUICHES

•Q•••H•
SQUISHY

•Q••••H
SQUELCH
SQUINCH

QI•••••
QINGDAO
QINTARS
QIVIUTS

Q•I••••
QUIBBLE
QUICHES
QUICKEN
QUICKER
QUICKIE
QUICKLY
QUIETED
QUIETEN
QUIETER
QUIETLY
QUIGLEY
QUILLED
QUILLER
QUILTED
QUILTER
QUINARY
QUINCES
QUININE
QUINOAS
QUINQUE
QUINTET
QUIPPED
QUIPPER
QUITTER
QUIVERS
QUIVERY
QUIXOTE
QUIZZED
QUIZZES

Q••I•••
QIVIUTS
QUAILED

Q•••I••
QUAKIER
QUAKILY
QUAKING
QUALIFY
QUALITY
QUERIED
QUERIER
QUERIES
QUERIST
QUEUING
QUININE
QUOTING

Q••••I•
QATARIS
QUENTIN
QUICKIE

•Q•I•••
AQUIFER
AQUINAS
AQUIVER
EQUINES
EQUINOX
SQUILLS
SQUINCH
SQUINTS
SQUINTY
SQUIRED
SQUIRES
SQUIRMS
SQUIRMY
SQUIRTS
SQUISHY

•Q•••I•
AQUARIA
AQUATIC
AQUAVIT
SQUALID

••Q•I••
ACQUIRE
ACQUITS
ENQUIRE
ENQUIRY
ESQUIRE
INQUIRE
INQUIRY
LIQUIDS
PIQUING
REQUIEM
REQUIRE
REQUITE
SEQUINS
TEQUILA

••Q••I•
SEQUOIA

•••Q•I•
JOAQUIN
JONQUIL
MARQUIS
YANQUIS

Q••K•••
QUAKERS
QUAKIER
QUAKILY
QUAKING
QUOKKAS

Q•••K••
QUACKED
QUICKEN
QUICKER
QUICKIE
QUICKLY
QUOKKAS

•Q•••K•
SQUAWKS
SQUAWKY
SQUEAKS
SQUEAKY

••Q•••K
UPQUARK

Q••L•••
QUALIFY
QUALITY
QUELLED
QUILLED
QUILLER
QUILTED
QUILTER

Q•••L••
QUAILED
QUELLED
QUIGLEY
QUILLED
QUILLER

Q••••L•
QUAKILY
QUEENLY
QUEERLY
QUIBBLE
QUICKLY
QUIETLY

Q•••••L
QUARREL
QUETZAL

•Q••L••
EQUALED
EQUALLY
SQUALID
SQUALLS
SQUALOR
SQUELCH
SQUILLS

•Q•••L•
EQUABLE
EQUABLY
EQUALLY
SQUALLS
SQUATLY
SQUEALS
SQUILLS

••Q••L•
SEQUELS
TEQUILA

•••Q••L
COEQUAL
JONQUIL
PREQUEL
RORQUAL
UNEQUAL

Q••••M•
QUORUMS

Q•••••M
QUANTUM

•Q•••M•
SQUIRMS
SQUIRMY

••Q•••M
REQUIEM

Q•N••••
QINGDAO
QINTARS

Q••N•••
QUANGOS
QUANTUM
QUENTIN
QUINARY
QUINCES
QUININE
QUINOAS
QUINQUE
QUINTET
QUONSET

Q•••N••
QUEENLY

Q••••N•
QUAKING
QUEUING
QUININE
QUOTING

Q•••••N
QUENTIN
QUICKEN
QUIETEN

•Q••N••
AQUINAS
EQUINES
EQUINOX
SQUANTO
SQUINCH
SQUINTS
SQUINTY

••Q••N•
PIQUANT
PIQUING
SEQUINS

••Q•••N
MCQUEEN

•••Q••N
JOAQUIN

Q•O••••
QUOKKAS
QUONSET
QUORUMS
QUOTERS
QUOTING

Q•••O••
QUAHOGS
QUINOAS
QUIXOTE

Q••••O•
QUANGOS
QUARTOS

Q•••••O
QINGDAO

•Q••O••
AQUEOUS

•Q•••O•
EQUATOR
EQUINOX
SQUALOR

•Q••••O
SQUANTO

••Q•O••
LIQUORS
PEQUOTS
SEQUOIA
UNQUOTE

••Q•••O
VAQUERO

Q••P•••
QUIPPED
QUIPPER

Q•••P••
QUIPPED
QUIPPER

Q•••••P
QUEUEUP

Q•••Q••
QUINQUE

Q••R•••
QUARREL
QUARTER
QUARTET
QUARTOS
QUERIED
QUERIER
QUERIES
QUERIST
QUORUMS

Q•••R••
QATARIS
QUARREL
QUEERED
QUEERER
QUEERLY

Q••••R•
QINTARS
QUAKERS
QUASARS
QUAVERS
QUAVERY
QUEUERS
QUINARY
QUIVERS
QUIVERY
QUOTERS

Q•••••R
QUAFFER
QUAKIER
QUARTER
QUEERER
QUERIER
QUICKER
QUIETER
QUILLER
QUILTER
QUIPPER
QUITTER

•Q••R••
AQUARIA
EQUERRY
SQUARED
SQUARER
SQUARES
SQUIRED
SQUIRES
SQUIRMS
SQUIRMY
SQUIRTS

•Q•••R•
EQUERRY

•Q••••R
AQUIFER
AQUIVER
EQUATOR
SQUALOR
SQUARER

••Q•R••
ACQUIRE
ENQUIRE
ENQUIRY
ESQUIRE
INQUIRE
INQUIRY
LIQUORS
REQUIRE
TSQUARE
UPQUARK
VAQUERO

••Q•••R
LIQUEUR

•••Q••R
CHEQUER
CONQUER
LACQUER

Q••S•••
QUASARS
QUASHED
QUASHES
QUESTED

Q•••S••
QUONSET

Q••••S•
QUERIST

Q•••••S
QATARIS
QINTARS
QIVIUTS
QUAGGAS
QUAHOGS
QUAKERS
QUANGOS
QUARTOS
QUASARS
QUASHES
QUAVERS
QUERIES
QUEUERS
QUICHES
QUINCES
QUINOAS
QUIVERS
QUIZZES
QUOKKAS
QUORUMS
QUOTERS

•Q••S••
IQTESTS
SQUISHY

•Q••••S
AQUEOUS
AQUINAS
EQUATES
EQUINES
IQTESTS
SQUALLS
SQUARES
SQUAWKS
SQUEAKS
SQUEALS
SQUILLS
SQUINTS
SQUIRES
SQUIRMS
SQUIRTS

••Q••S•
BEQUEST
INQUEST
REQUEST

••Q•••S
ACQUITS
LIQUIDS
LIQUORS
LOQUATS
PEQUOTS
SEQUELS
SEQUINS

•••Q••S
BASQUES
BISQUES
CAIQUES
CASQUES
CHEQUES
CIRQUES
CLAQUES
CLIQUES
CLOQUES
JACQUES
MARQUES
MARQUIS
MASQUES
MOSQUES
OPAQUES
PLAQUES
PULQUES
SACQUES
TORQUES
YANQUIS

•••••QS
POSSLQS
PSANDQS

Q•T••••
QATARIS

Q••T•••
QINTARS
QUETZAL
QUITTER
QUOTERS
QUOTING

Q•••T••
QUANTUM
QUARTER
QUARTET
QUARTOS
QUENTIN
QUESTED
QUIETED
QUIETEN
QUIETER
QUIETLY
QUILTED
QUILTER
QUINTET
QUITTER

Q••••T•
QIVIUTS
QUALITY
QUIXOTE

Q•••••T
QUARTET
QUERIST
QUINTET
QUONSET

•QT••••
IQTESTS

•Q••T••
AQUATIC
EQUATED
EQUATES
EQUATOR
SQUATLY
SQUATTY

•Q•••T•
IQTESTS
SQUANTO
SQUATTY
SQUINTS
SQUINTY
SQUIRTS

•Q••••T
AQUAVIT

••Q••T•
ACQUITS
LOQUATS
PEQUOTS
REQUITE
UNQUOTE

••Q•••T
BEQUEST
INQUEST
PIQUANT

REQUEST

•••Q••T
BANQUET
BOUQUET
BRIQUET
CROQUET
KUMQUAT
PARQUET
RACQUET

•••••QT
ONTHEQT

QU•••••
QUACKED
QUAFFED
QUAFFER
QUAGGAS
QUAHOGS
QUAILED
QUAKERS
QUAKIER
QUAKILY
QUAKING
QUALIFY
QUALITY
QUANGOS
QUANTUM
QUARREL
QUARTER
QUARTET
QUARTOS
QUASARS
QUASHED
QUASHES
QUAVERS
QUAVERY
QUECHUA
QUEENLY
QUEERED
QUEERER
QUEERLY
QUELLED
QUENTIN
QUERIED
QUERIER
QUERIES
QUERIST
QUESTED
QUETZAL
QUEUERS
QUEUEUP
QUEUING
QUIBBLE
QUICHES
QUICKEN
QUICKER
QUICKIE
QUICKLY
QUIETED
QUIETEN
QUIETER
QUIETLY
QUIGLEY
QUILLED
QUILLER
QUILTED
QUILTER
QUINARY
QUINCES
QUININE
QUINOAS
QUINQUE
QUINTET
QUIPPED
QUIPPER
QUITTER
QUIVERS
QUIVERY
QUIXOTE
QUIZZED
QUIZZES
QUOKKAS
QUONSET
QUORUMS
QUOTERS
QUOTING

Q••U•••
QUEUERS
QUEUEUP
QUEUING

Q•••U••
QIVIUTS
QUORUMS

Q••••U•
QUANTUM
QUECHUA
QUEUEUP
QUINQUE

•QU••••
AQUARIA
AQUATIC
AQUAVIT
AQUEOUS
AQUIFER
AQUINAS
AQUIVER
EQUABLE
EQUABLY
EQUALED
EQUALLY
EQUATED
EQUATES
EQUATOR
EQUERRY
EQUINES
EQUINOX
SQUALID
SQUALLS
SQUALOR
SQUANTO
SQUARED
SQUARER
SQUARES
SQUATLY
SQUATTY
SQUAWKS
SQUAWKY
SQUEAKS
SQUEAKY
SQUEALS
SQUEEZE
SQUELCH
SQUILLS
SQUINCH
SQUINTS
SQUINTY
SQUIRED
SQUIRES
SQUIRMS
SQUIRMY
SQUIRTS
SQUISHY

•Q•••U•
AQUEOUS

••QU•••
ACQUIRE
ACQUITS
BEQUEST
ENQUIRE
ENQUIRY
ESQUIRE
INQUEST
INQUIRE
INQUIRY
LIQUEFY
LIQUEUR
LIQUIDS
LIQUORS
LOQUATS
MCQUEEN
PEQUOTS
PIQUANT
PIQUING
REQUEST
REQUIEM
REQUIRE
REQUITE
SEQUELS
SEQUINS
SEQUOIA
TEQUILA
TSQUARE
UNQUOTE
UPQUARK
VAQUERO

••Q••U•
LIQUEUR

•••QU••
BANQUET
BASQUES
BISQUES
BOUQUET
BRIQUET
CAIQUES
CASQUED
CASQUES
CHEQUER
CHEQUES
CIRQUES
CLAQUES
CLIQUES
CLIQUEY
CLOQUES
COEQUAL
CONQUER
CROQUET
JACQUES
JOAQUIN
JONQUIL
KUMQUAT
LACQUER
MARQUEE
MARQUES
MARQUEZ
MARQUIS
MASQUES
MOSQUES
OPAQUES
PARQUET
PLAQUES
PREQUEL
PULQUES
RACQUET
RORQUAL
SACQUES
TORQUES
UNEQUAL
YANQUIS

••••QU•
ANTIQUE
BAROQUE
BEZIQUE
BRUSQUE
COMIQUE
DUBUQUE
LALIQUE
MACAQUE
MONIQUE
OBLIQUE
OBLOQUY
QUINQUE

Q•V••••
QIVIUTS

Q••V•••
QUAVERS
QUAVERY
QUIVERS
QUIVERY

•Q••V••
AQUAVIT
AQUIVER

•Q••W••
SQUAWKS
SQUAWKY

Q••X•••
QUIXOTE

•Q••••X
EQUINOX

Q•••••Y
QUAKILY
QUALIFY
QUALITY
QUAVERY
QUEENLY
QUEERLY
QUICKLY
QUIETLY
QUIGLEY
QUINARY
QUIVERY

•Q••••Y
EQUABLY
EQUALLY
EQUERRY
SQUATLY
SQUATTY
SQUAWKY
SQUEAKY
SQUINTY
SQUIRMY
SQUISHY

••Q•••Y
ENQUIRY
INQUIRY
LIQUEFY

•••Q••Y
CLIQUEY

••••Q•Y
OBLOQUY

Q••Z•••
QUIZZED
QUIZZES

Q•••Z••
QUETZAL
QUIZZED
QUIZZES

•Q•••Z•
SQUEEZE

•••Q••Z
MARQUEZ

RA•••••
RABBETS
RABBITS
RABBITT
RABBLES
RABIDLY
RACCOON
RACECAR
RACEMES
RACEWAY
RACIEST
RACKETS
RACKING
RACKSUP
RACQUET
RADDLED
RADDLES
RADIALS
RADIANS
RADIANT
RADIATE
RADICAL
RADICES
RADICLE
RADIOED
RADIXES
RADOMES
RADULAE
RAFFISH
RAFFLED
RAFFLER
RAFFLES
RAFTERS
RAFTING
RAGBAGS
RAGDOLL
RAGEFUL
RAGGEDY
RAGGING
RAGLANS
RAGMOPS
RAGOUTS
RAGRUGS
RAGTIME
RAGTOPS
RAGWEED
RAIDERS
RAIDING
RAILERS
RAILING
RAILSAT
RAILWAY
RAIMENT
RAINBOW
RAINHAT
RAINIER
RAINILY
RAINING
RAINMAN
RAINOUT
RAISERS
RAISEUP
RAISING
RAISINS
RAJPUTS
RAKEDIN
RAKEDUP
RAKEOFF
RAKESIN
RAKESUP
RALEIGH
RALLIED
RALLIER
RALLIES
RALLYTO
RALSTON
RAMADAN
RAMADAS
RAMBEAU
RAMBLED
RAMBLER
RAMBLES
RAMEKIN
RAMESES
RAMINTO
RAMJETS
RAMLIKE
RAMMING
RAMMISH
RAMPAGE
RAMPANT
RAMPART
RAMRODS
RANAWAY
RANCHED
RANCHER
RANCHES
RANCHOS
RANCOUR
RANDALL
RANDIER
RANDOWN
RANGERS
RANGIER
RANGING
RANGOFF
RANGOON
RANGOUT
RANINTO
RANKERS
RANKEST
RANKING
RANKISH
RANKLED
RANKLES
RANLATE
RANOVER
RANRIOT
RANSACK
RANSOMS
RANTERS
RANTING
RAPANUI
RAPHAEL
RAPIDER
RAPIDLY
RAPIERS
RAPINES
RAPPELS
RAPPERS
RAPPING
RAPPORT
RAPTORS
RAPTURE
RAREBIT
RAREGAS
RARITAN
RASCALS
RASHERS
RASHEST
RASPERS
RASPIER
RASPING
RASPISH
RASSLED
RASSLES
RASTERS
RATABLE
RATAFIA
RATATAT
RATBERT
RATCHET
RATFINK
RATHOLE
RATINGS
RATIONS
RATITES
RATLIKE
RATLINE
RATPACK
RATRACE
RATTAIL
RATTANS
RATTERS
RATTIER
RATTING
RATTISH
RATTLED
RATTLER
RATTLES
RATTRAP
RAUCOUS
RAVAGED
RAVAGER
RAVAGES
RAVELED
RAVENED
RAVENNA
RAVEUPS
RAVINES
RAVINGS
RAVIOLI
RAWDATA
RAWDEAL
RAWEGGS
RAWHIDE
RAWNESS
RAWSILK
RAYBURN
RAYGUNS
RAYKROC
RAYLIKE
RAYMOND
RAYOVAC
RAZORED
RAZZING

R•A••••
REACHED
REACHES
REACTED
REACTOR
REACTTO
READERS
READIED
READIER
READIES
READILY
READING
READMIT
READOUT
READSIN
REAFFIX
REAGENT
REAIMED
REAIRED
REALISE
REALISM
REALIST
REALITY
REALIZE
REALTOR
REAMASS
REAMERS
REAMING
REAPERS
REAPING
REAREND
REARERS
REARGUE
REARING
REARMED
REARSUP
REASONS
REAVAIL
RIANTLY
ROACHED
ROACHES
ROADBED
ROADHOG
ROADIES
ROADMAP
ROADWAY
ROAMERS
ROAMING
ROANOKE
ROARERS
ROARING
ROASTED
ROASTER
RUANDAN
RWANDAN

R••A•••
RAMADAN
RAMADAS
RANAWAY
RAPANUI
RATABLE
RATAFIA
RATATAT
RAVAGED
RAVAGER
RAVAGES
RDLAING
REBASTE
REBATED
REBATES
RECALLS
RECANED
RECANES
RECANTS
RECASTS
REDACTS
REDALGA
REDANTS
REDATED
REDATES
REFACED
REFACES
REGAINS
REGALED
REGALES
REGALIA
REGALLY
REGARDS
REGATTA
REHANGS
RELACED
RELACES
RELAPSE
RELATED
RELATES
RELAXED
RELAXES
RELAYED
REMAILS
REMAINS
REMAKES
REMANDS
REMARKS
REMARRY
RENAILS
RENAMED
RENAMES
RENARDS
RENAULT
REPAINT
REPAIRS
REPAPER
REPASTE
REPASTS
REPAVED
REPAVES
RERAISE
RERATED
RERATES
RESALES
RESALTS
RESANDS
RESAWED
RETAILS
RETAINS
RETAKEN
RETAKES
RETAPED
RETAPES
RETARDS
RETAXED
RETAXES
REVALUE
REVAMPS
REWARDS
REWARMS
REWAXED
REWAXES
RIBANDS
RICARDO
RIVALED
RIVALRY
ROBARDS
ROGAINE
ROLAIDS
ROMAINE
ROMANCE
ROMANIA
ROMANOV
ROMANSH
ROSALIE
ROSANNA
ROSANNE
ROSARIO
ROTATED
ROTATES
ROTATOR
ROXANNE
ROYALLY
ROYALTY
ROYALWE
RUBATOS
RUNAMOK
RUNAWAY
RURALLY

R•••A••
RADIALS
RADIANS
RADIANT
RADIATE
RAGBAGS
RAGLANS
RAMPAGE
RAMPANT
RAMPART
RANDALL
RANLATE
RANSACK
RAPHAEL
RASCALS
RATPACK
RATRACE
RATTAIL
RATTANS
RAWDATA
REAMASS
REAVAIL
RECHALK
RECLAIM
RECLAME
RECOATS
REDCAPS
REDEALS
REDEALT
REDHAIR
REDHATS
REDIALS
REDOAKS
REDRAWN
REDRAWS
REDTAPE
REENACT
REFLAGS
REFRACT
REFRAIN
REFRAME
REGNANT
REGRADE
REHEALS
REHEARD
REHEARS
REHEATS
RELEARN
RELEASE
RELIANT
RELOADS
REMNANT
RENTALS
REPEALS
REPEATS
REPLACE
REPLANS
REPLANT
REPLATE
REPLAYS
REREADS
RESCALE
RESEALS
RESEATS
RESTAGE
RESTAIN
RESTAMP
RESTART
RESTATE
RETEACH
RETEARS
RETIARY
RETRACE
RETRACK
RETRACT
RETRADE
RETRAIN
REVEALS
REWEAVE
REWRAPS
REXCATS
REYNARD
RHUBARB
RIBCAGE
RICHARD
RIMBAUD
RIOTACT
RIPRAPS
RIPSAWS
RITUALS
ROLVAAG
ROSEATE
ROSTAND
ROULADE
RUDYARD
RUMBAED
RUMMAGE
RUNBACK
RUNLATE
RUNWAYS
RUPIAHS

R••••A•
RACECAR
RACEWAY
RADICAL
RADULAE
RAILSAT
RAILWAY
RAINHAT
RAINMAN
RAMADAN
RAMADAS
RAMBEAU
RANAWAY
RAREGAS
RARITAN
RATATAT
RATTRAP
RAWDEAL
RAYOVAC
REBEKAH
RECITAL
RECLEAN
REDCOAT
REDFLAG
REDHEAD
REDHEAT
REDMEAT
REDSTAR
REFUSAL
REGULAR
REITMAN
REMORAS
REMOVAL
REMUDAS
RENEWAL
REPOMAN
RETINAE
RETINAL
RETINAS
RETREAD
RETREAT
RETRIAL
REVIVAL
RHUMBAS
RICERAT
RICHMAN
RICKMAN
RIDGWAY
ROADMAP
ROADWAY
ROLLBAR
ROLVAAG
ROMULAN
RONDEAU
RORQUAL
ROSEBAY
ROWBOAT
RUANDAN
RUFFIAN
RUFIYAA
RUNAWAY
RUSSIAN
RWANDAN

R•••••A
RATAFIA
RAVENNA
RAWDATA
REBECCA
REDALGA
REGALIA
REGATTA
REPLICA
RETSINA
RICKSHA
RICOTTA
RIGVEDA
RIORITA
RIVIERA
ROBERTA
ROBUSTA
ROMANIA
ROSANNA
ROSETTA
ROSSSEA
ROTUNDA
RUFIYAA

•RA••••
ARABIAN
ARACHNE
ARAFURA
ARALSEA
ARAMAIC
ARAMEAN
ARAPAHO
ARAWAKS
BRACERO
BRACERS
BRACEUP
BRACING
BRACKEN
BRACKET
BRADLEE
BRADLEY
BRAGGED
BRAGGER
BRAHMAN
BRAHMAS
BRAHMIN
BRAIDED
BRAIDER
BRAILLE
BRAINED
BRAISED
BRAISES
BRAKING
BRALESS
BRAMBLE
BRAMBLY
BRANAGH
BRANDED
BRANDER
BRANDON
BRANSON
BRASHER
BRASHLY
BRASSES
BRASSIE
BRAVADO
BRAVELY
BRAVERY
BRAVEST
BRAVING
BRAVOES
BRAVURA
BRAWLED
BRAWLER
BRAXTON
BRAYERS
BRAYING
BRAZIER
BRAZING
CRABBED
CRABBER
CRACKED
CRACKER
CRACKLE
CRACKLY
CRACKUP
CRADLED
CRADLES
CRAFTED
CRAFTER
CRAFTSY
CRAMMED
CRAMMER
CRAMPED
CRAMPON
CRANIAL
CRANING
CRANIUM
CRANKED
CRANKUP
CRAPPIE
CRASHED
CRASHES
CRASSER
CRASSLY
CRASSUS
CRATERS
CRATING
CRAVATS
CRAVENS
CRAVERS
CRAVING
CRAWDAD
CRAWLED
CRAWLER
CRAYOLA
CRAYONS
CRAZIER
CRAZIES
CRAZILY
CRAZING
DRABBER
DRACHMA
DRACHMS
DRACULA
DRAFTED
DRAFTEE
DRAGGED
DRAGGER
DRAGNET
DRAGONS
DRAGOON
DRAGOUT
DRAGSIN
DRAGSON
DRAINED
DRAINER
DRAPERS
DRAPERY
DRAPING
DRASTIC
DRATTED
DRAUGHT
DRAWBAR
DRAWERS
DRAWING
DRAWLED
DRAWNIN
DRAWNON
DRAWNUP
DRAWOUT
DRAWSIN
DRAWSON
DRAWSUP
DRAYAGE
DRAYING
ERASERS
ERASING
ERASMUS
ERASURE
FRACTAL
FRAGILE
FRAILER
FRAILLY
FRAILTY
FRAISES
FRAMEUP
FRAMING
FRANCES
FRANCIS
FRANKED
FRANKEN
FRANKER
FRANKIE
FRANKLY
FRANKOZ
FRANTIC
FRAPPES
FRASIER
FRAUGHT
FRAWLEY
FRAYING
FRAZIER
FRAZZLE
GRABBAG
GRABBED
GRABBER
GRABSAT
GRACIAS

GRACILE
GRACING
GRACKLE
GRADERS
GRADING
GRADUAL
GRAFTED
GRAFTON
GRAHAME
GRAHAMS
GRAINED
GRAMMAR
GRAMMER
GRAMMES
GRAMMYS
GRAMPAS
GRAMPUS
GRANADA
GRANARY
GRANDAM
GRANDEE
GRANDER
GRANDLY
GRANDMA
GRANDPA
GRANGER
GRANGES
GRANITE
GRANOLA
GRANTED
GRANTEE
GRANTOR
GRANULE
GRAPHED
GRAPHIC
GRAPIER
GRAPNEL
GRAPPAS
GRAPPLE
GRASPED
GRASSED
GRASSES
GRATERS
GRATIAS
GRATIFY
GRATING
GRAVELS
GRAVELY
GRAVERS
GRAVEST
GRAVIES
GRAVING
GRAVITY
GRAVURE
GRAYEST
GRAYING
GRAYISH
GRAYJAY
GRAYLAG
GRAYSON
GRAZERS
GRAZING
IRANIAN
IRATELY
IRATEST
KRATERS
KRATION
ORACLES
ORANGES
ORANGEY
ORATING
ORATION
ORATORS
ORATORY

PRAETOR
PRAIRIE
PRAISED
PRAISER
PRAISES
PRALINE
PRANCED
PRANCER
PRANCES
PRANGED
PRANKED
PRATERS
PRATING
PRATTLE
PRAYERS
PRAYFOR
PRAYING
PRAYSTO
TRABERT
TRACERS
TRACERY
TRACHEA
TRACING
TRACKED
TRACKER
TRACTOR
TRADEIN
TRADEON
TRADERS
TRADEUP
TRADING
TRADUCE
TRAFFIC
TRAGEDY
TRAILED
TRAILER
TRAINED
TRAINEE
TRAINER
TRAIPSE
TRAITOR
TRALALA
TRAMCAR
TRAMMEL
TRAMPAS
TRAMPED
TRAMPLE
TRANCES
TRANSIT
TRANSOM
TRAPEZE
TRAPPED
TRAPPER
TRASHED
TRASHES
TRAUMAS
TRAVAIL
TRAVELS
TRAVERS
TRAVOIS
TRAWLED
TRAWLER
TRAYFUL
URANITE
URANIUM
WRACKED
WRAITHS
WRANGLE
WRAPPED
WRAPPER
WRAPSUP
WRAPUPS
XRATING
XRAYING

•R•A•••

ARCADES
ARCADIA
ARCANUM
AREARUG
AREAWAY
ARIADNE
ARMADAS
ARRAIGN
ARRANGE
ARRASES
ARRAYED
BREADED
BREADTH
BREAKER
BREAKIN
BREAKUP
BREASTS
BREATHE
BREATHS
BREATHY
BRIARDS
BROADAX
BROADEN
BROADER
BROADLY
CREAKED
CREAMED
CREAMER
CREASED
CREASES
CREATED
CREATES
CREATOR
CROAKED
CROATIA
DREADED
DREAMED
DREAMER
DREAMON
DREAMUP
ERGATES
ERRANCY
ERRANDS
ERRATIC
ERRATUM
FREAKED
FRIABLE
GREASED
GREASER
GREASES
GREATER
GREATLY
GREAVES
GROANED
GROANER
MRMAGOO
ORDAINS
ORGANDY
ORGANIC
ORGANON
ORGANUM
ORGANZA
ORGATES
ORLANDO
ORMANDY
PREACHY
PREAMPS
TREACLE
TREACLY
TREADED
TREADER
TREADLE
TREASON
TREATED
TRUANCY
TRUANTS
URBANER
WREAKED
WREATHE
WREATHS

•R••A••

ARAMAIC
ARAPAHO
ARAWAKS
ARCHAIC
ARCLAMP
ARIKARA
ARMBAND
ARMYANT
ARREARS
ARTWARE
BRANAGH
BRAVADO
BRIDALS
BRIGADE
BRIGAND
BRITAIN
BROCADE
BROGANS
BROMATE
CRAVATS
CRETANS
CRUSADE
CRUSADO
CRUZADO
CRYBABY
DRAYAGE
DRYWALL
FRIDAYS
FRIGATE
FROMAGE
FROWARD
FRYPANS
GRAHAME
GRAHAMS
GRANADA
GRANARY
GRENADA
GRENADE
GRIMACE
IRELAND
IRONAGE
ORCHARD
ORDEALS
OREGANO
ORGEATS
ORIGAMI
ORLEANS
ORPHANS
PRECAST
PREDATE
PREDAWN
PREFABS
PREFACE
PRELATE
PREPAID
PREPARE
PREPAYS
PRESAGE
PRESALE
PRETAPE
PREVAIL
PREWASH
PRIMACY
PRIMARY
PRIMATE
PRIVACY
PRIVATE
PROBATE
PROFANE
PROPANE
PRORATA
PRORATE
PROSAIC
TRALALA
TRAVAIL
TREMAIN
TRENARY
TREPANS
TROCARS
TROJANS

•R•••A•

ARABIAN
ARAMEAN
ARCHWAY
AREAWAY
AREOLAE
AREOLAR
AREOLAS
ARISTAE
ARISTAS
ARMADAS
ARMLOAD
ARNICAS
AROUSAL
ARRIVAL
ARROBAS
ARSENAL
ARTISAN
BRAHMAN
BRAHMAS
BRENDAN
BRENNAN
BRIGHAM
BROADAX
BROSNAN
CRANIAL
CRAWDAD
CREWMAN
CRIMEAN
CROWBAR
CRUCIAL
CRYSTAL
DRAWBAR
DRIPPAN
DRISTAN
DRIVEAT
FRACTAL
FREEMAN
FREEWAY
FRENEAU
FRETSAW
FRIEDAN
FRISIAN
FROGMAN
FRONTAL
FROWNAT
GRABBAG
GRABSAT
GRACIAS
GRADUAL
GRAMMAR
GRAMPAS
GRANDAM
GRAPPAS
GRATIAS
GRAYJAY
GRAYLAG
GRECIAN
GRISHAM
IRANIAN
IRONMAN
MRCLEAN
ORBITAL
ORDINAL
ORPHEAN
ORTOLAN
PREHEAT
PRELOAD
PRESOAK
PROGRAM
PROPMAN
PROTEAN
TRAMCAR
TRAMPAS
TRAUMAS
TREERAT
TRIGRAM
TRISHAW
TRISTAN
TRISTAR
TRIVIAL
TROIKAS
TRUCIAL
TRUDEAU
URUGUAY

•R••••A

ARAFURA
ARALSEA
ARCADIA
ARIETTA
ARIKARA
ARIZONA
ARMENIA
ARUGULA
BRAVURA
CRAYOLA
CREMONA
CROATIA
DRACHMA
DRACULA
ERITREA
EROTICA
FREESIA
GRANADA
GRANDMA
GRANDPA
GRANOLA
GRENADA
KRISHNA
ORGANZA
PRORATA
PRUSSIA
TRACHEA
TRALALA

••RA•••

ABRADED
ABRADER
ABRADES
ABRAHAM
AERATED
AERATES
AERATOR
AFRAMES
AGRAFFE
AMRADIO
ARRAIGN
ARRANGE
ARRASES
ARRAYED
AURALEE
AURALLY
BARANOF
BERATED
BERATES
BORACIC
BORATES
CARABAO
CARACAL
CARACAS
CARAFES
CARAMBA
CARAMEL
CARAMIA
CARAVAN
CARAVEL
CARAWAY
CBRADIO
CERAMIC
CORAZON
CURACAO
CURATES
CURATOR
DERAILS
DURABLE
DURABLY
DURANCE
DURANGO
DURANTE
EARACHE
ENRAGED
ENRAGES
ERRANCY
ERRANDS
ERRATIC
ERRATUM
EURASIA
FARADAY
FARAWAY
FMRADIO
FORAGED
FORAGER
FORAGES
GARAGED
GARAGES
GERAINT
GERALDO
GIRAFFE
GIRASOL
GYRATED
GYRATES
GYRATOR
HERALDS
HIRABLE
HORATIO
HYRACES
HYRAXES
ISRAELI
KARACHI
KARAJAN
KARAKUL
KARAKUM
KARAOKE
KARASEA
KERATIN
LARAINE
LARAMIE
MARABOU
MARACAS
MARAUDS
MIRACLE
MIRADOR
MIRAGES
MIRAMAR
MIRAMAX
MIRANDA
MORAINE
MORALES
MORALLY
MORANIS
MORAVIA
OTRANTO
PARABLE
PARADED
PARADES
PARADOX
PARAGON
PARAPET
PARAPHS
PARASOL
PARATUS
PHRASAL
PHRASED
PHRASES
PIRAEUS
PIRANHA
PIRATED
PIRATES
PIRATIC
PYRAMID
PYRAMUS
RERAISE
RERATED
RERATES
RURALLY
SARACEN
SARALEE
SARANAC
SARAWAK
SARAZEN
SCRAGGY
SCRAPED
SCRAPER
SCRAPES
SCRAPPY
SCRATCH
SCRAWLS
SCRAWLY
SCRAWNY
SERAPES
SERAPHS
SERAPIS
SPRAINS
SPRAWLS
SPRAYED
SPRAYER
STRAFED
STRAFES
STRAINS
STRAITS
STRANDS
STRANGE
STRASSE
STRATUM
STRATUS
STRAUSS
STRAYED
TARANTO
TERAPHS
THRALLS
TIRADES
TYRANNY
TYRANTS
UKRAINE
UNRATED
UNRAVEL
UPRAISE
VERANDA
VIRAGOS

••R•A••

ABREAST
ACREAGE
AERIALS
AIRBAGS
AIRBALL
AIRBASE
AIRDAMS
AIRDATE
AIRFARE
AIRLANE
AIRMADA
AIRMAIL
AIRMASS
AIRRAID
AIRSACS
AIRTAXI
AIRWAVE
AIRWAYS
ALREADY
ARREARS
AUREATE
BARBARA
BARBARY
BARCARS
BARGAIN
BARMAID
BARNABY
BARNARD
BARRACK
BARRAGE
BARTABS
BARWARE
BEREAVE
BERNARD
BURBANK
BUREAUS
BURLAPS
BURMANS
BUROAKS
BURSARS
BURSARY
BYROADS
CARCASE
CARCASS
CARFARE
CARPALS
CARPARK
CARTAGE
CARWASH
CEREALS
CERTAIN
CORDAGE
CORDATE
CORKAGE
CORRALS
CORSAGE
CORSAIR
CUREALL
CURRANT
CURTAIL
CURTAIN
DORMANT
DORSALS
EARHART
EARMARK
FAREAST
FARRAGO
FERRARI
FERRARO
FERRATE
FIREANT
FIREARM
FORBADE
FOREARM
FORGAVE
FORMALS
FORMATS
FORSAKE
FORSALE
FORWARD
FURBALL
FURNACE
GARBAGE
GARLAND
GERMANE
GERMANS
GERMANY
HARVARD
HERBAGE
HERBALS
HERMANN
HURRAHS
INROADS
KIRMANS
KOREANS
LARIATS
MARCATO
MARGATE
MARGAUX
MARGAYS
MARIANA
MARMARA
MARSALA
MARYANN
MERMAID
MORDANT
MORGANA
MORGANS
MORTALS
MORTARS
MYRIADS
NARRATE
NARWALS
NIRVANA
NORMALS
NORMAND
NORMANS
OURGANG
PARFAIT
PARIAHS
PARKADE
PARLAYS
PARTAKE
PERCALE
PERHAPS
PERTAIN
PERVADE
PORTAGE
PORTALS
PURDAHS
REREADS
SARCASM
SCREAKS
SCREAMS
SERIALS
SERIATE
SERRATE
SERVALS
SERVANT
SORBATE
SPREADS
STREAKS
STREAKY
STREAMS
STRIATE
SURFACE
SURNAME
SURPASS
SYRIANS
TARBABY
TARMACS
TARSALS
TARTANS
TARTARE
TARTARS
TARZANA
TERNARY
TERNATE
TERRACE
TERRAIN
THREADS
THREADY
THREATS
THROATS
THROATY
TORNADO
TURBANS
UNREADY
UPROARS
VARIANT
VERBALS
VERDANT
WARFARE
WARGAME
WARPATH
WARRANT
YARDAGE
YARDARM
ZERMATT

••R••A•

ABRAHAM
ACROBAT
ADRENAL
AEROBAT
AFRICAN
AIRBOAT
AIRHEAD
AIRPLAY
ARRIVAL
ARROBAS
AURORAE
AURORAL
AURORAS
BARKSAT
BARSOAP
BERGMAN
BIRDMAN
BURGLAR
BYREMAN
CARABAO
CARACAL
CARACAS
CARAVAN
CARAWAY
CARCOAT
CARDIAC
CARINAS
CARLOAD
CARSEAT
CORDIAL
CORNEAL
CORNEAS
CORONAE
CORONAS
CURACAO
DARESAY
DARKMAN
EARFLAP
FARADAY
FARAWAY
FERNBAR
FIREMAN
FORBEAR
FORDHAM
FOREMAN
FOREPAW
FORERAN
FORESAW
FORREAL
FORTRAN
FURSEAL
GORDIAN
GURKHAS
HARDHAT
HARDPAN
HARTMAN
JERBOAS
KARAJAN
KEROUAC
KORUNAS
LORICAE
LYRICAL
MARACAS
MARCEAU
MARINAS
MARITAL
MARKHAM
MARKKAA
MARSHAL
MARTIAL
MARTIAN
MARYKAY
MIRAMAR
MIRAMAX
NARWHAL
PARKWAY
PARTIAL
PARTWAY
PERLMAN
PERSIAN
PERUSAL
PHRASAL
PORTMAN
PORTRAY
PURITAN
RAREGAS
RARITAN
RORQUAL
SARANAC
SARAWAK
SAROYAN
SERBIAN
SORORAL
SURCOAT
SURINAM
SURREAL
TERTIAL
THREEAM
THRUWAY
TURFWAR
VERITAS
VIRGOAN
VIRTUAL
WIRETAP
WORKDAY
WORKMAN
YARDMAN
YEREVAN
ZAREBAS

••R•••A

AGRIPPA
AIRMADA
AUREOLA
BARBARA
BARBUDA
BARETTA
BERETTA
BERMUDA
BIRETTA
BURKINA
CARAMBA
CARAMIA
CARIOCA
CARNERA
CEREBRA
CORDOBA
CORETTA
COROLLA
CORRIDA
CORSICA
ETRURIA
EURASIA
FORMICA
FORMOSA
FORMULA
FORTUNA
GORILLA
HERBTEA
KARASEA
LORETTA
MARIANA
MARIMBA
MARKKAA
MARKOVA
MARMARA
MARSALA
MARTINA
MIRANDA
MORAVIA
MORGANA
NIRVANA
NORIEGA
PARTITA
PERGOLA
PERSONA
PIRANHA
PORSENA
SYRINGA
TARZANA
VERANDA
VERBENA

•••RA••

AFFRAYS
AIRRAID
ANORAKS
ASHRAMS
ATTRACT
AVERAGE
AYNRAND
BAHRAIN
BARRACK
BARRAGE
BETRAYS
BUMRAPS
CHARADE
CHORALE
CHORALS
CITRATE
COMRADE
CORRALS
COURAGE
COURANT
CUIRASS
CURRANT
CUTRATE
DEFRAUD
DEFRAYS
DEGRADE
DEPRAVE
DETRACT
DETRAIN
DIGRAMS
DIGRAPH
DIORAMA
EMBRACE
EMERALD
EMIRATE
ENGRAFT
ENGRAMS
ENGRAVE
ENTRAIN
ENTRANT
ENTRAPS
ENWRAPS
ESTRADA
ESTRAYS
EXTRACT
FARRAGO
FERRARI
FERRARO
FERRATE
GOURAMI
GUARANI
HATRACK
HAYRACK
HEBRAIC
HURRAHS
HYDRANT
HYDRATE
INGRAIN
INGRATE
ITERANT
ITERATE
LEGRAND
LIBRARY
MACRAME
MALRAUX
MIGRANT
MIGRATE
MOORAGE
NARRATE
NITRATE
OFFRAMP
ONTRACK
OPERAND
OPERATE
OUTRACE
OUTRAGE
OUTRANK
OVERACT
OVERAGE
OVERALL
OVERATE
OVERAWE
PEERAGE
PHARAOH
PLURALS
PRORATA
PRORATE
RATRACE
REDRAWN
REDRAWS
REFRACT
REFRAIN
REFRAME
REGRADE
RETRACE
RETRACK
RETRACT
RETRADE

RETRAIN
REWRAPS
RIPRAPS
SATRAPS
SCARABS
SERRATE
SKIRACK
SOPRANO
SPIRALS
SPIRANT
STORAGE
SUCRASE
SUNRAYS
TAXRATE
TERRACE
TERRAIN
TETRADS
THERAPY
TIERACK
TITRATE
TOURACO
UMBRAGE
UNCRATE
UNDRAPE
UNDRAWN
UNTRAPS
UNWRAPS
UPBRAID
UPDRAFT
UPGRADE
USGRANT
VAGRANT
VIBRANT
VIBRATE
VIBRATO
WARRANT

•••R•A•

ACCRUAL
ANDREAS
ANYROAD
BEARCAT
BEARPAW
BOERWAR
CZARDAS
DIURNAL
DOORMAN
DOORMAT
DOORWAY
ENTREAT
ETERNAL
EXURBAN
FAIRWAY
FORREAL
FOURWAY
GETREAL
GLORIAM
GLORIAS
HADRIAN
HEARSAY
IBERIAN
JEERSAT
JOURDAN
JOURNAL
LEERSAT
LIPREAD
LOWROAD
MEGRYAN
MISREAD
NUTRIAS
OFFROAD
ONTRIAL
OVEREAT
OVERLAP
OVERLAY
OVERRAN
OVERSAW
OVERTAX
PATRIAL
PEERSAT
PHARLAP
RETREAD
RETREAT
RETRIAL
SAURIAN
SHERMAN
SHERPAS
SIERRAS
SPARTAN
SPIREAS
SPORRAN
STAREAT
STARMAN
STARMAP
STERNAL
STYRIAN
SURREAL
SWOREAT
TEARGAS
TEARSAT
THEREAT
THERMAL
THOREAU
THURMAN
UMBRIAN
UXORIAL
WHEREAS
WHEREAT
ZAIREAN
ZAIRIAN

•••R••A

ACEROLA
AMERICA
AMERIKA
CORRIDA
CZARINA
DIORAMA
EMERITA
ESTRADA
EXURBIA
FLORIDA
GEORGIA
INERTIA
KEDROVA
OCARINA
OVERSEA
PAPRIKA
PODRIDA
PRORATA
RIORITA
SABRINA
SUBROSA
THERESA
TSARINA
TZARINA

••••RA•

ADMIRAL
ALSORAN
AMSCRAY
ANAGRAM
ANGORAS
APPARAT
APTERAL
ASFARAS
ASHTRAY
AUGURAL
AURORAE
AURORAL
AURORAS
AUSTRAL
BETARAY
BUCKRAM
CAMERAS
CENTRAL
CHLORAL
COCHRAN
CONTRAS
DEBORAH
DIAGRAM
DISHRAG
ENTHRAL
EPIGRAM
FAYWRAY
FEDERAL
FEDORAS
FEMORAL
FLYTRAP
FORERAN
FORTRAN
GENERAL
HEGIRAS
HOFBRAU
HUMERAL
IMMORAL
KINGRAT
LATERAL
LATERAN
LIBERAL
LITERAL
MACGRAW
MALLRAT
MANTRAP
MANTRAS
MAYORAL
MENORAH
MINERAL
MISTRAL
MITHRAS
MUBARAK
MUSKRAT
NATURAL
NEUTRAL
NUMERAL
OUTDRAW
OVERRAN
PACKRAT
PANARAB
PORTRAY
PROGRAM
RATTRAP
REMORAS
RICERAT
SAHARAN
SAMPRAS
SAMURAI
SCLERAS
SEAGRAM
SENORAS
SEVERAL
SIERRAS
SNEERAT
SORORAL
SPORRAN
SWEARAT
TANGRAM
TEATRAY
TEHERAN
TELERAN
TREERAT
TRIGRAM
TUNDRAS
UNSTRAP
VENTRAL
VETERAN
WASHRAG
WOLFRAM

••••R•A

ALBERTA
ALFORJA
ALGERIA
ANDORRA
AQUARIA
ASSYRIA
ASTORIA
AUSTRIA
BAVARIA
BEGORRA
CIBORIA
DELIRIA
EMPORIA
ERITREA
ETRURIA
JAKARTA
LASORDA
LIBERIA
MAJORCA
MAZURKA
MINERVA
MINORCA
NIGERIA
ROBERTA
SAMARIA
SANGRIA
SCHIRRA
SCIORRA
SIBERIA
SOLARIA
TALARIA

•••••RA

ABEXTRA
ABINTRA
ALGEBRA
AMPHORA
ANDORRA
ARAFURA
ARIKARA
BARBARA
BEGORRA
BOKHARA
BRAVURA
CAESURA
CALDERA
CARNERA
CASCARA
CEREBRA
CHIMERA
CULEBRA
DYKSTRA
ELECTRA
ELEKTRA
GUEVARA
HONIARA
INTEGRA
ISADORA
LEMPIRA
LEONORA
MADEIRA
MARMARA
MASCARA
NIAGARA
OLESTRA
OVIPARA
OXYMORA
PANDORA
PHAEDRA
PLECTRA
RIVIERA
SAMSARA
SCHIRRA
SCIORRA
SINATRA
SPECTRA
SUMATRA
TANTARA
TEMPERA
TEMPURA
TESSERA
VAMPIRA
VENTURA
VISCERA
WOOMERA

R•B••••

RABBETS
RABBITS
RABBITT
RABBLES
RABIDLY
REBASTE
REBATED
REBATES
REBECCA
REBEKAH
REBENDS
REBINDS
REBIRTH
REBLOOM
REBOILS
REBOLTS
REBOOTS
REBOUND
REBOZOS
REBUFFS
REBUILD
REBUILT
REBUKED
REBUKES
REBUSES
RIBANDS
RIBBIES
RIBBING
RIBBONS
RIBCAGE
RIBEYES
RIBLESS
RIBLIKE
ROBARDS
ROBBERS
ROBBERY
ROBBING
ROBBINS
ROBERTA
ROBERTO
ROBERTS
ROBESON
ROBLOWE
ROBOCOP
ROBOTIC
ROBROYS
ROBUSTA
RUBATOS
RUBBERS
RUBBERY
RUBBING
RUBBISH
RUBBLES
RUBDOWN
RUBICON
RUBITIN
RUBRICS
RUBSOFF
RUBSOUT

R••B•••

RABBETS
RABBITS
RABBITT
RABBLES
RAGBAGS
RAMBEAU
RAMBLED
RAMBLER
RAMBLES
RATBERT
RAYBURN
REDBIRD
REDBOOK
REDBUDS
REUBENS
RHEBOKS
RHUBARB
RIBBIES
RIBBING
RIBBONS
RIMBAUD
ROBBERS
ROBBERY
ROBBING
ROBBINS
ROEBUCK
ROUBLES
ROWBOAT
RUBBERS
RUBBERY
RUBBING
RUBBISH
RUBBLES
RUMBAED
RUMBLED
RUMBLES
RUNBACK

R•••B••

RAINBOW
RAREBIT
RATABLE
RHOMBUS
RHUMBAS
RISIBLE
RISIBLY
ROADBED
ROLLBAR
ROSEBAY
ROSEBUD

R••••B•

REDOUBT
RESORBS
REVERBS
RIOLOBO

R•••••B

RHUBARB

•RB••••

ARBITER
ARBORED
ARBOURS
ARBUTUS
MRBONES
ORBISON
ORBITAL
ORBITED
ORBITER
ORBLESS
ORBLIKE
URBANER

•R•B•••

ARABIAN
ARMBAND
BRIBERY
BRIBING
BRUBECK
CRABBED
CRABBER
CRIBBED
CRYBABY
DRABBER
DRIBBLE
DRIBLET
DRUBBED
GRABBAG
GRABBED
GRABBER
GRABSAT
GRUBBED
PREBEND
PROBATE
PROBERS
PROBING
PROBITY
PROBLEM
PROBONO
TRABERT
TREBLED
TREBLES
TRIBUNE
TRIBUTE

•R••B••

ARROBAS
BRAMBLE
BRAMBLY
CRABBED
CRABBER
CRIBBED
CROWBAR
CRUMBLE
CRUMBLY
DRABBER
DRAWBAR
DRIBBLE
DRUBBED
FREEBEE
FREEBIE
FRIABLE
FRISBEE
GRABBAG
GRABBED
GRABBER
GRUBBED
GRUMBLE
GRUMBLY
TREMBLE
TREMBLY
TROUBLE

•R•••B•

ARECIBO
CRYBABY
DROPSBY
PREFABS

•R••••B

PROVERB

••RB•••

AIRBAGS
AIRBALL
AIRBASE
AIRBOAT
BARBARA
BARBARY
BARBELL
BARBELS
BARBERS
BARBING
BARBUDA
BERBERS
BURBANK
BURBLED
BURBLES
BURBOTS
CARBIDE
CARBINE
CARBONS
CARBOYS
CORBELS
CORBETT
CURBCUT
CURBING
DARBIES
DERBIES
FORBADE
FORBEAR
FORBIDS
FORBORE
FURBALL
FURBISH
GARBAGE
GARBING
GARBLED
GARBLES
GERBILS
HARBORS
HARBOUR
HARBURG
HERBAGE
HERBALS
HERBERT
HERBIER
HERBTEA
JERBOAS
MARBLED
MARBLES
NORBERT
PARBOIL
SERBIAN
SORBATE
SORBETS
TARBABY
TARBELL
TERBIUM
TURBANS
TURBINE
TURBITS
TURBOTS
VERBALS
VERBENA
VERBOSE
WARBLED
WARBLER
WARBLES

••R•B••

ACROBAT
AEROBAT
AEROBES
AEROBIC
ARROBAS
CARABAO
CARIBES
CARIBOU
CEREBRA
DURABLE
DURABLY
ENROBED
ENROBES
FERNBAR
FIREBOX
FIREBUG
HIRABLE
MARABOU
PARABLE
RAREBIT
SCRIBES
SCRUBBY
SCRUBUP
SHRUBBY
STROBES
UNROBED
UNROBES
VIRIBUS
ZAREBAS

••R••B•

BARNABY
BARTABS
CARAMBA
CORDOBA
EARLOBE
HORNSBY
MARIMBA
MORESBY
SCRUBBY
SHRUBBY
TARBABY

••R•••B

CORNCOB
PERTURB

•••RB••

ACERBIC
BOURBON
EXURBAN
EXURBIA
GEARBOX
INORBIT
OVERBIG
OVERBUY
POORBOX
POORBOY
SHERBET
THURBER

•••R•B•

ASCRIBE
CHERUBS
DISROBE
LAPROBE
MICROBE
MIDRIBS
NAIROBI
SCARABS
SWOREBY
THEREBY
WHEREBY

•••R••B

BEARCUB
OVERDUB

••••RB•

ABSORBS
ADSORBS
ADVERBS
RESORBS
REVERBS
SUBURBS
SWEARBY

••••R•B

BACKRUB
PANARAB

•••••RB

DISTURB
PERTURB
POTHERB
PROVERB
RHUBARB

R•C••••

RACCOON
RACECAR
RACEMES
RACEWAY
RACIEST
RACKETS
RACKING
RACKSUP
RACQUET
RECALLS
RECANED
RECANES
RECANTS
RECASTS
RECEDED
RECEDES
RECEIPT
RECEIVE
RECENCY
RECHALK
RECHECK
RECHOSE
RECIPES
RECITAL
RECITED
RECITER
RECITES
RECKONS
RECLAIM
RECLAME
RECLEAN
RECLINE
RECLUSE
RECOATS
RECODED
RECODES
RECOILS
RECOLOR
RECORDS
RECORKS
RECOUNT
RECOUPS
RECOVER
RECROOM
RECROSS
RECRUIT
RECTIFY
RECTORS
RECTORY
RECUSED
RECUSES
RECYCLE
RICARDO
RICERAT
RICHARD
RICHEST
RICHMAN
RICHTER
RICKETY
RICKEYS
RICKLES
RICKMAN
RICKSHA
RICOTTA
ROCHETS
ROCKERS
ROCKERY
ROCKETS
ROCKIER
ROCKIES
ROCKING
ROCKYII
ROCKYIV
RUCHING
RUCKING
RUCTION

R••C•••

RACCOON
RANCHED
RANCHER
RANCHES
RANCHOS
RANCOUR
RASCALS
RATCHET
RAUCOUS
REACHED
REACHES
REACTED
REACTOR
REACTTO
REDCAPS
REDCELL
REDCENT
REDCOAT
REOCCUR
RESCALE
RESCIND
RESCUED
RESCUER
RESCUES
REXCATS
RIBCAGE
RIPCORD
ROACHED
ROACHES

R•••C••

RACECAR
RADICAL
RADICES
RADICLE
REBECCA
RECYCLE
REDACTS
REDUCED
REDUCER
REDUCES
REFACED
REFACES
REFOCUS
REJECTS
RELACED
RELACES
RELICTS
RELOCKS
RELUCTS
REOCCUR
RESECTS
RETICLE
ROBOCOP
RUBICON

R••••C•

RANSACK
RATPACK
RATRACE
REBECCA
RECENCY
RECHECK
REELECT
REENACT
REFLECT
REFRACT
REGENCY
REJOICE
REPLACE
REPLICA
REPRICE
RESPECT
RESTOCK
RETEACH
RETOUCH
RETRACE
RETRACK
RETRACT
REVOICE
RIDDICK
RIOTACT
ROEBUCK
ROLLICK
ROMANCE
RUBRICS
RUNBACK
RUSTICS

R•••••C

RAYKROC
RAYOVAC
ROBOTIC

•RC••••

ARCADES
ARCADIA
ARCANUM
ARCHAIC
ARCHERS
ARCHERY
ARCHING
ARCHIVE
ARCHONS
ARCHWAY
ARCLAMP
ARCSINE
MRCHIPS
MRCLEAN
ORCHARD
ORCHIDS
URCHINS

•R•C•••

ARACHNE
ARECIBO
BRACERO
BRACERS
BRACEUP
BRACING
BRACKEN
BRACKET
BRICKED
BROCADE
CRACKED
CRACKER
CRACKLE
CRACKLY
CRACKUP
CRECHES
CRICKED
CRICKET
CROCHET
CRUCIAL
CRUCIFY
DRACHMA
DRACHMS
DRACULA
DRUCKER
DRYCELL
ERECTED
ERECTER
ERECTLY
ERECTOR
ERICSON
ERUCTED
FRACTAL
FRECKLE
FRECKLY
FRICKIE
FROCKED
FRYCOOK
GRACIAS
GRACILE
GRACING
GRACKLE
GRECIAN
GROCERS
GROCERY
IRECKON
ORACLES
PRECAST
PRECEDE
PRECEPT
PRECISE
PRECOOK
PRECOOL
PRICERS
PRICIER
PRICING
PRICKED
PRICKLE
PRICKLY
PROCEED
PROCESS
PROCTOR
PROCURE
PROCYON
TRACERS
TRACERY
TRACHEA
TRACING
TRACKED
TRACKER
TRACTOR
TRICEPS
TRICKED
TRICKER
TRICKLE
TRICORN
TRICOTS
TROCARS
TROCHEE
TROCHES
TRUCIAL
TRUCKED
TRUCKEE
TRUCKER
TRUCKLE
WRACKED
WRECKED
WRECKER

•R••C••

ARNICAS
ARTICLE
BRIOCHE
BRONCHI
BRONCOS
CREWCUT
CRUNCHY
FRANCES
FRANCIS
FRESCOS
GROUCHO
GROUCHY
PRANCED
PRANCER
PRANCES
PREACHY
PRINCES
TRAMCAR
TRANCES
TREACLE
TREACLY

•R•••C•

ARDENCY
ARMLOCK
ARTDECO
BRUBECK
CREVICE
CRITICS
DRSPOCK
DRYDOCK
EROTICA
ERRANCY
FROLICS
GRIMACE
MRSPOCK
ORIFICE
ORINOCO
PREDICT
PREFACE
PREFECT
PRIMACY
PRIVACY
PRODUCE
PRODUCT
PROJECT
PROTECT
TRADUCE
TRISECT
TROPICS
TROUNCE
TRUANCY
URGENCY

•R••••C

ARAMAIC
ARCHAIC
ARSENIC
CRYPTIC
DRASTIC
ERISTIC
ERRATIC
FRANTIC
FREDRIC
GRAPHIC

ORGANIC
PROSAIC
TRAFFIC
TROPHIC

••RC•••

AIRCOOL
AIRCREW
BARCARS
BARCODE
BIRCHED
BIRCHES
CARCASE
CARCASS
CARCOAT
CIRCLED
CIRCLES
CIRCLET
CIRCUIT
CIRCUSY
FARCING
FORCEPS
FORCERS
FORCING
GARCONS
HERCULE
KERCHOO
LARCENY
LARCHES
LURCHED
LURCHES
MARCATO
MARCEAU
MARCELS
MARCHED
MARCHER
MARCHES
MARCHON
MARCONI
MERCERS
MERCERY
MERCIES
MERCURY
PARCELS
PARCHED
PARCHES
PERCALE
PERCENT
PERCHED
PERCHES
PORCHES
PORCINE
PURCELL
SARCASM
SORCERY
SURCOAT
TERCELS
TERCETS
TORCHED
TORCHES
ZIRCONS

••R•C••

AFRICAN
APRICOT
AURICLE
AUROCHS
BORACIC
BORSCHT
CARACAL
CARACAS
CORNCOB
CURACAO
CURBCUT
DIRECTS
EARACHE
HARICOT
HYRACES
JERICHO
KARACHI
LORICAE
LYRICAL
MARACAS
MIRACLE
MOROCCO
PORSCHE
SARACEN
SIROCCO
SPRUCED
SPRUCER
SPRUCES
UTRECHT

••R••C•

AIRLOCK
AIRSACS
AIRSOCK
BARRACK
BERNICE
BURDOCK
CARIOCA
CARRICK
CORNICE
CORRECT
CORSICA
DERRICK
DORMICE
DURANCE
EARLOCK
EHRLICH
ERRANCY
FORMICA
FURNACE
GARRICK
HEROICS
MOROCCO
MURDOCH
NORDICS
NORELCO
OARLOCK
PARSECS
PERFECT
PORTICO
SCRATCH
SCREECH
SCRUNCH
SERPICO
SERVICE
SIROCCO
STRETCH
SURFACE
TARMACS
TERENCE
TERRACE
VERDICT
WARLOCK
WARWICK

••R•••C

ACRYLIC
AEROBIC
BORACIC
CARDIAC
CERAMIC
CHRONIC
ERRATIC
HERETIC
JURIDIC
KEROUAC
PHRENIC
PIRATIC
PYRRHIC
SARANAC

•••RC••

ALARCON
AMERCED
AMERCES
ANARCHY
APERCUS
BEARCAT
BEARCUB
COERCED
COERCER
COERCES
EPARCHS
EPARCHY
EXARCHS
FIERCER
HAIRCUT
PIERCED
PIERCES
SCARCER
SOURCED
SOURCES
STARCHY

•••R•C•

AGARICS
ALDRICH
AMERICA
ATTRACT
AVARICE
BARRACK
BEDROCK
CAPRICE
CARRICK
CHIRICO
CLARICE
CLERICS
CORRECT
DEFROCK
DERRICK
DETRACT
ELGRECO
EMBRACE
EXTRACT
FABRICS
GARRICK
HATRACK
HAYRACK
KUBRICK
MAURICE
METRICS
ONTRACK
OSTRICH
OUTRACE
OVERACT
PATRICE
PATRICK
PETROCK
RATRACE
REFRACT
REPRICE
RETRACE
RETRACK
RETRACT
RUBRICS
SECRECY
SKIRACK
TENRECS
TERRACE
TIERACK
TOURACO
UNFROCK

•••R••C

ACERBIC
HEBRAIC
PYRRHIC

••••RC•

BYFORCE
DIVORCE
ENFORCE
INFORCE
LAMARCK
MAJORCA
MINORCA
MONARCH

••••R•C

AELFRIC
AMHARIC
BALDRIC
CALORIC
CAMBRIC
CENTRIC
FREDRIC
GASTRIC
GENERIC
HOMERIC
LAUTREC
MANTRIC
NUMERIC
RAYKROC
SATIRIC

RD•••••

RDLAING

R•D••••

RADDLED
RADDLES
RADIALS
RADIANS
RADIANT
RADIATE
RADICAL
RADICES
RADICLE
RADIOED
RADIXES
RADOMES
RADULAE
REDACTS
REDALGA
REDANTS
REDATED
REDATES
REDBIRD
REDBOOK
REDBUDS
REDCAPS
REDCELL
REDCENT
REDCOAT
REDDEER
REDDENS
REDDEST
REDDING
REDDISH
REDDOGS
REDEALS
REDEALT
REDEEMS
REDEYED
REDEYES
REDFINS
REDFIRS
REDFLAG
REDFORD
REDGUMS
REDHAIR
REDHATS
REDHEAD
REDHEAT
REDHOTS
REDIALS
REDLINE
REDMEAT
REDNESS
REDOAKS
REDOING
REDOUBT
REDOUND
REDPINE
REDPOLL
REDRAWN
REDRAWS
REDRESS
REDROSE
REDSPOT
REDSTAR
REDTAPE
REDTOPS
REDUCED
REDUCER
REDUCES
REDWINE
REDWING
REDWOLF
REDWOOD
RIDDICK
RIDDING
RIDDLED
RIDDLER
RIDDLES
RIDEOFF
RIDEOUT
RIDGIER
RIDGING
RIDGWAY
RIDOTTO
RODDING
RODENTS
RODEOFF
RODEOUT
RODGERS
RODLESS
RODLIKE
RODOLFO
RUDDERS
RUDDIER
RUDDILY
RUDOLPH
RUDYARD

R••D•••

RADDLED
RADDLES
RAGDOLL
RAIDERS
RAIDING
RANDALL
RANDIER
RANDOWN
RAWDATA
RAWDEAL
READERS
READIED
READIER
READIES
READILY
READING
READMIT
READOUT
READSIN
REDDEER
REDDENS
REDDEST
REDDING
REDDISH
REDDOGS
REEDIER
REEDING
REEDITS
RENDERS
RENDING
RHODIUM
RIDDICK
RIDDING
RIDDLED
RIDDLER
RIDDLES
ROADBED
ROADHOG
ROADIES
ROADMAP
ROADWAY
RODDING
ROEDEER
RONDEAU
RONDELS
ROWDIER
ROWDIES
ROWDILY
RUBDOWN
RUDDERS
RUDDIER
RUDDILY
RUNDEEP
RUNDLES
RUNDOWN

R•••D••

RABIDLY
RAKEDIN
RAKEDUP
RAMADAN
RAMADAS
RAPIDER
RAPIDLY
RECEDED
RECEDES
RECODED
RECODES
REMODEL
REMUDAS
REORDER
REREDOS
RESIDED
RESIDES
RESIDUE
RIGIDLY
ROLODEX
ROPEDIN
ROUNDED
ROUNDER
ROUNDLY
ROUNDON
ROUNDUP
RUANDAN
RUNSDRY
RUSHDIE
RWANDAN

R••••D•

RAGGEDY
RAMRODS
RAWHIDE
REBENDS
REBINDS
RECORDS
REDBUDS
REFUNDS
REGARDS
REGRADE
RELOADS
REMANDS
REMENDS
REMINDS
REMOLDS
RENARDS
REREADS
RESANDS
RESEEDS
RESENDS
RETARDS
RETRADE
REWARDS
REWELDS
REWINDS
REWORDS
RIBANDS
RICARDO
RIGVEDA
RIPTIDE
ROBARDS
ROLAIDS
ROTUNDA
ROULADE

R•••••D

RADDLED
RADIOED
RAFFLED
RAGWEED
RALLIED
RAMBLED
RANCHED
RANKLED
RASSLED
RATTLED
RAVAGED
RAVELED
RAVENED
RAYMOND
RAZORED
REACHED
REACTED
READIED
REAIMED
REAIRED
REAREND
REARMED
REBATED
REBOUND
REBUILD
REBUKED
RECANED
RECEDED
RECITED
RECODED
RECUSED
REDATED
REDBIRD
REDEYED
REDFORD
REDHEAD
REDOUND
REDUCED
REDWOOD
REFACED
REFILED
REFINED
REFRIED
REFUSED
REFUTED
REGALED
REGLUED
REHEARD
REHIRED
REIFIED
REIGNED
REINKED
REKEYED
RELACED
RELATED
RELAXED
RELAYED
RELINED
RELIVED
RELUMED
REMIXED
REMOVED
REMOWED
RENAMED
RENEGED
RENEWED
RENOTED
REOILED
REPAVED
REPINED
REPLIED
REPOSED
REPUTED
RERATED
RESAWED
RESCIND
RESCUED
RESIDED
RESILED
RESOLED
RESOUND
RESPOND
RESUMED
RETAPED
RETAXED
RETILED
RETIMED
RETIRED
RETOWED
RETREAD
RETRIED
RETUNED
RETYPED
REUPPED
REVELED
REVERED
REVILED
REVISED
REVIVED
REVOKED
REWAXED
REWIRED
REWOUND
REYNARD
REZONED
RICHARD
RIDDLED
RIFFLED
RIGHTED
RIMBAUD
RIMPLED
RIPCORD
RIPENED
RIPPLED
RIVALED
RIVETED
ROACHED
ROADBED
ROASTED
ROOSTED
ROSEBUD
ROSERED
ROSTAND
ROTATED
ROUGHED
ROUNDED
ROUSTED
RUDYARD
RUFFLED
RUMBAED
RUMBLED
RUMORED
RUMPLED
RUSTLED

•RD••••

ARDENCY
ARDMORE
ARDOURS
ARDUOUS
MRDEEDS
ORDAINS
ORDEALS
ORDERED
ORDERER
ORDERLY
ORDINAL
ORDINES

•R•D•••

ARIDEST
ARIDITY
ARTDECO
BRADLEE
BRADLEY
BRIDALS
BRIDGED
BRIDGES
BRIDGET
BRIDLED
BRIDLES
CRADLED
CRADLES
CREDITS
CRUDELY
CRUDEST
CRUDITY
DREDGED
DREDGER
DREDGES
DRUDGED
DRUDGES
DRYDOCK
ERODENT
ERODING
ERUDITE
FREDDIE
FREDRIC
FRIDAYS
FRIDGES
GRADERS
GRADING
GRADUAL
GRIDDED
GRIDDER
GRIDDLE
GRODIER
GRUDGED
GRUDGES
IRIDIUM
PREDATE
PREDAWN
PREDICT
PRIDING
PRODDED
PRODDER
PRODIGY
PRODUCE
PRODUCT
PRUDENT
PRUDERY
PRUDHOE
PRUDISH
TRADEIN
TRADEON
TRADERS
TRADEUP
TRADING
TRADUCE
TRIDENT
TRODDEN
TRUDEAU
TRUDGED
TRUDGER
TRUDGES

•R••D••

ARCADES
ARCADIA
ARIADNE
ARLEDGE
ARMADAS
BRAIDED
BRAIDER
BRANDED
BRANDER
BRANDON
BREADED
BREADTH
BREEDER
BRENDAN
BRINDLE
BROADAX
BROADEN
BROADER
BROADLY
BROODED
BROODER
CRAWDAD
CROWDED
DREADED
DREIDEL
DRESDEN
DRIEDUP
DRIPDRY
FREDDIE
FREEDOM
FRIEDAN
GRANDAM
GRANDEE
GRANDER
GRANDLY
GRANDMA
GRANDPA
GRENDEL
GRIDDED
GRIDDER
GRIDDLE
GRINDER
PRODDED
PRODDER
PROUDER
PROUDLY
TREADED
TREADER
TREADLE
TRENDED
TRIEDON
TRIODES
TRODDEN
TRUNDLE

•R•••D•

BRAVADO
BRIARDS
BRIGADE
BROCADE
BROMIDE
CRUSADE
CRUSADO
CRUZADO
ERRANDS
FRIENDS
GRANADA
GRENADA
GRENADE
GROUNDS
MRDEEDS
ORCHIDS
ORGANDY
ORLANDO
ORMANDY
PRECEDE
PRELUDE
PREMEDS
PRESIDE
PROSODY
PROVIDE
TRAGEDY
TRIPODS

•R••••D

ARBORED
ARMBAND
ARMLOAD
ARMORED
AROUSED
ARRAYED
ARRIVED
BRAGGED
BRAIDED
BRAINED
BRAISED
BRANDED
BRAWLED
BREADED
BREEZED
BRICKED
BRIDGED
BRIDLED
BRIEFED
BRIGAND
BRIMMED
BROILED
BRONZED
BROODED
BROOKED
BROWNED
BROWSED
BRUISED
BRUITED
BRUSHED
CRABBED
CRACKED
CRADLED
CRAFTED
CRAMMED
CRAMPED
CRANKED
CRASHED
CRAWDAD
CRAWLED
CREAKED
CREAMED
CREASED
CREATED
CREEPED
CRESTED
CRIBBED
CRICKED
CRIMPED
CRINGED
CRINOID
CRISPED
CROAKED
CROOKED
CROONED
CROPPED
CROSSED
CROWDED
CROWNED
CRUISED
CRUSHED
CRUSTED
DRAFTED
DRAGGED
DRAINED
DRATTED
DRAWLED
DREADED
DREAMED
DREDGED
DRESSED
DRIFTED
DRILLED
DRIPPED
DROOLED
DROOPED
DROPPED
DROWNED
DROWSED
DRUBBED
DRUDGED
DRUGGED
DRUMMED
DRYEYED
ERECTED
ERUCTED
ERUPTED
FRANKED
FREAKED
FRETTED
FRILLED
FRINGED
FRISKED
FRITTED
FRIZZED
FROCKED
FRONTED
FROSTED
FROTHED
FROWARD
FROWNED
FRUITED
GRABBED
GRAFTED
GRAINED
GRANTED
GRAPHED
GRASPED
GRASSED
GREASED
GREENED
GREETED
GRIDDED
GRIEVED
GRILLED
GRINNED
GRIPPED
GRITTED
GROANED
GROOMED
GROOVED
GROSSED
GROUPED
GROUSED
GROUTED
GROWLED
GRUBBED
GRUDGED
GRUMPED
GRUNTED
IRELAND
ORBITED
ORCHARD
ORDERED
OROTUND
PRAISED
PRANCED
PRANGED
PRANKED
PREBEND
PREENED
PRELOAD
PREPAID
PRESSED
PRETEND
PRICKED
PRIMPED
PRINKED
PRINTED
PROCEED
PRODDED
PROGGED
PRONGED
PROOFED
PROPPED
PROWLED
TRACKED
TRAILED
TRAINED
TRAMPED
TRAPPED
TRASHED
TRAWLED
TREADED
TREATED
TREBLED
TREKKED
TRENDED
TRICKED
TRIFLED
TRIGGED
TRILLED
TRIMMED
TRIPLED
TRIPPED
TROLLED
TROOPED
TROTHED
TROTTED
TRUCKED
TRUDGED
TRUMPED
TRUSSED
TRUSTED
TRYSTED
WRACKED
WRAPPED
WREAKED
WRECKED
WRESTED
WRITHED
WRONGED

••RD•••

AIRDAMS
AIRDATE
AIRDROP
BARDISH
BIRDDOG
BIRDERS
BIRDIED
BIRDIES
BIRDING
BIRDMAN
BIRDMEN
BORDERS
BURDENS
BURDOCK
CARDERS
CARDIAC
CARDING
CARDOZO
CORDAGE
CORDATE
CORDELL
CORDERO
CORDIAL
CORDING
CORDITE
CORDOBA
CORDONS
CURDIER
CURDING
CURDLED
CURDLES
EARDROP
EARDRUM
FORDHAM
FORDING
GARDENS
GARDNER
GIRDERS
GIRDING
GIRDLED
GIRDLES
GORDIAN
HARDENS
HARDEST
HARDHAT
HARDHIT
HARDIER
HARDILY
HARDING
HARDPAN
HARDPUT
HARDSET
HARDTOP
HARDWON
HERDERS
HERDING

HURDLED
HURDLER
HURDLES
KURDISH
LARDERS
LARDIER
LARDING
LARDNER
LARDONS
LORDING
LORDJIM
MORDANT
MORDENT
MORDRED
MURDERS
MURDOCH
NERDIER
NORDICS
PARDNER
PARDONS
PERDIEM
PURDAHS
SARDINE
SORDINI
SORDINO
TARDIER
TARDILY
VERDANT
VERDICT
VERDOUX
VERDUGO
VERDURE
WARDENS
WARDERS
WARDING
WARDOFF
WORDIER
WORDILY
WORDING
WORDONE
YARDAGE
YARDARM
YARDMAN
YARDMEN

••R•D••

ABRADED
ABRADER
ABRADES
ABRIDGE
ACRIDLY
AMRADIO
BERIDOF
BIRDDOG
BOREDOM
BORODIN
CBRADIO
CCRIDER
CORNDOG
DERIDED
DERIDES
DIRNDLS
EARLDOM
FARADAY
FIREDOG
FIREDUP
FMRADIO
JURIDIC
LURIDLY
MIRADOR
PARADED
PARADES
PARADOX
PERIDOT
REREDOS
SERFDOM
STRIDER
STRIDES
STRUDEL
TEREDOS
TIRADES
TIREDER
TIREDLY
TIREDOF
WORKDAY
WORLDLY

••R••D•

AIRMADA
ALREADY
BARBUDA
BARCODE
BERMUDA
BYROADS
CARBIDE
CERVIDS
CORRIDA
CORRODE
ERRANDS
FORBADE
FORBIDS
GERALDO
GERUNDS
GIRONDE
HERALDS
INROADS
MARAUDS
MIRANDA
MYRIADS
NEREIDS
PARKADE
PERFIDY
PERIODS
PERVADE
REREADS
SCREEDS
SHROUDS
SPREADS
STRANDS
THREADS
THREADY
TORNADO
TOROIDS
TORPEDO
UNREADY
VERANDA
WARGODS

••R•••D

ABRADED
AERATED
AGROUND
AIRHEAD
AIRRAID
APRONED
ARRAYED
ARRIVED
BARMAID
BARNARD
BARTEND
BERATED
BERNARD
BERRIED
BERTHED
BIRCHED
BIRDIED
BIRTHED
BURBLED
BURGLED
CARLOAD
CAROLED
CAROMED
CAROTID
CARRIED
CIRCLED
CORNFED
CURDLED
CURRIED
DERIDED
DERIVED
DIRTIED
ENRAGED
ENROBED
FERRIED
FORAGED
FORFEND
FORGOOD
FORWARD
GARAGED
GARBLED
GARGLED
GARLAND
GIRDLED
GOROUND
GURGLED
GYRATED
HARRIED
HARVARD
HURDLED
HURRIED
HURTLED
LURCHED
MARBLED
MARCHED
MARRIED
MERITED
MERMAID
MORDRED
MORPHED
NORMAND
PARADED
PARCHED
PAROLED
PARRIED
PARTIED
PERCHED
PERSEID
PERUSED
PHRASED
PIRATED
PORTEND
PURFLED
PURPLED
PURSUED
PYRAMID
RERATED
SCRAPED
SCREWED
SERRIED
SORTIED
SPRAYED
SPRUCED
STRAFED
STRAYED
STREWED
STRIPED
STRIVED
STROKED
TARRIED
THRIVED
TORCHED
TURTLED
UNRATED
UNROBED
WARBLED
WARLORD
WORRIED
WORSTED

•••RD••

AWARDED
AWARDEE
AWARDER
BEARDED
BOARDED
BOARDER
CZARDAS
CZARDOM
DOORDIE
GEORDIE
GOURDES
GUARDED
GUARDEE
HAIRDOS
HAIRDYE
HEARDOF
HOARDED
HOARDER
JOURDAN
LOURDES
ONORDER
OVERDID
OVERDUB
OVERDUE
REORDER
STARDOM
THIRDLY
TOORDER
WEIRDER
WEIRDLY
WEIRDOS

•••R•D•

ACARIDS
ALFREDO
ASTRIDE
CHARADE
COMRADE
CORRIDA
CORRODE
DEGRADE
ESTRADA
EXTRUDE
FLORIDA
FLYRODS
HAYRIDE
HOTRODS
HYBRIDS
INTRUDE
JOYRIDE
NIMRODS
NITRIDE
OBTRUDE
PODRIDA
RAMRODS
REGRADE
RETRADE
TETRADS
TIERODS
UPGRADE
USERIDS

•••R••D

ABORTED
ACCRUED
ADORNED
AIRRAID
ALARMED
ALERTED
AMERCED
AMERIND
ANDROID
ANEROID
ANYROAD
AVERRED
AVERTED
AWARDED
AYKROYD
AYNRAND
BEARDED
BERRIED
BLURRED
BLURTED
BOARDED
CARRIED
CHARGED
CHARMED
CHARRED
CHARTED
CHIRPED
CHURNED
CLERKED
COERCED
CONRIED
COURSED
COURTED
CURRIED
DECREED
DECRIED
DEFRAUD
DWARFED
EMERALD
EMERGED
EMERSED
EVERTED
EXERTED
FERRIED
FLIRTED
GLORIED
GNARLED
GNARRED
GUARDED
HARRIED
HEARTED
HOARDED
HURRIED
IMBRUED
INBREED
KNURLED
LEARNED
LEGRAND
LIPREAD
LOWROAD
MARRIED
MISREAD
MOURNED
OFFROAD
OPERAND
OVERDID
PARRIED
PEARLED
PIERCED
QUERIED
REAREND
REARMED
REFRIED
RETREAD
RETRIED
SCARFED
SCARPED
SCARRED
SCORNED
SERRIED
SHARPED
SHIRKED
SHIRRED
SHORTED
SKIRLED
SKIRRED
SKIRTED
SLURPED
SLURRED
SMARTED
SMIRKED
SNARLED
SNORTED
SOURCED
SPARGED
SPARKED
SPARRED
SPORTED
SPURNED
SPURRED
SPURTED
STARRED
STARTED
STARVED
STEROID
STIRRED
STORIED
STORMED
SWARMED
SWERVED
SWIRLED
TARRIED
TWIRLED
UNARMED
UNTRIED
UPBRAID
USURPED
WEARIED
WHARFED
WHIRLED
WHIRRED
WHORLED
WORRIED
YEAREND
YEARNED

••••RD•

ACCORDS
AFFORDS
BACARDI
BOIARDO
BRIARDS
BYWORDS
CANARDS
COWARDS
DOTARDS
EDWARDS
ENGARDE
ENGIRDS
HAZARDS
HOWARDS
IDCARDS
INNARDS
INWARDS
IZZARDS
LASORDA
LIZARDS
MILORDS
ONWARDS
OXFORDS
PETARDS
PICARDY
RECORDS
REGARDS
RENARDS
RETARDS
REWARDS
REWORDS
RICARDO
ROBARDS
TABARDS
TOWARDS
UNDERDO
UNGIRDS
UPWARDS
WIZARDS

••••R•D

ABJURED
ADHERED
ADJURED
ADMIRED
ALLURED
ALTERED
ANGERED
ARBORED
ARMORED
ASPIRED
ASSURED
ATTIRED
AUGURED
AVERRED
BEMIRED
BLEARED
BLURRED
BOWERED
CAPERED
CATERED
CEDARED
CENTRED
CHAIRED
CHARRED
CHEERED
CLEARED
COHERED
COLORED
COVERED
COWERED
DESIRED
DOWERED
ENDURED
ENSURED
ENTERED
EUCHRED
EXPIRED
FAVORED
FIGURED
FLOORED
FLOURED
FUELROD
GLAIRED
GNARRED
HAVERED
HOMERED
HONORED
HOVERED
HUMORED
HUNDRED
IGNORED
ILLBRED
IMMURED
INHERED
INJURED
INSURED
KINDRED
LABORED
LAYERED
LEVERED
LOUVRED
LOWBRED
LOWERED
LUSTRED
MAITRED
MAJORED
MANFRED
MATURED
METERED
MILDRED
MINORED
MITERED
MORDRED
MOTORED
NATURED
OFFERED
ORDERED
OSIERED
PAPERED
PETERED
POWERED
QUEERED
RAZORED
REAIRED
REHIRED
RETIRED
REVERED
REWIRED
ROSERED
RUMORED
SAVORED
SCARRED
SCOURED
SECURED
SEESRED
SEVERED
SHEARED
SHEERED
SHIRRED
SKIRRED
SLURRED
SMEARED
SNEERED
SOBERED
SPARRED
SPEARED
SPURRED
SQUARED
SQUIRED
STARRED
STEERED
STIRRED
SUGARED
SUTURED
TAPERED
TENURED
TOWERED
TUTORED
UMPIRED
UNAIRED
USHERED
UTTERED
WAGERED
WATERED
WAVERED
WHIRRED
WILFRID
WINERED

•••••RD

ABELARD
ASHFORD
AWKWARD
BALLARD
BARNARD
BERNARD
BIGBIRD
BOMBARD
BUSTARD
BUZZARD
CATBIRD
COLLARD
CONCORD
COWBIRD
COWHERD
CUECARD
CUSTARD
DASTARD
DIEHARD
DILLARD
DISCARD
DISCORD
DULLARD
EDOUARD
FORWARD
FOULARD
FROWARD
GIFFORD
GIZZARD
GODDARD
HAGGARD
HALYARD
HARVARD
HAYWARD
HUBBARD
INAWORD
INBOARD
JAYBIRD
KEYCARD
KEYWORD
LAGGARD
LANFORD
LANYARD
LAWFORD
LEEWARD
LEONARD
LEOPARD
LEOTARD
LOLLARD
LOMBARD
MALLARD
MANSARD
MAYNARD
MILLARD
MISWORD
MITFORD
MUMFORD
MUSTARD
NIGGARD
ONBOARD
ONGUARD
ORCHARD
OUTWARD
PACKARD
PEPPARD
PICCARD
PLACARD
PONIARD
REDBIRD
REDFORD
REHEARD
REYNARD
RICHARD
RIPCORD
RUDYARD
SANFORD
SEABIRD
SEAWARD
SHEPARD
SKYWARD
STEWARD
TANKARD
UNHEARD
WARLORD
WAYWARD
WILFORD
WILLARD
WOODARD

RE•••••

REACHED
REACHES
REACTED
REACTOR
REACTTO
READERS
READIED
READIER
READIES
READILY
READING
READMIT
READOUT
READSIN
REAFFIX
REAGENT
REAIMED
REAIRED
REALISE
REALISM
REALIST
REALITY
REALIZE
REALTOR
REAMASS
REAMERS
REAMING
REAPERS
REAPING
REAREND
REARERS
REARGUE
REARING
REARMED
REARSUP
REASONS
REAVAIL
REBASTE
REBATED
REBATES
REBECCA
REBEKAH
REBENDS
REBINDS
REBIRTH
REBLOOM
REBOILS
REBOLTS
REBOOTS
REBOUND
REBOZOS
REBUFFS
REBUILD
REBUILT
REBUKED
REBUKES
REBUSES
RECALLS
RECANED
RECANES
RECANTS
RECASTS
RECEDED
RECEDES
RECEIPT
RECEIVE
RECENCY
RECHALK
RECHECK
RECHOSE
RECIPES
RECITAL
RECITED
RECITER
RECITES
RECKONS
RECLAIM
RECLAME
RECLEAN
RECLINE
RECLUSE
RECOATS
RECODED
RECODES
RECOILS
RECOLOR
RECORDS
RECORKS
RECOUNT
RECOUPS
RECOVER
RECROOM
RECROSS
RECRUIT
RECTIFY
RECTORS
RECTORY
RECUSED
RECUSES
RECYCLE
REDACTS
REDALGA
REDANTS
REDATED
REDATES
REDBIRD
REDBOOK
REDBUDS
REDCAPS
REDCELL
REDCENT
REDCOAT
REDDEER
REDDENS
REDDEST
REDDING
REDDISH
REDDOGS
REDEALS
REDEALT
REDEEMS
REDEYED
REDEYES
REDFINS
REDFIRS
REDFLAG
REDFORD
REDGUMS
REDHAIR
REDHATS
REDHEAD
REDHEAT
REDHOTS
REDIALS
REDLINE
REDMEAT
REDNESS
REDOAKS
REDOING
REDOUBT
REDOUND
REDPINE
REDPOLL
REDRAWN
REDRAWS
REDRESS
REDROSE
REDSPOT
REDSTAR
REDTAPE
REDTOPS
REDUCED
REDUCER
REDUCES
REDWINE
REDWING
REDWOLF
REDWOOD
REEDIER
REEDING
REEDITS
REEFERS
REEFING
REEKING
REELECT
REELING
REELOFF
REELSIN
REENACT
REENTER
REENTRY
REFACED
REFACES
REFEREE
REFERTO
REFFING
REFILED
REFILES
REFILLS
REFILMS
REFINED
REFINER
REFINES
REFIRES
REFLAGS
REFLECT
REFOCUS
REFORMS
REFRACT
REFRAIN
REFRAME
REFRESH
REFRIED
REFRIES
REFUELS
REFUGEE
REFUGES
REFUNDS
REFUSAL
REFUSED
REFUSER
REFUSES
REFUTED
REFUTER
REFUTES
REGAINS
REGALED
REGALES
REGALIA
REGALLY
REGARDS
REGATTA
REGENCY
REGENTS
REGIMEN
REGIMES
REGIONS
REGLETS
REGLUED
REGLUES
REGNANT
REGRADE
REGRESS
REGRETS
REGROUP
REGULAR
REGULUS
REHANGS
REHEALS
REHEARD
REHEARS
REHEATS
REHEELS
REHIRED
REHIRES
REHOOKS
REIFIED
REIFIES
REIGNED
REINING
REINKED
REINSIN
REISSUE
REITMAN
REJECTS
REJOICE
REJOINS
REKEYED
RELACED
RELACES
RELAPSE
RELATED
RELATES
RELAXED
RELAXES
RELAYED
RELEARN
RELEASE
RELENTS
RELIANT
RELICTS
RELIEFS
RELIEVE
RELIEVO
RELIGHT
RELINED
RELINES
RELISTS
RELIVED
RELIVES
RELLENO
RELOADS
RELOCKS
RELUCTS
RELUMED
RELUMES
RELYING
REMAILS
REMAINS
REMAKES
REMANDS
REMARKS
REMARRY
REMELTS
REMENDS
REMIGES
REMINDS
REMIXED
REMIXES
REMNANT
REMODEL
REMOLDS
REMORAS
REMORSE
REMOTER
REMOTES
REMOUNT
REMOVAL
REMOVED
REMOVER
REMOVES
REMOWED
REMUDAS
RENAILS
RENAMED
RENAMES
RENARDS
RENAULT
RENDERS
RENDING
RENEGED
RENEGER
RENEGES
RENEGUE
RENEWAL
RENEWED
RENEWER
RENNINS
RENOTED
RENOTES
RENTALS
RENTERS
RENTING
REOCCUR
REOILED
REOPENS
REORDER
REPAINT
REPAIRS
REPAPER
REPASTE
REPASTS
REPAVED
REPAVES
REPEALS
REPEATS
REPENTS
REPINED
REPINES
REPLACE
REPLANS
REPLANT
REPLATE
REPLAYS
REPLETE
REPLICA
REPLIED
REPLIES
REPLOWS
REPOLLS
REPOMAN
REPORTS
REPOSED
REPOSES
REPRESS

REPRICE
REPRINT
REPRISE
REPROOF
REPROVE
REPTILE
REPUGNS
REPULSE
REPUTED
REPUTES
REQUEST
REQUIEM
REQUIRE
REQUITE
RERAISE
RERATED
RERATES
REREADS
REREDOS
RERENTS
RERINSE
REROUTE
RESALES
RESALTS
RESANDS
RESAWED
RESCALE
RESCIND
RESCUED
RESCUER
RESCUES
RESEALS
RESEATS
RESECTS
RESEEDS
RESELLS
RESENDS
RESENTS
RESERVE
RESHIPS
RESHOES
RESHOOT
RESIDED
RESIDES
RESIDUE
RESIGNS
RESILED
RESILES
RESINGS
RESISTS
RESOLED
RESOLES
RESOLVE
RESORBS
RESORTS
RESOUND
RESPECT
RESPINS
RESPIRE
RESPITE
RESPOND
RESTAGE
RESTAIN
RESTAMP
RESTART
RESTATE
RESTERS
RESTFUL
RESTING
RESTIVE
RESTOCK
RESTORE
RESTSUP
RESTYLE
RESULTS
RESUMED
RESUMES
RESURGE
RETAILS
RETAINS
RETAKEN
RETAKES
RETAPED
RETAPES
RETARDS
RETAXED
RETAXES
RETEACH
RETEARS
RETELLS
RETESTS
RETHINK
RETIARY
RETICLE
RETILED
RETILES
RETIMED
RETIMES
RETINAE
RETINAL
RETINAS
RETINUE
RETIRED
RETIREE
RETIRES
RETITLE
RETOOLS
RETORTS
RETOUCH
RETOURS
RETOWED
RETRACE
RETRACK
RETRACT
RETRADE
RETRAIN
RETREAD
RETREAT
RETRIAL
RETRIED
RETRIES
RETRIMS
RETSINA
RETUNED
RETUNES
RETURNS
RETYPED
RETYPES
REUBENS
REUNIFY
REUNION
REUNITE
REUPPED
REUTERS
REUTHER
REVALUE
REVAMPS
REVEALS
REVELED
REVELER
REVELRY
REVENGE
REVENUE
REVERBS
REVERED
REVERES
REVERIE
REVERSE
REVERTS
REVIEWS
REVILED
REVILES
REVISED
REVISER
REVISES
REVISIT
REVIVAL
REVIVED
REVIVES
REVOICE
REVOKED
REVOKES
REVOLTS
REVOLVE
REVVING
REWARDS
REWARMS
REWAXED
REWAXES
REWEAVE
REWELDS
REWINDS
REWIRED
REWIRES
REWORDS
REWORKS
REWOUND
REWOVEN
REWRAPS
REWRITE
REWROTE
REXCATS
REYNARD
REZONED
REZONES

R•E••••

REEDIER
REEDING
REEDITS
REEFERS
REEFING
REEKING
REELECT
REELING
REELOFF
REELSIN
REENACT
REENTER
REENTRY
RHEBOKS
RHENISH
RHENIUM
RHETORS
ROEBUCK
ROEDEER

R••E•••

RACECAR
RACEMES
RACEWAY
RAGEFUL
RAKEDIN
RAKEDUP
RAKEOFF
RAKESIN
RAKESUP
RALEIGH
RAMEKIN
RAMESES
RAREBIT
RAREGAS
RAVELED
RAVENED
RAVENNA
RAVEUPS
RAWEGGS
REBECCA
REBEKAH
REBENDS
RECEDED
RECEDES
RECEIPT
RECEIVE
RECENCY
REDEALS
REDEALT
REDEEMS
REDEYED
REDEYES
REFEREE
REFERTO
REGENCY
REGENTS
REHEALS
REHEARD
REHEARS
REHEATS
REHEELS
REJECTS
REKEYED
RELEARN
RELEASE
RELENTS
REMELTS
REMENDS
RENEGED
RENEGER
RENEGES
RENEGUE
RENEWAL
RENEWED
RENEWER
REPEALS
REPEATS
REPENTS
REREADS
REREDOS
RERENTS
RESEALS
RESEATS
RESECTS
RESEEDS
RESELLS
RESENDS
RESENTS
RESERVE
RETEACH
RETEARS
RETELLS
RETESTS
REVEALS
REVELED
REVELER
REVELRY
REVENGE
REVENUE
REVERBS
REVERED
REVERES
REVERIE
REVERSE
REVERTS
REWEAVE
REWELDS
RIBEYES
RICERAT
RIDEOFF
RIDEOUT
RILESUP
RIPENED
RIVETED
RIVETER
ROBERTA
ROBERTO
ROBERTS
ROBESON
RODENTS
RODEOFF
RODEOUT
ROPEDIN
ROPESIN
ROPETOW
ROSEATE
ROSEBAY
ROSEBUD
ROSELLE
ROSEOIL
ROSERED
ROSETTA
ROSETTE
ROZELLE
RULEOUT
RULESON

R•••E••

RABBETS
RACIEST
RACKETS
RAFTERS
RAGGEDY
RAGWEED
RAIDERS
RAILERS
RAIMENT
RAISERS
RAISEUP
RAMBEAU
RAMJETS
RANGERS
RANKERS
RANKEST
RANTERS
RAPIERS
RAPPELS
RAPPERS
RASHERS
RASHEST
RASPERS
RASTERS
RATBERT
RATTERS
RAWDEAL
RAWNESS
READERS
REAGENT
REAMERS
REAPERS
REAREND
REARERS
RECHECK
RECLEAN
REDCELL
REDCENT
REDDEER
REDDENS
REDDEST
REDEEMS
REDHEAD
REDHEAT
REDMEAT
REDNESS
REDRESS
REEFERS
REELECT
REFLECT
REFRESH
REFUELS
REGLETS
REGRESS
REGRETS
REHEELS
RELIEFS
RELIEVE
RELIEVO
RELLENO
RENDERS
RENTERS
REOPENS
REPLETE
REPRESS
REQUEST
RESEEDS
RESPECT
RESTERS
RETREAD
RETREAT
REUBENS
REUTERS
REVIEWS
RHYMERS
RIBLESS
RICHEST
RICKETY
RICKEYS
RIFLERS
RIFLERY
RIGGERS
RIGVEDA
RILLETS
RIMIEST
RIMLESS
RINGERS
RIOTERS
RIPIENO
RIPPERS
RISKERS
RIVIERA
RIVIERE
ROAMERS
ROARERS
ROBBERS
ROBBERY
ROCHETS
ROCKERS
ROCKERY
ROCKETS
RODGERS
RODLESS
ROEDEER
ROGUERY
ROLLERS
ROMNEYS
ROMPERS
RONDEAU
RONDELS
ROOFERS
ROOKERY
ROOMERS
ROOTERS
ROPIEST
ROSIEST
ROSTERS
ROSWELL
ROTTERS
ROUSERS
ROUTERS
ROZZERS
RUBBERS
RUBBERY
RUDDERS
RUINERS
RUMLESS
RUNDEEP
RUNLETS
RUNNELS
RUNNERS
RUSHEES
RUSHERS
RUSSELL
RUSSETS
RUSSETY
RUTGERS

R••••E•

RABBLES
RACEMES
RACQUET
RADDLED
RADDLES
RADICES
RADIOED
RADIXES
RADOMES
RAFFLED
RAFFLER
RAFFLES
RAGWEED
RAINIER
RALLIED
RALLIER
RALLIES
RAMBLED
RAMBLER
RAMBLES
RAMESES
RANCHED
RANCHER
RANCHES
RANDIER
RANGIER
RANKLED
RANKLES
RANOVER
RAPHAEL
RAPIDER
RAPINES
RASPIER
RASSLED
RASSLES
RATCHET
RATITES
RATTIER
RATTLED
RATTLER
RATTLES
RAVAGED
RAVAGER
RAVAGES
RAVELED
RAVENED
RAVINES
RAZORED
REACHED
REACHES
REACTED
READIED
READIER
READIES
REAIMED
REAIRED
REARMED
REBATED
REBATES
REBUKED
REBUKES
REBUSES
RECANED
RECANES
RECEDED
RECEDES
RECIPES
RECITED
RECITER
RECITES
RECODED
RECODES
RECOVER
RECUSED
RECUSES
REDATED
REDATES
REDDEER
REDEYED
REDEYES
REDUCED
REDUCER
REDUCES
REEDIER
REENTER
REFACED
REFACES
REFEREE
REFILED
REFILES
REFINED
REFINER
REFINES
REFIRES
REFRIED
REFRIES
REFUGEE
REFUGES
REFUSED
REFUSER
REFUSES
REFUTED
REFUTER
REFUTES
REGALED
REGALES
REGIMEN
REGIMES
REGLUED
REGLUES
REHIRED
REHIRES
REIFIED
REIFIES
REIGNED
REINKED
REKEYED
RELACED
RELACES
RELATED
RELATES
RELAXED
RELAXES
RELAYED
RELINED
RELINES
RELIVED
RELIVES
RELUMED
RELUMES
REMAKES
REMIGES
REMIXED
REMIXES
REMODEL
REMOTER
REMOTES
REMOVED
REMOVER
REMOVES
REMOWED
RENAMED
RENAMES
RENEGED
RENEGER
RENEGES
RENEWED
RENEWER
RENOTED
RENOTES
REOILED
REORDER
REPAPER
REPAVED
REPAVES
REPINED
REPINES
REPLIED
REPLIES
REPOSED
REPOSES
REPUTED
REPUTES
REQUIEM
RERATED
RERATES
RESALES
RESAWED
RESCUED
RESCUER
RESCUES
RESHOES
RESIDED
RESIDES
RESILED
RESILES
RESOLED
RESOLES
RESUMED
RESUMES
RETAKEN
RETAKES
RETAPED
RETAPES
RETAXED
RETAXES
RETILED
RETILES
RETIMED
RETIMES
RETIRED
RETIREE
RETIRES
RETOWED
RETRIED
RETRIES
RETUNED
RETUNES
RETYPED
RETYPES
REUPPED
REUTHER
REVELED
REVELER
REVERED
REVERES
REVILED
REVILES
REVISED
REVISER
REVISES
REVIVED
REVIVES
REVOKED
REVOKES
REWAXED
REWAXES
REWIRED
REWIRES
REWOVEN
REZONED
REZONES
RIBBIES
RIBEYES
RICHTER
RICKLES
RIDDLED
RIDDLER
RIDDLES
RIDGIER
RIFFLED
RIFFLES
RIGHTED
RIGHTER
RIMPLED
RIMPLES
RINGLET
RIPENED
RIPPLED
RIPPLES
RISKIER
RITZIER
RIVALED
RIVETED
RIVETER
RIVULET
ROACHED
ROACHES
ROADBED
ROADIES
ROASTED
ROASTER
ROCKIER
ROCKIES
ROEDEER
ROILIER
ROISTER
ROLODEX
RONTGEN
ROOKIER
ROOKIES
ROOMIER
ROOMIES
ROOSTED
ROOSTER
ROOTIER
ROOTLET
ROSERED
ROSSSEA
ROTATED
ROTATES
ROTIFER
ROUBLES
ROUGHED
ROUGHEN
ROUGHER
ROUNDED
ROUNDER
ROUSTED
ROWDIER
ROWDIES
RUBBLES
RUDDIER
RUFFLED
RUFFLES
RUMBAED
RUMBLED
RUMBLES
RUMMIER
RUMORED
RUMPLED
RUMPLES
RUNDEEP
RUNDLES
RUNNIER
RUNOVER
RUNTIER
RUSHEES
RUSHIER
RUSTIER
RUSTLED
RUSTLER
RUSTLES
RUTTIER

R•••••E

RADIATE
RADICLE
RADULAE
RAGTIME
RAMLIKE
RAMPAGE
RANLATE
RAPTURE
RATABLE
RATHOLE
RATLIKE
RATLINE
RATRACE
RAWHIDE
RAYLIKE
REALISE
REALIZE
REARGUE
REBASTE
RECEIVE
RECHOSE
RECLAME
RECLINE
RECLUSE
RECYCLE
REDLINE
REDPINE
REDROSE
REDTAPE
REDWINE
REFEREE
REFRAME
REFUGEE
REGRADE
REISSUE
REJOICE
RELAPSE
RELEASE
RELIEVE
REMORSE
RENEGUE
REPASTE
REPLACE
REPLATE
REPLETE
REPRICE
REPRISE
REPROVE
REPTILE
REPULSE
REQUIRE
REQUITE
RERAISE
RERINSE
REROUTE
RESCALE
RESERVE
RESIDUE
RESOLVE
RESPIRE
RESPITE
RESTAGE
RESTATE
RESTIVE
RESTORE
RESTYLE
RESURGE
RETICLE
RETINAE
RETINUE
RETIREE
RETITLE
RETRACE
RETRADE
REUNITE
REVALUE
REVENGE
REVENUE
REVERIE
REVERSE
REVOICE
REVOLVE
REWEAVE
REWRITE
REWROTE
RHIZOME
RIBCAGE
RIBLIKE
RIPOSTE
RIPTIDE
RISIBLE
RISSOLE
RIVIERE
ROANOKE
ROBLOWE
RODLIKE
ROGAINE
ROMAINE
ROMANCE
ROSALIE
ROSANNE
ROSEATE
ROSELLE
ROSETTE
ROULADE
ROUTINE
ROXANNE
ROYALWE
ROZELLE
RUGLIKE
RUMMAGE
RUMPOLE
RUNHOME
RUNLATE
RUPTURE
RUSHDIE

•RE••••

AREARUG
AREAWAY
ARECIBO
AREOLAE
AREOLAR
AREOLAS
ARETINO
BREADED
BREADTH
BREAKER
BREAKIN
BREAKUP
BREASTS
BREATHE
BREATHS
BREATHY
BREEDER
BREEZED
BREEZES
BRENDAN
BRENNAN
BRENNER
BRERFOX
BRESLIN
BRETONS
BREVETS
BREVITY
BREWERS
BREWERY
BREWING
CREAKED
CREAMED
CREAMER
CREASED
CREASES
CREATED
CREATES
CREATOR
CRECHES
CREDITS
CREEPED
CREEPER
CREEPUP
CREMONA
CRENELS
CREOLES
CREOSOL
CRESSES
CRESTED
CRETANS
CRETINS
CREVICE
CREWCUT
CREWELS
CREWING
CREWMAN
CREWMEN
DREADED
DREAMED
DREAMER
DREAMON
DREAMUP
DREDGED
DREDGER
DREDGES
DREIDEL
DREISER
DRESDEN
DRESSED
DRESSER
DRESSES
DRESSUP
DREWOUT
DREYFUS
ERECTED
ERECTER
ERECTLY
ERECTOR
ERELONG
EREMITE
EREWHON
FREAKED
FRECKLE
FRECKLY
FREDDIE
FREDRIC
FREEBEE
FREEBIE
FREEDOM
FREEING
FREEMAN
FREEMEN
FREESIA
FREEWAY
FREEZER
FREEZES
FREIGHT
FREMONT
FRENEAU
FRESCOS
FRESHEN
FRESHER
FRESHET
FRESHLY
FRETFUL
FRETSAW
FRETTED
GREASED
GREASER
GREASES
GREATER
GREATLY
GREAVES
GRECIAN
GREELEY
GREENED
GREENER
GREETED
GREETER
GREGORY
GREMLIN
GRENADA
GRENADE
GRENDEL
GRETZKY
GREYEST
GREYHEN
GREYING
GREYISH
IRECKON
IRELAND
IRELESS
JREWING
KREMLIN
OREGANO
ORESTES
PREACHY
PREAMPS
PREBEND
PRECAST
PRECEDE
PRECEPT
PRECISE
PRECOOK
PRECOOL
PREDATE
PREDAWN

PREDICT
PREEMIE
PREEMPT
PREENED
PREENER
PREFABS
PREFACE
PREFECT
PREFERS
PREHEAT
PRELATE
PRELIMS
PRELOAD
PRELUDE
PREMEDS
PREMIER
PREMISE
PREMISS
PREMIUM
PRENUPS
PREPAID
PREPARE
PREPAYS
PREPPIE
PREQUEL
PRESAGE
PRESALE
PRESELL
PRESENT
PRESETS
PRESIDE
PRESLEY
PRESOAK
PRESORT
PRESSED
PRESSER
PRESSES
PRESSON
PRESSUP
PRESTON
PRESTOS
PRESUME
PRETAPE
PRETEEN
PRETEND
PRETEST
PRETEXT
PRETZEL
PREVAIL
PREVENT
PREVIEW
PREWASH
PREXIES
PREYSON
TREACLE
TREACLY
TREADED
TREADER
TREADLE
TREASON
TREATED
TREBLED
TREBLES
TREEING
TREERAT
TREETOP
TREFOIL
TREKKED
TREKKER
TREKKIE
TRELLIS
TREMAIN
TREMBLE
TREMBLY
TREMOLO
TREMORS
TRENARY
TRENDED
TRENTON
TREPANS
TRESSES
TRESTLE
TREVINO
WREAKED
WREATHE
WREATHS
WRECKED
WRECKER
WRESTED
WRESTLE

•R•E•••

ARDENCY
ARIETTA
ARLEDGE
ARMENIA
ARPENTS
ARREARS
ARRESTS
ARSENAL
ARSENIC
ARSENIO
ARTEMIS
ARTEMUS
BREEDER
BREEZED
BREEZES
BRIEFED
BRIEFER
BRIEFLY
BRUEGEL
CREEPED
CREEPER
CREEPUP
CROESUS
CRUELER
CRUELLY
CRUELTY
DRIEDUP
DRIESUP
DRSEUSS
DRYEYED
ERNESTO
FREEBEE
FREEBIE
FREEDOM
FREEING
FREEMAN
FREEMEN
FREESIA
FREEWAY
FREEZER
FREEZES
FRIEDAN
FRIENDS
FRIEZES
GREELEY
GREENED
GREENER
GREETED
GREETER
GRIEVED
GRIEVER
GRIEVES
MRDEEDS
ORDEALS
ORDERED
ORDERER
ORDERLY
ORGEATS
ORIENTE
ORIENTS
ORLEANS
ORNETTE
PRAETOR
PREEMIE
PREEMPT
PREENED
PREENER
PRIESTS
TREEING
TREERAT
TREETOP
TRIEDON
TRIESON
TRIESTE
TRUEING
URGENCY
URTEXTS

•R••E••

ARAMEAN
ARCHERS
ARCHERY
ARGUERS
ARIDEST
ARMLESS
ARMLETS
ARMREST
ARRIERE
ARTDECO
ARTIEST
ARTLESS
BRACERO
BRACERS
BRACEUP
BRALESS
BRAVELY
BRAVERY
BRAVEST
BRAYERS
BREVETS
BREWERS
BREWERY
BRIBERY
BROKEIN
BROKERS
BROKEUP
BRUBECK
BRUNETS
BRUTELY
CRATERS
CRAVENS
CRAVERS
CRENELS
CREWELS
CRIMEAN
CROWERS
CRUDELY
CRUDEST
DRAPERS
DRAPERY
DRAWERS
DRIVEAT
DRIVEIN
DRIVELS
DRIVERS
DRIVEUP
DRONERS
DROVERS
DRYCELL
DRYNESS
DRYWELL
ERASERS
ERODENT
EROSELY
FRAMEUP
FRENEAU
GRADERS
GRATERS
GRAVELS
GRAVELY
GRAVERS
GRAVEST
GRAYEST
GRAZERS
GREYEST
GRIPERS
GRIVETS
GROCERS
GROCERY
GROVELS
GROWERS
GRUYERE
IRATELY
IRATEST
IRELESS
IRONERS
KRATERS
MRCLEAN
MRDEEDS
ORBLESS
OROGENY
ORPHEAN
ORPHEUS
PRATERS
PRAYERS
PREBEND
PRECEDE
PRECEPT
PREFECT
PREFERS
PREHEAT
PREMEDS
PRESELL
PRESENT
PRESETS
PRETEEN
PRETEND
PRETEST
PRETEXT
PREVENT
PRICERS
PRIMERS
PRIVETS
PROBERS
PROCEED
PROCESS
PROFESS
PROGENY
PROJECT
PRONELY
PROPELS
PROSERS
PROTEAN
PROTECT
PROTEGE
PROTEIN
PROTEST
PROTEUS
PROVERB
PROVERS
PROWESS
PRUDENT
PRUDERY
PRUNERS
TRABERT
TRACERS
TRACERY
TRADEIN
TRADEON
TRADERS
TRADEUP
TRAGEDY
TRAPEZE
TRAVELS
TRAVERS
TRICEPS
TRIDENT
TRIJETS
TRIREME
TRISECT
TRITELY
TRITEST
TRIVETS
TROWELS
TROWERS
TRUDEAU
WRITEIN
WRITERS
WRITETO
WRITEUP
WROTEIN
WROTETO
WROTEUP
WRYNESS

•R•••E•

ARALSEA
ARBITER
ARBORED
ARCADES
ARGIVES
ARGYLES
ARMORED
ARMORER
ARMURES
AROUSED
AROUSES
ARRASES
ARRAYED
ARRISES
ARRIVED
ARRIVER
ARRIVES
ARTSIER
BRACKEN
BRACKET
BRADLEE
BRADLEY
BRAGGED
BRAGGER
BRAIDED
BRAIDER
BRAINED
BRAISED
BRAISES
BRANDED
BRANDER
BRASHER
BRASSES
BRAVOES
BRAWLED
BRAWLER
BRAZIER
BREADED
BREAKER
BREEDER
BREEZED
BREEZES
BRENNER
BRICKED
BRIDGED
BRIDGES
BRIDGET
BRIDLED
BRIDLES
BRIEFED
BRIEFER
BRIMLEY
BRIMMED
BRINGER
BRINIER
BRIQUET
BRISKER
BRISKET
BRITTEN
BROADEN
BROADER
BROGUES
BROILED
BROILER
BRONZED
BRONZES
BROODED
BROODER
BROOKED
BROTHER
BROWNED
BROWNER
BROWSED
BROWSER
BROWSES
BRUEGEL
BRUISED
BRUISER
BRUISES
BRUITED
BRUMMEL
BRUSHED
BRUSHES
BRYNNER
CRABBED
CRABBER
CRACKED
CRACKER
CRADLED
CRADLES
CRAFTED
CRAFTER
CRAMMED
CRAMMER
CRAMPED
CRANKED
CRASHED
CRASHES
CRASSER
CRAWLED
CRAWLER
CRAZIER
CRAZIES
CREAKED
CREAMED
CREAMER
CREASED
CREASES
CREATED
CREATES
CRECHES
CREEPED
CREEPER
CREOLES
CRESSES
CRESTED
CREWMEN
CRIBBED
CRICKED
CRICKET
CRIMPED
CRIMPER
CRINGED
CRINGES
CRISPED
CRISPER
CRITTER
CROAKED
CROCHET
CROFTER
CRONIES
CROOKED
CROONED
CROONER
CROPPED
CROPPER
CROQUET
CROSIER
CROSSED
CROSSER
CROSSES
CROWDED
CROWNED
CRUELER
CRUISED
CRUISER
CRUISES
CRULLER
CRUMPET
CRUSHED
CRUSHER
CRUSHES
CRUSTED
CRYOGEN
DRABBER
DRAFTED
DRAFTEE
DRAGGED
DRAGGER
DRAGNET
DRAINED
DRAINER
DRATTED
DRAWLED
DREADED
DREAMED
DREAMER
DREDGED
DREDGER
DREDGES
DREIDEL
DREISER
DRESDEN
DRESSED
DRESSER
DRESSES
DRIBLET
DRIFTED
DRIFTER
DRILLED
DRILLER
DRINKER
DRIPPED
DROLLER
DROOLED
DROOLER
DROOPED
DROPLET
DROPPED
DROPPER
DROWNED
DROWSED
DROWSES
DRUBBED
DRUCKER
DRUDGED
DRUDGES
DRUGGED
DRUMMED
DRUMMER
DRYEYED
ERECTED
ERECTER
ERGATES
ERITREA
ERMINES
ERUCTED
ERUPTED
FRAILER
FRAISES
FRANCES
FRANKED
FRANKEN
FRANKER
FRAPPES
FRASIER
FRAWLEY
FRAZIER
FREAKED
FREEBEE
FREEMEN
FREEZER
FREEZES
FRESHEN
FRESHER
FRESHET
FRETTED
FRIDGES
FRIEZES
FRILLED
FRINGED
FRINGES
FRIPPET
FRISBEE
FRISKED
FRITTED
FRITTER
FRIZZED
FRIZZES
FROCKED
FROGMEN
FRONTED
FROSTED
FROTHED
FROWNED
FROWNER
FRUITED
GRABBED
GRABBER
GRAFTED
GRAINED
GRAMMER
GRAMMES
GRANDEE
GRANDER
GRANGER
GRANGES
GRANTED
GRANTEE
GRAPHED
GRAPIER
GRAPNEL
GRASPED
GRASSED
GRASSES
GRAVIES
GREASED
GREASER
GREASES
GREATER
GREAVES
GREELEY
GREENED
GREENER
GREETED
GREETER
GRENDEL
GREYHEN
GRIDDED
GRIDDER
GRIEVED
GRIEVER
GRIEVES
GRIFFEY
GRIFTER
GRILLED
GRILLES
GRILLET
GRIMIER
GRIMMER
GRINDER
GRINNED
GRINNER
GRIPPED
GRIPPER
GRITTED
GROANED
GROANER
GRODIER
GROLIER
GROMMET
GROOMED
GROOMER
GROOVED
GROOVES
GROSSED
GROSSER
GROSSES
GROUPED
GROUPER
GROUSED
GROUSER
GROUSES
GROUTED
GROWLED
GROWLER
GRUBBED
GRUDGED
GRUDGES
GRUFFER
GRUMPED
GRUNGES
GRUNTED
IRONIES
IRONMEN
MRBONES
ORACLES
ORANGES
ORANGEY
ORBITED
ORBITER
ORDERED
ORDERER
ORDINES
ORESTES
ORGATES
ORIOLES
ORPHREY
ORPINES
PRAISED
PRAISER
PRAISES
PRANCED
PRANCER
PRANCES
PRANGED
PRANKED
PREENED
PREENER
PREMIER
PREQUEL
PRESLEY
PRESSED
PRESSER
PRESSES
PRETEEN
PRETZEL
PREVIEW
PREXIES
PRICIER
PRICKED
PRIMMER
PRIMPED
PRINCES
PRINKED
PRINTED
PRINTER
PRITHEE
PRIVIER
PRIVIES
PROBLEM
PROCEED
PRODDED
PRODDER
PROFFER
PROGGED
PRONGED
PROOFED
PROOFER
PROPHET
PROPJET
PROPMEN
PROPPED
PROPTER
PROSIER
PROSPER
PROUDER
PROWLED
PROWLER
PROXIES
TRACHEA
TRACKED
TRACKER
TRAILED
TRAILER
TRAINED
TRAINEE
TRAINER
TRAMMEL
TRAMPED
TRANCES
TRAPPED
TRAPPER
TRASHED
TRASHES
TRAWLED
TRAWLER
TREADED
TREADER
TREATED
TREBLED
TREBLES
TREKKED
TREKKER
TRENDED
TRESSES
TRICKED
TRICKER
TRIFLED
TRIFLER
TRIFLES
TRIGGED
TRIGGER
TRILLED
TRIMMED
TRIMMER
TRINKET
TRIODES
TRIPLED
TRIPLES
TRIPLET
TRIPLEX
TRIPPED
TRIPPER
TRIPPET
TRIUNES
TROCHEE
TROCHES
TRODDEN
TROLLED
TROLLEY
TROOPED
TROOPER
TROTHED
TROTTED
TROTTER
TROUPER
TROUPES
TROUSER
TRUCKED
TRUCKEE
TRUCKER
TRUDGED
TRUDGER
TRUDGES
TRUMPED
TRUMPET
TRUSSED
TRUSSES
TRUSTED
TRUSTEE
TRYSTED
TRYSTER
URBANER
WRACKED
WRAPPED
WRAPPER
WREAKED
WRECKED
WRECKER
WRESTED
WRIGLEY
WRINGER
WRITHED
WRITHES
WRITTEN
WRONGED
WRONGER

•R••••E

ARACHNE
ARCHIVE
ARCSINE
ARDMORE
AREOLAE
ARGONNE
ARIADNE
ARISTAE
ARLEDGE
ARMHOLE
ARMLIKE
ARMOIRE
ARRANGE
ARRIERE
ARTICLE
ARTISTE
ARTWARE
BRADLEE
BRAILLE
BRAMBLE
BRASSIE
BREATHE
BRIGADE
BRINDLE
BRIOCHE
BRISTLE
BRITTLE
BROCADE
BROMATE
BROMIDE
BROMINE
BROWNIE
BRUSQUE
CRACKLE
CRAPPIE
CREVICE
CRINKLE
CRUMBLE
CRUMPLE
CRUSADE
DRAFTEE
DRAYAGE
DRIBBLE
DRIZZLE
DRYHOLE
ERASURE
EREMITE
EROSIVE
ERSKINE
ERUDITE
FRAGILE
FRANKIE
FRAZZLE
FRECKLE
FREDDIE
FREEBEE
FREEBIE
FRIABLE
FRICKIE
FRIGATE
FRISBEE
FRIZZLE
FROMAGE
GRACILE
GRACKLE
GRAHAME
GRANDEE
GRANITE
GRANTEE
GRANULE
GRAPPLE
GRAVURE
GRENADE
GRIDDLE
GRIMACE
GRISTLE
GRIZZLE
GROUPIE
GRUMBLE
GRUYERE
IRKSOME
IRONAGE
IRONORE
KRINGLE
ORBLIKE
ORIENTE
ORIFICE
ORNETTE
OROURKE
ORVILLE
PRAIRIE
PRALINE
PRATTLE
PRECEDE
PRECISE
PREDATE
PREEMIE
PREFACE
PRELATE
PRELUDE
PREMISE
PREPARE
PREPPIE
PRESAGE
PRESALE
PRESIDE
PRESUME
PRETAPE
PRICKLE
PRIMATE
PRITHEE
PRIVATE
PROBATE
PROCURE
PRODUCE
PROFANE
PROFILE
PROFUSE
PROMISE
PROMOTE
PROPANE
PROPOSE
PRORATE
PROTEGE
PROVIDE
PROVOKE
PRUDHOE
TRADUCE
TRAINEE
TRAIPSE
TRAMPLE
TRAPEZE
TREACLE
TREADLE
TREKKIE
TREMBLE
TRESTLE
TRIBUNE
TRIBUTE
TRICKLE
TRIESTE
TRIREME
TRITONE
TROCHEE
TROUBLE
TROUNCE
TRUCKEE
TRUCKLE
TRUFFLE
TRUNDLE
TRUSTEE
URANITE
URNLIKE
WRANGLE
WREATHE
WRESTLE
WRIGGLE
WRINKLE

••RE•••

ABREAST
ACREAGE
ADRENAL
AFREETS
AGREETO
ALREADY
ARREARS
ARRESTS
AUREATE
AUREOLA
AUREOLE
BARENTS
BARETTA
BEREAVE
BERETTA
BIREMES
BIRETTA
BOREDOM
BOREOUT
BUREAUS
BURETTE
BYREMAN
BYREMEN
CAREENS
CAREERS
CAREFOR
CAREFUL
CEREALS
CEREBRA
CORELLI
CORETTA
CUREALL
DAREFUL
DARESAY
DARESTO
DIRECTS
DIREFUL
FAREAST
FIREANT
FIREARM
FIREBOX
FIREBUG
FIREDOG
FIREDUP
FIREFLY
FIRELIT
FIREMAN
FIREMEN
FIRENZE
FIREOFF
FIRESUP
FOREARM
FOREIGN
FORELEG
FOREMAN
FOREMEN
FOREPAW
FORERAN
FORERUN
FORESAW
FORESEE
FORESTS
FOREVER
GERENTS
GORETEX
GYRENES
HERETIC
HIRESON

KOREANS
LORELEI
LORENZO
LORETTA
MARENGO
MORELLO
MORESBY
NEREIDS
NORELCO
NUREYEV
OGREISH
PARENTS
PHRENIC
RAREBIT
RAREGAS
REREADS
REREDOS
RERENTS
SCREAKS
SCREAMS
SCREECH
SCREEDS
SCREENS
SCREWED
SCREWUP
SERENER
SPREADS
STREAKS
STREAKY
STREAMS
STREETS
STRETCH
STRETTO
STREWED
STREWER
TEREDOS
TERENCE
THREADS
THREADY
THREATS
THREEAM
THREEPM
THREERS
THREWIN
TIREDER
TIREDLY
TIREDOF
TIREOUT
TOREOFF
TOREOUT
TOREROS
TUREENS
UNREADY
UNREELS
UTRECHT
WIRETAP
WOREOFF
WOREOUT
YEREVAN
ZAREBAS

••R•E••

AERIEST
AFREETS
AGREETO
AIRHEAD
AIRIEST
AIRLESS
ARRIERE
BARBELL
BARBELS
BARBERS
BARGEIN
BARKEEP
BARKERS
BARLESS
BARLEYS
BARNEYS
BARRELS
BARRENS
BARRETT
BARTEND
BARTERS
BERBERS
BERGERE
BERMEJO
BERNESE
BERSERK
BIRDERS
BORDERS
BORNEUP
BURDENS
BURGEES
BURGEON
BURGERS
BURGESS
BURMESE
BURNERS
BURNETT
CARDERS
CAREENS
CAREERS
CARLESS
CARNERA
CARNETS
CARPELS
CARPERS
CARPETS
CARRELS
CARSEAT
CARTELS
CARTERS
CARVERS
CORBELS
CORBETT
CORDELL
CORDERO
CORKERS
CORNEAL
CORNEAS
CORNELL
CORNERS
CORNETS
CORRECT
CORSETS
CORTEGE
CURFEWS
CURLERS
CURLEWS
CURRENT
CURTEST
CURVETS
DARKENS
DARKEST
DARLENE
DARNERS
DARTERS
DORMERS
DORSETT
DURRELL
EARLESS
EARNERS
EARNEST
EERIEST
FARLEFT
FARMERS
FARMERY
FARWEST
FERMENT
FERRETS
FERVENT
FIRMEST
FORBEAR
FORCEPS
FORCERS
FORFEIT
FORFEND
FORGERS
FORGERY
FORGETS
FORKERS
FORREAL
FORRENT
FORREST
FORWENT
FURLESS
FURSEAL
GARDENS
GARMENT
GARNERS
GARNETS
GARRETS
GARRETT
GARTERS
GIRDERS
GORGETS
GORIEST
GURNEYS
HARDENS
HARDEST
HARKENS
HARNESS
HARPERS
HARVEST
HERBERT
HERDERS
HERSELF
HORNETS
HURLERS
HURLEYS
ISRAELI
JARLESS
JERSEYS
KERNELS
LARCENY
LARDERS
LARGELY
LARGESS
LARGEST
MARCEAU
MARCELS
MARKERS
MARKETS
MARLENE
MARTENS
MARVELS
MERCERS
MERCERY
MERGERS
MIRIEST
MORDENT
MORSELS
MURDERS
NORBERT
NORIEGA
NURSERS
NURSERY
OARLESS
OURSELF
PARCELS
PARGETS
PARLEYS
PARSECS
PARSEES
PARSERS
PARVENU
PERCENT
PERFECT
PERSEID
PERSEUS
PERTEST
PIRAEUS
PORKERS
PORSENA
PORTEND
PORTENT
PORTERS
PURCELL
PURRERS
PURSERS
PURVEYS
SARGENT
SCREECH
SCREEDS
SCREENS
SERPENT
SERVERS
SERVERY
SERVEUP
SHRIEKS
SORBETS
SORCERY
SORRELS
SORTERS
SPRIEST
SPRYEST
STREETS
SURFEIT
SURFERS
SURGEON
SURGERY
SURREAL
SURREYS
SURVEYS
TARBELL
TARGETS
TARHEEL
TARTEST
TERCELS
TERCETS
TERRENE
TERRETS
TERSELY
TERSEST
THREEAM
THREEPM
THREERS
TORMENT
TORPEDO
TORRENS
TORRENT
TUREENS
TURKEYS
TURNERS
TURNERY
TURRETS
UNREELS
VARIETY
VARLETS
VERBENA
VERGERS
VERMEER
VERMEIL
VERVETS
WARDENS
WARDERS
WARIEST
WARLESS
WARMEST
WARRENS
WIRIEST
WORKERS
WORSENS
WURLEYS

••R••E•

ABRADED
ABRADER
ABRADES
AERATED
AERATES
AEROBES
AFRAMES
AIRCREW
APRONED
ARRASES
ARRAYED
ARRISES
ARRIVED
ARRIVER
ARRIVES
AURALEE
BARKEEP
BARKIER
BARKLEY
BARMIER
BARONET
BARRIER
BERATED
BERATES
BERNSEN
BERRIED
BERRIES
BERTHED
BIRCHED
BIRCHES
BIRDIED
BIRDIES
BIRDMEN
BIREMES
BIRTHED
BORATES
BURBLED
BURBLES
BURGEES
BURGHER
BURGLED
BURGLES
BURLIER
BYREMEN
CARAFES
CARAMEL
CARAVEL
CARGOES
CARIBES
CARNIES
CAROLED
CAROLER
CAROMED
CARRIED
CARRIER
CARRIES
CARTIER
CCRIDER
CERUMEN
CHROMES
CIRCLED
CIRCLES
CIRCLET
CIRQUES
CORKIER
CORNFED
CORNIER
CORONET
CURATES
CURDIER
CURDLED
CURDLES
CURLIER
CURRIED
CURRIER
CURRIES
CURTSEY
CURVIER
DARBIES
DARNLEY
DERBIES
DERIDED
DERIDES
DERIVED
DERIVES
DERNIER
DIRTIED
DIRTIER
DIRTIES
EARLIER
EARTHEN
ENRAGED
ENRAGES
ENROBED
ENROBES
FARRIER
FARTHER
FERNIER
FERRIED
FERRIES
FERULES
FIREMEN
FIRRIER
FORAGED
FORAGER
FORAGES
FORELEG
FOREMEN
FORESEE
FOREVER
FORFREE
FORGOES
FORKIER
FORSTER
FORTIES
FURORES
FURRIER
FURTHER
GARAGED
GARAGES
GARBLED
GARBLES
GARDNER
GARGLED
GARGLES
GERMIER
GIRDLED
GIRDLES
GORETEX
GORSIER
GURGLED
GURGLES
GYRATED
GYRATES
GYRENES
HARDIER
HARDSET
HARPIES
HARRIED
HARRIER
HARRIES
HARRIET
HARSHEN
HARSHER
HERBIER
HERBTEA
HERSHEY
HORSIER
HURDLED
HURDLER
HURDLES
HURLIES
HURRIED
HURRIES
HURTLED
HURTLES
HYRACES
HYRAXES
JERKIER
KARASEA
KIRTLES
LARCHES
LARDIER
LARDNER
LORELEI
LORISES
LORRIES
LURCHED
LURCHES
MARBLED
MARBLES
MARCHED
MARCHER
MARCHES
MARGRET
MARINER
MARINES
MARQUEE
MARQUES
MARQUEZ
MARRIED
MARRIES
MARSHES
MERCIES
MERIMEE
MERITED
MERRIER
MIRAGES
MIRKIER
MORALES
MORDRED
MORPHED
MURKIER
MYRTLES
NARTHEX
NERDIER
NERVIER
NORTHER
NUREYEV
PARADED
PARADES
PARAPET
PARCHED
PARCHES
PARDNER
PAROLED
PAROLEE
PAROLES
PARQUET
PARRIED
PARRIER
PARRIES
PARSEES
PARSLEY
PARTIED
PARTIER
PARTIES
PARTNER
PARURES
PERCHED
PERCHES
PERDIEM
PERIGEE
PERKIER
PERPLEX
PERRIER
PERUKES
PERUSED
PERUSER
PERUSES
PHRASED
PHRASES
PIRATED
PIRATES
PORCHES
PORGIES
PORKIER
PURFLED
PURFLES
PURLIEU
PURPLED
PURPLES
PURSIER
PURSUED
PURSUER
PURSUES
PURVIEW
PYRITES
RERATED
RERATES
SARACEN
SARALEE
SARAZEN
SARKIER
SCRAPED
SCRAPER
SCRAPES
SCREWED
SCRIBES
SCRIVEN
SERAPES
SERENER
SERRIED
SHRIKES
SHRINER
SHRINES
SHRIVEL
SHRIVER
SHRIVES
SORITES
SORRIER
SORTIED
SORTIES
SPRAYED
SPRAYER
SPRITES
SPRUCED
SPRUCER
SPRUCES
STRAFED
STRAFES
STRAYED
STREWED
STREWER
STRIDER
STRIDES
STRIKER
STRIKES
STRIPED
STRIPER
STRIPES
STRIVED
STRIVEN
STRIVER
STRIVES
STROBES
STROKED
STROKES
STRUDEL
SURFIER
SURLIER
SURTSEY
TARDIER
TARHEEL
TARRIED
TARRIER
TARRIES
TARSIER
TERRIER
TERRIES
THRIVED
THRIVES
THRONES
THROWER
TIRADES
TIREDER
TORCHED
TORCHES
TORQUES
TURFIER
TURNKEY
TURTLED
TURTLES
UNRATED
UNRAVEL
UNROBED
UNROBES
UPRISEN
UPRISES
UPRIVER
VERMEER
VERNIER
VIRTUES
VIRUSES
WARBLED
WARBLER
WARBLES
WARTIER
WERNHER
WERTHER
WORDIER
WORKMEN
WORMIER
WORRIED
WORRIER
WORRIES
WORSTED
YARDMEN
YORKIES

••R•••E

ABRIDGE
ACREAGE
AGRAFFE
AIRBASE
AIRDATE
AIRFARE
AIRHOLE
AIRLANE
AIRLIKE
AIRLINE
AIRMILE
AIRTIME
AIRWAVE
ARRANGE
ARRIERE
AURALEE
AUREATE
AUREOLE
AURICLE
AURORAE
BARCODE
BARNONE
BAROQUE
BARRAGE
BARWARE
BEREAVE
BERGERE
BERNESE
BERNICE
BURETTE
BURMESE
CARBIDE
CARBINE
CARCASE
CARFARE
CARLYLE
CARMINE
CAROUSE
CARTAGE
CORDAGE
CORDATE
CORDITE
CORKAGE
CORNICE
CORONAE
CORRODE
CORSAGE
CORTEGE
CURLIKE
CURSIVE
DARLENE
DORMICE
DURABLE
DURANCE
DURANTE
EARACHE
EARLIKE
EARLOBE
ENROUTE
FARGONE
FERRATE
FERRITE
FERRULE
FERTILE
FIRENZE
FORBADE
FORBORE
FORESEE
FORFREE
FORGAVE
FORGIVE
FORGONE
FORLIFE
FORSAKE
FORSALE
FORSURE
FORTUNE
FURNACE
FURTIVE
GARBAGE
GARONNE
GERMANE
GIRAFFE
GIRONDE
HERBAGE
HERCULE
HEROINE
HIRABLE
HIRSUTE
HORMONE
KARAOKE
KIRSTIE
LARAINE
LARAMIE
LORICAE
MARGATE
MARLENE
MARLOWE
MARQUEE
MARRYME
MERIMEE
MIRACLE
MORAINE
MORTISE
NARRATE
NURTURE
OARLIKE
PARABLE
PARKADE
PAROLEE
PARTAKE
PARTITE
PERCALE
PERFUME
PERIGEE
PERJURE
PERLITE
PERVADE
PIROGUE
PORCINE
PORKPIE
PORSCHE
PORTAGE
PURPOSE
RERAISE
RERINSE
REROUTE
SARALEE
SARDINE
SCROOGE
SCRUPLE
SERIATE
SERRATE
SERVICE
SERVILE
SORBATE
STRANGE
STRASSE
STRIATE
STROPHE
SURFACE
SURMISE
SURNAME
SURVIVE
SYRINGE
TARTARE
TERENCE
TERHUNE
TERMITE
TERNATE
TERRACE
TERRENE
TURBINE
UKRAINE
UPRAISE
VERBOSE
VERDURE
VIRGULE
VIRTUTE
WARFARE
WARGAME
WARLIKE
WARTIME
WARZONE
WORDONE
YARDAGE

•••RE••

ACCRETE
ACTRESS
ADDRESS
ADORERS
AGGRESS
AIGRETS
ALFREDO
ANDREAS
ANDRESS
ANDREWS
ARMREST
AWAREOF
BARRELS
BARRENS
BARRETT
BEARERS
BEDREST
CARRELS
CLARETS
CLORETS
CORRECT
CURRENT
CYPRESS
DEAREST
DECREED
DECREES
DEGREES
DEPRESS
DIGRESS
DOUREST
DURRELL
ELGRECO
EMPRESS
ENTREAT
ENTREES
EVEREST
EVERETT
EXCRETE
EXPRESS
EXTREME
FAIREST
FEARERS
FERRETS
FLAREUP
FLORETS
FORREAL
FORRENT
FORREST
GARRETS
GARRETT
GETREAL
HEARERS
HEBREWS
HEIRESS
IMARETS
IMPRESS
INBREED
INGRESS
IPCRESS
JEERERS
LABRETS
LAURELS
LAURENT
LEERERS
LIPREAD
MAUREEN
MISREAD
NEAREST
OPPRESS
OSPREYS
OVEREAT
PEERESS
PETRELS
POOREST
POURERS
PUGREES
PURRERS
REAREND
REARERS
REDRESS
REFRESH
REGRESS
REGRETS
REPRESS
RETREAD
RETREAT
ROARERS
SANREMO
SCARERS
SCAREUP
SCORERS
SECRECY
SECRETE
SECRETS
SEERESS
SHAREIN
SHARERS
SNORERS
SOARERS
SOIREES
SORRELS
SOUREST
SPARELY
SPAREST
SPIREAS
STAREAT
STARERS
STARETS
STEREOS
STORERS
STOREUP
STOREYS
STYRENE
SUPREME
SUPREMO
SURREAL
SURREYS
SWOREAT
SWOREBY
SWOREIN
TENRECS
TERRENE
TERRETS
THEREAT
THEREBY
THEREIN
THERELL
THEREOF
THEREON
THERESA
THERETO
THOREAU
TIGRESS
TORRENS
TORRENT
TOURERS
TRIREME
TUAREGS
TURRETS
UNDRESS
USURERS
WARRENS
WEARERS
WHEREAS
WHEREAT
WHEREBY
WHEREIN
WHERELL
WHEREOF
WHERERE
WHERETO
WHEREVE
YEAREND
ZAIREAN

•••R•E•

ABORTED
ACCRUED
ACCRUES
ADORNED
ADORNER
ALARMED
ALARMER
ALERTED
ALERTER
AMBRIES
AMERCED
AMERCES
ANGRIER
APERIES
AVERRED
AVERTED
AWARDED
AWARDEE
AWARDER
BARRIER
BEARDED
BEERIER
BERRIED
BERRIES
BLARNEY
BLURRED
BLURTED
BOARDED
BOARDER
BOURREE
BOURSES
CARRIED
CARRIER
CARRIES
CHARGED
CHARGER
CHARGES
CHARIER
CHARLES
CHARLEY
CHARMED
CHARMER
CHARRED
CHARTED
CHARTER
CHIRPED
CHURNED
CITROEN
CLERKED
COARSEN
COARSER
COERCED
COERCER
COERCES
CONRIED

COURIER
COURSED
COURSER
COURSES
COURTED
COWRIES
CURRIED
CURRIER
CURRIES
DAIRIES
DEARIES
DEBRIEF
DECREED
DECREES
DECRIED
DECRIER
DECRIES
DEGREES
DEVRIES
DIARIES
DOORMEN
DOWRIES
DWARFED
DWARVES
EMERGED
EMERGES
EMERSED
ENTREES
ENTRIES
EVERTED
EXERTED
FAERIES
FAIRIES
FARRIER
FERRIED
FERRIES
FIERCER
FIERIER
FIRRIER
FLIRTED
FOURIER
FURRIER
GABRIEL
GEORGES
GLORIED
GLORIES
GNARLED
GNARRED
GOURDES
GOURMET
GUARDED
GUARDEE
HAARLEM
HAIRIER
HAIRNET
HARRIED
HARRIER
HARRIES
HARRIET
HEARKEN
HEARTED
HEARTEN
HOARDED
HOARDER
HOARIER
HOARSEN
HOARSER
HURRIED
HURRIES
IMBRUED
IMBRUES
INBREED
INBRIEF
IVORIES
JOURNEY
KEARNEY
KNURLED
LAERTES
LEARIER
LEARJET
LEARNED
LEARNER
LEERIER
LIERNES
LORRIES
LOURDES
MARRIED
MARRIES
MAUREEN
MERRIER
MOORHEN
MOORIER
MOURNED
ONORDER
OVERSEA
OVERSEE
PARRIED
PARRIER
PARRIES
PEARLED
PERRIER
PIERCED
PIERCES
PUGREES
QUARREL
QUARTER
QUARTET
QUERIED
QUERIER
QUERIES
REARMED
REFRIED
REFRIES
REORDER
RETRIED
RETRIES
SCARCER
SCARFED
SCARIER
SCARLET
SCARPED
SCARPER
SCARRED
SCARVES
SCORNED
SCORNER
SCURVES
SERRIED
SHARKEY
SHARPED
SHARPEI
SHARPEN
SHARPER
SHERBET
SHIRKED
SHIRKER
SHIRLEY
SHIRRED
SHORTED
SHORTEN
SHORTER
SKIRLED
SKIRRED
SKIRTED
SLURPED
SLURRED
SMARTED
SMARTEN
SMARTER
SMIRKED
SNARLED
SNORKEL
SNORTED
SNORTER
SOIREES
SORRIER
SOURCED
SOURCES
SPARGED
SPARGES
SPARKED
SPARRED
SPARSER
SPIRIER
SPORTED
SPURNED
SPURNER
SPURRED
SPURTED
STARKER
STARLET
STARRED
STARTED
STARTER
STARVED
STARVES
STERNER
STIRRED
STIRRER
STORIED
STORIES
STORMED
STURGES
SWARMED
SWERVED
SWERVES
SWIRLED
TARRIED
TARRIER
TARRIES
TEARIER
TERRIER
TERRIES
THURBER
TIERNEY
TOORDER
TOURNEY
TWIRLED
TWIRLER
UNARMED
UNTRIED
USURIES
USURPED
USURPER
VEERIES
WEARIED
WEARIER
WEARIES
WEIRDER
WHARFED
WHARVES
WHIRLED
WHIRRED
WHORLED
WORRIED
WORRIER
WORRIES
YEARNED
YEARNER

•••R••E

ACCRETE
ACEROSE
AMBROSE
APPRISE
APPRIZE
APPROVE
ASARULE
ASCRIBE
ASTRIDE
ATTRITE
AVARICE
AVERAGE
AWARDEE
AZURITE
BARRAGE
BEGRIME
BOURREE
CAPRICE
CHARADE
CHARLIE
CHORALE
CHORINE
CHORTLE
CITRATE
CITRINE
CLARICE
COMRADE
CORRODE
COURAGE
CUTRATE
DEGRADE
DEPRAVE
DEPRIVE
DHURRIE
DISROBE
DOORDIE
EMBRACE
EMIRATE
ENGRAVE
EPERGNE
EXCRETE
EXTREME
EXTRUDE
FEBRILE
FERRATE
FERRITE
FERRULE
GAGRULE
GEORDIE
GOBROKE
GUARDEE
HAIRDYE
HAYRIDE
HYDRATE
IMPROVE
INGRATE
INTRUDE
ITERATE
JOYRIDE
LAPROBE
LOWRISE
MACRAME
MARRYME
MAURICE
MELROSE
MICROBE
MIDRISE
MIGRATE
MISRULE
MOORAGE
NARRATE
NEURONE
NITRATE
NITRIDE
NITRITE
OBTRUDE
OLDROSE
OPERATE
OPEROSE
OUTRACE
OUTRAGE
OVERAGE
OVERATE
OVERAWE
OVERDUE
OVERLIE
OVERSEE
OVERUSE
PADRONE
PATRICE
PEERAGE
PRORATE
PUERILE
RATRACE
REARGUE
REDROSE
REFRAME
REGRADE
REPRICE
REPRISE
REPROVE
RETRACE
RETRADE
REWRITE
REWROTE
SECRETE
SERRATE
SPARKLE
STARTLE
STERILE
STORAGE
STYRENE
SUCRASE
SUCROSE
SUNRISE
SUPREME
TAURINE
TAXRATE
TEAROSE
TERRACE
TERRENE
TITRATE
TOWROPE
TRIREME
UMBRAGE
UNCRATE
UNDRAPE
UPGRADE
VIBRATE
WHERERE
WHEREVE

••••RE•

ABJURED
ABJURES
ADHERED
ADHERES
ADJURED
ADJURES
ADMIRED
ADMIRER
ADMIRES
AIRCREW
ALLURED
ALLURES
ALTERED
ALTERER
ALVAREZ
AMPERES
ANGERED
ANTARES
APPAREL
ARBORED
ARMORED
ARMORER
ARMURES
ASPIRED
ASPIRER
ASPIRES
ASSURED
ASSURES
ATTIRED
ATTIRES
AUGURED
AVERRED
BEMIRED
BEMIRES
BESTREW
BLEARED
BLURRED
BODEREK
BOURREE
BOWERED
BUGFREE
CABARET
CAPERED
CATERED
CATERER
CEDARED
CENTRED
CENTRES
CHAIRED
CHARRED
CHEERED
CHEVRES
CLEARED
CLEARER
COHERED
COHERES
COLORED
COMFREY
CONURES
COVERED
COWERED
DALTREY
DEMURER
DESIRED
DESIREE
DESIRES
DOLORES
DOWERED
EAGERER
ELMTREE
EMIGRES
EMPIRES
ENCORES
ENDURED
ENDURES
ENSURED
ENSURES
ENTERED
ERITREA
EUCHRED
EUCHRES
EXPIRED
EXPIRES
FABARES
FAVORED
FIACRES
FIGURED
FIGURER
FIGURES
FLOORED
FLOURED
FORFREE
FURORES
FUTURES
GAMBREL
GLAIRED
GNARRED
GODFREY
GUMTREE
HAVERED
HOMBRES
HOMERED
HONORED
HONOREE
HONORER
HOVERED
HOVERER
HUMORED
HUNDRED
ICEFREE
IGNORED
IGNORER
IGNORES
ILLBRED
IMMURED
IMMURES
IMPURER
INHERED
INHERES
INJURED
INJURES
INSURED
INSURER
INSURES
JEFFREY
JOFFREY
KESTREL
KINDRED
LABORED
LABORER
LAMPREY
LAUTREC
LAYERED
LETTRES
LEVERED
LEVERET
LOUVRED
LOUVRES
LOWBRED
LOWERED
LUSTRED
LUSTRES
MAIGRET
MAITRED
MAJORED
MANFRED
MARGRET
MATURED
MATURER
MATURES
MAYTREE
MEMOREX
METERED
MILDRED
MINARET
MINORED
MITERED
MONGREL
MORDRED
MOTORED
NATURED
NATURES
OAKTREE
OEUVRES
OFFERED
OFFERER
ORDERED
ORDERER
ORPHREY
OSIERED
OUTDREW
OUTGREW
PALFREY
PAPERED
PAPERER
PARURES
PETERED
POWERED
QUARREL
QUEERED
QUEERER
RAZORED
REAIRED
REFEREE
REFIRES
REHIRED
REHIRES
RETIRED
RETIREE
RETIRES
REVERED
REVERES
REWIRED
REWIRES
ROSERED
RUMORED
SATIRES
SAVORED
SCARRED
SCOURED
SCOURER
SECURED
SECURER
SECURES
SEESRED
SENORES
SEVERED
SEVERER
SHEARED
SHEARER
SHEERED
SHEERER
SHIRRED
SKIRRED
SLURRED
SMEARED
SNEERED
SNEERER
SOBERED
SOBERER
SPARRED
SPEARED
SPHERES
SPURRED
SQUARED
SQUARER
SQUARES
SQUIRED
SQUIRES
STARRED
STEERED
STEERER
STIRRED
STIRRER
SUGARED
SUTURED
SUTURES
SWEARER
TABORET
TAPERED
TAXFREE
TEATREE
TENURED
TENURES
THEOREM
TIMBRES
TOWERED
TUMBREL
TUTORED
UMPIRED
UMPIRES
UNAIRED
UNSCREW
UPATREE
USHERED
UTTERED
UTTERER
WAGERED
WAGERER
WASTREL
WATERED
WATERER
WAVERED
WAVERER
WHIRRED
WINERED
WINFREY

••••R•E

ADVERSE
ASPERSE
ASTARTE
ATLARGE
AURORAE
BIZARRE
BOURREE
BUGFREE
BYFORCE
CALORIE
CASERNE
COTERIE
DEBARGE
DEFARGE
DESERVE
DESIREE
DHURRIE
DIVERGE
DIVERSE
DIVORCE
ELMTREE
ENDORSE
ENFORCE
ENGARDE
ENGORGE
ENLARGE
EUTERPE
EXPARTE
FABERGE
FORFREE
GUMTREE
GUTHRIE
HONOREE
ICEFREE
IMMERSE
INDORSE
INFORCE
INTERSE
INVERSE
LAFARGE
LAPORTE
LAVERNE
LECARRE
LUCERNE
MAYTREE
MCENROE
NAVARRE
NOTTRUE
OAKTREE
OBSERVE
OBVERSE
ONSERVE
OROURKE
OSBORNE
PANURGE
PRAIRIE
REFEREE
REMORSE
RESERVE
RESURGE
RETIREE
REVERIE
REVERSE
SCOURGE
SPLURGE
TAXFREE
TEATREE
UNHORSE
UNNERVE
UPATREE
UPBORNE
UPSURGE
VALERIE

•••••RE

ACQUIRE
AFFAIRE
AIRFARE
ALLHERE
ANYMORE
ARDMORE
ARMOIRE
ARRIERE
ARTWARE
ASTAIRE
AUSTERE
BARWARE
BERGERE
BIZARRE
BONFIRE
BUSFARE
CALIBRE
CAPTURE
CARFARE
CELEBRE
CENSURE
CLOSURE
CLOTURE
COCHERE
COMPARE
COMPERE
CONJURE
COUTURE
CULTURE
DASYURE
DAYCARE
DAYMARE
DECLARE
DENTURE
DEPLORE
ENQUIRE
ENSNARE
EPICURE
ERASURE
ESQUIRE
ETAGERE
EXPLORE
EYESORE
FAILURE
FANFARE
FEATURE
FISSURE
FIXTURE
FORBORE
FORSURE
FOXFIRE
GESTURE
GRAVURE
GRUYERE
GUNFIRE
HAYWIRE
HECTARE
HILAIRE
HITHERE
HOTWIRE
IMPLORE
INQUIRE
INSPIRE
INSTORE
IRONORE
KILDARE
LECARRE
LECTURE
LEHAVRE
LEISURE
LUMIERE
MACABRE
MAGUIRE
MAJEURE
MCCLURE
MCGUIRE
MEASURE
MEMOIRE
MISFIRE
MIXTURE
MOLIERE
NAVARRE
NOTSURE
NOWHERE
NURTURE
OBSCURE
ONADARE
ONSHORE
OUTWORE
PASTURE
PERJURE
PHILTRE
PIASTRE
PICTURE
PISMIRE
POSTURE
PREPARE
PROCURE
RAPTURE
REQUIRE
RESPIRE
RESTORE
RIVIERE
RUPTURE
SCEPTRE
SEAFIRE
SEEHERE
SINCERE
SOTHERE
SPECTRE
STATURE
SUOJURE
TANGERE
TARTARE
TEXTURE
THEATRE
TINWARE
TONSURE
TOSPARE
TSQUARE
UNAWARE
VAMPIRE
VENTURE
VERDURE
VESTURE
VULTURE
WARFARE
WELFARE
WHERERE

R•F••••

RAFFISH
RAFFLED
RAFFLER
RAFFLES
RAFTERS
RAFTING
REFACED
REFACES
REFEREE
REFERTO
REFFING
REFILED
REFILES
REFILLS
REFILMS
REFINED
REFINER
REFINES
REFIRES
REFLAGS
REFLECT
REFOCUS
REFORMS
REFRACT
REFRAIN
REFRAME
REFRESH
REFRIED
REFRIES
REFUELS
REFUGEE
REFUGES
REFUNDS
REFUSAL
REFUSED
REFUSER
REFUSES
REFUTED
REFUTER
REFUTES
RIFFING
RIFFLED
RIFFLES
RIFLERS
RIFLERY
RIFLING
RIFTING
RUFFIAN
RUFFLED
RUFFLES
RUFIYAA

R••F•••

RAFFISH
RAFFLED
RAFFLER
RAFFLES
RATFINK
REAFFIX
REDFINS
REDFIRS
REDFLAG
REDFORD
REEFERS
REEFING
REFFING
REIFIED
REIFIES
RIFFING
RIFFLED
RIFFLES
ROOFERS
ROOFING
ROOFTOP
RUFFIAN
RUFFLED
RUFFLES

R•••F••

RAGEFUL
RATAFIA
REAFFIX
REBUFFS
RESTFUL
RIPOFFS
ROOMFUL
ROOTFOR
ROTIFER
RUNOFFS
RUNSFOR
RUTHFUL

R••••F•

RAKEOFF
RANGOFF
REBUFFS
RECTIFY
REELOFF
RELIEFS
REUNIFY
RIDEOFF
RINGOFF
RIPOFFS
RIPSOFF
RODEOFF
RODOLFO
RUBSOFF
RUNGOFF
RUNOFFS
RUNSOFF
RUSHOFF

R•••••F

RAKEOFF
RANGOFF
REDWOLF
REELOFF
REPROOF
RIDEOFF
RINGOFF
RIPSOFF
RODEOFF
RUBSOFF
RUNGOFF
RUNSOFF
RUSHOFF

•RF••••

MRFIXIT

•R•F•••

ARAFURA
ARMFULS
ARTFILM
ARTFORM
CRAFTED
CRAFTER
CRAFTSY
CROFTER
DRAFTED
DRAFTEE
DRIFTED
DRIFTER
GRAFTED
GRAFTON
GRIFFEY
GRIFFIN
GRIFFON
GRIFTER
GRUFFER
GRUFFLY
ORIFICE
PREFABS
PREFACE
PREFECT
PREFERS
PROFANE
PROFESS
PROFFER
PROFILE
PROFITS
PROFUSE
TRAFFIC
TREFOIL
TRIFLED
TRIFLER
TRIFLES
TRUFFLE

•R••F••

BRERFOX
BRIEFED
BRIEFER
BRIEFLY
BRIMFUL
DREYFUS
FRETFUL
GRIFFEY
GRIFFIN
GRIFFON
GRUFFER
GRUFFLY
PRAYFOR
PROFFER
PROOFED
PROOFER
TRAFFIC
TRAYFUL
TRUFFLE

•R•••F•

CRUCIFY
DROPOFF
GRATIFY

•R••••F

CRYWOLF
DROPOFF

••RF•••

AIRFARE
AIRFLOW
AIRFOIL
CARFARE
CARFULS
CURFEWS
EARFLAP

EARFULS
FORFEIT
FORFEND
FORFREE
JARFULS
NORFOLK
PARFAIT
PERFECT
PERFIDY
PERFORM
PERFUME
PURFLED
PURFLES
SERFDOM
SURFACE
SURFEIT
SURFERS
SURFIER
SURFING
TURFIER
TURFWAR
WARFARE

••R•F••
AGRAFFE
CARAFES
CAREFOR
CAREFUL
CORNFED
DAREFUL
DIREFUL
FIREFLY
FORKFUL
FORMFUL
GIRAFFE
HARMFUL
HURTFUL
SCRUFFS
SCRUFFY
SHRIFTS
STRAFED
STRAFES
TARIFFS
THRIFTS
THRIFTY
WORKFOR

••R••F•
AGRAFFE
AIRLIFT
CERTIFY
EARMUFF
FARLEFT
FIREOFF
FORLIFE
FORTIFY
GIRAFFE
HORRIFY
KARLOFF
MARKOFF
MORTIFY
SCRUFFS
SCRUFFY
TARIFFS
TERRIFY
TOREOFF
TORNOFF
TURNOFF
VERSIFY
WARDOFF
WOREOFF
WORKOFF
WORNOFF

••R•••F
AIRWOLF
BARANOF
BERIDOF
EARMUFF
FIREOFF
HERSELF
KARLOFF
MARKOFF
OURSELF
TIREDOF
TOREOFF
TORNOFF
TURNOFF
WARDOFF
WOREOFF
WORKOFF
WORNOFF

•••RF••
BRERFOX
DEERFLY
DWARFED
FEARFUL
ODORFUL
OVERFLY
SCARFED
STIRFRY
TEARFUL
WHARFED

•••R•F•
BEAROFF
CLARIFY
ENGRAFT
FAIROFF
GLORIFY
HORRIFY
MIDRIFF
PAIROFF
PETRIFY
SCARIFY
SHERIFF
TEAROFF
TERRIFY
UPDRAFT
VITRIFY
WEAROFF

•••R••F
AWAREOF
BEAROFF
DEBRIEF
FAIROFF
HEARDOF
HEARSOF
HIPROOF
INBRIEF
MIDRIFF
PAIROFF
REPROOF
SHERIFF
SHORTOF
SUNROOF
TEAROFF
THEREOF
WEAROFF
WHEREOF

•••••RF
NETSURF
WALDORF

R•G••••
RAGBAGS
RAGDOLL
RAGEFUL
RAGGEDY
RAGGING
RAGLANS
RAGMOPS
RAGOUTS
RAGRUGS
RAGTIME
RAGTOPS
RAGWEED
REGAINS
REGALED
REGALES
REGALIA
REGALLY
REGARDS
REGATTA
REGENCY
REGENTS
REGIMEN
REGIMES
REGIONS
REGLETS
REGLUED
REGLUES
REGNANT
REGRADE
REGRESS
REGRETS
REGROUP
REGULAR
REGULUS
RIGGERS
RIGGING
RIGHTED
RIGHTER
RIGHTLY
RIGHTON
RIGIDLY
RIGOURS
RIGVEDA
ROGAINE
ROGUERY
ROGUISH
RUGLIKE

R••G•••
RAGGEDY
RAGGING
RANGERS
RANGIER
RANGING
RANGOFF
RANGOON
RANGOUT
RAYGUNS
REAGENT
REDGUMS
REIGNED
RIDGIER
RIDGING
RIDGWAY
RIGGERS
RIGGING
RINGERS
RINGING
RINGLET
RINGOFF
RINGOUT
RINGSUP
RODGERS
ROUGHED
ROUGHEN
ROUGHER
ROUGHIT
ROUGHLY
ROUGHUP
ROUGING
RUNGOFF
RUNGOUT
RUTGERS

R•••G••
RAREGAS
RAVAGED
RAVAGER
RAVAGES
RAWEGGS
REARGUE
REFUGEE
REFUGES
RELIGHT
REMIGES
RENEGED
RENEGER
RENEGES
RENEGUE
REPUGNS
RESIGNS
RONTGEN

R••••G•
RAGBAGS
RAGRUGS
RALEIGH
RAMPAGE
RATINGS
RAVINGS
RAWEGGS
REDALGA
REDDOGS
REFLAGS
REHANGS
RESINGS
RESTAGE
RESURGE
REVENGE
RIBCAGE
RISINGS
RULINGS
RUMMAGE

R•••••G
RACKING
RAFTING
RAGGING
RAIDING
RAILING
RAINING
RAISING
RAMMING
RANGING
RANKING
RANTING
RAPPING
RASPING
RATTING
RAZZING
RDLAING
READING
REAMING
REAPING
REARING
REDDING
REDFLAG
REDOING
REDWING
REEDING
REEFING
REEKING
REELING
REFFING
REINING
RELYING
RENDING
RENTING
RESTING
REVVING
RHYMING
RIBBING
RIDDING
RIDGING
RIFFING
RIFLING
RIFTING
RIGGING
RIMMING
RINGING
RINSING
RIOTING
RIPPING
RISKING
ROADHOG
ROAMING
ROARING
ROBBING
ROCKING
RODDING
ROILING
ROLLING
ROLVAAG
ROMPING
ROOFING
ROOKING
ROOMING
ROOTING
ROTTING
ROUGING
ROUSING
ROUTING
RUBBING
RUCHING
RUCKING
RUINING
RUNNING
RUSHING
RUSTING

•RG••••
ARGIVES
ARGONNE
ARGUERS
ARGUING
ARGYLES
ERGATES
ORGANDY
ORGANIC
ORGANON
ORGANUM
ORGANZA
ORGATES
ORGEATS
URGENCY

•R•G•••
ARUGULA
BRAGGED
BRAGGER
BRIGADE
BRIGAND
BRIGHAM
BROGANS
BROGUES
DRAGGED
DRAGGER
DRAGNET
DRAGONS
DRAGOON
DRAGOUT
DRAGSIN
DRAGSON
DRUGGED
FRAGILE
FRIGATE
FRIGHTS
FROGMAN
FROGMEN
GREGORY
GRIGRIS
OREGANO
ORIGAMI
ORIGINS
OROGENY
PROGENY
PROGGED
PROGRAM
TRAGEDY
TRIGGED
TRIGGER
TRIGONS
TRIGRAM
TROGONS
URUGUAY
WRIGGLE
WRIGGLY
WRIGHTS
WRIGLEY

•R••G••
BRAGGED
BRAGGER
BRIDGED
BRIDGES
BRIDGET
BRINGER
BRINGIN
BRINGON
BRINGTO
BRINGUP
BROUGHT
BRUEGEL
CRINGED
CRINGES
CRYOGEN
DRAGGED
DRAGGER
DRAUGHT
DREDGED
DREDGER
DREDGES
DROUGHT
DRUDGED
DRUDGES
DRUGGED
FRAUGHT
FREIGHT
FRIDGES
FRINGED
FRINGES
GRANGER
GRANGES
GRUDGED
GRUDGES
GRUNGES
KRINGLE
MRMAGOO
MRRIGHT
ORANGES
ORANGEY
PRANGED
PROGGED
PRONGED
TRIGGED
TRIGGER
TROUGHS
TRUDGED
TRUDGER
TRUDGES
WRANGLE
WRIGGLE
WRIGGLY
WRINGER
WRONGED
WRONGER
WRONGLY
WROUGHT

•R•••G•
ARLEDGE
ARRAIGN
ARRANGE
BRANAGH
DRAYAGE
FROMAGE
IRONAGE
PRESAGE
PRODIGY
PROLOGS
PROTEGE
TRILOGY

•R••••G
ARCHING
AREARUG
ARGUING
ARISING
ARTSONG
BRACING
BRAKING
BRAVING
BRAYING
BRAZING
BREWING
BRIBING
BRINING
BRUXING
CRANING
CRATING
CRAVING
CRAZING
CREWING
CROWING
DRAPING
DRAWING
DRAYING
DRIVING
DRONING
ERASING
ERELONG
ERODING
FRAMING
FRAYING
FREEING
GRABBAG
GRACING
GRADING
GRATING
GRAVING
GRAYING
GRAYLAG
GRAZING
GREYING
GRIMING
GRIPING
GROPING
GROWING
IRONING
JREWING
ORATING
PRATING
PRAYING
PRICING
PRIDING
PRIMING
PRIZING
PROBING
PROLONG
PROSING
PROVING
PRUNING
TRACING
TRADING
TREEING
TRUEING
WRITING
XRATING
XRAYING

••RG•••
AIRGUNS
BARGAIN
BARGEIN
BARGING
BERGERE
BERGMAN
BERGSON
BURGEES
BURGEON
BURGERS
BURGESS
BURGHER
BURGLAR
BURGLED
BURGLES
BURGOOS
CARGOES
FARGONE
FORGAVE
FORGERS
FORGERY
FORGETS
FORGING
FORGIVE
FORGOES
FORGONE
FORGOOD
GARGLED
GARGLES
GORGETS
GORGING
GORGONS
GURGLED
GURGLES
JARGONS
JARGONY
LARGELY
LARGESS
LARGEST
LARGISH
MARGATE
MARGAUX
MARGAYS
MARGINS
MARGRET
MERGERS
MERGING
MORGANA
MORGANS
OURGANG
PARGETS
PERGOLA
PORGIES
PURGING
SARGENT
SORGHUM
SURGEON
SURGERY
SURGING
TARGETS
VERGERS
VERGING
VIRGINS
VIRGOAN
VIRGULE
WARGAME
WARGODS

••R•G••
ALRIGHT
BURPGUN
ENRAGED
ENRAGES
FORAGED
FORAGER
FORAGES
GARAGED
GARAGES
MIRAGES
MRRIGHT
PARAGON
PERIGEE
PIROGUE
RAREGAS
SCRAGGY
UPRIGHT
VIRAGOS

••R••G•
ABRIDGE
ACREAGE
AIRBAGS
AIRINGS
ARRAIGN
ARRANGE
BARONGS
BARRAGE
BOROUGH
CARTAGE
CORDAGE
CORKAGE
CORSAGE
CORTEGE
DURANGO
EARWIGS
FARRAGO
FIRINGS
FOREIGN
GARBAGE
HERBAGE
MARENGO
NORIEGA
PARINGS
PORTAGE
SARONGS
SCRAGGY
SCROOGE
SPRINGS
SPRINGY
STRANGE
STRINGS
STRINGY
SYRINGA
SYRINGE
THRONGS
THROUGH
VERDUGO
VERTIGO
YARDAGE

••R•••G
BARBING
BARGING
BARKING
BARRING
BIRDDOG
BIRDING
BIRLING
BURLING
BURNING
BURPING
BURYING
CARDING
CARKING
CARPING
CARTING
CARVING
CORDING
CORKING
CORNDOG
CORNING
CURBING
CURDING
CURLING
CURSING
CURVING
DARLING
DARNING
DARTING
DERRING
DURNING
EARNING
EARPLUG
EARRING
FARCING
FARMING
FIREBUG
FIREDOG
FIRMING
FORCING
FORDING
FORELEG
FORGING
FORKING
FORMING
FURLING
FURLONG
FURRING
GARBING
GIRDING
GIRNING
GORGING
HARBURG
HARDING
HARKING
HARMING
HARPING
HERDING
HERRING
HORNING
HORSING
HURLING
HURTING
JARRING
JERKING
JURYING
JURYRIG
KERNING
LARDING
LORDING
LURKING
MARKING
MARRING
MERGING
MORNING
NURSING
OURGANG
PARKING
PARRING
PARSING
PARTING
PERKING
PERMING
PURGING
PURLING
PURRING
PURSING
SERLING
SERVING
SORTING
SURFING
SURGING
TARRING
TERMING
TURNING
VARYING
VERGING
WARDING
WARMING
WARNING
WARPING
WARRING
WARTHOG
WORDING
WORKING
YARNING
YERKING
ZEROING

•••RG••
CHARGED
CHARGER
CHARGES
EMERGED
EMERGES
EPERGNE
GEORGES
GEORGIA
GIORGIO
GUARGUM
REARGUE
SPARGED
SPARGES
STURGES
TEARGAS

•••R•G•
AMERIGO
AVERAGE
BARRAGE
COURAGE
FARRAGO
MOORAGE
OILRIGS
OUTRAGE
OVERAGE
PEERAGE
RAGRUGS
STORAGE
TUAREGS
UMBRAGE

•••R••G
ADORING
BARRING
BEARHUG
BEARING
BLARING
DERRING
EARRING
ENURING
FAIRING
FEARING
FLARING
FURRING
GEARING
GLARING
GOWRONG
HEARING
HERRING
INURING
JARRING
JEERING
KEYRING
LEERING
MARRING
MITRING
MOORING
NEARING
OVERBIG
PAIRING
PARRING
PEERING
POURING
PURRING
REARING
ROARING
SCARING
SCORING
SEARING
SHARING
SHORING
SNARING
SNORING
SOARING
SOURING
SPARING
STARING
STORING
TARRING
TEARING
TIERING
TITRING
TOURING
VEERING
WARRING
WEARING

••••RG•
ALLERGY
ATLARGE
CYBORGS
DEBARGE
DEFARGE
DIVERGE
EMBARGO
ENGORGE
ENLARGE
FABERGE
LAFARGE
LITURGY
PANURGE
RESURGE
SCOURGE
SPLURGE
SYNERGY
THEURGY
UNDERGO
UPSURGE
ZYMURGY

••••R•G
AREARUG
DISHRAG
JURYRIG
WASHRAG

•••••RG
HAMBURG
HARBURG
HOMBURG
ICEBERG
SEABORG

RH•••••
RHEBOKS
RHENISH
RHENIUM
RHETORS
RHIZOME
RHODIUM
RHOMBUS
RHUBARB
RHUMBAS
RHYMERS
RHYMING
RHYTHMS

R•H••••
REHANGS
REHEALS
REHEARD
REHEARS
REHEATS
REHEELS
REHIRED
REHIRES
REHOOKS

R••H•••
RAPHAEL
RASHERS
RASHEST
RATHOLE
RAWHIDE
RECHALK
RECHECK
RECHOSE
REDHAIR
REDHATS
REDHEAD
REDHEAT
REDHOTS
RESHIPS
RESHOES
RESHOOT
RETHINK
RICHARD
RICHEST
RICHMAN
RICHTER
RIGHTED
RIGHTER
RIGHTLY
RIGHTON
ROCHETS
RUCHING
RUNHOME
RUSHDIE
RUSHEES
RUSHERS
RUSHIER
RUSHING
RUSHOFF
RUTHFUL

R•••H••
RAINHAT
RANCHED
RANCHER
RANCHES
RANCHOS
RATCHET
REACHED
REACHES
REUTHER
RHYTHMS
RIMSHOT
ROACHED
ROACHES
ROADHOG
ROUGHED
ROUGHEN
ROUGHER
ROUGHIT
ROUGHLY
ROUGHUP

R••••H•
RELIGHT
RICKSHA
RUPIAHS

R•••••H
RAFFISH
RALEIGH
RAMMISH
RANKISH
RASPISH
RATTISH
REBEKAH
REBIRTH
REDDISH
REFRESH
RETEACH
RETOUCH
RHENISH
ROGUISH
ROMANSH
ROMPISH
RUBBISH
RUDOLPH
RUNTISH
RUNWITH
RUTTISH

•R•H•••
ARCHAIC
ARCHERS
ARCHERY
ARCHING
ARCHIVE
ARCHONS
ARCHWAY
ARMHOLE
BRAHMAN

BRAHMAS
BRAHMIN
DRYHOLE
GRAHAME
GRAHAMS
MRCHIPS
ORCHARD
ORCHIDS
ORPHANS
ORPHEAN
ORPHEUS
ORPHREY
PREHEAT
URCHINS

•R••H••

ARACHNE
BRASHER
BRASHLY
BRIGHAM
BROTHER
BRUSHED
BRUSHES
BRUSHUP
CRASHED
CRASHES
CRECHES
CROCHET
CRUSHED
CRUSHER
CRUSHES
DRACHMA
DRACHMS
DROSHKY
EREWHON
FRESHEN
FRESHER
FRESHET
FRESHLY
FRIGHTS
FROTHED
GRAPHED
GRAPHIC
GREYHEN
GRISHAM
GRYPHON
KRISHNA
PRITHEE
PROPHET
PROSHOP
PRUDHOE
TRACHEA
TRASHED
TRASHES
TRISHAW
TROCHEE
TROCHES
TROPHIC
TROTHED
WRIGHTS
WRITHED
WRITHES

•R•••H•

ARAPAHO
BREATHE
BREATHS
BREATHY
BRIOCHE
BRONCHI
BROUGHT
CRUNCHY
DRAUGHT
DROUGHT
FRAUGHT
FREIGHT
GROUCHO
GROUCHY
GROWTHS
MRRIGHT
ORNITHO
PREACHY
TROUGHS
WRAITHS
WREATHE
WREATHS
WROUGHT

•R••••H

BRANAGH
BREADTH
BRINISH
BRITISH
BRUTISH
CRONISH
DRONISH
GRAYISH
GREYISH
PREWASH
PRUDISH
TRIUMPH

••RH•••

AIRHEAD
AIRHOLE
BARHOPS
CARHOPS
EARHART
PERHAPS
TARHEEL
TERHUNE

••R•H••

ABRAHAM
AIRSHIP
AIRSHOW
BERTHED
BIRCHED
BIRCHES
BIRTHED
BURGHER
EARSHOT
EARTHEN
EARTHLY
FARTHER
FORDHAM
FURTHER
GURKHAS
HARDHAT
HARDHIT
HARSHEN
HARSHER
HARSHLY
HERSHEY
KERCHOO
LARCHES
LURCHED
LURCHES
MARCHED
MARCHER
MARCHES
MARCHON
MARKHAM
MARKHOR
MARSHAL
MARSHES
MORPHED
NARTHEX
NARWHAL
NORTHER
PARCHED
PARCHES
PERCHED
PERCHES
PORCHES
PORTHOS
PYRRHIC
PYRRHUS
SORGHUM
TORCHED
TORCHES
WARSHIP
WARTHOG
WERNHER
WERTHER
WORSHIP

••R••H•

ALRIGHT
ATROPHY
AUROCHS
BORSCHT
CERIPHS
DOROTHY
EARACHE
HURRAHS
JERICHO
KARACHI
MRRIGHT
PARAPHS
PARIAHS
PIRANHA
PORSCHE
PURDAHS
SERAPHS
STROPHE
TERAPHS
UPRIGHT
UTRECHT

••R•••H

BARDISH
BOROUGH
BURNISH
CARWASH
CORINTH
CORNISH
CURRISH
DARKISH
DERVISH
EHRLICH
FORSYTH
FURBISH
FURNISH
GARNISH
GIRLISH
HORNISH
KURDISH
LARGISH
LARKISH
MURDOCH
OGREISH
PARRISH
PERKISH
PORKISH
SCRATCH
SCREECH
SCRUNCH
STRETCH
TARNISH
TARTISH
THROUGH
TORYISH
TURKISH
VARNISH
WARMISH
WARPATH
WORMISH
YERKISH

•••RH••

BEARHUG
MOORHEN
PYRRHIC
PYRRHUS

•••R•H•

ANARCHY
DEARTHS
EPARCHS
EPARCHY
EXARCHS
FOURTHS
HEARTHS
HURRAHS
STARCHY
SWARTHY

•••R••H

ALDRICH
BEARISH
BETROTH
BOARISH
BOORISH
BULRUSH
BUMRUSH
CHERISH
CURRISH
DIGRAPH
FAIRISH
INARUSH
INTRUTH
MOORISH
NOURISH
OSTRICH
PARRISH
PHARAOH
POORISH
REFRESH
SOURISH
TIGRISH
UNTRUTH

••••R•H

ALWORTH
DEBORAH
HOGARTH
MENORAH
MONARCH
REBIRTH
UNEARTH

RI•••••

RIANTLY
RIBANDS
RIBBIES
RIBBING
RIBBONS
RIBCAGE
RIBEYES
RIBLESS
RIBLIKE
RICARDO
RICERAT
RICHARD
RICHEST
RICHMAN
RICHTER
RICKETY
RICKEYS
RICKLES
RICKMAN
RICKSHA
RICOTTA
RIDDICK
RIDDING
RIDDLED
RIDDLER
RIDDLES
RIDEOFF
RIDEOUT
RIDGIER
RIDGING
RIDGWAY
RIDOTTO
RIFFING
RIFFLED
RIFFLES
RIFLERS
RIFLERY
RIFLING
RIFTING
RIGGERS
RIGGING
RIGHTED
RIGHTER
RIGHTLY
RIGHTON
RIGIDLY
RIGOURS
RIGVEDA
RILESUP
RILLETS
RIMBAUD
RIMIEST
RIMLESS
RIMMING
RIMPLED
RIMPLES
RIMSHOT
RINGERS
RINGING
RINGLET
RINGOFF
RINGOUT
RINGSUP
RINSING
RIOLOBO
RIORITA
RIOTACT
RIOTERS
RIOTING
RIOTOUS
RIPCORD
RIPENED
RIPIENO
RIPINTO
RIPOFFS
RIPOSTE
RIPPERS
RIPPING
RIPPLED
RIPPLES
RIPRAPS
RIPSAWS
RIPSOFF
RIPSOUT
RIPTIDE
RIPTORN
RISIBLE
RISIBLY
RISINGS
RISKERS
RISKIER
RISKILY
RISKING
RISOTTO
RISSOLE
RITUALS
RITZIER
RITZILY
RIVALED
RIVALRY
RIVETED
RIVETER
RIVIERA
RIVIERE
RIVULET

R•I••••

RAIDERS
RAIDING
RAILERS
RAILING
RAILSAT
RAILWAY
RAIMENT
RAINBOW
RAINHAT
RAINIER
RAINILY
RAINING
RAINMAN
RAINOUT
RAISERS
RAISEUP
RAISING
RAISINS
REIFIED
REIFIES
REIGNED
REINING
REINKED
REINSIN
REISSUE
REITMAN
RHIZOME
ROILIER
ROILING
ROISTER
RUINERS
RUINING
RUINOUS

R••I•••

RABIDLY
RACIEST
RADIALS
RADIANS
RADIANT
RADIATE
RADICAL
RADICES
RADICLE
RADIOED
RADIXES
RAMINTO
RANINTO
RAPIDER
RAPIDLY
RAPIERS
RAPINES
RARITAN
RATINGS
RATIONS
RATITES
RAVINES
RAVINGS
RAVIOLI
REAIMED
REAIRED
REBINDS
REBIRTH
RECIPES
RECITAL
RECITED
RECITER
RECITES
REDIALS
REFILED
REFILES
REFILLS
REFILMS
REFINED
REFINER
REFINES
REFIRES
REGIMEN
REGIMES
REGIONS
REHIRED
REHIRES
RELIANT
RELICTS
RELIEFS
RELIEVE
RELIEVO
RELIGHT
RELINED
RELINES
RELISTS
RELIVED
RELIVES
REMIGES
REMINDS
REMIXED
REMIXES
REOILED
REPINED
REPINES
RERINSE
RESIDED
RESIDES
RESIDUE
RESIGNS
RESILED
RESILES
RESINGS
RESISTS
RETIARY
RETICLE
RETILED
RETILES
RETIMED
RETIMES
RETINAE
RETINAL
RETINAS
RETINUE
RETIRED
RETIREE
RETIRES
RETITLE
REVIEWS
REVILED
REVILES
REVISED
REVISER
REVISES
REVISIT
REVIVAL
REVIVED
REVIVES
REWINDS
REWIRED
REWIRES
RIGIDLY
RIMIEST
RIPIENO
RIPINTO
RISIBLE
RISIBLY
RISINGS
RIVIERA
RIVIERE
ROPIEST
ROSIEST
ROTIFER
RUBICON
RUBITIN
RUFIYAA
RULINGS
RUNINTO
RUPIAHS

R•••I••

RABBITS
RABBITT
RACKING
RAFFISH
RAFTING
RAGGING
RAGTIME
RAIDING
RAILING
RAINIER
RAINILY
RAINING
RAISING
RAISINS
RALEIGH
RALLIED
RALLIER
RALLIES
RAMLIKE
RAMMING
RAMMISH
RANDIER
RANGIER
RANGING
RANKING
RANKISH
RANRIOT
RANTING
RAPPING
RASPIER
RASPING
RASPISH
RATFINK
RATLIKE
RATLINE
RATTIER
RATTING
RATTISH
RAWHIDE
RAWSILK
RAYLIKE
RAZZING
RDLAING
READIED
READIER
READIES
READILY
READING
REALISE
REALISM
REALIST
REALITY
REALIZE
REAMING
REAPING
REARING
REBOILS
REBUILD
REBUILT
RECEIPT
RECEIVE
RECLINE
RECOILS
RECTIFY
REDBIRD
REDDING
REDDISH
REDFINS
REDFIRS
REDLINE
REDOING
REDPINE
REDWINE
REDWING
REEDIER
REEDING
REEDITS
REEFING
REEKING
REELING
REFFING
REFRIED
REFRIES
REGAINS
REIFIED
REIFIES
REINING
REJOICE
REJOINS
RELYING
REMAILS
REMAINS
RENAILS
RENDING
RENNINS
RENTING
REPAINT
REPAIRS
REPLICA
REPLIED
REPLIES
REPRICE
REPRINT
REPRISE
REPTILE
REQUIEM
REQUIRE
REQUITE
RERAISE
RESCIND
RESHIPS
RESPINS
RESPIRE
RESPITE
RESTING
RESTIVE
RETAILS
RETAINS
RETHINK
RETRIAL
RETRIED
RETRIES
RETRIMS
RETSINA
REUNIFY
REUNION
REUNITE
REVOICE
REVVING
REWRITE
RHENISH
RHENIUM
RHODIUM
RHYMING
RIBBIES
RIBBING
RIBLIKE
RIDDICK
RIDDING
RIDGIER
RIDGING
RIFFING
RIFLING
RIFTING
RIGGING
RIMMING
RINGING
RINSING
RIORITA
RIOTING
RIPPING
RIPTIDE
RISKIER
RISKILY
RISKING
RITZIER
RITZILY
ROADIES
ROAMING
ROARING
ROBBING
ROBBINS
ROCKIER
ROCKIES
ROCKING
RODDING
RODLIKE
ROGAINE
ROGUISH
ROILIER
ROILING
ROLAIDS
ROLLICK
ROLLING
ROLLINS
ROMAINE
ROMPING
ROMPISH
ROOFING
ROOKIER
ROOKIES
ROOKING
ROOMIER
ROOMIES
ROOMILY
ROOMING
ROOTIER
ROOTING
ROSSINI
ROTTING
ROUGING
ROUSING
ROUTINE
ROUTING
ROWDIER
ROWDIES
ROWDILY
RUBBING
RUBBISH
RUBRICS
RUCHING
RUCKING
RUCTION
RUDDIER
RUDDILY
RUFFIAN
RUGLIKE
RUINING
RUMMIER
RUNNIER
RUNNING
RUNRIOT
RUNTIER
RUNTISH
RUNWITH
RUSHIER
RUSHING
RUSSIAN
RUSTICS
RUSTIER
RUSTILY
RUSTING
RUTTIER
RUTTISH

R••••I•

RAKEDIN
RAKESIN
RAMEKIN
RAREBIT
RATAFIA
RATTAIL
READMIT
READSIN
REAFFIX
REAVAIL
RECLAIM
RECRUIT
REDHAIR
REELSIN
REFRAIN
REGALIA
REINSIN
RESTAIN
RETRAIN
REVERIE
REVISIT
ROBOTIC
ROCKYII
ROCKYIV
ROLLSIN
ROMANIA
ROPEDIN
ROPESIN
ROSALIE
ROSARIO
ROSEOIL
ROUGHIT
RUBITIN
RUSHDIE

R•••••I

RAPANUI
RAVIOLI
ROCKYII
ROSSINI

•RI••••

ARIADNE
ARIDEST
ARIDITY
ARIETTA
ARIKARA
ARIOSOS
ARIOSTO
ARISING
ARISTAE
ARISTAS
ARISTOS
ARIZONA
BRIARDS
BRIBERY
BRIBING
BRICKED
BRIDALS
BRIDGED
BRIDGES
BRIDGET
BRIDLED
BRIDLES
BRIEFED
BRIEFER
BRIEFLY
BRIGADE
BRIGAND
BRIGHAM
BRIMFUL
BRIMLEY
BRIMMED
BRINDLE
BRINGER
BRINGIN
BRINGON
BRINGTO
BRINGUP
BRINIER
BRINING
BRINISH
BRIOCHE
BRIQUET
BRISKER
BRISKET
BRISKLY
BRISTLE
BRISTLY
BRISTOL
BRITAIN
BRITISH
BRITONS
BRITTEN
BRITTLE
BRITTON
CRIBBED
CRICKED
CRICKET
CRIMEAN
CRIMPED
CRIMPER
CRIMSON
CRINGED
CRINGES
CRINKLE
CRINKLY
CRINOID
CRIOLLO
CRISPED
CRISPER
CRISPIN
CRISPLY
CRISPUS
CRITICS
CRITTER
DRIBBLE
DRIBLET
DRIEDUP
DRIESUP
DRIFTED
DRIFTER
DRILLED
DRILLER
DRINKER
DRIPDRY
DRIPPAN
DRIPPED
DRISTAN
DRIVEAT
DRIVEIN
DRIVELS
DRIVERS
DRIVEUP
DRIVING
DRIZZLE
DRIZZLY
ERICSON
ERISTIC
ERITREA
FRIABLE
FRICKIE
FRIDAYS
FRIDGES
FRIEDAN
FRIENDS
FRIEZES
FRIGATE
FRIGHTS
FRILLED
FRINGED
FRINGES
FRIPPET
FRISBEE
FRISIAN
FRISKED
FRISSON
FRITTED
FRITTER
FRIZZED
FRIZZES
FRIZZLE
FRIZZLY
GRIDDED
GRIDDER
GRIDDLE
GRIEVED
GRIEVER
GRIEVES
GRIFFEY
GRIFFIN
GRIFFON
GRIFTER
GRIGRIS
GRILLED
GRILLES
GRILLET
GRIMACE
GRIMIER
GRIMILY
GRIMING
GRIMMER
GRINDER
GRINNED
GRINNER
GRIPERS
GRIPING
GRIPPED
GRIPPER
GRISHAM
GRISKIN
GRISSOM
GRISTLE
GRISTLY
GRITTED
GRIVETS
GRIZZLE
GRIZZLY
IRIDIUM
IRISOUT
KRINGLE
KRISHNA
ORIENTE
ORIENTS
ORIFICE
ORIGAMI
ORIGINS
ORINOCO
ORIOLES
ORISONS
PRICERS
PRICIER
PRICING
PRICKED
PRICKLE
PRICKLY
PRIDING
PRIESTS
PRIMACY
PRIMARY
PRIMATE
PRIMERS
PRIMING
PRIMMER
PRIMPED
PRINCES
PRINKED
PRINTED
PRINTER
PRIORTO
PRISONS
PRITHEE
PRIVACY
PRIVATE
PRIVETS
PRIVIER
PRIVIES
PRIVILY
PRIVITY
PRIZING
TRIBUNE
TRIBUTE
TRICEPS
TRICKED
TRICKER
TRICKLE
TRICORN
TRICOTS
TRIDENT
TRIEDON
TRIESON
TRIESTE
TRIFLED
TRIFLER
TRIFLES
TRIGGED
TRIGGER
TRIGONS
TRIGRAM
TRIJETS
TRILLED
TRILLIN
TRILOGY

TRIMMED
TRIMMER
TRINITY
TRINKET
TRIODES
TRIPLED
TRIPLES
TRIPLET
TRIPLEX
TRIPODS
TRIPOLI
TRIPPED
TRIPPER
TRIPPET
TRIPSUP
TRIREME
TRISECT
TRISHAW
TRISTAN
TRISTAR
TRITELY
TRITEST
TRITIUM
TRITONE
TRITONS
TRIUMPH
TRIUNES
TRIVETS
TRIVIAL
WRIGGLE
WRIGGLY
WRIGHTS
WRIGLEY
WRINGER
WRINKLE
WRINKLY
WRITEIN
WRITERS
WRITETO
WRITEUP
WRITHED
WRITHES
WRITING
WRITTEN

•R•I•••

ARBITER
ARGIVES
ARNICAS
ARRIERE
ARRISES
ARRIVAL
ARRIVED
ARRIVER
ARRIVES
ARTICLE
ARTIEST
ARTISAN
ARTISTE
ARTISTS
BRAIDED
BRAIDER
BRAILLE
BRAINED
BRAISED
BRAISES
BROILED
BROILER
BRUISED
BRUISER
BRUISES
BRUITED
CRUISED
CRUISER
CRUISES
DRAINED
DRAINER
DREIDEL
DREISER
ERMINES
FRAILER
FRAILLY
FRAILTY
FRAISES
FREIGHT
FRUITED
GRAINED
MRFIXIT
MRRIGHT
ORBISON
ORBITAL
ORBITED
ORBITER
ORDINAL
ORDINES
ORNITHO
ORPINES
ORVILLE
PRAIRIE
PRAISED
PRAISER
PRAISES
PRYINTO
TRAILED
TRAILER
TRAINED
TRAINEE
TRAINER
TRAIPSE
TRAITOR
TROIKAS
TROILUS
TRUISMS
WRAITHS

•R••I••

ARABIAN
ARCHING
ARCHIVE
ARCSINE
ARECIBO
ARETINO
ARGUING
ARIDITY
ARISING
ARMLIKE
ARMOIRE
ARMPITS
ARRAIGN
ARTFILM
ARTSIER
BRACING
BRAKING
BRAVING
BRAYING
BRAZIER
BRAZING
BREVITY
BREWING
BRIBING
BRINIER
BRINING
BRINISH
BRITISH
BROMIDE
BROMINE
BRUTISH
BRUXING
CRANIAL
CRANING
CRANIUM
CRATING
CRAVING
CRAZIER
CRAZIES
CRAZILY
CRAZING
CREDITS
CRETINS
CREVICE
CREWING
CRITICS
CRONIES
CRONISH
CROSIER
CROWING
CRUCIAL
CRUCIFY
CRUDITY
DRAPING
DRAWING
DRAYING
DRIVING
DRONING
DRONISH
DROPINS
ERASING
EREMITE
ERODING
EROSION
EROSIVE
EROTICA
ERSKINE
ERUDITE
FRAGILE
FRAMING
FRASIER
FRAYING
FRAZIER
FREEING
FRISIAN
FROLICS
GRACIAS
GRACILE
GRACING
GRADING
GRANITE
GRAPIER
GRATIAS
GRATIFY
GRATING
GRAVIES
GRAVING
GRAVITY
GRAYING
GRAYISH
GRAZING
GRECIAN
GREYING
GREYISH
GRIMIER
GRIMILY
GRIMING
GRIPING
GRODIER
GROLIER
GROPING
GROPIUS
GROWING
GRUNION
IRANIAN
IRIDIUM
IRONIES
IRONING
JREWING
KRATION
MRCHIPS
ORATING
ORATION
ORBLIKE
ORCHIDS
ORDAINS
ORIFICE
ORIGINS
PRALINE
PRATING
PRAYING
PRECISE
PREDICT
PRELIMS
PREMIER
PREMISE
PREMISS
PREMIUM
PRESIDE
PREVIEW
PREXIES
PRICIER
PRICING
PRIDING
PRIMING
PRIVIER
PRIVIES
PRIVILY
PRIVITY
PRIZING
PROBING
PROBITY
PRODIGY
PROFILE
PROFITS
PROMISE
PROSIER
PROSILY
PROSING
PROTIST
PROVIDE
PROVING
PROVISO
PROXIES
PROXIMO
PRUDISH
PRUNING
TRACING
TRADING
TREEING
TREVINO
TRINITY
TRITIUM
TRIVIAL
TROPICS
TROPISM
TRUCIAL
TRUEING
URANITE
URANIUM
URCHINS
URNLIKE
WRITING
XRATING
XRAYING

•R•••I•

ARAMAIC
ARCADIA
ARCHAIC
ARMENIA
ARSENIC
ARSENIO
ARTEMIS
BRAHMIN
BRASSIE
BREAKIN
BRESLIN
BRINGIN
BRITAIN
BROKEIN
BROWNIE
CRAPPIE
CRINOID
CRISPIN
CROATIA
CRYPTIC
DRAGSIN
DRASTIC
DRAWNIN
DRAWSIN
DRIVEIN
DROPSIN
DRUMLIN
DRYSUIT
ERISTIC
ERRATIC
FRANCIS
FRANKIE
FRANTIC
FREDDIE
FREDRIC
FREEBIE
FREESIA
FRICKIE
GRAPHIC
GREMLIN
GRIFFIN
GRIGRIS
GRISKIN
GROUPIE
KREMLIN
MRFIXIT
ORGANIC
PRAIRIE
PREEMIE
PREPAID
PREPPIE
PREVAIL
PROPRIO
PROSAIC
PROTEIN
PRUSSIA
TRADEIN
TRAFFIC
TRANSIT
TRAVAIL
TRAVOIS
TREFOIL
TREKKIE
TRELLIS
TREMAIN
TRILLIN
TROPHIC
WRITEIN
WROTEIN

•R••••I

BRONCHI
ORIGAMI
TRIPOLI

••RI•••

ABRIDGE
ACRIDLY
AERIALS
AERIEST
AFRICAN
AGRIPPA
AIRIEST
AIRINGS
ALRIGHT
AORISTS
APRICOT
APRIORI
ARRIERE
ARRISES
ARRIVAL
ARRIVED
ARRIVER
ARRIVES
ATRIUMS
AURICLE
BERIDOF
CARIBES
CARIBOU
CARINAS
CARIOCA
CCRIDER
CERIPHS
CHRISMS
CHRISTI
CHRISTO
CHRISTY
CORINTH
CURIOUS
DERIDED
DERIDES
DERIVED
DERIVES
DORITOS
EERIEST
FIRINGS
FORINTS
FURIOUS
GERITOL
GORIEST
GORILLA
HARICOT
HORIZON
JERICHO
JURIDIC
JURISTS
LARIATS
LORICAE
LORISES
LURIDLY
LYRICAL
LYRISTS
MARIANA
MARILYN
MARIMBA
MARINAS
MARINER
MARINES
MARITAL
MERIMEE
MERINOS
MERITED
MIRIEST
MRRIGHT
MURILLO
MYRIADS
NORIEGA
PARIAHS
PARINGS
PERIDOT
PERIGEE
PERIODS
PURISTS
PURITAN
PYRITES
RARITAN
RERINSE
SCRIBES
SCRIMPS
SCRIMPY
SCRIPPS
SCRIPTS
SCRIVEN
SERIALS
SERIATE
SERIOUS
SHRIEKS
SHRIFTS
SHRIKES
SHRILLS
SHRILLY
SHRIMPS
SHRINER
SHRINES
SHRINKS
SHRIVEL
SHRIVER
SHRIVES
SORITES
SPRIEST
SPRINGS
SPRINGY
SPRINTS
SPRITES
STRIATE
STRIDER
STRIDES
STRIKER
STRIKES
STRINGS
STRINGY
STRIPED
STRIPER
STRIPES
STRIVED
STRIVEN
STRIVER
STRIVES
SURINAM
SYRIANS
SYRINGA
SYRINGE
TARIFFS
THRIFTS
THRIFTY
THRILLS
THRIVED
THRIVES
UPRIGHT
UPRISEN
UPRISES
UPRIVER
UTRILLO
VARIANT
VARIETY
VARIOUS
VERISMO
VERITAS
VIRIBUS
WARIEST
WIRIEST

••R•I••

AIRKISS
AIRLIFT
AIRLIKE
AIRLINE
AIRMILE
AIRTIME
ARRAIGN
BARBING
BARDISH
BARGING
BARKIER
BARKING
BARMIER
BARRIER
BARRING
BARRIOS
BERLIOZ
BERLITZ
BERNICE
BERRIED
BERRIES
BIRDIED
BIRDIES
BIRDING
BIRLING
BURKINA
BURLIER
BURLING
BURNING
BURNISH
BURPING
BURRITO
BURYING
CARBIDE
CARBINE
CARDIAC
CARDING
CARKING
CARMINE
CARNIES
CARPING
CARRICK
CARRIED
CARRIER
CARRIES
CARRION
CARTIER
CARTING
CARVING
CERTIFY
CERVIDS
CORDIAL
CORDING
CORDITE
CORKIER
CORKING
CORNICE
CORNIER
CORNILY
CORNING
CORNISH
CORRIDA
CORSICA
CURBING
CURDIER
CURDING
CURLIER
CURLIKE
CURLING
CURRIED
CURRIER
CURRIES
CURRISH
CURSING
CURSIVE
CURTISS
CURVIER
CURVING
DARBIES
DARKISH
DARLING
DARNING
DARTING
DERAILS
DERBIES
DERNIER
DERRICK
DERRING
DERVISH
DIRTIED
DIRTIER
DIRTIES
DIRTILY
DORMICE
DURNING
EARLIER
EARLIKE
EARNING
EARRING
EARWIGS
EHRLICH
FARCING
FARMING
FARRIER
FERMIUM
FERNIER
FERRIED
FERRIES
FERRITE
FERTILE
FIRKINS
FIRMING
FIRRIER
FORBIDS
FORCING
FORDING
FOREIGN
FORGING
FORGIVE
FORKIER
FORKING
FORLIFE
FORMICA
FORMING
FORTIES
FORTIFY
FORTIUS
FURBISH
FURLING
FURNISH
FURRIER
FURRING
FURTIVE
GARBING
GARNISH
GARRICK
GERAINT
GERBILS
GERMIER
GIRDING
GIRLISH
GIRNING
GORDIAN
GORGING
GORSIER
HARDIER
HARDILY
HARDING
HARKING
HARMING
HARPIES
HARPING
HARPIST
HARRIED
HARRIER
HARRIES
HARRIET
HERBIER
HERDING
HERMITS
HEROICS
HEROINE
HEROISM
HERRING
HERRIOT
HORNING
HORNISH
HORNIST
HORRIFY
HORSIER
HORSING
HURLIES
HURLING
HURRIED
HURRIES
HURTING
JARRING
JERKIER
JERKILY
JERKING
JERKINS
JURYING
KERNING
KURDISH
LARAINE
LARDIER
LARDING
LARGISH
LARKISH
LORDING
LORRIES
LURKING
MARGINS
MARKING
MARLINS
MARMION
MARRIED
MARRIES
MARRING
MARTIAL
MARTIAN
MARTINA
MARTINI
MARTINO
MARTINS
MARXISM
MARXIST
MERCIES
MERGING
MERRIER
MERRILL
MERRILY
MIRKIER
MORAINE
MORNING
MORTIFY
MORTISE
MURKIER
MURKILY
NERDIER
NEREIDS
NERVIER
NERVILY
NORDICS
NURSING
OARLIKE
OGREISH
PARKING
PARRIED
PARRIER
PARRIES
PARRING
PARRISH
PARSING
PARTIAL
PARTIED
PARTIER
PARTIES
PARTING
PARTITA
PARTITE
PERDIEM
PERFIDY
PERKIER
PERKILY
PERKING
PERKINS
PERKISH
PERLITE
PERMING
PERMITS
PERRIER
PERSIAN
PERSIST
PERSIUS
PORCINE
PORGIES
PORKIER
PORKISH
PORTICO
PORTION
PURGING
PURLIEU
PURLING
PURLINS
PURRING
PURSIER
PURSING
PURVIEW
RERAISE
SARDINE
SARKIER
SERBIAN
SERLING
SERPICO
SERRIED
SERVICE
SERVILE
SERVING
SORDINI
SORDINO
SORRIER
SORRILY
SORTIED
SORTIES
SORTING
SORVINO
SPRAINS
STRAINS
STRAITS
SURFIER
SURFING
SURGING
SURLIER
SURLILY
SURMISE
SURVIVE
TARDIER
TARDILY
TARNISH
TARPITS
TARRIED
TARRIER
TARRIES
TARRING
TARSIER
TARTISH
TERBIUM
TERMING
TERMINI
TERMITE
TERRIER
TERRIES
TERRIFY
TERTIAL
TOROIDS
TORSION
TORYISH
TORYISM
TURBINE
TURBITS
TURFIER
TURKISH
TURNING
TURNIPS
UKRAINE
UPRAISE
VARMINT
VARNISH
VARSITY
VARYING
VERDICT
VERGING
VERNIER
VERSIFY
VERSION
VERTIGO
VIRGINS
WARDING
WARLIKE
WARMING
WARMISH
WARNING
WARPING
WARRING
WARRIOR
WARTIER
WARTIME
WARWICK
WORDIER
WORDILY
WORDING
WORKING
WORMIER
WORMISH
WORRIED
WORRIER
WORRIES
YARNING
YERKING
YERKISH
YORKIES
YORKIST
ZEROING

••R••I•

ACRYLIC
AEROBIC
AIRFOIL
AIRMAIL
AIRRAID
AIRSHIP
AMRADIO
BARGAIN
BARGEIN
BARMAID
BORACIC
BORODIN
BORZOIS
CARAMIA
CAROTID
CBRADIO
CERAMIC
CERTAIN
CHRONIC
CIRCUIT
CORNOIL
CORSAIR
CURTAIL
CURTAIN
ERRATIC
ETRURIA
EURASIA
FIRELIT
FMRADIO
FORFEIT
HARDHIT
HERETIC
HORATIO
HORNSIN
JURIDIC
JURYRIG
KERATIN
KIRSTIE
LARAMIE
LORDJIM
MARQUIS
MERMAID
MORANIS
MORAVIA
PARBOIL
PARFAIT
PARSNIP
PERSEID
PERTAIN
PHRENIC
PIRATIC
PORKPIE
PURLOIN
PURSUIT
PYRAMID
PYRRHIC
RAREBIT
SERAPIS
SIRLOIN
SURFEIT
TERRAIN
THREWIN
THROWIN
TURMOIL
TURNSIN
VERMEIL
WARSHIP
WORKSIN
WORSHIP

••R•••I

ABRUZZI
AIRTAXI
APRIORI
CHRISTI
CORELLI
FERRARI
ISRAELI
KARACHI
KAROLYI
LORELEI
MARCONI
MARTINI
SORDINI
TERMINI
TORTONI

•••RI••

ACARIDS
ADORING
AGARICS
ALDRICH
AMBRIES
AMERICA
AMERIGO
AMERIKA
AMERIND
ANGRIER
ANGRILY
APERIES
APPRISE
APPRIZE
ASCRIBE
ASTRIDE
ATTRITE
ATTRITS
AVARICE
AZURITE
BARRIER
BARRING
BARRIOS
BEARING
BEARISH
BEERIER
BEGRIME
BERRIED
BERRIES
BLARING
BLERIOT
BOARISH
BOORISH
BURRITO
CABRINI
CAPRICE
CARRICK
CARRIED
CARRIER
CARRIES
CARRION
CHARIER
CHARILY
CHARIOT
CHARITY
CHERISH
CHIRICO
CHORINE
CHORIZO
CITRINE
CLARICE
CLARIFY
CLARION
CLARITY
CLERICS
CLERISY
CONRIED
CORRIDA
COURIER
COWRIES
CURRIED
CURRIER
CURRIES
CURRISH
CYPRIOT
CZARINA

CZARISM
CZARIST
DAIRIES
DEARIES
DEBRIEF
DECRIED
DECRIER
DECRIES
DEPRIVE
DERRICK
DERRING
DEVRIES
DIARIES
DOWRIES
EARRING
EMERITA
EMERITI
ENTRIES
ENURING
FABRICS
FAERIES
FAIRIES
FAIRING
FAIRISH
FARRIER
FEARING
FEBRILE
FERRIED
FERRIES
FERRITE
FIBRILS
FIBRINS
FIERIER
FIERILY
FIRRIER
FLARING
FLORIDA
FLORINS
FLORIST
FOURIER
FURRIER
FURRING
GABRIEL
GARRICK
GEARING
GLARING
GLORIAM
GLORIAS
GLORIED
GLORIES
GLORIFY
HADRIAN
HAIRIER
HARRIED
HARRIER
HARRIES
HARRIET
HAYRIDE
HEARING
HERRING
HERRIOT
HOARIER
HOARILY
HORRIFY
HURRIED
HURRIES
HYBRIDS
IBERIAN
ICERINK
IMPRINT
INBRIEF
INPRINT
INURING
IVORIES
JARRING
JEERING
JOYRIDE
KEYRING
KUBRICK
LEARIER
LEERIER
LEERILY
LEERING
LORRIES
LOWRISE
MARRIED
MARRIES
MARRING
MAURICE
MEGRIMS
MERRIER
MERRILL
MERRILY
METRICS
MIDRIBS
MIDRIFF
MIDRISE
MITRING
MOORIER
MOORING
MOORISH
NATRIUM
NEARING
NITRIDE
NITRITE
NOURISH
NUTRIAS
OCARINA
OILRIGS
ONTRIAL
OSTRICH
PAIRING
PAPRIKA
PARRIED
PARRIER
PARRIES
PARRING
PARRISH
PATRIAL
PATRICE
PATRICK
PATRIOT
PEERING
PERRIER
PETRIFY
PODRIDA
POORIER
POORISH
POURING
PUERILE
PURRING
QUERIED
QUERIER
QUERIES
QUERIST
RANRIOT
REARING
REFRIED
REFRIES
REPRICE
REPRINT
REPRISE
RETRIAL
RETRIED
RETRIES
RETRIMS
REWRITE
RIORITA
ROARING
RUBRICS
RUNRIOT
SABRINA
SAURIAN
SCARIER
SCARIFY
SCARILY
SCARING
SCORING
SEARING
SERRIED
SHARING
SHERIFF
SHORING
SNARING
SNORING
SOARING
SORRIER
SORRILY
SOURING
SOURISH
SPARING
SPIRIER
SPIRITO
SPIRITS
STARING
STERILE
STORIED
STORIES
STORING
STYRIAN
SUNRISE
TARRIED
TARRIER
TARRIES
TARRING
TAURINE
TEARIER
TEARILY
TEARING
TERRIER
TERRIES
TERRIFY
THORIUM
TIERING
TIGRISH
TITRING
TOURING
TOURISM
TOURIST
TSARINA
TSARIST
TUGRIKS
TZARINA
UMBRIAN
UNTRIED
USERIDS
USURIES
UXORIAL
VEERIES
VEERING
VITRIFY
VITRIOL
WARRING
WARRIOR
WEARIED
WEARIER
WEARIES
WEARILY
WEARING
WORRIED
WORRIER
WORRIES
YTTRIUM
ZAIRIAN

•••R•I•

ACERBIC
AIRRAID
ANDROID
ANEROID
BAHRAIN
CHARLIE
CHARMIN
CHERVIL
DEARSIR
DETRAIN
DETROIT
DHURRIE
DOORDIE
EMBROIL
ENTRAIN
EXURBIA
FLORUIT
GEORDIE
GEORGIA
GHERKIN
GIORGIO
HAIRPIN
HEBRAIC
HENRYIV
INERTIA
INGRAIN
INORBIT
INTROIT
MAUROIS
OBERLIN
OCTROIS
OVERBIG
OVERDID
OVERLIE
PEERSIN
POURSIN
PYRRHIC
RECRUIT
REFRAIN
RETRAIN
SCORPIO
SHAREIN
SHERWIN
STARLIT
STCROIX
STEROID
STIRSIN
SWOREIN
TERRAIN
THEREIN
UPBRAID
WHEREIN

•••R••I

CABRINI
EMERITI
FERRARI
GOURAMI
GUARANI
NAIROBI
PADRONI
SHARPEI

••••RI•

AELFRIC
ALGERIA
AMHARIC
AQUARIA
ASPIRIN
ASSYRIA
ASTORIA
AUSTRIA
BALDRIC
BAVARIA
BEATRIX
CALORIC
CALORIE
CAMBRIC
CANTRIP
CENTRIC
CETERIS
CHAGRIN
CHEERIO
CIBORIA
CONBRIO
COTERIE
CULPRIT
DAYTRIP
DELIRIA
DEMERIT
DENARII
DEXTRIN
DHURRIE
EGOTRIP
EMPORIA
ESTORIL
ETRURIA
FREDRIC
GAGARIN
GASTRIC
GENERIC
GENERIS
GOFORIT
GONERIL
GRIGRIS
GUTHRIE
HENDRIX
HEPARIN
HOMERIC
HONORIS
IMPERIL
INHERIT
INTERIM
JURYRIG
KEYGRIP
LIBERIA
LITCRIT
MAHARIS
MANTRIC
NIGERIA
NOSTRIL
NUMERIC
ONTARIO
PILGRIM
POLARIS
PRAIRIE
PROPRIO
QATARIS
REVERIE
ROSARIO
SAFARIS
SAMARIA
SANGRIA
SATIRIC
SAVARIN
SIBERIA
SOLARIA
SWEARIN
TALARIA
TAMARIN
TENDRIL
TSOURIS
VALERIE
WILFRID

••••R•I

BACARDI
DENARII
HAVARTI
SAMURAI
SCHERZI

•••••RI

ALFIERI
APRIORI
CAMPARI
DIMITRI
FERRARI
MAESTRI
SALIERI
SHANGRI
SHASTRI
SHIKARI

R•J••••

RAJPUTS
REJECTS
REJOICE
REJOINS

R••J•••

RAMJETS

•R•J•••

PROJECT
TRIJETS
TROJANS

•R••J••

GRAYJAY
PROPJET

••RJ•••

PERJURE
PERJURY

••R•J••

KARAJAN
LORDJIM

••R••J•

BERMEJO

•••RJ••

LEARJET
OVERJOY

••••RJ•

ALFORJA

R•K••••

RAKEDIN
RAKEDUP
RAKEOFF
RAKESIN
RAKESUP
REKEYED

R••K•••

RACKETS
RACKING
RACKSUP
RANKERS
RANKEST
RANKING
RANKISH
RANKLED
RANKLES
RAYKROC
RECKONS
REEKING
RICKETY
RICKEYS
RICKLES
RICKMAN
RICKSHA
RISKERS
RISKIER
RISKILY
RISKING
ROCKERS
ROCKERY
ROCKETS
ROCKIER
ROCKIES
ROCKING
ROCKYII
ROCKYIV
ROOKERY
ROOKIER
ROOKIES
ROOKING
RUCKING

R•••K••

RAMEKIN
REBEKAH
REBUKED
REBUKES
REINKED
REMAKES
RETAKEN
RETAKES
REVOKED
REVOKES

R••••K•

RAMLIKE
RATLIKE
RAYLIKE
RECORKS
REDOAKS
REHOOKS
RELOCKS
REMARKS
REWORKS
RHEBOKS
RIBLIKE
ROANOKE
RODLIKE
RUGLIKE

R•••••K

RANSACK
RATFINK
RATPACK
RAWSILK
RECHALK
RECHECK
REDBOOK
RESTOCK
RETHINK
RETRACK
RIDDICK
ROEBUCK
ROLLICK
RUNAMOK
RUNBACK

•RK••••

IRKSOME

•R•K•••

ARIKARA
BRAKING
BROKEIN
BROKERS
BROKEUP
ERSKINE
TREKKED
TREKKER
TREKKIE

•R••K••

BRACKEN
BRACKET
BREAKER
BREAKIN
BREAKUP
BRICKED
BRISKER
BRISKET
BRISKLY
BROOKED
CRACKED
CRACKER
CRACKLE
CRACKLY
CRACKUP
CRANKED
CRANKUP
CREAKED
CRICKED
CRICKET
CRINKLE
CRINKLY
CROAKED
CROOKED
DRINKER
DRUCKER
FRANKED
FRANKEN
FRANKER
FRANKIE
FRANKLY
FRANKOZ
FREAKED
FRECKLE
FRECKLY
FRICKIE
FRISKED
FROCKED
GRACKLE
GRISKIN
IRECKON
PRANKED
PRICKED
PRICKLE
PRICKLY
PRINKED
TRACKED
TRACKER
TREKKED
TREKKER
TREKKIE
TRICKED
TRICKER
TRICKLE
TRINKET
TROIKAS
TRUCKED
TRUCKEE
TRUCKER
TRUCKLE
WRACKED
WREAKED
WRECKED
WRECKER
WRINKLE
WRINKLY

•R•••K•

ARAWAKS
ARMLIKE
DROSHKY
GRETZKY
GROMYKO
ORBLIKE
OROURKE
PROVOKE
TROTSKY
URNLIKE
VRONSKY

•R••••K

ARMLOCK
ARTWORK
BRUBECK
DRSPOCK
DRYDOCK
FRYCOOK
MRSPOCK
PRECOOK
PRESOAK

••RK•••

AIRKISS
BARKEEP
BARKERS
BARKIER
BARKING
BARKLEY
BARKSAT
BURKINA
CARKING
CORKAGE
CORKERS
CORKIER
CORKING
DARKENS
DARKEST
DARKISH
DARKMAN
FIRKINS
FORKERS
FORKFUL
FORKIER
FORKING
GURKHAS
HARKENS
HARKING
JERKIER
JERKILY
JERKING
JERKINS
LARKISH
LURKING
MARKERS
MARKETS
MARKHAM
MARKHOR
MARKING
MARKKAA
MARKOFF
MARKOVA
MARKSUP
MARKUPS
MIRKIER
MURKIER
MURKILY
PARKADE
PARKING
PARKWAY
PERKIER
PERKILY
PERKING
PERKINS
PERKISH
PERKSUP
PORKERS
PORKIER
PORKISH
PORKPIE
SARKIER
TURKEYS
TURKISH
WORKDAY
WORKERS
WORKFOR
WORKING
WORKMAN
WORKMEN
WORKOFF
WORKOUT
WORKSIN
WORKSON
WORKSUP
WORKUPS
YERKING
YERKISH
YORKIES
YORKIST

••R•K••

KARAKUL
KARAKUM
MARKKAA
MARYKAY
PERUKES
SHRIKES
STRIKER
STRIKES
STROKED
STROKES
TURNKEY

••R••K•

AIRLIKE
BUROAKS
CURLIKE
EARLIKE
FORSAKE
KARAOKE
OARLIKE
PARTAKE
SCREAKS
SHRIEKS
SHRINKS
STREAKS
STREAKY
WARLIKE

••R•••K

AIRLOCK
AIRSOCK
BARRACK
BERSERK
BURBANK
BURDOCK
CARPARK
CARRICK
DERRICK
EARLOCK
EARMARK
FORSOOK
GARRICK
NORFOLK
OARLOCK
PARTOOK
SARAWAK
WARLOCK
WARWICK

•••RK••

CLERKED
GHERKIN
HEARKEN
SHARKEY
SHIRKED
SHIRKER
SMIRKED
SNORKEL
SPARKED
SPARKLE
STARKER
STARKLY

•••R•K•

AMERIKA
ANORAKS
GOBROKE
PAPRIKA
TUGRIKS

•••R••K

BARRACK
BEDROCK
CARRICK
DEFROCK
DERRICK
GARRICK
HATRACK
HAYRACK
ICERINK
KUBRICK
ONTRACK
OUTRANK
PATRICK
PETROCK
RETRACK
SKIRACK
TIERACK
UNFROCK

••••RK•

AUTARKY
DEBARKS
EMBARKS
EXWORKS
MAZURKA
OROURKE
RECORKS
REMARKS
REWORKS
UNCORKS

••••R•K

BODEREK
DMYTRYK
LAMARCK
MASARYK
MUBARAK

•••••RK

ARTWORK
ATATURK
BERSERK
BULWARK
CARPARK
DEKLERK
DENMARK
DUNKIRK
EARMARK
HAUBERK
HAYFORK
HOLYARK
LEGWORK
NETWORK
NEWYORK
OUTWORK
SELKIRK
SKYLARK
TINWORK
UPQUARK
WAXWORK
WIDMARK

R•L••••

RALEIGH
RALLIED
RALLIER
RALLIES
RALLYTO
RALSTON
RDLAING
RELACED
RELACES
RELAPSE
RELATED
RELATES
RELAXED
RELAXES
RELAYED
RELEARN
RELEASE
RELENTS
RELIANT
RELICTS
RELIEFS
RELIEVE
RELIEVO
RELIGHT
RELINED
RELINES
RELISTS
RELIVED
RELIVES
RELLENO
RELOADS
RELOCKS
RELUCTS
RELUMED
RELUMES
RELYING
RILESUP
RILLETS
ROLAIDS
ROLLBAR
ROLLERS
ROLLICK
ROLLING
ROLLINS
ROLLOUT
ROLLSIN
ROLLSON
ROLLSUP
ROLLTOP
ROLODEX
ROLVAAG
RULEOUT
RULESON
RULINGS

R••L•••

RAGLANS
RAILERS
RAILING
RAILSAT
RAILWAY
RALLIED
RALLIER
RALLIES
RALLYTO
RAMLIKE
RANLATE
RATLIKE
RATLINE
RAYLIKE
REALISE
REALISM
REALIST
REALITY
REALIZE
REALTOR
REBLOOM
RECLAIM
RECLAME
RECLEAN
RECLINE
RECLUSE
REDLINE
REELECT
REELING
REELOFF
REELSIN
REFLAGS
REFLECT
REGLETS
REGLUED
REGLUES
RELLENO
REPLACE
REPLANS
REPLANT
REPLATE
REPLAYS
REPLETE
REPLICA
REPLIED
REPLIES
REPLOWS
RIBLESS
RIBLIKE
RIFLERS
RIFLERY
RIFLING
RILLETS
RIMLESS
RIOLOBO
ROBLOWE
RODLESS
RODLIKE
ROILIER
ROILING
ROLLBAR
ROLLERS
ROLLICK
ROLLING
ROLLINS
ROLLOUT
ROLLSIN
ROLLSON
ROLLSUP
ROLLTOP
ROULADE
RUGLIKE
RUMLESS
RUNLATE
RUNLETS

R•••L••

RABBLES
RADDLED
RADDLES
RADULAE
RAFFLED
RAFFLER
RAFFLES
RAMBLED
RAMBLER
RAMBLES
RANKLED
RANKLES
RASSLED
RASSLES
RATTLED
RATTLER
RATTLES
RAVELED
REBOLTS
RECALLS
RECOLOR
REDALGA
REDFLAG
REFILED
REFILES
REFILLS
REFILMS
REGALED
REGALES
REGALIA
REGALLY
REGULAR
REGULUS
REMELTS
REMOLDS
REOILED
REPOLLS
REPULSE
RESALES
RESALTS
RESELLS
RESILED
RESILES
RESOLED
RESOLES
RESOLVE
RESULTS
RETELLS
RETILED
RETILES
REVALUE
REVELED
REVELER
REVELRY
REVILED
REVILES
REVOLTS
REVOLVE
REWELDS
RICKLES
RIDDLED
RIDDLER
RIDDLES
RIFFLED
RIFFLES
RIMPLED
RIMPLES
RINGLET
RIPPLED
RIPPLES

RIVALED
RIVALRY
RIVULET
RODOLFO
ROMULAN
ROMULUS
ROOTLET
ROSALIE
ROSELLE
ROUBLES
ROYALLY
ROYALTY
ROYALWE
ROZELLE
RUBBLES
RUDOLPH
RUFFLED
RUFFLES
RUMBLED
RUMBLES
RUMPLED
RUMPLES
RUNDLES
RURALLY
RUSTLED
RUSTLER
RUSTLES

R••••L•

RABIDLY
RADIALS
RADICLE
RAGDOLL
RAINILY
RANDALL
RAPIDLY
RAPPELS
RASCALS
RATABLE
RATHOLE
RAVIOLI
RAWSILK
READILY
REBOILS
REBUILD
REBUILT
RECALLS
RECHALK
RECOILS
RECYCLE
REDCELL
REDEALS
REDEALT
REDIALS
REDPOLL
REDWOLF
REFILLS
REFUELS
REGALLY
REHEALS
REHEELS
REMAILS
RENAILS
RENAULT
RENTALS
REPEALS
REPOLLS
REPTILE
RESCALE
RESEALS
RESELLS
RESTYLE
RETAILS
RETELLS
RETICLE
RETITLE
RETOOLS
REVEALS
RIANTLY
RIGHTLY
RIGIDLY
RISIBLE
RISIBLY
RISKILY
RISSOLE
RITUALS
RITZILY
RONDELS
ROOMILY
ROSELLE
ROSWELL
ROUGHLY
ROUNDLY
ROWDILY
ROYALLY
ROZELLE
RUDDILY
RUMPOLE
RUNNELS
RURALLY
RUSSELL
RUSTILY

R•••••L

RADICAL
RAGDOLL
RAGEFUL
RANDALL
RAPHAEL
RATTAIL
RAWDEAL
REAVAIL
RECITAL
REDCELL
REDPOLL
REFUSAL
REMODEL
REMOVAL
RENEWAL
RESTFUL
RETINAL
RETRIAL
REVIVAL
ROOMFUL
RORQUAL
ROSEOIL
ROSWELL
RUSSELL
RUTHFUL

•RL••••

ARLEDGE
ORLANDO
ORLEANS

•R•L•••

ARALSEA
ARCLAMP
ARMLESS
ARMLETS
ARMLIKE
ARMLOAD
ARMLOCK
ARTLESS
BRALESS
CRULLER
DRILLED
DRILLER
DROLLER
ERELONG
FRILLED
FROLICS
GRILLED
GRILLES
GRILLET
GROLIER
IRELAND
IRELESS
MRCLEAN
ORBLESS
ORBLIKE
PRALINE
PRELATE
PRELIMS
PRELOAD
PRELUDE
PROLOGS
PROLONG
TRALALA
TRELLIS
TRILLED
TRILLIN
TRILOGY
TROLLED
TROLLEY
URNLIKE

•R••L••

AREOLAE
AREOLAR
AREOLAS
ARGYLES
BRADLEE
BRADLEY
BRAILLE
BRAWLED
BRAWLER
BRESLIN
BRIDLED
BRIDLES
BRIMLEY
BROILED
BROILER
CRADLED
CRADLES
CRAWLED
CRAWLER
CREOLES
CRIOLLO
CRUELER
CRUELLY
CRUELTY
CRULLER
DRAWLED
DRIBLET
DRILLED
DRILLER
DROLLER
DROOLED
DROOLER
DROPLET
DRUMLIN
FRAILER
FRAILLY
FRAILTY
FRAWLEY
FRILLED
GRAYLAG
GREELEY
GREMLIN
GRILLED
GRILLES
GRILLET
GROWLED
GROWLER
KREMLIN
ORACLES
ORIOLES
ORMOLUS
ORTOLAN
ORVILLE
PRESLEY
PROBLEM
PROWLED
PROWLER
TRAILED
TRAILER
TRAWLED
TRAWLER
TREBLED
TREBLES
TRELLIS
TRIFLED
TRIFLER
TRIFLES
TRILLED
TRILLIN
TRIPLED
TRIPLES
TRIPLET
TRIPLEX
TROILUS
TROLLED
TROLLEY
WRIGLEY

•R•••L•

ARMFULS
ARMHOLE
ARTFILM
ARTICLE
ARUGULA
BRAILLE
BRAMBLE
BRAMBLY
BRASHLY
BRAVELY
BRIDALS
BRIEFLY
BRINDLE
BRISKLY
BRISTLE
BRISTLY
BRITTLE
BROADLY
BRUTELY
CRACKLE
CRACKLY
CRASSLY
CRAYOLA
CRAZILY
CRENELS
CREWELS
CRINKLE
CRINKLY
CRIOLLO
CRISPLY
CROSSLY
CRUDELY
CRUELLY
CRUMBLE
CRUMBLY
CRUMPLE
CRUMPLY
CRYWOLF
DRACULA
DRIBBLE
DRIVELS
DRIZZLE
DRIZZLY
DRYCELL
DRYHOLE
DRYWALL
DRYWELL
ERECTLY
EROSELY
FRAGILE
FRAILLY
FRANKLY
FRAZZLE
FRECKLE
FRECKLY
FRESHLY
FRIABLE
FRIZZLE
FRIZZLY
GRACILE
GRACKLE
GRANDLY
GRANOLA
GRANULE
GRAPPLE
GRAVELS
GRAVELY
GREATLY
GRIDDLE
GRIMILY
GRISTLE
GRISTLY
GRIZZLE
GRIZZLY
GROSSLY
GROVELS
GRUFFLY
GRUMBLE
GRUMBLY
IRATELY
KRINGLE
ORDEALS
ORDERLY
ORVILLE
PRATTLE
PRESALE
PRESELL
PRICKLE
PRICKLY
PRIVILY
PROFILE
PRONELY
PROPELS
PROSILY
PROUDLY
TRALALA
TRAMPLE
TRAVELS
TREACLE
TREACLY
TREADLE
TREMBLE
TREMBLY
TREMOLO
TRESTLE
TRICKLE
TRIPOLI
TRITELY
TROUBLE
TROWELS
TRUCKLE
TRUFFLE
TRUNDLE
WRANGLE
WRESTLE
WRIGGLE
WRIGGLY
WRINKLE
WRINKLY
WRONGLY

•R••••L

AROUSAL
ARRIVAL
ARSENAL
BRIMFUL
BRISTOL
BRUEGEL
BRUMMEL
CRANIAL
CREOSOL
CRUCIAL
CRYSTAL
DREIDEL
DRYCELL
DRYWALL
DRYWELL
FRACTAL
FRETFUL
FRONTAL
GRADUAL
GRAPNEL
GRENDEL
ORBITAL
ORDINAL
PRECOOL
PREQUEL
PRESELL
PRETZEL
PREVAIL
TRAMMEL
TRAVAIL
TRAYFUL
TREFOIL
TRIVIAL
TRUCIAL

••RL•••

AIRLANE
AIRLESS
AIRLIFT
AIRLIKE
AIRLINE
AIRLOCK
BARLESS
BARLEYS
BERLIOZ
BERLITZ
BIRLING
BURLAPS
BURLIER
BURLING
CARLESS
CARLOAD
CARLSON
CARLTON
CARLYLE
CURLERS
CURLEWS
CURLIER
CURLIKE
CURLING
CURLSUP
DARLENE
DARLING
EARLDOM
EARLESS
EARLIER
EARLIKE
EARLOBE
EARLOCK
EARLYON
EHRLICH
FARLEFT
FORLIFE
FORLORN
FURLESS
FURLING
FURLONG
GARLAND
GIRLISH
HURLERS
HURLEYS
HURLIES
HURLING
JARLESS
KARLOFF
MARLENE
MARLINS
MARLOWE
MERLOTS
OARLESS
OARLIKE
OARLOCK
PARLAYS
PARLEYS
PARLORS
PARLOUR
PARLOUS
PERLITE
PERLMAN
PURLIEU
PURLING
PURLINS
PURLOIN
SERLING
SIRLOIN
SURLIER
SURLILY
VARLETS
WARLESS
WARLIKE
WARLOCK
WARLORD
WORLDLY
WURLEYS

••R•L••

ACRYLIC
AIRFLOW
AIRPLAY
AURALEE
AURALLY
BARKLEY
BURBLED
BURBLES
BURGLAR
BURGLED
BURGLES
CAROLED
CAROLER
CAROLUS
CAROLYN
CIRCLED
CIRCLES
CIRCLET
CORELLI
COROLLA
CURDLED
CURDLES
DARNLEY
EARFLAP
EARPLUG
ENROLLS
FERULES
FIRELIT
FORELEG
GARBLED
GARBLES
GARGLED
GARGLES
GERALDO
GIRDLED
GIRDLES
GORILLA
GURGLED
GURGLES
HERALDS
HURDLED
HURDLER
HURDLES
HURTLED
HURTLES
KAROLYI
KERPLOP
KIRTLES
LORELEI
MARBLED
MARBLES
MARILYN
MARYLOU
MORALES
MORALLY
MORELLO
MURILLO
MYRTLES
NORELCO
PAROLED
PAROLEE
PAROLES
PARSLEY
PERPLEX
PURFLED
PURFLES
PURPLED
PURPLES
RURALLY
SARALEE
SCROLLS
SHRILLS
SHRILLY
STROLLS
SURPLUS
THRALLS
THRILLS
TURTLED
TURTLES
UNROLLS
UTRILLO
WARBLED
WARBLER
WARBLES

••R••L•

ACRIDLY
AERIALS
AIRBALL
AIRHOLE
AIRMILE
AIRWOLF
AURALLY
AUREOLA
AUREOLE
AURICLE
BARBELL
BARBELS
BARRELS
BERTOLT
CARFULS
CARLYLE
CARPALS
CARPELS
CARRELS
CARROLL
CARTELS
CEREALS
CORBELS
CORDELL
CORELLI
CORNELL
CORNILY
COROLLA
CORRALS
CUREALL
DERAILS
DIRNDLS
DIRTILY
DORSALS
DURABLE
DURABLY
DURRELL
EARFULS
EARTHLY
ENROLLS
FERRULE
FERTILE
FIREFLY
FIRSTLY
FORMALS
FORMULA
FORSALE
FURBALL
GERBILS
GORILLA
HARDILY
HARSHLY
HERBALS
HERCULE
HERSELF
HIRABLE
ISRAELI
JARFULS
JERKILY
KERNELS
LARGELY
LURIDLY
MARCELS
MARSALA
MARVELS
MERRILL
MERRILY
MIRACLE
MORALLY
MORELLO
MORSELS
MORTALS
MURILLO
MURKILY
NARWALS
NERVILY
NORFOLK
NORMALS
OURSELF
PARABLE
PARCELS
PERCALE
PERGOLA
PERKILY
PORTALS
PURCELL
RURALLY
SCRAWLS
SCRAWLY
SCROLLS
SCRUPLE
SERIALS
SERVALS
SERVILE
SHRILLS
SHRILLY
SORRELS
SORRILY
SPRAWLS
STROLLS
SURLILY
TARBELL
TARDILY
TARSALS
TERCELS
TERSELY
THRALLS
THRILLS
TIREDLY
UNREELS
UNROLLS
UTRILLO
VERBALS
VIRGULE
WORDILY
WORLDLY

••R•••L

ADRENAL
AEROSOL
AIRBALL
AIRCOOL
AIRFOIL
AIRMAIL
ARRIVAL
AURORAL
BARBELL
BARNOWL
CARACAL
CARAMEL
CARAVEL
CAREFUL
CARPOOL
CARROLL
CORDELL
CORDIAL
CORNEAL
CORNELL
CORNOIL
CUREALL
CURTAIL
DAREFUL
DIREFUL
DURRELL
FORKFUL
FORMFUL
FORREAL
FURBALL
FURSEAL
GERITOL
GIRASOL
HARMFUL
HURTFUL
KARAKUL
LYRICAL
MARITAL
MARSHAL
MARTIAL
MERRILL
NARWHAL
PARASOL
PARBOIL
PARTIAL
PERUSAL
PHRASAL
PURCELL
RORQUAL
SHRIVEL
SORORAL
STRUDEL
SURREAL
TARBELL
TARHEEL
TERTIAL
TURMOIL
UNRAVEL
VERMEIL
VIRTUAL

•••RL••

CHARLES
CHARLEY
CHARLIE
GNARLED
HAARLEM
KNURLED
OBERLIN
OVERLAP
OVERLAY
OVERLIE
PEARLED
PHARLAP
SCARLET
SHIRLEY
SKIRLED
SNARLED
STARLET
STARLIT
SWIRLED
TWIRLED
TWIRLER
WHIRLED
WHORLED

•••R•L•

ACEROLA
ALERTLY
ANGRILY
ASARULE
BARRELS
BEDROLL
CARRELS
CARROLL
CHARILY
CHORALE
CHORALS
CHORTLE
CORRALS
COURTLY
DEERFLY
DURRELL
EGGROLL
EMERALD
FEBRILE
FERRULE
FIBRILS
FIERILY
GAGRULE
HOARILY
INERTLY
LAURELS
LEERILY
LOGROLL
MERRILL
MERRILY
MISRULE
ONAROLL
OVERALL
OVERFLY
OVERTLY
PATROLS
PAYROLL
PETRELS
PETROLS
PLURALS
PUERILE
SCARILY
SHARPLY
SHORTLY
SMARTLY
SORRELS
SORRILY
SPARELY
SPARKLE
SPIRALS
STARKLY
STARTLE
STERILE
STERNLY
STEROLS
TEARILY
THERELL
THIRDLY
WEARILY
WEIRDLY
WHERELL

•••R••L

ACCRUAL
BEDROLL
CARROLL
CHERVIL
DIURNAL
DURRELL
EGGROLL
EMBROIL
ETERNAL
FEARFUL
FORREAL
GABRIEL
GETREAL
JOURNAL
LOGROLL
MERRILL
ODORFUL
ONAROLL
ONTRIAL
OVERALL
PATRIAL
PAYROLL
QUARREL
RETRIAL
SNORKEL
STERNAL
SURREAL
TEARFUL
THERELL
THERMAL
UXORIAL
VITRIOL
WHERELL

••••RL•

BEVERLY
CLEARLY
DECARLO
EAGERLY
ELDERLY
LOVERLY
MISERLY
ORDERLY
QUEERLY
SHEERLY
SOBERLY
UNCURLS
UNFURLS
UTTERLY

••••R•L

ADMIRAL
APPAREL
APTERAL
AUGURAL
AURORAL
AUSTRAL
CENTRAL
CHLORAL
CLAIROL
CONTROL
DEMEROL
ENTHRAL
ESTORIL
FEDERAL
FEMORAL
GAMBREL
GENERAL
GONERIL
HUMERAL
IMMORAL
IMPERIL
KESTREL
LATERAL
LIBERAL
LITERAL
MAYORAL
MINERAL
MISTRAL
MONGREL
NATURAL
NEUTRAL
NOSTRIL
NUMERAL
QUARREL
SEVERAL
SORORAL
TENDRIL
TUMBREL
VENTRAL
WASTREL

•••••RL

BATGIRL
BUSGIRL
COWGIRL
ENSNARL
PINCURL
UNSNARL

R•M••••

RAMADAN
RAMADAS
RAMBEAU
RAMBLED
RAMBLER
RAMBLES
RAMEKIN
RAMESES
RAMINTO
RAMJETS
RAMLIKE
RAMMING
RAMMISH
RAMPAGE
RAMPANT
RAMPART
RAMRODS
REMAILS
REMAINS
REMAKES
REMANDS
REMARKS
REMARRY
REMELTS
REMENDS
REMIGES
REMINDS
REMIXED
REMIXES
REMNANT
REMODEL
REMOLDS
REMORAS
REMORSE
REMOTER
REMOTES
REMOUNT
REMOVAL
REMOVED
REMOVER
REMOVES
REMOWED
REMUDAS
RIMBAUD
RIMIEST
RIMLESS
RIMMING
RIMPLED
RIMPLES
RIMSHOT
ROMAINE
ROMANCE
ROMANIA
ROMANOV
ROMANSH
ROMNEYS
ROMPERS
ROMPING
ROMPISH
ROMULAN
ROMULUS
RUMBAED
RUMBLED
RUMBLES
RUMLESS
RUMMAGE
RUMMIER
RUMORED
RUMOURS
RUMPLED
RUMPLES
RUMPOLE

R••M•••

RAGMOPS
RAIMENT
RAMMING
RAMMISH
RAYMOND
REAMASS
REAMERS
REAMING
REDMEAT
RHOMBUS
RHUMBAS
RHYMERS

RHYMING
RIMMING
ROAMERS
ROAMING
ROOMERS
ROOMFUL
ROOMIER
ROOMIES
ROOMILY
ROOMING
RUMMAGE
RUMMIER

R•••M••
RACEMES
RADOMES
RAINMAN
READMIT
REAIMED
REARMED
REGIMEN
REGIMES
REITMAN
RELUMED
RELUMES
RENAMED
RENAMES
REPOMAN
RESUMED
RESUMES
RETIMED
RETIMES
REVAMPS
RICHMAN
RICKMAN
ROADMAP
RUNAMOK

R••••M•
RAGTIME
RANSOMS
RECLAME
REDEEMS
REDGUMS
REFILMS
REFORMS
REFRAME
RESTAMP
RETRIMS
REWARMS
RHIZOME
RHYTHMS
RUNHOME

R•••••M
REALISM
REBLOOM
RECLAIM
RECROOM
REQUIEM
RHENIUM
RHODIUM
ROSTRUM

•RM••••
ARMADAS
ARMBAND
ARMENIA
ARMFULS
ARMHOLE
ARMLESS
ARMLETS
ARMLIKE
ARMLOAD
ARMLOCK
ARMOIRE
ARMORED
ARMORER
ARMOURS
ARMOURY
ARMPITS
ARMREST
ARMURES
ARMYANT
ERMINES
MRMAGOO
ORMANDY
ORMOLUS

•R•M•••
ARAMAIC
ARAMEAN
ARDMORE
BRAMBLE
BRAMBLY
BRIMFUL
BRIMLEY
BRIMMED
BROMATE
BROMIDE
BROMINE
BRUMMEL
CRAMMED
CRAMMER
CRAMPED
CRAMPON
CREMONA
CRIMEAN
CRIMPED
CRIMPER
CRIMSON
CRUMBLE
CRUMBLY
CRUMPET
CRUMPLE
CRUMPLY
DRUMLIN
DRUMMED
DRUMMER
DRUMSUP
EREMITE
FRAMEUP
FRAMING
FREMONT
FROMAGE
GRAMMAR
GRAMMER
GRAMMES
GRAMMYS
GRAMPAS
GRAMPUS
GREMLIN
GRIMACE
GRIMIER
GRIMILY
GRIMING
GRIMMER
GROMMET
GROMYKO
GRUMBLE
GRUMBLY
GRUMPED
KREMLIN
PREMEDS
PREMIER
PREMISE
PREMISS
PREMIUM
PRIMACY
PRIMARY
PRIMATE
PRIMERS
PRIMING
PRIMMER
PRIMPED
PROMISE
PROMOTE
PROMPTS
TRAMCAR
TRAMMEL
TRAMPAS
TRAMPED
TRAMPLE
TREMAIN
TREMBLE
TREMBLY
TREMOLO
TREMORS
TRIMMED
TRIMMER
TRUMPED
TRUMPET
TRUMPUP

•R••M••
ARTEMIS
ARTEMUS
BRAHMAN
BRAHMAS
BRAHMIN
BRIMMED
BRUMMEL
CRAMMED
CRAMMER
CREAMED
CREAMER
CREWMAN
CREWMEN
DREAMED
DREAMER
DREAMON
DREAMUP
DRUMMED
DRUMMER
ERASMUS
FREEMAN
FREEMEN
FROGMAN
FROGMEN
GRAMMAR
GRAMMER
GRAMMES
GRAMMYS
GRIMMER
GROMMET
GROOMED
GROOMER
IRONMAN
IRONMEN
PREAMPS
PREEMIE
PREEMPT
PRIMMER
PROPMAN
PROPMEN
TRAMMEL
TRAUMAS
TRIMMED
TRIMMER
TRIUMPH

•R•••M•
ARCLAMP
DRACHMA
DRACHMS
GRAHAME
GRAHAMS
GRANDMA
IRKSOME
ORIGAMI
PRELIMS
PRESUME
PROXIMO
TRIREME
TRUISMS

•R••••M
ARCANUM
ARTFILM
ARTFORM
BRIGHAM
CRANIUM
ERRATUM
FREEDOM
GRANDAM
GRISHAM
GRISSOM
IRIDIUM
ORGANUM
PREMIUM
PROBLEM
PROGRAM
TRANSOM
TRIGRAM
TRITIUM
TROPISM
URANIUM

••RM•••
AIRMADA
AIRMAIL
AIRMASS
AIRMILE
BARMAID
BARMIER
BERMEJO
BERMUDA
BURMANS
BURMESE
CARMINE
DORMANT
DORMERS
DORMICE
EARMARK
EARMUFF
FARMERS
FARMERY
FARMING
FARMOUT
FERMENT
FERMIUM
FIRMEST
FIRMING
FIRMSUP
FORMALS
FORMATS
FORMFUL
FORMICA
FORMING
FORMOSA
FORMULA
GARMENT
GERMANE
GERMANS
GERMANY
GERMIER
HARMFUL
HARMING
HARMONY
HERMANN
HERMITS
HORMONE
KIRMANS
MARMARA
MARMION
MARMOTS
MERMAID
MORMONS
MURMURS
NORMALS
NORMAND
NORMANS
PERMING
PERMITS
SERMONS
SURMISE
TARMACS
TERMING
TERMINI
TERMITE
TORMENT
TURMOIL
VARMINT
VERMEER
VERMEIL
VERMONT
WARMEST
WARMING
WARMISH
WARMSUP
WARMUPS
WORMIER
WORMISH
ZERMATT

••R•M••
AFRAMES
BERGMAN
BIRDMAN
BIRDMEN
BIREMES
BYREMAN
BYREMEN
CARAMBA
CARAMEL
CARAMIA
CAROMED
CERAMIC
CERUMEN
CHROMES
DARKMAN
FIREMAN
FIREMEN
FOREMAN
FOREMEN
HARTMAN
LARAMIE
MARIMBA
MERIMEE
MIRAMAR
MIRAMAX
PERLMAN
PORTMAN
PYRAMID
PYRAMUS
SCRIMPS
SCRIMPY
SCRUMMY
SHRIMPS
WORKMAN
WORKMEN
YARDMAN
YARDMEN

••R••M•
AIRDAMS
AIRPUMP
AIRTIME
ATRIUMS
CHRISMS
MARRYME
PERFUME
SCREAMS
SCRUMMY
STREAMS
SURNAME
VERISMO
WARGAME
WARTIME

••R•••M
ABRAHAM
ACRONYM
BARROOM
BOREDOM
EARDRUM
EARLDOM
ERRATUM
FERMIUM
FIREARM
FORDHAM
FOREARM
HEROISM
KARAKUM
LORDJIM
MARKHAM
MARXISM
PERDIEM
PERFORM
SARCASM
SERFDOM
SORGHUM
STRATUM
SURINAM
TERBIUM
THREEAM
THREEPM
TORYISM
YARDARM
ZEROSUM

•••RM••
ALARMED
ALARMER
CHARMED
CHARMER
CHARMIN
DOORMAN
DOORMAT
DOORMEN
GOURMET
REARMED
SHERMAN
STARMAN
STARMAP
STORMED
SWARMED
THERMAL
THERMOS
THURMAN
UNARMED

•••R•M•
ALARUMS
ASHRAMS
BEGRIME
DIGRAMS
DIORAMA
ENGRAMS
EXTREME
GOURAMI
MACRAME
MARRYME
MEGRIMS
NOTRUMP
OFFRAMP
QUORUMS
REFRAME
RETRIMS
SANREMO
SUPREME
SUPREMO
TRIREME

•••R••M
BARROOM
BEDROOM
BOXROOM
CZARDOM
CZARISM
DAYROOM
GLORIAM
GUARGUM
GYPROOM
HAARLEM
LEGROOM
NATRIUM
RECROOM
STARDOM
STERNUM
SUNROOM
TAPROOM
TEAROOM
THORIUM
TOURISM
YTTRIUM

••••RM•
AFFIRMS
DEFORMS
DISARMS
INFORMS
PALERMO
REFORMS
REWARMS
SQUIRMS
SQUIRMY

••••R•M
ANAGRAM
BUCKRAM
CHETRUM
DECORUM
DIAGRAM
EARDRUM
EPIGRAM
FULCRUM
HUMDRUM
INTERIM
NOSTRUM
PILGRIM
PROGRAM
ROSTRUM
SEAGRAM
SISTRUM
TANGRAM
TANTRUM
THEOREM
TRIGRAM
WOLFRAM

•••••RM
ANTFARM
ARTFORM
CONFIRM
CONFORM
FIREARM
FOREARM
LONGARM
MIDTERM
PERFORM
SIDEARM
THEFIRM
TONEARM
UNIFORM
YARDARM

R•N••••
RANAWAY
RANCHED
RANCHER
RANCHES
RANCHOS
RANCOUR
RANDALL
RANDIER
RANDOWN
RANGERS
RANGIER
RANGING
RANGOFF
RANGOON
RANGOUT
RANINTO
RANKERS
RANKEST
RANKING
RANKISH
RANKLED
RANKLES
RANLATE
RANOVER
RANRIOT
RANSACK
RANSOMS
RANTERS
RANTING
RENAILS
RENAMED
RENAMES
RENARDS
RENAULT
RENDERS
RENDING
RENEGED
RENEGER
RENEGES
RENEGUE
RENEWAL
RENEWED
RENEWER
RENNINS
RENOTED
RENOTES
RENTALS
RENTERS
RENTING
RINGERS
RINGING
RINGLET
RINGOFF
RINGOUT
RINGSUP
RINSING
RONDEAU
RONDELS
RONTGEN
RUNAMOK
RUNAWAY
RUNBACK
RUNDEEP
RUNDLES
RUNDOWN
RUNGOFF
RUNGOUT
RUNHOME
RUNINTO
RUNLATE
RUNLETS
RUNNELS
RUNNERS
RUNNIER
RUNNING
RUNOFFS
RUNOUTS
RUNOVER
RUNRIOT
RUNSDRY
RUNSFOR
RUNSOFF
RUNSOUT
RUNTIER
RUNTISH
RUNWAYS
RUNWITH

R••N•••
RAINBOW
RAINHAT
RAINIER
RAINILY
RAINING
RAINMAN
RAINOUT
RAWNESS
REDNESS
REENACT
REENTER
REENTRY
REGNANT
REINING
REINKED
REINSIN
REMNANT
RENNINS
REUNIFY
REUNION
REUNITE
REYNARD
RHENISH
RHENIUM
RIANTLY
ROANOKE
ROMNEYS
ROUNDED
ROUNDER
ROUNDLY
ROUNDON
ROUNDUP
RUANDAN
RUINERS
RUINING
RUINOUS
RUNNELS
RUNNERS
RUNNIER
RUNNING
RWANDAN

R•••N••
RAMINTO
RANINTO
RAPANUI
RAPINES
RATINGS
RAVENED
RAVENNA
RAVINES
RAVINGS
REBENDS
REBINDS
RECANED
RECANES
RECANTS
RECENCY
REDANTS
REFINED
REFINER
REFINES
REFUNDS
REGENCY
REGENTS
REHANGS
REIGNED
RELENTS
RELINED
RELINES
REMANDS
REMENDS
REMINDS
REPENTS
REPINED
REPINES
RERENTS
RERINSE
RESANDS
RESENDS
RESENTS
RESINGS
RETINAE
RETINAL
RETINAS
RETINUE
RETUNED
RETUNES
REVENGE
REVENUE
REWINDS
REZONED
REZONES
RIBANDS
RIPENED
RIPINTO
RISINGS
RODENTS
ROMANCE
ROMANIA
ROMANOV
ROMANSH
ROSANNA
ROSANNE
ROTUNDA
ROXANNE
RULINGS
RUNINTO

R••••N•
RACKING
RADIANS
RADIANT
RAFTING
RAGGING
RAGLANS
RAIDING
RAILING
RAIMENT
RAINING
RAISING
RAISINS
RAMMING
RAMPANT
RANGING
RANKING
RANTING
RAPPING
RASPING
RATFINK
RATIONS
RATLINE
RATTANS
RATTING
RAVENNA
RAYGUNS
RAYMOND
RAZZING
RDLAING
READING
REAGENT
REAMING
REAPING
REAREND
REARING
REASONS
REBOUND
RECKONS
RECLINE
RECOUNT
REDCENT
REDDENS
REDDING
REDFINS
REDLINE
REDOING
REDOUND
REDPINE
REDWINE
REDWING
REEDING
REEFING
REEKING
REELING
REFFING
REGAINS
REGIONS
REGNANT
REINING
REJOINS
RELIANT
RELLENO
RELYING
REMAINS
REMNANT
REMOUNT
RENDING
RENNINS
RENTING
REOPENS
REPAINT
REPLANS
REPLANT
REPRINT
REPUGNS
RESCIND
RESIGNS
RESOUND
RESPINS
RESPOND
RESTING
RETAINS
RETHINK
RETSINA
RETURNS
REUBENS
REVVING
REWOUND
RHYMING
RIBBING
RIBBONS
RIDDING
RIDGING
RIFFING
RIFLING
RIFTING
RIGGING
RIMMING
RINGING
RINSING
RIOTING
RIPIENO
RIPPING
RISKING
ROAMING
ROARINS
ROBBING
ROBBINS
ROCKING
RODDING
ROGAINE
ROILING
ROLLING
ROLLINS
ROMAINE
ROMPING
ROOFING
ROOKING
ROOMING
ROOTING
ROSANNA
ROSANNE
ROSSINI
ROSTAND
ROTTING
ROUGING
ROUSING
ROUTINE
ROUTING
ROXANNE
RUBBING
RUCHING
RUCKING
RUINING
RUNNING
RUSHING
RUSTING

R•••••N
RACCOON
RAINMAN
RAKEDIN
RAKESIN
RALSTON
RAMADAN
RAMEKIN
RANDOWN
RANGOON
RARITAN
RAYBURN
READSIN
RECLEAN
REDRAWN
REELSIN
REFRAIN
REGIMEN
REINSIN
REITMAN
RELEARN
REPOMAN
RESTAIN
RETAKEN
RETRAIN
REUNION
REWOVEN
RICHMAN
RICKMAN
RIGHTON
RIPTORN
ROBESON
ROLLSIN
ROLLSON
ROMULAN
RONTGEN
ROPEDIN
ROPESIN
ROUGHEN
ROUNDON
RUANDAN
RUBDOWN
RUBICON
RUBITIN
RUCTION
RUFFIAN
RULESON
RUNDOWN
RUSSIAN
RWANDAN

•RN••••
ARNICAS
ERNESTO
ORNETTE
ORNITHO
URNLIKE

•R•N•••
BRANAGH
BRANDED
BRANDER
BRANDON
BRANSON
BRENDAN
BRENNAN
BRENNER
BRINDLE
BRINGER
BRINGIN
BRINGON
BRINGTO
BRINGUP
BRINIER
BRINING
BRINISH
BRONCHI
BRONCOS
BRONSON
BRONZED
BRONZES
BRUNETS
BRYNNER
CRANIAL
CRANING
CRANIUM
CRANKED
CRANKUP
CRENELS
CRINGED
CRINGES
CRINKLE
CRINKLY
CRINOID
CRONIES
CRONISH
CRUNCHY
DRINKER
DRONERS
DRONING
DRONISH
DRYNESS
FRANCES
FRANCIS
FRANKED
FRANKEN
FRANKER
FRANKIE
FRANKLY
FRANKOZ
FRANTIC
FRENEAU
FRINGED
FRINGES
FRONTAL
FRONTED
FRONTON
GRANADA
GRANARY
GRANDAM
GRANDEE
GRANDER
GRANDLY
GRANDMA
GRANDPA
GRANGER
GRANGES
GRANITE
GRANOLA
GRANTED
GRANTEE
GRANTOR
GRANULE
GRENADA
GRENADE
GRENDEL
GRINDER
GRINNED
GRINNER
GRUNGES
GRUNION
GRUNTED
IRANIAN
IRONAGE
IRONERS
IRONIES
IRONING
IRONMAN
IRONMEN
IRONONS
IRONORE
IRONOUT
KRINGLE
ORANGES
ORANGEY
ORINOCO
PRANCED
PRANCER
PRANCES

PRANGED
PRANKED
PRENUPS
PRINCES
PRINKED
PRINTED
PRINTER
PRONELY
PRONGED
PRONOUN
PRUNERS
PRUNING
TRANCES
TRANSIT
TRANSOM
TRENARY
TRENDED
TRENTON
TRINITY
TRINKET
TRUNDLE
URANITE
URANIUM
VRONSKY
WRANGLE
WRINGER
WRINKLE
WRINKLY
WRONGED
WRONGER
WRONGLY
WRYNESS

•R••N••

ARCANUM
ARDENCY
ARGONNE
ARMENIA
ARPENTS
ARRANGE
ARSENAL
ARSENIC
ARSENIO
BRAINED
BRENNAN
BRENNER
BROSNAN
BROWNED
BROWNER
BROWNIE
BRYNNER
CROONED
CROONER
CROWNED
DRAGNET
DRAINED
DRAINER
DRAWNIN
DRAWNON
DRAWNUP
DROWNED
ERMINES
ERRANCY
ERRANDS
FRIENDS
FROWNAT
FROWNED
FROWNER
GRAINED
GRAPNEL
GREENED
GREENER
GRINNED
GRINNER
GROANED
GROANER
GROUNDS
GROWNUP
MRBONES
ORDINAL
ORDINES
ORGANDY
ORGANIC
ORGANON
ORGANUM
ORGANZA
ORIENTE
ORIENTS
ORLANDO
ORMANDY
ORPINES
PREENED
PREENER
PRYINTO
TRAINED
TRAINEE
TRAINER
TRIUNES
TROUNCE
TRUANCY
TRUANTS
URBANER
URGENCY

•R•••N•

ARACHNE
ARCHING
ARCHONS
ARCSINE
ARETINO
ARGONNE
ARGUING
ARIADNE
ARISING
ARIZONA
ARMBAND
ARMYANT
ARTSONG
BRACING
BRAKING
BRAVING
BRAYING
BRAZING
BRETONS
BREWING
BRIBING
BRIGAND
BRINING
BRITONS
BROGANS
BROMINE
BRUXING
CRANING
CRATING
CRAVENS
CRAVING
CRAYONS
CRAZING
CREMONA
CRETANS
CRETINS
CREWING
CROWING
DRAGONS
DRAPING
DRAWING
DRAYING
DRIVING
DRONING
DROPINS
DRYRUNS
ERASING
ERELONG
ERODENT
ERODING
ERSKINE
FRAMING
FRAYING
FREEING
FREMONT
FRYPANS
GRACING
GRADING
GRATING
GRAVING
GRAYING
GRAZING
GREYING
GRIMING
GRIPING
GROPING
GROWING
IRELAND
IRONING
IRONONS
JREWING
KRISHNA
ORATING
ORDAINS
OREGANO
ORIGINS
ORISONS
ORLEANS
OROGENY
OROTUND
ORPHANS
PRALINE
PRATING
PRAYING
PREBEND
PRESENT
PRETEND
PREVENT
PRICING
PRIDING
PRIMING
PRISONS
PRIZING
PROBING
PROBONO
PROFANE
PROGENY
PROLONG
PROPANE
PROSING
PROTONS
PROVING
PRUDENT
PRUNING
TRACING
TRADING
TREEING
TREPANS
TREVINO
TRIBUNE
TRIDENT
TRIGONS
TRITONE
TRITONS
TROGONS
TROJANS
TRUEING
URCHINS
WRITING
XRATING
XRAYING

•R••••N

ARABIAN
ARAMEAN
ARRAIGN
ARTISAN
BRACKEN
BRAHMAN
BRAHMIN
BRANDON
BRANSON
BRAXTON
BREAKIN
BRENDAN
BRENNAN
BRESLIN
BRINGIN
BRINGON
BRITAIN
BRITTEN
BRITTON
BROADEN
BROKEIN
BRONSON
BROSNAN
CRAMPON
CREWMAN
CREWMEN
CRIMEAN
CRIMSON
CRISPIN
CROUTON
CRYOGEN
DRAGOON
DRAGSIN
DRAGSON
DRAWNIN
DRAWNON
DRAWSIN
DRAWSON
DREAMON
DRESDEN
DRIPPAN
DRISTAN
DRIVEIN
DROPSIN
DRUMLIN
EREWHON
ERICSON
EROSION
FRANKEN
FREEMAN
FREEMEN
FRESHEN
FRIEDAN
FRISIAN
FRISSON
FROGMAN
FROGMEN
FRONTON
GRAFTON
GRAYSON
GRECIAN
GREMLIN
GREYHEN
GRIFFIN
GRIFFON
GRISKIN
GROWSON
GRUNION
GRYPHON
IRANIAN
IRECKON
IRONMAN
IRONMEN
KRATION
KREMLIN
KRYPTON
MRCLEAN
ORATION
ORBISON
ORGANON
ORPHEAN
ORTOLAN
PREDAWN
PRESSON
PRESTON
PRETEEN
PREYSON
PROCYON
PRONOUN
PROPMAN
PROPMEN
PROTEAN
PROTEIN
TRADEIN
TRADEON
TREASON
TREMAIN
TRENTON
TRICORN
TRIEDON
TRIESON
TRILLIN
TRISTAN
TRODDEN
WRITEIN
WRITTEN
WROTEIN

••RN•••

BARNABY
BARNARD
BARNEYS
BARNONE
BARNOWL
BERNARD
BERNESE
BERNICE
BERNSEN
BORNEUP
BURNERS
BURNETT
BURNING
BURNISH
BURNOUT
BURNSUP
BURNTUP
CARNERA
CARNETS
CARNIES
CORNCOB
CORNDOG
CORNEAL
CORNEAS
CORNELL
CORNERS
CORNETS
CORNFED
CORNICE
CORNIER
CORNILY
CORNING
CORNISH
CORNOIL
CORNROW
DARNERS
DARNING
DARNLEY
DERNIER
DIRNDLS
DURNING
EARNERS
EARNEST
EARNING
FERNBAR
FERNIER
FURNACE
FURNISH
GARNERS
GARNETS
GARNISH
GIRNING
GURNEYS
HARNESS
HORNETS
HORNING
HORNISH
HORNIST
HORNSBY
HORNSIN
KERNELS
KERNING
MORNING
SURNAME
TARNISH
TERNARY
TERNATE
TORNADO
TORNOFF
TORNOUT
TURNERS
TURNERY
TURNING
TURNIPS
TURNKEY
TURNOFF
TURNOUT
TURNSIN
TURNSON
TURNSTO
TURNSUP
VARNISH
VERNIER
WARNING
WERNHER
WORNOFF
WORNOUT
YARNING

••R•N••

ACRONYM
ADRENAL
AIRINGS
APRONED
ARRANGE
BARANOF
BARENTS
BARONET
BARONGS
CARINAS
CHRONIC
CORINTH
CORONAE
CORONAS
CORONET
DURANCE
DURANGO
DURANTE
ERRANCY
ERRANDS
FIRENZE
FIRINGS
FORINTS
GARDNER
GARONNE
GERENTS
GERUNDS
GIRONDE
GYRENES
KORUNAS
LARDNER
LORENZO
MARENGO
MARINAS
MARINER
MARINES
MERINOS
MIRANDA
MORANIS
OTRANTO
PARDNER
PARENTS
PARINGS
PARSNIP
PARTNER
PHRENIC
PIRANHA
RERENTS
RERINSE
SARANAC
SARONGS
SCRUNCH
SERENER
SHRINER
SHRINES
SHRINKS
SPRINGS
SPRINGY
SPRINTS
STRANDS
STRANGE
STRINGS
STRINGY
SURINAM
SYRINGA
SYRINGE
TARANTO
TERENCE
THRONES
THRONGS
TORONTO
TYRANNY
TYRANTS
VERANDA

••R••N•

AGROUND
AIRGUNS
AIRLANE
AIRLINE
BARBING
BARGING
BARKING
BARNONE
BARRENS
BARRING
BARTEND
BARYONS
BIRDING
BIRLING
BURBANK
BURDENS
BURKINA
BURLING
BURMANS
BURNING
BURPING
BURYING
CARBINE
CARBONS
CARDING
CAREENS
CARKING
CARMINE
CARPING
CARTING
CARTONS
CARVING
CORDING
CORDONS
CORKING
CORNING
CURBING
CURDING
CURLING
CURRANT
CURRENT
CURSING
CURVING
DARKENS
DARLENE
DARLING
DARNING
DARTING
DERRING
DORMANT
DURNING
EARNING
EARRING
FARCING
FARGONE
FARMING
FERMENT
FERVENT
FIREANT
FIRKINS
FIRMING
FORCING
FORDING
FORFEND
FORGING
FORGONE
FORKING
FORMING
FORRENT
FORTUNA
FORTUNE
FORWENT
FURLING
FURLONG
FURRING
GARBING
GARCONS
GARDENS
GARLAND
GARMENT
GARONNE
GERAINT
GERMANE
GERMANS
GERMANY
GIRDING
GIRNING
GORGING
GORGONS
GOROUND
HARDENS
HARDING
HARKENS
HARKING
HARMING
HARMONY
HARPING
HERDING
HERMANN
HEROINE
HERRING
HORMONE
HORNING
HORSING
HURLING
HURTING
JARGONS
JARGONY
JARRING
JERKING
JERKINS
JURYING
KERNING
KIRMANS
KOREANS
LARAINE
LARCENY
LARDING
LARDONS
LORDING
LURKING
MARCONI
MARGINS
MARIANA
MARKING
MARLENE
MARLINS
MAROONS
MARRING
MARTENS
MARTINA
MARTINI
MARTINO
MARTINS
MARYANN
MERGING
MORAINE
MORDANT
MORDENT
MORGANA
MORGANS
MORMONS
MORNING
NIRVANA
NORMAND
NORMANS
NURSING
OURGANG
PARDONS
PARKING
PARRING
PARSING
PARSONS
PARTING
PARVENU
PERCENT
PERKING
PERKINS
PERMING
PERSONA
PERSONS
PORCINE
PORSENA
PORTEND
PORTENT
PURGING
PURLING
PURLINS
PURRING
PURSING
SARDINE
SARGENT
SCRAWNY
SCREENS
SERLING
SERMONS
SERPENT
SERVANT
SERVING
SORDINI
SORDINO
SORTING
SORVINO
SPRAINS
STRAINS
SURFING
SURGING
SYRIANS
TARPONS
TARRING
TARTANS
TARZANA
TERHUNE
TERMING
TERMINI
TERRENE
TORMENT
TORRENS
TORRENT
TORTONI
TURBANS
TURBINE
TUREENS
TURNING
TYRANNY
UKRAINE
VARIANT
VARMINT
VARYING
VERBENA
VERDANT
VERGING
VERMONT
VIRGINS
WARDENS
WARDING
WARMING
WARNING
WARPING
WARRANT
WARRENS
WARRING
WARZONE
WORDING
WORDONE
WORKING
WORSENS
YARNING
YERKING
ZEROING
ZIRCONS

••R•••N

AFRICAN
ARRAIGN
BARGAIN
BARGEIN
BERGMAN
BERGSON
BERNSEN
BIRDMAN
BIRDMEN
BORODIN
BURGEON
BURPGUN
BURSTYN
BYREMAN
BYREMEN
CARAVAN
CARLSON
CARLTON
CAROLYN
CARRION
CARRYON
CARTOON
CERTAIN
CERUMEN
CORAZON
CURTAIN
DARKMAN
EARLYON
EARTHEN
FIREMAN
FIREMEN
FOREIGN
FOREMAN
FOREMEN
FORERAN
FORERUN
FORLORN
FORTRAN
GORDIAN
HARDPAN
HARDWON
HARPOON
HARPSON
HARSHEN
HARTMAN
HERMANN
HIRESON
HORIZON
HORNSIN
KARAJAN
KERATIN
MARCHON
MARILYN
MARMION
MARTIAN
MARYANN
OURTOWN
PARAGON
PERLMAN
PERSIAN
PERTAIN
PORTION
PORTMAN
PURITAN
PURLOIN
RARITAN
SARACEN
SARAZEN
SAROYAN
SCRIVEN
SERBIAN
SIRLOIN
STRIVEN
SURGEON
TERRAIN
THREWIN
THROWIN
TORSION
TURNSIN
TURNSON
UPRISEN
VERSION
VIRGOAN
WORKMAN
WORKMEN
WORKSIN
WORKSON
YARDMAN
YARDMEN
YEREVAN

•••RN••

ADORNED
ADORNER
BLARNEY
CHURNED
DIURNAL
ETERNAL
HAIRNET
JOURNAL
JOURNEY
JOURNOS
KEARNEY
LEARNED
LEARNER
LIERNES
MOURNED
SCORNED
SCORNER
SPURNED
SPURNER
STERNAL
STERNER
STERNLY
STERNUM
TIERNEY
TOURNEY
YEARNED
YEARNER

•••R•N•

ADORING
AFFRONT
AMERIND
AYNRAND
BARRENS
BARRING
BEARING
BLARING
CABRINI
CHORINE
CITRINE
CITRONS
COURANT
CURRANT
CURRENT
CZARINA
DERRING
DRYRUNS
EARRING
ENDRUNS
ENTRANT
ENURING
EPERGNE
FAIRING
FEARING
FIBRINS
FLARING
FLORINS
FORRENT
FURRING
GEARING
GLARING
GOWRONG
GUARANI
HEARING
HERRING
HYDRANT
ICERINK
IMPRINT
INFRONT
INPRINT
INURING
ITERANT
JARRING
JEERING
KEYRING
LAURENT
LEERING
LEGRAND
MACRONS
MARRING
MATRONS
MICRONS
MIGRANT
MITRING
MOORING
NEARING
NEURONE
NEURONS
OCARINA
OPERAND
OUTRANK
OUTRUNS
PADRONE
PADRONI
PAIRING
PARRING
PATRONS
PEERING
PHARYNX
POURING
PURRING
REAREND
REARING
REPRINT
ROARING
SABRINA
SCARING
SCORING
SEARING
SHARING
SHORING
SKIRUNS
SNARING
SNORING
SOARING
SOPRANO
SOURING
SPARING
SPIRANT
STARING
STORING
STYRENE
TARRING
TAURINE
TEARING
TERRENE
TIERING
TITRING
TORRENS
TORRENT
TOURING
TSARINA
TZARINA
UPFRONT
USGRANT
VAGRANT
VEERING
VIBRANT
WARRANT
WARRENS
WARRING
WEARING
YEAREND

•••R••N

ALARCON
BAHRAIN
BEARSON
BOURBON
CARRION
CARRYON
CHARMIN
CITROEN
CLARION
COARSEN
DETRAIN
DOORMAN
DOORMEN
EMERSON
ENTRAIN
EXURBAN
GHERKIN
HADRIAN
HAIRPIN
HEARKEN
HEARTEN
HOARSEN
IBERIAN
INGRAIN
INGROWN
JOURDAN
MAUREEN
MEGRYAN
MOORHEN
OBERLIN
OVERRAN
OVERRUN
PATROON
PEARSON
PEERSIN
POURSIN
REDRAWN
REFRAIN
RETRAIN
SAURIAN
SHAREIN
SHARPEN
SHERMAN
SHERWIN
SHORTEN
SMARTEN
SPARTAN
SPORRAN
SPURSON
STARMAN
STIRSIN
STYRIAN
SWOREIN
TERRAIN
THEREIN
THEREON
THURMAN
UMBRIAN
UNDRAWN
WHARTON
WHEREIN
ZAIREAN
ZAIRIAN

••••RN•

AUBURNS
BYTURNS
CASERNE
CASERNS
CAVERNS
DEHORNS
EXTERNS
GOVERNS
INFERNO
INTERNS
LAVERNE
LIVORNO
LOCARNO
LUCERNE
MODERNS
OSBORNE
PATERNO
RETURNS
SALERNO
SUBORNS
SUKARNO
TAVERNS
UPBORNE
UPTURNS
WYVERNS

••••R•N

ACHERON
AILERON
ALSORAN
ANDIRON
ASPIRIN
BULLRUN
CALDRON
CAMERON
CHAGRIN
CHEVRON
COCHRAN
DENDRON
DEXTRIN
ENTERON
FORERAN
FORERUN
FORTRAN
GAGARIN
HEPARIN
HOMERUN
KATHRYN
LATERAN
LATERON
LEBARON
LONGRUN
MILKRUN
MILLRUN
NEUTRON
NONIRON
OMICRON
ONEIRON
OVERRAN
OVERRUN
PIGIRON
SAFFRON
SAHARAN
SAVARIN
SIXIRON
SPORRAN
SWEARIN
TAMARIN
TEHERAN
TELERAN
TWOIRON
VETERAN
WAITRON
WELLRUN

•••••RN

ADJOURN
BIGHORN
BITTERN
CISTERN
CLIBURN
COGBURN
CONCERN
DISCERN
EASTERN
FOGHORN
FORLORN
HEPBURN
INKHORN
LANTERN
LECTERN
LEGHORN
LOWBORN
MAXBORN
NEWBORN
NOCTURN
OAKFERN
OUTWORN
PASTERN
PATTERN
POPCORN
POSTERN
RAYBURN
RELEARN
RIPTORN
SAXHORN
SOJOURN
SOTHERN
SUNBURN
TINHORN
TINTERN
TRICORN
UNICORN
UNLEARN
UNSHORN
WAYWORN
WESTERN

RO•••••

ROACHED
ROACHES
ROADBED
ROADHOG
ROADIES
ROADMAP
ROADWAY
ROAMERS
ROAMING
ROANOKE
ROARERS
ROARING
ROASTED
ROASTER
ROBARDS
ROBBERS
ROBBERY
ROBBING
ROBBINS
ROBERTA
ROBERTO
ROBERTS
ROBESON
ROBLOWE
ROBOCOP
ROBOTIC
ROBROYS
ROBUSTA
ROCHETS
ROCKERS
ROCKERY
ROCKETS
ROCKIER
ROCKIES
ROCKING
ROCKYII
ROCKYIV
RODDING
RODENTS
RODEOFF
RODEOUT
RODGERS
RODLESS
RODLIKE
RODOLFO
ROEBUCK
ROEDEER
ROGAINE
ROGUERY
ROGUISH
ROILIER
ROILING
ROISTER
ROLAIDS
ROLLBAR
ROLLERS
ROLLICK
ROLLING
ROLLINS
ROLLOUT
ROLLSIN
ROLLSON
ROLLSUP
ROLLTOP
ROLODEX
ROLVAAG
ROMAINE
ROMANCE
ROMANIA
ROMANOV
ROMANSH
ROMNEYS
ROMPERS
ROMPING
ROMPISH
ROMULAN
ROMULUS
RONDEAU
RONDELS
RONTGEN
ROOFERS
ROOFING
ROOFTOP
ROOKERY
ROOKIER
ROOKIES
ROOKING
ROOMERS
ROOMFUL
ROOMIER
ROOMIES
ROOMILY
ROOMING
ROOSTED
ROOSTER
ROOTERS
ROOTFOR
ROOTIER
ROOTING
ROOTLET
ROOTOUT
ROPEDIN
ROPESIN
ROPETOW
ROPIEST
RORQUAL
ROSALIE
ROSANNA
ROSANNE
ROSARIO
ROSEATE
ROSEBAY
ROSEBUD
ROSELLE
ROSEOIL
ROSERED
ROSETTA
ROSETTE
ROSIEST
ROSSINI
ROSSSEA
ROSTAND
ROSTERS
ROSTRUM
ROSWELL
ROTATED
ROTATES
ROTATOR
ROTIFER
ROTTERS
ROTTING
ROTUNDA
ROUBLES
ROUGHED
ROUGHEN
ROUGHER
ROUGHIT
ROUGHLY
ROUGHUP
ROUGING
ROULADE
ROUNDED
ROUNDER
ROUNDLY
ROUNDON
ROUNDUP
ROUSERS
ROUSING
ROUSTED
ROUTERS
ROUTINE
ROUTING
ROWBOAT
ROWDIER
ROWDIES
ROWDILY
ROXANNE
ROYALLY
ROYALTY
ROYALWE
ROZELLE
ROZZERS

R•O••••

REOCCUR
REOILED
REOPENS
REORDER
RHODIUM
RHOMBUS
RIOLOBO
RIORITA
RIOTACT
RIOTERS
RIOTING
RIOTOUS
ROOFERS
ROOFING
ROOFTOP
ROOKERY
ROOKIER
ROOKIES
ROOKING
ROOMERS
ROOMFUL
ROOMIER
ROOMIES
ROOMILY
ROOMING
ROOSTED
ROOSTER
ROOTERS
ROOTFOR
ROOTIER
ROOTING
ROOTLET
ROOTOUT

R••O•••

RADOMES
RAGOUTS
RANOVER
RAYOVAC
RAZORED
REBOILS
REBOLTS
REBOOTS
REBOUND
REBOZOS
RECOATS
RECODED
RECODES
RECOILS
RECOLOR
RECORDS
RECORKS
RECOUNT
RECOUPS
RECOVER
REDOAKS
REDOING
REDOUBT
REDOUND
REFOCUS
REFORMS
REHOOKS
REJOICE
REJOINS
RELOADS
RELOCKS
REMODEL
REMOLDS
REMORAS
REMORSE
REMOTER
REMOTES
REMOUNT
REMOVAL
REMOVED
REMOVER
REMOVES
REMOWED
RENOTED
RENOTES
REPOLLS
REPOMAN
REPORTS
REPOSED
REPOSES
REROUTE
RESOLED
RESOLES
RESOLVE
RESORBS
RESORTS
RESOUND
RETOOLS
RETORTS
RETOUCH
RETOURS
RETOWED
REVOICE
REVOKED
REVOKES
REVOLTS
REVOLVE
REWORDS
REWORKS
REWOUND
REWOVEN
REZONED
REZONES
RICOTTA
RIDOTTO
RIGOURS
RIPOFFS
RIPOSTE
RISOTTO
ROBOCOP
ROBOTIC
RODOLFO
ROLODEX
RUDOLPH
RUMORED
RUMOURS
RUNOFFS
RUNOUTS
RUNOVER

R•••O••

RACCOON
RADIOED
RAGDOLL
RAGMOPS
RAGTOPS
RAINOUT
RAKEOFF
RAMRODS
RANCOUR
RANDOWN
RANGOFF
RANGOON
RANGOUT
RANSOMS
RAPPORT
RAPTORS
RATHOLE
RATIONS
RAUCOUS
RAVIOLI
RAYMOND
READOUT
REASONS
REBLOOM
REBOOTS
RECHOSE
RECKONS
RECROOM
RECROSS
RECTORS
RECTORY
REDBOOK
REDCOAT
REDDOGS
REDFORD
REDHOTS
REDPOLL
REDROSE
REDTOPS
REDWOLF
REDWOOD
REELOFF
REGIONS
REGROUP
REHOOKS
REPLOWS
REPROOF
REPROVE
RESHOES
RESHOOT
RESPOND
RESTOCK
RESTORE
RETOOLS
REWROTE
RHEBOKS
RHETORS
RHIZOME
RIBBONS
RIDEOFF
RIDEOUT
RINGOFF
RINGOUT
RIOLOBO
RIOTOUS
RIPCORD
RIPSOFF
RIPSOUT
RIPTORN
RISSOLE
ROANOKE
ROBLOWE
ROBROYS
RODEOFF
RODEOUT
ROLLOUT
ROOTOUT
ROSEOIL
ROWBOAT
RUBDOWN
RUBSOFF
RUBSOUT
RUINOUS
RULEOUT
RUMPOLE
RUNDOWN
RUNGOFF
RUNGOUT
RUNHOME
RUNSOFF
RUNSOUT
RUSHOFF

R••••O•

RACCOON
RAINBOW
RALSTON
RANCHOS
RANGOON
RANRIOT
RAYKROC
REACTOR
REALTOR
REBLOOM
REBOZOS
RECOLOR
RECROOM
REDBOOK
REDSPOT
REDWOOD
REPROOF
REREDOS
RESHOOT
REUNION
RIGHTON
RIMSHOT
ROADHOG
ROBESON
ROBOCOP
ROLLSON
ROLLTOP
ROMANOV
ROOFTOP
ROOTFOR
ROPETOW
ROTATOR
ROUNDON
RUBATOS
RUBICON
RUCTION
RULESON
RUNAMOK
RUNRIOT
RUNSFOR

R•••••O

RALLYTO
RAMINTO
RANINTO
REACTTO
REFERTO
RELIEVO
RELLENO
RICARDO
RIDOTTO
RIOLOBO
RIPIENO
RIPINTO
RISOTTO
ROBERTO
RODOLFO
ROSARIO
RUNINTO

•RO••••

AROUSAL
AROUSED
AROUSES
BROADAX
BROADEN
BROADER
BROADLY
BROCADE
BROGANS
BROGUES
BROILED
BROILER
BROKEIN
BROKERS
BROKEUP
BROMATE
BROMIDE
BROMINE
BRONCHI
BRONCOS
BRONSON
BRONZED
BRONZES
BROODED
BROODER
BROOKED
BROSNAN
BROTHER
BROUGHT
BROWNED
BROWNER
BROWNIE
BROWSED
BROWSER
BROWSES
CROAKED
CROATIA
CROCHET
CROESUS
CROFTER
CRONIES
CRONISH
CROOKED
CROONED
CROONER
CROPPED
CROPPER
CROPSUP
CROQUET
CROSIER
CROSSED
CROSSER
CROSSES
CROSSLY
CROSSUP
CROUTON
CROWBAR
CROWDED
CROWERS
CROWING
CROWNED
DROLLER
DRONERS
DRONING
DRONISH
DROOLED
DROOLER
DROOPED
DROPINS
DROPLET
DROPOFF
DROPOUT
DROPPED
DROPPER
DROPSBY
DROPSIN
DROSHKY
DROUGHT
DROVERS
DROWNED
DROWSED
DROWSES
ERODENT
ERODING
EROSELY
EROSION
EROSIVE
EROTICA
FROCKED
FROGMAN
FROGMEN
FROLICS
FROMAGE
FRONTAL
FRONTED
FRONTON
FROSTED
FROTHED
FROWARD
FROWNAT
FROWNED
FROWNER
FROWSTY
GROANED
GROANER
GROCERS
GROCERY
GRODIER
GROLIER
GROMMET
GROMYKO
GROOMED
GROOMER
GROOVED
GROOVES
GROPING
GROPIUS
GROSSED
GROSSER
GROSSES
GROSSLY
GROTTOS
GROUCHO
GROUCHY
GROUNDS
GROUPED
GROUPER
GROUPIE
GROUSED
GROUSER
GROUSES
GROUTED
GROVELS
GROWERS
GROWING
GROWLED
GROWLER
GROWNUP
GROWSON
GROWSUP
GROWTHS
IRONAGE
IRONERS
IRONIES
IRONING
IRONMAN
IRONMEN
IRONONS
IRONORE
IRONOUT
OROGENY
OROTUND
OROURKE
PROBATE
PROBERS
PROBING
PROBITY
PROBLEM
PROBONO
PROCEED
PROCESS
PROCTOR
PROCURE
PROCYON
PRODDED
PRODDER
PRODIGY
PRODUCE
PRODUCT
PROFANE
PROFESS
PROFFER
PROFILE
PROFITS
PROFUSE
PROGENY
PROGGED
PROGRAM
PROJECT
PROLOGS
PROLONG
PROMISE
PROMOTE
PROMPTS
PRONELY
PRONGED
PRONOUN
PROOFED
PROOFER
PROPANE
PROPELS
PROPHET
PROPJET
PROPMAN
PROPMEN
PROPOSE
PROPPED
PROPRIO
PROPSUP
PROPTER
PRORATA
PRORATE
PROSAIC
PROSERS
PROSHOP
PROSIER
PROSILY
PROSING
PROSODY
PROSPER
PROTEAN
PROTECT
PROTEGE
PROTEIN
PROTEST
PROTEUS
PROTIST
PROTONS
PROUDER
PROUDLY
PROVERB
PROVERS
PROVIDE
PROVING
PROVISO
PROVOKE
PROVOST
PROWESS
PROWLED
PROWLER
PROXIES
PROXIMO
TROCARS
TROCHEE
TROCHES
TRODDEN
TROGONS
TROIKAS
TROILUS
TROJANS
TROLLED
TROLLEY
TROOPED
TROOPER
TROPHIC
TROPICS
TROPISM
TROTHED
TROTOUT
TROTSKY
TROTTED
TROTTER
TROUBLE
TROUGHS
TROUNCE
TROUPER
TROUPES
TROUSER
TROWELS
TROWERS
VRONSKY
WRONGED
WRONGER
WRONGLY
WROTEIN
WROTETO
WROTEUP
WROUGHT

•R•O•••

ARBORED
ARBOURS
ARDOURS
AREOLAE
AREOLAR
AREOLAS
ARGONNE
ARIOSOS
ARIOSTO
ARMOIRE
ARMORED
ARMORER
ARMOURS
ARMOURY
ARROBAS
ARROYOS
BRIOCHE
BROODED
BROODER
BROOKED
CREOLES
CREOSOL
CRIOLLO
CROOKED
CROONED
CROONER
CRYOGEN
DROOLED
DROOLER
DROOPED
GROOMED
GROOMER
GROOVED
GROOVES
MRBONES
ORIOLES
ORMOLUS
ORTOLAN
PRIORTO
PROOFED
PROOFER
TRIODES
TROOPED
TROOPER
TRYOUTS

•R••O••

ARCHONS
ARDMORE
ARDUOUS
ARIZONA
ARMHOLE
ARMLOAD
ARMLOCK
ARTFORM
ARTSONG
ARTWORK
BRAVOES
BRETONS
BRITONS
CRAYOLA
CRAYONS
CREMONA
CRINOID
CRYWOLF
DRAGONS
DRAGOON
DRAGOUT
DRAWOUT
DREWOUT
DROPOFF
DROPOUT
DRSPOCK
DRYDOCK
DRYHOLE
DRYROTS
ERELONG
FREMONT
FRYCOOK
GRANOLA
GREGORY
IRISOUT
IRKSOME
IRONONS
IRONORE
IRONOUT
MRSPOCK
ORATORS
ORATORY
ORINOCO
ORISONS
PRECOOK
PRECOOL
PRELOAD
PRESOAK
PRESORT
PRISONS
PROBONO
PROLOGS
PROLONG
PROMOTE
PRONOUN
PROPOSE
PROSODY
PROTONS
PROVOKE
PROVOST
TRAVOIS
TREFOIL
TREMOLO
TREMORS
TRICORN
TRICOTS
TRIGONS
TRILOGY
TRIPODS
TRIPOLI
TRITONE
TRITONS
TROGONS
TROTOUT

•R•••O•

ARIOSOS
ARISTOS
ARROYOS
BRANDON
BRANSON
BRAXTON
BRERFOX
BRINGON
BRISTOL
BRITTON
BRONCOS
BRONSON
CRAMPON
CREATOR
CREOSOL
CRIMSON
CROUTON
CRYPTOS
DRAGOON
DRAGSON
DRAWNON
DRAWSON
DREAMON
ERECTOR
EREWHON
ERICSON
EROSION
FRANKOZ
FREEDOM
FRESCOS
FRISSON
FRONTON
FRYCOOK
GRAFTON
GRANTOR
GRAYSON
GRIFFON
GRISSOM
GROTTOS
GROWSON
GRUNION
GRYPHON
IRECKON
KRATION
KRYPTON
MRMAGOO
ORATION
ORBISON
ORGANON
PRAETOR
PRAYFOR
PRECOOK
PRECOOL
PRESSON
PRESTON
PRESTOS
PREYSON
PROCTOR
PROCYON
PROSHOP
PRUDHOE
TRACTOR
TRADEON
TRAITOR
TRANSOM
TREASON
TREETOP
TRENTON
TRIEDON
TRIESON

•R••••O

ARAPAHO
ARECIBO
ARETINO
ARIOSTO
ARSENIO
ARTDECO

BRACERO
BRAVADO
BRINGTO
CRIOLLO
CRUSADO
CRUZADO
ERNESTO
GROMYKO
GROUCHO
MRMAGOO
OREGANO
ORINOCO
ORLANDO
ORNITHO
PRAYSTO
PRIORTO
PROBONO
PROPRIO
PROVISO
PROXIMO
PRYINTO
TREMOLO
TREVINO
WRITETO
WROTETO

••RO•••

ACROBAT
ACRONYM
AEROBAT
AEROBES
AEROBIC
AEROSOL
AGROUND
APRONED
APROPOS
ARROBAS
ARROYOS
ATROPHY
AUROCHS
AURORAE
AURORAL
AURORAS
BARONET
BARONGS
BAROQUE
BORODIN
BOROUGH
BUROAKS
BYROADS
CAROLED
CAROLER
CAROLUS
CAROLYN
CAROMED
CAROTID
CAROUSE
CHROMES
CHRONIC
COROLLA
CORONAE
CORONAS
CORONET
DOROTHY
ENROBED
ENROBES
ENROLLS
ENROOTS
ENROUTE
FURORES
GARONNE
GIRONDE
GOROUND
HEROICS
HEROINE
HEROISM
INROADS
KAROLYI
KEROUAC
MAROONS
MOROCCO
PAROLED
PAROLEE
PAROLES
PIROGUE
REROUTE
SARONGS
SAROYAN
SCROLLS
SCROOGE
SHROUDS
SIROCCO
SORORAL
SPROUTS
STROBES
STROKED
STROKES
STROLLS
STROPHE
STROPPY
THROATS
THROATY
THRONES
THRONGS
THROUGH
THROWER
THROWIN
TOROIDS
TORONTO
UNROBED
UNROBES
UNROLLS
UPROARS
UPROOTS
ZEROING
ZEROSUM

••R•O••

AIRBOAT
AIRCOOL
AIRFOIL
AIRHOLE
AIRLOCK
AIRPORT
AIRSOCK
AIRSOUT
AIRWOLF
APRIORI
AUREOLA
AUREOLE
BARCODE
BARHOPS
BARNONE
BARNOWL
BARROOM
BARROWS
BARSOAP
BARYONS
BERTOLT
BOREOUT
BORROWS
BORZOIS
BURBOTS
BURDOCK
BURGOOS
BURNOUT
BURROWS
CARBONS
CARBOYS
CARCOAT
CARDOZO
CARGOES
CARHOPS
CARIOCA
CARLOAD
CARPOOL
CARPORT
CARROLL
CARROTS
CARTONS
CARTOON
CORDOBA
CORDONS
CORNOIL
CORRODE
CURIOUS
CURSORS
CURSORY
EARLOBE
EARLOCK
ENROOTS
FARGONE
FARMOUT
FARROWS
FERROUS
FERVORS
FERVOUR
FIREOFF
FORBORE
FORGOES
FORGONE
FORGOOD
FORLORN
FORMOSA
FORSOOK
FURIOUS
FURLONG
FURROWS
GARCONS
GORGONS
HARBORS
HARBOUR
HARMONY
HARPOON
HARROWS
HORMONE
HORRORS
JARGONS
JARGONY
JERBOAS
KARAOKE
KARLOFF
LARDONS
MARCONI
MARKOFF
MARKOVA
MARLOWE
MARMOTS
MAROONS
MARROWS
MERLOTS
MIRRORS
MORMONS
MORROWS
MURDOCH
NARROWS
NERVOUS
NORFOLK
OARLOCK
OURTOWN
PARBOIL
PARDONS
PARLORS
PARLOUR
PARLOUS
PARROTS
PARSONS
PARTOOK
PARTOUT
PERFORM
PERGOLA
PERIODS
PERSONA
PERSONS
PURLOIN
PURPORT
PURPOSE
SCROOGE
SERIOUS
SERMONS
SIRLOIN
SORROWS
SORTOUT
SURCOAT
TARPONS
TERRORS
TIREOUT
TOREOFF
TOREOUT
TORNOFF
TORNOUT
TORTONI
TURBOTS
TURMOIL
TURNOFF
TURNOUT
UPROOTS
VARIOUS
VERBOSE
VERDOUX
VERMONT
VIRGOAN
WARDOFF
WARGODS
WARLOCK
WARLORD
WARZONE
WORDONE
WOREOFF
WOREOUT
WORKOFF
WORKOUT
WORNOFF
WORNOUT
YARROWS
ZIRCONS

••R••O•

AERATOR
AEROSOL
AIRCOOL
AIRDROP
AIRFLOW
AIRSHOW
APRICOT
APROPOS
ARROYOS
BARANOF
BARRIOS
BARROOM
BARSTOW
BERGSON
BERIDOF
BERLIOZ
BIRDDOG
BOREDOM
BURGEON
BURGOOS
CAREFOR
CARIBOU
CARLSON
CARLTON
CARPOOL
CARRION
CARRYON
CARTOON
CORAZON
CORNCOB
CORNDOG
CORNROW
CURATOR
DORITOS
EARDROP
EARLDOM
EARLYON
EARSHOT
FIREBOX
FIREDOG
FORGOOD
FORSOOK
GERITOL
GIRASOL
GYRATOR
HARDTOP
HARDWON
HARICOT
HARPOON
HARPSON
HERRIOT
HIRESON
HORIZON
KERCHOO
KERPLOP
MARABOU
MARCHON
MARKHOR
MARMION
MARYLOU
MERINOS
MIRADOR
PARADOX
PARAGON
PARASOL
PARTOOK
PERIDOT
PORTHOS
PORTION
REREDOS
SERFDOM
SURGEON
TEREDOS
TIREDOF
TOREROS
TORSION
TURNSON
VERSION
VIRAGOS
WARRIOR
WARTHOG
WORKFOR
WORKSON

••R•••O

AGREETO
AMRADIO
BERMEJO
BURRITO
CARABAO
CARDOZO
CBRADIO
CHRISTO
CORDERO
CURACAO
DARESTO
DURANGO
FARRAGO
FERRARO
FMRADIO
GERALDO
HORATIO
JERICHO
KERCHOO
LORENZO
MARCATO
MARENGO
MARTINO
MORELLO
MOROCCO
MURILLO
NORELCO
OTRANTO
PORTICO
SERPICO
SIROCCO
SORDINO
SORVINO
STRETTO
TARANTO
TORNADO
TORONTO
TORPEDO
TURNSTO
UTRILLO
VERDUGO
VERISMO
VERTIGO

•••RO••

ACEROLA
ACEROSE
AFFRONT
AMBROSE
AMOROUS
ANDROID
ANEROID
ANYROAD
APPROVE
AYKROYD
BARROOM
BARROWS
BEAROFF
BEAROUT
BEDROCK
BEDROLL
BEDROOM
BETROTH
BORROWS
BOXROOM
BURROWS
CARROLL
CARROTS
CHEROOT
CITROEN
CITRONS
CITROUS
CORRODE
DAYROOM
DEFROCK
DEFROST
DETROIT
DISROBE
DRYROTS
EGGROLL
EMBROIL
ENGROSS
ENTROPY
ESCROWS
FAIROFF
FARROWS
FERROUS
FIBROUS
FLYRODS
FURROWS
GOBROKE
GOWRONG
GYPROOM
HARROWS
HEAROUT
HIPROOF
HORRORS
HOTRODS
HYDROUS
IMPROVE
INFRONT
INGROUP
INGROWN
INTROIT
KEDROVA
LAPROBE
LEGROOM
LOGROLL
LOWROAD
MACRONS
MARROWS
MATRONS
MAUROIS
MELROSE
MICROBE
MICRONS
MIRRORS
MORROWS
NAIROBI
NARROWS
NEURONE
NEURONS
NIMRODS
NITROUS
OCTROIS
ODOROUS
OFFROAD
OLDROSE
OLOROSO
ONAROLL
ONEROUS
OPEROSE
PADRONE
PADRONI
PAIROFF
PARROTS
PATROLS
PATRONS
PATROON
PAYROLL
PEEROUT
PETROCK
PETROLS
PETROUS
POUROUT
RAMRODS
RECROOM
RECROSS
REDROSE
REGROUP
REPROOF
REPROVE
REWROTE
ROBROYS
SORROWS
STCROIX
STEROID
STEROLS
SUBROSA
SUCROSE
SUNROOF
SUNROOM
TAPROOM
TAPROOT
TEAROFF
TEAROOM
TEAROSE
TEAROUT
TERRORS
THEROUX
TIERODS
TOWROPE
UNFROCK
UPFRONT
WEAROFF
WEAROUT
YARROWS

•••R•O•

ALARCON
AWAREOF
BARRIOS
BARROOM
BEARSON
BEDROOM
BLERIOT
BOURBON
BOXROOM
BRERFOX
CARRION
CARRYON
CHARIOT
CHEROOT
CLARION
CYPRIOT
CZARDOM
DAYROOM
EMBRYOS
EMERSON
GEARBOX
GYPROOM
HAIRDOS
HEARDOF
HEARSOF
HERRIOT
HIPROOF
INERROR
JOURNOS
LEGROOM
NEARYOU
OVERJOY
PATRIOT
PATROON
PEARSON
PHARAOH
PIERROT
POORBOX
POORBOY
QUARTOS
RANRIOT
RECROOM
REPROOF
RUNRIOT
SHORTOF
SPARROW
SPURSON
STARDOM
STEREOS
SUNROOF
SUNROOM
TAPROOM
TAPROOT
TEAROOM
THEREOF
THEREON
THERMOS
VITRIOL
WARRIOR
WEIRDOS
WHARTON
WHEREOF

•••R••O

ALFREDO
AMERIGO
BURRITO
CHIRICO
CHORIZO
ELGRECO
FARRAGO
FERRARO
GEARSTO
GIORGIO
OLOROSO
SANREMO
SCORPIO
SOPRANO
SPIRITO
SUPREMO
THERETO
TOURACO
VIBRATO
WHERETO

••••RO•

ACHERON
AILERON
AIRDROP
ANDIRON
ATECROW
BISTROS
BOLEROS
BOUTROS
CALDRON
CAMERON
CHEVRON
CLAIROL
COMOROS
CONTROL
CORNROW
DEMEROL
DENDRON
DESTROY
DEWDROP
DIDEROT
DOGTROT
EARDROP
EATCROW
EMPEROR
ENDUROS
ENTERON
EYEBROW
FOXTROT
FUELROD
GABBROS
GUMDROP
INERROR
LATERON
LEBARON
LOWBROW
MCENROE
NEMEROV
NEUTRON
NONIRON
OLDPROS
OMICRON
ONEIRON
OUTCROP
OUTGROW
PALTROW
PICAROS
PIERROT
PIGIRON
POTOROO
RAYKROC
SAFFRON
SIXIRON
SKIDROW
SPARROW
THECROW
TONEROW
TOREROS
TWOIRON
VICEROY
WAITRON
WINDROW
WOODROW

••••R•O

ALBERTO
BOIARDO
CATERTO
CHEERIO
CONBRIO
DECARLO
EMBARGO
ESPARTO
INFERNO
LIVORNO
LOCARNO
NOVARRO
ONTARIO
PALERMO
PATERNO
PIZARRO
POTOROO
PRIORTO
PROPRIO
REFERTO
RICARDO
ROBERTO
ROSARIO
SALERNO
SCHERZO
SUHARTO
SUKARNO
SWEARTO
UMBERTO
UNDERDO
UNDERGO

•••••RO

ALLEGRO
BRACERO
CORDERO
DEUTERO
ELECTRO
FERRARO
GENNARO
GOLFPRO
HHMUNRO
INVITRO
MAESTRO
MONTERO
NONZERO
NOVARRO
PIZARRO
SAGUARO
SAPPORO
SEMIPRO
SHAPIRO
SUBZERO
VAQUERO

R•P••••

RAPANUI
RAPHAEL
RAPIDER
RAPIDLY
RAPIERS
RAPINES
RAPPELS
RAPPERS
RAPPING
RAPPORT
RAPTORS
RAPTURE
REPAINT
REPAIRS
REPAPER
REPASTE
REPASTS
REPAVED
REPAVES
REPEALS
REPEATS
REPENTS
REPINED
REPINES
REPLACE
REPLANS
REPLANT
REPLATE
REPLAYS
REPLETE
REPLICA
REPLIED
REPLIES
REPLOWS
REPOLLS
REPOMAN
REPORTS
REPOSED
REPOSES
REPRESS
REPRICE
REPRINT
REPRISE
REPROOF
REPROVE
REPTILE
REPUGNS
REPULSE
REPUTED
REPUTES
RIPCORD
RIPENED
RIPIENO
RIPINTO
RIPOFFS
RIPOSTE
RIPPERS
RIPPING
RIPPLED
RIPPLES
RIPRAPS
RIPSAWS
RIPSOFF
RIPSOUT
RIPTIDE
RIPTORN
ROPEDIN
ROPESIN
ROPETOW
ROPIEST
RUPIAHS
RUPTURE

R••P•••

RAJPUTS
RAMPAGE
RAMPANT
RAMPART
RAPPELS
RAPPERS
RAPPING
RAPPORT
RASPERS
RASPIER
RASPING
RASPISH
RATPACK
REAPERS
REAPING
REDPINE
REDPOLL
REOPENS
RESPECT
RESPINS
RESPIRE
RESPITE
RESPOND
REUPPED
RIMPLED
RIMPLES
RIPPERS
RIPPING
RIPPLED
RIPPLES
ROMPERS
ROMPING
ROMPISH
RUMPLED
RUMPLES
RUMPOLE

R•••P••

RECIPES
REDSPOT
RELAPSE
REPAPER
RETAPED
RETAPES
RETYPED
RETYPES
REUPPED

R••••P•

RAGMOPS
RAGTOPS
RAVEUPS
RECEIPT
RECOUPS
REDCAPS
REDTAPE
REDTOPS
RESHIPS
REVAMPS
REWRAPS
RIPRAPS
RUDOLPH

R•••••P

RACKSUP
RAISEUP
RAKEDUP
RAKESUP
RATTRAP
REARSUP
REGROUP
RESTAMP
RESTSUP
RILESUP
RINGSUP
ROADMAP
ROBOCOP
ROLLSUP
ROLLTOP
ROOFTOP
ROUGHUP
ROUNDUP
RUNDEEP

•RP••••

ARPENTS
ORPHANS
ORPHEAN
ORPHEUS
ORPHREY
ORPINES

•R•P•••

ARAPAHO
ARMPITS
CRAPPIE
CROPPED
CROPPER
CROPSUP
CRYPTIC
CRYPTOS
DRAPERS
DRAPERY
DRAPING
DRIPDRY
DRIPPAN
DRIPPED
DROPINS
DROPLET
DROPOFF
DROPOUT
DROPPED
DROPPER
DROPSBY
DROPSIN
DRSPOCK
ERUPTED
FRAPPES
FRIPPET
FRYPANS
GRAPHED
GRAPHIC
GRAPIER
GRAPNEL
GRAPPAS
GRAPPLE
GRIPERS
GRIPING
GRIPPED
GRIPPER
GROPING
GROPIUS
GRYPHON
KRYPTON
MRSPOCK
PREPAID
PREPARE
PREPAYS
PREPPIE
PROPANE
PROPELS
PROPHET
PROPJET
PROPMAN
PROPMEN
PROPOSE
PROPPED
PROPRIO
PROPSUP
PROPTER
TRAPEZE
TRAPPED
TRAPPER
TREPANS
TRIPLED
TRIPLES
TRIPLET
TRIPLEX
TRIPODS
TRIPOLI
TRIPPED
TRIPPER
TRIPPET
TRIPSUP
TROPHIC
TROPICS
TROPISM
WRAPPED
WRAPPER
WRAPSUP
WRAPUPS

•R••P••

CRAMPED
CRAMPON
CRAPPIE
CREEPED
CREEPER
CREEPUP
CRIMPED
CRIMPER
CRISPED
CRISPER
CRISPIN
CRISPLY
CRISPUS
CROPPED
CROPPER
CRUMPET
CRUMPLE
CRUMPLY
DRIPPAN
DRIPPED
DROOPED
DROPPED
DROPPER
FRAPPES
FRIPPET
GRAMPAS
GRAMPUS
GRAPPAS
GRAPPLE
GRASPED
GRIPPED
GRIPPER
GROUPED
GROUPER
GROUPIE
GRUMPED
IRRUPTS
PREPPIE
PRIMPED
PROMPTS
PROPPED

PROSPER
TRAIPSE
TRAMPAS
TRAMPED
TRAMPLE
TRAPPED
TRAPPER
TRIPPED
TRIPPER
TRIPPET
TROOPED
TROOPER
TROUPER
TROUPES
TRUMPED
TRUMPET
TRUMPUP
WRAPPED
WRAPPER

•R•••P•

GRANDPA
MRCHIPS
PREAMPS
PRECEPT
PREEMPT
PRENUPS
PRETAPE
TRICEPS
TRIUMPH
WRAPUPS

•R••••P

ARCLAMP
BRACEUP
BREAKUP
BRINGUP
BROKEUP
BRUSHUP
CRACKUP
CRANKUP
CREEPUP
CROPSUP
CROSSUP
DRAWNUP
DRAWSUP
DREAMUP
DRESSUP
DRIEDUP
DRIESUP
DRIVEUP
DRUMSUP
FRAMEUP
GROWNUP
GROWSUP
PRESSUP
PROPSUP
PROSHOP
TRADEUP
TREETOP
TRIPSUP
TRUMPUP
WRAPSUP
WRITEUP
WROTEUP

••RP•••

AIRPLAY
AIRPORT
AIRPUMP
BURPGUN
BURPING
CARPALS
CARPARK
CARPELS
CARPERS
CARPETS
CARPING
CARPOOL
CARPORT
EARPLUG
HARPERS
HARPIES
HARPING
HARPIST
HARPOON
HARPSON
KERPLOP
MORPHED
PERPLEX
PURPLED
PURPLES
PURPORT
PURPOSE
SERPENT
SERPICO
SURPASS
SURPLUS
TARPITS
TARPONS
TORPEDO
WARPATH
WARPING

••R•P••

AGRIPPA
APROPOS
ATROPHY
CERIPHS
FOREPAW
HARDPAN
HARDPUT
IRRUPTS
PARAPET
PARAPHS
PORKPIE
SCRAPED
SCRAPER
SCRAPES
SCRAPPY
SCRIPPS
SCRIPTS
SCRUPLE
SERAPES
SERAPHS
SERAPIS
STRIPED
STRIPER
STRIPES
STROPHE
STROPPY
TERAPHS

••R••P•

AGRIPPA
BARHOPS
BURLAPS
CARHOPS
CORRUPT
FORCEPS
LARRUPS
MARKUPS
PERHAPS
SCRAPPY
SCRIMPS
SCRIMPY
SCRIPPS
SHRIMPS
STROPPY
THREEPM
TURNIPS
WARMUPS
WORKUPS

••R•••P

AIRDROP
AIRPUMP
AIRSHIP
BARKEEP
BARSOAP
BORNEUP
BURNSUP
BURNTUP
CURLSUP
EARDROP
EARFLAP
FIREDUP
FIRESUP
FIRMSUP
HARDTOP
HURRYUP
KERPLOP
MARKSUP
PARSNIP
PERKSUP
SCREWUP
SCRUBUP
SERVEUP
TURNSUP
WARMSUP
WARSHIP
WIRETAP
WORKSUP
WORSHIP

•••RP••

BEARPAW
CHIRPED
HAIRPIN
SCARPED
SCARPER
SCORPIO
SHARPED
SHARPEI
SHARPEN
SHARPER
SHARPLY
SHERPAS
SLURPED
USURPED
USURPER

•••R•P•

BUMRAPS
CORRUPT
DECRYPT
DIGRAPH
DISRUPT
ENCRYPT
ENTRAPS
ENTROPY
ENWRAPS
LARRUPS
REWRAPS
RIPRAPS
SATRAPS
THERAPY
TOWROPE
UNDRAPE
UNTRAPS
UNWRAPS

•••R••P

BEARSUP
FAIRSUP
FLAREUP
GEARSUP
HURRYUP
INGROUP
NOTRUMP
OFFRAMP
OVERLAP
PAIRSUP
PHARLAP
REARSUP
REGROUP
SCAREUP
STARMAP
STARTUP
STIRRUP
STIRSUP
STOREUP
TEARSUP

••••RP•

ESCARPS
EUTERPE
EXCERPT

••••R•P

AIRDROP
CANTRIP
CHEERUP
CLEARUP
COVERUP
DAYTRIP
DEWDROP
EARDROP
EGOTRIP
FLYTRAP
GUMDROP
KEYGRIP
MANTRAP
OUTCROP
RATTRAP
STIRRUP
UNSTRAP

•••••RP

ANTWERP
HANSARP
JEANARP

R•Q••••

REQUEST
REQUIEM
REQUIRE
REQUITE

R••Q•••

RACQUET
RORQUAL

•R•Q•••

BRIQUET
CROQUET
PREQUEL

•R••Q••

BRUSQUE

••RQ•••

CIRQUES
MARQUEE
MARQUES
MARQUEZ
MARQUIS
PARQUET
RORQUAL
TORQUES

••R•Q••

BAROQUE

R•R••••

RAREBIT
RAREGAS
RARITAN
RERAISE
RERATED
RERATES
REREADS
REREDOS
RERENTS
RERINSE
REROUTE
RORQUAL
RURALLY

R••R•••

RAGRUGS
RAMRODS
RANRIOT
RATRACE
REAREND
REARERS
REARGUE
REARING
REARMED
REARSUP
RECROOM
RECROSS
RECRUIT
REDRAWN
REDRAWS
REDRESS
REDROSE
REFRACT
REFRAIN
REFRAME
REFRESH
REFRIED
REFRIES
REGRADE
REGRESS
REGRETS
REGROUP
REORDER
REPRESS
REPRICE
REPRINT
REPRISE
REPROOF
REPROVE
RETRACE
RETRACK
RETRACT
RETRADE
RETRAIN
RETREAD
RETREAT
RETRIAL
RETRIED
RETRIES
RETRIMS
REWRAPS
REWRITE
REWROTE
RIORITA
RIPRAPS
ROARERS
ROARING
ROBROYS
RUBRICS
RUNRIOT

R•••R••

RATTRAP
RAYKROC
RAZORED
REAIRED
REBIRTH
RECORDS
RECORKS
REFEREE
REFERTO
REFIRES
REFORMS
REGARDS
REHIRED
REHIRES
REMARKS
REMARRY
REMORAS
REMORSE
RENARDS
REPORTS
RESERVE
RESORBS
RESORTS
RESURGE
RETARDS
RETIRED
RETIREE
RETIRES
RETORTS
RETURNS
REVERBS
REVERED
REVERES
REVERIE
REVERSE
REVERTS
REWARDS
REWARMS
REWIRED
REWIRES
REWORDS
REWORKS
RICARDO
RICERAT
ROBARDS
ROBERTA
ROBERTO
ROBERTS
ROSARIO
ROSERED
ROSTRUM
RUMORED

R••••R•

RAFTERS
RAIDERS
RAILERS
RAISERS
RAMPART
RANGERS
RANKERS
RANTERS
RAPIERS
RAPPERS
RAPPORT
RAPTORS
RAPTURE
RASHERS
RASPERS
RASTERS
RATBERT
RATTERS
RAYBURN
READERS
REAMERS
REAPERS
REARERS
RECTORS
RECTORY
REDBIRD
REDFIRS
REDFORD
REEFERS
REENTRY
REHEARD
REHEARS
RELEARN
REMARRY
RENDERS
RENTERS
REPAIRS
REQUIRE
RESPIRE
RESTART
RESTERS
RESTORE
RETEARS
RETIARY
RETOURS
REUTERS
REVELRY
REYNARD
RHETORS
RHUBARB
RHYMERS
RICHARD
RIFLERS
RIFLERY
RIGGERS
RIGOURS
RINGERS
RIOTERS
RIPCORD
RIPPERS
RIPTORN
RISKERS
RIVALRY
RIVIERA
RIVIERE
ROAMERS
ROARERS
ROBBERS
ROBBERY
ROCKERS
ROCKERY
RODGERS
ROGUERY
ROLLERS
ROMPERS
ROOFERS
ROOKERY
ROOMERS
ROOTERS
ROSTERS
ROTTERS
ROUSERS
ROUTERS
ROZZERS
RUBBERS
RUBBERY
RUDDERS
RUDYARD
RUINERS
RUMOURS
RUNNERS
RUNSDRY
RUPTURE
RUSHERS
RUTGERS

R•••••R

RACECAR
RAFFLER
RAINIER
RALLIER
RAMBLER
RANCHER
RANCOUR
RANDIER
RANGIER
RANOVER
RAPIDER
RASPIER
RATTIER
RATTLER
RAVAGER
REACTOR
READIER
REALTOR
RECITER
RECOLOR
RECOVER
REDDEER
REDHAIR
REDSTAR
REDUCER
REEDIER
REENTER
REFINER
REFUSER
REFUTER
REGULAR
REMOTER
REMOVER
RENEGER
RENEWER
REOCCUR
REORDER
REPAPER
RESCUER
REUTHER
REVELER
REVISER
RICHTER
RIDDLER
RIDGIER
RIGHTER
RISKIER
RITZIER
RIVETER
ROASTER
ROCKIER
ROEDEER
ROILIER
ROISTER
ROLLBAR
ROOKIER
ROOMIER
ROOSTER
ROOTFOR
ROOTIER
ROTATOR
ROTIFER
ROUGHER
ROUNDER
ROWDIER
RUDDIER
RUMMIER
RUNNIER
RUNOVER
RUNSFOR
RUNTIER
RUSHIER
RUSTIER
RUSTLER
RUTTIER

•RR••••

ARRAIGN
ARRANGE
ARRASES
ARRAYED
ARREARS
ARRESTS
ARRIERE
ARRISES
ARRIVAL
ARRIVED
ARRIVER
ARRIVES
ARROBAS
ARROYOS
ERRANCY
ERRANDS
ERRATIC
ERRATUM
IRRUPTS
MRRIGHT

•R•R•••

ARMREST
BRERFOX
DRYROTS
DRYRUNS
PRORATA
PRORATE
TRIREME

•R••R••

ARBORED
AREARUG
ARMORED
ARMORER
ARMURES
BRIARDS
ERITREA
FREDRIC
GRIGRIS
ORDERED
ORDERER
ORDERLY
OROURKE
ORPHREY
PRAIRIE
PRIORTO
PROGRAM
PROPRIO
TREERAT
TRIGRAM

•R•••R•

ARAFURA
ARBOURS
ARCHERS
ARCHERY
ARDMORE
ARDOURS
ARGUERS
ARIKARA
ARMOIRE
ARMOURS
ARMOURY
ARREARS
ARRIERE
ARTFORM
ARTWARE
ARTWORK
BRACERO
BRACERS
BRAVERY
BRAVURA
BRAYERS
BREWERS
BREWERY
BRIBERY
BROKERS
CRATERS
CRAVERS
CROWERS
DRAPERS
DRAPERY
DRAWERS
DRIPDRY
DRIVERS
DRONERS
DROVERS
ERASERS
ERASURE
FROWARD
GRADERS
GRANARY
GRATERS
GRAVERS
GRAVURE
GRAZERS
GREGORY
GRIPERS
GROCERS
GROCERY
GROWERS
GRUYERE
IRONERS
IRONORE
KRATERS
ORATORS
ORATORY
ORCHARD
PRATERS
PRAYERS
PREFERS
PREPARE
PRESORT
PRICERS
PRIMARY
PRIMERS
PROBERS
PROCURE
PROSERS
PROVERB
PROVERS
PRUDERY
PRUNERS
TRABERT
TRACERS
TRACERY
TRADERS
TRAVERS
TREMORS
TRENARY
TRICORN
TROCARS
TROWERS
WRITERS

•R••••R

ARBITER
AREOLAR
ARMORER
ARRIVER
ARTSIER
BRAGGER
BRAIDER
BRANDER
BRASHER
BRAWLER
BRAZIER
BREAKER
BREEDER
BRENNER
BRIEFER
BRINGER
BRINIER
BRISKER
BROADER
BROILER
BROODER
BROTHER
BROWNER
BROWSER
BRUISER
BRYNNER
CRABBER
CRACKER
CRAFTER
CRAMMER
CRASSER
CRAWLER
CRAZIER
CREAMER
CREATOR
CREEPER
CRIMPER
CRISPER
CRITTER
CROFTER
CROONER
CROPPER
CROSIER
CROSSER
CROWBAR
CRUELER
CRUISER
CRULLER
CRUSHER
DRABBER
DRAGGER
DRAINER
DRAWBAR
DREAMER
DREDGER
DREISER
DRESSER
DRIFTER
DRILLER
DRINKER
DROLLER
DROOLER
DROPPER
DRUCKER
DRUMMER
ERECTER
ERECTOR
FRAILER
FRANKER
FRASIER
FRAZIER
FREEZER
FRESHER
FRITTER
FROWNER
GRABBER
GRAMMAR
GRAMMER
GRANDER
GRANGER
GRANTOR
GRAPIER
GREASER
GREATER
GREENER
GREETER
GRIDDER
GRIEVER
GRIFTER
GRIMIER
GRIMMER
GRINDER
GRINNER
GRIPPER
GROANER
GRODIER
GROLIER
GROOMER
GROSSER
GROUPER
GROUSER
GROWLER
GRUFFER
ORBITER
ORDERER
PRAETOR
PRAISER
PRANCER
PRAYFOR
PREENER
PREMIER
PRESSER
PRICIER
PRIMMER
PRINTER
PRIVIER
PROCTOR
PRODDER
PROFFER
PROOFER
PROPTER
PROSIER
PROSPER
PROUDER
PROWLER
TRACKER
TRACTOR
TRAILER
TRAINER
TRAITOR
TRAMCAR
TRAPPER
TRAWLER
TREADER
TREKKER
TRICKER
TRIFLER
TRIGGER
TRIMMER
TRIPPER
TRISTAR
TROOPER
TROTTER
TROUPER
TROUSER
TRUCKER
TRUDGER
TRYSTER
URBANER
WRAPPER
WRECKER
WRINGER
WRONGER

••RR•••

AIRRAID
BARRACK
BARRAGE
BARRELS
BARRENS
BARRETT
BARRIER
BARRING
BARRIOS
BARROOM
BARROWS
BERRIED
BERRIES
BORROWS
BURRITO
BURROWS
CARRELS
CARRICK
CARRIED
CARRIER
CARRIES
CARRION
CARROLL
CARROTS
CARRYON
CORRALS
CORRECT
CORRIDA
CORRODE
CORRUPT
CURRANT
CURRENT
CURRIED
CURRIER
CURRIES
CURRISH
DERRICK
DERRING
DURRELL
EARRING
FARRAGO
FARRIER
FARROWS
FERRARI
FERRARO
FERRATE
FERRETS
FERRIED
FERRIES
FERRITE
FERROUS
FERRULE
FIRRIER
FORREAL
FORRENT
FORREST
FURRIER
FURRING
FURROWS
GARRETS
GARRETT
GARRICK
HARRIED
HARRIER
HARRIES
HARRIET
HARROWS
HERRING
HERRIOT
HORRIFY
HORRORS
HURRAHS
HURRIED
HURRIES
HURRYUP
JARRING
LARRUPS
LORRIES
MARRIED
MARRIES
MARRING
MARROWS
MARRYME
MERRIER
MERRILL
MERRILY
MIRRORS
MORROWS
NARRATE
NARROWS
PARRIED
PARRIER
PARRIES
PARRING
PARRISH
PARROTS
PERRIER
PURRERS
PURRING
PYRRHIC
PYRRHUS
SERRATE
SERRIED
SORRELS
SORRIER
SORRILY
SORROWS
SURREAL
SURREYS
TARRIED
TARRIER
TARRIES
TARRING
TERRACE
TERRAIN
TERRENE
TERRETS
TERRIER
TERRIES
TERRIFY
TERRORS
TORRENS
TORRENT
TURRETS
WARRANT
WARRENS
WARRING
WARRIOR
WORRIED
WORRIER
WORRIES
YARROWS

••R•R••

AIRCREW
AIRDROP
AURORAE
AURORAL
AURORAS
CORNROW

EARDROP
EARDRUM
ETRURIA
FORERAN
FORERUN
FORFREE
FORTRAN
FURORES
JURYRIG
MARGRET
MORDRED
PARURES
PORTRAY
SORORAL
TOREROS

••R••R•

AIRFARE
AIRPORT
APRIORI
ARREARS
ARRIERE
BARBARA
BARBARY
BARBERS
BARCARS
BARKERS
BARNARD
BARTERS
BARWARE
BERBERS
BERGERE
BERNARD
BERSERK
BIRDERS
BORDERS
BURGERS
BURNERS
BURSARS
BURSARY
CARDERS
CAREERS
CARFARE
CARNERA
CARPARK
CARPERS
CARPORT
CARTERS
CARVERS
CEREBRA
CORDERO
CORKERS
CORNERS
CURLERS
CURSORS
CURSORY
DARNERS
DARTERS
DORMERS
EARHART
EARMARK
EARNERS
FARMERS
FARMERY
FERRARI
FERRARO
FERVORS
FIREARM
FORBORE
FORCERS
FOREARM
FORGERS
FORGERY
FORKERS
FORLORN
FORSURE
FORWARD
GARNERS
GARTERS
GIRDERS
HARBORS
HARBURG
HARPERS
HARVARD
HERBERT
HERDERS
HORRORS
HURLERS
LARDERS
MARKERS
MARMARA
MARTYRS
MERCERS
MERCERY
MERCURY
MERGERS
MIRRORS
MORTARS
MURDERS
MURMURS
NORBERT
NURSERS
NURSERY
NURTURE
PARLORS
PARSERS
PERFORM
PERJURE
PERJURY
PERTURB
PORKERS
PORTERS
PURPORT
PURRERS
PURSERS
SERVERS
SERVERY
SORCERY
SORTERS
SURFERS
SURGERY
TARTARE
TARTARS
TERNARY
TERRORS
THREERS
TURNERS
TURNERY
UPROARS
VERDURE
VERGERS
WARDERS
WARFARE
WARLORD
WORKERS
YARDARM

••R•••R

ABRADER
AERATOR
ARRIVER
BARKIER
BARMIER
BARRIER
BURGHER
BURGLAR
BURLIER
CAREFOR
CAROLER
CARRIER
CARTIER
CCRIDER
CORKIER
CORNIER
CORSAIR
CURATOR
CURDIER
CURLIER
CURRIER
CURVIER
DERNIER
DIRTIER
EARLIER
FARRIER
FARTHER
FERNBAR
FERNIER
FERVOUR
FIRRIER
FORAGER
FORBEAR
FOREVER
FORKIER
FORSTER
FURRIER
FURTHER
GARDNER
GERMIER
GORSIER
GYRATOR
HARBOUR
HARDIER
HARRIER
HARSHER
HERBIER
HORSIER
HURDLER
JERKIER
LARDIER
LARDNER
MARCHER
MARINER
MARKHOR
MERRIER
MIRADOR
MIRAMAR
MIRKIER
MURKIER
NERDIER
NERVIER
NORTHER
PARDNER
PARLOUR
PARRIER
PARTIER
PARTNER
PERKIER
PERRIER
PERUSER
PORKIER
PURSIER
PURSUER
SARKIER
SCRAPER
SERENER
SHRINER
SHRIVER
SORRIER
SPRAYER
SPRUCER
STREWER
STRIDER
STRIKER
STRIPER
STRIVER
SURFIER
SURLIER
TARDIER
TARRIER
TARSIER
TERRIER
THROWER
TIREDER
TURFIER
TURFWAR
UPRIVER
VERMEER
VERNIER
WARBLER
WARRIOR
WARTIER
WERNHER
WERTHER
WORDIER
WORKFOR
WORMIER
WORRIER

•••RR••

AVERRED
BLURRED
BOURREE
CHARRED
DHURRIE
GNARRED
INERROR
OVERRAN
OVERRUN
PIERROT
QUARREL
SCARRED
SHIRRED
SIERRAS
SKIRRED
SLURRED
SPARRED
SPARROW
SPORRAN
SPURRED
STARRED
STIRRED
STIRRER
STIRRUP
WHIRRED

•••R•R•

ADORERS
BEARERS
FEARERS
FERRARI
FERRARO
HEARERS
HORRORS
JEERERS
LEERERS
LIBRARY
MIRRORS
POURERS
PURRERS
REARERS
ROARERS
SCARERS
SCORERS
SHARERS
SNORERS
SOARERS
STARERS
STIRFRY
STORERS
TERRORS
TOURERS
USURERS
WEARERS
WHERERE

•••R••R

ADORNER
ALARMER
ALERTER
ANGRIER
AWARDER
BARRIER
BEERIER
BOARDER
BOERWAR
CARRIER
CHARGER
CHARIER
CHARMER
CHARTER
COARSER
COERCER
COURIER
COURSER
CURRIER
DEARSIR
DECRIER
FARRIER
FIERCER
FIERIER
FIRRIER
FOURIER
FURRIER
HAIRIER
HARRIER
HOARDER
HOARIER
HOARSER
INERROR
LEARIER
LEARNER
LEERIER
MERRIER
MOORIER
ONORDER
PARRIER
PERRIER
QUARTER
QUERIER
REORDER
SCARCER
SCARIER
SCARPER
SCORNER
SHARPER
SHIRKER
SHORTER
SMARTER
SNORTER
SORRIER
SPARSER
SPIRIER
SPURNER
STARKER
STARTER
STERNER
STIRRER
TARRIER
TEARIER
TERRIER
THURBER
TOORDER
TWIRLER
USURPER
WARRIOR
WEARIER
WEIRDER
WORRIER
YEARNER

••••RR•

ANDORRA
BEGORRA
BIZARRE
DUBARRY
EQUERRY
IMSORRY
LECARRE
NAVARRE
NOVARRO
PIZARRO
REMARRY
SCHIRRA
SCIORRA

••••R•R

ADMIRER
ALTERER
ARMORER
ASPIRER
CATERER
CLEARER
DEMURER
EAGERER
EMPEROR
FIGURER
HONORER
HOVERER
IGNORER
IMPURER
INERROR
INSURER
LABORER
MATURER
OFFERER
ORDERER
PAPERER
QUEERER
SCOURER
SECURER
SEVERER
SHEARER
SHEERER
SNEERER
SOBERER
SQUARER
STEERER
STIRRER
SWEARER
UTTERER
WAGERER
WATERER
WAVERER

R•S••••

RASCALS
RASHERS
RASHEST
RASPERS
RASPIER
RASPING
RASPISH
RASSLED
RASSLES
RASTERS
RESALES
RESALTS
RESANDS
RESAWED
RESCALE
RESCIND
RESCUED
RESCUER
RESCUES
RESEALS
RESEATS
RESECTS
RESEEDS
RESELLS
RESENDS
RESENTS
RESERVE
RESHIPS
RESHOES
RESHOOT
RESIDED
RESIDES
RESIDUE
RESIGNS
RESILED
RESILES
RESINGS
RESISTS
RESOLED
RESOLES
RESOLVE
RESORBS
RESORTS
RESOUND
RESPECT
RESPINS
RESPIRE
RESPITE
RESPOND
RESTAGE
RESTAIN
RESTAMP
RESTART
RESTATE
RESTERS
RESTFUL
RESTING
RESTIVE
RESTOCK
RESTORE
RESTSUP
RESTYLE
RESULTS
RESUMED
RESUMES
RESURGE
RISIBLE
RISIBLY
RISINGS
RISKERS
RISKIER
RISKILY
RISKING
RISOTTO
RISSOLE
ROSALIE
ROSANNA
ROSANNE
ROSARIO
ROSEATE
ROSEBAY
ROSEBUD
ROSELLE
ROSEOIL
ROSERED
ROSETTA
ROSETTE
ROSIEST
ROSSINI
ROSSSEA
ROSTAND
ROSTERS
ROSTRUM
ROSWELL
RUSHDIE
RUSHEES
RUSHERS
RUSHIER
RUSHING
RUSHOFF
RUSSELL
RUSSETS
RUSSETY
RUSSIAN
RUSTICS
RUSTIER
RUSTILY
RUSTING
RUSTLED
RUSTLER
RUSTLES

R••S•••

RAISERS
RAISEUP
RAISING
RAISINS
RALSTON
RANSACK
RANSOMS
RASSLED
RASSLES
RAWSILK
REASONS
REDSPOT
REDSTAR
REISSUE
RETSINA
RIMSHOT
RINSING
RIPSAWS
RIPSOFF
RIPSOUT
RISSOLE
ROASTED
ROASTER
ROISTER
ROOSTED
ROOSTER
ROSSINI
ROSSSEA
ROUSERS
ROUSING
ROUSTED
RUBSOFF
RUBSOUT
RUNSDRY
RUNSFOR
RUNSOFF
RUNSOUT
RUSSELL
RUSSETS
RUSSETY
RUSSIAN

R•••S••

RACKSUP
RAILSAT
RAKESIN
RAKESUP
RAMESES
READSIN
REARSUP
REBASTE
REBUSES
RECASTS
RECUSED
RECUSES
REELSIN
REFUSAL
REFUSED
REFUSER
REFUSES
REINSIN
REISSUE
RELISTS
REPASTE
REPASTS
REPOSED
REPOSES
RESISTS
RESTSUP
RETESTS
REVISED
REVISER
REVISES
REVISIT
RICKSHA
RILESUP
RINGSUP
RIPOSTE
ROBESON
ROBUSTA
ROLLSIN
ROLLSON
ROLLSUP
ROPESIN
ROSSSEA
RULESON

R••••S•

RACIEST
RAFFISH
RAMMISH
RANKEST
RANKISH
RASHEST
RASPISH
RATTISH
RAWNESS
REALISE
REALISM
REALIST
REAMASS
RECHOSE
RECLUSE
RECROSS
REDDEST
REDDISH
REDNESS
REDRESS
REDROSE
REFRESH
REGRESS
RELAPSE
RELEASE
REMORSE
REPRESS
REPRISE
REPULSE
REQUEST
RERAISE
RERINSE
REVERSE
RHENISH
RIBLESS
RICHEST
RIMIEST
RIMLESS
RODLESS
ROGUISH
ROMANSH
ROMPISH
ROPIEST
ROSIEST
RUBBISH
RUMLESS
RUNTISH
RUTTISH

R•••••S

RABBETS
RABBITS
RABBLES
RACEMES
RACKETS
RADDLES
RADIALS
RADIANS
RADICES
RADIXES
RADOMES
RAFFLES
RAFTERS
RAGBAGS
RAGLANS
RAGMOPS
RAGOUTS
RAGRUGS
RAGTOPS
RAIDERS
RAILERS
RAISERS
RAISINS
RAJPUTS
RALLIES
RAMADAS
RAMBLES
RAMESES
RAMJETS
RAMRODS
RANCHES
RANCHOS
RANGERS
RANKERS
RANKLES
RANSOMS
RANTERS
RAPIERS
RAPINES
RAPPELS
RAPPERS
RAPTORS
RAREGAS
RASCALS
RASHERS
RASPERS
RASSLES
RASTERS
RATINGS
RATIONS
RATITES
RATTANS
RATTERS
RATTLES
RAUCOUS
RAVAGES
RAVEUPS
RAVINES
RAVINGS
RAWEGGS
RAWNESS
RAYGUNS
REACHES
READERS
READIES
REAMASS
REAMERS
REAPERS
REARERS
REASONS
REBATES
REBENDS
REBINDS
REBOILS
REBOLTS
REBOOTS
REBOZOS
REBUFFS
REBUKES
REBUSES
RECALLS
RECANES
RECANTS
RECASTS
RECEDES
RECIPES
RECITES
RECKONS
RECOATS
RECODES
RECOILS
RECORDS
RECORKS
RECOUPS
RECROSS
RECTORS
RECUSES
REDACTS
REDANTS
REDATES
REDBUDS
REDCAPS
REDDENS
REDDOGS
REDEALS
REDEEMS
REDEYES
REDFINS
REDFIRS
REDGUMS
REDHATS
REDHOTS
REDIALS
REDNESS
REDOAKS
REDRAWS
REDRESS
REDTOPS
REDUCES
REEDITS
REEFERS
REFACES
REFILES
REFILLS
REFILMS
REFINES
REFIRES
REFLAGS
REFOCUS
REFORMS
REFRIES
REFUELS
REFUGES
REFUNDS
REFUSES
REFUTES
REGAINS
REGALES
REGARDS
REGENTS
REGIMES
REGIONS
REGLETS
REGLUES
REGRESS
REGRETS
REGULUS
REHANGS
REHEALS
REHEARS
REHEATS
REHEELS
REHIRES
REHOOKS
REIFIES
REJECTS
REJOINS
RELACES
RELATES
RELAXES
RELENTS
RELICTS
RELIEFS
RELINES
RELISTS
RELIVES
RELOADS
RELOCKS
RELUCTS
RELUMES
REMAILS
REMAINS
REMAKES
REMANDS
REMARKS
REMELTS
REMENDS
REMIGES
REMINDS
REMIXES
REMOLDS
REMORAS
REMOTES
REMOVES
REMUDAS
RENAILS
RENAMES
RENARDS
RENDERS
RENEGES
RENNINS
RENOTES
RENTALS
RENTERS
REOPENS
REPAIRS
REPASTS
REPAVES
REPEALS
REPEATS
REPENTS
REPINES
REPLANS
REPLAYS
REPLIES
REPLOWS
REPOLLS
REPORTS
REPOSES
REPRESS
REPUGNS
REPUTES
RERATES
REREADS
REREDOS
RERENTS
RESALES
RESALTS
RESANDS
RESCUES
RESEALS
RESEATS
RESECTS
RESEEDS
RESELLS
RESENDS
RESENTS
RESHIPS
RESHOES
RESIDES
RESIGNS
RESILES
RESINGS
RESISTS
RESOLES
RESORBS
RESORTS
RESPINS
RESTERS
RESULTS
RESUMES
RETAILS
RETAINS
RETAKES
RETAPES
RETARDS
RETAXES
RETEARS
RETELLS
RETESTS
RETILES
RETIMES
RETINAS
RETIRES
RETOOLS
RETORTS
RETOURS
RETRIES
RETRIMS
RETUNES
RETURNS
RETYPES
REUBENS
REUTERS
REVAMPS
REVEALS
REVERBS
REVERES
REVERTS
REVIEWS
REVILES
REVISES
REVIVES
REVOKES
REVOLTS
REWARDS
REWARMS
REWAXES
REWELDS
REWINDS
REWIRES
REWORDS
REWORKS
REWRAPS
REXCATS
REZONES
RHEBOKS
RHETORS
RHOMBUS
RHUMBAS
RHYMERS
RHYTHMS
RIBANDS
RIBBIES
RIBBONS
RIBEYES
RIBLESS
RICKEYS
RICKLES
RIDDLES
RIFFLES
RIFLERS
RIGGERS
RIGOURS
RILLETS
RIMLESS
RIMPLES
RINGERS
RIOTERS
RIOTOUS
RIPOFFS
RIPPERS
RIPPLES
RIPRAPS
RIPSAWS
RISINGS
RISKERS
RITUALS
ROACHES
ROADIES
ROAMERS
ROARERS
ROBARDS
ROBBERS
ROBBINS
ROBERTS
ROBROYS
ROCHETS
ROCKERS
ROCKETS
ROCKIES
RODENTS
RODGERS
RODLESS
ROLAIDS
ROLLERS
ROLLINS
ROMNEYS
ROMPERS
ROMULUS
RONDELS
ROOFERS
ROOKIES
ROOMERS
ROOMIES
ROOTERS
ROSTERS
ROTATES
ROTTERS
ROUBLES

ROUSERS
ROUTERS
ROWDIES
ROZZERS
RUBATOS
RUBBERS
RUBBLES
RUBRICS
RUDDERS
RUFFLES
RUINERS
RUINOUS
RULINGS
RUMBLES
RUMLESS
RUMOURS
RUMPLES
RUNDLES
RUNLETS
RUNNELS
RUNNERS
RUNOFFS
RUNOUTS
RUNWAYS
RUPIAHS
RUSHEES
RUSHERS
RUSSETS
RUSTICS
RUSTLES
RUTGERS

•RS••••

ARSENAL
ARSENIC
ARSENIO
DRSEUSS
DRSPOCK
ERSKINE
MRSPOCK

•R•S•••

ARCSINE
ARISING
ARISTAE
ARISTAS
ARISTOS
ARTSIER
ARTSONG
BRASHER
BRASHLY
BRASSES
BRASSIE
BRESLIN
BRISKER
BRISKET
BRISKLY
BRISTLE
BRISTLY
BRISTOL
BROSNAN
BRUSHED
BRUSHES
BRUSHUP
BRUSQUE
CRASHED
CRASHES
CRASSER
CRASSLY
CRASSUS
CRESSES
CRESTED
CRISPED
CRISPER
CRISPIN
CRISPLY
CRISPUS
CROSIER
CROSSED
CROSSER
CROSSES
CROSSLY
CROSSUP
CRUSADE
CRUSADO
CRUSHED
CRUSHER
CRUSHES
CRUSTED
CRYSTAL
DRASTIC
DRESDEN
DRESSED
DRESSER
DRESSES
DRESSUP
DRISTAN
DROSHKY
DRYSUIT
ERASERS
ERASING
ERASMUS
ERASURE
ERISTIC
EROSELY
EROSION
EROSIVE
FRASIER
FRESCOS
FRESHEN
FRESHER
FRESHET
FRESHLY
FRISBEE
FRISIAN
FRISKED
FRISSON
FROSTED
GRASPED
GRASSED
GRASSES
GRISHAM
GRISKIN
GRISSOM
GRISTLE
GRISTLY
GROSSED
GROSSER
GROSSES
GROSSLY
IRISOUT
IRKSOME
KRISHNA
ORESTES
ORISONS
PRESAGE
PRESALE
PRESELL
PRESENT
PRESETS
PRESIDE
PRESLEY
PRESOAK
PRESORT
PRESSED
PRESSER
PRESSES
PRESSON
PRESSUP
PRESTON
PRESTOS
PRESUME
PRISONS
PROSAIC
PROSERS
PROSHOP
PROSIER
PROSILY
PROSING
PROSODY
PROSPER
PRUSSIA
TRASHED
TRASHES
TRESSES
TRESTLE
TRISECT
TRISHAW
TRISTAN
TRISTAR
TRUSSED
TRUSSES
TRUSTED
TRUSTEE
TRYSTED
TRYSTER
WRESTED
WRESTLE

•R••S••

ARALSEA
ARIOSOS
ARIOSTO
AROUSAL
AROUSED
AROUSES
ARRASES
ARRESTS
ARRISES
ARTISAN
ARTISTE
ARTISTS
BRAISED
BRAISES
BRANSON
BRASSES
BRASSIE
BREASTS
BRONSON
BROWSED
BROWSER
BROWSES
BRUISED
BRUISER
BRUISES
CRASSER
CRASSLY
CRASSUS
CREASED
CREASES
CREOSOL
CRESSES
CRIMSON
CROESUS
CROPSUP
CROSSED
CROSSER
CROSSES
CROSSLY
CROSSUP
CRUISED
CRUISER
CRUISES
DRAGSIN
DRAGSON
DRAWSIN
DRAWSON
DRAWSUP
DREISER
DRESSED
DRESSER
DRESSES
DRESSUP
DRIESUP
DROPSBY
DROPSIN
DROWSED
DROWSES
DRUMSUP
ERICSON
ERNESTO
FRAISES
FREESIA
FRETSAW
FRISSON
FROWSTY
GRABSAT
GRASSED
GRASSES
GRAYSON
GREASED
GREASER
GREASES
GRISSOM
GROSSED
GROSSER
GROSSES
GROSSLY
GROUSED
GROUSER
GROUSES
GROWSON
GROWSUP
ORBISON
PRAISED
PRAISER
PRAISES
PRAYSTO
PRESSED
PRESSER
PRESSES
PRESSON
PRESSUP
PREYSON
PRIESTS
PROPSUP
PRUSSIA
TRANSIT
TRANSOM
TREASON
TRESSES
TRIESON
TRIESTE
TRIPSUP
TROTSKY
TROUSER
TRUISMS
TRUSSED
TRUSSES
VRONSKY
WRAPSUP

•R•••S•

ARIDEST
ARMLESS
ARMREST
ARTIEST
ARTLESS
BRALESS
BRAVEST
BRINISH
BRITISH
BRUTISH
CRAFTSY
CRONISH
CRUDEST
DRONISH
DRSEUSS
DRYNESS
GRAVEST
GRAYEST
GRAYISH
GREYEST
GREYISH
IRATEST
IRELESS
ORBLESS
PRECAST
PRECISE
PREMISE
PREMISS
PRETEST
PREWASH
PROCESS
PROFESS
PROFUSE
PROMISE
PROPOSE
PROTEST
PROTIST
PROVISO
PROVOST
PROWESS
PRUDISH
TRAIPSE
TRITEST
TROPISM
WRYNESS

•R••••S

ARAWAKS
ARBOURS
ARBUTUS
ARCADES
ARCHERS
ARCHONS
ARDOURS
ARDUOUS
AREOLAS
ARGIVES
ARGUERS
ARGYLES
ARIOSOS
ARISTAS
ARISTOS
ARMADAS
ARMFULS
ARMLESS
ARMLETS
ARMOURS
ARMPITS
ARMURES
ARNICAS
AROUSES
ARPENTS
ARRASES
ARREARS
ARRESTS
ARRISES
ARRIVES
ARROBAS
ARROYOS
ARTEMIS
ARTEMUS
ARTISTS
ARTLESS
BRACERS
BRAHMAS
BRAISES
BRALESS
BRASSES
BRAVOES
BRAYERS
BREASTS
BREATHS
BREEZES
BRETONS
BREVETS
BREWERS
BRIARDS
BRIDALS
BRIDGES
BRIDLES
BRITONS
BROGANS
BROGUES
BROKERS
BRONCOS
BRONZES
BROWSES
BRUISES
BRUNETS
BRUSHES
CRADLES
CRASHES
CRASSUS
CRATERS
CRAVATS
CRAVENS
CRAVERS
CRAYONS
CRAZIES
CREASES
CREATES
CRECHES
CREDITS
CRENELS
CREOLES
CRESSES
CRETANS
CRETINS
CREWELS
CRINGES
CRISPUS
CRITICS
CROESUS
CRONIES
CROSSES
CROWERS
CRUISES
CRUSHES
CRYPTOS
DRACHMS
DRAGONS
DRAPERS
DRAWERS
DREDGES
DRESSES
DREYFUS
DRIVELS
DRIVERS
DRONERS
DROPINS
DROVERS
DROWSES
DRSEUSS
DRUDGES
DRYNESS
DRYROTS
DRYRUNS
ERASERS
ERASMUS
ERGATES
ERMINES
ERRANDS
FRAISES
FRANCES
FRANCIS
FRAPPES
FREEZES
FRESCOS
FRIDAYS
FRIDGES
FRIENDS
FRIEZES
FRIGHTS
FRINGES
FRIZZES
FROLICS
FRYPANS
GRACIAS
GRADERS
GRAHAMS
GRAMMES
GRAMMYS
GRAMPAS
GRAMPUS
GRANGES
GRAPPAS
GRASSES
GRATERS
GRATIAS
GRAVELS
GRAVERS
GRAVIES
GRAZERS
GREASES
GREAVES
GRIEVES
GRIGRIS
GRILLES
GRIPERS
GRIVETS
GROCERS
GROOVES
GROPIUS
GROSSES
GROTTOS
GROUNDS
GROUSES
GROVELS
GROWERS
GROWTHS
GRUDGES
GRUNGES
IRELESS
IRONERS
IRONIES
IRONONS
IRRUPTS
KRATERS
MRBONES
MRCHIPS
MRDEEDS
ORACLES
ORANGES
ORATORS
ORBLESS
ORCHIDS
ORDAINS
ORDEALS
ORDINES
ORESTES
ORGATES
ORGEATS
ORIENTS
ORIGINS
ORIOLES
ORISONS
ORLEANS
ORMOLUS
ORPHANS
ORPHEUS
ORPINES
PRAISES
PRANCES
PRATERS
PRAYERS
PREAMPS
PREFABS
PREFERS
PRELIMS
PREMEDS
PREMISS
PRENUPS
PREPAYS
PRESETS
PRESSES
PRESTOS
PREXIES
PRICERS
PRIESTS
PRIMERS
PRINCES
PRISONS
PRIVETS
PRIVIES
PROBERS
PROCESS
PROFESS
PROFITS
PROLOGS
PROMPTS
PROPELS
PROSERS
PROTEUS
PROTONS
PROVERS
PROWESS
PROXIES
PRUNERS
TRACERS
TRADERS
TRAMPAS
TRANCES
TRASHES
TRAUMAS
TRAVELS
TRAVERS
TRAVOIS
TREBLES
TRELLIS
TREMORS
TREPANS
TRESSES
TRICEPS
TRICOTS
TRIFLES
TRIGONS
TRIJETS
TRIODES
TRIPLES
TRIPODS
TRITONS
TRIUNES
TRIVETS
TROCARS
TROCHES
TROGONS
TROIKAS
TROILUS
TROJANS
TROPICS
TROUGHS
TROUPES
TROWELS
TROWERS
TRUANTS
TRUDGES
TRUISMS
TRUSSES
TRYOUTS
URCHINS
URTEXTS
WRAITHS
WRAPUPS
WREATHS
WRIGHTS
WRITERS
WRITHES
WRYNESS

••RS•••

AIRSACS
AIRSHIP
AIRSHOW
AIRSOCK
AIRSOUT
BARSOAP
BARSTOW
BERSERK
BORSCHT
BURSARS
BURSARY
BURSTYN
CARSEAT
CORSAGE
CORSAIR
CORSETS
CORSICA
CURSING
CURSIVE
CURSORS
CURSORY
DORSALS
DORSETT
EARSHOT
FIRSTLY
FORSAKE
FORSALE
FORSOOK
FORSTER
FORSURE
FORSYTH
FURSEAL
GORSIER
HARSHEN
HARSHER
HARSHLY
HERSELF
HERSHEY
HIRSUTE
HORSIER
HORSING
JERSEYS
KIRSTIE
MARSALA
MARSHAL
MARSHES
MORSELS
NURSERS
NURSERY
NURSING
OURSELF
PARSECS
PARSEES
PARSERS
PARSING
PARSLEY
PARSNIP
PARSONS
PERSEID
PERSEUS
PERSIAN
PERSIST
PERSIUS
PERSONA
PERSONS
PORSCHE
PORSENA
PURSERS
PURSIER
PURSING
PURSUED
PURSUER
PURSUES
PURSUIT
TARSALS
TARSIER
TERSELY
TERSEST
TORSION
VARSITY
VERSIFY
VERSION
WARSHIP
WORSENS
WORSHIP
WORSTED

••R•S••

AEROSOL
AORISTS
ARRASES
ARRESTS
ARRISES
BARKSAT
BERGSON
BERNSEN
BURNSUP
CARLSON
CHRISMS
CHRISTI
CHRISTO
CHRISTY
CURLSUP
CURTSEY
DARESAY
DARESTO
EURASIA
FIRESUP
FIRMSUP
FORESAW
FORESEE
FORESTS
GIRASOL
HARDSET
HARPSON
HIRESON
HORNSBY
HORNSIN
JURISTS
KARASEA
LORISES
LYRISTS
MARKSUP
MORESBY
PARASOL
PERKSUP
PERUSAL
PERUSED
PERUSER
PERUSES
PHRASAL
PHRASED
PHRASES
PURISTS
STRASSE
SURTSEY
THRUSTS
TURNSIN
TURNSON
TURNSTO
TURNSUP
UPRISEN
UPRISES
VERISMO
VIRUSES
WARMSUP
WORKSIN
WORKSON
WORKSUP
ZEROSUM

••R••S•

ABREAST
AERIEST
AIRBASE
AIRIEST
AIRKISS
AIRLESS
AIRMASS
BARDISH
BARLESS
BERNESE
BURGESS
BURMESE
BURNISH
CARCASE
CARCASS
CARLESS
CAROUSE
CARWASH
CIRCUSY
CORNISH
CURRISH
CURTEST
CURTISS
DARKEST
DARKISH
DERVISH
EARLESS
EARNEST
EERIEST
FAREAST
FARWEST
FIRMEST
FORMOSA
FORREST
FURBISH
FURLESS
FURNISH
GARNISH
GIRLISH
GORIEST
HARDEST
HARNESS
HARPIST
HARVEST
HEROISM
HORNISH
HORNIST
JARLESS
KURDISH
LARGESS
LARGEST
LARGISH
LARKISH
MARXISM
MARXIST
MIRIEST
MORTISE
OARLESS
OGREISH
PARRISH
PERKISH
PERSIST
PERTEST
PORKISH
PURPOSE
RERAISE
RERINSE
SARCASM
SPRIEST
SPRYEST
STRASSE
STRAUSS
SURMISE
SURPASS
TARNISH
TARTEST
TARTISH
TERSEST
TORYISH
TORYISM
TURKISH
UPRAISE
VARNISH
VERBOSE
WARIEST
WARLESS
WARMEST
WARMISH
WIRIEST
WORMISH
YERKISH
YORKIST

••R•••S

ABRADES
AERATES
AERIALS
AEROBES
AFRAMES
AFREETS
AIRBAGS
AIRDAMS
AIRGUNS
AIRINGS
AIRKISS
AIRLESS
AIRMASS
AIRSACS
AIRWAYS
AORISTS
APROPOS
ARRASES
ARREARS
ARRESTS
ARRISES
ARRIVES
ARROBAS
ARROYOS
ATRIUMS
AUROCHS
AURORAS
BARBELS
BARBERS
BARCARS
BARENTS
BARHOPS
BARKERS
BARLESS
BARLEYS
BARNEYS
BARONGS
BARRELS
BARRENS
BARRIOS
BARROWS
BARTABS
BARTERS
BARYONS
BERATES
BERBERS
BERRIES
BIRCHES
BIRDERS
BIRDIES
BIREMES
BORATES
BORDERS
BORROWS
BORZOIS
BURBLES
BURBOTS
BURDENS
BUREAUS
BURGEES
BURGERS
BURGESS
BURGLES
BURGOOS
BURLAPS
BURMANS
BURNERS
BUROAKS
BURROWS
BURSARS
BYROADS
CARACAS
CARAFES
CARBONS
CARBOYS
CARCASS
CARDERS
CAREENS
CAREERS
CARFULS
CARGOES
CARHOPS
CARIBES
CARINAS
CARLESS
CARNETS
CARNIES
CAROLUS
CARPALS
CARPELS
CARPERS
CARPETS
CARRELS
CARRIES
CARROTS
CARTELS
CARTERS
CARTONS
CARVERS
CEREALS
CERIPHS
CERVIDS
CHRISMS
CHROMES
CIRCLES
CIRQUES
CORBELS
CORDONS
CORKERS
CORNEAS
CORNERS
CORNETS
CORONAS
CORRALS
CORSETS
CURATES
CURDLES
CURFEWS
CURIOUS
CURLERS
CURLEWS
CURRIES
CURSORS
CURTISS
CURVETS
DARBIES
DARKENS
DARNERS
DARTERS
DERAILS
DERBIES
DERIDES
DERIVES
DIRECTS
DIRNDLS
DIRTIES
DORITOS
DORMERS
DORSALS
EARFULS
EARLESS
EARNERS
EARWIGS
ENRAGES
ENROBES
ENROLLS
ENROOTS
ERRANDS
FARMERS
FARROWS
FERRETS
FERRIES
FERROUS
FERULES
FERVORS
FIRINGS
FIRKINS
FORAGES
FORBIDS
FORCEPS
FORCERS
FORESTS
FORGERS
FORGETS
FORGOES
FORINTS
FORKERS

FORMALS
FORMATS
FORTIES
FORTIUS
FURIOUS
FURLESS
FURORES
FURROWS
GARAGES
GARBLES
GARCONS
GARDENS
GARGLES
GARNERS
GARNETS
GARRETS
GARTERS
GERBILS
GERENTS
GERMANS
GERUNDS
GIRDERS
GIRDLES
GORGETS
GORGONS
GURGLES
GURKHAS
GURNEYS
GYRATES
GYRENES
HARBORS
HARDENS
HARKENS
HARNESS
HARPERS
HARPIES
HARRIES
HARROWS
HERALDS
HERBALS
HERDERS
HERMITS
HEROICS
HORNETS
HORRORS
HURDLES
HURLERS
HURLEYS
HURLIES
HURRAHS
HURRIES
HURTLES
HYRACES
HYRAXES
INROADS
IRRUPTS
JARFULS
JARGONS
JARLESS
JERBOAS
JERKINS
JERSEYS
JURISTS
KERNELS
KIRMANS
KIRTLES
KOREANS
KORUNAS
LARCHES
LARDERS
LARDONS
LARGESS
LARIATS
LARRUPS
LORISES
LORRIES
LURCHES
LYRISTS
MARACAS
MARAUDS
MARBLES
MARCELS
MARCHES
MARGAYS
MARGINS
MARINAS
MARINES
MARKERS
MARKETS
MARKUPS
MARLINS
MARMOTS
MAROONS
MARQUES
MARQUIS
MARRIES
MARROWS
MARSHES
MARTENS
MARTINS
MARTYRS
MARVELS
MERCERS
MERCIES
MERGERS
MERINOS
MERLOTS
MIRAGES
MIRRORS
MORALES
MORANIS
MORGANS
MORMONS
MORROWS
MORSELS
MORTALS
MORTARS
MURDERS
MURMURS
MYRIADS
MYRTLES
NARROWS
NARWALS
NEREIDS
NERVOUS
NORDICS
NORMALS
NORMANS
NURSERS
OARLESS
PARADES
PARAPHS
PARATUS
PARCELS
PARCHES
PARDONS
PARENTS
PARGETS
PARIAHS
PARINGS
PARLAYS
PARLEYS
PARLORS
PARLOUS
PAROLES
PARRIES
PARROTS
PARSECS
PARSEES
PARSERS
PARSONS
PARTIES
PARURES
PERCHES
PERHAPS
PERIODS
PERKINS
PERMITS
PERSEUS
PERSIUS
PERSONS
PERUKES
PERUSES
PHRASES
PIRAEUS
PIRATES
PORCHES
PORGIES
PORKERS
PORTALS
PORTERS
PORTHOS
PURDAHS
PURFLES
PURISTS
PURLINS
PURPLES
PURRERS
PURSERS
PURSUES
PURVEYS
PYRAMUS
PYRITES
PYRRHUS
RAREGAS
RERATES
REREADS
REREDOS
RERENTS
SARONGS
SCRAPES
SCRAWLS
SCREAKS
SCREAMS
SCREEDS
SCREENS
SCRIBES
SCRIMPS
SCRIPPS
SCRIPTS
SCROLLS
SCRUFFS
SERAPES
SERAPHS
SERAPIS
SERIALS
SERIOUS
SERMONS
SERVALS
SERVERS
SHRIEKS
SHRIFTS
SHRIKES
SHRILLS
SHRIMPS
SHRINES
SHRINKS
SHRIVES
SHROUDS
SORBETS
SORITES
SORRELS
SORROWS
SORTERS
SORTIES
SPRAINS
SPRAWLS
SPREADS
SPRINGS
SPRINTS
SPRITES
SPROUTS
SPRUCES
STRAFES
STRAINS
STRAITS
STRANDS
STRATUS
STRAUSS
STREAKS
STREAMS
STREETS
STRIDES
STRIKES
STRINGS
STRIPES
STRIVES
STROBES
STROKES
STROLLS
SURFERS
SURPASS
SURPLUS
SURREYS
SURVEYS
SYRIANS
TARGETS
TARIFFS
TARMACS
TARPITS
TARPONS
TARRIES
TARSALS
TARTANS
TARTARS
TERAPHS
TERCELS
TERCETS
TEREDOS
TERRETS
TERRIES
TERRORS
THRALLS
THREADS
THREATS
THREERS
THRIFTS
THRILLS
THRIVES
THROATS
THRONES
THRONGS
THRUSTS
TIRADES
TORCHES
TOREROS
TOROIDS
TORQUES
TORRENS
TURBANS
TURBITS
TURBOTS
TUREENS
TURKEYS
TURNERS
TURNIPS
TURRETS
TURTLES
TYRANTS
UNREELS
UNROBES
UNROLLS
UPRISES
UPROARS
UPROOTS
VARIOUS
VARLETS
VERBALS
VERGERS
VERITAS
VERVETS
VIRAGOS
VIRGINS
VIRIBUS
VIRTUES
VIRUSES
WARBLES
WARDENS
WARDERS
WARGODS
WARLESS
WARMUPS
WARRENS
WORKERS
WORKUPS
WORRIES
WORSENS
WURLEYS
YARROWS
YORKIES
ZAREBAS
ZIRCONS

•••RS••

BEARSON
BEARSUP
BOURSES
COARSEN
COARSER
COURSED
COURSER
COURSES
DEARSIR
EMERSED
EMERSON
FAIRSUP
GEARSTO
GEARSUP
HEARSAY
HEARSOF
HOARSEN
HOARSER
JEERSAT
LEERSAT
OVERSAW
OVERSEA
OVERSEE
PAIRSUP
PEARSON
PEERSAT
PEERSIN
POURSIN
REARSUP
SPARSER
SPURSON
STIRSIN
STIRSUP
TEARSAT
TEARSUP
THIRSTS
THIRSTY

•••R•S•

ACEROSE
ACTRESS
ADDRESS
AGGRESS
AMBROSE
ANDRESS
APPRISE
ARMREST
BEARISH
BEDREST
BOARISH
BOORISH
BULRUSH
BUMRUSH
CHERISH
CLERISY
CUIRASS
CURRISH
CYPRESS
CZARISM
CZARIST
DEAREST
DEFROST
DEPRESS
DIGRESS
DOUREST
EMPRESS
ENCRUST
ENGROSS
ENTRUST
EVEREST
EXPRESS
FAIREST
FAIRISH
FLORIST
FORREST
HEIRESS
IMPRESS
INARUSH
INGRESS
INTRUST
IPCRESS
LOWRISE
MELROSE
MIDRISE
MOORISH
NEAREST
NOURISH
OLDROSE
OLOROSO
OPEROSE
OPPRESS
OVERUSE
PARRISH
PEERESS
POOREST
POORISH
QUERIST
RECROSS
REDRESS
REDROSE
REFRESH
REGRESS
REPRESS
REPRISE
SEERESS
SOUREST
SOURISH
SPAREST
SUBROSA
SUCRASE
SUCROSE
SUNRISE
TEAROSE
THERESA
TIGRESS
TIGRISH
TOURISM
TOURIST
TSARIST
UNDRESS

•••R••S

ACARIDS
ACCRUES
ACTRESS
ADDRESS
ADORERS
AFFRAYS
AGARICS
AGGRESS
AIGRETS
ALARUMS
AMBRIES
AMERCES
AMOROUS
ANDREAS
ANDRESS
ANDREWS
ANORAKS
APERCUS
APERIES
ASHRAMS
ATTRITS
BARRELS
BARRENS
BARRIOS
BARROWS
BEARERS
BERRIES
BETRAYS
BORROWS
BOURSES
BUMRAPS
BURROWS
CARRELS
CARRIES
CARROTS
CHARGES
CHARLES
CHERUBS
CHORALS
CITRONS
CITROUS
CLARETS
CLERICS
CLORETS
COERCES
CORRALS
COURSES
COWRIES
CUIRASS
CURRIES
CYPRESS
CZARDAS
DAIRIES
DEARIES
DEARTHS
DECREES
DECRIES
DEFRAYS
DEGREES
DEPRESS
DEVRIES
DIARIES
DIGRAMS
DIGRESS
DOWRIES
DRYROTS
DRYRUNS
DWARVES
EMBRYOS
EMERGES
EMPRESS
ENDRUNS
ENGRAMS
ENGROSS
ENTRAPS
ENTREES
ENTRIES
ENWRAPS
EPARCHS
ESCROWS
ESTRAYS
EXARCHS
EXPRESS
FABRICS
FAERIES
FAIRIES
FARROWS
FEARERS
FERRETS
FERRIES
FERROUS
FIBRILS
FIBRINS
FIBROUS
FLORETS
FLORINS
FLYRODS
FOURTHS
FURROWS
GARRETS
GEORGES
GLORIAS
GLORIES
GOURDES
HAIRDOS
HARRIES
HARROWS
HEARERS
HEARTHS
HEBREWS
HEIRESS
HORRORS
HOTRODS
HURRAHS
HURRIES
HYBRIDS
HYDROUS
IMARETS
IMBRUES
IMPRESS
INGRESS
IPCRESS
IVORIES
JEERERS
JOURNOS
LABRETS
LAERTES
LARRUPS
LAURELS
LEERERS
LIERNES
LORRIES
LOURDES
MACRONS
MARRIES
MARROWS
MATRONS
MAUROIS
MEGRIMS
METRICS
MICRONS
MIDRIBS
MIRRORS
MORROWS
NARROWS
NEURONS
NIMRODS
NITROUS
NUTRIAS
OCTROIS
ODOROUS
OILRIGS
ONEROUS
OPPRESS
OSPREYS
OUTRUNS
PARRIES
PARROTS
PATROLS
PATRONS
PEERESS
PETRELS
PETROLS
PETROUS
PIERCES
PLURALS
POURERS
PUGREES
PURRERS
PYRRHUS
QUARTOS
QUERIES
QUORUMS
RAGRUGS
RAMRODS
REARERS
RECROSS
REDRAWS
REDRESS
REFRIES
REGRESS
REGRETS
REPRESS
RETRIES
RETRIMS
REWRAPS
RIPRAPS
ROARERS
ROBROYS
RUBRICS
SATRAPS
SCARABS
SCARERS
SCARVES
SCORERS
SCURVES
SECRETS
SEERESS
SHARERS
SHERPAS
SIERRAS
SKIRUNS
SNORERS
SOARERS
SOIREES
SORRELS
SORROWS
SOURCES
SPARGES
SPIRALS
SPIREAS
SPIRITS
STARERS
STARETS
STARVES
STEREOS
STEROLS
STORERS
STOREYS
STORIES
STURGES
SUNRAYS
SURREYS
SWERVES
TARRIES
TEARGAS
TENRECS
TERRETS
TERRIES
TERRORS
TETRADS
THERMOS
THIRSTS
TIERODS
TIGRESS
TORRENS
TOURERS
TUAREGS
TUGRIKS
TURRETS
UNDRESS
UNTRAPS
UNWRAPS
USERIDS
USURERS
USURIES
VEERIES
WARRENS
WEARERS
WEARIES
WEIRDOS
WHARVES
WHEREAS
WORRIES
YARROWS

••••RS•

ACCURST
ADVERSE
AMHERST
ASPERSE
ATHIRST
ATWORST
DIVERSE
ENDORSE
IMMERSE
INDORSE
INTERSE
INVERSE
OBVERSE
REMORSE
REVERSE
UNHORSE

••••R•S

ABJURES
ABSORBS
ACCORDS
ADHERES
ADJURES
ADMIRES
ADSORBS
ADVERBS
ADVERTS
AFFIRMS
AFFORDS
ALLURES
AMPERES
ANGORAS
ANTARES
ARMURES
ASFARAS
ASPIRES
ASSERTS
ASSORTS
ASSURES
ATTIRES
AUBURNS
AURORAS
BEMIRES
BISTROS
BOLEROS
BOUTROS
BRIARDS
BYTURNS
BYWORDS
CAMERAS
CANARDS
CASERNS
CAVERNS
CAVORTS
CENTRES
CETERIS
CHEVRES
COHERES
COHORTS
COMOROS
CONTRAS
CONURES
COWARDS
CYBORGS
DEBARKS
DEFORMS
DEHORNS
DEPARTS
DEPORTS
DESERTS
DESIRES
DISARMS
DIVERTS
DOLORES
DOTARDS
EDWARDS
EFFORTS
EMBARKS
EMIGRES
EMPIRES
ENCORES
ENDURES
ENDUROS
ENGIRDS
ENSURES
ESCARPS
ESCORTS
EUCHRES
EXHORTS
EXPERTS
EXPIRES
EXPORTS
EXSERTS
EXTERNS
EXTORTS
EXWORKS
FABARES
FEDORAS
FIACRES
FIGURES
FURORES
FUTURES
GABBROS
GENERIS
GOCARTS
GOKARTS
GOVERNS
GRIGRIS
HAZARDS
HEGIRAS
HOMBRES
HONORIS
HOWARDS
HUMERUS
IDCARDS
IGNORES
IMMURES
IMPARTS
IMPORTS
INFORMS
INHERES
INJURES
INNARDS
INSERTS
INSURES
INTERNS
INVERTS
INWARDS
IZZARDS
JABIRUS
LAZARUS
LETTRES
LIZARDS
LOUVRES
LUSTRES
MAHARIS
MANTRAS
MATURES
MILORDS
MITHRAS
MODERNS
NATURES
OBVERTS
OEUVRES
OFSORTS
OLDPROS
ONWARDS
OXCARTS
OXFORDS
PAPYRUS
PARURES
PETARDS
PICAROS
POLARIS
QATARIS
RECORDS
RECORKS
REFIRES
REFORMS
REGARDS
REHIRES
REMARKS
REMORAS
RENARDS
REPORTS
RESORBS
RESORTS
RETARDS
RETIRES
RETORTS
RETURNS
REVERBS
REVERES
REVERTS
REWARDS
REWARMS
REWIRES
REWORDS
REWORKS
ROBARDS
ROBERTS
SAFARIS
SAMPRAS
SATIRES
SCLERAS
SECURES
SENORAS
SENORES
SIERRAS
SPHERES
SQUARES
SQUIRES
SQUIRMS
SQUIRTS
SUBORNS
SUBURBS
SUTURES
TABARDS
TAVERNS
TENURES
THWARTS
TIMBRES
TOREROS
TOWARDS
TOYSRUS
TSHIRTS
TSOURIS
TUNDRAS
UMPIRES
UNCORKS
UNCURLS
UNFURLS
UNGIRDS
UPTURNS
UPWARDS
WIZARDS
WYVERNS
YOGURTS

•••••RS

ABUSERS
ADORERS
AETHERS
AFFAIRS
ALGIERS
ALLEARS
AMBLERS
ANCHORS
ANGLERS
ANSWERS
ANTHERS
ANTLERS
APPEARS
ARBOURS
ARCHERS
ARDOURS
ARGUERS
ARMOURS
ARREARS
ASHLARS
AUPAIRS
AUTEURS
AUTHORS
AVATARS
AVOWERS
BACKERS
BADGERS
BAGGERS
BAILERS
BAILORS
BANKERS
BANNERS
BANTERS
BARBERS
BARCARS
BARKERS
BARTERS
BASTERS
BATHERS
BATTERS
BAWLERS
BAZAARS
BEAKERS
BEARERS
BEATERS
BEAVERS
BEEPERS
BEGGARS
BENDERS
BERBERS
BESTIRS
BETTERS
BETTORS
BEZIERS
BICKERS
BIDDERS
BIGGERS
BINDERS
BIRDERS
BITTERS
BLADERS
BLAZERS
BLOWERS
BOATERS
BOBBERS
BOILERS
BOMBERS
BONKERS
BOOMERS
BOPPERS
BORDERS
BOTHERS
BOVVERS
BOWLERS
BOWYERS
BOXCARS
BRACERS
BRAYERS
BREWERS
BROKERS
BUFFERS
BUGLERS
BULGARS
BUMMERS
BUMPERS
BUNKERS
BURGERS
BURNERS
BURSARS
BUSTERS
BUTLERS
BUTTERS
BUZZERS
CABLERS
CADGERS
CAESARS
CAHIERS
CALLERS
CAMBERS
CAMPERS
CANKERS
CANNERS
CANTERS

CANTORS
CAPPERS
CAPTORS
CARDERS
CAREERS
CARPERS
CARTERS
CARVERS
CASTERS
CAVIARS
CELLARS
CENSERS
CENSORS
CENTERS
CHASERS
CHEWERS
CHIDERS
CHOKERS
CINDERS
CIPHERS
CLAMORS
CLAWERS
CLOVERS
COALERS
COAXERS
COCKERS
CODGERS
COFFERS
COHEIRS
COINERS
COLLARS
COLOURS
COMBERS
CONCURS
CONDORS
CONFERS
CONGERS
CONKERS
CONNORS
COOKERS
COOLERS
COOPERS
COPIERS
COPPERS
COPTERS
CORKERS
CORNERS
COSTARS
COTTERS
COUGARS
CRATERS
CRAVERS
CROWERS
CULLERS
CULVERS
CURLERS
CURSORS
CUTLERS
CUTTERS
CYCLERS
CYPHERS
DAGGERS
DAMMARS
DAMPERS
DANCERS
DANDERS
DANGERS
DARNERS
DARTERS
DASHERS
DAUBERS
DEALERS
DEBEERS
DEBTORS

DEICERS
DELVERS
DENIERS
DEODARS
DETOURS
DEVOURS
DIALERS
DIAPERS
DICKERS
DIETERS
DIFFERS
DIGGERS
DIMMERS
DINNERS
DIPPERS
DISBARS
DITHERS
DOCKERS
DOCTORS
DODDERS
DODGERS
DOGEARS
DOLLARS
DOLOURS
DORMERS
DOSSERS
DOWNERS
DOWSERS
DRAPERS
DRAWERS
DRIVERS
DRONERS
DROVERS
DUBBERS
DUELERS
DUFFERS
DUNKERS
DUSTERS
EARNERS
EASTERS
ECLAIRS
EDITORS
ELATERS
ELIXIRS
ELOPERS
EMOTERS
ENAMORS
ENDEARS
ENVIERS
ERASERS
ETCHERS
EVADERS
EVOKERS
FABLERS
FACTORS
FALTERS
FARMERS
FATHERS
FAVOURS
FAWNERS
FEARERS
FEEDERS
FEELERS
FELLERS
FENCERS
FENDERS
FERVORS
FESTERS
FETTERS
FIBBERS
FILLERS
FILTERS
FINDERS
FINGERS

FISHERS
FITTERS
FLAKERS
FLAVORS
FLEXORS
FLOWERS
FODDERS
FOGGERS
FOLDERS
FOLGERS
FOOTERS
FORCERS
FORGERS
FORKERS
FOSTERS
FOWLERS
FUELERS
GABBERS
GADDERS
GAFFERS
GAINERS
GAITERS
GAMMERS
GANDERS
GANGERS
GAOLERS
GARNERS
GARTERS
GASPERS
GASSERS
GATHERS
GAUGERS
GAWKERS
GEEZERS
GENDERS
GEYSERS
GIBBERS
GILDERS
GINGERS
GIRDERS
GLAZERS
GLIDERS
GLOWERS
GNAWERS
GOLFERS
GOMPERS
GOOBERS
GOPHERS
GOUGERS
GRADERS
GRATERS
GRAVERS
GRAZERS
GRIPERS
GROCERS
GROWERS
GUITARS
GUNNERS
GUSHERS
GUTTERS
GYPPERS
HACKERS
HALTERS
HAMMERS
HAMPERS
HANGARS
HANGERS
HANKERS
HARBORS
HARPERS
HATTERS
HAULERS
HAWKERS
HAWSERS

HEADERS
HEALERS
HEARERS
HEATERS
HEAVERS
HECTORS
HEDGERS
HEELERS
HEIFERS
HELLERS
HELPERS
HEMMERS
HERDERS
HINDERS
HISSERS
HITTERS
HOAXERS
HOLDERS
HOLLERS
HONKERS
HONOURS
HOOFERS
HOOTERS
HOOVERS
HOPPERS
HORRORS
HOSIERS
HOTCARS
HOTWARS
HOWLERS
HUGGERS
HULLERS
HUMMERS
HUMOURS
HUNGERS
HUNKERS
HUNTERS
HURLERS
HUSKERS
HUSSARS
IMAGERS
IMPAIRS
INDOORS
INSTARS
INTEARS
IRONERS
ISOBARS
ISOMERS
ISSUERS
JABBERS
JAEGERS
JAGUARS
JAILERS
JAMMERS
JASPERS
JEERERS
JEFFERS
JESTERS
JIGGERS
JITTERS
JOBBERS
JOGGERS
JOINERS
JOSSERS
JUDDERS
JUICERS
JUMPERS
JUNIORS
JUNKERS
KAFFIRS
KAISERS
KEENERS
KEEPERS
KEGLERS

KICKERS
KIDDERS
KILLERS
KIPPERS
KISSERS
KOSHERS
KRATERS
LAAGERS
LABOURS
LADDERS
LADLERS
LAGGERS
LANCERS
LANDERS
LANGURS
LARDERS
LASHERS
LATHERS
LAWYERS
LEADERS
LEAKERS
LEANERS
LEAPERS
LEASERS
LECTORS
LEDGERS
LEERERS
LEKVARS
LENDERS
LESSORS
LETTERS
LEVIERS
LIBBERS
LICTORS
LIFTERS
LIMBERS
LIMNERS
LINGERS
LINKERS
LIQUORS
LITTERS
LOADERS
LOAFERS
LOANERS
LOBBERS
LOCKERS
LODGERS
LOGGERS
LOITERS
LOOKERS
LOOPERS
LOOTERS
LOPPERS
LOUVERS
LUBBERS
LUGGERS
LUMBARS
LUMBERS
LUMPERS
LUNKERS
LUSTERS
MADDERS
MAGYARS
MAILERS
MANGERS
MANNERS
MAPPERS
MARKERS
MARTYRS
MASHERS
MASKERS
MASTERS
MATHERS
MATTERS

MEMBERS
MEMOIRS
MENDERS
MENHIRS
MENTORS
MERCERS
MERGERS
METEORS
METIERS
MEWLERS
MILKERS
MILLERS
MINCERS
MINDERS
MINTERS
MIRRORS
MISTERS
MOANERS
MOCKERS
MOHAIRS
MOILERS
MOLDERS
MOLTERS
MONGERS
MOPPERS
MORTARS
MOSHERS
MOTHERS
MOUSERS
MUDDERS
MUGGERS
MULLERS
MUMMERS
MURDERS
MURMURS
MUSHERS
MUSTERS
MUTTERS
NABBERS
NAILERS
NAPPERS
NATTERS
NECKERS
NECTARS
NESTERS
NICKERS
NIPPERS
NODDERS
NOSHERS
NUDGERS
NUMBERS
NURSERS
NUTTERS
ONAGERS
OPENERS
OPINERS
ORATORS
OSTLERS
OUSTERS
OYSTERS
PACKERS
PADDERS
PALLORS
PALTERS
PAMPERS
PANDERS
PANNERS
PANZERS
PARLORS
PARSERS
PASSERS
PASTORS
PATTERS
PAUPERS

PAWNERS
PEDLARS
PEEKERS
PEELERS
PEEPERS
PELTERS
PENNERS
PEPPERS
PESTERS
PETTERS
PHASERS
PICKERS
PIECERS
PILFERS
PILLARS
PINCERS
PINNERS
PITIERS
PITTERS
PLACERS
PLANERS
PLATERS
PLAYERS
PLEXORS
PLOVERS
PLOWERS
POLDERS
POLLERS
PONDERS
POPLARS
POPPERS
PORKERS
PORTERS
POSEURS
POSTERS
POTHERS
POTTERS
POURERS
POUTERS
POWDERS
PRATERS
PRAYERS
PREFERS
PRICERS
PRIMERS
PROBERS
PROSERS
PROVERS
PRUNERS
PUCKERS
PUFFERS
PULSARS
PUMPERS
PUNKERS
PUNTERS
PURRERS
PURSERS
PUTTERS
QINTARS
QUAKERS
QUASARS
QUAVERS
QUEUERS
QUIVERS
QUOTERS
RAFTERS
RAIDERS
RAILERS
RAISERS
RANGERS
RANKERS
RANTERS
RAPIERS
RAPPERS

RAPTORS
RASHERS
RASPERS
RASTERS
RATTERS
READERS
REAMERS
REAPERS
REARERS
RECTORS
REDFIRS
REEFERS
REHEARS
RENDERS
RENTERS
REPAIRS
RESTERS
RETEARS
RETOURS
REUTERS
RHETORS
RHYMERS
RIFLERS
RIGGERS
RIGOURS
RINGERS
RIOTERS
RIPPERS
RISKERS
ROAMERS
ROARERS
ROBBERS
ROCKERS
RODGERS
ROLLERS
ROMPERS
ROOFERS
ROOMERS
ROOTERS
ROSTERS
ROTTERS
ROUSERS
ROUTERS
ROZZERS
RUBBERS
RUDDERS
RUINERS
RUMOURS
RUNNERS
RUSHERS
RUTGERS
SACKERS
SAILORS
SALTERS
SALVERS
SALVORS
SAMBARS
SANDERS
SANTIRS
SAPPERS
SASSERS
SAUCERS
SAVIORS
SAVOURS
SAWYERS
SCALARS
SCALERS
SCARERS
SCORERS
SCOTERS
SEALERS
SEATERS
SECTORS
SEEDERS

SEEKERS
SEINERS
SEIZERS
SELLERS
SENDERS
SENIORS
SENSORS
SERVERS
SETTERS
SHAKERS
SHAPERS
SHARERS
SHAVERS
SHINERS
SHIVERS
SHOFARS
SHOVERS
SHOWERS
SIFTERS
SIGHERS
SIGNERS
SILVERS
SIMMERS
SIMPERS
SINGERS
SINKERS
SINNERS
SIPPERS
SISTERS
SITTERS
SKATERS
SKEWERS
SKIVERS
SLAVERS
SLAYERS
SLICERS
SLIDERS
SLIVERS
SMILERS
SMOKERS
SNIPERS
SNORERS
SOAKERS
SOAPERS
SOARERS
SOBBERS
SOLDERS
SOLVERS
SOONERS
SORTERS
SPACERS
SPADERS
SPIDERS
SPIKERS
STAGERS
STARERS
STATORS
STEWERS
STOKERS
STONERS
STORERS
STUMERS
STUPORS
STYLERS
SUCCORS
SUCKERS
SUFFERS
SUITORS
SULKERS
SUMMERS
SUNDERS
SUPPERS
SURFERS
SUTLERS

SUTTERS
SWAYERS
SWIPERS
TACKERS
TAILORS
TALKERS
TAMPERS
TANKERS
TANNERS
TAPPERS
TARTARS
TASTERS
TATTERS
TEASERS
TEDDERS
TEENERS
TEETERS
TELLERS
TEMPERS
TENDERS
TENNERS
TENSORS
TENTERS
TERRORS
TESTERS
TETHERS
THALERS
THECARS
THENARS
THREERS
TICKERS
TILLERS
TILTERS
TIMBERS
TINDERS
TINEARS
TINKERS
TINNERS
TINTERS
TIPPERS
TITFERS
TITHERS
TITTERS
TOILERS
TOOTERS
TOPPERS
TOSSERS
TOTTERS
TOURERS
TOUTERS
TOWCARS
TOWNERS
TRACERS
TRADERS
TRAVERS
TREMORS
TROCARS
TROWERS
TUCKERS
TUGGERS
TURNERS
TUSKERS
TWOFERS
ULSTERS
UNITERS
UPROARS
USURERS
VALOURS
VAMPERS
VAPOURS
VECTORS
VELOURS
VENDORS
VENEERS

VENTERS
VERGERS
VESPERS
VETOERS
VICTORS
VIEWERS
VIGOURS
VIZIERS
WAILERS
WAITERS
WAIVERS
WALKERS
WALTERS
WANDERS
WARDERS
WASHERS
WASTERS
WEARERS
WEAVERS
WEEDERS
WEEPERS
WELDERS
WELTERS
WENDERS
WETBARS
WETHERS
WHALERS
WHINERS
WICKERS
WIENERS
WINCERS
WINDERS
WINGERS
WINKERS
WINNERS
WINTERS
WISHERS
WITHERS
WONDERS
WOOFERS
WORKERS
WOWSERS
WRITERS
YABBERS
YAKKERS
YAMMERS
YAPPERS
YAWNERS
YAWPERS
YELLERS
YELPERS
YONKERS
YOWLERS
ZAFFERS
ZANDERS
ZAPPERS
ZEDBARS
ZEPHYRS
ZINGERS
ZIPPERS
ZITHERS
ZONKERS

R•T••••

RATABLE
RATAFIA
RATATAT
RATBERT
RATCHET
RATFINK
RATHOLE
RATINGS
RATIONS
RATITES
RATLIKE
RATLINE
RATPACK
RATRACE
RATTAIL
RATTANS
RATTERS
RATTIER
RATTING
RATTISH
RATTLED
RATTLER
RATTLES
RATTRAP
RETAILS
RETAINS
RETAKEN
RETAKES
RETAPED
RETAPES
RETARDS
RETAXED
RETAXES
RETEACH
RETEARS
RETELLS
RETESTS
RETHINK
RETIARY
RETICLE
RETILED
RETILES
RETIMED
RETIMES
RETINAE
RETINAL
RETINAS
RETINUE
RETIRED
RETIREE
RETIRES
RETITLE
RETOOLS
RETORTS
RETOUCH
RETOURS
RETOWED
RETRACE
RETRACK
RETRACT
RETRADE
RETRAIN
RETREAD
RETREAT
RETRIAL
RETRIED
RETRIES
RETRIMS
RETSINA
RETUNED
RETUNES
RETURNS
RETYPED
RETYPES
RITUALS
RITZIER
RITZILY
ROTATED
ROTATES
ROTATOR
ROTIFER
ROTTERS
ROTTING
ROTUNDA
RUTGERS
RUTHFUL
RUTTIER
RUTTISH

R••T•••

RAFTERS
RAFTING
RAGTIME
RAGTOPS
RANTERS
RANTING
RAPTORS
RAPTURE
RASTERS
RATTAIL
RATTANS
RATTERS
RATTIER
RATTING
RATTISH
RATTLED
RATTLER
RATTLES
RATTRAP
RECTIFY
RECTORS
RECTORY
REDTAPE
REDTOPS
REITMAN
RENTALS
RENTERS
RENTING
REPTILE
RESTAGE
RESTAIN
RESTAMP
RESTART
RESTATE
RESTERS
RESTFUL
RESTING
RESTIVE
RESTOCK
RESTORE
RESTSUP
RESTYLE
REUTERS
REUTHER
RHETORS
RHYTHMS
RIFTING
RIOTACT
RIOTERS
RIOTING
RIOTOUS
RIPTIDE
RIPTORN
RONTGEN
ROOTERS
ROOTFOR
ROOTIER
ROOTING
ROOTLET
ROOTOUT
ROSTAND
ROSTERS
ROSTRUM
ROTTERS
ROTTING
ROUTERS
ROUTINE
ROUTING
RUCTION
RUNTIER
RUNTISH
RUPTURE
RUSTICS
RUSTIER
RUSTILY
RUSTING
RUSTLED
RUSTLER
RUSTLES
RUTTIER
RUTTISH

R•••T••

RALSTON
RARITAN
RATATAT
RATITES
REACTED
REACTOR
REACTTO
REALTOR
REBATED
REBATES
RECITAL
RECITED
RECITER
RECITES
REDATED
REDATES
REDSTAR
REENTER
REENTRY
REFUTED
REFUTER
REFUTES
REGATTA
RELATED
RELATES
REMOTER
REMOTES
RENOTED
RENOTES
REPUTED
REPUTES
RERATED
RERATES
RETITLE
RIANTLY
RICHTER
RICOTTA
RIDOTTO
RIGHTED
RIGHTER
RIGHTLY
RIGHTON
RISOTTO
RIVETED
RIVETER
ROASTED
ROASTER
ROBOTIC
ROISTER
ROLLTOP
ROOFTOP
ROOSTED
ROOSTER
ROPETOW
ROSETTA
ROSETTE
ROTATED
ROTATES
ROTATOR

ROUSTED
RUBATOS
RUBITIN

R••••T•

RABBETS
RABBITS
RABBITT
RACKETS
RADIATE
RAGOUTS
RAJPUTS
RALLYTO
RAMINTO
RAMJETS
RANINTO
RANLATE
RAWDATA
REACTTO
REALITY
REBASTE
REBIRTH
REBOLTS
REBOOTS
RECANTS
RECASTS
RECOATS
REDACTS
REDANTS
REDHATS
REDHOTS
REEDITS
REFERTO
REGATTA
REGENTS
REGLETS
REGRETS
REHEATS
REJECTS
RELENTS
RELICTS
RELISTS
RELUCTS
REMELTS
REPASTE
REPASTS
REPEATS
REPENTS
REPLATE
REPLETE
REPORTS
REQUITE
RERENTS
REROUTE
RESALTS
RESEATS
RESECTS
RESENTS
RESISTS
RESORTS
RESPITE
RESTATE
RESULTS
RETESTS
RETORTS
REUNITE
REVERTS
REVOLTS
REWRITE
REWROTE
REXCATS
RICKETY
RICOTTA
RIDOTTO
RILLETS
RIORITA
RIPINTO
RIPOSTE
RISOTTO
ROBERTA
ROBERTO
ROBERTS
ROBUSTA
ROCHETS
ROCKETS
RODENTS
ROSEATE
ROSETTA
ROSETTE
ROYALTY
RUNINTO
RUNLATE
RUNLETS
RUNOUTS
RUNWITH
RUSSETS
RUSSETY

R•••••T

RABBITT
RACIEST
RACQUET
RADIANT
RAILSAT
RAIMENT
RAINHAT
RAINOUT
RAMPANT
RAMPART
RANGOUT
RANKEST
RANRIOT
RAPPORT
RAREBIT
RASHEST
RATATAT
RATBERT
RATCHET
READMIT
READOUT
REAGENT
REALIST
REBUILT
RECEIPT
RECOUNT
RECRUIT
REDCENT
REDCOAT
REDDEST
REDEALT
REDHEAT
REDMEAT
REDOUBT
REDSPOT
REELECT
REENACT
REFLECT
REFRACT
REGNANT
RELIANT
RELIGHT
REMNANT
REMOUNT
RENAULT
REPAINT
REPLANT
REPRINT
REQUEST
RESHOOT
RESPECT
RESTART
RETRACT
RETREAT
REVISIT
RICERAT
RICHEST
RIDEOUT
RIMIEST
RIMSHOT
RINGLET
RINGOUT
RIOTACT
RIPSOUT
RIVULET
RODEOUT
ROLLOUT
ROOTLET
ROOTOUT
ROPIEST
ROSIEST
ROUGHIT
ROWBOAT
RUBSOUT
RULEOUT
RUNGOUT
RUNRIOT
RUNSOUT

•RT••••

ARTDECO
ARTEMIS
ARTEMUS
ARTFILM
ARTFORM
ARTICLE
ARTIEST
ARTISAN
ARTISTE
ARTISTS
ARTLESS
ARTSIER
ARTSONG
ARTWARE
ARTWORK
ORTOLAN
URTEXTS

•R•T•••

ARETINO
BRETONS
BRITAIN
BRITISH
BRITONS
BRITTEN
BRITTLE
BRITTON
BROTHER
BRUTELY
BRUTISH
CRATERS
CRATING
CRETANS
CRETINS
CRITICS
CRITTER
DRATTED
ERITREA
EROTICA
FRETFUL
FRETSAW
FRETTED
FRITTED
FRITTER
FROTHED
GRATERS
GRATIAS
GRATIFY
GRATING
GRETZKY
GRITTED
GROTTOS
IRATELY
IRATEST
KRATERS
KRATION
ORATING
ORATION
ORATORS
ORATORY
OROTUND
PRATERS
PRATING
PRATTLE
PRETAPE
PRETEEN
PRETEND
PRETEST
PRETEXT
PRETZEL
PRITHEE
PROTEAN
PROTECT
PROTEGE
PROTEIN
PROTEST
PROTEUS
PROTIST
PROTONS
TRITELY
TRITEST
TRITIUM
TRITONE
TRITONS
TROTHED
TROTOUT
TROTSKY
TROTTED
TROTTER
WRITEIN
WRITERS
WRITETO
WRITEUP
WRITHED
WRITHES
WRITING
WRITTEN
WROTEIN
WROTETO
WROTEUP
XRATING

•R••T••

ARBITER
ARBUTUS
ARIETTA
ARISTAE
ARISTAS
ARISTOS
BRAXTON
BREATHE
BREATHS
BREATHY
BRISTLE
BRISTLY
BRISTOL
BRITTEN
BRITTLE
BRITTON
BRUITED
CRAFTED
CRAFTER
CRAFTSY
CREATED
CREATES
CREATOR
CRESTED
CRITTER
CROATIA
CROFTER
CROUTON
CRUSTED
CRYPTIC
CRYPTOS
CRYSTAL
DRAFTED
DRAFTEE
DRASTIC
DRATTED
DRIFTED
DRIFTER
DRISTAN
ERECTED
ERECTER
ERECTLY
ERECTOR
ERGATES
ERISTIC
ERRATIC
ERRATUM
ERUCTED
ERUPTED
FRACTAL
FRANTIC
FRETTED
FRITTED
FRITTER
FRONTAL
FRONTED
FRONTON
FROSTED
FRUITED
GRAFTED
GRAFTON
GRANTED
GRANTEE
GRANTOR
GREATER
GREATLY
GREETED
GREETER
GRIFTER
GRISTLE
GRISTLY
GRITTED
GROTTOS
GROUTED
GROWTHS
GRUNTED
KRYPTON
ORBITAL
ORBITED
ORBITER
ORESTES
ORGATES
ORNETTE
ORNITHO
PRAETOR
PRATTLE
PRESTON
PRESTOS
PRINTED
PRINTER
PROCTOR
PROPTER
TRACTOR
TRAITOR
TREATED
TREETOP
TRENTON
TRESTLE
TRISTAN
TRISTAR
TROTTED
TROTTER
TRUSTED
TRUSTEE
TRYSTED
TRYSTER
WRAITHS
WREATHE
WREATHS
WRESTED
WRESTLE
WRITTEN

•R•••T•

ARIDITY
ARIETTA
ARIOSTO
ARMLETS
ARMPITS
ARPENTS
ARRESTS
ARTISTE
ARTISTS
BREADTH
BREASTS
BREVETS
BREVITY
BRINGTO
BROMATE
BRUNETS
CRAVATS
CREDITS
CRUDITY
CRUELTY
DRYROTS
EREMITE
ERNESTO
ERUDITE
FRAILTY
FRIGATE
FRIGHTS
FROWSTY
GRANITE
GRAVITY
GRIVETS
IRRUPTS
ORGEATS
ORIENTE
ORIENTS
ORNETTE
PRAYSTO
PREDATE
PRELATE
PRESETS
PRIESTS
PRIMATE
PRIORTO
PRIVATE
PRIVETS
PRIVITY
PROBATE
PROBITY
PROFITS
PROMOTE
PROMPTS
PRORATA
PRORATE
PRYINTO
TRIBUTE
TRICOTS
TRIESTE
TRIJETS
TRINITY
TRIVETS
TRUANTS
TRYOUTS
URANITE
URTEXTS
WRIGHTS
WRITETO
WROTETO

•R••••T

ARIDEST
ARMREST
ARMYANT
ARTIEST
BRACKET
BRAVEST
BRIDGET
BRIQUET
BRISKET
BROUGHT
CREWCUT
CRICKET
CROCHET
CROQUET
CRUDEST
CRUMPET
DRAGNET
DRAGOUT
DRAUGHT
DRAWOUT
DREWOUT
DRIBLET
DRIVEAT
DROPLET
DROPOUT
DROUGHT
DRYSUIT
ERODENT
FRAUGHT
FREIGHT
FREMONT
FRESHET
FRIPPET
FROWNAT
GRABSAT
GRAVEST
GRAYEST
GREYEST
GRILLET
GROMMET
IRATEST
IRISOUT
IRONOUT
MRFIXIT
MRRIGHT
PRECAST
PRECEPT
PREDICT
PREEMPT
PREFECT
PREHEAT
PRESENT
PRESORT
PRETEST
PRETEXT
PREVENT
PRODUCT
PROJECT
PROPHET
PROPJET
PROTECT
PROTEST
PROTIST
PROVOST
PRUDENT
TRABERT
TRANSIT
TREERAT
TRIDENT
TRINKET
TRIPLET
TRIPPET
TRISECT
TRITEST
TROTOUT
TRUMPET
WROUGHT

••RT•••

AIRTAXI
AIRTIME
BARTABS
BARTEND
BARTERS
BERTHED
BERTOLT
BIRTHED
CARTAGE
CARTELS
CARTERS
CARTIER
CARTING
CARTONS
CARTOON
CERTAIN
CERTIFY
CORTEGE
CURTAIL
CURTAIN
CURTEST
CURTISS
CURTSEY
DARTERS
DARTING
DIRTIED
DIRTIER
DIRTIES
DIRTILY
EARTHEN
EARTHLY
FARTHER
FERTILE
FORTIES
FORTIFY
FORTIUS
FORTRAN
FORTUNA
FORTUNE
FURTHER
FURTIVE
GARTERS
HARTMAN
HURTFUL
HURTING
HURTLED
HURTLES
KIRTLES
MARTENS
MARTIAL
MARTIAN
MARTINA
MARTINI
MARTINO
MARTINS
MARTYRS
MORTALS
MORTARS
MORTIFY
MORTISE
MYRTLES
NARTHEX
NORTHER
NURTURE
OURTOWN
PARTAKE
PARTIAL
PARTIED
PARTIER
PARTIES
PARTING
PARTITA
PARTITE
PARTNER
PARTOOK
PARTOUT
PARTWAY
PERTAIN
PERTEST
PERTURB
PORTAGE
PORTALS
PORTEND
PORTENT
PORTERS
PORTHOS
PORTICO
PORTION
PORTMAN
PORTRAY
SORTERS
SORTIED
SORTIES
SORTING
SORTOUT
SURTSEY
TARTANS
TARTARE
TARTARS
TARTEST
TARTISH
TERTIAL
TORTONI
TURTLED
TURTLES
VERTIGO
VIRTUAL
VIRTUES
VIRTUTE
WARTHOG
WARTIER
WARTIME
WERTHER

••R•T••

AERATED
AERATES
AERATOR
BARETTA
BARSTOW
BERATED
BERATES
BERETTA
BIRETTA
BORATES
BURETTE
BURNTUP
BURSTYN
CARLTON
CAROTID
CORETTA
CURATES
CURATOR
DORITOS
DOROTHY
ERRATIC
ERRATUM
FIRSTLY
FORSTER
GERITOL
GORETEX
GYRATED
GYRATES
GYRATOR
HARDTOP
HERBTEA
HERETIC
HORATIO
KERATIN
KIRSTIE
LORETTA
MARITAL
MERITED
PARATUS
PIRATED
PIRATES
PIRATIC
PURITAN
PYRITES
RARITAN
RERATED
RERATES
SCRATCH
SORITES
SPRITES
STRATUM
STRATUS
STRETCH
STRETTO
UNRATED
VERITAS
WIRETAP
WORSTED

••R••T•

AFREETS
AGREETO
AIRDATE
AORISTS
ARRESTS
AUREATE
BARENTS
BARETTA
BARRETT
BERETTA
BERLITZ
BIRETTA
BURBOTS
BURETTE
BURNETT
BURRITO
CARNETS
CARPETS
CARROTS
CHRISTI
CHRISTO
CHRISTY
CORBETT
CORDATE
CORDITE
CORETTA
CORINTH
CORNETS
CORSETS
CURVETS
DARESTO
DIRECTS
DORSETT
DURANTE
ENROOTS
ENROUTE
FERRATE
FERRETS
FERRITE
FORESTS
FORGETS
FORINTS
FORMATS
FORSYTH
GARNETS
GARRETS
GARRETT
GERENTS
GORGETS
HERMITS
HIRSUTE
HORNETS
IRRUPTS
JURISTS
LARIATS
LORETTA
LYRISTS
MARCATO
MARGATE
MARKETS
MARMOTS
MERLOTS
NARRATE
OTRANTO
PARENTS
PARGETS
PARROTS
PARTITA
PARTITE
PERLITE
PERMITS
PURISTS
RERENTS
REROUTE
SCRIPTS
SERIATE
SERRATE
SHRIFTS
SORBATE
SORBETS
SPRINTS
SPROUTS
STRAITS
STREETS
STRETTO
STRIATE
TARANTO
TARGETS
TARPITS
TERCETS
TERMITE
TERNATE
TERRETS
THREATS
THRIFTS
THRIFTY
THROATS
THROATY
THRUSTS
TORONTO
TURBITS
TURBOTS
TURNSTO
TURRETS
TYRANTS
UPROOTS
VARIETY
VARLETS
VARSITY
VERVETS
VIRTUTE
WARPATH
ZERMATT

••R•••T

ABREAST
ACROBAT
AERIEST
AEROBAT
AIRBOAT
AIRIEST
AIRLIFT
AIRPORT
AIRSOUT
ALRIGHT
APRICOT
BARKSAT
BARONET
BARRETT
BERTOLT
BOREOUT
BORSCHT
BURNETT
BURNOUT
CARCOAT
CARPORT
CARSEAT
CIRCLET
CIRCUIT
CORBETT
CORONET
CORRECT
CORRUPT
CURBCUT
CURRANT
CURRENT
CURTEST
DARKEST
DORMANT
DORSETT
EARHART
EARNEST
EARSHOT
EERIEST
FAREAST
FARLEFT
FARMOUT
FARWEST
FERMENT
FERVENT
FIREANT
FIRELIT
FIRMEST
FORFEIT
FORRENT
FORREST
FORWENT
GARMENT
GARRETT
GERAINT
GORIEST
HARDEST
HARDHAT
HARDHIT
HARDPUT
HARDSET
HARICOT
HARPIST
HARRIET
HARVEST
HERBERT
HERRIOT
HORNIST
LARGEST
MARGRET
MARXIST
MIRIEST
MORDANT
MORDENT
MRRIGHT
NORBERT
PARAPET
PARFAIT
PARQUET
PARTOUT
PERCENT
PERFECT
PERIDOT
PERSIST
PERTEST
PORTENT
PURPORT
PURSUIT
RAREBIT
SARGENT
SERPENT
SERVANT
SORTOUT
SPRIEST
SPRYEST
SURCOAT
SURFEIT
TARTEST
TERSEST
TIREOUT
TOREOUT
TORMENT
TORNOUT
TORRENT
TURNOUT
UPRIGHT
UTRECHT
VARIANT
VARMINT
VERDANT
VERDICT
VERMONT
WARIEST
WARMEST
WARRANT
WIRIEST
WOREOUT
WORKOUT
WORNOUT
YORKIST
ZERMATT

•••RT••

ABORTED
ALERTED
ALERTER
ALERTLY
AVERTED
BLURTED
CHARTED
CHARTER
CHORTLE
COURTED
COURTLY
DEARTHS
EVERTED
EXERTED
FLIRTED
FOURTHS
HEARTED
HEARTEN
HEARTHS
INERTIA
INERTLY
LAERTES
OVERTAX
OVERTLY
QUARTER
QUARTET
QUARTOS
SHORTED
SHORTEN
SHORTER
SHORTLY
SHORTOF
SKIRTED
SMARTED
SMARTEN
SMARTER
SMARTLY
SNORTED
SNORTER
SPARTAN
SPORTED
SPURTED
STARTED
STARTER
STARTLE
STARTUP
SWARTHY
WHARTON

•••R•T•

ACCRETE
AIGRETS
ATTRITE
ATTRITS
AZURITE
BARRETT
BETROTH
BURRITO
CARROTS
CHARITY
CITRATE
CLARETS
CLARITY
CLORETS
CUTRATE
DRYROTS
EMERITA
EMERITI
EMIRATE
EVERETT
EXCRETE
FERRATE
FERRETS
FERRITE
FLORETS
GARRETS
GARRETT
GEARSTO
HYDRATE

IMARETS
INGRATE
INTRUTH
ITERATE
LABRETS
MIGRATE
NARRATE
NITRATE
NITRITE
OPERATE
OVERATE
PARROTS
PRORATA
PRORATE
REGRETS
REWRITE
REWROTE
RIORITA
SECRETE
SECRETS
SERRATE
SPIRITO
SPIRITS
STARETS
TAXRATE
TERRETS
THERETO
THIRSTS
THIRSTY
TITRATE
TURRETS
UNCRATE
UNTRUTH
VIBRATE
VIBRATO
WHERETO

•••R••T

AFFRONT
ARMREST
ATTRACT
BARRETT
BEARCAT
BEAROUT
BEDREST
BLERIOT
CHARIOT
CHEROOT
CORRECT
CORRUPT
COURANT
CURRANT
CURRENT
CYPRIOT
CZARIST
DEAREST
DECRYPT
DEFROST
DETRACT
DETROIT
DISRUPT
DOORMAT
DOUREST
ENCRUST
ENCRYPT
ENGRAFT
ENTRANT
ENTREAT
ENTRUST
EVEREST
EVERETT
EXTRACT
FAIREST
FLORIST
FLORUIT
FORRENT
FORREST
GARRETT
GOURMET
HAIRCUT
HAIRNET
HARRIET
HEAROUT
HERRIOT
HYDRANT
IMPRINT
INFRONT
INORBIT
INPRINT
INTROIT
INTRUST
ITERANT
JEERSAT
LAURENT
LEARJET
LEERSAT
MIGRANT
NEAREST
OVERACT
OVEREAT
PATRIOT
PEEROUT
PEERSAT
PIERROT
POOREST
POUROUT
QUARTET
QUERIST
RANRIOT
RECRUIT
REFRACT
REPRINT
RETRACT
RETREAT
RUNRIOT
SCARLET
SHERBET
SOUREST
SPAREST
SPIRANT
STAREAT
STARLET
STARLIT
SWOREAT
TAPROOT
TEAROUT
TEARSAT
THEREAT
TORRENT
TOURIST
TSARIST
UPDRAFT
UPFRONT
USGRANT
VAGRANT
VIBRANT
WARRANT
WEAROUT
WHEREAT

••••RT•

ADVERTS
ALBERTA
ALBERTO
ALWORTH
ASSERTS
ASSORTS
ASTARTE
CATERTO
CAVORTS
COHORTS
DEPARTS
DEPORTS
DESERTS
DIVERTS
EFFORTS
ESCORTS
ESPARTO
EXHORTS
EXPARTE
EXPERTS
EXPORTS
EXSERTS
EXTORTS
GOCARTS
GOKARTS
HAVARTI
HOGARTH
IMPARTS
IMPORTS
INSERTS
INVERTS
JAKARTA
LAPORTE
LIBERTY
OBVERTS
OFSORTS
OXCARTS
POVERTY
PRIORTO
PUBERTY
REBIRTH
REFERTO
REPORTS
RESORTS
RETORTS
REVERTS
ROBERTA
ROBERTO
ROBERTS
SQUIRTS
SUHARTO
SWEARTO
THWARTS
TSHIRTS
UMBERTO
UNEARTH
YOGURTS

••••R•T

ACCURST
AMHERST
APPARAT
ATHIRST
ATWORST
CABARET
CULPRIT
DEMERIT
DIDEROT
DOGTROT
EXCERPT
FOXTROT
GOFORIT
INHERIT
KINGRAT
LEVERET
LITCRIT
MAIGRET
MALLRAT
MARGRET
MINARET
MUSKRAT
PACKRAT
PIERROT
RICERAT
SNEERAT
SWEARAT
TABORET
TREERAT

•••••RT

AIRPORT
ANTIART
ATHEART
ATHWART
BITPART
BYHEART
CALVERT
CARPORT
CATBERT
CLIPART
COLBERT
COMFORT
COMPORT
CONCERT
CONSORT
CONTORT
CONVERT
CULVERT
DESSERT
DILBERT
DISPORT
DISTORT
DOGBERT
DOGCART
EARHART
ECKHART
ELKHART
FILBERT
FINEART
FOLKART
GILBERT
HERBERT
INSHORT
JETPORT
JUNKART
LAMBERT
NEWHART
NEWPORT
NORBERT
OFASORT
PAYDIRT
POPTART
PRESORT
PURPORT
RAMPART
RAPPORT
RATBERT
RESTART
SEAGIRT
SEAPORT
SHUBERT
STEWART
SUBVERT
SUPPORT
TEACART
TRABERT
UPSTART
WALMART
YOGHURT

RU•••••

RUANDAN
RUBATOS
RUBBERS
RUBBERY
RUBBING
RUBBISH
RUBBLES
RUBDOWN
RUBICON
RUBITIN
RUBRICS
RUBSOFF
RUBSOUT
RUCHING
RUCKING
RUCTION
RUDDERS
RUDDIER
RUDDILY
RUDOLPH
RUDYARD
RUFFIAN
RUFFLED
RUFFLES
RUFIYAA
RUGLIKE
RUINERS
RUINING
RUINOUS
RULEOUT
RULESON
RULINGS
RUMBAED
RUMBLED
RUMBLES
RUMLESS
RUMMAGE
RUMMIER
RUMORED
RUMOURS
RUMPLED
RUMPLES
RUMPOLE
RUNAMOK
RUNAWAY
RUNBACK
RUNDEEP
RUNDLES
RUNDOWN
RUNGOFF
RUNGOUT
RUNHOME
RUNINTO
RUNLATE
RUNLETS
RUNNELS
RUNNERS
RUNNIER
RUNNING
RUNOFFS
RUNOUTS
RUNOVER
RUNRIOT
RUNSDRY
RUNSFOR
RUNSOFF
RUNSOUT
RUNTIER
RUNTISH
RUNWAYS
RUNWITH
RUPIAHS
RUPTURE
RURALLY
RUSHDIE
RUSHEES
RUSHERS
RUSHIER
RUSHING
RUSHOFF
RUSSELL
RUSSETS
RUSSETY
RUSSIAN
RUSTICS
RUSTIER
RUSTILY
RUSTING
RUSTLED
RUSTLER
RUSTLES
RUTGERS
RUTHFUL
RUTTIER
RUTTISH

R•U••••

RAUCOUS
REUBENS
REUNIFY
REUNION
REUNITE
REUPPED
REUTERS
REUTHER
RHUBARB
RHUMBAS
ROUBLES
ROUGHED
ROUGHEN
ROUGHER
ROUGHIT
ROUGHLY
ROUGHUP
ROUGING
ROULADE
ROUNDED
ROUNDER
ROUNDLY
ROUNDON
ROUNDUP
ROUSERS
ROUSING
ROUSTED
ROUTERS
ROUTINE
ROUTING

R••U•••

RADULAE
REBUFFS
REBUILD
REBUILT
REBUKED
REBUKES
REBUSES
RECUSED
RECUSES
REDUCED
REDUCER
REDUCES
REFUELS
REFUGEE
REFUGES
REFUNDS
REFUSAL
REFUSED
REFUSER
REFUSES
REFUTED
REFUTER
REFUTES
REGULAR
REGULUS
RELUCTS
RELUMED
RELUMES
REMUDAS
REPUGNS
REPULSE
REPUTED
REPUTES
REQUEST
REQUIEM
REQUIRE
REQUITE
RESULTS
RESUMED
RESUMES
RESURGE
RETUNED
RETUNES
RETURNS
RITUALS
RIVULET
ROBUSTA
ROGUERY
ROGUISH
ROMULAN
ROMULUS
ROTUNDA

R•••U••

RACQUET
RAGOUTS
RAGRUGS
RAJPUTS
RAPTURE
RAVEUPS
RAYBURN
RAYGUNS
REBOUND
RECLUSE
RECOUNT
RECOUPS
RECRUIT
REDBUDS
REDGUMS
REDOUBT
REDOUND
REGLUED
REGLUES
REMOUNT
RENAULT
REROUTE
RESCUED
RESCUER
RESCUES
RESOUND
RETOUCH
RETOURS
REWOUND
RIGOURS
ROEBUCK
RORQUAL
RUMOURS
RUNOUTS
RUPTURE

R••••U•

RACKSUP
RAGEFUL
RAINOUT
RAISEUP
RAKEDUP
RAKESUP
RANCOUR
RANGOUT
RAPANUI
RAUCOUS
READOUT
REARGUE
REARSUP
REFOCUS
REGROUP
REGULUS
REISSUE
RENEGUE
REOCCUR
RESIDUE
RESTFUL
RESTSUP
RETINUE
REVALUE
REVENUE
RHENIUM
RHODIUM
RHOMBUS
RIDEOUT
RILESUP
RIMBAUD
RINGOUT
RINGSUP
RIOTOUS
RIPSOUT
RODEOUT
ROLLOUT
ROLLSUP
ROMULUS
ROOMFUL
ROOTOUT
ROSEBUD
ROSTRUM
ROUGHUP
ROUNDUP
RUBSOUT
RUINOUS
RULEOUT
RUNGOUT
RUNSOUT
RUTHFUL

R•••••U

RAMBEAU
RONDEAU

•RU••••

ARUGULA
BRUBECK
BRUEGEL
BRUISED
BRUISER
BRUISES
BRUITED
BRUMMEL
BRUNETS
BRUSHED
BRUSHES
BRUSHUP
BRUSQUE
BRUTELY
BRUTISH
BRUXING
CRUCIAL
CRUCIFY
CRUDELY
CRUDEST
CRUDITY
CRUELER
CRUELLY
CRUELTY
CRUISED
CRUISER
CRUISES
CRULLER
CRUMBLE
CRUMBLY
CRUMPET
CRUMPLE
CRUMPLY
CRUNCHY
CRUSADE
CRUSADO
CRUSHED
CRUSHER
CRUSHES
CRUSTED
CRUZADO
DRUBBED
DRUCKER
DRUDGED
DRUDGES
DRUGGED
DRUMLIN
DRUMMED
DRUMMER
DRUMSUP
ERUCTED
ERUDITE
ERUPTED
FRUITED
GRUBBED
GRUDGED
GRUDGES
GRUFFER
GRUFFLY
GRUMBLE
GRUMBLY
GRUMPED
GRUNGES
GRUNION
GRUNTED
GRUYERE
PRUDENT
PRUDERY
PRUDHOE
PRUDISH
PRUNERS
PRUNING
PRUSSIA
TRUANCY
TRUANTS
TRUCIAL
TRUCKED
TRUCKEE
TRUCKER
TRUCKLE
TRUDEAU
TRUDGED
TRUDGER
TRUDGES
TRUEING
TRUFFLE
TRUISMS
TRUMPED
TRUMPET
TRUMPUP
TRUNDLE
TRUSSED
TRUSSES
TRUSTED
TRUSTEE
URUGUAY

•R•U•••

ARBUTUS
ARDUOUS
ARGUERS
ARGUING
ARMURES
AROUSAL
AROUSED
AROUSES
BROUGHT
CROUTON
DRAUGHT
DROUGHT
FRAUGHT
GROUCHO
GROUCHY
GROUNDS
GROUPED
GROUPER
GROUPIE
GROUSED
GROUSER
GROUSES
GROUTED
IRRUPTS
OROURKE
PROUDER
PROUDLY
TRAUMAS
TRIUMPH
TRIUNES
TROUBLE
TROUGHS
TROUNCE
TROUPER
TROUPES
TROUSER
WROUGHT

•R••U••

ARAFURA
ARBOURS
ARDOURS
ARMFULS
ARMOURS
ARMOURY
ARUGULA
BRAVURA
BRIQUET
BROGUES
CROQUET
DRACULA
DRSEUSS
DRYRUNS
DRYSUIT
ERASURE
GRADUAL
GRANULE
GRAVURE
OROTUND
PRELUDE
PRENUPS
PREQUEL
PRESUME
PROCURE
PRODUCE
PRODUCT
PROFUSE
TRADUCE
TRIBUNE
TRIBUTE
TRYOUTS
URUGUAY
WRAPUPS

•R•••U•

ARBUTUS
ARCANUM
ARDUOUS
AREARUG
ARTEMUS
BRACEUP
BREAKUP
BRIMFUL
BRINGUP
BROKEUP
BRUSHUP
BRUSQUE
CRACKUP
CRANIUM
CRANKUP
CRASSUS
CREEPUP
CREWCUT
CRISPUS
CROESUS
CROPSUP
CROSSUP
DRAGOUT
DRAWNUP
DRAWOUT
DRAWSUP
DREAMUP
DRESSUP
DREWOUT
DREYFUS
DRIEDUP
DRIESUP
DRIVEUP
DROPOUT
DRUMSUP
ERASMUS
ERRATUM
FRAMEUP
FRETFUL
GRAMPUS
GROPIUS
GROWNUP
GROWSUP
IRIDIUM
IRISOUT
IRONOUT
ORGANUM
ORMOLUS
ORPHEUS
PREMIUM
PRESSUP
PRONOUN
PROPSUP
PROTEUS
TRADEUP
TRAYFUL
TRIPSUP
TRITIUM
TROILUS
TROTOUT
TRUMPUP
URANIUM
WRAPSUP
WRITEUP
WROTEUP

•R••••U

FRENEAU
TRUDEAU

••RU•••

ABRUZZI
CERUMEN
ETRURIA
FERULES
GERUNDS
IRRUPTS
KORUNAS
PARURES
PERUKES
PERUSAL
PERUSED
PERUSER
PERUSES
SCRUBBY
SCRUBUP
SCRUFFS
SCRUFFY
SCRUMMY
SCRUNCH
SCRUPLE
SHRUBBY
SPRUCED
SPRUCER
SPRUCES
STRUDEL
THRUSTS
THRUWAY
VIRUSES

••R•U••

AGROUND
AIRGUNS
AIRPUMP
ATRIUMS
BARBUDA
BERMUDA
BOROUGH
CARFULS
CAROUSE
CIRCUIT
CIRCUSY
CIRQUES
CORRUPT
EARFULS
EARMUFF
ENROUTE
FERRULE
FORMULA
FORSURE
FORTUNA
FORTUNE
GOROUND
HARBURG
HERCULE
HIRSUTE
JARFULS
KEROUAC
LARRUPS
MARAUDS
MARKUPS
MARQUEE
MARQUES
MARQUEZ
MARQUIS
MERCURY
MURMURS
NURTURE
PARQUET
PERFUME
PERJURE
PERJURY
PERTURB
PURSUED
PURSUER
PURSUES
PURSUIT
REROUTE
RORQUAL
SHROUDS
SPROUTS
STRAUSS
TERHUNE
THROUGH
TORQUES
VERDUGO
VERDURE
VIRGULE
VIRTUAL
VIRTUES
VIRTUTE
WARMUPS
WORKUPS

••R••U•

AIRSOUT
BAROQUE
BOREOUT
BORNEUP
BUREAUS
BURNOUT
BURNSUP
BURNTUP
BURPGUN
CAREFUL
CAROLUS
CURBCUT
CURIOUS
CURLSUP
DAREFUL
DIREFUL
EARDRUM
EARPLUG
ERRATUM
FARMOUT
FERMIUM
FERROUS
FERVOUR
FIREBUG
FIREDUP
FIRESUP
FIRMSUP
FORERUN
FORKFUL
FORMFUL
FORTIUS
FURIOUS
HARBOUR
HARDPUT
HARMFUL
HURRYUP
HURTFUL
KARAKUL
KARAKUM
MARGAUX
MARKSUP
NERVOUS
PARATUS
PARLOUR
PARLOUS
PARTOUT
PERKSUP
PERSEUS
PERSIUS
PIRAEUS
PIROGUE
PYRAMUS
PYRRHUS
SCREWUP
SCRUBUP
SERIOUS
SERVEUP
SORGHUM
SORTOUT
STRATUM
STRATUS
SURPLUS
TERBIUM
TIREOUT
TOREOUT
TORNOUT
TURNOUT
TURNSUP
VARIOUS
VERDOUX
VIRIBUS
WARMSUP
WOREOUT
WORKOUT
WORKSUP
WORNOUT
ZEROSUM

••R•••U

CARIBOU
MARABOU
MARCEAU
MARYLOU
PARVENU
PURLIEU

•••RU••

ACCRUAL
ACCRUED
ACCRUES
ALARUMS
ASARULE
BULRUSH
BUMRUSH
CHERUBS
CORRUPT
DISRUPT
DRYRUNS
ENCRUST
ENDRUNS
ENTRUST
EXTRUDE
FERRULE
FLORUIT
GAGRULE
IMBRUED
IMBRUES
INARUSH
INTRUDE
INTRUST
INTRUTH
LARRUPS
MISRULE
NOTRUMP
OBTRUDE
OUTRUNS
OVERUSE
QUORUMS
RAGRUGS
RECRUIT
SKIRUNS
UNTRUTH

•••R•U•

AMOROUS
APERCUS
BEARCUB
BEARHUG
BEAROUT
BEARSUP

CITROUS
DEFRAUD
FAIRSUP
FEARFUL
FERROUS
FIBROUS
FLAREUP
GEARSUP
GUARGUM
HAIRCUT
HEAROUT
HURRYUP
HYDROUS
INGROUP
MALRAUX
NATRIUM
NITROUS
ODORFUL
ODOROUS
ONEROUS
OVERBUY
OVERDUB
OVERDUE
OVERRUN
PAIRSUP
PEEROUT
PETROUS
POUROUT
PYRRHUS
REARGUE
REARSUP
REGROUP
SCAREUP
STARTUP
STERNUM
STIRRUP
STIRSUP
STOREUP
TEARFUL
TEAROUT
TEARSUP
THEROUX
THORIUM
WEAROUT
YTTRIUM

•••R••U

NEARYOU
THOREAU

••••RU•

AREARUG
BACKRUB
BULLRUN
CHEERUP
CHETRUM
CLEARUP
COVERUP
DECORUM
EARDRUM
FORERUN
FULCRUM
HOMERUN
HUMDRUM
HUMERUS
JABIRUS
LAZARUS
LONGRUN
MILKRUN
MILLRUN
NOSTRUM
NOTTRUE
OVERRUN
PAPYRUS
ROSTRUM
SISTRUM
STIRRUP
TANTRUM
TOYSRUS
WELLRUN

••••R•U

HOFBRAU

R•V••••

RAVAGED
RAVAGER
RAVAGES
RAVELED
RAVENED
RAVENNA
RAVEUPS
RAVINES
RAVINGS
RAVIOLI
REVALUE
REVAMPS
REVEALS
REVELED
REVELER
REVELRY
REVENGE
REVENUE
REVERBS
REVERED
REVERES
REVERIE
REVERSE
REVERTS
REVIEWS
REVILED
REVILES
REVISED
REVISER
REVISES
REVISIT
REVIVAL
REVIVED
REVIVES
REVOICE
REVOKED
REVOKES
REVOLTS
REVOLVE
REVVING
RIVALED
RIVALRY
RIVETED
RIVETER
RIVIERA
RIVIERE
RIVULET

R••V•••

REAVAIL
REVVING
RIGVEDA
ROLVAAG

R•••V••

RANOVER
RAYOVAC
RECOVER
RELIVED
RELIVES
REMOVAL
REMOVED
REMOVER
REMOVES
REPAVED
REPAVES
REVIVAL
REVIVED
REVIVES
REWOVEN
RUNOVER

R••••V•

RECEIVE
RELIEVE
RELIEVO
REPROVE
RESERVE
RESOLVE
RESTIVE
REVOLVE
REWEAVE

R•••••V

ROCKYIV
ROMANOV

•RV••••

ORVILLE

•R•V•••

BRAVADO
BRAVELY
BRAVERY
BRAVEST
BRAVING
BRAVOES
BRAVURA
BREVETS
BREVITY
CRAVATS
CRAVENS
CRAVERS
CRAVING
CREVICE
DRIVEAT
DRIVEIN
DRIVELS
DRIVERS
DRIVEUP
DRIVING
DROVERS
GRAVELS
GRAVELY
GRAVERS
GRAVEST
GRAVIES
GRAVING
GRAVITY
GRAVURE
GRIVETS
GROVELS
PREVAIL
PREVENT
PREVIEW
PRIVACY
PRIVATE
PRIVETS
PRIVIER
PRIVIES
PRIVILY
PRIVITY
PROVERB
PROVERS
PROVIDE
PROVING
PROVISO
PROVOKE
PROVOST
TRAVAIL
TRAVELS
TRAVERS
TRAVOIS
TREVINO
TRIVETS
TRIVIAL

•R••V••

ARGIVES
ARRIVAL
ARRIVED
ARRIVER
ARRIVES
GREAVES
GRIEVED
GRIEVER
GRIEVES
GROOVED
GROOVES

•R•••V•

ARCHIVE
EROSIVE

••RV•••

CARVERS
CARVING
CERVIDS
CURVETS
CURVIER
CURVING
DERVISH
FERVENT
FERVORS
FERVOUR
HARVARD
HARVEST
MARVELS
NERVIER
NERVILY
NERVOUS
NIRVANA
PARVENU
PERVADE
PURVEYS
PURVIEW
SERVALS
SERVANT
SERVERS
SERVERY
SERVEUP
SERVICE
SERVILE
SERVING
SORVINO
SURVEYS
SURVIVE
VERVETS

••R•V••

ARRIVAL
ARRIVED
ARRIVER
ARRIVES
CARAVAN
CARAVEL
DERIVED
DERIVES
FOREVER
MORAVIA
SCRIVEN
SHRIVEL
SHRIVER
SHRIVES
STRIVED
STRIVEN
STRIVER
STRIVES
THRIVED
THRIVES
UNRAVEL
UPRIVER
YEREVAN

••R••V•

AIRWAVE
BEREAVE
CURSIVE
FORGAVE
FORGIVE
FURTIVE
MARKOVA
SURVIVE

••R•••V

NUREYEV

•••RV••

CHERVIL
DWARVES
SCARVES
SCURVES
STARVED
STARVES
SWERVED
SWERVES
WHARVES

•••R•V•

APPROVE
DEPRAVE
DEPRIVE
ENGRAVE
IMPROVE
KEDROVA
REPROVE
WHEREVE

•••R••V

HENRYIV

••••RV•

DESERVE
MINERVA
OBSERVE
ONSERVE
RESERVE
UNNERVE

••••R•V

NEMEROV

RW•••••

RWANDAN

R•W••••

RAWDATA
RAWDEAL
RAWEGGS
RAWHIDE
RAWNESS
RAWSILK
REWARDS
REWARMS
REWAXED
REWAXES
REWEAVE
REWELDS
REWINDS
REWIRED
REWIRES
REWORDS
REWORKS
REWOUND
REWOVEN
REWRAPS
REWRITE
REWROTE
ROWBOAT
ROWDIER
ROWDIES
ROWDILY

R••W•••

RAGWEED
REDWINE
REDWING
REDWOLF
REDWOOD
ROSWELL
RUNWAYS
RUNWITH

R•••W••

RACEWAY
RAILWAY
RANAWAY
REMOWED
RENEWAL
RENEWED
RENEWER
RESAWED
RETOWED
RIDGWAY
ROADWAY
RUNAWAY

R••••W•

RANDOWN
REDRAWN
REDRAWS
REPLOWS
REVIEWS
RIPSAWS
ROBLOWE
ROYALWE
RUBDOWN
RUNDOWN

R•••••W

RAINBOW
ROPETOW

•R•W•••

ARAWAKS
ARTWARE
ARTWORK
BRAWLED
BRAWLER
BREWERS
BREWERY
BREWING
BROWNED
BROWNER
BROWNIE
BROWSED
BROWSER
BROWSES
CRAWDAD
CRAWLED
CRAWLER
CREWCUT
CREWELS
CREWING
CREWMAN
CREWMEN
CROWBAR
CROWDED
CROWERS
CROWING
CROWNED
CRYWOLF
DRAWBAR
DRAWERS
DRAWING
DRAWLED
DRAWNIN
DRAWNON
DRAWNUP
DRAWOUT
DRAWSIN
DRAWSON
DRAWSUP
DREWOUT
DROWNED
DROWSED
DROWSES
DRYWALL
DRYWELL
EREWHON
FRAWLEY
FROWARD
FROWNAT
FROWNED
FROWNER
FROWSTY
GROWERS
GROWING
GROWLED
GROWLER
GROWNUP
GROWSON
GROWSUP
GROWTHS
JREWING
PREWASH
PROWESS
PROWLED
PROWLER
TRAWLED
TRAWLER
TROWELS
TROWERS

•R••W••

ARCHWAY
AREAWAY
FREEWAY

•R•••W•

PREDAWN

•R••••W

FRETSAW
PREVIEW
TRISHAW

••RW•••

AIRWAVE
AIRWAYS
AIRWOLF
BARWARE
CARWASH
EARWIGS
FARWEST
FORWARD
FORWENT
NARWALS
NARWHAL
WARWICK

••R•W••

CARAWAY
FARAWAY
HARDWON
PARKWAY
PARTWAY
SARAWAK
SCRAWLS
SCRAWLY
SCRAWNY
SCREWED
SCREWUP
SPRAWLS
STREWED
STREWER
THREWIN
THROWER
THROWIN
THRUWAY
TURFWAR

••R••W•

BARNOWL
BARROWS
BORROWS
BURROWS
CURFEWS
CURLEWS
FARROWS
FURROWS
HARROWS
MARLOWE
MARROWS
MORROWS
NARROWS
OURTOWN
SORROWS
YARROWS

••R•••W

AIRCREW
AIRFLOW
AIRSHOW
BARSTOW
CORNROW
FOREPAW
FORESAW
PURVIEW

•••RW••

BOERWAR
DOORWAY
FAIRWAY
FOURWAY
SHERWIN

•••R•W•

ANDREWS
BARROWS
BORROWS
BURROWS
ESCROWS
FARROWS
FURROWS
HARROWS
HEBREWS
INGROWN
MARROWS
MORROWS
NARROWS
OVERAWE
REDRAWN
REDRAWS
SORROWS
UNDRAWN
YARROWS

•••R••W

BEARPAW
OVERSAW
SPARROW

••••R•W

AIRCREW
ATECROW
BESTREW
CORNROW
EATCROW
EYEBROW
LOWBROW
MACGRAW
OUTDRAW
OUTDREW
OUTGREW
OUTGROW
PALTROW
SKIDROW
SPARROW
THECROW
TONEROW
UNSCREW
WINDROW
WOODROW

R•X••••

REXCATS
ROXANNE

R•••X••

RADIXES
RELAXED
RELAXES
REMIXED
REMIXES
RETAXED
RETAXES
REWAXED
REWAXES

R•••••X

REAFFIX
ROLODEX

•R•X•••

BRAXTON
BRUXING
PREXIES
PROXIES
PROXIMO

•R••X••

MRFIXIT
URTEXTS

•R•••X•

PRETEXT

•R••••X

BRERFOX
BROADAX
TRIPLEX

••RX•••

MARXISM
MARXIST

••R•X••

HYRAXES

••R••X•

AIRTAXI

••R•••X

FIREBOX
GORETEX
MARGAUX
MIRAMAX
NARTHEX
PARADOX
PERPLEX
VERDOUX

•••R••X

BRERFOX
GEARBOX
MALRAUX
OVERTAX
PHARYNX
POORBOX
STCROIX
THEROUX

••••R•X

BEATRIX
HENDRIX
MEMOREX

R•Y••••

RAYBURN
RAYGUNS
RAYKROC
RAYLIKE
RAYMOND
RAYOVAC
REYNARD
RHYMERS
RHYMING
RHYTHMS
ROYALLY
ROYALTY
ROYALWE

R••Y•••

RECYCLE
RELYING
RETYPED
RETYPES
RUDYARD

R•••Y••

RALLYTO
REDEYED
REDEYES
REKEYED
RELAYED
RESTYLE
RIBEYES
ROCKYII
ROCKYIV
RUFIYAA

R••••Y•

REPLAYS
RICKEYS
ROBROYS
ROMNEYS
RUNWAYS

R•••••Y

RABIDLY
RACEWAY
RAGGEDY
RAILWAY
RAINILY
RANAWAY
RAPIDLY
READILY
REALITY
RECENCY
RECTIFY
RECTORY
REENTRY
REGALLY
REGENCY
REMARRY
RETIARY
REUNIFY
REVELRY
RIANTLY
RICKETY
RIDGWAY
RIFLERY
RIGHTLY
RIGIDLY
RISIBLY
RISKILY
RITZILY
RIVALRY
ROADWAY
ROBBERY
ROCKERY
ROGUERY
ROOKERY
ROOMILY
ROSEBAY
ROUGHLY
ROUNDLY
ROWDILY
ROYALLY
ROYALTY
RUBBERY
RUDDILY
RUNAWAY
RUNSDRY
RURALLY
RUSSETY
RUSTILY

•RY••••

BRYNNER
CRYBABY
CRYOGEN
CRYPTIC
CRYPTOS
CRYSTAL
CRYWOLF
DRYCELL
DRYDOCK
DRYEYED
DRYHOLE
DRYNESS
DRYROTS
DRYRUNS
DRYSUIT
DRYWALL
DRYWELL
FRYCOOK
FRYPANS
GRYPHON
KRYPTON
PRYINTO
TRYOUTS
TRYSTED
TRYSTER
WRYNESS

•R•Y•••

ARGYLES
ARMYANT
BRAYERS
BRAYING
CRAYOLA
CRAYONS
DRAYAGE
DRAYING
DREYFUS
FRAYING
GRAYEST
GRAYING
GRAYISH
GRAYJAY
GRAYLAG
GRAYSON
GREYEST
GREYHEN
GREYING
GREYISH
GRUYERE
PRAYERS
PRAYFOR
PRAYING
PRAYSTO
PREYSON
TRAYFUL
XRAYING

•R••Y••

ARRAYED
ARROYOS
DRYEYED
GROMYKO
PROCYON

•R•••Y•

FRIDAYS
GRAMMYS
PREPAYS

•R••••Y

ARCHERY
ARCHWAY
ARDENCY
AREAWAY
ARIDITY
ARMOURY
BRADLEY
BRAMBLY
BRASHLY
BRAVELY
BRAVERY
BREATHY
BREVITY
BREWERY
BRIBERY
BRIEFLY
BRIMLEY
BRISKLY
BRISTLY
BROADLY
BRUTELY
CRACKLY
CRAFTSY
CRASSLY
CRAZILY
CRINKLY
CRISPLY
CROSSLY
CRUCIFY
CRUDELY
CRUDITY
CRUELLY
CRUELTY
CRUMBLY
CRUMPLY
CRUNCHY
CRYBABY
DRAPERY
DRIPDRY
DRIZZLY
DROPSBY
DROSHKY
ERECTLY
EROSELY
ERRANCY
FRAILLY
FRAILTY
FRANKLY
FRAWLEY
FRECKLY
FREEWAY
FRESHLY
FRIZZLY
FROWSTY
GRANARY
GRANDLY
GRATIFY
GRAVELY
GRAVITY
GRAYJAY
GREATLY
GREELEY
GREGORY
GRETZKY
GRIFFEY
GRIMILY
GRISTLY
GRIZZLY
GROCERY
GROSSLY
GROUCHY
GRUFFLY
GRUMBLY
IRATELY
ORANGEY
ORATORY
ORDERLY
ORGANDY
ORMANDY
OROGENY
ORPHREY
PREACHY
PRESLEY
PRICKLY
PRIMACY
PRIMARY
PRIVACY
PRIVILY
PRIVITY
PROBITY
PRODIGY
PROGENY
PRONELY
PROSILY
PROSODY
PROUDLY
PRUDERY
TRACERY
TRAGEDY
TREACLY
TREMBLY
TRENARY
TRILOGY
TRINITY
TRITELY
TROLLEY
TROTSKY
TRUANCY
URGENCY
URUGUAY
VRONSKY
WRIGGLY
WRIGLEY
WRINKLY
WRONGLY

••RY•••

ACRYLIC
BARYONS
BURYING
JURYING
JURYRIG
MARYANN
MARYKAY
MARYLOU
SPRYEST
TORYISH
TORYISM
VARYING

••R•Y••

ARRAYED
ARROYOS
CARLYLE
CARRYON
EARLYON
FORSYTH
HURRYUP
MARRYME
MARTYRS
NUREYEV
SAROYAN
SPRAYED
SPRAYER
STRAYED

••R••Y•

ACRONYM
AIRWAYS
BARLEYS
BARNEYS
BURSTYN
CARBOYS
CAROLYN
GURNEYS
HURLEYS
JERSEYS
KAROLYI
MARGAYS
MARILYN
PARLAYS
PARLEYS
PURVEYS
SURREYS
SURVEYS
TURKEYS
WURLEYS

••R•••Y

ACRIDLY
AIRPLAY

ALREADY
ATROPHY
AURALLY
BARBARY
BARKLEY
BARNABY
BURSARY
CARAWAY
CERTIFY
CHRISTY
CIRCUSY
CORNILY
CURSORY
CURTSEY
DARESAY
DARNLEY
DIRTILY
DOROTHY
DURABLY
EARTHLY
ERRANCY
FARADAY
FARAWAY
FARMERY
FIREFLY
FIRSTLY
FORGERY
FORTIFY
GERMANY
HARDILY
HARMONY
HARSHLY
HERSHEY
HORNSBY
HORRIFY
JARGONY
JERKILY
LARCENY
LARGELY
LURIDLY
MARYKAY
MERCERY
MERCURY
MERRILY
MORALLY
MORESBY
MORTIFY
MURKILY
NERVILY
NURSERY
PARKWAY
PARSLEY
PARTWAY
PERFIDY
PERJURY
PERKILY
PORTRAY
RURALLY
SCRAGGY
SCRAPPY
SCRAWLY
SCRAWNY
SCRIMPY
SCRUBBY
SCRUFFY
SCRUMMY
SERVERY
SHRILLY
SHRUBBY
SORCERY
SORRILY
SPRINGY
STREAKY
STRINGY
STROPPY
SURGERY
SURLILY
SURTSEY
TARBABY
TARDILY
TERNARY
TERRIFY
TERSELY
THREADY
THRIFTY
THROATY
THRUWAY
TIREDLY
TURNERY
TURNKEY
TYRANNY
UNREADY
VARIETY
VARSITY
VERSIFY
WORDILY
WORKDAY
WORLDLY

•••RY••

CARRYON
DECRYPT
EMBRYOS
ENCRYPT
HENRYIV
HURRYUP
MARRYME
MEGRYAN
NEARYOU
PHARYNX

•••R•Y•

AFFRAYS
AYKROYD
BETRAYS
DEFRAYS
ESTRAYS
HAIRDYE
OSPREYS
ROBROYS
STOREYS
SUNRAYS
SURREYS

•••R••Y

ALERTLY
ANARCHY
ANGRILY
BLARNEY
CHARILY
CHARITY
CHARLEY
CLARIFY
CLARITY
CLERISY
COURTLY
DEERFLY
DOORWAY
ENTROPY
EPARCHY
FAIRWAY
FIERILY
FOURWAY
GLORIFY
HEARSAY
HOARILY
HORRIFY
INERTLY
JOURNEY
KEARNEY
LEERILY
LIBRARY
MERRILY
OVERBUY
OVERFLY
OVERJOY
OVERLAY
OVERTLY
PETRIFY
POORBOY
SCARIFY
SCARILY
SECRECY
SHARKEY
SHARPLY
SHIRLEY
SHORTLY
SMARTLY
SORRILY
SPARELY
STARCHY
STARKLY
STERNLY
STIRFRY
SWARTHY
SWOREBY
TEARILY
TERRIFY
THERAPY
THEREBY
THIRDLY
THIRSTY
TIERNEY
TOURNEY
VITRIFY
WEARILY
WEIRDLY
WHEREBY

••••RY•

DMYTRYK
KATHRYN
MASARYK

••••R•Y

ALLERGY
AMSCRAY
ASHTRAY
AUTARKY
BETARAY
BEVERLY
CLEARLY
COMFREY
DALTREY
DESTROY
DUBARRY
EAGERLY
ELDERLY
EQUERRY
FAYWRAY
GODFREY
IMSORRY
JEFFREY
JOFFREY
LAMPREY
LIBERTY
LITURGY
LOVERLY
MISERLY
ORDERLY
ORPHREY
PALFREY
PICARDY
PORTRAY
POVERTY
PUBERTY
QUEERLY
REMARRY
SHEERLY
SOBERLY
SQUIRMY
SWEARBY
SYNERGY
TEATRAY
THEURGY
UTTERLY
VICEROY
WINFREY
ZYMURGY

•••••RY

ACTUARY
AMATORY
ARCHERY
ARMOURY
ASHBURY
BARBARY
BATTERY
BEANERY
BIGOTRY
BINDERY
BLOWDRY
BONEDRY
BRAVERY
BREWERY
BRIBERY
BURSARY
BUTTERY
CADBURY
CALGARY
CALVARY
CANNERY
CAVALRY
CENTURY
CHICORY
CINDERY
CONAKRY
CONNERY
COOKERY
COPPERY
COUNTRY
CURSORY
CUTLERY
DANBURY
DEANERY
DEEPFRY
DEVILRY
DIETARY
DITHERY
DRAPERY
DRIPDRY
DUBARRY
ELUSORY
ENQUIRY
EQUERRY
ESOTERY
ESTUARY
EXUPERY
FACTORY
FARMERY
FISHERY
FISHFRY
FLOWERY
FOOLERY
FOPPERY
FORGERY
FOUNDRY
GALLERY
GINGERY
GRANARY
GREGORY
GROCERY
GUNNERY
HELOTRY
HENNERY
HICKORY
HILLARY
HISTORY
HOSIERY
HUNGARY
IMAGERY
IMSORRY
INQUIRY
JANUARY
JEWELRY
JIGGERY
JITTERY
JOBBERY
JOINERY
KNAVERY
LANGTRY
LASTORY
LATHERY
LAUNDRY
LIBRARY
LOTTERY
MASONRY
MASTERY
MCHENRY
MERCERY
MERCURY
MIMICRY
MOCKERY
MUMMERY
MYSTERY
NEWBERY
NUNNERY
NURSERY
ORATORY
PALEDRY
PALMARY
PECCARY
PEPPERY
PERJURY
PIGGERY
PILLORY
PLENARY
POTTERY
POULTRY
POWDERY
PRIMARY
PRUDERY
PUFFERY
QUAVERY
QUINARY
QUIVERY
RECTORY
REENTRY
REMARRY
RETIARY
REVELRY
RIFLERY
RIVALRY
ROBBERY
ROCKERY
ROGUERY
ROOKERY
RUBBERY
RUNSDRY
SAVOURY
SCENERY
SENSORY
SERVERY
SHIVERY
SHOWERY
SILVERY
SLAVERY
SORCERY
SPICERY
SPIDERY
SPINDRY
STIRFRY
SUDBURY
SUMMARY
SUMMERY
SURGERY
SWELTRY
TANNERY
TERNARY
TOGGERY
TOPIARY
TOTTERY
TRACERY
TRENARY
TURNERY
UNITARY
VICTORY
WAGGERY
WINTERY
ZACHARY

R•Z••••

RAZORED
RAZZING
REZONED
REZONES
ROZELLE
ROZZERS

R••Z•••

RAZZING
RHIZOME
RITZIER
RITZILY
ROZZERS

R•••Z••

REBOZOS

R••••Z•

REALIZE

•R•Z•••

ARIZONA
BRAZIER
BRAZING
CRAZIER
CRAZIES
CRAZILY
CRAZING
CRUZADO
DRIZZLE
DRIZZLY
FRAZIER
FRAZZLE
FRIZZED
FRIZZES
FRIZZLE
FRIZZLY
GRAZERS
GRAZING
GRIZZLE
GRIZZLY
PRIZING

•R••Z••

BREEZED
BREEZES
BRONZED
BRONZES
DRIZZLE
DRIZZLY
FRAZZLE
FREEZER
FREEZES
FRIEZES
FRIZZED
FRIZZES
FRIZZLE
FRIZZLY
GRETZKY
GRIZZLE
GRIZZLY
PRETZEL

•R•••Z•

ORGANZA
TRAPEZE

•R••••Z

FRANKOZ

••RZ•••

BORZOIS
TARZANA
WARZONE

••R•Z••

ABRUZZI
CORAZON
HORIZON
SARAZEN

••R••Z•

ABRUZZI
CARDOZO
FIRENZE
LORENZO

••R•••Z

BERLIOZ
BERLITZ
MARQUEZ

•••R•Z•

APPRIZE
CHORIZO

••••RZ•

SCHERZI
SCHERZO

••••R•Z

ALVAREZ

SA•••••

SABBATH
SABINES
SABRINA
SACHEMS
SACHETS
SACKERS
SACKFUL
SACKING
SACKOUT
SACLIKE
SACQUES
SADDENS
SADDEST
SADDLED
SADDLER
SADDLES
SADNESS
SADSACK
SAFARIS
SAFFRON
SAGEHEN
SAGGIER
SAGGING
SAGINAW
SAGUARO
SAHARAN
SAILING
SAILORS
SAINTED
SAINTLY
SALAAMS
SALABLE
SALADIN
SALAMIS
SALAZAR
SALCHOW
SALERNO
SALIENT
SALIERI
SALINAS
SALLETS
SALLIED
SALLIES
SALLOWS
SALMONS
SALOONS
SALSIFY
SALSODA
SALTBOX
SALTERS
SALTIER
SALTILY
SALTINE
SALTING
SALTISH
SALUKIS
SALUTED
SALUTES
SALVAGE
SALVERS
SALVIAS
SALVING
SALVOES
SALVORS
SAMARIA
SAMBAED
SAMBALS
SAMBARS
SAMECHS
SAMEDAY
SAMHILL
SAMISEN
SAMITES
SAMLETS
SAMOANS
SAMOVAR
SAMOYED
SAMPANS
SAMPLED
SAMPLER
SAMPLES
SAMPRAS
SAMPSON
SAMSARA
SAMSUNG
SAMURAI
SANCTUM
SANDALS
SANDBAG
SANDBAR
SANDBOX
SANDERS
SANDFLY
SANDHOG
SANDIER
SANDING
SANDLOT
SANDMAN
SANDMEN
SANFORD
SANGOUT
SANGRIA
SANIBEL
SANJOSE
SANJUAN
SANLUIS
SANREMO
SANTAFE
SANTANA
SANTINI
SANTIRS
SAOTOME
SAPIENS
SAPIENT
SAPLESS
SAPLING
SAPPERS
SAPPIER
SAPPILY
SAPPING
SAPPORO
SAPSAGO
SARACEN
SARALEE
SARANAC
SARAWAK
SARAZEN
SARCASM
SARDINE
SARGENT
SARKIER
SARONGS
SAROYAN
SASHAYS
SASHBAR
SASHIMI
SASSERS
SASSIER
SASSIES
SASSILY
SASSING
SASSOON
SATCHEL
SATCHMO
SATDOWN
SATEENS
SATIATE
SATIETY
SATINET
SATIRES
SATIRIC
SATISFY
SATRAPS
SATSUMA
SAUCERS
SAUCIER
SAUCILY
SAUNTER
SAURIAN
SAUSAGE
SAUTEED
SAVABLE
SAVAGED
SAVAGER
SAVAGES
SAVALAS
SAVANNA
SAVANTS
SAVARIN
SAVEDUP
SAVELOY
SAVESUP
SAVINGS
SAVIORS
SAVIOUR
SAVORED
SAVOURS
SAVOURY
SAVVIER
SAVVILY
SAWBUCK
SAWDUST
SAWFISH
SAWLIKE
SAWLOGS
SAWMILL
SAWWOOD
SAWYERS
SAXHORN
SAYINGS
SAYWHEN
SAYYIDS

S•A••••

SCALARS
SCALDED
SCALENE
SCALERS
SCALIER
SCALING
SCALLOP
SCALPED
SCALPEL
SCALPER
SCAMMED
SCAMPED
SCAMPER
SCANDAL
SCANNED
SCANNER
SCANTED
SCANTER
SCANTLY
SCAPULA
SCARABS
SCARCER
SCARERS
SCAREUP
SCARFED
SCARIER
SCARIFY
SCARILY
SCARING
SCARLET
SCARPED
SCARPER
SCARRED
SCARVES
SCATHED
SCATHES
SCATTED
SCATTER
SEABAGS
SEABASS
SEABEDS
SEABEES
SEABIRD
SEABLUE
SEABORG
SEACOWS
SEADOGS
SEADUTY
SEAFANS
SEAFIRE
SEAFOOD
SEAGATE
SEAGIRT
SEAGRAM
SEAGULL
SEALABS
SEALANE
SEALANT
SEALEGS
SEALERS
SEALILY
SEALING
SEALION
SEALOFF
SEALSUP
SEAMIER
SEAMING
SEAMOSS
SEANCES
SEAPORT
SEARING
SEASALT
SEASICK
SEASIDE
SEASLUG
SEASONS
SEASTAR
SEATERS
SEATING
SEATTLE
SEAWALL
SEAWARD
SEAWAYS
SEAWEED
SEAWOLF
SHACKLE
SHADIER
SHADILY
SHADING
SHADOOF
SHADOWS
SHADOWY
SHAFFER
SHAFTED
SHAGGED
SHAHDOM
SHAKERS
SHAKEUP
SHAKIER
SHAKILY
SHAKING
SHAKOES
SHALALA
SHALLOT
SHALLOW
SHALOMS
SHAMANS
SHAMBLE
SHAMING
SHAMMED
SHAMPOO
SHANANA
SHANGRI
SHANKAR
SHANKED
SHANNON
SHANTEY
SHAPELY
SHAPERS
SHAPEUP
SHAPING
SHAPIRO
SHAPLEY
SHAREIN
SHARERS
SHARING
SHARKEY
SHARPED
SHARPEI
SHARPEN
SHARPER
SHARPLY
SHASTRI
SHATNER
SHATTER
SHAVERS
SHAVING
SHAWNEE
SHAWWAL
SIAMESE
SKANKED
SKANKER
SKATERS
SKATING
SLABBED
SLACKED
SLACKEN
SLACKER
SLACKLY
SLAKING
SLALOMS
SLAMMED
SLAMMER
SLANDER
SLANTED
SLAPPED
SLASHED
SLASHER
SLASHES
SLATHER
SLATIER
SLATING
SLATTED
SLAVERS
SLAVERY
SLAVEYS
SLAVING
SLAVISH
SLAYERS
SLAYTON
SMACKED
SMACKER
SMALLER
SMALTOS
SMARTED
SMARTEN
SMARTER
SMARTLY
SMASHED
SMASHER
SMASHES
SMASHUP
SMATTER
SNACKED
SNACKER
SNAFFLE
SNAFUED
SNAGGED
SNAKIER
SNAKILY
SNAKING
SNAPONS
SNAPPED
SNAPPER
SNAPPLE
SNAPSAT
SNAPSTO
SNAPSUP
SNARING
SNARLED
SOAKERS
SOAKING
SOAKSUP
SOANDSO
SOAPBOX
SOAPERS
SOAPIER
SOAPILY
SOAPING
SOARERS
SOARING
SPACERS
SPACIER
SPACING
SPACKLE
SPADERS
SPADING
SPALLED
SPAMMED
SPAMMER
SPANDEX
SPANGLE
SPANGLY
SPANIEL
SPANISH
SPANKED
SPANKER
SPANNED
SPANNER
SPARELY
SPAREST
SPARGED
SPARGES
SPARING
SPARKED
SPARKLE
SPARRED
SPARROW
SPARSER
SPARTAN
SPASSKY
SPATIAL
SPATTED
SPATTER
SPATULA
SPAVINS
SPAWNED
SPAYING
STABBED
STABILE
STABLED
STABLER
STABLES
STACKED
STACKUP
STADIUM
STAFFED
STAFFER
STAGERS
STAGGED
STAGGER
STAGIER
STAGILY
STAGING
STAIDER
STAIDLY
STAINED
STAINER
STAKING
STALAGS
STALELY
STALEST
STALKED
STALKER
STALLED
STAMENS
STAMINA
STAMMER
STAMPED
STANCES
STANDBY
STANDEE
STANDIN
STANDON
STANDUP
STANLEE
STANLEY
STANNIC
STANTON
STANZAS
STAPLED
STAPLER
STAPLES
STARCHY
STARDOM
STAREAT
STARERS
STARETS
STARING
STARKER
STARKLY
STARLET
STARLIT
STARMAN
STARMAP
STARRED
STARTED
STARTER
STARTLE
STARTUP
STARVED
STARVES
STASHED
STASHES
STASSEN
STATELY
STATICE
STATICS
STATING
STATION
STATIST
STATORS
STATUES
STATURE
STATUTE
STAUNCH
STAVING
STAYING
STAYPUT
STAYSUP
SUASION
SUAVELY
SUAVEST
SUAVITY
SWABBED
SWADDLE
SWAGGER

SWAHILI
SWALLET
SWALLOW
SWAMPED
SWANKED
SWANKER
SWANSEA
SWANSON
SWAPPED
SWAPPER
SWARMED
SWARTHY
SWATHED
SWATHES
SWATTED
SWATTER
SWAYERS
SWAYING

S••A•••

SAFARIS
SAHARAN
SALAAMS
SALABLE
SALADIN
SALAMIS
SALAZAR
SAMARIA
SARACEN
SARALEE
SARANAC
SARAWAK
SARAZEN
SAVABLE
SAVAGED
SAVAGER
SAVAGES
SAVALAS
SAVANNA
SAVANTS
SAVARIN
SCHATZI
SCRAGGY
SCRAPED
SCRAPER
SCRAPES
SCRAPPY
SCRATCH
SCRAWLS
SCRAWLY
SCRAWNY
SECANTS
SEDALIA
SEDATED
SEDATER
SEDATES
SEEABLE
SENATES
SENATOR
SERAPES
SERAPHS
SERAPIS
SESAMES
SHEARED
SHEARER
SHEATHE
SHEATHS
SHEAVED
SHEAVES
SHIATSU
SINATRA
SIZABLE
SIZABLY
SMEARED
SNEAKED
SNEAKER
SNEAKIN
SODAPOP
SOFABED
SOLACES
SOLARIA
SOMALIA
SOMALIS
SOMATIC
SONATAS
SPEAKER
SPEAKOF
SPEAKUP
SPEARED
SPLASHY
SPLAYED
SPRAINS
SPRAWLS
SPRAYED
SPRAYER
SQUALID
SQUALLS
SQUALOR
SQUANTO
SQUARED
SQUARER
SQUARES
SQUATLY
SQUATTY
SQUAWKS
SQUAWKY
STEALTH
STEAMED
STEAMER
STRAFED
STRAFES
STRAINS
STRAITS
STRANDS
STRANGE
STRASSE
STRATUM
STRATUS
STRAUSS
STRAYED
SUGARED
SUHARTO
SUKARNO
SUMATRA
SUSANNA
SUSANNE
SUZANNE
SWEARAT
SWEARBY
SWEARER
SWEARIN
SWEARTO
SWEATED
SWEATER
SYNAPSE

S•••A••

SABBATH
SADSACK
SAGUARO
SALAAMS
SALVAGE
SAMBAED
SAMBALS
SAMBARS
SAMOANS
SAMPANS
SAMSARA
SANDALS
SANTAFE
SANTANA
SAPSAGO
SARCASM
SASHAYS
SATIATE
SATRAPS
SAUSAGE
SCALARS
SCARABS
SCHNAPS
SCREAKS
SCREAMS
SEABAGS
SEABASS
SEAFANS
SEAGATE
SEALABS
SEALANE
SEALANT
SEASALT
SEAWALL
SEAWARD
SEAWAYS
SEESAWS
SELVAGE
SENSATE
SERIALS
SERIATE
SERRATE
SERVALS
SERVANT
SETBACK
SETSAIL
SEXTANS
SEXTANT
SFUMATO
SHALALA
SHAMANS
SHANANA
SHEBANG
SHEPARD
SHIKARI
SHOFARS
SIDEARM
SIGNALS
SIMIANS
SINKAGE
SIOUANS
SITUATE
SIXPACK
SKIMASK
SKIRACK
SKYCAPS
SKYJACK
SKYLARK
SKYWARD
SKYWAYS
SLOGANS
SLOVAKS
SMETANA
SNOCATS
SOCIALS
SOPRANO
SORBATE
SOUTANE
SPINACH
SPIRALS
SPIRANT
SPOKANE
SPREADS
SQUEAKS
SQUEAKY
SQUEALS
STALAGS
STEWARD
STEWART
STOMACH
STOMATA
STORAGE
STREAKS
STREAKY
STREAMS
STRIATE
SUBWAYS
SUCRASE
SULFATE
SULTANA
SULTANS
SUMMARY
SUNBATH
SUNDAES
SUNDAYS
SUNLAMP
SUNMAID
SUNRAYS
SUNTANS
SURFACE
SURNAME
SURPASS
SUSTAIN
SYLLABI
SYLVANS
SYRIANS

S••••A•

SAGINAW
SAHARAN
SALAZAR
SALINAS
SALVIAS
SAMEDAY
SAMOVAR
SAMPRAS
SAMURAI
SANDBAG
SANDBAR
SANDMAN
SANJUAN
SARANAC
SARAWAK
SAROYAN
SASHBAR
SAURIAN
SAVALAS
SCANDAL
SCHEMAS
SCHOLAR
SCLERAS
SEAGRAM
SEASTAR
SECULAR
SEMINAL
SEMINAR
SENECAS
SENEGAL
SENORAS
SENSUAL
SERBIAN
SEVENAM
SEVERAL
SHANKAR
SHAWWAL
SHEILAS
SHELLAC
SHERMAN
SHERPAS
SHIPMAN
SHOOTAT
SHOWMAN
SICHUAN
SICKBAY
SICKDAY
SICKPAY
SIDEBAR
SIDECAR
SIDEMAN
SIENNAS
SIERRAS
SIESTAS
SILICAS
SILKHAT
SIMILAR
SIOBHAN
SKIWEAR
SLOTCAR
SNAPSAT
SNEERAT
SNIFFAT
SNIPEAT
SNOWCAP
SNOWCAT
SNOWDAY
SNOWMAN
SOLEDAD
SOMEDAY
SOMEWAY
SONATAS
SORORAL
SOYBEAN
SPARTAN
SPATIAL
SPECIAL
SPIREAS
SPORRAN
SPOUSAL
STANZAS
STAREAT
STARMAN
STARMAP
STELLAR
STERNAL
STIGMAS
STOICAL
STOPGAP
STYGIAN
STYRIAN
SUBHEAD
SUNBEAM
SUNDIAL
SURCOAT
SURINAM
SURREAL
SWEARAT
SWOREAT
SYNGMAN
SYNODAL

S•••••A

SABRINA
SALSODA
SAMARIA
SAMSARA
SANGRIA
SANTANA
SATSUMA
SAVANNA
SCAPULA
SCHIRRA
SCIORRA
SEDALIA
SEGOVIA
SEQUOIA
SESTINA
SHALALA
SHANANA
SHOULDA
SIBERIA
SILESIA
SINATRA
SMETANA
SNOWPEA
SOLARIA
SOMALIA
SOYINKA
SPATULA
SPECTRA
SPINOZA
STAMINA
STLUCIA
STOMATA
SUBROSA
SULTANA
SULUSEA
SUMATRA
SUSANNA
SWANSEA
SYRINGA

•SA••••

ASARULE
ISADORA
PSALMED
PSALTER
PSANDQS
TSARINA
TSARIST

•S•A•••

ASFARAS
ASHAMED
ASHANTI
ASIATIC
ASKANCE
ASSAILS
ASSAULT
ASSAYED
ASSAYER
ASTAIRE
ASTARTE
ESCAPED
ESCAPEE
ESCAPES
ESCARPS
ESPANOL
ESPARTO
ESSAYED
ESTATES
ISLAMIC
ISLANDS
ISRAELI
USEABLE
USUALLY

•S••A••

ASHCANS
ASHLAND
ASHLARS
ASHRAMS
ASPHALT
ASSUAGE
ESPIALS
ESTRADA
ESTRAYS
ESTUARY
ISHMAEL
ISOBARS
ISOLATE
TSQUARE
TSUNAMI
USGRANT

•S•••A•

ASFARAS
ASHTRAY
ASOCIAL
ASSEGAI
ASTOLAT
ASUSUAL
ESCHEAT
ESPOSAS
ESTIVAL

•S••••A

ASSYRIA
ASTORIA
ESTONIA
ESTRADA
ISADORA
OSCEOLA
TSARINA

••SA•••

ABSALOM
ALSATIA
ASSAILS
ASSAULT
ASSAYED
ASSAYER
BASALLY
BASALTS
CASABAS
CASAVAS
DESALTS
DISABLE
DISARMS
DISAVOW
DOSAGES
ESSAYED
HOSANNA
LASAGNA
LASAGNE
LASALLE
MASARYK
MISALLY
MOSAICS
NASALLY
PESAWAS
POSADAS
RESALES
RESALTS
RESANDS
RESAWED
ROSALIE
ROSANNA
ROSANNE
ROSARIO
SESAMES
SUSANNA
SUSANNE
TISANES
UNSATED
VISAGES
VISAING
VISALIA
VISAVIS
WASATCH

••S•A••

ABSTAIN
ASSUAGE
ATSTAKE
BUSFARE
BUSTARD
CASCADE
CASCARA
CASSATT
CASSAVA
CASUALS
COSSACK
COSTAIN
COSTARS
CUSHAWS
CUSTARD
DASTARD
DESCANT
DESPAIR
DISBAND
DISBARS
DISCARD
DISDAIN
DISEASE
DISMAYS
DISTAFF
DISTANT
DOSSALS
ECSTASY
ENSLAVE
ENSNARE
ENSNARL
GASBAGS
GASCAPS
GASMAIN
GESTALT
GESTATE
GOSHAWK
HISPANO
HOSTAGE
HUSBAND
HUSHABY
HUSSARS
INSCAPE
INSEAMS
INSHAPE
INSPANS
INSTALL
INSTALS
INSTANT
INSTARS
INSTATE
LASCALA
LASCAUX
LESPAUL
MASCARA
MASSAGE
MASTABA
MESCALS
MESSAGE
MESSALA
MISCALL
MISCAST
MISDATE
MISHAPS
MISLAID
MISLAYS
MISMATE
MISNAME
MISSAID
MISSALS
MISSAYS
MISTAKE
MUSCATS
MUSTAFA
MUSTANG
MUSTARD
NASTASE
NESCAFE
ONSTAGE
PASSADO
PASSAGE
POSTAGE
RASCALS
RESCALE
RESEALS
RESEATS
RESTAGE
RESTAIN
RESTAMP
RESTART
RESTATE
ROSEATE
ROSTAND
SASHAYS
SUSTAIN
TOSCALE
TOSPARE
TOSTADA
TUSCANY
TUSSAUD
UNSEALS
UNSEATS
UNSNAGS
UNSNAPS
UNSNARL
UNSTACK
UPSCALE
UPSTAGE
UPSTART
UPSTATE
VASSALS
VISUALS
WASSAIL
WASTAGE
YESMAAM

••S••A•

ALSORAN
AMSCRAY
ARSENAL
ASSEGAI
AUSTRAL
BASEMAN
BASEPAY
BESMEAR
BESPEAK
BESTIAL
BESTMAN
BUSHMAN
CASABAS
CASAVAS
CASELAW
CASHBAR
CASPIAN
CASSIAS
DISHPAN
DISHRAG
DISPLAY
DUSTMAN
DUSTPAN
EASTMAN
FASCIAS
FUSTIAN
HESHVAN
HESSIAN
INSOFAR
INSTEAD
INSULAR
MESSIAH
MISDEAL
MISDIAL
MISHEAR
MISLEAD
MISPLAY
MISREAD
MISTRAL
MUSICAL
MUSKRAT
NOSEBAG
NOSEGAY
NOSWEAT
PASCHAL
PESAWAS
PESETAS
POSADAS
POSTBAG
POSTMAN
POSTWAR
ROSEBAY
RUSSIAN
SASHBAR
TASHMAN
TESTBAN
UNSTRAP
WASHRAG
WISEMAN
YASHMAK
YESDEAR
YESMAAM

••S•••A

ALSATIA
ASSYRIA
AUSTRIA
CASCARA
CASSAVA
FESTIVA
HOSANNA
JESSICA
LASAGNA
LASCALA
LASORDA
MASCARA
MASTABA
MESSALA
MESSINA
MESTIZA
MUSTAFA
PASTINA
ROSANNA
ROSETTA
ROSSSEA
SESTINA
SUSANNA
TESSERA
TOSHIBA
TOSTADA
VISALIA
VISCERA
VISTULA
YESHIVA

•••SA••

AGESAGO
AIRSACS
ANASAZI
BALSAMS
BOWSAWS
BURSARS
BURSARY
CAESARS
CASSATT
CASSAVA
CORSAGE
CORSAIR
COSSACK
CRUSADE
CRUSADO
DORSALS
DOSSALS
FORSAKE
FORSALE
GOESAPE
HANSARP
HUSSARS
IBNSAUD
JIGSAWS
KANSANS
MANSARD
MARSALA
MASSAGE
MESSAGE
MESSALA
MISSAID
MISSALS
MISSAYS
NAYSAID
NAYSAYS
OLDSAWS
OVISACS
PAISANO
PASSADO
PASSAGE
PEASANT
PITSAWS
PRESAGE
PRESALE
PROSAIC
PULSARS
PULSATE
QUASARS
RANSACK
RIPSAWS
SADSACK
SAMSARA
SAPSAGO
SAUSAGE
SEASALT
SEESAWS
SENSATE
SETSAIL
TAGSALE
TARSALS
TOPSAIL
TULSANS
TUSSAUD
UPPSALA
VASSALS
WASSAIL

•••S•A•

ABYSMAL
ALASKAN
ALLSTAR
AMISTAD
ARISTAE
ARISTAS
ASUSUAL
BARSOAP
BATSMAN
BEESWAX
BOXSEAT
BROSNAN
CAPSHAW
CAPSTAN
CARSEAT
CASSIAS
CATSCAN
CATSPAW
COASTAL
CRYSTAL
DAYSTAR
DOGSTAR
DRISTAN
ELYSIAN
ETESIAN
FIESTAS
FRISIAN
FURSEAL
GEISHAS
GLOSSAE
GOESBAD
GRISHAM
HEISMAN
HESSIAN
HOTSEAT
HOUSMAN
KEESHAN
KINSMAN
MARSHAL
MESSIAH
MIASMAS
NEWSDAY
NEWSMAN
ONESTAR
PERSIAN
PLASMAS
POTSDAM
PRESOAK
REDSTAR
RUSSIAN
SEASTAR
SENSUAL
SIESTAS
TELSTAR
THUSFAR
TINSTAR
TRISHAW
TRISTAN
TRISTAR
TUESDAY
TWOSTAR
UNUSUAL
VIZSLAS
ZOYSIAS

•••S••A

ANOSMIA
CAESURA
CASSAVA
CORSICA
DYKSTRA
JESSICA
KRISHNA
MARSALA
MESSALA
MESSINA
OLESTRA
PERSONA
PORSENA
PRUSSIA
RETSINA
ROSSSEA
SALSODA
SAMSARA
SATSUMA
TESSERA
UPPSALA

••••SA•

ALTOSAX
AROUSAL
ARTISAN
BABYSAT
BANDSAW
BARKSAT
BUCKSAW
BUZZSAW
COMESAT
DARESAY
DEPOSAL
ESPOSAS
FLIESAT
FLOTSAM
FORESAW
FRETSAW
GAINSAY
GANGSAW
GLOSSAE
GRABSAT
HACKSAW
HANDSAW
HEARSAY
HINTSAT
HOOTSAT
JEERSAT
JUMPSAT
KEEPSAT
LANDSAT
LEERSAT
LINDSAY
LOOKSAT
MEDUSAE
MEDUSAS
MIMOSAS
OVERSAW
PECKSAT
PEEKSAT
PEERSAT
PERUSAL
PHRASAL
PICKSAT
PINESAP
PLAYSAT
POKESAT
RAILSAT
REFUSAL
SNAPSAT
SPOUSAL
TALKSAT
TEARSAT
WHIPSAW
WINESAP
WINKSAT
YELLSAT

••••S•A

ALYOSHA
AMNESIA
ARALSEA
AUGUSTA
BATISTA
CANASTA
CELESTA
CHELSEA
DEADSEA
DEEPSEA
EURASIA
FREESIA
FUCHSIA
GANGSTA
JOCASTA
KARASEA
KENOSHA
LATOSCA
MELISSA
NATASHA
NICOSIA
OPENSEA
OVERSEA
PRUSSIA
RICKSHA
ROBUSTA
ROSSSEA
SILESIA
SULUSEA
SWANSEA
TUNISIA
VANESSA

•••••SA

FORMOSA
MELISSA
MOMBASA
SUBROSA
THERESA
VANESSA

S•B••••

SABBATH
SABINES
SABRINA
SIBERIA
SIBLING
SOBBERS
SOBBING
SOBERED
SOBERER
SOBERLY
SUBBING
SUBDEBS
SUBDUED
SUBDUER
SUBDUES
SUBHEAD
SUBJECT
SUBJOIN
SUBLETS
SUBLIME
SUBMITS
SUBORNS
SUBPLOT
SUBROSA
SUBSETS
SUBSIDE
SUBSIDY
SUBSIST
SUBSOIL
SUBSUME
SUBTEND
SUBTEXT
SUBTLER
SUBUNIT
SUBURBS
SUBVERT
SUBVOCE
SUBWAYS
SUBZERO

S••B•••

SABBATH
SAMBAED
SAMBALS
SAMBARS
SAWBUCK
SEABAGS
SEABASS

SEABEDS
SEABEES
SEABIRD
SEABLUE
SEABORG
SERBIAN
SETBACK
SHEBANG
SHUBERT
SIOBHAN
SKIBOBS
SKIBOOT
SKYBLUE
SLABBED
SLOBBER
SNUBBED
SOBBERS
SOBBING
SORBATE
SORBETS
SOWBUGS
SOYBEAN
STABBED
STABILE
STABLED
STABLER
STABLES
STUBBED
STUBBLE
STUBBLY
SUBBING
SUDBURY
SUNBATH
SUNBEAM
SUNBELT
SUNBOWL
SUNBURN
SWABBED
SWOBBED
SYMBOLS

S•••B••
SALABLE
SALTBOX
SANDBAG
SANDBAR
SANDBOX
SANIBEL
SASHBAR
SAVABLE
SCRIBES
SCRUBBY
SCRUBUP
SEEABLE
SEEDBED
SHAMBLE
SHERBET
SHOEBOX
SHOWBIZ
SHRUBBY
SICKBAY
SIDEBAR
SIDEBET
SIZABLE
SIZABLY
SLABBED
SLOBBER
SLUMBER
SNUBBED
SOAPBOX
SOFABED
SOLUBLE
STABBED
STEUBEN
STROBES
STUBBED
STUBBLE
STUBBLY
STUMBLE
SWABBED
SWOBBED

S••••B•
SCARABS
SCRUBBY
SEALABS
SHRUBBY
SKIBOBS
STANDBY
STOODBY
SUBDEBS
SUBURBS
SWEARBY
SWINGBY
SWOREBY
SYLLABI

S•••••B
SNOWJOB
SUCCUMB

•SB••••
OSBORNE

•S•B•••
ASHBURY
ISOBARS

•S••B••
USEABLE

•S•••B•
ASCRIBE

••SB•••
BUSBIES
BUSBOYS
DASBOOT
DISBAND
DISBARS
GASBAGS
HASBEEN
HUSBAND

••S•B••
BESTBOY
CASABAS
CASHBAR
CASHBOX
DISABLE
DISOBEY
DUSTBIN
NOSEBAG
POSTBAG
POSTBOX
RISIBLE
RISIBLY
ROSEBAY
ROSEBUD
SASHBAR
TESTBAN
VISIBLE
VISIBLY

••S••B•
ABSORBS
ADSORBS
DISROBE
HUSHABY
MASTABA
RESORBS
TOSHIBA

••S•••B
DISTURB
NOSEJOB
WASHTUB

•••SB••
FRISBEE
GEMSBOK
GOESBAD
NEWSBOY

•••S•B•
CLOSEBY

••••SB•
COMESBY
DROPSBY
HORNSBY
MORESBY

SC•••••
SCALARS
SCALDED
SCALENE
SCALERS
SCALIER
SCALING
SCALLOP
SCALPED
SCALPEL
SCALPER
SCAMMED
SCAMPED
SCAMPER
SCANDAL
SCANNED
SCANNER
SCANTED
SCANTER
SCANTLY
SCAPULA
SCARABS
SCARCER
SCARERS
SCAREUP
SCARFED
SCARIER
SCARIFY
SCARILY
SCARING
SCARLET
SCARPED
SCARPER
SCARRED
SCARVES
SCATHED
SCATHES
SCATTED
SCATTER
SCENDED
SCENERY
SCENTED
SCEPTER
SCEPTIC
SCEPTRE
SCHATZI
SCHEMAS
SCHEMED
SCHEMER
SCHEMES
SCHERZI
SCHERZO
SCHIRRA
SCHISMS
SCHLEPP
SCHLEPS
SCHLOCK
SCHMEER
SCHMIDT
SCHMOES
SCHMOOS
SCHNAPS
SCHOLAR
SCHOOLS
SCHULTZ
SCHWINN
SCIENCE
SCIORRA
SCISSOR
SCLERAS
SCOFFED
SCOFFER
SCOLDED
SCOLDER
SCONCES
SCOOPED
SCOOPER
SCOOTED
SCOOTER
SCOPING
SCORERS
SCORING
SCORNED
SCORNER
SCORPIO
SCOTERS
SCOTTIE
SCOURED
SCOURER
SCOURGE
SCOUSES
SCOUTED
SCOUTER
SCOWLED
SCOWLER
SCRAGGY
SCRAPED
SCRAPER
SCRAPES
SCRAPPY
SCRATCH
SCRAWLS
SCRAWLY
SCRAWNY
SCREAKS
SCREAMS
SCREECH
SCREEDS
SCREENS
SCREWED
SCREWUP
SCRIBES
SCRIMPS
SCRIMPY
SCRIPPS
SCRIPTS
SCRIVEN
SCROLLS
SCROOGE
SCRUBBY
SCRUBUP
SCRUFFS
SCRUFFY
SCRUMMY
SCRUNCH
SCRUPLE
SCUDDED
SCUFFED
SCUFFLE
SCULLED
SCULLER
SCULPTS
SCUPPER
SCURVES
SCUTTLE
SCYTHED
SCYTHES

S•C••••
SACHEMS
SACHETS
SACKERS
SACKFUL
SACKING
SACKOUT
SACLIKE
SACQUES
SECANTS
SECEDED
SECEDER
SECEDES
SECKELS
SECLUDE
SECONDS
SECRECY
SECRETE
SECRETS
SECTION
SECTORS
SECULAR
SECURED
SECURER
SECURES
SICCING
SICHUAN
SICKBAY
SICKDAY
SICKENS
SICKEST
SICKISH
SICKLES
SICKOUT
SICKPAY
SOCIALS
SOCIETY
SOCKETS
SOCKEYE
SOCKING
SOCKSIN
STCROIX
SUCCEED
SUCCESS
SUCCORS
SUCCOUR
SUCCUMB
SUCKERS
SUCKING
SUCKSIN
SUCRASE
SUCROSE
SUCTION

S••C•••
SALCHOW
SANCTUM
SARCASM
SATCHEL
SATCHMO
SAUCERS
SAUCIER
SAUCILY
SEACOWS
SEICHES
SHACKLE
SHOCKED
SHOCKER
SHUCKED
SHUCKER
SICCING
SINCERE
SITCOMS
SKYCAPS
SLACKED
SLACKEN
SLACKER
SLACKLY
SLICERS
SLICING
SLICKED
SLICKER
SLICKLY
SMACKED
SMACKER
SNACKED
SNACKER
SNICKER
SNOCATS
SNOCONE
SORCERY
SPACERS
SPACIER
SPACING
SPACKLE
SPECCED
SPECIAL
SPECIES
SPECIFY
SPECING
SPECKED
SPECKLE
SPECTER
SPECTOR
SPECTRA
SPECTRE
SPICERY
SPICEUP
SPICIER
SPICILY
SPICING
STACKED
STACKUP
STICHES
STICKER
STICKTO
STICKUP
STOCKED
STOCKUP
STUCCOS
STUCKTO
STUCKUP
SUCCEED
SUCCESS
SUCCORS
SUCCOUR
SUCCUMB
SUNCITY
SURCOAT
SYNCHED
SYNCHES
SYNCING

S•••C••
SAMECHS
SARACEN
SCARCER
SCONCES
SEANCES
SEDUCED
SEDUCER
SEDUCES
SELECTS
SENECAS
SHTICKS
SIDECAR
SILICAS
SILICON
SIROCCO
SKETCHY
SLOTCAR
SLOUCHY
SLUICED
SLUICES
SNITCHY
SNOWCAP
SNOWCAT
SOLACES
SOLICIT
SOUPCON
SOURCED
SOURCES
SPECCED
SPENCER
SPLICED
SPLICER
SPLICES
SPRUCED
SPRUCER
SPRUCES
STANCES
STARCHY
STENCIL
STLUCIA
STOICAL
STUCCOS

S••••C•
SADSACK
SAWBUCK
SCHLOCK
SCIENCE
SCRATCH
SCREECH
SCRUNCH
SEASICK
SECRECY
SELLECK
SERPICO
SERVICE
SETBACK
SHYLOCK
SILENCE
SIROCCO
SIXPACK
SKIRACK
SKYJACK
SPINACH
SPLOTCH
SQUELCH
SQUINCH
STATICE
STATICS
STAUNCH
STOMACH
STRETCH
SUBJECT
SUBVOCE
SUFFICE
SUNDECK
SUOLOCO
SURFACE
SUSPECT

S•••••C
SARANAC
SATIRIC
SCEPTIC
SEISMIC
SELENIC
SEMITIC
SHELLAC
SKEPTIC
SOMATIC
STANNIC
STYPTIC
SYNODIC

•SC••••
ASCENDS
ASCENTS
ASCETIC
ASCRIBE
BSCHOOL
ESCAPED
ESCAPEE
ESCAPES
ESCARPS
ESCHEAT
ESCHEWS
ESCORTS
ESCROWS
ESCUDOS
OSCEOLA
OSCINES

•S•C•••
ASHCANS
ASOCIAL
PSYCHED
PSYCHES
PSYCHIC
PSYCHUP

•S••C••
ASPECTS
OSSICLE

•S•••C•
ASKANCE
ESSENCE
OSTRICH

•S••••C
ASCETIC
ASEPTIC
ASIATIC
ISLAMIC
OSMOTIC
OSSIFIC
PSYCHIC

••SC•••
ABSCOND
AMSCRAY
BISCUIT
CASCADE
CASCARA
DESCANT
DESCEND
DESCENT
DISCARD
DISCERN
DISCOED
DISCORD
DISCUSS
FASCIAS
FESCUES
FISCHER
GASCAPS
GASCONS
GASCONY
INSCAPE
LASCALA
LASCAUX
MASCARA
MASCOTS
MESCALS
MISCALL
MISCAST
MISCUED
MISCUES
MUSCATS
MUSCLED
MUSCLES
MUSCOVY
NASCENT
NESCAFE
OBSCENE
OBSCURE
PASCHAL
PISCINE
PISCOPO
RASCALS
RESCALE
RESCIND
RESCUED
RESCUER
RESCUES
TOSCALE
TUSCANY
UNSCREW
UPSCALE
VISCERA
VISCOUS

••S•C••
BISECTS
CASHCOW
INSECTS
MUSICAL
OSSICLE
RESECTS

••S••C•
ABSENCE
AUSPICE
BESEECH
CASSOCK
COSSACK
DISSECT
DRSPOCK
ESSENCE
FOSDICK
FUSTICS
HASSOCK
HOSPICE
INSPECT
INSTOCK
IPSWICH
JESSICA
JUSTICE
MASTICS
MOSAICS
MRSPOCK
MYSTICS
RESPECT
RESTOCK
RUSTICS
SUSPECT
TUSSOCK
UNSTACK
UNSTICK
UNSTUCK
WASATCH

••S•••C
ARSENIC
GASTRIC
HASIDIC
MASONIC
OSSIFIC

•••SC••
BORSCHT
CATSCAN
FIASCOS
FRESCOS
KITSCHY
PORSCHE

•••S•C•
AIRSACS
AIRSOCK
CANSECO
CASSOCK
CORSICA
COSSACK
DISSECT
HASSOCK
JESSICA
OVISACS
PARSECS
PHYSICS
RANSACK
SADSACK
SEASICK
TRISECT
TUSSOCK

•••S••C
ANOSMIC
CAUSTIC
CLASSIC
DRASTIC
ELASTIC
ERISTIC
GNOSTIC
LIPSYNC
MIASMIC
PLASTIC
PROSAIC
SEISMIC

••••SC•
BELASCO
DEHISCE
ILIESCU
IONESCO
JALISCO
KLATSCH
LATOSCA
MENISCI
NABISCO
TABASCO

••••S•C
CLASSIC

•••••SC
MOLLUSC

S•D••••
SADDENS
SADDEST
SADDLED
SADDLER
SADDLES
SADNESS
SADSACK
SEDALIA
SEDATED
SEDATER
SEDATES
SEDGIER
SEDUCED
SEDUCER
SEDUCES
SIDEARM
SIDEBAR
SIDEBET
SIDECAR
SIDEMAN
SIDEMEN
SIDINGS
SIDLING
SODAPOP
SODDIER
SODDIES
SODDING
SODLESS
STDENIS
SUDBURY
SUDSIER
SUDSING

S••D•••
SADDENS
SADDEST
SADDLED
SADDLER
SADDLES
SANDALS
SANDBAG
SANDBAR
SANDBOX
SANDERS
SANDFLY
SANDHOG
SANDIER
SANDING
SANDLOT
SANDMAN
SANDMEN
SARDINE
SATDOWN
SAWDUST
SCUDDED
SEADOGS
SEADUTY
SEEDBED
SEEDERS
SEEDIER
SEEDILY
SEEDING
SEEDPOD
SEIDELS
SENDERS
SENDFOR
SENDING
SENDOFF
SENDOUT
SENDSIN
SENDSUP
SENDUPS
SETDOWN
SHADIER
SHADILY
SHADING
SHADOOF
SHADOWS
SHADOWY
SHODDEN
SHUDDER
SITDOWN
SKIDDED
SKIDDER
SKIDDOO
SKIDROW
SKYDIVE
SLEDDED
SLEDDER
SLEDDOG
SLEDGES
SLIDEIN
SLIDERS
SLIDING
SLUDGES
SMIDGEN
SMUDGED
SMUDGES
SNIDELY
SNIDEST
SODDIER
SODDIES
SODDING
SOLDERS
SOLDIER
SOLDOFF
SOLDOUT
SORDINI
SORDINO
SPADERS
SPADING
SPIDERS
SPIDERY
STADIUM
STUDDED
STUDENT
STUDIED
STUDIES
STUDIOS
SUBDEBS
SUBDUED
SUBDUER
SUBDUES
SUNDAES
SUNDAYS
SUNDECK
SUNDERS
SUNDEWS
SUNDIAL
SUNDOGS
SUNDOWN
SWADDLE
SWEDISH

S•••D••
SALADIN
SAMEDAY
SAVEDUP
SCALDED
SCANDAL
SCENDED
SCOLDED
SCOLDER
SCUDDED
SECEDED
SECEDER
SECEDES
SERFDOM
SEWEDON
SEWEDUP
SHAHDOM
SHELDON
SHINDIG
SHODDEN
SHOWDOG
SHUDDER
SICKDAY
SINEDIE
SIZEDUP
SKIDDED
SKIDDER
SKIDDOO
SLANDER
SLEDDED
SLEDDER
SLEDDOG
SLENDER
SMOLDER
SNOWDAY
SNOWDON
SOANDSO
SOLEDAD
SOLIDER
SOLIDLY
SOMEDAY
SOUNDED
SOUNDER
SOUNDLY
SPANDEX
SPEEDED
SPEEDER
SPEEDOS
SPEEDUP
SPENDER
SPIEDON
SPINDLE
SPINDLY
SPINDRY
SPONDEE
STAIDER
STAIDLY
STANDBY
STANDEE
STANDIN
STANDON
STANDUP
STARDOM
STOODBY
STOODIN
STOODUP
STRIDER
STRIDES
STRUDEL
STUDDED
SWADDLE
SWINDLE
SYNODAL
SYNODIC

S••••D•
SALSODA
SAYYIDS
SCHMIDT
SCREEDS
SEABEDS
SEASIDE
SECLUDE
SECONDS
SHIELDS
SHOULDA
SHROUDS
SPREADS
STRANDS
SUBSIDE
SUBSIDY
SULFIDE
SUNGODS

S•••••D
SADDLED
SAINTED
SALLIED
SALUTED
SAMBAED
SAMOYED
SAMPLED
SANFORD
SAUTEED
SAVAGED
SAVORED
SAWWOOD
SCALDED
SCALPED
SCAMMED
SCAMPED
SCANNED
SCANTED
SCARFED
SCARPED
SCARRED
SCATHED
SCATTED
SCENDED
SCENTED
SCHEMED
SCOFFED
SCOLDED
SCOOPED
SCOOTED
SCORNED
SCOURED
SCOUTED
SCOWLED
SCRAPED
SCREWED
SCUDDED
SCUFFED
SCULLED
SCYTHED
SEABIRD
SEAFOOD
SEAWARD
SEAWEED
SECEDED
SECURED
SEDATED
SEDUCED
SEEDBED
SEEDPOD
SEESRED
SEETHED
SERRIED
SETTLED
SEVERED
SHAFTED
SHAGGED
SHAMMED
SHANKED
SHARPED
SHEARED
SHEAVED
SHEERED

SHEETED
SHELLED
SHELVED
SHEPARD
SHIFTED
SHILLED
SHINNED
SHIPPED
SHIRKED
SHIRRED
SHOCKED
SHOPPED
SHORTED
SHOUTED
SHUCKED
SHUNNED
SHUNTED
SHUSHED
SIGHTED
SIGMUND
SINGLED
SIXFOLD
SIZZLED
SKANKED
SKIDDED
SKILLED
SKIMMED
SKIMPED
SKINNED
SKIPPED
SKIRLED
SKIRRED
SKIRTED
SKULKED
SKUNKED
SKYWARD
SLABBED
SLACKED
SLAMMED
SLANTED
SLAPPED
SLASHED
SLATTED
SLEDDED
SLEEKED
SLEETED
SLICKED
SLIMMED
SLINKED
SLIPPED
SLOGGED
SLOPPED
SLOSHED
SLOTTED
SLUGGED
SLUICED
SLUMMED
SLUMPED
SLURPED
SLURRED
SMACKED
SMARTED
SMASHED
SMEARED
SMELLED
SMELTED
SMIRKED
SMUDGED
SNACKED
SNAFUED
SNAGGED
SNAPPED
SNARLED
SNEAKED
SNEERED
SNEEZED
SNIFFED
SNIPPED
SNOGGED
SNOOPED
SNOOTED
SNOOZED
SNORTED
SNUBBED
SNUFFED
SOBERED
SOFABED
SOLEDAD
SOOTHED
SORTIED
SOUGHED
SOUNDED
SOURCED
SPALLED
SPAMMED
SPANKED
SPANNED
SPARGED
SPARKED
SPARRED
SPATTED
SPAWNED
SPEARED
SPECCED
SPECKED
SPEEDED
SPELLED
SPIELED
SPILLED
SPLAYED
SPLICED
SPOILED
SPONGED
SPOOFED
SPOOKED
SPOOLED
SPOONED
SPORTED
SPOTTED
SPOUTED
SPRAYED
SPRUCED
SPURNED
SPURRED
SPURTED
SQUALID
SQUARED
SQUIRED
STABBED
STABLED
STACKED
STAFFED
STAGGED
STAINED
STALKED
STALLED
STAMPED
STAPLED
STARRED
STARTED
STARVED
STASHED
STEAMED
STEELED
STEEPED
STEERED
STEMMED
STEPPED
STEROID
STETTED
STEWARD
STIFFED
STIFLED
STILLED
STILTED
STINTED
STIPEND
STIRRED
STOCKED
STOMPED
STOOKED
STOOPED
STOPPED
STORIED
STORMED
STRAFED
STRAYED
STREWED
STRIPED
STRIVED
STROKED
STUBBED
STUDDED
STUDIED
STUFFED
STUMPED
STUNNED
STUNTED
STYMIED
SUBDUED
SUBHEAD
SUBTEND
SUCCEED
SUGARED
SULLIED
SUNMAID
SUSPEND
SUTURED
SWABBED
SWAMPED
SWANKED
SWAPPED
SWARMED
SWATHED
SWATTED
SWEATED
SWELLED
SWERVED
SWIGGED
SWILLED
SWIRLED
SWISHED
SWOBBED
SWOONED
SWOOPED
SWOPPED
SYNCHED

•S•D•••

ISADORA

•S••D••

ASKEDIN
ASUNDER
ESCUDOS
PSANDQS

•S•••D•

ASCENDS
ASTRIDE
ESTRADA
ISLANDS
ISOPODS
USERIDS

•S••••D

ASHAMED
ASHFORD
ASHLAND
ASPIRED
ASSAYED
ASSUMED
ASSURED
ASTOUND
ESCAPED
ESSAYED
OSIERED
OSMOSED
OSTEOID
PSALMED
PSYCHED
USHERED
USURPED

••SD•••

DISDAIN
FOSDICK
MISDATE
MISDEAL
MISDEED
MISDIAL
MISDOES
MISDONE
YESDEAR

••S•D••

APSIDES
BESIDES
DOSIDOS
EASEDIN
EASEDUP
HASIDIC
HASIDIM
INSIDER
INSIDES
ONSIDES
PASTDUE
POSADAS
RESIDED
RESIDES
RESIDUE
RUSHDIE
WISEDUP

••S••D•

AXSEEDS
BUSHIDO
CASCADE
CASSIDY
CUSPIDS
CUSTODY
LASORDA
PASSADO
RESANDS
RESEEDS
RESENDS
TESTUDO
TOSTADA
VESPIDS

••S•••D

ABSCOND
ASSAYED
ASSUMED
ASSURED
BUSTARD
BUSTLED
CASQUED
CASTLED
CUSTARD
DASTARD
DESCEND
DESIRED
DESMOND
DISBAND
DISCARD
DISCOED
DISCORD
DISTEND
DISUSED
EASTEND
ENSILED
ENSKIED
ENSURED
ESSAYED
GUSSIED
HASSLED
HUSBAND
HUSTLED
INSIPID
INSTEAD
INSURED
JOSTLED
LASSOED
LUSTRED
MASTOID
MISCUED
MISDEED
MISLAID
MISLEAD
MISREAD
MISSAID
MISUSED
MISWORD
MOSEYED
MUSCLED
MUSTARD
NESTLED
PESTLED
POSITED
RASSLED
RESAWED
RESCIND
RESCUED
RESIDED
RESILED
RESOLED
RESOUND
RESPOND
RESUMED
ROSEBUD
ROSERED
ROSTAND
RUSTLED
SUSPEND
TUSSAUD
TUSSLED
UNSATED
UNSEWED
UNSOUND
VISITED
WESTEND

•••SD••

DRESDEN
GADSDEN
NEWSDAY
POTSDAM
RUNSDRY
TUESDAY

•••S•D•

BEDSIDE
CAPSIDS
CASSIDY
CRUSADE
CRUSADO
EPISODE
OFFSIDE
OUTSIDE
PASSADO
PRESIDE
PROSODY
SALSODA
SEASIDE
SUBSIDE
SUBSIDY
TOPSIDE
WAYSIDE

•••S••D

ABASHED
AMASSED
AMISTAD
ANISEED
BIASSED
BLASTED
BLESSED
BLUSHED
BOASTED
BOBSLED
BOOSTED
BRUSHED
CLASHED
CLASPED
CLASSED
COASTED
CRASHED
CRESTED
CRISPED
CROSSED
CRUSHED
CRUSTED
DOGSLED
DRESSED
EGESTED
ENISLED
EXISTED
FEASTED
FLASHED
FLESHED
FLOSSED
FLUSHED
FOISTED
FRISKED
FROSTED
GHOSTED
GLASSED
GLOSSED
GNASHED
GODSEND
GOESBAD
GRASPED
GRASSED
GROSSED
GUESSED
GUESTED
GUSSIED
HASSLED
HAYSEED
HEISTED
HOISTED
IBNSAUD
JOISTED
JOUSTED
LASSOED
LEASHED
LINSEED
MANSARD
MISSAID
MOUSSED
NAYSAID
NONSKID
OUTSOLD
PERSEID
PLASHED
PRESSED
PURSUED
QUASHED
QUESTED
RASSLED
ROASTED
ROOSTED
ROUSTED
SEESRED
SHUSHED
SLASHED
SLOSHED
SMASHED
STASHED
SWISHED
TOASTED
TOUSLED
TRASHED
TRUSSED
TRUSTED
TRYSTED
TUSSAUD
TUSSLED
TWISTED
UNASKED
WHISHED
WHISKED
WORSTED
WRESTED

••••SD•

MAKESDO

••••S•D

ACCUSED
ADVISED
AMASSED
APPOSED
AROUSED
AVULSED
BEMUSED
BIASSED
BLESSED
BLOUSED
BRAISED
BROWSED
BRUISED
CLASSED
COURSED
CREASED
CROSSED
CRUISED
DEBASED
DEFUSED
DEMISED
DEPOSED
DEVISED
DISUSED
DRESSED
DROWSED
EFFUSED
ELAPSED
EMERSED
ENCASED
EVULSED
EXCISED
EXCUSED
EXPOSED
FLENSED
FLOSSED
FOCUSED
GLASSED
GLOSSED
GRASSED
GREASED
GROSSED
GROUSED
GUESSED
ILLUSED
IMPOSED
INCASED
INCISED
INFUSED
IODISED
IONISED
LIAISED
MISUSED
MOUSSED
OPPOSED
OSMOSED
PERUSED
PHRASED
PLEASED
PRAISED
PRESSED
RECUSED
REFUSED
REPOSED
REVISED
TRUSSED
UNCASED

SE•••••

SEABAGS
SEABASS
SEABEDS
SEABEES
SEABIRD
SEABLUE
SEABORG
SEACOWS
SEADOGS
SEADUTY
SEAFANS
SEAFIRE
SEAFOOD
SEAGATE
SEAGIRT
SEAGRAM
SEAGULL
SEALABS
SEALANE
SEALANT
SEALEGS
SEALERS
SEALILY
SEALING
SEALION
SEALOFF
SEALSUP
SEAMIER
SEAMING
SEAMOSS
SEANCES
SEAPORT
SEARING
SEASALT
SEASICK
SEASIDE
SEASLUG
SEASONS
SEASTAR
SEATERS
SEATING
SEATTLE
SEAWALL
SEAWARD
SEAWAYS
SEAWEED
SEAWOLF
SECANTS
SECEDED
SECEDER
SECEDES
SECKELS
SECLUDE
SECONDS
SECRECY
SECRETE
SECRETS
SECTION
SECTORS
SECULAR
SECURED
SECURER
SECURES
SEDALIA
SEDATED
SEDATER
SEDATES
SEDGIER
SEDUCED
SEDUCER
SEDUCES
SEEABLE
SEEDBED
SEEDERS
SEEDIER
SEEDILY
SEEDING
SEEDPOD
SEEHERE
SEEKERS
SEEKING
SEEKOUT
SEEMING
SEENFIT
SEENOFF
SEENOUT
SEEPIER
SEEPING
SEEPSIN
SEERESS
SEESAWS
SEESFIT
SEESOFF
SEESOUT
SEESRED
SEETHED
SEETHES
SEETOIT
SEGMENT
SEGOVIA
SEICHES
SEIDELS
SEINERS
SEINING
SEISMIC
SEIZERS
SEIZING
SELECTS
SELENIC
SELFISH
SELKIRK
SELLECK
SELLERS
SELLFOR
SELLING
SELLOFF
SELLOUT
SELTZER
SELVAGE
SEMILOG
SEMINAL
SEMINAR
SEMIPRO
SEMITES
SEMITIC
SENATES
SENATOR
SENDERS
SENDFOR
SENDING
SENDOFF
SENDOUT
SENDSIN
SENDSUP
SENDUPS
SENECAS
SENEGAL
SENIORS
SENNETT
SENORAS
SENORES
SENSATE
SENSING
SENSORS
SENSORY
SENSUAL
SENTFOR
SENTOFF
SENTOUT
SENUFOS
SEPTETS
SEQUELS
SEQUINS
SEQUOIA
SERAPES
SERAPHS
SERAPIS
SERBIAN
SERENER
SERFDOM
SERIALS
SERIATE
SERIOUS
SERLING
SERMONS
SERPENT
SERPICO
SERRATE
SERRIED
SERVALS
SERVANT
SERVERS
SERVERY
SERVEUP
SERVICE
SERVILE
SERVING
SESAMES
SESSILE
SESSION
SESTETS
SESTINA
SETBACK
SETDOWN
SETINTO
SETLINE
SETSAIL
SETSOFF
SETSOUT
SETTEES
SETTERS
SETTING
SETTLED
SETTLER
SETTLES
SETUPON
SEVENAM
SEVENPM
SEVENTH
SEVENTY
SEVENUP
SEVERAL
SEVERED
SEVERER
SEVIGNE
SEVILLE
SEWEDON
SEWEDUP
SEXIEST
SEXISTS
SEXTANS
SEXTANT
SEXTETS
SEXTONS
SEYMOUR

S•E••••

SCENDED
SCENERY
SCENTED
SCEPTER
SCEPTIC
SCEPTRE
SEEABLE
SEEDBED
SEEDERS
SEEDIER
SEEDILY
SEEDING
SEEDPOD
SEEHERE
SEEKERS
SEEKING
SEEKOUT
SEEMING
SEENFIT
SEENOFF
SEENOUT
SEEPIER
SEEPING
SEEPSIN
SEERESS
SEESAWS
SEESFIT
SEESOFF
SEESOUT
SEESRED
SEETHED
SEETHES
SEETOIT
SHEARED
SHEARER
SHEATHE
SHEATHS
SHEAVED
SHEAVES
SHEBANG
SHEERED
SHEERER
SHEERLY
SHEETED
SHEIKHS
SHEILAS
SHEKELS
SHELDON
SHELLAC
SHELLED
SHELLER
SHELLEY
SHELTER
SHELTIE
SHELTON
SHELVED
SHELVES
SHEPARD
SHERBET
SHERIFF
SHERMAN
SHERPAS
SHERWIN
SHEWOLF
SIENNAS
SIERRAS
SIESTAS
SKEETER
SKEEZIX
SKELTER
SKELTON
SKEPTIC
SKETCHY
SKEWERS
SKEWING
SLEDDED
SLEDDER
SLEDDOG
SLEDGES
SLEEKED
SLEEKEN
SLEEKER
SLEEKLY
SLEEPER
SLEEPIN
SLEEPON
SLEETED
SLEEVES
SLEIGHS
SLEIGHT
SLENDER
SLEPTIN
SLEPTON
SLEUTHS
SMEARED
SMELLED
SMELTED
SMELTER
SMETANA
SNEAKED
SNEAKER
SNEAKIN
SNEERAT
SNEERED
SNEERER
SNEEZED
SNEEZER
SNEEZES
SNELLEN
SPEAKER
SPEAKOF
SPEAKUP
SPEARED
SPECCED
SPECIAL
SPECIES
SPECIFY
SPECING
SPECKED
SPECKLE
SPECTER
SPECTOR
SPECTRA
SPECTRE
SPEEDED
SPEEDER
SPEEDOS
SPEEDUP
SPELLED
SPELLER
SPELUNK
SPENCER
SPENDER
SPENSER
SPEWING
STEALTH
STEAMED
STEAMER
STEELED
STEELER
STEELIE
STEEPED
STEEPEN
STEEPER
STEEPLE
STEEPLY
STEERED
STEERER
STEIGER
STEINEM
STEINER
STELLAR
STEMMED
STENCIL
STENGEL
STENTOR
STEPHEN
STEPINS
STEPOUT
STEPPED
STEPPER
STEPPES
STEPSIN
STEPSON
STEPSUP
STEPUPS
STEREOS
STERILE
STERNAL
STERNER
STERNLY
STERNUM
STEROID
STEROLS
STETSON
STETTED
STEUBEN
STEVENS
STEWARD
STEWART
STEWERS
STEWING
SVELTER
SWEARAT
SWEARBY
SWEARER
SWEARIN
SWEARTO
SWEATED
SWEATER
SWEDISH
SWEENEY
SWEEPER
SWEEPUP
SWEETEN
SWEETER
SWEETIE
SWEETLY
SWEETON
SWELLED
SWELLUP
SWELTER
SWELTRY
SWEPTUP
SWERVED
SWERVES

S••E•••

SAGEHEN
SALERNO
SAMECHS
SAMEDAY
SATEENS
SAVEDUP
SAVELOY
SAVESUP
SCHEMAS
SCHEMED
SCHEMER
SCHEMES
SCHERZI
SCHERZO
SCIENCE
SCLERAS
SCREAKS
SCREAMS
SCREECH
SCREEDS
SCREENS
SCREWED
SCREWUP
SECEDED
SECEDER
SECEDES
SELECTS
SELENIC
SENECAS
SENEGAL
SERENER
SEVENAM
SEVENPM
SEVENTH
SEVENTY
SEVENUP
SEVERAL
SEVERED
SEVERER
SEWEDON
SEWEDUP
SHEERED
SHEERER
SHEERLY
SHEETED
SHIELDS
SHOEBOX
SHOEING
SIBERIA
SIDEARM
SIDEBAR
SIDEBET
SIDECAR

SIDEMAN
SIDEMEN
SILENCE
SILENTS
SILESIA
SIMENON
SINEDIE
SIZEDUP
SIZESUP
SKEETER
SKEEZIX
SLEEKED
SLEEKEN
SLEEKER
SLEEKLY
SLEEPER
SLEEPIN
SLEEPON
SLEETED
SLEEVES
SLOEGIN
SNEERAT
SNEERED
SNEERER
SNEEZED
SNEEZER
SNEEZES
SOBERED
SOBERER
SOBERLY
SOLEDAD
SOMEDAY
SOMEHOW
SOMEONE
SOMEWAY
SPEEDED
SPEEDER
SPEEDOS
SPEEDUP
SPHERES
SPIEDON
SPIEGEL
SPIELED
SPIELER
SPIESON
SPLEENS
SPREADS
SQUEAKS
SQUEAKY
SQUEALS
SQUEEZE
SQUELCH
STDENIS
STEELED
STEELER
STEELIE
STEEPED
STEEPEN
STEEPER
STEEPLE
STEEPLY
STEERED
STEERER
STIEGEL
STPETER
STREAKS
STREAKY
STREAMS
STREETS
STRETCH
STRETTO
STREWED
STREWER
SUZETTE
SWEENEY
SWEEPER
SWEEPUP
SWEETEN
SWEETER
SWEETIE
SWEETLY
SWEETON
SYNERGY

S•••E••

SACHEMS
SACHETS
SACKERS
SADDENS
SADDEST
SADNESS
SALIENT
SALIERI
SALLETS
SALTERS
SALVERS
SAMLETS
SANDERS
SANREMO
SAPIENS
SAPIENT
SAPLESS
SAPPERS
SARGENT
SASSERS
SATEENS
SATIETY
SAUCERS
SAUTEED
SAWYERS
SCALENE
SCALERS
SCARERS
SCAREUP
SCENERY
SCHLEPP
SCHLEPS
SCHMEER
SCORERS
SCOTERS
SCREECH
SCREEDS
SCREENS
SEABEDS
SEABEES
SEALEGS
SEALERS
SEATERS
SEAWEED
SECKELS
SECRECY
SECRETE
SECRETS
SEEDERS
SEEHERE
SEEKERS
SEERESS
SEGMENT
SEIDELS
SEINERS
SEIZERS
SELLECK
SELLERS
SENDERS
SENNETT
SEPTETS
SEQUELS
SERPENT
SERVERS
SERVERY
SERVEUP
SESTETS
SETTEES
SETTERS
SEXIEST
SEXTETS
SHAKERS
SHAKEUP
SHAPELY
SHAPERS
SHAPEUP
SHAREIN
SHARERS
SHAVERS
SHEKELS
SHINERS
SHIVERS
SHIVERY
SHOVELS
SHOVERS
SHOWERS
SHOWERY
SHRIEKS
SHUBERT
SHUTEYE
SHYNESS
SIAMESE
SICKENS
SICKEST
SIFTERS
SIGHERS
SIGNEES
SIGNERS
SIGNETS
SILVERS
SILVERY
SIMMERS
SIMPERS
SINCERE
SINGERS
SINKERS
SINLESS
SINNERS
SIPPERS
SIPPETS
SISTERS
SITTERS
SITWELL
SIXTEEN
SKATERS
SKEWERS
SKIVERS
SKIWEAR
SKYLESS
SLAVERS
SLAVERY
SLAVEYS
SLAYERS
SLICERS
SLIDEIN
SLIDERS
SLIVERS
SLOVENE
SLOVENS
SLOWEST
SLYNESS
SMILERS
SMOKERS
SNIDELY
SNIDEST
SNIPEAT
SNIPERS
SNIVELS
SNORERS
SOAKERS
SOAPERS
SOARERS
SOBBERS
SOCIETY
SOCKETS
SOCKEYE
SODLESS
SOFTENS
SOFTEST
SOIREES
SOLDERS
SOLFEGE
SOLVENT
SOLVERS
SONLESS
SONNETS
SOONERS
SOONEST
SORBETS
SORCERY
SORRELS
SORTERS
SOSUEME
SOTHERE
SOTHERN
SOUREST
SOVIETS
SOYBEAN
SPACERS
SPADERS
SPARELY
SPAREST
SPICERY
SPICEUP
SPIDERS
SPIDERY
SPIKERS
SPINELS
SPINETS
SPIREAS
SPLEENS
SPOKEOF
SPOKEUP
SPRIEST
SPRYEST
SQUEEZE
STAGERS
STALELY
STALEST
STAMENS
STAREAT
STARERS
STARETS
STATELY
STEREOS
STEVENS
STEWERS
STIPEND
STOKELY
STOKERS
STONERS
STORERS
STOREUP
STOREYS
STREETS
STUDENT
STUMERS
STUPEFY
STYLERS
STYLETS
STYRENE
SUAVELY
SUAVEST
SUBDEBS
SUBHEAD
SUBJECT
SUBLETS
SUBSETS
SUBTEND
SUBTEXT
SUBVERT
SUBZERO
SUCCEED
SUCCESS
SUCKERS
SUFFERS
SUGGEST
SULKERS
SUMLESS
SUMMERS
SUMMERY
SUNBEAM
SUNBELT
SUNDECK
SUNDERS
SUNDEWS
SUNLESS
SUNSETS
SUPPERS
SUPREME
SUPREMO
SURFEIT
SURFERS
SURGEON
SURGERY
SURREAL
SURREYS
SURVEYS
SUSPECT
SUSPEND
SUTLERS
SUTTERS
SWAYERS
SWIPERS
SWIVELS
SWIVETS
SWOREAT
SWOREBY
SWOREIN
SYSTEMS

S••••E•

SABINES
SACQUES
SADDLED
SADDLER
SADDLES
SAGEHEN
SAGGIER
SAINTED
SALLIED
SALLIES
SALTIER
SALUTED
SALUTES
SALVOES
SAMBAED
SAMISEN
SAMITES
SAMOYED
SAMPLED
SAMPLER
SAMPLES
SANDIER
SANDMEN
SANIBEL
SAPPIER
SARACEN
SARALEE
SARAZEN
SARKIER
SASSIER
SASSIES
SATCHEL
SATINET
SATIRES
SAUCIER
SAUNTER
SAUTEED
SAVAGED
SAVAGER
SAVAGES
SAVORED
SAVVIER
SAYWHEN
SCALDED
SCALIER
SCALPED
SCALPEL
SCALPER
SCAMMED
SCAMPED
SCAMPER
SCANNED
SCANNER
SCANTED
SCANTER
SCARCER
SCARFED
SCARIER
SCARLET
SCARPED
SCARPER
SCARRED
SCARVES
SCATHED
SCATHES
SCATTED
SCATTER
SCENDED
SCENTED
SCEPTER
SCHEMED
SCHEMER
SCHEMES
SCHMEER
SCHMOES
SCOFFED
SCOFFER
SCOLDED
SCOLDER
SCONCES
SCOOPED
SCOOPER
SCOOTED
SCOOTER
SCORNED
SCORNER
SCOURED
SCOURER
SCOUSES
SCOUTED
SCOUTER
SCOWLED
SCOWLER
SCRAPED
SCRAPER
SCRAPES
SCREWED
SCRIBES
SCRIVEN
SCUDDED
SCUFFED
SCULLED
SCULLER
SCUPPER
SCURVES
SCYTHED
SCYTHES
SEABEES
SEAMIER
SEANCES
SEAWEED
SECEDED
SECEDER
SECEDES
SECURED
SECURER
SECURES
SEDATED
SEDATER
SEDATES
SEDGIER
SEDUCED
SEDUCER
SEDUCES
SEEDBED
SEEDIER
SEEPIER
SEESRED
SEETHED
SEETHES
SEICHES
SELTZER
SEMITES
SENATES
SENORES
SERAPES
SERENER
SERRIED
SESAMES
SETTEES
SETTLED
SETTLER
SETTLES
SEVERED
SEVERER
SHADIER
SHAFFER
SHAFTED
SHAGGED
SHAKIER
SHAKOES
SHAMMED
SHANKED
SHANTEY
SHAPLEY
SHARKEY
SHARPED
SHARPEI
SHARPEN
SHARPER
SHATNER
SHATTER
SHAWNEE
SHEARED
SHEARER
SHEAVED
SHEAVES
SHEERED
SHEERER
SHEETED
SHELLED
SHELLER
SHELLEY
SHELTER
SHELVED
SHELVES
SHERBET
SHIFTED
SHIITES
SHILLED
SHIMMER
SHINIER
SHINNED
SHIPMEN
SHIPPED
SHIPPER
SHIRKED
SHIRKER
SHIRLEY
SHIRRED
SHOCKED
SHOCKER
SHODDEN
SHOOTER
SHOPPED
SHOPPER
SHOPPES
SHORTED
SHORTEN
SHORTER
SHOUTED
SHOUTER
SHOWIER
SHOWMEN
SHRIKES
SHRINER
SHRINES
SHRIVEL
SHRIVER
SHRIVES
SHUCKED
SHUCKER
SHUDDER
SHUNNED
SHUNTED
SHUSHED
SHUSHES
SHUTTER
SHYSTER
SICKLES
SIDEBET
SIDEMEN
SIGHTED
SIGNEES
SILKIER
SILLIER
SILLIES
SILTIER
SIMILES
SIMPLER
SIMPLEX
SINGLED
SINGLES
SINUSES
SISSIES
SIXTEEN
SIXTIES
SIZZLED
SIZZLES
SKANKED
SKANKER
SKEETER
SKELTER
SKIDDED
SKIDDER
SKILLED
SKILLET
SKIMMED
SKIMMER
SKIMPED
SKINNED
SKINNER
SKIPPED
SKIPPER
SKIRLED
SKIRRED
SKIRTED
SKITTER
SKOSHES
SKULKED
SKULKER
SKUNKED
SLABBED
SLACKED
SLACKEN
SLACKER
SLAMMED
SLAMMER
SLANDER
SLANTED
SLAPPED
SLASHED
SLASHER
SLASHES
SLATHER
SLATIER
SLATTED
SLEDDED
SLEDDER
SLEDGES
SLEEKED
SLEEKEN
SLEEKER
SLEEPER
SLEETED
SLEEVES
SLENDER
SLICKED
SLICKER
SLIMIER
SLIMMED
SLIMMER
SLINGER
SLINKED
SLIPPED
SLIPPER
SLITHER
SLOBBER
SLOGGED
SLOPPED
SLOSHED
SLOSHES
SLOTTED
SLUDGES
SLUGGED
SLUGGER
SLUICED
SLUICES
SLUMBER
SLUMMED
SLUMPED
SLURPED
SLURRED
SLUSHES
SMACKED
SMACKER
SMALLER
SMARTED
SMARTEN
SMARTER
SMASHED
SMASHER
SMASHES
SMATTER
SMEARED
SMELLED
SMELTED
SMELTER
SMIDGEN
SMIRKED
SMITTEN
SMOKIER
SMOKIES
SMOLDER
SMOTHER
SMUDGED
SMUDGES
SMUGGER
SNACKED
SNACKER
SNAFUED
SNAGGED
SNAKIER
SNAPPED
SNAPPER
SNARLED
SNEAKED
SNEAKER
SNEERED
SNEERER
SNEEZED
SNEEZER
SNEEZES
SNELLEN
SNICKER
SNIFFED
SNIFFER
SNIFTER
SNIGGER
SNIGLET
SNIPPED
SNIPPET
SNOGGED
SNOOKER
SNOOPED
SNOOPER
SNOOTED
SNOOZED
SNOOZES
SNORKEL
SNORTED
SNORTER
SNOWIER
SNOWMEN
SNOWPEA
SNUBBED
SNUFFED
SNUFFER
SNUGGER
SOAPIER
SOBERED
SOBERER
SODDIER
SODDIES
SOFABED
SOFTIES
SOGGIER
SOIGNEE
SOIREES
SOLACES
SOLDIER
SOLIDER
SOLUTES
SOOTHED
SOOTHER
SOOTHES
SOOTIER
SOPPIER
SORITES
SORRIER
SORTIED
SORTIES
SOUGHED
SOUNDED
SOUNDER
SOUPIER
SOURCED
SOURCES
SOUTHEY
SPACIER
SPALLED
SPAMMED
SPAMMER
SPANDEX
SPANIEL
SPANKED
SPANKER
SPANNED
SPANNER
SPARGED
SPARGES
SPARKED
SPARRED
SPARSER
SPATTED
SPATTER
SPAWNED
SPEAKER
SPEARED
SPECCED
SPECIES
SPECKED
SPECTER
SPEEDED
SPEEDER
SPELLED
SPELLER
SPENCER
SPENDER
SPENSER
SPHERES
SPICIER
SPIEGEL
SPIELED
SPIELER
SPIKIER
SPILLED
SPINIER
SPINNER
SPINNEY
SPIRIER
SPITZES
SPLAYED
SPLICED
SPLICER
SPLICES
SPLINES
SPOILED
SPOILER
SPONDEE
SPONGED
SPONGER
SPONGES
SPOOFED
SPOOFER
SPOOKED
SPOOLED
SPOONED
SPOONER
SPORTED
SPOTTED
SPOTTER
SPOUSES
SPOUTED
SPOUTER
SPRAYED
SPRAYER
SPRITES
SPRUCED
SPRUCER
SPRUCES
SPUMIER
SPURNED
SPURNER
SPURRED
SPURTED
SPUTTER
SQUARED
SQUARER
SQUARES
SQUIRED
SQUIRES
STABBED
STABLED
STABLER
STABLES
STACKED
STAFFED
STAFFER
STAGGED
STAGGER
STAGIER
STAIDER
STAINED
STAINER
STALKED
STALKER
STALLED
STAMMER
STAMPED
STANCES
STANDEE
STANLEE
STANLEY
STAPLED
STAPLER
STAPLES
STARKER
STARLET
STARRED
STARTED
STARTER
STARVED
STARVES
STASHED
STASHES
STASSEN
STATUES
STEAMED
STEAMER
STEELED
STEELER
STEEPED
STEEPEN
STEEPER
STEERED
STEERER
STEIGER
STEINEM
STEINER
STEMMED
STENGEL
STEPHEN
STEPPED
STEPPER
STEPPES
STERNER
STETTED
STEUBEN
STICHES
STICKER
STIEGEL
STIFFED
STIFFEN
STIFFER
STIFLED
STIFLES
STILLED
STILLER
STILTED
STINGER
STINKER
STINTED
STIRRED
STIRRER
STOCKED
STOGIES
STOLLEN
STOLLER
STOMPED
STONIER
STOOGES
STOOKED
STOOKEY
STOOPED
STOPPED
STOPPER
STORIED
STORIES
STORMED
STOUTEN
STOUTER
STPETER
STRAFED
STRAFES
STRAYED
STREWED
STREWER
STRIDER
STRIDES
STRIKER
STRIKES
STRIPED
STRIPER
STRIPES
STRIVED
STRIVEN
STRIVER
STRIVES
STROBES
STROKED
STROKES
STRUDEL
STUBBED
STUDDED
STUDIED
STUDIES
STUFFED
STUFFER
STUMPED
STUMPER
STUNNED
STUNNER
STUNTED
STURGES
STYMIED
STYMIES
SUBDUED
SUBDUER
SUBDUES
SUBTLER
SUCCEED
SUDSIER
SUGARED
SULKIER
SULKIES
SULLIED
SULLIES
SULUSEA
SUNDAES
SUNNIER
SUPPLER
SURFIER
SURLIER
SURTSEY
SUTURED
SUTURES
SVELTER
SWABBED
SWAGGER
SWALLET
SWAMPED
SWANKED
SWANKER
SWANSEA
SWAPPED
SWAPPER
SWARMED
SWATHED
SWATHES
SWATTED
SWATTER
SWEARER
SWEATED
SWEATER
SWEENEY
SWEEPER
SWEETEN
SWEETER
SWELLED
SWELTER
SWERVED
SWERVES
SWIFTER
SWIGGED
SWILLED
SWIMMER
SWINGER
SWIRLED
SWISHED
SWISHES
SWITZER
SWOBBED
SWOLLEN
SWONKEN
SWOONED
SWOOPED
SWOPPED
SYNCHED
SYNCHES
SYNFUEL

S•••••E

SACLIKE
SALABLE
SALTINE
SALVAGE
SANJOSE
SANTAFE

SAOTOME
SARALEE
SARDINE
SATIATE
SAUSAGE
SAVABLE
SAWLIKE
SCALENE
SCEPTRE
SCIENCE
SCOTTIE
SCOURGE
SCROOGE
SCRUPLE
SCUFFLE
SCUTTLE
SEABLUE
SEAFIRE
SEAGATE
SEALANE
SEASIDE
SEATTLE
SECLUDE
SECRETE
SEEABLE
SEEHERE
SELVAGE
SENSATE
SERIATE
SERRATE
SERVICE
SERVILE
SESSILE
SETLINE
SEVIGNE
SEVILLE
SHACKLE
SHAMBLE
SHAWNEE
SHEATHE
SHELTIE
SHINGLE
SHUFFLE
SHUTEYE
SHUTTLE
SIAMESE
SILENCE
SINCERE
SINEDIE
SINKAGE
SINLIKE
SISTINE
SITUATE
SIZABLE
SKIPOLE
SKITTLE
SKYBLUE
SKYDIVE
SKYLIKE
SKYLINE
SLOVENE
SMUGGLE
SNAFFLE
SNAPPLE
SNIFFLE
SNIGGLE
SNOCONE
SNUFFLE
SNUGGLE
SOCKEYE
SOIGNEE
SOLFEGE
SOLUBLE
SOMEONE
SONLIKE
SORBATE
SOSUEME
SOTHERE
SOUFFLE
SOUTANE
SOWLIKE
SPACKLE
SPANGLE
SPARKLE
SPECKLE
SPECTRE
SPINDLE
SPLURGE
SPOKANE
SPONDEE
SPUMONE
SQUEEZE
STABILE
STANDEE
STANLEE
STARTLE
STATICE
STATURE
STATUTE
STEELIE
STEEPLE
STERILE
STIPPLE
STOOLIE
STORAGE
STRANGE
STRASSE
STRIATE
STROPHE
STUBBLE
STUMBLE
STYLISE
STYLIZE
STYRENE
SUBLIME
SUBSIDE
SUBSUME
SUBVOCE
SUCRASE
SUCROSE
SUFFICE
SUFFUSE
SULFATE
SULFIDE
SULFITE
SUNLIKE
SUNRISE
SUOJURE
SUPPOSE
SUPREME
SURFACE
SURMISE
SURNAME
SURVIVE
SUSANNE
SUZANNE
SUZETTE
SWADDLE
SWEETIE
SWINDLE
SWIZZLE
SWOOSIE
SYNAPSE
SYRINGE
SYSTOLE

•SE••••

ASEPSIS
ASEPTIC
TSELIOT
TSETSES
USEABLE
USELESS
USERIDS

•S•E•••

ASCENDS
ASCENTS
ASCETIC
ASKEDIN
ASPECTS
ASPERSE
ASSEGAI
ASSENTS
ASSERTS
CSLEWIS
ESSENCE
ESSENES
ESTEEMS
ESTELLE
ESTEVEZ
OSCEOLA
OSIERED
OSSEOUS
OSTEOID
USHERED

•S••E••

ASHIEST
ASHLESS
ESCHEAT
ESCHEWS
ESOTERY
ESTEEMS
ESTHETE
ISOHELS
ISOMERS
ISRAELI
ISSUERS
OSPREYS
OSTLERS
USELESS
USOPENS
USSTEEL
USURERS

•S•••E•

ASHAMED
ASPIRED
ASPIRER
ASPIRES
ASSAYED
ASSAYER
ASSIZES
ASSUMED
ASSUMES
ASSURED
ASSURES
ASUNDER
ESCAPED
ESCAPEE
ESCAPES
ESSAYED
ESSENES
ESTATES
ESTEVEZ
ISHMAEL
OSCINES
OSIERED
OSMOSED
OSMOSES
PSALMED
PSALTER
PSYCHED
PSYCHES
TSETSES
USHERED
USSTEEL
USURIES
USURPED
USURPER

•S••••E

ASARULE
ASCRIBE
ASININE
ASKANCE
ASPERSE
ASSLIKE
ASSUAGE
ASTAIRE
ASTARTE
ASTRIDE
ESCAPEE
ESPOUSE
ESQUIRE
ESSENCE
ESTELLE
ESTHETE
ISOLATE
ISOTOPE
OSBORNE
OSSICLE
TSQUARE
USEABLE

••SE•••

ABSENCE
ABSENTS
ARSENAL
ARSENIC
ARSENIO
ASSEGAI
ASSENTS
ASSERTS
AXSEEDS
BASEHIT
BASEMAN
BASEMEN
BASENJI
BASEPAY
BESEECH
BESEEMS
BISECTS
CASELAW
CASERNE
CASERNS
DESERTS
DESERVE
DISEASE
DRSEUSS
EASEDIN
EASEDUP
EASEFUL
EASEOFF
EASEOUT
EASESIN
EASESUP
ESSENCE
ESSENES
EXSERTS
GASEOUS
GISELLE
INSEAMS
INSECTS
INSERTS
LISENTE
LOSEOUT
LOSESIT
LYSENKO
MISERLY
MOSELLE
MOSEYED
MUSEFUL
MUSETTE
MUSEUMS
NOSEBAG
NOSEEUM
NOSEGAY
NOSEJOB
NOSEOUT
OBSERVE
ONSERVE
OSSEOUS
PESETAS
POSEURS
RESEALS
RESEATS
RESECTS
RESEEDS
RESELLS
RESENDS
RESENTS
RESERVE
ROSEATE
ROSEBAY
ROSEBUD
ROSELLE
ROSEOIL
ROSERED
ROSETTA
ROSETTE
UNSEALS
UNSEATS
UNSEWED
WISEDUP
WISEGUY
WISEMAN
WISEMEN
WISESUP

••S•E••

ANSWERS
AUSTERE
AXSEEDS
BASKETS
BASSETS
BASTERS
BESEECH
BESEEMS
BESIEGE
BESMEAR
BESPEAK
BOSKETS
BOSWELL
BUSHELS
BUSIEST
BUSTERS
CASHEWS
CASTERS
CISTERN
COSIEST
COSSETS
DASHERS
DESCEND
DESCENT
DESSERT
DISCERN
DISPELS
DISSECT
DISSENT
DISTEND
DOSSERS
DUSTERS
EASIEST
EASTEND
EASTERN
EASTERS
EPSTEIN
FASTENS
FASTEST
FESTERS
FISHERS
FISHERY
FISHEYE
FOSTERS
GASJETS
GASKETS
GASLESS
GASPERS
GASSERS
GOSPELS
GOSSETT
GUSHERS
GUSSETS
HASBEEN
HASTENS
HISSERS
HOSIERS
HOSIERY
HOSTELS
HOSTESS
HUSKERS
HUSSEIN
INSPECT
INSTEAD
INSTEPS
ISSUERS
JASPERS
JESTERS
JOSSERS
KISSERS
KOSHERS
LASHERS
LESSEES
LESSENS
LISTEES
LISTELS
LISTENS
LUSHEST
LUSTERS
MASHERS
MASKERS
MASSEUR
MASTERS
MASTERY
MISDEAL
MISDEED
MISHEAR
MISLEAD
MISREAD
MISTERS
MOSHERS
MOSLEMS
MUSHERS
MUSKEGS
MUSKETS
MUSSELS
MUSTERS
MYSTERY
NASCENT
NESTEGG
NESTERS
NOSEEUM
NOSHERS
NOSIEST
NOSWEAT
OBSCENE
OUSTERS
OYSTERS
PASSELS
PASSERS
PASSEUL
PASTELS
PASTERN
PASTEUP
PASTEUR
PESTERS
POSHEST
POSSESS
POSSETS
POSTERN
POSTERS
RASHERS
RASHEST
RASPERS
RASTERS
RESEEDS
RESPECT
RESTERS
RISKERS
ROSIEST
ROSTERS
ROSWELL
RUSHEES
RUSHERS
RUSSELL
RUSSETS
RUSSETY
SASSERS
SESTETS
SISTERS
SOSUEME
SUSPECT
SUSPEND
SYSTEMS
TASSELS
TASTERS
TESSERA
TESTEES
TESTERS
TOSSERS
TUSKERS
ULSTERS
UNSPENT
UNSWEPT
UPSWEEP
UPSWEPT
USSTEEL
VASTEST
VESPERS
VESSELS
VESTEES
VISCERA
WASHERS
WASTERS
WESTEND
WESTERN
WISHERS
YESDEAR

••S••E•

APSIDES
ASSAYED
ASSAYER
ASSIZES
ASSUMED
ASSUMES
ASSURED
ASSURES
AUSSIES
BASEMEN
BASQUES
BESIDES
BESTMEN
BESTREW
BISQUES
BOSKIER
BOSSIER
BUSBIES
BUSHIER
BUSHMEN
BUSTLED
BUSTLES
CASHIER
CASQUED
CASQUES
CASTLED
CASTLES
COSINES
COSTNER
CUSHIER
CUSSLER
DESIRED
DESIREE
DESIRES
DESKSET
DISCOED
DISHIER
DISOBEY
DISUSED
DOSAGES
DOSSIER
DUSKIER
DUSTIER
DUSTMEN
ENSILED
ENSILES
ENSKIED
ENSKIES
ENSURED
ENSURES
ESSAYED
ESSENES
FESCUES
FISCHER
FISHIER
FISHNET
FUSSIER
FUSTIER
GASSIER
GESSOES
GUSHIER
GUSSIED
GUSSIES
GUSTIER
GUSTOES
HASBEEN
HASSLED
HASSLES
HASTIER
HOSTLER
HUSKIER
HUSKIES
HUSSIES
HUSTLED
HUSTLER
HUSTLES
INSIDER
INSIDES
INSOLES
INSURED
INSURER
INSURES
JOSTLED
JOSTLER
JOSTLES
KESTREL
KISHKES
LASSIES
LASSOED
LASSOER
LASSOES
LESSEES
LISTEES
LUSTIER
LUSTRED
LUSTRES
MASHIES
MASQUES
MASSIER
MESHIER
MESSIER
MISCUED
MISCUES
MISDEED
MISDOES
MISSIES
MISSTEP
MISTIER
MISUSED
MISUSES
MOSEYED
MOSQUES
MOSSIER
MUSCLED
MUSCLES
MUSHIER
MUSKIER
MUSKIES
MUSSIER
MUSTIER
MUSTSEE
NASTIER
NESTLED
NESTLER
NESTLES
ONSIDES
PASSKEY
PASTIER
PESKIER
PESTLED
PESTLES
POSITED
POSTMEN
PUSHIER
RASPIER
RASSLED
RASSLES
RESALES
RESAWED
RESCUED
RESCUER
RESCUES
RESHOES
RESIDED
RESIDES
RESILED
RESILES
RESOLED
RESOLES
RESUMED
RESUMES
RISKIER
ROSERED
ROSSSEA
RUSHEES
RUSHIER
RUSTIER
RUSTLED
RUSTLER
RUSTLES
SASSIER
SASSIES
SESAMES
SISSIES
TASTIER
TESTEES
TESTIER
TISANES
TISSUES
TUSSLED
TUSSLES
UNSATED
UNSCREW
UNSEWED
UPSWEEP
USSTEEL
VASTIER
VESTEES
VISAGES
VISITED
WASHIER
WASPIER
WASTREL
WISEMEN
WISPIER
ZESTIER

••S•••E

ABSENCE
ABSOLVE
ASSLIKE
ASSUAGE
ATSTAKE
AUSPICE
AUSTERE
BESIEGE
BESPOKE
BUSFARE
BUSLINE
CASCADE
CASERNE
CASTILE
COSTUME
DASYURE
DESERVE
DESIREE
DESPISE
DESPITE
DESTINE
DISABLE
DISEASE
DISLIKE
DISPOSE
DISPUTE
DISROBE
ENSLAVE
ENSNARE
ENSUITE
ERSKINE
ESSENCE
FASTONE
FESTIVE
FISHEYE
FISSILE
FISSURE
GESTATE
GESTURE
GISELLE
HOSPICE
HOSTAGE
HOSTILE
IFSTONE
INSCAPE
INSHAPE
INSPIRE
INSTATE
INSTORE
INSTYLE
JASMINE
JUSTICE
JUSTINE
LASAGNE
LASALLE
LISENTE
LISSOME
MASSAGE
MASSIVE
MCSWINE
MESSAGE
MISDATE
MISDONE
MISFILE
MISFIRE
MISLIKE
MISMATE
MISNAME
MISRULE
MISSILE
MISSIVE
MISTAKE
MISTYPE
MOSELLE
MUSETTE
MUSTSEE
NASTASE
NESCAFE
OBSCENE
OBSCURE
OBSERVE
ONSERVE
ONSHORE
ONSTAGE
OSSICLE
PASSAGE
PASSIVE
PASTDUE
PASTIME
PASTURE
PISCINE
PISMIRE
PISTOLE
POSTAGE
POSTURE
RESCALE
RESERVE
RESIDUE
RESOLVE
RESPIRE
RESPITE
RESTAGE
RESTATE
RESTIVE
RESTORE
RESTYLE
RESURGE
RISIBLE
RISSOLE
ROSALIE
ROSANNE
ROSEATE
ROSELLE
ROSETTE
RUSHDIE
SESSILE
SISTINE
SOSUEME
SUSANNE
SYSTOLE
TOSCALE
TOSPARE
UPSCALE
UPSTAGE
UPSTATE
UPSURGE
VESTIGE
VESTURE
VISIBLE
WASTAGE

•••SE••

ABUSERS
ANISEED
BASSETS
BERSERK
BOXSEAT
CANSECO
CARSEAT
CATSEYE
CENSERS
CHASERS
CHISELS
CLOSEBY
CLOSEIN
CLOSELY
CLOSEST
CLOSETS
CLOSEUP
CONSENT
CORSETS
COSSETS
DAMSELS
DANSEUR
DENSELY
DENSEST
DESSERT
DIESELS
DISSECT
DISSENT
DORSETT
DOSSERS
DOWSERS
ELYSEES
ERASERS
EROSELY
FALSELY
FALSEST
FURSEAL
GASSERS
GEYSERS
GINSENG
GODSEND
GOSSETT
GUSSETS
HAWSERS
HAYSEED
HERSELF
HIMSELF
HISSERS
HOTSEAT
HUSSEIN
JERSEYS
JOSSERS
KAISERS
KISSERS
LEASERS
LESSEES
LESSENS
LINSEED
LOOSELY
LOOSENS
LOOSEST
LOUSEUP
MASSEUR
MORSELS
MOUSERS
MUSSELS
NONSELF
NURSERS
NURSERY
OFFSETS
ONESELF
OURSELF
OUTSELL
OUTSETS
PARSECS
PARSEES
PARSERS
PASSELS
PASSERS
PASSEUL
PENSEES
PERSEID
PERSEUS
PHASEIN
PHASERS
PORSENA
POSSESS
POSSETS
PRESELL
PRESENT
PRESETS
PROSERS
PURSERS
RAISERS
RAISEUP
ROUSERS
RUSSELL
RUSSETS
RUSSETY
SASSERS
SUBSETS
SUNSETS
TASSELS
TEASELS
TEASERS
TEASETS
TENSELY
TENSEST
TENSEUP
TERSELY
TERSEST
TESSERA
THESEUS
THYSELF
TINSELS
TOSSERS
TRISECT
VESSELS
WEASELS
WORSENS
WOWSERS

•••S•E•

ABASHED
ABASHES
ABYSSES
AMASSED
AMASSER
AMASSES
ANISEED
ANTSIER
ARTSIER
AUSSIES
BANSHEE
BATSMEN
BIASSED
BITSIER
BLASTED
BLASTER
BLESSED
BLESSES
BLISTER
BLUSHED
BLUSHER
BLUSHES
BLUSTER
BOASTED
BOASTER
BOBSLED
BOLSTER
BOOSLER
BOOSTED
BOOSTER
BOSSIER
BOXSTEP
BRASHER
BRASSES
BRISKER
BRISKET
BRUSHED
BRUSHES
CHASSES
CHASTEN
CHASTER
CHESTER
CLASHED
CLASHES
CLASPED
CLASSED
CLASSES
CLUSTER
COASTED
COASTER
CRASHED
CRASHES
CRASSER
CRESSES
CRESTED
CRISPED
CRISPER
CROSIER
CROSSED
CROSSER
CROSSES
CRUSHED
CRUSHER
CRUSHES
CRUSTED
CUSSLER
DAISIES
DITSIER
DOGSLED
DOSSIER
DRESDEN
DRESSED
DRESSER
DRESSES
EDASNER
EGESTED
ELYSEES
ENISLED
ENISLES
EXISTED
FEASTED

FLASHED
FLASHER
FLASHES
FLESHED
FLESHES
FLOSSED
FLOSSES
FLUSHED
FLUSHES
FLUSTER
FOCSLES
FOISTED
FORSTER
FRASIER
FRESHEN
FRESHER
FRESHET
FRISBEE
FRISKED
FROSTED
FUBSIER
FUSSIER
GADSDEN
GAGSTER
GASSIER
GESSOES
GETSSET
GHOSTED
GIPSIES
GLASSED
GLASSES
GLISTEN
GLOSSED
GLOSSES
GNASHED
GNASHES
GOOSIER
GORSIER
GRASPED
GRASSED
GRASSES
GROSSED
GROSSER
GROSSES
GUESSED
GUESSER
GUESSES
GUESTED
GUSSIED
GUSSIES
GUTSIER
GYPSIES
HAMSTER
HARSHEN
HARSHER
HASSLED
HASSLES
HAYSEED
HEISTED
HEMSLEY
HERSHEY
HIPSTER
HOISTED
HOLSTER
HOOSIER
HORSIER
HUSSIES
INASTEW
JANSSEN
JOISTED
JOUSTED
JOUSTER
KAISHEK
KINSMEN

KNESSET
KNISHES
LAISSEZ
LASSIES
LASSOED
LASSOER
LASSOES
LEASHED
LEASHES
LEISTER
LESSEES
LETSSEE
LINSEED
LOBSTER
LOESSER
LOESSES
LOUSIER
MARSHES
MASSIER
MEASLES
MEISSEN
MEISTER
MESSIER
MISSIES
MISSTEP
MOBSTER
MOISTEN
MOISTER
MONSTER
MOSSIER
MOUSIER
MOUSSED
MOUSSES
MUSSIER
NEWSIER
NEWSIES
NEWSMEN
NOISIER
NUTSIER
ODYSSEY
OLDSTER
ONESTEP
ORESTES
OUTSTEP
PAISLEY
PANSIES
PARSEES
PARSLEY
PASSKEY
PATSIES
PENSEES
PIASTER
PILSNER
PLASHED
PLASHES
PLASTER
PLUSHER
PLUSHES
PLUSSES
POTSIER
PRESLEY
PRESSED
PRESSER
PRESSES
PROSIER
PROSPER
PUNSTER
PURSIER
PURSUED
PURSUER
PURSUES
QUASHED
QUASHES
QUESTED

RASSLED
RASSLES
ROASTED
ROASTER
ROISTER
ROOSTED
ROOSTER
ROSSSEA
ROUSTED
SASSIER
SASSIES
SEESRED
SHUSHED
SHUSHES
SHYSTER
SISSIES
SKOSHES
SLASHED
SLASHER
SLASHES
SLOSHED
SLOSHES
SLUSHES
SMASHED
SMASHER
SMASHES
STASHED
STASHES
STASSEN
SUDSIER
SWISHED
SWISHES
TANSIES
TAPSTER
TARSIER
TIPSIER
TIPSTER
TISSUES
TOASTED
TOASTER
TOUSLED
TOUSLES
TRASHED
TRASHES
TRESSES
TRUSSED
TRUSSES
TRUSTED
TRUSTEE
TRYSTED
TRYSTER
TUSSLED
TUSSLES
TWISTED
TWISTER
TWOSTEP
ULYSSES
UNASKED
WEBSTER
WHISHED
WHISHES
WHISKED
WHISKER
WHISKEY
WHISPER
WOOSTER
WORSTED
WRESTED

•••S••E
ABUSIVE
APOSTLE
ARCSINE
ARISTAE

ATISSUE
AWESOME
BANSHEE
BEASTIE
BEDSIDE
BRASSIE
BRISTLE
BRUSQUE
CAPSIZE
CAPSULE
CATSEYE
CENSURE
CLOSURE
CONSOLE
CONSUME
CORSAGE
CRUSADE
CUISINE
CURSIVE
ELUSIVE
EPISODE
EPISTLE
ERASURE
EROSIVE
EVASIVE
EYESORE
FISSILE
FISSURE
FORSAKE
FORSALE
FORSURE
FRISBEE
FULSOME
GLOSSAE
GOESAPE
GRISTLE
GUMSHOE
GYMSHOE
HIRSUTE
IRKSOME
KIRSTIE
LEISURE
LETSSEE
LISSOME
MASSAGE
MASSIVE
MEASURE
MESSAGE
MIDSIZE
MISSILE
MISSIVE
NETSUKE
NOISOME
NOTSURE
OFFSIDE
OFFSITE
OUTSIDE
OUTSIZE
PASSAGE
PASSIVE
PENSIVE
PIASTRE
PLOSIVE
PORSCHE
PRESAGE
PRESALE
PRESIDE
PRESUME
PULSATE
REISSUE
RISSOLE
SAUSAGE
SEASIDE
SENSATE

SESSILE
SUBSIDE
SUBSUME
TAGSALE
TENSILE
TENSIVE
THISTLE
TOESHOE
TONSURE
TOPSIDE
TRESTLE
TRUSTEE
TWOSOME
WAYSIDE
WEBSITE
WHISTLE
WINSOME
WRESTLE

••••SE•
ABYSSES
ACCUSED
ACCUSER
ACCUSES
ADVISED
ADVISER
ADVISES
ALIASES
ALUNSER
AMASSED
AMASSER
AMASSES
APHESES
APPOSED
APPOSES
ARALSEA
AROUSED
AROUSES
ARRASES
ARRISES
ATLASES
AVULSED
AVULSES
BEMUSED
BEMUSES
BENTSEN
BERNSEN
BETISES
BIASSED
BIGOSES
BLESSED
BLESSES
BLOUSED
BLOUSES
BOLUSES
BONESET
BONUSES
BOURSES
BRAISED
BRAISES
BRASSES
BROWSED
BROWSER
BROWSES
BRUISED
BRUISER
BRUISES
CAMISES
CAYUSES
CHAISES
CHASSES
CHEESES
CHELSEA
CHOOSER

CHOOSES
CLASSED
CLASSES
CLAUSES
COARSEN
COARSER
COUNSEL
COURSED
COURSER
COURSES
CRASSER
CREASED
CREASES
CRESSES
CROSSED
CROSSER
CROSSES
CRUISED
CRUISER
CRUISES
CURTSEY
DATASET
DEADSEA
DEADSET
DEBASED
DEBASES
DEEPSEA
DEEPSET
DEFUSED
DEFUSES
DEMISED
DEMISES
DEMPSEY
DEPOSED
DEPOSER
DEPOSES
DESKSET
DEVISED
DEVISES
DINESEN
DISUSED
DREISER
DRESSED
DRESSER
DRESSES
DROWSED
DROWSES
ECDYSES
EFFUSED
EFFUSES
ELAPSED
ELAPSES
EMERSED
ENCASED
ENCASES
ENDUSER
ENDUSES
EVULSED
EVULSES
EXCISED
EXCISES
EXCUSED
EXCUSES
EXPOSED
EXPOSES
FICUSES
FLENSED
FLENSES
FLOSSED
FLOSSES
FOCUSED
FOCUSES
FORESEE
FRAISES

GENESEE
GENESES
GETSSET
GLASSED
GLASSES
GLOSSED
GLOSSES
GRASSED
GRASSES
GREASED
GREASER
GREASES
GROSSED
GROSSER
GROSSES
GROUSED
GROUSER
GROUSES
GUESSED
GUESSER
GUESSES
HANDSET
HARDSET
HEADSET
HOARSEN
HOARSER
HOLYSEE
ILLUSED
ILLUSES
IMPOSED
IMPOSES
INCASED
INCASES
INCISED
INCISES
INFUSED
INFUSES
IODISED
IODISES
IONISED
IONISES
JANSSEN
JONESES
KARASEA
KNESSET
LAISSEZ
LETSSEE
LIAISED
LIAISES
LINDSEY
LOESSER
LOESSES
LOOKSEE
LORISES
LOTUSES
MALMSEY
MEIOSES
MEISSEN
MINDSET
MINUSES
MISUSED
MISUSES
MITOSES
MOONSET
MOUSSED
MOUSSES
MUSTSEE
NAILSET
NEMESES
NEXUSES
NIELSEN
NONUSER
OBTUSER
ODYSSEY

OPENSEA
OPPOSED
OPPOSER
OPPOSES
OSMOSED
OSMOSES
OVERSEA
OVERSEE
PAULSEN
PERUSED
PERUSER
PERUSES
PHRASED
PHRASES
PLEASED
PLEASER
PLEASES
PLUSSES
PRAISED
PRAISER
PRAISES
PRESSED
PRESSER
PRESSES
QUONSET
RAMESES
REBUSES
RECUSED
RECUSES
REFUSED
REFUSER
REFUSES
REPOSED
REPOSES
REVISED
REVISER
REVISES
ROSSSEA
SAMISEN
SCOUSES
SINUSES
SPARSER
SPENSER
SPOUSES
STASSEN
SULUSEA
SURTSEY
SWANSEA
TALUSES
TRESSES
TROUSER
TRUSSED
TRUSSES
TSETSES
TYPESET
ULYSSES
UNCASED
UNCASES
UNWISER
UPRISEN
UPRISES
VALISES
VIRUSES
WELLSET
WOOLSEY

••••S•E
ARTISTE
ATISSUE
AUGUSTE
BATISTE
BEATSME
BRASSIE
CELESTE

DEHISCE
DEMESNE
ENMASSE
FINESSE
FOOTSIE
FORESEE
GENESEE
GLOSSAE
HOLYSEE
IMPASSE
INHASTE
LACOSTE
LETSSEE
LOOKSEE
MAJESTE
MATISSE
MEDUSAE
MODISTE
MUSTSEE
OVERSEE
PELISSE
REBASTE
REISSUE
REPASTE
RIPOSTE
STRASSE
SWOOSIE
TOOTSIE
TRIESTE
WOEISME

•••••SE
ACEROSE
ADIPOSE
ADVERSE
AGONISE
AIRBASE
AMBROSE
AMYLASE
ANALYSE
ANODISE
APPEASE
APPRISE
ASPERSE
ATOMISE
BAPTISE
BECAUSE
BERNESE
BURMESE
BYANOSE
CABOOSE
CARCASE
CAROUSE
CHEMISE
CHINESE
CLEANSE
COCHISE
COMPOSE
CONCISE
CONFUSE
CONTUSE
DEFENSE
DELUISE
DESPISE
DIFFUSE
DIOCESE
DISEASE
DISPOSE
DIVERSE
DONJOSE
ECLIPSE
EGGCASE
ELLIPSE
ENCLOSE

ENDORSE
ENDWISE
ENMASSE
ENTHUSE
ESPOUSE
EXPANSE
EXPENSE
FINESSE
GENOESE
GLIMPSE
GLUCOSE
HELOISE
IDOLISE
IMMENSE
IMMERSE
IMPASSE
IMPULSE
INCENSE
INCLOSE
INDORSE
INHOUSE
INPHASE
INTENSE
INTERSE
INVERSE
ITEMISE
JACCUSE
LACTASE
LACTOSE
LAVALSE
LICENSE
LIONISE
LOWRISE
MALAISE
MALTESE
MALTOSE
MATISSE
MELROSE
MIDRISE
MORTISE
NASTASE
OBVERSE
OFFBASE
OFFENSE
OLDROSE
OPEROSE
OVERUSE
OXIDASE
OXIDISE
PAPOOSE
PELISSE
PRECISE
PREMISE
PROFUSE
PROMISE
PROPOSE
PUGNOSE
PURPOSE
REALISE
RECHOSE
RECLUSE
REDROSE
RELAPSE
RELEASE
REMORSE
REPRISE
REPULSE
RERAISE
RERINSE
REVERSE
SANJOSE
SIAMESE
STRASSE
STYLISE

SUCRASE
SUCROSE
SUFFUSE
SUNRISE
SUPPOSE
SURMISE
SYNAPSE
TEAROSE
TRAIPSE
TWOBASE
UNCLOSE
UNHORSE
UNLOOSE
UPCLOSE
UPRAISE
UTILISE
VAMOOSE
VERBOSE

SF•••••
SFUMATO

S•F••••
SAFARIS
SAFFRON
SIFTERS
SIFTING
SOFABED
SOFFITS
SOFTENS
SOFTEST
SOFTIES
SOFTISH
SOFTTOP
SUFFERS
SUFFICE
SUFFOLK
SUFFUSE

S••F•••
SAFFRON
SANFORD
SAWFISH
SCOFFED
SCOFFER
SCUFFED
SCUFFLE
SEAFANS
SEAFIRE
SEAFOOD
SELFISH
SERFDOM
SHAFFER
SHAFTED
SHIFTED
SHOFARS
SHUFFLE
SIXFOLD
SNAFFLE
SNAFUED
SNIFFAT
SNIFFED
SNIFFER
SNIFFLE
SNIFFLY
SNIFTER
SNUFFED
SNUFFER
SNUFFLE
SNUFFLY
SOFFITS
SOLFEGE
SOUFFLE
STAFFED

STAFFER
STIFFED
STIFFEN
STIFFER
STIFFLY
STIFLED
STIFLES
STUFFED
STUFFER
SUFFERS
SUFFICE
SUFFOLK
SUFFUSE
SULFATE
SULFIDE
SULFITE
SUNFISH
SURFACE
SURFEIT
SURFERS
SURFIER
SURFING
SWIFTER
SWIFTLY
SYNFUEL

S•••F••
SACKFUL
SANDFLY
SCARFED
SCOFFED
SCOFFER
SCRUFFS
SCRUFFY
SCUFFED
SCUFFLE
SEENFIT
SEESFIT
SELLFOR
SENDFOR
SENTFOR
SENUFOS
SHAFFER
SHOOFLY
SHOPFUL
SHOTFOR
SHRIFTS
SHUFFLE
SIGHFUL
SKILFUL
SKINFUL
SNAFFLE
SNIFFAT
SNIFFED
SNIFFER
SNIFFLE
SNIFFLY
SNUFFED
SNUFFER
SNUFFLE
SNUFFLY
SONGFUL
SOUFFLE
SOULFUL
SPOOFED
SPOOFER
STAFFED
STAFFER
STIFFED
STIFFEN
STIFFER
STIFFLY
STIRFRY
STRAFED

STRAFES
STUFFED
STUFFER

S••••F•
SALSIFY
SANTAFE
SATISFY
SCARIFY
SCRUFFS
SCRUFFY
SEALOFF
SEENOFF
SEESOFF
SELLOFF
SENDOFF
SENTOFF
SETSOFF
SHERIFF
SHOWOFF
SHUTOFF
SIGNIFY
SIGNOFF
SKILIFT
SOLDOFF
SPECIFY
SPINOFF
SPUNOFF
STOPOFF
STUPEFY

S•••••F
SEALOFF
SEAWOLF
SEENOFF
SEESOFF
SELLOFF
SENDOFF
SENTOFF
SETSOFF
SHADOOF
SHERIFF
SHEWOLF
SHORTOF
SHOWOFF
SHUTOFF
SIGNOFF
SOLDOFF
SPEAKOF
SPINOFF
SPOKEOF
SPUNOFF
STOPOFF
SUNROOF

•SF••••
ASFARAS

•S•F•••
ASHFORD
ASOFNOW

•S••F••
ASKSFOR
OSSIFIC

••SF•••
BUSFARE
MISFILE
MISFIRE
MISFITS

••S•F••
BASHFUL
DISHFUL
EASEFUL
FISHFRY
FISTFUL
HUSHFUL
INSOFAR
LUSTFUL
MUSEFUL
OSSIFIC
PASSFOR
PUSHFUL
RESTFUL
TESTFLY
WISHFUL
WISTFUL
ZESTFUL

••S••F•
CASTOFF
DASHOFF
DISTAFF
DUSTOFF
EASEOFF
EASYOFF
JUSTIFY
KISSOFF
MASSIFS
MASTIFF
MUSTAFA
MYSTIFY
NESCAFE
PASSOFF
PUSHOFF
RUSHOFF
TESTIFY
TOSSOFF
WASHOFF

••S•••F
CASTOFF
DASHOFF
DISTAFF
DUSTOFF
EASEOFF
EASYOFF
KISSOFF
MASTIFF
PASSOFF
PUSHOFF
RUSHOFF
TOSSOFF
WASHOFF

•••SF••
AIMSFOR
ASKSFOR
GOESFOR
GUNSFOR
LAYSFOR
LETSFLY
OPTSFOR
PASSFOR
PAYSFOR
RUNSFOR
SEESFIT
THUSFAR

•••S•F•
BEGSOFF
BUGSOFF
BUYSOFF
CUTSOFF
DIESOFF
FALSIFY

FOBSOFF
GETSOFF
GOESOFF
HOPSOFF
KISSOFF
LAYSOFF
LETSOFF
LOGSOFF
MASSIFS
NODSOFF
PASSOFF
PAYSOFF
POPSOFF
PUTSOFF
RIPSOFF
RUBSOFF
RUNSOFF
SALSIFY
SEESOFF
SETSOFF
TAPSOFF
TEESOFF
TIPSOFF
TOPSOFF
TOSSOFF
VERSIFY

•••S••F

BEGSOFF
BUGSOFF
BUYSOFF
CUTSOFF
DIESOFF
FOBSOFF
GETSOFF
GOESOFF
HERSELF
HIMSELF
HOPSOFF
KISSOFF
LAYSOFF
LETSOFF
LOGSOFF
NETSURF
NODSOFF
NONSELF
ONESELF
OURSELF
PASSOFF
PAYSOFF
POPSOFF
PUTSOFF
RIPSOFF
RUBSOFF
RUNSOFF
SEESOFF
SETSOFF
TAPSOFF
TEESOFF
THYSELF
TIPSOFF
TOPSOFF
TOSSOFF

••••SF•

SATISFY

••••S•F

HEARSOF
TELLSOF

S•G••••

SAGEHEN
SAGGIER
SAGGING
SAGINAW
SAGUARO
SEGMENT
SEGOVIA
SIGHERS
SIGHFUL
SIGHING
SIGHTED
SIGHTLY
SIGMUND
SIGNALS
SIGNEES
SIGNERS
SIGNETS
SIGNIFY
SIGNING
SIGNOFF
SIGNOUT
SIGNSIN
SIGNSON
SIGNSUP
SOGGIER
SOGGILY
SUGARED
SUGGEST

S••G•••

SAGGIER
SAGGING
SANGOUT
SANGRIA
SARGENT
SEAGATE
SEAGIRT
SEAGRAM
SEAGULL
SEDGIER
SHAGGED
SHOGUNS
SINGERS
SINGING
SINGLED
SINGLES
SINGOUT
SINGSTO
SIXGUNS
SLIGHTS
SLOGANS
SLOGGED
SLUGGED
SLUGGER
SMUGGER
SMUGGLE
SNAGGED
SNIGGER
SNIGGLE
SNIGLET
SNOGGED
SNUGGER
SNUGGLE
SOGGIER
SOGGILY
SOIGNEE
SONGFUL
SORGHUM
SOUGHED
SPIGOTS
STAGERS
STAGGED
STAGGER
STAGIER
STAGILY
STAGING
STIGMAS
STOGIES
STYGIAN
SUGGEST
SUNGODS
SURGEON
SURGERY
SURGING
SWAGGER
SWIGGED
SYNGMAN

S•••G••

SAVAGED
SAVAGER
SAVAGES
SCRAGGY
SENEGAL
SEVIGNE
SHAGGED
SHANGRI
SHINGLE
SHOTGUN
SLEDGES
SLEIGHS
SLEIGHT
SLINGER
SLOEGIN
SLOGGED
SLOUGHS
SLUDGES
SLUGGED
SLUGGER
SMIDGEN
SMUDGED
SMUDGES
SMUGGER
SMUGGLE
SNAGGED
SNIGGER
SNIGGLE
SNOGGED
SNUGGER
SNUGGLE
SPANGLE
SPANGLY
SPARGED
SPARGES
SPIEGEL
SPONGED
SPONGER
SPONGES
STAGGED
STAGGER
STEIGER
STENGEL
STIEGEL
STINGER
STINGOS
STOOGES
STOPGAP
STUNGUN
STURGES
SWAGGER
SWIGGED
SWINGBY
SWINGER

S••••G•

SALVAGE
SAPSAGO
SARONGS
SAUSAGE
SAVINGS
SAWLOGS
SAYINGS
SCOURGE
SCRAGGY
SCROOGE
SEABAGS
SEADOGS
SEALEGS
SELVAGE
SIDINGS
SINKAGE
SIZINGS
SKYHIGH
SOLFEGE
SOWBUGS
SPLURGE
SPRINGS
SPRINGY
STALAGS
STORAGE
STRANGE
STRINGS
STRINGY
SUNDOGS
SYNERGY
SYRINGA
SYRINGE

S•••••G

SACKING
SAGGING
SAILING
SALTING
SALVING
SAMSUNG
SANDBAG
SANDHOG
SANDING
SAPLING
SAPPING
SASSING
SCALING
SCARING
SCOPING
SCORING
SEABORG
SEALING
SEAMING
SEARING
SEASLUG
SEATING
SEEDING
SEEKING
SEEMING
SEEPING
SEINING
SEIZING
SELLING
SEMILOG
SENDING
SENSING
SERLING
SERVING
SETTING
SHADING
SHAKING
SHAMING
SHAPING
SHARING
SHAVING
SHEBANG
SHINDIG
SHINING
SHOEING
SHOOING
SHORING
SHOVING
SHOWDOG
SHOWING
SIBLING
SICCING
SIDLING
SIFTING
SIGHING
SIGNING
SILOING
SILTING
SINGING
SINKING
SIPPING
SITTING
SKATING
SKEWING
SLAKING
SLATING
SLAVING
SLEDDOG
SLICING
SLIDING
SLOPING
SLOWING
SMILING
SMITING
SMOKING
SNAKING
SNARING
SNIPING
SNORING
SNOWING
SOAKING
SOAPING
SOARING
SOBBING
SOCKING
SODDING
SOILING
SOLOING
SOLVING
SOPPING
SORTING
SOURING
SPACING
SPADING
SPARING
SPAYING
SPECING
SPEWING
SPICING
SPIKING
SPITING
SPOKING
SPUMING
STAGING
STAKING
STARING
STATING
STAVING
STAYING
STEWING
STOKING
STONING
STORING
STOWING
STYLING
SUBBING
SUCKING
SUDSING
SUITING
SULKING
SUMMING
SUNNING
SUPPING
SURFING
SURGING
SUSSING
SWAYING
SWIPING
SYNCING

•SG••••

USGRANT

•S•G•••

ISOGONS

•S••G••

ASSEGAI
ASSIGNS
USINGUP

•S•••G•

ASSUAGE

•S••••G

ESPYING
ISSUING

••SG•••

BUSGIRL
DISGUST

••S•G••

ASSEGAI
ASSIGNS
COSIGNS
DESIGNS
DOSAGES
ENSIGNS
INSIGHT
KOSYGIN
LASAGNA
LASAGNE
NOSEGAY
ONSIGHT
RESIGNS
VISAGES
WISEGUY

••S••G•

ASSUAGE
BESIEGE
CASINGS
GASBAGS
GASLOGS
HOSTAGE
MASSAGE
MESSAGE
MUSKEGS
NESTEGG
ONSTAGE
PASSAGE
POSTAGE
RESINGS
RESTAGE
RESURGE
RISINGS
UNSNAGS
UPSTAGE
UPSURGE
VESTIGE
WASTAGE

••S•••G

BASHING
BASKING
BASTING
BESTING
BOSSING
BUSHHOG
BUSHING
BUSHPIG
BUSKING
BUSSING
BUSTING
BUSYING
CASHING
CASTING
CESSING
COSHING
COSTING
CUSHING
CUSSING
DASHING
DISHING
DISHRAG
DISSING
DUSTING
ENSUING
FASTING
FESSING
FISHING
FUSSING
GASHING
GASPING
GOSLING
GUSHING
GUSTING
HASHING
HASPING
HASTING
HISSING
HOSTING
HUSHING
HUSKING
ISSUING
JESTING
JOSHING
KISSING
LASHING
LASTING
LESSING
LISPING
LISTING
LUSTING
MASHING
MASKING
MASSING
MESHING
MESSING
MISSING
MISTING
MOSHING
MOSSING
MUSHING
MUSSING
MUSTANG
NESTEGG
NESTING
NOSEBAG
NOSHING
OUSTING
PASSING
PASTING
POSTBAG
POSTING
PUSHING
RASPING
RESTING
RISKING
RUSHING
RUSTING
SASSING
SUSSING
TASKING
TASTING
TESTING
TOSSING
UPSWING
VESTING
VISAING
WASHING
WASHRAG
WASTING
WISHING
WISPING
WYSIWYG
YESSING

•••SG••

GLASGOW

•••S•G•

AGESAGO
CONSIGN
CORSAGE
HEXSIGN
MASSAGE
MESSAGE
PASSAGE
PRESAGE
SAPSAGO
SAUSAGE

•••S••G

ABASING
ABUSING
AMUSING
ARISING
ARTSONG
BIASING
BOSSING
BOUSING
BUSSING
CAUSING
CEASING
CENSING
CESSING
CHASING
CLOSING
CURSING
CUSSING
DISSING
DOUSING
DOWSING
ERASING
FESSING
FUSSING
GINSENG
GOOSING
HISSING
HORSING
HOUSING
KISSING
LANSING
LAPSING
LEASING
LESSING
LOOSING
LOUSING
MASSING
MESSING
MISSING
MOSSING
MOUSING
MUSSING
NOISING
NOOSING
NURSING
PARSING
PASSING
PAUSING
PHASING
POISING
PROSING
PULSING
PURSING
RAISING
RINSING
ROUSING
SAMSUNG
SASSING
SEASLUG
SENSING
SUDSING
SUSSING
TEASING
TENSING
TOSSING
YESSING

SH•••••

SHACKLE
SHADIER
SHADILY
SHADING
SHADOOF
SHADOWS
SHADOWY
SHAFFER
SHAFTED
SHAGGED
SHAHDOM
SHAKERS
SHAKEUP
SHAKIER
SHAKILY
SHAKING
SHAKOES
SHALALA
SHALLOT
SHALLOW
SHALOMS
SHAMANS
SHAMBLE
SHAMING
SHAMMED
SHAMPOO
SHANANA
SHANGRI
SHANKAR
SHANKED
SHANNON
SHANTEY
SHAPELY
SHAPERS
SHAPEUP
SHAPING
SHAPIRO
SHAPLEY
SHAREIN
SHARERS
SHARING
SHARKEY
SHARPED
SHARPEI
SHARPEN
SHARPER
SHARPLY
SHASTRI
SHATNER
SHATTER
SHAVERS
SHAVING
SHAWNEE
SHAWWAL
SHEARED
SHEARER
SHEATHE
SHEATHS
SHEAVED
SHEAVES
SHEBANG
SHEERED
SHEERER
SHEERLY
SHEETED
SHEIKHS
SHEILAS
SHEKELS
SHELDON
SHELLAC
SHELLED
SHELLER
SHELLEY
SHELTER
SHELTIE
SHELTON
SHELVED
SHELVES
SHEPARD
SHERBET
SHERIFF
SHERMAN
SHERPAS
SHERWIN
SHEWOLF
SHIATSU
SHIELDS
SHIFTED
SHIHTZU
SHIITES
SHIKARI
SHIKOKU
SHILLED
SHIMMER
SHINDIG
SHINERS
SHINGLE
SHINIER
SHINILY
SHINING
SHINNED
SHIPMAN
SHIPMEN
SHIPOUT
SHIPPED
SHIPPER
SHIRKED
SHIRKER
SHIRLEY
SHIRRED
SHIVERS
SHIVERY
SHOCKED
SHOCKER
SHODDEN
SHOEBOX
SHOEING
SHOFARS
SHOGUNS
SHOOFLY
SHOOING
SHOOINS
SHOOKUP
SHOOTAT
SHOOTER
SHOOTUP
SHOPFUL
SHOPPED
SHOPPER
SHOPPES
SHORING
SHORTED
SHORTEN
SHORTER
SHORTLY
SHORTOF
SHOTFOR
SHOTGUN
SHOTOUT
SHOTPUT
SHOULDA
SHOUTED
SHOUTER
SHOVELS
SHOVERS
SHOVING
SHOWBIZ
SHOWDOG
SHOWERS
SHOWERY
SHOWIER
SHOWILY
SHOWING
SHOWMAN
SHOWMEN
SHOWNIN
SHOWOFF
SHOWOUT
SHOWSIN
SHOWSUP
SHRIEKS
SHRIFTS
SHRIKES
SHRILLS
SHRILLY
SHRIMPS
SHRINER
SHRINES
SHRINKS
SHRIVEL
SHRIVER
SHRIVES
SHROUDS
SHRUBBY
SHTICKS
SHUBERT
SHUCKED
SHUCKER
SHUDDER
SHUFFLE
SHUNNED
SHUNTED
SHUSHED
SHUSHES
SHUTEYE
SHUTINS
SHUTOFF
SHUTOUT
SHUTSIN
SHUTSUP
SHUTTER
SHUTTLE
SHYLOCK
SHYNESS
SHYSTER

S•H••••

SAHARAN
SCHATZI
SCHEMAS
SCHEMED
SCHEMER
SCHEMES
SCHERZI
SCHERZO
SCHIRRA
SCHISMS
SCHLEPP
SCHLEPS
SCHLOCK
SCHMEER
SCHMIDT
SCHMOES
SCHMOOS
SCHNAPS
SCHOLAR
SCHOOLS
SCHULTZ
SCHWINN
SPHERES
SUHARTO

S••H•••

SACHEMS
SACHETS
SAMHILL
SASHAYS
SASHBAR
SASHIMI
SAXHORN
SEEHERE
SHAHDOM
SHIHTZU
SICHUAN
SIGHERS
SIGHFUL
SIGHING
SIGHTED
SIGHTLY
SIKHISM
SIPHONS
SKYHIGH
SKYHOOK
SOPHISM
SOPHIST
SOTHERE
SOTHERN
SUBHEAD
SWAHILI
SYPHONS

S•••H••

SAGEHEN
SALCHOW
SANDHOG
SATCHEL
SATCHMO
SAYWHEN
SCATHED
SCATHES
SCYTHED
SCYTHES
SEETHED
SEETHES
SEICHES
SHUSHED
SHUSHES
SILKHAT
SIOBHAN
SIXTHLY
SKOSHES
SLASHED
SLASHER
SLASHES
SLATHER
SLIGHTS
SLITHER
SLOSHED
SLOSHES
SLUSHES
SMASHED
SMASHER
SMASHES
SMASHUP
SMOTHER
SOMEHOW
SOOTHED
SOOTHER
SOOTHES
SORGHUM
SOUGHED
SOUTHEY
STASHED
STASHES
STEPHEN
STICHES
STJOHNS
SULPHUR
SWATHED
SWATHES
SWISHED
SWISHES
SYNCHED
SYNCHES

S••••H•

SAMECHS
SERAPHS
SHEATHE
SHEATHS
SHEIKHS
SKETCHY
SLEIGHS
SLEIGHT
SLEUTHS
SLOUCHY
SLOUGHS
SMOOTHS
SMOOTHY
SNITCHY
SPLASHY
SQUISHY
STARCHY
STROPHE
SWARTHY

S•••••H

SABBATH
SALTISH
SAWFISH
SCRATCH
SCREECH
SCRUNCH
SELFISH
SEVENTH
SICKISH
SKYHIGH
SLAVISH
SOFTISH
SOPWITH
SOTTISH
SOURISH
SPANISH
SPINACH
SPLOTCH
SQUELCH
SQUINCH
STAUNCH
STEALTH
STOMACH
STRETCH
STYLISH
SUNBATH
SUNFISH
SWEDISH
SWINISH

•SH••••

ASHAMED
ASHANTI
ASHBURY
ASHCANS
ASHFORD
ASHIEST
ASHLAND
ASHLARS
ASHLESS
ASHRAMS
ASHTRAY
ISHMAEL
OSHKOSH
TSHIRTS
USHERED

•S•H•••

ASPHALT
BSCHOOL
ESCHEAT
ESCHEWS
ESTHETE
ISOHELS
ISTHMUS

•S••H••

PSYCHED
PSYCHES
PSYCHIC
PSYCHUP
USOSHOW

•S••••H

OSHKOSH
OSTRICH

••SH•••

BASHFUL
BASHING
BISHOPS
BUSHELS
BUSHHOG
BUSHIDO
BUSHIER
BUSHILY
BUSHING
BUSHMAN
BUSHMEN
BUSHPIG
CASHBAR
CASHBOX
CASHCOW
CASHEWS
CASHIER
CASHING

CASHOUT
COSHING
CUSHAWS
CUSHIER
CUSHING
CUSHION
DASHERS
DASHIKI
DASHING
DASHOFF
DISHFUL
DISHIER
DISHING
DISHOUT
DISHPAN
DISHRAG
FASHION
FISHERS
FISHERY
FISHEYE
FISHFRY
FISHIER
FISHILY
FISHING
FISHNET
FISHOUT
GASHING
GOSHAWK
GUSHERS
GUSHIER
GUSHILY
GUSHING
HASHING
HESHVAN
HUSHABY
HUSHFUL
HUSHING
INSHAPE
INSHORT
JOSHING
KASHMIR
KISHKES
KOSHERS
LASHERS
LASHING
LASHUPS
LUSHEST
MASHERS
MASHIES
MASHING
MESHIER
MESHING
MISHAPS
MISHEAR
MISHITS
MOSHERS
MOSHING
MOSHPIT
MUSHERS
MUSHIER
MUSHILY
MUSHING
NOSHERS
NOSHING
NOSHOWS
ONSHORE
POSHEST
PUSHFUL
PUSHIER
PUSHILY
PUSHING
PUSHKIN
PUSHOFF
PUSHPIN
PUSHUPS
RASHERS
RASHEST
RESHIPS
RESHOES
RESHOOT
RUSHDIE
RUSHEES
RUSHERS
RUSHIER
RUSHING
RUSHOFF
SASHAYS
SASHBAR
SASHIMI
TASHLIN
TASHMAN
TOSHIBA
TVSHOWS
UNSHORN
UPSHOTS
WASHERS
WASHIER
WASHING
WASHOFF
WASHOUT
WASHRAG
WASHTUB
WASHUPS
WISHERS
WISHFUL
WISHING
YASHMAK
YESHIVA

••S•H••

BASEHIT
BUSHHOG
FISCHER
GASOHOL
PASCHAL

••S••H•

INSIGHT
LESOTHO
ONSIGHT

••S•••H

BESEECH
BISMUTH
DUSKISH
IPSWICH
MESSIAH
MISSISH
NESMITH
RASPISH
WASATCH
WASPISH

•••SH••

ABASHED
ABASHES
AIRSHIP
AIRSHOW
APISHLY
BANSHEE
BIGSHOT
BLUSHED
BLUSHER
BLUSHES
BLUSHON
BOLSHOI
BRASHER
BRASHLY
BRUSHED
BRUSHES
BRUSHUP
CAPSHAW
CATSHOW
CLASHED
CLASHES
CRASHED
CRASHES
CRUSHED
CRUSHER
CRUSHES
DOGSHOW
DROSHKY
EARSHOT
EYESHOT
FLASHED
FLASHER
FLASHES
FLESHED
FLESHES
FLESHLY
FLUSHED
FLUSHES
FRESHEN
FRESHER
FRESHET
FRESHLY
GEISHAS
GNASHED
GNASHES
GRISHAM
GUMSHOE
GUNSHOT
GYMSHOE
HARSHEN
HARSHER
HARSHLY
HERSHEY
HOTSHOT
ICESHOW
KAISHEK
KEESHAN
KINSHIP
KNISHES
KRISHNA
LAKSHMI
LEASHED
LEASHES
MARSHAL
MARSHES
MUGSHOT
ONESHOT
PLASHED
PLASHES
PLUSHER
PLUSHES
PLUSHLY
POTSHOT
PROSHOP
QUASHED
QUASHES
RIMSHOT
SHUSHED
SHUSHES
SKOSHES
SLASHED
SLASHER
SLASHES
SLOSHED
SLOSHES
SLUSHES
SMASHED
SMASHER
SMASHES
SMASHUP
STASHED
STASHES
SWISHED
SWISHES
TEASHOP
TOESHOE
TOYSHOP
TRASHED
TRASHES
TRISHAW
USOSHOW
WARSHIP
WHISHED
WHISHES
WORSHIP

•••S•H•

BORSCHT
KITSCHY
PORSCHE
WHOSWHO

•••S••H

FORSYTH
MESSIAH
MISSISH

••••SH•

ALYOSHA
BELUSHI
COCKSHY
KENOSHA
NATASHA
RICKSHA
SPLASHY
SQUISHY

••••S•H

KLATSCH

•••••SH

ABOLISH
BABYISH
BADDISH
BALDISH
BARDISH
BEAMISH
BEARISH
BEAUISH
BIGGISH
BLEMISH
BLUEISH
BOARISH
BOGGISH
BONEASH
BOOKISH
BOORISH
BRINISH
BRITISH
BRUTISH
BULLISH
BULRUSH
BUMRUSH
BURNISH
CADDISH
CARWASH
CATFISH
CATTISH
CHERISH
CLAYISH
COCKISH
CODFISH
COLDISH
COLTISH
COOLISH
CORNISH
CRONISH
CUBBISH
CULTISH
CURRISH
DAMPISH
DARKISH
DAWKISH
DERVISH
DOGFISH
DOGGISH
DOLLISH
DOLTISH
DONNISH
DRONISH
DULLISH
DUMPISH
DUNCISH
DUSKISH
ENGLISH
EVANISH
EYELASH
EYEWASH
FADDISH
FAIRISH
FATTISH
FINNISH
FLEMISH
FLYFISH
FOGYISH
FOLKISH
FOOLISH
FOPPISH
FURBISH
FURNISH
GARNISH
GAULISH
GAWKISH
GIRLISH
GNOMISH
GOATISH
GOODISH
GOULASH
GOUTISH
GRAYISH
GREYISH
HAGGISH
HAWKISH
HELLISH
HENNISH
HOGGISH
HOGWASH
HORNISH
HUFFISH
HUNNISH
INARUSH
JETWASH
JIGGISH
KADDISH
KENTISH
KIDDISH
KNAVISH
KURDISH
LADDISH
LADYISH
LAPPISH
LARGISH
LARKISH
LAZYISH
LETTISH
LOGGISH
LONGISH
LOUDISH
LOUTISH
LUMPISH
MADDISH
MAIDISH
MANNISH
MAWKISH
MINXISH
MISSISH
MOBBISH
MONKISH
MOONISH
MOORISH
NAGGISH
NEBBISH
NOURISH
OGREISH
OMIGOSH
OSHKOSH
PANFISH
PARRISH
PAYCASH
PEAKISH
PECKISH
PEEVISH
PELTISH
PERKISH
PETTISH
PICTISH
PIGGISH
PINKISH
PIXYISH
PLANISH
POORISH
PORKISH
PREWASH
PRUDISH
PUBLISH
PUCKISH
PUGGISH
RAFFISH
RAMMISH
RANKISH
RASPISH
RATTISH
REDDISH
REFRESH
RHENISH
ROGUISH
ROMANSH
ROMPISH
RUBBISH
RUNTISH
RUTTISH
SALTISH
SAWFISH
SELFISH
SICKISH
SLAVISH
SOFTISH
SOTTISH
SOURISH
SPANISH
STYLISH
SUNFISH
SWEDISH
SWINISH
TALLISH
TANNISH
TARNISH
TARTISH
TIGRISH
TOADISH
TONNISH
TORYISH
TOWNISH
TURKISH
UNLEASH
VAMPISH
VARNISH
VOGUISH
WAGGISH
WANNISH
WARMISH
WASPISH
WEAKISH
WENDISH
WETTISH
WHEYISH
WHITISH
WILDISH
WIMPISH
WOLFISH
WORMISH
YERKISH
YIDDISH
ZANYISH

SI•••••

SIAMESE
SIBERIA
SIBLING
SICCING
SICHUAN
SICKBAY
SICKDAY
SICKENS
SICKEST
SICKISH
SICKLES
SICKOUT
SICKPAY
SIDEARM
SIDEBAR
SIDEBET
SIDECAR
SIDEMAN
SIDEMEN
SIDINGS
SIDLING
SIENNAS
SIERRAS
SIESTAS
SIFTERS
SIFTING
SIGHERS
SIGHFUL
SIGHING
SIGHTED
SIGHTLY
SIGMUND
SIGNALS
SIGNEES
SIGNERS
SIGNETS
SIGNIFY
SIGNING
SIGNOFF
SIGNOUT
SIGNSIN
SIGNSON
SIGNSUP
SIKHISM
SILENCE
SILENTS
SILESIA
SILICAS
SILICON
SILKHAT
SILKIER
SILKILY
SILLIER
SILLIES
SILOING
SILTIER
SILTING
SILVERS
SILVERY
SIMENON
SIMIANS
SIMILAR
SIMILES
SIMMERS
SIMMONS
SIMPERS
SIMPLER
SIMPLEX
SIMPSON
SINATRA
SINCERE
SINEDIE
SINGERS
SINGING
SINGLED
SINGLES
SINGOUT
SINGSTO
SINKAGE
SINKERS
SINKING
SINKSIN
SINLESS
SINLIKE
SINNERS
SINUOUS
SINUSES
SIOBHAN
SIOUANS
SIPHONS
SIPPERS
SIPPETS
SIPPING
SIRLOIN
SIROCCO
SISKINS
SISSIES
SISTERS
SISTINE
SISTRUM
SITCOMS
SITDOWN
SITSOUT
SITTERS
SITTING
SITUATE
SITWELL
SIXFOLD
SIXGUNS
SIXIRON
SIXPACK
SIXTEEN
SIXTHLY
SIXTIES
SIZABLE
SIZABLY
SIZEDUP
SIZESUP
SIZINGS
SIZZLED
SIZZLES

S•I••••

SAILING
SAILORS
SAINTED
SAINTLY
SCIENCE
SCIORRA
SCISSOR
SEICHES
SEIDELS
SEINERS
SEINING
SEISMIC
SEIZERS
SEIZING
SHIATSU
SHIELDS
SHIFTED
SHIHTZU
SHIITES
SHIKARI
SHIKOKU
SHILLED
SHIMMER
SHINDIG
SHINERS
SHINGLE
SHINIER
SHINILY
SHINING
SHINNED
SHIPMAN
SHIPMEN
SHIPOUT
SHIPPED
SHIPPER
SHIRKED
SHIRKER
SHIRLEY
SHIRRED
SHIVERS
SHIVERY
SKIBOBS
SKIBOOT
SKIDDED
SKIDDER
SKIDDOO
SKIDROW
SKIJUMP
SKILFUL
SKILIFT
SKILLED
SKILLET
SKIMASK
SKIMMED
SKIMMER
SKIMPED
SKINFUL
SKINNED
SKINNER
SKIPOLE
SKIPOUT
SKIPPED
SKIPPER
SKIRACK
SKIRLED
SKIRRED
SKIRTED
SKIRUNS
SKISUIT
SKITOWS
SKITTER
SKITTLE
SKIVERS
SKIWEAR
SLICERS
SLICING
SLICKED
SLICKER
SLICKLY
SLIDEIN
SLIDERS
SLIDING
SLIGHTS
SLIMIER
SLIMILY
SLIMJIM
SLIMMED
SLIMMER
SLINGER
SLINKED
SLIPONS
SLIPOUT
SLIPPED
SLIPPER
SLIPSIN
SLIPSON
SLIPSUP
SLIPUPS
SLITHER
SLIVERS
SMIDGEN
SMILERS
SMILING
SMIRKED
SMITING
SMITTEN
SNICKER
SNIDELY
SNIDEST
SNIFFAT
SNIFFED
SNIFFER
SNIFFLE
SNIFFLY
SNIFTER
SNIGGER
SNIGGLE
SNIGLET
SNIPEAT
SNIPERS
SNIPING
SNIPPED
SNIPPET
SNITCHY
SNIVELS
SOIGNEE
SOILING
SOIREES
SPICERY
SPICEUP
SPICIER
SPICILY
SPICING
SPIDERS
SPIDERY
SPIEDON
SPIEGEL
SPIELED
SPIELER
SPIESON
SPIGOTS
SPIKERS
SPIKIER
SPIKILY
SPIKING
SPILLED
SPINACH
SPINDLE
SPINDLY
SPINDRY
SPINELS
SPINETS
SPINIER
SPINNER
SPINNEY
SPINOFF
SPINOUT
SPINOZA
SPIRALS
SPIRANT
SPIREAS
SPIRIER
SPIRITO
SPIRITS
SPITING
SPITZES
STICHES
STICKER
STICKTO
STICKUP
STIEGEL
STIFFED
STIFFEN
STIFFER
STIFFLY
STIFLED
STIFLES
STIGMAS
STILLED
STILLER
STILTED
STILTON
STIMULI
STINGER
STINGOS
STINKER
STINTED
STIPEND
STIPPLE
STIRFRY
STIRRED
STIRRER
STIRRUP
STIRSIN
STIRSUP
SUITING
SUITORS
SUITSUP
SWIFTER
SWIFTLY
SWIGGED
SWILLED
SWIMMER
SWINDLE
SWINGBY
SWINGER
SWINISH
SWIPERS
SWIPING
SWIRLED
SWISHED
SWISHES
SWITZER
SWIVELS
SWIVETS
SWIZZLE

S••I•••

SABINES
SAGINAW
SALIENT
SALIERI
SALINAS
SAMISEN
SAMITES
SANIBEL
SAPIENS
SAPIENT
SATIATE
SATIETY
SATINET
SATIRES
SATIRIC
SATISFY
SAVINGS
SAVIORS
SAVIOUR
SAYINGS
SCHIRRA
SCHISMS
SCRIBES
SCRIMPS
SCRIMPY
SCRIPPS
SCRIPTS
SCRIVEN
SEMILOG
SEMINAL
SEMINAR
SEMIPRO
SEMITES
SEMITIC
SENIORS
SERIALS
SERIATE
SERIOUS
SETINTO
SEVIGNE
SEVILLE
SEXIEST
SEXISTS
SHEIKHS
SHEILAS
SHIITES
SHRIEKS
SHRIFTS
SHRIKES
SHRILLS
SHRILLY
SHRIMPS
SHRINER
SHRINES
SHRINKS
SHRIVEL
SHRIVER
SHRIVES
SHTICKS
SIDINGS
SILICAS
SILICON
SIMIANS
SIMILAR
SIMILES
SIXIRON
SIZINGS
SLEIGHS
SLEIGHT
SLUICED
SLUICES
SOCIALS
SOCIETY
SOLICIT
SOLIDER
SOLIDLY
SORITES
SOVIETS
SOYINKA
SPLICED
SPLICER
SPLICES
SPLINES
SPLINTS
SPLITUP
SPOILED
SPOILER
SPRIEST
SPRINGS
SPRINGY
SPRINTS
SPRITES
SQUILLS
SQUINCH
SQUINTS
SQUINTY
SQUIRED
SQUIRES
SQUIRMS
SQUIRMY
SQUIRTS
SQUISHY
STAIDER
STAIDLY
STAINED
STAINER
STEIGER
STEINEM
STEINER
STKITTS
STOICAL
STRIATE
STRIDER
STRIDES
STRIKER
STRIKES
STRINGS
STRINGY
STRIPED
STRIPER
STRIPES
STRIVED
STRIVEN
STRIVER
STRIVES
SURINAM
SYRIANS
SYRINGA
SYRINGE

S•••I••

SABRINA
SACKING
SACLIKE
SAGGIER
SAGGING
SAILING
SALLIED
SALLIES
SALSIFY
SALTIER
SALTILY
SALTINE
SALTING
SALTISH
SALVIAS
SALVING
SAMHILL
SANDIER
SANDING
SANTINI
SANTIRS
SAPLING
SAPPIER
SAPPILY
SAPPING
SARDINE
SARKIER
SASHIMI
SASSIER
SASSIES
SASSILY
SASSING
SAUCIER
SAUCILY
SAURIAN
SAVVIER
SAVVILY
SAWFISH
SAWLIKE
SAWMILL
SAYYIDS
SCALIER
SCALING
SCARIER
SCARIFY
SCARILY
SCARING
SCHMIDT
SCHWINN
SCOPING
SCORING
SEABIRD
SEAFIRE
SEAGIRT
SEALILY
SEALING
SEALION
SEAMIER
SEAMING
SEARING
SEASICK
SEASIDE
SEATING
SECTION
SEDGIER
SEEDIER
SEEDILY
SEEDING
SEEKING
SEEMING
SEEPIER
SEEPING
SEINING
SEIZING
SELFISH
SELKIRK
SELLING
SENDING
SENSING
SEQUINS
SERBIAN
SERLING
SERPICO
SERRIED
SERVICE
SERVILE
SERVING
SESSILE
SESSION
SESTINA
SETLINE
SETTING
SHADIER
SHADILY

SHADING
SHAKIER
SHAKILY
SHAKING
SHAMING
SHAPING
SHAPIRO
SHARING
SHAVING
SHERIFF
SHINIER
SHINILY
SHINING
SHOEING
SHOOING
SHOOINS
SHORING
SHOVING
SHOWIER
SHOWILY
SHOWING
SHUTINS
SIBLING
SICCING
SICKISH
SIDLING
SIFTING
SIGHING
SIGNIFY
SIGNING
SIKHISM
SILKIER
SILKILY
SILLIER
SILLIES
SILOING
SILTIER
SILTING
SINGING
SINKING
SINLIKE
SIPPING
SISKINS
SISSIES
SISTINE
SITTING
SIXTIES
SKATING
SKEWING
SKILIFT
SKYDIVE
SKYHIGH
SKYLIKE
SKYLINE
SLAKING
SLATIER
SLATING
SLAVING
SLAVISH
SLICING
SLIDING
SLIMIER
SLIMILY
SLOPING
SLOWING
SMILING
SMITING
SMOKIER
SMOKIES
SMOKILY
SMOKING
SNAKIER
SNAKILY
SNAKING
SNARING
SNIPING
SNORING
SNOWIER
SNOWILY
SNOWING
SOAKING
SOAPIER
SOAPILY
SOAPING
SOARING
SOBBING
SOCKING
SODDIER
SODDIES
SODDING
SOFFITS
SOFTIES
SOFTISH
SOGGIER
SOGGILY
SOILING
SOLDIER
SOLOING
SOLOIST
SOLVING
SONLIKE
SOOTIER
SOOTILY
SOPHISM
SOPHIST
SOPPIER
SOPPING
SOPWITH
SORDINI
SORDINO
SORRIER
SORRILY
SORTIED
SORTIES
SORTING
SORVINO
SOTTISH
SOUPIER
SOURING
SOURISH
SOWLIKE
SPACIER
SPACING
SPADING
SPANIEL
SPANISH
SPARING
SPATIAL
SPAVINS
SPAYING
SPECIAL
SPECIES
SPECIFY
SPECING
SPEWING
SPICIER
SPICILY
SPICING
SPIKIER
SPIKILY
SPIKING
SPINIER
SPIRIER
SPIRITO
SPIRITS
SPITING
SPOKING
SPRAINS
SPUMIER
SPUMING
STABILE
STADIUM
STAGIER
STAGILY
STAGING
STAKING
STAMINA
STARING
STATICE
STATICS
STATING
STATION
STATIST
STAVING
STAYING
STEPINS
STERILE
STEWING
STOGIES
STOKING
STONIER
STONILY
STONING
STORIED
STORIES
STORING
STOWING
STRAINS
STRAITS
STUDIED
STUDIES
STUDIOS
STYGIAN
STYLING
STYLISE
STYLISH
STYLIST
STYLIZE
STYMIED
STYMIES
STYRIAN
SUASION
SUAVITY
SUBBING
SUBLIME
SUBMITS
SUBSIDE
SUBSIDY
SUBSIST
SUCKING
SUCTION
SUDSIER
SUDSING
SUFFICE
SUITING
SULFIDE
SULFITE
SULKIER
SULKIES
SULKILY
SULKING
SULLIED
SULLIES
SUMMING
SUMMITS
SUNCITY
SUNDIAL
SUNFISH
SUNKIST
SUNLIKE
SUNNIER
SUNNILY
SUNNING
SUNRISE
SUPPING
SURFIER
SURFING
SURGING
SURLIER
SURLILY
SURMISE
SURVIVE
SUSLIKS
SUSSING
SWAHILI
SWAYING
SWEDISH
SWINISH
SWIPING
SYNCING

S••••I•

SAFARIS
SALADIN
SALAMIS
SALUKIS
SAMARIA
SANGRIA
SANLUIS
SATIRIC
SAVARIN
SCEPTIC
SCORPIO
SCOTTIE
SEDALIA
SEENFIT
SEEPSIN
SEESFIT
SEETOIT
SEGOVIA
SEISMIC
SELENIC
SEMITIC
SENDSIN
SEQUOIA
SERAPIS
SETSAIL
SHAREIN
SHELTIE
SHERWIN
SHINDIG
SHOWBIZ
SHOWNIN
SHOWSIN
SHUTSIN
SIBERIA
SIGNSIN
SILESIA
SINEDIE
SINKSIN
SIRLOIN
SKEEZIX
SKEPTIC
SKISUIT
SLEEPIN
SLEPTIN
SLIDEIN
SLIMJIM
SLIPSIN
SLOEGIN
SNEAKIN
SNOWSIN
SOCKSIN
SOLARIA
SOLICIT
SOMALIA
SOMALIS
SOMATIC
SPOTLIT
SPUTNIK
SQUALID
STANDIN
STANNIC
STARLIT
STCROIX
STDENIS
STEELIE
STENCIL
STEPSIN
STEROID
STIRSIN
STLOUIS
STLUCIA
STOODIN
STOOLIE
STOPSIN
STYPTIC
SUBJOIN
SUBSOIL
SUBUNIT
SUCKSIN
SUNMAID
SUNSUIT
SURFEIT
SUSTAIN
SWEARIN
SWEETIE
SWOOSIE
SWOREIN
SYNODIC

S•••••I

SALIERI
SAMURAI
SANTINI
SASHIMI
SCHATZI
SCHERZI
SHANGRI
SHARPEI
SHASTRI
SHIKARI
SORDINI
SPUMONI
STIMULI
SWAHILI
SYLLABI

•SI••••

ASIATIC
ASININE
OSIERED
USINGUP

•S•I•••

ASHIEST
ASPIRED
ASPIRER
ASPIRES
ASPIRIN
ASSIGNS
ASSISTS
ASSIZES
ESKIMOS
ESPIALS
ESTIVAL
OSCINES
OSSICLE
OSSIFIC
TSHIRTS
USTINOV

•S••I••

ASCRIBE
ASININE
ASOCIAL
ASSAILS
ASSLIKE
ASTAIRE
ASTRIDE
ESPYING
ESQUIRE
ISSUING
OSTRICH
TSARINA
TSARIST
TSELIOT
USERIDS
USURIES

•S•••I•

ASCETIC
ASEPSIS
ASEPTIC
ASIATIC
ASKEDIN
ASPIRIN
ASSYRIA
ASTORIA
CSLEWIS
ESTONIA
ESTORIL
ISLAMIC
OSMOSIS
OSMOTIC
OSSIFIC
OSTEOID
PSYCHIC
TSOURIS

•S••••I

ASHANTI
ASSEGAI
ISRAELI
TSUNAMI

••SI•••

APSIDES
ASSIGNS
ASSISTS
ASSIZES
BESIDES
BESIEGE
BUSIEST
CASINGS
CASINOS
COSIEST
COSIGNS
COSINES
DESIGNS
DESIRED
DESIREE
DESIRES
DESISTS
DOSIDOS
EASIEST
ENSIGNS
ENSILED
ENSILES
EPSILON
HASIDIC
HASIDIM
HOSIERS
HOSIERY
INSIDER
INSIDES
INSIGHT
INSIPID
INSISTS
MUSICAL
NOSIEST
ONSIDES
ONSIGHT
OSSICLE
OSSIFIC
POSITED
RESIDED
RESIDES
RESIDUE
RESIGNS
RESILED
RESILES
RESINGS
RESISTS
RISIBLE
RISIBLY
RISINGS
ROSIEST
UPSILON
VISIBLE
VISIBLY
VISIONS
VISITED
VISITOR
WYSIWYG

••S•I••

ASSAILS
ASSLIKE
AUSPICE
AUSSIES
BASHING
BASKING
BASSIST
BASTING
BASTION
BESTIAL
BESTING
BESTIRS
BOSKIER
BOSSIER
BOSSILY
BOSSING
BUSBIES
BUSGIRL
BUSHIDO
BUSHIER
BUSHILY
BUSHING
BUSKING
BUSKINS
BUSLINE
BUSSING
BUSTING
BUSYING
CASHIER
CASHING
CASPIAN
CASSIAS
CASSIDY
CASSINI
CASSINO
CASSIUS
CASTILE
CASTING
CESSING
CESSION
COSHING
COSTING
CUSHIER
CUSHING
CUSHION
CUSPIDS
CUSSING
DASHIKI
DASHING
DESPISE
DESPITE
DESTINE
DESTINY
DISHIER
DISHING
DISLIKE
DISMISS
DISSING
DISTILL
DISTILS
DOSSIER
DUSKIER
DUSKILY
DUSKISH
DUSTIER
DUSTILY
DUSTING
ENSKIED
ENSKIES
ENSUING
ENSUITE
ERSKINE
FASCIAS
FASHION
FASTING
FESSING
FESTIVA
FESTIVE
FISHIER
FISHILY
FISHING
FISSILE
FISSION
FOSDICK
FOSSILS
FUSSIER
FUSSILY
FUSSING
FUSTIAN
FUSTICS
FUSTIER
FUSTILY
GASHING
GASKINS
GASPING
GASSIER
GOSLING
GOSSIPS
GOSSIPY
GUSHIER
GUSHILY
GUSHING
GUSSIED
GUSSIES
GUSTIER
GUSTILY
GUSTING
HASHING
HASPING
HASTIER
HASTILY
HASTING
HESSIAN
HISSING
HOSKINS
HOSPICE
HOSTILE
HOSTING
HUSHING
HUSKIER
HUSKIES
HUSKILY
HUSKING
HUSSIES
INSPIRE
INSTILL
INSTILS
IPSWICH
ISSUING
JASMINE
JESSICA
JESTING
JESUITS
JOSHING
JOSKINS
JUSTICE
JUSTIFY
JUSTINE
KISSING
LASHING
LASSIES
LASTING
LESSING
LISPING
LISTING
LUSTIER
LUSTILY
LUSTING
MASHIES
MASHING
MASKING
MASSIER
MASSIFS
MASSING
MASSIVE
MASTICS
MASTIFF
MCSWINE
MESHIER
MESHING
MESSIAH
MESSIER
MESSILY
MESSINA
MESSING
MESTIZA
MESTIZO
MISDIAL
MISFILE
MISFIRE
MISFITS
MISHITS
MISLIKE
MISSIES
MISSILE
MISSING
MISSION
MISSISH
MISSIVE
MISTIER
MISTILY
MISTING
MOSAICS
MOSHING
MOSSIER
MOSSING
MUSHIER
MUSHILY
MUSHING
MUSKIER
MUSKIES
MUSLIMS
MUSLINS
MUSSIER
MUSSILY
MUSSING
MUSTIER
MUSTILY
MYSTICS
MYSTIFY
NASTIER
NASTILY
NESMITH
NESTING
NOSHING
OUSTING
PASSING
PASSION
PASSIVE
PASTIER
PASTIME
PASTINA
PASTING
PESKIER
PESKILY
PISCINE
PISMIRE
PISTILS
POSTING
POSTITS
PUSHIER
PUSHILY
PUSHING
RASPIER
RASPING
RASPISH
RESCIND
RESHIPS
RESPINS
RESPIRE
RESPITE
RESTING
RESTIVE
RISKIER
RISKILY
RISKING
ROSSINI
RUSHIER
RUSHING
RUSSIAN
RUSTICS
RUSTIER
RUSTILY
RUSTING
SASHIMI
SASSIER
SASSIES
SASSILY
SASSING
SESSILE
SESSION
SESTINA
SISKINS
SISSIES
SISTINE
SUSLIKS
SUSSING
TASKING
TASTIER
TASTILY
TASTING
TESTIER
TESTIFY
TESTILY
TESTING
TOSHIBA
TOSSING
UNSTICK
UPSWING
VASTIER
VESPIDS
VESTIGE
VESTING
VISAING
WASHIER
WASHING
WASPIER
WASPILY
WASPISH
WASTING
WESKITS
WISHING
WISPIER
WISPILY
WISPING
YESHIVA
YESSING
ZESTIER

••S••I•

ABSTAIN
ALSATIA
ARSENIC
ARSENIO
ASSYRIA
AUSTRIA
BASEHIT
BISCUIT
BUSHPIG
COSTAIN
DESPAIR
DESPOIL
DISDAIN
DISJOIN
DUSTBIN
EASEDIN
EASESIN
EPSTEIN
GASMAIN
GASTRIC
HASIDIC
HASIDIM
HUSSEIN
INSIPID
INSULIN
KASHMIR
KOSYGIN
LOSESIT
MASONIC
MASTOID
MESSKIT
MISLAID
MISSAID
MOSHPIT
NOSTRIL
OSSIFIC
PUSHKIN
PUSHPIN
RESTAIN
ROSALIE
ROSARIO
ROSEOIL
RUSHDIE
SUSTAIN
TASHLIN
VISALIA
VISAVIS
WASSAIL

••S•••I

ASSEGAI
BASENJI
CASSINI
DASHIKI
ROSSINI
SASHIMI

•••SI••

ABASING
ABUSING
ABUSIVE
AMUSING
ANTSIER
ARCSINE
ARISING
ARTSIER
AUSSIES
BASSIST
BEDSIDE
BIASING
BITSIER
BOSSIER
BOSSILY
BOSSING
BOUSING
BUSSING
CAESIUM
CAPSIDS
CAPSIZE
CASSIAS
CASSIDY
CASSINI
CASSINO
CASSIUS
CAUSING
CEASING
CELSIUS
CENSING
CESSING
CESSION
CHASING
CLOSING
CONSIGN
CONSIST
CORSICA
COUSINS
CROSIER
CUISINE
CURSING
CURSIVE
CUSSING
DAISIES
DAYSINN
DENSITY
DISSING
DITSIER
DOGSITS
DOSSIER
DOUSING
DOWSING
ELISION
ELUSIVE
ELYSIAN
ELYSIUM
ERASING
EROSION
EROSIVE
ETESIAN
EVASION
EVASIVE
FALSIFY
FALSITY
FESSING
FISSILE
FISSION
FOSSILS
FRASIER
FRISIAN
FUBSIER
FUSSIER
FUSSILY
FUSSING
GASSIER
GIPSIES
GOOSIER
GOOSING
GORSIER
GOSSIPS
GOSSIPY
GUSSIED
GUSSIES
GUTSIER
GUTSILY
GYPSIES
HESSIAN
HEXSIGN
HISSING
HOOSIER
HORSIER
HORSING
HOUSING
HUSSIES
JESSICA
KISSING
LANSING
LAPSING
LASSIES
LEASING
LESSING
LOOSING
LOUSIER
LOUSILY
LOUSING
MANSION
MASSIER
MASSIFS
MASSING
MASSIVE
MESSIAH
MESSIER
MESSILY
MESSINA
MESSING
MIDSIZE
MISSIES
MISSILE
MISSING
MISSION
MISSISH
MISSIVE
MOSSIER
MOSSING
MOUSIER
MOUSING
MUSSIER
MUSSILY
MUSSING
NEWSIER
NEWSIES
NOISIER
NOISILY
NOISING
NOOSING
NURSING
NUTSIER
OFFSIDE
OFFSITE
OUTSIDE
OUTSIZE
PANSIES
PARSING
PASSING
PASSION
PASSIVE
PATSIES
PAUSING
PENSION
PENSIVE
PEPSINS
PERSIAN
PERSIST
PERSIUS
PHASING
PHYSICS
PLOSION
PLOSIVE
POISING
POTSIER
PRESIDE
PROSIER
PROSILY
PROSING
PULSING
PURSIER
PURSING
RAISING
RAISINS
RAWSILK
RETSINA
RINSING
ROSSINI
ROUSING
RUSSIAN
SALSIFY
SASSIER
SASSIES
SASSILY
SASSING
SEASICK
SEASIDE
SENSING
SESSILE
SESSION
SISSIES
SUASION
SUBSIDE
SUBSIDY
SUBSIST
SUDSIER
SUDSING
SUSSING
TANSIES
TARSIER
TEASING
TENSILE
TENSING
TENSION
TENSIVE
TIPSIER
TIPSILY
TOCSINS
TONSILS
TOPSIDE
TORSION
TOSSING
VARSITY
VERSIFY
VERSION
WAYSIDE

WEBSITE
YESSING
ZOYSIAS

•••S•I•
AGASSIZ
AIRSHIP
ANOSMIA
ANOSMIC
BEASTIE
BONSOIR
BRASSIE
BRESLIN
CATSUIT
CAUSTIC
CHASSIS
CLASSIC
CLOSEIN
CORSAIR
COWSLIP
CRISPIN
DOESKIN
DRASTIC
DRYSUIT
EELSKIN
ELASTIC
ERISTIC
GNOSTIC
GRISKIN
HUSSEIN
INASNIT
INASPIN
JETSKIS
KIDSKIN
KINSHIP
KIRSTIE
KTOSLIN
LAWSUIT
LETSLIP
MESSKIT
MIASMIC
MISSAID
NAYSAID
NONSKID
NONSLIP
OILSKIN
ONASSIS
PARSNIP
PERSEID
PHASEIN
PIGSKIN
PLASTIC
PROSAIC
PRUSSIA
PURSUIT
SEESFIT
SEISMIC
SETSAIL
SKISUIT
SUBSOIL
SUNSUIT
THESPIS
TOPSAIL
TOPSOIL
WARSHIP
WASSAIL
WETSUIT
WORSHIP

•••S••I
ANASAZI
BOLSHOI
CASSINI
LAKSHMI
MAESTRI
ROSSINI
SHASTRI
TOLSTOI

••••SI•
AGASSIZ
AMNESIA
ASEPSIS
BABYSIT
BACKSIN
BEATSIT
BLOWSIN
BLOWSIT
BOXESIN
BRASSIE
BUTTSIN
CALLSIN
CAVESIN
CHASSIS
CHIPSIN
CLASSIC
CLUESIN
COMESIN
COOLSIT
DEALSIN
DEARSIR
DEEPSIX
DEPOSIT
DINESIN
DIVESIN
DRAGSIN
DRAWSIN
DROPSIN
EASESIN
ECDYSIS
EDGESIN
EURASIA
FADESIN
FALLSIN
FILLSIN
FLIESIN
FOOTSIE
FREESIA
FUCHSIA
GENESIS
GIVESIN
HANDSIN
HANGSIN
HEADSIN
HOLDSIN
HOOFSIT
HORNSIN
JOINSIN
JUMPSIN
KEEPSIN
KICKSIN
LEADSIN
LIVESIN
LOOKSIN
LOSESIT
MAILSIN
MAKESIT
MEIOSIS
MIMESIS
MITOSIS
MIXESIN
MOVESIN
NAILSIN
NEMESIS
NICOSIA
ONASSIS
OSMOSIS
PEERSIN
PILESIN
PLUGSIN
POURSIN
PRUSSIA
PULLSIN
RAKESIN
READSIN
REELSIN
REINSIN
REVISIT
ROLLSIN
ROPESIN
SEEPSIN
SENDSIN
SHOWSIN
SHUTSIN
SIGNSIN
SILESIA
SINKSIN
SLIPSIN
SNOWSIN
SOCKSIN
STEPSIN
STIRSIN
STOPSIN
SUCKSIN
SWOOSIE
TAKESIN
THATSIT
TOOTSIE
TRANSIT
TUCKSIN
TUNESIN
TUNISIA
TURNSIN
UTENSIL
VOTESIN
WADESIN
WANTSIN
WAVESIN
WINGSIT
WORKSIN
YELTSIN
ZOOMSIN

••••S•I
BELUSHI
CHRISTI
COLOSSI
ELMISTI
MENISCI
PULASKI

•••••SI
COLOSSI
PACHISI
TBILISI

S•J••••
SOJOURN
STJOHNS

S••J•••
SANJOSE
SANJUAN
SKIJUMP
SKYJACK
SUBJECT
SUBJOIN
SUOJURE

S•••J••
SLIMJIM
SNOWJOB

••SJ•••
DISJOIN
GASJETS

••S•J••
NOSEJOB

••S••J•
BASENJI

SK•••••
SKANKED
SKANKER
SKATERS
SKATING
SKEETER
SKEEZIX
SKELTER
SKELTON
SKEPTIC
SKETCHY
SKEWERS
SKEWING
SKIBOBS
SKIBOOT
SKIDDED
SKIDDER
SKIDDOO
SKIDROW
SKIJUMP
SKILFUL
SKILIFT
SKILLED
SKILLET
SKIMASK
SKIMMED
SKIMMER
SKIMPED
SKINFUL
SKINNED
SKINNER
SKIPOLE
SKIPOUT
SKIPPED
SKIPPER
SKIRACK
SKIRLED
SKIRRED
SKIRTED
SKIRUNS
SKISUIT
SKITOWS
SKITTER
SKITTLE
SKIVERS
SKIWEAR
SKOOKUM
SKOSHES
SKULKED
SKULKER
SKUNKED
SKYBLUE
SKYCAPS
SKYDIVE
SKYHIGH
SKYHOOK
SKYJACK
SKYLARK
SKYLESS
SKYLIKE
SKYLINE
SKYWARD
SKYWAYS

S•K••••
SIKHISM
STKITTS
SUKARNO

S••K•••
SACKERS
SACKFUL
SACKING
SACKOUT
SARKIER
SECKELS
SEEKERS
SEEKING
SEEKOUT
SELKIRK
SHAKERS
SHAKEUP
SHAKIER
SHAKILY
SHAKING
SHAKOES
SHEKELS
SHIKARI
SHIKOKU
SICKBAY
SICKDAY
SICKENS
SICKEST
SICKISH
SICKLES
SICKOUT
SICKPAY
SILKHAT
SILKIER
SILKILY
SINKAGE
SINKERS
SINKING
SINKSIN
SISKINS
SLAKING
SMOKERS
SMOKIER
SMOKIES
SMOKILY
SMOKING
SNAKIER
SNAKILY
SNAKING
SOAKERS
SOAKING
SOAKSUP
SOCKETS
SOCKEYE
SOCKING
SOCKSIN
SOUKOUS
SPIKERS
SPIKIER
SPIKILY
SPIKING
SPOKANE
SPOKEOF
SPOKEUP
SPOKING
STAKING
STOKELY
STOKERS
STOKING
SUCKERS
SUCKING
SUCKSIN
SULKERS
SULKIER
SULKIES
SULKILY
SULKING
SUNKIST

S•••K••
SALUKIS
SHACKLE
SHANKAR
SHANKED
SHARKEY
SHEIKHS
SHIRKED
SHIRKER
SHOCKED
SHOCKER
SHOOKUP
SHRIKES
SHUCKED
SHUCKER
SKANKED
SKANKER
SKOOKUM
SKULKED
SKULKER
SKUNKED
SLACKED
SLACKEN
SLACKER
SLACKLY
SLEEKED
SLEEKEN
SLEEKER
SLEEKLY
SLICKED
SLICKER
SLICKLY
SLINKED
SMACKED
SMACKER
SMIRKED
SNACKED
SNACKER
SNEAKED
SNEAKER
SNEAKIN
SNICKER
SNOOKER
SNORKEL
SPACKLE
SPANKED
SPANKER
SPARKED
SPARKLE
SPEAKER
SPEAKOF
SPEAKUP
SPECKED
SPECKLE
SPOOKED
STACKED
STACKUP
STALKED
STALKER
STARKER
STARKLY
STICKER
STICKTO
STICKUP
STINKER
STOCKED
STOCKUP
STOOKED
STOOKEY
STRIKER
STRIKES
STROKED
STROKES
STUCKTO
STUCKUP
SWANKED
SWANKER
SWONKEN

S••••K•
SACLIKE
SAWLIKE
SCREAKS
SHIKOKU
SHRIEKS
SHRINKS
SHTICKS
SINLIKE
SKYLIKE
SLOVAKS
SONLIKE
SOWLIKE
SOYINKA
SPASSKY
SQUAWKS
SQUAWKY
SQUEAKS
SQUEAKY
STREAKS
STREAKY
SUNLIKE
SUSLIKS

S•••••K
SADSACK
SARAWAK
SAWBUCK
SCHLOCK
SEASICK
SELKIRK
SELLECK
SETBACK
SHYLOCK
SIXPACK
SKIMASK
SKIRACK
SKYHOOK
SKYJACK
SKYLARK
SPELUNK
SPUTNIK
SUFFOLK
SUNDECK

•SK••••
ASKANCE
ASKEDIN
ASKSFOR
ASKSOUT
ESKIMOS

•S•K•••
OSHKOSH

•S•••K•
ASSLIKE

••SK•••
BASKETS
BASKING
BOSKETS
BOSKIER
BUSKING
BUSKINS
DESKSET
DESKTOP
DUSKIER
DUSKILY
DUSKISH
ENSKIED
ENSKIES
ERSKINE
GASKETS
GASKINS
HOSKINS
HUSKERS
HUSKIER
HUSKIES
HUSKILY
HUSKING
JOSKINS
MASKERS
MASKING
MUSKEGS
MUSKETS
MUSKIER
MUSKIES
MUSKRAT
PESKIER
PESKILY
RISKERS
RISKIER
RISKILY
RISKING
SISKINS
TASKING
TUSKERS
WESKITS

••S•K••
KISHKES
MESSKIT
PASSKEY
PUSHKIN

••S••K•
ASSLIKE
ATSTAKE
BESPOKE
DASHIKI
DISLIKE
KUSPUKS
LYSENKO
MISLIKE
MISTAKE
SUSLIKS

••S•••K
BESPEAK
CASSOCK
COSSACK
DRSPOCK
FOSDICK
GOSHAWK
HASSOCK
INSTOCK
MASARYK
MISTOOK
MRSPOCK
RESTOCK
TUSSOCK
UNSTACK
UNSTICK
UNSTUCK
YASHMAK

•••SK••
ALASKAN
BRISKER
BRISKET
BRISKLY
DOESKIN
EELSKIN
FRISKED
GRISKIN
JETSKIS
KIDSKIN
MESSKIT
NONSKID
OILSKIN
PASSKEY
PIGSKIN
UNASKED
WHISKED
WHISKER
WHISKEY

•••S•K•
DROSHKY
FORSAKE
NETSUKE
SPASSKY

•••S••K
AIRSOCK
BERSERK
CASSOCK
COSSACK
FORSOOK
GEMSBOK
HASSOCK
KAISHEK
PRESOAK
RANSACK
RAWSILK
SADSACK
SEASICK
TUSSOCK

••••SK•
BLUESKY
CHOMSKY
DAMASKS
PULASKI
SPASSKY
TROTSKY
UNMASKS
VRONSKY

•••••SK
MOLLUSK
OBELISK
OKHOTSK
SKIMASK
YAKUTSK

SL•••••
SLABBED
SLACKED
SLACKEN
SLACKER
SLACKLY
SLAKING
SLALOMS
SLAMMED
SLAMMER
SLANDER
SLANTED
SLAPPED
SLASHED
SLASHER
SLASHES
SLATHER
SLATIER
SLATING
SLATTED
SLAVERS
SLAVERY
SLAVEYS
SLAVING
SLAVISH
SLAYERS
SLAYTON
SLEDDED
SLEDDER
SLEDDOG
SLEDGES
SLEEKED
SLEEKEN
SLEEKER
SLEEKLY
SLEEPER
SLEEPIN
SLEEPON
SLEETED
SLEEVES
SLEIGHS
SLEIGHT
SLENDER
SLEPTIN
SLEPTON
SLEUTHS
SLICERS
SLICING
SLICKED
SLICKER
SLICKLY
SLIDEIN
SLIDERS
SLIDING
SLIGHTS
SLIMIER
SLIMILY
SLIMJIM
SLIMMED
SLIMMER
SLINGER
SLINKED
SLIPONS
SLIPOUT
SLIPPED
SLIPPER
SLIPSIN
SLIPSON
SLIPSUP
SLIPUPS
SLITHER
SLIVERS
SLOBBER
SLOEGIN
SLOGANS
SLOGGED
SLOPING
SLOPPED
SLOSHED
SLOSHES
SLOTCAR
SLOTTED
SLOUCHY
SLOUGHS
SLOVAKS
SLOVENE
SLOVENS
SLOWEST
SLOWING
SLOWSUP
SLOWUPS
SLUDGES
SLUGGED
SLUGGER
SLUICED
SLUICES
SLUMBER
SLUMMED
SLUMPED
SLURPED
SLURRED
SLUSHES
SLYNESS

S•L••••
SALAAMS
SALABLE
SALADIN
SALAMIS
SALAZAR
SALCHOW
SALERNO
SALIENT
SALIERI
SALINAS
SALLETS
SALLIED
SALLIES
SALLOWS
SALMONS
SALOONS
SALSIFY
SALSODA
SALTBOX
SALTERS
SALTIER
SALTILY
SALTINE
SALTING
SALTISH
SALUKIS
SALUTED
SALUTES
SALVAGE
SALVERS
SALVIAS
SALVING
SALVOES
SALVORS
SCLERAS
SELECTS
SELENIC
SELFISH
SELKIRK
SELLECK
SELLERS
SELLFOR
SELLING
SELLOFF
SELLOUT
SELTZER
SELVAGE
SILENCE
SILENTS
SILESIA
SILICAS
SILICON
SILKHAT
SILKIER
SILKILY
SILLIER
SILLIES
SILOING
SILTIER
SILTING
SILVERS
SILVERY
SOLACES
SOLARIA
SOLDERS
SOLDIER
SOLDOFF
SOLDOUT
SOLEDAD
SOLFEGE
SOLICIT
SOLIDER
SOLIDLY
SOLOING
SOLOIST
SOLOMON
SOLUBLE
SOLUTES
SOLVENT
SOLVERS
SOLVING
SPLASHY
SPLAYED
SPLEENS
SPLICED
SPLICER
SPLICES
SPLINES
SPLINTS
SPLITUP
SPLOTCH
SPLURGE
STLOUIS
STLUCIA
SULFATE
SULFIDE
SULFITE
SULKERS
SULKIER
SULKIES
SULKILY
SULKING
SULLIED
SULLIES
SULPHUR
SULTANA
SULTANS
SULUSEA
SYLLABI
SYLVANS

S••L•••
SACLIKE
SAILING
SAILORS
SALLETS
SALLIED
SALLIES
SALLOWS
SAMLETS
SANLUIS
SAPLESS
SAPLING
SAWLIKE
SAWLOGS
SCALARS
SCALDED
SCALENE
SCALERS
SCALIER
SCALING
SCALLOP
SCALPED
SCALPEL
SCALPER
SCHLEPP
SCHLEPS
SCHLOCK
SCOLDED
SCOLDER
SCULLED
SCULLER
SCULPTS
SEALABS
SEALANE
SEALANT
SEALEGS
SEALERS
SEALILY
SEALING
SEALION
SEALOFF
SEALSUP
SECLUDE
SELLECK
SELLERS
SELLFOR
SELLING
SELLOFF
SELLOUT
SERLING
SETLINE
SHALALA
SHALLOT
SHALLOW
SHALOMS
SHELDON
SHELLAC
SHELLED
SHELLER
SHELLEY
SHELTER
SHELTIE
SHELTON
SHELVED
SHELVES
SHILLED
SHYLOCK
SIBLING
SIDLING
SILLIER
SILLIES
SINLESS
SINLIKE
SIRLOIN
SKELTER
SKELTON
SKILFUL
SKILIFT
SKILLED
SKILLET
SKULKED
SKULKER
SKYLARK
SKYLESS
SKYLIKE
SKYLINE
SLALOMS
SMALLER
SMALTOS
SMELLED
SMELTED
SMELTER
SMILERS
SMILING
SMOLDER
SNELLEN
SODLESS
SOILING
SONLESS
SONLIKE
SOULFUL
SOWLIKE
SPALLED
SPELLED
SPELLER
SPELUNK
SPILLED
STALAGS
STALELY
STALEST
STALKED
STALKER
STALLED
STELLAR
STILLED
STILLER
STILTED
STILTON
STOLLEN
STOLLER
STOLONS
STYLERS
STYLETS
STYLING
STYLISE
STYLISH
STYLIST
STYLIZE
SUBLETS
SUBLIME
SULLIED
SULLIES
SUMLESS
SUNLAMP
SUNLESS
SUNLIKE
SUOLOCO
SURLIER
SURLILY
SUSLIKS
SUTLERS
SVELTER
SWALLET
SWALLOW
SWELLED
SWELLUP
SWELTER
SWELTRY
SWILLED
SWOLLEN
SYLLABI

S•••L••
SADDLED
SADDLER
SADDLES
SAMPLED
SAMPLER
SAMPLES
SANDLOT
SARALEE
SAVALAS
SAVELOY
SCALLOP
SCARLET
SCHOLAR
SCHULTZ
SCOWLED

SCOWLER
SCROLLS
SCULLED
SCULLER
SEABLUE
SEASLUG
SECULAR
SEDALIA
SEMILOG
SETTLED
SETTLER
SETTLES
SEVILLE
SHALLOT
SHALLOW
SHAPLEY
SHEILAS
SHELLAC
SHELLED
SHELLER
SHELLEY
SHIELDS
SHILLED
SHIRLEY
SHOULDA
SHRILLS
SHRILLY
SICKLES
SIMILAR
SIMILES
SIMPLER
SIMPLEX
SINGLED
SINGLES
SIZZLED
SIZZLES
SKILLED
SKILLET
SKIRLED
SKYBLUE
SMALLER
SMELLED
SNARLED
SNELLEN
SNIGLET
SOMALIA
SOMALIS
SPALLED
SPELLED
SPELLER
SPIELED
SPIELER
SPILLED
SPOILED
SPOILER
SPOOLED
SPOTLIT
SQUALID
SQUALLS
SQUALOR
SQUELCH
SQUILLS
STABLED
STABLER
STABLES
STALLED
STANLEE
STANLEY
STAPLED
STAPLER
STAPLES
STARLET
STARLIT
STEALTH
STEELED
STEELER
STEELIE
STELLAR
STIFLED
STIFLES
STILLED
STILLER
STOLLEN
STOLLER
STOOLIE
STROLLS
SUBPLOT
SUBTLER
SUPPLER
SURPLUS
SWALLET
SWALLOW
SWELLED
SWELLUP
SWILLED
SWIRLED
SWOLLEN

S••••L•

SAINTLY
SALABLE
SALTILY
SAMBALS
SAMHILL
SANDALS
SANDFLY
SAPPILY
SASSILY
SAUCILY
SAVABLE
SAVVILY
SAWMILL
SCANTLY
SCAPULA
SCARILY
SCHOOLS
SCRAWLS
SCRAWLY
SCROLLS
SCRUPLE
SCUFFLE
SCUTTLE
SEAGULL
SEALILY
SEASALT
SEATTLE
SEAWALL
SEAWOLF
SECKELS
SEEABLE
SEEDILY
SEIDELS
SEQUELS
SERIALS
SERVALS
SERVILE
SESSILE
SEVILLE
SHACKLE
SHADILY
SHAKILY
SHALALA
SHAMBLE
SHAPELY
SHARPLY
SHEERLY
SHEKELS
SHEWOLF
SHINGLE
SHINILY
SHOOFLY
SHORTLY
SHOVELS
SHOWILY
SHRILLS
SHRILLY
SHUFFLE
SHUTTLE
SIGHTLY
SIGNALS
SILKILY
SITWELL
SIXFOLD
SIXTHLY
SIZABLE
SIZABLY
SKIPOLE
SKITTLE
SLACKLY
SLEEKLY
SLICKLY
SLIMILY
SMARTLY
SMOKILY
SMUGGLE
SNAFFLE
SNAKILY
SNAPPLE
SNIDELY
SNIFFLE
SNIFFLY
SNIGGLE
SNIVELS
SNOWILY
SNUFFLE
SNUFFLY
SNUGGLE
SOAPILY
SOBERLY
SOCIALS
SOGGILY
SOLIDLY
SOLUBLE
SOOTILY
SORRELS
SORRILY
SOUFFLE
SOUNDLY
SPACKLE
SPANGLE
SPANGLY
SPARELY
SPARKLE
SPATULA
SPECKLE
SPICILY
SPIKILY
SPINDLE
SPINDLY
SPINELS
SPIRALS
SPRAWLS
SQUALLS
SQUATLY
SQUEALS
SQUILLS
STABILE
STAGILY
STAIDLY
STALELY
STARKLY
STARTLE
STATELY
STEEPLE
STEEPLY
STERILE
STERNLY
STEROLS
STIFFLY
STIMULI
STIPPLE
STOKELY
STONILY
STOUTLY
STROLLS
STUBBLE
STUBBLY
STUMBLE
SUAVELY
SUFFOLK
SULKILY
SUNBELT
SUNNILY
SURLILY
SWADDLE
SWAHILI
SWEETLY
SWIFTLY
SWINDLE
SWIVELS
SWIZZLE
SYMBOLS
SYSTOLE

S•••••L

SACKFUL
SAMHILL
SANIBEL
SATCHEL
SAWMILL
SCALPEL
SCANDAL
SEAGULL
SEAWALL
SEMINAL
SENEGAL
SENSUAL
SETSAIL
SEVERAL
SHAWWAL
SHOPFUL
SHRIVEL
SIGHFUL
SITWELL
SKILFUL
SKINFUL
SNORKEL
SONGFUL
SORORAL
SOULFUL
SPANIEL
SPATIAL
SPECIAL
SPIEGEL
SPOUSAL
STENCIL
STENGEL
STERNAL
STIEGEL
STOICAL
STRUDEL
SUBSOIL
SUNBOWL
SUNDIAL
SURREAL
SYNFUEL
SYNODAL

•SL••••

CSLEWIS
ISLAMIC
ISLANDS

•S•L•••

ASHLAND
ASHLARS
ASHLESS
ASSLIKE
ASYLUMS
ISOLATE
OSTLERS
PSALMED
PSALTER
TSELIOT
USELESS

•S••L••

ASTOLAT
ESTELLE
USUALLY

•S•••L•

ASARULE
ASPHALT
ASSAILS
ASSAULT
ESPIALS
ESTELLE
ISOHELS
ISRAELI
OSCEOLA
OSSICLE
USEABLE
USUALLY

•S••••L

ASOCIAL
ASUSUAL
BSCHOOL
ESPANOL
ESTIVAL
ESTORIL
ISHMAEL
USSTEEL

••SL•••

ASSLIKE
BUSLINE
DISLIKE
ENSLAVE
GASLESS
GASLOGS
GOSLING
GOSLOWS
MISLAID
MISLAYS
MISLEAD
MISLIKE
MOSLEMS
MUSLIMS
MUSLINS
SUSLIKS

••S•L••

ABSALOM
ABSOLUT
ABSOLVE
BASALLY
BASALTS
BUSTLED
BUSTLES
CASELAW
CASTLED
CASTLES
CUSSLER
DESALTS
DISPLAY
ENSILED
ENSILES
EPSILON
GISELLE
HASSLED
HASSLES
HOSTLER
HUSTLED
HUSTLER
HUSTLES
INSOLES
INSULAR
INSULIN
INSULTS
JOSTLED
JOSTLER
JOSTLES
LASALLE
MISALLY
MISPLAY
MOSELLE
MUSCLED
MUSCLES
NASALLY
NESTLED
NESTLER
NESTLES
PESTLED
PESTLES
POSSLQS
RASSLED
RASSLES
RESALES
RESALTS
RESELLS
RESILED
RESILES
RESOLED
RESOLES
RESOLVE
RESULTS
ROSALIE
ROSELLE
RUSTLED
RUSTLER
RUSTLES
TASHLIN
TUSSLED
TUSSLES
UPSILON
VISALIA

••S••L•

ASSAILS
ASSAULT
BASALLY
BOSSILY
BOSWELL
BUSHELS
BUSHILY
CASTILE
CASUALS
DISABLE
DISPELS
DISTILL
DISTILS
DOSSALS
DUSKILY
DUSTILY
ENSOULS
FISHILY
FISSILE
FOSSILS
FUSSILY
FUSTILY
GESTALT
GISELLE
GOSPELS
GUSHILY
GUSTILY
HASTILY
HOSTELS
HOSTILE
HUSKILY
INSTALL
INSTALS
INSTILL
INSTILS
INSTYLE
LASALLE
LASCALA
LISTELS
LUSTILY
MESCALS
MESSALA
MESSILY
MISALLY
MISCALL
MISERLY
MISFILE
MISRULE
MISSALS
MISSILE
MISTILY
MOSELLE
MUSHILY
MUSSELS
MUSSILY
MUSTILY
NASALLY
NASTILY
OSSICLE
PASSELS
PASTELS
PESKILY
PISTILS
PISTOLE
PISTOLS
PUSHILY
RASCALS
RESCALE
RESEALS
RESELLS
RESTYLE
RISIBLE
RISIBLY
RISKILY
RISSOLE
ROSELLE
ROSWELL
RUSSELL
RUSTILY
SASSILY
SESSILE
SYSTOLE
TASSELS
TASTILY
TESTFLY
TESTILY
TOSCALE
UNSEALS
UPSCALE
VASSALS
VESSELS
VISIBLE
VISIBLY
VISTULA
VISUALS
WASPILY
WISPILY

••S•••L

ARSENAL
AUSTRAL
BASHFUL
BESTIAL
BOSWELL
BUSGIRL
DESPOIL
DISHFUL
DISTILL
EASEFUL
ENSNARL
FISTFUL
GASOHOL
HUSHFUL
INSTALL
INSTILL
KESTREL
LESPAUL
LUSTFUL
MISCALL
MISDEAL
MISDIAL
MISTRAL
MUSEFUL
MUSICAL
NOSTRIL
PASCHAL
PASSEUL
PUSHFUL
RESTFUL
ROSEOIL
ROSWELL
RUSSELL
UNSNARL
USSTEEL
WASSAIL
WASTREL
WISHFUL
WISTFUL
ZESTFUL

•••SL••

BOBSLED
BOOSLER
BRESLIN
COWSLIP
CUSSLER
DOGSLED
ENISLED
ENISLES
FOCSLES
HASSLED
HASSLES
HEMSLEY
KTOSLIN
LAYSLOW
LETSLIP
LIESLOW
MEASLES
NONSLIP
PAISLEY
PARSLEY
POSSLQS
PRESLEY
RASSLED
RASSLES
SEASLUG
TOUSLED
TOUSLES
TUSSLED
TUSSLES
VIZSLAS
WINSLOW

•••S•L•

APISHLY
APOSTLE
BEASTLY
BOSSILY
BRASHLY
BRISKLY
BRISTLE
BRISTLY
CAPSULE
CHISELS
CLOSELY
CONSOLE
CONSULS
CONSULT
CRASSLY
CRISPLY
CROSSLY
DAMSELS
DENSELY
DIESELS
DORSALS
DOSSALS
EPISTLE
EROSELY
FALSELY
FIRSTLY
FISSILE
FLESHLY
FORSALE
FOSSILS
FRESHLY
FUSSILY
GHASTLY
GHOSTLY
GRISTLE
GRISTLY
GROSSLY
GUTSILY
HANSOLO
HARSHLY
HERSELF
HIMSELF
LETSFLY
LOOSELY
LOUSILY
MARSALA
MESSALA
MESSILY
MISSALS
MISSILE
MOISTLY
MORSELS
MUSSELS
MUSSILY
NOISILY
NONSELF
ONESELF
OURSELF
OUTSELL
OUTSOLD
PASSELS
PLUSHLY
PRESALE
PRESELL
PROSILY
RAWSILK
RISSOLE
RUSSELL
SASSILY
SEASALT
SESSILE
TAGSALE
TARSALS
TASSELS
TEASELS
TENSELY
TENSILE
TERSELY
THISTLE
THISTLY
THYSELF
TINSELS
TIPSILY
TONSILS
TRESTLE
UPPSALA
VASSALS
VESSELS
WEASELS
WHISTLE
WRESTLE

•••S••L

ABYSMAL
ASUSUAL
BRISTOL
COASTAL
CRYSTAL
FURSEAL
MARSHAL
OUTSELL
PASSEUL
PRESELL
RUSSELL
SENSUAL
SETSAIL
SUBSOIL
TOPSAIL
TOPSOIL
UNUSUAL
WASSAIL

••••SL•

CRASSLY
CROSSLY
GROSSLY
PIOUSLY

••••S•L

AEROSOL
AROUSAL
COUNSEL
CREOSOL
DEPOSAL
GIRASOL
PARASOL
PERUSAL
PHRASAL
REFUSAL
SPOUSAL
UTENSIL

SM•••••

SMACKED
SMACKER
SMALLER
SMALTOS
SMARTED
SMARTEN
SMARTER
SMARTLY
SMASHED
SMASHER
SMASHES
SMASHUP
SMATTER
SMEARED
SMELLED
SMELTED
SMELTER
SMETANA
SMIDGEN
SMILERS
SMILING
SMIRKED
SMITING
SMITTEN
SMOKERS
SMOKIER
SMOKIES
SMOKILY
SMOKING
SMOLDER
SMOOTHS
SMOOTHY
SMOTHER
SMUDGED
SMUDGES
SMUGGER
SMUGGLE

S•M••••

SAMARIA
SAMBAED
SAMBALS
SAMBARS
SAMECHS
SAMEDAY
SAMHILL
SAMISEN
SAMITES
SAMLETS
SAMOANS
SAMOVAR
SAMOYED
SAMPANS
SAMPLED
SAMPLER
SAMPLES
SAMPRAS
SAMPSON
SAMSARA
SAMSUNG
SAMURAI
SEMILOG
SEMINAL
SEMINAR
SEMIPRO
SEMITES
SEMITIC
SIMENON
SIMIANS
SIMILAR
SIMILES
SIMMERS
SIMMONS
SIMPERS
SIMPLER
SIMPLEX
SIMPSON
SOMALIA
SOMALIS
SOMATIC
SOMEDAY
SOMEHOW
SOMEONE
SOMEWAY
SUMATRA
SUMLESS
SUMMARY
SUMMERS
SUMMERY
SUMMING
SUMMITS
SUMMONS
SYMBOLS
SYMPTOM

S••M•••

SALMONS
SAWMILL
SCAMMED
SCAMPED
SCAMPER
SCHMEER
SCHMIDT
SCHMOES
SCHMOOS
SEAMIER
SEAMING
SEAMOSS
SEEMING
SEGMENT
SERMONS
SEYMOUR
SFUMATO
SHAMANS
SHAMBLE
SHAMING
SHAMMED
SHAMPOO
SHIMMER
SIAMESE
SIGMUND
SIMMERS
SIMMONS
SKIMASK
SKIMMED
SKIMMER
SKIMPED
SLAMMED
SLAMMER
SLIMIER
SLIMILY
SLIMJIM
SLIMMED
SLIMMER
SLUMBER
SLUMMED
SLUMPED
SPAMMED
SPAMMER
SPUMIER
SPUMING
SPUMONE
SPUMONI
SPUMOUS
STAMENS
STAMINA
STAMMER
STAMPED
STEMMED
STIMULI
STOMACH
STOMATA
STOMPED
STUMBLE
STUMERS
STUMPED
STUMPER
STYMIED
STYMIES
SUBMITS
SUMMARY
SUMMERS
SUMMERY
SUMMING
SUMMITS
SUMMONS
SUNMAID
SURMISE
SWAMPED
SWIMMER

S•••M••

SALAMIS
SANDMAN
SANDMEN
SCAMMED
SCHEMAS
SCHEMED
SCHEMER
SCHEMES
SCRIMPS
SCRIMPY
SCRUMMY
SEISMIC
SESAMES
SHAMMED
SHERMAN
SHIMMER
SHIPMAN
SHIPMEN
SHOWMAN
SHOWMEN
SHRIMPS
SIDEMAN
SIDEMEN
SKIMMED
SKIMMER
SLAMMED
SLAMMER
SLIMMED
SLIMMER
SLUMMED
SNOWMAN
SNOWMEN
SOLOMON
SPAMMED
SPAMMER
STAMMER
STARMAN
STARMAP
STEAMED
STEAMER
STEMMED
STIGMAS
STORMED
SWARMED
SWIMMER
SYNGMAN

S••••M•

SACHEMS
SALAAMS
SANREMO
SAOTOME
SASHIMI
SATCHMO
SATSUMA
SCHISMS
SCREAMS
SCRUMMY
SHALOMS
SITCOMS
SKIJUMP
SLALOMS
SOSUEME
SQUIRMS
SQUIRMY
STREAMS
SUBLIME
SUBSUME
SUCCUMB
SUNLAMP
SUPREME
SUPREMO
SURNAME
SYSTEMS

S•••••M

SANCTUM
SARCASM
SEAGRAM
SERFDOM
SEVENAM
SEVENPM
SHAHDOM
SIDEARM
SIKHISM
SISTRUM
SKOOKUM
SLIMJIM
SOPHISM
SORGHUM
STADIUM
STARDOM
STEINEM
STERNUM
STRATUM
SUNBEAM
SUNROOM
SURINAM
SYMPTOM
SYNONYM

•SM••••

OSMOSED
OSMOSES
OSMOSIS
OSMOTIC

•S•M•••

ISHMAEL
ISOMERS

•S••M••

ASHAMED
ASSUMED
ASSUMES
ESKIMOS
ISLAMIC
ISTHMUS
PSALMED

•S•••M•

ASHRAMS
ASYLUMS
ESTEEMS
ISONOMY
TSUNAMI

••SM•••
BESMEAR
BISMUTH
DESMOND
DISMAYS
DISMISS
GASMAIN
JASMINE
MISMATE
NESMITH
PISMIRE
YESMAAM

••S•M••
ASSUMED
ASSUMES
BASEMAN
BASEMEN
BESTMAN
BESTMEN
BUSHMAN
BUSHMEN
DUSTMAN
DUSTMEN
DUSTMOP
EASTMAN
KASHMIR
POSTMAN
POSTMEN
RESUMED
RESUMES
SESAMES
TASHMAN
WISEMAN
WISEMEN
YASHMAK

••S••M•
BESEEMS
COSTUME
CUSTOMS
DISARMS
GASPUMP
INSEAMS
LISSOME
MISNAME
MOSLEMS
MUSEUMS
MUSLIMS
PASTIME
POSSUMS
RESTAMP
SASHIMI
SOSUEME
SYSTEMS

••S•••M
ABSALOM
HASIDIM
NOSEEUM
NOSTRUM
ROSTRUM
SISTRUM
YESMAAM

•••SM••
ABYSMAL
ANOSMIA
ANOSMIC
BATSMAN
BATSMEN
ERASMUS
HEISMAN
HOUSMAN
KINSMAN
KINSMEN
MIASMAS
MIASMIC
NEWSMAN
NEWSMEN
PLASMAS
SEISMIC

•••S•M•
AWESOME
BALSAMS
CONSUME
FULSOME
HANSOMS
IRKSOME
LAKSHMI
LISSOME
NOISOME
POSSUMS
PRESUME
RANSOMS
SATSUMA
SUBSUME
TWOSOME
WINSOME

•••S••M
ALYSSUM
BLOSSOM
CAESIUM
ELYSIUM
GRISHAM
GRISSOM
OPOSSUM
POTSDAM

••••SM•
BEATSME
CHRISMS
SCHISMS
TRUISMS
VERISMO
WOEISME

••••S•M
ALYSSUM
BLOSSOM
FLOTSAM
GRISSOM
LUMPSUM
OPOSSUM
TRANSOM
ZEROSUM

•••••SM
ANIMISM
ATAVISM
ATHEISM
BAPTISM
CULTISM
CZARISM
DADAISM
EGOTISM
ELITISM
FADDISM
FAUVISM
FOGYISM
HEROISM
JUDAISM
LAMAISM
MARXISM
PIANISM
PIETISM
REALISM
SARCASM
SIKHISM
SOPHISM
TORYISM
TOURISM
TROPISM

SN•••••
SNACKED
SNACKER
SNAFFLE
SNAFUED
SNAGGED
SNAKIER
SNAKILY
SNAKING
SNAPONS
SNAPPED
SNAPPER
SNAPPLE
SNAPSAT
SNAPSTO
SNAPSUP
SNARING
SNARLED
SNEAKED
SNEAKER
SNEAKIN
SNEERAT
SNEERED
SNEERER
SNEEZED
SNEEZER
SNEEZES
SNELLEN
SNICKER
SNIDELY
SNIDEST
SNIFFAT
SNIFFED
SNIFFER
SNIFFLE
SNIFFLY
SNIFTER
SNIGGER
SNIGGLE
SNIGLET
SNIPEAT
SNIPERS
SNIPING
SNIPPED
SNIPPET
SNITCHY
SNIVELS
SNOCATS
SNOCONE
SNOGGED
SNOOKER
SNOOPED
SNOOPER
SNOOTED
SNOOZED
SNOOZES
SNORERS
SNORING
SNORKEL
SNORTED
SNORTER
SNOWCAP
SNOWCAT
SNOWDAY
SNOWDON
SNOWIER
SNOWILY
SNOWING
SNOWJOB
SNOWMAN
SNOWMEN
SNOWPEA
SNOWSIN
SNUBBED
SNUFFED
SNUFFER
SNUFFLE
SNUFFLY
SNUGGER
SNUGGLE

S•N••••
SANCTUM
SANDALS
SANDBAG
SANDBAR
SANDBOX
SANDERS
SANDFLY
SANDHOG
SANDIER
SANDING
SANDLOT
SANDMAN
SANDMEN
SANFORD
SANGOUT
SANGRIA
SANIBEL
SANJOSE
SANJUAN
SANLUIS
SANREMO
SANTAFE
SANTANA
SANTINI
SANTIRS
SENATES
SENATOR
SENDERS
SENDFOR
SENDING
SENDOFF
SENDOUT
SENDSIN
SENDSUP
SENDUPS
SENECAS
SENEGAL
SENIORS
SENNETT
SENORAS
SENORES
SENSATE
SENSING
SENSORS
SENSORY
SENSUAL
SENTFOR
SENTOFF
SENTOUT
SENUFOS
SINATRA
SINCERE
SINEDIE
SINGERS
SINGING
SINGLED
SINGLES
SINGOUT
SINGSTO
SINKAGE
SINKERS
SINKING
SINKSIN
SINLESS
SINLIKE
SINNERS
SINUOUS
SINUSES
SONATAS
SONGFUL
SONLESS
SONLIKE
SONNETS
SUNBATH
SUNBEAM
SUNBELT
SUNBOWL
SUNBURN
SUNCITY
SUNDAES
SUNDAYS
SUNDECK
SUNDERS
SUNDEWS
SUNDIAL
SUNDOGS
SUNDOWN
SUNFISH
SUNGODS
SUNKIST
SUNLAMP
SUNLESS
SUNLIKE
SUNMAID
SUNNIER
SUNNILY
SUNNING
SUNRAYS
SUNRISE
SUNROOF
SUNROOM
SUNSETS
SUNSPOT
SUNSUIT
SUNTANS
SYNAPSE
SYNCHED
SYNCHES
SYNCING
SYNERGY
SYNFUEL
SYNGMAN
SYNODAL
SYNODIC
SYNONYM

S••N•••
SADNESS
SAINTED
SAINTLY
SAUNTER
SCANDAL
SCANNED
SCANNER
SCANTED
SCANTER
SCANTLY
SCENDED
SCENERY
SCENTED
SCHNAPS
SCONCES
SEANCES
SEENFIT
SEENOFF
SEENOUT
SEINERS
SEINING
SENNETT
SHANANA
SHANGRI
SHANKAR
SHANKED
SHANNON
SHANTEY
SHINDIG
SHINERS
SHINGLE
SHINIER
SHINILY
SHINING
SHINNED
SHUNNED
SHUNTED
SHYNESS
SIENNAS
SIGNALS
SIGNEES
SIGNERS
SIGNETS
SIGNIFY
SIGNING
SIGNOFF
SIGNOUT
SIGNSIN
SIGNSON
SIGNSUP
SINNERS
SKANKED
SKANKER
SKINFUL
SKINNED
SKINNER
SKUNKED
SLANDER
SLANTED
SLENDER
SLINGER
SLINKED
SLYNESS
SOANDSO
SONNETS
SOONERS
SOONEST
SOUNDED
SOUNDER
SOUNDLY
SPANDEX
SPANGLE
SPANGLY
SPANIEL
SPANISH
SPANKED
SPANKER
SPANNED
SPANNER
SPENCER
SPENDER
SPENSER
SPINACH
SPINDLE
SPINDLY
SPINDRY
SPINELS
SPINETS
SPINIER
SPINNER
SPINNEY
SPINOFF
SPINOUT
SPINOZA
SPONDEE
SPONGED
SPONGER
SPONGES
SPONSOR
SPUNOFF
SPUNOUT
STANCES
STANDBY
STANDEE
STANDIN
STANDON
STANDUP
STANLEE
STANLEY
STANNIC
STANTON
STANZAS
STENCIL
STENGEL
STENTOR
STINGER
STINGOS
STINKER
STINTED
STONERS
STONIER
STONILY
STONING
STUNGUN
STUNNED
STUNNER
STUNTED
SUNNIER
SUNNILY
SUNNING
SURNAME
SWANKED
SWANKER
SWANSEA
SWANSON
SWINDLE
SWINGBY
SWINGER
SWINISH
SWONKEN

S•••N••
SABINES
SAGINAW
SALINAS
SARANAC
SARONGS
SATINET
SAVANNA
SAVANTS
SAVINGS
SAYINGS
SCANNED
SCANNER
SCIENCE
SCORNED
SCORNER
SCRUNCH
SECANTS
SECONDS
SELENIC
SEMINAL
SEMINAR
SERENER
SETINTO
SEVENAM
SEVENPM
SEVENTH
SEVENTY
SEVENUP
SHANNON
SHATNER
SHAWNEE
SHINNED
SHOWNIN
SHRINER
SHRINES
SHRINKS
SHUNNED
SIDINGS
SIENNAS
SILENCE
SILENTS
SIMENON
SIZINGS
SKINNED
SKINNER
SOIGNEE
SOYINKA
SPANNED
SPANNER
SPAWNED
SPINNER
SPINNEY
SPLINES
SPLINTS
SPOONED
SPOONER
SPRINGS
SPRINGY
SPRINTS
SPURNED
SPURNER
SPUTNIK
SQUANTO
SQUINCH
SQUINTS
SQUINTY
STAINED
STAINER
STANNIC
STAUNCH
STDENIS
STEINEM
STEINER
STERNAL
STERNER
STERNLY
STERNUM
STRANDS
STRANGE
STRINGS
STRINGY
STUNNED
STUNNER
SUBUNIT
SURINAM
SUSANNA
SUSANNE
SUZANNE
SWEENEY
SWOONED
SYNONYM
SYRINGA
SYRINGE

S••••N•
SABRINA
SACKING
SADDENS
SAGGING
SAILING
SALERNO
SALIENT
SALMONS
SALOONS
SALTINE
SALTING
SALVING
SAMOANS
SAMPANS
SAMSUNG
SANDING
SANTANA
SANTINI
SAPIENS
SAPIENT
SAPLING
SAPPING
SARDINE
SARGENT
SASSING
SATEENS
SAVANNA
SCALENE
SCALING
SCARING
SCHWINN
SCOPING
SCORING
SCRAWNY
SCREENS
SEAFANS
SEALANE
SEALANT
SEALING
SEAMING
SEARING
SEASONS
SEATING
SEEDING
SEEKING
SEEMING
SEEPING
SEGMENT
SEINING
SEIZING
SELLING
SENDING
SENSING
SEQUINS
SERLING
SERMONS
SERPENT
SERVANT
SERVING
SESTINA
SETLINE
SETTING
SEVIGNE
SEXTANS
SEXTANT
SEXTONS
SHADING
SHAKING
SHAMANS
SHAMING
SHANANA
SHAPING
SHARING
SHAVING
SHEBANG
SHINING
SHOEING
SHOGUNS
SHOOING
SHOOINS
SHORING
SHOVING
SHOWING
SHUTINS
SIBLING
SICCING
SICKENS
SIDLING
SIFTING
SIGHING
SIGMUND
SIGNING
SILOING
SILTING
SIMIANS
SIMMONS
SINGING
SINKING
SIOUANS
SIPHONS
SIPPING
SISKINS
SISTINE
SITTING
SIXGUNS
SKATING
SKEWING
SKIRUNS
SKYLINE
SLAKING
SLATING
SLAVING
SLICING
SLIDING
SLIPONS
SLOGANS
SLOPING
SLOVENE
SLOVENS
SLOWING
SMETANA
SMILING
SMITING
SMOKING
SNAKING
SNAPONS
SNARING
SNIPING
SNOCONE
SNORING
SNOWING
SOAKING
SOAPING
SOARING
SOBBING
SOCKING
SODDING
SOFTENS
SOILING
SOLOING
SOLVENT
SOLVING
SOMEONE
SOPPING
SOPRANO
SORDINI
SORDINO
SORTING
SORVINO
SOURING
SOUTANE
SPACING
SPADING
SPARING
SPAVINS
SPAYING
SPECING
SPELUNK
SPEWING
SPICING
SPIKING
SPIRANT
SPITING
SPLEENS
SPOKANE
SPOKING
SPRAINS
SPUMING
SPUMONE
SPUMONI
STAGING
STAKING
STAMENS
STAMINA
STARING
STATING
STAVING
STAYING
STEPINS
STEVENS
STEWING
STIPEND
STJOHNS
STOKING
STOLONS
STONING
STORING
STOWING
STRAINS
STUDENT
STYLING
STYRENE
SUBBING
SUBORNS
SUBTEND
SUCKING
SUDSING
SUITING
SUKARNO
SULKING
SULTANA
SULTANS
SUMMING
SUMMONS
SUNNING
SUNTANS
SUPPING
SURFING
SURGING
SUSANNA
SUSANNE
SUSPEND
SUSSING
SUZANNE
SWAYING
SWIPING
SYLVANS
SYNCING
SYPHONS
SYRIANS

S•••••N
SAFFRON
SAGEHEN
SAHARAN
SALADIN
SAMISEN
SAMPSON
SANDMAN
SANDMEN
SANJUAN
SARACEN
SARAZEN
SAROYAN
SASSOON
SATDOWN
SAURIAN
SAVARIN
SAXHORN
SAYWHEN
SCHWINN
SCRIVEN
SEALION
SECTION
SEEPSIN
SENDSIN
SERBIAN
SESSION
SETDOWN
SETUPON
SEWEDON
SHANNON
SHAREIN
SHARPEN
SHELDON
SHELTON
SHERMAN
SHERWIN
SHIPMAN
SHIPMEN
SHODDEN
SHORTEN
SHOTGUN
SHOWMAN
SHOWMEN
SHOWNIN
SHOWSIN
SHUTSIN
SICHUAN
SIDEMAN
SIDEMEN
SIGNSIN
SIGNSON
SILICON
SIMENON
SIMPSON
SINKSIN
SIOBHAN
SIRLOIN
SITDOWN
SIXIRON
SIXTEEN
SKELTON
SLACKEN
SLAYTON
SLEEKEN
SLEEPIN
SLEEPON
SLEPTIN
SLEPTON
SLIDEIN
SLIPSIN
SLIPSON
SLOEGIN
SMARTEN
SMIDGEN
SMITTEN
SNEAKIN
SNELLEN
SNOWDON
SNOWMAN
SNOWMEN
SNOWSIN
SOCKSIN
SOJOURN
SOLOMON
SOTHERN
SOUPCON
SOYBEAN
SPARTAN
SPIEDON
SPIESON
SPORRAN
SPURSON
STANDIN
STANDON
STANTON
STARMAN
STASSEN
STATION
STEEPEN
STEPHEN
STEPSIN
STEPSON
STETSON
STEUBEN
STIFFEN
STILTON
STIRSIN
STOLLEN
STOODIN
STOPSIN
STOUTEN
STRIVEN
STUNGUN
STYGIAN
STYRIAN
SUASION
SUBJOIN
SUCKSIN
SUCTION
SUNBURN
SUNDOWN
SURGEON
SUSTAIN
SWANSON
SWEARIN
SWEETEN
SWEETON
SWOLLEN
SWONKEN
SWOREIN
SYNGMAN

•S•N•••
ASININE
ASUNDER
ISONOMY
PSANDQS
TSUNAMI
USINGUP

•S••N••
ASCENDS
ASCENTS
ASHANTI
ASKANCE
ASOFNOW
ASSENTS
ESPANOL
ESSENCE
ESSENES
ESTONIA
ISLANDS
OSCINES
USTINOV

•S•••N•
ASHCANS
ASHLAND
ASININE
ASSIGNS
ASTOUND
ESPYING
ISOGONS
ISSUING
OSBORNE
TSARINA
USGRANT
USOPENS

•S••••N
ASKEDIN
ASPIRIN

••SN•••
ENSNARE
ENSNARL
MISNAME
UNSNAGS
UNSNAPS
UNSNARL

••S•N••
ABSENCE
ABSENTS
ARSENAL
ARSENIC
ARSENIO
ASSENTS
BASENJI
CASINGS
CASINOS
COSINES
COSTNER
ESSENCE
ESSENES
FISHNET
HOSANNA
JUSTNOW
LISENTE
LYSENKO
MASONIC
MASONRY
RESANDS
RESENDS
RESENTS
RESINGS
RISINGS
ROSANNA
ROSANNE
SUSANNA
SUSANNE
TISANES

••S••N•
ABSCOND
ASSIGNS
BASHING
BASKING
BASTING
BESTING
BOSSING

BUSHING
BUSKING
BUSKINS
BUSLINE
BUSSING
BUSTING
BUSYING
CASERNE
CASERNS
CASHING
CASSINI
CASSINO
CASTING
CESSING
COSHING
COSIGNS
COSTING
CUSHING
CUSSING
DASHING
DESCANT
DESCEND
DESCENT
DESIGNS
DESMOND
DESTINE
DESTINY
DISBAND
DISHING
DISOWNS
DISSENT
DISSING
DISTANT
DISTEND
DUSTING
EASTEND
ENSIGNS
ENSUING
ERSKINE
FASTENS
FASTING
FASTONE
FESSING
FISHING
FUSSING
GASCONS
GASCONY
GASHING
GASKINS
GASPING
GOSLING
GUSHING
GUSTING
HASHING
HASPING
HASTENS
HASTING
HISPANO
HISSING
HOSANNA
HOSKINS
HOSTING
HUSBAND
HUSHING
HUSKING
IFSTONE
INSPANS
INSTANT
ISSUING
JASMINE
JESTING
JOSHING
JOSKINS
JUSTINE
KISSING
LASAGNA
LASAGNE
LASHING
LASTING
LESSENS
LESSING
LESSONS
LISPING
LISTENS
LISTING
LUSTING
MASHING
MASKING
MASSING
MCSWINE
MESHING
MESSINA
MESSING
MISDONE
MISSING
MISTING
MOSHING
MOSSING
MUSHING
MUSLINS
MUSSING
MUSTANG
NASCENT
NESTING
NOSHING
OBSCENE
OUSTING
PASSING
PASTINA
PASTING
PISCINE
PISTONS
POSTING
PUSHING
RASPING
RESCIND
RESIGNS
RESOUND
RESPINS
RESPOND
RESTING
RISKING
ROSANNA
ROSANNE
ROSSINI
ROSTAND
RUSHING
RUSTING
SASSING
SESTINA
SISKINS
SISTINE
SUSANNA
SUSANNE
SUSPEND
SUSSING
TASKING
TASTING
TESTING
TOSSING
TUSCANY
UNSOUND
UNSPENT
UPSWING
VESTING
VISAING
VISIONS
WASHING
WASTING
WESTEND
WISHING
WISPING
YESSING

••S•••N

ABSTAIN
ALSORAN
BASEMAN
BASEMEN
BASSOON
BASTION
BESTMAN
BESTMEN
BUSHMAN
BUSHMEN
CASPIAN
CESSION
CISTERN
COSTAIN
CUSHION
DISCERN
DISDAIN
DISHPAN
DISJOIN
DUSTBIN
DUSTMAN
DUSTMEN
DUSTPAN
EASEDIN
EASESIN
EASTERN
EASTMAN
EPSILON
EPSTEIN
FASHION
FESTOON
FISSION
FUSTIAN
GASMAIN
HASBEEN
HESHVAN
HESSIAN
HUSSEIN
INSULIN
KOSYGIN
MISSION
PASSION
PASTERN
POSTERN
POSTMAN
POSTMEN
PUSHKIN
PUSHPIN
RESTAIN
RUSSIAN
SASSOON
SESSION
SUSTAIN
TASHLIN
TASHMAN
TESTBAN
UNSHORN
UPSILON
WESTERN
WISEMAN
WISEMEN

•••SN••

BROSNAN
EDASNER
INASNIT
PARSNIP
PILSNER

•••S•N•

ABASING
ABUSING
AMUSING
ARCSINE
ARISING
ARTSONG
BIASING
BOSSING
BOUSING
BUSSING
CASSINI
CASSINO
CAUSING
CEASING
CENSING
CESSING
CHASING
CLOSING
CONSENT
COUSINS
CUISINE
CURSING
CUSSING
DAMSONS
DAYSINN
DISSENT
DISSING
DOUSING
DOWSING
ERASING
FESSING
FUSSING
GINSENG
GODSEND
GODSONS
GOOSING
HISSING
HORSING
HOUSING
JETSONS
KANSANS
KISSING
KMESONS
KRISHNA
LANSING
LAPSING
LEASING
LESSENS
LESSING
LESSONS
LIPSYNC
LOOSENS
LOOSING
LOUSING
MASSING
MESSINA
MESSING
MISSING
MOSSING
MOUSING
MUSSING
NELSONS
NOISING
NOOSING
NURSING
ORISONS
PAISANO
PARSING
PARSONS
PASSING
PAUSING
PEASANT
PEPSINS
PERSONA
PERSONS
PHASING
POISING
POISONS
PORSENA
PRESENT
PRISONS
PROSING
PULSING
PURSING
RAISING
RAISINS
REASONS
RETSINA
RINSING
ROSSINI
ROUSING
SAMSUNG
SASSING
SEASONS
SENSING
SUDSING
SUSSING
TEASING
TENSING
TOCSINS
TOSSING
TULSANS
UNISONS
WORSENS
YESSING

•••S••N

ALASKAN
ALLSTON
ANDSOON
ANISTON
BASSOON
BATSMAN
BATSMEN
BLUSHON
BRESLIN
BROSNAN
BURSTYN
CAISSON
CAPSTAN
CATSCAN
CESSION
CHASTEN
CLOSEIN
CONSIGN
CRISPIN
DAYSINN
DOESKIN
DRESDEN
DRISTAN
EELSKIN
ELISION
ELYSIAN
EROSION
ETESIAN
EVASION
FISSION
FRESHEN
FRISIAN
FRISSON
GADSDEN
GLISTEN
GRISKIN
HALSTON
HARSHEN
HEISMAN
HESSIAN
HEXSIGN
HOUSMAN
HOUSTON
HUSSEIN
INASPIN
JANSSEN
KEESHAN
KIDSKIN
KINSMAN
KINSMEN
KTOSLIN
MANSION
MEISSEN
MISSION
MOISTEN
MONSOON
NEWSMAN
NEWSMEN
NILSSON
OILSKIN
PASSION
PENSION
PERSIAN
PHASEIN
PIGSKIN
PLOSION
POISSON
PRESSON
PRESTON
RALSTON
RUSSIAN
SASSOON
SESSION
STASSEN
SUASION
TENSION
TORSION
TRISTAN
VERSION
WALSTON
WINSTON

••••SN•

DEMESNE

••••S•N

ACHESON
ADAMSON
ADDISON
ALLISON
ALLYSON
ARTISAN
BACKSIN
BANKSON
BEARSON
BENISON
BENTSEN
BERGSON
BERNSEN
BLOUSON
BLOWSIN
BOXESIN
BRANSON
BRONSON
BUTTSIN
CAISSON
CALLSIN
CALLSON
CARLSON
CAVESIN
CHANSON
CHIPSIN
CLEMSON
CLUESIN
COARSEN
COMESIN
COMESON
CRIMSON
DAWNSON
DEALSIN
DINESEN
DINESIN
DINESON
DIVESIN
DODGSON
DOTESON
DRAGSIN
DRAGSON
DRAWSIN
DRAWSON
DROPSIN
EASESIN
EDGESIN
ELEISON
ELLISON
EMERSON
ERICSON
FADESIN
FALLSIN
FALLSON
FEEDSON
FILLSIN
FLIESIN
FRISSON
GAINSON
GIVESIN
GLEASON
GLUESON
GOODSON
GRAYSON
GROWSON
HANDSIN
HANDSON
HANGSIN
HANGSON
HARPSON
HEADSIN
HIRESON
HOARSEN
HOLDSIN
HOLDSON
HORNSIN
JACKSON
JAMESON
JANSSEN
JEWISON
JOHNSON
JOINSIN
JUMPSIN
JUMPSON
KEEPSIN
KEEPSON
KICKSIN
LEADSIN
LEADSON
LEANSON
LIAISON
LIVESIN
LIVESON
LOCKSON
LOOKSIN
LOOKSON
MADISON
MAILSIN
MEISSEN
MIXESIN
MOVESIN
MOVESON
MUMESON
NAILSIN
NIELSEN
NILSSON
ORBISON
PAULSEN
PEARSON
PEERSIN
PICKSON
PILESIN
PILESON
PIMESON
PLANSON
PLAYSON
PLUGSIN
POISSON
POURSIN
PRESSON
PREYSON
PULLSIN
PULLSON
RAKESIN
READSIN
REELSIN
REINSIN
ROBESON
ROLLSIN
ROLLSON
ROPESIN
RULESON
SAMISEN
SAMPSON
SEEPSIN
SENDSIN
SHOWSIN
SHUTSIN
SIGNSIN
SIGNSON
SIMPSON
SINKSIN
SLIPSIN
SLIPSON
SNOWSIN
SOCKSIN
SPIESON
SPURSON
STASSEN
STEPSIN
STEPSON
STETSON
STIRSIN
STOPSIN
SUCKSIN
SWANSON
TACKSON
TAKESIN
TAKESON
TELLSON
THOMSON
TREASON
TRIESON
TUCKSIN
TUNESIN
TURNSIN
TURNSON
UPRISEN
VENISON
VOTESIN
WADESIN
WAITSON
WALKSON
WANTSIN
WAVESIN
WILLSON
WORKSIN
WORKSON
YELTSIN
ZOOMSIN

SO•••••

SOAKERS
SOAKING
SOAKSUP
SOANDSO
SOAPBOX
SOAPERS
SOAPIER
SOAPILY
SOAPING
SOARERS
SOARING
SOBBERS
SOBBING
SOBERED
SOBERER
SOBERLY
SOCIALS
SOCIETY
SOCKETS
SOCKEYE
SOCKING
SOCKSIN
SODAPOP
SODDIER
SODDIES
SODDING
SODLESS
SOFABED
SOFFITS
SOFTENS
SOFTEST
SOFTIES
SOFTISH
SOFTTOP
SOGGIER
SOGGILY
SOIGNEE
SOILING
SOIREES
SOJOURN
SOLACES
SOLARIA
SOLDERS
SOLDIER
SOLDOFF
SOLDOUT
SOLEDAD
SOLFEGE
SOLICIT
SOLIDER
SOLIDLY
SOLOING
SOLOIST
SOLOMON
SOLUBLE
SOLUTES
SOLVENT
SOLVERS
SOLVING
SOMALIA
SOMALIS
SOMATIC
SOMEDAY
SOMEHOW
SOMEONE
SOMEWAY
SONATAS
SONGFUL
SONLESS
SONLIKE
SONNETS
SOONERS
SOONEST
SOOTHED
SOOTHER
SOOTHES
SOOTIER
SOOTILY
SOPHISM
SOPHIST
SOPPIER
SOPPING
SOPRANO
SOPWITH
SORBATE
SORBETS
SORCERY
SORDINI
SORDINO
SORGHUM
SORITES
SORORAL
SORRELS
SORRIER
SORRILY
SORROWS
SORTERS
SORTIED
SORTIES
SORTING
SORTOUT
SORVINO
SOSUEME
SOTHERE
SOTHERN
SOTTISH
SOUFFLE
SOUGHED
SOUKOUS
SOULFUL
SOUNDED
SOUNDER
SOUNDLY
SOUPCON
SOUPIER
SOUPSUP
SOURCED
SOURCES
SOUREST
SOURING
SOURISH
SOUTANE
SOUTHEY
SOVIETS
SOWBUGS
SOWLIKE
SOYBEAN
SOYINKA

S•O••••

SAOTOME
SCOFFED
SCOFFER
SCOLDED
SCOLDER
SCONCES
SCOOPED
SCOOPER
SCOOTED
SCOOTER
SCOPING
SCORERS
SCORING
SCORNED
SCORNER
SCORPIO
SCOTERS
SCOTTIE
SCOURED
SCOURER
SCOURGE
SCOUSES
SCOUTED
SCOUTER
SCOWLED
SCOWLER
SHOCKED
SHOCKER
SHODDEN
SHOEBOX
SHOEING
SHOFARS
SHOGUNS
SHOOFLY
SHOOING
SHOOINS
SHOOKUP
SHOOTAT
SHOOTER
SHOOTUP
SHOPFUL
SHOPPED
SHOPPER
SHOPPES
SHORING
SHORTED
SHORTEN
SHORTER
SHORTLY
SHORTOF
SHOTFOR
SHOTGUN
SHOTOUT
SHOTPUT
SHOULDA
SHOUTED
SHOUTER
SHOVELS
SHOVERS
SHOVING
SHOWBIZ
SHOWDOG
SHOWERS
SHOWERY
SHOWIER
SHOWILY
SHOWING
SHOWMAN
SHOWMEN
SHOWNIN
SHOWOFF
SHOWOUT
SHOWSIN
SHOWSUP
SIOBHAN
SIOUANS
SKOOKUM
SKOSHES
SLOBBER
SLOEGIN
SLOGANS
SLOGGED
SLOPING
SLOPPED
SLOSHED
SLOSHES
SLOTCAR
SLOTTED
SLOUCHY
SLOUGHS
SLOVAKS
SLOVENE
SLOVENS
SLOWEST
SLOWING
SLOWSUP
SLOWUPS
SMOKERS
SMOKIER
SMOKIES
SMOKILY
SMOKING
SMOLDER
SMOOTHS
SMOOTHY
SMOTHER
SNOCATS
SNOCONE
SNOGGED
SNOOKER
SNOOPED
SNOOPER
SNOOTED
SNOOZED
SNOOZES
SNORERS
SNORING
SNORKEL
SNORTED
SNORTER
SNOWCAP
SNOWCAT
SNOWDAY
SNOWDON
SNOWIER
SNOWILY
SNOWING
SNOWJOB
SNOWMAN
SNOWMEN
SNOWPEA
SNOWSIN
SOONERS
SOONEST
SOOTHED
SOOTHER
SOOTHES
SOOTIER
SOOTILY
SPOILED
SPOILER
SPOKANE
SPOKEOF
SPOKEUP
SPOKING
SPONDEE
SPONGED
SPONGER
SPONGES
SPONSOR
SPOOFED
SPOOFER
SPOOKED
SPOOLED
SPOONED
SPOONER
SPORRAN
SPORTED
SPOTLIT
SPOTTED
SPOTTER
SPOUSAL
SPOUSES
SPOUTED
SPOUTER
STOCKED
STOCKUP
STOGIES
STOICAL
STOKELY
STOKERS
STOKING
STOLLEN
STOLLER
STOLONS
STOMACH
STOMATA
STOMPED
STONERS
STONIER
STONILY
STONING
STOODBY
STOODIN
STOODUP
STOOGES
STOOKED
STOOKEY
STOOLIE
STOOPED
STOPGAP
STOPOFF
STOPPED
STOPPER
STOPSIN
STOPSUP
STORAGE
STORERS
STOREUP
STOREYS
STORIED
STORIES
STORING
STORMED
STOUTEN
STOUTER
STOUTLY
STOWING
SUOJURE
SUOLOCO
SWOBBED
SWOLLEN
SWONKEN
SWOONED
SWOOPED
SWOOSIE
SWOPPED
SWOREAT
SWOREBY
SWOREIN

S••O•••

SALOONS
SAMOANS
SAMOVAR
SAMOYED
SARONGS
SAROYAN
SAVORED
SAVOURS
SAVOURY
SCHOLAR
SCHOOLS
SCIORRA
SCOOPED
SCOOPER
SCOOTED
SCOOTER
SCROLLS
SCROOGE
SECONDS
SEGOVIA
SENORAS
SENORES
SHOOFLY
SHOOING
SHOOINS
SHOOKUP
SHOOTAT
SHOOTER
SHOOTUP
SHROUDS
SILOING
SIROCCO
SKOOKUM
SMOOTHS
SMOOTHY
SNOOKER
SNOOPED
SNOOPER
SNOOTED
SNOOZED
SNOOZES
SOJOURN
SOLOING
SOLOIST
SOLOMON
SORORAL
SPLOTCH
SPOOFED
SPOOFER
SPOOKED
SPOOLED
SPOONED
SPOONER
SPROUTS
STJOHNS
STLOUIS
STOODBY
STOODIN
STOODUP
STOOGES
STOOKED
STOOKEY
STOOLIE
STOOPED
STROBES
STROKED
STROKES
STROLLS
STROPHE
STROPPY
SUBORNS
SWOONED
SWOOPED
SWOOSIE
SYNODAL
SYNODIC
SYNONYM

S•••O••

SACKOUT
SAILORS
SALLOWS
SALMONS
SALOONS

SALSODA
SALVOES
SALVORS
SANFORD
SANGOUT
SANJOSE
SAOTOME
SAPPORO
SASSOON
SATDOWN
SAVIORS
SAVIOUR
SAWLOGS
SAWWOOD
SAXHORN
SCHLOCK
SCHMOES
SCHMOOS
SCHOOLS
SCROOGE
SEABORG
SEACOWS
SEADOGS
SEAFOOD
SEALOFF
SEAMOSS
SEAPORT
SEASONS
SEAWOLF
SECTORS
SEEKOUT
SEENOFF
SEENOUT
SEESOFF
SEESOUT
SEETOIT
SELLOFF
SELLOUT
SENDOFF
SENDOUT
SENIORS
SENSORS
SENSORY
SENTOFF
SENTOUT
SEQUOIA
SERIOUS
SERMONS
SETDOWN
SETSOFF
SETSOUT
SEXTONS
SEYMOUR
SHADOOF
SHADOWS
SHADOWY
SHAKOES
SHALOMS
SHEWOLF
SHIKOKU
SHIPOUT
SHOTOUT
SHOWOFF
SHOWOUT
SHUTOFF
SHUTOUT
SHYLOCK
SICKOUT
SIGNOFF
SIGNOUT
SIMMONS
SINGOUT
SINUOUS
SIPHONS

SIRLOIN
SITCOMS
SITDOWN
SITSOUT
SIXFOLD
SKIBOBS
SKIBOOT
SKIPOLE
SKIPOUT
SKITOWS
SKYHOOK
SLALOMS
SLIPONS
SLIPOUT
SNAPONS
SNOCONE
SOLDOFF
SOLDOUT
SOMEONE
SORROWS
SORTOUT
SOUKOUS
SPIGOTS
SPINOFF
SPINOUT
SPINOZA
SPUMONE
SPUMONI
SPUMOUS
SPUNOFF
SPUNOUT
STATORS
STCROIX
STEPOUT
STEROID
STEROLS
STOLONS
STOPOFF
STUPORS
SUBJOIN
SUBROSA
SUBSOIL
SUBVOCE
SUCCORS
SUCCOUR
SUCROSE
SUFFOLK
SUITORS
SUMMONS
SUNBOWL
SUNDOGS
SUNDOWN
SUNGODS
SUNROOF
SUNROOM
SUOLOCO
SUPPORT
SUPPOSE
SURCOAT
SYMBOLS
SYPHONS
SYSTOLE

S••••O•
SAFFRON
SALCHOW
SALTBOX
SAMPSON
SANDBOX
SANDHOG
SANDLOT
SASSOON
SAVELOY
SAWWOOD

SCALLOP
SCHMOOS
SCISSOR
SEAFOOD
SEALION
SECTION
SEEDPOD
SELLFOR
SEMILOG
SENATOR
SENDFOR
SENTFOR
SENUFOS
SERFDOM
SESSION
SETUPON
SEWEDON
SHADOOF
SHAHDOM
SHALLOT
SHALLOW
SHAMPOO
SHANNON
SHELDON
SHELTON
SHOEBOX
SHORTOF
SHOTFOR
SHOWDOG
SIGNSON
SILICON
SIMENON
SIMPSON
SIXIRON
SKELTON
SKIBOOT
SKIDDOO
SKIDROW
SKYHOOK
SLAYTON
SLEDDOG
SLEEPON
SLEPTON
SLIPSON
SMALTOS
SNOWDON
SNOWJOB
SOAPBOX
SODAPOP
SOFTTOP
SOLOMON
SOMEHOW
SOUPCON
SPARROW
SPEAKOF
SPECTOR
SPEEDOS
SPIEDON
SPIESON
SPOKEOF
SPONSOR
SPURSON
SQUALOR
STANDON
STANTON
STARDOM
STATION
STENTOR
STEPSON
STEREOS
STETSON
STILTON
STINGOS
STUCCOS

STUDIOS
SUASION
SUBPLOT
SUCTION
SUNROOF
SUNROOM
SUNSPOT
SURGEON
SWALLOW
SWANSON
SWEETON
SYMPTOM

S•••••O
SAGUARO
SALERNO
SANREMO
SAPPORO
SAPSAGO
SATCHMO
SCHERZO
SCORPIO
SEMIPRO
SERPICO
SETINTO
SFUMATO
SHAMPOO
SHAPIRO
SINGSTO
SIROCCO
SKIDDOO
SNAPSTO
SOANDSO
SOPRANO
SORDINO
SORVINO
SPIRITO
SQUANTO
STICKTO
STRETTO
STUCKTO
SUBZERO
SUHARTO
SUKARNO
SUOLOCO
SUPREMO
SWEARTO

•SO••••
ASOCIAL
ASOFNOW
ESOTERY
ISOBARS
ISOGONS
ISOHELS
ISOLATE
ISOMERS
ISONOMY
ISOPODS
ISOTOPE
TSOURIS
USOPENS
USOSHOW

•S•O•••
ASSORTS
ASTOLAT
ASTORIA
ASTOUND
ESCORTS
ESPOSAS
ESPOSOS
ESPOUSE
ESTONIA

ESTORIL
OSBORNE
OSMOSED
OSMOSES
OSMOSIS
OSMOTIC

•S••O••
ASHFORD
ASKSOUT
BSCHOOL
ESCROWS
ISADORA
ISOGONS
ISONOMY
ISOPODS
ISOTOPE
OSCEOLA
OSHKOSH
OSSEOUS
OSTEOID

•S•••O•
ASKSFOR
ASOFNOW
BSCHOOL
ESCUDOS
ESKIMOS
ESPANOL
ESPOSOS
TSELIOT
USOSHOW
USTINOV

•S••••O
ESPARTO

••SO•••
ABSOLUT
ABSOLVE
ABSORBS
ADSORBS
ALSORAN
ASSORTS
DESOTOS
DISOBEY
DISOWNS
ENSOULS
GASOHOL
IMSORRY
INSOFAR
INSOLES
LASORDA
LESOTHO
MASONIC
MASONRY
OFSORTS
RESOLED
RESOLES
RESOLVE
RESORBS
RESORTS
RESOUND
RISOTTO
UNSOUND

••S•O••
ABSCOND
BASSOON
BESPOKE
BESTOWS
BISHOPS
BUSBOYS
BUSTOUT

CASHOUT
CASSOCK
CASTOFF
CASTOUT
CUSTODY
CUSTOMS
DASBOOT
DASHOFF
DESMOND
DESPOIL
DESPOTS
DISCOED
DISCORD
DISHOUT
DISJOIN
DISPORT
DISPOSE
DISROBE
DISTORT
DRSPOCK
DUSTOFF
EASEOFF
EASEOUT
EASYOFF
FASTONE
FESTOON
FISHOUT
GASCONS
GASCONY
GASEOUS
GASLOGS
GESSOES
GOSLOWS
GUSTOES
HASSOCK
HISTORY
HYSSOPS
IFSTONE
INSHORT
INSPOTS
INSTOCK
INSTORE
KISSOFF
LASSOED
LASSOER
LASSOES
LASTORY
LESSONS
LESSORS
LISSOME
LOSEOUT
LOSTOUT
MASCOTS
MASTOID
MISDOES
MISDONE
MISSOUT
MISTOOK
MISWORD
MRSPOCK
MUSCOVY
NOSEOUT
NOSHOWS
ONSHORE
OSSEOUS
PASSOFF
PASSOUT
PASTORS
PISCOPO
PISTOLE
PISTOLS
PISTONS
PUSHOFF
RESHOES

RESHOOT
RESPOND
RESTOCK
RESTORE
RISSOLE
ROSEOIL
RUSHOFF
SASSOON
SYSTOLE
TESTOUT
TOSSOFF
TOSSOUT
TUSSOCK
TVSHOWS
UNSHORN
UNSTOPS
UPSHOTS
VISCOUS
VISIONS
WASHOFF
WASHOUT

••S••O•
ABSALOM
BASSOON
BASTION
BESTBOY
BISTROS
BUSHHOG
BUSSTOP
CASHBOX
CASHCOW
CASINOS
CESSION
CUSHION
DASBOOT
DESKTOP
DESOTOS
DESTROY
DISAVOW
DOSIDOS
DUSTMOP
EPSILON
FASHION
FESTOON
FISSION
FUSSPOT
GASOHOL
JUSTNOW
MISSION
MISTOOK
NOSEJOB
PASSFOR
PASSION
POSTBOX
RESHOOT
SASSOON
SESSION
UPSILON
VISITOR

••S•••O
ARSENIO
BUSHIDO
CASSINO
HISPANO
LESOTHO
LYSENKO
MESTIZO
PASSADO
PISCOPO
RISOTTO
ROSARIO
TESTUDO

•••SO••
ACESOUT
ACTSOUT
AIRSOCK
AIRSOUT
ANDSOON
ARTSONG
ASKSOUT
AWESOME
BARSOAP
BASSOON
BEGSOFF
BONSOIR
BOWSOUT
BUGSOFF
BUGSOUT
BUMSOUT
BUYSOFF
BUYSOUT
CASSOCK
CENSORS
CONSOLE
CONSORT
COPSOUT
CURSORS
CURSORY
CUTSOFF
CUTSOUT
DAMSONS
DIESOFF
DIESOUT
DIGSOUT
EATSOUT
EKESOUT
ELUSORY
EPISODE
EYESORE
FANSOUT
FOBSOFF
FORSOOK
FULSOME
GESSOES
GETSOFF
GETSOUT
GODSONS
GOESOFF
GOESOUT
HANSOLO
HANSOMS
HASSOCK
HITSOUT
HOPSOFF
HYSSOPS
ICESOUT
IRISOUT
IRKSOME
JETSONS
KISSOFF
KMESONS
LASSOED
LASSOER
LASSOES
LAYSOFF
LAYSOUT
LESSONS
LESSORS
LETSOFF
LETSOUT
LISSOME
LOGSOFF
LOGSOUT
MISSOUT
MONSOON
NELSONS

NODSOFF
NOISOME
OFASORT
OPTSOUT
ORISONS
OUTSOLD
PANSOUT
PARSONS
PASSOFF
PASSOUT
PAYSOFF
PAYSOUT
PEASOUP
PERSONA
PERSONS
PIGSOUT
POISONS
POPSOFF
POPSOUT
PRESOAK
PRESORT
PRISONS
PROSODY
PUTSOFF
PUTSOUT
RANSOMS
REASONS
RIPSOFF
RIPSOUT
RISSOLE
RUBSOFF
RUBSOUT
RUNSOFF
RUNSOUT
SALSODA
SASSOON
SEASONS
SEESOFF
SEESOUT
SENSORS
SENSORY
SETSOFF
SETSOUT
SITSOUT
SUBSOIL
TAGSOUT
TAPSOFF
TAPSOUT
TEESOFF
TENSORS
TIPSOFF
TOPSOFF
TOPSOIL
TOPSOUT
TOSSOFF
TOSSOUT
TUSSOCK
TWOSOME
UNISONS
WIGSOUT
WINSOME
WINSOUT

•••S•O•
AIMSFOR
AIRSHOW
ALLSTON
ANDSOON
ANISTON
ARISTOS
ASKSFOR
BARSTOW
BASSOON
BIGSHOT

BLOSSOM
BLUSHON
BOLSHOI
BRISTOL
BUSSTOP
CAISSON
CATSHOW
CESSION
DOGSHOW
EARSHOT
ELISION
EROSION
EVASION
EYESHOT
FIASCOS
FISSION
FORSOOK
FRESCOS
FRISSON
FUSSPOT
GEMSBOK
GLASGOW
GOESFOR
GRISSOM
GUMSHOE
GUNSFOR
GUNSHOT
GYMSHOE
HALSTON
HOTSHOT
HOTSPOT
HOUSTON
ICESHOW
INASPOT
INKSPOT
KNOSSOS
LAYSFOR
LAYSLOW
LIESLOW
MANSION
MISSION
MONSOON
MUGSHOT
NEWSBOY
NILSSON
NONSTOP
ONESHOT
OPTSFOR
PASSFOR
PASSION
PAYSFOR
PENSION
PITSTOP
PLOSION
POISSON
POTSHOT
PRESSON
PRESTON
PRESTOS
PROSHOP
RALSTON
REDSPOT
RIMSHOT
RUNSFOR
SASSOON
SCISSOR
SESSION
SUASION
SUNSPOT
TEASHOP
TENSION
TENSPOT
TOESHOE
TOLSTOI

TOLSTOY
TORSION
TOYSHOP
USOSHOW
VERSION
WALSTON
WINSLOW
WINSTON

•••S••O
AGESAGO
CANSECO
CASSINO
CRUSADO
HANSOLO
MAESTRO
PAISANO
PASSADO
SAPSAGO
WHOSWHO
ZEMSTVO

••••SO•
ACHESON
ADAMSON
ADDISON
ADVISOR
AEROSOL
ALLISON
ALLYSON
ARIOSOS
BANKSON
BEARSON
BENISON
BERGSON
BLOSSOM
BLOUSON
BRANSON
BRONSON
CAISSON
CALLSON
CARLSON
CHANSON
CLEMSON
COMESON
CREOSOL
CRIMSON
DAWNSON
DINESON
DIVISOR
DODGSON
DOTESON
DRAGSON
DRAWSON
ELEISON
ELLISON
EMERSON
ERICSON
ESPOSOS
FALLSON
FEEDSON
FRISSON
GAINSON
GIRASOL
GLEASON
GLUESON
GOODSON
GRAYSON
GRISSOM
GROWSON
HANDSON
HANGSON
HARPSON
HEARSOF

HIRESON
HOLDSON
INCISOR
JACKSON
JAMESON
JEWISON
JOHNSON
JUMPSON
KEEPSON
KNOSSOS
LEADSON
LEANSON
LIAISON
LIVESON
LOCKSON
LOOKSON
MADISON
MILKSOP
MOVESON
MUMESON
NILSSON
ORBISON
PARASOL
PEARSON
PICKSON
PILESON
PIMESON
PLANSON
PLAYSON
POISSON
PRESSON
PREYSON
PULLSON
ROBESON
ROLLSON
RULESON
SAMPSON
SCISSOR
SIGNSON
SIMPSON
SLIPSON
SPIESON
SPONSOR
SPURSON
STEPSON
STETSON
SWANSON
TACKSON
TAKESON
TELLSOF
TELLSON
THOMSON
TRANSOM
TREASON
TRIESON
TURNSON
VENISON
WAITSON
WALKSON
WILLSON
WINDSOR
WORKSON

••••S•O
ARIOSTO
BELASCO
CHRISTO
COMESTO
DARESTO
ERNESTO
FALLSTO
GEARSTO
GIVESTO
HOLDSTO

IMPASTO
IONESCO
JALISCO
KEEPSTO
LEADSTO
LOOKSTO
MAKESDO
MODESTO
NABISCO
PICASSO
PRAYSTO
SINGSTO
SNAPSTO
TABASCO
TAKESTO
TALKSTO
TENDSTO
TURNSTO
VERISMO
WANTSTO

•••••SO
ALFONSO
CALYPSO
OLOROSO
PICASSO
PROVISO
SOANDSO

SP•••••
SPACERS
SPACIER
SPACING
SPACKLE
SPADERS
SPADING
SPALLED
SPAMMED
SPAMMER
SPANDEX
SPANGLE
SPANGLY
SPANIEL
SPANISH
SPANKED
SPANKER
SPANNED
SPANNER
SPARELY
SPAREST
SPARGED
SPARGES
SPARING
SPARKED
SPARKLE
SPARRED
SPARROW
SPARSER
SPARTAN
SPASSKY
SPATIAL
SPATTED
SPATTER
SPATULA
SPAVINS
SPAWNED
SPAYING
SPEAKER
SPEAKOF
SPEAKUP
SPEARED
SPECCED
SPECIAL
SPECIES

SPECIFY
SPECING
SPECKED
SPECKLE
SPECTER
SPECTOR
SPECTRA
SPECTRE
SPEEDED
SPEEDER
SPEEDOS
SPEEDUP
SPELLED
SPELLER
SPELUNK
SPENCER
SPENDER
SPENSER
SPEWING
SPHERES
SPICERY
SPICEUP
SPICIER
SPICILY
SPICING
SPIDERS
SPIDERY
SPIEDON
SPIEGEL
SPIELED
SPIELER
SPIESON
SPIGOTS
SPIKERS
SPIKIER
SPIKILY
SPIKING
SPILLED
SPINACH
SPINDLE
SPINDLY
SPINDRY
SPINELS
SPINETS
SPINIER
SPINNER
SPINNEY
SPINOFF
SPINOUT
SPINOZA
SPIRALS
SPIRANT
SPIREAS
SPIRIER
SPIRITO
SPIRITS
SPITING
SPITZES
SPLASHY
SPLAYED
SPLEENS
SPLICED
SPLICER
SPLICES
SPLINES
SPLINTS
SPLITUP
SPLOTCH
SPLURGE
SPOILED
SPOILER
SPOKANE
SPOKEOF
SPOKEUP

SPOKING
SPONDEE
SPONGED
SPONGER
SPONGES
SPONSOR
SPOOFED
SPOOFER
SPOOKED
SPOOLED
SPOONED
SPOONER
SPORRAN
SPORTED
SPOTLIT
SPOTTED
SPOTTER
SPOUSAL
SPOUSES
SPOUTED
SPOUTER
SPRAINS
SPRAWLS
SPRAYED
SPRAYER
SPREADS
SPRIEST
SPRINGS
SPRINGY
SPRINTS
SPRITES
SPROUTS
SPRUCED
SPRUCER
SPRUCES
SPRYEST
SPUMIER
SPUMING
SPUMONE
SPUMONI
SPUMOUS
SPUNOFF
SPUNOUT
SPURNED
SPURNER
SPURRED
SPURSON
SPURTED
SPUTNIK
SPUTTER

S•P••••

SAPIENS
SAPIENT
SAPLESS
SAPLING
SAPPERS
SAPPIER
SAPPILY
SAPPING
SAPPORO
SAPSAGO
SEPTETS
SIPHONS
SIPPERS
SIPPETS
SIPPING
SOPHISM
SOPHIST
SOPPIER
SOPPING
SOPRANO
SOPWITH
STPETER
SUPPERS
SUPPING
SUPPLER
SUPPORT
SUPPOSE
SUPREME
SUPREMO
SYPHONS

S••P•••

SAMPANS
SAMPLED
SAMPLER
SAMPLES
SAMPRAS
SAMPSON
SAPPERS
SAPPIER
SAPPILY
SAPPING
SAPPORO
SCAPULA
SCEPTER
SCEPTIC
SCEPTRE
SCOPING
SCUPPER
SEAPORT
SEEPIER
SEEPING
SEEPSIN
SERPENT
SERPICO
SHAPELY
SHAPERS
SHAPEUP
SHAPING
SHAPIRO
SHAPLEY
SHEPARD
SHIPMAN
SHIPMEN
SHIPOUT
SHIPPED
SHIPPER
SHOPFUL
SHOPPED
SHOPPER
SHOPPES
SIMPERS
SIMPLER
SIMPLEX
SIMPSON
SIPPERS
SIPPETS
SIPPING
SIXPACK
SKEPTIC
SKIPOLE
SKIPOUT
SKIPPED
SKIPPER
SLAPPED
SLEPTIN
SLEPTON
SLIPONS
SLIPOUT
SLIPPED
SLIPPER
SLIPSIN
SLIPSON
SLIPSUP
SLIPUPS
SLOPING
SLOPPED
SNAPONS
SNAPPED
SNAPPER
SNAPPLE
SNAPSAT
SNAPSTO
SNAPSUP
SNIPEAT
SNIPERS
SNIPING
SNIPPED
SNIPPET
SOAPBOX
SOAPERS
SOAPIER
SOAPILY
SOAPING
SOPPIER
SOPPING
SOUPCON
SOUPIER
SOUPSUP
STAPLED
STAPLER
STAPLES
STEPHEN
STEPINS
STEPOUT
STEPPED
STEPPER
STEPPES
STEPSIN
STEPSON
STEPSUP
STEPUPS
STIPEND
STIPPLE
STOPGAP
STOPOFF
STOPPED
STOPPER
STOPSIN
STOPSUP
STUPEFY
STUPORS
STYPTIC
SUBPLOT
SULPHUR
SUPPERS
SUPPING
SUPPLER
SUPPORT
SUPPOSE
SURPASS
SURPLUS
SUSPECT
SUSPEND
SWAPPED
SWAPPER
SWEPTUP
SWIPERS
SWIPING
SWOPPED
SYMPTOM

S•••P••

SCALPED
SCALPEL
SCALPER
SCAMPED
SCAMPER
SCARPED
SCARPER
SCOOPED
SCOOPER
SCORPIO
SCRAPED
SCRAPER
SCRAPES
SCRAPPY
SCRIPPS
SCRIPTS
SCRUPLE
SCULPTS
SCUPPER
SEEDPOD
SEMIPRO
SERAPES
SERAPHS
SERAPIS
SETUPON
SHAMPOO
SHARPED
SHARPEI
SHARPEN
SHARPER
SHARPLY
SHERPAS
SHIPPED
SHIPPER
SHOPPED
SHOPPER
SHOPPES
SHOTPUT
SICKPAY
SKIMPED
SKIPPED
SKIPPER
SLAPPED
SLEEPER
SLEEPIN
SLEEPON
SLIPPED
SLIPPER
SLOPPED
SLUMPED
SLURPED
SNAPPED
SNAPPER
SNAPPLE
SNIPPED
SNIPPET
SNOOPED
SNOOPER
SNOWPEA
SODAPOP
STAMPED
STAYPUT
STEEPED
STEEPEN
STEEPER
STEEPLE
STEEPLY
STEPPED
STEPPER
STEPPES
STIPPLE
STOMPED
STOOPED
STOPPED
STOPPER
STRIPED
STRIPER
STRIPES
STROPHE
STROPPY
STUMPED
STUMPER
SUNSPOT
SWAMPED
SWAPPED
SWAPPER
SWEEPER
SWEEPUP
SWOOPED
SWOPPED
SYNAPSE

S••••P•

SATRAPS
SCHLEPP
SCHLEPS
SCHNAPS
SCRAPPY
SCRIMPS
SCRIMPY
SCRIPPS
SENDUPS
SEVENPM
SHRIMPS
SKYCAPS
SLIPUPS
SLOWUPS
STEPUPS
STROPPY

S•••••P

SAVEDUP
SAVESUP
SCALLOP
SCAREUP
SCHLEPP
SCREWUP
SCRUBUP
SEALSUP
SENDSUP
SERVEUP
SEVENUP
SEWEDUP
SHAKEUP
SHAPEUP
SHOOKUP
SHOOTUP
SHOWSUP
SHUTSUP
SIGNSUP
SIZEDUP
SIZESUP
SKIJUMP
SLIPSUP
SLOWSUP
SMASHUP
SNAPSUP
SNOWCAP
SOAKSUP
SODAPOP
SOFTTOP
SOUPSUP
SPEAKUP
SPEEDUP
SPICEUP
SPLITUP
SPOKEUP
STACKUP
STANDUP
STARMAP
STARTUP
STAYSUP
STEPSUP
STICKUP
STIRRUP
STIRSUP
STOCKUP
STOODUP
STOPGAP
STOPSUP
STOREUP
STUCKUP
SUITSUP
SUNLAMP
SWEEPUP
SWELLUP
SWEPTUP

•SP••••

ASPECTS
ASPERSE
ASPHALT
ASPIRED
ASPIRER
ASPIRES
ASPIRIN
ESPANOL
ESPARTO
ESPIALS
ESPOSAS
ESPOSOS
ESPOUSE
ESPYING
OSPREYS

•S•P•••

ASEPSIS
ASEPTIC
ISOPODS
USOPENS

•S••P••

ESCAPED
ESCAPEE
ESCAPES
USURPED
USURPER

•S•••P•

ESCARPS
ISOTOPE

•S••••P

PSYCHUP
USINGUP

••SP•••

AUSPICE
BESPEAK
BESPOKE
CASPIAN
CUSPIDS
DESPAIR
DESPISE
DESPITE
DESPOIL
DESPOTS
DISPELS
DISPLAY
DISPORT
DISPOSE
DISPUTE
DRSPOCK
GASPERS
GASPING
GASPUMP
GOSPELS
HASPING
HISPANO
HOSPICE
INSPANS
INSPECT
INSPIRE
INSPOTS
JASPERS
KUSPUKS
LESPAUL
LISPING
MISPLAY
MRSPOCK
RASPERS
RASPIER
RASPING
RASPISH
RESPECT
RESPINS
RESPIRE
RESPITE
RESPOND
SUSPECT
SUSPEND
TOSPARE
UNSPENT
VESPERS
VESPIDS
WASPIER
WASPILY
WASPISH
WISPIER
WISPILY
WISPING

••S•P••

BASEPAY
BUSHPIG
DISHPAN
DUSTPAN
FUSSPOT
INSIPID
MOSHPIT
PUSHPIN

••S••P•

BISHOPS
DISRUPT
DUSTUPS
GASCAPS
GOSSIPS
GOSSIPY
HYSSOPS
INSCAPE
INSHAPE
INSTEPS
LASHUPS
MISHAPS
MISTYPE
PISCOPO
PUSHUPS
RESHIPS
TOSSUPS
UNSNAPS
UNSTOPS
UNSWEPT
UPSWEPT
WASHUPS

••S•••P

BUSSTOP
DESKTOP
DUSTMOP
EASEDUP
EASESUP
GASPUMP
GUSSYUP
MISSTEP
PASTEUP
RESTAMP
RESTSUP
UNSTRAP
UPSWEEP
WISEDUP
WISESUP

•••SP••

CATSPAW
CLASPED
CRISPED
CRISPER
CRISPIN
CRISPLY
CRISPUS
FUSSPOT
GRASPED
HOTSPOT
HOTSPUR
INASPIN
INASPOT
INKSPOT
PROSPER
REDSPOT
SUNSPOT
TENSPOT
THESPIS
WHISPER

•••S•P•

GOESAPE
GOSSIPS
GOSSIPY
HYSSOPS
TOSSUPS

•••S••P

AIRSHIP
BARSOAP
BOOSTUP
BOXSTEP
BRUSHUP
BUSSTOP
CLOSEUP
COWSLIP
CROSSUP
DRESSUP
GUSSYUP
HANSARP
KINSHIP
LETSLIP
LOUSEUP
MISSTEP
NONSLIP
NONSTOP
ONESTEP
OUTSTEP
PARSNIP
PEASOUP
PITSTOP
PRESSUP
PROSHOP
RAISEUP
SMASHUP
TEASHOP
TENSEUP
TOYSHOP
TWOSTEP
WARSHIP
WORSHIP

••••S•P

ANTESUP
BACKSUP
BALLSUP
BANGSUP
BEADSUP
BEAMSUP
BEARSUP
BEATSUP
BEEFSUP
BINDSUP
BLOWSUP
BONESUP
BOOTSUP
BOXESUP
BUCKSUP
BUMPSUP
BUOYSUP
BURNSUP
CALLSUP
CHATSUP
CHEWSUP
CLAMSUP
CLOGSUP
COILSUP
COMESUP
COOKSUP
COOPSUP
CROPSUP
CROSSUP
CURLSUP
DOLLSUP
DRAWSUP
DRESSUP
DRIESUP
DRUMSUP
EASESUP
EVENSUP
FAIRSUP
FILLSUP
FIRESUP
FIRMSUP
FIXESUP
FOLDSUP
FOULSUP
GANGSUP
GEARSUP
GIVESUP
GOOFSUP
GROWSUP
HANDSUP
HANGSUP
HAULSUP
HEADSUP
HEATSUP
HIKESUP
HOLDSUP
HOLESUP
HOOKSUP
HYPESUP
JACKSUP
JOINSUP
JUMPSUP
KEEPSUP
KICKSUP
KNEESUP
LACESUP
LEADSUP
LIFTSUP
LINESUP
LOCKSUP
LOOKSUP
MAKESUP
MARKSUP
MILKSOP
MIXESUP
MOVESUP
MUCKSUP
OPENSUP
PACKSUP
PAIRSUP
PERKSUP
PICKSUP
PILESUP
PINESAP
PIPESUP
PLAYSUP
PRESSUP
PROPSUP
PULLSUP
PUMPSUP
RACKSUP
RAKESUP
REARSUP
RESTSUP
RILESUP
RINGSUP
ROLLSUP
SAVESUP
SEALSUP
SENDSUP
SHOWSUP
SHUTSUP
SIGNSUP
SIZESUP
SLIPSUP
SLOWSUP
SNAPSUP
SOAKSUP
SOUPSUP
STAYSUP
STEPSUP
STIRSUP
STOPSUP
SUITSUP
TAKESUP
TALKSUP
TANKSUP
TEAMSUP
TEARSUP
TIMESUP
TONESUP
TOOLSUP
TRIPSUP
TUNESUP
TURNSUP
TYPESUP
WAITSUP
WAKESUP
WALLSUP
WARMSUP
WELLSUP
WHIPSUP
WINDSUP
WINESAP
WIPESUP
WISESUP
WORKSUP
WRAPSUP

•••••SP

UNCLASP

SQ•••••

SQUALID
SQUALLS
SQUALOR
SQUANTO
SQUARED
SQUARER
SQUARES
SQUATLY
SQUATTY
SQUAWKS
SQUAWKY
SQUEAKS
SQUEAKY
SQUEALS
SQUEEZE
SQUELCH
SQUILLS
SQUINCH
SQUINTS
SQUINTY
SQUIRED
SQUIRES
SQUIRMS
SQUIRMY
SQUIRTS
SQUISHY

S•Q••••

SEQUELS
SEQUINS
SEQUOIA

S••Q•••

SACQUES

•SQ••••

ESQUIRE
TSQUARE

•S•••Q•

PSANDQS

••SQ•••

BASQUES
BISQUES
CASQUED
CASQUES
MASQUES
MOSQUES

••S••Q•

POSSLQS

•••SQ••

BRUSQUE

•••S•Q•

POSSLQS

S•R••••

SARACEN
SARALEE
SARANAC
SARAWAK
SARAZEN
SARCASM
SARDINE
SARGENT
SARKIER
SARONGS
SAROYAN
SCRAGGY
SCRAPED
SCRAPER
SCRAPES
SCRAPPY
SCRATCH
SCRAWLS
SCRAWLY
SCRAWNY
SCREAKS
SCREAMS
SCREECH
SCREEDS
SCREENS
SCREWED
SCREWUP
SCRIBES
SCRIMPS
SCRIMPY
SCRIPPS
SCRIPTS
SCRIVEN
SCROLLS
SCROOGE
SCRUBBY
SCRUBUP
SCRUFFS
SCRUFFY
SCRUMMY
SCRUNCH
SCRUPLE
SERAPES
SERAPHS
SERAPIS
SERBIAN
SERENER
SERFDOM
SERIALS
SERIATE
SERIOUS
SERLING
SERMONS
SERPENT
SERPICO
SERRATE
SERRIED
SERVALS
SERVANT
SERVERS
SERVERY
SERVEUP
SERVICE
SERVILE
SERVING
SHRIEKS
SHRIFTS
SHRIKES
SHRILLS
SHRILLY
SHRIMPS
SHRINER
SHRINES
SHRINKS
SHRIVEL
SHRIVER
SHRIVES
SHROUDS
SHRUBBY
SIRLOIN
SIROCCO
SORBATE
SORBETS
SORCERY
SORDINI
SORDINO
SORGHUM
SORITES
SORORAL
SORRELS
SORRIER
SORRILY
SORROWS
SORTERS
SORTIED
SORTIES
SORTING
SORTOUT
SORVINO
SPRAINS
SPRAWLS
SPRAYED
SPRAYER
SPREADS
SPRIEST
SPRINGS
SPRINGY
SPRINTS
SPRITES
SPROUTS
SPRUCED
SPRUCER
SPRUCES
SPRYEST
STRAFED
STRAFES
STRAINS
STRAITS
STRANDS
STRANGE
STRASSE
STRATUM
STRATUS
STRAUSS
STRAYED
STREAKS
STREAKY
STREAMS
STREETS
STRETCH
STRETTO
STREWED
STREWER
STRIATE
STRIDER
STRIDES
STRIKER
STRIKES
STRINGS
STRINGY
STRIPED
STRIPER
STRIPES
STRIVED
STRIVEN
STRIVER
STRIVES
STROBES
STROKED
STROKES
STROLLS
STROPHE
STROPPY
STRUDEL
SURCOAT
SURFACE
SURFEIT
SURFERS
SURFIER
SURFING
SURGEON
SURGERY
SURGING
SURINAM
SURLIER
SURLILY
SURMISE
SURNAME
SURPASS
SURPLUS
SURREAL
SURREYS
SURTSEY
SURVEYS
SURVIVE
SYRIANS
SYRINGA
SYRINGE

S••R•••

SABRINA
SANREMO
SATRAPS
SAURIAN
SCARABS
SCARCER
SCARERS
SCAREUP
SCARFED
SCARIER
SCARIFY
SCARILY
SCARING
SCARLET
SCARPED
SCARPER
SCARRED
SCARVES
SCORERS
SCORING
SCORNED
SCORNER
SCORPIO
SCURVES
SEARING
SECRECY
SECRETE
SECRETS
SEERESS
SERRATE
SERRIED
SHAREIN
SHARERS
SHARING
SHARKEY
SHARPED
SHARPEI
SHARPEN
SHARPER
SHARPLY
SHERBET
SHERIFF
SHERMAN
SHERPAS
SHERWIN
SHIRKED
SHIRKER
SHIRLEY
SHIRRED
SHORING
SHORTED
SHORTEN
SHORTER
SHORTLY
SHORTOF
SIERRAS
SKIRACK
SKIRLED
SKIRRED
SKIRTED

SKIRUNS
SLURPED
SLURRED
SMARTED
SMARTEN
SMARTER
SMARTLY
SMIRKED
SNARING
SNARLED
SNORERS
SNORING
SNORKEL
SNORTED
SNORTER
SOARERS
SOARING
SOIREES
SOPRANO
SORRELS
SORRIER
SORRILY
SORROWS
SOURCED
SOURCES
SOUREST
SOURING
SOURISH
SPARELY
SPAREST
SPARGED
SPARGES
SPARING
SPARKED
SPARKLE
SPARRED
SPARROW
SPARSER
SPARTAN
SPIRALS
SPIRANT
SPIREAS
SPIRIER
SPIRITO
SPIRITS
SPORRAN
SPORTED
SPURNED
SPURNER
SPURRED
SPURSON
SPURTED
STARCHY
STARDOM
STAREAT
STARERS
STARETS
STARING
STARKER
STARKLY
STARLET
STARLIT
STARMAN
STARMAP
STARRED
STARTED
STARTER
STARTLE
STARTUP
STARVED
STARVES
STCROIX
STEREOS
STERILE

STERNAL
STERNER
STERNLY
STERNUM
STEROID
STEROLS
STIRFRY
STIRRED
STIRRER
STIRRUP
STIRSIN
STIRSUP
STORAGE
STORERS
STOREUP
STOREYS
STORIED
STORIES
STORING
STORMED
STURGES
STYRENE
STYRIAN
SUBROSA
SUCRASE
SUCROSE
SUNRAYS
SUNRISE
SUNROOF
SUNROOM
SUPREME
SUPREMO
SURREAL
SURREYS
SWARMED
SWARTHY
SWERVED
SWERVES
SWIRLED
SWOREAT
SWOREBY
SWOREIN

S•••R••
SAFARIS
SAFFRON
SAHARAN
SALERNO
SAMARIA
SAMPRAS
SAMURAI
SANGRIA
SATIRES
SATIRIC
SAVARIN
SAVORED
SCARRED
SCHERZI
SCHERZO
SCHIRRA
SCIORRA
SCLERAS
SCOURED
SCOURER
SCOURGE
SEAGRAM
SECURED
SECURER
SECURES
SEESRED
SENORAS
SENORES
SEVERAL
SEVERED

SEVERER
SHEARED
SHEARER
SHEERED
SHEERER
SHEERLY
SHIRRED
SIBERIA
SIERRAS
SISTRUM
SIXIRON
SKIDROW
SKIRRED
SLURRED
SMEARED
SNEERAT
SNEERED
SNEERER
SOBERED
SOBERER
SOBERLY
SOLARIA
SORORAL
SPARRED
SPARROW
SPEARED
SPHERES
SPLURGE
SPORRAN
SPURRED
SQUARED
SQUARER
SQUARES
SQUIRED
SQUIRES
SQUIRMS
SQUIRMY
SQUIRTS
STARRED
STEERED
STEERER
STIRRED
STIRRER
STIRRUP
SUBORNS
SUBURBS
SUGARED
SUHARTO
SUKARNO
SUTURED
SUTURES
SWEARAT
SWEARBY
SWEARER
SWEARIN
SWEARTO
SYNERGY

S••••R•
SACKERS
SAGUARO
SAILORS
SALIERI
SALTERS
SALVERS
SALVORS
SAMBARS
SAMSARA
SANDERS
SANFORD
SANTIRS
SAPPERS
SAPPORO
SASSERS

SAUCERS
SAVIORS
SAVOURS
SAVOURY
SAWYERS
SAXHORN
SCALARS
SCALERS
SCARERS
SCENERY
SCEPTRE
SCHIRRA
SCIORRA
SCORERS
SCOTERS
SEABIRD
SEABORG
SEAFIRE
SEAGIRT
SEALERS
SEAPORT
SEATERS
SEAWARD
SECTORS
SEEDERS
SEEHERE
SEEKERS
SEINERS
SEIZERS
SELKIRK
SELLERS
SEMIPRO
SENDERS
SENIORS
SENSORS
SENSORY
SERVERS
SERVERY
SETTERS
SHAKERS
SHANGRI
SHAPERS
SHAPIRO
SHARERS
SHASTRI
SHAVERS
SHEPARD
SHIKARI
SHINERS
SHIVERS
SHIVERY
SHOFARS
SHOVERS
SHOWERS
SHOWERY
SHUBERT
SIDEARM
SIFTERS
SIGHERS
SIGNERS
SILVERS
SILVERY
SIMMERS
SIMPERS
SINATRA
SINCERE
SINGERS
SINKERS
SINNERS
SIPPERS
SISTERS
SITTERS
SKATERS
SKEWERS

SKIVERS
SKYLARK
SKYWARD
SLAVERS
SLAVERY
SLAYERS
SLICERS
SLIDERS
SLIVERS
SMILERS
SMOKERS
SNIPERS
SNORERS
SOAKERS
SOAPERS
SOARERS
SOBBERS
SOJOURN
SOLDERS
SOLVERS
SOONERS
SORCERY
SORTERS
SOTHERE
SOTHERN
SPACERS
SPADERS
SPECTRA
SPECTRE
SPICERY
SPIDERS
SPIDERY
SPIKERS
SPINDRY
STAGERS
STARERS
STATORS
STATURE
STEWARD
STEWART
STEWERS
STIRFRY
STOKERS
STONERS
STORERS
STUMERS
STUPORS
STYLERS
SUBVERT
SUBZERO
SUCCORS
SUCKERS
SUDBURY
SUFFERS
SUITORS
SULKERS
SUMATRA
SUMMARY
SUMMERS
SUMMERY
SUNBURN
SUNDERS
SUOJURE
SUPPERS
SUPPORT
SURFERS
SURGERY
SUTLERS
SUTTERS
SWAYERS
SWELTRY
SWIPERS

S•••••R
SADDLER
SAGGIER
SALAZAR
SALTIER
SAMOVAR
SAMPLER
SANDBAR
SANDIER
SAPPIER
SARKIER
SASHBAR
SASSIER
SAUCIER
SAUNTER
SAVAGER
SAVIOUR
SAVVIER
SCALIER
SCALPER
SCAMPER
SCANNER
SCANTER
SCARCER
SCARIER
SCARPER
SCATTER
SCEPTER
SCHEMER
SCHMEER
SCHOLAR
SCISSOR
SCOFFER
SCOLDER
SCOOPER
SCOOTER
SCORNER
SCOURER
SCOUTER
SCOWLER
SCRAPER
SCULLER
SCUPPER
SEAMIER
SEASTAR
SECEDER
SECULAR
SECURER
SEDATER
SEDGIER
SEDUCER
SEEDIER
SEEPIER
SELLFOR
SELTZER
SEMINAR
SENATOR
SENDFOR
SENTFOR
SERENER
SETTLER
SEVERER
SEYMOUR
SHADIER
SHAFFER
SHAKIER
SHANKAR
SHARPER
SHATNER
SHATTER
SHEARER
SHEERER
SHELLER
SHELTER

SHIMMER
SHINIER
SHIPPER
SHIRKER
SHOCKER
SHOOTER
SHOPPER
SHORTER
SHOTFOR
SHOUTER
SHOWIER
SHRINER
SHRIVER
SHUCKER
SHUDDER
SHUTTER
SHYSTER
SIDEBAR
SIDECAR
SILKIER
SILLIER
SILTIER
SIMILAR
SIMPLER
SKANKER
SKEETER
SKELTER
SKIDDER
SKIMMER
SKINNER
SKIPPER
SKITTER
SKIWEAR
SKULKER
SLACKER
SLAMMER
SLANDER
SLASHER
SLATHER
SLATIER
SLEDDER
SLEEKER
SLEEPER
SLENDER
SLICKER
SLIMIER
SLIMMER
SLINGER
SLIPPER
SLITHER
SLOBBER
SLOTCAR
SLUGGER
SLUMBER
SMACKER
SMALLER
SMARTER
SMASHER
SMATTER
SMELTER
SMOKIER
SMOLDER
SMOTHER
SMUGGER
SNACKER
SNAKIER
SNAPPER
SNEAKER
SNEERER
SNEEZER
SNICKER
SNIFFER
SNIFTER
SNIGGER

SNOOKER
SNOOPER
SNORTER
SNOWIER
SNUFFER
SNUGGER
SOAPIER
SOBERER
SODDIER
SOGGIER
SOLDIER
SOLIDER
SOOTHER
SOOTIER
SOPPIER
SORRIER
SOUNDER
SOUPIER
SPACIER
SPAMMER
SPANKER
SPANNER
SPARSER
SPATTER
SPEAKER
SPECTER
SPECTOR
SPEEDER
SPELLER
SPENCER
SPENDER
SPENSER
SPICIER
SPIELER
SPIKIER
SPINIER
SPINNER
SPIRIER
SPLICER
SPOILER
SPONGER
SPONSOR
SPOOFER
SPOONER
SPOTTER
SPOUTER
SPRAYER
SPRUCER
SPUMIER
SPURNER
SPUTTER
SQUALOR
SQUARER
STABLER
STAFFER
STAGGER
STAGIER
STAIDER
STAINER
STALKER
STAMMER
STAPLER
STARKER
STARTER
STEAMER
STEELER
STEEPER
STEERER
STEIGER
STEINER
STELLAR
STENTOR
STEPPER
STERNER

STICKER
STIFFER
STILLER
STINGER
STINKER
STIRRER
STOLLER
STONIER
STOPPER
STOUTER
STPETER
STREWER
STRIDER
STRIKER
STRIPER
STRIVER
STUFFER
STUMPER
STUNNER
SUBDUER
SUBTLER
SUCCOUR
SUDSIER
SULKIER
SULPHUR
SUNNIER
SUPPLER
SURFIER
SURLIER
SVELTER
SWAGGER
SWANKER
SWAPPER
SWATTER
SWEARER
SWEATER
SWEEPER
SWEETER
SWELTER
SWIFTER
SWIMMER
SWINGER
SWITZER

•SR••••
ISRAELI

•S•R•••
ASARULE
ASCRIBE
ASHRAMS
ASTRIDE
ESCROWS
ESTRADA
ESTRAYS
OSPREYS
OSTRICH
TSARINA
TSARIST
USERIDS
USGRANT
USURERS
USURIES
USURPED
USURPER

•S••R••
ASFARAS
ASHTRAY
ASPERSE
ASPIRED
ASPIRER
ASPIRES
ASPIRIN

ASSERTS
ASSORTS
ASSURED
ASSURES
ASSYRIA
ASTARTE
ASTORIA
ESCARPS
ESCORTS
ESPARTO
ESTORIL
OSBORNE
OSIERED
TSHIRTS
TSOURIS
USHERED

•S•••R•
ASHBURY
ASHFORD
ASHLARS
ASTAIRE
ESOTERY
ESQUIRE
ESTUARY
ISADORA
ISOBARS
ISOMERS
ISSUERS
OSTLERS
TSQUARE
USURERS

•S••••R
ASKSFOR
ASPIRER
ASSAYER
ASUNDER
PSALTER
USURPER

••SR•••
DISROBE
DISRUPT
MISREAD
MISRULE

••S•R••
ABSORBS
ADSORBS
ALSORAN
AMSCRAY
ASSERTS
ASSORTS
ASSURED
ASSURES
ASSYRIA
AUSTRAL
AUSTRIA
BESTREW
BISTROS
CASERNE
CASERNS
DESERTS
DESERVE
DESIRED
DESIREE
DESIRES
DESTROY
DISARMS
DISHRAG
ENSURED
ENSURES
EXSERTS

GASTRIC
IMSORRY
INSERTS
INSURED
INSURER
INSURES
KESTREL
LASORDA
LUSTRED
LUSTRES
MASARYK
MISERLY
MISTRAL
MUSKRAT
NOSTRIL
NOSTRUM
OBSERVE
OFSORTS
ONSERVE
RESERVE
RESORBS
RESORTS
RESURGE
ROSARIO
ROSERED
ROSTRUM
SISTRUM
UNSCREW
UNSTRAP
UPSURGE
WASHRAG
WASTREL

••S••R•
ANSWERS
AUSTERE
BASTERS
BESTIRS
BUSFARE
BUSGIRL
BUSTARD
BUSTERS
CASCARA
CASTERS
CISTERN
COSTARS
CUSTARD
DASHERS
DASTARD
DASYURE
DESSERT
DISBARS
DISCARD
DISCERN
DISCORD
DISPORT
DISTORT
DISTURB
DOSSERS
DUSTERS
EASTERN
EASTERS
ENSNARE
ENSNARL
FESTERS
FISHERS
FISHERY
FISHFRY
FISSURE
FOSTERS
GASPERS
GASSERS
GESTURE
GUSHERS

HISSERS
HISTORY
HOSIERS
HOSIERY
HUSKERS
HUSSARS
IMSORRY
INSHORT
INSPIRE
INSTARS
INSTORE
ISSUERS
JASPERS
JESTERS
JOSSERS
KISSERS
KOSHERS
LASHERS
LASTORY
LESSORS
LUSTERS
MASCARA
MASHERS
MASKERS
MASONRY
MASTERS
MASTERY
MISFIRE
MISTERS
MISWORD
MOSHERS
MUSHERS
MUSTARD
MUSTERS
MYSTERY
NESTERS
NOSHERS
OBSCURE
ONSHORE
OUSTERS
OYSTERS
PASSERS
PASTERN
PASTORS
PASTURE
PESTERS
PISMIRE
POSEURS
POSTERN
POSTERS
POSTURE
RASHERS
RASPERS
RASTERS
RESPIRE
RESTART
RESTERS
RESTORE
RISKERS
ROSTERS
RUSHERS
SASSERS
SISTERS
TASTERS
TESSERA
TESTERS
TOSPARE
TOSSERS
TUSKERS
ULSTERS
UNSHORN
UNSNARL
UPSTART
VESPERS

VESTURE
VISCERA
WASHERS
WASTERS
WESTERN
WISHERS

••S•••R
ASSAYER
BESMEAR
BOSKIER
BOSSIER
BUSHIER
CASHBAR
CASHIER
COSTNER
CUSHIER
CUSSLER
DESPAIR
DISHIER
DOSSIER
DUSKIER
DUSTIER
FISCHER
FISHIER
FUSSIER
FUSTIER
GASSIER
GUSHIER
GUSTIER
HASTIER
HOSTLER
HUSKIER
HUSTLER
INSIDER
INSOFAR
INSULAR
INSURER
JOSTLER
KASHMIR
LASSOER
LUSTIER
MASSEUR
MASSIER
MESHIER
MESSIER
MISHEAR
MISTIER
MOSSIER
MUSHIER
MUSKIER
MUSSIER
MUSTIER
NASTIER
NESTLER
PASSFOR
PASTEUR
PASTIER
PESKIER
POSTWAR
PUSHIER
RASPIER
RESCUER
RISKIER
RUSHIER
RUSTIER
RUSTLER
SASHBAR
SASSIER
TASTIER
TESTIER
VASTIER
VISITOR
WASHIER

WASPIER
WISPIER
YESDEAR
ZESTIER

•••SR••
SEESRED
TOYSRUS

•••S•R•
ABUSERS
BERSERK
BURSARS
BURSARY
CAESARS
CAESURA
CENSERS
CENSORS
CENSURE
CHASERS
CLOSURE
CONSORT
CURSORS
CURSORY
DESSERT
DOSSERS
DOWSERS
DYKSTRA
ELUSORY
ERASERS
ERASURE
EYESORE
FISSURE
FORSURE
GASSERS
GEYSERS
HANSARP
HAWSERS
HISSERS
HUSSARS
JOSSERS
KAISERS
KISSERS
LEASERS
LEISURE
LESSORS
MAESTRI
MAESTRO
MANSARD
MEASURE
MOUSERS
NETSURF
NOTSURE
NURSERS
NURSERY
OFASORT
OLESTRA
PARSERS
PASSERS
PHASERS
PIASTRE
PRESORT
PROSERS
PULSARS
PURSERS
QUASARS
RAISERS
ROUSERS
RUNSDRY
SAMSARA
SASSERS
SENSORS
SENSORY
SHASTRI

TEASERS
TENSORS
TESSERA
TONSURE
TOSSERS
WOWSERS

•••S••R

AIMSFOR
ALLSTAR
AMASSER
ANTSIER
ARTSIER
ASKSFOR
BITSIER
BLASTER
BLISTER
BLUSHER
BLUSTER
BOASTER
BOLSTER
BONSOIR
BOOSLER
BOOSTER
BOSSIER
BRASHER
BRISKER
CHASTER
CHESTER
CLUSTER
COASTER
CORSAIR
CRASSER
CRISPER
CROSIER
CROSSER
CRUSHER
CUSSLER
DANSEUR
DAYSTAR
DITSIER
DOGSTAR
DOSSIER
DRESSER
EDASNER
FLASHER
FLUSTER
FORSTER
FRASIER
FRESHER
FUBSIER
FUSSIER
GAGSTER
GASSIER
GOESFOR
GOOSIER
GORSIER
GROSSER
GUESSER
GUNSFOR
GUTSIER
HAMSTER
HARSHER
HIPSTER
HOLSTER
HOOSIER
HORSIER
HOTSPUR
JOUSTER
LASSOER
LAYSFOR
LEISTER
LOBSTER
LOESSER
LOUSIER
MASSEUR
MASSIER
MEISTER
MESSIER
MOBSTER
MOISTER
MONSTER
MOSSIER
MOUSIER
MUSSIER
NEWSIER
NOISIER
NUTSIER
OLDSTER
ONESTAR
OPTSFOR
PASSFOR
PAYSFOR
PIASTER
PILSNER
PLASTER
PLUSHER
POTSIER
PRESSER
PROSIER
PROSPER
PUNSTER
PURSIER
PURSUER
REDSTAR
ROASTER
ROISTER
ROOSTER
RUNSFOR
SASSIER
SCISSOR
SEASTAR
SHYSTER
SLASHER
SMASHER
SUDSIER
TAPSTER
TARSIER
TELSTAR
THUSFAR
TINSTAR
TIPSIER
TIPSTER
TOASTER
TRISTAR
TRYSTER
TWISTER
TWOSTAR
WEBSTER
WHISKER
WHISPER
WOOSTER

••••S•R

ACCUSER
ADVISER
ADVISOR
ALUNSER
AMASSER
BROWSER
BRUISER
CHOOSER
COARSER
COURSER
CRASSER
CROSSER
CRUISER
DEARSIR
DEPOSER
DIVISOR
DREISER
DRESSER
ENDUSER
GREASER
GROSSER
GROUSER
GUESSER
HOARSER
INCISOR
LOESSER
NONUSER
OBTUSER
OPPOSER
PERUSER
PLEASER
PRAISER
PRESSER
REFUSER
REVISER
SCISSOR
SPARSER
SPENSER
SPONSOR
TROUSER
UNWISER
WINDSOR

S•S••••

SASHAYS
SASHBAR
SASHIMI
SASSERS
SASSIER
SASSIES
SASSILY
SASSING
SASSOON
SESAMES
SESSILE
SESSION
SESTETS
SESTINA
SISKINS
SISSIES
SISTERS
SISTINE
SISTRUM
SOSUEME
SUSANNA
SUSANNE
SUSLIKS
SUSPECT
SUSPEND
SUSSING
SUSTAIN
SYSTEMS
SYSTOLE

S••S•••

SADSACK
SALSIFY
SALSODA
SAMSARA
SAMSUNG
SAPSAGO
SASSERS
SASSIER
SASSIES
SASSILY
SASSING
SASSOON
SATSUMA
SAUSAGE
SCISSOR
SEASALT
SEASICK
SEASIDE
SEASLUG
SEASONS
SEASTAR
SEESAWS
SEESFIT
SEESOFF
SEESOUT
SEESRED
SEISMIC
SENSATE
SENSING
SENSORS
SENSORY
SENSUAL
SESSILE
SESSION
SETSAIL
SETSOFF
SETSOUT
SHASTRI
SHUSHED
SHUSHES
SHYSTER
SIESTAS
SISSIES
SITSOUT
SKISUIT
SKOSHES
SLASHED
SLASHER
SLASHES
SLOSHED
SLOSHES
SLUSHES
SMASHED
SMASHER
SMASHES
SMASHUP
SPASSKY
STASHED
STASHES
STASSEN
SUASION
SUBSETS
SUBSIDE
SUBSIDY
SUBSIST
SUBSOIL
SUBSUME
SUDSIER
SUDSING
SUNSETS
SUNSPOT
SUNSUIT
SUSSING
SWISHED
SWISHES

S•••S••

SAMISEN
SAMPSON
SATISFY
SAVESUP
SCHISMS
SCISSOR
SCOUSES
SEALSUP
SEEPSIN
SENDSIN
SENDSUP
SEXISTS
SHOWSIN
SHOWSUP
SHUTSIN
SHUTSUP
SIGNSIN
SIGNSON
SIGNSUP
SILESIA
SIMPSON
SINGSTO
SINKSIN
SINUSES
SIZESUP
SLIPSIN
SLIPSON
SLIPSUP
SLOWSUP
SNAPSAT
SNAPSTO
SNAPSUP
SNOWSIN
SOAKSUP
SOCKSIN
SOUPSUP
SPARSER
SPASSKY
SPENSER
SPIESON
SPLASHY
SPONSOR
SPOUSAL
SPOUSES
SPURSON
SQUISHY
STASSEN
STAYSUP
STEPSIN
STEPSON
STEPSUP
STETSON
STIRSIN
STIRSUP
STOPSIN
STOPSUP
STRASSE
SUCKSIN
SUITSUP
SULUSEA
SURTSEY
SWANSEA
SWANSON
SWOOSIE

S••••S•

SADDEST
SADNESS
SALTISH
SANJOSE
SAPLESS
SARCASM
SAWDUST
SAWFISH
SEABASS
SEAMOSS
SEERESS
SELFISH
SEXIEST
SHIATSU
SHYNESS
SIAMESE
SICKEST
SICKISH
SIKHISM
SINLESS
SKIMASK
SKYLESS
SLAVISH
SLOWEST
SLYNESS
SNIDEST
SOANDSO
SODLESS
SOFTEST
SOFTISH
SOLOIST
SONLESS
SOONEST
SOPHISM
SOPHIST
SOTTISH
SOUREST
SOURISH
SPANISH
SPAREST
SPRIEST
SPRYEST
STALEST
STATIST
STRASSE
STRAUSS
STYLISE
STYLISH
STYLIST
SUAVEST
SUBROSA
SUBSIST
SUCCESS
SUCRASE
SUCROSE
SUFFUSE
SUGGEST
SUMLESS
SUNFISH
SUNKIST
SUNLESS
SUNRISE
SUPPOSE
SURMISE
SURPASS
SWEDISH
SWINISH
SYNAPSE

S•••••S

SABINES
SACHEMS
SACHETS
SACKERS
SACQUES
SADDENS
SADDLES
SADNESS
SAFARIS
SAILORS
SALAAMS
SALAMIS
SALINAS
SALLETS
SALLIES
SALLOWS
SALMONS
SALOONS
SALTERS
SALUKIS
SALUTES
SALVERS
SALVIAS
SALVOES
SALVORS
SAMBALS
SAMBARS
SAMECHS
SAMITES
SAMLETS
SAMOANS
SAMPANS
SAMPLES
SAMPRAS
SANDALS
SANDERS
SANLUIS
SANTIRS
SAPIENS
SAPLESS
SAPPERS
SARONGS
SASHAYS
SASSERS
SASSIES
SATEENS
SATIRES
SATRAPS
SAUCERS
SAVAGES
SAVALAS
SAVANTS
SAVINGS
SAVIORS
SAVOURS
SAWLOGS
SAWYERS
SAYINGS
SAYYIDS
SCALARS
SCALERS
SCARABS
SCARERS
SCARVES
SCATHES
SCHEMAS
SCHEMES
SCHISMS
SCHLEPS
SCHMOES
SCHMOOS
SCHNAPS
SCHOOLS
SCLERAS
SCONCES
SCORERS
SCOTERS
SCOUSES
SCRAPES
SCRAWLS
SCREAKS
SCREAMS
SCREEDS
SCREENS
SCRIBES
SCRIMPS
SCRIPPS
SCRIPTS
SCROLLS
SCRUFFS
SCULPTS
SCURVES
SCYTHES
SEABAGS
SEABASS
SEABEDS
SEABEES
SEACOWS
SEADOGS
SEAFANS
SEALABS
SEALEGS
SEALERS
SEAMOSS
SEANCES
SEASONS
SEATERS
SEAWAYS
SECANTS
SECEDES
SECKELS
SECONDS
SECRETS
SECTORS
SECURES
SEDATES
SEDUCES
SEEDERS
SEEKERS
SEERESS
SEESAWS
SEETHES
SEICHES
SEIDELS
SEINERS
SEIZERS
SELECTS
SELLERS
SEMITES
SENATES
SENDERS
SENDUPS
SENECAS
SENIORS
SENORAS
SENORES
SENSORS
SENUFOS
SEPTETS
SEQUELS
SEQUINS
SERAPES
SERAPHS
SERAPIS
SERIALS
SERIOUS
SERMONS
SERVALS
SERVERS
SESAMES
SESTETS
SETTEES
SETTERS
SETTLES
SEXISTS
SEXTANS
SEXTETS
SEXTONS
SHADOWS
SHAKERS
SHAKOES
SHALOMS
SHAMANS
SHAPERS
SHARERS
SHAVERS
SHEATHS
SHEAVES
SHEIKHS
SHEILAS
SHEKELS
SHELVES
SHERPAS
SHIELDS
SHIITES
SHINERS
SHIVERS
SHOFARS
SHOGUNS
SHOOINS
SHOPPES
SHOVELS
SHOVERS
SHOWERS
SHRIEKS
SHRIFTS
SHRIKES
SHRILLS
SHRIMPS
SHRINES
SHRINKS
SHRIVES
SHROUDS
SHTICKS
SHUSHES
SHUTINS
SHYNESS
SICKENS
SICKLES
SIDINGS
SIENNAS
SIERRAS
SIESTAS
SIFTERS
SIGHERS
SIGNALS
SIGNEES
SIGNERS
SIGNETS
SILENTS
SILICAS
SILLIES
SILVERS
SIMIANS
SIMILES
SIMMERS
SIMMONS
SIMPERS
SINGERS
SINGLES
SINKERS
SINLESS
SINNERS
SINUOUS
SINUSES
SIOUANS
SIPHONS
SIPPERS
SIPPETS
SISKINS
SISSIES
SISTERS
SITCOMS
SITTERS
SIXGUNS
SIXTIES
SIZINGS
SIZZLES
SKATERS
SKEWERS
SKIBOBS
SKIRUNS
SKITOWS
SKIVERS
SKOSHES
SKYCAPS
SKYLESS
SKYWAYS
SLALOMS
SLASHES
SLAVERS
SLAVEYS
SLAYERS
SLEDGES
SLEEVES
SLEIGHS
SLEUTHS
SLICERS
SLIDERS
SLIGHTS
SLIPONS
SLIPUPS
SLIVERS
SLOGANS
SLOSHES
SLOUGHS
SLOVAKS
SLOVENS
SLOWUPS
SLUDGES
SLUICES
SLUSHES
SLYNESS
SMALTOS
SMASHES
SMILERS
SMOKERS
SMOKIES
SMOOTHS
SMUDGES
SNAPONS
SNEEZES
SNIPERS
SNIVELS
SNOCATS
SNOOZES
SNORERS
SOAKERS
SOAPERS
SOARERS
SOBBERS
SOCIALS
SOCKETS
SODDIES
SODLESS
SOFFITS
SOFTENS
SOFTIES
SOIREES
SOLACES
SOLDERS
SOLUTES
SOLVERS
SOMALIS
SONATAS
SONLESS
SONNETS
SOONERS
SOOTHES
SORBETS
SORITES
SORRELS
SORROWS
SORTERS
SORTIES
SOUKOUS
SOURCES
SOVIETS
SOWBUGS
SPACERS
SPADERS
SPARGES
SPAVINS
SPECIES
SPEEDOS
SPHERES
SPIDERS
SPIGOTS
SPIKERS
SPINELS
SPINETS
SPIRALS
SPIREAS
SPIRITS
SPITZES
SPLEENS
SPLICES
SPLINES
SPLINTS
SPONGES
SPOUSES
SPRAINS
SPRAWLS
SPREADS
SPRINGS
SPRINTS
SPRITES
SPROUTS
SPRUCES
SPUMOUS
SQUALLS
SQUARES
SQUAWKS
SQUEAKS
SQUEALS
SQUILLS
SQUINTS
SQUIRES
SQUIRMS
SQUIRTS
STABLES
STAGERS
STALAGS
STAMENS
STANCES
STANZAS
STAPLES
STARERS
STARETS
STARVES
STASHES
STATICS
STATORS
STATUES
STDENIS
STEPINS
STEPPES
STEPUPS
STEREOS
STEROLS
STEVENS
STEWERS
STICHES
STIFLES
STIGMAS
STINGOS
STJOHNS
STKITTS
STLOUIS
STOGIES
STOKERS
STOLONS
STONERS
STOOGES
STORERS
STOREYS
STORIES
STRAFES
STRAINS
STRAITS
STRANDS
STRATUS
STRAUSS
STREAKS
STREAMS
STREETS
STRIDES
STRIKES
STRINGS
STRIPES
STRIVES
STROBES
STROKES
STROLLS
STUCCOS
STUDIES
STUDIOS
STUMERS
STUPORS
STURGES
STYLERS
STYLETS
STYMIES
SUBDEBS
SUBDUES
SUBLETS
SUBMITS
SUBORNS
SUBSETS
SUBURBS
SUBWAYS
SUCCESS
SUCCORS
SUCKERS
SUFFERS
SUITORS
SULKERS
SULKIES
SULLIES
SULTANS
SUMLESS
SUMMERS
SUMMITS
SUMMONS
SUNDAES
SUNDAYS
SUNDERS
SUNDEWS
SUNDOGS
SUNGODS
SUNLESS
SUNRAYS
SUNSETS
SUNTANS
SUPPERS
SURFERS
SURPASS
SURPLUS
SURREYS
SURVEYS
SUSLIKS
SUTLERS
SUTTERS
SUTURES
SWATHES
SWAYERS
SWERVES
SWIPERS
SWISHES
SWIVELS
SWIVETS
SYLVANS
SYMBOLS
SYNCHES
SYPHONS
SYRIANS
SYSTEMS

•SS••••

ASSAILS
ASSAULT
ASSAYED
ASSAYER
ASSEGAI
ASSENTS
ASSERTS
ASSIGNS
ASSISTS
ASSIZES
ASSLIKE
ASSORTS
ASSUAGE
ASSUMED
ASSUMES
ASSURED
ASSURES
ASSYRIA
ESSAYED
ESSENCE
ESSENES
ISSUERS
ISSUING
OSSEOUS
OSSICLE
OSSIFIC
USSTEEL

•S•S•••

ASKSFOR
ASKSOUT
ASUSUAL
USOSHOW

•S••S••

ASEPSIS
ASSISTS
ESPOSAS
ESPOSOS
OSMOSED
OSMOSES
OSMOSIS
TSETSES

•S•••S•

ASHIEST
ASHLESS
ASPERSE
ESPOUSE
OSHKOSH
TSARIST
USELESS

•S••••S

ASCENDS
ASCENTS
ASEPSIS
ASFARAS
ASHCANS
ASHLARS
ASHLESS
ASHRAMS
ASPECTS
ASPIRES
ASSAILS
ASSENTS
ASSERTS
ASSIGNS
ASSISTS
ASSIZES
ASSORTS
ASSUMES
ASSURES
ASYLUMS
CSLEWIS
ESCAPES
ESCARPS
ESCHEWS
ESCORTS
ESCROWS
ESCUDOS
ESKIMOS
ESPIALS
ESPOSAS
ESPOSOS
ESSENES
ESTATES
ESTEEMS
ESTRAYS
ISLANDS
ISOBARS
ISOGONS
ISOHELS
ISOMERS
ISOPODS
ISSUERS
ISTHMUS
OSCINES
OSMOSES
OSMOSIS
OSPREYS
OSSEOUS
OSTLERS
PSANDQS
PSYCHES
TSETSES
TSHIRTS
TSOURIS
USELESS
USERIDS
USOPENS
USURERS
USURIES

••SS•••

AUSSIES
BASSETS
BASSIST
BASSOON
BOSSIER
BOSSILY
BOSSING
BUSSING
BUSSTOP
CASSATT
CASSAVA
CASSIAS
CASSIDY
CASSINI
CASSINO
CASSIUS
CASSOCK
CESSING
CESSION
COSSACK

COSSETS
CUSSING
CUSSLER
DESSERT
DISSECT
DISSENT
DISSING
DOSSALS
DOSSERS
DOSSIER
FESSING
FISSILE
FISSION
FISSURE
FOSSILS
FUSSIER
FUSSILY
FUSSING
FUSSPOT
GASSERS
GASSIER
GESSOES
GOSSETT
GOSSIPS
GOSSIPY
GUSSETS
GUSSIED
GUSSIES
GUSSYUP
HASSLED
HASSLES
HASSOCK
HESSIAN
HISSERS
HISSING
HUSSARS
HUSSEIN
HUSSIES
HYSSOPS
JESSICA
JOSSERS
KISSERS
KISSING
KISSOFF
LASSIES
LASSOED
LASSOER
LASSOES
LESSEES
LESSENS
LESSING
LESSONS
LESSORS
LISSOME
MASSAGE
MASSEUR
MASSIER
MASSIFS
MASSING
MASSIVE
MESSAGE
MESSALA
MESSIAH
MESSIER
MESSILY
MESSINA
MESSING
MESSKIT
MISSAID
MISSALS
MISSAYS
MISSIES
MISSILE
MISSING
MISSION
MISSISH
MISSIVE
MISSOUT
MISSTEP
MOSSIER
MOSSING
MUSSELS
MUSSIER
MUSSILY
MUSSING
PASSADO
PASSAGE
PASSELS
PASSERS
PASSEUL
PASSFOR
PASSING
PASSION
PASSIVE
PASSKEY
PASSOFF
PASSOUT
POSSESS
POSSETS
POSSLQS
POSSUMS
RASSLED
RASSLES
RISSOLE
ROSSINI
ROSSSEA
RUSSELL
RUSSETS
RUSSETY
RUSSIAN
SASSERS
SASSIER
SASSIES
SASSILY
SASSING
SASSOON
SESSILE
SESSION
SISSIES
SUSSING
TASSELS
TESSERA
TISSUES
TOSSERS
TOSSING
TOSSOFF
TOSSOUT
TOSSUPS
TUSSAUD
TUSSLED
TUSSLES
TUSSOCK
VASSALS
VESSELS
WASSAIL
YESSING

••S•S••

ASSISTS
DESISTS
DESKSET
DISUSED
EASESIN
EASESUP
INSISTS
LOSESIT
MISUSED
MISUSES
MUSTSEE
RESISTS
RESTSUP
ROSSSEA
WISESUP

••S••S•

BASSIST
BUSIEST
COSIEST
DESPISE
DISCUSS
DISEASE
DISGUST
DISMISS
DISPOSE
DRSEUSS
DUSKISH
EASIEST
ECSTASY
FASTEST
GASLESS
HOSTESS
LUSHEST
MISCAST
MISSISH
NASTASE
NOSIEST
POSHEST
POSSESS
RASHEST
RASPISH
ROSIEST
VASTEST
WASPISH

••S•••S

ABSENTS
ABSORBS
ADSORBS
ANSWERS
APSIDES
ASSAILS
ASSENTS
ASSERTS
ASSIGNS
ASSISTS
ASSIZES
ASSORTS
ASSUMES
ASSURES
AUSSIES
AXSEEDS
BASALTS
BASKETS
BASQUES
BASSETS
BASTERS
BESEEMS
BESIDES
BESTIRS
BESTOWS
BISECTS
BISHOPS
BISQUES
BISTROS
BOSKETS
BUSBIES
BUSBOYS
BUSHELS
BUSKINS
BUSTERS
BUSTLES
CASABAS
CASAVAS
CASERNS
CASHEWS
CASINGS
CASINOS
CASQUES
CASSIAS
CASSIUS
CASTERS
CASTLES
CASUALS
COSIGNS
COSINES
COSSETS
COSTARS
CUSHAWS
CUSPIDS
CUSTOMS
DASHERS
DESALTS
DESERTS
DESIGNS
DESIRES
DESISTS
DESOTOS
DESPOTS
DISARMS
DISBARS
DISCUSS
DISMAYS
DISMISS
DISOWNS
DISPELS
DISTILS
DOSAGES
DOSIDOS
DOSSALS
DOSSERS
DRSEUSS
DUSTERS
DUSTUPS
EASTERS
ENSIGNS
ENSILES
ENSKIES
ENSOULS
ENSURES
ESSENES
EXSERTS
FASCIAS
FASTENS
FESCUES
FESTERS
FISHERS
FOSSILS
FOSTERS
FUSTICS
GASBAGS
GASCAPS
GASCONS
GASEOUS
GASJETS
GASKETS
GASKINS
GASLESS
GASLOGS
GASPERS
GASSERS
GESSOES
GOSLOWS
GOSPELS
GOSSIPS
GUSHERS
GUSSETS
GUSSIES
GUSTOES
HASSLES
HASTENS
HISSERS
HOSIERS
HOSKINS
HOSTELS
HOSTESS
HUSKERS
HUSKIES
HUSSARS
HUSSIES
HUSTLES
HYSSOPS
INSEAMS
INSECTS
INSERTS
INSIDES
INSISTS
INSOLES
INSPANS
INSPOTS
INSTALS
INSTARS
INSTEPS
INSTILS
INSULTS
INSURES
ISSUERS
JASPERS
JESTERS
JESUITS
JOSKINS
JOSSERS
JOSTLES
KISHKES
KISSERS
KOSHERS
KUSPUKS
LASHERS
LASHUPS
LASSIES
LASSOES
LESSEES
LESSENS
LESSONS
LESSORS
LISTEES
LISTELS
LISTENS
LUSTERS
LUSTRES
MASCOTS
MASHERS
MASHIES
MASKERS
MASQUES
MASSIFS
MASTERS
MASTICS
MESCALS
MISCUES
MISDOES
MISFITS
MISHAPS
MISHITS
MISLAYS
MISSALS
MISSAYS
MISSIES
MISTERS
MISUSES
MOSAICS
MOSHERS
MOSLEMS
MOSQUES
MUSCATS
MUSCLES
MUSEUMS
MUSHERS
MUSKEGS
MUSKETS
MUSKIES
MUSLIMS
MUSLINS
MUSSELS
MUSTERS
MYSTICS
NESTERS
NESTLES
NOSHERS
NOSHOWS
OFSORTS
ONSIDES
OSSEOUS
OUSTERS
OYSTERS
PASSELS
PASSERS
PASTELS
PASTORS
PESAWAS
PESETAS
PESTERS
PESTLES
PISTILS
PISTOLS
PISTONS
POSADAS
POSEURS
POSSESS
POSSETS
POSSLQS
POSSUMS
POSTERS
POSTITS
PUSHUPS
RASCALS
RASHERS
RASPERS
RASSLES
RASTERS
RESALES
RESALTS
RESANDS
RESCUES
RESEALS
RESEATS
RESECTS
RESEEDS
RESELLS
RESENDS
RESENTS
RESHIPS
RESHOES
RESIDES
RESIGNS
RESILES
RESINGS
RESISTS
RESOLES
RESORBS
RESORTS
RESPINS
RESTERS
RESULTS
RESUMES
RISINGS
RISKERS
ROSTERS
RUSHEES
RUSHERS
RUSSETS
RUSTICS
RUSTLES
SASHAYS
SASSERS
SASSIES
SESAMES
SESTETS
SISKINS
SISSIES
SISTERS
SUSLIKS
SYSTEMS
TASSELS
TASTERS
TESTEES
TESTERS
TISANES
TISSUES
TOSSERS
TOSSUPS
TUSKERS
TUSSLES
TVSHOWS
ULSTERS
UNSEALS
UNSEATS
UNSNAGS
UNSNAPS
UNSTOPS
UPSHOTS
VASSALS
VESPERS
VESPIDS
VESSELS
VESTEES
VISAGES
VISAVIS
VISCOUS
VISIONS
VISUALS
WASHERS
WASHUPS
WASTERS
WESKITS
WISHERS

•••SS••

ABYSSES
AGASSIZ
ALYSSUM
AMASSED
AMASSER
AMASSES
ATISSUE
BIASSED
BLESSED
BLESSES
BLOSSOM
BRASSES
BRASSIE
CAISSON
CHASSES
CHASSIS
CLASSED
CLASSES
CLASSIC
CRASSER
CRASSLY
CRASSUS
CRESSES
CROSSED
CROSSER
CROSSES
CROSSLY
CROSSUP
DRESSED
DRESSER
DRESSES
DRESSUP
FLOSSED
FLOSSES
FRISSON
GETSSET
GLASSED
GLASSES
GLOSSAE
GLOSSED
GLOSSES
GRASSED
GRASSES
GRISSOM
GROSSED
GROSSER
GROSSES
GROSSLY
GUESSED
GUESSER
GUESSES
JANSSEN
KNESSET
KNOSSOS
LAISSEZ
LETSSEE
LOESSER
LOESSES
MEISSEN
MOUSSED
MOUSSES
NILSSON
ODYSSEY
ONASSIS
OPOSSUM
PLUSSES
POISSON
PRESSED
PRESSER
PRESSES
PRESSON
PRESSUP
PRUSSIA
REISSUE
ROSSSEA
SCISSOR
SPASSKY
STASSEN
TRESSES
TRUSSED
TRUSSES
ULYSSES

•••S•S•

BASSIST
CLOSEST
CONSIST
DENSEST
FALSEST
LOOSEST
MISSISH
PERSIST
POSSESS
SUBSIST
TENSEST
TERSEST

•••S••S

ABASHES
ABUSERS
ABYSSES
AIRSACS
AMASSES
ARISTAS
ARISTOS
AUSSIES
BALSAMS
BASSETS
BLESSES
BLUSHES
BOWSAWS
BRASSES
BRUSHES
BURSARS
CAESARS
CAPSIDS
CASSIAS
CASSIUS
CELSIUS
CENSERS
CENSORS
CHASERS
CHASSES
CHASSIS
CHISELS
CLASHES
CLASSES
CLOSETS
CONSULS
CORSETS
COSSETS
COUSINS
CRASHES
CRASSUS
CRESSES
CRISPUS
CROSSES
CRUSHES
CURSORS
DAISIES
DAMSELS
DAMSONS
DIESELS
DOGSITS
DORSALS
DOSSALS
DOSSERS
DOWSERS
DRESSES
ELYSEES
ENISLES
ERASERS
ERASMUS
FAUSTUS
FIASCOS
FIESTAS
FLASHES
FLESHES
FLOSSES
FLUSHES
FOCSLES
FOSSILS
FRESCOS
GASSERS
GEISHAS
GESSOES
GEYSERS
GIPSIES
GLASSES
GLOSSES
GNASHES
GODSONS
GOSSIPS
GRASSES
GROSSES
GUESSES
GUSSETS
GUSSIES
GYPSIES
HANSOMS
HASSLES
HAWSERS
HISSERS
HUSSARS
HUSSIES
HYSSOPS
JERSEYS
JETSKIS
JETSONS
JIGSAWS
JOSSERS
KAISERS
KANSANS
KISSERS
KMESONS
KNISHES
KNOSSOS
LASSIES
LASSOES
LEASERS
LEASHES
LESSEES
LESSENS
LESSONS
LESSORS
LOESSES
LOOSENS
MARSHES
MASSIFS
MEASLES
MIASMAS
MISSALS
MISSAYS
MISSIES
MORSELS
MOUSERS
MOUSSES
MUSSELS
NAYSAYS
NELSONS
NEWSIES
NURSERS
OFFSETS
OLDSAWS
ONASSIS
ORESTES
ORISONS
OUTSETS
OVISACS
PANSIES
PARSECS
PARSEES
PARSERS
PARSONS
PASSELS
PASSERS
PATSIES
PENSEES
PEPSINS
PERSEUS
PERSIUS
PERSONS
PHASERS
PHYSICS
PITSAWS
PLASHES
PLASMAS
PLUSHES
PLUSSES
POISONS
POSSESS
POSSETS
POSSLQS
POSSUMS
PRESETS
PRESSES
PRESTOS
PRISONS
PROSERS
PULSARS
PURSERS
PURSUES
QUASARS
QUASHES
RAISERS
RAISINS
RANSOMS
RASSLES
REASONS
RIPSAWS
ROUSERS
RUSSETS
SASSERS
SASSIES
SEASONS
SEESAWS
SENSORS
SHUSHES
SIESTAS
SISSIES
SKOSHES
SLASHES
SLOSHES
SLUSHES
SMASHES
STASHES
SUBSETS
SUNSETS
SWISHES
TANSIES
TARSALS
TASSELS
TEASELS
TEASERS
TEASETS
TENSORS
THESEUS
THESPIS
TINSELS
TISSUES
TOCSINS
TONSILS
TOSSERS
TOSSUPS
TOUSLES
TOYSRUS
TRASHES
TRESSES
TRUSSES
TULSANS
TUSSLES
ULYSSES
UNISONS
VASSALS
VESSELS
VIZSLAS
WEASELS
WHISHES
WORSENS
WOWSERS
ZOYSIAS

••••SS•

BABASSU
COLOSSI
DEBUSSY
EMBASSY
ENMASSE
FINESSE
IMPASSE
MATISSE
MELISSA
PELISSE
PICASSO
STRASSE
VANESSA

••••S•S

ABYSSES
ACCOSTS
ACCUSES
ADJUSTS
ADVISES
AGEISTS
ALIASES
AMASSES
AORISTS
APHESES
APPOSES
ARIOSOS
AROUSES
ARRASES
ARRESTS
ARRISES
ARTISTS
ASEPSIS
ASSISTS
ATLASES
ATTESTS
AVULSES
BEHESTS
BEMUSES
BETISES
BIGOSES
BLESSES
BLOUSES
BOLUSES
BONUSES
BOURSES
BRAISES
BRASSES
BREASTS
BROWSES
BRUISES
CAMISES
CAYUSES
CHAISES
CHASSES
CHASSIS
CHEESES
CHOOSES
CHRISMS
CLASSES
CLAUSES
COHOSTS
COURSES
CRASSUS
CREASES
CRESSES
CROESUS
CROSSES
CRUISES
CUBISTS
DAMASKS
DEBASES
DEFUSES
DEGUSTS
DELISTS
DEMISES
DEPOSES
DESISTS
DETESTS
DEVISES
DIGESTS
DIVESTS
DRESSES
DROWSES
DYNASTS
ECDYSES
ECDYSIS
EFFUSES
EGOISTS
ELAPSES
ENCASES
ENDUSES
ENLISTS
ESPOSAS
ESPOSOS
EVULSES
EXCISES
EXCUSES
EXPOSES
FICUSES
FLENSES
FLOSSES
FOCUSES
FORESTS
FRAISES
GENESES
GENESIS
GLASSES
GLOSSES
GRASSES
GREASES
GROSSES
GROUSES
GUESSES
HOLISTS
ILLUSES
IMPOSES
IMPOSTS
INCASES
INCISES
INFESTS
INFUSES
INGESTS
INSISTS
INVESTS
IODISES
IONISES
IQTESTS
JONESES
JURISTS
KNOSSOS
LEGISTS
LIAISES
LOCUSTS
LOESSES
LORISES
LOTUSES
LUTISTS
LYRISTS
MAOISTS
MEDUSAS
MEIOSES
MEIOSIS
MIMESIS
MIMOSAS
MINUSES
MISUSES
MITOSES
MITOSIS
MOLESTS
MOUSSES
NEMESES
NEMESIS
NEXUSES
NUDISTS
OBLASTS
OBOISTS
ONASSIS
OPPOSES
OSMOSES
OSMOSIS
PEGASUS
PERUSES
PHRASES
PLEASES
PLUSSES
PRAISES
PRESSES
PRIESTS
PURISTS
RAMESES
REBUSES
RECASTS
RECUSES
REFUSES
RELISTS
REPASTS
REPOSES
RESISTS
RETESTS
REVISES
SCHISMS
SCOUSES
SEXISTS
SINUSES
SPOUSES
TALUSES
TAOISTS
THEISTS
THIRSTS
THRUSTS
TRESSES
TRUISMS
TRUSSES
TSETSES
TUBISTS
TYPISTS
ULYSSES
UNCASES
UNMASKS
UPRISES
VALISES
VIRUSES

•••••SS

ACTRESS
ADDRESS
AGELESS
AGGRESS
AIDLESS
AIMLESS
AIRKISS
AIRLESS
AIRMASS
ANDRESS
APTNESS

ARMLESS ARTLESS ASHLESS ATALOSS AWELESS AWNLESS BADNESS BARLESS BEDLESS BIBLESS BIGNESS BIOMASS BITLESS BOWLESS BRALESS BUDLESS BURGESS CANVASS CAPLESS CARCASS CARLESS COMPASS CONFESS COYNESS CUIRASS CURTISS CUTLASS CYPRESS DECLASS DEGAUSS DEPRESS DEWLESS DIGRESS DIMNESS DISCUSS DISMISS DOGLESS DRSEUSS DRYNESS DUCHESS EARLESS EGGLESS EMPRESS ENDLESS ENGROSS EXPRESS EYELESS FATLESS FATNESS FEELESS FITNESS FLYLESS FOGLESS FURLESS GAPLESS GASLESS GEMLESS GODDESS GODLESS GUMLESS GUNLESS GUTLESS HAPLESS HARNESS HATLESS HEIRESS HIPLESS HIPNESS HITLESS HOSTESS HOTNESS HUELESS ICELESS ICINESS

ILLNESS IMPRESS INAMESS INGRESS INKLESS INNLESS IPCRESS IRELESS JACKASS JAGLESS JARLESS JAWLESS JOBLESS JOYLESS KEYLESS KINLESS LARGESS LAWLESS LAXNESS LEGLESS LIDLESS LIONESS LIPLESS LOWNESS MADNESS MANLESS MATLESS NAPLESS NEWNESS OAKMOSS OARLESS ODDNESS OILLESS OLDNESS OLEMISS ONENESS OPPRESS ORBLESS PATNESS PEERESS PEGLESS PINLESS PITBOSS POSSESS PREMISS PROCESS PROFESS PROWESS PUNLESS RAWNESS REAMASS RECROSS REDNESS REDRESS REGRESS REPRESS RIBLESS RIMLESS RODLESS RUMLESS SADNESS SAPLESS SEABASS SEAMOSS SEERESS SHYNESS SINLESS SKYLESS SLYNESS SODLESS SONLESS STRAUSS SUCCESS SUMLESS

SUNLESS SURPASS TAXLESS TEALESS TIELESS TIGRESS TIPLESS TOELESS TOYLESS TUGLESS UNDRESS USELESS VOWLESS WANNESS WARLESS WAYLESS WEBLESS WETNESS WIGLESS WITLESS WITNESS WRYNESS

ST•••••

STABBED STABILE STABLED STABLER STABLES STACKED STACKUP STADIUM STAFFED STAFFER STAGERS STAGGED STAGGER STAGIER STAGILY STAGING STAIDER STAIDLY STAINED STAINER STAKING STALAGS STALELY STALEST STALKED STALKER STALLED STAMENS STAMINA STAMMER STAMPED STANCES STANDBY STANDEE STANDIN STANDON STANDUP STANLEE STANLEY STANNIC STANTON STANZAS STAPLED STAPLER STAPLES STARCHY STARDOM STAREAT STARERS STARETS

STARING STARKER STARKLY STARLET STARLIT STARMAN STARMAP STARRED STARTED STARTER STARTLE STARTUP STARVED STARVES STASHED STASHES STASSEN STATELY STATICE STATICS STATING STATION STATIST STATORS STATUES STATURE STATUTE STAUNCH STAVING STAYING STAYPUT STAYSUP STCROIX STDENIS STEALTH STEAMED STEAMER STEELED STEELER STEELIE STEEPED STEEPEN STEEPER STEEPLE STEEPLY STEERED STEERER STEIGER STEINEM STEINER STELLAR STEMMED STENCIL STENGEL STENTOR STEPHEN STEPINS STEPOUT STEPPED STEPPER STEPPES STEPSIN STEPSON STEPSUP STEPUPS STEREOS STERILE STERNAL STERNER STERNLY STERNUM STEROID STEROLS STETSON

STETTED STEUBEN STEVENS STEWARD STEWART STEWERS STEWING STICHES STICKER STICKTO STICKUP STIEGEL STIFFED STIFFEN STIFFER STIFFLY STIFLED STIFLES STIGMAS STILLED STILLER STILTED STILTON STIMULI STINGER STINGOS STINKER STINTED STIPEND STIPPLE STIRFRY STIRRED STIRRER STIRRUP STIRSIN STIRSUP STJOHNS STKITTS STLOUIS STLUCIA STOCKED STOCKUP STOGIES STOICAL STOKELY STOKERS STOKING STOLLEN STOLLER STOLONS STOMACH STOMATA STOMPED STONERS STONIER STONILY STONING STOODBY STOODIN STOODUP STOOGES STOOKED STOOKEY STOOLIE STOOPED STOPGAP STOPOFF STOPPED STOPPER STOPSIN STOPSUP STORAGE STORERS STOREUP

STOREYS STORIED STORIES STORING STORMED STOUTEN STOUTER STOUTLY STOWING STPETER STRAFED STRAFES STRAINS STRAITS STRANDS STRANGE STRASSE STRATUM STRATUS STRAUSS STRAYED STREAKS STREAKY STREAMS STREETS STRETCH STRETTO STREWED STREWER STRIATE STRIDER STRIDES STRIKER STRIKES STRINGS STRINGY STRIPED STRIPER STRIPES STRIVED STRIVEN STRIVER STRIVES STROBES STROKED STROKES STROLLS STROPHE STROPPY STRUDEL STUBBED STUBBLE STUBBLY STUCCOS STUCKTO STUCKUP STUDDED STUDENT STUDIED STUDIES STUDIOS STUFFED STUFFER STUMBLE STUMERS STUMPED STUMPER STUNGUN STUNNED STUNNER STUNTED STUPEFY STUPORS STURGES

STYGIAN STYLERS STYLETS STYLING STYLISE STYLISH STYLIST STYLIZE STYMIED STYMIES STYPTIC STYRENE STYRIAN

S•T••••

SATCHEL SATCHMO SATDOWN SATEENS SATIATE SATIETY SATINET SATIRES SATIRIC SATISFY SATRAPS SATSUMA SETBACK SETDOWN SETINTO SETLINE SETSAIL SETSOFF SETSOUT SETTEES SETTERS SETTING SETTLED SETTLER SETTLES SETUPON SHTICKS SITCOMS SITDOWN SITSOUT SITTERS SITTING SITUATE SITWELL SOTHERE SOTHERN SOTTISH SUTLERS SUTTERS SUTURED SUTURES

S••T•••

SALTBOX SALTERS SALTIER SALTILY SALTINE SALTING SALTISH SANTAFE SANTANA SANTINI SANTIRS SAOTOME SAUTEED SCATHED SCATHES SCATTED

SCATTER SCOTERS SCOTTIE SCUTTLE SCYTHED SCYTHES SEATERS SEATING SEATTLE SECTION SECTORS SEETHED SEETHES SEETOIT SELTZER SENTFOR SENTOFF SENTOUT SEPTETS SESTETS SESTINA SETTEES SETTERS SETTING SETTLED SETTLER SETTLES SEXTANS SEXTANT SEXTETS SEXTONS SHATNER SHATTER SHOTFOR SHOTGUN SHOTOUT SHOTPUT SHUTEYE SHUTINS SHUTOFF SHUTOUT SHUTSIN SHUTSUP SHUTTER SHUTTLE SIFTERS SIFTING SILTIER SILTING SISTERS SISTINE SISTRUM SITTERS SITTING SIXTEEN SIXTHLY SIXTIES SKATERS SKATING SKETCHY SKITOWS SKITTER SKITTLE SLATHER SLATIER SLATING SLATTED SLITHER SLOTCAR SLOTTED SMATTER SMETANA SMITING SMITTEN

SMOTHER SNITCHY SOFTENS SOFTEST SOFTIES SOFTISH SOFTTOP SOOTHED SOOTHER SOOTHES SOOTIER SOOTILY SORTERS SORTIED SORTIES SORTING SORTOUT SOTTISH SOUTANE SOUTHEY SPATIAL SPATTED SPATTER SPATULA SPITING SPITZES SPOTLIT SPOTTED SPOTTER SPUTNIK SPUTTER STATELY STATICE STATICS STATING STATION STATIST STATORS STATUES STATURE STATUTE STETSON STETTED SUBTEND SUBTEXT SUBTLER SUCTION SUITING SUITORS SUITSUP SULTANA SULTANS SUNTANS SURTSEY SUSTAIN SUTTERS SWATHED SWATHES SWATTED SWATTER SWITZER SYSTEMS SYSTOLE

S•••T••

SAINTED SAINTLY SALUTED SALUTES SAMITES SANCTUM SAUNTER SCANTED SCANTER

SCANTLY SCATTED SCATTER SCENTED SCEPTER SCEPTIC SCEPTRE SCHATZI SCOOTED SCOOTER SCOTTIE SCOUTED SCOUTER SCRATCH SCUTTLE SEASTAR SEATTLE SEDATED SEDATER SEDATES SEMITES SEMITIC SENATES SENATOR SHAFTED SHANTEY SHASTRI SHATTER SHEATHE SHEATHS SHEETED SHELTER SHELTIE SHELTON SHIATSU SHIFTED SHIHTZU SHIITES SHOOTAT SHOOTER SHOOTUP SHORTED SHORTEN SHORTER SHORTLY SHORTOF SHOUTED SHOUTER SHUNTED SHUTTER SHUTTLE SHYSTER SIESTAS SIGHTED SIGHTLY SINATRA SKEETER SKELTER SKELTON SKEPTIC SKIRTED SKITTER SKITTLE SLANTED SLATTED SLAYTON SLEETED SLEPTIN SLEPTON SLEUTHS SLOTTED SMALTOS SMARTED SMARTEN

SMARTER SMARTLY SMATTER SMELTED SMELTER SMITTEN SMOOTHS SMOOTHY SNIFTER SNOOTED SNORTED SNORTER SOFTTOP SOLUTES SOMATIC SONATAS SORITES SPARTAN SPATTED SPATTER SPECTER SPECTOR SPECTRA SPECTRE SPLITUP SPLOTCH SPORTED SPOTTED SPOTTER SPOUTED SPOUTER SPRITES SPURTED SPUTTER SQUATLY SQUATTY STANTON STARTED STARTER STARTLE STARTUP STENTOR STETTED STILTED STILTON STINTED STKITTS STOUTEN STOUTER STOUTLY STPETER STRATUM STRATUS STRETCH STRETTO STUNTED STYPTIC SUMATRA SUZETTE SVELTER SWARTHY SWATTED SWATTER SWEATED SWEATER SWEETEN SWEETER SWEETIE SWEETLY SWEETON SWELTER SWELTRY SWEPTUP SWIFTER

SWIFTLY SYMPTOM

S••••T•

SABBATH SACHETS SALLETS SAMLETS SATIATE SATIETY SAVANTS SCHULTZ SCRIPTS SCULPTS SEADUTY SEAGATE SECANTS SECRETE SECRETS SELECTS SENNETT SENSATE SEPTETS SERIATE SERRATE SESTETS SETINTO SEVENTH SEVENTY SEXISTS SEXTETS SFUMATO SHRIFTS SIGNETS SILENTS SINGSTO SIPPETS SITUATE SLIGHTS SNAPSTO SNOCATS SOCIETY SOCKETS SOFFITS SONNETS SOPWITH SORBATE SORBETS SOVIETS SPIGOTS SPINETS SPIRITO SPIRITS SPLINTS SPRINTS SPROUTS SQUANTO SQUATTY SQUINTS SQUINTY SQUIRTS STARETS STATUTE STEALTH STICKTO STKITTS STOMATA STRAITS STREETS STRETTO STRIATE STUCKTO STYLETS SUAVITY

SUBLETS SUBMITS SUBSETS SUHARTO SULFATE SULFITE SUMMITS SUNBATH SUNCITY SUNSETS SUZETTE SWEARTO SWIVETS

S•••••T

SACKOUT SADDEST SALIENT SANDLOT SANGOUT SAPIENT SARGENT SATINET SAWDUST SCARLET SCHMIDT SEAGIRT SEALANT SEAPORT SEASALT SEEKOUT SEENFIT SEENOUT SEESFIT SEESOUT SEETOIT SEGMENT SELLOUT SENDOUT SENNETT SENTOUT SERPENT SERVANT SETSOUT SEXIEST SEXTANT SHALLOT SHERBET SHIPOUT SHOOTAT SHOTOUT SHOTPUT SHOWOUT SHUBERT SHUTOUT SICKEST SICKOUT SIDEBET SIGNOUT SILKHAT SINGOUT SITSOUT SKIBOOT SKILIFT SKILLET SKIPOUT SKISUIT SLEIGHT SLIPOUT SLOWEST SNAPSAT SNEERAT SNIDEST SNIFFAT

SNIGLET SNIPEAT SNIPPET SNOWCAT SOFTEST SOLDOUT SOLICIT SOLOIST SOLVENT SOONEST SOPHIST SORTOUT SOUREST SPAREST SPINOUT SPIRANT SPOTLIT SPRIEST SPRYEST SPUNOUT STALEST STAREAT STARLET STARLIT STATIST STAYPUT STEPOUT STEWART STUDENT STYLIST SUAVEST SUBJECT SUBPLOT SUBSIST SUBTEXT SUBUNIT SUBVERT SUGGEST SUNBELT SUNKIST SUNSPOT SUNSUIT SUPPORT SURCOAT SURFEIT SUSPECT SWALLET SWEARAT SWOREAT

•ST••••

ASTAIRE ASTARTE ASTOLAT ASTORIA ASTOUND ASTRIDE ESTATES ESTEEMS ESTELLE ESTEVEZ ESTHETE ESTIVAL ESTONIA ESTORIL ESTRADA ESTRAYS ESTUARY ISTHMUS OSTEOID OSTLERS OSTRICH USTINOV

•S•T•••
ASHTRAY
ESOTERY
ISOTOPE
TSETSES
USSTEEL

•S••T••
ASCETIC
ASEPTIC
ASIATIC
ESTATES
OSMOTIC
PSALTER

•S•••T•
ASCENTS
ASHANTI
ASPECTS
ASSENTS
ASSERTS
ASSISTS
ASSORTS
ASTARTE
ESCORTS
ESPARTO
ESTHETE
ISOLATE
TSHIRTS

•S••••T
ASHIEST
ASKSOUT
ASPHALT
ASSAULT
ASTOLAT
ESCHEAT
TSARIST
TSELIOT
USGRANT

••ST•••
ABSTAIN
ATSTAKE
AUSTERE
AUSTRAL
AUSTRIA
BASTERS
BASTING
BASTION
BESTBOY
BESTIAL
BESTING
BESTIRS
BESTMAN
BESTMEN
BESTOWS
BESTREW
BISTROS
BUSTARD
BUSTERS
BUSTING
BUSTLED
BUSTLES
BUSTOUT
CASTERS
CASTILE
CASTING
CASTLED
CASTLES
CASTOFF
CASTOUT
CISTERN
COSTAIN
COSTARS
COSTING
COSTNER
COSTUME
CUSTARD
CUSTODY
CUSTOMS
DASTARD
DESTINE
DESTINY
DESTROY
DISTAFF
DISTANT
DISTEND
DISTILL
DISTILS
DISTORT
DISTURB
DUSTBIN
DUSTERS
DUSTIER
DUSTILY
DUSTING
DUSTMAN
DUSTMEN
DUSTMOP
DUSTOFF
DUSTPAN
DUSTUPS
EASTEND
EASTERN
EASTERS
EASTMAN
ECSTASY
EPSTEIN
FASTENS
FASTEST
FASTING
FASTONE
FESTERS
FESTIVA
FESTIVE
FESTOON
FISTFUL
FOSTERS
FUSTIAN
FUSTICS
FUSTIER
FUSTILY
GASTRIC
GESTALT
GESTATE
GESTURE
GUSTIER
GUSTILY
GUSTING
GUSTOES
HASTENS
HASTIER
HASTILY
HASTING
HISTORY
HOSTAGE
HOSTELS
HOSTESS
HOSTILE
HOSTING
HOSTLER
HUSTLED
HUSTLER
HUSTLES
IFSTONE
INSTALL
INSTALS
INSTANT
INSTARS
INSTATE
INSTEAD
INSTEPS
INSTILL
INSTILS
INSTOCK
INSTORE
INSTYLE
JESTERS
JESTING
JOSTLED
JOSTLER
JOSTLES
JUSTICE
JUSTIFY
JUSTINE
JUSTNOW
KESTREL
LASTING
LASTORY
LISTEES
LISTELS
LISTENS
LISTING
LOSTOUT
LUSTERS
LUSTFUL
LUSTIER
LUSTILY
LUSTING
LUSTRED
LUSTRES
MASTABA
MASTERS
MASTERY
MASTICS
MASTIFF
MASTOID
MESTIZA
MESTIZO
MISTAKE
MISTERS
MISTIER
MISTILY
MISTING
MISTOOK
MISTRAL
MISTYPE
MUSTAFA
MUSTANG
MUSTARD
MUSTERS
MUSTIER
MUSTILY
MUSTSEE
MYSTERY
MYSTICS
MYSTIFY
NASTASE
NASTIER
NASTILY
NESTEGG
NESTERS
NESTING
NESTLED
NESTLER
NESTLES
NOSTRIL
NOSTRUM
ONSTAGE
OUSTERS
OUSTING
OYSTERS
PASTDUE
PASTELS
PASTERN
PASTEUP
PASTEUR
PASTIER
PASTIME
PASTINA
PASTING
PASTORS
PASTURE
PESTERS
PESTLED
PESTLES
PISTILS
PISTOLE
PISTOLS
PISTONS
POSTAGE
POSTBAG
POSTBOX
POSTERN
POSTERS
POSTING
POSTITS
POSTMAN
POSTMEN
POSTURE
POSTWAR
RASTERS
RESTAGE
RESTAIN
RESTAMP
RESTART
RESTATE
RESTERS
RESTFUL
RESTING
RESTIVE
RESTOCK
RESTORE
RESTSUP
RESTYLE
ROSTAND
ROSTERS
ROSTRUM
RUSTICS
RUSTIER
RUSTILY
RUSTING
RUSTLED
RUSTLER
RUSTLES
SESTETS
SESTINA
SISTERS
SISTINE
SISTRUM
SUSTAIN
SYSTEMS
SYSTOLE
TASTERS
TASTIER
TASTILY
TASTING
TESTBAN
TESTEES
TESTERS
TESTFLY
TESTIER
TESTIFY
TESTILY
TESTING
TESTOUT
TESTUDO
TOSTADA
ULSTERS
UNSTACK
UNSTICK
UNSTOPS
UNSTRAP
UNSTUCK
UPSTAGE
UPSTART
UPSTATE
USSTEEL
VASTEST
VASTIER
VESTEES
VESTIGE
VESTING
VESTURE
VISTULA
WASTAGE
WASTERS
WASTING
WASTREL
WESTEND
WESTERN
WISTFUL
ZESTFUL
ZESTIER

••S•T••
ALSATIA
BUSSTOP
DESKTOP
DESOTOS
LESOTHO
MISSTEP
MUSETTE
PESETAS
POSITED
RISOTTO
ROSETTA
ROSETTE
UNSATED
VISITED
VISITOR
WASATCH
WASHTUB

••S••T•
ABSENTS
ASSENTS
ASSERTS
ASSISTS
ASSORTS
BASALTS
BASKETS
BASSETS
BISECTS
BISMUTH
BOSKETS
CASSATT
COSSETS
DESALTS
DESERTS
DESISTS
DESPITE
DESPOTS
DISPUTE
ENSUITE
EXSERTS
GASJETS
GASKETS
GESTATE
GOSSETT
GUSSETS
INSECTS
INSERTS
INSISTS
INSPOTS
INSTATE
INSULTS
JESUITS
LISENTE
MASCOTS
MISDATE
MISFITS
MISHITS
MISMATE
MUSCATS
MUSETTE
MUSKETS
NESMITH
OFSORTS
POSSETS
POSTITS
RESALTS
RESEATS
RESECTS
RESENTS
RESISTS
RESORTS
RESPITE
RESTATE
RESULTS
RISOTTO
ROSEATE
ROSETTA
ROSETTE
RUSSETS
RUSSETY
SESTETS
UNSEATS
UPSHOTS
UPSTATE
WESKITS

••S•••T
ABSOLUT
ASSAULT
BASEHIT
BASSIST
BISCUIT
BUSIEST
BUSTOUT
CASHOUT
CASSATT
CASTOUT
COSIEST
DASBOOT
DESCANT
DESCENT
DESKSET
DESSERT
DISGUST
DISHOUT
DISPORT
DISRUPT
DISSECT
DISSENT
DISTANT
DISTORT
EASEOUT
EASIEST
FASTEST
FISHNET
FISHOUT
FUSSPOT
GESTALT
GOSSETT
INSHORT
INSIGHT
INSPECT
INSTANT
LOSEOUT
LOSESIT
LOSTOUT
LUSHEST
MESSKIT
MISCAST
MISSOUT
MOSHPIT
MUSKRAT
NASCENT
NOSEOUT
NOSIEST
NOSWEAT
ONSIGHT
PASSOUT
POSHEST
RASHEST
RESHOOT
RESPECT
RESTART
ROSIEST
SUSPECT
TESTOUT
TOSSOUT
UNSPENT
UNSWEPT
UPSTART
UPSWEPT
VASTEST
WASHOUT

•••ST••
ALLSTAR
ALLSTON
AMISTAD
ANISTON
APOSTLE
ARISTAE
ARISTAS
ARISTOS
BARSTOW
BEASTIE
BEASTLY
BLASTED
BLASTER
BLISTER
BLUSTER
BOASTED
BOASTER
BOLSTER
BOOSTED
BOOSTER
BOOSTUP
BOXSTEP
BRISTLE
BRISTLY
BRISTOL
BURSTYN
BUSSTOP
CAPSTAN
CAUSTIC
CHASTEN
CHASTER
CHESTER
CLUSTER
COASTAL
COASTED
COASTER
CRESTED
CRUSTED
CRYSTAL
DAYSTAR
DOGSTAR
DRASTIC
DRISTAN
DYKSTRA
EGESTED
ELASTIC
EPISTLE
ERISTIC
EXISTED
FAUSTUS
FEASTED
FIESTAS
FIRSTLY
FLUSTER
FOISTED
FORSTER
FROSTED
GAGSTER
GHASTLY
GHOSTED
GHOSTLY
GLISTEN
GNOSTIC
GRISTLE
GRISTLY
GUESTED
HALSTON
HAMSTER
HEISTED
HIPSTER
HOISTED
HOLSTER
HOUSTON
INASTEW
JOISTED
JOUSTED
JOUSTER
KIRSTIE
LEISTER
LOBSTER
MAESTRI
MAESTRO
MEISTER
MISSTEP
MOBSTER
MOISTEN
MOISTER
MOISTLY
MONSTER
NONSTOP
OLDSTER
OLESTRA
ONESTAR
ONESTEP
ORESTES
OUTSTEP
PIASTER
PIASTRE
PITSTOP
PLASTER
PLASTIC
PRESTON
PRESTOS
PUNSTER
QUESTED
RALSTON
REDSTAR
ROASTED
ROASTER
ROISTER
ROOSTED
ROOSTER
ROUSTED
SEASTAR
SHASTRI
SHYSTER
SIESTAS
TAPSTER
TELSTAR
THISTLE
THISTLY
TINSTAR
TIPSTER
TOASTED
TOASTER
TOLSTOI
TOLSTOY
TRESTLE
TRISTAN
TRISTAR
TRUSTED
TRUSTEE
TRYSTED
TRYSTER
TWISTED
TWISTER
TWOSTAR
TWOSTEP
WALSTON
WEBSTER
WHISTLE
WINSTON
WOOSTER
WORSTED
WRESTED
WRESTLE
ZEMSTVO

•••S•T•
BASSETS
CASSATT
CLOSETS
CORSETS
COSSETS
DENSITY
DOGSITS
DORSETT
FALSITY
FORSYTH
GOSSETT
GUSSETS
HIRSUTE
OFFSETS
OFFSITE
OUTSETS
POSSETS
PRESETS
PULSATE
RUSSETS
RUSSETY
SENSATE
SUBSETS
SUNSETS
TEASETS
VARSITY
WEBSITE

•••S••T
ACESOUT
ACTSOUT
AIRSOUT
ASKSOUT
BASSIST
BIGSHOT
BORSCHT
BOWSOUT
BOXSEAT
BRISKET
BUGSOUT
BUMSOUT
BUYSOUT
CARSEAT
CASSATT
CATSUIT
CLOSEST
CONSENT
CONSIST
CONSORT
CONSULT
COPSOUT
CUTSOUT
DENSEST
DESSERT
DIESOUT
DIGSOUT
DISSECT
DISSENT
DORSETT
DRYSUIT
EARSHOT
EATSOUT
EKESOUT
EYESHOT
FALSEST
FANSOUT
FRESHET
FUSSPOT
GETSOUT
GETSSET
GOESOUT
GOSSETT
GUNSHOT
HITSOUT
HOTSEAT
HOTSHOT
HOTSPOT
ICESOUT
INASNIT
INASPOT
INKSPOT
IRISOUT
KNESSET
LAWSUIT
LAYSOUT
LETSOUT
LOGSOUT
LOOSEST
MESSKIT
MISSOUT
MUGSHOT
OFASORT
ONESHOT
OPTSOUT
PANSOUT
PASSOUT
PAYSOUT
PEASANT
PERSIST
PIGSOUT
POPSOUT
POTSHOT
PRESENT
PRESORT
PURSUIT
PUTSOUT
REDSPOT
RIMSHOT
RIPSOUT
RUBSOUT
RUNSOUT
SEASALT
SEESFIT
SEESOUT
SETSOUT
SITSOUT
SKISUIT
SUBSIST
SUNSPOT
SUNSUIT
TAGSOUT
TAPSOUT
TENSEST
TENSPOT
TERSEST
TOPSOUT
TOSSOUT
TRISECT
WETSUIT
WIGSOUT
WINSOUT

••••ST•
ACCOSTS
ADJUSTS
AGEISTS
AMNESTY
AORISTS
ARIOSTO
ARRESTS
ARTISTE
ARTISTS
ASSISTS
ATTESTS
AUGUSTA
AUGUSTE
BATISTA
BATISTE
BEHESTS
BREASTS
CANASTA
CELESTA
CELESTE
CHRISTI
CHRISTO
CHRISTY
COHOSTS
COMESTO
CUBISTS
DARESTO
DEGUSTS
DELISTS
DESISTS
DETESTS
DIGESTS
DIVESTS
DYNASTS
DYNASTY
EGOISTS
ELMISTI
ENLISTS
ERNESTO
FALLSTO
FORESTS
FROWSTY
GANGSTA
GEARSTO
GIVESTO
HOLDSTO
HOLISTS
HONESTY
IMPASTO
IMPOSTS
INFESTS
INGESTS
INHASTE
INSISTS
INVESTS
IQTESTS
JOCASTA
JURISTS
KEEPSTO
LACOSTE
LEADSTO
LEGISTS
LOCUSTS
LOOKSTO
LUTISTS
LYRISTS
MAJESTE
MAJESTY
MAOISTS
MODESTO
MODESTY
MODISTE
MOLESTS
NUDISTS
OBLASTS
OBOISTS
PRAYSTO
PRIESTS
PURISTS
REBASTE
RECASTS
RELISTS
REPASTE
REPASTS
RESISTS
RETESTS
RIPOSTE
ROBUSTA
SEXISTS
SINGSTO
SNAPSTO
TAKESTO
TALKSTO
TAOISTS
TENDSTO
THEISTS
THIRSTS
THIRSTY
THRUSTS
TRIESTE
TUBISTS
TURNSTO
TYPISTS
WANTSTO

••••S•T
BABYSAT
BABYSIT
BARKSAT
BEATSIT
BLOWSIT
BONESET
COMESAT
COOLSIT
DATASET
DEADSET
DEEPSET
DEPOSIT
DESKSET
FLIESAT
GETSSET
GRABSAT
HANDSET
HARDSET
HEADSET
HINTSAT
HOOFSIT
HOOTSAT
JEERSAT
JUMPSAT
KEEPSAT
KNESSET
LANDSAT
LEERSAT
LOOKSAT
LOSESIT
MAKESIT
MINDSET
MOONSET
NAILSET
PECKSAT
PEEKSAT
PEERSAT
PICKSAT
PLAYSAT
POKESAT
QUONSET
RAILSAT
REVISIT
SNAPSAT
TALKSAT
TEARSAT
THATSIT
TRANSIT
TYPESET
WELLSET
WINGSIT
WINKSAT
YELLSAT

•••••ST
ABREAST
ACCURST
ACHIEST
AERIEST
AGAINST
AGONIST
AIRIEST
AMHERST
AMONGST
AMPLEST
ANALYST
ANAPEST
ANIMIST
ARIDEST
ARMREST
ARTIEST
ASHIEST
ATAVIST
ATHEIST
ATHIRST
ATLEAST
ATWORST
BADDEST
BALDEST
BALLAST
BAPTIST
BASSIST
BEDPOST
BEDREST
BELFAST
BEQUEST
BIGGEST
BOLDEST
BOMBAST
BONIEST
BOXIEST
BRAVEST
BUSIEST
CAGIEST
CAKIEST
CALMEST
CANIEST
CELLIST
CHEMIST
CLOSEST
COEXIST
COKIEST
COLDEST
COMBUST
COMPOST
CONGEST
CONSIST
CONTEST
COOLEST
COPYIST
COSIEST
COZIEST
CRUDEST
CULTIST
CURTEST
CYCLIST
CZARIST
DADAIST
DAFTEST
DAMPEST
DANKEST
DARKEST
DEAFEST
DEAREST
DEEPEST
DEFROST
DEFTEST
DENSEST
DENTIST
DICIEST
DIMMEST
DISGUST
DOPIEST
DOUREST
DOZIEST
DUELIST
DULLEST
DUMBEST
EARNEST
EASIEST
EDGIEST
EELIEST
EERIEST
EGGIEST
EGOTIST
ELEGIST
ELITIST
ENCRUST
ENDMOST
ENTRUST
EPEEIST
EVENEST
EVEREST
EVILEST
EXHAUST
FADDIST
FAIREST
FALSEST
FAREAST
FARWEST
FASTEST
FATTEST
FAUVIST
FIRMEST
FITTEST
FLORIST

FLUTIST
FLYCAST
FLYPAST
FONDEST
FORREST
FOULEST
FOXIEST
FULLEST
FUMIEST
FUNFEST
GABFEST
GAMIEST
GETLOST
GLUIEST
GOOIEST
GORIEST
GOTLOST
GRAVEST
GRAYEST
GREYEST
GYMNAST
HARDEST
HARPIST
HARVEST
HAZIEST
HEPPEST
HIGHEST
HIPPEST
HITLIST
HOKIEST
HOLIEST
HOMIEST
HORNIST
HOTTEST
ICKIEST
IFFIEST
INANEST
INKIEST
INQUEST
INTRUST
IRATEST
JIVIEST
JOKIEST
JUDOIST
KEENEST
KEYWEST
KINDEST
LACIEST
LAKIEST
LAMAIST
LANKEST
LARGEST
LAZIEST
LEANEST
LEFTIST
LEWDEST
LIMIEST
LIMPEST
LINIEST
LITHEST
LOGIEST
LONGEST
LOOSEST
LOUDEST
LOWCOST
LUSHEST
MADDEST
MAEWEST
MARXIST
MAZIEST
MEANEST
MEEKEST
MIDEAST
MIDMOST
MIDWEST
MILDEST
MIRIEST
MISCAST
MOPIEST
NEAREST
NEATEST
NIGHEST
NOBLEST
NOSIEST
NUMBEST
OCULIST
OILIEST
OLDWEST
OOZIEST
OUTCAST
OUTLAST
OUTPOST
PALIEST
PALMIST
PAULIST
PERSIST
PERTEST
PIANIST
PIETIST
PINIEST
PINKEST
PIPIEST
POKIEST
POLOIST
POOREST
POSHEST
PRECAST
PRETEST
PROTEST
PROTIST
PROVOST
PUNIEST
QUERIST
RACIEST
RANKEST
RASHEST
REALIST
REDDEST
REQUEST
RICHEST
RIMIEST
ROPIEST
ROSIEST
SADDEST
SAWDUST
SEXIEST
SICKEST
SLOWEST
SNIDEST
SOFTEST
SOLOIST
SOONEST
SOPHIST
SOUREST
SPAREST
SPRIEST
SPRYEST
STALEST
STATIST
STYLIST
SUAVEST
SUBSIST
SUGGEST
SUNKIST
TALLEST
TANNEST
TARTEST
TAUTEST
TEMPEST
TENSEST
TERSEST
TIDIEST
TINIEST
TITLIST
TONIEST
TOPMAST
TOPMOST
TOURIST
TRITEST
TSARIST
TUBAIST
TYPIEST
UGLIEST
UNBLEST
UNTWIST
VAGUEST
VAINEST
VASTEST
VINIEST
VIOLIST
WANIEST
WANNEST
WARIEST
WARMEST
WAVIEST
WAXIEST
WEAKEST
WETTEST
WHITEST
WILDEST
WILIEST
WINIEST
WIRIEST
YORKIST
ZANIEST

SU•••••

SUASION
SUAVELY
SUAVEST
SUAVITY
SUBBING
SUBDEBS
SUBDUED
SUBDUER
SUBDUES
SUBHEAD
SUBJECT
SUBJOIN
SUBLETS
SUBLIME
SUBMITS
SUBORNS
SUBPLOT
SUBROSA
SUBSETS
SUBSIDE
SUBSIDY
SUBSIST
SUBSOIL
SUBSUME
SUBTEND
SUBTEXT
SUBTLER
SUBUNIT
SUBURBS
SUBVERT
SUBVOCE
SUBWAYS
SUBZERO
SUCCEED
SUCCESS
SUCCORS
SUCCOUR
SUCCUMB
SUCKERS
SUCKING
SUCKSIN
SUCRASE
SUCROSE
SUCTION
SUDBURY
SUDSIER
SUDSING
SUFFERS
SUFFICE
SUFFOLK
SUFFUSE
SUGARED
SUGGEST
SUHARTO
SUITING
SUITORS
SUITSUP
SUKARNO
SULFATE
SULFIDE
SULFITE
SULKERS
SULKIER
SULKIES
SULKILY
SULKING
SULLIED
SULLIES
SULPHUR
SULTANA
SULTANS
SULUSEA
SUMATRA
SUMLESS
SUMMARY
SUMMERS
SUMMERY
SUMMING
SUMMITS
SUMMONS
SUNBATH
SUNBEAM
SUNBELT
SUNBOWL
SUNBURN
SUNCITY
SUNDAES
SUNDAYS
SUNDECK
SUNDERS
SUNDEWS
SUNDIAL
SUNDOGS
SUNDOWN
SUNFISH
SUNGODS
SUNKIST
SUNLAMP
SUNLESS
SUNLIKE
SUNMAID
SUNNIER
SUNNILY
SUNNING
SUNRAYS
SUNRISE
SUNROOF
SUNROOM
SUNSETS
SUNSPOT
SUNSUIT
SUNTANS
SUOJURE
SUOLOCO
SUPPERS
SUPPING
SUPPLER
SUPPORT
SUPPOSE
SUPREME
SUPREMO
SURCOAT
SURFACE
SURFEIT
SURFERS
SURFIER
SURFING
SURGEON
SURGERY
SURGING
SURINAM
SURLIER
SURLILY
SURMISE
SURNAME
SURPASS
SURPLUS
SURREAL
SURREYS
SURTSEY
SURVEYS
SURVIVE
SUSANNA
SUSANNE
SUSLIKS
SUSPECT
SUSPEND
SUSSING
SUSTAIN
SUTLERS
SUTTERS
SUTURED
SUTURES
SUZANNE
SUZETTE

S•U••••

SAUCERS
SAUCIER
SAUCILY
SAUNTER
SAURIAN
SAUSAGE
SAUTEED
SCUDDED
SCUFFED
SCUFFLE
SCULLED
SCULLER
SCULPTS
SCUPPER
SCURVES
SCUTTLE
SFUMATO
SHUBERT
SHUCKED
SHUCKER
SHUDDER
SHUFFLE
SHUNNED
SHUNTED
SHUSHED
SHUSHES
SHUTEYE
SHUTINS
SHUTOFF
SHUTOUT
SHUTSIN
SHUTSUP
SHUTTER
SHUTTLE
SKULKED
SKULKER
SKUNKED
SLUDGES
SLUGGED
SLUGGER
SLUICED
SLUICES
SLUMBER
SLUMMED
SLUMPED
SLURPED
SLURRED
SLUSHES
SMUDGED
SMUDGES
SMUGGER
SMUGGLE
SNUBBED
SNUFFED
SNUFFER
SNUFFLE
SNUFFLY
SNUGGER
SNUGGLE
SOUFFLE
SOUGHED
SOUKOUS
SOULFUL
SOUNDED
SOUNDER
SOUNDLY
SOUPCON
SOUPIER
SOUPSUP
SOURCED
SOURCES
SOUREST
SOURING
SOURISH
SOUTANE
SOUTHEY
SPUMIER
SPUMING
SPUMONE
SPUMONI
SPUMOUS
SPUNOFF
SPUNOUT
SPURNED
SPURNER
SPURRED
SPURSON
SPURTED
SPUTNIK
SPUTTER
SQUALID
SQUALLS
SQUALOR
SQUANTO
SQUARED
SQUARER
SQUARES
SQUATLY
SQUATTY
SQUAWKS
SQUAWKY
SQUEAKS
SQUEAKY
SQUEALS
SQUEEZE
SQUELCH
SQUILLS
SQUINCH
SQUINTS
SQUINTY
SQUIRED
SQUIRES
SQUIRMS
SQUIRMY
SQUIRTS
SQUISHY
STUBBED
STUBBLE
STUBBLY
STUCCOS
STUCKTO
STUCKUP
STUDDED
STUDENT
STUDIED
STUDIES
STUDIOS
STUFFED
STUFFER
STUMBLE
STUMERS
STUMPED
STUMPER
STUNGUN
STUNNED
STUNNER
STUNTED
STUPEFY
STUPORS
STURGES

S••U•••

SAGUARO
SALUKIS
SALUTED
SALUTES
SAMURAI
SCHULTZ
SCOURED
SCOURER
SCOURGE
SCOUSES
SCOUTED
SCOUTER
SCRUBBY
SCRUBUP
SCRUFFS
SCRUFFY
SCRUMMY
SCRUNCH
SCRUPLE
SECULAR
SECURED
SECURER
SECURES
SEDUCED
SEDUCER
SEDUCES
SENUFOS
SEQUELS
SEQUINS
SEQUOIA
SETUPON
SHOULDA
SHOUTED
SHOUTER
SHRUBBY
SINUOUS
SINUSES
SIOUANS
SITUATE
SLEUTHS
SLOUCHY
SLOUGHS
SOLUBLE
SOLUTES
SOSUEME
SPLURGE
SPOUSAL
SPOUSES
SPOUTED
SPOUTER
SPRUCED
SPRUCER
SPRUCES
STAUNCH
STEUBEN
STLUCIA
STOUTEN
STOUTER
STOUTLY
STRUDEL
SUBUNIT
SUBURBS
SULUSEA
SUTURED
SUTURES

S•••U••

SACQUES
SAMSUNG
SANJUAN
SANLUIS
SATSUMA
SAVOURS
SAVOURY
SAWBUCK
SAWDUST
SCAPULA
SEADUTY
SEAGULL
SECLUDE
SENDUPS
SENSUAL
SHOGUNS
SHROUDS
SICHUAN
SIGMUND
SIXGUNS
SKIJUMP
SKIRUNS
SKISUIT
SLIPUPS
SLOWUPS
SNAFUED
SOJOURN
SOWBUGS
SPATULA
SPELUNK
SPROUTS
STATUES
STATURE
STATUTE
STEPUPS
STIMULI
STLOUIS
STRAUSS
SUBDUED
SUBDUER
SUBDUES
SUBSUME
SUCCUMB
SUDBURY
SUFFUSE
SUNBURN
SUNSUIT
SUOJURE
SYNFUEL

S••••U•

SACKFUL
SACKOUT
SANCTUM
SANGOUT
SAVEDUP
SAVESUP
SAVIOUR
SCAREUP
SCREWUP
SCRUBUP
SEABLUE
SEALSUP
SEASLUG
SEEKOUT
SEENOUT
SEESOUT
SELLOUT
SENDOUT
SENDSUP
SENTOUT
SERIOUS
SERVEUP
SETSOUT
SEVENUP
SEWEDUP
SEYMOUR
SHAKEUP
SHAPEUP
SHIPOUT
SHOOKUP
SHOOTUP
SHOPFUL
SHOTGUN
SHOTOUT
SHOTPUT
SHOWOUT
SHOWSUP
SHUTOUT
SHUTSUP
SICKOUT
SIGHFUL
SIGNOUT
SIGNSUP
SINGOUT
SINUOUS
SISTRUM
SITSOUT
SIZEDUP
SIZESUP
SKILFUL
SKINFUL
SKIPOUT
SKOOKUM
SKYBLUE
SLIPOUT
SLIPSUP
SLOWSUP
SMASHUP
SNAPSUP
SOAKSUP
SOLDOUT
SONGFUL
SORGHUM
SORTOUT
SOUKOUS
SOULFUL
SOUPSUP
SPEAKUP
SPEEDUP
SPICEUP
SPINOUT
SPLITUP
SPOKEUP
SPUMOUS
SPUNOUT
STACKUP
STADIUM
STANDUP
STARTUP
STAYPUT
STAYSUP
STEPOUT
STEPSUP
STERNUM
STICKUP
STIRRUP
STIRSUP
STOCKUP
STOODUP
STOPSUP
STOREUP
STRATUM
STRATUS
STUCKUP
STUNGUN
SUCCOUR
SUITSUP
SULPHUR
SURPLUS
SWEEPUP
SWELLUP
SWEPTUP

S•••••U

SHIATSU
SHIHTZU
SHIKOKU

•SU••••

ASUNDER
ASUSUAL
TSUNAMI
USUALLY
USURERS
USURIES
USURPED
USURPER

•S•U•••

ASSUAGE
ASSUMED
ASSUMES
ASSURED
ASSURES
ESCUDOS
ESQUIRE
ESTUARY
ISSUERS
ISSUING
TSOURIS
TSQUARE

•S••U••

ASARULE
ASHBURY
ASSAULT
ASTOUND
ASUSUAL
ASYLUMS
ESPOUSE

•S•••U•

ASKSOUT
ISTHMUS
OSSEOUS
PSYCHUP
USINGUP

••SU•••

ASSUAGE
ASSUMED
ASSUMES
ASSURED
ASSURES
CASUALS
DISUSED
ENSUING
ENSUITE
ENSURED
ENSURES
INSULAR
INSULIN
INSULTS
INSURED
INSURER
INSURES
ISSUERS
ISSUING
JESUITS
MISUSED
MISUSES
RESULTS
RESUMED
RESUMES
RESURGE
SOSUEME
UPSURGE
VISUALS

••S•U••

ASSAULT
BASQUES
BISCUIT
BISMUTH
BISQUES
CASQUED
CASQUES
COSTUME
DASYURE
DISCUSS
DISGUST
DISPUTE
DISRUPT
DISTURB
DRSEUSS
DUSTUPS
ENSOULS
FESCUES
FISSURE
GASPUMP
GESTURE
KUSPUKS
LASHUPS
MASQUES
MISCUED
MISCUES
MISRULE
MOSQUES
MUSEUMS
OBSCURE
PASTURE
POSEURS
POSSUMS
POSTURE
PUSHUPS
RESCUED
RESCUER
RESCUES
RESOUND
TESTUDO
TISSUES
TOSSUPS
UNSOUND
UNSTUCK
VESTURE
VISTULA
WASHUPS

••S••U•

ABSOLUT
BASHFUL
BUSTOUT
CASHOUT
CASSIUS
CASTOUT
DISHFUL
DISHOUT
EASEDUP
EASEFUL
EASEOUT
EASESUP
FISHOUT
FISTFUL
GASEOUS
GUSSYUP
HUSHFUL
LASCAUX
LESPAUL
LOSEOUT
LOSTOUT
LUSTFUL
MASSEUR
MISSOUT
MUSEFUL
NOSEEUM
NOSEOUT
NOSTRUM
OSSEOUS
PASSEUL
PASSOUT
PASTDUE
PASTEUP
PASTEUR
PUSHFUL
RESIDUE
RESTFUL
RESTSUP
ROSEBUD
ROSTRUM
SISTRUM
TESTOUT
TOSSOUT
TUSSAUD
VISCOUS
WASHOUT
WASHTUB
WISEDUP
WISEGUY
WISESUP
WISHFUL
WISTFUL
ZESTFUL

•••SU••

ASUSUAL
CAESURA
CAPSULE
CATSUIT
CENSURE
CLOSURE
CONSULS
CONSULT
CONSUME
DRYSUIT
ERASURE
FISSURE
FORSURE
HIRSUTE
LAWSUIT
LEISURE
MEASURE
NETSUKE
NETSURF
NOTSURE
POSSUMS
PRESUME
PURSUED
PURSUER
PURSUES
PURSUIT
SAMSUNG
SATSUMA
SENSUAL
SKISUIT
SUBSUME
SUNSUIT
TISSUES
TONSURE
TOSSUPS
UNUSUAL
WETSUIT

•••S•U•

ACESOUT
ACTSOUT
AIRSOUT
ALYSSUM
ASKSOUT
ATISSUE
BOOSTUP
BOWSOUT
BRUSHUP
BRUSQUE
BUGSOUT
BUMSOUT
BUYSOUT
CAESIUM
CASSIUS
CELSIUS
CLOSEUP
COPSOUT
CRASSUS
CRISPUS
CROSSUP
CUTSOUT
DANSEUR
DIESOUT
DIGSOUT
DRESSUP
EATSOUT
EKESOUT
ELYSIUM
ERASMUS
FANSOUT
FAUSTUS
GETSOUT
GOESOUT
GUSSYUP
HITSOUT
HOTSPUR
IBNSAUD
ICESOUT
IRISOUT
LAYSOUT
LETSOUT
LOGSOUT
LOUSEUP
MASSEUR
MISSOUT
OPOSSUM
OPTSOUT
PANSOUT
PASSEUL
PASSOUT
PAYSOUT
PEASOUP
PERSEUS
PERSIUS
PIGSOUT
POPSOUT
PRESSUP
PUTSOUT
RAISEUP
REISSUE
RIPSOUT
RUBSOUT
RUNSOUT
SEASLUG
SEESOUT
SETSOUT
SITSOUT
SMASHUP
TAGSOUT
TAPSOUT
TENSEUP
THESEUS
TOPSOUT
TOSSOUT
TOYSRUS
TUSSAUD
WIGSOUT
WINSOUT

••••SU•

ALYSSUM
ANTESUP
ATISSUE
BACKSUP
BALLSUP
BANGSUP
BEADSUP
BEAMSUP
BEARSUP
BEATSUP
BEEFSUP
BINDSUP
BLOWSUP
BONESUP
BOOTSUP
BOXESUP
BUCKSUP
BUMPSUP
BUOYSUP
BURNSUP
CALLSUP
CHATSUP
CHEWSUP
CLAMSUP
CLOGSUP
COILSUP
COMESUP

COOKSUP
COOPSUP
CRASSUS
CROESUS
CROPSUP
CROSSUP
CURLSUP
DOLLSUP
DRAWSUP
DRESSUP
DRIESUP
DRUMSUP
EASESUP
EVENSUP
FAIRSUP
FILLSUP
FIRESUP
FIRMSUP
FIXESUP
FOLDSUP
FOULSUP
GANGSUP
GEARSUP
GIVESUP
GOOFSUP
GROWSUP
HANDSUP
HANGSUP
HAULSUP
HEADSUP
HEATSUP
HIKESUP
HOLDSUP
HOLESUP
HOOKSUP
HYPESUP
JACKSUP
JOINSUP
JUMPSUP
KEEPSUP
KICKSUP
KNEESUP
LACESUP
LEADSUP
LIFTSUP
LINESUP
LOCKSUP
LOOKSUP
LUMPSUM
MAKESUP
MARKSUP
MIXESUP
MOVESUP
MUCKSUP
OPENSUP
OPOSSUM
PACKSUP
PAIRSUP
PEGASUS
PERKSUP
PICKSUP
PILESUP
PIPESUP
PLAYSUP
PRESSUP
PROPSUP
PULLSUP
PUMPSUP
RACKSUP
RAKESUP
REARSUP
REISSUE
RESTSUP
RILESUP
RINGSUP
ROLLSUP
SAVESUP
SEALSUP
SENDSUP
SHOWSUP
SHUTSUP
SIGNSUP
SIZESUP
SLIPSUP
SLOWSUP
SNAPSUP
SOAKSUP
SOUPSUP
STAYSUP
STEPSUP
STIRSUP
STOPSUP
SUITSUP
TAKESUP
TALKSUP
TANKSUP
TEAMSUP
TEARSUP
TIMESUP
TONESUP
TOOLSUP
TRIPSUP
TUNESUP
TURNSUP
TYPESUP
WAITSUP
WAKESUP
WALLSUP
WARMSUP
WELLSUP
WHIPSUP
WINDSUP
WIPESUP
WISESUP
WORKSUP
WRAPSUP
ZEROSUM

••••S•U
BABASSU
ILIESCU

•••••SU
BABASSU
FUJITSU
JUJITSU
KOMATSU
SHIATSU

SV•••••
SVELTER

S•V••••
SAVABLE
SAVAGED
SAVAGER
SAVAGES
SAVALAS
SAVANNA
SAVANTS
SAVARIN
SAVEDUP
SAVELOY
SAVESUP
SAVINGS
SAVIORS
SAVIOUR
SAVORED
SAVOURS
SAVOURY
SAVVIER
SAVVILY
SEVENAM
SEVENPM
SEVENTH
SEVENTY
SEVENUP
SEVERAL
SEVERED
SEVERER
SEVIGNE
SEVILLE
SOVIETS

S••V•••
SALVAGE
SALVERS
SALVIAS
SALVING
SALVOES
SALVORS
SAVVIER
SAVVILY
SELVAGE
SERVALS
SERVANT
SERVERS
SERVERY
SERVEUP
SERVICE
SERVILE
SERVING
SHAVERS
SHAVING
SHIVERS
SHIVERY
SHOVELS
SHOVERS
SHOVING
SILVERS
SILVERY
SKIVERS
SLAVERS
SLAVERY
SLAVEYS
SLAVING
SLAVISH
SLIVERS
SLOVAKS
SLOVENE
SLOVENS
SNIVELS
SOLVENT
SOLVERS
SOLVING
SORVINO
SPAVINS
STAVING
STEVENS
SUAVELY
SUAVEST
SUAVITY
SUBVERT
SUBVOCE
SURVEYS
SURVIVE
SWIVELS
SWIVETS
SYLVANS

S•••V••
SAMOVAR
SCARVES
SCRIVEN
SCURVES
SEGOVIA
SHEAVED
SHEAVES
SHELVED
SHELVES
SHRIVEL
SHRIVER
SHRIVES
SLEEVES
STARVED
STARVES
STRIVED
STRIVEN
STRIVER
STRIVES
SWERVED
SWERVES

S••••V•
SKYDIVE
SURVIVE

•S••V••
ESTEVEZ
ESTIVAL

•S••••V
USTINOV

••S•V••
CASAVAS
DISAVOW
HESHVAN
VISAVIS

••S••V•
ABSOLVE
CASSAVA
DESERVE
ENSLAVE
FESTIVA
FESTIVE
MASSIVE
MISSIVE
MUSCOVY
OBSERVE
ONSERVE
PASSIVE
RESERVE
RESOLVE
RESTIVE
YESHIVA

•••S•V•
ABUSIVE
CASSAVA
CURSIVE
ELUSIVE
EROSIVE
EVASIVE
MASSIVE
MISSIVE
PASSIVE
PENSIVE
PLOSIVE
TENSIVE
ZEMSTVO

SW•••••
SWABBED
SWADDLE
SWAGGER
SWAHILI
SWALLET
SWALLOW
SWAMPED
SWANKED
SWANKER
SWANSEA
SWANSON
SWAPPED
SWAPPER
SWARMED
SWARTHY
SWATHED
SWATHES
SWATTED
SWATTER
SWAYERS
SWAYING
SWEARAT
SWEARBY
SWEARER
SWEARIN
SWEARTO
SWEATED
SWEATER
SWEDISH
SWEENEY
SWEEPER
SWEEPUP
SWEETEN
SWEETER
SWEETIE
SWEETLY
SWEETON
SWELLED
SWELLUP
SWELTER
SWELTRY
SWEPTUP
SWERVED
SWERVES
SWIFTER
SWIFTLY
SWIGGED
SWILLED
SWIMMER
SWINDLE
SWINGBY
SWINGER
SWINISH
SWIPERS
SWIPING
SWIRLED
SWISHED
SWISHES
SWITZER
SWIVELS
SWIVETS
SWIZZLE
SWOBBED
SWOLLEN
SWONKEN
SWOONED
SWOOPED
SWOOSIE
SWOPPED
SWOREAT
SWOREBY
SWOREIN

S•W••••
SAWBUCK
SAWDUST
SAWFISH
SAWLIKE
SAWLOGS
SAWMILL
SAWWOOD
SAWYERS
SEWEDON
SEWEDUP
SOWBUGS
SOWLIKE

S••W•••
SAWWOOD
SAYWHEN
SCHWINN
SCOWLED
SCOWLER
SEAWALL
SEAWARD
SEAWAYS
SEAWEED
SEAWOLF
SHAWNEE
SHAWWAL
SHEWOLF
SHOWBIZ
SHOWDOG
SHOWERS
SHOWERY
SHOWIER
SHOWILY
SHOWING
SHOWMAN
SHOWMEN
SHOWNIN
SHOWOFF
SHOWOUT
SHOWSIN
SHOWSUP
SITWELL
SKEWERS
SKEWING
SKIWEAR
SKYWARD
SKYWAYS
SLOWEST
SLOWING
SLOWSUP
SLOWUPS
SNOWCAP
SNOWCAT
SNOWDAY
SNOWDON
SNOWIER
SNOWILY
SNOWING
SNOWJOB
SNOWMAN
SNOWMEN
SNOWPEA
SNOWSIN
SOPWITH
SPAWNED
SPEWING
STEWARD
STEWART
STEWERS
STEWING
STOWING
SUBWAYS

S•••W••
SARAWAK
SCRAWLS
SCRAWLY
SCRAWNY
SCREWED
SCREWUP
SHAWWAL
SHERWIN
SOMEWAY
SPRAWLS
SQUAWKS
SQUAWKY
STREWED
STREWER

S••••W•
SALLOWS
SATDOWN
SEACOWS
SEESAWS
SETDOWN
SHADOWS
SHADOWY
SITDOWN
SKITOWS
SORROWS
SUNBOWL
SUNDEWS
SUNDOWN

S•••••W
SAGINAW
SALCHOW
SHALLOW
SKIDROW
SOMEHOW
SPARROW
SWALLOW

•S••W••
CSLEWIS

•S•••W•
ESCHEWS
ESCROWS

•S••••W
ASOFNOW
USOSHOW

••SW•••
ANSWERS
BOSWELL
IPSWICH
MCSWINE
MISWORD
NOSWEAT
ROSWELL
UNSWEPT
UPSWEEP
UPSWEPT
UPSWING

••S•W••
DISOWNS
PESAWAS
POSTWAR
RESAWED
UNSEWED
WYSIWYG

••S••W•
BESTOWS
CASHEWS
CUSHAWS
GOSHAWK
GOSLOWS
NOSHOWS
TVSHOWS

••S•••W
BESTREW
CASELAW
CASHCOW
DISAVOW
JUSTNOW
UNSCREW

•••SW••
BEESWAX
WHOSWHO

•••S•W•
BOWSAWS
JIGSAWS
OLDSAWS
PITSAWS
RIPSAWS
SEESAWS

•••S••W
AIRSHOW
BARSTOW
CAPSHAW
CATSHOW
CATSPAW
DOGSHOW
GLASGOW
ICESHOW
INASTEW
LAYSLOW
LIESLOW
TRISHAW
USOSHOW
WINSLOW

••••S•W
BANDSAW
BUCKSAW
BUZZSAW
FORESAW
FRETSAW
GANGSAW
HACKSAW
HANDSAW
OVERSAW
WHIPSAW

S•X••••
SAXHORN
SEXIEST
SEXISTS
SEXTANS
SEXTANT
SEXTETS
SEXTONS
SIXFOLD
SIXGUNS
SIXIRON
SIXPACK
SIXTEEN
SIXTHLY
SIXTIES

S••••X•
SUBTEXT

S•••••X
SALTBOX
SANDBOX
SHOEBOX
SIMPLEX
SKEEZIX
SOAPBOX
SPANDEX
STCROIX

••S•••X
CASHBOX
LASCAUX
POSTBOX

•••S••X
BEESWAX

••••S•X
ALTOSAX
DEEPSIX

SY•••••
SYLLABI
SYLVANS
SYMBOLS
SYMPTOM
SYNAPSE
SYNCHED
SYNCHES
SYNCING
SYNERGY
SYNFUEL
SYNGMAN
SYNODAL
SYNODIC
SYNONYM
SYPHONS
SYRIANS
SYRINGA
SYRINGE
SYSTEMS
SYSTOLE

S•Y••••
SAYINGS
SAYWHEN
SAYYIDS
SCYTHED
SCYTHES
SEYMOUR
SHYLOCK
SHYNESS
SHYSTER
SKYBLUE
SKYCAPS
SKYDIVE
SKYHIGH
SKYHOOK
SKYJACK
SKYLARK
SKYLESS
SKYLIKE
SKYLINE
SKYWARD
SKYWAYS
SLYNESS
SOYBEAN
SOYINKA
STYGIAN
STYLERS
STYLETS
STYLING
STYLISE
STYLISH
STYLIST
STYLIZE
STYMIED
STYMIES
STYPTIC
STYRENE
STYRIAN

S••Y•••
SAWYERS
SAYYIDS
SLAYERS
SLAYTON
SPAYING
SPRYEST
STAYING
STAYPUT
STAYSUP
SWAYERS
SWAYING

S•••Y••
SAMOYED
SAROYAN
SPLAYED
SPRAYED
SPRAYER
STRAYED

S••••Y•
SASHAYS
SEAWAYS
SHUTEYE
SKYWAYS
SLAVEYS
SOCKEYE
STOREYS
SUBWAYS
SUNDAYS
SUNRAYS
SURREYS
SURVEYS
SYNONYM

S•••••Y
SAINTLY
SALSIFY
SALTILY
SAMEDAY
SANDFLY
SAPPILY
SASSILY
SATIETY
SATISFY
SAUCILY
SAVELOY
SAVOURY
SAVVILY
SCANTLY
SCARIFY
SCARILY
SCENERY
SCRAGGY
SCRAPPY
SCRAWLY
SCRAWNY
SCRIMPY
SCRUBBY
SCRUFFY
SCRUMMY
SEADUTY
SEALILY
SECRECY
SEEDILY
SENSORY
SERVERY
SEVENTY
SHADILY
SHADOWY
SHAKILY
SHANTEY
SHAPELY
SHAPLEY
SHARKEY
SHARPLY
SHEERLY
SHELLEY
SHINILY
SHIRLEY
SHIVERY
SHOOFLY
SHORTLY
SHOWERY
SHOWILY
SHRILLY
SHRUBBY
SICKBAY
SICKDAY
SICKPAY
SIGHTLY
SIGNIFY
SILKILY
SILVERY
SIXTHLY
SIZABLY
SKETCHY
SLACKLY
SLAVERY
SLEEKLY
SLICKLY
SLIMILY
SLOUCHY
SMARTLY
SMOKILY
SMOOTHY
SNAKILY
SNIDELY
SNIFFLY
SNITCHY
SNOWDAY
SNOWILY
SNUFFLY
SOAPILY
SOBERLY
SOCIETY
SOGGILY
SOLIDLY
SOMEDAY
SOMEWAY
SOOTILY
SORCERY
SORRILY
SOUNDLY
SOUTHEY
SPANGLY
SPARELY
SPASSKY
SPECIFY
SPICERY
SPICILY
SPIDERY
SPIKILY
SPINDLY
SPINDRY
SPINNEY
SPLASHY
SPRINGY
SQUATLY
SQUATTY
SQUAWKY
SQUEAKY
SQUINTY
SQUIRMY
SQUISHY
STAGILY
STAIDLY
STALELY
STANDBY
STANLEY
STARCHY
STARKLY
STATELY
STEEPLY
STERNLY
STIFFLY
STIRFRY
STOKELY
STONILY
STOODBY
STOOKEY
STOUTLY
STREAKY
STRINGY
STROPPY
STUBBLY
STUPEFY
SUAVELY
SUAVITY
SUBSIDY
SUDBURY
SULKILY
SUMMARY
SUMMERY
SUNCITY
SUNNILY
SURGERY
SURLILY
SURTSEY
SWARTHY
SWEARBY
SWEENEY
SWEETLY
SWELTRY
SWIFTLY
SWINGBY
SWOREBY
SYNERGY

•SY••••
ASYLUMS
PSYCHED
PSYCHES
PSYCHIC
PSYCHUP

•S•Y•••
ASSYRIA
ESPYING

•S••Y••
ASSAYED
ASSAYER
ESSAYED

•S•••Y•
ESTRAYS
OSPREYS

•S••••Y
ASHBURY
ASHTRAY
ESOTERY
ESTUARY
ISONOMY
USUALLY

••SY•••
ASSYRIA
BUSYING
DASYURE
EASYOFF
KOSYGIN

••S•Y••
ASSAYED
ASSAYER
ESSAYED
GUSSYUP
INSTYLE
MISTYPE
MOSEYED
RESTYLE

••S••Y•
BUSBOYS
DISMAYS
FISHEYE
MASARYK
MISLAYS
MISSAYS
SASHAYS
WYSIWYG

••S•••Y
AMSCRAY
BASALLY
BASEPAY
BESTBOY
BOSSILY
BUSHILY
CASSIDY
CUSTODY
DESTINY
DESTROY
DISOBEY
DISPLAY
DUSKILY
DUSTILY
ECSTASY
FISHERY
FISHFRY
FISHILY
FUSSILY
FUSTILY
GASCONY
GOSSIPY
GUSHILY
GUSTILY
HASTILY
HISTORY
HOSIERY
HUSHABY
HUSKILY
IMSORRY
JUSTIFY
LASTORY
LUSTILY
MASONRY
MASTERY
MESSILY
MISALLY
MISERLY
MISPLAY
MISTILY
MUSCOVY
MUSHILY
MUSSILY
MUSTILY
MYSTERY
MYSTIFY
NASALLY
NASTILY
NOSEGAY
PASSKEY
PESKILY
PUSHILY
RISIBLY
RISKILY
ROSEBAY
RUSSETY
RUSTILY
SASSILY
TASTILY
TESTFLY
TESTIFY
TESTILY
TUSCANY
VISIBLY
WASPILY
WISEGUY
WISPILY

•••SY••
FORSYTH
GUSSYUP
LIPSYNC

•••S•Y•
BURSTYN
CATSEYE
JERSEYS
MISSAYS
NAYSAYS

•••S••Y
APISHLY
BEASTLY
BOSSILY
BRASHLY
BRISKLY
BRISTLY
BURSARY
CASSIDY
CLOSEBY
CLOSELY
CRASSLY
CRISPLY
CROSSLY
CURSORY
DENSELY
DENSITY
DROSHKY
ELUSORY
EROSELY
FALSELY
FALSIFY
FALSITY
FIRSTLY
FLESHLY
FRESHLY
FUSSILY
GHASTLY
GHOSTLY
GOSSIPY
GRISTLY
GROSSLY
GUTSILY
HARSHLY
HEMSLEY
HERSHEY
KITSCHY
LETSFLY

LOOSELY
LOUSILY
MESSILY
MOISTLY
MUSSILY
NEWSBOY
NEWSDAY
NOISILY
NURSERY
ODYSSEY
PAISLEY
PARSLEY
PASSKEY
PLUSHLY
PRESLEY
PROSILY
PROSODY
RUNSDRY
RUSSETY
SALSIFY
SASSILY
SENSORY
SPASSKY
SUBSIDY
TENSELY
TERSELY
THISTLY
TIPSILY
TOLSTOY
TUESDAY
VARSITY
VERSIFY
WHISKEY

••••S•Y

AMNESTY
BLUESKY
CHOMSKY
CHRISTY
COCKSHY
COMESBY
CRASSLY
CROSSLY
CURTSEY
DARESAY
DEBUSSY
DEMPSEY
DROPSBY
DYNASTY
EMBASSY
FROWSTY
GAINSAY
GROSSLY
HEARSAY
HONESTY
HORNSBY
LINDSAY
LINDSEY
MAJESTY
MALMSEY
MODESTY
MORESBY
ODYSSEY
PIOUSLY
SATISFY
SPASSKY
SPLASHY
SQUISHY
SURTSEY
THIRSTY
TROTSKY
VRONSKY
WOOLSEY

•••••SY

CIRCUSY
CLERISY
CRAFTSY
DEBUSSY
ECSTASY
EMBASSY
FANTASY
GEODESY

S•Z••••

SIZABLE
SIZABLY
SIZEDUP
SIZESUP
SIZINGS
SIZZLED
SIZZLES
SUZANNE
SUZETTE

S••Z•••

SEIZERS
SEIZING
SIZZLED
SIZZLES
SUBZERO
SWIZZLE

S•••Z••

SALAZAR
SARAZEN
SELTZER
SKEEZIX
SNEEZED
SNEEZER
SNEEZES
SNOOZED
SNOOZES
SPITZES
STANZAS
SWITZER
SWIZZLE

S••••Z•

SCHATZI
SCHERZI
SCHERZO
SHIHTZU
SPINOZA
SQUEEZE
STYLIZE

S•••••Z

SCHULTZ
SHOWBIZ

•S••Z••

ASSIZES

•S••••Z

ESTEVEZ

••S•Z••

ASSIZES

••S••Z•

MESTIZA
MESTIZO

•••S•Z•

ANASAZI
CAPSIZE
MIDSIZE
OUTSIZE

•••S••Z

AGASSIZ
LAISSEZ

••••S•Z

AGASSIZ
LAISSEZ

TA•••••

TABARDS
TABASCO
TABBIES
TABBING
TABITHA
TABLEAU
TABLETS
TABLING
TABLOID
TABORET
TABULAR
TACITLY
TACITUS
TACKERS
TACKIER
TACKILY
TACKING
TACKLED
TACKLER
TACKLES
TACKSON
TACTFUL
TACTICS
TACTILE
TADPOLE
TAFFETA
TAFFIES
TAGALOG
TAGENDS
TAGGANT
TAGGING
TAGLIKE
TAGLINE
TAGSALE
TAGSOUT
TAGTEAM
TAILEND
TAILFIN
TAILING
TAILLES
TAILOFF
TAILORS
TAINTED
TAIPANS
TAKEAIM
TAKENIN
TAKENON
TAKEOFF
TAKEONE
TAKEOUT
TAKESIN
TAKESON
TAKESTO
TAKESUP
TAKETEN
TALARIA
TALCUMS
TALENTS
TALKBIG
TALKERS
TALKIER
TALKIES
TALKING
TALKOUT
TALKSAT
TALKSTO
TALKSUP
TALLEST
TALLIED
TALLIER
TALLIES
TALLINN
TALLISH
TALLOWS
TALLYHO
TALLYUP
TALONED
TALUSES
TAMABLE
TAMALES
TAMARIN
TAMBALA
TAMBOUR
TAMMANY
TAMPERS
TAMPICO
TAMPING
TAMTAMS
TANAGER
TANDEMS
TANGELO
TANGENT
TANGERE
TANGIER
TANGLED
TANGLES
TANGOED
TANGRAM
TANKARD
TANKERS
TANKFUL
TANKING
TANKSUP
TANKTOP
TANLINE
TANNERS
TANNERY
TANNEST
TANNING
TANNINS
TANNISH
TANOAKS
TANSIES
TANTARA
TANTIVY
TANTRUM
TAOISTS
TAPEMAN
TAPEMEN
TAPERED
TAPINGS
TAPINTO
TAPIOCA
TAPPERS
TAPPETS
TAPPING
TAPROOM
TAPROOT
TAPSOFF
TAPSOUT
TAPSTER
TARANTO
TARBABY
TARBELL
TARDIER
TARDILY
TARGETS
TARHEEL
TARIFFS
TARMACS
TARNISH
TARPITS
TARPONS
TARRIED
TARRIER
TARRIES
TARRING
TARSALS
TARSIER
TARTANS
TARTARE
TARTARS
TARTEST
TARTISH
TARZANA
TASHLIN
TASHMAN
TASKING
TASSELS
TASTERS
TASTIER
TASTILY
TASTING
TATAMIS
TATIANA
TATTERS
TATTIER
TATTILY
TATTING
TATTLED
TATTLER
TATTLES
TATTOOS
TAUNTED
TAURINE
TAUTENS
TAUTEST
TAVERNS
TAWNIER
TAWNILY
TAXABLE
TAXFREE
TAXICAB
TAXIING
TAXIMAN
TAXIMEN
TAXIWAY
TAXLESS
TAXRATE

T•A••••

TEABAGS
TEABALL
TEACAKE
TEACART
TEACHER
TEACHES
TEACHIN
TEACUPS
TEALEAF
TEALESS
TEAMING
TEAMSUP
TEAPOTS
TEAPOYS
TEARFUL
TEARGAS
TEARIER
TEARILY
TEARING
TEAROFF
TEAROOM
TEAROSE
TEAROUT
TEARSAT
TEARSUP
TEASELS
TEASERS
TEASETS
TEASHOP
TEASING
TEATIME
TEATRAY
TEATREE
THALERS
THANKED
THATCHY
THATSIT
THAWING
TIANJIN
TOADIED
TOADIES
TOADISH
TOASTED
TOASTER
TRABERT
TRACERS
TRACERY
TRACHEA
TRACING
TRACKED
TRACKER
TRACTOR
TRADEIN
TRADEON
TRADERS
TRADEUP
TRADING
TRADUCE
TRAFFIC
TRAGEDY
TRAILED
TRAILER
TRAINED
TRAINEE
TRAINER
TRAIPSE
TRAITOR
TRALALA
TRAMCAR
TRAMMEL
TRAMPAS
TRAMPED
TRAMPLE
TRANCES
TRANSIT
TRANSOM
TRAPEZE
TRAPPED
TRAPPER
TRASHED
TRASHES
TRAUMAS
TRAVAIL
TRAVELS
TRAVERS
TRAVOIS
TRAWLED
TRAWLER
TRAYFUL
TSARINA
TSARIST
TUAREGS
TWADDLE
TWANGED
TZARINA

T••A•••

TABARDS
TABASCO
TAGALOG
TALARIA
TAMABLE
TAMALES
TAMARIN
TANAGER
TARANTO
TATAMIS
TAXABLE
TELAVIV
TENABLE
TENABLY
TENACES
TENANCY
TENANTS
TERAPHS
TETANUS
THEATER
THEATRE
THRALLS
THWACKS
THWARTS
TIRADES
TISANES
TITANIA
TITANIC
TOBACCO
TONALLY
TOPAZES
TOTALED
TOTALLY
TOWARDS
TOWAWAY
TREACLE
TREACLY
TREADED
TREADER
TREADLE
TREASON
TREATED
TRUANCY
TRUANTS
TUBAIST
TWEAKED
TYRANNY
TYRANTS

T•••A••

TAGGANT
TAGSALE
TAIPANS
TAKEAIM
TAMBALA
TAMMANY
TAMTAMS
TANKARD
TANOAKS
TANTARA
TARBABY
TARMACS
TARSALS
TARTANS
TARTARE
TARTARS
TARZANA
TATIANA
TAXRATE
TEABAGS
TEABALL
TEACAKE
TEACART
TEDMACK
TEENAGE
TELLALL
TERNARY
TERNATE
TERRACE
TERRAIN
TETRADS
THEBABE
THECARS
THENARS
THERAPY
THINAIR
THREADS
THREADY
THREATS
THROATS
THROATY
TICTACS
TIERACK
TIETACK
TIFFANY
TILLAGE
TIMBALE
TIMBALS
TINCANS
TINEARS
TINHATS
TINTACK
TINWARE
TITRATE
TOCCATA
TOECAPS
TOENAIL
TOETAPS
TOMCATS
TONEARM
TONGANS
TONNAGE
TOPHATS
TOPIARY
TOPKAPI
TOPMAST
TOPSAIL
TORNADO
TOSCALE
TOSPARE
TOSTADA
TOUCANS
TOURACO
TOWCARS
TOWPATH
TOYLAND
TRALALA
TRAVAIL
TREMAIN
TRENARY
TREPANS
TROCARS
TROJANS
TSQUARE
TSUNAMI
TULSANS
TURBANS
TUSCANY
TUSSAUD
TWOBASE
TWOLANE
TYMPANA
TYMPANI

T••••A•

TABLEAU
TABULAR
TAGTEAM
TALKSAT
TANGRAM
TAPEMAN
TASHMAN
TAXICAB
TAXIMAN
TAXIWAY
TEALEAF
TEARGAS
TEARSAT
TEATRAY
TEHERAN
TELERAN
TELSTAR
TEMPLAR
TERTIAL
TESTBAN
TEXTUAL
THEREAT
THERMAL
THOREAU
THREEAM
THRUWAY
THURMAN
THUSFAR
TIBETAN
TIMELAG
TINSTAR
TITULAR
TOLLWAY
TONNEAU
TOPCOAT
TOPICAL
TOTEBAG
TOWAWAY
TOWHEAD
TRAMCAR
TRAMPAS
TRAUMAS
TREERAT
TRIGRAM
TRISHAW
TRISTAN
TRISTAR
TRIVIAL
TROIKAS
TRUCIAL
TRUDEAU
TUBULAR
TUCHMAN
TUESDAY
TUGBOAT
TUNDRAS
TURFWAR
TUTELAR
TWOSTAR
TYPICAL

T•••••A

TABITHA
TAFFETA
TALARIA
TAMBALA
TANTARA
TAPIOCA
TARZANA
TATIANA
TEMPERA
TEMPURA
TEQUILA
TESSERA
THERESA
TIJUANA
TITANIA
TOCCATA
TOMBOLA
TOSHIBA
TOSTADA
TRACHEA
TRALALA
TSARINA
TUNISIA
TYMPANA
TZARINA

•TA••••

ATACAMA
ATALOSS
ATAMANS
ATATURK
ATAVISM
ATAVIST
ETAGERE
ETAMINE
ITALIAN
ITALICS
STABBED
STABILE
STABLED
STABLER
STABLES
STACKED
STACKUP
STADIUM
STAFFED
STAFFER
STAGERS
STAGGED
STAGGER
STAGIER
STAGILY
STAGING
STAIDER
STAIDLY
STAINED
STAINER
STAKING
STALAGS
STALELY
STALEST
STALKED
STALKER
STALLED
STAMENS
STAMINA
STAMMER
STAMPED
STANCES
STANDBY
STANDEE
STANDIN
STANDON
STANDUP
STANLEE
STANLEY
STANNIC
STANTON
STANZAS
STAPLED
STAPLER
STAPLES
STARCHY
STARDOM
STAREAT
STARERS
STARETS
STARING
STARKER
STARKLY
STARLET
STARLIT
STARMAN
STARMAP
STARRED
STARTED
STARTER
STARTLE
STARTUP
STARVED
STARVES
STASHED
STASHES
STASSEN
STATELY
STATICE
STATICS
STATING
STATION
STATIST
STATORS
STATUES
STATURE
STATUTE
STAUNCH
STAVING
STAYING
STAYPUT
STAYSUP
UTAHANS

•T•A•••

ATFAULT
ATLANTA
ATLARGE
ATLASES
ATLATLS
ATTABOY
ATTACHE
ATTACKS
ATTAINS
ETHANOL
ITHACAN
OTRANTO
OTTAWAS
STEALTH
STEAMED
STEAMER
STRAFED
STRAFES
STRAINS
STRAITS
STRANDS
STRANGE
STRASSE
STRATUM
STRATUS
STRAUSS
STRAYED

•T••A••

ATACAMA
ATAMANS
ATHEART
ATHWART
ATLEAST
ATPEACE
ATSTAKE
ATTRACT
ETCHANT
ITERANT
ITERATE
PTBOATS
STALAGS
STEWARD
STEWART
STOMACH
STOMATA
STORAGE
STREAKS
STREAKY
STREAMS
STRIATE
UTAHANS

•T•••A•

ETERNAL
ETESIAN
ETHICAL
ETONIAN
ITALIAN
ITHACAN
OTTAWAS
OTTOMAN
STANZAS
STAREAT
STARMAN
STARMAP
STELLAR
STERNAL
STIGMAS
STOICAL
STOPGAP
STYGIAN
STYRIAN
UTOPIAN
UTOPIAS

•T••••A

ATACAMA
ATLANTA
ETRURIA
STAMINA
STLUCIA
STOMATA

••TA•••

ACTABLE
ACTAEON
ANTACID
ANTAEUS
ANTARES
ASTAIRE
ASTARTE
ATTABOY
ATTACHE
ATTACKS
ATTAINS
AUTARKY
BETAKEN
BETAKES
BETAMAX
BETARAY
BUTANOL
CATALAN
CATALOG
CATALPA
CATAWBA
CITABLE
CITADEL
CUTAWAY
DATASET
DETAILS
DETAINS
DOTARDS
EATABLE
EATAWAY
ENTAILS
ESTATES
GETAWAY
GOTAWAY
HITACHI
INTAKES
MATADOR
METATES
MUTABLE
MUTABLY
MUTAGEN
MUTANTS
MUTATED
MUTATES
NATALIA
NATALIE
NATASHA
NOTABIT
NOTABLE
NOTABLY
NOTATED
NOTATES
NUTATED
NUTATES
OBTAINS
OCTAGON
OCTANES
OCTANTS
OCTAVES
OCTAVIA
OCTAVOS
ONTARIO
OTTAWAS
OUTACTS
OUTAGES
PATACAS
PETALED
PETARDS
PITAPAT
POTABLE
POTAGES
PUTAMEN
PUTAWAY
QATARIS
RATABLE
RATAFIA
RATATAT
RETAILS
RETAINS
RETAKEN
RETAKES
RETAPED
RETAPES
RETARDS
RETAXED
RETAXES
ROTATED
ROTATES
ROTATOR
TATAMIS
TETANUS
TITANIA
TITANIC
TOTALED
TOTALLY
UNTACKS
UNTAMED
UNTAPED
UPTAKES
VITALLY
VITAMIN

••T•A••

ACTUARY
ACTUATE
ANTFARM
ANTIART
ARTWARE
ATTRACT
BATEAUX
BETHANY
BETRAYS
BITMAPS
BITPART
CATCALL
CATHAIR
CATNAPS
CATTAIL
CATWALK
CITRATE
COTTAGE
CUTBACK
CUTLASS
CUTRATE
DETRACT
DETRAIN
DITTANY
ENTRAIN
ENTRANT
ENTRAPS
ESTRADA
ESTRAYS
ESTUARY
EXTRACT
FATBACK
FATCATS
GATEAUX
GETBACK
GOTBACK
GOTLAND
HATBAND
HATRACK
HETMANS
HOTCAKE
HOTCAPS
HOTCARS
HOTWARS
INTEARS
JETWASH
JETWAYS
JUTLAND
KITBAGS
METHANE
MUTUALS
NITRATE
NITTANY
ONTRACK
OUTBACK
OUTCAST
OUTEATS
OUTFACE
OUTLAID
OUTLAND
OUTLAST
OUTLAWS
OUTLAYS
OUTPACE
OUTRACE
OUTRAGE
OUTRANK
OUTTAKE
OUTTALK
OUTWARD
PETNAME

PITFALL
PITSAWS
POTTAGE
RATPACK
RATRACE
RATTAIL
RATTANS
RETEACH
RETEARS
RETIARY
RETRACE
RETRACK
RETRACT
RETRADE
RETRAIN
RITUALS
SATIATE
SATRAPS
SETBACK
SETSAIL
SITUATE
TATIANA
TETRADS
TITRATE
UNTRAPS
VITIATE
WATTAGE
WETBARS
WETLAND

••T••A•

ALTOSAX
ANTBEAR
ANTITAX
ANTIWAR
APTERAL
ARTISAN
ASTOLAT
AUTOMAT
AZTECAN
BATEMAN
BATHMAT
BATSMAN
BETAMAX
BETARAY
CATALAN
CATBOAT
CATENAE
CATHEAD
CATSCAN
CATSPAW
CUTAWAY
EATAWAY
EATENAT
ENTHRAL
ENTREAT
ESTIVAL
FATHEAD
GATEMAN
GATEWAY
GETAWAY
GETREAL
GOTAWAY
GOTCHAS
HOTHEAD
HOTSEAT
JETBOAT
KETCHAM
KUTENAI
LATERAL
LATERAN
LATIFAH
LATINAS
LATVIAN
LITERAL
MATEWAN
MATHIAS
MATTHAU
MITHRAS
MITZVAH
NATURAL
NOTEPAD
NUTMEAT
NUTRIAS
OATMEAL
ONTRIAL
OPTICAL
OPTIMAL
ORTOLAN
OTTAWAS
OTTOMAN
OUTDRAW
OUTPLAY
OUTWEAR
PATACAS
PATHWAY
PATINAS
PATRIAL
PITAPAT
PITTMAN
POTOMAC
POTSDAM
PUTAWAY
PYTHIAN
PYTHIAS
RATATAT
RATTRAP
RETINAE
RETINAL
RETINAS
RETREAD
RETREAT
RETRIAL
TITULAR
TOTEBAG
TUTELAR
ULTIMAS
UPTOPAR
VATICAN
VETERAN
WATTEAU
YITZHAK

••T•••A

ALTOONA
ANTENNA
ANTIGUA
ANTONIA
ASTORIA
BATISTA
BOTHNIA
CATALPA
CATAWBA
ESTONIA
ESTRADA
INTEGRA
LATOSCA
LETITIA
MATILDA
NATALIA
NATASHA
OCTAVIA
PATELLA
PETUNIA
RATAFIA
RETSINA
ROTUNDA
SATSUMA
TATIANA
TITANIA

•••TA••

ABSTAIN
ACETATE
AGITATE
AGITATO
AIRTAXI
ATSTAKE
AVATARS
BANTAMS
BARTABS
BELTANE
BIGTALK
BLATANT
BOBTAIL
BOITANO
BRITAIN
BUSTARD
CAFTANS
CANTATA
CAPTAIN
CARTAGE
CATTAIL
CENTAUR
CENTAVO
CERTAIN
CONTACT
CONTAIN
COSTAIN
COSTARS
COTTAGE
CRETANS
CURTAIL
CURTAIN
CUSTARD
DASTARD
DELTAIC
DENTATE
DICTATE
DIETARY
DIKTATS
DISTAFF
DISTANT
DITTANY
DOGTAGS
ECSTASY
FANTAIL
FANTASY
FOOTAGE
FOXTAIL
GAUTAMA
GESTALT
GESTATE
GUITARS
HECTARE
HEPTADS
HOSTAGE
IMITATE
INSTALL
INSTALS
INSTANT
INSTARS
INSTATE
KAFTANS
LACTASE
LACTATE
LANTANA
LEOTARD
MAITAIS
MASTABA
MISTAKE
MONTAGE
MONTANA
MONTAND
MONTANE
MONTANI
MORTALS
MORTARS
MUSTAFA
MUSTANG
MUSTARD
NASTASE
NECTARS
NITTANY
ONSTAGE
OUTTAKE
OUTTALK
PARTAKE
PELTATE
PENTADS
PEPTALK
PERTAIN
PIGTAIL
PINTAIL
POPTART
PORTAGE
PORTALS
POSTAGE
POTTAGE
PRETAPE
QINTARS
RATTAIL
RATTANS
REDTAPE
RENTALS
RESTAGE
RESTAIN
RESTAMP
RESTART
RESTATE
RIOTACT
ROSTAND
SANTAFE
SANTANA
SEXTANS
SEXTANT
SMETANA
SOUTANE
SULTANA
SULTANS
SUNTANS
SUSTAIN
TAMTAMS
TANTARA
TARTANS
TARTARE
TARTARS
TICTACS
TIETACK
TINTACK
TOETAPS
TOSTADA
UNITARY
UNSTACK
UPSTAGE
UPSTART
UPSTATE
VANTAGE
VINTAGE
VOLTAGE
VOLTAIC
WAGTAIL
WANTADS
WASTAGE
WATTAGE
WENTAPE

•••T•A•

ABUTTAL
ASHTRAY
AUSTRAL
BELTBAG
BELTWAY
BENTHAM
BESTIAL
BESTMAN
BOATMAN
CENTRAL
CHATEAU
CHATHAM
COCTEAU
CONTRAS
CULTJAM
DUSTMAN
DUSTPAN
EASTMAN
FACTUAL
FLATCAR
FLATTAX
FLOTSAM
FLYTRAP
FOOTMAN
FOOTPAD
FOOTWAY
FORTRAN
FRETSAW
FUSTIAN
GENTIAN
GLOTTAL
GODTHAB
GRATIAS
HAITIAN
HARTMAN
HINTSAT
HOOTSAT
INITIAL
INSTEAD
LACTEAL
LAOTIAN
MANTRAP
MANTRAS
MARTIAL
MARTIAN
MATTHAU
MISTRAL
NEUTRAL
NUPTIAL
ONATEAR
PARTIAL
PARTWAY
PITTMAN
PLATEAU
PONTIAC
PORTMAN
PORTRAY
POSTBAG
POSTMAN
POSTWAR
PROTEAN
QUETZAL
RATTRAP
REITMAN
SLOTCAR
SPATIAL
TAGTEAM
TEATRAY
TERTIAL
TESTBAN
TEXTUAL
UNSTRAP
VENTRAL
VICTUAL
VIETNAM
VIRTUAL
WATTEAU
WENTBAD
WHITMAN
XANTHAN
YEATEAM

•••T••A

AUSTRIA
BOOTHIA
CANTATA
CANTINA
CYNTHIA
DAYTONA
ERITREA
EROTICA
EXOTICA
FESTIVA
FONTINA
FORTUNA
GAUTAMA
LANTANA
MARTINA
MASTABA
MESTIZA
MONTANA
MONTOYA
MUSTAFA
PARTITA
PASTINA
SANTANA
SESTINA
SMETANA
SPATULA
SULTANA
TANTARA
TOSTADA
VENTURA
VISTULA

••••TA•

ABUTTAL
ALLSTAR
AMISTAD
ANTITAX
ARISTAE
ARISTAS
BENATAR
CAPITAL
CAPITAN
CAPSTAN
CHEETAH
CHOCTAW
COALTAR
COASTAL
CRYSTAL
DAKOTAN
DAKOTAS
DAYSTAR
DIGITAL
DOGSTAR
DRISTAN
EIGHTAM
EXACTAS
FAJITAS
FIESTAS
FLATTAX
FRACTAL
FRONTAL
GLOTTAL
HABITAT
HEELTAP
JACKTAR
LAKOTAS
MARITAL
MULETAS
NAMETAG
ONESTAR
ORBITAL
OVERTAX
PALATAL
PELOTAS
PESETAS
PINATAS
PINETAR
PIVOTAL
PLANTAR
POLLTAX
PULLTAB
PURITAN
RARITAN
RATATAT
RECITAL
REDSTAR
SEASTAR
SHOOTAT
SIESTAS
SONATAS
SPARTAN
TELSTAR
TIBETAN
TINSTAR
TRISTAN
TRISTAR
TWOSTAR
VEGETAL
VERITAS
WIRETAP
YUCATAN

••••T•A

ABEXTRA
ABINTRA
ALSATIA
ARIETTA
BARETTA
BEEFTEA
BERETTA
BIRETTA
CORETTA
CROATIA
DYKSTRA
ELECTRA
ELEKTRA
GALATEA
GALATIA
HERBTEA
HIGHTEA
ICEDTEA
INERTIA
LAMOTTA
LETITIA
LORETTA
MAHATMA
MILITIA
MINUTIA
NAPHTHA
OLESTRA
PLECTRA
REGATTA
RICOTTA
ROSETTA
SINATRA
SPECTRA
SUMATRA
TABITHA

•••••TA

ALBERTA
ALMAATA
ARIETTA
ATLANTA
AUGUSTA
BARETTA
BATISTA
BERETTA
BIRETTA
CANASTA
CANTATA
CELESTA
CONDITA
CORETTA
DOGMATA
EMERITA
GANGSTA
INFANTA
JAKARTA
JOCASTA
LAMOTTA
LAPLATA
LORETTA
MAGENTA
MINOLTA
PARTITA
POLENTA
PRORATA
RAWDATA
REGATTA
RICOTTA
RIORITA
ROBERTA
ROBUSTA
ROSETTA
STOMATA
TAFFETA
TOCCATA
VEDANTA
WICHITA

TB•••••

TBILISI

T•B••••

TABARDS
TABASCO
TABBIES
TABBING
TABITHA
TABLEAU
TABLETS
TABLING
TABLOID
TABORET
TABULAR
TIBETAN
TOBACCO
TUBAIST
TUBBIER
TUBISTS
TUBLIKE
TUBULAR

T••B•••

TABBIES
TABBING
TAMBALA
TAMBOUR
TARBABY
TARBELL
TEABAGS
TEABALL
TEMBLOR
TERBIUM
THEBABE
THEBLOB
TIDBITS
TIMBALE
TIMBALS
TIMBERS
TIMBRES
TITBITS
TOMBOLA
TOMBOYS
TRABERT
TREBLED
TREBLES
TRIBUNE
TRIBUTE
TUBBIER
TUGBOAT
TUMBLED
TUMBLER
TUMBLES
TUMBREL
TURBANS
TURBINE
TURBITS
TURBOTS
TWOBASE
TWOBITS

T•••B••

TALKBIG
TAMABLE
TAXABLE
TENABLE
TENABLY
TESTBAN
THIMBLE
THUMBED
THURBER
TOOLBOX
TOTEBAG
TOYNBEE
TREMBLE
TREMBLY
TROUBLE
TWINBED

T••••B•

TARBABY
THEBABE
THEREBY
TOSHIBA

T•••••B

TAXICAB
THEBLOB

•TB••••

PTBOATS

•T•B•••

STABBED
STABILE
STABLED
STABLER
STABLES
STUBBED
STUBBLE
STUBBLY

•T••B••

ATTABOY
STABBED
STEUBEN
STROBES
STUBBED
STUBBLE
STUBBLY
STUMBLE

•T•••B•

STANDBY
STOODBY

••TB•••

ANTBEAR
BATBOYS
CATBERT
CATBIRD
CATBOAT
CUTBACK
FATBACK
GETBACK
GOTBACK
HATBAND
HOTBEDS
JETBOAT
KITBAGS
OUTBACK
OUTBIDS
PITBOSS
PITBULL
RATBERT
SETBACK
TITBITS
WETBARS

••T•B••

ACTABLE
ANTIBES
ATTABOY
CITABLE
EATABLE
ENTEBBE
MUTABLE
MUTABLY
NOTABIT
NOTABLE
NOTABLY
OCTOBER
POTABLE
RATABLE
TOTEBAG

••T••B•

BYTHEBY
CATAWBA
ENTEBBE
HOTTUBS
LETITBE

••T•••B

BATHTUB
HOTCOMB
POTHERB

•••TB••

BELTBAG
BESTBOY
DUSTBIN
FLATBED
HAUTBOY
PEATBOG
POSTBAG
POSTBOX
SALTBOX
TESTBAN
WENTBAD

•••T•B•

ABITIBI
BARTABS
HOTTUBS
MASTABA

•••T••B

DISTURB
GODTHAB
PERTURB

••••TB•

LETITBE

••••T•B

BATHTUB
PULLTAB
WASHTUB

T•C••••

TACITLY
TACITUS
TACKERS
TACKIER
TACKILY
TACKING
TACKLED
TACKLER
TACKLES
TACKSON
TACTFUL
TACTICS
TACTILE
TECHIER
TECHIES
TICKERS
TICKETS
TICKETY
TICKING
TICKLED
TICKLER
TICKLES
TICKOFF
TICTACS
TOCCATA
TOCSINS
TUCHMAN
TUCKERS
TUCKING
TUCKSIN
TYCOONS

T••C•••

TALCUMS
TEACAKE
TEACART
TEACHER
TEACHES
TEACHIN
TEACUPS
TEICHER
TENCENT
TERCELS
TERCETS
TETCHED
THECARS
THECROW
THICKEN
THICKER
THICKET
THICKLY
TIECLIP
TINCANS
TOCCATA
TOECAPS
TOMCATS
TOPCOAT
TORCHED
TORCHES
TOSCALE
TOUCANS
TOUCHED
TOUCHES
TOUCHON
TOUCHUP
TOWCARS
TRACERS
TRACERY
TRACHEA
TRACING
TRACKED
TRACKER
TRACTOR
TRICEPS
TRICKED
TRICKER
TRICKLE
TRICORN
TRICOTS
TROCARS
TROCHEE
TROCHES
TRUCIAL
TRUCKED
TRUCKEE
TRUCKER
TRUCKLE
TUSCANY

T•••C••

TAXICAB
TENACES
THATCHY
THWACKS
TIMECOP
TOBACCO
TOPICAL
TRAMCAR
TRANCES
TREACLE
TREACLY
TUNICLE
TWITCHY
TYPICAL

T••••C•

TABASCO
TACTICS
TAMPICO
TAPIOCA
TARMACS
TEDMACK
TENANCY
TENRECS
TERENCE
TERRACE
THINICE
TICTACS
TIERACK
TIETACK
TINTACK
TITMICE
TOBACCO
TOLTECS
TOPKICK
TOURACO
TRADUCE
TRISECT
TROPICS
TROUNCE
TRUANCY
TUSSOCK

T•••••C

TITANIC
TONELOC
TOTEMIC
TRAFFIC
TROPHIC

•TC••••

ETCHANT
ETCHERS
ETCHING
ITCHIER
ITCHING
STCROIX

•T•C•••

ATACAMA
ATECROW
STACKED
STACKUP
STICHES
STICKER
STICKTO
STICKUP
STOCKED
STOCKUP
STUCCOS
STUCKTO
STUCKUP

•T••C••

ATTACHE
ATTACKS
ATTICUS
ATTUCKS
ETHICAL
ITHACAN
STANCES
STARCHY
STENCIL
STLUCIA
STOICAL
STUCCOS
UTRECHT

•T•••C•

ATPEACE
ATTRACT
ETHNICS
ITALICS
STATICE
STATICS
STAUNCH
STOMACH
STRETCH

•T••••C

STANNIC
STYPTIC

••TC•••

AITCHES
ANTCOWS
BATCHED
BATCHES
BOTCHED
BOTCHES
BOTCHUP
BUTCHER
CATCALL
CATCHER
CATCHES
CATCHON
CATCHUP
DITCHED
DITCHES
EATCROW
FATCATS
FATCITY
FETCHED
FETCHES
FITCHES
GOTCHAS
HATCHED
HATCHER
HATCHES
HATCHET
HITCHED
HITCHER
HITCHES
HOTCAKE
HOTCAPS
HOTCARS
HOTCOMB
HUTCHES
KETCHAM
KETCHES
KETCHUP
KITCHEN
KUTCHIN
LATCHED
LATCHES
LITCHIS
LITCRIT
MATCHED
MATCHES
MATCHUP
MITCHUM
NATCHEZ
NOTCHED
NOTCHES
OUTCAST
OUTCOME
OUTCROP
PATCHED
PATCHES
PATCHUP
PETCOCK
PITCHED
PITCHER
PITCHES
PITCHIN
RATCHET
SATCHEL
SATCHMO
SITCOMS
TETCHED
VETCHES
WATCHED
WATCHER
WATCHES
WATCHIT
WETCELL
WITCHES

••T•C••

ANTACID
ARTICLE
ATTACHE
ATTACKS
ATTICUS

ATTUCKS
AZTECAN
CATSCAN
CUTICLE
DETECTS
ENTICED
ENTICER
ENTICES
HITACHI
KITSCHY
LATICES
NOTICED
NOTICES
OPTICAL
OUTACTS
PATACAS
RETICLE
SHTICKS
UNTACKS
UPTICKS
VATICAN
VOTECHS

••T••C•
ANTIOCH
ARTDECO
ATTRACT
CUTBACK
DETRACT
EXTINCT
EXTRACT
FATBACK
FETLOCK
GETBACK
GOTBACK
GOTHICS
HATRACK
LATENCY
LATOSCA
LATTICE
LETTUCE
MATLOCK
MATTOCK
METRICS
NITPICK
ONTRACK
OSTRICH
OUTBACK
OUTFACE
OUTPACE
OUTRACE
PATRICE
PATRICK
PETCOCK
PETROCK
POTENCY
POTLUCK
RATPACK
RATRACE
RETEACH
RETOUCH
RETRACE
RETRACK
RETRACT
SETBACK
TITMICE

••T•••C
ACTINIC
MITOTIC
POTOMAC
SATIRIC
TITANIC
TOTEMIC

•••TC••
BLOTCHY
FLATCAR
SKETCHY
SLOTCAR
SNITCHY
THATCHY
TWITCHY

•••T•C•
CALTECH
CELTICS
CONTACT
CRITICS
DIPTYCH
DNOTICE
EROTICA
EXOTICA
EXOTICS
FUSTICS
INSTOCK
JUSTICE
KLATSCH
LATTICE
LETTUCE
LOWTECH
MASTICS
MATTOCK
MYSTICS
NOETICS
PHOTICS
POETICS
PORTICO
PROTECT
RESTOCK
RIOTACT
RUSTICS
STATICE
STATICS
TACTICS
TICTACS
TIETACK
TINTACK
TOLTECS
UNSTACK
UNSTICK
UNSTUCK

•••T••C
CENTRIC
DELTAIC
GASTRIC
LAUTREC
MANTRIC
PONTIAC
VOLTAIC
XANTHIC

••••TC•
ABBOTCY
BEWITCH
GODUTCH
INDUTCH
SCRATCH
SPLOTCH
STRETCH
UNHITCH
UNLATCH
WASATCH

••••T•C
AQUATIC
ASCETIC
ASEPTIC
ASIATIC
CAUSTIC
CHAOTIC
CRYPTIC
DRASTIC
ELASTIC
ERISTIC
ERRATIC
FANATIC
FRANTIC
GENETIC
GNOSTIC
HAMITIC
HEPATIC
HERETIC
IDENTIC
IDIOTIC
KINETIC
LUNATIC
MEIOTIC
MIMETIC
MITOTIC
OSMOTIC
PIRATIC
PLASTIC
POLITIC
ROBOTIC
SCEPTIC
SEMITIC
SKEPTIC
SOMATIC
STYPTIC
ZAPOTEC

T•D••••
TADPOLE
TEDDERS
TEDDIES
TEDDING
TEDIOUS
TEDIUMS
TEDMACK
TIDBITS
TIDIEST
TIDINGS
TIDYING
TODDIES
TODDLED
TODDLER
TODDLES

T••D•••
TANDEMS
TARDIER
TARDILY
TEDDERS
TEDDIES
TEDDING
TEEDOFF
TENDERS
TENDING
TENDONS
TENDRIL
TENDSTO
THEDEEP
THUDDED
TIEDOWN
TIEDYED
TIEDYES
TINDERS
TOADIED
TOADIES
TOADISH
TODDIES
TODDLED
TODDLER
TODDLES
TOLDOFF
TOPDOGS
TOPDOWN
TOYDOGS
TRADEIN
TRADEON
TRADERS
TRADEUP
TRADING
TRADUCE
TRIDENT
TRODDEN
TRUDEAU
TRUDGED
TRUDGER
TRUDGES
TUNDRAS
TWADDLE
TWIDDLE

T•••D••
TEPIDLY
TEREDOS
THIRDLY
THUDDED
THUNDER
TIMIDER
TIMIDLY
TIRADES
TIREDER
TIREDLY
TIREDOF
TONEDUP
TOORDER
TOTIDEM
TREADED
TREADER
TREADLE
TRENDED
TRIEDON
TRIODES
TRODDEN
TRUNDLE
TUESDAY
TUNEDIN
TUNEDUP
TUXEDOS
TWADDLE
TWIDDLE
TYPEDUP

T••••D•
TABARDS
TAGENDS
TESTUDO
TETRADS
THREADS
THREADY
TIERODS
TOPSIDE
TORNADO
TOROIDS
TORPEDO
TOSTADA
TOWARDS
TRAGEDY
TRIPODS
TVGUIDE

T•••••D
TABLOID
TACKLED
TAILEND
TAINTED
TALLIED
TALONED
TANGLED
TANGOED
TANKARD
TAPERED
TARRIED
TATTLED
TAUNTED
TEETHED
TELEXED
TEMPTED
TENFOLD
TENONED
TENURED
TETCHED
THANKED
THIEVED
THINNED
THRIVED
THUDDED
THUMBED
THUMPED
TICKLED
TIEDYED
TINGLED
TINKLED
TIPPLED
TIPTOED
TOADIED
TOASTED
TODDLED
TOEHOLD
TOGGLED
TOKENED
TONGUED
TOOTHED
TOOTLED
TOPPLED
TORCHED
TOTALED
TOUCHED
TOUSLED
TOWELED
TOWERED
TOWHEAD
TOYLAND
TRACKED
TRAILED
TRAINED
TRAMPED
TRAPPED
TRASHED
TRAWLED
TREADED
TREATED
TREBLED
TREKKED
TRENDED
TRICKED
TRIFLED
TRIGGED
TRILLED
TRIMMED
TRIPLED
TRIPPED
TROLLED
TROOPED
TROTHED
TROTTED
TRUCKED
TRUDGED
TRUMPED
TRUSSED
TRUSTED
TRYSTED
TUMBLED
TURTLED
TUSSAUD
TUSSLED
TUTORED
TWANGED
TWEAKED
TWEETED
TWEEZED
TWILLED
TWINBED
TWINGED
TWINNED
TWIRLED
TWISTED
TWITTED
TWOFOLD

•TD••••
STDENIS

•T•D•••
STADIUM
STUDDED
STUDENT
STUDIED
STUDIES
STUDIOS

•T••D••
STAIDER
STAIDLY
STANDBY
STANDEE
STANDIN
STANDON
STANDUP
STARDOM
STOODBY
STOODIN
STOODUP
STRIDER
STRIDES
STRUDEL
STUDDED

•T•••D•
ATTENDS
STRANDS

•T••••D
ATTIRED
ATTUNED
STABBED
STABLED
STACKED
STAFFED
STAGGED
STAINED
STALKED
STALLED
STAMPED
STAPLED
STARRED
STARTED
STARVED
STASHED
STEAMED
STEELED
STEEPED
STEERED
STEMMED
STEPPED
STEROID
STETTED
STEWARD
STIFFED
STIFLED
STILLED
STILTED
STINTED
STIPEND
STIRRED
STOCKED
STOMPED
STOOKED
STOOPED
STOPPED
STORIED
STORMED
STRAFED
STRAYED
STREWED
STRIPED
STRIVED
STROKED
STUBBED
STUDDED
STUDIED
STUFFED
STUMPED
STUNNED
STUNTED
STYMIED
UTTERED

••TD•••
ARTDECO
CUTDOWN
GETDOWN
GOTDOWN
HOTDOGS
LETDOWN
OUTDOES
OUTDONE
OUTDOOR
OUTDRAW
OUTDREW
PUTDOWN
SATDOWN
SETDOWN
SITDOWN

••T•D••
ACTEDON
ACTEDUP
ANTEDUP
BETIDED
BETIDES
CITADEL
DATEDLY
DOTEDON
FETIDLY
KATYDID
MATADOR
NOTEDLY
POTSDAM
TOTIDEM
VOTEDIN

••T••D•
ASTRIDE
ATTENDS
CATHODE
DOTARDS
ESTRADA
EXTENDS
EXTRUDE
HOTBEDS
HOTRODS
INTENDS
INTRUDE
MATILDA
METHODS
NITRIDE
OBTRUDE
OBTUNDS
OUTBIDS
OUTSIDE
PETARDS
RETARDS
RETRADE
ROTUNDA
TETRADS

••T•••D
ALTERED
ANTACID
ASTOUND
ATTIRED
ATTUNED
BATCHED
BATIKED
BATTLED
BETIDED
BOTCHED
BOTTLED
CATBIRD
CATERED
CATFOOD
CATHEAD
DITCHED
DITTOED
ENTERED
ENTICED
FATHEAD
FETCHED
GOTLAND
HATBAND
HATCHED
HITCHED
HOTHEAD
INTONED
JUTLAND
JUTTIED
KATYDID
LATCHED
MATCHED
MATURED
METERED
MITERED
MITFORD
MOTORED
MOTTLED
MUTATED
NATURED
NETTLED
NOTATED
NOTCHED
NOTEPAD
NOTICED
NUTATED
OCTOPOD
OSTEOID
OUTLAID
OUTLAND
OUTLOUD
OUTSOLD
OUTWARD
PATCHED
PETALED
PETERED
PITCHED
PUTTIED
RATTLED
RETAPED
RETAXED
RETILED
RETIMED
RETIRED
RETOWED
RETREAD
RETRIED
RETUNED
RETYPED
ROTATED
SETTLED
SUTURED
TATTLED
TETCHED
TOTALED
TUTORED
UNTAMED
UNTAPED
UNTRIED
UNTUNED
UTTERED
WATCHED
WATERED
WETLAND

•••TD••
PASTDUE

•••T•D•
CUSTODY
EBBTIDE
HEPTADS
LEETIDE
LOWTIDE
MALTEDS
PENTADS
PEPTIDE
RIPTIDE
TESTUDO
TOSTADA
WANTADS

•••T••D
ABETTED
ABUTTED
ALLTOLD
BARTEND
BATTLED
BERTHED
BIRTHED
BLATTED
BLITZED
BLOTTED
BOTTLED
BUSTARD
BUSTLED
CASTLED
CENTRED
CHATTED
CLOTHED
CLOTTED
CONTEND
CUSTARD
DASTARD
DELTOID
DIRTIED
DISTEND
DITTOED
DRATTED
EASTEND
EMITTED
EMPTIED
FACTOID
FLATBED
FLATTED
FLITTED
FOOTPAD
FRETTED
FRITTED
FROTHED
GENTLED
GLITZED
GLUTTED
GOATEED
GRITTED
HOGTIED
HURTLED
HUSTLED
INSTEAD
JOSTLED
JUTTIED
KNITTED
KNOTTED
LEOTARD
LOATHED
LUSTRED
MAITRED
MANTLED
MASTOID
MONTAND
MOTTLED
MOUTHED
MUSTARD
NESTLED
NETTLED
OMITTED
OROTUND
PARTIED
PESTLED
PHOTOED
PLOTTED
PORTEND
PRETEND
PUTTIED
RATTLED
ROSTAND
RUSTLED
SAUTEED
SCATHED
SCATTED
SCYTHED
SEETHED
SETTLED
SLATTED
SLOTTED
SOOTHED
SORTIED
SPATTED
SPOTTED
STETTED
SUBTEND
SWATHED
SWATTED
TATTLED
TEETHED
TIPTOED
TOOTHED
TOOTLED
TROTHED
TROTTED
TURTLED
TWITTED
WALTZED
WEBTOED
WENTBAD
WESTEND
WHETTED
WRITHED

••••T•D
ABETTED
ABLATED
ABORTED
ABUTTED
ADAPTED
ADOPTED
AERATED
ALERTED
AMISTAD
AUDITED
AVERTED
AVIATED
AWAITED
BELATED
BERATED
BIGOTED
BLASTED
BLATTED
BLEATED
BLOATED
BLOTTED
BLUNTED
BLURTED
BOASTED
BOOSTED
BRUITED
CAROTID
CHANTED
CHARTED
CHATTED
CHEATED
CLOTTED
CLOUTED
COASTED
COOPTED
COUNTED
COURTED
COVETED
CRAFTED
CREATED
CRESTED
CRUSTED
DAUNTED
DEBATED
DEBITED
DEBUTED
DELETED
DEMOTED
DENOTED
DEPUTED
DEVOTED
DILATED
DILUTED
DONATED
DOUBTED
DRAFTED
DRATTED
DRIFTED
EGESTED
EJECTED
ELECTED
EMITTED
ENACTED
EQUATED
ERECTED
ERUCTED
ERUPTED
EVERTED
EVICTED
EXACTED
EXALTED
EXCITED
EXERTED
EXISTED
EXULTED
FACETED
FAGOTED
FAINTED
FAULTED
FEASTED
FEINTED
FIXATED
FLATTED
FLIRTED
FLITTED
FLOATED
FLOUTED
FOISTED
FRETTED
FRITTED
FRONTED
FROSTED
FRUITED
GHOSTED
GLINTED
GLOATED
GLUTTED
GRAFTED
GRANTED
GREETED
GRITTED
GROUTED
GRUNTED
GUESTED
GYRATED
HABITED
HAUNTED
HEARTED
HEISTED
HOISTED
IDEATED
IGNITED
IMPUTED
INCITED
INDITED
INVITED
JAUNTED
JOINTED
JOISTED
JOUSTED
KNITTED
KNOTTED
KNOUTED
LIGATED
LIGHTED
LIMITED
LOCATED
LUXATED
MERITED
MOULTED
MOUNTED
MULCTED
MUTATED
NEGATED
NOTATED
NUTATED
OMITTED
ORBITED
PAINTED
PILOTED
PIRATED
PIVOTED
PLAITED
PLANTED
PLEATED
PLOTTED
POINTED
POSITED
PRINTED
QUESTED
QUIETED
QUILTED
REACTED
REBATED
RECITED
REDATED
REFUTED
RELATED
RENOTED
REPUTED
RERATED
RIGHTED
RIVETED
ROASTED
ROOSTED
ROTATED
ROUSTED
SAINTED
SALUTED
SCANTED
SCATTED
SCENTED
SCOOTED
SCOUTED
SEDATED
SHAFTED
SHEETED
SHIFTED
SHORTED
SHOUTED
SHUNTED
SIGHTED
SKIRTED
SLANTED
SLATTED
SLEETED
SLOTTED
SMARTED
SMELTED
SNOOTED
SNORTED
SPATTED
SPORTED
SPOTTED
SPOUTED
SPURTED
STARTED
STETTED
STILTED
STINTED
STUNTED
SWATTED
SWEATED
TAINTED
TAUNTED
TEMPTED
TOASTED
TREATED
TROTTED
TRUSTED
TRYSTED
TWEETED
TWISTED
TWITTED
UNDATED
UNRATED
UNSATED
UPDATED
VACATED
VAULTED
VAUNTED
VISITED
WHETTED
WORSTED
WRESTED
YACHTED

TE•••••
TEABAGS
TEABALL
TEACAKE
TEACART
TEACHER
TEACHES
TEACHIN
TEACUPS
TEALEAF
TEALESS
TEAMING
TEAMSUP
TEAPOTS
TEAPOYS
TEARFUL
TEARGAS
TEARIER
TEARILY
TEARING
TEAROFF
TEAROOM
TEAROSE
TEAROUT
TEARSAT
TEARSUP
TEASELS
TEASERS
TEASETS
TEASHOP
TEASING
TEATIME
TEATRAY
TEATREE
TECHIER
TECHIES
TEDDERS
TEDDIES
TEDDING
TEDIOUS
TEDIUMS
TEDMACK
TEEDOFF
TEEMING
TEENAGE
TEENERS
TEENIER
TEEPEES
TEESOFF
TEETERS
TEETHED
TEETHER
TEETHES
TEETIME
TEHERAN
TEICHER
TEKTITE
TELAVIV

TELERAN
TELEXED
TELEXES
TELLALL
TELLERS
TELLIES
TELLING
TELLOFF
TELLSOF
TELLSON
TELSTAR
TEMBLOR
TEMPEHS
TEMPERA
TEMPERS
TEMPEST
TEMPLAR
TEMPLES
TEMPTED
TEMPTER
TEMPURA
TENABLE
TENABLY
TENACES
TENANCY
TENANTS
TENCENT
TENDERS
TENDING
TENDONS
TENDRIL
TENDSTO
TENFOLD
TENFOUR
TENNERS
TENNIEL
TENONED
TENPINS
TENRECS
TENSELY
TENSEST
TENSEUP
TENSILE
TENSING
TENSION
TENSIVE
TENSORS
TENSPOT
TENTERS
TENTHLY
TENTING
TENUITY
TENUOUS
TENURED
TENURES
TENZING
TEPIDLY
TEQUILA
TERAPHS
TERBIUM
TERCELS
TERCETS
TEREDOS
TERENCE
TERHUNE
TERMING
TERMINI
TERMITE
TERNARY
TERNATE
TERRACE
TERRAIN
TERRENE
TERRETS

TERRIER
TERRIES
TERRIFY
TERRORS
TERSELY
TERSEST
TERTIAL
TESSERA
TESTBAN
TESTEES
TESTERS
TESTFLY
TESTIER
TESTIFY
TESTILY
TESTING
TESTOUT
TESTUDO
TETANUS
TETCHED
TETHERS
TETRADS
TEUTONS
TEXTILE
TEXTUAL
TEXTURE

T•E••••

TEEDOFF
TEEMING
TEENAGE
TEENERS
TEENIER
TEEPEES
TEESOFF
TEETERS
TEETHED
TEETHER
TEETHES
TEETIME
THEATER
THEATRE
THEBABE
THEBLOB
THECARS
THECROW
THEDEEP
THEFIRM
THEFONZ
THEISTS
THENARS
THEOMEN
THEOREM
THEPITS
THERAPY
THEREAT
THEREBY
THEREIN
THERELL
THEREOF
THEREON
THERESA
THERETO
THERMAL
THERMOS
THEROUX
THESEUS
THESPIS
THEURGY
THEWIER
TIECLIP
TIEDOWN
TIEDYED
TIEDYES

TIEINTO
TIELESS
TIELINE
TIEPINS
TIEPOLO
TIERACK
TIERING
TIERNEY
TIERODS
TIETACK
TOECAPS
TOEHOLD
TOELESS
TOELIKE
TOELOOP
TOENAIL
TOESHOE
TOETAPS
TREACLE
TREACLY
TREADED
TREADER
TREADLE
TREASON
TREATED
TREBLED
TREBLES
TREEING
TREERAT
TREETOP
TREFOIL
TREKKED
TREKKER
TREKKIE
TRELLIS
TREMAIN
TREMBLE
TREMBLY
TREMOLO
TREMORS
TRENARY
TRENDED
TRENTON
TREPANS
TRESSES
TRESTLE
TREVINO
TSELIOT
TSETSES
TUESDAY
TWEAKED
TWEETED
TWEETER
TWEEZED
TWEEZES
TWELFTH
TWELVES

T••E•••

TAGENDS
TAKEAIM
TAKENIN
TAKENON
TAKEOFF
TAKEONE
TAKEOUT
TAKESIN
TAKESON
TAKESTO
TAKESUP
TAKETEN
TALENTS
TAPEMAN
TAPEMEN

TAPERED
TAVERNS
TEHERAN
TELERAN
TELEXED
TELEXES
TEREDOS
TERENCE
THIEVED
THIEVES
THREADS
THREADY
THREATS
THREEAM
THREEPM
THREERS
THREWIN
TIBETAN
TIMECOP
TIMELAG
TIMEOFF
TIMEOUT
TIMESUP
TINEARS
TIREDER
TIREDLY
TIREDOF
TIREOUT
TOKENED
TONEARM
TONEDUP
TONELOC
TONEROW
TONESUP
TOREOFF
TOREOUT
TOREROS
TOTEBAG
TOTEMIC
TOWELED
TOWERED
TREEING
TREERAT
TREETOP
TRIEDON
TRIESON
TRIESTE
TRUEING
TUNEDIN
TUNEDUP
TUNEFUL
TUNEOUT
TUNESIN
TUNESUP
TUNEUPS
TUPELOS
TUREENS
TUTELAR
TUXEDOS
TWEETED
TWEETER
TWEEZED
TWEEZES
TYLENOL
TYPEDUP
TYPESET
TYPESUP

T•••E••

TABLEAU
TABLETS
TACKERS
TAFFETA
TAGTEAM

TAILEND
TALKERS
TALLEST
TAMPERS
TANDEMS
TANGELO
TANGENT
TANGERE
TANKERS
TANNERS
TANNERY
TANNEST
TAPPERS
TAPPETS
TARBELL
TARGETS
TARHEEL
TARTEST
TASSELS
TASTERS
TATTERS
TAUTENS
TAUTEST
TAXLESS
TEALEAF
TEALESS
TEASELS
TEASERS
TEASETS
TEDDERS
TEENERS
TEEPEES
TEETERS
TELLERS
TEMPEHS
TEMPERA
TEMPERS
TEMPEST
TENCENT
TENDERS
TENNERS
TENRECS
TENSELY
TENSEST
TENSEUP
TENTERS
TERCELS
TERCETS
TERRENE
TERRETS
TERSELY
TERSEST
TESSERA
TESTEES
TESTERS
TETHERS
THALERS
THEDEEP
THEREAT
THEREBY
THEREIN
THERELL
THEREOF
THEREON
THERESA
THERETO
THESEUS
THOREAU
THREEAM
THREEPM
THREERS
THYSELF
TICKERS
TICKETS

TICKETY
TIDIEST
TIELESS
TIGRESS
TILLERS
TILTERS
TIMBERS
TINDERS
TINIEST
TINKERS
TINNERS
TINSELS
TINTERN
TINTERS
TIPLESS
TIPPERS
TIPPETS
TITFERS
TITHERS
TITTERS
TOELESS
TOFFEES
TOGGERY
TOILERS
TOILETS
TOLTECS
TOLUENE
TONIEST
TONNEAU
TOOTERS
TOPPERS
TORMENT
TORPEDO
TORRENS
TORRENT
TOSSERS
TOTTERS
TOTTERY
TOUPEES
TOURERS
TOUTERS
TOWHEAD
TOWHEES
TOWNERS
TOYLESS
TRABERT
TRACERS
TRACERY
TRADEIN
TRADEON
TRADERS
TRADEUP
TRAGEDY
TRAPEZE
TRAVELS
TRAVERS
TRICEPS
TRIDENT
TRIJETS
TRIREME
TRISECT
TRITELY
TRITEST
TRIVETS
TROWELS
TROWERS
TRUDEAU
TUAREGS
TUCKERS
TUFFETS
TUGGERS
TUGLESS
TUNNELS
TUREENS

TURKEYS
TURNERS
TURNERY
TURRETS
TUSKERS
TWOFERS
TYPIEST

T••••E•

TABBIES
TABORET
TACKIER
TACKLED
TACKLER
TACKLES
TAFFIES
TAILLES
TAINTED
TAKETEN
TALKIER
TALKIES
TALLIED
TALLIER
TALLIES
TALONED
TALUSES
TAMALES
TANAGER
TANGIER
TANGLED
TANGLES
TANGOED
TANSIES
TAPEMEN
TAPERED
TAPSTER
TARDIER
TARHEEL
TARRIED
TARRIER
TARRIES
TARSIER
TASTIER
TATTIER
TATTLED
TATTLER
TATTLES
TAUNTED
TAWNIER
TAXFREE
TAXIMEN
TEACHER
TEACHES
TEARIER
TEATREE
TECHIER
TECHIES
TEDDIES
TEENIER
TEEPEES
TEETHED
TEETHER
TEETHES
TEICHER
TELEXED
TELEXES
TELLIES
TEMPLES
TEMPTED
TEMPTER
TENACES
TENNIEL
TENONED
TENURED

TENURES
TERRIER
TERRIES
TESTEES
TESTIER
TETCHED
THANKED
THEATER
THEDEEP
THEOMEN
THEOREM
THEWIER
THICKEN
THICKER
THICKET
THIEVED
THIEVES
THINKER
THINNED
THINNER
THITHER
THRIVED
THRIVES
THRONES
THROWER
THUDDED
THUMBED
THUMPED
THUMPER
THUNDER
THURBER
TICKLED
TICKLER
TICKLES
TIEDYED
TIEDYES
TIERNEY
TIGHTEN
TIGHTER
TIMBRES
TIMIDER
TINGLED
TINGLES
TINKLED
TINKLES
TINNIER
TIPPIER
TIPPLED
TIPPLER
TIPPLES
TIPSIER
TIPSTER
TIPTOED
TIPTOES
TIRADES
TIREDER
TISANES
TISSUES
TITTLES
TIZZIES
TOADIED
TOADIES
TOASTED
TOASTER
TODDIES
TODDLED
TODDLER
TODDLES
TOFFEES
TOFFLER
TOGGLED
TOGGLES
TOKENED
TOLKIEN

TOLLIES
TONGUED
TONGUES
TOOKTEN
TOONIES
TOORDER
TOOTHED
TOOTLED
TOOTLES
TOPAZES
TOPPLED
TOPPLES
TORCHED
TORCHES
TORQUES
TOTALED
TOTIDEM
TOUCHED
TOUCHES
TOUGHEN
TOUGHER
TOUPEES
TOURNEY
TOUSLED
TOUSLES
TOWELED
TOWERED
TOWHEES
TOWNIES
TOYNBEE
TRACHEA
TRACKED
TRACKER
TRAILED
TRAILER
TRAINED
TRAINEE
TRAINER
TRAMMEL
TRAMPED
TRANCES
TRAPPED
TRAPPER
TRASHED
TRASHES
TRAWLED
TRAWLER
TREADED
TREADER
TREATED
TREBLED
TREBLES
TREKKED
TREKKER
TRENDED
TRESSES
TRICKED
TRICKER
TRIFLED
TRIFLER
TRIFLES
TRIGGED
TRIGGER
TRILLED
TRIMMED
TRIMMER
TRINKET
TRIODES
TRIPLED
TRIPLES
TRIPLET
TRIPLEX
TRIPPED
TRIPPER

TRIPPET
TRIUNES
TROCHEE
TROCHES
TRODDEN
TROLLED
TROLLEY
TROOPED
TROOPER
TROTHED
TROTTED
TROTTER
TROUPER
TROUPES
TROUSER
TRUCKED
TRUCKEE
TRUCKER
TRUDGED
TRUDGER
TRUDGES
TRUMPED
TRUMPET
TRUSSED
TRUSSES
TRUSTED
TRUSTEE
TRYSTED
TRYSTER
TSETSES
TUBBIER
TUFTIER
TUMBLED
TUMBLER
TUMBLES
TUMBREL
TUMMIES
TUNNIES
TURFIER
TURNKEY
TURTLED
TURTLES
TUSSLED
TUSSLES
TUTORED
TWANGED
TWEAKED
TWEETED
TWEETER
TWEEZED
TWEEZES
TWELVES
TWILLED
TWINBED
TWINGED
TWINGES
TWINNED
TWIRLED
TWIRLER
TWISTED
TWISTER
TWITTED
TWITTER
TWOSTEP
TYPESET

T•••••E

TACTILE
TADPOLE
TAGLIKE
TAGLINE
TAGSALE
TAKEONE
TAMABLE

TANGERE
TANLINE
TARTARE
TAURINE
TAXABLE
TAXFREE
TAXRATE
TEACAKE
TEAROSE
TEATIME
TEATREE
TEENAGE
TEETIME
TEKTITE
TENABLE
TENSILE
TENSIVE
TERENCE
TERHUNE
TERMITE
TERNATE
TERRACE
TERRENE
TEXTILE
TEXTURE
THEATRE
THEBABE
THIMBLE
THINICE
THISTLE
THYMINE
TIELINE
TILLAGE
TIMBALE
TINLIKE
TINTYPE
TINWARE
TITMICE
TITRATE
TOELIKE
TOESHOE
TOLUENE
TONNAGE
TONSURE
TONTINE
TOOTSIE
TOPHOLE
TOPSIDE
TOSCALE
TOSPARE
TOUGHIE
TOWROPE
TOYLIKE
TOYNBEE
TRADUCE
TRAINEE
TRAIPSE
TRAMPLE
TRAPEZE
TREACLE
TREADLE
TREKKIE
TREMBLE
TRESTLE
TRIBUNE
TRIBUTE
TRICKLE
TRIESTE
TRIREME
TRITONE
TROCHEE
TROUBLE
TROUNCE
TRUCKEE

TRUCKLE
TRUFFLE
TRUNDLE
TRUSTEE
TSQUARE
TUBLIKE
TUNICLE
TURBINE
TVGUIDE
TWADDLE
TWIDDLE
TWINKLE
TWOBASE
TWOLANE
TWOONIE
TWOSOME
TWOTIME
TWOTONE

•TE••••

ATECROW
ATELIER
ETERNAL
ETESIAN
ITEMISE
ITEMIZE
ITERANT
ITERATE
STEALTH
STEAMED
STEAMER
STEELED
STEELER
STEELIE
STEEPED
STEEPEN
STEEPER
STEEPLE
STEEPLY
STEERED
STEERER
STEIGER
STEINEM
STEINER
STELLAR
STEMMED
STENCIL
STENGEL
STENTOR
STEPHEN
STEPINS
STEPOUT
STEPPED
STEPPER
STEPPES
STEPSIN
STEPSON
STEPSUP
STEPUPS
STEREOS
STERILE
STERNAL
STERNER
STERNLY
STERNUM
STEROID
STEROLS
STETSON
STETTED
STEUBEN
STEVENS
STEWARD
STEWART
STEWERS

STEWING
UTENSIL

•T•E•••

ATHEART
ATHEISM
ATHEIST
ATLEAST
ATPEACE
ATTEMPT
ATTENDS
ATTESTS
ETIENNE
OTHELLO
STDENIS
STEELED
STEELER
STEELIE
STEEPED
STEEPEN
STEEPER
STEEPLE
STEEPLY
STEERED
STEERER
STIEGEL
STPETER
STREAKS
STREAKY
STREAMS
STREETS
STRETCH
STRETTO
STREWED
STREWER
UTRECHT
UTTERED
UTTERER
UTTERLY

•T••E••

ATHLETE
ETAGERE
ETCHERS
PTOLEMY
STAGERS
STALELY
STALEST
STAMENS
STAREAT
STARERS
STARETS
STATELY
STEREOS
STEVENS
STEWERS
STIPEND
STOKELY
STOKERS
STONERS
STORERS
STOREUP
STOREYS
STREETS
STUDENT
STUMERS
STUPEFY
STYLERS
STYLETS
STYRENE

•T•••E•

ATELIER
ATHOMES

ATLASES
ATOMIES
ATONIES
ATTIMES
ATTIRED
ATTIRES
ATTUNED
ATTUNES
ETOILES
ITCHIER
STABBED
STABLED
STABLER
STABLES
STACKED
STAFFED
STAFFER
STAGGED
STAGGER
STAGIER
STAIDER
STAINED
STAINER
STALKED
STALKER
STALLED
STAMMER
STAMPED
STANCES
STANDEE
STANLEE
STANLEY
STAPLED
STAPLER
STAPLES
STARKER
STARLET
STARRED
STARTED
STARTER
STARVED
STARVES
STASHED
STASHES
STASSEN
STATUES
STEAMED
STEAMER
STEELED
STEELER
STEEPED
STEEPEN
STEEPER
STEERED
STEERER
STEIGER
STEINEM
STEINER
STEMMED
STENGEL
STEPHEN
STEPPED
STEPPER
STEPPES
STERNER
STETTED
STEUBEN
STICHES
STICKER
STIEGEL
STIFFED
STIFFEN
STIFFER
STIFLED

STIFLES
STILLED
STILLER
STILTED
STINGER
STINKER
STINTED
STIRRED
STIRRER
STOCKED
STOGIES
STOLLEN
STOLLER
STOMPED
STONIER
STOOGES
STOOKED
STOOKEY
STOOPED
STOPPED
STOPPER
STORIED
STORIES
STORMED
STOUTEN
STOUTER
STPETER
STRAFED
STRAFES
STRAYED
STREWED
STREWER
STRIDER
STRIDES
STRIKER
STRIKES
STRIPED
STRIPER
STRIPES
STRIVED
STRIVEN
STRIVER
STRIVES
STROBES
STROKED
STROKES
STRUDEL
STUBBED
STUDDED
STUDIED
STUDIES
STUFFED
STUFFER
STUMPED
STUMPER
STUNNED
STUNNER
STUNTED
STURGES
STYMIED
STYMIES
UTTERED
UTTERER

•T•••E

ATHLETE
ATINGLE
ATISSUE
ATLARGE
ATOMISE
ATOMIZE
ATPEACE
ATSTAKE
ATTACHE
ATTRITE
ETAGERE
ETAMINE
ETIENNE
ITEMISE
ITEMIZE
ITERATE
STABILE
STANDEE
STANLEE
STARTLE
STATICE
STATURE
STATUTE
STEELIE
STEEPLE
STERILE
STIPPLE
STOOLIE
STORAGE
STRANGE
STRASSE
STRIATE
STROPHE
STUBBLE
STUMBLE
STYLISE
STYLIZE
STYRENE
UTILISE
UTILIZE

••TE•••

ACTEDON
ACTEDUP
ALTERED
ALTERER
ANTEDUP
ANTEING
ANTENNA
ANTESUP
APTERAL
ARTEMIS
ARTEMUS
ATTEMPT
ATTENDS
ATTESTS
AUTEURS
AZTECAN
BATEAUX
BATEMAN
BITEOFF
CATENAE
CATERED
CATERER
CATERTO
CETERIS
COTERIE
DATEDLY
DETECTS
DETENTE
DETESTS
DOTEDON
DOTESON
DUTEOUS
EATENAT
EATENUP
ENTEBBE
ENTENTE
ENTERED
ENTERON
ESTEEMS
ESTELLE
ESTEVEZ
EUTERPE
EXTENDS
EXTENTS
EXTERNS
FATEFUL
GATEAUX
GATELEG
GATEMAN
GATEMEN
GATEWAY
GETEVEN
GOTEVEN
HATEFUL
INTEARS
INTEGER
INTEGRA
INTENDS
INTENSE
INTENTS
INTERIM
INTERNS
INTERSE
IQTESTS
KUTENAI
LATEENS
LATENCY
LATENTS
LATERAL
LATERAN
LATERON
LATEXES
LITERAL
MATELOT
MATEWAN
METEORS
METEOUT
METERED
MITERED
NOTEDLY
NOTEPAD
OFTENER
OSTEOID
OUTEATS
PATELLA
PATENTS
PATERNO
PETERED
PITEOUS
POTENCY
RETEACH
RETEARS
RETELLS
RETESTS
SATEENS
TOTEBAG
TOTEMIC
TUTELAR
UPTEMPO
URTEXTS
UTTERED
UTTERER
UTTERLY
VETERAN
VOTECHS
VOTEDIN
VOTEFOR
VOTEOUT
VOTESIN
WATERED
WATERER

••T•E••

ACTAEON
ACTRESS
AETHERS
ANTAEUS
ANTBEAR
ANTHEMS
ANTHERS
ANTLERS
ANTWERP
APTNESS
ARTDECO
ARTIEST
ARTLESS
BATHERS
BATTELS
BATTENS
BATTERS
BATTERY
BETHELS
BETTERS
BETWEEN
BITLESS
BITTERN
BITTERS
BOTHERS
BUTLERS
BUTTERS
BUTTERY
BYTHEBY
CATBERT
CATHEAD
CATSEYE
COTTERS
CUTLERS
CUTLERY
CUTLETS
CUTTERS
DITHERS
DITHERY
ENTREAT
ENTREES
ESTEEMS
ESTHETE
EXTREME
FATHEAD
FATHERS
FATLESS
FATNESS
FATTENS
FATTEST
FETTERS
FITNESS
FITTERS
FITTEST
GATHERS
GETREAL
GETWELL
GOTWELL
GUTLESS
GUTTERS
HATLESS
HATTERS
HITHERE
HITLESS
HITTERS
HOTBEDS
HOTHEAD
HOTNESS
HOTSEAT
HOTTEST
JITNEYS
JITTERS
JITTERY
KITTENS
LATEENS
LATHERS
LATHERY
LATTENS
LETTERS
LITHELY
LITHEST
LITTERS
LOTTERY
MATHERS
MATHEWS
MATLESS
MATTERS
METIERS
MITTENS
MOTHERS
MUTTERS
NATTERS
NOTWELL
NUTLETS
NUTMEAT
NUTMEGS
NUTTERS
OATMEAL
ONTHEGO
ONTHEQT
OSTLERS
OUTLETS
OUTSELL
OUTSETS
OUTWEAR
PATIENT
PATNESS
PATTENS
PATTERN
PATTERS
PETRELS
PETTERS
PITIERS
PITTERS
POTHERB
POTHERS
POTTERS
POTTERY
PUTTEES
PUTTERS
RATBERT
RATTERS
RETREAD
RETREAT
ROTTERS
RUTGERS
SATEENS
SATIETY
SETTEES
SETTERS
SITTERS
SITWELL
SOTHERE
SOTHERN
SUTLERS
SUTTERS
TATTERS
TETHERS
TITFERS
TITHERS
TITTERS
TOTTERS
TOTTERY
VETOERS
WATTEAU
WETCELL
WETHERS
WETNESS
WETTEST
WITHERS
WITLESS
WITNESS
ZITHERS

••T••E•

ACTIVES
AITCHES
ALTERED
ALTERER
ANTARES
ANTIBES
ANTIGEN
ANTSIER
ARTSIER
ATTIMES
ATTIRED
ATTIRES
ATTUNED
ATTUNES
BATCHED
BATCHES
BATIKED
BATSMEN
BATTIER
BATTLED
BATTLER
BATTLES
BATTUES
BETAKEN
BETAKES
BETIDED
BETIDES
BETIMES
BETISES
BETOKEN
BETWEEN
BITSIER
BITTIER
BITUMEN
BOTCHED
BOTCHES
BOTTLED
BOTTLER
BOTTLES
BUTCHER
BUTTIES
CATCHER
CATCHES
CATERED
CATERER
CATTIER
CITADEL
CITIZEN
CITROEN
CNTOWER
DATASET
DITCHED
DITCHES
DITSIER
DITTIES
DITTOED
DITZIER
DOTTIER
DOTTLES
ECTYPES
ENTERED
ENTICED
ENTICER
ENTICES
ENTREES
ENTRIES
ESTATES
ESTEVEZ
FATTIER
FETCHED
FETCHES
FETTLES
FITCHES
FUTURES
GATELEG
GATEMEN
GETEVEN
GETOVER
GETSSET
GOTEVEN
GOTOVER
GUTSIER
GUTTIER
HATCHED
HATCHER
HATCHES
HATCHET
HITCHED
HITCHER
HITCHES
HUTCHES
INTAKES
INTEGER
INTONED
INTONER
INTONES
JETTIES
JUTTIED
JUTTIES
KETCHES
KETONES
KETTLES
KITCHEN
KITTIES
LATCHED
LATCHES
LATEXES
LATICES
LETSSEE
LETTRES
LITOTES
LITTLER
LOTUSES
MATCHED
MATCHES
MATINEE
MATTHEW
MATURED
MATURER
MATURES
METATES
METERED
METOOER
METTLES
MITERED
MITOSES
MOTHIER
MOTIVES
MOTORED
MOTTLED
MOTTLES
MOTTOES
MUTAGEN
MUTATED
MUTATES
NATCHEZ
NATIVES
NATTIER
NATURED
NATURES
NETIZEN
NETTLED
NETTLES
NITTIER
NOTATED
NOTATES
NOTCHED
NOTCHES
NOTICED
NOTICES
NUTATED
NUTATES
NUTSIER
NUTTIER
OBTUSER
OCTANES
OCTAVES
OCTOBER
OFTENER
OUTAGES
OUTDOES
OUTDREW
OUTGOES
OUTGREW
OUTSTEP
PATCHED
PATCHES
PATSIES
PATTIES
PETALED
PETERED
PETITES
PETTIER
PITCHED
PITCHER
PITCHES
PITHIER
POTAGES
POTPIES
POTSIER
POTTIER
POTTLES
PUTAMEN
PUTOVER
PUTTEES
PUTTIED
PUTTIES
RATCHET
RATITES
RATTIER
RATTLED
RATTLER
RATTLES
RETAKEN
RETAKES
RETAPED
RETAPES
RETAXED
RETAXES
RETILED
RETILES
RETIMED
RETIMES
RETIRED
RETIREE
RETIRES
RETOWED
RETRIED
RETRIES
RETUNED
RETUNES
RETYPED
RETYPES
RITZIER
ROTATED
ROTATES
ROTIFER
RUTTIER
SATCHEL
SATINET
SATIRES
SETTEES
SETTLED
SETTLER
SETTLES
SUTURED
SUTURES
TATTIER
TATTLED
TATTLER
TATTLES
TETCHED
TITTLES
TOTALED
TOTIDEM
TUTORED
UNTAMED
UNTAPED
UNTRIED
UNTUNED
UNTUNES
UPTAKES
UTTERED
UTTERER
VETCHES
VITTLES
WATCHED
WATCHER
WATCHES
WATERED
WATERER
WATTLES
WITCHES
WITHIER
WITHIES
WITTIER
ZATOPEK

••T•••E

ACTABLE
ACTFIVE
ACTUATE
ANTIQUE
ANTLIKE
ANTOINE
ARTICLE
ARTISTE
ARTWARE
ASTAIRE
ASTARTE
ASTRIDE
ATTACHE
ATTRITE
BATISTE
BATLIKE
CATENAE
CATHODE
CATLIKE
CATSEYE
CITABLE
CITRATE
CITRINE
COTERIE
COTTAGE
CUTICLE
CUTRATE
CUTTIME
DETENTE
DOTLIKE
EATABLE
ENTEBBE
ENTENTE
ENTHUSE
ENTITLE
ENTWINE
ESTELLE
ESTHETE
EUTERPE
EXTREME
EXTRUDE
FATIGUE
FATLIKE
GUTHRIE
HATLIKE
HITHERE
HITTITE
HOTCAKE
HOTLINE
HOTWIRE
HUTLIKE
INTENSE
INTERSE
INTRUDE
LATTICE
LETITBE
LETSSEE
LETTUCE
MATINEE
MATISSE
METHANE
MUTABLE
NATALIE
NETLIKE
NETSUKE
NITRATE
NITRIDE
NITRITE
NOTABLE
NOTSURE
NOTTRUE
NUTLIKE
OATLIKE
OBTRUDE
OCTUPLE
OUTCOME
OUTDONE
OUTFACE
OUTLINE
OUTLIVE
OUTPACE
OUTRACE
OUTRAGE
OUTSIDE
OUTSIZE
OUTTAKE
OUTVOTE
OUTWORE
PATRICE
PETIOLE
PETNAME
POTABLE
POTHOLE
POTTAGE
RATABLE
RATHOLE
RATLIKE
RATLINE
RATRACE
RETICLE
RETINAE
RETINUE
RETIREE
RETITLE
RETRACE
RETRADE
SATIATE
SETLINE
SITUATE
SOTHERE
TITMICE
TITRATE
VITIATE
WATTAGE

•••TE••

ACUTELY
AMATEUR
AUSTERE
BANTERS
BARTEND
BARTERS
BASTERS
BATTELS
BATTENS
BATTERS
BATTERY
BEATERS
BETTERS
BITTERN
BITTERS
BOATELS
BOATERS
BOOTEES
BRUTELY
BUSTERS
BUTTERS
BUTTERY
CALTECH
CANTEEN
CANTERS
CARTELS
CARTERS
CASTERS
CENTERS
CHATEAU
CISTERN
COCTEAU
CONTEMN
CONTEND
CONTENT
CONTEST
CONTEXT
COPTERS
CORTEGE
COTTERS
CRATERS
CURTEST
CUTTERS
DAFTEST
DARTERS
DEFTEST
DEUTERO
DIETERS
DISTEND
DUSTERS
EASTEND
EASTERN
EASTERS
ELATERS
EMOTERS
EPSTEIN
ESOTERY
FALTERS
FASTENS
FASTEST
FATTENS
FATTEST
FESTERS
FETTERS
FIFTEEN
FILTERS
FITTERS
FITTEST
FONTEYN
FOOTERS
FOSTERS
GAITERS
GARTERS
GENTEEL
GOATEED
GOATEES
GRATERS
GUTTERS
HALTERS
HASTENS
HATTERS
HAUTEUR
HEATERS
HITTERS
HOOTERS
HOSTELS
HOSTESS
HOTTEST
HUNTERS
INSTEAD
INSTEPS
IRATELY
IRATEST
JESTERS
JITTERS
JITTERY
KITTENS
KRATERS
LACTEAL
LANTERN
LATTENS
LECTERN
LETTERS
LIFTERS
LINTELS
LISTEES
LISTELS
LISTENS
LITTERS
LOITERS
LOOTERS
LOTTERY
LOWTECH
LUSTERS
MALTEDS
MALTESE
MANTELS
MARTENS
MASTERS
MASTERY
MATTERS
MIDTERM
MINTERS
MISTERS
MITTENS
MOLTERS
MONTEGO
MONTERO
MUSTERS
MUTTERS
MYSTERY
NATTERS
NEATENS
NEATEST
NESTEGG
NESTERS
NUTTERS
ONATEAR
OUSTERS
OYSTERS
PALTERS
PASTELS
PASTERN
PASTEUP
PASTEUR
PATTENS
PATTERN
PATTERS
PELTERS
PERTEST
PESTERS
PETTERS
PITTERS
PLATEAU
PLATENS
PLATERS
PORTEND
PORTENT
PORTERS
POSTERN
POSTERS
POTTERS
POTTERY
POUTERS
PRATERS
PRETEEN
PRETEND
PRETEST
PRETEXT
PROTEAN
PROTECT
PROTEGE
PROTEIN
PROTEST
PROTEUS
PUNTERS
PUPTENT
PUTTEES
PUTTERS
QUOTERS
RAFTERS
RANTERS
RASTERS
RATTERS
RENTERS
RESTERS
REUTERS
RIOTERS
ROOTERS
ROSTERS
ROTTERS
ROUTERS
SALTERS
SAUTEED
SCOTERS
SEATERS
SEPTETS
SESTETS
SETTEES
SETTERS
SEXTETS
SHUTEYE
SIFTERS
SISTERS
SITTERS
SIXTEEN
SKATERS
SOFTENS
SOFTEST
SORTERS
STATELY
SUBTEND
SUBTEXT
SUTTERS
SYSTEMS
TAGTEAM
TARTEST
TASTERS
TATTERS
TAUTENS
TAUTEST
TEETERS
TENTERS
TESTEES
TESTERS
TILTERS
TINTERN
TINTERS
TITTERS
TOLTECS
TOOTERS
TOTTERS
TOTTERY
TOUTERS
TRITELY
TRITEST
ULSTERS
UMPTEEN
UNITERS
USSTEEL
VASTEST
VENTERS
VESTEES
WAITERS
WALTERS
WASTERS
WATTEAU
WELTERS
WESTEND
WESTERN
WETTEST
WHITENS
WHITEST
WINTERS
WINTERY
WRITEIN
WRITERS
WRITETO
WRITEUP
WROTEIN
WROTETO
WROTEUP
YEATEAM

•••T•E•

ABETTED
ABUTTED
ANOTHER
APOTHEM
AUNTIES
BATTIER
BATTLED
BATTLER
BATTLES
BATTUES
BEATLES
BEETLES
BENTLEY
BENTSEN
BERTHED
BESTMEN
BESTREW
BIGTOES
BIRTHED
BITTIER
BLATHER

BLATTED
BLITHER
BLITZED
BLITZEN
BLITZES
BLOTTED
BLOTTER
BOATMEN
BOOTEES
BOOTIES
BOOTLEG
BOTTLED
BOTTLER
BOTTLES
BOWTIES
BRITTEN
BROTHER
BUSTLED
BUSTLES
BUTTIES
CANTEEN
CANTLES
CARTIER
CASTLED
CASTLES
CATTIER
CENTRED
CENTRES
CHATTED
CHATTEL
CHATTER
CHITTER
CHUTNEY
CLATTER
CLOTHED
CLOTHES
CLOTTED
CLUTTER
COOTIES
COSTNER
CRITTER
CURTSEY
DALTREY
DEITIES
DIRTIED
DIRTIER
DIRTIES
DITTIES
DITTOED
DOTTIER
DOTTLES
DRATTED
DUSTIER
DUSTMEN
EARTHEN
ELMTREE
EMITTED
EMITTER
EMPTIED
EMPTIER
EMPTIES
EPITHET
ERITREA
FARTHER
FATTIER
FEATHER
FETTLES
FIFTEEN
FIFTIES
FLATBED
FLATLET
FLATTED
FLATTEN
FLATTER
FLITTED
FLITTER
FLUTIER
FLUTTER
FOOTMEN
FORTIES
FRETTED
FRITTED
FRITTER
FROTHED
FURTHER
FUSTIER
GANTLET
GENTEEL
GENTLED
GENTLER
GENTLES
GLITTER
GLITZED
GLITZES
GLUTTED
GOATEED
GOATEES
GOUTIER
GRITTED
GUMTREE
GUNTHER
GUSTIER
GUSTOES
GUTTIER
HASTIER
HEATHEN
HEATHER
HEATTER
HEFTIER
HOGTIED
HOGTIES
HOSTLER
HUNTLEY
HURTLED
HURTLES
HUSTLED
HUSTLER
HUSTLES
JETTIES
JOLTIER
JOSTLED
JOSTLER
JOSTLES
JUTTIED
JUTTIES
KESTREL
KETTLES
KILTIES
KIRTLES
KITTIES
KLUTZES
KNITTED
KNITTER
KNOTTED
LAUTREC
LEATHER
LEFTIES
LETTRES
LINTIER
LISTEES
LITTLER
LOATHED
LOATHES
LOFTIER
LUSTIER
LUSTRED
LUSTRES
MAITRED
MALTIER
MANTLED
MANTLES
MATTHEW
MAYTREE
MEATIER
METTLES
MINTIER
MISTIER
MOTTLED
MOTTLES
MOTTOES
MOUTHED
MUSTIER
MUSTSEE
MYRTLES
NARTHEX
NASTIER
NATTIER
NEITHER
NESTLED
NESTLER
NESTLES
NETTLED
NETTLES
NIFTIER
NITTIER
NORTHER
NUTTIER
OAKTREE
OMITTED
OMITTER
PANTHER
PARTIED
PARTIER
PARTIES
PARTNER
PASTIER
PATTIES
PEATIER
PESTLED
PESTLES
PETTIER
PHOTOED
PIETIES
PLATIER
PLATTER
PLOTTED
PLOTTER
POITIER
POSTMEN
POTTIER
POTTLES
POUTIER
PRETEEN
PRETZEL
PRITHEE
PUNTIES
PUTTEES
PUTTIED
PUTTIES
QUITTER
RATTIER
RATTLED
RATTLER
RATTLES
REUTHER
RONTGEN
ROOTIER
ROOTLET
RUNTIER
RUSTIER
RUSTLED
RUSTLER
RUSTLES
RUTTIER
SALTIER
SAUTEED
SCATHED
SCATHES
SCATTED
SCATTER
SCYTHED
SCYTHES
SEETHED
SEETHES
SELTZER
SETTEES
SETTLED
SETTLER
SETTLES
SHATNER
SHATTER
SHUTTER
SILTIER
SIXTEEN
SIXTIES
SKITTER
SLATHER
SLATIER
SLATTED
SLITHER
SLOTTED
SMATTER
SMITTEN
SMOTHER
SOFTIES
SOOTHED
SOOTHER
SOOTHES
SOOTIER
SORTIED
SORTIES
SOUTHEY
SPATTED
SPATTER
SPITZES
SPOTTED
SPOTTER
SPUTTER
STATUES
STETTED
SUBTLER
SURTSEY
SWATHED
SWATHES
SWATTED
SWATTER
SWITZER
TASTIER
TATTIER
TATTLED
TATTLER
TATTLES
TEATREE
TEETHED
TEETHER
TEETHES
TESTEES
TESTIER
THITHER
TIPTOED
TIPTOES
TITTLES
TOOTHED
TOOTLED
TOOTLES
TROTHED
TROTTED
TROTTER
TSETSES
TUFTIER
TURTLED
TURTLES
TWITTED
TWITTER
UMPTEEN
UNITIES
UPATREE
USSTEEL
VASTIER
VESTEES
VINTNER
VIRTUES
VITTLES
WALTZED
WALTZER
WALTZES
WARTIER
WASTREL
WATTLES
WEATHER
WEBTOED
WERTHER
WHETHER
WHETTED
WHITHER
WHITIER
WHITNEY
WITTIER
WRITHED
WRITHES
WRITTEN
YAHTZEE
ZESTIER

•••T••E

ACETATE
ACETONE
AGITATE
AIRTIME
ALLTIME
AMATIVE
ANATOLE
ANYTIME
APATITE
ATSTAKE
AUSTERE
BAPTISE
BAPTIZE
BEATSME
BEATTIE
BEDTIME
BELTANE
BIGTIME
BRITTLE
BUYTIME
CAPTIVE
CAPTURE
CARTAGE
CASTILE
CENTIME
CLOTURE
CONTUSE
CORTEGE
COSTUME
COTTAGE
COUTURE
CULTURE
CUTTIME
DAYTIME
DENTATE
DENTINE
DENTURE
DESTINE
DICTATE
DNOTICE
DUCTILE
EBBTIDE
ELMTREE
EMOTIVE
EPITOME
FASTONE
FEATURE
FERTILE
FESTIVE
FICTIVE
FIXTURE
FOOTAGE
FOOTSIE
FORTUNE
FURTIVE
GENTILE
GESTATE
GESTURE
GUMTREE
HECTARE
HITTITE
HOSTAGE
HOSTILE
IFSTONE
IMITATE
INSTATE
INSTORE
INSTYLE
INUTILE
ISOTOPE
JUSTICE
JUSTINE
LACTASE
LACTATE
LACTOSE
LATTICE
LECTURE
LEETIDE
LETTUCE
LOWTIDE
MALTESE
MALTOSE
MAYTIME
MAYTREE
MISTAKE
MISTYPE
MIXTURE
MONTAGE
MONTANE
MORTISE
MUSTSEE
NAPTIME
NASTASE
NEPTUNE
NOTTRUE
NURTURE
OAKTREE
OLDTIME
ONETIME
ONSTAGE
OUTTAKE
PARTAKE
PARTITE
PASTDUE
PASTIME
PASTURE
PELTATE
PEPTIDE
PICTURE
PISTOLE
PONTINE
PORTAGE
POSTAGE
POSTURE
POTTAGE
PRATTLE
PRETAPE
PRITHEE
PROTEGE
RAGTIME
RAPTURE
REDTAPE
REPTILE
RESTAGE
RESTATE
RESTIVE
RESTORE
RESTYLE
RIPTIDE
ROUTINE
RUPTURE
SALTINE
SANTAFE
SAOTOME
SCOTTIE
SCUTTLE
SEATTLE
SHUTEYE
SHUTTLE
SISTINE
SKITTLE
SOUTANE
STATICE
STATURE
STATUTE
SYSTOLE
TACTILE
TARTARE
TEATIME
TEATREE
TEETIME
TEKTITE
TEXTILE
TEXTURE
TINTYPE
TONTINE
TOOTSIE
TRITONE
TWOTIME
TWOTONE
UNITIVE
UPATREE
UPSTAGE
UPSTATE
VANTAGE
VENTURE
VESTIGE
VESTURE
VINTAGE
VIRTUTE
VOLTAGE
VULTURE
WARTIME
WASTAGE
WATTAGE
WENTAPE
WHITTLE
YAHTZEE

••••TE•

ABETTED
ABLATED
ABLATES
ABORTED
ABUTTED
ACHATES
ADAPTED
ADAPTER
ADOPTED
ADOPTEE
ADOPTER
AERATED
AERATES
AGNATES
ALERTED
ALERTER
AMMETER
ARBITER
AUDITED
AVERTED
AVIATED
AVIATES
AWAITED
BAINTER
BEEFTEA
BELATED
BERATED
BERATES
BIGOTED
BLASTED
BLASTER
BLATTED
BLEATED
BLISTER
BLOATED
BLOTTED
BLOTTER
BLUNTED
BLUNTER
BLURTED
BLUSTER
BOASTED
BOASTER
BOLSTER
BOOSTED
BOOSTER
BORATES
BOXSTEP
BRITTEN
BRUITED
CHANTED
CHANTER
CHANTEY
CHAPTER
CHARTED
CHARTER
CHASTEN
CHASTER
CHATTED
CHATTEL
CHATTER
CHEATED
CHEATER
CHESTER
CHITTER
CHUNTER
CLATTER
CLOTTED
CLOUTED
CLUSTER
CLUTTER
COASTED
COASTER
COOPTED
COULTER
COUNTED
COUNTER
COURTED
COVETED
COYOTES
CRAFTED
CRAFTER
CREATED
CREATES
CRESTED
CRITTER
CROFTER
CRUSTED
CURATES
DAUNTED
DEBATED
DEBATER
DEBATES
DEBITED
DEBUTED
DELETED
DELETES
DEMETER
DEMOTED
DEMOTES
DENOTED
DENOTES
DEPUTED
DEPUTES
DEVOTED
DEVOTEE
DEVOTES
DILATED
DILATES
DILUTED
DILUTER
DILUTES
DIOPTER
DONATED
DONATES
DOUBTED
DOUBTER
DRAFTED
DRAFTEE
DRATTED
DRIFTED
DRIFTER
EGESTED
EJECTED
ELECTED
ELECTEE
EMITTED
EMITTER
ENACTED
EQUATED
EQUATES
ERECTED
ERECTER
ERGATES
ERUCTED
ERUPTED
ESTATES
EVERTED
EVICTED
EXACTED
EXACTER
EXALTED
EXCITED
EXCITES
EXERTED
EXISTED
EXULTED
FACETED
FAGOTED
FAINTED
FAINTER
FAULTED
FEASTED
FEINTED
FIGHTER
FIXATED
FIXATES
FLATTED
FLATTEN
FLATTER
FLEETER
FLIRTED
FLITTED
FLITTER
FLOATED
FLOATER
FLOUTED
FLUSTER
FLUTTER
FOISTED
FORSTER
FRETTED
FRITTED
FRITTER
FRONTED
FROSTED
FRUITED
GAGSTER
GALATEA
GAMETES
GAUNTER
GEMOTES
GHOSTED
GLINTED
GLISTEN
GLITTER
GLOATED
GLUTTED
GOAFTER
GOLFTEE
GORETEX
GRAFTED
GRANTED
GRANTEE
GREATER
GREETED
GREETER
GRIFTER
GRITTED
GROUTED
GRUNTED
GUESTED
GYRATED
GYRATES
HABITED
HALITES
HAMITES
HAMSTER
HANGTEN
HAUNTED
HEARTED
HEARTEN
HEATTER
HEISTED
HERBTEA
HIGHTEA
HIPSTER
HOISTED
HOLSTER
ICEDTEA
IDEATED
IDEATES
IGNITED
IGNITER
IGNITES
IMPUTED
IMPUTES
INAPTER
INASTEW
INCITED
INCITER
INCITES
INDITED
INDITES
INMATES
INVITED
INVITES
IODATES
JAUNTED
JOINTED
JOISTED
JOUSTED
JOUSTER
JUPITER
KNITTED
KNITTER
KNOTTED
KNOUTED
LAERTES
LEGATEE
LEGATES
LEISTER
LEVITES
LIGATED
LIGATES
LIGHTED
LIGHTEN
LIGHTER
LIMITED
LITOTES
LOBSTER
LOCATED
LOCATER
LOCATES
LUXATED
LUXATES
MANATEE
MEISTER
MERITED
METATES
MINUTES
MISSTEP
MOBSTER
MOISTEN
MOISTER
MONSTER
MOULTED
MOUNTED
MULCTED
MUTATED
MUTATES
NEGATED
NEGATER
NEGATES
NOTATED
NOTATES
NUTATED
NUTATES
OBLATES
OLDSTER
OLEATES
OMITTED
OMITTER
ONESTEP
OOCYTES
OOLITES
OPHITES
OPIATES
ORBITED
ORBITER
ORESTES
ORGATES
OUTSTEP
PAINTED
PAINTER
PAIUTES
PALATES
PENATES
PETITES
PHILTER
PIASTER
PILOTED
PIRATED
PIRATES
PIVOTED
PLAITED
PLANTED
PLANTER
PLASTER
PLATTER
PLEATED
PLOTTED
PLOTTER
POINTED
POINTER
POLITER
POSITED
PRINTED
PRINTER
PROPTER
PSALTER
PUNSTER
PYRITES
QUARTER
QUARTET
QUESTED
QUIETED
QUIETEN
QUIETER
QUILTED
QUILTER
QUINTET
QUITTER
RATITES
REACTED
REBATED
REBATES
RECITED
RECITER
RECITES
REDATED
REDATES
REENTER
REFUTED
REFUTER
REFUTES
RELATED
RELATES
REMOTER
REMOTES
RENOTED
RENOTES
REPUTED
REPUTES
RERATED
RERATES
RICHTER
RIGHTED
RIGHTER
RIVETED
RIVETER
ROASTED
ROASTER
ROISTER
ROOSTED
ROOSTER
ROTATED
ROTATES
ROUSTED
SAINTED
SALUTED
SALUTES
SAMITES
SAUNTER
SCANTED
SCANTER
SCATTED
SCATTER
SCENTED
SCEPTER
SCOOTED
SCOOTER
SCOUTED
SCOUTER
SEDATED
SEDATER
SEDATES
SEMITES
SENATES
SHAFTED
SHANTEY
SHATTER
SHEETED
SHELTER
SHIFTED
SHIITES
SHOOTER
SHORTED
SHORTEN
SHORTER
SHOUTED
SHOUTER
SHUNTED
SHUTTER
SHYSTER
SIGHTED
SKEETER
SKELTER
SKIRTED
SKITTER
SLANTED
SLATTED
SLEETED
SLOTTED
SMARTED
SMARTEN
SMARTER
SMATTER
SMELTED
SMELTER
SMITTEN
SNIFTER
SNOOTED
SNORTED
SNORTER
SOLUTES
SORITES
SPATTED
SPATTER
SPECTER
SPORTED
SPOTTED
SPOTTER
SPOUTED
SPOUTER
SPRITES
SPURTED
SPUTTER
STARTED
STARTER
STETTED
STILTED
STINTED
STOUTEN
STOUTER
STPETER
STUNTED
SVELTER
SWATTED
SWATTER
SWEATED
SWEATER
SWEETEN
SWEETER
SWELTER
SWIFTER
TAINTED
TAKETEN
TAPSTER
TAUNTED
TEMPTED
TEMPTER
THEATER
TIGHTEN
TIGHTER
TIPSTER
TOASTED
TOASTER
TOOKTEN
TREATED
TROTTED
TROTTER
TRUSTED
TRUSTEE
TRYSTED
TRYSTER
TWEETED
TWEETER
TWISTED
TWISTER
TWITTED
TWITTER
TWOSTEP
UNDATED
UNEATEN
UNRATED
UNSATED
UPDATED
UPDATES
VACATED
VACATES
VAULTED
VAULTER
VAUNTED
VAUNTER
VISITED
WEBSTER
WHETTED
WOOSTER
WORSTED
WRESTED
WRITTEN
YACHTED
ZAPATEO
ZAPOTEC
ZYGOTES

••••T•E

ADOPTEE
ANNETTE
APOSTLE

ARISTAE
BABETTE
BEASTIE
BEATTIE
BOLOTIE
BREATHE
BRISTLE
BRITTLE
BURETTE
CADETTE
CHORTLE
COLETTE
CULOTTE
DEVOTEE
DINETTE
DRAFTEE
ELECTEE
ENTITLE
EPISTLE
GAVOTTE
GAZETTE
GOLFTEE
GRANTEE
GRISTLE
HABITUE
KIRSTIE
LAFITTE
LAYETTE
LEGATEE
LETITBE
MANATEE
MOUNTIE
MUSETTE
NANETTE
NECKTIE
NIGHTIE
OPENTOE
ORNETTE
PALETTE
PHILTRE
PIASTRE
PIPETTE
PRATTLE
RETITLE
ROSETTE
SCEPTRE
SCOTTIE
SCUTTLE
SEATTLE
SHEATHE
SHELTIE
SHUTTLE
SKITTLE
SPECTRE
STARTLE
SUZETTE
SWEETIE
THEATRE
THISTLE
TRESTLE
TRUSTEE
WHISTLE
WHITTLE
WREATHE
WRESTLE
WYNETTE
YANGTZE

•••••TE

ACCRETE
ACETATE
ACOLYTE
ACONITE
ACTUATE
ADAMITE
ADULATE
AGITATE
AIRDATE
ALDENTE
ANDANTE
ANIMATE
ANNETTE
APATITE
ARTISTE
ASTARTE
ATHLETE
ATTRITE
AUGUSTE
AUREATE
AZURITE
BABETTE
BATISTE
BAUXITE
BOXKITE
BROMATE
BURETTE
CADETTE
CALCITE
CELESTE
CILIATE
CITRATE
CLIMATE
COGNATE
COLETTE
COLGATE
COLLATE
COMMUTE
COMPETE
COMPOTE
COMPUTE
CONFUTE
CONNOTE
CORDATE
CORDITE
CULOTTE
CUTRATE
DEFLATE
DENTATE
DEPLETE
DESPITE
DETENTE
DEVIATE
DICTATE
DINETTE
DISPUTE
DUEDATE
DURANTE
EBONITE
EBWHITE
EDUCATE
EGALITE
ELEVATE
EMANATE
EMIRATE
EMULATE
ENROUTE
ENSUITE
ENTENTE
EREMITE
ERUDITE
ESTHETE
EXCRETE
EXECUTE
EXPARTE
EXPIATE
FERRATE
FERRITE
FOLIATE
FRIGATE
GAVOTTE
GAZETTE
GEFILTE
GESTATE
GRANITE
HIRSUTE
HITTITE
HYDRATE
IMAMATE
IMITATE
INFLATE
INGRATE
INHASTE
INSTATE
ISOLATE
ITERATE
JADEITE
KEYNOTE
LABIATE
LACOSTE
LACTATE
LAFITTE
LAPORTE
LAYETTE
LIGNITE
LINEATE
LISENTE
LUDDITE
MACHETE
MAGNATE
MAJESTE
MALEATE
MANDATE
MARGATE
MEDIATE
MIGRATE
MISDATE
MISMATE
MODISTE
MUSETTE
NAIVETE
NANETTE
NARRATE
NEONATE
NEWGATE
NITRATE
NITRITE
OBVIATE
OFFSITE
ONADATE
ONENOTE
OPERATE
ORIENTE
ORNETTE
OUTVOTE
OVERATE
PALETTE
PALMATE
PAPEETE
PARTITE
PELTATE
PENNATE
PERLITE
PICANTE
PINNATE
PIPETTE
PLACATE
POLLUTE
PREDATE
PRELATE
PRIMATE
PRIVATE
PROBATE
PROMOTE
PRORATE
PULSATE
QUIXOTE
RADIATE
RANLATE
REBASTE
REPASTE
REPLATE
REPLETE
REQUITE
REROUTE
RESPITE
RESTATE
REUNITE
REWRITE
REWROTE
RIPOSTE
ROSEATE
ROSETTE
RUNLATE
SATIATE
SEAGATE
SECRETE
SENSATE
SERIATE
SERRATE
SITUATE
SORBATE
STATUTE
STRIATE
SULFATE
SULFITE
SUZETTE
TAXRATE
TEKTITE
TERMITE
TERNATE
TITRATE
TRIBUTE
TRIESTE
ULULATE
UNCRATE
UNQUOTE
UPSTATE
URANITE
VALUATE
VALVATE
VIBRATE
VIOLATE
VIRTUTE
VITIATE
VULGATE
WEBSITE
WYNETTE

T•F••••

TAFFETA
TAFFIES
TIFFANY
TIFFING
TIFFINS
TOFFEES
TOFFLER
TUFFETS
TUFTIER
TUFTING

T••F•••

TAFFETA
TAFFIES
TAXFREE
TENFOLD
TENFOUR
THEFIRM
THEFONZ
TIFFANY
TIFFING
TIFFINS
TINFOIL
TITFERS
TOFFEES
TOFFLER
TOMFOOL
TRAFFIC
TREFOIL
TRIFLED
TRIFLER
TRIFLES
TRUFFLE
TUFFETS
TURFIER
TURFWAR
TWOFERS
TWOFOLD

T•••F••

TACTFUL
TAILFIN
TANKFUL
TARIFFS
TEARFUL
TESTFLY
THRIFTS
THRIFTY
THUSFAR
TIPOFFS
TOILFUL
TRAFFIC
TRAYFUL
TRUFFLE
TUNEFUL
TWELFTH

T••••F•

TAILOFF
TAKEOFF
TAPSOFF
TARIFFS
TEAROFF
TEEDOFF
TEESOFF
TELLOFF
TERRIFY
TESTIFY
TICKOFF
TIMEOFF
TIPOFFS
TIPSOFF
TOLDOFF
TOOKOFF
TOPSOFF
TOREOFF
TORNOFF
TOSSOFF
TURNOFF

T•••••F

TAILOFF
TAKEOFF
TAPSOFF
TEALEAF
TEAROFF
TEEDOFF
TEESOFF
TELLOFF
TELLSOF
THEREOF
THINKOF
THYSELF
TICKOFF
TIMEOFF
TIPSOFF
TIREDOF
TOLDOFF
TOOKOFF
TOPSOFF
TOREOFF
TORNOFF
TOSSOFF
TURNOFF

•TF••••

ATFAULT

•T•F•••

STAFFED
STAFFER
STIFFED
STIFFEN
STIFFER
STIFFLY
STIFLED
STIFLES
STUFFED
STUFFER

•T••F••

STAFFED
STAFFER
STIFFED
STIFFEN
STIFFER
STIFFLY
STIRFRY
STRAFED
STRAFES
STUFFED
STUFFER

•T•••F•

STOPOFF
STUPEFY

•T••••F

STOPOFF

••TF•••

ACTFIVE
ACTFOUR
ANTFARM
ARTFILM
ARTFORM
CATFISH
CATFOOD
HOTFOOT
MITFORD
OUTFACE
OUTFITS
OUTFLOW
PITFALL
POTFULS
RATFINK
TITFERS
VATFULS

••T•F••

ANTIFOG
CUTOFFS
DUTIFUL
FATEFUL
HATEFUL
LATIFAH
LETSFLY
OPTSFOR
OUTOFIT
PITIFUL
RATAFIA
ROTIFER
RUTHFUL
VOTEFOR

••T••F•

BITEOFF
CUTOFFS
CUTSOFF
GETSOFF
LETSOFF
PETRIFY
PUTSOFF
SATISFY
SETSOFF
VITRIFY

••T•••F

BITEOFF
CUTSOFF
GETSOFF
LETSOFF
NETSURF
ONTOPOF
PUTSOFF
SETSOFF

•••TF••

FACTFUL
FELTFOR
FISTFUL
FRETFUL
HEATFUL
HURTFUL
LUSTFUL
PLOTFUL
POUTFUL
RESTFUL
ROOTFOR
SENTFOR
SHOTFOR
TACTFUL
TESTFLY
WAITFOR
WENTFOR
WHATFOR
WISTFUL
ZESTFUL

•••T•F•

BEATIFY
CASTOFF
CERTIFY
DISTAFF
DUSTOFF
FORTIFY
GRATIFY
JUSTIFY
KEPTOFF
LEFTOFF
LIFTOFF
MASTIFF
MORTIFY
MUSTAFA
MYSTIFY
PONTIFF
RECTIFY
SANTAFE
SENTOFF
SHUTOFF
TESTIFY
WENTOFF

•••T••F

CASTOFF
DISTAFF
DUSTOFF
KEPTOFF
LEFTOFF
LIFTOFF
MASTIFF
PONTIFF
SENTOFF
SHUTOFF
WENTOFF

••••T•F

SHORTOF

T•G••••

TAGALOG
TAGENDS
TAGGANT
TAGGING
TAGLIKE
TAGLINE
TAGSALE
TAGSOUT
TAGTEAM
TIGHTEN
TIGHTER
TIGHTLY
TIGLONS
TIGRESS
TIGRISH
TOGGERY
TOGGING
TOGGLED
TOGGLES
TUGBOAT
TUGGERS
TUGGING
TUGLESS
TUGRIKS
TVGUIDE

T••G•••

TAGGANT
TAGGING
TANGELO
TANGENT
TANGERE
TANGIER
TANGLED
TANGLES
TANGOED
TANGRAM
TARGETS
TINGING
TINGLED
TINGLES
TOGGERY
TOGGING
TOGGLED
TOGGLES
TONGANS
TONGUED
TONGUES
TOPGUNS
TOUGHEN
TOUGHER
TOUGHIE
TOUGHLY
TRAGEDY
TRIGGED
TRIGGER
TRIGONS
TRIGRAM
TROGONS
TUGGERS
TUGGING
TUNGOIL

T•••G••

TANAGER
TEARGAS
THOUGHT
TLINGIT
TONIGHT
TRIGGED
TRIGGER
TROUGHS
TRUDGED
TRUDGER
TRUDGES
TWANGED
TWINGED
TWINGES
TYINGIN
TYINGUP

T••••G•

TAPINGS
TEABAGS
TEENAGE
THEURGY
THRONGS
THROUGH
TIDINGS
TILINGS
TILLAGE
TIMINGS
TONNAGE
TOPDOGS
TOYDOGS
TRILOGY
TUAREGS

T•••••G

TABBING
TABLING
TACKING
TAGALOG
TAGGING
TAILING
TALKBIG
TALKING
TAMPING
TANKING
TANNING
TAPPING
TARRING
TASKING
TASTING
TATTING
TAXIING
TEAMING
TEARING
TEASING
TEDDING
TEEMING
TELLING
TENDING
TENSING
TENTING
TENZING
TERMING
TESTING
THAWING
TICKING
TIDYING
TIERING
TIFFING
TILLING
TILTING
TIMELAG
TINGING
TINTING
TIPPING
TITHING
TITLING
TITRING
TOGGING
TOILING
TOLLING
TOOLING
TOOTING
TOPPING
TOSSING
TOTEBAG
TOTTING
TOURING
TOUTING
TRACING
TRADING
TREEING
TRUEING
TUCKING
TUFTING
TUGGING
TUMMING
TURNING
TWINING

•T•G•••

ETAGERE
STAGERS
STAGGED
STAGGER
STAGIER
STAGILY
STAGING
STIGMAS
STOGIES
STYGIAN

•T••G••

ATINGLE
STAGGED
STAGGER
STEIGER
STENGEL
STIEGEL
STINGER
STINGOS
STOOGES
STOPGAP
STUNGUN
STURGES

•T•••G•

ATLARGE
STALAGS
STORAGE
STRANGE
STRINGS
STRINGY

•T••••G

ATONING
ETCHING
ITCHING
STAGING
STAKING
STARING
STATING
STAVING
STAYING
STEWING
STOKING
STONING
STORING
STOWING
STYLING

••TG•••

BATGIRL
JETGUNS
OUTGOES
OUTGREW
OUTGROW
OUTGUNS
RUTGERS

••T•G••

ANTIGEN
ANTIGUA
FATIGUE
INTEGER
INTEGRA
LITHGOW
MUTAGEN
OCTAGON
OUTAGES
POTAGES
UPTIGHT

••T••G•

COTTAGE
HOTDOGS
KITBAGS
LITURGY
NUTMEGS
ONTHEGO
OUTINGS
OUTRAGE
POTTAGE
RATINGS
WATTAGE

••T•••G

ANTEING
ANTIFOG
ANTILOG
ARTSONG
BATHING
BATTING
BATWING
BETTING
BITTING
BUTTING
CATALOG
CATTING
CUTTING
DOTTING
FITTING
FUTZING
GATELEG
GATLING
GETTING
GUTTING
HATTING
HITTING
JETTING
JOTTING
JUTTING
LATHING
LETTING
LOTTING
MATTING
MITRING
NETTING
NOTHING
NUTTING
PATTING
PETTING
PITHING
PITTING
PITYING
POTTING
PUTTING
RATTING
ROTTING
SETTING
SITTING
TATTING
TITHING
TITLING
TITRING
TOTEBAG
TOTTING
UNTYING
VATTING
VETOING
VETTING
WETTING
WITTING

•••TG••

RONTGEN
SHOTGUN

•••T•G•

CARTAGE
CORTEGE
COTTAGE
DOGTAGS
FOOTAGE
HOSTAGE
LENTIGO
MONTAGE
MONTEGO
NESTEGG
ONSTAGE
PHOTOGS
PORTAGE
POSTAGE
POTTAGE
PROTEGE
RESTAGE
UPSTAGE
VANTAGE
VERTIGO
VESTIGE
VINTAGE
VOLTAGE
WASTAGE
WATTAGE

•••T••G

ABATING
ACHTUNG
BAITING
BASTING
BATTING
BEATING
BELTBAG
BELTING
BESTING
BETTING
BITTING
BOATING
BOLTING
BOOTING
BOOTLEG
BUNTING
BUSTING
BUTTING
CANTING
CARTING
CASTING
CATTING
COATING
COSTING
CRATING
CUTTING
DARTING
DENTING
DIETING
DOTTING
DUCTING
DUSTING
EDITING
ELATING
ELUTING
EMOTING
EXITING
FASTING
FITTING
FLUTING
FOOTING
GAITING
GETTING
GRATING
GUSTING
GUTTING
HAFTING
HALTING
HASTING
HATTING
HEATING
HEFTING
HENTING
HINTING
HITTING
HOOTING
HOSTING
HUNTING
HURTING
JESTING
JETTING
JILTING
JOLTING
JOTTING
JUTTING
KILTING
LASTING
LETTING
LIFTING
LILTING
LISTING
LOFTING
LOOTING
LOTTING
LUSTING
MALTING
MATTING
MEETING
MELTING
MINTING
MISTING
MOLTING
MUSTANG
NESTEGG
NESTING
NETTING
NUTTING
ORATING
OUSTING
PANTING
PARTING
PASTING
PATTING
PEATBOG
PELTING
PETTING
PITTING
PLATING
POSTBAG
POSTING
POTTING
POUTING
PRATING
PUNTING
PUTTING
QUOTING
RAFTING
RANTING
RATTING
RENTING
RESTING
RIFTING
RIOTING
ROOTING
ROTTING
ROUTING
RUSTING
SALTING
SEATING
SETTING
SIFTING
SILTING
SITTING
SKATING
SLATING
SMITING
SORTING
SPITING
STATING
SUITING
TASTING
TATTING
TENTING
TESTING
TILTING
TINTING
TOOTING
TOTTING
TOUTING
TUFTING
UNITING
VATTING
VENTING
VESTING
VETTING
WAFTING
WAITING
WANTING
WARTHOG
WASTING
WELTING
WETTING
WHITING
WILTING
WITTING
WRITING
XRATING

ZEITUNG

••••T•G
NAMETAG

TH•••••
THALERS
THANKED
THATCHY
THATSIT
THAWING
THEATER
THEATRE
THEBABE
THEBLOB
THECARS
THECROW
THEDEEP
THEFIRM
THEFONZ
THEISTS
THENARS
THEOMEN
THEOREM
THEPITS
THERAPY
THEREAT
THEREBY
THEREIN
THERELL
THEREOF
THEREON
THERESA
THERETO
THERMAL
THERMOS
THEROUX
THESEUS
THESPIS
THEURGY
THEWIER
THICKEN
THICKER
THICKET
THICKLY
THIEVED
THIEVES
THIMBLE
THIMPHU
THINAIR
THINICE
THINKER
THINKOF
THINKUP
THINNED
THINNER
THIRDLY
THIRSTS
THIRSTY
THISTLE
THISTLY
THITHER
THOMSON
THOREAU
THORIUM
THOUGHT
THRALLS
THREADS
THREADY
THREATS
THREEAM
THREEPM
THREERS
THREWIN
THRIFTS
THRIFTY
THRILLS
THRIVED
THRIVES
THROATS
THROATY
THRONES
THRONGS
THROUGH
THROWER
THROWIN
THRUSTS
THRUWAY
THUDDED
THULIUM
THUMBED
THUMPED
THUMPER
THUNDER
THURBER
THURMAN
THUSFAR
THWACKS
THWARTS
THYMINE
THYSELF

T•H••••
TEHERAN
TSHIRTS

T••H•••
TARHEEL
TASHLIN
TASHMAN
TECHIER
TECHIES
TERHUNE
TETHERS
TIGHTEN
TIGHTER
TIGHTLY
TINHATS
TINHORN
TITHERS
TITHING
TOEHOLD
TOPHATS
TOPHOLE
TOSHIBA
TOWHEAD
TOWHEES
TUCHMAN
TVSHOWS
TYPHOON

T•••H••
TEACHER
TEACHES
TEACHIN
TEASHOP
TEETHED
TEETHER
TEETHES
TEICHER
TENTHLY
TETCHED
THITHER
TOESHOE
TOOTHED
TORCHED
TORCHES
TOUCHED
TOUCHES
TOUCHON
TOUCHUP
TOUGHEN
TOUGHER
TOUGHIE
TOUGHLY
TOYSHOP
TRACHEA
TRASHED
TRASHES
TRISHAW
TROCHEE
TROCHES
TROPHIC
TROTHED

T••••H•
TABITHA
TALLYHO
TEMPEHS
TERAPHS
THATCHY
THIMPHU
THOUGHT
TIMOTHY
TONIGHT
TROUGHS
TWITCHY

T•••••H
TALLISH
TANNISH
TARNISH
TARTISH
THROUGH
TIGRISH
TOADISH
TONNISH
TORYISH
TOWNISH
TOWPATH
TRIUMPH
TURKISH
TWELFTH

•TH••••
ATHEART
ATHEISM
ATHEIST
ATHIRST
ATHLETE
ATHOMES
ATHWART
ETHANOL
ETHICAL
ETHNICS
ITHACAN
OTHELLO

•T•H•••
ETCHANT
ETCHERS
ETCHING
ITCHIER
ITCHING
UTAHANS

•T••H••
STASHED
STASHES
STEPHEN
STICHES
STJOHNS

•T•••H•
ATROPHY
ATTACHE
STARCHY
STROPHE
UTRECHT

•T••••H
STAUNCH
STEALTH
STOMACH
STRETCH
STYLISH

••TH•••
AETHERS
ANTHEMS
ANTHERS
ANTHILL
ANTHONY
AUTHORS
BATHERS
BATHING
BATHMAT
BATHOIL
BATHTUB
BETHANY
BETHELS
BETHINK
BOTHERS
BOTHNIA
BYTHEBY
CATHAIR
CATHEAD
CATHODE
DITHERS
DITHERY
ENTHRAL
ENTHUSE
ESTHETE
FATHEAD
FATHERS
FATHOMS
GATHERS
GOTHICS
GUTHRIE
HITHERE
HOTHEAD
ISTHMUS
KATHRYN
LATHERS
LATHERY
LATHING
LITHELY
LITHEST
LITHGOW
LITHIUM
MATHERS
MATHEWS
MATHIAS
METHANE
METHODS
MITHRAS
MOTHERS
MOTHIER
NOTHING
ONTHEGO
ONTHEQT
OUTHITS
PATHWAY
PITHIER
PITHILY
PITHING
POTHERB
POTHERS
POTHOLE
POTHOOK
PYTHIAN
PYTHIAS
PYTHONS
RATHOLE
RETHINK
RUTHFUL
SOTHERE
SOTHERN
TETHERS
TITHERS
TITHING
WETHERS
WITHERS
WITHIER
WITHIES
WITHOUT
ZITHERS

••T•H••
AITCHES
BATCHED
BATCHES
BOTCHED
BOTCHES
BOTCHUP
BUTCHER
CATCHER
CATCHES
CATCHON
CATCHUP
CATSHOW
DITCHED
DITCHES
FETCHED
FETCHES
FITCHES
GOTCHAS
HATCHED
HATCHER
HATCHES
HATCHET
HITCHED
HITCHER
HITCHES
HOTSHOT
HUTCHES
KETCHAM
KETCHES
KETCHUP
KITCHEN
KUTCHIN
LATCHED
LATCHES
LITCHIS
MATCHED
MATCHES
MATCHUP
MATTHAU
MATTHEW
MITCHUM
NATCHEZ
NOTCHED
NOTCHES
PATCHED
PATCHES
PATCHUP
PITCHED
PITCHER
PITCHES
PITCHIN
POTSHOT
RATCHET
SATCHEL
SATCHMO
TETCHED
VETCHES
WATCHED
WATCHER
WATCHES
WATCHIT
WITCHES
YITZHAK

••T••H•
ATTACHE
HITACHI
KITSCHY
MATZOHS
NATASHA
UPTIGHT
VOTECHS

••T•••H
ANTIOCH
BETROTH
CATFISH
CATTISH
FATTISH
INTRUTH
JETWASH
LATIFAH
LETTISH
MITZVAH
OSTRICH
PETTISH
RATTISH
RETEACH
RETOUCH
RUTTISH
SOTTISH
UNTRUTH
WETTISH

•••TH••
ANOTHER
APOTHEM
BENTHAM
BERTHED
BIRTHED
BLATHER
BLITHER
BOOTHIA
BROTHER
CHATHAM
CLOTHED
CLOTHES
CYNTHIA
EARTHEN
EARTHLY
EPITHET
FARTHER
FEATHER
FIFTHLY
FROTHED
FURTHER
GODTHAB
GUNTHER
HEATHEN
HEATHER
LEATHER
LOATHED
LOATHES
MALTHUS
MATTHAU
MATTHEW
MENTHOL
MONTHLY
MOUTHED
NARTHEX
NEITHER
NINTHLY
NORTHER
PANTHER
PORTHOS
PRITHEE
REUTHER
RHYTHMS
SCATHED
SCATHES
SCYTHED
SCYTHES
SEETHED
SEETHES
SIXTHLY
SLATHER
SLITHER
SMOTHER
SOOTHED
SOOTHER
SOOTHES
SOUTHEY
SWATHED
SWATHES
TEETHED
TEETHER
TEETHES
TENTHLY
THITHER
TOOTHED
TROTHED
WARTHOG
WEATHER
WERTHER
WHETHER
WHITHER
WRITHED
WRITHES
XANTHAN
XANTHIC

•••T•H•
BLOTCHY
SKETCHY
SNITCHY
THATCHY
TWITCHY

•••T••H
BRITISH
BRUTISH
CALTECH
CATTISH
COLTISH
CULTISH
DIPTYCH
DOLTISH
FATTISH
GOATISH
GOUTISH
KENTISH
KLATSCH
LETTISH
LOUTISH
LOWTECH
PELTISH
PETTISH
PICTISH
RATTISH
RUNTISH
RUTTISH
SALTISH
SOFTISH
SOTTISH
TARTISH
WETTISH
WHITISH

••••TH•
ACANTHI
BREATHE
BREATHS
BREATHY
BYPATHS
DALETHS
DEARTHS
DOROTHY
EIGHTHS
EMPATHY
EOLITHS
FOURTHS
GROWTHS
HEALTHY
HEARTHS
IOMOTHS
LENGTHS
LENGTHY
LESOTHO
NAPHTHA
OOLITHS
ORNITHO
PLINTHS
SHEATHE
SHEATHS
SLEUTHS
SMOOTHS
SMOOTHY
SWARTHY
TABITHA
TIMOTHY
WEALTHY
WRAITHS
WREATHE
WREATHS
ZENITHS

••••T•H
BEWITCH
CHEETAH
GODUTCH
INDUTCH
SCRATCH
SPLOTCH
STRETCH
UNHITCH
UNLATCH
WASATCH

•••••TH
ALWORTH
AZIMUTH
BENEATH
BETROTH
BISMUTH
BREADTH
CORINTH
DOZENTH
FORSYTH
GOLIATH
GWYNETH
HOGARTH
INDEPTH
INTRUTH
JACINTH
JAPHETH
KENNETH
KLAMATH
MACBETH
MAMMOTH
NCWYETH
NEOLITH
NESMITH
NEWMATH
REBIRTH
RUNWITH
SABBATH
SEVENTH
SOPWITH
STEALTH
SUNBATH
TOWPATH
TWELFTH
UNCOUTH
UNEARTH
UNTRUTH
WARPATH

TI•••••
TIANJIN
TIBETAN
TICKERS
TICKETS
TICKETY
TICKING
TICKLED
TICKLER
TICKLES
TICKOFF
TICTACS
TIDBITS
TIDIEST
TIDINGS
TIDYING
TIECLIP
TIEDOWN
TIEDYED
TIEDYES
TIEINTO
TIELESS
TIELINE
TIEPINS
TIEPOLO
TIERACK
TIERING
TIERNEY
TIERODS
TIETACK
TIFFANY
TIFFING
TIFFINS
TIGHTEN
TIGHTER
TIGHTLY
TIGLONS
TIGRESS
TIGRISH
TIJUANA
TILINGS
TILLAGE
TILLERS
TILLING
TILTERS
TILTING
TIMBALE
TIMBALS
TIMBERS
TIMBRES
TIMECOP
TIMELAG
TIMEOFF
TIMEOUT
TIMESUP
TIMIDER
TIMIDLY
TIMINGS
TIMMINS
TIMOTHY
TINCANS
TINDERS
TINEARS
TINFOIL
TINGING
TINGLED
TINGLES
TINHATS
TINHORN
TINIEST
TINKERS
TINKLED
TINKLES
TINLIKE
TINNERS
TINNIER
TINNILY
TINSELS
TINSTAR
TINTACK
TINTERN
TINTERS
TINTING
TINTYPE
TINWARE
TINWORK
TINYTIM
TIOMKIN
TIPLESS
TIPOFFS
TIPPERS
TIPPETS
TIPPIER
TIPPING
TIPPLED
TIPPLER
TIPPLES
TIPSIER
TIPSILY
TIPSOFF
TIPSTER
TIPTOED
TIPTOES
TIPTOPS
TIRADES
TIREDER
TIREDLY
TIREDOF
TIREOUT
TISANES
TISSUES
TITANIA
TITANIC
TITBITS
TITFERS
TITHERS
TITHING
TITLING
TITLIST
TITMICE
TITRATE
TITRING
TITTERS
TITTLES
TITTUPS
TITULAR
TIZZIES

T•I••••
TAILEND
TAILFIN
TAILING
TAILLES
TAILOFF
TAILORS
TAINTED
TAIPANS
TBILISI
TEICHER
THICKEN
THICKER
THICKET
THICKLY
THIEVED
THIEVES
THIMBLE
THIMPHU
THINAIR
THINICE
THINKER
THINKOF
THINKUP
THINNED
THINNER
THIRDLY
THIRSTS
THIRSTY
THISTLE
THISTLY
THITHER
TLINGIT
TOILERS
TOILETS
TOILFUL
TOILING
TRIBUNE
TRIBUTE
TRICEPS
TRICKED
TRICKER
TRICKLE
TRICORN
TRICOTS
TRIDENT
TRIEDON
TRIESON
TRIESTE
TRIFLED
TRIFLER
TRIFLES
TRIGGED
TRIGGER
TRIGONS
TRIGRAM
TRIJETS
TRILLED
TRILLIN
TRILOGY
TRIMMED
TRIMMER
TRINITY
TRINKET
TRIODES
TRIPLED
TRIPLES
TRIPLET
TRIPLEX
TRIPODS
TRIPOLI
TRIPPED
TRIPPER
TRIPPET
TRIPSUP
TRIREME
TRISECT
TRISHAW
TRISTAN
TRISTAR
TRITELY
TRITEST
TRITIUM
TRITONE
TRITONS
TRIUMPH
TRIUNES
TRIVETS
TRIVIAL
TUITION
TWIDDLE
TWILLED
TWINBED
TWINGED
TWINGES
TWINING
TWINKLE
TWINKLY
TWINNED
TWIRLED
TWIRLER
TWISTED
TWISTER
TWITCHY
TWITTED
TWITTER
TYINGIN
TYINGUP

T••I•••
TABITHA
TACITLY
TACITUS
TAOISTS
TAPINGS
TAPINTO
TAPIOCA
TARIFFS
TATIANA
TAXICAB
TAXIING
TAXIMAN
TAXIMEN
TAXIWAY
TEDIOUS
TEDIUMS
TEPIDLY
THEISTS
THRIFTS
THRIFTY
THRILLS
THRIVED
THRIVES
TIDIEST
TIDINGS
TIEINTO
TILINGS
TIMIDER
TIMIDLY
TIMINGS
TINIEST
TONIEST
TONIGHT
TOPIARY
TOPICAL
TOTIDEM
TRAILED
TRAILER
TRAINED
TRAINEE
TRAINER
TRAIPSE
TRAITOR
TROIKAS
TROILUS
TRUISMS
TSHIRTS
TUBISTS
TUNICLE
TUNISIA
TWOIRON
TYPICAL
TYPIEST
TYPISTS

T•••I••
TABBIES
TABBING
TABLING
TACKIER
TACKILY
TACKING
TACTICS
TACTILE
TAFFIES
TAGGING
TAGLIKE
TAGLINE
TAILING
TALKIER
TALKIES
TALKING
TALLIED
TALLIER
TALLIES
TALLINN
TALLISH
TAMPICO
TAMPING
TANGIER
TANKING
TANLINE
TANNING
TANNINS
TANNISH
TANSIES
TANTIVY
TAPPING
TARDIER
TARDILY
TARNISH
TARPITS
TARRIED
TARRIER
TARRIES
TARRING
TARSIER
TARTISH
TASKING
TASTIER
TASTILY
TASTING
TATTIER
TATTILY
TATTING
TAURINE
TAWNIER
TAWNILY
TAXIING
TBILISI
TEAMING
TEARIER
TEARILY
TEARING
TEASING
TEATIME
TECHIER
TECHIES
TEDDIES
TEDDING
TEEMING
TEENIER
TEETIME
TEKTITE
TELLIES
TELLING
TENDING
TENNIEL
TENPINS
TENSILE
TENSING
TENSION
TENSIVE
TENTING
TENUITY
TENZING
TEQUILA
TERBIUM
TERMING
TERMINI
TERMITE
TERRIER
TERRIES
TERRIFY
TERTIAL
TESTIER
TESTIFY
TESTILY
TESTING
TEXTILE
THAWING
THEFIRM
THEPITS
THEWIER
THINICE
THORIUM
THULIUM
THYMINE
TICKING
TIDBITS
TIDYING
TIELINE
TIEPINS
TIERING
TIFFING
TIFFINS
TIGRISH
TILLING
TILTING
TIMMINS
TINGING
TINLIKE
TINNIER
TINNILY
TINTING
TIPPIER
TIPPING
TIPSIER
TIPSILY
TITBITS
TITHING
TITLING
TITLIST

TITMICE
TITRING
TIZZIES
TOADIED
TOADIES
TOADISH
TOCSINS
TODDIES
TOELIKE
TOGGING
TOILING
TOLKIEN
TOLLIES
TOLLING
TOMTITS
TONNISH
TONSILS
TONTINE
TOOLING
TOONIES
TOOTING
TOPKICK
TOPPING
TOPSIDE
TOROIDS
TORSION
TORYISH
TORYISM
TOSHIBA
TOSSING
TOTTING
TOURING
TOURISM
TOURIST
TOUTING
TOWNIES
TOWNISH
TOYLIKE
TRACING
TRADING
TREEING
TREVINO
TRINITY
TRITIUM
TRIVIAL
TROPICS
TROPISM
TRUCIAL
TRUEING
TSARINA
TSARIST
TSELIOT
TUBAIST
TUBBIER
TUBLIKE
TUCKING
TUFTIER
TUFTING
TUGGING
TUGRIKS
TUITION
TUMMIES
TUMMING
TUNNIES
TURBINE
TURBITS
TURFIER
TURKISH
TURNING
TURNIPS
TVGUIDE
TWINING
TWOBITS
TWOTIME
TZARINA

T••••I•

TABLOID
TAILFIN
TAKEAIM
TAKENIN
TAKESIN
TALARIA
TALKBIG
TAMARIN
TASHLIN
TATAMIS
TEACHIN
TELAVIV
TENDRIL
TERRAIN
THATSIT
THEREIN
THESPIS
THINAIR
THREWIN
THROWIN
TIANJIN
TIECLIP
TINFOIL
TINYTIM
TIOMKIN
TITANIA
TITANIC
TLINGIT
TOENAIL
TOOTSIE
TOPSAIL
TOPSOIL
TOTEMIC
TOUGHIE
TRADEIN
TRAFFIC
TRANSIT
TRAVAIL
TRAVOIS
TREFOIL
TREKKIE
TRELLIS
TREMAIN
TRILLIN
TROPHIC
TSOURIS
TUCKSIN
TUNEDIN
TUNESIN
TUNGOIL
TUNISIA
TURMOIL
TURNSIN
TWOONIE
TYINGIN

T•••••I

TBILISI
TERMINI
TOLSTOI
TOPKAPI
TORTONI
TRIPOLI
TSUNAMI
TYMPANI

•TI••••

ATINGLE
ATISSUE
ETIENNE
STICHES
STICKER
STICKTO
STICKUP
STIEGEL
STIFFED
STIFFEN
STIFFER
STIFFLY
STIFLED
STIFLES
STIGMAS
STILLED
STILLER
STILTED
STILTON
STIMULI
STINGER
STINGOS
STINKER
STINTED
STIPEND
STIPPLE
STIRFRY
STIRRED
STIRRER
STIRRUP
STIRSIN
STIRSUP
UTILISE
UTILITY
UTILIZE

•T•I•••

ATHIRST
ATRIUMS
ATTICUS
ATTIMES
ATTIRED
ATTIRES
ETHICAL
ETOILES
STAIDER
STAIDLY
STAINED
STAINER
STEIGER
STEINEM
STEINER
STKITTS
STOICAL
STRIATE
STRIDER
STRIDES
STRIKER
STRIKES
STRINGS
STRINGY
STRIPED
STRIPER
STRIPES
STRIVED
STRIVEN
STRIVER
STRIVES
UTRILLO

•T••I••

ATAVISM
ATAVIST
ATELIER
ATHEISM
ATHEIST
ATOMIES
ATOMISE
ATOMIZE
ATONIES
ATONING
ATTAINS
ATTRITE
ATTRITS
ETAMINE
ETCHING
ETESIAN
ETHNICS
ETONIAN
ITALIAN
ITALICS
ITCHIER
ITCHING
ITEMISE
ITEMIZE
STABILE
STADIUM
STAGIER
STAGILY
STAGING
STAKING
STAMINA
STARING
STATICE
STATICS
STATING
STATION
STATIST
STAVING
STAYING
STEPINS
STERILE
STEWING
STOGIES
STOKING
STONIER
STONILY
STONING
STORIED
STORIES
STORING
STOWING
STRAINS
STRAITS
STUDIED
STUDIES
STUDIOS
STYGIAN
STYLING
STYLISE
STYLISH
STYLIST
STYLIZE
STYMIED
STYMIES
STYRIAN
UTILISE
UTILITY
UTILIZE
UTOPIAN
UTOPIAS
YTTRIUM

•T•••I•

ETRURIA
KTOSLIN
STANDIN
STANNIC
STARLIT
STCROIX
STDENIS
STEELIE
STENCIL
STEPSIN
STEROID
STIRSIN
STLOUIS
STLUCIA
STOODIN
STOOLIE
STOPSIN
STYPTIC
UTENSIL

•T••••I

STIMULI

••TI•••

ACTINIC
ACTIONS
ACTIVES
ANTIART
ANTIBES
ANTIFOG
ANTIGEN
ANTIGUA
ANTILOG
ANTIOCH
ANTIQUE
ANTITAX
ANTIWAR
ARTICLE
ARTIEST
ARTISAN
ARTISTE
ARTISTS
ATTICUS
ATTIMES
ATTIRED
ATTIRES
BATIKED
BATISTA
BATISTE
BETIDED
BETIDES
BETIMES
BETISES
CATIONS
CITIZEN
CUTICLE
CUTINTO
DUTIFUL
ENTICED
ENTICER
ENTICES
ENTITLE
ESTIVAL
EXTINCT
FATIGUE
FETIDLY
GETINTO
GETITON
GOTINTO
GOTITON
LATICES
LATIFAH
LATINAS
LATINOS
LETINON
LETITBE
LETITIA
LITINTO
LOTIONS
LUTISTS
MATILDA
MATINEE
MATISSE
METIERS
MOTIONS
MOTIVES
NATIONS
NATIVES
NETIZEN
NOTICED
NOTICES
NOTIONS
OPTICAL
OPTIMAL
OPTIMUM
OPTIONS
OUTINGS
PATIENT
PATINAS
PETIOLE
PETITES
PITIERS
PITIFUL
POTIONS
PUTITTO
RATINGS
RATIONS
RATITES
RETIARY
RETICLE
RETILED
RETILES
RETIMED
RETIMES
RETINAE
RETINAL
RETINAS
RETINUE
RETIRED
RETIREE
RETIRES
RETITLE
ROTIFER
SATIATE
SATIETY
SATINET
SATIRES
SATIRIC
SATISFY
SETINTO
SHTICKS
TATIANA
TOTIDEM
ULTIMAS
UPTICKS
UPTIGHT
USTINOV
VATICAN
VITIATE

••T•I••

ACTFIVE
ANTEING
ANTHILL
ANTLIKE
ANTLION
ANTOINE
ANTSIER
ARTFILM
ARTSIER
ASTAIRE
ASTRIDE
ATTAINS
ATTRITE
ATTRITS
BATGIRL
BATHING
BATLIKE
BATTIER
BATTING
BATWING
BETHINK
BETTING
BETWIXT
BITSIER
BITTIER
BITTING
BUTTIES
BUTTING
CATBIRD
CATFISH
CATKINS
CATLIKE
CATNIPS
CATTIER
CATTILY
CATTING
CATTISH
CITRINE
CUTTIME
CUTTING
DETAILS
DETAINS
DITSIER
DITTIES
DITZIER
DOTLIKE
DOTTIER
DOTTILY
DOTTING
ENTAILS
ENTRIES
ENTWINE
FATCITY
FATLIKE
FATTIER
FATTILY
FATTISH
FATUITY
FITTING
FUTZING
GATLING
GETTING
GOTHICS
GUTSIER
GUTSILY
GUTTIER
GUTTING
HATLIKE
HATPINS
HATTING
HITLIST
HITTING
HITTITE
HOTLINE
HOTLINK
HOTLIPS
HOTTIPS
HOTWIRE
HUTLIKE
INTUITS
JETTIES
JETTING
JOTTING
JUTTIED
JUTTIES
JUTTING
KITTIES
LATHING
LATTICE
LATVIAN
LETTING
LETTISH
LITHIUM
LOTTING
MATHIAS
MATTING
METRICS
MITRING
MOTHIER
NATRIUM
NATTIER
NATTILY
NETLIKE
NETTING
NITPICK
NITRIDE
NITRITE
NITTIER
NITWITS
NOTHING
NUTLIKE
NUTRIAS
NUTSIER
NUTTIER
NUTTILY
NUTTING
OATLIKE
OBTAINS
ONTRIAL
OSTRICH
OUTBIDS
OUTFITS
OUTHITS
OUTLINE
OUTLIVE
OUTSIDE
OUTSIZE
OUTWITS
PATRIAL
PATRICE
PATRICK
PATRIOT
PATSIES
PATTIES
PATTING
PETRIFY
PETTIER
PETTILY
PETTING
PETTISH
PITHIER
PITHILY
PITHING
PITTING
PITYING
POTPIES
POTSIER
POTTIER
POTTING
PUTTIED
PUTTIES
PUTTING
PYTHIAN
PYTHIAS
RATFINK
RATLIKE
RATLINE
RATTIER
RATTING
RATTISH
RETAILS
RETAINS
RETHINK
RETRIAL
RETRIED
RETRIES
RETRIMS
RETSINA
RITZIER
RITZILY
ROTTING
RUTTIER
RUTTISH
SETLINE
SETTING
SITTING
SOTTISH
TATTIER
TATTILY
TATTING
TITBITS
TITHING
TITLING
TITLIST
TITMICE
TITRING
TOTTING
UNTRIED
UNTWIST
UNTYING
VATTING
VETOING
VETTING
VITRIFY
VITRIOL
WETTING
WETTISH
WITHIER
WITHIES
WITTIER
WITTILY
WITTING
YTTRIUM

••T••I•

ACTINIC
ANTACID
ANTONIA
ANTONIN
ANTONIO
ARTEMIS
ASTORIA
BATHOIL
BOTHNIA
BUTTSIN
CATHAIR
CATSUIT
CATTAIL
CETERIS
COTERIE
DETRAIN
DETROIT
ENTRAIN
ESTONIA
ESTORIL
GUTHRIE
INTERIM
INTROIT
JETSKIS
KATYDID
KUTCHIN
LETITIA
LETSLIP
LITCHIS
LITCRIT
MITOSIS
MITOTIC
NATALIA
NATALIE
NOTABIT
OCTAVIA
OCTROIS
ONTARIO
OSTEOID
OUTLAID
OUTOFIT
PETUNIA
PITCHIN
QATARIS
RATAFIA
RATTAIL
RETRAIN
SATIRIC
SETSAIL
TATAMIS
TITANIA
TITANIC
TOTEMIC
VITAMIN
VOTEDIN
VOTESIN
WATCHIT
WETSUIT

••T•••I

HITACHI
KUTENAI

•••TI••

ABATING
ABITIBI
AIRTIME
ALLTIME
AMATIVE
ANYTIME
APATITE
ARETINO
AUCTION
AUNTIES
BAITING
BAPTISE
BAPTISM
BAPTIST
BAPTIZE
BASTING
BASTION
BATTIER
BATTING
BEATIFY
BEATING
BEDTIME
BELTING
BESTIAL
BESTING
BESTIRS
BETTING
BIGTIME
BITTIER
BITTING
BOATING
BOLTING
BOOTIES
BOOTING
BOWTIES
BRITISH
BRUTISH
BUNTING
BUSTING
BUTTIES
BUTTING
BUYTIME
CANTILY
CANTINA
CANTING
CAPTION
CAPTIVE
CARTIER
CARTING
CASTILE
CASTING
CATTIER
CATTILY
CATTING
CATTISH
CAUTION
CELTICS
CENTIME
CENTIMO
CERTIFY
COATING
COLTISH
COOTIES
COSTING
CRATING
CRETINS
CRITICS
CULTISH
CULTISM
CULTIST
CURTISS
CUTTIME
CUTTING
DARTING
DAYTIME
DEITIES
DENTINE
DENTING
DENTIST
DESTINE
DESTINY
DICTION
DIETING
DIRTIED
DIRTIER
DIRTIES
DIRTILY
DISTILL
DISTILS
DITTIES
DNOTICE
DOLTISH
DOTTIER
DOTTILY
DOTTING
DUCTILE
DUCTING
DUSTIER
DUSTILY
DUSTING
EBBTIDE
EDITING
EDITION
EGOTISM
EGOTIST
ELATING
ELATION
ELITISM
ELITIST
ELUTING
ELUTION
EMOTING
EMOTION
EMOTIVE
EMPTIED
EMPTIER
EMPTIES
EMPTILY
EROTICA
EXITING
EXOTICA
EXOTICS
FACTION
FASTING
FATTIER
FATTILY
FATTISH
FERTILE
FESTIVA
FESTIVE
FICTION
FICTIVE
FIFTIES
FITTING
FLUTIER
FLUTING
FLUTIST
FONTINA
FOOTING
FORTIES
FORTIFY
FORTIUS
FURTIVE
FUSTIAN
FUSTICS
FUSTIER
FUSTILY
GAITING
GENTIAN
GENTILE
GETTING
GOATISH
GOUTIER
GOUTILY
GOUTISH
GRATIAS
GRATIFY
GRATING
GUSTIER
GUSTILY
GUSTING
GUTTIER
GUTTING
HAFTING
HAITIAN
HALTING
HASTIER
HASTILY
HASTING
HATTING
HEATING
HEFTIER
HEFTILY
HEFTING
HENTING
HINTING
HITTING
HITTITE
HOGTIED
HOGTIES
HOOTING
HOSTILE
HOSTING
HOTTIPS
HUNTING
HURTING
INITIAL
INSTILL
INSTILS
INUTILE
JESTING
JETTIES
JETTING
JILTING
JOLTIER
JOLTING
JOTTING
JUSTICE
JUSTIFY
JUSTINE
JUTTIED
JUTTIES
JUTTING
KENTISH
KILTIES
KILTING
KITTIES
KONTIKI
KRATION
LAOTIAN
LASTING
LATTICE
LEETIDE
LEFTIES
LEFTIST
LENTIGO
LENTILS
LETTING
LETTISH
LIFTING
LILTING
LINTIER
LISTING
LOFTIER
LOFTILY
LOFTING
LOOTING
LOTTING
LOUTISH
LOWTIDE
LUSTIER
LUSTILY
LUSTING
MALTIER
MALTING
MARTIAL
MARTIAN
MARTINA
MARTINI
MARTINO
MARTINS
MASTICS
MASTIFF
MATTING
MAYTIME
MEATIER
MEATILY
MEETING
MELTING
MENTION
MESTIZA
MESTIZO
MINTIER
MINTING
MISTIER
MISTILY
MISTING
MOLTING
MORTIFY
MORTISE
MUNTINS
MUSTIER
MUSTILY
MYSTICS
MYSTIFY
NAPTIME
NASTIER
NASTILY
NATTIER
NATTILY
NESTING
NETTING
NIFTIER
NIFTILY
NITTIER
NOETICS
NUPTIAL
NUTTIER
NUTTILY
NUTTING
OLDTIME
ONETIME
ORATING
ORATION
OUSTING
OVATION
PANTING
PARTIAL
PARTIED
PARTIER
PARTIES
PARTING
PARTITA
PARTITE
PASTIER
PASTIME
PASTINA
PASTING
PATTIES
PATTING
PEATIER
PECTINS
PELTING
PELTISH
PENTIUM
PEPTIDE
PETTIER
PETTILY
PETTING
PETTISH
PHOTICS
PICTISH
PIETIES
PIETINS
PIETISM
PIETIST
PISTILS
PITTING
PLATIER
PLATING
POETICS
POITIER
PONTIAC
PONTIFF
PONTINE
PONTIUS
PORTICO
PORTION
POSTING
POSTITS
POTTIER
POTTING
POUTIER
POUTING
PRATING
PROTIST
PUNTIES
PUNTING

PUTTIED
PUTTIES
PUTTING
QUOTING
RAFTING
RAGTIME
RANTING
RATTIER
RATTING
RATTISH
RECTIFY
RENTING
REPTILE
RESTING
RESTIVE
RIFTING
RIOTING
RIPTIDE
ROOTIER
ROOTING
ROTTING
ROUTINE
ROUTING
RUCTION
RUNTIER
RUNTISH
RUSTICS
RUSTIER
RUSTILY
RUSTING
RUTTIER
RUTTISH
SALTIER
SALTILY
SALTINE
SALTING
SALTISH
SANTINI
SANTIRS
SEATING
SECTION
SESTINA
SETTING
SHUTINS
SIFTING
SILTIER
SILTING
SISTINE
SITTING
SIXTIES
SKATING
SLATIER
SLATING
SMITING
SOFTIES
SOFTISH
SOOTIER
SOOTILY
SORTIED
SORTIES
SORTING
SOTTISH
SPATIAL
SPITING
STATICE
STATICS
STATING
STATION
STATIST
SUCTION
SUITING
TACTICS
TACTILE
TANTIVY
TARTISH
TASTIER
TASTILY
TASTING
TATTIER
TATTILY
TATTING
TEATIME
TEETIME
TEKTITE
TENTING
TERTIAL
TESTIER
TESTIFY
TESTILY
TESTING
TEXTILE
TILTING
TINTING
TOMTITS
TONTINE
TOOTING
TOTTING
TOUTING
TRITIUM
TUFTIER
TUFTING
TUITION
TWOTIME
UNCTION
UNITIES
UNITING
UNITIVE
UNSTICK
VASTIER
VATTING
VENTING
VERTIGO
VESTIGE
VESTING
VETTING
VICTIMS
WAFTING
WAITING
WANTING
WARTIER
WARTIME
WASTING
WELTING
WETTING
WETTISH
WHITIER
WHITING
WHITISH
WILTING
WITTIER
WITTILY
WITTING
WRITING
XRATING
ZESTIER

•••T•I•

ABSTAIN
AUSTRIA
BEATNIK
BEATRIX
BEATSIT
BEATTIE
BOBTAIL
BOOTHIA
BRITAIN
BUTTSIN
CANTRIP
CAPTAIN
CATTAIL
CENTRIC
CERTAIN
CONTAIN
COSTAIN
CURTAIL
CURTAIN
CYNTHIA
DAYTRIP
DELTAIC
DELTOID
DEXTRIN
DUSTBIN
EGOTRIP
EPSTEIN
FACTOID
FANTAIL
FOOTSIE
FOXTAIL
GASTRIC
GLOTTIS
HOPTOIT
MAITAIS
MANTRIC
MASTOID
NOSTRIL
PERTAIN
PIGTAIL
PINTAIL
PROTEIN
RATTAIL
RESTAIN
SCOTTIE
SEETOIT
SHUTSIN
SPOTLIT
SPUTNIK
SUSTAIN
THATSIT
TOOTSIE
VOLTAIC
WAGTAIL
WANTSIN
WRITEIN
WROTEIN
XANTHIC
YELTSIN

•••T••I

ABITIBI
AIRTAXI
KONTIKI
MARTINI
MONTANI
PLATYPI
SANTINI
TORTONI

••••TI•

AGOUTIS
ALSATIA
AQUATIC
ASCETIC
ASEPTIC
ASIATIC
BEASTIE
BEATTIE
BOLOTIE
BUILTIN
CAROTID
CAUSTIC
CHAOTIC
CHEATIN
COEPTIS
CROATIA
CRYPTIC
DEALTIN
DRASTIC
ELASTIC
ERISTIC
ERRATIC
FANATIC
FOULTIP
FRANTIC
GALATIA
GELATIN
GELATIS
GENETIC
GLOTTIS
GNOSTIC
HAMITIC
HEPATIC
HERETIC
HORATIO
IDENTIC
IDIOTIC
INERTIA
KERATIN
KINETIC
KIRSTIE
LETITIA
LUNATIC
MEIOTIC
MILITIA
MIMETIC
MINUTIA
MITOTIC
MOUNTIE
NECKTIE
NIGHTIE
OSMOTIC
PIRATIC
PLASTIC
POLITIC
QUENTIN
ROBOTIC
RUBITIN
SCEPTIC
SCOTTIE
SEMITIC
SHELTIE
SKEPTIC
SLEPTIN
SOMATIC
STYPTIC
SWEETIE
TINYTIM
WAPITIS
WINGTIP

••••T•I

ACANTHI
DIMITRI
MAESTRI
MENOTTI
SCHATZI
SHASTRI
TOLSTOI

•••••TI

ASHANTI
CHAPATI
CHIANTI
CHRISTI
DELICTI
ELMISTI
EMERITI
HAVARTI
KUWAITI
MENOTTI

T•J••••

TIJUANA

T••J•••

TRIJETS
TROJANS

T•••J••

TIANJIN

•TJ••••

STJOHNS

••TJ•••

OUTJUMP

•••TJ••

CULTJAM

T•K••••

TAKEAIM
TAKENIN
TAKENON
TAKEOFF
TAKEONE
TAKEOUT
TAKESIN
TAKESON
TAKESTO
TAKESUP
TAKETEN
TEKTITE
TOKENED

T••K•••

TACKERS
TACKIER
TACKILY
TACKING
TACKLED
TACKLER
TACKLES
TACKSON
TALKBIG
TALKERS
TALKIER
TALKIES
TALKING
TALKOUT
TALKSAT
TALKSTO
TALKSUP
TANKARD
TANKERS
TANKFUL
TANKING
TANKSUP
TANKTOP
TASKING
TICKERS
TICKETS
TICKETY
TICKING
TICKLED
TICKLER
TICKLES
TICKOFF
TINKERS
TINKLED
TINKLES
TOLKIEN
TOOKOFF
TOOKOUT
TOOKTEN
TOPKAPI
TOPKICK
TOPKNOT
TREKKED
TREKKER
TREKKIE
TUCKERS
TUCKING
TUCKSIN
TURKEYS
TURKISH
TUSKERS

T•••K••

THANKED
THICKEN
THICKER
THICKET
THICKLY
THINKER
THINKOF
THINKUP
TIOMKIN
TRACKED
TRACKER
TREKKED
TREKKER
TREKKIE
TRICKED
TRICKER
TRICKLE
TRINKET
TROIKAS
TRUCKED
TRUCKEE
TRUCKER
TRUCKLE
TURNKEY
TWEAKED
TWINKLE
TWINKLY

T••••K•

TAGLIKE
TANOAKS
TEACAKE
THWACKS
TINLIKE
TOELIKE
TOYLIKE
TROTSKY
TUBLIKE
TUGRIKS

T•••••K

TEDMACK
TIERACK
TIETACK
TINTACK
TINWORK
TOPKICK
TUSSOCK

•TK••••

STKITTS

•T•K•••

STAKING
STOKELY
STOKERS
STOKING

•T••K••

STACKED
STACKUP
STALKED
STALKER
STARKER
STARKLY
STICKER
STICKTO
STICKUP
STINKER
STOCKED
STOCKUP
STOOKED
STOOKEY
STRIKER
STRIKES
STROKED
STROKES
STUCKTO
STUCKUP

•T•••K•

ATSTAKE
ATTACKS
ATTUCKS
STREAKS
STREAKY

•T••••K

ATATURK

••TK•••

CATKINS

••T•K••

BATIKED
BETAKEN
BETAKES
BETOKEN
INTAKES
JETSKIS
RETAKEN
RETAKES
UPTAKES

••T••K•

ANTLIKE
ATTACKS
ATTUCKS
AUTARKY
BATLIKE
CATLIKE
DOTLIKE
FATLIKE
HATLIKE
HOTCAKE
HUTLIKE
NETLIKE
NETSUKE
NUTLIKE
OATLIKE
OUTTAKE
RATLIKE
SHTICKS
UNTACKS
UPTICKS

••T•••K

ARTWORK
BETHINK
CATWALK
CUTBACK
FATBACK
FETLOCK
GETBACK
GOTBACK
HATRACK
HOTLINK
MATLOCK
MATTOCK
NETWORK
NITPICK
ONTRACK
OUTBACK
OUTLOOK
OUTRANK
OUTTALK
OUTWORK
PATRICK
PETCOCK
PETROCK
POTHOOK
POTLUCK
RATFINK
RATPACK
RETHINK
RETRACK
SETBACK
YITZHAK
ZATOPEK

•••T•K•

ATSTAKE
GRETZKY
KONTIKI
MISTAKE
OUTTAKE
PARTAKE
TROTSKY

•••T••K

ATATURK
BEATNIK
BIGTALK
DMYTRYK
INSTOCK
MATTOCK
MISTOOK
OUTTALK
PARTOOK
PEPTALK
RESTOCK
SPUTNIK
TIETACK
TINTACK
UNSTACK
UNSTICK
UNSTUCK

••••T•K

GANGTOK
OKHOTSK
YAKUTSK

TL•••••

TLINGIT

T•L••••

TALARIA
TALCUMS
TALENTS
TALKBIG
TALKERS
TALKIER
TALKIES
TALKING
TALKOUT
TALKSAT
TALKSTO
TALKSUP
TALLEST
TALLIED
TALLIER
TALLIES
TALLINN
TALLISH
TALLOWS
TALLYHO
TALLYUP
TALONED
TALUSES
TELAVIV
TELERAN
TELEXED
TELEXES
TELLALL
TELLERS
TELLIES
TELLING
TELLOFF
TELLSOF
TELLSON
TELSTAR
TILINGS
TILLAGE
TILLERS
TILLING
TILTERS
TILTING
TOLDOFF
TOLKIEN
TOLLIES
TOLLING
TOLLWAY
TOLSTOI
TOLSTOY
TOLTECS
TOLUENE
TULSANS
TYLENOL

T••L•••

TABLEAU
TABLETS
TABLING
TABLOID
TAGLIKE
TAGLINE
TAILEND
TAILFIN
TAILING
TAILLES
TAILOFF
TAILORS
TALLEST
TALLIED
TALLIER
TALLIES
TALLINN
TALLISH
TALLOWS
TALLYHO
TALLYUP
TANLINE
TAXLESS
TBILISI
TEALEAF
TEALESS
TELLALL
TELLERS
TELLIES
TELLING
TELLOFF
TELLSOF
TELLSON
THALERS
THULIUM
TIELESS
TIELINE
TIGLONS
TILLAGE
TILLERS
TILLING
TINLIKE
TIPLESS
TITLING
TITLIST
TOELESS
TOELIKE
TOELOOP
TOILERS
TOILETS
TOILFUL
TOILING
TOLLIES
TOLLING
TOLLWAY
TOOLBOX
TOOLING
TOOLSUP
TOYLAND
TOYLESS
TOYLIKE
TRALALA
TRELLIS
TRILLED
TRILLIN
TRILOGY
TROLLED
TROLLEY
TSELIOT
TUBLIKE
TUGLESS
TWELFTH
TWELVES
TWILLED
TWOLANE

T•••L••

TABULAR
TACKLED
TACKLER
TACKLES
TAGALOG
TAILLES
TAMALES
TANGLED
TANGLES
TASHLIN
TATTLED
TATTLER
TATTLES
TEMBLOR
TEMPLAR
TEMPLES
THEBLOB
THRALLS
THRILLS
TICKLED
TICKLER
TICKLES
TIECLIP
TIMELAG
TINGLED
TINGLES
TINKLED
TINKLES
TIPPLED
TIPPLER
TIPPLES
TITTLES
TITULAR
TODDLED
TODDLER
TODDLES
TOFFLER
TOGGLED
TOGGLES
TONALLY
TONELOC
TOOTLED
TOOTLES
TOPPLED
TOPPLES
TOTALED
TOTALLY
TOUSLED
TOUSLES
TOWELED
TRAILED
TRAILER
TRAWLED
TRAWLER
TREBLED
TREBLES
TRELLIS
TRIFLED
TRIFLER
TRIFLES
TRILLED
TRILLIN
TRIPLED
TRIPLES
TRIPLET
TRIPLEX
TROILUS
TROLLED
TROLLEY
TUBULAR
TUMBLED
TUMBLER
TUMBLES
TUMULTS
TUMULUS
TUPELOS
TURTLED
TURTLES
TUSSLED
TUSSLES
TUTELAR
TWILLED
TWIRLED
TWIRLER

T••••L•

TACITLY
TACKILY
TACTILE
TADPOLE
TAGSALE
TAMABLE
TAMBALA
TANGELO
TARBELL
TARDILY
TARSALS
TASSELS
TASTILY
TATTILY
TAWNILY
TAXABLE
TEABALL
TEARILY
TEASELS
TELLALL
TENABLE
TENABLY
TENFOLD
TENSELY
TENSILE
TENTHLY
TEPIDLY
TEQUILA
TERCELS
TERSELY
TESTFLY
TESTILY
TEXTILE
THERELL
THICKLY
THIMBLE
THIRDLY
THISTLE
THISTLY
THRALLS
THRILLS
THYSELF
TIEPOLO
TIGHTLY
TIMBALE
TIMBALS
TIMIDLY
TINNILY
TINSELS
TIPSILY
TIREDLY
TOEHOLD
TOMBOLA
TONALLY
TONSILS
TOPHOLE
TOSCALE
TOTALLY
TOUGHLY
TRALALA
TRAMPLE
TRAVELS
TREACLE
TREACLY
TREADLE
TREMBLE
TREMBLY
TREMOLO
TRESTLE
TRICKLE
TRIPOLI
TRITELY
TROUBLE
TROWELS
TRUCKLE
TRUFFLE
TRUNDLE
TUNICLE
TUNNELS
TWADDLE
TWIDDLE
TWINKLE
TWINKLY
TWOFOLD

T•••••L

TACTFUL
TANKFUL
TARBELL
TARHEEL
TEABALL
TEARFUL
TELLALL
TENDRIL
TENNIEL
TERTIAL
TEXTUAL
THERELL
THERMAL
TINFOIL
TOENAIL
TOILFUL
TOMFOOL
TOPICAL
TOPSAIL
TOPSOIL
TRAMMEL
TRAVAIL
TRAYFUL
TREFOIL
TRIVIAL
TRUCIAL
TUMBREL
TUNEFUL
TUNGOIL
TURMOIL
TYLENOL
TYPICAL

•TL••••

ATLANTA
ATLARGE
ATLASES
ATLATLS
ATLEAST
STLOUIS
STLUCIA

•T•L•••

ATALOSS
ATELIER
ATHLETE
ITALIAN
ITALICS
PTOLEMY
STALAGS
STALELY
STALEST
STALKED
STALKER
STALLED
STELLAR
STILLED
STILLER
STILTED
STILTON
STOLLEN
STOLLER
STOLONS
STYLERS
STYLETS
STYLING
STYLISE
STYLISH
STYLIST
STYLIZE
UTILISE
UTILITY
UTILIZE

•T••L••

ETOILES
KTOSLIN
OTHELLO
STABLED
STABLER
STABLES
STALLED
STANLEE
STANLEY
STAPLED
STAPLER
STAPLES
STARLET
STARLIT
STEALTH
STEELED
STEELER
STEELIE
STELLAR
STIFLED
STIFLES
STILLED
STILLER
STOLLEN
STOLLER
STOOLIE
STROLLS
UTRILLO

•T•••L•

ATFAULT
ATINGLE
ATLATLS
OTHELLO
STABILE
STAGILY
STAIDLY
STALELY
STARKLY
STARTLE
STATELY
STEEPLE
STEEPLY
STERILE
STERNLY
STEROLS
STIFFLY
STIMULI
STIPPLE
STOKELY
STONILY
STOUTLY
STROLLS
STUBBLE
STUBBLY
STUMBLE
UTRILLO
UTTERLY

•T••••L

ETERNAL
ETHANOL
ETHICAL
STENCIL
STENGEL
STERNAL
STIEGEL
STOICAL
STRUDEL
UTENSIL

••TL•••

ANTLERS

ANTLIKE
ANTLION
ARTLESS
BATLIKE
BITLESS
BUTLERS
CATLIKE
CUTLASS
CUTLERS
CUTLERY
CUTLETS
DOTLIKE
FATLESS
FATLIKE
FETLOCK
GATLING
GETLOST
GOTLAND
GOTLOST
GUTLESS
HATLESS
HATLIKE
HITLESS
HITLIST
HOTLINE
HOTLINK
HOTLIPS
HUTLIKE
JUTLAND
MATLESS
MATLOCK
NETLIKE
NUTLETS
NUTLIKE
OATLIKE
OSTLERS
OUTLAID
OUTLAND
OUTLAST
OUTLAWS
OUTLAYS
OUTLETS
OUTLINE
OUTLIVE
OUTLOOK
OUTLOUD
POTLUCK
RATLIKE
RATLINE
SETLINE
SUTLERS
TITLING
TITLIST
WETLAND
WITLESS

••T•L••

ANTILOG
ASTOLAT
BATTLED
BATTLER
BATTLES
BOTTLED
BOTTLER
BOTTLES
CATALAN
CATALOG
CATALPA
DOTTLES
ESTELLE
FETTLES
GATELEG
KETTLES
LETSLIP
LITTLER
MATELOT
MATILDA
METTLES
MOTTLED
MOTTLES
NATALIA
NATALIE
NETTLED
NETTLES
ORTOLAN
OUTFLOW
OUTPLAY
PATELLA
PETALED
POTTLES
RATTLED
RATTLER
RATTLES
RETELLS
RETILED
RETILES
SETTLED
SETTLER
SETTLES
TATTLED
TATTLER
TATTLES
TITTLES
TITULAR
TOTALED
TOTALLY
TUTELAR
VITALLY
VITTLES
WATTLES

••T••L•

ACTABLE
ANTHILL
ARTFILM
ARTICLE
BATTELS
BETHELS
CATCALL
CATTILY
CATWALK
CITABLE
CUTICLE
DATEDLY
DETAILS
DOTTILY
EATABLE
ENTAILS
ENTITLE
ESTELLE
FATTILY
FETIDLY
GETWELL
GOTWELL
GUTSILY
LETSFLY
LITHELY
MUTABLE
MUTABLY
MUTUALS
NATTILY
NOTABLE
NOTABLY
NOTEDLY
NOTWELL
NUTTILY
OCTUPLE
OUTPOLL
OUTSELL
OUTSOLD
OUTTALK
PATELLA
PATROLS
PETIOLE
PETRELS
PETROLS
PETTILY
PITBULL
PITFALL
PITHILY
POTABLE
POTFULS
POTHOLE
RATABLE
RATHOLE
RETAILS
RETELLS
RETICLE
RETITLE
RETOOLS
RITUALS
RITZILY
SITWELL
TATTILY
TOTALLY
UTTERLY
VATFULS
VITALLY
WETCELL
WITTILY

••T•••L

ANTHILL
APTERAL
BATGIRL
BATHOIL
BUTANOL
CATCALL
CATTAIL
CITADEL
DUTIFUL
ENTHRAL
ESTIVAL
ESTORIL
FATEFUL
GETREAL
GETWELL
GOTWELL
HATEFUL
LATERAL
LITERAL
NATURAL
NOTWELL
OATMEAL
ONTRIAL
OPTICAL
OPTIMAL
OUTPOLL
OUTSELL
PATRIAL
PITBULL
PITFALL
PITIFUL
RATTAIL
RETINAL
RETRIAL
RUTHFUL
SATCHEL
SETSAIL
SITWELL
VITRIOL
WETCELL

•••TL••

BATTLED
BATTLER
BATTLES
BEATLES
BEETLES
BENTLEY
BOOTLEG
BOTTLED
BOTTLER
BOTTLES
BUSTLED
BUSTLES
CANTLES
CASTLED
CASTLES
DOTTLES
FETTLES
FIATLUX
FLATLET
GANTLET
GENTLED
GENTLER
GENTLES
HOSTLER
HUNTLEY
HURTLED
HURTLES
HUSTLED
HUSTLER
HUSTLES
JOSTLED
JOSTLER
JOSTLES
KETTLES
KIRTLES
LITTLER
MANTLED
MANTLES
METTLES
MOTTLED
MOTTLES
MYRTLES
NESTLED
NESTLER
NESTLES
NETTLED
NETTLES
PESTLED
PESTLES
POTTLES
RATTLED
RATTLER
RATTLES
ROOTLET
RUSTLED
RUSTLER
RUSTLES
SETTLED
SETTLER
SETTLES
SPOTLIT
SUBTLER
TATTLED
TATTLER
TATTLES
TITTLES
TOOTLED
TOOTLES
TURTLED
TURTLES
VITTLES
WATTLES

•••T•L•

ACUTELY
ALLTOLD
ANATOLE
BATTELS
BERTOLT
BIGTALK
BOATELS
BRITTLE
BRUTELY
CANTILY
CARTELS
CASTILE
CATTILY
DACTYLS
DIRTILY
DISTILL
DISTILS
DOTTILY
DUCTILE
DUSTILY
EARTHLY
EMPTILY
FATTILY
FERTILE
FIFTHLY
FUSTILY
GENTILE
GESTALT
GOUTILY
GUSTILY
HASTILY
HEFTILY
HOSTELS
HOSTILE
INSTALL
INSTALS
INSTILL
INSTILS
INSTYLE
INUTILE
IRATELY
LENTILS
LINTELS
LISTELS
LOFTILY
LUSTILY
MANTELS
MEATILY
MISTILY
MONTHLY
MORTALS
MUSTILY
NASTILY
NATTILY
NIFTILY
NINTHLY
NUTTILY
OUTTALK
PASTELS
PEPTALK
PETTILY
PISTILS
PISTOLE
PISTOLS
PORTALS
PRATTLE
RENTALS
REPTILE
RESTYLE
RUSTILY
SALTILY
SCUTTLE
SEATTLE
SHUTTLE
SIXTHLY
SKITTLE
SOOTILY
SPATULA
STATELY
SYSTOLE
TACTILE
TASTILY
TATTILY
TENTHLY
TESTFLY
TESTILY
TEXTILE
TRITELY
VISTULA
WHITTLE
WITTILY

•••T••L

ABUTTAL
AUSTRAL
BESTIAL
BOBTAIL
CATTAIL
CENTRAL
CHATTEL
CONTROL
CURTAIL
DISTILL
FACTFUL
FACTUAL
FANTAIL
FISTFUL
FOXTAIL
FRETFUL
GENTEEL
GLOTTAL
HEATFUL
HOOTOWL
HURTFUL
INITIAL
INSTALL
INSTILL
KESTREL
LACTEAL
LUSTFUL
MARTIAL
MENTHOL
MISTRAL
NEUTRAL
NOSTRIL
NUPTIAL
PARTIAL
PIGTAIL
PINTAIL
PLOTFUL
POUTFUL
PRETZEL
QUETZAL
RATTAIL
RESTFUL
SPATIAL
TACTFUL
TERTIAL
TEXTUAL
USSTEEL
VENTRAL
VICTUAL
VIRTUAL
WAGTAIL
WASTREL
WISTFUL
ZESTFUL

••••TL•

ADEPTLY
ADULTLY
ALERTLY
APOSTLE
ATLATLS
BEASTLY
BLUNTLY
BRISTLE
BRISTLY
BRITTLE
CHORTLE
COURTLY
ENTITLE
EPISTLE
ERECTLY
EXACTLY
FAINTLY
FIRSTLY
FLEETLY
GAUNTLY
GHASTLY
GHOSTLY
GREATLY
GRISTLE
GRISTLY
INAPTLY
INEPTLY
INERTLY
JOINTLY
LICITLY
LIGHTLY
MOISTLY
NIGHTLY
OVERTLY
PRATTLE
QUIETLY
RETITLE
RIANTLY
RIGHTLY
SAINTLY
SCANTLY
SCUTTLE
SEATTLE
SHORTLY
SHUTTLE
SIGHTLY
SKITTLE
SMARTLY
SQUATLY
STARTLE
STOUTLY
SWEETLY
SWIFTLY
TACITLY
THISTLE
THISTLY
TIGHTLY
TRESTLE
UNAPTLY
WHISTLE
WHITTLE
WRESTLE

••••T•L

ABUTTAL
BRISTOL
CAPITAL
CAPITOL
CHATTEL
COASTAL
CRYSTAL
DIGITAL
FRACTAL
FRONTAL
GERITOL
GLOTTAL
MARITAL
ORBITAL
PALATAL
PIVOTAL
RECITAL
VEGETAL

•••••TL

AXOLOTL
NAHUATL

T•M••••

TAMABLE
TAMALES
TAMARIN
TAMBALA
TAMBOUR
TAMMANY
TAMPERS
TAMPICO
TAMPING
TAMTAMS
TEMBLOR
TEMPEHS
TEMPERA
TEMPERS
TEMPEST
TEMPLAR
TEMPLES
TEMPTED
TEMPTER
TEMPURA
TIMBALE
TIMBALS
TIMBERS
TIMBRES
TIMECOP
TIMELAG
TIMEOFF
TIMEOUT
TIMESUP
TIMIDER
TIMIDLY
TIMINGS
TIMMINS
TIMOTHY
TOMBOLA
TOMBOYS
TOMCATS
TOMFOOL
TOMTITS
TOMTOMS
TUMBLED
TUMBLER
TUMBLES
TUMBREL
TUMMIES
TUMMING
TUMULTS
TUMULUS
TYMPANA
TYMPANI

T••M•••

TAMMANY
TARMACS
TEAMING
TEAMSUP
TEDMACK
TEEMING
TERMING
TERMINI
TERMITE
THIMBLE
THIMPHU
THOMSON
THUMBED
THUMPED
THUMPER
THYMINE
TIMMINS
TIOMKIN
TITMICE
TOPMAST
TOPMOST
TORMENT
TRAMCAR
TRAMMEL
TRAMPAS
TRAMPED
TRAMPLE
TREMAIN
TREMBLE
TREMBLY
TREMOLO
TREMORS
TRIMMED
TRIMMER
TRUMPED
TRUMPET
TRUMPUP
TUMMIES
TUMMING
TURMOIL

T•••M••

TAPEMAN
TAPEMEN
TASHMAN
TATAMIS
TAXIMAN
TAXIMEN
THEOMEN
THERMAL
THERMOS
THURMAN
TOTEMIC
TRAMMEL
TRAUMAS
TRIMMED
TRIMMER
TRIUMPH
TUCHMAN

T••••M•

TALCUMS
TAMTAMS
TANDEMS
TEATIME
TEDIUMS
TEETIME
TOMTOMS
TRIREME
TRUISMS
TSUNAMI
TWOSOME
TWOTIME

T•••••M

TAGTEAM
TAKEAIM
TANGRAM
TANTRUM
TAPROOM
TEAROOM
TERBIUM
THEFIRM
THEOREM
THORIUM
THREEAM
THREEPM
THULIUM
TINYTIM
TONEARM
TORYISM
TOTIDEM
TOURISM
TRANSOM
TRIGRAM
TRITIUM
TROPISM

•T•M•••

ATAMANS
ATOMIES
ATOMISE
ATOMIZE
ETAMINE
ITEMISE
ITEMIZE
STAMENS
STAMINA
STAMMER
STAMPED
STEMMED
STIMULI
STOMACH
STOMATA
STOMPED
STUMBLE
STUMERS
STUMPED
STUMPER
STYMIED
STYMIES

•T••M••

ATHOMES
ATTEMPT
ATTIMES
OTTOMAN
STAMMER
STARMAN
STARMAP
STEAMED
STEAMER
STEMMED
STIGMAS
STORMED

•T•••M•

ATACAMA
ATRIUMS
PTOLEMY
STREAMS

•T••••M

ATAVISM
ATHEISM
STADIUM
STARDOM
STEINEM
STERNUM
STRATUM
YTTRIUM

••TM•••

BITMAPS
HETMANS
NUTMEAT
NUTMEGS
OATMEAL
TITMICE
WETMOPS

••T•M••

ARTEMIS
ARTEMUS
ATTEMPT
ATTIMES
AUTOMAT
AUTUMNS
BATEMAN
BATHMAT
BATSMAN
BATSMEN
BETAMAX
BETIMES
BITUMEN
GATEMAN
GATEMEN
ISTHMUS
OPTIMAL
OPTIMUM
OTTOMAN
PITTMAN
POTOMAC
PUTAMEN
RETIMED
RETIMES
TATAMIS
TOTEMIC
ULTIMAS
UNTAMED
UPTEMPO
VITAMIN

••T••M•

ANTHEMS
BOTTOMS
CUTTIME
ESTEEMS
EXTREME
FATHOMS
HOTCOMB
NOTRUMP
OUTCOME
OUTJUMP
PETNAME
RETRIMS
SATCHMO
SATSUMA
SITCOMS

••T•••M

ANTFARM
ANTONYM
ARTFILM
ARTFORM
INTERIM
KETCHAM
LITHIUM
MITCHUM
NATRIUM
OPTIMUM
POTSDAM
TOTIDEM
YTTRIUM

•••TM••

BESTMAN
BESTMEN
BOATMAN
BOATMEN
DUSTMAN
DUSTMEN
DUSTMOP
EASTMAN
FOOTMAN
FOOTMEN
HARTMAN
PITTMAN
PORTMAN
POSTMAN
POSTMEN
REITMAN
WHITMAN

•••T•M•

AIRTIME
ALLTIME
ANATOMY
ANYTIME
BANTAMS
BEATSME
BEDTIME
BIGTIME
BOTTOMS
BUYTIME
CENTIME
CENTIMO
CONTEMN
COSTUME
CUSTOMS
CUTTIME
DAYTIME
DIATOMS
DICTUMS
EPITOME
GAUTAMA
MAYTIME
NAPTIME
OLDTIME
ONETIME
PASTIME
RAGTIME
RESTAMP
RHYTHMS
SAOTOME
SYSTEMS
TAMTAMS
TEATIME
TEETIME
TOMTOMS
TWOTIME
VICTIMS
WARTIME

•••T••M

APOTHEM
BAPTISM
BENTHAM
CHATHAM
CHETRUM
CULTISM
CULTJAM
EGOTISM
ELITISM
FLOTSAM
MIDTERM
NOSTRUM
PENTIUM
PIETISM
ROSTRUM
SISTRUM
TAGTEAM
TANTRUM
TRITIUM
VIETNAM
YEATEAM

••••TM•

MAHATMA

••••T•M

EIGHTAM
EIGHTPM
ERRATUM
OMENTUM
PHANTOM
PINETUM
QUANTUM
SANCTUM
STRATUM
SYMPTOM
TINYTIM

T•N••••

TANAGER
TANDEMS
TANGELO
TANGENT
TANGERE
TANGIER
TANGLED
TANGLES
TANGOED
TANGRAM
TANKARD
TANKERS
TANKFUL
TANKING
TANKSUP
TANKTOP
TANLINE
TANNERS
TANNERY
TANNEST
TANNING
TANNINS
TANNISH
TANOAKS
TANSIES
TANTARA
TANTIVY
TANTRUM
TENABLE
TENABLY
TENACES
TENANCY
TENANTS
TENCENT
TENDERS
TENDING
TENDONS
TENDRIL
TENDSTO
TENFOLD
TENFOUR
TENNERS
TENNIEL
TENONED
TENPINS
TENRECS
TENSELY
TENSEST
TENSEUP
TENSILE
TENSING
TENSION
TENSIVE
TENSORS
TENSPOT
TENTERS
TENTHLY
TENTING
TENUITY
TENUOUS
TENURED
TENURES
TENZING
TINCANS
TINDERS
TINEARS
TINFOIL
TINGING
TINGLED
TINGLES
TINHATS
TINHORN
TINIEST
TINKERS
TINKLED
TINKLES
TINLIKE
TINNERS
TINNIER
TINNILY
TINSELS
TINSTAR
TINTACK
TINTERN
TINTERS
TINTING
TINTYPE
TINWARE
TINWORK
TINYTIM
TONALLY
TONEARM
TONEDUP
TONELOC
TONEROW
TONESUP
TONGANS
TONGUED
TONGUES
TONIEST
TONIGHT
TONNAGE
TONNEAU
TONNISH
TONSILS
TONSURE
TONTINE
TUNDRAS
TUNEDIN
TUNEDUP
TUNEFUL
TUNEOUT
TUNESIN
TUNESUP
TUNEUPS
TUNGOIL
TUNICLE
TUNISIA
TUNNELS
TUNNIES

T••N•••

TAINTED
TANNERS
TANNERY
TANNEST
TANNING

TANNINS
TANNISH
TARNISH
TAUNTED
TAWNIER
TAWNILY
TEENAGE
TEENERS
TEENIER
TENNERS
TENNIEL
TERNARY
TERNATE
THANKED
THENARS
THINAIR
THINICE
THINKER
THINKOF
THINKUP
THINNED
THINNER
THUNDER
TIANJIN
TINNERS
TINNIER
TINNILY
TLINGIT
TOENAIL
TONNAGE
TONNEAU
TONNISH
TOONIES
TORNADO
TORNOFF
TORNOUT
TOWNERS
TOWNIES
TOWNISH
TOYNBEE
TRANCES
TRANSIT
TRANSOM
TRENARY
TRENDED
TRENTON
TRINITY
TRINKET
TRUNDLE
TSUNAMI
TUNNELS
TUNNIES
TURNERS
TURNERY
TURNING
TURNIPS
TURNKEY
TURNOFF
TURNOUT
TURNSIN
TURNSON
TURNSTO
TURNSUP
TWANGED
TWINBED
TWINGED
TWINGES
TWINING
TWINKLE
TWINKLY
TWINNED
TYINGIN
TYINGUP

T•••N••

TAGENDS
TAKENIN
TAKENON
TALENTS
TALONED
TAPINGS
TAPINTO
TARANTO
TENANCY
TENANTS
TENONED
TERENCE
TETANUS
THINNED
THINNER
THRONES
THRONGS
TIDINGS
TIEINTO
TIERNEY
TILINGS
TIMINGS
TISANES
TITANIA
TITANIC
TOKENED
TOPKNOT
TORONTO
TOURNEY
TRAINED
TRAINEE
TRAINER
TRIUNES
TROUNCE
TRUANCY
TRUANTS
TWINNED
TWOONIE
TYLENOL
TYRANNY
TYRANTS

T••••N•

TABBING
TABLING
TACKING
TAGGANT
TAGGING
TAGLINE
TAILEND
TAILING
TAIPANS
TAKEONE
TALKING
TALLINN
TAMMANY
TAMPING
TANGENT
TANKING
TANLINE
TANNING
TANNINS
TAPPING
TARPONS
TARRING
TARTANS
TARZANA
TASKING
TASTING
TATIANA
TATTING
TAURINE
TAUTENS
TAVERNS
TAXIING
TEAMING
TEARING
TEASING
TEDDING
TEEMING
TELLING
TENCENT
TENDING
TENDONS
TENPINS
TENSING
TENTING
TENZING
TERHUNE
TERMING
TERMINI
TERRENE
TESTING
TEUTONS
THAWING
THEFONZ
THYMINE
TICKING
TIDYING
TIELINE
TIEPINS
TIERING
TIFFANY
TIFFING
TIFFINS
TIGLONS
TIJUANA
TILLING
TILTING
TIMMINS
TINCANS
TINGING
TINTING
TIPPING
TITHING
TITLING
TITRING
TOCSINS
TOGGING
TOILING
TOLLING
TOLUENE
TONGANS
TONTINE
TOOLING
TOOTING
TOPGUNS
TOPPING
TORMENT
TORRENS
TORRENT
TORTONI
TOSSING
TOTTING
TOUCANS
TOURING
TOUTING
TOYLAND
TRACING
TRADING
TREEING
TREPANS
TREVINO
TRIBUNE
TRIDENT
TRIGONS
TRITONE
TRITONS
TROGONS
TROJANS
TRUEING
TSARINA
TUCKING
TUFTING
TUGGING
TULSANS
TUMMING
TURBANS
TURBINE
TUREENS
TURNING
TUSCANY
TWINING
TWOLANE
TWOTONE
TYCOONS
TYMPANA
TYMPANI
TYRANNY
TZARINA

T•••••N

TACKSON
TAILFIN
TAKENIN
TAKENON
TAKESIN
TAKESON
TAKETEN
TALLINN
TAMARIN
TAPEMAN
TAPEMEN
TASHLIN
TASHMAN
TAXIMAN
TAXIMEN
TEACHIN
TEHERAN
TELERAN
TELLSON
TENSION
TERRAIN
TESTBAN
THEOMEN
THEREIN
THEREON
THICKEN
THOMSON
THREWIN
THROWIN
THURMAN
TIANJIN
TIBETAN
TIEDOWN
TIGHTEN
TINHORN
TINTERN
TIOMKIN
TOLKIEN
TOOKTEN
TOPDOWN
TORSION
TOUCHON
TOUGHEN
TRADEIN
TRADEON
TREASON
TREMAIN
TRENTON
TRICORN
TRIEDON
TRIESON
TRILLIN
TRISTAN
TRODDEN
TUCHMAN
TUCKSIN
TUITION
TUNEDIN
TUNESIN
TURNSIN
TURNSON
TWOIRON
TYINGIN
TYPHOON

•T•N•••

ATINGLE
ATONIES
ATONING
ETHNICS
ETONIAN
STANCES
STANDBY
STANDEE
STANDIN
STANDON
STANDUP
STANLEE
STANLEY
STANNIC
STANTON
STANZAS
STENCIL
STENGEL
STENTOR
STINGER
STINGOS
STINKER
STINTED
STONERS
STONIER
STONILY
STONING
STUNGUN
STUNNED
STUNNER
STUNTED
UTENSIL

•T••N••

ATLANTA
ATTENDS
ATTUNED
ATTUNES
ETERNAL
ETHANOL
ETIENNE
OTRANTO
STAINED
STAINER
STANNIC
STAUNCH
STDENIS
STEINEM
STEINER
STERNAL
STERNER
STERNLY
STERNUM
STRANDS
STRANGE
STRINGS
STRINGY
STUNNED
STUNNER

•T•••N•

ATAMANS
ATONING
ATTAINS
ETAMINE
ETCHANT
ETCHING
ETIENNE
ITCHING
ITERANT
STAGING
STAKING
STAMENS
STAMINA
STARING
STATING
STAVING
STAYING
STEPINS
STEVENS
STEWING
STIPEND
STJOHNS
STOKING
STOLONS
STONING
STORING
STOWING
STRAINS
STUDENT
STYLING
STYRENE
UTAHANS

•T••••N

ETESIAN
ETONIAN
ITALIAN
ITHACAN
KTOSLIN
OTTOMAN
STANDIN
STANDON
STANTON
STARMAN
STASSEN
STATION
STEEPEN
STEPHEN
STEPSIN
STEPSON
STETSON
STEUBEN
STIFFEN
STILTON
STIRSIN
STOLLEN
STOODIN
STOPSIN
STOUTEN
STRIVEN
STUNGUN
STYGIAN
STYRIAN
UTOPIAN

••TN•••

APTNESS
CATNAPS
CATNIPS
FATNESS
FITNESS
HOTNESS
JITNEYS
PATNESS
PETNAME
WETNESS
WITNESS

••T•N••

ACTINIC
ANTENNA
ANTONIA
ANTONIN
ANTONIO
ANTONYM
ATTENDS
ATTUNED
ATTUNES
BOTHNIA
BUTANOL
CATENAE
CUTINTO
DETENTE
EATENAT
EATENUP
ENTENTE
ESTONIA
EXTENDS
EXTENTS
EXTINCT
GETINTO
GOTINTO
INTENDS
INTENSE
INTENTS
INTONED
INTONER
INTONES
KETONES
KUTENAI
LATENCY
LATENTS
LATINAS
LATINOS
LETINON
LITINTO
MATINEE
MUTANTS
OBTUNDS
OCTANES
OCTANTS
OFTENER
OUTINGS
PATENTS
PATINAS
PETUNIA
POTENCY
RATINGS
RETINAE
RETINAL
RETINAS
RETINUE
RETUNED
RETUNES
ROTUNDA
SATINET
SETINTO
TETANUS
TITANIA
TITANIC
UNTUNED
UNTUNES
UPTONOW
USTINOV

••T••N•

ACTIONS
ALTOONA
ANTEING
ANTENNA
ANTHONY
ANTOINE
ARTSONG
ASTOUND
ATTAINS
AUTUMNS
BATHING
BATTENS
BATTING
BATWING
BETHANY
BETHINK
BETTING
BITTING
BUTTING
BUTTONS
BYTURNS
CATIONS
CATKINS
CATTING
CITRINE
CITRONS
COTTONS
COTTONY
CUTTING
DETAINS
DITTANY
DOTTING
ENTRANT
ENTWINE
EXTERNS
FATTENS
FITTING
FUTZING
GATLING
GETTING
GOTLAND
GUTTING
HATBAND
HATPINS
HATTING
HETMANS
HITTING
HOTLINE
HOTLINK
INTERNS
JETGUNS
JETSONS
JETTING
JOTTING
JUTLAND
JUTTING
KITTENS
LATEENS
LATHING
LATTENS
LETTING
LOTIONS
LOTTING
MATRONS
MATTING
METHANE
MITRING
MITTENS
MOTIONS
MUTTONS
NATIONS
NETTING
NITTANY
NOTHING
NOTIONS
NUTTING
OBTAINS
OPTIONS
OUTDONE
OUTGUNS
OUTLAND
OUTLINE
OUTRANK
OUTRUNS
PATERNO
PATIENT
PATRONS
PATTENS
PATTING
PETTING
PITHING
PITTING
PITYING
POTIONS
POTTING
PUTTING
PYTHONS
RATFINK
RATIONS
RATLINE
RATTANS
RATTING
RETAINS
RETHINK
RETSINA
RETURNS
ROTTING
SATEENS
SETLINE
SETTING
SITTING
TATIANA
TATTING
TITHING
TITLING
TITRING
TOTTING
UNTYING
UPTURNS
VATTING
VETOING
VETTING
WETLAND
WETTING
WITTING

••T•••N

ACTAEON
ACTEDON
ACTUPON
ANTIGEN
ANTLION
ANTONIN
ARTISAN
AZTECAN
BATEMAN
BATSMAN
BATSMEN
BETAKEN
BETOKEN
BETWEEN
BITTERN
BITUMEN
BUTTSIN
CATALAN
CATCHON
CATSCAN
CITIZEN
CITROEN
CUTDOWN
DETRAIN
DOTEDON
DOTESON
ENTERON
ENTRAIN
GATEMAN
GATEMEN
GETDOWN
GETEVEN
GETITON
GOTDOWN
GOTEVEN
GOTITON
KATHRYN
KITCHEN
KUTCHIN
LATERAN
LATERON
LATVIAN
LETDOWN
LETINON
LETUPON
MATEWAN
MUTAGEN
NETIZEN
OCTAGON
ORTOLAN
OTTOMAN
OUTWORN
PATROON
PATTERN
PITCHIN
PITTMAN
PUTAMEN
PUTDOWN
PUTUPON
PYTHIAN
RETAKEN
RETRAIN
SATDOWN
SETDOWN
SETUPON
SITDOWN
SOTHERN
VATICAN
VETERAN
VITAMIN
VOTEDIN
VOTESIN

•••TN••

BEATNIK
CHUTNEY
COSTNER
JUSTNOW
PARTNER
SHATNER
SPUTNIK
VIETNAM
VINTNER
WHATNOT
WHITNEY

•••T•N•

ABATING
ACETONE
ACHTUNG
ARETINO
BAITING
BARTEND
BASTING
BATTENS
BATTING
BEATING
BELTANE
BELTING
BESTING
BETTING
BITTING
BLATANT
BOATING
BOITANO
BOLTING
BOOTING
BRETONS
BRITONS
BUNTING
BUSTING
BUTTING
BUTTONS
CAFTANS
CANTINA
CANTING
CANTONS
CARTING
CARTONS
CASTING
CATTING
COATING
CONTEND
CONTENT
COSTING
COTTONS
COTTONY
CRATING
CRETANS
CRETINS
CUTTING
DARTING
DAYTONA
DENTINE
DENTING
DESTINE
DESTINY
DIETING
DISTANT
DISTEND
DITTANY
DOTTING
DUCTING
DUSTING
EASTEND
EDITING
ELATING
ELUTING
EMOTING
EXITING
FASTENS
FASTING
FASTONE
FATTENS
FITTING
FLUTING
FONTINA
FOOTING
FORTUNA
FORTUNE
GAITING
GETTING
GRATING
GUSTING
GUTTING
HAFTING
HALTING
HASTENS
HASTING
HATTING
HEATING
HEFTING
HENTING
HINTING
HITTING
HOOTING
HOSTING
HUNTING
HURTING
IFSTONE
INSTANT
JESTING
JETTING
JILTING
JOLTING
JOTTING
JUSTINE
JUTTING
KAFTANS
KILTING
KITTENS
LANTANA
LASTING
LATTENS
LEPTONS
LETTING
LIFTING
LILTING
LISTENS
LISTING
LOFTING
LOOTING
LOTTING
LUSTING
MALTING
MARTENS
MARTINA
MARTINI
MARTINO
MARTINS
MATTING
MEETING
MELTING
MINTING
MISTING
MITTENS
MOLTING
MONTANA
MONTAND
MONTANE
MONTANI
MOUTONS
MUNTINS
MUSTANG
MUTTONS
NEATENS
NEPTUNE
NESTING
NETTING
NEWTONS
NITTANY
NUTTING
ORATING
OROTUND
OUSTING
PANTING
PARTING
PASTINA
PASTING
PATTENS
PATTING
PECTINS
PELTING
PETTING
PHOTONS
PIETINS
PISTONS
PITTING
PLATENS
PLATING
PONTINE
PORTEND
PORTENT
POSTING
POTTING
POUTING
PRATING
PRETEND
PROTONS
PUNTING
PUPTENT
PUTTING
QUOTING
RAFTING
RANTING
RATTANS
RATTING
RENTING
RESTING
RIFTING
RIOTING
ROOTING
ROSTAND
ROTTING
ROUTINE
ROUTING
RUSTING
SALTINE
SALTING
SANTANA
SANTINI
SEATING
SESTINA
SETTING
SEXTANS
SEXTANT
SEXTONS
SHUTINS
SIFTING
SILTING
SISTINE
SITTING
SKATING
SLATING
SMETANA
SMITING
SOFTENS
SORTING
SOUTANE
SPITING
STATING
SUBTEND
SUITING
SULTANA
SULTANS
SUNTANS
TARTANS
TASTING
TATTING
TAUTENS
TENTING
TESTING
TEUTONS
TILTING
TINTING
TONTINE
TOOTING
TORTONI
TOTTING
TOUTING
TRITONE
TRITONS
TUFTING
TWOTONE
UNITING
VATTING
VENTING
VESTING
VETTING
WAFTING
WAITING
WANTING
WASTING
WELTING
WESTEND
WETTING
WHITENS
WHITING
WILTING
WITTING
WONTONS
WRITING
XRATING
ZEITUNG

•••T••N

ABSTAIN
AUCTION
BASTION
BENTSEN
BESTMAN
BESTMEN
BITTERN
BLITZEN
BOATMAN
BOATMEN
BRITAIN
BRITTEN
BRITTON
BUTTSIN
CANTEEN
CAPTAIN
CAPTION
CARTOON
CAUTION
CERTAIN
CISTERN
CONTAIN
CONTEMN
COSTAIN
COWTOWN
CURTAIN
DEXTRIN
DICTION
DUSTBIN
DUSTMAN
DUSTMEN
DUSTPAN
EARTHEN
EASTERN
EASTMAN
EDITION
ELATION
ELUTION
EMOTION
EPSTEIN
FACTION
FESTOON
FICTION
FIFTEEN

FLATTEN FONTEYN FOOTMAN FOOTMEN FORTRAN FUSTIAN GENTIAN GLUTTON HAITIAN HARTMAN HEATHEN KRATION LANTERN LAOTIAN LECTERN MARTIAN MENTION MIDTOWN NEUTRON NEWTOWN NOCTURN ORATION OURTOWN OVATION PASTERN PATTERN PERTAIN PITTMAN PLATOON PONTOON PORTION PORTMAN POSTERN POSTMAN POSTMEN PRETEEN PROTEAN PROTEIN REITMAN RESTAIN RIPTORN RONTGEN RUCTION SECTION SHOTGUN SHUTSIN SIXTEEN SMITTEN STATION STETSON SUCTION SUSTAIN TESTBAN TINTERN TUITION UMPTEEN UNCTION WAITRON WAITSON WANTSIN WESTERN WHITMAN WRITEIN WRITTEN WROTEIN XANTHAN YELTSIN ANISTON BALATON BRAXTON BRITTEN BRITTON BUILTIN BURSTYN CAPITAN CAPSTAN CARLTON CHASTEN CHEATIN CLAPTON CLAYTON CLIFTON CLINTON COUNTON CROUTON DAKOTAN DEALTIN DRISTAN FLATTEN FRONTON GELATIN GETITON GLISTEN GLUTTON GOTITON GRAFTON HALSTON HAMPTON HANGTEN HEARTEN HOUSTON KERATIN KILOTON KRYPTON LAYITON LIGHTEN LONGTON MOISTEN PHAETON PRESTON PURITAN QUENTIN QUIETEN RALSTON RARITAN RIGHTON RUBITIN SHELTON SHORTEN SKELTON SLAYTON SLEPTIN SLEPTON SMARTEN SMITTEN SPARTAN STANTON STILTON STOUTEN SWEETEN SWEETON TAKETEN TIBETAN TIGHTEN TOOKTEN TRENTON TRISTAN UNEATEN WALSTON WHARTON WHEATON WINSTON WRITTEN YANKTON YUCATAN

••••TN•

MIGHTNT OUGHTNT

••••T•N

ALLSTON

TO•••••

TOADIED TOADIES TOADISH TOASTED TOASTER TOBACCO TOCCATA TOCSINS TODDIES TODDLED TODDLER TODDLES TOECAPS TOEHOLD TOELESS TOELIKE TOELOOP TOENAIL TOESHOE TOETAPS TOFFEES TOFFLER TOGGERY TOGGING TOGGLED TOGGLES TOILERS TOILETS TOILFUL TOILING TOKENED TOLDOFF TOLKIEN TOLLIES TOLLING TOLLWAY TOLSTOI TOLSTOY TOLTECS TOLUENE TOMBOLA TOMBOYS TOMCATS TOMFOOL TOMTITS TOMTOMS TONALLY TONEARM TONEDUP TONELOC TONEROW TONESUP TONGANS TONGUED TONGUES TONIEST TONIGHT TONNAGE TONNEAU TONNISH TONSILS TONSURE TONTINE TOOKOFF TOOKOUT TOOKTEN TOOLBOX TOOLING TOOLSUP TOONIES TOORDER TOOTERS TOOTHED TOOTING TOOTLED TOOTLES TOOTSIE TOPAZES TOPCOAT TOPDOGS TOPDOWN TOPGUNS TOPHATS TOPHOLE TOPIARY TOPICAL TOPKAPI TOPKICK TOPKNOT TOPMAST TOPMOST TOPPERS TOPPING TOPPLED TOPPLES TOPSAIL TOPSIDE TOPSOFF TOPSOIL TOPSOUT TORCHED TORCHES TOREOFF TOREOUT TOREROS TORMENT TORNADO TORNOFF TORNOUT TOROIDS TORONTO TORPEDO TORQUES TORRENS TORRENT TORSION TORTONI TORYISH TORYISM TOSCALE TOSHIBA TOSPARE TOSSERS TOSSING TOSSOFF TOSSOUT TOSSUPS TOSTADA TOTALED TOTALLY TOTEBAG TOTEMIC TOTIDEM TOTTERS TOTTERY TOTTING TOUCANS TOUCHED TOUCHES TOUCHON TOUCHUP TOUGHEN TOUGHER TOUGHIE TOUGHLY TOUPEES TOURACO TOURERS TOURING TOURISM TOURIST TOURNEY TOUSLED TOUSLES TOUTERS TOUTING TOWARDS TOWAWAY TOWCARS TOWELED TOWERED TOWHEAD TOWHEES TOWNERS TOWNIES TOWNISH TOWPATH TOWROPE TOYDOGS TOYLAND TOYLESS TOYLIKE TOYNBEE TOYSHOP TOYSRUS

T•O••••

TAOISTS THOMSON THOREAU THORIUM THOUGHT TIOMKIN TOOKOFF TOOKOUT TOOKTEN TOOLBOX TOOLING TOOLSUP TOONIES TOORDER TOOTERS TOOTHED TOOTING TOOTLED TOOTLES TOOTSIE TROCARS TROCHEE TROCHES TRODDEN TROGONS TROIKAS TROILUS TROJANS TROLLED TROLLEY TROOPED TROOPER TROPHIC TROPICS TROPISM TROTHED TROTOUT TROTSKY TROTTED TROTTER TROUBLE TROUGHS TROUNCE TROUPER TROUPES TROUSER TROWELS TROWERS TSOURIS TWOBASE TWOBITS TWOFERS TWOFOLD TWOIRON TWOLANE TWOONIE TWOSOME TWOSTAR TWOSTEP TWOTIME TWOTONE

T••O•••

TABORET TALONED TANOAKS TENONED THEOMEN THEOREM THROATS THROATY THRONES THRONGS THROUGH THROWER THROWIN TIMOTHY TIPOFFS TOROIDS TORONTO TRIODES TROOPED TROOPER TRYOUTS TUTORED TWOONIE TYCOONS

T•••O••

TABLOID TADPOLE TAGSOUT TAILOFF TAILORS TAKEOFF TAKEONE TAKEOUT TALKOUT TALLOWS TAMBOUR TANGOED TAPIOCA TAPROOM TAPROOT TAPSOFF TAPSOUT TARPONS TATTOOS TEAPOTS TEAPOYS TEAROFF TEAROOM TEAROSE TEAROUT TEDIOUS TEEDOFF TEESOFF TELLOFF TENDONS TENFOLD TENFOUR TENSORS TENUOUS TERRORS TESTOUT TEUTONS THEFONZ THEROUX TICKOFF TIEDOWN TIEPOLO TIERODS TIGLONS TIMEOFF TIMEOUT TINFOIL TINHORN TINWORK TIPSOFF TIPTOED TIPTOES TIPTOPS TIREOUT TOEHOLD TOELOOP TOLDOFF TOMBOLA TOMBOYS TOMFOOL TOMTOMS TOOKOFF TOOKOUT TOPCOAT TOPDOGS TOPDOWN TOPHOLE TOPMOST TOPSOFF TOPSOIL TOPSOUT TOREOFF TOREOUT TORNOFF TORNOUT TORTONI TOSSOFF TOSSOUT TOWROPE TOYDOGS TRAVOIS TREFOIL TREMOLO TREMORS TRICORN TRICOTS TRIGONS TRILOGY TRIPODS TRIPOLI TRITONE TRITONS TROGONS TROTOUT TUGBOAT TUNEOUT TUNGOIL TURBOTS TURMOIL TURNOFF TURNOUT TUSSOCK TVSHOWS TWOFOLD TWOSOME TWOTONE TYCOONS TYPHOON

T••••O•

TACKSON TAGALOG TAKENON TAKESON TANKTOP TAPROOM TAPROOT TATTOOS TEAROOM TEASHOP TELLSOF TELLSON TEMBLOR TENSION TENSPOT TEREDOS THEBLOB THECROW THEREOF THEREON THERMOS THINKOF THOMSON TIMECOP TIREDOF TOELOOP TOESHOE TOLSTOI TOLSTOY TOMFOOL TONELOC TONEROW TOOLBOX TOPKNOT TOREROS TORSION TOUCHON TOYSHOP TRACTOR TRADEON TRAITOR TRANSOM TREASON TREETOP TRENTON TRIEDON TRIESON TSELIOT TUITION TUPELOS TURNSON TUXEDOS TWOIRON TYLENOL TYPHOON

T•••••O

TABASCO TAKESTO TALKSTO TALLYHO TAMPICO TANGELO TAPINTO TARANTO TENDSTO TESTUDO THERETO TIEINTO TIEPOLO TOBACCO TORNADO TORONTO TORPEDO TOURACO TREMOLO TREVINO TURNSTO

•TO••••

ATOMIES ATOMISE ATOMIZE ATONIES ATONING ETOILES ETONIAN KTOSLIN PTOLEMY STOCKED STOCKUP STOGIES STOICAL STOKELY STOKERS STOKING STOLLEN STOLLER STOLONS STOMACH STOMATA STOMPED STONERS STONIER STONILY STONING STOODBY STOODIN STOODUP STOOGES STOOKED STOOKEY STOOLIE STOOPED STOPGAP STOPOFF STOPPED STOPPER STOPSIN STOPSUP STORAGE STORERS STOREUP STOREYS STORIED STORIES STORING STORMED STOUTEN STOUTER STOUTLY STOWING UTOPIAN UTOPIAS

•T•O•••

ATHOMES ATROPHY ATWORST OTTOMAN PTBOATS STJOHNS STLOUIS STOODBY STOODIN STOODUP STOOGES STOOKED STOOKEY STOOLIE STOOPED STROBES STROKED STROKES STROLLS STROPHE STROPPY

•T••O••

ATALOSS STATORS STCROIX STEPOUT STEROID STEROLS STOLONS STOPOFF STUPORS

•T•••O•

ATECROW ATTABOY ETHANOL STANDON STANTON STARDOM STATION STENTOR STEPSON STEREOS STETSON STILTON STINGOS STUCCOS STUDIOS

•T••••O

OTHELLO OTRANTO STICKTO STRETTO STUCKTO UTRILLO

••TO•••

ALTOONA ALTOSAX ANTOINE ANTONIA ANTONIN ANTONIO ANTONYM ASTOLAT ASTORIA ASTOUND AUTOMAT BETOKEN CNTOWER CUTOFFS CUTOUTS DETOURS ESTONIA ESTORIL EXTORTS GETOVER GOTOPOT GOTOVER INTONED INTONER INTONES KETONES LATOSCA LITOTES METOOER MITOSES MITOSIS MITOTIC MOTORED OCTOBER OCTOPOD OCTOPUS ONTOPOF ORTOLAN OTTOMAN OUTOFIT POTOMAC POTOROO PUTOUTS PUTOVER RETOOLS RETORTS RETOUCH RETOURS RETOWED TUTORED UPTONOW UPTOPAR VETOERS VETOING ZATOPEK

••T•O••

ACTFOUR ACTIONS ACTSOUT ALTOONA ANTCOWS ANTHONY ANTIOCH ARTFORM ARTSONG ARTWORK AUTHORS BATBOYS BATHOIL BETROTH BETTORS BITEOFF BOTTOMS BUTTONS BUTTOUT CATBOAT CATFOOD CATHODE CATIONS CITROEN CITRONS CITROUS COTTONS COTTONY CUTDOWN CUTSOFF CUTSOUT DETROIT DITTOED DUTEOUS EATSOUT ENTROPY FATHOMS FATUOUS FETLOCK GETDOWN GETLOST GETSOFF GETSOUT GOTDOWN GOTLOST HITSOUT HOTCOMB HOTDOGS HOTFOOT HOTPOTS HOTRODS INTROIT JETBOAT JETPORT JETSONS LETDOWN LETSOFF LETSOUT LOTIONS MATLOCK MATRONS MATTOCK MATZOHS METEORS METEOUT METHODS METOOER MITFORD MOTIONS MOTTOES MUTTONS NATIONS NETWORK NITROUS NOTIONS OCTROIS OPTIONS OPTSOUT OSTEOID OUTCOME OUTDOES OUTDONE OUTDOOR OUTGOES OUTLOOK OUTLOUD OUTPOLL OUTPOST OUTSOLD OUTVOTE OUTWORE OUTWORK OUTWORN PATROLS PATRONS PATROON PETCOCK PETIOLE PETROCK PETROLS PETROUS PITBOSS PITEOUS POTHOLE POTHOOK POTIONS PUTDOWN PUTSOFF PUTSOUT PYTHONS RATHOLE RATIONS RETOOLS SATDOWN SETDOWN SETSOFF SETSOUT SITCOMS SITDOWN SITSOUT TATTOOS VOTEOUT WETMOPS WITHOUT

••T••O•

ACTAEON ACTEDON ACTUPON ANTIFOG ANTILOG ANTLION ATTABOY BUTANOL CATALOG CATCHON CATFOOD CATSHOW DOTEDON DOTESON EATCROW ENTERON GETITON GOTITON GOTOPOT HOTFOOT HOTSHOT HOTSPOT LATERON LATINOS LETINON LETUPON LITHGOW MATADOR MATELOT OCTAGON OCTAVOS OCTOPOD ONTOPOF OPTSFOR OUTCROP OUTDOOR OUTFLOW OUTGROW OUTLOOK PATRIOT PATROON PITSTOP POTHOOK POTOROO POTSHOT PUTUPON ROTATOR SETUPON TATTOOS UPTONOW USTINOV VITRIOL VOTEFOR

••T•••O

ANTONIO ARTDECO CATERTO CUTINTO GETINTO GOTINTO LITINTO ONTARIO ONTHEGO PATERNO POTOROO PUTITTO SATCHMO SETINTO UPTEMPO

•••TO••

ACETONE ALLTOLD AMATORY ANATOLE ANATOMY BEATOUT BERTOLT BESTOWS BETTORS BIGTOES BIGTOPS BLOTOUT BOOTOUT BOTTOMS BOXTOPS BRETONS BRITONS BUSTOUT BUTTONS BUTTOUT CANTONS CANTORS CAPTORS CARTONS CARTOON CASTOFF CASTOUT CONTORT CONTOUR COTTONS COTTONY COWTOWN CUSTODY CUSTOMS DAYTONA DEBTORS DELTOID DIATOMS DISTORT DITTOED DOCTORS DUSTOFF EDITORS EDITOUT EPITOME FACTOID FACTORS FACTORY FASTONE FELTOUT FESTOON FLATOUT GUSTOES HECTORS HISTORY HOOTOWL

HOPTOIT
IFSTONE
INSTOCK
INSTORE
ISOTOPE
KEPTOFF
KEPTOUT
KOWTOWS
LACTOSE
LAPTOPS
LASTORY
LECTORS
LEFTOFF
LEFTOUT
LEPTONS
LICTORS
LIFTOFF
LOSTOUT
MALTOSE
MASTOID
MATTOCK
MENTORS
MIDTOWN
MISTOOK
MONTOYA
MOPTOPS
MOTTOES
MOUTONS
MUTTONS
NEWTONS
NEWTOWN
ORATORS
ORATORY
OURTOWN
PARTOOK
PARTOUT
PASTORS
PEGTOPS
PHOTOED
PHOTOGS
PHOTONS
PHOTOOP
PISTOLE
PISTOLS
PISTONS
PLATOON
PONTOON
POPTOPS
PROTONS
RAGTOPS
RAPTORS
RECTORS
RECTORY
REDTOPS
RESTOCK
RESTORE
RHETORS
RIOTOUS
RIPTORN
ROOTOUT
SAOTOME
SECTORS
SEETOIT
SENTOFF
SENTOUT
SEXTONS
SHOTOUT
SHUTOFF
SHUTOUT
SKITOWS
SORTOUT
STATORS
SUITORS
SYSTOLE
TATTOOS
TESTOUT
TEUTONS
TIPTOED
TIPTOES
TIPTOPS
TOMTOMS
TORTONI
TRITONE
TRITONS
TROTOUT
TWOTONE
UNSTOPS
VECTORS
VICTORS
VICTORY
WAITOUT
WANTOUT
WEBTOED
WENTOFF
WENTOUT
WONTONS
YOMTOVS

•••T•O•
ABETTOR
AUCTION
BASTION
BESTBOY
BISTROS
BOUTROS
BRITTON
CAPTION
CARTOON
CAUTION
CONTROL
DESTROY
DICTION
DOGTROT
DUSTMOP
EDITION
ELATION
ELUTION
EMOTION
FACTION
FELTFOR
FESTOON
FICTION
FLATTOP
FOXTROT
GHETTOS
GLUTTON
GROTTOS
HAUTBOY
JUSTNOW
KRATION
MENTHOL
MENTION
MISTOOK
NEUTRON
ORATION
OVATION
PALTROW
PARTOOK
PEATBOG
PHOTOOP
PLATOON
PONTOON
PORTHOS
PORTION
POSTBOX
ROOTFOR
RUCTION
SALTBOX
SECTION
SENTFOR
SHOTFOR
SOFTTOP
STATION
STETSON
SUCTION
TATTOOS
TUITION
UNCTION
WAITFOR
WAITRON
WAITSON
WARTHOG
WENTFOR
WHATFOR
WHATNOT

•••T••O
AGITATO
ARETINO
BOITANO
CENTAVO
CENTIMO
DEUTERO
LENTIGO
MARTINO
MESTIZO
MONTEGO
MONTERO
PORTICO
TESTUDO
VERTIGO
WANTSTO
WRITETO
WROTETO

••••TO•
ABETTOR
ADAPTOR
AERATOR
ALLSTON
ANISTON
ARISTOS
AUDITOR
AVIATOR
BALATON
BARSTOW
BIENTOT
BONITOS
BRAXTON
BRISTOL
BRITTON
BUSSTOP
CAPITOL
CARLTON
CHEETOS
CHEWTOY
CLAPTON
CLAYTON
CLIFTON
CLINTON
COOKTOP
COUNTON
CREATOR
CROUTON
CRYPTOS
CURATOR
DESKTOP
DESOTOS
DONATOR
DORITOS
ELECTOR
ENACTOR
EQUATOR
ERECTOR
EXACTOR
FLATTOP
FRONTON
GANGTOK
GERITOL
GETITON
GHETTOS
GLUTTON
GOTITON
GRAFTON
GRANTOR
GROTTOS
GYRATOR
HALSTON
HAMPTON
HARDTOP
HIGHTOP
HILLTOP
HOUSTON
JANITOR
KILOTON
KRYPTON
LAYITON
LEANTOS
LEGATOS
LOCATOR
LONGTON
MAINTOP
MANITOU
MOLOTOV
MONITOR
NEGATOR
NONSTOP
ONLYTOO
OPENTOE
PALMTOP
PHAETON
PHANTOM
PITSTOP
PRAETOR
PRESTON
PRESTOS
PROCTOR
QUARTOS
RALSTON
REACTOR
REALTOR
RIGHTON
ROLLTOP
ROOFTOP
ROPETOW
ROTATOR
RUBATOS
SENATOR
SHELTON
SHORTOF
SKELTON
SLAYTON
SLEPTON
SMALTOS
SOFTTOP
SPECTOR
STANTON
STENTOR
STILTON
SWEETON
SYMPTOM
TANKTOP
TOLSTOI
TOLSTOY
TRACTOR
TRAITOR
TREETOP
TRENTON
VISITOR
WALSTON
WHARTON
WHEATON
WINSTON
YANKTON

••••T•O
ADMITTO
ANNATTO
CAVETTO
ELECTRO
HORATIO
INPETTO
INVITRO
LESOTHO
MAESTRO
ONLYTOO
ORNITHO
POINTTO
PUTITTO
REACTTO
RIDOTTO
RISOTTO
STRETTO
ZAPATEO
ZEMSTVO

•••••TO
ADDEDTO
ADDONTO
ADDUPTO
ADMITTO
AGITATO
AGREETO
AIMEDTO
AKIHITO
ALBERTO
ANIMATO
ANNATTO
ARIOSTO
BANDITO
BRINGTO
BURRITO
CATERTO
CAVETTO
CHRISTO
COMESTO
CONMOTO
CUTINTO
DARESTO
DEFACTO
ERNESTO
ESPARTO
EXFACTO
FALLSTO
FLOCKTO
GEARSTO
GETINTO
GIVENTO
GIVESTO
GOTINTO
HAEMATO
HEAVETO
HOLDSTO
IMPASTO
INPETTO
KEEPSTO
LAYINTO
LEADSTO
LEDUPTO
LEPANTO
LITINTO
LOOKSTO
LYINGTO
MAGNETO
MARCATO
MEMENTO
MODESTO
OTRANTO
OWINGTO
PIMENTO
POINTTO
PRAYSTO
PRIORTO
PRYINTO
PUTITTO
RALLYTO
RAMINTO
RANINTO
REACTTO
REFERTO
RIDOTTO
RIPINTO
RISOTTO
ROBERTO
RUNINTO
SETINTO
SFUMATO
SINGSTO
SNAPSTO
SPIRITO
SQUANTO
STICKTO
STRETTO
STUCKTO
SUHARTO
SWEARTO
TAKESTO
TALKSTO
TAPINTO
TARANTO
TENDSTO
THERETO
TIEINTO
TORONTO
TURNSTO
UMBERTO
VIBRATO
WANTSTO
WHERETO
WRITETO
WROTETO

T•P••••
TAPEMAN
TAPEMEN
TAPERED
TAPINGS
TAPINTO
TAPIOCA
TAPPERS
TAPPETS
TAPPING
TAPROOM
TAPROOT
TAPSOFF
TAPSOUT
TAPSTER
TEPIDLY
TIPLESS
TIPOFFS
TIPPERS
TIPPETS
TIPPIER
TIPPING
TIPPLED
TIPPLER
TIPPLES
TIPSIER
TIPSILY
TIPSOFF
TIPSTER
TIPTOED
TIPTOES
TIPTOPS
TOPAZES
TOPCOAT
TOPDOGS
TOPDOWN
TOPGUNS
TOPHATS
TOPHOLE
TOPIARY
TOPICAL
TOPKAPI
TOPKICK
TOPKNOT
TOPMAST
TOPMOST
TOPPERS
TOPPING
TOPPLED
TOPPLES
TOPSAIL
TOPSIDE
TOPSOFF
TOPSOIL
TOPSOUT
TUPELOS
TYPEDUP
TYPESET
TYPESUP
TYPHOON
TYPICAL
TYPIEST
TYPISTS

T••P•••
TADPOLE
TAIPANS
TAMPERS
TAMPICO
TAMPING
TAPPERS
TAPPETS
TAPPING
TARPITS
TARPONS
TEAPOTS
TEAPOYS
TEEPEES
TEMPEHS
TEMPERA
TEMPERS
TEMPEST
TEMPLAR
TEMPLES
TEMPTED
TEMPTER
TEMPURA
TENPINS
THEPITS
TIEPINS
TIEPOLO
TIPPERS
TIPPETS
TIPPIER
TIPPING
TIPPLED
TIPPLER
TIPPLES
TOPPERS
TOPPING
TOPPLED
TOPPLES
TORPEDO
TOSPARE
TOUPEES
TOWPATH
TRAPEZE
TRAPPED
TRAPPER
TREPANS
TRIPLED
TRIPLES
TRIPLET
TRIPLEX
TRIPODS
TRIPOLI
TRIPPED
TRIPPER
TRIPPET
TRIPSUP
TROPHIC
TROPICS
TROPISM
TYMPANA
TYMPANI

T•••P••
TENSPOT
TERAPHS
THESPIS
THIMPHU
THUMPED
THUMPER
TRAIPSE
TRAMPAS
TRAMPED
TRAMPLE
TRAPPED
TRAPPER
TRIPPED
TRIPPER
TRIPPET
TROOPED
TROOPER
TROUPER
TROUPES
TRUMPED
TRUMPET
TRUMPUP

T••••P•
TEACUPS
THERAPY
THREEPM
TINTYPE
TIPTOPS
TITTUPS
TOECAPS
TOETAPS
TOPKAPI
TOSSUPS
TOWROPE
TRICEPS
TRIUMPH
TUNEUPS
TURNIPS

T•••••P
TAKESUP
TALKSUP
TALLYUP
TANKSUP
TANKTOP
TEAMSUP
TEARSUP
TEASHOP
TENSEUP
THEDEEP
THINKUP
TIECLIP
TIMECOP
TIMESUP
TOELOOP
TONEDUP
TONESUP
TOOLSUP
TOUCHUP
TOYSHOP
TRADEUP
TREETOP
TRIPSUP
TRUMPUP
TUNEDUP
TUNESUP
TURNSUP
TWOSTEP
TYINGUP
TYPEDUP
TYPESUP

•TP••••
ATPEACE
STPETER

•T•P•••
STAPLED
STAPLER
STAPLES
STEPHEN
STEPINS
STEPOUT
STEPPED
STEPPER
STEPPES
STEPSIN
STEPSON
STEPSUP
STEPUPS
STIPEND
STIPPLE
STOPGAP
STOPOFF
STOPPED
STOPPER
STOPSIN
STOPSUP
STUPEFY
STUPORS
STYPTIC
UTOPIAN
UTOPIAS

•T••P••
ATROPHY
STAMPED
STAYPUT
STEEPED
STEEPEN
STEEPER
STEEPLE
STEEPLY
STEPPED
STEPPER
STEPPES
STIPPLE
STOMPED
STOOPED
STOPPED
STOPPER
STRIPED
STRIPER
STRIPES
STROPHE
STROPPY
STUMPED
STUMPER

•T•••P•
ATTEMPT
STEPUPS
STROPPY

•T••••P
STACKUP
STANDUP
STARMAP
STARTUP
STAYSUP
STEPSUP
STICKUP
STIRRUP
STIRSUP
STOCKUP
STOODUP
STOPGAP
STOPSUP
STOREUP
STUCKUP

••TP•••
BITPART
HATPINS
HOTPOTS
JETPORT
NITPICK
OUTPACE
OUTPLAY
OUTPOLL
OUTPOST
OUTPUTS
POTPIES
PUTPUTS
RATPACK

••T•P••
ACTUPON
CATSPAW
ECTYPES
GOTOPOT
HOTSPOT
HOTSPUR
LETUPON
NOTEPAD
OCTOPOD
OCTOPUS
OCTUPLE
ONTOPOF
PITAPAT
PUTUPON
RETAPED
RETAPES
RETYPED
RETYPES
SETUPON
UNTAPED
UPTOPAR
ZATOPEK

••T••P•
ATTEMPT
BITMAPS
CATALPA
CATNAPS
CATNIPS
ENTRAPS
ENTROPY
EUTERPE
HOTCAPS
HOTLIPS
HOTTIPS
SATRAPS
TITTUPS
UNTRAPS
UPTEMPO
WETMOPS

••T•••P
ACTEDUP
ANTEDUP
ANTESUP
ANTWERP
BOTCHUP
CATCHUP
EATENUP
KETCHUP
LETSLIP
MATCHUP
NOTRUMP
OUTCROP
OUTJUMP
OUTSTEP
PATCHUP
PITSTOP
RATTRAP

•••TP••
DUSTPAN
FOOTPAD
SHOTPUT

•••T•P•
BIGTOPS
BOXTOPS
DUSTUPS
HOTTIPS
INSTEPS
ISOTOPE
LAPTOPS
MISTYPE
MOPTOPS
PEGTOPS
PLATYPI
POPTOPS
PRETAPE
RAGTOPS
REDTAPE
REDTOPS
TINTYPE
TIPTOPS
TITTUPS
TOETAPS
UNSTOPS
WENTAPE

•••T••P
BEATSUP
BOOTSUP
CANTRIP
CHATSUP
DAYTRIP
DUSTMOP
EGOTRIP
FLATTOP
FLYTRAP
HEATSUP
LIFTSUP
MANTRAP
PASTEUP
PHOTOOP
RATTRAP
RESTAMP
RESTSUP
SHUTSUP
SOFTTOP
SUITSUP
UNSTRAP
WAITSUP
WRITEUP
WROTEUP

••••TP•
EIGHTPM

••••T•P
BOOSTUP
BOXSTEP
BUILTUP
BURNTUP
BUSSTOP
COOKTOP
DESKTOP
FLATTOP
FOULTIP
HAMITUP
HARDTOP
HEELTAP
HIGHTOP
HILLTOP
LIGHTUP
MAINTOP
MISSTEP
MIXITUP
NONSTOP
ONESTEP
OUTSTEP
PALMTOP
PITSTOP
ROLLTOP
ROOFTOP
SHOOTUP
SOFTTOP
SPLITUP
STARTUP
SWEPTUP
TANKTOP
TREETOP
TWOSTEP
WINGTIP
WIRETAP

T•Q••••
TEQUILA
TSQUARE

T••Q•••
TORQUES

••T•Q••
ANTIQUE

••T••Q•
ONTHEQT

TR•••••
TRABERT
TRACERS
TRACERY
TRACHEA
TRACING
TRACKED
TRACKER
TRACTOR
TRADEIN
TRADEON
TRADERS
TRADEUP
TRADING
TRADUCE
TRAFFIC
TRAGEDY
TRAILED
TRAILER
TRAINED
TRAINEE
TRAINER
TRAIPSE
TRAITOR
TRALALA
TRAMCAR
TRAMMEL
TRAMPAS
TRAMPED
TRAMPLE
TRANCES
TRANSIT
TRANSOM
TRAPEZE
TRAPPED
TRAPPER
TRASHED
TRASHES
TRAUMAS
TRAVAIL
TRAVELS
TRAVERS
TRAVOIS
TRAWLED
TRAWLER
TRAYFUL
TREACLE
TREACLY
TREADED
TREADER
TREADLE
TREASON
TREATED
TREBLED
TREBLES
TREEING
TREERAT
TREETOP
TREFOIL
TREKKED
TREKKER
TREKKIE
TRELLIS
TREMAIN
TREMBLE
TREMBLY
TREMOLO
TREMORS
TRENARY
TRENDED
TRENTON
TREPANS
TRESSES
TRESTLE
TREVINO
TRIBUNE
TRIBUTE
TRICEPS
TRICKED
TRICKER
TRICKLE
TRICORN
TRICOTS
TRIDENT
TRIEDON
TRIESON
TRIESTE
TRIFLED
TRIFLER
TRIFLES
TRIGGED
TRIGGER
TRIGONS
TRIGRAM
TRIJETS
TRILLED
TRILLIN
TRILOGY
TRIMMED
TRIMMER
TRINITY
TRINKET
TRIODES
TRIPLED
TRIPLES
TRIPLET
TRIPLEX
TRIPODS
TRIPOLI
TRIPPED
TRIPPER
TRIPPET
TRIPSUP
TRIREME
TRISECT
TRISHAW
TRISTAN
TRISTAR
TRITELY
TRITEST
TRITIUM
TRITONE
TRITONS
TRIUMPH
TRIUNES
TRIVETS
TRIVIAL
TROCARS
TROCHEE
TROCHES
TRODDEN
TROGONS
TROIKAS
TROILUS
TROJANS
TROLLED
TROLLEY
TROOPED
TROOPER
TROPHIC
TROPICS
TROPISM
TROTHED
TROTOUT
TROTSKY
TROTTED
TROTTER
TROUBLE
TROUGHS
TROUNCE
TROUPER

TROUPES
TROUSER
TROWELS
TROWERS
TRUANCY
TRUANTS
TRUCIAL
TRUCKED
TRUCKEE
TRUCKER
TRUCKLE
TRUDEAU
TRUDGED
TRUDGER
TRUDGES
TRUEING
TRUFFLE
TRUISMS
TRUMPED
TRUMPET
TRUMPUP
TRUNDLE
TRUSSED
TRUSSES
TRUSTED
TRUSTEE
TRYOUTS
TRYSTED
TRYSTER

T•R•••••

TARANTO
TARBABY
TARBELL
TARDIER
TARDILY
TARGETS
TARHEEL
TARIFFS
TARMACS
TARNISH
TARPITS
TARPONS
TARRIED
TARRIER
TARRIES
TARRING
TARSALS
TARSIER
TARTANS
TARTARE
TARTARS
TARTEST
TARTISH
TARZANA
TERAPHS
TERBIUM
TERCELS
TERCETS
TEREDOS
TERENCE
TERHUNE
TERMING
TERMINI
TERMITE
TERNARY
TERNATE
TERRACE
TERRAIN
TERRENE
TERRETS
TERRIER
TERRIES
TERRIFY
TERRORS
TERSELY
TERSEST
TERTIAL
THRALLS
THREADS
THREADY
THREATS
THREEAM
THREEPM
THREERS
THREWIN
THRIFTS
THRIFTY
THRILLS
THRIVED
THRIVES
THROATS
THROATY
THRONES
THRONGS
THROUGH
THROWER
THROWIN
THRUSTS
THRUWAY
TIRADES
TIREDER
TIREDLY
TIREDOF
TIREOUT
TORCHED
TORCHES
TOREOFF
TOREOUT
TOREROS
TORMENT
TORNADO
TORNOFF
TORNOUT
TOROIDS
TORONTO
TORPEDO
TORQUES
TORRENS
TORRENT
TORSION
TORTONI
TORYISH
TORYISM
TURBANS
TURBINE
TURBITS
TURBOTS
TUREENS
TURFIER
TURFWAR
TURKEYS
TURKISH
TURMOIL
TURNERS
TURNERY
TURNING
TURNIPS
TURNKEY
TURNOFF
TURNOUT
TURNSIN
TURNSON
TURNSTO
TURNSUP
TURRETS
TURTLED
TURTLES
TYRANNY
TYRANTS

T••R•••

TAPROOM
TAPROOT
TARRIED
TARRIER
TARRIES
TARRING
TAURINE
TAXRATE
TEARFUL
TEARGAS
TEARIER
TEARILY
TEARING
TEAROFF
TEAROOM
TEAROSE
TEAROUT
TEARSAT
TEARSUP
TENRECS
TERRACE
TERRAIN
TERRENE
TERRETS
TERRIER
TERRIES
TERRIFY
TERRORS
TETRADS
THERAPY
THEREAT
THEREBY
THEREIN
THERELL
THEREOF
THEREON
THERESA
THERETO
THERMAL
THERMOS
THEROUX
THIRDLY
THIRSTS
THIRSTY
THOREAU
THORIUM
THURBER
THURMAN
TIERACK
TIERING
TIERNEY
TIERODS
TIGRESS
TIGRISH
TITRATE
TITRING
TOORDER
TORRENS
TORRENT
TOURACO
TOURERS
TOURING
TOURISM
TOURIST
TOURNEY
TOWROPE
TRIREME
TSARINA
TSARIST
TUAREGS
TUGRIKS
TURRETS
TWIRLED
TWIRLER
TZARINA

T•••R••

TABARDS
TABORET
TALARIA
TAMARIN
TANGRAM
TANTRUM
TAPERED
TAVERNS
TAXFREE
TEATRAY
TEATREE
TEHERAN
TELERAN
TENDRIL
TENURED
TENURES
THECROW
THEOREM
THEURGY
THWARTS
TIMBRES
TONEROW
TOREROS
TOWARDS
TOWERED
TOYSRUS
TREERAT
TRIGRAM
TSHIRTS
TSOURIS
TUMBREL
TUNDRAS
TUTORED
TWOIRON

T••••R•

TACKERS
TAILORS
TALKERS
TAMPERS
TANGERE
TANKARD
TANKERS
TANNERS
TANNERY
TANTARA
TAPPERS
TARTARE
TARTARS
TASTERS
TATTERS
TEACART
TEASERS
TEDDERS
TEENERS
TEETERS
TELLERS
TEMPERA
TEMPERS
TEMPURA
TENDERS
TENNERS
TENSORS
TENTERS
TERNARY
TERRORS
TESSERA
TESTERS
TETHERS
TEXTURE
THALERS
THEATRE
THECARS
THEFIRM
THENARS
THREERS
TICKERS
TILLERS
TILTERS
TIMBERS
TINDERS
TINEARS
TINHORN
TINKERS
TINNERS
TINTERN
TINTERS
TINWARE
TINWORK
TIPPERS
TITFERS
TITHERS
TITTERS
TOGGERY
TOILERS
TONEARM
TONSURE
TOOTERS
TOPIARY
TOPPERS
TOSPARE
TOSSERS
TOTTERS
TOTTERY
TOURERS
TOUTERS
TOWCARS
TOWNERS
TRABERT
TRACERS
TRACERY
TRADERS
TRAVERS
TREMORS
TRENARY
TRICORN
TROCARS
TROWERS
TSQUARE
TUCKERS
TUGGERS
TURNERS
TURNERY
TUSKERS
TWOFERS

T•••••R

TABULAR
TACKIER
TACKLER
TALKIER
TALLIER
TAMBOUR
TANAGER
TANGIER
TAPSTER
TARDIER
TARRIER
TARSIER
TASTIER
TATTIER
TATTLER
TAWNIER
TEACHER
TEARIER
TECHIER
TEENIER
TEETHER
TEICHER
TELSTAR
TEMBLOR
TEMPLAR
TEMPTER
TENFOUR
TERRIER
TESTIER
THEATER
THEWIER
THICKER
THINAIR
THINKER
THINNER
THITHER
THROWER
THUMPER
THUNDER
THURBER
THUSFAR
TICKLER
TIGHTER
TIMIDER
TINNIER
TINSTAR
TIPPIER
TIPPLER
TIPSIER
TIPSTER
TIREDER
TITULAR
TOASTER
TODDLER
TOFFLER
TOORDER
TOUGHER
TRACKER
TRACTOR
TRAILER
TRAINER
TRAITOR
TRAMCAR
TRAPPER
TRAWLER
TREADER
TREKKER
TRICKER
TRIFLER
TRIGGER
TRIMMER
TRIPPER
TRISTAR
TROOPER
TROTTER
TROUPER
TROUSER
TRUCKER
TRUDGER
TRYSTER
TUBBIER
TUBULAR
TUFTIER
TUMBLER
TURFIER
TURFWAR
TUTELAR
TWEETER
TWIRLER
TWISTER
TWITTER
TWOSTAR

•TR••••

ATRIUMS
ATROPHY
ETRURIA
OTRANTO
STRAFED
STRAFES
STRAINS
STRAITS
STRANDS
STRANGE
STRASSE
STRATUM
STRATUS
STRAUSS
STRAYED
STREAKS
STREAKY
STREAMS
STREETS
STRETCH
STRETTO
STREWED
STREWER
STRIATE
STRIDER
STRIDES
STRIKER
STRIKES
STRINGS
STRINGY
STRIPED
STRIPER
STRIPES
STRIVED
STRIVEN
STRIVER
STRIVES
STROBES
STROKED
STROKES
STROLLS
STROPHE
STROPPY
STRUDEL
UTRECHT
UTRILLO

•T•R•••

ATTRACT
ATTRITE
ATTRITS
ETERNAL
ITERANT
ITERATE
STARCHY
STARDOM
STAREAT
STARERS
STARETS
STARING
STARKER
STARKLY
STARLET
STARLIT
STARMAN
STARMAP
STARRED
STARTED
STARTER
STARTLE
STARTUP
STARVED
STARVES
STCROIX
STEREOS
STERILE
STERNAL
STERNER
STERNLY
STERNUM
STEROID
STEROLS
STIRFRY
STIRRED
STIRRER
STIRRUP
STIRSIN
STIRSUP
STORAGE
STORERS
STOREUP
STOREYS
STORIED
STORIES
STORING
STORMED
STURGES
STYRENE
STYRIAN
YTTRIUM

•T••R••

ATECROW
ATHIRST
ATLARGE
ATTIRED
ATTIRES
ATWORST
ETRURIA
STARRED
STEERED
STEERER
STIRRED
STIRRER
STIRRUP
UTTERED
UTTERER
UTTERLY

•T•••R•

ATATURK
ATHEART
ATHWART
ETAGERE
ETCHERS
STAGERS
STARERS
STATORS
STATURE
STEWARD
STEWART
STEWERS
STIRFRY
STOKERS
STONERS
STORERS
STUMERS
STUPORS
STYLERS

•T••••R

ATELIER
ITCHIER
STABLER
STAFFER
STAGGER
STAGIER
STAIDER
STAINER
STALKER
STAMMER
STAPLER
STARKER
STARTER
STEAMER
STEELER
STEEPER
STEERER
STEIGER
STEINER
STELLAR
STENTOR
STEPPER
STERNER
STICKER
STIFFER
STILLER
STINGER
STINKER
STIRRER
STOLLER
STONIER
STOPPER
STOUTER
STPETER
STREWER
STRIDER
STRIKER
STRIPER
STRIVER
STUFFER
STUMPER
STUNNER
UTTERER

••TR•••

ACTRESS
ASTRIDE
ATTRACT
ATTRITE
ATTRITS
BETRAYS
BETROTH
CITRATE
CITRINE
CITROEN
CITRONS
CITROUS
CUTRATE
DETRACT
DETRAIN
DETROIT
ENTRAIN
ENTRANT
ENTRAPS
ENTREAT
ENTREES
ENTRIES
ENTROPY
ENTRUST
ESTRADA
ESTRAYS
EXTRACT
EXTREME
EXTRUDE
GETREAL
HATRACK
HOTRODS
INTROIT
INTRUDE
INTRUST
INTRUTH
MATRONS
METRICS
MITRING
NATRIUM
NITRATE
NITRIDE
NITRITE
NITROUS
NOTRUMP
NUTRIAS
OBTRUDE
OCTROIS
ONTRACK
ONTRIAL
OSTRICH
OUTRACE
OUTRAGE
OUTRANK
OUTRUNS
PATRIAL
PATRICE
PATRICK
PATRIOT
PATROLS
PATRONS
PATROON
PETRELS
PETRIFY
PETROCK
PETROLS
PETROUS
RATRACE
RETRACE
RETRACK
RETRACT
RETRADE
RETRAIN
RETREAD
RETREAT
RETRIAL
RETRIED
RETRIES
RETRIMS
SATRAPS
TETRADS
TITRATE
TITRING
UNTRAPS
UNTRIED
UNTRUTH
VITRIFY
VITRIOL
YTTRIUM

••T•R••

ALTERED
ALTERER
ANTARES
APTERAL
ASTARTE
ASTORIA
ATTIRED
ATTIRES
AUTARKY
BETARAY
BYTURNS
CATERED
CATERER
CATERTO
CETERIS
COTERIE
DOTARDS
EATCROW
ENTERED
ENTERON
ENTHRAL
ESTORIL
EUTERPE
EXTERNS
EXTORTS
FUTURES
GUTHRIE
INTERIM
INTERNS
INTERSE
KATHRYN
LATERAL
LATERAN
LATERON
LETTRES
LITCRIT
LITERAL
LITURGY
MATURED
MATURER
MATURES
METERED
MITERED
MITHRAS
MOTORED
NATURAL
NATURED
NATURES
NOTTRUE
ONTARIO
OUTCROP
OUTDRAW
OUTDREW
OUTGREW
OUTGROW
PATERNO
PETARDS
PETERED
POTOROO
QATARIS
RATTRAP
RETARDS
RETIRED
RETIREE
RETIRES
RETORTS
RETURNS
SATIRES
SATIRIC
SUTURED
SUTURES
TUTORED
UPTURNS
UTTERED
UTTERER
UTTERLY
VETERAN
WATERED
WATERER

••T••R•

ACTUARY
AETHERS
ANTFARM
ANTHERS
ANTIART
ANTLERS
ANTWERP
ARTFORM
ARTWARE
ARTWORK
ASTAIRE
AUTEURS
AUTHORS
BATGIRL
BATHERS
BATTERS
BATTERY
BETTERS
BETTORS
BITPART
BITTERN
BITTERS
BOTHERS
BUTLERS
BUTTERS
BUTTERY
CATBERT
CATBIRD
COTTERS
CUTLERS
CUTLERY
CUTTERS
DETOURS
DITHERS
DITHERY
ESTUARY
FATHERS
FETTERS
FITTERS
GATHERS
GUTTERS
HATTERS
HITHERE
HITTERS
HOTCARS
HOTWARS
HOTWIRE
INTEARS
INTEGRA
JETPORT
JITTERS
JITTERY
LATHERS
LATHERY
LETTERS
LITTERS
LOTTERY
MATHERS
MATTERS
METEORS
METIERS
MITFORD
MOTHERS
MUTTERS
NATTERS
NETSURF
NETWORK
NOTSURE
NUTTERS
OSTLERS
OUTWARD
OUTWORE
OUTWORK
OUTWORN
PATTERN
PATTERS
PETTERS
PITIERS
PITTERS
POTHERB
POTHERS
POTTERS
POTTERY
PUTTERS
RATBERT
RATTERS
RETEARS
RETIARY
RETOURS
ROTTERS
RUTGERS
SETTERS
SITTERS
SOTHERE
SOTHERN
SUTLERS
SUTTERS
TATTERS
TETHERS
TITFERS
TITHERS
TITTERS
TOTTERS
TOTTERY
VETOERS
WETBARS
WETHERS
WITHERS
ZITHERS

••T•••R

ACTFOUR
ALTERER
ANTBEAR
ANTIWAR
ANTSIER
ARTSIER
BATTIER
BATTLER
BITSIER
BITTIER
BOTTLER
BUTCHER
CATCHER
CATERER
CATHAIR
CATTIER
CNTOWER
DITSIER
DITZIER
DOTTIER
ENTICER
FATTIER
GETOVER
GOTOVER
GUTSIER
GUTTIER
HATCHER
HITCHER
HOTSPUR
INTEGER
INTONER
LITTLER
MATADOR
MATURER
METOOER
MOTHIER
NATTIER
NITTIER
NUTSIER
NUTTIER
OBTUSER
OCTOBER
OFTENER
OPTSFOR
OUTDOOR
OUTWEAR
PETTIER
PITCHER
PITHIER
POTSIER
POTTIER
PUTOVER
RATTIER
RATTLER
RITZIER
ROTATOR
ROTIFER
RUTTIER
SETTLER
TATTIER
TATTLER
TITULAR
TUTELAR
UPTOPAR
UTTERER
VOTEFOR
WATCHER
WATERER
WITHIER
WITTIER

•••TR••

ASHTRAY
AUSTRAL
AUSTRIA
BEATRIX
BESTREW
BISTROS
BOUTROS
CANTRIP
CENTRAL
CENTRED
CENTRES
CENTRIC
CHETRUM
CONTRAS
CONTROL
DALTREY
DAYTRIP
DESTROY
DEXTRIN
DMYTRYK
DOGTROT
EGOTRIP
ELMTREE
ERITREA
FLYTRAP
FORTRAN
FOXTROT
GASTRIC
GUMTREE
KESTREL
LAUTREC
LETTRES
LUSTRED
LUSTRES
MAITRED
MANTRAP
MANTRAS
MANTRIC
MAYTREE
MISTRAL
NEUTRAL
NEUTRON
NOSTRIL
NOSTRUM
NOTTRUE

OAKTREE
PALTROW
PORTRAY
RATTRAP
ROSTRUM
SISTRUM
TANTRUM
TEATRAY
TEATREE
UNSTRAP
UPATREE
VENTRAL
WAITRON
WASTREL

•••T•R•

AMATORY
ATATURK
AUSTERE
AVATARS
BANTERS
BARTERS
BASTERS
BATTERS
BATTERY
BEATERS
BESTIRS
BETTERS
BETTORS
BITTERN
BITTERS
BOATERS
BUSTARD
BUSTERS
BUTTERS
BUTTERY
CANTERS
CANTORS
CAPTORS
CAPTURE
CARTERS
CASTERS
CENTERS
CENTURY
CISTERN
CLOTURE
CONTORT
COPTERS
COSTARS
COTTERS
COUTURE
CRATERS
CULTURE
CUSTARD
CUTTERS
DARTERS
DASTARD
DEBTORS
DENTURE
DEUTERO
DIETARY
DIETERS
DISTORT
DISTURB
DOCTORS
DUSTERS
EASTERN
EASTERS
EDITORS
ELATERS
EMOTERS
ESOTERY
FACTORS
FACTORY
FALTERS
FEATURE
FESTERS
FETTERS
FILTERS
FITTERS
FIXTURE
FOOTERS
FOSTERS
GAITERS
GARTERS
GESTURE
GRATERS
GUITARS
GUTTERS
HALTERS
HATTERS
HEATERS
HECTARE
HECTORS
HISTORY
HITTERS
HOOTERS
HUNTERS
INSTARS
INSTORE
JESTERS
JITTERS
JITTERY
KRATERS
LANTERN
LASTORY
LECTERN
LECTORS
LECTURE
LEOTARD
LETTERS
LICTORS
LIFTERS
LITTERS
LOITERS
LOOTERS
LOTTERY
LUSTERS
MARTYRS
MASTERS
MASTERY
MATTERS
MENTORS
MIDTERM
MINTERS
MISTERS
MIXTURE
MOLTERS
MONTERO
MORTARS
MUSTARD
MUSTERS
MUTTERS
MYSTERY
NATTERS
NECTARS
NESTERS
NOCTURN
NURTURE
NUTTERS
ORATORS
ORATORY
OUSTERS
OYSTERS
PALTERS
PASTERN
PASTORS
PASTURE
PATTERN
PATTERS
PELTERS
PERTURB
PESTERS
PETTERS
PICTURE
PITTERS
PLATERS
POPTART
PORTERS
POSTERN
POSTERS
POSTURE
POTTERS
POTTERY
POUTERS
PRATERS
PUNTERS
PUTTERS
QINTARS
QUOTERS
RAFTERS
RANTERS
RAPTORS
RAPTURE
RASTERS
RATTERS
RECTORS
RECTORY
RENTERS
RESTART
RESTERS
RESTORE
REUTERS
RHETORS
RIOTERS
RIPTORN
ROOTERS
ROSTERS
ROTTERS
ROUTERS
RUPTURE
SALTERS
SANTIRS
SCOTERS
SEATERS
SECTORS
SETTERS
SIFTERS
SISTERS
SITTERS
SKATERS
SORTERS
STATORS
STATURE
SUITORS
SUTTERS
TANTARA
TARTARE
TARTARS
TASTERS
TATTERS
TEETERS
TENTERS
TESTERS
TEXTURE
TILTERS
TINTERN
TINTERS
TITTERS
TOOTERS
TOTTERS
TOTTERY
TOUTERS
ULSTERS
UNITARY
UNITERS
UPSTART
VECTORS
VENTERS
VENTURA
VENTURE
VESTURE
VICTORS
VICTORY
VULTURE
WAITERS
WALTERS
WASTERS
WELTERS
WESTERN
WINTERS
WINTERY
WRITERS

•••T••R

ABETTOR
AMATEUR
ANOTHER
BATTIER
BATTLER
BITTIER
BLATHER
BLITHER
BLOTTER
BOTTLER
BROTHER
CARTIER
CATTIER
CENTAUR
CHATTER
CHITTER
CLATTER
CLUTTER
CONTOUR
COSTNER
CRITTER
DIRTIER
DOTTIER
DUSTIER
EMITTER
EMPTIER
FARTHER
FATTIER
FEATHER
FELTFOR
FLATCAR
FLATTER
FLITTER
FLUTIER
FLUTTER
FRITTER
FURTHER
FUSTIER
GENTLER
GLITTER
GOUTIER
GUNTHER
GUSTIER
GUTTIER
HASTIER
HAUTEUR
HEATHER
HEATTER
HEFTIER
HOSTLER
HUSTLER
JOLTIER
JOSTLER
KNITTER
LEATHER
LINTIER
LITTLER
LOFTIER
LUSTIER
MALTIER
MEATIER
MINTIER
MISTIER
MUSTIER
NASTIER
NATTIER
NEITHER
NESTLER
NIFTIER
NITTIER
NORTHER
NUTTIER
OMITTER
ONATEAR
PANTHER
PARTIER
PARTNER
PASTEUR
PASTIER
PEATIER
PETTIER
PLATIER
PLATTER
PLOTTER
POITIER
POSTWAR
POTTIER
POUTIER
QUITTER
RATTIER
RATTLER
REUTHER
ROOTFOR
ROOTIER
RUNTIER
RUSTIER
RUSTLER
RUTTIER
SALTIER
SCATTER
SELTZER
SENTFOR
SETTLER
SHATNER
SHATTER
SHOTFOR
SHUTTER
SILTIER
SKITTER
SLATHER
SLATIER
SLITHER
SLOTCAR
SMATTER
SMOTHER
SOOTHER
SOOTIER
SPATTER
SPOTTER
SPUTTER
SUBTLER
SWATTER
SWITZER
TASTIER
TATTIER
TATTLER
TEETHER
TESTIER
THITHER
TROTTER
TUFTIER
TWITTER
VASTIER
VINTNER
WAITFOR
WALTZER
WARTIER
WEATHER
WENTFOR
WERTHER
WHATFOR
WHETHER
WHITHER
WHITIER
WITTIER
ZESTIER

••••TR•

ABEXTRA
ABINTRA
BIGOTRY
COUNTRY
DIMITRI
DYKSTRA
ELECTRA
ELECTRO
ELEKTRA
HELOTRY
INVITRO
LANGTRY
MAESTRI
MAESTRO
OLESTRA
PHILTRE
PIASTRE
PLECTRA
POULTRY
REENTRY
SCEPTRE
SHASTRI
SINATRA
SPECTRA
SPECTRE
SUMATRA
SWELTRY
THEATRE

••••T•R

ABETTOR
ADAPTER
ADAPTOR
ADOPTER
AERATOR
ALERTER
ALLSTAR
AMMETER
ARBITER
AUDITOR
AVIATOR
BAINTER
BENATAR
BLASTER
BLISTER
BLOTTER
BLUNTER
BLUSTER
BOASTER
BOLSTER
BOOSTER
CHANTER
CHAPTER
CHARTER
CHASTER
CHATTER
CHEATER
CHESTER
CHITTER
CHUNTER
CLATTER
CLUSTER
CLUTTER
COALTAR
COASTER
COULTER
COUNTER
CRAFTER
CREATOR
CRITTER
CROFTER
CURATOR
DAYSTAR
DEBATER
DECATUR
DEMETER
DILUTER
DIOPTER
DOGSTAR
DONATOR
DOUBTER
DRIFTER
ELECTOR
EMITTER
ENACTOR
EQUATOR
ERECTER
ERECTOR
EXACTER
EXACTOR
FAINTER
FIGHTER
FLATTER
FLEETER
FLITTER
FLOATER
FLUSTER
FLUTTER
FORSTER
FRITTER
GAGSTER
GAUNTER
GLITTER
GOAFTER
GRANTOR
GREATER
GREETER
GRIFTER
GYRATOR
HAMSTER
HEATTER
HIPSTER
HOLSTER
IGNITER
INAPTER
INCITER
JACKTAR
JANITOR
JOUSTER
JUPITER
KNITTER
LEISTER
LIGHTER
LOBSTER
LOCATER
LOCATOR
MEISTER
MOBSTER
MOISTER
MONITOR
MONSTER
NEGATER
NEGATOR
OLDSTER
OMITTER
ONESTAR
ORBITER
PAINTER
PHILTER
PIASTER
PINETAR
PLANTAR
PLANTER
PLASTER
PLATTER
PLOTTER
POINTER
POLITER
PRAETOR
PRINTER
PROCTOR
PROPTER
PSALTER
PUNSTER
QUARTER
QUIETER
QUILTER
QUITTER
REACTOR
REALTOR
RECITER
REDSTAR
REENTER
REFUTER
REMOTER
RICHTER
RIGHTER
RIVETER
ROASTER
ROISTER
ROOSTER
ROTATOR
SAUNTER
SCANTER
SCATTER
SCEPTER
SCOOTER
SCOUTER
SEASTAR
SEDATER
SENATOR
SHATTER
SHELTER
SHOOTER
SHORTER
SHOUTER
SHUTTER
SHYSTER
SKEETER
SKELTER
SKITTER
SMARTER
SMATTER
SMELTER
SNIFTER
SNORTER
SPATTER
SPECTER
SPECTOR
SPOTTER
SPOUTER
SPUTTER
STARTER
STENTOR
STOUTER
STPETER
SVELTER
SWATTER
SWEATER
SWEETER
SWELTER
SWIFTER
TAPSTER
TELSTAR
TEMPTER
THEATER
TIGHTER
TINSTAR
TIPSTER
TOASTER
TRACTOR
TRAITOR
TRISTAR
TROTTER
TRYSTER
TWEETER
TWISTER
TWITTER
TWOSTAR
VAULTER
VAUNTER
VISITOR
WEBSTER
WOOSTER

TS•••••

TSARINA
TSARIST
TSELIOT
TSETSES
TSHIRTS
TSOURIS
TSQUARE
TSUNAMI

T•S••••

TASHLIN
TASHMAN
TASKING
TASSELS
TASTERS
TASTIER
TASTILY
TASTING
TESSERA
TESTBAN
TESTEES
TESTERS
TESTFLY
TESTIER
TESTIFY
TESTILY
TESTING
TESTOUT
TESTUDO
TISANES
TISSUES
TOSCALE
TOSHIBA
TOSPARE
TOSSERS
TOSSING
TOSSOFF
TOSSOUT
TOSSUPS
TOSTADA
TUSCANY
TUSKERS
TUSSAUD
TUSSLED
TUSSLES
TUSSOCK
TVSHOWS

T••S•••

TAGSALE
TAGSOUT
TANSIES
TAPSOFF
TAPSOUT
TAPSTER
TARSALS
TARSIER
TASSELS
TEASELS
TEASERS
TEASETS
TEASHOP
TEASING
TEESOFF
TELSTAR
TENSELY
TENSEST
TENSEUP
TENSILE
TENSING
TENSION
TENSIVE
TENSORS
TENSPOT
TERSELY
TERSEST
TESSERA
THESEUS
THESPIS
THISTLE
THISTLY
THUSFAR
THYSELF
TINSELS
TINSTAR
TIPSIER
TIPSILY
TIPSOFF
TIPSTER
TISSUES
TOASTED
TOASTER
TOCSINS
TOESHOE
TOLSTOI
TOLSTOY
TONSILS
TONSURE
TOPSAIL
TOPSIDE
TOPSOFF
TOPSOIL
TOPSOUT
TORSION
TOSSERS
TOSSING
TOSSOFF
TOSSOUT
TOSSUPS
TOUSLED
TOUSLES
TOYSHOP
TOYSRUS
TRASHED
TRASHES
TRESSES
TRESTLE
TRISECT
TRISHAW
TRISTAN
TRISTAR
TRUSSED
TRUSSES
TRUSTED
TRUSTEE
TRYSTED
TRYSTER
TUESDAY
TULSANS
TUSSAUD
TUSSLED
TUSSLES
TUSSOCK
TWISTED
TWISTER
TWOSOME
TWOSTAR
TWOSTEP

T•••S••

TABASCO
TACKSON
TAKESIN
TAKESON
TAKESTO
TAKESUP
TALKSAT
TALKSTO
TALKSUP
TALUSES
TANKSUP
TAOISTS
TEAMSUP
TEARSAT
TEARSUP
TELLSOF
TELLSON
TENDSTO
THATSIT
THEISTS
THIRSTS
THIRSTY
THOMSON
THRUSTS
TIMESUP
TONESUP
TOOLSUP
TOOTSIE
TRANSIT
TRANSOM
TREASON
TRESSES
TRIESON
TRIESTE
TRIPSUP
TROTSKY
TROUSER
TRUISMS
TRUSSED
TRUSSES
TSETSES
TUBISTS
TUCKSIN
TUNESIN
TUNESUP
TUNISIA
TURNSIN
TURNSON
TURNSTO
TURNSUP
TYPESET
TYPESUP
TYPISTS

T••••S•

TALLEST
TALLISH
TANNEST
TANNISH
TARNISH
TARTEST
TARTISH
TAUTEST
TAXLESS
TBILISI
TEALESS
TEAROSE
TEMPEST
TENSEST
TERSEST
THERESA
TIDIEST
TIELESS
TIGRESS
TIGRISH
TINIEST
TIPLESS
TITLIST
TOADISH
TOELESS
TONIEST
TONNISH
TOPMAST
TOPMOST
TORYISH
TORYISM
TOURISM
TOURIST
TOWNISH
TOYLESS
TRAIPSE
TRITEST
TROPISM
TSARIST
TUBAIST
TUGLESS
TURKISH
TWOBASE
TYPIEST

T•••••S

TABARDS
TABBIES
TABLETS
TACITUS
TACKERS
TACKLES
TACTICS
TAFFIES
TAGENDS
TAILLES
TAILORS
TAIPANS
TALCUMS
TALENTS
TALKERS
TALKIES
TALLIES
TALLOWS
TALUSES
TAMALES
TAMPERS
TAMTAMS
TANDEMS
TANGLES
TANKERS
TANNERS
TANNINS
TANOAKS
TANSIES
TAOISTS
TAPINGS
TAPPERS
TAPPETS
TARGETS
TARIFFS
TARMACS
TARPITS
TARPONS
TARRIES
TARSALS
TARTANS
TARTARS
TASSELS
TASTERS
TATAMIS
TATTERS
TATTLES
TATTOOS
TAUTENS
TAVERNS
TAXLESS
TEABAGS
TEACHES
TEACUPS
TEALESS
TEAPOTS
TEAPOYS
TEARGAS
TEASELS
TEASERS
TEASETS
TECHIES
TEDDERS
TEDDIES
TEDIOUS
TEDIUMS
TEENERS
TEEPEES
TEETERS
TEETHES
TELEXES
TELLERS
TELLIES
TEMPEHS
TEMPERS
TEMPLES
TENACES
TENANTS
TENDERS
TENDONS
TENNERS
TENPINS
TENRECS
TENSORS
TENTERS
TENUOUS
TENURES
TERAPHS
TERCELS
TERCETS
TEREDOS
TERRETS
TERRIES
TERRORS
TESTEES
TESTERS
TETANUS
TETHERS
TETRADS
TEUTONS
THALERS
THECARS
THEISTS
THENARS
THEPITS
THERMOS
THESEUS
THESPIS
THIEVES
THIRSTS
THRALLS
THREADS
THREATS
THREERS
THRIFTS
THRILLS
THRIVES
THROATS
THRONES
THRONGS
THRUSTS
THWACKS
THWARTS
TICKERS
TICKETS
TICKLES
TICTACS
TIDBITS
TIDINGS
TIEDYES
TIELESS
TIEPINS
TIERODS
TIFFINS
TIGLONS
TIGRESS
TILINGS
TILLERS
TILTERS
TIMBALS
TIMBERS
TIMBRES
TIMINGS
TIMMINS
TINCANS
TINDERS
TINEARS
TINGLES
TINHATS
TINKERS
TINKLES
TINNERS
TINSELS
TINTERS
TIPLESS
TIPOFFS
TIPPERS
TIPPETS
TIPPLES
TIPTOES
TIPTOPS
TIRADES
TISANES
TISSUES
TITBITS
TITFERS

TITHERS
TITTERS
TITTLES
TITTUPS
TIZZIES
TOADIES
TOCSINS
TODDIES
TODDLES
TOECAPS
TOELESS
TOETAPS
TOFFEES
TOGGLES
TOILERS
TOILETS
TOLLIES
TOLTECS
TOMBOYS
TOMCATS
TOMTITS
TOMTOMS
TONGANS
TONGUES
TONSILS
TOONIES
TOOTERS
TOOTLES
TOPAZES
TOPDOGS
TOPGUNS
TOPHATS
TOPPERS
TOPPLES
TORCHES
TOREROS
TOROIDS
TORQUES
TORRENS
TOSSERS
TOSSUPS
TOTTERS
TOUCANS
TOUCHES
TOUPEES
TOURERS
TOUSLES
TOUTERS
TOWARDS
TOWCARS
TOWHEES
TOWNERS
TOWNIES
TOYDOGS
TOYLESS
TOYSRUS
TRACERS
TRADERS
TRAMPAS
TRANCES
TRASHES
TRAUMAS
TRAVELS
TRAVERS
TRAVOIS
TREBLES
TRELLIS
TREMORS
TREPANS
TRESSES
TRICEPS
TRICOTS
TRIFLES
TRIGONS
TRIJETS
TRIODES
TRIPLES
TRIPODS
TRITONS
TRIUNES
TRIVETS
TROCARS
TROCHES
TROGONS
TROIKAS
TROILUS
TROJANS
TROPICS
TROUGHS
TROUPES
TROWELS
TROWERS
TRUANTS
TRUDGES
TRUISMS
TRUSSES
TRYOUTS
TSETSES
TSHIRTS
TSOURIS
TUAREGS
TUBISTS
TUCKERS
TUFFETS
TUGGERS
TUGLESS
TUGRIKS
TULSANS
TUMBLES
TUMMIES
TUMULTS
TUMULUS
TUNDRAS
TUNEUPS
TUNNELS
TUNNIES
TUPELOS
TURBANS
TURBITS
TURBOTS
TUREENS
TURKEYS
TURNERS
TURNIPS
TURRETS
TURTLES
TUSKERS
TUSSLES
TUTTUTS
TUXEDOS
TVSHOWS
TWEEZES
TWELVES
TWINGES
TWOBITS
TWOFERS
TYCOONS
TYPISTS
TYRANTS

•TS••••

ATSTAKE

•T•S•••

ATISSUE
ETESIAN
KTOSLIN
STASHED
STASHES
STASSEN

•T••S••

ATISSUE
ATLASES
ATTESTS
STASSEN
STAYSUP
STEPSIN
STEPSON
STEPSUP
STETSON
STIRSIN
STIRSUP
STOPSIN
STOPSUP
STRASSE
UTENSIL

•T•••S•

ATALOSS
ATAVISM
ATAVIST
ATHEISM
ATHEIST
ATHIRST
ATLEAST
ATOMISE
ATWORST
ITEMISE
STALEST
STATIST
STRASSE
STRAUSS
STYLISE
STYLISH
STYLIST
UTILISE

•T••••S

ATALOSS
ATAMANS
ATHOMES
ATLASES
ATLATLS
ATOMIES
ATONIES
ATRIUMS
ATTACKS
ATTAINS
ATTENDS
ATTESTS
ATTICUS
ATTIMES
ATTIRES
ATTRITS
ATTUCKS
ATTUNES
ETCHERS
ETHNICS
ETOILES
ITALICS
OTTAWAS
PTBOATS
STABLES
STAGERS
STALAGS
STAMENS
STANCES
STANZAS
STAPLES
STARERS
STARETS
STARVES
STASHES
STATICS
STATORS
STATUES
STDENIS
STEPINS
STEPPES
STEPUPS
STEREOS
STEROLS
STEVENS
STEWERS
STICHES
STIFLES
STIGMAS
STINGOS
STJOHNS
STKITTS
STLOUIS
STOGIES
STOKERS
STOLONS
STONERS
STOOGES
STORERS
STOREYS
STORIES
STRAFES
STRAINS
STRAITS
STRANDS
STRATUS
STRAUSS
STREAKS
STREAMS
STREETS
STRIDES
STRIKES
STRINGS
STRIPES
STRIVES
STROBES
STROKES
STROLLS
STUCCOS
STUDIES
STUDIOS
STUMERS
STUPORS
STURGES
STYLERS
STYLETS
STYMIES
UTAHANS
UTOPIAS

••TS•••

ACTSOUT
ANTSIER
ARTSIER
ARTSONG
BATSMAN
BATSMEN
BITSIER
CATSCAN
CATSEYE
CATSHOW
CATSPAW
CATSUIT
CUTSOFF
CUTSOUT
DITSIER
EATSOUT
GETSOFF
GETSOUT
GETSSET
GUTSIER
GUTSILY
HITSOUT
HOTSEAT
HOTSHOT
HOTSPOT
HOTSPUR
JETSKIS
JETSONS
KITSCHY
LETSFLY
LETSLIP
LETSOFF
LETSOUT
LETSSEE
NETSUKE
NETSURF
NOTSURE
NUTSIER
OPTSFOR
OPTSOUT
OUTSELL
OUTSETS
OUTSIDE
OUTSIZE
OUTSOLD
OUTSTEP
PATSIES
PITSAWS
PITSTOP
POTSDAM
POTSHOT
POTSIER
PUTSOFF
PUTSOUT
RETSINA
SATSUMA
SETSAIL
SETSOFF
SETSOUT
SITSOUT
WETSUIT

••T•S••

ALTOSAX
ANTESUP
ARTISAN
ARTISTE
ARTISTS
ATTESTS
BATISTA
BATISTE
BETISES
BUTTSIN
DATASET
DETESTS
DOTESON
GETSSET
IQTESTS
LATOSCA
LETSSEE
LOTUSES
LUTISTS
MATISSE
MITOSES
MITOSIS
NATASHA
OBTUSER
RETESTS
SATISFY
VOTESIN

••T••S•

ACTRESS
APTNESS
ARTIEST
ARTLESS
BITLESS
CATFISH
CATTISH
CUTLASS
ENTHUSE
ENTRUST
FATLESS
FATNESS
FATTEST
FATTISH
FITNESS
FITTEST
GETLOST
GOTLOST
GUTLESS
HATLESS
HITLESS
HITLIST
HOTNESS
HOTTEST
INTENSE
INTERSE
INTRUST
JETWASH
LETTISH
LITHEST
MATISSE
MATLESS
OUTCAST
OUTLAST
OUTPOST
PATNESS
PETTISH
PITBOSS
RATTISH
RUTTISH
SOTTISH
TITLIST
UNTWIST
WETNESS
WETTEST
WETTISH
WITLESS
WITNESS

••T•••S

ACTIONS
ACTIVES
ACTRESS
AETHERS
AITCHES
ANTAEUS
ANTARES
ANTCOWS
ANTHEMS
ANTHERS
ANTIBES
ANTLERS
APTNESS
ARTEMIS
ARTEMUS
ARTISTS
ARTLESS
ATTACKS
ATTAINS
ATTENDS
ATTESTS
ATTICUS
ATTIMES
ATTIRES
ATTRITS
ATTUCKS
ATTUNES
AUTEURS
AUTHORS
AUTUMNS
BATBOYS
BATCHES
BATHERS
BATTELS
BATTENS
BATTERS
BATTLES
BATTUES
BETAKES
BETHELS
BETIDES
BETIMES
BETISES
BETRAYS
BETTERS
BETTORS
BITLESS
BITMAPS
BITTERS
BOTCHES
BOTHERS
BOTTLES
BOTTOMS
BUTLERS
BUTTERS
BUTTIES
BUTTONS
BYTURNS
CATCHES
CATIONS
CATKINS
CATNAPS
CATNIPS
CETERIS
CITRONS
CITROUS
COTTERS
COTTONS
CUTLASS
CUTLERS
CUTLETS
CUTOFFS
CUTOUTS
CUTTERS
DETAILS
DETAINS
DETECTS
DETESTS
DETOURS
DITCHES
DITHERS
DITTIES
DOTARDS
DOTTLES
DUTEOUS
ECTYPES
ENTAILS
ENTICES
ENTRAPS
ENTREES
ENTRIES
ESTATES
ESTEEMS
ESTRAYS
EXTENDS
EXTENTS
EXTERNS
EXTORTS
FATCATS
FATHERS
FATHOMS
FATLESS
FATNESS
FATTENS
FATUOUS
FETCHES
FETTERS
FETTLES
FITCHES
FITNESS
FITTERS
FUTURES
GATHERS
GOTCHAS
GOTHICS
GUTLESS
GUTTERS
HATCHES
HATLESS
HATPINS
HATTERS
HETMANS
HITCHES
HITLESS
HITTERS
HOTBEDS
HOTCAPS
HOTCARS
HOTDOGS
HOTLIPS
HOTNESS
HOTPOTS
HOTRODS
HOTTIPS
HOTTUBS
HOTWARS
HUTCHES
INTAKES
INTEARS
INTENDS
INTENTS
INTERNS
INTONES
INTUITS
IQTESTS
ISTHMUS
JETGUNS
JETSKIS
JETSONS
JETTIES
JETWAYS
JITNEYS
JITTERS
JUTTIES
KETCHES
KETONES
KETTLES
KITBAGS
KITTENS
KITTIES
LATCHES
LATEENS
LATENTS
LATEXES
LATHERS
LATICES
LATINAS
LATINOS
LATTENS
LETTERS
LETTRES
LITCHIS
LITOTES
LITTERS
LOTIONS
LOTUSES
LUTISTS
MATCHES
MATHERS
MATHEWS
MATHIAS
MATLESS
MATRONS
MATTERS
MATURES
MATZOHS
METATES
METEORS
METHODS
METIERS
METRICS
METTLES
MITHRAS
MITOSES
MITOSIS
MITTENS
MOTHERS
MOTIONS
MOTIVES
MOTTLES
MOTTOES
MUTANTS
MUTATES
MUTTERS
MUTTONS
MUTUALS
NATIONS
NATIVES
NATTERS
NATURES
NETTLES
NITROUS
NITWITS
NOTATES
NOTCHES
NOTICES
NOTIONS
NUTATES
NUTLETS
NUTMEGS
NUTRIAS
NUTTERS
OBTAINS
OBTUNDS
OCTANES
OCTANTS
OCTAVES
OCTAVOS
OCTOPUS
OCTROIS
OPTIONS
OSTLERS
OTTAWAS
OUTACTS
OUTAGES
OUTBIDS
OUTDOES
OUTEATS
OUTFITS
OUTGOES
OUTGUNS
OUTHITS
OUTINGS
OUTLAWS
OUTLAYS
OUTLETS
OUTPUTS
OUTRUNS
OUTSETS
OUTWITS
PATACAS
PATCHES
PATENTS
PATINAS
PATNESS
PATROLS
PATRONS
PATSIES
PATTENS
PATTERS
PATTIES
PETARDS
PETITES
PETRELS
PETROLS
PETROUS
PETTERS
PITBOSS
PITCHES
PITEOUS
PITIERS
PITSAWS
PITTERS
POTAGES
POTFULS
POTHERS
POTIONS
POTPIES
POTTERS
POTTLES
PUTOUTS
PUTPUTS
PUTTEES
PUTTERS
PUTTIES
PYTHIAS
PYTHONS
QATARIS
RATINGS
RATIONS
RATITES
RATTANS
RATTERS
RATTLES
RETAILS
RETAINS
RETAKES
RETAPES
RETARDS
RETAXES
RETEARS
RETELLS
RETESTS
RETILES
RETIMES
RETINAS
RETIRES
RETOOLS
RETORTS
RETOURS
RETRIES
RETRIMS
RETUNES
RETURNS
RETYPES
RITUALS
ROTATES
ROTTERS
RUTGERS
SATEENS
SATIRES
SATRAPS
SETTEES
SETTERS
SETTLES
SHTICKS
SITCOMS
SITTERS
SUTLERS
SUTTERS
SUTURES
TATAMIS
TATTERS
TATTLES
TATTOOS
TETANUS
TETHERS
TETRADS
TITBITS
TITFERS
TITHERS
TITTERS
TITTLES
TITTUPS
TOTTERS
TUTTUTS
ULTIMAS
UNTACKS
UNTRAPS
UNTUNES
UPTAKES
UPTICKS
UPTURNS
URTEXTS
VATFULS
VETCHES
VETOERS
VITTLES
VOTECHS
WATCHES
WATTLES
WETBARS
WETHERS
WETMOPS
WETNESS
WITCHES
WITHERS
WITHIES
WITLESS
WITNESS
ZITHERS

•••TS••

BEATSIT
BEATSME
BEATSUP
BENTSEN
BOOTSUP
BUTTSIN
CHATSUP
CURTSEY
FLOTSAM
FOOTSIE
FRETSAW
HEATSUP
HINTSAT
HOOTSAT
KLATSCH
LIFTSUP
MUSTSEE
RESTSUP
SHUTSIN
SHUTSUP
STETSON
SUITSUP
SURTSEY
THATSIT
TOOTSIE
TROTSKY
TSETSES
WAITSON
WAITSUP
WANTSIN
WANTSTO
YELTSIN

•••T•S•

BAPTISE
BAPTISM
BAPTIST
BRITISH
BRUTISH
CATTISH
COLTISH
CONTEST
CONTUSE
CULTISH
CULTISM
CULTIST
CURTEST
CURTISS
DAFTEST
DEFTEST
DENTIST
DOLTISH
ECSTASY
EGOTISM
EGOTIST
ELITISM
ELITIST
FANTASY
FASTEST
FATTEST
FATTISH
FITTEST
FLUTIST
GOATISH
GOUTISH
HOSTESS
HOTTEST
IRATEST
KENTISH
LACTASE
LACTOSE
LEFTIST
LETTISH
LOUTISH
MALTESE
MALTOSE
MORTISE
NASTASE
NEATEST
PELTISH
PERTEST
PETTISH
PICTISH
PIETISM
PIETIST
PRETEST
PROTEST
PROTIST
RATTISH
RUNTISH
RUTTISH
SALTISH
SOFTEST
SOFTISH
SOTTISH
STATIST
TARTEST
TARTISH
TAUTEST
TRITEST
VASTEST
WETTEST
WETTISH
WHITEST
WHITISH

•••T••S

AUNTIES
AVATARS
BANTAMS
BANTERS
BARTABS
BARTERS
BASTERS
BATTELS
BATTENS
BATTERS
BATTLES
BATTUES
BEATERS
BEATLES
BEETLES
BESTIRS
BESTOWS
BETTERS
BETTORS
BIGTOES
BIGTOPS
BISTROS
BITTERS
BLITZES
BOATELS
BOATERS
BOOTEES
BOOTIES
BOTTLES
BOTTOMS
BOUTROS
BOWTIES
BOXTOPS
BRETONS
BRITONS
BUSTERS
BUSTLES
BUTTERS
BUTTIES
BUTTONS
CAFTANS
CANTERS
CANTLES
CANTONS
CANTORS
CAPTORS
CARTELS
CARTERS
CARTONS
CASTERS
CASTLES
CELTICS
CENTERS
CENTRES
CLOTHES
CONTRAS
COOTIES
COPTERS
COSTARS
COTTERS
COTTONS
CRATERS
CRETANS
CRETINS
CRITICS
CURTISS
CUSTOMS
CUTTERS
DACTYLS
DARTERS
DEBTORS
DEITIES
DIATOMS
DICTUMS
DIETERS
DIKTATS
DIRTIES
DISTILS
DITTIES
DOCTORS
DOGTAGS
DOTTLES
DUSTERS
DUSTUPS
EASTERS
EDITORS
ELATERS
EMOTERS
EMPTIES
EXOTICS
FACTORS
FALTERS
FASTENS
FATTENS
FESTERS
FETTERS
FETTLES
FIFTIES
FILTERS
FITTERS
FOOTERS
FORTIES
FORTIUS
FOSTERS
FUSTICS
GAITERS
GARTERS
GENTLES
GHETTOS
GLITZES
GLOTTIS
GOATEES
GRATERS
GRATIAS
GROTTOS
GUITARS
GUSTOES
GUTTERS
HALTERS
HASTENS
HATTERS
HEATERS
HECTORS
HEPTADS
HITTERS
HOGTIES
HOOTERS
HOSTELS
HOSTESS
HOTTIPS
HOTTUBS
HUNTERS
HURTLES
HUSTLES
INSTALS

INSTARS
INSTEPS
INSTILS
JESTERS
JETTIES
JITTERS
JOSTLES
JUTTIES
KAFTANS
KETTLES
KILTIES
KIRTLES
KITTENS
KITTIES
KLUTZES
KOWTOWS
KRATERS
LAPTOPS
LATTENS
LECTORS
LEFTIES
LENTILS
LEPTONS
LETTERS
LETTRES
LICTORS
LIFTERS
LINTELS
LISTEES
LISTELS
LISTENS
LITTERS
LOATHES
LOITERS
LOOTERS
LUSTERS
LUSTRES
MAITAIS
MALTEDS
MALTHUS
MANTELS
MANTLES
MANTRAS
MARTENS
MARTINS
MARTYRS
MASTERS
MASTICS
MATTERS
MENTORS
METTLES
MINTERS
MISTERS
MITTENS
MOLTERS
MOPTOPS
MORTALS
MORTARS
MOTTLES
MOTTOES
MOUTONS
MUNTINS
MUSTERS
MUTTERS
MUTTONS
MYRTLES
MYSTICS
NATTERS
NEATENS
NECTARS
NESTERS
NESTLES
NETTLES
NEWTONS

NOETICS
NUTTERS
ORATORS
OUSTERS
OYSTERS
PALTERS
PARTIES
PASTELS
PASTORS
PATTENS
PATTERS
PATTIES
PECTINS
PEGTOPS
PELTERS
PENTADS
PESTERS
PESTLES
PETTERS
PHOTICS
PHOTOGS
PHOTONS
PIETIES
PIETINS
PISTILS
PISTOLS
PISTONS
PITTERS
PLATENS
PLATERS
POETICS
PONTIUS
POPTOPS
PORTALS
PORTERS
PORTHOS
POSTERS
POSTITS
POTTERS
POTTLES
POUTERS
PRATERS
PROTEUS
PROTONS
PUNTERS
PUNTIES
PUTTEES
PUTTERS
PUTTIES
QINTARS
QUOTERS
RAFTERS
RAGTOPS
RANTERS
RAPTORS
RASTERS
RATTANS
RATTERS
RATTLES
RECTORS
REDTOPS
RENTALS
RENTERS
RESTERS
REUTERS
RHETORS
RHYTHMS
RIOTERS
RIOTOUS
ROOTERS
ROSTERS
ROTTERS
ROUTERS
RUSTICS

RUSTLES
SALTERS
SANTIRS
SCATHES
SCOTERS
SCYTHES
SEATERS
SECTORS
SEETHES
SEPTETS
SESTETS
SETTEES
SETTERS
SETTLES
SEXTANS
SEXTETS
SEXTONS
SHUTINS
SIFTERS
SISTERS
SITTERS
SIXTIES
SKATERS
SKITOWS
SOFTENS
SOFTIES
SOOTHES
SORTERS
SORTIES
SPITZES
STATICS
STATORS
STATUES
SUITORS
SULTANS
SUNTANS
SUTTERS
SWATHES
SYSTEMS
TACTICS
TAMTAMS
TARTANS
TARTARS
TASTERS
TATTERS
TATTLES
TATTOOS
TAUTENS
TEETERS
TEETHES
TENTERS
TESTEES
TESTERS
TEUTONS
TICTACS
TILTERS
TINTERS
TIPTOES
TIPTOPS
TITTERS
TITTLES
TITTUPS
TOETAPS
TOLTECS
TOMTITS
TOMTOMS
TOOTERS
TOOTLES
TOTTERS
TOUTERS
TRITONS
TSETSES
TURTLES
TUTTUTS

ULSTERS
UNITERS
UNITIES
UNSTOPS
VECTORS
VENTERS
VESTEES
VICTIMS
VICTORS
VIRTUES
VITTLES
WAITERS
WALTERS
WALTZES
WANTADS
WASTERS
WATTLES
WELTERS
WHITENS
WINTERS
WONTONS
WRITERS
WRITHES
YOMTOVS

••••TS•

CRAFTSY
FUJITSU
JUJITSU
KOMATSU
OKHOTSK
SHIATSU
YAKUTSK

••••T•S

ABLATES
ACHATES
AERATES
AGNATES
AGOUTIS
ARBUTUS
ARISTAS
ARISTOS
ATLATLS
AVIATES
BERATES
BONITOS
BORATES
BREATHS
BYPATHS
CHEETOS
COEPTIS
COYOTES
CREATES
CRYPTOS
CURATES
DAKOTAS
DALETHS
DEARTHS
DEBATES
DELETES
DEMOTES
DENOTES
DEPUTES
DESOTOS
DEVOTES
DILATES
DILUTES
DONATES
DORITOS
EIGHTHS
EOLITHS
EQUATES
ERGATES

ESTATES
EXACTAS
EXCITES
FAJITAS
FAUSTUS
FIESTAS
FIXATES
FOURTHS
GAMETES
GELATIS
GEMOTES
GHETTOS
GLOTTIS
GROTTOS
GROWTHS
GYRATES
HALITES
HAMITES
HEARTHS
IDEATES
IGNITES
IMPETUS
IMPUTES
INCITES
INDITES
INMATES
INVITES
IODATES
IOMOTHS
LAERTES
LAKOTAS
LEANTOS
LEGATES
LEGATOS
LENGTHS
LEVITES
LIGATES
LITOTES
LOCATES
LUXATES
METATES
MINUTES
MULETAS
MUTATES
NEGATES
NOTATES
NUTATES
OBLATES
OLEATES
OOCYTES
OOLITES
OOLITHS
OPHITES
OPIATES
ORESTES
ORGATES
PAIUTES
PALATES
PARATUS
PELOTAS
PENATES
PESETAS
PETITES
PINATAS
PIRATES
PLAUTUS
PLINTHS
PRESTOS
PYRITES
QUARTOS
RATITES
REBATES
RECITES
REDATES

REFUTES
RELATES
REMOTES
RENOTES
REPUTES
RERATES
ROTATES
RUBATOS
SALUTES
SAMITES
SEDATES
SEMITES
SENATES
SHEATHS
SHIITES
SIESTAS
SLEUTHS
SMALTOS
SMOOTHS
SOLUTES
SONATAS
SORITES
SPRITES
STKITTS
STRATUS
TACITUS
UPDATES
VACATES
VERITAS
WAPITIS
WRAITHS
WREATHS
ZENITHS
ZYGOTES

•••••TS

ABDUCTS
ABLAUTS
ABSENTS
ACCENTS
ACCEPTS
ACCOSTS
ACQUITS
ADDUCTS
ADJUSTS
ADVENTS
ADVERTS
AFFECTS
AFREETS
AGEISTS
AIGRETS
ALIGHTS
AMOUNTS
AMULETS
ANKLETS
ANOINTS
AORISTS
APPLETS
ARMLETS
ARMPITS
ARPENTS
ARRESTS
ARTISTS
ASCENTS
ASPECTS
ASSENTS
ASSERTS
ASSISTS
ASSORTS
ATTESTS
ATTRITS
AUKLETS
AVOCETS
BALLETS

BALLOTS
BANDITS
BARENTS
BASALTS
BASKETS
BASSETS
BEHESTS
BILLETS
BISECTS
BLIGHTS
BOBCATS
BONMOTS
BONNETS
BOSKETS
BREASTS
BREVETS
BRUNETS
BUCKETS
BUDGETS
BUFFETS
BULLETS
BURBOTS
BUYOUTS
CACHETS
CAHOOTS
CAPLETS
CAPNUTS
CARNETS
CARPETS
CARROTS
CAVEATS
CAVORTS
CEMENTS
CHALETS
CLARETS
CLIENTS
CLORETS
CLOSETS
COEDITS
COHORTS
COHOSTS
COLLETS
COMBATS
COMFITS
COMMITS
COPOUTS
CORNETS
CORSETS
COSSETS
CRAVATS
CREDITS
CUBISTS
CURVETS
CUTLETS
CUTOUTS
CYGNETS
DECANTS
DECEITS
DECOCTS
DEDUCTS
DEFEATS
DEFECTS
DEGUSTS
DEJECTS
DELICTS
DELISTS
DEPARTS
DEPICTS
DEPORTS
DESALTS
DESERTS
DESISTS
DESPOTS
DETECTS

DETESTS
DIDACTS
DIGESTS
DIKTATS
DIMOUTS
DIMWITS
DIRECTS
DIVERTS
DIVESTS
DOCENTS
DOCKETS
DOGSITS
DOPANTS
DRYROTS
DUGOUTS
DYNASTS
EAGLETS
EFFECTS
EFFORTS
EGOISTS
ELICITS
ENLISTS
ENROOTS
ESCORTS
EXCEPTS
EXEMPTS
EXHORTS
EXPECTS
EXPERTS
EXPORTS
EXSERTS
EXTENTS
EXTORTS
EYELETS
FANJETS
FANOUTS
FATCATS
FAUCETS
FERRETS
FIDGETS
FILLETS
FLAUNTS
FLIGHTS
FLORETS
FLYNETS
FOMENTS
FORESTS
FORGETS
FORINTS
FORMATS
FRIGHTS
GADGETS
GALOOTS
GAMBITS
GANNETS
GARNETS
GARRETS
GASJETS
GASKETS
GERENTS
GIBBETS
GIBLETS
GIMLETS
GOBLETS
GOCARTS
GODWITS
GOKARTS
GORGETS
GRIVETS
GULLETS
GUSSETS
HAMLETS
HEIGHTS
HELMETS

HENBITS
HEPCATS
HERMITS
HEXNUTS
HOBBITS
HOGGETS
HOLISTS
HORNETS
HOTPOTS
IMARETS
IMPACTS
IMPARTS
IMPORTS
IMPOSTS
INCANTS
INCEPTS
INDENTS
INDICTS
INDUCTS
INFANTS
INFECTS
INFESTS
INGESTS
INJECTS
INSECTS
INSERTS
INSISTS
INSPOTS
INSULTS
INTENTS
INTUITS
INVENTS
INVERTS
INVESTS
IQTESTS
IRRUPTS
JACKETS
JENNETS
JESUITS
JOBLOTS
JUNKETS
JURISTS
KNIGHTS
LABRETS
LAMENTS
LANCETS
LAPPETS
LARIATS
LATENTS
LAYOUTS
LEGISTS
LEVANTS
LIMPETS
LINNETS
LIONETS
LOCKETS
LOCUSTS
LOQUATS
LUGNUTS
LUTISTS
LYRISTS
MAGNETS
MAHOUTS
MALLETS
MAOISTS
MARKETS
MARMOTS
MASCOTS
MERLOTS
MIDGETS
MILLETS
MINUETS
MISFITS
MISHITS

MODELTS
MOLESTS
MOMENTS
MOPPETS
MUDCATS
MULLETS
MUPPETS
MUSCATS
MUSKETS
MUTANTS
NAUGHTS
NITWITS
NOUGATS
NOUGHTS
NUDISTS
NUGGETS
NUMBATS
NUTLETS
OBJECTS
OBLASTS
OBOISTS
OBVERTS
OCCULTS
OCELOTS
OCTANTS
ODDLOTS
OFFSETS
OFSORTS
OMELETS
ORGEATS
ORIENTS
OUTACTS
OUTEATS
OUTFITS
OUTHITS
OUTLETS
OUTPUTS
OUTSETS
OUTWITS
OXCARTS
PACKETS
PALLETS
PANDITS
PARENTS
PARGETS
PARROTS
PATENTS
PAYOUTS
PEANUTS
PEDANTS
PELLETS
PENULTS
PEQUOTS
PERMITS
PICKETS
PIGLETS
PIGNUTS
PIOLETS
PLAINTS
PLANETS
PLIGHTS
POCKETS
POPPETS
POSSETS
POSTITS
PRESETS
PRIESTS
PRIVETS
PROFITS
PROMPTS
PTBOATS
PULLETS
PULPITS
PUNDITS

PUNNETS
PUPPETS
PURISTS
PUTOUTS
PUTPUTS
QIVIUTS
RABBETS
RABBITS
RACKETS
RAGOUTS
RAJPUTS
RAMJETS
REBOLTS
REBOOTS
RECANTS
RECASTS
RECOATS
REDACTS
REDANTS
REDHATS
REDHOTS
REEDITS
REGENTS
REGLETS
REGRETS
REHEATS
REJECTS
RELENTS
RELICTS
RELISTS
RELUCTS
REMELTS
REPASTS
REPEATS
REPENTS
REPORTS
RERENTS
RESALTS
RESEATS
RESECTS
RESENTS
RESISTS
RESORTS
RESULTS
RETESTS
RETORTS
REVERTS
REVOLTS
REXCATS
RILLETS
ROBERTS
ROCHETS
ROCKETS
RODENTS
RUNLETS
RUNOUTS
RUSSETS
SACHETS
SALLETS
SAMLETS
SAVANTS
SCRIPTS
SCULPTS
SECANTS
SECRETS
SELECTS
SEPTETS
SESTETS
SEXISTS
SEXTETS
SHRIFTS
SIGNETS
SILENTS
SIPPETS

SLIGHTS
SNOCATS
SOCKETS
SOFFITS
SONNETS
SORBETS
SOVIETS
SPIGOTS
SPINETS
SPIRITS
SPLINTS
SPRINTS
SPROUTS
SQUINTS
SQUIRTS
STARETS
STKITTS
STRAITS
STREETS
STYLETS
SUBLETS
SUBMITS
SUBSETS
SUMMITS
SUNSETS
SWIVETS
TABLETS
TALENTS
TAOISTS
TAPPETS
TARGETS
TARPITS
TEAPOTS
TEASETS
TENANTS
TERCETS
TERRETS
THEISTS
THEPITS
THIRSTS
THREATS
THRIFTS
THROATS
THRUSTS
THWARTS
TICKETS
TIDBITS
TINHATS
TIPPETS
TITBITS
TOILETS
TOMCATS
TOMTITS
TOPHATS
TRICOTS
TRIJETS
TRIVETS
TRUANTS
TRYOUTS
TSHIRTS
TUBISTS
TUFFETS
TUMULTS
TURBITS
TURBOTS
TURRETS
TUTTUTS
TWOBITS
TYPISTS
TYRANTS
UMLAUTS
UNBOLTS
UNKNITS
UNKNOTS

UNSEATS
UPBEATS
UPLIFTS
UPROOTS
UPSHOTS
URTEXTS
VARLETS
VEIGHTS
VELVETS
VERVETS
VIOLETS
WALLETS
WALNUTS
WEIGHTS
WESKITS
WICKETS
WIDGETS
WIGLETS
WILLETS
WOMBATS
WRIGHTS
YOGURTS
ZEALOTS

T•T••••

TATAMIS
TATIANA
TATTERS
TATTIER
TATTILY
TATTING
TATTLED
TATTLER
TATTLES
TATTOOS
TETANUS
TETCHED
TETHERS
TETRADS
TITANIA
TITANIC
TITBITS
TITFERS
TITHERS
TITHING
TITLING
TITLIST
TITMICE
TITRATE
TITRING
TITTERS
TITTLES
TITTUPS
TITULAR
TOTALED
TOTALLY
TOTEBAG
TOTEMIC
TOTIDEM
TOTTERS
TOTTERY
TOTTING
TUTELAR
TUTORED
TUTTUTS

T••T•••

TACTFUL
TACTICS
TACTILE
TAGTEAM
TAMTAMS
TANTARA
TANTIVY

TANTRUM
TARTANS
TARTARE
TARTARS
TARTEST
TARTISH
TASTERS
TASTIER
TASTILY
TASTING
TATTERS
TATTIER
TATTILY
TATTING
TATTLED
TATTLER
TATTLES
TATTOOS
TAUTENS
TAUTEST
TEATIME
TEATRAY
TEATREE
TEETERS
TEETHED
TEETHER
TEETHES
TEETIME
TEKTITE
TENTERS
TENTHLY
TENTING
TERTIAL
TESTBAN
TESTEES
TESTERS
TESTFLY
TESTIER
TESTIFY
TESTILY
TESTING
TESTOUT
TESTUDO
TEUTONS
TEXTILE
TEXTUAL
TEXTURE
THATCHY
THATSIT
THITHER
TICTACS
TIETACK
TILTERS
TILTING
TINTACK
TINTERN
TINTERS
TINTING
TINTYPE
TIPTOED
TIPTOES
TIPTOPS
TITTERS
TITTLES
TITTUPS
TOETAPS
TOLTECS
TOMTITS
TOMTOMS
TONTINE
TOOTERS
TOOTHED
TOOTING
TOOTLED

TOOTLES
TOOTSIE
TORTONI
TOSTADA
TOTTERS
TOTTERY
TOTTING
TOUTERS
TOUTING
TRITELY
TRITEST
TRITIUM
TRITONE
TRITONS
TROTHED
TROTOUT
TROTSKY
TROTTED
TROTTER
TSETSES
TUFTIER
TUFTING
TUITION
TURTLED
TURTLES
TUTTUTS
TWITCHY
TWITTED
TWITTER
TWOTIME
TWOTONE

T•••T••

TABITHA
TACITLY
TACITUS
TAINTED
TAKETEN
TANKTOP
TAPSTER
TAUNTED
TELSTAR
TEMPTED
TEMPTER
THEATER
THEATRE
THISTLE
THISTLY
TIBETAN
TIGHTEN
TIGHTER
TIGHTLY
TIMOTHY
TINSTAR
TINYTIM
TIPSTER
TOASTED
TOASTER
TOLSTOI
TOLSTOY
TOOKTEN
TRACTOR
TRAITOR
TREATED
TREETOP
TRENTON
TRESTLE
TRISTAN
TRISTAR
TROTTED
TROTTER
TRUSTED
TRUSTEE
TRYSTED
TRYSTER
TWEETED
TWEETER
TWISTED
TWISTER
TWITTED
TWITTER
TWOSTAR
TWOSTEP

T••••T•

TABLETS
TAFFETA
TAKESTO
TALENTS
TALKSTO
TAOISTS
TAPINTO
TAPPETS
TARANTO
TARGETS
TARPITS
TAXRATE
TEAPOTS
TEASETS
TEKTITE
TENANTS
TENDSTO
TENUITY
TERCETS
TERMITE
TERNATE
TERRETS
THEISTS
THEPITS
THERETO
THIRSTS
THIRSTY
THREATS
THRIFTS
THRIFTY
THROATS
THROATY
THRUSTS
THWARTS
TICKETS
TICKETY
TIDBITS
TIEINTO
TINHATS
TIPPETS
TITBITS
TITRATE
TOCCATA
TOILETS
TOMCATS
TOMTITS
TOPHATS
TORONTO
TOWPATH
TRIBUTE
TRICOTS
TRIESTE
TRIJETS
TRINITY
TRIVETS
TRUANTS
TRYOUTS
TSHIRTS
TUBISTS
TUFFETS
TUMULTS
TURBITS
TURBOTS
TURNSTO
TURRETS
TUTTUTS
TWELFTH
TWOBITS
TYPISTS
TYRANTS

T•••••T

TABORET
TAGGANT
TAGSOUT
TAKEOUT
TALKOUT
TALKSAT
TALLEST
TANGENT
TANNEST
TAPROOT
TAPSOUT
TARTEST
TAUTEST
TEACART
TEAROUT
TEARSAT
TEMPEST
TENCENT
TENSEST
TENSPOT
TERSEST
TESTOUT
THATSIT
THEREAT
THICKET
THOUGHT
TIDIEST
TIMEOUT
TINIEST
TIREOUT
TITLIST
TLINGIT
TONIEST
TONIGHT
TOOKOUT
TOPCOAT
TOPKNOT
TOPMAST
TOPMOST
TOPSOUT
TOREOUT
TORMENT
TORNOUT
TORRENT
TOSSOUT
TOURIST
TRABERT
TRANSIT
TREERAT
TRIDENT
TRINKET
TRIPLET
TRIPPET
TRISECT
TRITEST
TROTOUT
TRUMPET
TSARIST
TSELIOT
TUBAIST
TUGBOAT
TUNEOUT
TURNOUT
TYPESET
TYPIEST

•TT••••

ATTABOY
ATTACHE
ATTACKS
ATTAINS
ATTEMPT
ATTENDS
ATTESTS
ATTICUS
ATTIMES
ATTIRED
ATTIRES
ATTRACT
ATTRITE
ATTRITS
ATTUCKS
ATTUNED
ATTUNES
OTTAWAS
OTTOMAN
UTTERED
UTTERER
UTTERLY
YTTRIUM

•T•T•••

ATATURK
ATSTAKE
STATELY
STATICE
STATICS
STATING
STATION
STATIST
STATORS
STATUES
STATURE
STATUTE
STETSON
STETTED

•T••T••

ATLATLS
STANTON
STARTED
STARTER
STARTLE
STARTUP
STENTOR
STETTED
STILTED
STILTON
STINTED
STKITTS
STOUTEN
STOUTER
STOUTLY
STPETER
STRATUM
STRATUS
STRETCH
STRETTO
STUNTED
STYPTIC

•T•••T•

ATHLETE
ATLANTA
ATTESTS
ATTRITE
ATTRITS
ITERATE
OTRANTO
PTBOATS
STARETS
STATUTE
STEALTH
STICKTO
STKITTS
STOMATA
STRAITS
STREETS
STRETTO
STRIATE
STUCKTO
STYLETS
UTILITY

•T••••T

ATAVIST
ATFAULT
ATHEART
ATHEIST
ATHIRST
ATHWART
ATLEAST
ATTEMPT
ATTRACT
ATWORST
ETCHANT
ITERANT
STALEST
STAREAT
STARLET
STARLIT
STATIST
STAYPUT
STEPOUT
STEWART
STUDENT
STYLIST
UTRECHT

••TT•••

BATTELS
BATTENS
BATTERS
BATTERY
BATTIER
BATTING
BATTLED
BATTLER
BATTLES
BATTUES
BETTERS
BETTING
BETTORS
BITTERN
BITTERS
BITTIER
BITTING
BOTTLED
BOTTLER
BOTTLES
BOTTOMS
BUTTERS
BUTTERY
BUTTIES
BUTTING
BUTTONS
BUTTOUT
BUTTSIN
CATTAIL
CATTIER
CATTILY
CATTING
CATTISH
COTTAGE
COTTERS
COTTONS
COTTONY
CUTTERS
CUTTIME
CUTTING
DITTANY
DITTIES
DITTOED
DOTTIER
DOTTILY
DOTTING
DOTTLES
FATTENS
FATTEST
FATTIER
FATTILY
FATTISH
FETTERS
FETTLES
FITTERS
FITTEST
FITTING
GETTING
GUTTERS
GUTTIER
GUTTING
HATTERS
HATTING
HITTERS
HITTING
HITTITE
HOTTEST
HOTTIPS
HOTTUBS
JETTIES
JETTING
JITTERS
JITTERY
JOTTING
JUTTIED
JUTTIES
JUTTING
KETTLES
KITTENS
KITTIES
LATTENS
LATTICE
LETTERS
LETTING
LETTISH
LETTRES
LETTUCE
LITTERS
LITTLER
LOTTERY
LOTTING
MATTERS
MATTHAU
MATTHEW
MATTING
MATTOCK
METTLES
MITTENS
MOTTLED
MOTTLES
MOTTOES
MUTTERS
MUTTONS
NATTERS
NATTIER
NATTILY
NETTING
NETTLED
NETTLES
NITTANY
NITTIER
NOTTRUE
NUTTERS
NUTTIER
NUTTILY
NUTTING
OUTTAKE
OUTTALK
PATTENS
PATTERN
PATTERS
PATTIES
PATTING
PETTERS
PETTIER
PETTILY
PETTING
PETTISH
PITTERS
PITTING
PITTMAN
POTTAGE
POTTERS
POTTERY
POTTIER
POTTING
POTTLES
PUTTEES
PUTTERS
PUTTIED
PUTTIES
PUTTING
RATTAIL
RATTANS
RATTERS
RATTIER
RATTING
RATTISH
RATTLED
RATTLER
RATTLES
RATTRAP
ROTTERS
ROTTING
RUTTIER
RUTTISH
SETTEES
SETTERS
SETTING
SETTLED
SETTLER
SETTLES
SITTERS
SITTING
SOTTISH
SUTTERS
TATTERS
TATTIER
TATTILY
TATTING
TATTLED
TATTLER
TATTLES
TATTOOS
TITTERS
TITTLES
TITTUPS
TOTTERS
TOTTERY
TOTTING
TUTTUTS
VATTING
VETTING
VITTLES
WATTAGE
WATTEAU
WATTLES
WETTEST
WETTING
WETTISH
WITTIER
WITTILY
WITTING

••T•T••

ANTITAX
BATHTUB
ENTITLE
ESTATES
GETITON
GOTITON
LETITBE
LETITIA
LITOTES
METATES
MITOTIC
MUTATED
MUTATES
NOTATED
NOTATES
NUTATED
NUTATES
OUTSTEP
PETITES
PITSTOP
PUTITTO
RATATAT
RATITES
RETITLE
ROTATED
ROTATES
ROTATOR

••T••T•

ACTUATE
ARTISTE
ARTISTS
ASTARTE
ATTESTS
ATTRITE
ATTRITS
BATISTA
BATISTE
BETROTH
CATERTO
CITRATE
CUTINTO
CUTLETS
CUTOUTS
CUTRATE
DETECTS
DETENTE
DETESTS
ENTENTE
ESTHETE
EXTENTS
EXTORTS
FATCATS
FATCITY
FATUITY
GETINTO
GOTINTO
HITTITE
HOTPOTS
INTENTS
INTRUTH
INTUITS
IQTESTS
LATENTS
LITINTO
LUTISTS
MUTANTS
NITRATE
NITRITE
NITWITS
NUTLETS
OCTANTS
OUTACTS
OUTEATS
OUTFITS
OUTHITS
OUTLETS
OUTPUTS
OUTSETS
OUTVOTE
OUTWITS
PATENTS
PUTITTO
PUTOUTS
PUTPUTS
RETESTS
RETORTS
SATIATE
SATIETY
SETINTO
SITUATE
TITBITS
TITRATE
TUTTUTS
UNTRUTH
URTEXTS
VITIATE

••T•••T

ACTSOUT
ANTIART
ARTIEST
ASTOLAT
ATTEMPT
ATTRACT
AUTOMAT
BATHMAT
BETWIXT
BITPART
BUTTOUT
CATBERT
CATBOAT
CATSUIT
CUTSOUT
DATASET
DETRACT
DETROIT
EATENAT
EATSOUT
ENTRANT
ENTREAT
ENTRUST
EXTINCT
EXTRACT
FATTEST
FITTEST
GETLOST
GETSOUT
GETSSET
GOTLOST
GOTOPOT
HATCHET
HITLIST
HITSOUT
HOTFOOT
HOTSEAT
HOTSHOT
HOTSPOT
HOTTEST
INTROIT
INTRUST
JETBOAT
JETPORT
LETSOUT
LITCRIT
LITHEST
MATELOT
METEOUT
NOTABIT
NUTMEAT
ONTHEQT
OPTSOUT
OUTCAST
OUTLAST
OUTOFIT
OUTPOST
PATIENT
PATRIOT
PITAPAT
POTSHOT
PUTSOUT
RATATAT
RATBERT
RATCHET
RETRACT
RETREAT
SATINET
SETSOUT
SITSOUT
TITLIST
UNTWIST
UPTIGHT
VOTEOUT
WATCHIT
WETSUIT
WETTEST
WITHOUT

•••TT••

ABETTED
ABETTOR
ABUTTAL
ABUTTED
BEATTIE
BLATTED
BLOTTED
BLOTTER
BRITTEN
BRITTLE
BRITTON
CHATTED
CHATTEL
CHATTER
CHITTER
CLATTER
CLOTTED
CLUTTER
CRITTER
DRATTED
EMITTED
EMITTER
FLATTAX
FLATTED
FLATTEN
FLATTER
FLATTOP
FLITTED
FLITTER
FLUTTER
FRETTED
FRITTED
FRITTER
GHETTOS
GLITTER
GLOTTAL
GLOTTIS
GLUTTED
GLUTTON
GRITTED
GROTTOS
HEATTER
KNITTED
KNITTER
KNOTTED
OMITTED
OMITTER
PLATTER
PLOTTED
PLOTTER
PRATTLE
QUITTER
SCATTED
SCATTER
SCOTTIE
SCUTTLE
SEATTLE
SHATTER
SHUTTER
SHUTTLE
SKITTER
SKITTLE
SLATTED
SLOTTED
SMATTER
SMITTEN
SOFTTOP
SPATTED
SPATTER
SPOTTED
SPOTTER
SPUTTER
STETTED
SWATTED
SWATTER
TROTTED
TROTTER
TWITTED
TWITTER
WHETTED
WHITTLE
WRITTEN

•••T•T•

ACETATE
AGITATE
AGITATO
APATITE
CANTATA
DENTATE
DICTATE
DIKTATS
GESTATE
HITTITE
IMITATE
INSTATE
LACTATE
PARTITA
PARTITE
PELTATE
POSTITS
RESTATE
SEPTETS
SESTETS
SEXTETS
STATUTE
TEKTITE
TOMTITS
TUTTUTS
UPSTATE
VIRTUTE
WANTSTO
WRITETO
WROTETO

•••T••T

BAPTIST
BEATOUT
BEATSIT
BERTOLT
BLATANT
BLOTOUT
BOOTOUT
BUSTOUT
BUTTOUT
CASTOUT
CONTACT
CONTENT
CONTEST
CONTEXT
CONTORT
CULTIST
CURTEST
DAFTEST
DEFTEST
DENTIST
DISTANT
DISTORT
DOGTROT
EDITOUT
EGOTIST
ELITIST
EPITHET
FASTEST
FATTEST
FELTOUT
FITTEST
FLATLET
FLATOUT
FLUTIST
FOXTROT
GANTLET
GESTALT
HINTSAT
HOOTSAT
HOPTOIT
HOTTEST
INSTANT
IRATEST
KEPTOUT
LEFTIST
LEFTOUT
LOSTOUT
NEATEST
PARTOUT
PERTEST
PIETIST
POPTART
PORTENT
PRETEST
PRETEXT
PROTECT
PROTEST
PROTIST
PUPTENT
RESTART
RIOTACT
ROOTLET
ROOTOUT
SEETOIT
SENTOUT
SEXTANT
SHOTOUT
SHOTPUT
SHUTOUT
SOFTEST
SORTOUT
SPOTLIT
STATIST
SUBTEXT
TARTEST
TAUTEST
TESTOUT
THATSIT
TRITEST
TROTOUT
UPSTART
VASTEST
WAITOUT
WANTOUT
WENTOUT
WETTEST
WHATNOT
WHITEST

••••TT•

ADMITTO
ANNATTO
ANNETTE
ARIETTA
BABETTE
BARETTA
BERETTA
BIRETTA
BURETTE
CADETTE
CAVETTO
COLETTE
CORETTA
CULOTTE
DINETTE
GAVOTTE
GAZETTE
INPETTO
LAFITTE
LAMOTTA
LAYETTE
LORETTA
MENOTTI
MUSETTE
NANETTE
ORNETTE
PALETTE
PIPETTE
POINTTO
PUTITTO
REACTTO
REGATTA
RICOTTA
RIDOTTO
RISOTTO
ROSETTA
ROSETTE
SQUATTY
STKITTS
STRETTO
SUZETTE
WYNETTE

••••T•T

BIENTOT
HABITAT
KINGTUT
MIGHTNT
OUGHTNT
QUARTET
QUINTET
RATATAT
SHOOTAT

•••••TT

BABBITT
BARRETT
BECKETT
BENNETT
BOYCOTT
BUFFETT
BULLITT
BURNETT
CASSATT
CORBETT
DORSETT
ELLIOTT
EVERETT
FAWCETT
FOLLETT
GANNETT
GARRETT
GOSSETT
HACKETT
HAMMETT
HEWLETT
MILLETT
PICKETT
PUCKETT
RABBITT
SENNETT
WALCOTT
ZERMATT

TU•••••

TUAREGS
TUBAIST
TUBBIER
TUBISTS
TUBLIKE
TUBULAR
TUCHMAN
TUCKERS
TUCKING
TUCKSIN
TUESDAY
TUFFETS
TUFTIER
TUFTING
TUGBOAT
TUGGERS
TUGGING
TUGLESS
TUGRIKS
TUITION
TULSANS
TUMBLED
TUMBLER
TUMBLES
TUMBREL
TUMMIES
TUMMING
TUMULTS
TUMULUS
TUNDRAS
TUNEDIN
TUNEDUP
TUNEFUL
TUNEOUT
TUNESIN

TUNESUP
TUNEUPS
TUNGOIL
TUNICLE
TUNISIA
TUNNELS
TUNNIES
TUPELOS
TURBANS
TURBINE
TURBITS
TURBOTS
TUREENS
TURFIER
TURFWAR
TURKEYS
TURKISH
TURMOIL
TURNERS
TURNERY
TURNING
TURNIPS
TURNKEY
TURNOFF
TURNOUT
TURNSIN
TURNSON
TURNSTO
TURNSUP
TURRETS
TURTLED
TURTLES
TUSCANY
TUSKERS
TUSSAUD
TUSSLED
TUSSLES
TUSSOCK
TUTELAR
TUTORED
TUTTUTS
TUXEDOS

T•U••••
TAUNTED
TAURINE
TAUTENS
TAUTEST
TEUTONS
THUDDED
THULIUM
THUMBED
THUMPED
THUMPER
THUNDER
THURBER
THURMAN
THUSFAR
TOUCANS
TOUCHED
TOUCHES
TOUCHON
TOUCHUP
TOUGHEN
TOUGHER
TOUGHIE
TOUGHLY
TOUPEES
TOURACO
TOURERS
TOURING
TOURISM
TOURIST
TOURNEY
TOUSLED
TOUSLES
TOUTERS
TOUTING
TRUANCY
TRUANTS
TRUCIAL
TRUCKED
TRUCKEE
TRUCKER
TRUCKLE
TRUDEAU
TRUDGED
TRUDGER
TRUDGES
TRUEING
TRUFFLE
TRUISMS
TRUMPED
TRUMPET
TRUMPUP
TRUNDLE
TRUSSED
TRUSSES
TRUSTED
TRUSTEE
TSUNAMI

T••U•••
TABULAR
TALUSES
TENUITY
TENUOUS
TENURED
TENURES
TEQUILA
THEURGY
THOUGHT
THRUSTS
THRUWAY
TIJUANA
TITULAR
TOLUENE
TRAUMAS
TRIUMPH
TRIUNES
TROUBLE
TROUGHS
TROUNCE
TROUPER
TROUPES
TROUSER
TSOURIS
TSQUARE
TUBULAR
TUMULTS
TUMULUS
TVGUIDE

T•••U••
TALCUMS
TEACUPS
TEDIUMS
TEMPURA
TERHUNE
TESTUDO
TEXTUAL
TEXTURE
THROUGH
TISSUES
TITTUPS
TONGUED
TONGUES
TONSURE
TOPGUNS
TORQUES
TOSSUPS
TRADUCE
TRIBUNE
TRIBUTE
TRYOUTS
TUNEUPS
TUTTUTS

T••••U•
TACITUS
TACTFUL
TAGSOUT
TAKEOUT
TAKESUP
TALKOUT
TALKSUP
TALLYUP
TAMBOUR
TANKFUL
TANKSUP
TANTRUM
TAPSOUT
TEAMSUP
TEARFUL
TEAROUT
TEARSUP
TEDIOUS
TENFOUR
TENSEUP
TENUOUS
TERBIUM
TESTOUT
TETANUS
THEROUX
THESEUS
THINKUP
THORIUM
THULIUM
TIMEOUT
TIMESUP
TIREOUT
TOILFUL
TONEDUP
TONESUP
TOOKOUT
TOOLSUP
TOPSOUT
TOREOUT
TORNOUT
TOSSOUT
TOUCHUP
TOYSRUS
TRADEUP
TRAYFUL
TRIPSUP
TRITIUM
TROILUS
TROTOUT
TRUMPUP
TUMULUS
TUNEDUP
TUNEFUL
TUNEOUT
TUNESUP
TURNOUT
TURNSUP
TUSSAUD
TYINGUP
TYPEDUP
TYPESUP

T•••••U
TABLEAU
THIMPHU
THOREAU
TONNEAU
TRUDEAU

•TU••••
STUBBED
STUBBLE
STUBBLY
STUCCOS
STUCKTO
STUCKUP
STUDDED
STUDENT
STUDIED
STUDIES
STUDIOS
STUFFED
STUFFER
STUMBLE
STUMERS
STUMPED
STUMPER
STUNGUN
STUNNED
STUNNER
STUNTED
STUPEFY
STUPORS
STURGES

•T•U•••
ATTUCKS
ATTUNED
ATTUNES
ETRURIA
STAUNCH
STEUBEN
STLUCIA
STOUTEN
STOUTER
STOUTLY
STRUDEL

•T••U••
ATATURK
ATFAULT
ATRIUMS
STATUES
STATURE
STATUTE
STEPUPS
STIMULI
STLOUIS
STRAUSS

•T•••U•
ATISSUE
ATTICUS
STACKUP
STADIUM
STANDUP
STARTUP
STAYPUT
STAYSUP
STEPOUT
STEPSUP
STERNUM
STICKUP
STIRRUP
STIRSUP
STOCKUP
STOODUP
STOPSUP
STOREUP
STRATUM
STRATUS
STUCKUP
STUNGUN
YTTRIUM

••TU•••
ACTUARY
ACTUATE
ACTUPON
ATTUCKS
ATTUNED
ATTUNES
AUTUMNS
BITUMEN
BYTURNS
ESTUARY
FATUITY
FATUOUS
FUTURES
INTUITS
LETUPON
LITURGY
LOTUSES
MATURED
MATURER
MATURES
MUTUALS
NATURAL
NATURED
NATURES
OBTUNDS
OBTUSER
OCTUPLE
PETUNIA
PUTUPON
RETUNED
RETUNES
RETURNS
RITUALS
ROTUNDA
SETUPON
SITUATE
SUTURED
SUTURES
TITULAR
UNTUNED
UNTUNES
UPTURNS

••T•U••
ASTOUND
AUTEURS
BATTUES
CATSUIT
CUTOUTS
DETOURS
ENTHUSE
ENTRUST
EXTRUDE
HOTTUBS
INTRUDE
INTRUST
INTRUTH
JETGUNS
LETTUCE
NETSUKE
NETSURF
NOTRUMP
NOTSURE
OBTRUDE
OUTGUNS
OUTJUMP
OUTPUTS
OUTRUNS
PITBULL
POTFULS
POTLUCK
PUTOUTS
PUTPUTS
RETOUCH
RETOURS
SATSUMA
TITTUPS
TUTTUTS
UNTRUTH
VATFULS
WETSUIT

••T••U•
ACTEDUP
ACTFOUR
ACTSOUT
ANTAEUS
ANTEDUP
ANTESUP
ANTIGUA
ANTIQUE
ARTEMUS
ATTICUS
BATEAUX
BATHTUB
BOTCHUP
BUTTOUT
CATCHUP
CITROUS
CUTSOUT
DUTEOUS
DUTIFUL
EATENUP
EATSOUT
FATEFUL
FATIGUE
FATUOUS
GATEAUX
GETSOUT
HATEFUL
HITSOUT
HOTSPUR
ISTHMUS
KETCHUP
LETSOUT
LITHIUM
MATCHUP
METEOUT
MITCHUM
NATRIUM
NITROUS
NOTTRUE
OCTOPUS
OPTIMUM
OPTSOUT
OUTLOUD
PATCHUP
PETROUS
PITEOUS
PITIFUL
PUTSOUT
RETINUE
RUTHFUL
SETSOUT
SITSOUT
TETANUS
VOTEOUT
WITHOUT
YTTRIUM

••T•••U
MATTHAU
WATTEAU

•••TU••
ACHTUNG
ATATURK
BATTUES
CAPTURE
CENTURY
CLOTURE
CONTUSE
COSTUME
COUTURE
CULTURE
DENTURE
DICTUMS
DISTURB
DUSTUPS
FACTUAL
FEATURE
FIXTURE
FORTUNA
FORTUNE
GESTURE
HOTTUBS
LECTURE
LETTUCE
MIXTURE
NEPTUNE
NOCTURN
NURTURE
OROTUND
PASTURE
PERTURB
PICTURE
POSTURE
RAPTURE
RUPTURE
SPATULA
STATUES
STATURE
STATUTE
TESTUDO
TEXTUAL
TEXTURE
TITTUPS
TUTTUTS
UNSTUCK
VENTURA
VENTURE
VESTURE
VICTUAL
VIRTUAL
VIRTUES
VIRTUTE
VISTULA
VULTURE
ZEITUNG

•••T•U•
AMATEUR
BEATOUT
BEATSUP
BLOTOUT
BOOTOUT
BOOTSUP
BUSTOUT
BUTTOUT
CASTOUT
CENTAUR
CHATSUP
CHETRUM
CONTOUR
EDITOUT
FACTFUL
FELTOUT
FIATLUX
FISTFUL
FLATOUT
FORTIUS
FRETFUL
HAUTEUR
HEATFUL
HEATSUP
HURTFUL
KEPTOUT
LEFTOUT
LIFTSUP
LOSTOUT
LUSTFUL
MALTHUS
NOSTRUM
NOTTRUE
PARTOUT
PASTDUE
PASTEUP
PASTEUR
PENTIUM
PLOTFUL
PONTIUS
POUTFUL
PROTEUS
RESTFUL
RESTSUP
RIOTOUS
ROOTOUT
ROSTRUM
SENTOUT
SHOTGUN
SHOTOUT
SHOTPUT
SHUTOUT
SHUTSUP
SISTRUM
SORTOUT
SUITSUP
TACTFUL
TANTRUM
TESTOUT
TRITIUM
TROTOUT
WAITOUT
WAITSUP
WANTOUT
WENTOUT
WISTFUL
WRITEUP
WROTEUP
ZESTFUL

•••T••U
CHATEAU
COCTEAU
MATTHAU
PLATEAU
WATTEAU

••••TU•
ARBUTUS
BATHTUB
BOOSTUP
BUILTUP
BURNTUP
DECATUR
ERRATUM
FAUSTUS
HABITUE
HAMITUP
IMPETUS
KINGTUT
LIGHTUP
MIXITUP
OMENTUM
PARATUS
PINETUM
PLAUTUS
QUANTUM
SANCTUM
SHOOTUP
SPLITUP
STARTUP
STRATUM
STRATUS
SWEPTUP
TACITUS
WASHTUB

••••T•U
FUJITSU
JUJITSU
KOMATSU
MANITOU
SHIATSU
SHIHTZU

•••••TU
VANUATU

TV•••••
TVGUIDE
TVSHOWS

T•V••••
TAVERNS

T••V•••
TRAVAIL
TRAVELS
TRAVERS
TRAVOIS
TREVINO
TRIVETS
TRIVIAL

T•••V••
TELAVIV
THIEVED
THIEVES
THRIVED
THRIVES
TWELVES

T••••V•
TANTIVY
TENSIVE

T•••••V
TELAVIV

•T•V•••
ATAVISM
ATAVIST
STAVING
STEVENS

•T••V••
STARVED
STARVES
STRIVED
STRIVEN
STRIVER
STRIVES

••TV•••
LATVIAN
OUTVOTE

••T•V••
ACTIVES
ESTEVEZ
ESTIVAL
GETEVEN
GETOVER
GOTEVEN
GOTOVER
MITZVAH
MOTIVES
NATIVES
OCTAVES
OCTAVIA
OCTAVOS
PUTOVER

••T••V•
ACTFIVE
OUTLIVE

••T•••V
USTINOV

•••T•V•
AMATIVE
CAPTIVE
CENTAVO
EMOTIVE
FESTIVA
FESTIVE
FICTIVE
FURTIVE
RESTIVE
TANTIVY
UNITIVE
YOMTOVS

••••TV•
ZEMSTVO

••••T•V
MOLOTOV

•••••TV
CABLETV

TW•••••
TWADDLE
TWANGED
TWEAKED
TWEETED
TWEETER
TWEEZED
TWEEZES
TWELFTH
TWELVES
TWIDDLE
TWILLED
TWINBED
TWINGED
TWINGES
TWINING
TWINKLE
TWINKLY
TWINNED
TWIRLED
TWIRLER
TWISTED
TWISTER
TWITCHY
TWITTED
TWITTER
TWOBASE
TWOBITS
TWOFERS
TWOFOLD
TWOIRON
TWOLANE
TWOONIE
TWOSOME
TWOSTAR
TWOSTEP
TWOTIME
TWOTONE

T•W••••
TAWNIER
TAWNILY
THWACKS
THWARTS
TOWARDS
TOWAWAY
TOWCARS
TOWELED
TOWERED
TOWHEAD
TOWHEES
TOWNERS
TOWNIES
TOWNISH
TOWPATH
TOWROPE

T••W•••
THAWING
THEWIER
TINWARE
TINWORK
TRAWLED
TRAWLER
TROWELS
TROWERS

T•••W••
TAXIWAY
THREWIN
THROWER
THROWIN
THRUWAY
TOLLWAY
TOWAWAY
TURFWAR

T••••W•
TALLOWS
TIEDOWN
TOPDOWN
TVSHOWS

T•••••W
THECROW
TONEROW
TRISHAW

•TW••••
ATWORST

•T•W•••
ATHWART
STEWARD
STEWART
STEWERS
STEWING
STOWING

•T••W••
OTTAWAS
STREWED
STREWER

•T••••W
ATECROW

••TW•••
ANTWERP
ARTWARE
ARTWORK
BATWING
BETWEEN
BETWIXT
CATWALK
ENTWINE
GETWELL
GOTWELL
HOTWARS
HOTWIRE
JETWASH
JETWAYS
NETWORK
NITWITS
NOTWELL
OUTWARD
OUTWEAR
OUTWITS
OUTWORE
OUTWORK
OUTWORN
SITWELL
UNTWIST

••T•W••
ANTIWAR
CATAWBA
CNTOWER
CUTAWAY
EATAWAY
GATEWAY
GETAWAY
GOTAWAY
MATEWAN
OTTAWAS
PATHWAY
PUTAWAY
RETOWED

••T••W•
ANTCOWS
CUTDOWN
GETDOWN
GOTDOWN
LETDOWN
MATHEWS
OUTLAWS
PITSAWS
PUTDOWN
SATDOWN
SETDOWN
SITDOWN

••T•••W
CATSHOW
CATSPAW
EATCROW
LITHGOW
MATTHEW
OUTDRAW
OUTDREW
OUTFLOW
OUTGREW
OUTGROW
UPTONOW

•••TW••
BELTWAY
FOOTWAY
PARTWAY
POSTWAR

•••T•W•
BESTOWS
COWTOWN
HOOTOWL
KOWTOWS
MIDTOWN
NEWTOWN
OURTOWN
SKITOWS

•••T••W
BESTREW
FRETSAW
JUSTNOW
MATTHEW
PALTROW

••••T•W
BARSTOW
CHOCTAW
INASTEW
ROPETOW

T•X••••
TAXABLE
TAXFREE
TAXICAB
TAXIING
TAXIMAN
TAXIMEN
TAXIWAY
TAXLESS
TAXRATE
TEXTILE
TEXTUAL
TEXTURE
TUXEDOS

T•••X••
TELEXED
TELEXES

T•••••X
THEROUX
TOOLBOX
TRIPLEX

•T••••X
STCROIX

••T•X••
LATEXES
RETAXED
RETAXES
URTEXTS

••T••X•
BETWIXT

••T•••X
ALTOSAX
ANTITAX
BATEAUX
BETAMAX
GATEAUX

•••T•X•
AIRTAXI
CONTEXT
PRETEXT
SUBTEXT

•••T••X
BEATRIX
FIATLUX
FLATTAX
NARTHEX
POSTBOX
SALTBOX

••••T•X
ANTITAX
FLATTAX
GORETEX
OVERTAX
POLLTAX

TY•••••
TYCOONS
TYINGIN
TYINGUP
TYLENOL
TYMPANA
TYMPANI
TYPEDUP
TYPESET
TYPESUP
TYPHOON
TYPICAL
TYPIEST
TYPISTS
TYRANNY
TYRANTS

T•Y••••
THYMINE
THYSELF
TOYDOGS
TOYLAND
TOYLESS
TOYLIKE
TOYNBEE
TOYSHOP
TOYSRUS
TRYOUTS
TRYSTED
TRYSTER

T••Y•••
TIDYING
TINYTIM
TORYISH
TORYISM
TRAYFUL

T•••Y••
TALLYHO
TALLYUP
TIEDYED
TIEDYES
TINTYPE

T••••Y•
TEAPOYS
TOMBOYS
TURKEYS

T•••••Y
TACITLY
TACKILY
TAMMANY
TANNERY
TANTIVY
TARBABY
TARDILY
TASTILY
TATTILY
TAWNILY
TAXIWAY
TEARILY
TEATRAY
TENABLY
TENANCY
TENSELY
TENTHLY
TENUITY
TEPIDLY
TERNARY
TERRIFY
TERSELY
TESTFLY
TESTIFY
TESTILY
THATCHY
THERAPY
THEREBY
THEURGY
THICKLY
THIRDLY
THIRSTY
THISTLY
THREADY
THRIFTY
THROATY
THRUWAY
TICKETY
TIERNEY
TIFFANY
TIGHTLY
TIMIDLY
TIMOTHY
TINNILY
TIPSILY
TIREDLY
TOGGERY
TOLLWAY
TOLSTOY
TONALLY
TOPIARY
TOTALLY
TOTTERY
TOUGHLY
TOURNEY
TOWAWAY
TRACERY
TRAGEDY
TREACLY
TREMBLY
TRENARY
TRILOGY
TRINITY
TRITELY
TROLLEY
TROTSKY
TRUANCY
TUESDAY
TURNERY
TURNKEY
TUSCANY
TWINKLY
TWITCHY
TYRANNY

•TY••••
STYGIAN
STYLERS
STYLETS
STYLING
STYLISE
STYLISH
STYLIST
STYLIZE
STYMIED
STYMIES
STYPTIC
STYRENE
STYRIAN

•T•Y•••
STAYING
STAYPUT
STAYSUP

•T••Y••
STRAYED

•T•••Y•
STOREYS

•T••••Y
ATROPHY
ATTABOY
PTOLEMY
STAGILY
STAIDLY
STALELY
STANDBY
STANLEY
STARCHY
STARKLY
STATELY
STEEPLY
STERNLY
STIFFLY
STIRFRY
STOKELY
STONILY
STOODBY
STOOKEY
STOUTLY
STREAKY
STRINGY
STROPPY
STUBBLY
STUPEFY
UTILITY
UTTERLY

••TY•••
ECTYPES
KATYDID
PITYING
RETYPED
RETYPES
UNTYING

••T••Y•
ANTONYM
BATBOYS
BETRAYS
CATSEYE
ESTRAYS
JETWAYS
JITNEYS
KATHRYN
OUTLAYS

••T•••Y
ACTUARY
ANTHONY
ATTABOY
AUTARKY
BATTERY
BETARAY
BETHANY
BUTTERY
BYTHEBY
CATTILY
COTTONY
CUTAWAY
CUTLERY
DATEDLY
DITHERY
DITTANY
DOTTILY
EATAWAY
ENTROPY
ESTUARY
FATCITY
FATTILY
FATUITY
FETIDLY
GATEWAY
GETAWAY
GOTAWAY
GUTSILY
JITTERY
KITSCHY
LATENCY
LATHERY
LETSFLY
LITHELY
LITURGY
LOTTERY
MUTABLY
NATTILY
NITTANY
NOTABLY
NOTEDLY
NUTTILY
OUTPLAY
PATHWAY
PETRIFY
PETTILY
PITHILY
POTENCY
POTTERY
PUTAWAY
RETIARY
RITZILY
SATIETY
SATISFY
TATTILY
TOTALLY
TOTTERY
UTTERLY
VITALLY
VITRIFY
WITTILY

•••TY••
DACTYLS
DIPTYCH
INSTYLE
MARTYRS
MISTYPE
PLATYPI
RESTYLE
TINTYPE

•••T•Y•
DMYTRYK
FONTEYN
MONTOYA
SHUTEYE

•••T••Y
ACUTELY
AMATORY
ANATOMY
ASHTRAY
BATTERY
BEATIFY
BELTWAY
BENTLEY
BESTBOY
BLOTCHY
BRUTELY
BUTTERY
CANTILY
CATTILY
CENTURY
CERTIFY
CHUTNEY
COTTONY
CURTSEY
CUSTODY
DALTREY
DESTINY
DESTROY
DIETARY
DIRTILY
DITTANY
DOTTILY
DUSTILY
EARTHLY
ECSTASY
EMPTILY
ESOTERY
FACTORY
FANTASY
FATTILY
FIFTHLY
FOOTWAY
FORTIFY
FUSTILY
GOUTILY
GRATIFY
GRETZKY
GUSTILY
HASTILY
HAUTBOY
HEFTILY
HISTORY
HUNTLEY
IRATELY
JITTERY
JUSTIFY
LASTORY
LOFTILY
LOTTERY
LUSTILY
MASTERY
MEATILY
MISTILY
MONTHLY
MORTIFY
MUSTILY
MYSTERY
MYSTIFY
NASTILY
NATTILY
NIFTILY
NINTHLY
NITTANY
NUTTILY
ORATORY
PARTWAY
PETTILY
PORTRAY
POTTERY
RECTIFY
RECTORY
RUSTILY
SALTILY
SIXTHLY
SKETCHY
SNITCHY
SOOTILY
SOUTHEY
STATELY
SURTSEY
TANTIVY
TASTILY
TATTILY
TEATRAY
TENTHLY
TESTFLY
TESTIFY
TESTILY
THATCHY
TOTTERY
TRITELY
TROTSKY
TWITCHY
UNITARY
VICTORY
WHITNEY
WINTERY
WITTILY

••••TY•
BURSTYN

••••T•Y
ABBOTCY
ADEPTLY
ADULTLY
ALERTLY
BEASTLY
BIGOTRY
BLUNTLY
BREATHY
BRISTLY
CHANTEY
CHEWTOY
CHINTZY
COUNTRY
COURTLY
CRAFTSY
DOROTHY
EMPATHY
ERECTLY
EXACTLY
FAINTLY
FIRSTLY
FLEETLY
GAUNTLY
GHASTLY
GHOSTLY
GREATLY
GRISTLY
HEALTHY
HELOTRY
INAPTLY
INEPTLY
INERTLY
JOINTLY
LANGTRY
LENGTHY
LICITLY
LIGHTLY
MOISTLY
NIGHTLY
OVERTLY
POULTRY
QUIETLY
REENTRY
RIANTLY
RIGHTLY
SAINTLY
SCANTLY
SHANTEY
SHORTLY
SIGHTLY
SMARTLY
SMOOTHY
SQUATLY
SQUATTY
STOUTLY
SWARTHY
SWEETLY
SWELTRY
SWIFTLY
TACITLY
THISTLY
TIGHTLY
TIMOTHY
TOLSTOY
UNAPTLY
WEALTHY

•••••TY
ABILITY
ACIDITY
AGILITY
AMENITY
AMNESTY
ANNUITY
ANXIETY
APLENTY
ARIDITY
AVIDITY
BAYCITY
BLIGHTY
BREVITY
CHARITY
CHRISTY
CLARITY
CRUDITY
CRUELTY
DENSITY
DIGNITY
DOUGHTY
DUALITY
DUBIETY
DYNASTY
EDACITY
FACULTY
FALSITY
FATCITY
FATUITY
FIDGETY
FLAUNTY
FLIGHTY
FRAILTY
FROWSTY
GADGETY
GRAVITY
HAUGHTY
HONESTY
IMPIETY
INANITY
JOLLITY
KKKKATY
LIBERTY
LOYALTY
MAJESTY
MODESTY
NAIVETY
NAUGHTY
NIMIETY
NOVELTY
NULLITY
OFFDUTY
OPACITY
PAUCITY
PENALTY
POVERTY
PRIVITY
PROBITY
PUBERTY
QUALITY
REALITY
RICKETY
ROYALTY
RUSSETY
SATIETY
SEADUTY
SEVENTY
SOCIETY
SQUATTY
SQUINTY
SUAVITY
SUNCITY
TENUITY
THIRSTY
THRIFTY
THROATY
TICKETY
TRINITY
UTILITY
VACUITY
VARIETY
VARSITY
VELVETY
WEIGHTY

TZ•••••
TZARINA

T•Z••••
TIZZIES

T••Z•••
TARZANA
TENZING
TIZZIES

T•••Z••
TOPAZES
TWEEZED
TWEEZES

T••••Z•
TRAPEZE

T•••••Z
THEFONZ

•T••Z••
STANZAS

•T•••Z•
ATOMIZE
ITEMIZE
STYLIZE
UTILIZE

••TZ•••
DITZIER
FUTZING
MATZOHS
MITZVAH
RITZIER
RITZILY
YITZHAK

••T•Z••
CITIZEN
NETIZEN

••T••Z•
OUTSIZE

••T•••Z
ESTEVEZ
NATCHEZ

•••TZ••
BLITZED
BLITZEN
BLITZES
GLITZED
GLITZES
GRETZKY
KLUTZES
PRETZEL
QUETZAL
SELTZER
SPITZES
SWITZER
WALTZED
WALTZER
WALTZES
YAHTZEE

•••T•Z•
BAPTIZE
MESTIZA
MESTIZO

••••TZ•
CHINTZY
SCHATZI
SHIHTZU
YANGTZE

•••••TZ
BERLITZ
HEIFETZ
KIBBUTZ
SCHULTZ

U•A••••
UGANDAN
ULALUME
ULANOVA
UNAIDED
UNAIMED
UNAIRED
UNALIKE
UNAMUNO
UNAPTLY
UNARMED
UNASKED
UNAVOCE
UNAWARE
UNAWFUL
UPATREE
URANITE
URANIUM
UTAHANS

U••A•••
UKRAINE
ULYANOV
UMLAUTS
UNBAKED
UNCAGED
UNCAGES
UNCANNY
UNCASED
UNCASES
UNDATED
UNEARTH
UNEATEN
UNFAZED
UNHANDS
UNHANDY
UNHAPPY
UNLACED
UNLACES
UNLADES
UNLATCH
UNMAKES
UNMASKS
UNNAMED
UNPACKS
UNPAVED
UNRATED
UNRAVEL
UNSATED
UNTACKS
UNTAMED
UNTAPED
UPDATED
UPDATES
UPLANDS
UPRAISE
UPTAKES
UPWARDS
URBANER
USEABLE
USUALLY

U•••A••
ULLMANN
ULULANT
ULULATE
UMBRAGE
UNAWARE
UNCHAIN
UNCIALS
UNCLASP
UNCRATE
UNDRAPE
UNDRAWN
UNHEARD
UNITARY
UNLEARN
UNLEASH
UNLOADS
UNREADY
UNSEALS
UNSEATS
UNSNAGS
UNSNAPS
UNSNARL
UNSTACK
UNTRAPS
UNWEAVE
UNWRAPS
UPBEATS
UPBRAID
UPDRAFT
UPGRADE
UPLOADS
UPPSALA
UPQUARK
UPROARS
UPSCALE
UPSTAGE
UPSTART
UPSTATE
USGRANT
UTAHANS

U••••A•
UGANDAN
ULTIMAS
UMBRIAN
UNCLEAN
UNCLEAR
UNCLOAK
UNEQUAL
UNSTRAP
UNUSUAL
UPTOPAR
URUGUAY
UTOPIAN
UTOPIAS
UXORIAL

U•••••A
ULANOVA
UPPSALA

•UA••••
DUALITY
GUANACO
GUANINE
GUARANI
GUARDED
GUARDEE
GUARGUM
MUAMMAR
NUANCED
NUANCES
QUACKED
QUAFFED
QUAFFER
QUAGGAS
QUAHOGS
QUAILED
QUAKERS
QUAKIER
QUAKILY
QUAKING
QUALIFY
QUALITY
QUANGOS
QUANTUM
QUARREL
QUARTER
QUARTET
QUARTOS
QUASARS
QUASHED
QUASHES
QUAVERS
QUAVERY
RUANDAN
SUASION
SUAVELY
SUAVEST
SUAVITY
TUAREGS

•U•A•••
AUBADES
AUPAIRS
AURALEE
AURALLY
AUTARKY
BUGABOO
BUGALOO
BUTANOL
BUYABLE
CURACAO
CURATES
CURATOR
CUTAWAY
DUBARRY
DUKAKIS
DUNAWAY
DURABLE
DURABLY
DURANCE
DURANGO
DURANTE
EURASIA
HUMANLY
HUMANUM
JUDAISM
JUMANJI
KUWAITI
LUNATIC
LUXATED
LUXATES
MUBARAK
MUTABLE
MUTABLY
MUTAGEN
MUTANTS
MUTATED
MUTATES
NUTATED
NUTATES
OUTACTS
OUTAGES
PULASKI
PUTAMEN
PUTAWAY
RUBATOS
RUNAMOK
RUNAWAY
RURALLY
SUGARED
SUHARTO
SUKARNO
SUMATRA
SUSANNA
SUSANNE
SUZANNE
TUBAIST
YUCATAN

•U••A••
AUREATE
BUFFALO
BULGARS
BULWARK
BUMRAPS
BUOYANT
BURBANK
BUREAUS
BURLAPS
BURMANS
BUROAKS
BURSARS
BURSARY
BUSFARE
BUSTARD
BUZZARD
CUEBALL
CUECARD
CUIRASS
CUPCAKE
CUREALL
CURRANT
CURTAIL
CURTAIN
CUSHAWS
CUSTARD
CUTBACK
CUTLASS
CUTRATE
DUEDATE
DULLARD
FUNFAIR
FURBALL
FURNACE
GUANACO
GUARANI
GUEVARA
GUFFAWS
GUITARS
GULLAHS
GUMBALL
GUNWALE
HUBBARD
HUBCAPS
HUNGARY
HUNYADY
HURRAHS
HUSBAND
HUSHABY
HUSSARS
HUZZAHS
JUGBAND
JULIANA
JUNKART
JUTLAND
LUCIANO
LUGGAGE
LULLABY
LUMBAGO
LUMBARS
MUDCATS
MUDPACK
MULLAHS
MUNDANE
MUSCATS
MUSTAFA
MUSTANG
MUSTARD
MUTUALS
NUBIANS
NULLAHS
NUMBATS
OURGANG
OUTBACK
OUTCAST
OUTEATS
OUTFACE
OUTLAID
OUTLAND
OUTLAST
OUTLAWS
OUTLAYS
OUTPACE
OUTRACE
OUTRAGE
OUTRANK
OUTTAKE
OUTTALK
OUTWARD
PULSARS
PULSATE
PUNJABI
PUNKAHS
PURDAHS
QUASARS
QUINARY
RUDYARD
RUMBAED
RUMMAGE
RUNBACK
RUNLATE
RUNWAYS
RUPIAHS
SUBWAYS
SUCRASE
SULFATE
SULTANA
SULTANS
SUMMARY
SUNBATH
SUNDAES
SUNDAYS
SUNLAMP
SUNMAID
SUNRAYS
SUNTANS
SURFACE
SURNAME
SURPASS
SUSTAIN
TULSANS
TURBANS
TUSCANY
TUSSAUD
VULCANS
VULGATE

•U•••A•
AUGURAL
AURORAE
AURORAL
AURORAS
AUSTRAL
AUTOMAT
BUCKRAM
BUCKSAW
BUDDHAS
BUGBEAR
BURGLAR
BUSHMAN
BUZZSAW
CULTJAM
CUPOLAS
CURACAO
CUTAWAY
DUENNAS
DUNAWAY
DUSTMAN
DUSTPAN
FUNCHAL
FURSEAL
FUSTIAN
GUINEAS
GUNBOAT
GUNPLAY
GURKHAS
HULLOAS
HUMERAL
JUGHEAD
JUGULAR
JUMPSAT
JUNKMAN
JUVENAL
KUMQUAT
KUTENAI
LUNGEAT
MUAMMAR
MUBARAK
MULETAS
MUSICAL
MUSKRAT
NUCLEAR
NUMERAL
NUPTIAL
NUTMEAT
NUTRIAS
OUTDRAW
OUTPLAY
OUTWEAR
PULLMAN
PULLTAB
PURITAN
PUTAWAY
QUAGGAS
QUETZAL
QUINOAS
QUOKKAS
RUANDAN
RUFFIAN
RUFIYAA
RUNAWAY
RUSSIAN
SUBHEAD
SUNBEAM
SUNDIAL
SURCOAT
SURINAM
SURREAL
TUBULAR
TUCHMAN
TUESDAY
TUGBOAT
TUNDRAS
TURFWAR
TUTELAR
YUCATAN

•U••••A
AUGUSTA
AUREOLA
AUSTRIA
BURKINA
CULEBRA
DUODENA
EURASIA
FUCHSIA
GUEVARA
JULIANA
JUNKDNA
MUSTAFA
QUECHUA
RUFIYAA
SUBROSA
SULTANA
SULUSEA
SUMATRA
SUSANNA
TUNISIA

••UA•••
AQUARIA
AQUATIC
AQUAVIT
ECUADOR
EQUABLE
EQUABLY
EQUALED
EQUALLY
EQUATED
EQUATES
EQUATOR
GOUACHE
IGUANAS
SQUALID
SQUALLS
SQUALOR
SQUANTO
SQUARED
SQUARER
SQUARES
SQUATLY
SQUATTY
SQUAWKS
SQUAWKY
TRUANCY
TRUANTS
USUALLY
ZOUAVES

••U•A••
ABUBAKR
ADULATE
AOUDADS
BAUHAUS
COUGARS
COURAGE
COURANT
CRUSADE
CRUSADO
CRUZADO
EDUCATE
EMULATE
FOULARD
GAUTAMA
GOULASH
GOURAMI
HAULAGE
MAUMAUS
MOULAGE
NOUGATS
PLUMAGE
PLURALS
RHUBARB
ROULADE
SAUSAGE
SFUMATO
SOUTANE
SQUEAKS
SQUEAKY
SQUEALS
TOUCANS
TOURACO
TSUNAMI
ULULANT
ULULATE
YOUMANS

••U••A•
ABUTTAL
ALUMNAE
ALUMNAL
AQUINAS
ASUSUAL
BLUEJAY
BLUELAW
CHUKKAS
CLUBCAR
CRUCIAL
DIURNAL
DOUGLAS
EXURBAN
FAUXPAS
FLUVIAL
FOURWAY
HOUSMAN
HYUNDAI
IGUANAS
JOURDAN
JOURNAL
KAUFMAN
KLUGMAN
LAUGHAT
MAUGHAM
NEUTRAL
NOUVEAU
NYUNGAR
PLUVIAL
RHUMBAS
SAURIAN
THURMAN
THUSFAR
TRUCIAL
TRUDEAU
UNUSUAL
URUGUAY
VAUGHAN
ZEUGMAS

••U•••A
AQUARIA
ARUGULA
EXURBIA
GAUTAMA
LOUELLA
PAULINA
PRUSSIA

•••UA••
ACTUARY
ACTUATE
ANNUALS
ASSUAGE
CASUALS
CEBUANO
EDOUARD
ESTUARY
JAGUARS
JANUARY
LOQUATS
MANUALS
MUTUALS
NAHUATL
ONGUARD
PADUANS
PAPUANS
PIQUANT
RITUALS
SAGUARO
SIOUANS
SITUATE
TIJUANA
TSQUARE
UPQUARK
VALUATE
VANUATU
VISUALS

•••U•A•
ANGULAR
ANNULAR
AROUSAL
AUGURAL
CAYUGAS
COPULAE
COPULAS
FACULAE
FIBULAE
FIBULAS
HANUKAH
INHUMAN
INSULAR
JOCULAR
JUGULAR
KAHUNAS
KORUNAS
LACUNAE
LACUNAL
LACUNAS
LAGUNAS
MACULAE
MCLUHAN
MEDUSAE
MEDUSAS
MODULAR
NATURAL
NEBULAE
NEBULAR
NEBULAS
NODULAR
OLDUVAI
PADUCAH
PERUSAL
POPULAR
RADULAE
REFUSAL
REGULAR
REMUDAS
ROMULAN
SAMURAI
SECULAR
SPOUSAL
TABULAR
THRUWAY
TITULAR
TRAUMAS
TUBULAR
VICUNAS
YAKUZAS

•••U••A
ALLUVIA
AUGUSTA
CLAUDIA
ETRURIA
FELUCCA
MAZURKA
MEDULLA
MINUTIA
PETUNIA
ROBUSTA
ROTUNDA
SEQUOIA
SHOULDA
STLUCIA
SULUSEA
TEQUILA
TIJUANA

••••UA•
ACCRUAL
ANAHUAC
ASUSUAL
BIVOUAC
COEQUAL
DONJUAN
FACTUAL
GRADUAL
KEROUAC
KUMQUAT
LINGUAL
RORQUAL
SANJUAN
SENSUAL
SICHUAN
TEXTUAL
UNEQUAL
UNUSUAL
URUGUAY
VICTUAL
VIRTUAL

••••U•A
ARAFURA
ARUGULA
BARBUDA
BERMUDA
BLACULA
BRAVURA
CAESURA
DRACULA
FORMULA
FORTUNA
INOCULA
KILAUEA
SATSUMA
SCAPULA
SPATULA
TEMPURA
VENTURA
VISTULA

•••••UA
ANTIGUA
MANAGUA
QUECHUA

U•B••••
UMBERTO
UMBRAGE
UMBRIAN
UNBAKED
UNBENDS
UNBINDS
UNBLEST
UNBLOCK
UNBOLTS
UNBOUND
UNBOWED
UNBOXED
UNBOXES
UPBEATS
UPBORNE
UPBRAID
URBANER

U•••B••
UNROBED
UNROBES
USEABLE

•UB••••
AUBADES
AUBURNS
BUBBLED
BUBBLES
CUBBIES
CUBBISH
CUBICLE
CUBISTS
DUBARRY
DUBBERS
DUBBING
DUBIETY
DUBIOUS
DUBUQUE
FUBBING
FUBSIER
HUBBARD
HUBBELL
HUBBIES
HUBBUBS
HUBCAPS
JUBILEE
KUBRICK
LUBBERS
LUBBOCK
LUBEJOB
MUBARAK
NUBBIER
NUBBINS
NUBBLES
NUBIANS
PUBERTY
PUBLICS
PUBLISH
RUBATOS
RUBBERS
RUBBERY
RUBBING
RUBBISH
RUBBLES
RUBDOWN
RUBICON
RUBITIN
RUBRICS
RUBSOFF
RUBSOUT
SUBBING
SUBDEBS
SUBDUED
SUBDUER
SUBDUES
SUBHEAD
SUBJECT
SUBJOIN
SUBLETS
SUBLIME
SUBMITS
SUBORNS
SUBPLOT
SUBROSA
SUBSETS
SUBSIDE
SUBSIDY
SUBSIST
SUBSOIL
SUBSUME
SUBTEND
SUBTEXT
SUBTLER
SUBUNIT
SUBURBS
SUBVERT
SUBVOCE
SUBWAYS
SUBZERO
TUBAIST
TUBBIER
TUBISTS
TUBLIKE
TUBULAR

•U•B•••
BUBBLED
BUBBLES
BUGBEAR
BULBLET
BULBOUS
BULBULS
BUMBLED
BUMBLER
BUMBLES
BURBANK
BURBLED
BURBLES
BURBOTS
BUSBIES
BUSBOYS
CUBBIES
CUBBISH
CUEBALL
CUIBONO
CURBCUT
CURBING
CUTBACK
DUBBERS
DUBBING
DUMBEST
DUMBING
FUBBING
FUMBLED
FUMBLER
FUMBLES
FURBALL
FURBISH
GUMBALL
GUNBOAT
HUBBARD
HUBBELL
HUBBIES
HUBBUBS
HUMBLED
HUMBLER
HUMBLES
HUMBUGS
HUSBAND
JUGBAND
JUMBLED
JUMBLES
LUBBERS
LUBBOCK
LUMBAGO
LUMBARS
LUMBERS
MUMBLED
MUMBLER
MUMBLES
NUBBIER
NUBBINS
NUBBLES
NUMBATS
NUMBERS
NUMBEST
NUMBING
OUTBACK
OUTBIDS
PUEBLOS
QUIBBLE
RUBBERS
RUBBERY
RUBBING
RUBBISH
RUBBLES
RUMBAED
RUMBLED
RUMBLES
RUNBACK
SUBBING
SUDBURY
SUNBATH
SUNBEAM
SUNBELT
SUNBOWL
SUNBURN
TUBBIER
TUGBOAT
TUMBLED
TUMBLER
TUMBLES
TUMBREL
TURBANS
TURBINE
TURBITS
TURBOTS

•U••B••
AUDIBLE
AUDIBLY
AUDUBON
BUGABOO
BUNKBED
BUYABLE
CULEBRA
DURABLE
DURABLY
DUSTBIN
JUJUBES
JUKEBOX
JUNEBUG
MUTABLE
MUTABLY
QUIBBLE

•U•••B•
HUBBUBS
HUSHABY
LULLABY
PUNJABI
SUBDEBS
SUBURBS

•U••••B
LUBEJOB
PULLTAB
SUCCUMB

••UB•••
ABUBAKR
BAUBLES
BLUBBER
BRUBECK
CLUBBED
CLUBCAR
DAUBERS
DAUBING
DOUBLED
DOUBLES
DOUBLET
DOUBLEU
DOUBTED
DOUBTER
DRUBBED
FLUBBED
FLUBBER
GRUBBED
HAUBERK
REUBENS
RHUBARB
ROUBLES
SHUBERT
SNUBBED
STUBBED
STUBBLE
STUBBLY

••U•B••
BLUBBER
BLUEBOY
BOURBON
CLUBBED
CRUMBLE
CRUMBLY
DRUBBED
EQUABLE
EQUABLY
EXURBAN
EXURBIA
FLUBBED
FLUBBER
FNUMBER
GRUBBED
GRUMBLE
GRUMBLY
HAUTBOY
PLUMBED
PLUMBER
RHUMBAS
SLUMBER
SNUBBED
STUBBED
STUBBLE
STUBBLY
STUMBLE
THUMBED
THURBER

••U••B•
WOULDBE

••U•••B
COULOMB
RHUBARB

•••UB••
AUDUBON
JUJUBES
SCRUBBY
SCRUBUP
SHRUBBY
SOLUBLE
STEUBEN
TROUBLE
VOLUBLE
VOLUBLY

•••U•B•
BENUMBS
COLUMBO
SCRUBBY
SHRUBBY
SUBURBS

••••UB•
BEDAUBS
CHERUBS
HOTTUBS
HUBBUBS
ICECUBE
INDOUBT
NODOUBT
REDOUBT

••••U•B
DIMBULB
DISTURB
PERTURB
SUCCUMB

•••••UB
BACKRUB
BATHTUB
BEARCUB
FANCLUB
KEYCLUB
LIONCUB
OVERDUB
WASHTUB

UC•••••
UCCELLO

U•C••••
UCCELLO
UNCAGED
UNCAGES
UNCANNY
UNCASED
UNCASES
UNCHAIN
UNCIALS
UNCIVIL
UNCLASP
UNCLEAN
UNCLEAR
UNCLOAK
UNCLOGS
UNCLOSE
UNCOILS
UNCORKS
UNCOUTH
UNCOVER
UNCRATE
UNCTION
UNCURLS
UPCLOSE
URCHINS

U••C•••
UNICORN
UNSCREW
UPSCALE

U•••C••
UNLACED
UNLACES
UNLOCKS
UNLUCKY
UNPACKS
UNTACKS
UPTICKS
UTRECHT

U••••C•
UNAVOCE
UNBLOCK
UNFROCK
UNHITCH
UNLATCH
UNSTACK
UNSTICK
UNSTUCK
URGENCY

•UC••••
AUCTION
BUCKETS
BUCKEYE
BUCKING
BUCKLED
BUCKLER
BUCKLES
BUCKLEY
BUCKOES
BUCKRAM
BUCKSAW
BUCKSUP
BUCOLIC
CUCKOOS
DUCHESS
DUCHIES
DUCKIER
DUCKING
DUCKPIN
DUCTILE
DUCTING
EUCHRED
EUCHRES
FUCHSIA
KUCHENS
LUCENCY
LUCERNE
LUCIANO
LUCIDLY
LUCIFER
LUCILLE
LUCKIER
LUCKILY
LUCKING
LUCKOUT
MUCKIER
MUCKILY
MUCKING
MUCKSUP
NUCLEAR
NUCLEIC
NUCLEON
NUCLEUS
NUCLIDE
PUCCINI
PUCKERS
PUCKETT
PUCKISH
RUCHING
RUCKING
RUCTION
SUCCEED
SUCCESS
SUCCORS
SUCCOUR
SUCCUMB
SUCKERS
SUCKING
SUCKSIN
SUCRASE
SUCROSE
SUCTION
TUCHMAN
TUCKERS
TUCKING
TUCKSIN
YUCATAN
YUCKIER

•U•C•••
BUNCHED
BUNCHES
BUNCOED
BUTCHER
CUECARD
CUPCAKE
DULCIFY
DUNCISH
FULCRUM
FUNCHAL
GULCHES
HUBCAPS
HUNCHED
HUNCHES
HUTCHES
JUICERS
JUICEUP
JUICIER
JUICILY
JUICING
JUNCOES
KUTCHIN
LUNCHED
LUNCHES
LURCHED
LURCHES
MUDCATS
MULCHED
MULCHES
MULCTED
MUNCHED
MUNCHER
MUNCHES
MUSCATS
MUSCLED
MUSCLES
MUSCOVY
NUNCIOS
OUTCAST
OUTCOME
OUTCROP
PUCCINI
PUNCHED
PUNCHER
PUNCHES
PUNCHIN
PUNCHUP
PURCELL
QUACKED
QUECHUA
QUICHES
QUICKEN
QUICKER
QUICKIE
QUICKLY
SUCCEED
SUCCESS
SUCCORS
SUCCOUR
SUCCUMB
SUNCITY
SURCOAT
TUSCANY
VULCANS

•U••C••
AURICLE
AUROCHS
CUBICLE
CURACAO
CURBCUT
CUTICLE
JUMPCUT
MUSICAL
NUANCED
NUANCES
OUTACTS
PUMICES
QUINCES
RUBICON
TUNICLE

•U•••C•
AUSPICE
BULLOCK
BURDOCK
CUTBACK
DUNNOCK
DURANCE
FURNACE
FUSTICS
GUANACO
GUNLOCK
HUMMOCK
JUSTICE
KUBRICK
LUBBOCK
LUCENCY
MUDPACK
MURDOCH
OUTBACK
OUTFACE
OUTPACE
OUTRACE
PUBLICS
PUDENCY
RUBRICS
RUNBACK
RUSTICS
SUBJECT
SUBVOCE
SUFFICE
SUNDECK
SUOLOCO
SURFACE
SUSPECT
TUSSOCK

•U••••C
BUCOLIC
JURIDIC
LUNATIC
NUCLEIC
NUMERIC

••UC•••
CHUCKED
CHUCKLE
CLUCKED
COUCHED
COUCHES
CRUCIAL
CRUCIFY
DRUCKER
EDUCATE
EDUCING
ERUCTED
FAUCETS
GAUCHER
GAUCHOS
GLUCOSE
KNUCKLE
LEUCINE
PAUCITY
PLUCKED
POUCHED
POUCHES
RAUCOUS
SAUCERS
SAUCIER
SAUCILY
SHUCKED
SHUCKER
STUCCOS
STUCKTO
STUCKUP
TOUCANS
TOUCHED
TOUCHES
TOUCHON
TOUCHUP
TRUCIAL
TRUCKED
TRUCKEE
TRUCKER
TRUCKLE
VOUCHED
VOUCHER
VOUCHES

••U•C••
BOUNCED
BOUNCER
BOUNCES
CLUBCAR
COUNCIL
CRUNCHY
GOUACHE
JOUNCED
JOUNCES
PAUNCHY
POUNCED
POUNCER
POUNCES
SLUICED
SLUICES
SOUPCON
SOURCED
SOURCES
STUCCOS

••U••C•
BRUBECK
FLUENCY
MAURICE
SQUELCH
SQUINCH
TOURACO
TRUANCY

••U•••C
AQUATIC
CAUSTIC
LAUTREC
POULENC
YOUNGMC

•••UC••
ABDUCTS
ADDUCED
ADDUCES
ADDUCTS
ATTUCKS
CADUCEI
CHAUCER
DEDUCED
DEDUCES
DEDUCTS
FELUCCA
GROUCHO
GROUCHY
INDUCED
INDUCER
INDUCES
INDUCTS
NOGUCHI
PADUCAH
PENUCHE
REDUCED
REDUCER
REDUCES
RELUCTS
SEDUCED
SEDUCER
SEDUCES
SLOUCHY
SPRUCED
SPRUCER
SPRUCES
STLUCIA
UNLUCKY

•••U•C•
ADJUNCT
DEFUNCT
ENOUNCE
FELUCCA
FLOUNCE
FLOUNCY
GODUTCH
INDUTCH
SCRUNCH
STAUNCH
TROUNCE

••••UC•
CONDUCE
CONDUCT
DEBAUCH
DEBOUCH
LETTUCE
POTLUCK
PRODUCE
PRODUCT
RETOUCH
ROEBUCK
SAWBUCK
TRADUCE
UNSTUCK
VIADUCT

••••U•C
ANAHUAC
BIVOUAC
KEROUAC
MOLLUSC

•••••UC
JEANLUC

U•D••••
UNDATED
UNDERDO
UNDERGO
UNDOING
UNDRAPE
UNDRAWN
UNDRESS
UNDYING
UPDATED
UPDATES
UPDRAFT

U•••D••
UGANDAN
UNAIDED
UNENDED
UNGODLY
UNLADES
UPENDED

U••••D•
UNBENDS
UNBINDS
UNDERDO
UNFOLDS
UNGIRDS
UNHANDS
UNHANDY
UNIPODS
UNLOADS
UNREADY
UNWINDS
UPGRADE
UPHOLDS
UPLANDS
UPLOADS
UPWARDS
USERIDS

U•••••D
UMPIRED
UNAIDED
UNAIMED
UNAIRED
UNARMED
UNASKED
UNBAKED
UNBOUND
UNBOWED
UNBOXED
UNCAGED
UNCASED
UNDATED
UNENDED
UNFAZED
UNFIXED
UNGLUED
UNHEARD
UNIFIED
UNLACED
UNLIKED
UNLINED
UNLOVED
UNMOVED
UNNAMED
UNOILED
UNPAVED
UNPILED
UNRATED
UNROBED
UNSATED
UNSEWED
UNSOUND
UNTAMED
UNTAPED
UNTRIED
UNTUNED
UNWOUND
UNYOKED
UNZONED
UPBRAID
UPDATED
UPENDED
USHERED
USURPED
UTTERED

•UD••••
AUDIBLE
AUDIBLY
AUDILES
AUDITED
AUDITOR
AUDUBON
BUDDHAS
BUDDIES
BUDDING
BUDDYUP
BUDGETS
BUDGIES
BUDGING
BUDLESS
BUDLIKE
CUDDIES
CUDDLED
CUDDLES
CUDGELS
DUDEDUP
DUDGEON
FUDDLED
FUDDLES
FUDGING
HUDDLED
HUDDLES
JUDAISM
JUDDERS
JUDGING
JUDOIST
LUDDITE
MUDCATS
MUDDERS
MUDDIED
MUDDIER
MUDDIES
MUDDILY
MUDDLED
MUDDLER
MUDDLES
MUDEELS
MUDHENS
MUDPACK
MUDPIES
NUDGERS
NUDGING
NUDISTS
NUDNIKS
PUDDING
PUDDLED
PUDDLES
PUDENCY
PUDGIER
PUDGILY
RUDDERS
RUDDIER
RUDDILY
RUDOLPH
RUDYARD
SUDBURY
SUDSIER
SUDSING

•U•D•••
BUDDHAS
BUDDIES
BUDDING
BUDDYUP
BUNDLED
BUNDLES
BURDENS
BURDOCK
CUDDIES
CUDDLED
CUDDLES
CURDIER
CURDING
CURDLED
CURDLES
CUTDOWN
DUEDATE
DUMDUMS
DUODENA
FUDDLED
FUDDLES
FUNDING
GUIDING
GUIDONS
GUMDROP
GUNDOGS
HUDDLED
HUDDLES
HUMDRUM
HUNDRED
HURDLED
HURDLER
HURDLES
JUDDERS
KURDISH
LUDDITE
MUDDERS
MUDDIED
MUDDIER
MUDDIES
MUDDILY
MUDDLED
MUDDLER
MUDDLES
MUNDANE
MURDERS
MURDOCH
OUTDOES
OUTDONE
OUTDOOR
OUTDRAW
OUTDREW
PUDDING
PUDDLED
PUDDLES
PUNDITS
PURDAHS
PUTDOWN
RUBDOWN
RUDDERS
RUDDIER
RUDDILY
RUNDEEP
RUNDLES
RUNDOWN
SUBDEBS
SUBDUED
SUBDUER
SUBDUES
SUNDAES
SUNDAYS
SUNDECK
SUNDERS
SUNDEWS
SUNDIAL
SUNDOGS
SUNDOWN
TUNDRAS

•U••D••
AUBADES
BUILDER
BUILDIN
BUILDUP
BULLDOG
DUDEDUP
DUKEDOM
GUARDED
GUARDEE
GUILDER
HUMIDLY
HUMIDOR
JUNKDNA
JURIDIC
LUCIDLY
LURIDLY
RUANDAN
RUNSDRY
RUSHDIE
TUESDAY
TUNEDIN
TUNEDUP
TUXEDOS

•U•••D•
AUGENDS
BUSHIDO
CUSPIDS
CUSTODY
HUNYADY
NUCLIDE
OUTBIDS
OUTSIDE
SUBSIDE
SUBSIDY
SULFIDE
SUNGODS

•U••••D
AUDITED
AUGURED
BUBBLED
BUCKLED
BUGEYED
BULLIED
BUMBLED
BUNCHED
BUNCOED
BUNDLED
BUNGLED
BUNKBED
BUNKOED
BURBLED
BURGLED
BUSTARD
BUSTLED
BUZZARD
CUDDLED
CUECARD
CULLIED
CURDLED
CURRIED
CUSTARD
DULLARD
DUMMIED
EUCHRED
FUDDLED
FUELLED
FUELROD
FUMBLED
GUARDED
GUESSED
GUESTED
GURGLED
GUSSIED
GUZZLED
HUBBARD
HUDDLED
HULLOED
HUMBLED
HUMORED
HUNCHED
HUNDRED
HURDLED
HURRIED
HURTLED
HUSBAND
HUSTLED
JUGBAND
JUGGLED
JUGHEAD
JUMBLED
JUTLAND
JUTTIED
LUNCHED
LURCHED
LUSTRED
LUXATED
MUDDIED
MUDDLED
MUFFLED
MULCHED
MULCTED
MUMBLED
MUMFORD
MUNCHED
MUSCLED
MUSTARD
MUTATED
MUZZLED
NUANCED
NUTATED
NUZZLED
OUTLAID
OUTLAND
OUTLOUD
OUTSOLD
OUTWARD
PUDDLED
PUNCHED
PURFLED
PURPLED
PURSUED
PUTTIED
PUZZLED
QUACKED
QUAFFED
QUAILED
QUASHED
QUEERED
QUELLED
QUERIED
QUESTED
QUIETED
QUILLED
QUILTED
QUIPPED
QUIZZED
RUDYARD
RUFFLED
RUMBAED
RUMBLED
RUMORED
RUMPLED
RUSTLED
SUBDUED
SUBHEAD
SUBTEND
SUCCEED
SUGARED
SULLIED
SUNMAID
SUSPEND
SUTURED
TUMBLED
TURTLED
TUSSAUD
TUSSLED
TUTORED

••UD•••
AOUDADS
BOUDOIR
CAUDLES
CRUDELY
CRUDEST
CRUDITY
DRUDGED
DRUDGES
ELUDING
ERUDITE
EXUDING
FEUDING
GAUDIER
GAUDILY
GRUDGED
GRUDGES
HOUDINI
KLUDGES
LAUDING
LOUDEST
LOUDISH
MAUDLIN
PRUDENT
PRUDERY
PRUDHOE
PRUDISH
SCUDDED
SHUDDER
SLUDGES
SMUDGED
SMUDGES
STUDDED
STUDENT
STUDIED
STUDIES
STUDIOS
THUDDED
TRUDEAU
TRUDGED
TRUDGER
TRUDGES

••U•D••
ASUNDER
BLUNDER
BOULDER
BOUNDED
BOUNDER
BOUNDUP
CLUEDIN
COULDNT
ECUADOR
FLUIDLY
FOUNDED
FOUNDER
FOUNDRY
GLUEDON
GOUNDER
GOURDES
HOUNDED
HYUNDAI
JOURDAN
LAUNDER
LAUNDRY
LOURDES
MAULDIN
MAUNDER
MOULDED
MOULDER
MOUNDED
PLUNDER
POUNDED
POUNDER
ROUNDED
ROUNDER
ROUNDLY
ROUNDON
ROUNDUP
SCUDDED
SHUDDER
SOUNDED
SOUNDER
SOUNDLY
STUDDED
THUDDED
THUNDER
TRUNDLE
WOULDBE
WOULDNT
WOUNDED
WOUNDUP

••U••D•
AOUDADS
CRUSADE
CRUSADO
CRUZADO
ROULADE

••U•••D
ABUTTED
AVULSED
BAULKED
BLUFFED
BLUNTED
BLURRED
BLURTED
BLUSHED
BOUNCED
BOUNDED
BRUISED
BRUITED
BRUSHED
CAULKED
CHUCKED
CHUGGED
CHUMMED
CHURNED
CLUBBED
CLUCKED
CLUMPED
CLUNKED
COUCHED
COUGHED
COUNTED
COUPLED
COURSED
COURTED
CRUISED
CRUSHED
CRUSTED
DAUNTED
DOUBLED
DOUBTED
DRUBBED
DRUDGED
DRUGGED
DRUMMED
EQUALED
EQUATED
ERUCTED
ERUPTED
EVULSED
EXULTED
FAULTED
FLUBBED
FLUFFED
FLUNKED
FLUSHED
FOULARD
FOUNDED
FRUITED
GLUGGED
GLUTTED
GRUBBED
GRUDGED
GRUMPED
GRUNTED
HAUNTED
HOUGHED
HOUNDED
JAUNTED
JOUNCED
JOUSTED
KNURLED
LAUGHED
LOUNGED
LOUVRED
MOULDED
MOULTED
MOUNDED
MOUNTED
MOURNED
MOUSSED
MOUTHED
PLUCKED
PLUGGED
PLUMBED
PLUMPED
PLUNGED
PLUNKED
POUCHED
POUNCED
POUNDED
REUPPED
ROUGHED
ROUNDED
ROUSTED
SAUTEED
SCUDDED
SCUFFED
SCULLED
SHUCKED
SHUNNED
SHUNTED
SHUSHED
SKULKED
SKUNKED
SLUGGED
SLUICED
SLUMMED
SLUMPED
SLURPED
SLURRED
SMUDGED
SNUBBED
SNUFFED
SOUGHED
SOUNDED
SOURCED
SPURNED
SPURRED
SPURTED
SQUALID
SQUARED
SQUIRED
STUBBED
STUDDED
STUDIED
STUFFED
STUMPED
STUNNED
STUNTED
TAUNTED
THUDDED
THUMBED
THUMPED
TOUCHED
TOUSLED
TRUCKED
TRUDGED
TRUMPED
TRUSSED
TRUSTED
USURPED
VAULTED
VAUNTED
VOUCHED
WHUPPED
WOUNDED

•••UD••
ADJUDGE
ALLUDED
ALLUDES
CLAUDIA
CLAUDIO
CLOUDED
DELUDED
DELUDES
DENUDED
DENUDES
ESCUDOS
ILLUDED
ILLUDES
INCUDES
PLAUDIT
PROUDER
PROUDLY
REMUDAS
STRUDEL
WHAUDEN

•••U•D•
ABOUNDS
ALBUNDY
GERUNDS
GROUNDS
LIQUIDS
OBTUNDS
REFUNDS
ROTUNDA
SHOULDA
TVGUIDE
YAOUNDE

•••U••D
ABJURED
ACCUSED
ADDUCED
ADJURED
ALLUDED
ALLURED
AROUSED
ASSUMED
ASSURED
ATTUNED
AUGURED
BEMUSED
BLOUSED
CLOUDED
CLOUTED
DEBUTED
DEDUCED
DEFUSED
DELUDED
DELUGED
DENUDED
DEPUTED
DILUTED
DISUSED
EDOUARD
EFFUSED
ENDURED
ENSURED
EXCUSED
FIGURED
FLOURED
FLOUTED
FOCUSED
GROUPED
GROUSED
GROUTED
ILLUDED
ILLUMED
ILLUSED
IMMURED
IMPUTED
INDUCED
INFUSED
INJURED
INSURED
KNOUTED
MATURED
MINUEND
MISUSED
NATURED
ONGUARD
PERUSED
REBUILD
REBUKED
RECUSED
REDUCED
REFUSED
REFUTED
RELUMED
REPUTED
RESUMED
RETUNED
SALUTED
SCOURED
SCOUTED
SECURED
SEDUCED
SHOUTED
SPOUTED
SPRUCED
SUTURED
TENURED
UNTUNED

••••UD•
BARBUDA
BERMUDA
COLLUDE
EXCLUDE
EXTRUDE
HEYJUDE
INCLUDE
INTRUDE
MARAUDS
OBTRUDE
OCCLUDE
PRELUDE
REDBUDS
SECLUDE
SHROUDS
TESTUDO

••••U•D
ACCRUED
AGROUND
ASTOUND
CASQUED
ENGLUND
EXPOUND
GOROUND
IMBRUED
IMPOUND
INBOUND
LANGUID
MISCUED
OROTUND
PLAGUED
PURSUED
REBOUND
REDOUND
REGLUED
RESCUED
RESOUND
REWOUND
SIGMUND
SNAFUED
SUBDUED
TONGUED
UNBOUND
UNGLUED
UNSOUND
UNWOUND

•••••UD
APPLAUD
BECLOUD
DEFRAUD
GIELGUD
IBNSAUD
MALAMUD
MCCLOUD
MILHAUD
OUTLOUD
RIMBAUD
ROSEBUD
TUSSAUD

U•E••••
UNEARTH
UNEATEN
UNENDED
UNEQUAL
UPENDED
USEABLE
USELESS
USERIDS
UTENSIL

U••E•••
UCCELLO
UMBERTO
UNBENDS
UNDERDO
UNDERGO
UNHEARD
UNKEMPT
UNLEARN
UNLEASH
UNNERVE
UNREADY
UNREELS
UNSEALS
UNSEATS
UNSEWED
UNVEILS
UNWEAVE
UPBEATS
UPTEMPO
URGENCY
URTEXTS
USHERED
UTRECHT
UTTERED
UTTERER
UTTERLY

U•••E••
UGLIEST
UKULELE
ULSTERS
UMPTEEN
UNBLEST
UNCLEAN
UNCLEAR
UNDRESS
UNGUENT
UNITERS
UNREELS
UNSPENT
UNSWEPT
UPSWEEP
UPSWEEP
UPSWEPT
USELESS
USOPENS
USSTEEL
USSTEEL
USURERS

U••••E•
ULYSSES
UMPIRED
UMPIRES
UMPTEEN
UNAIDED
UNAIMED
UNAIRED
UNARMED
UNASKED
UNBAKED
UNBOWED
UNBOXED
UNBOXES
UNCAGED
UNCAGES
UNCASED
UNCASES
UNCOVER
UNDATED
UNEATEN
UNENDED
UNFAZED
UNFIXED
UNGLUED
UNIFIED
UNIFIER
UNIFIES
UNITIES
UNLACED
UNLACES
UNLADES
UNLIKED
UNLINED
UNLOVED
UNMAKES
UNMOVED
UNNAMED
UNOILED
UNPAVED
UNPILED
UNPILES
UNRATED
UNRAVEL
UNROBED
UNROBES
UNSATED
UNSCREW
UNSEWED
UNTAMED
UNTAPED
UNTRIED
UNTUNED
UNTUNES
UNWISER
UNWOVEN
UNYOKED
UNYOKES
UNZONED
UPATREE
UPDATED
UPDATES
UPENDED
UPRISEN
UPRISES
UPRIVER
UPSWEEP
UPTAKES
URBANER
USHERED
USSTEEL
USURIES
USURPED
USURPER
UTTERED
UTTERER

U•••••E
UKRAINE
UKULELE
ULALUME
ULULATE
UMBRAGE
UNALIKE
UNAVOCE
UNAWARE
UNCLOSE
UNCRATE
UNDRAPE
UNHORSE
UNITIVE
UNLOOSE
UNNERVE
UNQUOTE
UNWEAVE
UPATREE
UPBORNE
UPCLOSE
UPGRADE
UPRAISE
UPSCALE
UPSTAGE
UPSTATE
UPSURGE
URANITE
URNLIKE
USEABLE
UTILISE
UTILIZE

•UE••••
CUEBALL
CUECARD
DUEDATE
DUELERS
DUELING
DUELIST
DUENNAS
FUELERS
FUELING
FUELLED
FUELOIL
FUELROD
GUELPHS
GUESSED
GUESSER
GUESSES
GUESTED
GUEVARA
HUELESS
MUEZZIN
PUEBLOS
PUERILE
QUECHUA
QUEENLY
QUEERED
QUEERER
QUEERLY
QUELLED
QUENTIN
QUERIED
QUERIER
QUERIES
QUERIST
QUESTED
QUETZAL
QUEUERS
QUEUEUP
QUEUING
TUESDAY

•U•E•••
AUGENDS
AUREATE
AUREOLA
AUREOLE
AUTEURS
BUGEYED
BUREAUS
BURETTE
CULEBRA
CUREALL
DUDEDUP
DUKEDOM
DUTEOUS
EUGENIE
EUTERPE
HUMERAL
HUMERUS
JUKEBOX
JUNEBUG
JUVENAL
KUTENAI
LUBEJOB
LUCENCY
LUCERNE
MUDEELS
MULETAS
MUMESON
MUSEFUL
MUSETTE
MUSEUMS
NUMERAL
NUMERIC
NUREYEV
OUTEATS
PUBERTY
PUDENCY
QUEENLY

QUEERED
QUEERER
QUEERLY
QUIETED
QUIETEN
QUIETER
QUIETLY
RULEOUT
RULESON
SUZETTE
TUNEDIN
TUNEDUP
TUNEFUL
TUNEOUT
TUNESIN
TUNESUP
TUNEUPS
TUPELOS
TUREENS
TUTELAR
TUXEDOS
YULELOG

•U••E••

AUGMENT
AUKLETS
AUSTERE
BUCKETS
BUCKEYE
BUDGETS
BUDLESS
BUFFERS
BUFFETS
BUFFETT
BUGBEAR
BUGLERS
BULLETS
BUMMERS
BUMPERS
BUNGEES
BUNKERS
BURDENS
BURGEES
BURGEON
BURGERS
BURGESS
BURMESE
BURNERS
BURNETT
BUSHELS
BUSIEST
BUSTERS
BUTLERS
BUTTERS
BUTTERY
BUZZERS
CUDGELS
CULLERS
CULVERS
CULVERT
CURFEWS
CURLERS
CURLEWS
CURRENT
CURTEST
CURVETS
CUTLERS
CUTLERY
CUTLETS
CUTTERS
DUBBERS
DUBIETY
DUCHESS
DUDGEON
DUELERS
DUFFELS
DUFFERS
DULLEST
DUMBEST
DUNGEON
DUNKERS
DUODENA
DURRELL
DUSTERS
FUELERS
FULGENT
FULLEST
FUMIEST
FUNFEST
FUNNELS
FURLESS
FURSEAL
GUINEAS
GULLETS
GUMLESS
GUNLESS
GUNNELS
GUNNERS
GUNNERY
GURNEYS
GUSHERS
GUSSETS
GUTLESS
GUTTERS
HUBBELL
HUELESS
HUGGERS
HULLERS
HUMMERS
HUMVEES
HUNGERS
HUNKERS
HUNTERS
HURLERS
HURLEYS
HUSKERS
HUSSEIN
HUYGENS
JUDDERS
JUGHEAD
JUICERS
JUICEUP
JUMPERS
JUNKERS
JUNKETS
KUCHENS
LUBBERS
LUGGERS
LUMBERS
LUMIERE
LUMPERS
LUNGEAT
LUNKERS
LUSHEST
LUSTERS
MUDDERS
MUDEELS
MUDHENS
MUGGERS
MULLEIN
MULLERS
MULLETS
MUMMERS
MUMMERY
MUPPETS
MURDERS
MUSHERS
MUSKEGS
MUSKETS
MUSSELS
MUSTERS
MUTTERS
NUCLEAR
NUCLEIC
NUCLEON
NUCLEUS
NUDGERS
NUGGETS
NUMBERS
NUMBEST
NUNNERY
NURSERS
NURSERY
NUTLETS
NUTMEAT
NUTMEGS
NUTTERS
OURSELF
OUSTERS
OUTLETS
OUTSELL
OUTSETS
OUTWEAR
PUCKERS
PUCKETT
PUFFERS
PUFFERY
PUGREES
PULLETS
PULLEYS
PUMMELS
PUMPERS
PUNGENT
PUNIEST
PUNKERS
PUNLESS
PUNNETS
PUNTERS
PUPPETS
PUPTENT
PURCELL
PURRERS
PURSERS
PURVEYS
PUTTEES
PUTTERS
QUAKERS
QUAVERS
QUAVERY
QUEUERS
QUEUEUP
QUIVERS
QUIVERY
QUOTERS
RUBBERS
RUBBERY
RUDDERS
RUINERS
RUMLESS
RUNDEEP
RUNLETS
RUNNELS
RUNNERS
RUSHEES
RUSHERS
RUSSELL
RUSSETS
RUSSETY
RUTGERS
SUAVELY
SUAVEST
SUBDEBS
SUBHEAD
SUBJECT
SUBLETS
SUBSETS
SUBTEND
SUBTEXT
SUBVERT
SUBZERO
SUCCEED
SUCCESS
SUCKERS
SUFFERS
SUGGEST
SULKERS
SUMLESS
SUMMERS
SUMMERY
SUNBEAM
SUNBELT
SUNDECK
SUNDERS
SUNDEWS
SUNLESS
SUNSETS
SUPPERS
SUPREME
SUPREMO
SURFEIT
SURFERS
SURGEON
SURGERY
SURREAL
SURREYS
SURVEYS
SUSPECT
SUSPEND
SUTLERS
SUTTERS
TUAREGS
TUCKERS
TUFFETS
TUGGERS
TUGLESS
TUNNELS
TUREENS
TURKEYS
TURNERS
TURNERY
TURRETS
TUSKERS
WURLEYS

•U•••E•

AUBADES
AUDILES
AUDITED
AUGURED
AUNTIES
AURALEE
AUSSIES
BUBBLED
BUBBLES
BUCKLED
BUCKLER
BUCKLES
BUCKLEY
BUCKOES
BUDDIES
BUDGIES
BUGEYED
BUGFREE
BUGGIER
BUGGIES
BUILDER
BULBLET
BULGIER
BULKIER
BULLIED
BULLIES
BULLPEN
BUMBLED
BUMBLER
BUMBLES
BUMPIER
BUNCHED
BUNCHES
BUNCOED
BUNDLED
BUNDLES
BUNGEES
BUNGLED
BUNGLER
BUNGLES
BUNKBED
BUNKOED
BUNNIES
BURBLED
BURBLES
BURGEES
BURGHER
BURGLED
BURGLES
BURLIER
BUSBIES
BUSHIER
BUSHMEN
BUSTLED
BUSTLES
BUTCHER
BUTTIES
CUBBIES
CUDDIES
CUDDLED
CUDDLES
CULLIED
CULLIES
CURATES
CURDIER
CURDLED
CURDLES
CURLIER
CURRIED
CURRIER
CURRIES
CURTSEY
CURVIER
CUSHIER
CUSSLER
DUCHIES
DUCKIER
DUMMIED
DUMMIES
DUMPIER
DUSKIER
DUSTIER
DUSTMEN
EUCHRED
EUCHRES
FUBSIER
FUDDLED
FUDDLES
FUELLED
FUMBLED
FUMBLER
FUMBLES
FUNGOES
FUNKIER
FUNNIER
FUNNIES
FURORES
FURRIER
FURTHER
FUSSIER
FUSTIER
FUTURES
FUZZIER
GUARDED
GUARDEE
GUESSED
GUESSER
GUESSES
GUESTED
GUILDER
GUIMPES
GULCHES
GULLIES
GULPIER
GUMMIER
GUMTREE
GUNKIER
GUNNIES
GUNTHER
GUPPIES
GURGLED
GURGLES
GUSHIER
GUSSIED
GUSSIES
GUSTIER
GUSTOES
GUTSIER
GUTTIER
GUZZLED
GUZZLER
GUZZLES
HUBBIES
HUDDLED
HUDDLES
HUFFIER
HULLOED
HUMBLED
HUMBLER
HUMBLES
HUMORED
HUMPIER
HUMVEES
HUNCHED
HUNCHES
HUNDRED
HUNKIER
HUNTLEY
HURDLED
HURDLER
HURDLES
HURLIES
HURRIED
HURRIES
HURTLED
HURTLES
HUSKIER
HUSKIES
HUSSIES
HUSTLED
HUSTLER
HUSTLES
HUTCHES
JUBILEE
JUGGLED
JUGGLER
JUGGLES
JUICIER
JUJUBES
JUMBLED
JUMBLES
JUMPIER
JUNCOES
JUNGLES
JUNIPER
JUNKIER
JUNKIES
JUPITER
JUTTIED
JUTTIES
LUCIFER
LUCKIER
LUMPIER
LUNCHED
LUNCHES
LUPINES
LURCHED
LURCHES
LUSTIER
LUSTRED
LUSTRES
LUXATED
LUXATES
MUCKIER
MUDDIED
MUDDIER
MUDDIES
MUDDLED
MUDDLER
MUDDLES
MUDPIES
MUFFLED
MUFFLER
MUFFLES
MUGGIER
MULCHED
MULCHES
MULCTED
MUMBLED
MUMBLER
MUMBLES
MUMMIES
MUNCHED
MUNCHER
MUNCHES
MURKIER
MUSCLED
MUSCLES
MUSHIER
MUSKIER
MUSKIES
MUSSIER
MUSTIER
MUSTSEE
MUTAGEN
MUTATED
MUTATES
MUZZIER
MUZZLED
MUZZLES
NUANCED
NUANCES
NUBBIER
NUBBLES
NUREYEV
NUTATED
NUTATES
NUTSIER
NUTTIER
NUZZLED
NUZZLER
NUZZLES
OUTAGES
OUTDOES
OUTDREW
OUTGOES
OUTGREW
OUTSTEP
PUDDLED
PUDDLES
PUDGIER
PUFFIER
PUGREES
PULPIER
PULQUES
PUMICES
PUNCHED
PUNCHER
PUNCHES
PUNKIER
PUNKIES
PUNNIER
PUNSTER
PUNTIES
PUPPIES
PURFLED
PURFLES
PURLIEU
PURPLED
PURPLES
PURSIER
PURSUED
PURSUER
PURSUES
PURVIEW
PUSHIER
PUTAMEN
PUTOVER
PUTTEES
PUTTIED
PUTTIES
PUZZLED
PUZZLER
PUZZLES
QUACKED
QUAFFED
QUAFFER
QUAILED
QUAKIER
QUARREL
QUARTER
QUARTET
QUASHED
QUASHES
QUEERED
QUEERER
QUELLED
QUERIED
QUERIER
QUERIES
QUESTED
QUICHES
QUICKEN
QUICKER
QUIETED
QUIETEN
QUIETER
QUIGLEY
QUILLED
QUILLER
QUILTED
QUILTER
QUINCES
QUINTET
QUIPPED
QUIPPER
QUITTER
QUIZZED
QUIZZES
QUONSET
RUBBLES
RUDDIER
RUFFLED
RUFFLES
RUMBAED
RUMBLED
RUMBLES
RUMMIER
RUMORED
RUMPLED
RUMPLES
RUNDEEP
RUNDLES
RUNNIER
RUNOVER
RUNTIER
RUSHEES
RUSHIER
RUSTIER
RUSTLED
RUSTLER
RUSTLES
RUTTIER
SUBDUED
SUBDUER
SUBDUES
SUBTLER
SUCCEED
SUDSIER
SUGARED
SULKIER
SULKIES
SULLIED
SULLIES
SULUSEA
SUNDAES
SUNNIER
SUPPLER
SURFIER
SURLIER
SURTSEY
SUTURED
SUTURES
TUBBIER
TUFTIER
TUMBLED
TUMBLER
TUMBLES
TUMBREL
TUMMIES
TUNNIES
TURFIER
TURNKEY
TURTLED
TURTLES
TUSSLED
TUSSLES
TUTORED
YUCKIER
YUMMIER
YUPPIES

•U••••E

AUDIBLE
AUGUSTE
AURALEE
AUREATE
AUREOLE
AURICLE
AURORAE
AUSPICE
AUSTERE
BUCKEYE
BUDLIKE
BUGFREE
BURETTE
BURMESE
BUSFARE
BUSLINE
BUYABLE
BUYTIME
CUBICLE
CUISINE
CULOTTE
CULTURE
CUPCAKE
CUPLIKE
CURLIKE
CURSIVE
CUTICLE
CUTRATE
CUTTIME
DUBUQUE
DUCTILE
DUEDATE
DURABLE
DURANCE
DURANTE
EUGENIE
EUTERPE
FULSOME
FURNACE
FURTIVE
GUANINE
GUARDEE
GUMLIKE
GUMSHOE
GUMTREE
GUNFIRE
GUNWALE
GUTHRIE
HUNLIKE
HUTLIKE
JUBILEE
JUGWINE
JUSTICE
JUSTINE
LUCERNE
LUCILLE
LUDDITE
LUGGAGE
LUMIERE
MUNDANE
MUSETTE
MUSTSEE
MUTABLE
NUCLIDE
NUNLIKE
NURTURE
NUTLIKE
OUTCOME
OUTDONE
OUTFACE
OUTLINE
OUTLIVE
OUTPACE
OUTRACE
OUTRAGE
OUTSIDE
OUTSIZE
OUTTAKE
OUTVOTE
OUTWORE
PUERILE
PUGNOSE
PULSATE
PURPOSE
QUIBBLE
QUICKIE
QUININE
QUINQUE
QUIXOTE
RUGLIKE
RUMMAGE
RUMPOLE
RUNHOME
RUNLATE
RUPTURE
RUSHDIE
SUBLIME
SUBSIDE
SUBSUME
SUBVOCE
SUCRASE
SUCROSE
SUFFICE
SUFFUSE
SULFATE
SULFIDE
SULFITE
SUNLIKE
SUNRISE
SUOJURE
SUPPOSE
SUPREME
SURFACE
SURMISE
SURNAME
SURVIVE
SUSANNE
SUZANNE
SUZETTE
TUBLIKE
TUNICLE
TURBINE
VULGATE
VULPINE
VULTURE

••UE•••

AQUEOUS
BLUEBOY
BLUEFIN
BLUEFOX
BLUEGUM
BLUEING
BLUEISH
BLUEJAY
BLUELAW
BLUESKY
BRUEGEL
CLUEDIN
CLUEING
CLUESIN
CRUELER
CRUELLY
CRUELTY
EQUERRY
FLUENCY
GLUEDON
GLUESON
LOUELLA
SQUEAKS
SQUEAKY
SQUEALS
SQUEEZE
SQUELCH
TRUEING

••U•E••

ABUSERS
ACUMENS
ACUTELY
AMULETS
BRUBECK
BRUNETS
BRUTELY
COULEES
CRUDELY
CRUDEST
DAUBERS
DEUTERO
DOUREST
EXUPERY
FAUCETS
FOULEST
GAUGERS
GLUIEST
GOUGERS
GRUYERE
HAUBERK
HAULERS
HAUTEUR
LAURELS
LAURENT
LOUDEST
LOUSEUP
LOUVERS
MAUREEN
MOUSERS
NOUVEAU
OPULENT
PAUPERS
PEUGEOT
POULENC
POURERS
POUTERS
PRUDENT
PRUDERY
PRUNERS
REUBENS
REUTERS
ROUSERS
ROUTERS
SAUCERS
SAUTEED
SHUBERT
SHUTEYE
SOUREST
SQUEEZE
STUDENT
STUMERS
STUPEFY
TAUTENS
TAUTEST
TOUPEES
TOURERS
TOUTERS
TRUDEAU
UKULELE
USURERS

••U••E•

ABUTTED
ALUNSER
AQUIFER
AQUIVER
ASUNDER
AVULSED
AVULSES
BAUBLES
BAULKED
BLUBBER
BLUFFED
BLUFFER
BLUNDER
BLUNTED
BLUNTER
BLURRED
BLURTED
BLUSHED
BLUSHER
BLUSHES
BLUSTER
BOULDER
BOULLES
BOUNCED
BOUNCER
BOUNCES
BOUNDED
BOUNDER
BOUQUET
BOURREE
BOURSES
BRUEGEL
BRUISED
BRUISER
BRUISES
BRUITED
BRUMMEL
BRUSHED
BRUSHES
CAUDLES
CAULKED
CAULKER
CHUCKED
CHUGGED
CHUKKER
CHUMMED
CHUNNEL
CHUNTER
CHURNED
CHUTNEY
CLUBBED
CLUCKED
CLUMPED
CLUNKED
CLUNKER
CLUSTER
CLUTTER
COUCHED
COUCHES
COUGHED
COULEES
COULTER
COUNSEL
COUNTED
COUNTER
COUPLED
COUPLES
COUPLET
COURIER
COURSED
COURSER
COURSES
COURTED
CRUELER
CRUISED
CRUISER
CRUISES
CRULLER
CRUMPET
CRUSHED
CRUSHER
CRUSHES
CRUSTED
DAUMIER
DAUNTED
DOUBLED
DOUBLES
DOUBLET
DOUBLEU
DOUBTED
DOUBTER
DRUBBED
DRUCKER
DRUDGED
DRUDGES
DRUGGED
DRUMMED
DRUMMER
EQUALED
EQUATED
EQUATES
EQUINES
ERUCTED
ERUPTED
EVULSED
EVULSES
EXULTED
FAULTED
FLUBBED
FLUBBER
FLUFFED
FLUKIER
FLUNKED
FLUSHED
FLUSHES
FLUSTER
FLUTIER
FLUTTER
FNUMBER
FOUNDED
FOUNDER
FOURIER
FRUITED
GAUCHER
GAUDIER
GAUNTER
GAUZIER
GLUGGED
GLUMMER
GLUTTED
GOUNDER
GOURDES
GOURMET
GOUTIER
GRUBBED
GRUDGED
GRUDGES
GRUFFER
GRUMPED
GRUNGES
GRUNTED
HAUNTED
HOUGHED
HOUNDED
JAUNTED
JOUNCED
JOUNCES
JOURNEY
JOUSTED
JOUSTER
KLUDGES
KLUTZES
KNURLED
LAUGHED
LAUGHER
LAUNDER
LAUTREC
LOUNGED

LOUNGER
LOUNGES
LOURDES
LOUSIER
LOUVRED
LOUVRES
MAUNDER
MAUREEN
MOULDED
MOULDER
MOULTED
MOUNDED
MOUNTED
MOURNED
MOUSIER
MOUSSED
MOUSSES
MOUTHED
OEUVRES
PAULSEN
PLUCKED
PLUGGED
PLUGGER
PLUMBED
PLUMBER
PLUMIER
PLUMMER
PLUMMET
PLUMPED
PLUMPER
PLUNDER
PLUNGED
PLUNGER
PLUNGES
PLUNKED
PLUSHER
PLUSHES
PLUSSES
POUCHED
POUCHES
POUNCED
POUNCER
POUNCES
POUNDED
POUNDER
POUTIER
REUPPED
REUTHER
ROUBLES
ROUGHED
ROUGHEN
ROUGHER
ROUNDED
ROUNDER
ROUSTED
SAUCIER
SAUNTER
SAUTEED
SCUDDED
SCUFFED
SCULLED
SCULLER
SCUPPER
SCURVES
SHUCKED
SHUCKER
SHUDDER
SHUNNED
SHUNTED
SHUSHED
SHUSHES
SHUTTER
SKULKED
SKULKER
SKUNKED
SLUDGES
SLUGGED
SLUGGER
SLUICED
SLUICES
SLUMBER
SLUMMED
SLUMPED
SLURPED
SLURRED
SLUSHES
SMUDGED
SMUDGES
SMUGGER
SNUBBED
SNUFFED
SNUFFER
SNUGGER
SOUGHED
SOUNDED
SOUNDER
SOUPIER
SOURCED
SOURCES
SOUTHEY
SPUMIER
SPURNED
SPURNER
SPURRED
SPURTED
SPUTTER
SQUARED
SQUARER
SQUARES
SQUIRED
SQUIRES
STUBBED
STUDDED
STUDIED
STUDIES
STUFFED
STUFFER
STUMPED
STUMPER
STUNNED
STUNNER
STUNTED
STURGES
TAUNTED
THUDDED
THUMBED
THUMPED
THUMPER
THUNDER
THURBER
TOUCHED
TOUCHES
TOUGHEN
TOUGHER
TOUPEES
TOURNEY
TOUSLED
TOUSLES
TRUCKED
TRUCKEE
TRUCKER
TRUDGED
TRUDGER
TRUDGES
TRUMPED
TRUMPET
TRUSSED
TRUSSES
TRUSTED
TRUSTEE
USURIES
USURPED
USURPER
VAULTED
VAULTER
VAUNTED
VAUNTER
VOUCHED
VOUCHER
VOUCHES
WHUPPED
WOUNDED
YOUNGER
ZOUAVES

••U•••E

ABUSIVE
ADULATE
ALUMNAE
AZURITE
BAUXITE
BOURREE
BRUSQUE
CHUCKLE
COURAGE
COUTURE
CRUMBLE
CRUMPLE
CRUSADE
DHURRIE
EDUCATE
ELUSIVE
EMULATE
EQUABLE
ERUDITE
GLUCOSE
GOUACHE
GRUMBLE
GRUYERE
HAULAGE
INUTILE
KNUCKLE
LEUCINE
MAURICE
MOULAGE
MOUNTIE
NEURONE
PAULINE
PLUMAGE
PRUDHOE
REUNITE
ROULADE
ROUTINE
SAUSAGE
SCUFFLE
SCUTTLE
SHUFFLE
SHUTEYE
SHUTTLE
SMUGGLE
SNUFFLE
SNUGGLE
SOUFFLE
SOUTANE
SPUMONE
SQUEEZE
STUBBLE
STUMBLE
TAURINE
TOUGHIE
TRUCKEE
TRUCKLE
TRUFFLE
TRUNDLE
TRUSTEE
UKULELE
ULULATE
WOULDBE

•••UE••

ARGUERS
BEQUEST
INQUEST
ISSUERS
LIQUEFY
LIQUEUR
MAGUEYS
MCQUEEN
MINUEND
MINUETS
QUEUERS
QUEUEUP
REFUELS
REQUEST
ROGUERY
SEQUELS
SOSUEME
TOLUENE
UNGUENT
VAGUELY
VAGUEST
VAQUERO

•••U•E•

ABJURED
ABJURES
ACCUSED
ACCUSER
ACCUSES
ADDUCED
ADDUCES
ADJURED
ADJURES
ALBUMEN
ALLUDED
ALLUDES
ALLURED
ALLURES
AMPULES
ARMURES
AROUSED
AROUSES
ASSUMED
ASSUMES
ASSURED
ASSURES
ATTUNED
ATTUNES
AUGURED
BEMUSED
BEMUSES
BITUMEN
BLOUSED
BLOUSES
BOLUSES
BONUSES
CADUCEI
CALUMET
CAPULET
CAYUSES
CERUMEN
CHAUCER
CLAUSES
CLOUDED
CLOUTED
CONURES
COZUMEL
DEBUTED
DEDUCED
DEDUCES
DEFUSED
DEFUSES
DELUDED
DELUDES
DELUGED
DELUGES
DEMURER
DENUDED
DENUDES
DEPUTED
DEPUTES
DILUTED
DILUTER
DILUTES
DISUSED
EFFUSED
EFFUSES
ENDURED
ENDURES
ENDUSER
ENDUSES
ENSURED
ENSURES
EPAULET
EXCUSED
EXCUSES
FERULES
FICUSES
FIGURED
FIGURER
FIGURES
FLOURED
FLOUTED
FOCUSED
FOCUSES
FUTURES
GROUPED
GROUPER
GROUSED
GROUSER
GROUSES
GROUTED
ILLUDED
ILLUDES
ILLUMED
ILLUMES
ILLUSED
ILLUSES
IMMURED
IMMURES
IMPURER
IMPUTED
IMPUTES
INCUDES
INDUCED
INDUCER
INDUCES
INFUSED
INFUSES
INJURED
INJURES
INSURED
INSURER
INSURES
JUJUBES
KNOUTED
LEGUMES
LOBULES
LOTUSES
MATURED
MATURER
MATURES
MCQUEEN
MINUSES
MINUTES
MISUSED
MISUSES
MODULES
NATURED
NATURES
NEXUSES
NODULES
NONUSER
OBTUSER
PAIUTES
PARURES
PERUKES
PERUSED
PERUSER
PERUSES
PROUDER
REBUKED
REBUKES
REBUSES
RECUSED
RECUSES
REDUCED
REDUCER
REDUCES
REFUGEE
REFUGES
REFUSED
REFUSER
REFUSES
REFUTED
REFUTER
REFUTES
RELUMED
RELUMES
REPUTED
REPUTES
REQUIEM
RESUMED
RESUMES
RETUNED
RETUNES
RIVULET
SALUTED
SALUTES
SCOURED
SCOURER
SCOUSES
SCOUTED
SCOUTER
SECURED
SECURER
SECURES
SEDUCED
SEDUCER
SEDUCES
SHOUTED
SHOUTER
SINUSES
SOLUTES
SPOUSES
SPOUTED
SPOUTER
SPRUCED
SPRUCER
SPRUCES
STEUBEN
STOUTEN
STOUTER
STRUDEL
SULUSEA
SUTURED
SUTURES
TALUSES
TENURED
TENURES
TRIUNES
TROUPER
TROUPES
TROUSER
UNTUNED
UNTUNES
VIRUSES
VOLUMES
WHAUDEN

•••U••E

ACQUIRE
ACTUATE
ADJUDGE
ASSUAGE
AUGUSTE
BEGUILE
BEGUINE
COPULAE
DELUISE
DIVULGE
DUBUQUE
ENOUNCE
ENQUIRE
ENSUITE
ESQUIRE
EXPUNGE
FACULAE
FIBULAE
FLOUNCE
GENUINE
GROUPIE
IMPULSE
INDULGE
INQUIRE
LACUNAE
MACULAE
MAGUIRE
MCGUIRE
MEDUSAE
NEBULAE
OCTUPLE
OROURKE
PANURGE
PENUCHE
RADULAE
REFUGEE
REPULSE
REQUIRE
REQUITE
RESURGE
SCOURGE
SCRUPLE
SITUATE
SOLUBLE
SOSUEME
SPLURGE
TOLUENE
TROUBLE
TROUNCE
TSQUARE
TVGUIDE
UNQUOTE
UPSURGE
VACUOLE
VALUATE
VOLUBLE
YAOUNDE

••••UE•

ACCRUED
ACCRUES
AVENUES
BANQUET
BASQUES
BATTUES
BISQUES
BOUQUET
BRIQUET
BROGUES
CAIQUES
CASQUED
CASQUES
CHEQUER
CHEQUES
CIRQUES
CLAQUES
CLIQUES
CLIQUEY
CLOQUES
CONQUER
CROQUET
EMANUEL
EVACUEE
FESCUES
FONDUES
GIBLUES
IMBRUED
IMBRUES
JACQUES
KILAUEA
LACQUER
LEAGUES
LONGUES
MARQUEE
MARQUES
MARQUEZ
MASQUES
MISCUED
MISCUES
MOSQUES
OPAQUES
PARQUET
PLAGUED
PLAGUES
PLAQUES
PREQUEL
PULQUES
PURSUED
PURSUER
PURSUES
RACQUET
REGLUED
REGLUES
RESCUED
RESCUER
RESCUES
SACQUES
SNAFUED
STATUES
SUBDUED
SUBDUER
SUBDUES
SYNFUEL
TISSUES
TONGUED
TONGUES
TORQUES
UNGLUED
VIRTUES

••••U•E

AMPOULE
ASARULE
BECAUSE
CAPSULE
CAPTURE
CAROUSE
CENSURE
CLOSURE
CLOTURE
COLLUDE
COMMUNE
COMMUTE
COMPUTE
CONDUCE
CONFUSE
CONFUTE
CONJURE
CONSUME
CONTUSE
COSTUME
COUTURE
CULTURE
DASYURE
DENEUVE
DENTURE
DIFFUSE
DISPUTE
ENROUTE
ENTHUSE
EPICURE
ERASURE
ESPOUSE
EVACUEE
EXCLUDE
EXECUTE
EXTRUDE
FAILURE
FEATURE
FERRULE
FISSURE
FIXTURE
FORSURE
FORTUNE
GAGRULE
GESTURE
GLOBULE
GRANULE
GRAVURE
HERCULE
HEYJUDE
HIRSUTE
ICECUBE
INCLUDE
INHOUSE
INTRUDE
JACCUSE
LECTURE
LEISURE
LETTUCE
MAJEURE
MARQUEE
MCCLURE
MEASURE
MISRULE
MIXTURE
NEPTUNE
NETSUKE
NOTSURE
NURTURE
OBSCURE
OBTRUDE
OCCLUDE
OVERUSE
PASTURE
PERFUME
PERJURE
PICTURE
POLLUTE
POSTURE
PRELUDE
PRESUME
PROCURE
PRODUCE
PROFUSE
RAPTURE
RECLUSE
REROUTE
RUPTURE
SECLUDE
STATURE
STATUTE
SUBSUME
SUFFUSE
SUOJURE
TERHUNE
TEXTURE
TONSURE
TRADUCE
TRIBUNE
TRIBUTE
ULALUME
VENTURE
VERDURE
VESTURE
VIRGULE
VIRTUTE
VULTURE

•••••UE

AMIBLUE
ANTIQUE
ATISSUE
BAROQUE
BEZIQUE
BRUSQUE
CAMEDUE
COMEDUE
COMIQUE
DEVALUE
DONAHUE
DUBUQUE
ECLOGUE
FATIGUE
HABITUE
ICEBLUE
INGENUE
INVOGUE
LALIQUE
MACAQUE
MONIQUE
NOTTRUE
OBLIQUE
OVERDUE
PASTDUE
PIROGUE
QUINQUE
REARGUE
REISSUE
RENEGUE
RESIDUE
RETINUE
REVALUE
REVENUE
SEABLUE
SKYBLUE

U•F••••

UNFAZED
UNFIXED
UNFOLDS
UNFROCK
UNFURLS
UPFRONT

U••F•••

UNIFIED
UNIFIER
UNIFIES
UNIFORM

U•••F••

UNAWFUL
UPLIFTS

U••••F•

UPDRAFT

•UF••••

BUFFALO
BUFFERS
BUFFETS
BUFFETT
BUFFING
BUFFOON
CUFFING
DUFFELS
DUFFERS
GUFFAWS
HUFFIER
HUFFILY
HUFFING
HUFFISH
LUFFING
MUFFING
MUFFINS
MUFFLED
MUFFLER
MUFFLES
PUFFERS
PUFFERY
PUFFIER
PUFFILY
PUFFING
PUFFINS
RUFFIAN
RUFFLED
RUFFLES
RUFIYAA
SUFFERS
SUFFICE
SUFFOLK
SUFFUSE
TUFFETS
TUFTIER
TUFTING

•U•F•••

BUFFALO
BUFFERS
BUFFETS
BUFFETT
BUFFING
BUFFOON
BUGFREE
BUSFARE
CUFFING
CUPFULS
CURFEWS
DUFFELS
DUFFERS
FULFILL
FULFILS
FUNFAIR
FUNFEST
GUFFAWS
GULFING
GUNFIRE
HUFFIER
HUFFILY
HUFFING
HUFFISH
JUGFULS
LUFFING
MUFFING
MUFFINS
MUFFLED
MUFFLER
MUFFLES
MUMFORD
OUTFACE
OUTFITS
OUTFLOW
PUFFERS
PUFFERY
PUFFIER
PUFFILY
PUFFING
PUFFINS
PURFLED
PURFLES
QUAFFED
QUAFFER
RUFFIAN
RUFFLED
RUFFLES
SUFFERS
SUFFICE
SUFFOLK
SUFFUSE
SULFATE
SULFIDE
SULFITE
SUNFISH
SURFACE
SURFEIT
SURFERS
SURFIER
SURFING
TUFFETS
TURFIER
TURFWAR

•U••F••

CUTOFFS
DUTIFUL
GUNSFOR
HURTFUL
HUSHFUL
LUCIFER
LUSTFUL
MUSEFUL
OUTOFIT
PULLFOR
PUSHFUL
QUAFFED
QUAFFER
RUNOFFS
RUNSFOR
RUTHFUL
TUNEFUL

•U•••F•

BUGSOFF
BUYSOFF
BUZZOFF
CUTOFFS
CUTSOFF
DULCIFY
DUSTOFF
JUMPOFF
JUSTIFY
MUSTAFA
NULLIFY
PULLOFF
PUSHOFF
PUTSOFF
QUALIFY
RUBSOFF
RUNGOFF
RUNOFFS
RUNSOFF
RUSHOFF
TURNOFF

•U••••F

BUGSOFF
BUYSOFF
BUZZOFF
CUTSOFF
DUSTOFF
JUMPOFF
OURSELF
PULLOFF
PUSHOFF
PUTSOFF
RUBSOFF
RUNGOFF
RUNSOFF
RUSHOFF
SUNROOF
TURNOFF

••UF•••

BLUFFED
BLUFFER
BLUFFLY
FLUFFED
GRUFFER
GRUFFLY
KAUFMAN
MOUFLON
SCUFFED
SCUFFLE
SHUFFLE
SNUFFED
SNUFFER
SNUFFLE
SNUFFLY
SOUFFLE
STUFFED
STUFFER
TRUFFLE

••U•F••

AQUIFER
BLUEFIN
BLUEFOX
BLUFFED
BLUFFER
BLUFFLY
FLUFFED
GRUFFER
GRUFFLY
POUTFUL
SCUFFED
SCUFFLE
SHUFFLE
SNUFFED
SNUFFER
SNUFFLE
SNUFFLY
SOUFFLE
SOULFUL
STUFFED
STUFFER
THUSFAR
TRUFFLE

••U••F•

CRUCIFY
HAULOFF
REUNIFY
SHUTOFF
SPUNOFF
STUPEFY

••U•••F

HAULOFF
SHUTOFF
SPUNOFF

•••UF••

REBUFFS
SCRUFFS
SCRUFFY
SENUFOS

•••U•F•

ENGULFS
LIQUEFY
REBUFFS
SCRUFFS
SCRUFFY

••••UF•

EARMUFF
MACDUFF

••••U•F

BEOWULF
EARMUFF
MACDUFF
NETSURF

UG•••••

UGANDAN
UGLIEST

U•G••••

UNGIRDS
UNGLUED
UNGODLY
UNGUENT
UPGRADE
URGENCY
USGRANT

U••G•••

URUGUAY

U•••G••

UNCAGED
UNCAGES
UPRIGHT
UPTIGHT
USINGUP

U••••G•

UMBRAGE
UNCLOGS
UNDERGO
UNPLUGS
UNSNAGS
UPSTAGE
UPSURGE

U•••••G
UNDOING
UNDYING
UNITING
UNTYING
UPSWING

•UG••••
AUGENDS
AUGMENT
AUGURAL
AUGURED
AUGUSTA
AUGUSTE
BUGABOO
BUGALOO
BUGBEAR
BUGEYED
BUGFREE
BUGGIER
BUGGIES
BUGGING
BUGLERS
BUGLING
BUGSOFF
BUGSOUT
DUGONGS
DUGOUTS
EUGENIE
HUGGERS
HUGGING
HUGGINS
JUGBAND
JUGFULS
JUGGING
JUGGINS
JUGGLED
JUGGLER
JUGGLES
JUGHEAD
JUGULAR
JUGWINE
LUGGAGE
LUGGERS
LUGGING
LUGNUTS
MUGGERS
MUGGIER
MUGGING
MUGSHOT
MUGWUMP
NUGGETS
OUGHTNT
PUGGISH
PUGNOSE
PUGREES
RUGLIKE
SUGARED
SUGGEST
TUGBOAT
TUGGERS
TUGGING
TUGLESS
TUGRIKS

•U•G•••
BUDGETS
BUDGIES
BUDGING
BUGGIER
BUGGIES
BUGGING
BULGARS
BULGHUR
BULGIER
BULGING
BUNGEES
BUNGING
BUNGLED
BUNGLER
BUNGLES
BURGEES
BURGEON
BURGERS
BURGESS
BURGHER
BURGLAR
BURGLED
BURGLES
BURGOOS
BUSGIRL
CUDGELS
DUDGEON
DUNGEON
FUDGING
FULGENT
FULGHUM
FUNGOES
GURGLED
GURGLES
HUGGERS
HUGGING
HUGGINS
HUNGARY
HUNGERS
HUNGOUT
HUYGENS
JUDGING
JUGGING
JUGGINS
JUGGLED
JUGGLER
JUGGLES
JUNGLES
LUGGAGE
LUGGERS
LUGGING
LUNGEAT
LUNGING
MUGGERS
MUGGIER
MUGGING
NUDGERS
NUDGING
NUGGETS
OURGANG
OUTGOES
OUTGREW
OUTGROW
OUTGUNS
PUDGIER
PUDGILY
PUGGISH
PUNGENT
PURGING
QUAGGAS
QUIGLEY
RUNGOFF
RUNGOUT
RUTGERS
SUGGEST
SUNGODS
SURGEON
SURGERY
SURGING
TUGGERS
TUGGING
TUNGOIL
VULGATE

•U••G••
BURPGUN
GUARGUM
MUTAGEN
OUTAGES
QUAGGAS
QUANGOS

•U•••G•
DUGONGS
DURANGO
GUNDOGS
HUMBUGS
LUGGAGE
LUMBAGO
MUSKEGS
NUTMEGS
OUTINGS
OUTRAGE
QUAHOGS
RULINGS
RUMMAGE
SUNDOGS
TUAREGS

•U••••G
BUCKING
BUDDING
BUDGING
BUFFING
BUGGING
BUGLING
BULGING
BULKING
BULLDOG
BULLING
BUMMING
BUMPING
BUNGING
BUNKING
BUNTING
BUOYING
BURLING
BURNING
BURPING
BURYING
BUSHHOG
BUSHING
BUSHPIG
BUSKING
BUSSING
BUSTING
BUSYING
BUTTING
BUZZING
CUFFING
CULLING
CUNNING
CUPPING
CURBING
CURDING
CURLING
CURSING
CURVING
CUSHING
CUSSING
CUTTING
DUBBING
DUCKING
DUCTING
DUELING
DULLING
DUMBING
DUMPING
DUNKING
DUNNING
DURNING
DUSTING
FUBBING
FUDGING
FUELING
FUNDING
FUNKING
FUNNING
FURLING
FURLONG
FURRING
FUSSING
FUTZING
FUZZING
GUIDING
GULFING
GULLING
GULPING
GUMMING
GUNNING
GUSHING
GUSTING
GUTTING
HUFFING
HUGGING
HULKING
HULLING
HUMMING
HUNTING
HURLING
HURTING
HUSHING
HUSKING
JUDGING
JUGGING
JUICING
JUMPING
JUNEBUG
JUNKING
JURYING
JURYRIG
JUTTING
LUCKING
LUFFING
LUGGING
LULLING
LUMPING
LUNGING
LURKING
LUSTING
MUCKING
MUFFING
MUGGING
MULLING
MUMMING
MUMPING
MUSHING
MUSSING
MUSTANG
MUZZING
NUDGING
NULLING
NUMBING
NURSING
NUTTING
OURGANG
OUSTING
PUDDING
PUFFING
PULLING
PULSING
PUMPING
PUNNING
PUNTING
PURGING
PURLING
PURRING
PURSING
PUSHING
PUTTING
QUAKING
QUEUING
QUOTING
RUBBING
RUCHING
RUCKING
RUINING
RUNNING
RUSHING
RUSTING
SUBBING
SUCKING
SUDSING
SUITING
SULKING
SUMMING
SUNNING
SUPPING
SURFING
SURGING
SUSSING
TUCKING
TUFTING
TUGGING
TUMMING
TURNING
YULELOG

••UG•••
ARUGULA
CHUGGED
COUGARS
COUGHED
COUGHUP
DOUGHTY
DOUGLAS
DRUGGED
GAUGERS
GAUGING
GAUGUIN
GLUGGED
GOUGERS
GOUGING
HAUGHTY
HOUGHED
KLUGMAN
LAUGHAT
LAUGHED
LAUGHER
LAUGHIN
MAUGHAM
NAUGHTS
NAUGHTY
NOUGATS
NOUGHTS
PEUGEOT
PLUGGED
PLUGGER
PLUGINS
PLUGSIN
ROUGHED
ROUGHEN
ROUGHER
ROUGHIT
ROUGHLY
ROUGHUP
ROUGING
SLUGGED
SLUGGER
SMUGGER
SMUGGLE
SNUGGER
SNUGGLE
SOUGHED
TOUGHEN
TOUGHER
TOUGHIE
TOUGHLY
URUGUAY
VAUGHAN
ZEUGMAS

••U•G••
BLUEGUM
BRUEGEL
CHUGGED
DRUDGED
DRUDGES
DRUGGED
GLUGGED
GRUDGED
GRUDGES
GRUNGES
KLUDGES
LOUNGED
LOUNGER
LOUNGES
NYUNGAR
PLUGGED
PLUGGER
PLUNGED
PLUNGER
PLUNGES
SLUDGES
SLUGGED
SLUGGER
SMUDGED
SMUDGES
SMUGGER
SMUGGLE
SNUGGER
SNUGGLE
STUNGUN
STURGES
TRUDGED
TRUDGER
TRUDGES
YOUNGER
YOUNGMC
YOUNGUN

••U••G•
COURAGE
HAULAGE
MOULAGE
PLUMAGE
SAUSAGE

••U•••G
ABUSING
AMUSING
BLUEING
BOUSING
BRUXING
CAUSING
CLUEING
DAUBING
DOUSING
EDUCING
ELUDING
ELUTING
ENURING
EXUDING
FEUDING
FLUTING
FLUXING
FOULING
GAUGING
GAUMING
GOUGING
HAULING
HOUSING
INURING
LAUDING
LOUSING
MAULING
MOUSING
PAULING
PAUSING
PLUMING
POURING
POUTING
PRUNING
ROUGING
ROUSING
ROUTING
SOURING
SPUMING
TOURING
TOUTING
TRUEING

•••UG••
ABOUGHT
BROUGHT
CAYUGAS
DELUGED
DELUGES
DRAUGHT
DROUGHT
FRAUGHT
IMPUGNS
OPPUGNS
PLOUGHS
REFUGEE
REFUGES
REPUGNS
SLOUGHS
THOUGHT
TROUGHS
WROUGHT

•••U•G•
ADJUDGE
ASSUAGE
DIVULGE
EXPUNGE
INDULGE
LITURGY
PANURGE
RESURGE
SCOURGE
SPLURGE
THEURGY
UPSURGE
ZYMURGY

•••U••G
ARGUING
ENDUING
ENSUING
IMBUING
ISSUING
PIQUING
QUEUING
VALUING

••••UG•
BEDBUGS
BOROUGH
HUMBUGS
RAGRUGS
SOWBUGS
THROUGH
UNPLUGS
VERDUGO

••••U•G
ACHTUNG
CYYOUNG
HAMBURG
HARBURG
HOMBURG
SAMSUNG
ZEITUNG

•••••UG
AREARUG
BEARHUG
EARPLUG
FIREBUG
GOLDBUG
JUNEBUG
LADYBUG
LOVEBUG
PILLBUG
SEASLUG

U•H••••
UNHANDS
UNHANDY
UNHAPPY
UNHEARD
UNHITCH
UNHOOKS
UNHORSE
UPHOLDS
USHERED

U••H•••
UNCHAIN
UNSHORN
UPSHOTS
URCHINS
UTAHANS

U•••H••
USOSHOW

U••••H•
UPRIGHT
UPTIGHT
UTRECHT

U•••••H
UNCOUTH
UNEARTH
UNHITCH
UNLATCH
UNLEASH
UNTRUTH

•UH••••
SUHARTO

•U•H•••
AUTHORS
BUSHELS
BUSHHOG
BUSHIDO
BUSHIER
BUSHILY
BUSHING
BUSHMAN
BUSHMEN
BUSHPIG
CUSHAWS
CUSHIER
CUSHING
CUSHION
DUCHESS
DUCHIES
EUCHRED
EUCHRES
EUPHONY
FUCHSIA
GUSHERS
GUSHIER
GUSHILY
GUSHING
GUTHRIE
HUSHABY
HUSHFUL
HUSHING
JUGHEAD
KUCHENS
LUSHEST
MUDHENS
MUSHERS
MUSHIER
MUSHILY
MUSHING
MUZHIKS
OUGHTNT
OUTHITS
PUSHFUL
PUSHIER
PUSHILY
PUSHING
PUSHKIN
PUSHOFF
PUSHPIN
PUSHUPS
QUAHOGS
RUCHING
RUNHOME
RUSHDIE
RUSHEES
RUSHERS
RUSHIER
RUSHING
RUSHOFF
RUTHFUL
SUBHEAD
TUCHMAN

•U••H••
BUDDHAS
BULGHUR
BUNCHED
BUNCHES
BURGHER
BUSHHOG
BUTCHER
FULGHUM
FUNCHAL
FURTHER
GULCHES
GUMSHOE
GUNSHOT
GUNTHER
GURKHAS
HUNCHED
HUNCHES
HUTCHES
KUTCHIN
LUNCHED
LUNCHES
LURCHED
LURCHES
MUGSHOT
MULCHED
MULCHES
MUNCHED
MUNCHER
MUNCHES
PUNCHED
PUNCHER
PUNCHES
PUNCHIN
PUNCHUP
QUASHED
QUASHES
QUECHUA
QUICHES
SULPHUR

•U•••H•
AUROCHS
GUELPHS
GULLAHS
HURRAHS
HUZZAHS
MULLAHS
NULLAHS
PUNKAHS
PURDAHS
RUPIAHS

•U••••H
BULLISH
BULRUSH
BUMRUSH
BURNISH
CUBBISH
CULTISH
CURRISH
DULLISH
DUMPISH
DUNCISH
DUSKISH
FURBISH
FURNISH
HUFFISH
HUNNISH
KURDISH
LUMPISH
MURDOCH
PUBLISH
PUCKISH
PUGGISH
RUBBISH
RUDOLPH
RUNTISH
RUNWITH
RUTTISH
SUNBATH
SUNFISH
TURKISH

••UH•••
BAUHAUS

••U•H••
BLUSHED
BLUSHER
BLUSHES
BLUSHON
BRUSHED
BRUSHES
BRUSHUP
COUCHED
COUCHES
COUGHED
COUGHUP
CRUSHED
CRUSHER
CRUSHES
DAUPHIN
DOUGHTY
FLUSHED
FLUSHES
GAUCHER
GAUCHOS
HAUGHTY
HOUGHED
LAUGHAT
LAUGHED
LAUGHER
LAUGHIN
MAUGHAM
MOUTHED
NAUGHTS
NAUGHTY
NOUGHTS
PLUSHER
PLUSHES
PLUSHLY
POUCHED
POUCHES
PRUDHOE
REUTHER
ROUGHED
ROUGHEN
ROUGHER
ROUGHIT
ROUGHLY
ROUGHUP
SHUSHED
SHUSHES
SLUSHES
SOUGHED
SOUTHEY
TOUCHED
TOUCHES
TOUCHON
TOUCHUP
TOUGHEN
TOUGHER
TOUGHIE
TOUGHLY
VAUGHAN
VOUCHED
VOUCHER
VOUCHES

••U••H•
CRUNCHY
FOURTHS
GOUACHE
PAUNCHY
SQUISHY

••U•••H
BLUEISH
BRUTISH
GAULISH
GOULASH
GOUTISH
LOUDISH
LOUTISH
NOURISH
PRUDISH
SOURISH
SQUELCH
SQUINCH

•••UH••
MCLUHAN
MENUHIN

•••U•H•
ABOUGHT
BELUSHI
BROUGHT
DRAUGHT
DROUGHT
FRAUGHT
GROUCHO
GROUCHY
NOGUCHI
PENUCHE
PLOUGHS
SLEUTHS
SLOUCHY
SLOUGHS
THOUGHT
TROUGHS
WROUGHT

•••U••H
ANOUILH
BEAUISH
GALUMPH
GODUTCH
HANUKAH
INDUTCH
PADUCAH
ROGUISH
SCRUNCH
STAUNCH
TRIUMPH
VOGUISH

••••UH•
NIEBUHR

••••U•H
AZIMUTH
BISMUTH
BOROUGH
BULRUSH
BUMRUSH
DEBAUCH
DEBOUCH
INARUSH
INTRUTH
RETOUCH
THROUGH
UNCOUTH
UNTRUTH

U•I••••
UNICORN
UNIFIED
UNIFIER
UNIFIES
UNIFORM
UNIPODS
UNISONS
UNITARY
UNITERS
UNITIES
UNITING
UNITIVE
USINGUP
UTILISE
UTILITY
UTILIZE

U••I•••
UGLIEST
ULTIMAS
UMPIRED
UMPIRES
UNAIDED
UNAIMED
UNAIRED
UNBINDS
UNCIALS
UNCIVIL
UNFIXED
UNGIRDS
UNHITCH
UNKINKS
UNLIKED
UNLINED
UNLINKS
UNOILED
UNPILED
UNPILES
UNWINDS
UNWISER
UPLIFTS
UPLINKS
UPRIGHT
UPRISEN
UPRISES
UPRIVER
UPSILON
UPTICKS
UPTIGHT
USTINOV
UTRILLO

U•••I••
UKRAINE
UMBRIAN
UNALIKE
UNCOILS
UNCTION
UNDOING
UNDYING
UNIFIED
UNIFIER
UNIFIES
UNITIES
UNITING
UNITIVE
UNKNITS
UNSTICK
UNTRIED
UNTWIST
UNTYING
UNVEILS
UPRAISE
UPSWING
URANITE
URANIUM
URCHINS
URNLIKE
USERIDS
USURIES
UTILISE
UTILITY
UTILIZE
UTOPIAN
UTOPIAS
UXORIAL

U••••I•
UNCHAIN
UNCIVIL
UPBRAID
UTENSIL

•UI••••
BUILDER
BUILDIN
BUILDUP
BUILTIN
BUILTUP
CUIBONO
CUIRASS
CUISINE
GUIDING
GUIDONS
GUILDER
GUIMPES
GUINEAS
GUITARS
JUICERS
JUICEUP
JUICIER
JUICILY
JUICING
QUIBBLE
QUICHES
QUICKEN
QUICKER
QUICKIE
QUICKLY
QUIETED
QUIETEN
QUIETER
QUIETLY
QUIGLEY
QUILLED
QUILLER
QUILTED
QUILTER
QUINARY
QUINCES
QUININE
QUINOAS
QUINQUE
QUINTET
QUIPPED
QUIPPER
QUITTER
QUIVERS
QUIVERY
QUIXOTE
QUIZZED
QUIZZES
RUINERS
RUINING
RUINOUS
SUITING
SUITORS
SUITSUP
TUITION

•U•I•••
AUDIBLE
AUDIBLY
AUDILES
AUDITED
AUDITOR

AURICLE
BUNIONS
BUSIEST
CUBICLE
CUBISTS
CURIOUS
CUTICLE
CUTINTO
DUBIETY
DUBIOUS
DUTIFUL
FUJITSU
FUMIEST
FURIOUS
HUMIDLY
HUMIDOR
JUBILEE
JUJITSU
JULIANA
JUNIORS
JUNIPER
JUPITER
JURIDIC
JURISTS
LUCIANO
LUCIDLY
LUCIFER
LUCILLE
LUMIERE
LUPINES
LURIDLY
LUTISTS
MURILLO
MUSICAL
NUBIANS
NUDISTS
OUTINGS
PUMICES
PUNIEST
PURISTS
PURITAN
PUTITTO
QUAILED
RUBICON
RUBITIN
RUFIYAA
RULINGS
RUNINTO
RUPIAHS
SURINAM
TUBISTS
TUNICLE
TUNISIA

•U••I••

AUCTION
AUNTIES
AUPAIRS
AUSPICE
AUSSIES
BUCKING
BUDDIES
BUDDING
BUDGIES
BUDGING
BUDLIKE
BUFFING
BUGGIER
BUGGIES
BUGGING
BUGLING
BULGIER
BULGING
BULKIER
BULKING
BULLIED
BULLIES
BULLING
BULLION
BULLISH
BULLITT
BUMMING
BUMPIER
BUMPILY
BUMPING
BUNGING
BUNKING
BUNNIES
BUNTING
BUNYIPS
BUOYING
BURKINA
BURLIER
BURLING
BURNING
BURNISH
BURPING
BURRITO
BURYING
BUSBIES
BUSGIRL
BUSHIDO
BUSHIER
BUSHILY
BUSHING
BUSKING
BUSKINS
BUSLINE
BUSSING
BUSTING
BUSYING
BUTTIES
BUTTING
BUYTIME
BUZZING
CUBBIES
CUBBISH
CUDDIES
CUFFING
CUISINE
CULLIED
CULLIES
CULLING
CULTISH
CULTISM
CULTIST
CUNNING
CUPLIKE
CUPPING
CURBING
CURDIER
CURDING
CURLIER
CURLIKE
CURLING
CURRIED
CURRIER
CURRIES
CURRISH
CURSING
CURSIVE
CURTISS
CURVIER
CURVING
CUSHIER
CUSHING
CUSHION
CUSPIDS
CUSSING
CUTTIME
CUTTING
DUALITY
DUBBING
DUCHIES
DUCKIER
DUCKING
DUCTILE
DUCTING
DUELING
DUELIST
DULCIFY
DULLING
DULLISH
DUMBING
DUMMIED
DUMMIES
DUMPIER
DUMPING
DUMPISH
DUNCISH
DUNKING
DUNKIRK
DUNLINS
DUNNING
DURNING
DUSKIER
DUSKILY
DUSKISH
DUSTIER
DUSTILY
DUSTING
FUBBING
FUBSIER
FUDGING
FUELING
FULFILL
FULFILS
FUNDING
FUNKIER
FUNKILY
FUNKING
FUNNIER
FUNNIES
FUNNILY
FUNNING
FURBISH
FURLING
FURNISH
FURRIER
FURRING
FURTIVE
FUSSIER
FUSSILY
FUSSING
FUSTIAN
FUSTICS
FUSTIER
FUSTILY
FUTZING
FUZZIER
FUZZILY
FUZZING
GUANINE
GUIDING
GULFING
GULLIES
GULLING
GULPIER
GULPING
GUMLIKE
GUMMIER
GUMMING
GUNFIRE
GUNKIER
GUNNIES
GUNNING
GUPPIES
GUSHIER
GUSHILY
GUSHING
GUSSIED
GUSSIES
GUSTIER
GUSTILY
GUSTING
GUTSIER
GUTSILY
GUTTIER
GUTTING
HUBBIES
HUFFIER
HUFFILY
HUFFING
HUFFISH
HUGGING
HUGGINS
HULKING
HULLING
HUMMING
HUMPIER
HUNKIER
HUNLIKE
HUNNISH
HUNTING
HURLIES
HURLING
HURRIED
HURRIES
HURTING
HUSHING
HUSKIER
HUSKIES
HUSKILY
HUSKING
HUSSIES
HUTLIKE
JUDAISM
JUDGING
JUDOIST
JUGGING
JUGGINS
JUGWINE
JUICIER
JUICILY
JUICING
JUMPIER
JUMPILY
JUMPING
JUNKIER
JUNKIES
JUNKING
JURYING
JUSTICE
JUSTIFY
JUSTINE
JUTTIED
JUTTIES
JUTTING
KUBRICK
KURDISH
KUWAITI
LUCKIER
LUCKILY
LUCKING
LUDDITE
LUFFING
LUGGING
LULLING
LUMPIER
LUMPILY
LUMPING
LUMPISH
LUNGING
LURKING
LUSTIER
LUSTILY
LUSTING
MUCKIER
MUCKILY
MUCKING
MUDDIED
MUDDIER
MUDDIES
MUDDILY
MUDPIES
MUFFING
MUFFINS
MUGGIER
MUGGING
MULLING
MULLION
MUMMIES
MUMMING
MUMPING
MUNTINS
MURKIER
MURKILY
MUSHIER
MUSHILY
MUSHING
MUSKIER
MUSKIES
MUSLIMS
MUSLINS
MUSSIER
MUSSILY
MUSSING
MUSTIER
MUSTILY
MUZHIKS
MUZZIER
MUZZILY
MUZZING
NUBBIER
NUBBINS
NUCLIDE
NUDGING
NUDNIKS
NULLIFY
NULLING
NULLITY
NUMBING
NUNCIOS
NUNLIKE
NUPTIAL
NURSING
NUTLIKE
NUTRIAS
NUTSIER
NUTTIER
NUTTILY
NUTTING
OUSTING
OUTBIDS
OUTFITS
OUTHITS
OUTLINE
OUTLIVE
OUTSIDE
OUTSIZE
OUTWITS
PUBLICS
PUBLISH
PUCCINI
PUCKISH
PUDDING
PUDGIER
PUDGILY
PUERILE
PUFFIER
PUFFILY
PUFFING
PUFFINS
PUGGISH
PULLING
PULLINS
PULPIER
PULPITS
PULSING
PUMPING
PUNDITS
PUNKIER
PUNKIES
PUNNIER
PUNNILY
PUNNING
PUNTIES
PUNTING
PUPPIES
PURGING
PURLIEU
PURLING
PURLINS
PURRING
PURSIER
PURSING
PURVIEW
PUSHIER
PUSHILY
PUSHING
PUTTIED
PUTTIES
PUTTING
QUAKIER
QUAKILY
QUAKING
QUALIFY
QUALITY
QUERIED
QUERIER
QUERIES
QUERIST
QUEUING
QUININE
QUOTING
RUBBING
RUBBISH
RUBRICS
RUCHING
RUCKING
RUCTION
RUDDIER
RUDDILY
RUFFIAN
RUGLIKE
RUINING
RUMMIER
RUNNIER
RUNNING
RUNRIOT
RUNTIER
RUNTISH
RUNWITH
RUSHIER
RUSHING
RUSSIAN
RUSTICS
RUSTIER
RUSTILY
RUSTING
RUTTIER
RUTTISH
SUASION
SUAVITY
SUBBING
SUBLIME
SUBMITS
SUBSIDE
SUBSIDY
SUBSIST
SUCKING
SUCTION
SUDSIER
SUDSING
SUFFICE
SUITING
SULFIDE
SULFITE
SULKIER
SULKIES
SULKILY
SULKING
SULLIED
SULLIES
SUMMING
SUMMITS
SUNCITY
SUNDIAL
SUNFISH
SUNKIST
SUNLIKE
SUNNIER
SUNNILY
SUNNING
SUNRISE
SUPPING
SURFIER
SURFING
SURGING
SURLIER
SURLILY
SURMISE
SURVIVE
SUSLIKS
SUSSING
TUBAIST
TUBBIER
TUBLIKE
TUCKING
TUFTIER
TUFTING
TUGGING
TUGRIKS
TUITION
TUMMIES
TUMMING
TUNNIES
TURBINE
TURBITS
TURFIER
TURKISH
TURNING
TURNIPS
VULPINE
YUCKIER
YUMMIER
YUPPIES

•U•••I•

AUSTRIA
BUCOLIC
BUILDIN
BUILTIN
BUMPKIN
BUSHPIG
BUTTSIN
CULPRIT
CURTAIL
CURTAIN
DUCKPIN
DUKAKIS
DUSTBIN
EUGENIE
EURASIA
FUCHSIA
FUELOIL
FUNFAIR
GUTHRIE
HUSSEIN
JUMPSIN
JURIDIC
JURYRIG
KUTCHIN
LUNATIC
MUEZZIN
MULLEIN
NUCLEIC
NUMERIC
OUTLAID
OUTOFIT
PULLSIN
PUMPKIN
PUNCHIN
PURLOIN
PURSUIT
PUSHKIN
PUSHPIN
QUENTIN
QUICKIE
RUBITIN
RUSHDIE
SUBJOIN
SUBSOIL
SUBUNIT
SUCKSIN
SUNMAID
SUNSUIT
SURFEIT
SUSTAIN
TUCKSIN
TUNEDIN
TUNESIN
TUNGOIL
TUNISIA
TURMOIL
TURNSIN

•U••••I

GUARANI
JUMANJI
KUTENAI
KUWAITI
PUCCINI
PULASKI
PUNJABI

••UI•••

AQUIFER
AQUINAS
AQUIVER
BRUISED
BRUISER
BRUISES
BRUITED
CRUISED
CRUISER
CRUISES
EQUINES
EQUINOX
FLUIDLY
FRUITED
GLUIEST
SLUICED
SLUICES
SQUILLS
SQUINCH
SQUINTS
SQUINTY
SQUIRED
SQUIRES
SQUIRMS
SQUIRMY
SQUIRTS
SQUISHY
TRUISMS

••U•I••

ABUSING
ABUSIVE
AMUSING
AZURITE
BAUXITE
BLUEING
BLUEISH
BOUSING
BRUTISH
BRUXING
CAUSING
CAUTION
CLUEING
COURIER
COUSINS
CRUCIAL
CRUCIFY
CRUDITY
DAUBING
DAUMIER
DOUSING
EDUCING
ELUDING
ELUSIVE
ELUTING
ELUTION
ELUVIUM
ENURING
ERUDITE
EXUDING
FAUVISM
FAUVIST
FEUDING
FLUKIER
FLUTIER
FLUTING
FLUTIST
FLUVIAL
FLUXING
FOULING
FOURIER
GAUDIER
GAUDILY
GAUGING
GAULISH
GAUMING
GAUZIER
GAUZILY
GOUGING
GOUTIER
GOUTILY
GOUTISH
GRUNION
HAULING
HOUDINI
HOUSING
INURING
INUTILE
LAUDING
LEUCINE
LOUDISH
LOUSIER
LOUSILY
LOUSING
LOUTISH
MAULING
MAURICE
MOUSIER
MOUSING
NOURISH
OCULIST
PAUCITY
PAULINA
PAULINE
PAULING
PAULIST
PAUSING
PLUGINS
PLUMIER
PLUMING
PLUVIAL
POURING
POUTIER
POUTING
PRUDISH
PRUNING
REUNIFY
REUNION
REUNITE
ROUGING
ROUSING
ROUTINE
ROUTING
SAUCIER
SAUCILY
SAURIAN
SHUTINS
SOUPIER
SOURING
SOURISH
SPUMIER
SPUMING
STUDIED
STUDIES
STUDIOS
TAURINE
THULIUM
TOURING
TOURISM
TOURIST
TOUTING
TRUCIAL
TRUEING
USURIES

••U••I•

AQUARIA
AQUATIC
AQUAVIT
BLUEFIN
BOUDOIR
CAUSTIC
CLUEDIN
CLUESIN
COUNCIL
DAUPHIN
DHURRIE
DRUMLIN
EXURBIA
FOULTIP
GAUGUIN
LAUGHIN
MAUDLIN
MAULDIN
MAUROIS
MOUNTIE
PLUGSIN
POURSIN
PRUSSIA
ROUGHIT
SHUTSIN
SPUTNIK
SQUALID
TOUGHIE

••U•••I

GOURAMI
HOUDINI
HYUNDAI
SPUMONI
TSUNAMI

•••UI••

ACQUIRE
ACQUITS
ANNUITY
ANOUILH
ARGUING
BEAUISH
BEGUILE
BEGUINE
DELUISE
ENDUING
ENQUIRE
ENQUIRY
ENSUING
ENSUITE
ESQUIRE
FATUITY
GENUINE
IMBUING
INQUIRE
INQUIRY
INTUITS
ISSUING
JESUITS
LIQUIDS
MAGUIRE
MCGUIRE
PIQUING
QUEUING
REBUILD
REBUILT
REQUIEM
REQUIRE
REQUITE
ROGUISH
SEQUINS
TENUITY
TEQUILA
TVGUIDE
VACUITY
VALUING
VOGUISH

•••U•I•

AGOUTIS
ALBUMIN
ALLUVIA
CLAUDIA
CLAUDIO
ETRURIA
GROUPIE
INSULIN
KABUKIS
MANUMIT
MENUHIN
MINUTIA
PETUNIA
PLAUDIT
SALUKIS
SEQUOIA
STLUCIA
SUBUNIT
TSOURIS

•••U••I

ABRUZZI
BELUSHI
CADUCEI
JACUZZI
NOGUCHI
OLDUVAI
SAMURAI

••••UI•

BEDOUIN
BISCUIT
CATSUIT
CIRCUIT
CONDUIT
DRYSUIT
FLORUIT
GAUGUIN
JOAQUIN
JONQUIL
LANGUID
LAWSUIT
MARQUIS
PENGUIN
PURSUIT
RECRUIT
SANLUIS
SKISUIT
STLOUIS
SUNSUIT
WETSUIT
YANQUIS

••••U•I

STIMULI

•••••UI

RAPANUI

•UJ••••

FUJITSU
JUJITSU
JUJUBES

•U•J•••

OUTJUMP
PUNJABI
SUBJECT
SUBJOIN
SUOJURE

•U••J••

CULTJAM
LUBEJOB

•U•••J•

JUMANJI

••U•J••

BLUEJAY

UK•••••

UKRAINE
UKULELE

U•K••••

UNKEMPT
UNKINKS
UNKNITS
UNKNOTS
UNKNOWN

U•••K••

UNASKED
UNBAKED
UNLIKED
UNMAKES
UNYOKED
UNYOKES
UPTAKES

U••••K•

UNALIKE
UNCORKS
UNHOOKS
UNKINKS
UNLINKS
UNLOCKS
UNLUCKY
UNMASKS
UNPACKS
UNTACKS
UPLINKS
UPTICKS
URNLIKE

U•••••K

UNBLOCK
UNCLOAK
UNFROCK
UNSTACK
UNSTICK
UNSTUCK
UPQUARK

•UK••••

AUKLETS
DUKAKIS
DUKEDOM
JUKEBOX
MUKLUKS
SUKARNO

•U•K•••

BUCKETS
BUCKEYE
BUCKING
BUCKLED
BUCKLER
BUCKLES
BUCKLEY
BUCKOES
BUCKRAM
BUCKSAW
BUCKSUP
BULKIER
BULKING
BUNKBED
BUNKERS
BUNKING
BUNKOED
BURKINA
BUSKING
BUSKINS
CUCKOOS
DUCKIER
DUCKING
DUCKPIN
DUNKERS
DUNKING
DUNKIRK
DUSKIER
DUSKILY
DUSKISH
FUNKIER
FUNKILY
FUNKING
GUNKIER
GURKHAS
HULKING
HUNKERS
HUNKIER
HUSKERS
HUSKIER
HUSKIES
HUSKILY
HUSKING
JUNKART
JUNKDNA
JUNKERS
JUNKETS
JUNKIER
JUNKIES
JUNKING
JUNKMAN
LUCKIER
LUCKILY
LUCKING
LUCKOUT
LUNKERS
LURKING
MUCKIER
MUCKILY
MUCKING
MUCKSUP
MURKIER
MURKILY
MUSKEGS
MUSKETS
MUSKIER
MUSKIES
MUSKRAT
PUCKERS
PUCKETT
PUCKISH
PUNKAHS
PUNKERS
PUNKIER
PUNKIES
QUAKERS
QUAKIER
QUAKILY
QUAKING
QUOKKAS
RUCKING
SUCKERS
SUCKING
SUCKSIN
SULKERS
SULKIER
SULKIES
SULKILY
SULKING

SUNKIST
TUCKERS
TUCKING
TUCKSIN
TURKEYS
TURKISH
TUSKERS
YUCKIER

•U••K••

BUMPKIN
DUKAKIS
PUMPKIN
PUSHKIN
QUACKED
QUICKEN
QUICKER
QUICKIE
QUICKLY
QUOKKAS
TURNKEY

•U•••K•

AUTARKY
BUDLIKE
BUROAKS
CUPCAKE
CUPLIKE
CURLIKE
GUMLIKE
HUNLIKE
HUTLIKE
KUSPUKS
MUKLUKS
MUZHIKS
NUDNIKS
NUNLIKE
NUTLIKE
OUTTAKE
PULASKI
RUGLIKE
SUNLIKE
SUSLIKS
TUBLIKE
TUGRIKS

•U••••K

BULLOCK
BULWARK
BURBANK
BURDOCK
CUTBACK
DUNKIRK
DUNNOCK
GUNLOCK
HUMMOCK
KUBRICK
LUBBOCK
MUBARAK
MUDPACK
OUTBACK
OUTLOOK
OUTRANK
OUTTALK
OUTWORK
RUNAMOK
RUNBACK
SUFFOLK
SUNDECK
TUSSOCK

••UK•••

CHUKKAS
CHUKKER
FLUKIER
SOUKOUS
YOUKNOW

••U•K••

BAULKED
CAULKED
CAULKER
CHUCKED
CHUCKLE
CHUKKAS
CHUKKER
CLUCKED
CLUNKED
CLUNKER
DRUCKER
FLUNKED
KNUCKLE
PLUCKED
PLUNKED
SHUCKED
SHUCKER
SKULKED
SKULKER
SKUNKED
STUCKTO
STUCKUP
TRUCKED
TRUCKEE
TRUCKER
TRUCKLE

••U••K•

ABUBAKR
BLUESKY
SQUAWKS
SQUAWKY
SQUEAKS
SQUEAKY

••U•••K

BRUBECK
HAUBERK
SPUTNIK

•••UK••

HANUKAH
KABUKIS
PERUKES
REBUKED
REBUKES
SALUKIS

•••U•K•

ATTUCKS
DEBUNKS
MAZURKA
OROURKE
UNLUCKY

•••U••K

UPQUARK
YAKUTSK

••••UK•

DYBBUKS
KUSPUKS
MUKLUKS
NETSUKE

••••U•K

ATATURK
MOLLUSK
POTLUCK
ROEBUCK
SAWBUCK
SPELUNK
UNSTUCK

UL•••••

ULALUME
ULANOVA
ULLMANN
ULSTERS
ULTIMAS
ULULANT
ULULATE
ULYANOV
ULYSSES

U•L••••

UGLIEST
ULLMANN
UMLAUTS
UNLACED
UNLACES
UNLADES
UNLATCH
UNLEARN
UNLEASH
UNLIKED
UNLINED
UNLINKS
UNLOADS
UNLOCKS
UNLOOSE
UNLOVED
UNLUCKY
UPLANDS
UPLIFTS
UPLINKS
UPLOADS

U••L•••

UKULELE
ULALUME
ULULANT
ULULATE
UNALIKE
UNBLEST
UNBLOCK
UNCLASP
UNCLEAN
UNCLEAR
UNCLOAK
UNCLOGS
UNCLOSE
UNGLUED
UNPLUGS
UPCLOSE
URNLIKE
USELESS
UTILISE
UTILITY
UTILIZE

U•••L••

UCCELLO
UNBOLTS
UNFOLDS
UNOILED
UNPILED
UNPILES
UNROLLS
UPHOLDS
UPSILON
USUALLY
UTRILLO

U••••L•

UCCELLO
UKULELE
UNAPTLY
UNCIALS
UNCOILS
UNCURLS
UNFURLS
UNGODLY
UNREELS
UNROLLS
UNSEALS
UNVEILS
UPPSALA
UPSCALE
USEABLE
USUALLY
UTRILLO
UTTERLY

U•••••L

UNAWFUL
UNCIVIL
UNEQUAL
UNRAVEL
UNSNARL
UNUSUAL
USSTEEL
UTENSIL
UXORIAL

•UL••••

BULBLET
BULBOUS
BULBULS
BULGARS
BULGHUR
BULGIER
BULGING
BULKIER
BULKING
BULLDOG
BULLETS
BULLIED
BULLIES
BULLING
BULLION
BULLISH
BULLITT
BULLOCK
BULLPEN
BULLRUN
BULRUSH
BULWARK
CULEBRA
CULLERS
CULLIED
CULLIES
CULLING
CULOTTE
CULPRIT
CULTISH
CULTISM
CULTIST
CULTJAM
CULTURE
CULVERS
CULVERT
DULCIFY
DULLARD
DULLEST
DULLING
DULLISH
FULCRUM
FULFILL
FULFILS
FULGENT
FULGHUM
FULLEST
FULSOME
GULCHES
GULFING
GULLAHS
GULLETS
GULLIES
GULLING
GULPIER
GULPING
HULKING
HULLERS
HULLING
HULLOAS
HULLOED
JULIANA
LULLABY
LULLING
MULCHED
MULCHES
MULCTED
MULETAS
MULLAHS
MULLEIN
MULLERS
MULLETS
MULLING
MULLION
NULLAHS
NULLIFY
NULLING
NULLITY
PULASKI
PULLETS
PULLEYS
PULLFOR
PULLING
PULLINS
PULLMAN
PULLOFF
PULLONS
PULLOUT
PULLSIN
PULLSON
PULLSUP
PULLTAB
PULLUPS
PULPIER
PULPITS
PULQUES
PULSARS
PULSATE
PULSING
RULEOUT
RULESON
RULINGS
SULFATE
SULFIDE
SULFITE
SULKERS
SULKIER
SULKIES
SULKILY
SULKING
SULLIED
SULLIES
SULPHUR
SULTANA
SULTANS
SULUSEA
TULSANS
VULCANS
VULGATE
VULPINE
VULTURE
YULELOG

•U•L•••

AUKLETS
BUDLESS
BUDLIKE
BUGLERS
BUGLING
BUILDER
BUILDIN
BUILDUP
BUILTIN
BUILTUP
BULLDOG
BULLETS
BULLIED
BULLIES
BULLING
BULLION
BULLISH
BULLITT
BULLOCK
BULLPEN
BULLRUN
BURLAPS
BURLIER
BURLING
BUSLINE
BUTLERS
CULLERS
CULLIED
CULLIES
CULLING
CUPLIKE
CURLERS
CURLEWS
CURLIER
CURLIKE
CURLING
CURLSUP
CUTLASS
CUTLERS
CUTLERY
CUTLETS
DUALITY
DUELERS
DUELING
DUELIST
DULLARD
DULLEST
DULLING
DULLISH
DUNLINS
FUELERS
FUELING
FUELLED
FUELOIL
FUELROD
FULLEST
FURLESS
FURLING
FURLONG
GUELPHS
GUILDER
GULLAHS
GULLETS
GULLIES
GULLING
GUMLESS
GUMLIKE
GUNLESS
GUNLOCK
GUTLESS
HUELESS
HULLERS
HULLING
HULLOAS
HULLOED
HUNLIKE
HURLERS
HURLEYS
HURLIES
HURLING
HUTLIKE
JUTLAND
LULLABY
LULLING
MUKLUKS
MULLAHS
MULLEIN
MULLERS
MULLETS
MULLING
MULLION
MUSLIMS
MUSLINS
NUCLEAR
NUCLEIC
NUCLEON
NUCLEUS
NUCLIDE
NULLAHS
NULLIFY
NULLING
NULLITY
NUNLIKE
NUTLETS
NUTLIKE
OUTLAID
OUTLAND
OUTLAST
OUTLAWS
OUTLAYS
OUTLETS
OUTLINE
OUTLIVE
OUTLOOK
OUTLOUD
PUBLICS
PUBLISH
PULLETS
PULLEYS
PULLFOR
PULLING
PULLINS
PULLMAN
PULLOFF
PULLONS
PULLOUT
PULLSIN
PULLSON
PULLSUP
PULLTAB
PULLUPS
PUNLESS
PURLIEU
PURLING
PURLINS
PURLOIN
QUALIFY
QUALITY
QUELLED
QUILLED
QUILLER
QUILTED
QUILTER
RUGLIKE
RUMLESS
RUNLATE
RUNLETS
SUBLETS
SUBLIME
SULLIED
SULLIES
SUMLESS
SUNLAMP
SUNLESS
SUNLIKE
SUOLOCO
SURLIER
SURLILY
SUSLIKS
SUTLERS
TUBLIKE
TUGLESS
WURLEYS

•U••L••

AUDILES
AURALEE
AURALLY
BUBBLED
BUBBLES
BUCKLED
BUCKLER
BUCKLES
BUCKLEY
BUCOLIC
BUGALOO
BULBLET
BUMBLED
BUMBLER
BUMBLES
BUNDLED
BUNDLES
BUNGLED
BUNGLER
BUNGLES
BURBLED
BURBLES
BURGLAR
BURGLED
BURGLES
BUSTLED
BUSTLES
CUDDLED
CUDDLES
CUMULUS
CUPOLAS
CURDLED
CURDLES
CUSSLER
FUDDLED
FUDDLES
FUELLED
FUMBLED
FUMBLER
FUMBLES
GUNPLAY
GURGLED
GURGLES
GUZZLED
GUZZLER
GUZZLES
HUDDLED
HUDDLES
HUMBLED
HUMBLER
HUMBLES
HUNTLEY
HURDLED
HURDLER
HURDLES
HURTLED
HURTLES
HUSTLED
HUSTLER
HUSTLES
JUBILEE
JUGGLED
JUGGLER
JUGGLES
JUGULAR
JUMBLED
JUMBLES
JUNGLES
LUCILLE
MUDDLED
MUDDLER
MUDDLES
MUFFLED
MUFFLER
MUFFLES
MUMBLED
MUMBLER
MUMBLES
MURILLO
MUSCLED
MUSCLES
MUZZLED
MUZZLES
NUBBLES
NUZZLED
NUZZLER
NUZZLES
OUTFLOW
OUTPLAY
PUDDLED
PUDDLES
PUEBLOS
PURFLED
PURFLES
PURPLED
PURPLES
PUZZLED
PUZZLER
PUZZLES
QUAILED
QUELLED
QUIGLEY
QUILLED
QUILLER
RUBBLES
RUDOLPH
RUFFLED
RUFFLES
RUMBLED
RUMBLES
RUMPLED
RUMPLES
RUNDLES
RURALLY
RUSTLED
RUSTLER
RUSTLES
SUBPLOT
SUBTLER
SUPPLER
SURPLUS
TUBULAR
TUMBLED
TUMBLER
TUMBLES
TUMULTS
TUMULUS
TUPELOS
TURTLED
TURTLES
TUSSLED
TUSSLES
TUTELAR
YULELOG

•U•••L•

AUDIBLE
AUDIBLY
AURALLY
AUREOLA
AUREOLE
AURICLE
BUFFALO
BULBULS
BUMPILY
BUSHELS
BUSHILY
BUYABLE
CUBICLE
CUDGELS
CUEBALL
CUPFULS
CUREALL
CUTICLE
DUCTILE
DUFFELS
DURABLE
DURABLY
DURRELL
DUSKILY
DUSTILY
FULFILL
FULFILS
FUNKILY
FUNNELS
FUNNILY
FURBALL
FUSSILY
FUSTILY
FUZZILY
GUMBALL
GUNMOLL
GUNNELS
GUNWALE
GUSHILY
GUSTILY
GUTSILY
HUBBELL
HUFFILY
HUMANLY
HUMIDLY
HUSKILY
JUGFULS
JUICILY
JUMPILY
LUCIDLY
LUCILLE
LUCKILY
LUMPILY
LURIDLY
LUSTILY
MUCKILY
MUDDILY
MUDEELS
MURILLO
MURKILY
MUSHILY
MUSSELS
MUSSILY
MUSTILY
MUTABLE
MUTABLY
MUTUALS
MUZZILY
NUTTILY
OURSELF
OUTPOLL
OUTSELL
OUTSOLD
OUTTALK
PUDGILY
PUERILE
PUFFILY
PUMMELS
PUNNILY
PURCELL
PUSHILY
QUAKILY
QUEENLY
QUEERLY
QUIBBLE
QUICKLY
QUIETLY
RUDDILY
RUMPOLE
RUNNELS
RURALLY
RUSSELL
RUSTILY
SUAVELY
SUFFOLK
SULKILY
SUNBELT
SUNNILY
SURLILY
TUNICLE
TUNNELS

•U••••L

AUGURAL
AURORAL
AUSTRAL
BUSGIRL
BUTANOL
CUEBALL
CUREALL
CURTAIL
DURRELL
DUTIFUL
FUELOIL
FULFILL
FUNCHAL
FURBALL
FURSEAL
GUMBALL
GUNMOLL
HUBBELL
HUMERAL
HURTFUL
HUSHFUL
JUVENAL
LUSTFUL
MUSEFUL
MUSICAL
NUMERAL
NUPTIAL
OUTPOLL
OUTSELL
PURCELL
PUSHFUL
QUARREL
QUETZAL
RUSSELL
RUTHFUL
SUBSOIL
SUNBOWL
SUNDIAL
SURREAL
TUMBREL
TUNEFUL
TUNGOIL
TURMOIL

••UL•••

ADULATE
ADULTLY
AMULETS
AVULSED
AVULSES
BAULKED
BOULDER
BOULLES
CAULKED
CAULKER
COULDNT
COULEES
COULOMB
COULTER
CRULLER
EMULATE
EVULSED
EVULSES
EXULTED
FAULTED
FOULARD
FOULEST
FOULING
FOULOUT
FOULSUP
FOULTIP
FOULUPS
GAULISH
GOULASH
HAULAGE
HAULERS
HAULING
HAULOFF
HAULSUP
MAULDIN
MAULING
MOULAGE
MOULDED
MOULDER
MOULTED
OCULIST
OPULENT
PAULINA
PAULINE
PAULING
PAULIST
PAULSEN
POULENC
POULTRY
ROULADE
SCULLED
SCULLER
SCULPTS
SKULKED
SKULKER
SOULFUL
THULIUM
UKULELE
ULULANT
ULULATE
VAULTED
VAULTER
WOULDBE
WOULDNT

••U•L••

BAUBLES
BLUELAW
BOULLES
CAUDLES
COUPLED
COUPLES
COUPLET
CRUELER
CRUELLY
CRUELTY
CRULLER
DOUBLED
DOUBLES
DOUBLET
DOUBLEU
DOUGLAS
DRUMLIN
EQUALED
EQUALLY
KNURLED
LOUELLA
MAUDLIN
MOUFLON
ROUBLES
SCULLED
SCULLER
SQUALID
SQUALLS
SQUALOR
SQUELCH
SQUILLS
TOUSLED
TOUSLES
USUALLY

••U••L•

ACUTELY
ADULTLY
ARUGULA
BLUFFLY
BLUNTLY
BRUTELY
CHUCKLE
COURTLY
CRUDELY
CRUELLY
CRUMBLE
CRUMBLY
CRUMPLE
CRUMPLY
EQUABLE
EQUABLY
EQUALLY
FLUIDLY
GAUDILY
GAUNTLY
GAUZILY
GOUTILY
GRUFFLY
GRUMBLE
GRUMBLY
INUTILE
KNUCKLE
LAURELS
LOUELLA
LOUSILY
PLUMPLY
PLURALS
PLUSHLY
ROUGHLY
ROUNDLY
SAUCILY
SCUFFLE
SCUTTLE
SHUFFLE
SHUTTLE
SMUGGLE
SNUFFLE
SNUFFLY
SNUGGLE
SOUFFLE
SOUNDLY
SQUALLS
SQUATLY
SQUEALS
SQUILLS
STUBBLE
STUBBLY
STUMBLE
TOUGHLY
TRUCKLE
TRUFFLE
TRUNDLE
UKULELE
USUALLY

••U•••L

ABUTTAL
ALUMNAL
ASUSUAL
BRUEGEL
BRUMMEL
CHUNNEL
COUNCIL
COUNSEL
CRUCIAL
DIURNAL
FLUVIAL
JOURNAL
NEUTRAL
PLUVIAL
POUTFUL
SOULFUL
TRUCIAL
UNUSUAL

•••UL••

AMPULES
ANGULAR
ANNULAR
ANNULUS
AWFULLY
CAPULET
COPULAE
COPULAS
CUMULUS
DIVULGE
ENGULFS
EPAULET
FACULAE
FACULTY
FAMULUS
FERULES
FIBULAE
FIBULAS
IMPULSE
INDULGE
INSULAR
INSULIN
INSULTS
JOCULAR
JUGULAR
LOBULES

MACULAE
MEDULLA
MODULAR
MODULES
NEBULAE
NEBULAR
NEBULAS
NODULAR
NODULES
OCCULTS
PABULUM
PENULTS
POPULAR
POPULUS
RADULAE
REGULAR
REGULUS
REPULSE
RESULTS
RIVULET
ROMULAN
ROMULUS
SCHULTZ
SECULAR
SHOULDA
TABULAR
TITULAR
TUBULAR
TUMULTS
TUMULUS
ZEBULON

•••U•L•

ANNUALS
ANOUILH
AWFULLY
BEGUILE
CASUALS
MANUALS
MEDULLA
MUTUALS
OCTUPLE
PIOUSLY
PROUDLY
REBUILD
REBUILT
REFUELS
RITUALS
SCRUPLE
SEQUELS
SOLUBLE
STOUTLY
TEQUILA
TROUBLE
UNCURLS
UNFURLS
VACUOLE
VAGUELY
VISUALS
VOLUBLE
VOLUBLY

•••U••L

AROUSAL
AUGURAL
COZUMEL
LACUNAL
NAHUATL
NATURAL
PERUSAL
REFUSAL
SPOUSAL
STRUDEL

••••UL•

AMPOULE
ARMFULS
ARUGULA
ASARULE
ASSAULT
ATFAULT
BAGFULS
BEFOULS
BEOWULF
BLACULA
BOXFULS
BULBULS
CANFULS
CAPFULS
CAPSULE
CARFULS
CONSULS
CONSULT
CUPFULS
DEFAULT
DIMBULB
DRACULA
EARFULS
ENSOULS
EYEFULS
FERRULE
FORMULA
GAGRULE
GLOBULE
GRANULE
HERCULE
INHAULS
INOCULA
JARFULS
JUGFULS
LAPFULS
LEGPULL
MISRULE
NOFAULT
PANFULS
PITBULL
POTFULS
RENAULT
SCAPULA
SEAGULL
SPATULA
STIMULI
VATFULS
VIRGULE
VISTULA

••••U•L

ACCRUAL
ASUSUAL
COEQUAL
EMANUEL
FACTUAL
GRADUAL
JONQUIL
LEGPULL
LINGUAL
PINCURL
PITBULL
PREQUEL
RORQUAL
SEAGULL
SENSUAL
SYNFUEL
TEXTUAL
UNEQUAL
UNUSUAL
VICTUAL
VIRTUAL

•••••UL

BALEFUL
BANEFUL
BASHFUL
BOWLFUL
BRIMFUL
CAREFUL
DAREFUL
DIREFUL
DISHFUL
DOLEFUL
DOOMFUL
DUTIFUL
EASEFUL
FACTFUL
FATEFUL
FEARFUL
FISTFUL
FORKFUL
FORMFUL
FRETFUL
GAINFUL
GLEEFUL
HANDFUL
HARMFUL
HATEFUL
HEATFUL
HEEDFUL
HELPFUL
HOPEFUL
HURTFUL
HUSHFUL
KARAKUL
LESPAUL
LIFEFUL
LUSTFUL
MINDFUL
MOANFUL
MUSEFUL
NEEDFUL
ODORFUL
PAGEFUL
PAILFUL
PAINFUL
PASSEUL
PIPEFUL
PITIFUL
PLAYFUL
PLOTFUL
POUTFUL
PUSHFUL
RAGEFUL
RESTFUL
ROOMFUL
RUTHFUL
SACKFUL
SHOPFUL
SIGHFUL
SKILFUL
SKINFUL
SONGFUL
SOULFUL
TACTFUL
TANKFUL
TEARFUL
TOILFUL
TRAYFUL
TUNEFUL
UNAWFUL
WAILFUL
WAKEFUL
WILLFUL
WISHFUL
WISTFUL
YAWNFUL
ZESTFUL

UM•••••

UMBERTO
UMBRAGE
UMBRIAN
UMLAUTS
UMPIRED
UMPIRES
UMPTEEN

U•M••••

UNMAKES
UNMASKS
UNMOVED

U••M•••

ULLMANN
UNAMUNO

U•••M••

ULTIMAS
UNAIMED
UNARMED
UNKEMPT
UNNAMED
UNTAMED
UPTEMPO

U••••M•

ULALUME

U•••••M

UNIFORM
URANIUM

•UM••••

BUMBLED
BUMBLER
BUMBLES
BUMMERS
BUMMING
BUMPERS
BUMPIER
BUMPILY
BUMPING
BUMPKIN
BUMPSUP
BUMRAPS
BUMRUSH
BUMSOUT
CUMULUS
DUMBEST
DUMBING
DUMDUMS
DUMMIED
DUMMIES
DUMMYUP
DUMPIER
DUMPING
DUMPISH
FUMBLED
FUMBLER
FUMBLES
FUMIEST
GUMBALL
GUMDROP
GUMLESS
GUMLIKE
GUMMIER
GUMMING
GUMSHOE
GUMTREE
HUMANLY
HUMANUM
HUMBLED
HUMBLER
HUMBLES
HUMBUGS
HUMDRUM
HUMERAL
HUMERUS
HUMIDLY
HUMIDOR
HUMMERS
HUMMING
HUMMOCK
HUMORED
HUMOURS
HUMPIER
HUMVEES
JUMANJI
JUMBLED
JUMBLES
JUMPCUT
JUMPERS
JUMPIER
JUMPILY
JUMPING
JUMPOFF
JUMPSAT
JUMPSIN
JUMPSON
JUMPSUP
KUMQUAT
LUMBAGO
LUMBARS
LUMBERS
LUMIERE
LUMPERS
LUMPIER
LUMPILY
LUMPING
LUMPISH
LUMPSUM
MUMBLED
MUMBLER
MUMBLES
MUMESON
MUMFORD
MUMMERS
MUMMERY
MUMMIES
MUMMING
MUMPING
NUMBATS
NUMBERS
NUMBEST
NUMBING
NUMERAL
NUMERIC
PUMICES
PUMMELS
PUMPERS
PUMPING
PUMPKIN
PUMPSUP
RUMBAED
RUMBLED
RUMBLES
RUMLESS
RUMMAGE
RUMMIER
RUMORED
RUMOURS
RUMPLED
RUMPLES
RUMPOLE
SUMATRA
SUMLESS
SUMMARY
SUMMERS
SUMMERY
SUMMING
SUMMITS
SUMMONS
TUMBLED
TUMBLER
TUMBLES
TUMBREL
TUMMIES
TUMMING
TUMULTS
TUMULUS
YUMMIER

•U•M•••

AUGMENT
BUMMERS
BUMMING
BURMANS
BURMESE
DUMMIED
DUMMIES
DUMMYUP
GUIMPES
GUMMIER
GUMMING
GUNMOLL
HUMMERS
HUMMING
HUMMOCK
MUAMMAR
MUMMERS
MUMMERY
MUMMIES
MUMMING
MURMURS
MUUMUUS
NUTMEAT
NUTMEGS
PUMMELS
RUMMAGE
RUMMIER
SUBMITS
SUMMARY
SUMMERS
SUMMERY
SUMMING
SUMMITS
SUMMONS
SUNMAID
SURMISE
TUMMIES
TUMMING
TURMOIL
YUMMIER

•U••M••

AUTOMAT
AUTUMNS
BUSHMAN
BUSHMEN
DUSTMAN
DUSTMEN
DUSTMOP
JUNKMAN
MUAMMAR
PULLMAN
PUTAMEN
RUNAMOK
TUCHMAN

•U•••M•

BUYTIME
CUSTOMS
CUTTIME
DUMDUMS
FULSOME
MUGWUMP
MUSEUMS
MUSLIMS
OUTCOME
OUTJUMP
QUORUMS
RUNHOME
SUBLIME
SUBSUME
SUCCUMB
SUNLAMP
SUPREME
SUPREMO
SURNAME

•U••••M

BUCKRAM
CULTISM
CULTJAM
DUKEDOM
FULCRUM
FULGHUM
GUARGUM
HUMANUM
HUMDRUM
JUDAISM
LUMPSUM
QUANTUM
SUNBEAM
SUNROOM
SURINAM

••UM•••

ACUMENS
ALUMNAE
ALUMNAL
ALUMNUS
BRUMMEL
CHUMMED
CLUMPED
CRUMBLE
CRUMBLY
CRUMPET
CRUMPLE
CRUMPLY
DAUMIER
DRUMLIN
DRUMMED
DRUMMER
DRUMSUP
FLUMMOX
FNUMBER
GAUMING
GLUMMER
GRUMBLE
GRUMBLY
GRUMPED
MAUMAUS
MUUMUUS
PLUMAGE
PLUMBED
PLUMBER
PLUMIER
PLUMING
PLUMMER
PLUMMET
PLUMPED
PLUMPER
PLUMPLY
RHUMBAS
SFUMATO
SLUMBER
SLUMMED
SLUMPED
SPUMIER
SPUMING
SPUMONE
SPUMONI
SPUMOUS
STUMBLE
STUMERS
STUMPED
STUMPER
THUMBED
THUMPED
THUMPER
TRUMPED
TRUMPET
TRUMPUP
YOUMANS

••U•M••

BRUMMEL
CHUMMED
DRUMMED
DRUMMER
FLUMMOX
GLUMMER
GOURMET
HOUSMAN
KAUFMAN
KLUGMAN
PLUMMER
PLUMMET
SLUMMED
THURMAN
ZEUGMAS

••U••M•

COULOMB
GAUTAMA
GOURAMI
SQUIRMS
SQUIRMY
TRUISMS
TSUNAMI
YOUNGMC

••U•••M

BLUEGUM
ELUVIUM
FAUVISM
MAUGHAM
THULIUM
TOURISM

•••UM••

ALBUMEN
ALBUMIN
ASSUMED
ASSUMES
AUTUMNS
BENUMBS
BITUMEN
CALUMET
CALUMNY
CERUMEN
COLUMBO
COLUMNS
COZUMEL
GALUMPH
GAZUMPS
ILLUMED
ILLUMES
INHUMAN
LEGUMES
MANUMIT
RELUMED
RELUMES
RESUMED
RESUMES
SCRUMMY
TRAUMAS
TRIUMPH
VOLUMES

•••U•M•

SCRUMMY
SOSUEME
VACUUMS

•••U••M

JEJUNUM
PABULUM
REQUIEM

••••UM•

AIRPUMP
ALARUMS
ASYLUMS
ATRIUMS
BEEGUMS
CONSUME
COSTUME
DICTUMS
DUMDUMS
GASPUMP
LYCEUMS
MAGNUMS
MEDIUMS
MUGWUMP
MUSEUMS
NOTRUMP
OUTJUMP
PABLUMS
PEPLUMS
PERFUME
PLENUMS
PODIUMS
POSSUMS
PRESUME
QUORUMS
REDGUMS
SATSUMA
SKIJUMP
SUBSUME
SUCCUMB
TALCUMS
TEDIUMS
ULALUME
VACUUMS
VELLUMS

•••••UM

ALYSSUM
ARCANUM
BELGIUM
BLUEGUM
CADMIUM
CAESIUM
CALCIUM
CAMBIUM
CHETRUM
CRANIUM
DECORUM
DIVINUM
EARDRUM
ELUVIUM
ELYSIUM
ERRATUM
FERMIUM
FULCRUM
FULGHUM
GALLIUM
GUARGUM
HAFNIUM
HAHNIUM
HOLMIUM
HOODLUM
HUMANUM
HUMDRUM
IRIDIUM
JEJUNUM
KARAKUM
LITHIUM
LUMPSUM
MAXIMUM
MINIMUM
MITCHUM
MODICUM
NATRIUM
NIOBIUM
NOSEEUM
NOSTRUM
OMENTUM
OPOSSUM
OPTIMUM
ORGANUM
PABULUM
PALLIUM
PENTIUM
PINETUM
PREMIUM
QUANTUM
RHENIUM
RHODIUM
ROSTRUM
SANCTUM
SISTRUM
SKOOKUM
SORGHUM
STADIUM
STERNUM
STRATUM
TANTRUM
TERBIUM
THORIUM
THULIUM
TRITIUM
URANIUM
YTTRIUM
ZEROSUM

UN•••••

UNAIDED
UNAIMED
UNAIRED
UNALIKE
UNAMUNO
UNAPTLY
UNARMED
UNASKED
UNAVOCE
UNAWARE
UNAWFUL
UNBAKED
UNBENDS
UNBINDS
UNBLEST
UNBLOCK
UNBOLTS
UNBOUND
UNBOWED
UNBOXED
UNBOXES
UNCAGED
UNCAGES
UNCANNY
UNCASED
UNCASES
UNCHAIN
UNCIALS
UNCIVIL
UNCLASP
UNCLEAN
UNCLEAR
UNCLOAK
UNCLOGS
UNCLOSE
UNCOILS
UNCORKS
UNCOUTH
UNCOVER
UNCRATE
UNCTION
UNCURLS
UNDATED
UNDERDO
UNDERGO
UNDOING
UNDRAPE
UNDRAWN
UNDRESS
UNDYING
UNEARTH
UNEATEN
UNENDED
UNEQUAL
UNFAZED
UNFIXED
UNFOLDS
UNFROCK
UNFURLS
UNGIRDS
UNGLUED
UNGODLY
UNGUENT
UNHANDS
UNHANDY
UNHAPPY
UNHEARD
UNHITCH
UNHOOKS
UNHORSE
UNICORN
UNIFIED
UNIFIER
UNIFIES
UNIFORM
UNIPODS
UNISONS
UNITARY
UNITERS
UNITIES
UNITING
UNITIVE
UNKEMPT
UNKINKS
UNKNITS
UNKNOTS
UNKNOWN
UNLACED
UNLACES
UNLADES
UNLATCH
UNLEARN
UNLEASH
UNLIKED
UNLINED
UNLINKS
UNLOADS
UNLOCKS
UNLOOSE
UNLOVED
UNLUCKY
UNMAKES
UNMASKS
UNMOVED
UNNAMED
UNNERVE
UNOILED
UNPACKS
UNPAVED
UNPILED
UNPILES
UNPLUGS
UNQUOTE
UNRATED
UNRAVEL
UNREADY
UNREELS
UNROBED
UNROBES
UNROLLS
UNSATED
UNSCREW
UNSEALS
UNSEATS
UNSEWED
UNSHORN
UNSNAGS
UNSNAPS
UNSNARL
UNSOUND
UNSPENT
UNSTACK
UNSTICK
UNSTOPS
UNSTRAP
UNSTUCK
UNSWEPT
UNTACKS
UNTAMED
UNTAPED
UNTRAPS
UNTRIED
UNTRUTH
UNTUNED
UNTUNES
UNTWIST
UNTYING
UNUSUAL
UNVEILS
UNWEAVE
UNWINDS
UNWISER
UNWOUND
UNWOVEN
UNWRAPS
UNYOKED
UNYOKES
UNZONED

U•N••••

UNNAMED
UNNERVE
URNLIKE

U••N•••

UGANDAN
ULANOVA
UNENDED
UNKNITS
UNKNOTS
UNKNOWN
UNSNAGS
UNSNAPS
UNSNARL
UPENDED
URANITE
URANIUM
USINGUP
UTENSIL

U•••N••

ULYANOV
UNBENDS
UNBINDS
UNCANNY
UNHANDS
UNHANDY
UNKINKS
UNLINED
UNLINKS
UNTUNED
UNTUNES
UNWINDS
UNZONED
UPLANDS
UPLINKS
UPTONOW
URBANER
URGENCY
USTINOV

U••••N•

UKRAINE
ULLMANN
ULULANT
UNAMUNO
UNBOUND
UNCANNY
UNDOING
UNDYING
UNGUENT
UNISONS
UNITING
UNSOUND
UNSPENT
UNTYING
UNWOUND
UPBORNE
UPFRONT
UPSWING
UPTURNS
URCHINS
USGRANT
USOPENS
UTAHANS

U•••••N

UGANDAN
ULLMANN
UMBRIAN
UMPTEEN
UNCHAIN
UNCLEAN
UNCTION
UNDRAWN
UNEATEN
UNICORN
UNKNOWN
UNLEARN
UNSHORN
UNWOVEN
UPRISEN
UPSILON
UTOPIAN

•UN••••

AUNTIES
BUNCHED
BUNCHES
BUNCOED
BUNDLED
BUNDLES
BUNGEES
BUNGING
BUNGLED
BUNGLER
BUNGLES
BUNIONS
BUNKBED
BUNKERS
BUNKING
BUNKOED
BUNNIES
BUNTING
BUNYIPS
CUNNING
DUNAWAY
DUNCISH
DUNGEON
DUNKERS
DUNKING
DUNKIRK
DUNLINS
DUNNING
DUNNOCK
FUNCHAL
FUNDING
FUNFAIR
FUNFEST
FUNGOES
FUNKIER
FUNKILY
FUNKING
FUNNELS
FUNNIER
FUNNIES
FUNNILY
FUNNING
GUNBOAT
GUNDOGS
GUNFIRE
GUNKIER
GUNLESS
GUNLOCK
GUNMOLL
GUNNELS
GUNNERS
GUNNERY
GUNNIES
GUNNING
GUNPLAY
GUNSFOR
GUNSHOT
GUNTHER
GUNWALE
HUNCHED
HUNCHES
HUNDRED
HUNGARY
HUNGERS

HUNGOUT
HUNKERS
HUNKIER
HUNLIKE
HUNNISH
HUNTERS
HUNTING
HUNTLEY
HUNYADY
JUNCOES
JUNEBUG
JUNGLES
JUNIORS
JUNIPER
JUNKART
JUNKDNA
JUNKERS
JUNKETS
JUNKIER
JUNKIES
JUNKING
JUNKMAN
LUNATIC
LUNCHED
LUNCHES
LUNGEAT
LUNGING
LUNKERS
MUNCHED
MUNCHER
MUNCHES
MUNDANE
MUNTINS
NUNCIOS
NUNLIKE
NUNNERY
PUNCHED
PUNCHER
PUNCHES
PUNCHIN
PUNCHUP
PUNDITS
PUNGENT
PUNIEST
PUNJABI
PUNKAHS
PUNKERS
PUNKIER
PUNKIES
PUNLESS
PUNNETS
PUNNIER
PUNNILY
PUNNING
PUNSTER
PUNTERS
PUNTIES
PUNTING
RUNAMOK
RUNAWAY
RUNBACK
RUNDEEP
RUNDLES
RUNDOWN
RUNGOFF
RUNGOUT
RUNHOME
RUNINTO
RUNLATE
RUNLETS
RUNNELS
RUNNERS
RUNNIER
RUNNING
RUNOFFS
RUNOUTS
RUNOVER
RUNRIOT
RUNSDRY
RUNSFOR
RUNSOFF
RUNSOUT
RUNTIER
RUNTISH
RUNWAYS
RUNWITH
SUNBATH
SUNBEAM
SUNBELT
SUNBOWL
SUNBURN
SUNCITY
SUNDAES
SUNDAYS
SUNDECK
SUNDERS
SUNDEWS
SUNDIAL
SUNDOGS
SUNDOWN
SUNFISH
SUNGODS
SUNKIST
SUNLAMP
SUNLESS
SUNLIKE
SUNMAID
SUNNIER
SUNNILY
SUNNING
SUNRAYS
SUNRISE
SUNROOF
SUNROOM
SUNSETS
SUNSPOT
SUNSUIT
SUNTANS
TUNDRAS
TUNEDIN
TUNEDUP
TUNEFUL
TUNEOUT
TUNESIN
TUNESUP
TUNEUPS
TUNGOIL
TUNICLE
TUNISIA
TUNNELS
TUNNIES

•U•N•••

BUNNIES
BURNERS
BURNETT
BURNING
BURNISH
BURNOUT
BURNSUP
BURNTUP
CUNNING
DUENNAS
DUNNING
DUNNOCK
DURNING
FUNNELS
FUNNIER
FUNNIES
FUNNILY
FUNNING
FURNACE
FURNISH
GUANACO
GUANINE
GUINEAS
GUNNELS
GUNNERS
GUNNERY
GUNNIES
GUNNING
GURNEYS
HUNNISH
LUGNUTS
NUANCED
NUANCES
NUDNIKS
NUNNERY
PUGNOSE
PUNNETS
PUNNIER
PUNNILY
PUNNING
QUANGOS
QUANTUM
QUENTIN
QUINARY
QUINCES
QUININE
QUINOAS
QUINQUE
QUINTET
QUONSET
RUANDAN
RUINERS
RUINING
RUINOUS
RUNNELS
RUNNERS
RUNNIER
RUNNING
SUNNIER
SUNNILY
SUNNING
SURNAME
TUNNELS
TUNNIES
TURNERS
TURNERY
TURNING
TURNIPS
TURNKEY
TURNOFF
TURNOUT
TURNSIN
TURNSON
TURNSTO
TURNSUP

•U••N••

AUGENDS
BUTANOL
CUTINTO
DUENNAS
DUGONGS
DURANCE
DURANGO
DURANTE
EUGENIE
HUMANLY
HUMANUM
JUMANJI
JUSTNOW
JUVENAL
KUTENAI
LUCENCY
LUPINES
MUTANTS
OUTINGS
PUDENCY
QUEENLY
RULINGS
RUNINTO
SUBUNIT
SURINAM
SUSANNA
SUSANNE
SUZANNE

•U•••N•

AUBURNS
AUGMENT
AUTUMNS
BUCKING
BUDDING
BUDGING
BUFFING
BUGGING
BUGLING
BULGING
BULKING
BULLING
BUMMING
BUMPING
BUNGING
BUNIONS
BUNKING
BUNTING
BUOYANT
BUOYING
BURBANK
BURDENS
BURKINA
BURLING
BURMANS
BURNING
BURPING
BURYING
BUSHING
BUSKING
BUSKINS
BUSLINE
BUSSING
BUSTING
BUSYING
BUTTING
BUTTONS
BUZZING
CUFFING
CUIBONO
CUISINE
CULLING
CUNNING
CUPPING
CURBING
CURDING
CURLING
CURRANT
CURRENT
CURSING
CURVING
CUSHING
CUSSING
CUTTING
DUBBING
DUCKING
DUCTING
DUELING
DULLING
DUMBING
DUMPING
DUNKING
DUNLINS
DUNNING
DUODENA
DURNING
DUSTING
EUPHONY
FUBBING
FUDGING
FUELING
FULGENT
FUNDING
FUNKING
FUNNING
FURLING
FURLONG
FURRING
FUSSING
FUTZING
FUZZING
GUANINE
GUARANI
GUIDING
GUIDONS
GULFING
GULLING
GULPING
GUMMING
GUNNING
GUSHING
GUSTING
GUTTING
HUFFING
HUGGING
HUGGINS
HULKING
HULLING
HUMMING
HUNTING
HURLING
HURTING
HUSBAND
HUSHING
HUSKING
HUYGENS
JUDGING
JUGBAND
JUGGING
JUGGINS
JUGWINE
JUICING
JULIANA
JUMPING
JUNKDNA
JUNKING
JURYING
JUSTINE
JUTLAND
JUTTING
KUCHENS
LUCERNE
LUCIANO
LUCKING
LUFFING
LUGGING
LULLING
LUMPING
LUNGING
LURKING
LUSTING
MUCKING
MUDHENS
MUFFING
MUFFINS
MUGGING
MULLING
MUMMING
MUMPING
MUNDANE
MUNTINS
MUSHING
MUSLINS
MUSSING
MUSTANG
MUTTONS
MUZZING
NUBBINS
NUBIANS
NUDGING
NULLING
NUMBING
NURSING
NUTTING
OUGHTNT
OURGANG
OUSTING
OUTDONE
OUTGUNS
OUTLAND
OUTLINE
OUTRANK
OUTRUNS
PUCCINI
PUDDING
PUFFING
PUFFINS
PULLING
PULLINS
PULLONS
PULSING
PUMPING
PUNGENT
PUNNING
PUNTING
PUPTENT
PURGING
PURLING
PURLINS
PURRING
PURSING
PUSHING
PUTTING
QUAKING
QUEUING
QUININE
QUOTING
RUBBING
RUCHING
RUCKING
RUINING
RUNNING
RUSHING
RUSTING
SUBBING
SUBORNS
SUBTEND
SUCKING
SUDSING
SUITING
SUKARNO
SULKING
SULTANA
SULTANS
SUMMING
SUMMONS
SUNNING
SUNTANS
SUPPING
SURFING
SURGING
SUSANNA
SUSANNE
SUSPEND
SUSSING
SUZANNE
TUCKING
TUFTING
TUGGING
TULSANS
TUMMING
TURBANS
TURBINE
TUREENS
TURNING
TUSCANY
VULCANS
VULPINE

•U••••N

AUCTION
AUDUBON
BUFFOON
BUILDIN
BUILTIN
BULLION
BULLPEN
BULLRUN
BUMPKIN
BURGEON
BURPGUN
BURSTYN
BUSHMAN
BUSHMEN
BUTTSIN
CURTAIN
CUSHION
CUTDOWN
DUCKPIN
DUDGEON
DUNGEON
DUSTBIN
DUSTMAN
DUSTMEN
DUSTPAN
FUSTIAN
HUSSEIN
JUMPSIN
JUMPSON
JUNKMAN
KUTCHIN
MUEZZIN
MULLEIN
MULLION
MUMESON
MUTAGEN
NUCLEON
OURTOWN
OUTWORN
PULLMAN
PULLSIN
PULLSON
PUMPKIN
PUNCHIN
PURITAN
PURLOIN
PUSHKIN
PUSHPIN
PUTAMEN
PUTDOWN
PUTUPON
QUENTIN
QUICKEN
QUIETEN
RUANDAN
RUBDOWN
RUBICON
RUBITIN
RUCTION
RUFFIAN
RULESON
RUNDOWN
RUSSIAN
SUASION
SUBJOIN
SUCKSIN
SUCTION
SUNBURN
SUNDOWN
SURGEON
SUSTAIN
TUCHMAN
TUCKSIN
TUITION
TUNEDIN
TUNESIN
TURNSIN
TURNSON
YUCATAN

••UN•••

ALUNSER
ASUNDER
BLUNDER
BLUNTED
BLUNTER
BLUNTLY
BOUNCED
BOUNCER
BOUNCES
BOUNDED
BOUNDER
BOUNDUP
BRUNETS
CHUNNEL
CHUNTER
CLUNKED
CLUNKER
COUNCIL
COUNSEL
COUNTED
COUNTER
COUNTON
COUNTRY
CRUNCHY
DAUNTED
FLUNKED
FOUNDED
FOUNDER
FOUNDRY
GAUNTER
GAUNTLY
GOUNDER
GRUNGES
GRUNION
GRUNTED
HAUNTED
HOUNDED
HYUNDAI
JAUNTED
JOUNCED
JOUNCES
LAUNDER
LAUNDRY
LOUNGED
LOUNGER
LOUNGES
MAUNDER
MOUNDED
MOUNTED
MOUNTIE
NYUNGAR
PAUNCHY
PLUNDER
PLUNGED
PLUNGER
PLUNGES
PLUNKED
POUNCED
POUNCER
POUNCES
POUNDED
POUNDER
PRUNERS
PRUNING
REUNIFY
REUNION
REUNITE
ROUNDED
ROUNDER
ROUNDLY
ROUNDON
ROUNDUP
SAUNTER
SHUNNED
SHUNTED
SKUNKED
SOUNDED
SOUNDER
SOUNDLY
SPUNOFF
SPUNOUT
STUNGUN
STUNNED
STUNNER
STUNTED
TAUNTED
THUNDER
TRUNDLE
TSUNAMI
VAUNTED
VAUNTER
WOUNDED
WOUNDUP
YOUNGER
YOUNGMC
YOUNGUN

••U•N••

ALUMNAE
ALUMNAL
ALUMNUS
AQUINAS
CHUNNEL
CHURNED
CHUTNEY
DIURNAL
EQUINES
EQUINOX
FLUENCY
IGUANAS
JOURNAL
JOURNEY
JOURNOS
MOURNED
SHUNNED
SPURNED
SPURNER
SPUTNIK
SQUANTO
SQUINCH
SQUINTS
SQUINTY
STUNNED
STUNNER
TOURNEY
TRUANCY
TRUANTS
YOUKNOW

••U••N•

ABUSING
ACUMENS
AMUSING
BLUEING
BOUSING
BRUXING
CAUSING
CLUEING
COULDNT
COUPONS
COURANT
COUSINS
DAUBING
DOUSING
EDUCING
ELUDING
ELUTING
ENURING
EXUDING
FEUDING
FLUTING
FLUXING
FOULING
GAUGING
GAUMING
GOUGING
HAULING
HOUDINI
HOUSING
INURING
LAUDING
LAURENT
LEUCINE
LOUSING
MAULING
MOUSING
MOUTONS
NEURONE
NEURONS
OPULENT
PAULINA
PAULINE
PAULING
PAUSING
PLUGINS
PLUMING
POULENC
POURING
POUTING
PRUDENT
PRUNING
REUBENS
ROUGING
ROUSING
ROUTINE
ROUTING
SHUTINS
SOURING
SOUTANE
SPUMING
SPUMONE
SPUMONI
STUDENT
TAURINE
TAUTENS
TEUTONS
TOUCANS
TOURING
TOUTING
TRUEING
ULULANT
WOULDNT
YAUPONS
YOUMANS

••U•••N

BLUEFIN
BLUSHON
BOURBON
CAUTION
CLUEDIN
CLUESIN
COUNTON
DAUPHIN
DRUMLIN
ELUTION
EXURBAN
GAUGUIN
GLUEDON
GLUESON
GLUTTON
GRUNION
HOUSMAN
HOUSTON
JOURDAN
KAUFMAN
KLUGMAN
LAUGHIN
MAUDLIN
MAULDIN
MAUREEN
MOUFLON
NEUTRON
PAULSEN
PLUGSIN
POURSIN
REUNION
ROUGHEN
ROUNDON
SAURIAN
SHUTSIN
SOUPCON
SPURSON
STUNGUN
THURMAN
TOUCHON
TOUGHEN
VAUGHAN
YOUNGUN

•••UN••

ABOUNDS
ADJUNCT
ALBUNDY
AMOUNTS
ATTUNED
ATTUNES
DEBUNKS
DEFUNCT
ENOUNCE
EXPUNGE
FLAUNTS
FLAUNTY
FLOUNCE
FLOUNCY
GERUNDS
GODUNOV
GROUNDS
HHMUNRO
JEJUNUM
KAHUNAS
KORUNAS
LACUNAE
LACUNAL
LACUNAS
LAGUNAS
OBTUNDS
PETUNIA
REFUNDS
RETUNED
RETUNES
ROTUNDA
SCRUNCH
STAUNCH
SUBUNIT
TRIUNES
TROUNCE
UNTUNED
UNTUNES
VICUNAS
YAOUNDE

•••U•N•

ARGUING
AUBURNS
AUTUMNS
BEGUINE
BYTURNS
CALUMNY
CEBUANO
COLUMNS
ENDUING
ENSUING
GENUINE
IMBUING
IMPUGNS
ISSUING
MINUEND
OPPUGNS
PADUANS
PAPUANS
PIQUANT
PIQUING
QUEUING
REPUGNS
RETURNS
SEQUINS
SIOUANS
TIJUANA
TOLUENE
UNGUENT
UPTURNS
VALUING

•••U••N

ACTUPON
ALBUMEN
ALBUMIN
AUDUBON
BITUMEN
BLOUSON
CERUMEN
CROUTON
INHUMAN
INSULIN
LETUPON
MCLUHAN
MCQUEEN
MENUHIN
PUTUPON
ROMULAN
SETUPON
STEUBEN
STOUTEN
WHAUDEN
ZEBULON

••••UN•

ACCOUNT
ACHTUNG
AGROUND
AIRGUNS
ASTOUND
BIGGUNS
CAPGUNS
COMMUNE
CYYOUNG
DRYRUNS
ENDRUNS
ENGLUND
EXPOUND
FORTUNA
FORTUNE
GOROUND
IMPOUND
INBOUND
JETGUNS
JOBHUNT
MANHUNT
NEPTUNE
OROTUND
OUTGUNS
OUTRUNS
POPGUNS
RAYGUNS
REBOUND
RECOUNT
REDOUND
REMOUNT
RESOUND
REWOUND
SAMSUNG
SHOGUNS
SIGMUND
SIXGUNS
SKIRUNS
SPELUNK
TERHUNE
TOPGUNS
TRIBUNE
UNAMUNO
UNBOUND
UNSOUND
UNWOUND
ZEITUNG

••••U•N

ADJOURN
BEDOUIN
CLIBURN
COGBURN
DONJUAN
GAUGUIN
HEPBURN
JOAQUIN
NOCTURN
PENGUIN
RAYBURN
SANJUAN
SICHUAN
SOJOURN
SUNBURN

•••••UN

BELAKUN
BLOWGUN
BULLRUN
BURPGUN
CALHOUN
ELAAIUN
FORERUN
HANDGUN
HOMERUN
LONGRUN
MILKRUN
MILLRUN
OVERRUN
POKEFUN
PRONOUN
SHOTGUN
STUNGUN
WELLRUN
YOUNGUN

U•O••••

UNOILED
USOPENS
USOSHOW
UTOPIAN
UTOPIAS
UXORIAL

U••O•••

UNBOLTS
UNBOUND
UNBOWED
UNBOXED
UNBOXES
UNCOILS
UNCORKS
UNCOUTH
UNCOVER
UNDOING
UNFOLDS
UNGODLY
UNHOOKS
UNHORSE
UNLOADS
UNLOCKS
UNLOOSE
UNLOVED
UNMOVED
UNROBED
UNROBES
UNROLLS
UNSOUND
UNWOUND
UNWOVEN
UNYOKED
UNYOKES
UNZONED
UPBORNE
UPHOLDS
UPLOADS
UPROARS
UPROOTS
UPTONOW
UPTOPAR

U•••O••

ULANOVA
UNAVOCE
UNBLOCK
UNCLOAK
UNCLOGS

UNCLOSE
UNFROCK
UNHOOKS
UNICORN
UNIFORM
UNIPODS
UNISONS
UNKNOTS
UNKNOWN
UNLOOSE
UNQUOTE
UNSHORN
UNSTOPS
UPCLOSE
UPFRONT
UPROOTS
UPSHOTS

U••••O•
ULYANOV
UNCTION
UPSILON
UPTONOW
USOSHOW
USTINOV

U•••••O
UCCELLO
UMBERTO
UNAMUNO
UNDERDO
UNDERGO
UPTEMPO
UTRILLO

•UO••••
BUOYANT
BUOYING
BUOYSUP
DUODENA
QUOKKAS
QUONSET
QUORUMS
QUOTERS
QUOTING
SUOJURE
SUOLOCO

•U•O•••
AUROCHS
AURORAE
AURORAL
AURORAS
AUTOMAT
BUCOLIC
BUROAKS
BUYOUTS
CULOTTE
CUPOLAS
CUTOFFS
CUTOUTS
DUGONGS
DUGOUTS
FURORES
HUMORED
HUMOURS
JUDOIST
OUTOFIT
PUTOUTS
PUTOVER
RUDOLPH
RUMORED
RUMOURS
RUNOFFS
RUNOUTS
RUNOVER
SUBORNS
TUTORED

•U••O••
AUREOLA
AUREOLE
AUTHORS
BUCKOES
BUFFOON
BUGSOFF
BUGSOUT
BULBOUS
BULLOCK
BUMSOUT
BUNCOED
BUNIONS
BUNKOED
BURBOTS
BURDOCK
BURGOOS
BURNOUT
BURROWS
BUSBOYS
BUSTOUT
BUTTONS
BUTTOUT
BUYSOFF
BUYSOUT
BUZZOFF
CUCKOOS
CUIBONO
CURIOUS
CURSORS
CURSORY
CUSTODY
CUSTOMS
CUTDOWN
CUTSOFF
CUTSOUT
DUBIOUS
DUNNOCK
DUSTOFF
DUTEOUS
EUPHONY
FUELOIL
FULSOME
FUNGOES
FURIOUS
FURLONG
FURROWS
GUIDONS
GUNBOAT
GUNDOGS
GUNLOCK
GUNMOLL
GUSTOES
HULLOAS
HULLOED
HUMMOCK
HUNGOUT
JUMPOFF
JUNCOES
JUNIORS
LUBBOCK
LUCKOUT
MUMFORD
MURDOCH
MUSCOVY
MUTTONS
OURTOWN
OUTCOME
OUTDOES
OUTDONE
OUTDOOR
OUTGOES
OUTLOOK
OUTLOUD
OUTPOLL
OUTPOST
OUTSOLD
OUTVOTE
OUTWORE
OUTWORK
OUTWORN
PUGNOSE
PULLOFF
PULLONS
PULLOUT
PURLOIN
PURPORT
PURPOSE
PUSHOFF
PUTDOWN
PUTSOFF
PUTSOUT
QUAHOGS
QUINOAS
QUIXOTE
RUBDOWN
RUBSOFF
RUBSOUT
RUINOUS
RULEOUT
RUMPOLE
RUNDOWN
RUNGOFF
RUNGOUT
RUNHOME
RUNSOFF
RUNSOUT
RUSHOFF
SUBJOIN
SUBROSA
SUBSOIL
SUBVOCE
SUCCORS
SUCCOUR
SUCROSE
SUFFOLK
SUITORS
SUMMONS
SUNBOWL
SUNDOGS
SUNDOWN
SUNGODS
SUNROOF
SUNROOM
SUOLOCO
SUPPORT
SUPPOSE
SURCOAT
TUGBOAT
TUNEOUT
TUNGOIL
TURBOTS
TURMOIL
TURNOFF
TURNOUT
TUSSOCK

•U•••O•
AUCTION
AUDITOR
AUDUBON
BUFFOON
BUGABOO
BUGALOO
BULLDOG
BULLION
BURGEON
BURGOOS
BUSHHOG
BUSSTOP
BUTANOL
CUCKOOS
CURATOR
CUSHION
DUDGEON
DUKEDOM
DUNGEON
DUSTMOP
FUELROD
FUSSPOT
GUMDROP
GUMSHOE
GUNSFOR
GUNSHOT
HUMIDOR
JUKEBOX
JUMPSON
JUSTNOW
LUBEJOB
MUGSHOT
MULLION
MUMESON
NUCLEON
NUNCIOS
OUTCROP
OUTDOOR
OUTFLOW
OUTGROW
OUTLOOK
PUEBLOS
PULLFOR
PULLSON
PUTUPON
QUANGOS
QUARTOS
RUBATOS
RUBICON
RUCTION
RULESON
RUNAMOK
RUNRIOT
RUNSFOR
SUASION
SUBPLOT
SUCTION
SUNROOF
SUNROOM
SUNSPOT
SURGEON
TUITION
TUPELOS
TURNSON
TUXEDOS
YULELOG

•U••••O
BUFFALO
BUGABOO
BUGALOO
BURRITO
BUSHIDO
CUIBONO
CURACAO
CUTINTO
DURANGO
GUANACO
LUCIANO
LUMBAGO
MURILLO
PUTITTO
RUNINTO
SUBZERO
SUHARTO
SUKARNO
SUOLOCO
SUPREMO
TURNSTO

••U•O••
AQUEOUS
BOUDOIR
COULOMB
COUPONS
ELUSORY
FOULOUT
GLUCOSE
HAULOFF
MAUROIS
MOUTONS
NEURONE
NEURONS
POUROUT
RAUCOUS
SHUTOFF
SHUTOUT
SOUKOUS
SPUMONE
SPUMONI
SPUMOUS
SPUNOFF
SPUNOUT
STUPORS
TEUTONS
YAUPONS

••U••O•
BLUEBOY
BLUEFOX
BLUSHON
BOURBON
BOUTROS
CAUTION
COUNTON
ECUADOR
ELUTION
EQUATOR
EQUINOX
FLUMMOX
GAUCHOS
GLUEDON
GLUESON
GLUTTON
GRUNION
HAUTBOY
HOUSTON
JOURNOS
MOUFLON
NEUTRON
PEUGEOT
PRUDHOE
REUNION
ROUNDON
SOUPCON
SPURSON
SQUALOR
STUCCOS
STUDIOS
TOUCHON
YOUKNOW

••U•••O
CRUSADO
CRUZADO
DEUTERO
SFUMATO
SQUANTO
STUCKTO
TOURACO

•••UO••
ARDUOUS
FATUOUS
LIQUORS
NOCUOUS
PEQUOTS
SEQUOIA
SINUOUS
TENUOUS
UNQUOTE
VACUOLE
VACUOUS

•••U•O•
ACTUPON
AUDUBON
BLOUSON
CROUTON
ENDUROS
ESCUDOS
GODUNOV
LETUPON
PUTUPON
SENUFOS
SETUPON
ZEBULON

•••U••O
ADDUPTO
CEBUANO
CLAUDIO
COLUMBO
GROUCHO
HHMUNRO
LEDUPTO
SAGUARO
VAQUERO

••••UO•
LANGUOR

••••U•O
TESTUDO
UNAMUNO
VERDUGO

•••••UO
INVACUO

UP•••••
UPATREE
UPBEATS
UPBORNE
UPBRAID
UPCLOSE
UPDATED
UPDATES
UPDRAFT
UPENDED
UPFRONT
UPGRADE
UPHOLDS
UPLANDS
UPLIFTS
UPLINKS
UPLOADS
UPPSALA
UPQUARK
UPRAISE
UPRIGHT
UPRISEN
UPRISES
UPRIVER
UPROARS
UPROOTS
UPSCALE
UPSHOTS
UPSILON
UPSTAGE
UPSTART
UPSTATE
UPSURGE
UPSWEEP
UPSWEPT
UPSWING
UPTAKES
UPTEMPO
UPTICKS
UPTIGHT
UPTONOW
UPTOPAR
UPTURNS
UPWARDS

U•P••••
UMPIRED
UMPIRES
UMPTEEN
UNPACKS
UNPAVED
UNPILED
UNPILES
UNPLUGS
UPPSALA

U••P•••
UNAPTLY
UNIPODS
UNSPENT
USOPENS
UTOPIAN
UTOPIAS

U•••P••
UNHAPPY
UNTAPED
UPTOPAR
USURPED
USURPER

U••••P•
UNDRAPE
UNHAPPY
UNKEMPT
UNSNAPS
UNSTOPS
UNSWEPT
UNTRAPS
UNWRAPS
UPSWEPT
UPTEMPO

U•••••P
UNCLASP
UNSTRAP
UPSWEEP
USINGUP

•UP••••
AUPAIRS
CUPCAKE
CUPFULS
CUPLIKE
CUPOLAS
CUPPING
EUPHONY
GUPPIES
JUPITER
LUPINES
MUPPETS
NUPTIAL
PUPPETS
PUPPIES
PUPTENT
RUPIAHS
RUPTURE
SUPPERS
SUPPING
SUPPLER
SUPPORT
SUPPOSE
SUPREME
SUPREMO
TUPELOS
YUPPIES

•U•P•••
AUSPICE
BUMPERS
BUMPIER
BUMPILY
BUMPING
BUMPKIN
BUMPSUP
BURPGUN
BURPING
CULPRIT
CUPPING
CUSPIDS
DUMPIER
DUMPING
DUMPISH
GULPIER
GULPING
GUNPLAY
GUPPIES
HUMPIER
JUMPCUT
JUMPERS
JUMPIER
JUMPILY
JUMPING
JUMPOFF
JUMPSAT
JUMPSIN
JUMPSON
JUMPSUP
KUSPUKS
LUMPERS
LUMPIER
LUMPILY
LUMPING
LUMPISH
LUMPSUM
MUDPACK
MUDPIES
MUMPING
MUPPETS
OUTPACE
OUTPLAY
OUTPOLL
OUTPOST
OUTPUTS
PULPIER
PULPITS
PUMPERS
PUMPING
PUMPKIN
PUMPSUP
PUPPETS
PUPPIES
PURPLED
PURPLES
PURPORT
PURPOSE
PUTPUTS
QUIPPED
QUIPPER
RUMPLED
RUMPLES
RUMPOLE
SUBPLOT
SULPHUR
SUPPERS
SUPPING
SUPPLER
SUPPORT
SUPPOSE
SURPASS
SURPLUS
SUSPECT
SUSPEND
VULPINE
YUPPIES

•U••P••
BULLPEN
BUSHPIG
DUCKPIN
DUSTPAN
FUSSPOT
GUELPHS
GUIMPES
JUNIPER
PUSHPIN
PUTUPON
QUIPPED
QUIPPER
SUNSPOT

•U•••P•
BUMRAPS
BUNYIPS
BURLAPS
DUSTUPS
EUTERPE
HUBCAPS
PULLUPS
PUSHUPS
RUDOLPH
TUNEUPS
TURNIPS

•U••••P
BUCKSUP
BUDDYUP
BUILDUP
BUILTUP
BUMPSUP
BUOYSUP
BURNSUP
BURNTUP
BUSSTOP
CURLSUP
DUDEDUP
DUMMYUP
DUSTMOP
GUMDROP
GUSSYUP
HURRYUP
JUICEUP
JUMPSUP
MUCKSUP
MUGWUMP
OUTCROP
OUTJUMP
OUTSTEP
PULLSUP
PUMPSUP
PUNCHUP
QUEUEUP
RUNDEEP
SUITSUP
SUNLAMP
TUNEDUP
TUNESUP
TURNSUP

••UP•••
COUPLED
COUPLES
COUPLET
COUPONS
DAUPHIN
ERUPTED
EXUPERY
PAUPERS
REUPPED
SCUPPER
SOUPCON
SOUPIER
SOUPSUP
STUPEFY
STUPORS
TOUPEES
WHUPPED
YAUPONS

••U•P••
CLUMPED
CRUMPET
CRUMPLE
CRUMPLY
FAUXPAS
GRUMPED
PLUMPED
PLUMPER
PLUMPLY
REUPPED
SCULPTS
SCUPPER
SLUMPED
SLURPED
STUMPED
STUMPER
THUMPED
THUMPER
TRUMPED
TRUMPET
TRUMPUP
USURPED
USURPER
WHUPPED

••U••P•
FOULUPS

••U•••P
BOUNDUP
BRUSHUP
COUGHUP
DRUMSUP
FOULSUP
FOULTIP
HAULSUP
LOUSEUP
ROUGHUP
ROUNDUP
SHUTSUP
SOUPSUP
STUCKUP
TOUCHUP
TRUMPUP
WOUNDUP

•••UP••
ACTUPON
ADDUPTO
GROUPED
GROUPER
GROUPIE
IRRUPTS
LEDUPTO
LETUPON
OCTUPLE
PUTUPON
SCRUPLE
SETUPON
TROUPER
TROUPES

•••U•P•
GALUMPH
GAZUMPS
TRIUMPH

•••U••P
QUEUEUP
SCRUBUP

••••UP•
BACKUPS
BLOWUPS
CHINUPS
CORRUPT
DISRUPT
DUSTUPS
EGGCUPS
EYECUPS
FILLUPS
FLIPUPS
FOLDUPS
FOULUPS
GIVEUPS
GOOFUPS
HANGUPS
HICCUPS
HOLDUPS
HOOKUPS
KICKUPS
LARRUPS
LASHUPS
LINEUPS
LINKUPS
LOCKUPS
LOOKUPS
MAKEUPS
MARKUPS
MOCKUPS
PICKUPS
PILEUPS
PRENUPS
PULLUPS
PUSHUPS
RAVEUPS
RECOUPS
SENDUPS
SLIPUPS
SLOWUPS
STEPUPS
TEACUPS
TITTUPS
TOSSUPS
TUNEUPS
WALKUPS
WARMUPS
WASHUPS
WINDUPS
WORKUPS
WRAPUPS

••••U•P
AIRPUMP
GASPUMP
MUGWUMP
NOTRUMP
OUTJUMP
SKIJUMP

•••••UP
ACTEDUP
ADDEDUP
ANTEDUP
ANTESUP
BACKSUP
BALLSUP
BANGSUP
BEADSUP
BEAMSUP
BEARSUP
BEATSUP
BEEFSUP
BELLYUP
BINDSUP
BLOWNUP
BLOWSUP
BONEDUP
BONESUP
BOOSTUP
BOOTSUP
BORNEUP
BOTCHUP
BOUNDUP
BOXEDUP
BOXESUP
BRACEUP
BREAKUP
BRINGUP
BROKEUP
BRUSHUP
BUCKSUP
BUDDYUP
BUILDUP
BUILTUP
BUMPSUP
BUOYSUP
BURNSUP
BURNTUP
CALLSUP
CATCHUP
CHALKUP
CHATSUP
CHECKUP
CHEERUP
CHEWSUP
CHOKEUP
CLAMSUP
CLEANUP
CLEARUP
CLOGSUP
CLOSEUP
COILSUP
COMESUP
COOKSUP
COOPSUP
COUGHUP
COVERUP
CRACKUP
CRANKUP
CREEPUP
CROPSUP
CROSSUP
CURLSUP
DOINGUP
DOLLSUP
DRAWNUP
DRAWSUP
DREAMUP
DRESSUP
DRIEDUP
DRIESUP
DRIVEUP
DRUMSUP
DUDEDUP
DUMMYUP
EASEDUP
EASESUP
EATENUP
ENDEDUP
EVENSUP
FAIRSUP
FILLSUP
FIREDUP
FIRESUP
FIRMSUP
FIXEDUP
FIXESUP
FLAREUP
FOLDSUP
FOULSUP
FRAMEUP
GANGSUP
GEARSUP
GIDDYUP
GIVENUP
GIVESUP
GOINGUP
GOOFSUP
GROWNUP
GROWSUP
GUSSYUP
HAMITUP
HANDSUP
HANGSUP
HAULSUP
HEADSUP
HEATSUP
HIKEDUP
HIKESUP
HOLDSUP
HOLEDUP
HOLESUP
HOOKSUP
HURRYUP
HYPEDUP
HYPESUP
ICINGUP
IGIVEUP
INGROUP
JACKSUP
JOINSUP
JUICEUP
JUMPSUP
KEEPSUP
KETCHUP
KEYEDUP
KICKSUP
KNEESUP
LACEDUP
LACESUP
LEADSUP
LIFTSUP
LIGHTUP
LINEDUP
LINESUP
LOCKSUP
LOOKSUP
LOUSEUP
MAKESUP
MARKSUP
MATCHUP
MIXEDUP
MIXESUP
MIXITUP
MOVEDUP
MOVESUP
MUCKSUP
OPENSUP
OWNEDUP
PACKSUP
PAIRSUP
PASTEUP
PATCHUP
PEASOUP
PERKSUP
PICKSUP
PILEDUP
PILESUP
PIPEDUP
PIPESUP
PLAYSUP
PRESSUP
PROPSUP
PSYCHUP
PULLSUP
PUMPSUP
PUNCHUP
QUEUEUP
RACKSUP
RAISEUP
RAKEDUP
RAKESUP
REARSUP
REGROUP
RESTSUP
RILESUP
RINGSUP
ROLLSUP
ROUGHUP
ROUNDUP
SAVEDUP
SAVESUP
SCAREUP
SCREWUP
SCRUBUP
SEALSUP
SENDSUP
SERVEUP
SEVENUP
SEWEDUP
SHAKEUP
SHAPEUP
SHOOKUP
SHOOTUP
SHOWSUP
SHUTSUP

SIGNSUP
SIZEDUP
SIZESUP
SLIPSUP
SLOWSUP
SMASHUP
SNAPSUP
SOAKSUP
SOUPSUP
SPEAKUP
SPEEDUP
SPICEUP
SPLITUP
SPOKEUP
STACKUP
STANDUP
STARTUP
STAYSUP
STEPSUP
STICKUP
STIRRUP
STIRSUP
STOCKUP
STOODUP
STOPSUP
STOREUP
STUCKUP
SUITSUP
SWEEPUP
SWELLUP
SWEPTUP
TAKESUP
TALKSUP
TALLYUP
TANKSUP
TEAMSUP
TEARSUP
TENSEUP
THINKUP
TIMESUP
TONEDUP
TONESUP
TOOLSUP
TOUCHUP
TRADEUP
TRIPSUP
TRUMPUP
TUNEDUP
TUNESUP
TURNSUP
TYINGUP
TYPEDUP
TYPESUP
USINGUP
WAITSUP
WAKESUP
WALLSUP
WARMSUP
WELLSUP
WHIPSUP
WICKIUP
WINDSUP
WIPEDUP
WIPESUP
WISEDUP
WISESUP
WOKENUP
WORKSUP
WOUNDUP
WRAPSUP
WRITEUP
WROTEUP

U•Q••••

UNQUOTE
UPQUARK

U••Q•••

UNEQUAL

•U•Q•••

KUMQUAT
PULQUES

•U••Q••

DUBUQUE
QUINQUE

••UQ•••

BOUQUET

••U•Q••

BRUSQUE

•••UQ••

DUBUQUE

UR•••••

URANITE
URANIUM
URBANER
URCHINS
URGENCY
URNLIKE
URTEXTS
URUGUAY

U•R••••

UKRAINE
UNRATED
UNRAVEL
UNREADY
UNREELS
UNROBED
UNROBES
UNROLLS
UPRAISE
UPRIGHT
UPRISEN
UPRISES
UPRIVER
UPROARS
UPROOTS
UTRECHT
UTRILLO

U••R•••

UMBRAGE
UMBRIAN
UNARMED
UNCRATE
UNDRAPE
UNDRAWN
UNDRESS
UNFROCK
UNTRAPS
UNTRIED
UNTRUTH
UNWRAPS
UPBRAID
UPDRAFT
UPFRONT
UPGRADE
USERIDS
USGRANT
USURERS
USURIES
USURPED
USURPER
UXORIAL

U•••R••

UMBERTO
UMPIRED
UMPIRES
UNAIRED
UNCORKS
UNCURLS
UNDERDO
UNDERGO
UNEARTH
UNFURLS
UNGIRDS
UNHORSE
UNNERVE
UNSCREW
UNSTRAP
UPATREE
UPBORNE
UPSURGE
UPTURNS
UPWARDS
USHERED
UTTERED
UTTERER
UTTERLY

U••••R•

ULSTERS
UNAWARE
UNHEARD
UNICORN
UNIFORM
UNITARY
UNITERS
UNLEARN
UNSHORN
UNSNARL
UPQUARK
UPROARS
UPSTART
USURERS

U•••••R

UNCLEAR
UNCOVER
UNIFIER
UNWISER
UPRIVER
UPTOPAR
URBANER
USURPER
UTTERER

•UR••••

AURALEE
AURALLY
AUREATE
AUREOLA
AUREOLE
AURICLE
AUROCHS
AURORAE
AURORAL
AURORAS
BURBANK
BURBLED
BURBLES
BURBOTS
BURDENS
BURDOCK
BUREAUS
BURETTE
BURGEES
BURGEON
BURGERS
BURGESS
BURGHER
BURGLAR
BURGLED
BURGLES
BURGOOS
BURKINA
BURLAPS
BURLIER
BURLING
BURMANS
BURMESE
BURNERS
BURNETT
BURNING
BURNISH
BURNOUT
BURNSUP
BURNTUP
BUROAKS
BURPGUN
BURPING
BURRITO
BURROWS
BURSARS
BURSARY
BURSTYN
BURYING
CURACAO
CURATES
CURATOR
CURBCUT
CURBING
CURDIER
CURDING
CURDLED
CURDLES
CUREALL
CURFEWS
CURIOUS
CURLERS
CURLEWS
CURLIER
CURLIKE
CURLING
CURLSUP
CURRANT
CURRENT
CURRIED
CURRIER
CURRIES
CURRISH
CURSING
CURSIVE
CURSORS
CURSORY
CURTAIL
CURTAIN
CURTEST
CURTISS
CURTSEY
CURVETS
CURVIER
CURVING
DURABLE
DURABLY
DURANCE
DURANGO
DURANTE
DURNING
DURRELL
EURASIA
FURBALL
FURBISH
FURIOUS
FURLESS
FURLING
FURLONG
FURNACE
FURNISH
FURORES
FURRIER
FURRING
FURROWS
FURSEAL
FURTHER
FURTIVE
GURGLED
GURGLES
GURKHAS
GURNEYS
HURDLED
HURDLER
HURDLES
HURLERS
HURLEYS
HURLIES
HURLING
HURRAHS
HURRIED
HURRIES
HURRYUP
HURTFUL
HURTING
HURTLED
HURTLES
JURIDIC
JURISTS
JURYING
JURYRIG
KURDISH
LURCHED
LURCHES
LURIDLY
LURKING
MURDERS
MURDOCH
MURILLO
MURKIER
MURKILY
MURMURS
NUREYEV
NURSERS
NURSERY
NURSING
NURTURE
OURGANG
OURSELF
OURTOWN
PURCELL
PURDAHS
PURFLED
PURFLES
PURGING
PURISTS
PURITAN
PURLIEU
PURLING
PURLINS
PURLOIN
PURPLED
PURPLES
PURPORT
PURPOSE
PURRERS
PURRING
PURSERS
PURSIER
PURSING
PURSUED
PURSUER
PURSUES
PURSUIT
PURVEYS
PURVIEW
RURALLY
SURCOAT
SURFACE
SURFEIT
SURFERS
SURFIER
SURFING
SURGEON
SURGERY
SURGING
SURINAM
SURLIER
SURLILY
SURMISE
SURNAME
SURPASS
SURPLUS
SURREAL
SURREYS
SURTSEY
SURVEYS
SURVIVE
TURBANS
TURBINE
TURBITS
TURBOTS
TUREENS
TURFIER
TURFWAR
TURKEYS
TURKISH
TURMOIL
TURNERS
TURNERY
TURNING
TURNIPS
TURNKEY
TURNOFF
TURNOUT
TURNSIN
TURNSON
TURNSTO
TURNSUP
TURRETS
TURTLED
TURTLES
WURLEYS

•U•R•••

BULRUSH
BUMRAPS
BUMRUSH
BURRITO
BURROWS
CUIRASS
CURRANT
CURRENT
CURRIED
CURRIER
CURRIES
CURRISH
CUTRATE
DURRELL
FURRIER
FURRING
FURROWS
GUARANI
GUARDED
GUARDEE
GUARGUM
HURRAHS
HURRIED
HURRIES
HURRYUP
KUBRICK
NUTRIAS
OUTRACE
OUTRAGE
OUTRANK
OUTRUNS
PUERILE
PUGREES
PURRERS
PURRING
QUARREL
QUARTER
QUARTET
QUARTOS
QUERIED
QUERIER
QUERIES
QUERIST
QUORUMS
RUBRICS
RUNRIOT
SUBROSA
SUCRASE
SUCROSE
SUNRAYS
SUNRISE
SUNROOF
SUNROOM
SUPREME
SUPREMO
SURREAL
SURREYS
TUAREGS
TUGRIKS
TURRETS

•U••R••

AUBURNS
AUGURAL
AUGURED
AURORAE
AURORAL
AURORAS
AUSTRAL
AUSTRIA
AUTARKY
BUCKRAM
BUGFREE
BULLRUN
CULPRIT
DUBARRY
EUCHRED
EUCHRES
EUTERPE
FUELROD
FULCRUM
FURORES
FUTURES
GUMDROP
GUMTREE
GUTHRIE
HUMDRUM
HUMERAL
HUMERUS
HUMORED
HUNDRED
JURYRIG
LUCERNE
LUSTRED
LUSTRES
MUBARAK
MUSKRAT
NUMERAL
NUMERIC
OUTCROP
OUTDRAW
OUTDREW
OUTGREW
OUTGROW
PUBERTY
QUARREL
QUEERED
QUEERER
QUEERLY
RUMORED
SUBORNS
SUBURBS
SUGARED
SUHARTO
SUKARNO
SUTURED
SUTURES
TUMBREL
TUNDRAS
TUTORED

•U•••R•

AUPAIRS
AUSTERE
AUTEURS
AUTHORS
BUFFERS
BUGLERS
BULGARS
BULWARK
BUMMERS
BUMPERS
BUNKERS
BURGERS
BURNERS
BURSARS
BURSARY
BUSFARE
BUSGIRL
BUSTARD
BUSTERS
BUTLERS
BUTTERS
BUTTERY
BUZZARD
BUZZERS
CUECARD
CULEBRA
CULLERS
CULTURE
CULVERS
CULVERT
CURLERS
CURSORS
CURSORY
CUSTARD
CUTLERS
CUTLERY
CUTTERS
DUBARRY
DUBBERS
DUELERS
DUFFERS
DULLARD
DUNKERS
DUNKIRK
DUSTERS
FUELERS
GUEVARA
GUITARS
GUNFIRE
GUNNERS
GUNNERY
GUSHERS
GUTTERS
HUBBARD
HUGGERS
HULLERS
HUMMERS
HUMOURS
HUNGARY
HUNGERS
HUNKERS
HUNTERS
HURLERS
HUSKERS
HUSSARS
JUDDERS
JUICERS
JUMPERS
JUNIORS
JUNKART
JUNKERS
LUBBERS
LUGGERS
LUMBARS
LUMBERS
LUMIERE
LUMPERS
LUNKERS
LUSTERS
MUDDERS
MUGGERS
MULLERS
MUMFORD
MUMMERS
MUMMERY
MURDERS
MURMURS
MUSHERS
MUSTARD
MUSTERS
MUTTERS
NUDGERS
NUMBERS
NUNNERY
NURSERS
NURSERY
NURTURE
NUTTERS
OUSTERS
OUTWARD
OUTWORE
OUTWORK
OUTWORN
PUCKERS
PUFFERS
PUFFERY
PULSARS
PUMPERS
PUNKERS
PUNTERS
PURPORT
PURRERS
PURSERS
PUTTERS
QUAKERS
QUASARS
QUAVERS
QUAVERY
QUEUERS
QUINARY
QUIVERS
QUIVERY
QUOTERS
RUBBERS
RUBBERY
RUDDERS
RUDYARD
RUINERS
RUMOURS
RUNNERS
RUNSDRY
RUPTURE
RUSHERS
RUTGERS
SUBVERT
SUBZERO
SUCCORS
SUCKERS
SUDBURY
SUFFERS
SUITORS
SULKERS
SUMATRA
SUMMARY
SUMMERS
SUMMERY
SUNBURN
SUNDERS
SUOJURE
SUPPERS
SUPPORT
SURFERS
SURGERY
SUTLERS
SUTTERS
TUCKERS
TUGGERS
TURNERS
TURNERY
TUSKERS
VULTURE

•U••••R

AUDITOR
BUCKLER
BUGBEAR
BUGGIER
BUILDER
BULGHUR
BULGIER
BULKIER
BUMBLER
BUMPIER
BUNGLER
BURGHER
BURGLAR
BURLIER
BUSHIER
BUTCHER
CURATOR
CURDIER
CURLIER
CURRIER
CURVIER
CUSHIER
CUSSLER
DUCKIER
DUMPIER
DUSKIER
DUSTIER
FUBSIER
FUMBLER
FUNFAIR
FUNKIER
FUNNIER
FURRIER
FURTHER
FUSSIER
FUSTIER
FUZZIER
GUESSER
GUILDER
GULPIER
GUMMIER
GUNKIER
GUNSFOR
GUNTHER
GUSHIER
GUSTIER
GUTSIER
GUTTIER
GUZZLER
HUFFIER
HUMBLER
HUMIDOR
HUMPIER
HUNKIER
HURDLER
HUSKIER
HUSTLER
JUGGLER
JUGULAR
JUICIER
JUMPIER
JUNIPER
JUNKIER
JUPITER
LUCIFER
LUCKIER
LUMPIER
LUSTIER
MUAMMAR
MUCKIER
MUDDIER
MUDDLER
MUFFLER
MUGGIER
MUMBLER
MUNCHER
MURKIER
MUSHIER
MUSKIER
MUSSIER
MUSTIER
MUZZIER
NUBBIER
NUCLEAR
NUTSIER
NUTTIER
NUZZLER
OUTDOOR
OUTWEAR
PUDGIER
PUFFIER
PULLFOR
PULPIER
PUNCHER
PUNKIER
PUNNIER
PUNSTER
PURSIER
PURSUER
PUSHIER
PUTOVER
PUZZLER
QUAFFER
QUAKIER
QUARTER
QUEERER
QUERIER
QUICKER
QUIETER
QUILLER
QUILTER
QUIPPER
QUITTER
RUDDIER
RUMMIER
RUNNIER
RUNOVER
RUNSFOR
RUNTIER
RUSHIER
RUSTIER
RUSTLER
RUTTIER
SUBDUER
SUBTLER
SUCCOUR
SUDSIER
SULKIER
SULPHUR
SUNNIER
SUPPLER
SURFIER
SURLIER
TUBBIER
TUBULAR
TUFTIER
TUMBLER
TURFIER
TURFWAR
TUTELAR
YUCKIER
YUMMIER

••UR•••

AZURITE
BLURRED
BLURTED
BOURBON
BOURREE
BOURSES
CHURNED
COURAGE
COURANT
COURIER
COURSED
COURSER
COURSES
COURTED
COURTLY
DHURRIE
DIURNAL
DOUREST
ENURING
EXURBAN
EXURBIA
FOURIER
FOURTHS
FOURWAY
GOURAMI
GOURDES
GOURMET
INURING
JOURDAN
JOURNAL
JOURNEY
JOURNOS
KNURLED
LAURELS
LAURENT
LOURDES
MAUREEN
MAURICE
MAUROIS
MOURNED
NEURONE
NEURONS
NOURISH
PLURALS
POURERS
POURING
POUROUT
POURSIN
SAURIAN
SCURVES
SLURPED
SLURRED
SOURCED
SOURCES
SOUREST
SOURING
SOURISH
SPURNED
SPURNER
SPURRED
SPURSON
SPURTED
STURGES
TAURINE
THURBER
THURMAN
TOURACO
TOURERS
TOURING
TOURISM
TOURIST
TOURNEY
USURERS
USURIES
USURPED
USURPER

••U•R••

AQUARIA
BLURRED
BOURREE
BOUTROS
DHURRIE
EQUERRY
LAUTREC
LOUVRED
LOUVRES
NEUTRAL
NEUTRON
OEUVRES
SLURRED
SPURRED
SQUARED
SQUARER
SQUARES
SQUIRED
SQUIRES
SQUIRMS
SQUIRMY
SQUIRTS

••U••R•

ABUSERS
COUGARS
COUNTRY
COUTURE
DAUBERS
DEUTERO
ELUSORY
EQUERRY
EXUPERY
FOULARD
FOUNDRY
GAUGERS
GOUGERS
GRUYERE
HAUBERK
HAULERS
LAUNDRY
LOUVERS
MOUSERS
PAUPERS
POULTRY
POURERS
POUTERS
PRUDERY
PRUNERS
REUTERS
RHUBARB
ROUSERS
ROUTERS
SAUCERS
SHUBERT
STUMERS
STUPORS
TOURERS
TOUTERS
USURERS

••U•••R

ABUBAKR
ALUNSER
AQUIFER
AQUIVER
ASUNDER
BLUBBER
BLUFFER
BLUNDER
BLUNTER
BLUSHER
BLUSTER
BOUDOIR
BOULDER
BOUNCER
BOUNDER
BRUISER
CAULKER
CHUKKER
CHUNTER
CLUBCAR
CLUNKER
CLUSTER
CLUTTER
COULTER
COUNTER
COURIER
COURSER
CRUELER
CRUISER
CRULLER
CRUSHER
DAUMIER
DOUBTER
DRUCKER
DRUMMER

ECUADOR
EQUATOR
FLUBBER
FLUKIER
FLUSTER
FLUTIER
FLUTTER
FNUMBER
FOUNDER
FOURIER
GAUCHER
GAUDIER
GAUNTER
GAUZIER
GLUMMER
GOUNDER
GOUTIER
GRUFFER
HAUTEUR
JOUSTER
LAUGHER
LAUNDER
LOUNGER
LOUSIER
MAUNDER
MOULDER
MOUSIER
NYUNGAR
PLUGGER
PLUMBER
PLUMIER
PLUMMER
PLUMPER
PLUNDER
PLUNGER
PLUSHER
POUNCER
POUNDER
POUTIER
REUTHER
ROUGHER
ROUNDER
SAUCIER
SAUNTER
SCULLER
SCUPPER
SHUCKER
SHUDDER
SHUTTER
SKULKER
SLUGGER
SLUMBER
SMUGGER
SNUFFER
SNUGGER
SOUNDER
SOUPIER
SPUMIER
SPURNER
SPUTTER
SQUALOR
SQUARER
STUFFER
STUMPER
STUNNER
THUMPER
THUNDER
THURBER
THUSFAR
TOUGHER
TRUCKER
TRUDGER
USURPER
VAULTER
VAUNTER
VOUCHER
YOUNGER

•••UR••

ABJURED
ABJURES
ACCURST
ADJURED
ADJURES
ALLURED
ALLURES
ARMURES
ASSURED
ASSURES
AUBURNS
AUGURAL
AUGURED
BYTURNS
CONURES
DEMURER
ENDURED
ENDURES
ENDUROS
ENSURED
ENSURES
ETRURIA
FIGURED
FIGURER
FIGURES
FLOURED
FUTURES
IMMURED
IMMURES
IMPURER
INJURED
INJURES
INSURED
INSURER
INSURES
LITURGY
MATURED
MATURER
MATURES
MAZURKA
NATURAL
NATURED
NATURES
OROURKE
PANURGE
PARURES
RESURGE
RETURNS
SAMURAI
SCOURED
SCOURER
SCOURGE
SECURED
SECURER
SECURES
SPLURGE
SUBURBS
SUTURED
SUTURES
TENURED
TENURES
THEURGY
TSOURIS
UNCURLS
UNFURLS
UPSURGE
UPTURNS
YOGURTS
ZYMURGY

•••U•R•

ACQUIRE
ACTUARY
ARGUERS
EDOUARD
ENQUIRE
ENQUIRY
ESQUIRE
ESTUARY
HHMUNRO
INQUIRE
INQUIRY
ISSUERS
JAGUARS
JANUARY
LIQUORS
MAGUIRE
MCGUIRE
ONGUARD
QUEUERS
REQUIRE
ROGUERY
SAGUARO
TSQUARE
UPQUARK
VAQUERO

•••U••R

ACCUSER
ANGULAR
ANNULAR
CHAUCER
DEMURER
DILUTER
ENDUSER
FIGURER
GROUPER
GROUSER
IMPURER
INDUCER
INSULAR
INSURER
JOCULAR
JUGULAR
LIQUEUR
MATURER
MODULAR
NEBULAR
NODULAR
NONUSER
OBTUSER
PERUSER
POPULAR
PROUDER
REDUCER
REFUSER
REFUTER
REGULAR
SCOURER
SCOUTER
SECULAR
SECURER
SEDUCER
SHOUTER
SPOUTER
SPRUCER
STOUTER
TABULAR
TITULAR
TROUPER
TROUSER
TUBULAR

••••UR•

ADJOURN
ARAFURA
ARBOURS
ARDOURS
ARMOURS
ARMOURY
ASHBURY
ATATURK
AUTEURS
BRAVURA
CADBURY
CAESURA
CAPTURE
CENSURE
CENTURY
CLIBURN
CLOSURE
CLOTURE
COGBURN
COLOURS
CONCURS
CONJURE
COUTURE
CULTURE
DANBURY
DASYURE
DENTURE
DETOURS
DEVOURS
DISTURB
DOLOURS
EPICURE
ERASURE
FAILURE
FAVOURS
FEATURE
FISSURE
FIXTURE
FORSURE
GESTURE
GRAVURE
HAMBURG
HARBURG
HEPBURN
HOMBURG
HONOURS
HUMOURS
LABOURS
LANGURS
LECTURE
LEISURE
MAJEURE
MCCLURE
MEASURE
MERCURY
MIXTURE
MURMURS
NETSURF
NOCTURN
NOTSURE
NURTURE
OBSCURE
PASTURE
PERJURE
PERJURY
PERTURB
PICTURE
PINCURL
POSEURS
POSTURE
PROCURE
RAPTURE
RAYBURN
RETOURS
RIGOURS
RUMOURS
RUPTURE
SAVOURS
SAVOURY
SOJOURN
STATURE
SUDBURY
SUNBURN
SUOJURE
TEMPURA
TEXTURE
TONSURE
VALOURS
VAPOURS
VELOURS
VENTURA
VENTURE
VERDURE
VESTURE
VIGOURS
VULTURE
YOGHURT

••••U•R

CHEQUER
CONQUER
LACQUER
LANGUOR
NIEBUHR
PURSUER
RESCUER
SUBDUER

•••••UR

ACTFOUR
AMATEUR
BALFOUR
BONJOUR
BULGHUR
CANDOUR
CENTAUR
CLAMOUR
CONTOUR
DANSEUR
DECATUR
ENAMOUR
FAKEFUR
FERVOUR
FLANEUR
FLAVOUR
GLAMOUR
HARBOUR
HAUTEUR
HOTSPUR
LIQUEUR
MANHOUR
MASSEUR
OFFHOUR
PARLOUR
PASTEUR
PAVIOUR
RANCOUR
REOCCUR
SAVIOUR
SEYMOUR
SUCCOUR
SULPHUR
TAMBOUR
TENFOUR

US•••••

USEABLE
USELESS
USERIDS
USGRANT
USHERED
USINGUP
USOPENS
USOSHOW
USSTEEL
USTINOV
USUALLY
USURERS
USURIES
USURPED
USURPER

U•S••••

ULSTERS
UNSATED
UNSCREW
UNSEALS
UNSEATS
UNSEWED
UNSHORN
UNSNAGS
UNSNAPS
UNSNARL
UNSOUND
UNSPENT
UNSTACK
UNSTICK
UNSTOPS
UNSTRAP
UNSTUCK
UNSWEPT
UPSCALE
UPSHOTS
UPSILON
UPSTAGE
UPSTART
UPSTATE
UPSURGE
UPSWEEP
UPSWEPT
UPSWING
USSTEEL

U••S•••

ULYSSES
UNASKED
UNISONS
UNUSUAL
UPPSALA
USOSHOW

U•••S••

ULYSSES
UNCASED
UNCASES
UNMASKS
UNWISER
UPRISEN
UPRISES
UTENSIL

U••••S•

UGLIEST
UNBLEST
UNCLASP
UNCLOSE
UNDRESS
UNHORSE
UNLEASH
UNLOOSE
UNTWIST
UPCLOSE
UPRAISE
USELESS
UTILISE

U•••••S

ULSTERS
ULTIMAS
ULYSSES
UMLAUTS
UMPIRES
UNBENDS
UNBINDS
UNBOLTS
UNBOXES
UNCAGES
UNCASES
UNCIALS
UNCLOGS
UNCOILS
UNCORKS
UNCURLS
UNDRESS
UNFOLDS
UNFURLS
UNGIRDS
UNHANDS
UNHOOKS
UNIFIES
UNIPODS
UNISONS
UNITERS
UNITIES
UNKINKS
UNKNITS
UNKNOTS
UNLACES
UNLADES
UNLINKS
UNLOADS
UNLOCKS
UNMAKES
UNMASKS
UNPACKS
UNPILES
UNPLUGS
UNREELS
UNROBES
UNROLLS
UNSEALS
UNSEATS
UNSNAGS
UNSNAPS
UNSTOPS
UNTACKS
UNTRAPS
UNTUNES
UNVEILS
UNWINDS
UNWRAPS
UNYOKES
UPBEATS
UPDATES
UPHOLDS
UPLANDS
UPLIFTS
UPLINKS
UPLOADS
UPRISES
UPROARS
UPROOTS
UPSHOTS
UPTAKES
UPTICKS
UPTURNS
UPWARDS
URCHINS
URTEXTS
USELESS
USERIDS
USOPENS
USURERS
USURIES
UTAHANS
UTOPIAS

•US••••

AUSPICE
AUSSIES
AUSTERE
AUSTRAL
AUSTRIA
BUSBIES
BUSBOYS
BUSFARE
BUSGIRL
BUSHELS
BUSHHOG
BUSHIDO
BUSHIER
BUSHILY
BUSHING
BUSHMAN
BUSHMEN
BUSHPIG
BUSIEST
BUSKING
BUSKINS
BUSLINE
BUSSING
BUSSTOP
BUSTARD
BUSTERS
BUSTING
BUSTLED
BUSTLES
BUSTOUT
BUSYING
CUSHAWS
CUSHIER
CUSHING
CUSHION
CUSPIDS
CUSSING
CUSSLER
CUSTARD
CUSTODY
CUSTOMS
DUSKIER
DUSKILY
DUSKISH
DUSTBIN
DUSTERS
DUSTIER
DUSTILY
DUSTING
DUSTMAN
DUSTMEN
DUSTMOP
DUSTOFF
DUSTPAN
DUSTUPS
FUSSIER
FUSSILY
FUSSING
FUSSPOT
FUSTIAN
FUSTICS
FUSTIER
FUSTILY
GUSHERS
GUSHIER
GUSHILY
GUSHING
GUSSETS
GUSSIED
GUSSIES
GUSSYUP
GUSTIER
GUSTILY
GUSTING
GUSTOES
HUSBAND
HUSHABY
HUSHFUL
HUSHING
HUSKERS
HUSKIER
HUSKIES
HUSKILY
HUSKING
HUSSARS
HUSSEIN
HUSSIES
HUSTLED
HUSTLER
HUSTLES
JUSTICE
JUSTIFY
JUSTINE
JUSTNOW
KUSPUKS
LUSHEST
LUSTERS
LUSTFUL
LUSTIER
LUSTILY
LUSTING
LUSTRED
LUSTRES
MUSCATS
MUSCLED
MUSCLES
MUSCOVY
MUSEFUL
MUSETTE
MUSEUMS
MUSHERS
MUSHIER
MUSHILY
MUSHING
MUSICAL
MUSKEGS
MUSKETS
MUSKIER
MUSKIES
MUSKRAT
MUSLIMS
MUSLINS
MUSSELS
MUSSIER
MUSSILY
MUSSING
MUSTAFA
MUSTANG
MUSTARD
MUSTERS
MUSTIER
MUSTILY
MUSTSEE
OUSTERS
OUSTING
PUSHFUL
PUSHIER
PUSHILY
PUSHING
PUSHKIN
PUSHOFF
PUSHPIN
PUSHUPS
RUSHDIE
RUSHEES
RUSHERS
RUSHIER
RUSHING
RUSHOFF
RUSSELL
RUSSETS
RUSSETY
RUSSIAN
RUSTICS
RUSTIER
RUSTILY
RUSTING
RUSTLED
RUSTLER
RUSTLES
SUSANNA
SUSANNE
SUSLIKS
SUSPECT
SUSPEND
SUSSING
SUSTAIN
TUSCANY
TUSKERS
TUSSAUD
TUSSLED
TUSSLES
TUSSOCK

•U•S•••

AUSSIES
BUGSOFF
BUGSOUT
BUMSOUT
BURSARS
BURSARY
BURSTYN
BUSSING
BUSSTOP
BUYSOFF
BUYSOUT
CUISINE
CURSING
CURSIVE
CURSORS
CURSORY
CUSSING
CUSSLER
CUTSOFF
CUTSOUT
FUBSIER
FULSOME
FURSEAL
FUSSIER
FUSSILY
FUSSING
FUSSPOT
GUESSED
GUESSER
GUESSES
GUESTED
GUMSHOE
GUNSFOR
GUNSHOT
GUSSETS
GUSSIED
GUSSIES
GUSSYUP
GUTSIER
GUTSILY
HUSSARS
HUSSEIN
HUSSIES
MUGSHOT
MUSSELS
MUSSIER
MUSSILY
MUSSING
NURSERS
NURSERY
NURSING
NUTSIER
OURSELF
OUTSELL
OUTSETS
OUTSIDE
OUTSIZE
OUTSOLD
OUTSTEP
PULSARS
PULSATE
PULSING
PUNSTER
PURSERS
PURSIER
PURSING
PURSUED
PURSUER
PURSUES
PURSUIT
PUTSOFF
PUTSOUT
QUASARS
QUASHED
QUASHES
QUESTED
RUBSOFF
RUBSOUT
RUNSDRY
RUNSFOR
RUNSOFF
RUNSOUT
RUSSELL
RUSSETS
RUSSETY
RUSSIAN
SUASION
SUBSETS
SUBSIDE
SUBSIDY
SUBSIST
SUBSOIL
SUBSUME
SUDSIER
SUDSING
SUNSETS
SUNSPOT
SUNSUIT
SUSSING
TUESDAY
TULSANS
TUSSAUD
TUSSLED
TUSSLES
TUSSOCK

•U••S••

AUGUSTA
AUGUSTE
BUCKSAW
BUCKSUP
BUMPSUP
BUOYSUP
BURNSUP
BUTTSIN
BUZZSAW
CUBISTS
CURLSUP
CURTSEY
EURASIA
FUCHSIA
GUESSED
GUESSER
GUESSES
JUMPSAT
JUMPSIN
JUMPSON
JUMPSUP
JURISTS
LUMPSUM
LUTISTS
MUCKSUP
MUMESON
MUSTSEE
NUDISTS
PULASKI
PULLSIN
PULLSON
PULLSUP
PUMPSUP
PURISTS
QUONSET
RULESON
SUCKSIN
SUITSUP
SULUSEA
SURTSEY
TUBISTS
TUCKSIN
TUNESIN
TUNESUP
TUNISIA
TURNSIN
TURNSON
TURNSTO
TURNSUP

•U•••S•

BUDLESS
BULLISH
BULRUSH
BUMRUSH
BURGESS
BURMESE
BURNISH
BUSIEST
CUBBISH
CUIRASS
CULTISH
CULTISM
CULTIST
CURRISH
CURTEST
CURTISS
CUTLASS
DUCHESS
DUELIST
DULLEST
DULLISH
DUMBEST
DUMPISH
DUNCISH
DUSKISH
FUJITSU
FULLEST
FUMIEST
FUNFEST
FURBISH
FURLESS
FURNISH
GUMLESS
GUNLESS
GUTLESS
HUELESS
HUFFISH
HUNNISH
JUDAISM
JUDOIST
JUJITSU
KURDISH
LUMPISH
LUSHEST
NUMBEST
OUTCAST
OUTLAST
OUTPOST
PUBLISH
PUCKISH
PUGGISH
PUGNOSE
PUNIEST
PUNLESS
PURPOSE
QUERIST
RUBBISH
RUMLESS
RUNTISH
RUTTISH
SUAVEST
SUBROSA
SUBSIST
SUCCESS
SUCRASE
SUCROSE
SUFFUSE
SUGGEST
SUMLESS
SUNFISH
SUNKIST
SUNLESS
SUNRISE
SUPPOSE
SURMISE
SURPASS
TUBAIST
TUGLESS
TURKISH

•U••••S

AUBADES
AUBURNS
AUDILES
AUGENDS
AUKLETS
AUNTIES
AUPAIRS
AUROCHS
AURORAS
AUSSIES
AUTEURS
AUTHORS
AUTUMNS
BUBBLES
BUCKETS
BUCKLES
BUCKOES
BUDDHAS
BUDDIES
BUDGETS
BUDGIES
BUDLESS
BUFFERS
BUFFETS
BUGGIES
BUGLERS
BULBOUS
BULBULS
BULGARS
BULLETS
BULLIES
BUMBLES
BUMMERS
BUMPERS
BUMRAPS
BUNCHES
BUNDLES
BUNGEES
BUNGLES
BUNIONS
BUNKERS
BUNNIES
BUNYIPS
BURBLES
BURBOTS
BURDENS
BUREAUS
BURGEES
BURGERS
BURGESS
BURGLES
BURGOOS
BURLAPS
BURMANS
BURNERS
BUROAKS
BURROWS
BURSARS
BUSBIES
BUSBOYS
BUSHELS
BUSKINS
BUSTERS
BUSTLES
BUTLERS
BUTTERS
BUTTIES
BUTTONS
BUYOUTS
BUZZERS
CUBBIES
CUBISTS
CUCKOOS
CUDDIES
CUDDLES
CUDGELS
CUIRASS
CULLERS
CULLIES
CULVERS
CUMULUS
CUPFULS
CUPOLAS
CURATES
CURDLES
CURFEWS
CURIOUS
CURLERS
CURLEWS
CURRIES
CURSORS

CURTISS
CURVETS
CUSHAWS
CUSPIDS
CUSTOMS
CUTLASS
CUTLERS
CUTLETS
CUTOFFS
CUTOUTS
CUTTERS
DUBBERS
DUBIOUS
DUCHESS
DUCHIES
DUELERS
DUENNAS
DUFFELS
DUFFERS
DUGONGS
DUGOUTS
DUKAKIS
DUMDUMS
DUMMIES
DUNKERS
DUNLINS
DUSTERS
DUSTUPS
DUTEOUS
EUCHRES
FUDDLES
FUELERS
FULFILS
FUMBLES
FUNGOES
FUNNELS
FUNNIES
FURIOUS
FURLESS
FURORES
FURROWS
FUSTICS
FUTURES
GUELPHS
GUESSES
GUFFAWS
GUIDONS
GUIMPES
GUINEAS
GUITARS
GULCHES
GULLAHS
GULLETS
GULLIES
GUMLESS
GUNDOGS
GUNLESS
GUNNELS
GUNNERS
GUNNIES
GUPPIES
GURGLES
GURKHAS
GURNEYS
GUSHERS
GUSSETS
GUSSIES
GUSTOES
GUTLESS
GUTTERS
GUZZLES
HUBBIES
HUBBUBS
HUBCAPS

HUDDLES
HUELESS
HUGGERS
HUGGINS
HULLERS
HULLOAS
HUMBLES
HUMBUGS
HUMERUS
HUMMERS
HUMOURS
HUMVEES
HUNCHES
HUNGERS
HUNKERS
HUNTERS
HURDLES
HURLERS
HURLEYS
HURLIES
HURRAHS
HURRIES
HURTLES
HUSKERS
HUSKIES
HUSSARS
HUSSIES
HUSTLES
HUTCHES
HUYGENS
HUZZAHS
JUDDERS
JUGFULS
JUGGINS
JUGGLES
JUICERS
JUJUBES
JUMBLES
JUMPERS
JUNCOES
JUNGLES
JUNIORS
JUNKERS
JUNKETS
JUNKIES
JURISTS
JUTTIES
KUCHENS
KUSPUKS
LUBBERS
LUGGERS
LUGNUTS
LUMBARS
LUMBERS
LUMPERS
LUNCHES
LUNKERS
LUPINES
LURCHES
LUSTERS
LUSTRES
LUTISTS
LUXATES
MUDCATS
MUDDERS
MUDDIES
MUDDLES
MUDEELS
MUDHENS
MUDPIES
MUFFINS
MUFFLES
MUGGERS
MUKLUKS

MULCHES
MULETAS
MULLAHS
MULLERS
MULLETS
MUMBLES
MUMMERS
MUMMIES
MUNCHES
MUNTINS
MUPPETS
MURDERS
MURMURS
MUSCATS
MUSCLES
MUSEUMS
MUSHERS
MUSKEGS
MUSKETS
MUSKIES
MUSLIMS
MUSLINS
MUSSELS
MUSTERS
MUTANTS
MUTATES
MUTTERS
MUTTONS
MUTUALS
MUUMUUS
MUZHIKS
MUZZLES
NUANCES
NUBBINS
NUBBLES
NUBIANS
NUCLEUS
NUDGERS
NUDISTS
NUDNIKS
NUGGETS
NULLAHS
NUMBATS
NUMBERS
NUNCIOS
NURSERS
NUTATES
NUTLETS
NUTMEGS
NUTRIAS
NUTTERS
NUZZLES
OUSTERS
OUTACTS
OUTAGES
OUTBIDS
OUTDOES
OUTEATS
OUTFITS
OUTGOES
OUTGUNS
OUTHITS
OUTINGS
OUTLAWS
OUTLAYS
OUTLETS
OUTPUTS
OUTRUNS
OUTSETS
OUTWITS
PUBLICS
PUCKERS
PUDDLES
PUEBLOS

PUFFERS
PUFFINS
PUGREES
PULLETS
PULLEYS
PULLINS
PULLONS
PULLUPS
PULPITS
PULQUES
PULSARS
PUMICES
PUMMELS
PUMPERS
PUNCHES
PUNDITS
PUNKAHS
PUNKERS
PUNKIES
PUNLESS
PUNNETS
PUNTERS
PUNTIES
PUPPETS
PUPPIES
PURDAHS
PURFLES
PURISTS
PURLINS
PURPLES
PURRERS
PURSERS
PURSUES
PURVEYS
PUSHUPS
PUTOUTS
PUTPUTS
PUTTEES
PUTTERS
PUTTIES
PUZZLES
QUAGGAS
QUAHOGS
QUAKERS
QUANGOS
QUARTOS
QUASARS
QUASHES
QUAVERS
QUERIES
QUEUERS
QUICHES
QUINCES
QUINOAS
QUIVERS
QUIZZES
QUOKKAS
QUORUMS
QUOTERS
RUBATOS
RUBBERS
RUBBLES
RUBRICS
RUDDERS
RUFFLES
RUINERS
RUINOUS
RULINGS
RUMBLES
RUMLESS
RUMOURS
RUMPLES
RUNDLES
RUNLETS

RUNNELS
RUNNERS
RUNOFFS
RUNOUTS
RUNWAYS
RUPIAHS
RUSHEES
RUSHERS
RUSSETS
RUSTICS
RUSTLES
RUTGERS
SUBDEBS
SUBDUES
SUBLETS
SUBMITS
SUBORNS
SUBSETS
SUBURBS
SUBWAYS
SUCCESS
SUCCORS
SUCKERS
SUFFERS
SUITORS
SULKERS
SULKIES
SULLIES
SULTANS
SUMLESS
SUMMERS
SUMMITS
SUMMONS
SUNDAES
SUNDAYS
SUNDERS
SUNDEWS
SUNDOGS
SUNGODS
SUNLESS
SUNRAYS
SUNSETS
SUNTANS
SUPPERS
SURFERS
SURPASS
SURPLUS
SURREYS
SURVEYS
SUSLIKS
SUTLERS
SUTTERS
SUTURES
TUAREGS
TUBISTS
TUCKERS
TUFFETS
TUGGERS
TUGLESS
TUGRIKS
TULSANS
TUMBLES
TUMMIES
TUMULTS
TUMULUS
TUNDRAS
TUNEUPS
TUNNELS
TUNNIES
TUPELOS
TURBANS
TURBITS
TURBOTS
TUREENS

TURKEYS
TURNERS
TURNIPS
TURRETS
TURTLES
TUSKERS
TUSSLES
TUTTUTS
TUXEDOS
VULCANS
WURLEYS
YUPPIES

••US•••

ABUSERS
ABUSING
ABUSIVE
AMUSING
ASUSUAL
BLUSHED
BLUSHER
BLUSHES
BLUSHON
BLUSTER
BOUSING
BRUSHED
BRUSHES
BRUSHUP
BRUSQUE
CAUSING
CAUSTIC
CLUSTER
COUSINS
CRUSADE
CRUSADO
CRUSHED
CRUSHER
CRUSHES
CRUSTED
DOUSING
ELUSIVE
ELUSORY
FAUSTUS
FLUSHED
FLUSHES
FLUSTER
HOUSING
HOUSMAN
HOUSTON
JOUSTED
JOUSTER
LOUSEUP
LOUSIER
LOUSILY
LOUSING
MOUSERS
MOUSIER
MOUSING
MOUSSED
MOUSSES
PAUSING
PLUSHER
PLUSHES
PLUSHLY
PLUSSES
PRUSSIA
ROUSERS
ROUSING
ROUSTED
SAUSAGE
SHUSHED
SHUSHES
SLUSHES
THUSFAR

TOUSLED
TOUSLES
TRUSSED
TRUSSES
TRUSTED
TRUSTEE
UNUSUAL

••U•S••

ALUNSER
AVULSED
AVULSES
BLUESKY
BOURSES
BRUISED
BRUISER
BRUISES
CLUESIN
COUNSEL
COURSED
COURSER
COURSES
CRUISED
CRUISER
CRUISES
DRUMSUP
EVULSED
EVULSES
FOULSUP
GLUESON
HAULSUP
MOUSSED
MOUSSES
PAULSEN
PLUGSIN
PLUSSES
POURSIN
PRUSSIA
SHUTSIN
SHUTSUP
SOUPSUP
SPURSON
SQUISHY
TRUISMS
TRUSSED
TRUSSES

••U••S•

BLUEISH
BRUTISH
CRUDEST
DOUREST
FAUVISM
FAUVIST
FLUTIST
FOULEST
GAULISH
GLUCOSE
GLUIEST
GOULASH
GOUTISH
LOUDEST
LOUDISH
LOUTISH
NOURISH
OCULIST
PAULIST
PRUDISH
SOUREST
SOURISH
TAUTEST
TOURISM
TOURIST

••U•••S

ABUSERS
ACUMENS
ALUMNUS
AMULETS
AOUDADS
AQUEOUS
AQUINAS
AVULSES
BAUBLES
BAUHAUS
BLUSHES
BOULLES
BOUNCES
BOURSES
BOUTROS
BRUISES
BRUNETS
BRUSHES
CAUDLES
CHUKKAS
COUCHES
COUGARS
COULEES
COUPLES
COUPONS
COURSES
COUSINS
CRUISES
CRUSHES
DAUBERS
DOUBLES
DOUGLAS
DRUDGES
EQUATES
EQUINES
EVULSES
FAUCETS
FAUSTUS
FAUXPAS
FLUSHES
FOULUPS
FOURTHS
GAUCHOS
GAUGERS
GOUGERS
GOURDES
GRUDGES
GRUNGES
HAULERS
IGUANAS
JOUNCES
JOURNOS
KLUDGES
KLUTZES
LAURELS
LOUNGES
LOURDES
LOUVERS
LOUVRES
MAUMAUS
MAUROIS
MOUSERS
MOUSSES
MOUTONS
MUUMUUS
NAUGHTS
NEURONS
NOUGATS
NOUGHTS
OEUVRES
PAUPERS
PLUGINS
PLUNGES

PLURALS
PLUSHES
PLUSSES
POUCHES
POUNCES
POURERS
POUTERS
PRUNERS
RAUCOUS
REUBENS
REUTERS
RHUMBAS
ROUBLES
ROUSERS
ROUTERS
SAUCERS
SCULPTS
SCURVES
SHUSHES
SHUTINS
SLUDGES
SLUICES
SLUSHES
SMUDGES
SOUKOUS
SOURCES
SPUMOUS
SQUALLS
SQUARES
SQUAWKS
SQUEAKS
SQUEALS
SQUILLS
SQUINTS
SQUIRES
SQUIRMS
SQUIRTS
STUCCOS
STUDIES
STUDIOS
STUMERS
STUPORS
STURGES
TAUTENS
TEUTONS
TOUCANS
TOUCHES
TOUPEES
TOURERS
TOUSLES
TOUTERS
TRUANTS
TRUDGES
TRUISMS
TRUSSES
USURERS
USURIES
VOUCHES
YAUPONS
YOUMANS
ZEUGMAS
ZOUAVES

•••US••

ACCUSED
ACCUSER
ACCUSES
ADJUSTS
AROUSAL
AROUSED
AROUSES
AUGUSTA
AUGUSTE
BELUSHI

BEMUSED
BEMUSES
BLOUSED
BLOUSES
BLOUSON
BOLUSES
BONUSES
CAYUSES
CLAUSES
DEBUSSY
DEFUSED
DEFUSES
DEGUSTS
DISUSED
EFFUSED
EFFUSES
ENDUSER
ENDUSES
EXCUSED
EXCUSES
FICUSES
FOCUSED
FOCUSES
GROUSED
GROUSER
GROUSES
ILLUSED
ILLUSES
INFUSED
INFUSES
LOCUSTS
LOTUSES
MEDUSAE
MEDUSAS
MINUSES
MISUSED
MISUSES
NEXUSES
NONUSER
OBTUSER
PERUSAL
PERUSED
PERUSER
PERUSES
PIOUSLY
REBUSES
RECUSED
RECUSES
REFUSAL
REFUSED
REFUSER
REFUSES
ROBUSTA
SCOUSES
SINUSES
SPOUSAL
SPOUSES
SULUSEA
TALUSES
THRUSTS
TROUSER
VIRUSES

•••U•S•

ACCURST
BEAUISH
BEQUEST
DEBUSSY
DELUISE
IMPULSE
INQUEST
REPULSE
REQUEST
ROGUISH

VAGUEST
VOGUISH
YAKUTSK

•••U••S

ABDUCTS
ABJURES
ABOUNDS
ACCUSES
ACQUITS
ADDUCES
ADDUCTS
ADJURES
ADJUSTS
AGOUTIS
ALLUDES
ALLURES
AMOUNTS
AMPULES
ANNUALS
ANNULUS
ARBUTUS
ARDUOUS
ARGUERS
ARMURES
AROUSES
ASSUMES
ASSURES
ATTUCKS
ATTUNES
AUBURNS
AUTUMNS
BEMUSES
BENUMBS
BLOUSES
BOLUSES
BONUSES
BYTURNS
CASUALS
CAYUGAS
CAYUSES
CLAUSES
COLUMNS
CONURES
COPULAS
CUMULUS
DEBUNKS
DEDUCES
DEDUCTS
DEFUSES
DEGUSTS
DELUDES
DELUGES
DENUDES
DEPUTES
DILUTES
EFFUSES
ENDURES
ENDUROS
ENDUSES
ENGULFS
ENSURES
ESCUDOS
EXCUSES
FAMULUS
FATUOUS
FERULES
FIBULAS
FICUSES
FIGURES
FLAUNTS
FOCUSES
FUTURES
GAZUMPS

GERUNDS
GROUNDS
GROUSES
ILLUDES
ILLUMES
ILLUSES
IMMURES
IMPUGNS
IMPUTES
INCUDES
INDUCES
INDUCTS
INFUSES
INJURES
INSULTS
INSURES
INTUITS
IRRUPTS
ISSUERS
JAGUARS
JESUITS
JUJUBES
KABUKIS
KAHUNAS
KIKUYUS
KORUNAS
LACUNAS
LAGUNAS
LEGUMES
LIQUIDS
LIQUORS
LOBULES
LOCUSTS
LOQUATS
LOTUSES
MAGUEYS
MANUALS
MATURES
MEDUSAS
MINUETS
MINUSES
MINUTES
MISUSES
MODULES
MUTUALS
NATURES
NEBULAS
NEXUSES
NOCUOUS
NODULES
OBTUNDS
OCCULTS
OPPUGNS
PADUANS
PAIUTES
PAPUANS
PARURES
PENULTS
PEQUOTS
PERUKES
PERUSES
PLAUTUS
PLOUGHS
POPULUS
QUEUERS
REBUFFS
REBUKES
REBUSES
RECUSES
REDUCES
REFUELS
REFUGES
REFUNDS
REFUSES

REFUTES
REGULUS
RELUCTS
RELUMES
REMUDAS
REPUGNS
REPUTES
RESULTS
RESUMES
RETUNES
RETURNS
RITUALS
ROMULUS
SALUKIS
SALUTES
SCOUSES
SCRUFFS
SECURES
SEDUCES
SENUFOS
SEQUELS
SEQUINS
SINUOUS
SINUSES
SIOUANS
SLEUTHS
SLOUGHS
SOLUTES
SPOUSES
SPRUCES
SUBURBS
SUTURES
TALUSES
TENUOUS
TENURES
THRUSTS
TRAUMAS
TRIUNES
TROUGHS
TROUPES
TSOURIS
TUMULTS
TUMULUS
UNCURLS
UNFURLS
UNTUNES
UPTURNS
VACUOUS
VACUUMS
VICUNAS
VIRUSES
VISUALS
VOLUMES
YAKUZAS
YOGURTS

••••US•

BECAUSE
BULRUSH
BUMRUSH
CAROUSE
CIRCUSY
COMBUST
CONFUSE
CONTUSE
DEGAUSS
DIFFUSE
DISCUSS
DISGUST
DRSEUSS
ENCRUST
ENTHUSE
ENTRUST
ESPOUSE

EXHAUST
INARUSH
INHOUSE
INTRUST
JACCUSE
MOLLUSC
MOLLUSK
OVERUSE
PROFUSE
RECLUSE
SAWDUST
STRAUSS
SUFFUSE

••••U•S

ABLAUTS
ACCRUES
AIRGUNS
ALARUMS
ARBOURS
ARDOURS
ARMFULS
ARMOURS
ASYLUMS
ATRIUMS
AUTEURS
AVENUES
BACKUPS
BADGUYS
BAGFULS
BASQUES
BATTUES
BEDAUBS
BEDBUGS
BEEGUMS
BEFOULS
BIGGUNS
BISQUES
BLOWUPS
BOXFULS
BROGUES
BULBULS
BUYOUTS
CAIQUES
CANFULS
CAPFULS
CAPGUNS
CAPNUTS
CARFULS
CASQUES
CHEQUES
CHERUBS
CHINUPS
CIRQUES
CLAQUES
CLIQUES
CLOQUES
COLOURS
CONCURS
CONSULS
COPOUTS
CUPFULS
CUTOUTS
DEGAUSS
DETOURS
DEVOURS
DICTUMS
DIMOUTS
DISCUSS
DOLOURS
DRSEUSS
DRYRUNS
DUGOUTS
DUMDUMS

DUSTUPS
DYBBUKS
EARFULS
EGGCUPS
ENDRUNS
ENSOULS
EYECUPS
EYEFULS
FANOUTS
FAVOURS
FESCUES
FILLUPS
FLIPUPS
FOLDUPS
FONDUES
FOULUPS
GIBLUES
GILGUYS
GIVEUPS
GOOFUPS
HANGUPS
HEXNUTS
HICCUPS
HOLDUPS
HONOURS
HOOKUPS
HOTTUBS
HUBBUBS
HUMBUGS
HUMOURS
IMBRUES
INHAULS
JACQUES
JARFULS
JETGUNS
JUGFULS
KICKUPS
KUSPUKS
LABOURS
LANGURS
LAPFULS
LARRUPS
LASHUPS
LAYOUTS
LEAGUES
LINEUPS
LINKUPS
LOCKUPS
LONGUES
LOOKUPS
LUGNUTS
LYCEUMS
MAGNUMS
MAHOUTS
MAKEUPS
MARAUDS
MARKUPS
MARQUES
MARQUIS
MASQUES
MEDIUMS
MISCUES
MOCKUPS
MOSQUES
MUKLUKS
MURMURS
MUSEUMS
MUUMUUS
OPAQUES
OUTGUNS
OUTPUTS
OUTRUNS
PABLUMS
PANFULS
PAYOUTS
PEANUTS
PEPLUMS
PICKUPS
PIGNUTS
PILEUPS
PLAGUES
PLAQUES
PLENUMS
PODIUMS
POPGUNS
POSEURS
POSSUMS
POTFULS
PRENUPS
PULLUPS
PULQUES
PURSUES
PUSHUPS
PUTOUTS
PUTPUTS
QIVIUTS
QUORUMS
RAGOUTS
RAGRUGS
RAJPUTS
RAVEUPS
RAYGUNS
RECOUPS
REDBUDS
REDGUMS
REGLUES
RESCUES
RETOURS
RIGOURS
RUMOURS
RUNOUTS
SACQUES
SANLUIS
SAVOURS
SENDUPS
SHOGUNS
SHROUDS
SIXGUNS
SKIRUNS
SLIPUPS
SLOWUPS
SOWBUGS
SPROUTS
STATUES
STEPUPS
STLOUIS
STRAUSS
SUBDUES
TALCUMS
TEACUPS
TEDIUMS
TISSUES
TITTUPS
TONGUES
TOPGUNS
TORQUES
TOSSUPS
TRYOUTS
TUNEUPS
TUTTUTS
UMLAUTS
UNPLUGS
VACUUMS
VALOURS
VAPOURS
VATFULS
VELLUMS
VELOURS
VIGOURS
VIRTUES
WALKUPS
WALNUTS
WARMUPS
WASHUPS
WINDUPS
WORKUPS
WRAPUPS
YANQUIS

•••••US

ALUMNUS
AMADEUS
AMOROUS
ANGELUS
ANNULUS
ANTAEUS
ANXIOUS
APERCUS
AQUEOUS
ARBUTUS
ARDUOUS
ARTEMUS
ATTICUS
BACCHUS
BAUHAUS
BILIOUS
BULBOUS
BUREAUS
CACHOUS
CALLOUS
CANOPUS
CAROLUS
CASSIUS
CELSIUS
CEPHEUS
CITROUS
COLOBUS
COPIOUS
CRASSUS
CRISPUS
CROESUS
CUMULUS
CURIOUS
DEDALUS
DEVIOUS
DOMINUS
DONIMUS
DREYFUS
DUBIOUS
DUTEOUS
ECHINUS
ENVIOUS
ERASMUS
FAMULUS
FATUOUS
FAUSTUS
FERROUS
FIBROUS
FORTIUS
FURIOUS
GASEOUS
GIBBOUS
GRAMPUS
GROPIUS
HEINOUS
HIDEOUS
HUMERUS
HYDROUS
IGNEOUS
IMPETUS
IMPIOUS
INFOCUS
ISTHMUS
JABIRUS
JEALOUS
KIKUYUS
LANDAUS
LAZARUS
MALTHUS
MAUMAUS
MAXIMUS
MILIEUS
MINIBUS
MUUMUUS
NERVOUS
NITROUS
NOCUOUS
NONPLUS
NOXIOUS
NUCLEUS
OBVIOUS
OCEANUS
OCELLUS
OCTOPUS
ODOROUS
OEDIPUS
OLYMPUS
OMINOUS
OMNIBUS
ONEROUS
ORMOLUS
ORPHEUS
OSSEOUS
OZONOUS
PAILOUS
PAPYRUS
PARATUS
PARLOUS
PEGASUS
PERSEUS
PERSIUS
PETROUS
PHOEBUS
PIRAEUS
PITEOUS
PLAUTUS
POMPOUS
PONTIUS
POPULUS
PROTEUS
PYRAMUS
PYRRHUS
RAUCOUS
REFOCUS
REGULUS
RHOMBUS
RIOTOUS
ROMULUS
RUINOUS
SERIOUS
SINUOUS
SOUKOUS
SPUMOUS
STRATUS
SURPLUS
TACITUS
TEDIOUS
TENUOUS
TETANUS
THESEUS
TOYSRUS
TROILUS
TUMULUS
VACUOUS
VARIOUS
VICIOUS
VILNIUS
VIRIBUS
VISCOUS
ZEALOUS

UT•••••

UTAHANS
UTENSIL
UTILISE
UTILITY
UTILIZE
UTOPIAN
UTOPIAS
UTRECHT
UTRILLO
UTTERED
UTTERER
UTTERLY

U•T••••

ULTIMAS
UNTACKS
UNTAMED
UNTAPED
UNTRAPS
UNTRIED
UNTRUTH
UNTUNED
UNTUNES
UNTWIST
UNTYING
UPTAKES
UPTEMPO
UPTICKS
UPTIGHT
UPTONOW
UPTOPAR
UPTURNS
URTEXTS
USTINOV
UTTERED
UTTERER
UTTERLY

U••T•••

ULSTERS
UMPTEEN
UNCTION
UNITARY
UNITERS
UNITIES
UNITING
UNITIVE
UNSTACK
UNSTICK
UNSTOPS
UNSTRAP
UNSTUCK
UPATREE
UPSTAGE
UPSTART
UPSTATE
USSTEEL

U•••T••

UNAPTLY
UNDATED
UNEATEN
UNHITCH
UNLATCH
UNRATED
UNSATED
UPDATED
UPDATES

U••••T•

ULULATE
UMBERTO
UMLAUTS
UNBOLTS
UNCOUTH
UNCRATE
UNEARTH
UNKNITS
UNKNOTS
UNQUOTE
UNSEATS
UNTRUTH
UPBEATS
UPLIFTS
UPROOTS
UPSHOTS
UPSTATE
URANITE
URTEXTS
UTILITY

U•••••T

UGLIEST
ULULANT
UNBLEST
UNGUENT
UNKEMPT
UNSPENT
UNSWEPT
UNTWIST
UPDRAFT
UPFRONT
UPRIGHT
UPSTART
UPSWEPT
UPTIGHT
USGRANT
UTRECHT

•UT••••

AUTARKY
AUTEURS
AUTHORS
AUTOMAT
AUTUMNS
BUTANOL
BUTCHER
BUTLERS
BUTTERS
BUTTERY
BUTTIES
BUTTING
BUTTONS
BUTTOUT
BUTTSIN
CUTAWAY
CUTBACK
CUTDOWN
CUTICLE
CUTINTO
CUTLASS
CUTLERS
CUTLERY
CUTLETS
CUTOFFS
CUTOUTS
CUTRATE
CUTSOFF
CUTSOUT
CUTTERS
CUTTIME
CUTTING
DUTEOUS
DUTIFUL
EUTERPE
FUTURES
FUTZING
GUTHRIE
GUTLESS
GUTSIER
GUTSILY
GUTTERS
GUTTIER
GUTTING
HUTCHES
HUTLIKE
JUTLAND
JUTTIED
JUTTIES
JUTTING
KUTCHIN
KUTENAI
LUTISTS
MUTABLE
MUTABLY
MUTAGEN
MUTANTS
MUTATED
MUTATES
MUTTERS
MUTTONS
MUTUALS
NUTATED
NUTATES
NUTLETS
NUTLIKE
NUTMEAT
NUTMEGS
NUTRIAS
NUTSIER
NUTTERS
NUTTIER
NUTTILY
NUTTING
OUTACTS
OUTAGES
OUTBACK
OUTBIDS
OUTCAST
OUTCOME
OUTCROP
OUTDOES
OUTDONE
OUTDOOR
OUTDRAW
OUTDREW
OUTEATS
OUTFACE
OUTFITS
OUTFLOW
OUTGOES
OUTGREW
OUTGROW
OUTGUNS
OUTHITS
OUTINGS
OUTJUMP
OUTLAID
OUTLAND
OUTLAST
OUTLAWS
OUTLAYS
OUTLETS
OUTLINE
OUTLIVE
OUTLOOK
OUTLOUD
OUTOFIT
OUTPACE
OUTPLAY
OUTPOLL
OUTPOST
OUTPUTS
OUTRACE
OUTRAGE
OUTRANK
OUTRUNS
OUTSELL
OUTSETS
OUTSIDE
OUTSIZE
OUTSOLD
OUTSTEP
OUTTAKE
OUTTALK
OUTVOTE
OUTWARD
OUTWEAR
OUTWITS
OUTWORE
OUTWORK
OUTWORN
PUTAMEN
PUTAWAY
PUTDOWN
PUTITTO
PUTOUTS
PUTOVER
PUTPUTS
PUTSOFF
PUTSOUT
PUTTEES
PUTTERS
PUTTIED
PUTTIES
PUTTING
PUTUPON
RUTGERS
RUTHFUL
RUTTIER
RUTTISH
SUTLERS
SUTTERS
SUTURED
SUTURES
TUTELAR
TUTORED
TUTTUTS

•U•T•••

AUCTION
AUNTIES
AUSTERE
AUSTRAL
AUSTRIA
BUNTING
BUSTARD
BUSTERS
BUSTING
BUSTLED
BUSTLES
BUSTOUT
BUTTERS
BUTTERY
BUTTIES
BUTTING
BUTTONS
BUTTOUT
BUTTSIN
BUYTIME
CULTISH
CULTISM
CULTIST
CULTJAM
CULTURE
CURTAIL
CURTAIN
CURTEST
CURTISS
CURTSEY
CUSTARD
CUSTODY
CUSTOMS
CUTTERS
CUTTIME
CUTTING
DUCTILE
DUCTING
DUSTBIN
DUSTERS
DUSTIER
DUSTILY
DUSTING
DUSTMAN
DUSTMEN
DUSTMOP
DUSTOFF
DUSTPAN
DUSTUPS
FURTHER
FURTIVE
FUSTIAN
FUSTICS
FUSTIER
FUSTILY
GUITARS
GUMTREE
GUNTHER
GUSTIER
GUSTILY
GUSTING
GUSTOES
GUTTERS
GUTTIER
GUTTING
HUNTERS
HUNTING
HUNTLEY
HURTFUL
HURTING
HURTLED
HURTLES
HUSTLED
HUSTLER
HUSTLES
JUSTICE
JUSTIFY
JUSTINE
JUSTNOW
JUTTIED
JUTTIES
JUTTING
LUSTERS
LUSTFUL
LUSTIER
LUSTILY
LUSTING
LUSTRED
LUSTRES
MUNTINS
MUSTAFA
MUSTANG
MUSTARD
MUSTERS
MUSTIER
MUSTILY
MUSTSEE
MUTTERS
MUTTONS
NUPTIAL
NURTURE
NUTTERS
NUTTIER
NUTTILY
NUTTING
OURTOWN
OUSTERS
OUSTING
OUTTAKE
OUTTALK
PUNTERS
PUNTIES
PUNTING
PUPTENT
PUTTEES
PUTTERS
PUTTIED
PUTTIES
PUTTING
QUETZAL
QUITTER
QUOTERS
QUOTING
RUCTION
RUNTIER
RUNTISH
RUPTURE
RUSTICS
RUSTIER
RUSTILY
RUSTING
RUSTLED
RUSTLER
RUSTLES
RUTTIER
RUTTISH
SUBTEND
SUBTEXT
SUBTLER
SUCTION
SUITING
SUITORS
SUITSUP
SULTANA
SULTANS
SUNTANS
SURTSEY
SUSTAIN
SUTTERS
TUFTIER
TUFTING
TUITION
TURTLED
TURTLES
TUTTUTS
VULTURE

•U••T••

AUDITED
AUDITOR
BUILTIN
BUILTUP
BURETTE
BURNTUP
BURSTYN
BUSSTOP
CULOTTE
CURATES
CURATOR
FUJITSU
GUESTED
JUJITSU
JUPITER
LUNATIC
LUXATED
LUXATES
MULCTED
MULETAS
MUSETTE
MUTATED
MUTATES
NUTATED
NUTATES
OUGHTNT
OUTSTEP
PULLTAB
PUNSTER
PURITAN
PUTITTO
QUANTUM
QUARTER
QUARTET
QUARTOS
QUENTIN
QUESTED
QUIETED
QUIETEN
QUIETER
QUIETLY
QUILTED
QUILTER
QUINTET
QUITTER
RUBATOS
RUBITIN
SUMATRA
SUZETTE
YUCATAN

•U•••T•

AUGUSTA
AUGUSTE
AUKLETS
AUREATE
BUCKETS
BUDGETS
BUFFETS
BUFFETT
BULLETS
BULLITT
BURBOTS
BURETTE
BURNETT
BURRITO
BUYOUTS
CUBISTS
CULOTTE
CURVETS
CUTINTO
CUTLETS
CUTOUTS
CUTRATE
DUALITY
DUBIETY
DUEDATE
DUGOUTS
DURANTE
GULLETS
GUSSETS
JUNKETS
JURISTS
KUWAITI
LUDDITE
LUGNUTS
LUTISTS
MUDCATS
MULLETS
MUPPETS
MUSCATS
MUSETTE
MUSKETS
MUTANTS
NUDISTS
NUGGETS
NULLITY
NUMBATS
NUTLETS
OUTACTS
OUTEATS
OUTFITS
OUTHITS
OUTLETS
OUTPUTS
OUTSETS
OUTVOTE
OUTWITS
PUBERTY
PUCKETT
PULLETS
PULPITS
PULSATE
PUNDITS
PUNNETS
PUPPETS
PURISTS
PUTITTO
PUTOUTS
PUTPUTS
QUALITY
QUIXOTE
RUNINTO
RUNLATE
RUNLETS
RUNOUTS
RUNWITH
RUSSETS
RUSSETY
SUAVITY
SUBLETS
SUBMITS
SUBSETS
SUHARTO
SULFATE
SULFITE
SUMMITS
SUNBATH
SUNCITY
SUNSETS
SUZETTE
TUBISTS
TUFFETS
TUMULTS
TURBITS
TURBOTS
TURNSTO
TURRETS
TUTTUTS
VULGATE

•U••••T

AUGMENT
AUTOMAT
BUFFETT
BUGSOUT
BULBLET
BULLITT
BUMSOUT
BUOYANT
BURNETT
BURNOUT
BUSIEST
BUSTOUT
BUTTOUT
BUYSOUT
CULPRIT
CULTIST
CULVERT
CURBCUT
CURRANT
CURRENT
CURTEST
CUTSOUT
DUELIST
DULLEST
DUMBEST
FULGENT
FULLEST
FUMIEST
FUNFEST
FUSSPOT
GUNBOAT
GUNSHOT
HUNGOUT
JUDOIST
JUMPCUT
JUMPSAT
JUNKART
KUMQUAT
LUCKOUT
LUNGEAT
LUSHEST
MUGSHOT
MUSKRAT
NUMBEST
NUTMEAT
OUGHTNT
OUTCAST
OUTLAST
OUTOFIT
OUTPOST
PUCKETT
PULLOUT
PUNGENT
PUNIEST
PUPTENT
PURPORT
PURSUIT
PUTSOUT
QUARTET
QUERIST
QUINTET
QUONSET
RUBSOUT
RULEOUT
RUNGOUT
RUNRIOT
RUNSOUT
SUAVEST
SUBJECT
SUBPLOT
SUBSIST
SUBTEXT
SUBUNIT
SUBVERT
SUGGEST
SUNBELT
SUNKIST
SUNSPOT
SUNSUIT
SUPPORT
SURCOAT
SURFEIT
SUSPECT
TUBAIST
TUGBOAT
TUNEOUT
TURNOUT

••UT•••

ABUTTAL
ABUTTED
ACUTELY
BOUTROS
BRUTELY
BRUTISH
CAUTION
CHUTNEY
CLUTTER
COUTURE
DEUTERO
ELUTING
ELUTION
FLUTIER
FLUTING
FLUTIST
FLUTTER
GAUTAMA
GLUTTED
GLUTTON
GOUTIER
GOUTILY
GOUTISH
HAUTBOY
HAUTEUR
INUTILE
KLUTZES
LAUTREC
LOUTISH
MOUTHED
MOUTONS
NEUTRAL
NEUTRON
POUTERS
POUTFUL
POUTIER
POUTING
REUTERS
REUTHER
ROUTERS
ROUTINE
ROUTING
SAUTEED
SCUTTLE
SHUTEYE
SHUTINS
SHUTOFF
SHUTOUT
SHUTSIN
SHUTSUP
SHUTTER
SHUTTLE
SOUTANE
SOUTHEY
SPUTNIK
SPUTTER
TAUTENS
TAUTEST
TEUTONS
TOUTERS
TOUTING

••U•T••

ABUTTAL
ABUTTED
ADULTLY

AQUATIC
BLUNTED
BLUNTER
BLUNTLY
BLURTED
BLUSTER
BRUITED
CAUSTIC
CHUNTER
CLUSTER
CLUTTER
COULTER
COUNTED
COUNTER
COUNTON
COUNTRY
COURTED
COURTLY
CRUSTED
DAUNTED
DOUBTED
DOUBTER
EQUATED
EQUATES
EQUATOR
ERUCTED
ERUPTED
EXULTED
FAULTED
FAUSTUS
FLUSTER
FLUTTER
FOULTIP
FOURTHS
FRUITED
GAUNTER
GAUNTLY
GLUTTED
GLUTTON
GRUNTED
HAUNTED
HOUSTON
JAUNTED
JOUSTED
JOUSTER
MOULTED
MOUNTED
MOUNTIE
POULTRY
ROUSTED
SAUNTER
SCUTTLE
SHUNTED
SHUTTER
SHUTTLE
SPURTED
SPUTTER
SQUATLY
SQUATTY
STUNTED
TAUNTED
TRUSTED
TRUSTEE
VAULTED
VAULTER
VAUNTED
VAUNTER

••U••T•

ADULATE
AMULETS
AZURITE
BAUXITE
BRUNETS
CRUDITY
CRUELTY
DOUGHTY
EDUCATE
EMULATE
ERUDITE
FAUCETS
HAUGHTY
NAUGHTS
NAUGHTY
NOUGATS
NOUGHTS
PAUCITY
REUNITE
SCULPTS
SFUMATO
SQUANTO
SQUATTY
SQUINTS
SQUINTY
SQUIRTS
STUCKTO
TRUANTS
ULULATE

••U•••T

AQUAVIT
BOUQUET
COULDNT
COUPLET
COURANT
CRUDEST
CRUMPET
DOUBLET
DOUREST
FAUVIST
FLUTIST
FOULEST
FOULOUT
GLUIEST
GOURMET
LAUGHAT
LAURENT
LOUDEST
OCULIST
OPULENT
PAULIST
PEUGEOT
PLUMMET
POUROUT
PRUDENT
ROUGHIT
SHUBERT
SHUTOUT
SOUREST
SPUNOUT
STUDENT
TAUTEST
TOURIST
TRUMPET
ULULANT
WOULDNT

•••UT••

AGOUTIS
ARBUTUS
CLOUTED
CROUTON
DEBUTED
DEPUTED
DEPUTES
DILUTED
DILUTER
DILUTES
FLOUTED
GODUTCH
GROUTED
IMPUTED
IMPUTES
INDUTCH
KNOUTED
MINUTES
MINUTIA
PAIUTES
PLAUTUS
REFUTED
REFUTER
REFUTES
REPUTED
REPUTES
SALUTED
SALUTES
SCOUTED
SCOUTER
SHOUTED
SHOUTER
SLEUTHS
SOLUTES
SPOUTED
SPOUTER
STOUTEN
STOUTER
STOUTLY
YAKUTSK

•••U•T•

ABDUCTS
ACQUITS
ACTUATE
ADDUCTS
ADDUPTO
ADJUSTS
AMOUNTS
ANNUITY
AUGUSTA
AUGUSTE
DEDUCTS
DEGUSTS
ENSUITE
FACULTY
FATUITY
FLAUNTS
FLAUNTY
INDUCTS
INSULTS
INTUITS
IRRUPTS
JESUITS
LEDUPTO
LOCUSTS
LOQUATS
MINUETS
NAHUATL
OCCULTS
PENULTS
PEQUOTS
RELUCTS
REQUITE
RESULTS
ROBUSTA
SCHULTZ
SITUATE
TENUITY
THRUSTS
TUMULTS
UNQUOTE
VACUITY
VALUATE
VANUATU
YOGURTS

•••U••T

ABOUGHT
ACCURST
ADJUNCT
BEQUEST
BROUGHT
CALUMET
CAPULET
DEFUNCT
DRAUGHT
DROUGHT
EPAULET
FRAUGHT
INQUEST
MANUMIT
PIQUANT
PLAUDIT
REBUILT
REQUEST
RIVULET
SUBUNIT
THOUGHT
UNGUENT
VAGUEST
WROUGHT

••••UT•

ABLAUTS
AZIMUTH
BISMUTH
BUYOUTS
CAPNUTS
COMMUTE
COMPUTE
CONFUTE
COPOUTS
CUTOUTS
DIMOUTS
DISPUTE
DUGOUTS
ENROUTE
EXECUTE
FANOUTS
HEXNUTS
HIRSUTE
INTRUTH
KIBBUTZ
LAYOUTS
LUGNUTS
MAHOUTS
OFFDUTY
OUTPUTS
PAYOUTS
PEANUTS
PIGNUTS
POLLUTE
PUTOUTS
PUTPUTS
QIVIUTS
RAGOUTS
RAJPUTS
REROUTE
RUNOUTS
SEADUTY
SPROUTS
STATUTE
TRIBUTE
TRYOUTS
TUTTUTS
UMLAUTS
UNCOUTH
UNTRUTH
VIRTUTE
WALNUTS

••••U•T

ACCOUNT
ASSAULT
ATFAULT
BANQUET
BISCUIT
BOUQUET
BRIQUET
CATSUIT
CIRCUIT
COMBUST
CONDUCT
CONDUIT
CONSULT
CORRUPT
CROQUET
DEFAULT
DISGUST
DISRUPT
DRYSUIT
ENCRUST
ENTRUST
EXHAUST
FLORUIT
INDOUBT
INTRUST
JOBHUNT
KUMQUAT
LAWSUIT
MANHUNT
NODOUBT
NOFAULT
PARQUET
PRODUCT
PURSUIT
RACQUET
RECOUNT
RECRUIT
REDOUBT
REMOUNT
RENAULT
SAWDUST
SKISUIT
SUNSUIT
VIADUCT
WETSUIT
YOGHURT

•••••UT

ABSOLUT
ACEDOUT
ACESOUT
ACTSOUT
AIRSOUT
ASKSOUT
BACKOUT
BAILOUT
BAWLOUT
BEAROUT
BEATOUT
BLEWOUT
BLOTOUT
BLOWOUT
BOOTOUT
BOREOUT
BOWSOUT
BUGSOUT
BUMSOUT
BURNOUT
BUSTOUT
BUTTOUT
BUYSOUT
CALLOUT
CAMEOUT
CAMPOUT
CASHOUT
CASTOUT
CHEWOUT
COCONUT
COLDCUT
COMEOUT
CONKOUT
COOKOUT
COPSOUT
CREWCUT
CURBCUT
CUTSOUT
DEALOUT
DECKOUT
DIEDOUT
DIESOUT
DIGSOUT
DISHOUT
DOLEOUT
DOPEOUT
DRAGOUT
DRAWOUT
DREWOUT
DROPOUT
EASEOUT
EATSOUT
EDGEOUT
EDITOUT
EKEDOUT
EKESOUT
EVENOUT
FADEOUT
FALLOUT
FANSOUT
FARMOUT
FEELOUT
FELLOUT
FELTOUT
FILLOUT
FINDOUT
FISHOUT
FLATOUT
FLIPOUT
FOLDOUT
FOULOUT
GAVEOUT
GETSOUT
GIVEOUT
GOABOUT
GOESOUT
HAIRCUT
HALIBUT
HANDOUT
HANGOUT
HARDPUT
HEADOUT
HEAROUT
HELDOUT
HELPOUT
HIDEOUT
HITSOUT
HOLDOUT
HOLEOUT
HUNGOUT
ICEDOUT
ICESOUT
IRISOUT
IRONOUT
JUMPCUT
KEPTOUT
KICKOUT
KINGTUT
LAIDOUT
LAYSOUT
LEADOUT
LEFTOUT
LETSOUT
LIVEOUT
LOCKNUT
LOCKOUT
LOGSOUT
LOOKOUT
LOSEOUT
LOSTOUT
LUCKOUT
MADEOUT
MAILOUT
MAKEOUT
METEOUT
MISSOUT
MOVEOUT
NOSEOUT
OCCIPUT
OPTSOUT
PAIDOUT
PANSOUT
PARTOUT
PASSOUT
PAYSOUT
PEEKOUT
PEEROUT
PICKOUT
PIGSOUT
PINENUT
PLANOUT
PLAYOUT
POOPOUT
POPSOUT
POUROUT
PULLOUT
PUTSOUT
RAINOUT
RANGOUT
READOUT
RIDEOUT
RINGOUT
RIPSOUT
RODEOUT
ROLLOUT
ROOTOUT
RUBSOUT
RULEOUT
RUNGOUT
RUNSOUT
SACKOUT
SANGOUT
SEEKOUT
SEENOUT
SEESOUT
SELLOUT
SENDOUT
SENTOUT
SETSOUT
SHIPOUT
SHOTOUT
SHOTPUT
SHOWOUT
SHUTOUT
SICKOUT
SIGNOUT
SINGOUT
SITSOUT
SKIPOUT
SLIPOUT
SOLDOUT
SORTOUT
SPINOUT
SPUNOUT
STAYPUT
STEPOUT
TAGSOUT
TAKEOUT
TALKOUT
TAPSOUT
TEAROUT
TESTOUT
TIMEOUT
TIREOUT
TOOKOUT
TOPSOUT
TOREOUT
TORNOUT
TOSSOUT
TROTOUT
TUNEOUT
TURNOUT
VOTEOUT
WAITOUT
WALKOUT
WANTOUT
WASHOUT
WEAROUT
WEEDOUT
WENTOUT
WIGSOUT
WINGNUT
WINKOUT
WINSOUT
WIPEOUT
WITHOUT
WOODCUT
WOREOUT
WORKOUT
WORNOUT
XINGOUT
ZONKOUT

U•U••••

UKULELE
ULULANT
ULULATE
UNUSUAL
URUGUAY
USUALLY
USURERS
USURIES
USURPED
USURPER

U••U•••

UNCURLS
UNFURLS
UNGUENT
UNLUCKY
UNQUOTE
UNTUNED
UNTUNES
UPQUARK
UPSURGE
UPTURNS

U•••U••

ULALUME
UMLAUTS
UNAMUNO
UNBOUND
UNCOUTH
UNEQUAL
UNGLUED
UNPLUGS
UNSOUND
UNSTUCK
UNTRUTH
UNUSUAL
UNWOUND
URUGUAY

U••••U•

UNAWFUL
URANIUM
USINGUP

•UU••••

MUUMUUS

•U•U•••

AUBURNS
AUDUBON
AUGURAL
AUGURED
AUGUSTA
AUGUSTE
AUTUMNS
CUMULUS
DUBUQUE
FUTURES
JUGULAR
JUJUBES
MUTUALS
PUTUPON
QUEUERS
QUEUEUP
QUEUING
SUBUNIT
SUBURBS
SULUSEA
SUTURED
SUTURES
TUBULAR
TUMULTS
TUMULUS

•U••U••

AUTEURS
BULBULS
BULRUSH
BUMRUSH
BUYOUTS
CULTURE
CUPFULS
CUTOUTS
DUGOUTS
DUMDUMS
DUSTUPS
HUBBUBS
HUMBUGS
HUMOURS
JUGFULS
KUMQUAT
KUSPUKS
LUGNUTS
MUGWUMP
MUKLUKS
MURMURS
MUSEUMS
MUUMUUS
NURTURE
OUTGUNS
OUTJUMP
OUTPUTS
OUTRUNS
PULLUPS
PULQUES
PURSUED
PURSUER
PURSUES
PURSUIT
PUSHUPS
PUTOUTS
PUTPUTS
QUORUMS
RUMOURS
RUNOUTS
RUPTURE
SUBDUED
SUBDUER
SUBDUES
SUBSUME
SUCCUMB
SUDBURY
SUFFUSE
SUNBURN
SUNSUIT
SUOJURE
TUNEUPS
TUTTUTS
VULTURE

•U•••U•

BUCKSUP
BUDDYUP
BUGSOUT
BUILDUP
BUILTUP
BULBOUS
BULGHUR
BULLRUN
BUMPSUP
BUMSOUT
BUOYSUP
BUREAUS
BURNOUT
BURNSUP
BURNTUP
BURPGUN
BUSTOUT
BUTTOUT
BUYSOUT
CUMULUS
CURBCUT
CURIOUS
CURLSUP
CUTSOUT
DUBIOUS
DUBUQUE
DUDEDUP
DUMMYUP
DUTEOUS
DUTIFUL
FULCRUM
FULGHUM
FURIOUS
GUARGUM
GUSSYUP
HUMANUM
HUMDRUM
HUMERUS
HUNGOUT
HURRYUP
HURTFUL
HUSHFUL
JUICEUP
JUMPCUT
JUMPSUP
JUNEBUG
LUCKOUT
LUMPSUM
LUSTFUL
MUCKSUP
MUSEFUL
MUUMUUS
NUCLEUS
OUTLOUD
PULLOUT
PULLSUP
PUMPSUP
PUNCHUP
PUSHFUL
PUTSOUT
QUANTUM
QUECHUA
QUEUEUP
QUINQUE
RUBSOUT
RUINOUS
RULEOUT
RUNGOUT
RUNSOUT
RUTHFUL
SUCCOUR
SUITSUP
SULPHUR
SURPLUS
TUMULUS
TUNEDUP
TUNEFUL
TUNEOUT
TUNESUP
TURNOUT
TURNSUP
TUSSAUD

•U••••U

FUJITSU
JUJITSU
PURLIEU

••U•U••

ARUGULA
ASUSUAL
BOUQUET
COUTURE
FOULUPS
GAUGUIN
MUUMUUS
UNUSUAL
URUGUAY

••U••U•

ALUMNUS
AQUEOUS
BAUHAUS
BLUEGUM
BOUNDUP
BRUSHUP
BRUSQUE
COUGHUP
DRUMSUP
ELUVIUM
FAUSTUS
FOULOUT
FOULSUP
HAULSUP
HAUTEUR
LOUSEUP
MAUMAUS
MUUMUUS
POUROUT
POUTFUL
RAUCOUS
ROUGHUP
ROUNDUP
SHUTOUT
SHUTSUP
SOUKOUS
SOULFUL
SOUPSUP
SPUMOUS
SPUNOUT
STUCKUP
STUNGUN
THULIUM
TOUCHUP
TRUMPUP
WOUNDUP
YOUNGUN

••U•••U

DOUBLEU
NOUVEAU
TRUDEAU

•••UU••

VACUUMS

•••U•U•

ANNULUS
ARBUTUS
ARDUOUS
CUMULUS
DUBUQUE
FAMULUS
FATUOUS
JEJUNUM
KIKUYUS
LIQUEUR
NOCUOUS
PABULUM
PLAUTUS
POPULUS
QUEUEUP
REGULUS
ROMULUS
SCRUBUP
SINUOUS
TENUOUS
TUMULUS
VACUOUS

•••U••U

VANUATU

••••UU•

MUUMUUS

U•V••••

UNVEILS

U••V•••

UNAVOCE

U•••V••

UNCIVIL
UNCOVER
UNLOVED
UNMOVED
UNPAVED
UNRAVEL
UNWOVEN
UPRIVER

U••••V•

ULANOVA
UNITIVE
UNNERVE
UNWEAVE

U•••••V

ULYANOV
USTINOV

•UV••••

JUVENAL

•U•V•••

CULVERS
CULVERT
CURVETS
CURVIER
CURVING
GUEVARA
HUMVEES
OUTVOTE
PURVEYS
PURVIEW
QUAVERS
QUAVERY
QUIVERS
QUIVERY
SUAVELY
SUAVEST
SUAVITY
SUBVERT
SUBVOCE
SURVEYS
SURVIVE

•U••V••

PUTOVER
RUNOVER

•U•••V•

CURSIVE
FURTIVE
MUSCOVY
OUTLIVE
SURVIVE

•U••••V

NUREYEV

••UV•••

ELUVIUM
FAUVISM
FAUVIST
FLUVIAL
LOUVERS
LOUVRED
LOUVRES
NOUVEAU
OEUVRES
PLUVIAL

••U•V••

AQUAVIT
AQUIVER
SCURVES
ZOUAVES

••U••V•

ABUSIVE
ELUSIVE

•••UV••

ALLUVIA
OLDUVAI

•••U••V

GODUNOV

••••UV•

DENEUVE

U•W••••

UNWEAVE
UNWINDS
UNWISER
UNWOUND
UNWOVEN
UNWRAPS
UPWARDS

U••W•••

UNAWARE
UNAWFUL
UNSWEPT
UNTWIST
UPSWEEP
UPSWEPT
UPSWING

U•••W••

UNBOWED
UNSEWED

U••••W•

UNDRAWN
UNKNOWN

U•••••W

UNSCREW
UPTONOW
USOSHOW

•UW••••

KUWAITI

•U•W•••

BULWARK
GUNWALE
JUGWINE
MUGWUMP
OUTWARD
OUTWEAR
OUTWITS
OUTWORE
OUTWORK
OUTWORN
RUNWAYS
RUNWITH
SUBWAYS

•U••W••

CUTAWAY
DUNAWAY
PUTAWAY
RUNAWAY
TURFWAR

•U•••W•

BURROWS
CURFEWS
CURLEWS
CUSHAWS
CUTDOWN
FURROWS
GUFFAWS
OURTOWN
OUTLAWS
PUTDOWN
RUBDOWN

RUNDOWN
SUNBOWL
SUNDEWS
SUNDOWN

•U••••W
BUCKSAW
BUZZSAW
JUSTNOW
OUTDRAW
OUTDREW
OUTFLOW
OUTGREW
OUTGROW
PURVIEW

••U•W••
FOURWAY
SQUAWKS
SQUAWKY

••U•••W
BLUELAW
YOUKNOW

•••UW••
THRUWAY

UX•••••
UXORIAL

U•••X••
UNBOXED
UNBOXES
UNFIXED
URTEXTS

•UX••••
LUXATED
LUXATES
TUXEDOS

•U•X•••
QUIXOTE

•U•••X•
SUBTEXT

•U••••X
JUKEBOX

••UX•••
BAUXITE
BRUXING
FAUXPAS
FLUXING

••U•••X
BLUEFOX
EQUINOX
FLUMMOX

•••••UX
BATEAUX
BENELUX
FIATLUX
GATEAUX
LASCAUX
LEMIEUX
MALRAUX
MARGAUX
MILIEUX
MIMIEUX
THEROUX
VERDOUX

U•Y••••
ULYANOV
ULYSSES
UNYOKED
UNYOKES

U••Y•••
UNDYING
UNTYING

U•••••Y
UNAPTLY
UNCANNY
UNGODLY
UNHANDY
UNHAPPY
UNITARY
UNLUCKY
UNREADY
URGENCY
URUGUAY
USUALLY
UTILITY
UTTERLY

•UY••••
BUYABLE
BUYOUTS
BUYSOFF
BUYSOUT
BUYTIME
HUYGENS

•U•Y•••
BUNYIPS
BUOYANT
BUOYING
BUOYSUP
BURYING
BUSYING
HUNYADY
JURYING
JURYRIG
RUDYARD

•U••Y••
BUDDYUP
BUGEYED
DUMMYUP
GUSSYUP
HURRYUP
NUREYEV
RUFIYAA

•U•••Y•
BUCKEYE
BURSTYN
BUSBOYS
GURNEYS
HURLEYS
OUTLAYS
PULLEYS
PURVEYS
RUNWAYS
SUBWAYS
SUNDAYS
SUNRAYS
SURREYS
SURVEYS
TURKEYS
WURLEYS

•U••••Y
AUDIBLY
AURALLY
AUTARKY
BUCKLEY
BUMPILY
BURSARY
BUSHILY
BUTTERY
CURSORY
CURTSEY
CUSTODY
CUTAWAY
CUTLERY
DUALITY
DUBARRY
DUBIETY
DULCIFY
DUNAWAY
DURABLY
DUSKILY
DUSTILY
EUPHONY
FUNKILY
FUNNILY
FUSSILY
FUSTILY
FUZZILY
GUNNERY
GUNPLAY
GUSHILY
GUSTILY
GUTSILY
HUFFILY
HUMANLY
HUMIDLY
HUNGARY
HUNTLEY
HUNYADY
HUSHABY
HUSKILY
JUICILY
JUMPILY
JUSTIFY
LUCENCY
LUCIDLY
LUCKILY
LULLABY
LUMPILY
LURIDLY
LUSTILY
MUCKILY
MUDDILY
MUMMERY
MURKILY
MUSCOVY
MUSHILY
MUSSILY
MUSTILY
MUTABLY
MUZZILY
NULLIFY
NULLITY
NUNNERY
NURSERY
NUTTILY
OUTPLAY
PUBERTY
PUDENCY
PUDGILY
PUFFERY
PUFFILY
PUNNILY
PUSHILY
PUTAWAY
QUAKILY
QUALIFY
QUALITY
QUAVERY
QUEENLY
QUEERLY
QUICKLY
QUIETLY
QUIGLEY
QUINARY
QUIVERY
RUBBERY
RUDDILY
RUNAWAY
RUNSDRY
RURALLY
RUSSETY
RUSTILY
SUAVELY
SUAVITY
SUBSIDY
SUDBURY
SULKILY
SUMMARY
SUMMERY
SUNCITY
SUNNILY
SURGERY
SURLILY
SURTSEY
TUESDAY
TURNERY
TURNKEY
TUSCANY

••UY•••
GRUYERE

••U••Y•
SHUTEYE

••U•••Y
ACUTELY
ADULTLY
BLUEBOY
BLUEJAY
BLUESKY
BLUFFLY
BLUNTLY
BRUTELY
CHUTNEY
COUNTRY
COURTLY
CRUCIFY
CRUDELY
CRUDITY
CRUELLY
CRUELTY
CRUMBLY
CRUMPLY
CRUNCHY
DOUGHTY
ELUSORY
EQUABLY
EQUALLY
EQUERRY
EXUPERY
FLUENCY
FLUIDLY
FOUNDRY
FOURWAY
GAUDILY
GAUNTLY
GAUZILY
GOUTILY
GRUFFLY
GRUMBLY
HAUGHTY
HAUTBOY
JOURNEY
LAUNDRY
LOUSILY
NAUGHTY
PAUCITY
PAUNCHY
PLUMPLY
PLUSHLY
POULTRY
PRUDERY
REUNIFY
ROUGHLY
ROUNDLY
SAUCILY
SNUFFLY
SOUNDLY
SOUTHEY
SQUATLY
SQUATTY
SQUAWKY
SQUEAKY
SQUINTY
SQUIRMY
SQUISHY
STUBBLY
STUPEFY
TOUGHLY
TOURNEY
TRUANCY
URUGUAY
USUALLY

•••UY••
KIKUYUS

•••U•Y•
MAGUEYS

•••U••Y
ACTUARY
ALBUNDY
ANNUITY
AWFULLY
CALUMNY
DEBUSSY
ENQUIRY
ESTUARY
FACULTY
FATUITY
FLAUNTY
FLOUNCY
GROUCHY
INQUIRY
JANUARY
LIQUEFY
LITURGY
PIOUSLY
PROUDLY
ROGUERY
SCRUBBY
SCRUFFY
SCRUMMY
SHRUBBY
SLOUCHY
STOUTLY
TENUITY
THEURGY
THRUWAY
UNLUCKY
VACUITY
VAGUELY
VOLUBLY
ZYMURGY

••••UY•
BADGUYS
GILGUYS

••••U•Y
ARMOURY
ASHBURY
CADBURY
CENTURY
CIRCUSY
CLIQUEY
DANBURY
MERCURY
OFFDUTY
PERJURY
SAVOURY
SEADUTY
SUDBURY
URUGUAY

•••••UY
FALLGUY
OBLOQUY
OVERBUY
WISEGUY

U•Z••••
UNZONED

U•••Z••
UNFAZED

U••••Z•
UTILIZE

•UZ••••
BUZZARD
BUZZERS
BUZZING
BUZZOFF
BUZZSAW
FUZZIER
FUZZILY
FUZZING
GUZZLED
GUZZLER
GUZZLES
HUZZAHS
MUZHIKS
MUZZIER
MUZZILY
MUZZING
MUZZLED
MUZZLES
NUZZLED
NUZZLER
NUZZLES
PUZZLED
PUZZLER
PUZZLES
SUZANNE
SUZETTE

•U•Z•••
BUZZARD
BUZZERS
BUZZING
BUZZOFF
BUZZSAW
FUTZING
FUZZIER
FUZZILY
FUZZING
GUZZLED
GUZZLER
GUZZLES
HUZZAHS
MUEZZIN
MUZZIER
MUZZILY
MUZZING
MUZZLED
MUZZLES
NUZZLED
NUZZLER
NUZZLES
PUZZLED
PUZZLER
PUZZLES
QUIZZED
QUIZZES
SUBZERO

•U••Z••
MUEZZIN
QUETZAL
QUIZZED
QUIZZES

•U•••Z•
OUTSIZE

••UZ•••
CRUZADO
GAUZIER
GAUZILY

••U•Z••
KLUTZES

••U••Z•
SQUEEZE

•••UZ••
ABRUZZI
JACUZZI
YAKUZAS

•••U•Z•
ABRUZZI
JACUZZI

•••U••Z
SCHULTZ

••••U•Z
KIBBUTZ
MARQUEZ

VA•••••
VACANCY
VACATED
VACATES
VACCINE
VACUITY
VACUOLE
VACUOUS
VACUUMS
VAGRANT
VAGUELY
VAGUEST
VAINEST
VALANCE
VALENCE
VALENCY
VALERIE
VALIANT
VALIDLY
VALISES
VALJEAN
VALLEJO
VALLEYS
VALOURS
VALUATE
VALUING
VALVATE
VAMOOSE
VAMPERS
VAMPING
VAMPIRA
VAMPIRE
VAMPISH
VANDALS
VANDINE
VANDYCK
VANDYKE
VANESSA
VANEYCK
VANGOGH
VANILLA
VANILLI
VANPOOL
VANTAGE
VANUATU
VAPIDLY
VAPOURS
VAQUERO
VARIANT
VARIETY
VARIOUS
VARLETS
VARMINT
VARNISH
VARSITY
VARYING
VASSALS
VASTEST
VASTIER
VATFULS
VATICAN
VATTING
VAUGHAN
VAULTED
VAULTER
VAUNTED
VAUNTER

V•A••••
VEALIER
VIADUCT

V••A•••
VACANCY
VACATED
VACATES
VALANCE
VEDANTA
VENALLY
VERANDA
VIDALIA
VIRAGOS
VISAGES
VISAING
VISALIA
VISAVIS
VITALLY
VITAMIN
VIVALDI
VOCALIC
VOCALLY
VOYAGED
VOYAGER
VOYAGES

V•••A••
VAGRANT
VALIANT
VALUATE
VALVATE
VANDALS
VANTAGE
VANUATU
VARIANT
VASSALS
VEEJAYS
VERBALS
VERDANT
VIBRANT
VIBRATE
VIBRATO
VILLAGE
VILLAIN
VINTAGE
VIOLATE
VISUALS
VITIATE
VOLCANO
VOLTAGE
VOLTAIC
VULCANS
VULGATE

V••••A•
VALJEAN
VATICAN
VAUGHAN
VEGETAL
VENTRAL
VERITAS
VETERAN
VICTUAL
VICUNAS
VIETNAM
VINEGAR
VIRGOAN
VIRTUAL
VIZSLAS

V•••••A
VAMPIRA
VANESSA
VANILLA
VEDANTA
VENTURA
VERANDA
VERBENA
VIDALIA
VISALIA
VISCERA
VISTULA

•VA••••
AVAILED
AVARICE
AVATARS
EVACUEE
EVADERS
EVADING
EVANDER
EVANGEL
EVANISH
EVASION
EVASIVE
IVANHOE
IVANOVO
OVATION

•V•A•••
AVIANCA
AVIATED
AVIATES
AVIATOR

•V••A••
AVATARS
AVERAGE
AVOCADO
AVOWALS
OVERACT
OVERAGE
OVERALL
OVERATE
OVERAWE
OVIPARA
OVISACS

•V•••A•
OVEREAT
OVERLAP
OVERLAY
OVERRAN
OVERSAW
OVERTAX
OVOIDAL

•V••••A
AVIANCA
AVONLEA
OVERSEA
OVIPARA

••VA•••
ADVANCE
ALVAREZ
BAVARIA
BIVALVE
CAVALRY
DEVALUE
HAVARTI
INVACUO
INVADED
INVADER
INVADES
INVALID
JAVAMAN
LAVALSE
LEVANTS
LIVABLE
LOVABLE
LOVABLY
MOVABLE
MOVABLY
NAVAHOS
NAVAJOS
NAVARRE
NEVADAN
NOVARRO
PAVANES
RAVAGED
RAVAGER
RAVAGES
REVALUE
REVAMPS
RIVALED
RIVALRY
SAVABLE
SAVAGED
SAVAGER
SAVAGES
SAVALAS
SAVANNA
SAVANTS
SAVARIN
VIVALDI

••V•A••
CAVEATS
CAVIARS
DEVIANT
DEVIATE
GAVIALS
HOVLANE
OBVIATE
REVEALS

••V••A•
BIVOUAC
CAVEMAN
GAVEWAY
GIVEWAY
JAVAMAN
JUVENAL
LIVEOAK
NEVADAN
NOVENAS
PIVOTAL
REVIVAL
SAVALAS
SEVENAM
SEVERAL

••V•••A
BAVARIA
LAVINIA
NOVELLA
PAVLOVA
RAVENNA
RIVIERA
SAVANNA

•••VA••
BRAVADO
CALVARY
CANVASS
COEVALS
CRAVATS
ELEVATE
GALVANI
GUEVARA
HALVAHS
HARVARD
LEKVARS
NIRVANA
PERVADE
PREVAIL
PRIVACY
PRIVATE
REAVAIL
ROLVAAG
SALVAGE
SELVAGE
SERVALS
SERVANT
SLOVAKS
SYLVANS
TRAVAIL
VALVATE
ZHIVAGO

•••V•A•
DRIVEAT
FLUVIAL
LATVIAN
NOUVEAU
PLUVIAL
ROLVAAG
SALVIAS
TRIVIAL

•••V••A
BOBVILA
BRAVURA
GUEVARA
NIRVANA
RIGVEDA

••••VA•
ARRIVAL
BOLIVAR
CARAVAN
CASAVAS
DONOVAN
ESTIVAL
HESHVAN
MEDEVAC
MINIVAN
MITZVAH
OLDUVAI
RAYOVAC
REMOVAL
REVIVAL
SAMOVAR
YEREVAN

••••V•A
ALLUVIA
BOLIVIA
MORAVIA
OCTAVIA
SEGOVIA

•••••VA
BAKLAVA
CASSAVA
FESTIVA
GINGIVA
KEDROVA
MARKOVA
MINERVA
MOLDOVA
PAVLOVA
ULANOVA
YESHIVA

V•B••••
VIBRANT
VIBRATE
VIBRATO

V••B•••
VERBALS
VERBENA
VERBOSE

V•••B••
VIRIBUS
VISIBLE
VISIBLY
VOLUBLE
VOLUBLY

•V••B••
OVERBIG
OVERBUY

•V••••B
OVERDUB

••V•B••
LIVABLE
LOVABLE
LOVABLY
LOVEBUG
MOVABLE
MOVABLY
SAVABLE

••V••B•
ADVERBS
REVERBS

•••V••B
PROVERB

V•C••••
VACANCY
VACATED
VACATES
VACCINE
VACUITY
VACUOLE
VACUOUS
VACUUMS
VECTORS
VICEROY
VICIOUS
VICTIMS
VICTORS
VICTORY
VICTUAL
VICUNAS
VOCALIC
VOCALLY

V••C•••
VACCINE
VETCHES
VINCENT
VISCERA
VISCOUS
VOICING
VOLCANO
VOUCHED
VOUCHER
VOUCHES
VULCANS

V•••C••
VATICAN
VEHICLE
VOTECHS

V••••C•
VACANCY
VALANCE
VALENCE
VALENCY
VANDYCK
VANEYCK
VEENECK
VERDICT
VIADUCT

V•••••C
VOCALIC
VOLTAIC

•V•C•••
AVOCADO
AVOCETS
EVACUEE
EVICTED

•V••C••
EVINCED
EVINCES

•V•••C•
AVARICE
AVIANCA
OVERACT
OVISACS

••V•C••
DEVICES
DOVECOT
INVACUO
NOVICES

••V••C•
ADVANCE
DAVINCI
DIVORCE
INVOICE
REVOICE

••V•••C
BIVOUAC

•••V•C•
CONVICT
CREVICE
PRIVACY
SERVICE
SUBVOCE
UNAVOCE

••••V•C
MEDEVAC
RAYOVAC

V•D••••
VEDANTA
VIDALIA

V••D•••
VANDALS
VANDINE
VANDYCK
VANDYKE
VENDING
VENDORS
VERDANT
VERDICT
VERDOUX
VERDUGO
VERDURE
VIADUCT
VOIDING
VOODOOS

V•••D••
VALIDLY
VAPIDLY
VEXEDLY
VIVIDER
VIVIDLY
VOTEDIN

V••••D•
VERANDA

VESPIDS
VIVALDI
VIVENDI

V•••••D
VACATED
VAULTED
VAUNTED
VISITED
VOUCHED
VOYAGED

•V•D•••
AVIDITY
EVADERS
EVADING
EVIDENT

•V••D••
AVOIDED
EVANDER
OVERDID
OVERDUB
OVERDUE
OVOIDAL

•V•••D•
AVOCADO
TVGUIDE

•V••••D
AVAILED
AVENGED
AVERRED
AVERTED
AVIATED
AVOIDED
AVULSED
EVERTED
EVICTED
EVINCED
EVOLVED
EVULSED
OVERDID

••V•D••
CAVEDIN
DIVIDED
DIVIDER
DIVIDES
INVADED
INVADER
INVADES
LIVEDIN
LIVEDON
LIVIDLY
MOVEDIN
MOVEDON
MOVEDUP
NEVADAN
SAVEDUP
VIVIDER
VIVIDLY
WAVEDIN

••V••D•
VIVALDI
VIVENDI

••V•••D
ADVISED
BEVELED
CAVILED
COVERED
COVETED
DEVILED
DEVISED
DEVOTED
DIVIDED
DIVINED
DIVVIED
FAVORED
GAVELED
HAVERED
HOVERED
INVADED
INVALID
INVITED
INVOKED
LEVELED
LEVERED
LIVENED
PIVOTED
RAVAGED
RAVELED
RAVENED
REVELED
REVERED
REVILED
REVISED
REVIVED
REVOKED
RIVALED
RIVETED
SAVAGED
SAVORED
SEVERED
WAVERED

•••V•D•
BRAVADO
CERVIDS
PERVADE
PROVIDE
RIGVEDA

•••V••D
CHEVIED
DIVVIED
HARVARD
LOUVRED

••••V•D
ARRIVED
BEHAVED
BEHOVED
BELOVED
CLEAVED
DERIVED
EVOLVED
GRIEVED
GROOVED
RELIVED
REMOVED
REPAVED
REVIVED
SHEAVED
SHELVED
STARVED
STRIVED
SWERVED
THIEVED
THRIVED
UNLOVED
UNMOVED
UNPAVED

VE•••••
VEALIER
VECTORS
VEDANTA
VEEJAYS
VEENECK
VEERIES
VEERING
VEGETAL
VEGGIES
VEGGING
VEHICLE
VEIGHTS
VEILING
VEINIER
VEINING
VELLUMS
VELOURS
VELVETS
VELVETY
VENALLY
VENDING
VENDORS
VENEERS
VENISON
VENTERS
VENTING
VENTRAL
VENTURA
VENTURE
VERANDA
VERBALS
VERBENA
VERBOSE
VERDANT
VERDICT
VERDOUX
VERDUGO
VERDURE
VERGERS
VERGING
VERISMO
VERITAS
VERMEER
VERMEIL
VERMONT
VERNIER
VERSIFY
VERSION
VERTIGO
VERVETS
VESPERS
VESPIDS
VESSELS
VESTEES
VESTIGE
VESTING
VESTURE
VETCHES
VETERAN
VETOERS
VETOING
VETTING
VEXEDLY

V•E••••
VEEJAYS
VEENECK
VEERIES
VEERING
VIETNAM
VIEWERS
VIEWIER
VIEWING

V••E•••
VALENCE
VALENCY
VALERIE
VANESSA
VANEYCK
VEGETAL
VENEERS
VETERAN
VEXEDLY
VICEROY
VINEGAR
VIVENDI
VOTECHS
VOTEDIN
VOTEFOR
VOTEOUT
VOTESIN

V•••E••
VAGUELY
VAGUEST
VAINEST
VALJEAN
VALLEJO
VALLEYS
VAMPERS
VAQUERO
VARIETY
VARLETS
VASTEST
VEENECK
VELVETS
VELVETY
VENEERS
VENTERS
VERBENA
VERGERS
VERMEER
VERMEIL
VERVETS
VESPERS
VESSELS
VESTEES
VETOERS
VIEWERS
VILLEIN
VINCENT
VINIEST
VIOLENT
VIOLETS
VISCERA
VIZIERS
VOLLEYS
VOWLESS

V••••E•
VACATED
VACATES
VALISES
VASTIER
VAULTED
VAULTER
VAUNTED
VAUNTER
VEALIER
VEERIES
VEGGIES
VEINIER
VERMEER
VERNIER
VESTEES
VETCHES
VIEWIER
VINTNER
VIRTUES
VIRUSES
VISAGES
VISITED
VITTLES
VIVIDER
VOLUMES
VOUCHED
VOUCHER
VOUCHES
VOYAGED
VOYAGER
VOYAGES

V•••••E
VACCINE
VACUOLE
VALANCE
VALENCE
VALERIE
VALUATE
VALVATE
VAMOOSE
VAMPIRE
VANDINE
VANDYKE
VANTAGE
VEHICLE
VENTURE
VERBOSE
VERDURE
VESTIGE
VESTURE
VIBRATE
VILLAGE
VINTAGE
VIOLATE
VIRGULE
VIRTUTE
VISIBLE
VITIATE
VOLPONE
VOLTAGE
VOLUBLE
VULGATE
VULPINE
VULTURE

•VE••••
AVENGED
AVENGER
AVENGES
AVENUES
AVERAGE
AVERRED
AVERTED
EVENEST
EVENING
EVENKIS
EVENOUT
EVENSUP
EVEREST
EVERETT
EVERTED
OVERACT
OVERAGE
OVERALL
OVERATE
OVERAWE
OVERBIG
OVERBUY
OVERDID
OVERDUB
OVERDUE
OVEREAT
OVERFLY
OVERJOY
OVERLAP
OVERLAY
OVERLIE
OVERRAN
OVERRUN
OVERSAW
OVERSEA
OVERSEE
OVERTAX
OVERTLY
OVERUSE
SVELTER

•V••E••
AVOCETS
AVOWERS
EVADERS
EVENEST
EVEREST
EVERETT
EVIDENT
EVILEST
EVILEYE
EVOKERS
OVEREAT

•V•••E•
AVAILED
AVENGED
AVENGER
AVENGES
AVENUES
AVERRED
AVERTED
AVIATED
AVIATES
AVOIDED
AVONLEA
AVULSED
AVULSES
EVACUEE
EVANDER
EVANGEL
EVERTED
EVICTED
EVILLER
EVINCED
EVINCES
EVOLVED
EVOLVES
EVULSED
EVULSES
EVZONES
IVORIES
OVERSEA
OVERSEE
SVELTER

•V••••E
AVARICE
AVERAGE
EVACUEE
EVASIVE
EVILEYE
IVANHOE
IVYLIKE
OVERAGE
OVERATE
OVERAWE
OVERDUE
OVERLIE
OVERSEE
OVERUSE
TVGUIDE

••VE•••
ADVENTS
ADVERBS
ADVERSE
ADVERTS
ALVEOLI
BEVELED
BEVERLY
CAVEATS
CAVEDIN
CAVEINS
CAVEMAN
CAVEMEN
CAVERNS
CAVESIN
CAVETTO
COVERED
COVERUP
COVETED
DEVEINS
DEVELOP
DIVERGE
DIVERSE
DIVERTS
DIVESIN
DIVESTS
DOVECOT
ENVELOP
GAVELED
GAVEOFF
GAVEOUT
GAVEWAY
GIVENIN
GIVENTO
GIVENUP
GIVEOFF
GIVEOUT
GIVESIN
GIVESTO
GIVESUP
GIVEUPS
GIVEWAY
GOVERNS
HAVENOT
HAVERED
HOVERED
HOVERER
INVEIGH
INVENTS
INVERSE
INVERTS
INVESTS
JAVELIN
JUVENAL
LAVERNE
LEVELED
LEVELER
LEVELLY
LEVERED
LEVERET
LIVEDIN
LIVEDON
LIVENED
LIVEOAK
LIVEONE
LIVEOUT
LIVESIN
LIVESON
LOVEBUG
LOVEINS
LOVERLY
MOVEDIN
MOVEDON
MOVEDUP
MOVEOUT
MOVESIN
MOVESON
MOVESUP
NOVELLA
NOVELLE
NOVELTY
NOVENAS
OBVERSE
OBVERTS
POVERTY
RAVELED
RAVENED
RAVENNA
RAVEUPS
REVEALS
REVELED
REVELER
REVELRY
REVENGE
REVENUE
REVERBS
REVERED
REVERES
REVERIE
REVERSE
REVERTS
RIVETED
RIVETER
SAVEDUP
SAVELOY
SAVESUP
SEVENAM
SEVENPM
SEVENTH
SEVENTY
SEVENUP
SEVERAL
SEVERED
SEVERER
TAVERNS
UNVEILS
VIVENDI
WAVEDIN
WAVELET
WAVEOFF
WAVERED
WAVERER
WAVESIN
WYVERNS

••V•E••
BOVVERS
ENVIERS
JIVIEST
LEVIERS
REVIEWS
RIVIERA
RIVIERE
SOVIETS
WAVIEST
YEVGENY

••V••E•
ADVISED
ADVISER
ADVISES
ALVAREZ
BEVELED
BOVINES
CAVEMEN
CAVILED
CAVILER
CIVVIES
COVERED
COVETED
DEVICES
DEVILED
DEVISED
DEVISES
DEVOTED
DEVOTEE
DEVOTES
DEVRIES
DIVIDED
DIVIDER
DIVIDES
DIVINED
DIVINER
DIVINES
DIVVIED
DIVVIES
FAVORED
GAVELED
HAVERED
HOVERED
HOVERER
INVADED
INVADER
INVADES
INVITED
INVITES
INVOKED
INVOKER
INVOKES
LEVELED
LEVELER
LEVERED
LEVERET
LEVITES
LIVENED
NAVVIES
NOVICES
PAVANES
PIVOTED
RAVAGED
RAVAGER
RAVAGES
RAVELED
RAVENED
RAVINES
REVELED
REVELER
REVERED
REVERES
REVILED
REVILES
REVISED
REVISER
REVISES
REVIVED
REVIVES
REVOKED
REVOKES
RIVALED
RIVETED
RIVETER
RIVULET
SAVAGED
SAVAGER
SAVAGES
SAVORED
SAVVIER
SEVERED
SEVERER
VIVIDER
WAVELET
WAVERED
WAVERER

••V•••E
ADVANCE
ADVERSE
BIVALVE
DEVALUE
DEVIATE
DEVILLE
DEVOLVE
DEVOTEE
DIVERGE
DIVERSE
DIVORCE
DIVULGE
GAVOTTE
HOVLANE
INVERSE
INVOGUE
INVOICE
INVOLVE
LAVALSE
LAVERNE
LIVABLE
LIVEONE
LOVABLE
MOVABLE
NAVARRE
NEVILLE
NOVELLE
OBVERSE
OBVIATE
ORVILLE
REVALUE
REVENGE
REVENUE
REVERIE
REVERSE
REVOICE
REVOLVE
RIVIERE
SAVABLE
SEVIGNE
SEVILLE

•••VE••
BEAVERS
BOVVERS
BRAVELY
BRAVERY
BRAVEST
BREVETS
CALVERT
CARVERS
CLAVELL
CLOVERS
CONVENE
CONVENT
CONVERT
CONVEYS
CRAVENS
CRAVERS
CULVERS
CULVERT
CURVETS
DELVERS
DRIVEAT
DRIVEIN
DRIVELS
DRIVERS
DRIVEUP
DROVERS
ELEVENS
FERVENT
GRAVELS
GRAVELY
GRAVERS
GRAVEST
GRIVETS
GROVELS
HARVEST
HEAVEHO
HEAVENS
HEAVERS
HEAVETO
HOOVERS
HUMVEES
IGIVEUP
JAYVEES
KNAVERY
LEAVEIN
LEAVENS
LOUVERS
MARVELS
NAIVELY
NAIVETE
NAIVETY
NOUVEAU
PARVENU
PEAVEYS
PLOVERS
PREVENT
PRIVETS
PROVERB
PROVERS
PURVEYS
QUAVERS
QUAVERY
QUIVERS
QUIVERY
RIGVEDA
SALVERS
SERVERS
SERVERY
SERVEUP
SHAVERS
SHIVERS
SHIVERY
SHOVELS
SHOVERS
SILVERS
SILVERY
SKIVERS
SLAVERS
SLAVERY
SLAVEYS
SLIVERS
SLOVENE
SLOVENS
SNIVELS
SOLVENT
SOLVERS
STEVENS
SUAVELY
SUAVEST
SUBVERT
SURVEYS
SWIVELS
SWIVETS
TRAVELS
TRAVERS
TRIVETS
VELVETS
VELVETY
VERVETS
WAIVERS
WEAVERS

•••V•E•
BMOVIES
BRAVOES
CHEVIED
CHEVIES
CHEVRES
CIVVIES
CLAVIER
CURVIER
DIVVIED
DIVVIES
FLIVVER
GRAVIES
HEAVIER
HEAVIES
HUMVEES
JANVIER
JAYVEES
LOUVRED
LOUVRES
NAVVIES
NERVIER
OEUVRES
OLIVIER
PREVIEW
PRIVIER
PRIVIES
PURVIEW
SALVOES
SAVVIER

•••V••E
CONVENE
CONVOKE
CREVICE
ELEVATE
GRAVURE
NAIVETE
OLIVINE
OUTVOTE
PERVADE
PRIVATE
PROVIDE
PROVOKE
SALVAGE
SELVAGE
SERVICE
SERVILE
SLOVENE
SUBVOCE
SURVIVE
UNAVOCE
VALVATE

••••VE•
ACTIVES
ALCOVES
ALLOVER
ANDOVER
AQUIVER
ARGIVES
ARRIVED
ARRIVER
ARRIVES
BEHAVED
BEHAVES
BEHOVED
BEHOVES
BELOVED
BILEVEL
CARAVEL
CHEEVER
CLEAVED
CLEAVER
CLEAVES
DELIVER
DERIVED
DERIVES
DIDOVER
DWARVES
ENDIVES
ENLIVEN
ESTEVEZ
EVOLVED
EVOLVES
EXWIVES
FLIVVER
FLYOVER
FOREVER
GETEVEN
GETOVER
GOTEVEN
GOTOVER
GREAVES
GRIEVED
GRIEVER
GRIEVES
GROOVED
GROOVES
HANOVER
HOPOVER
HOWEVER
KNIEVEL
LAYOVER
LIEOVER
MINIVER
MOTIVES
NATIVES
NINEVEH
OCTAVES
PALAVER
POPOVER
PUTOVER
RANOVER
RECOVER
RELIVED
RELIVES
REMOVED
REMOVER
REMOVES
REPAVED
REPAVES
REVIVED
REVIVES
REWOVEN
RUNOVER
SCARVES
SCRIVEN
SCURVES
SHEAVED
SHEAVES
SHELVED
SHELVES
SHRIVEL
SHRIVER
SHRIVES
SLEEVES
STARVED
STARVES
STRIVED
STRIVEN
STRIVER
STRIVES
SWERVED
SWERVES
THIEVED
THIEVES
THRIVED
THRIVES
TWELVES
UNCOVER
UNLOVED
UNMOVED
UNPAVED
UNRAVEL
UNWOVEN
UPRIVER
WHARVES
WHOEVER
ZOUAVES

••••V•E
LEHAVRE

•••••VE
ABSOLVE
ABUSIVE
ACHIEVE
ACTFIVE
AIRWAVE
AMATIVE
APPROVE
ARCHIVE
BEEHIVE
BEHOOVE
BELIEVE
BEREAVE
BIVALVE
CAPTIVE
COMMOVE
CONCAVE
CONNIVE
CURSIVE
DECEIVE
DENEUVE
DEPRAVE
DEPRIVE
DESERVE
DEVOLVE
ELUSIVE
EMOTIVE
ENCLAVE
ENGRAVE
ENSLAVE
EROSIVE
EVASIVE
FESTIVE
FICTIVE
FORGAVE
FORGIVE
FURTIVE
IMPROVE
INVOLVE
MASSIVE
MISSIVE
NEWWAVE
OBSERVE
ONLEAVE
ONSERVE
OUTLIVE
PASSIVE
PENSIVE
PLOSIVE
RECEIVE
RELIEVE
REPROVE
RESERVE

RESOLVE
RESTIVE
REVOLVE
REWEAVE
SKYDIVE
SURVIVE
TENSIVE
UNITIVE
UNNERVE
UNWEAVE
WHEREVE

V••F•••
VATFULS

V•••F••
VOTEFOR

V••••F•
VERSIFY
VITRIFY

•V••F••
OVERFLY

••V••F•
GAVEOFF
GIVEOFF
WAVEOFF

••V•••F
GAVEOFF
GIVEOFF
WAVEOFF

V•G••••
VAGRANT
VAGUELY
VAGUEST
VEGETAL
VEGGIES
VEGGING
VIGOURS
VOGUISH

V••G•••
VANGOGH
VAUGHAN
VEGGIES
VEGGING
VEIGHTS
VERGERS
VERGING
VIRGINS
VIRGOAN
VIRGULE
VULGATE

V•••G••
VINEGAR
VIRAGOS
VISAGES
VOYAGED
VOYAGER
VOYAGES

V••••G•
VANGOGH
VANTAGE
VERDUGO
VERTIGO
VESTIGE
VIKINGS
VILLAGE
VINTAGE
VOLTAGE

V•••••G
VALUING
VAMPING
VARYING
VATTING
VEERING
VEGGING
VEILING
VEINING
VENDING
VENTING
VERGING
VESTING
VETOING
VETTING
VIEWING
VISAING
VOICING
VOIDING

•VG••••
TVGUIDE

•V•G•••
AVIGNON

•V••G••
AVENGED
AVENGER
AVENGES
EVANGEL

•V•••G•
AVERAGE
OVERAGE

•V••••G
AVOWING
EVADING
EVENING
EVOKING
OVERBIG

••VG•••
YEVGENY

••V•G••
INVOGUE
RAVAGED
RAVAGER
RAVAGES
SAVAGED
SAVAGER
SAVAGES
SEVIGNE

••V••G•
DIVERGE
DIVULGE
INVEIGH
LIVINGS
RAVINGS
REVENGE
SAVINGS

••V•••G
ENVYING
LEVYING
LOVEBUG
REVVING

•••V•G•
SALVAGE
SELVAGE
ZHIVAGO

•••V••G
BRAVING
CALVING
CARVING
CRAVING
CURVING
DELVING
DRIVING
GRAVING
HALVING
HEAVING
LEAVING
PEEVING
PROVING
REVVING
ROLVAAG
SALVING
SERVING
SHAVING
SHOVING
SLAVING
SOLVING
STAVING
WAIVING
WEAVING

V•H••••
VEHICLE

V••H•••
VAUGHAN
VEIGHTS
VETCHES
VOUCHED
VOUCHER
VOUCHES

V••••H•
VOTECHS

V•••••H
VAMPISH
VANGOGH
VARNISH
VOGUISH

•V•H•••
TVSHOWS

•V••H••
IVANHOE

•V••••H
EVANISH

••V•H••
NAVAHOS

••V•••H
INVEIGH
SEVENTH

•••V•H•
HALVAHS
HEAVEHO

•••V••H
DERVISH
KNAVISH
PEEVISH
SLAVISH

••••V•H
MITZVAH
NINEVEH

VI•••••
VIADUCT
VIBRANT
VIBRATE
VIBRATO
VICEROY
VICIOUS
VICTIMS
VICTORS
VICTORY
VICTUAL
VICUNAS
VIDALIA
VIETNAM
VIEWERS
VIEWIER
VIEWING
VIGOURS
VIKINGS
VILLAGE
VILLAIN
VILLEIN
VILNIUS
VINCENT
VINEGAR
VINIEST
VINTAGE
VINTNER
VIOLATE
VIOLENT
VIOLETS
VIOLINS
VIOLIST
VIRAGOS
VIRGINS
VIRGOAN
VIRGULE
VIRIBUS
VIRTUAL
VIRTUES
VIRTUTE
VIRUSES
VISAGES
VISAING
VISALIA
VISAVIS
VISCERA
VISCOUS
VISIBLE
VISIBLY
VISIONS
VISITED
VISITOR
VISTULA
VISUALS
VITALLY
VITAMIN
VITIATE
VITRIFY
VITRIOL
VITTLES
VIVALDI
VIVENDI
VIVIDER
VIVIDLY
VIZIERS
VIZSLAS

V•I••••
VAINEST
VEIGHTS
VEILING
VEINIER
VEINING
VOICING
VOIDING

V••I•••
VALIANT
VALIDLY
VALISES
VANILLA
VANILLI
VAPIDLY
VARIANT
VARIETY
VARIOUS
VATICAN
VEHICLE
VENISON
VERISMO
VERITAS
VICIOUS
VIKINGS
VINIEST
VIRIBUS
VISIBLE
VISIBLY
VISIONS
VISITED
VISITOR
VITIATE
VIVIDER
VIVIDLY
VIZIERS

V•••I••
VACCINE
VACUITY
VALUING
VAMPING
VAMPIRA
VAMPIRE
VAMPISH
VANDINE
VARMINT
VARNISH
VARSITY
VARYING
VASTIER
VATTING
VEALIER
VEERIES
VEERING
VEGGIES
VEGGING
VEILING
VEINIER
VEINING
VENDING
VENTING
VERDICT
VERGING
VERNIER
VERSIFY
VERSION
VERTIGO
VESPIDS
VESTIGE
VESTING
VETOING
VETTING
VICTIMS
VIEWIER
VIEWING
VILNIUS
VIOLINS
VIOLIST
VIRGINS
VISAING
VITRIFY
VITRIOL
VOGUISH
VOICING
VOIDING
VULPINE

V••••I•
VALERIE
VERMEIL
VIDALIA
VILLAIN
VILLEIN
VISALIA
VISAVIS
VITAMIN
VOCALIC
VOLTAIC
VOTEDIN
VOTESIN

V•••••I
VANILLI
VIVALDI
VIVENDI

•VI••••
AVIANCA
AVIATED
AVIATES
AVIATOR
AVIDITY
AVIGNON
EVICTED
EVIDENT
EVILEST
EVILEYE
EVILLER
EVINCED
EVINCES
OVIPARA
OVISACS

•V•I•••
AVAILED
AVOIDED
OVOIDAL

•V••I••
AVARICE
AVIDITY
AVOWING
EVADING
EVANISH
EVASION
EVASIVE
EVENING
EVOKING
IVORIES
IVYLIKE
OVATION
TVGUIDE

•V•••I•
EVENKIS
OVERBIG
OVERDID
OVERLIE

••VI•••
ADVISED
ADVISER
ADVISES
ADVISOR
BOVINES
CAVIARS
CAVILED
CAVILER
CIVILLY
DAVINCI
DEVIANT
DEVIATE
DEVICES
DEVILED
DEVILLE
DEVILRY
DEVIOUS
DEVISED
DEVISES
DIVIDED
DIVIDER
DIVIDES
DIVINED
DIVINER
DIVINES
DIVINUM
DIVISOR
ENVIERS
ENVIOUS
GAVIALS
INVITED
INVITES
INVITRO
JIVIEST
LAVINIA
LEVIERS
LEVITES
LIVIDLY
LIVINGS
NEVILLE
NOVICES
OBVIATE
OBVIOUS
ORVILLE
PAVIOUR
QIVIUTS
RAVINES
RAVINGS
RAVIOLI
REVIEWS
REVILED
REVILES
REVISED
REVISER
REVISES
REVISIT
REVIVAL
REVIVED
REVIVES
RIVIERA
RIVIERE
SAVINGS
SAVIORS
SAVIOUR
SEVIGNE
SEVILLE
SOVIETS
VIVIDER
VIVIDLY
WAVIEST

••V•I••
CAVEINS
CIVVIES
DEVEINS
DEVRIES
DIVVIED
DIVVIES
ENVYING
INVEIGH
INVOICE
LEVYING
LOVEINS
NAVVIES
REVOICE
REVVING
SAVVIER
SAVVILY
UNVEILS

••V••I•
BAVARIA
CAVEDIN
CAVESIN
DIVESIN
GIVENIN
GIVESIN
INVALID
JAVELIN
LAVINIA
LIVEDIN
LIVESIN
MOVEDIN
MOVESIN
REVERIE
REVISIT
SAVARIN
WAVEDIN
WAVESIN

••V•••I
ALVEOLI
DAVINCI
HAVARTI
RAVIOLI
VIVALDI
VIVENDI

•••VI••
ATAVISM
ATAVIST
BMOVIES
BOBVILA
BRAVING
BREVITY
CALVING
CARVING
CERVIDS
CHEVIED
CHEVIES
CHEVIOT
CIVVIES
CLAVIER
CONVICT
CRAVING
CREVICE
CURVIER
CURVING
DELVING
DERVISH
DIVVIED
DIVVIES
DRIVING
ELUVIUM
FAUVISM
FAUVIST
FLUVIAL
GRAVIES
GRAVING
GRAVITY
HALVING
HEAVIER
HEAVIES
HEAVILY
HEAVING
JANVIER
KNAVISH
LATVIAN
LEAVING
NAVVIES
NERVIER
NERVILY
OLIVIER
OLIVINE
PEEVING
PEEVISH
PLUVIAL
PREVIEW
PRIVIER
PRIVIES
PRIVILY
PRIVITY
PROVIDE
PROVING
PROVISO
PURVIEW
REVVING
SALVIAS
SALVING
SAVVIER
SAVVILY
SERVICE
SERVILE
SERVING
SHAVING
SHOVING
SLAVING
SLAVISH
SOLVING
SORVINO
SPAVINS
STAVING
SUAVITY
SURVIVE
TREVINO
TRIVIAL
WAIVING
WEAVING
WEEVILS

•••V•I•
DRIVEIN
LEAVEIN
PREVAIL
REAVAIL
TRAVAIL
TRAVOIS

•••V••I
GALVANI

••••VI•
ALLUVIA
AQUAVIT
BEDEVIL
BOLIVIA
CHERVIL
INCIVIL
MCGAVIN
MORAVIA
OCTAVIA
SEGOVIA
TELAVIV
UNCIVIL
VISAVIS

••••V•I
OLDUVAI

•••••VI
BONJOVI
PAHLAVI

V••J•••
VALJEAN
VEEJAYS

V••••J•
VALLEJO

•V••J••
OVERJOY

••V•J••
NAVAJOS

V•K••••
VIKINGS

V••••K•
VANDYKE
VRONSKY

V•••••K
VANDYCK
VANEYCK
VEENECK

•V•K•••
EVOKERS
EVOKING

•V••K••
EVENKIS

•V•••K•
IVYLIKE

••V•K••
INVOKED
INVOKER
INVOKES
REVOKED
REVOKES

••V•••K
LIVEOAK

•••V•K•
CONVOKE
PROVOKE
SLOVAKS

V•L••••
VALANCE
VALENCE
VALENCY
VALERIE
VALIANT
VALIDLY
VALISES
VALJEAN
VALLEJO
VALLEYS
VALOURS
VALUATE
VALUING
VALVATE
VELLUMS
VELOURS
VELVETS
VELVETY
VILLAGE
VILLAIN
VILLEIN
VILNIUS
VOLCANO
VOLLEYS
VOLPONE
VOLTAGE
VOLTAIC
VOLUBLE
VOLUBLY
VOLUMES
VULCANS
VULGATE
VULPINE
VULTURE

V••L•••
VALLEJO
VALLEYS
VARLETS
VAULTED
VAULTER
VEALIER
VEILING
VELLUMS
VILLAGE
VILLAIN
VILLEIN
VIOLATE
VIOLENT
VIOLETS
VIOLINS
VIOLIST
VOLLEYS
VOWLESS

V•••L••
VANILLA
VANILLI
VENALLY
VIDALIA
VISALIA
VITALLY
VITTLES
VIVALDI
VIZSLAS
VOCALIC
VOCALLY

V••••L•
VACUOLE
VAGUELY
VALIDLY
VANDALS
VANILLA
VANILLI
VAPIDLY
VASSALS
VATFULS
VEHICLE
VENALLY
VERBALS
VESSELS
VEXEDLY
VIRGULE
VISIBLE
VISIBLY
VISTULA
VISUALS
VITALLY
VIVIDLY
VOCALLY
VOLUBLE
VOLUBLY

V•••••L
VANPOOL
VEGETAL
VENTRAL
VERMEIL
VICTUAL
VIRTUAL
VITRIOL

•V•L•••
AVULSED
AVULSES
EVILEST
EVILEYE
EVILLER
EVOLVED
EVOLVES
EVULSED
EVULSES
IVYLIKE
SVELTER

•V••L••
AVAILED
AVONLEA
EVILLER
OVERLAP
OVERLAY
OVERLIE

•V•••L•
AVOWALS
OVERALL
OVERFLY
OVERTLY

•V••••L
EVANGEL
OVERALL
OVOIDAL

••VL•••
HOVLANE
PAVLOVA

••V•L••
BEVELED
BIVALVE
CAVALRY
CAVILED
CAVILER
CIVILLY
DEVALUE
DEVELOP
DEVILED
DEVILLE
DEVILRY
DEVOLVE
DIVULGE
ENVELOP
GAVELED
INVALID
INVOLVE
JAVELIN
LAVALSE
LEVELED
LEVELER
LEVELLY
NEVILLE
NOVELLA
NOVELLE
NOVELTY
ORVILLE
RAVELED
REVALUE
REVELED
REVELER
REVELRY
REVILED
REVILES
REVOLTS
REVOLVE
RIVALED
RIVALRY
RIVULET
SAVALAS
SAVELOY
SEVILLE
VIVALDI
WAVELET

••V••L•
ALVEOLI
BEVERLY
CIVILLY
DEVILLE
GAVIALS
LEVELLY
LIVABLE
LIVIDLY
LOVABLE
LOVABLY
LOVERLY
MOVABLE
MOVABLY
NEVILLE
NOVELLA
NOVELLE
ORVILLE
RAVIOLI
REVEALS
SAVABLE
SAVVILY
SEVILLE
UNVEILS
VIVIDLY

••V•••L
JUVENAL
PIVOTAL
REVIVAL
SEVERAL

•••V•L•
BOBVILA
BRAVELY
CLAVELL
COEVALS
DRIVELS
GRAVELS
GRAVELY
GROVELS
HEAVILY
MARVELS
NAIVELY
NERVILY
PRIVILY
SAVVILY
SERVALS
SERVILE
SHOVELS
SNIVELS
SUAVELY
SWIVELS
TRAVELS
WEEVILS

•••V••L
CLAVELL
FLUVIAL
PLUVIAL
PREVAIL
REAVAIL
TRAVAIL
TRIVIAL

••••V•L
ARRIVAL
BEDEVIL
BILEVEL
CARAVEL
CHERVIL
ESTIVAL
INCIVIL
KNIEVEL
REMOVAL
REVIVAL
SHRIVEL
UNCIVIL
UNRAVEL

V•M••••
VAMOOSE
VAMPERS
VAMPING
VAMPIRA
VAMPIRE
VAMPISH

V••M•••
VARMINT
VERMEER
VERMEIL
VERMONT

V•••M••
VITAMIN
VOLUMES

V••••M•
VACUUMS
VELLUMS
VERISMO
VICTIMS

V•••••M
VIETNAM

••V•M••
CAVEMAN
CAVEMEN
JAVAMAN
REVAMPS

••V•••M
DIVINUM
SEVENAM
SEVENPM

•••V••M
ATAVISM

ELUVIUM
FAUVISM

V•N••••
VANDALS
VANDINE
VANDYCK
VANDYKE
VANESSA
VANEYCK
VANGOGH
VANILLA
VANILLI
VANPOOL
VANTAGE
VANUATU
VENALLY
VENDING
VENDORS
VENEERS
VENISON
VENTERS
VENTING
VENTRAL
VENTURA
VENTURE
VINCENT
VINEGAR
VINIEST
VINTAGE
VINTNER

V••N•••
VAINEST
VARNISH
VAUNTED
VAUNTER
VEENECK
VEINIER
VEINING
VERNIER
VILNIUS
VRONSKY

V•••N••
VACANCY
VALANCE
VALENCE
VALENCY
VEDANTA
VERANDA
VICUNAS
VIETNAM
VIKINGS
VINTNER
VIVENDI

V••••N•
VACCINE
VAGRANT
VALIANT
VALUING
VAMPING
VANDINE
VARIANT
VARMINT
VARYING
VATTING
VEERING
VEGGING
VEILING
VEINING
VENDING
VENTING
VERBENA
VERDANT
VERGING
VERMONT
VESTING
VETOING
VETTING
VIBRANT
VIEWING
VINCENT
VIOLENT
VIOLINS
VIRGINS
VISAING
VISIONS
VOICING
VOIDING
VOLCANO
VOLPONE
VULCANS
VULPINE

V•••••N
VALJEAN
VATICAN
VAUGHAN
VENISON
VERSION
VETERAN
VILLAIN
VILLEIN
VIRGOAN
VITAMIN
VOTEDIN
VOTESIN

•V•N•••
AVENGED
AVENGER
AVENGES
AVENUES
AVONLEA
EVANDER
EVANGEL
EVANISH
EVENEST
EVENING
EVENKIS
EVENOUT
EVENSUP
EVINCED
EVINCES
IVANHOE
IVANOVO

•V••N••
AVIANCA
AVIGNON
EVZONES

•V•••N•
AVOWING
EVADING
EVENING
EVIDENT
EVOKING

•V••••N
AVIGNON
EVASION
OVATION
OVERRAN
OVERRUN

••V•N••
ADVANCE
ADVENTS
BOVINES
DAVINCI
DIVINED
DIVINER
DIVINES
DIVINUM
GIVENIN
GIVENTO
GIVENUP
HAVENOT
INVENTS
JUVENAL
LAVINIA
LEVANTS
LIVENED
LIVINGS
NOVENAS
PAVANES
RAVENED
RAVENNA
RAVINES
RAVINGS
REVENGE
REVENUE
SAVANNA
SAVANTS
SAVINGS
SEVENAM
SEVENPM
SEVENTH
SEVENTY
SEVENUP
VIVENDI

••V••N•
CAVEINS
CAVERNS
DEVEINS
DEVIANT
ENVYING
GOVERNS
HOVLANE
LAVERNE
LEVYING
LIVEONE
LIVORNO
LOVEINS
RAVENNA
REVVING
SAVANNA
SEVIGNE
TAVERNS
WYVERNS
YEVGENY

••V•••N
CAVEDIN
CAVEMAN
CAVEMEN
CAVESIN
DIVESIN
GIVENIN
GIVESIN
JAVAMAN
JAVELIN
LIVEDIN
LIVEDON
LIVESIN
LIVESON
MOVEDIN
MOVEDON
MOVESIN
MOVESON
NEVADAN
SAVARIN
WAVEDIN
WAVESIN

•••V•N•
BRAVING
CALVING
CARVING
CONVENE
CONVENT
CRAVENS
CRAVING
CURVING
DELVING
DRIVING
ELEVENS
FERVENT
GALVANI
GRAVING
HALVING
HEAVENS
HEAVING
LEAVENS
LEAVING
NIRVANA
OLIVINE
PARVENU
PEEVING
PREVENT
PROVING
REVVING
SALVING
SERVANT
SERVING
SHAVING
SHOVING
SLAVING
SLOVENE
SLOVENS
SOLVENT
SOLVING
SORVINO
SPAVINS
STAVING
STEVENS
SYLVANS
TREVINO
WAIVING
WEAVING

•••V••N
CHEVRON
DRIVEIN
LATVIAN
LEAVEIN

••••V•N
CARAVAN
CLEAVON
DONOVAN
ENLIVEN
GETEVEN
GOTEVEN
HESHVAN
MCGAVIN
MINIVAN
REWOVEN
SCRIVEN
STRIVEN
UNWOVEN
YEREVAN

VO•••••
VOCALIC
VOCALLY
VOGUISH
VOICING
VOIDING
VOLCANO
VOLLEYS
VOLPONE
VOLTAGE
VOLTAIC
VOLUBLE
VOLUBLY
VOLUMES
VOODOOS
VOTECHS
VOTEDIN
VOTEFOR
VOTEOUT
VOTESIN
VOUCHED
VOUCHER
VOUCHES
VOWLESS
VOYAGED
VOYAGER
VOYAGES

V•O••••
VIOLATE
VIOLENT
VIOLETS
VIOLINS
VIOLIST
VOODOOS
VRONSKY

V••O•••
VALOURS
VAMOOSE
VAPOURS
VELOURS
VETOERS
VETOING
VIGOURS

V•••O••
VACUOLE
VACUOUS
VAMOOSE
VANGOGH
VANPOOL
VARIOUS
VECTORS
VENDORS
VERBOSE
VERDOUX
VERMONT
VICIOUS
VICTORS
VICTORY
VIRGOAN
VISCOUS
VISIONS
VOLPONE
VOODOOS
VOTEOUT

V••••O•
VANPOOL
VENISON
VERSION
VICEROY
VIRAGOS
VISITOR
VITRIOL
VOODOOS
VOTEFOR

V•••••O
VALLEJO
VAQUERO
VERDUGO
VERISMO
VERTIGO
VIBRATO
VOLCANO

•VO••••
AVOCADO
AVOCETS
AVOIDED
AVONLEA
AVOWALS
AVOWERS
AVOWING
EVOKERS
EVOKING
EVOLVED
EVOLVES
IVORIES
OVOIDAL

•V•O•••
EVZONES

•V••O••
EVENOUT
IVANOVO
TVSHOWS

•V•••O•
AVIATOR
AVIGNON
EVASION
IVANHOE
OVATION
OVERJOY

•V••••O
AVOCADO
IVANOVO

••VO•••
BIVOUAC
CAVORTS
DEVOLVE
DEVOTED
DEVOTEE
DEVOTES
DEVOURS
DIVORCE
FAVORED
FAVOURS
GAVOTTE
INVOGUE
INVOICE
INVOKED
INVOKER
INVOKES
INVOLVE
LIVORNO
PIVOTAL
PIVOTED
REVOICE
REVOKED
REVOKES
REVOLTS
REVOLVE
SAVORED
SAVOURS
SAVOURY

••V•O••
ALVEOLI
DEVIOUS
ENVIOUS
GAVEOFF
GAVEOUT
GIVEOFF
GIVEOUT
LIVEOAK
LIVEONE
LIVEOUT
MOVEOUT
OBVIOUS
PAVIOUR
PAVLOVA
RAVIOLI
SAVIORS
SAVIOUR
WAVEOFF

••V••O•
ADVISOR
DEVELOP
DIVISOR
DOVECOT
ENVELOP
HAVENOT
LIVEDON
LIVESON
MOVEDON
MOVESON
NAVAHOS
NAVAJOS
SAVELOY

••V•••O
CAVETTO
GIVENTO
GIVESTO
INVACUO
INVITRO
LIVORNO
NOVARRO

•••VO••
BRAVOES
CONVOKE
CONVOYS
FERVORS
FERVOUR
FLAVORS
FLAVOUR
NERVOUS
OUTVOTE
PROVOKE
PROVOST
SALVOES
SALVORS
SUBVOCE
TRAVOIS
UNAVOCE

•••V•O•
CHEVIOT
CHEVRON

•••V••O
BRAVADO
HEAVEHO
HEAVETO
PROVISO
SORVINO
TREVINO
ZHIVAGO

••••VO•
CLEAVON
DISAVOW
INFAVOR
OCTAVOS

•••••VO
CENTAVO
IVANOVO
RELIEVO
ZEMSTVO

V•P••••
VAPIDLY
VAPOURS

V••P•••
VAMPERS
VAMPING
VAMPIRA
VAMPIRE
VAMPISH
VANPOOL
VESPERS
VESPIDS
VOLPONE
VULPINE

•V•P•••
OVIPARA

•V••••P
EVENSUP
OVERLAP

••V••P•
GIVEUPS
RAVEUPS
REVAMPS
SEVENPM

••V•••P
COVERUP
DEVELOP
ENVELOP
GIVENUP
GIVESUP
MOVEDUP
MOVESUP
SAVEDUP
SAVESUP
SEVENUP

•••V••P
DRIVEUP
IGIVEUP
SERVEUP

V•Q••••
VAQUERO

VR•••••
VRONSKY

V•R••••
VARIANT
VARIETY
VARIOUS
VARLETS
VARMINT
VARNISH
VARSITY
VARYING
VERANDA
VERBALS
VERBENA
VERBOSE
VERDANT
VERDICT
VERDOUX
VERDUGO
VERDURE
VERGERS
VERGING
VERISMO
VERITAS
VERMEER
VERMEIL
VERMONT
VERNIER
VERSIFY
VERSION
VERTIGO
VERVETS
VIRAGOS
VIRGINS
VIRGOAN
VIRGULE
VIRIBUS
VIRTUAL
VIRTUES
VIRTUTE
VIRUSES

V••R•••
VAGRANT
VEERIES
VEERING
VIBRANT
VIBRATE
VIBRATO
VITRIFY
VITRIOL

V•••R••
VALERIE
VENTRAL
VETERAN
VICEROY

V••••R•
VALOURS
VAMPERS
VAMPIRA
VAMPIRE
VAPOURS
VAQUERO
VECTORS
VELOURS
VENDORS
VENEERS
VENTERS
VENTURA
VENTURE
VERDURE
VERGERS
VESPERS
VESTURE
VETOERS
VICTORS
VICTORY
VIEWERS
VIGOURS
VISCERA
VIZIERS
VULTURE

V•••••R
VASTIER
VAULTER
VAUNTER
VEALIER
VEINIER
VERMEER
VERNIER
VIEWIER
VINEGAR
VINTNER
VISITOR
VIVIDER
VOTEFOR
VOUCHER
VOYAGER

•V•R•••
AVARICE
AVERAGE
AVERRED
AVERTED
EVEREST
EVERETT
EVERTED
IVORIES
OVERACT
OVERAGE
OVERALL
OVERATE
OVERAWE
OVERBIG
OVERBUY
OVERDID
OVERDUB
OVERDUE
OVEREAT
OVERFLY
OVERJOY
OVERLAP
OVERLAY
OVERLIE
OVERRAN
OVERRUN
OVERSAW
OVERSEA
OVERSEE
OVERTAX
OVERTLY
OVERUSE

•V••R••
AVERRED
OVERRAN
OVERRUN

•V•••R•
AVATARS
AVOWERS
EVADERS
EVOKERS
OVIPARA

•V••••R
AVENGER
AVIATOR
EVANDER
EVILLER
SVELTER

••VR•••
DEVRIES

••V•R••
ADVERBS
ADVERSE
ADVERTS
ALVAREZ
BAVARIA
BEVERLY
CAVERNS
CAVORTS
COVERED
COVERUP
DIVERGE
DIVERSE
DIVERTS
DIVORCE
FAVORED
GOVERNS
HAVARTI
HAVERED
HOVERED
HOVERER
INVERSE
INVERTS
LAVERNE
LEVERED
LEVERET
LIVORNO
LOVERLY
NAVARRE
NOVARRO
OBVERSE
OBVERTS
POVERTY
REVERBS
REVERED
REVERES
REVERIE
REVERSE
REVERTS
SAVARIN
SAVORED
SEVERAL
SEVERED
SEVERER
TAVERNS
WAVERED
WAVERER
WYVERNS

••V••R•
BOVVERS
CAVALRY
CAVIARS
DEVILRY
DEVOURS
ENVIERS
FAVOURS
INVITRO
LEVIERS
NAVARRE
NOVARRO
REVELRY
RIVALRY
RIVIERA
RIVIERE
SAVIORS
SAVOURS
SAVOURY

••V•••R
ADVISER
ADVISOR
CAVILER
DIVIDER
DIVINER
DIVISOR
HOVERER
INVADER
INVOKER
LEVELER
PAVIOUR
RAVAGER
REVELER
REVISER
RIVETER
SAVAGER
SAVIOUR
SAVVIER
SEVERER
VIVIDER
WAVERER

•••VR••
CHEVRES
CHEVRON
LOUVRED
LOUVRES
OEUVRES

•••V•R•
BEAVERS
BOVVERS
BRAVERY
BRAVURA
CALVARY
CALVERT
CARVERS
CLOVERS
CONVERT
CRAVERS
CULVERS
CULVERT
DELVERS
DRIVERS
DROVERS
FERVORS
FLAVORS
GRAVERS
GRAVURE
GUEVARA
HARVARD
HEAVERS
HOOVERS
KNAVERY
LEKVARS
LOUVERS
PLOVERS
PROVERB
PROVERS
QUAVERS
QUAVERY
QUIVERS
QUIVERY
SALVERS
SALVORS
SERVERS
SERVERY
SHAVERS
SHIVERS
SHIVERY
SHOVERS
SILVERS
SILVERY
SKIVERS
SLAVERS
SLAVERY
SLIVERS
SOLVERS
SUBVERT
TRAVERS
WAIVERS
WEAVERS

•••V••R
CLAVIER
CURVIER
FERVOUR
FLAVOUR
FLIVVER
HEAVIER
JANVIER
NERVIER
OLIVIER
PRIVIER
SAVVIER

••••VR•
LEHAVRE

••••V•R
ALLOVER
ANDOVER
AQUIVER
ARRIVER
BOLIVAR
CHEEVER
CLEAVER
DELIVER
DIDOVER
FLIVVER
FLYOVER
FOREVER
GETOVER
GOTOVER
GRIEVER
HANOVER
HOPOVER
HOWEVER
INFAVOR
LAYOVER
LIEOVER
MINIVER
PALAVER
POPOVER
PUTOVER
RANOVER
RECOVER
REMOVER
RUNOVER
SAMOVAR
SHRIVER
STRIVER
UNCOVER
UPRIVER
WHOEVER

V•S••••
VASSALS
VASTEST
VASTIER
VESPERS
VESPIDS
VESSELS
VESTEES
VESTIGE
VESTING
VESTURE
VISAGES
VISAING
VISALIA
VISAVIS
VISCERA
VISCOUS
VISIBLE
VISIBLY
VISIONS
VISITED
VISITOR
VISTULA
VISUALS

V••S•••
VARSITY
VASSALS
VERSIFY
VERSION
VESSELS
VIZSLAS

V•••S••
VALISES
VANESSA
VENISON
VERISMO
VIRUSES
VOTESIN
VRONSKY

V••••S•
VAGUEST
VAINEST
VAMOOSE
VAMPISH
VANESSA
VARNISH
VASTEST
VERBOSE
VINIEST
VIOLIST
VOGUISH
VOWLESS

V•••••S
VACATES
VACUOUS
VACUUMS
VALISES
VALLEYS
VALOURS
VAMPERS
VANDALS
VAPOURS
VARIOUS
VARLETS
VASSALS
VATFULS
VECTORS
VEEJAYS
VEERIES
VEGGIES
VEIGHTS
VELLUMS
VELOURS
VELVETS
VENDORS
VENEERS
VENTERS
VERBALS
VERGERS
VERITAS
VERVETS
VESPERS
VESPIDS

VESSELS
VESTEES
VETCHES
VETOERS
VICIOUS
VICTIMS
VICTORS
VICUNAS
VIEWERS
VIGOURS
VIKINGS
VILNIUS
VIOLETS
VIOLINS
VIRAGOS
VIRGINS
VIRIBUS
VIRTUES
VIRUSES
VISAGES
VISAVIS
VISCOUS
VISIONS
VISUALS
VITTLES
VIZIERS
VIZSLAS
VOLLEYS
VOLUMES
VOODOOS
VOTECHS
VOUCHES
VOWLESS
VOYAGES
VULCANS

•VS••••
TVSHOWS

•V•S•••
EVASION
EVASIVE
OVISACS

•V••S••
AVULSED
AVULSES
EVENSUP
EVULSED
EVULSES
OVERSAW
OVERSEA
OVERSEE

•V•••S•
EVANISH
EVENEST
EVEREST
EVILEST
OVERUSE

•V••••S
AVATARS
AVENGES
AVENUES
AVIATES
AVOCETS
AVOWALS
AVOWERS
AVULSES
EVADERS
EVENKIS
EVINCES
EVOKERS
EVOLVES
EVULSES
EVZONES
IVORIES
OVISACS
TVSHOWS

••V•S••
ADVISED
ADVISER
ADVISES
ADVISOR
CAVESIN
DEVISED
DEVISES
DIVESIN
DIVESTS
DIVISOR
GIVESIN
GIVESTO
GIVESUP
INVESTS
LIVESIN
LIVESON
MOVESIN
MOVESON
MOVESUP
REVISED
REVISER
REVISES
REVISIT
SAVESUP
WAVESIN

••V••S•
ADVERSE
DIVERSE
INVERSE
JIVIEST
LAVALSE
OBVERSE
REVERSE
WAVIEST

••V•••S
ADVENTS
ADVERBS
ADVERTS
ADVISES
BOVINES
BOVVERS
CAVEATS
CAVEINS
CAVERNS
CAVIARS
CAVORTS
CIVVIES
DEVEINS
DEVICES
DEVIOUS
DEVISES
DEVOTES
DEVOURS
DEVRIES
DIVERTS
DIVESTS
DIVIDES
DIVINES
DIVVIES
ENVIERS
ENVIOUS
FAVOURS
GAVIALS
GIVEUPS
GOVERNS
INVADES
INVENTS
INVERTS
INVESTS
INVITES
INVOKES
LEVANTS
LEVIERS
LEVITES
LIVINGS
LOVEINS
NAVAHOS
NAVAJOS
NAVVIES
NOVENAS
NOVICES
OBVERTS
OBVIOUS
PAVANES
QIVIUTS
RAVAGES
RAVEUPS
RAVINES
RAVINGS
REVAMPS
REVEALS
REVERBS
REVERES
REVERTS
REVIEWS
REVILES
REVISES
REVIVES
REVOKES
REVOLTS
SAVAGES
SAVALAS
SAVANTS
SAVINGS
SAVIORS
SAVOURS
SOVIETS
TAVERNS
UNVEILS
WYVERNS

•••V•S•
ATAVISM
ATAVIST
BRAVEST
CANVASS
DERVISH
FAUVISM
FAUVIST
GRAVEST
HARVEST
KNAVISH
PEEVISH
PROVISO
PROVOST
SLAVISH
SUAVEST

•••V••S
BEAVERS
BMOVIES
BOVVERS
BRAVOES
BREVETS
CANVASS
CARVERS
CERVIDS
CHEVIES
CHEVRES
CIVVIES
CLOVERS
COEVALS
CONVEYS
CONVOYS
CRAVATS
CRAVENS
CRAVERS
CULVERS
CURVETS
DELVERS
DIVVIES
DRIVELS
DRIVERS
DROVERS
ELEVENS
FERVORS
FLAVORS
GRAVELS
GRAVERS
GRAVIES
GRIVETS
GROVELS
HALVAHS
HEAVENS
HEAVERS
HEAVIES
HOOVERS
HUMVEES
JAYVEES
LEAVENS
LEKVARS
LOUVERS
LOUVRES
MARVELS
NAVVIES
NERVOUS
OEUVRES
PEAVEYS
PLOVERS
PRIVETS
PRIVIES
PROVERS
PURVEYS
QUAVERS
QUIVERS
SALVERS
SALVIAS
SALVOES
SALVORS
SERVALS
SERVERS
SHAVERS
SHIVERS
SHOVELS
SHOVERS
SILVERS
SKIVERS
SLAVERS
SLAVEYS
SLIVERS
SLOVAKS
SLOVENS
SNIVELS
SOLVERS
SPAVINS
STEVENS
SURVEYS
SWIVELS
SWIVETS
SYLVANS
TRAVELS
TRAVERS
TRAVOIS
TRIVETS
VELVETS
VERVETS
WAIVERS
WEAVERS
WEEVILS

••••V•S
ACTIVES
ALCOVES
ARGIVES
ARRIVES
BEHAVES
BEHOVES
CASAVAS
CLEAVES
DERIVES
DWARVES
ENDIVES
EVOLVES
EXWIVES
GREAVES
GRIEVES
GROOVES
MOTIVES
NATIVES
OCTAVES
OCTAVOS
RELIVES
REMOVES
REPAVES
REVIVES
SCARVES
SCURVES
SHEAVES
SHELVES
SHRIVES
SLEEVES
STARVES
STRIVES
SWERVES
THIEVES
THRIVES
TWELVES
VISAVIS
WHARVES
ZOUAVES

•••••VS
YOMTOVS

V•T••••
VATFULS
VATICAN
VATTING
VETCHES
VETERAN
VETOERS
VETOING
VETTING
VITALLY
VITAMIN
VITIATE
VITRIFY
VITRIOL
VITTLES
VOTECHS
VOTEDIN
VOTEFOR
VOTEOUT
VOTESIN

V••T•••
VANTAGE
VASTEST
VASTIER
VATTING
VECTORS
VENTERS
VENTING
VENTRAL
VENTURA
VENTURE
VERTIGO
VESTEES
VESTIGE
VESTING
VESTURE
VETTING
VICTIMS
VICTORS
VICTORY
VICTUAL
VIETNAM
VINTAGE
VINTNER
VIRTUAL
VIRTUES
VIRTUTE
VISTULA
VITTLES
VOLTAGE
VOLTAIC
VULTURE

V•••T••
VACATED
VACATES
VAULTED
VAULTER
VAUNTED
VAUNTER
VEGETAL
VERITAS
VISITED
VISITOR

V••••T•
VACUITY
VALUATE
VALVATE
VANUATU
VARIETY
VARLETS
VARSITY
VEDANTA
VEIGHTS
VELVETS
VELVETY
VERVETS
VIBRATE
VIBRATO
VIOLATE
VIOLETS
VIRTUTE
VITIATE
VULGATE

V•••••T
VAGRANT
VAGUEST
VAINEST
VALIANT
VARIANT
VARMINT
VASTEST
VERDANT
VERDICT
VERMONT
VIADUCT
VIBRANT
VINCENT
VINIEST
VIOLENT
VIOLIST
VOTEOUT

•V•T•••
AVATARS
OVATION

•V••T••
AVERTED
AVIATED
AVIATES
AVIATOR
EVERTED
EVICTED
OVERTAX
OVERTLY
SVELTER

•V•••T•
AVIDITY
AVOCETS
EVERETT
OVERATE

•V••••T
EVENEST
EVENOUT
EVEREST
EVERETT
EVIDENT
EVILEST
OVERACT
OVEREAT

••V•T••
CAVETTO
COVETED
DEVOTED
DEVOTEE
DEVOTES
GAVOTTE
INVITED
INVITES
INVITRO
LEVITES
PIVOTAL
PIVOTED
RIVETED
RIVETER

••V••T•
ADVENTS
ADVERTS
CAVEATS
CAVETTO
CAVORTS
DEVIATE
DIVERTS
DIVESTS
GAVOTTE
GIVENTO
GIVESTO
HAVARTI
INVENTS
INVERTS
INVESTS
LEVANTS
NOVELTY
OBVERTS
OBVIATE
POVERTY
QIVIUTS
REVERTS
REVOLTS
SAVANTS
SEVENTH
SEVENTY
SOVIETS

••V•••T
DEVIANT
DOVECOT
GAVEOUT
GIVEOUT
HAVENOT
JIVIEST
LEVERET
LIVEOUT
MOVEOUT
REVISIT
RIVULET
WAVELET
WAVIEST

•••V•T•
BREVETS
BREVITY
CRAVATS
CURVETS
ELEVATE
GRAVITY
GRIVETS
HEAVETO
NAIVETE
NAIVETY
OUTVOTE
PRIVATE
PRIVETS
PRIVITY
SUAVITY
SWIVETS
TRIVETS
VALVATE
VELVETS
VELVETY
VERVETS

•••V••T
ATAVIST
BRAVEST
CALVERT
CHEVIOT
CONVENT
CONVERT
CONVICT
CULVERT
DRIVEAT
FAUVIST
FERVENT
GRAVEST
HARVEST
PREVENT
PROVOST
SERVANT
SOLVENT
SUAVEST
SUBVERT

••••V•T
AQUAVIT

VU•••••
VULCANS
VULGATE
VULPINE
VULTURE

V•U••••
VAUGHAN
VAULTED
VAULTER
VAUNTED
VAUNTER
VOUCHED
VOUCHER
VOUCHES

V••U•••
VACUITY
VACUOLE
VACUOUS
VACUUMS
VAGUELY
VAGUEST
VALUATE
VALUING
VANUATU
VAQUERO
VICUNAS
VIRUSES
VISUALS
VOGUISH
VOLUBLE
VOLUBLY
VOLUMES

V•••U••
VACUUMS
VALOURS
VAPOURS
VATFULS
VELLUMS
VELOURS
VENTURA
VENTURE
VERDUGO
VERDURE
VESTURE
VIADUCT
VICTUAL
VIGOURS
VIRGULE
VIRTUAL
VIRTUES
VIRTUTE
VISTULA
VULTURE

V••••U•
VACUOUS
VARIOUS
VERDOUX
VICIOUS
VILNIUS
VIRIBUS
VISCOUS
VOTEOUT

V•••••U
VANUATU

•VU••••
AVULSED
AVULSES
EVULSED
EVULSES

•V•U•••
TVGUIDE

•V••U••
AVENUES
EVACUEE
OVERUSE

•V•••U•
EVENOUT
EVENSUP
OVERBUY
OVERDUB
OVERDUE
OVERRUN

••VU•••
DIVULGE
RIVULET

••V•U••
BIVOUAC
DEVOURS
FAVOURS
GIVEUPS
QIVIUTS
RAVEUPS
SAVOURS
SAVOURY

••V••U•
COVERUP
DEVALUE
DEVIOUS
DIVINUM
ENVIOUS
GAVEOUT
GIVENUP
GIVEOUT
GIVESUP
INVACUO
INVOGUE
LIVEOUT
LOVEBUG
MOVEDUP
MOVEOUT
MOVESUP
OBVIOUS
PAVIOUR
REVALUE
REVENUE
SAVEDUP
SAVESUP
SAVIOUR
SEVENUP

•••VU••
BRAVURA
GRAVURE

•••V•U•
DRIVEUP
ELUVIUM
FERVOUR
FLAVOUR
IGIVEUP
NERVOUS
SERVEUP

•••V••U
NOUVEAU
PARVENU

V•V••••
VIVALDI
VIVENDI
VIVIDER
VIVIDLY

V••V•••
VALVATE
VELVETS
VELVETY
VERVETS

V•••V••
VISAVIS

•V••V••
EVOLVED
EVOLVES

•V•••V•
EVASIVE
IVANOVO

••VV•••
BOVVERS
CIVVIES
DIVVIED
DIVVIES
NAVVIES
REVVING
SAVVIER
SAVVILY

••V•V••
REVIVAL
REVIVED
REVIVES

••V••V•
BIVALVE
DEVOLVE
INVOLVE
PAVLOVA
REVOLVE

•••VV••
FLIVVER

•••V•V•
SURVIVE

••••V•V
TELAVIV

V•W••••
VOWLESS

V••W•••
VIEWERS
VIEWIER
VIEWING

•V•W•••
AVOWALS
AVOWERS
AVOWING

•V•••W•
OVERAWE
TVSHOWS

•V••••W
OVERSAW

••V•W••
GAVEWAY
GIVEWAY

••V••W•
REVIEWS

•••V••W
PREVIEW
PURVIEW

••••V•W
DISAVOW

V•X••••
VEXEDLY

V•••••X
VERDOUX

•V••••X
OVERTAX

V•Y••••
VOYAGED
VOYAGER
VOYAGES

V••Y•••
VARYING

V•••Y••
VANDYCK
VANDYKE
VANEYCK

V••••Y•
VALLEYS
VEEJAYS
VOLLEYS

V•••••Y
VACANCY
VACUITY
VAGUELY
VALENCY
VALIDLY
VAPIDLY
VARIETY
VARSITY
VELVETY
VENALLY
VERSIFY
VEXEDLY
VICEROY
VICTORY
VISIBLY
VITALLY
VITRIFY
VIVIDLY
VOCALLY
VOLUBLY
VRONSKY

•VY••••
IVYLIKE

•V•••Y•
EVILEYE

•V••••Y
AVIDITY
OVERBUY
OVERFLY
OVERJOY
OVERLAY
OVERTLY

••VY•••
ENVYING
LEVYING

••V•••Y
BEVERLY
CAVALRY
CIVILLY
DEVILRY
GAVEWAY
GIVEWAY
LEVELLY
LIVIDLY
LOVABLY
LOVERLY
MOVABLY
NOVELTY
POVERTY
REVELRY
RIVALRY
SAVELOY
SAVOURY
SAVVILY
SEVENTY
VIVIDLY
YEVGENY

•••V•Y•
CONVEYS
CONVOYS
PEAVEYS
PURVEYS
SLAVEYS
SURVEYS

•••V••Y
BRAVELY
BRAVERY
BREVITY
CALVARY
GRAVELY
GRAVITY
HEAVILY
KNAVERY
NAIVELY
NAIVETY
NERVILY
PRIVACY
PRIVILY
PRIVITY
QUAVERY
QUIVERY
SAVVILY
SERVERY
SHIVERY
SILVERY
SLAVERY
SUAVELY
SUAVITY
VELVETY

•••••VY
ANCHOVY
MUSCOVY
TANTIVY

V•Z••••
VIZIERS
VIZSLAS

•VZ••••
EVZONES

••V•••Z
ALVAREZ

••••V•Z
ESTEVEZ

WA•••••
WACKIER
WACKILY
WADDIES
WADDING
WADDLED
WADDLER
WADDLES
WADEDIN
WADESIN
WAFFLED
WAFFLER
WAFFLES
WAFTING
WAGERED
WAGERER
WAGGERY
WAGGING
WAGGISH
WAGGLED
WAGGLES
WAGGONS
WAGONER
WAGTAIL
WAHINES
WAIKIKI
WAILERS
WAILFUL
WAILING
WAITERS
WAITFOR
WAITING
WAITOUT
WAITRON
WAITSON
WAITSUP
WAIVERS
WAIVING
WAKEFUL
WAKENED
WAKENER
WAKESUP
WALCOTT
WALDORF
WALKERS
WALKING
WALKINS
WALKMAN
WALKONS
WALKOUT
WALKSON
WALKUPS
WALKWAY
WALLABY
WALLACE
WALLACH
WALLETS
WALLEYE
WALLING
WALLOON
WALLOPS
WALLOWS
WALLSUP
WALMART
WALNUTS

WALPOLE
WALSTON
WALTERS
WALTZED
WALTZER
WALTZES
WAMBLED
WAMBLES
WANDERS
WANGLED
WANGLER
WANGLES
WANIEST
WANNABE
WANNESS
WANNEST
WANNISH
WANTADS
WANTING
WANTOUT
WANTSIN
WANTSTO
WAPITIS
WARBLED
WARBLER
WARBLES
WARDENS
WARDERS
WARDING
WARDOFF
WARFARE
WARGAME
WARGODS
WARIEST
WARLESS
WARLIKE
WARLOCK
WARLORD
WARMEST
WARMING
WARMISH
WARMSUP
WARMUPS
WARNING
WARPATH
WARPING
WARRANT
WARRENS
WARRING
WARRIOR
WARSHIP
WARTHOG
WARTIER
WARTIME
WARWICK
WARZONE
WASATCH
WASHERS
WASHIER
WASHING
WASHOFF
WASHOUT
WASHRAG
WASHTUB
WASHUPS
WASPIER
WASPILY
WASPISH
WASSAIL
WASTAGE
WASTERS
WASTING
WASTREL
WATCHED
WATCHER
WATCHES
WATCHIT
WATERED
WATERER
WATTAGE
WATTEAU
WATTLES
WAVEDIN
WAVELET
WAVEOFF
WAVERED
WAVERER
WAVESIN
WAVIEST
WAXBEAN
WAXIEST
WAXLIKE
WAXWING
WAXWORK
WAYBILL
WAYCOOL
WAYLAID
WAYLAYS
WAYLESS
WAYSIDE
WAYWARD
WAYWORN

W•A••••

WEAKENS
WEAKEST
WEAKISH
WEALTHY
WEANING
WEAPONS
WEARERS
WEARIED
WEARIER
WEARIES
WEARILY
WEARING
WEAROFF
WEAROUT
WEASELS
WEATHER
WEAVERS
WEAVING
WHACKED
WHALERS
WHALING
WHAMMED
WHANGED
WHARFED
WHARTON
WHARVES
WHATFOR
WHATNOT
WHAUDEN
WRACKED
WRAITHS
WRANGLE
WRAPPED
WRAPPER
WRAPSUP
WRAPUPS
WYANDOT

W••A•••

WASATCH
WCHANDY
WHEATON
WIZARDS
WOMANLY
WREAKED
WREATHE
WREATHS

W•••A••

WAGTAIL
WALLABY
WALLACE
WALLACH
WALMART
WANNABE
WANTADS
WARFARE
WARGAME
WARPATH
WARRANT
WASSAIL
WASTAGE
WATTAGE
WAYLAID
WAYLAYS
WAYWARD
WEBPAGE
WELFARE
WELLAND
WENTAPE
WETBARS
WETLAND
WHYDAHS
WIDMARK
WIGWAGS
WIGWAMS
WILLARD
WOMBATS
WOODARD

W••••A•

WALKMAN
WALKWAY
WASHRAG
WATTEAU
WAXBEAN
WEEKDAY
WELLMAN
WENTBAD
WHEREAS
WHEREAT
WHIPSAW
WHITMAN
WILDCAT
WILLIAM
WINDBAG
WINEBAR
WINESAP
WINKSAT
WIRETAP
WISEMAN
WOLFGAL
WOLFMAN
WOLFRAM
WORKDAY
WORKMAN
WOZNIAK

W•••••A

WICHITA
WOOMERA
WYNONNA

•WA••••

AWAITED
AWAKENS
AWAKING
AWARDED
AWARDEE
AWARDER
AWAREOF
DWARFED
DWARVES
KWACHAS
KWANZAS
RWANDAN
SWABBED
SWADDLE
SWAGGER
SWAHILI
SWALLET
SWALLOW
SWAMPED
SWANKED
SWANKER
SWANSEA
SWANSON
SWAPPED
SWAPPER
SWARMED
SWARTHY
SWATHED
SWATHES
SWATTED
SWATTER
SWAYERS
SWAYING
TWADDLE
TWANGED

•W•A•••

SWEARAT
SWEARBY
SWEARER
SWEARIN
SWEARTO
SWEATED
SWEATER
TWEAKED

•W••A••

AWKWARD
TWOBASE
TWOLANE

•W•••A•

KWACHAS
KWANZAS
RWANDAN
SWEARAT
SWOREAT
TWOSTAR

•W••••A

IWOJIMA
SWANSEA

••WA•••

BEWAILS
BYWAYOF
COWARDS
DOWAGER
EDWARDS
HOWARDS
INWARDS
KIWANIS
KUWAITI
NEWAGER
ONWARDS
REWARDS
REWARMS
REWAXED
REWAXES
THWACKS
THWARTS
TOWARDS
TOWAWAY
UPWARDS

••W•A••

BOWSAWS
COWHAND
DEWLAPS
ENWRAPS
GEWGAWS
HAWHAWS
HOWDAHS
LOWBALL
LOWLAND
LOWPAID
NEWGATE
NEWHART
NEWMATH
NEWWAVE
PAWPAWS
RAWDATA
REWEAVE
REWRAPS
TOWCARS
TOWPATH
UNWEAVE
UNWRAPS

••W••A•

COWPEAS
DEWCLAW
DOWNPAT
LOWBEAM
LOWGEAR
LOWROAD
NEWDEAL
NEWSDAY
NEWSMAN
NEWYEAR
PAWEDAT
RAWDEAL
ROWBOAT
TOWAWAY
TOWHEAD

••W•••A

RAWDATA

•••WA••

AIRWAVE
AIRWAYS
ARAWAKS
ARTWARE
ATHWART
AVOWALS
AWKWARD
BARWARE
BULWARK
CARWASH
CATWALK
DRYWALL
ENDWAYS
EYEWASH
FLYWAYS
FORWARD
FROWARD
GUNWALE
HAYWARD
HOGWASH
HOTWARS
JAYWALK
JETWASH
JETWAYS
LEEWARD
MIDWAYS
NARWALS
NEWWAVE
OUTWARD
PEDWAYS
PINWALE
PREWASH
RUNWAYS
SEAWALL
SEAWARD
SEAWAYS
SKYWARD
SKYWAYS
STEWARD
STEWART
SUBWAYS
TINWARE
UNAWARE
WAYWARD
WIGWAGS
WIGWAMS

•••W•A•

CRAWDAD
CREWMAN
CROWBAR
DRAWBAR
FAYWRAY
FLOWNAT
FROWNAT
NARWHAL
NOSWEAT
OUTWEAR
PLOWMAN
SHAWWAL
SHOWMAN
SKIWEAR
SNOWCAP
SNOWCAT
SNOWDAY
SNOWMAN

•••W••A

SNOWPEA

••••WA•

ALLOWAY
ANTIWAR
ARCHWAY
AREAWAY
BEESWAX
BELTWAY
BIKEWAY
BOERWAR
CARAWAY
COLDWAR
CUTAWAY
DOORWAY
DUNAWAY
EATAWAY
FAIRWAY
FARAWAY
FLYAWAY
FOLKWAY
FOOTWAY
FOURWAY
FREEWAY
GANGWAY
GATEWAY
GAVEWAY
GETAWAY
GIVEWAY
GOTAWAY
HALFWAY
HALLWAY
HEADWAY
HIGHWAY
HOLYWAR
INNOWAY
JANEWAY
LAYAWAY
MADEWAY
MAKEWAY
MANOWAR
MATEWAN
OJIBWAS
OJIBWAY
OTTAWAS
PARKWAY
PARTWAY
PATHWAY
PESAWAS
POSTWAR
PUTAWAY
RACEWAY
RAILWAY
RANAWAY
RENEWAL
RIDGWAY
ROADWAY
RUNAWAY
SARAWAK
SHAWWAL
SOMEWAY
TAXIWAY
THRUWAY
TOLLWAY
TOWAWAY
TURFWAR
WALKWAY

••••W•A

CATAWBA

•••••WA

OKINAWA

W•B••••

WEBBIER
WEBBING
WEBFEET
WEBFOOT
WEBLESS
WEBLIKE
WEBPAGE
WEBSITE
WEBSTER
WEBTOED
WOBBLED
WOBBLES
WOBEGON

W••B•••

WAMBLED
WAMBLES
WARBLED
WARBLER
WARBLES
WAXBEAN
WAYBILL
WEBBIER
WEBBING
WETBARS
WIMBLED
WIMBLES
WOBBLED
WOBBLES
WOMBATS

W•••B••

WENTBAD
WINDBAG
WINEBAR

W••••B•

WALLABY
WANNABE
WHEREBY
WOULDBE

W•••••B

WASHTUB

•W•B•••

SWABBED
SWOBBED
TWOBASE
TWOBITS

•W••B••

SWABBED
SWOBBED
TWINBED

•W•••B•

SWEARBY
SWINGBY
SWOREBY

••WB•••

COWBELL
COWBIRD
COWBOYS
HOWBEIT
JAWBONE
LOWBALL
LOWBEAM
LOWBLOW
LOWBORN
LOWBOYS
LOWBRED
LOWBROW
NEWBERY
NEWBORN
ROWBOAT
SAWBUCK
SOWBUGS

••W•B••

DOWNBOW
NEWSBOY

•••WB••

CROWBAR
DRAWBAR
PLOWBOY
SHOWBIZ

•••W•B•

COBWEBS

•••W••B

SNOWJOB

••••WB•

CATAWBA

••••W•B

FOODWEB

WC•••••

WCHANDY

W•C••••

WACKIER
WACKILY
WICHITA
WICKERS
WICKETS
WICKIUP
WYCHELM

W••C•••

WALCOTT
WATCHED
WATCHER
WATCHES
WATCHIT
WAYCOOL
WELCHED
WELCHES
WELCOME
WENCHES
WETCELL
WHACKED
WINCERS
WINCHED
WINCHES
WINCING
WITCHES
WRACKED
WRECKED
WRECKER

W•••C••

WILDCAT
WOODCUT

W••••C•

WALLACE
WALLACH
WARLOCK
WARWICK
WASATCH
WEDLOCK
WOZZECK

•W•C•••

KWACHAS

•W••C••

TWITCHY

••WC•••

DEWCLAW
FAWCETT
HOWCOME
LOWCOST
TOWCARS

••W•C••

THWACKS

••W••C•

BEWITCH
COWLICK
LOWNECK
LOWTECH
SAWBUCK

•••WC••

CREWCUT
SNOWCAP
SNOWCAT

•••W•C•

IPSWICH
WARWICK

W•D••••

WADDIES
WADDING
WADDLED
WADDLER
WADDLES
WADEDIN
WADESIN
WEDDING
WEDGIER
WEDGIES
WEDGING
WEDLOCK
WIDENED
WIDGEON
WIDGETS
WIDMARK
WIDOWED
WIDOWER

W••D•••

WADDIES
WADDING
WADDLED
WADDLER
WADDLES
WALDORF
WANDERS
WARDENS
WARDERS
WARDING
WARDOFF
WEDDING
WEEDERS
WEEDIER
WEEDILY
WEEDING
WEEDOUT
WELDERS
WELDING
WENDELL
WENDERS
WENDING
WENDISH
WHYDAHS
WILDCAT
WILDEST
WILDING
WILDISH
WILDONE
WINDBAG
WINDERS
WINDIER
WINDILY
WINDING
WINDOWS
WINDROW
WINDSOR
WINDSUP
WINDUPS
WONDERS
WOODARD
WOODCUT
WOODIER
WOODIES
WOODLOT
WOODROW
WORDIER
WORDILY
WORDING
WORDONE

W•••D••

WADEDIN
WAVEDIN
WEEKDAY
WEIRDER
WEIRDLY
WEIRDOS
WHAUDEN
WHEEDLE
WIELDED
WIPEDUP
WISEDUP
WORKDAY
WORLDLY
WOULDBE
WOULDNT
WOUNDED
WOUNDUP
WYANDOT

W••••D•

WANTADS
WARGODS
WAYSIDE
WCHANDY
WIZARDS

W•••••D

WADDLED
WAFFLED
WAGERED
WAGGLED
WAKENED
WALTZED
WAMBLED
WANGLED
WARBLED
WARLORD
WATCHED
WATERED
WAVERED
WAYLAID
WAYWARD
WEARIED
WEBTOED
WEEKEND
WEIGHED
WELCHED
WELLAND
WELLFED
WENTBAD
WESTEND
WETLAND
WHACKED
WHAMMED
WHANGED
WHARFED
WHEELED
WHEEZED
WHELMED
WHELPED
WHETTED
WHIFFED
WHIPPED
WHIRLED
WHIRRED
WHISHED
WHISKED
WHIZKID
WHIZZED
WHOMPED
WHOOPED
WHOPPED
WHORLED
WHUPPED
WIDENED
WIDOWED
WIELDED
WIGGLED
WILFORD
WILFRID
WILLARD
WIMBLED
WIMPLED
WINCHED
WINERED
WINKLED
WIZENED
WOBBLED
WOODARD
WORRIED
WORSTED
WOUNDED
WRACKED
WRAPPED
WREAKED
WRECKED
WRESTED
WRITHED
WRONGED

•W•D•••

SWADDLE
SWEDISH
TWADDLE
TWIDDLE

•W••D••

AWARDED
AWARDEE
AWARDER
DWINDLE
OWNEDUP
RWANDAN
SWADDLE
SWINDLE
TWADDLE
TWIDDLE

•W••••D

AWAITED
AWARDED
AWKWARD
DWARFED
DWELLED
SWABBED
SWAMPED
SWANKED
SWAPPED
SWARMED
SWATHED
SWATTED
SWEATED
SWELLED
SWERVED
SWIGGED
SWILLED
SWIRLED
SWISHED
SWOBBED
SWOONED
SWOOPED
SWOPPED
TWANGED
TWEAKED
TWEETED
TWEEZED
TWILLED
TWINBED
TWINGED
TWINNED
TWIRLED
TWISTED
TWITTED
TWOFOLD

••WD•••

BAWDIER
BAWDILY
BOWDLER
DAWDLED
DAWDLER
DAWDLES
DEWDROP
DOWDIER
DOWDILY
HOWDAHS
LEWDEST
LOWDOWN
MOWDOWN
NEWDEAL
POWDERS
POWDERY
RAWDATA
RAWDEAL
ROWDIER
ROWDIES
ROWDILY
SAWDUST

••W•D••

NEWSDAY
PAWEDAT
SEWEDON
SEWEDUP

••W••D•

BYWORDS
COWARDS
COWHIDE
EDWARDS
HOWARDS
INWARDS
LOWTIDE
ONWARDS
RAWHIDE
REWARDS
REWELDS
REWINDS
REWORDS
TOWARDS
UNWINDS
UPWARDS

••W•••D

BOWERED
COWBIRD
COWERED
COWHAND
COWHERD
DAWDLED
DOWERED
JEWELED
LAWFORD
LOWBRED
LOWERED
LOWLAND
LOWPAID
LOWROAD
POWERED
REWAXED
REWIRED
REWOUND
SAWWOOD
TOWELED
TOWERED
TOWHEAD
UNWOUND

•••WD••

BLOWDRY
CHOWDER
CLOWDER
CRAWDAD
CROWDED
SHOWDOG
SNOWDAY
SNOWDON

•••W••D

AWKWARD
BOXWOOD
BRAWLED
BROWNED
BROWSED
CLOWNED
CRAWDAD
CRAWLED
CROWDED
CROWNED
DAGWOOD
DOGWOOD
DRAWLED
DROWNED
DROWSED
FORWARD
FROWARD
FROWNED
GROWLED
HAYWARD
HEYWOOD
HOGWILD
ILLWIND
INAWORD
KEYWORD
LEEWARD
MISWORD
OUTWARD
PLYWOOD
PROWLED
RAGWEED
REDWOOD
SAWWOOD
SCOWLED
SEAWARD
SEAWEED
SKYWARD
SPAWNED
STEWARD
TRAWLED
WAYWARD

••••W•D

ALLOWED
BEDEWED
ELBOWED
ENDOWED
REMOWED
RENEWED
RESAWED
RETOWED
SCREWED
STREWED
UNBOWED

UNSEWED
WIDOWED

WE•••••
WEAKENS
WEAKEST
WEAKISH
WEALTHY
WEANING
WEAPONS
WEARERS
WEARIED
WEARIER
WEARIES
WEARILY
WEARING
WEAROFF
WEAROUT
WEASELS
WEATHER
WEAVERS
WEAVING
WEBBIER
WEBBING
WEBFEET
WEBFOOT
WEBLESS
WEBLIKE
WEBPAGE
WEBSITE
WEBSTER
WEBTOED
WEDDING
WEDGIER
WEDGIES
WEDGING
WEDLOCK
WEEDERS
WEEDIER
WEEDILY
WEEDING
WEEDOUT
WEEKDAY
WEEKEND
WEENIER
WEENIES
WEEPERS
WEEPIER
WEEPIES
WEEPING
WEEVILS
WEIGHED
WEIGHIN
WEIGHTS
WEIGHTY
WEIRDER
WEIRDLY
WEIRDOS
WELCHED
WELCHES
WELCOME
WELDERS
WELDING
WELFARE
WELKINS
WELLAND
WELLFED
WELLING
WELLMAN
WELLOFF
WELLRUN
WELLSET
WELLSUP
WELTERS
WELTING
WENCHES
WENDELL
WENDERS
WENDING
WENDISH
WENTAPE
WENTBAD
WENTFOR
WENTOFF
WENTOUT
WERNHER
WERTHER
WESKITS
WESTEND
WESTERN
WETBARS
WETCELL
WETHERS
WETLAND
WETMOPS
WETNESS
WETSUIT
WETTEST
WETTING
WETTISH

W•E••••
WEEDERS
WEEDIER
WEEDILY
WEEDING
WEEDOUT
WEEKDAY
WEEKEND
WEENIER
WEENIES
WEEPERS
WEEPIER
WEEPIES
WEEPING
WEEVILS
WHEATON
WHEEDLE
WHEELED
WHEELER
WHEELIE
WHEEZED
WHEEZER
WHEEZES
WHELMED
WHELPED
WHEREAS
WHEREAT
WHEREBY
WHEREIN
WHERELL
WHEREOF
WHERERE
WHERETO
WHEREVE
WHETHER
WHETTED
WHEYISH
WIELDED
WIENERS
WIENIES
WOEISME
WREAKED
WREATHE
WREATHS
WRECKED
WRECKER
WRESTED
WRESTLE

W••E•••
WADEDIN
WADESIN
WAGERED
WAGERER
WAKEFUL
WAKENED
WAKENER
WAKESUP
WATERED
WATERER
WAVEDIN
WAVELET
WAVEOFF
WAVERED
WAVERER
WAVESIN
WHEEDLE
WHEELED
WHEELER
WHEELIE
WHEEZED
WHEEZER
WHEEZES
WHOEVER
WIDENED
WINEBAR
WINERED
WINESAP
WIPEDUP
WIPEOUT
WIPESUP
WIRETAP
WISEDUP
WISEGUY
WISEMAN
WISEMEN
WISESUP
WIZENED
WOBEGON
WOKENUP
WOREOFF
WOREOUT
WYNETTE
WYVERNS

W•••E••
WAGGERY
WAILERS
WAITERS
WAIVERS
WALKERS
WALLETS
WALLEYE
WALTERS
WANDERS
WANIEST
WANNESS
WANNEST
WARDENS
WARDERS
WARIEST
WARLESS
WARMEST
WARRENS
WASHERS
WASTERS
WATTEAU
WAVIEST
WAXBEAN
WAXIEST
WAYLESS
WEAKENS
WEAKEST
WEARERS
WEASELS
WEAVERS
WEBFEET
WEBLESS
WEEDERS
WEEKEND
WEEPERS
WELDERS
WELTERS
WENDELL
WENDERS
WESTEND
WESTERN
WETCELL
WETHERS
WETNESS
WETTEST
WHALERS
WHEREAS
WHEREAT
WHEREBY
WHEREIN
WHERELL
WHEREOF
WHERERE
WHERETO
WHEREVE
WHINERS
WHITENS
WHITEST
WICKERS
WICKETS
WIDGEON
WIDGETS
WIENERS
WIGLESS
WIGLETS
WILDEST
WILHELM
WILIEST
WILLETS
WINCERS
WINDERS
WINGERS
WINIEST
WINKERS
WINNERS
WINTERS
WINTERY
WIRIEST
WISHERS
WITHERS
WITLESS
WITNESS
WONDERS
WOOFERS
WOOLENS
WOOMERA
WORKERS
WORSENS
WOWSERS
WOZZECK
WRITEIN
WRITERS
WRITETO
WRITEUP
WROTEIN
WROTETO
WROTEUP
WRYNESS
WURLEYS
WYCHELM

W••••E•
WACKIER
WADDIES
WADDLED
WADDLER
WADDLES
WAFFLED
WAFFLER
WAFFLES
WAGERED
WAGERER
WAGGLED
WAGGLES
WAGONER
WAHINES
WAKENED
WAKENER
WALTZED
WALTZER
WALTZES
WAMBLED
WAMBLES
WANGLED
WANGLER
WANGLES
WARBLED
WARBLER
WARBLES
WARTIER
WASHIER
WASPIER
WASTREL
WATCHED
WATCHER
WATCHES
WATERED
WATERER
WATTLES
WAVELET
WAVERED
WAVERER
WEARIED
WEARIER
WEARIES
WEATHER
WEBBIER
WEBFEET
WEBSTER
WEBTOED
WEDGIER
WEDGIES
WEEDIER
WEENIER
WEENIES
WEEPIER
WEEPIES
WEIGHED
WEIRDER
WELCHED
WELCHES
WELLFED
WELLSET
WENCHES
WERNHER
WERTHER
WHACKED
WHAMMED
WHANGED
WHARFED
WHARVES
WHAUDEN
WHEELED
WHEELER
WHEEZED
WHEEZER
WHEEZES
WHELMED
WHELPED
WHETHER
WHETTED
WHIFFED
WHIMPER
WHINIER
WHIPPED
WHIPPET
WHIRLED
WHIRRED
WHISHED
WHISHES
WHISKED
WHISKER
WHISKEY
WHISPER
WHITHER
WHITIER
WHITNEY
WHIZZED
WHIZZER
WHIZZES
WHOEVER
WHOMPED
WHOOPED
WHOOPEE
WHOPPED
WHOPPER
WHORLED
WHUPPED
WIDENED
WIDOWED
WIDOWER
WIELDED
WIENIES
WIGGIER
WIGGLED
WIGGLER
WIGGLES
WILLIES
WIMBLED
WIMBLES
WIMPIER
WIMPLED
WIMPLES
WINCHED
WINCHES
WINDIER
WINERED
WINFREY
WINKLED
WINKLER
WINKLES
WISEMEN
WISPIER
WITCHES
WITHIER
WITHIES
WITTIER
WIZENED
WOBBLED
WOBBLES
WOLFMEN
WONKIER
WOODIER
WOODIES
WOOKIES
WOOLIER
WOOLIES
WOOLLEN
WOOLLEY
WOOLSEY
WOOSTER
WOOZIER
WORDIER
WORKMEN
WORMIER
WORRIED
WORRIER
WORRIES
WORSTED
WOUNDED
WRACKED
WRAPPED
WRAPPER
WREAKED
WRECKED
WRECKER
WRESTED
WRIGLEY
WRINGER
WRITHED
WRITHES
WRITTEN
WRONGED
WRONGER

W•••••E
WALLACE
WALLEYE
WALPOLE
WANNABE
WARFARE
WARGAME
WARLIKE
WARTIME
WARZONE
WASTAGE
WATTAGE
WAXLIKE
WAYSIDE
WEBLIKE
WEBPAGE
WEBSITE
WELCOME
WELFARE
WENTAPE
WHEEDLE
WHEELIE
WHERERE
WHEREVE
WHISTLE
WHITTLE
WHOOPEE
WIGLIKE
WILDONE
WILLKIE
WIMPOLE
WINSOME
WOEISME
WORDONE
WOULDBE
WRANGLE
WREATHE
WRESTLE
WRIGGLE
WRINKLE
WYNETTE

•WE••••
AWELESS
AWESOME
DWEEZIL
DWELLED
DWELLER
SWEARAT
SWEARBY
SWEARER
SWEARIN
SWEARTO
SWEATED
SWEATER
SWEDISH
SWEENEY
SWEEPER
SWEEPUP
SWEETEN
SWEETER
SWEETIE
SWEETLY
SWEETON
SWELLED
SWELLUP
SWELTER
SWELTRY
SWEPTUP
SWERVED
SWERVES
TWEAKED
TWEETED
TWEETER
TWEEZED
TWEEZES
TWELFTH
TWELVES

•W•E•••
DWEEZIL
OWNEDUP
SWEENEY
SWEEPER
SWEEPUP
SWEETEN
SWEETER
SWEETIE
SWEETLY
SWEETON
TWEETED
TWEETER
TWEEZED
TWEEZES

•W••E••
AWAKENS
AWAREOF
AWELESS
AWNLESS
GWYNETH
SWAYERS
SWIPERS
SWIVELS
SWIVETS
SWOREAT
SWOREBY
SWOREIN
TWOFERS

•W•••E•
AWAITED
AWARDED
AWARDEE
AWARDER
DWARFED
DWARVES
DWELLED
DWELLER
SWABBED
SWAGGER
SWALLET
SWAMPED
SWANKED
SWANKER
SWANSEA
SWAPPED
SWAPPER
SWARMED
SWATHED
SWATHES
SWATTED
SWATTER
SWEARER
SWEATED
SWEATER
SWEENEY
SWEEPER
SWEETEN
SWEETER
SWELLED
SWELTER
SWERVED
SWERVES
SWIFTER
SWIGGED
SWILLED
SWIMMER
SWINGER
SWIRLED
SWISHED
SWISHES
SWITZER
SWOBBED
SWOLLEN
SWONKEN
SWOONED
SWOOPED
SWOPPED
TWANGED
TWEAKED
TWEETED
TWEETER
TWEEZED
TWEEZES
TWELVES
TWILLED
TWINBED
TWINGED
TWINGES
TWINNED
TWIRLED
TWIRLER
TWISTED
TWISTER
TWITTED
TWITTER
TWOSTEP

•W••••E
AWARDEE
AWESOME
DWINDLE
OWLLIKE
SWADDLE
SWEETIE
SWINDLE
SWIZZLE
SWOOSIE
TWADDLE
TWIDDLE
TWINKLE
TWOBASE
TWOLANE
TWOONIE
TWOSOME
TWOTIME
TWOTONE

••WE•••
BOWERED
COWERED
DOWERED
HGWELLS
HOWELLS
HOWEVER
JEWELED
JEWELER
JEWELRY
LOWERED
PAWEDAT
POWERED
RAWEGGS
REWEAVE
REWELDS
SEWEDON
SEWEDUP
TOWELED
TOWERED
UNWEAVE

••W•E••
BAWLERS
BOWLERS
BOWLESS
BOWYERS
COWBELL
COWHERD
COWPEAS
DEWLESS
DOWNERS
DOWSERS
FAWCETT
FAWNERS
FOWLERS
GAWKERS
HAWKERS
HAWKEYE
HAWSERS
HEWLETT
HOWBEIT
HOWLERS
JAWLESS
LAWLESS
LAWYERS
LEWDEST
LOWBEAM
LOWGEAR
LOWHEEL
LOWNECK
LOWNESS
LOWTECH
MEWLERS
NCWYETH
NEWBERY
NEWDEAL
NEWLEFT
NEWNESS
NEWYEAR
NOWHERE
PAWNEES
PAWNERS
POWDERS
POWDERY
RAWDEAL
RAWNESS
SAWYERS
TOWHEAD
TOWHEES
TOWNERS
VOWLESS
WOWSERS
YAWNERS
YAWPERS
YOWLERS

••W••E•
BAWDIER
BOWDLER
BOWERED
BOWTIES
COWERED
COWRIES
DAWDLED
DAWDLER
DAWDLES
DOWAGER
DOWDIER
DOWERED
DOWNIER
DOWRIES
EXWIVES
GAWKIER
HOWEVER
JEWELED
JEWELER
JOWLIER
KEWPIES
LOWBRED
LOWERED
LOWHEEL
LOWLIER
NEWAGER
NEWSIER
NEWSIES
NEWSMEN
PAWKIER
PAWNEES
POWERED
REWAXED
REWAXES
REWIRED
REWIRES
REWOVEN
ROWDIER
ROWDIES
TAWNIER
TOWELED
TOWERED
TOWHEES
TOWNIES
UNWISER
UNWOVEN

••W•••E
BOWLIKE
BOWLINE
COWHIDE
COWLIKE
COWPOKE
DEWLINE
EBWHITE
HAWKEYE
HOWCOME
JAWBONE
JAWLIKE
JAWLINE
LAWLIKE
LOWLIFE
LOWRISE
LOWTIDE
NEWGATE
NEWWAVE
NOWHERE
RAWHIDE
REWEAVE
REWRITE
REWROTE
SAWLIKE
SOWLIKE
TOWROPE
UNWEAVE

•••WE••
ANSWERS
ANTWERP
AVOWERS
BETWEEN
BLOWERS
BOSWELL
BREWERS
BREWERY
CHEWERS
CLAWERS
COBWEBS
CREWELS
CROWERS
DRAWERS
DRYWELL
FALWELL
FARWEST
FLOWERS
FLOWERY
FORWENT
GETWELL
GLOWERS
GNAWERS
GOTWELL
GROWERS
INAWEOF
INDWELL
INKWELL
KEYWEST
MAEWEST
MAXWELL
MIDWEEK
MIDWEST
NOSWEAT
NOTWELL
OILWELL
OLDWEST
OUTWEAR
PEEWEES
PLOWERS
PROWESS
RAGWEED
ROSWELL
SEAWEED
SHOWERS
SHOWERY
SITWELL
SKEWERS
SKIWEAR
SLOWEST
STEWERS
TROWELS
TROWERS
UNSWEPT
UPSWEEP
UPSWEPT
VIEWERS

•••W•E•
BETWEEN
BLOWIER
BRAWLED
BRAWLER
BROWNED
BROWNER
BROWSED
BROWSER
BROWSES
CHEWIER
CHOWDER
CLOWDER
CLOWNED
CRAWLED
CRAWLER
CREWMEN
CROWDED
CROWNED
DRAWLED
DROWNED
DROWSED
DROWSES
FRAWLEY
FROWNED
FROWNER
GROWLED
GROWLER
MIDWEEK
PEEWEES
PLOWMEN
PROWLED
PROWLER
RAGWEED
SAYWHEN
SCOWLED
SCOWLER
SEAWEED
SHAWNEE
SHOWIER
SHOWMEN
SNOWIER
SNOWMEN
SNOWPEA
SPAWNED
THEWIER
TRAWLED
TRAWLER
UPSWEEP
VIEWIER

•••W••E
AIRWAVE
ALEWIFE
ARTWARE
BARWARE
BROWNIE
ENDWISE
ENTWINE
GUNWALE
HAYWIRE
HOTWIRE
JUGWINE
MAYWINE
MCSWINE
MIDWIFE
NEWWAVE
OUTWORE
PINWALE
REDWINE
SHAWNEE
TINWARE
UNAWARE

••••WE•
ALLOWED
BEDEWED
CNTOWER
ELBOWED
EMPOWER
ENDOWED
FOODWEB
INPOWER
REMOWED
RENEWED
RENEWER
RESAWED
RETOWED
SCREWED
STREWED
STREWER
THROWER
UNBOWED
UNSEWED
WIDOWED
WIDOWER

•••••WE
MARLOWE
OVERAWE
ROBLOWE
ROYALWE

W•F••••
WAFFLED
WAFFLER
WAFFLES
WAFTING

W••F•••
WAFFLED
WAFFLER
WAFFLES
WARFARE
WEBFEET
WEBFOOT
WELFARE
WHIFFED
WILFORD
WILFRID
WINFREY
WOLFGAL
WOLFING
WOLFISH
WOLFMAN
WOLFMEN
WOLFRAM
WOOFERS
WOOFING

W•••F••
WAILFUL
WAITFOR
WAKEFUL
WELLFED
WENTFOR
WHARFED
WHATFOR
WHIFFED
WILLFUL
WISHFUL
WISTFUL
WORKFOR

W••••F•
WARDOFF
WASHOFF
WAVEOFF
WEAROFF
WELLOFF
WENTOFF
WOREOFF

WORKOFF
WORNOFF

W•••••F
WALDORF
WARDOFF
WASHOFF
WAVEOFF
WEAROFF
WELLOFF
WENTOFF
WHEREOF
WOREOFF
WORKOFF
WORNOFF

•WF••••
AWFULLY

•W•F•••
SWIFTER
SWIFTLY
TWOFERS
TWOFOLD

•W••F••
DWARFED
TWELFTH

•W••••F
AWAREOF

••WF•••
BOWFINS
LAWFORD
SAWFISH

••W•F••
BOWLFUL
YAWNFUL

••W••F•
LOWLIFE
NEWLEFT
PAWNOFF

••W•••F
BYWAYOF
PAWNOFF

•••WF••
BLOWFLY
UNAWFUL

•••W•F•
ALEWIFE
BLEWOFF
BLOWOFF
MIDWIFE
SHOWOFF

•••W••F
AIRWOLF
BEOWULF
BLEWOFF
BLOWOFF
CRYWOLF
INAWEOF
REDWOLF
SEAWOLF
SHEWOLF
SHOWOFF

W•G••••
WAGERED
WAGERER
WAGGERY
WAGGING
WAGGISH
WAGGLED
WAGGLES
WAGGONS
WAGONER
WAGTAIL
WIGGIER
WIGGLED
WIGGLER
WIGGLES
WIGLESS
WIGLETS
WIGLIKE
WIGSOUT
WIGWAGS
WIGWAMS

W••G•••
WAGGERY
WAGGING
WAGGISH
WAGGLED
WAGGLES
WAGGONS
WANGLED
WANGLER
WANGLES
WARGAME
WARGODS
WEDGIER
WEDGIES
WEDGING
WEIGHED
WEIGHIN
WEIGHTS
WEIGHTY
WIDGEON
WIDGETS
WIGGIER
WIGGLED
WIGGLER
WIGGLES
WINGERS
WINGING
WINGNUT
WINGSIT
WINGTIP
WRIGGLE
WRIGGLY
WRIGHTS
WRIGLEY

W•••G••
WHANGED
WISEGUY
WOBEGON
WOLFGAL
WRANGLE
WRIGGLE
WRIGGLY
WRINGER
WRONGED
WRONGER
WRONGLY
WROUGHT

W••••G•
WASTAGE
WATTAGE
WEBPAGE
WIGWAGS

W•••••G
WADDING
WAFTING
WAGGING
WAILING
WAITING
WAIVING
WALKING
WALLING
WANTING
WARDING
WARMING
WARNING
WARPING
WARRING
WARTHOG
WASHING
WASHRAG
WASTING
WAXWING
WEANING
WEARING
WEAVING
WEBBING
WEDDING
WEDGING
WEEDING
WEEPING
WELDING
WELLING
WELTING
WENDING
WETTING
WHALING
WHILING
WHINING
WHITING
WILDING
WILLING
WILTING
WINCING
WINDBAG
WINDING
WINGING
WINKING
WINNING
WISHING
WISPING
WITTING
WOLFING
WOOFING
WORDING
WORKING
WRITING
WYOMING
WYSIWYG

•W•G•••
SWAGGER
SWIGGED

•W••G••
OWINGTO
SWAGGER
SWIGGED
SWINGBY
SWINGER
TWANGED
TWINGED
TWINGES
ZWINGLI

•W•••G•
AWNINGS

•W••••G
AWAKING
SWAYING
SWIPING
TWINING

••WG•••
COWGIRL
GEWGAWS
LOWGEAR
NEWGATE

••W•G••
DOWAGER
NEWAGER
RAWEGGS

••W••G•
RAWEGGS
SAWLOGS
SOWBUGS

••W•••G
BAWLING
BOWLING
COWLING
DAWNING
DOWNING
DOWSING
FAWNING
FOWLING
GAWKING
GAWPING
GOWRONG
HAWKING
HOWLING
MEWLING
PAWNING
YAWNING
YAWPING
YOWLING

•••WG••
BLOWGUN

•••W•G•
BIGWIGS
EARWIGS
WIGWAGS

•••W••G
AVOWING
BATWING
BLOWING
BREWING
CHEWING
CLAWING
CREWING
CROWING
DRAWING
FLAWING
FLOWING
GLOWING
GNAWING
GROWING
JREWING
KNOWING
LAPWING
MEOWING
PLOWING
REDWING
SHOWDOG
SHOWING
SKEWING
SLOWING
SNOWING
SPEWING
STEWING
STOWING
THAWING
UPSWING
VIEWING
WAXWING

••••W•G
WYSIWYG

WH•••••
WHACKED
WHALERS
WHALING
WHAMMED
WHANGED
WHARFED
WHARTON
WHARVES
WHATFOR
WHATNOT
WHAUDEN
WHEATON
WHEEDLE
WHEELED
WHEELER
WHEELIE
WHEEZED
WHEEZER
WHEEZES
WHELMED
WHELPED
WHEREAS
WHEREAT
WHEREBY
WHEREIN
WHERELL
WHEREOF
WHERERE
WHERETO
WHEREVE
WHETHER
WHETTED
WHEYISH
WHIFFED
WHILING
WHIMPER
WHINERS
WHINIER
WHINING
WHIPPED
WHIPPET
WHIPSAW
WHIPSUP
WHIRLED
WHIRRED
WHISHED
WHISHES
WHISKED
WHISKER
WHISKEY
WHISPER
WHISTLE
WHITENS
WHITEST
WHITHER
WHITIER
WHITING
WHITISH
WHITMAN
WHITNEY
WHITTLE
WHIZKID
WHIZZED
WHIZZER
WHIZZES
WHOEVER
WHOMPED
WHOOPED
WHOOPEE
WHOPPED
WHOPPER
WHORLED
WHOSWHO
WHUPPED
WHYDAHS

W•H••••
WAHINES
WCHANDY

W••H•••
WASHERS
WASHIER
WASHING
WASHOFF
WASHOUT
WASHRAG
WASHTUB
WASHUPS
WETHERS
WICHITA
WILHELM
WISHERS
WISHFUL
WISHING
WITHERS
WITHIER
WITHIES
WITHOUT
WYCHELM

W•••H••
WARSHIP
WARTHOG
WATCHED
WATCHER
WATCHES
WATCHIT
WEATHER
WEIGHED
WEIGHIN
WEIGHTS
WEIGHTY
WELCHED
WELCHES
WENCHES
WERNHER
WERTHER
WHETHER
WHISHED
WHISHES
WHITHER
WINCHED
WINCHES
WITCHES
WORSHIP
WRIGHTS
WRITHED
WRITHES

W••••H•
WEALTHY
WHOSWHO
WHYDAHS
WRAITHS
WREATHE
WREATHS
WROUGHT

W•••••H
WAGGISH
WALLACH
WANNISH
WARMISH
WARPATH
WASATCH
WASPISH
WEAKISH
WENDISH
WETTISH
WHEYISH
WHITISH
WILDISH
WIMPISH
WOLFISH
WORMISH

•W•H•••
SWAHILI

•W••H••
KWACHAS
SWATHED
SWATHES
SWISHED
SWISHES

•W•••H•
SWARTHY
TWITCHY

•W••••H
GWYNETH
SWEDISH
SWINISH
TWELFTH

••WH•••
COWHAND
COWHERD
COWHIDE
EBWHITE
HAWHAWS
LOWHEEL
NEWHART
NOWHERE
RAWHIDE
TOWHEAD
TOWHEES

••W••H•
HOWDAHS

••W•••H
ALWORTH
BEWITCH
DAWKISH
GAWKISH
HAWKISH
LOWTECH
MAWKISH
NCWYETH
NEWMATH
SAWFISH
TOWNISH
TOWPATH

•••WH••
EREWHON
GEEWHIZ
KNOWHOW
NARWHAL
SAYWHEN

•••W•H•
GROWTHS

•••W••H
CARWASH
EYEWASH
HOGWASH
IPSWICH
JETWASH
PREWASH
RUNWITH
SOPWITH

••••WH•
WHOSWHO

WI•••••
WICHITA
WICKERS
WICKETS
WICKIUP
WIDENED
WIDGEON
WIDGETS
WIDMARK
WIDOWED
WIDOWER
WIELDED
WIENERS
WIENIES
WIGGIER
WIGGLED
WIGGLER
WIGGLES
WIGLESS
WIGLETS
WIGLIKE
WIGSOUT
WIGWAGS
WIGWAMS
WILDCAT
WILDEST
WILDING
WILDISH
WILDONE
WILFORD
WILFRID
WILHELM
WILIEST
WILLARD
WILLETS
WILLFUL
WILLIAM
WILLIES
WILLING
WILLKIE
WILLOWS
WILLOWY
WILLSON
WILTING
WIMBLED
WIMBLES
WIMPIER
WIMPISH
WIMPLED
WIMPLES
WIMPOLE
WINCERS
WINCHED
WINCHES
WINCING
WINDBAG
WINDERS
WINDIER
WINDILY
WINDING
WINDOWS
WINDROW
WINDSOR
WINDSUP
WINDUPS
WINEBAR
WINERED
WINESAP
WINFREY
WINGERS
WINGING
WINGNUT
WINGSIT
WINGTIP
WINIEST
WINKERS
WINKING
WINKLED
WINKLER
WINKLES
WINKOUT
WINKSAT
WINNERS
WINNING
WINNOWS
WINSLOW
WINSOME
WINSOUT
WINSTON
WINTERS
WINTERY
WIPEDUP
WIPEOUT
WIPESUP
WIRETAP
WIRIEST
WISEDUP
WISEGUY
WISEMAN
WISEMEN
WISESUP
WISHERS
WISHFUL
WISHING
WISPIER
WISPILY
WISPING
WISTFUL
WITCHES
WITHERS
WITHIER
WITHIES
WITHOUT
WITLESS
WITNESS
WITTIER
WITTILY
WITTING
WIZARDS
WIZENED

W•I••••
WAIKIKI
WAILERS
WAILFUL
WAILING
WAITERS
WAITFOR
WAITING
WAITOUT
WAITRON
WAITSON
WAITSUP
WAIVERS
WAIVING
WEIGHED
WEIGHIN
WEIGHTS
WEIGHTY
WEIRDER
WEIRDLY
WEIRDOS
WHIFFED
WHILING
WHIMPER
WHINERS
WHINIER
WHINING
WHIPPED
WHIPPET
WHIPSAW
WHIPSUP
WHIRLED
WHIRRED
WHISHED
WHISHES
WHISKED
WHISKER
WHISKEY
WHISPER
WHISTLE
WHITENS
WHITEST
WHITHER
WHITIER
WHITING
WHITISH
WHITMAN
WHITNEY
WHITTLE
WHIZKID
WHIZZED
WHIZZER
WHIZZES
WRIGGLE
WRIGGLY
WRIGHTS
WRIGLEY
WRINGER
WRINKLE
WRINKLY
WRITEIN
WRITERS
WRITETO
WRITEUP
WRITHED
WRITHES
WRITING
WRITTEN

W••I•••
WAHINES
WANIEST
WAPITIS
WARIEST
WAVIEST
WAXIEST
WILIEST
WINIEST
WIRIEST
WOEISME
WRAITHS
WYSIWYG

W•••I••
WACKIER
WACKILY
WADDIES
WADDING
WAFTING
WAGGING
WAGGISH
WAIKIKI
WAILING
WAITING
WAIVING
WALKING
WALKINS
WALLING
WANNISH
WANTING
WARDING
WARLIKE
WARMING
WARMISH
WARNING
WARPING
WARRING
WARRIOR
WARTIER
WARTIME
WARWICK
WASHIER
WASHING
WASPIER
WASPILY
WASPISH
WASTING
WAXLIKE
WAXWING
WAYBILL
WAYSIDE
WEAKISH
WEANING
WEARIED
WEARIER
WEARIES
WEARILY
WEARING
WEAVING
WEBBIER
WEBBING
WEBLIKE
WEBSITE
WEDDING
WEDGIER
WEDGIES
WEDGING
WEEDIER
WEEDILY
WEEDING
WEENIER
WEENIES
WEEPIER
WEEPIES
WEEPING
WEEVILS
WELDING
WELKINS
WELLING
WELTING
WENDING
WENDISH
WESKITS
WETTING
WETTISH
WHALING
WHEYISH
WHILING
WHINIER
WHINING
WHITIER
WHITING
WHITISH
WICHITA
WICKIUP
WIENIES
WIGGIER
WIGLIKE
WILDING
WILDISH
WILLIAM
WILLIES
WILLING
WILTING
WIMPIER
WIMPISH
WINCING
WINDIER
WINDILY
WINDING
WINGING
WINKING
WINNING
WISHING
WISPIER
WISPILY
WISPING
WITHIER
WITHIES
WITTIER
WITTILY
WITTING
WOLFING
WOLFISH
WONKIER
WOODIER
WOODIES
WOOFING
WOOKIES
WOOLIER
WOOLIES
WOOZIER
WOOZILY
WORDIER
WORDILY
WORDING
WORKING
WORMIER
WORMISH
WORRIED
WORRIER
WORRIES
WOZNIAK
WRITING
WYOMING

W••••I•
WADEDIN
WADESIN
WAGTAIL
WANTSIN
WAPITIS
WARSHIP
WASSAIL
WATCHIT
WAVEDIN
WAVESIN
WAYLAID
WEIGHIN
WETSUIT
WHEELIE
WHEREIN
WHIZKID
WILFRID
WILLKIE
WINGSIT
WINGTIP
WORKSIN
WORSHIP
WRITEIN
WROTEIN

W•••••I
WAIKIKI

•WI••••
DWINDLE
OWINGTO
SWIFTER
SWIFTLY
SWIGGED
SWILLED
SWIMMER
SWINDLE
SWINGBY
SWINGER
SWINISH
SWIPERS
SWIPING
SWIRLED
SWISHED
SWISHES
SWITZER
SWIVELS
SWIVETS
SWIZZLE
TWIDDLE
TWILLED
TWINBED
TWINGED
TWINGES
TWINING
TWINKLE
TWINKLY
TWINNED
TWIRLED
TWIRLER
TWISTED
TWISTER
TWITCHY
TWITTED
TWITTER
ZWINGLI

•W•I•••
AWAITED
AWNINGS
TWOIRON

•W••I••
AWAKING
IWOJIMA
OWLLIKE
SWAHILI
SWAYING
SWEDISH
SWINISH
SWIPING
TWINING
TWOBITS
TWOTIME

•W•••I•
DWEEZIL
SWEARIN
SWEETIE
SWOOSIE
SWOREIN
TWOONIE

•W••••I
SWAHILI
ZWINGLI

••WI•••
BEWITCH
EXWIVES
JEWISON
REWINDS
REWIRED
REWIRES
UNWINDS
UNWISER

••W•I••
BAWDIER
BAWDILY
BAWLING
BEWAILS
BOWFINS
BOWLIKE
BOWLINE
BOWLING
BOWTIES
COWBIRD
COWGIRL
COWHIDE
COWLICK
COWLIKE
COWLING
COWRIES
DAWKISH
DAWNING
DEWLINE
DOWDIER
DOWDILY
DOWNIER
DOWNING
DOWRIES
DOWSING
EBWHITE
FAWNING
FOWLING
GAWKIER
GAWKILY
GAWKING
GAWKISH
GAWPING
HAWKING
HAWKINS
HAWKISH
HOWLING
JAWLIKE
JAWLINE
JOWLIER
KEWPIES
KUWAITI
LAWLIKE
LOWLIER
LOWLIFE

LOWRISE
LOWTIDE
MAWKISH
MEWLING
NEWSIER
NEWSIES
PAWKIER
PAWNING
RAWHIDE
RAWSILK
REWRITE
ROWDIER
ROWDIES
ROWDILY
SAWFISH
SAWLIKE
SAWMILL
SOWLIKE
TAWNIER
TAWNILY
TOWNIES
TOWNISH
YAWNING
YAWPING
YOWLING

••W••I•

COWSLIP
HOWBEIT
KIWANIS
LAWSUIT
LOWPAID

••W•••I

KUWAITI

•••WI••

ALEWIFE
AVOWING
BATWING
BETWIXT
BIGWIGS
BLOWIER
BLOWING
BREWING
CHEWIER
CHEWING
CLAWING
CREWING
CROWING
DIMWITS
DRAWING
EARWIGS
ENDWISE
ENTWINE
FLAWING
FLOWING
GLOWING
GNAWING
GODWITS
GROWING
HAYWIRE
HOGWILD
HOTWIRE
ILLWILL
ILLWIND
IPSWICH
JREWING
JUGWINE
KNOWING
LAPWING
MAYWINE
MCSWINE
MEOWING
MIDWIFE
NITWITS
OUTWITS
PLOWING
REDWINE
REDWING
RUNWITH
SCHWINN
SHOWIER
SHOWILY
SHOWING
SKEWING
SLOWING
SNOWIER
SNOWILY
SNOWING
SOPWITH
SPEWING
STEWING
STOWING
THAWING
THEWIER
UNTWIST
UPSWING
VIEWIER
VIEWING
WARWICK
WAXWING

•••W•I•

BLOWSIN
BLOWSIT
BROWNIE
DRAWNIN
DRAWSIN
FLOWNIN
GEEWHIZ
SHOWBIZ
SHOWNIN
SHOWSIN
SNOWSIN

••••WI•

BALDWIN
CSLEWIS
GOODWIN
HALFWIT
SHERWIN
THREWIN
THROWIN

•W•J•••

IWOJIMA

•••WJ••

SNOWJOB

W•K••••

WAKEFUL
WAKENED
WAKENER
WAKESUP
WOKENUP

W••K•••

WACKIER
WACKILY
WAIKIKI
WALKERS
WALKING
WALKINS
WALKMAN
WALKONS
WALKOUT
WALKSON
WALKUPS
WALKWAY
WEAKENS
WEAKEST
WEAKISH
WEEKDAY
WEEKEND
WELKINS
WESKITS
WICKERS
WICKETS
WICKIUP
WINKERS
WINKING
WINKLED
WINKLER
WINKLES
WINKOUT
WINKSAT
WONKIER
WOOKIES
WORKDAY
WORKERS
WORKFOR
WORKING
WORKMAN
WORKMEN
WORKOFF
WORKOUT
WORKSIN
WORKSON
WORKSUP
WORKUPS

W•••K••

WHACKED
WHISKED
WHISKER
WHISKEY
WHIZKID
WILLKIE
WRACKED
WREAKED
WRECKED
WRECKER
WRINKLE
WRINKLY

W••••K•

WAIKIKI
WARLIKE
WAXLIKE
WEBLIKE
WIGLIKE

W•••••K

WARLOCK
WARWICK
WAXWORK
WEDLOCK
WIDMARK
WOZNIAK
WOZZECK

•WK••••

AWKWARD

•W•K•••

AWAKENS
AWAKING

•W••K••

SWANKED
SWANKER
SWONKEN
TWEAKED
TWINKLE
TWINKLY

•W•••K•

OWLLIKE

••WK•••

BOWKNOT
DAWKISH
GAWKERS
GAWKIER
GAWKILY
GAWKING
GAWKISH
HAWKERS
HAWKEYE
HAWKING
HAWKINS
HAWKISH
MAWKISH
PAWKIER

••W••K•

BOWLIKE
COWLIKE
COWPOKE
EXWORKS
JAWLIKE
LAWLIKE
REWORKS
SAWLIKE
SOWLIKE
THWACKS

••W•••K

COWLICK
LOWNECK
NEWLOOK
NEWYORK
RAWSILK
SAWBUCK

•••W•K•

ARAWAKS

•••W••K

ARTWORK
BULWARK
CATWALK
JAYWALK
LEGWORK
MIDWEEK
NETWORK
OUTWORK
TINWORK
WARWICK
WAXWORK

••••WK•

MOHAWKS
SQUAWKS
SQUAWKY

••••W•K

SARAWAK

•••••WK

GOSHAWK

W•L••••

WALCOTT
WALDORF
WALKERS
WALKING
WALKINS
WALKMAN
WALKONS
WALKOUT
WALKSON
WALKUPS
WALKWAY
WALLABY
WALLACE
WALLACH
WALLETS
WALLEYE
WALLING
WALLOON
WALLOPS
WALLOWS
WALLSUP
WALMART
WALNUTS
WALPOLE
WALSTON
WALTERS
WALTZED
WALTZER
WALTZES
WELCHED
WELCHES
WELCOME
WELDERS
WELDING
WELFARE
WELKINS
WELLAND
WELLFED
WELLING
WELLMAN
WELLOFF
WELLRUN
WELLSET
WELLSUP
WELTERS
WELTING
WILDCAT
WILDEST
WILDING
WILDISH
WILDONE
WILFORD
WILFRID
WILHELM
WILIEST
WILLARD
WILLETS
WILLFUL
WILLIAM
WILLIES
WILLING
WILLKIE
WILLOWS
WILLOWY
WILLSON
WILTING
WOLFGAL
WOLFING
WOLFISH
WOLFMAN
WOLFMEN
WOLFRAM

W••L•••

WAILERS
WAILFUL
WAILING
WALLABY
WALLACE
WALLACH
WALLETS
WALLEYE
WALLING
WALLOON
WALLOPS
WALLOWS
WALLSUP
WARLESS
WARLIKE
WARLOCK
WARLORD
WAXLIKE
WAYLAID
WAYLAYS
WAYLESS
WEALTHY
WEBLESS
WEBLIKE
WEDLOCK
WELLAND
WELLFED
WELLING
WELLMAN
WELLOFF
WELLRUN
WELLSET
WELLSUP
WETLAND
WHALERS
WHALING
WHELMED
WHELPED
WHILING
WIELDED
WIGLESS
WIGLETS
WIGLIKE
WILLARD
WILLETS
WILLFUL
WILLIAM
WILLIES
WILLING
WILLKIE
WILLOWS
WILLOWY
WILLSON
WITLESS
WOOLENS
WOOLIER
WOOLIES
WOOLLEN
WOOLLEY
WOOLSEY
WORLDLY
WOULDBE
WOULDNT
WURLEYS

W•••L••

WADDLED
WADDLER
WADDLES
WAFFLED
WAFFLER
WAFFLES
WAGGLED
WAGGLES
WAMBLED
WAMBLES
WANGLED
WANGLER
WANGLES
WARBLED
WARBLER
WARBLES
WATTLES
WAVELET
WHEELED
WHEELER
WHEELIE
WHIRLED
WHORLED
WIGGLED
WIGGLER
WIGGLES
WIMBLED
WIMBLES
WIMPLED
WIMPLES
WINKLED
WINKLER
WINKLES
WINSLOW
WOBBLED
WOBBLES
WOODLOT
WOOLLEN
WOOLLEY
WRIGLEY

W••••L•

WACKILY
WALPOLE
WASPILY
WAYBILL
WEARILY
WEASELS
WEEDILY
WEEVILS
WEIRDLY
WENDELL
WETCELL
WHEEDLE
WHERELL
WHISTLE
WHITTLE
WILHELM
WIMPOLE
WINDILY
WISPILY
WITTILY
WOMANLY
WOOZILY
WORDILY
WORLDLY
WRANGLE
WRESTLE
WRIGGLE
WRIGGLY
WRINKLE
WRINKLY
WRONGLY
WYCHELM

W•••••L

WAGTAIL
WAILFUL
WAKEFUL
WASSAIL
WASTREL
WAYBILL
WAYCOOL
WENDELL
WETCELL
WHERELL
WILLFUL
WISHFUL
WISTFUL
WOLFGAL

•WL••••

OWLLIKE

•W•L•••

AWELESS
AWNLESS
DWELLED
DWELLER
OWLLIKE
SWALLET
SWALLOW
SWELLED
SWELLUP
SWELTER
SWELTRY
SWILLED
SWOLLEN
TWELFTH
TWELVES
TWILLED
TWOLANE

•W••L••

AWFULLY
DWELLED
DWELLER
SWALLET
SWALLOW
SWELLED
SWELLUP
SWILLED
SWIRLED
SWOLLEN
TWILLED
TWIRLED
TWIRLER

•W•••L•

AWFULLY
DWINDLE
SWADDLE
SWAHILI
SWEETLY
SWIFTLY
SWINDLE
SWIVELS
SWIZZLE
TWADDLE
TWIDDLE
TWINKLE
TWINKLY
TWOFOLD
ZWINGLI

•W••••L

DWEEZIL

••WL•••

BAWLERS
BAWLING
BAWLOUT
BOWLERS
BOWLESS
BOWLFUL
BOWLIKE
BOWLINE
BOWLING
COWLICK
COWLIKE
COWLING
DEWLAPS
DEWLESS
DEWLINE
FOWLERS
FOWLING
HEWLETT
HOWLERS
HOWLING
JAWLESS
JAWLIKE
JAWLINE
JOWLIER
KOWLOON
LAWLESS
LAWLIKE
LOWLAND
LOWLIER
LOWLIFE
MEWLERS
MEWLING
NEWLEFT
NEWLOOK
SAWLIKE
SAWLOGS
SOWLIKE
VOWLESS
YOWLERS
YOWLING

••W•L••

BOWDLER
COWSLIP
DAWDLED
DAWDLER
DAWDLES
DEWCLAW
HGWELLS
HOWELLS
JEWELED
JEWELER
JEWELRY
LOWBLOW
REWELDS
TOWELED

••W••L•

BAWDILY
BEWAILS
COWBELL
DOWDILY
GAWKILY
HGWELLS
HOWELLS
LOWBALL
RAWSILK
ROWDILY
SAWMILL
TAWNILY

••W•••L

BOWLFUL
COWBELL
COWGIRL
LOWBALL
LOWHEEL
NEWDEAL
RAWDEAL
SAWMILL
YAWNFUL

•••WL••

BRAWLED
BRAWLER
CRAWLED
CRAWLER
DRAWLED
FRAWLEY
GROWLED
GROWLER
PROWLED
PROWLER
SCOWLED
SCOWLER
TRAWLED
TRAWLER

•••W•L•

AIRWOLF
AVOWALS
BEOWULF
BLOWFLY
BOSWELL
CATWALK
CREWELS
CRYWOLF
DRYWALL
DRYWELL
FALWELL
GETWELL
GOTWELL
GUNWALE
HOGWILD
ILLWILL
INDWELL
INKWELL
JAYWALK
MAXWELL
NARWALS
NOTWELL
OILWELL
PINWALE
REDWOLF
ROSWELL
SEAWALL
SEAWOLF
SHEWOLF
SHOWILY
SITWELL
SNOWILY
TROWELS

•••W••L

BOSWELL
DRYWALL
DRYWELL
FALWELL
GETWELL
GOTWELL
ILLWILL
INDWELL
INKWELL
MAXWELL
NARWHAL
NOTWELL
OILWELL
ROSWELL
SEAWALL
SHAWWAL
SITWELL
UNAWFUL

••••WL•

SCRAWLS
SCRAWLY
SPRAWLS

••••W•L

RENEWAL
SHAWWAL

•••••WL

BARNOWL
HOOTOWL
PEAFOWL
SUNBOWL

W•M••••

WAMBLED
WAMBLES
WIMBLED
WIMBLES
WIMPIER
WIMPISH
WIMPLED
WIMPLES
WIMPOLE
WOMANLY
WOMBATS

W••M•••

WALMART
WARMEST
WARMING
WARMISH
WARMSUP
WARMUPS
WETMOPS
WHAMMED
WHIMPER
WHOMPED
WIDMARK
WOOMERA
WORMIER
WORMISH
WYOMING

W•••M••

WALKMAN
WELLMAN
WHAMMED
WHELMED
WHITMAN
WISEMAN
WISEMEN
WOLFMAN
WOLFMEN
WORKMAN
WORKMEN

W••••M•

WARGAME
WARTIME
WELCOME
WIGWAMS
WINSOME
WOEISME

W•••••M

WILHELM
WILLIAM
WOLFRAM
WYCHELM

•W•M•••

SWAMPED
SWIMMER

•W••M••

SWARMED
SWIMMER

•W•••M•

AWESOME
IWOJIMA
TWOSOME
TWOTIME

••WM•••

NEWMATH
NEWMOON
NEWMOWN
SAWMILL

••W•M••

NEWSMAN
NEWSMEN

••W••M•

HOWCOME
REWARMS

••W•••M

LOWBEAM

•••WM••

CREWMAN
CREWMEN
PLOWMAN
PLOWMEN
SHOWMAN
SHOWMEN
SNOWMAN
SNOWMEN

•••W•M•

MUGWUMP
WIGWAMS

W•N••••

WANDERS
WANGLED
WANGLER
WANGLES
WANIEST
WANNABE
WANNESS
WANNEST
WANNISH
WANTADS
WANTING
WANTOUT
WANTSIN
WANTSTO
WENCHES
WENDELL
WENDERS
WENDING
WENDISH
WENTAPE
WENTBAD
WENTFOR
WENTOFF
WENTOUT
WINCERS
WINCHED
WINCHES
WINCING
WINDBAG
WINDERS
WINDIER
WINDILY
WINDING
WINDOWS
WINDROW
WINDSOR
WINDSUP
WINDUPS
WINEBAR
WINERED
WINESAP
WINFREY
WINGERS
WINGING
WINGNUT
WINGSIT
WINGTIP
WINIEST
WINKERS
WINKING
WINKLED
WINKLER
WINKLES
WINKOUT
WINKSAT
WINNERS
WINNING
WINNOWS
WINSLOW
WINSOME
WINSOUT
WINSTON
WINTERS
WINTERY
WONDERS
WONKIER
WONTONS
WYNETTE
WYNONNA

W••N•••

WALNUTS
WANNABE
WANNESS
WANNEST
WANNISH
WARNING
WEANING
WEENIER
WEENIES
WERNHER
WETNESS
WHANGED
WHINERS
WHINIER
WHINING
WIENERS
WIENIES
WINNERS
WINNING
WINNOWS
WITNESS
WORNOFF
WORNOUT
WOUNDED
WOUNDUP
WOZNIAK
WRANGLE
WRINGER
WRINKLE
WRINKLY
WRONGED
WRONGER
WRONGLY
WRYNESS
WYANDOT

W•••N••

WAGONER
WAHINES
WAKENED
WAKENER
WCHANDY
WHATNOT
WHITNEY
WIDENED
WINGNUT
WIZENED
WOKENUP
WOMANLY
WYNONNA

W••••N•

WADDING
WAFTING
WAGGING
WAGGONS
WAILING
WAITING
WAIVING
WALKING
WALKINS
WALKONS
WALLING
WANTING
WARDENS
WARDING
WARMING
WARNING
WARPING
WARRANT
WARRENS
WARRING
WARZONE
WASHING
WASTING
WAXWING
WEAKENS
WEANING
WEAPONS
WEARING
WEAVING
WEBBING
WEDDING
WEDGING
WEEDING
WEEKEND
WEEPING
WELDING
WELKINS
WELLAND
WELLING
WELTING
WENDING
WESTEND
WETLAND
WETTING
WHALING
WHILING
WHINING
WHITENS
WHITING
WILDING
WILDONE
WILLING
WILTING
WINCING
WINDING
WINGING
WINKING
WINNING

WISHING
WISPING
WITTING
WOLFING
WONTONS
WOOFING
WOOLENS
WORDING
WORDONE
WORKING
WORSENS
WOULDNT
WRITING
WYNONNA
WYOMING
WYVERNS

W•••••N
WADEDIN
WADESIN
WAITRON
WAITSON
WALKMAN
WALKSON
WALLOON
WALSTON
WANTSIN
WAVEDIN
WAVESIN
WAXBEAN
WAYWORN
WEIGHIN
WELLMAN
WELLRUN
WESTERN
WHARTON
WHAUDEN
WHEATON
WHEREIN
WHITMAN
WIDGEON
WILLSON
WINSTON
WISEMAN
WISEMEN
WOBEGON
WOLFMAN
WOLFMEN
WOOLLEN
WORKMAN
WORKMEN
WORKSIN
WORKSON
WRITEIN
WRITTEN
WROTEIN

•WN••••
AWNINGS
AWNLESS
OWNEDUP

•W•N•••
DWINDLE
GWYNETH
KWANZAS
OWINGTO
RWANDAN
SWANKED
SWANKER
SWANSEA
SWANSON
SWINDLE
SWINGBY
SWINGER
SWINISH
SWONKEN
TWANGED
TWINBED
TWINGED
TWINGES
TWINING
TWINKLE
TWINKLY
TWINNED
ZWINGLI

•W••N••
AWNINGS
SWEENEY
SWOONED
TWINNED
TWOONIE

•W•••N•
AWAKENS
AWAKING
SWAYING
SWIPING
TWINING
TWOLANE
TWOTONE

•W••••N
RWANDAN
SWANSON
SWEARIN
SWEETEN
SWEETON
SWOLLEN
SWONKEN
SWOREIN
TWOIRON

••WN•••
DAWNING
DAWNSON
DOWNBOW
DOWNERS
DOWNIER
DOWNING
DOWNPAT
FAWNERS
FAWNING
LOWNECK
LOWNESS
NEWNESS
PAWNEES
PAWNERS
PAWNING
PAWNOFF
RAWNESS
TAWNIER
TAWNILY
TOWNERS
TOWNIES
TOWNISH
YAWNERS
YAWNFUL
YAWNING

••W•N••
BOWKNOT
KIWANIS
REWINDS
UNWINDS

••W••N•
BAWLING
BOWFINS
BOWLINE
BOWLING
COWHAND
COWLING
COWPONY
DAWNING
DEWLINE
DOWNING
DOWSING
FAWNING
FOWLING
GAWKING
GAWPING
GOWRONG
HAWKING
HAWKINS
HOWLING
JAWBONE
JAWLINE
LOWLAND
MEWLING
NEWTONS
PAWNING
REWOUND
UNWOUND
YAWNING
YAWPING
YOWLING

••W•••N
COWTOWN
DAWNSON
JEWISON
KOWLOON
LOWBORN
LOWDOWN
MOWDOWN
NEWBORN
NEWMOON
NEWMOWN
NEWSMAN
NEWSMEN
NEWTOWN
REWOVEN
SEWEDON
UNWOVEN

•••WN••
BLOWNUP
BROWNED
BROWNER
BROWNIE
CLOWNED
CROWNED
DRAWNIN
DRAWNON
DRAWNUP
DROWNED
FLOWNAT
FLOWNIN
FROWNAT
FROWNED
FROWNER
GROWNUP
SHAWNEE
SHOWNIN
SPAWNED

•••W•N•
AVOWING
BATWING
BLOWING
BREWING
CHEWING
CLAWING
CREWING
CROWING
DRAWING
ENTWINE
FLAWING
FLOWING
FORWENT
GLOWING
GNAWING
GROWING
ILLWIND
JREWING
JUGWINE
KNOWING
LAPWING
MAYWINE
MCSWINE
MEOWING
PLOWING
REDWINE
REDWING
SCHWINN
SHOWING
SKEWING
SLOWING
SNOWING
SPEWING
STEWING
STOWING
THAWING
UPSWING
VIEWING
WAXWING

•••W••N
BETWEEN
BLOWGUN
BLOWSIN
CREWMAN
CREWMEN
DRAWNIN
DRAWNON
DRAWSIN
DRAWSON
EREWHON
FLOWNIN
GROWSON
OUTWORN
PLOWMAN
PLOWMEN
SAYWHEN
SCHWINN
SHOWMAN
SHOWMEN
SHOWNIN
SHOWSIN
SNOWDON
SNOWMAN
SNOWMEN
SNOWSIN
WAYWORN

••••WN•
DISOWNS
SCRAWNY

••••W•N
BALDWIN
GOLDWYN
GOODWIN
HARDWON
MATEWAN
SHERWIN
THREWIN
THROWIN

•••••WN
BEDDOWN
BOGDOWN
COWTOWN
CUTDOWN
DIEDOWN
GETDOWN
GOTDOWN
HOEDOWN
INGROWN
LAYDOWN
LETDOWN
LIEDOWN
LOWDOWN
MIDTOWN
MOWDOWN
NEWMOWN
NEWTOWN
OAKLAWN
OURTOWN
PINDOWN
PREDAWN
PUTDOWN
RANDOWN
REDRAWN
RUBDOWN
RUNDOWN
SATDOWN
SETDOWN
SITDOWN
SUNDOWN
TIEDOWN
TOPDOWN
UNDRAWN
UNKNOWN

WO•••••
WOBBLED
WOBBLES
WOBEGON
WOEISME
WOKENUP
WOLFGAL
WOLFING
WOLFISH
WOLFMAN
WOLFMEN
WOLFRAM
WOMANLY
WOMBATS
WONDERS
WONKIER
WONTONS
WOODARD
WOODCUT
WOODIER
WOODIES
WOODLOT
WOODROW
WOOFERS
WOOFING
WOOKIES
WOOLENS
WOOLIER
WOOLIES
WOOLLEN
WOOLLEY
WOOLSEY
WOOMERA
WOOSTER
WOOZIER
WOOZILY
WORDIER
WORDILY
WORDING
WORDONE
WOREOFF
WOREOUT
WORKDAY
WORKERS
WORKFOR
WORKING
WORKMAN
WORKMEN
WORKOFF
WORKOUT
WORKSIN
WORKSON
WORKSUP
WORKUPS
WORLDLY
WORMIER
WORMISH
WORNOFF
WORNOUT
WORRIED
WORRIER
WORRIES
WORSENS
WORSHIP
WORSTED
WOULDBE
WOULDNT
WOUNDED
WOUNDUP
WOWSERS
WOZNIAK
WOZZECK

W•O••••
WHOEVER
WHOMPED
WHOOPED
WHOOPEE
WHOPPED
WHOPPER
WHORLED
WHOSWHO
WOODARD
WOODCUT
WOODIER
WOODIES
WOODLOT
WOODROW
WOOFERS
WOOFING
WOOKIES
WOOLENS
WOOLIER
WOOLIES
WOOLLEN
WOOLLEY
WOOLSEY
WOOMERA
WOOSTER
WOOZIER
WOOZILY
WRONGED
WRONGER
WRONGLY
WROTEIN
WROTETO
WROTEUP
WROUGHT
WYOMING

W••O•••
WAGONER
WHOOPED
WHOOPEE
WIDOWED
WIDOWER
WYNONNA

W•••O••
WAGGONS
WAITOUT
WALCOTT
WALDORF
WALKONS
WALKOUT
WALLOON
WALLOPS
WALLOWS
WALPOLE
WANTOUT
WARDOFF
WARGODS
WARLOCK
WARLORD
WARZONE
WASHOFF
WASHOUT
WAVEOFF
WAXWORK
WAYCOOL
WAYWORN
WEAPONS
WEAROFF
WEAROUT
WEBFOOT
WEBTOED
WEDLOCK
WEEDOUT
WELCOME
WELLOFF
WENTOFF
WENTOUT
WETMOPS
WIGSOUT
WILDONE
WILFORD
WILLOWS
WILLOWY
WIMPOLE
WINDOWS
WINKOUT
WINNOWS
WINSOME
WINSOUT
WIPEOUT
WITHOUT
WONTONS
WORDONE
WOREOFF
WOREOUT
WORKOFF
WORKOUT
WORNOFF
WORNOUT

W••••O•
WAITFOR
WAITRON
WAITSON
WALKSON
WALLOON
WALSTON
WARRIOR
WARTHOG
WAYCOOL
WEBFOOT
WEIRDOS
WENTFOR
WHARTON
WHATFOR
WHATNOT
WHEATON
WHEREOF
WIDGEON
WILLSON
WINDROW
WINDSOR
WINSLOW
WINSTON
WOBEGON
WOODLOT
WOODROW
WORKFOR
WORKSON
WYANDOT

W•••••O
WANTSTO
WHERETO
WHOSWHO
WRITETO
WROTETO

•WO••••
IWOJIMA
SWOBBED
SWOLLEN
SWONKEN
SWOONED
SWOOPED
SWOOSIE
SWOPPED
SWOREAT
SWOREBY
SWOREIN
TWOBASE
TWOBITS
TWOFERS
TWOFOLD
TWOIRON
TWOLANE
TWOONIE
TWOSOME
TWOSTAR
TWOSTEP
TWOTIME
TWOTONE

•W•O•••
SWOONED
SWOOPED
SWOOSIE
TWOONIE

•W••O••
AWESOME
TWOFOLD
TWOSOME
TWOTONE

•W•••O•
AWAREOF
SWALLOW
SWANSON
SWEETON
TWOIRON

•W••••O
OWINGTO
SWEARTO

••WO•••
ALWORTH
ATWORST
BYWORDS
EXWORKS
REWORDS
REWORKS
REWOUND
REWOVEN
UNWOUND
UNWOVEN

••W•O••
BAWLOUT
BOWSOUT
BOWWOWS
COWBOYS
COWPOKE
COWPONY
COWTOWN
GOWRONG
HOWCOME
JAWBONE
KOWLOON
KOWTOWS
LAWFORD
LOWBORN
LOWBOYS
LOWCOST
LOWDOWN
LOWROAD
MOWDOWN
NEWBORN
NEWLOOK
NEWMOON
NEWMOWN
NEWPORT
NEWTONS
NEWTOWN
NEWYORK
PAWNOFF
POWWOWS
REWROTE
ROWBOAT
SAWLOGS
SAWWOOD
TOWROPE

••W••O•
BOWKNOT
BYWAYOF
DAWNSON
DEWDROP
DOWNBOW
JEWISON
KOWLOON
LOWBLOW
LOWBROW
NEWLOOK
NEWMOON
NEWSBOY
SAWWOOD
SEWEDON

•••WO••
AIRWOLF
ARTWORK
BLEWOFF
BLEWOUT
BLOWOFF
BLOWOUT
BOWWOWS
BOXWOOD
CHEWOUT
CRYWOLF
DAGWOOD
DOGWOOD
DRAWOUT
DREWOUT
HEYWOOD
INAWORD
KEYWORD
LEGWORK
MISWORD
NETWORK
OUTWORE
OUTWORK
OUTWORN
PLYWOOD
POWWOWS
REDWOLF
REDWOOD
SAWWOOD
SEAWOLF
SHEWOLF
SHOWOFF
SHOWOUT
TINWORK
WAXWORK
WAYWORN

•••W•O•
BOXWOOD
CHEWTOY
DAGWOOD
DOGWOOD
DRAWNON
DRAWSON
EREWHON
GROWSON
HEYWOOD
INAWEOF
KNOWHOW
PLOWBOY
PLYWOOD
REDWOOD
SAWWOOD
SHOWDOG
SNOWDON
SNOWJOB

••••WO•
HARDWON

••••W•O
WHOSWHO

W•P••••
WAPITIS
WIPEDUP
WIPEOUT
WIPESUP

W••P•••
WALPOLE
WARPATH
WARPING
WASPIER
WASPILY
WASPISH
WEAPONS
WEBPAGE
WEEPERS
WEEPIER
WEEPIES
WEEPING
WHIPPED
WHIPPET
WHIPSAW
WHIPSUP
WHOPPED
WHOPPER
WHUPPED
WIMPIER
WIMPISH
WIMPLED
WIMPLES
WIMPOLE
WISPIER
WISPILY
WISPING
WRAPPED
WRAPPER
WRAPSUP
WRAPUPS

W•••P••
WHELPED
WHIMPER
WHIPPED
WHIPPET
WHISPER
WHOMPED
WHOOPED
WHOOPEE
WHOPPED
WHOPPER
WHUPPED
WRAPPED
WRAPPER

W••••P•
WALKUPS
WALLOPS
WARMUPS
WASHUPS
WENTAPE
WETMOPS
WINDUPS
WORKUPS
WRAPUPS

W•••••P
WAITSUP
WAKESUP
WALLSUP
WARMSUP
WARSHIP
WELLSUP
WHIPSUP
WICKIUP
WINDSUP
WINESAP
WINGTIP
WIPEDUP
WIPESUP
WIRETAP
WISEDUP
WISESUP
WOKENUP
WORKSUP
WORSHIP
WOUNDUP
WRAPSUP
WRITEUP
WROTEUP

•W•P•••
SWAPPED
SWAPPER
SWEPTUP
SWIPERS
SWIPING
SWOPPED

•W••P••
SWAMPED
SWAPPED
SWAPPER
SWEEPER
SWEEPUP
SWOOPED
SWOPPED

•W••••P
OWNEDUP
SWEEPUP
SWELLUP
SWEPTUP
TWOSTEP

••WP•••
COWPEAS
COWPOKE
COWPONY
GAWPING
KEWPIES
LOWPAID
NEWPORT
PAWPAWS
TOWPATH
YAWPERS
YAWPING

••W•P••
DOWNPAT

••W••P•
DEWLAPS
ENWRAPS
REWRAPS
TOWROPE
UNWRAPS

••W•••P
COWSLIP
DEWDROP
SEWEDUP

•••WP••
SNOWPEA

•••W•P•
BLOWUPS
SLOWUPS
UNSWEPT
UPSWEPT

•••W••P
ANTWERP
BLOWNUP
BLOWSUP
CHEWSUP
DRAWNUP
DRAWSUP
GROWNUP
GROWSUP
MUGWUMP
SHOWSUP
SLOWSUP
SNOWCAP
UPSWEEP

••••W•P
SCREWUP

WR•••••
WRACKED
WRAITHS
WRANGLE
WRAPPED
WRAPPER
WRAPSUP
WRAPUPS
WREAKED
WREATHE
WREATHS
WRECKED
WRECKER
WRESTED
WRESTLE
WRIGGLE
WRIGGLY
WRIGHTS
WRIGLEY
WRINGER
WRINKLE
WRINKLY
WRITEIN
WRITERS
WRITETO
WRITEUP
WRITHED
WRITHES
WRITING
WRITTEN
WRONGED
WRONGER
WRONGLY
WROTEIN
WROTETO
WROTEUP
WROUGHT
WRYNESS

W•R••••
WARBLED
WARBLER
WARBLES
WARDENS
WARDERS
WARDING
WARDOFF
WARFARE
WARGAME
WARGODS
WARIEST
WARLESS
WARLIKE
WARLOCK
WARLORD
WARMEST
WARMING
WARMISH
WARMSUP
WARMUPS
WARNING
WARPATH
WARPING
WARRANT
WARRENS
WARRING
WARRIOR
WARSHIP
WARTHOG
WARTIER
WARTIME
WARWICK
WARZONE
WERNHER
WERTHER
WIRETAP
WIRIEST
WORDIER
WORDILY
WORDING
WORDONE
WOREOFF
WOREOUT
WORKDAY
WORKERS
WORKFOR
WORKING
WORKMAN
WORKMEN
WORKOFF
WORKOUT
WORKSIN
WORKSON
WORKSUP
WORKUPS
WORLDLY
WORMIER
WORMISH
WORNOFF
WORNOUT
WORRIED
WORRIER
WORRIES
WORSENS
WORSHIP
WORSTED
WURLEYS

W••R•••
WARRANT
WARRENS
WARRING
WARRIOR
WEARERS
WEARIED
WEARIER
WEARIES
WEARILY
WEARING
WEAROFF
WEAROUT
WEIRDER
WEIRDLY
WEIRDOS
WHARFED
WHARTON
WHARVES
WHEREAS
WHEREAT
WHEREBY
WHEREIN
WHERELL
WHEREOF
WHERERE
WHERETO
WHEREVE
WHIRLED
WHIRRED
WHORLED
WORRIED
WORRIER

WORRIES

W•••R••
WAGERED
WAGERER
WAITRON
WASHRAG
WASTREL
WATERED
WATERER
WAVERED
WAVERER
WELLRUN
WHIRRED
WILFRID
WINDROW
WINERED
WINFREY
WIZARDS
WOLFRAM
WOODROW
WYVERNS

W••••R•
WAGGERY
WAILERS
WAITERS
WAIVERS
WALDORF
WALKERS
WALMART
WALTERS
WANDERS
WARDERS
WARFARE
WARLORD
WASHERS
WASTERS
WAXWORK
WAYWARD
WAYWORN
WEARERS
WEAVERS
WEEDERS
WEEPERS
WELDERS
WELFARE
WELTERS
WENDERS
WESTERN
WETBARS
WETHERS
WHALERS
WHERERE
WHINERS
WICKERS
WIDMARK
WIENERS
WILFORD
WILLARD
WINCERS
WINDERS
WINGERS
WINKERS
WINNERS
WINTERS
WINTERY
WISHERS
WITHERS
WONDERS
WOODARD
WOOFERS
WOOMERA
WORKERS
WOWSERS
WRITERS

W•••••R
WACKIER
WADDLER
WAFFLER
WAGERER
WAGONER
WAITFOR
WAKENER
WALTZER
WANGLER
WARBLER
WARRIOR
WARTIER
WASHIER
WASPIER
WATCHER
WATERER
WAVERER
WEARIER
WEATHER
WEBBIER
WEBSTER
WEDGIER
WEEDIER
WEENIER
WEEPIER
WEIRDER
WENTFOR
WERNHER
WERTHER
WHATFOR
WHEELER
WHEEZER
WHETHER
WHIMPER
WHINIER
WHISKER
WHISPER
WHITHER
WHITIER
WHIZZER
WHOEVER
WHOPPER
WIDOWER
WIGGIER
WIGGLER
WIMPIER
WINDIER
WINDSOR
WINEBAR
WINKLER
WISPIER
WITHIER
WITTIER
WONKIER
WOODIER
WOOLIER
WOOSTER
WOOZIER
WORDIER
WORKFOR
WORMIER
WORRIER
WRAPPER
WRECKER
WRINGER
WRONGER

•W•R•••
AWARDED
AWARDEE
AWARDER
AWAREOF
DWARFED
DWARVES
SWARMED
SWARTHY
SWERVED
SWERVES
SWIRLED
SWOREAT
SWOREBY
SWOREIN
TWIRLED
TWIRLER

•W••R••
SWEARAT
SWEARBY
SWEARER
SWEARIN
SWEARTO
TWOIRON

•W•••R•
AWKWARD
SWAYERS
SWELTRY
SWIPERS
TWOFERS

•W••••R
AWARDER
DWELLER
SWAGGER
SWANKER
SWAPPER
SWATTER
SWEARER
SWEATER
SWEEPER
SWEETER
SWELTER
SWIFTER
SWIMMER
SWINGER
SWITZER
TWEETER
TWIRLER
TWISTER
TWITTER
TWOSTAR

••WR•••
COWRIES
DOWRIES
ENWRAPS
GOWRONG
LOWRISE
LOWROAD
REWRAPS
REWRITE
REWROTE
TOWROPE
UNWRAPS

••W•R••
ALWORTH
ATWORST
BOWERED
BYWORDS
COWARDS
COWERED
DEWDROP
DOWERED
EDWARDS
EXWORKS
HOWARDS
INWARDS
LOWBRED
LOWBROW
LOWERED
ONWARDS
POWERED
REWARDS
REWARMS
REWIRED
REWIRES
REWORDS
REWORKS
THWARTS
TOWARDS
TOWERED
UPWARDS

••W••R•
BAWLERS
BOWLERS
BOWYERS
COWBIRD
COWGIRL
COWHERD
DOWNERS
DOWSERS
FAWNERS
FOWLERS
GAWKERS
HAWKERS
HAWSERS
HOWLERS
JEWELRY
LAWFORD
LAWYERS
LOWBORN
MEWLERS
NEWBERY
NEWBORN
NEWHART
NEWPORT
NEWYORK
NOWHERE
PAWNERS
POWDERS
POWDERY
SAWYERS
TOWCARS
TOWNERS
WOWSERS
YAWNERS
YAWPERS
YOWLERS

••W•••R
BAWDIER
BOWDLER
DAWDLER
DOWAGER
DOWDIER
DOWNIER
GAWKIER
HOWEVER
JEWELER
JOWLIER
LOWGEAR
LOWLIER
NEWAGER
NEWSIER
NEWYEAR
PAWKIER
ROWDIER
TAWNIER
UNWISER

•••WR••
FAYWRAY

•••W•R•
ANSWERS
ANTWERP
ARTWARE
ARTWORK
ATHWART
AVOWERS
AWKWARD
BARWARE
BLOWDRY
BLOWERS
BREWERS
BREWERY
BULWARK
CHEWERS
CLAWERS
CROWERS
DRAWERS
FLOWERS
FLOWERY
FORWARD
FROWARD
GLOWERS
GNAWERS
GROWERS
HAYWARD
HAYWIRE
HOTWARS
HOTWIRE
INAWORD
KEYWORD
LEEWARD
LEGWORK
MISWORD
NETWORK
OUTWARD
OUTWORE
OUTWORK
OUTWORN
PLOWERS
SEAWARD
SHOWERS
SHOWERY
SKEWERS
SKYWARD
STEWARD
STEWART
STEWERS
TINWARE
TINWORK
TROWERS
UNAWARE
VIEWERS
WAXWORK
WAYWARD
WAYWORN

•••W••R
BLOWIER
BRAWLER
BROWNER
BROWSER
CHEWIER
CHOWDER
CLOWDER
CRAWLER
CROWBAR
DRAWBAR
FROWNER
GROWLER
OUTWEAR
PROWLER
SCOWLER
SHOWIER
SKIWEAR
SNOWIER
THEWIER
TRAWLER
VIEWIER

••••W•R
ANTIWAR
BOERWAR
CNTOWER
COLDWAR
EMPOWER
HOLYWAR
INPOWER
MANOWAR
POSTWAR
RENEWER
STREWER
THROWER
TURFWAR
WIDOWER

W•S••••
WASATCH
WASHERS
WASHIER
WASHING
WASHOFF
WASHOUT
WASHRAG
WASHTUB
WASHUPS
WASPIER
WASPILY
WASPISH
WASSAIL
WASTAGE
WASTERS
WASTING
WASTREL
WESKITS
WESTEND
WESTERN
WISEDUP
WISEGUY
WISEMAN
WISEMEN
WISESUP
WISHERS
WISHFUL
WISHING
WISPIER
WISPILY
WISPING
WISTFUL
WYSIWYG

W••S•••
WALSTON
WARSHIP
WASSAIL
WAYSIDE
WEASELS
WEBSITE
WEBSTER
WETSUIT
WHISHED
WHISHES
WHISKED
WHISKER
WHISKEY
WHISPER
WHISTLE
WHOSWHO
WIGSOUT
WINSLOW
WINSOME
WINSOUT
WINSTON
WOOSTER
WORSENS
WORSHIP
WORSTED
WOWSERS
WRESTED
WRESTLE

W•••S••
WADESIN
WAITSON
WAITSUP
WAKESUP
WALKSON
WALLSUP
WANTSIN
WANTSTO
WARMSUP
WAVESIN
WELLSET
WELLSUP
WHIPSAW
WHIPSUP
WILLSON
WINDSOR
WINDSUP
WINESAP
WINGSIT
WINKSAT
WIPESUP
WISESUP
WOEISME
WOOLSEY
WORKSIN
WORKSON
WORKSUP
WRAPSUP

W••••S•
WAGGISH
WANIEST
WANNESS
WANNEST
WANNISH
WARIEST
WARLESS
WARMEST
WARMISH
WASPISH
WAVIEST
WAXIEST
WAYLESS
WEAKEST
WEAKISH
WEBLESS
WENDISH
WETNESS
WETTEST
WETTISH
WHEYISH
WHITEST
WHITISH
WIGLESS
WILDEST
WILDISH
WILIEST
WIMPISH
WINIEST
WIRIEST
WITLESS
WITNESS
WOLFISH
WORMISH
WRYNESS

W•••••S
WADDIES
WADDLES
WAFFLES
WAGGLES
WAGGONS
WAHINES
WAILERS
WAITERS
WAIVERS
WALKERS
WALKINS
WALKONS
WALKUPS
WALLETS
WALLOPS
WALLOWS
WALNUTS
WALTERS
WALTZES
WAMBLES
WANDERS
WANGLES
WANNESS
WANTADS
WAPITIS
WARBLES
WARDENS
WARDERS
WARGODS
WARLESS
WARMUPS
WARRENS
WASHERS
WASHUPS
WASTERS
WATCHES
WATTLES
WAYLAYS
WAYLESS
WEAKENS
WEAPONS
WEARERS
WEARIES
WEASELS
WEAVERS
WEBLESS
WEDGIES
WEEDERS
WEENIES
WEEPERS
WEEPIES
WEEVILS
WEIGHTS
WEIRDOS
WELCHES
WELDERS
WELKINS
WELTERS
WENCHES
WENDERS
WESKITS
WETBARS
WETHERS
WETMOPS
WETNESS
WHALERS
WHARVES
WHEEZES
WHEREAS
WHINERS
WHISHES
WHITENS
WHIZZES
WHYDAHS
WICKERS
WICKETS
WIDGETS
WIENERS
WIENIES
WIGGLES
WIGLESS
WIGLETS
WIGWAGS
WIGWAMS
WILLETS
WILLIES
WILLOWS
WIMBLES
WIMPLES
WINCERS
WINCHES
WINDERS
WINDOWS
WINDUPS
WINGERS
WINKERS
WINKLES
WINNERS
WINNOWS
WINTERS
WISHERS
WITCHES
WITHERS
WITHIES
WITLESS
WITNESS
WIZARDS
WOBBLES
WOMBATS
WONDERS
WONTONS
WOODIES
WOOFERS
WOOKIES
WOOLENS
WOOLIES
WORKERS
WORKUPS
WORRIES
WORSENS
WOWSERS
WRAITHS
WRAPUPS
WREATHS
WRIGHTS
WRITERS
WRITHES
WRYNESS
WURLEYS
WYVERNS

•W•S•••
AWESOME
SWISHED
SWISHES
TWISTED
TWISTER
TWOSOME
TWOSTAR
TWOSTEP

•W••S••
SWANSEA
SWANSON
SWOOSIE

•W•••S•
AWELESS
AWNLESS
SWEDISH
SWINISH
TWOBASE

•W••••S
AWAKENS
AWELESS
AWNINGS
AWNLESS
DWARVES
KWACHAS
KWANZAS
SWATHES
SWAYERS
SWERVES
SWIPERS
SWISHES
SWIVELS
SWIVETS
TWEEZES
TWELVES
TWINGES
TWOBITS
TWOFERS

••WS•••
BOWSAWS
BOWSOUT
COWSLIP
DOWSERS
DOWSING
HAWSERS
LAWSUIT
NEWSBOY
NEWSDAY
NEWSIER
NEWSIES
NEWSMAN
NEWSMEN
RAWSILK
WOWSERS

••W•S••
DAWNSON
JEWISON
UNWISER

••W••S•
ATWORST
BOWLESS
DAWKISH
DEWLESS
GAWKISH
HAWKISH
JAWLESS
LAWLESS
LEWDEST
LOWCOST
LOWNESS
LOWRISE
MAWKISH
NEWNESS
RAWNESS
SAWDUST
SAWFISH
TOWNISH
VOWLESS

••W•••S
BAWLERS
BEWAILS
BOWFINS
BOWLERS
BOWLESS
BOWSAWS
BOWTIES
BOWWOWS
BOWYERS
BYWORDS
COWARDS
COWBOYS
COWPEAS
COWRIES
DAWDLES
DEWLAPS
DEWLESS
DOWNERS
DOWRIES
DOWSERS
EDWARDS
ENWRAPS
EXWIVES
EXWORKS
FAWNERS
FOWLERS
GAWKERS
GEWGAWS
HAWHAWS
HAWKERS
HAWKINS
HAWSERS
HGWELLS
HOWARDS
HOWDAHS
HOWELLS
HOWLERS
INWARDS
JAWLESS
KEWPIES
KIWANIS
KOWTOWS
LAWLESS
LAWYERS
LOWBOYS
LOWNESS
MEWLERS
NEWNESS
NEWSIES
NEWTONS
ONWARDS
PAWNEES
PAWNERS
PAWPAWS
POWDERS
POWWOWS
RAWEGGS
RAWNESS
REWARDS
REWARMS
REWAXES
REWELDS
REWINDS
REWIRES
REWORDS
REWORKS
REWRAPS
ROWDIES
SAWLOGS
SAWYERS
SOWBUGS
THWACKS
THWARTS
TOWARDS
TOWCARS
TOWHEES
TOWNERS
TOWNIES
UNWINDS
UNWRAPS
UPWARDS
VOWLESS
WOWSERS
YAWNERS
YAWPERS
YOWLERS

•••WS••
BLOWSIN
BLOWSIT
BLOWSUP
BROWSED
BROWSER
BROWSES
CHEWSUP
DRAWSIN
DRAWSON
DRAWSUP
DROWSED
DROWSES
FROWSTY
GROWSON
GROWSUP
SHOWSIN
SHOWSUP
SLOWSUP
SNOWSIN

•••W•S•
CARWASH
ENDWISE
EYEWASH
FARWEST
HOGWASH
JETWASH
KEYWEST
MAEWEST
MIDWEST
OLDWEST
PREWASH
PROWESS
SLOWEST
UNTWIST

•••W••S
AIRWAYS
ANSWERS
ARAWAKS
AVOWALS
AVOWERS
BIGWIGS
BLOWERS
BLOWUPS
BOWWOWS
BREWERS
BROWSES
CHEWERS
CLAWERS
COBWEBS
CREWELS
CROWERS
DIMWITS
DRAWERS
DROWSES
EARWIGS
ENDWAYS
FLOWERS
FLYWAYS
GLOWERS
GNAWERS
GODWITS
GROWERS
GROWTHS
HOTWARS
JETWAYS
MIDWAYS
NARWALS
NITWITS
OUTWITS
PEDWAYS
PEEWEES
PLOWERS
POWWOWS
PROWESS
RUNWAYS
SEAWAYS
SHOWERS
SKEWERS
SKYWAYS
SLOWUPS
STEWERS
SUBWAYS
TROWELS
TROWERS
VIEWERS
WIGWAGS
WIGWAMS

••••W•S
CSLEWIS
DISOWNS
MOHAWKS
OJIBWAS
OTTAWAS
PESAWAS
SCRAWLS
SPRAWLS
SQUAWKS

•••••WS
ANDREWS
ANTCOWS
BARROWS
BELLOWS
BESTOWS
BILLOWS
BORROWS
BOWSAWS
BOWWOWS
BURROWS
CASHEWS
CURFEWS
CURLEWS
CUSHAWS
ESCHEWS
ESCROWS
FALLOWS
FARROWS
FELLOWS
FOGBOWS
FOLLOWS
FURROWS
GAGLAWS
GEEGAWS
GEWGAWS
GOSLOWS
GUFFAWS
HALLOWS
HARROWS
HAWHAWS
HAYMOWS
HEBREWS
HEEHAWS
HOLLOWS
INFLOWS
JIGSAWS
KOWTOWS
MALLOWS
MARROWS
MATHEWS
MEADOWS
MELLOWS
MILDEWS
MINNOWS
MORROWS
NARROWS
NEPHEWS
NOSHOWS
OLDNEWS
OLDSAWS
OUTLAWS
PAWPAWS
PILLOWS
PITSAWS
POWWOWS
REDRAWS
REPLOWS
REVIEWS
RIPSAWS
SALLOWS
SEACOWS
SEESAWS
SHADOWS
SKITOWS
SORROWS
SUNDEWS
TALLOWS
TVSHOWS
WALLOWS
WILLOWS
WINDOWS
WINNOWS
YARROWS
YELLOWS

W•T••••
WATCHED
WATCHER
WATCHES
WATCHIT
WATERED
WATERER
WATTAGE
WATTEAU
WATTLES
WETBARS
WETCELL
WETHERS
WETLAND
WETMOPS
WETNESS
WETSUIT
WETTEST
WETTING
WETTISH
WITCHES

WITHERS
WITHIER
WITHIES
WITHOUT
WITLESS
WITNESS
WITTIER
WITTILY
WITTING

W••T•••
WAFTING
WAGTAIL
WAITERS
WAITFOR
WAITING
WAITOUT
WAITRON
WAITSON
WAITSUP
WALTERS
WALTZED
WALTZER
WALTZES
WANTADS
WANTING
WANTOUT
WANTSIN
WANTSTO
WARTHOG
WARTIER
WARTIME
WASTAGE
WASTERS
WASTING
WASTREL
WATTAGE
WATTEAU
WATTLES
WEATHER
WEBTOED
WELTERS
WELTING
WENTAPE
WENTBAD
WENTFOR
WENTOFF
WENTOUT
WERTHER
WESTEND
WESTERN
WETTEST
WETTING
WETTISH
WHATFOR
WHATNOT
WHETHER
WHETTED
WHITENS
WHITEST
WHITHER
WHITIER
WHITING
WHITISH
WHITMAN
WHITNEY
WHITTLE
WILTING
WINTERS
WINTERY
WISTFUL
WITTIER
WITTILY
WITTING

WONTONS
WRITEIN
WRITERS
WRITETO
WRITEUP
WRITHED
WRITHES
WRITING
WRITTEN
WROTEIN
WROTETO
WROTEUP

W•••T••
WALSTON
WAPITIS
WASATCH
WASHTUB
WEALTHY
WEBSTER
WHARTON
WHEATON
WHETTED
WHISTLE
WHITTLE
WINGTIP
WINSTON
WIRETAP
WOOSTER
WORSTED
WRAITHS
WREATHE
WREATHS
WRESTED
WRESTLE
WRITTEN
WYNETTE

W••••T•
WALCOTT
WALLETS
WALNUTS
WANTSTO
WARPATH
WEBSITE
WEIGHTS
WEIGHTY
WESKITS
WHERETO
WICHITA
WICKETS
WIDGETS
WIGLETS
WILLETS
WOMBATS
WRIGHTS
WRITETO
WROTETO
WYNETTE

W•••••T
WAITOUT
WALCOTT
WALKOUT
WALMART
WANIEST
WANNEST
WANTOUT
WARIEST
WARMEST
WARRANT
WASHOUT
WATCHIT
WAVELET

WAVIEST
WAXIEST
WEAKEST
WEAROUT
WEBFEET
WEBFOOT
WEEDOUT
WELLSET
WENTOUT
WETSUIT
WETTEST
WHATNOT
WHEREAT
WHIPPET
WHITEST
WIGSOUT
WILDCAT
WILDEST
WILIEST
WINGNUT
WINGSIT
WINIEST
WINKOUT
WINKSAT
WINSOUT
WIPEOUT
WIRIEST
WITHOUT
WOODCUT
WOODLOT
WOREOUT
WORKOUT
WORNOUT
WOULDNT
WROUGHT
WYANDOT

•W•T•••
SWATHED
SWATHES
SWATTED
SWATTER
SWITZER
TWITCHY
TWITTED
TWITTER
TWOTIME
TWOTONE

•W••T••
AWAITED
SWARTHY
SWATTED
SWATTER
SWEATED
SWEATER
SWEETEN
SWEETER
SWEETIE
SWEETLY
SWEETON
SWELTER
SWELTRY
SWEPTUP
SWIFTER
SWIFTLY
TWEETED
TWEETER
TWISTED
TWISTER
TWITTED
TWITTER
TWOSTAR
TWOSTEP

•W•••T•
GWYNETH
OWINGTO
SWEARTO
SWIVETS
TWELFTH
TWOBITS

•W••••T
SWALLET
SWEARAT
SWOREAT

••WT•••
BOWTIES
COWTOWN
KOWTOWS
LOWTECH
LOWTIDE
NEWTONS
NEWTOWN

••W•T••
BEWITCH

••W••T•
ALWORTH
EBWHITE
FAWCETT
HEWLETT
KUWAITI
NCWYETH
NEWGATE
NEWMATH
RAWDATA
REWRITE
REWROTE
THWARTS
TOWPATH

••W•••T
ATWORST
BAWLOUT
BOWKNOT
BOWSOUT
DOWNPAT
FAWCETT
HEWLETT
HOWBEIT
LAWSUIT
LEWDEST
LOWCOST
NEWHART
NEWLEFT
NEWPORT
PAWEDAT
ROWBOAT
SAWDUST

•••WT••
CHEWTOY
GROWTHS

•••W•T•
DIMWITS
FROWSTY
GODWITS
NITWITS
OUTWITS
RUNWITH
SOPWITH

•••W••T
ATHWART

BETWIXT
BLEWOUT
BLOWOUT
BLOWSIT
CHEWOUT
CREWCUT
DRAWOUT
DREWOUT
FARWEST
FLOWNAT
FORWENT
FROWNAT
KEYWEST
MAEWEST
MIDWEST
NOSWEAT
OLDWEST
SHOWOUT
SLOWEST
SNOWCAT
STEWART
UNSWEPT
UNTWIST
UPSWEPT

••••W•T
HALFWIT

WU•••••
WURLEYS

W•U••••
WHUPPED
WOULDBE
WOULDNT
WOUNDED
WOUNDUP

W••U•••
WHAUDEN
WROUGHT

W•••U••
WALKUPS
WALNUTS
WARMUPS
WASHUPS
WETSUIT
WINDUPS
WORKUPS
WRAPUPS

W••••U•
WAILFUL
WAITOUT
WAITSUP
WAKEFUL
WAKESUP
WALKOUT
WALLSUP
WANTOUT
WARMSUP
WASHOUT
WASHTUB
WEAROUT
WEEDOUT
WELLRUN
WELLSUP
WENTOUT
WHIPSUP
WICKIUP
WIGSOUT
WILLFUL
WINDSUP

WINGNUT
WINKOUT
WINSOUT
WIPEDUP
WIPEOUT
WIPESUP
WISEDUP
WISEGUY
WISESUP
WISHFUL
WISTFUL
WITHOUT
WOKENUP
WOODCUT
WOREOUT
WORKOUT
WORKSUP
WORNOUT
WOUNDUP
WRAPSUP
WRITEUP
WROTEUP

W•••••U
WATTEAU

•W•U•••
AWFULLY

•W•••U•
OWNEDUP
SWEEPUP
SWELLUP
SWEPTUP

••W•U••
LAWSUIT
REWOUND
SAWBUCK
SAWDUST
SOWBUGS
UNWOUND

••W••U•
BAWLOUT
BOWLFUL
BOWSOUT
SEWEDUP
YAWNFUL

•••WU••
BEOWULF
BLOWUPS
MUGWUMP
SLOWUPS

•••W•U•
BLEWOUT
BLOWGUN
BLOWNUP
BLOWOUT
BLOWSUP
CHEWOUT
CHEWSUP
CREWCUT
DRAWNUP
DRAWOUT
DRAWSUP
DREWOUT
GROWNUP
GROWSUP
SHOWOUT
SHOWSUP
SLOWSUP

UNAWFUL

••••WU•
SCREWUP

W•V••••
WAVEDIN
WAVELET
WAVEOFF
WAVERED
WAVERER
WAVESIN
WAVIEST
WYVERNS

W••V•••
WAIVERS
WAIVING
WEAVERS
WEAVING
WEEVILS

W•••V••
WHARVES
WHOEVER

W••••V•
WHEREVE

•W•V•••
SWIVELS
SWIVETS

•W••V••
DWARVES
SWERVED
SWERVES
TWELVES

••W•V••
EXWIVES
HOWEVER
REWOVEN
UNWOVEN

••W••V•
NEWWAVE
REWEAVE
UNWEAVE

•••W•V•
AIRWAVE
NEWWAVE

W•W••••
WOWSERS

W••W•••
WARWICK
WAXWING
WAXWORK
WAYWARD
WAYWORN
WIGWAGS
WIGWAMS

W•••W••
WALKWAY
WHOSWHO
WIDOWED
WIDOWER
WYSIWYG

W••••W•
WALLOWS
WILLOWS
WILLOWY
WINDOWS
WINNOWS

W•••••W
WHIPSAW
WINDROW
WINSLOW
WOODROW

•W•W•••
AWKWARD

•W••••W
SWALLOW

••WW•••
BOWWOWS
NEWWAVE
POWWOWS
SAWWOOD

••W•W••
TOWAWAY

••W••W•
BOWSAWS
BOWWOWS
COWTOWN
GEWGAWS
HAWHAWS
KOWTOWS
LOWDOWN
MOWDOWN
NEWMOWN
NEWTOWN
PAWPAWS
POWWOWS

••W•••W
DEWCLAW
DOWNBOW
LOWBLOW
LOWBROW

•••WW••
SHAWWAL

•••W•W•
BOWWOWS
POWWOWS

•••W••W
KNOWHOW

W•X••••
WAXBEAN
WAXIEST
WAXLIKE
WAXWING
WAXWORK

••W•X••
REWAXED
REWAXES

•••W•X•
BETWIXT

••••W•X
BEESWAX

WY•••••
WYANDOT
WYCHELM
WYNETTE
WYNONNA
WYOMING
WYSIWYG
WYVERNS

W•Y••••
WAYBILL
WAYCOOL
WAYLAID
WAYLAYS
WAYLESS
WAYSIDE
WAYWARD
WAYWORN
WHYDAHS
WRYNESS

W••Y•••
WHEYISH

W••••Y•
WALLEYE
WAYLAYS
WURLEYS
WYSIWYG

W•••••Y
WACKILY
WAGGERY
WALKWAY
WALLABY
WASPILY
WCHANDY
WEALTHY
WEARILY
WEEDILY
WEEKDAY
WEIGHTY
WEIRDLY
WHEREBY
WHISKEY
WHITNEY
WILLOWY
WINDILY
WINFREY
WINTERY
WISEGUY
WISPILY
WITTILY
WOMANLY
WOOLLEY
WOOLSEY
WOOZILY
WORDILY
WORKDAY
WORLDLY
WRIGGLY
WRIGLEY
WRINKLY
WRONGLY

•WY••••
GWYNETH

•W•Y•••
SWAYERS
SWAYING

•W••••Y
AWFULLY

SWARTHY
SWEARBY
SWEENEY
SWEETLY
SWELTRY
SWIFTLY
SWINGBY
SWOREBY
TWINKLY
TWITCHY

••WY•••
BOWYERS
LAWYERS
NCWYETH
NEWYEAR
NEWYORK
SAWYERS

••W•Y••
BYWAYOF

••W••Y•
COWBOYS
HAWKEYE
LOWBOYS

••W•••Y
BAWDILY
COWPONY
DOWDILY
GAWKILY
JEWELRY
NEWBERY
NEWSBOY
NEWSDAY
POWDERY
ROWDILY
TAWNILY
TOWAWAY

•••W•Y•
AIRWAYS
ENDWAYS
FLYWAYS
JETWAYS
MIDWAYS
PEDWAYS
RUNWAYS
SEAWAYS
SKYWAYS
SUBWAYS

•••W••Y
BLOWDRY
BLOWFLY
BREWERY
CHEWTOY
FAYWRAY
FLOWERY
FRAWLEY
FROWSTY
PLOWBOY
SHOWERY
SHOWILY
SNOWDAY
SNOWILY

••••WY•
GOLDWYN
WYSIWYG

••••W•Y
ALLOWAY

ARCHWAY
AREAWAY
BELTWAY
BIKEWAY
CARAWAY
CUTAWAY
DOORWAY
DUNAWAY
EATAWAY
FAIRWAY
FARAWAY
FLYAWAY
FOLKWAY
FOOTWAY
FOURWAY
FREEWAY
GANGWAY
GATEWAY
GAVEWAY
GETAWAY
GIVEWAY
GOTAWAY
HALFWAY
HALLWAY
HEADWAY
HIGHWAY
INNOWAY
JANEWAY
LAYAWAY
MADEWAY
MAKEWAY
OJIBWAY
PARKWAY
PARTWAY
PATHWAY
PUTAWAY
RACEWAY
RAILWAY
RANAWAY
RIDGWAY
ROADWAY
RUNAWAY
SCRAWLY
SCRAWNY
SOMEWAY
SQUAWKY
TAXIWAY
THRUWAY
TOLLWAY
TOWAWAY
WALKWAY

•••••WY
BILLOWY
MEADOWY
MILDEWY
PILLOWY
SHADOWY
WILLOWY
YELLOWY

W•Z••••
WIZARDS
WIZENED
WOZNIAK
WOZZECK

W••Z•••
WARZONE
WHIZKID
WHIZZED
WHIZZER
WHIZZES
WOOZIER

WOOZILY
WOZZECK

W•••Z••
WALTZED
WALTZER
WALTZES
WHEEZED
WHEEZER
WHEEZES
WHIZZED
WHIZZER
WHIZZES

•W•Z•••
SWIZZLE

•W••Z••
DWEEZIL
KWANZAS
SWITZER
SWIZZLE
TWEEZED
TWEEZES

•••W••Z
GEEWHIZ
SHOWBIZ

XA•••••
XANTHAN
XANTHIC

X•A••••
XRATING
XRAYING

X••••A•
XANTHAN

•XA••••
EXACTAS
EXACTED
EXACTER
EXACTLY
EXACTOR
EXALTED
EXAMINE
EXAMPLE
EXANIMO
EXARCHS

•X•A•••
AXIALLY
EXFACTO
EXHALED
EXHALES
EXHAUST
EXPANDS
EXPANSE
EXPARTE
OXCARTS

•X••A••
EXCLAIM
EXPIATE
EXPLAIN
EXTRACT
OXIDANT
OXIDASE

•X•••A•
AXILLAE
EXACTAS

EXURBAN
OXONIAN
UXORIAL

•X••••A
EXOTICA
EXURBIA
OXYMORA

••XA•••
FIXABLE
FIXATED
FIXATES
HEXAGON
LUXATED
LUXATES
MIXABLE
ROXANNE
TAXABLE

••X•A••
BOXCARS
FOXTAIL
MAXBAER
REXCATS
SEXTANS
SEXTANT
SIXPACK
TAXRATE

••X••A•
BOXSEAT
LEXICAL
MAXIMAL
MEXICAN
TAXICAB
TAXIMAN
TAXIWAY
TEXTUAL
WAXBEAN

••X•••A
MAXILLA
NOXZEMA

•••XA••
INEXACT

•••X•A•
COAXIAL
FAUXPAS
MANXCAT
MANXMAN

•••X••A
ABEXTRA

•XB••••
OXBLOOD

•X••B••
EXHIBIT
EXURBAN
EXURBIA

••XB•••
MAXBAER
MAXBORN
WAXBEAN

••X•B••
FIXABLE
MIXABLE
TAXABLE

••X•••B
COXCOMB
TAXICAB

X•••••C
XANTHIC

•XC••••
EXCEEDS
EXCEPTS
EXCERPT
EXCISED
EXCISES
EXCITED
EXCITES
EXCLAIM
EXCLUDE
EXCRETE
EXCUSED
EXCUSES
OXCARTS

•X•C•••
EXACTAS
EXACTED
EXACTER
EXACTLY
EXACTOR
EXECUTE

•X••C••
EXARCHS
EXFACTO
EXPECTS

•X•••C•
EXOTICA
EXOTICS
EXTINCT
EXTRACT

••XC•••
BOXCARS
COXCOMB
REXCATS

••X•C••
LEXICAL
LEXICON
MEXICAN
TAXICAB

••X••C•
SIXPACK

•••XC••
MANXCAT

•••X•C•
INEXACT

•X•D•••
EXUDING
OXIDANT
OXIDASE
OXIDISE
OXIDIZE

•X•••D•
AXSEEDS
EXCEEDS
EXCLUDE
EXPANDS
EXPENDS

EXPLODE
EXTENDS
EXTRUDE
OXFORDS

•X••••D
EXACTED
EXALTED
EXCISED
EXCITED
EXCUSED
EXERTED
EXHALED
EXISTED
EXPIRED
EXPOSED
EXPOUND
EXULTED
OXBLOOD

••X•D••
BOXEDIN
BOXEDUP
FIXEDLY
FIXEDUP
MIXEDIN
MIXEDUP
PYXIDES
TUXEDOS
VEXEDLY

••X•••D
BOXWOOD
FIXATED
LUXATED
SIXFOLD

•••X•D•
DIOXIDE

••••X•D
ADMIXED
AFFIXED
ANNEXED
IMMIXED
INDEXED
RELAXED
REMIXED
RETAXED
REWAXED
TELEXED
UNBOXED
UNFIXED

X•E••••
XHEIGHT

•XE••••
EXECUTE
EXEMPLI
EXEMPTS
EXERTED

•X•E•••
AXSEEDS
EXCEEDS
EXCEPTS
EXCERPT
EXPECTS
EXPENDS
EXPENSE
EXPERTS
EXSERTS
EXTENDS
EXTENTS
EXTERNS

•X••E••
AXSEEDS
EXCEEDS
EXCRETE
EXIGENT
EXPRESS
EXTREME
EXUPERY

•X•••E•
EXACTED
EXACTER
EXALTED
EXCISED
EXCISES
EXCITED
EXCITES
EXCUSED
EXCUSES
EXERTED
EXHALED
EXHALES
EXISTED
EXPIRED
EXPIRES
EXPOSED
EXPOSES
EXULTED
EXWIVES

•X••••E
AXILLAE
EXAMINE
EXAMPLE
EXCLUDE
EXCRETE
EXECUTE
EXPANSE
EXPARTE
EXPENSE
EXPIATE
EXPLODE
EXPLORE
EXPUNGE
EXTREME
EXTRUDE
OXIDASE
OXIDISE
OXIDIZE

••XE•••
BOXEDIN
BOXEDUP
BOXESIN
BOXESUP
FIXEDLY
FIXEDUP
FIXESUP
LEXEMES
MIXEDIN
MIXEDUP
MIXESIN
MIXESUP
TUXEDOS
VEXEDLY

••X•E••
ANXIETY
BOXIEST
BOXSEAT
FOXIEST
LAXNESS
MAXWELL
NOXZEMA
SEXIEST
SEXTETS
SIXTEEN
TAXLESS
WAXBEAN
WAXIEST

••X••E•
BOXSTEP
FIXATED
FIXATES
LEXEMES
LUXATED
LUXATES
MAXBAER
NEXUSES
PYXIDES
SIXTEEN
SIXTIES
TAXFREE
TAXIMEN

••X•••E
BOXKITE
BOXLIKE
FIXABLE
FIXTURE
FOXFIRE
FOXHOLE
FOXLIKE
MIXABLE
MIXTURE
ROXANNE
TAXABLE
TAXFREE
TAXRATE
TEXTILE
TEXTURE
WAXLIKE

•••XE••
COAXERS
HOAXERS

•••X•E•
EPOXIES
FLAXIER
FLEXNER
MANXMEN
PREXIES
PROXIES

•••X••E
BAUXITE
DIOXIDE
QUIXOTE

••••XE•
ADMIXED
ADMIXES
AFFIXED
AFFIXES
ANNEXED
ANNEXES
CALYXES
HELIXES
HYRAXES
ICEAXES
IMMIXED
IMMIXES
INBOXES
INDEXED
INDEXES
LATEXES
PHLOXES
POBOXES
RADIXES
RELAXED
RELAXES
REMIXED
REMIXES
RETAXED
RETAXES
REWAXED
REWAXES
TELEXED
TELEXES
UNBOXED
UNBOXES
UNFIXED

•••••XE
PICKAXE
POLEAXE

•XF••••
EXFACTO
OXFORDS

••XF•••
BOXFULS
FOXFIRE
SIXFOLD
TAXFREE

X••G•••
XINGOUT

X•••G••
XHEIGHT

X•••••G
XRATING
XRAYING

•X•G•••
EXIGENT

•X•••G•
EXPUNGE

•X••••G
EXILING
EXITING
EXUDING

••XG•••
SIXGUNS

••X•G••
HEXAGON

••X••G•
FIXINGS
HEXSIGN

••X•••G
TAXIING
WAXWING

•••X••G
BRUXING
COAXING
FLEXING
FLUXING
HOAXING
JINXING

XH•••••
XHEIGHT

X•••H••
XANTHAN
XANTHIC

X••••H•
XHEIGHT

•XH••••
EXHALED
EXHALES
EXHAUST
EXHIBIT
EXHORTS

•X•••H•
EXARCHS

••XH•••
FOXHOLE
SAXHORN

••X•H••
SIXTHLY

••X•••H
PIXYISH

•••X••H
MINXISH

XI•••••
XINGOUT

X••I•••
XHEIGHT

X•••I••
XRATING
XRAYING

X••••I•
XANTHIC

•XI••••
AXIALLY
AXILLAE
EXIGENT
EXILING
EXISTED
EXITING
OXIDANT
OXIDASE
OXIDISE
OXIDIZE

•X•I•••
EXCISED
EXCISES
EXCITED
EXCITES
EXHIBIT
EXPIATE
EXPIRED
EXPIRES
EXTINCT
EXWIVES

•X••I••
EXAMINE
EXANIMO
EXILING
EXITING
EXOTICA
EXOTICS
EXUDING
OXIDISE
OXIDIZE
OXONIAN
UXORIAL

•X•••I•
EXCLAIM
EXHIBIT
EXPLAIN
EXPLOIT
EXURBIA

•X••••I
EXEMPLI

••XI•••
ANXIETY
ANXIOUS
BOXIEST
FIXINGS
FOXIEST
LEXICAL
LEXICON
MAXILLA
MAXIMAL
MAXIMUM
MAXIMUS
MEXICAN
MIXITUP
NOXIOUS
PYXIDES
SEXIEST
SEXISTS
SIXIRON
TAXICAB
TAXIING
TAXIMAN
TAXIMEN
TAXIWAY
WAXIEST

••X•I••
BOXKITE
BOXLIKE
FOXFIRE
FOXLIKE
HEXSIGN
PIXYISH
SIXTIES
TAXIING
TEXTILE
WAXLIKE
WAXWING

••X••I•
BOXEDIN
BOXESIN
DEXTRIN
FOXTAIL
MIXEDIN
MIXESIN

•••XI••
BAUXITE
BRUXING
COAXIAL
COAXING
COEXIST
DIOXIDE
ELIXIRS
EPOXIES
FLAXIER
FLEXING
FLUXING
HOAXING
JINXING
MARXISM
MARXIST
MINXISH
PREXIES
PROXIES
PROXIMO

••••XI•
MRFIXIT

•••••XI
AIRTAXI

•X•••K•
EXWORKS

••XK•••
BOXKITE

••X••K•
BOXLIKE
FOXLIKE
WAXLIKE

••X•••K
SIXPACK
WAXWORK

•X•L•••
AXILLAE
AXOLOTL
EXALTED
EXCLAIM
EXCLUDE
EXILING
EXPLAIN
EXPLODE
EXPLOIT
EXPLORE
EXULTED
OXBLOOD

•X••L••
AXIALLY
AXILLAE
EXHALED
EXHALES

•X•••L•
AXIALLY
EXACTLY
EXAMPLE
EXEMPLI

•X••••L
AXOLOTL
UXORIAL

••XL•••
BOXLIKE
FOXLIKE
TAXLESS
WAXLIKE

••X•L••
MAXILLA

••X••L•
BOXFULS
FIXABLE
FIXEDLY
FOXHOLE
MAXILLA
MAXWELL
MIXABLE
SIXFOLD
SIXTHLY
TAXABLE
TEXTILE
VEXEDLY

••X•••L
FOXTAIL
LEXICAL
MAXIMAL
MAXWELL
TEXTUAL

•••X••L
COAXIAL

•X•M•••
EXAMINE
EXAMPLE
EXEMPLI
EXEMPTS
OXYMORA

•X•••M•
EXANIMO
EXTREME

•X••••M
EXCLAIM

••X•M••
LEXEMES
MAXIMAL
MAXIMUM
MAXIMUS
TAXIMAN
TAXIMEN

••X••M•
COXCOMB
NOXZEMA

••X•••M
BOXROOM
MAXIMUM

•••XM••
MANXMAN
MANXMEN

•••X•M•
PROXIMO

•••X••M
MARXISM

X•N••••
XANTHAN
XANTHIC
XINGOUT

X••••N•
XRATING
XRAYING

X•••••N
XANTHAN

•X•N•••
EXANIMO
OXONIAN

•X••N••
EXPANDS
EXPANSE
EXPENDS
EXPENSE
EXPUNGE
EXTENDS
EXTENTS
EXTINCT

•X•••N•
EXAMINE
EXIGENT
EXILING
EXITING
EXPOUND
EXTERNS
EXUDING
OXIDANT

•X••••N
EXPLAIN
EXURBAN
OXONIAN

••XN•••
HEXNUTS
LAXNESS

••X•N••
FIXINGS
ROXANNE

••X••N•
ROXANNE
SEXTANS
SEXTANT
SEXTONS
SIXGUNS
TAXIING
WAXWING

••X•••N
BOXEDIN
BOXESIN
DEXTRIN
HEXAGON
HEXSIGN
LEXICON
MEXICAN
MIXEDIN
MIXESIN
SAXHORN
SIXIRON
SIXTEEN
TAXIMAN
TAXIMEN
WAXBEAN

•••XN••
FLEXNER

•••X•N•
BRUXING
COAXING
FLEXING
FLUXING
HOAXING
JINXING
KLAXONS

•••X••N
BRAXTON
MANXMAN
MANXMEN

X•••O••
XINGOUT

•XO••••
AXOLOTL
EXOTICA
EXOTICS
OXONIAN
UXORIAL

•X•O•••
EXHORTS
EXPORTS
EXPOSED
EXPOSES
EXPOUND
EXTORTS
EXWORKS
OXFORDS

•X••O••
AXOLOTL
EXPLODE
EXPLOIT
EXPLORE
OXBLOOD
OXYMORA

•X•••O•
EXACTOR
OXBLOOD

•X••••O
EXANIMO
EXFACTO

••X•O••
ANXIOUS
BOXROOM
BOXTOPS
BOXWOOD
COXCOMB
FOXHOLE
MAXBORN
NOXIOUS
SAXHORN
SEXTONS
SIXFOLD
WAXWORK

••X••O•
BOXROOM
BOXWOOD
FOXTROT
HEXAGON
LEXICON
SIXIRON
TUXEDOS

•••XO••
FLEXORS
KLAXONS
PLEXORS
QUIXOTE

•••X•O•
BRAXTON

•••X••O
PROXIMO

•XP••••
EXPANDS
EXPANSE
EXPARTE
EXPECTS
EXPENDS
EXPENSE
EXPERTS
EXPIATE
EXPIRED
EXPIRES
EXPLAIN
EXPLODE
EXPLOIT
EXPLORE
EXPORTS
EXPOSED
EXPOSES
EXPOUND
EXPRESS
EXPUNGE

•X•P•••
EXUPERY

•X••P••
EXAMPLE
EXCEPTS
EXEMPLI
EXEMPTS

•X•••P•
EXCERPT

••XP•••
SIXPACK

••X••P•
BOXTOPS

••X•••P
BOXEDUP
BOXESUP
BOXSTEP
FIXEDUP
FIXESUP
MIXEDUP
MIXESUP
MIXITUP

•••XP••
FAUXPAS

XR•••••
XRATING
XRAYING

•X•R•••
EXARCHS
EXCRETE
EXERTED
EXPRESS
EXTRACT
EXTREME
EXTRUDE
EXURBAN
EXURBIA
UXORIAL

•X••R••
EXCERPT
EXHORTS
EXPARTE
EXPERTS
EXPIRED
EXPIRES
EXPORTS
EXSERTS
EXTERNS
EXTORTS
EXWORKS
OXCARTS
OXFORDS

•X•••R•
EXPLORE
EXUPERY
OXYMORA

•X••••R
EXACTER
EXACTOR

••XR•••
BOXROOM
TAXRATE

••X•R••
DEXTRIN
FOXTROT
SIXIRON
TAXFREE

••X••R•
BOXCARS
FIXTURE
FOXFIRE
MAXBORN
MIXTURE
SAXHORN
TEXTURE
WAXWORK

••X•••R
MAXBAER

•••X•R•
ABEXTRA
COAXERS
ELIXIRS
FLEXORS
HOAXERS
PLEXORS

•••X••R
FLAXIER
FLEXNER

•XS••••
AXSEEDS
EXSERTS

•X•S•••
EXISTED

•X••S••
EXCISED
EXCISES
EXCUSED
EXCUSES
EXPOSED
EXPOSES

•X•••S•
EXHAUST
EXPANSE
EXPENSE
EXPRESS
OXIDASE
OXIDISE

•X••••S
AXSEEDS
EXACTAS
EXARCHS
EXCEEDS
EXCEPTS
EXCISES
EXCITES
EXCUSES
EXEMPTS
EXHALES
EXHORTS
EXOTICS
EXPANDS
EXPECTS
EXPENDS
EXPERTS
EXPIRES
EXPORTS
EXPOSES
EXPRESS
EXSERTS
EXTENDS
EXTENTS
EXTERNS
EXTORTS
EXWIVES
EXWORKS
OXCARTS
OXFORDS

••XS•••
BOXSEAT
BOXSTEP
HEXSIGN

••X•S••
BOXESIN
BOXESUP
FIXESUP
MIXESIN
MIXESUP
NEXUSES
SEXISTS

••X••S•
BOXIEST
FOXIEST
LAXNESS
PIXYISH
SEXIEST
TAXLESS
WAXIEST

••X•••S
ANXIOUS
BOXCARS
BOXFULS
BOXTOPS
FIXATES
FIXINGS
HEXNUTS
LAXNESS
LEXEMES
LUXATES
MAXIMUS
NEXUSES
NOXIOUS
PYXIDES
REXCATS
SEXISTS
SEXTANS
SEXTETS
SEXTONS
SIXGUNS
SIXTIES
TAXLESS
TUXEDOS

•••X•S•
COEXIST
MARXISM
MARXIST
MINXISH

•••X••S
COAXERS
ELIXIRS
EPOXIES
FAUXPAS
FLEXORS
HOAXERS
KLAXONS
PLEXORS
PREXIES
PROXIES

••••X•S
ADMIXES
AFFIXES
ANNEXES
CALYXES
HELIXES
HYRAXES
ICEAXES
IMMIXES
INBOXES
INDEXES
LATEXES
PHLOXES
POBOXES
RADIXES
RELAXES
REMIXES
RETAXES
REWAXES
TELEXES
UNBOXES
URTEXTS

X••T•••
XANTHAN
XANTHIC
XRATING

X•••••T
XHEIGHT
XINGOUT

•XT••••
EXTENDS
EXTENTS
EXTERNS
EXTINCT
EXTORTS
EXTRACT

EXTREME
EXTRUDE

•X•T•••
EXITING
EXOTICA
EXOTICS

•X••T••
EXACTAS
EXACTED
EXACTER
EXACTLY
EXACTOR
EXALTED
EXCITED
EXCITES
EXERTED
EXISTED
EXULTED

•X•••T•
AXOLOTL
EXCEPTS
EXCRETE
EXECUTE
EXEMPTS
EXFACTO
EXHORTS
EXPARTE
EXPECTS
EXPERTS
EXPIATE
EXPORTS
EXSERTS
EXTENTS
EXTORTS
OXCARTS

•X••••T
EXCERPT
EXHAUST
EXHIBIT
EXIGENT
EXPLOIT
EXTINCT
EXTRACT
OXIDANT

••XT•••
BOXTOPS
DEXTRIN
FIXTURE
FOXTAIL
FOXTROT
MIXTURE
SEXTANS
SEXTANT
SEXTETS
SEXTONS
SIXTEEN
SIXTHLY
SIXTIES
TEXTILE
TEXTUAL
TEXTURE

••X•T••
BOXSTEP
FIXATED
FIXATES
LUXATED
LUXATES
MIXITUP

••X••T•
ANXIETY
BOXKITE
HEXNUTS
REXCATS
SEXISTS
SEXTETS
TAXRATE

••X•••T
BOXIEST
BOXSEAT
FOXIEST
FOXTROT
SEXIEST
SEXTANT
WAXIEST

•••XT••
ABEXTRA
BRAXTON

•••X•T•
BAUXITE
QUIXOTE

•••X••T
COEXIST
INEXACT
MANXCAT
MARXIST

••••XT•
URTEXTS

••••X•T
MRFIXIT

•••••XT
BETWIXT
CONTEXT
PRETEXT
SUBTEXT

X••••U•
XINGOUT

•XU••••
EXUDING
EXULTED
EXUPERY
EXURBAN
EXURBIA

•X•U•••
EXCUSED
EXCUSES
EXPUNGE

•X••U••
EXCLUDE
EXECUTE
EXHAUST
EXPOUND
EXTRUDE

••XU•••
NEXUSES

••X•U••
BOXFULS
FIXTURE
HEXNUTS
MIXTURE
SIXGUNS
TEXTUAL
TEXTURE

••X••U•
ANXIOUS
BOXEDUP
BOXESUP
FIXEDUP
FIXESUP
MAXIMUM
MAXIMUS
MIXEDUP
MIXESUP
MIXITUP
NOXIOUS

•X••V••
EXWIVES

•XW••••
EXWIVES
EXWORKS

••XW•••
BOXWOOD
MAXWELL
WAXWING
WAXWORK

••X•W••
TAXIWAY

X••Y•••
XRAYING

•XY••••
OXYMORA

•X••••Y
AXIALLY
EXACTLY
EXUPERY

••XY•••
PIXYISH

••X•••Y
ANXIETY
FIXEDLY
SIXTHLY
TAXIWAY
VEXEDLY

•X•••Z•
OXIDIZE

••XZ•••
NOXZEMA

YA•••••
YABBERS
YACHTED
YACKING
YAHTZEE
YAKIMAS
YAKKERS
YAKKING
YAKUTSK
YAKUZAS
YAMMERS
YANGTZE
YANKEES
YANKING
YANKTON
YANQUIS
YAOUNDE
YAPPERS
YAPPING
YARDAGE
YARDARM
YARDMAN
YARDMEN
YARNING
YARROWS
YASHMAK
YAUPONS
YAWNERS
YAWNFUL
YAWNING
YAWPERS
YAWPING

Y•A••••
YEANING
YEAREND
YEARNED
YEARNER
YEATEAM

Y••A•••
YUCATAN

Y•••A••
YARDAGE
YARDARM
YESMAAM
YOUMANS

Y••••A•
YAKIMAS
YAKUZAS
YARDMAN
YASHMAK
YEATEAM
YELLSAT
YEREVAN
YESDEAR
YESMAAM
YITZHAK
YUCATAN

Y•••••A
YESHIVA

•YA••••
BYANDBY
BYANOSE
HYALINE
MYANMAR
WYANDOT

•Y•A•••
AYEAYES
BYPATHS
BYWAYOF
DYNAMIC
DYNAMOS
DYNASTS
DYNASTY
GYRATED
GYRATES
GYRATOR
HYRACES
HYRAXES
MYMAMMY
PYJAMAS
PYRAMID
PYRAMUS
SYNAPSE
TYRANNY
TYRANTS

•Y••A••
AYNRAND
BYHEART
BYPLAYS
BYROADS
CYMBALS
EYEBALL
EYEBANK
EYELASH
EYEWASH
GYMBAGS
GYMNAST
HYDRANT
HYDRATE
HYMNALS
MYRIADS
SYLLABI
SYLVANS
SYRIANS
TYMPANA
TYMPANI

•Y•••A•
BYREMAN
CYNICAL
HYUNDAI
LYRICAL
MYANMAR
NYUNGAR
PYJAMAS
PYTHIAN
PYTHIAS
SYNGMAN
SYNODAL
TYPICAL

•Y••••A
CYNTHIA
DYKSTRA
HYGIEIA
SYRINGA
TYMPANA
WYNONNA

••YA•••
BUYABLE
FLYAWAY
KAYAKED
KAYAKER
LAYAWAY
LOYALLY
LOYALTY
MAYALIN
PAYABLE
ROYALLY
ROYALTY
ROYALWE
ULYANOV
VOYAGED
VOYAGER
VOYAGES

••Y•A••
AMYLASE
CAYMANS
CRYBABY
DAYCAMP
DAYCARE
DAYMARE
DRYWALL
FLYBALL
FLYCAST
FLYPAST
FLYWAYS
FRYPANS
HAYRACK
HAYWARD
HEYDAYS
JAYWALK
KEYCARD
KEYPADS
LAYBACK
MAYDAYS
MAYFAIR
MAYNARD
NAYSAID
NAYSAYS
PAYCASH
PAYDAYS
REYNARD
SKYCAPS
SKYJACK
SKYLARK
SKYWARD
SKYWAYS
TOYLAND
WAYLAID
WAYLAYS
WAYWARD
WHYDAHS

••Y••A•
ABYSMAL
ALYKHAN
ANYROAD
BAYLEAF
CAYUGAS
CRYSTAL
DAYSTAR
ELYSIAN
FAYWRAY
FEYNMAN
FLYAWAY
FLYLEAF
FLYTRAP
LAYAWAY
MAYORAL
PAYLOAD
PAYOLAS
RAYOVAC
SOYBEAN
STYGIAN
STYRIAN
ZOYSIAS

••Y•••A
ALYOSHA
DAYTONA
OLYMPIA
OXYMORA
SOYINKA

•••YA••
ABEYANT
ARMYANT
BANYANS
BUOYANT
DRAYAGE
HALYARD
HOLYARK
HUNYADY
KENYANS
LANYARD
LIBYANS
MAGYARS
MARYANN
MINYANS
PLAYACT
RUDYARD

•••Y•A•
BABYSAT
BODYFAT
COPYCAT
GRAYJAY
GRAYLAG
HOLYDAY
HOLYWAR
INKYCAP
KHAYYAM
LADYDAY
LILYPAD
MANYEAR
MARYKAY
MIDYEAR
NEWYEAR
OFFYEAR
PLAYSAT

•••Y••A
ASSYRIA
CRAYOLA

••••YA•
GIDDYAP
KHAYYAM
MALAYAN
MEGRYAN
MIAOYAO
PAPAYAS
RUFIYAA
SAROYAN

••••Y•A
RUFIYAA

•••••YA
MONTOYA

Y•B••••
YABBERS

Y••B•••
YABBERS

•YB••••
CYBORGS
DYBBUKS
HYBRIDS

•Y•B•••
CYMBALS
DYBBUKS
EYEBALL
EYEBANK
EYEBOLT
EYEBROW
GYMBAGS
SYMBOLS

•Y•••B•
BYANDBY
BYTHEBY
SYLLABI

••YB•••
ANYBODY
CRYBABY
DAYBEDS
DAYBOOK
DAYBOYS
FLYBALL
FLYBOYS
JAYBIRD
LAYBACK
RAYBURN
SKYBLUE
SOYBEAN
WAYBILL

••Y•B••
BUYABLE
PAYABLE
TOYNBEE

••Y••B•
CRYBABY
DAYJOBS

••Y•••B
KEYCLUB

•••YB••
COPYBOY
LADYBUG
PLAYBOY

Y•C••••
YACHTED
YACKING
YUCATAN
YUCKIER

Y•••••C
YOUNGMC

•YC••••
CYCLERS
CYCLING
CYCLIST
CYCLONE
CYCLOPS
LYCEUMS
TYCOONS
WYCHELM

•Y•C•••
EYECUPS
PYNCHON
SYNCHED
SYNCHES
SYNCING

•Y••C••
CYNICAL
HYRACES
LYRICAL
TYPICAL
ZYDECOS

•Y•••C•
BYFORCE
MYSTICS

•Y••••C
DYNAMIC
PYRRHIC
SYNODIC

••YC•••
BAYCITY
BOYCOTT
DAYCAMP
DAYCARE
DRYCELL
FLYCAST
FRYCOOK
JAYCEES
KEYCARD
KEYCLUB
PAYCASH
PSYCHED
PSYCHES
PSYCHIC
PSYCHUP
SKYCAPS
WAYCOOL

••Y••C•
DRYDOCK
HAYRACK
LAYBACK
PHYSICS
SHYLOCK
SKYJACK

••Y•••C
CRYPTIC
IDYLLIC
OLYMPIC
PSYCHIC
RAYKROC
RAYOVAC
STYPTIC

•••YC••
BICYCLE
CALYCES
COPYCAT
HOLYCOW
INKYCAP
RECYCLE

•••Y•C•
PLAYACT

•••Y••C
ACRYLIC

••••YC•
DIPTYCH
VANDYCK
VANEYCK

••••Y•C
LIPSYNC

Y•D••••
YIDDISH
YODELED
YODELER

Y••D•••
YARDAGE
YARDARM
YARDMAN
YARDMEN
YESDEAR
YIDDISH

Y•••D••
YIELDED

Y••••D•
YAOUNDE

Y•••••D
YACHTED
YEAREND
YEARNED
YIELDED
YODELED

•YD••••
HYDRANT
HYDRATE
HYDROUS
ZYDECOS

•Y•D•••
PYEDOGS

•Y••D••
BYANDBY
HYPEDUP
HYUNDAI
PYXIDES
SYNODAL
SYNODIC
TYPEDUP
WYANDOT

•Y•••D•
BYROADS
BYWORDS
EYELIDS
HYBRIDS
HYMNODY
MYRIADS

•Y••••D
AYKROYD
AYNRAND
BYLINED
GYRATED
PYRAMID
SYNCHED

••YD•••
DRYDOCK
HEYDAYS
HOYDENS
LAYDOWN
MAYDAYS
PAYDAYS
PAYDIRT
SKYDIVE
TOYDOGS
WHYDAHS

••Y•D••
KEYEDIN
KEYEDUP

••Y••D•
ANYBODY
DAYBEDS
FLYRODS
HAYRIDE
HEYJUDE
JOYRIDE
KEYPADS
SAYYIDS
WAYSIDE

••Y•••D
ANYROAD
BOYHOOD
DRYEYED
HAYSEED
HAYWARD
HEYWOOD
JAYBIRD
KAYAKED
KEYCARD
KEYWORD
LAYERED
MAYNARD
NAYSAID
PAYLOAD
PLYWOOD
PSYCHED
RAYMOND
REYNARD
SCYTHED
SKYWARD
STYMIED
TOYLAND
TRYSTED
UNYOKED
VOYAGED
WAYLAID
WAYWARD

•••YD••
HOLYDAY
KATYDID
LADYDAY
PLAYDOH

•••Y•D•
HUNYADY
SAYYIDS

•••Y••D
HALYARD
KATYDID
LANYARD
LILYPAD
RETYPED
RUDYARD

••••Y•D
ALLAYED
ALLOYED
ANNOYED
ARRAYED
ASSAYED
BELAYED
BOGEYED
BUGEYED
DECAYED
DECOYED
DELAYED
DRYEYED
EMBAYED
ENJOYED
ESSAYED
HONEYED
MONEYED
MOSEYED
ONEEYED
POPEYED
REDEYED
REKEYED
RELAYED
SAMOYED
SPLAYED
SPRAYED
STRAYED
TIEDYED

•••••YD
AYKROYD

YE•••••
YEANING
YEAREND
YEARNED
YEARNER
YEATEAM
YELLERS
YELLING
YELLOWS
YELLOWY
YELLSAT
YELPERS
YELPING
YELTSIN
YEMENIS
YEREVAN
YERKING
YERKISH
YESDEAR
YESHIVA
YESMAAM
YESSING
YEVGENY

Y•E••••
YIELDED

Y••E•••
YEMENIS
YEREVAN
YODELED
YODELER
YULELOG

Y•••E••
YABBERS
YAKKERS
YAMMERS
YANKEES
YAPPERS
YAWNERS
YAWPERS
YEAREND
YEATEAM
YELLERS
YELPERS
YESDEAR
YEVGENY
YONKERS
YOWLERS

Y••••E•
YACHTED
YAHTZEE
YANKEES
YARDMEN
YEARNED
YEARNER
YIELDED
YODELED
YODELER
YORKIES
YOUNGER
YUCKIER
YUMMIER
YUPPIES

Y•••••E
YAHTZEE
YANGTZE
YAOUNDE
YARDAGE

•YE••••
AYEAYES
EYEBALL
EYEBANK
EYEBOLT
EYEBROW
EYECUPS
EYEFULS
EYEHOLE
EYELASH
EYELESS
EYELETS
EYELIDS
EYELIKE
EYESHOT
EYESORE
EYEWASH
PYEDOGS

•Y•E•••
BYHEART
BYREMAN
BYREMEN
GYRENES
HYPEDUP
HYPESUP
LYCEUMS
LYSENKO
SYNERGY
TYLENOL
TYPEDUP
TYPESET
TYPESUP
WYNETTE
WYVERNS
ZYDECOS

•Y••E••
BYTHEBY
CYCLERS
CYGNETS
CYPHERS
CYPRESS
EYELESS
EYELETS
GYPPERS
HYGIEIA
HYGIENE
HYPHENS
MYNHEER
MYSTERY
OYSTERS
SYSTEMS
TYPIEST
WYCHELM

•Y•••E•
AYEAYES
BYGONES
BYLINED
BYLINES
BYREMEN
GYPSIES
GYRATED
GYRATES
GYRENES
HYRACES
HYRAXES
KYLIKES
MYNHEER
MYRTLES
PYGMIES
PYRITES
PYXIDES
SYNCHED
SYNCHES
SYNFUEL
TYPESET
ZYGOTES

•Y••••E
BYANOSE
BYFORCE
CYCLONE
EYEHOLE
EYELIKE
EYESORE
GYMSHOE
HYALINE
HYDRATE
HYGIENE
SYNAPSE
SYRINGE
SYSTOLE
WYNETTE

••YE•••
CAYENNE
DOYENNE
DRYEYED
KEYEDIN
KEYEDUP
LAYERED
LAYETTE

••Y•E••
BAYLEAF
COYNESS
DAYBEDS
DRYCELL
DRYNESS
DRYWELL
ELYSEES
FLYLEAF
FLYLESS
FLYNETS
GEYSERS
GWYNETH
HAYSEED
HOYDENS
HUYGENS
JAYCEES
JAYLENO
JAYVEES
JOYLESS
KEYLESS
KEYWEST
MAYHEMS
PAYMENT
RHYMERS
SHYNESS
SKYLESS
SLYNESS
SOYBEAN
STYLERS
STYLETS
STYRENE
THYSELF
TOYLESS
WAYLESS
WRYNESS

••Y••E•
ABYSSES
ANYONES
BAYONET
BRYNNER
CAYUSES

COYOTES
CRYOGEN
DRYEYED
ELYSEES
FLYOVER
HAYSEED
JAYCEES
JAYVEES
KAYAKED
KAYAKER
LAYERED
LAYOPEN
LAYOVER
MAYTREE
ODYSSEY
PSYCHED
PSYCHES
SAYWHEN
SCYTHED
SCYTHES
SHYSTER
STYMIED
STYMIES
TOYNBEE
TRYSTED
TRYSTER
ULYSSES
UNYOKED
UNYOKES
VOYAGED
VOYAGER
VOYAGES

••Y•••E
AMYLASE
ANYMORE
ANYTIME
BUYABLE
BUYTIME
CAYENNE
DAYCARE
DAYMARE
DAYTIME
DOYENNE
DRYHOLE
HAYRIDE
HAYWIRE
HEYJUDE
IVYLIKE
JOYRIDE
KEYHOLE
KEYLIME
KEYNOTE
LAYETTE
MAYPOLE
MAYTIME
MAYTREE
MAYWINE
PAYABLE
RAYLIKE
ROYALWE
SKYBLUE
SKYDIVE
SKYLIKE
SKYLINE
STYLISE
STYLIZE
STYRENE
THYMINE
TOYLIKE
TOYNBEE
WAYSIDE

•••YE••
BOWYERS
BRAYERS
GRAYEST
GREYEST
GRUYERE
LAWYERS
MANYEAR
MIDYEAR
NCWYETH
NEWYEAR
OFFYEAR
PLAYERS
PRAYERS
SAWYERS
SLAYERS
SPRYEST
SWAYERS

•••Y•E•
ARGYLES
CALYCES
CALYXES
CLAYIER
ECDYSES
ECTYPES
ENZYMES
GREYHEN
HOLYSEE
OOCYTES
PLAYLET
PLAYPEN
POLYMER
RETYPED
RETYPES

•••Y••E
BICYCLE
DASYURE
DRAYAGE
GRUYERE
HOLYOKE
HOLYSEE
RECYCLE

••••YE•
ALLAYED
ALLAYER
ALLEYES
ALLOYED
ANNOYED
ARRAYED
ASSAYED
ASSAYER
AYEAYES
AZODYES
BELAYED
BIGEYES
BOGEYED
BUGEYED
COLLYER
DECAYED
DECOYED
DELAYED
DELAYER
DRYEYED
EMBAYED
ENJOYED
ESSAYED
HONEYED
LOBBYER
MONEYED
MOSEYED
NUREYEV
ONEEYED
POPEYED
REDEYED
REDEYES
REKEYED
RELAYED
RIBEYES
SAMOYED
SPLAYED
SPRAYED
SPRAYER
STRAYED
TIEDYED
TIEDYES

••••Y•E
ACOLYTE
ANALYSE
ANALYZE
ANODYNE
CARLYLE
INSTYLE
MARRYME
MISTYPE
RESTYLE
TINTYPE
VANDYKE

•••••YE
BUCKEYE
CATSEYE
DEADEYE
EMPLOYE
EVILEYE
FISHEYE
GLADEYE
GOODBYE
HAIRDYE
HAWKEYE
SHUTEYE
SOCKEYE
WALLEYE

Y•••F••
YAWNFUL

•YF••••
BYFORCE

•Y•F•••
EYEFULS
SYNFUEL

•Y•••F•
MYSTIFY

•Y••••F
BYWAYOF

••YF•••
FLYFISH
HAYFORK
MAYFAIR

••Y•F••
LAYOFFS
LAYSFOR
PAYOFFS
PAYSFOR

••Y••F•
BUYSOFF
HAYLOFT
LAYOFFS
LAYSOFF
PAYOFFS
PAYSOFF

••Y•••F
BAYLEAF
BUYSOFF
CRYWOLF
FLYLEAF
LAYSOFF
PAYSOFF
THYSELF

•••YF••
BODYFAT
DREYFUS
PLAYFUL
PRAYFOR
TRAYFUL

•••Y•F•
EASYOFF
PLAYOFF

•••Y••F
EASYOFF
PLAYOFF

••••Y•F
BYWAYOF

Y•G••••
YOGHURT
YOGURTS

Y••G•••
YANGTZE
YEVGENY

Y•••G••
YOUNGER
YOUNGMC
YOUNGUN

Y••••G•
YARDAGE

Y•••••G
YACKING
YAKKING
YANKING
YAPPING
YARNING
YAWNING
YAWPING
YEANING
YELLING
YELPING
YERKING
YESSING
YIPPING
YOWLING
YOYOING
YULELOG

•YG••••
BYGOLLY
BYGONES
CYGNETS
HYGIEIA
HYGIENE
PYGMIES
ZYGOTES

•Y•G•••
SYNGMAN

•Y••G••
LYINGTO
NYUNGAR
TYINGIN
TYINGUP

•Y•••G•
CYBORGS
GYMBAGS
PYEDOGS
SYNERGY
SYRINGA
SYRINGE
ZYMURGY

•Y••••G
CYCLING
CYYOUNG
GYPPING
HYPOING
SYNCING
WYOMING
WYSIWYG

••YG•••
HUYGENS
KEYGRIP
RAYGUNS
STYGIAN

••Y•G••
CAYUGAS
CRYOGEN
VOYAGED
VOYAGER
VOYAGES

••Y••G•
FLYHIGH
SAYINGS
SKYHIGH
TOYDOGS

••Y•••G
CYYOUNG
DAYLONG
KAYOING
KEYRING
RHYMING
STYLING
YOYOING

•••YG••
KOSYGIN
POLYGON

•••Y•G•
DRAYAGE

•••Y••G
ALLYING
BABYING
BELYING
BRAYING
BUOYING
BURYING
BUSYING
CLOYING
COPYING
COZYING
DEFYING
DENYING
DRAYING
EDDYING
ENVYING
ESPYING
FLAYING
FLEYING
FRAYING
GRAYING
GRAYLAG
GREYING
JURYING
JURYRIG
LADYBUG
LEVYING
OBEYING
OKAYING
PITYING
PLAYING
PONYING
PRAYING
RELYING
SPAYING
STAYING
SWAYING
TIDYING
UNDYING
UNTYING
VARYING
XRAYING

•••••YG
WYSIWYG

Y•H••••
YAHTZEE

Y••H•••
YACHTED
YASHMAK
YESHIVA
YOGHURT

Y•••H••
YITZHAK

Y•••••H
YERKISH
YIDDISH

•YH••••
BYHEART

•Y•H•••
BYTHEBY
CYPHERS
EYEHOLE
HYPHENS
MYNHEER
PYTHIAN
PYTHIAS
PYTHONS
SYPHONS
TYPHOON
WYCHELM

•Y••H••
CYNTHIA
EYESHOT
GYMSHOE
PYNCHON
PYRRHIC
PYRRHUS
SYNCHED
SYNCHES

•Y•••H•
BYPATHS

•Y••••H
EYELASH
EYEWASH

••YH•••
BOYHOOD
DRYHOLE
FLYHIGH
KEYHOLE
MAYHEMS
SKYHIGH
SKYHOOK

••Y•H••
ALYKHAN
GRYPHON
PSYCHED
PSYCHES
PSYCHIC
PSYCHUP
RHYTHMS
SAYWHEN
SCYTHED
SCYTHES
TOYSHOP

••Y••H•
ALYOSHA
WHYDAHS

••Y•••H
FLYFISH
FLYHIGH
GWYNETH
PAYCASH
SKYHIGH
STYLISH

•••YH••
GREYHEN

•••Y••H
BABYISH
CLAYISH
FOGYISH
GRAYISH
GREYISH
LADYISH
LAZYISH
NCWYETH
PIXYISH
PLAYDOH
TORYISH
WHEYISH
ZANYISH

••••YH•
TALLYHO

••••Y•H
DIPTYCH
FORSYTH

YI•••••
YIDDISH
YIELDED
YIPPING
YITZHAK

Y••I•••
YAKIMAS

Y•••I••
YACKING
YAKKING
YANKING
YAPPING
YARNING
YAWNING
YAWPING
YEANING
YELLING
YELPING
YERKING
YERKISH
YESHIVA
YESSING
YIDDISH
YIPPING
YORKIES
YORKIST
YOWLING
YOYOING
YTTRIUM
YUCKIER
YUMMIER
YUPPIES

Y••••I•
YANQUIS
YELTSIN
YEMENIS

•YI••••
LYINGTO
TYINGIN
TYINGUP

•Y•I•••
BYLINED
BYLINES
CYNICAL
HYGIEIA
HYGIENE
KYLIKES
LYRICAL
LYRISTS
MYRIADS
PYRITES
PYXIDES
SYRIANS
SYRINGA
SYRINGE
TYPICAL
TYPIEST
TYPISTS
WYSIWYG

•Y••I••
CYCLING
CYCLIST
CYPRIOT
EYELIDS
EYELIKE
GYPPING
GYPSIES
HYALINE
HYBRIDS
HYPOING
MYSTICS
MYSTIFY
PYGMIES
PYTHIAN
PYTHIAS
SYNCING
WYOMING

•Y•••I•
CYNTHIA
DYNAMIC
HYGIEIA
PYRAMID
PYRRHIC
SYNODIC
TYINGIN

•Y••••I
HYUNDAI
SYLLABI
TYMPANI

••YI•••
LAYINTO
LAYITON
PRYINTO
SAYINGS
SOYINKA

••Y•I••
ANYTIME
BAYCITY
BUYTIME
DAYLILY
DAYSINN
DAYTIME
ELYSIAN
ELYSIUM
FLYFISH
FLYHIGH
HAYRIDE
HAYWIRE
IVYLIKE
JAYBIRD
JOYRIDE
KAYOING
KEYLIME
KEYRING
MAYTIME
MAYWINE
PAYDIRT
PHYSICS
RAYLIKE
RHYMING
SAYYIDS
SKYDIVE
SKYHIGH
SKYLIKE
SKYLINE
STYGIAN
STYLING
STYLISE
STYLISH
STYLIST
STYLIZE
STYMIED
STYMIES
STYRIAN
THYMINE
TOYLIKE
WAYBILL
WAYSIDE
YOYOING
ZOYSIAS

••Y••I•
CRYPTIC
DAYTRIP
DRYSUIT
IDYLLIC
KEYEDIN
KEYGRIP
MAYALIN
MAYFAIR
NAYSAID
OLYMPIA
OLYMPIC
PHYLLIS
PSYCHIC
STYPTIC
WAYLAID

•••YI••
ALLYING
BABYING
BABYISH
BELYING
BRAYING
BUNYIPS
BUOYING
BURYING
BUSYING
CLAYIER
CLAYISH
CLOYING
COPYING
COPYIST
COZYING
DEFYING
DENYING
DRAYING
EDDYING
ENVYING
ESPYING
FLAYING
FLEYING
FOGYISH
FOGYISM
FRAYING
GRAYING
GRAYISH
GREYING
GREYISH
JURYING
LADYISH
LAZYISH
LEVYING
OBEYING
OKAYING
PITYING
PIXYISH
PLAYING
PONYING
PRAYING
RELYING
SAYYIDS
SPAYING
STAYING
SWAYING
TIDYING
TORYISH
TORYISM
UNDYING
UNTYING
VARYING
WHEYISH
XRAYING
ZANYISH

•••Y•I•
ACRYLIC
ASSYRIA
BABYSIT
ECDYSIS
JURYRIG
KATYDID
KOSYGIN
TINYTIM

••••YI•
HENRYIV
ROCKYII
ROCKYIV

••••Y•I
PLATYPI
ROCKYII

•••••YI
KAROLYI

•YJ••••
PYJAMAS

••YJ•••
DAYJOBS
HEYJUDE
SKYJACK

•••YJ••
GRAYJAY

Y•K••••
YAKIMAS
YAKKERS
YAKKING
YAKUTSK
YAKUZAS
YOKOONO

Y••K•••
YACKING
YAKKERS
YAKKING
YANKEES
YANKING
YANKTON
YERKING
YERKISH
YONKERS
YORKIES
YORKIST
YOUKNOW
YUCKIER

Y•••••K
YAKUTSK
YASHMAK
YITZHAK

•YK••••
AYKROYD
DYKSTRA

•Y••K••
KYLIKES

•Y•••K•
DYBBUKS
EYELIKE
LYSENKO

•Y••••K
EYEBANK

••YK•••
ALYKHAN
RAYKROC

••Y•K••
KAYAKED
KAYAKER
UNYOKED
UNYOKES

••Y••K•
IVYLIKE
RAYLIKE
SKYLIKE
SOYINKA
TOYLIKE

••Y•••K
DAYBOOK
DMYTRYK
DRYDOCK
FRYCOOK
HAYFORK
HAYRACK
JAYWALK
LAYBACK
SHYLOCK
SKYHOOK
SKYJACK
SKYLARK

•••YK••
MARYKAY

•••Y•K•
HOLYOKE

•••Y••K
HOLYARK
NEWYORK

••••YK•
GROMYKO
VANDYKE

••••Y•K
VANDYCK
VANEYCK

•••••YK
DMYTRYK
MASARYK

Y•L••••
YELLERS
YELLING
YELLOWS
YELLOWY
YELLSAT
YELPERS
YELPING
YELTSIN
YULELOG

Y••L•••
YELLERS
YELLING
YELLOWS
YELLOWY
YELLSAT
YIELDED
YOWLERS
YOWLING

Y•••L••
YODELED
YODELER
YULELOG

Y•••••L
YAWNFUL

•YL••••
BYLINED
BYLINES
KYLIKES
SYLLABI
SYLVANS
TYLENOL

•Y•L•••
BYPLAYS
CYCLERS
CYCLING
CYCLIST
CYCLONE
CYCLOPS
EYELASH
EYELESS
EYELETS
EYELIDS
EYELIKE
HYALINE
SYLLABI

•Y••L••
BYGOLLY
MYRTLES

•Y•••L•
BYGOLLY
CYMBALS
EYEBALL
EYEBOLT
EYEFULS
EYEHOLE
HYMNALS
SYMBOLS
SYSTOLE
WYCHELM

•Y••••L
CYNICAL
EYEBALL
LYRICAL
SYNFUEL
SYNODAL
TYLENOL
TYPICAL

••YL•••
AMYLASE
ASYLUMS
BAYLEAF
DAYLILY
DAYLONG
FLYLEAF
FLYLESS
HAYLOFT
IDYLLIC
IVYLIKE
JAYLENO
JOYLESS
KEYLESS
KEYLIME
PAYLOAD
PHYLLIS
RAYLIKE
SHYLOCK
SKYLARK
SKYLESS
SKYLIKE
SKYLINE
STYLERS
STYLETS
STYLING
STYLISE
STYLISH
STYLIST
STYLIZE
TOYLAND
TOYLESS
TOYLIKE
WAYLAID
WAYLAYS
WAYLESS

••Y•L••
IDYLLIC
KEYCLUB
LAYSLOW
LOYALLY
LOYALTY
MAYALIN
PAYOLAS
PHYLLIS
ROYALLY
ROYALTY
ROYALWE
SKYBLUE

••Y••L•
BUYABLE
CRYWOLF
DAYLILY
DRYCELL
DRYHOLE
DRYWALL
DRYWELL
FLYBALL
JAYWALK
KEYHOLE
LOYALLY
MAYPOLE
PAYABLE
PAYROLL
ROYALLY
THYSELF
WAYBILL

••Y•••L
ABYSMAL
CRYSTAL
DRYCELL
DRYWALL
DRYWELL
FLYBALL
MAYORAL
PAYROLL
WAYBILL
WAYCOOL

•••YL••
ACRYLIC
ARGYLES
BABYLON
EMMYLOU
GRAYLAG
MARYLOU
PLAYLET

•••Y•L•
BICYCLE
CRAYOLA
RECYCLE

•••Y••L
PLAYFUL
TRAYFUL

••••YL•
CARLYLE
DACTYLS
INSTYLE
RESTYLE

Y•M••••
YAMMERS
YEMENIS
YOMTOVS
YUMMIER

Y••M•••
YAMMERS
YESMAAM
YOUMANS
YUMMIER

Y•••M••
YAKIMAS
YARDMAN
YARDMEN
YASHMAK

Y••••M•
YOUNGMC

Y•••••M
YARDARM
YEATEAM
YESMAAM
YTTRIUM

•YM••••
CYMBALS
GYMBAGS
GYMNAST
GYMSHOE
HYMNALS
HYMNODY
MYMAMMY
SYMBOLS
SYMPTOM
TYMPANA
TYMPANI
ZYMURGY

•Y•M•••
PYGMIES
WYOMING

•Y••M••
BYREMAN
BYREMEN
DYNAMIC
DYNAMOS
MYANMAR
MYMAMMY
PYJAMAS
PYRAMID
PYRAMUS
SYNGMAN

•Y•••M•
LYCEUMS
MYMAMMY
SYSTEMS

•Y••••M
GYPROOM
HYPONYM
SYMPTOM
SYNONYM
WYCHELM

••YM•••
ANYMORE
CAYMANS
DAYMARE
HAYMOWS
OLYMPIA
OLYMPIC
OLYMPUS
OXYMORA
PAYMENT
RAYMOND
RHYMERS
RHYMING
SEYMOUR
STYMIED
STYMIES
THYMINE

••Y•M••
ABYSMAL
FEYNMAN

••Y••M•
ANYTIME
ASYLUMS
BUYTIME
DAYCAMP
DAYTIME
KEYLIME
MAYHEMS
MAYTIME
RHYTHMS

••Y•••M
ALYSSUM
DAYROOM
ELYSIUM

•••YM••
ENZYMES
POLYMER

•••Y••M
FOGYISM
KHAYYAM
TINYTIM
TORYISM

••••YM•
ANONYMS
EPONYMS
EPONYMY
MARRYME

••••Y•M
KHAYYAM

•••••YM
ACRONYM
ANTONYM
HOMONYM
HYPONYM
SYNONYM

Y•N••••
YANGTZE
YANKEES
YANKING
YANKTON
YANQUIS
YONKERS

Y••N•••
YARNING
YAWNERS
YAWNFUL
YAWNING
YEANING
YOUNGER
YOUNGMC
YOUNGUN

Y•••N••
YAOUNDE
YEARNED
YEARNER
YEMENIS
YOUKNOW

Y••••N•
YACKING
YAKKING
YANKING
YAPPING
YARNING
YAUPONS
YAWNING
YAWPING
YEANING
YEAREND
YELLING
YELPING
YERKING
YESSING
YEVGENY
YIPPING
YOKOONO
YOUMANS
YOWLING
YOYOING

Y•••••N
YANKTON
YARDMAN
YARDMEN
YELTSIN
YEREVAN
YOUNGUN
YUCATAN

•YN••••
AYNRAND
CYNICAL
CYNTHIA
DYNAMIC
DYNAMOS
DYNASTS
DYNASTY
MYNHEER
PYNCHON
SYNAPSE
SYNCHED
SYNCHES
SYNCING
SYNERGY
SYNFUEL
SYNGMAN
SYNODAL
SYNODIC
SYNONYM
WYNETTE
WYNONNA

•Y•N•••
BYANDBY
BYANOSE
CYGNETS
GYMNAST
HYMNALS
HYMNODY
HYUNDAI
LYINGTO
MYANMAR
NYUNGAR
TYINGIN
TYINGUP
WYANDOT

•Y••N••
BYGONES
BYLINED
BYLINES
GYRENES
HYPONYM
LYSENKO
SYNONYM
SYRINGA
SYRINGE
TYLENOL
TYRANNY
TYRANTS
WYNONNA

•Y•••N•
AYNRAND
BYTURNS
CYCLING
CYCLONE
CYYOUNG
EYEBANK
GYPPING
HYALINE
HYDRANT
HYGIENE
HYPHENS
HYPOING
PYTHONS
SYLVANS
SYNCING
SYPHONS
SYRIANS
TYCOONS
TYMPANA
TYMPANI
TYRANNY
WYNONNA
WYOMING
WYVERNS

•Y••••N
BYREMAN
BYREMEN
PYNCHON
PYTHIAN
SYNGMAN
TYINGIN
TYPHOON

••YN•••
BRYNNER
COYNESS
DRYNESS
FEYNMAN
FLYNETS
GWYNETH
KEYNOTE
MAYNARD
REYNARD
SHYNESS
SLYNESS
TOYNBEE
WRYNESS

••Y•N••
ANYONES
BAYONET
BRYNNER
CAYENNE
DOYENNE
LAYINTO
PRYINTO
SAYINGS
SOYINKA
ULYANOV

••Y••N•
CAYENNE
CAYMANS
CYYOUNG
DAYLONG
DAYSINN
DAYTONA
DOYENNE
DRYRUNS
FRYPANS
HOYDENS
HUYGENS
JAYLENO
KAYOING
KEYRING
MAYWINE
PAYMENT
RAYGUNS
RAYMOND
RHYMING
SKYLINE
STYLING
STYRENE
THYMINE
TOYLAND
YOYOING

••Y•••N
ALYKHAN
CRYOGEN
DAYSINN
ELYSIAN
FEYNMAN
GRYPHON
KEYEDIN
KRYPTON
LAYDOWN
LAYITON
LAYOPEN
MAYALIN
RAYBURN
SAYWHEN
SOYBEAN
STYGIAN
STYRIAN
WAYWORN

•••Y•N•
ABEYANT
ALLYING
ARMYANT
BABYING
BANYANS
BARYONS
BELYING
BRAYING
BUOYANT
BUOYING
BURYING
BUSYING
CANYONS
CLOYING
COPYING
COZYING
CRAYONS
DEFYING
DENYING
DRAYING
EDDYING
ENVYING
ESPYING
FLAYING
FLEYING
FRAYING
GRAYING
GREYING
JURYING
KENYANS
LEVYING
LIBYANS
MARYANN
MINYANS
OBEYING
OKAYING
PITYING
PLAYING
PONYING
PRAYING
RELYING
SPAYING
STAYING
SWAYING
TIDYING
UNDYING
UNTYING
VARYING
XRAYING

•••Y••N
ALLYSON
BABYLON
CLAYTON
GRAYSON
GREYHEN
KOSYGIN
MARYANN
PLAYPEN
PLAYSON
POLYGON
PREYSON
SLAYTON

••••YN•
ANODYNE
LIPSYNC
PHARYNX

••••Y•N
CARRYON
EARLYON
HALCYON
MALAYAN
MEGRYAN
PROCYON
SAROYAN

•••••YN
BURSTYN
CAROLYN
FONTEYN
GOLDWYN
KATHRYN
MARILYN

YO•••••
YODELED
YODELER
YOGHURT
YOGURTS
YOKOONO
YOMTOVS
YONKERS
YORKIES
YORKIST
YOUKNOW
YOUMANS
YOUNGER
YOUNGMC
YOUNGUN
YOWLERS
YOWLING
YOYOING

Y•O••••
YAOUNDE

Y••O•••
YOKOONO
YOYOING

Y•••O••
YARROWS
YAUPONS
YELLOWS
YELLOWY
YOKOONO
YOMTOVS

Y••••O•
YANKTON
YOUKNOW
YULELOG

Y•••••O
YOKOONO

•YO••••
WYOMING

•Y•O•••
BYFORCE
BYGOLLY
BYGONES
BYROADS
BYWORDS
CYBORGS
CYYOUNG
HYPOING
HYPONYM
SYNODAL
SYNODIC
SYNONYM
TYCOONS
WYNONNA
ZYGOTES

•Y••O••
AYKROYD
BYANOSE
CYCLONE
CYCLOPS
EYEBOLT
EYEHOLE
EYESORE
GYPROOM
HYDROUS
HYMNODY
HYSSOPS
PYEDOGS
PYTHONS
SYMBOLS
SYPHONS
SYSTOLE
TYCOONS
TYPHOON

•Y•••O•
BYWAYOF
CYPRIOT
DYNAMOS
EYEBROW
EYESHOT
GYMSHOE
GYPROOM
GYRATOR
PYNCHON
SYMPTOM
TYLENOL
TYPHOON
WYANDOT
ZYDECOS

•Y••••O
LYINGTO
LYSENKO

••YO•••
ALYOSHA
ANYONES
BAYONET
BUYOUTS
COYOTES
CRYOGEN
CYYOUNG
FLYOVER
KAYOING
LAYOFFS
LAYOPEN
LAYOUTS
LAYOVER
MAYORAL
PAYOFFS
PAYOLAS
PAYOUTS
RAYOVAC
TRYOUTS
UNYOKED
UNYOKES
YOYOING

••Y•O••
ANYBODY
ANYMORE
ANYROAD
BOYCOTT
BOYHOOD
BUYSOFF
BUYSOUT
CRYWOLF
DAYBOOK
DAYBOYS
DAYJOBS
DAYLONG
DAYROOM
DAYTONA
DRYDOCK
DRYHOLE
DRYROTS
FLYBOYS
FLYRODS
FRYCOOK
HAYFORK
HAYLOFT
HAYMOWS
HEYWOOD
KEYHOLE
KEYNOTE
KEYWORD
LAYDOWN
LAYSOFF
LAYSOUT
MAYPOLE
OXYMORA
PAYLOAD
PAYROLL
PAYSOFF
PAYSOUT
PLYWOOD
RAYMOND
SEYMOUR
SHYLOCK
SKYHOOK
TOYDOGS
WAYCOOL
WAYWORN

••Y••O•
BOYHOOD
CRYPTOS
DAYBOOK
DAYROOM
FRYCOOK
GRYPHON
HEYWOOD
KRYPTON
LAYITON
LAYSFOR
LAYSLOW
PAYSFOR
PLYWOOD
RAYKROC
SKYHOOK
TOYSHOP
ULYANOV
WAYCOOL

••Y•••O
JAYLENO
LAYINTO
PRYINTO

•••YO••
BARYONS
CANYONS
CRAYOLA
CRAYONS
EASYOFF
HOLYOKE
NEWYORK
PLAYOFF
PLAYOUT

•••Y•O•
ALLYSON
BABYLON
CLAYTON
COPYBOY
EMMYLOU
GRAYSON
HOLYCOW
MARYLOU
ONLYTOO
ONLYYOU
PLAYBOY
PLAYDOH
PLAYSON
POLYGON
PRAYFOR
PREYSON
SLAYTON

•••Y••O
CALYPSO
ONLYTOO
PRAYSTO

••••YO•
ARROYOS
BYWAYOF
CARRYON
EARLYON
EMBRYOS
HALCYON
NEARYOU
ONLYYOU
PROCYON

••••Y•O
GROMYKO
MIAOYAO
RALLYTO
TALLYHO

Y•P••••
YAPPERS
YAPPING
YIPPING
YUPPIES

Y••P•••
YAPPERS
YAPPING
YAUPONS
YAWPERS
YAWPING
YELPERS
YELPING
YIPPING
YUPPIES

•YP••••
BYPATHS
BYPLAYS
CYPHERS
CYPRESS
CYPRIOT
GYPPERS
GYPPING
GYPROOM
GYPSIES
HYPEDUP
HYPESUP
HYPHENS
HYPOING
HYPONYM
SYPHONS
TYPEDUP
TYPESET
TYPESUP
TYPHOON
TYPICAL
TYPIEST
TYPISTS

•Y•P•••
GYPPERS
GYPPING
SYMPTOM
TYMPANA
TYMPANI

•Y••P••
SYNAPSE

•Y•••P•
CYCLOPS
EYECUPS
HYSSOPS

•Y••••P
HYPEDUP
HYPESUP
TYINGUP
TYPEDUP
TYPESUP

••YP•••
CRYPTIC
CRYPTOS
FLYPAST
FRYPANS
GRYPHON
KEYPADS
KRYPTON
MAYPOLE
STYPTIC

••Y•P••
LAYOPEN
OLYMPIA
OLYMPIC
OLYMPUS

••Y••P•
SKYCAPS

••Y•••P
DAYCAMP
DAYTRIP
FLYTRAP
KEYEDUP
KEYGRIP
PSYCHUP
TOYSHOP

•••YP••
CALYPSO
ECTYPES
LILYPAD
PLAYPEN
RETYPED
RETYPES
STAYPUT

•••Y•P•
BUNYIPS

•••Y••P
BUOYSUP
INKYCAP
PLAYSUP
STAYSUP

••••YP•
DECRYPT
ENCRYPT
MISTYPE
PLATYPI
TINTYPE

••••Y•P
BELLYUP
BUDDYUP
DUMMYUP
GIDDYAP
GIDDYUP
GUSSYUP
HURRYUP
TALLYUP

Y••Q•••
YANQUIS

Y•R••••
YARDAGE
YARDARM
YARDMAN
YARDMEN
YARNING
YARROWS
YEREVAN
YERKING
YERKISH
YORKIES
YORKIST

Y••R•••
YARROWS
YEAREND
YEARNED
YEARNER
YTTRIUM

Y•••R••
YOGURTS

Y••••R•
YABBERS
YAKKERS
YAMMERS
YAPPERS
YARDARM
YAWNERS
YAWPERS
YELLERS
YELPERS
YOGHURT
YONKERS
YOWLERS

Y•••••R
YEARNER
YESDEAR
YODELER
YOUNGER
YUCKIER
YUMMIER

•YR••••
BYREMAN
BYREMEN
BYROADS
GYRATED
GYRATES
GYRATOR
GYRENES
HYRACES
HYRAXES
LYRICAL
LYRISTS
MYRIADS
MYRTLES
PYRAMID
PYRAMUS
PYRITES
PYRRHIC
PYRRHUS
SYRIANS
SYRINGA
SYRINGE
TYRANNY
TYRANTS

•Y•R•••
AYKROYD
AYNRAND
CYPRESS
CYPRIOT
GYPROOM
HYBRIDS
HYDRANT
HYDRATE
HYDROUS
PYRRHIC
PYRRHUS

•Y••R••
BYFORCE
BYTURNS
BYWORDS
CYBORGS
EYEBROW
SYNERGY
WYVERNS
ZYMURGY

•Y•••R•
BYHEART
CYCLERS
CYPHERS
DYKSTRA
EYESORE
GYPPERS
MYSTERY
OYSTERS

•Y••••R
GYRATOR
MYANMAR
MYNHEER
NYUNGAR

••YR•••
ANYROAD
DAYROOM
DRYROTS
DRYRUNS
FLYRODS
HAYRACK
HAYRIDE
JOYRIDE
KEYRING
PAYROLL
STYRENE
STYRIAN

••Y•R••
DAYTRIP
DMYTRYK
FAYWRAY
FLYTRAP
KEYGRIP
LAYERED
MAYORAL
MAYTREE
RAYKROC
TOYSRUS

••Y••R•
ANYMORE
DAYCARE
DAYMARE
GEYSERS
HAYFORK
HAYWARD
HAYWIRE
JAYBIRD
KEYCARD
KEYWORD
MAYNARD
OXYMORA
PAYDIRT
RAYBURN
REYNARD
RHYMERS
SKYLARK
SKYWARD
STYLERS
WAYWARD
WAYWORN

••Y•••R
BRYNNER
DAYSTAR
FLYOVER
KAYAKER
LAYOVER
LAYSFOR
MAYFAIR
PAYSFOR
SEYMOUR
SHYSTER
TRYSTER
VOYAGER

•••YR••
ASSYRIA
JURYRIG
PAPYRUS

•••Y•R•
BOWYERS
BRAYERS
DASYURE
GRUYERE
HALYARD
HOLYARK
LANYARD
LAWYERS
MAGYARS
NEWYORK
PLAYERS
PRAYERS
RUDYARD
SAWYERS
SLAYERS
SWAYERS

•••Y••R
CLAYIER
HOLYWAR
MANYEAR
MIDYEAR
NEWYEAR
OFFYEAR
POLYMER
PRAYFOR

••••YR•
MARTYRS
ZEPHYRS

••••Y•R
ALLAYER
ASSAYER
COLLYER
DELAYER
LOBBYER
SPRAYER

Y•S••••
YASHMAK
YESDEAR
YESHIVA
YESMAAM
YESSING

Y••S•••
YESSING

Y•••S••
YELLSAT
YELTSIN

Y••••S•
YAKUTSK
YERKISH
YIDDISH
YORKIST

Y•••••S
YABBERS
YAKIMAS
YAKKERS
YAKUZAS
YAMMERS
YANKEES
YANQUIS
YAPPERS
YARROWS
YAUPONS
YAWNERS
YAWPERS
YELLERS
YELLOWS
YELPERS
YEMENIS
YOGURTS
YOMTOVS
YONKERS
YORKIES
YOUMANS
YOWLERS
YUPPIES

•YS••••
HYSSOPS
LYSENKO
MYSTERY
MYSTICS
MYSTIFY
OYSTERS
SYSTEMS
SYSTOLE
WYSIWYG

•Y•S•••
DYKSTRA
EYESHOT
EYESORE
GYMSHOE
GYPSIES
HYSSOPS

•Y••S••
DYNASTS
DYNASTY
HYPESUP
LYRISTS
TYPESET
TYPESUP
TYPISTS

•Y•••S•
BYANOSE
CYCLIST
CYPRESS
EYELASH
EYELESS
EYEWASH
GYMNAST
SYNAPSE
TYPIEST

•Y••••S
AYEAYES
BYGONES
BYLINES
BYPATHS
BYPLAYS
BYROADS
BYTURNS
BYWORDS
CYBORGS
CYCLERS
CYCLOPS
CYGNETS
CYMBALS
CYPHERS
CYPRESS
DYBBUKS
DYNAMOS
DYNASTS
EYECUPS
EYEFULS
EYELESS
EYELETS
EYELIDS
GYMBAGS
GYPPERS
GYPSIES
GYRATES
GYRENES
HYBRIDS
HYDROUS
HYMNALS
HYPHENS
HYRACES
HYRAXES
HYSSOPS
KYLIKES
LYCEUMS
LYRISTS
MYRIADS
MYRTLES
MYSTICS
OYSTERS
PYEDOGS
PYGMIES
PYJAMAS
PYRAMUS
PYRITES
PYRRHUS
PYTHIAS
PYTHONS
PYXIDES
SYLVANS
SYMBOLS
SYNCHES
SYPHONS
SYRIANS
SYSTEMS
TYCOONS
TYPISTS
TYRANTS
WYVERNS
ZYDECOS
ZYGOTES

••YS•••
ABYSMAL
ABYSSES
ALYSSUM
BUYSOFF
BUYSOUT
CRYSTAL
DAYSINN
DAYSTAR
DRYSUIT
ELYSEES
ELYSIAN
ELYSIUM
GEYSERS
HAYSEED
LAYSFOR
LAYSLOW
LAYSOFF
LAYSOUT
NAYSAID
NAYSAYS
ODYSSEY
PAYSFOR
PAYSOFF
PAYSOUT
PHYSICS
SHYSTER
THYSELF
TOYSHOP
TOYSRUS
TRYSTED
TRYSTER
ULYSSES
WAYSIDE
ZOYSIAS

••Y•S••
ABYSSES
ALYOSHA
ALYSSUM
CAYUSES
ODYSSEY
ULYSSES

••Y••S•
AMYLASE
COYNESS
DRYNESS
FLYCAST
FLYFISH
FLYLESS
FLYPAST
JOYLESS
KEYLESS
KEYWEST
PAYCASH
SHYNESS
SKYLESS
SLYNESS
STYLISE
STYLISH
STYLIST
TOYLESS
WAYLESS
WRYNESS

••Y•••S
ABYSSES
ANYONES
ASYLUMS
BUYOUTS
CAYMANS
CAYUGAS
CAYUSES
COYNESS
COYOTES
CRYPTOS
DAYBEDS
DAYBOYS
DAYJOBS
DRYNESS
DRYROTS
DRYRUNS
ELYSEES
FLYBOYS
FLYLESS
FLYNETS
FLYRODS
FLYWAYS
FRYPANS
GEYSERS
HAYMOWS
HEYDAYS
HOYDENS
HUYGENS
JAYCEES
JAYVEES
JOYLESS
KEYLESS
KEYPADS
LAYOFFS
LAYOUTS
MAYDAYS
MAYHEMS
NAYSAYS
OLYMPUS
PAYDAYS
PAYOFFS
PAYOLAS
PAYOUTS
PHYLLIS
PHYSICS
PSYCHES
RAYGUNS
RHYMERS
RHYTHMS
SAYINGS
SAYYIDS
SCYTHES
SHYNESS
SKYCAPS
SKYLESS
SKYWAYS
SLYNESS
STYLERS
STYLETS
STYMIES
TOYDOGS
TOYLESS
TOYSRUS
TRYOUTS
ULYSSES
UNYOKES
VOYAGES
WAYLAYS
WAYLESS
WHYDAHS
WRYNESS
ZOYSIAS

•••YS••
ALLYSON
BABYSAT
BABYSIT
BUOYSUP
ECDYSES
ECDYSIS
GRAYSON
HOLYSEE
PLAYSAT
PLAYSON
PLAYSUP
PRAYSTO
PREYSON
STAYSUP

•••Y•S•
BABYISH
CALYPSO
CLAYISH
COPYIST
FOGYISH
FOGYISM
GRAYEST
GRAYISH
GREYEST
GREYISH
LADYISH
LAZYISH
PIXYISH
SPRYEST
TORYISH
TORYISM
WHEYISH
ZANYISH

•••Y••S
ARGYLES
BANYANS
BARYONS
BOWYERS
BRAYERS
BUNYIPS
CALYCES
CALYXES
CANYONS
CRAYONS
DREYFUS
ECDYSES
ECDYSIS
ECTYPES
ENZYMES
KENYANS
LAWYERS
LIBYANS
MAGYARS
MINYANS
OOCYTES
PAPYRUS
PLAYERS
PRAYERS
RETYPES
SAWYERS
SAYYIDS
SLAYERS
SWAYERS

••••YS•
ANALYSE
ANALYST

••••Y•S
ALLEYES
ANONYMS
ARROYOS
AYEAYES
AZODYES
BIGEYES
DACTYLS
EMBRYOS
EPONYMS
KIKUYUS
MARTYRS
PAPAYAS
REDEYES
RIBEYES
TIEDYES
ZEPHYRS

•••••YS
AFFRAYS
AIRWAYS
BADBOYS
BADGUYS
BAILEYS
BARLEYS
BARNEYS
BATBOYS
BETRAYS
BIGBOYS
BUSBOYS
BYPLAYS
CARBOYS
CONVEYS
CONVOYS
COWBOYS
DAYBOYS
DEEJAYS
DEFRAYS
DEPLOYS
DICKEYS
DISMAYS
DOGDAYS
DONKEYS
EMPLOYS
ENDWAYS
ESTRAYS
FLYBOYS
FLYWAYS
FRIDAYS
GALLEYS
GILGUYS
GOODBYS
GRAMMYS
GURNEYS
HEYDAYS
HURLEYS
JACKEYS
JERSEYS
JETWAYS
JITNEYS
JOCKEYS
KIDNEYS
LACKEYS
LOONEYS
LOWBOYS
MAGUEYS
MANDAYS
MARGAYS
MAYDAYS
MEDLEYS
MICKEYS
MIDDAYS
MIDWAYS
MISLAYS
MISSAYS
MONDAYS
MONKEYS
NAYSAYS
NOBODYS
OLDDAYS
OSPREYS
OUTLAYS
PARLAYS
PARLEYS
PAYDAYS
PEAVEYS
PEDWAYS
PHONEYS
PREPAYS
PULLEYS
PURVEYS
REPLAYS
RICKEYS
ROBROYS
ROMNEYS
RUNWAYS
SASHAYS
SEAWAYS
SKYWAYS
SLAVEYS
STOREYS
SUBWAYS
SUNDAYS
SUNRAYS
SURREYS
SURVEYS
TEAPOYS
TOMBOYS
TURKEYS
VALLEYS
VEEJAYS
VOLLEYS
WAYLAYS
WURLEYS

YT•••••
YTTRIUM

Y•T••••
YITZHAK
YTTRIUM

Y••T•••
YAHTZEE
YEATEAM
YELTSIN
YOMTOVS

Y•••T••
YACHTED
YAKUTSK
YANGTZE
YANKTON
YUCATAN

Y••••T•
YOGURTS

Y•••••T
YELLSAT
YOGHURT
YORKIST

•YT••••
BYTHEBY
BYTURNS
PYTHIAN
PYTHIAS
PYTHONS

•Y•T•••
CYNTHIA
MYRTLES
MYSTERY
MYSTICS
MYSTIFY
OYSTERS
SYSTEMS
SYSTOLE

•Y••T••
BYPATHS
DYKSTRA
GYRATED
GYRATES
GYRATOR
PYRITES
SYMPTOM
WYNETTE
ZYGOTES

•Y•••T•
CYGNETS
DYNASTS
DYNASTY
EYELETS
HYDRATE
LYINGTO
LYRISTS
TYPISTS
TYRANTS
WYNETTE

•Y••••T
BYHEART
CYCLIST
CYPRIOT
EYEBOLT
EYESHOT
GYMNAST
HYDRANT
TYPESET
TYPIEST
WYANDOT

••YT•••
ANYTIME
BUYTIME
DAYTIME
DAYTONA
DAYTRIP
DMYTRYK
FLYTRAP
MAYTIME
MAYTREE
RHYTHMS
SCYTHED
SCYTHES

••Y•T••
COYOTES
CRYPTIC
CRYPTOS
CRYSTAL
DAYSTAR
KRYPTON
LAYETTE
LAYITON
SHYSTER
STYPTIC
TRYSTED
TRYSTER

••Y••T•
BAYCITY
BOYCOTT
BUYOUTS
DRYROTS
FLYNETS
GWYNETH
KEYNOTE
LAYETTE
LAYINTO
LAYOUTS
LOYALTY
PAYOUTS
PRYINTO
ROYALTY
STYLETS
TRYOUTS

••Y•••T
BAYONET
BOYCOTT
BUYSOUT
DRYSUIT
FLYCAST
FLYPAST
HAYLOFT
KEYWEST
LAYSOUT
PAYDIRT
PAYMENT
PAYSOUT
STYLIST

•••YT••
CLAYTON
ONLYTOO
OOCYTES
SLAYTON
TINYTIM

•••Y•T•
NCWYETH
PRAYSTO

•••Y••T
ABEYANT
ARMYANT
BABYSAT
BABYSIT
BODYFAT
BUOYANT
COPYCAT
COPYIST
GRAYEST
GREYEST
PLAYACT
PLAYLET
PLAYOUT
PLAYSAT
SPRYEST
STAYPUT

••••YT•
ACOLYTE
FORSYTH
RALLYTO

••••Y•T
ANALYST
DECRYPT
ENCRYPT

YU•••••
YUCATAN
YUCKIER
YULELOG
YUMMIER
YUPPIES

Y•U••••
YAUPONS
YOUKNOW
YOUMANS
YOUNGER
YOUNGMC
YOUNGUN

Y••U•••
YAKUTSK
YAKUZAS
YAOUNDE
YOGURTS

Y•••U••
YANQUIS
YOGHURT

Y••••U•
YAWNFUL
YOUNGUN
YTTRIUM

•YU••••
HYUNDAI
NYUNGAR

•Y•U•••
BYTURNS
ZYMURGY

•Y••U••
CYYOUNG
DYBBUKS
EYECUPS
EYEFULS
LYCEUMS
SYNFUEL

•Y•••U•
HYDROUS
HYPEDUP
HYPESUP
PYRAMUS
PYRRHUS
TYINGUP
TYPEDUP
TYPESUP

••YU•••
CAYUGAS
CAYUSES

••Y•U••
ASYLUMS
BUYOUTS
CYYOUNG
DRYRUNS
DRYSUIT
HEYJUDE
LAYOUTS
PAYOUTS
RAYBURN
RAYGUNS
TRYOUTS

••Y••U•
ALYSSUM
BUYSOUT
ELYSIUM
KEYCLUB
KEYEDUP
LAYSOUT
OLYMPUS
PAYSOUT
PSYCHUP
SEYMOUR
SKYBLUE
TOYSRUS

•••YU••
DASYURE

•••Y•U•
BUOYSUP
DREYFUS
LADYBUG
PAPYRUS
PLAYFUL
PLAYOUT
PLAYSUP
STAYPUT
STAYSUP
TRAYFUL

•••Y••U
EMMYLOU
MARYLOU
ONLYYOU

••••YU•
BELLYUP
BUDDYUP
DUMMYUP
GIDDYUP
GUSSYUP
HURRYUP
KIKUYUS
TALLYUP

••••Y•U
NEARYOU
ONLYYOU

Y•V••••
YEVGENY

Y•••V••
YEREVAN

Y••••V•
YESHIVA
YOMTOVS

•YV••••
WYVERNS

•Y•V•••
SYLVANS

••YV•••
JAYVEES

••Y•V••
FLYOVER
LAYOVER
RAYOVAC

••Y••V•
SKYDIVE

••Y•••V
ULYANOV

••••Y•V
HENRYIV
NUREYEV
ROCKYIV

Y•W••••
YAWNERS
YAWNFUL
YAWNING
YAWPERS
YAWPING
YOWLERS
YOWLING

Y••••W•
YARROWS
YELLOWS
YELLOWY

Y•••••W
YOUKNOW

•YW••••
BYWAYOF
BYWORDS

•Y•W•••
EYEWASH

•Y••W••
WYSIWYG

•Y••••W
EYEBROW

••YW•••
CRYWOLF
DRYWALL
DRYWELL
FAYWRAY
FLYWAYS
HAYWARD
HAYWIRE
HEYWOOD
JAYWALK
KEYWEST
KEYWORD
MAYWINE
PLYWOOD
SAYWHEN
SKYWARD
SKYWAYS
WAYWARD
WAYWORN

••Y•W••
FLYAWAY
LAYAWAY

••Y••W•
HAYMOWS
LAYDOWN
ROYALWE

••Y•••W
LAYSLOW

•••YW••
HOLYWAR

•••Y••W
HOLYCOW

•YX••••
PYXIDES

•Y••X••
HYRAXES

•••YX••
CALYXES

••••Y•X
PHARYNX

Y•Y••••
YOYOING

Y•••••Y
YELLOWY
YEVGENY

•YY••••
CYYOUNG

•Y••Y••
AYEAYES
BYWAYOF

•Y•••Y•
AYKROYD
BYPLAYS
HYPONYM
SYNONYM
WYSIWYG

•Y••••Y
BYANDBY
BYGOLLY
BYTHEBY
DYNASTY
HYMNODY
MYMAMMY
MYSTERY
MYSTIFY
SYNERGY
TYRANNY
ZYMURGY

••YY•••
SAYYIDS

••Y•Y••
DRYEYED

••Y••Y•
DAYBOYS
DMYTRYK
FLYBOYS
FLYWAYS
HEYDAYS
MAYDAYS
NAYSAYS
PAYDAYS
SKYWAYS
WAYLAYS

••Y•••Y
ANYBODY
BAYCITY
CRYBABY
DAYLILY
FAYWRAY
FLYAWAY
LAYAWAY
LOYALLY
LOYALTY
ODYSSEY
ROYALLY
ROYALTY

•••YY••
KHAYYAM
ONLYYOU

•••Y••Y
COPYBOY
GRAYJAY
HOLYDAY
HUNYADY
LADYDAY
MARYKAY
PLAYBOY

••••Y•Y
EPONYMY

Y••Z•••
YITZHAK

Y•••Z••
YAHTZEE
YAKUZAS

Y••••Z•
YANGTZE

••Y••Z•
STYLIZE

••••YZ•
ANALYZE

ZA•••••
ZACHARY
ZAFFERS
ZAGGING
ZAIREAN
ZAIRIAN
ZAMBEZI
ZAMBIAN
ZAMBONI
ZANDERS
ZANIEST
ZANYISH
ZAPATEO
ZAPOTEC
ZAPPERS
ZAPPIER
ZAPPING
ZAREBAS
ZATOPEK

Z•A••••
ZEALAND
ZEALOTS
ZEALOUS

Z••A•••
ZAPATEO
ZENANAS
ZONALLY
ZOUAVES

Z•••A••
ZACHARY
ZEALAND
ZEDBARS

ZERMATT
ZHIVAGO
ZIGZAGS
ZODIACS

Z••••A•
ZAIREAN
ZAIRIAN
ZAMBIAN
ZAREBAS
ZENANAS
ZEUGMAS
ZINNIAS
ZOYSIAS

Z•••••A
ZENOBIA

•ZA••••
AZALEAS
CZARDAS
CZARDOM
CZARINA
CZARISM
CZARIST
TZARINA

•Z•A•••
IZZARDS

•Z•••A•
AZALEAS
AZTECAN
CZARDAS

•Z••••A
CZARINA
TZARINA

••ZA•••
BAZAARS
BIZARRE
CEZANNE
HAZARDS
IZZARDS
KAZAKHS
LAZARUS
LIZARDS
PIZARRO
SIZABLE
SIZABLY
SUZANNE
WIZARDS

••Z•A••
BAZAARS
BUZZARD
GIZZARD
HUZZAHS
JAZZAGE
PIZZAZZ

••Z••A•
BUZZSAW
JAZZMAN
VIZSLAS
WOZNIAK

••Z•••A
BAZOOKA
MAZURKA

•••ZA••
BUZZARD
CINZANO
CRUZADO
GIZZARD
HUZZAHS
JAZZAGE
PIZZAZZ
TARZANA
ZIGZAGS

•••Z•A•
BUZZSAW
JAZZMAN
MITZVAH
PIAZZAS
YITZHAK

•••Z••A
ARIZONA
NOXZEMA
TARZANA

••••ZA•
ALCAZAR
KWANZAS
PIAZZAS
QUETZAL
SALAZAR
STANZAS
YAKUZAS

•••••ZA
BONANZA
CADENZA
MENDOZA
MESTIZA
ORGANZA
SPINOZA

Z•B••••
ZEBULON

Z••B•••
ZAMBEZI
ZAMBIAN
ZAMBONI
ZEDBARS
ZOMBIES
ZOMBIFY

Z•••B••
ZAREBAS
ZENOBIA

••Z•B••
GAZEBOS
JEZEBEL
SIZABLE
SIZABLY

Z•C••••
ZACHARY

Z••C•••
ZILCHES
ZIPCODE
ZIRCONS

Z•••C••
ZYDECOS

Z••••C•
ZODIACS

Z•••••C
ZAPOTEC

•Z••C••
AZTECAN

••Z••C•
WOZZECK

•••Z•C•
WOZZECK

Z•D••••
ZEDBARS
ZODIACS
ZYDECOS

Z••D•••
ZANDERS

Z••••D•
ZIPCODE

Z•••••D
ZEALAND

•Z•D•••
AZODYES

•Z••D••
CZARDAS
CZARDOM

•Z•••D•
IZZARDS

••Z•D••
DAZEDLY
SIZEDUP

••Z••D•
HAZARDS
IZZARDS
LIZARDS
WIZARDS

••Z•••D
BUZZARD
COZENED
DAZZLED
DIZENED
DIZZIED
FIZZLED
GIZZARD
GUZZLED
MIZZLED
MUZZLED
NUZZLED
PUZZLED
RAZORED
REZONED
SIZZLED
UNZONED
WIZENED

•••Z•D•
CRUZADO

•••Z••D
BUZZARD
DAZZLED
DIZZIED
FIZZLED
FOOZLED
FRIZZED
GIZZARD
GUZZLED
MIZZLED
MUZZLED
NUZZLED
PUZZLED
QUIZZED
SIZZLED
WHIZKID
WHIZZED

••••Z•D
BLITZED
BREEZED
BRONZED
FRIZZED
GLITZED
IODIZED
IONIZED
QUIZZED
SNEEZED
SNOOZED
TWEEZED
UNFAZED
WALTZED
WHEEZED
WHIZZED

ZE•••••
ZEALAND
ZEALOTS
ZEALOUS
ZEBULON
ZEDBARS
ZEITUNG
ZEMSTVO
ZENANAS
ZENITHS
ZENOBIA
ZEPHYRS
ZERMATT
ZEROING
ZEROSUM
ZESTFUL
ZESTIER
ZEUGMAS

Z•E••••
ZOELLER

Z••E•••
ZAREBAS
ZYDECOS

Z•••E••
ZAFFERS
ZAIREAN
ZAMBEZI
ZANDERS
ZANIEST
ZAPPERS
ZINGERS
ZIPPERS
ZITHERS
ZONKERS

Z••••E•
ZAPATEO
ZAPOTEC
ZAPPIER
ZATOPEK
ZESTIER
ZILCHES
ZINGIER
ZIPPIER
ZOELLER
ZOMBIES
ZOUAVES
ZYGOTES

Z•••••E
ZIPCODE

•ZE••••
EZEKIEL

•Z•E•••
AZTECAN

•Z••E••
AZALEAS

•Z•••E•
AZODYES
EZEKIEL

•Z••••E
AZURITE

••ZE•••
COZENED
DAZEDLY
DIZENED
DOZENTH
DOZEOFF
GAZEBOS
GAZELLE
GAZETTE
JEZEBEL
LOZENGE
ROZELLE
SIZEDUP
SIZESUP
SUZETTE
WIZENED

••Z•E••
BEZIERS
BUZZERS
COZIEST
COZZENS
DOZIEST
HAZIEST
LAZIEST
MAZIEST
MIZZENS
OOZIEST
ROZZERS
VIZIERS
WOZZECK

••Z••E•
COZENED
COZUMEL
DAZZLED
DAZZLER
DAZZLES
DIZENED
DIZZIED
DIZZIER
DIZZIES
ENZYMES
EVZONES
FIZZIER
FIZZLED
FIZZLES
FUZZIER
GUZZLED
GUZZLER
GUZZLES
JAZZIER
JAZZMEN
JEZEBEL
MIZZLED
MIZZLES
MUZZIER
MUZZLED
MUZZLES
NOZZLES
NUZZLED
NUZZLER
NUZZLES
PUZZLED
PUZZLER
PUZZLES
RAZORED
REZONED
REZONES
SIZZLED
SIZZLES
TIZZIES
UNZONED
WIZENED

••Z•••E
BEZIQUE
BIZARRE
CEZANNE
GAZELLE
GAZETTE
JAZZAGE
LOZENGE
ROZELLE
SIZABLE
SUZANNE
SUZETTE

•••ZE••
BENZENE
BLAZERS
BUZZERS
COZZENS
GEEZERS
GLAZERS
GRAZERS
MIZZENS
NONZERO
NOXZEMA
PANZERS
ROZZERS
SEIZERS
SUBZERO
WOZZECK

•••Z•E•
BRAZIER
CRAZIER
CRAZIES
DAZZLED
DAZZLER
DAZZLES
DITZIER
DIZZIED
DIZZIER
DIZZIES
DOOZIES
FIZZIER
FIZZLED
FIZZLES
FOOZLED
FOOZLES
FRAZIER
FRIZZED
FRIZZES
FUZZIER
GAUZIER
GLAZIER
GUZZLED
GUZZLER
GUZZLES
JAZZIER
JAZZMEN
MENZIES
MIZZLED
MIZZLES
MUZZIER
MUZZLED
MUZZLES
NOZZLES
NUZZLED
NUZZLER
NUZZLES
PUZZLED
PUZZLER
PUZZLES
QUIZZED
QUIZZES
RITZIER
SIZZLED
SIZZLES
TIZZIES
WHIZZED
WHIZZER
WHIZZES
WOOZIER

•••Z••E
BENZENE
CALZONE
CANZONE
DRIZZLE
ENDZONE
FANZINE
FRAZZLE
FRIZZLE
GRIZZLE
JAZZAGE
RHIZOME
SWIZZLE
WARZONE

••••ZE•
ASSIZES
BEDIZEN
BLITZED
BLITZEN
BLITZES
BREEZED
BREEZES
BRONZED
BRONZES
CITIZEN
DENIZEN
FREEZER
FREEZES
FRIEZES
FRIZZED
FRIZZES
GLITZED
GLITZES
IODIZED
IODIZES
IONIZED
IONIZER
IONIZES
KLUTZES
NETIZEN
PRETZEL
QUIZZED
QUIZZES
SARAZEN
SELTZER
SNEEZED
SNEEZER
SNEEZES
SNOOZED
SNOOZES
SPITZES
SWITZER
TOPAZES
TWEEZED
TWEEZES
UNFAZED
WALTZED
WALTZER
WALTZES
WHEEZED
WHEEZER
WHEEZES
WHIZZED
WHIZZER
WHIZZES
YAHTZEE

••••Z•E
DRIZZLE
FRAZZLE
FRIZZLE
GRIZZLE
SWIZZLE
YAHTZEE

•••••ZE
AGONIZE
ANALYZE
ANODIZE
APPRIZE
ATOMIZE
BAPTIZE
CAPSIZE
FIRENZE
IDOLIZE
INADAZE
ITEMIZE
LIONIZE
MIDSIZE
OUTSIZE
OXIDIZE
REALIZE
SQUEEZE
STYLIZE
TRAPEZE
UTILIZE
YANGTZE

Z•F••••
ZAFFERS

Z••F•••
ZAFFERS

Z•••F••
ZESTFUL

Z••••F•
ZOMBIFY

••Z••F•
BUZZOFF
DOZEOFF

••Z•••F
BUZZOFF
DOZEOFF

•••Z•F•
BUZZOFF

•••Z••F
BUZZOFF

Z•G••••
ZAGGING
ZIGGING
ZIGZAGS
ZYGOTES

Z••G•••
ZAGGING
ZEUGMAS
ZIGGING
ZINGERS
ZINGIER
ZINGING

Z•••G••
ZWINGLI

Z••••G•
ZHIVAGO
ZIGZAGS
ZOOLOGY
ZYMURGY

Z•••••G
ZAGGING
ZAPPING
ZEITUNG
ZEROING
ZIGGING
ZINGING
ZIPPING
ZONKING
ZOOMING

••ZG•••
FIZGIGS

••Z•G••
FIZGIGS
HAZINGS
JAZZAGE
LOZENGE
SIZINGS

••Z•••G
BUZZING
COZYING
FIZZING
FUZZING
JAZZING
MUZZING
RAZZING

•••Z•G•
JAZZAGE
ZIGZAGS

•••Z••G
AMAZING
BLAZING
BRAZING
BUZZING
CRAZING
FIZZING
FUTZING
FUZZING
GLAZING
GLOZING
GRAZING
JAZZING
MUZZING
PRIZING
RAZZING
SEIZING
TENZING

••••Z•G
LEIPZIG

ZH•••••
ZHIVAGO

Z••H•••
ZACHARY
ZEPHYRS
ZITHERS

Z•••H••
ZILCHES

Z••••H•
ZENITHS

Z•••••H
ZANYISH

•Z••••H
AZIMUTH

••ZH•••
MUZHIKS

••Z••H•
HUZZAHS
KAZAKHS

••Z•••H
DOZENTH
LAZYISH

•••ZH••
YITZHAK

•••Z•H•
HUZZAHS
MATZOHS

•••Z••H
MITZVAH

ZI•••••
ZIGGING
ZIGZAGS
ZILCHES
ZILLION
ZINGERS
ZINGIER
ZINGING
ZINNIAS
ZIPCODE
ZIPPERS
ZIPPIER
ZIPPING
ZIRCONS
ZITHERS

Z•I••••
ZAIREAN
ZAIRIAN
ZEITUNG
ZHIVAGO
ZWINGLI

Z••I•••
ZANIEST
ZENITHS
ZODIACS

Z•••I••
ZAGGING
ZAIRIAN
ZAMBIAN
ZANYISH
ZAPPIER
ZAPPING
ZEROING
ZESTIER
ZIGGING
ZILLION
ZINGIER
ZINGING
ZINNIAS
ZIPPIER
ZIPPING
ZOMBIES
ZOMBIFY
ZONKING
ZOOMING
ZOYSIAS

Z••••I•
ZENOBIA
ZOOMSIN

Z•••••I
ZAMBEZI
ZAMBONI
ZWINGLI

•ZI••••
AZIMUTH

•Z•I•••
AZURITE
CZARINA
CZARISM
CZARIST
EZEKIEL
TZARINA

••ZI•••
BEZIERS
BEZIQUE
COZIEST
DOZIEST
HAZIEST
HAZINGS
LAZIEST
MAZIEST
OOZIEST
SIZINGS
VIZIERS

••Z•I••
BUZZING
COZYING
DIZZIED
DIZZIER
DIZZIES
DIZZILY
FIZGIGS
FIZZIER
FIZZING
FUZZIER
FUZZILY
FUZZING
JAZZIER
JAZZILY
JAZZING
LAZYISH
MUZHIKS
MUZZIER
MUZZILY
MUZZING
RAZZING
TIZZIES
WOZNIAK

•••ZI••
AMAZING
BLAZING
BRAZIER
BRAZING
BUZZING
CRAZIER
CRAZIES
CRAZILY
CRAZING
DITZIER
DIZZIED
DIZZIER
DIZZIES
DIZZILY
DOOZIES
FANZINE
FIZZIER
FIZZING
FRAZIER
FUTZING
FUZZIER
FUZZILY
FUZZING
GAUZIER
GAUZILY
GLAZIER
GLAZING
GLOZING
GRAZING
JAZZIER
JAZZILY
JAZZING
MENZIES
MUZZIER
MUZZILY
MUZZING
PRIZING
RAZZING
RITZIER
RITZILY
SEIZING
TENZING
TIZZIES
WOOZIER
WOOZILY

•••Z•I•
BORZOIS
MUEZZIN
WHIZKID

••••ZI•
BENAZIR
DWEEZIL
LEIPZIG
MUEZZIN
SKEEZIX

••••Z•I
ABRUZZI
JACUZZI
PALAZZI

•••••ZI
ABRUZZI
ANASAZI
JACUZZI
PALAZZI
SCHATZI
SCHERZI
ZAMBEZI

Z••K•••
ZONKERS
ZONKING
ZONKOUT

Z•••••K
ZATOPEK

•Z•K•••
EZEKIEL

••Z•K••
KAZAKHS

••Z••K•
BAZOOKA
MAZURKA
MUZHIKS

••Z•••K
WOZNIAK
WOZZECK

•••ZK••
WHIZKID

•••Z••K
WOZZECK
YITZHAK

••••ZK•
GRETZKY

Z•L••••
ZILCHES
ZILLION

Z••L•••
ZEALAND
ZEALOTS
ZEALOUS
ZILLION
ZOELLER
ZOOLOGY

Z•••L••
ZEBULON
ZOELLER
ZONALLY

Z••••L•
ZONALLY
ZWINGLI

Z•••••L
ZESTFUL

•Z•L•••
AZALEAS

•Z••••L
EZEKIEL

••Z•L••
DAZZLED
DAZZLER
DAZZLES
FIZZLED
FIZZLES
GAZELLE
GUZZLED
GUZZLER
GUZZLES
MIZZLED
MIZZLES
MUZZLED
MUZZLES
NOZZLES
NUZZLED
NUZZLER
NUZZLES
PUZZLED
PUZZLER
PUZZLES
ROZELLE
SIZZLED
SIZZLES
VIZSLAS

••Z••L•
DAZEDLY
DIZZILY
FUZZILY
GAZELLE
JAZZILY
MUZZILY
ROZELLE
SIZABLE
SIZABLY

••Z•••L
COZUMEL
JEZEBEL

•••ZL••
DAZZLED
DAZZLER
DAZZLES
FIZZLED
FIZZLES
FOOZLED
FOOZLES
GUZZLED
GUZZLER
GUZZLES
MIZZLED
MIZZLES
MUZZLED
MUZZLES
NOZZLES
NUZZLED
NUZZLER
NUZZLES
PUZZLED
PUZZLER
PUZZLES
SIZZLED
SIZZLES

•••Z•L•
CRAZILY

DIZZILY
DRIZZLE
DRIZZLY
FRAZZLE
FRIZZLE
FRIZZLY
FUZZILY
GAUZILY
GRIZZLE
GRIZZLY
JAZZILY
MUZZILY
RITZILY
SWIZZLE
WOOZILY

••••ZL•
DRIZZLE
DRIZZLY
FRAZZLE
FRIZZLE
FRIZZLY
GRIZZLE
GRIZZLY
SWIZZLE

••••Z•L
DWEEZIL
PRETZEL
QUETZAL

Z•M••••
ZAMBEZI
ZAMBIAN
ZAMBONI
ZEMSTVO
ZOMBIES
ZOMBIFY
ZYMURGY

Z••M•••
ZERMATT
ZOOMING
ZOOMSIN

Z•••M••
ZEUGMAS

Z•••••M
ZEROSUM

•Z•M•••
AZIMUTH

•Z••••M
CZARDOM
CZARISM

••Z•M••
COZUMEL
ENZYMES
GAZUMPS
JAZZMAN
JAZZMEN

•••ZM••
JAZZMAN
JAZZMEN

•••Z•M•
NOXZEMA
RHIZOME

Z•N••••
ZANDERS
ZANIEST
ZANYISH
ZENANAS
ZENITHS
ZENOBIA
ZINGERS
ZINGIER
ZINGING
ZINNIAS
ZONALLY
ZONKERS
ZONKING
ZONKOUT

Z••N•••
ZINNIAS
ZWINGLI

Z•••N••
ZENANAS

Z••••N•
ZAGGING
ZAMBONI
ZAPPING
ZEALAND
ZEITUNG
ZEROING
ZIGGING
ZINGING
ZIPPING
ZIRCONS
ZONKING
ZOOMING

Z•••••N
ZAIREAN
ZAIRIAN
ZAMBIAN
ZEBULON
ZILLION
ZOOMSIN

•Z•N•••
OZONOUS

•Z••N••
CZARINA
TZARINA

•Z••••N
AZTECAN

••ZN•••
WOZNIAK

••Z•N••
CEZANNE
COZENED
DIZENED
DOZENTH
EVZONES
HAZINGS
LOZENGE
REZONED
REZONES
SIZINGS
SUZANNE
UNZONED
WIZENED

••Z••N•
BUZZING
CEZANNE
COZYING
COZZENS
FIZZING
FUZZING
JAZZING
MIZZENS
MUZZING
RAZZING
SUZANNE

••Z•••N
JAZZMAN
JAZZMEN

•••Z•N•
AMAZING
AMAZONS
ARIZONA
BENZENE
BLAZING
BLAZONS
BRAZING
BUZZING
CALZONE
CANZONE
CINZANO
COZZENS
CRAZING
ENDZONE
FANZINE
FIZZING
FUTZING
FUZZING
GLAZING
GLOZING
GRAZING
JAZZING
MIZZENS
MUZZING
PRIZING
RAZZING
SEIZING
TARZANA
TENZING
WARZONE

•••Z••N
JAZZMAN
JAZZMEN
MUEZZIN

••••Z•N
BEDIZEN
BLITZEN
CITIZEN
CORAZON
DENIZEN
HORIZON
MUEZZIN
NETIZEN
SARAZEN

ZO•••••
ZODIACS
ZOELLER
ZOMBIES
ZOMBIFY
ZONALLY
ZONKERS
ZONKING
ZONKOUT
ZOOLOGY
ZOOMING
ZOOMSIN
ZOUAVES
ZOYSIAS

Z•O••••
ZOOLOGY
ZOOMING
ZOOMSIN

Z••O•••
ZAPOTEC
ZATOPEK
ZENOBIA
ZEROING
ZEROSUM
ZYGOTES

Z•••O••
ZAMBONI
ZEALOTS
ZEALOUS
ZIPCODE
ZIRCONS
ZONKOUT
ZOOLOGY

Z••••O•
ZEBULON
ZILLION
ZYDECOS

Z•••••O
ZAPATEO
ZEMSTVO
ZHIVAGO

•ZO••••
AZODYES
OZONOUS

•Z••O••
OZONOUS

•Z•••O•
CZARDOM

••ZO•••
BAZOOKA
EVZONES
RAZORED
REZONED
REZONES
UNZONED

••Z•O••
BAZOOKA
BUZZOFF
DOZEOFF

••Z••O•
GAZEBOS

••Z•••O
PIZARRO

•••ZO••
AMAZONS
ARIZONA
BLAZONS
BORZOIS
BUZZOFF
CALZONE
CANZONE
ENDZONE
MATZOHS
RHIZOME
WARZONE

•••Z••O
CINZANO
CRUZADO
NONZERO
SUBZERO

••••ZO•
CORAZON
HORIZON
REBOZOS

••••Z•O
PALAZZO

•••••ZO
CARDOZO
CHORIZO
LORENZO
MESTIZO
PALAZZO
SCHERZO

Z••P•••
ZAPPERS
ZAPPIER
ZAPPING
ZIPPERS
ZIPPIER
ZIPPING

Z•••P••
ZATOPEK

••Z••P•
GAZUMPS

••Z•••P
SIZEDUP
SIZESUP

••Z•Q••
BEZIQUE

Z•R••••
ZAREBAS
ZERMATT
ZEROING
ZEROSUM
ZIRCONS

Z••R•••
ZAIREAN
ZAIRIAN

Z•••R••
ZYMURGY

Z••••R•
ZACHARY
ZAFFERS
ZANDERS
ZAPPERS
ZEDBARS
ZEPHYRS
ZINGERS
ZIPPERS
ZITHERS
ZONKERS

Z•••••R
ZAPPIER
ZESTIER
ZINGIER
ZIPPIER
ZOELLER

Z•P••••
ZAPATEO
ZAPOTEC
ZAPPERS
ZAPPIER
ZAPPING
ZEPHYRS
ZIPCODE
ZIPPERS
ZIPPIER
ZIPPING

•Z•R•••
AZURITE
CZARDAS
CZARDOM
CZARINA
CZARISM
CZARIST
TZARINA

•Z••R••
IZZARDS

••Z•R••
BIZARRE
HAZARDS
IZZARDS
LAZARUS
LIZARDS
MAZURKA
PIZARRO
RAZORED
WIZARDS

••Z••R•
BAZAARS
BEZIERS
BIZARRE
BUZZARD
BUZZERS
GIZZARD
PIZARRO
ROZZERS
VIZIERS

••Z•••R
DAZZLER
DIZZIER
FIZZIER
FUZZIER
GUZZLER
JAZZIER
MUZZIER
NUZZLER
PUZZLER

•••Z•R•
BLAZERS
BUZZARD
BUZZERS
GEEZERS
GIZZARD
GLAZERS
GRAZERS
NONZERO
PANZERS
ROZZERS
SEIZERS
SUBZERO

•••Z••R
BRAZIER
CRAZIER
DAZZLER
DITZIER
DIZZIER
FIZZIER
FRAZIER
FUZZIER
GAUZIER
GLAZIER
GUZZLER
JAZZIER
MUZZIER
NUZZLER
PUZZLER
RITZIER
WHIZZER
WOOZIER

••••Z•R
ALCAZAR
BENAZIR
FREEZER
IONIZER
SALAZAR
SELTZER
SNEEZER
SWITZER
WALTZER
WHEEZER
WHIZZER

Z•S••••
ZESTFUL
ZESTIER

Z••S•••
ZEMSTVO
ZOYSIAS

Z•••S••
ZEROSUM
ZOOMSIN

Z••••S•
ZANIEST
ZANYISH

Z•••••S
ZAFFERS
ZANDERS
ZAPPERS
ZAREBAS
ZEALOTS
ZEALOUS
ZEDBARS
ZENANAS
ZENITHS
ZEPHYRS
ZEUGMAS
ZIGZAGS
ZILCHES
ZINGERS
ZINNIAS
ZIPPERS
ZIRCONS
ZITHERS
ZODIACS
ZOMBIES
ZONKERS
ZOUAVES
ZOYSIAS
ZYDECOS
ZYGOTES

•Z•••S•
CZARISM
CZARIST

•Z••••S
AZALEAS
AZODYES
CZARDAS
IZZARDS
OZONOUS

••ZS•••
VIZSLAS

••Z•S••
BUZZSAW
SIZESUP

••Z••S•
COZIEST
DOZIEST
HAZIEST
LAZIEST
LAZYISH
MAZIEST
OOZIEST

••Z•••S
BAZAARS
BEZIERS
BUZZERS
COZZENS
DAZZLES
DIZZIES
ENZYMES
EVZONES
FIZGIGS
FIZZLES
GAZEBOS
GAZUMPS
GUZZLES
HAZARDS
HAZINGS
HUZZAHS
IZZARDS
KAZAKHS
LAZARUS
LIZARDS
MIZZENS
MIZZLES
MUZHIKS
MUZZLES
NOZZLES
NUZZLES
PUZZLES
REZONES
ROZZERS
SIZINGS
SIZZLES
TIZZIES
VIZIERS
VIZSLAS
WIZARDS

•••ZS••
BUZZSAW

•••Z••S
AMAZONS
BLAZERS
BLAZONS
BORZOIS
BUZZERS
COZZENS
CRAZIES
DAZZLES
DIZZIES
DOOZIES
FIZZLES
FOOZLES
FRIZZES
GEEZERS
GLAZERS
GRAZERS
GUZZLES
HUZZAHS
MATZOHS
MENZIES
MIZZENS
MIZZLES
MUZZLES
NOZZLES
NUZZLES
PANZERS
PIAZZAS
PUZZLES
QUIZZES
ROZZERS
SEIZERS
SIZZLES
TIZZIES
WHIZZES
ZIGZAGS

••••Z•S
ASSIZES
BLITZES
BREEZES
BRONZES
FREEZES
FRIEZES
FRIZZES
GLITZES
IODIZES
IONIZES
KLUTZES
KWANZAS
PIAZZAS
QUIZZES
REBOZOS
SNEEZES
SNOOZES
SPITZES
STANZAS
TOPAZES
TWEEZES
WALTZES
WHEEZES
WHIZZES
YAKUZAS

Z•T••••
ZATOPEK
ZITHERS

Z••T•••
ZEITUNG
ZESTFUL
ZESTIER

Z•••T••
ZAPATEO
ZAPOTEC
ZEMSTVO
ZENITHS
ZYGOTES

Z••••T•
ZEALOTS
ZERMATT

Z•••••T
ZANIEST
ZERMATT
ZONKOUT

•ZT••••
AZTECAN

•Z•••T•
AZIMUTH
AZURITE

•Z••••T
CZARIST

••Z•T••
GAZETTE
SUZETTE

••Z••T•
DOZENTH
GAZETTE
SUZETTE

••Z•••T
COZIEST
DOZIEST
HAZIEST
LAZIEST
MAZIEST
OOZIEST

Z•U••••
ZEUGMAS
ZOUAVES

Z••U•••
ZEBULON
ZYMURGY

Z•••U••
ZEITUNG

Z••••U•
ZEALOUS
ZEROSUM
ZESTFUL
ZONKOUT

•ZU••••
AZURITE

•Z••U••
AZIMUTH

•Z•••U•
OZONOUS

••ZU•••
COZUMEL
GAZUMPS
MAZURKA

••Z••U•
BEZIQUE
LAZARUS
SIZEDUP
SIZESUP

•••••ZU
SHIHTZU

Z••V•••
ZHIVAGO

Z•••V••
ZOUAVES

Z••••V•
ZEMSTVO

•••ZV••
MITZVAH

ZW•••••
ZWINGLI

••Z•••W
BUZZSAW

•••Z••W
BUZZSAW

••••Z•X
SKEEZIX

ZY•••••
ZYDECOS
ZYGOTES
ZYMURGY

Z•Y••••
ZOYSIAS

Z••Y•••
ZANYISH

Z•••Y••
ZEPHYRS

Z•••••Y
ZACHARY
ZOMBIFY
ZONALLY
ZOOLOGY
ZYMURGY

•Z••Y••
AZODYES

••ZY•••
COZYING
ENZYMES
LAZYISH

••Z•••Y
DAZEDLY
DIZZILY
FUZZILY
JAZZILY
MUZZILY
SIZABLY

•••Z••Y
CRAZILY
DIZZILY
DRIZZLY
FRIZZLY
FUZZILY
GAUZILY
GRIZZLY
JAZZILY
MUZZILY
RITZILY
WOOZILY

••••Z•Y
DRIZZLY
FRIZZLY
GRETZKY
GRIZZLY

•••••ZY
CHINTZY

Z••Z•••
ZIGZAGS

Z••••Z•
ZAMBEZI

•ZZ••••
IZZARDS

••ZZ•••
BUZZARD
BUZZERS
BUZZING
BUZZOFF
BUZZSAW
COZZENS
DAZZLED
DAZZLER
DAZZLES
DIZZIED
DIZZIER
DIZZIES
DIZZILY
FIZZIER
FIZZING
FIZZLED
FIZZLES
FUZZIER
FUZZILY
FUZZING
GIZZARD
GUZZLED
GUZZLER
GUZZLES
HUZZAHS
JAZZAGE
JAZZIER
JAZZILY
JAZZING
JAZZMAN
JAZZMEN
MIZZENS
MIZZLED
MIZZLES
MUZZIER
MUZZILY
MUZZING
MUZZLED
MUZZLES
NOZZLES
NUZZLED
NUZZLER
NUZZLES
PIZZAZZ
PUZZLED
PUZZLER
PUZZLES
RAZZING
ROZZERS
SIZZLED
SIZZLES
TIZZIES
WOZZECK

••Z••Z•
PIZZAZZ

••Z•••Z
PIZZAZZ

•••ZZ••
DRIZZLE
DRIZZLY
FRAZZLE
FRIZZED
FRIZZES
FRIZZLE
FRIZZLY
GRIZZLE
GRIZZLY
MUEZZIN
PIAZZAS
QUIZZED
QUIZZES
SWIZZLE
WHIZZED
WHIZZER
WHIZZES

•••Z•Z•
PIZZAZZ

•••Z••Z
PIZZAZZ

••••ZZ•
ABRUZZI
JACUZZI
PALAZZI
PALAZZO

•••••ZZ
GINFIZZ
PIZZAZZ